HALLIWELL'S
WHO'S WHO
IN THE MOVIES

Also available from HarperCollins*Publishers*

Halliwell's Film & Video Guide

HALLIWELL'S WHO'S WHO IN THE MOVIES

LESLIE HALLIWELL

13th EDITION

Edited by
JOHN WALKER

HarperCollins*Entertainment*

An Imprint of HarperCollins*Publishers*

HarperCollins*Entertainment*
An Imprint of HarperCollins*Publishers*
77–85 Fulham Palace Road,
Hammersmith, London W6 8JB
www.**fire**and**water**.com

Thirteenth edition published by HarperCollins*Publishers* 1999
3 5 7 9 10 8 6 4 2

First published in Great Britain as *Halliwell's Filmgoer's Companion* by
MacGibbon & Kee Ltd 1965
Second edition 1967
Third edition 1970
Fourth edition by Granada publishing 1974
Fifth edition (revised and reset in paperback) 1976
Sixth edition 1977
Seventh edition 1980
Eighth edition 1984
Ninth edition by Grafton Books 1988
Ninth edition (paperback) by Paladin Books 1989
Tenth edition by HarperCollins*Publishers* 1993
Eleventh edition by HarperCollins*Publishers* 1995
Twelfth edition by HarperCollins*Publishers* 1997

A catalogue record for this book is
available from the British Library

ISBN 0 00 255905 6

Set in Linotype Goudy and Frutiger by
Rowland Phototypesetting Ltd, Bury St Edmunds, Suffolk

Printed and bound in Great Britain by
Caledonian International Book Manufacturing Ltd, Glasgow

Contents

Preface

This book is for people who like movies. And who want to know more about the people involved: the stars of today, yesterday and tomorrow, the bit players and character actors, the directors and producers, writers, cinematographers, composers, editors and all the other talents involved.

It tries to be both concise and comprehensive. Apart from its A–Z of who's who in the movies, there are sections on movie sequels, series, remakes, themes and genres, taking in fictional and cartoon characters from Ali Baba to Zorro; on the studios, production companies and creative organizations; and on movies around the world. There are year-by-year listings of the winners of Oscars, of leading festivals, and of critics' awards. There is a dictionary of film terms, a brief history of the movies from their beginnings until today, a listing of many of the best movie periodicals and books, as well as a guide to some of the immense resources to be found on the Internet.

One unusual aspect of this reference book is the inclusion of quotes, either by the subjects themselves, or by others about them. They are not only apposite and often witty, but add a human dimension to the recital of facts and figures; they are also revealing of character, both of those making the remarks, and of those about whom they are made.

The book is based on an old favourite, *Halliwell's Filmgoer's Companion*, which here has been fully updated, improved and newly arranged, to make its information more easily accessible. More than 200,000 words have been added to the *Companion's* database, which has grown ever larger and more all-embracing through its twelve editions, published over thirty years. As much information as possible about movie-making is packed between its covers, except for reviews of the movies themselves. For those, you need the annually updated *Halliwell's Film & Video Guide*.

I'm grateful to the many people who have written to me with their suggestions. They include: Gregg Brownless, Allen Dace, Jeff Fendall, Douglas Ferguson, John Glynn, David Hattenstone, Erik Holst, David Johnson, Jacques Lefort, Andrew Ross, Nando Schellen, Basil Somner, Anthony Thomas, Tom Veilleux, A. D. Watson and Ian Wilkinson (and my apologies to any whose names I may have overlooked). I'm grateful also to fellow film professionals who have freely provided help, including Alan Goble, author of the *Complete Index to World Film*, Bob Mastrangelo, Alex Patterson, Michael Thornton, and Wes Walker. I owe a greater debt of gratitudeTo William C. Clogston for giving me the benefit of his knowledge, to my editor, Ian Paten, for his skills, to the support of Val Hudson and Andrea Henry at HarperCollins, and to my agents Gloria Ferris and Rivers Scott for their kindness and encouragement. My love and admiration goes to my own particular star, my wife Barbara.

John Walker (e-mail: film@dial.pipex.com)

Explanatory Notes

Alphabetical order

The main section of this book (Section 1, Who's Who in the Movies) is an A–Z of actors, directors, producers, writers and other key personnel involved in the movies, where all entries are in alphabetical order, on normal dictionary lines. Mac and Mc are treated as one, although the spelling is of course kept distinct. Names such as Von Stroheim come under 'V' and Cecil B. De Mille under 'D'. All names, whatever their nationality, are treated as if the last name were the surname, e.g. Zhang Yimou will be found under Yimou, Zhang. Fictional characters can be found in Section 2 (Movie Remakes, Series, Themes and Genres). They are listed under their complete names, so that Antoine Doinel is under 'A' and Sherlock Holmes is under 'S'.

Personal dates

The birth year of an actor or actress is often obscured beyond the powers of a crystal ball, and in some cases is impossible to discover in an industry that is averse to ageing. In general, the earliest date in print is the one preferred as most likely to be accurate.

Doubtful dates are prefaced by 'c.' (*circa*).

(*) indicates that the person has died, but the date of death is uncertain.

Film titles

The title by which the film is known in its English-speaking country of origin is given. Foreign-language titles are generally translated when the film has been released in English-speaking countries, with the original title following.

Film dates

It can be as difficult to ascertain the correct date of a film as it is to determine the personal dates of its stars. Some films sit on the shelf for several years before being released, while frequently more than 12 months can pass between an American film's release in its home country and in Britain. There is an undoubted area of confusion: *Casablanca*, for instance, was given a 50th-anniversary re-release in 1992, yet the film was not officially released until 1943, and also bears a 1943 copyright date. But it was shown to critics in November 1942, so it can also qualify as a movie from the earlier year. The aim here is to give wherever possible the date when the film was first publicly shown in its country of origin.

Filmographies

Complete filmographies are indicated by the symbol ■. A complete entry should not necessarily be taken as a sign of eminence or as a seal of approval. Some people simply made very few films or had compact typical careers which are worth detailing as instances of what goes on in the film industry: the gradual climb, the good cameo role, the star period, the two or three 'dogs' in a row, the gradual decline, the cheap exploitation movie. Filmographies cannot be completed for several major directors and stars because not all of their earlier films can be traced.

Incomplete lists normally end with 'etc.', which means that there may be up to as many films again as have been listed, while 'many others' indicates that the list has only scratched the surface. These lists usually include either the first film or the most significant role of the subject, and end up with his or her most recent work, with dates coming closest together over the most prolific and significant period.

A subject's most significant films are indicated by italics. The reader may interpret 'significant' as meaning commercial, artistic, critical or personal success.

Short films (less than 50 minutes or so) are not normally accounted for unless the subject worked chiefly in this field.

Almost every performer and director now works in TV as well as films, and many make their reputations these days on the small screen. For this reason, significant appearances in television series are also listed after the filmographies. The main lists also include some, but not all, of a subject's TV movies, made for any of its forms from cable to satellite, and are indicated by '(TV)' after the title. The majority of the TV movies listed have also been released on video-cassette.

Quotes

These are introduced by the symbol **❝**. Quotes by the subject are indicated by his or her initials; from other sources by the person's name.

Rosettes (⊚)

These are bestowed for significant work in a particular field over a sizeable period of film history, upon people with remarkable talents which are not easily duplicated. For rosette winners, one film is singled out in which the person concerned was at his or her peak.

Abbreviations

The main ones used are:

a	actor	fx	special effects
ed	editor	m	musical score
AA	Academy Award,	md	musical director
	indicating the winning of a	oa	original author
	Hollywood Oscar, awarded	orig sp	original screenplay
	annually by the Academy of	p	producer, which covers all the
	Motion Picture Arts and		many varieties of the breed,
	Sciences		from executive producer to
AAN	indicates a nomination for		associate producer,
	an Academy Award		co-producer, etc.
BFA	indicates the winning of a	d	director
	British Film Academy	pd	production designer
	award, awarded by the	ph	cinematographer
	British Academy of Film	s	song(s)
	and Television Arts	w	screenwriter
ch	choreographer	wd	writer and director

Where more than one person is involved in an activity, it is indicated by co-, so that co-w means that at least two writers scripted a particular film.

The symbol '&' means that the function abbreviated is in addition to that normally expected of the subject. In an actor's list, '& wd' would mean that he or she also wrote and directed.

Abbreviations for countries include:

Aus.	Australia	Gr.	Greece
Aust.	Austria	Hol.	Netherlands
Braz.	Brazil	Ire.	Ireland
Can.	Canada	It.	Italy
Den.	Denmark	Nor.	Norway
Fr.	France	Swe.	Sweden
GB	Great Britain	Swiss	Switzerland
Ger.	Germany	US	United States of America

Cross-References

People or organizations with their own significant entries are indicated by the use of SMALL CAPITALS.

1
Who's Who in the Movies

An A–Z of Personalities

A

Aaker, Lee (1943–).
Child actor whose career faded in his early teens, when he quit the profession.
The Atomic City 52. Desperate Search 52. No Room for the Groom 52. My Son John 52. Jeopardy 52. Take Me to Town 53. Arena 53. Hondo 53. Rin Tin Tin, Hero of the West 55, etc.
TV series: Adventures of Rin Tin Tin 54–59.

Aames, Willie (1960–) (William Upton).
American leading actor, who began as a clean-cut teenager on television, but has found worthwhile adult roles harder to find.
Frankenstein (TV) 73. Scavenger Hunt 79. Paradise 82. Zapped! 82. Cut and Run (It.) 85. Killing Machine (Sp.) 86. Eight Is Enough: A Family Reunion (TV) 87. Eight Is Enough: Wedding (TV) 89, etc.
TV series: We'll Get By 75. Swiss Family Robinson 75–76. Eight Is Enough 77–81. We're Movin' 82. Charles in Charge 84–85.

Aaron, Caroline (1954–).
American actress.
Baby, It's You 82. Heartburn 86. Crimes and Misdemeanors 89. Edward Scissorhands 90. Alice 90. This Is My Life 92. Mr 247 94. House Arrest 96. Big Night 96. A Modern Affair 96. Deconstructing Harry 97. Weapons of Mass Distraction (TV) 97. Primary Colors 98. There's No Fish Food in Heaven 98, etc.

Aaron, Sidney.
Pseudonym used by Paddy Chayefsky for his last film script, *Altered States*.

Abady, Temple (1903–1970).
British composer, from the theatre.
The Woman in the Hall 47. Miranda 48. All over the Town 49. Folly to Be Wise 52. Kill Me Tomorrow 57, etc.

Abatantuono, Diego (1955–).
Italian leading actor and screenwriter, born in Milan; he is frequently in the films of Gabriele SALVATORES.
Attila 80. Il Tango Della Gelosia 81. Christmas Present/Regalo di Natale 86. Marrakech Express 88. On Tour/Turne 90. Mediterraneo 91. The Dark Continent/Nel Continente Nero 92. Puerto Escondido (& w) 93. The Bull/El Toro 95. The Best Man/Il Testimone dello Sposo 97, etc.

Abbott, Bud (1895–1974) (William Abbott).
American comedian, the brusque and slightly shifty 'straight man' half of Abbott and Costello, cross-talking vaudevillians of long standing who became Universal's top stars of the early 40s. Bud, seldom seen without his hat, was the bully who left the dirty work for his partner, never believed his tall but true stories of crooks and monsters, and usually avoided the pie in the face.
■ *One Night in the Tropics* (their only supporting roles) 40. *Buck Privates* 41. In The Navy 41. *Hold That Ghost* 41. Keep 'Em Flying 41. Ride 'Em Cowboy 41. Rio Rita 42. Pardon My Sarong 42. Who Done It? 42. It Ain't Hay 43. Hit the Ice 43. Lost In A Harem 44. *In Society* 44. Here Come the Co-Eds 45. *The Naughty Nineties* (featuring their famous 'Who's On First' routine) 45. Abbott and Costello in Hollywood 45. The Little Giant (a doomed attempt to work separately within the same film) 46. The Time of Their Lives (an interesting failure) 46. Buck Privates Come Home 47. The Wistful Widow of Wagon Gap 47. The Noose Hangs High 48. *Abbott and Costello Meet Frankenstein* 48. Mexican Hayride 48. Africa Screams 49. Abbott and Costello Meet the Killer 49. Abbott and Costello in the Foreign Legion 50. Abbott and Costello Meet the Invisible Man 51. Comin' Round the Mountain 51. Jack and the Beanstalk 52. Abbott and Costello Lost in Alaska 52. Abbott and Costello Meet Captain Kidd 52. Abbott and Costello Go to Mars 53. *Abbott and Costello Meet Dr Jekyll and Mr Hyde* 53. Abbott and Costello Meet the Keystone Kops 54. Abbott and Costello Meet the Mummy 55. Dance with Me Henry 56.
After a TV series (1953) using up all their old routines, the team split and Abbott retired. See COSTELLO, Lou. In 1975 there was published *Who's On First*, a selection of frame-by-frame routines, by Richard J. Anobile. Bob Thomas's biography, *Bud and Lou*, was published in 1977, and appeared in 1978 as a TV movie, with Harvey Korman and Buddy Hackett.
~All Abbott and Costello movies depended for their effectiveness on the number of old vaudeville routines included, such as the following: 'All Because You Don't Like Mustard' and 'Jonah and the Whale' (*One Night in the Tropics*); 'Drill' (*Buck Privates*); 'Bussing the Bee' and 'Seven Times Thirteen Is Twenty-Eight' (*In the Navy*); 'The Moving Candle' (*Hold That Ghost*, *Meet Frankenstein*); 'Don't Order Anything' (*Keep 'Em Flying*, borrowed from Laurel and Hardy's *Man o' War*); 'Poker Game' (*Ride 'Em Cowboy*); 'Ten Dollars You're Not There' (*Rio Rita*); 'The Poisoned Drink' (*Pardon My Sarong*); 'The Telephone Call' (*Who Done It*); 'Bagel Street' (*In Society*); 'The Magic Act' and 'Slowly I Turned' (*Lost in a Harem*); 'The Mirror' and 'Who's on First' (*The Naughty Nineties*); 'Hole in the Wall' (*The Noose Hangs High*); 'Identification' and 'Silver Ore' (*Mexican Hayride*); 'The Gorilla' (*Africa Screams*); 'The Shovel Is My Pick' (*Meet the Mummy*).
✪ For bringing authentic vaudeville to Hollywood in a few imperishable routines; and for cheering up a generation at war. *Abbott and Costello Meet Frankenstein*.
❝ Abbott and Costello's comedy depended on caricature and contrast: the fat and the thin, the nervous and the foolhardy, the stupid and the stupider. Their work falls into well-remembered routines and reactions. There is chubby, terrified Costello calling after his partner:
Ch-ch-ch-ch-ch-i-ck!
There is his shy admission:
I'm a ba-a-a-ad boy!
There is the old pantomime gag of his seeing something alarming and running to tell his partner; by the time the latter returns the thing has naturally disappeared. There are repetitive routines such as the 'Slowly I Turned' scene from *Lost in a Harem*, with its Laurel and Hardy-like inevitability. Most memorably there is skilful nightclub cross-talk, seen at its best in the 'Who's On First' sketch which first brought them to fame. Here is part of it:
A: You know, these days they give ballplayers very peculiar names. Take the St Louis team: Who's on first, What's on second, I Don't Know is on third . . .
C: That's what I want to find out. I want you to tell me the names of the fellows on the St Louis team.
I'm telling you. Who's on first. What's on second, I Don't Know is on third.
– Who's playing first?
Yes.
– I mean, the fellow's name on first base.
Who.
– The fellow playing first base.
Who.
– The guy on first base.
Who is on first.
– Well, what are you asking me for?
I'm not asking you, I'm telling you. Who is on first.
– I'm asking you – who is on first?
That's the man's name.
– That's who's name?
Yes.
– Well, go ahead, tell me.
Who!
– All I'm trying to find out is, what's the guy's name on first base.
Oh no, What is on second.
– I'm not asking you who's on second.
Who's on first.
– That's what I'm trying to find out!
What's the guy's name on first base?
What's the guy's name on second base.
– I'm not asking who's on second.
Who's on first.
– I Don't Know.
He's on third . . .
And so on, for another five minutes.

Abbott, Diahnne (1945–).
American actress. Her second husband was Robert de Niro (1976–78).
Taxi Driver 76. New York New York 77. Welcome to L.A. 77. The King of Comedy 83. Love Streams 84. Jo Jo Dancer, Your Life Is Calling 86, etc.

Abbott, George (1887–1995).
American playwright and producer of lively commercial properties. He sporadically invaded Hollywood to supervise their filming, and stayed briefly to perform other services.
Autobiography: 1963, *Mister Abbott*.
AS ORIGINAL AUTHOR: Four Walls 28. Coquette 28. *Broadway* 29 (and 42). *Three Men on a Horse* 36. On Your Toes 39. The Boys from Syracuse 40. *The Pajama Game* (& co-d) 57. *Damn Yankees* (& co-d) 58, etc.
AS PRODUCER: *Boy Meets Girl* 38. Room Service 38. The Primrose Path 40. *The Pajama Game* 57. *Damn Yankees* 58, etc.
AS DIRECTOR: Why Bring That Up? 29. The Sea God 30. Stolen Heaven 31. Secrets of a Secretary 31. My Sin 31. Too Many Girls 40, etc.
❝ I must confess that one of my main defects as a director has always been an incurable impatience. – G.A.
Many great minds have made a botch of matters because their emotions fettered their thinking. – G.A.

Abbott, John (1905–1996).
British character actor, specializing in eccentric parts. Born in London, he began as a commercial artist, and made his professional debut on stage in 1934, before joining the Old Vic company to play Shakespearean roles, including Malvolio in *Twelfth Night*.
Mademoiselle Docteur 37. The Return of the Scarlet Pimpernel 37. The Saint in London 39. The Shanghai Gesture 41. Mrs Miniver 42. They Got Me Covered 42. The London Blackout Murders (lead) 42. Jane Eyre 43. The Vampire's Ghost 45. Deception 47. *The Woman in White* 48 (a memorable performance, as the grotesque invalid Frederick Fairlie). The Merry Widow 52. Public Pigeon Number One 57. Gigi 58. Who's Minding the Store? 63. Gambit 66. The Store 66. 2000 Years Later 69. The Black Bird 75. Slapstick 84. Lady Jane 85, many others.

Abbott, Philip (1923–).
American 'second lead' of the 50s.
Bachelor Party 57. *Sweet Bird of Youth* 62. The Spiral Road 62. Miracle of the White Stallions 63. Those Calloways 65. Tail Gunner Joe (TV) 77. Savannah Smiles 82. The First Power 90, etc.
TV series: *The F.B.I.* 65–73. Rich Man, Poor Man – Book II 76–77.

Abdul-Jabbar, Kareem (1947–) (Lew Alcindor).
Lanky American actor, a former star basketball player.
Game of Death 78. The Fish that Saved Pittsburgh 79. Airplane! 80. Fletch 85. Purple People Eater 88. D2: The Mighty Ducks (as himself) 94. Slam Dunk Ernest 95, etc.

Abel, Alfred (1880–1937).
German character actor of weighty personality, in films from 1913.
Dr Mabuse 22. Phantom 22. Metropolis 26. Gold 28. Narkose (& d) 29. Congress Dances 31. Salon Dora Greene 33. Das Hofkonzert 36. Kater Lampe 36. Frau Sylvelin 38, etc.

Abel, Walter (1898–1987).
American character actor with stage experience. Made his Hollywood debut as D'Artagnan, but later settled enjoyably into variations on a single performance of harassment and nervousness, whether as father, friend of the family or professional man. Born in St Paul, Minnesota, he studied at the American Academy of Dramatic Art in New York, and began on stage and in vaudeville.
■ Liliom 30. *The Three Musketeers* 35. The Lady Consents 36. Two in the Dark 36. The Witness Chair 36. Fury 36. We Went to College 36. Second Wife 36. Portia on Trial 37. Wise Girl 37. Law of the Underworld 38. Racket Busters 38. Men with Wings 38. King of the Turf 39. Miracle on Main Street 40. Dance Girl Dance 40. *Arise My Love* (which provided him with a key line: 'I'm not happy. I'm not happy at all') 40. Michael Shayne Private Detective 40. Who Killed Aunt Maggie? 40. *Hold Back the Dawn* 41. Skylark 41. Glamour Boy 41. *Beyond the Blue Horizon* 42. *Star Spangled Rhythm* 42. *Holiday Inn* 42. Wake Island 42. So Proudly We Hail 43. Fired Wife 43. Follow the Boys 44. *Mr Skeffington* 44. An American Romance 44. *The Affairs of Susan* 45. Duffy's Tavern 45. *Kiss and Tell* 45. The Kid from Brooklyn 46. 13 Rue Madeleine 46. The Fabulous Joe 47. *Dream Girl* 48. That Lady in Ermine 48. Island in the Sky 53. So This is Love 53. Night People 54. The Indian Fighter 55. The Steel Jungle 56. *Bernardine* 57. Raintree County 57. Handle with Care 58. Mirage 65. Quick Let's Get Married 65. Zora 71. The Man without a Country (TV) 74. Silent Night, Bloody Night 74. The Ultimate Solution of Grace Quigley 84.
Famous line *Arise My Love*: 'I'm not happy. I'm not happy at all!'

Abraham, F. Murray (1940–).
Intense American character actor, who has found effective film roles hard to come by, despite his Oscar. Born in Pittsburgh, Pennsylvania, of Italian and Syrian parents, he was brought up in El Paso, Texas, and educated at the University of Texas, beginning on stage in 1965. His finest performance remains that of Salieri in *Amadeus*.
They Might Be Giants 71. Serpico 73. The Sunshine Boys 75. All the President's Men 76. The Ritz 76. The Big Fix 78. Scarface 83. *Amadeus* (AA) 84. The Name of the Rose 86. Personal Choice 88. An Innocent Man 89. La Nuit du Serail 89. Russicum 89. Slipstream 89. La Batalla de los Tres Reyes 90. Bonfire of the Vanities 90. Cadence 90. Mobsters 91. National Lampoon's Loaded Weapon 1 93. Sweet Killing 93. The Last Action Hero 93. Surviving the Game 94. Jamila 94. L'Affaire (Fr.) 94. Nostradamus 94. Mighty Aphrodite 95. Children of the Revolution (as Stalin) 96. Looking for Richard 96. Larry

McMurtry's Dead Man's Walk (TV) 96. Baby Face Nelson 97. Mimic 97. Falcone 98. Star Trek: Insurrection 98, etc.

Abrahams, Jim (1944–).
American director, screenwriter and actor, usually in collaboration with Jerry and David Zucker.
The Kentucky Fried Movie (a, co-w) 77. Airplane! (a, co-wd) 80. Top Secret! (co-wd) 84. Ruthless People (co-d) 86. The Naked Gun: From the Files of Police Squad (co-w) 88. Big Business (d) 88. Welcome Home Roxy Carmichael (d) 91. Hot Shots! (co-w, d) 91. Hot Shots! Part Deux (co-w, d) 93. First Do No Harm (TV) 97. Mafia!/Jane Austen's Mafia! 98, etc.

Abrams, Jeffrey.
American scriptwriter.
Taking Care of Business/Filofax 90. Regarding Henry (& a) 91. Forever Young 92. Six Degrees of Separation (a) 93. Gone Fishin' 97, etc.

Abril, Victoria (1959–).
Spanish leading actress, who moved to France in the early 80s.
Mother, Dearly Loved/Mater Amatisima 79. The Beehive/La Colmena 81. The Moon in the Gutter/La Lune dans le Caniveau 83. On the Line/Rio Abajo 84. Our Father/Padre Nuestro 84. The Witching Hour/La Hora Bruja 85. Max, Mon Amour 86. Time of Silence/Tiempo de Silencio 86. Baton Rouge 88. Tie Me Up! Tie Me Down!/¡Atame! 89. Lovers/Amantes 91. High Heels/Tacones Lejanos 91. Wonderful Times/Une Epoque Formidable 91. Too Much Heart/Demasiado Corazón 92. Kika 93. Intruso 93. Jimmy Hollywood 94. French Twist/Gazon Maudit 95. Nobody Will Talk about Us When We're Dead/Nadie Hablará de Nosotros Cuando Haramos Muertos 95. Libertarias 96. Entre las Piernas 98, etc.

Abuladze, Tengiz (1924–1994).
Russian film director and screenwriter. Born in Georgia, he studied film in Moscow before returning to Georgia to work.
Magdana's Donkey/Magdanas Lurdzha (co-d) 55. Somebody Else's Children/Skhvisi Shvilebi 58. The Invocation/Vedreba 68. A Necklace for My Beloved/Samkauli Satr Posatvis 73. The Wishing Tree/Natvris Khe 76. *Repentance*/Monanieba 84, etc.

Achard, Marcel (1899–1974) (Marcel-Auguste Ferréol).
French dramatist, screenwriter and occasional director. Born in Ste-Foy-les-Lyon, and educated at the University of Lyon, he was active as a playwright of sentimental romances from the early 20s to the mid-60s.
The Merry Widow 34. Mayerling 36. Alibi (oa) 37. The Strange Monsieur Victor 38. Untel Père et Fils 40. Monsieur la Souris 43. The Paris Waltz (d only) 50. Madame De 53. La Garçonne 57. A Woman Like Satan 59. A Shot in the Dark (oa) 64.

Acheson, James.
English costume designer, now in international films.
Time Bandits 81. Water 84. Brazil 85. Highlander 86. The Last Emperor (AA) 87. Dangerous Liaisons (AA) 88. The Sheltering Sky 90. Little Buddha 93. Mary Shelley's Frankenstein 94. Restoration (AA) 94, etc.

Acker, Jean (1893–1978).
American screen and stage actress, the first wife of Rudolph Valentino (1919–21).
Are You a Mason? 15. Arabian Knight 20. Brewster's Millions 21. The Woman in Chains 23. The Girl Habit 31. No More Ladies 35. My Favorite Wife 40. The Thin Man Goes Home 44. Spellbound 45. Something to Live For 52, etc.

Acker, Sharon (1935–).
Anglo-American leading lady.
Lucky Jim (GB) 57. Waiting For Caroline (Can.) 67. Point Blank 67. The First Time 68. Act of the Heart 70. A Clear and Present Danger (TV) 70. Hec Ramsey (TV) 72. The Stranger (TV) 73. The Hanged Man (TV) 74. Our Man Flint: Dead On Target (TV) 76. The Hostage Heart (TV) 77. The Murder That Wouldn't Die (TV) 79. Happy Birthday to Me 80.
TV series: The Senator 70. Perry Mason 73. Executive Suite 76.

Ackerman, Bettye (1928–).
American general purpose actress.
Face of Fire 59. Companions in Nightmare (TV) 68. Rascal 69. M*A*S*H. 70, etc.
TV series: *Ben Casey* 60–64.

Ackerman, Thomas.
American cinematographer, a former camera operator. Born in Iowa, he was educated at the University of Iowa.
New Year's Evil 81. Roadhouse 66 84. Frankenweenie 84. Girls Just Want to Have Fun 85. Back to School 86. Beetlejuice 88. National Lampoon's Christmas Vacation 89. True Identity 91. Dennis the Menace/Dennis 93. Baby's Day Out 94. Jumanji 95. The Eighteenth Angel 97. George of the Jungle 97, etc.

Ackland, Joss (1928–).
British actor of larger-than-life personality; much on TV. Born in London, he studied at the Central School of Dramatic Art and was on stage from 1946.
Autobiography: 1989, *I Must Be in There Somewhere*.
Seven Days to Noon 49. The Ghost Ship 53. Rasputin the Mad Monk 65. Crescendo 70. Mr Forbush and the Penguins 71. The House That Dripped Blood 71. Villain 71. England Made Me 72. The Happiness Cage (US) 72. Hitler: The Last Ten Days 73. Penny Gold 73. The Three Musketeers 73. The Black Windmill 74. S.P.Y.S. 74. Great Expectations 75. Royal Flash 75. Operation Daybreak 75. Silver Bears 78. Who is Killing the Great Chefs of Europe? 78. Saint Jack 79. The Apple 80. Rough Cut 80. Dangerous Davies (TV) 81. A Zed and Two Noughts 85. Lady Jane 86. White Mischief 87. It Couldn't Happen Here 88. Popielusko 88. Lethal Weapon 2 89. To Forget Palermo/Dimenticare Palermo 89. The Bridge 90. The Hunt for Red October 90. Tre Colonne in Cronaca 90. The Object of Beauty 91. Bill & Ted's Bogus Journey 91. Once Upon a Crime 92. The Mighty Ducks 92. The Princess and the Goblin (voice) 92. Nowhere to Run 92. Mad Dogs and Englishmen 95. Occhiopinocchio (It.) 95. Citizen X (US) 95. Daisies in December (TV) 95. Surviving Picasso 96. D3: Mighty Ducks (US) 96. To the Ends of Time (US) 96. Amy Foster/Swept from the Sea 97, etc.
TV series: Kipling 64. Further Adventures of the Three Musketeers 67. The Crezz 76. Thicker Than Water 81. Ashenden 91.

Ackland, Rodney (1908–1991).
British writer, sporadically in films from 1930, usually in association with other scenarists.
Autobiography: 1954, *The Celluloid Mistress*.
Shadows 31. Number Seventeen 32. The Case of Gabriel Perry (a only) 35. Bank Holiday 38. Young Man's Fancy 39. 49th Parallel (co-w, AAN) 41. Dangerous Moonlight 41. Hatter's Castle 41. Thursday's Child (& d) 42. Wanted for Murder 46. Temptation Harbour 47. Queen of Spades 48, etc.

Acord, Art (1890–1931).
American star of silent westerns. Sound ended his career and he committed suicide.
The Squaw Man 13. A Man Afraid of His Wardrobe 15. The Moon Riders 20. In the Days of Buffalo Bill 21. The Oregon Trail 23. The Call of Courage 25. Rustler's Ranch 26. Sky High Corral 26. Hard Fists 27. Loco Luck 27. Two Gun O'Brien 28. Bullets and Justice 29. Wyoming Tornado 29, etc.

Acosta, Rodolfo (1920–1974).
Cold-eyed Mexican-American character actor, a frequent western villain or henchman.
The Fugitive 48. One Way Street 50. Yankee Buccaneer 52. Hondo 54. Bandido 56. The Tijuana Story (leading role) 57. Flaming Star 60. How the West Was Won 62. Rio Conchos 64. Return of the Seven 66. Flap 70. The Great White Hope 70. The Magnificent Seven Ride 72, many others.
TV series: High Chaparral 67.

Acres, Birt (1854–1918).
British cinematograph pioneer, American born, later projector manufacturer. Claimed to be the first producer of cinema films in Britain.
Haycart Crossing, Hadley 94. The Derby 95. Boxing Kangaroo 96. A Visit to the Zoo 96. Princess Maud's Wedding 96. An Unfriendly Call 97, etc.

Acuff, Eddie (1908–1956).
American supporting comedian, remembered as the postman in the 'Blondie' series.
Shipmates Forever 35. The Petrified Forest 36. The Boys from Syracuse 40. Hellzapoppin 41. Guadalcanal Diary 43. It Happened Tomorrow 44. The Flying Serpent 45. Blondie's Big Moment 47, many others.

Adair, Jean (1873–1953).
American stage actress best remembered by film fans as one of the sweetly murderous aunts in *Arsenic and Old Lace*.
■ In the Name of the Law 22. Advice to the Lovelorn 33. *Arsenic and Old Lace* 44. Something in the Wind 46. Living in a Big Way 47.

Adair, Robert (1900–1954).
English character actor, from the American stage. Born in San Francisco, he was educated at Harrow, made his screen debut as Captain Hardy in *Journey's End*, and spent his mid-career in Hollywood.
Journey's End 30. Raffles 32. King of the Jungle 33. Limehouse Blues 35. The Prince and the Pauper 37. Brilliant Marriage 38. Jamaica Inn 39. Man on the Run 49. The Gambler and the Lady 52. Meet Mr Callaghan 54, etc.

Adam, Alfred (1909–1982).
French character actor, usually of weak or villainous roles.
La Kermesse Héroique 35. Carnet de Bal 37. Boule de Suif 45. La Ferme du Pendu 46. The Witches of Salem 56. Maigret Sets a Trap 57. Le Président 61. Vivre sa Vie 62. La Vie Conjugale 63. Les Fêtes Galantes 65. Que la Fête Commence 74, etc.

Adam, Ken (1921–) (Klaus Adam).
German-born art director, in films from 1947. Born in Berlin, he was in Britain from the mid-30s. The 60s were for him a period of spectacular inventiveness.
Queen of Spades 48. Around the World in Eighty Days (AAN) 56. The Trials of Oscar Wilde 60. *Dr Strangelove* 63. *Goldfinger* 64. The Ipcress File 65. Thunderball 65. Funeral in Berlin 66. *You Only Live Twice* 67. Chitty Chitty Bang Bang 68. Goodbye Mr Chips 69. The Owl and the Pussycat 70. Sleuth 72. Live and Let Die 73. Barry Lyndon (AA) 75. The Seven Per Cent Solution 76. The Spy Who Loved Me (AAN) 77. Moonraker 79. Pennies from Heaven 80. King David 84. Agnes of God 85. Crimes of the Heart 86. The Deceivers 88. Dead-Bang 89. The Freshman 90. The Doctor 91. Undercover Blues 93. Addams Family Values (AAN) 93. The Madness of King George (AA) 94. Bogus 96. In and Out 97, etc.

Adam, Ronald (1896–1979).
English character actor and playwright. Born in Worcestershire, he trained as a chartered accountant and began as a theatre manager in the mid-20s, turning to acting in the 30s. He specialized in well-bred but stuffy professional men. Married twice.
Autobiography: 1938, *Overture and Beginners*.
Inspector Hornleigh 36. Strange Boarders 38. The Drum 38. Escape to Danger 43. Journey Together 44. Take My Life 47. Bonnie Prince Charles 48. The Case of Charles Peace 49. Seven Days to Noon 50. My Daughter Joy 50. Laughter in Paradise 51. The Late Edwina Black 51. Hindle Wakes 52. Top Secret 52. Private's Progress 55. Reach for the Sky 56. Assignment Redhead 56. Carry On Admiral 57. The Golden Disc 58, etc.

Adams, Beverly (1945–).
Canadian-born leading lady in Hollywood films. Formerly married to hairdresser and businessman Vidal Sassoon. Retired to raise a family and write books on beauty.
Winter a GoGo 63. The New Interns 64. *The Silencers* 66. Birds Do It 66. Murderers' Row 66. The Torture Garden (GB) 67. The Ambushers 67, etc.

Adams, Brooke (1949–).
American leading lady of the *jolie laide* type; showed more promise than performance.
Shock Waves 77. Invasion of the Body Snatchers 78. *Days of Heaven* 78. The First Great Train Robbery 79. A Man, a Woman and a Bank 79. Cuba 79. Tell Me a Riddle 80. The Dead Zone 83. Almost You 84. Key Exchange 84. The Stuff 85. Man on Fire 87. The Unborn 91. Stephen King's Sometimes They Come Back 91. Gas Food Lodging 91. The Last Hit (TV) 93. The Baby-Sitters Club 95, etc.
TV series: O.K. Crackerby 65–66.

Adams, Casey (1917–).
See under Max Showalter (his real name, which he has recently used).

Adams, Claire (1900–1978).
Canadian-born leading lady of silent films. She retired early and in 1938 moved to Australia following her second marriage.
Riders of the Dawn 20. The Penalty 20. The Killer 21. Just Tony 22. Stepping Fast 23. Where the North Begins 23. Oh, You Tony! 24. The Fast Set 24. The Big Parade 25. The Sea Wolf 26. Married Alive 27, etc.

Adams, Don (1926–).
American comedian, from night-clubs and television, best known for his Emmy-winning performance as Maxwell Smart in the spy spoof *Get Smart*.
The Nude Bomb 80. Jimmy the Kid 82. Back to the Beach 87, etc.
TV series: Kraft Music Hall 61–63. Bill Dana Show 63–65. Get Smart 65–70. The Partners 71–72. Don Adams' Screen Test 75. Check It Out 85–88.

Adams, Dorothy (1900–1988).
American character actress, usually of timorous or sullen ladies.
Broadway Musketeers 38. The Flame of New Orleans 41. Laura 44. The Best Years of Our Lives 46. The Foxes of Harrow 48. Carrie 52. Three for Jamie Dawn 56. The Big Country 58. From the Terrace 60. Peeper 76, etc.

Adams, Edie (1927–) (Elizabeth Edith Enke).
Pert American singer-comedienne, widow of Ernie Kovacs.
■ *The Apartment* 60. Lover Come Back 61. Call Me Bwana 62. It's a Mad Mad Mad Mad World 63. Under the Yum Yum Tree 63. *Love with the Proper Stranger* 64. The Best Man 64. Made in Paris 66. The Oscar 66. *The Honey Pot* 66. Box Office 82. The Haunting of Harrington House 82. Shooting Stars 85. Adventures Beyond Belief 87.
TV work includes: Evil Roy Slade 71. The Return of Joe Forrester 75. Word Games/Mrs Columbo 79.

Adams, Ernie (1885–1947).
Short American character actor, from the stage, most often in westerns.
A Regular Girl 19. The Pony Express 25. The Main Event 27. The Tip-Off 31. Breed of the Border 33. Gun Lords of Stirrup Basin 37. Ridin' the Lone Trail 37. The Man Who Came to Dinner 41. The Perils of Pauline 47. Return of the Bad Men 48, etc.

Adams, Gerald Drayson (1904–).
Canadian screenwriter, former literary agent.
Dead Reckoning 47. The Big Steal 49. The Golden Horde 51. Flaming Feather 51. The Black Sleep 56. Kissing Cousins 64. Harum Scarum 65, many others.

Adams, Jane (1921–).
American actress of the 40s.
House of Dracula 45. Gunman's Code 46. The Brute Man 46. Batman and Robin 49. Rising Son (TV) 90. Vital Signs 90. Light Sleeper 91. I Love Trouble 94. Mrs Parker and the Vicious Circle 94, etc.

Adams, Jill (1930–).
Pert British leading lady, former model, who decorated a number of lightweight films in the 50s.
The Young Lovers 54. Doctor at Sea 55. Private's Progress 56. The Green Man 56. Brothers in Law 57. Carry On Constable 60. Doctor in Distress 63. Promise Her Anything 66, etc.

Adams, Joey Lauren (1971–).
American actress, in independent films, sometimes credited as Joey Adams. Born in Little Rock, Arkansas, she began her career in television. She has been romantically linked to director Kevin SMITH and actor Vince VAUGHN.
Dazed and Confused 93. Coneheads 93. The Program 93. SFW 94. Sleep with Me 94. Mallrats 95. Bio-Dome 96. Michael 96. Chasing Amy 97. A Cool Dry Place 98, etc.
TV series: Top of the Heap 91. Vinnie and Bobby 92.

Adams, Julie (formerly Julia) (1926–) (Betty May Adams).
American leading lady in Hollywood from 1947. Her essentially soft and sympathetic nature made the slight change of first name seem especially apt.
Hollywood Story 51. Bright Victory 51. Bend of the River 52. Mississippi Gambler 53. The Creature from the Black Lagoon 54. One Desire 55. Away All Boats 56. Slaughter on Tenth Avenue 57. Raymie 60. Tickle Me 65. Valley of Mystery 67. The Last Movie 71. McQ 74. The McCullochs 75. Killer Force 76. The Killer Inside Me 76. Black Roses 88. Catchfire/Backtrack 89, etc.
TV series: Yancy Derringer 58–59. The Jimmy Stewart Show 71. Code Red 81.

Adams, Maud (Maude) (1945–) (Maud Wikstrom).
Persistently promising Swedish-American leading lady of the 70s.
The Boys in the Band 70. The Christian Licorice Store 71. Rollerball 74. The Man with the Golden Gun 74. Killer Force 76. Tattoo 80. Octopussy 83. Playing for Time (TV) 80. Nairobi Affair (TV) 85. Hell Hunters 86. The Women's Club 87. Jane and the Lost City 88. Deadly Intent 88. Ski School 89. Soda Cracker 89. The Kill Reflex 90. Initiation: Silent Night, Deadly Night 4 90, etc.
TV series: Chicago Story 82. Emerald Point N.A.S. 83–84.

Adams, Nick (1931–1968) (Nicholas Adamschock).
American leading man who usually played neurotic or aggressive types; never quite made the big time. Died of a drug overdose.
Somebody Loves Me (debut) 52. Mister Roberts 55. *No Time for Sergeants* 58. Pillow Talk 59. Hell is for Heroes 62. The Hook 62. Twilight of Honor (AAN) 63. Young Dillinger 64. Monster of Terror (GB) 66. Frankenstein Conquers the World (Jap.) 66. Fever Heat 67, etc.
TV series: The Rebel 59–60. Saints and Sinners 62–63.

Adams, Richard (1920–).
British best-selling novelist who sees the world from the animals' point of view. His *Watership Down* and *The Plague Dogs* were somewhat unsatisfactorily turned into cartoon features.

Adams, Robert (1906–).
West Indian actor, former teacher, prominent in British films of the 40s.
Sanders of the River (debut) 35. King Solomon's Mines 37. Caesar and Cleopatra 45. Men of Two Worlds (leading role) 46. Old Mother Riley's Jungle Treasure 52. Man of Africa 52. Sapphire 59, etc.

Adams, Stanley (1915–1977).
American character actor. Committed suicide.
The Atomic Kid 54. Hell on Frisco Bay 56. Breakfast at Tiffany's 61. Nevada Smith 66. The Clones 74, etc.

Adams, Tom (1938–).
Burly British leading man whose career might have flourished better in the 50s.
The Great Escape 63. Licensed to Kill 65. Where the Bullets Fly 66. The Fighting Prince of Donegal 66. Fathom 67. Subterfuge 68. The Fast Kill 72. The Onedin Line (TV) 79. Mask of the Devil (TV) 84. The Pyrates (TV) 85.
TV series: Spy Trap 75.

Adamson, Al (1929–1995).
American director of exploitation movies noted for their high level of sex, violence and general incompetence which gained a new audience following their release on video. Many exist in various versions under different titles. A former actor, known as Rick Adams, he was born in Hollywood, the son of silent western star, producer and director Denver DIXON, and turned to directing in the 60s, with films that tended to star actors past their prime, such as Lon Chaney Jnr and John Carradine. He was murdered.
AS ACTOR: Halfway to Hell 55.
AS DIRECTOR: Blood of Dracula's Castle/ Dracula's Castle 69. Five Bloody Graves/The Gun Riders 69. Satan's Sadists 69. The Fakers 69. Vampire Men of the Lost Planet/Horror of the Blood Monsters 70. Dracula vs Frankenstein/Blood of Frankenstein 71. The Female Bunch (co-d) 71. Brain of Blood/The Creature's Revenge 71. Angels' Wild Women 72. Blood of Ghastly Horror 72. Man with the Synthetic Brain/Psycho a Go-Go 72. The Naughty Stewardesses 73. I Spit on Your Corpse 74. Jessie's Girls 75. Texas Layover 75. Blazing Stewardesses 75. Wanted Women 76. Nurse Sherri 77. Dr Dracula 77. Black Samurai 77. Cinderella 2000 77. Hospital of Terror 78. Sunset Cove 78. Carnival Magic 82, etc.

Adamson, Harold (1906–1980).
American lyricist, usually with Jimmy McHugh.
Dancing Lady 33. Kid Millions 34. Suzy 36. That Certain Age 38. Nob Hill 45. If You Knew Susie 48. Gentlemen Prefer Blondes 52. An Affair to Remember 57, many others.

Adamson, Joy (1910–1980).
Austrian-born wild-life expert who wrote *Born Free* and *Living Free*. A long-time resident of Kenya, she was mysteriously murdered.
Biography: 1996, *Joy Adamson: Behind the Mask* by Caroline Cass.

Addams, Charles (1912–1988).
American cartoonist of ghoulish humour, much in the *New Yorker* from 1940. TV in 1964–65 ran *The Addams Family*, about creepy characters in a cobwebby house, which became the basis of successful feature films in the 90s. With regard to films he is best remembered for his remark on attending the premiere of *Cleopatra*: 'I only came to see the asp.'

Addams, Dawn (1930–1985).
Smart and glamorous British leading lady in international films. Films mainly unremarkable.
Night into Morning 51. Plymouth Adventure 52. The Robe 53. The Moon Is Blue 53. Khyber Patrol 54. A King in New York 57. The Silent Enemy 58. The Two Faces of Dr Jekyll 60. The Black Tulip 64. Ballad in Blue 65. Where the Bullets Fly 66. Vampire Lovers 70. Sappho 70. Vault of Horror 73, etc.
TV series: Star Maidens 77.

Addinsell, Richard (1904–1977).
British composer.
The Amateur Gentleman 36. Fire over England 37. Goodbye Mr Chips 39. Gaslight 40. *Dangerous Moonlight* (including 'Warsaw Concerto') 40. Love on the Dole 41. Blithe Spirit 45. Scrooge 51. Beau Brummell 54. The Prince and the Showgirl 57. The Admirable Crichton 57. The Waltz of the Toreadors 62, etc.

Addison, John (1920–).
British composer, in films from 1948. He studied at the Royal College of Music, where he also taught in the 50s, and began his film career through a friendship with producer-director Roy BOULTING, who admired his compositions. In the mid-70s, he moved to Los Angeles and scored many TV movies.
The Guinea Pig 49. Seven Days to Noon 50. The Man Between 53. Private's Progress 55. *Reach for the Sky* 56. Lucky Jim 57. I Was Monty's Double 58. Look Back in Anger 59. The Entertainer 60. A Taste of Honey 61. The Loneliness of the Long Distance Runner 62. *Tom Jones* (AA) 63. Guns at Batasi 64. Moll Flanders 65. Torn Curtain 66. A Fine Madness 66. The Honey Pot 67. Smashing Time 67. Country Dance 70. Mr Forbush and the Penguins 71. Sleuth 72. Dead Cert 74. A Bridge Too Far 77. The Seven Per Cent Solution 77. Centennial (TV) 78. Pearl (TV) 80. Strange Invaders 83. The Ultimate Solution of Grace Quigley 84. Code Name: Emerald 85. Phantom of the Opera (TV) 90, etc.

Addy, Wesley (1913–).
Thin American character actor, usually of humourless or sinister appearance. He married actress Celeste Holm in 1966.
The First Legion 51. My Six Convicts 52. Kiss Me Deadly 55. The Big Knife 55. Timetable 57. The Garment Jungle 58. Ten Seconds to Hell 59. Whatever Happened to Baby Jane? 62. *Seconds* 66. Mister Buddwing 66. The Grissom Gang 71. Network 76. The Europeans 79. The Verdict 82. The Bostonians 84. Mr 247 94. Hiroshima (TV) 95. Before and After 96. A Modern Affair 96, etc.
TV series: Loving 83–91, 94–95.

Adjani, Isabelle (1955–).
Franco-German leading lady of international films. She has a son by actor Daniel DAY-LEWIS.
Faustine 71. The Slap 74. *The Story of Adèle H* (AAN) 75. The Tenant 76. Barocco 77. The Driver 78. Nosferatu 78. The Brontë Sisters 79. Clara et les Chics Types 80. Possession 80. Quartet 81. One Deadly Summer 83. Subway 85. Maladie d'Amour 86. Ishtar 87. Camille Claudel (AAN) 88. La Reine Margot 94. Diabolique (US) 96, etc.

Adler, Buddy (1906–1960) (Maurice Adler).
American producer, with Columbia from 1948, Fox from 1954 (head of studio from 1956).
The Dark Past 48. No Sad Songs for Me 50. Salome 53. *From Here to Eternity* (AA) 53. Violent Saturday 55. *Love is a Many Splendored Thing* 55. The Left Hand of God 55. Bus Stop 56. Anastasia 56. A Hatful of Rain 57. South Pacific 58. *The Inn of the Sixth Happiness* 58, etc.

Adler, Gilbert.
American director, screenwriter and producer.
Home Movies (p) 80. A Certain Fury (p) 85. Children of the Corn II: The Final Sacrifice (co-w) 93. Tales from the Crypt Presents Demon Knight (p) 95. Tales from the Crypt Presents Bordello of Blood (co-w, d) 96, etc.

Adler, Jay (1896–1978).
American character actor, brother of Luther Adler; usually played hoboes, small-time gangsters, etc.
No Time to Marry 38. My Six Convicts 52. 99 River Street 54. The Big Combo 55. Sweet Smell of Success 57. The Brothers Karamazov 58. Seven Guns to Mesa 60. The Family Jewels 65, many others.

Adler, Larry (1914–).
American harmonica virtuoso whose chief contribution to films is the score of *Genevieve* 53; also composed for *The Hellions* 61. *The Hook* 63. *King and Country* 63. *High Wind in Jamaica* 64; and appeared in *St Martin's Lane* 38. *Music for Millions* 44.
Autobiography: 1985, *It Ain't Necessarily So.*

Adler, Luther (1903–1984) (Lutha Adler).
Heavy-featured American character actor, member of well-known theatrical family (brother Jay, sister Stella).
■ Lancer Spy 37. Cornered 45. Saigon 48. The Loves of Carmen 48. *Wake of the Red Witch* 48. House of Strangers 49. D.O.A. 50. South Sea Sinner 50. Under My Skin 50. Kiss Tomorrow Goodbye 50. M 51. The Magic Face (as Hitler) 51. The Desert Fox 51. Hoodlum Empire 52. The Tall Texan 53. The Miami Story 54. Crashout 55. The Girl in the Red Velvet Swing 55. Hot Blood 56. The Last Angry Man 59. Cast a Giant Shadow 66. *The Brotherhood* 68. Crazy Joe 74. Murph the Surf 74. The Man in the Glass Booth 75. Mean Johnny Barrows 75. Voyage of the Damned 76. Absence of Malice 81.
TV series: The Psychiatrist 71. Also many guest appearances, especially in Naked City.

Adler, Richard (1921–).
American composer and lyricist who with his partner Jerry Ross (1926–55) (Jerold Rosenberg) wrote *The Pajama Game* and *Damn Yankees*.

Adler, Stella (1902–1992).
American stage actress, sister of Luther and Jay Adler. Known at one time as Stella Ardler.
Love on Toast 38. Shadow of the Thin Man 41. My Girl Tisa 48, etc.

Adlon, Percy (1935–).
German producer-director and screenwriter. A former actor, broadcaster and documentary film-maker, he founded his own production company in 1978. His international success came in 1987 with *Bagdad Café*, which made a star of Marianne Sägebrecht and subsequently became the basis for a TV series starring Whoopi Goldberg.
Celeste 81. Five Last Days/Letz Funf Tage 82. The Swing/Die Schaukel 83. Sugar Baby/ Zuckerbaby 86. Bagdad Café 87. Rosalie Goes Shopping 89. Salmonberries 91. Younger and Younger 93, etc.

Adolfi, John G. (1888–1933).
American director at his peak in the transitional period between silent and sound. Began as an actor, but quickly turned to directing and found steady work. Three years before his death he formed an association with George Arliss and filmed the star's stage successes.
A Man and His Mate 15. The Sphinx 16. A Modern Cinderella 17. A Child of the Wild 17. Queen of the Sea 18. Who's Your Brother? 19. The Darling of the Rich 22. The Little Red Schoolhouse 23. Chalk Marks 24. The Phantom Express 25. The Checkered Flag 26. Husband Hunters 27. The Little Snob 28. Fancy Baggage 29. The Show of Shows 29. Dumbbells in Ermine 30. Sinner's Holiday 30. College Lovers 30. The Millionaire 31. Alexandra Hamilton 31. Compromised 31. The Man Who Played God 32. A Successful Calamity 32. Central Park 32. The King's Vacation 33. The Working Man 33. Voltaire 33, many others.

Adoree, Renee (1898–1933) (Jeanne de la Fonté).
French leading lady, former circus bareback rider, who became an exotic star of Hollywood films in the 20s but could not transfer to sound and died of tuberculosis. The first of her two husbands was actor Tom Moore (1921–24).
The Strongest 20. Made in Heaven 21. Monte Cristo 22. The Eternal Struggle 23. Women Who Give 24. The Bandolero 24. Man and Maid 25. Exchange of Wives 25. *The Big Parade* 25. La Bohème 26. The Exquisite Sinner 26. Tin Gods 26. The Flaming Forest 26. Heaven on Earth 27. Mr Wu 27. On ze Boulevard 27. Back to God's Country 27. The Cossacks 28. The Michigan Kid 28. The Mating Call 28. The Pagan 29. Tide of Empire 29. Redemption 30. Call of the Flesh 30.

Adorf, Mario (1930–).
Swiss actor in European films.
The Girl Rosemarie 59. Station Six Sahara 63. Major Dundee (US) 65. Ten Little Indians 66. The Red Tent 71. Journey to Vienna 73. Fedora 78. The Tin Drum 79. L'Empreinte des géants 80. Lola 81. Smiley's People (TV) 80. Marco Polo (TV) 81. The Holcroft Covenant 85. Momo 86. Quiet Days in Clichy 90. Money 91. Smilla's Sense of Snow/Smilla's Feeling for Snow 96, etc.

Adreon, Franklin (1902–).
American second feature director.
Canadian Mounties vs Atomic Invaders (serial) 53. No Man's Woman 55. This Man Is Armed 56. Hell's Crossroads 57. The Steel Whip 58. The Nun and the Sergeant 62. Cyborg 2087 66. Dimension Five 66, etc.

Adrian (1903–1959) (Adrian Adolph Greenberg).
American costume designer, with MGM 1927–42 and credited with the authentic images of Garbo, Shearer, Harlow, etc. Married Janet Gaynor; quit films after being forced to create ordinary clothes for Garbo in *Two-Faced Woman*, a film that also ended Garbo's career. He opened his own successful fashion house and then retired to a ranch in Brazil, returning only to design the costumes for the stage version of *Camelot*. Committed suicide.
❝ If I'm copied, it's because of my clothes and Adrian does those. – *Joan Crawford*

Adrian, Iris (1912–1994) (I. A. Hostetter)
American character actress, former Ziegfeld Follies dancer, familiar from the early 30s as wisecracking or tawdry blonde.
Paramount on Parade 30. Rumba 35. Our Relations 37. Professional Bride 41. The G-String Murders 42. Spotlight Scandals 44. I'm from Arkansas 45. Road to Alcatraz 46. The Paleface 48. G.I. Jane 51. Highway Dragnet 54. The Buccaneer 59. That Darn Cat 65. The Odd Couple 68. Scandalous John 71. The Shaggy D.A. 76. Murder Can Hurt You (TV) 78. Herbie Goes Bananas 80, many others.
TV series: The Ted Knight Show 78.

Adrian, Max (1903–1973) (Max Bor).
Irish stage actor of high camp personality; latterly a star of mischievous revue and an impersonator of Bernard Shaw. Too richly flavoured to star in films, but made occasional character appearances.

■ The Primrose Path 34. Eight Cylinder Love 34. A Touch of the Moon 36. To Catch a Thief 36. Nothing Like Publicity 36. The Happy Family 37. When the Devil Was Well 37. Why Pick on Me? 37. Macushla 38. Merely Mr Hawkins 38. *Kipps* 41. Penn of Pennsylvania 41. *The Young Mr Pitt* 42. Talk About Jacqueline 42. Henry V 45. Her Favorite Husband 50. Pool of London 51. The Pickwick Papers 52. *Dr Terror's House of Horrors* 65. *The Deadly Affair* 66. Funeral in Berlin 66. Julius Caesar 70. The Music Lovers 70. The Devils 71. *The Boy Friend* 71.

Affleck, Ben (1972–).
American leading actor and screenwriter. Born in Berkeley, California, and brought up in Cambridge, Massachusetts, he made a breakthrough to wide recognition in *Chasing Amy*, and by writing *Good Will Hunting* with his friend Matt Damon. He began acting on television at the age of eight. He has been romantically linked with actress Gwyneth Paltrow. Current asking price: around $600,000.

Hands of a Stranger (TV) 87. School Ties 92. Dazed and Confused 93. Last Call 95. Mallrats 95. Glory Daze 96. Going All the Way 97. Chasing Amy 97. *Good Will Hunting* (& co-w) (AANw) 97. Armageddon 98. Shakespeare in Love 98. Phantoms 98. Dogma 98. Forces of Nature 99, etc.

TV series: Against the Grain 93.

Agar, John (1921–).
American leading man, once married to Shirley Temple; mainly in low-budgeters.

Fort Apache 48. Sands of Iwo Jima 49. The Magic Carpet 52. The Golden Mistress 53. Bait 54, Joe Butterfly 56. Daughter of Dr Jekyll 57. The Brain from Planet Arous 58. Journey to the Seventh Planet 61. Of Love and Desire 63. Cavalry Command 65. Waco 66. The St Valentine's Day Massacre 67. The Curse of the Swamp Creature 67. The Undefeated 69. Big Jake 71. King Kong 76. How's Your Love Life? 77. The Amazing Mr No-Legs 78. Perfect Victims 88. Miracle Mile 89. Fear 89. The Perfect Bride 91, etc.

Agate, James (1877–1947).
British drama critic with a passion for Sarah Bernhardt. He performed some reluctant stints of film reviewing, and the results are compiled in two volumes of *Around Cinema*. They show him as a highbrow waffler rather than a wit, and no real appreciation of the art of film comes through.

Autobiographies: *Ego* (Vols 1–9, 1935–49).

Biography: 1986, *Agate* by James Harding.

❝ What I want in the cinema is something that can't possibly happen to me. –*J.A.*

The fact remains that if a young man has a good photogenic profile one picture will make him a star even if he hasn't enough acting talent to carry in the tea-things in a play at Kew. –*J.A.*

A professional is a man who can do his job when he doesn't feel like it. An amateur is a man who can't do his job when he does feel like it. –*J.A.*

James Agate, the dean of English critics, said in one of his early reviews, 'Charles Laughton is a genius.' Then, about a year later in a review, Agate said, 'This so-called genius . . .' And then, some time later he said, 'This self-styled genius . . .' – *Elsa Lanchester*

Agee, James (1909–1955).
One of America's most respected film critics, he also wrote novels and screenplays (e.g. *The African Queen* 51). A posthumous collection of his reviews was published under the title *Agee on Film*, and the screenplays followed. His novel *A Death in the Family* was filmed in 1963 as *All the Way Home*.

✪ For his brief, witty, incisive reviews which perfectly encapsulate hundreds of 40s films.

Ager, Cecelia (1898–1981).
American critic for various New York magazines in the 30s. Wrote a book of essays, *Let's Go to the Pictures*.

Ager, Milton (1893–1979).
American composer and former vaudeville accompanist who, with lyricist Jack Yellen, wrote the score for Sophie Tucker's first movie, *Honky Tonk* 29. The partnership's biggest hit was that movie's 'Happy Days Are Here Again', which has also turned up in *Beau James* 57, *This Earth Is Mine* 59, and *The Night of the Iguana* 64.

Chasing Rainbows (s) 30. King of Jazz (s) 30. They Learned about Women (s) 30, etc.

Aghayan, Ray (1934–).
Iranian-born costume designer, in America.

Father Goose 64. Do Not Disturb 65. The Glass Bottom Boat 66. Caprice 67. Doctor Dolittle 67. Gaily, Gaily (AAN) 69. Hannie Calder 72. Lady Sings the Blues (AAN) 72. Funny Lady (AAN) 75, etc.

Agland, Phil (1950–).
English director, from television documentaries. Born in Weymouth, he studied geography at Hull University.

China: Beyond the Clouds (doc) 94. The Woodlanders 98.

Agnew, Robert (1899–1983).
American leading juvenile of silent pictures. Born in Louisville, Kentucky, he began on the stage and retired soon after the coming of sound to work at Warner Brothers as an assistant director.

The Valley of Doubt 20. The Passion Flower 21. Without Fear 22. The Spanish Dancer 23. Wine of Youth 24. The Great Love 25. She's My Baby 26. The Heart of Salome 27. The Heart of Broadway 28. Extravagance 30. The Naughty Flirt 31. Gold Diggers of 1933 33, etc.

Agostini, Philippe (1910–).
French director. Born in Paris, he was formerly a leading cinematographer of the 40s, who worked with such directors as Bresson, Carné and Ophuls.

as cinematographer: Carnet de Bal (co-ph) 37. Les Anges du Péché 43. Les Dames du Bois de Boulogne 44. Les Portes de la Nuit 46. Pattes Blanches 48. Le Plaisir (co-ph) 51. Rififi 55, etc.

as director: Le Naif aux 40 Enfants 57. Tu es Pierre 58. Le Dialogue des Carmélites 59. La Soupe aux Poulets 63. La Petite Fille Qui Cherche le Printemps 71, etc.

Agresti, Alejandro (1961–).
Argentinian director and screenwriter, a former cameraman, now based in Holland.

El Hombre que Ganó la Razón 86. Love is a Fat Woman/El Amor es una Mujer Gorda 88. Secret Wedding/Boda Secreta 89. City Life (co-d) 89. The Night of the Wild Donkeys/De Nacht de Wilde Ezels (a, p) 89. Luba 91. How to Survive a Broken Heart (a) 91. Modern Crimes (& a) 92. Just Good Friends 92. Pieces of Love 93. El Acto en Cuestión 93. Buenos Aires Vice Versa 96. Wind with the Gone/El Viento Se Llevó lo Que (wd) 98, etc.

Agutter, Jenny (1952–).
British actress who came to leading roles as a teenager.

East of Sudan 64. Gates to Paradise 67. Star! 68. I Start Counting 69. *The Railway Children* 70. Walkabout 70. The Snow Goose (TV) 71. A War of Children (TV) 72. Logan's Run 76. The Eagle Has Landed 77. Equus 77. Dominique 78. China Nine Liberty Thirty Seven 78. The Riddle of the Sands 79. Sweet William 79. The Survivor 80. Amy 81. An American Werewolf in London 81. Secret Places 84. Silas Marner (TV) 85. Dark Tower 87. King of the Wind 89. Child's Play 2 90. Darkman 90. Freddie as FR07 (voice) 92. The Buccaneers (TV) 95. A Respectable Trade (TV) 98, etc.

Aherne, Brian (1902–1986).
Gentle-mannered British leading man of stage and screen; resident from 1933 in Hollywood and New York, where he became the American ideal of the charming Britisher. A child actor who trained under Italia Conti, he was on stage from the age of nine. His first wife was Joan Fontaine.

Autobiography: 1969, *A Proper Job*. Also published a memoir of George Sanders: 1979, *A Dreadful Man*.

■ The Eleventh Commandment 24. King of the Castle 25. The Squire of Long Hadley 26. Safety First 26. A Woman Redeemed 27. *Shooting Stars* 28. Underground 29. The W Plan 30. Madame Guillotine 31. *I Was A Spy* 33. *Song of Songs* 33. What Every Woman Knows 34. The Fountain 34. *The Constant Nymph* 34. Sylvia Scarlett 35. I Live My Life 35. *Beloved Enemy* 36. *The Great Garrick* 37. Merrily We Live 38. Captain Fury 39. *Juarez* (as Emperor Maximilian) (AAN) 39. Vigil in the Night 40. *The Lady In Question* 40. Hired Wife 40. *My Son My Son* 40. The Man Who Lost Himself 41. Skylark 41. Smilin' Through 41. My Sister Eileen 42. Forever and a Day 43. A Night to Remember 43. First Comes Courage 43. What a Woman! 43. The Locket 46. Smart Woman 48. Angel on the Amazon 48. *I Confess* 53. Titanic 53. Prince Valiant 54. A Bullet is Waiting 54. *The Swan* (first comic character role) 56. The Best of Everything 59. Susan Slade 61. *Lancelot and Guinevere* (as King Arthur) 63. The Waltz King 64. The Cavern 65. Rosie 67.

Aherne, Patrick (1901–1970).
Irish light actor, brother of Brian Aherne; in America from 1936. He was married to Renee Houston.

A Daughter in Revolt 25. Huntingtower 27. The Game Chicken 31. Trouble Ahead 36. Green Dolphin Street 47. The Paradine Case 48. Bwana Devil 52. The Court Jester 56, etc.

Ahlberg, Mac (1931–).
Swedish director who later worked as a cinematographer in America.

as director: I, a Woman 65. I, a Woman II 68. Nana/Take Me, Love Me 70. Flossie 74. Around the World with Fanny Hill 74. Justine and Juliet 75. Bel Ami 76. Sex in Sweden/Molly 77, etc.

as cinematographer: Nocturna 78. Hell Night 81. Parasite 82. My Tutor 82. The Dungeon Master 84. Ghoulies 84. Trancers 84. Re-Animator 85. Eliminators 86. House 86. House II 87. Innocent Blood 92. My Boyfriend's Back 93. Striking Distance 93. Beverly Hills Cop III 94. The Brady Bunch Movie 95. A Very Brady Sequel 96, etc.

Ahlstedt, Börje (1939–).
Swedish character actor, best known internationally in the role of Uncle Carl in three films based on Ingmar Bergman's memories of his childhood.

I am Curious – Yellow/Jar Ar Nyfiken – Gul 67. I Am Curious – Blue/Jar Ar Nyfiken – Bla 68. Made in Sweden 69. Troll 71. Fanny and Alexander 83. Ronja Roverdatter 84. Amorosa 86. Emma's Shadow/Skyggen Af Emma 88. Fallgropen 89. The Best Intentions/Den Goda Viljan 92. Sunday's Children 92. Belma 95. Autumn in Paradise/Host I Paradiset 95, etc.

Ahn, Philip (1911–1978).
American actor of Korean parentage, seen in Hollywood films as an assortment of Asiatic types.

The General Died at Dawn 36. Thank You Mr Moto 38. Charlie Chan in Honolulu 38. They Got Me Covered 42. China Sky 45. Rogues' Regiment 48. I was an American Spy 51. Love is a Many Splendored Thing 55. Never So Few 59. Diamond Head 63. Thoroughly Modern Millie 67. The World's Greatest Athlete 73. Voodoo Heartbeat 75, many others.

TV series: Kung Fu 71–75.

Aidman, Charles (1925–1993).
American character actor, mostly on TV. He was narrator of the TV series *The Twilight Zone* 85–87.

The Hour of the Gun 67. Countdown 67. Kotch 72. Dirty Little Billy 72. Amelia Earhart (TV) 76. Twilight's Last Gleaming 77. Zoot Suit 81. Prime Suspect (TV) 81. Uncommon Valor 83, etc.

Aiello, Danny (1935–).
American actor.

The Front 76. Fingers 77. Bloodbrothers 78. Fort Apache, the Bronx 81. Once Upon a Time in America 84. The Purple Rose of Cairo 84. The Stuff 85. Man on Fire 87. Moonstruck 87. The Pick-Up Artist 87. Radio Days 87. The January Man 88. White Hot 88. Do the Right Thing (AAN) 89. Harlem Nights 89. Russicum 89. Jacob's Ladder 90. Once Around 90. Hudson Hawk 91. The Closer 91. The Pickle 92. Ruby 92. 29th Street 92. Mistress 92. The Cemetery Club 93. The Pickle 93. Me and the Kid 93. Leon/The Professional (Fr.) 94. Prêt-à-Porter/Ready to Wear 94. City Hall 96. Two Days in the Valley 96. Two Much 96. Mojave Moon 96. The Last Don (TV) 97. Bring Me the Head of Mavis Davies 98. The Last Don II (TV) 98, etc.

TV series: Lady Blue 85–86. Dellaventura 97–98.

Aimée, Anouk (1932–)
(Françoise Sorya Dreyfus).
Svelte French leading lady who captured many hearts in the days when she was known simply as 'Anouk'. She has subsequently lent her poise to many routine pictures.

La Maison sous la Mer 47. *Les Amants de Vérone* 49. The Golden Salamander (GB) 49. Le Rideau Cramoisi 51. The Man Who Watched Trains Go By (GB) 52. Les Mauvaises Rencontres 55. Contraband Spain (GB) 55. Pot Bouille 56. Montparnasse 19 58. La Tête Contre les Murs 58. Les Dragueurs 59. The Journey (US) 59. La Dolce Vita 60. *Lola* 61. Sodom and Gomorrah 61. Eight and a Half 63. La Fuga 65. *Un Homme et une Femme* (AAN) 66. Justine (US) 69. The Model Shop (US) 69. The Appointment (US) 69. Si C'était à Refaire 76. Mon Premier Amour 78. The Tragedy of a Ridiculous Man 81. General of the Dead Army 83. Success is the Best Revenge 84. Long Live Life 84. A Man and a Woman: 20 Years Later 86. Arrivederci e Grazie 88. La Table Tournante 88. Bethune: The Making of a Hero 90. Il y a des Jours . . . et des Lunes 90. Ruptures 92. Les Marmottes 93. Prêt-à-Porter 94. LA without a Map (as herself) 98, etc.

Aimos, Raymond (1889–1944).
French general-purpose actor of the 30s; died from war injuries.

Vingt Ans Après 22. Quatorze Juillet 32. Le Dernier Milliardaire 34. Mayerling 36. Le Golem 36. La Belle Equipe 36. Quai des Brumes 38. De Mayerling à Sarajevo 40. Lumière d'Eté 42. Les Petites du Quai aux Fleurs 43, etc.

Ainley, Henry (1879–1945).
British stage actor in occasional films, a former accountant.

She Stoops to Conquer 14. The Prisoner of Zenda 15. Rupert of Hentzau 15. The Great Adventure 15. The Manxman 16. Quinneys 19. The Prince and the Beggarmaid 21. Sweet Lavender 23. The Good Companions 32. The First Mrs Fraser 32. As You Like It 36, etc.

Ainley, Richard (1910–1967).
British-born actor, son of Henry Ainley.

As You Like It 36. The Frog 37. A Stolen Life 39. Lady with Red Hair 40. The Smiling Ghost 41. White Cargo 42. Above Suspicion 43. Passage to Hong Kong 49, etc.

Aitken, Maria (1945–).
Lanky British comedy actress, popular on TV. Her second husband was actor Nigel Davenport (1972–80).

Some Girls Do 69. Mary, Queen of Scots 71. Half Moon Street 87. A Fish Called Wanda 88. The Grotesque 95. Jinnah (Pak.) 98, etc.

TV series: Company and Co. 80. Poor Little Rich Girls 84.

Aitken, Spottiswoode (1869–1933) (Frank Aitken).
Scottish-born character actor, usually as benign old men, in silent films in Hollywood, from the stage. He appeared in several of D. W. Griffith's films, including the role of Dr Cameron in *The Birth of a Nation*.

The Battle 11. The Avenging Conscience 14. The Birth of a Nation 15. Intolerance 15. Stage Struck 17. Her Kingdom of Dreams 19. Nomads of the North 20. The Unknown Wife 21. Manslaughter 22. The Young Rajah 22. Six Days 23. The Eagle 25. The Goose Woman 25. Roaring Fires 27, many others.

Aked, Muriel (1887–1955).
British character actress usually seen as comedy spinster or gossip.

A Sister to Assist 'Er 22 and 47. The Mayor's Nest 32. *Rome Express* 32. Friday the Thirteenth 33. Cottage to Let 41. Two Thousand Women 44. The Wicked Lady 45. *The Happiest Days of Your Life* 50. The Story of Gilbert and Sullivan 53, etc.

Akeley, Carl E. (1864–1926).
American taxidermist and photographer, inventor in the early 20s of a tripod camera which first made steady panning possible.

Akerman, Chantal (1950–).
Belgian director and screenwriter who learned her craft in New York in the early 70s.

Saute Ma Ville 68. La Chambre 72. News from Home 76. Dis Moi 80. L'Homme à la Valise 83. The Golden Eighties 86. Seven Women, Seven Sins (co-d) 87. Histoires d'Amérique 89. Night and Day/Nuit et Jour 91. Window Shopping 92. D'Est 93. A Couch in New York 96, etc.

Akins, Claude (1918–1994).
Solidly built American character actor who was usually cast as a western villain until it was realized that he could just as well play a burly middle-aged hero, Wallace Beery-style. In the late 70s he was much in demand as a TV star.
■ *From Here to Eternity* 53. Bitter Creek 54. The Caine Mutiny 54. The Raid 54. The Human Jungle 54. Down Three Dark Streets 54. Shield for Murder 54. The Sea Chase 55. Battle Stations 56. The Proud and Profane 56. Johnny Concho 56. The Burning Hills 56. The Sharkfighters 56. Hot Summer Night 57. The Kettles on Old Macdonald's Farm 57. The Lonely Man 57. Joe Dakota 57. The Defiant Ones 58. Onionhead 58. Rio Bravo 59. Don't Give Up the Ship 59. *Porgy and Bess* 59. Yellowstone Kelly 59. The Hound Dog Man 59. Comanche Station 60. Inherit the Wind 60. Claudelle Inglish 61. Merrill's Marauders 62. How the West Was Won 62. Black Gold 63. A Distant Trumpet 64. The Killers 64. Ride Beyond Vengeance 64. Return of the Seven 66. Incident at Phantom Hill 66. First to Fight 67. Waterhole Three 67. The Devil's Brigade 68. The Great Bank Robbery 69. Flap 70. A Man Called Sledge 71. The Night Stalker (TV) 71. Skyjacked 72. Battle for the Planet of the Apes 73. In Tandem (TV) 73. Timber Tramps 75. Tentacles 77. Tarantulas: The Deadly Cargo 77. Monster in the Closet 86. Sherlock Holmes: The Incident at Victoria Falls (TV) 91. Falling from Grace 92.
TV series as star: *Movin' On* 74–75. B.J. and the Bear 79. The Misadventures of Sheriff Lobo 79–81. Legmen 84.

Akins, Zoë (1886–1958).
American playwright and screenwriter. Born in Humansville, Missouri, she became a successful playwright in 1919 and remained one through the 20s, going to Hollywood in the 30s to write screenplays. By the end of the decade, her work no longer attracted much of an audience on stage or screen.
Daddy's Gone a-Hunting (oa) 25. Her Private Life (oa) 29. The Right to Love 30. Sarah and Son 30. Anybody's Woman 30. Once a Lady 31. *The Greeks Had a Word for Them* (oa) 32. Morning Glory (oa) 33. Christopher Strong 33. Outcast Lady 34. Lady of Secrets 36. Accused 36. Camille 37. The Toy Wife 38. Zaza 38. The Old Maid (oa) 39. Desire Me 47. How to Marry a Millionaire 53. Stage Struck (oa) 58, etc.
❝ A woman with a career is a tragedy. Women are not fitted for careers. I, who have one, say it! – Z.A.

Akkad, Moustapha.
Syrian producer and director.
Mohammad, Messenger of God (p, d) 77. Lion of the Desert (p, d) 81. Appointment with Fear 85 (p). Free Ride 86. Halloween 5 (p) 89, etc.

Akst, Albert (c. 1890–1958).
American editor, long at MGM.
The Raven 35. Johnny Eager 42. Meet Me in St Louis 44. Ziegfeld Follies 46. Easter Parade 48. Annie Get Your Gun 50. Royal Wedding 52. The Band Wagon 53. Moonfleet 55. Somebody Up There Likes Me 56, many others.

Akst, Harry (1894–1963).
American composer and pianist. Born in New York, he worked in vaudeville and was staff pianist for Irving BERLIN's publishing company before heading for Hollywood, where he wrote many songs for the studios, notably for Fox and Warner. He was also accompanist to Al JOLSON. His best-known songs include 'Am I Blue?', 'Baby Face' and 'Dinah'.
The Squall 29. On with the Show 29. So Long, Letty 29. Song of the Flame 30. Leathernecking 30. Stand Up and Cheer 34. Bright Lights 35. Can This Be Dixie? 36. The Music Goes Round 36. Star for a Night 36. The Holy Terror 37. Sing and Be Happy 37. Rascals 38. Harvest Melody 43, etc.

Alazraki, Benito (1923–).
Mexican director best known abroad for his 1955 film of Indian life, *Roots*. Born in Mexico City, he moved to Spain in the early 60s, where he worked mainly in television, returning to Mexico in the early 70s. He began directing films again in the late 80s.
Roots/Raices 54. Los Amantes 57. Café Colon 58. Lost Souls/Infierno de Almas 58. The Karambazo Sisters/Las Hermanas Karambazo 59. Black Bull/Toro Negro 60. The Time and the Touch (US) 62. Los Jóvenes Amantes (Sp.) 70. Las Tres Perfectas Casadas (Sp.) 72. El Rey de los Taxistas 87. Objetos Sexuales 89, etc.

Alba, Maria (1905–) (Maria Casajuana).
Spanish actress and dancer, born in Barcelona, who was in American films of the late 20s and 30s.
Girl in Every Port 28. Hell's Heroes 30. Mr Robinson Crusoe 32. Chandu on the Magic Island 34. Return of Chandu 34, etc.

Albee, Edward (1928–).
American playwright whose only significant contribution to cinema was *Who's Afraid of Virginia Woolf?* 66. *A Delicate Balance* however was filmed in 1973.
❝ 'I have a fine sense of the ridiculous but no sense of humour.' – *Quote from Who's Afraid of Virginia Woolf?*

Alberghetti, Anna Maria (1936–).
Italian-American operatic singer who came to films as a teenager and has made occasional appearances. Born in Pesaro, Italy, she retired from the screen in the early 60s. Married director Claudio Guzman.
Here Comes the Groom 51. The Stars Are Singing 53. The Medium 54. The Last Command 55. Ten Thousand Bedrooms 57. Cinderfella 60, etc.

Alberni, Luis (1887–1962).
Spanish-American character actor who played countless small film roles, usually featuring his mangled English.
Santa Fe Trail 30. Svengali 31. The Kid from Spain 32. Topaze 33. Flying Down to Rio 33. Roberta 35. Anthony Adverse 36. The Housekeeper's Daughter 39. That Hamilton Woman 42. Captain Carey USA 49. What Price Glory 52. The Ten Commandments 57, etc.

Albers, Hans (1892–1960).
Leading German actor with broad experience. Born in Hamburg, he began as a vaudeville comedian and dancer, and was in films from 1911. In the late 20s, he appeared in Max REINHARDT's stage productions and established himself as the leading German film actor of his time, gaining an international reputation with his performance in *The Blue Angel*.
Irene d'Or 23. A Midsummer Night's Dream 25. Rasputin 29. The Blue Angel 30. Drei Tage Liebe 31. FP 1 32. Gold 33. Peer Gynt 35. Casanova 36. Baron Munchausen 43. The White Hell of Pitz Palu 53. Der Greifer 58. Kein Engel ist so Rein 60, etc.

Albert, Eddie (1908– (Eddie Albert Heimberger).
American character actor with radio and stage experience: for nearly forty years he has been playing honest Joes, nice guys and best friends, seldom winning the girl but allowing himself an occasional meaty role out of character.
■ *Brother Rat* 38. On Your Toes 39. *Four Wives* 39. Brother Rat and a Baby 40. An Angel from Texas 40. My Love Came Back 40. A Dispatch from Reuters 40. Four Mothers 41. The Wagons Roll at Night 41. Out of the Fog 41. Thieves Fall Out 41. The Great Mr Nobody 41. Treat 'Em Rough 42. Eagle Squadron 42. Ladies' Day 43. Lady Bodyguard 43. Bombardier 43. Strange Voyage 45. Rendezvous with Annie 46. The Perfect Marriage 46. *Smash Up* 47. Time out of Mind 47. Hit Parade of 1947 47. The Dude Goes West 48. You Gotta Stay Happy 48. The Fuller Brush Girl 50. Meet Me After the Show 51. You're in the Navy Now 51. Actors and Sin 52. *Carrie* 52. *Roman Holiday* (AAN) 53. The Girl Rush 55. *Oklahoma!* 55. *I'll Cry Tomorrow* 55. *Attack!* (his most serious role) 56. *The Teahouse of the August Moon* 56. The Sun Also Rises 57. The Joker is Wild 57. The Gun Runners 58. *The Roots of Heaven* 58. *Orders to Kill* (GB) 58. Beloved Infidel 59. The Young Doctors 61. The Two Little Bears 61. Madison Avenue 62. The Longest Day 62. Who's Got the Action? 62. The Party's Over (GB) 63. Miracle of the White Stallions 65. Captain Newman MD 63. Seven Women 65. See the Man Run (TV) 71. Fireball Forward (TV) 72. McQ 72. The Take 72. The Heartbreak Kid (AAN) 72. *The Longest Yard* 74. Escape to Witch Mountain 75. The Devil's Rain 75. Promise Him Anything (TV) 75. Hustle 76. Whiffs 76. Birch Interval 76. Moving Violation 76. The Word (TV) 78. Airport 80 The Concorde 79. Foolin' Around 80. How to Beat the High Cost of Living 80. Take This Job and Shove It 81. Yes Giorgio 82. Yesterday 80. This Time Forever 81. The Act 84. Dreamscape 84. Goliath Awaits (TV) 84. Head Office 85. Stitches 85. In Like Flynn (TV) 85. Turnaround 86. Head Office 86. The Big Picture 88. Brenda Starr 89. Return to Green Acres (TV) 90. The Girl from Mars 91. Brenda Starr 92.
TV series: *Leave It to Larry* 52. *Green Acres* 65–71. *Switch* 75–78. Falcon Crest 86. Beauty and The Beast 89–90.

Albert, Edward (1951–).
American light actor, son of Eddie Albert; his career to date has been somewhat disappointing.
The Fool Killer 65. Butterflies Are Free 72. Forty Carats 73. Midway 76. The Domino Principle 77. The Purple Taxi 77. The Greek Tycoon 78. The Word (TV) 78. Silent Victory (TV) 79. The Last Convertible (TV) 79. When Time Ran Out 80. Galaxy of Terror 81. Butterfly 81. The Squeeze 81. Blood Feud (TV) 81. The House Where Evil Dwells 82. Ellie 84. Getting Even 86. Distortions 87. Terminal Entry 87. The Underachievers 88. Fist Fighter 88. The Rescue 88. Mindgames 89. Wild Zone 89. Exiled in America 90. Body Language 92. Shootfighter: Fight to the Death 93. The Ice Runner 93. Guarding Tess 94. Space Marines 96. The Secret Agent Club 96. The Man in the Iron Mask 97, etc.
TV series: The Yellow Rose 83–84. Falcon Crest 86.

Albert, Marvin H (1924–).
American screenwriter.
Duel at Diablo 66. Rough Night in Jericho (co-w) 67. Lady in Cement (co-w) 68. A Twist of Sand 68, etc.

Albertson, Frank (1909–1964).
American light leading man, later character actor, in films since 1922 when he began as extra and prop boy.
Prep and Pep 28. Just Imagine 31. A Connecticut Yankee 31. Dangerous Crossroad 33. Alice Adams 35. Fury 36. The Plainsman 37. *Room Service* 38. *Bachelor Mother* 39. The Man from Headquarters 40. Man Made Monster 41. Mystery Broadcast 43. Arson Squad 45. The Hucksters 47. The Last Hurrah 58. Bye Bye Birdie 63, many others.

Albertson, Jack (1907–1981).
American character actor who started as a straight man in burlesque.
Miracle on 34th Street 47. Top Banana 54. The Harder They Fall 56. Man of a Thousand Faces 57. The Shaggy Dog 59. Period of Adjustment 62. A Tiger Walks 64. How to Murder Your Wife 65. *The Subject Was Roses* (AA) 68. Justine 69. Rabbit Run 70. *Willy Wonka and the Chocolate Factory* 71. The Poseidon Adventure 72. Pick Up on 101 72. Charlie's Balloon (TV) 78. Dead and Buried 81, etc.
TV series: Ensign O'Toole 62–64. Dr Simon Locke 72. *Chico and the Man* 74–77. Grandpa Goes to Washington 78.

Albertson, Mabel (1901–1982).
American character comedienne, typically cast as nosy neighbour or wise and witty grandma.
Mutiny on the Blackhawk 39. She's Back on Broadway 53. Ransom 56. Forever Darling 56. *The Long Hot Summer* 58. *Home Before Dark* 58. *The Gazebo* 60. Period of Adjustment 62. *Barefoot in the Park* 67. On a Clear Day You Can See Forever 70. What's Up Doc? 72, etc.
TV series: That's My Boy 54–55. Those Whiting Girls 57. The Tom Ewell Show 60–61.

Albicocco, Jean-Gabriel (1936–).
French director with a pictorial eye.
■ The Girl with the Golden Eyes 61. Le Rat d'Amérique 62. *Le Grand Meaulnes* 67. L'Amour au Féminin (part) 68. Le Coeur Fou 70. Le Petit Matin 71.

Albright, Hardie (1903–1975) (Hardy Albrecht).
Underused American leading man of the 30s, of Scottish and Jewish parentage.
■ Young Sinners 31. Hush Money 31. Skyline 31. Heartbreak 31. A Successful Calamity 32. So Big 32. The Purchase Price 32. Jewel Robbery 32. The Crash 32. Three on a Match 32. Cabin in the Cotton 32. This Sporting Age 32. The Match King 32. The Working Man 32. Song of Songs 33. *Three Cornered Moon* 33. The House on 56th Street 33. Nana 34. Crimson Romance 34. The Ninth Guest 34. White Heat 34. Beggar's Holiday 34. The Scarlet Letter 34. Two Heads on a Pillow 34. The Silver Streak 34. Sing Sing Nights 34. Women Must Dress 35. Ladies Love Danger 35. Calm Yourself 35. Champagne for Breakfast 35. Red Salute 35. Granny Get Your Gun 40. Ski Patrol 40. Carolina Moon 40. Flight from Destiny 41. Men of the Timberland 41. Bachelor Daddy 41. Marry the Boss's Daughter 41. The Loves of Edgar Allan Poe 42. Lady in a Jam 42. Pride of the Yankees 42. Army Wives 44. Captain Tugboat Annie 45. The Jade Mask 45. Sunset in Eldorado 45. Angel on My Shoulder 46. Mom and Dad 57.

Albright, Lola (1925–).
Stylish, tough-talking American leading lady; roles for her Stanwyck-like personality were hard to find.
Champion 49. The Good Humour Man 50. Arctic Flight 52. The Tender Trap 56. The Monolith Monsters 57. Seven Guns to Mesa 60. *A Cold Wind in August* 61. Kid Galahad 62. The Love Cage 65. Lord Love a Duck 66. The Way West 67. Where Were You When the Lights Went Out? 68. The Impossible Years 68, etc.
TV series: *Peter Gunn* 58–60.

Albright, Wally (1925–).
Curly-haired American juvenile actor, in films from the age of one, who appeared in Our Gang shorts and quit in 1954 to follow business interests.
Thunder 29. East Lynne 31. The Prodigal 31. Zoo in Budapest 33. The Count of Monte Cristo 34. Black Fury 35. The Woman I Love 37. What Price Vengeance 37. The Wild One 54, etc.

Alcott, John (1931–1986).
British cinematographer.
A Clockwork Orange 71. Barry Lyndon (AA) 75. March or Die 77. Someone Is Killing the Great Chefs of Europe 78. The Shining 79. Terror Train 80. Fort Apache, the Bronx 81. Greystoke: The Legend of Tarzan, Lord of the Apes 84. Baby 85. No Way Out 87. White Water Summer 87, etc.

Alcott, Louisa M. (1832–1888).
American novelist whose cosy family tales LITTLE WOMEN and *Little Men* have been frequently plundered by movie-makers.

Alda, Alan (1936–).
American leading actor and director, son of Robert Alda.
Gone Are the Days 63. The Extraordinary Seaman 68. Paper Lion 68. Catch 22 70. Jenny 70. The Mephisto Waltz 71. To Kill A Clown 72. The Glass House (TV) 72. The Moonshine War 74. Kill Me if You Can (as Caryl Chessman) (TV) 77. *Same Time Next Year* 78. California Suite 78. The Seduction of Joe Tynan (& w) 79. *The Four Seasons* (& w, d) 81. Sweet Liberty (& w, d) 86. A New Life (& w, d) 88. Crimes and Misdemeanors 89. Betsy's Wedding (& w, d) 90. Whispers in the Dark 92. Manhattan Murder Mystery 93. And the Band Played On (TV) 94. White Mile (TV) 94. Canadian Bacon 95. Flirting with Disaster 96. Everyone Says I Love You 96. Murder at 1600 97. Mad City 97. The Object of My Affection 98, etc.
TV series: M*A*S*H 72–82.
❝ I wouldn't live in California. All that sun makes you sterile. – A.A.

Alda, Robert (1914–1986) (Alphonso d'Abruzzo).
American actor with radio and stage experience.
Rhapsody in Blue (as George Gershwin) 45. Cloak and Dagger 46. The Beast with Five Fingers 47. Nora Prentiss 47. April Showers 48. Tarzan and the Slave Girl 50. Two Gals and a Guy 51. Beautiful but Dangerous (It.) 55. Imitation of Life 59. Cleopatra's Daughter 63. The Girl Who Knew Too Much 68. I Will, I Will, for Now 76. Bittersweet Love 76, etc.
TV series: Secret File, U.S.A. 54–55. Supertrain 79.

Alden, Mary (1883–1946).
American actress, from the stage, best known for her work with D. W. Griffith.
The Battle of the Sexes 14. The Old Maid 14. Home, Sweet Home 14. Birth of a Nation 15. The Good-Bad Man 16. The Unpardonable Sin 19. Milestone 20. Trust Your Wife 21. Man with Two Mothers 22. Pleasure Mad 23. Babbitt 24. Soiled 24. The Plastic Age 25. Brown of Harvard 26. Twin Flappers 27. Ladies of the Mob 28. Sawdust Paradise 28. Girl Overboard 29. Hell's House 32. Strange Interlude 32, etc.

Alden, Norman (1924–).
American character actor.
Operation Bottleneck 60. Man's Favorite Sport 63. The Devil's Brigade 68. Tora Tora Tora 70. Kansas City Bomber 72. Semi-Tough 77. I Never Promised You a Rose Garden 77. Borderline 80. Back to the Future 85. Off the Mark 87. Ed Wood 94, etc.
TV series: Hennessy 60–62. Rango 67. Fay 75–76.

Alderton, John (1940–).
British light leading man, a popular figure in several long-running TV series including *Emergency Ward Ten*, *Please Sir*, *Upstairs Downstairs*, *Thomas and Sarah*, *My Wife Next Door* and *Father's Day*. Married to actress Pauline Collins.
The System 64. Duffy 68. Hannibal Brooks 69. Please Sir 71. Zardoz 74. It Shouldn't Happen to a Vet 76. Clockwork Mice 95, etc.

Aldo, G. R. (1902–1953) (Aldo Graziati).
Italian cinematographer. He was killed in a car crash while working on *Senso*.
La Chartreuse de Parme 47. La Terra Trema 48. The Last Days of Pompeii 49. *Miracle in Milan* 51. Othello 51. Umberto D 52. Indiscretion 53. La Provinciale 53. Senso 54.

Aldon, Mari (1930–).
American leading lady of the 50s; former ballet dancer.
Distant Drums 51. This Woman Is Dangerous 52. The Barefoot Contessa 54. Summertime 55. The Mad Trapper 72, etc.

Aldredge, Theoni V. (1932–).
Greek costume designer, in America, from the stage.
Girl of the Night 60. No Way to Treat a Lady 68. The Great Gatsby (AA) 74. Eyes of Laura Mars 78. Can't Stop the Music 80. Rich and Famous 81. Annie 82. Ghostbusters 84. Moonstruck 87. We're No Angels 89. Stanley & Iris 90. Other People's Money 91. Milk Money 94. Mrs Winterbourne 96. The First Wives Club 96. The Mirror Has Two Faces 96, etc.

Aldrich, Robert (1918–1983).
American director and producer of tough and often sensational features, more appreciated in Europe than America. Born in Cranston, Rhode Island, he studied law and economics at the University of Virginia and began working for RKO as a production clerk, progressing to assistant director. In the mid-40s, he also worked with Jean Renoir on *The Southerner*. By the early 50s, he was directing TV dramas, and set up his own production company in 1955. He worked in Europe in the late 50s and early 60s, before returning to Hollywood and establishing his own studio following the success of *The Dirty Dozen*; but he was forced to sell in the mid-70s, dying soon after from kidney failure.
Biography: 1995, *Whatever Happened to Robert Aldrich?: His Life and His Films* by Alain Silver, James Ursini.
■ Big Leaguer 53. World for Ransom 53. *Apache* 54. *Vera Cruz* 54. *Kiss Me Deadly* (& p) 55. The Big Knife (& p) 55. Autumn Leaves 56. *Attack!* (& p) 57. Ten Seconds to Hell 59. The Angry Hills 59. The Last Sunset 60. Sodom and Gomorrah (co-d) 63. *Whatever Happened to Baby Jane?* 62. Four For Texas 63. Hush Hush Sweet Charlotte 64. The Flight of the Phoenix 65. *The Dirty Dozen* 66. The Killing of Sister George 68. The Legend of Lylah Clare 69. Too Late the Hero 69. The Grissom Gang 71. Ulzana's Raid 72. Emperor of the North Pole 73. The Longest Yard 75. Hustle 76. Twilight's Last Gleaming 77. The Choirboys 77. The Frisco Kid 79. All the Marbles 81.
❝ A director is a ringmaster, a psychiatrist and a referee. – *R.A.*
His films are invariably troubled by intimations of decadence and disorder. – *Andrew Sarris, 1968*

Aldridge, Michael (1920–1994).
English character actor, with a nice line in suave comedy and aristocratic vagueness.
Bank Holiday Luck 47. Murder in the Cathedral 51. Mouse on the Moon 63. Chimes at Midnight 66. Follow Me/The Public Eye 71. Tinker, Tailor, Soldier, Spy (TV) 80. The Barchester Chronicles (TV) 82. Bullshot 83. Turtle Diary 85. Mussolini – The Untold Story (TV) 85. Shanghai Surprise 86. Clockwise 86, etc.
TV series: The Man in Room 17 65–66. Love for Lydia 77. Charlie 84. Charters and Caldicott 85. Last of the Summer Wine 85–89.

Alea, Tomás Gutiérrez (1928–1996).
Leading Cuban film director and screenwriter. Born in Havana, he studied law and then went to Rome to study cinema before returning to Cuba where he was one of the founders of ICAIC, the country's film institute set up to create a national cinema following Castro's revolution.
Stories of the Revolution/Historias de la Revolución 60. Cumbite 64. *Death of a Bureaucrat*/La Muerte de un Burocrata 66. *Memories of Underdevelopment*/Memorias del Subdesarrollo 68. El Arte del Tobaco 74. The Last Supper/La Última Cena 76. The Survivors/Los Sobrevivientes 79. Up to a Point/Hasta Cierto Punto 83. Letters from the Park/Cartas del Parque 88. *Strawberry and Chocolate*/Fresa y Chocolate (AAN) 94. Guantanamera (co-w, co-d) 95, etc.

Aleandro, Norma (1936–).
Argentinian leading actress, now in international films, from the stage and television. She won the best actress award at the Cannes Film Festival for her role in *The Official Story*.
La Muerte en las Calles 52. La Fiaca 68. Guemes, the Land in Arms 71. The Truce/La Tregua 74. Don't Touch the Girl 76. The Official Story/La Historia Oficial 85. Gaby – A True Story (US) (AAN) 87. Cousins (US) 89. Dark Holiday (US) (TV) 89. Vital Signs (US) 90. One Man's War (GB) 91. The Tombs (Sp.) 91, etc.

Aleichem, Sholem (1859–1916) (Solomon Rabinovitch).
Russian/Jewish storyteller whose *Tevye the Milkman* was much filmed in Yiddish and finally emerged as *Fiddler on the Roof*.

Alekan, Henri (1909–).
French cinematographer.
Mademoiselle Docteur 37. La Bataille du Rail 44. *La Belle et la Bête* 46. Les Maudits 47. *Une Si Jolie Petite Plage* 48. Anna Karenina 48. Juliette ou la Clef des Songes 50. Austerlitz 60. Topkapi 64. Lady L 65. Triple Cross 66. Mayerling 68. Red Sun 71. The Territory 81. La Belle Captive 83. Esther 86. *Wings of Desire*/Der Mimmel über Berlin 87. Jerusalem 89. Bilitis, My Love 91, etc.

Alessandrini, Goffredo (1904–1978).
Italian director and occasional screenwriter of popular films who scored a local success with his pro-fascist war films from the mid-30s. Born in Cairo, he began in Italy as an assistant to director Alessandro Blasetti, and then went to Hollywood to supervise the Italian versions of MGM films, before returning to Italy to work as a director. Married (1938–40) actress Anna Magnani.
La Segretaria Privata 31. Seconda B (& co-w) 34. Don Bosco 35. *Cavalleria* 36. Luciano Serra, Pilote 38. Abuna Messias 39. Caravaggio 41. Nozze di Sangue 41. Giarabub 42. We, the Living/Noi Vivi 42. Furia 47. Rapture 49. Gli Amanti del Deserto (co-d) 56, etc.

Alexander, Ben (1911–1969) (Nicholas Benton Alexander).
American boy actor of silent days; later character man.
The Little Americans 17. Little Orphan Annie 18. Hearts of the World 18. Tangled Threads 19. Family Honor 20. Boy of Mine 23. Penrod and Sam 23. Pampered Youth 25. Scotty of the Scouts 26. All Quiet on the Western Front 30. Are These Our Children? 31. Tom Brown of Culver 33. Stage Mother 33. Flirtation 34. Annapolis Farewell 35. Born to Gamble 35. Splendor 35. Red Lights Ahead 37. Shall We Dance? 37. Western Gold 37. The Leather Pushers 40. Criminals Within 41. Dragnet 54. Man in the Shadow 57, many others.
TV series: *Dragnet* 51–58. The Felony Squad 66–68.

Alexander, Jane (1939–) (Jane Quigley).
American stage actress in occasional films. Born in Boston, she studied at the University of Edinburgh. Her second husband was director Edward Sherin.
■ The Great White Hope (AAN) 70. A Gunfight 71. Welcome Home Johnny Bristol (TV) 71. The New Centurions 72. Miracle on 34th Street (TV) 73. This Is the West That Was (TV) 74. Death Be Not Proud (TV) 75. *All the President's Men* (AAN) 76. *Eleanor and Franklin* (TV) (as Eleanor Roosevelt) 76. The Betsy 78. Kramer versus Kramer (AAN) 79. Brubaker 80. Playing for Time (TV) 80. Night Crossing 82. Testament (AAN) 83. City Heat 84. Malice in Wonderland (TV) (as Hedda Hopper) 85. Sweet Country 86, Blood and Orchids (TV) 86. Square Dance 86. Building Bombs 89. Glory 89. An American Place 89. Stay the Night 92.
❝ I never thought of myself as pretty as a child, and I have tried to bring that awareness to my roles. – *J.A.*
Things come up suddenly these days, but that's all right because I work better under pressure. – *J.A.*

Alexander, Jason (1959–) (Jay Greenspan).
American actor, from juvenile roles on television. He is best known for his role as George Costanza in the TV sitcom *Seinfeld*, for which he reportedly earned $60,000 an episode.
Pretty Woman 89. White Palace 90. I Don't Buy Kisses Anymore 92. Coneheads 93. The Paper 94. North 94. Blankman 94. Dunston Checks In 96. The Hunchback of Notre Dame (voice) 96. The Last Supper 96. Love! Valour! Compassion! 97. Cinderella (TV) 97, etc.
TV series: E/R 84–85. Seinfeld 90–98.

Alexander, Jeff (1910–1989).
American composer.
Westward the Women 51. Escape from Fort Bravo 53. The Tender Trap 55. Gun Glory 57. Ask Any Girl 59. Kid Galahad 61. The Rounders 65. Speedway 68. Dirty Dingus Magee 70. The Sex Symbol (TV) 74. Kate Bliss and the Tickertape Kid (TV) 78. The Sea Gypsies 78, many others.

Alexander, John (1897–1982).
Portly American stage actor with amiable personality.
The Petrified Forest 36. Flowing Gold 41. A Tree Grows in Brooklyn 44. *Arsenic and Old Lace* (as Uncle Teddy) 44. Mr Skeffington 45. The Jolson Story 46. Summer Holiday 48. Fancy Pants (as Theodore Roosevelt) 50. The Marrying Kind 52. The Man in the Net 59. One Foot in Hell 60, etc.

Alexander, Katherine (1901–1981).
American actress specializing in sympathetic second leads.
The Barretts of Wimpole Street 34. The Painted Veil 34. The Dark Angel 36. Double Wedding 37. The Great Man Votes 39. The Hunchback of Notre Dame 39. The Vanishing Virginian 42. The Human Comedy 42. Kiss and Tell 45. John Loves Mary 49, etc.

Alexander, Richard (1903–1989).
Massive character actor who played villains in many serials and westerns and was also Prince Barin, rightful ruler of Mongo, in the serials *Flash Gordon* 36 and *Flash Gordon's Trip to Mars* 38.

Alexander, Ross (1907–1937).
American leading man of the early 30s. Born in Brooklyn, New York, he was on-stage from his teens. Married actresses Aleta Freel and Anne Nagel. Shot himself.
■ The Wiser Sex 32. Flirtation Walk 34. Gentlemen Are Born 34. Loudspeaker Lowdown 34. Social Register 34. Shipmates Forever 35. A Midsummer Night's Dream 35. Captain Blood 35. We're in the Money 35. Going Highbrow 35. Maybe It's Love 35. Brides Are Like That 36. I Married a Doctor 36. Hot Money 36. Here Comes Carter 36. Boulder Dam 36. China Clipper 36. Ready Willing and Able 37.

Alexander, Scott.
American screenwriter, usually in collaboration with Larry Karaszewski. The pair worked uncredited on *Mars Attacks!* 96.
Spaced Invaders 89. Problem Child 90. Problem Child 2 91. Ed Wood 94. *The People vs. Larry Flynt* 96. That Darn Cat 96, etc.

Alexander, Terence (1923–).
British light leading man of the 50s, often in ineffectual roles; by the 80s he was a popular character support in the TV series *Bergerac*.
The Woman with No Name 51. The Gentle Gunman 52. The Runaway Bus 54. Portrait of Alison 55. The One That Got Away 57. Danger Within 59. The League of Gentlemen 60. The Fast Lady 62. The Long Duel 67. Waterloo 70. Vault of Horror 73. The Internecine Project 74. Ike (TV) 79. That Englishwoman 90, many others.
TV series: Garry Halliday 59–62. Devenish 77–78. Bergerac 81–91. The New Statesman 87–90.

Alexander the Great (356–322 BC).
A mighty warrior who became king of Macedonia at the age of 20 and quickly overran most of the Mediterranean before he died of fever at the age of 33. He was played by Richard Burton in Robert Rossen's rather stolid 1956 biopic; William Shatner took over in a failed TV pilot of 1963; and 1980 brought forth a mini-series.

Alexandrov, Grigori (1903–1983) (G. Mormonenko).
Distinguished Russian director, former assistant to Eisenstein.
Internationale 32. *Jazz Comedy* 34. *Circus* 36. *Volga-Volga* 38. The Bright Road 40. Spring 47. Glinka 52. From Man to Man 58. Lenin in Poland 61. Before October 65.

Alexieff, Alexandre (1901–1982).
Franco-Russian animator who devised a method of illuminating pins stuck through a screen at various levels to produce a picture. Chief examples are *A Night on a Bare Mountain* 33, and the titles for *The Trial* 62.

Algar, James (1912–).
American writer-director of Disney's *True Life Adventures* and associated productions.
The Living Desert 53. *The Vanishing Prairie* 54. The African Lion 55. White Wilderness 58. Jungle Cat 60. The Legend of Lobo 63. *The Incredible Journey* 63. The Gnome-Mobile 67, etc.

Algren, Nelson (1909–1981).
American novelist who wrote of life's seamy side. He served as a model for the novelist Lewis Brogan in Simone de Beauvoir's *The Mandarins*.
Books included *The Man with the Golden Arm* and *A Walk on the Wild Side*.

Ali, Muhammed (1942–) (Cassius Clay).
American heavyweight boxing champion, internationally known for his cheerfully boastful manner, for staying too long at the top, and for converting to Islam. Tried playing himself in *The Greatest* 77; also starred in a TV mini-series, *Freedom Road*.
❝ When you're as great as I am, it's hard to be humble. – *M.A.*

Alison, Dorothy (1925–1992).
Australian actress resident in Britain.
Mandy 52. Turn the Key Softly 53. The Maggie 54. Reach for the Sky 56. The Long Arm 56. The Scamp 57. Life in Emergency Ward Ten 59. Georgy Girl 66. Pretty Polly 68. Blind Terror 71. The Amazing Mr Blunden 72. A Town Like Alice (TV) 80. A Cry in the Dark 88, etc.

Allan, Elizabeth (1910–1990).
British leading lady with stage experience; adept at delicate or aristocratic heroines.
Alibi 31. Black Coffee 31. Michael and Mary 32. Nine Till Six 32. The Lodger 33. Java Head 34. *David Copperfield* (US) 34. Mark of the Vampire (US) 35. *A Tale of Two Cities* (US) 36. Camille (US) 36. Michael Strogoff (US) 37. Inquest 38. Saloon Bar 40. The Great Mr Handel 42. Went the Day Well? 42. He Stoops to Conquer 44. No Highway 51. The Heart of the Matter 54. The Brain Machine 55. Grip of the Strangler 58, etc.

Allan, Ted (1916–1995).
Canadian playwright and screenwriter, a former journalist.
Lies My Father Told Me (AAN) 75. Falling in Love Again (co-w) 80. Love Streams (oa, co-w) 84. Bethune – The Making of a Hero 90, etc.

Alland, William (1916–).
American actor, originally with Orson Welles' Mercury Theatre: played the enquiring reporter in *Citizen Kane* 41. Later became staff producer for Universal-International: *It Came from Outer Space* 53. *This Island Earth* 56. *The Lady Takes a Flyer* 58. *The Rare Breed* 65, etc. Independently produced and directed *Look in Any Window* 61.

Allbritton, Louise (1920–1979).
American leading lady of the 40s, mainly in light comedy. Born in Oklahoma City and educated at the University of Oklahoma, she retired soon after her marriage in 1946. Died from cancer.
■ Danger in the Pacific 42. Parachute Nurse 42. Pittsburgh 42. Who Done It? 42. Fired Wife 43. Good Morning Judge 43. It Comes Up Love 43. *Son of Dracula* 43. Bowery to Broadway 44. Follow the Boys 44. Her Primitive Man 44. San Diego I Love You 44. This is the Life 44. Men in Her Diary 45. That Night with You 45. Tangier 46. The Egg and I 47. Don't Trust Your Husband 48. Sitting Pretty 48. Walk a Crooked Mile 48. The Doolins of Oklahoma 49. Felicia (Puerto Rico) 64.

Allégret, Marc (1900–1973).
French director of superior commercial films. Born in Switzerland, he began as a documentary film-maker.
Mam'zelle Nitouche 31. Fanny 32. Lac Aux Dames 34. Les Beaux Yeux 35. Gribouille 37. Orage 38. Entrée des Artistes 38. L'Arlésienne 42. Petrus 46. Blanche Fury (GB) 47. Maria Chapdelaine 50. Blackmailed (GB) 51. Futures Vedettes 55. Lady Chatterley's Lover 55. En Effeuillant La Marguerite 56. Un Drôle de Dimanche 58. L'Abominable Homme des Douanes 62. Le Bal du Comte d'Orgel 69, etc.

Allégret, Yves (1907–1987).
French director, brother of Marc Allégret. He began as an assistant to Jean Renoir and came to notice in the late 40s with thrillers in the *film noir* tradition.
Les Deux Timides 41. *Dédée d'Anvers* 47. *Une Si Jolie Petite Plage* 48. Manèges 49. Les Orgueilleux 53. Oasis 54. Germinal 62. Don't Bite, We Love You 76, etc.

Allen, Adrianne (1907–1993).
British light actress, mostly on stage. Mother of Daniel Massey, ex-wife of Raymond.
Loose Ends 31. Black Coffee 31. The Morals of Marcus 35. The October Man 47. Vote for Huggett 49. The Final Test 53. Meet Mr Malcolm 54, etc.

Allen, Barbara Jo (1905–1974) (also known as *Vera Vague*).
American comedy actress, well known on radio with Bob Hope.
Village Barn Dance 40. Ice Capades 41. Mrs Wiggs of the Cabbage Patch 42. In Rosie's Room 44. Snafu 45. Square Dance Katy 50. The Opposite Sex 56, etc.

Allen, Bob 'Tex':
see ALLEN, Robert.

Allen, Chesney (1894–1982).
British light comedian, for many years teamed with Bud FLANAGAN and the CRAZY GANG, from whose more violent antics he stood somewhat aloof. He retired in the 40s for health reasons, but long outlived the other gang members, and in 1982 was still singing and reminiscing on TV. Born in London, he was on-stage from 1919.
■ A Fire Has Been Arranged 35. Underneath the Arches 37. Okay for Sound 37. *Alf's Button Afloat* 38. *The Frozen Limits* 39. Gasbags 40. We'll Smile Again 42. Theatre Royal 43. Here Comes the Sun 44. Dreaming 44. Life Is a Circus 58. Dunkirk 58.

Allen, Chet (1940–1984).
Child star who sang the title role in the first performance of Menotti's television opera *Amahl and the Night Vistors* 51, and made one film before lapsing into obscurity. Committed suicide.
Meet Me at the Fair 52.
TV series: Bonino 53. The Troubleshooters 59–60.

Allen, Corey (1934–).
American supporting actor, specializing in depraved adolescents, who turned director in the 70s, mainly of TV films.
The Mad Magician 54. Night of the Hunter 55. Rebel without a Cause 55. The Shadow on the Window 57. Party Girl 58. Private Property (lead) 60. Sweet Bird of Youth 62. The Chapman Report 62. Thunder and Lightning (d only) 77. Avalanche (d, co-w) 78. Stone (TV) 79. Brass (TV) 85. The Last Fling (TV) 87. Star Trek: The Next Generation (TV) 87. The Ann Jillian Story (TV) 88, etc.

Allen, Dede (1924–).
American editor.
Odds Against Tomorrow 59. The Hustler 61. America America 63. *Bonnie and Clyde* 67. Little Big Man 70. Serpico 73. Dog Day Afternoon (AAN) 75. The Missouri Breaks 76. Slapshot 77. The Wiz 78. Reds (& co-p, AAN) 81. The Breakfast Club 85. The Milagro Beanfield War 88. Let It Ride 89. Henry and June 90. The Addams Family 91, etc.

Allen, Elizabeth (1934–) (Elizabeth Gillease).
American leading lady with stage experience.
From the Terrace 60. Diamond Head 63. Donovan's Reef 63. Cheyenne Autumn 64. Star Spangled Girl 71. The Carey Treatment 72, etc.
TV series: Bracken's World 69. The Paul Lynde Show 72. C.P.O. Sharkey 76–77.

Allen, Fred (1894–1956) (John F. Sullivan).
Baggy-eyed American radio comedian: very occasional films. Born in Cambridge, Massachusetts, and educated at Boston University, he began in vaudeville before becoming a success on radio. Married actress Portland Hoffa, who partnered him on stage and radio.
Autobiography: 1954, *Treadmill to Oblivion*.
■ *Thanks a Million* 35. Sally, Irene and Mary 38. Love Thy Neighbour 41. *It's in the Bag* 45. We're Not Married 52. O. Henry's Full House 53.
❝ My eyes look as though they are peeping over two dirty ping pong balls. – *F.A.*
California's a great place . . . if you happen to be an orange. – *F.A.*
You can count on the thumb of one hand the American who is at once a comedian, a humourist, a wit and a satirist, and his name is Fred Allen. – *James Thurber*

Allen, Gracie (1902/6–1964).
American comedienne who projected a scatterbrained image for 30 years on radio, TV and films, usually with her husband George Burns.
■ The Big Broadcast 32. College Humor 33. International House 33. Six of a Kind 34. *We're Not Dressing* 34. The Big Broadcast of 1936 35. Here Comes Cookie 35. Love in Bloom 35. The Big Broadcast of 1937 36. College Holiday 36. *A Damsel in Distress* 37. College Swing 38. *The Gracie Allen Murder Case* 39. Honolulu 39. Mr and Mrs North 41. *Two Girls and a Sailor* 44.

Allen, Henry Wilson 'Heck' (1912–1991).
Prolific writer, under the pseudonyms of Will Henry and Clay Fisher, of western novels, seven of which were filmed. Previously, from 1943–55, he worked for MGM's cartoon unit and wrote the stories for many of Tex Avery's cartoons.
The Tall Men (oa) 55. Santa Fe Passage (oa) 55. Pillars of the Sky (oa) 56. Yellowstone Kelly (oa) 59. Journey to Shiloh (oa) 68. Young Billy Young (oa) 69. Mackenna's Gold (oa) 69.
❝ Being an intellectual is a helluva handicap, in almost anything. It's always been a handicap to me. – *H.A.*

Allen, Hervey (1888–1949).
Popular American novelist whose mammoth *Anthony Adverse*, published in 1933, was filmed three years later.

Allen, Irving (1905–1987).
Polish-American producer. Hollywood experience from 1929.
Avalanche (d) 47. Sixteen Fathoms Deep (d) 50. New Mexico (p) 51. Slaughter Trail (d, p) 51. In Britain from early 50s as co-founder of Warwick Films (Cockleshell Heroes, Zarak, etc.). The Trials of Oscar Wilde 60. The Hellions 61. The Long Ships 64. Genghis Khan 65. The Silencers 66. The Ambushers 67. Hammerhead 68. Cromwell 70, etc.
TV series: Matt Helm 75.

Allen, Irwin (1916–1991).
American writer-producer who began with semi-instructional entertainments and then switched to fantasy and disaster movies.
The Sea Around Us (AAN) 50. The Animal World 56. The Story of Mankind (& d) 57. The Big Circus 59. The Lost World (& d) 61. A Voyage to the Bottom of the Sea (& d) 62. Five Weeks in a Balloon (& d) 63. The Poseidon Adventure 72. The Towering Inferno (& co-d) 74. The Time Travelers (TV) 76. Swarm 78. Hanging by a Thread (TV) 79. Beyond the Poseidon Adventure 79. When Time Ran Out 80, etc.
TV series in similar vein: Voyage to the Bottom of the Sea 64–68. Lost in Space 65–68. Time Tunnel 66–67. Land of the Giants 68–70. The Swiss Family Robinson 75–75, etc.
❝ If I can't blow up the world in the first ten seconds, then the show is a flop. – *I.A.*

Allen, Jay Presson (1922–).
American screenwriter with literary aspirations.
The Prime of Miss Jean Brodie (AAN) 69. Cabaret (AAN) 72. Travels with My Aunt 72. Just Tell Me What You Want 79. Prince of the City (AAN) 81. Deathtrap 82. Lord of the Flies 90, etc.

Allen, Jim (1926–).
English television playwright and screenwriter of working-class life, often for director Ken Loach. A former building worker and miner, he began as a scriptwriter for the television soap opera *Coronation Street*.
The Lump (TV) 67. Days of Hope (TV) 76. The Spongers (TV) 78. United Kingdom (TV) 81. The Gathering Seed (TV) 83. Hidden Agenda 90. *Raining Stones* 93. *Land and Freedom* 95, etc.

Allen, Joan (1956–).
American actress.
All My Sons (TV) 86. Fat Guy Goes Nutzoid 86. Manhunter 86. Peggy Sue Got Married 86. Tucker: The Man and His Dream 88. In Country 89. Without Warning: The James Brady Story (TV) 89. Mad Love 95. *Nixon* (AAN, as Pat Nixon) 95. *The Crucible* (AAN) 96. Face/Off 97. The Ice Storm 97. Pleasantville 98, etc.

Allen, Karen (1951–).
American leading lady.
Animal House 78. Manhattan 79. The Wanderers 79. Raiders of the Lost Ark 81. Shoot the Moon 82. Split Image 82. Starman 84. Backfire 87. The Glass Menagerie 87. Scrooged 88. Secret Places of the Heart 89. Exile 89. Sweet Talker 91. King of the Hill 93. Ghost in the Machine 94, etc.
TV series: The Road Home 94.

Allen, Keith (1953–).
British stand-up comic and character actor, usually in menacing roles.
Crystal Gazing 82. Loose Connections 83. The Supergrass 85. Comrades 86. Chicago Joe and the Showgirl 90. Kafka 91. Rebecca's Daughters 92. Carry On Columbus 92. Shallow Grave 94. *Martin Chuzzlewit* (TV) 94. Beyond Bedlam 94. Second Best 94. Captives 94. Blue Juice 95. Loch Ness 96. Trainspotting 96. Twin Town 97. The Life and Crimes of William Palmer (TV) 98, etc.
TV series: Making Out 89–90. Jackson Pace: The Great Years 90. Class Act 94–95. Born to Run 97.
❝ What defines you as an actor is never what you're doing in front of the camera or on stage – it's what you're doing when you're *not* on stage and you're *not* in front of the camera – *that's* the stuff. That's what makes you good. – *K.A.*

Allen, Lewis (1905–1986).
British director in Hollywood; his career started well but spluttered out.
■ Our Hearts were Young and Gay 44. *The Uninvited* 44. The Unseen 45. Those Endearing Young Charms 46. The Perfect Marriage 46. The Imperfect Lady 46. Desert Fury 47. So Evil My Love 48. Sealed Verdict 48. Chicago Deadline 49. Valentino 51. Appointment with Danger 51. At Sword's Point 52. Suddenly 54. A Bullet For Joey 55. Illegal 56. Another Time Another Place 58. Whirlpool (GB) 59. Decision at Midnight (MRA film) 63.

Allen, Lewis M. (1922–).
American producer with theatrical experience. He is married to screenwriter Jay Presson ALLEN.
■ The Connection 60. The Balcony 63. Lord of the Flies 64. Fahrenheit 451 66. The Queen 68. Fortune and Men's Eyes 71. Never Cry Wolf 83. On Valentine's Day 86. End of the Line 87. O.C. and Stiggs 87. Swimming to Cambodia 87. Miss Firecracker 89. Lord of the Flies 90.

Allen, Nancy (1950–).
American leading lady, former wife of Brian de Palma.
The Last Detail 73. Carrie 76. 1941 79. Home Movies 79. Dressed to Kill 80. Blowout 81. Strange Invaders 83. The Buddy System 84. Not for Publication 84. The Philadelphia Experiment 84. Robocop 87. Sweet Revenge 87. Poltergeist III 88. Limit Up 89. Robocop 2 90. Robocop 3 93. Acting on Impulse 93. Les Patriotes (Fr.) 94. The Man Who Wouldn't Die 95. Out of Sight 98, etc.

Allen, Patrick (1927–).
Lantern-jawed British leading man who after playing assorted villains and heroes in routine films established himself as TV's tough guy *Crane*, 63–65.
1984 55. High Tide at Noon 57. The Long Haul 57–8. Dunkirk 58. Tread Softly Stranger 58. I Was Monty's Double 58. Never Take Sweets from a Stranger 60. The Traitors 62. Captain Clegg 62. The Night of the Generals 66. Night of the Big Heat 67. When Dinosaurs Ruled the Earth 69. Puppet On a Chain 71. Diamonds on Wheels 73. Persecution 74. Hard Times (TV) 78. The Wild Geese 78. The Sea Wolves 80. Who Dares Wins 82. The Thirteenth Day of Christmas (TV) 85. Full Metal Ninja 89. Body & Soul (TV) 93. Bullet to Beijing 95, etc.
TV series: Body and Soul 93.

Allen, Rex (1922–).
American singing cowboy, popular on radio, in vaudeville and in second features.
Arizona Cowboy 50. Under Mexicali Stars 50. The Old Overland Trail 53. The Phantom Stallion 53, etc.
TV series: Frontier Doctor 58.

Allen, Robert (1906–1998) (Irving Theodore Baehr).
American actor who divided his time between playing leads and, later, character roles in features and starring in Columbia's series of 'Texas Ranger' 'B' westerns as Bob 'Tex' Allen. Born in Mount Vernon, New York, he studied at the University of Virginia. The first of his two wives was actress Evelyn Pierce.
Mr Potter of Texas 22. The Perils of Pauline (serial) 33. Crime and Punishment 35. I'll Love You Always 35. Law Beyond the Range 35. Love Me Forever 35. The Revenge Rider 35. Rio Grande Ranger 36. Craig's Wife 36. The Awful Truth 37. The Rangers Step In 37. The Unknown Ranger 37. Ranger Courage 38. Reckless Ranger 38. Everybody's Baby 39. City of Chance 40. Death Valley Rangers 43. Terror in the City 66. Dirtymouth 70. Raiders of the Living Dead 86. Night Game 89, etc.

Allen, Sian Barbara (1946–).
American actress of the 70s.
You'll Like My Mother 72. The Family Rico (TV) 72. Scream Pretty Peggy (TV) 73. Billy Two Hats 73. Eric (TV) 75. Smash-Up On Interstate 5 (TV) 76. The Lindbergh Kidnapping Case (TV) 76, etc.

Allen, Steve (1921–).
American radio and TV personality, in occasional films.
Autobiography: 1992, *Hi-Ho Steverino! My Adventures in the Wonderful Wacky World of TV*.
■ Down Memory Lane 49. I'll Get By 51. *The Benny Goodman Story* 56. The Big Circus 59. College Confidential 60. Don't Worry, We'll Think of a Title 66. A Man Called Dagger 67. Warning Shot 67. Now You See It, Now You Don't (TV) 67. Where were You When the Lights Went Out? 68. The Comic 69. The Sunshine Boys 75. Heartbeat 79. The Ratings Game (TV) 84.
❝ When I can't sleep, I read a book by Steve Allen. – *Oscar Levant*
I'm fond of Steve Allen, but not so much as he is. – *Jack Paar*

Allen, Tim (1953–) (Tim Allen Dick).
American comic actor, from television. Born in Denver, Colorado, he studied television production at Western Michigan University and began as a stand-up comedian. He has revealed that he served a prison term for possession and distribution of narcotics in the early 80s. Disney paid him $1.25m an episode to make the eighth season of his *Home Improvement* sitcom.
Autobiographies: 1994, *Don't Stand Too Close to a Naked Man*; 1996, *I'm Not Really Here*.
The Santa Clause 94. Toy Story (voice) 95. Jungle 2 Jungle 96. For Richer or Poorer 97, etc.
TV series: Home Improvement 93–99.

Allen, Woody (1935–) (Allen Stewart Konigsberg).
Bespectacled American actor, director and screenwriter, a former night-club comedian of smart one-liners and neurotic imaginings. His second wife was actress Louise Lasser (1966–71), and he has a son by actress Mia Farrow.

Biography: 1991, *Woody Allen* by Eric Lax.

He was played by Dennis Boutsikaris in the TV biopic *The Mia Farrow Story: Love and Betrayal* 95.

■ What's New Pussycat (& w) 65. *Casino Royale* (& co-w) 67. What's Up Tiger Lily? (& w) 67. Take the Money and Run (& w, d) 69. Don't Drink the Water (w only) 69. *Bananas* (& co-w, d) 71. Everything You Always Wanted to Know About Sex (& wpd) 72. *Play It Again Sam* (& w) 72. Sleeper (& co-w, d) 73. *Love and Death* (co-w, d) 76. The Front 76. *Annie Hall* (& co-w, d) (AAwd, best picture, AANa) 77. *Interiors* (w, d only) (AANw, d) 78. *Manhattan* (& w, d) (AANw, BFA) 79. Stardust Memories (& w, d) 80. A Midsummer Night's Sex Comedy (& w, d) 82. Zelig (& w, d) 83. Broadway Danny Rose (& w, d) (AAw, AANd) 84. The Purple Rose of Cairo (w, d only) (AAw, BFAw) 85. *Hannah and Her Sisters* (& w, AANd) 86. Radio Days (w, d only) 87. September (w, d only) 87. Another Woman (w, d only) 88. Crimes and Misdemeanors (& w, d) (AANw, d) 89. New York Stories (& w, d) 89. Alice (w, d only) 90. Scenes from a Mall 91. Shadows and Fog (& w, d) 92. Manhattan Murder Mystery (& co-w, d) 93. Bullets over Broadway (wd) (AANd) 94. Mighty Aphrodite (a, wd) 95. Everyone Says I Love You (a, wd) 96. Deconstructing Harry (a, wd) (AANw) 97. Celebrity (a, wd) 98. Antz (voice) 98, etc.

✪ For creating the most individual body of work in American cinema and capturing the stressful pleasures of modern urban living. *Manhattan.*

❝ With me, it's just a genetic dissatisfaction with everything. – *W.A.*

To me, American serious pictures always have one foot in entertainment, and I like more personal drama, though there may not be a market for it. – *W.A.*

I don't want to achieve immortality through my work. I want to achieve it through not dying. – *W.A.*

Most of the time I don't have much fun. The rest of the time I don't have any fun at all. – *W.A.*

I don't believe in an afterlife, but I'm bringing along a change of underwear. – *W.A.*

It's not that I'm afraid to die. I just don't want to be there when it happens. – *W.A.*

If only God would give me a sign. Such as making a large deposit in my name in a Swiss bank. – *W.A.*

Love is the answer, but while you're waiting for the answer, sex raises some pretty good questions. – *W.A.*

Life is divided into the horrible and the miserable. – *W.A.*

Don't knock masturbation: it's sex with someone you love. – *W.A.*

I was suicidal, and would have killed myself, but I was in analysis with a strict Freudian, and if you kill yourself they make you pay for the lessons you miss. – *W.A.*

Basketball or baseball or any sport is as dearly important as life itself. After all, why is it such a big deal to work and love and strive and have children and then die and decompose into eternal nothingness? – *W.A.*

He has a face that convinces you that God is a cartoonist. – *Jack Kroll*

The only thing Woody Allen has in common with Ingmar Bergman is Sven Nykvist. – *Joe Queenan*

Alley, Kirstie (1955–).
American actress. She was formerly married to actor Parker Stevenson and has been romantically linked with actor James Wilder.

Star Trek II 82. Blind Date 83. Champions 83. Runaway 84. North and South (TV) 85. Summer School 87. Shoot to Kill/Deadly Pursuit 87. Look Who's Talking 89. Loverboy 89. Madhouse 90. Sibling Rivalry 90. Look Who's Talking Too 90. Look Who's Talking Now 93. David's Mother (TV) 94. It Takes Two 95. Village of the Damned 95. Sticks and Stones 96. The Last Don (TV) 97. Toothless 97. For Richer or Poorer 97. Deconstructing Harry 97, etc.

TV series: Masquerade 83–84. North and South 85. Cheers 87–92. Veronica's Closet 97– .

Allgeier, Sepp (1890–1968).
German cinematographer.

Best-known films include: *Diary of a Lost Girl* 29. *The White Hell of Pitz Palu* 29. *William Tell* 33.

Allgood, Sara (1883–1950).
Irish character actress, long with the Abbey Theatre and from 1940 in Hollywood. Born in Dublin, she toured with W. G. Fay before joining the Abbey Theatre when it opened, later creating there the role of Juno in Sean O'Casey's *Juno and the Paycock*, a part she repeated in Hitchcock's film version. Her sister was actress Maire O'Neill. She gave up the stage on going to Hollywood and became an American citizen in 1945.

■ *Blackmail* 29. *Juno and the Paycock* 30. The World, the Flesh and the Devil 32. The Fortunate Fool 33. Irish Hearts 34. Lily of Killarney 34. The Passing of the Third Floor Back 35. Riders to the Sea 35. Lazybones 35. Peg of Old Drury 35. It's Love Again 36. Pot Luck 36. Southern Roses 36. *Storm in a Teacup* 37. The Sky's the Limit 37. The Londonderry Air 38. Kathleen Mavourneen 38. *That Hamilton Woman* 41. *How Green Was My Valley* (AAN) 41. Dr Jekyll and Mr Hyde 41. Lydia 41. The War Against Mrs Hadley 42. Roxie Hart 42. This Above All 42. It Happened in Flatbush 42. Life Begins at 8.30 42. City without Men 43. Jane Eyre 44. *The Lodger* 44. *Between Two Worlds* 44. The Keys of the Kingdom 44. The Strange Affair of Uncle Harry 45. Cluny Brown 46. Kitty 46. The Spiral Staircase 46. Mother Wore Tights 47. The Fabulous Dorseys 47. Ivy 47. Mourning Becomes Electra 47. My Wild Irish Rose 47. One Touch of Venus 48. The Man from Texas 48. The Girl from Manhattan 48. The Accused 48. Challenge to Lassie 49. Sierra 50. Cheaper by the Dozen 50.

Allio, René (1925–1995).
Thoughtful French director and screenwriter with sparse output, from the theatre, a former artist and set designer.

■ Les Ames Mortes 60. La Meule 63. *The Shameless Old Lady* 65. L'Une et l'Autre (& w) 67. Pierre et Paul 69. Les Camisards 72. Rude Journée pour la Reine 73. Moi, Pierre Rivière, Ayant Égorgé Ma Mère, Ma soeur, Mon frère 76. Retour à Marseille 80. L'Heure Exquise 81. Le Matelot 512 84. Un Médecin des Lumières 88. Transit (& co-w) 91. Against Oblivion (co-d 92).

Allison, May (1895–1989).
Blonde American leading lady in silent pictures, often as a romantic lead opposite Harold Lockwood. In two years, they appeared together in more than 20 films. She retired in the 20s.

A Fool There Was 15. The Masked Rider 16. The River of Romance 16. Big Tremaine 16. The Promise 17. The Hidden Children 17. Peggy Does Her Darndest 19. In for Thirty Days 19. Extravagance 21. Flapper Wives 24. The City 26. The Telephone Girl 27, etc.

Allister, Claud (1891–1970) (Claud Palmer).
British character actor associated with monocled silly-ass roles.

Bulldog Drummond (US) 29. The Private Life of Henry VIII 32. The Private Life of Don Juan 34. Dracula's Daughter (US) 36. Captain Fury (US) 39. Charley's Aunt (US) 41. Kiss the Bride Goodbye 44. Gaiety George 46. Quartet 48. Kiss Me Kate (US) 53, etc.

Allman, Greg (1947–).
American rock musician and actor. He formed The Allman Brothers band in the late 60s and was briefly married to Cher in 1975 – she filed for divorce nine days after the wedding.

Rush Week 91. Rush 91.

Allouache, Merzak (1944–).
Algerian director who studied film in Paris at IDHEC.

Omar Gatlato 76. Les Aventures d'un Héros 78. Al Radjoul Oun Na Fitta 82. Un Amour à Paris (Fr.) 87. *Bab el-Oued City* 94. Salut Cousin 96. Algiers-Beirut: A Souvenir 98, etc.

Allwyn, Astrid (1909–1978).
Swedish-American leading lady of minor movies in the 30s.

Reputation 32. Only Yesterday 33. Follow the Fleet 36. Dimples 37. Love Affair 39. Mr Smith Goes to Washington 39. Unexpected Uncle 41. No Hands on the Clock 41. Hit Parade of 1943 43, etc.

Allyson, June (1917–) (Ella Geisman).
Husky-voiced American leading lady who could play a tomboy or a tease, and was equally ready with a smile or a tear. Started in 1937 two-reelers, then spent five years as a Broadway chorus dancer before making her Hollywood feature debut. Her cute sexiness kept her popular for fifteen years. Married to Dick Powell 1945–63.

Autobiography: 1982, *June Allyson*.

■ Best Foot Forward 43. Girl Crazy 43. Thousands Cheer 43. Meet the People 44. *Two Girls and a Sailor* 44. *Music For Millions* 44. Her Highness and the Bellboy 45. The Sailor Takes a Wife 45. Two Sisters from Boston 45. Till the Clouds Roll By 46. The Secret Heart 46. High Barbaree 47. Good News 47. The Bride Goes Wild 48. The Three Musketeers 48. Words and Music (singing 'Thou Swell') 48. *Little Women* (as Jo) 49. The Stratton Story 49. The Reformer and the Redhead 50. Right Cross 50. Too Young to Kiss 51. The Girl in White 52. Battle Circus 53. Remains to be Seen 53. *The Glenn Miller Story* 54. Executive Suite 54. Woman's World 54. Strategic Air Command 55. *The Shrike* (her most dramatic role) 55. The McConnell Story 56. The Opposite Sex 56. You Can't Run Away from It 56. Interlude 57. My Man Godfrey 57. Stranger in My Arms 59. They Only Kill Their Masters 72. See the Man Run (TV) 72. Letters from Three Lovers (TV) 73. Blackout 77. Vegas (TV pilot) 78. The Kid with the Broken Halo (TV) 82. That's Entertainment III 94.

TV series: *The June Allyson Show* 59–61.

❝ MGM was my mother and father, mentor and guide, my all-powerful and benevolent crutch. When I left them, it was like walking into space. – *J.A.*

In real life I'm a poor dressmaker and a terrible cook–anything in fact but the perfect wife. – *J.A.*

Almendros, Nestor (1930–1992).
Spanish-American cinematographer.

Autobiography: 1984, *A Man with a Camera*.

La Collectionneuse 66. Ma Nuit Chez Maud 68. Claire's Knee 70. L'Enfant Sauvage 69. Two English Girls 71. Love in the Afternoon 72. Cockfighter 74. The Story of Adèle H 75. Madame Rosa 77. *Days of Heaven* (AA) 78. Going South 78. Love on the Run 79. Kramer vs Kramer 79. The Blue Lagoon 80. The Last Metro 81. Still of the Night 82. Sophie's Choice 82. Vivement Dimanche 83. Pauline at the Beach 83. Places in the Heart 84. Heartburn 86. Nadine 87. New York Stories 89. Billy Bathgate 91, etc.

Almereyda, Michael (1960–).
American experimental film-maker. His *Another Girl Another Planet* was shot using a Fisher-Price Pixel toy video camera.

A Hero of Our Time 85. Twister 89. Another Girl Another Planet 92. Search and Destroy (w) 95. Nadja (wd) 95. Trance 98, etc.

See also: Pixelvision.

Almodóvar, Pedro (1951–).
Spanish producer and director of camp comedies. He began as a cartoonist and stage actor with an experimental group.

Laberinto de Pasiones/Labyrinth of Passions 82. Dark Habits/Entre Tinieblas 84. What Have I Done to Deserve This? 85. Matador 86. Law of Desire/La Ley del Deseo 87. *Women on the Verge of a Nervous Breakdown*/Mujeres al Borde de un Ataque de Nervios 88. Tie Me Up! Tie Me Down!/¡Atame! 90. High Heels/Tacones Lejanos 91. Kika 93. Acción Mutante (p) 93. The Flower of My Secret/La Flor de Mi Secreto 95. *Live Flesh/Carne Tremula* 97. All about My Mother 99, etc.

❝ Absolutely all of my life is in my films. The way in which I do my autobiography is never direct. I am behind, in the shadow, of everything. – *P.A.*

I am a good confessor. I think you need to be, to be a good director. – *P.A.*

I am very worried about what's happening on Spanish television, with so much reality-based programming. There's so much interest in rapists and murderers that soon they'll have to get agents. – *P.A.*

Almond, Paul (1931–).
Canadian director, from TV.

■ Isabel 68. Act of the Heart 70. The Journey 72. Final Assignment 81. Up and Down 83. Captive Hearts 87. The Dance Goes On 92.

Alonso, Chelo.
Italian cabaret dancer and actress who added decorative interest to Italian epics of the late 50s and early 60s.

Sign of the Gladiator/Nel Segno di Roma 59. Morgan the Pirate/Morgan il Pirata 60. The Cyclops/Maciste nella Terra dei Ciclopi 61. The Huns/La Regina dei Tartari 62. Son of Samson/Maciste nella Valle dei Re 62. The Good, the Bad and the Ugly/Il Buono, il Brutto, il Cattivo 66, etc.

Alonso, Maria Conchita (1957–).
Cuban-born leading actress, in America from the mid-80s.

Moscow on the Hudson 84. Fear City 85. A Fine Mess 86. Touch and Go 86. Blood Ties 87. Extreme Prejudice 87. The Running Man 87. Colors 88. Vampire's Kiss 88. Predator 2 90. McBain 91. The House of the Spirits 93. James A. Michener's Texas (TV) 94. Roosters 95. Caught 96. Footsteps 98. Shout Out/El Grito en El Cielo 98, etc.

Alonzo, John A. (1934–).
Mexican-American cinematographer.

Bloody Mama 70. *Vanishing Point* 71. Sounder 72. Lady Sings the Blues 72. Hit! 73. The Naked Ape 73. Conrack 74. Chinatown 74. Once Is Not Enough 75. The Fortune 75. *Farewell My Lovely* 75. The Bad News Bears 76. Black Sunday 77. Close Encounters of the Third Kind (co-ph) 77. F.M. (d) 78. Norma Rae 79. Tom Horn 80. Back Roads 81. Zorro the Gay Blade 81. Blue Thunder 83. Cross Creek 83. Scarface 83. Runaway 84. Out of Control 85. Nothing in Common 86. Overboard 87. Real Men 87. Steel Magnolias 89. The Guardian 90. Internal Affairs 90. Navy SEALS 90. Housesitter 92. The Meteor Man 93. Clifford 94. Star Trek Generations 94. The Grass Harp 95, etc.

Alper, Murray (1904–).
American small-part character actor often seen as cab driver, soldier, etc.

The Royal Family of Broadway 30. The Girl Habit 31. Seven Keys to Baldpate 35. Winterset 36. Cocoanut Grove 38. The Roaring Twenties 39. Black Friday 40. The Maltese Falcon 41. The Big Shot 42. Mug Town 43. Wing and a Prayer 44. Angel on My shoulder 46. Sleep My Love 48. Lost Continent 51. Devil's Canyon 53. Tanganyika 54. Calypso Joe 57. The Leech Woman 60. The Nutty Professor 63. The Outlaws is Coming 65, many others.

Alperson, Edward L. (1896–1969).
American independent producer, mainly of hokum pictures; former film salesman.

Black Beauty 47. Dakota Lil 50. Invaders from Mars 53. New Faces 54. The Magnificient Matador 56. I Mobster 59. September Storm 60, many others.

Alpert, Hollis (1916–).
American critic.

Books include *The Dreams and the Dreamers* 62; *The Barrymores* 64.

Alt, Carol (1960–).
American actress and model.

Portfolio 88. Bye Bye Baby (It.) 89. My First Forty Years (It.) 89. My Wonderful Life 90. A Family Matter/Vendetta (TV) 91. Ring of Steel 93. Deadly Past 95. Private Parts 96. Hostage Train 97. Body Armour 97, etc.

Altman, Robert (1925–).
American director who had a big commercial success with M*A*S*H. He followed with some successful large-scale ensemble works, but dwindling commercial success led him to small-scale films, often adaptations of stage plays. He made a triumphant return to critical and some commercial success in 92 with *The Player*, a satire on Hollywood.

Book: 1992, *Robert Altman's America* by Helene Keyssar.

Biography: 1995, *Robert Altman: Hollywood Survivor* by Daniel O'Brien.

■ The Delinquents (& wp) 55. The James Dean Story (co-d & p) 57. Nightmare in Chicago 64.

Countdown 68. That Cold Day in the Park 68. M*A*S*H (AAN) 70. Brewster McCloud 71. McCabe and Mrs Miller 71. Images 72. The Long Goodbye 72. Thieves Like Us 73. California Split 74. *Nashville* (AAN) 75. Buffalo Bill and the Indians 76. The Late Show (p only) 77. Welcome to L.A. (p only) 78. 3 Women (& wp) 78. A *Wedding* (& co-w, p) 78. Remember My Name (p only) 78. Quintet (& co-w, p) 78. A Perfect Couple (& co-w, p) 79. Rich Kids (p only) 79. Health (& co-w, p) 79. Popeye 80. Come Back to the Five and Dime, Jimmy Dean, Jimmy Dean 82. Streamers 83. Secret Honor 84. Fool for Love 85. Beyond Therapy 87. O.C. and Stiggs 87. Aria (co-d) 87. Vincent and Theo 90. *The Player* 92. *Short Cuts* (AAN) 93. Mrs Parker and the Vicious Circle (p) 94. Prêt-à-Porter/Ready-to-Wear (co-w, d) 94. Kansas City 96. The Gingerbread Man 97.

❝ Film-making is a chance to live many lifetimes. – *R.A.*

What is a cult? It just means not enough people to make a minority. – *R.A.*

The majors don't want to make the same pictures I do, and I'm too old to change. – *R.A. 1986*

It's very hard to find anyone with any decency in the business. They all hide behind the corporate structure. They're like landlords who kick people out of tenement buildings. There's no compassion, and there's certainly no interest in the arts. – *R.A.*

Altman, Stephen.
American production designer, the son of Robert Altman.
Fool for Love 85. Aria 87. Beyond Therapy 87. Near Dark 87. Vincent & Theo 90. The Player 92. Short Cuts 93. What's Love Got to Do with It 93. Ready to Wear/Prêt-à-Porter 94. Kansas City 96. Grosse Point Blank 97. The Gingerbread Man 98, etc.

Alton, John (1901–1996).
Hungarian-born cinematographer, in Hollywood from 1924. Noted for the quickness of his work and a distinctive, dramatic chiaroscuro approach, influenced by Rembrandt, that helped define *film noir*, he retired at the peak of his career. He won an Oscar for his colour work, shooting the ballet sequence in *An American in Paris* 51. He wrote the first text-book on cinematography, *Painting with Light*, 1949.
Courageous Dr Christian 40. Atlantic City 44. T-Men 47. He Walked by Night 48. The Black Book 49. Father of the Bride 50. *An American in Paris* (AA) 51. The People Against O'Hara 51. Battle Circus 53. The Big Combo 55. Tea and Sympathy 56. The Teahouse of the August Moon 56. The Brothers Karamazov 58. Elmer Gantry 60, etc.

❝ I stopped because I wanted to live. That was no life, to work at the studio, get up at six every morning and fight the producers. I had enough. I looked at my bank book and I said, 'That's it!' – *J.A.*

He gave you quality and suggestions like no other cameraman that I ever worked with, and I've worked with the best of them. – *Joseph H. Lewis*

He recognised that shadows were just as important as the light. – *Bernard Vorhaus*

Alton was not afraid of the dark. – *Todd McCarthy*

Alton, Robert (1897–1957) (Robert Alton Hart).
American director, mainly of musical sequences:
Strike Me Pink 36. Showboat 51. There's No Business Like Show Business 55, many others. Directed features: Merton of the Movies 47. Pagan Love Song 50.

Alvarado, Don (1900–1967) (José Paige).
American 'Latin lover' of the 20s; later appeared in character roles.
The Loves of Carmen 26. Drums of Love 27. The Battle of the Sexes 28. The Bridge of San Luis Rey 29. Rio Rita 29. Morning Glory 33. The Devil Is a Woman 35. The Big Steal 49, etc.

Alvarado, Trini (1967–).
American actress.
Times Square 80. Sweet Lorraine 87. Satisfaction 88. The Chair/The Hot Seat 89. Stella 90. American Blue Note 90. American Friends 91. The Babe 92. Little Women 94. The Perez Family 95. The Frighteners 96. Paulie 98, etc.

Alves, Joe (1938–).
American production designer.
Winning 69. Pufnstuf 70. Sugarland Express 74. Jaws 75. Close Encounters of the Third Kind (AAN) 77. Jaws II 78. Escape from New York 81. Jaws 3-D (& d) 83. Starman 84. Everybody's All-American 88. Freejack 92. Geronimo: An American Legend 93. Drop Zone 94. Shadow Conspiracy 97, etc.

Alwyn, William (1905–1985).
Prolific British composer who progressed from documentary scoring to fictional narrative. Born in Northampton, he studied at the Royal Academy of Music, where he also taught from the mid-20s to the mid-50s. Married composer Doreen Carwithen.
Fires Were Started 42. World of Plenty 43. The Way Ahead 44. *The True Glory* 45. The Rake's Progress 45. Odd Man Out 46. Captain Boycott 47. *The Fallen Idol* 48. The History of Mr Polly 49. The Magic Box 51. The Card 52. The Crimson Pirate 53. The Million Pound Note 54. The Ship That Died of Shame 55. Geordie 55. Manuela 57. Carve Her Name With Pride 58. A Night to Remember 58. The Swiss Family Robinson 60. The Running Man 63, etc.

Alyn, Kirk (1910–).
American leading man, chiefly remembered for playing Superman in the 1948 serial version. Other roles in Lucky Jordan 42. Sweet Genevieve 47. Radar Patrol vs Spy King (serial) 50. Scalps 82, etc.

Alzado, Lyle (1949–1992).
American actor, a former football player, in action movies. He played for the Denver Broncos, Cleveland Browns and L.A. Raiders, before appearing in films from the late 70s. Married twice; died of cancer of the brain.
The Double McGuffin 79. Oceans of Fire 86. Ernest Goes to Camp 87. Tapeheads 88. Destroyer 88. Learning the Ropes 88. Who's Harry Crumb? 89. Zapped Again 89. Club Fed 91. Comrades in Arms 91. Neon City 92, etc.

Amado, Jorge (1912–).
Prolific Brazilian novelist whose works have been adapted for many films and television series.
Dona Flor and Her Two Husbands 78. Otalia de Bahia 77. Tent of Miracles/Tenda dos Milagres 77. Jubiaba 86. Tieta do Agreste 96, etc.

Amadori, Luis Cesar (1903–1977).
Prolific Argentinian director, dramatist and composer, a former journalist and music critic. Born in Italy, he moved to Argentina as a child and was also a theatrical producer before beginning to direct films in his mid-30s. He made more than 60 and worked in Spain for a decade from 1958, following the overthrow of Perón.
Puerto Nuevo (co-d) 36. Napoleon 41. Carmen 43. Mosquita Muerta 46. Albéniz 47. Don Juan Tenorio 49. Nacha Regules 50. El Gritto Sagrado 54. Amor Prohibido 58. Mi Último Tango 60. Como Dos Gotas de Agua 63. Cristina Guzmán 68. Amor en el Aire 68, etc.

Amann, Betty (1907–1990).
Leading actress, born in Bavaria of American parents, who trained for the stage in America, began her career in German films, and worked in England in the 30s before going to Hollywood in 1939 to appear in a few minor films.
Temptation 29. The Perfect Lady 31. Rich and Strange 31. Strictly Business 32. Pyjamas Preferred 32. Daughter of Today 33. McGlusky the Sea Rover 35. In Old Mexico 39. Nancy Drew – Reporter 39. Isle of Forgotten Sins 44, etc.

Amaral, Suzana (1933–).
Brazilian director, from television.
Hour of the Star/A Hora dele Estrela 85.

Amateau, Rod (1923–).
American radio writer who in the early 50s briefly became a film director and then turned his attention to half-hour comedy TV films, of which he has since made many hundreds.
The Rebel 51. Monsoon 52. Pussycat Pussycat I Love You 70. The Statue 70. Where Does It Hurt? (& co-p, co-w) 72. Drive in 76. Loveliness 84. The Garbage Pail Kids Movie 87, etc.

Amato, Giuseppe (1899–1964) (Giuseppe Vasaturo).
Italian producer.
Four Steps in the Clouds (& w) 42. Open City 45. Shoe Shine 46. Bicycle Thieves 49. Umberto D 52. Don Camillo 52. La Dolce Vita 59, many others.

Ambler, Eric (1909–1998).
English thriller writer and screenwriter, a former advertising copywriter. He turned to film-making as a writer-producer in the late 40s, working for the Rank Organization, and later spent 10 years in Hollywood. His second wife was writer-producer Joan Harrison.
Autobiographies: 1985, *Here Lies*; 1993, *The Story So Far: Memories and Other Fictions*.
Background to Danger (oa) 43. Journey into Fear (oa) 43. The Way Ahead (oa, co-w) 44. Hotel Reserve (oa) 44. The Mask of Dimitrios (oa) 44. The October Man (p, w) 47. The Purple Plain (w) 54. Yangtse Incident/Battle Hell (w) 57. The Passionate Friends (p, co-w) 58. Highly Dangerous (w) 50. Encore (co-w) 51. The Magic Box (w) 51. The Card/The Promoter (w) 52. The Cruel Sea (w) (AAN) 52. Rough Shoot 53. Lease of Life (w) 54. *A Night to Remember* (w) 58. The Eye of Truth (TV) 58. The Wreck of the Mary Deare (w) 59. Mutiny on the Bounty (uncredited) 62. Topkapi (oa) 64, etc.

❝ Mr Ambler is our greatest thriller writer. – *Graham Greene*

Doesn't everyone want to be able to lie successfully? – *E.A.*

Ambler, Joss (1900–1959).
British character actor, often seen as heavy father or police inspector.
Captain's Orders 37. Meet Mr Penny 38. Come On George 39. Contraband 40. Penn of Pennsylvania 41. The Big Blockade 42. The Next of Kin 42. The Silver Fleet 43. Candles at Nine 44. The Agitator 45. The Years Between 46. Mine Own Executioner 47. Who Goes There 52. Miss Tulip Stays the Night 55. The Long Arm 56. Soho Incident 56, many others.

Ambrose (1896–1971).
British bandleader of the 30s and later.
■ Soft Lights and Sweet Music 36. Kicking the Moon Around 38.

Ameche, Don (1908–1993) (Dominic Felix Amici).
American leading man with stage and radio experience. Born in Kenosha, Wisconsin, he read law at the University of Wisconsin. Married dietician Honore Prendergast in 1932; he had four sons and two adopted daughters. A pleasant light hero of mainly trivial films, he returned to Broadway in the 60s and became popular on TV as a circus ringmaster. His film career revived with *Trading Places*.
■ Sins of Man 36. *Ramona* 36. Ladies in Love 36. One in a Million 37. Love is News 37. Fifty Roads to Town 37. You Can't Have Everything 37. Love Under Fire 37. *In Old Chicago* 38. Happy Landing 38. Josette 38. *Alexander's Ragtime Band* 38. Gateway 38. *The Three Musketeers* (musical version; as D'Artagnan) 39. *Midnight* 39. *The Story of Alexander Graham Bell* (which started a long-standing joke about Ameche inventing the telephone) 39. Hollywood Cavalcade 39. *Swanee River* (as Stephen Foster) 39. Lillian Russell 40. *Four Sons* 40. Down Argentine Way 40. *That Night in Rio* (dual role) 41. Moon over Miami 41. Kiss the Boys Goodbye 41. The Feminine Touch 41. Confirm or Deny 41. The Magnificent Dope 42. Girl Trouble 43. *Heaven Can Wait* (under Lubitsch, his best acting performance) 43. *Happy Land* 43. Something to Shout About 43. Wing and a Prayer 44. Greenwich Village 44. It's In the Bag 45. Guest Wife 45. So Goes My Love 46. That's My Man 47. Sleep My Love 48. Slightly French 49. Phantom Caravan 54. Fire One 55. A Fever in the Blood 61. Rings Around the World 66. Picture Mommy Dead 66. Shadow Over Elveron (TV) 68. Suppose They Gave a War and Nobody Came 70. The Boatniks 70. Gidget Gets Married (TV) 71. Trading Places 83. *Cocoon* (AA) 84. A Masterpiece of Murder (TV) 85. Harry and the Hendersons 87. Cocoon: The Return 88. Coming to America 88. *Things Change* 88. Oscar 91. Folks! 92. Sunstroke 92. Corrina, Corrina 94.
TV series: Holiday Hotel 50–51. Coke Time with Eddie Fisher 53. International Showtime 61–65.

Amelio, Gianni (1945–).
Italian director.
La Fine del Gioco (TV) 70. Colpire al Cuore 82. I Ragazzi di Via Panisperna 88. Open Doors (AAN) 90. Stolen Children/Il Ladro di Bambini 92. Lamerica 94. The Way They Laughed/Cosi Ridevano (wd) 98, etc.

Amendola, Claudio (1963–).
Italian leading actor, in international productions.
Far From Where?/Lontano da Dove? 83. American Holidays/Vacanze in America 84. The Firemen/I Pompieri 85. Forever Mary/Mery per Sempre 89. Ultra 91. The Escort/La Scorta 93. Queen Margot/La Reine Margot (Fr.) 94. Horseman on the Roof/Le Hussard sur le Toit (Fr.) 95. Poliziotti 95. Nostromo (TV) 97, etc.

Ames, Adrienne (1907–1947) (Adrienne Ruth McClure).
American light leading lady of the 30s. Her third husband was actor Bruce Cabot (1934–37). Died of cancer.
Girls About Town 31. Husband's Holiday 32. A Bedtime Story 33. You're Telling Me 34. Woman Wanted 35. City Girl 38. Panama Patrol 39, etc.

Ames, Leon (1903–1993) (Leon Wycoff).
American character actor, a specialist in harassed or kindly fathers and suave professional men.
Murders in the Rue Morgue 32. 13 Women 32. Parachute Jumper 33. The Count of Monte Cristo 34. Reckless 35. Stowaway 36. Charlie Chan on Broadway 37. Mysterious Mr Moto 38. Code of the Streets 39. Ellery Queen and the Murder Ring 41. Crime Doctor 43. *Meet Me In St Louis* 44. Thirty Seconds Over Tokyo 44. Son of Lassie 45. Weekend at the Waldorf 45. Yolanda and the Thief 45. Song of the Thin Man 47. A Date with Judy 48. *Little Women* 49. Battleground 49. Crisis 50. *On Moonlight Bay* 51. Let's Do It Again 53. Peyton Place 57. *From the Terrace* 60. The Absent-minded Professor 61. The Monkey's Uncle 65. On a Clear Day You Can See Forever 70. Hammersmith is Out 72. Just You and Me, Kid 79. Testament 83. Jake Speed 86. Peggy Sue Got Married 86, many others.
TV series: Life with Father 53–55. Frontier Judge 56. Father of the Bride 61–62. Mr Ed 63–65.

Ames, Preston (1905–1983).
American art director, with MGM from the mid-30s to the late 60s. He studied architecture in France and was at his best when working on films directed by Vincente Minnelli.
An American in Paris (AA) 51. The Story of Three Loves (AAN) 53. The Band Wagon 53. Brigadoon (AAN) 54. Kismet 55. *Lust for Life* (AAN) 56. Designing Woman 57. *Gigi* (AA) 58. The Bells Are Ringing 60. Billy Rose's Jumbo 62. The Unsinkable Molly Brown (AAN) 64. Airport (AAN) 70. Brewster McCloud 70. Lost Horizon 73. Earthquake (AAN) 74. Rooster Cogburn 75. Beyond the Poseidon Adventure 79. Oh God, Book Two 80. The Pursuit of D.B. Cooper 81, etc.

Ames, Ramsay (1924–) (Ramsay Philips).
American leading lady who started as a Universal starlet but didn't make much of a mark.
Ali Baba and the Forty Thieves 44. The Mummy's Tomb 44. Calling Dr Death 44. A Wave, a WAC and a Marine 44. Alexander the Great 56. The Running Man 63, etc.

Amfitheatrof, Daniele (1901–1983).
Russian-born composer and arranger, in Hollywood. Born in St Petersburg, he studied in Rome and worked as a conductor in Europe before arriving in Hollywood in 1938, where he was first contracted to MGM.
La Signora di Tutti (It.) 34. Fast and Furious 39. Northwest Passage 40. Dr Gillespie's Criminal Case 43. Lassie Come Home 43. A Stranger in Town 43. Cry Havoc 43. I'll Be Seeing You 44. Guest Wife (AAN) 45. The Virginian 46. *Song of the South* (AAN) 46. Temptation 46. The Lost Moment 47. The Senator Was Indiscreet 47. An Act of Murder 48. Letter from an Unknown Woman 48. House of Strangers 49. The Fan 49. Sand 49. The Capture 50. The Damned Don't Cry 50. Storm Warning 50. Bird of Paradise 51. Angels in the Outfield 51. Tomorrow Is Another Day 51. The Painted Hills 51. The Desert Fox 51. The Naked Jungle 53. Salome 53. Human Desire 54. The Last Hunt 55. Trial 55. Spanish Affair 57. The Unholy Wife 57. From Hell to Texas 58. Fraulein 58. Edge

of Eternity 59. Heller in Pink Tights 60. Major Dundee 64, many others.

Amick, Mädchen (1970–).
American leading actress who gained fame as Shelly in the TV series *Twin Peaks*.
The Borrower 89. I'm Dangerous Tonight 90. Don't Tell Her It's Me 90. Sleepwalkers 92. Twin Peaks: Fire Walk with Me 92. Dream Lover 94. Love, Cheat & Steal 94. Trapped in Paradise 94. French Exit 95, etc.
TV series: Twin Peaks 90. Central Park West 95– . Fantasy Island 98– .

Amidei, Sergio (1904–1981).
Italian scriptwriter, associated with neo-realism.
Pietro Micca 38. Rome, Open City (AAN) 45. Paisa 47. Domenica d'Agosto 50. The Bed/Il Letto 54. General Della Rivere/Il Generale Della Rivere 59. La Fuga 64. Fumo di Londri 66. Maigret a Pigalle 67. Why?/Detenuto in Attesa di Giudizio 71. Tales of Ordinary Madness/Storie di Ordinaria Follia 81. La Nuit de Varennes 82, etc.

Amiel, Jon (1948–).
British director from television.
The Singing Detective (TV) 87. Queen of Hearts 89. Tune in Tomorrow/Aunt Julia and the Scriptwriter 90. Sommersby 93. Copycat 95. The Man Who Knew Too Little 97, etc.
❛❛ Good producers are as rare as rocking horse doo doo. – *J.A.*

Amis, Sir Kingsley (1922–1995).
British light novelist. Films of his books include: Lucky Jim 57. Only Two Can Play/That Uncertain Feeling 62. Take a Girl Like You 70.

Amis, Martin (1949–).
English novelist, journalist and screenwriter who was briefly a child actor. He is the son of novelist Sir Kingsley Amis.
A High Wind in Jamaica (a) 65. Saturn 3 (w) 80. The Rachel Papers (oa) 89.

Amis, Suzy (1958–).
American leading actress.
Fandango 85. Big Town 87. Plain Clothes 88. Rocket Gibraltar 88. Twister 89. Where the Heart Is 90. Rich in Love 92. Watch It 93. The Ballad of Little Joe 93. Two Small Bodies 93. Blown Away 94. The Usual Suspects 95. Cadillac Ranch 96. Titanic 97. Firestorm 97, etc.

Amos, John (1940–).
American actor, best known for his role as Kunte Kinte in *Roots*.
Sweet Sweetback's Baadasssss Song 71. World's Greatest Athlete 73. Let's Do It Again 75. Future Cop 76. Willa (TV) 79. To Elvis, with Love/Touched by Love 80. Beastmaster 82. American Flyers 85. Coming to America 88. Lock Up 89. Die Hard 2 90. Ricochet 91. Mac 92. Mardi Gras for the Devil 93. Hologram Man 95. For Better or Worse (TV) 95. The Players Club 98, etc.
TV series: The Mary Tyler Moore Show 70–73. Maude 73–74. Good Times 74–76. Roots 77. Hunter 84–85.

Amram, David (1933–).
American composer.
Pull My Daisy 57. The Young Savages 60. Splendor in the Grass 61. The Manchurian Candidate 62. The Arrangement 69, etc.

Amy, George J. (1900–1986).
American editor.
The Gorilla 30. Underworld 31. Doctor X 32. Footlight Parade 33. The Mystery of the Wax Museum 33. Dames 34. Lady Killer 34. Captain Blood 35. The Charge of the Light Brigade 36. Green Pastures 36. Dodge City 39. The Letter 40. The Sea Hawk 40. The Sea Wolf 41. Yankee Doodle Dandy 42. Air Force 43. Confidential Agent 45. Three Strangers 46. Life with Father 47. The Sound of Fury 50. Clash by Night 52. A Lion is in the Streets 53, many others.

Amyes, Julian (1917–1992).
British director who became a TV executive.
A Hill in Korea 56. Miracle in Soho 56. Great Expectations (TV) 81. Jane Eyre (TV) 83, etc.

Anand, Chetan (1915–1997).
Indian director and actor, a former lecturer.
Lowly City/Neecha Nagar 45. Afsar 50. Aandhian 52. Taxi Driver 54. Funtoosh 56. Kinare Kinare 63. Reality/Haqeeqat 64. Heer Ranjha 70. Hindustan Ki Kasam 73. Kudrat 81. Haathon Ki Lakeeren 86. Param Veer Chakra 88, etc.

Anchia, Juan Ruiz:
see Ruiz-Anchia, Juan.

Anders, Allison (1954–).
American director.
Border Radio (co-d) 88. Gas Food Lodging 92. Mi Vida Loca 93. Four Rooms (co-d) 95. Grace of My Heart 96, etc.

Anders, Glenn (1889–1981)
American stage actor who made occasional film appearances, usually sinister.
Laughter 30. By Your Leave 35. Nothing but the Truth 41. *The Lady from Shanghai* 48. M 51. Behave Yourself 51, etc.

Anders, Luana (1940–).
American leading lady of minor movies of the 60s.
Life Begins at Seventeen 58. The Pit and the Pendulum 61. The Young Racers 63. Dementia 13 63. *That Cold Day in the Park* 68. B.J. Presents 71. When the Legends Die 72. Shampoo 75. The Missouri Breaks 76. Goin' South 78. Personal Best 81. Movers and Shakers 84. Border Radio 87. Limit Up 89. American Strays 96, etc.

Anders, Merry (1932–).
American light leading lady.
Les Misérables 52. Phffft 54. The Dalton Girls 57. Violent Road 58. The Hypnotic Eye 60. 20,000 Eyes 61. House of the Damned 63. Tickle Me 65. Legacy of Blood 71, etc.
TV series: The Stu Erwin Show 54. It's Always Jan 55. How to Marry a Millionaire 58. The Time Travellers 64, etc.

Anders, Rudolph (1895–1987).
German-born character actor who also acted under the names Rudolph Amendt and Robert O. Davis (1939–44). In Hollywood from the 30s, and often cast as a German agent.
The Fountain 34. I Met Him in Paris 37. Confessions of a Nazi Spy 39. The Great Dictator 40. To Be or Not to Be 42. Watch on the Rhine 43. Escape in the Desert 45. Under Nevada Skies 46. Actors and Sin 51. Phantom from Space 53. She Demons 58. On the Double 61. The Pigeon that Took Rome 62. The Prize 63, etc.

Andersen, Hans Christian (1805–1875).
Danish writer of fairy tales, impersonated by Danny Kaye in Goldwyn's 1952 biopic. Many of his tales were filmed by Disney as *Silly Symphonies*, and one of them was the basis of *The Red Shoes* 48.

Anderson, Barbara (1945–).
American leading lady, chiefly remembered as Ironside's pretty assistant in the TV series.
Visions (TV) 72. Don't Be Afraid of the Dark (TV) 73. Strange Honeymoon (TV) 74. You Lie So Deep My Love (TV) 75. Doctors' Private Lives (TV) 79, etc.
TV series: A Man Called Ironside 67–71. Mission: Impossible 72–73.

Anderson, Carl.
American art director and production designer, with Columbia for much of the 40s and 50s.
Riders of the Northwest Mounted 43. Tell It to the Judge 49. The Traveling Saleswoman 50. Ten Tall Men 51. Miss Sadie Thompson 53. The Buster Keaton Story 56. Secret of Treasure Mountain 66. Gunmen from Laredo 58. The Last Angry Man (AAN) 59. All the Young Men 60. The Wackiest Ship in the Army 60. Hatari! 61. A Raisin in the Sun 61. Spencer's Mountain 63. El Dorado 66. Lt Robin Crusoe USN 66. Counterpoint 67. 100 Rifles 68. Chisum 70. Big Jake 71. Lady Sings the Blues (AAN) 72. The Culpepper Cattle Co. 72. Against a Crooked Sky 76. The Villain 79. . . . All the Marbles 81, etc.

Anderson, Daphne (1922–) (Daphne Scrutton).
British light actress chiefly associated with the stage.
Trottie True 49. The Beggar's Opera 52. Hobson's Choice 54. A Kid for Two Farthings 55. The Prince and the Showgirl 57. Snowball 60. Captain Clegg 62. The Scarlet Pimpernel (TV) 82.

Anderson, Donna (1938–).
American leading lady.
On the Beach 59. Inherit the Wind 60.

Anderson, Eddie 'Rochester' (1905–1977).
Comedian long associated with Jack Benny on radio and TV. His gravel voice and rolling eyes were familiar in the 30s and 40s, but his amiable stereotype became unpopular in a race-conscious age. As he said in a 1970 TV appearance, when invited to resume his old role of butler, 'Massah Benny, we don' do dat no mo' . . .'
What Price Hollywood 30. Three Men on a Horse 35. *Green Pastures* 36. Jezebel 38. *You Can't Take It With You* 38. *Gone With the Wind* 39. *Topper Returns* 41. Tales of Manhattan 42. The Meanest Man in the World 42. *Cabin In The Sky* (leading role) 43. Broadway Rhythm 44. The Show-Off 46. It's a Mad Mad Mad Mad World 63, many others.
TV series: *The Jack Benny Show* 50–65.

Anderson, Ernest
American character actor.
In This Our Life 42. Three for Bedroom C 52. The Well 52. Whatever Happened to Baby Jane? 62, etc.

Anderson, G. M. ('Bronco Billy') (1882–1971) (Max Aronson).
American silent actor, an unsuccessful vaudeville performer who drifted into films in *The Great Train Robbery* 03. Later co-founded the Essanay company and made nearly four hundred one-reel westerns starring himself. Retired in 1920; reappeared in 1965 in *The Bounty Killer*. Special Academy Award 1957 'for his contribution to the development of motion pictures'.

Anderson, Gene (1931–1965).
British actress. Born in London, she studied at the Central School of Dramatic Art. Married actor Edward Judd.
The Intruder 53. Flannelfoot 53. A Tale of Three Women 54. The Immigrant 55. Laughing in the Sunshine (Swe.) 56. Yangtse Incident 57. The Long Haul 57. The Shakedown 60. The Day the Earth Caught Fire 61. The Break 62. The Madras House (TV) 65. Women Beware Women (TV) 65, etc.

Anderson, Gerry (1929–).
British puppeteer who via his Century 21 productions made TV series such as *Four Feather Falls*, *Supercar*, *Fireball XL5*, *Captain Scarlet*, *Joe 90*, *Thunderbirds*. Less successfully he moved into gimmicky live-action with *UFO* and *Space 1999*, and into feature films with *Journey to the Far Side of the Sun*.

Anderson, Gillian (1968–).
American actress, best known for the role of Dana Scully in the TV series *The X Files*. Born in Chicago, she lived in London as a child, then studied acting at Chicago's DePaul University and began in off-Broadway theatre.
The Turning 92. The X Files Movie 98. Playing by Heart 98. The Mighty 98, etc.
TV series: Future Fantastic (narrator) 96.

Anderson, Herbert (1917–1994).
Mild-mannered American actor.
Till We Meet Again 40. The Body Disappears 41. The Male Animal 42. I Bury the Living 58. Sunrise at Campobello 60. Rascal 69, etc.
TV series: *Dennis the Menace* 59–63.

Anderson, James (1921–1969).
American general-purpose supporting actor.
Sergeant York 41. The Great Sinner 49. Donovan's Brain 53. I Married a Monster from Outer Space 57. The Ballad of Cable Hogue 70, many others.

Anderson, Jean (1908–).
British stage and screen actress often cast as sympathetic nurse, tired mother, or spinster aunt.
The Mark of Cain 47. Elizabeth of Ladymead 49. White Corridors 51. The Franchise Affair 51. A Town Like Alice 56. Heart of a Child 57. Robbery Under Arms 57. Solomon and Sheba 59. Half a Sixpence 67. The Night Digger 71. The Lady Vanishes 79. Screamtime 83. The Uninvited (TV) 97, many others.
TV series: *The Brothers* 71–76.

Anderson, John (1922–1992).
Tall, thin, pale-eyed American character actor.
The True Story of Lynn Stuart 58. Psycho 60. Ride the High Country 62. The Satan Bug 65. Welcome to Hard Times 69. Soldier Blue 70. The Hancocks (TV) 76. The Lincoln Conspiracy (as Lincoln) 78. The Deerslayer 78. Donner Pass – the Road to Survival (TV) 84. Firehouse 87, etc.
TV series: The Life and Legend of Wyatt Earp 59–61. Rich Man, Poor Man – Book II 76–77.

Anderson, John Murray (1886–1954).
Canadian-born director, producer, writer, lyricist and choreographer, mainly for stage revues, a former ballroom dancer and art dealer. Educated at Edinburgh Academy and Lausanne University, he studied at RADA under Sir Herbert Beerbohm-Tree and began writing and staging his own productions in New York from 1919, as well as directing Ziegfeld Follies and musicals in New York and London. In the cinema, his main achievement was devising, co-writing and directing the innovative musical revue *The King of Jazz* 30.
Autobiography: 1954, *On without My Rubbers*.
Lilies of Broadway 31. Bathing Beauty (water ballet) 44. New Faces (deviser) 54, etc.

Anderson, Dame Judith (1898–1992) (Frances Margaret Anderson).
Australian stage actress whose splendidly icy presence made her a hit on Broadway and gave her a long career there. Her occasional movies were seldom notable, but she will be remembered for her inimitable Mrs Danvers in *Rebecca*.
■ Blood Money 33. *Rebecca* (AAN) 40. Forty Little Mothers 40. Kings Row 41. Free and Easy 41. Lady Scarface 41. All Through the Night 42. Edge of Darkness 43. Stage Door Canteen 43. Laura 44. And Then There Were None 45. The Diary of a Chambermaid 46. The Strange Love of Martha Ivers 46. The Specter of the Rose 46. Tycoon 47. The Red House 47. Pursued 47. The Furies 50. Salome 53. The Ten Commandments 56. Cat on a Hot Tin Roof 58. Cinderfella 60. Macbeth (TV) 60. Don't Bother to Knock 61. A Man Called Horse 70. Inn of the Damned 74. Star Trek III: The Search for Spock 84.
~In 1984, at the age of 86, she made her TV soap opera debut as the grand dame in Santa Barbara (which happens to be her home town).
❛❛ I have not myself a very serene temperament. –*J.A.*
Famous line (*And Then There Were None*): 'Very stupid to kill the servants: now we don't even know where to find the marmalade.'

Anderson, Kevin (1960–).
American leading actor, from the stage. He was a member of Chicago's Steppenwolf Theater.
Risky Business 83. Pink Nights 87. Orphans 87. Miles from Home 88. In Country 89. Orpheus Descending (TV) 91. Liebestraum 91. Sleeping with the Enemy 91. Hoffa 92. The Night We Never Met 93. Rising Sun 93. The Wrong Man 93. A Thousand Acres 97. Eye of God 97, etc.

Anderson, Lindsay (1923–1994).
Maverick British director of stage and screen, a former critic. Born in Bangalore, India, he was educated at Oxford University and co-founded the film magazine *Sequence*. Beginning as a documentary film-maker and a member of the Free Cinema group, he worked as a theatre director before making features. His closest collaboration was with writer David Storey, directing 12 of his plays and his screenplays *This Sporting Life* and *In Celebration* (from Storey's play). He was the author of a book on the work of John Ford.
O Dreamland 53. Thursday's Children 54. Every Day Except Christmas 57. *This Sporting Life* 63. The White Bus 67. *If* 68. *O Lucky Man* 72. In Celebration 74. The Old Crowd (TV) 79. Chariots of Fire (as actor) 81. Britannia Hospital 82. The Whales of August 87. Blame It on the Bellboy (as actor) 92. Is That All There Is (TV doc) 92, etc.
❛❛ He's a prime example of somebody who, once he has created something, tries to support it with a scaffolding of theory. But it's all rubbish: either it's worked or it hasn't. – *Tony Richardson*
To make a film is to create a world. – *L.A.*
I suppose I'm the boy who stood on the burning deck whence all but he had fled. The trouble is I

don't know whether the boy was a hero or a bloody idiot. – *L.A.*

He was a loner. There was an absoluteness of stance about him, an uncompromising quality which gave him many disciples, but also hundreds of enemies. – *Karel Reisz*

One of the most remarkable creative personalities of our time and, in some respects, possibly the most remarkable. – *David Storey*

Anderson, Loni (1946–).
Blonde American leading lady.
The Magnificent Magical Magnet of Santa Mesa (TV) 77. The Jayne Mansfield Story (title role) 80. Sizzle (TV) 81. Stroker Ace 83. All Dogs Go to Heaven (voice) 89. Sorry, Wrong Number (TV) 89. Blown Away 90. White Hot: Mysterious Murder of Thelma Todd (TV) 91. Munchie 92. Three Ninjas: High Noon at Mega Mountain 97. A Night at the Roxbury 98, etc.
TV series: WKRP in Cincinatti 78–82. Partners in Crime 84. Easy Street 86–87.

Anderson, Mary (1920–).
American supporting actress. While making *Lifeboat*, she asked the director, 'Which do you think is my best side, Mr Hitchcock?' 'My dear, you're sitting on it,' he said.
Gone with the Wind 39. Cheers for Miss Bishop 41. Lifeboat 43. *The Song of Bernadette* 44. Wilson 44. To Each His Own 46. Underworld Story 50. I The Jury 53. Dangerous Crossing 53, etc.

Anderson, Max (1914–1959).
British documentary director, with the GPO Film Unit from 1936, later Crown Film Unit, Best known for *The Harvest Shall Come* 41. *Daybreak in Udi* 48.

Anderson, Maxwell (1888–1959).
American middlebrow playwright, many of whose plays were filmed.
What Price Glory? 27 & 52. *All Quiet on the Western Front* (screenplay) 30. Mary of Scotland 36. Winterset 37. Elizabeth and Essex/Elizabeth the Queen 39. The Eve of St Mark 44. Key Largo 48. Joan of Arc/Joan of Lorraine 48. The Wrong Man (orig sp) 56. The Bad Seed 56. Anne of the Thousand Days 70.

Anderson, Michael (1920–).
British director who graduated to the international scene.
■ Waterfront 50. Hell Is Sold Out 51. Night Was Our Friend 52. Will Any Gentleman? 53. House of the Arrow 54. *The Dam Busters* 55. *1984* 55. *Around the World in Eighty Days* (AAN) 56. Yangtse Incident 56. Chase a Crooked Shadow 57. Shake Hands with the Devil 59. The Wreck of the Mary Deare 59. All the Fine Young Cannibals 60. The Naked Edge 61. Flight from Ashiya 62. Wild and Wonderful 63. Operation Crossbow 65. *The Quiller Memorandum* 66. *The Shoes of the Fisherman* 68. Pope Joan 72. Doc Savage 75. Conduct Unbecoming 75. Logan's Run 76. Orca 77. Dominique 78. The Martian Chronicles (TV) 79. Bells 79. Murder by Phone 82. Second Time Lucky 83. Separate Vacations 86. Sword of Gideon (TV) 86. The Jeweller's Shop 88. Millennium 89. Young Catherine (TV) 91. The Sea Wolf (TV) 93. Summer of the Monkey (Can.) 98.

Anderson, Michael, Jnr (1943–).
British juvenile lead, former child actor, son of director Michael Anderson.
The Moonraker 57. The Sundowners 60. In Search of the Castaways 61. Play It Cool 62. The Greatest Story Ever Told 65. Major Dundee 65. The Sons of Katie Elder 65. The Glory Guys 65. WUSA 69. The Last Movie 71. Sunset Grill 92, etc.
TV series: The Monroes 66.

Anderson, Paul.
British director and screenwriter, in Hollywood.
Shopping (wd) 94. Mortal Kombat (d) 95. Event Horizon (US) 97. Soldier (US) 98, etc.

Anderson, Paul Thomas (1970–).
American director and screenwriter who began working as a production assistant on music videos.
Cigarettes and Coffee (short) 93. Hard Eight 97. Boogie Nights (AAN) 97, etc.

Anderson, Philip W. (1915–1980).
American editor.
Sayonara 57. Cash McCall 59. The FBI Story 59. Ocean's Eleven 60. The Parent Trap 61. Gypsy 62. A Man Called Horse 70, many others.

Anderson, Richard (1926–).
Thoughtful-looking American supporting actor.
The People Against O'Hara 51. The Story of Three Lovers 53. Escape from Fort Bravo 54. Forbidden Planet 56. *Paths of Glory* 57. *The Long Hot Summer* 58. Compulsion 59. Seven Days in May 64. Seconds 66. Macho Callahan 70. Doctors' Wives 71. The Honkers 72. The Glass Shield 95, etc.
TV series: Mama Rosa 50. Bus Stop 61. Perry Mason 65–66. Dan August 70. Six Million Dollar Man 73–78. Bionic Woman 76–77. Cover Up 84. Dynasty 86–87.

Anderson, Robert (1917–).
American playwright who became an occasional Hollywood scriptwriter.
Tea and Sympathy (from his play) 56. Until They Sail 57. The Nun's Story 59. The Sand Pebbles 66. I Never Sang for My Father (from his play) (AAN) 70.

Anderson, Roland.
American art director, mainly working for Paramount, often in collaboration with Hans Dreier or Hal Pereira.
A Farewell to Arms (AAN) 32. Cleopatra 34. Lives of a Bengal Lancer (AAN) 34. The Plainsman 37. Souls at Sea (AAN) 37. The Buccaneer 38. Northwest Mounted Police (AAN) 40. Reap the Wild Wind (AAN) 42. Love Letters (AAN) 45. To Each His Own 46. The Big Clock 48. Carrie (AAN) 52. Red Garters (AAN) 54. The Country Girl 54. White Christmas 54. The Court Jester 55. The Joker Is Wild 57. It Started in Naples (AAN) 60. Breakfast at Tiffany's (AAN) 61. The Pigeon that Took Rome (AAN) 62. Come Blow Your Horn (AAN) 63. Will Penny 67. The Sterile Cuckoo 69, etc.

Anderson, Rona (1926–).
Scottish actress whose film career has been desultory.
Sleeping Car to Trieste 48. Poet's Pub 49. Home to Danger 51. Black Thirteen 54. The Flaw 55. Stock Car 55. Man with a Gun 58. Devils of Darkness 65. *The Prime of Miss Jean Brodie* 69, etc.

Anderson, Warner (1911–1976).
American supporting actor of solid presence but no outstanding personality.
This Is the Army 43. Destination Tokyo 43. Objective Burma 45. Abbott and Costello in Hollywood 45. Weekend at the Waldorf 45. Bad Bascomb 46. Dark Delusion 47. Song of the Thin Man 47. Command Decision 48. The Doctor and the Girl 49. *Destination Moon* (leading role) 50. The Blue Veil 51. *Detective Story* 51. Only the Valiant 51. A Lion is in the Streets 53. The Caine Mutiny 54. Drum Beat 54. The Blackboard Jungle 55. The Line-Up 58. Armored Command 61. Rio Conchos 64, many others.
TV series: The Doctors 52. The Line-Up 59. *Peyton Place* (as the newspaper editor) 64–68.

Anderson, William M.
Australian editor, in Hollywood.
Don's Party 76. The Getting of Wisdom 77. Money Movers 78. Breaker Morant 80. The Club 80. Gallipoli 81. Puberty Blues 83. The Year of Living Dangerously 83. Tender Mercies 83. Stanley 84. Razorback 84. King David 85. Big Shots 87. 1969 88. Signs of Life 89. Dead Poets Society 89. Old Gringo 89. Robocop 2 90. Green Card 90. At Play in the Fields of the Lord 91. 1492: Conquest of Paradise 92. City Slickers II: The Legend of Curly's Gold 94. Down Periscope 96, etc.

Andersson, Bibi (1935–).
Swedish actress who has ventured into international films.
Smiles of a Summer Night 55. *The Seventh Seal* 56. *Wild Strawberries* 57. The Face 58. So Close to Life 60. The Devil's Eye 61. Square of Violence 63. Now About These Women 64. My Sister My Love 66. Duel at Diablo 66. *Persona* 66. A Question of Rape 67. The Story of a Woman 69. *The Kremlin Letter* 69. A Passion 70. The Touch 71. My Husband, His Mistress and I 76. I Never Promised You a Rose Garden 77. An Enemy of the People 78. Quintet 79. Airport 79 – the Concorde 79. Exposed 83. The Last Summer 84. Poor Butterfly 86. Babette's Feast 87. Fordringsagare 89. The Butterfly's Dream/Il Sogno della Farfalla (It.) 94. Dreamplay/Dromspel 94, etc.

Andersson, Harriet (1932–).
Swedish actress, a member of Ingmar Bergman's company.
Summer with Monika 52. *Sawdust and Tinsel* 53. A Lesson in Love 54. *Smiles of a Summer Night* 55. Through a Glass Darkly 62. To Love 64. Now About These Women 64. The Deadly Affair (GB) 66. *Cries and Whispers* 72. The White Wall/Den Vita Väggen 75. The Sabina 79. Fanny and Alexander 82. Summer Nights/Sommarkvaller Pa Jorden 87. Blankt Vapen 90, etc.

Andes, Keith (1920–).
American light actor, usually in secondary roles.
The Farmer's Daughter 47. Clash by Night 52. Blackbeard the Pirate 52. Back from Eternity 56. The Girl Most Likely 58. Tora! Tora! Tora! 70. The Ultimate Impostor (TV) 79, etc.
TV series: This Man Dawson 59. Glynis 63. Search 73.

Andresen, Bjorn (1955–).
Swedish actor, best known for playing the beautiful boy in *Death in Venice* 71.
Bluff Stop 77. Summer's Ending 90, etc.

Andress, Ursula (1936–).
Swiss-born glamour star, in international films. Formerly married to actor and director John Derek (1957–66), she has a son (b. 1979) by actor Harry Hamlin.
The Loves of Casanova (It.) 54. *Dr No* 62. Four for Texas 63. Fun in Acapulco 64. *She* 64. Nightmare in the Sun 64. *What's New Pussycat?* 65. Up to His Ears 65. The Tenth Victim 65. Once Before I Die 66. The Blue Max 66. Casino Royale 67. The Southern Star 69. Perfect Friday 70. Red Sun 71. Five Against Capricorn 72. The Life and Times of Scaramouche 76. Loaded Guns 76. The Fifth Musketeer 77. The Clash of the Titans 81. Mexico in Flames 82. Big Man 88. The Chinatown Murders (TV) 89, etc.

Andrews, Anthony (1948–).
British leading actor who graduated through TV.
QB VII (TV) 74. A War of Children (TV) 74. Take Me High 74. David Copperfield (TV) 74. Percy's Progress 75. Operation Daybreak 76. Les Adolescentes 76. The Scarlet Pimpernel (title role) (TV) 82. Ivanhoe (TV) 82. Sparkling Cyanide (TV) 83. Under the Volcano 84. The Holcroft Covenant 85. The Second Victory 86. Suspicion (TV) 87. The Lighthorsemen 87. Hanna's War 88. The Strange Case of Dr Jekyll and Mr Hyde (TV) 89. Lost in Siberia 91. Haunted 95, etc.
TV series: *Danger UXB* 78. *Brideshead Revisited* 81.

Andrews, Dana (1909–1992) (Carver Daniel Andrews).
American leading man who showed promise in a wide variety of 40s roles, but whose somewhat hard and immobile features limited him in middle age.
■ The Westerner 40. Lucky Cisco Kid 40. Sailor's Lady 40. Kit Carson 40. Tobacco Road 41. Belle Starr 41. Swamp Water 41. Ball of Fire 41. Berlin Correspondent 42. Crash Dive 43. *The Ox Bow Incident* 43. North Star 43. *The Purple Heart* 44. Wing and a Prayer 44. Up in Arms 44. *Laura* 44. State Fair 45. Fallen Angel 45. *A Walk in the Sun* 45. Canyon Passage 46. *The Best Years of Our Lives* 46. *Boomerang* 47. Night Song 47. Daisy Kenyon 47. The Iron Curtain 48. Deep Waters 48. No Minor Vices 48. Britannia Mews 48. Sword in the Desert 49. *My Foolish Heart* 50. Where the Sidewalk Ends 50. Edge of Doom 50. The Frogmen 50. Sealed Cargo 51. I Want You 51. Assignment Paris 52. Elephant Walk 53. Duel in the Jungle 54. Three Hours to Kill 54. Smoke Signal 55. Strange Lady in Town 55. Comanche 56. While the City Sleeps 56. Beyond a Reasonable Doubt 56. Night of the Demon 57. Spring Reunion 57. Zero Hour 57. The Fearmakers 58. Enchanted Island 58. The Crowded Sky 60. Madison Avenue 62. Crack in the World 65. The Satan Bug 65. In Harm's Way 65. Brainstorm 65. Town Tamer 65. The Loved One 65. Battle of the Bulge 65. Johnny Reno 66. Spy in Your Eye 66. Hot Rods to Hell 67. The Frozen Dead 67. Cobra 67. Ten Million-Dollar Grab 68. The Devil's Brigade 68. The Failing of Raymond (TV) 71. Innocent Bystanders 72. The First 36 Hours of Dr Durant (TV) 75. Airport 75 75. Take a Hard Ride 75. Shadow in the Streets (TV) 76. The Last Tycoon 76. Ike (TV) 79. Good Guys Wear Black 79. Born Again 79. The Pilot 79. Prince Jack 84.
TV series: Bright Promise (daily soap opera) 71. The American Girls 78. Falcon Crest 82.

Andrews, Edward (1914–1985).
Beaming, bespectacled American character actor who could effortlessly become hearty, hen-pecked or sinister.
■ *The Phenix City Story* 55. The Harder They Fall 56. Tea and Sympathy 56. These Wilder Years 56. *The Unguarded Moment* 56. Tension at Table Rock 56. Three Brave Men 57. Hot Summer Night 57. The Tattered Dress 57. Trooper Hook 57. The Fiend That Walked the West 58. Night of the Quarter Moon 59. *Elmer Gantry* 60. The Absent-Minded Professor 61. The Young Savages 61. Love in a Goldfish Bowl 61. The Young Doctors 61. Advise and Consent 62. Forty Pounds of Trouble 62. Son of Flubber 62. The Thrill of It All 63. A Tiger Walks 64. The Brass Bottle 64. Good Neighbor Sam 64. Kisses for My President 64. Youngblood Hawke 64. Send Me No Flowers 64. The Man from Galveston 64. Fluffy 65. The Glass Bottom Boat 66. Birds Do It 66. Tora! Tora! Tora! 70. The Trouble with Girls 70. The Million Dollar Duck 71. How to Frame a Figg 71. Now You See Him Now You Don't 72. Avanti 72. Charley and the Angel 73. The Photographer 75. Gremlins 84. Sixteen Candles 84.
TV series: Broadside 64. Supertrain 79.

Andrews, Harry (1911–1989).
Tough-looking British stage and screen actor. Often played sergeant-majors or other no-nonsense characters.
The Red Beret (debut) 52. The Black Knight 54. Helen of Troy 55. *A Hill in Korea* 56. Alexander the Great 56. Moby Dick 56. Saint Joan 57. *Ice Cold in Alex* 58. The Devil's Disciple 59. Solomon and Sheba 59. Circle of Deception 60. The Best of Enemies 62. Lisa 62. 55 Days at Peking 62. Barabbas 62. The Informers 63. The System 64. *The Hill* 65. Sands of the Kalahari 65. The Agony and the Ecstasy 65. Modesty Blaise 66. *The Deadly Affair* 66. The Jokers 67. Danger Route 67. The Charge of the Light Brigade 68. The Night They Raided Minsky's (US) 68. The Seagull 68. A Nice Girl Like Me 69. The Battle of Britain 69. Country Dance 70. Entertaining Mr Sloane 70. Wuthering Heights 70. Burke and Hare 71. Nicholas and Alexandra 71. I Want What I Want 71. The Ruling Class 72. Man of La Mancha 72. Theatre of Blood 73. The Mackintosh Man 74. Man at the Top 74. The Bluebird 76. Equus 77. The Four Feathers (TV) 78. Death on the Nile 78. The Big Sleep 78. Superman 78. SOS Titanic (TV) 80. The Curse of King Tut's Tomb (TV) 80. Hawk the Slayer 80. The Seven Dials Mystery (TV) 83, etc.

Andrews, Julie (1935–) (Julia Wells).
British star of Hollywood films. A singing stage performer from childhood who became the original stage Eliza of *My Fair Lady* but failed to get the film role. She zoomed to international stardom the same year but her refreshingly old-fashioned image seemed to pall rather quickly. She is married to director Blake Edwards. In 1995, she starred on Broadway in a musical version of her film *Victor/Victoria*. Blake Edwards announced in 1998 that, following surgery in 1997 to remove throat nodules, she may never sing again.
Biographies: 1996, *Julie Andrews* by James Arntz and Thomas S. Wilson; 1997, *Julie Andrews* by Robert Windeler.
Mary Poppins (AA) 64. *The Americanization of Emily* 64. *The Sound of Music* (AAN) 65. Torn Curtain 66. Hawaii 66. *Thoroughly Modern Millie* 67. *Star!* 68. Darling Lili 69. The Tamarind Seed 74. '10' 79. Little Miss Marker 80. S.O.B. 81. Victor/Victoria (AAN) 82. The Man Who Loved Women 83. Duet for One 86. That's Life 86. Tchin-Tchin 91. Our Sons (TV) 91, etc.

❝ One senses that she is realistic enough to have enjoyed the good times while they lasted, and to fall from grace gracefully. But she may fight. After *The Sound of Music*, Christopher Plummer said that:

Working with her is like being hit over the head with a Valentine's card.

And some anonymous gentleman described her as:

Like a nun with a switchblade.

Moss Hart said:

She has that wonderful British strength that makes you wonder why they lost India.

Miss Andrews does seem to merit the suggestion of steel beneath the velvet. When she accepted her Oscar, which many thought went to her out of sympathy because Warners refused her the film of *My Fair Lady*, her little speech ran:

I'd like to thank all those who made this possible – especially Jack Warner.

Having got to the top by being sweet and old-fashioned, she quickly showed signs of disliking her own image.

I don't want to be thought of as wholesome,

she said in 1966, and promptly proved it by accepting a sexy role. She was also seen wearing a badge which read:

Mary Poppins is a junkie.

But her serene self-confidence may be something of a sham. She once said:

Films are much more my level. On stage I never feel quite enough . . .

One way or another, she achieved, briefly, a worldwide image best expressed by a *Time* magazine interviewer:

She's everybody's tomboy tennis partner and their daughter, their sister, their mum . . . She is Christmas carols in the snow, a companion by the fire, a laughing clown at charades, a girl to read poetry to on a cold winter's night . . .

Andrews, Lois (1924–1968).
American light leading lady.
Dixie Dugan 43. Roger Touhy Gangster 44. The Desert Hawk 50. Meet Me After the Show 51, etc.

Andrews, Naveen (1969–).
Anglo-Asian actor.
London Kills Me 91. Wild West 92. The Buddha of Suburbia (TV) 93. *The English Patient* 96. Kama Sutra: A Tale of Love 96, etc.

Andrews, Robert Hardy (1903–1976).
American screenwriter.
If I Had a Million (oa) 32. Bataan 44. The Cross of Lorraine 44. The Hairy Ape 44. Tarzan Goes to India 62, etc.

The Andrews Sisters: *Patty* (1920–1992), *Maxene* (1918–1995), *Laverne* (1915–1967).
American close harmony singing group, popular in light musicals of the 40s.
■ Argentine Nights 40. In The Navy 41. Buck Privates 41. Hold That Ghost 41. Give Out Sisters 42. Private Buckaroo 42. What's Cookin'? 42. Always a Bridesmaid 43. How's About It? 43. Follow the Boys 44. Hollywood Canteen 44. Moonlight and Cactus 44. Swingtime Johnny 44. Her Lucky Night 45. Make Mine Music (voices) 46. Road to Rio 47. Melody Time (voices) 48.

Andrews, Stanley (1892–1969).
American character actor, often seen as grizzled western veteran. He more or less ended his career as the 'old ranger' host of TV's *Death Valley Days* 52–65.
Evelyn Prentice 34. Mississippi 35. Murder Man 35. Pennies from Heaven 36. Desire 36. Madame X 37. Nancy Steele Is Missing 37. Hold That Co-Ed 38. Alexander's Ragtime Band 38. Kentucky 38. Beau Geste 39. Union Pacific 39. The Blue Bird 40. Meet John Doe 41. My Gal Sal 42. Murder My Sweet 44. Adventure 45. It's a Wonderful Life 46. Robin Hood of Texas 47. Northwest Stampede 48. The Last Bandit 49. Arizona Cowboy 50. Vengeance Valley 51. Woman of the North Country 52. Ride Vaquero 52. Dawn at Socorro 54. The Treasure of Ruby Hills 55. Frontier Gambler 56. Cry Terror 58, many others.

Andrews, Tige (1924–) (Tiger Androwaous).
Lebanese-American supporting actor, usually an amiable tough.
Mr Roberts 55. The Wings of Eagles 57. Imitation General 58. China Doll 58. A Private Affair 59. The Last Tycoon 76, etc.
TV series: *The Detectives* 59–62. *The Mod Squad* 68–73.

Andrews, Tod (1920–1972).
Burly American leading man of minor action films; previously known as Michael Ames.
Now Voyager 42. Action in the North Atlantic 43. From Hell It Came 60. In Harm's Way 64, etc.
TV series: The Gray Ghost 57.

Andreyev, Boris (1915–).
Russian leading actor.
Tractor Drivers 39. Two Soldiers 43. The Last Hill 44. Song of Siberia 47. The Fall of Berlin 49. Ilya Muromets 56. The Gordeyev Family 59. The Cossacks 61. Aladdin 67, many others.

Andrien, Jean-Jacques (1944–).
Belgian producer, director and screenwriter.
La Pierre Qui Flotte (w) 71. Le Fils d'Amour Est Mort (co-w, d) 75. Le Grand Paysage d'Alexis Droeven (co-w, d) 81. Mémoires (co-w, d) 84. Australia (co-w, d) 89, etc.

Andriot, Lucien (1897–1979).
French American cinematographer long in Hollywood.
Two Lives 15. Oh Boy 19. Why Trust Your Husband 21. Hell's Hole 23. Gigolo 26. White Gold 27. The Valiant 28. Hallelujah I'm a Bum 33. Anne of Green Gables 34. The Gay Desperado 36. The Lady in Question 40. The Hairy Ape 44. The Southerner 45. And Then There Were None 45. Dishonored Lady 47. Outpost in Morocco 49. Borderline 50. Home Town Story 51, many others. Later in television.

Angel, Danny (Daniel M.) (1911–).
British producer, in films from 1945.
Mr Drake's Duck 50. Albert R.N. 53. The Sea Shall Not Have Them 54. Reach for the Sky 56. Carve Her Name with Pride 57. The Sheriff of Fractured Jaw 58. West Eleven 63, etc.

Angel, Heather (1909–1986).
British-born leading lady of the 30s; in Hollywood from 1933.
City of Song 30. *Berkeley Square* 33. The Informer 35. The Mystery of Edwin Drood 35. Last of the Mohicans 36. Army Girl 38. Pride and Prejudice 40. Time to Kill 42. Lifeboat 43. In the Meantime, Darling 44. The Saxon Charm 48. The Premature Burial 62.
TV series: Peyton Place 64–69.

Angeli, Pier (1932–1971) (Anna Maria Pierangeli).
Sensitive-looking Italian actress who after some stage experience at home moved to Hollywood but found only occasional worthy roles. Twin sister of Marisa Pavan, she was married to singer Vic Damone. Committed suicide.
■ Tomorrow Is Too Late (It.) 50. Tomorrow Is Another Day (It.) 51. *Teresa* 51. The Light Touch 51. The Devil Makes Three 52. The Story of Three Loves 52. Sombrero 53. The Flame and the Flesh 54. The Silver Chalice 54. Santerella (It.) 54. Somebody Up There Likes Me 56. Port Afrique 56. The Vintage 57. Merry Andrew 58. SOS Pacific 60. The Angry Silence 60. Musketeers of the Sea (It.) 62. White Slave Ship 62. Sodom and Gomorrah 63. Battle of the Bulge 65. Spy in Your Eye 66. Missione Morte (It.) 66. Per Mille Dollari al Giorno (It.) 66. Shadow of Evil 67. Red Roses for the Fuehrer (It.) 67. One Step to Hell 68. Vive America (Sp.) 68. Les Enemoniades (Sp.) 70. Every Bastard a King 70. Adio Alexandra (It.) 71. Nelle Pieghe Della Carne 71. Octaman 72.

Angelo, Yves (1956–).
French cinematographer who turned to directing in the mid-90s. He studied at the Conservatoire de Musique in Paris before studying film at the L'École Lumière and then working as an assistant cameraman and cameraman.
AS CINEMATOGRAPHER: Baxter 88. Nocturne Indien 89. Tumultes 90. *Tous les Matins du Monde* 91. The Accompanist/L'Accompagnatrice 92. A Heart in Winter/Un Coeur en Hiver 92. *Germinal* 93, etc.
AS DIRECTOR: Colonel Chabert/Le Colonel Chabert 94. Un Air Si Pur 97. Stolen Life/Voleur de Vie (& co-w) 98, etc.

Angelopoulos, Theodoros (1936–).
Greek director whose *The Travelling Players* was widely praised in 1975.
The Broadcast/Ekpombi 68. Reconstruction/Anaparastassi 70. The Hunters/I Kynighi 77. Alexander the Great/O Megalexandros 80. Athens 1982 82. Voyage to Cythera/Taxidi Sta Kythera 84. The Beekeeper/O Melissokomos 86. Landscape in the Mist/Topio Stin Omichli 88. The Suspended Step of the Stork/To Meteoro Vima To Pelargou 91. Le Regard d'Ulysse 95. Eternity and a Day 98, etc.

Angelus, Muriel (1909–) (M. A. Findlay).
Blonde English leading actress who went to Hollywood for a brief career in the late 30s and retired in the United States. Born in London, she was on-stage from 1924. Married actor John STUART and conductor Paul Lavalle.
Sailors Don't Care 28. The Ringer 28. No Exit 30. The Ringer (remake) 31. Hindle Wakes 31. Blind Spot 32. So You Won't Talk 35. The Light that Failed (US) 39. The Great McGinty (US) 40. The Way of All Flesh (US) 40. Safari (US) 40, etc.

Anger, Kenneth (1932–).
American independent film-maker who grew up in Hollywood and also wrote *Hollywood Babylon*, scurrilous exposés of the private lives of its stars. His films are mainly short, inscrutable and Freudian.
Biography: 1996, *Anger: The Unauthorized Biography of Kenneth Anger* by Bill Landis.
Fireworks 47. Eaux d'Artifice 53. Inauguration of the Pleasure Dome 54. Scorpio Rising 64. Kustom Kar Kommandos 65. Invocation of My Demon Brother 69. Lucifer Rising 80, etc.

Angers, Avril (1922–).
British character comedienne whose film appearances have been infrequent.
Skimpy in the Navy 50. Lucky Mascot 51. The Green Man 56. Devils of Darkness 65. The Family Way 66. Two a Penny 68, etc.

Anglade, Jean-Hugues (1955–).
French leading actor, on stage from 1978.
L'Indiscrétion 82. Subway 85. Betty Blue 90. Nikita/La Femme Nikita 90. Jona Che Visse nella Balena 93. Les Marmottes 93. Queen Margot/La Reine Margot 94. Killing Zoe 94. Les Menteurs 95. Say Yes/Dis-Moi Oui 95. Nelly & Mr Arnaud 95. Maximum Risk (US) 96. Ceux Qui m'Aiment Prendront le Train 98, etc.

Anhalt, Edward (1914–).
American middlebrow scriptwriter.
With his then wife *Edna Anhalt* (1914–):
Bulldog Drummond Strikes Back 48. Panic in the Streets 50. The Sniper (AAN) 52. Not as a Stranger 54. The Pride and the Passion 56. The Young Lions 58, etc.
Alone: A Girl Named Tamiko 63. Becket (AA) 64. Hour of the Gun 67. The Boston Strangler 68. The Mad Woman of Chaillot 69. Jeremiah Johnson (co-w) 72. Luther 74. The Man in the Glass Booth 76. Escape to Athena 79. The Holcroft Covenant 85. The Take 90. Alexander the Great (TV) 91, etc.

Aniston, Jennifer 1969–).
American actress, best known for her role in the TV sitcom *Friends*. Born in Sherman Oaks, California, she studied at New York's High School of the Performing Arts, and first acted in off-Broadway productions. She is the daughter of actor John Aniston. She has been romantically linked with actors Tate Donovan and Brad PITT. Current asking price: around $3m.
Leprachaun 93. She's the One 96. Dream for an Insomniac 96. Picture Perfect 97. 'Til There Was You 97. The Object of My Affection 98, etc.
TV series: Molloy 90. Ferris Bueller 90. The Edge 92. Friends 94– .

Anka, Paul (1941–).
Canadian pop singer of the 60s, subject of the documentary *Lonely Boy* 62. Also acted the same year in *The Longest Day*, and composed the theme song.
Look in Any Window 61. Captain Ron 92. Mad Dog Time/Trigger Happy 96, etc.

Ankers, Evelyn (1918–1985).
British leading lady who did not so much act as react. She also looked decorative, and after going to Hollywood in 1940 she appeared as the well-bred heroine of innumerable co-features. Married Richard Denning.
The Villiers Diamond 33. Rembrandt 36. Knight without Armour 37. Over the Moon 39. Hold that Ghost 41. Bachelor Daddy 41. *The Wolf Man* 41. The Ghost of Frankenstein 42. The Great Impersonation 42. The Mad Ghoul 43. Hers to Hold 43. His Butler's Sister 43. Ladies Courageous 44. Weird Woman 44. The Frozen Ghost 45. The French Key 46. The Lone Wolf In London 47. The Texan Meets Calamity Jane 50. No Greater Love 60, etc.

Ankrum, Morris (1896–1964) (Morris Nussbaum).
American stage actor seen in innumerable films as lawyer, judge or western villain.
Buck Benny Rides Again 40. Light of the Western Stars 40. Tales of Manhattan 42. *Tennessee Johnson* 42. Let's Face It 43. Barbary Coast Gent 44. The Hidden Eye 45. The Harvey Girls 46. Joan of Arc 48. Rocketship XM 50. My Favourite Spy 51. Son of Ali Baba 52. Apache 54. Earth Versus the Flying Saucers 56. Badman's Country 59. The Most Dangerous Man Alive 61, many others.

Annabella (1909–1996) (Suzanne Charpentier).
French leading lady of the 30s, in international films. She began as a dancer before being groomed for stardom by director René CLAIR in the 30s. In the late 30s and 40s she was signed by Twentieth Century-Fox and went first to Britain, where she made three films, and then to Hollywood, but without notable success, partly owing to disputes with Darryl ZANUCK, who tried to prevent her marrying Tyrone POWER, her third husband (1939–48). Her second husband was actor Jean Murat.
Napoleon 26. Le Million 32. Le Quatorze Juillet 33. Under the Red Robe 36. Dinner at the Ritz 37. Wings of the Morning 37. Suez 38, Hôtel du Nord 38. Bridal Suite 39. Bomber's Moon 42. Tonight We Raid Calais 43. 13 Rue Madeleine 46. Don Juan (sp) 50, etc.

Annakin, Ken (1914–).
British director of very variable output. Formerly a journalist.
■ Holiday Camp 47. Here Come the Huggetts 47. Broken Journey 48. Miranda 48. Quartet (part) 48. Vote for Huggett 49. Landfall 49. Double Confession 50. Trio (part) 50. The Huggetts Abroad 51. Hotel Sahara 51. Robin Hood 52. The Planter's Wife 52. The Seekers 53. The Sword and the Rose 53. You Know What Sailors Are 53. Value for Money 55. Three Men in a Boat 56. Loser Takes All 56. Across the Bridge 57. Nor the Moon by Night 58. *The Swiss Family Robinson* 60. Third Man on the Mountain 61. *Very Important Person* 61. The Longest Day 62. The Hellions 62. Crooks Anonymous 62. The Informers 63. *The Fast Lady* 63. *Those Magnificent Men in Their Flying Machines* 64. Battle of the Bulge 65. The Biggest Bundle of Them All 66. The Long Duel 67. Monte Carlo or Bust 69. Call of the Wild 72. Paper Tiger 75. The Fifth Musketeer 78. The Pirate (TV) 79. Cheaper to Keep Her 80. The Pirate Movie 82. Pippi Longstocking 88.

Annaud, Jean-Jacques (1943–).
French director and screenwriter who began his career with educational films for the army, and TV commercials.
Black and White in Color/La Victoire en Chantant (AA) 78. Hot Head/Coup de Tête 80. Quest for Fire 82. The Name of the Rose 86. The Bear/L'Ours 88. The Lover/L'Amant 92. Wings of Courage (3-D Imax) 95. Seven Years in Tibet 97, etc.

Annis, Francesca (1945–).
British leading lady, former juvenile player.
The Cat Gang 58. Cleopatra 62. The Eyes of Annie Jones 63. Flipper and the Pirates (US) 64. The Pleasure Girls 65. Run with the Wind 66. The Walking Stick 69. Macbeth 71. Krull 83. Coming Out of the Ice (TV) 83. The Secret Adversary (TV) 83. Dune 86. I'll Take Manhattan (TV) 86. Under the Cherry Moon 86. Doomsday Gun (TV) 94. Deadly Summer (TV) 97, etc.
TV series: *Lillie* (title role) 78. Partners in Crime 83. Reckless 97.

Ann-Margret (1941–) (Ann-Margret Olsson).
Swedish-American sex symbol and formidable cabaret performer; a hard worker who gradually became a good actress.
Autobiography: 1994, *Ann-Margret: My Story* (with Todd Gold).
■ Pocketful of Miracles 61. *State Fair* 62. *Bye Bye Birdie* 62. Viva Las Vegas 64. Kitten with a Whip 64. Bus Riley's Back in Town 65. The Pleasure Seekers 65. Once a Thief 65. *The Cincinnati Kid* 65. Made in Paris 66. The Swinger 66. Stagecoach

66. Murderers' Row 66. The Tiger and the Pussycat 67. Mr Kinky 68. Rebus (It.) 68. Seven Men and One Brain (It.) 69. C.C. and Co. 70. *Carnal Knowledge* (AAN) 71. R.P.M. 71. The Train Robbers 73. The Outside Man 73. Tommy (AAN) 75. The Twist 76. Joseph Andrews 76. The Last Remake of Beau Geste 77. The Cheap Detective 78. Magic 78. The Villain 79. Middle Age Crazy 80. I Ought to Be in Pictures 82. Lookin' to Get Out 82. The Return of the Soldier 82. Who Will Love My Children? (TV) 83. Twice in a Lifetime 85. The Two Mrs Grevilles (TV) 86. 52 Pick-Up 86. A Tiger's Tale 87. A New Life 88. Newsies/Newsboys 92. Queen (TV) 93. Grumpy Old Men 93. Nobody's Children 94. Grumpier Old Men 95.

Anouilh, Jean (1910–1987).
Skilful and versatile French playwright who worked in the cinema as a screenwriter and director. Several of his plays have also been filmed.
Les Dégourdis de la Onzième (w) 36. Le Voyageur sans Bagage (d, oa) 43. Monsieur Vincent (w) 47. Anna Karenina (GB) (w) 47. Pattes Blanches (w) 48. Caroline Chérie (w) 50. Deux Sous de Violette (d) 51. Le Chevalier de la Nuit (w) 53. Waltz of the Toreadors (oa) 62. La Ronde (w) 64. Becket (oa) 64, etc.

Ansara, Michael (1922–).
Tall, swarthy American character actor, from the stage, often in westerns, frequently as an Indian. Married actress Barbara Eden (1958–73).
Action in Arabia 44. New Orleans 47. Only the Valiant 50. Soldiers Three 51. Brave Warrior 52. The Robe (as Judas) 53. Julius Caesar 53. Sign of the Pagan 54. Voyage to the Bottom of the Sea 61. The Comancheros 61. The Greatest Story Ever Told 65. Texas across the River 66. Guns of the Magnificent Seven 68. Stand Up and Be Counted 71. It's Alive 74. The Bears and I 74. Day of the Animals 76. Knights of the City 85. Assassination 86, etc.
TV series: Broken Arrow (as Cochise) 56–58. Law of the Plainsman 59–60. Centennial 78–79. Buck Rogers in the 25th Century 79–80.

Anschutz, Ottomar (1846–1907).
Polish inventor who devised a motion-picture camera and patented his Elektrotachyscope, a device for showing his pictures, in 1887.

Anspach, Susan (1945–).
American leading lady, from the stage. She has a son (b. 1970) by actor Jack Nicholson.
■ The Landlord 70. Five Easy Pieces 70. Play It Again Sam 72. Blume in Love 72. Nashville 75. The Big Fix 78. Running 79. The Devil and Max Devlin 81. Gas 81. Montenegro 82. Misunderstood 84. Blue Monkey 87. Into the Fire 87. Blood Red 89. Back to Back 90. The Rutanga Tapes 90. Killer Instinct 90.
TV series: The Yellow Rose 83.

Anspaugh, David.
American director.
Hoosiers/Best Shot 86. Fresh Horses 88. Rudy 93. Moonlight and Valentino 96, etc.

Anstey, Edgar (1907–1987).
British documentary producer (Housing Problems 35. Enough to Eat 36, etc.). Long-time Chief Films Officer for British Transport.

Anstey, F. (1856–1934) (Thomas Anstey Guthrie).
British humorous novelist. Works filmed: *Vice Versa* 48 and 88. The Brass Bottle 64.

Ant, Adam (1954–) (Stuart Leslie Goddard).
British rock singer of the 80s who became an actor as his popularity waned at the end of the decade.
Jubilee 78. Nomads 86. Slamdance 87. Cold Steel 87. Spellcaster 88. World Gone Wild 88. Trust Me 89. Midnight Heat 91. Acting on Impulse 93. Drop Dead Rock 96. Lover's Knot 96. Face Down 97, etc.

Antheil, George (1900–1959).
American composer, former concert pianist.
The Plainsman 37. The Buccaneer 38. Angels over Broadway 40. Specter of the Rose 46. Knock on Any Door 49. The Fighting Kentuckian 49. In a Lonely Place 50. The Sniper 51. Actors and Sin 52. The Juggler 53. Not as a Stranger 55. The Pride and the Passion 57, etc.

Anthony, Joseph (1912–1993) (J. A. Deuster).
American director from stage and TV; former small part actor and dancer.
■ The Rainmaker 56. The Matchmaker 58. Career 59. All in a Night's Work 61. The Captive City 63. Tomorrow 72.

Anthony, Lysette (1963–).
English leading actress.
Ivanhoe (TV) 82. Oliver Twist (TV) 82. Krull 83. The House on Kirov Street 87. Looking for Eileen 87. Without a Clue 88. Switch 91. Husbands and Wives 92. The Hour of the Pig 93. Look Who's Talking Now 93. The Hard Truth 94. Dr Jekyll and Ms Hyde 95. Dracula: Dead and Loving It 95. Trilogy of Terror 2 (TV) 96. Dead Cold 96. Misbegotten 98, etc.
TV series: Dark Shadows 91.

Anthony, Tony (1937–).
American leading man who had some success in tough Italian westerns.
A Stranger in Town 67. The Stranger Returns 68. Samurai on a Horse 69. Blindman 71. Comin' at Ya 81. Treasure of the Four Crowns 82, etc.

Antin, Manuel (1926–).
Argentinian director, producer, screenwriter, novelist, poet and playwright.
La Cifra Impar 62. Los Venerables Todos (& oa) 62. Circe 64. Don Segundo Sombre 69. Juan Manuel de Rosas 78. Far Away and Long Ago/Allá Lejos y Hace Tiempo 78. La Invitación 82, etc.

Anton, Susan (1950–).
American actress, tipped for stardom in the 90s.
Goldengirl 79. Spring Fever 81. Cannonball Run II 84. Options 88. Lena's Holiday 91, etc.
TV series: Presenting Susan Anton 79. Stop Susan Williams 79.

Antonelli, Laura (1941–).
Sultry Italian leading actress.
A Man Called Sledge 70. Divine Nymph 71. High Heels/Docteur Popaul 72. How Funny Can Sex Be?/Sessomatto 73. Malicious/Malizia 73. Till Marriage Do Us Part 77. The Innocent/L'Innocente 77. Tigers in Lipstick/Wild Beds 78. Passion of Love/Passione d'Amore 82. Rimini, Rimini 87, etc.

Antonio, Lou (1934–).
Tough-looking American character actor who has dabbled successfully in TV direction.
America America 63. Hawaii 66. Cool Hand Luke 67. Sole Survivor (TV) 69. The Phynx 70. Partners in Crime (TV) 73. Someone I Touched (TV) 75. The Gypsy Warriors (TV) 78. Breaking Up Is Hard to Do (TV) 79. Between Friends (TV) 83. Mayflower Madam (TV) 87, etc.
TV series: The Snoop Sisters 73. Dog and Cat 77.

Antonioni, Michelangelo (1912–).
Italian director whose reputation was boosted in the 50s by the ardent support of highbrow film magazines. Co-scripts all his own films, which largely jettison narrative in favour of vague incident and relentless character study. He was awarded an honorary Oscar in 1995.
Book: 1995, *Antonioni: The Poet of Images* by William Arrowsmith.
Cronaca di un Amore 50. Le Amiche 55. Il Grido 57. *L'Avventura* 59. *La Notte* 60. L'Eclisse 62. *The Red Desert* 64. *Blow-Up* (GB) (AAN) 67. Zabriskie Point (US) 69. The Passenger 74. The Oberwald Mystery 81. Identification of a Woman 82. Beyond the Clouds (co-d) 95, etc.
❝ I feel like a father towards my old films. You bring children into the world, then they grow up and go off on their own. From time to time you get together, and it's always a pleasure to see them again. – M.A.
Actors are like cows. You have to lead them through a fence. – M.A.

Antonutti, Omero. (1935–).
Italian leading actor.
Italy: Year One 74. *Padre Padrone* 77. Night of the Shooting Stars 82. Basileus Quartet 82. Good Morning Babylon 87. *The Fencing Master* 92. Whistle Stop/Una Estación de Paso 92. The Greek Labyrinth 92. Genesis: The Creation and the Flood/Genesi: La Creazione e il Diluvio 94. Un Eroe Borghese 95. Farinelli the Castrato 95, etc.

Antony, Scott (1950–) (Anthony Scott).
British leading juvenile of the early 70s.
Baxter 72. Savage Messiah 73. Dead Cert 73. The Mutations 74.

Anwar, Gabrielle (1969–).
English leading actress.
Manifesto 88. If Looks Could Kill 91. Wild Hearts Can't Be Broken 91. Scent of a Woman 92. Body Snatchers 93. The Three Musketeers 93. In Pursuit of Honor (TV) 95. Things to Do in Denver When You're Dead 95. The Grave 96, etc.

Apfel, Oscar (1874–1938).
American character actor.
Ten Nights in a Bar Room 22. The Social Code 23. Perils of the Coastguard 26. Code of the Cow Country 27. Not Quite Decent 29. Five Star Final 31. Wicked 31. The Maltese Falcon 31. High Pressure 32. Make Me a Star 32. Before Dawn 33. The House of Rothschild 34. Bordertown 35. The Plot Thickens 36. The Toast of New York 37, many others.

Applebaum, Louis (1918–).
Canadian composer who spent time in Hollywood.
Tomorrow the World 44. The Story of GI Joe (AA) 45. Lost Boundaries 48. Teresa 51. The Whistle at Eaton Falls 51. Walk East on Beacon 52. The Mask 61, etc.

Applegate, Christina (1972–).
American actress, on-screen as a teenager.
Jaws of Satan/King Cobra 85. Streets 90. Don't Tell Mom the Babysitter's Dead 91. Wild Bill 95. Nowhere 96. Mars Attacks! 96. The Big Hit 98. Jane Austen's Mafia/Mafia! 98. Claudine's Return 98, etc.
TV series: Heart of the City 86–87. Married . . . with Children 87–89. Jesse 98– .

Apted, Michael (1941–).
British director, from TV.
Triple Echo 72. Stardust 74. The Squeeze 77. Agatha 79. *Coal Miner's Daughter* 80. Continental Divide 81. P'tang Yang Kipperbang (TV) 82. Gorky Park 83. First Born 84. 28 Up 84. Bring on the Night 85. Critical Condition 87. Gorillas in the Mist 88. The Long Way Home 89. Class Action 91. Thunderheart 92. Incident at Oglala (doc) 92. Crossroads (TV) 92. Blink 94. Nell 94. Extreme Measures 96. Always Outnumbered 98, etc.

Aquanetta (1920–) (Burnu Davenport).
Exotic American leading lady of easterns and horrors in the early 40s.
Arabian Nights 42. Jungle Captive 43. Jungle Woman 44. Dead Man's Eyes 44. Tarzan and the Leopard Woman 46, etc.

Araki, Gregg. (1959–).
American director of movies on homosexual themes.
The Long Weekend 89. The Living End 92. Totally F***ed Up 93. *The Doom Generation* 95. Nowhere 97, etc.

Aranda, Vicente (1926–).
Spanish director and screenwriter. Born in Barcelona, he spent most of the 50s in Venezuela before returning to the city to form his own production company in the mid-60s.
Brilliant Future/Brillante Porvenir 64. Fata Morgana 66. The Cruel Women/Las Crueles 69. The Bloody Bride/La Novia Ensangrenada 72. Clara Is the Price/Clara Es el Precio 74. Sex Change/Cambio de Sexo 77. The Girl in the Golden Panties/La Muchacha de las Bragas de Oro 80. Murder in the Central Committee/Asesinato en el Comité Central 82. Fanny Pelopaja 84. Time of Silence/Tiempo de Silencio 86. El Lute 87. El Lute II 88. Si Te Dicen Que Cai 89. *Lovers*/Amantes 91. Intruder/Intruso 93. Turkish Passion/Pasiones Turcas 94. Libertarias 96. The Naked Eye/La Miranda del Otro 98, etc.

Arau, Alfonso (1932–).
Mexican actor, director and producer. Best known internationally as an actor as the bandit El Guapo in *Three Amigos!*, in the 50s he performed in the song-and-dance act Arau and Corona, and spent the early 60s in Cuba. He is married to the Mexican screenwriter and novelist Laura ESQUIVEL.MD4 *Like Water for Chocolate*, from his wife's novel and screenplay, was one of the few Mexican films of recent years to find a worldwide audience.
The Barefoot Eagle (d) 67. The Wild Bunch (a) 69. Scandalous John (a) 71. El Rincón de las Virgenes (a) 72. Calzonzin Inspector (a, d) 74. Tivoli (a) 74. Posse (a) 75. Mojado Power (d) 80. Used Cars (a) 80. Chido Guan (d) 84. Romancing the Stone (a) 84. Three Amigos! (a) 86. Walker (a) 87. Stones for Ibarra (a) (TV) 88. Dynamite and Gold/Where the Hell's the Gold? (a) (TV) 88. *Like Water for Chocolate*/Como Agua para Chocolate (p, d) 92. Estrellita Marinera (d) 94. A Walk in the Clouds (d) 95, etc.

Arbeid, Ben (1924–1992).
British producer.
The Barber of Stamford Hill 62. *Private Potter* 63. Children of the Damned 64. Murder Most Foul 65. The Jokers 67. Assignment K 68. Hoffman 70. The Hireling 71. The Water Babies 76. Eagle's Wing 79.

Arbogast, Thierry.
French cinematographer.
Nikita/La Femme Nikita 90. I Don't Kiss/J'Embrasse Pas 91. The Girl in the Air/La Fille de l'Air 92. My Favourite Season/Ma Saison Préferée 93. The Professional/Leon 94. The Horseman on the Roof/Le Hussard sur le Toit 95. Ridicule 96. L'Appartement 96. The Fifth Element 97. She's So Lovely (US) 97, etc.

Arbuckle, Roscoe 'Fatty' (1887–1933).
Grown-up fat boy of American silent cinema. His highly successful career, mainly in two-reelers, came to grief after a sensational murder trial in 1921, and his only subsequent films were a few two-reelers in the early 30s; he also directed a few films as William Goodrich. The first of his three wives was actress Minta Durfee (1908–23).
Biographies: 1976, *The Day the Laughter Stopped* by David A. Yallop. 1990, *Frame-Up! The Untold Story of Roscoe 'Fatty' Arbuckle* by Andy Edmonds.
In the Clutches of the Gang (as a Keystone Kop) 13. Fatty and Mabel's Simple Life 15. Mabel and Fatty's Married Life 16. Fatty's Flirtation 16. Fickle Fatty's Fall 17. His Wedding Night 17. Out West 17. The Bell Boy 17. The Round Up 20. The Life of the Party (feature) 20. The Travelling Salesman (feature) 21. Gasoline Gus (feature) 21, many others.
❝ Roscoe always said, I'll make it, darling, and you spend it. – *Minta Durfee (wife)*
He could throw two pies at once in different directions, but he was not precise in this feat. – *Mack Sennett*

Arcand, Denys (1941–).
French-Canadian director. He began as a director of commercials and documentaries.
La Maudite Galette 72. Réjeanne Padovani 73. Gina 74. Le Crime d'Ovide Plouffe (TV) 83. The Decline of the American Empire (AAN) 86. *Jesus of Montreal* 89. Montreal Sextet (co-d) 91. Love and Human Remains 93, etc.

Archainbaud, George (1890–1959).
American director, mainly of routine westerns.
Fool's Gold 19. The Shadow of Rosalie Byrnes 20. Single Wives 24. Men of Steel 26. College Coquette 29. The Lost Squadron 32. The Return of Sophie Lang 36. Her Jungle Love 38. Thanks for the Memory 38. Untamed 40. The Kansan 43. Woman of the Town 44. King of the Wild Horses 47. Hunt the Man Down 51. Last of the Pony Riders 53, many others.

Archard, Bernard (1916–).
Lean, incisive British actor with repertory experience: became famous on TV as *Spycatcher*.
Village of the Damned 60. The List of Adrian Messenger 63. Face of a Stranger 66. Song of Norway 70. The Horror of Frankenstein 70. The Purple Twilight (TV) 79. The Sea Wolves 80. Krull 83. King Solomon's Mines 85. Hidden Agenda 90, etc.

Archer, Anne (1947–).
American leading lady, the daughter of John Archer and Marjorie Lord.
The All-American Boy 70. The Honkers 72. Cancel My Reservation 72. Trackdown 76. Paradise Alley 78. Green Ice 80. Waltz Across Texas 82. The Naked Face 84. The Check is in the Mail 85. Fatal Attraction (AAN) 87. Love at Large 90. Narrow Margin 90. Eminent Domain 91. Nails 92. Patriot Games 92. Family Prayers 93.

Body of Evidence 93. Short Cuts 93. Clear and Present Danger 94. Mojave Moon 96, etc.
TV series: Bob and Carol and Ted and Alice 73. Seventh Avenue 77. The Family Tree 83. Falcon Crest 85.

Archer, John (1915–) (Ralph Bowman).
American leading man of routine second features.
Flaming Frontier 38. Gangs Inc. 41. Crash Dive 43. The Last Moment 47. White Heat 49. Destination Moon 50. A Yank in Indo-China 52. Rodeo 53. The Stars Are Singing 53. No Man's Woman 55. Emergency Hospital 59. Blue Hawaii 62. Apache Rifles 64. I Saw What You Did 65. How to Frame a Figg 71, etc.

Archibugi, Francesca (1961–).
Italian director.
Mignon Has Left/Mignon è Partita 87. Towards Evening/Verso Sera 90. The Great Pumpkin/Il Grande Cocomero 92. The Wind 97. The Pear Tree 98. Shooting the Moon/L'Albero delle Pere (wd) 98, etc.

Ardant, Fanny (1949–).
French leading lady.
Les Chiens 79. Les Uns et les Autres 80. The Woman Next Door 81. *Vivement Dimanche* 82. Benvenuta 83. Sun and Night 84. Swann in Love 84. Desiderio 84. Family Business/Conseil de Famille 86. Australia 89. Three Sisters/Paura e amore 90. La Femme du Déserteur 91. Nothing but Lies/Rien que des Mensonges 91. The Deserter's Wife 92. Afraid of the Dark 92. Amok 93. Le Colonel Chabert 94. Beyond the Clouds 95. Desire 96. Ridicule 96. Elizabeth (GB) 98, etc.

Arden, Eve (1908–1990) (Eunice Quedens).
American comedy actress, a tall, cool lady who spent a generation as the wisecracking friend of the heroine. Originally a Ziegfeld girl. Married twice, though the love of her life seems to have been Danny Kaye.
Autobiography: 1985, *Three Faces of Eve.*
Song of Love 29. Dancing Lady 33. Oh Doctor 37. *Stage Door* 37. Having Wonderful Time 38. At the Circus 39. Comrade X 40. Ziegfeld Girl 41. That Uncertain Feeling 41. Whistling in the Dark 41. Let's Face It 43. *Cover Girl* 44. *The Doughgirls* 44. *Mildred Pierce* (AAN) 45. Night and Day 46. The Unfaithful 47. *The Voice of the Turtle* 47. The Lady Takes a Sailor 49. *Paid in Full* 50. Curtain Call at Cactus Creek 50. *Tea for Two* 50. *Three Husbands* 50. *We're Not Married* 52. The Lady Wants Mink 53. Our Miss Brooks 56. *Anatomy of a Murder* 59. *The Dark at the Top of the Stairs* 60. Sergeant Deadhead 65. A Very Missing Person (TV) 71. All My Darling Daughters (TV) 72. *Grease* 78. Under the Rainbow 81. Grease II 82, etc.
TV series: *Our Miss Brooks* 52–56. The Eve Arden Show 59. Mothers-in-Law 67–69.
✪ For patenting the comic image of the cool, sophisticated but usually manless career woman. *Mildred Pierce.*

Arden, Robert (1921–).
Anglo-American actor resident in Britain; former vocalist.
Two Thousand Women 44. No Orchids for Miss Blandish 48. *Confidential Report* 56, etc.
TV series: Saber of London 58–60.

Ardolino, Emile. (1953–1993).
American director from TV and dance theatre, a former actor. Died of AIDS.
He Makes Me Feel Like Dancin' (doc) (AA) 83. Dirty Dancing 87. Chances Are 89. Three Men and a Little Lady 90. Sister Act 92. George Balanchine's The Nutcracker 93. Gypsy (TV) 93, etc.

Ardrey, Robert (1907–1980).
American screenwriter, novelist and playwright.
They Knew What They Wanted 40. *Thunder Rock* (& oa) 43. The Green Years 46. The Three Musketeers 48. Madame Bovary 49. Quentin Durward 56. The Wonderful Country 58. The Four Horsemen of the Apocalypse 62. Khartoum (AAN) 66, etc.

Argento, Asia (1975–).
Italian leading actress, the daughter of director Dario Argento and actress Daria Nicolodi.
Dreams and Needs/Sogni e Bisogni 85. Demons 2 86. The Zoo 88. The Church 89. Palombella Rossa 89. Close Friends/L'Amiche del Cuore 92. Trauma 93. Perdiamoci di Vista 94. Queen Margot/La Reine Margot 94. The Stendhal Syndrome 96. Bits and Pieces 96. New Rose Hotel (US) 98. B Monkey (GB/US) 98. The Phantom of the Opera 98, etc.

Argento, Dario (1940–).
Italian thriller director and screenwriter. Born in Rome, he began as a film critic and actor, then became a scriptwriter after working with Sergio Leone on *Once Upon a Time in the West* 69. Married actress Daria Nicolodi; their daughter is actress Asia Argento.
Book: *Broken Mirrors/Broken Minds: The Dark Dreams of Dario Argento* by Maitland McDonagh (1991).
The Bird with Crystal Plumage (& w) 70. One Night at Dinner (& w) 70. Cat O'Nine Tails (& w) 71. Four Flies on Grey Velvet 71. Le Cinque Giornate 73. Deep Red (& w) 77. Suspiria (& w) 77. Inferno 79. Unsane/Tenebrae (& m, w) 82. Creepers (& w) 85. Demons/Demoni (w) 85. Demons 2/Demoni 2 (w) 86. Opera (& w) 87. Two Evil Eyes/Due Occhi Diabolici (co-w, co-d) 89. The Sect/La Setta (w) 91. Trauma (& co-w) 93. The Stendhal Syndrome 96. Bits and Pieces (a) 96. House of Wax (p, co-w) 97, etc.
❝ There's nothing gratuitous about my films. – *D.A.*

Argo, Victor.
American character actor, usually as a tough guy.
Boxcar Bertha 72. Mean Streets 73. The Don Is Dead 73. Taxi Driver 76. Hot Tomorrows 78. The Rose 79. Falling in Love 84. Desperately Seeking Susan 85. The Last Temptation of Christ (as Peter) 88. New York Stories 89. Crimes and Misdemeanors 89. King of New York 90. Shadows and Fog 90. Bad Lieutenant 92. Snake Eyes 93. Household Saints 93. Men Lie 94. Blue in the Face 95. The Funeral 96. Next Stop Wonderland 97, etc.
TV series: Dream Street 89.

Argyle, John F. (1911–1962).
British director.
Paradise Alley 31. Smiling Along 31. Mutiny on the Elsinore (p only) 36. Tower of Terror (p only) 41. Send for Paul Temple (& p) 46. Once a Sinner (p only) 50, etc.

Aristaráin, Adolfo (1943–).
Argentinian director, screenwriter and producer, a former film actor. Born in Buenos Aires, he went to Spain in the late 60s and spent six years there, working as an assistant director on films by Sergio Leone, Melvin Frank, Lewis Gilbert, Peter Collinson and others before returning home. His output includes political thrillers and musicals.
The Lion's Share/La Parte del León 78. La Playa del Amor 79. La Discoteca del Amor 80. Time for Revenge/Tiempo de Revancha 81. The Last Days of the Victim/Los Últimos Días de la Víctima 82. The Stranger (US) (d only) 87. A Place in the World/Un Lugar en el Mundo 92. The Law of the Frontier/La Ley de la Frontera 95. Martin/Hache 97, etc.

Arkin, Alan (1934–).
American leading character actor, from Broadway.
Autobiography: 1979, *Halfway through the Door: An Actor's Journey toward the Self.*
The Russians Are Coming, The Russians Are Coming (AAN) 66. Woman Times Seven 67. *Wait Until Dark* 67. Inspector Clouseau 68. *The Heart Is a Lonely Hunter* (AAN) 68. Popi 69. The Monitors 69. *Catch 22* 70. *Little Murders* (& d) 71. Deadhead Miles 72. Last of the Red Hot Lovers 72. Freebie and the Bean 74. Rafferty and the Gold Dust Twins 75. Hearts of the West 75. The Seven Per Cent Solution (as Freud) 76. *The Other Side of Hell* (TV) 77. Fire Sale (& d) 77. The In-Laws 79. The Magician of Lublin 79. Simon 79. Improper Channels 80. Chu Chu and the Philly Flash 81. Full Moon High 81. Deadhead Miles 82. The Return of Captain Invincible 83. Big Trouble 84. Joshua Then and Now 85. Bad Medicine 85. Coupe de Ville 90. Edward Scissorhands 90. Havana 90. The Rocketeer 91. Glengarry Glen Ross 92. Cooperstown (TV) 93. Indian Summer 93. North 94. Steal Big, Steal Little 95. Mother Night 96. Grosse Point Blank 97. Gattaca 97. Four Days in September (Braz.) 97. The Slums of Beverly Hills 98, etc.

Arkoff, Samuel Z. (1918–).
American executive producer, co-founder with James H. Nicholson of American International Pictures.
Autobiography: 1992, *Flying Through Hollywood by the Seat of My Pants* (with Richard Trubo).

Arlen, Alice.
American screenwriter.
Silkwood (co-w, AAN) 83. Alamo Bay 85. Cookie (co-w) 89, etc.

Arlen, Harold (1905–1986) (Hyman Arluck).
American song composer ('Happiness Is Just a Thing Called Joe', 'That Old Black Magic', 'Blues in the Night', 'Stormy Weather', 'Accentuate the Positive', many others).
Film scores include: Strike Me Pink 36. Love Affair 39. The Wizard of Oz (AA for 'Over the Rainbow') 39. Cabin in the Sky 43. A Star Is Born 54. I Could Go On Singing 63, etc.

Arlen, Michael (1895–1956) (Dikran Kuyumjian).
Armenian novelist, educated in England. In the 20s his *The Green Hat* was the basis for Garbo's *A Woman of Affairs*, and in 1948 his short story 'A Gentleman from America' became The Fatal Night.
❝ My forebears were successful crooks living on the slopes of Mount Ararat. – M.A.
For all his reputation, Arlen is not a bounder. He is every other inch a gentleman. – *Alexander Woollcott*

Arlen, Richard (1899–1976) (Cornelius van Mattemore).
Rugged American leading man who rose from extra to star in the 20s, became the durable hero of scores of 'B' pictures, and later played bits. The second of his three wives was actress Jobyna Ralston (1927–45).
In the Name of Love 25. Rolled Stockings 27. *Wings* 27. *The Four Feathers* 28. Thunderbolt 29. *The Virginian* 29. The Sea God 30. Touchdown 31. College Humor 33. Three-Cornered Moon 33. She Made Her Bed 34. Heldorado 35. Secret Valley 36. Murder in Greenwich Village 37. Call of the Yukon 38. Mutiny on the Blackhawk 39. Legion of Lost Flyers 39. Hot Steel 40. Men of the Timberland 41. Torpedo Boat 42. Alaska Highway 43. Minesweeper 43. The Lady and the Monster 44. Storm over Lisbon 44. The Phantom Speaks 45. Accomplice 46. Speed to Spare 48. Grand Canyon 49. Kansas Raiders 50. Flaming Feather 52. Sabre Jet 53. Devil's Harbour 54. The Mountain 56. Raymie 60. Cavalry Command 63. Law of the Lawless 64. The Human Duplicators 65. Apache Uprising 66. Red Tomahawk 67. Buckskin 68. Won Ton Ton 76, many others.

Arletty (1898–1992) (Leonie Bathiat).
Celebrated French actress of stage and screen adept at the portrayal of world-weary, sophisticated women.
■ Un Chien Qui Rapporte 31. Don't Walk About in the Nude 32. Enlevez Moi 32. Un Fil à la Patte 33. Feue la Mère de Madame 33. La Belle Aventure 33. Une Idée Folle 33. Un Soir de Réveillon 34. Je Te Confie Ma Femme 34. Le Voyage de Monsieur Perrichon 34. La Guerre des Valses 35. Pension Mimosas 35. La Fille de Madame Angot 35. L'Ecole des Cocottes 36. Amants et Voleurs 36. La Garçonne 36. Un Mari Rêve 36. Aventure à Paris 36. Faisons un Rêve 36. Messieurs les Ronds-de-Cuir 36. Les Perles de la Couronne 37. Aloha 37. Mirages 37. Desire 37. Le Petit Chose 38. La Chaleur du Sein 38. *Hôtel du Nord* 38. *Le Jour Se Lève* 39. Fric Frac 39. Circonstances Atténuantes 39. Tempête 40. Madame Sans Gêne 41. The Woman I Loved the Most 42. Boléro 42. L'Amant de Borneo 42. *Les Visiteurs du Soir* 43. *Les Enfants du Paradis* 44. Portrait d'un Assassin 49. L'Amour, Madame 52. Gibier de Potence 52. Le Père de Mademoiselle 53. Le Grand Jeu 54. L'Air de Paris 55. Huis Clos 55. Mon Curé Chez les Pauvres 56. Vacances Explosives 57. Le Passager Clandestin 58. Et Ta Soeur? 59. Maxime 59. Drôle de Dimanche 60. La Gamberge 61. Les Petits Matins 61. La Loi des Hommes 61. The Longest Day 62. Tempo di Roma 63. Le Voyage à Biarritz 63.

Arling, Arthur E. (1906–1991).
American cinematographer.
Gone with the Wind (co-ph) 39. The Yearling (AA) 46. The Homestretch 47. You're My Everything 49. Wabash Avenue 50. Red Garters 54. I'll Cry Tomorrow 55. Pay the Devil 57. The Story of Ruth 60. Notorious Landlady 62. My Six Loves 63. Straitjacket 63. The Secret Invasion 64, many others.

Arliss, Florence (1871–1950).
British character actress who appeared in a few of the films of her husband George Arliss, from *The Devil* to *The House of Rothschild*.

Arliss, George (1868–1946) (George Augustus Andrews).
Distinguished British stage actor of the old school who in middle age was persuaded to face the cameras and unexpectedly became a star both in Britain and America, presenting a gallery of kings, statesmen, rajahs, eccentric millionaires and rather unconvincing hoboes. Born in London, he was on-stage from the 1890s and in 1901 accompanied Mrs Patrick Campbell to America, where he remained. Married actress Florence Montgomery (aka Florence Arliss) in 1899. Their son was writer-director Leslie Arliss.
Autobiographies: 1926, *On The Stage*. 1927, *Up the Years from Bloomsbury*. 1940, *My Ten Years in the Studios*.
■ The Devil 21. *Disraeli* 21. *The Green Goddess* 23. The Ruling Passion 23. *Disraeli* (AA) 29. *The Green Goddess* (sound) (AAN) 30. Old English 30. Millionaire 31. Alexander Hamilton 31. The Man Who Played God 32. Successful Calamity 32. The King's Vacation 33. The Working Man 33. Voltaire 33. *The House of Rothschild* 34. The Tunnel 34. The Last Gentleman 34. Cardinal Richelieu 35. The Iron Duke 35. The Guvnor 35. East Meets West 36. His Lordship 37. Dr Syn 37.
✪ For the sheer autocratic determination which made him a world star despite his very limited and inflexible talent. *The House of Rothschild*.
❝ His small dark eyes held an ancient sadness; but his taut triangular mouth seemed always to be repressing an irrepressible mirth. – *Bette Davis*
The talking picture is like a dress rehearsal in the theatre. It never gets those moments of inspiration when an audience lifts an actor out of himself. So I say that no player in pictures can ever be seen at his best. – G.A.

Arliss, Leslie (1901–1987).
British writer who worked on Orders Is Orders 32. Jack Ahoy 34. Rhodes of Africa 36. Pastor Hall 39. The Foreman Went to France 42. Then turned director and made some of the popular Gainsborough costume melodramas of the 40s. He was the son of George and Florence Arliss.
The Night Has Eyes 42. The Man in Grey 43. Love Story 44. The Wicked Lady 45. A Man about the House 47. Idol of Paris 48. The Woman's Angle 52. Miss Tulip Stays the Night 55. See How They Run 55, etc.

Armendariz, Pedro (1912–1963).
Massive Mexican actor with expansive personality; became a star in his own country, then moved on to Hollywood and Europe. Committed suicide.
Rosario 36. Isle of Passion 41. *Maria Candelaria* 43. The Pearl 46. The Fugitive 47. Maclovia 48. Fort Apache 48. Three Godfathers 48. Tulsa 48. We Were Strangers 49. The Torch 50. *El Bruto* 52. Lucretia Borgia 52. Border River 54. The Conqueror 56. Manuela 57. The Wonderful Country 59. Francis of Assisi 61. Captain Sinbad 63. *From Russia with Love* 63, etc.

Armendariz, Pedro, Jnr (1930–).
Mexican-American character actor.
The Magnificent Seven Ride 72. The Deadly Trackers 73. Earthquake 74. La Chevre 81. Treasure Island 90. Tombstone 94. The Mask of Zorro 98, etc.

Armetta, Henry (1888–1945).
Italian-born character actor, long in US, where he was on stage before going to Hollywood. Typecast as excitable, gesticulating foreigner.
My Cousin 18. The Silent Command 23. Street Angel 28. Romance 30. Strangers May Kiss 31. The Unholy Garden 31. Prosperity 32. What! No Beer? 33. The Man Who Reclaimed His Head 34. After Office Hours 35. Poor Little Rich Girl 36. Make a Wish 37. Everybody Sing 38. Dust be my Destiny 39. *The Big Store* 41. Anchors Aweigh 45. Colonel Effingham's Raid 46, many others.

Armida (1913–) (Armida Vendrell).
Mexican actress, performing as a singer and a dancer as a child, who went on to appear in many westerns.
The International Revue 29. Border Romance 30. Gaiety 43. Fiesta 47. Jungle Goddess 49, etc.

Armitage, George B.
American director and screenwriter.
Gas-s-s-! Or It Became Necessary to Destroy the World in Order to Save It! (w) 70. Vigilante Force (wd) 76. The Last of the Finest (co-w) 90. Miami Blues (wd) 90. The Late Shift (w) (TV) 96. Grosse Pointe Blank 97, etc.

Armstrong, Alun (1946–).
British Shakespearean character actor, occasionally in films.
The Duellists 77. A Bridge Too Far 77. Krull 83. The French Lieutenant's Woman 83. Billy the Kid and the Green Baize Vampire 85. White Hunter, Black Heart 90. London Kills Me 91. Split Second 92. Blue Ice 92. Goodbye Cruel World (TV) 92. Patriot Games 92. Black Beauty 94. Braveheart 95. The Saint 97. Breaking the Code (TV) 97, etc.
TV series: Underworld 97.

Armstrong, Bess (1953–).
American leading lady.
Jekyll and Hyde Together Again 82. High Road to China 83. Jaws 3-D 83. Nothing in Common 86. Second Sight 89. The Skateboard Kid 93. Dream Lover 94. My So-Called Life (TV) 94. That Darn Cat 96, etc.
TV series: On Our Own 77–78. All Is Forgiven 86. Married People 90–91. Forever Love 98– .

Armstrong, Gillian (1950–).
Australian director. Born in Melbourne, she worked for Fred Schepisi's production company before studying at the Australian Film and Television School. She began as an art director and a documentary film-maker.
My Brilliant Career 80. Starstruck 82. Mrs Soffel (US) 84. High Tide 87. The Last Days of Chez Nous 91. Fires Within 91. *Little Women* 94. Not 14 Again (doc) 96. Oscar and Lucinda 97, etc.

Armstrong, Louis (1900–1971).
Gravel-voiced American jazz trumpeter and singer, affectionately known as 'Satchmo' (satchel mouth). Sporadic screen appearances, chiefly in guest spots.
Biography: 1997, *Louis Armstrong: An Extravagant Life* by Laurence Bergreen.
■ Pennies from Heaven 36. Every Day's a Holiday 37. Dr Rhythm 38. Artists and Models 38. Going Places 39. *The Birth of the Blues* 41. Cabin in the Sky 43. Jam Session 44. Atlantic City 44. Hollywood Canteen 44. *New Orleans* 47. A Song Is Born 48. The Strip 51. *Here Comes The Groom* 51. Glory Alley 51. *The Glenn Miller Story* 54. *High Society* 56. *Satchmo The Great* 57. The Beat Generation 59. *The Five Pennies* 59. *Paris Blues* 61. *Jazz On A Summer's Day* 61. When the Boys Meet the Girls 62. A Man Called Adam 66. Hello Dolly 69.

Armstrong, R. G. (1917–).
Tough, serious-looking American supporting actor.
Never Love a Stranger 58. *Ride The High Country* 62. Major Dundee 66. El Dorado 66. The Great White Hope 71. Stay Hungry 76. Heaven Can Wait 78. Reds 81. Hammett 82. Evilspeak 82. Angels Die Hard 84. Children of the Corn 84. The Best of Times 86. Bulletproof 88. Dick Tracy 90. Invasion of Privacy 96, etc.
TV series: T.H.E. Cat 66–67.

Armstrong, Robert (1890–1973) (Donald Robert Smith).
Tough American character actor often seen as cop, sheriff, trail boss or shady investigator.
The Main Event 27. Big Money 30. The Tip-Off 31. The Most Dangerous Game 32. *King Kong* (his best role, as foolhardy film producer Carl Denham) 33. Son of Kong 33. G-Men 35. Mystery Man 37. Sky Raiders 41. Outside the Law 41. Dive Bomber 41. The Mad Ghoul 43. Gangs of the Waterfront 45. *Mighty Joe Young* (a continuation of his Kong role) 49. Las Vegas Shakedown 55. For Those Who Think Young 63, many others.
Famous line (*King Kong*): 'Oh no, it wasn't the airplanes. It was beauty killed the beast.'

Armstrong, Todd (1939–).
Stalwart American leading man of the 60s.
Walk on the Wild Side 62. Jason and the Argonauts 63. King Rat 65. A Time for Killing 68, etc.
TV series: Manhunt 60–61.

Arnall, Julia (1931–).
Austrian-born actress resident in Britain.
Man of the Moment 54. I Am a Camera 55. Lost 56. House of Secrets 56. Man without a Body 57. Mark of the Phoenix 59. The Quiller Memorandum 66. The Double Man 67, etc.

Arnatt, John (1917–).
Solid, pipe-smoking British character actor, mostly on TV.
Only Two Can Play 62. Dr Crippen 63. Licensed to Kill 66. The Breaking of Bumbo 70. Crucible of Terror 71. Bluebell (TV) 85. House of Cards (TV) 90, many others.
TV series: Robin Hood (as the hero's perpetual adversary) 55–59.

Arnaud, Léon (1904–).
French composer (and conductor) in Hollywood.
Babes in Arms 39. The Big Store 41. Dubarry Was a Lady 43. Easter Parade 48. Three Little Words 50. Sombrero 53. Seven Brides for Seven Brothers 54. Blue 68, etc.

Arnaud, Yvonne (1892–1958).
French actress and pianist, long popular on the British stage.
■ Desire 20. The Temptress 20. Canaries Sometimes Sing 30. Tons of Money 31. On Approval 31. *A Cuckoo in the Nest* 33. Princess Charming 34. Lady in Danger 34. Widow's Might 36. The Gay Adventure 36. The Improper Duchess 36. Stormy Weather 36. Neutral Port 40. Tomorrow We Live 42. Woman to Woman 46. The Ghosts of Berkeley Square 47. Mon Oncle 58.

Arnaz, Desi (1917–1986) (Desiderio Alberto Arnaz y de Acha).
Diminutive but explosive Cuban who began his career as a singer and later formed his own Latin-American band. Performed in minor film musicals during 40s, then married Lucille Ball, founded Desilu Studios, and appeared in the long-running TV series *I Love Lucy* 50–61. Later films include *The Long Long Trailer* 54. *Forever Darling* 56. *The Escape Artist* 82. Produced TV series *The Mothers-in-Law* 57–58.

Arnaz, Desi, Jnr (1953–).
American juvenile lead of the 70s, son of Desi Arnaz and Lucille Ball. Had years of training on his mother's TV series.
Red Sky at Morning 70. Marco 73. Billy Two Hats 74. She Lives (TV) 74. Joyride 77. How to Pick Up Girls (TV) 78. A Wedding 79. The Night the Bridge Fell Down (TV) 80. The House of Long Shadows 83. The Mambo Kings (playing his father) 92, etc.
TV series: Here's Lucy 68–71. Automan 83–84.

Arnaz, Lucie (1951–).
American leading lady, daughter of Lucille Ball and Desi Arnaz.
Who Is the Black Dahlia? (TV) 75. Billy Jack Goes to Washington 77. Death Scream (TV) 78. The Mating Season 80. Second Thoughts 83.
TV series: Here's Lucy 68–74. The Lucie Arnaz Show 85.

Arne, Peter (1920–1983) (Peter Arne Albrecht).
Unsmiling Anglo-American actor in British films, usually as dastardly villain. He was murdered, clubbed to death in his London flat.
Time Slip 55. The Purple Plain 55. *The Moonraker* 57. Ice Cold in Alex 57. *Danger Within* 58. *The Hellfire Club* 61. The Black Torment 64. Khartoum 66. Battle Beneath the Earth 68. Murders in the Rue Morgue 71. Straw Dogs 71. Antony and Cleopatra 72. Providence 77. Victor/Victoria 82, etc.

Arnell, Richard (1917–).
British composer. Born in London, he studied at the Royal College of Music.
The Land 40. The Third Secret 63. The Visit 64. The Man Outside 67. Black Panther 77, etc.

Arness, James (1923–) (James Aurness).
Giant-size American leading man who found his greatest fame on TV. Brother of Peter Graves.
The Farmer's Daughter 47. Battleground 49. Wagonmaster 51. The Thing (title role) 52. Big Jim McLain 53. Them 54. The Sea Chase 55. The First Traveling Saleslady 56. The Alamo: Thirteen Days to Glory (TV) 87. Gunsmoke: Return to Dodge (TV) 87. Gunsmoke: The Long Ride (TV) 93, many others.
TV series: Gunsmoke (as Marshal Dillon) 55–75. How the West Was Won 76–79. McLain's Law 81–82.
❝ I just wanted to see California. I wasn't thinking of acting. – *J.A.*
The greatest spirtual cleansing I can imagine is to dive into a big surf. – *J.A.*

Arnheim, Rudolf (1904–).
German-American critic whose published writings include *Film as Art* 32 and *Art and Visual Perception* 58.

Arno, Sig (1895–1975) (Siegfried Aron).
German comedy actor in US from early 30s; latterly typecast as funny foreigner.
Manon Lescaut 26. Pandora's Box 28. The Loves of Jeanne Ney 28. Diary of a Lost Girl 29. The Star Maker 38. The Great Dictator 40. The Palm Beach Story 42. Up In Arms 44. The Great Lover 48. On Moonlight Bay 51. The Great Diamond Robbery 53, many others.
TV series: My Friend Irma 52–53.

Arnold, David (1962–).
English composer. Born in Luton, Bedfordshire, he began by working with director Danny Cannon.
The Young Americans 93. StarGate 94. Judge Dredd 95. Last of the Dogmen 95. Independence Day 96, etc.

Arnold, Edward (1890–1956) (Guenther Schneider).
Rotund but dynamic American actor who played go-getter leading roles in the 30s. Although he later became typed as kindly father/apoplectic business man, he never lost his popularity.
Autobiography: 1940, *Lorenzo Goes To Hollywood*.
■ When the Man Speaks 16. The Wrong Way 17. Rasputin and the Empress 32. Okay, America 32. Afraid to Talk 32. Three on a Match 32. Whistling in the Dark 33. The White Sister 33. The Barbarian 33. Jennie Gerhardt 33. Her Bodyguard 33. The Secret of the Blue Room 33. *I'm No Angel* 33. *Roman Scandals* 33. Madame Spy 34. Sadie McKee 34. Thirty Day Princess 34. Unknown Blonde 34. Hideout 34. Million Dollar Ransom 34. The President Vanishes 34. Wednesday's Child 34. Biography of a Bachelor Girl 35. Cardinal Richelieu 35. *The Glass Key* 35. *Diamond Jim* 35. *Crime and Punishment* 35. Remember Last Night? 35. Sutter's Gold 36. *Meet Nero Wolfe* 36. *Come and Get It* 36. John Meade's Woman 37. *The Toast of New York* 37. Easy Living 37. Blossoms on Broadway 37. The Crowd Roars 38. *You Can't Take It With You* 38. Let Freedom Ring 39. Idiot's Delight 39. Man About Town 39. *Mr Smith Goes To Washington* 39. Slightly Honourable 40. The Earl of Chicago 40. Johnny Apollo 40. Lillian Russell 40. The Penalty 41. The Lady from Cheyenne 41. Meet John Doe 41. Nothing But the Truth 41. Unholy Partners 41. Design for Scandal 41. Johnny Eager 41. *All That Money Can Buy* (as Daniel Webster) 41. The War Against Mrs Hadley 42. *Eyes in The Night* 42. The Youngest Profession 42. Standing Room Only 44. Janie 44. *Kismet* 44. Mrs Parkington 44. Main Street After Dark 44. Weekend at the Waldorf 45. The Hidden Eye 45. Ziegfeld Follies 46. Janie Gets Married 46. *Three Wise Fools* 46. No Leave No Love 46. The Mighty McGurk 46. My Brother Talks to Horses 46. *Dear Ruth* 47. *The Hucksters* 47. Three Daring Daughters 48. Big City 48. Wallflower 48. Command Decision 48. John Loves Mary 49. Take Me Out to the Ball Game 49. Big Jack 49. Dear Wife 49. The Yellow Cab Man 50. Annie Get Your Gun 50. The Skipper Surprised His Wife 50. Dear Brat 51. Belles on Their Toes 52. City That Never Sleeps 53. Man of Conflict 53. Living It Up 54. The Houston Story 56. The Ambassador's Daughter 56. Miami Exposé 56.
✪ For maintaining an ebullient star personality through two decades of talkies, despite his unromantic physique. *Diamond Jim*.

Arnold, Jack (1916–1992).
American director.
It Came from Outer Space 53. The Glass Web 53. Girls in the Night 53. The Creature from the Black Lagoon 54. Tarantula 55. Red Sundown 56. The Tattered Dress 57. *The Incredible Shrinking Man* 57. Pay the Devil 57. The Lady Takes a Flyer 58. High School Confidential 58. The Mouse That Roared (GB) 59. No Name on the Bullet 59. Bachelor in Paradise 61. A Global Affair 63. Hello Down There 68. Black Eye 73. The Swiss Conspiracy 76, etc.

Arnold, Sir Malcolm (1921–).
British composer, musician and conductor. Born in Northampton, he played trumpet in the London Philharmonic Orchestra before writing scores for documentary films in the mid-40s.
Your Witness 50. The Ringer 52. Stolen Face 52. *The Sound Barrier* 52. Wings of Danger 52. The Captain's Paradise 53. Albert RN 53. Four Sided Triangle 53. Hobson's Choice 53. The Sea Shall Not Have Them 54. The Belles of St Trinian's 54. You Know What Sailors Are 54. Devil on Horseback 54. The Night My Number Came Up 54. The Sleeping Tiger 54. A Prize of Gold 55. I Am a Camera 55. The Constant Husband 55. The Deep Blue Sea 55. 1984 55. Value for Money 55. Trapeze (US) 56. A Hill in Korea 56. Wicked as They Come 56. Port Afrique 56. Island in the Sun 57. Blue Murder at St Trinian's 57. *The Bridge on the River Kwai* (AA) 57. The Inn of the Sixth Happiness 58. *The Roots of Heaven* (US) 58. Dunkirk 58. *The Key* 58. Suddenly Last Summer 59. The Angry Silence 60. Tunes of Glory 60. No Love for Johnnie 60. Whistle Down the Wind 61. The Inspector/Lisa 61. On the Fiddle/Operation Snafu 61. Nine Hours to Rama 62. Tamahine 62. The Chalk Garden 64. The Thin Red Line (US) 64. The Heroes of the Telemark 65. Sky West and Crooked/Gypsy Girl 65. The Great St Trinian's Train Robbery 66. Africa Texas Style 67. The Reckoning 69. David Copperfield (TV) 70, etc.

Arnold, Tom.
American actor and producer. Formerly married to Roseanne Barr. He was played by Stephen Lee in the made-for-TV biopic *Roseanne and Tom: Behind the Scenes* 95, concerned with the couple's brief and stormy marriage.
Backfield in Motion (TV) 91. Hero/Accidental Hero 92. The Woman Who Loved Elvis (TV) 93. Undercover Blues 93. True Lies 94. Nine Months 95. The Stupids 96. Carpool 96. McHale's Navy 97. Austin Powers: International Man of Mystery 97, etc.
TV series: Roseanne 89–94. The Tom Show 97– .

Arnold, Wilfred.
British art director who worked on Hitchcock's early films.
The Pleasure Garden 25. The Lodger 26. The Ring 27. *Blackmail* 29. The Outsider 31. Rich and Strange 32. When Knights Were Bold 36. The Saint in London 39. Old Mother Riley, Detective 43. Twilight Hour 44. Old Mother Riley, Headmistress 50. Worm's Eye View 51. Horrors of the Black Museum 59. Konga 60. The Password Is Courage 62. Shadow of Fear 63. Walk a Crooked Path 69, etc.

Arnoul, Françoise (1931–) (Françoise Gautsch).
Sultry French leading lady of sex melodramas in the 50s.
Quai de Grenelle 50. Forbidden Fruit 52. Companions of the Night 53. La Rage au Corps 53. The Sheep Has Five Legs 54. French Can-Can 55. The Face of the Cat 57. The Devil and the Ten Commandments 61. Le Dimanche de la Vie 66. The Little Theatre of Jean Renoir 69. La Garçonne 73. Violette et François 76. Ronde de Nuit 83. Nuit Docile 87. Temps de Chien 96. Post Coitum Animal Triste 97, etc.

Arnt, Charles (1908–1990).
American character actor often seen as snoop, suspicious character, or just plain ordinary fellow.
Ladies Should Listen 34. The Witness Chair 36. Remember the Night 40. Blossoms in the Dust 41. Twin Beds 42. Up in Arms 44. Cinderella Jones 46. *Dangerous Intruder* 46. That Brennan Girl 47. Wabash Avenue 50. Veils of Baghdad 53. Miracle of the Hills 59. Sweet Bird of Youth 62, many others.

Arquette, Alexis (1970–).
American actor, the brother of Rosanna and Patricia Arquette.
Last Exit to Brooklyn 89. Jumpin' at the Boneyard 92. Miracle Beach 92. Jack Be Nimble 93. Threesome 94. Don't Do It 94. Pulp Fiction 94. Grief 94. Paradise Framed (Hol.) 95. Dead Weekend 95. Things I Never Told You 96. Never Met Picasso 96. Frisk 96. The Wedding Singer 97. Bride of Chucky 98. Cleopatra's Second Husband 98. Love Kills 98, etc.

Arquette, Cliff (1905–1974).
American comedy actor familiar on radio and TV as hillbilly Charlie Weaver. Appeared with Abbott and Costello in *Comin' Round the Mountain*.

Arquette, David (1972–).
American actor, brother of Alexis, Patricia and Rosanna ARQUETTE.
Where the Day Takes You 92. Buffy the Vampire Slayer 92. Ghost Brigade 93. Airheads 94. The Road Killers 94. Fall Time 95. Wild Bill 95. Johns 96. Larry McMurtry's 'Dead Man's Walk' (TV) 96. Beautiful Girls 96. Scream 96. Dream with the Fishes (& co-p) 97. Scream 2 97. The Alarmist 98, etc.
TV series: The Outsiders 90. Parenthood 90.

Arquette, Lewis.
American character actor, the son of Cliff Arquette and father of Rosanna, Patricia and Alexis.
Loose Shoes 80. Nobody's Fool 86. The Horror Show 89. Syngenor 90. Book of Love 91. The Linguini Incident 92. Sleep with Me 94. Kiss and Tell 96. Waiting for Guffman 96. Scream 2 97, etc.
TV series: The Waltons 78–81.

Arquette, Patricia (1968–).
American leading actress, in routine movies until *True Romance*. She is the sister of Rosanna Arquette. Married actor Nicolas Cage.
A Nightmare on Elm Street Part Three: Dream Warriors 87. Pretty Smart 87. Far North 88. Indian Runner 91. Prayer of the Rollerboys 91. Trouble Bound 93. Ethan Frome 93. *True Romance* 94. Holy Matrimony 94. Ed Wood 94. Beyond Rangoon 95. Flirting with Disaster 96. Secret Agent 96. Lost Highway 97. Infinity 96. Joseph Conrad's Secret Agent (GB) 96. Lost Highway 97. Deceiver 97. Trading Favours 97. Hope Floats 98. Goodbye, Lover 98. The Hi-Lo Country 98, etc.
❝ I never had a huge need to be a big movie star or a billionaire. – *P.A.*
I think raising my baby is the most artistic thing you can do. – *P.A.*

Arquette, Rosanna (1959–).
American leading lady of the 80s, usually in sultry roles. Married composer James Newton HOWARD (1986–88).
Harvest Home (TV) 78. More American Graffiti 79. Gorp 80. S.O.B. 81. *Johnny Belinda* (TV) 82. *The Executioner's Song* (TV) 83. Baby It's You 83. Off the Wall 84. Desperately Seeking Susan (BFA) 85. 8 Million Ways to Die 85. The Aviator 85. Silverado 85. After Hours 85. Nobody's Fool 86. Amazon Women on the Moon 87. The Big Blue 88. Black Rainbow 89. New York Stories 89. Wendy Cracked a Walnut 90. Flight of the Intruder 91. Son of the Morning Star (TV) 91. Sweet Revenge 91. The Linguini Incident 92. The Wrong Man 93. Nowhere to Run 93. Pulp Fiction 94. Search and Destroy 95. Crash 97. Gone Fishin' 97. Buffalo '66 97. Hope Floats (uncredited) 98. I'm Losing You 98, etc.
TV series: Shirley 79–80.

Arrabal, Fernando (1932–).
Spanish playwright and occasional screenwriter and director, who moved to live in France. Born in Morocco, he often wrote to shock, describing his work as *Théâtre Panique*.
Viva la Meurtre (Fr.) 70. J'Irai comme Un Cheval Fou 73. The Emperor of Peru (wd) 82. Le Cimetière de Voitures 82, etc.

Arrighi, Luciana.
Australian production designer.
My Brilliant Career 80. Privates on Parade 84. The Ploughman's Lunch 84. Mrs Soffel 84. The Return of the Soldier 85. Madame Sousatzka 88. The Rainbow 89. Close My Eyes 91. Howards End (AA) 92. The Remains of the Day (AAN) 93. Only You 94. Sense and Sensibility 95, etc.

Arrighi, Nike (1946–).
Italian-Australian leading lady.
Don't Raise the Bridge, Lower the River 67. The Devil Rides Out 68. One Plus One 68. Women in Love 69. Countess Dracula 70. Day for Night 73, etc.

Artaud, Antonin (1896–1948).
French drama critic and writer who dabbled in films.
Napoleon (a) 26. The Passion of Joan of Arc (a) 28. *The Seashell and the Clergyman* (w) 28.

Artemyev, Eduard.
Russian composer, associated with the films of Andrei Tarkovsky and Nikita Mikhalkov.
Solaris 72. At Home among Strangers 74. A Slave of Love 76. Platanov 77. Stalker 79. Urga/Close to Eden 91. The Inner Circle 92. Limita 94. Burnt by the Sun 94. The Odyssey (TV) 97, etc.

Arthur, Beatrice (1923–) (Bernice Frankel).
Dominant American comedy actress, a big TV hit 1972–76 as 'Maude'.
That Kind of Woman 58. Lovers and Other Strangers 69. *Mame* 73. History of the World: Part I 81, etc.
TV series: *Maude* 72–76 (after occasional stints as the character in All in the Family). Amanda's 83. *The Golden Girls* 85–92.
❝ All this time I've just wanted to be blonde, beautiful, and 5 feet 2 inches tall. (She's 5 feet 11 inches). – *B.A.*
Famous line (*Auntie Mame*): 'Oh my God – somebody's been sleeping in my dress!'

Arthur, George K. (1889–1985) (G. K. A. Brest).
Small but gamy hero of the British silent screen, popular in such films as *Kipps* 21. *A Dear Fool* 22. Went to Hollywood and was popular for a while. Became a financier and distributor of art shorts.
Madness of Youth 23. Lights of Old Broadway 25. The Salvation Hunters 25. Irene 26. The Boy Friend 26. Rookies (first of a series of comedies with Karl Dane) 27. Baby Mine 28. The Last of Mrs Cheyney 29. Chasing Rainbows 30. Oliver Twist 33. Riptide 34. Vanessa 35. That's Entertainment III 94.

Arthur, Jean (1905–1991) (Gladys Greene).
Petite, squeaky-voiced American leading actress who, after a long and dreary apprenticeship, was especially notable as the determined feminist heroine of social comedies in the 30s and 40s. Born in New York, she began as a model before being offered a contract by Fox, then spending more than a decade in small roles in undistinguished films at Paramount and elsewhere before leaving films to learn her craft on stage. She returned in the mid-30s to work for Columbia and became a star, though her years there were marked by continual battles with studio head Harry COHN. When her contract ended in 1944 she ran through the streets shouting, 'I'm free! I'm free!' Garson KANIN wrote *Born Yesterday* for her, but she withdrew from the play, and the role made Judy HOLLIDAY a Broadway and Hollywood star. Her first marriage in 1928, to photographer Julian Anker, was annulled after a day, and she later married singer and producer Frank Ross, Jnr (1932–49).
Biography: 1997, *Jean Arthur: The Actress Nobody Knew* by John Oller.
■ Cameo Kirby 23. The Temple of Venus 24. Fast and Fearless 24. Seven Chances 25. The Drug Store Cowboy 25. A Man of Nerve 25. Tearing Loose 25. Thundering Through 26. Born to Battle 26. The Hurricane Horseman 26. The Fighting Cheat 26. The Cowboy Cop 26. Twisted Triggers 26. The College Boob 26. The Block Signal 26. Husband Hunters 27. The Broken Gate 27. Horseshoes 27. The Poor Nut 27. Flying Luck 27. The Masked Menace 27. Wallflowers 28. Easy Come Easy Go 28. Warming Up 28. Brotherly Love 28. Sins of the Fathers 29. The Canary Murder Case 29. Stairs of Sand 29. The Mysterious Dr Fu Manchu 29. *The Greene Murder Case* 29. *The Saturday Night Kid* 29. Halfway to Heaven 29. Street of Chance 30. Young Eagles 30. Paramount on Parade 30. The Return of Dr Fu Manchu 30. Danger Lights 30. The Silver Horde 30. The Gang Buster 31. Virtuous Husband 31. The Lawyer's Secret 31. Ex-Bad Boy 31. Get That Venus 33. The Past of Mary Holmes 33. Whirlpool 34. The Defense Rests 34. The Most Precious Thing in Life 34. *The Whole Town's Talking* 35. Public Hero Number One 35. Party Wife 35. *Diamond Jim* 35. The Public Menace 35. *If You Could Only Cook* 35. *Mr Deeds Goes to Town* 36. The Ex Mrs Bradford 36. Adventure in Manhattan 36. *The Plainsman* (as Calamity Jane) 36. More Than a Secretary 36. *History is Made at Night* 37. *Easy Living* 37. *You Can't Take It With You* 38. Only Angels Have Wings 39. *Mr Smith Goes to Washington* 39. Too Many Husbands 40. Arizona 40. *The Devil and Miss Jones* 41. *The Talk of the Town* 42. *The More the Merrier* (AAN) 43. A Lady Takes a Chance 43. The Impatient Years 44. *A Foreign Affair* 48. *Shane* 53.
TV series: The Jean Arthur Show 66.
❝ You can't get her in front of the cameras without her crying, whining, vomiting, all that shit she does. But then when she *does* get in front of the camera, and you turn on the lights – wow! All of that disappears and out comes a strong-minded woman. Then when she finishes the scene, she runs back to the dressing room and hides. – *Frank Capra*

Arthur, Johnny (1883–1951) (John Williams).
American character actor, mainly in comedies, including Our Gang shorts, and often as a downtrodden little man. His best, and least characteristic, role was as the villain Sakima in the serial *The Masked Marvel* 43.
The Unknown Purple 23. The Desert Song 29. It's a Wise Child 31. Traveling Saleslady 35. Crime and Punishment 35. The King Steps Out 36. Danger on the Air 38. Road to Singapore 40. Henry Aldrich Gets Glamour 43, etc.

Arthur, Robert (1909–1986) (R. A. Feder).
American producer, mainly with Universal.
Buck Privates Come Home 46. Abbott and Costello Meet Frankenstein 48. The Big Heat 53. Man of a Thousand Faces 57. The Great Impostor 60. Lover Come Back 60. That Touch of Mink 62. Father Goose 64. Shenandoah 65. Blindfold 66. Hellfighters 68. Sweet Charity 69. One More Train to Rob 73, many others.

Arthur, Robert (1925–) (Robert Arthaud).
American actor, former radio announcer, in general supporting roles since 1945.
Roughly Speaking 45. Twelve O'Clock High 49. Ace in the Hole 51. Young Bess 54. Top of the World 55. Hellcats 57. Young and Wild 58, many others.

Arundell, Denis (1898–1987).
British character actor (radio's Dr Morelle).
The Show Goes On 35. The Return of Carol Deane 38. Pimpernel Smith 41. Colonel Blimp 43. Carnival 46. The History of Mr Polly 49. Something Money Can't Buy 52, etc.

Arvanitis, Georgos (1941–).
Greek cinematographer, associated with the films of director Theodoros ANGELOPOULOS.
Reconstruction/Anaparastassi 70. Days of 36/Imeres Tou 36 72. The Travelling Players/O Thiassos 75. Assault to Agathon 75. Iphigenia 76. The Huntsman/The Hunters)/I Kynighi 77. Alexander the Great/O Megalexandros 80. Voyage to Cythera/Taxidi Sta Kithira 84. *The Beekeeper*/O Melissokomos 86. Komitas 87. *Landscape in the Mist*/Topio Stin Omichli 88. Australia 89. The Suspended Step of the Stork/To Meteoro Vima To Pelargou 91. The Butterfly's Dream/Il Sogno della Farfalla 94. Total Eclipse 95. Someone Else's America 96. Bent (US) 97. Train of Life/Train de Vie (Fr./Bel./Rom./Hol.) 98, etc.

Arvidson, Linda (1884–1949).
American silent actress, first wife of D. W. Griffith; she played leads in a few of his early shorts, then retired.

Arzner, Dorothy (1900–1979).
A former editor who became Hollywood's only woman director of the 30s.
Biography: 1994, *Directed by Dorothy Arzner* by Judith Mayne.
■ Fashions for Women 27. Get Your Man 27. Ten Modern Commandments 27. Manhattan Cocktail 28. The Wild Party 29. Sarah and Son 30. Paramount on Parade (part) 30. Anybody's Woman 30. Honour Among Lovers 31. Working Girls 31. *Merrily We Go to Hell* 32. Christopher Strong 33. *Nana* 34. *Craig's Wife* 36. The Bride Wore Red 37. *Dance Girl Dance* 40. First Comes Courage 43.

Asche, Oscar (1871–1936).
Heavily built, powerful Australian-born actor-manager and playwright, of Scandinavian descent. Author of the libretto for the musical *Chu Chin Chow*, which ran for 2,238 performances in London and has been filmed twice, as a silent and in 1934. He was on the London stage from 1893, often in Shakespeare, and appeared in a few British films of the 30s.
Autobiography: 1929, *Life*.
Don Quixote 33. My Lucky Star 33. Two Hearts in Waltz Time 34. Scrooge 35. Eliza Comes to Stay 36. Robber Symphony 36, etc.
❝ How I would like that fellow to play Desdemona to my Othello, because I should enjoy strangling the life out of his carcase. – O.A. *on a fellow actor*

Ashbrook, Dana (1967–).
American actor.
Waxwork 88. Return of the Living Dead Part II 88. Girlfriend from Hell 89. Ghost Dad 90. Twin Peaks: Firewalk with Me 92, etc.

Ashby, Hal (1929–1988).
American director who tended to smother his undoubted talent under layers of oblique approaches, and often outstayed his welcome.
AS EDITOR: The Russians Are Coming, The Russians Are Coming 66. In the Heat of the Night (AA) 67. The Thomas Crown Affair 68, etc.
AS DIRECTOR: The Landlord 70. Harold and Maude 71. The Last Detail 73. Shampoo 75. Bound for Glory 76. *Coming Home* (AAN) 78. Being There 79. Second Hand Hearts 80. Lookin' to Get Out 82. Let's Spend the Night Together 83. The Slugger's Wife 85. Eight Million Ways to Die 85.

Ashcroft, Dame Peggy (1907–1991).
Distinguished British stage actress who appeared in films only occasionally.
The Wandering Jew 33. *The Thirty-Nine Steps* 35. Rhodes of Africa 36. *Quiet Wedding* 40. The Nun's Story 58. Secret Ceremony 68. Sunday Bloody Sunday 71. Joseph Andrews 77. Hullaballoo over Bonnie and George's Pictures 78. *A Passage to India* (AA, BFA) 84, etc.
TV series: Edward and Mrs Simpson (as Queen Mary) 78. *The Jewel in the Crown* 84.

Asher, Jack (1916–1991).
British cinematographer, brother of director Robert Asher. He began with Gainsborough in 1930 as an assistant cameraman.
Lili Marlene 42. Jassy 47. The Good Die Young 53. The Young Lovers 54. Reach for the Sky 56. Dracula 58. She'll Have to Go (& co-p) 61. The Intelligence Men 65. The Early Bird 65. That Riviera Touch 66, many others.

Asher, Jane (1946–).
British leading lady, former child performer in films from 1951. She is also a novelist and cookbook author, noted for her elaborate cakes. Married cartoonist and artist Gerald SCARFE.
Mandy 52. The Greengage Summer 60. The Girl in the Headlines 63. The Masque of the Red Death 64. Alfie 66. *Deep End* 71. Henry VIII and His Six Wives 72. Runners 83. Success is the Best Revenge 84. Dreamchild 85. Paris by Night 88, etc.
TV series: Wish Me Luck 89–90. Eats for Treats 91. The Choir 95.

Asher, Max (1880–1957).
American silent film comedian, from vaudeville. He was known as 'the funniest Dutch comedian in pictures', starring in dozens of shorts, and also played Mike in the popular Mike and Jake series of comedy shorts. He played character parts in the late 20s and early 30s before retiring to become a make-up man.
Mike and Jake at the Beach 13. Mike and Jake in Mexico 13. Mike and Jake at College 13. In the Year 2014 14. Pete's Awful Crime 15. When Hiram Went to the City 15. Hiram's Inheritance 15. Suds of Love 17. Rip Van Winkle 21. The Courtship of Miles Standish 23. The Shooting of Dan McGrew 24. The Carnival Girl 26. Painting the Town 27. Show Boat 29. Sweethearts on Parade 30. The Perils of Pauline (serial) 33. Little Man, What Now? 34, many others.

Asher, Robert (1915–1979).
British director.
Follow a Star 59. Make Mine Mink 60. The Bulldog Breed 60. She'll Have to Go (co-p, co-w, co-d) 61. On the Beat 62. A Stitch in Time 63. The Intelligence Men 65. The Early Bird 65. Press for Time 66.

Asher, William (1919–).
American 'B' director.
■ Leather Gloves (co-d) 48. The Shadow on the Window 57. The Twenty-Seventh Day 57. *Beach Party* 63. Johnny Cool 63. Muscle Beach Party 64. Bikini Beach 64. Beach Blanket Bingo 65. How to Stuff a Wild Bikini 65. Fireball 500 66. Night Warning 83. Movers and Shakers 84.

Asherson, Renée (1920–).
British stage actress in occasional films. Married actor Robert Donat (1953–58).
Henry V 44. The Way Ahead 44. The Way to the Stars 44. The Small Back Room 49. The Cure for Love 50. The Day the Earth Caught Fire 62. Rasputin the Mad Monk 65. The Smashing Bird I Used to Know 68. Memento Mori (TV) 92. Harnessing Peacocks (TV) 93, etc.

Ashley, Edward (1904–) (E. A. Cooper).
British leading man who went to Hollywood but never did better than third leads.
Men of Steel 33. Underneath the Arches 37. Spies of the Air 39. *Pride and Prejudice* 40. Bitter Sweet 41. The Black Swan 42. Nocturne 46. The Other Love 47. Tarzan and the Mermaids 48. Macao 52. The Court Jester (as the Fox) 56. Herbie Rides Again 73. Won Ton Ton 76. Beyond the Next Mountain 87, etc.

Ashley, Elizabeth (1939–) (Elizabeth Cole).
Cool American leading lady who makes sporadic appearances. Formerly married to actors James Farentino (1962–65) and George Peppard (1966–72).
Autobiography: 1978, *Actress: Postcards from the Road.*
The Carpetbaggers 64. Ship of Fools 65. The Third Day 65. Harpy (TV) 70. Marriage of a Young Stockbroker 71. When Michael Calls (TV) 71. The Face of Fear (TV) 71. Second Chance (TV) 71. Your Money or Your Wife (TV) 72. The Heist (TV) 73. The Magician (TV) 73. Golden Needles 74. Paperback Hero 75. Rancho de Luxe 75. 92 in the Shade 75. One of my Wives is Missing 76. The Great Scout and Cathouse Thursday 76. Fire in the Sky (TV) 77. Coma 78. Windows 80. Split Image 82. Svengali (TV) 82. Dragnet 87. Dangerous Curves 88. Happiness 98, etc.

Ashman, Howard (1951–1991).
American lyricist, in collaboration with composer Alan Menken. Died of AIDS.

Ashton, John.
American character actor.
Breaking Away 79. Borderline 80. Beverly Hills Cop 84. King Kong Lives 86. Some Kind of Wonderful 87. Beverly Hills Cop II 87. Midnight Run 88. She's Having a Baby 88. L.A. Gangs Rising 89. Curly Sue 91. The Tommyknockers (TV) 93. Trapped in Paradise 94. Little Big League 94. Meet the Deedles 98, etc.
TV series: Dallas 78–79. Breaking Away 80–81. Hardball 89–90.

Ashton, Roy (1918–1995).
British make-up artist.
Curse of Frankenstein 57. Dracula 58. The Mummy 59. Curse of the Werewolf 61. The Reptile 66. Vault of Horror 73. The Monster Club 81, etc.

Askew, Luke (1937–).
American character actor, usually in westerns.
Cool Hand Luke 67. The Green Berets 68. Easy Rider 69. The Great Northfield Minnesota Raid 72. The Culpepper Cattle Company 72. Posse 75. Rolling Thunder 77. Wanda Nevada 79. The Warrior and the Sorceress 84. Back to Back 90. Dune Warriors 91. Traveller 96, etc.

Askey, Arthur (1900–1982).
Diminutive (5'2" British comedian with music-hall experience; gained fame as 'Big Hearted Arthur' in radio shows.
Autobiography: 1975, *Before Your Very Eyes.*
■ Calling All Stars 37. Band Wagon 39. Charley's Big-Hearted Aunt 40. *The Ghost Train* 41. I Thank You 41. Back Room Boy 42. King Arthur Was a Gentleman 42. Miss London Ltd 43. Bees in Paradise 44. The Love Match 54. Ramsbottom Rides Again 56. Make Mine a Million 58. Friends and Neighbours 59. The Alf Garnett Saga 72.

Askin, Leon (1907–).
Rotund American supporting actor who often plays sinister or comic Russians.
Autobiography: 1990, *Quietude and Quest.*
Road to Bali 52. Knock on Wood 54. Son of Sinbad 55. My Gun Is Quick 58. One Two Three 61. Do Not Disturb 65. The Maltese Bippy 69. Dr Death 73, many others.
TV series: The Charlie Farrell Show 56.

Askwith, Robin (1950–).
British leading man of 70s low comedy, most recently on stage in London, New Zealand and Australia.
If 68. Bartleby 70. Nicholas and Alexandra 71. The Four Dimensions of Greta 71. Bless this House 73. Confessions of a Window Cleaner 74. Confessions of a Pop Performer 75. Confessions of a Driving Instructor 76. Stand Up Virgin Soldiers 77. Let's Get Laid 78, etc.
TV series: Bottle Boys 83–86.

Aslan, Grégoire (1908–1982) (Kridor Aslanian).
Armenian character actor, usually in comic or villainous roles.
Sleeping Car to Trieste 48. Occupe-Toi d'Amélie 49. Last Holiday 50. Cage of Gold 50. Confidential Report 53. He Who Must Die 56. Roots of Heaven 56. The Criminal 60. Cleopatra 62. Paris When It Sizzles 64. The High Bright Sun 65. Moment to Moment 65. Our Man in Marrakesh 66. Lost Command 66. A Flea in Her Ear 68. You Can't Win Them All 70. The Golden Voyage of Sinbad 73, many others.

Asner, Edward (1929–).
Chubby American character actor who usually plays tough guys, sometimes with a heart of gold. He was a provocative union leader in a long-running actors' strike, and his successful series *Lou Grant* was cancelled allegedly because of his political views.
Kid Galahad 62. The Satan Bug 65. The Slender Thread 65. El Dorado 66. The Venetian Affair 67. Gunn 67. The Todd Killings 70. The Skin Game 71. Rich Man Poor Man (TV) 76. Hey I'm Alive (TV) 76. Gus 76. The Life and Assassination of the Kingfish (as Huey Long) (TV) 77. Roots (TV) 77. The Gathering (TV) 78. Fort Apache, the Bronx 82. O'Hara's Wife 82. Anatomy of an Illness (TV) 83. Daniel 83. The Christmas Star (TV) 86. Bronx Zoo (TV) 87. JFK 91. Heads (TV) 94. Hard Rain 97, etc.
TV series: Slattery's People 64. *The Mary Tyler Moore Show* 70–74. *Lou Grant* 77–82. Off the Rack 85. Thunder Alley 94.
❝ I really wanted to be an adventurer, to lay pipeline in South America or be a cabin boy . . . but I didn't have the guts. – *E.A.*
I don't know him well, but he seems an extremely angry and short-tempered man. He's enormously sensitive to criticism. – *Charlton Heston*

Asp, Anna (1946–).
Swedish production designer, noted for her work with Ingmar Bergman.
Face to Face 76. Autumn Sonata 78. Fanny and Alexander (AA) 82. After the Rehearsal 84. The Sacrifice 86. Pelle the Conqueror 87. Katinka 88. The Best Intentions 92. The House of the Spirits 94. Les Misérables (US) 98, etc.

Asquith, Anthony (1902–1968).
British director, son of Lord Oxford and Asquith, nicknamed 'Puffin'. His films were always civilized and usually entertaining but both the early experiments in technique and the later upper-class comedies and dramas suffered from the same lack of warmth and humanity.
Biography: 1973, *'Puffin' Asquith* by R. J. Minney.
■ *Shooting Stars* (co-d) 28. *Underground* 30. A Cottage on Dartmoor 30. The Runaway Princess 30. Tell England 31. Dance Pretty Lady 31. Marry Me 32. The Window Cleaner 32. Lucky Number 33. Unfinished Symphony 34. Moscow Nights 35. Forever England 35. *Pygmalion* (co-d) 37. *French Without Tears* 39. Freedom Radio 40. *Quiet Wedding* 40. Cottage to Let 41. Uncensored 42. We Dive at Dawn 43. *The Demi-Paradise* 43. Welcome to Britain (doc) 43. Two Fathers 44. *Fanny by Gaslight* 44. *The Way to the Stars* 45. While the Sun Shines 46. *The Winslow Boy* 48. The Woman in Question 50. *The Browning Version* 50. *The Importance of Being Earnest* 51. The Net 53. The Final Test 53. The Young Lovers 54. Carrington VC 55. On Such a Night (doc) 56. *Orders to Kill* 58. The Doctors' Dilemma 59. Libel 60. The Millionairess 61. Guns of Darkness 62. Two Living One Dead 62. *The VIPS* 63. The Yellow Rolls-Royce 64.

Assante, Armand (1949–).
American leading man.
The Lords of Flatbush 74. Paradise Alley 78. Prophecy 79. Lady of the House (TV) 79. Private Benjamin 80. Love and Money 82. I the Jury 83. Unfaithfully Yours 84. Belizaire the Cajun 85. The Penitent 88. Animal Behavior 89. Eternity 90. Q & A 90. The Marrying Man/Too Hot to Handle 91. Hoffa 92. The Mambo Kings 92. 1492 92. Triple Indemnity 93. Fatal Instinct 93. Trial by Jury 94. Judge Dredd 95. Striptease 96. Gotti (TV) 96. The Odyssey (TV) 97, etc.

Assayas, Olivier (1955–).
French screenwriter and director, often dealing with the problems of the young. Born in Paris, he studied literature and painting and in the early 80s was an editor of the film journal *Cahiers du Cinéma*. After making some short films, he wrote with André Téchiné the scripts for the latter's *Rendezvous* 85 and *Scene of the Crime* 86, and then turned to directing features.
A former critic, he is the co-author of the 1990 book *Conversations with Ingmar Bergman.*
Désordre 86. L'Enfant de L'Hiver 89. Paris at Dawn/Paris S'Éveille 91. A New Life/Une Nouvelle Vie 93. Cold Water/L'Eau Froide 94. Irma Vep (wd) 96. HHH: A Portrait of Hou Hsiao-Hsien (doc) 97. Late August, Early September/Fin Août, Debut Septembre 98, etc.

Asta.
A wire-haired fox-terrier who appeared (impersonated by several dogs) in *The Thin Man* and other films between 1934 and 1947.

Astaire, Fred (1899–1987) (Frederick Austerlitz).
American dancing star whose inimitable finesse and good humour delighted two generations. His half-spoken singing was almost equally delightful, and the films in which he was teamed with Ginger Rogers(*) have a magic all their own. Academy Award 1949 'for his unique artistry and his unique contribution to the techniques of motion pictures'. He was born in Omaha, Nebraska, and began in vaudeville before appearing in Broadway musicals, working with his sister Adele. When she retired in the early 30s to marry into the English aristocracy, he became a solo turn and was signed, and then released, by Goldwyn, before being put under contract by RKO, which began his successful partnership with Ginger Rogers. He married twice.
Autobiography: 1959, *Steps in Time.*
Biographies: 1979, *Fred Astaire* by Benny Green; 1984, *A Tribute to Fred Astaire* by Peter Carrick; 1984, *Astaire: The Man, the Dancer* by Bob Thomas.
Book: 1972, *The Fred Astaire and Ginger Rogers Book* by Arlene Croce.
■ Dancing Lady 33. **Flying Down to Rio* 33. **The Gay Divorcee* 34. **Roberta* 35. **Top Hat* 35. **Follow the Fleet* 36. **Swing Time* 36. **Shall We Dance?* 37. A Damsel in Distress 37. **Carefree* 38. **The Story of Vernon and Irene Castle* 39. Broadway Melody 40. Second Chorus 40. *You'll Never Get Rich* 41. *Holiday Inn* 42. You Were Never Lovelier 42. The Sky's the Limit 43. Yolanda and the Thief 45. *Ziegfeld Follies* 46. *Blue Skies* 46. *Easter Parade* 48. **The Barkleys of Broadway* 48. Three Little Words 50. Let's Dance 50. Royal Wedding 51. The Belle of New York 52. *The Band Wagon* 53. Daddy Long Legs 55. *Funny Face* 57. Silk Stockings 57. *On the Beach* (dramatic role) 59. *The Pleasure of His Company* (dr) 61. Notorious Landlady (dr) 62. *Finian's Rainbow* 68. The Midas Run (dr) 69. The Over The Hill Gang Rides Again (dr: TV film) 71. That's Entertainment 74. The Towering Inferno (dr) (AAN) 75. The Amazing Dobermans (dr) 76. The Purple Taxi (dr) 77. A Family Upside Down (dr) (TV) 78. The Man in the Santa Claus Suit (dr) (TV) 80. Ghost Story (dr) 81. That's Entertainment III 94.
TV series: Alcoa Premiere 61–63. It Takes a Thief 65–70.
✪ For his apparently lighter-than-air constitution, his brilliantly inventive dancing, his breezy elegance, his unlikely but effective voice, and his pleasing longevity. *Top Hat.*
❝ The most famous quote about the screen's nimblest dancer is the report of the studio talent scout on his first screen test:
Can't act. Can't sing. Slightly bald. Can dance a little.
In later years, when he was a household name around the world, he tried to match that for humility:
I have no desire to prove anything by dancing. I have never used it as an outlet or as a means of expressing myself. I just dance.
And:
I just put my feet in the air and move them around.
But in another mood, he did once confess:
I suppose I made it look easy, but gee whiz, did I work and worry.
Gene Kelly summed up his appeal:
He can give the audience pleasure just by walking across the floor.
And Mr Kelly graciously added:
If I'm the Marlon Brando of dancing, he's Cary Grant.
Graham Greene put it another way:
The nearest we are ever likely to get to a human Mickey Mouse.
C. A. Lejeune produced this analysis:
I have never met anyone who did not like Fred Astaire. Somewhere in his sad monkey-sad face, his loose legs, his shy grin, or perhaps the anxious diffidence of his manner, he has found the secret of persuading the world.
André Sennwald, in a review of *The Gay Divorcee*, was equally percipient:
The audience meets Mr Astaire and the film at their best when he is adjusting his cravat to an elaborate dance routine or saying delicious things with his flashing feet that a lyricist would have difficulty putting into words.
While Fred Astaire said in his 80s:
When they review my shows, they don't say whether they're good or bad – they just write about how old I am.

Asther, Nils (1897–1981).
Suave, exotic Swedish leading man in Hollywood from the mid-20s. He was married to Vivian Duncan.
Topsy and Eva 27. *Sorrell and Son* 27. The Blue Danube 28. Laugh Clown Laugh 28. The Cossacks 28. Loves of an Actress 28. The Cardboard Lover 28. *Our Dancing Daughters* 28. Dream of Love 28. Wild Orchids 29. *The Single Standard* 29. The Wrath of the Seas 29. Letty Lynton 32. The Washington Masquerade 32. *The Bitter Tea of General Yen* 32. Storm at Daybreak 33. The Right to Romance 33. By *Candlelight* 34. Madame Spy 34. The Crime Doctor 34. The Love Captive 34. *Abdul the Damned* (GB) 35. Make Up (GB) 37. Dr Kildare's Wedding Day 41. The Night Before the Divorce 41. The Night of January 16th 41. Sweater Girl 42. Night Monster 42. The Hour Before Dawn 44. *The Man in Half Moon Street* 44. Son of Lassie 45. Jealousy 45. The Feathered Serpent 49. That Man from Tangier 50. Vita Frun 62. Gudrun 63.

Astin, John (1930–).
American comic actor with stage experience. He was formerly married to actress Patty Duke.
West Side Story 61. That Touch of Mink 62. Candy 68. Viva Max 68. Evil Roy Slade (TV) 72. Get to Know Your Rabbit 72. The Brothers O'Toole 73. Freaky Friday 77. Body Slam 87. Gremlins 2: The New Batch 90. The Silence of the Hams (It.) 94. The Frighteners 96, etc.
TV series: I'm Dickens He's Fenster 63. The Addams Family 64. Operation Petticoat 77. Mary 85–86.

Astin, MacKenzie (1973–).
American actor, the son of John Astin and Patty Duke and brother of Sean Astin.
The Garbage Pail Kids Movie 87. Iron Will 94. Wyatt Earp 94. Dream for an Insomniac 96. Evening Star 96. In Love and War 96. The Last Days of Disco 98, etc.
TV series: The Facts of Life 85–88.

Astin, Sean (1971–).
American adolescent actor, the son of John Astin and Patty Duke.
The Goonies 85. Like Father Like Son 87. White

Water Summer 87. Staying Together 89. The War of the Roses 89. Memphis Belle 90. Toy Soldiers 91. Encino Man/California Man 92. Where the Day Takes You 92. Rudy 93. Safe Passage 94. The Low Life 95. Harrison Bergeron (TV) 95. Courage under Fire 96. Bulworth 98. Boy Meets Girl 98, etc.

Astley, Edwin.
Prolific British composer of the 50s and 60s, mainly of documentaries and 'B' features, many for the DANZIGER brothers.

Devil Girl from Mars 54. Star of My Night 54. To Paris with Love 54. What Every Woman Wants 54. The Gay Dog 54. The Crowded Day 54. The Happiness of Three Women 54. Alias John Preston 55. Fun at St Fanny's 55. Diamond Expert 55. Final Column 55. The Schemer 56. Stars in Your Eyes 56. At the Stroke of Nine 57. The Heart Within 57. Woman Eater 57. A Woman of Mystery 57. Three Sundays to Live 57. Kill Her Gently 57. Dublin Nightmare 58. The Man Who Liked Funerals 58. Innocent Meeting 58. A Woman Possessed 58. Three Crooked Men 58. The Day They Robbed the Bank of England 59. The Crowning Touch 59. In the Wake of a Stranger 59. The Great Van Robbery 59. The Mouse that Roared 59. Faces in the Dark 60. Let's Get Married 60. Visa to Canton/Passport to China 60. Follow That Man 61. The Last Rhino 61. A Matter of Who 61. The Phantom of the Opera 62. The World Ten Times Over 63. The Syndicate 67. All at Sea 69, etc.

Astor, Gertrude (1887–1977).
American silent screen actress, on stage from the age of 13.

Uncle Tom's Cabin 27. The Cat and the Canary 28. Camille 36. How Green Was My Valley 40. The Man Who Shot Liberty Valance 62, many others.

Astor, Mary (1906–1987) (Lucille Langehanke).
American leading lady who despite a stormy and well-publicized private life remained a star from the mid-20s to the mid-40s and remained in demand for character roles. Born in Quincy, Illinois, and a teenage beauty queen whose father was determined to get her into films, she found success when she appeared in *Beau Brummell* with John BARRYMORE, who became her lover. Her career not only survived a scandal in the mid-30s, when excerpts from her diary about her love affair with playwright George S. KAUFMAN were read out in divorce court and leaked to the press, but also her alcoholism in the 40s and 50s. She married four times, first in 1928 to director Kenneth Hawks, who died in a plane crash in 1930.

Autobiographies: 1959, *My Story*. 1971, *A Life on Film*. Novels include: *Image of Kate* 1966. *A Place Called Saturday* 1969.

SILENT FILMS: *The Beggar Maid* 21. The Bright Shawl 23. Puritan Passions 23. *Beau Brummell* 24. Inez from Hollywood 25. *Don Q Son of Zorro* 25. *Don Juan* 26. Rose of the Golden West 27. Two Arabian Knights 27. Heart to Heart 28. Romance of the Underworld 29, etc.

■ SOUND: Ladies Love Brutes 30. The Runaway Bride 30. Holiday 30. The Lash 30. The Sin Ship 30. The Royal Bed 30. Other Men's Women 31. Behind Office Doors 31. White Shoulders 31. Smart Woman 31. Men of Chance 31. The Lost Squadron 32. A Successful Calamity 32. Those We Love 32. *Red Dust* 32. The Little Giant 33. Jennie Gerhardt 33. The Kennel Murder Case 33. Convention City 33. The World Changes 33. Easy to Love 34. The Man with Two Faces 34. Return of the Terror 34. Upper World 34. The Case of the Howling Dog 34. I am a Thief 34. Man of Iron 35. Red Hot Tires 35. Straight from the Heart 35. Dinky 35. Page Miss Glory 35. The Murder of Dr Harrigan 35. The Lady from Nowhere 36. And So They Were Married 36. *Dodsworth* 36. Trapped by Television 36. *The Prisoner of Zenda* 37. *The Hurricane* 37. Paradise for Three 38. No Time to Marry 38. There's Always a Woman 38. Woman against Woman 38. Listen Darling 39. *Midnight* 39. *Turnabout* 40. Brigham Young 40. *The Great Lie* (AA) (her most splendid bitchy performance) 41. *The Maltese Falcon* 41. *Across the Pacific* 42. *The Palm Beach Story* 42. Young Ideas 43. Thousands Cheer 43. *Meet Me in St Louis* 44. Blonde Fever 44. Claudia and David 46. Desert Fury 47. Cynthia 47. Fiesta 47. *Act of Violence* 49. Cass Timberlane 49. *Little Women* (as Marmee) 49. Any Number Can Play 49. A Kiss Before Dying 56. The Power and the Prize 56. The Devil's Hairpin 56. This Happy Feeling 58. Stranger in my Arms 59. *Return to Peyton Place* 61. *Youngblood Hawke* 64. Hush Hush Sweet Charlotte 64.

✪ For amiably sending herself up in half a dozen portraits of mature but fallible women between 1936 and 1942; and for sheer durability. *The Great Lie*.

❝ I was never totally involved in movies. I was making my father's dream come true. – *M.A.*

Famous line (*The Great Lie*): 'If I didn't think you meant so well, I'd feel like slapping your face.'

Astruc, Alexandre (1923–).
French director, former film critic.

The Crimson Curtain 51. Les Mauvaises Rencontres 54. Une Vie 56. La Proie Pour l'Ombre 61. L'Education Sentimentale 61. La Longue Marche 65. Flammes sur L'Adriatique 67. Charlotte/La Jeune Fille Assassinée 74. Sartre by Himself (doc) 76, etc.

❝ The fundamental problem of the cinema is how to express thought. – *A.A.*

Atchley, Hooper (1887–1943).
American character actor, from the stage. Committed suicide.

Love at First Sight 29. The Santa Fe Trail 30. Arizona Terror 31. Trouble in Paradise 32. Gun Justice 33. The Three Musketeers (serial) 34. Mystery Mountain (serial) 34. Law beyond the Range 35. Ace Drummond (serial) 36. A Day at the Races 37. Mr Wong, Detective 38. Pirates of the Skies 39. The Gay Caballero 40. Adventures of Red Ryder (serial) 40. Dick Tracy vs Crime, Inc (serial) 41. The Little Foxes 41. Gentleman Jim 42. Mission to Moscow 43. G-Men versus the Black Dragon (serial) 43. The Song of Bernadette 43, etc.

Ates, Roscoe (1892–1962).
Short, stuttering American character actor, on stage from 1915 and films from 1929. A former violinist and vaudeville performer, he played Eddie Dean's sidekick in many second-feature westerns.

South Sea Rose 29. Billy the Kid 30. Cimarron 31. Renegades of the West 33. Alice in Wonderland 33. Riders of the Black Hills 38. Gone with the Wind 39. Chad Hanna 40. Bad Men of Missouri 41. Sullivan's Travels 42. Stars over Texas 46. West to Glory 47. Black Hills 48. Thunder in the Pines 49. The Blazing Forest 52. The Stranger Wore a Gun 53. Abbott and Costello Meet the Keystone Cops 53. Meet Me in Las Vegas 56. The Birds and the Bees 57. The Ladies' Man 61, etc.

TV series: The Marshal of Gunsight Pass 50.

Atherton, William (1947–) (William Knight).
American actor with stage background.

The New Centurions 72. Class of '44 73. The Sugarland Express 74. The Day of the Locust 74. The Hindenburg 76. Looking for Mr Goodbar 77. Malibu (TV) 83. Ghostbusters 84. Real Genius 85. No Mercy 86. Intrigue 90. Die Hard 2 90. Oscar 91. Chrome Soldiers 92. The Pelican Brief 93. Saints and Sinners 95. Broken Trust (TV) 95. Bio-Dome 96. Mad City 97, etc.

Atkins, Christopher (1961–).
American actor who began by starring opposite Brooke Shields in *The Blue Lagoon*.

The Blue Lagoon 80. The Pirate Movie 82. A Night in Heaven 83. Mortuary Academy 88. Listen to Me 89. Shakma 90. Exchange Lifeguards 93. Signal One (Aus) 95. It's My Party 96, etc.

TV series: Dallas 83–84.

Atkins, Eileen (1934–).
British character actress, highly regarded on stage. She was co-creator of the TV series *Upstairs, Downstairs* and *The House of Elliott*. Formerly married to actor Julian Glover.

Inadmissible Evidence 68. I Don't Want to Be Born 75. Equus 77. She Fell Among Thieves (TV) 78. The Dresser 83. Let Him Have It 91. The Lost Language of Cranes (TV) 91. Wolf 94. Cold Comfort Farm (TV) 95. Mrs Dalloway (w) 97. Vita and Virginia (& w) 97. The Avengers 98, etc.

Atkinson, Rowan (1955–).
English actor and comedian, best known as the hapless Mr Bean, which from 1990 to 1995 revived silent slapstick comedy on television. He studied electrical engineering at Newcastle University and then went to Oxford University, where he appeared in the Oxford Revue and then performed a one-man show before teaming with Mel Smith and Griff Rhys Jones in the TV series *Not the Nine O'Clock News*.

Never Say Never Again 83. The Tall Guy 89. The Appointments of Dennis Jennings (short) 89. The Witches 90. Hot Shots! Part Deux 93. Four Weddings and a Funeral 94. The Lion King (voice of Zazu) 94. Dr Bean 97. Bean (& co-w) 97, etc.

TV series: Not the Nine O'Clock News 81–82. Blackadder 83–84. Blackadder II 85. Blackadder III 87–88. Blackadder Goes Forth 89–90. The Thin Blue Line 95–96.

❝ It is better to make no films than bad films. I see the film world as a big bag of worry. – *R.A.*

Atsumi, Kiyoshi (1928–1996) (Yasuo Tadokoro).
Japanese leading comic actor, best known for playing Tora-san, an itinerant pedlar, in a long-running series which began on television in 1968 and encompassed 48 films from 1969 to 1995, mostly directed by Yoji YAMADA.

Attanasio, Paul (1959–).
American screenwriter who also created the mid-90s TV series *Homicide: Life on the Street*. Born in New York, he studied law at Harvard and, in the 1980s, was a film critic for the *Washington Post*.

Quiz Show (AAN) 94. Disclosure 94. Donnie Brasco 97, etc.

❝ Films could return full circle to having just a lot of silent action and title cards – pure spectacle. It seems where the audience is going. – *P.A.*

Little guys aren't lovable. Chaplin's little tramp is not lovable. The little guy's usually mean and vindictive, because he's been made that way. – *P.A.*

Attenborough, Richard (1923–) (Lord Attenborough).
British character actor who escaped from early typecasting as a young coward, revealed an ambitious range of characterizations, and went on to produce and direct. He became a life peer in 1993. Married to actress Sheila Sim in 1945.

In Which We Serve 42. Schweik's New Adventures 42. The Hundred Pound Window 43. Journey Together 43. A Matter of Life and Death 46. School for Secrets 46. The Man Within 47. Dancing with Crime 47. *Brighton Rock* 47. London Belongs to Me 48. *The Guinea Pig* (as a 13-year-old) 49. The Lost People 50. Boys in Brown 50. Morning Departure 50. Hell is Sold Out 51. The Magic Box 51. The Gift Horse 52. Father's Doing Fine 53. Eight O'Clock Walk 54. The Ship that Died of Shame 54. *Private's Progress* 55. The Baby and the Battleship 56. Brothers in Law 56. The Scamp 58. Dunkirk 58. *The Man Upstairs* 58. Danger Within 58. I'm All Right Jack 58. Sea of Sand 58. Jetstorm 59. SOS Pacific 59. *The Angry Silence* (& co-p) 59. *The League of Gentlemen* (& co-p) 59. Only Two Can Play 62. *Whistle Down the Wind* (p only) 62. The Dock Brief 62. All Night Long 62. *The Great Escape* (US) 63. *Seance on a Wet Afternoon* (& p) 64. The Third Secret 64. *Guns at Batasi* (BFA) 64. The Flight of the Phoenix (US) 65. The Sand Pebbles (US) 66. Doctor Dolittle 67. The Bliss of Mrs Blossom 68. The Last Grenade 68. Only When I Larf 68. *Oh What a Lovely War* (co-p and d only) 69. David Copperfield 69. The Magic Christian 70. A Severed Head 70. *Loot* 71. 10 Rillington Place 71. Young Winston (d only) 72. Conduct Unbecoming 75. Rosebud 75. Brannigan 75. And Then There Were None 75. A Bridge Too Far (d only) 77. The Chess Players (India) 78. Magic (d only) 78. The Human Factor 79. *Gandhi* (p, d only) (AA) 82. A Chorus Line (d only) 85. Cry Freedom (d only) 87. Chaplin (d) 92. Jurassic Park (a) 93. *Shadowlands* (p, d) 93. Miracle on 34th Street (a) 94. In Love and War (p, d) 96. Hamlet (a) 96. In Love and War (d) 97. Elizabeth (a) 98. Grey Owl (p, d) 98, etc.

✪ For being a prime mover in most aspects of British entertainment for half a century and demonstrating in an age of hyperbole and bluster the effectiveness of understatement. *Shadowlands*.

Atterbury, Malcolm (1907–1992).
American character actor.

Dragnet 54. I Was a Teenage Werewolf 57. Blood of Dracula 57. Rio Bravo 59. The Birds 63. Seven Days in May 64. The Learning Tree 69. The Emperor of the North Pole 73. Day of Terror, Night of Fear (TV) 77, etc.

TV series: Thicker than Water 73. Apple's Way 74–75.

Atwater, Barry (1918–1978).
American character actor.

Nightmare 56. Pork Chop Hill 59. Sweet Bird of Youth 62. Return of the Gunfighter (TV) 66. The Night Stalker (TV) 72, etc.

Atwater, Edith (1911–1986).
American character actress, usually as a helpmeet – secretary, nurse or mother. Born in Chicago, Illinois, she was married to actors Joseph Allen, Jnr, Hugh MARLOWE and Kent SMITH.

We Went to College 36. The Body Snatcher 45. The Sweet Smell of Success 57. It Happened at the World's Fair 63. Strait Jacket 64. Strange Bedfellows 64. True Grit 69. Pieces of Dreams 70. Stand Up and Be Counted 71. Die Sister Die 74. Family Plot 76, etc.

Atwill, Lionel (1885–1946).
Incisive but rather stolid British actor who went to Hollywood in 1932 and stayed to play teutonic villians, mad doctors and burgomasters.

■ Eve's Daughter 18. For Sale 18. The Marriage Price 19. The Highest Bidder 21. Indiscretion 21. The Silent Witness 32. *Doctor X* 32. The Vampire Bat 33. The Secret of Madame Blanche 33. *The Mystery of the Wax Museum* 33. Murders in the Zoo 33. The Sphinx 33. Song of Songs 33. The Secret of the Blue Room 33. The Solitaire Man 33. *Nana* 34. Beggars in Ermine 34. Stamboul Quest 34. One More River 34. The Age of Innocence 34. The Firebird 34. The Man Who Reclaimed His Head 35. Mark of the Vampire 35. *The Devil is a Woman* 35. The Murder Man 35. Rendezvous 35. Captain Blood 35. Lady of Secrets 36. Absolute Quiet 36. Till We Meet Again 36. *The Road Back* 37. The High Command 37. Last Train from Madrid 37. The Great Garrick 37. Lancer Spy 37. Three Comrades 38. The Great Waltz 38. *Son of Frankenstein* (memorable as the one-armed police chief) 39. *The Three Musketeers* 39. *The Hound of the Baskervilles* 39. The Gorilla 39. The Sun Never Sets 39. Mr Moto Takes a Vacation 39. The Secret of Dr Kildare 39. Balalaika 39. Charlie Chan in Panama 39. The Mad Empress 40. Johnny Apollo 40. Charlie Chan's Murder Cruise 40. The Girl in 313 40. Boom Town 40. The Great Profile 40. *Man Made Monster* 41. The Mad Doctor of Market Street 42. *To Be Or Not To Be* 42. The Strange Case of Dr RX 42. The Ghost of Frankenstein 42. Pardon My Sarong 42. Cairo 42. Night Monster 42. Junior G-Men of the Air (serial) 42. *Sherlock Holmes and the Secret Weapon* (as Moriarty) 42. Frankenstein Meets the Wolf Man 43. House of Frankenstein 44. Captain America (serial) 44. Raiders of Ghost City (serial) 44. Lady in the Death House 44. Secrets of Scotland Yard 44. Fog Island 45. Genius at Work 45. Crime Incorporated 45. *House of Dracula* 45. Lost City of the Jungle (serial) 46.

❝ See, one side of my face is gentle and kind, incapable of anything but love of my fellow man. The other profile is cruel and predatory and evil, incapable of anything but lusts and dark passions. It all depends which side of my face is turned towards you – or the camera. – *L.A.*

One doesn't easily forget, Herr Baron, an arm torn out by the roots. – *L.A. in Son of Frankenstein*

My dear, why are you so pitifully afraid? Immortality has been the dream, the inspiration of mankind through the ages. And I am going to give you immortality! – *L.A. in The Mystery of the Wax Museum*

Atwood, Colleen.
American costume designer; she began on *Ragtime* as an assistant to production designer Patrizia VON BRANDENSTEIN.

Firstborn 84. Manhunter 86. The Pick-Up Artist 87. Someone to Watch Over Me 87. Married to the Mob 88. Torch Song Trilogy 88. Edward Scissorhands 90. Joe versus the Volcano 90. Hider in the House 91. Silence of the Lambs 91. Love Field 92. Rush 92. Lorenzo's Oil 92. Born Yesterday 93. Philadelphia 93. Cabin Boy 94. Ed Wood 94. Wyatt Earp 94. Little Women (AAN) 94. The Juror 96. Mars Attacks! 96. Gattaca 97. Head above Water 97. Fallen 98. Beloved 98, etc.

Auberjonois, René (1940–).
American character actor.

M*A*S*H 70. Brewster McCloud 71. McCabe and Mrs Miller 71. Images 72. Pete 'n Tillie 72. Panache (TV) 76. The Hindenburg 76. King Kong 76. Eyes of Laura Mars 78. Where the Buffalo Roam 80. The Christmas Star (TV) 86. Walker

87. Police Academy 5: Assignment Miami Beach 88. The Little Mermaid (voice) 89. The Feud 90. The Lost Language of Cranes (TV) 91. The Player 92. The Ballad of Little Joe 93. Batman Forever 95. Los Locos 97, etc.

TV series: Benson 80–85. Star Trek: Deep Space Nine 93– .

Aubert, Lenore (1913–).
Yugoslavian actress in Hollywood from the late 30s, usually in sinister roles.

Bluebeard's Eighth Wife 38. They Got Me Covered 43. Action in Arabia 44. *Wife of Monte Cristo* 46. The Other Love 47. Return of the Whistler 48. *Abbott and Costello Meet Frankenstein* 48. Abbott and Costello Meet the Killer 49. Une Fille sur la Route 52, etc.

Aubrey, Anne (1937–).
British leading lady of a few comedies and adventures in the late 50s.

No Time To Die 58. The Man Inside 58. The Secret Man 58. The Bandit of Zhobe 59. Idle on Parade 59. Killers of Kilimanjaro 59. Jazzboat 60. In the Nick 60. Let's Get Married 60. The Hellions 61. Assignment Munich (TV) 72. The Carey Treatment 73.

Aubrey, James T. (1918–1994).
Production executive, nicknamed 'The Smiling Cobra'. He was president of CBS-TV at the height of its success (1959–65), and, from 1969–73, in charge of MGM, during which period he cut costs by cancelling movies and selling many of the studio's assets, including its wardrobe and props from its classic films. Then became an independent producer, mainly of TV movies. Married actress Phyllis Thaxter (1944–63).

Futureworld 76. The Hunger 83, etc.

❝ I don't want to hear any more bullshit about the old MGM. The old MGM is gone. – *J.T.A.*

Jim Aubrey doesn't know as much about film as a first-year cinema student. – *Blake Edwards*

No man in history ever had such a lock on such an enormous audience. – *Life magazine on Aubrey at CBS*

Aubrey, Jimmy (1887–1983).
English music-hall comedian and actor. Born in Liverpool, he was a member of Fred Karno's troupe that toured America and also included Charlie Chaplin and Stan Laurel. He starred in silent comedy shorts, with Oliver Hardy as the heavy, and had bit parts in a few Laurel and Hardy comedies before becoming a character actor in early talkies.

Footlights and Fakers 17. She Laughs Last 20. Their Purple Moment 28. That's My Wife 29. Courage in the North 35. Aces and Eights 36, etc.

Aubrey, Skye (1945–).
American leading lady of a few 70s films: daughter of James Aubrey, TV executive, and actress Phyllis Thaxter.

Vanished (TV) 71. The Carey Treatment 72. The Longest Night (TV) 72. The Phantom of Hollywood (TV) 73, etc.

Aubry, Cécile (1929–) (Anne-José Benard).
Petite French leading lady of the early 50s. Now a children's author.

Manon 49. The Black Rose 50. Bluebeard 51. La Ironia 54, etc.

Auclair, Michel (1922–1988) (Vladimir Vujovic).
French leading man.

La Belle et la Bête 46. Les Maudits 47. Manon 49. Justice Est Faite 50. Henriette 52. Funny Face (US) 56. The Fanatics 57. Rendezvous de Minuit 61. Symphony for a Massacre 64. The Day of the Jackal 73, etc.

Audiard, Jacques (1952–).
French screenwriter and director, the son of writer-director Michel AUDIARD, with whom he wrote his first scripts, *The Professional/Le Professionnel* 81 and *Mortel Randonnée* 82.

Vive le Sociale 83. La Cage aux Folles III (co-w) 85. Angel Dust/Poussière d'Ange 87. Australia (co-w) 89. Baxter (co-w) 89. Barjo (co-w) 93. See How They Fall/Regard les Hommes Tomber (wd) 94. A *Self-Made Hero*/Un Héro Très Discret (wd) 95, etc.

Audiard, Michel (1920–1985).
French writer-director.

Mr Peek-a-Boo (w) 51. Gas Oil (w) 55. Les Misérables (w) 57. Babette Goes to War (w) 60. A Monkey in Winter (w) 62. Mélodie en Sous-Sol (w) 63. Tendre Voyou (w) 66. Opération Léontine (wd) 68. Le Drapeau Noir (wd) 71. Tendre Poulet (wd) 78. Le Cavaleur (wd) 79, many others.

Audley, Maxine (1923–1992).
British stage actress who made occasional film appearances.

The Sleeping Tiger 54. The Barretts of Wimpole Street 57. The Vikings 58. Our Man in Havana 59. The Trials of Oscar Wilde 60. Hell Is a City 60. A Jolly Bad Fellow 64. Here We Go Round the Mulberry Bush 67. Frankenstein Must Be Destroyed 69, etc.

Audran, Stéphane (1933–).
Cool French leading actress, in international films. Married Jean-Louis Trintignant and Claude Chabrol.

La Bonne Tisane 58. Les Cousins 59. Les Bonnes Femmes 60. Les Godelureaux 61. Le Signe du Lion 62. Landru 63. Le Tigre Aime la Chair Fraîche 64. Paris vu Par 65. The Champagne Murders 67. *Les Biches* 68. La Femme Infidèle 69. The Lady in the Car with Glasses and a Gun 70. Just Before Nightfall 71. Without Apparent Motive 71. *The Discreet Charm of the Bourgeoisie* 72. Les Noces Rouges 73. Dead Pigeon on Beethoven Street 73. And Then There Were None 74. The Black Bird 75. Vincent, Paul, François and the Others 76. Folies Bourgeoises 76. Silver Bears 77. Violette Nozière 78. The Prisoner of Zenda 79. Eagle's Wing 79. Le Coeur à l'Envers 80. The Big Red One 80. Brideshead Revisited (TV) 80. Blood Relatives 81. Coup de Torchon 82. The Blood of Others 84. Cop au Vin 84. Mistral's Daughter (TV) 84. Les Plouffe 85. The Gypsy 85. Babette's Feast 87. Quiet Days in Clichy 90. Betty 92. Au Petit Marguery 95. Maximum Risk (US) 96, etc.

Audry, Jacqueline (1908–1977).
French director whose films were usually written by her husband, Pierre Laroche.

Gigi 49. L'Ingénue Libertine 50. *Olivia* 51. Huis Clos 54. In Six Easy Lessons 57. Mitsou 57. Les Petits Matins 62. Soledad 66. Le Lis de Mer 70, etc.

Audsley, Mick.
British editor.

The Hit 85. Dance with a Stranger 85. My Beautiful Laundrette 86. Prick Up Your Ears 87. Sammy and Rosie Get Laid 87. Dangerous Liaisons 88. Soursweet 88. We're No Angels 89. The Grifters 90. Hero/Accidental Hero 92. Interview with the Vampire 94. 12 Monkeys 95. The Van 96. The Avengers 98, etc.

Auer, John H. (1909–1975).
Hungarian-born American director, turning out 'B' films since the 30s.

■ Frankie and Johnnie 35. The Crime of Dr Crespi 35. Rhythm in the Clouds 37. Circus Girl 37. Outside of Paradise 38. Invisible Enemy 38. I Stand Accused 38. A Desperate Adventure 38. Orphans of the Street 38. Forged Passport 39. SOS Tidal Wave 39. Smuggled Cargo 39. Calling All Marines 39. Thou Shalt Not Kill 40. Women in War 40. Hit Parade of 1941 40. A Man Betrayed 41. The Devil Pays Off 41. Pardon My Stripes 42. Moonlight Masquerade 42. Johnny Doughboy 42. Tahiti Honey 43. *Gangway for Tomorrow* 43. Seven Days Ashore 44. Moonlight in Manhattan 44. Pan Americana 45. Beat the Band 47. The Flame 48. I Jane Doe 48. Angel on the Amazon 48. The Avengers 50. Hit Parade of 1951 50. Thunderbirds 52. *City that Never Sleeps* (& p) 53. Hell's Half Acre (& p) 54. The Eternal Sea (& p) 55. Johnny Trouble (& p) 57.

Then to TV.

Auer, Mischa (1905–1967) (Mischa Ounskowsky).
Lanky Russian comedy actor with prominent eyes and wild gestures. Went to Broadway after the revolution, and in 1928 arrived in Hollywood; after several false starts found himself much in demand for noble idiot roles in broken English.

■ Something Always Happens 28. Marquis Preferred 28. The Benson Murder Case 30. Inside the Lines 30. Just Imagine 30. Women Love Once 30. The Unholy Garden 31. The Yellow Ticket 31. Delicious 31. The Midnight Patrol 32. No Greater Love 32. Mata Hari 32. Scarlet Dawn 32. The Monster Walks 32. Dangerously Yours 33. Sucker Money 33. Infernal Machine 33. Corruption 33. After Tonight 33. Cradle Song 33. Girl Without a Room 33. Wharf Angel 34. Bulldog Drummond Strikes Back 34. Stamboul Quest 34. I Dream too Much 34. The Crusades 35. Mystery Woman 35. Lives of a Bengal Lancer 35. Clive of India 35. Sons of Guns 36. Murder in the Fleet 36. The House of a Thousand Candles 36. One Rainy Afternoon 36. The Princess Comes Across 36. My *Man Godfrey* (in which his gorilla impersonation really put him on the map) (AAN) 36. *The Gay Desperado* 36. Winterset 36. That Girl from Paris 37. Three Smart Girls 37. Top of the Town 37. We Have Our Moments 37. Pick a Star 37. Marry the Girl 37. Vogues of 1938 37. *100 Men and a Girl* 37. Merry Go Round 37. It's All Yours 38. Rage of Paris 38. *You Can't Take It With You* 38. Service de Luxe 38. Little Tough Guys in Society 38. *Sweethearts* 38. *East Side of Heaven* 39. Unexpected Father 39. *Destry Rides Again* 39. Alias the Deacon 40. Sandy is a Lady 40. Public Deb Number One 40. *Spring Parade* 40. Seven Sinners 40. Trail of the Vigilantes 40. The Flame of New Orleans 41. Hold That Ghost 41. Moonlight in Hawaii 41. *Hellzapoppin* 41. Cracked Nuts 41. *Twin Beds* 42. Around the World 43. *Lady in the Dark* 44. *Up in Mabel's Room* 44. *A Royal Scandal* 45. Brewster's Millions 45. And Then There Were None 45. Sentimental Journey 46. She Wrote the Book 46. Sofia 48. The Sky is Red 52. Song of Paris 52. *Confidential Report* 55. Futures Vedettes 55. The Monte Carlo Story 58. Mam'zelle Pigalle 58. The Foxiest Girl in Paris 58. A Dog a Mouse and a Sputnik 60. We Joined the Navy 62. Ladies First 63. The Christmas that Almost Wasn't 66. Drop Dead Darling 66.

✪ For assuring the world that Russians could be fun. *Twin Beds*.

Famous line (*Lady in the Dark*): 'This is the end! The absolute end!'

Auger, Claudine (1942–).
French leading lady, in occasional films abroad.

In the French Style 63. Thunderball 65. Triple Cross 66. Jeu de Massacre 67. The Devil in Love 67. The Bastard 68. The Crimebuster 77. Travels with Anita 79. Fantastica 80. Lovers and Liars 81. The Associate 82. Secret Places 84, etc.

August, Bille (1948–).
Danish director and screenwriter, a former cinematographer. He has won the Palme d'Or at the Cannes Film Festival with *Pelle the Conqueror* and *The Best Intentions*.

In My Life 78. Zappa (wd) 83. Twist and Shout (wd) 84. Buster's World (TV) 85. Pelle the Conqueror/Pelle Erobreren (wd) 88. The Best Intentions/Den Goda Viljan (d) 92. The House of the Spirits (wd) 93. Jerusalem (wd) 96. Smilla's Sense of Snow/Smilla's Feeling for Snow (d) 97. Les Misérables (d) (US) 98, etc.

August, Joseph (1890–1947).
Distinguished American cinematographer.

SELECTED SILENTS: The Narrow Trail 17. Tiger Man 18. Square Deal Sanderson 19. Sand 20. O'Malley of the Mounted 21. *Travellin' On* 22. Madness of Youth 23. *Dante's Inferno* 24. *Tumbleweeds* 25. *The Road to Glory* 26. *The Beloved Rogue* 26. Fig Leaves 26. Two Arabian Knights 27. Honor Bound 28. The Black Watch 29.

■ SOUND FILMS: Men Without Women 30. Double Crossroads 30. On Your Back 30. Up the River 30. Seas Beneath 31. Mr Lemon of Orange 31. Quick Millions 31. The Brat 31. Heartbreak 31. Charlie Chan's Chance 31. Silent Witness 32. Mystery Ranch 32. Vanity Street 32. No More Orchids 32. That's My Boy 32. *Man's Castle* 33. Master of Men 33. As the Devil Commands 33. Cocktail Hour 33. Circus Queen Murder 33. The Captain Hates the Sea 34. Among the Missing 34. The Defense Rests 34. Black Moon 34. Twentieth Century 34. No Greater Glory 34. Sylvia Scarlett 35. After the Dance 35. *The Informer* 35. I'll Love You Always 35. The Whole Town's Talking 35. The Plough and the Stars 36. *Mary of Scotland* 36. Every Saturday Night 36. A Damsel in Distress 37. Music for Madame 37. Super Sleuth 37. Fifty Roads to Town 37. *Michael Strogoff* 37. Sea Devils 37. Gun Law 37. This Marriage Business 38. The Saint in New York 38. *The Hunchback of Notre Dame* 39. *Gunga Din* 39. Nurse Edith Cavell 40. Man of Conquest 40. Melody Ranch 40. Primrose Path 40. *All that Money Can Buy* 41. They Were Expendable 45. *Portrait of Jennie* 48.

✪ For the imperishable visuals of his half-dozen melodramatic masterpieces. *Portrait of Jennie*.

Auld, Georgie (1919–1990) (John Altwerger).
Jazz tenor saxophonist and occasional actor. Best known for his recordings with Benny Goodman in the 40s, he played a bandleader and dubbed Robert De Niro's saxophone playing in Martin Scorsese's *New York, New York* 77. He also dubbed fellow saxophonist Dexter Gordon's playing in *Unchained* 55.

Aulin, Ewa (1949–).
Scandinavian leading lady in international films.

Candy 68. Start the Revolution without Me 69. This Kind of Love 72, etc.

Ault, Marie (1870–1951) (Mary Cragg).
British character actress of stage and screen, usually in dialect comedy roles.

Woman to Woman 24. The Lodger 26. Hobson's Choice 31. *Major Barbara* 40. *Love on the Dole* 41. We Dive at Dawn 43. I See a Dark Stranger 46. Madness of the Heart 49, many others.

Aumont, Jean-Pierre (1909–) (J.-P. Salomons).
French leading man, in films from 1931, Hollywood from 1941. His three wives include actresses Maria MONTEZ and Marisa PAVAN.

Autobiography: 1977, *Sun and Shadow*.

Jean de la Lune 32. Maria Chapdelaine 35. Drôle de Drame 36. *Hôtel du Nord* 38. The Cross of Lorraine 42. Assignment in Brittany 43. Heartbeat 46. Song of Scheherazade 48. The First Gentleman (GB) 48. Charge of the Lancers 53. *Lili* 53. Hilda Crane 56. The Seventh Sin 57. The Devil at Four O'Clock 61. Five Miles to Midnight 63. Castle Keep 69. *La Nuit Américaine* 73. The Happy Hooker 75. Catherine and Company 75. Seven Suspects for Murder 77. Nana 83. Shadow Dance 83. The Blood of Others 84. Sweet Country 86. Johnny Monroe 87. A Notre Regrettable Époux 88. Becoming Colette 92. Au Petit Marguery 95. Jefferson in Paris (US) 95. The Proprietor 96, etc.

Aurel, Jean (1925–).
French writer-director, originally of documentary shorts.

14–18 (d) 63. La Bataille de France (d) 64. De l'Amour (wd) 65. Manon 70 (wd) 68. Les Femmes (wd) 69. Comme un Pot de Fraises (wd) 74. The Woman Next Door 81. Vivement Dimanche (w) 83. Confidentially Yours (w) 84, etc.

Aurenche, Jean (1904–1992).
French writer who with Pierre Bost (1901–1975) wrote many well-known films.

Hôtel du Nord 38. Sylvie et le Fantôme 45. La Symphonie Pastorale 46. *Le Diable au Corps* 46. Occupe-Toi d'Amélie 49. Dieu A Besoin des Hommes 50. *The Red Inn* 51. *Les Jeux Interdits* 51. Ripening Seed 53. Gervaise 56. En Cas de Malheur 57. L'Affaire d'Une Nuit 60. The Clockmaker 76. De Guerre Lasse 87. Fucking Fernand 87. Le Palanquin des Larmes 88, etc. Aurenche worked alone on the screenplay of *Woman in White* 65.

Auric, Georges (1899–1983).
French composer who became director of the Paris Opéra.

Autobiography: 1974, *Quand J'étais Là*.

Le Sang d'un Poète 30. *À Nous la Liberté* 31. Lac aux Dames 34. L'Alibi 37. Orage 38. L'Eternel Retour 43. Dead of Night 45. Caesar and Cleopatra 45. La Belle et la Bête 46. It Always Rains on Sunday 47. Corridor of Mirrors 48. Passport to Pimlico 49. *Orphée* 49. *Belles de Nuit* 52. Roman Holiday 53. The Wages of Fear 53. Father Brown 54. Rififi 55. The Witches of Salem 56. Gervaise 56. The Picasso Mystery 56. Bonjour Tristesse 57. La Chambre Ardente 62. The Mind Benders 63. Thomas the Impostor 65. Therese and Isabelle 68. The Christmas Tree 69, many others.

Aurthur, Robert Alan (1922–1978).
American novelist and screenwriter.

Edge of the City 56. Warlock 59. For Love of Ivy 68. The Lost Man 70, etc.

Austen, Jane (1775–1817).
After years of being neglected by film-makers, the most delightful of English novelists enjoyed great popularity in the 90s, as part of the cycle of British

period films, possibly in emulation of the successful films of Merchant-Ivory, who had turned the Edwardian novels of E. M. Forster into box-office successes.

Pride and Prejudice 40. *Clueless* (an update of Emma) 95. Persuasion 95. Pride and Prejudice (TV) 95. *Sense and Sensibilty* 95. Emma 96. Emma (TV) 96. Mansfield Park 99, etc.

Auster, Paul.
American minimalist novelist and screenwriter.
Autobiography: 1997, *Hand to Mouth: A Chronicle of Early Failure.*
The Music of Chance (oa) 93. Smoke (w) 95. Blue in the Face (co-w, co-d) 95. Lulu on the Bridge (wd) 98.

Austin, Albert (1855–1953).
English actor and director in Hollywood, from music hall. Born in Birmingham, he became a member of Fred Karno's group, touring America before making his film debut, working with Chaplin on his two-reel comedies for Mutual.
The Floorwalker 16. The Fireman 16. The Vagabond 16. One A.M. 16. The Count 16. The Pawnshop 16. Behind the Screen 16. The Rink 16. Easy Street 17. The Cure 17. The Immigrant 17. The Adventurer 17. A Dog's Life 18. Shoulder Arms 18. A Day's Pleasure 19. The Kid 21. Pay Day 22. Trouble (d) 22. A Prince of a King (d) 23. The Gold Rush 25. City Lights 31, etc.

Austin, Charles (1878–1944).
English music-hall comedian who made a few films. He was on the halls from 1896, notably as cockney policeman Parker P.C.
Parker's Weekend 16. The Exploits of Parker 18. Hot Heir 31. It's a Cop (co-w) 34. School for Stars (story) 35, etc.

Austin, Charlotte (1933–).
American leading lady who moved from musicals to monsters in the 50s.
Sunny Side of the Street 51. The Farmer Takes a Wife 53. How to Marry a Millionaire 53. Gorilla at Large 54. Desirée 54. Daddy Long Legs 55. How to Be Very Very Popular 55. Bride of the Beast 58, etc.

Austin, Jerry (1892–1976).
Dwarf American actor.
Saratoga Trunk 43. Adventures of Don Juan 47, etc.

Austin, Ray (1932–).
British director, mostly of TV episodes, in America from the early 50s.
House of the Living Dead 73. Sword of Justice (TV) 79. Salvage I (TV) 79. Tales of the Gold Monkey (TV) 82. The Zany Adventures of Robin Hood (TV) 84. Return of the Six Million Dollar Man and the Bionic Woman (TV) 87. The New Zorro (TV) 92, etc.

Austin, Ron
American screenwriter.
The Happening 67. Harry in Your Pocket 73, etc.

Austin, William (1891–1975).
English character actor, mainly in Hollywood. Born in Georgetown, British Guiana, he trained in London but made his stage debut in Los Angeles in 1919.
Ruggles of Red Gap 21. Silk Stockings 24. Mysterious Dr Fu Manchu 29. Return of Dr Fu Manchu 31. High Society 32. Three Men in a Boat 33. Alice in Wonderland (as the Gryphon) 33. The Private Life of Henry VIII 33. The Gay Divorcee 35. Dr Rhythm 38. Sherlock Holmes 40. Charley's Aunt 41. Return of Monte Cristo 46. The Ghost & Mrs Muir 47. Batman 50, etc.

Autant-Lara, Claude (1903–).
French director, usually of stylish romantic dramas; former assistant to René Clair.
Ciboulette 33. L'Affaire du Courrier de Lyon 37. *Fric Frac* 39. Lettres d'Amour 42. Douce 43. Sylvie et le Fantôme 45. *Le Diable au Corps* 46. *Occupe-Toi d'Amélie* 49. *The Red Inn* 51. Ripening Seed 53. Le Rouge et le Noir 54. Marguerite de la Nuit 55. La Traversée de Paris 56. *En Cas de Malheur* 57. The Green Marc's Nest 59. Le Bois des Amants 60. The Count of Monte Cristo 61. Le Meurtrier 62. Thou Shalt Not Kill 62. The Woman in White 65. Les Patates 69. Le Rouge et le Blanc 70. Gloria 77, etc.
❝ The director must consider himself surrounded by enemies; what I mean is that, in a business where the taste of one man must prevail, he is surrounded by people who want to do nothing but impose their own tastes. – *C.A-L.*

Auteuil, Daniel (1950–).
French leading actor, from the stage, where he played with the Théâtre National Populaire. His early parts tended to be comic, although since *Jean de Florette* brought him to international attention he has played more varied roles.
Le Sex Shop 73. Jean de Florette 87. *Manon des Sources* 87. Romuald et Juliette 89. *A Heart in Winter*/Un Coeur en Hiver 91. The Elegant Criminal/Lacenaire 92. My Favourite Season/Ma Saison Préférée 93. Queen Margot/La Reine Margot 94. Une Femme Française 95. According to Pereira 95. Thieves/Les Voleurs 96. The Eighth Day 96. On Guard! 97. The Lost Son 98, etc.

Autry, Gene (1907–).
Easy-going Texan who made innumerable minor westerns 1934–54 as singing cowboy, usually with his horse Champion. Beginning as a singer on radio, billed as 'Oklahoma's Yodeling Cowboy', he presented a clean-living image: he refused to hit anyone smaller than himself and would not smoke or drink on-screen. He made 56 features for Republic, often with his sidekick from radio, Lester 'Smiley' Burnette, or his later partner Pat Buttram. From 1937–42, he was the top western star, turning to TV in the 50s and retiring in 1960. Spin-offs he produced from his own TV series included *The Adventures of Champion* 55–56, and *Annie Oakley* 54–56, featuring his frequent movie co-star Gail Davis.
Autobiography: 1978, *Back in the Saddle Again.*
In Old Sante Fe 34. The Phantom Empire (serial) 35. Tumbling Tumbleweeds 35. The Big Show 36. Red River Valley 36. The Singing Cowboy 36. Boots and Saddles 37. Springtime in the Rockies 37. Rhythm of the Saddle 38. Home on the Range 39. Mexicali Rose 39. Shooting High 40. Melody Ranch 40. Back in the Saddle 41. The Singing Hills 41. Cowboy Serenade 42. Bells of Capistrano 42. Sioux City Sue 46. Robin Hood of Texas 47. The Strawberry Roan 48. Riders of the Whistling Pines 49. Riders in the Sky 49. Mule Train 50. Gene Autry and the Mounties 51. Valley of Fire 51. The Old West 52. On Top of Old Smoky 53. Last of the Pony Riders 53. Alias Jesse James 59, many others.
TV series: The Gene Autry Show 50–55.
❝ In my day, most people thought dance hall girls actually danced. – *G.A.*
Autry used to ride off into the sunset. Now he owns it. – *Pat Buttram*

Avakian, Aram (1926–1987).
American director.
■ Lad – a Dog 62. The End of the Road 69. Cops and Robbers 73. 11 Harrowhouse 74.

Avalon, Frankie (1939–) (Francis Avallone).
American light leading man and pop singer, former trumpeter.
Guns of the Timberland 60. The Alamo 60. Voyage to the Bottom of the Sea 62. Beach Blanket Bingo 65. I'll Take Sweden 65. Sergeant Deadhead 66. Fireball 500 66. Pajama Party in a Haunted House 66. How to Stuff a Wild Bikini 66. Skidoo 68. The Take 74. Grease 78. Back to the Beach 87. A Dream Is a Wish Your Heart Makes: The Annette Funicello Story (TV) (as himself) 95. Casino (as himself) 95, etc.

Avary, Roger (1965–).
American screenwriter and director.
Pulp Fiction (co-w) 94. Killing Zoe (wd) 94.

Avati, Pupi (1938–) (Giuseppe Avati).
Italian director. He is a former jazz musician and factory worker who decided to work in films after seeing Fellini's 8½.
Balsamus l'Uomo di Satana 68. Thomas the Possessed/Thomas . . . gli Indemoniati 69. La Mazurka del Barone 74. Bordella 75. Le Strelle nel Fosso 78. Zeder 83. Us Three/Noi Tre 84. Fiesta di Laurea 85. The Last Minute 87. Boys and Girls/Storia di Ragazzi e Ragazze 89. Bix 91. Brothers and Sisters 92. Magnificat 93. Declarations of Love 94. The Arcane Enchanter 95. Festival 96. The Best Man/Il Testimone dello Sposo (AAN) 97, etc.

Avedon, Doe (1928–).
American leading lady who had a very short career before retiring to marry. She is the former wife of the director Don Siegel.
■ *The High and the Mighty* 54. Deep in My Heart 55. The Boss 56.
TV series: Big Town 55.

Averback, Hy (1925–).
American director with much TV experience, especially in comedy series.
Chamber of Horrors 66. Where Were You When the Lights Went Out? 68. *I Love You Alice B. Toklas* 68. The Great Bank Robbery 69. Suppose They Gave a War and Nobody Came 70. Where the Boys Are 84, etc.

Avery, Margaret
American character actress.
Magnum Force 73. Which Way Is Up? 77. The Fish that Saved Pittsburgh 79. The Lathe of Heaven 80. The Color Purple (AAN) 85. Blueberry Hill 88. Riverbend 89, etc.

Avery, Tex (1907–1980) (Fred Avery).
American animator, best known for MGM cartoons which combined savagery with hilarity. He created Droopy.
Biography: 1975, *Tex Avery: King of Cartoons* by Joe Adamson.

Avery, Val
American character actor.
King Creole 58. Too Late Blues 61. Hud 63. The Hallelujah Trail 65. The Pink Jungle 68. The Travelling Executioner 70. The Laughing Policeman 73. Let's Do It Again 75. Heroes 77. The Wanderers 79. Choices 81. Courage (TV) 86, etc.

Avildsen, John G. (1935–).
American director and screenwriter.
■ Turn on to Love 67. OK Bill 68. Guess What We Learned at School Today 69. *Joe* 70. Cry Uncle 71. Roger the Stoolie 72. Save the Tiger 73. WW and the Dixie Dance Kings 75. Foreplay (co-d) 75. *Rocky* (AA) 76. Slow Dancing in the Big City 78. The Formula 80. The President's Women 81. Neighbors 81. A Night in Heaven 83. The Karate Kid 84. The Karate Kid II 86. Happy New Year 87. For Keeps 88. The Karate Kid Part III 89. Lean on Me 89. Rocky V 90. The Power of One 92. Lane Frost 93. 8 Seconds 94.

Avital, Mili (1972–).
Israeli actress, in Hollywood. After winning awards for her performances in Israeli films, she moved to the US in 1993, first working as a waitress before landing the role of Sha'uri in *Stargate*.
Me'Ever Layam 91. Stargate 94. Dead Man 96. Invasion of Privacy 96. The End of Violence (Ger.) 97. Kissing a Fool 98. Polish Wedding 98, etc.

Avnet, Jon (1949–).
American director, producer and screenwriter.
Outlaw Blues (p) 77. Risky Business (p) 83. Between Two Women (co-w, d) (TV) 86. Less than Zero (p) 87. Men Don't Leave (p, d) 90. Fried Green Tomatoes (p, co-w, d) 91. The Mighty Ducks (p) 92. D2: The Mighty Ducks (p) 94. When a Man Loves a Woman (p) 94. The War (p, d) 94. Up Close and Personal (p, d) 96. D3: The Mighty Ducks (p) 96. The Red Corner (co-p, d) 97, etc.

Axel, Gabriel (1918–).
French-born director and screenwriter who makes movies in Denmark. He mainly works as a stage actor and director in Denmark and France.
Guld Og Gronne Skove 59. Den Rode Kappe 67. Med Kaerlig Hilsen 71. Familien Gyldenkaal 75. *Babette's Feast* (AA) 87. Christian 89. Prince of Denmark (& co-w) 93, etc.

Axelrod, George (1922–).
American comedy writer.
■ Phffft 54. The Seven Year Itch (oa) 55. Bus Stop 56. Will Success Spoil Rock Hunter? (oa) 57. Breakfast at Tiffany's 61. The Manchurian Candidate 62. Paris When It Sizzles 64. Goodbye Charlie 64. How to Murder Your Wife (& p) 65. Lord Love a Duck (& pd) 66. The Secret Life of an American Wife (& pd) 68. The Lady Vanishes 79. The Holcroft Covenant 85. The Fourth Protocol 87, etc.

Axt, Dr William (1888–1959).
American composer, almost entirely for MGM in the 30s.
Don Juan 26. Ben Hur 26. White Shadows of the South Seas 28. Smilin' Through 32. Dinner at Eight 33. The Thin Man 34. David Copperfield 35. Piccadilly Jim 36. Parnell 37. Yellow Jack 38. Stand Up and Fight 39, many others.

Axton, Hoyt (1938–).
American character actor, singer and songwriter.
The Black Stallion 79. Cloud Dancer 79. Endangered Species 82. Heart Like a Wheel 82. Liar's Moon 84. Gremlins 84. Dixie Lanes 88. Retribution 88. We're No Angels 89. Disorganised Crime 89. The Rousters (TV) 90. Season of Change 94, etc.
TV series: The Rousters 83–84. Domestic Life 84.

Ayala, Fernando (1920–).
Argentinian producer, director and screenwriter. In the late 50s, together with Hector Olivera, he founded Aries, the country's most successful and longest-surviving production company. His early films dealt with social problems; his later ones concentrate more on entertainment.
Ayer Fue Primavera 55. El Jefe 58. El Candidato 59. Paula Cautiva 63. Primero Yo 64. Las Locas del Conventillo 65. La Fiaca 68. El Profesor Hippie 69. Argentisima (co-d) 71. Argentisima II (co-d) 72. Los Médicos 78. Plata Dulce 82. Sobredosis 86. Dios los Cria 91, etc.

Ayckbourn, Alan (1939–).
English playwright and theatre director whose work has been relatively neglected by the cinema. Born in London, he began as a stage manager and actor with Sir Donald WOLFIT, and became Britain's most commercially successful and performed dramatist, writing more than 50 plays, most of them increasingly dark, and technically complex, comedies of middle-class life.
Biography: 1981, *Conversations with Ayckbourn* by Ian Watson.
A Chorus of Disapproval 89. *Smoking/No Smoking* (Fr.) 93. The Revenger's Comedies 98.
❝ All my characters seem to have this terrible disappointment, this terrible gap between what they meant to achieve and what they did achieve. – *A.A.*

Aykroyd, Dan (1952–).
Canadian revue comedian who made his name on *Saturday Night Live*. Married actress Donna Dixon, his second wife, in 1983.
1941 79. Mr Mike's Mondo Video 79. The Blues Brothers 80. Neighbours 81. Dr Detroit 82. Nothing Lasts Forever 82. Twilight Zone 83. Trading Places 83. Ghostbusters 84. Into the Night 84. Spies Like Us 85. Dragnet 87. Caddyshack II 88. The Couch Trip 88. The Great Outdoors 88. My Stepmother Is an Alien 88. Driving Miss Daisy (AAN) 89. Ghostbusters II (& w) 89. Loose Cannons 90. Nothing But Trouble (& wd) 91. My Girl 91. This Is My Life 92. Charlie 92. Sneakers 92. Coneheads (& co-w) 93. My Girl 2 94. North 94. Exit to Eden 94. Tommy Boy 95. Sgt Bilko 96. Getting Away with Murder 96. Celtic Pride 96. Feeling Minnesota 96. Rainbow 96. My Fellow Americans 97. Susan's Plan 98. Antz (voice) 98, etc.
TV series: Soul Man 97.
❝ I have this kind of mild nice-guy exterior, but inside, my heart is like a steel trap. I'm really quite robotic. – *D.A.*
The entertainment business is not the be-all and end-all for me. – *D.A.*

Aylmer, Sir Felix (1889–1979) (Felix Edward Aylmer Jones).
Distinguished British stage character actor, a respected industry figure who from 1950 was president of Equity, the actors' trade union. In films he mainly played schoolmasters, bankers, bishops, etc.
The Wandering Jew 33. The Iron Duke 35. Tudor Rose 36. As You Like It 36. *Victoria the Great* 37. The Citadel 38. Saloon Bar 40. *The Ghost of St Michael's* 41. Mr Emmanuel 44. Henry V 44. The Ghost of Berkeley Square 47. *Hamlet* (as Polonius) 48. Edward My Son 49. Quo Vadis 51. Ivanhoe 52. The Master of Ballantrae 53. Knights of the Round Table 54. The Angel Who Pawned Her Harp 54. Saint Joan 57. *Separate Tables* 58. *Never Take Sweets from a Stranger* 60. Exodus 60. The Chalk

Garden 64. Becket 64. Decline and Fall 68. Hostile Witness 68, many others.

Aylward, Gladys (1901–1970).
British missionary whose exploits in China were fictionalized in *Inn of the Sixth Happiness*, in which she was played by Ingrid Bergman.

Ayres, Agnes (1898–1940) (Agnes Hinkle).
American leading lady of the silent screen.
Forbidden Fruit 19. The Affairs of Anatol 20. *The Sheik* 21. Racing Hearts 23. When a Girl Loves 24. Morals for Men 25. Her Market Value 26. Son of the Sheik 26. Eve's Love Letters 29, many others.

Ayres, Lew (1908–1996) (Lewis Ayer).
Boyish American leading man of the 30s; he occasionally got a chance to prove himself a comfortable and friendly actor, but his career suffered during World War II when he declared himself a conscientious objector. Born in Minneapolis, he studied medicine at the University of Arizona and became a singer and bandleader before entering films. The first two of his three wives were Lola Lane (1931–33) and Ginger ROGERS (1934–41). He enjoyed success in the 30s as Dr Kildare in a series of films.
■ *The Kiss* 29. The Sophomore 29. Many a Slip 30. *All Quiet on the Western Front* 30. Common Clay 30. East is West 30. Doorway to Hell 30. Iron Man 31. Up for Murder 31. The Spirit of Notre Dame 31. Heaven on Earth 31. The Impatient Maiden 32. Night World 32. Okay America 32. *State Fair* 33. Don't Bet On Love 33. My Weakness 33. Cross Country Cruise 34. She Learned About Sailors 34. Servants' Entrance 34. Let's Be Ritzy 34. Lottery Lover 35. The Silk Hat Kid 35. The Leathernecks have Landed 36. Panic on the Air 36. Shakedown 36. Lady be Careful 36. Murder with Pictures 36. The Crime Nobody Saw 36. *Last Train from Madrid* 37. Hold 'Em Navy 37. Scandal Street 38. King of the Newsboys 38. *Holiday* (a key performance as Katharine Hepburn's drunken brother) 38. Rich Man Poor Girl 38. *Young Dr Kildare* 38. Spring Madness 38. Ice Follies 39. Broadway Serenade 39. Calling Dr Kildare 39. These Glamour Girls 39. The Secret of Dr Kildare 39. Remember? 39. Dr Kildare's Strange Case 40. Dr Kildare Goes Home 40. The Golden Fleecing 40. Dr Kildare's Crisis 40. Maisie Was a Lady 41. The People vs Dr Kildare 41. Dr Kildare's Wedding Day 41. Fingers at the Window 42. Dr Kildare's Victory 42. *The Dark Mirror* 46. The Unfaithful 47. *Johnny Belinda* (AAN) 48. The Capture 50. New Mexico 51. No Escape 53. Donovan's Brain 54. *Advise and Consent* 61. *The Carpetbaggers* 64. Hawaii Five-O (TV pilot) 68. Marcus Welby MD (TV pilot) 68. Earth II (TV) 71. She Waits (TV) 72. The Man (TV) 72. The Biscuit Eater 72. The Stranger (TV) 72. The Questor Tapes (TV) 73. Battle For Planet of the Apes 73. Heatwave (TV) 74. Francis Gary Powers (TV) 76. End of the World 77. Greatest Heroes of the Bible (TV) (as Noah) 78. Damien-Omen II 78. Of Mice and Men (TV) 81. Cast the First Stone (TV) 89.
TV series: Hawkins 74. Lime Street 85.

Ayres, Robert (1914–1968).
Canadian actor of strong silent types, long resident in Britain.
They Were Not Divided 49. Cosh Boy 52. Contraband Spain 55. It's Never Too Late 55. A Night to Remember 57. The Sicilians 63. Battle Beneath the Earth 68, many others.

Ayrton, Randle (1869–1940).
British character actor.
My Sweetheart 18. The Wonderful Year 21. Chu Chin Chow 23. Southern Love 24. Nell Gwynne 26. Passion Island 26. Glorious Youth 28. Comets 30. Dreyfus 31. Jew Süss 34. Me and Marlborough 35. Talk of the Devil 36, etc.

Azaria, Hank (1964–).
American stand-up comedian and actor.
Pretty Woman 90. Quiz Show 94. Heat 95. If Not for You 95. The Birdcage 96. Homegrown 97. Grosse Point Blanke 97. Great Expectations 97. Godzilla 98. Celebrity 98, etc.
TV series: The Simpsons (voices) 89. Herman's Head 91–94. Mad About You 93– .

Aznavour, Charles (1924–) (Shahnour Aznavurjan).
Armenian leading man of the small but rugged school, but better known as a singer-songwriter.
Autobiography: 1972, *Aznavour by Aznavour*.
Passage du Rhin 61. Cloportes 65. Candy 68. The Adventures 70. The Games 70. Un Beau Monstre 70. And Then There Were None 75. Sky Riders 76. Folies Bourgeoises 76. The Tin Drum 79. Les Fantômes du Chapelier 82. Der Zauberberg 82. Yiddish Connection (& w) 86. Migrations 88. Il Maestro 89. Les Années Campagne 91, etc.
66 Love now. Tomorrow, who knows? – C.A.

B

Babbitt, Art (1907–1992).
Leading animator, whose career began in the 20s. He worked for Disney, animating the Wicked Queen in *Snow White* and the dance of the mushrooms in *Fantasia*, for Warner's Looney Tunes, UPA and Hanna-Barbera. Married dancer Marjorie Belcher (later Marge Champion).
Snow White and the Seven Dwarfs 37. Pinocchio 40. Fantasia 40. The Thief and the Cobbler 93, etc.

Babcock, Barbara (1937–).
American character actress.
Heaven with a Gun 68. The Last Child (TV) 71. Bang the Drum Slowly 73. Chosen Survivors (TV) 74. Salem's Lot (TV) 79. The Lords of Discipline 82. Heart of Dixie 89. Happy Together 90. Far and Away 92, etc.
TV series: Dallas 78–82. Hill Street Blues 81–85. The Four Seasons 84. Mr Sunshine 86.

Babenco, Hector (1946–).
Argentinian-born director who worked in Brazil and then, declaring that Brazilian cinema was dead, moved to Hollywood.
Lucio Flavio 78. Pixote 81. Kiss of the Spider Woman (AAN) 85. Ironweed 87. At Play in the Fields of the Lord 91. Foolish Heart 98, etc.

Baby Le Roy (1931–) (Le Roy Overacker).
American toddler who appeared to general delight in comedies of the early 30s. The story goes that W. C. Fields once spiked his orange juice with gin . . .
A Bedtime Story 33. Tillie and Gus 33. Miss Fane's Baby is Stolen 33. The Old Fashioned Way 34. The Lemon Drop Kid 34. It's a Gift 35. etc.

Baby Peggy (1917–) (Peggy Montgomery).
American child star of the 20s. Later appeared under her own name, and in the 70s published two books, *The Hollywood Posse* and *Hollywood Children*.
Peggy Behave 22. Captain January 23. The Law Forbids 24. The Speed Demon 25. April Fool 26. The Sonora Kid 27, etc.

Baby Sandy (1938–) (Sandra Henville).
American infant performer who made money for Universal in the early 40s.
■ East Side of Heaven 39. Unexpected Father 39. Little Accident 39. Sandy Is a Lady 40. Sandy Gets Her Man 40. Sandy Steps Out 41. Bachelor Daddy 41. Melody Lane 41. Johnny Doughboy 42.

Bacall, Lauren (1924–) (Betty Joan Perske).
Sultry American leading actress who after stage experience made her film debut opposite Humphrey Bogart ('If you want anything, just whistle . . .') and subsequently married him. Her image gradually changed to that of an astringent and resourceful woman of the world, and in 1970 she made a triumphant return to the Broadway stage in *Applause*. Her second husband was Jason Robards Jnr (1961–69).
Autobiography: 1978, *Lauren Bacall*.
Biography: 1976, *Bogey's Baby* by Howard Greenberger.
To Have and Have Not 45. Confidential Agent 45. *The Big Sleep* 46. Dark Passage 47. Key Largo 48. *Young Man with a Horn* 50. Bright Leaf 50. *How to Marry a Millionaire* 53. Woman's World 54. The Cobweb 55. Blood Alley 55. Written on the Wind 56. Designing Woman 57. The Gift of Love 58. Northwest Frontier (GB) 59. Shock Treatment 64. Sex and the Single Girl 64. *Harper* 66. Murder on the Orient Express 74. The Shootist 76. Health 79. The Fan 81. Appointment with Death 88. Mr North 88. Misery 90. Dinner at Eight (TV) 90. Innocent Victim 90. Star for Two 91. All I Want For Christmas 91. The Portrait (TV) 93. A Foreign Field (TV) 93. Prêt-à-Porter 94. My Fellow Americans 96. *The Mirror Has Two Faces* (AAN) 96. The Day and the Night/Le Jour et la Nuit 97, etc.
~She made an uncredited cameo appearance in *Two Guys from Milwaukee* 46.
❝ Slinky! Sultry! Sensational! – *1944 promotion for L.B.*
I used to tremble from nerves so badly that the only way I could hold my head steady was to lower my chin practically to my chest and look up at Bogie. That was the beginning of The Look. – *L.B.*
I was not a woman of the world. I'd lived with Mother all my life. – *L.B.*
What I learned from Mr Bogart I learned from a master, and that, God knows, has stood me in very good stead. – *L.B.*

Bacalov, Luis Enrique.
Prolific Spanish-born composer and pianist, working in Italy. In the 60s he formed a guitar-dominated rock group, Luis Enrique and his Electronic Men.
La Banda del Buco 60. The Gospel According to St Matthew (AAN) 65. Django 66. A Bullet for the General/Quién Sabe? 66. L'Amica 69. Roma Bene 71. La Rosa Rossa 73. Le Maestro 79. City of Women 80. Entre Nous/Coupe de Foudre 83. Le Juge 83. Le Transfuge 85. The Postman/Il Postino (AA) 94, many others.

Baccaloni, Salvatore (1900–1969).
Italian opera singer who played some comedy roles in American films.
■ Full of Life 56. Merry Andrew 58. Rock a Bye Baby 58. Fanny 61. The Pigeon That Took Rome 62.

Bach, Barbara (1947–) (Barbara Goldbach).
American leading lady, first in Italian films, who played the female lead in *The Spy Who Loved Me* 77. Married former Beatle Ringo Starr.
Force Ten from Navarone 78. The Humanoid 79. Up the Academy 80. Caveman 81. The Unseen 81. Give My Regards to Broad Street 84, etc.

Bacharach, Burt (1929–).
American composer and songwriter (usually with lyricist Hal David), a former accompanist to Marlene Dietrich. The second of his three wives was actress Angie Dickinson.
Lizzie (s) 57. What's New Pussycat? (AANs) 65. Alfie (AANs) 66. Casino Royale (AANs, m) 67. *Butch Cassidy and the Sundance Kid* (AAs, m) 69. The April Fools (m) 69. Lost Horizon (s) 73. Together? 79. Arthur (AAs) 81. Night Shift 82. Best Defence 84. Arthur 2: On the Rocks 88, etc.
❝ The groovy thing about pop music is that it's wide open. Anything can happen. – *B.B.*

Bachelor, Stephanie (1924–).
American leading lady of 40s 'B' pictures.
Lady of Burlesque 43. Her Primitive Man 44. Lake Placid Serenade 44. Scotland Yard Investigator 45. I've Always Loved You 46. Blackmail 47. King of the Gamblers 48, etc.

Back, Frédéric.
French-born animator who moved to Canada in the mid-40s.
Tout Rien 80. CRAC (AA) 81. The Man Who Planted Trees (AA) 87. The Mighty River/Le Fleuve aux Grandes Eaux 94, etc.

Backus, Jim (1913–1989).
Burly American character comedian, perhaps most famous as the voice of Mr Magoo in UPA cartoons of the 50s. Stock, vaudeville and radio experience.
Autobiography: 1958, *Rocks on the Roof*.
The Great Lover 49. Hollywood Story 51. His Kind of Woman 51. I Want You 51. Pat and Mike 52. Androcles and the Lion 53. *Rebel Without a Cause* 55. The Great Man 56. Man of a Thousand Faces 57. Macabre 58. Ice Palace 60. Boys' Night Out 62. *It's A Mad Mad Mad Mad World* 63. Advance to the Rear 64. Billie 65. Where Were You When the Lights Went Out? 68. Now You See Him Now You Don't 72. Pete's Dragon 77. There Goes the Bride 80, etc.
TV series: *I Married Joan* 52–56. Hot off the Wire 60. *Gilligan's Island* 64–66. Blondie 68.

Baclanova, Olga (1899–1974).
Russian actress who played leads in a few American films.
Street of Sin 27. Docks of New York 28. *Freaks* 32. Billion Dollar Scandal 32. Claudia 43, etc.

Bacon, Irving (1893–1965).
American character actor in films from 1920, often as not-so-dumb country type or perplexed official.
Street of Chance 30. Million Dollar Legs 32. Private Worlds 35. Sing You Sinners 38. Meet John Doe 41. Pin Up Girl 44. Monsieur Verdoux 47. Room for One More 52. A Star is Born 54. Fort Massacre 58, many others.

Bacon, Kevin (1958–).
American actor. Born in Philadelphia, Pennsylvania, he trained for the stage at Circle in the Square Theater in New York and the Manning Street Actors Theatre in Philadelphia. In the mid-90s he also formed a folk-rock group, the Bacon Brothers, with his brother Michael. Married actress Kyra Sedgwick.
National Lampoon's Animal House 78. Starting Over 79. Friday the 13th 80. Hero at Large 80. Only When I Laugh 81. Diner 82. Forty Deuce 82. Enormous Changes at the Last Minute 83. Footloose 84. Quicksilver 86. Planes, Trains and Automobiles 87. She's Having a Baby 88. The Big Picture 88. Criminal Law 89. Tremors 89. Flatliners 90. JFK 91. A Few Good Men 92. The Air Up There 94. The River Wild 94. Apollo 13 95. Murder in the First 95. Balto (voice) 95. Losing Chase (d only, TV) 96. Sleepers 96. Telling Lies in America 97. Picture Perfect 97. Wild Things 98, etc.
❝ I've been a film star so long that I don't know what it would feel like not to be one. – *K.B.*

Bacon, Lloyd (1890–1955).
American director, long under contract to Warner. Born in San Jose, California, he began as a stage actor in 1911, later acting in silents before beginning to direct in the early 20s, working at Warner's from the mid-20s to the mid-40s, and then moving to Twentieth Century-Fox until the early 50s. Competent rather than brilliant, he nevertheless handled several memorable films among the mass of routine.
■ Private Izzy Murphy 26. Fingerprints 26. Broken Hearts of Hollywood 26. The Heart of Maryland 26. White Flannels 27. A Sailor's Sweetheart 27. Brass Knuckles 27. Pay As You Enter 28. The Lion and the Mouse 28. Women They Talk About 28. *The Singing Fool* 28. Stark Mad 29. Honky Tonk 29. No Defense 29. Say It with Songs 29. So Long Lefty 30. She Couldn't Say No 30. A Notorious Affair 30. The Other Tomorrow 30. Moby Dick 30. The Office Wife 30. Kept Husbands 31. Sit Tight 31. Fifty Million Frenchmen 31. Gold Dust Gertie 31. Honor of the Family 31. Manhattan Parade 31. Fireman Save my Child 32. Alias the Doctor 32. The Famous Ferguson Case 32. *Miss Pinkerton* 32. Crooner 32. You Said a Mouthful 32. *42nd Street* 33. Footlight Parade 33. *Picture Snatcher* 33. Mary Stevens MD 33. Son of a Sailor 33. *Wonder Bar* 34. A Very Honorable Guy 34. He Was Her Man 34. Six Day Bike Rider 34. *Here Comes the Navy* 34. *Devil Dogs of the Air* 35. In Caliente 35. Broadway Gondolier 35. The Irish In Us 35. Frisco Kid 35. Sons of Guns 36. Cain and Mabel 36. Gold Diggers of 1937 36. *Marked Woman* 37. Ever Since Eve 37. *San Quentin* 37. Submarine D1 37. *A Slight Case of Murder* 38. Cowboy from Brooklyn 38. *Boy Meets Girl* 38. Racket Busters 38. Wings of the Navy 38. *The Oklahoma Kid* 39. Indianapolis Speedway 39. Espionage Agent 39. A Child Is Born 39. Invisible Stripes 39. Three Cheers for the Irish 40. *Brother Orchid* 40. Knute Rockne, All American 40. Honeymoon for Three 41. Footsteps in the Dark 41. Navy Blues 41. Affectionately Yours 41. Honeymoon for Three 41. Larceny Inc 42. Wings for the Eagle 42. Silver Queen 42. Action in the North Atlantic 43. The Sullivans 44. *Sunday Dinner for a Soldier* 44. Captain Eddie 45. Home Sweet Homicide 46. Wake Up and Dream 46. I Wonder Who's Kissing Her Now 47. You were Meant for Me 48. Give My Regards to Broadway 48. Don't Trust Your Husband 48. Mother Is a Freshman 48. It Happens Every Spring 49. Miss Grant Takes Richmond 49. Kill The Umpire 50. The Good Humor Man 50. The Fuller Brush Girl 50. Call Me Mister 51. Golden Girl 51. The Frogmen 51. The I Don't Care Girl 53. The Great Sioux Uprising 53. Walking My Baby Back Home 53. The French Line 53. She Couldn't Say No 54.

Bacon, Max (1904–1969).
Plump English character actor, usually in cockney roles. He was a former drummer and singer with Ambrose's Orchestra.
Soft Lights and Sweet Music 36. Calling All Stars 37. Kicking the Moon Around 38. King Arthur Was a Gentleman 42. Bees in Paradise 43. Pool of London 51. The Gambler and the Lady 52. Espresso Bongo 59. The Entertainer 60. Crooks in Cloisters 63. The Sandwich Man 66. Privilege 67. Chitty Chitty Bang Bang 68, etc.

Badalamenti, Angelo. (1937–).
American composer.
Gordon's War 73. Law and Disorder 74. Across the Great Divide 76. Blue Velvet 86. Nightmare on Elm Street III 87. Tough Guys Don't Dance 87. Weeds 87. Cousins 89. Twin Peaks (TV) 90. The Comfort of Strangers 90. Wild at Heart 90. Wait Until Spring, Bandini 90. Shattered 91. Other People's Money 91. Twin Peaks: Fire Walk with Me 92. Hotel Room (TV) 93. Naked in New York 93. City of Lost Children (Fr.) 95. Invasion of Privacy 96, etc.

Baddeley, Angela (1904–1976).
British stage character actress, sister of Hermione Baddeley. Popular on TV as Mrs Bridges in *Upstairs Downstairs* 70–75. Married theatre director Glen Byam Shaw.
■ The Speckled Band 31. The Ghost Train 31. The Safe 32. Arms and the Man 32. Those Were the Days 34. The Citadel 38. Quartet 48. Zoo Baby 57. Tom Jones 63.

Baddeley, Hermione (1906–1986).
British character comedienne, adept at blowsy roles; long stage experience. Born in Shropshire, she was performing from the age of 14 and at 16 was a star in the play *The Likes of 'Er*, going on to work in Cochran's revues in London's West End.

Married twice. Her lovers included actor Laurence Harvey.

Autobiography: 1984, *The Unsinkable Hermione Baddeley*.

■ A Daughter in Revolt 27. The Guns of Loos 27. Caste 30. Love Life and Laughter 34. Royal Cavalcade 35. Kipps 41. It Always Rains on Sunday 47. *Brighton Rock* 47. No Room at the Inn 48. Quartet 48. *Passport to Pimlico* 49. Dear Mr Prohack 49. The Woman in Question 49. There is Another Sun 51. Tom Brown's Schooldays 51. Hell is Sold Out 51. Scrooge 51. Song of Paris 52. Time Gentlemen Please 52. *The Pickwick Papers* 52. Cosh Boy 52. Counterspy 53. The Belles of St Trinian's 54. Women without Men 56. *Room at the Top* (AAN) 58. Jetstorm 59. Espresso Bongo 59. Let's Get Married 60. Midnight Lace 60. Information Received 61. Rag Doll 61. Mary Poppins 64. The Unsinkable Molly Brown 64. Do Not Disturb 65. Harlow 65. Marriage on the Rocks 65. Bullwhip Griffin 65. The Happiest Millionaire 67. Up the Front 72. The Black Windmill 74. Chomps 79. There Goes the Bride 80. The Secret of Nimh (voice) 82.

TV series: Camp Runamuck 65–66. The Good Life (US) 71. Maude 74–77.

❝ I have spent most of my life working in the theatre – which is always my greatest love, but the films and television were the providers of the little luxuries of life. – *H.B.*

Badel, Alan (1923–1982).
British stage and screen actor of considerable sensitivity, not easy to cast in leading roles.

The Stranger Left No Card 52. Salome 53. *Three Cases of Murder* 54. Magic Fire 54. This Sporting Life 63. Children of the Damned 64. *Arabesque* 66. Otley 68. Where's Jack? 69. *The Adventurers* 70. The Day of the Jackal 73. Luther 73. Telefon 77. Force Ten From Navarone 78. The Riddle of the Sands 79. Nijinsky 80. Shogun (TV) 82, etc.

Baden-Semper, Nina (1945–).
West Indian leading lady, popular on British TV.

Kongi's Harvest 73. Love Thy Neighbour 73.

Badger, Clarence (1880–1964).
American director at his peak in the 20s.

Jubilo 19. Doubling for Romeo 21. Miss Brewster's Millions 26. *It* 27. Hot News 28. Three Weekends 28. No No Nanette 30. The Bad Man 32. Rangle River 39, etc.

Badham, John (1939–).
American director with a sharp visual style. Born in England, he is a graduate of Yale University and the Yale School of Drama.

The Impatient Heart (TV) 71. Isn't It Shocking? (TV) 73. The Godchild (TV) 74. *The Law* (TV) 74. The Gun (TV) 74. Reflections of Murder (TV) 74. The Keegans (TV) 76. The Bingo Long All Stars and Travelling Motor Kings 76. *Saturday Night Fever* 77. Dracula 79. Whose Life Is It Anyway? 81. War Games 83. Blue Thunder 83. American Flyers 85. Short Circuit 86. Stakeout 87. Bird on a Wire 90. The Hard Way 91. Point of No Return 93. Another Stakeout 93. Drop Zone 94. Nick of Time 95. Incognito 97, etc.

Badham, Mary (1952–).
American teenage actress.

■ To Kill a Mockingbird (AAN) 62. This Property Is Condemned 66. Let's Kill Uncle 66.

Badiyi, Reza S. (1936–).
Iranian-born director in America, from TV, where he came to fame by devising the title sequence for Hawaii Five-O.

The Eyes of Charles Sand (TV) 72. Trader Horn 73. Of Mice and Men (TV) 81. Blade in Hong Kong (TV) 85, etc.

Baer, Buddy (1915–1986) (Jacob Henry Baer).
American heavyweight prizefighter, brother of Max.

Africa Screams 49. Quo Vadis 51. Jack and the Beanstalk 52. Slightly Scarlet 56. Snow White and the Three Stooges 61, etc.

Baer, Max (1909–1959).
Former American world heavyweight champion who made several films.

The Prizefighter and the Lady 33. Riding High 50. The Iron Road 55. The Harder They Fall 56. Over She Goes 58, etc.

Baer, Max, Jnr (1937–).
American actor who spent nine years playing Jethro in TV's The Beverly Hillbillies, then became an independent producer.

Macon County Line 73. The McCulloughs (& a, d) 75. Ode to Billy Joe (d only) 76. Hometown, USA (d only) 79, etc.

Baer, Parley
American character actor, usually as professional type.

Comanche Territory 50. Deadline USA 52. D-Day Sixth of June 56. Cash McCall 60. Gypsy 62. Fluffy 65. Counterpoint 67. Young Billy Young 69. Punch and Jody (TV) 74. The Amazing Dobermans 77. Rodeo Girl 80. White Dog 82, etc.

TV series: The Adventures of Ozzie and Harriet 55–61. The Andy Griffith Show 62–63. Double Life of Henry Phyfe 66.

Bagdadi, Maroun (1948–1993).
Lebanese director who studied film in Paris in the mid-70s.

Little Wars 82. L'Homme Voilé 87. Hors la Vie 91. *La Fille de l'Air* 92, etc.

Baggott, King (1874–1948).
Tall, powerful American leading man of silent adventure dramas. Made a few early talkies, then retired.

Lady Audley's Secret 12. Ivanhoe 12. Dr Jekyll and Mr Hyde 13. The Corsican Brothers 15. Moonlight Follies 21. Going Straight 22. Tumbleweeds (d only) 25. Notorious Lady 27. The Czar of Broadway 30. Once a Gentleman 30. Scareheads 32. Romance in the Rain 34. Mississippi 35. Come Live with Me 41. Abbott and Costello in Hollywood 45, many others.

Baigelman, Steven (1961–).
Canadian director and screenwriter. Born in Toronto, he studied acting under Sanford Meisner in New York and has also exhibited his paintings in the US and Europe.

Feeling Minnesota 96.

Bailey, John (1942–).
American cinematographer.

Welcome to L.A. 77. Boulevard Nights 79. American Gigolo 80. Ordinary People 80. Honky Tonk Freeway 81. Racing with the Moon 84. Silverado 85. Brighton Beach Memoirs 86. Crossroads 86. Swimming to Cambodia 87. The Accidental Tourist 88. My Blue Heaven 90. In the Line of Fire 93. Groundhog Day 93. China Moon (d) 94. Nobody's Fool 94. As Good as It Gets 97. Living Out Loud 98, etc.

Bailey, Pearl (1918–1990).
American entertainer and Broadway star.

Autobiography: 1968, *The Raw Pearl*.

Variety Girl 47. Isn't It Romantic? 48. Carmen Jones 54. That Certain Feeling 56. St Louis Blues 58. Porgy and Bess 59. All the Fine Young Cannibals 60. The Landlord 70. Norman, Is That You? 76, etc.

Bailey, Raymond (1905–1980).
American small part actor, often a crook or lawyer.

Secret Service of the Air 39. Tidal Wave 40. I Want to Live 55. Picnic 56. The Incredible Shrinking Man 57. Vertigo 58. Al Capone 59. From the Terrace 60, many others.

TV series: My Sister Eileen 59. The Many Loves of Dobie Gillis 61–62. *The Beverly Hillbillies* (as Drysdale) 62–70.

Bailey, Robin (1919–1999).
British comedy character actor with a penchant for dialects as well as the extremes of 'Oxford English'. A television star in such series as *I Didn't Know You Cared, Sorry I'm a Stranger Here Myself, Potter*.

School for Secrets 46. Private Angelo 49. Glory at Sea 52. Just My Luck 57. Hell Drivers 58. The Spy with the Cold Nose 66. You Only Live Twice 67. The Four Feathers (TV) 78. Screamtime 83. Jane and the Lost City 88, etc.

TV series: I Didn't Know You Cared 75–79. Sorry I'm a Stranger Here Myself 81–82. Potter 83. Charters and Caldicott 85.

Bain, Barbara (1931–).
American leading lady, once married to Martin Landau. Best known on TV in series Mission Impossible (66–69). Space 1999 (75–76).

Murder Once Removed (TV) 71. Goodnight My Love 72. A Summer Without Boys (TV) 73. Destination Moonbase Alpha 75. Skinheads 88. Trust Me 89, etc.

Bainbridge, Beryl (1934–).
English novelist and playwright, a former actress.

Adult Fun (a) 72. Sweet William (oa) 80. The Dressmaker (oa) 89. An Awfully Big Adventure (oa) 94.

Bainter, Fay (1892–1968).
American character actress who came to films from the stage in 1934 and specialized in stalwart but sympathetic matrons.

■ This Side of Heaven 34. *Quality Street* 37. The Soldier and the Lady 37. Make Way for Tomorrow 37. *Jezebel* (AA) 38. *White Banners* (AAN) 38. Mother Carey's Chickens 38. The Arkansas Traveller 38. The Shining Hour 38. Yes My Darling Daughter 39. The Lady and the Mob 39. Daughters Courageous 39. Our Neighbours the Carters 39. Young Tom Edison 40. *Our Town* 40. A Bill of Divorcement 40. Maryland 40. Babes on Broadway 41. Woman of the Year 42. *The War Against Mrs Hadley* 42. *Mrs Wiggs of the Cabbage Patch* 42. Journey for Margaret 43. *The Human Comedy* 43. Presenting Lily Mars 43. Salute to the Marines 43. Cry Havoc 43. The Heavenly Body 43. *Dark Waters* (rare villainous role) 44. Three is a Family 44. *State Fair* 45. The Virginian 46. The Kid from Brooklyn 46. *The Secret Life of Walter Mitty* 47. Deep Valley 47. Give My Regards to Broadway 48. *June Bride* 48. Close to My Heart 51. The President's Lady 53. *The Children's Hour* (AAN) 62. Bon Voyage 62.

Baio, Scott (1961–).
American actor who briefly became a star in his teens and is best remembered for the role of Chachi Arcola in the TV series *Happy Days*. Born in Brooklyn, New York, he began in commercials at the age of nine. He was once engaged to actress Pamela Anderson.

Bugsy Malone 76. Foxes 80. The Boy Who Drank Too Much (TV) 81. Something for Joey (TV) 81. Zapped! 82. Evil Laugh 88. Mixed Blessings (TV) 95. Detonator 97, etc.

TV series: Happy Days 77–84. Joanie Loves Chaci 82–83. Charles in Charge 84–85. Baby Talk 91. Diagnosis Murder 94–96.

Baird, Stuart (1948–).
Leading British editor, now working in Hollywood. He was a creative consultant at Warner 1989–92 after being called in to rescue *Tango and Cash*. He also worked uncredited on the final cuts of *Predator, New Jack City, Scrooged* and *Robin Hood: Prince of Thieves*.

Tommy 75. Lisztomania 75. The Omen 76. Valentino 77. Superman (AAN) 78. Superman II 80. Altered States 80. Outland 81. Five Days One Summer 82. Revolution 85. Ladyhawke 85. Lethal Weapon 87. Gorillas in the Mist (AAN) 88. Lethal Weapon II 89. Tango & Cash 89. Die Hard 2 90. Radio Flyer 92. *Demolition Man* 93. Maverick 94, etc.

❝ If your megapic doesn't click, call Baird. – *Variety*

Baird, Teddy.
British producer, in films from 1928 after journalistic experience.

The Browning Version 51. The Importance of Being Earnest 52. Carrington V.C. 56. Two Living One Dead 62, etc.

Bakaleinikoff, Constantin (1898–1966).
Russian-born musical director and composer, in Hollywood. Born in Moscow, he studied at the Moscow Conservatory of Music, and first worked in the USA with the Los Angeles Philharmonic Orchestra. He became musical director of the Grauman Theatre Corp., before working in a similar capacity for Paramount and MGM. In 1941, he became head of RKO's music department, staying until 1952.

Father and Son 29. A Date with the Falcon 41. The Big Street 42. The Tuttles of Tahiti 42. Here We Go Again 42. Cat People 43. Around the World 43. The Seventh Victim 43. I Walked with a Zombie 43. Tarzan Triumphs 43. Tarzan's Desert Mystery 43. Murder My Sweet 44. Step Lively 44. The Curse of the Cat People 44. Betrayal from the East 45. Isle of the Dead 45. Johnny Angel 45. The Falcon in San Francisco 45. Those Endearing Young Charms 45. The Body Snatcher 45. George White's Scandals 45. Deadline at Dawn 46. Sister Kenny 46. Notorious 46. Lady Luck 46. Bedlam 46. Magic Town 47. Mourning Becomes Electra 47. Blood on the Moon 48. Mr Blandings Builds His Dream House 48. If You Knew Susie 48. I Remember Mama 48. Caught 48. Adventure in Baltimore 49. She Wore a Yellow Ribbon 49. Easy Living 49. The Big Steal 49. Where Danger Lives 50. His Kind of Woman 51. At Sword's Point 52. The Big Sky 52. Androcles and the Lion – The Conqueror 56. The Bachelor Party 56, etc.

Bakaleinikoff, Mischa (1890–1960).
Russian-born musical director and composer, in Hollywood. Many of his own scores were for westerns and horror movies.

The Threat 42. One Mysterious Night 44. Cry of the Werewolf 44. Louisiana Hayride 44. Mysterious Intruder (serial) 46. Boston Blackie and the Law 46. The Lone Wolf in London 47. Bulldog Drummond Strikes Back 47. The Last of the Redmen 47. Devil Ship 47. The Prince of Thieves 48. My Dog Rusty 48. Riders in the Sky 49. Barbary Pirate 49. Ace Lucky 49. Prison Warden 49. Chinatown at Midnight 49. Batman and Robin (serial) 49. Blondie's Hero 50. Mule Train 50. Mark of the Gorilla 50. The Adventures of Sir Galahad 50. Captain Video (serial) 51. Harem Girl 51. Gasoline Alley 51. Jungle Manhunt 51. Smuggler's Gold 51. When the Redskins Rode 51. Night Stage to Galveston 52. Thief of Damascus 52. The Kid from Broken Gun 52. The Big Heat 53. Savage Mutiny 53. Serpent of the Nile 53. Prince of Pirates 53. Gun Fury 53. Conquest of Cochise 53. Cannibal Attack 54. It Came from Beneath the Sea 55. Devil Goddess 55. Women's Prison 55. Seminole Uprising 55. Creature with the Atom Brain 55. Earth vs the Flying Saucers 56. The Werewolf 56. Fury at Gunsight Pass 56. The Tall T 57. 20 Million Miles to Earth 57. The Tijuana Story 57. The Phantom Stagecoach 57. The Giant Claw 57. Hellcats of the Navy 57. Zombies of Mora-Tau 57. Screaming Mimi 58. The Lineup 58. Crash Landing 58. Apache Territory 58. The Flying Fontaines 59. The Enemy General 60. Comanche Station 60, many others.

Bakalyan, Richard (1941–).
American character actor, usually as villain.

The Brothers Rico 57. Up Periscope 59. Panic in Year Zero 62. Von Ryan's Express 65. The St Valentine's Day Massacre 67. Chinatown 74. Return from Witch Mountain 78, etc.

Baker, Art (1898–1966) (Arthur Shank).
American general-purpose actor.

Once Upon a Time 44. Spellbound 45. The Farmer's Daughter 47. *Cover Up* 48. Take One False Step 49. Cause for Alarm 51. Living It Up 54. Twelve Hours to Kill 60. Young Dillinger 65. The Wild Angels 66, etc.

Baker, Blanche (1956–).
American actress, the daughter of Carroll Baker.

The Seduction of Joe Tynan 79. French Postcards 79. Mary and Joseph: A Story of Faith (TV) 79. The Awakening of Candra (TV) 81. Cold Feet 84. Sixteen Candles 84. Raw Deal 86. Shakedown 88. The Handmaid's Tale 90, etc.

Baker, Buddy (1918–).
American composer for Walt Disney films.

Summer Magic 63. A Tiger Walks 64. The Gnome-Mobile 67. Napoleon and Samantha (AAN) 72. The Apple Dumpling Gang 75. The Shaggy D.A. 76. Hot Lead and Cold Feet 78. The Apple Dumpling Gang Rides Again 79. The Devil and Max Devlin 81. The Fox and the Hound 81, etc.

Baker, Carroll (1931–).
American leading lady who tried to vary her sex-symbol status via roles of melodramatic intensity. After her Hollywood career fizzled she made many exploitation pictures in Italy. Married director Jack Garfein (1955–69) and actor Donald Burton.

Autobiography: 1984, *Baby Doll*.

Easy to Love 53. *Giant* 56. *Baby Doll* (AAN) 56. The Big Country 58. The Miracle 59. But Not for Me 59. Something Wild 61. Bridge to the Sun 61. How the West Was Won 62. *The Carpetbaggers* 64. Station Six Sahara 64. Cheyenne Autumn 64. Sylvia 64. The Greatest Story Ever Told 65. Mr Moses 65. *Harlow* 65. Jack of Diamonds 67. The Sweet Body of Deborah 68. Paranoia 68. The Harem 68. The Spider 70. The Fourth Mrs Anderson 71.

Captain Apache 71. Bloody Mary 72. Baba Yaga Devil Witch 74. Andy Warhol's Bad 76. The Devil Has Seven Faces 77. The World Is Full of Married Men 79. The Watcher in the Woods 80. Star 80 83. The Secret Diary of Sigmund Freud 84. Native Son 86. Ironweed 87. Blonde Fist 91. Cybereden (It.) 93. North Shore Fish 97. The Game 97. Heart Full of Rain (TV) 97, etc.

❝ More bomb than bombshell. – *Judith Crist*

Baker, Chet (1929–88) (Chesney H. Baker).
Cool American jazz trumpeter and singer who made his name playing with the Gerry Mulligan Quartet in the early 50s. His later career was hampered by his drug addiction and he moved to Europe in the 60s, dying after a fall from a hotel window in Amsterdam. He was the subject of a documentary, *Let's Get Lost* 89.

Baker, Diane (1938–).
Demure-looking American leading actress who can also handle unsympathetic roles. Many TV guest appearances.

The Diary of Anne Frank 59. The Best of Everything 59. Journey to the Centre of the Earth 59. Tess of the Storm Country 60. Hemingway's Adventures of a Young Man 62. The 300 Spartans 62. Nine Hours to Rama 63. Stolen Hours 63. *Strait Jacket* 63. *The Prize* 63. Della (TV) 64. *Marnie* 64. *Mirage* 65. Sands of Beersheba 66. The Dangerous Days of Kiowa Jones (TV) 66. Krakatoa, East of Java 68. The Horse in the Grey Flannel Suit 69. Murder One (TV) 69. The Badge or the Cross (TV) 70. Do You Take This Stranger? (TV) 70. Wheeler and Murdoch (TV) 70. The Old Man Who Cried Wolf (TV) 70. A Little Game (TV) 71. Killer By Night (TV) 71. Congratulations, It's A Boy (TV) 71. A Tree Grows in Brooklyn (TV) 74. The Dream Makers (TV) 75. The Last Survivors (TV) 75. Baker's Hawk 76. The Summer of Sixty-Nine (TV) 77. Danger in the Skies 79. The Pilot 82. The Closer 90. The Silence of the Lambs 91. The Haunted (TV) 91. Twenty Bucks (TV) 93. The Joy Luck Club 93. Imaginary Crimes 94. The Net 95. The Cable Guy 96. Murder at 1600 97, etc.

TV series: *Here We Go Again* 73. The Blue and the Grey 82.

Baker, Eddie (1897–1968) (Edward King).
American comic actor, one of the original Keystone Kops.

Hold Your Breath 24. All at Sea 29. City Lights 31. Monkey Business 31. Babes in Toyland 34. Land of Fury 55, etc.

Baker, George (1929–).
British leading man, also on stage and TV; best known for his role as Inspector Wexford in the TV series *The Ruth Rendell Mysteries* 87–92.

The Intruder 52. The Dam Busters 55. A Hill in Korea 56. The Woman for Joe 56. *The Moonraker* 57. Tread Softly Stranger 58. No Time for Tears 59. Lancelot and Guinevere 62. Curse of the Fly 65. Mr Ten Per Cent 67. Justine 69. On Her Majesty's Secret Service 69. The Spy Who Loved Me 77. I, Claudius (TV) 77. Print Out (TV) 79. North Sea Hijack 79. Hopscotch 80. The Secret Adversary (TV) 82. Goodbye Mr Chips (TV) 84. A Woman of Substance (TV) 84. For Queen and Country 88. Simisola (TV) 96, etc.

TV series: Bowler 73. No Job for a Lady 90–91.

Baker, Graham
American director.

The Final Conflict 81. Impulse 84. Alien Nation 88. Born to Ride 91. Beowulf 98, etc.

Baker, Hylda (1908–1986).
British comedienne in northern music-hall tradition.

■ Saturday Night and Sunday Morning 60. She Knows You Know 61. Up the Junction 67. Oliver! 68. Nearest and Dearest 73.

Baker, Ian.
Australian cinematographer, associated with the films of Fred Schepisi.

Libido 73. The Devil's Playground 76. The Chant of Jimmy Blacksmith 78. Barbarosa 81. The Clinic 82. Iceman 84. Plenty 85. Roxanne 87. A Cry in the Dark 88. The Punisher 89. Everybody Wins 90. The Russia House 90. Six Degrees of Separation 93. I.Q. 94. The Chamber 96. Fierce Creatures 97, etc.

Baker, Joe Don (1936–).
Tough American leading man.

Cool Hand Luke 67. Guns of the Magnificent Seven 69. Adam at Six a.m. 70. Wild Rovers 71. Mongo's Back in Town (TV) 71. Welcome Home Soldier Boys 72. Junior Bonner 72. *Charley Varrick* 73. *Walking Tall* 73. The Outfit 74. Golden Needles 74. Mitchell 74. Framed 75. Crash 76. The Pack 77. To Kill a Cop (TV) 77. Power (TV) 79. Joysticks 83. The Natural 84. Fletch 85. Getting Even 85. The Killing Time 87. The Living Daylights 87. Criminal Law 89. The Children 90. Cape Fear 91. The Distinguished Gentleman 92. Ring of Steel 93. Reality Bites 94. Congo 95. The Underneath 95. Panther 95. The Grass Harp 95. GoldenEye 95. Congo 95. Mars Attacks! 96. Tomorrow Never Dies 97, etc.

TV series: Eischied/Chief of Detectives 79.

Baker, Josephine. (1906–1975) (Josephine Carson).
American dancer, singer and actress. Born in the slums of St Louis, Missouri, she began in vaudeville, causing a sensation when she performed in Paris at the Folies Bergère. She became a French citizen in the early 40s and, in the 50s, established a home for children she had found on her various tours, though she was rarely free of financial difficulties. Married four times; her lovers included novelist Georges SIMENON.

La Sirène des Tropiques 27. Zou Zou 34. Princesse Tam Tam 35. Moulin Rouge 44. The French Way 52. Ten on Every Finger/An Jedem Finger Zehn 54, etc.

Baker, Kathy (1950–).
American leading actress who began as a child and then spent time in France, studying Cordon Bleu cookery.

The Right Stuff 83. The Killing Affair 86. My Sister's Keeper 86. Street Smart (AAN) 87. Clean and Sober 88. Permanent Record 88. Dad 89. Jacknife 89. Edward Scissorhands 90. Article 99 92. Mad Dog and Glory 92. Lush Life 93. To Gillian on Her 37th Birthday 96. Inventing the Abbots 97. Weapons of Mass Distraction (TV) 97, etc.

TV series: Picket Fences 92.

Baker, Kenny (1912–1985).
American crooner, popular in the late 30s but subsequently little heard of.

King of Burlesque 35. The Goldwyn Follies 38. The Mikado (GB: as Nanki Poo) 39. 52nd Street 39. At the Circus 39. Hit Parade of 1941 40. Silver Skates 42. Doughboys in Ireland 43. The Harvey Girls 46. That's Entertainment III 94, etc.

Baker, Lenny (1945–1982).
American actor of stage and screen. He died of cancer.

The Hospital 71. The Paper Chase 73. *Next Stop, Greenwich Village* 76, etc.

Baker, Phil (1896–1963).
American radio personality who appeared in a few films.

Gift of Gab 34. The Goldwyn Follies 38. The Gang's All Here 43. *Take It or Leave It* 44, etc.

Baker, Rick (1950–).
American make-up and special effects artist.

Octaman 71. Schlock 72. The Thing with Two Heads 72. It's Alive 74. King Kong 76. *Star Wars* 77. The Incredible Melting Man 77. *An American Werewolf in London* (AA) 81. Greystoke (AAN) 84. Teen Wolf 85. Harry and the Hendersons (AA) 87. Coming to America (AAN) 88. Gorillas in the Mist 88. Gremlins 2: The New Batch 90. Wolf 94. Ed Wood (AA) 94. Baby's Day Out 94. The Frighteners 96. Escape from L.A. 96. The Nutty Professor (AA) 96. Men in Black (AA) 97. Mighty Joe Young 98, etc.

Baker, Robert S. (1916–).
British producer: co-founder with Monty Berman of Tempean Films, which since 1948 has produced many co-features, also *The Saint* and other TV series.

■ AS DIRECTOR: Melody Club 49. Blackout 50. 13 East Street 52. The Steel Key 53. Passport to Treason 56. Jack the Ripper 58. The Siege of Sidney Street 60. The Hellfire Club 60. The Treasure of Monte Cristo 61.

Baker, Roy Ward (1916–).
Notable British director whose career declined in the 60s. Served apprenticeship at Gainsborough 1934–39, then war service.

The October Man 47. The Weaker Sex 48. *Morning Departure* 50. I'll Never Forget You (US) 51. *Inferno* (US) 52. Don't Bother to Knock (US) 52. Passage Home 54. Jacqueline 56. Tiger in the Smoke 56. *The One That Got Away* 57. *A Night to Remember* 58. The Singer Not the Song (& p) 60. Flame in the Streets (& p) 61. The Valiant 61. Two Left Feet 64. *Quatermass and the Pit* 67. The Anniversary 68. Moon Zero Two 69. The Vampire Lovers 70. Scars of Dracula 70. Dr Jekyll and Sister Hyde 71. Asylum 72. And Now the Screaming Starts 73. Vault of Horror 73. The Legend of the Seven Golden Vampires 74. The Monster Club 80. The Flame Trees of Thika (TV) 81, etc.

Baker, Sir Stanley (1927–1976).
Virile Welsh actor who rose from character roles to stardom, projecting honesty or villainy with equal ease.

Biography: 1977, *Portrait of an Actor* by Anthony Storey.

■ Undercover 41. All Over the Town 48. Obsession 49. Your Witness 50. The Rossiter Case 51. Cloudburst 51. Captain Horatio Hornblower 51. Home to Danger 51. Whispering Smith Hits London 52. Lili Marlene 52. *The Cruel Sea* 53. The Red Beret 53. Knights of the Round Table 53. *Hell Below Zero* 54. The Good Die Young 54. Beautiful Stranger 54. Helen of Troy 55. Alexander the Great 55. *Richard III* (as Henry Tudor) 55. Child in the House 56. A Hill in Korea 56. Checkpoint 56. *Campbell's Kingdom* 57. *Hell Drivers* 57. Violent Playground 58. Sea Fury 58. The Angry Hills 59. Hell Is a City 59. Blind Date 60. Jet Storm 60. Yesterday's Enemy 60. *The Criminal* 60. The Guns of Navarone 61. A Prize of Arms 61. Sodom and Gomorrah 62. The Man Who Finally Died 62. Eva 62. In the French Style 62. *Zulu* (& co-p) 64. Dingaka 65. Sands of the Kalahari (& co-p) 65. *Accident* 67. Robbery (& co-p) 67. Code Name: Heraclitus (TV) 67. Girl with Pistol 68. Where's Jack? 69. The Last Grenade 69. The Games 70. Perfect Friday 70. Popsy Pop 71. Schizoid 71. Who Killed Lamb? (TV) 72. Innocent Bystanders 72. Graceless Go I (TV) 74. Zorro 75.

TV series: How Green Was My Valley 76.

Baker, Tom (1936–).
British character actor with a larger-than-life air. On TV as Doctor Who 74–82. The second of his three wives was actress Lalla Ward.

Autobiography: 1997, *Who on Earth Is Tom Baker?*

Nicholas and Alexandra (as Rasputin) 71. Luther 73. Vault of Horror 73. The Golden Voyage of Sinbad 73. The Mutations 74. Angels Die Hard 84. The Zany Adventures of Robin Hood 84, etc.

TV series: Medics 91–95.

❝ Doctor Who was the most wonderful part – I was a madman to give it up. They wouldn't give me the film, would they? They won't know how to do it. Popular films are tawdry, about images and not about thinking. – *T.B.*

The Doctor Who Society in America have conventions and I go among them and lay on hands. Middle-aged ladies stick their tongues in my ear under the pretext of listening. The odd thing is that after the age of 47 chunky little females have tongues like shrapnel. It makes me slightly deaf. A blessing in disguise in our business. – *T.B.*

I like the dead. They're so uncritical. – *T.B.*

Bakewell, William (1908–1993).
American general-purpose actor. Married actress Jennifer HOLT.

The Heart Thief 27. All Quiet on the Western Front 30. Spirit of Notre Dame 31. Three Cornered Moon 33. Cheers for Miss Bishop 41. Davy Crockett 55, many others.

TV series: The Pinky Lee Show 50.

Bakshi, Ralph (1938–).
American director of animated features. Born in Palestine, he became a director of Terrytoons cartoons from 1964, including creating the *Sad Cat* series 65–68, directing a series of 17 James Hound cartoons 66–67, spoofing James Bond, and a series of 10 *The Mighty Heroes* 69–71, with such characters as Diaper Man and Cuckoo Man. He also directed for Famous Studios two of the *Go-Go Toons* series 67, and three of the *Fractured Fables* series 68. His first animated features featured sex and drugs, his later ones concentrated on sword and sorcery, while *Cool World* mixed animation and live action.

Book: 1989, *The Animated Art of Ralph Bakshi.*

Fritz the Cat (wd) 71. Heavy Traffic (wd) 73. Coonskin/Streetfight (wd) 75. Hey, Good Lookin' (p, wd) 75 (released 82). Wizards (d) 77. Lord of the Rings (d) 78. American Pop (d) 81. Fire and Ice (d) 83. Cool World 92, etc.

Bakula, Scott (1954–).
American leading actor, best known for his role as Dr Sam Beckett in the 90s TV series *Quantum Leap*.

The Last Fling (TV) 86. Sibling Rivalry 90. Necessary Roughness 91. Color of Night 94. A Passion to Kill 94. My Family/Mi Familia 95. Lord of Illusions 95. The Invaders (TV) 95, etc.

TV series: Gung Ho 86–87. Eisenhower & Lutz 88.

Balaban, Barney (1888–1971).
American executive, former exhibitor, president of Paramount 1936–64.

Balaban, Burt (1922–1965).
American director, son of Barney Balaban.

Stranger from Venus (GB) 54. Lady of Vengeance 57. High Hell 58. Murder Inc. 60. Mad Dog Coll 61. The Gentle Rain 66, etc.

Balaban, Robert (Bob) (1945–).
American character actor turned director.

Midnight Cowboy 69. Me Natalie 69. Close Encounters of the Third Kind 78. Altered States 80. Prince of the City 81. Absence of Malice 81. Whose Life Is It Anyway? 81. End of the Line 88. Parents (d) 88. Dead Bang 89. Bob Roberts 92. For Love or Money 93. Amos & Andrew 93. My Boyfriend's Back (d) 93. The Last Good Time (d) 94. Greedy/Greed (a) 94. Pie in the Sky 95. The Late Shift (TV) 97. Deconstructing Harry 97. Clockwatchers 97, etc.

Balanchine, George (1904–1983).
Distinguished Russian-born American choreographer who worked occasionally in Hollywood.

Dark Red Roses 29. The Goldwyn Follies 38. I Was an Adventuress 40. George Balanchine's The Nutcracker 93.

Balasko, Josiane (1952–).
French actress, screenwriter, dramatist and director, of Yugoslavian descent. She is best known internationally for her role as the plump and homely secretary for whom Gérard Depardieu's car dealer abandons his beautiful wife in *Too Beautiful for You*.

Le Locataire (a) 76. Une Fille Unique (a) 76. Dites-Lui que Je l'Aime (a) 77. Pardon Mon Affaire, Too/Nous Irons Tous au Paradis (a) 77. Les Bronzes Font du Ski (a) 78. L'Année Prochaine Si Tout Va Bien (co-w) 81. Clara et les Chics Types (a) 81. Hotel des Amériques (a) 81. Le Père Noel Est une Ordure (a) 82. P'tit Con (a) 84. La Vengeance du Serpent à Plumes (a) 84. Nuit d'Ivresse (a, w) 86. Les Keufs (a, wd) 87. *Too Beautiful for You*/Trop Belle pour Toi (a) 89. Ma Vie Est un Enfer (a, wd) 91. A Shadow of a Doubt/L'Ombre du Doute (a) 93. Grosse Fatigue (a) 94. *French Twist*/Gauzon Maudit (a, wd) 95. A Great Shout of Love/Un Grand Cri d'Amour (a, wd) 98, etc.

Balazs, Bela (1884–1949) (Hubert Bauer).
Hungarian writer. Wrote book, *Theory of the Film*.

Die Dreigroschenoper 31. *The Blue Light* 31.

Balch, Antony (1937–1980).
British producer, director, screenwriter, editor and distributor, mainly of avant-garde films. His own short films featured writer William BURROUGHS, but his two commercial features stuck to the clichés of their genres while also parodying them. Died of cancer.

Towers Open Fire (short) 63. The Cut-Ups (short) 67. Secrets of Sex/Bizarre (co-w, p, d) 69. Bill & Tony (short) 72. Horror Hospital (co-w, d) 73.

Balchin, Nigel (1908–1970).
British novelist and screenwriter. Educated at Cambridge University, he was also a businessman and during the Second World War became Scientific Adviser to the Army Council. Married twice.

Fame Is the Spur 47. Mine Own Executioner (& oa) 47. The Small Back Room (& oa) 48. Mandy 52. Malta Story 53. Josephine and Men (& story) 55. The Man Who Never Was 55. 23 Paces to Baker Street (US) 56. The Blue Angel (US) 59. Circle of Deception 60. Suspect (& oa) 60. The Singer Not the Song 60. Barabbas (It.) 61, etc.

Balcon, Jill (1925–).
British actress, daughter of Sir Michael Balcon. She is the mother of Daniel Day-Lewis.
Nicholas Nickleby 47. Good Time Girl 48. Highly Dangerous 50. Edward II 91, etc.

Balcon, Sir Michael (1896–1977).
British executive producer. During a long and distinguished career he headed Gainsborough, Gaumont-British, MGM-British, Ealing, Bryanston and independent production companies, and was directly responsible for the planning and production of many famous films. He served as a model for the character of the mill-owner, played by Cecil Parker, in *The Man in the White Suit*.
Autobiography: 1969, *A Lifetime of Films*.
His more personal projects include: Woman to Woman 23. The Pleasure Garden 25. The Lodger 26. Easy Virtue 27. Man of Aran 33. The Man Who Knew Too Much 34. The 39 Steps 35. Sabotage 37. A Yank at Oxford 38. The Citadel 38. Goodbye Mr Chips 39. Convoy 40. The Next of Kin 42. The Bells Go Down 42. Champagne Charlie 44. Dead of Night 45. The Captive Heart 46. Hue and Cry 46. Nicholas Nickleby 47. It Always Rains on Sunday 48. Scott of the Antarctic 48. Kind Hearts and Coronets 49. Whisky Galore 49. Passport to Pimlico 49. The Blue Lamp 50. The Man in the White Suit 51. The Lavender Hill Mob 51. The Cruel Sea 53. The Ladykillers 55. Dunkirk 58. Saturday Night and Sunday Morning 60. Tom Jones 63.
❂ For steering his part of the British film industry in very much the right way, and for refusing to lower his standards. *Dead of Night*.
❝ I always look for people whose ideas coincide with mine, and then I'm ready to give them a chance to make a name for themselves. – M.B.
We made films at Ealing that were good, bad and indifferent, but they were indisputably British. They were rooted in the soil of the country. – M.B.

Balderston, John (1899–1954).
Anglo-American screenwriter, usually in collaboration, with a penchant for romantic and fantastic themes.
Frankenstein 31. *The Mummy* 32. Smilin' Through 32 and 41. *Berkeley Square* (oa) 33. Lives of a Bengal Lancer (AAN) 34. The Mystery of Edwin Drood 35. *Mad Love* 35. *Bride of Frankenstein* 35. Beloved Enemy 36. *The Prisoner of Zenda* 37. Victory 40. Tennessee Johnson 42. Gaslight (AAN) 44. Red Planet Mars 52, many others.

Baldi, Ferdinando (1927–).
Italian director.
David and Goliath (co-d) 59. Duel of the Champions 71. Blindman 71. Get Mean 76. My Name Is Trinity 76. The Sicilian Connection 77. Comin' at Ya 81. Treasure of the Four Crowns 83. War Bus 86, etc.

Baldwin, Adam (1962–).
American actor.
My Bodyguard 80. Ordinary People 80. D.C. Cab 83. Reckless 84. Hadley's Rebellion 84. Love on the Run (TV) 85. Bad Guys 86. Full Metal Jacket 87. Cohen and Tate 88. Next of Kin 89. Internal Affairs 90. Predator 2 90. Radio Flyer 92. Bitter Harvest 93. Eight Hundred Leagues down the Amazon 93. Wyatt Earp 94. Lover's Knot 96. Independence Day 96, etc.
TV series: The Cape 96– .

Baldwin, Alec (1958–).
American leading actor. Born in New York, he studied at George Washington University, New York University, and New York's Lee Strasberg Institute. He is partner in the production company Eldorado Pictures. Married actress Kim Basinger. He is the brother of actors Daniel, Stephen and William Baldwin.
Ghosts of Mississippi 96. Heaven's Prisoners 96. The Edge 97. Mercury Rising 98. Outside Providence 99, etc.
TV series: Cutter to Houston 83.

❝ I'm starting to feel I have to cure my addiction to Hollywood money, because while it's delightful, it's also insidious. – *A.B., 1997*

Baldwin, Daniel (1961–).
American actor, the brother of Alec Baldwin.
The Heroes of Desert Storm 91. Nothing but Trouble 91. Harley Davidson and the Marlboro Man 91. Car 54, Where Are You? 94. Bodily Harm 95. Mulholland Falls 96. Trees Lounge 96. John Carpenter's Vampires 98. Love Kills 98, etc.
TV series: Homicide: Life on the Street 93.

Baldwin, Faith (1893–1978).
American novelist.
Scenario credits include: The Moon's Our Home 36. Men Are Such Fools 37. Apartment for Peggy 50. Queen for a Day 51.

Baldwin, Stephen (1966–).
American leading actor, the brother of Alec Baldwin.
The Beast 88. Born on the Fourth of July 89. Bitter Harvest 93. Posse 93. Threesome 94. 8 Seconds 94. A Simple Twist of Fate 94. Mrs Parker and the Vicious Circle 94. Fall Time 95. The Usual Suspects 95. Dead Weekend 95. Bio-Dome 96. Fled 96. Half-Baked 97. One Tough Cop 98. Friends and Lovers 98, etc.
TV series: The Young Riders 89–92.
❝ If there's one thing I learned in the business, it's at least have your package looking good. – *S.B.*

Baldwin, Walter (1887–1977).
American character actor, often in owlish or countrified roles.
Angels Over Broadway 40. All That Money Can Buy 41. Kings Row 42. Happy Land 43. I'll Be Seeing You 44. The Lost Weekend 45. The Best Years of Our Lives 46. Mourning Becomes Electra 47. The Man from Colorado 48. Cheaper by the Dozen 50. Carrie 52. Scandal at Scourie 53. Glory 55. Cheyenne Autumn 64. Rosemary's Baby 68, many others.

Baldwin, William (1963–).
American actor, the brother of actor Alec Baldwin.
Born on the Fourth of July 89. Internal Affairs 90. Flatliners 90. Backdraft 91. Three of Hearts 92. Sliver 93. A Pyromaniac's Love Story 95. Fair Game 95. Curdled 96. Virus 98. Shattered Image 98, etc.

Bale, Christian (1974–).
Welsh actor who made his screen debut as a teenager in the leading role in *Empire of the Sun*.
Empire of the Sun 87. Land of Faraway 88. Henry V 89. Treasure Island (TV) 90. Newsies/News Boys 92. Swing Kids 93. Little Women 94. The Portrait of a Lady 96. Joseph Conrad's Secret Agent 96. Velvet Goldmine 98. All the Little Animals 98, etc.

Balfour, Betty (1903–1978).
British comedienne of silent days, a popular favourite of the 20s as pert heroine of *Cinders*, *Love Life and Laughter* and the *Squibs* series.
The Brat 30. The Vagabond Queen 30. Paddy the Next Best Thing 33. Evergreen 34. Squibs (remake) 35. 29 Acacia Avenue 45, etc.

Balfour, Michael (1918–1997).
English character actor, frequently as a taxi-driver, serviceman or dumb gangster. Born in Kent, he began in repertory theatre in 1936, and from the mid-40s assumed an American identity as a Detroit-born former child actor to obtain a role in the London production of Garson Kanin's play *Born Yesterday*. He was also a sculptor and painter; from the late 70s to the mid-90s, he also worked as a circus clown.
Just William's Luck 47. The Front Page (TV) 48. No Orchids for Miss Blandish 48. Cosh Boy/The Slasher 52. Genevieve 53. Albert RN 53. The Sea Shall Not Have Them 54. Meet Mr Callaghan 54. The Belles of St Trinian's 54. Gentlemen Marry Brunettes 55. Reach for the Sky 56. Quatermass II/Enemy from Space 57. Look Back in Anger 59. Carry On Constable 60. Sink the Bismarck! 60. The Hellfire Club 61. The Sicilians 64. Alfie 64. Fahrenheit 451 66. The Oblong Box 69. The Private Life of Sherlock Holmes 70. Macbeth 71. Joseph Andrews 76. Candleshoe 77. Prisoner of Zenda 79. The Holcroft Covenant 85. Revenge of Billy the Kid 91, many others.

TV series: Mark Saber 55–56. The Splendid Spur 60.

Balin, Ina (1937–1990) (Ina Rosenberg).
American leading lady, with stage experience.
Compulsion 58. The Black Orchid 58. The Comancheros 61. The Patsy 64. The Greatest Story Ever Told 65. Run Like a Thief 68. Charro 69. The Projectionist 71. The Don is Dead 73, etc.

Balin, Mireille (1909–1968).
French leading lady.
Don Quixote 33. Pépé le Moko 36. Gueule d'Amour 37, etc.

Balk, Fairuza (1974–).
American actress. Born in Point Reyes, California, she moved with her mother to England in the early 80s and studied at the Bush Davies Performing Arts School before appearing in *Return to Oz*, returning to live in Vancouver, Canada, in the late 80s.
Return to Oz (as Dorothy) 85. Valmont 89. Gas Food Lodging 91. Imaginary Crimes 94. Tollbooth 94. Things to Do in Denver When You're Dead 95. The Craft 96. What Is It? (voice) 96. The Island of Dr Moreau 96. The Maker 97. American Perfekt 97. American History X 98. The Waterboy 98. There's No Fish Food in Heaven 98. Great Sex 99, etc.

Ball, Lucille (1911–1989).
American comedienne, a former Goldwyn girl who after a generally unrewarding youth in the movies, turned in middle age to TV and became known as one of the world's great female clowns and a highly competent production executive. She was formerly married to actor Desi Arnaz. Their children were actors Desi Arnaz Jnr and Lucie Arnaz. Desilu, the production company she set up with Arnaz, was responsible not only for *I Love Lucy*, but also such series as *December Bride*, *The Untouchables* and *Mannix*. It was sold to Paramount in 1967 for some $20m. She was played by Frances Fisher in the TV movie *Lucy and Desi: Before the Laughter* 91.
Autobiography: 1996, *Love, Lucy*.
Biographies: 1973, *Lucy: The Bittersweet Life of Lucille Ball* by Joe Morella and Edward Z. Epstein; 1994, *Lucille: The Life of Lucille Ball* by Kathleen Brady.
■ Broadway Thru a Keyhole 33. Blood Money 33. Roman Scandals 33. Moulin Rouge 33. Nana 34. Bottoms Up 34. Hold that Girl 34. Bulldog Drummond Strikes Back 34. The Affairs of Cellini 34. Kid Millions 34. Broadway Bill 34. Jealousy 34. Men of the Night 34. Fugitive Lady 34. Carnival (first billed role) 34. Roberta 35. Old Man Rhythm 35. Top Hat 35. The Three Musketeers 35. I Dream Too Much 35. Chatterbox 36. Follow the Fleet 36. The Farmer in the Dell 36. Bunker Bean 36. That Girl from Paris 36. Don't Tell the Wife 37. *Stage Door* 37. Joy of Living 38. Go Chase Yourself 38. Having A Wonderful Time 38. *The Affairs of Annabel* 38. Room Service 38. The Next Time I Marry 38. Annabel Takes a Tour 39. Beauty for the Asking 39. Twelve Crowded Hours 39. Panama Lady 39. *Five Came Back* 39. That's Right You're Wrong 39. The Marines Fly High 40. You Can't Fool Your Wife 40. Dance Girl Dance 40. Too Many Girls 40. A Guy, a Girl and Gob 40. Look Who's Laughing 41. Valley of the Sun 42. *The Big Street* (serious role) 42. Seven Days Leave 42. *Du Barry was a Lady* 43. Best Foot Forward 43. Thousands Cheer 43. Meet the People 44. *Without Love* 45. Abbott and Costello in Hollywood 45. Ziegfeld Follies 46. The Dark Corner 46. *Easy to Wed* 46. Two Smart People 46. Lover Come Back 46. Lured 47. *Her Husband's Affairs* 47. *Sorrowful Jones* 49. Easy Living 49. Miss Grant Takes Richmond 49. *Fancy Pants* 50. The Fuller Brush Girl 50. The Magic Carpet 51. *The Long Long Trailer* 54. Forever Darling 56. *The Facts of Life* 60. Critic's Choice 63. A Guide for the Married Man 67. *Yours Mine and Ours* 68. Mame 74. Stone Pillow (TV) 85.
TV series: *I Love Lucy* 51–55. *The Lucy Show* 62–68. *Here's Lucy* 68–73. Life with Lucy 86.

Ball, Suzan (1933–1955).
American leading lady of the early 50s.
Untamed Frontier 52. East of Sumatra 53. City Beneath the Sea 53. War Arrow 54. Chief Crazy Horse 54, etc.

Ball, Vincent (1924–).
Australian actor, in England for a time.
A Town Like Alice 56. Robbery under Arms 57. Danger Within 58. Identity Unknown 60. Where Eagles Dare 68. Oh What a Lovely War 69. Deadline (Aus) 81. Phar Lap (Aus) 83. The Year My Voice Broke (Aus) 87, etc.

Ballard, Carroll (1937–).
American director with a flair for wild life.
The Black Stallion 80. Never Cry Wolf 83. Nutcracker: The Motion Picture 86. Wind 92. Fly Away Home 96, etc.

Ballard, J. G. (1930–).
English writer, mainly of science fiction in an avant garde manner. Born in Shanghai, his childhood experiences in a Japanese prison camp during the Second World War formed the basis for his best-known novel, *Empire of the Sun*, which was filmed by Steven Spielberg. He studied medicine before becoming a full-time writer in 1962.
When Dinosaurs Ruled the Earth (treatment) 70. Empire of the Sun (oa) 87. Crash (oa) 96.
❝ I'm very proud that my first screen credit was for what is, without doubt, the worst film ever made. – *J.G.B.*
Film, for most of this century, has been a far more serious medium than the novel. – *J.G.B*

Ballard, Kay(e) (1926–) (Catherine Balotta).
American comedienne with stage experience.
The Girl Most Likely 58. A House is Not a Home 64. Freaky Friday 77. Falling in Love Again 80. Tiger Warshaw 87. Modern Love 90. Eternity 90, etc.
TV series: The Mothers-in-Law 67–68. The Doris Day Show 70–71.

Ballard, Lucien (1908–1988).
Distinguished American cinematographer. He was married to actress Merle Oberon (1945–49).
Crime and Punishment 35. The King Steps Out 36. Craig's Wife 36. The Shadow 37. Penitentiary 38. *Blind Alley* 39. The Villain Still Pursued Her 40. Wild Geese Calling 41. The Undying Monster 42. Orchestra Wives 42. Holy Matrimony 43. *The Lodger* 44. *Laura* (co-ph) 44. This Love of Ours 45. Temptation 46. Night Song 47. Berlin Express 48. The House on Telegraph Hill 51. O. Henry's Full House 52. *Inferno* (3-D) 53. New Faces 54. White Feather 55. The Proud Ones 56. *The Killing* 56. Band of Angels 57. Murder by Contract 58. Al Capone 59. Pay or Die 60. The Parent Trap 61. Ride the High Country 62. *The Caretakers* (AAN) 63. The New Interns 64. Boeing Boeing 65. Nevada Smith 66. *Hour of the Gun* 67. Will Penny 68. *The Wild Bunch* 69. True Grit 69. The Ballad of Cable Hogue 70. The Hawaiians 70. What's the Matter with Helen? 71. Junior Bonner 72. The Getaway 72. Breakout 75. Breakheart Pass 76. St Ives 76, etc.

Ballhaus, Michael (1935–).
German cinematographer who worked on many of Fassbinder's films before moving to Hollywood in the 80s.
Whity 70. Adele Spitzeder 72. The Bitter Tears of Petra von Kant/Die Bitteren Tränen der Petra von Kant 72. Adolf und Marlene 77. Despair 78. The Marriage of Maria Braun/Die Ehe der Maria Braun 79. Malou 81. Reckless 84. Heartbreakers 84. After Hours 85. The Color of Money 86. Under the Cherry Moon 86. Broadcast News (AAN) 87. The House on Carroll Street 88. Dirty Rotten Scoundrels 88. The Last Temptation of Christ 88. Working Girl 88. The Fabulous Baker Boys (AAN) 89. GoodFellas 90. Postcards from the Edge 90. Guilty by Suspicion 90. What about Bob? 91. The Mambo Kings 92. Bram Stoker's Dracula 92. The Age of Innocence 93. I'll Do Anything 94. Quiz Show 94. Outbreak 95. Sleepers 96. Air Force One 97. Primary Colors 98, etc.

Ballin, Hugo (1879–1956).
American director and art director of silents. He studied in Rome and was a noted portrait and mural painter. Many of the films he directed starred his wife Mabel Ballin (1885–1958). Retired from films in the late 20s.
Baby Mine (co-d) 17. Jane Eyre 21. East Lynne 21. Vanity Fair 23. The Shining Adventure 25. *The Love of Sunya* (art d only) 27. The Princess and the Pirate (art consultant) 44, etc.

Balmain, Pierre (1914–1982).
French fashion designer who set up his own couture business in the 50s and worked on more than 70 films.
Sabrina (US) 54. Funny Face (US) 56. Bonsoir Paris 56. The Glass Tower/Der Glaserne Turm (Ger.) 57. Paris Holiday (US) 57. The Reluctant Debutante (US) 58. The Millionairess (GB) 60. The Roman Spring of Mrs Stone (GB) 61. Tender Is the Night (GB) 61. Two Weeks in Another Town (US) 62. Love Is a Funny Thing/Un Homme qui Me Plaît 69, etc.

Balsam, Martin (1919–1996).
American character actor of quiet and comfortable presence: range varies from executive to stagecoach driver.
■ On the Waterfront 54. *Twelve Angry Men* 57. *Time Limit* 57. Marjorie Morningstar 58. Al Capone 59. Middle of the Night 59. Everybody Go Home (It.) 60. *Psycho* (as the ill-fated private detective) 60. Ada 61. Breakfast at Tiffany's 61. Cape Fear 61. The Captive City 63. Who's Been Sleeping in My Bed? 63. *The Carpetbaggers* (as the Louis B. Mayer type studio chief) 64. Youngblood Hawke 64. *Seven Days in May* 64. Harlow 65. The Bedford Incident 65. *A Thousand Clowns* (AA) 65. After the Fox 66. Hombre 67. Me Natalie 69. Trilogy (TV) 69. *The Good Guys and the Bad Guys* 69. Tora! Tora! Tora! 70. Catch 22 70. Little Big Man 70. The Old Man Who Cried Wolf (TV) 70. Hunters Are for Killing (TV) 70. *The Anderson Tapes* 71. Confessions of a Police Commissioner (It.) 71. The Man (TV) 72. Night of Terror (TV) 72. *Summer Wishes Winter Dreams* 73. The Stone Killer 73. Six Million Dollar Man (TV) 73. Money to Burn (TV) 74. Trapped Beneath the Sea (TV) 74. The Taking of Pelham 123 74. Murder on the Orient Express 74. Miles to Go Before I Sleep (TV) 75. Corruption in the Halls of Justice (It.) 75. Mitchell 75. Death Among Friends (TV) 75. All the President's Men 76. Two Minute Warning 76. The Sentinel 76. Raid on Entebbe (TV) 77. Silver Bears 77. Rainbow (TV) 78. The Seeding of Sarah Burns (TV) 79. The House on Garibaldi Street (TV) 79. Aunt Mary (TV) 79. The Love Tapes (TV) 79. Cuba 79. There Goes the Bride 80. The Salamander 81. Little Gloria . . . Happy at Last (TV) 82. The Goodbye People 84. St Elmo's Fire 85. Death Wish 3 85. Delta Force 86. Space (TV) 87. Queenie (TV) 87. Private Investigations 87. Two Evil Eyes/Due Occhi Diabolici 89. Cape Fear 91. Innocent Prey 92. The Silence of the Hams (It.) 94.
TV series: Archie Bunker's Place 79–81.

Balser, Ewald (1898–1978).
Austrian character actor in German films.
Rembrandt (title role) 42. The Last Act 48. Eroica (as Beethoven) 49. William Tell 56. Jedermann 62, many others.

Balto (1921–1933).
The lead husky in a sled team that brought an anti-diphtheria vaccine to the stricken town of Nome, Alaska, in 1925, he and the other dogs starred in a silent film, *Balto's Race to Nome*. They were briefly a vaudeville and sideshow attraction before spending the remainder of their lives at Cleveland Zoo. *Balto*, an animated feature in which he is depicted as a cross-breed between wolf and dog, was released in 1995, directed by Simon Wells. A commemorative statue to Balto stands in New York's Central Park.

Bancroft, Anne (1931–) (Anna Maria Italiano).
Warm, ambitious and effective American leading actress who after TV experience went to Hollywood in 1952 and made inferior routine films; fled to Broadway stage and after triumph in *The Miracle Worker* returned to films as a star. She married Mel Brooks in 1964.
Don't Bother to Knock 52. Treasure of the Golden Condor 52. Tonight We Sing 53. The Kid from Left Field 53. Demetrius and the Gladiators 54. The Raid 54. Gorilla at Large 54. A Life in the Balance 54. New York Confidential 55. The Naked Street 55. Walk the Proud Land 56. Nightfall 56. Savage Wilderness/The Last Frontier 56. The Restless Breed 57. The Girl in Black Stockings 57. So Soon to Die (TV) 57. *The Miracle Worker* (AA, BFA) 62. *The Pumpkin Eater* (AAN, BFA) 64. *The Slender Thread* 65. Seven Women 66. *The Graduate* (AAN) 67. *Young Winston* 72. The Prisoner of Second Avenue 75. The Hindenburg 76. Lipstick 76. Silent Movie 76. Jesus of Nazareth (TV) 77. *The Turning Point* (AAN) 77. The Elephant Man 80. Fatso (also directed) 80. Marco Polo (TV) 81. To Be or Not to Be 83. Garbo Talks 84. Agnes of God (AAN) 85. Night Mother 86. *84 Charing Cross Road* 86. Torch Song Trilogy 88. Bert Rigby, You're a Fool 89. Broadway Bound (TV) 91. Honeymoon in Vegas 92. Love Potion No. 9 92. Malice 93. Point of No Return 93. Mr Jones 93. Oldest Living Confederate Widow Tells All (TV) 94. How to Make an American Quilt 95. Home for the Holidays 95. Dracula: Dead and Loving It 95. The Sunchaser 96. Great Expectations 97. G.I. Jane 97. Critical Care 97. Antz (voice) 98, etc.

Bancroft, George (1882–1956).
Burly American actor who after a period in the Navy became popular in Broadway musicals and straight plays. Went to Hollywood in the 20s and found his strong masculine personality much in demand for tough or villainous roles, almost always in run-of-the-mill films.
The Journey's End 21. *Driven* 21. *Pony Express* 25. *Code of the West* 25. *Old Ironsides* 26. *Underworld* 27. White Gold 27. Docks of New York 28. Thunderbolt (AAN) 29. Derelict 30. Ladies Love Brutes 30. Scandal Sheet 31. Lady and Gent 33. Blood Money 33. Mr Deeds Goes to Town 36. John Meade's Woman 37. Angels with Dirty Faces 38. *Stagecoach* 39. Each Dawn I Die 39. Young Tom Edison 40. Texas 41. Syncopation 41. Whistling in Dixie 42, many others.
❝ When words roll from his tongue, you expect them to be punctuated by lightning. – *N.Y. Times, 1929*

Band, Albert (1924–) (Alfredo Antonini).
Italian-born director and producer, in Hollywood since the 40s.
The Young Guns 56. I Bury the Living (& p) 57. Face of Fire 59. I Pascali Rossi 63. The Tramplers (& p) 66. A Minute to Pray, a Second to Die (p, co-w only) 68. Dracula's Dog 77. She Came to the Valley 79. Ghoulies II 88. Honey, I Blew Up the Kid (p) 92. Prehysteria (co-d) 93. Dragon World (co-p) 93, etc.

Band, Charles (1952–).
American producer and director of low-budget horror movies, many of them released direct to video. The son of Albert Band, he is founder of the production company Full Moon Entertainment.
AS PRODUCER: Ghoulies 85. Re-Animator 85. Crawlspace (ex p) 86. Troll (ex p) 86. Eliminators 86. Catacombs 87. Puppetmaster 89. Puppetmaster II 90. Puppetmaster III 91. Netherworld 91. Bad Channels 91. Demonic Toys 91. Arcade 92. Dragon World 93. Oblivion (& story) 94, etc.
AS DIRECTOR: Crash! 77. Parasite 82. Metalstorm: The Destruction of Jared-Syn 83. The Dungeonmaster (co-d) 85. Future Cop 85. Trancers 85. Pulsepounders 88. Meridian: Kiss of the Beast 90. Trancers II 91. Doctor Modrid (co-d) 91. Trancers III 92. Prehysteria (co-d) 93, etc.

Band, Richard H. (1953–).
American composer, the son of Albert Band.
Laserblast 78. The Day Time Ended 79. Dr Heckle and Mr Hype 80. Parasite 82. Time Walker 83. Ghoulies 85. Re-Animator 85. Eliminators 86. Terrorvision 86. Troll 86. Dolls 87. Prison 88. Puppet Master 89. Bride of Re-Animator 90. Doctor Mordrid: Master of the Unknown 90. Crash and Burn 90. The Resurrected 91. The Pit and the Pendulum 91. Remote 93. Doll vs Demonic Toys 93. Shrunken Heads 94. Dragonworld 94. Magic Island 95. Castle Freak 95. Head of the Family 96. Hideous 97, etc.

Banderas, Antonio (1960–).
Spanish leading actor, associated with the films of Pedro Almodóvar. Married actress Melanie Griffith in 1996.
Labyrinth of Passion/Laberinto de Pasiones 82. The Stilts/Los Zancos 84. Matador 86. The Law of Desire/La Ley del Deseo 87. Baton Rouge 88. Women on the Verge of a Nervous Breakdown/Mujeres al Borde de un Ataque de Nervios 88. Baton Rouge 88. Tie Me Up! Tie Me Down!/¡Atame!) 90. Cuentos de Borges I 91. The Mambo Kings 92. A Woman in the Rain/Una Mujer bajo la Lluvia 92. Il Giovane Mussolini (as Mussolini) 93. ¡Dispara! 93. Philadelphia 93. Of Love and Shadows 94. Interview with the Vampire 94. Miami Rhapsody 95. Desperado 95. Four Rooms 95. Assassins 95. Never Talk to Strangers 95. Two Much 96. Evita (as Che Guevara) 96. The Mask of Zorro 98, etc.

Banerjee, Victor (1946–).
Indian leading actor, occasionally in international films.
The Chess Players/Shatranj Ke Khilari 77. The Home and the World/Ghare Baire 84. Hullabaloo over Georgie and Bonnie's Pictures 78. A Passage to India 84. Foreign Body 86. World Within, World Without/Mahaprithivi 91. Bitter Moon 92, etc.

Bankhead, Tallulah (1903–1968).
Gravel-voiced, highly theatrical leading lady of American stage and screen. The daughter of an eminent politician, she titillated Broadway and London in the 20s by her extravagant performance on stage and off, and later tended to fritter away her considerable talents by living too dangerously. Films never managed to contain her. Married actor John Emery (1937–41).
Autobiography: 1952, *Tallulah*.
Biographies: 1972, *Miss Tallulah Bankhead* by Lee Israel; 1972, *Tallulah, Darling of the Gods: An Intimate Portrait* by Kieran Tunney; 1979, *Tallulah: A Memory* by Eugenia Rawls; 1996, *A Scandalous Life* by David Bret.
■ When Men Betray 18. Thirty a Week 18. A Woman's Law 28. His House in Order 28. *Tarnished Lady* 31. My Sin 31. The Cheat 31. Thunder Below 32. The Devil and the Deep 32. Faithless 32. Make Me a Star 32. Stage Door Canteen 43. *Lifeboat* 43. *A Royal Scandal* 45. Main Street to Broadway 53. *Fanatic* (GB) 65.
❝ She said of herself:
I'm as pure as the driven slush.
What one remembers about Miss Bankhead is not her merit as a performer, which in her heyday was considerable, but rather her well-publicized lifestyle, which kept her in the headlines throughout the 20s and 30s. As Mrs Patrick Campbell said:
Tallulah is always skating on thin ice. Everyone wants to be there when it breaks.
The lady herself issued such statements as:
Cocaine isn't habit-forming. I should know – I've been using it for years.
As a result, in her later years:
They used to photograph Shirley Temple through gauze. They should photograph me through linoleum.
But it was more sad than funny when someone asked:
Are you really the famous Tallulah?
and got the answer:
What's left of her.
She concluded:
The only thing I regret about my past is the length of it. If I had it to live over again I'd make the same mistakes, only sooner.
Sooner or later she alienated most of her friends. Howard Dietz was the one who said:
A day away from Tallulah is like a month in the country.

Bankolé, Isaach de (1958–).
Ivory Coast-born actor and comedian.
Black and White/Noir et Blanc (Fr.) 86. Chocolate/Chocolat (Fr.) 88. How to Make Love to a Negro without Getting Tired/Comment Faire l'Amour avec un Nègre sans Se Fatiguer 89. S'en Fout la Mort (Fr.) 90. Night on Earth (US) 92. Heart of Darkness (US) (TV) 92. Down to Earth/Casa de Lava 94. The Keeper (US) 96, etc.

Banks, Don (1923–1981).
Australian composer in Britain.
Captain Clegg 62. The Punch and Judy Man 62. Hysteria 65. Die Monster Die 65. The Reptile 66. The Mummy's Shroud 67. The Torture Garden 68, etc.

Banks, Leslie (1890–1952).
Distinguished British stage actor who after unsuccessful experiments in home-grown silent films started his film career in Hollywood. His sophistication seemed to be enhanced by his war-scarred profile.
■ *The Most Dangerous Game* 32. Strange Evidence 32. The Fire-Raisers 33. I am Suzanne 33. Night of the Party 34. The Red Ensign 34. *The Man Who Knew Too Much* 34. The Tunnel 35. *Sanders of the River* 35. Debt of Honour 36. The Three Maxims 37. Fire over England 37. Farewell Again 37. Wings of the Morning 37. *Twenty-one Days* 37. Jamaica Inn 39. Dead Man's Shoes 39. The Arsenal Stadium 39. Sons of the Sea 39. Busman's Honeymoon 40. The Door with Seven Locks 40. Neutral Port 40. Ships with Wings 41. Cottage to Let 41. The Big Blockade 42. Went the Day Well? 42. *Henry V* (as Chorus) 44. Mrs Fitzherbert 47. The Small Back Room 49. Madeleine 49. Your Witness 50.

Banks, Lionel.
American art director who worked for Columbia from the mid-30s.
Public Hero 35. Holiday (AAN) 38. Mr Smith Goes to Washington (AAN) 39. You Can't Take It with You 38. Golden Boy 39. Coast Guard 39. Before I Hang 40. Arizona (AAN) 40. Too Many Husbands 40. Ladies in Retirement (AAN) 41. The Blonde from Singapore 41. The Devil Commands 41. You'll Never Get Rich 41. Cadets on Parade 42. Hello, Annapolis 42. The Talk of the Town (AAN) 42. A Night to Remember 42. You Were Never Lovelier 42. The Devil's Trail 43. Is Everybody Happy? 43. The Return of the Vampire 43. Address Unknown (AAN) 44. Cover Girl (AAN) 44. Guest Wife 45. So Goes My Love 46. Magic Town 47. Moonrise 48, etc.

Banks, Monty (1897–1950) (Mario Bianchi).
Italian comic dancer who appeared in many silent two-reel comedies of the 20s then moved to Britain and later turned director. He was married to Gracie Fields.
Atlantic 30. Weekend Wives 31. Almost a Honeymoon (d) 31. Tonight's the Night (d) 32. No Limit (d) 35. We're Going to be Rich (d) 38. Great Guns (US) (d) 41, etc.

Banks, Russell (1940–).
American novelist and academic. Born in Newton, Massachusetts, and brought up in New Hampshire, he graduated from the University of North Carolina.
The Sweet Hereafter (oa) 97. Affliction (oa) 98. Continental Drift (w, oa) 99, etc.

Banky, Vilma (1898–1991) (Vilma Lonchit).
Austro-Hungarian star of American silents, discovered by Sam Goldwyn during a European holiday. Popular in the 20s but could not make the transition to sound. Married Rod la Rocque.
■ Im Letzen Augenblick (Hung.) 20. Galathea (Hung.) 21. Tavaszi Szerelem (Hung.) 21. Veszelyben a Pokol (Hung.) 21. Kauft Mariett-Aktien (Ger.) 22. Das Auge des Toten (Ger.) 22. Schattenkinder des Glucks (Ger.) 22. Die Letzte Stinde (Ger.) 23. The Forbidden Land (Aust.) 24. Clown aus Liebe (Aust.) 24. The Lady from Paris (Ger.) 24. Das Bildnis (Aust.) 25. Sollman Heiraten (Ger.) 25. *The Dark Angel* 25. The Eagle 25. Son of the Sheik 26. The Winning of Barbara Worth 26. The Night of Love 27. The Magic Flame 27. Two Lovers 28. The Awakening 28. This Is Heaven 29. A Lady to Love 30. De Sehnsucht Jeder Frau (Ger.) 30. The Rebel (Ger.) 33.
❝ She spoke no English at all: for their love scenes in *The Dark Angel*, she spoke in her own language while co-star Ronald Colman chatted away about cricket. – *John Baxter, The Hollywood Exiles*

Bannen, Ian (1928–).
British stage and TV actor who has been effective in several films.
Private's Progress 56. The Birthday Present 57. Carlton Browne of the F.O. 58. Macbeth 59. *A French Mistress* 60. *Suspect* 60. On Friday at Eleven 60. Station Six Sahara 62. Rotten to the Core 65. *The Hill* 65. The Flight of the Phoenix (AAN) 65. Sailor from Gibraltar 66. Penelope 67. Lock Up Your Daughters 69. Too Late the Hero 69. Fright 71. Doomwatch 72. The Offence 72. The Mackintosh Man 73. Bite the Bullet 75. The Sweeney 76. Bastards Without Glory (It.) 78. The Watcher in the Woods 80. Eye of the Needle 81. Gandhi 82. Night Crossing 82. Gorky Park 83. Defence of the Realm 85. Lamb 86. Hope and Glory 87. The Courier 88. George's Island 89. Ghost Dad 90. The Big Man 90. Damage 92. A Pin for the Butterfly 94. The Politician's Wife (TV) 95. Braveheart 95. To Walk with Lions 98. Waking Ned Devine 98, etc.
TV series: Doctor Finlay 93– .

Banner, John (1910–1973).
American character actor of Polish origin; usually played explosive Europeans.
Once Upon a Honeymoon 42. The Fallen Sparrow 43. Black Angel 47. My Girl Tisa 48. The Juggler 53. The Rains of Ranchipur 56. The

Story of Ruth 60. Hitler 63. Thirty-six Hours 64, etc.

TV series: *Hogan's Heroes* 65–70. Chicago Teddy Bears 71.

Bannerman, Celia (1944–).
English actress and theatre director.

The Tamarind Seed 74. Biddy (title role) 83. Little Dorrit 87. As You Like It 92, etc.

Bannon, Jim (1911–1984).
American actor with radio experience: played second feature leads in the 40s and starred in a western series as 'Red Ryder' in the 50s.

The Missing Juror 44. I Love a Mystery 45. The Thirteenth Hour 47. Daughter of the Jungle 49. The Man from Colorado 49. Rodeo 53. Chicago Confidential 58. Madame X 65, many others.

TV series: Adventures of Champion 55–56.

Banton, Travis (1894–1958).
American costume designer, long at Paramount, noted for dressing Mae West and Marlene Dietrich. Because of his heavy drinking, he was forced to leave the studio in 1938.

The Wild Party 29. Morocco 29. The Vagabond King 30. Dishonored 31. Shanghai Express 32. *The Scarlet Empress* 34. *The Devil Is a Woman* 35. The Crusades 35. Maid of Salem 37. Angel 37. Letter from an Unknown Woman 48, etc.

Bar, Jacques (1921–).
French producer, often in association with American companies.

Where the Hot Wind Blows 60. Vie Privée 61. A Monkey in Winter 62. Joy House 64. Once a Thief 65. The Guns of San Sebastian 67. The Mysterious Island of Captain Nemo 73, etc.

Bara, Nina (1925–1990).
Argentinian actress, best remembered for her role as Tonga in TV's children's series *Space Patrol* 51–52.

Missile to the Moon 58, etc.

Bara, Theda (1890–1955) (Theodosia Goodman).
American actress, the first to be called a 'vamp' (because of her absurdly vampirish, man-hungry screen personality). An extra in 1915, she was whisked to stardom on some highly imaginary publicity statistics (she was the daughter of an Eastern potentate, her name was an anagram of 'Arab death', etc.). *A Fool There Was* 15 is remembered for its classic sub-title, 'Kiss Me, My Fool!'; in 1919, her popularity waning, she forsook Hollywood for the Broadway stage, and when she returned in 1925 was forced to accept parts burlesquing her former glories, e.g. *Madame Mystery* 26. Wisely, she soon retired. Married director Charles Brabin in 1921.

Biography: 1998, *Vamp: The Rise and Fall of Theda Bara* by Eve Golden.

■ The Two Orphans 15. The Clemenceau Case 15. The Stain 15. Lady Audley's Secret 15. *A Fool There Was* 15. The Vixen 16. Sin 16. Carmen 16. Romeo and Juliet 16. The Light 16. Destruction 16. Gold and the Woman 16. The Serpent 16. Eternal Sappho 16. East Lynne 16. Her Double Life 16. *Cleopatra* 17. Madame Du Barry 17. Under Two Flags 17. Camille 17. Heart and Soul 17. The Tiger Woman 17. Salome 18. When a Woman Sins 18. The Forbidden Path 18. The She Devil 18. Rose of the Blood 18. Kathleen Mavourneen 19. La Belle Russe 19. When Men Desire 19. The Siren's Song 19. A Woman There Was 20. The Price of Silence 21. Her Greatest Love 21. The Hunchback of Notre Dame 23. The Unchastened Woman 25. Madame Mystery 26. The Dancer of Paris 26.

❝ She was divinely, hysterically, insanely malevolent. – *Bette Davis*

She made voluptuousness a common American commodity, as accessible as chewing gum. – *Lloyd Morris*

Baranski, Christine (1952–).
American actress, best known for her Emmy-winning role in the TV sitcom *Cybill*. Born in Buffalo, New York, she studied at the Juilliard School; married actor Matthew Cowles.

Crackers 83. Lovesick 83. 9½ Weeks 84. Legal Eagles 86. House of Blue Leaves 87. Reversal of Fortune 90. The Night We Never Met 93. The Ref/Hostile Hostages 94. The War 94. New Jersey Drive 95. Jeffrey 95. The Birdcage 96. The Odd Couple II 98. Bulworth 98, etc.

TV series: Cybill 95–98.

Baratier, Jacques (1918–).
French director of shorts and occasional features, a former theatre critic.

Paris la Nuit 55. Goha 57. La Poupée 62. Dragées au Poivre 63. L'Or du Duc 65. Le Désordre à Vingt Ans 67. La Décharge 70, etc.

Barbara (1930–1997) (Monique Serf).
French cabaret singer and composer, and occasional actress. Born in Paris, the daughter of a Polish mother and a Russian father, she studied voice and piano at the Paris Conservatoire before working in Brussels and Paris as a singer, often performing her own songs, which were typically about the end of a love affair.

Franz 71. Das Ganze Leben (Swiss) 83. The Book (US) 90, etc.

Barbeau, Adrienne (1945–).
American leading lady, mostly on TV. Married director John Carpenter (1979–84).

Red Alert (TV) 77. Someone's Watching Me (TV) 78. The Disappearance of Flight 401 (TV) 79. The Fog 79. Escape from New York 81. Swamp Thing 81. Creep Show 82. The Next One 84. Seduced 85. Back to School 86. Two Evil Eyes/Due Occhi Diabolici 89. Cannibal Women in the Avocado Jungle of Death 89. Doublecrossed (TV) 91. Silk Degrees 94. Burial of the Rats (TV) 95, etc.

TV series: Maude 72–78.

Barber, Frances (1958–).
English actress, born in Wolverhampton, Staffordshire.

The Missionary 81. Zed and Two Noughts 85. Castaway 86. Prick Up Your Ears 87. Sammy and Rosie Get Laid 87. We Think the World of You 88. The Grasscutter 89. Secret Friends 91. Young Soul Rebels 91. Soft Top, Hard Shoulder 92. Germaine et Benjamin (Fr.) 94. Rhodes (TV) 97. The Ice House (TV) 97, etc.

Barber, Glynis (1955–).
South African leading lady in Britain. Became popular on TV in Dempsey and Makepeace 85.

The Wicked Lady 83. Edge of Sanity 88. Déjà Vu (US) 98, etc.

Barbera, Joe (1911–).
American animator who with William Hanna created Tom and Jerry at MGM in 1937 and controlled the output until 1957: 'the cinema's purest representation of pure energy'. Later formed an independent company which produced dozens of 'semi-animated' cartoon series for TV, including the adventures of Yogi Bear, Huckleberry Hound, the Jetsons, the Flintstones, Magilla Gorilla, Scooby Doo and Snagglepuss.

Barbier, George (1865–1945).
American character actor remembered in talkies as a blustery but essentially kindly old man.

Monsieur Beaucaire 24. The Big Pond 30. The Sap from Syracuse 30. The Smiling Lieutenant 31. No Man of her Own 32. One Hour with You 32. Million Dollar Legs 32. The Big Broadcast 32. Mama Loves Papa 33. Tillie and Gus 34. Ladies Should Listen 34. *The Merry Widow* 34. The Crusades 35. The Cat's Paw 35. The Milky Way 36. The Princess Comes Across 36. *On the Avenue* 37. Hotel Haywire 37. Tarzan's Revenge 38. Little Miss Broadway 38. Sweethearts 38. News is Made at Night 39. The Return of Frank James 40. *The Man Who Came to Dinner* 41. Weekend in Havana 41. The Magnificent Dope 42. Song of the Islands 42. Hello Frisco Hello 43. Weekend Pass 44. Her Lucky Night 45, many others.

Barbieri, Gato (1934–) (Leandro Barbieri).
Argentinian jazz saxophonist and composer. Born in Rosario, he moved to Rome in the early 60s and worked in Europe for a decade before returning to Buenos Aires.

Before the Revolution (It.) 64. Last Tango in Paris (& a) (It.) 73. The Pig's War 75. Firepower (GB) 79. Stranger's Kiss (US) 83. Diario di un Vizio (It.) 93. Manhattan by Numbers 94, etc.

Barclay, Don (1892–1975).
Chubby American character actor, on screen from 1914.

Frisco Kid 35. Man Hunt 36. I Cover the War 37. Outlaw Express 38. The Oklahoma Kid 39. The Falcon's Brother 42. Frankenstein Meets the Wolf Man 43. Shine On Harvest Moon 44. My Darling Clementine 46. Mr Perrin and Mr Traill 48. The Long Gray Line 55. A Hundred and One Dalmatians (voice) 61. Mary Poppins 64. Half a Sixpence 68, etc.

Barcroft, Roy (1902–1969) (Howard H. Ravenscroft).
American character actor, usually as a villain in westerns. Born in Crab Orchard, Nebraska, he worked in various jobs, as a soldier, sailor, truck driver and musician, before turning to acting in his thirties. He made more than 200 westerns as a heavy, mellowing into a crotchety bystander in his later movies. Died of cancer.

Mata Hari 32. Dick Tracy (serial) 37. The Frontiersmen 38. Renegade Trail 39. Ragtime Cowboy Joe 40. Flash Gordon Conquers the Universe (serial) 40. The Showdown 40. Jesse James at Bay 41. They Died with Their Boots On 41. Sunset Serenade 42. Sagebrush Law 43. Calling Wild Bill Elliott 43. Hoppy Serves a Writ 43. Cheyenne Wildcat 44. Wagon Wheels Westward 45. The Purple Monster Strikes (serial) 45. Alias Billy the Kid 46. My Pal Trigger 46. Stagecoach to Reno 47. Jesse James Rides Again (serial) 47. Son of Zorro (serial) 47. Sundown at Santa Fe 48. San Antone Ambush 49. North of the Great Divide 50. The Vanishing Westerner 50. Dakota Kid 51. Flying Disc Men from Mars (serial) 51. Oklahoma Annie 52. Marshall of Cedar Rock 53. Two Guns and a Badge 54. Man without a Star 55. The Last Hunt 56. Billy the Kid vs Dracula 65. Texas across the River 66. The Way West 67. Bandolero! 68. The Reivers 69. Gaily, Gaily 69, many others.

❝ I liked the roles best where I could be the dirtiest, meanest, unkempt individual possible. – *R.B.*

Bardem, Juan-Antonio (1922–).
Spanish director and screenwriter, jailed in the 70s for political activities as a member of the Communist party; until the mid-80s he was unable to find work in Spain.

Welcome Mr Marshall (w) 52. *Death of a Cyclist* 54. Calle Mayor 56. Vengeance 57. Sonatas 59. Los Inocentes 62. Los Pianos Mecanicos 64. The Uninhibited 68. Variétés 71. Behind the Shutters 74. The Dog 77. Lorca, la Muerta de un Poeta 87, etc.

Bardette, Trevor (1902–1977).
American character actor, usually seen as western villain.

They Won't Forget 37. The Oklahoma Kid 39. Dark Command 40. The Moon Is Down 43. The Whistler 44. The Big Sleep 46. Song of India 49. The Texas Rangers 51. Lone Star 52. The Desert Song 53. Destry 54. The Man from Bitter Ridge 55. The Hard Man 57. The Mating Game 59. Papa's Delicate Condition 63. Mackenna's Gold 69, many others.

Bardot, Brigitte (1934–).
Pulchritudinous French pin-up girl who, given world publicity as a 'sex kitten', used her small but significant talents to make some routine movies very profitable. Her early career was orchestrated by her first husband, director Roger Vadim. Later she was often a reluctant star and attempted suicide on at least one occasion, becoming reclusive and, in 1986, setting up a foundation to care for the welfare of animals. (In 1997, she was fined 10,000 francs for inciting racial hatred, after criticizing the Muslim ritual slaughter of sheep.) Married actor Jacques Charrier, millionaire Gunter Sachs, and Bernard d'Ormale, who had connections with the right-wing National Front. Her lovers included singers Serge Gainsbourg and Sacha Distel and actor Jean-Louis Trintignant.

Biography: 1994, *Bardot: Two Lives* by Jeffrey Robinson.

Act of Love 54. Doctor at Sea (GB) 55. *The Light Across the Street* 55. Helen of Troy 55. *And God Created Woman* 57. Heaven Fell That Night 58. Une Parisienne 57. Please Mr Balzac 57. *En Cas de Malheur* 58. The Devil is a Woman 58. Mam'zelle Pigalle 58. Babette Goes to War 59. Please Not Now 61. *The Truth* 61. *Vie Privée* 61. *Love on a Pillow* 62. *Contempt* 63. Dear Brigitte 65. *Viva Maria* 65. Two Weeks in September 67. Shalako 68. *The Novices* 70. The Legend of Frenchy King 72. Don Juan 73, etc.

❝ For twenty years I was cornered and hounded like an animal. I didn't throw myself off my balcony only because I knew people would photograph me lying dead. – *B.B.*

I started out as a lousy actress and have remained one. – *B.B.*

France's most ogled export. – *Time 1956*

It was the first time on the screen that a woman was shown as really free on a sexual level, with none of the guilt attached to nudity or carnal pleasure. – *Roger Vadim*

The cinema means nothing to me. I cannot remember it. – *BB in 1994*

Bare, Richard (1909–).
American director who moved into TV.

Smart Girls Don't Talk 48. Flaxy Martin 48. The House Across the Street 49. Return of the Frontiersman 50. This Side of the Law 51. Prisoners of the Casbah 53. Shoot-Out at Medicine Bend 57. This Rebel Breed 60. I Sailed to Tahiti with an All-Girl Crew 67. Wicked, Wicked 73, etc.

Bari, Lynn (1913–1989) (Marjorie Fisher; aka Marjorie Bitzer).
Pert American 'second lead', often in 'other woman' roles. A chorus graduate, she was given plenty of work in the 30s and 40s but almost all of it was routine.

Dancing Lady 33. Stand Up and Cheer 34. Thanks a Million 35. Sing Baby Sing 36. Wee Willie Winkie 37. Josette 38. Return of the Cisco Kid 39. Hollywood Cavalcade 39. Earthbound 40. *Sun Valley Serenade* 41. *Moon Over Her Shoulder* 41. *The Magnificent Dope* 42. *Orchestra Wives* 42. Hello Frisco Hello 43. *The Bridge of San Luis Rey* 44. Tampico 44. Captain Eddie 45. Shock 45. *Margie* 46. The Man from Texas 48. On the Loose 51. Has Anybody Seen My Gal? 52. Francis Joins the WACS 54. Women of Pitcairn Island 56. Damn Citizen 58. Trauma 64. The Young Runaways 68, many others.

TV series: Boss Lady 52.

Baring, Norah (1907–) (Norah Baker).
British leading lady.

Underground 28. Cottage on Dartmoor 29. At the Villa Rose 30. Murder 30. The Lyons Mail 31. The House of Trent 33, etc.

Barker, Bradley (1883–1951).
American actor in silent films and animal impersonator who first supplied the roars for Leo, the MGM's trademark lion.

Erstwhile Susan 19. Adam and Eva 23. Into the Net (serial) 24. The Early Bird 25. The Brown Derby 26. The Potters 27. The Ape 28, etc.

Barker, Clive (1952–).
British horror author, screenwriter and director.

Underworld (co-w) 85. Rawhead Rex (oa) 87. Hellraiser (wd) 87. Transmutations (w) 88. Nightbreed (wd) 89. Sleepwalkers (a) 92. Candy Man (oa) 92. Hellraiser III: Hell on Earth (p) 92. Candyman: Farewell to the Flesh (ex p, story) 95. Lord of Illusions (wd) 95. Hellraiser: Bloodline (ex p) 96, etc.

TV series: Clive Barker's A–Z of Horror 97.

❝ True horror is seeing my stories turned into poor films. – *C.B.*

Barker, Eric (1912–1990).
British character comedian long popular on radio with his wife Pearl Hackney. A stroke in his early fifties brought his film career to an end.

Autobiography: 1956, *Steady Barker*.

Carry On London 37. Concert Party 37. On Velvet 38. *Brothers in Law* 57. Happy Is the Bride 58. Blue Murder at St Trinian's 58. Carry On Sergeant 58. Left, Right and Centre 59. Carry On Constable 60. Heavens Above 63. The Bargee 65. The Great St Trinian's Train Robbery 66. Maroc 7 67. There's a Girl in My Soup 70, etc.

Barker, Jess (1914–).
Lightweight American leading man of minor 40s films. He was formerly married to Susan Hayward.

Cover Girl 44. Keep Your Powder Dry 44. This Love of Ours 45. Take One False Step 49. Shack Out on 101 56. The Night Walker 65, etc.

Barker, Lex (1919–1973).
Blond, virile-looking American actor who in 1948 was signed to play Tarzan. After five films the role passed to another actor and Barker's stock slumped, but he continued to make routine action adventures. His five wives included actresses Arlene Dahl (1951–53) and Lana Turner (1953–57). Died of a heart attack.

Battles of Chief Pontiac 52. The Price of Fear

56. Jungle Heat 57. The Girl in the Kremlin 57. Terror of the Red Mask 59. La Dolce Vita 60. Robin Hood and the Pirates 60. Winnetou I 63. Victim Five 63. Old Shatterhand 64. Winnetou II 64. Kali-Yug, Goddess of Vengeance 64. Winnetou III 65. Dynamite Morgan 67. Woman Times Seven 67. Winnetou and Shatterhand 68, etc.

Barker, Ma (1880–1935) (Kate Barker).
Notorious American outlaw of the 30s, who with her four sons terrorized the central states before being shot in Florida. She was played by Jean Harvey in *Guns Don't Argue* 55, Lurene Tuttle in *Ma Barker's Killer Brood* 60, Shelley Winters in *Bloody Mama* 70, and Claire Trevor in an episode of *The Untouchables*. So-called fictional variants were played by Blanche Yurka in *Queen of the Mob* 40, Irene Dailey in *The Grissom Gang* 71 and Angie Dickinson in *Big Bad Mama* 74.

Barker, Ronnie (1929–).
Portly but versatile British TV comedian, rarely seen in films; immensely popular in *The Two Ronnies* and *Porridge*. He retired in 1988.
Biography: 1998, *Ronnie Barker, the Authorized Biography* by Bob McCabe.
Doctor in Distress 63. The Bargee 64. The Man Outside 67. *Futtock's End* 70. Robin and Marian 76. Porridge 79, etc.

Barker, Sir Will G. (1867–1951).
Pioneer British producer of the cinema's fairground days. A former salesman and cameraman, he founded the original Ealing studio.
Henry VIII 11. Jim the Fireman 12. Sixty Years a Queen 13. Greater Love Hath No Man 13. The Fighting Parson 14. Jane Shore 15, many others.

Barkin, Ellen (1954–).
American leading actress, usually in sexy roles. Born in the Bronx, New York, she studied at Hunter College and began on stage. She was married to actor Gabriel Byrne (1988–94).
Diner 82. Tender Mercies 82. Daniel 83. Eddie and the Cruisers 83. Enormous Changes at the Last Minute 83. The Adventures of Buckaroo Banzai Across the Eighth Dimension 84. Harry & Son 84. Terminal Choice 85. The Big Easy 86. Desert Bloom 86. Down by Law 86. Made in Heaven 87. Siesta 87. Clinton and Nadine/Blood Money (TV) 88. Johnny Handsome 89. Sea of Love 89. Switch 91. Man Trouble 92. This Boy's Life 93. Bad Company 95. Wild Bill 95. The Fan 96. Mad Dog Time/Trigger Happy 96. Fear and Loathing in Las Vegas 98, etc.

Barkworth, Peter (1929–).
Smooth British comedy actor, mostly on TV; very popular in diffident roles.
A Touch of Larceny 61. Tiara Tahiti 62. No Love for Johnnie 63. Where Eagles Dare 69. Escape from the Dark 76. Champions 84, etc.
TV series: *Telford's Change* 78.

Barnard, Ivor (1887–1953).
British character actor of stage and screen, often of henpecked or nosey parker types, on stage from 1908.
Waltz Time 33. The Wandering Jew 34. Storm in a Teacup 37. Pygmalion 38. The Saint's Vacation 41. Hotel Reserve 44. The Wicked Lady 45. Great Expectations 46. Oliver Twist 48. *Beat the Devil* (his last and best role, as a vicious killer) 53, many others.

Barnes, Barry K. (1906–1965) (Nelson Barnes).
Stylish British stage actor, in occasional films. Born in London, he worked in his father's store-fitting business before training for the stage at RADA. He was on stage from 1927 and in films from 1937. His second wife was actress Diana Churchill.
The Return of the Scarlet Pimpernel 38. *This Man is News* 38. The Ware Case 38. Prison without Bars 39. The Midas Touch 40. Spies of the Air 40. The Girl in the News 41. Dancing with Crime 46. Bedelia 46, etc.

Barnes, Binnie (1905–1998) (Gitelle Barnes).
Self-confident British light actress who, after varied experience, made a few early British talkies, then went to Hollywood in 1934 and played mainly smart, wise-cracking ladies. Married Mike Frankovich.
Love Lies 31. Murder at Covent Garden 31. Heads We Go 33. *The Private Life of Henry VIII* (as Katherine Howard) 33. The Private Life of Don Juan 34. Diamond Jim 35. The Last of the Mohicans 35. The Magnificent Brute 36. *Three Smart Girls* 37. The Adventures of Marco Polo 38. Three Blind Mice 38. The Divorce of Lady X 38. *The Three Musketeers* 39. Till We Meet Again 40. Tight Shoes 41. Skylark 41. *Three Girls About Town* 41. The Man from Down Under 43. Barbary Coast Gent 44. *Up in Mabel's Room* 44. *It's in the Bag* 45. The Spanish Main 45. If Winter Comes 47. My Own True Love 48. Shadow of the Eagle 50. Fugitive Lady 51. Decameron Nights 53. *The Trouble with Angels* 66. Where Angels Go, Trouble Follows 68. Forty Carats 72, many others.

Barnes, George (c. 1880–1949).
American actor whose claim to fame was playing the outlaw who, in close-up, fired his revolver directly at the audience at the end (or, in some versions, the beginning) of *The Great Train Robbery* 03.

Barnes, George (1893–1953).
Distinguished American cinematographer. Married actress Joan Blondell (1933–35).
The Haunted Bedroom 19. Silk Hosiery 21. Hairpins 22. Dusk to Dawn 24. *The Eagle* 25. *Son of the Sheik* 26. Janice Meredith 27. Sadie Thompson 28. Our Dancing Daughters 28. *Bulldog Drummond* 29. The Trespasser 29. *Condemned* 29. Raffles 30. Five and Ten 31. The Unholy Garden 31. Street Scene 31. The Wet Parade 32. Sherlock Holmes 32. Peg O' My Heart 33. *Footlight Parade* 33. Massacre 34. *Dames* 34. Flirtation Walk 34. In Caliente 35. The Singing Kid 36. Black Legion 36. *Marked Woman* 37. Hollywood Hotel 37. Gold Diggers in Paris 38. *Jesse James* 39. *Rebecca* (AA) 40. Devil's Island 40. Hudson's Bay 40. *Meet John Doe* 41. *Ladies in Retirement* 41. Rings on Her Fingers 42. Once Upon a Honeymoon 42. Mr Lucky 43. *Frenchman's Creek* 44. *Jane Eyre* 44. None But the Lonely Heart 44. *Spellbound* 45. The Spanish Main 45. The Bells of St Mary's 45. *From This Day Forward* 46. Sinbad the Sailor 47. Mourning Becomes Electra 47. The Emperor Waltz 48. The Boy with Green Hair 48. *Force of Evil* 49. Let's Dance 50. Mr Music 50. Riding High 50. Here Comes the Groom 51. Something to Live For 52. *The War of the Worlds* 53. Little Boy Lost 53, etc.

Barnes, Joanna (1934–).
American actress occasionally seen in cool supporting roles. Also a novelist.
Home Before Dark 58. Spartacus 60. The Parent Trap 61. Goodbye Charlie 64. The War Wagon 67. B.S. I Love You 70. I Wonder Who's Killing Her Now? 76, etc.

Barnes, Peter (1931–).
British dramatist and screenwriter, a former film critic and story editor.
Offbeat 60. Ring of Spies/Ring of Treason 63. The Ruling Class 72. Enchanted April 91. Voices 95, etc.

Barnes, T. Roy (1880–1937).
English-born actor who went to America as a child. He spent 12 years in vaudeville in a comedy act with his wife, Bessie Crawford, and was on stage from 1914.
Scratch My Back 20. Adam and Eva 23. The Great White Way 24. Seven Chances 25. Body and Soul 27. Chicago 27. Dangerous Curves 29. Kansas City Princess 34. It's a Gift 34. The Virginia Judge 35, etc.

Barnet, Charlie (1913–1991).
American bandleader and jazz saxophonist, in films usually as himself. Born in New York, to a wealthy family, he resisted becoming a lawyer to lead a popular swing band in the 30s and 40s. He also made several shorts and soundies. Married many times.
Autobiography: 1984, *Those Swinging Years* (with Stanley Dance).
Love and Hisses (a) 37. Sally, Irene and Mary (a) 38. Juke Box Jenny 42. Syncopation 42. Jam Session (playing his hit recording of 'Cherokee') 44. Music in Manhattan 44. Freddie Steps Out 46. Idea Girl 46. The Fabulous Dorseys 47. A Song Is Born 48. Make Believe Ballroom 49. Bright and Breezy (short) 56. The Big Beat 57. The Swingin' Singin' Years (TV) 60, etc.

Barnett, Vince (1902–1977).
American character actor, usually of minor gangsters or downtrodden little men, from vaudeville. He was previously a professional insulter, hired to be be rude to people at parties. Born in Pittsburgh, Pennsylvania, he was educated at Duquesne University.
Her Man 30. *Scarface* 32. I Cover the Waterfront 33. Dancing Feet 36. A Star Is Born 37. Overland Trail 39. East Side Kids 40. A Dangerous Game 41. Baby Face Morgan 42. Kid Dynamite 43. The Killers 46. Big Town Scandal 48. Mule Train 50. Carson City 52. Springfield Rifle 52. The Quiet Gun 57. The Rookie 59. Dr Goldfoot and the Bikini Machine 65. The Big Mouth 67. Crazy Mama 75, many others.

Barnum, Phineas T. (1810–1891).
American showman who is alleged to have said 'There's one born every minute' of the people who flocked to see his freak shows. He became a multi-millionaire and co-founded the famous Barnum and Bailey Circus. He was played in *A Lady's Morals* 30 and *The Mighty Barnum* 35 by Wallace Beery; in *Rocket to the Moon* 67 by Burl Ives.

Baron, Auguste (1853–1938).
French inventor who patented a method of talking pictures (1896–99) and two multiscreen processes, Cinématorama in 1896 and Multirama in 1912, but failed to find backing for his ideas.

Baron Munchausen.
There has been a longish line of movies about the tall story-teller. Méliès made a version in 1911; Emile Cole in 1913; Hans Albers starred in a German version in 1943. Karl Zeman made a semi-animated fantasy in 1962, and John Neville starred in Terry Gilliam's expensive version in 1989. The real Baron (1720–97) was a German army officer, but the collection of stories written by Rudolph Raspe, first published in English in 1785, included much material from other sources.

Baroncelli, Jacques de (1881–1951).
French director, a former journalist, who made more than 80 films in a career that ran from the silent era until the late 40s.
La Maison de l'Espoir 15. Le Père Goriot 21. La Femme et le Pantin 29. Michel Strogoff 37. La Duchesse de Langeais 42. Rocambole 48, etc.

Barr, Douglas (1931–).
English juvenile actor who also starred in the BBC's first radio comedy series aimed at teenagers, *It's Fine to Be Young* 48.
Hue and Cry 46. Fortune Lane 47. The Last Load 48. Dance Hall 50. Madeleine 50. One Good Turn 51, etc.

Barr, Jean-Marc (1960–).
French leading actor in international films. Bilingual, he has a French mother and an American father and trained as an actor in London.
The Frog Prince 85. King David 85. Hope and Glory 87. The Big Blue/Le Grand Bleu 88. Le Brasier 90. Europa 91. The Plague/La Peste 92. Iron Horsemen 94. Les Faussaires 94. Breaking the Waves (Den.) 96. Close Shave 96. Preference 98. What I Did for Love 98. Don't Let Me Die on a Sunday 98, etc.

Barr, Patrick (1908–1985).
British stage, screen and TV actor who played solid, dependable types from the 30s.
Norah O'Neale 34. The Return of the Scarlet Pimpernel 38. The Frightened Lady 41. The Blue Lagoon 48. Robin Hood 52. Singlehanded 53. Crest of the Wave 54. Saint Joan 57. Next to No Time 60. The Longest Day 62. Billy Liar 63. Ring of Spies 64. House of Whipcord 74, many others.

Barr, Roseanne (1952–).
Plump, outspoken American actress, a former stand-up comic, who is a star on TV but not, so far, on film. Formerly married to actor Tom Arnold. She was played by Patrika Darbo in the made-for-TV biopic *Roseanne and Tom: Behind the Scenes* 95, concerned with the couple's brief and stormy marriage.
Autobiography. 1990, *My Life as a Woman*.
She Devil 89. Into the Deep Woods (TV) 92. The Woman Who Loved Elvis (TV) 93. Even Cowgirls Get the Blues 94. Blue in the Face 95, etc.
TV series: Roseanne 88–97. The Roseanne Show 98– .

Barrat, Robert (1891–1970).
American character actor in films from silent days, usually as heavy western villain. In 1934 alone he appeared in 19 films.
Mayor of Hell 33. Wild Boys of the Road 33. Dark Hazard 34. Wonder Bar 34. Captain Blood 35. Dr Socrates 35. Trail of the Lonesome Pine 36. The Charge of the Light Brigade 36. The Life of Emile Zola 37. Souls at Sea 37. The Buccaneer 38. Union Pacific 39. Return of the Cisco Kid 39. Go West 40. Captain Caution 40. Riders of the Purple Sage 41. American Empire 42. They Came to Blow Up America 43. The Adventures of Mark Twain 44. Road to Utopia 45. They Were Expendable 45. The Time of Their Lives 46. Road to Rio 47. Joan of Arc 48. Canadian Pacific 49. The Baron of Arizona 50. Flight to Mars 51. Double Crossbones 51. Son of Ali Baba 52. Tall Man Riding 55, many others.

Barrault, Jean-Louis (1910–1994).
Celebrated French stage actor, in a few rewarding film roles. He was married to actress Madeleine Renaud.
Mademoiselle Docteur 36. *Drôle de Drame* 36. *La Symphonie Fantastique* 42. *Les Enfants du Paradis* 44. D'Homme à Hommes 48. La Ronde 50. Le Testament du Docteur Cordelier 59. The Longest Day 62. La Nuit de Varennes 83, etc.

Barrault, Marie-Christine (1944–).
French actress, best known for her work with Eric Rohmer. She is the niece of Jean-Louis Barrault.
My Night at Maud's/Ma Nuit Chez Maud 68. Lancelot of the Lake/Lancelot du Lac 74. Cousin Cousine (AAN) 75. Perceval 78. The Medusa Touch 78. Stardust Memories 80. Table for Five 83. A Love in Germany/Eine Liebe in Deutschland 83. Swann in Love/Un Amour de Swann 83. The Abyss/L'Oeuvre au Noir 88. Gallant Ladies/Dames Galantes 91. Necessary Love/L'Amore Necessario 91. La Prossima Volta Il Fuoco 93. Mad Love/Amour Fou 94. Obsession 97, etc.

Barreto, Bruno (1955–).
Brazilian director and screenwriter. The son of leading Brazilian producers Luis Carlos Barreto and Lucy Barreto, he began as a youth making experimental shorts before achieving an international success with *Dona Flor and Her Two Husbands*. He married actress Amy Irving and is now based in America.
Tati, a Garota 73. Dona Flor and Her Two Husbands/Dona Flor e Seus Dois Maridos 76. Amor Bandido 78. Lucia 81. Gabriela 83. Felizes para Sempre 84. A Show of Force 89. The Story of Fausta 92. Carried Away 95. Four Days in September (AAN) 97. One Tough Cop 98, etc.

Barreto, Lima (1905–1982).
Brazilian film director and screenwriter, a former actor and journalist. Born in Casa Branca, he became a documentary film-maker in the 40s and 50s before making his feature debut with the first Brazilian film to gain an international reputation.
The Bandit/O Cangaçeiro 53. A Primeira Missa 61, etc.

Barrett, Edith (1912–1977).
American character actress, usually in fey roles.
Ladies in Retirement 41. Jane Eyre 43. I Walked with a Zombie 43. The Song of Bernadette 43. The Swan 56, etc.

Barrett, James Lee (1929–1989).
American screenwriter. Born in Charlotte, North Carolina, he was educated at Penn State University and began as a writer working for Stanley Kramer and Universal.
The D.I. 58. The Greatest Story Ever Told (co-w) 65. The Truth About Spring 65. Shenandoah 65. Bandolero 68. The Green Berets 68. The Cheyenne Social Club (& p) 70. Smokey and the Bandit (co-w) 77, etc.

Barrett, Jane (1923–1969).
British leading actress. Born in London, she was on stage from 1938, and then worked for the BBC Repertory Company in the early 40s.
The Captive Heart 45. Eureka Stockade 48. Time Gentlemen Please 52. The Sword and the Rose 53, etc.

Barrett, Judith (1914–). (Lucille Kelly).
American leading lady of a few 30s films.
Flying Hostess 36. Let Them Live 37. Armored Car 37. Illegal Traffic 38. Television Spy 39. The Great Victor Herbert 39. Road to Singapore 40. Women without Names 40, etc.

Barrett, Ray (1926–).
Australian leading actor in British TV and films.
The Sundowners 60. Touch of Death 62. Jigsaw 63. The Reptile 65. Revenge 71. Waterfront 83. Where the Green Ants Dream 84. Rebel 86. Hotel Sorrento 94. Dad and Dave on Our Selection 95. Brilliant Lies 96. Heaven's Burning 97. In the Winter Dark 98, etc.
TV series: *The Troubleshooters* 66–71.

Barrett, Rona (1934–) (Rona Burnstein).
American gossip columnist who, centred in Hollywood for the television networks, has more or less inherited the mantle of Hedda and Louella.
Autobiography: 1974, *Miss Rona*.
❝ I'm not friends with the stars, because if I were I couldn't tell the truth about them. – *R.B.*
I'm really a pussycat – with an iron tail. – *R.B.*

Barrie, Amanda (1939–) (Amanda Broadbent).
British leading lady with TV experience. Born in Ashton-under-Lyne, Lancashire, she performed from infancy, trained as a ballet dancer and began as a chorus girl in London at the age of 14.
Doctor in Distress 63. Carry On Cabby 63. Carry On Cleo 64. I Gotta Horse 65. One of Our Dinosaurs Is Missing 75, etc.
TV series: Mood In 61. Bulldog Breed 62. It's Tarbuck! 64–65. The Reluctant Romeo 67. Time of My Life 80. Coronation Street 81. L for Lester 82. Coronation Street 89– .

Barrie, Barbara (1931–) (Barbara Berman).
Pert American character actress. Born in Chicago, Illinois.
One Potato Two Potato 64. Summer of My German Soldier (TV) 78. The Bell Jar 79. Breaking Away (AAN) 79. Private Benjamin 80. Real Men 87. End of the Line 88, etc.
TV series: Diana 73–74. Barney Miller 75–76. Breaking Away 80–81. Tucker's Witch 82–83. Reggie 83. Double Trouble 84–85.

Barrie, Sir J. M. (1860–1937).
British playwright whose work usually had a recognizable fey quality, which even survived the film versions.
The Admirable Crichton 17. Peter Pan 24 and 53. The Little Minister 34. What Every Woman Knows 34. Quality Street 37. Darling How Could You? ('Alice Sit by the Fire') 51. Forever Female ('Rosalind') 53, etc.

Barrie, John (1917–1980).
Heavily built British character actor with long repertory experience. Played *Sergeant Cork* on TV, and in the cinema is best remembered as the police inspector in *Victim* 63.

Barrie, Mona (1909–1964) (Mona Smith).
English actress, born in London, who began her career on stage in Australia, and was in Hollywood from the early 30s, playing second leads.
Carolina 34. The House of Connelly 34. A Message to Garcia 36. I Met Him in Paris 37. When Ladies Meet 41. Cairo 42. Storm over Lisbon 44. I Cover Big Town 47. Strange Fascination 52. Plunder of the Sun 53, many others.

Barrie, Wendy (1912–1978) (Wendy Jenkins).
Bright British leading lady who went to Hollywood in 1934 but found only mediocre roles. Had her own TV show in 1948, and was later active in local radio.
It's a Boy (GB) 32. *The Private Life of Henry VIII* (GB) 32. For Love or Money 34. A Feather in Her Hat 35. Love on a Bet 36. Dead End 37. I Am the Law 38. The Hound of the Baskervilles 39. Five Came Back 39. The Saint Takes Over 40. Who Killed Aunt Maggie? 40. The Gay Falcon 41. Eyes of the Underworld 42. Women in War 42. Forever and a Day 43. It Could Happen to You (guest appearance) 53. Summer Holiday 63. The Moving Finger 63, etc.

Barrier, Edgar (1907–1964).
American character actor with stage experience.
Escape 40. Arabian Nights 42. Phantom of the Opera 43. Flesh and Fantasy 44. *A Game of Death* 45. Macbeth 48. To the Ends of the Earth 48. Cyrano de Bergerac 50. Princess of the Nile 54. On the Double 61. Irma la Douce 63, many others.

Barron, Keith (1934–).
British leading actor of the angry young man type; mostly on TV.
Baby Love 69. Melody 70. The Fire Chasers 70. The Man Who Had Power Over Women 70. She'll Follow You Anywhere 71. Nothing but the Night 73. The Land that Time Forgot 75. Voyage of the Damned 76. The Elephant Man 80. Close Relations (TV) 98. This Could Be the Last Time (TV) 98, etc.
TV series: The Odd Man 62–63. It's Dark Outside 64–65. The New Adventures of Lucky Jim 67. Joint Account 69. My Good Woman 72. Brotherly Love 74. No Strings 74. Telford's Change 79. Leaving 84–85. Duty Free 84–86. Room at the Bottom 86–88. Late Expectations 87. Haggard 90–92. All Night Long 94.

Barron, Steve (1956–).
British director who began with pop videos. Born in Dublin, he worked in films from the early 70s. He is the son of Zelda Barron.
Electric Dreams 84. Bulldance 89. Teenage Mutant Ninja Turtles 90. Coneheads 93. The Adventures of Pinocchio 96. Merlin (TV) 98.

Barron, Zelda.
British director. She first worked in production and as a script supervisor.
Secret Places 84. Shag 88.

Barry, Don (1912–1980) (Donald Barry d'Acosta).
Rugged American actor, in Hollywood from 1939 after stage experience and immediately popular as hero of second-feature westerns. Sometimes known as Donald 'Red' Barry. Committed suicide.
Night Waitress 36. The Crowd Roars 38. Calling All Marines 39. Remember Pearl Harbor 42. The Chicago Kid 45. The Dalton Gang 49. Jesse James' Women (& d) 53. I'll Cry Tomorrow 55. Walk on the Wild Side 62. Fort Utah 66. Bandolero 68. Shalako 68. Dirty Dingus Magee 70. Junior Bonner 72. Hustle 75. Orca 77. The Swarm 78, etc.
TV series: Surfside Six 60. Mr Novak 63.

Barry, Gene (1921–) (Eugene Klass).
Poised and debonair American leading man who also does a song and dance act. Films routine, but TV has kept him busy. Married actress Betty Claire.
■ The Atomic City 52. The Girls of Pleasure Island 52. *The War of the Worlds* 53. Those Redheads from Seattle 53. Alaska Seas 54. *Red Garters* 54. *Naked Alibi* 54. Soldier of Fortune 55. The Purple Mask 55. The Houston Story 56. Back From Eternity 56. The 27th Day 57. China Gate 57. Ain't No Time for Glory (TV) 57. Forty Guns 57. Hong Kong Confidential 58. *Thunder Road* 58. Maroc 7 67. Prescription Murder (TV) 67. Istanbul Express (TV) 68. Subterfuge 69. Do You Take This Stranger? (TV) 70. The Devil and Miss Sarah (TV) 71. The Second Coming of Suzanne 73. Guyana, Crime of the Century 79. The Adventures of Nellie Bly (TV) 81. The Girl, The Gold Watch and Dynamite (TV) 81.
TV series: Our Miss Brooks 55. *Bat Masterson* 58–61. *Burke's Law* 63–66. *The Name of the Game* 68–71. The Adventurer 72. Aspen 77. Burke's Law 94–95.

Barry, Iris (1895–1969).
Founder-member of the London Film Society (1925); director of New York Museum of Modern Art Film Library from 1935; president of the International Federation of Film Archives 1946; author of books on the film.
❝ Film is a machine for seeing more than meets the eye. – *I.B.*

Barry, Joan (1903–1989).
British leading lady of the early 30s, chiefly known for dubbing Anny Ondra's voice in *Blackmail*.
The Card 22. The Rising Generation 28. The Outsider 31. Rich and Strange 31. Ebb Tide 32. Sally Bishop 32. Rome Express 32. Mrs Dane's Defence 34, etc.

Barry, John (1933–) (J. B. Prendergast).
British composer and musician, best known for writing the music to the James Bond movies and for his arrangement of the theme music. Born in York, the son of a cinema owner, he began by leading his own group, the John Barry Seven. Formerly married to actress Jane BIRKIN.
Biography: 1998, *John Barry: A Sixties Theme* by Eddi Fiegel.
Beat Girl 59. Never Let Go 60. Dr No (md) 62. The Amorous Prawn 62. The L-shaped Room 62. *From Russia with Love* 63. Zulu 63. The Man in the Middle 64. Goldfinger 64. The Ipcress File 65. The Knack 65. Thunderball 65. King Rat 65. The Chase 66. *Born Free* (AA) 66. The Wrong Box 66. The Quiller Memorandum 66. Petulia 68. Boom 68. Deadfall 68. The Lion in Winter (AA) 68. Midnight Cowboy 69. Murphy's War 71. They Might Be Giants 71. Mary, Queen of Scots (AAN) 71. Diamonds Are Forever 72. The Tamarind Seed 73. The Man with the Golden Gun 74. King Kong 76. The Deep 77. The White Buffalo 77. The Betsy 78. Moonraker 79. The Black Hole 79. Raise the Titanic 80. Somewhere in Time 80. Body Heat 81. Hammett 82. Frances 82. Octopussy 83. Out of Africa (AA) 85. Jagged Edge 86. Peggy Sue got Married 86. The Living Daylights 87. Hearts of Fire 87. Masquerade 88. Dances with Wolves (AA) 90. Chaplin (AAN) 92. My Life 93. Indecent Proposal 93. Ruby Cairo 93. The Specialist 94. The Scarlet Letter 95. Swept from the Sea/Amy Foster 97. Mercury Rising 98, etc.

Barry, John (1935–1979).
Anglo-American production designer.
A Clockwork Orange 73. Phase IV 73. Lucky Lady 75. Star Wars 77. Superman 78. Superman 2 80. The Empire Strikes Back 80, etc.

Barry, Julian.
American screenwriter.
Secret Agent Fireball 66. Rhinoceros 74. Lenny (AAN) 74. The River 84, etc.

Barry, Philip (1896–1949).
American playwright, several of whose sophisticated comedies have been filmed.
Holiday 30 and 38. The Animal Kingdom 32 (remade as One More Tomorrow 46). The Philadelphia Story 40. Without Love 45.

Barry, Tony (1941–).
Australian actor, usually in tough roles.
Break of Day 76. The Picture Show Man 77. Newsfront 78. Hard Knocks 80. Goodbye Pork Pie 81. We of the Never Never 82. With Prejudice 82. The Coca-Cola Kid 85. Two Friends 86. Never Say Die 88. Return to Snowy River 88. Deadly 90. Jack Be Nimble 92. The Last Tattoo 94. Country Life 94, etc.
TV series: Skippy 66.

Barry, Wesley (1908–1994).
American child actor, on screen from the age of six, who later became an assistant director of 'B' movies and retired in the 40s.
Rebecca of Sunnybrook Farm 13. The Country Kid 23. Battling Bunyon 24. Sunny Skies 30. Daddy Long Legs 31. Night Life of the Gods 35. The Plough and the Stars 36, etc.

Barrymore, Diana (1921–1960).
American actress, daughter of John Barrymore. She made a few mediocre films in the early 40s but was not a successful leading lady and later succumbed to alcoholism. Her autobiography *Too Much Too Soon* was filmed in 1958 with Dorothy Malone (and Errol Flynn as John Barrymore).
■ Eagle Squadron 42. *Between Us Girls* 42. Nightmare 42. Frontier Badmen 43. Fired Wife 43. *Ladies Courageous* 44.

Barrymore, Drew (1975–).
American leading actress who was in films from the age of five. Born in Los Angeles, the daughter of John BARRYMORE, Jnr, she first came to notice in *E.T. the Extra-Terrestrial*, but problems with drugs and alcohol derailed her career in her teens. She then wrote a book about her experiences, cleaned up her act, and began to make the transition to adult roles.
Autobiography: 1989, *Little Girl Lost*, with Todd Gold.
E.T. 82. Firestarter 84. Irreconcilable Differences 84. Cat's Eye 84. A Conspiracy of Love (TV) 87. Far from Home 89. See You in the Morning 89. Guncrazy 92. Doppelganger 92. Motorama 92. Poison Ivy 92. Beyond Control: The Amy Fisher Story (TV) 93. Wayne's World 2 93. Bad Girls 94. Inside the Goldmine 94. Mad Love 95. Boys on the Side 95. Batman Forever 95. Scream 96. Everyone Says I Love You 96. The Wedding Singer 97. Ever After 98. Home Fries 98, etc.
TV series: 2000 Malibu Road 92.

Barrymore, Ethel (1879–1959) (Edith Blythe).
Distinguished American actress of regal presence. The sister of Lionel and John, and daughter of leading stage actors Maurice Barrymore and Georgiana Drew Barrymore, she was born in Philadelphia and was on stage from 1893, becoming a Broadway star in 1901. She made a few silents but had contempt for Hollywood, alienating MGM when she went to work there in the 30s, when she was drinking heavily and had financial problems. She remained on Broadway until 1944, when she made her home in Hollywood. Her greatest role came after more than 40 years in the theatre: as Miss Moffat in Emlyn WILLIAMS's *The Corn Is Green*, a part that went to Bette DAVIS when it was filmed. Always conscious of her position as the most admired stage actress of her time, when a young actor pointed out that if he went where she directed him to stand he would be upstage of her, she replied, 'Oh, my dear, don't worry about me. Wherever I am is centre stage.' She was courted by Winston Churchill, engaged to actor Gerald DU MAURIER, and had affairs, possibly platonic, with actors Conway TEARLE and Henry DANIELL. Married millionaire Russell Colt and had three children: Ethel (1912–1977), who became an opera singer and actress; the alcoholic John Drew (1913–1975); and Samuel (1910–1986). Both boys also occasionally acted, though without any particular distinction. She, her daughter, her brother John and her mother were satirized in George KAUFMAN and Edna FERBER's 1927 Broadway hit *The Royal Family*.
Autobiography: 1955, *Memories*.
Biographies: 1964, *The Barrymores* by Hollis Alpert; 1981, *The Barrymores: The Royal Family in Hollywood* by James Kotsilibas-Davis; 1990, *The House of Barrymore* by Margot Peters.
■ The Nightingale 14. The Final Judgement 15. The Awakening of Helen Ritchie 16. Kiss of Hate 16. The White Raven 17. The Lifted Veil 17. The Eternal Mother 17. The American Widow 17. Life's Whirlpool 17. The Call of Her People 17. Our Miss McChesney 18. The Divorcee 19. Rasputin and the Empress (only film appearance with her brothers) 32. *None but the Lonely Heart* (AA) 44. The Spiral Staircase (AAN) 46. *The Farmer's Daughter* 47. Moss Rose 47. The Paradine Case (AAN) 48. Night Song 48. Moonrise 49. Portrait of Jennie 49. The Great Sinner 49. That Midnight Kiss 49. Pinky (AAN) 49. The Red Danube 49. The Secret of Convict Lake 51. *Kind Lady* 51. It's a Big Country 52. *Deadline* 52. Just for You 52. The Story of Three Loves 53. Main Street to Broadway 53. *Young at Heart* 54. Johnny Trouble 57.
❝ That's all there is, there isn't any more! – *E.B.'s farewell line, delivered after her curtain calls*
✪ For spending her later years portraying Hollywood's idea of the indomitable old lady with a heart of gold. *The Farmer's Daughter*.

Barrymore, John (1882–1942) (John Blythe).
Celebrated, self-destructive American stage and screen actor, the brother of Ethel and Lionel BARRYMORE, and son of leading stage actors Maurice Barrymore and Georgiana Drew Barrymore. Born in Philadelphia, he studied at the Slade School of Art and worked first as an illustrator and cartoonist before following the family occupation from 1900. An undisciplined talent, he quickly became bored with repeating his performances night after night and, after triumphing on Broadway and in London in *Hamlet* in the early 20s, he quit the stage when Warner Bros offered him a three-picture contract at $76,250 a picture plus plenty of perks. Plans to film his *Hamlet*, made at various times by WARNER's, SELZNICK and Alexander KORDA, went awry (though a colour test he later made in 1933 allegedly remains in New York's Museum of Modern Art). An irresistible matinee idol with a 'great profile', he became a romantic movie hero in the 20s, but thereafter abused his talent. When Warner's refused to renew his contract in the early 30s, he worked for MGM, though that studio also tired of him. Alcoholism often dampened his film

performances and he became too erratic to employ. He was fired from the role of the drunken actor Norman Maine in the 1934 version of *A Star Is Born* and finished playing parodies of himself on stage (in *My Dear Children*) and screen (*The Great Profile*). His second wife was poet, playwright and occasional actress Michael Strange, by whom he had a daughter, Diana; his third, actress Dolores Costello, by whom he had a daughter and a son, John Drew, Jnr; his fourth, Elaine Barrie, briefly became an actress. His lovers included Evelyn Nesbit and Mary Astor. He was played by Errol Flynn in *Too Much, Too Soon* 58, based on the autobiography of his daughter Diana, and by Jack Cassidy in *W. C. Fields and Me* 76.

Autobiography: 1926, *Confessions of an Actor*.

Biographies: 1941, *John Barrymore: The Legend and the Man* by Alma Power-Walters; 1943, *Goodnight, Sweet Prince* by Gene Fowler; 1964, *The Barrymores* by Hollis Alpert; 1977, *Damned in Paradise: The Life of John Barrymore* by John Kobler; 1981, *The Barrymores: The Royal Family in Hollywood* by James Kotsilibas-Davis; 1990, *The House of Barrymore* by Margot Peters.

Book: 1980, *The Film Acting of John Barrymore* by Joseph Garton.

■ Are You a Mason? 13. An American Citizen 13. The Man from Mexico 14. The Dictator 15. The Incorrigible Dukane 16. The Lost Bridegroom 16. The Red Widow 16. *Raffles* 17. On the Quiet 18. Here Comes the Bride 18. Test of Honour 19. *Dr Jekyll and Mr Hyde* 20. The Lotus Eater 21. *Sherlock Holmes* 22. *Beau Brummell* 24. *The Sea Beast* 26. *Don Juan* 26. When a Man Loves 27. *The Beloved Rogue* 27. *Tempest* 28. Eternal Love 29. *Show of Shows* (first talkie: recites Richard III) 29. General Crack 29. The Man from Blankley's 30. *Moby Dick* 30. *Svengali* 31. The Mad Genius 31. *Arsène Lupin* 32. *Grand Hotel* 32. State's Attorney 32. *A Bill of Divorcement* 32. *Rasputin and the Empress* 32. *Topaze* 33. *Reunion In Vienna* 33. *Dinner at Eight* 33. Night Flight 33. *Counsellor at Law* 33. Long Lost Father 34. *Twentieth Century* 34. *Romeo and Juliet* (as Mercutio) 36. *Maytime* 37. *Bulldog Drummond Comes Back* (as the inspector) 37. Night Club Scandal 37. Bulldog Drummond's Revenge 37. Bulldog Drummond's Peril 37. *True Confession* 38. Romance in the Dark 38. *Marie Antoinette* 38. *Spawn of the North* 38. *Hold that Co-Ed* 38. *The Great Man Votes* 39. *Midnight* 39. The Great Profile 40. Invisible Woman 41. World Premiere 41. Playmates 42.

✪ For a few performances of fine swashbucking, for a few more of ripe ham, and as an awful warning of what can happen to a star who becomes too sure that the world is his oyster. *Twentieth Century*.

❝ I like to be introduced as America's foremost actor. It saves the necessity of further effort. – *J.B.*

My head is buried in the sands of tomorrow, while my tail feathers are singed by the hot sun of today. – *J.B.*

I'm fifty years old and I want to look like Jackie Cooper's grandson. – *J.B.*

If you stay in front of the movie camera long enough, it will show you not only what you had for breakfast but who your ancestors were. – *J.B.*

I've done everything three times. The fourth time around becomes monotonous. – *J.B.*

The good die young – because they see no point in living if you have to be good. – *J. B.*

Student to lecturer: Tell me, Mr Barrymore, in your view did Ophelia ever sleep with Hamlet?' J.B. to student, after much thought: 'Only in the Chicago company . . .'

Katharine Hepburn after finishing *A Bill of Divorcement:* 'Thank goodness I don't have to act with you any more!' J.B., sweetly: 'I didn't know you ever had, darling . . .'

J.B., flinging a fish at a coughing audience: 'Busy yourselves with that, you damned walruses, while the rest of us get on with the play!'

A producer's wife at a Hollywood party, finding J.B. relieving himself in a corner of the ladies' room: 'Mr Barrymore, this is for ladies!' J.B., turning around without buttoning up: 'So, madam, is this!'

'My memory is full of beauty: Hamlet's soliloquies, Queen Mab's speech, the Song of Solomon. Do you expect me to clutter up all that with this horse shit?' (When asked why he required idiot boards in the studio, having perfect recall elsewhere).

He moved through a movie scene like an exquisite paper knife. – *Heywood Broun*

Die? I should say not, old fellow. No Barrymore would allow such a conventional thing to happen to him. – *J.B. during his last illness*

This is a man who went through all the genres, starting with vaudeville – he was a song and dance man – classical theatre, the great American Hamlet, the silent movies, straight through into talking pictures. Nobody else did all that. Nobody. – *Nicol Williamson*

What I really have in common with Jack Barrymore is a lack of vocation. He himself played the part of an actor because that was the role he'd been given. – *Orson Welles*

Perhaps the most cynical actor who ever rattled rafters. – *William Redfield*

Famous line (*Twentieth Century*): 'I close the iron door on you!'

Barrymore, John, Jnr (1932–) (John Drew Barrymore).
American actor, son of John Barrymore and Dolores Costello. Usually plays weaklings. He is the father of actress Drew Barrymore.

The Sundowners 50. The Big Night 51. Thunderbirds 52. While the City Sleeps 56. Night of the Quarter Moon 59. The Boatmen 59. The Cossacks 60. Nights of Rasputin 61. War of the Zombies 63, etc.

Barrymore, Lionel (1878–1954) (Lionel Blythe).
Accomplished American character actor, the brother of Ethel and John Barrymore, and son of leading stage actors Maurice Barrymore and Georgiana Drew Barrymore. Born in Philadelphia, he first appeared on stage with his grandmother, the London-born actress Mrs John Drew, in 1893, and was a Broadway star by 1918, combining stage roles with screen appearances. Often reluctant to follow the family acting tradition, he preferred composing music and painting and etching, which he had studied in Paris, subsidized by Ethel. He turned his back on the stage to concentrate on movies after stage failures in the mid-20s. With the onset of sound, he also directed, including *Redemption* and *His Glorious Night*, the two films that destroyed the career of John Gilbert, and claimed to have invented the sound boom, by tying a microphone onto the end of a fishing rod. An addiction to morphine and cocaine hampered his screen career, as did his later confinement to a wheelchair, as the result of a fall or, possibly, syphilis. From the early 30s he was a familiar and well-loved member of the MGM galaxy, playing sentimental, crotchety grandpas, churlish millionaires and, in a long and successful series of films, Dr Gillespie. He was the author of a novel, *Mr Cantonwine, a Moral Tale*. Married actresses Doris Rankin and Irene Fenwick.

Autobiography: 1951, *We Barrymores*.

Biographies: 1964, *The Barrymores* by Hollis Alpert; 1981, *The Barrymores: The Royal Family in Hollywood* by James Kotsilibas-Davis; 1990, *The House of Barrymore* by Margot Peters.

■ Friends 09. Fighting Blood 11. Judith of Bethulia 11. The New York Hat 12. The Seats of the Mighty 14. Under the Gaslight 14. Wildfire 15. A Modern Magdalen 15. The Curious Conduct 15. The Flaming Sword 15. Dora 15. A Yellow Streak 15. The Exploits of Elaine 15. Dorian's Divorce 16. The Quitter 16. The Upheaval 16. The Brand of Cowardice 16. His Father's Son 17. The End of the Tour 17. The Millionaire's Double 17. Life's Whirlpool 17. The Valley of Night 19. The Devil's Garden 20. The Copperhead 20. The Master Mind 20. Jim the Penman 21. The Great Adventure 21. Face in the Fog 22. Boomerang 22. Enemies of Women 23. Unseeing Eyes 23. The Eternal City 24. America 24. Meddling Women 24. The Iron Man 25. Children of the Whirlwind 25. The Girl Who Wouldn't Work 25. Fifty Fifty 25. I am the Man 25. The Wrongdoers 25. The Barrier 26. *The Bells* 26. The Splendid Road 26. The Temptress 26. Brooding Eyes 26. The Lucky Lady 26. Paris at Midnight 26. Women Love Diamonds 27. The Show 27. Body and Soul 27. The 13th Hour 27. Drums of Love 27. Love 27. *Sadie Thompson* 28. West of Zanzibar 28. Decameron Nights 28. The Lion and the Mouse 28. Roadhouse 28. The River Woman 28. Alias Jimmy Valentine (first talkie) 29. Mysterious Island 29. Hollywood Revue 29. Confession (d only) 29. Madame X (AAN d only) 29. His Glorious Night (d only) 29. The Unholy Night (d only) 29. The Rogue Song (d only) 30. Free and Easy 30. Ten Cents a Dance (d only) 31. *A Free Soul* (AA) 31. The Yellow Ticket 31. Guilty Hands 31. Mata Hari 31. *The Man I Killed* 32. *Arsène Lupin* 32. *Grand Hotel* 32. Washington Masquerade 32. *Rasputin and the Empress* (as Rasputin) 32. Sweepings 33. Looking Forward 33. The Stranger's Return 33. Dinner at Eight 33. One Man's Journey 33. Night Flight 33. Christopher Bean 33. Should Ladies Behave? 33. This Side of Heaven 34. Carolina 34. The Girl from Missouri 34. Treasure Island 34. David Copperfield 34. The Little Colonel 35. Mark of the Vampire 35. Public Hero Number One 35. The Return of Peter Grimm 35. *Ah Wilderness* 35. The Voice of Bugle Ann 36. The Road to Glory 36. *The Devil Doll* 36. The Gorgeous Hussy 36. *Camille* 37. *A Family Affair* (first of Hardy Family series) 37. Captains Courageous 37. Saratoga 37. Navy Blue and Gold 37. A Yank at Oxford 38. Test Pilot 38. *You Can't Take It With You* 38. *Young Dr Kildare* (start of series, as Dr Gillespie) 38. Let Freedom Ring 39. Calling Dr Kildare 39. *On Borrowed Time* 39. The Secret of Dr Kildare 39. Dr Kildare's Strange Case 40. Dr Kildare Goes Home 40. Dr Kildare's Crisis 40. The Bad Man 41. The Penalty 41. The People vs Dr Kildare 41. Dr Kildare's Wedding Day 41. Lady Be Good 41. Dr Kildare's Victory 41. *Calling Dr Gillespie* 42. Dr Gillespie's New Assistant 42. Tennessee Johnson 43. Dr Gillespie's Criminal Case 43. Thousands Cheer 43. A Guy Named Joe 43. Three Men in White 44. Since You Went Away 44. Between Two Women 45. The Valley of Decision 45. *Three Wise Fools* 46. *It's a Wonderful Life* 46. The Secret Heart 46. *Duel in the Sun* 46. Dark Delusion 47. *Key Largo* 48. Down to the Sea in Ships 49. Malaya 50. Right Cross 50. Bannerline 51. Lone Star 52. Main Street to Broadway 53.

❝ I never played with him that I didn't envy his consummate art. – *Marie Dressler*

This is the age of insincerity. The movies had the misfortune to come along in the twentieth century, and because they appeal to the masses there can be no sincerity in them. Hollywood is tied hand and foot to the demands for artificiality of the masses all over the world. – *L.B.*

As my brother Lionel says in every single picture to some ingenue: 'You have spirit – I like that!' – *John Barrymore*

✪ For having a go at everything in sight, even female impersonation; and for becoming Hollywood's omnipresent crotchety grandpa. *You Can't Take It with You.*

Barsacq, Léon (1906–1969).
Russian art director and set designer, long in France. He studied architecture and decorative arts in Paris before beginning work as an assistant designer, later collaborating with Alexandre Trauner and others.

La Marseillaise 38. Lumière d'Eté 43. *Les Enfants du Paradis* 44. L'Idiot 46. Le Silence est d'Or 47. *La Beauté du Diable* 50. Les Belles de Nuit 52. Les Diaboliques 55. Les Grandes Maneuvres 55. The Ambassador's Daughter (US) 56. Porte des Lilas 57. The Longest Day 62. The Visit 64. Phèdre 69, many others.

Barsi, Judith (1977–1988).
American child actress. Killed by her father.

Eye of the Tiger 86. Jaws: The Revenge 87. Slamdance 87. The Land before Time (voice) 88. All Dogs Go to Heaven (voice) 89, etc.

Barstow, Stan (1928–).
British north country novelist whose *A Kind of Loving* was successfully filmed. Some of his other material has been adapted for television.

Bart (1978–).
American grizzly bear who has given fearsome performances in many films, frequently better than those of his co-stars. He stands 9 ft 6 ins tall and weighs 1480 lbs.

Clan of the Cave Bear 85. The Bear 89. White Fang 90. The Great Outdoors 88. Legends of the Fall 94. The Edge 97, etc.

Bart, Lionel (1930–) (Lionel Begleiter).
London-born lyricist and composer who can't read music but was phenomenally successful with West End musicals such as *Fings Ain't What They Used To Be*, *Oliver!*, *Blitz* and *Maggie May*.

The Tommy Steele Story (s) 57. The Duke Wore Jeans (story) 58. Tommy the Toreador (s) 59. In the Nick (s) 59. Sparrows Can't Sing (title s) 62. From Russia with Love (title s) 63. Man in the Middle (m) 63. *Oliver!* (oa) 69. Lock Up Your Daughters! (oa) 69. Black Beauty (m) 71, etc.

Bartel, Paul (1938–).
American actor and director. Born in Brooklyn, New York, he studied at UCLA and at Rome's Centro Sperimentale di Cinematografica. Recently, he has been more active as a character actor than as a director.

Private Parts (d) 72. Death Race 2000 (d) 75. Eat My Dust (a) 76. Cannonball (adw) 76. Grand Theft Auto (a) 77. Eating Raoul (ad) 81. Lust in the Dust 84. Not for Publication 84. Longshot 85. Scenes from the Class Struggle in Beverly Hills 89. Gremlins 2: The New Batch (a) 89. The Pope Must Die/The Pope Must Diet (a) 91. Desire and Hell at Sunset Motel (a) 92. Shelf Life (a) 93. Acting on Impulse (a) 93. Grief (a) 94. The Usual Suspects (a) 95. Basquiat (a) 96. Lewis and Clark and George (a) 97, etc.

Barthelmess, Richard (1895–1963).
Presentable American leading man who went straight from college into silent films. Griffith used him memorably, and in 1921 he formed his own company and was popular until the advent of talkies, which made his innocent image seem old-fashioned and condemned him to insipid character roles.

■ Gloria's Romance 16. Camille 17. The Eternal Sin 17. The Moral Code 17. Rich Man Poor Man 18. The Hope Chest 19. Boots 19. The Girl Who Stayed Home 19. Three Men and a Girl 19. Peppy Polly 19. *Broken Blossoms* 19. I'll Get Him Yet 19. Scarlet Days 19. The Idol Dancer 20. The Love Flower 20. Way Down East 20. Experience 21. *Tol'able David* 21. The Seventh Day 22. Sonny 22. The Bond Boy 22. The Bright Shawl 23. The Fighting Blade 23. Twenty One 24. *The Enchanted Cottage* 24. Classmates 24. New Toys 25. Soul Fire 25. Shore Leave 25. The Beautiful City 25. Just Suppose 26. Ranson's Folly 26. The Amateur Gentleman 26. The White Black Sheep 26. *The Patent Leather Kid* (AAN) 27. The Drop Kick 27. The Noose (AAN) 28. Kentucky Courage 28. Wheels of Chance 28. Out of the Ruins 28. Scarlet Seas 28. Weary River 29. Drag 29. Young Nowheres 29. Show of Shows 29. Son of the Gods 30. *The Dawn Patrol* 30. The Lash 31. Way Down East 31. The Finger Points 31. The Last Flight 31. Alias the Doctor 32. *The Cabin in the Cotton* 32. Central Airport 33. Heroes for Sale 33. Massacre 33. *A Modern Hero* 34. Midnight Alibi 34. Spy of Napoleon 35. Four Hours to Kill 35. *Only Angels Have Wings* 39. The Man Who Talked Too Much 40. The Mayor of 44th Street 42. *The Spoilers* 42.

❝ He has the most beautiful face of any man who ever went before a camera. – *Lillian Gish*

Bartholomew, Freddie (1924–1992) (Frederick Llewellyn).
Impeccably well-bred British child actor whose success in Hollywood films of the 30s delighted elderly aunts the world over. His somewhat toffee-nosed image fell from favour during the war and as an adult he moved out of show business into advertising.

■ Fascination (GB) 30. Lily Christine (GB) 32. *David Copperfield* 35. Anna Karenina 35. Professional Soldier 35. *Little Lord Fauntleroy* 36. The Devil is a Sissy 36. Lloyds of London 36. *Captains Courageous* 37. *Kidnapped* 38. Lord Jeff 38. Listen Darling 38. Spirit of Culver 38. Two Bright Boys 39. *The Swiss Family Robinson* 40. *Tom Brown's Schooldays* 40. Naval Academy 41. Cadets on Parade 42. A Yank at Eton 42. The Town Went Wild 44. Sepia Cinderella 47. St Benny the Dip 51.

Bartkowiak, Andrzej (1950–).
Polish-born cinematographer who studied at the Lodz Film School and emigrated to the US in 1972, where he first worked in commercials.

Deadly Hero 76. Prince of the City 81. Deathtrap 82. The Verdict 82. Daniel 83. Terms of Endearment 83. Prizzi's Honor 85. Power 86. Nuts 87. Twins 88. Q & A 90. Falling Down 92. A Good Man in Africa 94. Speed 94. Losing Isaiah 95. Species 95. The Mirror Has Two Faces 96. Dante's Peak 97. The Devil's Advocate 97, etc.

Bartlam, Dorothy (1908–).
English leading actress and novelist, a former dancer who began in films as an extra in 1925. As a result of winning a beauty contest, she obtained leading roles with British Lion in the late 20s, retiring in the mid-30s, soon after her first novel, *Contrary-Wise*, was published.

The Flying Squad 29. The Ringer 31. Birds of a Feather 31. We Dine at Seven 31. The Fires of

Fate 32. Call Me Mame 33. Up for the Derby 33. On Thin Ice 33, etc.

Bartlett, Hall (1922–1993).
American independent producer, director and screenwriter whose films seldom seem quite good enough to be independent about. Married Rhonda Fleming (1966–71).
■ *Navajo* 52. Unchained (& wd) 55. *Drango* (& wd) 56. Zero Hour (& d) 57. All the Young Men (& d) 60. *The Caretakers* (& d) 64. A Global Affair 64. Sol Madrid 68. Changes (d) 69. The Wild Pack (d) 72. Jonathan Livingston Seagull (& d, co-w) 73. The Children of Sanchez (d) 78. Leaving Home (d) 86.

Bartlett, Richard (1922–1994).
American director.
The Lonesome Trail 55. I've Lived Before 56. Rock Pretty Baby 56. Joe Dakota 57. Slim Carter 57. Money, Women and Guns 58. The Gentle People and the Quiet Land 71. A Christmas Story (TV) 88, etc.

Bartlett, Sy (1900–1978) (Sacha Baraniev).
American screenwriter and producer, a former journalist. Born in Kansas City, Missouri, and educated at Yale University, he began as a writer and later set up a production company with actor Gregory PECK, ending his career under contract to Twentieth Century-Fox.
The Big Brain (w) 33. Boulder Dam (w) 35. Coconut Grove 38. Road to Zanzibar (co-w) 41. Bullet Scars 42. The Princess and the Pirate 44. 13 Rue Madeleine 46. Down to the Sea in Ships 49. *Twelve O'Clock High* (w) 49. That Lady (wp) 55. *The Big Country* (w) 57. A Gathering of Eagles (wp) 63. Che (p) 69, etc.

Bartok, Eva (1926–1998) (Eva Sjöke).
Glamorous Hungarian-born actress in international films. Born in Kecskemet, she came to England in the mid-40s and was put under contract by Alexander KORDA. In the early 50s, she moved to Europe and married actor Curt JURGENS, her fourth husband; after their divorce, she had a daughter by, she claimed, Frank SINATRA. She returned to England in the mid-80s, where she died, forgotten and penniless.
Autobiography: 1959, *Worth Living For*.
A Tale of Five Cities 51. Venetian Bird 52. The Crimson Pirate 52. Front Page Story 54. Ten Thousand Bedrooms 57. Operation Amsterdam 59. SOS Pacific 60. Beyond the Curtain 60. Blood and Black Lace 64, etc.
❝ I have made a mess of my life. I have been a sentimental fool. – *E.B.*

Barton, Buzz (1914–1980).
American character actor, a child star in early westerns, from rodeo.
The Boy Rider 28. Apache Kid's Escape 30. The Lone Defender (serial) 32. Mystery Trooper 32. Powersmoke Range 35. The Tonto Kid 35. In the Heat of the Night 67. In Cold Blood 67, etc.

Barton, Charles (1902–1981).
Routine American director, long at Universal.
■ Wagon Wheels 34. Car 99 35. Rocky Mountain Mystery 35. The Last Outpost (co-d) 35. Timothy's Quest 36. And Sudden Death 36. Nevada 36. Rose Bowl 36. Murder with Pictures 36. The Crime Nobody Saw 37. Forlorn River 37. Thunder Train 37. Born to the West 38. Behind Prison Gates 39. Five Little Peppers and How They Grew 39. My Son is Guilty 40. Five Little Peppers at Home 40. Island of Doomed Men 40. Babies for Sale 40. Out West with the Peppers 40. Five Little Peppers in Trouble 40. Nobody's Children 40. The Phantom Submarine 40. The Big Boss 41. The Richest Man in Town 41. Harmon of Michigan 41. Two Latins from Manhattan 41. Sing for your Supper 41. Honolulu Lu 41. Shut My Big Mouth 42. Tramp Tramp Tramp 42. Hello Anapolis 42. Parachute Nurse 42. Sweetheart of the Fleet 42. A Man's World 42. Lucky Legs 42. The Spirit of Stanford 42. Laugh Your Blues Away 42. *Reveille with Beverly* 43. Let's Have Fun 43. She Has What It Takes 43. What's Buzzin Cousin 43. Is Everybody Happy 43. What a Woman 43. Beautiful but Broke 44. Hey Rookie 44. Jam Session 44. Louisiana Hayride 44. Men in her Diary 45. White Tie and Tails 45. *The Time of Their Lives* 46. Smooth as Silk 46. The Wistful Widow of Wagon Gap 47. Buck Privates Come Home 47. Mexican Hayride 48. *Abbott and Costello Meet Frankenstein* 48. The Noose Hangs High 48. Free for All 49. Africa Screams 49. Abbott and Costello Meet the Killer 49. The Milkman 50. Double Crossbones 50. Ma and Pa Kettle at the Fair 52. Dance with Me Henry 56. The Shaggy Dog 59. Toby Tyler 60. Swinging Along 62.

Barton, Dee.
American composer.
Play Misty for Me 71. High Plains Drifter 73. Thunderbolt and Lightfoot 74, etc.

Barton, James (1890–1962).
Grizzled, good-humoured American character actor, a veteran of burlesque and Broadway.
Captain Hurricane 35. Shepherd of the Hills 41. *The Time of Your Life* 48. Yellow Sky 49. The Daughter of Rosie O'Grady 50. Wabash Avenue 50. Here Comes the Groom 51. Golden Girl 51. The Naked Hills 57. Quantez 57. *The Misfits* 61, etc.

Bartosch, Berthold (1893–1968).
Austro-Hungarian animator, best known for his symbolic *L'Idée* 34.

Barty, Billy (1925–) (William Bertanzetti).
American dwarf actor, 3 feet 9 inches high, in films from the age of three. A former member of Spike Jones's City Slickers, he was noted for singing 'I'm in the Mood for Love', a parody of Liberace, complete with exploding candelabra, which he recorded with the band in 1954.
Gold Diggers of 1933 33. Mickey's Minstrels 34. Harum Scarum 65. Pufnstuf 70. The Day of the Locust 74. Won Ton Ton, The Dog Who Saved Hollywood 75. W. C. Fields and Me 76. Under the Rainbow 81. Legend 85. Masters of the Universe 87. Willow 88. Lobster Man from Mars 89. Life Stinks 91. Radioland Murders 94, etc.
TV series: The Spike Jones Show 54. Circus Boy 56–58. The Spike Jones Show 57. Ace Crawford, Private Eye 82.

Barwood, Hal (1940–).
American director and screenwriter, most recently involved in designing video games for George Lucas's software company LucasArts, including *Indiana Jones and the Fate of Atlantis*.
The Sugarland Express (co-w) 74. The Bingo Long Traveling All-Stars & Motor Kings (co-w) 76. MacArthur (co-w) 77. Corvette Summer (co-w) 78. Dragonslayer (co-w) 81. Warning Sign (co-w, d) 85, etc.

Baryshnikov, Mikhail (1948–).
Latvian ballet dancer who made his American film debut in *The Turning Point* (AAN) 77 and consolidated this in *White Nights* 85, *Dancers* 87. The Cabinet of Dr Ramirez 91. Company Business 91.
❝ I'm not the first straight dancer or the last. Anyway, it has nothing to do with art. – *M.B.*

Barzman, Ben (1911–1989).
Canadian screenwriter, a former journalist and novelist. Born in Toronto and educated at Reed College, he began working in Hollywood but was blacklisted in the early 50s. (He later said that he had been approached by lawyer Martin Gang, who told him that for a payment of $16,000 a congressman would prevent his name going on the list.) He moved to France and worked with other US exiles in Europe, including director Joseph LOSEY.
True to Life 42. The Boy with Green Hair 48. He Who Must Die 56. Time without Pity 57. Blind Date 59. The Ceremony 63. The Heroes of Telemark 65. The Blue Max 66, etc.

Basehart, Richard (1914–1984).
Thoughtful American leading actor who somehow never achieved his expected stardom; equally adept at honesty, villainy and mental disturbance. Many TV appearances. He was married to Valentina CORTESE.
■ Cry Wolf 47. Repeat Performance 47. *He Walked by Night* 48. Roseanna McCoy 49. *The Black Book* 49. Tension 49. Outside the Wall 50. *Fourteen Hours* 51. The House on Telegraph Hill 51. Fixed Bayonets 51. Decision Before Dawn 51. The Stranger's Hand 53. Titanic 53. La Strada 54. The Good Die Young 54. La Reprise de Justice 54. La Vena d'Oro 55. Cartouche 55. Canyon Crossroads 55. Il Bidone/The Swindlers 55. The Extra Day 56. *Moby Dick* 56. The Intimate Stranger 56. *Time Limit* 57. So Soon to Die (TV) 57. Arrivederci Dimas 57. *The Brothers Karamazov* 58. L'Ambiteuse 58. Jons und Erdme 59. Five Branded Women 60. Portrait in Black 60. For the Love of Mike 60. Passport to China 61. The Savage Guns 61. Tierra Brutal 62. *Hitler* (title role) 63. Kings of the Sun 63. The Satan Bug 65. The Sole Survivor (TV) 69. The Death of Me Yet (TV) 71. City Beneath the Sea/One Hour to Doomsday (TV) 71. Assignment Munich (TV) 72. The Bounty Man (TV) 72. Escape of the Birdmen (TV) 72. Chato's Land 72. Rage 72. Maneater (TV) 73. And Millions Will Die 73. How the West Was Won (TV) 75. Mansion of the Doomed 76. The Island of Dr Moreau 77. WEB (TV) 78. The Bastard (TV) 78. Being There 79. The Great Georgia Bank Hoax 79. Marilyn, the Untold Story (TV) 80. Knight Rider (TV) 82.
TV series: *Voyage to the Bottom of the Sea* 64–67.

Basevi, James
Anglo-American art director and special effects wizard, at Fox from the mid-20s.
The Big Parade 25. The Hurricane 38. Wuthering Heights (AAN) 39. The Long Voyage Home 40. The Westerner (AAN) 40. Tobacco Road 41. The Ox-Bow Incident 43. The Gang's All Here (AAN) 43. The Song of Bernadette (AA) 43. Lifeboat 44. Jane Eyre 44. Spellbound 45. The Keys of the Kingdom (AAN) 45. Duel in the Sun 46. My Darling Clementine 46. Boomerang! 47. Fort Apache 48. Mighty Joe Young 49. She Wore a Yellow Ribbon 49. My Man and I 52. East of Eden 54. The Searchers 56, many others.

Basinger, Kim (1953–).
Sultry American leading actress, often in oversexed roles. She is married to Alec Baldwin.
Hard Country 81. Killjoy (TV) 81. Mother Lode 82. The Man Who Loved Women 83. Never Say Never Again 83. The Natural 84. Fool for Love 85. Nine and a Half Weeks 85. No Mercy 86. Blind Date 87. Nadine 87. My Stepmother Is an Alien 88. Batman 89. The Marrying Man/Too Hot to Handle 91. Final Analysis 92. The Real McCoy 93. Wayne's World 2 93. The Getaway 94. Prêt-à-Porter 94. *LA Confidential* (AA) 97, etc.
TV series: Dog and Cat 79. From Here to Eternity 80.
❝ You have to be a little unreal to be in this business. – *K.B.*
I don't have any friends in this business at all. That Mafia guy John Gotti's best friend is the one who stabbed him in the back. Hollywood is a lot like that. It's like the Mafia. – *K.B.*

Baskett, James (1904–1948).
American character actor best known for his performance as Uncle Remus in *Song of the South* 48.

Basler, Marianne (1964–).
Blonde Swiss leading actress, in French and international films.
Alexina 85. La Soule 88. A Soldier's Tale 88. Dames Galantes 90. Overseas 90. Eline Vere 91. Blanc d'Ébene 91. Farinelli the Castrato 94, etc.

Basquette, Lina (1907–1994).
American leading lady of the 20s, former child star and dancer. Her lively private life included seven husbands.
Autobiography: 1990, *Lina: DeMille's Godless Girl*.
Juvenile Dancer 16. Prince for a Day 17. Penrod 22. Ranger of the North 27. Wheel of Chance 28. Show Folks 28. *The Godless Girl* 29. Dude Wrangler 30. Hard Hombre 31. Morals for Women 31. Phantom Express 32. Ebb Tide 37. Four Men and a Prayer 38, etc.

Basquiat, Jean-Michael (1960–1988).
American artist, commemorated in the biopic *Basquiat*, directed by fellow-artist Julian SCHNABEL. Of middle-class Haitian and Puerto Rican descent, he first made his mark as a street graffiti artist, signing his work with the tag Samo (for Same old shit) before being promoted by influential dealers and galleries. He had a much-publicized affair with singer MADONNA in the mid-80s. Died from a heroin overdose. In the biopic he is played by Jeffrey Wright, with David BOWIE in the role of Andy Warhol and Gary OLDMAN as Schnabel. Basquiat's father refused permission for his paintings to be used, so those shown in the film were done by Schnabel.

Bass, Alfie (1920–1987).
Pint-sized British character comedian, adept at cockney/Jewish roles.
Johnny Frenchman 45. Holiday Camp 47. It Always Rains on Sunday 47. The Hasty Heart 49. *The Lavender Hill Mob* 51. *The Bespoke Overcoat* 55. A Kid for Two Farthings 55. A Tale of Two Cities 57. I Only Arsked 59. The Millionairess 60. Alfie 66. The Fearless Vampire Killers 67. The Magnificent Seven Deadly Sins 72. Moonraker 79, etc.
TV series: The Army Game 57–62. Bootsie and Snudge 60–63. Are You Being Served? 79.

Bass, Ronald.
American screenwriter, a former attorney. He signed a six-picture deal worth $8m with Tri-Star Pictures in 1996, and includes in his contracts the clause that no one may rewrite his scripts.
Code Name: Emerald 85. Black Widow 87. Gardens of Stone 87. Rain Man (co-w, AA) 88. Joy Luck Club (co-w) 93. When a Man Loves a Woman (co-w) 94. Dangerous Minds 95. My Best Friend's Wedding 97. How Stella Got Her Groove Back (co-w) 98. What Dreams May Come 98, etc.

Bass, Sam (1851–1878).
American western adventurer, played by Howard Duff in *Calamity Jane and Sam Bass*.

Bass, Saul (1921–1996).
American graphic designer and director, best known for creating title sequences for some 50 films, including many by Otto Preminger. He also designed the detailed storyboards for Hitchcock's *Psycho*, directed racing scenes for John Frankenheimer's *Grand Prix* and the final battle in *Spartacus*.
AS DIRECTOR: Why Man Creates (short) (AA) 68. Phase IV 74, etc.
AS TITLE DESIGNER: Carmen Jones 54. The Shrike 55. The Man with the Golden Arm 55. The Seven Year Itch 55. Around the World in 80 Days (closing animated credit sequence) 56. Vertigo 58. The Big Country 58. Bonjour Tristesse 58. North by Northwest 59. Anatomy of a Murder 59. Psycho 60. Exodus 60. Ocean's Eleven 60. A Walk on the Wild Side 62. It's a Mad Mad Mad Mad World 63. Nine Hours to Rama 63. Bunny Lake Is Missing 65. The Human Factor 79. Broadcast News 87. Big 88. The War of the Roses 89. Cape Fear 91. The Age of Innocence 93, etc.

Basserman, Albert (1867–1952).
Distinguished German stage actor who came to Hollywood as refugee in 1939 and played sympathetic roles.
■ Der Andere 13. Voruntersuchung 31. The Last Days Before the War 32. Kadetten 33. Ein Gewisser Herr Gran 33. Alraune 33. Letzte Liebe 38. Le Famille Lefrancois 39. Dr Ehrlich's Magic Bullet 40. *Foreign Correspondent* (AAN) 40. A Dispatch from Reuters 40. Moon Over Burma 40. Knute Rockne 40. Escape 40. *The Shanghai Gesture* 41. The Great Awakening 41. New Wine 41. A Woman's Face 41. The Moon and Sixpence 42. Invisible Agent 42. Once Upon a Honeymoon 42. Fly by Night 42. Desperate Journey 42. Good Luck Mr Yates 43. Passport to Heaven 43. Reunion in France 43. Madame Curie 44. Since You Went Away 44. *Rhapsody in Blue* 45. Strange Holiday 46. The Searching Wind 46. The Private Affairs of Bel Ami 47. Escape Me Never 47. *The Red Shoes* (GB) 48.
✪ For bringing to Hollywood a suggestion of the unique strength of the European theatre. *The Shanghai Gesture*.

Bassett, Angela (1958–).
American leading actress, from the stage. She played Tina TURNER in the biopic *What's Love Got to Do with It?* Married actor Courtney B. Vance in 1997.
FX 86. Kindergarten Cop 90. Boyz N The Hood 91. Innocent Blood 92. Passion Fish 92. Malcolm X 93. *What's Love Got to Do with It?* (AAN) 93. Strange Days 95. Vampire in Brooklyn 95. Waiting to Exhale 95. Contact 97. How Stella Got Her Groove Back 98. Supernova 99, etc.

Bassey, Shirley (1937–).
Torrid British-born cabaret singer whose film appearances have always been as a performer. She sang the title songs of the James Bond movies *Goldfinger* 64, *Diamonds Are Forever* 71, and *Moonraker* 79.

Bassler, Robert (1903–).
American producer. Born in Washington, he was educated at George Washington University, and was in films from 1924, first in Paramount's research department and later as an editor. He became a literary agent in the early 30s, and was European story editor for Twentieth Century-Fox before becoming a producer from the 40s, and later working in television.
My Gal Sal 42. *The Black Swan* 43. The Lodger 44. Hangover Square 45. Thunder in the Valley 47. *The Snake Pit* 48. Thieves' Highway 49. Halls of Montezuma 50. Kangaroo 52. Beneath the Twelve-Mile Reef 53. Suddenly 54, etc.

Bassman, George (1914–).
American composer, working for MGM from the mid-30s and 40s.
A Day at the Races 37. Babes in Arms 39. Go West 40. Lady Be Good 41. The Big Store 41. The Canterville Ghost 44. The Clock 45. The Postman Always Rings Twice 46. Little Mister Jim 47. The Joe Louis Story 53. Ride the High Country 62. Mail Order Bride 63, etc.

Bastedo, Alexandra (1946–).
Leading lady of Canadian, Italian and English ancestry.
Thirteen Frightened Girls 63. Inside Daisy Clover 66. Casino Royale 67. The Ghoul 75. The Blood-Spattered Bride 80, etc.
TV series: *The Champions* 67.

Batchelor, Joy (1914–1991).
British animator, wife of John Halas and co-founder of Halas and Batchelor Cartoon Films.

Bate, Anthony (1929–).
Smooth English character actor, mostly on television. He trained at the Central School of Speech and Drama and was on stage from 1953.
Stopover Forever 64. Act of Murder 64. Ghost Story/Madhouse Mansion 74. Bismarck 76. Philby, Burgess and Maclean (TV) 80. Give My Regards to Broad Street 83. War and Remembrance 89. Eminent Domain 90. Prime Suspect 4: Inner Circles (TV) 95. Rebecca (TV) 97, etc.
TV series: Game, Set, and Match 88.

Bateman, Jason (1969–).
American actor, from television as a juvenile. He is the brother of Justine Bateman.
Can You Feel Me Dancing? 85. Teen Wolf Too 87. Breaking the Rules 92. A Taste for Killing 92, etc.
TV series: Little House on the Prairie 81–82. Silver Spoons 82–84. It's Your Move 84–85. Valerie 86–87. The Hogan Family 88–91.

Bateman, Justine (1966–).
American actress, from television as a juvenile. She is the sister of Jason Bateman.
Can You Feel Me Dancing? 85. Satisfaction 88. The Fatal Image (TV) 90. The Closer 91. Primary Motive 92. Deadbolt 92. The Night We Never Met 93, etc.
TV series: Family Ties 82–89.

Bates, Alan (1934–).
Leading British actor of stage and screen: tends to play thoughtful toughs with soft centres. Born in Allestree, Derbyshire, he trained at RADA and was on stage from 1955, first gaining fame in various roles at the Royal Court theatre.
■ The Entertainer 59. *A Kind of Loving* 62. *Whistle Down the Wind* 62. The Caretaker 63. The Running Man 63. *Nothing But the Best* 64. *Zorba the Greek* 65. Georgy Girl 66. King of Hearts 67. *Far from the Madding Crowd* 67. The Fixer (AAN) 68. *Women in Love* 69. Three Sisters 70. The Go-Between 70. *A Day in the Death of Joe Egg* 71. Impossible Object 73. Butley 73. In Celebration 74. Royal Flash 75. The Collection (TV) 76. An Unmarried Woman 77. The Shout 78. The Rose 79. Very Like a Whale (TV) 80. Nijinsky 80. Quartet 81. The Return of the Soldier 82. Britannia Hospital 82. An Englishman Abroad (TV) 83. A Voyage Around My Father (TV) 83. Dr Fischer of Geneva (TV) 83. Duet For One 86. A Prayer for the Dying 87. We Think the World of You 88. Force Majeure 89. 102 Boulevard Haussman (TV) 90. Docteur M. 90. Hamlet 90. Mister Frost 90. Secret Friends 91. Silent Tongue 93. The Grotesque 95.

Bates, Barbara (1925–1969).
American leading lady, former model and ballet dancer. Committed suicide.
This Love of Ours 45. The Fabulous Joe 48. June Bride 48. *The Inspector General* 49. Cheaper by the Dozen 49. All About Eve 50. Belles on Her Toes 52. Rhapsody 54. House of Secrets (GB) 56. Town on Trial (GB) 57. Apache Territory 58, etc.
TV series: It's a Great Life 54–55

Bates, Florence (1888–1954) (Florence Rabe).
American character actress, adept at friendly or monstrous matrons. Born in San Antonio, Texas, she became the state's first woman lawyer in 1914, and was later a businesswoman. She trained at the Pasadena Playhouse in her late 40s, and was persuaded by Alfred Hitchcock to play the role of Mrs Van Hopper in *Rebecca*, for which she is best remembered; she remained in demand for the rest of her career.
■ The Man in Blue 37. *Rebecca* 40. Calling All Husbands 40. Son of Monte Cristo 40. Hudson's Bay 40. Kitty Foyle 40. Road Show 41. Love Crazy 41. The Chocolate Soldier 41. Strange Alibi 41. The Devil and Miss Jones 41. The Tuttles of Tahiti 42. *The Moon and Sixpence* 42. My Heart Belongs to Daddy 42. Mexican Spitfire at Sea 42. We Were Dancing 42. Slightly Dangerous 43. His Butler's Sister 43. They Got Me Covered 43. Mister Big 43. Heaven Can Wait 43. Mr Lucky 43. Since You Went Away 44. The Mask of Dimitrios 44. Kismet 44. Belle of the Yukon 44. The Racket Man 44. Saratoga Trunk 45. Tahiti Nights 45. *Tonight and Every Night* 45. Sanantonio 45. Out of This World 45. Claudia and David 46. Cluny Brown 46. The Diary of a Chambermaid 46. Whistle Stop 46. The Time the Place and the Girl 46. *The High Window* 47. Love and Learn 47. Desire Me 47. *The Secret Life of Walter Mitty* 47. Texas Brooklyn and Heaven 48. Winter Meeting 48. The Inside Story 48. River Lady 48. My Dear Secretary 48. Portrait of Jennie 48. *I Remember Mama* 48. A Letter to Three Wives 48. The Judge Steps Out 49. The Girl from Jones Beach 49. On the Town 49. Belle of Old Mexico 50. *County Fair* 50. The Second Woman 51. Lullaby of Broadway 51. The Tall Target 51. Havana Rose 51. Father Takes the Air 51. The Whistle at Eaton Falls 51. The San Francisco Story 52. Les Miserables 52. Paris Model 53. Main Street to Broadway 53.

Bates, Granville (1882–1940).
American general purpose supporting actor of the 30s: storekeepers, doctors and grandpas.
Jealousy 29. The Smiling Lieutenant 31. Woman Wanted 35. 13 Hours by Air 36. They Won't Forget 37. Nancy Steele is Missing 37. Wells Fargo 37. Go Chase Yourself 38. Gold is Where You Find It 38. The Great Man Votes 39. Pride of the Blue Grass 39. Of Mice and Men 39. Jesse James 39. My Favorite Wife 40. The Mortal Storm 40. Brother Orchid 40, many others.

Bates, H. E. (1905–1974).
British novelist who dabbled in the cinema. *The Purple Plain* was filmed; *The Darling Buds of May* was filmed as *The Mating Season* and formed the basis of a successful TV series from 1990. *Fair Stood the Wind for France* was done on television; and he co-scripted *Summer Madness*. In 1995 came *Feast of July*, directed by Christopher Menaul, and *A Month by the Lake*, directed by John Irvin.

Bates, Kathy (1948–).
American character actress, notable as the crazed fan in *Misery*. Born in Memphis, Tennessee, and educated at the Southern Methodist University, she first came to notice in the theatre.
Straight Time 78. Come Back to the Five and Dime, Jimmy Dean, Jimmy Dean 82. Summer Heat 87. Arthur 2: On the Rocks 88. High Stakes/Melanie Rose 89. Signs of Life 89. Men Don't Leave 90. Dick Tracy 90. White Palace 90. *Misery* (AA) 90. Fried Green Tomatoes at the Whistle Stop Café 91. The Road to Mecca 91. At Play in the Fields of the Lord 91. Shadows and Fog 92. Prelude to a Kiss 92. A Home of Our Own 93. North 94. Curse of the Starving Class 94. Angus 95. Diabolique 96. The War at Home 96. The Late Shift (TV) 96. Titanic 97. Amy Foster/Swept from the Sea 97. Primary Colors 98. The Waterboy 98. A Civil Action 98, etc.

Bates, Michael (1920–1978).
British character actor who specialized in stupid policemen and other caricatures.
Carrington VC 55. I'm All Right Jack 59. Bedazzled 67. *Here We Go Round the Mulberry Bush* 67. Salt and Pepper 68. Don't Raise the Bridge Lower the River 68. Hammerhead 68. Patton 70. The Rise and Rise of Michael Rimmer 70. A *Clockwork Orange* 71. No Sex Please, We're British 73, etc.
TV series: It Ain't Half Hot Mum 73–77.

Bates, Ralph (1940–1991).
Incisive British character actor who played Caligula on TV and took the natural step to Hammer horrors.
The Horror of Frankenstein 70. Lust for a Vampire 70. Dr Jekyll and Sister Hyde 71. Fear in the Night 73. Persecution 74. I Don't Want to be Born 75. Letters to an Unknown Lover 84, etc.
TV series: Poldark, Penmarric, Dear John.

Bath, Hubert (1883–1945).
British composer. Born in Barnstaple, Devon, he spent much of his career from the early 30s as a composer and arranger for Gaumont-British, where his work was frequently uncredited. His best-known composition was the concerto *Cornish Rhapsody* played by pianist Harriet Cohen, dubbing for Stewart Granger, in *Love Story*.
Kitty 29. Blackmail 29. The Plaything 29. Under the Greenwood Tree 29. Waltzes from Vienna 34. Chu Chin Chow (conductor) 34. The Thirty-Nine Steps 35. Rhodes of Africa 36. The Great Barrier 37. A Yank at Oxford 37. Yellow Sands 38. A Place of One's Own 44. *Love Story* 44, etc.

Báthory, Countess Elisabeth (1560–1614).
Hungarian aristocrat who is alleged to have killed more than 600 girls and women, and to have bathed in the blood of virgins to keep her skin white; though it is also claimed that these stories were inventions of her enemies at her trial, at which she was not present. Arrested in 1610, she was kept under house arrest until her death. So far, four films have been based on her legend, most notably Hammer's *Countess Dracula* 70.
Biography: 1997, *Countess Dracula: The Life and Times of Elisabeth Báthory the Blood Countess* by Tony Thorne.
Le Rouge aux Lèvres (Bel.) 71. Ceremonia Sangrienta (Sp./It.) 72. Immoral Tales/Contes Immoraux (Fr.) 74.

Bators, Stiv (1950–1990) (Steve Bators).
American singer with the 70s punk group Dead Boys and occasional actor. Died after being hit by a car.
Polyester 81. Tapeheads 89.

Battle, John Tucker.
American screenwriter.
Irish Eyes Are Smiling 44. Captain Eddie 45. So Dear to My Heart 48. The Frogmen 51. A Man Alone 55. Lisbon 56. Shootout at Medicine Bend 57, etc.

Bauchau, Patrick.
Belgian leading actor; he quit the profession in the mid-60s for a time to continue a career as an artist.
Suzanne's Career/La Carrière de Suzanne 63. Paris Vu Par 64. The Collector/La Collectionneuse 66. Guns 80. Winter Journey/Le Voyage d'Hiver 82. The State of Things 82. Enigma 82. Entre Nous 83. Choose Me (US) 83. Coup de Foudre 83. Emmanuelle IV 84. Phenomena/Creepers 84. A View to a Kill (GB) 85. Cross 87. Comèdie d'Amour 89. The Rapture (US) 91. Double Identity 91. Chain of Desire (US) 92. Crystal Gazing (GB) 92. Acting on Impulse (US) 93. And the Band Played On (TV) 93. Every Breath (US) 93. The New Age (US) 94. The Dark Side of Genius (US) 94. Day of Reckoning (US) 94. Lisbon Story 95. Jenipapo 95. We Free Kings/I Magi Randagi 96, etc.

Bauchens, Anne (1882–1967).
American editor, almost always for De Mille.
The Squaw Man 18. Don't Change Your Husband 19. The Affairs of Anatol 21. The Ten Commandments 23. King of Kings 27. Dynamite 29. The Sign of the Cross 32. Cleopatra (AAN) 34. The Crusade 35. The Buccaneer 38. North West Mounted Police (AA) 40. Reap the Wild Wind 42. Love Letters 45. Unconquered 47. Samson and Delilah 49. The Greatest Show on Earth (AAN) 52. The Ten Commandments (AAN) 56, many others.

Bauer, Belinda (1956–).
Australian actress, a former model, in American films, usually in off-beat roles.
Winter Kills 79. Success 79. Fugitive from the Empire (TV) 81. Sins of Dorian Gray (TV) 82. Timerider 83. Flashdance 83. Samson and Delilah (TV) 84. The Rosary Murders 87. The Game of Love 87. UHF 89. Act of Piracy 90. Robocop 2 90. Necronomicon 93, etc.

Bauer, Steven (1956–) (Steven Echevarria).
Cuban character actor in Hollywood. Married actress Melanie Griffith (1983–85).
Scarface 83. Thief of Hearts 84. Running Scared 86. Sword of Gideon 86. The Beast 88. Gleaming the Cube 89. A Row of Crows 90. Sweet Poison 91. False Arrest (TV) 91. Raising Caine 92. Snapdragon 93. Improper Conduct 94. Body Count 95. Primal Fear 96. Navajo Blues 97, etc.

Baum, L. Frank (1856–1919).
American author of *The Wizard of Oz*, 1900, and other adventures set in the mythical kingdom. He brought out the book himself after every publisher turned it down, adapted it as a Broadway musical and financed early silent film versions, setting up the Oz Film Manufacturing Company in 1914 and briefly opening his own studio in Hollywood.
The Wizard of Oz 08. The Road to Oz 09. His Majesty the Tin Scarecrow of Oz 14. The Patchwork Girl of Oz 14. The Magic Cloak of Oz 14. The Wizard of Oz 25. The Wizard of Oz 39. The Wiz 78, etc.

Baum, Vicki (1896–1960).
Austrian novelist whose chief gift to Hollywood was the much-filmed and well imitated *Grand Hotel*, which she herself revamped as *Hotel Berlin*.
Autobiography: 1964, *It Was All Quite Different*.

Baur, Harry (1880–1943).
Celebrated French actor of stage and screen.
Shylock 10. La Voyante 23. David Golder 31. Poil de Carotte 32. Golgotha 34. Moscow Nights 35. Crime and Punishment 35. Taras Bulba 35. Un Carnet de Bal 37. The Rebel Son 38. Volpone 39. L'Assassinat du Père Noël 41. Symphonie eines Lebens 42, etc.

Bava, Lamberto (1944–).
Italian director of horror and action movies, the son of Mario Bava. Born in Rome, he began working as an assistant on his father's films, and later was an assistant director on Dario Argento's films in the early 80s.
Macabre/Macabro 80. Blastfighter 84. Monster Shark/Shark Rosso nell'Oceano 84. Demons/Demoni 85. Demons 2/Demoni 2 86. Le Foto di Gioia 87. Black Sabbath 89. Body Puzzle/Misteria 93, etc.

Bava, Mario (1914–1980).
Italian director, former photographer, of period muscleman epics and pseudo-British horror stories, revered by the *cognoscenti* for his tongue-in-cheek attitude towards some of them.
Black Sunday (wd, ph) 60. Hercules in the Centre of the Earth (wd, ph) 61. Erik the Conqueror (wd) 63. The Evil Eye (wd, ph) 63. *Black Sabbath* (wd) 63. *Blood and Black Lace* (wd, ph) 64. Planet of Blood (d) 65. Dr Goldfoot and the Girl Bombs (d) 66. Curse of the Dead (wd) 67. *Diabolik* (wd) 68. The Antecedent (d) 71, etc.

Bavier, Frances (1903–1989).
Motherly American actress, mainly on TV and best known for her Emmy award-winning performance as Aunt Bee on *The Andy Griffith Show* 60–68.
The Day the Earth Stood Still 51. The Lady Says No 51. Horizons West 52. Benji 74, etc.
TV series: It's a Great Life 54–56. The Eve Arden Show 57–58. Mayberry R.F.D. 68–70.

Bax, Sir Arnold (1883–1953).
British composer in a romantic style who scored occasional films. Born in London, he studied at the Royal Academy of Music. He was knighted in 1937 and became Master of the King's Music in 1942.

■ Malta GC 43. Oliver Twist 48. Journey into History 48.

Baxley, Barbara (1927–1990).
American character actress.
The Badlanders 58. The Savage Eye 60. All Fall Down 62. Countdown 67. No Way to Treat a Lady 68. The Impostor (TV) 74. Nashville 75. Norma Rae 79, etc.

Baxley, Craig R.
American director of action films.
Action Jackson 88. I Come in Peace/Dark Angel 91. Stone Cold 91, etc.

Baxter, Alan (1908–1976).
Cold-eyed American second lead of the 40s; graduated to colonels and tough executives.
Mary Burns Fugitive 35. The Last Gangster 37. Gangs of New York 38. Each Dawn I Die 39. Santa Fe Trail 40. Saboteur 42. Submarine Base 43. Winged Victory 44. The Set Up 49. The Devil's Weed 49. End of the Line (in Britain) 56. The True Story of Jesse James 57. The Mountain Road 60. Judgment at Nuremburg 61. This Property is Condemned 66. Willard 71, etc.

Baxter, Anne (1923–1985).
American leading lady who usually played shy and innocent but proved equally at home as a schemer. Trained for the stage but was starring in Hollywood at seventeen. After 1960 found the going tough. The first of her three husbands was actor John Hodiak (1946–53).
Autobiography: 1977, *Intermission*.
■ Twenty Mule Team 40. The Great Profile 40. Charley's Aunt 41. Swamp Water 41. The Pied Piper 42. *The Magnificent Ambersons* 42. Crash Dive 43. *Five Graves to Cairo* 43. North Star 43. The Sullivans 44. The Eve of St Mark 44. Sunday Dinner for a Soldier 44. *Guest in the House* 45. A Royal Scandal 45. Smoky 46. Angel on My Shoulder 46. *The Razor's Edge* (AA) 46. Blaze of Noon 47. Homecoming 48. The Walls of Jericho 48. The Luck of the Irish 48. Yellow Sky 48. You're My Everything 49. A Ticket to Tomahawk 49. *All About Eve* (AAN) 50. Follow the Sun 51. The Outcasts of Poker Flat 52. My Wife's Best Friend 52. Full House 52. I Confess 53. The Blue Gardenia 53. Carnival Story 54. Bedevilled 55. One Desire 55. The Spoilers 55. The Come On 56. The Ten Commandments 56. Three Violent People 57. *Chase a Crooked Shadow* 57. Summer of the Seventeenth Doll 60. Mix Me a Person 61. Cimarron 61. A Walk on the Wild Side 62. The Family Jewels 65. Frontier Woman 66. The Busy Body 67. Companions in Nightmare (TV) 67. Stranger on the Run (TV) 68. The Challengers (TV) 68. The Tall Women 68. Marcus Welby MD (TV pilot) 69. Ritual of Evil 69. The Catcher (TV) 71. Fools Parade 71. The Late Liz 71. If Tomorrow Comes (TV) 71. Lisa Bright and Dark (TV) 72. The Moneychangers (TV) 76. Jane Austen in Manhattan 80. East of Eden (TV) 81.
TV series: Marcus Welby, MD 69–70. Hotel 83–85.

Baxter, Beryl (1926–) (Beryl Ivory).
British leading lady who was groomed for stardom but starred in only one film, and that notoriously poor *Idol of Paris* 46.
Subsequently: The Man with the Twisted Lip 51. Counterspy 53.

Baxter, Jane (1909–) (Feodora Forde).
Gentle-mannered British actress of stage and screen.
The Constant Nymph 32. The Clairvoyant 34. We Live Again (US) 35. The Ware Case 39. Ships with Wings 41. The Flemish Farm 43. Death of an Angel 51, etc.

Baxter, John (1896–1975).
Influential British producer-director of vigorous rough-and-ready dramas and comedies of the 30s and 40s which pointed the way to 50s realism and had an amiable style of their own.
Doss House 32. *Song of the Plough* 32. Lest We Forget 34. Music Hall 35. Say It with Flowers 36. Men of Yesterday 37. Crooks Tour 39. *Love on the Dole* 40. *The Common Touch* 41. *Let the People Sing* 42. *When We are Married* 43. The Shipbuilders 45. The Second Mate 50. Judgment Deferred 51. Ramsbottom Rides Again 56, many others including Old Mother Riley and Flanagan & Allen comedies.

Baxter, Les (1922–1996).
American composer and musical director. He began as a jazz saxophonist and singer, and was md for many Capitol Records albums from the 40s to the 60s.
Hot Blood 55. The Black Sleep 56. Macabre 58. Goliath and the Barbarians 59. *House of Usher* 60. The Pit and the Pendulum 61. Panic in Year Zero 62. Tales of Terror 62. *The Raven* 63. The Comedy of Terrors 63. Muscle Beach Party 64. Dr G and the Bikini Machine 65. Wild in the Streets 68. Flare Up 69. The Dunwich Horror 70. Cry of the Banshee 70. Frogs 72. I Escaped from Devil's Island 73. Savage Sisters 74. Born Again 78. The Beast Within 82, etc.

Baxter, Meredith:
see Birney, Meredith Baxter.

Baxter, Stanley (1926–).
Rubber-faced Scottish comedian and impressionist of stage, screen and TV.
■ Geordie 55. *Very Important Person* 61. Crooks Anonymous 62. *The Fast Lady* 63. And Father Came Too 63. Joey Boy 65.
TV series: On the Bright Side 59–60. The Stanley Baxter Show 63, 67–68, 71. Baxter On . . . 64. The Stanley Baxter Picture Show 72. The Stanley Baxter Series 81.
❝ I'm the best known anonymity in the business. – *S.B.*

Baxter, Warner (1891–1951).
Distinguished-looking American leading man with stage experience. A popular hero of silent melodrama, he survived transition to talkies. Born in Columbus, Ohio, he worked as a salesman before turning to acting, and became a star in the late 20s playing the Cisco Kid in *Old Arizona*, a role he was to repeat in three more movies. After leaving Twentieth Century-Fox at the beginning of the 40s, he had a nervous breakdown and returned to make the 'B' picture series Crime Doctor for Columbia, which required no more than eight weeks' work a year. He suffered from severe arthritis and died of pneumonia following surgery.
■ Her Own Money 14. All Woman 18. Lombardi Ltd. 19. Cheated Hearts 21. First Love 21. The Love Charm 21. Sheltered Daughters 22. If I were Queen 22. The Girl in His Room 22. A Girl's Desire 22. The Ninety and Nine 22. Her Own Money (remake) 22. Blow Your Own Horn 23. In Search of a Thrill 23. St Elmo 23. Alimony 23. Christine of the Hungry Heart 24. The Female 24. The Garden of Weeds 24. His Forgotten Wife 24. Those Who Dance 24. The Golden Bed 25. Air Mail 25. The Awful Truth 25. The Best People 25. Rugged Water 25. A Son of His Father 25. Welcome Home 25. Mannequin 26. Miss Brewster's Millions 26. Mismates 26. Aloma of the South Seas 26. *The Great Gatsby* 26. The Runaway 26. The Telephone Girl 27. The Coward 27. Drums of the Desert 27. Singed 27. Danger Street 28. Three Sinners 28. *Ramona* 28. Craig's Wife 28. The Tragedy of Youth 28. A Woman's Way 28. Linda 29. Far Call 29. Thru Different Eyes 29. Behind that Curtain 29. Romance of the Rio Grande 29. *In Old Arizona* (AA) 29. West of Zanzibar 29. Happy Days 29. The Arizona Kid 30. Renegades 30. Such Men are Dangerous 30. The Cisco Kid 31. The Squaw Man 31. Doctors' Wives 31. Their Mad Moment 31. *Daddy Long Legs* 31. Surrender 31. Six Hours to Live 32. Man About Town 32. Amateur Daddy 32. Paddy the Next Best Thing 33. *42nd Street* 33. Dangerously Yours 34. I Loved You Wednesday 34. Penthouse 34. Stand Up and Cheer 34. *Broadway Bill* 34. As Husbands Go 34. Such Women are Dangerous 34. Grand Canary 35. Hell in the Heavens 35. Under the Pampas Moon 35. *One More Spring* 35. King of Burlesque 35. *Prisoner of Shark Island* 36. *The Road to Glory* 36. To Mary with Love 36. White Hunter 36. Robin Hood of El Dorado 36. Slave Ship 37. Vogues of 1938 37. Wife Doctor and Nurse 37. Kidnapped 38. I'll Give a Million 38. Wife Husband and Friend 39. Barricade 39. The Return of the Cisco Kid 39. Earthbound 40. Adam Had Four Sons 41. Crime Doctor 43. The Crime Doctor's Strangest Case 43. Lady in the Dark 44. Shadows in the Night 44. The Crime Doctor's Courage 45. The Crime Doctor's Warning 45. Just Before Dawn 46. The Crime Doctor's Man Hunt 46. The Millerson Case 47. The Crime Doctor's Gamble 47. A Gentleman from Nowhere 48. Prison Warden 49. The Devil's Henchman 49. The Crime Doctor's Diary 49. State Penitentiary 50.

Bay, Michael.
American director, from music videos, including several for Meat Loaf. In 1996, after the box-office success of *The Rock*, Disney contracted him to direct two pictures for a reported $12m.
Bad Boys 95. The Rock 96. *Armageddon* 98, etc.

Baye, Nathalie (1948–).
French leading actress.
Day for Night 73. The Green Room 78. A Girl from Lorraine 80. La Balance 82. The Return of Martin Guerre 82. Beethoven's Nephew 85. De Guerre Lasse 87. Massacre Play/Gioco al Massacro 89. C'est la Vie/La Baule-les-pins 90. La Voix 92. Mensonge 93. And the Band Played On (TV) 93, etc.

Bayes, Nora (1880–1928) (Dora Goldberg).
American vaudeville singer, impersonated by Ann Sheridan in the biopic *Shine On Harvest Moon* 44.

Bayldon, Geoffrey (1924–).
Lanky British character actor with a penchant for absent-minded or eccentric types.
The Stranger Left No Card 53. Dracula 58. Libel 60. The Webster Boy 62. A Jolly Bad Fellow 64. King Rat 65. *Sky West and Crooked* 65. *To Sir With Love* 66. Casino Royale 67. Otley 69. The Raging Moon 70. Scrooge 71. Asylum 72. Bullshot 83. Madame Sousatzka 88. The Necessary Love (It.) 91. Tom and Viv 94. Asterix in America (voice, as Getafix) 94, etc.
TV series: Catweazle (title role) 70–71. Worzel Gummidge (as the Crowman) 79–81.

Bayne, Beverly (1894–1982) (Pearl von Name).
American silent screen star, especially when married to Francis X. Bushman.
Graustark 15. A Virginia Romance 16. Romeo and Juliet 16. The Voice of Conscience 17. The Age of Innocence 24. Eve's Loves 25, etc.

Bazelli, Bojan.
American cinematographer.
China Girl 87. Patty Hearst 88. Tapeheads 88. King of New York 90. The Rapture 91. Deep Cover 92. Body Snatchers 93. Kalifornia 93. Sugar Hill 93. Surviving the Game 94. Body Snatchers 94, etc.

Bazin, André (1918–1958).
French critic who wrote books on Welles, de Sica and Renoir: 'the spiritual father of the New Wave'. Founded 'Cahiers du Cinéma'.
Book: 1997, *Bazin at Work: Major Essays and Reviews from the Forties and Fifties*, ed. Bert Cardullo.

Bazlen, Brigid (1944–1989).
Israeli leading lady of a few international films.
King of Kings (as Salome) 61. The Honeymoon Machine 61. How the West Was Won 62.
TV series: Too Young to Go Steady 59.

Beach, Rex (1877–1949).
American novelist whose books set in the Klondike, where he lived for a while, have attracted film-makers hoping to strike it rich. *The Spoilers/Alaska* has been filmed five times: in 14, 23, 30, 42 and 55.
The Silver Horde 30. Son of the Gods 30 and 42. The Avengers (from Don Careless) 50. The World in His Arms 52.

Beacham, Stephanie (1947–).
British leading actress. Born in Casablanca, she trained at RADA and is now based in the United States. She was formerly married to actor John McEnery.
The Games 69. The Nightcomers 71. Dracula AD 1972 72. House of Whipcord 76. Schizo 77. Inseminoid 80. The Wolves of Willoughby Chase 88. Troop Beverly Hills 89. Foreign Affairs (TV) 93. Wedding Bell Blues 96, etc.
TV series: Tenko 82. Sorrell and Son 84. Connie 85. The Colbys 85. Napoleon and Josephine 87. Dynasty 88–89. Sister Kate 89–90. No Bananas 96.

Beal, John (1909–1997) (Alexander Bliedung).
American stage actor whose look of boyish innocence was useful in the 30s but tended to hamper him subsequently. Married stage actress Helen Craig in 1934.
Another Language 33. Hat Coat and Glove 34. *The Little Minister* 34. Les Misérables 35. *Laddie* 35. Break of Hearts 35. The Man Who Found Himself 37. Double Wedding 37. Port of Seven Seas 38. I Am The Law 38. *The Cat and the Canary* 39. Ellery Queen and the Perfect Crime 41. The Great Commandment 42. Edge of Darkness 43. Key Witness 47. Alimony 49. My Six Convicts 52. Remains to be Seen 53. That Night 57. The Vampire 57. Ten Who Dared 61. Amityville 3-D 83. The Firm 93, etc.
TV series: The Nurses 62–67. Another World 64. The Adams Chronicles 67.

Beals, Jennifer (1963–).
American leading lady. Married director Alexandre Rockwell.
Flashdance (in which she did *not* do the dancing) 83. The Bride 85. The Gamble/La Partita 88. Split Decisions 88. Vampire's Kiss 88. Sons 89. Docteur M. 90. Blood and Concrete 91. Day of Atonement/Le Grand Pardon 2 92. In the Soup 92. Indecency 92. Terror Stalks the Class Reunion 93. Dear Diary/Caro Diario 93. Mrs Parker and the Vicious Circle 94. Devil in a Blue Dress 95. Arabian Knight (voice) 95. Four Rooms 95. Let It Be Me 95. The Twilight of the Golds (TV) 97. Last Days of Disco 98, etc.
TV series: 2000 Malibu Road 92.

Bean, Judge Roy (1823–1902).
American Western badman, a self-appointed lawmaker who kept himself in whisky from his fines. Played by Walter Brennan in *The Westerner* 40; by Edgar Buchanan in a TV series, *Judge Roy Bean* 50; and by Paul Newman in *The Life and Times of Judge Roy Bean* 72.

Bean, Sean (1958–).
English leading actor, much on television; he is best known for playing Sharpe, a soldier serving in Wellington's armies who works his way up from the ranks, in a series of TV movies. Born in Sheffield, he trained at RADA and was on stage with the Royal Shakespeare Company. Married actress Melanie Hill.
Caravaggio 86. Stormy Monday 88. War Requiem 88. The Field 90. Clarissa (TV) 91. Patriot Games 92. Sharpe's Rifles (TV) 93. Sharpe's Eagle (TV) 93. Lady Chatterley (TV) 93. A Woman's Guide to Adultery (TV) 93. Sharpe's Company (TV) 94. Shopping 94. Black Beauty 94. GoldenEye 95. When Saturday Comes 96. Leo Tolstoy's Anna Karenina 97. Ronin 98. Bravo Two Zero (TV) 98, etc.

Beard, John.
English production designer.
The Wildcats of St Trinians 80. An Unsuitable Job for a Woman 81. Digital Dreams 83. Eureka 83. Brazil 83. Absolute Beginners 86. Siesta 87. The Last Temptation of Christ 88. Erik the Viking 89. Splitting Heirs 93. The Browning Version 94, etc.

Beard, Matthew 'Stymie' (1925–1981).
American actor, as a child in the Our Gang comedy shorts of the late 20s and 30s, and later in supporting roles.
Uncle Tom's Cabin 27. Two Gun Man from Harlem 38. Broken Strings 40. The Return of Jesse James 40. Fallen Angel 45. Truck Turner 74. The Buddy Holly Story 78. East of Eden 80, etc.

Béart, Emmanuelle (1965–).
French leading actress. She is the daughter of French singer Guy Béart. She has a daughter by French actor Daniel Auteuil.
Manon des Sources 87. Date with an Angel 87. Captain Fracassa's Journey/Il Viàggio di Capitan Fracassa 90. La Belle Noiseuse 91. I Don't Kiss/J'Embrasse Pas 91. Un Coeur en Hiver 91. Ruptures 93. *L'Enfer* 94. Haute Epoque 94. Une Femme Française 95. Nelly and Mr Arnaud 95. Mission: Impossible 96. Stolen Life/Voleur de Vie 98, etc.
❝ There is no Hollywood now. – *E.B.*
I could never become a slave to the movie machine. I must be captain of my own ship. That to me is the only imperative. – *E.B.*

The Beatles.
This Liverpudlian pop group achieved astonishing popularity in the early 60s, but the pressures of success caused a split and the members went their rich but somewhat malcontented ways. They were *John Lennon* (1940–1980), *George Harrison* (1943–), *Paul McCartney* (1942–) and *Ringo Starr* (Richard Starkey) (1940–). A biopic, *Backbeat*, about the group's earliest days in Hamburg,

was released in 1995, directed by Iain Softley.
Biography: 1968, *The Beatles: The Authorized Biography* by Hunter Davies.
Books: 1992, *The Ultimate Beatles Encyclopedia* by Bill Harry; 1997, *The Beatles Movies* by Bob Neaverson.
FILMS TOGETHER: *A Hard Day's Night* 64. Help! 65. Let It Be (AAs) 70. They also lent their music and cartoon images to *Yellow Submarine* 67 and a subsequent TV series.
SEPARATELY: Lennon was in *How I Won The War* 67; Starr in *Candy* 68, *The Magic Christian* 70, *That'll Be the Day* 73, *Caveman* 81, *Give My Regards to Broad Street* 84, together with the film's producer, Paul McCartney.
❝ I see the Beatles have arrived from England. They were forty pounds overweight, and that was just their hair. – *Bob Hope, 1964*

Beaton, Sir Cecil (1904–1980).
English society photographer, artist, diarist and designer who worked mainly in the theatre and occasionally in films, where his greatest achievements were *Gigi* 58 and the costumes for *My Fair Lady* 64. In the early 30s, he fell in love with Greta Garbo and, despite their homosexual predilections, tried unavailingly to persuade her to marry him, a romance he described in *The Happy Years*. His lovers included Coral BROWNE, and he also claimed to have had an affair with Gary COOPER.
Autobiographies: 1961, *The Wandering Years*; 1965, *The Years Between*; 1972, *The Happy Years*; 1973, *The Strenuous Years*; 1976, *The Restless Years*; 1978, *The Parting Years*; 1979, *Self Portrait with Friends – The Selected Diaries of Cecil Beaton*, ed Richard Buckle.
Biographies: 1985, *Cecil Beaton* by Hugo Vickers; 1994, *Greta and Cecil* by Diana Southam; 1995, *Loving Garbo* by Hugo Vickers.
Kipps 41. Major Barbara 41. Anna Karenina 47. An Ideal Husband 48. The Doctor's Dilemma 59. On a Clear Day You Can See Forever 70.
❝ The camera not only picks up shoddiness but it detects lack of sincerity or shallowness of feeling. This applies ubiquitously to the work of director, performer or designer. – C.B.

Beatty, Clyde (1903–1965).
American animal trainer and circus owner who made a few film appearances.
■ The Big Cage 33. The Lost Jungle 34. Darkest Africa 36. Africa Screams 49. Ring of Fear 54.

Beatty, Ned (1937–).
Chubby American character actor.
Deliverance 72. The Life and Times of Judge Roy Bean 72. Footsteps (TV) 72. The Thief Who Came to Dinner 73. White Lightning 73. The Marcus-Nelson Murders (TV) 73. Dying Room Only (TV) 73. The Execution of Private Slovik (TV) 74. The Last American Hero 74. Attack on Terror (TV) 75. The Deadly Tower (TV) 75. W. W. and the Dixie Dancekings 75. Nashville 75. All the President's Men 76. *Network* (AAN) 76. Silver Streak 76. The Big Bus 76. Mikey and Nicky 76. Alambrista 77. Tail Gunner Joe (TV) 77. Lucan (TV) 77. Exorcist II 77. Shenanigans 77. Gray Lady Down 78. Superman 78. A Question of Love 78. Promises in the Dark 79. Wise Blood 79. *Friendly Fire* (TV) 79. 1941 79. Success 79. Guyana Tragedy (TV) 80. Hopscotch 80. The Incredible Shrinking Woman 81. Superman 2 81. The Toy 82. A Woman Called Golda (TV) 82. Stroker Ace 83. Touched 83. Restless Natives 84. Back to School 86. The Big Easy 86. The Fourth Protocol 87. Rolling Vengeance 87. The Trouble with Spies 87. After the Rain 88. Midnight Crossing 88. Physical Evidence 88. Purple People Eater 88. Shadows in the Storm 88. Switching Channels 88. The Unholy 88. Ministry of Vengeance 89. Time Trackers 89. Twist of Fate 89. Chattahoochee 89. Tennessee Nights 89. Big Bad John 90. Captain America 90. A Cry in the Wild 90. Repossessed 90. Going Under 90. *Hear My Song* 91. Angel Street 91. Illusions 91. Prelude to a Kiss 92. Ed and His Dead Mother 93. Rudy 93. Radioland Murders 94. Just Cause 95. Gulliver's Travels (TV) 95. Larry McMurtry's Streets of Laredo 95. The Affair (TV) 96. Crazy Horse (TV) 96. He Got Game 98, etc.
TV series: Szysznyk 77–78. Homicide: Life on the Street 93.

Beatty, Robert (1909–1992).
Rugged, good-humoured Canadian leading man long resident in Britain.
San Demetrio, London 43. Appointment with Crime 46. *Odd Man Out* 46. *Against the Wind* 47. Counterblast 48. Another Shore 48. Captain Horatio Hornblower R.N. 51. The Square Ring 53. *Albert R.N.* 53. The Gentle Gunman 53. Tarzan and the Lost Safari 57. Something of Value 57. The Shakedown 59. The Amorous Prawn 62. 2001: A Space Odyssey 68. Where Eagles Dare 69. Man at the Top 73. Golden Rendezvous 77. The Spaceman and King Arthur 79. The Amateur 81. Superman III 83. Meeting at Reykjavik (TV) (as Ronald Reagan) 87, etc.
TV series: *Dial* 999 57–58.

Beatty, Warren (1937–) (Warren Beaty).
Unruly American leading actor of the post-Brando school, with a flair for psychological maladjustment. Brother of Shirley Maclaine. He married actress Annette Bening in 1992.
Biography: 1987, *Warren Beatty: A Life and a Story* by David Thomson.
■ *Splendour in the Grass* 61. The Roman Spring of Mrs Stone 61. *All Fall Down* 62. *Lilith* 65. *Mickey One* 65. Promise Her Anything 66. Kaleidoscope 66. *Bonnie and Clyde* (& p) (AAN) 67. The Only Game in Town 69. McCabe and Mrs Miller 71. Dollars 72. The Parallax View 74. *Shampoo* (& p, co-w) (AAN) 75. The Fortune 75. *Heaven Can Wait* (& p, w, co-d) (AAN) 78. *Reds* (& pd, co-w) (AANd, AANa, AANw) 81. Ishtar 87. Dick Tracy (& pd) 90. Bugsy (AAN) 91. Love Affair (& d) 94. Bulworth (& co-w, d) 98.
TV series: The Many Loves of Dobie Gillis 55–59.
❝ I'm old, I'm young, I'm intelligent, I'm stupid. My tide goes in and out. – *W.B.*
Movies are fun, but they're not a cure for cancer. – *W.B.*
Warren has an interesting psychology. He has always fallen in love with girls who have just won, or just been nominated for, an Oscar . . . Anyone who comes close to him loses a few feathers. He tends to maul you. – *Leslie Caron*
He was insatiable. Three, four, five times a day was not unusual for him, and he was able to accept telephone calls at the same time. – *Joan Collins*
If I come back in another life, I want to be Warren Beatty's fingertips. – *Woody Allen*
Not having sex with Warren is like going to Rome and not seeing the Pope. – *Sonia Braga*

Beaudine, William (1892–1970).
Prolific American director of silent family films and, later, second features. In two years in England in the 30s he directed 13 films.
Penrod and Sam 23. Little Annie Rooney 25. *Sparrows* 26. The Life of Riley 27. The Cohens and Kellys in Paris 28. Home James 28. The Girl from Woolworth's 29. The Lady Who Dared 31. *Penrod and Sam* 31. Three Wise Girls 32. The Crime of the Century 33. The Old-Fashioned Way 34. Says O'Reilly to Macnab (in Britain) 37. Torchy Gets Her Man 38. Torchy Blane in Chinatown 39. Broadway Big Shot 42. The Mystery of the 13th Guest 43. Black Market Babies 46. Kidnapped 48. Blue Grass of Kentucky 50. Westward Ho the Wagons 56. Lassie's Greatest Adventure 63. Billy the Kid versus Dracula 66, etc.
❝ I've been moderate in everything. I never set out to break any records. – *W.B.*

Beaumont, Charles (1929–1967).
American writer, chiefly of science fiction.
Queen of Outer Space 58. The Intruder 61. Night of the Eagle 62. The Haunted Palace 63. Seven Faces of Dr Lao 64. Mister Moses 65, etc.

Beaumont, Harry (1888–1966).
American director, at his peak in the 20s.
A Man and His Money 19. Lord and Lady Algy 19. *Main Street* 23. *Beau Brummell* 24. *Babbitt* 24. The Lover of Camille 24. *His Majesty Bunker Bean* 25. *Our Dancing Daughters* 28. *Broadway Melody* (AAN) 29. Lord Byron of Broadway 30. The Florodora Girl 30. Our Blushing Brides 30. Dance Fools Dance 31. Faithless 32. *When Ladies Meet* 33. Enchanted April 35. The Girl on the Front Page 36. When's Your Birthday? 37. Maisie Goes to Reno 44. Twice Blessed 45. The Show-Off 47, many others.

Beaumont, Hugh (1909–1982).
American second lead and second-feature hero.
Flight Lieutenant 42. The Seventh Victim 43. Objective Burma 45. The Blue Dahlia 46. Bury Me Dead 47. Railroaded 49. Mr Belvedere Rings the Bell 52. Mississippi Gambler 53. The Mole People 57. The Human Duplicators 65, etc.
TV series: Leave It To Beaver 57–63.

Beaumont, Lucy (1873–1937).
English character actress, from the London and New York stage, in Hollywood from the 20s.
Ashes of Vengeance 23. The Crowd 28. Sonny Boy 29. A Free Soul 31. Condemned to Live 35. The Devil Doll 36. The Maid of Salem 37, etc.

Beaumont, Susan (1936–) (Susan Black).
British leading lady of a few 50s films.
Jumping for Joy 55. High Tide at Noon 57. Innocent Sinners 58. Carry On Nurse 59. Web of Suspicion 59, etc.

Beavers, Louise (1902–1962).
American actress who played innumerable happy housekeepers.
Coquette 29. Girls About Town 32. What Price Hollywood 32. She Done Him Wrong 33. *Imitation of Life* (her best role) 35. Rainbow on the River 36. The Last Gangster 37. Made For Each Other 39. No Time for Comedy 40. Reap the Wild Wind 42. Dubarry was a Lady 43. Delightfully Dangerous 46. *Mr Blandings Builds His Dream House* 48. My Blue Heaven 50. Teenage Rebel 56. The Goddess 58. The Facts of Life 61, many others.
TV series: *Beulah* 50.
Famous line (*Mr Blandings*): 'If you ain't eatin' Wham, you ain't eatin' ham!'

Beck, James (1932–1973).
English character actor, best known for his role as Private James Walker, the black marketeer of the TV sitcom *Dad's Army*.
The Outsider (US) 61. Forty Guns to Apache Pass (US) 67. Groupie Girl 70. Dad's Army 71. Troll 86, etc.
TV series: Dad's Army 68–73. Romany Jones 72–73.

Beck, John (1943–).
American leading man.
The Silent Gun (TV) 69. Lawman 71. The Unexpected Mrs Pollifax 72. Pat Garrett and Billy the Kid 73. Sidekicks (TV) 74. The Law (TV) 74. The Call of the Wild (TV) 76. The Big Bus 76. Sky Riders 76. Audrey Rose 77. The Other Side of Midnight 77. Wheels (TV) 78. The Time Machine (TV) 78. The Great American Traffic Jam (TV) 80. Deadly Illusion 87. Fire and Rain (TV) 89. A Row of Crows 90. Last Time Out 94. Suspect Device (TV) 95. Black Day Blue Night 95, etc.
TV series: Flamingo Road 80–82. Dallas 83–85.

Beck, Michael (1948–).
American leading man.
Holocaust (TV) 77. Mayflower (TV) 78. The Warriors 79. Xanadu 80. Alcatraz (TV) 81. Triumphs of a Man Called Horse 84. Rear View Mirror (TV) 84. Blackout 85. Deadly Game (TV) 91. Fade to Black 93, etc.

Beck, Thomas (1909–1995).
American leading man of the 30s, a somewhat bland hero of mainly 'B' features. Retired in the late 30s to become a property developer.
Charlie Chan in Egypt 35. Charlie Chan in Paris 35. Champagne Charlie 36. Crack-Up 36. White Fang 36. Heidi 37. Thank You, Mr Moto 37. I Stand Accused 38. The Family Next Door 39. They Asked for It 39, etc.

Becker, Harold (1928–).
American director, a former photographer.
The Onion Field 79. The Black Marble 80. Taps 81. Vision Quest 85. The Boost 88. Sea of Love 89. Malice 93. City Hall 96. Mercury Rising 98, etc.

Becker, Jacques (1906–1960).
French director, mainly of civilized comedies, an assistant to Jean Renoir for most of the 30s.
Goupi Mains Rouges 42. Falbalas 44. *Antoine et Antoinette* 47. Rendezvous de Juillet 49. *Edouard et Caroline* 50. *Casque d'Or* 51. Rue de l'Estrapade 52. *Touchez Pas au Grisbi* 53. Ali Baba 55. The Adventures of Arsène Lupin 56. Montparnasse Nineteen 57. The Hole 60, etc.

Becker, Jean (1933–).
French director, son of Jacques Becker.
Echappement Libre 62. Pas de Caviar pour Tante Olga 64. Tendre Voyou 66, etc.

Beckett, Samuel (1906–1989).
Irish playwright and novelist of bleak dramas on the purposelessness of human existence. Born in Dublin, he lived in Paris from the mid-30s, gaining international fame with his play *Waiting for Godot* in 1953. *Film* was writen for Jack MacGowran, but when he was unable to perform it because of other commitments, Beckett suggested Buster Keaton for the role.
Biography: 1996, *Damned to Fame: The Life of Samuel Beckett* by James Knolwson.
Tous Ceux Qui Tombent 63. Acte sans Parole (short) 64. Beginning to End (short) 65. *Film* (short) 65. Film 79. Happy Days (TV) 79, etc.

Beckett, Scotty (1929–1968).
Soulful-looking American child actor of the 30s and 40s; one-time member of 'Our Gang'. Problems surfaced in the 50s, when he was arrested three times on various charges, including possessing dangerous drugs. He made an unsuccessful suicide attempt in the early 60s; died from an overdose of sleeping pills, a probable suicide.
Whom the Gods Destroy 34. Dante's Inferno 35. The Charge of the Light Brigade 36. Marie Walewska 38. *The Bluebird* 40. *Kings Row* 42. The Youngest Profession 43. *Ali Baba and the Forty Thieves* 43. Junior Miss 45. *The Jolson Story* (as young Jolson) 46. A Date with Judy 48. Battleground 49. Corky 51. Three for Jamie Dawn 56, many others.

Beckinsale, Kate (1974–).
English actress, the daughter of actor Richard Beckinsale. She made her first film while still a student at Oxford University.
One against the Wind (TV) 91. Much Ado about Nothing 93. Uncovered 94. Cold Comfort Farm (TV) 95. Marie-Louise (Fr.) 95. Haunted 95. Emma (TV) 96. Shooting Fish 97. The Last Days of Disco (US) 98, etc.

Beckinsale, Richard (1947–1979).
British comedy leading man, in several TV series. Three for All 74. Porridge 79.
Film: The Lovers 72.

Beckley, Tony (1928–1980).
British actor, often seen as young thug.
The Penthouse 67. Chimes at Midnight 67. The Long Day's Dying 68. The Lost Continent 68. Get Carter 71. Sitting Target 72. Gold 74. The Return of the Pink Panther 74. Diagnosis Murder 75. Revenge of the Pink Panther 78. When a Stranger Calls 79, etc.

Beckwith, Reginald (1908–1965).
Chubby British character actor, whose high voice and impeccable timing were a constant delight. Also wrote successful plays, e.g. *Boys in Brown*, *A Soldier for Christmas*.
Voice in the Night 41. *Scott of the Antarctic* 48. Another Man's Poison 51. Mr Drake's Duck 52. *Genevieve* 53. *The Runaway Bus* 54. Dance Little Lady 55. *The Captain's Table* 58. The Thirty-Nine Steps 59. Double Bunk 61. The Password is Courage 62. Never Put It in Writing 64. A Shot in the Dark 64. Mister Moses 65, many others.

Beddoe, Don (1903–1991).
American character actor with genial, sometimes startled, look; in hundreds of films, often as sheriff, reporter or cop.
Golden Boy 39. *The Face Behind the Mask* 41. Talk of the Town 42. Crime Inc. 45. O.S.S. 46. The Best Years of Our Lives 46. The Farmer's Daughter 47. Dancing in the Dark 49. Carrie 51. Night of the Hunter 55. *Saintly Sinners* (lead role) 61. *Jack the Giant Killer* (as a leprechaun) 62. Texas Across the River 66. The Impossible Years 68. Generation 69. How Do I Love Thee 70. Nickel Mountain 85, many others.

Bedelia, Bonnie (1946–) (Bonnie Bedelia Culkin).
American leading lady.
The Gypsy Moths 69. They Shoot Horses Don't They? 70. *Lovers and Other Strangers* 70. The Strange Vengeance of Rosalie 72. Hawkins on Murder (TV) 73. The Big Fix 78. Heart Like a Wheel 83. Between Friends (TV) 83. Death of an Angel 85. The Stranger 87. Die Hard 88. Fat Man and Little

Boy/The Shadowmakers 89. Die Hard 2 90. Presumed Innocent 90. Somebody Has to Shoot the Picture 91. The Fire Next Time (TV) 93. Needful Things 93. Speechless 94. Judicial Consent 94. Homecoming (TV) 96, etc.

Bedford, Brian (1935–).
British stage actor who has been in a few films.
Miracle in Soho 58. The Angry Silence 59. The Punch and Judy Man 63. The Pad 66. Grand Prix 67. Robin Hood (voice) 73. Scarlett (TV) 94. Nixon 95, etc.
TV series: Coronet Blue 67.

Bedi, Kabir (1945–).
Stalwart Indian leading man of the late 70s.
Swashbuckler 76. The Thief of Baghdad (TV) 78. Ashanti 78. Octopussy 83. Terminal Entry 87. The Beast 88. Lie Down with Lions (TV) 94, etc.
TV series: Sandokan the Great 76.

Bedoya, Alfonso (1904–1957).
Mexican character actor whose beaming face could provide comedy or menace.
The Treasure of the Sierra Madre (as the bandit) 47. The Pearl 48. Streets of Laredo 49. The Black Rose 50. Sombrero 52. California Conquest 52. The Stranger Wore a Gun 53. Ten Wanted Men 55. *The Big Country* 57, etc.

The Bee Gees.
Three British brothers who as pop singers challenged the record of the Beatles and had an even more extravagant life style. A succession of hits culminated in their original score for *Saturday Night Fever*, which put them in the multi-millionaire category. They are *Barry* (born Douglas) (1947–), *Maurice* and *Robin* (both born 1949). Sergeant Pepper's Lonely Hearts Club Band 78.

Bee, Kenny (Zhang Chentau).
Hong Kong leading actor and singer.
The Spooky Bunch/Zhuang Dao Zheng 80. Shanghai Blues/Shanghai Zhi Ye 84. And Now, What's Your Name? 84. Green, Green Grass of Home/Zai Na Hepan Qing Cao Qing 85. The Armour of God/Long Xiong Hu Di 86. 100 Ways to Murder Your Wife (d) 86. Happy Bigamist 87. A Fishy Story/Battutmatdik Yan 90. Saviour of the Soul 91. Mary from Beijing/Mungsing Sifan 93. Rose, Rose I Love You 93. Moon Warriors 93. The Chinese Feast/Gamyuk Muntong 95. What a Wonderful Life 96, etc.

Beebe, Ford (1888–1978).
American director of low-budget westerns, second features and serials – over 200 of them from 1916.
Laughing at Life 33. *Flash Gordon's Trip to Mars* 38. *Riders of Death Valley* 41. Night Monster 42. The Invisible Man's Revenge 44. Enter Arsène Lupin 44. Bomba the Jungle Boy 49, etc.

Beecher, Janet (1884–1955) (J. B. Meysenburg).
American character actress usually seen in ladylike roles. Retired 1943.
Gallant Lady 33. The President Vanishes 34. The Mighty Barnum 34. The Dark Angel 35. Love Before Breakfast 36. The Thirteenth Chair 37. Rosalie 37. Judge Hardy's Children 38. Yellow Jack 38. Man of Conquest 39. The Mark of Zorro 40. Bitter Sweet 40. The Lady Eve 41. Silver Queen 42. Reap the Wild Wind 42. Mrs Wiggs of the Cabbage Patch 42. Henry Aldrich Gets Glamour 43, many others.

Beecroft, Jeffrey.
American production designer.
The Wizard of Loneliness 88. Midnight Caller 88. Dances with Wolves (AAN) 90. The Bodyguard 92. Pontiac Moon 94. 12 Monkeys 95. Head above Water 96, etc.

Beeny, Christopher (1941–).
Self-effacing English character actor who began on stage in 1951 and was in films as a child. Born in London, he played Lennie, the young son, in Britain's first TV soap opera, *The Grove Family*. He gave up acting in the 60s, returning in the 70s.
The Kidnappers 53. The Long Memory 53. Trouble in Store 53. Child's Play 54. Doctor in Distress 63, etc.
TV series: The Grove Family 54–57. Upstairs Downstairs 71–75. Miss Jones and Son 77–78. The Rag Trade 77–79. In Loving Memory 79–86.

Beery, Noah (1884–1946).
American character actor, half-brother of Wallace Beery and one of the silent screen's most celebrated villains.
The Mormon Maid 18. *The Mark of Zorro* 20. The Sea Wolf 20. Tol'able David 21. The Spoilers 22. The Coming of Amos 25. Beau Geste 26. *Don Juan* 26. Beau Sabreur 27. The Four Feathers 29. Noah's Ark 29. Tol'able David 30. The Drifter 31. Out of Singapore 32. She Done Him Wrong 33. King of the Damned (GB) 35. Our Fighting Navy (GB) 37. The Girl of the Golden West 38. Isle of Missing Men 42. This Man's Navy 45, many others.

Beery, Noah, Jnr (1913–1994).
American character actor, son of Noah Beery. Started as child actor, and later played easy-going country cousins.
The Mark of Zorro 20. Heroes of the West 26. Father and Son 29. Jungle Madness 31. The Road Back 37. Only Angels Have Wings 39. Of Mice and Men 40. Riders of Death Valley 41. Prairie Chickens 43. Gung Ho 44. Red River 48. Rocketship XM 50. White Feather 55. Inherit the Wind 60. The Seven Faces of Dr Lao 64. Incident at Phantom Hill 65. Little Fauss and Big Halsy 70. Walking Tall 73. The Best Little Whorehouse in Texas 82, many others.
TV series: Circus Boy 56–57. Custer 67. Doc Elliot 74. The Rockford Files 74–80. The Quest 83.

Beery, Wallace (1885–1949).
American character star with circus and musical comedy experience, long under contract to MGM. Started as a grotesque female impersonator and tried every kind of part before acquiring his best remembered persona: tough, ugly, slow-thinking and easy-going. Half-brother of Noah Beery. The first of his two wives was actress Gloria Swanson (1916–18).
SELECTED SILENT FILMS: Teddy at the Throttle 16. The Unpardonable Sin 19. The Virgin of Stamboul 20. The Last of the Mohicans 21. *Robin Hood* (as King Richard) 22. *Richard the Lion-Hearted* 23. The Sea Hawk 24. So Big 24. *The Lost World* (as Professor Challenger) 25. The Wanderer 25. Volcano 26. We're in the Navy Now 26. Casey at the Bat 27. Fireman Save My Child 27. Partners of Crime 28. Beggars of Life 28, many others.
■ SOUND FILMS: Chinatown Nights 29. River of Romance 29. *The Big House* (AAN) 30. Way for a Sailor 30. Billy the Kid 30. A Lady's Morals 30. *Min and Bill* 30. The Secret Six 31. Hell Divers 31. *The Champ* (AA) 31. *Grand Hotel* 32. Flesh 32. *Dinner at Eight* 33. *Tugboat Annie* 33. *The Bowery* 33. *Viva Villa* 34. *Treasure Island* (as Long John Silver) 34. *The Mighty Barnum* 34. West Point of the Air 35. China Seas 35. O'Shaughnessy's Boy 35. *Ah Wilderness* 35. A Message to Garcia 36. Old Hutch 36. Good Old Soak 37. *Slave Ship* 37. Bad Man of Brimstone 38. Port of Seven Seas 38. Stablemates 38. Sergeant Madden 39. *Stand Up and Fight* 39. Thunder Afloat 39. The Man from Dakota 40. Twenty Mule Team 40. Wyoming 40. Barnacle Bill 41. The Bad Man 41. The Bugle Sounds 42. Jackass Mail 42. Salute to the Marines 43. Rationing 44. *Barbary Coast Gent* 44. This Man's Navy 45. Bad Bascomb 46. The Mighty McGurk 47. A Date with Judy 48. Alias a Gentleman 48. Big Jack 49.
❝ I never let anyone sucker me, not even for a nickel. – *W.B.*
Like my dear old friend Marie Dressler, my ugly mug has been my fortune. – *W.B.*
He always made me feel uncomfortable. – *Jackie Cooper*
Beery's a son of a bitch, but he's *our* son of a bitch. – *Louis B. Mayer*

Beeson, Paul (1921–).
British cinematographer.
Dunkirk 58. Greyfriars Bobby 61. In Search of the Castaways 62. The Moonspinners 64. To Sir with Love 66. Moon Zero Two 69. Kidnapped 70. Jane Eyre 71. A Warm December 73. The Mutations 74. One of our Dinosaurs is Missing 75. Escape from the Dark 76. Candleshoe 77. The Spaceman and King Arthur 79. Silver Dream Racer 80. Hawk the Slayer 80. Raiders of the Lost Ark 81. Never Say Never Again 83. Indiana Jones and the Temple of Doom 84. Santa Claus 85. Jane and the Lost City 87, etc.

Beethoven, Ludwig van (1770–1827).
German classical composer who in view of his total deafness and unattractive physique has been surprisingly frequently portrayed in movies: by Harry Baur in *Beethoven* 36; Albert Basserman in *New Wine* 41; Rene Deltgen in *Whom the Gods Love* 41; Karl Bochm in *The Magnificent Rebel* 60 and Wolfgang Reichmann in *Beethoven's Nephew* 88; Gary Oldman in *Imortal Beloved* 95.

Begelman, David (1921–1995).
American producer and executive, a former agent and co-founder of Creative Management Associates. President of Columbia Pictures from 1973 to 1978, during the studio's upturn in its fortunes, he was forced to resign following the discovery of his embezzlement of studio funds, including forging actor Cliff Robertson's and director Martin Ritt's names on cheques. Became head of MGM in 1980 and of United Artists the following year. Ousted in 1982, he went into independent production. Committed suicide after legal action over further financial irregularities, including the theft of $2m. He was a model for agent Lyon Burke in Jacqueline Susann's novel *Valley of the Dolls*.
Book: 1982, *Indecent Exposure* by David McClintick (on the scandal at Columbia).
Angel Death (doc) 79. Wholly Moses 80. The Sicilian 87. Mannequin 87. Weekend at Bernie's 89, etc.
❝ One of the most skilled negotiators of deals in the entertainment business – perhaps the most skilled without exception. – *David McClintick*
He was the embodiment of the best and worst traits of Hollywood power players. There was hardly a moment in his life when he was not at once stunningly successful, yet also teetering on the brink of abject humiliation. – *Variety*
Life is hard, death is easy. – *D.B.*

Begley, Ed (1901–1970).
Blustery American character actor with radio and stage experience; usually seen as jovial uncle or man at the end of his tether.
■ Big Town 47. Boomerang 47. Deep Waters 48. Sitting Pretty 48. The Street with No Name 48. Sorry Wrong Number 48. Tulsa 49. It Happens Every Spring 49. The Great Gatsby 49. Backfire 50. Stars in my Crown 50. Wyoming Mail 50. Convicted 50. Saddle Tramp 50. Dark City 50. Lady from Texas 51. On Dangerous Ground 51. You're In the Navy Now 51. Deadline 52. Boots Malone 52. The Turning Point 52. What Price Glory 52. Lone Star 52. *Patterns* 56. *Twelve Angry Men* 57. *Odds Against Tomorrow* 59. The Green Helmet 61. *Sweet Bird of Youth* (AA) 62. The Unsinkable Molly Brown 64. The Oscar 66. Warning Shot 66. *Billion Dollar Brain* 67. Firecreek 67. Wild in the Streets 68. Hang 'Em High 68. The Violent Enemy 69. The Silent Gun (TV) 69. The Dunwich Horror 69. The Road to Salina 71.
TV series: Leave It to Larry 52.

Begley, Ed, Jnr (1949–).
American character actor.
Now You See Him Now You Don't 72. Cockfighter 74. Stay Hungry 76. Blue Collar 78. The Concorde–Airport 79 79. This is Spinal Tap 80. The In-Laws 81. Young Doctors in Love 82. Protocol 84. Streets of Fire 85. Amazon Women on the Moon 87. The Accidental Tourist 88. Scenes from the Class Struggle in Beverly Hills 89. She-Devil 89. Meet the Applegates 91. Dark Horse 92. Greedy/Greed 94. Even Cowgirls Get the Blues 94. Renaissance Man 94. The Pagemaster 94. The Late Shift (TV) 96. Not in This Town (TV) 97. Joey 98. I'm Losing You 98, etc.
TV series: Roll Out! 73–74. St Elsewhere 82–88. The Ed Begley Jnr Show 89. Parenthood 92. Maggie Day 98– .

Behan, Brendan (1923–1964).
Irish dramatist whose flamboyant behaviour often hit the headlines in the 50s; his only play to be filmed was *The Quare Fellow*.
❝ I have a total irreverence for anything concerned with society except that which makes the roads safer, the beer stronger, the food cheaper, and old men and women warmer in the winter and happier in the summer. – *B.B.*

Behrman, S. N. (1893–1973).
American playwright and screenwriter.
He Knew Women (oa) 30. *Queen Christina* 33. Cavalcade 33. *Anna Karenina* 35. Biography of a Bachelor Girl (oa) 35. A Tale of Two Cities 35. Parnell 37. Conquest 37. *No Time for Comedy* (oa) 40. Waterloo Bridge 40. Two-Faced Woman 41. The Pirate (oa) 48. Quo Vadis 51. *Me and the Colonel* (& oa) 56, etc.

Beich, Albert (1919–1996).
American radio and film writer.
Girls in Chains 44. The Perils of Pauline 47. The Bride Goes Wild 48. Key to the City 50. The Lieutenant Wore Skirts 55. Dead Ringer 64, etc.

Beiderbecke, Leon Bix (1903–1931).
Jazz cornettist, also a pianist and composer, who played with the Wolverines and the Paul Whiteman orchestra. A legendary figure for his brilliant improvisations and short, alcoholic life, he was the subject of a biopic, *Bix*, made by Italian director Pupi Avati in 1991, and a documentary, *Bix*, made by Brigette Berman in 1981. Dorothy Baker's novel *Young Man with a Horn*, filmed by Michael Curtiz in 1950, is very loosely based on his life, apart from the happy ending, although the soundtrack trumpet by Harry James is closer to that of the equally alcoholic and almost as accomplished jazz trumpeter Bunny Berigan (1908–42), who replaced Beiderbecke in Whiteman's orchestra.

Beineix, Jean-Jacques (1946–).
Chic French director. He gave up medical studies to become an assistant director and also directs TV commercials.
Diva 82. The Moon in the Gutter 83. Betty Blue 86. Roselyne and the Lions 88. IP5: The Island of Pachyderms 92. Otaku 94, etc.
❝ I'm an anxious person in an anxious world. – *J-J.B.*

Bekassy, Stephen (1910–).
Hungarian stage actor who came to Hollywood in the 40s.
A Song to Remember (as Liszt) 45. Arch of Triumph 48. Black Magic 49. Fair Wind to Java 53. Hell and High Water 54. Interrupted Melody 55. The Light in the Forest 58. Bachelor Flat 61. The Four Horsemen of the Apocalypse 62, etc.

Bel Geddes, Barbara (1922–) (Barbara Geddes Lewis).
American stage actress who makes occasional films, usually as nice placid girls.
■ The Gangster 47. The Long Night 47. *I Remember Mama* (AAN) 48. Blood on the Moon 48. Caught 49. Panic in the Streets 50. *Fourteen Hours* 51. Vertigo 58. The Five Pennies 59. Five Branded Women 60. By Love Possessed 61. The Todd Killings 70. Summertree 71.
TV series: Dallas 78–90.

Belafonte, Harry (1927–).
Handsome American ballad singer who has acted strikingly in several films.
Bright Road 53. *Carmen Jones* 54. *Island in the Sun* 57. The World the Flesh and the Devil 59. *Odds Against Tomorrow* 59. The Angel Levine 70. Buck and the Preacher 72. Uptown Saturday Night 74. First Look 84. The Player (as himself) 92. Prêt-à-Porter/Ready to Wear 94. White Man's Burden 95. Kansas City 96, etc.

Belasco, Leon (1902–1988).
Wiry Russian-born small-part player of excitable balletmasters, head-waiters, landlords, etc.
The Best People (debut) 26. Topper Takes a Trip 39. The Mummy's Hand 40. Nothing But the Truth 41. Pin-Up Girl 44. The New Adventures of Don Juan 48. Call Me Madam 53, many others.
TV series: My Sister Eileen 60-61.

Belita (1924–) (Gladys Jepson-Turner).
British ice-skating and dancing star who made a few Hollywood films.
Ice Capades 41. Silver Skates 43. Suspense 46. The Hunted 47. Never Let Me Go 53. Invitation to the Dance 56. Silk Stockings 57, etc.

Bell, Ann (1939–).
British character actress who was always welcome but never reached the top.
Flat Two 62. Dr Terror's House of Horrors 64. To Sir with Love 66. The Witches 66. The Shuttered Room 66. The Reckoning 69. The Statue 70. Spectre (TV) 77. Very Like a Whale (TV) 80. Champions 84. When Saturday Comes 96, etc.
TV series: Tenko 81–84. Double First 88. Head over Heels 93.

Bell, James (1891–1973).
American character actor, usually in benevolent roles.
I Am a Fugitive from a Chain Gang 32. White Woman 33. I Walked with a Zombie 42. The Spiral Staircase 45. Brute Force 47. The Violent Hour 50. The Glenn Miller Story 54. The Lonely Man 57. Twilight of Honor 63, many others.

Bell, Marie (1900–1985) (Marie-Jeanne Bellon-Downey).
Distinguished French actress who appeared in a few well-remembered films.
Madame Récamier 28. *Le Grand Jeu* 34. La Garçonne 35. *Carnet de Bal* 37. La Charrette Fantôme 40. Le Colonel Chabert 43. La Bonne Soupe 64. Hotel Paradiso 66, etc.

Bell, Marshall.
American character actor. Born in Tulsa, Oklahoma, he is a former consultant in training businessmen in public speaking.
Birdy 84. A Nightmare on Elm Street II: Freddy's Revenge 85. Stand by Me 86. Twins 88. Tucker 88. Total Recall 90. Air America 90. Innocent Blood 92. Undercover Blues 93. Airheads 94. The Chase 94. The Puppet Masters 94. Natural Born Killers 94. Operation Dumbo Drop 95. Things to Do in Denver When You're Dead 95. Starship Troopers 97, etc.

Bell, Monta (1891–1958).
American director whose peak was in the 20s.
A Woman of Paris (co-d) 23. Broadway after Dark 24. The Snob 24. *The Torrent* 25. The King on Main Street 27. After Midnight (& w) 27. Man Woman and Sin (& w) 27. The Bellamy Trial 29. East is West 30. Men in White 33. West Point of the Air 35. China's Little Devils 45, etc.

Bell, Rex (1905–1962) (George F. Beldam).
American cowboy star of the 30s: left Hollywood to become Lieut.-Governor of Nevada. Married Clara Bow.
Pleasure Crazed 29. True to the Navy 30. Lightnin' 30. Tombstone 42. Lone Star 52, many others.
TV series: Cowboys and Injuns 50.

Bell, Tom (1932–).
Gaunt British leading man.
The Kitchen 61. *Payroll* 61. HMS Defiant 62. *The L-Shaped Room* 62. A Prize of Arms 63. Ballad in Blue 65. *He Who Rides a Tiger* 66. The Long Day's Dying 68. In Enemy Country (US) 68. Lock Up Your Daughters 69. *All the Right Noises* 69. Quest for Love 71. The Spy's Wife 71. Royal Flash 75. Holocaust (TV) 78. Wish You Were Here 87. Resurrected 88. Red King, White Knight (TV) 89. The Krays 90. Let Him Have It 91. Prospero's Books 91. Angels (TV) 92. Prime Suspect 3 (TV) 93. Feast of July 95, etc.
TV series: *Out* 78. Hope It Rains 91–92. No Bananas 96.

Bellah, James Warner (1899–1976).
American screenwriter, mainly on historical themes; former war correspondent.
Fort Apache 48. She Wore a Yellow Ribbon 49. Rio Grande 50. Rio Bravo 55. The Sea Chase (co-w) 55. Sergeant Rutledge 59. A Thunder of Drums 61. The Man Who Shot Liberty Valance (co-w) 62, etc.

Bellamy, Earl (1917–).
Routine American director, much involved in TV series.
Blackjack Ketchum, Desperado 56. Fluffy 65. Gunpoint 65. Incident at Phantom Hill 66. Seven Alone 74. Part Two Walking Tall 75. Sidewinder One 77. Speedtrap 78. Magnum Thrust 81, etc.

Bellamy, Madge (1899–1990) (Margaret Philpott).
American general-purpose actress of the 20s, a former dancer and beauty queen.
Autobiography: 1990, *Darling of the Twenties*.
Soft Living 28. Riot Squad 32. White Zombie 32. Charlie Chan in London 34. The Great Hotel Murder 35. Champagne Charlie 36. Northwest Trail 45, etc.

Bellamy, Ralph (1904–1991).
Soft-voiced, serious-looking American leading man of stage and screen who in the 30s became typecast as the simple-minded rich man who never got the girl. In fact he played most kinds of parts, including detectives and villains, and later became a highly respected stage actor. He was given an honorary Oscar in 1987.
Autobiography: 1979, *When the Smoke Hit the Fan*.
■ The Secret Six 31. The Magnificent Lie 31. Surrender 31. Forbidden 32. West of Broadway 32. Disorderly Conduct 32. Young America 32. Rebecca of Sunnybrook Farm 32. The Woman in Room 13 32. Wild Girl 32. Air Mail 32. Almost Married 32. Second Hand Wife 32. Parole Girl 33. Destination Unknown 33. Picture Snatcher 33. Narrow Corner 33. Below the Sea 33. Headline Shooters 33. Flying Devils 33. Blind Adventure 33. Ace of Aces 33. Ever in My Heart 33. Spitfire 34. This Man Is Mine 34. Once to Every Woman 34. One Is Guilty 34. Before Midnight 34. The Crime of Helen Stanley 34. Girl in Danger 34. Woman in the Dark 34. Helldorado 35. The Wedding Night 35. Rendezvous at Midnight 35. Air Hawks 35. Eight Bells 35. The Healer 35. Gigolette 35. Navy Wife 35. Hands Across the Table 35. Dangerous Intrigue 36. The Final Hour 36. Roaming Lady 36. Straight from the Shoulder 36. Wild Brian Kent 36. Counterfeit Lady 37. The Man Who Lived Twice 37. *The Awful Truth* (in which his 'other man' stereotype was sealed) (AAN) 37. Let's Get Married 37. The Crime of Dr Hallet 38. Fools for Scandal 38. Boy Meets Girl 38. Carefree 38. Girls' School 38. Trade Winds 38. Let Us Live 38. *Blind Alley* 39. Smashing the Spy Ring 39. Coast Guard 39. *His Girl Friday* (in which the Ralph Bellamy type was amiably mocked) 40. Flight Angels 40. Brother Orchid 40. Queen of the Mob 40. Dance Girl Dance 40. Public Deb Number One 40. Ellery Queen Master Detective (title role) 40. Meet the Wildcat 40. Ellery Queen's Penthouse Mystery 41. Footsteps in the Dark 41. Affectionately Yours 41. Ellery Queen and the Perfect Crime 41. Dive Bomber 41. Ellery Queen and the Murder Ring 41. The Wolf Man 41. The Ghost of Frankenstein 42. Lady in a Jam 42. Men of Texas 42. The Great Impersonation 42. Stage Door Canteen 43. Guest in the House 44. Delightfully Dangerous 45. Lady on a Train 45. The Court Martial of Billy Mitchell 55. *Sunrise at Campobello* (as FDR) 60. The Professionals 66. Rosemary's Baby 68. Wings of Fire (TV) 68. The Immortal (TV) 69. Doctors' Wives 71. Cancel My Reservation 72. Something Evil (TV) 72. The Log of the Black Pearl (TV) 75. Adventures of the Queen (TV) 75. Search for the Gods (TV) 75. Murder on Flight 502 (TV) 75. McNaughton's Daughter (TV) 76. Nightmare in Badham County (TV) 76. The Boy in the Plastic Bubble (TV) 76. Once an Eagle (TV) 76. The Moneychangers (TV) 76. Testimony of Two Men (TV) 77. Charlie Cobb: Nice Night for a Hanging (TV) 77. Westside Medical (TV) 77. Oh God 77. Wheels (TV) 78. The Clone Master (TV) 78. The Millionaire (TV) 78. Billion Dollar Threat (TV) 79. Condominium (TV) 79. Power (TV) 79. The Memory of Eva Ryker (TV) 83. *The Winds of War* (TV) 83. *Trading Places* 83. Space (TV) 85. Disorderlies 87.
TV series: Man Against Crime 49–53. The Eleventh Hour 64. The Survivors 69. The Most Deadly Game 69. Hunter 77.
✪ For solid service and the occasional gleam of brilliance.
❝ One day in Hollywood I read a script in which the character was described as 'charming but dull – a typical Ralph Bellamy type'. I promptly headed for New York to find a part with guts. – *R.B.*

Bellaver, Harry (1905–1993).
American character actor, often seen as cop, small-time gangster or cabby.
Another Thin Man 40. The House on 92nd Street 45. No Way Out 50. The Lemon Drop Kid 51. From Here to Eternity 53. Love Me or Leave Me 55. Serenade 56. Slaughter on Tenth Avenue 57. The Old Man and the Sea 58. One Potato Two Potato 64. A Fine Madness 66. Madigan 67. God Told Me To 76. Demon 77. Blue Collar 78. Hero at Large 80, etc.
TV series: *Naked City* 58–63.

Beller, Kathleen (1955–).
American leading lady.
Godfather II 74. The Betsy 78. Mary White (TV) 79. Something for Joey (TV) 80. Are You in the House Alone? (TV) 82. Touched by Love 83. Surfacing 84. Cloud Waltzing (TV) 87. Time Trackers 88, etc.
TV series: Dynasty 82–84.

Bellocchio, Marco (1939–).
Italian director.
Fists in the Pocket 65. China is Near 67. In the Name of the Father 71. Triumphal March 76. Les Yeux Fertiles 77. Salto nel Vuoto 79. Henry IV 84. Devil in the Flesh 85. La Visione del Sabba 87. The Sentence/La Condanna 91. Il Sogno della Farfalla 94. Portrait of a Romantic Hero 96.

Bellon, Yannick (1924–).
French director and screenwriter, a former editor. Although she made shorts from the mid-40s, she did not direct her first feature until 1972. Her films tend to deal with the troubled lives of women.
Quelque Part, Quelqu'un 72. La Femme de Jean 74. Rape of Love/L'Amour Violé 78. La Triche 84. Les Enfants du Désordre 89, etc.

Bellows, Gil.
American actor.
The Shawshank Redemption 94. Love and a 45 94. Black Day Blue Knight 95. Miami Rhapsody 95. The Substance of Fire 96. Snow White: A Tale of Terror 97, etc.

Bellucci, Monica (1968–).
Italian leading actress and model, in international films. She has been romantically linked with actor Vincent Cassel.
Briganti 90. Bram Stoker's Dracula (US) 92. I Mitici 94. As You Want Me/Come Mi Vuoi 96. Palla di Neve 96. L'Appartement (Fr.) 96. Mauvais Genre (Fr.) 97. Comme un Poisson dans l'Eau (Fr.) 98. La Saison des Amours (Fr.) 98, etc.

Belmondo, Jean-Paul (1933–).
Interesting but unhandsome French leading actor.
Dimanche . . . Nous Volerons 56. Les Tricheurs 58. Un Drôle de Dimanche 58. Sois Belle et Tais-Toi 58. A Double Tour 59. *A Bout de Souffle* 59. Moderato Cantabile 60. La Viaccia 60. Leon Morin, Priest 61. Two Women 61. Cartouche 62. *Un Singe en Hiver* 62. Cent Mille Dollars au Soleil 63. *That Man from Rio* 64. Weekend in Dunkirk 65. Pierrot le Fou 65. Les Tribulations d'un Chinois en Chine 65. Is Paris Burning? 66. Tendre Voyou 66. Le Voleur 67. The Brain 68. Ho! 68. The Mississippi Mermaid 69. A Man I Like 69. Le Casse 71. Scoundrel in White 72. Le Magnifique 73. Stavisky 74. The Night Caller 75. L'Alpagueur 76. Le Corps de Mon Ennemi 76. L'Animal 77. Le Guignolo 80. Le Marginal 83. Vultures 83. Hold-Up 85. Le Solitaire 86. Der Glückspitz 88. L'Inconnu dans la Maison 92. Les Misérables du XXème Siècle 95. Desire 96, etc.
❝ Hell, everybody knows that an ugly guy with a good line gets the chicks. – *J.P.B.*
New blood, new looks, new vitality, new fluidism, new eroticism, new normality for that malady-ridden strain of today's neurotic actors. – *Marlene Dietrich*
Wrong or right I suppose he represents France. – *Daniel Boulander*

Belmont, Vera (1931–).
French actress, director and producer.
Sursis pour un Espion (a) 64. The Young Wolves (p) 67. The Sin of Father Mouret (p) 70. Les Oeillets Rouges d'Avril (d, doc) 74. Quest for Fire (co-p) 81. Rouge Baiser (co-w, d) 85. Milena (p, wd) 90. Farinelli the Castrato (p) 94. Marquise (co-w, d) 97, etc.

Belmore, Bertha (1882–1953).
Ample British character comedienne, a British Margaret Dumont whose dignity was inevitably shattered.
Are You a Mason? 33. Going Gay 34. Broken Blossoms 36. In the Soup 37. Over She Goes 38. Yes Madam 39, etc.

Belmore, Lionel (1867–1953).
Portly British character actor in Hollywood in the 30s.
The Antique Dealer 15. Madame X 20. Oliver Twist 22. Red Lights 23. The Sea Hawk 24. Never the Twain Shall Meet 25. Bardelys the Magnificent 26. Sorrell and Son 27. King of Kings 27. Rose Marie 28. The Love Parade 29. Monte Carlo 30. Alexander Hamilton 31. Frankenstein 31. Vanity Fair 32. So Big 32. The Vampire Bat 33. Cleopatra 34. Vanessa 34. The Count of Monte Cristo 34. Cardinal Richelieu 35. Clive of India 35. Little Lord Fauntleroy 36. Maid of Salem 37. The Prince and the Pauper 37. Tower of London 39. Son of Frankenstein 39. My Son My Son 40, many others.

Beloin, Edmund (1910–1992).
American comedy writer with radio experience.
Buck Benny Rides Again 40. Love Thy Neighbour 40. Because of Him 45. The Great Lover (& p) 49. A Connecticut Yankee in King Arthur's Court 49. The Sad Sack 57. G.I. Blues 60. All in a Night's Work 61, etc.

Belson, Jerry.
American screenwriter and director.
How Sweet It Is 68. Smile 76. Fun with Dick and Jane 77. The End 78. Smokey and the Bandit II (co-w) 80. Jekyll and Hyde . . . Together Again 82 (wd). Surrender (wd) 87. Always 89, etc.

Belushi, James (1954–).
American leading man whose popularity does not travel much beyond America. He is the brother of John Belushi.
Mutant Video 76. Thief 81. Trading Places 83. Man with One Red Shoe 85. Salvador 85. About Last Night . . . 86. Little Shop of Horrors 86. Jumpin' Jack Flash 86. The Principal 87. Real Men 87. Red Heat 88. K-9 89. Who's Harry Crumb? 89. Homer and Eddie 89. To Forget Palermo/Dimenticare Palermo 89. Mr Destiny 90. Taking Care of Business/Filofax 90. Only the Lonely 91. Curly Sue 91. Once Upon a Crime 92. Traces of Red 92. Diary of a Hit Man 92. Once Upon a Crime 92. Royce 94. Parallel Lives (TV) 94. The Pebble and the Penguin (voice) 95. Destiny Turns on the Radio 95. Separate Lives 95. Race the Sun 96. Sahara 96. Jingle All the Way 96. Angel's Dance 98, etc.
TV series: Working Stiffs 79. Wild Palms 93. Total Security 97.

Belushi, John (1949–1982).
Overweight American comic actor from television satire shows. Died from an overdose of drugs. A biography, *Wired*, by Bob Woodward, was filmed in 1989 with Michael Chiklis as Belushi.
■ National Lampoon's Animal House 78. Going South 78. 1941 79. Old Boyfriends 79. The Blues Brothers 80. Continental Divide 81. Neighbours 81.
❝ A good man, but a bad boy. – *Dan Aykroyd*

Bemberg, Maria Luisa (1917–1995).
Argentinian film director and screenwriter on feminist themes who made her first feature film when she was in her 50s. She was active in the theatre as a producer.
■ Crónica de una Señora (w) 70. Triángulo de Cuatro (w) 74. Moments/Momentos 80. Nobody's Wife/Señora de Nadie 82. Camila (AAN) 84. Miss Mary 86. I, the Worst of All/Yo, la Peor de Todas 90. We Don't Want to Talk about It/De Eso No Se Habla 93.

Benacerraf, Margot (1926–).
Venezuelan film director who studied in Paris and made two acclaimed films in the 50s before retiring, despite offers of work.
■ Reveron (doc) 52. Araya 58.

Benchley, Peter (1940–).
American novelist, fashionable in Hollywood for his one real hit. Grandson of Robert Benchley.
Jaws 75. The Deep 77. The Island 80. Peter Benchley's 'The Beast' (TV) 96.

Benchley, Robert (1889–1945).
American magazine humourist who exploited the small problems of twentieth-century living. He appeared in many films as a lovable bumbler, usually trying to explain something very complicated or to control a patently unmanageable situation. Benchley made many amusing shorts consisting of lectures by him on matters of science or domestic harmony. One of them, *How to Sleep* (1935), won an Academy Award. In *Mrs Parker and the Vicious Circle* (1994) he is played by Campbell Scott.
Biography: 1946, *Robert Benchley* by his son Nathaniel.
■ Feature appearances: Headline Shooter 33. Dancing Lady 33. Rafter Romance 34. Social Register 34. China Seas 35. Piccadilly Jim 36. Live Love and Learn 37. Broadway Melody of 1938 37. Hired Wife 40. *Foreign Correspondent* 40. Nice Girl 41. *The Reluctant Dragon* 41. You'll Never Get Rich 41. Three Girls about Town 41. Bedtime

Story 41. Take a Letter Darling 42. The Major and the Minor 42. *I Married a Witch* 42. Flesh and Fantasy 43. Young and Willing 43. Song of Russia 43. The Sky's the Limit 43. Her Primitive Man 44. National Barn Dance 44. See Here Private Hargrove 44. Practically Yours 44. Janie 44. Pan Americana 45. *It's In the Bag* 45. Weekend at the Waldorf 45. Kiss and Tell 45. Duffy's Tavern 45. The Stork Club 45. *Road to Utopia* 45. The Bride Wore Boots 46. Snafu 46. Janie Gets Married 46. Blue Skies 46.

✪ For assuming a subtly fantasticated screen version of his own cosmopolitan personality, and delighting the world by doing so. *Road to Utopia*.

❝ In Milwaukee last month a man died laughing at one of his own jokes. That's what makes it so tough for us outsiders. We have to fight home competition. – *R.B.*

It took me fifteen years to discover that I had no talent for writing. But by then I couldn't give it up because I was too famous. – *R.B.*

The reason for Benchley's success as a satirist was that he did not have to invent either the clown face or the commonplace. He wore them both like a pair of mismated socks. All the ineptitudes and foolish ignorances he needed as targets for his satire were right under his nose, in himself. – *Ben Hecht*

Benchley tended to spend his later years drinking in Hollywood's Garden of Allah hotel. When he finally left to go east he pointedly refrained from favouring a hated doorman. 'Sir,' said the man, 'aren't you going to remember me?' 'Sure,' said Benchley, 'I'll write you every day.'

Leaving a restaurant, Benchley approached what appeared to be a uniformed commissionaire and muttered: 'Get me a taxi.' The man bridled and said: 'Sir, I am a rear admiral in the United States Navy.' 'Really,' said Benchley. 'Then get me a battleship.'

Bender, Lawrence (1958–).
American producer, a former actor, associated with Quentin Tarantino and other new talents.
Eva's Dream (a) 82. Reservoir Dogs 92. Fresh 94. Pulp Fiction 94. Killing Zoe 94. White Man's Burden 95. Four Rooms 95. From Dusk till Dawn 96. *Good Will Hunting* (AAN) 97. *Jackie Brown* 97. A Price above Rubies 98, etc.

Bendix, William (1906–1964).
Familiar American character actor who usually played the tough guy with the heart of gold; his broken nose, raucous Brooklyn accent and air of amiable stupidity endeared him to a generation.
■ Woman of the Year 42. The McGuerins from Brooklyn 42. Brooklyn Orchid 42. Wake Island (AAN) 42. *The Glass Key* (as a murderous thug) 42. Who Done It? 42. Star Spangled Rhythm 42. The Crystal Ball 43. Taxi Mister 43. China 43. Hostages 43. Guadalcanal Diary 43. *Lifeboat* 43. *The Hairy Ape* 44. Abroad with Two Yanks 44. Greenwich Village 44. It's in the Bag 45. Don Juan Quilligan 45. A Bell for Adano 45. Sentimental Journey 45. *The Blue Dahlia* 46. The Dark Corner 46. Two Years Before the Mast 46. White Tie and Tails 46. I'll Be Yours 46. Blaze of Noon 47. Calcutta 47. The Web 47. Where There's Life 47. Variety Girl 47. *The Time of Your Life* 48. Race Street 48. The Babe Ruth Story 48. *The Life of Riley* 49. A Connecticut Yankee in King Arthur's Court 49. *The Big Steal* 49. Streets of Laredo 49. Cover Up 49. Johnny Holiday 49. Kill the Umpire 50. Gambling House 50. Submarine Command 51. *Detective Story* 51. Macao 52. A Girl in Every Port 52. Blackbeard the Pirate 52. Dangerous Mission 54. Crashout 55. Battle Stations 56. The Deep Six 58. Idol on Parade (GB) 59. The Rough and the Smooth (GB) 59. Boy's Night Out 62. Johnny Nobody (GB) 62. The Young and the Brave 63. For Love or Money 63. Law of the Lawless 64. The Phony American 64. Young Fury 65.
TV series: *The Life of Riley* 53–58. Overland Stage 60.
❝ Neanderthal man reincarnated in Brooklyn. – *David Shipman*

Benedek, Barbara.
American screenwriter.
The Big Chill (co-w, AAN) 83. Immediate Family 89. Men Don't Leave (co-w) 90. Sabrina (co-w) 95, etc.

Benedek, Laslo (1907–1992).
Hungarian director in Hollywood; output surprisingly meagre.
■ The Kissing Bandit 48. Port of New York 49. Storm over the Tiber 52. *Death of a Salesman* 52. *The Wild One* 54. Bengal Brigade 54. Kinder Mütter und ein General (Ger.) 55. Affair in Havana 57. Moment of Danger (GB) 62. Namu the Killer Whale (& p) 66. The Daring Game 68. The Night Visitor 71. Assault on Agathon 74.

Benedict, Billy (1906–).
American character actor who in his youth was one of the original 'Bowery Boys'; now plays cabbies, bartenders, etc.
Doubting Thomas 35. Way Down East 35. Ramona 36. Libeled Lady 36. That I May Live 37. King of the Newsboys 38. Little Tough Guys in Society 38. Newsboys' Home 39. Code of the Streets 39. Call a Messenger 39. The Bowery Boy 40. My Little Chickadee 40. The Mad Doctor 41. Lady in a Jam 42. Clancy Street Boys 43. Adventures of the Flying Cadets 43. Follow the Leader 44. Docks of New York 45. Hollywood and Vine 45. Spook Busters 46. The Hucksters 47. Hard Boiled Mahoney 47. Fighting Fools 49. Ghost Chasers 51. Last Train from Gun Hill 59. Lover Come Back 61. The Hallelujah Trail 65. Hello Dolly 69. The Sting 73. Farewell My Lovely 75. Won Ton Ton 76. Born Again 78. Computercide (TV) 82, many others.

Benedict, Dirk (1945–) (D. Niewoehner).
Standard-type American leading man with mainly television experience.
Journey from Darkness (TV) 75. Cruise into Terror (TV) 78. Scavenger Hunt 79. Underground Aces 81. Body Slam 87. Blue Tornado 90. Shadow Force 92, etc.
TV series: Chopper One 74. Battlestar Galactica 78. The A Team 83–87.

Benedict, Richard (1916–1984) (Riccardo Benedetto).
American leading man, usually in second features; sometimes played the heavy.
Till the End of Time 46. Crossfire 47. City Across the River 49. State Penitentiary 50. Ace in the Hole 51. Okinawa 52. The Juggler 53. Hoodlum Empire 55. The Shrike 55. Monkey on my Back 57. Ocean's Eleven 60, etc.

Benet, Stephen Vincent (1898–1943).
American poet and novelist whose *The Devil and Daniel Webster* was filmed as *All that Money Can Buy*. His *The Sobbin' Women* was the basis of the musical *Seven Brides for Seven Brothers*, filmed in 1954.

Benigni, Roberto (1952–).
Italian comedian, director, screenwriter and actor who was picked to star in a new *Pink Panther* movie. His *Johnny Stecchino* set box-office records in Italy.
I Love You Berlinguer/Berlinguer ti Voglio Bene (a) 77. Tu mi Turbi (a, wd) 83. Non ci Resta che Piangere (a, wd) 84. Down by Law (a) 86. The Little Devil/Il Piccolo Diavolo 87 (a, wd). The Voice of the Moon/La Voce della Luna (a) 90. Johnny Stecchino (a, wd) 91. Night on Earth (a) 91. Son of the Pink Panther (a) 93. The Monster/Le Monstre (a, co-w, d) 94. *Life Is Beautiful/La Vita è Bella* (a, co-w, d) 98, etc.

Bening, Annette (1958–).
American leading actress. She is married to actor and director Warren Beatty.
The Great Outdoors 88. Valmont 89. Grifters (AAN) 90. Postcards from the Edge 90. Guilty by Suspicion 90. Regarding Henry 91. Bugsy 91. Love Affair 94. The American President 95. Richard III 95. Mars Attacks! 96. The Siege 98, etc.

Benjamin, Arthur (1893–1960).
Anglo-Australian composer.
The Man Who Knew Too Much 34. The Scarlet Pimpernel 34. Turn of the Tide 35. Under the Red Robe 36. Master of Bankdam 47. An Ideal Husband 48. Above Us the Waves 55. Naked Earth 57, etc.

Benjamin, Richard (1938–).
Diffident-seeming American leading man who now concentrates on directing. Married Paula Prentiss in 1961.
AS ACTOR: Thunder over the Plains 53. *Goodbye Columbus* 69. Catch 22 70. *Diary of a Mad Housewife* 70. Marriage of a Young Stockbroker 71. Portnoy's Complaint 72. The Last of Sheila 73. Westworld 73. The Sunshine Boys 76. House Calls 78. Scavenger Hunt 79. The First Family 80. How to Beat the High Cost of Living 80. The Last Married Couple in America 80. Saturday the 14th 81. Deconstructing Harry 97. The Pentagon Wars (TV) 98, etc.
AS DIRECTOR: My Favorite Year 82. Racing with the Moon 83. City Heat 84. The Money Pit 85. Little Nikita 88. My Stepmother Is an Alien 88. Downtown 90. Mermaids 90. Made in America 93. Milk Money 94. Mrs Winterbourne 96, etc.
TV series: *He and She* 67. Quark 78.
❝ If you are married to an actress and your wife is getting all the calls, it's very hard on the ego. – *R.B.*

Bennent, David (1966–).
Swiss child actor, best known for playing the boy Oskar in *The Tin Drum* 79.
Canicule 83. Legend 86, etc.

Bennet, Spencer Gordon (1893–1987).
American silent actor and stuntman who became a famous director of serials and made 52 in all.
Rogue of the Rio Grande 30. Mysterious Pilot 37. Arizona Bound 42. Batman and Robin 48. Atom Man vs Superman 50. Adventures of Sir Galahad 51. Brave Warrior (feature) 52. The Atomic Submarine (feature) 60. The Bounty Killer (feature) 65, many others.

Bennett, Alan (1934–).
British dramatist, screenwriter and occasional actor who first gained fame as one of the four performers in *Beyond the Fringe*, a satirical revue of the 60s that also featured Peter Cook, Dudley Moore and Jonathan Miller.
Autobiography: 1994, *Writing Home*.
AS WRITER: An Englishman Abroad (TV) 83. A Private Function 84. Prick Up Your Ears 87. 102 Boulevard Haussmann (TV) 90. A Question of Attribution (TV) 91. The Madness of King George (AAN) 95.
AS ACTOR: The Wind in the Willows (voice, as Mole) 96. A Dance to the Music of Time (TV) 97.
❝ My claim to literary fame is that I used to deliver meat to a woman who became T.S. Eliot's mother-in-law. – *A.B.*

Bennett, Alma (1889–1958).
American silent-screen vamp.
Why Men Leave Home 14. The Silent Lover 16. The Dawn of a Tomorrow 19. Smiling Jim 22. Three Jumps Ahead 23. The Face on the Barroom Floor 23. Why Men Leave Home 24. The Lost World 25. The Light of Western Stars 25. Don Juan's Three Nights 26. Long Pants 27. Compassion 27. The Grain of Dust 28. Two Men and a Maid 29. Midnight Daddies 30, etc.

Bennett, Arnold (1867–1931).
British novelist, little of whose work has been filmed. *Buried Alive* has, however, been seen in several versions, under its own title, as *The Great Adventure*, as *His Double Life*, and as *Holy Matrimony*. British studios filmed *The Card* with Alec Guinness, and less successfully *Dear Mr Prohack* with Cecil Parker.

Bennett, Barbara (1902–1958).
American leading lady of a few 20s films. Sister of Constance and Joan Bennett.
Syncopation 29. Mother's Boy 29. Love Among the Millionaires 30, etc.

Bennett, Belle (1891–1932).
American leading lady of the silent screen.
A Soul in Trust 18. His Supreme Moment 25. If Marriage Fails 25. *Stella Dallas* 25. The Fourth Commandment 27. The Way of All Flesh 27. Mother Machree 28. The Iron Mask 29. Courage 30. Recaptured Love 31. The Big Shot 31, etc.

Bennett, Bill (1953–).
Australian director, screenwriter and producer. Born in Sydney, he began as a journalist, directing and writing television documentaries in the early 80s. His best films have involved improvisations with the actors.
A Street to Die (p, wd) 85. *Backlash* (wd) 86. Dear Cardholder 86 (not released, and then to video 89). Jilted (co-p, wd) 87 (not released, and then to video 90). Malpractice (d) (TV) 88. Mortgage (wd) (TV) 89. Spider & Rosie (wd) 93. Two If by Sea (US) 96. *Kiss or Kill* (wd) 98, In a Savage Land 99, etc.

Bennett, Billy (1887–1942).
English music-hall comedian and monologuist, billed as 'Almost a Gentleman', who appeared in films of the 20s and 30s. Born in Liverpool, the son of an acrobat, he also partnered James Carew and, later, Albert Whelan, in a black-face act, Alexander and Mose, on radio and in the halls.
Robin Hood 22. The Amateur Gentleman 26. Radio Parade of 1935 35. Soft Lights and Sweet Music 36. Calling All Stars 37. Almost a Gentleman 38. Young Man's Fancy 39, etc.
❝ Nobody who ever saw him is likely to forget that rubicund, unaesthetic countenance, that black, plastered quiff, that sergeant-major's moustache, that dreadful dinner-jacket, that well-used dickey and seedy collar, the too-short trousers, the hobnail boots, the red silk handkerchief tucked into the waistcoat, the continual perspiration which was the outward and visible sign of a mind struggling for expression – these things will not be forgotten – *James Agate*

Bennett, Bruce (1909–) (Herman Brix).
Athletic American leading man who started in films by playing Tarzan and subsequently settled down as a familiar flannel-suited second lead. Used his own name until 1940.
Student Tour 34. *The New Adventures of Tarzan* 35 (re-edited 1938 as *Tarzan and the Green Goddess*). Danger Patrol 37. Before I Hang 40. Atlantic Convoy 42. The More the Merrier 43. Sahara 43. Mildred Pierce 45. The Treasure of the Sierra Madre 47. Silver River 48. Task Force 49. The Doctor and the Girl 49. Without Honor 50. Sudden Fear 52. Dream Wife 53. Strategic Air Command 55. Three Violent People 57. The Outsider 61. Lost Island of Kioga (TV) 66. Deadhead Miles 72, many others.

Bennett, Charles (1899–1995).
British screenwriter who worked on some of Hitchcock's 30s films and later moved to Hollywood. Usually worked in collaboration. In the 90s he rewrote *Blackmail* for a forthcoming remake. He claimed to be 'the oldest working screenwriter of all time'.
Blackmail 29. The Man Who Knew Too Much 34. *The Thirty-nine Steps* 35. Secret Agent 36. Sabotage 37. King Solomon's Mines 37. The Young in Heart 38. Balalaika 39. *Foreign Correspondent* (AAN) 40. Joan of Paris 42. Reap the Wild Wind 42. The Story of Dr Wassell 44. Ivy 47. Madness of the Heart (& d) 48. Black Magic 49. Where Danger Lives 51. The Green Glove 52. No Escape (& d) 53. The Story of Mankind 57. The Lost World 60. Five Weeks in a Balloon 62. War Gods of the Deep 65, etc.

Bennett, Compton (1900–1974) (Robert Compton-Bennett).
British director, former editor.
■ *The Seventh Veil* 45. The Years Between 46. Daybreak 48. My Own True Love 49. *That Forsyte Woman* 49. *King Solomon's Mines* 50. So Little Time 52. The Gift Horse 52. It Started in Paradise 52. Desperate Moment 53. That Woman Opposite 57. After the Ball 57. The Flying Scot 57. Beyond the Curtain 60. How to Undress in Public Without Undue Embarrassment 65.

Bennett, Constance (1904–1965).
Glamorous American star of the 30s, adept at worldly roles; sister of Barbara and Joan Bennett. The fourth of her five husbands was actor Gilbert Roland (1941–45).
■ Reckless Youth 22. Evidence 22. What's Wrong with the Women? 22. Cytherea 24. Into the Net 24. *The Goose Hangs High* 25. Married 25. Code of the West 25. My Son 25. My Wife and I 25. *The Goose Woman* 25. Sally Irene and Mary 25. Wandering Fires 25. The Pinch Hitter 26. This Thing Called Love 29. Son of the Gods 30. Rich People 30. Common Clay 30. *Three Faces East* 30. Sin Takes a Holiday 30. The Easiest Way 31. Born to Love 31. The Common Law 31. Bought 31. Lady with a Past 32. *What Price Hollywood?* 32. Two Against the World 32. Rockabye 32. Our Betters 33. Bed of Roses 33. After Tonight 33. *Moulin Rouge* 33. Affairs of Cellini 34. Outcast Lady 34. After Office Hours 35. Everything is Thunder (GB) 36. Ladies in Love 36. *Topper* (as a ghost) 37. *Merrily We Live* 38. Service de Luxe 38. Topper Takes a Trip 38. Tailspin 39. *Escape to Glory* 40.

Law of the Tropics 41. *Two-Faced Woman* 41. Wild Bill Hickok Rides 41. Sin Town 42. Madame Spy 42. Paris Underground 46. Centennial Summer 46. *The Unsuspected* 47. Smart Woman 48. Angel on the Amazon 49. As Young as You Feel 51. It Should Happen to You 53. *Madame X* 65.

❝ She seemed to me the quintessence of a movie star. Everything about her shone – her burnished head, her jewels, her famous smile, her lovely long legs, and the highly publicised fact that she pulled down 30,000 bucks a week. – *David Niven*

Bennett, Enid (1895–1969).
Australian leading lady in Hollywood films of the 20s. Married director Fred Niblo.
Princess in the Dark 17. The Vamp 18. The Haunted Bedroom 19. Hairpins 20. Her Husband's Friend 21. Robin Hood 22. Scandalous Tongues 22. The Courtship of Miles Standish 23. The Sea Hawk 24. A Woman's Heart 26. The Wrong Mr Wright 27. Good Medicine 29. Skippy 31. Meet Dr Christian 39. Strike Up the Band 40, many others.

Bennett, Hywel (1944–).
Welsh leading man who has usually played roles requiring a feigning of innocence.
■ *The Family Way* 66. Twisted Nerve 68. *The Virgin Soldiers* 69. The Buttercup Chain 70. Loot 71. Percy 71. Endless Night 72. Alice's Adventures in Wonderland 72. The Love Ban 72. Malice Aforethought (TV) 79. Tinker Tailor Soldier Spy (TV) 79. Murder Elite (TV) 85. Deadline 87. Deadly Advice 94. Karaoke (TV) 96. Harpur and Iles (TV) 96.
TV series: *Shelley* 80–85.

Bennett, Jill (1930–1990).
Unusual-looking British actress who generally played emancipated roles. Committed suicide. She was formerly married to John Osborne (1970–77).
Autobiography: 1983, *Godfrey: A Special Time Remembered* (about her relationship with actor Sir Godfrey Tearle).
Moulin Rouge 53. Hell Below Zero 54. *Lust for Life* 56. The Criminal 60. The Skull 65. *The Nanny* 65. *Inadmissible Evidence* 68. *The Charge of the Light Brigade* 68. Julius Caesar 70. I Want What I Want 71. Mister Quilp 75. Full Circle 77. For Your Eyes Only 81. Britannia Hospital 82. Lady Jane 86. Hawks 89. The Sheltering Sky 90, etc.

❝ My idea of heaven is to be eternally rehearsing. – *J.B.*

Bennett, Joan (1910–1990).
Popular American leading lady of the 30s and 40s, one of the most attractive stars of her time. Sister of Barbara and Constance Bennett. She was formerly married to producer Walter Wanger.
Autobiography: 1970, *The Bennett Playbill*.
■ The Valley of Decision 15. Power 28. The Divine Lady 29. Bulldog Drummond 29. Three Live Ghosts 29. Disraeli 29. Mississippi Gambler 29. Puttin' On the Ritz 30. Crazy that Way 30. Moby Dick 30. Maybe It's Love 30. Scotland Yard 30. Many a Slip 31. Doctors' Wives 31. Hush Money 31. She Wanted a Millionaire 32. Careless Lady 32. The Trial of Vivienne Ware 32. Weekends Only 32. Wild Girl 32. Me and My Gal 32. Arizona to Broadway 32. *Little Women* 33. The Pursuit of Happiness 34. The Man Who Reclaimed His Head 34. *Private Worlds* 35. Mississippi 35. Two for Tonight 35. The Man Who Broke the Bank at Monte Carlo 35. She Couldn't Take It 35. Thirteen Hours by Air 36. Big Brown Eyes 36. Two in a Crowd 36. Wedding Present 36. Vogues of 1938 37. I Met My Love Again 38. The Texans 38. Artists and Models Abroad 38. Trade Winds 39. The Man in the Iron Mask 39. *The Housekeeper's Daughter* 39. Green Hell 40. The House across the Bay 40. The Man I Married 40. Son of Monte Cristo 40. She Knew All the Answers 41. *Man Hunt* 41. Wild Geese Calling 41. Confirm or Deny 42. Twin Beds 42. The Wife Takes a Flyer 42. Girl Trouble 42. Margin for Error 43. *The Woman in the Window* 44. Nob Hill 45. *Scarlet Street* 45. Colonel Effingham's Raid 46. *The Macomber Affair* 47. The Secret Beyond the Door 47. The Woman on the Beach 47. The Scar 47. *The Reckless Moment* 49. *Father of the Bride* 50. For Heaven's Sake 50. Father's Little Dividend 51. The Guy Who Came Back 51. Highway Dragnet 54. We're No Angels 55. There's Always Tomorrow 56. Navy Wife 56. Desire in the Dust 60. House of Dark Shadows 70. Inn of the Damned 71. Gidget Gets Married (TV) 71. The Eyes of Charles Sand (TV) 72. Suspiria 77. Suddenly, Love (TV) 78. Divorce Wars (TV) 82.
TV series: Too Young to Go Steady 59. Dark Shadows 66–71.

❝ The golden age is gone, and with it most of the people of great taste. It doesn't seem to be fun any more. – *J.B.*, 1984.
My film career faded. A man can go on playing certain roles till he's 60. But not a woman. – *J.B.*

Bennett, John (1928–).
Swarthy British character actor.
The Challenge 59. *The Barber of Stamford Hill* 62. Kaleidoscope 66. The Forsyte Saga (TV) 68. The House that Dripped Blood 70. The House in Nightmare Park 73. Hitler, the Last Ten Days (as Goebbels) 74. The Message 77. Eye of the Needle 81. Antonia and Jane (TV) 91, etc.

Bennett, Marjorie (1894–1982).
American character actress, in films since early silent experience as a bathing beauty.
Monsieur Verdoux 47. Limelight 52. Young at Heart 55. *Whatever Happened to Baby Jane?* 62. Mary Poppins 64. Charley Varrick 73. Mother, Jugs and Speed 76, many others.

Bennett, Richard (1873–1944).
Dapper American stage actor, a leading figure of his day; father of Barbara, Constance and Joan Bennett. Film appearances rare.
The Eternal City 23. The Home Towners 28. Arrowsmith 32. *If I Had a Million* (as the millionaire) 32. Nana 34. *The Magnificent Ambersons* 42. Journey into Fear 43, etc.

Bennett, Richard Rodney (1936–).
British composer and pianist, based in New York, who holds the international chair of composition at the Royal Academy of Music.
Interpol 57. Indiscreet 58. Only Two Can Play 61. Billy Liar 63. One Way Pendulum 64. The Nanny 65. Far from the Madding Crowd (AAN) 67. Secret Ceremony 68. Figures in a Landscape 70. Nicholas and Alexandra (AAN) 71. Lady Caroline Lamb 72. Voices 73. Murder on the Orient Express (AAN) 74. Permission to Kill 75. Sherlock Holmes in New York 77. Equus 77. Yanks 79. The Brink's Job 79. The Return of the Soldier 82. Murder with Mirrors (TV) 84. The Ebony Tower (TV) 84. Enchanted April 91. Four Weddings and a Funeral 94. Swann 96, etc.

❝ All I need in order to write a film score are the parameters of budget and length. Then, when the film is made, I require a time-coded video to work from. I don't need, or want, to be part of the production team. – *R.R.B*

Bennett, Tony (1926–) (Antonio Benedetto).
Heavyweight Italian-American ballad singer, famous for leaving his heart in San Francisco. Principal film appearance in *The Oscar*.

Benny, Jack (1894–1974) (Benjamin Kubelsky).
Celebrated American comedian of radio, TV and occasional films. His inimitable reproachful look, his pretence of meanness and his much maligned violin are among the trademarks which kept him popular for forty years. He graduated from burlesque, and later married his radio leading lady Mary Livingstone (Sadye Marks). His violin, which was made in Paris in 1845, was sold at auction in 1997 for $84,300.
Biographies: 1976, *Jack Benny* by Irving Fein. 1978, *Jack Benny* by Mary Livingstone Marks and others.
Autobiography: 1990, *Sunday Nights at Seven: The Jack Benny Story*.
■ *Hollywood Revue of 1929* 29. Chasing Rainbows 30. Medicine Man 30. Transatlantic Merry-Go-Round 34. Broadway Melody of 1936 35. It's in the Air 35. The Big Broadcast of 1937 36. College Holiday 36. Artists and Models 37. Artists and Models Abroad 38. Man About Town 39. Buck Benny Rides Again 39. Love Thy Neighbour 40. *Charley's Aunt* 41. *To Be or Not To Be* (an outstanding performance) 42. George Washington Slept Here 42. The Meanest Man in the World 43. Hollywood Canteen 44. *It's in the Bag* 45. *The Horn Blows at Midnight* 45. A Guide for the Married Man 67.
TV series: *The Jack Benny Show* 50–65.
~Benny also made gag appearances in Without Reservations 47. Beau James 57. It's a Mad Mad Mad Mad World 63.

❝ Hold-up Man: 'Your money or your life! Come on, come on, hurry up!' Benny: 'I'm thinking it over!'
He couldn't ad-lib a belch after a Hungarian dinner. – *Fred Allen* (in jest)
He didn't just stand on the stage. He owned it. – *Bob Hope*

Benoît-Lévy, Jean (1883–1959).
French director who also wrote books on cinema.
La Maternelle 33. Hélène 37. La Mort du Cygne 38. Fire in the Straw 43, etc.

Benson, George (1911–1983).
British character actor of stage, screen and TV, the nervous 'little man' of countless films.
Keep Fit 37. Convoy 40. The October Man 48. Pool of London 50. The Man in the White Suit 51. The Captain's Paradise 53. Doctor in the House 54. Value for Money 56. Dracula 58. A Jolly Bad Fellow 64. A Home of Your Own 65. The Creeping Flesh 72, etc.

Benson, Lucille (1914–1984).
American character actress.
The Fugitive Kind 60. Little Fauss and Big Halsy 70. Duel 71. Cactus in the Snow 72. Tom Sawyer 73. Huckleberry Finn 74. Reflections of Murder 74, etc.
TV series: Nashville 99 77. Bosom Buddies 80–81.

Benson, Martin (1918–).
British character actor often seen as a smooth foreign-looking crook.
The Blind Goddess 49. West of Zanzibar 54. The King and I (US) 56. Windom's Way 58. The Three Worlds of Gulliver 60. Cleopatra 62. Behold a Pale Horse 64. Goldfinger 64. The Secret of My Success 65. Pope Joan 72. The Omen 76. Mohammed 77. The Sea Wolves 80. Sphinx 81, many others.
TV series: Sword of Freedom 57.

Benson, Robby (1956–) (Robert Segal).
American leading man, on stage from the age of five. He is the son of screenwriter Jerry Segal.
Jory 73. *Jeremy* 73. *Death Be Not Proud* (TV) 75. Lucky Lady 76. The Death of Richie (TV) 76. One on One (& co-w) 77. The End 78. Ice Castles 78. Walk Proud 79. Die Laughing 80. Tribute 80. The Chosen 81. National Lampoon Goes to the Movies 82. City Limits 85. Rent-A-Cop 88. White Hot (& d) 88. Modern Love (& wd) 90. Beauty and the Beast (voice) 91. Invasion of Privacy 92. The Webbers 93, etc.
TV series: Tough Cookies 86.

❝ I was into show business straight from the womb. – *R.B.*
Cute as Bambi and twice as smarmy. – *An anonymous critic*

Benson, Sally (1900–1972).
American screenwriter, former film critic and novelist.
Shadow of a Doubt (co-w) 43. Meet Me in St Louis (oa) 44. Junior Miss (oa) 45. Anna and the King of Siam (co-w, AAN) 46. Come to the Stable (co-w) 49. No Man of Her Own (co-w) 50. The Farmer Takes a Wife (co-w) 53. Summer Magic (co-w) 63. Joy in the Morning (co-w) 65. The Singing Nun (co-w) 66.

Bentine, Michael (1922–1996).
Anglo-Peruvian comedian, popular on stage and TV, who has made several unsuccessful attempts to film his goonish style of humour, for example in *The Sandwich Man* 66.

Bentivoglio, Fabrizio (1957–).
Italian leading actor, from the stage.
Masoch 80. Salomè 85. Via Montenapoleone 85. Marrakech Express 88. Turné 89. Italia-Germania 4 a 3 90. Americano Rosso 91, The End Is Known/La Fine, Nota 93. Like Two Crocodiles/Come Due Coccodrilli 94. An Ordinary Hero/Un Eroe Borghese 95. La Strage Del Gallo 96. Livers Ain't Cheap (US) 97. Notes Of Love/La Parola Amore Esiste 98, etc.

Bentley, Irene (1904–1965).
American leading actress of the 30s who made a few films and then suddenly dropped from sight.
My Weakness 33. Smoky 33. Frontier Marshal 33.

Bentley, John (1916–).
British leading man who left the stage in 1946 to play in innumerable low-budget crime dramas, including series about Paul Temple and The Toff.
Hills of Donegal 47. Calling Paul Temple 48. The Happiest Days of Your Life 49. The Lost Hours 51. The Scarlet Spear 53. Golden Ivory 55. Istanbul (US) 58. Submarine Seahawk 59. The Singer Not the Song 60. Mary Had a Little 61. The Fur Collar 63, many others.
TV series: African Patrol 59.

Bentley, Thomas (c. 1880–195*).
British director, former Dickensian impersonator, who began in films by making silent versions of several Dickens novels.
Young Woodley 30. *Hobson's Choice* 31. The Scotland Yard Mystery 33. *Those Were the Days* 34. The Old Curiosity Shop 35. Music Hath Charms 35. Marigold 38. The Middle Watch 39. Lucky to Me 39. Old Mother Riley's Circus 41, many others.

Benton, Robert (1932–).
American magazine writer and art director who teamed up with David Newman to become co-screenwriter of such movies as *Bonnie and Clyde* (AAN), There Was a Crooked Man, What's Up Doc, and Superman.
AS DIRECTOR: Bad Company (& co-w) 70. The Late Show (& co-w) (AAN) 77. *Kramer vs Kramer* (AA) 79. Still of the Night 82. Places of the Heart (AAw, AANd) 84. Nadine (wd) 87. The House on Carroll Street 88. Billy Bathgate 91. Nobody's Fool (wd, AANw) 94. Twilight (co-w,d) 98.

❝ The success of *Bonnie and Clyde* made me very miserable. It's some deep-seated neurosis I have. – *R.B.*

Benzali, Daniel (1950–).
American actor, best known for his role as lawyer Ted Hoffman in the TV series *Murder One* 96. Born in Rio de Janeiro, he began in the New York and London theatre. Married actress Kim CATTRALL in 1997.
A View to a Kill 85. White Knights 85. Insignificance 85. Defence of the Realm (GB) 85. Whoops Apocalypse (GB) 86. A Day in October (Den.) 91. The Last of His Tribe 92. The Distinguished Gentleman 92. Murder at 1600 97. All the Little Animals 98, etc.

Beranger, André (1895–1973).
Australian Shakespearean actor who joined D. W. Griffith in Hollywood and appeared in mainly silent films.
The Birth of a Nation 15. Intolerance 16. Manhattan Madness 16. Broken Blossoms 19. The Bright Shawl 23. Beau Brummell 24. The Grand Duchess and the Waiter 26. Fig Leaves 26. Strange Cargo 29. Surrender 31. Mama Loves Papa 33. Over My Dead Body 42. Road House 48, many others.

Bérard, Christian (1902–1949).
Noted French theatrical designer who was responsible for the art direction of three of Cocteau's films.
La Belle et la Bête 47. L'Aigle à Deux Têtes 47. Les Parents Terribles 48.

Berenger, Tom (1950–).
Brooding American leading man in the John Garfield mould.
Johnny We Hardly Knew Ye (TV) 77. Butch and Sundance 79. Flesh and Blood (TV) 80. The Dogs of War 81. The Big Chill 83. Eddie and the Cruisers 83. Platoon (AAN) 86. Someone to Watch Over Me 87. Betrayed 88. Last Rites 88. Shoot to Kill 88. Born on the Fourth of July 89. The Field 90. Shattered 91. At Play in the Fields of the Lord 91. Sniper 93. Sliver 93. Gettysburg 93. Major League II 94. Chasers 94. Last of the Dogmen 95. The Substitute 96. An Occasional Hell 96. Rough Riders (TV) 97. The Gingerbread Man 97. One Man's Hero (Mex) 98, etc.

Berens, Harold (1903–1995).
English comedian and character actor, much on the radio, especially the long-running show *Ignorance Is Bliss* (1946–53).
Candelight in Algeria 43. The Man from Morocco 45. Up for the Cup 50. A Kid for Two Farthings 55. The Big Money 56. The Pure Hell of St Trinian's 59. What a Whopper! 61. Live Now, Pay Later 62. Mozambique 66. The Magic

Christian 70. Straight On till Morning 72. Trail of the Pink Panther 82. *Hear My Song* 91, etc.
~Catchphrase: What a geezer!

Berenson, Marisa (1947–).
International fashion model who has appeared in films.
Death in Venice 72. Cabaret 72. Barry Lyndon 75. Killer Fish 78. Naked Sun 80. S.O.B. 81. Secret Diary of Sigmund Freud 84. Night of the Cyclone 90. White Hunter, Black Heart 90. Night of the White Rabbit 92. The Fugitives 93. The Great White of Lamberene 95. Elles (Lux) 97, etc.
❝ My ultimate goal is to become a saint. – M.B.

Beresford, Bruce (1940–).
Australian director and screenwriter.
The Adventures of Barry Mackenzie 72. Barry Mackenzie Holds His Own 74. Side by Side 75. Don's Party 76. *The Getting of Wisdom* 77. Money Movers 78. *Breaker Morant* (AAN) 80. The Club 80. Puberty Blues 81. Tender Mercies (AAN) 82. King David 84. The Fringe Dwellers 85. Crimes of the Heart 86. Aria (co-d) 87. *Driving Miss Daisy* (d) (AA) 89. Her Alibi (d) 89. *Mister Johnson* (wd) 90. *Black Robe* (d) 91. Rich in Love (d) 93. A Good Man in Africa 94. Silent Fall 94. Last Dance 96. Paradise Road 97, etc.

Beresford, Harry (1864–1944).
British general-purpose actor in Hollywood from silent days.
The Quarterback 26. Charles Chan Carries On 31. So Big 32. Dr X 32. The Sign of the Cross 32. Murders in the Zoo 33. Dinner at Eight 33. Cleopatra 34. The Little Minister 34. Seven Keys To Baldpate 35. David Copperfield 35. Follow the Fleet 36. The Prince and the Pauper 37. They Won't Forget 37, many others.

Berg, Gertrude (1899–1966) (Gertrude Edelstein).
Plump American character actress famous on TV and radio as Molly of the Goldberg family. She appeared in a film version, *Molly* 51, also in another TV series, *Mrs G Goes to College* 61.

Berg, Peter (1964–).
American actor, best known as Dr Billy Kronk in the TV series *Chicago Hope*, who turned to directing and screenwriting in the late 90s. Born in New York City, he studied theatre at Macalaster College in St Paul, Minnesota.
Shocker 89. Crooked Hearts 91. Late for Dinner 91. A Midnight Clear 92. Aspen Extreme 93. Fire in the Sky 93. FTW 94. The Last Seduction 94. Girl 6 96. The Great White Hype 96. Cop Land 97. Very Bad Things (wd) 98, etc.
TV series: Chicago Hope 95– .
❝ Where writers live and die by their wit, actors more or less live and die by their muscle definition. – P.B.

Bergdahl, Victor (1878–1939).
Swedish animator of the silent era.

Bergen, Candice (1946–).
Stylish American leading lady, daughter of Edgar Bergen. She married film director Louis Malle in 1980.
Autobiography: 1984, *Knock Wood.*
■ *The Group* 66. The Sand Pebbles 66. The Day the Fish Came Out 67. Vivre Pour Vivre 67. The Magus 68. Getting Straight 70. Soldier Blue 70. The Adventures 70. *Carnal Knowledge* 71. The Hunting Party 71. T R Baskin 72. 11 Harrowhouse 74. Bite the Bullet 75. The Wind and the Lion 76. The Cassandra Crossing 76. The Domino Principle 77. A Night Full of Rain 77. Oliver's Story 78. Starting Over (AAN) 79. Rich and Famous 81. Gandhi 82. Stick 84. Hollywood Wives (TV) 85.
TV series: Murphy Brown 88–.
❝ There are moments when I perceive us as being on the brink of another dark age, a media blitzkrieg of mindlessness. – C.B.
It takes a long time to grow up. Longer than they tell you. – C.B.

Bergen, Edgar (1903–1978).
Mild-mannered Swedish-American ventriloquist, manipulator of Charlie McCarthy and Mortimer Snerd (special AA 1937); latterly a character actor.
The Goldwyn Follies 38. Letter of Introduction 38. *You Can't Cheat an Honest Man* 39. *Charlie McCarthy Detective* 39. Look Who's Laughing 41. Here We Go Again 42. Stage Door Canteen 43. Song of the Open Road 44. *I Remember Mama* 48. The Hanged Man 64. One Way Wahine 66. Don't Make Waves 67. The Homecoming (TV) 70, etc.

Bergen, Polly (1930–) (Nellie Burgin).
American singer of stage, radio and TV; also pleasing light actress in several films.
■ Across the Rio Grande 49. At War with the Army 50. That's My Boy 51. Warpath 51. The Stooge 53. Cry of the Hunted 53. Arena 53. Half a Hero 54. Fast Company 54. Escape from Fort Bravo 54. *Cape Fear* 62. Belle Sommers (TV) 62. The Caretakers 63. *Move Over Darling* 63. *Kisses for My President* 64. A Guide for the Married Man 67. Death Cruise (TV) 75. Murder on Flight 502 75. Million Dollar Face (TV) 81. Born Beautiful (TV) 82. *The Winds of War* (TV) 83. Making Mr Right 86. War and Remembrance (TV) 88. The Haunting of Sarah Hardy (TV) 89. Cry-Baby 90. One Upon a Time . . . When We Were Colored 96.
❝ I'm one of those people who always needs a mountain to climb. When I get up a mountain as far as I think I'm going to get, I try to find another mountain. – P.B.

Berger, Helmut (1944–) (Helmut Steinberger).
Handsome Austrian actor who gives a sinister edge to his performances.
The Damned 69. *Un Beau Monstre* 70. The Garden of the Finzi-Continis 71. Dorian Gray 72. Ash Wednesday 73. Ludwig 73. Conversation Piece 75. The Romantic Englishwoman 75. Madam Kitty 77. Roses of Danzig 79. Heroin 80. Victory 83. Code Name Emerald 85. Tunnel 85. Les Prédateurs de la Nuit 87. Er-Sie-Es 89. Never in Life/Nie im Leben (& co-w, d) 91. The Laughter of Maca Daracs/Das Lachen der Maca Daracs 91. Once Arizona/Einamal Arizona 91. Ludwig 1881 93, etc.
TV series: Dynasty 83–84.

Berger, Ludwig (1892–1969) (Ludwig Bamberger).
German director who made some international films.
Ein Glas Wasser 22. The Waltz Dream 26. The Woman from Moscow (US) 28. Sins of the Fathers 29. Die Meistersinger 29. The Vagabond King (US) 30. Playboy of Paris 30. Waltz Time in Vienna 33. Three Waltzes 39. The Thief of Baghdad (GB/US) 40. Ballerina (Fr.) 50, etc.

Berger, Nicole (1934–1967).
French leading lady. Killed in a car crash.
Juliette 52. Game of Love 54. Le Premier Mai 57. Love is My Profession 58. Les Dragueurs 59. Shoot the Pianist 62, etc.

Berger, Senta (1941–).
Austrian leading lady in international films.
Die Lindenwirtin vom Donaus Trand (debut) 57. The Journey 59. The Secret Ways 61. The Good Soldier Schweik 62. Sherlock Holmes and the Deadly Necklace 62. The Victors 63. Major Dundee 65. The Glory Guys 65. Cast a Giant Shadow 66. The Quiller Memorandum 67. Our Man in Marrakesh 67. The Ambushers 67. Treasure of San Gennaro 68. De Sade 69. Ludwig 72. The Scarlet Letter 72. Der Reigen 73. The Swiss Conspiracy 75. Cross of Iron 77. The Two Lives of Mattia Pascal/Le Due Vite di Mattia Pascal 84. The Flying Devils 85. Killing Cars 86. Swiss Cheese 87. Am I Beautiful?/Bin Ich Schon? 98, etc.

Berger, Thomas (1924–).
American novelist whose books are occasionally filmed.
Little Big Man (oa) 70. Neighbors (oa) 81.

Berger, William (1928–).
Austrian-born leading actor, mainly in Italian films.
The Man with the Balloons (It.) 65. The Murder Clinic (It.) 66. The Day the Fish Came Out (Ger.) 67. Every Bastard a King (It.) 70. Sabata (It.) 70. Today We Kill, Tomorrow We Die (It.) 71. Superfly TNT (US) 73. Three Tough Guys (It.) 74. Oil (It.) 78. Hercules (It.) 83. Day of the Cobra (It.) 84. Hercules II (It.) 85. Tex and the Lord of the Deep (It.) 85. The Berlin Affair (Ger.) 85. Hell Hunters 87, etc.

Bergerac, Jacques (1927–).
French leading man, former lawyer, in Hollywood from 1953. He was formerly married to actresses Ginger Rogers and Dorothy Malone.
Les Girls 57. Gigi 58. Thunder in the Sun 59. The Hypnotic Eye 60. Taffy and the Jungle Hunter 65, etc.

Bergere, Ouida (1885–1974).
American scriptwriter of the 20s (*On with the Dance, The Cheat,* etc.) who also acted in a few films before marrying Basil Rathbone and becoming Hollywood's most lavish hostess.

Berggren, Thommy (1937–).
Swedish leading actor.
Sunday in September 63. Raven's End 63. *Elvira Madigan* 67. The Adventurers 70. Joe Hill 71. Giliap 73. Kristoffers Hus 79. Broken Sky 82. The Mountain on the Other Side of the Moon 83. *Strindberg* (TV) 85. *Gosta Berlings Saga* (TV) 86. Sunday's Child 92, etc.

Berghof, Herbert (1909–1990).
Austrian character actor long on American stage, also as drama teacher; films rare.
Assignment Paris 52. *Five Fingers* 52. Red Planet Mars 52. Fräulein 58. Cleopatra 62. Harry and Tonto 74. Those Lips Those Eyes 80. Times Square 83. Target 85, etc.

Bergin, Patrick (1954–).
Irish leading actor in international films, a former teacher.
The Courier 87. Taffin 88. Mountains of the Moon 90. Robin Hood 90. Sleeping with the Enemy 91. Highway to Hell 91. The Humming-Bird (TV) 92. Map of the Human Heart 92. Love Crimes 92. Patriot Games 92. Highway to Hell 92. Frankenstein (TV) 93. Map of the Human Heart 93. Triplecross 95. Lawnmower Man 2: Beyond Cyberspace 96. The Proposition 96. One Man's Hero (Mex) 98, etc.

Berglund, Sven (1881–1937).
Swedish inventor with claims to be the first person to record sound on film by an optical process, which he worked on from 1906–11 and demonstrated in the 20s in Stockholm and Berlin. He also worked on stereoscopic film in the 30s before committing suicide.

Bergman, Alan (1925–).
Lyricist and songwriter in collaboration with his wife Marilyn.
The Thomas Crown Affair (AA) 68. The Happy Ending (AAN) 69. Pieces of Dreams (AAN) 70. Sometimes a Great Notion (AAN) 71. The Life and Times of Judge Roy Bean (AAN) 71. The Way We Were (AA) 73. Ode to Billy Joe 75. Same Time Next Year (AAN) 78. The Promise (AAN) 79. Best Friends (AAN) 82. Tootsie (AAN) 82. Yes, Giorgio (AAN) 82. Never Say Never Again 83. Yentl (AA) 83. Micki and Maude 84. Big 88. Shirley Valentine (AAN) 89. Welcome Home 89, many others.

Bergman, Andrew (1945–).
American screenwriter and director. He is the author of *We're in the Money: Depression America and Its Films* (1971), which was first written as a doctoral thesis at the University of Wisconsin.
Blazing Saddles (co-w) 74. The In-Laws (w) 79. So Fine (wd) 81. Oh God! You Devil (w) 84. Fletch (w) 85. Big Trouble (w) 86. Fletch Lives 89. The Freshman (wd) 90. Soapdish (co-w) 91. Honeymoon in Vegas (wd) 92. It Could Happen to You 94. The Scout (co-w) 94. Striptease (wd) 96, etc.

Bergman, Daniel (1962–).
Swedish director, the son of Ingmar Bergman.
Sunday's Child 92.

Bergman, Henry (1868–1946).
American comedy actor, the heavy villain in many a Chaplin film from *His New Job* in 1915 to *The Great Dictator* in 1940.

Bergman, Ingmar (1918–).
Swedish writer-director who divides his time between stage and film. In the late 50s his films had world-wide impact because of their semi-mystic, under-explained themes and bravura presentation by a repertory of excellent actors and cameramen; his work later became more austere and withdrawn. When he was accused of tax avoidance in the mid-70s, he suffered a brief breakdown. Married four times; his lovers include actresses Harriet Anderson and Bibi Andersson, and he has a daughter with actress Liv Ullmann. At the 50th Cannes Film Festival he was awarded, in absentia, the Palme de Palme D'Or.
Autobiography: 1988, *The Magic Lantern*; 1994, Images: *My Life in Film.*
Biographies include: 1962, *Ingmar Bergman* by Peter Cowie. 1964, *The Personal Vision of Ingmar Bergman* by Jorn Donner. 1968, *Ingmar Bergman* by Brigitta Steene. 1969, *The Silence of God* by Arthur Gibson. 1969, *Ingmar Bergman* by Robin Wood. 1971, *Cinema Borealis* by Vernon Young. Various screenplays have been published.
■ Crisis 45. It Rains on Our Love 46. A Ship Bound for India 47. Night is Our Future 47. Port of Call 48. *Prison* 48. *Thirst* 49. Till Gladje 49. Summer Interlude 50. Sant Hander inte Har 50. Waiting Women 52. Summer with Monika 52. *Sawdust and Tinsel* 53. A Lesson in Love 54. Journey into Autumn 55. *Smiles of a Summer Night* 55. *The Seventh Seal* 56. *Wild Strawberries* (AAN) 57. So Close to Life 58. *The Face/The Magician* 58. *The Virgin Spring* (AA) 59. The Devil's Eye 60. *Through a Glass Darkly* (AA) 61. *Winter Light* 62. *The Silence* 63. Now About these Women 64. *Persona* 66. The Hour of the Wolf 67. The Shame 68. The Rite (TV) 69. The Touch 70. A Passion 70. *Cries and Whispers* (AAN) 72. Scenes from a Marriage (TV) 74. The Magic Flute (TV) 75. Face to Face (TV) (AAN) 76. The Serpent's Egg 77. Autumn Sonata (AAN) 78. From the Life of the Marionettes 80. *Fanny and Alexander* (AAN) 82. After the Rehearsal 84. The Best Intentions (w) 92. Sunday's Child (w) 92. In the Presence of a Clown/Larmar Och Gor Sig Tag 98.
✪ For his obsessional realization of a bleak but bracing vision of the world. *The Seventh Seal.*
❝ The theatre is like a faithful wife. The film is the great adventure – the costly, exacting mistress. – I.B.
I have a morbid sense of humour. I'm very open and frank, and sometimes that is a mistake. – I.B.
To shoot a film is to organize a complete universe. – I.B.
I'm not a writer. My plays and scripts are skeletons awaiting sinew. – I.B.
I don't remember much about my private life, if I'm to be perfectly honest. I can't remember when my children were born. I don't know how old they are. If I want to date something, I do it with reference to films or plays. – I.B.

Bergman, Ingrid (1915–1982).
Gifted Swedish leading actress who went to Hollywood in 1938 and became an international star. In 1948 her romance with Roberto Rossellini caused a return to Europe where she appeared in mainly inferior films; Hollywood's door opened to her again in 1956. Her lovers included director Victor Fleming, musician Larry Adler, and war photographer Robert Capa, a relationship Hitchcock used in *Rear Window.*
Autobiography: 1972, My Story.
Biography: 1986, *As Time Goes By* by Laurence Leamer. 1997, *Notorious: The Life of Ingrid Bergman* by Donald Spoto.
■ Munkbrogreven 34. Branningar 35. Swedenhielms 35. Valborgsmassoafton 35. Pa Solsidan 36. *Intermezzo* 36. *En Kvinnas Ansikte* 38. En Enda Natt 38. Dollar 38. Die Vier Gesellen 38. *Intermezzo* (US remake) 39. Juninatten 40. Rage in Heaven 41. Adam Had Four Sons 41. Dr Jekyll and Mr Hyde 41. *Casablanca* 42. *For Whom the Bell Tolls* (AAN) 43. *Gaslight* (AA) 44. *The Bells of St Mary's* (AAN) 45. *Spellbound* 45. *Saratoga Trunk* 45. *Notorious* 46. Arch of Triumph 48. *Joan of Arc* (AAN) 48. Under Capricorn 49. Stromboli 50. Europa 51. We the Women 53. Journey to Italy 54. Joan at the Stake 54. Fear 54. *Anastasia* (AA) 56. Paris Does Strange Things 57. *Indiscreet* 58. *The Inn of the Sixth Happiness* 58. Goodbye Again 61. The Visit 64. The Yellow Rolls-Royce 64. Fugitive in Vienna 67. *Cactus Flower* 69. A Walk in the Spring Rain 70. From the Mixed Up Files of Mrs Basil E. Frankweiler 74. Murder on the Orient Express (AA, BFA) 74. A Matter of Time 76. Autumn Sonata (AAN) 78. A Woman Called Golda (TV) 82.
✪ For the ease with which in the 40s she conquered international audiences with her presentation of innocent strength and beauty. *Spellbound.*

❝ I have no regrets. I wouldn't have lived my life the way I did if I was going to worry about what people were going to say. – *I.B.*

It's not whether you really cry. It's whether the audience thinks you are crying. – *I.B.*

Sweden's greatest export since Garbo! – *publicity*

Famous line (from *For Whom the Bell Tolls*): 'Where do the noses go?'

Famous line (from *Indiscreet*): 'How dare he make love to me and not be a married man?'

Bergman, Marilyn (1929–).
Lyricist and songwriter in collaboration with her husband Alan.

The Thomas Crown Affair (AA) 68. The Happy Ending (AAN) 69. Pieces of Dreams (AAN) 70. Sometimes a Great Notion (AAN) 71. The Life and Times of Judge Roy Bean (AAN) 71. The Way We Were (AA) 73. Ode to Billy Joe 75. Same Time Next Year (AAN) 78. The Promise (AAN) 79. Best Friends (AAN) 82. Tootsie (AAN) 82. Yes, Giorgio (AAN) 82. Never Say Never Again 83. Yentl (AA) 83. Micki and Maude 84. Big 88. Shirley Valentine (AAN) 89. Welcome Home 89, many others.

Bergman, Sandahl (1951–).
American actress.

All That Jazz 79. Xanadu 80. Conan the Barbarian 82. She 83. Getting Physical 84. Red Sonja 85. Programmed to Kill 86. Stewardess School 86. Kandyland 87. Hell Comes to Frogtown 88. Raw Nerve 91. Loving Lulu 92. Lipstick Camera 93. Ice Cream Man 95. The P.A.C.K. 96, etc.

Bergner, Elisabeth (1898–1986) (Elizabeth Ettel).
German leading actress who settled in Britain in the 30s and married Paul CZINNER. Her fey gamine character quickly dated, but she was an undoubted star.

■ Der Evangelimann 24. Nju 24. Der Geiger von Florenz 26. Liebe 27. Queen Louisa 28. Dona Juana 28. Fraulein Else 29. Ariane 31. *Der Traumende Mund* 32. Ariane (GB) 33. *Catherine the Great* (GB) 34. *Escape Me Never* (GB) (AAN) 35. As You Like It (GB) 36. Dreaming Lips (GB) 37. Stolen Life (GB) 39. Paris Calling (US) 41. Die Glucklichen Jahre der Thorwalds (Ger.) 62. Cry of the Banshee (GB) 70. Courier to the Tsar (GB) 71. Der Fussganger (Ger.) 73. Whitsun Holiday (Ger.) 79.

Bergstrom, Helena (1964–).
Swedish leading actress, frequently the star of films directed by her husband, Colin NUTLEY.

The Women on the Roof 89. 1939 89. Blackjack 90. *House of Angels/Anglagård* 92. The Last Dance/ Sista Dansen 94. The Ferris Wheel/Pariserhjulet 94. House of Angels: The Second Summer/ Anglagård: Andra Sommaren 94. Jagarna 96. Such is Life/Sånt är Livet 96. Still Crazy 98, etc.

Berke, William (1903–1958).
American director of second features.

Minesweeper 43. The Falcon in Mexico 44. Splitface 46. Jungle Jim 48. Deputy Marshal 49. Zamba the Gorilla 49. I Shot Billy the Kid (& p) 50. Four Boys and a Gun (& p) 55. Cop Hater (& p) 57, etc.

Berkeley, Ballard (1904–1988).
British light actor of stage and screen.

The Chinese Bungalow 30. London Melody 35. The Outsider 38. In Which We Serve 42. They Made Me a Fugitive 47. The Long Dark Hall 51. Three Steps to the Gallows 56. See How They Run 57. Star! 68. The Wildcats of St Trinian's 80. Bullshot 83. National Lampoon's European Vacation 85, etc.

Berkeley, Busby (1895–1976) (William Berkeley Enos).
American song and dance director who in the early 30s invaded Hollywood from Broadway and developed the spectacular, kaleidoscopic girlie numbers which became a feature of all musicals, quickly dated, and were joyously rediscovered in the 60s. Below, (m) signifies that Berkeley directed the musical sequences only. His occasional dramatic films were inconsiderable.

■ *Whoopee* (m) 30. Kiki (m) 31. Palmy Days (m) 31. Flying High (m) 31. Night World (m) 32. Bird of Paradise (m) 32. *The Kid from Spain* (m) 32. *Forty Second Street* (m) 33. *Gold Diggers of 1933* (m) 33. She Had to Say Yes 33. *Footlight Parade* (m) 33. *Roman Scandals* (m) 33. *Wonder Bar* (m) 34. *Fashions of 1934* (m) 34. Twenty Million Sweethearts (m) 34. *Dames* (m) 34. *Gold Diggers of 1935* 35. Go into Your Dance (m) 35. Bright Lights 35. In Caliente (m) 35. I Live for Love 35. Stars Over Broadway 35. Stage Struck 36. Gold Diggers of 1937 (m) 37. The Go-Getter 37. The Singing Marine (m) 37. Varsity Show (m) 37. Hollywood Hotel 37. Men are Such Fools 38. Gold Diggers in Paris (m) 38. Garden of the Moon 38. Comet over Broadway 38. They Made Me a Criminal 39. Broadway Serenade (m) 39. *Babes In Arms* 39. Fast and Furious 39. Forty Little Mothers 40. *Strike Up the Band* 40. Blonde Inspiration 41. *Ziegfeld Girl* (m) 41. *Lady Be Good* (m) 41. Babes on Broadway 41. Born to Sing (m) 41. *For Me and My Gal* 42. Girl Crazy (m) 43. *The Gang's All Here* 43. Cinderella Jones 46. Romance on the High Seas (m) 48. *Take Me Out to the Ball Game* 49. Two Weeks with Love (m) 50. Call Me Mister (m) 51. Two Tickets to Broadway (m) 51. Million Dollar Mermaid (m) 52. Small Town Girl (m) 53. Easy to Love (m) 53. Rose Marie (m) 54. Jumbo (m) 62.

✪ For pushing to the limit the decorative possibilities of chorus girls, grand pianos, and optical processes. *Dames*.

❝ In an era of breadlines, depression and wars, I tried to help people get away from all the misery . . . to turn their minds to something else. I wanted to make people happy, if only for an hour. – *B.B.*

His vitality and ingenuity transcended the limitations of his sensibility, and he bequeathed to posterity an entertaining record of the audacity of an escapist era. – *Andrew Sarris, 1968*

If anybody wants to know what can be done with the camera, tell him to study every shot Busby Berkeley ever made. – *Gene Kelly*

Berkeley, Sir Lennox (1903–1989).
British composer.

Only feature film score: Hotel Reserve 44.

Berkley, Elizabeth (1973–).
American actress, from television, who made her screen debut in the most reviled film of 1995.

Showgirls 95. First Wives Club 97. The Real Blonde 97, etc.

TV series: Saved by the Bell 89–93.

Berkoff, Steven (1937–).
Intense British dramatist, writer and actor, often in villainous roles on screen.

Autobiography: 1994, *Overview* (essays); 1996, *Free Association*.

A Clockwork Orange 71. Nicholas and Alexandra 71. Barry Lyndon 75. The Passenger 75. Outland 81. Octopussy 83. Beverly Hills Cop 84. Rambo: First Blood II 85. Revolution 85. Absolute Beginners 86. Under the Cherry Moon 86. Underworld 86. Prisoner of Rio 88. Streets of Yesterday 89. The Krays 90. My Forgotten Man (a) 93. Decadence (a, wd) 94. Fair Game 95, etc.

❝ I often think of myself as a beautiful woman walking through a provincial village and being spat on by the locals. – *S.B.*

Berlanga, Luis (1921–).
Spanish director.

Welcome Mr Marshall 52. Calabuch 56. The Executioner 63. Vivan los Novios 70. Life Size 77. Nacional III 83. La Vaquilla 85. Moros y Cristianos 87. Todos a la Carcel 94, etc.

Berle, Milton (1908–) (Mendel Berlinger).
Brash American vaudeville and TV comedian who never quite found his niche in the movies. In silents from 1914 (as the child clinging to Marie Dressler's knee in *Tillie's Punctured Romance*).

Autobiography: 1974, *Milton Berle, an Autobiography*.

New Faces of 1937 37. Radio City Revels 38. Tall Dark and Handsome 41. Sun Valley Serenade 41. Rise and Shine 41. A Gentleman at Heart 42. Whispering Ghosts 42. Over My Dead Body 42. *Margin for Error* 43. *Always Leave Them Laughing* (based on his autobiography) 49. Let's Make Love 60. *It's a Mad Mad Mad Mad World* 63. The Oscar 65. The Loved Ones 65. Don't Worry We'll Think of a Title 66. The Happening 67. Who's Minding the Mint? 67. Where Angels Go Trouble Follows 68. For Singles Only 68. Hieronymus Merkin 69. Seven in Darkness (TV) 70. Evil Roy Slade (TV) 71. Lepke 75. The Legend of Valentino (TV) 75. Won Ton Ton 76. The Muppet Movie 80. Broadway Danny Rose 84. Smorgasbord 85. Driving Me Crazy 92, etc.

❝ The thief of bad gags. – *Anon*

He's been on TV for years and I finally figured out the reason for his success. He never improved. – *Steve Allen*

Berlin, Irving (1888–1989) (Israel Baline).
Prolific American composer and lyricist of tuneful popular songs.

Biography: 1990, *As Thousands Cheer* by Laurence Bergreen.

The Awakening 28. The Cocoanuts 29. Hallelujah 29. Putting on the Ritz 30. Mammy 30. Reaching for the Moon 31. Kid Millions 34. *Top Hat* 35. *Follow the Fleet* 36. *On the Avenue* 37. *Alexander's Ragtime Band* (AAN) 38. Carefree 38. Second Fiddle 39. Louisiana Purchase 42. Holiday Inn (AAN, story) 42. *This Is the Army* (in which he also appeared and sang 'Oh How I Hate to Get Up in the Morning') 43. *Blue Skies* 46. *Easter Parade* 48. *Annie Get Your Gun* 50. *Call Me Madam* 53. *There's No Business Like Show Business* 54. *White Christmas* 54. Sayonara 57, etc.

✪ For dominating three decades of musicals with an apparently endless barrage of tuneful melodies. *Alexander's Ragtime Band*.

Berlin, Jeannie (1949–)
American actress, daughter of Elaine May.

■ On a Clear Day You Can See Forever 70. Getting Straight 70. Move 70. The Strawberry Statement 70. The Baby Maker 70. Bone 72. Why 72. Portnoy's Complaint 71. *The Heartbreak Kid* (AAN) 73. Sheila Levine 75. In the Spirit (& co-w) 90.

Berling, Charles.
French leading actor.

Salt on Our Skin 92. Just Friends 93. Consentement Mutuel 94. Dernier Stade 94. Petits Arrangements avec les Morts 94. Nelly et Monsieur Arnaud 95. Ridicule 96. Ceux Qui M'Aiment Prendront le Train 98, etc.

Berlinger, Warren (1937–).
American stage and film actor, usually seen as chubby innocent.

Teenage Rebel 56. Three Brave Men 57. Platinum High School 60. The Wackiest Ship in the Army 61. All Hands on Deck 61. Billie 65. Thunder Valley 67. The Shaggy D.A. 76. The Magician of Lublin 79. The World According to Garp 82. Free Ride 86. Take Two 87. Outlaw Force 88. Going Bananas 88. Ten Little Indians 90. Hero/Accidental Hero 92, etc.

TV series: The Joey Bishop Show 61–62. The Funny Side 71. A Touch of Grace 73. Operation Petticoat 78–79. Small & Frye 83.

Berman, Monty (1913–).
British producer and cinematographer, co-founder with Robert S. BAKER of Tempean Films, producers of second features. In the 50s the company enjoyed some success with horror movies, following the example of Hammer; in the 60s, they turned to producing TV series: *The Saint*, *The Baron*, while Berman was co-creator of *The Champions*, *Department S*, *Randall and Hopkirk (Deceased)*, etc.

Some Day (ph only) 35. The Edge of the World (co-ph only) 37. Melody Club (& co-d) 49. 13 East Street 52. The Gilded Cage 54. Escape by Night 54. Murder on Approval 56. The Trollenberg Terror 58. Blood of the Vampire 58. Sea of Sand (p only) 58. Jack the Ripper (& co-d) 58. *The Hellfire Club* (& co-d) 60. The Siege of Sidney Street (& co-d) 60. The Flesh and the Fiends/Mania 61. What a Carve Up! 62, many others.

TV series: *The Saint*, *Gideon's Way*, The Baron, The Champions, Department S, Randall and Hopkirk (Deceased), The Adventurer, etc.

Berman, Pandro S. (1905–1996).
Distinguished American producer who spent many years at both RKO and MGM, and maintained a high standard of product.

Morning Glory 32. *The Gay Divorcee* 34. The Little Minister 34. *Top Hat* 35. Sylvia Scarlett 36. Mary of Scotland 36. *Winterset* 36. Quality Street 37. *Stage Door* 37. Room Service 38. *The Hunchback of Notre Dame* 39. *Ziegfeld Girl* 41. Somewhere I'll Find You 42. The Seventh Cross 44. National Velvet 44. Undercurrent 46. *The Three Musketeers* 48. Madame Bovary 49. *Father of the Bride* 50. Ivanhoe 52. The Prisoner of Zenda 52. *The Blackboard Jungle* 55. Tea and Sympathy 56. Jailhouse Rock 57. The Brothers Karamazov 58. Butterfield 8 60. Sweet Bird of Youth 62. *The Prize* 63. A Patch of Blue 65, many others.

✪ For a lifetime of unobtrusive professionalism. *The Hunchback of Notre Dame*.

Berman, Shelley (1926–).
American cabaret monologuist who has made a few film appearances.

■ *The Best Man* 64. The Wheeler Dealers 64. Divorce American Style 67. Every Home Should Have One (GB) 70. Son of Blob 72. Think Dirty 78. Rented Lips 88. Teen Witch 89.

TV series: Mary Hartman, Mary Hartman 77–78.

Bern, Paul (1889–1932) (Paul Levy).
Short, slightly-built German-born director and screenwriter of silents, and MGM executive. Born in Wandsbek, he emigrated as a child to New York, and studied at the American Academy of Dramatic Arts, briefly working as an actor and stage manager. He is remembered because of the controversy surrounding his death by gunshot soon after his marriage to Jean HARLOW and his enigmatic suicide note, which read: 'Dearest dear: Unfortunately this is the only way to make good the frightful wrong I have done you and to wipe out my abject humiliation. Paul. You understand that last night was only a comedy.' According to Harlow's biographer Irving SHULMAN, who had access to the papers and reminiscences of her agent, Bern was physiologically semi-impotent, and had beaten Harlow so badly on their wedding night that he damaged her kidneys, which later contributed to her death; while Louis B. MAYER insisted that Bern was homosexual. After his death, it was discovered that he was also maintaining a common-law wife, Dorothy Millette, who drowned herself on the night he died. Samuel Marx, who worked for MGM at the time, claimed that Millette murdered Bern. He was romantically involved with actress Barbara LA MARR. In the bio-pic *Harlow*, he was played by Peter LAWFORD.

Book: 1990, *Deadly Illusions: Jean Harlow and the Murder of Paul Bern* by Samuel Marx and Joyce Vanderveen.

The North Wind's Malice 20. Worldly Goods 24. Tomorrow's Love 25. The Dressmaker from Paris 25. Grounds for Divorce 25, etc.

❝ You understand that last night was only a comedy. – *from P.B.'s suicide note*

Bernard, James (1925–).
British composer with a predilection for horror themes. Co-authored film script, *Seven Days to Noon* 50.

The Quatermass Experiment 55. X the Unknown 56. The Curse of Frankenstein 57. Dracula 58. Windom's Way 58. The Hound of the Baskervilles 59. Kiss of the Vampire 62. The Gorgon 64. The Plague of the Zombies 65. She 65. The Torture Garden 67. Scars of Dracula 70. Frankenstein and the Monster from Hell 72. The Legend of the Seven Golden Vampires 73. Murder Elite (TV) 85, etc.

Bernard, Raymond (1891–1977).
French director.

Le Petit Café 19. Le Miracle des Loups 24. The Chess Player 27. Tarkanova 30. Les Misérables 34. Le Coupable 37. J'étais Une Aventurière 38. Les Otages 39. Un Ami Viendra Ce Soir 46. Maya 50. Le Jugement de Dieu 52. La Dame aux Camélias 53. Les Fruits de l'Eté 55. Le Septième Commandement 57. Le Septième Ciel 58, etc.

Bernardi, Herschel (1923–1986).
Balding, beaming American general-purpose actor, often seen as cop or gangster.

Green Fields 37. Crime Inc. 45. Miss Susie Slagle's 46. Stakeout on Dope Street 58. The Savage Eye 60. A Cold Wind in August 61. Irma La Douce 63. The Honey Pot 67. But I Don't Want to Get Married (TV) 71. No Place to Run (TV) 72. No Deposit No Return 76. The Front 76, etc.

TV series: Peter Gunn 58–60. *Arnie* 70–71. Hail to the Chief 85.

Bernds, Edward (1905–).
American second feature director, former sound mixer.

Blondie Hits the Jackpot 49. Harem Girl (& w) 52. Spy Chasers 55. World Without End (& w) 56.

Quantrill's Raiders 58. Return of the Fly (& w) 59. The Three Stooges in Orbit 62. Tickle Me (w only) 65. Prehistoric Valley 66, many others.

Berners, Lord (1883–1950).
British composer.
■ Halfway House 44. Champagne Charlie (song arrangement only) 44. Nicholas Nickleby 47.

Bernhard, Jack (1913–).
American second feature director.
Decoy 46. Appointment with Murder 48. Search for Danger 49. Alaska Patrol 49. The Second Face 50, etc.

Bernhard, Sandra (1955–).
American comedian, actress, singer, model, satirist and exhibitionist. *Without You I'm Nothing* is a film of her off-Broadway one-woman show.
Autobiography: 1988, *Confessions of a Pretty Lady*.
King of Comedy 82. Track 29 88. Casual Sex? 88. Without You I'm Nothing (& co-w) 90. Hudson Hawk 91. Truth or Dare/In Bed with Madonna 91. Dallas Doll 94. Freaky Friday (TV) 95. An Alan Smithee Film: Burn, Hollywood, Burn 97. Plump Fiction 98. I Woke Up Early the Day I Died 98, etc.

Bernhardt, Curtis (Kurt) (1899–1981).
German director; on arrival in Hollywood in 1940, he was generally assigned to 'women's pictures' and approached them with variable style.
Three Loves 29. Thirteen Men and a Girl 31. Die Letzte Kompagnie 32. The Beloved Vagabond (GB) 36. My Love Came Back 40. Lady with Red Hair 40. Million Dollar Baby 41. Juke Girl 42. Happy Go Lucky 43. *Devotion* 44. Conflict 45. My Reputation 45. *A Stolen Life* 46. *Possessed* 47. High Wall 47. The Doctor and the Girl 49. Payment on Demand (& w) 51. Sirocco 51. The Blue Veil 51. Miss Sadie Thompson 53. *Beau Brummell* 54. Interrupted Melody 55. Gaby 56. Stefanie in Rio 60. *Kisses for My President* (& p) 64, etc.

Bernhardt, Sarah (1844–1923) (Rosalie Bernard).
Famous French stage tragedienne who lent dignity if nothing else to early silent films, and even continued working in them after her leg was amputated. After seeing herself in *Queen Elizabeth*, which in America helped found the fortunes of Paramount, she is reputed to have said: 'Mr Zukor, you have put me in pickle for all time!' She was played in *The Incredible Sarah* by Glenda Jackson.
Biography: 1976, *Sarah Bernhardt* by William Emboden.
■ Hamlet's Duel 00. Tosca 08. La Dame aux Camélias 11. *Queen Elizabeth* 12. Adrienne Lecouvreur 13. Jeanne Doré 14. Mères Françaises 17. La Voyante 23.
❝ The film audience could see her only as a figure of fun, a dumb creature jerking her sawdust heart around in a puppet world. – *Alistair Cooke*

Bernie, Ben (1891–1943) (Benjamin Anzelvitz).
American bandleader who worked up a publicity feud with Walter Winchell and consequently appeared in a film or two.
■ Shoot the Works 34. Stolen Harmony 35. *Wake Up and Live* 37. Love and Hisses 37.

Bernsen, Corbin (1955–).
American leading actor, from television.
Eat My Dust! 76. King Kong 76. S.O.B. 81. Dead Aim 87. Hello Again 87. Disorganised Crime 89. Major League 89. Bert Rigby, You're a Fool 89. Shattered 91. Frozen Assets 92. Guns of Honor (TV) 94. Major League II 94. The New Age 94. Radioland Murders 94. Tales from the Hood 95. The Great White Hype 96. The Dentist 96. Bloodhounds (TV) 96. Major League 3: Back to the Minors 98, etc.
TV series: L.A. Law 86–93. The Cape 96– .

Bernstein, Charles (1943–).
American composer, mostly for TV films.
Hex 73. White Lightning 73. Mr Majestyk 74. Trackdown 76. Gator 76. Viva Knieval 77. Love at First Bite 79. The Entity 82. Cujo 83. A Nightmare on Elm Street 84. Deadly Friend 86. Dudes 87. Too Young to Die (TV) 90. The Ivory Hunters (TV) 90. The Sea Wolf (TV) 93. Excessive Force 93. Rumpelstiltskin 96. Miss Evers' Boys (TV) 97, etc.

Bernstein, Elmer (1922–).
American composer-conductor.
Saturday's Hero 51. Sudden Fear 52. Cat Women of the Moon 53. *The Man with the Golden Arm* (AAN) 55. The Ten Commandments 56. *The Sweet Smell of Success* 57. The Tin Star 57. God's Little Acre 58. The Buccaneer 59. *The Magnificent Seven* 60. Summer and Smoke (AAN) 61. A Walk on the Wild Side 62. To Kill a Mockingbird (AAN) 62. Baby the Rain Must Fall 65. The Sons of Katie Elder 65. The Reward 65. Return of the Seven (AAN) 66. Hawaii (AAN) 66. *Thoroughly Modern Millie* (AA) 67. A Cannon for Cordoba 70. The Shootist 76. National Lampoon's Animal House 76. Zulu Dawn 79. Airplane 80. The Great Santini 80. Saturn Three 80. An American Werewolf in London 81. Honky Tonk Freeway 81. Going Ape 81. Five Days One Summer 82. The Chosen 82. Class 82. Trading Places (AAN) 83. Ghostbusters 84. Legal Eagles 85. A Night in the Life of Jimmy Reardon 85. Spies Like Us 86. The Black Cauldron 86. Three Amigos! 86. Funny Farm 88. The Good Mother 88. Dad 88. My Left Foot 89. The Grifters 90. The Field 90. Oscar 91. Rambling Rose 91. Cape Fear (md) 91. The Babe 92. The Cemetery Club 93. Mad Dog and Glory 93. Lost in Yonkers 93. The Age of Innocence (AAN) 93. The Good Son 93. Search and Destroy 95. Roommates 95. Canadian Bacon 95. Devil in a Blue Dress 95. Frankie Starlight 95. Hoodlum 96. Bulletproof 96. John Grisham's The Rainmaker 97. Buddy 97. Twilight 98, etc.

Bernstein, Leonard (1918–1990).
American concert musician, conductor and composer.
Biographies: 1987, *Bernstein* by Joan Peyser; 1994, *Bernstein* by Humphrey Burton.
On the Town 49. On the Waterfront (AAN) 54. West Side Story 61.

Bernstein, Lord (1899–1993) (Sidney Bernstein).
British executive and producer, founder and chairman of the Granada group, including a television station and a cinema circuit. Founder member of the Film Society (1924). First to institute Saturday morning shows for children and to research audience preferences. During World War II, films adviser to the Ministry of Information and SHAEF.
Produced three films with Alfred Hitchcock as director: *Rope* 48, *Under Capricorn* 49. *I Confess* 52.

Bernstein, Walter (1919–).
American screenwriter.
That Kind of Woman 59. A Breath of Scandal 60. *Fail Safe* 64. The Train (co-w) 64. The Money Trap 66. The Molly Maguires 70. The Front (AAN) 76. Semi Tough 77. The Betsy 78. Yanks 79. Little Miss Marker (d only) 80. The House on Carroll Street 88. Doomsday Gun (TV) 94. The Affair (TV) 95. Miss Evers' Boys (TV) 97, etc.

Berri, Claude (1934–).
French writer-director and producer, usually of stories with a Jewish background. Acted in some of them.
Les Baisers (one episode) 64. La Chance et l'Amour 64. *Le Vieil Homme et l'Enfant* 67. Mazel Tov 68. Le Pistonné 70. Le Cinéma de Papa 71. Le Sex Shop 72. Male of the Century 75. La Première Fois 76. Un Moment d'Egarement 78. Tess (p, AAN) 79. Je Vous Aime 80. *Jean de Florette* 86. *Manon des Sources* 86. Uranus 90. *Germinal* 93. Lucie Aubrac 97, etc.

Berry, Chuck (1926–) (Charles Edward Berry).
American singer, guitarist and songwriter of rhythm and blues and rock music. In films playing himself.
Rock, Rock, Rock 56. Mr Rock and Roll 57. Go, Johnny Go! 58. Jazz on a Summer's Day (concert) 59. Let the Good Times Roll (concert) 73. American Hot Wax 78. Chuck Berry Hail! Hail! Rock 'n' Roll (concert) 87, etc.

Berry, Halle (1968–).
American leading actress, a former model and beauty queen, who was Miss USA in 1987.
The Last Boy Scout 91. Jungle Fever 91. Boomerang 91. Queen (TV) 91. Strictly Business 91. Father Hood 93. The Program 93. The Flintstones 94. Solomon & Sheba (TV) 95. Losing Isaiah 95. Executive Decision 96. Girl 6 96. Race the Sun 96. The Rich Man's Wife 96. B.A.P.s 97. Why Do Fools Fall in Love 98. Bulworth 98. Dorothy Dandridge (TV) 99, etc.
TV series: Living Dolls 89.

Berry, John (1917–).
American director with stage experience. Blacklisting in the 50s kept him away from Hollywood for a decade.
■ Cross My Heart 45. From This Day Forward 46. Miss Susie Slagle's 46. Casbah 48. Tension 49. He Ran All the Way 51. C'est Arrivé à Paris 52. Ça Va Barder (Fr.) 55. The Great Lover/Don Juan (Fr.) 55. Je Suis un Sentimental (Fr.) 55. Tamango 57. Oh Que Mambo (It.) 59. Maya 66. A Tout Casser 67. Claudine 74. Thieves 77. The Bad News Bears Go to Japan 78. Angel on My Shoulder (TV) 80. Sister, Sister (TV) 82. Honeyboy (TV) 82. Le Voyage à Paimpol 85. Maldonne 85. A Captive in the Land 90.

Berry, Jules (1883–1951) (Jules Paufichet).
Saturnine French character actor.
The Crime of Monsieur Lange 34. Carrefour 39. *Le Jour Se Lève* 39. *Les Visiteurs du Soir* 42. La Symphonie Fantastique 47, etc.

Berry, Ken (1933–).
American actor often seen on TV as birdlike comic hero.
Wake Me When The War Is Over (TV) 70. The Reluctant Heroes (TV) 71. Herbie Rides Again 74. Mountain Man 77. The Cat from Outer Space 78, etc.
TV series: F Troop 65–67. Mayberry RFD 68–71. Mama's Family 83–89.

Berry, Richard (1950–).
Saturnine French leading actor. He studied at the Paris Conservatoire and worked with La Comédie Française before concentrating on films from the 80s.
La Gifle 74. La Balance 82. Le Grand Pardon 82. Une Chambre en Ville 83. Caged Heart 85. L'Addition 85. A Man and a Woman: 20 Years Later 86. Honeymoon 87. Mayrig 91. Day of Atonement/Le Grand Pardon II 92. Adultère Mode d'Emploi 95. Fresh Bait/L'Appat 95. What a Drag 96. A Great Shout of Love/Un Grand Cri d'Amour 98, etc.

Berthomieu, André (1903–1960).
French director, former assistant to Julien Duvivier and author of a book on cinema grammar.
Ces Dames aux Chapeaux Verts 29. *Le Crime de Sylvestre Bonnard* 30. Mon Ami Victor 31. L'Aristo 34. La Flamme 36. The Girl in the Taxi (GB) 37. Les Nouveaux Riches 38. L'Inconnue de Monte Carlo 39. La Neige sur le Pas 41. L'Ange de la Nuit 44. J'ai 17 Ans 45. Gringalet 46. La Femme Nue 49. Chacun son Tour 51. Scènes de Ménage 54. La Joyeuse Prison 56. Préméditation 60, many others.

Berti, Marina (1928–).
Italian leading lady in occasional international films.
Prince of Foxes 49. Deported 50. Quo Vadis 51. Queen of Sheba 53. Abdullah the Great 56. Ben Hur 59. Tyrant of Syracuse 62. Cleopatra 62. Swordsman of Siena 63. Moses (TV) 76. Jesus of Nazareth (TV) 77.

Bertini, Francesca (1888–1985) (Elena Vitiello).
Italian leading lady of the silent period, a model of screen beauty and fashion.
La Dea del Mare 04. Il Trovatore 09. Salome 13. Assunta Spina 15. Tosca 17. Romeo and Juliet 20. Resurrection 20. La Donna Nuda 22. Monte Carlo 28. Odette 28. Dora 43, many others.

Berto, Juliet (1947–1990).
French leading actress and occasional screenwriter who turned to directing before her death from cancer.
Two or Three Things I Know About Her 66. La Chinoise 67. Weekend 67. Le Gai Savoir 68. Camarades 70. The Big Shots 72. Celine and Julie Go Boating (& w) 73. Summer Run 74. Mr Klein 76. Bastien, Bastienne 79. Snow/Neige (& wd) 81. Cap Canaille (& d) 83. Havre (wd) 86. Un Amour à Paris 87. Une Vie Suspendue 88, etc.

Bertolucci, Bernardo (1940–).
Italian writer-director, a former romanticist and poet who turned increasingly to censorable themes.
■ The Grim Reaper 62. *Before the Revolution* 64. Love and Anger (part) 67. Partner 68. *The Spider's Stratagem* 70. *The Conformist* (AANw) 70. *Last Tango in Paris* (AAN) 72. *1900* 76. La Luna 79. Tragedy of a Ridiculous Man 81. *The Last Emperor* (AA) 87. The Sheltering Sky 90. Little Buddha 93. Stealing Beauty 96. Besieged 98.

Bertolucci, Giuseppe (1947–).
Italian director and screenwriter. The younger brother of Bernardo Bertolucci, he began as a documentary film-maker and has worked on the scripts of some of his brother's films.
1900 (co-w) 76. I Love You Berlinguer/Berlinguer ti Voglio Bene 77. La Luna (co-w) 79. Secrets Secrets/Segreti Segreti 85. It's an Odd Life/Strana la Vita 88. The Camels/I Cammelli 88. Love at Work/Amori in Corso 89. Especially on Sundays/La Domenica Specialmente (co-d) 91, etc.

Bertrand, Paul (1915–1994).
French art director, a former assistant to Alexander Trauner.
Les Maudits 47. Gunman in the Streets 50. Forbidden Games/Jeux Interdits 52. Thérèse Raquin 53. Une Vie 58. Purple Noon/Plein Soleil 60, etc.

Besch, Bibi (1942–1996) (Bibiara Besch).
Austrian-born character actress, in America. She is the daughter of actress Gusti Huber (1914–1993) and the mother of actress Samantha Mathis.
Peter Lundy and the Medicine Hat Stallion (TV) 77. The Pack 77. Hardcore 79. Meteor 79. The Promise 79. Death of a Centrefold (TV) 81. Star Trek II: The Wrath of Khan 82. The Beast Within 82. The Lonely Lady 83. Date with an Angel 87. Tremors 89. Kill Me Again 89. Crazy from the Heart (TV) 91, etc.
TV series: Secrets of Midland Heights 80–81. The Hamptons 83. Melrose Place 96.

Beshara, Khairi (1947–).
Egyptian director.
The Collar and the Bracelet/Al-Tauq Wal-Iswira 86. Sweet Days, Bitter Days/Yoom Helw . . . Yoom Mor 88, etc.

Bessell, Ted (1935–1996).
American comic character actor.
Billie 65. Don't Drink the Water 69. Two on a Bench (TV) 71. Your Money or Your Wife (TV) 72. Breaking Up Is Hard to Do (TV) 79, etc.
TV series: It's a Man's World 62. Gomer Pyle 65–66. That Girl 66–71. Hail to the Chief 85.

Besser, Joe (1907–1988).
Rotund American burlesque comic who in the 50s became one of the Three Stooges in their declining days.

Besserer, Eugenie (1870–1934).
American character actress.
The Count of Monte Cristo 12. Scarlet Days 19. The Sin of Martha Queed 21. The Rosary 22. Her Reputation 23. The Price She Paid 24. A Fool and His Money 25. The Millionaire Policeman 26. *The Jazz Singer* (as Jolson's mother) 27. Two Lovers 28. Madame X 29. Thunderbolt 29. In Gay Madrid 30. To the Last Man 33, many others.

Bessie, Alvah (1904–1985).
American screenwriter, blacklisted in 1949 as one of the Hollywood Ten.
The Very Thought of You 44. Hotel Berlin 45. Objective Burma (AAN) 45, etc.

Besson, Luc (1959–).
French director and screenwriter with a fascination for the sea. In 1996, he issued the director's cut of *Leon*, which was 26 minutes longer than the version released in 1994, restoring scenes cut when it previewed in the US.
Autobiography: 1998, *The Story of the Fifth Element*.
The Last Battle/Le Dernier Combat 83. Subway 85. Kamikaze (co-d) 87. The Big Blue 88. Nikita/La Femme Nikita 90. Atlantis 91. Leon/The Professional 94. The Fifth Element (wd) 97. Joan of Arc (wd) 99, etc.

Best, Edna (1900–1974).
Soft-spoken, maternal British actress, once married to Herbert Marshall. Went to Hollywood in 1939 and stayed.
Tilly of Bloomsbury 21. A Couple of Down and Outs 23. Escape 30. *Tilly of Bloomsbury* 30. The Calendar 31. *Michael and Mary* 32. The Faithful

Heart 32. *The Man Who Knew Too Much* 34. Sleeping Partners 37. *South Riding* 38. Prison without Bars 39. *Intermezzo* 39. *The Swiss Family Robinson* 40. A Dispatch from Reuters 40. The Late George Apley 46. The Ghost and Mrs Muir 47. The Iron Curtain 48, etc.

Best, James (1926–).
American general-purpose actor, often in westerns as sly ranch-hand.
Winchester 73 50. Kansas Raiders 51. Francis Goes to West Point 52. Seven Angry Men 55. Gaby 56. The Left Handed Gun 58. The Mountain Road 60. Shock Corridor 63. Three on a Couch 66. Firecreek 67. Ode to Billy Joe 76. Rolling Thunder 77. The End 78. Hooper 78, etc.
TV series: The Dukes of Hazzard 79.

Best, Marjorie O. (1903–1997).
American costume designer with a penchant for period films. Born in Jacksonville, Illinois, she studied at the Chouinard School of Art in Los Angeles and also taught there.
The Adventures of Don Juan (AA) 49. Dallas 50. West Point Story 50. On Moonlight Bay 51. Distant Drums 51. Room for One More 52. Giant (AAN) 56. Rio Bravo 58. Left-Handed Gun 58. The Nun's Story 59. The Miracle 59. Yellowstone Kelly 59. Sunrise at Campobello (AAN) 60. Sergeant Rutledge 60. Sins of Rachel Cade 60. The Dark at the Top of the Stairs 60. Tender Is the Night 61. Comancheros 61. State Fair 62. Spencer's Mountain 63. *The Greatest Story Ever Told* (AAN) 65, etc.

Best, Richard (1916–).
British editor.
Desert Victory 43. Fame is the Spur 47. Mine Own Executioner 48. The Magic Box 51. The Dam Busters 54. Ice Cold in Alex 58. The Double Man 66. Otley 68. Please Sir 71. Dominique 77.

Best, Willie (1916–1962).
Goggle-eyed American comedian, once known as Sleep'n Eat and later the prototype frightened manservant.
Feet First 30. The Monster Walks 32. Kentucky Kernels 33. Little Miss Marker 34. Murder on a Honeymoon 35. Jalna 35. The Littlest Rebel 35. Mummy's Boys 36. Thank You Jeeves 36. Super Sleuth 37. Blondie 38. Merrily We Live 38. Vivacious Lady 38. At the Circus 39. I Take This Woman 40. *The Ghost Breakers* 40. Road Show 41. High Sierra 41. The Body Disappears 41. The Smiling Ghost 41. Busses Roar 42. The Hidden Hand 42. Cabin in the Sky 43. Thank Your Lucky Stars 43. Home in Indiana 44. Hold That Blonde 45. The Bride Wore Boots 46. Red Stallion 47. The Shanghai Chest 48. South of Caliente 51, many others.
TV series: My Little Margie 52–54. Trouble with Father 50–55.

Beswick, Martine (1941–).
British pin-up, decorative in occasional films.
From Russia with Love 62. Thunderball 65. One Million Years BC 66. The Penthouse 67. Dr Jekyll and Sister Hyde 71. Seizure 74. The Happy Hooker Goes to Hollywood 80. Melvin and Howard 80. Balboa 86. Cyclone 87. Evil Spirits 91. Trancers II 91. Wide Sargasso Sea 93, etc.

Bettger, Lyle (1915–).
American screen actor who started in 1946 as leading man but seemed more at home in villainous roles.
No Man of Her Own 50. Union Station 50. The First Legion 51. All I Desire 53. The Greatest Show on Earth 53. The Sea Chase 55. Gunfight at the OK Corral 57. Guns of the Timberland 60. Town Tamer 65. Nevada Smith 66. The Fastest Guitar Alive 68. The Seven Minutes 71. M Station Hawaii (TV) 80. many others.
TV series: Court of Last Resort 57. Grand Jury 58–59.

Betti, Laura (1934–).
Italian actress, associated with the films of Pasolini.
La Dolce Vita 60. Teorema 68. A Man Called Sledge 71. The Canterbury Tales 71. Last Tango in Paris 73. Drama of the Rich 75. Salo 75. 1900 76. La Luna 79. La Nuit de Varennes 82. Courage Mountain 89. Dames Galantes 90. Mario, Maria and Mario 94. With Closed Eyes 94. Un Eroe Borghese 95. Marianna Ucria 97, etc.

Betuel, Jonathan.
American director and screenwriter. *Theodore Rex*, starring Whoopi Goldberg, had the dubious distinction of being the most expensive film ($35m) to be released direct to video in the US.
The Last Starfighter (w) 84. My Science Project (wd) 85. Theodore Rex (wd) 96.

Betz, Carl (1920–1978).
American leading man who moved from films to TV.
The President's Lady 53. Inferno 53. Vicki 53. Dangerous Crossing 53. Spinout 66, etc.
TV series: *The Donna Reed Show* 58–65. *Judd for the Defense* 67–68.

Bevan, Billy (1887–1957) (William Bevan Harris).
Wide-eyed, moustachioed silent screen comedian, an Australian who moved to Hollywood and became one of Mack Sennett's troupe. Later played many small parts, often that of a bewildered policeman.
Easy Pickings 27. Riley the Cop 28. *Journey's End* 30. Sky Devils 32. *Cavalcade* 33. Alice in Wonderland 33. Limehouse Blues 34. *Dracula's Daughter* 36. Captain Fury 39. The Long Voyage Home 40. Dr Jekyll and Mr Hyde 41. The Picture of Dorian Gray 45. Cluny Brown 46. The Black Arrow 48, many others.

Bevan, Timothy (1958–).
British-based, New Zealand-born producer, a co-founder of Working Title Films. He was formerly married to actress Joely Richardson.
My Beautiful Laundrette 85. Wish You Were Here 87. A World Apart 88. For Queen and Country 88. Paperhouse 89. Chicago Joe and the Showgirl 90. Dakota Road 90. The Tall Guy 90. Robin Hood 91. Posse 93. Four Weddings and a Funeral 95. French Kiss 95. Moonlight and Valentino 95. Dead Man Walking 95. Fargo 96. Bean 97. The Borrowers 97. The Big Lebowski 98. Elizabeth 98. Plunkett & MacLeane 98. The Hi-Lo Country 98, etc.

Bevans, Clem (1879–1963) (Clement Blevins).
Long-faced and latterly white-haired American character actor who played a long succession of grandfathers, doorkeepers, oldest inhabitants and gold prospectors.
Way Down East 35. Of Human Hearts 38. Abe Lincoln in Illinois 40. *Saboteur* 42. The Human Comedy 43. Captain Eddie 45. The Yearling 46. The Paleface 48. Streets of Laredo 49. *Harvey* 50. The Stranger Wore a Gun 53. The Kentuckian 55, etc.

Bewes, Rodney (1937–).
Chubby British comedy actor.
Billy Liar 63. Decline and Fall 68. Spring and Port Wine 70. Alice's Adventures in Wonderland 72. The Likely Lads 76. Jabberwocky 77. The Spaceman and King Arthur 79. Saint Jack 79, etc.
TV series: *The Likely Lads* 64–66. Dear Mother Love Albert 70–72. *Whatever Happened to the Likely Lads* 73–74.

Bey, Turhan (1920–) (Turhan Selahattin Sahultavy Bey).
Dapper Turkish leading man who had a good run in Hollywood during World War II in the absence on war service of more dynamic stars. Later became a stills photographer and moved to Vienna.
Footsteps in the Dark 41. Drums of the Congo 42. The Mummy's Tomb 42. Arabian Nights 42. White Savage 43. Background to Danger 43. The Mad Ghoul 43. Ali Baba and the Forty Thieves 43. Dragon Seed 44. Bowery to Broadway 44. The Climax 44. Frisco Sal 44. A Night in Paradise 46. Out of the Blue 47. Adventures of Casanova 48. Song of India 49. Prisoners of the Casbah 53. Stolen Identity (p only) 53, etc.

Beymer, Richard (1939–).
American child actor who in the early 60s seemed about to turn into a major juvenile lead, but somehow never made it. Also a TV director.
So Big 52. Indiscretion of an American Wife 52. Johnny Tremain 57. The Diary of Anne Frank 59. High Time 60. *West Side Story* 61. Five Finger Exercise 62. *Hemingway's Adventures of a Young Man* 62. The Longest Day 62. The Stripper 62. Cross Country 83. Silent Night, Deadly Night 3: Better Watch Out! 89. My Girl 2 94. Foxfire 96, etc.
TV series: Paper Dolls 84. Twin Peaks 90.

Bezzerides, A. I. (1908–) (Albert Isaac Bezzerides).
American screenwriter.
They Drive by Night 40. Northern Pursuit 43. *Thieves' Highway* 49. Sirocco 51. On Dangerous Ground 52. Beneath the 12 Mile Reef 53. Track of the Cat 54. *Kiss Me Deadly* 55. The Angry Hills 59, etc.

Bianchi, Daniela (1942–).
Italian leading lady.
Love is My Profession 59. Sword of El Cid 62. *From Russia With Love* 63. The Balearic Caper 66. Weekend Italian Style 68. The Dirty Heroes 68, etc.

Biao, Yuen.
Hong Kong star of martial arts movies who began with the Seven Little Fortunes performance troupe that also included Jackie Chan, Samo Hung and Yuen Wah.
Heroes of Shaolin 79. The Prodigal Son 83. Warriors from the Magic Mountain 83. Wheels on Meals 84. Twinkle, Twinkle Lucky Stars 85. Mr Vampire 2 85. Eastern Condors 86. Shanghai Express 86. Those Merry Souls 87. Peacock King 88. Iceman Cometh/Time Warriors 89. Once Upon a Time in China 91. Kid from Tibet 92. Hero 97, etc.

Biberman, Abner (1909–1977).
American character actor who spent many years playing Red Indian braves and dastardly dagoes before turning into a director. He worked mainly as a TV director from the 50s.
Gunga Din 39. His Girl Friday 40. South of Pago Pago 40. South of Tahiti 41. Broadway 42. The Leopard Man 43. Salome Where She Danced 45. Captain Kidd 45. Back to Bataan 50. Elephant Walk 54. The Golden Mistress 54. The Price of Fear (d) 56. Above All Things 57. Gun for a Coward (d) 57, many others especially in TV.

Biberman, Herbert J. (1900–1971).
American director whose career was harmed by his political convictions. Married Gale Sondergaard.
One Way Ticket 35. Meet Nero Wolfe 36. King of Chinatown (w only) 38. *The Master Race* (& d) 44. New Orleans (w only) 47. Abilene Town (p only) 46. Salt of the Earth (& w) 53. Slaves (& w) 69, etc.

Bickford, Charles (1889–1967).
Rugged American character actor who sometimes played stubborn or unscrupulous roles but more often projected sincerity and warmth.
Autobiography: 1965, *Bulls, Balls, Bicycles and Actors*.
■ Dynamite 29. South Sea Rose 29. Hell's Heroes 29. *Anna Christie* 30. The Sea Bat 30. Passion Flower 30. River's End 31. The Squaw Man 31. East of Borneo 31. Pagan Lady 31. Men in Her Life 31. Panama Flo 32. *Thunder Below* 32. Scandal for Sale 32. The Last Man 32. Vanity Street 32. No Other Woman 33. Song of the Eagle 33. This Day and Age 33. White Woman 33. Little Miss Marker 34. A Wicked Woman 34. A Notorious Gentleman 35. Under Pressure 35. The Farmer Takes a Wife 35. East of Java 35. The Littlest Rebel 35. Rose of the Rancho 35. Pride of the Marines 36. The Plainsman 36. Night Club Scandal 37. Thunder Trail 37. Daughter of Shanghai 37. High, Wide and Handsome 37. Gangs of New York 38. Valley of the Giants 38. The Storm 39. Stand Up and Fight 39. Romance of the Redwoods 39. Street of Missing Men 39. Our Leading Citizen 39. One Hour to Live 39. Mutiny in the Big House 39. Thou Shalt Not Kill 39. *Of Mice and Men* 40. The Girl from God's Country 40. South to Karanga 40. Queen of the Yukon 40. *Riders of Death Valley* (serial) 41. Burma Convoy 41. Reap the Wild Wind 42. Tarzan's New York Adventure 42. Mr Lucky 43. *The Song of Bernadette* (AAN) 43. Wing and a Prayer 44. Captain Eddie 45. Fallen Angel 45. *Duel in the Sun* 46. *The Farmer's Daughter* (AAN) 47. The Woman on the Beach 47. *Brute Force* 47. The Babe Ruth Story 47. Four Faces West 48. *Johnny Belinda* (AAN) 48. Command Decision 48. Roseanna McCoy 49. Whirlpool 49. *Treason* (as Cardinal Mindzenty) 49. Branded 50. Riding High 50. Jim Thorpe – All American 51. The Raging Tide 51. Elopement 51. The Last Posse 53. *A Star is Born* 54. Prince of Players 55. Not as a Stranger 55. The Court Martial of Billy Mitchell 55. You Can't Run Away from It 56. Mister Cory 57. So Soon to Die (TV) 57. *The Big Country* 58. The Unforgiven 60. Days of Wine and Roses 62. Della (TV) 64. *A Big Hand for the Little Lady* 66.

Biddle, Adrian.
British cinematographer.
The Duellists 77. Aliens 86. The Princess Bride 87. Willow 88. The Tall Guy 90. Thelma and Louise (AAN) 91. 1492: Conquest of Paradise 92. Judge Dredd 95. 101 Dalmatians (US) 96. Fierce Creatures 97. The Butcher Boy 97. Event Horizon (US) 97. Holy Man (US) 98, etc.

Biehn, Michael (1956–).
American character actor, often in action films. Born in Anniston, Alaska, he grew up in Lincoln, Nebraska, and studied drama at the University of Arizona at Tucson.
Coach 78. Hog Wild 80. The Fan 81. Lords of Discipline 83. The Terminator 84. Aliens 86. Rampage 87. In a Shallow Grave 88. The Seventh Sign 88. The Abyss 90. Navy SEALS 90. Terminator 2 91. K2 91. Timebomb 91. A Taste for Killing 92. Deadfall 93. Tombstone 94. Jade 95. The Rock 96. Mojave Moon 96. Silver Wolf (Can.) 98. Susan's Plan 98, etc.
TV series: The Runaways 78. The Magnificent Seven 97– .

Bigas Luna (1946–) (José Juan Bigas Luna).
Spanish writer and director. Born in Barcelona, he worked as a graphic designer and wrote fiction before beginning to make short films in the early 70s. His feature films tend to be low-budget and are often on sexual themes.
Tatoo/Tatuaje 76. Bilbao, una Historia del Amor (wd) 78. Poodle/Caniche (wd) 79. Reborn/Renacer 82. Lola 85. Anguish/Angoixa 87. Las Edades de Lulu 91. Jamón, Jamón 92. Golden Balls/Huevos de Oro 93. The Tit and the Moon/La Tita y la Luna 94. Bombola 96. The Chambermaid/La Camarera del Titanic 98. The Naked Maja/Volaverunt 99, etc.
❝ Society can be reliably divided into garlic eaters (surrealists) and those who abstain (sad realists). – *B.L.*

Bigelow, Kathryn (1951–).
American director and screenwriter who began as an artist. Formerly married to director James Cameron.
The Loveless (co-d) 81. Near Dark 87. Blue Steel 89. Point Break 91. Strange Days 95, etc.
❝ Movies can be cathartic. I think that they can transform you, they're kind of windows on to another universe that you can't experience in any other context. – *K.B.*
Rules are meant to be broken, boundaries are meant to be invaded, envelopes meant to be pushed, preconceptions challenged. – *K.B.*

Biggers, Earl Derr (1884–1933).
American crime novelist, whose chief gift to the movies was Charlie Chan. Also wrote original story of *The Millionaire* 31, and the much filmed play *Seven Keys to Baldpate*.

Bikel, Theodore (1924–).
Heavily-built Viennese actor, guitarist and singer; can play most nationalities. International stage, TV, cabaret and film work.
The African Queen 51. The Love Lottery 54. The Pride and the Passion 57. The Defiant Ones (AAN) 58. The Blue Angel 59. A Dog of Flanders 60. My Fair Lady 64. Sands of the Kalahari 65. The Russians Are Coming, The Russians Are Coming 66. My Side of the Mountain 68. Darker than Amber 70. The Little Ark 71. Victory at Entebbe (TV) 76. Very Close Quarters 84. See You in the Morning 89. Shattered 91. Benefit of the Doubt 93. Shadow Conspiracy 97, etc.

Bill, Tony (1940–).
American light leading man, now concentrating on producing and directing.
Come Blow Your Horn 63. None But the Brave 65. Marriage on the Rocks 66. Ice Station Zebra 68. Castle Keep 69. Flap 70. Shampoo 75. Pee-Wee's Big Adventure 85, etc.
As producer: Deadhead Miles 70. Steelyard Blues 70. The Sting 73. Hearts of the West 75. Shampoo 75, etc.
As director: My Bodyguard 80. Six Weeks 82. Love Thy Neighbour (TV) 84. Five Corners (& p) 87. Heist (TV) 89. Crazy People 90. Baboon Heart (& p) 92. Untamed Heart (& p) 93. A Home of Our Own 93. Next Door (TV) 94. Beyond

the Call (TV) 96. Oliver Twist (TV) 97, etc.
AS ACTOR: Barb Wire 96.

Billingsley, Barbara (1922–).
American actress, best known for playing the mother in the long-running sitcom LEAVE IT TO BEAVER.
Secret Heart 46. I Cheated the Law 49. Pretty Baby 50. Tall Target 51. The Lady Wants Mink 53. Airplane! 80. Still the Beaver (TV) 83. Eye of the Demon (TV) 87, etc.
TV series: Professional Father 55. Leave It to Beaver 57–63. Still the Beaver 85–86. The New Leave It to Beaver 86–89.

Billington, Kevin (1933–).
British director, from TV.
Interlude 68. The Rise and Rise of Michael Rimmer 70. The Light at the Edge of the World 71. And No One Could Save Her (TV) 72. Voices 74. The Good Soldier (TV) 83, etc.

Billy the Kid,
the historical, homicidal western gunslinger, has frequently been turned by the movies into some kind of hero. A favourite character of the silents, he has been seen also in numerous talkie versions. Johnny Mack Brown played him on the wide screen in *Billy the Kid* 30; pious Roy Rogers was the star of *Billy the Kid Returns* 39; in 1940 Robert Taylor was *Billy the Kid;* and in 1943 (or so) came *The Outlaw*, with a happy ending for Jack Buetel who played Billy. In 1949 Audie Murphy played Billy in *The Kid from Texas;* 1950 brought *I Shot Billy the Kid* with Don Barry; 1954 *The Law Versus Billy the Kid* with Scott Brady; 1955 *The Parson and the Outlaw* with Anthony Dexter; 1958 *The Left-Handed Gun* with Paul Newman; in 1966 we were even offered *Billy the Kid Meets Dracula;* and in 1974 Sam Peckinpah's *Pat Garrett and Billy the Kid* added new refinements of violence. He was turned into a teen hero by Emilio Estevez in *Young Guns* and *Young Guns II* in 1989–90. There were also scores of second features in the 30s and 40s, with Bob Steele or Buster Crabbe as Billy; whose real name incidentally was William Bonney and who died in 1881 at the age of 21.

Bilon, Michael (1948–1983).
American dwarf actor who played the title role in some of the scenes of *E.T. – the Extra-Terrestrial*.
Under the Rainbow 81.

Binder, Maurice (1925–1991).
American title artist in Britain, chiefly known for designing the graphics of the James Bond films.
Indiscreet 58. The Mouse that Roared 59. The Grass is Greener 60. *Dr No* 62. Repulsion 64. The Chase 66. Bedazzled 67. The Private Life of Sherlock Holmes 71. Gold 74. Shout at the Devil 76. The Sea Wolves 80, etc.

Bing, Herman (1889–1947).
Plump, explosive German comedy actor, former assistant to F. W. Murnau; in Hollywood from 1929. Committed suicide.
Married in Hollywood 29. The Guardsman 31. Dinner at Eight 33. The Black Cat 34. Rose Marie 36. The Great Ziegfeld 36. Champagne Waltz 37. The Great Waltz 38. Sweethearts 38. The Devil with Hitler 42. Where Do We Go from Here? 45. Rendezvous 24 46, many others.

Binns, Edward (Ed) (1916–1990).
Solid but unremarkable American character actor.
Teresa 51. The Scarlet Hour 56. Twelve Angry Men 57. Compulsion 59. North by Northwest 59. Fail Safe 64. Chubasco 67. Patton 69. Oliver's Story 79, etc.
TV series: Brenner 59–64. The Nurses 62–64. It Takes a Thief 69–70.

Binoche, Juliette (1964–).
French actress in international films. She is also an artist and in 1994 exhibited work done in collaboration with designer Christian Fenouillat. Born in Paris, she was on stage from 1977, and in films from 1981, first attracting attention in André TÉCHINÉ's *Rendezvous*, and gaining an international reputation with *The Unbearable Lightness of Being*, directed by Philip KAUFMAN. She won the best actress award at the 1993 Venice Film Festival and a French César for *Three Colours: Blue*. She was romantically involved with director Leos CARAX.
Liberty Belle 81. Les Nanas 84. Family Life 84. Rendezvous 85. Bad Blood/Mauvais Sang 86. The Unbearable Lightness of Being 88. Les Amants du Pont-Neuf 91. Damage 92. Trois Couleurs: Rouge 92. Wuthering Heights 92. *Three Colours: Blue/* Trois Couleurs: Bleu 93. Three Colours: White/ Trois Couleurs: Blanc 94. The Horseman on the Roof 95. A Couch in New York 96. The English Patient (AA) (US) 96. Alice and Martin/Alice et Martin 98, etc.

Binyon, Claude (1905–1978).
American writer-director.
The Gilded Lily (w) 35. I Met Him in Paris (w) 37. Sing You Sinners (w) 38. Arizona (w) 40. Suddenly It's Spring (w) 44. *The Saxon Charm* (wd) 48. Family Honeymoon (wd) 49. Mother Didn't Tell Me (w) 50. Stella (wd) 50. Aaron Slick from Punkin Crick (wd) 52. *Dreamboat* (wd) 52. You Can't Run Away from It (w) 56. North to Alaska (w) 60. Satan Never Sleeps (w) 62. Kisses for My President (w) 64, etc.

Birch, Paul (c. 1900–1969).
Burly American character actor.
The War of the Worlds 53. Rebel without a Cause 55. When Gangland Strikes 56. *Not of This Earth* 57. The Dark at the Top of the Stairs 60. The Man Who Shot Liberty Valance 62. It's a Mad Mad Mad Mad World 63. Welcome to Hard Times 67, etc.
TV series: Cannonball 58.

Birch, Thora (1982–).
American child actress, in commercials from the age of four.
Purple People Eater 88. Paradise 91. All I Want for Christmas 91. Patriot Games 92. Hocus Pocus 93. Monkey Trouble 94. Clear and Present Danger 94. Now and Then 95. Alaska 96. Election 98, etc.
TV series: Day by Day 88–89. Parenthood 90.

Bird, Antonia.
English director, from the theatre. She worked at the Royal Court Theatre for six years before moving to television.
Submariners (TV) 83. The Men's Room (TV) 91. Safe (TV) 93. *Priest* 94. Mad Love 95. Face 97, etc.

Bird, Norman (1919–).
British character actor, usually of underdogs.
An Inspector Calls 54. *The League of Gentlemen* 59. *Victim* 62. The Hill 65. Sky West and Crooked 65. The Wrong Box 66. A Dandy in Aspic 68. The Virgin and the Gypsy 70. The Rise and Rise of Michael Rimmer 70. Ooh . . . You Are Awful 73. The Slipper and the Rose 76. The Medusa Touch 77. The Final Conflict 81. Queenie (TV) 87, many others.

Bird, Richard (1895–).
British light actor who played genial middle-aged roles in the 30s, from the stage.
Tilly of Bloomsbury 31. Mimi 35. Sensation 37. The Terror (& d) 38. The Door with Seven Locks 40. Halfway House 44. Forbidden 49. Alive and Kicking 58. Death Trap 62. Dr Strangelove 63. Masque of the Red Death 64. The Knack 65, many others.

Birell, Tala (1908–1959) (Natalie Bierle).
Viennese leading actress, of German and Polish extraction, a protégée of Max Reinhardt, who began in German films before her unsuccessful Hollywood career, often in second features, after which she retired and returned to Europe.
Man in a Cage (GB) 30. Doomed Battalion 32. The Captain Hates the Sea 34. Crime and Punishment 35. Bringing Up Baby 38. Seven Miles from Alcatraz 42. The Song of Bernadette 43. Mrs Parkington 44. Song of Love 47. The House of Tao Ling 47, etc.

Birkett, Michael (1929–) (Lord Birkett).
British producer, mainly of specialized entertainments.
The Caretaker 63. The Soldier's Tale 64. Modesty Blaise (associate) 66. The Marat/ Sade 66. A Midsummer Night's Dream 68. King Lear 70, etc.

Birkin, Andrew (1945–).
British screenwriter and director, the brother of Jane Birkin. He worked as an assistant to Stanley Kubrick in the mid-60s, during the making of *2001: A Space Odyssey*, and began writing screenplays from the 70s. He is also the author of *J. M. Barrie and the Lost Boys*, a biography of the creator of Peter Pan.
The Pied Piper (co-w) 71. Flame (w) 74. *The Lost Boys* (TV) 78. Sredni Vashtar (p, wd, short BFA, AAN) 79. The Final Conflict (w) 81. La Pirate (w) 84. King David (co-w) 85. The Name of the Rose (co-w) 86. Burning Secret (wd) 88. Shattered (co-w) 91. Salt on Our Skin (co-w, d) 93. The Cement Garden (wd) 93, etc.

Birkin, Jane (1946–).
English leading lady, former model, who has been seen to most advantage in continental productions. She was formerly married to composer John Barry and is the mother of Charlotte Gainsbourg. Married French director Jacques Doillon.
Blow Up 66. Les Chemins de Katmandou 69. Romance of a Horsethief 71. Don Juan 73. Private Projection 73. Sept Morts sur Ordonnance 75. Catherine and Co. 75. Le Diable au Coeur 75. Death on the Nile 78. Evil Under the Sun 82. Love on the Ground/L'Amour par Terre 84. Beethoven's Nephew 85. Dust 85. Leave All Fair 85. These Foolish Things/Daddy Nostalgie 90. La Belle Noiseuse 91. Black for Remembrance 96. Same Old Song/On Connaît la Chanson 97, etc.

Birney, David (1939–).
American leading man.
Caravan to Vaccares 74. Trial by Combat 76. Prettykill 87.
TV series: Bridget Loves Bernie 73. Serpico 76. St Elsewhere 82. Glitter 84.

Birney, Meredith Baxter (1947–).
American leading actress, mostly on TV. Formerly known as Meredith Baxter, she changed her name on her marriage to actor David Birney, reverting to her original name after her divorce.
Stand Up and Be Counted 71. Ben 72. The Cat Creature (TV) 73. The Stranger Who Looks Like Me (TV) 74. The Night That Panicked America (TV) 75. Target Risk (TV) 75. All the President's Men 76. The November Plan (TV) 76. Bittersweet Love 76. Beulah Land (TV) 80. Take Your Best Shot (TV) 82. Broken Badge (TV) 85. The Kissing Place (TV) 90. Till Murder Do Us Part (TV) 92, etc.
TV series: *Bridget Loves Bernie* 72. Family 76. *Family Ties* 82–89.

Biro, Lajos (1880–1948).
Hungarian screenwriter with Hollywood experience in the 20s followed by much work for Korda in Britain.
Forbidden Paradise 24. The Last Command (AAN) 27. The Way of All Flesh 28. Service for Ladies 32. *The Private Life of Henry VIII* 32. Catherine the Great 34. *The Scarlet Pimpernel* 34. Sanders of the River 35. The Divorce of Lady X 37. The Drum 38. The Four Feathers 39. *The Thief of Baghdad* 40. Five Graves to Cairo 43. A Royal Scandal 45, etc.: mostly in collaboration.

Biroc, Joseph F. (1903–1996).
American cinematographer.
It's a Wonderful Life (co-ph) 46. Magic Town 47. Roughshod 49. Without Warning 52. The Tall Texan 53. Down Three Dark Streets 54. Nightmare 56. Run of the Arrow 56. Attack 57. The Ride Back 57. The Amazing Colossal Man 57. Home Before Dark 58. Hitler 61. The Devil at Four o'Clock 61. Bye Bye Birdie 63. Bullet for a Badman 64. Hush Hush Sweet Charlotte 64. I Saw What You Did 65. The Flight of the Phoenix 65. The Russians Are Coming, The Russians Are Coming 66. The Killing of Sister George 68. Whatever Happened to Aunt Alice? 69. Too Late the Hero 69. The Legend of Lylah Clare 69. The Grissom Gang 71. The Organization 71. Emperor of the North Pole 73. Blazing Saddles 74. The Longest Yard 74. The Towering Inferno (co-ph, AA) 74. The Choirboys 77. Beyond the Poseidon Adventure 79. Airplane 80. All the Marbles 81. Airplane 2: the Sequel 82. Hammett 82. Father of Hell Town (TV) 85. A Winner Never Quits (TV) 86, etc.

Birri, Fernando (1925–).
Argentinian director in the neo-realist tradition; also a poet, and a former puppeteer and stage director. He studied at the Centro Sperimentale di Cinematografia in Rome and worked in Italy before returning to his homeland. There, he founded a documentary film school, La Escuela Documental de Santa Fé, and made films about the lives of the dispossessed, which the Argentinian government tried to ban and prevent from being shown abroad. In the mid-60s he left Argentina to work in Brazil and Italy, before teaching film in Cuba.
Alfabeto Notturno (co-d) (It.) 53. Selinunte, i Tempi Coricati (It.) 55. *Throw Us a Dime*/Tire Die 59. *The Inundated*/Los Inundados 61. Rafael Alberti, un Retrato del Poeta por Fernando Birri (It.) 83. A Very Old Man with Enormous Wings/ Un Señor Muy Viejo con unas Alas Enormes (& a, co-w) (Cuba/It.) 88, etc.
❝ There are basically two kinds of filmmakers: one invents an imaginary reality; the other confronts an existing reality and attempts to understand it. – *F.B.*

Birt, Daniel (1907–1955).
British director, former editor: busy in late 40s.
The Three Weird Sisters 48. No Room at the Inn 49. The Interrupted Journey 49. Circumstantial Evidence 52. Background 53, etc.

Bischoff, Samuel (1890–1975).
American producer, with Warners in 30s, Columbia in 40s, subsequently independent.
The Charge of the Light Brigade 36. A Slight Case of Murder 37. Submarine Zone 41. You'll Never Get Rich 41. Appointment in Berlin 43. None Shall Escape 44. Mr District Attorney 47. Pitfall 48. Mrs Mike 50. The System 53. The Phenix City Story 55. Operation Eichmann 61. King of the Roaring Twenties 61. The Strangler 64, many others.

Bishop, Ed (1942–).
American leading man in Great Britain. Starred in TV's *UFO* series and subsequently served as a handy transatlantic voice.
The War Lover 62. The Mouse on the Moon 63. 2001: A Space Odyssey 68. Doppelganger/Journey to the Far Side of the Sun 69. Diamonds Are Forever 71. The Devil's Web 74. Brass Target 78. Saturn 3 80. The Lords of Discipline 83. Restless Natives 85, etc.

Bishop, Joey (1918–) (Joseph Abraham Gottlieb).
American TV comedian who has made few film appearances.
The Naked and the Dead 58. Sergeants Three 63. Texas Across the River 66. A Guide for the Married Man 67. Who's Minding the Mint? 67. The Delta Force 86. Betsy's Wedding 90, etc.
TV series: The Joey Bishop Show 61–64, 67–69.

Bishop, Julie (1914–) (Jacqueline Brown).
American leading lady of routine films; also known as Jacqueline Wells.
Alice in Wonderland 33. The Bohemian Girl 36. The Nurse's Secret 41. Northern Pursuit 43. Rhapsody in Blue 45. Sands of Iwo Jima 49. Westward the Women 52. The High and the Mighty 54. The Big Land 57, many others.
TV series: My Hero 52.

Bishop, Larry (1947–).
American actor who turned to directing and screenwriting. The son of comedian Joey Bishop, in his younger days he performed in a comedy act with Rob REINER.
Wild in the Streets (a) 68. The Savage Seven (a) 68. The Devil's Eight (a) 69. Chrome and Hot Leather 71. Angel Unchained 70. How Come Nobody's on Our Side? (a) 73. Soul Hustler (a) 76. The Big Fix (a) 78. The Miracle Man 82. Underworld (w) 96. Trigger Happy (d) 96. Mad Dog Time (a, wd) 96, etc.

Bishop, Terry (1917–1981).
British director. Much TV work.
You're Only Young Twice 52. Jim Driscoll's Donkey 54. Light Fingers 57. Model for Murder 58. Cover Girl Killer 59. Danger Tomorrow 60. The Unstoppable Man 61, etc.

Bishop, William (1918–1959).
American leading man, mostly in routine features.
Pillow to Post 46. The Romance of Rosy Ridge 47. Anna Lucasta 49. Lorna Doone 51. Cripple Creek 52. The Boss 56. The Oregon Trail 59, etc.
TV series: It's a Great Life 54.

Bissell, James D. (1951–).
American production designer.
E.T. – the Extra-Terrestrial 82. The Last Starfighter 84. The Falcon and the Snowman 85. Harry and the Hendersons 87. Twins 88. Always 89. Arachnophobia 90. The Rocketeer 91. Dennis the Menace/Dennis 93. Jumanji 95, etc.

Bissell, Whit (1909–1996).
American character actor who played anything from attorneys to garage attendants.
Holy Matrimony 43. Another Part of the Forest 47. It Should Happen to You 53. The Young Stranger 57. I Was a Teenage Frankenstein 58. The Time Machine 60. Hud 63. Seven Days in May 64. Covenant with Death 67. Airport 69. The Salzburg Connection 72. Soylent Green 73. Psychic Killer 75. Casey's Shadow 78, many others.
TV series: Bachelor Father 59–61. Time Tunnel 66.

Bisset, Jacqueline (1944–).
British leading lady, in American films.
The Knack 64. Arrivederci Baby 65. Cul de Sac 66. Casino Royale 67. Two for the Road 67. The Sweet Ride 67. Capetown Affair 67. The Detective 68. Bullitt 68. The First Time 68. L'Echelle Blanche (Fr.) 69. Secret World 69. Airport 69. *The Grasshopper* 70. The Mephisto Waltz 71. Believe in Me 71. Secrets 71. Judge Roy Bean 72. Stand Up and Be Counted 72. Le Magnifique 73. La Nuit Américaine 73. The Thief Who Came to Dinner 73. Murder on the Orient Express 74. The Spiral Staircase 75. End of the Game 76. St Ives 76. The Sunday Woman 76. The Deep 77. The Greek Tycoon 78. Someone Is Killing the Great Chefs of Europe 78. When Time Ran Out 80. Rich and Famous 81. Together 81. Inchon 82. Class 83. Under the Volcano 84. Anna Karenina (TV) 84. Forbidden (TV) 85. High Season 87. La Maison de Jade 88. Amoureuse 89. Scenes from the Class Struggle in Beverly Hills 89. Wild Orchid 90. The Maid 91. C'e Kim Novak al Telefono 92. Les Marmottes (Fr.) 93. Crimebroker 94. A Judgment in Stone/La Cérémonie 95. Dangerous Beauty 98. Let the Devil Wear Black 98, etc.
❝ I'm fascinated by a man with a twinkle in his eye. – *J.B.*

Bitzer, Billy (1874–1944) (George William Bitzer).
American cameraman who worked with D. W. Griffith on his most important films and is credited with several major photographic developments.
The New York Hat 12. Judith of Bethulia 13. *Birth of a Nation* 15. *Intolerance* 16. *Hearts of the World* 18. *Broken Blossoms* 19. *Way Down East* 21. *America* 24. The Struggle 30, many others.

Bixby, Bill (1934–1993).
Diffident American light leading man who turned to directing TV movies.
Lonely Are the Brave 62. Irma la Douce 63. Under the Yum Yum Tree 64. Ride Beyond Vengeance 66. Spinout 67. Speedway 68. Congratulations It's a Boy (TV) 71. The Couple Takes a Wife (TV) 72. Barbary Coast (pilot) (& d) (TV) 75. The Apple Dumpling Gang 75. The Invasion of Johnson County (TV) 76. Kentucky Fried Movie 77. The Incredible Hulk (TV) 77. The Incredible Hulk Returns (TV) 88. Trial of the Incredible Hulk (TV) (& d) 89. Death of the Incredible Hulk (TV) (& d) 90. Baby of the Bride (TV) (d) 91. Another Pair of Aces: Three of a Kind (TV) (d) 91. The Woman Who Loved Elvis (TV) (d) 93, etc.
TV series: The Joey Bishop Show 62. My *Favourite Martian* 63–66. The Courtship of Eddie's Father 69–70. The Magician 73. The Incredible Hulk 79–81. Goodnight Beantown 83.

Biziou, Peter.
Welsh cinematographer now working in Hollywood. He began in advertising, shooting commercials for director Alan Parker.
Hier, Aujourd'hui, Demain 68. Bugsy Malone 76. Monty Python's Life of Brian 79. Time Bandits 81. Pink Floyd – The Wall 82. Another Country 84. 9½ Weeks 86. Mississippi Burning (AA) 88. A World Apart 88. Rosencrantz and Guildenstern Are Dead 91. City of Joy 92. Damage 92. In the Name of the Father 93. The Road to Wellville 94. Richard III 95. The Truman Show 98, etc.

Bjork, Anita (1923–).
Swedish actress who made only two English-speaking appearances.
Road to Heaven 42. Woman without a Face 47. The Realm of Men 49. *Miss Julie* 51. Secrets of Women 51. Night People (US) 52. Song of the Scarlet Flower 56. Of Love and Lust 57. The Phantom Carriage 58. Good Friends and Faithful Neighbours 60. The Lady in White 62. Square of Violence 63. Loving Couples 64. Adalen 31 69, etc.

Bjornstrand, Gunnar (1909–1986).
Distinguished Swedish character actor.
The False Millionaire 31. Panic 39. An Adventurer 42. A Night in the Harbour 43. Frenzy 44. It Rains on Our Love 46. Night Is My Future 47. The White Cat 50. Waiting Women 52. Sawdust and Tinsel 53. *Smiles of a Summer Night* 55. Seventh Heaven 56. *The Seventh Seal* 57. Wild Strawberries 57. *The Face* 58. The Devil's Eye 60. Through a Glass Darkly 61. Winter Light 63. Loving Couples 64. Persona 66. The Sadist 66. The Red Mantle 67. The Shame 68. The Rite 69. The Pistol 74. Face to Face 76. Tabu 77. Autumn Sonata 78. The Farewell 81. Fanny and Alexander 82, etc.

Black, Ian Stuart (1915–1997).
British novelist, playwright and screenwriter. Born in London, of Scottish parents, he studied philosophy at Manchester University and worked as an actor with Sir Donald Wolfit's company before becoming a script editor with Rank in the late 40s. His greatest successes came in television, where he helped to create such series of the 50s and 60s as *Fabian of the Yard, Danger Man, Sir Francis Drake, The Sentimental Agent* and *The Man in Room 17*. He also wrote scripts for the TV series H. G. *Wells' Invisible Man, The Saint, Doctor Who* and *Star Maidens*. Married actress Anne Brooke; his four children include actress Isobel Black.
Shadow of the Past (w) 50. Soho Incident (w) 56. The Long Knife (w) 58. In the Wake of a Stranger (oa) 59. She'll Have to Go (oa) 61. The High Bright Sun (w, oa) 65. Redgauntlet (TV) 70, etc.

Black, Isobel (1943–).
British character actress.
Kiss of the Vampire 62. The Magnificent Two 67. David Copperfield (TV) 70. 10 Rillington Place 70. Twins of Evil 71, etc.

Black, Karen (1942–) (Karen Ziegler).
American leading actress whose best roles were in the 70s. Born in Park Ride, Illinois, she studied at Northwestern University and the Actors Studio. Her third husband was screenwriter-actor L. M. Kit Carson.
You're a Big Boy Now 67. Hard Contract 68. Easy Rider 69. Five Easy Pieces (AAN) 70. A Gunfight 71. Drive He Said 71. Born to Win 71. Cisco Pike 71. Portnoy's Complaint 72. The Pyx 73. Rhinoceros 73. The Outfit 73. Little Laura and Big John 73. The Great Gatsby 74. Airport 75 75. Law and Disorder 75. Trilogy of Terror (TV) 75. The Day of the Locust 75. Nashville 75. Family Plot 76. Ace Up My Sleeve 76. Burnt Offerings 76. Killer Fish 78. Capricorn One 78. The Last Word 79. The Rip-Off 79. In Praise of Older Women 79. The Number 79. The Naked Sun 79. Separate Ways 81. Chanel Solitaire 81. Come Back to the Five and Dime, Jimmy Dean, Jimmy Dean 82. Can She Bake a Cherry Pie 83. Growing Pains 83. Martin's Day 84. Savage Dawn 84. Invaders from Mars 86. It's Alive III: Island of the Alive 87. Eternal Evil 87. Hostage 87. Dixie Lanes 88. The Invisible Kid 88. Homer and Eddie 89. Out of the Dark 89. Zapped Again 89. Twisted Justice 90. Night Angel 90. Judgement 91. Evil Spirits 91. Rubin and Ed 91. Club Fed 91. Blood Money 91. Haunting Fear 91. The Player 92. Caged Fear 92. Children of the Night 92. The Double O Kid 92. The Trust 93. Plan 10 from Outer Space 96. Sister Island 96. Children of the Corn 4: The Gathering 96. Cries of Silence 97. The Hunger (TV) 97, etc.
❝ My God, there aren't any more movie stars, which is terrific with me, it's very healthy. A lot of love now occurs in this business, people helping each other to do good work, getting high on each other's success. Isn't that great? – *K.B.*
When you start at the top, which is what happened to me, and then you're no longer at the top, you can't expect anyone else to pull you back up. You have to do it yourself. – *K.B.*

Black, Noel (1937–).
American director who graduated to features from shorts.
Pretty Poison 68. Cover Me Babe 70. Jennifer on My Mind 71. A Man, a Woman and a Bank 79. The Other Victim (TV) 81. Private School 83. Quarterback Princess (TV) 83. A Conspiracy of Love (TV) 87, etc.

Black, Shane (1962–).
American screenwriter and occasional actor who is among the highest paid in the business: he was paid $1.45m for *The Last Boy Scout* and $3.5m for *The Long Kiss Goodnight*.
Lethal Weapon 87. The Monster Squad 87. Lethal Weapon 2 (story) 89. The Last Boy Scout 92. The Last Action Hero (co-w) 93. The Long Kiss Goodnight 96. As Good As It Gets (a) 97, etc.

Black, Stanley (1913–).
British bandleader and composer, responsible for scoring nearly 200 films.
Rhythm Racketeers 38. Mrs Fitzherbert 47. It Always Rains on Sunday 47. The Fatal Night 48. The Monkey's Paw 48. Come Dance with Me 50. Paul Temple's Triumph 50. Lilli Marlene 50. Shadow of the Past 50. Laughter in Paradise 51. One Wild Oat 51. Hindle Wakes 52. Top Secret 52. 3 Steps to the Gallows 53. Escape by Night 53. Recoil 53. Happy Ever After 54. An Alligator Named Daisy 55. Tiger by the Tail 55. Impulse 55. Now and Forever 55. No Smoking 55. As Long as They're Happy 55. A Yank in Ermine 55. The Gilded Cage 55. Breakaway 56. Passport to Treason 56. My Teenage Daughter 56. The High Terrace 56. Bond of Fear 56. The Man Who Wouldn't Talk 57. Time Lock 57. These Dangerous Years 57. The Naked Truth 57. Stranger in Town 57. The Vicious Circle 57. The Flying Scot 57. Hour of Decision 57. Wonderful Things 57. Blood of the Vampire 58. The Trollenberg Terror 58. Jack the Ripper 58. Violent Moment 58. Further Up the Creek 58. Operation Cupid 59. Bottoms Up 59. Broth of a Boy 59. Too Many Crooks 59. Tommy the Toreador 59. Hell Is a City 59. The Battle of the Sexes 59. Make Mine a Million 59. The Flesh and the Fiends 59. Double Bunk 60. The Siege of Sidney Street 60. The Rebel 60. Follow That Horse! 60. Sword of Sherwood Forest 60. Sands of the Desert 60. The Full Treatment 60. The Long and the Short and the Tall 60. Petticoat Pirates 61. The Day the Earth Caught Fire 61. The Young Ones 61. House of Mystery 61. Five Golden Hours 61. The Pot Carriers 62. The Punch and Judy Man 62. Summer Holiday 62. Sparrows Can't Sing 62. 80,000 Suspects 63. What a Crazy World 63. West 11 63. The Cracksman 63. Crooks in Cloisters 64. Ballad in Blue 64. The System 64. Rattle of a Simple Man 64. Wonderful Life 64. The City under the Sea 65. The Double Man 67. Crossplot 69. Valentino 77. The Wicked Lady 83, etc.

Blackman, Honor (1926–).
British leading lady, a Rank 'charm school' product submerged in 'English rose' roles from 1946 until a TV series fitted her up with kinky suits and judo tactics. Her second husband was actor Maurice Kaufmann (1962–75). She is the author of the 1997 book *How to Look and Feel Half Your Age for the Rest of Your Life*.
Fame is the Spur 47. Quartet 48. Diamond City 49. So Long at the Fair 50. The Rainbow Jacket 53. Breakaway 55. A Night to Remember 58. The Square Peg 58. A Matter of Who 61. *Goldfinger* 64. The Secret of My Success 65. *Life at the Top* 65. Moment to Moment 65. A Twist of Sand 68. Shalako 68. The Last Grenade 69. The Virgin and the Gypsy 70. Fright 71. Something Big 71. To the Devil a Daughter 75. The Cat and the Canary 78. To Walk with Lions 98, etc.
TV series: *The Avengers* 60–63. Robin's Nest 77–78. Never the Twain 81–91. The Upper Hand 90–95.

Blackman, Joan (1938–).
American leading lady of the 60s.
Visit to a Small Planet 61. The Great Imposter 61. Blue Hawaii 62. Twilight of Honor 63. Intimacy 66. Daring Game 68. Macon County Line 74, etc.

Blackmer, Sidney (1895–1973).
Suave American character actor, often seen as politician or high-class crook but also capable of sympathetic roles.
A Most Immoral Lady 29. Kismet 30. Little Caesar 30. Once a Sinner 31. Cocktail Hour 33. The Count of Monte Cristo 34. The President Vanishes 34. The Little Colonel 35. Smart Girl 35. Early to Bed 36. A Doctor's Diary 37. This is My Affair 37. Charlie Chan at Monte Carlo 37. The Last Gangster 37. Trade Winds 38. Hotel for Women 39. I Want a Divorce 40. Love Crazy 41. The Feminine Touch 41. The Panther's Claw 42. Quiet Please Murder 42. Murder in Times Square 43. Duel in the Sun 46. My Girl Tisa (as Teddy Roosevelt) 48. People Will Talk 51. Johnny Dark 54. High Society 56. Tammy and the Bachelor 57. How to Murder Your Wife 65. Covenant with Death 67. Rosemary's Baby 68, many others.

Blackton, J. Stuart (1875–1941) (James Stewart Blackton).
British pioneer producer who spent years in America working with Edison. He was one of the founders of Vitagraph, an important producer in the first days of cinema. Born in Sheffield, he emigrated as a child with his mother to the USA.
Raffles 05. The Life of Moses 10. The Battle Cry of Peace 15. Womanhood 16. The Glorious Adventure (in Prizmacolour) 21. On the Banks of the Wabash 23. The Clean Heart 24. The Beloved Brute 24. Gypsy Cavalier 24. Tides of Passion 25. The Happy Warrior 25. Bride of the Storm 30, many others.

Blackwell, Carlyle (1888–1955).
American stage matinée idol, in demand for romantic roles during the 20s; his declamatory style could scarcely survive the coming of sound.
Uncle Tom's Cabin 09. The Key to Yesterday 14. The Restless Sex 20. Sherlock Holmes 22. The Beloved Vagabond 23. Bulldog Drummond 23. She 25. The Wrecker 29. The Crooked Billet 30. The Calling of Dan Matthews 35, many others.

Blades, Ruben (1948–).
Panamanian leading actor, screenwriter, musician and composer, in America. He studied law and has political ambitions to become a future president of his country.
The Last Fight 83. Beat Street 84. Crossover Dreams 85. Critical Condition 87. Fatal Beauty 87. Homeboy 88. The Milagro Beanfield War 88. Oliver and Company (s) 88. Disorganized Crime 89. The Heart of the Deal 90. Mo' Better Blues 90. Predator 2 90. The Two Jakes 90. Crazy from the Heart 91. Color of Night 94. A Million to Juan 94. Scorpion Spring 95. The Devil's Own 96. Chinese Box 97, etc.

Blain, Gérard (1930–).
French leading actor once thought of as a continental equivalent of James Dean. After a period of retirement he emerged again as a serious director.
Les Fruits Sauvages 54. Le Temps des Assassins 56. Crime and Punishment 56. Les Mistons 58. *Le Beau Serge* 58. *Les Cousins* 59. The Hunchback of Notre Dame 60. The Dauphins 60. Gold of Rome 61. Hatari (US) 62. La Bonne Soupe 64. Un Homme de Trop 67. Les Amis (w, d only) 71. Le Pélican (& w, d) 73. The American Friend 77. Utopia (w, d only) 78. Le Rebelle (w, d only) 80. La Derelitta (a) 81. Angel Dust/Poussière d'Ange (a) 87. Natalia (a) 88. Jour après Jour 89. The Raft of the Medusa/Le Radeau de la Meduse (a) (TV) 95, etc.

Blaine, Vivian (1921–1995) (Vivienne Stapleton).
Vivacious American leading lady and personable songstress. Made comparatively few films, her greatest success being on Broadway.
■ Thru Different Eyes 42. Girl Trouble 42. He Hired the Boss 43. Jitterbugs 43. Greenwich Village 44. Something for the Boys 44. Nob Hill 45. *State Fair* 45. Doll Face 45. If I'm Lucky 46. *Three Little Girls in Blue* 46. Skirts Ahoy 52. Main Street to Broadway 53. *Guys and Dolls* 55. Public Pigeon Number One 57. Katie, Portrait of a Centerfold (TV) 78. The Dark 78. The Cracker Factory (TV) 79. Sooner or Later (TV) 79. Parasite 82. I'm Going to Be Famous 83.
❝ I put all my intelligence, such as it is, into playing dumb blondes. – *V.B.*

Blair, Betsy (1923–) (Elizabeth Boger).
American character actress who often plays shy or nervous women.
■ The Guilt of Janet Ames 47. A Double Life 47. *Another Part of the Forest* 48. The Snake Pit 48.

Mystery Street 50. Kind Lady 51. *Marty* (BFA, AAN) 55. Calle Mayor (Sp.) 56. Il Grido (It.) 57. The Halliday Brand 57. All Night Long (GB) 61. A Delicate Balance 73.

Blair, George (1906–1970).
American second feature director.
Duke of Chicago 49. Flaming Fury 49. Daughter of the Jungle 49. Insurance Investigator 51. Jaguar 55. The Hypnotic Eye 60, many others.

Blair, Janet (1921–) (Martha Lafferty).
Vivacious American leading lady of co-features in the 40s.
■ *Three Girls About Town* 41. Blondie Goes to College 42. Two Yanks in Trinidad 42. Broadway 42. *My Sister Eileen* 42. Something to Shout About 43. Once Upon a Time 44. Tonight and Every Night 45. Tars and Spars 46. Gallant Journey 46. The Fabulous Dorseys 47. I Love Trouble 48. The Black Arrow 48. The Fuller Brush Man 48. Public Pigeon Number One 57. Boys' Night Out 62. *Night of the Eagle* (GB) 62. The One and Only Genuine Original Family Band 68.
TV series: Caesar's Hour 56–57. *The Smith Family* 71–72.

Blair, Linda (1959–).
American juvenile lead of the 70s who made a spectacular beginning as a possessed child.
The Sporting Club 71. *The Exorcist* (AAN) 74. Born Innocent (TV) 74. Sarah T, Portrait of a Teenage Alcoholic (TV) 75. Airport 75 75. Sweet Hostage (TV) 76. Victory at Entebbe (TV) 76. Exorcist II: The Heretic 78. Roller Boogie 79. Hell Night 81. Chained Heat 81. Savage Streets 82. Night Patrol 82. Red Heat 83. Savage Island 85. Nightforce 87. Grotesque 88. Silent Assassins 88. Up Your Alley 88. Bad Blood 89. Witchcraft 89. A Woman Obsessed 89. The Chilling 89. Moving Target 89. Zapped Again 89. Bail Out 90. Repossessed 90. Moving Target 90. Dead Sleep 90. The Fatal Bond 91. Prey of the Jaguar 96, etc.

Blake, Amanda (1929–1989) (Beverly Neill).
American supporting actress. Died of AIDS.
Duchess of Idaho 50. Stars in My Crown 50. Lili 53. Sabre Jet 53. A Star is Born 54. About Mrs Leslie 54. High Society 56. Betrayal (TV) 74, etc.
TV series: *Gunsmoke* (as Kitty) 55–75.

Blake, Howard (1938–).
British composer, pianist and conductor; he studied at the Royal Academy of Music.
Ride of the Valkyrie 67. An Elephant Called Slowly 69. Some Will – Some Won't 69. All the Way Up 70. Endless Night 72. Blood Relatives/Les Liens de Sang (Can./Fr.) 77. The Duellists 77. The Odd Job 78. Riddle of the Sands 78. The Changeling (Can.) 79. Flash Gordon (co-m) 80. The Lords of Discipline (US) 82. Victor/Victoria 82. The Hunger (US) 83. Amityville 3-D (US) 83. Scream for Help (US) 84. A Month in the Country 87. Granpa (TV) 89, etc.

Blake, Katherine (1928–1991).
South African actress in Britain, mostly on TV: Anne of the Thousand Days 69, etc.
Assassin for Hire 51. Hammer the Toff 52. To Have and to Hold 63.

Blake, Madge (1900–1969).
American supporting actress.
Between Midnight and Dawn 50. Singin' in the Rain 52. The Long Long Trailer 54. Batman 66, etc.

Blake, Marie (1896–1978) (Blossom MacDonald).
American small-part actress, sister of Jeanette MacDonald. Played the receptionist in the Dr Kildare movie series of the early 40s. Changed her billing to her married name, Blossom Rock, in the 50s.
Mannequin 37. Young Dr Kildare 38. The Women 39. They Knew What They Wanted 39. A Child Is Born 40. I Married a Witch 42. Abbott and Costello in Hollywood 45. The Snake Pit 49. Love Nest 51. From the Terrace 60, many others.
TV series: The Addams Family (as Grandmama) 64–66.

Blake, Robert (1933–) (Michael Gubitosi).
American child actor who later attracted some unusual adult roles.
Andy Hardy's Double Life 43. The Horn Blows at Midnight 45. Treasure of Sierra Madre 47. Revolt in the Big House 58. Battle Flame 59. The Purple Gang 60. The Greatest Story Ever Told 65. *In Cold Blood* 67. *Tell Them Willie Boy Is Here* 69. Corky 72. Electra Glide in Blue 73. Coast to Coast 80. Second Hand Hearts 80. Blood Feud (TV) 83, etc.
TV series: The Richard Boone Show 64. *Baretta* 74–77. Hell Town 85.

Blake, Whitney.
American character actress, mother of Meredith Baxter.
Deadline Midnight 59. The Boy Who Stole the Elephant (TV) 70. Strange Homecoming (TV) 74. The Betsy 78, etc.
TV series: Hazel 61–65.

Blakeley, John E. (1889–1958).
British producer-director of low-budget Lancashire comedies.
■ Dodging the Dole 36. Somewhere in England 40. Somewhere in Camp 42. Somewhere on Leave 42. Demobbed 44. Under New Management 46. Home Sweet Home 46. Cup Tie Honeymoon 48. Holiday with Pay 48. Somewhere in Politics 49. What a Carry On 49. School for Randle 49. Over the Garden Wall 50. Let's Have a Murder 50. It's a Grand Life 53.

Blakeley, Tom (1918–1984).
British producer of second features.
Love's a Luxury 58. Tomorrow at Ten 62. Devils of Darkness 65. Island of Terror 66, etc.

Blakely, Colin (1930–1987).
Stocky British stage actor, in occasional films.
Saturday Night and Sunday Morning 60. This Sporting Life 62. The Informers 63. The Long Ships 64. A Man for All Seasons 66. The Spy with a Cold Nose 67. *The Day the Fish Came Out* 67. Charlie Bubbles 67. The Vengeance of She 68. *Decline and Fall* 68. Alfred the Great 69. *The Private Life of Sherlock Holmes* (as Watson) 70. Something to Hide 72. Young Winston 72. Murder on the Orient Express 74. Galileo 74. Love Among the Ruins (TV) 74. It Shouldn't Happen to a Vet 76. Equus 77. The Day Christ Died (TV) 80. Loophole 80. Nijinsky 80. The Dogs of War 81. Evil Under the Sun 82. The Red Monarch (TV) 83. Paradise Postponed (TV) 86.

Blakely, Susan (1948–).
American leading lady; former model.
■ Savages 72. The Lords of Flatbush 74. The Towering Inferno 74. Report to the Commissioner 75. Shampoo 75. Capone 75. *Rich Man Poor Man* (TV) 76. Secrets (TV) 77. Savages 78. Make Me an Offer (TV) 80. A Cry for Love (TV) 80. Oklahoma City Dolls (TV) 80. The Concorde – Airport 79 79. The Bunker (TV) 81. Will There Really be a Morning? (TV) 83. Over the Top 87. Out of Sight, Out of Her Mind 89. My Mom's a Werewolf 89. Wildflower (TV) 91. Tous les Jours Dimanche (Fr.) 94.

Blakemore, Michael (1928–).
Australian director, mostly on English stage.
A Personal History of the Australian Surf 81. Privates on Parade 82. Country Life (a, wd) 94.

Blakley, Ronee (1946–).
American pop singer who has made acting appearances.
Nashville (AAN) 75. Renaldo and Clara 78. The Driver 78. She Came to the Valley 79. The Baltimore Bullet 80. Lightning Over Water 81. The Private Files of J. Edgar Hoover 77. Good Luck Miss Wyckoff 79. A Nightmare on Elm Street 84. I Played for You 85. Return to Salem's Lot 87. Someone to Love 87. Student Confidential 87. Murder by Numbers 90, etc.

Blanc, Jean-Pierre (1942–).
French director.
La Vieille Fille 71. Un Ange au Paradis 73. D'Amour et d'Eau Fraîche 75, etc.

Blanc, Mel (1908–1989).
The voice of Warner Brothers' cartoon characters, including Bugs Bunny, Sylvester and Tweetie Pie. Made occasional cameo appearances in films.
Autobiography: 1988, *That's Not All, Folks!*
Neptune's Daughter 49. Kiss Me Stupid 64, etc.
TV series: The Jack Benny Show 50–65. The Bugs Bunny Show (voices) 60–62. The Flintstones (voices of Barney Rubble and Dino) 60–66. The Jetsons (voices) 63–63. Where's Huddles (voice) 70. The Bugs Bunny/Roadrunner Show (voices) 76. Buck Rogers in the 25th Century (voice of Twiki) 79–81.

Blanc, Michel (1952–).
Balding leading French actor, from the theatre, who made his reputation in comic roles. He is also a writer and director. He won the screenplay award at the 1994 Cannes Film Festival for *Grosse Fatigue*.
Walk in the Shadow/Marche à l'Ombre (d) 84. The Fugitives/Les Fugitifs 86. Evening Dress/Tenue de Soirée 86. I Hate Actors! 86. Story of Women/Une Affaire de Femmes 88. Monsieur Hire 89. Chambre à Part 89. Strike It Rich 90. Uranus 90. Merci la Vie 91. Prospero's Books 91. The Favour, the Watch and the Very Big Fish/Rue Saint-Sulpice 91. Toxic Affair 93. Grosse Fatigue (& d) 94. The Grand Dukes 95, etc.

Blanchar, Pierre (1892–1963).
Distinguished French screen and stage actor.
Jocelyn 23. *L'Atlantide* 31. Le Diable en Bouteille 34. Crime and Punishment 35. Mademoiselle Docteur 36. L'Affaire du Courrier de Lyon 37. *Un Carnet de Bal* 37. La Symphonie Pastorale 40. Pontcarral 42. Rififi Chez les Femmes 58, etc.

Blanchard, Mari (1927–1970) (Mary Blanchard).
Decorative American leading lady of 50s co-features.
Mr Music 50. Ten Tall Men 51. Veils of Baghdad 53. Black Horse Canyon 54. *Destry* 55. The Crooked Web 56. The Return of Jack Slade 56. Jungle Heat 57. No Place to Land 58. Don't Knock the Twist 62. McLintock 63. Twice Told Tales 64, etc.

Blanchard, Terence (1962–).
American composer and jazz trumpeter who has scored four of Spike Lee's films. Born in New Orleans, he played with Art Blakey's Jazz Messengers in the 80s before leading his own band.
School Daze 87. Do the Right Thing 89. Jungle Fever 91. Malcolm X 92. Sugar Hill 94. The Inkwell 94. Crooklyn 94. Trial by Jury 94. Clockers 95. Till There Was You 96. Get on the Bus 96. Eve's Bayou 97. Gia (TV) 98. The Color of Courage 98, etc.

Blanchett, Cate (1970–).
Australian leading actress, from the stage. Brought up in Melbourne, of American and Australian parents, she studied at the National Institute for Dramatic Art and began her career with the Sydney Theatre Company.
Paradise Road 97. Oscar and Lucinda 97. Thank God He Met Lizzie 97. Elizabeth (GB) 98. Pushing Tin 98. The Talented Mr Ripley 99. An Ideal Husband 99, etc.
❝ It's not my job as an actor to like or dislike the character I'm playing. That way lies sentimentality. – C.B.

Blandick, Clara (1880–1962).
American character actress, often seen as sensible servant or no-nonsense aunt. Committed suicide.
The Girl Said No 30. Huckleberry Finn 31. The Wet Parade 32. One Sunday Afternoon 33. Broadway Bill 34. The Gorgeous Hussy 36. A Star is Born 37. Huckleberry Finn 39. *The Wizard of Oz* (as Aunt Em) 39. It Started with Eve 41. Can't Help Singing 44. A Stolen Life 46. Life with Father 47. The Bride Goes Wild 48. Love That Brute 50, many others.

Blane, Ralph (1914–1995) (Ralph Uriah Hunsecker).
American composer and lyricist, a former singer, who worked with Hugh Martin (1914–) and wrote lyrics for such composers as Harold Arlen and Harry Warren.
Best Foot Forward (with Martin) 43. *Meet Me in St Louis* (with Martin) 44. Summer Holiday 48. My Dream Is Yours 49. My Blue Heaven 50. Skirts Ahoy! 52. Down among the Sheltering Palms 52. Athena 54. The Girl Rush (with Martin) 55. The Girl Most Likely (with Martin) 58, etc.

Blane, Sally (1910–1997) (Elizabeth Jung).
American leading lady of the early 30s; sister of Loretta Young.
Sirens of the Sea 27. Rolled Stockings 27. The Vagabond Lover 29. Little Accident 30. Once a Sinner 31. Ten Cents a Dance 31. Disorderly Conduct 31. I am a Fugitive from a Chain Gang 32. Advice to the Lovelorn 33. The Silver Streak 35. One Mile from Heaven 37. Charlie Chan at Treasure Island 39. A Bullet for Joey 54, many others.

Blangsted, Folmar (1904–1982).
American editor.
The Doughgirls 44. Rhapsody in Blue 45. Cry Wolf 47. Flamingo Road 49. Distant Drums 51. The Charge at Feather River 53. A Star is Born 54. A Cry in the Night 56. Rio Bravo 59. Taras Bulba 63. The War Lord 65. Camelot 67. The Forbin Project 70. Man of La Mancha 72. Oklahoma Crude 73, many others.

Blanke, Henry (1901–1981).
German-American producer, long at Warner.
Female 33. *The Story of Louis Pasteur* 35. Satan Met a Lady 36. The Petrified Forest 36. Green Pastures 36. The Life of Emile Zola 37. Jezebel 38. *The Adventures of Robin Hood* 38. Juarez 39. The Old Maid 39. The Sea Hawk 40. *The Maltese Falcon* 41. Old Acquaintance 43. The Mask of Dimitrios 44. Deception 46. The Treasure of the Sierra Madre 47. The Fountainhead 49. Come Fill the Cup 51. King Richard and the Crusaders 54. Serenade 56. Too Much Too Soon 58. *The Nun's Story* 59. Ice Palace 60. Hell is for Heroes 62, many others.

Blankfort, Michael (1907–1982).
American screenwriter, former Princeton professor.
Blind Alley 39. Adam Had Four Sons 40. Texas 41. Flight Lieutenant 42. An Act of Murder 48. Broken Arrow 50. Halls of Montezuma 51. My Six Convicts 52. The Juggler (from his novel) 53. Untamed 55. Tribute to a Bad Man 56. The Vintage 57. The Other Man (TV) 70. A Fire in the Sky (TV) 78, etc.

Blasetti, Alessandro (1900–1987).
Italian director mainly associated with comedy and spectaculars.
Sole 29. Nero 30. Resurrection 31. The Old Guard 33. The Countess of Parma 37. *Four Steps in the Clouds* 42. A Day of Life 46. Fabiola 48. *First Communion* 50. Altri Tempi/Infidelity 52. Europe by Night 59. I Love You Love 61, many others.

Blatt, Edward A. (1905–1991).
Russian-born American stage director who worked briefly for Warners in the 40s.
■ Between Two Worlds 44. Escape in the Desert 45. Smart Woman 48.

Blatty, William Peter (1928–).
American screenwriter.
The Man from the Diners' Club 63. A Shot in the Dark 64. John Goldfarb Please Come Home 65. Promise Her Anything 66. What Did You Do in the War Daddy? 66. Gunn 67. The Great Bank Robbery 69. Darling Lili 69. The Exorcist (& w, p, oa) (AA script) 73. The Ninth Configuration (& w, oa) 80. 'Killer' Kane (wd) 80. The Exorcist III (wd) 90, etc.

Blaustein, Julian (1913–1995).
American producer.
Broken Arrow 50. Mister 880 50. Take Care of My Little Girl 51. Desiree 54. Storm Center 56. Bell Book and Candle 58. The Wreck of the Mary Deare 59. Two Loves 61. The Four Horsemen of the Apocalypse 62. Khartoum 66. Three into Two Won't Go 69, etc.

Blech, Hans Christian (1925–).
German character actor, occasionally in international films.
L'Affaire Blum 49. Decision Before Dawn 51. The Longest Day 62. The Visit 63. The Saboteur 65. Battle of the Bulge 65. The Bridge at Remagen 69. Dirty Hands/Les Innocents aux Main Sales 76. The Wrong Move 78, etc.

Blees, Robert (1922–).
American screenwriter and producer who has also written for many television series.
Paid in Full (co-w) 49. The Glass Web (co-w) 53. Playgirl (w) 54. Cattle Queen of Montana (co-w) 54. *Magnificent Obsession* (w) 54. One Desire (co-w) 54. From the Earth to the Moon (co-w) 54. Slightly Scarlet (w) 55. Autumn Leaves (co-w) 56. Screaming Mimi (w) 58. High School Confidential (co-w) 58. Whoever Slew Auntie Roo? (GB) (co-w) 71. Frogs (co-w) 72. Dr Phibes Rises Again (GB) (co-w) 72, etc.

Blessed, Brian (1937–).
Massive British character actor, originally 'Fancy Smith' in TV's *Z Cars*.
Brotherly Love 70. The Trojan Women 71. Man of La Mancha 72. Henry VIII and His Six Wives 73. I Claudius (TV) 76. Flash Gordon 80. High Road to China 83. War and Remembrance (TV) 88. Henry V 89. Robin Hood: Prince of Thieves 91. Prisoners of Honor 92. Back in the USSR 92. Chasing the Deer 95. Catherine the Great (TV) 95. Tom Jones (TV) 97, etc.

Bletcher, William (Billy) (1894–1979).
Small, deep-voiced American comic actor, from vaudeville. He made his film debut in 1913, was in many of Mack Sennett's two-reel comedies and partnered Billy Gilbert in some 30s shorts. He also appeared in Our Gang comedies as Spanky McFarland's father and supplied the voice of the Big Bad Wolf for Walt Disney's *Three Little Pigs*.
Billy Jim 22. The Dude Cowboy 26. Top Speed 30. The Midnight Patrol 33. Babes in Toyland 34. Destry Rides Again 39. Boss of Rawhide 51. The Patsy 64. Hello Dolly! 69, etc.

Blethyn, Brenda (1946–).
English character actress, much on TV. She trained at the Guildhall School of Drama and acted at the Royal National Theatre from the mid-70s.
The Witches 89. A River Runs through It 92. *Secrets and Lies* (AAN) 96. Girls' Night 98. In the Winter Dark (Aus.) 98. Little Voice 98, etc.
TV series: Chance in a Million 84–86. The Labours of Erica 89–90. All Good Things 91. Outside Edge 94.

Blier, Bernard (1916–1989).
French actor who made a virtue of his plumpness and baldness.
Hôtel du Nord 38. *Quai des Orfèvres* 47. *Dédée d'Anvers* 47. L'École Buissonnière 48. Manèges/The Wanton 49. Souvenirs Perdus 50. Les Misérables 57. Les Grandes Familles 58. Le Cave se Rebiffe 61. Les Saintes Nitouches 63. A Question of Honour (It.) 66. Breakdown (& d) 67. Catch Me a Spy 71. The Tall Blond Man with One Black Shoe 74. Chez Victor 76. Le Compromis 78. Buffet Froid 80. Passione d'Amore 82, etc.

Blier, Bertrand (1939–).
French director, son of Bernard BLIER.
Hitler Connais Pas 62. Les Valseuses 74. Femmes Fatales 76. *Préparez Vos Mouchoirs* (AA) 78. *Buffet Froid* 80. Beau Père 81. My Best Friend's Girl 83. Separate Rooms/Notre Histoire 84. Ménage/Tenue de Soirée 86. Trop Belle pour Toi 89. Merci la Vie 91. Un, Deux, Trois, Soleil 93. Grosse Fatigue (story) 94. My Man (wd) 96, etc.

Blinn, Holbrook (1872–1928).
American silent star.
Rosita 23. Janice Meredith 24. Yolanda 25. Zander the Great 27, many others.

Bliss, Sir Arthur (1891–1975).
British composer who occasionally scored films.
■ *Things to Come* 36. Conquest of the Air 38. Men of Two Worlds 46. Christopher Columbus 49. The Beggar's Opera 53. Welcome the Queen 54. Seven Waves Away 56.

Blitzstein, Marc (1905–1964).
American composer. Film music for documentaries, including Spanish Earth 38, Native Land 42.

Bloch, Robert (1917–1994).
American screenwriter dealing almost exclusively in horror themes with trick endings.
Psycho (oa) 60. The Cabinet of Caligari 62. Strait Jacket 63. *The Night Walker* 64. The Psychopath 66. The Deadly Bees 66. The Torture Garden 67. The House that Dripped Blood 70. Asylum 72, etc.

Blocker, Dan (1928–1972).
Heavyweight American character actor.
Come Blow Your Horn 63. Lady in Cement 68. The Cockeyed Cowboys of Calico County 69, etc.
TV series: Cimarron City 58. *Bonanza* (as Hoss Cartwright) 59–72.

Blomberg, Erik (1913–).
Finnish director, a former cinematographer, whose first feature won the prize for the best fairy-tale film at the Cannes Film Festival in 1953. From the mid-60s, he worked in television.
The White Reindeer/Valkoinen Peura 52. The Engagement/Kilhaus 55. The Wedding Night/Hääyö 62, etc.

Blomfield, Derek (1920–1964).
British boy actor of the 30s.
Emil and the Detectives 35. Turn of the Tide 35. The Ghost of St Michael's 41. Alibi 42. Night and the City 50. Hobson's Choice 54. It's Great to be Young 56. Carry On Admiral 57, etc.

Blondell, Joan (1909–1979).
Amiable American comedienne who played reporters, gold-diggers or the heroine's dizzy friend in innumerable comedies and musicals of the 30s. Later graduated to occasional character roles. Married cinematographer George Barnes (1933–35), actor Dick Powell (1936–44) and producer Mike Todd (1947–50).
Autobiographical novel 1972: *Center Door Fancy*.
■ Sinner's Holiday 30. The Office Wife 30. Other Men's Women 30. Illicit 31. My Past 31. Millie 31. The Reckless Hour 31. Big Business Girl 31. Night Nurse 31. Public Enemy 31. Blonde Crazy 31. Union Depot 32. The Crowd Roars 32. The Famous Ferguson Case 32. *Miss Pinkerton* 32. Big City Blues 32. Make Me a Star 32. The Greeks Had a Word for Them 32. Three on a Match 32. Central Park 32. Broadway Bad 33. Lawyer Man 33. Blondie Johnson 33. *Gold Diggers of 1933* 33. Goodbye Again 33. *Footlight Parade* 33. Havana Widows 33. *Convention City* 33. Kansas City Princess 34. Smarty 34. I've Got Your Number 34. He Was Her Man 34. *Dames* 34. The Travelling Saleslady 34. Broadway Gondolier 35. We're in the Money 35. Miss Pacific Fleet 35. Colleen 36. Sons o' Guns 36. Bullets or Ballots 36. *Stage Struck* 36. *Three Men on a Horse* 36. Gold Diggers of 1937 37. The King and the Chorus Girl 37. The Perfect Specimen 37. Back in Circulation 37. *Stand-In* 37. There's Always a Woman 38. Off the Record 38. East Side of Heaven 39. The Kid from Kokomo 39. Good Girls Go to Paris 39. The Amazing Mr Williams 39. Two Girls on Broadway 40. I Want a Divorce 40. *Topper Returns* 41. Model Wife 41. *Three Girls Around Town* 42. Lady for a Night 42. Cry Havoc 43. *A Tree Grows in Brooklyn* 44. Don Juan Quilligan 45. Adventure 46. The Corpse Came COD 47. Nightmare Alley 47. Christmas Eve 47. For Heaven's Sake 50. The Blue Veil (AAN) 51. The Opposite Sex 56. Lizzie 57. This Could Be the Night 57. The Desk Set 58. Will Success Spoil Rock Hunter 58. Angel Baby 61. Advance to the Rear 63. The Cincinatti Kid 66. Paradise Road 66. Ride Beyond Vengeance 66. Waterhole Three 67. Stay Away Joe 68. Kona Coast 68. The Phynx 70. Support Your Local Gunfighter 71. Winner Take All 75. Death at Love House (TV) 76. Opening Night 77. Battered (TV) 78. The Rebels (TV) 78. Grease 79. The Champ 79.
TV series: Here Come the Brides 68–69. Banyon 72.

Bloom, Claire (1931–) (Patricia Claire Blume).
British leading actress who came to the screen via the Old Vic. Married to novelist Philip Roth 1990–95; previous husbands were Rod Steiger (1959–69) and producer Hillard Elkins (1969–72).
Autobiographies: 1982, *Limelight and After: The Education of an Actress*; 1996, *Leaving a Doll's House*.
The Blind Goddess 48. *Limelight* 52. Innocents in Paris 52. The Man Between 53. Richard III 56. Alexander the Great 56. The Brothers Karamazov 58. *Look Back in Anger* 59. The Buccaneer 59. Brainwashed (Ger.) 60. The Chapman Report 61. The Wonderful World of the Brothers Grimm 63. *The Haunting* 63. 80,000 Suspects 63. Il Maestro di Vigevano 64. The Outrage 64. High Infidelity 65. *The Spy Who Came in from the Cold* 66. Charly 68. Three into Two Won't Go 69. The Illustrated Man 69. A Severed Head 69. The Going Up of David Lev (TV) 71. Red Sky at Morning 71. A Doll's House 73. Islands in the Stream 77. Backstairs at the White House (TV) 79. Clash of the Titans 81. Brideshead Revisited (TV) 81. Shadowlands (TV) 85. Hold the Dream (TV) 86. Queenie (TV) 87. Sammy and Rosie Get Laid 87. Crimes and Misdemeanors 89. The Princess and the Goblin (voice) 92. Mighty Aphrodite 95. Daylight 96. Family Money (TV) 97. Imogen's Face (TV) 98. Wrestling with Alligators 99, etc.

❝ I think that few professions have so much to do with chance and so little to do with the calculation of will. – *C.B.*
She could not be more beautiful without upsetting the balance of nature. – *Walter Kerr*

Bloom, Harold Jack.
American screenwriter.
The Naked Spur (co-w) 53. Magnificent Obsession 54. Last of the Pharaohs (co-w) 55. A Gunfight 71. Hardcase (co-w) 72.

Bloom, Jeffrey.
American screenwriter and director.
Snow Job (co-w) 72. Dogpound Shuffle (w) 74. 11 Harrowhouse (w) 74. Swashbuckler (w) 76. The Stick Up (wd) 78. Blood Beach (wd) 81. Nightmares (co-w) 83. Flowers in the Attic (wd) 87, etc.

Bloom, John (1935–).
English film editor, a former script reader for Rank. He is the brother of Claire Bloom.
Funeral in Berlin 66. Georgy Girl 67. The Lion in Winter 68. Travels with My Aunt 72. The Ritz 76. Orca 77. Who'll Stop the Rain/Dog Soldiers 78. Magic 79. Dracula 79. The French Lieutenant's Woman (AAN) 81. Gandhi (AA) 82. Betrayal 83. A Chorus Line (AAN) 85. Black Widow 87. Bright Lights, Big City 88. Jacknife 89. Everybody Wins 90. Air America 90. Prague 91. Damage 92. A Foreign Field (TV) 93. Nobody's Fool 94. Last Dance 96, etc.

Bloom, Verna (1939–).
American leading lady.
Medium Cool 69. The Hired Hand 71. High Plains Drifter 72. Badge 373 73. Where Have All the People Gone? (TV) 74. Sarah T (TV) 75. The Blue Knight (TV) 75. Heroes 77. Contract on Cherry Street (TV) 77. National Lampoon's Animal House 78. Playing for Time (TV) 80. The Journey of Natty Gann 85. After Hours 85. The Last Temptation of Christ 89, etc.

Blore, Eric (1887–1959).
British comic actor who went to Hollywood and played unctuous/insulting butlers and eccentric types in many films. Born in London, he began as an insurance agent and was on stage from 1908. He also wrote a few plays and many lyrics for revues and musical comedies. Married twice.
■ A Night Out and a Day In 20. The Great Gatsby 26. Laughter 30. My Sin 31. Tarnished Lady 31. Flying Down to Rio 33. *The Gay Divorcee* 34. Limehouse Blues 34. Behold My Wife 34. Folies Bergère 34. To Beat the Band 35. The Good Fairy 35. Diamond Jim 35. The Casino Murder Case 35. I Live My Life 35. *Top Hat* 35. I Dream Too Much 35. Seven Keys to Baldpate 35. Two in the Dark 36. The Ex Mrs Bradford 36. Swing Time 36. The Smartest Girl in Town 36. Sons o' Guns 36. Piccadilly Jim 36. The Soldier and the Lady 37. Quality Street 37. Shall We Dance? 37. Breakfast for Two 37. Hitting a New High 37. *It's Love I'm After* 37. Joy of Living 38. Swiss Miss 38. A Desperate Adventure 38. Island of Lost Men 39. 1000 Dollars a Touchdown 39. A Gentleman's Gentleman 39. Music in My Heart 40. The Man Who Wouldn't Talk 40. The Lone Wolf Strikes 40 (and ten other Lone Wolf adventures 40–47, all as the butler). Till We Meet Again 40. South of Suez 40. The Boys from Syracuse 40. The Earl of Puddlestone 40. *The Lady Eve* 41. Road to Zanzibar 41. Redhead 41. Lady Scarface 41. New York Town 41. The Shanghai Gesture 41. Sullivan's Travels 41. Three Girls About Town 41. *The Moon and Sixpence* 42. Confirm or Deny 42. Happy Go Lucky 43. The Sky's the Limit 43. Forever and a Day 43. Holy Matrimony 43. Submarine Base 43. San Diego I Love You 44. Penthouse Rhythm 45. Men in Her Diary 45. Easy to Look At 45. Kitty 45. Two Sisters from Boston 46. Abie's Irish Rose 46. Winter Wonderland 47. Romance on the High Seas 48. Love Happy 49. Ichabod and Mr Toad (voice of Toad) 49. *Fancy Pants* 50. Bowery to Bagdad 54.
Famous line (*Top Hat*): 'We are Jones, sir.'

Blue, Ben (1901–1975) (Benjamin Bernstein).
Lanky, rubber-limbed American comedian with vaudeville experience; sporadically in films, usually in cameos.
College Rhythm 33. Follow Your Heart 36. High Wide and Handsome 37. College Swing 38. Paris Honeymoon 39. For Me and My Gal 42. Thousands Cheer 43. Easy to Wed 46. One Sunday Afternoon 48. It's a Mad Mad Mad Mad World 63. *The Russians are Coming, The Russians are Coming* 66. *A Guide for the Married Man* 67. Where Were You When the Lights Went Out? 68, etc.

Blue, Monte (1890–1963).
Burly American silent hero who later appeared in innumerable bit roles.
Intolerance 16. Till I Come Back to You 18. Pettigrew's Girl 19. The Affairs of Anatol 21. Orphans of the Storm 22. Main Street 23. *The Marriage Circle* 24. The Black Swan 24. Other Women's Husbands 26. Other Men's Wives 26. So This is Paris 26. Wolf's Clothing 27. *White Shadows of the South Seas* 28. Tiger Rose 29. Isle of Escape 30. The Flood 31. The Stoker 32. Wagon Wheels 34. Lives of a Bengal Lancer 34. G Men 35. Souls at Sea 37. Dodge City 39. Geronimo 39. Across the Pacific 42. The Mask of Dimitrios 44. Life with Father 47. The Iroquois Trail 50. Apache 54, many others.

Blum, Daniel (1900–1965).
American writer, editor and collector; annually produced *Theatre World* and *Screen World* annuals.

Bluteau, Lothaire.
French-Canadian leading actor.
Jesus of Montreal 90. Black Robe 91. The Touch 92. Orlando 92. Other Voices, Other Rooms 95. I Shot Andy Warhol 96. The Confessional 96. Bent 97. Shot through the Heart (TV) 98. Conquest 98, etc.

Bluth, Don (1938–).
Director of animation who first worked for Disney before setting up his own company in the 80s to restore old-fashioned standards to the medium, with mixed results. In 1994, he signed a long-term deal with Fox.
Pete's Dragon 77. The Rescuers 77. The Secret of Nimh 82. An American Tail 86. The Land Before Time 88. All Dogs Go to Heaven 89. Rock-a-Doodle 91. Thumbelina 94. A Troll in Central Park (p, co-d) 95. The Pebble and the Penguin 95. Anastasia 97, etc.

Blyden, Larry (1925–1975).
American comic actor, on TV and in supporting roles.
The Bachelor Party 57. Kiss Them for Me 57. On a Clear Day You Can See Forever 70, etc.
TV series: Harry's Girls 63.

Blystone, John G. (1892–1938).
American director, former actor.
Dick Turpin 25. *Seven Chances* 25. Ankles Preferred 27. Mother Knows Best 28. The Sky Hawk 29. Tol'able David 30. Charlie Chan's Chance 32. Shanghai Madness 33. Hell in the Heavens 34. The Magnificent Brute 36. Woman Chases Man 37. Swiss Miss 38. *Blockheads* 38, many others.

Blyth, Ann (1928–).
Diminutive American songstress and leading lady who after opera training got her screen break in Donald O'Connor musicals, then graduated to dramatic roles.
■ Chip Off the Old Block 44. The Merry Monahans 44. Babes on Swing Street 44. Bowery to Broadway 44. *Mildred Pierce* (as the abominable daughter) (AAN) 45. Swell Guy 46. Brute Force 47. Killer McCoy 47. A Woman's Vengeance 47. *Another Part of the Forest* 48. *Mr Peabody and the Mermaid* 48. Red Canyon 49. Once More My Darling 49. Top o' the Morning 49. Free For All 49. Our Very Own 50. *The Great Caruso* 51. Katie Did It 51. Thunder on the Hill 51. I'll Never Forget You 51. The Golden Horde 51. The World in his Arms 51. One Minute to Zero 52. Sally and Saint Anne 52. All the Brothers were Valiant 53. *Rose Marie* 54. The Student Prince 54. The King's Thief 55. Kismet 55. Slander 57. The Buster Keaton Story 57. *The Helen Morgan Story* 57.

Blythe, Betty (1893–1972) (Elizabeth Blythe Slaughter).
American leading lady of the silent era.
Nomads of the North 20. Queen of Sheba 21. Chu Chin Chow 23. The Folly of Vanity 24. She 25. The Girl from Gay Paree 27. Glorious Betsy

28. A Daughter of Israel 28. Eager Lips 30. Tom Brown of Culver 32. Only Yesterday 33. Ever Since Eve 34. The Gorgeous Hussy 36. Gangster's Boy 38. Honky Tonk 41. Jiggs and Maggie in Society 47. My Fair Lady 64, many others.

Blythe, John (1921–1993).
British character actor, often of spiv types.
This Happy Breed 44. Holiday Camp 48. Vote for Huggett 49. Worm's Eye View 51. The Gay Dog 54. Foxhole in Cairo 60. A Stitch in Time 64. The Bed Sitting Room 69, many others.

Boam, Jeffrey.
American screenwriter.
Straight Time 78. The Dead Zone 83. Innerspace 87. The Lost Boys 87. Funny Farm 88. Indiana Jones and the Last Crusade 89. Lethal Weapon 2 89. Lethal Weapon 3 92, etc.

Boardman, Chris.
American composer.
The Color Purple (co-m, AAN) 85. Johnny Ryan (TV) 90, etc.

Boardman, Eleanor (1898–1991).
Sympathetic American leading lady of the late silent period, who never seemed happy in sound films and retired in 1934. Was married variously to King Vidor and Harry D'Abbadie D'Arrast.
■ The Stranger's Banquet 22. Gimme 23. Souls for Sale 23. Vanity Fair (as Amelia Sedley) 23. Three Wise Fools 23. Day of Faith 23. True as Steel 24. Wine of Youth 24. The Turmoil 24. Sinners in Silk 24. So This Is Marriage 24. The Silent Accuser 24. Wife of the Centaur 24. The Way of a Girl 25. Proud Flesh 25. Exchange of Wives 25. The Only Thing 25. The Circle 25. Memory Lane 26. The Auction Block 26. Bardeleys the Magnificent 26. Tell It to the Marines 26. *The Crowd* 28. Diamond Handcuffs 28. She Goes to War 29. Mamba 30. Redemption 30. *The Great Meadow* 31. The Flood 31. Women Love Once 31. The Squaw Man 31. It Happened in Spain 34.

Bochner, Hart (1956–).
Canadian character actor, the son of Lloyd Bochner.
Islands in the Stream 76. Breaking Away 79. Rich and Famous 81. The Wild Life 84. Supergirl 84. Apartment Zero 88. Die Hard 88. Fellow Traveller 90. Mr Destiny 90. And the Sea Will Tell (TV) 91. Mad at the Moon 92. The Innocent 93. Batman: Mask of the Phantasm (voice) 94. PCU (d only) 94. High School High (d) 96, etc.

Bochner, Lloyd (1924–).
Canadian leading man, mostly on TV but in occasional films.
Drums of Africa 63. The Night Walker 64. Sylvia 65. Harlow 65. Point Blank 67. Tony Rome 67. The Detective 68. The Young Runaways 68. The Horse in the Grey Flannel Suit 69. Ulzana's Raid 72. Mazes and Monsters (TV) 83. The Lonely Lady 87. Crystal Heart 87. Millennium 89. The Naked Gun 2½: The Smell of Fear 91. Morning Glory 93, etc.
TV series: Hong Kong 60. The Richard Boone Show 64. Dynasty 81–82.

Bock, Jerry (1928–).
American song composer who with lyricist Sheldon Harnick (1924–) wrote *Fiddler on the Roof*.

Bodard, Mag (1927–).
Swedish producer in France.
The Umbrellas of Cherbourg 64. The Young Girls of Rochefort 66. *Le Bonheur* 66. Mouchette 67. Benjamin 67. Le Viol 68. La Chinoise 68. *Peau d'Ane* 71, etc.

Boddey, Martin (1908–1975).
English character actor.
A Song for Tomorrow 48. Seven Days to Noon 50. Laughter in Paradise 51. Appointment with Venus 51. The Magic Box 51. Cry the Beloved Country 52. Doctor in the House 54. Forbidden Cargo 54. The Iron Petticoat 56. The Square Peg 58. Idol on Parade 58. Carry on Nurse 59. Oscar Wilde 60. The Prince and the Pauper 62. The Wrong Arm of the Law 62. A Man for All Seasons 66, etc.

Bode, Ralph (Ralf D. Bode).
American cinematographer.
Saturday Night Fever 77. Slow Dancing in the Big City 78. Rich Kids 79. Coal Miner's Daughter (AAN) 80. Dressed to Kill 80. Raggedy Man 81. A Little Sex 82. Gorky Park 83. Firstborn 84. Bring on the Night 85. Violets Are Blue 86. The Whoopee Boys 86. The Big Town 87. Critical Condition 87. The Accused 88. Distant Thunder 88. Cousins 89. The Long Way Home 89. Uncle Buck 89. One Good Cop 91. Leaving Normal 92. Love Field 92. Made in America 93. George Balanchine's The Nutcracker 93. Gypsy (TV) 93. Bad Girls 94. Safe Passage 94. Don Juan DeMarco 95. The Big Green 95. A Streetcar Named Desire (TV) 95. A Simple Wish 97, etc.

Bodeen, De Witt (1908–1988).
American screenwriter.
The Seventh Victim 43. *The Curse of the Cat People* 44. The Enchanted Cottage 44. *I Remember Mama* 47. Mrs Mike 50. Twelve to the Moon 58. Billy Budd 62, etc.

Bodrov, Sergei (1948–).
Russian director and screenwriter.
Sweet Dreams in the Grass/Sladkij Sok Vnutri Travy (wd) 84. My House on the Green Hills/Moj Dom Na Seljonych Cholmach (co-w) 86. The Nonprofessionals/Neprofessionaly (d) 88. Ser (wd) 89. The Cheater (co-w, d) 90. I Wanted to See Angels/Ya Hatiella Oovedit Angelov (co-w, d) 92. Roi Blanc, Dame Rouge 93. Somebody to Love (co-w) (US) 94. Prisoner of the Mountains/Kavkazskii Plennik (AAN) 96, etc.

Bodrov, Sergei, Jnr.
Leading Russian actor, the son of Sergei Bodrov.
Prisoner of the Mountains/Kavkazskii Plennik 96. Brother 97, etc.

Boehm, Karlheinz (1927–).
German leading actor who appeared in British and American films during the 60s.
Peeping Tom 60. Too Hot to Handle 60. Come Fly with Me 62. The Magnificent Rebel 62. The Wonderful World of the Brothers Grimm 62. Forever My Love 62. Rififi in Tokyo 63. The Venetian Affair 67. Martha 74. Fox and his Friends 75. Die Tannerhütt 76, etc.

Boehm, Sydney (1908–1990).
American screenwriter, a reliable hand at crime stories.
High Wall 48. *The Undercover Man* 49. Side Street 50. Mystery Street 50. *Union Station* 50. When Worlds Collide 52. The Savage 53. *The Big Heat* 53. The Secret of the Incas 54. Rogue Cop 54. Black Tuesday 54. Violent Saturday 55. The Tall Men 55. Hell on Frisco Bay 55. The Revolt of Mamie Stover 56. Harry Black 58. A Woman Obsessed (& p) 59. *Seven Thieves* (& p) 60. Shock Treatment 64. Sylvia 65. Rough Night in Jericho 67, etc.

Boetticher, Budd (1916–) (Oscar Boetticher).
American director, former bullfighter. Has not risen above a few striking co-features, but cineastes have made him the centre of a cult.
Autobiography: 1971, *When in Disgrace*.
The Missing Juror 44. Assigned to Danger 47. Sword of D'Artagnan 51. *The Bullfighter and the Lady* (& wp) (AANw) 51. Red Ball Express 52. Bronco Buster 52. Horizons West 52. East of Sumatra 53. Wings of the Hawk 53. The Man from the Alamo 53. The Magnificent Matador (& w) 55. The Killer is Loose 56. Seven Men from Now 56. Decision at Sundown 57. The Tall T 57. Buchanan Rides Alone 58. Ride Lonesome 59. Westbound 59. *The Rise and Fall of Legs Diamond* 60. *Arruza* 68. A Time for Dying 69. Two Mules for Sister Sara (w) 70, etc.

Bogarde, Sir Dirk (1921–) (Derek Van Den Bogaerd).
British leading actor of Dutch descent. In the 60s he moved to France and became a star of films by Visconti, Fassbinder, Cavani and other European directors. At the beginning of his career, he turned down an offer from Fox, who wanted to turn him into its new Spanish star and marry him off to one of its starlets, and instead signed a contract with Rank. He is also a novelist.
Autobiographies: 1977, *A Postillion Struck by Lightning*; 1978, *Snakes and Ladders*; 1983, *An Orderly Man*; 1986, *Backcloth*; 1989, *A Particular Friendship*; 1994, *A Short Walk from Harrods*; 1997, *Cleared for Take-Off*.
Biographies: 1974, *The Films of Dirk Bogarde* by Margaret Hinxman. 1996, *Dirk Bogarde, Rank Outsider* by Sheridan Morley.
Book: 1998, *For the Time Being* (collected journalism).
■ Esther Waters 47. Once a Jolly Swagman 48. *Quartet* 48. Dear Mr Prohack 49. Boys in Brown 49. So Long at the Fair 49. The Woman in Question 50. The Blue Lamp 50. Blackmailed 51. Penny Princess 51. The Gentle Gunman 52. Hunted 52. *Doctor in the House* 53. Appointment in London 53. They Who Dare 53. Desperate Moment 53. Simba 54. The Sea Shall Not Have Them 54. *The Sleeping Tiger* 54. For Better For Worse 54. Doctor at Sea 55. *Cast a Dark Shadow* 55. Doctor at Large 56. *The Spanish Gardener* 56. Ill Met By Moonlight 57. Campbell's Kingdom 58. The Wind Cannot Read 58. *A Tale of Two Cities* 58. The Doctor's Dilemma 59. Libel 59. Song Without End (as Liszt) (US) 60. The Angel Wore Red 60. The Singer Not the Song 60. *Victim* 61. We Joined the Navy (cameo) 62. HMS Defiant 62. The Password is Courage 63. I Could Go On Singing 63. The Mind Benders 63. *The Servant* (BFA) 63. Hot Enough for June 64. Doctor in Distress 64. *King and Country* 64. The High Bright Sun 65. *Darling* (BFA) 65. Modesty Blaise 66. Accident 67. Our Mother's House 67. Sebastian 67. The Fixer 68. Oh What a Lovely War 69. *The Damned* 69. Justine 69. *Death in Venice* 70. The Serpent 72. The Night Porter 74. Permission to Kill 75. Providence 77. A Bridge Too Far 77. Despair 78. The Patricia Neal Story (TV) 81. May We Borrow Your Husband? (TV) 85. The Vision 87. These Foolish Things/Daddy Nostalgie 90.
❝ I love the camera and it loves me. Well, not very much sometimes. But we're good friends – *D.B.*
I'll only work with new people. If you stick with your contemporaries, you're dead. – *D.B.*
I'm still in the shell, and you're not going to crack it, ducky. – *D.B. to Russell Harty in TV interview, 1986*
I've got a good left profile and a very bad right profile. I was the Loretta Young of my day. I was only ever photographed on the left-hand profile. – *D.B.*
I was as scrawny as a plucked hen. The Rank Organization did supply me with dumb-bells. All I did was put on two sweaters and then put my shirt on. – *D.B.*
Famous line (*Darling*): 'Your idea of fidelity is not having more than one man in bed at the same time.'

Bogart, Humphrey (1899–1957).
American leading actor who became one of Hollywood's imperishable personalities, a cynical but amiable tough guy in a trench coat who summed up all the *films noirs* of the 40s, after a long apprenticeship playing gangsters. His second wife was actress Mary Philips (1928–37), his third actress Mayo Methot (1938–45), and his fourth Lauren Bacall. Died from cancer.
Biographies: 1965, *Bogart* by Richard Gehman; 1965, *Bogey: The Good Bad Guy* by Ezra Goodman; 1974, *Humphrey Bogart* by Alan G. Barbour; 1975, *Humphrey Bogart* by Nathaniel Benchley; 1994, *Bogart: In Search of My Father* by Stephen Bogart; 1997, *Bogart* by A. M. Sperber and Eric Lax; 1997, *Bogart: A Life in Hollywood* by Jeffrey Meyers.
■ A Devil with Women 30. Up the River 30. Body and Soul 30. Bad Sister 30. Women of All Nations 31. A Holy Terror 31. Love Affair 32. Big City Blues 32. Three on a Match 32. Midnight 34. *The Petrified Forest* (his stage role as gangster Duke Mantee) 36. Two Against the World 36. Bullets or Ballots 36. China Clipper 36. Isle of Fury 36. The Great O'Malley 37. Black Legion 37. San Quentin 37. *Marked Woman* 37. Kid Galahad 37. *Dead End* 37. Stand In 37. Swing Your Lady 38. Men Are Such Fools 38. The Amazing Dr Clitterhouse 38. Racket Busters 38. *Angels with Dirty Faces* 38. Crime School 38. King of the Underworld 39. The Oklahoma Kid 39. Dark Victory 39. You Can't Get Away with Murder 39. *The Roaring Twenties* 39. The Return of Dr X (as a vampire) 39. Invisible Stripes 39. Virginia City 40. It All Came True 40. Brother Orchid 40. They Drive by Night 40. *High Sierra* 41. The Wagons Roll at Night 41. *The Maltese Falcon* (his archetypal performance) 41. All Through the Night 42. The Big Shot 42. *Across the Pacific* 42. *Casablanca* (AAN) 42. Action in the North Atlantic 43. Thank Your Lucky Stars 43. *Sahara* 43. *To Have and Have Not* 43. Passage to Marseilles 44. Conflict 45. *The Big Sleep* 46. The Two Mrs Carrolls 47. Dead Reckoning 47. Dark Passage 47. *The Treasure of the Sierra Madre* 47. *Key Largo* 48. Knock on any Door 49. Tokyo Joe 49. Chain Lightning 50. In a Lonely Place 50. *The Enforcer* 51. Sirocco 51. *The African Queen* (AA) 52. Deadline 52. Battle Circus 53. *Beat the Devil* 54. *The Caine Mutiny* (AAN) 54. Sabrina 54. *The Barefoot Contessa* 54. We're No Angels 55. The Left Hand of God 55. The Desperate Hours 55. The Harder they Fall 56.
~ Bogart also appeared in a 1930 short, *Broadway's Like That*; and he made uncredited gag appearances in *Two Guys from Milwaukee* 46, *Always Together* 48, *Road to Bali* 52, *The Love Lottery* 53.
✪ For contriving to represent both Action Man and Thinking Man of the early 40s; and for taking both these roles with a large pinch of salt. *Casablanca*.
❝ To some extent Bogart tended to live his film roles. As Dave Chase the Hollywood restaurateur once said:
Bogart's a helluva nice guy till 11.30 p.m. After that he thinks he's Bogart.
So in a way his aptest quotes are from his movies. As Rick in *Casablanca*:
I stick my neck out for nobody.
Or as Sam Spade in *The Maltese Falcon*:
Don't be so sure I'm as crooked as I'm supposed to be.
Truman Capote commented:
He was an actor without theories (well, one: that he should be highly paid), without temper but not without temperament; and because he understood that discipline was the better part of artistic survival, he lasted, he left his mark.
Stanley Kramer saw through him:
He was playing Bogart all the time, but he was really just a big sloppy bowl of mush.
One feels that this hits the nail pretty squarely on the head: Bogie was a nice guy who enjoyed a good grouch. About, for instance, the untrained beefcake stars of the early 50s, many of them picked up for tests from sidewalks and gas stations:
Shout 'gas' around the studios today, and half the young male stars will come running.
About acting theorists:
Do I subscribe to the Olivier school of acting? Ah, nuts. I'm an actor. I just do what comes naturally.
About the industry:
I don't hurt the industry. The industry hurts itself, by making so many lousy movies – as if General Motors deliberately put out a bad car.
And:
I made more lousy pictures than any actor in history.
And about life:
The trouble with the world is that everybody in it is about three drinks behind.
Other actors, perhaps, knew him better than he knew himself. Edward G. Robinson:
I always felt sorry for him – sorry that he had imposed upon himself the character with which he had become identified.
And Katharine Hepburn:
His yes meant yes, his no meant no. There was no bunkum about Bogart.
Famous lines:
(*The Maltese Falcon*) 'Don't be so sure I'm as crooked as I'm supposed to be.'
'Let's talk about the black bird.'
'We didn't exactly believe your story, Miss O'Shea, we believed your 200 dollars. You paid us more than if you'd been telling the truth, and enough more to make it all right.'
'Yes, angel, I'm gonna send you over.'
(*Across the Pacific*) 'When you're slapped, you're gonna take it and like it.'
(*Casablanca*) 'I came to Casablanca for the waters.' 'But we're in the middle of the desert.' 'I was misinformed.'
'Louis, I think this is the beginning of a beautiful friendship.'
(*The Big Sleep*) 'I don't mind if you don't like my manners. I don't like them myself. They're pretty bad. I grieve over them on long winter evenings.'

Bogart, Paul (1919–).
American director.
■ Halls of Anger 68. Marlowe 69. In Search of America (TV) 70. The Skin Game 71. Cancel My Reservation 71. Class of '44 73. Tell Me Where It Hurts (TV) 74. Winner Take All (TV) 75. Mr Ricco 75. Oh God You Devil 84. Torch Song

Trilogy 88. Broadway Bound (TV) 91. Gift of Love (TV) 94.

Bogdanovich, Peter (1939–).
American director with a penchant for reworking traditional themes; former film critic. He went bankrupt in the mid-80s after spending $5m of his own money on releasing and distributing *They All Laughed*, which grossed under $1m, and again declared himself bankrupt in the mid-90s. Married production designer, screenwriter and producer Polly Platt (1962–70); their daughter is actress Antonia Bogdanovich. He had a long relationship with actress Cybill SHEPHERD (1969–77). He also had a relationship with actress and *Playboy* model Dorothy STRATTEN, who was murdered in 1980 by her estranged husband, who then killed himself; later, he married her sister.
Autobiography: 1984, *The Killing of the Unicorn* (about the death of Stratten).
Books: 1992, *This Is Orson Welles*; 1997, *Who the Devil Made It?*
Biography: 1992, *Picture Shows: The Life and Films of Peter Bogdanovich* by Andrew Yule.
■ Voyage to the Planet of Prehistoric Women (as 'Derek Thomas') 68. *Targets* (& w) 68. *The Last Picture Show* (& w, AAN) 71. Directed by John Ford (doc) 71. *What's Up Doc?* (& w) 72. Paper Moon 73. Daisy Miller (& p) 74. At Long Last Love 75. Nickelodeon 77. Saint Jack 79. They All Laughed 81. Mask 85. Illegally Yours 88. Texasville 90. Noises Off 92. The Thing Called Love 93. To Sir with Love II (TV) 96.
❝ It isn't true that Hollywood is a bitter place, divided by hatred, greed and jealousy. All it takes to bring the community together is a flop by Peter Bogdanovich. – *Billy Wilder*

Bogeaus, Benedict (1904–1968).
American independent producer, formerly in real estate; his films were mildly interesting though eccentric.
The Bridge of San Luis Rey 44. Captain Kidd 45. The Diary of a Chambermaid 45. Christmas Eve 47. The Macomber Affair 47. Johnny One Eye 49. Passion 54. Slightly Scarlet 56. The Most Dangerous Man Alive 61, etc.

Bogosian, Eric (1953–).
American dramatist, actor and screenwriter, noted for his one-man shows.
Born in Flames 82. Special Effects 85. Funhouse (concert) 87. Talk Radio (co-w) 88. Suffering Bastards 89. Sex, Drugs, Rock & Roll (& w) 91. Naked in New York (as himself) 94. Dolores Claiborne 95. Under Siege 2: Dark Territory 95. The Substance of Fire 96. SubUrbia 97, etc.

Bohem, Leslie (1952–).
American screenwriter, a former rock musician.
The Horror Show/House III 89. A Nightmare on Elm Street: The Dream Child 89. Kid 90. Nowhere to Run 92. Twenty Bucks 93. Daylight 96. Dante's Peak 97, etc.

Bohnen, Roman (1894–1949).
German-born character actor, in Hollywood, usually in roles as a hard-working immigrant. Educated in Munich and at the University of Minnesota, he was on stage in Chicago from 1928, becoming a member of the Group Theatre in the early 30s. He was in films from 1937.
Vogues of 1938 37. Of Mice and Men 40. So Ends Our Night 41. Appointment for Love 41. Edge of Darkness 43. Mission to Moscow 43. The Song of Bernadette 43. *The Hitler Gang* 44. A Bell for Adano 45. The Strange Love of Martha Ivers 46. Mr Ace 46. The Best Years of Our Lives 46. Brute Force 47. Arch of Triumph 48. Night Has a Thousand Eyes 48, etc.

Bohr, José (1901–1994).
Chilean leading actor, screenwriter, director and songwriter. Born in Bonn, Germany, he worked in Chile at the transition from silent to sound films, starred in the first Spanish-language film made in Hollywood, *Shadows of Glory*, and spent the 30s and 40s making films in Mexico before working in Venezuela, Cuba and Argentina.
Como por un Tubo 19. Shadows of Glory/Sombras de Gloria 29. Marijuana, the Green Monster/Mariguana, El Mónstruo Verde 35. Flor del Carmen 44. My Silver Spurs/Mis Espuelas de Plata 48. La Cadena Infinita 49. El Gran Circo Chamorro 55. Un Chileno en España 62, many more.

Bohringer, Richard (1942–).
French leading actor, screenwriter and novelist. He began directing in the 90s.
L'Italien des Roses 72. Beau Masque (w) 72. Les Conquistadores 75. The Last Metro 80. Diva 81. La Bête Noire 83. Cap Canaille 83. Cent Francs l'Amour 85. Subway 85. Kamikaze 86. Le Grand Chemin 87. La Soule 88. The Cook, the Thief, His Wife and Her Lover 89. Stan the Flasher 90. Dien Bien Phu 91. Vézaz 91. La Reine Blanche 91. Gallant Ladies/Dames Galantes 91. City for Sale/Ville à Vendre 91. Wonderful Times/Une Epoque Formidable 91. L'Accompagnatrice 92. C'est Beau une Ville la Nuit (wd) 93. Tango 93. La Lumière des Etoiles Mortes 94. Le Parfum d'Yvonne 94. L'Amour Est un Jeu d'Enfant 94. The Smile/Le Sourire 94. Le Cri du Coeur 94. Fric-Frac 95. God, My Mother's Lover, and the Butcher's Son 95. Portraits Chinois 96. The Boxing Promoter/Le Montreur de Boxe 96. Wild Games/Combat de Fauves 97, etc.

Bohringer, Romane (1973–).
French leading actress, the daughter of Richard Bohringer.
Savage Nights 93. A Cause d'Elle 93. Mina Tannenbaum 94. Adultère Mode d'Emploi 95. Total Eclipse 95. Portraits Chinois 96. The Apartment/L'Appartement 96. The Chambermaid/La Femme de Chambre du Titanic 97. Vigo: Passion for Life (GB) 98, etc.

Bois, Curt (1900–1991).
Dapper German comedy actor, long in Hollywood playing head-waiters and pompous clerks.
Tovarich 37. Hollywood Hotel 38. *The Great Waltz* 38. Boom Town 40. Bitter Sweet 40. Hold Back the Dawn 41. Casablanca 42. The Desert Song 43. The Spanish Main 45. *The Woman in White* 48. The Great Sinner 49. Fortunes of Captain Blood 50. *Herr Puntilla and His Servant Matti* (Ger.) 54. Wings of Desire 87, many others.

Boisrond, Michel (1921–).
French director.
Mamzelle Pigalle 56. Une Parisienne 57. Come Dance with Me 59. Love and the Frenchwoman 60. Comment Réussir en Amour 62. Comment Epouser un Premier Ministre 64. L'Homme Qui Valait des Milliards 68. The Tender Moment 69. On Est Toujours Trop Bon avec les Femmes 71. Le Petit Poucet 72. Tell Me You Love Me 74. Catherine and Company 75, etc.

Boisset, Yves (1939–).
French director.
A Cop 70. Cobra 71. L'Attentat 72. Coplan Saves His Skin 72. Une Folle à Tuer 75. The Sheriff 76. The Purple Taxi 78. La Femme Flick 80. Le Prix du Danger 83. Canicule 84. Radio Corbeau 88. The Predators/Les Carnassiers 91. Double Identity 91. La Nuit du Herrison 93, etc.

Bolam, James (1938–).
Gritty English actor, mainly on television. Born in Sunderland, he trained at the Central School of Speech and Drama.
The Kitchen 61. A Kind of Loving 62. Otley 69. Crucible of Terror 71. Straight on Till Morning 72. O Lucky Man 73. In Celebration 74. The Likely Lads 76. The Limbo Connection (TV) 79. As You Like It (TV) 80. The Plague Dogs (voice) 82. Clockwork Mice 95. Eleven Men against Eleven (TV) 96. Stella Does Tricks 96. Have Your Cake and Eat It (TV) 97, etc.
TV series: *The Likely Lads* 64–66. *Whatever Happened to the Likely Lads?* 73–74. *When the Boat Comes In* 76–77. *Only When I Laugh* 79–83. The Beiderbecke Affair 85. Room at the Bottom 86–87. The Beiderbecke Tapes 87. The Beiderbecke Connection 88. Second Thoughts 92–94.

Boland, Bridget (1904–1988).
British playwright and screenwriter.
Gaslight 39. Spies of the Air 40. The Lost People 48. The Prisoner 54. War and Peace 56. Anne of the Thousand Days (co-w, AAN) 69, etc.

Boland, Mary (1880–1965).
American stage tragedienne who in middle age settled in Hollywood and played innumerable fluttery matrons: appeared in a series of domestic comedies with Charles Ruggles. Born in Philadelphia, she was on stage from 1901.
The Edge of the Abyss 16. His Temporary Wife 18. Personal Maid 31. *If I Had a Million* 32. *Three-Cornered Moon* 33. Four Frightened People 34. *Down to Their Last Yacht* 34. *Ruggles of Red Gap* 35. Early to Bed 36. Wives Never Know 36. Mama Runs Wild 37. Little Tough Guys in Society 38. *The Women* 39. New Moon 40. *Pride and Prejudice* (as Mrs Bennet) 40. In Our Time 44. Nothing But Trouble 44. Julia Misbehaves 48. Guilty Bystander 50, many others.

Boles, John (1895–1969).
American operetta singer who apart from musicals proved himself useful to Hollywood as a well-behaved 'other man'. Born in Greenville, Texas, he studied at the University of Texas, intending to become a doctor, but settled for the stage instead, making his debut in 1923.
■ So This Is Marriage 24. Excuse Me 25. The Loves of Sunya 27. The Shepherd of the Hills 28. We Americans 28. The Bride of the Colorado 28. Fazil 28. The Water Hole 28. Virgin Lips 28. Man-made Woman 28. Romance of the Underworld 28. The Last Warning 29. *The Desert Song* 29. Scandal 29. *Rio Rita* 29. Song of the West 30. Captain of the Guard 30. *The King of Jazz* 30. One Heavenly Night 30. Resurrection 31. Seed 31. Frankenstein (as Victor, friend of the family) 31. Good Sport 31. Careless Lady 31. *Back Street* 32. Six Hours to Live 32. Child of Manhattan 32. My Lips Betray 33. *Only Yesterday* 33. I Believed in You 34. Music in the Air 34. Beloved 34. Bottoms Up 34. Stand Up and Cheer 34. The Life of Vergie Winters 34. Wild Gold 34. The Age of Innocence 34. The White Parade 34. Orchids to You 34. Curly Top 35. Redheads on Parade 35. The Littlest Rebel 35. Rose of the Rancho 36. A Message to Garcia 36. Craig's Wife 36. As Good as Married 37. *Stella Dallas* 37. Fight for Your Lady 37. She Married an Artist 38. Romance in the Dark 38. Sinners in Paradise 38. The Road to Happiness 42. Between Us Girls 42. Thousands Cheer 43. Babes in Bagdad 52.

Boleslawski, Richard (1889–1937) (Boleslaw Ryszart Srzednicki).
Polish stage director, formerly with the Moscow Arts Theatre, who came to Hollywood in 1930 and made a few stylish movies.
■ Three Meetings (USSR) 17. Treasure Girl 30. The Last of the Lone Wolf 31. Woman Pursued 31. The Gay Diplomat 31. Rasputin and the Empress 32. Storm at Daybreak 33. Beauty for Sale 33. Fugitive Lovers 33. Men in White 34. Operator 13 34. *The Painted Veil* 34. *Clive of India* 35. *Les Misérables* 35. O'Shaughnessy's Boy 35. *Metropolitan* 35. Three Godfathers 36. *Theodora Goes Wild* 36. *The Garden of Allah* 36. The Last of Mrs Cheyney 37.

Bolger, Ray (1904–1987).
Rubber-legged American eccentric dancer, a stage star who made too few films.
■ The Great Ziegfeld 36. *Rosalie* 37. Sweethearts 38. *The Wizard of Oz* (as the scarecrow) 39. Sunny 41. Stage Door Canteen 43. Four Jacks and a Jill 44. *The Harvey Girls* 46. *Look for the Silver Lining* 49. *Where's Charley?* 52. April in Paris 52. Babes in Toyland 60. The Daydreamer 66. The Entertainer (TV) 75. The Captains and the Kings (TV) 76. Heaven Only Knows (TV) 79. The Runner Stumbles 79. Just You and Me Kid 79. That's Dancing 84. That's Entertainment III 94.
TV series: Where's Raymond 52.

Bolkan, Florinda (1941–) (Florinda Suares Bulcao).
Spanish-Indian leading lady.
Candy 68. The Damned 69. Investigation of a Citizen 70. The Last Valley 70. The Anonymous Venetian 71. Detective Belli 71. Romance 71. The Island 72. A Man to Respect 72. Lizard in a Woman's Skin 72. Hearts and Minds 74. Royal Flash 75. The Right to Love 76. Day that Shook the World 78. The Word 78. Collector's Item 89. Miliardi 91. Bela Donna 98, etc.

Bolling, Claude (1930–).
French composer and jazz pianist.
Bonjour Cinéma 55. Men and Women/L'Homme à Femmes 60. The Hands of Orlac 62. Cadet d'Eau Douce 69. Borsalino 70. Catch Me a Spy 71. Borsalino and Co. 74. Tell Me You Love Me/Dis-moi que Tu M'Aimes 74. Le Gitan 75. Les Passagers 76. Silver Bears 78. California Suite 78. The Awakening 80. Willie and Phil 80. Le Léopard 83. Bay Boy 84. On ne Meurt que Deux Fois 85. La Rumba 87. Luck or Coincidence/Hasards ou Coincidences (co-m) 98, etc.

Bolling, Tiffany (1947–).
American leading lady.
Kingdom of the Spiders 77. Bonnie's Kids 82. Ecstasy 84. Love Scenes 84, etc.
TV series: The New People 69–70.

Bologna, Joseph (1936–).
American actor who with his wife Renee Taylor usually writes his own material.
Lovers and Other Strangers (co-w only) (AANw) 70. Made for Each Other 71. Honor Thy Father (TV) 73. Mixed Company 74. Woman of the Year (TV) 75. The Big Bus 76. Chapter Two 79. Blame It On Rio 84. The Woman in Red 84. Transylvania 6–5000 85. It Had To Be You (wd) 89. Coup de Ville 90. Alligator II: The Mutation 91. Revenge of the Nerds IV: Nerds in Love (TV) 94. Love Is All There Is (& wd) 96, etc.
TV series: Rags to Riches 87.

Bolognini, Mauro (1922–).
Italian director.
Wild Love 55. Young Husbands 58. La Notte Brava 59. Il Bell'Antonio 60. La Viaccia 61. Senilita 62. Le Bambole 65. I Tre Volti 65. The Oldest Profession 67. Arabella 67. That Splendid November 68. Metello 70. Bubu 71. Down the Ancient Stairs 75. Black Journal 77. La Vera Storia della Signora delle Camelie 80. La Venexiana 85. Mosca Addio 87. A Time of Indifference (TV) 88. Husbands and Lovers 92, etc.

Bolt, Ben (1952–).
English director, the son of Robert Bolt.
Rainy Day Woman (TV) 86. The Big Town 87. Scarlet and Black (TV) 93, etc.

Bolt, Robert (1924–1995).
British playwright who turned to screenwriting and direction. Actress Sarah Miles was his second wife (1967–1976) and his fourth in 1988.
Biography: 1998, *Robert Bolt: Scenes from Two Lives* by Adrian Turner.
Lawrence of Arabia (AA) 62. *Doctor Zhivago* (AA) 65. *A Man For All Seasons* (AA) 66. Ryan's Daughter 70. Lady Caroline Lamb (& d) 72. The Bounty 84. The Mission 86.

Bolton, Guy (1884–1979).
English-born playwright, novelist and screenwriter. Born in Broxbourne, Hertfordshire, of American parents, he began as an architect before collaborating on his first play in 1911. He is best known for his association with P. G. WODEHOUSE on plays and musicals. He became an American citizen in 1956. Married four times.
Autobiography: 1953, *Bring On the Girls* (with P. G. Wodehouse).
Grounds for Divorce 25. The Love Doctor 29. The Love Parade 30. Girl Crazy (oa) 32. Ladies Should Listen (oa) 34. Anything Goes (oa) 35. Rosalie (oa) 37. Weekend at the Waldorf 45. Anastasia (oa) 56, etc.
❝ Bolton, as George Jean Nathan would say, knows his job from the first spoonful of soup to the final walnut. – *P. G. Wodehouse*

Bon Jovi, Jon (1962–) (John Bongiovi).
American rock singer, composer and actor, leader of the hard rock group Bon Jovi.
Young Guns II (a, s) 90. Moonlight and Valentino (a) 95. The Leading Man (a) 97.

Bonaduce, Danny (1959–).
American child actor, best known for his role as Danny in TV's *The Partridge Family* 70–74. Later worked in radio.
Corvette Summer 78. H.O.T.S. 79. Deadly Intruder 85, etc.
TV series: The Partridge Family, 2200 A.D. (voice) 74–75.
❝ What we often fail to appreciate is that being little and cute may have been our only skill. – *D.B.*

Bonanova, Fortunio (1893–1969).
Spanish opera singer and impresario who after managing his own repertory company in America in the 30s, settled in Hollywood to play excitable foreigners.
Careless Lady 32. Podoroso Caballero 36. Tropic Holiday 38. La Immaculada 39. I Was an Adventuress 40. *Citizen Kane* (as the music teacher) 41. Blood and Sand 41. The Black Swan 42. Five Graves to Cairo 43. For Whom the Bell Tolls 43. Going My Way 44. Double Indemnity 44.

Monsieur Beaucaire 46. The Fugitive 47. Whirlpool 50. September Affair 51. The Moon is Blue 53. An Affair to Remember 57. Thunder in the Sun 59. The Running Man 63. Million Dollar Collar 69, many others.

Bond, Derek (1919–).
British light leading man with varied pre-film experience including the Grenadier Guards.
The Captive Heart 46. *Nicholas Nickleby* (title role) 47. *Scott of the Antarctic* 48. Broken Journey 48. The Weaker Sex 48. Christopher Columbus 49. Marry Me 49. Uncle Silas 50. The Hour of Thirteen 52. Stranger from Venus 54. Svengali 55. Trouble in Store 55. Gideon's Day 58. The Hand 60. Saturday Night Out 64. Wonderful Life 64. Press for Time 66. When Eight Bells Toll 71, etc.

Bond, Gary (1940–1995).
British leading man, mainly on the stage. Died of cancer. His lovers included actor Jeremy Brett.
Zulu 64. Anne of the Thousand Days 70. *Outback* 70, etc.
TV series: Frontier 68.

Bond, James, III.
American actor, screenwriter and producer-director.
The Fish that Saved Pittsburgh (a) 79. The Sky Is Gray (a) (TV) 80. Def by Temptation (a, p, wd) 90, etc.

Bond, Julian (1930–).
British writer, mainly for TV. *A Man of Our Times*, Love for Lydia, Fair Stood the Wind for France, The Far Pavilions, Strangers and Brothers.
Films: The Shooting Party 84. The Whistle Blower 87.

Bond, Lilian (1910–1991).
British leading lady in American films of the 30s.
Just a Gigolo 31. Fireman Save My Child 32. *The Old Dark House* 32. Hot Pepper 33. Affairs of a Gentleman 34. China Seas 35. The Housekeeper's Daughter 39. The Westerner 40. The Picture of Dorian Gray 45. Man in the Attic 54. Pirates of Tripoli 55, etc.

Bond, Sudie (1923–1984).
American character actress in wisecracking roles.
A Thousand Clowns 65. Cold Turkey 70. They Might Be Giants 72. Come Back to the 5 and Dime Jimmy Dean, Jimmy Dean 82. Tomorrow 83. Silkwood 83. I Am the Cheese 83, etc.
TV series: Temperatures Rising 73–74. Flo 80–81.

Bond, Tommy (1927–).
American child actor who played Butch in the Our Gang comedies of the 30s; he also appeared in a few features before quitting acting in the early 50s.
Kid Millions 34. City Streets 38. A Little Bit of Heaven 40. Man from Frisco 44. Call Me Mister 51, etc.

Bond, Ward (1903–1960).
Burly American actor who from the coming of sound distinguished himself in small roles, especially in John Ford films; but it took TV to make him a star. Died of a heart attack.
The Big Trail 30. When Strangers Marry 33. Devil Dogs of the Air 35. You Only Live Once 37. The Oklahoma Kid 39. Young Mr Lincoln 39. Gone with the Wind 39. The Grapes of Wrath 40. *Tobacco Road* 41. The Maltese Falcon 41. Gentleman Jim 42. A Guy Named Joe 43. They Were Expendable 45. My Darling Clementine 46. Fort Apache 48. *Wagonmaster* 50. *The Quiet Man* 52. *Blowing Wild* 53. The Long Gray Line 55. *The Searchers* 56. *The Wings of Eagles* 57. *The Halliday Brand* 57. *Rio Bravo* 59, many others.
TV series: *Wagon Train* 57–60.

Bondarchuk, Sergei (1920–1994).
Russian actor and director.
The Young Guards (a) 48. The Grasshopper (a) 55. Othello (a) 56. *Destiny of a Man* (ad) 59. *War and Peace* (ad) (AA) 64. *Waterloo* (d) 70. They Fought for Their Country 75. The Steppe 78. Ten Days That Shook the World 82. Boris Godunov 86. Quiet Flows the Don 92, etc.

Bondi, Beulah (1888–1981) (Beulah Bondy).
Distinguished American character actress who from early middle age played cantankerous or kindly old ladies.
■ Street Scene 31. Arrowsmith 31. Rain 32. The Stranger's Return 33. Christopher Bean 33. Finishing School 34. The Painted Veil 34. Two Alone 34. Registered Nurse 34. Ready for Love 34. Bad Boy 35. The Good Fairy 35. The Invisible Ray 36. The Trail of the Lonesome Pine 36. The Moon's Our Home 36. The Case Against Mrs Ames 36. Hearts Divided 36. The Gorgeous Hussy (AAN) 36. *Maid of Salem* 37. *Make Way for Tomorrow* 37. The Buccaneer 38. Of Human Hearts (AAN) 38. Vivacious Lady 38. The Sisters 38. On Borrowed Time 39. Mr Smith Goes to Washington 39. The Underpup 39. Remember the Night 40. *Our Town* 40. The Captain is a Lady 40. Penny Serenade 41. Shepherd of the Hills 41. One Foot in Heaven 41. Tonight We Raid Calais 43. Watch on the Rhine 43. I Love a Soldier 44. She's a Soldier Too 44. Our Hearts Were Young and Gay 44. And Now Tomorrow 44. The Very Thought of You 44. *The Southerner* 45. Back to Bataan 45. Breakfast in Hollywood 46. Sister Kenny 46. *It's a Wonderful Life* 46. High Conquest 47. The Sainted Sisters 48. The Snake Pit 48. So Dear to My Heart 48. The Life of Riley 49. Reign of Terror 49. Mr Soft Touch 49. The Baron of Arizona 50. The Furies 50. Lone Star 52. Latin Lovers 53. *Track of the Cat* 54. Back from Eternity 56. The Unholy Wife 57. The Big Fisherman 59. A Summer Place 59. *Tammy Tell Me True* 61. The Wonderful World of the Brothers Grimm 62. Tammy and the Doctor 63. She Waits (TV) 71.
~B.B. always said that her great regret was being passed over for the role of Ma Joad in *The Grapes of Wrath*.

Bonerz, Peter (1938–).
American comic actor and director.
Funnyman (a, co-w) 67. Medium Cool (a) 69. Catch-22 (a) 70. Fuzz (a) 72. Serial (a) 80. Nobody's Perfekt (a, d) 81. Police Academy VI: City Under Siege (d) 89, etc.
TV series: The Bob Newhart Show 72–78. 9 to 5 82–83.

Bonet, Lisa (1967–).
American actress, born in San Francisco. She is best known for her television role as Denise in *The Cosby Show*.
Angel Heart 87. Bank Robber 93. Lights Out 93. Enemy of the State 98, etc.
TV series: The Cosby Show 84–91. A Different World 87–88.

Bonham Carter, Helena (1966–).
British leading lady. She has been romantically linked with actor-director Kenneth Branagh.
Lady Jane 84. A Room with a View 85. Maurice 87. The Vision 87. La Maschera 88. Francesco 89. Getting It Right 89. Hamlet 90. Where Angels Fear to Tread 91. Howards End 92. Mary Shelley's Frankenstein 94. Mighty Aphrodite 95. Twelfth Night 96. Portraits Chinois (Fr.) 96. Margaret's Museum 95. The Wings of the Dove (AAN) 97. Merlin (TV) 98. The Theory of Flight 98, etc.
❝ I hate this image of me as a prim Edwardian. I want to shock everyone. – *H.B.C.*

Bonnaire, Sandrine (1967–).
French leading actress.
To Our Loves/A Nos Amours 83. Sans Toit ni Loi 85. Police 85. Sous le Soleil de Satan 87. Monsieur Hire 89. Prisoner of the Desert/La Captive du Désert 90. Towards Evening/Verso Sera 90. The Sky Above Paris/Le Ciel de Paris 91. Prague 92. The Plague/La Peste 92. Jeanne la Pucelle 94. Confidences d'un Inconnu 95. La Nuit des Cerfs-Volants 95. A Judgment in Stone/La Cérémonie 95. Secrets Shared with a Stranger 95. Secret Défense 97. Stolen Life/Voleur de Vie 98, etc.

Bonnell, Lee (1919–1986).
American actor who won a talent contest and an RKO contract in the late 30s, when he was briefly known as Terry Belmont before reverting to his own name. He quit movies to become a successful insurance executive. Married actress Gale Storm.
Men against the Sky 40. Lady Scarface 41. Look Who's Laughing 41. Army Surgeon 42. Criminal Court 46. San Quentin 46. Smart Woman 48, etc.

Bonner, Margerie (1905–1988).
American actress, in silent films, often westerns, as a juvenile. She was the second wife (1940–57) of novelist Malcolm Lowry, serving as a model for the character of Yvonne, a former film star, in his novel *Under the Volcano*, filmed in 1984 with Jacqueline Bisset in the role, and for Primrose Wilderness in his posthumously published *Dark as the Grave wherein My Friend Is Laid*.

Bonner, Priscilla (1899–1996).
American leading lady of silent films, the sister of Margerie Bonner. Retired in 1928.
The Man Who Had Everything 20. Custer's Last Stand 21. Chalk Marks 24. Red Kimono 25. Charley's Aunt 25. Three Bad Men 26. It 27. Golden Shackles 28, etc.

Bonnot, Françoise (1939–).
French editor, now working in international films.
Guns for San Sebastian 68. Z (AA) 69. The Confession 70. State of Siege 73. Special Section 75. The Tenant 76. Black and White and in Colour 76. The Cassandra Crossing 77. I Sent a Letter to My Love 80. Missing 82. Hannah K 83. Swann in Love 84. Year of the Dragon 85. The Sicilian 87. Fat Man and Little Boy/The Shadowmakers 89. 1492: Conquest of Paradise 92. The Apartment/L'Appartement 96. Mad City (US) 97. Place Vendôme 98, etc.

Bono, Sonny (1935–1998) (Salvatore Bono).
American actor, a former pop singer and songwriter. Together with his then-wife Cher he had several hits as Sonny and Cher. He later became mayor of Palm Springs, and in 1994 a Republican Congressman.
Good Times 67. Murder on Flight 502 (TV) 75. Escape to Athena 79. Airplane II: The Sequel 82. Balboa (TV) 82. Troll 85. Dirty Laundry 87. Hairspray 88. Under the Boardwalk 89, etc.
TV series: The Sonny and Cher Comedy Show 71–74. The Sonny Comedy Revue 74. The Sonny and Cher Show 76–77.
❝ Sonny is perfectly at home there [Congress]. Politicians are one step below used-car salesmen. – *Cher*

Bonomo, Joe (1902–1978).
Muscular American strongman of silent pictures, often in serials. In films from 1911, he retired with the coming of sound and turned to merchandising physical fitness.
Autobiography: 1968, *The Strongman*.
The Hunchback of Notre Dame 23. Beasts of Paradise (serial) 23. The Iron Man (serial) 24. The Flaming Frontier 26. Heroes of the Wild (serial) 27. The Phantom of the West (serial) 31. Island of Lost Souls 33, etc.

Booke, Sorrell (1926–1994).
Chubby American character actor.
Gone are the Days 63. Fail Safe 64. Black Like Me 64. Lady in a Cage 64. Up the Down Staircase 67. Slaughterhouse Five 71. The Take 72. The Iceman Cometh 73. Bank Shot 74. Special Delivery 76. Freaky Friday 77. The Other Side of Midnight 77, etc.
TV series: The Dukes of Hazzard 79–85.

Boone, Daniel (1734–1820).
American pioneer and Indian scout who helped to open up Kentucky and Missouri. He has been frequently portrayed in films, notably by George O'Brien (*Daniel Boone*, 1936), David Bruce (*Young Daniel Boone*, 1950) and Bruce Bennett (*Daniel Boone, Trail Blazer*, 1956). In 1964 began a long-running TV series, *Daniel Boone*, starring Fess Parker.

Boone, Pat (1934–).
Gentle-mannered American pop singer of the 50s; never quite made it as a straight actor, perhaps because he paraded his lack of private vices.
■ *Bernardine* 57. April Love 57. Mardi Gras 58. *Journey to the Centre of the Earth* 59. All Hands on Deck 61. State Fair 62. The Yellow Canary 63. The Main Attraction 63. The Horror of it All (GB) 63. Never Put it in Writing (GB) 64. Goodbye Charlie 64. The Greatest Story Ever Told 65. The Perils of Pauline 67. The Pigeon (TV) 69. The Cross and the Switchblade 70.

Boone, Richard (1917–1981).
Craggy American character actor, often in menacing roles.
■ Halls of Montezuma 51. Call Me Mister 51. The Desert Fox 51. Return of the Texan 52. Red Skies of Montana 52. Kangaroo 52. The Way of a Gaucho 52. Man on a Tightrope 53. *Vicki* 53. *The Robe* 53. City of Bad Men 53. Beneath the Twelve-Mile Reef 53. The Siege at Red River 54. Dragnet 54. The Raid 54. Battle Stations 55. *Man Without a Star* 55. Ten Wanted Men 55. Robbers' Roost 55. Star in the Dust 56. Away All Boats 56. Lizzie 57. Garment Center 57. The Tall T 57. I Bury the Living 58. *The Alamo* 60. A Thunder of Drums 61. *Rio Conchos* 64. *The War Lord* 65. Hombre 67. Kona Coast 68. The Night of the Following Day 69. *The Arrangement* 69. Madron 70. *The Kremlin Letter* 70. Big Jake 71. In Broad Daylight (TV) 72. A Tattered Web (TV) 72. Goodnight My Love (TV) 72. Deadly Harvest (TV) 72. The Great Niagara (TV) 74. Against a Crooked Sky 75. The Shootist 76. God's Gun 77. The Big Sleep 78. Winter Kills 79. The Bushido Blade 79.
TV series: *Medic* 54–55. *Have Gun Will Travel* 57–62. *The Richard Boone Show* 63. Hec Ramsey 72–74.

Boorman, John (1933–).
British director, from TV.
Autobiography: 1985, *Money into Light: The Emerald Forest, a Diary*.
Catch Us if You Can 65. *Point Blank* (US) 67. *Hell in the Pacific* (US) 69. Leo the Last 70. *Deliverance* (AAN) 72. Zardoz (& w) 74. Exorcist II: The Heretic 77. Long Shot (as actor, in the role of himself) 78. Excalibur 81. Dream One (p only) 82. The Emerald Forest (& p) 85. *Hope and Glory* (& p) (AAN) 87. Where the Heart Is (p, wd) 90. I Dreamt I Woke Up (doc) 91. Beyond Rangoon 95. The General (Ire.) 98, etc.

Booth, Anthony (1937–).
British general-purpose actor: everything from Nazis to layabouts.
Mix Me a Person 62. The L-Shaped Room 62. Of Human Bondage 64. Till Death Us Do Part 68. Girl With a Pistol 69. The Garnett Saga 72, etc.
TV series: *Till Death Us Do Part* 67–71.

Booth, Connie (1941–).
American actress in Britain, formerly married to John Cleese, with whom she wrote, and starred in, the TV sitcom *Fawlty Towers*.
Monty Python and the Holy Grail 74. Little Lord Fauntleroy (TV) 80. The Hound of the Baskervilles 83. 84 Charing Cross Road 86. Hawks 88. American Friends 91. Smack and Thistle 91. Leon the Pig Farmer 92. The Buccaneers (TV) 95, etc.

Booth, Edwina (1909–1991) (Josephine Constance Woodruff).
American leading lady of the late 20s, best known for catching jungle fever while filming in Africa for *Trader Horn* 30. She retired shortly after.

Booth, Harry.
British director, former editor.
Blitz on Britain 59. A King's Story 64. On the Buses 71. Mutiny on the Buses 72. Go for a Take 72, etc.

Booth, James (1930–) (David Geeves-Booth).
British character actor who can play innocent or villainous, now in America.
The Trials of Oscar Wilde 60. The Hellions 61. In the Doghouse 62. Sparrows Can't Sing 63. French Dressing 63. *Zulu* 64. The Secret of My Success 65. Ninety Degrees in the Shade 66. *Robbery* 67. The Bliss of Mrs Blossom 68. The Man Who Had Power Over Women 70. Darker Than Amber 70. Macho Callahan 71. Revenge 71. That'll Be the Day 74. Brannigan 75. Airport 77 77. Wheels (TV) 78. It's Not the Size that Counts 79. The Jazz Singer 80. Zorro the Gay Blade 81. The Cowboy and the Ballerina (TV) 84. Bad Guys 85. Programmed to Kill 87. American Ninja 4: The Annihilator 91, etc.

Booth, Karin (1923–1992) (aka Katherine Booth).
American leading lady of second features.
Big City 48. Last of the Buccaneers 50. The Texas Rangers 50. Cripple Creek 52. Let's Do It Again 53. Seminole Uprising 55. The Crooked Sky (GB) 56. Beloved Infidel 59, etc.

Booth, Margaret (1898–).
Distinguished American editor, long at MGM, latterly as supervisor. She was given an honorary Oscar in 1977.
Memory Lane 26. The Bridge of San Luis Rey 29. Cuban Love Song 31. New Moon 31. Susan Lenox 31. Strange Interlude 31. Bombshell 33.

Dancing Lady 33. The Barretts of Wimpole Street 34. Mutiny on the Bounty 35. Camille 36. Romeo and Juliet 36. The Way We Were 73. The Sunshine Boys 76. Murder by Death 76. California Suite 78. Annie 82, many others.

Booth, Shirley (1907–1992) (Thelma Ford Booth).
Distinguished American stage actress who came to the screen for a few middle-aged roles.
■ *Come Back Little Sheba* (AA) 52. About Mrs Leslie 53. Main Street to Broadway 53. Hot Spell 57. *The Matchmaker* 59. The Smugglers (TV) 68.
TV series: *Hazel* 61–65. A Touch of Grace 73.

Boothe, Powers (1949–).
Powerful American lead actor, on TV in the mid-80s as Philip Marlowe.
A Cry for Love (TV) 80. Cruising 81. *Guyana Tragedy* (TV) 81. Southern Comfort 81. Chandlertown (TV) 83. Red Dawn 84. The Emerald Forest 85. Extreme Prejudice 87. By Dawn's Early Light 89. Tombstone 94. Blue Sky (made 91) 94. Nixon 95. Sudden Death 95. True Women (TV) 97. U-Turn 97, etc.

Borchers, Cornell (1925–) (Cornelia Bruch).
German leading actress, in a few international films.
The Big Lift 50. The Divided Heart (BFA) 55. Never Say Goodbye 56. Istanbul 57. Oasis 60, etc.

Borden, Lizzie (1954–).
American director and screenwriter of independent films, a former editor.
Born in Flames 82. Working Girls 86. Love Crimes 92. Erotique (co-d) 94.

Borden, Olive (1907–1947) (Sybil Tinkle).
American leading lady of the 20s. She failed to make the transition to sound and died in poverty, an alcoholic.
Dressmaker from Paris 25. Three Bad Men 26. Fig Leaves 26. The Joy Girl 26. Pajamas 26. Gang War 28. Virgin Lips 28. Love in the Desert 29. Dance Hall 29. Hello Sister 30, etc.

Bordoni, Irene (1895–1953).
Corsican-American revue comedienne who left Broadway to make only three films.
■ Show of Shows 28. Paris 30. Louisiana Purchase 42.

Borg, Carl Oscar (1878–1947).
Swedish-born art director, a former merchant seaman, in the US from the early 1900s; also a painter.
The Black Pirate 26. The Winning of Barbara Worth 26. The Magic Flame 27. *The Night of Love* 27. The Gaucho 28, etc.

Borg, Veda Ann (1915–1973).
American character actress, the archetypal hard-boiled blonde of a hundred second features.
Three Cheers for Love 36. Alcatraz Island 37. She Loved a Fireman 38. Café Hostess 39. Glamour for Sale 40. The Pittsburgh Kid 41. Duke of the Navy 42. Isle of Forgotten Sins 43. Smart Guy 44. What a Blonde 45. Mildred Pierce 45. Accomplice 46. Big Town 47. Blonde Savage 48. Forgotten Women 49. The Kangaroo Kid 50. Big Jim McLain 52. Three Sailors and a Girl 53. Bitter Creek 54. Guys and Dolls 55. Frontier Gambler 56. The Fearmakers 58. Thunder in the Sun 59. The Alamo 60, many others.

Borgia, Cesare (1476–1507) and ½Lucretia½ (1480–1519).
The son and daughter of Pope Alexander VI were suspected of several family murders. On screen they have been played as melodramatic figures, notably by MacDonald Carey and Paulette Goddard (*Bride of Vengeance* 49), Orson Welles (*Prince of Foxes* 49), Pedro Armendariz and Martine Carol (*Lucretia Borgia* 52), and Franco Fabrizi and Belinda Lee (*Nights of Lucretia Borgia* 59). In 1981 the BBC produced a risible mini-series on the subject, with Adolfo Celi unintelligible as the founder of the clan.

Borgnine, Ernest (1917–) (Ermes Borgnino).
Forceful American character actor who after stage and TV work was typecast by Hollywood as a heavy until *Marty* gave him star status. His wives include actresses Katy Jurado (1959–64) and Ethel Merman (1964).
China Corsair 51. The Whistle at Eaton Falls 51. The Mob 51. *From Here to Eternity* 53. The Stranger Wore a Gun 53. Demetrius and the Gladiators 54. The Bounty Hunter 54. Johnny Guitar 54. Vera Cruz 54. *Bad Day at Black Rock* 54. Run for Cover 55. *Marty* (AA, BFA) 55. Violent Saturday 55. The Last Command 55. The Square Jungle 56. Jubal 56. *The Catered Affair* 56. *The Best Things in Life Are Free* 56. Three Brave Men 57. *The Vikings* 58. The Badlanders 58. Torpedo Run 58. The Rabbit Trap 58. Man on a String 60. *Pay or Die* 60. Go Naked in the World 61. Summer of the Seventeenth Doll 61. Les Guerrilleros (Sp.) 61. Il Re de Poggioreale (It.) 61. Il Giudizio Universale (It.) 61. Seduction of the South (It.) 62. Barabbas 62. McHale's Navy 64. The Flight of the Phoenix 65. The Oscar 66. *The Dirty Dozen* 67. Chuka 67. *Ice Station Zebra* 68. The Split 68. The Legend of Lylah Clare 68. The Wild Bunch 69. Suppose They Gave a War and Nobody Came 69. Vengeance is Mine (It.) 69. The Adventurers 70. Bunny O'Hare 71. Hannie Caulder 71. Rain for a Dusty Summer 71. The Trackers (TV) 71. Willard 71. Tough Guy 72. The Revengers 72. What Happened to the Mysterious Mr Foster? (TV) 72. The Poseidon Adventure 72. Emperor of the North Pole 73. The Neptune Factor 73. Law and Disorder 74. Sunday in the Country 74. Twice in a Lifetime (TV) 74. The Devil's Rain 75. Cleaver and Haven (TV) 76. Hustle 76. Shoot 76. The Prince and the Pauper 77. Jesus of Nazareth (TV) 77. The Greatest 77. Convoy 78. The Black Hole 79. The Double McGuffin 79. All Quiet on the Western Front (TV) 79. When Time Ran Out 80. Escape from New York 81. High Risk 81. Deadly Blessing 81. Superfuzz 81. Blood Feud (TV) 82. Young Warriors 83. Masquerade (TV) 83. Airwolf (TV) 84. The Last Days of Pompeii (TV) 84. Codename Wildgeese 84. The Manhunt 84. The Dirty Dozen – The Next Mission (TV) 85. Skeleton Coast 88. Spike of Bensonhurst 88. Laser Mission 89. Turnaround 89. Ski School 89. Any Man's Death 90. Moving Target 90. Appearances (TV) 90. Mistress (as himself) 92. The Legend of O. B. Taggart 94. Eighth Day 96. McHale's Navy 97. Baseketball 98. Small Soldiers (voice) 98. 12 Bucks 98. An All Dogs Christmas Carol 98, etc.
TV series: *McHale's Navy* 62–65. Future Cop 76. Airwolf 84–86. The Single Guy 95– .

Boris, Robert.
American screenwriter and director.
Electra Glide in Blue (w) 73. Some Kind of Hero (co-w) 82. Doctor Detroit (co-w) 83. Oxford Blues (wd) (GB) 84. Steele Justice (wd) 87. Buy and Cell (d) 89. Frank and Jesse (wd) 94, etc.

Bornedal, Ole (1959–).
Danish director and screenwriter, who remade his first feature for Hollywood.
Nightwatch/Nattevagten 94. Nightwatch (US) 97. Mimic (US) (p only) 97, etc.

Boros, Ferike (1880–1951).
Hungarian actress in Hollywood.
Little Caesar 30. Svengali 31. Huddle 32. Humanity 33. The Fountain 34. Make Way for Tomorrow 37. Love Affair 39. Argentine Nights 40. Caught in the Draft 41. Once Upon a Honeymoon 42. The Doughgirls 44. The Specter of the Rose 46, etc.

Borowczyk, Walerian (1923–).
Polish writer-director, formerly animator, living in France.
The Theatre of M. and Mme Kobal 67. Goto, Island of Love 68. *Blanche* 72. Immoral Tales 74. The Story of Sin 74. La Bête 75. The Streetwalker 76. Dr Jekyll and the Women 81. L'Art d'Aimer 83. Emmanuelle 5 86. Cérémonie d'Amour 86, etc.

Borradaile, Osmond (1898–).
Canadian cinematographer, in Hollywood from 1916 and later in Britain.
The Private Life of Henry VIII (2nd unit) 33. Sanders of the River (2nd unit) 35. The Scarlet Pimpernel (2nd unit) 35. Elephant Boy (2nd unit) 36. The Drum (2nd unit) 38. *The Four Feathers* (2nd unit) 39. *The Thief of Bagdad* (co-ph) 40. *The Overlanders* 46. The Macomber Affair 47. Bonnie Prince Charlie 48. *Scott of the Antarctic* 48. I Was a Male War Bride 49. The Trap 66, etc.

Borsche, Dieter (1909–1982).
German character actor.
Alles weg'n dem Hund (debut) 35. Die Nachtwache 49. Die Grosse Versuchung 52. Ali Baba (Fr.) 54. Die Barrings 55. A Time to Love and a Time to Die (US) 58. Scotland Yard vs Dr Mabuse 63. Lady Hamilton 63, etc.

Borsos, Phillip (1953–1995).
Canadian director. Died from leukemia.
The Grey Fox 83. The Mean Season 84. One Magic Christmas 85. Bethune 89. Far From Home: The Adventures of Yellow Dog 95, etc.

Borzage, Frank (1893–1962).
American director who favoured a soft, sentimental approach to romantic dramas.
SILENT FILMS INCLUDE: Humoresque 20. Get Rich Quick Wallingford 21. Children of the Dust 23. Secrets 24. The Circle 25. The Marriage Licence 26. Seventh Heaven (AA) 27. Street Angel 28. The River 29.
■ SOUND FILMS: Song o' My Heart 30. *Liliom* 30. Doctors' Wives 31. Young as You Feel 31. Bad Girl (AA) 32. After Tomorrow 32. Young America 32. *A Farewell to Arms* 32. Secrets 33. *Man's Castle* 33. No Greater Glory 34. Little Man What Now? 34. Flirtation Walk 34. Living on Velvet 35. Stranded 35. Shipmates Forever 35. *Desire* 36. Hearts Divided 36. The Green Light 37. *History Is Made at Night* 37. Big City 38. Mannequin 38. *Three Comrades* 38. The Shining Hour 39. Disputed Passage 39. *Strange Cargo* 40. *The Mortal Storm* 40. Flight Command 41. *Smilin' Through* 41. The Vanishing Virginian 42. Seven Sweethearts 42. Stage Door Canteen 43. His Butler's Sister 43. Till We Meet Again 44. The Spanish Main 45. I've Always Loved You 46. Magnificent Doll 46. That's My Man 47. *Moonrise* 49. China Doll 58. The Big Fisherman 59.
❝ *History Is Made at Night* is not only the most romantic tragedy in the history of the cinema but also a profound exposition of Borzage's commitment to love over probability. – *Andrew Sarris, 1968*

Bosco, Philip (1930–).
American character actor. Born in Jersey City, he is a noted New York stage actor.
Requiem for a Heavyweight 62. A Lovely Way to Die 68. Trading Places 83. The Pope of Greenwich Village 84. Heaven Help Us 85. Flanagan 85. Walls of Glass 85. The Money Pit 86. Children of a Lesser God 86. Suspect 87. Three Men and a Baby 87. Another Woman 88. Working Girl 88. The Dream Team 89. The Luckiest Man in the World 89. Blue Steel 90. Quick Change 90. FX/2 – The Deadly Art of Illusion 91. True Colors 91. Angie 94. Milk Money 94. Nobody's Fool 94. Safe Passage 94. It Takes Two 95. The First Wives Club 96. My Best Friend's Wedding 97. Deconstructing Harry 97. Critical Care 97, etc.

Bose, Lucia (1931–).
Italian leading lady, former beauty queen.
No Peace Among the Olives 50. Cronaca di un Amore 51. Girls of the Spanish Steps 52. Death of a Cyclist (Sp.) 54. Le Testament d'Orphée 61. Lumière 76, etc.

Bosley, Tom (1927–).
Plump American character actor with stage and TV experience.
The Street with No Name 46. Call Northside 777 48. The World of Henry Orient 64. *Love with the Proper Stranger* 64. Divorce American Style 67. The Secret War of Harry Frigg 67. Yours Mine and Ours 68. To Find a Man 72. Gus 76. O'Hara's Wife 81. The Jesse Owens Story (TV) 84. Private Sessions (TV) 85. Million Dollar Mystery 87. Fire and Rain 89. Wicked Stepmother 89, etc.
TV series: *Debbie Reynolds Show* 69–70. Sandy Duncan Show 72. Happy Days 74–84. Father Dowling Mysteries 89–91.

Bost, Pierre:
see AURENCHE, Jean.

The Boston Strangler:
see DESALVO, Albert.

Bostwick, Barry (1945–).
Personable, easy-going leading man of the 70s, sometimes with a startling resemblance to James Stewart.
Jennifer on My Mind 71. Janice 72. The Chadwick Family (TV) 74. The Rocky Horror Picture Show 75. The Wrong Damn Film 75. The Quinns (TV) 77. Movie Movie 78. Murder by Natural Causes (TV) 79. Once Upon a Family (TV) 80. Moviola (TV) (as John Gilbert) 80. Scruples (TV) 80. Megaforce 82. George Washington (title role) (TV) 84. A Woman of Substance (TV) 84. Deceptions (TV) 85. Jailbait: Betrayed by Innocence (TV) 90. Weekend at Bernie's II 93. Praying Mantis (TV) 93. Eight Hundred Leagues down the Amazon 93. Danielle Steel's Once in a Lifetime (TV) 94. Spy Hard 96, etc.
TV series: Foul Play 80. War and Remembrance 88.

Bosustow, Stephen (1911–1981).
Founder of UPA cartoons (1943) after working as artist for Disney and others. Later won Academy Awards for creation of Gerald McBoing Boing and Mr Magoo.

Boswell, Connee (1907–1976).
American band singer, a polio victim who recovered sufficiently to continue her career.
Artist and Models 37. Kiss the Boys Goodbye 40. Syncopation 41, etc.

Bosworth, Hobart (1867–1943).
American character actor with stage experience: films from 1909.
The Country Mouse 14. Joan the Woman 16. Oliver Twist 16. Below the Surface 20. Vanity Fair 23. Captain January 24. Zander the Great 25. The Big Parade 25. The Blood Ship 27. A Woman of Affairs 29. Mammy 30. The Miracle Man 32. Lady for a Day 33. The Crusades 35. Bullets for O'Hara 41. Sin Town 42, many others.

Boteler, Wade (1891–1943).
American general-purpose small-part actor.
An Old Fashioned Boy 19. The Ghost Patrol 23. High School Hero 26. Top Sergeant Mulligan 28. College Lovers 30. Death Kiss 32. Belle of the Nineties 34. Whipsaw 36. You Only Live Once 37. In Old Chicago 38. Thunder Afloat 39. Castle on the Hudson 40. Kathleen 41. I Was Framed 42. Hi Buddy 43. The Last Ride 44, many others.

Botkin, Perry, Jnr (1933–).
American composer.
Bless the Beasts and Children (co-ph) 72. Skyjacked 72. Lady Ice 72. Your Three Minutes Are Up 73. Tarzan the Ape Man 81. Dance of the Dwarfs 83. Silent Night, Deadly Night 84. Weekend Warriors 86. Ordinary Heroes 86. Windmill of the Gods (TV) 88, etc.

Bottin, Rob (1959–).
American special effects and make-up designer. He worked with Rick Baker before setting up on his own.
Piranha 78. Rock 'n' Roll High School 79. The Fog (& a) 80. Humanoids from the Deep 80. The Howling 81. The Thing 82. Explorers 85. Legend (AAN) 86. Innerspace 87. Robocop 87. Witches of Eastwick 87. The Great Outdoors 88. Robocop 2 90. Total Recall (AA) 90. Bugsy 91. Basic Instinct 92. Robocop 3 93. Mission: Impossible 96. The Devil's Advocate 97. Mimic 97. Deep Rising 98. Fear and Loathing in Las Vegas 98, etc.

Bottoms, Joseph (1954–).
American juvenile of the 70s.
The Dove 74. Crime and Passion 76. Holocaust (TV) 78. The Black Hole 79. Cloud Dancer 80. King of the Mountain 81. Surfacing 84. Blind Date 84. Celebrity 85. Open House 86. Born to Race 88. Inner Sanctum 91. Liars Edge 92, etc.

Bottoms, Sam (1955–).
American leading man, youngest of the Bottoms brothers.
The Last Picture Show 71. Class of '44 73. Zandy's Bride 74. Savages (TV) 74. The Outlaw Josey Wales 76. Cage without a Key (TV) 77. Apocalypse Now 79. Bronco Billy 80. Prime Risk 84. After School 88. Hunter's Blood 87. Return to Eden 89. Ragin' Cajun 90. Dolly Dearest 92. The Trust 93. Sugar Hill 94, etc.

Bottoms, Timothy (1951–).
Leading American juvenile actor of the early 70s who has found few comparable adult roles.

Johnny Got His Gun 71. *The Last Picture Show* 71. Love, Pain and the Whole Damned Thing 73. The Paper Chase 73. The White Dawn 74. The Crazy World of Julius Vrooder 74. The Moneychangers (TV) 76. Operation Daybreak 76. A Small Town in Texas 76. Rollercoaster 77. Return Engagement (TV) 78. Hurricane 79. The Other Side of the Mountain Part Two 79. *East of Eden* (TV) 80. The High Country 81. Hambone and Hillie 83. Love Leads the Way (TV) 85. Invaders from Mars 86. The Land of Faraway 87. The Drifter 88. Husbands, Wives, Money and Murder 89. Return to the River Kwai 89. The Fantasist 89. The Gift of Love 90. Istanbul 90. Texasville 90. Digger 93, etc.

Bouchet, Barbara (1943–) (Barbara Gutscher).
German-American glamour girl.
In Harm's Way 65. Agent for HARM 66. Casino Royale 67. Danger Route 68. Down the Ancient Stairs 75. House of a Thousand Pleasures 76, etc.

Bouchey, Willis (1895–1977).
American character actor, often seen as judge or reluctant sheriff.
Elopement 51. Suddenly 54. Johnny Concho 56. The Last Hurrah 58. Sergeant Rutledge 60. Where Love has Gone 64. Support Your Local Sheriff 69, many others.

Bouchier, Chili (1909–) (Dorothy Irene Bouchier).
British leading lady, mainly on the London stage, where she was still active in her 80s.
Autobiographies: 1968, *For Dogs and Angels*; 1995, *Shooting Star*.
■ A Woman in Pawn 27. Shooting Stars 28. Maria Marten 28. Dawn 28. Chick 28. Palais de Danse 28. You Know What Sailors Are 28. Warned Off 28. The Silver King 29. City of Play 29. Downstream 29. Enter the Queen 30. The Call of the Sea 30. Kissing Cup's Race 30. Brown Sugar 31. *Carnival* 31. *The Blue Danube* 32. Ebb Tide 32. The King's Cup 33. Summer Lightning 33. Purse Strings 33. It's a Cop 34. To Be a Lady 34. The Office Wife 34. Death Drives Through 35. Royal Cavalcade 35. The Mad Hatters 35. Honours Easy 35. Lucky Days 35. Get Off My Foot 35. Mr Cohen Takes a Walk 35. The Ghost Goes West 36. Faithful 36. Where's Sally 36. Southern Roses 36. Gypsy 36. Mayfair Melody 37. The Minstrel Boy 37. Change for a Sovereign 37. The Singing Cop 38. The Dark Stairway 38. *Mr Satan* 38. The Return of Carol Deane 38. Everything Happens to Me 38. The Mind of Mr Reeder 39. My Wife's Family 41. Facing the Music 41. Murder in Reverse 45. The Laughing Lady 46. Mrs Fitzherbert 47. *The Case of Charles Peace* 48. Old Mother Riley's New Venture 49. The Wallet 52. The Counterfeit Plan 57. The Boy and the Bridge 59. Dead Lucky 60. Catch a Fallen Star (TV) 87.
TV series: Flip 91.

Boulting, Ingrid (1947–) (Ingrid Munnik).
South African leading lady who made less than a dazzling impact in *The Last Tycoon* 76.
Deadly Passion 85.

Boulting, John (1913–1985) and **Roy** (1913–).
Twin Britishers who after varied experience set up as writer-producer-directors of films with something to say. After World War II they became somewhat more conventional, and the early 50s were barren, but then they came up with a highly successful series of comedies pillorying national institutions. In the 60s they became directors of British Lion Films, with commercially successful but otherwise disappointing results. (Although they have produced and directed alternately, neither showed a particular style, and their films below are treated as joint efforts unless mentioned otherwise.)
Autobiography: *Double Exposure: Adventures of the Boulting Brothers in Wonderland*.
■ Consider Your Verdict 37. Inquest 38. Trunk Crime 38. *Pastor Hall* 39. *Thunder Rock* 42. *Desert Victory* (Roy) 44. Burma Victory (Roy) 45. *Journey Together* (John) 45. *Fame is the Spur* 46. *Brighton Rock* 46. *The Guinea Pig* 49. *Seven Days to Noon* 50. The Magic Box 51. High Treason (Roy) 52. Sailor of the King (Roy) 53. Seagulls Over Sorrento 54. Josephine and Men 54. *Private's Progress* 55. *Brothers in Law* 56. Run for the Sun (Roy) 56. *Lucky Jim* 57. Happy is the Bride 57. Carlton Browne of the F.O. 58. *I'm All Right Jack* 59. Suspect 60. A French Mistress 61. *Heavens Above* 63. Rotten to the Core 65. The Family Way 66. Twisted Nerve 68. There's a Girl in My Soup (Roy) 70. Endless Night 72. Soft Beds and Hard Battles (Roy) 73. The Last Word (Roy) 79.
✪ For raising the sights of British films in the 40s, and later for devising a strain of satirical comedy. *I'm All Right Jack*.

Boulton, David (1911–1989).
British cinematographer.
The Password Is Courage 62. The Haunting 63. Children of the Damned 65. The Secret of My Success 65. It 66. The Great Waltz 72, etc.

Bouquet, Carole (1957–).
French leading actress and model of classic beauty.
That Obscure Object of Desire 77. Buffet Froid 79. For Your Eyes Only 81. Le Bon Roi Dagobert 84. Rive Droite, Rive Gauche 85. Special Police 85. New York Stories 89. Trop Belle pour Toi/Too Beautiful for You 89. Tango 93. A Business Affair 94. Grosse Fatigue 94. Lucie Aubrac 97, etc.

Bouquet, Michel (1926–).
French general-purpose actor, notably in the films of Claude Chabrol.
Monsieur Vincent 47. Manon 49. La Tour de Nesle 55. Katia 60. An Orchid for the Tiger 65. The Road to Corinth 67. The Bride Wore Black 68. The Mississippi Mermaid 69. Borsalino 70. Just Before Nightfall 71. Malpertuis 72. The Serpent 73. Les Suspects 74. Beyond Fear 75. Le-Jouet 77. La Raison d'Etat 78. Toto Le Héros 91, etc.

Bourgoin, Jean (1913–).
French cinematographer.
La Marseillaise 38. Goupi Mains Rouges 43. Voyage Surprise 46. Dedée d'Anvers 47. Manèges 50. Justice est Faite 50. Nous Sommes Tous des Assassins 52. Confidential Report 55. *Mon Oncle* 58. *Black Orpheus* 59. The Counterfeit Traitor 62. Gigot 62. The Longest Day 62. Germinal 63. Pas Question le Samedi 65. Qui 70. La Chambre Rouge 73, many others.

Bourguignon, Serge (1928–).
French director of style but little substance.
Sundays and Cybele (AA) 62. The Reward 65. Two Weeks in September 67. The Picasso Summer 69. My Kingdom for a Horse (doc) 86. The Fascination 87, etc.

Bourne, Mel (1923–).
Production designer, often for Woody Allen's films.
Annie Hall 77. Interiors (AAN) 78. The Greek Tycoon 78. Manhattan 79. Stardust Memories 80. Windows 80. Thief 81. A Midsummer Night's Sex Comedy 82. Zelig 83. Broadway Danny Rose 84. The Natural (AAN) 84. Manhunter 86. F/X 86. Fatal Attraction 87. Cocktail 89. Rude Awakening 89. Reversal of Fortune 90. The Fisher King 91. Man Trouble 92. Indecent Proposal 93. Angie 94. Kiss of Death 95. Something to Talk About 95. Striptease 96, etc.

Bourneuf, Philip (1912–1979).
American supporting stage actor of the older school. Films few.
Winged Victory 44. Joan of Arc 49. The Big Night 51. Beyond a Reasonable Doubt 56. Hemingway's Adventures of a Young Man 62. The Arrangement 69. The Molly Maguires 70, etc.

Bourvil (1917–1970) (André Raimbourg).
Diminutive, expressive French comic actor.
La Ferme du Pendu 45. Mr Peek-a-boo 51. *La Traversée de Paris* 56. The Mirror Has Two Faces 58. The Green Mare's Nest 69. Tout l'Or du Monde 62. Heaven Sent 63. The Secret Agents 65. The Big Spree 66. *The Sucker* 66. Don't Look Now 67. The Brain 68. Monte Carlo or Bust 69. The Red Circle 70, many others.

Bouzid, Nouri (1945–).
Tunisian director and screenwriter.
Man of Ashes/Rih Essed 86. The Golden Horseshoes/Sfayah Min Dhahab 89. Halfouine (co-w only) 90. Bezness 92. L'Homme de Cendres 94. The Silences of the Palace (co-w only) 94. Tunisiennes (wd) 98, etc.

Bow, Clara (1905–1965).
American leading lady, the 'It' girl of the 20s: her films depicted the gay young flapper generation and her wide-eyed vivacity was tremendously popular for a time, but she came to grief through trying to parallel her screen image in her private life. She was notorious for her promiscuity, and her lovers included Gary Cooper, Victor Fleming, Gilbert Roland and Harry Richman. Revelations of her affairs, and of an orgy with a football team, came out during a court case in 1931, when she sued her former secretary, who had embezzled her money and tried to blackmail her. The scandal finished her career at Paramount and her later pictures failed to draw. Married cowboy actor turned politician Rex Bell in 1932.
Biography: 1989, *Clara Bow: Running Wild* by David Stenn.
■ Beyond the Rainbow 22. Down to the Sea in Ships 22. Enemies of Women 23. Maytime 23. The Daring Years 23. Grit 24. Black Oxen 24. Poisoned Paradise 24. Daughters of Pleasure 24. Wine 24. Empty Hearts 24. This Woman 24. Black Lightning 24. Capital Punishment 25. Helen's Babies 25. The Adventurous Sex 25. My Lady's Lips 25. Parisian Love 25. Eve's Lover 25. Kiss Me Again 25. The Scarlet West 25. The Primrose Path 25. The Plastic Age 25. The Keeper of the Bees 25. Free to Love 25. The Best Bad Man 25. Lawful Cheaters 25. Two Can Play 26. The Runaway 26. *Mantrap* 26. Kid Boots 26. The Ancient Mariner 26. My Lady of Whim 26. Dancing Mothers 26. The Shadow of the Law 26. *It* 27. Children of Divorce 27. Rough House Rosie 27. *Wings* 27. Hula 27. Get Your Man 27. Red Hair 28. Ladies of the Mob 28. The Fleet's In 28. Three Weekends 28. The Wild Party 29. The Saturday Night Kid 29. Dangerous Curves 29. Paramount on Parade 30. True to the Navy 30. Love Among the Millionaires 30. Her Wedding Night 30. No Limit 31. Kick In 31. Call Her Savage 32. Hoopla 33.
❝ She danced even when her feet were not moving. – *Adolph Zukor*
Being a sex symbol is a heavy load to carry, especially when one is tired, hurt and bewildered. – C.B.
Her life and career still seem to have been dreamed up by one of her scriptwriters. – *David Shipman*

Bowdon, Dorris (1915–).
American leading lady who abruptly retired to marry Nunnally Johnson.
■ Down on the Farm 38. Young Mr Lincoln 39. Drums Along the Mohawk 39. *The Grapes of Wrath* (as Rosasharn) 40. The Moon Is Down 42.

Bower, Dallas (1907–).
British producer. Originally sound recordist, editor and writer, he became director of BBC TV 1936–39, supervisor of Ministry of Information film production 1940–42. Associate producer *As You Like It* 36, *Henry V* 44, etc.; produced *Sir Lancelot*, TV series.
AS DIRECTOR: Alice in Wonderland (Fr.) 50. The Second Mrs Tanqueray 52. Doorway to Suspicion 57.

Bowers, William (1916–1987).
American screenwriter.
My Favorite Spy 42. Night and Day 46. *The Web* 47. Black Bart 48. Larceny 48. *The Gunfighter* 50. Cry Danger 51. *The Mob* 51. Split Second 53. *Five Against the House* 55. The Best Things in Life are Free 56. *The Sheepman* 58. Alias Jesse James 59. *The Last Time I Saw Archie* 61. Advance to the Rear 64. *Support Your Local Sheriff* 69, etc.

Bowie, David (1947–) (David Robert Jones).
Bizarrely decorated British pop singer who makes curious forays into film acting. Married Somalian model and occasional actress Iman in 1992. In 1997, the *Sunday Times* estimated his fortune at £150m.
■ The Man Who Fell to Earth 76. Just a Gigolo 78. The Hunger 83. Merry Christmas Mr Lawrence 83. Ziggy Stardust and the Spiders from Mars 83 (recorded 73). Into the Night 84. Absolute Beginners 85. Labyrinth 86. The Last Temptation of Christ 88. When the Wind Blows (title song) 88. UHF 89. The Linguini Incident 92. Twin Peaks: Fire Walk with Me 92. Basquiat (as Andy Warhol) 95. Everybody Loves Sunshine 98.
❝ I get offered so many bad movies. And they're all raging queens or transvestites or Martians. – *D.B., 1983*
I'm an instant star. Just add water and stir. – *D.B.*

Bowie, Jim (1796–1836).
American folk hero who invented the Bowie knife and died at the Alamo. He was played in *The Iron Mistress* by Alan Ladd, in *The Last Command* by Sterling Hayden, in *The First Texan* by Jeff Morrow, in *Davy Crockett* by Kenneth Tobey, in *Man of Conquest* by Robert Armstrong, in *Comanche Territory* by Macdonald Carey, and in *The Alamo* by Richard Widmark. A TV series called *The Adventures of Jim Bowie* 60 starred Scott Forbes.

Bowie, Les (1913–1979).
British special effects technician especially noted for matte shots.
Great Expectations 46. The Red Shoes 48. Star Wars 76. Superman 78. Many Hammer films.

Bowker, Judi (1954–).
British leading lady.
Brother Sun Sister Moon 73. Count Dracula (TV) 78. Clash of the Titans 81. East of Elephant Rock 81. The Shooting Party 85, etc.

Bowles, Paul (1910–).
American novelist, short-story writer and composer who has lived in Morocco for much of his life. At least two documentary films have been made about him: *Paul Bowles in Morocco* 70 and *Paul Bowles: The Complete Outsider* 94.
Biography: 1989, *An Invisible Spectator* by Christopher Sawyer-Lauçanno.
Bride of Samoa (m) 33. America's Disinherited (m) 36. Congo (m) 44. Dreams that Money Can Buy (m) 47. Senso (co-dialogue) 54. You Are Not I (oa) 81. *The Glass Menagerie* (theme) 87. The Sheltering Sky (narrator, oa) 90. Paul Bowles Halbmond (oa) 94, etc.

Bowles, Peter (1936–).
Suave English actor, much on TV.
Blowup 66. The Assassination Bureau 68. The Charge of the Light Brigade 68. Laughter in the Dark 69. A Day in the Death of Joe Egg 70. The Legend of Hell House 73. Try This One for Size 89. The Steal 95, etc.
TV series: Good Girl 74. The Crezz 76. Rumpole of the Bailey 78–80, 87–88. Only When I Laugh 79–83. To the Manor Born 79–81. The Bounder 82–83. The Irish RM 83–85. Lytton's Diary (& co-created) 85–86. Perfect Scoundrels (& co-created) 90–92.

Bowman, Lee (1910–1979).
Well-groomed American light leading man with stage experience; found a desultory career in films.
Three Men in White 36. *I Met Him in Paris* 37. Love Affair 39. Miracles for Sale 39. Florian 40. Buck Privates 41. *Kid Glove Killer* 42. Three Hearts for Julia 43. Cover Girl 44. *The Impatient Years* 44. Tonight and Every Night 45. The Walls Came Tumbling Down 46. Smash-Up 47. The House by the River 50. Double Barrel Miracle 55. Youngblood Hawke 64, etc.
TV series: Ellery Queen 50.

Box, Betty E. (1920–1999).
British producer, sister of Sydney Box and once assistant to him. For many years she turned out comedies and dramas with box office appeal but little cinematic flavour, usually in association with director Ralph Thomas.
Miranda 48. Here Come the Huggetts 49. *Doctor in the House* 53. The Iron Petticoat 56. A Tale of Two Cities 58. The Thirty-nine Steps 59. No Love for Johnnie 61. A Pair of Briefs 63. No My Darling Daughter 63. The High Bright Sun 65. Deadlier than the Male 66. The High Commissioner 68. Percy 70. The Love Ban 72. Percy's Progress 74, many others.

Box, John (1920–).
British production designer.
Lawrence of Arabia (AA) 62. *Doctor Zhivago* (AA) 65. *A Man For All Seasons* 66. *Oliver* (AA) 68. The Looking Glass War (p only) 69. *Nicholas and Alexandra* (AA) 71. Travels with my Aunt (AAN) 73. Rollerball 74. *The Great Gatsby* 74. Sorcerer 76. A Passage to India 84. Murder by the Book (TV) 90. Black Beauty 94. First Knight 95, etc.

Box, Muriel (1905–1991).
British director, producer and screenwriter, also a playwright, novelist and publisher. Having failed to become a professional actress, she began as a continuity girl, started directing documentaries in

the 40s and feature films from 1950. She was married to producer and screenwriter Sydney Box (1935–68) and Lord Gardiner, a former Lord Chancellor.
Autobiography: 1974, *Odd Woman Out*.
AS SCREENWRITER (with Sydney Box): 29 Acacia Avenue 45. *The Seventh Veil* (AA) 45. The Years Between 46. The Man Within (& p) 47. Dear Murderer (& p) 47. Holiday Camp 47. The Brothers 47. Easy Money 48. Daybreak 48. A Girl in a Million (& p) 50, etc.
AS DIRECTOR: The Happy Family (& w) 52. Street Corner (& w) 53. The Beachcomber 54. To Dorothy a Son 54. Simon and Laura 55. A Novel Affair (Passionate Stranger) (& w) 56. The Truth about Women (& w) 57. Subway in the Sky 58. Too Young to Love (& w) 59. Rattle of a Simple Man 64, etc.

Box, Sydney (1907–1983).
British writer-producer who had considerable success in the decade after World War II.
The Seventh Veil (co-w, AA) 46. The Years Between 47. *Holiday Camp* 47. Jassy 47. *The Brothers* 48. Dear Murderer 48. *Quartet* 48. Don't Take It to Heart (p only) 48. Broken Journey 48. Daybreak 49. A Girl in a Million 50. So Long at the Fair (p only) 51. *The Prisoner* 55, etc.

Boxleitner, Bruce (1950–).
American leading man, mostly on TV.
Six Pack Annie 75. Kiss Me Kill Me (TV) 76. Tron 82. Diplomatic Immunity 91. Breakaway 91. Murderous Vision 91. Kuffs 92. The Babe 92. The Secret 93. Wyatt Earp; Return to Tombstone (TV) 94, etc.
TV series: How the West Was Won 76. Bring 'em Back Alive 82. Scarecrow and Mrs King 83. Babylon 5 95– .

Boyd, Don (1948–).
British independent producer and director.
AS PRODUCER: Sweet William 78. Hussy 78. The Tempest 78. Blue Suede Shoes 79. Scum 79. Great Rock and Roll Swindle 80. Honky Tonk Freeway 81. Scrubbers 82. Unsuitable Job for a Woman 83. Captive 85. Aria 86. Last of England 87. War Requiem 89, etc.
AS DIRECTOR: Intimate Reflections 75. East of Elephant Rock 76. Twenty-One 91. Kleptomania 93. Lucia (wd) 98, etc.

Boyd, Dorothy (1907–).
English leading actress of the 30s, who began as an extra.
Easy Virtue 27. The Constant Nymph 28. Too Many Crooks 30. Third Time Lucky 31. The Girl in the Night 31. A Shot in the Dark 33. Ace of Spades 35. Ticket of Leave 36. Pearls Bring Tears 37. Shadowed Eyes 39, etc.

Boyd, Russell (1944–).
Australian cinematographer.
The Man from Hong Kong 75. Picnic at Hanging Rock 75. Summer of Secrets 76. Break of Day 77. The Last Wave 77. Dawn 79. Chain Reaction 80. Gallipoli 81. Starstruck 82. The Year of Living Dangerously 82. Tender Mercies 83. Phar Lap 84. A Soldier's Story 84. Mrs Soffel 85. Between Wars 85. Crocodile Dundee 86. High Tide 87. Burke and Wills 87. The Rescue 88. Crocodile Dundee II 88. In Country 89. Almost an Angel 90. Sweet Talker 91. White Men Can't Jump 92. Cobb 94. Operation Dumbo Drop 95. Tin Cup 96. Liar Liar 97, etc.

Boyd, Stephen (1928–1977) (William Millar).
Irish leading man in international films; fairly popular during the 60s.
■ Born for Trouble 55. An Alligator Named Daisy 55. A Hill in Korea 56. *The Man Who Never Was* (as the German spy) 56. Seven Waves Away 57. Island in the Sun 57. Seven Thunders 57. Heaven Fell That Night 57. The Bravados 58. *Ben Hur* (as Messala) 59. Woman Obsessed 59. The Best of Everything 59. The Big Gamble 61. The Inspector 62. Jumbo 62. Imperial Venus 63. *The Fall of the Roman Empire* 64. The Third Secret 64. Genghis Khan 64. The Oscar 66. Fantastic Voyage 66. The Bible 66. The Caper of the Golden Bulls 67. Assignment K 68. Shalako 68. Slaves 69. Carter's Army (TV) 71. The Hands of Cormac Joyce (TV) 71. Key West (TV) 72. Hannie Caulder 72. The Man Called Noon 73. Marta 74. Kill, Kill, Kill 74. Those Dirty Dogs 74. Evil in the Deep 75. The Lives of Jenny Dolan (TV) 75. Left Hand of the Law 76. The Squeeze 77. The Devil Has Seven Faces 77. Impossible Love 77.

Boyd, William (1895–1972).
Unassuming American leading man, in films from 1919, internationally famous from 1934 as cowboy hero Hopalong Cassidy, in which guise he made scores of second features and TV episodes.
Why Change Your Wife? 19. The Temple of Venus 23. Changing Husbands 24. The Volga Boatman 26. King of Kings 27. *Two Arabian Knights* 27. Skyscraper 28. The Leatherneck 29. The Benson Murder Case 30. The Spoilers 30. The Painted Desert 31. Murder by the Clock 31. Lucky Devils 33. Port of Lost Dreams 34. *Hopalong Cassidy* 35, many others, but all subsequent films as Cassidy; last in 1948.

Boyd, William (1952–).
English novelist and screenwriter.
Stars and Bars 88. Tune in Tomorrow/Aunt Julia and the Scriptwriter 90. Mister Johnson 91. Chaplin 92. A Good Man in Africa (from his novel) 94.

Boyd, William 'Stage' (1890–1935).
American stage actor, so known to distinguish him from his Hopalong Cassidy namesake.
Sky Devils 32. Painted Woman 32. *Oliver Twist* (as Sikes) 33, etc.

Boyer, Charles (1899–1978).
Gentlemanly French romantic actor in international films: went to Hollywood first in 1929, and later gained a reputation as the screen's 'great lover'. Committed suicide following the death of his wife of 44 years.
Biography: 1964, *Charles Boyer* by Larry Swindell.
■ L'Homme du Large 20. Chantelouve 21. Le Grillon du Foyer 22. L'Esclave 23. La Ronde Infernale 27. Le Capitaine Fracasse 27. *La Barcarolle d'Amour* 28. Le Procès de Mary Dugan 28. The Big House (French version) 30. The Magnificent Lie 31. Tumultes 31. *Red-headed Woman* 32. The Man from Yesterday 32. F.P.I. (French version) 32. The Only Girl 33. L'Impervier 33. The Battle (as a Japanese) 34. *Caravan* 34. Liliom 35. Private Worlds 35. Break of Hearts 35. Shanghai 35. Le Bonheur 36. *The Garden of Allah* 36. *Mayerling* 37. *Tovarich* 37. *Conquest* (as Napoleon) (AAN) 37. *History is Made at Night* 37. *Algiers* (AAN) 38. Orage 38. *Love Affair* 39. When Tomorrow Comes 39. Le Corsaire 39. *All This and Heaven Too* 40. Les Amoureux 40. Back Street 41. *Hold Back the Dawn* 41. Appointment for Love 41. Tales of Manhattan 42. The Constant Nymph 43. Flesh and Fantasy (& p) 43. *Gaslight* (AAN) 44. Confidential Agent 45. Together Again 45. Cluny Brown 46. Arch of Triumph 48. A Woman's Vengeance 48. The Thirteenth Letter 51. The First Legion 52. *The Happy Time* 52. Thunder in the East 53. *Madame de . . .* 53. The Cobweb 55. Lucky to Be a Woman 55. Paris Palace Hotel 56. Nana 56. Around the World in Eighty Days 56. La Parisienne 58. The Buccaneer 58. Maxime 58. *Fanny* (AAN) 62. The Four Horsemen of the Apocalypse 62. Les Démons de Minuit 62. Love is a Ball 63. Adorable Julia 64. *A Very Special Favour* 64. How to Steal a Million 66. Is Paris Burning? 66. Casino Royale 67. *Barefoot in the Park* 68. The April Fools 69. The Madwoman of Chaillot 69. The Day the Hot Line Got Hot 69. Lost Horizon 73. Stavisky 74. A Matter of Time 76.
TV series: *Four Star Theatre* 56. *The Rogues* 64.
✪ For capitalizing on the accepted image of the romantic Frenchman and proving that he could also act. *Love Affair*.
❝ We got a French actor here on a 6-month option, but I'm letting him go home because nobody can understand the guy's accent.–*Irving Thalberg, 1932*.
Famous line (which he never actually said in *Algiers*): 'Come with me to the Casbah.'

Boyer, François (1920–).
French screenwriter, also novelist.
Le Point du Jour 49. *Jeux Interdits* (& oa) 52. Chiens Perdus sans Collier 55. Le Joueur 58. Les Magiciennes 60. Un Singe en Hiver 62. War of the Buttons 62. Weekend in Dunkirk 64. The 25th Hour 67. Mords Pas On t'Aime 76, etc.

Boyer, Jean (1901–1965).
French director.
Monsieur, Madame et Bibi 32. Un Mauvais Garçon 36. Circonstances Atténuantes 39. Serenade 40. Romance de Paris 41. Bolero 42. La Bonne Etoile 43. La Femme Fatale 45. Les Aventures de Casanova 47. All Roads Lead to Rome 49. Le Rosier de Madame Husson 50. Le Passe-Muraille 51. Coiffeur pour Dames 52. Femmes de Paris 53. J'avais Sept Filles 54. Fernandel the Dressmaker 56. Sénéchal le Magnifique 57. Nina 58. Coup de Bambou 62. Relaxe-toi Chérie 64, many others.

Boyer, Myriam (1953–).
French actress of stage, screen and television, and occasional director.
Jonah Who Will Be 25 in the Year 2000 76. La Communion Solennelle 77. Holiday Hotel/ L'Hotel de la Plage 78. Série Noire 79. Golden 80s/Les Années 80 83. Too Beautiful for You/Trop Belle pour Toi! 89. Uranus 90. A Heart in Winter/ Un Coeur en Hiver 91. Tous les Matins du Monde 92. Un Deux Trois Soleil 93. Those Were the Days/ Le Plus Bel Age 95. Mother Christian/La Mère Christian (p, wd, a) 98, etc.

Boyle, Catherine (1929–) (Caterina di Francavilla).
Winsome Italian-English TV personality who has made a few film appearances.
Not Wanted on Voyage 52. Intent to Kill 56. The Truth About Women 57, etc.

Boyle, Danny (1956–).
British director, from television and theatre.
Shallow Grave 94. *Trainspotting* 95. A Life Less Ordinary 97. The Beach 99, etc.

Boyle, Lara Flynn (1970–).
American actress.
Poltergeist III 88. How I Got into College 89. Dead Poets Society 89. The Rookie 90. May Wine 91. Mobsters 91. Eyes of the Storm 91. Wayne's World 92. Equinox 92. The Dark Backward 92. Where the Day Takes You 92. Red Rock West 93. The Temp 93. Threesome 94. Baby's Day Out 94. The Road to Wellville 94. Farmer and Chase 95. The Big Squeeze 96. Maybe 96. Dogwater 97. Happiness 98. Susan's Plan 98, etc.
TV series: Twin Peaks 90.
❝ I don't mind playing 'the girlfriend'. I figure I'll go from girlfriend parts to wife parts to mother parts to grandmother parts. That's how it works, isn't it? –*L.F.B.*

Boyle, Peter (1933–).
Rotund, balding American character actor, a former Christian Brother who became a key performer in fashionable films of his time.
The Virgin President 68. Medium Cool 69. *Joe* 70. Diary of a Mad Housewife 70. T.R. Baskin 71. *The Candidate* 72. Steelyard Blues 73. Slither 73. Kid Blue 73. The Friends of Eddie Coyle 73. The Man Who Could Talk to Kids (TV) 73. Crazy Joe 74. *Young Frankenstein* (as the monster) 74. Taxi Driver 76. Swashbuckler 76. *Tail Gunner Joe* (TV) (as Senator Joe McCarthy) 77. FIST 78. Superman 78. Beyond the Poseidon Adventure 79. From Here to Eternity (TV) 79. Hardcore 79. In God We Trust 80. Where the Buffalo Roam 80. Outland 81. Hammett 82. Yellowbeard 83. Johnny Dangerously 84. Morons from Outer Space 85. Turk 182 85. The In Crowd 87. Surrender 87. Walker 87. Funny 88. Red Heat 88. The Dream Team 89. Speed Zone 89. Men of Respect 90. Solar Crisis 90. Kickboxer II 91. Rubin & Ed 91. Royce 94. Killer 94. The Shadow 94. The Santa Clause 94. Born to Be Wild 95. While You Were Sleeping 95. Milk & Money 96, etc.
TV series: Comedy Tonight 70. Joe Bash 86. Midnight Caller 88–91.

Boyle, Robert (1910–).
American production designer.
North by Northwest (AAN) 59. The Thrill of it All 63. The Birds 63. Marnie 64. The Russians are Coming, The Russians are Coming 66. How to Succeed in Business 67. In Cold Blood 67. The Thomas Crown Affair 68. Gaily Gaily (AAN) 69. The Landlord 70. Fiddler on the Roof (AAN) 71. Portnoy's Complaint 72. Mame 74. The Shootist (AAN) 76. The Big Fox 78. Winter Kills 79. Private Benjamin 80. The Best Little Whorehouse in Texas 82. Table for Five 83. Staying Alive 83. Rhinestone 84. Explorers 85. Jumpin' Jack Flash 86. Dragnet 87. Troop Beverly Hills 89, etc.

Bozzuffi, Marcel (1929–1988).
Balding French character actor.
Z 69. The American 69. The Lady in the Car 70. The French Connection 71. Images 72. Nightmare for a Killer 72. Caravan to Vaccares 76. La Grande Bourgeoise 77. *La Cage aux Folles* 79. La Cage aux Folles II 81, etc.

Brabin, Charles (1883–1957).
British film director who made a career in Hollywood but retired early. Married actress Theda Bara in 1921.
Stella Maris 18. *So Big* 23. Twinkletoes 26. Hard Boiled Haggerty 27. The Bridge of San Luis Rey 29. Call of the Flesh 30. Sporting Blood 31. Beast of the City 32. *The Mask of Fu Manchu* 32. Stage Mother 33. A Wicked Woman 34, many others.

Brabourne, John (1924–) (Lord Brabourne).
British producer, in films from 1950.
Harry Black 58. Sink the Bismarck 60. HMS Defiant 62. The Mikado 66. Tales of Beatrix Potter 71. *Murder on the Orient Express* 74. Death on the Nile 78. The Mirror Crack'd 80. Evil Under the Sun 82. A Passage to India 84. Little Dorrit 87, etc.

Bracco, Lorraine (1954–).
American leading actress and former model. She was formerly married to actor Harvey Keitel, and subsequently married Edward James Olmos.
The Pickup Artist 87. Someone to Watch Over Me 87. The Dream Team 89. GoodFellas (AAN) 90. Switch 91. Talent for the Game 91. Medicine Man 92. Radio Flyer 92. Traces of Red 92. Scam 93. Even Cowgirls Get the Blues 93. Being Human 94. The Basketball Diaries 95. Les Menteurs (Fr.) 95. Hackers 95, etc.

Brach, Gérard (1927–).
French screenwriter who has often worked with Roman Polanski.
Repulsion 65. Cul-de-Sac 66. The Fearless Vampire Killers 67. The Tenant 76. Tess 79. I Sent a Letter to My Love/Chère Inconnue 80. The Quest for Fire 81. L'Africain 83. Maria's Lovers 85. Jean de Florette 86. Manon des Sources 86. The Name of the Rose 86. Pirates 86. Shy People 87. Frantic 88. The Bear/L'Ours 89. The Lover/ L'Amant 91. I Divertimenti della Vita Privata 91. Bitter Moon 92, etc.

Bracken, Eddie (1920–).
American comic actor, popular in the 40s as the nervous hayseed type; made his best films for Preston Sturges. Later found stage success.
■ Too Many Girls 40. Life with Henry 41. Reaching for the Sun 41. Caught in the Draft 41. Sweater Girl 42. The Fleet's In 42. Star Spangled Rhythm 42. Happy Go Lucky 43. Young and Willing 43. *The Miracle of Morgan's Creek* 43. *Hail the Conquering Hero* 44. Rainbow Island 44. Out of This World 45. Bring on the Girls 45. Duffy's Tavern 45. Hold That Blonde 45. Ladies' Man 47. Fun on a Weekend 47. The Girl from Jones Beach 49. Summer Stock 50. Two Tickets to Broadway 51. We're Not Married 52. About Face 52. A Slight Case of Larceny 53. National Lampoon's Vacation 83. Oscar 91. Home Alone 2: Lost in New York 92. Rookie of the Year 93. Baby's Day Out 94.

Brackett, Charles (1892–1969).
American writer-producer, of generally sophisticated material; enjoyed long association with Billy Wilder.
Tomorrow's Love (oa) 25. Pointed Heels (oa) 29. Secrets of a Secretary (oa) 31. Enter Madame (w) 35. Piccadilly Jim (w) 36. Bluebeard's Eighth Wife (w) 38. Midnight (w) 39. Ninotchka (w, AAN) 39. Arise My Love (w) 40. Hold Back the Dawn (co-w, AAN) 41. The Major and the Minor (w) 42. *Five Graves to Cairo* (wp) 43. *The Uninvited* (p) 43. *The Lost Weekend* (wp) (AA) 45. To Each His Own (wp, AAN) 46. *A Foreign Affair* (wp, AAN) 48. *Sunset Boulevard* (wp) (AA) 50. Niagara (wp) 52. Titanic (wp) 52. Woman's World (p) 54. The King and I (p) 56. Ten North Frederick (p) 58. Journey to the Centre of the Earth (wp) 59. State Fair (p) 61, many others.

Brackett, Leigh (1915–1978).
American lady screenwriter.
The Big Sleep 46. Rio Bravo 59. 13 West Street 62. Hatari 62. El Dorado 67. Rio Lobo 70. The

Long Goodbye 73. The Empire Strikes Back 80, etc.

Brackman, Jacob.
American screenwriter.
The King of Marvin Gardens 72. Times Square 80, etc.

Bradbury, Ray (1920–).
American science fiction writer who has dabbled in films.
It Came from Outer Space (oa) 53. The Beast from 20,000 Fathoms (oa) 54. Moby Dick (w) 56. Fahrenheit 451 (oa) 66. The Illustrated Man (oa) 69. Something Wicked This Way Comes 83. Little Nemo: Adventures in Slumberland 92, etc.

Bradbury, Robert North (1886–1949).
American director and screenwriter of low-budget action films, mainly westerns and including many of John Wayne's early films. He was the father of western actor Bob Steele, who also starred in some of his films.
The Faith of the Strong 19. Desert Rider 23. Davy Crockett at the Fall of the Alamo 26. Hidden Valley 32. Breed of the Border 33. Blue Steel 34. Man from Utah 34. Alias John Law 35. Dawn Rider 35. Desert Trail 35. Headin' for the Rio Grande 36. Riders of the Rockies 37. Trouble in Texas 37, many others.

Braddell, Maurice (1901–1990).
English leading actor, dancer, playwright, screenwriter and producer. Born in Singapore and educated at Charterhouse and Oxford, he studied at RADA and toured America with Mrs Patrick Campbell's company, trying and failing to find work in Hollywood. On his return to London, he worked as an assistant producer on *The Battles of Coronel and Falkland Islands* 27, before becoming a film actor and writer, retiring after the Second World War to settle in New York as a picture restorer, and briefly returning to the screen in some Andy Warhol movies.
A Window in Piccadilly 28. Dawn 28. Not Quite a Lady 28. Master and Man 29. Wolves 30. School for Scandal 30. Her Reputation 31. *Men of Tomorrow* 32. This Week of Grace (co-w) 33. Love, Life and Laughter (co-w) 34. Things to Come 36. It's You I Want (oa) 36. Where's That Fire (story) 39. Sleep Walk 64. Flesh 68. Women in Revolt 72, etc.

Braden, Bernard (1916–1993).
Canadian TV personality, in Britain since 1938. Occasional film appearances. Long married to Barbara Kelly.
Autobiography: 1990, *The Kindness of Strangers*.
Love in Pawn 52. The Full Treatment 61. The Day the Earth Caught Fire 62. The War Lover 63, etc.

Bradford, Jesse. (1979–).
American actor.
Falling in Love 84. Presumed Innocent 90. My Blue Heaven 90. King of the Hill 93. Far from Home: The Adventures of Yellow Dog 94. Hackers 95. William Shakespeare's Romeo and Juliet 96. A Soldier's Daughter Never Cries 98, etc.

Bradford, Richard.
Thickset American character actor.
The Chase 66. The Missouri Breaks 76. Goin' South 78. More American Graffiti 79. Panic on Page One (TV) 79. Running Hot/Highway to Hell 83. The Trip to Bountiful 85. Legend of Billie Jean 85. The Untouchables 87. Little Nikita 88. The Milagro Beanfield War 88. Night Game 89. The Heart of Dixie 89. Internal Affairs 90. Ambition 91. Cold Heaven 92, etc.
TV series: Man in a Suitcase 68.

Bradley, Buddy (1908–*) (Robert Bradley).
American choreographer and dancer, mainly in Britain. Born in Harrisburg, Pennsylvania, he made his New York stage debut in 1926, in a revue with Florence Mills, and came to England to choreograph the stage musical *Evergreen* in 1930. He remained to work in theatre and films, and to open his own school of dancing.
Radio Parade of 1935 34. *Evergreen* 34. Brewsters Millions 35. It's Love Again 36. *This'll Make You Whistle* 36. Gangway 37. Head over Heels 37. Sailing Along 38. Fiddlers Three 44. Flight from Folly 44. Walking on Air 46, etc.

❝ Britain's answer to Busby Berkeley. – *Ken Russell*

Bradley, David (1919–).
American director who showed promise as an amateur but never seemed to make it professionally.
■ Peer Gynt 41. Julius Caesar 50. Talk About a Stranger 52. Dragstrip Riot 58. Twelve to the Moon 60. Madmen of Mandoras 64.

Bradley, Doug (1954–).
English actor, known for playing the Cenobite Pinhead in the *Hellraiser* series of horror films. Born in Liverpool, he began in experimental theatre.
Hellraiser 87. Hellbound: Hellraiser II 88. Hellraiser III: Hell on Earth 92. Proteus 95. Hellraiser: Bloodline 96, etc.

Bradley, Scott.
American musical director and composer, scoring cartoons, especially *Tom and Jerry*, after joining MGM in 1934.

Bradna, Olympe (1920–).
Slightly built French circus performer who had a brief Hollywood career following a stage tour, and retired on marriage to an American.
■ Three Cheers for Love 36. College Holiday 36. Last Train from Madrid 37. *Souls at Sea* 37. Stolen Heaven 38. Say It in French 38. The Night of Nights 39. South of Pago Pago 40. Highway West 41. Knockout 41. International Squadron 41.

Brady, Alice (1892–1939).
American stage actress who in her last few years made many films, either as a fluttery society matron or as a drab housewife. Died of cancer.
■ As Ye Sow 14. The Boss 15. The Cup of Chance 15. The Lure of Women 15. La Bohème 16. Bought and Paid for 16. Betsy Ross 17. Maternity 17. Woman and Wife 18. A Dark Lantern 19. The Fear Market 19. Out of the Chorus 21. Little Italy 21. The Land of Hope 21. Dawn of the East 21. Hush Money 21. Anna Ascends 21. Missing Millions 21. The Snow Bride 23. The Leopardess 23. *When Ladies Meet* 33. Broadway to Hollywood 33. Beauty for Sale 33. Stage Mother 33. Should Ladies Behave? 33. Miss Fane's Baby is Stolen 34. *The Gay Divorcee* 34. Let 'em Have It 34. Gold Diggers of 1935 35. Lady Tubbs 35. Metropolitan 35. The Harvester 35. *My Man Godfrey* (AAN) 36. Go West Young Man 36. Mind Your Own Business 36. *Three Smart Girls* 37. Call It a Day 37. Mama Steps Out 37. Mr Dodd Takes the Air 37. One Hundred Men and a Girl 37. Merry Go Round of 1938 38. *In Old Chicago* (AA) 38. Joy of Living 38. Goodbye Broadway 38. Zenobia 39. *Young Mr Lincoln* 39.

Brady, Scott (1924–1985) (Gerald Tierney).
Tough-looking American leading man of the 50s, brother of Lawrence Tierney.
Canon City 48. He Walked by Night 48. Port of New York 49. Undercover Girl 50. Kansas Raiders 51. *The Model and the Marriage Broker* 52. Perilous Journey 53. Johnny Guitar 54. Gentlemen Marry Brunettes 55. Mohawk 56. The Maverick Queen 56. They Were So Young 58. Battle Flame 59. Black Spurs 65. Castle of Evil 66. Red Tomahawk 67. Doctors' Wives 70. Nightmare in Wax 70. Dollars 71. The China Syndrome 79. The Winds of War (TV) 83, many others.
TV series: Shotgun Slade 59–60.

Braeden, Eric (1942–) (Hans Gudegast).
German general-purpose actor in international films.
Colossus of Rhodes 57. The Law and Jake Wade 59. Escape from the Planet of the Apes 70. Lady Ice 73. The Ultimate Thrill 74. Death Scream 75. The Adulteress 77. Happily Ever After 82. The Ambulance 90, etc.
TV series: The Rat Patrol 66–68.

Braga, Sonia (1950–).
Brazilian leading actress in international films and a star of stage and TV in her native country.
Dona Flor and Her Two Husbands 77. I Love You 81. Gabriela 83. Kiss of the Spider Woman 85. The Man Who Broke 1,000 Chains (TV) 87. The Milagro Beanfield War 88. Moon over Parador 88. The Rookie 90. Roosters 93. The Burning Season (TV) 94. Two Deaths (GB) 95, etc.

Bragaglia, Carlo Ludovico (1894–1998).
Italian director, screenwriter and poet. Born in Frosinone, he began in avant-garde theatre in Rome, but was best known for his films with comedian Toto and, in his later years, for his historical epics.
O La Borsa o la Vita 33. Amore 36. Animali Pazzi 39. Alessandro Sei Grande 41. Casanova Farebbe Cosi! 42. Torna a Sorrento 45. Il Flaco Rosso 49. Totò le Moko 49. Don Lorenzo 52. Orient-Express 54. The Queen of Babylon/La Cortigiana di Babilonia 56. The Sword and the Cross/La Spada e La Croce 59. The Loves of Hercules/Gli Amori di Ercole 60. Hannibal (co-d, uncredited) 60. The Mighty Crusaders/La Gerusalemme Liberata 60. Valley of the Lions/ Ursus nella Valle dei Leoni 61. Amazons of Rome/ Le Virgini di Roma 62. The Four Musketeers/I Quattro Moschettieri 63, many others.

Bragg, Melvyn (1939–) (Lord Bragg).
English screenwriter, novelist and television presenter. He became a Labour Peer in 1998.
Isadora (co-w) 68. Play Dirty (co-w) 69. The Music Lovers (w) 71. Jesus Christ Superstar (co-w) 73. A Time to Dance (oa) (TV) 92.

Brahm, John (1893–1982) (Hans Brahm).
German director who in the 30s moved first to Britain, then to Hollywood. Films generally competent, but routine.
■ ENGLISH-SPEAKING FILMS: Scrooge 35. The Last Journey 35. *Broken Blossoms* (British remake) 36. Counsel for Crime 37. Penitentiary 38. Girls' School 38. Let Us Live 39. Rio 39. *Escape to Glory* 40. Wild Geese Calling 41. *The Undying Monster* 42. Tonight We Raid Calais 42. Wintertime 43. The Lodger 44. *Hangover Square* 44. Guest in the House 44. *The Locket* 46. *The Brasher Doubloon* 47. Singapore 47. The Thief of Venice 49. Face to Face 52. The Miracle of Fatima 52. The Diamond Queen 53. The Mad Magican 54. Special Delivery 55. Bengazi 55. So Soon to Die (TV) 57. A Death of Princes (TV) 61. Hot Rods to Hell 67.
❝ His quiet virtues of visual tastefulness and dramatic balance were unable to sustain his career. – *Andrew Sarris, 1968*

Braithwaite, Dame Lilian (1873–1948).
Distinguished British stage actress in occasional films. Born in Ramsgate, she began in amateur theatricals, making her professional debut in 1897.
■ The World's Desire 15. The Climax 15. Masks and Faces 15. The Woman Who Was Nothing 16. Justice 16. The Gay Lord Quex 16. Dombey and Son 16. Because 18. The Chinese Puzzle 19. General Post 20. Castles in Spain 20. Downhill 27. Carnival 31. Man of Mayfair 31. The Chinese Puzzle 32. *A Man About the House* 47.

Brakhage, Stan (1933–).
American underground film-maker.
Interim 51. Desistfilm 54. Nightcats 56. Flesh of Morning 57. An Intercourse 59. The Dead 60. Mothlight 63. Black Vision 65. Lovemaking 68. Sexual Meditations 70. Fox Fire Child Watch 71, many others.

Brambell, Wilfrid (1912–1985).
Irish character actor, specializing in grotesques. Born in Dublin, he was on stage as a child, and later with the Abbey Theatre, moving to England in the late 40s. Celebrated on TV as old Steptoe in *Steptoe and Son* 64–73; film appearances usually cameos.
Autobiography: 1976, *All Above Board*.
39 Steps 35. Another Shore 48. Dry Rot 56. Serious Charge 58. What a Whopper 61. *In Search of the Castaways* 62. The Three Lives of Thomasina 63. *A Hard Day's Night* 64. Crooks in Cloisters 64. Where the Bullets Fly 66. Witchfinder General 68. Steptoe and Son 72. Steptoe and Son Ride Again 73. Holiday on the Buses 74. Sword of the Valiant 83, etc.
❝ Acting (which is, let us face it, the least of the arts in that it is uncreative and merely interpretive) is primarily an art of the emotions rather than of the mind. – *W.B.*

Bramble, A. V. (c. 1880–1963).
British director, former actor.
Fatal Fingers 16. Wuthering Heights 18. The Will 21. The Card 22. Chick 28. Shooting Stars (p & co-d) 28. The Man Who Changed His Name 29. Mrs Dane's Defence 33. An Outcast of the Islands (a only) 51, etc.

Branagh, Kenneth (1960–).
Belfast-born British leading actor, director and dramatist. In 1998, he set up the Shakespeare Film Co. to film Shakespeare's plays, beginning with a musical version of *Love's Labours Lost*, set in the 1930s. Formerly married to actress Emma Thompson, he has been romantically linked with actress Helena Bonham Carter.
Autobiography: 1989, *In the Beginning*.
Biography: 1994, *Ken & Em* by Ian Shuttleworth.
Fortunes of War (TV) 87. A Month in the Country 87. *Henry V* (a, d) (AAN) 89. Dead Again (a, d) 91. Peter's Friends (a, d) 92. Swing Kids (a) 92. *Much Ado about Nothing* (a, d) 93. Mary Shelley's Frankenstein (a, d) 94. The Shadow of a Gunman (a, TV) 95. In the Bleak Midwinter (wd) 95. Othello (as Iago) 95. Hamlet (title role, & wd) (AANw) 96. Celebrity 98. The Proposition 98. The Theory of Flight 98, etc.

Branch, Sarah (1938–).
British leading lady of the early 60s.
Sands of the Desert 60. Hell is a City 61. Sword of Sherwood Forest 61, etc.

Brand, Max (1892–1944) (Frederick Faust).
American popular novelist whose major bequests to Hollywood were *Destry Rides Again* and the Dr Kildare books. Killed in action as a war correspondent.

Brand, Neville (1921–1992).
Thickset American actor with stage and TV experience; often seen as Red Indian or gangster. In films from 1948 after ten years in the US Army: he was the fourth most decorated soldier.
D.O.A. 49. Halls of Montezuma 51. Stalag 17 53. *Riot in Cell Block Eleven* 54. Mohawk 55. The Tin Star 57. Cry Terror 58. Five Gates to Hell 59. *The Scarface Mob* (as Al Capone) 60. Huckleberry Finn 60. Birdman of Alcatraz 62. That Darn Cat 65. The Desperados 69. The Train Robbers 73. Scalawag 74. The Mad Bomber 75. Eaten Alive 76. The Quest (TV) 76. Captains Courageous (TV) 77. The Ninth Configuration 80. Without Warning 80. Alligator 80. Evils of the Night 85, many others.
TV series: The Untouchables 59–62 (as Al Capone). Laredo 66–67.

Brandauer, Klaus Maria (1944–).
Austrian actor and director, in international films.
Mephisto 82. Never Say Never Again 83. *Colonel Redl* 85. *Out of Africa* (AAN) 85. Quo Vadis (TV) 85. Streets of Gold 86. The Lightship 86. Burning Secret 89. Hanussen 89. Seven Minutes (& d) 89. The Russia House 90. White Fang 91. Becoming Colette 92. Mario and the Magician/Mario und der Zauberer (d) 94, etc.

Brando, Jocelyn (1919–).
American character actress, sister of Marlon Brando; film appearances rare.
The Big Heat 53. China Venture 53. Nightfall 56. The Explosive Generation 61. The Ugly American 63. Bus Riley's Back in Town 65. The Chase 66. A Question of Love (TV) 78, etc.

Brando, Marlon (1924–).
Unsmiling American leading actor whose prototype is the primitive modern male; he has however attempted a wide range of parts which have not always suited his 'method' technique and mumbling accent. Married actresses Anna Kashfi, Movita and Tarita Tariipaia.
Autobiography: 1994, *Brando: Songs My Mother Never Taught Me*.
Biographies: 1974, *Brando* by René Jordan. 1991, *Conversations with Brando* by Lawrence Grobel. 1991, *Brando: A Life in Our Times* by Richard Schickel. 1994, *Brando: The Biography* by Peter Manso. 1994, *Marlon Brando: A Portrait* by Paul Ryan.
The Men 50. *A Streetcar Named Desire* (AAN) 51. *Viva Zapata* (BFA, AAN) 52. *Julius Caesar* (as Mark Antony) (BFA, AAN) 53. *The Wild One* 53. *On the Waterfront* (AA, BFA) 54. Desirée (as Napoleon) 54. Guys and Dolls 55. *The Teahouse of the August Moon* 56. Sayonara (AAN) 57. *The Young Lions* 58. The Fugitive Kind 60. One Eyed Jacks (also directed) 60. Mutiny on the Bounty (as Fletcher Christian) 62. The Ugly American 63. Bedtime Story 64. The Saboteur 65. *The Chase* 66. The Appaloosa 66. A Countess from Hong Kong 67. Reflections in a Golden Eye 67. Candy 68. The Night of the Following Day 68. Queimada

70. The Nightcomers 71. *The Godfather* (AA) 72. *Last Tango in Paris* (AAN) 72. The Missouri Breaks 76. Superman 78. Roots: the New Generations (TV) 79. Apocalypse Now 79. The Formula 80. A Dry White Season (AAN) 89. The Freshman 90. Christopher Columbus: The Discovery 92. Don Juan DeMarco 95. The Island of Dr Moreau 96. The Brave 97, etc.

❝ Acting is an empty and useless profession. – M.B.

Most of the time he sounds like he has a mouth full of wet toilet paper. – *Rex Reed*

I have eyes like those of a dead pig. – M.B.

Acting is the expression of a neurotic impulse. It's a bum's life. Quitting acting, that's the sign of maturity. – M.B.

Once you're a star actor, people start asking you questions about politics, astronomy, archaeology, and birth control. – M.B.

An actor's a guy who, if you ain't talking about him, ain't listening. – M.B.

I'm not interested in making an assessment of myself and stripping myself for the general public to view. – M.B.

I think I would have liked to be a caveman, a neolithic person. – M.B.

Too much success can ruin you as surely as too much failure. – M.B.

I've never had any respect for Hollywood. It stands for avarice, phoniness, greed, crassness and bad taste, but when you act in a movie, you only have to work three months a year, then you can do as you please for the rest. – M.B.

He was deeply rebellious against the bourgeois spirit, the over-ordering of life. – *Elia Kazan*

Democracy is a fine way to run a country, but it's a hell of a way to make pictures. – *Lillian Hellman after working with Brando on The Chase*

An angel as a man, a monster as an actor. – *Bernardo Bertolucci*

He was in a unique position. He could have done anything. But he didn't choose to. – *Rod Steiger*

No actor of my generation has possessed greater natural gifts; but none other has transported intellectual falsity to higher levels of hilarious pretension. – *Truman Capote*

The once-beautiful, most distinguished actor of our time has turned into a self-loathing slob and left a lot of human wreckage in his wake. – *Peter Manso*

Famous line (*On the Waterfront*): 'I coulda had class. I coulda been a contender.'

Brandon, Henry (1912–1990) (Henry Kleinbach).
American character actor, a reliable menace for thirty years.

Babes in Toyland (as Barnaby) 34. The Garden of Allah 36. I Promise to Pay 37. Son of Monte Cristo 40. Edge of Darkness 43. Canon City 48. Scarlet Angel 52. Scared Stiff 53. Vera Cruz 54. The Searchers 56. The Buccaneer 58. Two Rode Together 61. *Where the North Wind Blows* 75, many others.

Brandon, Michael (1945–).
American leading man.

Lovers and Other Strangers 70. Four Flies on Grey Velvet 73. FM 78. A Vacation in Hell 79. Between Two Brothers (TV) 81. Deadly Messages (TV) 83. Déjà Vu 98, etc.

TV series: Emerald Point 83. Dempsey and Makepeace 84–86.

Brantford, Mrs Aggie (1884–*).
English character actress, on the stage from the age of seven, who made child stars of her two children, Aggie (1915–), whose career lasted from the age of two to 12, usually in films with her mother; and Mickey BRANTFORD, who started at the age of three.

A Will and a Way 22. Second to None 26. Heroes of the Mine 32. Everything Is Rhythm 36. Jacqueline 56, etc.

Brantford, Mickey (1911–).
Athletic English juvenile star of the 20s and 30s, in films from 1915. He was the son of Mrs Aggie BRANTFORD.

The Man the Army Made 15. The Road to Heaven 22. The Knockout 23. Afraid of Love 25. The Rolling Road 27. Sexton Blake, Gambler 28. Suspense 30. A 'Yell' of a Night 32. My Old Dutch 34. The Phantom Light 35. The Last Journey 35. Twice Branded 36. Darby and Joan 37, etc.

Brass, Tinto (1933–).
Italian director, mainly of soft-core porn, whose best-known film is *Caligula*.

Book: 1981, *Ultimate Porno* by PierNico Solinas (on the making of *Caligula*).

Chi Lavora è Perduto 63. La Mia Signora (co-d) 64. Yankee 66. Nerosubianco 69. Dropout 72. L'Urlo 72. Salon Kitty 76. Caligula 77. Action 79. La Chiave 85. Miranda 85. Snack Bar Budapest 88. Paprika 91. Cosi Fan Tutte 92. The Voyeur/ L'Uomo che Guarda (& a) 94. P.O. Box Tinto Brass (a, co-w, d) 95. Frivolous Lola 97, etc.

❝ All directors are voyeurs. Anybody who looks at the world through a hole is a voyeur. By definition. – *T.B.*

The difference between pornography and eroticism is not whether you see a penetration or you don't see it; it is how you show it. – *T.B.*

I put two big balls and a big cock between the legs of Italian cinema. – *T.B.*

First I look at the bottom of an actress. A bottom never lies. – *T.B.*

Brasselle, Keefe (1923–1981).
American light leading man who made little headway in movies but later, with the help of James Aubrey of CBS, became a television producer with several unsuccessful shows such as *The Baileys of Balboa* and *Mr Broadway*. He wrote a bitter novel about his experiences and called it *The Cannibals*.

■ Janie 44. River Gang 45. Railroaded 47. Not Wanted 48. Dial 1119 50. A Place in the Sun 51. Bannerline 51. It's a Big Country 52. Skirts Ahoy 52. *The Eddie Cantor Story* (title role) 53. Three Young Texans 54. Mad at the World 55. Battle Stations 56. West of Suez 57. If You Don't Stop It You'll Go Blind 77.

Brasseur, Claude (1936–).
French actor, son of Pierre Brasseur.

Eyes without a Face 60. Les Menteurs 61. The Vanishing Corporal 62. Germinal 63. Bande à Part 64. Un Homme de Trop 67. Portrait of Marianne 70. Such a Gorgeous Kid Like Me 72. Seins de Glace 74. Aggression 75. Pardon Mon Affaire 76. Une Histoire Simple 78. Ils Sont Grands Ces Petits 79. Josepha 81. La Boum 2 82. La Crime 83. Palace 84. Dandin 88. Dancing Machine 90. Dirty Like an Angel/Sale comme un Ange 91. Ville à Vendre 91. Le Souper 93. A Linha do Horizonte 93. Délit Mineur 94. Marriages/Matrimoni 98, many others.

Brasseur, Pierre (1903–1972) (P. Espinasse).
Distinguished French stage actor in occasional films from 1925.

Claudine à l'École 28. Café de Paris 33. *Quai des Brumes* 38. Lumière d'Été 42. *Les Enfants du Paradis* 44. Les Portes de la Nuit 46. Julie de Carneilhan 50. Bluebeard 51. Porte des Lilas 55. Eyes without a Face 59. Il Bell' Antonio 60. Deux Heures à Tuer 65. A New World 66. King of Hearts 67. Birds in Peru 68, etc.

Braugher, Andre (1969–).
American actor, best known for his role as Detective Frank Pembleton in the TV series *Homicide: Life on the Street*. Born in Chicago, Illinois, he studied at Stanford University.

Glory 89. The Court-Martial of Jackie Robinson (TV) 90. Murder in Mississippi 90. Somebody Has to Shoot the Picture (TV) 90. Striking Distance 93. The Tuskagee Airmen (TV) 95. Primal Fear 96. Get on the Bus 96. Thick as Thieves 98. City of Angels 98, etc.

TV series: Homicide: Life on the Streets 93–98.

Braunstein, Joseph:
see LARRAZ, José Ramón.

Bray, Robert (1917–1983).
American actor of the strong silent type.

Blood on the Moon 48. Warpath 52. Bus Stop 56. The Wayward Bus 57. My Gun is Quick (as Mike Hammer) 58. Never So Few 60, etc.

TV series: Man from Blackhawk 54. Stagecoach West 60. Lassie 67–68.

Brazzi, Rossano (1916–1994).
Handsome Italian romantic lead who apart from local work appeared in some successful international films.

Volcano 48. *Little Women* 49. *Three Coins in the Fountain* 54. The Barefoot Contessa 54. *Summertime* 55. The Story of Esther Costello 57. Legend of the Lost 57. Interlude 57. *South Pacific* 58. A Certain Smile 58. Count Your Blessings 59. The Light in the Piazza 62. Rome Adventure 62. Dark Purpose 64. The Battle of the Villa Fiorita 65. The Christmas That Almost Wasn't (& d) 66. The Bobo 67. Woman Times Seven 67. Krakatoa 68. The Italian Job 69. Honeymoon with a Stranger (TV) 69. The Survivors (TV 69. The Adventures 70. Psychout for Murder 70. The Great Waltz 72. Master of Love 74. The White Telephone 76. The Final Conflict 81. The Voice 82. Fear City 84. Final Justice 85. Formula for a Murder 86. The Third Solution 89. Christopher Columbus 91, etc.

TV series: The Survivors 69–70.

Breakston, George (1922–1973).
American who, born in France, went to Hollywood as a child and acted for several years; later went to Africa and produced many routine adventure films and TV series, usually with British backing.

AS ACTOR: Great Expectations 34. Mrs Wiggs of the Cabbage Patch 34. The Dark Angel 35. Love Finds Andy Hardy 38. Jesse James 39. The Courtship of Andy Hardy 42, etc.

AS PRODUCER: Urubu 48. Tokyo File 212 51. The Scarlet Spear (& d) 54. Golden Ivory 55. Escape in the Sun 56. Woman and the Hunter 57. Shadow of Treason (& d) 63. The Boy Cried Murder (& d) 66, etc.

Brecher, Irving (1914–).
American radio writer who moved on to Hollywood and received solo credit for two Marx Brothers scripts.

New Faces of 1937 37. *At the Circus* 39. Go West 40. Shadow of the Thin Man 41. Dubarry was a Lady 53. *Meet Me in St Louis* (AAN) 44. Yolanda and the Thief 45. Summer Holiday 47. The Life of Riley (& pd) 49. Somebody Loves Me (& d) 52. Cry for Happy 61. Sail a Crooked Ship (& d) 61. Bye Bye Birdie 63, etc.

TV series: The People's Choice 56–58.

Brecht, Bertolt (1898–1956).
German poet and playwright whose 'alienation method' (by which audiences are forced by various theatrical devices to remember that they are watching a play) has been influential on films from *Citizen Kane* to *Alfie*. His *Dreigroschenoper*, based on *The Beggar's Opera*, has been filmed twice; films have also been made of *Mother Courage*, *Herr Puntila* and *Galileo*. His sole Hollywood credit is for the script of *Hangmen Also Die*. His greatest cinematic achievement was *Kuhle Wampe* 32, for which he wrote the screenplay with Ernst Ottwald and, with the aid of director Slaten Dudow, cinematographer Gunter KRAMPF and composer Hanns EISLER, organized a collective to make it. The film depicted the plight of a working-class family in Berlin during the Depression.

Breck, Peter (1930–).
American general-purpose actor.

The Beatniks 60. Shock Corridor 63. The Crawling Hand 63. A Man for Hanging 72. Benji 74. Highway 61 91, etc.

TV series: Black Saddle 58–59. The Big Valley 65–68. The Secret Empire 79. Also episodes of Maverick (as Bat Masterson).

Bredin, Patricia.
English singer and leading actress of the late 50s, from the stage. She performed the first British entry, 'All', in the TV Eurovision Song Contest in 1957.

Geordie 55. The Bridal Path 59. Make Mine a Million 59. Desert Mice 59. Left, Right and Centre 59. The Treasure of Monte Cristo 61. To Have and To Hold 63, etc.

Breen, Bobby (1927–).
American boy singer of the 30s; later gave up films for night club work.

Let's Sing Again 36. Rainbow on the River 36. Make a Wish 37. Hawaii Calls 37. Breaking the Ice 38. Fisherman's Wharf 39. Way Down South 39. Johnny Doughboy 43, etc.

Breen, Joseph (1890–1965).
American executive, for many years administrator of the Production Code. See: CENSORSHIP

Breen, Richard L. (1919–1967).
American scenarist. Former president of Screenwriters' Guild.

A Foreign Affair (co-w, AAN) 48. Miss Tatlock's Millions 49. The Model and the Marriage Broker 51. Niagara 53. Titanic (AA) 53. Dragnet 54. Pete Kelly's Blues 55. Stopover Tokyo (& d) 57. Wake Me When It's Over 60. Captain Newman 63. Do Not Disturb 65. Tony Rome 67, many others.

Breese, Edmund (1871–1936).
American character actor, from the stage.

The Song of the Wage Slave 15. Luck 23. The Brown Derby 26. Sonny Boy 29. Tol'able David 30. All Quiet on the Western Front 30. Mata Hari 32. The Cabin in the Cotton 32. International House 33. Duck Soup 33. Treasure Island 34. The Marriage Bargain 35, etc.

Bregman, Martin (1926–).
American producer. In 1992 he formed M & M Productions with Michael Caine.

Serpico 73. Dog Day Afternoon 75. The Next Man 76. The Seduction of Joe Tynan 79. Simon 80. The Four Seasons 81. Venom 82. Eddie Macon's Run 83. Scarface 83. Sweet Liberty 86. A New Life 88. Sea of Love 89. Betsy's Wedding 90. Blue Ice 92. Carlito's Way 93, etc.

Breil, Joseph Carl (1870–1926).
American composer who wrote and arranged the music to accompany silent films, including several by D. W. Griffith. In the process he created the first hit song from a movie score: the love theme from *The Birth of a Nation* for scenes between the Little Colonel and Elsie Stoneman, published as 'The Perfect Song', which later became the theme tune of the radio show *Amos 'n' Andy*.

Queen Elizabeth 12. The Prisoner of Zenda 13. The Birth of a Nation 15. The Lily and the Rose 15. Intolerance 16. The Dramatic Life of Abraham Lincoln 23. America 24, etc.

Bremer, Lucille (1922–1996).
American dancer. MGM groomed her for stardom in the 40s, but her career was brief.

■ Meet Me in St Louis 44. *Yolanda and the Thief* 45. *Ziegfeld Follies* 45. Till the Clouds Roll By 46. Dark Delusion 47. Adventures of Casanova 48. Ruthless 48. Behind Locked Doors 48.

Bremner, Ewen.
Scottish actor.

Heavenly Pursuits 86. Conquest of the South Pole 89. Naked 93. The Prince of Jutland 94. *Trainspotting* 96. Mojo 97. The Life of Stuff 97. The Acid House 98, etc.

Brendel, El (1890–1964).
Mild-mannered American comic actor, a fake Swede from vaudeville with an attractive way of fracturing the English language.

The Campus Flirt 26. Wings 27. *Sunny Side Up* 29. The Big Trail 30. *Just Imagine* 30. Mr Lemon of Orange 30. Delicious 31. Hot Pepper 32. My Lips Betray 33. God's Country and the Woman 37. Little Miss Broadway 38. *If I Had My Way* 40. Captain Caution 40. Machine Gun Mama 44. The Beautiful Blonde from Bashful Bend 49. The She Creature 56, many others.

~Catchphrase: 'Yumping Yiminy!'

Brennan, Eileen (1935–).
Brassy American character actress.

Divorce American Style 67. The Last Picture Show 71. Playmates (TV) 72. The Blue Knight (TV) 73. Scarecrow 73. The Sting 73. Daisy Miller 74. My Father's House (TV) 75. The Night That Panicked America (TV) 75. At Long Last Love 75. Hustle 75. Murder by Death 76. The Death of Richie (TV) 77. All That Glitters (TV) 77. Last of the Cowboys 77. The Great Smokey Roadblock 78. FM 78. The Cheap Detective 78. My Old Man (TV). 79. Black Beauty (TV) 79. *Private Benjamin* (AAN) 80. When the Circus Came to Town (TV) 80. The Funny Farm 82. Pandemonium 82. Clue 85. The Fourth Wise Man 85. Blood Vows – the Story of a Mafia Wife (TV) 87. The New Adventures of Pippi Longstocking 88. Rented Lips 88. Sticky Fingers 88. It Had To Be You 89. Stella 90. Texasville 90. White Palace 90. Reckless 95. Changing Habits 97, etc.

TV series: All that Glitters 77. 13 Queens Boulevard 79. A New Kind of Family 79–80. Private Benjamin 81–82 (cancelled because of her car accident). Off the Rack 85. Blossom 91.

Brennan, Michael (1912–1982).
'Tough guy' British supporting actor, in films from 1932.

The Clouded Yellow 50. Ivanhoe 52. Trouble in

Store 56. The Day They Robbed the Bank of England 60. Thunderball 65. Lust for a Vampire 70, many others.

Brennan, Walter (1894–1974).
Popular American character actor who played toothless old men in his 30s, and was still a star in his 70s. Best remembered as a countrified wit, he also played villains and city slickers.
■ The Long Long Trail 29. The Shannons of Broadway 29. Smiling Guns 29. King of Jazz 30. One Hysterical Night 30. Dancing Dynamite 31. Neck and Neck 31. Law and Order 32. Texas Cyclone 32. Two Fisted Law 32. All American 32. Parachute Jumper 32. The Fourth Horseman 32. Strange Justice 32. Man of Action 33. Fighting for Justice 33. Sing Sinner Sing 33. Strange People 33. Silent Men 33. One Year Later 33. Goldie Gets Along 33. The Invisible Man 33. Good Dame 34. Half a Sinner 34. Great Expectations 34. The Crosby Case 34. Northern Frontier 35. The Wedding Night 35. Bride of Frankenstein 35. Lady Tubbs 35. Man on the Flying Trapeze 35. Metropolitan 35. Barbary Coast 35. Seven Keys to Baldpate 35. These Three 36. Three Godfathers 36. The Moon's Our Home 36. Fury 36. The Prescott Kid 36. *Come and Get It* (AA) 36. Banjo on My Knee 36. She's Dangerous 36. When Love Is Young 37. The Affair of Cappy Ricks 37. Wild and Woolly 37. *The Adventures of Tom Sawyer* 38. The Buccaneer 38. The Texans 38. Mother Carey's Chickens 38. *Kentucky* (AA) 38. The Cowboy and the Lady 38. The Story of Vernon and Irene Castle 38. They Shall Have Music 39. *Stanley and Livingstone* 39. Joe and Ethel Turp Call on the President 39. Northwest Passage 40. Maryland 40. *The Westerner* (as Judge Roy Bean) (AA) 40. This Woman Is Mine 41. Nice Girl 41. *Meet John Doe* 41. *Sergeant York* (AAN) 41. *Swamp Water* 41. Rise and Shine 41. Pride of the Yankees 42. Stand by for Action 42. Slightly Dangerous 43. Hangmen Also Die 43. North Star 43. Home in Indiana 43. *To Have and Have Not* 44. The Princess and the Pirate 44. Dakota 45. A Stolen Life 46. Centennial Summer 46. Nobody Lives Forever 46. *My Darling Clementine* (as Old Clanton) 46. Driftwood 47. Scudda Hoo Scudda Hay 48. Red River 48. Blood on the Moon 48. The Green Promise 49. The Great Dan Patch 49. Brimstone 49. Task Force 49. Singing Guns 50. A Ticket to Tomahawk 50. Curtain Call at Cactus Creek 50. The Showdown 50. Surrender 50. Best of the Bad Men 51. Along the Great Divide 51. The Wild Blue Yonder 51. Return of the Texan 52. Lure of the Wilderness 52. Sea of Lost Ships 53. The Far Country 54. Drums Across the River 54. Four Guns to the Border 54. At Gunpoint 55. Bad Day at Black Rock 55. *Come Next Spring* 56. Glory 56. Goodbye My Lady 56. The Proud Ones 56. Tammy and the Bachelor 57. The Way to the Gold 57. God Is My Partner 57. *Rio Bravo* 59. How the West Was Won 62. Those Calloways 64. The Oscar 66. *Who's Minding the Mint?* 67. The Gnome-mobile 67. The One and Only Genuine Original Family Band 67. Support Your Local Sheriff 69. The Over the Hill Gang (TV) 70. The Young Country (TV) 70. Two for the Money (TV) 71. The Over the Hill Gang Rides Again (TV) 71. Smoke in the Wind 71. Home for the Holidays (TV) 72.
TV series: *The Real McCoys* 57–63. Tycoon 64. *The Guns of Will Sonnett* 67–68. To Rome with Love 69.
✪ For long and spirited service, with and without his teeth. *The Westerner*.

Brenneman, Amy (1964–).
American leading actress, best known for her role as Janice Licalsi in the TV series *NYPD Blue*. She studied comparative religion at Harvard before joining the American Repertory Company. Married director Brad Silberling.
Middle Ages 92. Bye Bye Love 95. Casper 95. Heat 95. Fear 96. Daylight 96. Your Friends and Neighbors 98, etc.
TV series: NYPD Blue 93–94.

Brenner, Albert. (1926–).
American production designer.
The Hustler 61. The Pawnbroker 65. Point Blank 67. Bullitt 68. Monte Walsh 70. Summer of '42 71. Scarecrow 73. The Sunshine Boys (AAN) 75. The Missouri Breaks 76. Silent Movie 76. The Turning Point (AAN) 77. California Suite (AAN) 78. Only When I Laugh 81. Two of a Kind 83. Unfaithfully Yours 84. 2010 (AAN) 84. Sweet Dreams 85. Monster Squad 87. The Presidio 88. Baja Oklahoma 88. Beaches (AAN) 88. Pretty Woman 90. Backdraft 91. Frankie and Johnny 91. Mr Saturday Night 92. The Program 93. Under Siege 2: Dark Territory 95. Dear God 96, etc.

Brenner, Jules.
American cinematographer.
Johnny Got His Gun 71. The Glass House (TV) 72. Dillinger 73. Posse 75. Outlaw Blues 77. When You Comin' Back Red Ryder? 79. The Last Word 79. The Return of the Living Dead 85. Teen Wolf Too 87. 1969 88. Sins of the Mother (TV) 91, etc.

Brenon, Herbert (1880–1958).
Irish director, in Hollywood after stage experience: a big name of the 20s.
Ivanhoe 13. The Kreuzer Sonata 15. War Brides 16. The Passing of the Third Floor Back 18. The Sign on the Door 21. The Spanish Dancer 23. *Peter Pan* 24. A Kiss for Cinderella 24. *Beau Geste* 26. *Sorrell and Son* (GB) (AAN) 27. The Great Gatsby 27. Laugh Clown Laugh 28. The Rescue 29. Beau Ideal 29. Oliver Twist 33. Wine Women and Song 34. The Housemaster (GB) 38. At the Villa Rose (GB) 38. Yellow Sands (GB) 38. The Flying Squadron (GB) 40, etc.

Brent, Eve (1930–).
American leading lady who played Jane in *Tarzan's Fight for Life* 55. *Tarzan and the Trappers* 57.

Brent, Evelyn (1899–1975) (Mary Elizabeth Riggs).
American leading lady of the silent era; made a few talkies, then retired apart from some bit parts in the 40s.
The Other Man's Wife 19. The Shuttle of Life (GB) 20. Sybil (GB) 21. Married to a Mormon (GB) 22. Silk Stocking Sal 24. Smooth as Satin 25. Love 'Em and Leave 'Em 26. Queen of Diamonds 26. *Underworld* 27. Beau Sabreur 28. A Night of Mystery 28. The Mating Call 28. *Broadway* 29. *Slightly Scarlet* 30. Madonna of the Streets 30. The Pagan Lady 31. The World Gone Mad 33. Home on the Range 35. Night Club Scandal 37. Mr Wong Detective 38. The Mad Empress 40. The Seventh Victim 43. Bowery Champs 44. The Golden Eye 48, many others.

Brent, George (1904–1979) (George Brent Nolan).
Irishman who went to Hollywood and after years as a tough hero developed into a light leading man very effective against strong actresses such as Bette Davis and Myrna Loy. His five wives included actresses Ruth Chatterton (1932–34) and Ann Sheridan (1942–43).
■ SOUND FILMS: Under Suspicion 30. Lightning Warrior 31. Homicide Squad 31. Once a Sinner 31. Fair Warning 31. Charlie Chan Carries On 31. Ex Bad Boy 31. So Big 32. The Rich Are Always With Us 32. Weekend Marriage 32. Miss Pinkerton 32. Purchase Price 32. The Crash 32. They Call It Sin 32. Luxury Liner 33. *Forty Second Street* 33. The Keyhole 33. Lilly Turner 33. Baby Face 33. Female 33. Stamboul Quest 34. Housewife 34. Desirable 34. *The Painted Veil* 34. Living on Velvet 35. Stranded 35. *Front Page Woman* 35. The Goose and the Gander 35. Special Agent 35. In Person 35. The Right to Live 35. Snowed Under 36. The Golden Arrow 36. The Case Against Mrs Ames 36. Give Me Your Heart 36. More than a Secretary 36. God's Country and the Woman 37. The Go-getter 37. Mountain Justice 37. Gold Is Where You Find It 37. Submarine D-1 37. *Jezebel* 38. Racket Busters 38. Secrets of an Actress 38. Wings of the Navy 39. *Dark Victory* 39. The Old Maid 39. *The Rains Came* 39. The Man Who Talked Too Much 40. Till We Meet Again 40. The Fighting 69th 40. South of Suez 40. Adventure in Diamonds 40. Honeymoon for Three 41. *The Great Lie* 41. They Dare Not Love 41. International Lady 41. Twin Beds 42. The Gay Sisters 42. In This Our Life 42. You Can't Escape Forever 42. Silver Queen 42. Experiment Perilous 44. *The Affairs of Susan* 45. My Reputation 45. *The Spiral Staircase* 45. Tomorrow Is Forever 46. Lover Come Back 46. Temptation 46. Slave Girl 47. Out of the Blue 47. The Corpse Came COD 47. Christmas Eve 47. Luxury Liner 48. Angel on the Amazon 48. Red Canyon 49. Illegal Entry 49. Kid from Cleveland 49. Bride for Sale 49. FBI Girl 51. The Dark Page (GB) 51. Montana Belle 52. Tangier Incident 53. Born Again 78.
TV series: Wire Service 56.
✪ For behaving like the perfect gentleman in company with some extremely difficult ladies. *The Rains Came*.

Brent, Romney (1902–1976) (Romulo Larralde).
Dapper Mexican actor in British films in the 30s, later elsewhere.
East Meets West 36. Dreaming Lips 37. School for Husbands 37. Under the Red Robe 37. Dinner at the Ritz (& w) 37. Let George Do It 40. The Adventures of Don Juan 48. The Virgin Queen 55. Don't Go Near the Water 57. The Sign of Zorro 58, etc.

Brenta, Mario (1942–).
Italian director and screenwriter, from television documentaries.
Vermisat 74. Maicol 88. Barnabo of the Mountains/Barnabo della Montagna 94, etc.

Breon, Edmund (1882–1951) (Edmund McLaverty).
Beaming, monocled British stage actor, often seen as amiable bumbler. In Hollywood from late 20s, Britain 1933–42.
The Dawn Patrol 30. I Like Your Nerve 31. *Three Men in a Boat* 33. No Funny Business 33. The Scarlet Pimpernel 35. Keep Fit 37. A Yank at Oxford 38. Goodbye Mr Chips 39. The Outsider 39. She Shall Have Music 42. Gaslight 44. Casanova Brown 44. *The Woman in the Window* 45. *Dressed To Kill* 46. Forever Amber 47. Enchantment 48. Challenge to Lassie 50. At Sword's Point 51, etc.

Bresler, Jerry (1912–1977).
American independent producer.
Main Street after Dark 44. Bewitched 45. The Web 47. *Another Part of the Forest* 48. The Flying Missile 50. The Mob 51. Assignment Paris 52. Lizzie 57. *The Vikings* 58. Gidget Goes Hawaiian 61. Diamond Head 63. Major Dundee 65. Pussycat Pussycat I Love You 70, etc.

Bressart, Felix (1890–1949).
German character actor in Hollywood from late 30s, usually in downtrodden comic roles; a genuine original.
■ Drei von der Tankstelle 31. Der Wahre Jakob 31. Das Alte Lied 31. Nie Weider Liebe 31. Eine Freundin so Goldig wie Du 31. Der Schrecken der Garnison 32. Hirsekorn Greift Ein 32. Der Herr Buerovorsteher 32. Holzapfel Weiss Alles 33. Drei Tage Mittelarrest 33. Der Sohn der Weissen Berge 33. Der Glueckszylinger 34. Und Wer Kuesst Mich? 35. Three Smart Girls Grow Up 39. Bridal Suite 39. Swanee River 39. *Ninotchka* 39. The Shop Around the Corner 40. It All Came True 40. Edison the Man 40. Third Finger Left Hand 40. Bitter Sweet 40. Comrade X 40. Escape 40. Ziegfeld Girl 40. Blossoms in the Dust 41. Married Bachelor 41. Kathleen 41. Mr and Mrs North 41. *To Be or Not to Be* 42. Crossroads 42. Iceland 42. Three Hearts for Julia 43. Song of Russia 43. Above Suspicion 43. Greenwich Village 44. The Seventh Cross 44. Blonde Fever 44. Dangerous Partners 44. Without Love 45. Ding Dong Williams 46. I've Always Loved You 46. The Thrill of Brazil 46. Her Sister's Secret 46. A Song Is Born 48. Portrait of Jennie 48. Take One False Step 49.

Bresslaw, Bernard (1933–1993).
British comic actor who sprang to fame as giant-sized dope in TV series *The Army Game* 57–62 but proved lacking in big-screen star quality.
I Only Arsked 57. Too Many Crooks 58. The Ugly Duckling 59. Morgan 66. Carry On Screaming 66. Up Pompeii 70. Vampira 74. One of our Dinosaurs is Missing 76. Hawk the Slayer 80. Krull 83, many others in small roles.

Bresson, Robert (1907–).
Elusive French writer-director of austere, introspective, low-budget films.
■ Les Anges du Péché 43. *Les Dames du Bois de Boulogne* 44. *Le Journal d'un Curé de Campagne* 50. Un Condamné à Mort s'est Echappé 56. Pickpocket 59. The Trial of Joan of Arc 62. Au Hasard Balthazar 66. Mouchette 67. Une Femme Douce 69. Quatre Nuits d'un Rêveur 71. Lancelot du Lac 74. Le Diable Probablement 77. L'Argent 83.
❝ A film is not a spectacle: it is pre-eminently a style. – *R.B.*

Brest, Martin (1951–).
American director.
Hot Tomorrows 78. Going in Style 79. Beverly Hills Cop 84. *Midnight Run* 88. Scent of a Woman (AAN) 92. Meet Joe Black 98, etc.

Bretherton, David.
American film editor, on the staff of Twentieth Century-Fox for 20 years.
The Living Swamp 55. The Dark Wave 56. Peyton Place 57. Ten North Frederick 58. Let's Make Love 60. Return to Peyton Place 61. State Fair 62. The Sandpiper 65. Villa Rides 68. On a Clear Day You Can See Forever 69. Lovers and Other Strangers 70. Cabaret (AA) 72. Slither 73. Westworld 74. The Man in the Glass Booth 75. Silver Streak 76. Coma 78. Winter Kills 79. The Big Red One 80. Cannery Row 82. Love Lines 84. Clue 85. Lionheart 86. The Pick-Up Artist 87. Sea of Love 89. Malice 93, etc.

Bretherton, Howard (1896–1969).
American director of second features.
Hills of Kentucky 27. The Redeeming Sin 29. Isle of Escape 30. The Match King 32. Ladies They Talk About 33. The Return of the Terror 34. The Leathernecks Have Landed 36. It Happened Out West 37. The Girl Who Dared 44. Prince of Thieves 48. Whip Law 50, many others.

Brett, Jeremy (1935–1995) (Jeremy Huggins).
British light leading man. Educated at Eton, he changed his name, at his father's insistence, to hide the social disgrace of having an actor in the family. A highly regarded theatre actor, he found his polished style out of tune with the times and had his greatest success on television as Sherlock Holmes, a role that he grew to hate. Married actress Anna MASSEY (1958–62). His lovers included actor Gary BOND.
Biography: 1997, *The Man Who Became Sherlock Holmes* by Terry Manners.
War and Peace 56. The Wild and the Willing 61. The Very Edge 63. *My Fair Lady* 64. The Medusa Touch 77. Florence Nightingale (TV) 84. Deceptions (TV) 84. Mad Dogs and Englishmen 95. Moll Flanders 96, etc.
❝ He was terribly good-looking and always suffered for it. – *Robert Stephens*

Brialy, Jean-Claude (1933–).
French leading man.
Éléna et les Hommes 56. Lift to the Scaffold 57. Le Beau Serge 58. The Four Hundred Blows 59. Tire au Flanc 61. La Chambre Ardente 62. The Devil and Ten Commandments 62. La Ronde 64. Un Homme de Trop 67. King of Hearts 67. Le Rouge et le Noir 70. Claire's Knee 71. The Phantom of Liberty 74. Catherine and Company 75. Le Point de Mire 77. Robert et Robert 78. La Banquière 80. The Judge and the Assassin 81. The Demon of the Isle 83. Sarah 83. Pinot, Simple Flic 84. Grand Guignol 86. Inspector Lavardin 86. Les Innocents 87. Le Cop 2/Ripoux contre Ripoux 89. S'en Fout La Mort 89. August/Août 91. Queen Margot/La Reine Margot 94. Une Femme Française 95, etc.
ALSO DIRECTED: Eglantine 72. Closed Shutters 73. Un Amour de Pluie 74, etc.

Brian, David (1914–1993).
Stalwart American second lead, a former song-and-dance man who came to Hollywood in 1949 and sank into a groove of toughness and reliability, with a streak of villainy when required.
Flamingo Road 49. Beyond the Forest 49. *Intruder in the Dust* 49. The Damned Don't Cry 50. Breakthrough 50. Inside Straight 51. This Woman is Dangerous 52. Million Dollar Mermaid 52. The High and the Mighty 54. Timberjack 55. The First Travelling Saleslady 56. The Rabbit Trap 59. A Pocketful of Miracles 61. How the West was Won 62. The Rare Breed 68. The Destructors 69. The Seven Minutes 71, many others.
TV series: *Mr District Attorney* 54–55. The Immortal 70.

Brian, Mary (1908–) (Louise Dantzler).
Charming American leading lady of the 20s; her roles diminished with sound and finally petered out.
Peter Pan (as Wendy) 24. The Little French Girl 25. Brown of Harvard 26. Beau Geste 26. Running Wild 27. Shanghai Bound 27. Harold Teen 28. Varsity 28. The Man I Love 29. *The Virginian* 29. The Light of Western Stars 30. *The Royal Family of Broadway* 30. *The Front Page* 31. Blessed Event 32. Girl Missing 33. College Rhythm 34. Charlie Chan in Paris 35. Killer at Large 36. The Amazing Quest of Ernest Bliss (GB) 36. Navy Bound 37. Calaboose 43. The Dragnet 48, many others.

Briant, Shane (1946–).
British general-purpose actor, mainly in Australia.
Demons of the Mind 70. Straight on till Morning 71. Captain Kronos 72. Frankenstein and the Monster from Hell 72. Moving Targets 87. True Colors 87. Cassandra 87. Grievous Bodily Harm 89. Till There Was You 90. Tunnel Vision 95, etc.

Brice, Fanny (1891–1951) (Fanny Borach).
American Jewish entertainer who made a virtue of her plainness. Screen appearances rare, but four films were based on her life: *Broadway thro' a Keyhole* 33, *Rose of Washington Square* 38, *Funny Girl* 68, *Funny Lady* 75.
Biography: 1992, *Fanny Brice – the Original Funny Girl* by Herbert G. Goldman.
■ My Man 28. Night Club 29. Be Yourself 30. The Great Ziegfeld 36. Everybody Sing 38. Ziegfeld Follies 45.

Brickman, Marshall (1941–).
American screenwriter and director.
Sleeper (co-w) 73. *Annie Hall* (co-w) (AA) 77. *Manhattan* (co-w) (AAN) 79. Simon (& d) 80. Lovesick (& d) 83. The Manhattan Project (& d) 86. For the Boys (d) 91. Manhattan Murder Mystery (co-w) 93. Intersection (co-w) 94, etc.

Brickman, Paul (1949–).
American screenwriter and director.
The Bad News Bears in Breaking Training (w) 77. Citizen's Band/Handle with Care (w) 77. Risky Business (d) 83. Deal of the Century (w) 83. Men Don't Leave (co-w, d) 90.

Bricusse, Leslie (1931–).
British lyricist and composer.
Charley Moon 56. Stop the World I Want to Get Off 65. Doctor Dolittle (AA) 67. Goodbye Mr Chips (AAN) 69. Scrooge (AAN) 70. Willie Wonka and the Chocolate Factory (AAN) 71. Revenge of the Pink Panther 78. Superman 78. The Sea Wolves 80. Victor/Victoria 82. Babes in Toyland (TV) 86. Bullseye! 91, etc.

Bridge, Al (1891–1957).
Gravel-voiced American character actor chiefly memorable in Preston Sturges comedies.
Christmas in July 40. The Palm Beach Story 42. *Hail the Conquering Hero* 44, etc.

Bridges, Alan (1927–).
British director, from TV.
■ *An Act of Murder* 65. *Invasion* 66. The Lie (TV) 70. The Hireling 73. Brief Encounter (TV) 75. Out of Season 75. Summer Rain (Can.) 76. The Return of the Soldier 82. The Shooting Party 84. Displaced Person (TV) 85. Apt Pupil 88.

Bridges, Beau (1941–).
American leading man, son of Lloyd Bridges.
Force of Evil 48. The Red Pony 49. The Incident 67. For Love of Ivy 68. *Gaily Gaily* 69. *The Landlord* 70. Adam's Woman 70. The Christian Licorice Store 71. Hammersmith is Out 72. Child's Play 72. Loving Molly 73. The Other Side of the Mountain 75. Medical Story (TV) 75. One Summer Love 76. Swashbuckler 76. Two Minute Warning 76. Greased Lightning 77. The Fifth Musketeer 77. The Four Feathers (TV) 78. The President's Mistress (TV) 78. Norma Rae 79. The Child Stealer (TV) 79. The Runner Stumbles (TV) 79. Honky Tonk Freeway (TV) 81. Love Child 82. Night Crossing 82. Dangerous Company (TV) 82. Heart Like a Wheel 83. Witness for the Prosecution (TV) 84. Space (TV) 85. The Red Light Sting (TV) 86. The Wild Pair (& d) 87. Seven Hours to Judgement (& d) 88. The Fabulous Baker Boys 89. The Iron Triangle 89. Signs of Life 89. Daddy's Dyin', Who's Got the Will? 90. Married to It 91. The Positively True Adventures of the Alleged Texas Cheerleader-Murdering Mom (TV) 93. Sidekicks 93. Secret Sins of the Father (& d) (TV) 94. Kissinger and Nixon (TV, as Nixon) 95. Losing Chase 96. Hidden in America (TV) 96, etc.
TV series: Ensign O'Toole 62–64. United States 80. Harts of the West 93. Maximum Bob 98.

Bridges, James (1936–1993).
American writer-director, a former actor.
■ The Appaloosa (co-w only) 66. The Forbin Project (w only) 70. The Baby Maker 70. The Paper Chase (AANw) 73. September 30, 1955 77. The China Syndrome (AANw) 79. Urban Cowboy 80. Mike's Murder 82. Perfect 84. Bright Lights, Big City 88. White Hunter, Black Heart (w) 90.

Bridges, Jeff (1949–).
American leading man, son of Lloyd Bridges.
Halls of Anger 70. In Search of America (TV) 70. The Last Picture Show (AAN) 71. Fat City 71. Bad Company 72. The Last American Hero 73. Lolly Madonna XXX 73. The Iceman Cometh 73. Thunderbolt and Lightfoot (AAN) 74. Rancho de Luxe 75. *Hearts of the West* 75. Stay Hungry 76. King Kong 76. Somebody Killed Her Husband 79. Winter Kills 79. Success 79. Heaven's Gate 80. Cutter's Way 81. Tron 82. Kiss Me Goodbye 82. Against All Odds 83. Starman (AAN) 84. Jagged Edge 85. 8 Million Ways to Die 85. The Morning After 86. Nadine 87. Tucker: The Man and His Dream 88. The Fabulous Baker Boys 89. See You in the Morning 89. Texasville 90. The Fisher King 91. American Heart 92. The Vanishing 93. Fearless 93. Blown Away 94. Wild Bill 95. White Squall 96. The Mirror Has Two Faces 96. Hidden in America (TV) 96. Arlington Road 98. The Muse 99, etc.

Bridges, Lloyd (1913–1998).
American general-purpose actor and sometimes leading man who, over 30 years, has brought a sense of integrity to many westerns and melodramas.
Here Comes Mr Jordan 41. The Lone Wolf Takes a Chance 41. Atlantic Convoy 42. The Heat's On 43. The Master Race 44. Strange Confession 45. Miss Susie Slagle's 46. Canyon Passage 46. Ramrod 47. Sixteen Fathoms Deep 48. Moonrise 49. *Home of the Brave* 49. Trapped 49. Rocketship XM 50. The White Tower 50. *Try and Get Me* 51. Little Big Horn 51. The Whistle at Eaton Falls 51. High Noon 52. Plymouth Adventure 52. City of Bad Men 53. The Tall Texan 53. The Limping Man (GB) 54. Apache Woman 55. Wetbacks 56. The Rainmaker 56. *The Goddess* 58. Around the World Under the Sea 66. Attack on the Iron Coast 68. *The Love War* (TV) 70. The Silent Gun (TV) 70. To Find a Man 72. Haunts of the Very Rich (TV) 72. Trouble Comes to Town (TV) 73. Running Wild 73. Crime Club (TV) 73. Death Race (TV) 73. Stowaway to the Moon (TV) 75. The Return of Joe Forrester (TV) 75. Roots (TV) 77. Telethon (TV) 77. The Great Wallendas (TV) 78. The Critical List (TV) 78. Airplane 80. Grace Kelly (TV) 82. Weekend Warriors 86. The Wild Pair 87. Cousins 89. Joe Versus the Volcano 90. Hot Shots! 91. Devlin 92. Honey, I Blew Up the Kid 92. Hot Shoes! Part Deux 93. Run of Hearts 93. Secret Sins of the Father (TV) 94. Blown Away 94. Mafia!/Jane Austen's Mafia 98, etc.
TV series: *Sea Hunt* 57–60. The Lloyd Bridges Show 62. *The Loner* 65. San Francisco International 70. Joe Forrester 75. Paper Dolls 85. Harts of the West 93.

Bridie, James (1888–1951) (Osborne Henry Mavor).
Pawky Scottish dramatist whose works were more suited to stage than screen. Two films which did result were *Flesh and Blood* (from *A Sleeping Clergyman*) and *Folly to Be Wise* (from *It Depends What You Mean*).

Briers, Richard (1934–).
British comic character actor, a farceur who inherited the mantle of Ralph Lynn and was popular on TV.
Girls at Sea 58. The Girl on the Boat 62. Fathom 67. Rentadick 72. A Chorus of Disapproval 89. Henry V 90. Much Ado about Nothing 93. Skallagrigg (TV) 94. Mary Shelley's Frankenstein 94. In the Bleak Midwinter 95. P. G. Wodehouse's Heavy Weather (TV) 95. A Respectable Trade (TV) 98, etc.
TV series: Marriage Lines 63–66. Birds on the Wing 71. The Good Life 75–78. The Other One 77–79. Goodbye Mr Kent 82. Ever Decreasing Circles 84–89. All in Good Faith 85–88. If You See God, Tell Him 93.
❝ At drama school I played Hamlet and all the usual things one does. Then I got into the real world and realised I only had a one-string fiddle, a single talent – an instinctive sense of comedy timing. – *R.B.*
I know the word 'bumbling' often comes up when people discuss me. I don't mind, but I prefer 'obsessive'. – *R.B.*

Briggs, Harlan (1880–1952).
American small-part actor.
Dodsworth 36. A Family Affair 37. One Wild Night 38. Calling Dr Kildare 39. Abe Lincoln in Illinois 40. One Foot in Heaven 41. Tennessee Johnson 43. State Fair 45. A Double Life 48. Carrie 52, many others.

Briggs, Johnny (1935–).
British character actor, often a cockney on the wrong side of the law, best known for the role of Mike Baldwin in the TV soap opera *Coronation Street*.
Hue and Cry 47. Cosh Boy 53. Diplomatic Corpse 58. Light Up the Sky 60. 633 Squadron 64. Perfect Friday 70. Carry On Behind 75, etc.

Briley, John (1925–).
American-born screenwriter in Britain.
Postman's Knock 61. Children of the Damned 64. Pope Joan 72. That Lucky Touch 75. Eagle's Wing 79. *Gandhi* (AA) 82. Cry Freedom 87. Christopher Columbus: The Discovery 92. The Populist 97. Father Damien 99, etc.

Brimley, Wilford (1934–).
American character actor who plays wise, rough-edged old gents and hovers just below the star level.
The Electric Horseman 79. Brubaker 79. Borderline 80. The China Syndrome 80. Heaven's Gate 80. Death Valley 82. Absence of Malice 82. Tender Mercies 83. Ten to Midnight 83. Country 84. Hotel New Hampshire 84. The Natural 84. American Justice 85. Cocoon 85. Remo Williams 85. Act of Vengeance (TV) 86. American Justice/Jackals 86. Thompson's Last Run (TV) 86. End of the Line 87. Cocoon: The Return 88. Eternity 90. The Firm 93. Hard Target 93. The Good Old Boys 95. Tom Clancy's Op Center (TV) 95. In & Out 97. Summer of the Monkey (Can.) 98, etc.
TV series: *Our House* 86–88.

Brinegar, Paul (1917–1995).
American character actor, a long-time mainstay of television westerns, including the trail cook Wishbone in *Rawhide*.
Larceny 48. The Gal Who Took the West 49. The Captive City 51. Human Desire 54. How to Make a Monster 58. Charro! 69. High Plains Drifter 73. Maverick 94, etc.
TV series: The Life and Legend of Wyatt Earp 56–58. Rawhide 59–66. Lancer 69–70. Matt Houston 82–83.

Brinton, Ralph (1895–).
British art director, a former architect, in films from the mid-30s.
All at Sea 35. Wings of the Morning 37. Odd Man Out 47. Uncle Silas 47. The Chiltern Hundreds 49. Eye Witness 50. Scrooge 51. The Knave of Hearts 54. Moby Dick 56. The Gypsy and the Gentleman 58. Room at the Top 58. The Entertainer 60. A Taste of Honey 61. The Loneliness of the Long Distance Runner 62. *Tom Jones* (AAN) 63. Isadora 68, etc.

Brissac, Virginia (1894–1979).
American supporting actress, a familiar face in mother and neighbour roles.
A Tree Grows in Brooklyn 44. Monsieur Verdoux 47. The Snake Pit 48. Cheaper by the Dozen 50. Rebel Without a Cause 55, many others.

Brisson, Carl (1895–1958) (Carl Pedersen).
Danish leading man who made films in Britain.
The Ring 28. The Manxman 29. The American Prisoner 29. Song of Soho 30. Murder at the Vanities 34. All the King's Horses 35, etc.

Brisson, Frederick (1912–1984).
Danish producer with long experience in Britain (pre-39) and Hollywood. Married Rosalind Russell and subsequently masterminded her appearances.
■ The Velvet Touch 48. Never Wave at a WAC 53. The Girl Rush 55. The Pajama Game 57. Damn Yankees 58. Five Finger Exercise 62. Under the Yum Yum Tree 63. Generation 69. Mrs Pollifax – Spy 71.

Britt, May (1933–) (Maybritt Wilkens).
Swedish leading lady, in a few Hollywood films. She was married to Sammy Davis Jnr (1960–68).
Affairs of a Model 52. La Lupa 54. *The Young Lions* 58. The Hunters 58. The Blue Angel 59. Murder Inc. 60. Secrets of Woman 61. Haunts 77, etc.

Brittany, Morgan (1951–) (Suzanne Caputo).
American child actress, later leading lady.
Gypsy 62. The Birds 63. Marnie 64. Yours, Mine and Ours 68. The Day of the Locust 75. Gable and Lombard 76. Samurai (TV) 79. Death Car on the Freeway (TV) 79. Stunt Seven (TV) 80. The Prodigal 83. LBJ: The Early Years (TV) 88, etc.
TV series: Dallas 81–84. Glitter 84–85.

Britten, Baron Benjamin of Aldeburgh (1913–1976).
Distinguished English composer, pianist and co-founder of the Aldeburgh Festival, who scored several documentaries in the 30s and one feature film. He was made a life peer in 1976.
Coal Face (doc) 35. Night Mail (doc) 36. Love from a Stranger 37. Village Harvest (doc) 38, etc.

Britton, Barbara (1920–1980) (Barbara Brantingham Czukor).
American leading lady of the 40s who went straight from college to Hollywood.
Secret of the Wastelands 40. Louisiana Purchase 41. Wake Island 42. Reap the Wild Wind 42. So Proudly We Hail 43. *Till We Meet Again* 44. The Story of Dr Wassell 44. The Great John L. 45. Captain Kidd 45. The Virginian 46. The Fabulous Suzanne 47. Gunfighters 47. Albuquerque 48. I Shot Jesse James 49. Champagne for Caesar 50. Bandit Queen 50. The Raiders 52. Bwana Devil 53. The Spoilers 55, etc.
TV series: Mr and Mrs North 52–54.

Britton, Pamela (1923–1974).
Lightweight American actress, mainly familiar as TV's *Blondie* and in the My *Favorite Martian* series.
Anchors Aweigh 45. Key to the City 50. If It's Tuesday This Must Be Belgium 74, etc.

Britton, Tony (1924–).
British stage, screen and TV actor of quiet and polished style.
Salute the Toff 52. Loser Take All 57. The Birthday Present 57. Operation Amsterdam 58. The Rough and the Smooth 59. Suspect 60. Stork Talk 61. The Break 63. There's a Girl in My Soup 70. Sunday Bloody Sunday 71. The Day of the Jackal 73. Night Watch 74. The People That Time Forgot 76. Agatha 79, etc.
TV Series: Father Dear Father 68–73. Robin's Nest 77–81. Don't Wait Up 83–84.

Broadbent, Jim.
English character actor.
The Good Father 87. Life Is Sweet 91. *The Crying Game* 92. Enchanted April 92. Wide-Eyed and Legless (TV) 93. Widow's Peak 94. The Wedding Gift 94. Princess Caraboo 94. *Bullets over Broadway* 94. Rough Magic 95. Richard III 95. Joseph Conrad's Secret Agent 96. Smilla's Sense of Snow/Smilla's Feeling for Snow 96. The Borrowers 97. The Avengers 98. Little Voice 98, etc.
TV series: Gone to the Dogs 91. Gone to See 92. The Peter Principle 97.

Broccoli, Albert R. ('Cubby') (1909–1996).
American independent producer resident in London since 1951; successful as co-chief of Warwick Productions and later the James Bond films.
Autobiography: 1998, *When the Snow Melts* (with Donald Zec).
Hell Below Zero 54. The Black Knight 54. Cockleshell Heroes 55. Zarak 56. Fire Down Below 57. The Man Inside 59. *Dr No* 62. Call Me Bwana 63. From Russia with Love 63 (and subsequent Bond films). Chitty Chitty Bang Bang 68, many others.

Brocka, Lino (1940–1991).
Leading Filipino director whose best films focus on social deprivation in his homeland. He gained international recognition in 1978 when *Insiang* was shown at the Cannes Film Festival. He died in a car crash.
Wanted: Perfect Mother 70. Cherry Blossoms 72. Manila in the Claws of Light 75. Insiang 77. Jaguar 79. Hello Young Lovers 81. Caught in the Act 82. My Country: In Desperate Straits 84. Macho Dancer 88. I Carry the World 88, many others.

Brockwell, Gladys (1894–1929).
American leading actress of silent films. Died as a result of a car crash.
Double Trouble 15. Oliver Twist 22. The Hunchback of Notre Dame 23. Unmarried Wives 24. The Last Frontier 26. Seventh Heaven 27. Lights of New York 28. The Argyle Case 29. The Drake Case 29, etc.

Broderick, Helen (1890–1959).
Wry-faced American stage comedienne whose wisecracks enlivened many 30s comedies. Mother of Broderick Crawford.
■ Fifty Million Frenchmen 31. *Top Hat* 35. To Beat the Band 35. Love on a Bet 36. Murder on the Bridle Path 36. Swing Time 36. The Bride Walks Out 36. Smartest Girl in Town 36. We're on the Jury 37. Meet the Missus 37. Life of the Party 37. Radio City Revels 38. She's Got Everything 38. The Rage of Paris 38. The Road to Reno 38. Service de Luxe 38. Stand Up and Fight 39. Naughty but Nice 39. Honeymoon in Bali 39. The Captain Is a Lady 40. No No Nanette 40. Virginia 41. Nice Girl 41. Father Takes a Wife 41. Are Husbands Necessary 42. Stage Door Canteen 43. Chip Off the Old Block 44. Her Primitive Man 44. Three Is a Family 44. Love Honor and Goodbye 45. Because of Him 46.

Broderick, James (1927–1982).
Worried-looking American character actor.
The Group 66. Alice's Restaurant 69. The Taking of Pelham One Two Three 74. Dog Day Afternoon 75. The Shadow Box (TV) 80, etc.
TV series: Brenner 59. *Family* 76–80.

Broderick, Matthew (1962–).
American leading actor, from the stage. He is the son of James Broderick. Married actress Sarah Jessica PARKER in 1997.
Max Dugan Returns 82. *War Games* 83. Ladyhawke 84. On Valentine's Day 85. Ferris Bueller's Day Off 86. Project X 87. Biloxi Blues 88. Torch Song Trilogy 88. Family Business 89. Glory 89. The Freshman 90. Out on a Limb 92. The Night We Never Met 93. A Life in the Theatre 93. Mrs Parker and the Vicious Circle 94. The Lion King (voice) 94. The Road to Wellville 94. Arabian Knight (voice) 95. The Cable Guy 96. Infinity (a, co-w, d) 96. Addicted to Love 96. Godzilla 98. The Lion King II: Simba's Pride (voice) 98. Election 98, etc.

Brodie, Steve (1919–1992) (John Stevens).
Tough-looking American leading man and character actor, mainly in second features.
This Man's Navy 45. Young Wife 46. Trail Street 47. Home of the Brave 49. Winchester 73 50. Only the Valiant 51. Lady in the Iron Mask 52. The Beast from Twenty Thousand Fathoms 53. The Caine Mutiny 54. Gun Duel in Durango 57. Three Came to Kill 60. Of Love and Desire 63, etc.

Brodine, Norbert (1893–1970).
Distinguished American cinematographer.
SELECTED SILENT FILMS: Almost a Husband 19. The Invisible Power 21. A Blind Bargain 22. Brass 23. *The Sea Hawk* 24. The Eagle of the Sea 25. Paris at Midnight 26. The Clown 27. Beware of Bachelors 28. Her Private Affair 29.
■ SOUND FILMS: Rich People 29. This Thing Called Love 29. The Divorcee 30. Holiday 30. Let Us Be Gay 30. Beyond Victory 31. The Guardsman 31. Pagan Lady 31. The Passionate Plumber 32. Beast of the City 32. Night Court 32. Bachelor's Affairs 32. Unashamed 32. Wild Girl 32. Uptown New York 32. The Death Kiss 32. Whistling in the Dark 33. Clear All Wires 33. Made on Broadway 33. Broadway to Hollywood 33. Deluge 33. Counsellor at Law 33. The Crosby Case 34. Love Birds 34. *Little Man What Now* 34. The Human Side 34. There's Always Tomorrow 34. Cheating Cheaters 34. The Good Fairy 35. Princess O'Hara 35. She Gets Her Man 35. Lady Tubbs 35. The Affair of Susan 36. Don't Get Personal 36. Nobody's Fool 36. *Libeled Lady* 36. Nobody's Baby 37. Pick a Star 37. *Topper* 37. *Merrily We Live* 37. Swiss Miss 38. There Goes My Heart 38. Topper Takes a Trip 39. Captain Fury 39. The Housekeeper's Daughter 39. Of Mice and Men 39. *One Million Years BC* 40. Turnabout 40. Captain Caution 40. Model Wife 41. Road Show 41. Lady for a Night 41. Dr Gillespie's Criminal Case 43. The Dancing Masters 43. The Bullfighters 45. Don Juan Quilligan 45. *The House on 92nd Street* 45. Sentimental Journey 46. Somewhere in the Night 46. *Thirteen Rue Madeleine* 46. *Kiss of Death* 47. *Boomerang* 47. Sitting Pretty 48. I Was a Male War Bride 49. *Thieves' Highway* 49. *The Frogmen* 51. The Desert Fox 51. Five Fingers 52.

Brodney, Oscar (1905–).
American comedy writer, former lawyer. With Universal from the 40s, working mainly on routine series and light costume dramas.
When Johnny Comes Marching Home 43. Are You With It? 48. Yes Sir That's My Baby 49. Francis 50. Little Egypt 53. The Glenn Miller Story 54. Lady Godiva 55. Tammy and the Bachelor 57. Bobbikins (GB) (& p) 59. Tammy and the Doctor 63. The Brass Bottle 64. I'd Rather Be Rich 64. The Sword of Ali Baba 65. Ghost Fever 87, etc.

Brodszky, Nicholas (1905–1958).
Russian-born composer, long in America and Britain.
French Without Tears 39. Quiet Wedding 40. The Way to the Stars 45. A Man About the House 47. The Toast of New Orleans 50. Latin Lovers 53. The Opposite Sex 56, etc.

Brody, Estelle (1900–1995).
American actress and dancer who became a star of British silent films in the late 20s, returning as a character actress in the 50s. She was billed as a French-Canadian during her time in Britain, despite being born in New York.
White Heat 26. *Mademoiselle from Armentieres* 26. Hindle Wakes 27. Sailors Don't Care 28. Kitty 29. Me and the Boys 29. The Plaything 29. Lili Marlene 51. Safari 56. The Story of Esther Costello 57. Never Take Sweets from a Stranger 60, etc.

Brolin, James (1940–) (J. Bruderlin).
Tall, dark American leading man. Born in Los Angeles and educated at UCLA, he began in television, and was best known for playing Dr Steven Kiley in the TV series *Marcus Welby, MD*. Married singer-director Barbra STREISAND in 1998.
Take Her She's Mine 63. Goodbye Charlie 64. Von Ryan's Express 65. Morituri 65. Our Man Flint 67. The Boston Strangler 68. Short Walk to Daylight (TV) 72. Skyjacked 72. Westworld 73. Trapped (TV) 73. Class of 63 (TV) 73. *Gable and Lombard* (as Gable) 76. The Car 77. Steel Cowboy (TV) 78. The Amityville Horror 79. High Risk 81. Pee-Wee's Big Adventure 85. Bad Jim 89. Finish Line 89. Backstab 90. And the Sea Will Tell (TV) 91. Gas Food Lodging 92. Paper Hearts 93. Ted & Venus 93. Gunsmoke: The Long Ride (TV) 93. Relative Fear 94. Parallel Lives (TV) 94. Tracks of a Killer 95. The Fighter 95. The Haunted Sea 97. Lewis and Clark and George 97, etc.
TV series: *Marcus Welby MD* 69–75. Hotel 83–88.

Brolin, Josh (1968–) (J. Bruderlin).
American actor, the son of James BROLIN.
The Goonies 85. Thrashin' 86. Blue Hotel 87. Prison for Children (TV) 87. Private Eye 87. Finish Line (TV) 89. Roadflower 93. Bed of Roses 96. Flirting with Disaster 96. Nightwatch 96. Mimic 97, etc.
TV series: Private Eye 87–88. The Young Riders 89–92. Winnetka 94.

Bromberg, J. Edward (1903–1951).
Plump, wide-eyed Hungarian actor, in America from infancy; usually in gentle roles.
■ Under Two Flags 36. Sins of Man 36. The Crime of Dr Forbes 36. Girls' Dormitory 36. Star for a Night 36. Ladies in Love 36. Reunion 36. Stowaway 36. Fair Warning 37. That I May Live 37. Seventh Heaven 37. Charlie Chan on Broadway 37. Second Honeymoon 37. Mr Moto Takes a Chance 37. The Baroness and the Butler 38. One Wild Night 38. Four Men and a Prayer 38. Sally, Irene and Mary 38. Rebecca of Sunnybrook Farm 38. I'll Give a Million 38. *Suez* 38. Jesse James 39. Wife, Husband and Friend 39. *Hollywood Cavalcade* 39. Three Sons 39. Strange Cargo 40. The Return of Frank James 40. *The Mark of Zorro* 40. Hurricane Smith 41. Dance Hall 41. The Devil Pays Off 41. Pacific Blackout 42. Invisible Agent 42. Life Begins at 8.30 42. Tennessee Johnson 42. Reunion in France 42. Halfway to Shanghai 42. Lady of Burlesque 43. Phantom of the Opera 43. Son of Dracula 43. Chip Off the Old Block 44. Voice in the Wind 44. Easy to Look At 45. The Missing Corpse 45. Pillow of Death 45. Salome Where She Danced 45. The Walls Came Tumbling Down 46. Tangier 46. Cloak and Dagger 46. Queen of the Amazons 47. Arch of Triumph 48. *A Song Is Born* 48. I Shot Jesse James 49. Guilty Bystander 50.

Bromberger, Hervé (1918–1993).
French director, a former journalist; influenced later 'New Wave' directors, including Godard and Truffaut.
Identité Judiciaire 51. Les Fruits Sauvages 54. Les Loups dans la Bergerie 60. Mort Où Est Ta Victoire? 64, etc.

Bromfield, John (1922–) (Farron Bromfield).
American second lead; leading man of second features. He was formerly married to actress Corinne Calvet.
Harpoon 48. Rope of Sand 49. Paid in Full 50. The Furies 50. Flat Top 52. Easy to Love 53. Ring of Fear 53. Crime Against Joe 55. Manfish 56. Hot Cars 57, etc.
TV series: Sheriff of Cochise 56–57. U.S. Marshal 58–59.

Bromfield, Louis (1896–1956).
American popular novelist. *The Rains Came* was twice filmed; *Mrs Parkington* once. *It All Came True* and *Johnny Vagabond* were both taken from Bromfield stories.

Bromiley, Dorothy (1935–).
British leading lady of very few films.
The Girls of Pleasure Island (US) 53. It's Great to be Young 55. A Touch of the Sun 56. The Criminal 60, etc.

Bron, Eleanor (1934–).
Bloomsburyish British TV revue actress.
Help 65. Alfie 66. Two for the Road 67. Women in Love 69. Turtle Diary 85. Deadly Advice 94. Black Beauty 94. A Little Princess 95. Saint-Ex 96, etc.

Bronfman, Edgar, Jnr (1955–).
American motion picture executive and producer who bought 80 per cent of MCA/Universal for $5.7 billion from Matsushita in 1995. He is also a songwriter and head of the liquor company Seagram, founded by his grandfather. Seagram has a substantial interest in Time Warner.
Melody (GB) 71. The Blockhouse (GB) 73. The Border 82, etc.
❝ Money doesn't make you smart, but it doesn't necessarily make you stupid, either. – *E.B.*

Bronsky, Brick.
American wrestler turned actor, usually in the low-budget horrors of TROMA productions. He was born in Bethlehem, Pennsylvania.
Class of Nukem High II: Subhumanoid Meltdown 91. Class of Nukem High III: The Good, the Bad and the Subhumanoid 95. Sgt Kabukiman: NYPD 96. The Quest 96. Dark Dreams 97, etc.

Bronson, Betty (1906–1971) (Elizabeth Bronson).
Lively American leading lady of the 20s; did not succeed in talkies.
Peter Pan (title role) 24. The Golden Princess 25. Are Parents People? 25. A Kiss for Cinderella 26. *Ben Hur* 26. The Cat's Pajamas 26. Everybody's Acting 27. Brass Knuckles 27. *The Singing Fool* 28. Companionate Marriage 28. Sonny Boy 29. The Locked Door 29. Medicine Man 30. The Yodelling Kid from Pine Ridge 37. Who's Got the Action? 62. Blackbeard's Ghost 67. Evel Knievel 71, etc.

Bronson, Charles (1920–) (Charles Buchinski).
Sombre-looking, deep-featured American character actor who can deal with a variety of types, from Russian to Red Indian, from villainous to sturdily heroic. At the age of fifty he suddenly became a star. Married actress Jill IRELAND.
You're In the Navy Now 51. Pat and Mike 52. House of Wax 53. Apache 54. *Drumbeat* 54. Vera Cruz 54. Target Zero 55. Jubal 56. Run of the Arrow 57. Machine Gun Kelly 57. When Hell Broke Loose 58. Never So Few 59. *The Magnificent Seven* 60. A Thunder of Drums 61. Lonely are the Brave 62. The Great Escape 63. The Sandpiper 65. Battle of the Bulge 65. This Property is Condemned 66. *The Dirty Dozen* 67. Guns for San Sebastian 68. Adieu l'Ami 68. Once Upon a Time in the West 69. Rider in the Rain 69. Twinky 69. Violent City (It.) 70. You Can't Win Them All 70. Cold Sweat 71. *Chato's Land* 72. The Mechanic 72. *The Valachi Papers* 72. Wild Horses 73. The Stone Killer 73. Mr Majestyk 74. *Death Wish* 74. Breakout 75. *Hard Times* 75. Breakheart Pass 76. From Noon Till Three 76. St Ives 76. Raid on Entebbe (TV) 76. Telefon 77. The White Buffalo 77. Love and Bullets 79. Cabo Blanco 80. Borderline 80. Death Hunt 81. Death Wish II 82. Ten to Midnight 83. The Evil That Men Do 84. Death Wish III 85. Assassination 86. Death Wish IV 87. Messenger of Death 88. Kinjite 89. The Indian Runner 91. No Return 91. The Sea Wolf (TV) 93. Death Wish V: The Face of Death 94, etc.
TV series: Man with a Camera 58–59. Redigo 63. The Travels of Jamie McPheeters 64.
❝ Someday I'd like a part where I can lean my elbow against a mantelpiece and have a cocktail. – *C.B.*
I guess I look like a rock quarry that someone has dynamited – *C.B.*
Acting is the easiest thing I've ever done. I guess that's why I'm stuck with it. – *C.B.*

Bronson, Lillian (1902–1995).
American character actress.
Happy Land 43. A Tree Grows in Brooklyn 44. The Hucksters 47. The Next Voice You Hear 51. Walk on the Wild Side 62. The Americanization of Emily 64. The Over-the-Hill Gang (TV) 69. The Devil's Daughter (TV) 72. Medical Story (TV) 75, many others.
TV series: Kings Row 55–56. Date With the Angels 57–58.

Bronston, Samuel (1909–1994).
Russian-born American independent producer who in 1959 set up a studio in Madrid and made several international epics but ran into financial difficulty.
Jack London 43. A Walk in the Sun 46. John Paul Jones 59. King of Kings 61. El Cid 61. Fifty Five Days at Peking 62. The Fall of the Roman Empire 64. Circus World 64. Savage Pampas (co-p) 66, etc.

Brontë, Charlotte (1816–1855).
British novelist whose *Jane Eyre* has been frequently filmed, most recently in 1934 with Virginia Bruce and Colin Clive, in 1944 with Joan Fontaine and Orson Welles, in 1971 with Susannah York and George C. Scott, and in 1996 with Charlotte Gainsbourg. Its central situation, of a governess in the house of a mysterious but romantic tyrant, has also been frequently plagiarized.

Brontë, Emily (1818–1848).
British novelist, sister of Charlotte Brontë, and author of *Wuthering Heights*, much filmed in Britain before the definitive 1939 version. A somewhat romantic film about the sisters was filmed in 1943 under the title *Devotion*, with Olivia de Havilland as Charlotte and Ida Lupino as Emily.

Brook, Claudio (1927–).
Mexican leading actor whose work ranges from the films of Luis Buñuel to low-budget horrors.
Daniel Boone, Trail Blazer (US) 56. The Young One/La Joven 61. Neutron and the Black Mask 61. The Exterminating Angel 62. Samson in the Wax Museum/Santo en el Museo de Cera 63. Viva Maria! (Fr.) 65. *Simon of the Desert* 65. The Milky Way 68. The Peking Blonde/La Blonde de Pekin (Fr.) 68. Alucarda 72. Sisters of Satan 75. The Devil's Rain (US) 75. Dr Tarr's Torture Dungeon 75. The Return of a Man Called Horse (US) 76. Foxtrot 76. Eagle's Wing 78. Only Once in a Lifetime 79. Frida 85. La Mansion de la Locura 87. Cronos 94, etc.

Brook, Clive (1887–1974) (Clifford Brook).
Distinguished British leading man of stage and screen, for forty years the perfect gentleman (with very occasional caddish lapses). Popular in Hollywood in the 20s and early 30s.
■ A Debt of Honour 19. Trent's Last Case 20. Kissing Cup's Race 20. Her Penalty 20. The Loudwater Mystery 21. Daniel Deronda 21. A Sportsman's Wife 21. Sonia 21. Christie Johnstone 21. Woman to Woman 21. Through Fire and Water 22. This Freedom 22. Out to Win 22. The Reverse of the Medal 23. The Royal Oak 23. The Money Habit 24. The White Sheik 24. Recoil 24. The Wine of Life 24. The Passionate Adventure 24. Human Desires 24. Christine of the Hungry Heart 24. The Mirage 24. When Love Grows Cold 25. Enticement 25. The Social Exile 25. Playing

With Souls 25. If Marriage Fails 25. The Woman Hater 25. Compromise 25. Seven Sinners 25. The Home Maker 25. The Pleasure Buyers 25. Three Faces East 26. Why Girls Go Back Home 26. For Alimony Only 26. You Never Know Women 26. The Popular Sin 26. Afraid to Love 27. Barbed Wire 27. *Underworld* 27. Hula 27. The Devil Dancer 27. French Dressing 27. Midnight Madness 28. The Yellow Lily 28. The Perfect Crime 28. Forgotten Faces 28. Interference 29. A Dangerous Woman 29. *The Four Feathers* 29. Charming Sinners 29. The Return of Sherlock Holmes 29. The Laughing Lady 29. Slightly Scarlet 30. Paramount on Parade 30. Sweethearts and Wives 30. Anybody's Woman 30. Scandal Sheet 31. East Lynne 31. Tarnished Lady 31. The Lawyer's Secret 31. Silence 31. Twenty Four Hours 31. Husband's Holiday 31. *Shanghai Express* 32. The Man from Yesterday 32. The Night of June 13th 32. *Sherlock Holmes* 32. Make Me a Star 32. *Cavalcade* 33. Midnight Club 33. Gallant Lady 33. If I Were Free 34. Where Sinners Meet 34. Let's Try Again 34. The Love Affair of the Dictator 35. Dressed to Thrill 35. The Lonely Road 36. Love in Exile 36. *Action for Slander* 37. The Ware Case 38. *Return to Yesterday* 40. Convoy 40. Freedom Radio 41. Breach of Promise 41. The Flemish Farm 43. Shipbuilders 43. *On Approval* 44 (also d). The List of Adrian Messenger 63.

❝ Hollywood is a chain gang and we lose the will to escape. The links of the chain are forged not with cruelties but with luxuries. – *C.B. 1933*

Brook, Faith (1922–).
British actress of stage, screen and TV; daughter of Clive Brook.
Jungle Book 42. Uneasy Terms 48. Wicked as They Come 56. Chase a Crooked Shadow 57. The Thirty-Nine Steps 59. To Sir With Love 66. North Sea Hijack 80. The Sea Wolves 80. The Razor's Edge 83. Sins (TV) 86. The Two Mrs Grenvilles (TV) 86, etc.

Brook, Lesley (1916–).
British leading lady of a few sentimental dramas of the 40s.
The Vulture 37. Dead Men Tell No Tales 39. Rose of Tralee 41. Variety Jubilee 42. I'll Walk Beside You 43. The Trojan Brothers 46. House of Darkness 48, etc.

Brook, Lyndon (1926–).
British actor of stage, screen and TV; son of Clive Brook.
Train of Events 49. The Purple Plain 54. Reach for the Sky 56. Innocent Sinners 58. Song Without End (US) 60. Invasion 66. Pope Joan 72. The Hireling 73. Plenty 85. Defence of the Realm 85, etc.

Brook, Sir Peter (1925–).
British stage director whose film experiments have been largely unsuccessful.
■ The Beggar's Opera 52. Moderato Cantabile 60. Lord of the Flies 63. The Marat-Sade 66. Tell Me Lies 67. King Lear 70. Meetings with Remarkable Men 77. Carmen 83. The Mahabharata 89.
❝ We've had an enormous amount of trips into people's private visions. They're played out: it's exactly what's true of nudity, when you've seen one you've seen them all. – *P.B.*

Brook-Jones, Elwyn (1911–1962).
Thickset British character actor usually seen in villainous roles.
Dangerous Moonlight 40. Tomorrow We Live 42. Odd Man Out 46. The Three Weird Sisters 48. I'll Get You For This 50. Beau Brummell 54. The Pure Hell of St Trinian's 61, etc.

Brooke, Hillary (1914–) (Beatrice Peterson).
Statuesque, blonde American leading lady of 40s co-features; on TV in the 50s in the much revived Abbott and Costello series.
New Faces of 1937. Eternally Yours 39. Unfinished Business 41. Sherlock Holmes and the Voice of Terror 42. Lady in the Dark 44. Practically Yours 44. Ministry of Fear 44. *The Woman in Green* 45. Road to Utopia 45. Strange Journey 46. Big Town 47. Big Town After Dark 47. Let's Live Again 48. Africa Screams 49. The Admiral was a Lady 50. Insurance Investigator 51. Confidence Girl 52. Abbott and Costello Meet Captain Kidd 52. Mexican Manhunt 53. Dragon's Gold 54. The House Across the Lake (GB) 54. Bengazi 55. Spoilers of the Forest 57, many others.
TV series: My Little Margie 52–55. The Abbott and Costello Show 53–54.

Brooke-Taylor, Tim (1940–).
British light comedian, one of The Goodies. Mostly on radio and TV.
Twelve Plus One 70. The Statue 70. Willy Wonka and the Chocolate Factory 70.

Brooks, Albert (1947–) (Albert Einstein).
American director, actor and screenwriter of sharply observed comedies. He is the son of radio comedian Parkyakarkus (Harry Einstein).
Taxi Driver (a) 76. Real Life 79. Private Benjamin (a) 80. Modern Romance 81. Twilight Zone: The Movie (a) 83. Unfaithfully Yours (a) 84. Lost in America 85. Broadcast News (a) (AAN) 87. Defending Your Life 91. I'll Do Anything 94. The Scout (& co-w) 94. Mother (a, wd) 96. Critical Care (a) 97. Out of Sight (a) 98. The Muse (co-w, d) 99, etc.

Brooks, Geraldine (1925–1977) (Geraldine Stroock).
Intense young American actress of the 40s; never fulfilled her promise. She was married to writer Budd Schulberg. Died from cancer.
Possessed 47. *Cry Wolf* 47. The Younger Brothers 49. *The Reckless Moment* 49. Challenge for Lassie 50. Volcano 50. The Green Glove 52. Street of Sinners 56. Johnny Tiger 66, etc.
TV series: Faraday and Co. 73. The Dumplings 76.

Brooks, Hazel (1924–).
American second lead of the mid-40s. She was formerly married to art director Cedric Gibbons.
Body and Soul 47. Sleep My Love 48.

Brooks, James L. (1940–).
American writer-director and producer.
Terms of Endearment (AAw, AAd) 83. Broadcast News (wd) (AAN) 87. Big (p) 88. Say Anything (p) 89. The War of the Roses (p) 89. I'll Do Anything (p, wd) 94. Jerry Maguire (AANp) 96. *As Good as It Gets* (AANp, AANw) 97, etc.

Brooks, Jean (1921–).
Stylish-looking American leading lady who worked briefly for RKO in the 40s.
The Seventh Victim 43. The Leopard Man 43. The Falcon and the Co-Eds 44. Two O'Clock Courage 46. The Falcon's Alibi 46, etc.

Brooks, Leslie (1922–) (Leslie Gettman).
American leading lady of the 40s.
Undercover Agent 42. Nine Girls 44. Tonight and Every Night 45. The Cobra Strikes 48. Romance on the High Seas 48, etc.

Brooks, Louise (1906–1985).
American leading lady of the 20s who made her best films in Germany and remained an attractive critical enigma. The first of her two husbands was director Edward Sutherland (1926–28).
Autobiography: 1982, *Lulu in Hollywood* (with Hollis Alpert).
■ The Street of Forgotten Men 25. The American Venus 26. A Social Celebrity 26. It's the Old Army Game 26. The Show Off 26. Just Another Blonde 26. Love 'em and Leave 'em 27. Evening Clothes 27. Rolled Stockings 27. The City Gone Wild 27. Now We're in the Air 27. *A Girl in Every Port* 28. *Beggars of Life* 28. *Pandora's Box* (Ger.) 29. The Canary Murder Case 29. *Diary of a Lost Girl* (Ger.) 30. Prix de Beauté (Fr.) 30. It Pays to Advertise 31. God's Gift to Women 31. Empty Saddles 36. When You're in Love 36. King of Gamblers 37. Overland Stage Raiders 38.
❝ Not one woman exerted more magic, not one had her genius of interpretation. – *Ado Kyrou, 1957*
Her favourite form of exercise was walking off a movie set, which she did with the insouciance of a little girl playing hopscotch. – *Anita Loos*
A beautiful nothing. – *George Cukor*

Brooks, Mel (1926–) (Melvin Kaminsky).
American writer-producer-director of off-beat comedies. Married actress Anne Bancroft in 1964.
■ The Producers (AAw) 68. Putney Swope (a only) 69. The Twelve Chairs (also acted) 70. *Blazing Saddles* (also acted) 74. *Young Frankenstein* (AANw) 74. Silent Movie (also acted) 76. High Anxiety (also acted) 78. The Muppet Movie (a only) 79. History of the World Part One (also acted) 81. To Be or Not to Be 83. Spaceballs 87. Life Stinks 91. Robin Hood: Men in Tights (a, p, wd) 93. The Little Rascals (a) 94. Dracula: Dead and Loving It (a, co-w, d) 95.
❝ If you got it, flaunt it. – M.B.
When I write, I keep Tolstoy around because I want great limits. I want big thinking. – M.B.
The death of Hollywood is Mel Brooks and special effects. If Mel Brooks had come up in my time he wouldn't have qualified to be a busboy. – *Joseph L. Mankiewicz*

Brooks, Phyllis (1914–1995) (Phyllis Weiler).
Blonde American leading lady of co-features in the 30s and 40s.
I've Been Around 34. McFadden's Flats 35. You Can't Have Everything 37. Rebecca of Sunnybrook Farm 38. Charlie Chan in Reno 39. Slightly Honourable 40. *The Shanghai Gesture* 41. Hi Ya Sailor 43. The Unseen 45. High Powered 45, etc.

Brooks, Rand (1918–).
American leading man, usually in minor films.
Gone with the Wind 39. Florian 40. Son of Monte Cristo 41. Joan of Arc 47. The Steel Fist 52. Man from the Black Hills 56. Comanche Station 60. The Sex Symbol (TV) 74, etc.
TV series: Rin Tin Tin 54–56.

Brooks, Ray (1939–).
British leading man with repertory experience.
HMS Defiant 62. Play it Cool 62. Some People 63. *The Knack* 65. Daleks Invasion Earth 2150 AD 66. Alice's Adventures in Wonderland 72. Tiffany Jones 73. House of Whipcord 74. Death of an Expert Witness (TV) 85, etc.
TV series: Growing Pains 92–93.

Brooks, Richard (1912–1992) (Ruben Sax).
American writer-director whose reputation was somewhat higher than his films seem to justify. However, he wrote one of the best novels about Hollywood, *The Producer*. Married actress Jean Simmons (1961–77).
■ White Savage (w only) 42. Cobra Woman (w only) 44. Swell Guy (w only) 46. The Killers (co-w only) 46. Brute Force (w only) 47. Crossfire (oa only) 47. To the Victor (w only) 48. Key Largo (w only) 48. Any Number Can Play (w only) 49. *Crisis* 50. Mystery Street (w only) 50. Storm Warning (co-w only) 50. The Light Touch 51. Deadline 52. Battle Circus 52. The Last Time I Saw Paris (d only) 54. Take the High Ground (d only) 54. The Flame and the Flesh (d only) 54. *The Blackboard Jungle* (AANw) 55. *The Last Hunt* 56. The Catered Affair (d only) 56. Something of Value 57. The Brothers Karamazov 58. Cat on a Hot Tin Roof (AANw, d) 58. *Elmer Gantry* (AAw) 60. Sweet Bird of Youth 62. Lord Jim (& p) 65. The Professionals (& p) (AANw, d) 66. *In Cold Blood* (& p) (AANw, d) 67. The Happy Ending (& p) 70. Dollars (& p) 72. Bite The Bullet (& p) 75. Looking for Mr Goodbar 77. Wrong Is Right 82. Fever Pitch 85.
❝ Although most of his films display something of value on first viewing, none can take the high ground in retrospect. – *Andrew Sarris, 1968*

Brophy, Edward S. (1895–1960).
American character actor, often a gangster or a very odd kind of valet: a rotund, cigar-chewing little man in a bowler hat, oddly likeable despite his pretence of toughness.
Those Three French Girls 30. *The Champ* 31. Freaks 32. What, No Beer? 33. *The Thin Man* 34. Death on the Diamond 34. Mad Love (miscast as a murderer) 35. Remember Last Night 35. Strike Me Pink 36. Kelly the Second 36. *A Slight Case of Murder* 37. You Can't Cheat an Honest Man 39. Calling Philo Vance 40. Buy Me That Town 41. All Through the Night 42. Broadway 42. Cover Girl 44. The Thin Man Goes Home 44. The Falcon in San Francisco (and series) 45. *Wonder Man* 45. It Happened on Fifth Avenue 47. *The Last Hurrah* 58, many others.

Brosnan, Pierce (1951–).
Polished Irish leading man who took over the role of James Bond in 1994. Born in Navan, County Meath, he studied at London's Drama Centre and began on the stage. Married actress Cassandra Harris (d. 1991). His asking price: around $5m a movie.
Biography: 1997, *Pierce Brosnan* by York Membery.
The Long Good Friday 80. The Manions of America (TV) 81. Nancy Astor (TV) 81. Nomads 85. The Fourth Protocol 86. Noble House (TV) 87. The Deceivers 88. Taffin 88. The Heist (TV) 89. Mister Johnson 90. Victim of Love 91. Murder 101 (TV) 91. The Lawnmower Man 92. Live Wire 92. Mrs Doubtfire 93. Don't Talk to Strangers (TV) 94. Love Affair 94. *GoldenEye* 95. The Mirror Has Two Faces 96. Mars Attacks! 96. Dante's Peak 97. Quest for Camelot (voice) 98. The Nephew 98. Grey Owl 98, etc.
TV series: Remington Steele 82–87.
❝ I don't see myself as a hunk of the month – *P.B.*
A new Cary Grant, sexy but suave, manly though mannered, with subtlety instead of slapstick. – *People*

Brough, Mary (1863–1934).
British character comedienne usually seen as battleaxe or suspicious landlady, especially in the Aldwych farces. In films from 1914.
The Amazing Quest of Ernest Bliss 20. Squibs Wins the Calcutta Sweep 22. A Sister to Assist 'er 22 and 27. Dawn 28. *Rookery Nook* 30. On Approval 30. Tons of Money 31. Plunder 31. A Night Like This 32. Thark 32. *A Cuckoo in the Nest* 33. Up to the Neck 33. Turkey Time 33, etc.

Broughton, Bruce (1945–).
American composer, from television.
Ice Pirates 83. The Prodigal 84. Silverado (AAN) 85. Young Sherlock Holmes 85. Sweet Liberty 86. The Monster Squad 87. Square Dance 87. Harry and the Hendersons 87. Big Shots 87. The Presidio 88. The Rescue 88. Moonwalker 88. Last Rites 88. Jacknife 89. Betsy's Wedding 90. The Rescuers Down Under 90. All I Want for Christmas 91. Honey, I Blew Up The Kid 92. Homeward Bound: The Incredible Journey 93. So I Married an Axe Murderer 93. Holy Matrimony 94. Tombstone 94. Baby's Day Out 94. House Arrest 96. Carried Away 96. Homeward Bound II: Lost in San Francisco 96. Infinity 96. A Simple Wish 97. Shadow Conspiracy 97. Lost in Space 98. Krippendorf's Tribe 98. One Tough Cop 98, etc.

Brown, Barbara (1907–1975).
American character actress of the 40s and 50s, usually as an upper-class wife or matron.
You Were Never Lovelier 42. The Fighting Sullivans 42. Hollywood Canteen 44. Mildred Pierce 45. The Beast with Five Fingers 46. Ma and Pa Kettle Go to Town 50. Born Yesterday 50. Home Town Story 51. You for Me 52. My Sister Eileen 55. Sincerely Yours 55, etc.

Brown, Barry (1951–1978).
American leading man who shot himself.
Flesh 68. Halls of Anger 70. Escape of the Birdmen (TV) 71. The Great Northfield Minnesota Raid 71. Bad Company 72. Daisy Miller 74. The Disappearance of Aimee (TV) 76. Piranha 78, etc.

Brown, Blair (1948–).
American leading lady. Formerly married to actor Richard Jordan.
The Choirboys 77. Wheels (TV) 78. And I Alone Survived (TV) 78. The Child Stealer (TV) 79. Altered States 80. One Trick Pony 80. Continental Divide 81. Kennedy (TV) (as Jackie) 83. A Flash of Green 84. Stealing Home 88. Strapless 88. Passed Away 92, etc.

Brown, Bruce (1938–).
American director, cinematographer and editor, mainly of surfing documentaries, from 1958. *The Endless Summer* was a surprising box-office success, earning more than $30 million.
The Endless Summer 66. On Any Sunday (AAN) 71. The Endless Summer II 94.

Brown, Bryan (1947–).
Australian leading actor. He is married to actress Rachel Ward.
Newsfront 79. Breaker Morant 79. The Chant of Jimmie Blacksmith 80. Winter of Our Dreams 81. A Town Like Alice (TV) 81. Far East 82. The Thorn Birds (TV) 83. Kim (TV) 83. Give My Regards to Broad Street 84. Parker 85. Eureka Stockade (TV) 85. The Empty Beach 85. F/X 85. Rebel 85. The Good Wife 86, Taipan 86. The Shiralee (TV) 87. Cocktail 88. Gorillas in the Mist 88. Blood Oath 90. Sweet Talker (& story) 91. FX2 – the Deadly Art of Illusion 91. Blame It On The Bellboy 92. Devlin 92. The Last Hit (TV) 93.

Full Body Massage 95. Dead Heart 96. Dear Claudia 98, etc.

Brown, Charles D. (1887–1948).
Bland-faced American character actor who played scores of detectives, officials and executives.
The Dance of Life 29. Murder by the Clock 31. The Woman I Stole 33. It Happened One Night 34. Thoroughbreds Don't Cry 37. Charlie Chan in Reno 39. The Grapes of Wrath 39. Fingers at the Window 42. Jam Session 44. The Killers 46. Merton of the Movies 47, many others.

Brown, Clarence (1890–1987).
American director, with MGM and Garbo for many years; most at home with sentimental themes and busy pictorial values.
■ The Great Redeemer 20. The Last of the Mohicans 20. The Light in the Dark 22. Don't Marry for Money 23. The Acquittal 23. The Signal Tower 24. Butterfly 24. Smouldering Fires 25. *The Eagle* 25. *The Goose Woman* 25. Kiki 26. *Flesh and the Devil* 26. Trail of 98 28. A Woman of Affairs 29. Wonder of Women 29. Navy Blues 29. *Anna Christie* (AAN) 30. Romance (AAN) 30. Inspiration 31. A Free Soul (AAN) 31. Possessed 31. Emma 32. Letty Lynton 32. The Son Daughter 32. Looking Forward 33. Night Flight 33. Sadie McKee 34. Chained 34. *Anna Karenina* 35. *Ah Wilderness* 35. Wife Versus Secretary 36. The Gorgeous Hussy 36. *Conquest* 37. Of Human Hearts 38. Idiot's Delight 38. *The Rains Came* 39. *Edison the Man* 40. Come Live with Me (& p) 41. They Met in Bombay 41. *The Human Comedy* (& p) (AAN) 43. The White Cliffs of Dover 44. National Velvet (AAN) 44. *The Yearling* (AAN) 46. Song of Love (& p) 47. *Intruder in the Dust* (& p) 49. To Please a Lady (& p) 50. Angels in the Outfield (& p) 51. It's a Big Country (part) 51. When in Rome (& p) 51. Plymouth Adventure 52. Never Let Me Go (p only) 53.
✪ For persuading a commercially minded studio to let his films represent its cultural pretensions. *Intruder in the Dust*.
❝ His career is not without a certain amiability in its evolution from German Expressionism to American Gothic. – *Andrew Sarris, 1968*

Brown, David (1916–).
American producer, a New York journalist who became story editor at Fox and later joined Richard Zanuck in Zanuck-Brown, which made *The Sting* and *Jaws*.
Jaws 2 78. The Island 80. The Verdict (AAN) 82. Cocoon 85. Cocoon: The Return 88. Driving Miss Daisy (AA) 89. Deep Impact 98, etc.

Brown, Ed.
American cinematographer.
The Hot Rock 72. Lovin' Molly 74. The Education of Sonny Carson 74, etc.

Brown, George H. (1913–).
British producer, former production manager.
Sleeping Car to Trieste 48. The Chiltern Hundreds 50. The Seekers 54. Jacqueline 56. Dangerous Exile 57. Tommy the Toreador 60. Murder at the Gallop 63. Guns at Batasi 64. The Trap 66. Finders Keepers 66. Assault 70. Revenge 71. Innocent Bystanders 72. Open Season 74, etc.

Brown, Georg Stanford (1943–).
American character actor and TV director.
The Comedians 67. Dayton's Devils 68. Bullitt 68. The Forbin Project 70. The Man 72. Wild in the Sky 72. Roots (TV) 77. The Night the City Screamed (TV) 80. In Defense of Kids (TV) 83. The Jesse Owens Story (TV) 84, etc.
TV series: The Rookies 72–74.

Brown, Georgia (1933–1992) (Lilian Klot).
British cabaret songstress in occasional films.
The Fixer 67. Lock Up Your Daughters 69. The Raging Moon 71. Nothing but the Night 73. The Bawdy Adventures of Tom Jones 76. The Seven Per Cent Solution 77, etc.

Brown, Harry (1917–1986).
American novelist and screenwriter, mainly on war themes. Educated at Harvard, he was also a poet and playwright. Married twice.
The True Glory (co-w) 45. A Walk in the Sun (oa) 46. Arch of Triumph 48. Sands of Iwo Jima (AAN) 49. A Place in the Sun (co-w, AA) 51. Bugles in the Afternoon 52. The Sniper (co-w) 52. Eight Iron Men 52. All the Brothers Were Valiant (co-w) 53. D-Day Sixth of June (co-w) 56. Between Heaven and Hell (co-w) 57. El Dorado (oa) 66, etc.

Brown, Harry Joe (1892–1972).
American producer with long experience in all branches of show business; latterly concentrated on Randolph Scott westerns.
Parade of the West (d only) 30. Madison Square Garden (d only) 32. Sitting Pretty (d only) 33. Captain Blood 35. Alexander's Ragtime Band 38. The Rains Came 39. Young People 40. Western Union 41. *Knickerbocker Holiday* (& d) 44. Gunfighters 47. Fortunes of Captain Blood 50. Hangman's Knot 52. Three Hours to Kill 54. Screaming Mimi 58. Ride Lonesome 59, many others.

Brown, Hilyard (1910–).
American art director.
Abbott and Costello Meet Frankenstein 48. Flame of Araby 51. Creature from the Black Lagoon 54. *The Night of the Hunter* 55. Man of the West 58. Al Capone 59. *Cleopatra* (AA) 63. Von Ryan's Express 65. Finian's Rainbow 68. Fuzz 73. Freebie and the Bean 74. Hooper 78. Six Weeks 82, etc.

Brown, James (1920–1992).
Stalwart American supporting actor, in many westerns of the 40s and 50s.
The Forest Rangers 42. Corvette K225 44. Objective Burma 45. The Fabulous Texan 47. Sands of Iwo Jima 50. Springfield Rifle 52. The Woman They Almost Lynched 53. A Star Is Born 54. The Police Dog Story 61. Irma La Douce 63. Town Tamer 65. Whiffs 75. Mean Johnny Barrows 76, etc.
TV series: Rin Tin Tin 54–56.

Brown, Jim (1935–).
American leading man, former athlete.
Rio Conchos 64. The Dirty Dozen 67. Dark of the Sun 68. The Split 68. Ice Station Zebra 68. Riot 68. *100 Rifles* 69. Tick Tick Tick 70. The Grasshopper 70. El Condor 70. Kenner 71. Black Gunn 72. Slaughter 72. Slaughter's Big Rip-off 73. I Escaped from Devil's Island 73. The Slams 74. Three the Hard Way 74. Take a Hard Ride 75. Kid Vengeance 77. Fingers 78. One Down Two to Go 81. Pacific Inferno 84. Slam Dunk 87. The Running Man 87. I'm Gonna Git You Sucka 88. L.A. Heat 88. Crack House 89. L.A. Vice 89. Twisted Justice 90. Deadly Avenger 92. Original Gangstas 96. Mars Attacks! 96. He Got Game 98, etc.

Brown, Joe (1941–).
Amiable British pop singer, in occasional films.
What a Crazy World 63. Three Hats for Lisa 65, etc.

Brown, Joe E. (1892–1973).
Wide-mouthed American star comedian of the 30s, with background in circus, vaudeville and basketball.
Autobiography: 1956, *Laughter is a Wonderful Thing*.
■ Crooks Can't Wait 28. Me, Gangster 28. Road House 28. Dressed to Kill 28. The Circus Kid 28. Hit of the Show 28. Take Me Home 28. Burlesque 28. Don't Be Jealous 28. In Old Arizona 29. Sunny Side Up 29. Molly and Me 29. *Sally* 29. My Lady's Past 29. On with the Show 29. Painted Faces 29. The Cockeyed World 29. The Ghost Talks 29. Protection 29. Up the River 30. Maybe It's Love 30. Song of the West 30. Born Reckless 30. City Girl 30. Hold Everything 30. The Lottery Bride 30. Top Speed 30. Going Wild 31. Local Boy Makes Good 31. Broadminded 31. Sit Tight 31. *The Tenderfoot* 32. Fireman Save My Child 32. *You Said a Mouthful* 32. Elmer the Great 32. Son of a Sailor 32. The Circus Clown 34. Six Day Bike Rider 34. A Very Honourable Guy 34. *A Midsummer Night's Dream* 35. Alibi Ike 35. *Bright Lights* 36. Polo Joe 36. Sons of Guns 36. Earthworm Tractors 36. Fit for a King 37. When's Your Birthday 37. Flirting with Fate 38. The Gladiator 38. Wide Open Faces 38. Beware Spooks 39. One Thousand Dollars a Touchdown 39. So You Won't Talk 40. Shut My Big Mouth 42. The Daring Young Man 42. Joan of Ozark 42. Chatterbox 43. Pin Up Girl 44. Hollywood Canteen 44. Casanova in Burlesque 44. *The Tender Years* 49. *Showboat* 51. Around the World in 80 Days 56. *Some Like It Hot* 59. A Comedy of Terrors 63. It's a Mad Mad Mad Mad World 63.

Brown, John (Johnny) Mack (1904–1974).
American leading man of the 30s, former football star.
The Bugle Call 26. The Divine Woman 27. *Our Dancing Daughters* 28. Coquette 29. Jazz Heaven 29. *Billy the Kid* 30. The Secret Six 31. *The Last Flight* 31. Saturday's Millions 33. Female 33. Belle of the Nineties 34. Riding the Apache Trail 36. Wells Fargo 37. Bad Man from Red Butte 40. Ride 'Em Cowboy 41. The Right to Live 45. Stampede 49. Short Grass 50. The Bounty Killer 65. Apache Uprising 65, many others.

Brown, John Moulder:
see MOULDER BROWN, John.

Brown, Julie (1958–).
American actress, singer, screenwriter and TV producer and director.
Any Which Way You Can 80. The Incredible Shrinking Woman 81. Police Academy 2 85. Earth Girls Are Easy (a, co-w) 88. Shakes the Clown 91. Clueless 95, etc.
TV series: The Edge 92–93.

Brown, Karl (1897–1990).
American cinematographer of the 20s; retired early.
Autobiography: 1976, *Adventures with D.W. Griffith*.
The Birth of a Nation (2nd unit) 15. The Fourteenth Man 20. Gasoline Gus 21. The Dictator 22. *The Covered Wagon* 23. Ruggles of Red Gap 23. Merton of the Movies 24. Beggar on Horseback 25. *Pony Express* 25. Mannequin 26, etc.

Brown, Lew (1893–1958) (Louis Brownstein).
American lyricist, notably in partnership with Buddy DE SYLVA and Ray HENDERSON, though he also collaborated with Harry AKST, Harold ARLEN, Sammy FAIN and Nacio Herb BROWN. Born in New Haven, Connecticut, and brought up in New York, he began writing for Broadway in the mid-20s and for films from 1929. Songs he collaborated on include 'Button Up Your Overcoat', 'Don't Sit under the Apple Tree', 'If I Had a Talking Picture of You', 'Life Is Just a Bowl of Cherries', and 'You're the Cream in My Coffee'. In the biopic of De Sylva, Brown and Henderson, *The Best Things in Life Are Free* 56, he was played by Ernest BORGNINE.
The Singing Fool (song: 'Sonny Boy') 28. Say It with Songs (s) 29. Sunny Side Up (co-w, s) 29. Good News (s) 30. Follow Thru (co-w, s) 30. Just Imagine (co-w, s) 30. Indiscreet (co-w, s) 31. Stand Up and Cheer (s) 34. Strike Me Pink (s) 35. The Music Goes Round (s) 36. New Faces of 1937 (s) 37. Private Buckaroo 42. Yokel Boy (oa) 42. Swing Fever (s) 43. Good News (s) 47. Jolson Sings Again (s) 49, etc.

Brown, Naçio Herb (1896–1964).
American light composer who usually supplied the music for Arthur Freed's lyrics: 'Broadway Melody', 'Singin' in the Rain', 'Good Morning', 'You Are My Lucky Star', many others.
The Broadway Melody 29. Good News 30. Going Hollywood 33. Student Tour 34. Broadway Melody of 1936 35. Broadway Melody of 1938 37. Greenwich Village 44. Singin' in the Rain 52, etc.

Brown, Pamela (1917–1975).
British stage actress in occasional films, usually in haughty or eccentric roles. She was married to Peter Copley.
One of Our Aircraft Is Missing 42. *I Know Where I'm Going* 45. Tales of Hoffman 51. The Second Mrs Tanqueray 52. Personal Affair 53. Richard III 56. The Scapegoat 59. Becket 64. Secret Ceremony 68. Wuthering Heights 70. On a Clear Day You Can See Forever 70. Lady Caroline Lamb 72. Dracula (TV) 73, etc.

Brown, Phil (1916–).
American second lead, usually in diffident roles; moved to Europe in 1950.
I Wanted Wings 41. Calling Dr Gillespie 42. The Impatient Years 44. Without Reservations 46. The Killers 46. If You Knew Susie 48. Moonrise 49. *Obsession* 50. The Green Scarf 54. Camp on Blood Island 58. The Bedford Incident 65. Tropic of Cancer 69. Valdez Is Coming 70. Scalawag 73. The Romantic Englishwoman 75. The Pink Panther Strikes Again 76. Star Wars 77. Twilight's Last Gleaming 77. Superman 78. Chaplin 92, etc.

Brown, Reynold (1917–1991).
American illustrator who designed and painted posters for more than 250 Hollywood films in the 50s and 60s, including *The Creature from the Black Lagoon*, *Mutiny on the Bounty*, *Ben Hur*, *How the West Was Won*, and *The Incredible Shrinking Man*. He was the subject of a 1996 TV documentary, *The Man Who Drew Bug-Eyed Monsters*.

Brown, Robert (c. 1918–).
Burly British actor of stage, TV and film who played 'M' in the Bond films of the 80s.
Helen of Troy 55. A Hill in Korea 56. Campbell's Kingdom 57. Ben Hur 59. Sink the Bismarck 60. The Masque of the Red Death 64. One Million Years BC 66. Private Road 71. Warlords of Atlantis 78. Octopussy 83. A View to a Kill 85. The Living Daylights 87. Licence to Kill 89, etc.
TV series: Ivanhoe 57.

Brown, Robert N. (aka Toby Brown).
American editor.
The Mack 73. Damien: Omen II 78. The Amityville Horror 79. Brubaker 80. The Beast Within 82. The Pope of Greenwich Village 84. The Lost Boys 87. Cousins 89. Vital Signs 90. Flatliners 90. Dying Young 91. Lethal Weapon 3 92, etc.

Brown, Rowland (1901–1963).
American director whose career waned curiously after a promising start.
■ *Quick Millions* 31. Hell's Highway 32. Blood Money 33. The Devil is a Sissy (co-w only) 37.

Brown, Roy 'Chubby' (1945–) (Royston Vasey).
Northern English comic, a former drummer, billed as 'the rudest, crudest, filthiest comedian in the world'. He made his first film, which was publicized as 'the most offensive movie known to man', following the success of three videos of his stage act, which are said to have sold 750,000 copies.
UFO: The Movie 93.
❝ All I want to do is make people laugh, and I've found if you tell men about the size of women's tits and arses, they laugh; if you tell women about men's sexual exploits, their little bollocks, not being circumcised, women laugh. – *R.C.B.*

Brown, Tom (1913–1990).
American juvenile lead of the 30s; the 'boy next door' type. Re-emerged in the 60s as one of the villagers in the long-running TV series *Gunsmoke*.
The Hoosier Schoolmaster 24. The Lady Lies 29. Queen High 30. *Tom Brown of Culver* 32. Three Cornered Moon 33. Judge Priest 34. Anne of Green Gables 34. *Freckles* 35. I'd Give My Life 36. Maytime 37. In Old Chicago 38. Duke of West Point 38. Sergeant Madden 39. Sandy is a Lady 40. The Pay Off 43. The House on 92nd Street 45. Buck Privates Come Home 47. Duke of Chicago 49. The Quiet Gun 57, many others.
TV series: Mr Lucky 59–60.

Brown, Vanessa (1928–) (Smylla Brind).
American juvenile leading lady of a few late 40s films; usually demure.
Margie 46. *The Late George Apley* 47. Mother Wore Tights 47. The Foxes of Harrow 47. The Heiress 49. Tarzan and the Slave Girl 50. The Bad and the Beautiful 52. Rosie 68. Bless the Beasts and Children 71. The Witch Who Came from the Sea 76, etc.
TV series: My Favourite Husband 54. Rosie 67. Bless the Beasts and Children 71. The Witch Who Came from the Sea 75, etc.

Brown, Wally (1898–1961).
American comedian, a fast-talking vaudevillian who teamed with Alan CARNEY in a few comedy second features of the 40s.
Adventures of a Rookie 44. Rookies in Burma 44. Step Lively 44. Zombies on Broadway 45. Genius at Work 45. As Young As You Feel 51. The High and the Mighty 54. The Absent-minded Professor 61, etc.
TV series: Cimarron City 58.

Browne, Coral (1913–1991).
Australian stage actress long in Britain, usually in worldly comedy roles; films few. She married actor Vincent PRICE in 1974. She was also romantically involved with actor Jack BUCHANAN and photographer Cecil BEATON.
The Amateur Gentleman 36. Black Limelight 38. Let George Do It 40. Piccadilly Incident 46.

Auntie Mame (US) 58. The Roman Spring of Mrs Stone 61. Dr Crippen 64. *The Killing of Sister George* 68. Theatre of Blood 73. The Drowning Pool 75. An Englishman Abroad (TV) 83. American Dreamer 84. *Dreamchild* 85, etc.
TV series: Time Express 79.

Browne, Irene (1891–1965).
British stage actress, usually in dignified roles; films few.
The Letter 29. Cavalcade 33. Berkeley Square 33. The Amateur Gentleman 36. Pygmalion 38. The Prime Minister 40. *Quartet* 48. Madeleine 50. All at Sea 57. Rooney 58, etc.

Browne, Leslie (1958–).
American ballet dancer and occasional actress.
The Turning Point (AAN) 77. Nijinsky 80. Dancers 87, etc.

Browne, Roscoe Lee (1925–).
American character actor, a former athlete.
The Connection 62. The Cool World 64. *Topaz* 69. *The Liberation of L. B. Jones* 70. The Cowboys 72. Cisco Pike 72. Superfly Two 73. Logan's Run 76. Twilight's Last Gleaming 77. Nothing Personal 80. Jumpin' Jack Flash 86. Legal Eagles 86. Moon 44 91. The Mambo Kings 92. Eddie Presley 93. Naked in New York 93. The Pompatus of Love 95. Dear God 96, etc.
TV series: McCoy 75–76. Miss Winslow and Son 79. Soap 80–81. Falcon Crest 88.

Browning, Ricou (1930–).
American diver and stuntman who became a specialist in underwater direction for Ivan Tors.
The Creature from the Black Lagoon (also played title role) 54. Flipper 63. Around the World Under the Sea 66. Lady in Cement 68, etc.

Browning, Tod (1882–1962).
American director remembered chiefly for his horror films of the 20s and early 30s; revaluation has made them less striking than once was thought.
The Brazen Beauty 18. The Virgin of Stamboul 20. Under Two Flags 22. The White Tiger 23. The Unholy Three 25. The Mystic (& w) 25. The Unknown 27. *London After Midnight* 27. West of Zanzibar 28. Where East is East 29. The Thirteenth Chair 29. The Unholy Three (sound remake) 30. *Dracula* 30. Iron Man 31. *Freaks* 32. Fast Workers 33. Mark of the Vampire 35. *The Devil Doll* 36. Miracles for Sale 39, etc.

Brownlow, Kevin (1938–).
British producer-director who made his first film, *It Happened Here*, on a shoestring budget over seven years. It was released in 1966. Published 1969 *The Parade's Gone By*, a collection of interviews with silent movie stars. His 1975 film *Winstanley* was a clever but cheerless historical reconstruction; his 1979 book *The War, The West and The Wilderness* was another classic tome of research into silent filming.
TV series: *Hollywood* 79.

Bruce, Brenda (1918–).
British stage, TV and occasionally screen actress.
Millions Like Us 43. They Came to a City 45. Piccadilly Incident 46. My Brother's Keeper 48. Marry Me 52. The Final Test 53. Law and Disorder 57. Nightmare 63. The Uncle 65. That'll Be the Day 73. Swallows and Amazons 74. All Creatures Great and Small 74. Steaming 81. December Bride 90. Splitting Heirs 93. Harnessing Peacocks (TV) 93, etc.

Bruce, David (1914–1976) (Marden McBroom).
American light leading man familiar in Universal films during World War II.
The Sea Hawk 40. Singapore Woman 42. The Mad Ghoul 43. Ladies Courageous 44. Christmas Holiday 44. Can't Help Singing 44. Salome Where She Danced 45. Lady on a Train 45. Prejudice 48. Masterson of Kansas 55, etc.
TV series: Beulah 52.

Bruce, George (1898–).
American screenwriter.
Navy Blue and Gold 37. The Crowd Roars 38. The Duke of West Point 38. The Man in the Iron Mask 39. Son of Monte Cristo 40. South of Pago Pago 40. The Corsican Brothers 41. Miss Annie Rooney 42. Stand By for Action 43. Salute to the Marines 43. Two Years Before the Mast 46. Killer McCoy 47. Walk a Crooked Mile 48. Rogues of Sherwood Forest 50. Lorna Doone 51. Valentino 51. Kansas City Confidential 53. Solomon and Sheba 59, many others.

Bruce, Lenny (1926–1966) (Leonard Alfred Schneider).
Dirty-talking American nightclub comedian, a nine-day wonder who was impersonated on film by Dustin Hoffman in *Lenny*.
❝ Lenny, despite what his cultists and the Hoffman movie said, was dirty and sick. He had no redeeming social values. – *James Bacon*

Bruce, Nigel (1895–1953).
Tubby British comedy actor, mainly in Hollywood from 1934; usually played well-meaning upper-class buffoons, and was the screen's most memorable Dr Watson.
■ Red Aces 29. Birds of Prey 30. The Squeaker 31. Escape 31. The Calendar 31. Lord Camber's Ladies 32. The Midshipmaid 32. Channel Crossing 32. I Was a Spy 33. Springtime for Henry 34. Stand Up and Cheer 34. Coming Out Party 34. Murder in Trinidad 34. The Lady is Willing 34. Treasure Island 34. The Scarlet Pimpernel 35. *Becky Sharp* 35. Jalna 35. *She* 35. The Man Who Broke the Bank at Monte Carlo 35. The Trail of the Lonesome Pine 36. Under Two Flags 36. The White Angel 36. The Charge of the Light Brigade 36. Follow Your Heart 36. Make Way for a Lady 36. The Man I Married 36. Thunder in the City 37. The Last of Mrs Cheyney 37. The Baroness and the Butler 38. Kidnapped 38. Suez 38. *The Hound of the Baskervilles* 39. The Adventures of Sherlock Holmes 39. The Rains Came 39. *Rebecca* 40. Adventure in Diamonds 40. *The Bluebird* 40. Susan and God 40. Lillian Russell 40. A Dispatch from Reuters 40. Hudson's Bay 40. Playgirl 41. Free and Easy 41. The Chocolate Soldier 41. This Woman is Mine 41. Suspicion 41. Roxie Hart 42. This Above All 42. Eagle Squadron 42. Sherlock Holmes and the Voice of Terror 42. Sherlock Holmes and the Secret Weapon 42. Journey for Margaret 42. Sherlock Holmes in Washington 43. Crazy House (cameo) 43. Forever and a Day 43. Lassie Come Home 43. Sherlock Holmes Faces Death 43. Follow the Boys 44. The Pearl of Death 44. Spider Woman 44. Gypsy Wildcat 44. *The Scarlet Claw* 44. *Frenchman's Creek* 44. Son of Lassie 45. *House of Fear* 45. The Corn is Green 45. The Woman in Green 45. Pursuit to Algiers 45. Terror by Night 46. Dressed to Kill 46. The Two Mrs Carrolls 47. The Exile 47. Julia Misbehaves 48. Vendetta 50. Savage Drums 51. Hong Kong 51. Bwana Devil 53. *Limelight* 53. World for Ransom 53.
✪ For regrettably but amusingly fixing the image of the upper-class English dodderer. *Rebecca*.

Bruce, Tony (1910–1937).
Scottish leading actor, who left the Navy to star in Anthony Asquith's *Tell England* 31.
Mr Bill the Conqueror 32. Brother Alfred 32. Lucky Girl 32. Diamond Cut Diamond 32. Men of Tomorrow 32. Windjammer 35, etc.

Bruce, Virginia (1910–1982) (Helen Virginia Briggs).
American light leading lady of the 30s. The first of her three husbands was actor John Gilbert (1932–34).
Woman Trap 29. The Love Parade 29. Safety in Numbers 30. Hell Divers 31. The Wet Parade 32. Kongo 32. *Jane Eyre* (title role) 34. Dangerous Corner 34. Escapade 35. Metropolitan 35. The Great Ziegfeld 36. Born to Dance 36. Between Two Women 37. Arsène Lupin Returns 38. Yellow Jack 38. Society Lawyer 39. Flight Angels 40. Invisible Woman 41. Pardon My Sarong 42. Careful Soft Shoulders 42. Action in Arabia 44. Love Honour and Goodbye 45. Night Has a Thousand Eyes 48. The Reluctant Bride (GB) 52. Strangers When We Meet 60, many others.

Bruckheimer, Jerry.
American producer, formerly in advertising. Born in Detroit, he graduated from the University of Arizona and first worked for an advertising agency. With his partner Don Simpson, with whom he teamed up in 1983, he headed a company that produced some of the biggest box-office successes of the 80s for Paramount Pictures, a partnership that ended shortly before Simpson's death in 1996.
Farewell My Lovely 75. March or Die 77. American Gigolo 80. Defiance 80. Thief 81. Cat People 82. Young Doctors in Love 82. Armageddon 98. Enemy of the State 98. Max Q (TV) 98, etc.
CO-PRODUCTIONS (with Don Simpson): Flashdance 83. Beverly Hills Cop 84. Thief of Hearts 84. Top Gun 86. Beverly Hills Cop II 87. Days of Thunder 90. The Ref 94. Bad Boys 95. The Rock 96, etc.
❝ I make movies I want to see. – *J.B.*

Bruckman, Clyde (1894–1955).
American writer-director of many silent comedies, especially associated with Buster Keaton, Harold Lloyd, and W. C. Fields. Born in San Bernadino, California, he began as a journalist before joining Warner's as a screenwriter. Alcoholism hampered his career from the mid-30s, as did his habit of recycling gags from other movies. Committed suicide with a .45 Colt automatic that he borrowed from Keaton.
Sherlock Jnr (w) 24. *The Navigator* (w) 24. *The General* (wd) 27. *Feet First* (wd) 30. *Movie Crazy* (d) 32. The Man on the Flying Trapeze (d) 35, many others.

Bruel, Patrick (1959–).
Leading French actor, born in Tlemcen, Algeria.
Le Coup de Sirocco 78. Les Diplomes du Dernier Rang 82. Mariage Blues 85. La Maison Assassinée 87. Force Majeure 89. Band of Brothers/L'Union Sacrée 89. Profil Bas 94. Queen Margot/La Reine Margot 94. Sabrina (US) 95, etc.

Brummell, Beau (1778–1840).
A famous British dandy and politician who has been the subject of two biopics: in 1924 with John Barrymore (directed by Harry Beaumont) and in 1954 with Stewart Granger (directed by Curtis Bernhardt).

Brunel, Adrian (1892–1958).
British director with pleasant reputation in the 20s as an intellectual at large.
Autobiography: 1952, *Nice Work*.
Book: 1933, *Filmcraft*.
Bookworms (short) 20. The Bump (short) 20. *The Man without Desire* 23. Crossing the Great Sagrada (short) 24. *Blighty* 27. *The Constant Nymph* 27. The Vortex 28. While Parents Sleep 35. The City of Beautiful Nonsense 35. Prison Breaker 36. The Lion Has Wings 39. The Girl Who Forgot 40, etc.

Brunius, Jacques (1906–1967).
French actor, once critic and assistant to Clair and Renoir; later resident in Britain.
L'Age d'Or 30. Partie de Campagne 37. Sea Devils 53. To Paris with Love 55. Orders to Kill 58, etc.

Bruns, George (1913–).
American composer whose film scores have almost all been for Disney.
Davy Crockett, King of the Wild Frontier 55. Sleeping Beauty (AAN) 59. One Hundred and One Dalmatians 60. Babes in Toyland (AAN) 61. The Sword in the Stone (AAN) 63. The Jungle Book 67. The Love Bug 69. The Aristocats 70. Robin Hood 73. Herbie Rides Again 74, etc.

Bryan, Dora (1923–) (Dora Broadbent).
British stage and film comedienne, specializing in warm-hearted tarts of the cockney or northern variety.
Autobiography: 1987, *According to Dora*.
Odd Man Out 46. The Fallen Idol 48. The Cure for Love 48. The Blue Lamp 50. High Treason 51. Lady Godiva Rides Again 51. Mother Riley Meets the Vampire 52. Time Gentlemen Please 53. Fast and Loose 54. See How They Run 55. Cockleshell Heroes 56. The Green Man 57. Desert Mice 59. The Night We Got the Bird 60. *A Taste of Honey* (BFA: leading role) 61. The Great St Trinian's Train Robbery 66. The Sandwich Man 66. Two a Penny 68. Hands of the Ripper 71. Up the Front 72. Screamtime 83. Apartment Zero 88, etc.
TV series: Mother's Ruin 94.

Bryan, Jane (1918–) (Jane O'Brien).
Sympathetic American leading lady of the later 30s.
■ The Case of the Black Cat 36. Marked Woman 37. Kid Galahad 37. Confession 37. A Slight Case of Murder 38. *The Sisters* 38. Girls on Probation 38. Brother Rat 38. Each Dawn I Die 39. The Old Maid 39. These Glamour Girls 39. *We are Not Alone* 39. Invisible Stripes 40. Brother Rat and a Baby 40.

Bryan, John (1911–1969).
British producer and production designer.
Great Expectations (des) (AA) 46. Pandora and the Flying Dutchman (des) 51. *The Card* 52. The Purple Plain 54. The Spanish Gardener (& w) 56. Windom's Way 57. The Horse's Mouth 58. There Was a Crooked Man 60. Tamahine 62. After the Fox 66. The Touchables 68, etc.

Bryant, Michael (1928–).
Serious-looking British character actor of stage and TV; films occasional.
Life for Ruth 62. The Mindbenders 63. Goodbye Mr Chips 69. Nicholas and Alexandra (as Lenin) 71. Gandhi 81. Sakharov (TV) 84. Girly 87. Hamlet 96, etc.

Bryant, Nana (1888–1955).
Dignified but friendly American character actress who usually played middle-class mums or rich patrons.
A Feather in Her Hat 35. Theodora Goes Wild 36. Mad About Music 38. Espionage Agent 39. Nice Girl 41. Calling Dr Gillespie 42. The Song of Bernadette 43. Brewster's Millions 45. The Unsuspected 47. Harvey 50. Bright Victory 51. About Mrs Leslie 54. The Private War of Major Benson 55, many others.
TV series: Our Miss Brooks 55.

Brynner, Yul (1915–1985) (Youl Bryner).
Bald-headed international star of somewhat mysterious background: variously alleged to have originated in Switzerland and Russia, but assuredly American by adoption. A Broadway stage success, especially as the king in *The King and I*; long dominant in films though not easy to cast.
■ Port of New York 49. *The King and I* (AA) 56. The Ten Commandments 56. *Anastasia* 56. *The Brothers Karamazov* 58. The Buccaneer 58. The Journey 58. The Sound and the Fury 59. Solomon and Sheba 59. Once More with Feeling 60. Surprise Package 60. *The Magnificent Seven* 60. The Testament of Orpheus 60. Escape from Zahrain 62. *Taras Bulba* 62. Kings of the Sun 63. Flight from Ashiya 64. *Invitation to a Gunfighter* 64. The Saboteur 65. Cast a Giant Shadow 66. Return of the Seven 66. The Poppy is Also a Flower 66. Triple Cross 66. The Double Man 67. The Long Duel 67. Villa Rides 68. The Madwoman of Chaillot 69. The File of the Golden Goose 69. The Battle of Neretva 70. Indio Black 70. The Magic Christian 70. The Light at the Edge of the World 71. Romance of a Horsethief 71. Catlow 72. Fuzz 72. The Serpent 72. Westworld 73. The Ultimate Warrior 74. Futureworld 76. Anger in his Eyes (It.) 76.
TV series: *Anna and the King* 72.
✪ For proving that bald is beautiful at the box-office. *The Magnificent Seven*.
❝ People don't know my real self and they're not about to find out. – *Y.B.*

Bubbles, John W. 1902–1984 (John 'Bubber' Sublett).
American singer and tap-dancer, usually appearing as part of the duo 'Buck and Bubbles' with Ford Lee 'Buck' Washington. Born in Louisville, Kentucky, he devised a new style of tap-dancing in the 20s, appeared on Broadway, and created the role of Sportin' Life in Gershwin's *Porgy and Bess*. His vaudeville partnership with Washington lasted from 1912 to the early 50s.
Darktown Follies 30. Calling All Stars (GB) 37. Cabin in the Sky 43. Buck and Bubbles Laugh Jamboree 45. Mantan Messes Up 46. A Song Is Born 48. No Maps on My Taps (doc) 78, etc.

Buchan, John (1875–1940).
British adventure novelist oddly neglected by the cinema apart from *The Thirty-nine Steps*, no version of which bears much resemblance to the original; and a 1927 version of *Huntingtower*.

Buchanan, Edgar (1902–1979).
Jovial American character actor, in innumerable westerns and rustic dramas as hayseed, crooked judge, comic side-kick or straight villain.
My Son is Guilty 39. Arizona 40. The Richest Man in Town 41. The Desperados 42. Destroyer 43. Buffalo Bill 44. The Fighting Guardsman 45. Abilene Town 46. Framed 47. The Black Arrow 48. The Best Man Wins 48. Red Canyon 49. Devil's Doorway 50. The Great Missouri Raid 51. The Big Trees 52. Shane 53. Human Desire 54. Day of the Badman 57. The Sheepman 58. Edge of

Eternity 60. Cimarron 61. Ride the High Country 62. McLintock 63. The Rounders 65. Welcome to Hard Times 67. Benji 75, many others.
TV series: Hopalong Cassidy 51–52. Judge Roy Bean 53. Petticoat Junction 63–69. Cade's County 71.

Buchanan, Jack (1891–1957).
Debonair British entertainer, a memorable song-and-dance man of stage and screen in the 20s and 30s: good-looking, long-legged, nasal of voice and debonair in appearance.
Biography: 1978, *Top Hat and Tails* by Michael Marshall.
■ Bulldog Drummond's Third Round 25. Happy Landing 25. Toni 27. Confetti 28. Paris 29. Show of Shows 29. *Monte Carlo* 30. Goodnight Vienna 32. A Man of Mayfair 32. *Yes Mr Brown* 32. Magic Night 32. *Brewster's Millions* 33. That's a Good Girl 33. That Girl 34. Come out of the Pantry 35. Sons o'Guns 35. When Knights were Bold 36. Limelight 36. Smash and Grab 37. Break the News 37. This'll Make You Whistle 37. The Sky's the Limit 38. *The Gang's All Here* 39. Alias the Bulldog 39. The Middle Watch 39. Bulldog Sees It Through 40. *The Band Wagon* 53. As Long as They're Happy 53. Josephine and Men 55. The Diary of Major Thompson 56. That's Entertainment! III 94.

Buchholz, Horst (1932–).
German leading man, in occasional international films.
Marianne de Ma Jeunesse (debut) 54. Himmel Ohne Sterne 55. King in Shadow 56. The Confessions of Felix Krull 57. Resurrection 58. *Tiger Bay* 59. *The Magnificent Seven* 60. Fanny 61. *One Two Three* 61. Nine Hours to Rama 63. The Empty Canvas 64. Marco the Magnificent 65. That Man in Istanbul 66. Cervantes 66. L'Astragale 68. The Great Waltz 72. The Catamount Killing 75. Raid on Entebbe (TV) 77. Avalanche Express 79. Aphrodite 81. Sahara 83. Code Name: Emerald 85. Aces: Iron Eagle III 92. Faraway, So Close!/In Weiter Ferne, So Nah 93, etc.

Buchman, Sidney (1902–1975).
American writer-producer of good commercial films.
Matinée Ladies (oa) 27. *The Sign of the Cross* (co-w) 32. I'll Love You Always (w) 35. The King Steps Out (w) 36. *Theodora Goes Wild* (w) 36. *Mr Smith Goes to Washington* (w) 39. The Howards of Virginia (w) 40. *Here Comes Mr Jordan* (w) (AA) 41. *The Talk of the Town* (co-w, AAN) 42. *A Song to Remember* (wp) 45. Over 21 (p) 45. Jolson Sings Again (wp, AANw) 49. Saturday's Hero (w) 51. Cleopatra (w) 63. *The Group* (wp) 66, many others.

Buck and Bubbles:
see Washington, Ford Lee 'Buck', and Bubbles, John W.

Buck, Frank (1888–1950).
American explorer who made several animal films. In 1982 Buck was impersonated by Bruce Boxleitner in a short-lived TV series called *Bring 'Em Back Alive*, based in 1939 Singapore and involving Buck with spies as well as animals.
Appeared in *Africa Screams* 50.
Bring 'Em Back Alive 32. Fang and Claw 36. Jungle Menace 37. Jacare, Killer of the Amazon 42, etc.

Buck, Jules (1917–).
American producer who in the late 50s came to Britain and founded Keep Films with Peter O'Toole.
Fixed Bayonets 51. Treasure of the Golden Condor 53. The Day They Robbed the Bank of England 60. *Becket* 64. Great Catherine 66. The Ruling Class 71, etc.

Buck, Pearl (1892–1973).
American novelist and missionary to the Far East. Works filmed include *The Good Earth, Dragon Seed, Satan Never Sleeps*.

Buckland, Wilfred (1866–1946).
American art director, with claims to be the first so employed in films. A successful stage designer, he joined Famous Players Lasky in 1914 and worked on Cecil B. De Mille's early films, becoming involved not only in design but in using lighting for dramatic effect. Committed suicide after killing his mentally ill son.
Squaw Man 14. The Ghost Breaker 14. The Virginian 14. Carmen 15. Joan the Woman 16. Stella Maris 18. The Squaw Man 18. Conrad in Search of His Youth 20. Adam's Rib 23. Almost Human 27, many others.

Buckler, Hugh (1870–1936).
English actor, in Hollywood from the 30s. He was the father of actor John Buckler. Both were drowned in a car accident.
The Garden of Resurrection 19. Duke's Son 20. Guy Fawkes 23. Crash Donovan 36. Last of the Mohicans 36. Jungle Princess 36. Lost Horizon 37, etc.

Buckler, John (1896–1936).
English actor who accompanied his father Hugh Buckler to Hollywood in the 30s and died with him in a car accident.
David Copperfield 35. Eight Bells 35. The Black Room 35. Tarzan Escapes 36. The Unguarded Hour 36.

Buckley, Betty (1947–).
American actress and singer, from the Broadway stage.
Carrie 76. Tender Mercies 83. Frantic 88. Another Woman 88. Wyatt Earp 94. Critical Choices 97, etc.
TV series: Eight Is Enough 77–81.

Buckner, Robert (1906–).
American screenwriter, later producer.
Gold is Where You Find It 38. Jezebel 38. The Oklahoma Kid 39. *Dodge City* 39. Virginia City 39. *Santa Fe Trail* 40. Dive Bomber 41. Yankee Doodle Dandy (AAN) 42. Gentleman Jim (p) 42. Mission to Moscow (p) 43. Confidential Agent (& p) 45. Rogues' Regiment (& p) 48. Sword in the Desert (& p) 49. Bright Victory (& p) 51. Love Me Tender 56. From Hell to Texas (& p) 58. Return of the Gunfighter 68, etc.

Bucquet, Harold S. (1891–1946).
English director in Hollywood.
Young Dr Kildare 39. *On Borrowed Time* 39. The Secret of Dr Kildare 39. We Who Are Young 40. Dr Kildare Goes Home 40. The Penalty 41. Kathleen 41. Calling Dr Gillespie 42. The War Against Mrs Hadley 42. The Adventures of Tartu (GB) 43. Dragon Seed 44. Without Love 45, etc.

Budd, Roy (1949–1993).
British composer and jazz pianist.
Soldier Blue 70. Zeppelin 71. Get Carter 71. Flight of the Doves 71. Pulp 72. The Stone Killer 73. The Internecine Project 74. Paper Tiger 75. Sinbad and the Eye of the Tiger 77. The Wild Geese 78. The Sea Wolves 80. Who Dares Wins 82. Wild Geese II 85. Field of Honor 86, etc.

Buddy (1990–1998).
Basketball-playing golden retriever, who was the star of the Disney movie *Air Bud* 97. Shortly after filming finished, his right rear leg was amputated when the cancer that was to kill him was first diagnosed.

Buetel, Jack (1917–1989).
American western leading man who was little seen after a highly publicized debut.
The Outlaw (as Billy the Kid) 43. Best of the Badmen 51. The Half Breed 52. Jesse James' Women 54. Mustang 59, etc.
TV series: Judge Roy Bean 53.

Buff, Conrad.
American film and special effects editor.
The Empire Strikes Back 80. ET, the Extra-Terrestrial 82. Poltergeist 82. 2010 84. Ghost Busters 84. Jagged Edge 85. Solarbabies 86. Spaceballs 87. Short Circuit 2 88. Side Out 90. True Lies 94. The Getaway 94. Species 95. Titanic (AA) 97, etc.

Bujold, Geneviève (1942–).
French-Canadian leading lady.
French Can Can 56. La Guerre est Finie 63. King of Hearts 67. Isabel 67. Act of the Heart 70. *Anne of the Thousand Days* (as Anne Boleyn) (AAN) 70. Earthquake 74. Obsession 76. Swashbuckler 76. Alex and the Gypsy 76. Another Man, Another Chance 77. Murder by Decree 78. Coma 78. Final Assignment 80. Monsignor 81. Tightrope 84. Choose Me 85. Trouble in Mind 85. Dead Ringers 88. The Moderns 88. False Identity 90. Rue du Bac 91. The Dance Goes On 91. Paper Wedding 91. Oh, What a Night 92. An Ambush of Ghosts 93. Mon Amie Max 94. The Adventures of Pinocchio 96. The House of Yes 97. You Can Thank Me Later 98, etc.

Bukowski, Charles (1920–1994).
Hard-drinking American poet, chronicler of the low life, and occasional screenwriter.
Tales of Ordinary Madness (oa) 83. Love Is a Dog From Hell (oa) 87. Barfly (w) 87. Cold Moon (oa) 91.

Bull, Peter (1912–1984).
Portly British character actor often in haughty, aggressive or explosively foreign roles.
Autobiography: 1959, *I Know the Face but . . .*
Sabotage 37. The Ware Case 39. The Turners of Prospect Road 47. Oliver Twist 48. Saraband for Dead Lovers 48. The African Queen 51. The Malta Story 53. Footsteps in the Fog 55. Tom Jones 63. Dr Strangelove 63. The Old Dark House 63. Dr Dolittle 67. Lock Up Your Daughters 69. The Executioner 70. Up the Front 72. Alice's Adventures in Wonderland 72. Joseph Andrews 77. The Brute 78. Yellowbeard 83, many others.

Bullock, Sandra (1966–).
American actress. Born in Washington to a German mother and an American father, she spent her childhood in Nuremberg. Her price per movie went up from $500,000 (*Speed*) to $6m (*A Time to Kill*) and to around $11m for *Speed II* 97.
Who Shot Pat?/Who Shot Patakango? 90. Bionic Showdown: The Six-Million Dollar Man and the Bionic Woman (TV) 91. Fire on the Amazon 91. Love Potion #9 92. Demolition Man 93. The Vanishing 93. The Thing Called Love 93. Wrestling Ernest Hemingway 93. Speed 94. Me and the Mob 94. While You Were Sleeping 95. The Net 95. Two If by Sea/Stolen Hearts 96. A Time to Kill 96. Lost Paradise (made 90) 97. In Love and War 97. Speed 2: Cruise Control 97. Hope Floats 98. Practical Magic 98. Prince of Egypt (voice) 98, etc.
TV series: Working Girl 90.
❝ My goal is to create small films that we are crazy about. – *S.B.*

Buloff, Joseph (1899–1985).
American actor of stage and screen. Born in Lithuania, he went to America in the late 20s and first worked with the Yiddish Art Theatre in New York.
Let's Make Music 40. Carnegie Hall 47. The Loves of Carmen 48. A Kiss in the Dark 49. Somebody Up There Likes Me 56. Silk Stockings 57, etc.

Bumstead, Henry (1915–).
American production designer.
The Man Who Knew Too Much 56. Vertigo (AAN) 58. The Great Impostor 60. To Kill a Mockingbird (AA) 62. Father Goose 64. The War Lord 65. Tell Them Willie Boy Is Here 69. Topaz 69. Slaughterhouse Five 71. High Plains Drifter 73. The Sting (AA) 73. The Front Page 74. Family Plot 76. Slapshot 77. Same Time Next Year 78. A Little Romance 79. The Concorde – Airport '79 79. The World According to Garp 82. The Little Drummer Girl 84. Psycho III 86. A Time of Destiny 88. Ghost Dad 90. Almost an Angel 90. Cape Fear 91. Unforgiven 92. A Perfect World 93. The Stars Fell on Henrietta 95. Absolute Power 97. Home Alone 3 97. Midnight in the Garden of Good and Evil 97, many others.

Bunker, Eddie (1933–).
American screenwriter, thriller writer, and character actor, a former convict. The youngest-ever inmate of San Quentin prison at the age of 17, he was encouraged to write by actress Louise Fazenda.
Straight Time (co-w from his novel No Beast So Fierce, a) 78. The Long Riders (a) 80. Runaway Train (co-w) 85. Shy People (a) 87. American Heart (technical adviser) 92. Reservoir Dogs (as Mr Blue) 92, etc.
❝ I would rather do business with a straight-up bank robber than most agents. – *E.B.*

Bunnage, Avis (1923–1990).
Exuberant English character actress, from the stage.
Espresso Bongo 59. Saturday Night and Sunday Morning 60. Loneliness of the Long Distance Runner 62. Sparrows Can't Sing 63. Tom Jones 63. A Study in Terror 65. The Wrong Box 66. Gandhi 82. The Krays 90, etc.

Bunny, John (1863–1915).
British actor who became the funny fat man of early American silent comedy; made more than 150 shorts, usually with Flora Finch.

Buñuel, Juan (1934–).
French-born film director whose style is much influenced by that of his father, Luis Buñuel; he worked as an assistant director on several of his father's films from the 60s.
Au Rendez-vous de la Mort Joyeuse 73. *The Lady in Red Boots*/La Femme aux Bottes Rouges 74. Leonor 75. The Island of Passion 84. La Rebelión de los Colgados 87, etc.

Buñuel, Luis (1900–1983).
Spanish writer-director who worked in France in the 20s and 30s, made many films in Mexico 1945–60, then returned to Europe. A once-notorious surrealist, his later films mocked hypocrisy and the shows of religion.
Autobiography: 1984, *My Last Breath*.
Biographies: 1963, by Adonis Kyrou. 1967, by Raymond Durgnat. 1993, *Objects of Desire: Conversations with Luis Buñuel* by José de la Colina and Tomás Pérez.
Book: 1995, *The Films of Luis Buñuel* by Peter William Evans.
■ Un Chien Andalou 28. *L'Age d'Or* 30. Land without Bread 32. Grand Casino 46. El Gran Calavera 49. *Los Olvidados* 50. Suzana la Perverse 50. La Hija del Engaño 51. Una Mujer Sin Amor 51. Subida al Cielo 51. The Brute 52. Wuthering Heights 52. *Robinson Crusoe* 52. *El* 53. La Ilusión Viaja en Tranvia 53. El Rio y la Muerte 54. The Criminal Life of Archibaldo de la Cruz 55. La Mort en ce Jardin 56. Cela S'Appelle L'Aurore 58. La Fièvre Monte à El Pao 59. Nazarin 59. The Young One 60. *Viridiana* 61. *The Exterminating Angel* 62. Diary of a Chambermaid 64. *Belle de Jour* 66. Simon of the Desert 66. The Milky Way 69. Tristana (AAN) 70. *The Discreet Charm of the Bourgeoisie* (AAN) 72. *The Phantom of Liberty* 74. *That Obscure Object of Desire* 77.
✪ For making surrealism irresistible by mixing it with deft film-making techniques and suave direction of actors. *The Discreet Charm of the Bourgeoisie*.
I've always found insects exciting. – *L.B.*

Buono, Victor (1938–1982).
Massively bulky American character actor who moved to films via the amateur theatre.
■ *Whatever Happened to Baby Jane?* (AAN) 62. Four for Texas 63. *The Strangler* 64. Robin and the Seven Hoods 64. The Greatest Story Ever Told 65. Hush Hush Sweet Charlotte 65. Young Dillinger 65. The Silencers 66. Who's Minding the Mint? 67. Beneath the Planet of the Apes 69. In the Name of our Father (It.) 69. The Wrath of God 72. The Mad Butcher 72. Crime Club (TV) 72. Goodnight My Love (TV) 72. Northeast of Seoul 74. Arnold 75. Brenda Starr (TV) 75. High Risk (TV) 76. Man from Atlantis (TV) 77. The Evil 78. Return of the Mod Squad (TV) 79. Backstairs at the White House (TV) 79. The Man with Bogart's Face 80.

Burden, Hugh (1913–1985).
British character actor.
One of Our Aircraft is Missing 41. The Way Ahead 44. Fame is the Spur 46. Sleeping Car to Trieste 48. The Malta Story 53. No Love for Johnnie 61. Funeral in Berlin 66. The Statue 71. Blood from the Mummy's Tomb 71. The House in Nightmare Park 73, etc.

Burge, Stuart (1918–).
British director, from TV.
■ There Was a Crooked Man 60. Uncle Vanya 63. Othello 65. The Mikado 67. Julius Caesar 70.

Burgess, Anthony (1917–1993) (John Burgess Wilson).
British novelist whose chief contribution to the cinema is *A Clockwork Orange*.

Burgess, Don.
American cinematographer.
The Night Stalker 87. Blind Fury 89. Mo' Money 92. Josh and S.A.M. 93. Forrest Gump (AAN) 94. Richie Rich 95, etc.

Burgess, Dorothy (1907–1961).
American actress, from the New York stage, who went to Hollywood to star opposite Warner Baxter in *In Old Arizona* 29. Subsequently, she played leading roles in second features.
Cleopatra 30. Malay Nights 32. Orient Express 34. Manhattan Butterfly 35. I Want a Divorce 40. Lady for a Night 41. The Lone Star Ranger 42. Girls in Chains 43, etc.

Burgon, Geoffrey (1941–).
British composer.
Life of Brian 79. Dogs of War 80. Brideshead Revisited (TV) 82. Turtle Diary 85. Bleak House (TV) 85. Robin Hood 91. A Foreign Field (TV) 93. Martin Chuzzlewit (TV) 94, etc.

Burke, Alfred (1918–).
British stage, screen and TV actor usually in cold, unsympathetic or other-worldly roles.
Touch and Go 56. The Man Upstairs 58. The Angry Silence 59. Children of the Damned 64. The Nanny 65. One Day in the Life of Ivan Denisovich 71. The House on Garibaldi Street (TV) 79, etc.
TV series: Public Eye 69–73.

Burke, Billie (1885–1970) (Mary William Ethelbert Appleton Burke).
American stage star who married Florenz Ziegfeld; Myrna Loy played her in *The Great Ziegfeld*. After a few early silents she settled in Hollywood in the 30s and played variations on the dithery matron role she made her own.
Autobiographies: 1949, *With a Feather on my Nose*. 1959, *With Powder on My Nose*.
■ Gloria's Romance 16. Peggy 16. The Land of Promise 17. The Mysterious Miss Terry 17. Arms and the Girl 18. Eve's Daughter 18. Let's Get a Divorce 18. In Pursuit of Polly 18. The Make Believe Wife 18. Good Gracious Annabelle 19. The Misleading Widow 19. Sadie Love 19. Wanted, a Husband 19. Away Goes Prudence 20. The Frisky Mrs Johnson 21. The Education of Elizabeth 21. *A Bill of Divorcement* 32. Christopher Strong 33. *Dinner at Eight* 33. Only Yesterday 33. Finishing School 34. Where Sinners Meet 34. We're Rich Again 34. Forsaking all Others 34. Society Doctor 35. After Office Hours 35. Becky Sharp 35. Doubting Thomas 35. *A Feather in Her Hat* 35. She Couldn't Take It 35. Splendour 35. My American Wife 36. Piccadilly Jim 36. Craig's Wife 36. Parnell 36. *Topper* 37. The Bride Wore Red 37. Navy Blue and Gold 37. Everybody Sing 38. *Merrily We Live* (AAN) 38. *The Young in Heart* 38. Topper Takes a Trip 38. Zenobia 39. Bridal Suite 39. The Wizard of Oz 39. Eternally Yours 39. Remember 39. And One Was Beautiful 40. Irene 40. Dulcy 40. Hullaballoo 40. The Captain is a Lady 40. The Ghost Comes Home 40. The Wild Man of Borneo 41. Topper Returns 41. One Night in Lisbon 41. *The Man Who Came to Dinner* 41. What's Cookin'? 42. In This Our Life 42. They All Kissed the Bride 42. Girl Trouble 42. Hi Diddle Diddle 42. Gildersleeve on Broadway 43. You're a Lucky Fellow Mr Smith 43. So's Your Uncle 44. *The Cheaters* 45. Swing Out Sister 45. Breakfast in Hollywood 46. The Bachelor's Daughters 46. The Barkleys of Broadway 49. And Baby Makes Three 49. Father of the Bride 50. The Boy from Indiana 50. Three Husbands 51. Father's Little Dividend 51. Small Town Girl 53. The Young Philadelphians 59. Sergeant Rutledge 60. Pepe 60.
TV series: Doc Corkle 52.
Famous line (*The Wizard of Oz*): 'Close your eyes and tap your heels together three times. And think to yourself, there's no place like home.'

Burke, Kathy.
English character actress; she won the best actress award at the Cannes Film Festival in 1997 for her performance in *Nil by Mouth*.
Scrubbers 83. Sid and Nancy 86. Mr Wroe's Virgins (TV) 93. Nil by Mouth 97. Tom Jones (TV) 97. Elizabeth 98. Dancing at Lughnasa 98, etc.
TV series: Harry Enfield's Television Programme 90. Harry Enfield and Chums 94, 97.
❝ When you are called a character actress it's because you are too ugly to be called a leading lady. – K.B.

Burke, James (1886–1968).
Irish-American character actor who played more New York cops than he could count.
A Lady's Profession 33. Little Miss Marker 34. Ruggles of Red Gap 35. Song and Dance Man 36. Dead End 37. Dawn Patrol 38. At the Circus 39. Ellery Queen Master Detective 40. The Maltese Falcon 41. Army Surgeon 42. A Night to Remember 43. The Horn Blows at Midnight 45. Two Years Before the Mast 46. Nightmare Alley 47. June Bride 48. Copper Canyon 50. Lone Star 52. Lucky Me 54, many others.

Burke, Johnny (1908–1964).
American songwriter who often supplied lyrics for Jimmy Van Heusen's music. 'Pennies from Heaven', 'Moonlight Becomes You', 'Swinging on a Star' (AA 44), many others.

Burke, Kathleen (1913–1980).
American leading lady who made a few 30s appearances after being dubbed 'the panther woman' in 1932's *Island of Lost Souls*.

Burke, Marie (1894–1988) (Marie Holt).
British actress, mostly on stage.
After the Ball 33. Odette 50. The Constant Husband 55. The Snorkel 58. Rattle of a Simple Man 64, etc.

Burke, Martyn.
Canadian director.
The Clown Murders 76. Power Play 78. The Last Chase 81. Top Secret! 84. Sugartime (TV) 95. The Second Civil War (TV) 97, etc.

Burke, Patricia (1917–).
British actress, daughter of Marie Burke.
The Lisbon Story 45. The Trojan Brothers 45. Love Story 46. While I Live 47. Forbidden 49. The Happiness of Three Women 54. Spider's Web 60. The Day the Fish Came Out 67, etc.

Burke, Paul (1926–).
American leading man, who on TV projected integrity with great success but has done few movies.
South Sea Woman 53. Screaming Eagles 56. *Valley of the Dolls* 67. The Thomas Crown Affair 68. Daddy's Gone a-Hunting 69. Lt Schuster's Wife (TV) 72. Psychic Killer 75. Little Ladies of the Night (TV) 77. Wild and Wooly (TV) 78. Beach Patrol (TV) 79. The Red Light Sting 84, etc.
TV series: Harbormaster 57. Five Fingers 59. Noah's Ark 60. Naked City 60–63. Twelve o'Clock High 67. Dynasty 83. Hot Shots 86–87.

Burke, Robert John (1961–).
American actor.
The Unbelievable Truth 90. Rambling Rose 91. Dust Devil 92. Robocop 3 92. A Far Off Place 93. Tombstone 94. Stephen King's Thinner 96, etc.

Burke, Thomas (1886–1945).
English novelist and essayist, noted for his stories set in Limehouse, London's Chinese quarter. His essay 'The Comedian' in his *City of Encounters* was described by Chaplin's biographer David Robinson as 'the most searching and perceptive portrait ever written' of Charlie Chaplin.
Broken Blossoms (from The Chink and the Child) 19 and 36. Dream Street (from Gina of Chinatown) 21. Curlytop (from Twelve Golden Curls) 24, etc.

Burks, Robert (1910–1968).
American cinematographer.
■ Make Your Own Bed 44. Escape in the Desert 45. To the Victor 48. A Kiss in the Dark 49. *The Fountainhead* 49. Beyond the Forest 49. Task Force 49. The Glass Menagerie 50. Close to My Heart 51. *Strangers on a Train* 51. Tomorrow Is Another Day 51. *Come Fill the Cup* 51. *The Enforcer* 51. The Miracle of Our Lady of Fatima 52. Room for One More 52. Mara Maru 52. The Desert Song 53. This Is Love 53. Hondo 53. *I Confess* 53. The Boy from Oklahoma 54. Dial M for Murder 54. *Rear Window* 54. *To Catch a Thief* (AA) 55. The Trouble with Harry 56. The Man Who Knew Too Much 56. The Vagabond King 56. The Wrong Man 57. The Spirit of St Louis (co-ph) 58. *Vertigo* 58. The Black Orchid 59. *North by Northwest* 59. But Not for Me 59. The Rat Race 60. The Great Impostor 61. The Pleasure of His Company 61. *The Music Man* 62. *The Birds* 63. Marnie 64. Once a Thief 65. A Patch of Blue 66. A Covenant with Death 67. Waterhole Three 67.

Burlinson, Tom (1956–).
Australian leading actor.
The Man from Snowy River 82. Phar Lap 84. Flesh Blood 85. King Solomon's Mines 86. Windrider 86. The Time Guardian 87. Return to Snowy River 88. Showdown at Williams Creek 91, etc.

Burnaby, Davy (1881–1949).
Heavyweight, monocled British entertainer.
The Co-optimists 29. Three Men in a Boat 33. Are You a Mason? 34. Boys Will Be Boys 35. Feather Your Nest 37. Many Tanks Mr Atkins 39. etc.

Burness, Pete (1910–).
American animator who worked his way through *The Little King* and *Tom and Jerry* to U.P.A. and *Bullwinkle*.

Burnett, Carol (1933–).
Lanky, long-faced American revue and television star who, despite being a household word at home, hasn't made much of an impression in the overseas market.
■ Who's Been Sleeping in My Bed? 63. Pete 'n' Tillie 72. The Front Page 74. A Wedding 78. The Grass Is Always Greener Over the Septic Tank (TV) 78. *Friendly Fire* (TV) 79. Health 80. The Four Seasons 81. Chu Chu and the Philly Flash 81. Annie 82. Between Friends 83. Noises Off 92. Seasons of the Heart (TV) 94.
TV series: Stanley 56. The Garry Moore Show 60s. *The Carol Burnett Show* 70s. Mama's Family 83–84.
❝ How many people do you know who can make a lot of money by crossing their eyes and doing pratfalls? – C.B.
Celebrity was a long time in coming; it will go away. Everything goes away. – C.B.

Burnett, Charles (1944–).
American director and screenwriter.
Killer of Sheep 77. My Brother's Wedding 83. Bless Their Little Hearts 84. To Sleep with Anger 90. The Glass Shield (wd) 94. Nightjohn 96. The Wedding (TV) 98, etc.

Burnett, Frances Hodgson (1849–1924).
English novelist whose screen contributions include the much-filmed children's stories *Little Lord Fauntleroy* and *The Secret Garden*. *A Little Princess* made a solid vehicle for Shirley Temple. It was stylishly remade in 1995, directed by Alfonso Cuaron.

Burnett, Murray (1911–1997).
American playwright, co-author, with Joan Allison, of *Everybody Comes to Rick's*, an unproduced play for which Warner's paid £20,000, and which formed the basis of the film *Casablanca*, directed by Michael CURTIZ and starring Humphrey BOGART and Ingrid BERGMAN. The play was briefly presented at Rhode Island in 1948 and produced in London in 1991, but ran for only six weeks. A former teacher, he also worked as a radio and television writer, producer and director.

Burnett, W. R. (1899–1982).
American writer of gangster novels and screenplays which have been influential.
Little Caesar (oa) 30. *Scarface* (oa) 32. Dr Socrates (oa) 35. *High Sierra* (oa) 40. Wake Island (co-w, AAN) 42. Crash Dive (w) 43. Nobody Lives Forever (w) 46. The Asphalt Jungle (oa) 50. Captain Lightfoot (w) 54. Sergeants Three (w) 62, many others.

Burnette, Smiley (1911–1967) (Lester Alvin Burnette).
Tubby American character comedian who for many years made low-budget westerns as the sidekick of Charles STARRETT, Gene AUTRY and, occasionally, Roy ROGERS, usually wearing a battered hat and riding a white horse with a black circle around its left eye. Born in Summumm, Illinois, he began as a musician and was also a songwriter. He appeared in more than 200 films. Died from leukaemia.
In Old Santa Fe 34. Tumbling Tumbleweeds 35. Doughnuts and Society 36. The Old Corral 36. The Big Show 36. Comin' round the Mountain 36. Git Along Little Dogies 37. Yodelin' Kid from Pine Ridge 37. Guns and Guitars 37. Rootin' Tootin' Rhythm 37. Dick Tracy (serial) 37. Rhythm of the Saddle 38. Gold Mine in the Sky 38. Under Western Stars 38. Billy the Kid Returns 38. Blue Montana Skies 39. Home on the Prairie 39. South of the Border 39. Mexicali Rose 39. Colorado Sunset 39. Carolina Moon 40. Back in the Saddle 41. Down Mexico Way 41. Heart of the Golden West 42. King of the Cowboys 43. Call of the Canyon 43. Silver Spurs 43. Code of the Prairie 44. The Fighting Frontiersman 46. Last Days of Boot Hill 47. Blazing across the Pecos 48. State Police 48. Across the Badlands 50. Texas Dynamo 50. Lightning Guns 50. Bonanza Town 51. Cyclone Fury 51. Pecos River 51. Lost River 52. The Kid from Broken Gun 52. Whirlwind 52. Last of the Pony Riders 53. On Top of Old Smoky 53. Saginaw Trail 53, many others.

Burns, Bob ('Bazooka') (1893–1956).
Folksy American comedian and humorist who after radio success appeared in several light films.
The Big Broadcast of 1937 37. Waikiki Wedding 37. Wells Fargo 37. The Arkansas Traveler 38. Tropic Holiday 38. Our Leading Citizen 39. Alias the Deacon 40. Belle of the Yukon 44, etc.

Burns, Catherine (1945–).
American young character actress of the 70s.
■ Me Natalie 69. *Last Summer* (AAN) 69. Red Sky at Morning 71. The Catcher (TV) 71. Night of Terror (TV) 72. Two for the Money (TV) 72. Amelia Earhart (TV) 76. The Word (TV) 78.

Burns, David (1902–1971).
American character actor who often played the hero's buddy, the villain's henchman, or a fast-talking agent.
The Queen's Affair (GB) 34. The Sky's the Limit (GB) 38. A Girl Must Live (GB) 38. Knock On Wood 54. Deep in My Heart 55. Let's Make Love 60. The Tiger Makes Out 67. Who is Harry Kellerman? 71, etc.

Burns, Edward (1968–).
American director, screenwriter and producer. His first feature won the Grand Jury prize at the 1995 Sundance Film Festival. Born in New York City, he studied film at Hunter College and first worked in television.
The Brothers McMullen 95. She's the One 96.

Burns, George (1896–1996) (Nathan Birnbaum).
American vaudeville comedian who married his partner Gracie ALLEN and spent many successful years on radio and TV, puffing philosophically at his cigar as he suffered her harebrained schemes. At the age of eighty he again became a big star and a national institution.
Autobiographies: 1955, *I Love Her, That's Why*. 1976, *Living It Up*.
■ The Big Broadcast 32. College Humor 33. International House 33. Six of a Kind 34. We're Not Dressing 34. Many Happy Returns 34. Love in Bloom 35. The Big Broadcast of 1936 35. Here Comes Cookie 35. College Holiday 36. A Damsel in Distress 37. College Swing 38. Honolulu 39. *The Sunshine Boys* (AA) 75. *Oh God* 77. Sergeant Pepper's Lonely Hearts Club Band 78. Just You and Me Kid 79. Two of a Kind 79. Oh God Book Two 80. Going in Style 80. Oh God! You Devil 84. 18 Again! 88.
TV series: The Burns and Allen Show 50–57. The George Burns Show 59–60. Wendy and Me 64.
❝ My husband will never chase another woman. He's too fine, too decent, too old. – *Gracie Allen, 1960*
Acting is all about honesty. If you can fake that, you've got it made. – G.B.

Burns, Mark (1936–).
British leading man.
The Charge of the Light Brigade 67. The Adventures of Gerard 70. A Day on the Beach 70. Death in Venice 70. A Time for Loving 72. Juggernaut 74. The Maids 75. The Stud 78. The Bitch 79. The Wicked Lady 83, etc.

Burns, Michael (1947–).
American leading man of the 60s.
The Wizard of Baghdad 60. Mr Hobbs Takes a Vacation 62. The Raiders 64. Forty Guns to Apache Pass 66. The Mad Room 68. Thumb Tripping 72. The Magnificent Magical Magnet of Santa Mesa (TV) 77, etc.
TV series: Wagon Train 63–65.

Burns, Ralph (1922–).
American musical director and composer, a former jazz pianist and arranger for bandleader Woody Herman.
Cabaret (md) (AA) 72. Lenny 74. Lucky Lady 75. New York, New York 77. Movie Movie 78.

All That Jazz (md) (AA) 79. Urban Cowboy 80. Annie (md) (AAN) 82. My Favorite Year 82. National Lampoon's Vacation 83. Star 80 83. The Muppets Take Manhattan 84. Perfect 85. A Chorus Line (md) 85. Moving Violations 85. In the Mood/The Woo Woo Kid 87. Bert Rigby, You're a Fool 89. All Dogs Go to Heaven 89, etc.

Burns, Wilfred (1917–).
English composer and conductor who began in films as assistant music director to Hans MAY at British National Films.

Fools Rush In 49. Emergency Call/Emergency! 52. The Broken Horseshoe 53. The Black Rider 54. The Love Match 55. Stock Car 55. Not So Dusty 56. The Crooked Sky 56. You Pay Your Money 57. Morning Call 57. Mark of the Phoenix 57. Booby Trap 57. Man from Tangier 57. The Hand 60. The Man Who Couldn't Walk 60. Enter Inspector Duval 61. A Question of Suspense 61. Murder in Eden 61. Ambush in Leopard Street 62. Hornblower (TV) 63. Breath of Life 63. The Runaway 64. Till Death Us Do Part 69. Love Is a Splendid Illusion 69. Dad's Army 71. Adolf Hitler – My Part in His Downfall 72, etc.

Burr, Raymond (1917–1993).
Heavily-built Canadian leading man who for years played Hollywood heavies and then achieved TV stardom as Perry Mason.

■ Without Reservations 46. San Quentin 46. Code of the West 47. Desperate 47. Pitfall 48. Raw Deal 48. Fighting Father Dunne 48. Ruthless 48. Sleep My Love 48. The Adventures of Don Juan 48. Walk a Crooked Mile 48. Station West 48. I Love Trouble 48. Criss Cross 49. Bride of Vengeance 49. Black Magic 49. Abandoned 49. The Red Light 49. Love Happy 49. Unmasked 50. Borderline 50. Key to the City 50. *A Place in the Sun* 51. His Kind of Woman 51. Bride of the Gorilla 51. New Mexico 51. M 51. FBI Girl 51. The Whip Hand 51. Meet Danny Wilson 52. Mara Maru 52. Horizons West 52. The Blue Gardenia 53. Fort Algiers 53. Bandits of Corsica 53. Tarzan and the She Devil 53. Serpent of the Nile 54. Casanova's Big Night 54. Gorilla at Large 54. Khyber Patrol 54. *Rear Window* 54. Passion 54. Thunder Pass 54. They Were So Young 55. You're Never Too Young 55. Count Three and Pray 55. A Man Alone 55. The Brass Legend 56. Please Murder Me 56. Godzilla 56. Great Day in the Morning 56. The Secret of Treasure Mountain 56. A Cry in the Night 56. Ride the High Iron 56. Crime of Passion 57. Affair in Havana 57. Desire in the Dust 60. P.J. 68. 77 Park Avenue (TV) 77. The Jordan Chance (TV) 78. Tomorrow Never Comes 78. Love's Savage Fury (TV) 79. Out of the Blue 80. The Curse of King Tut's Tomb (TV) 80. The Return 80. The Night the City Screamed (TV) 80. Peter and Paul (TV) 81. Airplane II: the Sequel 82. Perry Mason Returns (TV) 85 (and several subsequent TV movies). Gojira 85. Delirious 91.

TV series: *Perry Mason* 57–65. *Ironside* 67–74. Kingston: Confidential 77. Centennial 78.

Burroughs, Edgar Rice (1875–1950).
American novelist, the creator (in 1914) of *Tarzan of the Apes*.

❝ I am one of those fellows who have few adventures. I always get to the fire after it's out. – *E.R.B.*

Burroughs, William S. (1914–1997).
American novelist whose *Naked Lunch* was filmed by David Cronenberg in 1991. An influential, experimental writer, using cinematic techniques in his work, he has featured in documentaries about the Beat generation and made cameo appearances as an actor. He also scripted and appeared in some short underground films directed by Antony Balch in the 60s: *Towers Open Fire, The Cut-Ups, Bill and Tony*, and *William Buys a Parrot*, which have been released on video-cassette.

AS HIMSELF: This Song for Jack 83. Burroughs 83. Heavy Petting 83. What Happened to Kerouac? 85. The Beat Generation – an American Dream 87. Even Cowgirls Get the Blues 94. Condo Painting 98.

AS ACTOR: Chappaqua 66. Twister 89. Drugstore Cowboy 89. The Bloodhounds of Broadway 89. Wax, or the Discovery of Television among the Bees 92.

❝ The cut-up method brings to writers the collage, which has been used by painters for fifty years, and used by the moving and still camera. In fact all street shots from movie or still cameras are by the unpredictable factors of passers-by and juxtaposition cut-ups. – *W.B.*

I went through about six analysts. I was too much for them. I wore 'em out. – *W.B.*

Burrows, Abe (1910–1985) (Abram Borowitz).
American librettist: *Guys and Dolls, Can Can, Silk Stockings, How to Succeed in Business*, etc.

Burstall, Tim (1929–).
English producer, director and screenwriter in Australia who began as a documentary film-maker.

Two Thousand Weeks 69. Stork 71. Alvin Purple 73. Petersen 74. End Play (& w) 75. Eliza Fraser 76. The Last of the Knucklemen (& w) 79. Attack Force Z 82. Duet for Four 82. The Naked Country 84. Kangaroo 86. Great Expectations – the Untold Story 87. Nightmare at Bitter Creek (TV) 88, etc.

Burstyn, Ellen (1932–) (Edna Gilhooley).
Leading American actress, acting under the name of Ellen McRae in the 60s.

Goodbye Charlie 64. For Those Who Think Young 65. Pit Stop 69. Tropic of Cancer 69. Alex in Wonderland 70. The Last Picture Show (AAN) 71. The King of Marvin Gardens 72. Thursday's Game (TV) 73. *The Exorcist* (AAN) 73. Harry and Tonto 74. *Alice Doesn't Live Here Any More* (AA) 75. Providence 77. Same Time Next Year (AAN) 78. A Dream of Passion 78. Resurrection (AAN) 80. Silence of the North 82. The People vs Jean Harris (TV) 83. The Ambassador 84. Surviving (TV) 85. Twice in a Lifetime 85. Dear America 87. Hello Actors Studio 87. Hanna's War 88. Dying Young 91. Grand Isle 91. The Cemetery Club 93. When a Man Loves a Woman 94. Getting Out (TV) 94. Getting Gotti (TV) 94. Roommates 95. My Brother's Keeper (TV) 95. How to Make an American Quilt 95. Care of the Spitfire Grill 96. Deceiver 97. You Can Thank Me Later (Can.) 98. Playing by Heart 98, etc.

TV series: The Iron Horse 67–68. The Ellen Burstyn Show 86–87.

❝ Acting feels like a congenital condition to me – it's in my genes. – *E.B.*

Burton, Geoff.
Australian cinematographer turned director, associated with the films of John Duigan.

The Fourth Wish 75. Storm Boy 76. Born to Run 76. The Picture Show Man 77. Blue Fin 78. Stir 80. The Year My Voice Broke 87. The Time Guardian 87. Romero 89. Bangkok Hilton (TV) 90. Flirting 92. Wide Sargasso Sea 93. Bedevil 93. The Nostradamus Kid 93. Frauds 93. Sirens 94. The Sum of Us (& co-d) 94. Hotel Sorrento 95. Peter Benchley's 'The Beast' (TV) 96. Brilliant Lies 96, etc.

Burton, Kate (1957–).
English actress, born in Geneva, Switzerland, the daughter of Richard BURTON.

Ellis Island (TV) 84. Evergreen (TV) 84. Big Trouble in Little China 86. Life with Mickey 93. August 95. Looking for Richard 96. The Ice Storm 97, etc.

Burton, LeVar (1957–).
American character actor who played the young Kunta Kinte in TV's *Roots*.

Billy: Portrait of a Street Kid (TV) 77. Looking for Mr Goodbar 77. Guyana Tragedy (TV) 80. The Hunter 80. The Supernaturals 86. The Midnight Hour 86. Star Trek Generations 94, etc.

Burton, Richard (1925–1984) (Richard Jenkins).
Welsh leading actor whose dark, brooding good looks did not bring him immediate film success either in Britain or in Hollywood. His 1963 marriage to Elizabeth Taylor, however, helped him climb to the crest of what these days passes for stardom, as did their subsequent divorces and reunions. High living and a kind of contempt for his work kept him from the heights of both serious achievement and popular acclaim.

Biography: 1986, *Burton, the Man Behind the Myth* by Penny Junor; 1988, *Rich: The Life of Richard Burton* by Melvyn Bragg.

■ The Last Days of Dolwyn 48. Now Barabbas was a Robber 49. Waterfront 50. The Woman with No Name 50. Green Grow the Rushes 51. *My Cousin Rachel* (AAN) 52. The Robe (AAN) 53. The Desert Rats 53. Prince of Players 54. The Rains of Ranchipur 55. *Alexander the Great* 56. Seawife 57. Bitter Victory 58. *Look Back in Anger* 59. The Bramble Bush 59. Ice Palace 60. The Longest Day 62. *Cleopatra* 62. *The V.I.P.s* 63. *Becket* (AAN) 64. *The Night of the Iguana* 64. The Sandpiper 65. *The Spy Who Came in from the Cold* (AAN) 65. *Who's Afraid of Virginia Woolf?* (AAN) 66. *The Taming of the Shrew* 67. Dr Faustus (& co-d) 67. The Comedians 67. Boom 68. Where Eagles Dare 68. Candy 68. *Staircase* 69. *Anne of the Thousand Days* (as Henry VIII) (AAN) 70. Raid on Rommel 71. Villain 71. Under Milk Wood 71. The Assassination of Trotsky 72. Hammersmith is Out 72. Bluebeard 72. Divorce His, Divorce Hers (TV) 73. Sutjeska (Yug.) 73. Massacre in Rome 74. The Klansman 74. The Voyage 74. Brief Encounter (TV) 75. Exorcist II: The Heretic 77. Equus (AAN) 77. The Medusa Touch 77. The Wild Geese 78. Sergeant Steiner 79. Absolution 79. Tristan and Isolt 80. Circle of Two 80. Wagner, 83. 1984 84. Ellis Island (TV) 84.

❝ I've done the most awful rubbish in order to have somewhere to go in the morning. – *R.B.*

When I played drunks I had to remain sober because I didn't know how to play them when I was drunk. – *R.B.*

An actor is something less than a man, while an actress is something more than a woman. – *R.B.*

Certainly most movie executives were making love to the starlets. But then, so were most of us actors. – *R.B. of Hollywood in the 50s*

I was up to, I'm told, because, of course, you don't remember if you drink that much, about two-and-a-half to three bottles of hard liquor a day . . . Fascinating idea, of course, drink on that scale. It's rather nice to have gone through it and to have survived – *R.B. in 1974*

The Burtons offered me a drink and rolled in a liquor cart from the bedroom which was its permanent abode, and the conversation afterwards was limited to a discussion of twentieth-century poetry. – *William Fadiman*

There is no longer any novelty in watching the sad disintegration of his acting career. – *Roger Ebert*

Who could take that scruffy arrogant buffoon seriously? – *Eddie Fisher*

Cable from Laurence Olivier to Burton at the height of the *Cleopatra* scandal: 'Make up your mind, dear heart. Do you want to be a great actor or a household word?' – Burton, replying: 'Both.'

Burton, Robert (1895–1964).
American character actor who played many executives, sheriffs and detectives.

Inferno 53. The Big Heat 54. Riot in Cell Block Eleven 56. Spirit of St Louis 57. Birdman of Alcatraz 62, many others.

TV series: Kings Row 55.

Burton, Tim (1960–).
American director, a former Disney animator.

Book: *Burton on Burton*, edited by Mark Salisbury.

Pee-Wee's Big Adventure 85. Beetlejuice 88. *Batman* 89. *Edward Scissorhands* 90. Batman Returns 92. Tim Burton's The Nightmare Before Christmas (p, story, characters) 93. Cabin Boy (p) 94. *Ed Wood* (p, d) 94. Mars Attacks! (p, d) 96, etc.

Burton, Wendell (1947–).
American character actor.

The Sterile Cuckoo 69. Fortune and Men's Eyes 70. Being There 79. East of Eden (TV) 81, etc.

Burum, Stephen H.
American cinematographer.

Pacific High 80. Death Valley 82. The Escape Artist 82. The Entity 83. The Outsiders 83. Something Wicked This Way Comes 83. Rumble Fish 83. Uncommon Valor 83. Body Double 84. St Elmo's Fire 85. The Bride 85. 8 Million Ways to Die 86. Nutcracker: The Motion Picture 86. The Untouchables 87. Arthur 2: On the Rocks 88. Casualties of War 89. War of the Roses 89. He Said, She Said 91. Man Trouble 92. Carlito's Way 93. The Shadow 94. Mission: Impossible 96. Fathers' Day 97. Snake Eyes 98, etc.

Burwell, Carter.
American composer, associated with the films of the Coen brothers.

Blood Simple 84. Psycho III 86. Raising Arizona 87. Pass the Ammo 88. It Takes Two 88. Beat 88. Checking Out 89. Miller's Crossing 90. Doc Hollywood 91. Barton Fink 91. Storyville 92. Buffy the Vampire Slayer 92. Waterland 92. This Boy's Life 93. Kalifornia 93. A Dangerous Woman 93. Wayne's World 2 93. The Hudsucker Proxy 94. It Could Happen to You 94. Rob Roy 95. Fargo 96. Joe's Apartment 96. The Chamber 96. The Spanish Prisoner 97. The Locusts 97. The Jackal 97. Conspiracy Theory 97. The Big Lebowski 97, etc.

Buscemi, Steve (1957–).
Thin, nervy American character actor and occasional director, in oddball and often violent roles. Born in Brooklyn, New York, he studied acting at New York's Lee Strasberg Institute. In his early days, between acting jobs, he worked as a fireman. Married choreographer Jo Andres.

No Picnic 86. Parting Glances 86. Sleepwalk 86. Force of Circumstance 87. Heart 87. Heart of Midnight 88. Vibes 88. Bloodhounds of Broadway 89. Mystery Train 89. New York Stories 89. Slaves of New York 89. King of New York 90. Miller's Crossing 90. Zandalee 90. Tales from the Darkside: The Movie 90. Billy Bathgate 91. Barton Fink 91. Reservoir Dogs 92. In the Soup 92. Crisscross 92. Ed and His Dead Mother 93. Rising Sun 93. Airheads 94. Floundering 94. The Hudsucker Proxy 94. Somebody to Love 94. Pulp Fiction 94. Desperado 95. Someone to Love 95. Things to Do in Denver When You're Dead 95. *Living in Oblivion* 95. Desperado 95. *Fargo* 96. Kansas City 96. Escape from L.A. 96. The Search for One-Eyed Jimmy (made 93) 96. Trees Lounge (& wd) 96. Con Air 97. The Big Lebowski 97. The Wedding Singer 97. Armageddon 98. The Imposters 98, etc.

Busch, Mae (1897–1946).
Cynical-looking Australian-born leading lady of Hollywood silents who later became an excellent foil for Laurel and Hardy in some of their best two-reelers.

The Grim Game 19. The Devil's Pass-key 20. *Foolish Wives* 21. The Christian (GB) 23. Nellie the Beautiful Cloak Model 24. Married Flirts 24. The Unholy Three 25. San Francisco Nights 27. While the City Sleeps 28. A Man's Man 29. Wicked 31. *Come Clean* 31. Scarlet Dawn 32. Their First Mistake 32. Sucker Money 33. Sons of the Desert 33. The Private Life of Oliver the Eighth 34. The Bohemian Girl 36. Daughter of Shanghai 37. Prison Farm 38. Women without Names 40. Ziegfeld Girl 40. The Blue Dahlia 46. Ladies' Man 47, many others.

Busch, Niven (1903–1991).
American novelist and screenwriter. He left Hollywood in 1952 to teach. He was married to actress Teresa Wright (1942–52).

Babbitt (w) 34. In Old Chicago (w, AAN) 38. The Westerner (w) 40. Duel in the Sun (oa) 46. Pursued (w) 47. The Furies (oa) 50. The Moonlighter (oa & w) 52. Treasure of Pancho Villa (w) 56, etc.

Busey, Gary (1944–).
American leading actor. He began as a singer with the group Carp, and was also a drummer with the Rubber Band 63–70.

Dirty Little Billy 72. Lolly Madonna XXX 73. The Last American Hero 73. The Execution of Private Slovik (TV) 74. Thunderbolt and Lightfoot 74. The Law (TV) 74. The Gumball Rally 76. A Star Is Born 76. Straight Time 77. Big Wednesday 78. The Buddy Holly Story (AAN) 78. Carny 80. D.C. Cab 83. The Bear 84. Insignificance 85. Silver Bullet 85. Eye of the Tiger 86. Lethal Weapon 87. Let's Get Harry 87. Bulletproof 87. Hider in the House 89. Predator 2 90. Point Break 91. Ganglands 91. Wild Texas Wind 91. My Heroes Have Always Been Cowboys 91. You and Me 91. Canvas 92. South Beach 92. The Player 92. Vengeance 93. The Firm 93. Rookie of the Year 93. Surviving the Game 94. Chasers 94. Drop Zone 94. Man with a Gun 95. Black Sheep 95. Carried Away 96. Liver's Ain't Cheap 96. Sticks and Stones 96. Fear and Loathing in Las Vegas 98. The Girl Next Door 98. Jacob Two Two Meets the Hooded Fang (Can.) 98. Soldier 98, etc.

TV series: The Texas Wheelers 74.

Busey, Jake (1972–).
American actor, the son of Gary BUSEY, born in Los Angeles.

Straight Time 78. Barbarosa 82. I'll Do Anything 94. The Stoned Age 94. S.F.W. 95. Twister 96. The Frighteners 96. Contact 97. Starship Troopers 97. Enemy of the State 98. Home Fries 98, etc.

Bush, Billy 'Green'.
American character actor of the 70s.
40 Carats 73. Electra Glide in Blue 74. Alice Doesn't Live Here Any More 74. Mackintosh and T. J. 75. Tom Horn 80. The River 84. Critters 86. The Deliberate Stranger (TV) 86. Elvis and Me (TV) 88. Friday the Thirteenth Part IX: Jason Goes to Hell 93, etc.

Bush, Dick (1931–).
British cinematographer.
Savage Messiah 73. Mahler 74. Tommy 74. In Celebration 74. The Legacy 78. Yanks 79. One Trick Pony 80. Little Gloria . . . Happy At Last (TV) 82. Victor Victoria 83. Crimes of Passion 85. The Journey of Natty Gann 85. Nazi Hunter (TV) 86. The Lair of the White Worm 88. Little Monsters 89. Staying Together 89. Switch 91, etc.

Bushell, Anthony (1904–1997).
Bland-faced British leading man of the 30s who started his career in Hollywood; later turned to playing occasional brigadiers and concentrated his efforts on production.
Disraeli 29. *Journey's End* 30. Three Faces East 30. Five Star Final 31. A Woman Commands 32. I Was a Spy 33. The Ghoul 33. Soldiers of the King 33. The Scarlet Pimpernel 34. Dark Journey 37. Farewell Again 37. The Return of the Scarlet Pimpernel 38. The Lion Has Wings 39. Hamlet (co-p only) 48. The Angel with the Trumpet (& d) 49. The Miniver Story 50. The Long Dark Hall (& pd) 51. High Treason 51. Who Goes There? 52. The Red Beret 53. The Purple Plain 54. The Battle of the River Plate 56. Richard III (co-p only) 56. The Wind Cannot Read 57. The Terror of the Tongs 61. The Queen's Guards 63, etc.

Bushman, Francis X. (1883–1966).
Heavily-built American leading actor of the silent era, once known as the handsomest man in the world. Born in Norfolk, Virginia, his was on stage as a child, became a wrestler and sculptor's model and entered films in 1911. A year later he was voted the most popular screen actor in America by *Motion Picture Story*, and his earnings soon soared to around $1m a year. In 1915, he joined Metro, but his career faltered when he left his wife to marry his frequent co-star Beverly Bayne. Coupled with accusations that he beat his wife and children, it was an act that earned him the hatred of Louis B. Mayer. When he walked away from the troubled *Ben-Hur*, Mayer dumped him as soon as his contract ended, and his days of stardom were over. (In the 40s, when a man with grievances against Mayer was charged with threatening to kill him, Bushman told the court that Mayer had ruined his career by blacklisting him.) After he lost his fortune in the 1929 Wall Street crash, he returned to the stage, making only occasional films, including some in Britain in the 30s, and ending with bit parts in unsuitable films of the 60s. His greatest role was as Messala in *Ben-Hur*, which was also notable for his handling of the horses in its spectacular chariot race. His son Ralph (1903–1978) acted in films of the 20s and 30s, sometimes billed as Francis X. Bushman, Jnr.
The Magic Wand 12. The Spy's Defeat 13. One Wonderful Night. 14. Under Royal Patronage 14. Graustark 15. The Return of Richard Neal 15. Romeo and Juliet 15. The Great Secret 16. Red White and Blue Blood 17. Social Quicksands 18. The Masked Bride 25. *Ben Hur* (as Messala) 26. The Lady in Ermine 27. The Thirteenth Juror 27. The Grip of the Yukon 29. Once a Gentleman 30. Hollywood Boulevard 36. David and Bathsheba 51. Sabrina 54. The Story of Mankind 57. The Ghost in the Invisible Bikini 66, many others.
❛❛ All the people love you, but I can't even have the love of half the people. – *President Taft*
His is the best known name and face in the world. – *Arthur Brisbane*

Bussières, Raymond (1907–1982).
Long-faced, mournful-looking French character actor.
Nous les Gosses 41. Les Portes de la Nuit 46. Quai des Orfèvres 47. Alice au Pays des Merveilles 51. Ma Pomme 51. Casque d'Or 52. Justice est Faite 52. Belles de Nuit 54. Porte des Lilas 55. Paris Palace Hotel 58. Fanny 61. Paris When It Sizzles 64. Up from the Beach 65. Drôles de Zèbres 77. Les Sous-Doués 80, many others.

Butcher, Ernest (1885–1965).
British character actor who spent a lifetime playing mild little men.
Variety Jubilee 42. Tawny Pipit 43. My Brother Jonathan 48, many others.

Butler, Artie.
American composer.
The Harrad Experiment 73. For Pete's Sake 74. It's Showtime 76. The Rescuers 78. Angel on My Shoulder (TV) 80. American Dream (TV) 81. Grease 2 82. O'Hara's Wife 82. Copacabana (TV) 85. Classified Love (TV) 86, etc.

Butler, Bill (1931–).
American cinematographer.
The Rain People 69. Drive He Said 71. The Conversation 74. *Jaws* 75. *One Flew over the Cuckoo's Nest* (AAN) 75. Alex and the Gypsy 76. Demon Seed 77. Damien: Omen II 78. Capricorn One 78. Grease 78. Rocky II 78. Can't Stop the Music 80. Stripes 81. A Little Sex 82. Rocky III 82. The Sting II 83. Beer 85. Rocky IV 85. Big Trouble 86. Biloxi Blues 88. Child's Play 88. Graffiti Bridge 90. Hot Shots! 91. Cop and a Half 93. Sniper 93. Beethoven's 2nd 93. Flipper 96. Anaconda 97. Don King: Only in America (TV) 97, etc.

Butler, David (1894–1979).
American director of light entertainments: occasional promise but little fulfilment. Former actor.
High School Hero 27. Win That Girl 28. *Sunny Side Up* 29. *Just Imagine* 30. *A Connecticut Yankee* 31. Business and Pleasure 32. Hold Me Tight 33. Bottoms Up 34. Bright Eyes 34. The Little Colonel 35. The Littlest Rebel 35. Captain January 36. White Fang 36. Ali Baba Goes to Town 37. Kentucky 38. East Side of Heaven 39. That's Right You're Wrong (& p) 39. If I Had My Way (& p) 40. You'll Find Out (& p) 40. *Caught in the Draft* 41. *Road to Morocco* (AAN) 42. Wake Island (AAN) 42. They Got Me Covered 43. *Thank Your Lucky Stars* 43. Shine on Harvest Moon 44. The Princess and the Pirate 44. San Antonio 45. Two Guys from Milwaukee 46. My Wild Irish Rose 47. Two Guys from Texas 48. Look for the Silver Lining 49. The Daughter of Rosie O'Grady 50. Tea for Two 50. Lullaby of Broadway 51. Painting the Clouds with Sunshine 51. Where's Charley? 52. By the Light of the Silvery Moon 53. *Calamity Jane* 53. King Richard and the Crusaders 54. Glory (& p) 56. The Right Approach 61. C'mon Let's Live a Little 67, etc.

Butler, Frank (1890–1967).
British-born writer, long in Hollywood.
College Humor 33. Babes in Toyland 34. Strike Me Pink 36. Road to Singapore 40. Road to Morocco (AAN) 42. Wake Island (AAN) 42. Going My Way (AA) 44. Incendiary Blonde 45. The Perils of Pauline 47. Whispering Smith 49. Strange Lady in Town 55, many others.

Butler, Hugo (1914–1968).
Canadian-born screenwriter, in Hollywood. Born in Calgary, Alberta, he studied at the University of Washington and began as a journalist. He was in Hollywood from 1937 and was blacklisted in the 50s, after which he worked in Mexico and Europe.
The Big City 37. A Christmas Carol 38. Huckleberry Finn 39. Society Lawyer 39. Wyoming 40. Edison the Man 40. Young Tom Edison 40. A Yank on the Burma Road 41. Barnacle Bill 41. The Omaha Trail 42. Lassie Come Home 43. From This Day Forward 46. Miss Susie Slagle's 46. Roughshod 49. Your Witness 50. The Prowler 50. He Ran All the Way 51. The Adventures of Robinson Crusoe (as Philip Roll) (Mex.) 53. Autumn Leaves 55. The Young One (Mex.) 61. Eva (Fr./It.) 62. A Face in the Rain 63. Sodom and Gomorrah (It./Fr.) 63. The Legend of Lylah Clare 66, etc.

Butler, Michael (1944–).
American cinematographer.
Charley Varrick 74. Harry and Tonto 74. The Car 77. The Gauntlet 77. Telefon 77. Wanda Nevada 79. A Small Circle of Friends 80. The Cannonball Run 81. Megaforce 82. Dance of the Dwarfs 83, etc.

Butler, Robert (1927–).
American director, from TV.
Guns in the Heather 69. The Computer Wore Tennis Shoes 69. The Barefoot Executive 71. Scandalous John 71. Death Takes a Holiday (TV) 71. Now You See Him Now You Don't 71. The Blue Knight (TV) 73. James Dean (TV) 76. In the Glitter Palace (TV) 77. Hot Lead and Cold Feet 78. Night of the Juggler 80. Up the Creek 83. Moonlighting (TV) 85. Out on a Limb (TV) 87. Out of Time (TV) 88. White Mile (TV) 94. Turbulence 97, etc.

Butrick, Merritt (1960–1989).
American actor, best known for playing William Shatner's son in two *Star Trek* movies. He died of AIDS.
Zapped! 82. Star Trek II: The Wrath of Khan 82. Star Trek III: The Search for Spock 84. Wired to Kill 86. When the Bough Breaks 86. Shy People 87. Death Spa 87, etc.

Butterworth, Charles (1896–1946).
Balding American comic actor who through the 30s played his own style of shy upper-class bachelor, never getting the girl and sometimes drowning his sorrows in drink. Died in a car crash.
■ The Life of the Party 30. Illicit 30. The Bargain 31. Side Show 31. The Mad Genius 31. Beauty and the Boss 32. *Love Me Tonight* 32. Manhattan Parade 32. The Nuisance 33. Penthouse 33. My Weakness 33. The Cat and the Fiddle 34. Student Tour 34. Forsaking All Others 34. *Bulldog Drummond Strikes Back* (as Algy) 34. Hollywood Party 34. *Ruggles of Red Gap* 34. The Night Is Young 35. Baby-Face Harrington 35. Orchids to You 35. Magnificent Obsession 35. The Moon's Our Home 36. Half Angel 36. We Went to College 36. Rainbow on the River 36. Swing High Swing Low 37. Every Day's a Holiday 37. Thanks for the Memory 38. Let Freedom Ring 39. The Boys from Syracuse 40. Second Chorus 40. Road Show 41. Blonde Inspiration 41. Sis Hopkins 41. What's Cookin' 42. A Night in New Orleans 42. Give Out Sisters 42. Always a Bridesmaid 43. The Sultan's Daughter 43. This Is the Army 43. The Bermuda Mystery 44. Dixie Jamboree 44. Follow the Boys 44.
I fell flat on my flute. – C.B. *in Love Me Tonight*

Butterworth, Donna (1956–).
American child actress.
The Family Jewels 65. Paradise Hawaiian Style 66.

Butterworth, Peter (1919–1979).
British comedian usually seen as well-meaning bumbler.
William Comes to Town 49. Penny Princess 51. Mr Drake's Duck 52. Carry On series 58–77. The Ritz 76. Carry On Emmanuelle 78, many others.

Buttolph, David (1902–).
American composer.
Show Them No Mercy 35. Nancy Steele is Missing 37. Four Sons 40. *The Mark of Zorro* 40. *Tobacco Road* 41. Moontide 42. My Favorite Blonde 42. Crash Dive 43. The Hitler Gang 44. The House on 92nd Street 45. Somewhere in the Night 46. Kiss of Death 47. Rope 48. Roseanna McCoy 49. Three Secrets 50. The Enforcer 51. My Man and I 52. *House of Wax* 53. Secret of the Incas 54. The Lone Ranger 56. The Big Land 57. The Horse Soldiers 59. Guns of the Timberland 60. The Man from Galveston 64, many others.

Buttons, Red (1919–) (Aaron Chwatt).
American vaudeville and TV comic who graduated to strong supporting roles in occasional movies.
■ Winged Victory 44. *Sayonara* (AA) 57. Imitation General 58. The Big Circus 59. One, Two, Three 61. Hatari 62. Five Weeks in a Balloon 62. The Longest Day 62. A Ticklish Affair 63. Your Cheatin' Heart 64. Up from the Beach 65. Harlow 65. Stagecoach 66. Breakout (TV) 67. *They Shoot Horses Don't They?* 69. Who Killed Mary What's'ername? 71. The Poseidon Adventure 72. Louis Armstrong, Chicago Style 75. The New Original Wonder Woman (TV) 75. Gable and Lombard 76. Viva Knievel 77. Pete's Dragon 77. Telethon (TV) 78. Vegas (TV pilot) 78. Movie Movie 78. The Users (TV) 78. C.H.O.M.P.S. 79. When Time Ran Out 80. The Dream Merchants (TV) 80. Reunion at Fairborough (TV) 85. 18 Again! 88. Into Thin Air 89. The Ambulance 90. It Could Happen to You 94.
TV series: *The Red Buttons Show* 52. The Double Life of Henry Phyfe 66. Knots Landing 87.

Buttram, Pat (1917–1994).
American comic character actor who usually plays hayseeds. He replaced Smiley Burnette as Gene Autry's sidekick in his later westerns. Married actress Sheila Ryan in 1952.
National Barn Dance 44. Beyond the Purple Hills 50. Mule Train 50. Blue Canadian Rockies 52. Twilight of Honor 63. Roustabout 64. The Sweet Ride 67. The Gatling Gun/King Gun 72. Robin Hood (voice) 73. Choices 81. Back to the Future III 90, etc.
TV series: Gene Autry Show 50–56. Green Acres 65–71.

Butts, Dale (1910–1991).
American composer, almost entirely for Republic.
Flame of the Barbary Coast 45. Catman of Paris 46. The Plunderers 48. Sea of Lost Ships 53. Santa Fe Passage 55. Affair in Reno 57, many others.

Buzzell, Edward (1897–1985).
American director of competent but not very individual output; former musical comedy actor. Married (1926–30) actress Ona Munson.
Virtue 32. Ann Carver's Profession 33. Cross Country Cruise 34. Transient Lady 35. The Luckiest Girl in the World 36. As Good as Married 37. Fast Company 38. Honolulu 39. *At the Circus* 39. Go West 40. Married Bachelor 41. Ship Ahoy 42. The Youngest Profession 43. Keep Your Powder Dry 45. *Easy to Wed* 46. Three Wise Fools 46. Song of the Thin Man 47. Neptune's Daughter 49. A Woman of Distinction 50. Confidentially Connie 53. Ain't Misbehavin' (& w) 55. Mary Had a Little (GB) 61, etc.

Buzzi, Ruth (1936–).
American comedienne who came to the fore as the frustrated spinster in TV's *Laugh-In*.
Freaky Friday 77. The Villain 79. Chu Chu and the Philly Flash 81. The Being 83. Surf II 84. Bad Guys 86. Dixie Lanes 88. My Mom's a Werewolf 89. Up Your Alley 89. Digging Up Business 91. Wishful Thinking 92. Boys Will Be Boys 97, etc.
TV series: That Girl 67–68.

Bygraves, Max (1922–).
British entertainer who has played in several films.
Autobiography: 1976, *I Wanna Tell You a Story*.
Skimpy in the Navy 49. Tom Brown's Schooldays 50. Charley Moon 56. A Cry from the Streets 57. Bobbikins 59. Spare the Rod 61. The Alf Garnett Saga 72, etc.

Byington, Spring (1893–1971).
American stage actress who settled in Hollywood in the 30s and played a long succession of bird-brained wives, scatty matrons, gossip columnists, and loving mums.
Little Women (as Marmee) 33. Werewolf of London 35. Way Down East 35. Mutiny on the Bounty 35. Ah Wilderness 35. Every Saturday Night (and ensuing Jones Family series) 36. Dodsworth 36. Theodora Goes Wild 36. It's Love I'm After 37. The Adventures of Tom Sawyer 38. Jezebel 38. *You Can't Take It with You* (AAN) 38. The Story of Alexander Graham Bell 39. A Child is Born 40. The Bluebird 40. Meet John Doe 41. The Devil and Miss Jones 41. When Ladies Meet 41. Roxie Hart 42. *Rings on Her Fingers* 42. Presenting Lily Mars 43. Heaven Can Wait 43. The Heavenly Body 44. I'll Be Seeing You 45. The Enchanted Cottage 45. Dragonwyck 46. Singapore 47. BF's Daughter 48. In the Good Old Summertime 49. Louisa 50. Walk Softly Stranger 50. According to Mrs Hoyle 51. Angels in the Outfield 51. Because You're Mine 52. The Rocket Man 54. Please Don't Eat the Daisies 60, many others.
TV series: *December Bride* 54–58. Laramie 59–62.
❛❛ TV keeps me young because it keeps me busy, keeps my mind alert, my senses sharp and my interest up. – *S.B., 1959*

Byrd, Ralph (1909–1952).
Tough-looking American leading man, mainly in second features.
Hell Ship Morgan 31. Dick Tracy 38. Desperate Cargo 41. Guadalcanal Diary 43. Mark of the Claw 47. The Redhead and the Cowboy 51, etc.
TV series: Dick Tracy 51.

Byrne, David (1952–).
Scottish-born musician, composer and director, in America. He was vocalist and leader of the rock band Talking Heads.

Something Wild (s) 86. True Stories (a, wd, m) 86. The Last Emperor (co-m, AA) 87. Married to the Mob (m) 88. David Byrne Live: Between the Teeth (concert) (co-d, m) 93.

Byrne, Eddie (1911–1981).
Irish character actor, in British films.

Odd Man Out 46. The Gentle Gunman 52. *Time Gentlemen Please* (leading role) 53. A Kid for Two Farthings 55. The Admirable Crichton 57. The Mummy 59. The Bulldog Breed 60. Mutiny on the Bounty 62. Devils of Darkness 65. Island of Terror 66. Stardust 74, many others.

Byrne, Gabriel (1950–).
Irish leading actor, producer and occasional screenwriter and director. Born in Dublin, he planned to be a priest, but instead studied at University College, Dublin. He worked on archaeological digs and as a teacher before deciding to become an actor at the age of 29, soon landing a role on an Irish TV soap opera. In the late 80s, he moved to America to broaden his career. Formerly married to Ellen BARKIN (1988–94), he has been romantically linked with actress Julia ORMOND.

The Outsider 79. Excalibur 81. The Keep 83. Hannah K 83. Reflections 83. Christopher Columbus (TV) 83. Defence of the Realm 85. Gothic 86. Lionheart 87. Siesta 87. Julia and Julia 87. Hello Again 87. The Courier 87. A Soldier's Tale 88. Diamond Skulls 89. Miller's Crossing 90. Shipwrecked/Haakon Haaakonsen 91. Christopher Columbus 91. Cool World 92. Into the West 92. A Dangerous Woman 93. Point of No Return 93. In the Name of the Father (p) 93. A Simple Twist of Fate 94. Trial by Jury 94. Little Women 94. Dead Man 95. The Usual Suspects 95. Frankie Starlight 95. Buffalo Girls (TV) 95. The Lark in the Clear Air (p, wd) 96. Mad Dog Time/Trigger Happy 96. The Last of the High Kings (& ex p, co-w) 96. Weapons of Mass Distraction (TV) 97. The End of Violence 97. Smilla's Sense of Snow/ Smilla's Feeling for Snow 97. Quest for Camelot (voice) 98. The Man in the Iron Mask 98. Enemy of the State 98. Polish Wedding 98, etc.

Byrne, John (1939?–).
Scottish playwright, screenwriter and director. He trained at Glasgow's School of Art and worked as a graphic designer in TV, and as a stage designer. He is the partner of actress Tilda SWINTON.

The Slab Boys (wd) 97.
TV series: Tutti Frutti (w) 87. Your Cheating Heart (w) 90.

Byrnes, Edd (1933–) (Edward Breitenberger).
American TV juvenile of the 50s; never quite made it in movies.

Autobiography: 1996, *Edd Byrnes: Kookie No More*.

Darby's Rangers 58. Up Periscope 59. Yellowstone Kelly 59. The Secret Invasion 64. Payment in Blood 69. Twirl (TV) 81. Erotic Images 85. Back to the Beach 87. Mankillers 87, etc.

TV series: *77 Sunset Strip* 58–63. Sweepstakes 79.

Byron, Arthur (1872–1943).
American character actor.

The Mummy 32. Mayor of Hell 33. Marie Galante 34. Fog Over Frisco 34. Oil for the Lamps of China 35. Prisoner of Shark Island 36, many others.

Byron, Lord (1788–1824) (George Gordon).
English poet who has been played on the screen by Dennis Price in *The Bad Lord Byron*, by Richard Chamberlain in *Lady Caroline Lamb*, by Gavin Gordon in *The Bride of Frankenstein*, and by Noel Willman in *Beau Brummell*. Gabriel Byrne played him in *Gothic*, the story of his time in Switzerland with Shelley and Mary Shelley which resulted in her creation of Frankenstein, which has also been the subject of two further films, *Frankenstein Unbound* and *Rowing with the Wind*.

Byron, Kathleen (1922–).
British leading actress of the 40s; on stage and screen.

The Young Mr Pitt 41. The Silver Fleet 43. A Matter of Life and Death 46. *Black Narcissus* (as a mad nun) 46. The Small Back Room 48. Madness of the Heart 49. The Reluctant Widow 50. Four Days 51. The Gambler and the Lady 52. Hand in Hand 60. Night of the Eagle 62. Private Road 71. Twins of Evil 71. One of Our Dinosaurs Is Missing 76. Les Misérables (US) 98, etc.

Byron, Marion (1911–1985) (Miriam Bilenkin).
American leading actress whose first role was opposite Buster Keaton in *Steamboat Bill Jnr* 28; retired at the end of the 30s.

Broadway Babies 29. Forward Pass 29. Playing Around 30. The Matrimonial Bed/A Matrimonial Problem 30. The Heart of New York 32. Love Me Tonight 32. Five of a Kind 38, etc.

Byron, Walter (1899–1972) (Walter Butler).
British leading man who had success in America.

White Heat 26. Passion Island 27. The Awakening 28. The Sacred Flame 29. Queen Kelly 29. Not Damaged 30. The Dancers 30. The Last Flight 31. Roar of the Dragon 32. Society Girl 32. British Agent 34. Folies Bergere 35. Mary of Scotland 36. Trade Winds 38, many others.

Byrum, John (1947–).
American writer-director. He created the TV sitcom *Winnetka Road* 94.

■ Inserts (GB) 75. Mahogany (w only) 75. Harry and Walter Go to New York (w only) 76. Heartbeat 79. Sphinx (w only) 81. The Razor's Edge 84. The Whoopee Boys 86.

C

Caan, James (1939–).
American leading man who has not quite made the front rank, but continues promising.
Irma La Douce 63. Lady in a Cage 64. The Glory Guys 65. Red Line 7000 65. El Dorado 67. Games 67. Journey to Shiloh 68. Countdown 68. Submarine XI 68. The Rain People 69. Rabbit Run 70. Man Without Mercy 70. *Brian's Song* (TV) 71. T. R. Baskin 72. *The Godfather* (AAN) 72. Slither 73. Cinderella Liberty 75. Freebie and the Bean 75. The Gambler 75. Funny Lady 75. Godfather Two (cameo) 74. Rollerball 75. The Killer Elite 76. Harry and Walter Go to New York 76. A Bridge Too Far 77. Another Man, Another Chance 77. Comes a Horseman 78. Chapter Two 79. Hide in Plain Sight (& d) 80. Les Uns et les Autres 81. Thief 81. Bolero 81. Kiss Me Goodbye 82. Gardens of Stone 87. Alien Nation 88. Dick Tracy 90. Misery 90. The Dark Backward 91. For the Boys 91. Honeymoon in Vegas 92. The Program 93. A Boy Called Hate 95. Eraser 96. Bulletproof 96. North Star 96. Poodle Springs (TV) 98, etc.
❝ My acting technique is to look up at God just before the camera rolls and say, 'Give me a break.' – *J.C.*

Cabanne, Christy (1888–1950).
American silent film director for Griffith and Fairbanks; declined to second features when talkies came.
Enoch Arden 15. Flirting with Fate 16. Reckless Youth 22. Youth for Sale 24. The Masked Bride 27. Altars of Desire 27. Hotel Continental 32. Daring Daughters 33. A Girl of the Limberlost 34. Keeper of the Bees 35. The Last Outlaw 36. Criminal Lawyer 37. Mutiny on the Blackhawk 39. The Mummy's Hand 40. Scattergood Baines 41. Drums of the Congo 42. Keep 'Em Slugging 43. Scared to Death 46. Robin Hood of Monterey 47. Back Trail 48, many others.

Cabot, Bruce (1904–1972) (Etienne Pelissier de Bujac).
Square-jawed American hero of many a 30s action adventure; later turned up as a western villain. Born in Carlsbad, New Mexico, he was educated at the University of the South and began under contract to RKO, finishing his career as part of the regular company gathered together by his friend and drinking companian John Wayne. Married three times, including to actress Adrienne Ames (1934–37). Died from lung and throat cancer.
Confessions of the Coed 31. What Price Hollywood? 32. Flying Devils 33. Lucky Devils 33. The Great Jasper 33. *King Kong* 33. Ann Vickers 33. Their Big Moment 34. Finishing School 34. Murder on the Blackboard 35. Let 'em Have It 35. Show Them No Mercy 35. Robin Hood of El Dorado 36. Fury 36. The Last of the Mohicans 36. Sinner Take All 37. Sinners in Paradise 38. Homicide Bureau 38. Dodge City 39. Susan and God 40. Captian Caution 40. Sundown 41. Wild Bill Hickok Rides 41. The Flame of New Orleans 41. Silver Queen 42. Pierre of the Plains 42. The Desert Song 43. Divorce 45. Fallen Angel 45. Salty O'Rourke 45. Angel and the Badman 46. Smoky 46. Gunfighters 47. The Gallant Legion 48. Sorrowful Jones 49. Fancy Pants 50. Best of the Badmen 51. Abbott and Costello Lost in Alaska 52. The Quiet American 57. The Sheriff of Fractured Jaw 58. John Paul Jones 59. Goliath and the Barbarians 59. The Comancheros 61. Hatari! 62. The Law of the Lawless 63. McLintock 63. In Harm's Way 65. The War Wagon 67. The Green Berets 68. Hellfighters 68. Chisum 70. WUSA 70. Big Jake 71. Diamonds Are Forever 71, etc.

Cabot, Sebastian (1918–1977).
Weighty British character actor who became popular on American TV as the incarnation of the pompous but amiable Englishman.
Secret Agent 36. Love on the Dole 41. The Agitator 45. They Made Me a Fugitive 47. Dick Barton Strikes Back 48. Old Mother Riley's Jungle Treasure 50. Ivanhoe 52. Babes in Baghdad 52. Romeo and Juliet 54. *Kismet* 55. Dragoon Wells Massacre 57. Terror in a Texas Town 58. The Time Machine 60. Twice Told Tales 63. The Family Jewels 65, etc.
TV series: *Checkmate* 59–61. *A Family Affair* 66–71. Ghost Story 73.

Cabot, Susan (1927–1986) (Harriet Shapiro).
Dark-haired American leading actress of the 50s, often cast as an Indian in westerns. She was beaten to death, her son (by actor Christopher Jones) being convicted of involuntary manslaughter.
The Enforcer 50. Flame of Araby 51. Battle at Apache Pass 52. Duel at Silver Creek 52. Ride Clear of Diablo 54. Fort Massacre 58. The Wasp Woman 60, etc.

Cabrera, Sergio.
Colombian film director. *The Strategy of a Snail* was the biggest box-office success of the year in Colombia, out-drawing *Jurassic Park*.
The Strategy of a Snail/La Estrategia del Caracol 93. Ilona Arrives with the Rain 96. Golpe de Estadio 98, etc.

Cacavas, John (1930–).
American composer.
Redneck 72. Horror Express 72. The Satanic Rites of Dracula 74. Airport 75 75. Airport 77 77. Murder at the World Series (TV) 77. Superdome (TV) 78. Hangar 18 80. Separate Ways 81. The Executioner's Song (TV) 82. A Time to Die 83. They're Playing with Fire 84. Jessie (TV) 84. The Dirty Dozen: The Deadly Mission (TV) 87. The Dirty Dozen: The Fatal Mission (TV) 88. Colombo Goes to the Guillotine (TV) 89. Murder in Paradise (TV) 90, etc.

Cacoyannis, Michael (1922–).
Greek director, trained in England.
Windfall in Athens 53. Stella 54. A Girl in Black 55. A Matter of Dignity 57. One Last Spring 59. The Wastrel 61. Electra 62. *Zorba the Greek* (AAN) 64. The Day the Fish Came Out 67. The Trojan Women 71. Iphigenia 76. Sweet Country (b & w) 86. Up, Down and Sideways 92. Pano Kato Ke Plagios 93, etc.

Cadell, Jean (1884–1967).
Sharp-faced Scottish character actress, typically cast as acidulous spinster and latterly dowager.
The Loves of Robert Burns 30. Fires of Fate 33. *David Copperfield* (as Mrs Micawber) 34. Love from a Stranger 37. *Pygmalion* 38. Quiet Wedding 40. The Young Mr Pitt 42. Dear Octopus 43. I Know Where I'm Going 45. Jassy 47. *Whisky Galore* 48. Madeleine 50. The Late Edwina Black 51. Marry Me 52. Rockets Galore 56. *A Taste of Money* (leading role) 62, many others.

Caesar, Adolph (1934–1986).
American actor who made an impression in *A Soldier's Story* 85, and received an Academy Award nomination.
The Color Purple 85. Club Paradise 86.

Caesar, Arthur (1892–1953).
American screenwriter and playwright, a former journalist. Born in Romania, he came to America as a child and was educated at Yale University. He was the brother of Irving Caesar.
Napoleon's Barber (oa) 28. The Aviator 29. Three Faces East 30. Life of the Party 30. The Tenderfoot 31. Her Majesty Love 31. Heart of New York 32. Fireman Save My Child 32. The Chief 33. Their Big Moment 34. Manhattan Melodrama (AA story) 34. McFadden's Flats 35. Alias Mary Dow 35. The Star Maker 39. Adventure in Washington 41. Arson Inc. 49. Anne of the Indies 51, etc.
❝ Getting through Yale at all had been a little short of a financial miracle. On Graduation Day the gilded youth in his class were getting fabulous presents – Mercer cars, trips to Europe, power launches. Well, Arthur's mother couldn't manage anything like that. But she wasn't going to let Arthur be without a present. She brought him a dozen white carnations. All the rest of his life, in memory of that gesture of hers, he wore a white carnation in his buttonhole. – *Charles Brackett*
I don't want to be right: I just want to keep on working. – *A.C.'s sign on his desk*
We are not punished *for* our sins but *by* them. – A.C.

Caesar, David.
Australian director and screenwriter, a former documentary film-maker, who studied at the Australian Film, Television and Radio School.
Bodyworks (doc) 88. Greenkeeping 91. The Feds (TV) 93. Idiot Box 96, etc.

Caesar, Irving (1895–1996) (Isadore Caesar).
American songwriter and composer who wrote lyrics for the musical *No No Nanette*, which was filmed three times. He also wrote the lyrics for such songs as 'Crazy Rhythm', 'Just a Gigolo', 'Swanee', and 'Animal Crackers in My Soup', which was sung by Shirley Temple in *Curly Top* 34.
No No Nanette 30. George White's Scandals 34. No No Nanette 40. Tea for Two (from No No Nanette) 50. Hit the Deck 54, etc.

Caesar, Sid (1922–).
American comedian, seldom in films but a big TV hit of the 50s, especially in *Your Show of Shows*.
■ Tars and Spars 45. The Guilt of Janet Ames 47. It's a Mad Mad Mad Mad World 63. A Guide for the Married Man 67. The Busy Body 67. Ten from Your Show of Shows 74. Airport 75 75. Silent Movie 76. The Cheap Detective 78. Grease 78. The Fiendish Plot of Fu Manchu 80. History of the World Part One 81. Grease 2 82. Cannonball Run 2 83. Over the Brooklyn Bridge 83. Stoogemania 86. The Emperor's New Clothes 87.

Cage, Nicolas (1964–) (N. Coppola).
American leading actor. He is the nephew of director Francis Ford Coppola. Married actress Patricia Arquette. Current asking price: around $15m a movie.
Biography: 1997, *Uncaged* by Douglas Thompson.
Rumblefish 83. Racing with the Moon 83. The Cotton Club 84. Birdy 85. Raising Arizona 87. Vampire's Kiss 88. Time to Kill/Tempo di Uccudere 89. Firebirds 90. Wild at Heart 90. Zandalee 90. Le Raccourci 91. Honeymoon in Vegas 92. Red Rock West 93. Amos & Andrew 93. Deadfall 93. Guarding Tess 94. It Could Happen to You 94. Trapped in Paradise 94. *Leaving Las Vegas* (AA) 95. The Rock 96. Face/Off 97. Con Air 97. City of Angels 98. Snake Eyes 98, etc.

Cagney, James (1899–1986).
American leading actor whose cocky walk and punchy personality took him out of the vaudeville chorus to become one of the most memorable stars of the 30s and 40s.
Autobiography: 1976, *Cagney by Cagney*.
Biography: 1998, *Cagney* by John McCabe.
■ Sinners' Holiday 30. Doorway to Hell 30. The Steel Highway 30. The Millionaire 31. Other Men's Women 31. *The Public Enemy* 31. Smart Money 31. Blonde Crazy 31. Taxi 32. The Crowd Roars 32. Winner Take All 32. Hard to Handle 33. The Picture Snatcher 33. Mayor of Hell 33. *Footlight Parade* 33. *Lady Killer* 33. Jimmy the Gent 34. He was her Man 34. Here Comes the Navy 34. The St Louis Kid 34. *Devil Dogs of the Air* 35. G-Men 35. The Irish in Us 35. *A Midsummer Night's Dream* (as Bottom) 35. The Frisco Kid 35. Ceiling Zero 35. Great Guy 36. Something to Sing About 37. *Boy Meets Girl* 38. *Angels with Dirty Faces* (AAN) 38. The Oklahoma Kid 39. Each Dawn I Die 39. *The Roaring Twenties* 39. The Fighting 69th 40. Torrid Zone 40. City for Conquest 40. *Strawberry Blonde* 41. The Bride Came C.O.D. 41. Captains of the Clouds 42. *Yankee Doodle Dandy* (AA; as George M. Cohan) 42. Johnny Come Lately 43. Blood on the Sun 45. 13 Rue Madeleine 46. *The Time of Your Life* 48. *White Heat* 49. West Point Story 50. Kiss Tomorrow Goodbye 50. Come Fill the Cup 51. Starlift 51. What Price Glory? 52. A Lion is in the Streets 53. Run for Cover 55. Love Me or Leave Me (AAN) 55. The Seven Little Foys (guest) 55. *Mister Roberts* 55. Tribute to a Bad Man 56. These Wilder Years 56. *Man of a Thousand Faces* (as Lon Chaney) 57. Short Cut to Hell (d only) 58. Never Steal Anything Small 59. Shake Hands with the Devil 59. The Gallant Hours 60. *One Two Three* 61. Arizona Bushwhackers (narrator only) 68. Ragtime 81. Terrible Joe Moran (TV) 84.
✪ For refining the image of the irrepressible Irishman; for inventing a unique form of dancing; and, whether as gangster or cop, for providing work for a thousand imitators. *Yankee Doodle Dandy*.
❝ He can't even put a telephone receiver back on the hook without giving the action some special spark of life. – *Time*
There's not much to say about acting but this. Never settle back on your heels. Never relax. If you relax, the audience relaxes. And always mean everything you say. – *J.C.*
Cagney has an inspired sense of timing, an arrogant style, a pride in the control of his body and a conviction and lack of self-consciousness that is unique in the deserts of the American cinema. – *Lincoln Kirstein, 1932*
He can do nothing which is not worth watching. – *Graham Greene*
I'm sick of carrying guns and beating up women. – *J.C., 1931.*
I admire him for quitting when he was at the top. – *Robert Redford*
Famous line (*White Heat*): 'Made it, Ma – top of the world!'
Famous line (*Yankee Doodle Dandy*): 'My mother thanks you, my father thanks you, my sister thanks you – and I thank you.'

Cagney, Jeanne (1919–1984) (Jean Cagney).
American actress, in occasional films: sister of James Cagney.
Golden Gloves 40. Yankee Doodle Dandy 42. The Time of Your Life 48. Don't Bother to Knock 52. A Lion is in the Streets 53. Man of a Thousand Faces 57. Town Tamer 65, etc.

Cagney, William (1902–1988).
American producer, brother of James Cagney.
Johnny Come Lately 43. Blood on the Sun 45. The Time of Your Life 48. Kiss Tomorrow Goodbye 50. A Lion is in the Streets 53, etc.

Cahn, Edward L. (1899–1963).
American director of second features.
Homicide Squad 31. *Law and Order* 32 (his best film, with Walter Huston as Wyatt Earp).

Confidential 35. Main Street After Dark 44. The Checkered Coat 48. Prejudice 48. Experiment Alcatraz (& p) 51. The Creature with the Atom Brain 55. Girls in Prison 56. Curse of the Faceless Man 58. Guns, Girls and Gangsters 58. It, The Terror from Beyond Space 58. Riot in a Juvenile Prison 61. Beauty and the Beast 62. Incident in an Alley 63, many others.

Cahn, Sammy (1913–1993) (Samuel Cohen).
American lyricist who has written many film songs, usually with James Van Heusen. Won Academy Awards for four songs: 'Three Coins in the Fountain', 'High Hopes', 'All the Way' and 'Call Me Irresponsible'.
Autobiography: 1974, *I Should Care*.
Youth on Parade (AANs) 42. Follow the Boys (AANs) 44. Tonight and Every Night (AANs) 45. Anchors Aweigh (AANs) 45. Romance on the High Seas (AANs) 48. It's a Great Feeling (AANs) 49. Toast of New Orleans (AANs) 50. Rich Young and Pretty (AANs) 51. Because You're Mine (AANs) 52. Three Coins in the Fountain (AAs) 54. Love Me or Leave Me (AANs) 55. The Tender Trap (AANs) 55. The Court Jester 55. Written on the Wind (AANs) 56. The Joker Is Wild (AAs) 57. Some Came Running (AANs) 58. The Best of Everything (AANs) 59. A Hole in the Head (AAs) 59. High Time (AANs) 60. Pocketful of Miracles (AANs) 61. Papa's Delicate Condition (AAs) 63. Robin and the Seven Hoods (AANs) 64. Where Love Has Gone (AAN) 64. Thoroughly Modern Millie (AANs) 67. Star! (AANs) 68. Touch of Class (AANs) 73. Whiffs (AANs) 75, etc.

Cain, Christopher (1943–) (Bruce Doggett).
American director and screenwriter.
Brother, My Song 76. The Buzzard 76. Grand Jury 77. Sixth and Main 77. The Stone Boy 84. That Was Then . . . This Is Now 85. Where the River Runs Black 86. The Principal 87. Young Guns 88. Pure Country 92. The Next Karate Kid 94. The Amazing Panda Machine 95. Gone Fishin' 97, etc.

Cain, James M. (1892–1977).
American novelist of the hard-boiled school; also worked in Hollywood.
She Made Her Bed (oa) 34. Stand Up and Fight (w) 38. When Tomorrow Comes (oa) 39. *Double Indemnity* (oa) 44. Gypsy Wildcat (w) 44. *Mildred Pierce* (oa) 45. *The Postman Always Rings Twice* (oa) 46, 81. Serenade (oa) 56. Butterfly 85. Girl in the Cadillac (from *The Enchanted Isle*) 95, etc.

Cain, Syd.
British art director and production designer.
The Road to Hong Kong 61. Lolita 61. Dr No 62. Summer Holiday 62. From Russia with Love 63. Fahrenheit 451 66. Billion Dollar Brain 67. On Her Majesty's Secret Service 69. Frenzy 72. Live and Let Die 73. Shout at the Devil 76. Wild Geese 78. The Sea Wolves 80. Supergirl 84. Wild Geese II 85, etc.

Caine, Michael (1933–) (Maurice Micklewhite).
British light leading man with effective mild manner and deliberately unconcealed cockney origin. Played for years in second features before his international appeal was discovered. He now runs his own production company, M & M Productions, in partnership with Martin Bregman. In 1998, the *Sunday Times* estimated his wealth, which includes interests in six restaurants, at £30m.
Autobiography: 1993, *What's It All About*.
A Hill in Korea 56. How to Murder a Rich Uncle 57. Blind Spot 58. The Key 58. Passport to Shame 58. The Wrong Arm of the Law 62. Solo for Sparrow 62. *Zulu* 64. *The Ipcress File* 65. *Alfie* (AAN) 66. The Wrong Box 66. Gambit 66. Funeral in Berlin 67. Woman Times Seven 67. Hurry Sundown 67. Billion Dollar Brain 67. Deadfall 68. The Magus 68. Play Dirty 68. The Italian Job 69. The Battle of Britain 69. Too Late the Hero 69. The Last Valley 70. *Get Carter* 71. Zee and Co 71. Kidnapped 71. Pulp 72. *Sleuth* (AAN) 72. The Black Windmill 74. The Marseilles Contract 74. The Wilby Conspiracy 75. Peeper 75. The Romantic Englishwoman 75. The Man Who Would Be King 75. Harry and Walter Go To New York 76. The Eagle Has Landed 76. A Bridge Too Far 77. Silver Bears 77. Swarm 78. *California Suite* 78. Ashanti 79. Beyond the Poseidon Adventure 79. Dressed to Kill 80. The Island 80. The Hand 81. Victory 81. Deathtrap 82. *Educating Rita* (AAN) 83. The Honorary Consul 83. Blame It On Rio 83. Water 85. The Holcroft Covenant 85. The Jigsaw Man 85. *Hannah and Her Sisters* (AA) 86. Sweet Liberty 86. Half Moon Street 86. The Whistle Blower 86. Mona Lisa 86. The Fourth Protocol 87. Jaws – The Revenge 87. Surrender 87. Dirty Rotten Scoundrels 88. Without a Clue 88. Mr Destiny 90. A Shock to the System 90. Bullseye! 91. Noises Off 92. Blue Ice 92. A Muppet Christmas Carol 92. On Deadly Ground 93. Blood and Wine 96. Bullet to Beijing 96. Midnight in St Petersburg 97. Mandela and de Klerk (TV) 97. Little Voice 98, etc.
❝ I'll always be there because I'm a skilled professional actor. Whether or not I've any talent is beside the point. – M.C.
John Wayne once advised me, talk low, talk slow and don't talk too much. And then I went and made *Sleuth*. – M.C.
I'm a sort of boy next door. If that boy has a good scriptwriter. – M.C.
You get paid the same for a bad film as you do for a good one. – M.C.

Calamity Jane (c. 1848–1903) (Martha Jane Canary).
This rootin' tootin' shootin' woman of the Old West has been glamorized many times for the movies, notably by Jean Arthur in *The Plainsman* 36, Frances Farmer in *Badlands of Dakota* 41, Jane Russell in *The Paleface* 48, Yvonne de Carlo in *Calamity Jane and Sam Bass* 49, Evelyn Ankers in *The Texan Meets Calamity Jane* 50, Doris Day in *Calamity Jane* 53, Judi Meredith in *The Raiders* 64, Abby Dalton in *The Plainsman* 66, Catherine O'Hara in *Tall Tale: The Unbelievable Adventures of Pecos Bill* 94, Anjelica Huston in *Buffalo Girls* (TV) 95, and Ellen Barkin in *Wild Bill* 95.

Calder, David (1946–).
English actor, from the stage.
Superman 78. Moonlighting 82. Defence of the Realm 85. American Friends 91, etc.
TV series: Star Cops 87. Widows 87–88. Bramwell 95–96.

Calder-Marshall, Anna (1949–).
British leading actress.
Pussycat Pussycat I Love You 70. *Wuthering Heights* 70. Zulu Dawn 79. Two Faces of Evil 82, etc.

Caldwell, Erskine (1903–1987).
American novelist who attacked social injustice in several novels which by their sensationalism earned him a fortune. *Tobacco Road* was filmed as a farce; *God's Little Acre* had to be taken straight.

Cale, John (1940–).
Welsh composer, singer and musician. He studied at Goldsmith's College before going to New York to study with Aaron Copland and found the avant-garde rock group Velvet Underground with Lou Reed in the mid-60s. With singer Nico, they became Andy Warhol's house band. Cale left the group in the late 60s.
Caged Heat 74. Something Wild 86. La Naissance de l'Amour 93. I Shot Andy Warhol 96, etc.

Calhern, Louis (1895–1956) (Carl Vogt).
Distinguished American stage actor who was in films occasionally from silent days and later became one of MGM's elder statesmen.
■ What's Worth While? 21. The Blot 21. Too Wise Wives 21. Women, Wake Up 22. The Last Moment 23. Stolen Heaven 31. Road to Singapore 31. Blonde Crazy 31. They Call It Sin 32. Night After Night 32. Okay America 32. Afraid to Talk 32. The Woman Accused 33. 20,000 Years in Sing Sing 33. Frisco Jenny 33. Strictly Personal 33. World Gone Mad 33. Diplomaniacs 33. Duck Soup 33. Affairs of Cellini 34. Man with Two Faces 34. The Count of Monte Cristo 34. Sweet Adeline 34. The Arizonian 34. Woman Wanted 35. The Last Days of Pompeii 35. The Gorgeous Hussy 36. Her Husband Lies 36. The Life of Emile Zola 37. Fast Company 38. Juarez 39. Fifth Avenue Girl 39. Charlie McCarthy Detective 39. I Take this Woman 40. Dr Ehrlich's Magic Bullet 40. Heaven Can Wait 43. Nobody's Darling 43. Up in Arms 44. The Bridge of San Luis Rey 44. Notorious 46. Arch of Triumph 48. The Red Pony 49. The Red Danube 49. *Annie Get Your Gun* (as Buffalo Bill) 50. Nancy Goes to Rio 50. *The Asphalt Jungle* 50. Devil's Doorway 50. A Life of Her Own 50. *The Magnificent Yankee* (AAN) 50. Two Weeks with Love 50. Man with a Cloak 51. It's a Big Country 51. Invitation 52. We're Not Married 52. Washington Story 52. *The Prisoner of Zenda* 52. Confidentially Connie 53. Remains To Be Seen 53. Julius Caesar (title role) 53. Latin Lovers 53. Main Street to Broadway 53. Rhapsody 54. Executive Suite 54. The Student Prince 54. Men of the Fighting Lady 54. Betrayed 54. Athena 54. The Blackboard Jungle 55. The Prodigal 55. Forever Darling 56. High Society 56.

Calhoun, Rory (1922–) (Francis Timothy Durgin).
Amiable American leading man of 50s action films; did not make the first rank.
Something for the Boys 44. The Red House 47. Miraculous Journey 48. Massacre River 49. Rogue River 50. I'd Climb the Highest Mountain 51. *With a Song in My Heart* 52. Powder River 53. *How to Marry a Millionaire* 53. Four Guns to the Border 54. Dawn at Socorro 54. Treasure of Pancho Villa 55. The Spoilers 55. Raw Edge 56. The Big Caper 57. The Hired Gun 57. The Colossus of Rhodes 60. Marco Polo 61. A Face in the Rain 62. The Gun Hawk 64. Apache Uprising 65. Finger on the Trigger 67. Dayton's Devils 68. Night of the Lepus 72. Avenging Angel 84. Hell Comes to Frogtown 88. Pure Country 92, many others.
TV series: The Texan 58–59. The Blue and the Grey 82.

Callahan, Gene (1908–1990).
American production designer.
America, America (AA) 63. The Cardinal (AAN) 63. The Group 65. The Last Tycoon (AAN) 76. Julia 77. Eyes of Laura Mars 78. Bloodbrothers 79. Whose Life Is It, Anyway? 81. Grease 2 82. Jagged Edge 85. Children of a Lesser God 86. Black Widow 87. Little Nikita 88. Arthur 2: On the Rocks 88. Steel Magnolias 89. The Man in the Moon 91, etc.

Callan, Michael (1935–) (Martin Calinift).
American leading man, former dancer.
They Came to Cordura 58. The Flying Fontaines 59. Mysterious Island 61. Bon Voyage 62. The Interns 63. The Victors 63. Cat Ballou 65. You Must Be Joking 65. Lepke 75. The Cat and the Canary 78. Freeway 88, etc.
TV series: Occasional Wife 66.

Callard, Kay.
Canadian leading lady in Britain in the 50s.
They Who Dare 54. Find the Lady 56. Intent to Kill 58. Freedom to Die 62, etc.
TV series: Knight Errant 58–60.

Callas, Maria (1923–1977) (Maria Kalogeropolos).
Celebrated Greek-American opera singer who in 1971 played the non-singing role of *Medea*.

Calleia, Joseph (1897–1975) (Joseph Spurin-Calleja).
Humorous but often sinister Maltese character actor who after world tours as an opera singer settled in Hollywood in the 30s and played several distinguished roles.
His Woman 31. Public Hero Number One 35. After the Thin Man 36. Winner Take All 37. *Algiers* 38. Juarez 39. *Five Came Back* 39. *Golden Boy* 39. My Little Chickadee 40. The Monster and the Girl 41. Jungle Book 42. *The Glass Key* 42. For Whom the Bell Tolls 43. The Conspirators 44. *Gilda* 46. Lured 47. Four Faces West 48. Noose (GB) 48. Vendetta 50. Branded 51. Valentino 51. When in Rome 52. Treasure of Pancho Villa 55. Hot Blood 56. Serenade 56. Wild is the Wind 57. Touch of Evil 58. Cry Tough 59. The Alamo 60. Johnny Cool 63, many others.

Calley, John (1930–).
American production executive who was appointed president of United Artists in 1993. He was president of production at Warner Brothers from 1975–80. Married actress Meg Tilley in 1995.
The Wheeler Dealers 63. The Americanization of Emily (co-p) 64. Topkapi (co-p) 64. The Cincinatti Kid (co-p) 65. The Loved One (co-p) 65. Don't Make Waves 67. Ice Station Zebra 68. Catch 22 (co-p) 70. Postcards from the Edge (co-p) 90, etc.

Callow, Simon (1949–).
British stage actor, in occasional films. He now concentrates on directing, mainly for the stage. He is the author of a biography of Charles Laughton 87 and *Being An Actor* 85, a book that challenged the autocracy of directors.
Autobiography: 1991, *Shooting the Actor*.
Amadeus 84. A Room with a View 86. Maurice 87. Mr & Mrs Bridge 90. Postcards from the Edge 90. The Ballad of the Sad Café (d) 91. Soft Top, Hard Shoulder 92. Howards End 92. Femme Fatale (TV) 93. Four Weddings and a Funeral 94. Street Fighter 94. England, My England (TV) 95. Jefferson in Paris 95. Ace Ventura: When Nature Calls 95. James and the Giant Peach (voice) 96. Shakespeare in Love 98, etc.
TV series: Little Napoleons 94.

Calloway, Cab (1907–1994) (Cabell Calloway).
High-spirited American bandleader and entertainer, in occasional films. Born in Rochester, New York, and brought up in Baltimore, he came to prominence in the 30s as an extravagantly dressed novelty vocalist, known as 'the King of Hi-De-Ho', and leader of a big jazz band. From the 50s, he led small groups and acted in musicals, gaining a new audience from his appearance in *The Blues Brothers*. He was played by Larry Marshall in *The Cotton Club* 84, and Madison McKoy in *Radioland Murders* 94. He was caricatured in several cartoons, including Vitaphone's *Clean Pastures* 37 and *Have You Got Any Castles?* 38, MGM's *The Old Mill Pond* 36 and *Minnie the Moocher's Wedding Day* 37, Walt Disney's *Mother Goose Goes to Hollywood* 38, Warner's *Porky at the Crocadero* 38, *Wholly Smoke* 38, and *The Swooner Crooner* 44. George GERSHWIN is said to have had him in mind for the role of Sportin' Life in his opera *Porgy and Bess*.
Autobiography: 1976, *Of Minnie the Moocher and Me*.
The Big Broadcast 32. International House 33. The Singing Kid 36. Manhattan Merry Go Round 37. *Stormy Weather* 43. Sensations of 1945 44. St Louis Blues 58. The Cincinnati Kid 65. A Man Called Adam 66. The Blues Brothers 80, etc.

Calthrop, Donald (1888–1940).
Slightly built British stage actor whose film appearances were usually as nervy villains. An alcoholic, he died of a heart attack during the filming of *Major Barbara* while drowning his sorrows, having been told that one of his sons had been killed.
The Gay Lord Quex 18. Nelson 19. *Shooting Stars* 27. *Blackmail* 29. Atlantic 30. Murder 30. The Bells 31. Number Seventeen 32. The Ghost Train 32. Rome Express 32. I Was a Spy 33. Friday the Thirteenth 33. Sorrell and Son 34. The Clairvoyant 34. Scrooge 35. Broken Blossoms 36. Fire Over England 36. Dreaming Lips 37. Let George Do It 40. Major Barbara 40, etc.

Calvert, E. H. (1873–1941).
American silent screen director who later had a second career as an actor, usually in military roles.
AS DIRECTOR: One Wonderful Night 14. The Slim Princess 15. The Man Trail 15. The Outer Edge 15. A Daughter of the City 15, etc.
AS ACTOR: The House of Pride 12. Vultures of Society 16. The Silent Partner 23. Inez from Hollywood 24. Sally 25. Ella Cinders 26. Rookies 27. The Wizard 27. Legion of the Condemned 28. The Canary Murder Case 29. The Virginian 29. The Love Parade 30. The Benson Murder Case 30. Beyond Victory 31. The Mysterious Rider 33. Here Comes the Groom 34. The Oregon Trail 36, many others.

Calvert, Phyllis (1915–) (Phyllis Bickle).
British leading lady of the forties, former child actress; usually played good girls.
Two Days to Live 39. They Came by Night 39. Charley's Big-hearted Aunt 40. Let George Do It 40. *Kipps* 41. The Young Mr Pitt 42. Uncensored 42. *The Man in Grey* 43. *Fanny by Gaslight* 44. Two Thousand Women 44. *Madonna of the Seven Moons* 44. They Were Sisters 45. Men of Two Worlds 46. The Magic Bow 46. The Root of All Evil 47. Time Out of Mind (US) 47. *My Own True Love* (US) 48. Broken Journey 48. Appointment with Danger (US) 49. The Golden Madonna 49. The Woman with No Name 50. Mr Denning Drives North 51. *Mandy* 52. The Net 53. It's Never Too Late 55. Child in the House 56. Indiscreet 58. Oscar Wilde 60. The Battle of the Villa Fiorita 65. Twisted Nerve 68. Oh What a Lovely War 69. The Walking Stick 70. Across the Lake (TV) 88. Mrs Dalloway 97, etc.
TV series: *Kate* 71.

Calvet, Corinne (1925–) (Corinne Dibos).
French leading lady, a statuesque blonde who had some success in Hollywood in the early 50s.
Autobiography: 1983, *Has Corinne Been a Good Girl?*
La Part de l'Ombre 45. Rope of Sand 49. When Willie Comes Marching Home 50. On the Riviera 51. What Price Glory? 52. Powder River 53. Flight to Tangier 53. The Far Country 54. So This Is Paris 55. The Plunderers of Painted Flats 58. Bluebeard's Ten Honeymoons 60. Hemingway's Adventures of a Young Man 62. Apache Uprising 65. Dr Heckle and Mr Hype 80. The Death of the Heart 86, etc.

Calvin, Henry (1918–1975) (Wimberly Calvin Goodman Jnr).
Rotund American comedy actor who for a while appeared in Disney films imitating Oliver Hardy.
Babes in Toyland 60. Toby Tyler 63.
TV series: Zorro.

Cambern, Donn.
American editor.
2000 Years Later 69. Easy Rider 69. The Last Picture Show 71. Blume in Love 73. The Hindenberg 75. Hooper 78. Time after Time 79. The Cannonball Run 81. Romancing the Stone (AAN) 84. Harry and the Hendersons 87. Twins 88. Ghostbusters II 89. The Bodyguard 92. Major League II 94. Little Giants 94. The Glimmer Man 96, etc.

Cambridge, Godfrey (1929–1976).
American comic actor.
The Last Angry Man 59. Gone are the Days 63. The Busy Body 67. The President's Analyst 67. Bye Bye Braverman 68. The Biggest Bundle of Them All 68. *Watermelon Man* 70. *Cotton Comes to Harlem* 70. The Biscuit Eater 72. Come Back Charleston Blue 72. Whiffs 75, etc.

Camerini, Mario (1895–1981).
Italian director of the old commercial school.
The House of Pulcini 24. Kiff Tebbi 27. Rotaie 29. Giallo 33. Il Grande Appello 36. Il Signor Max 37. Il Documento Fatale 39. Una Romantica Avventura 40. I Promessi Sposi 41. Due Lettere Anonime 45. The Captain's Daughter 47. Molti Sogni per le Strade 48. Il Brigante Musolino 50. Wife for a Night 51. Ulysses 54. The Miller's Wife 55. Primo Amore 58. Via Margutta 60. And Suddenly It's Murder 60. Kali-Yug Goddess of Vengeance 63. Don Camillo and Modern Youth 72, many others.

Cameron, Allan.
British production designer and art director, in Hollywood. He began in television.
Edward and Mrs Simpson (TV) 80. Nineteen Eighty-Four 84. Lady Jane 86. Highlander 86. The Fourth Protocol 87. Willow 88. Air America 90. Far and Away 92. Swing Kids 93. No Escape 94. The Jungle Book 94. Showgirls 95. Pinocchio 96. Starship Troopers 97. Tomorrow Never Dies 97, etc.

Cameron, Earl (1925–).
Jamaican actor seen in many British films.
Pool of London 50. Emergency Call 51. The Heart of the Matter 53. Simba 55. Safari 56. Sapphire 59. Flame in the Streets 61. Guns at Batasi 64. Thunderball 65. Battle beneath the Earth 68. Mohammed 77. Cuba 79. The Great Kandinsky (TV) 95. NeverWhere (TV) 96, etc.

Cameron, James (1954–).
Canadian-born action film director and screenwriter who began as an art director for Roger Corman. He runs his own production company, Lightstorm Entertainment, with his partner, producer Lawrence Kasanoff, and signed a five-year deal in 1992 with Fox to produce 12 films. He was formerly married to producer Gale Anne Hurd and director Kathryn Bigelow. He has a daughter by actress Linda Hamilton. Founded his own computer effects company, Digital Domain, in the mid-90s.
Biography: 1998, *Titanic and the Making of James Cameron* by Paula Parisi.
Piranha II: The Spawning 83. *The Terminator* 84. Rambo: First Blood Part II (w) 85. Aliens 86. The Abyss 89. *Terminator 2: Judgment Day* 91. True Lies (p, wd) 94. Strange Days (co-w) 95. *Titanic* (AAp, AAd, AAed) 97, etc.
❝ I would never do anything as merciful as firing anyone. – *J.C.*
So does this prove, once and for all, that size does matter? – *J.C., when accepting the Golden Globe award for Titanic*
If you're going to hang out with Jim, you better have your life insurance. – *Bill Paxton*
The high priest of Hollywood bloat. He is also the movies' mad toymaker. He keeps falling in love with an imposing machine (a cyborg, an alien, a submarine, a Harrier jet, an ocean liner) that he then spends great amounts of time and energy destroying. – *Richard Corliss, Time*

Cameron, John (1944–).
British composer.
Poor Cow 67. The Ruling Class 68. Kes 70. Every Home Should Have One 70. All the Right Noises 71. A Touch of Class (AAN) 73. Scalawag 73. Night Watch 73. Out of Season 75. Great Scout and Cathouse Thursday 76. Nasty Habits 77. The Thief of Baghdad 78. Sunburn 79. Lost and Found 79. The Mirror Crack'd 80. Who? 82. The Jigsaw Man 84. Jack the Ripper (TV) 88. Jekyll and Hyde (TV) 90. Frankenstein (TV) 93. Driftwood 95, etc.

Cameron, Rod (1910–1983) (Nathan Cox).
Rugged Canadian star of many a Hollywood second feature; originally labourer, engineer, and stand-in for Fred MacMurray.
Christmas in July 40. Northwest Mounted Police 40. The Monster and the Girl 41. The Remarkable Andrew 42. Wake Island 42. Gung Ho 43. Boss of Boom Town 44. Salome Where She Danced 45. The Runaround 46. The Bride Wasn't Willing 46. The Plunderers 48. Panhandle 49. The Sea Hornet 51. Ride the Man Down 53. Escapement (GB) 57. The Gun Hawk 63. The Bounty Killer 65. Old Firehand (Ger.) 66. The Last Movie 71. Evel Knievel 71. Jessie's Girls 76, many others.
TV series: City Detective 53–54. Coronado 9 59. State Trooper 57–59.

Cammell, Donald (1934–1996).
Scottish director and screenwriter. Born in Edinburgh, he studied at the Royal Academy of Art and was a portrait artist before beginning as a screenwriter. He moved to Los Angeles in the 70s, where he worked on many projects that never reached fulfilment. He had his director's credit removed from his last movie, *Wild Side*, and is said to have been depressed when it was recut by the production company and shown on cable television. Shot himself.
Duffy 68. *Performance* (co-d) 70. Demon Seed (d) 77. Tilt (w) 79. White of the Eye (wd) 87. Centrifuge (w) 90. Wild Side (co-w, d) 96, etc.

Camp, Colleen (1953–).
American actress.
Battle for the Planet of the Apes 73. Smile 75. Funny Lady 75. Apocalypse Now 79. Game of Death 79. They All Laughed 82. Valley Girls 83. Joy of Sex 84. Police Academy 2: Their First Assignment 85. D.A.R.Y.L. 85. Clue 85. Police Academy 3: Back in Training 86. Police Academy 4: Citizens on Patrol 87. Track 29 88. Wicked Stepmother 89. The Vagrant 91. Wayne's World 92. Greedy/Greed 94. Naked in New York 95. Die Hard with a Vengeance 95. Speed 2: Cruise Control 97. Plump Fiction 98, etc.

Camp, Joe (1939–).
American director of independent family films: *Benji, For the Love of Benji*, etc.

Campanella, Joseph (1927–).
American stage and TV actor who makes occasional film appearances.
Murder Inc. 61. The Young Lovers 64. The St Valentine's Day Massacre 67. Ben 72. Journey from Darkness (TV) 75. Meteor 79. Plutonium Incident (TV) 80. Steele Justice 87. Down the Drain 89. Body Chemistry 90. Club Fed 91. No Retreat No Surrender 3: Blood Brothers 91. Ninja Dragons 92, etc.
TV series: The Nurses 64–65. Mannix 67–68. The Lawyers 69–72. The Colbys 85–86.

Campanile, Pasquale Festa (1927–1986).
Italian screenwriter and director, often in collaboration with Massimo Franciosa.
The Chastity Belt 67. The Girl and the General 68. The Libertine 69. La Calandria 72. When Women Lost Their Tails 72. Rugantino 73. Soldier of Fortune 75. Autostop 77. Amante 78. Gege Bellevita 79, etc.

Campbell, Beatrice (1923–1980).
British leading lady.
Wanted for Murder 46. Things Happen at Night 48. Silent Dust 48. Last Holiday 50. The Mudlark 50. Laughter in Paradise 51. Grand National Night 53. Cockleshell Heroes 55, etc.

Campbell, Bill (1960–).
American leading actor.
Checkered Flag 90. Rocketeer 91. Bram Stoker's Dracula 92. The Night We Never Met 93. Out There (TV) 95. Lover's Knot 96. The Brylcreem Boys (GB) 96. Rudyard Kipling's The Second Jungle Book: Mowgli and Baloo 98. Max Q (TV) 98, etc.

Campbell, Bruce (1958–).
American actor and producer, most familiar as the clean-cut hero of horror movies. Born in Royal Oak, Michigan, he began acting in his early teens. After a brief period studying drama at Western Michigan University, he worked for a commercials company and began making films with his school-friend, director Sam Raimi. He has had recurring roles in the TV series *Xena: Warrior Princess* and *Hercules: The Legendary Journeys*, and also directed some episodes of the latter. His second wife is costume designer Ida Gearon.
Evil Dead (& co-ex p) 83. Going Back 83. Crimewave (& co-p) 85. Evil Dead 2 (& co-p) 87. Moontrap 88. Maniac Cop 88. Sundown: The Vampire in Retreat 89. Lunatics: A Love Story (& p) 89. Maniac Cop 2 89. Mindwarp 90. Waxwork 2: Lost in Time 91. Army of Darkness (& co-p) 93. The Hudsucker Proxy 94. The Quick & the Dead 94. Congo 95. Fargo 96. Tornado! (TV) 96. Escape from LA 96. McHale's Navy 97. In the Line of Duty: Blaze of Glory (TV) 97. Assault on Dome 4 (TV) 97. The Love Bug (TV) 98. Dusk till Dawn 2: Texas Blood Money 98. Running Time 99. La Patinoire (Fr.) 99, etc.
TV series: The Adventures of Brisco County Jnr 93–94. Ellen 96.

Campbell, Colin (1883–1966).
Diminutive Scottish character actor, long in Hollywood.
Tillie's Tomato Surprise 15. Where Lights are Low 21. The Grail 23. The White Monkey 25. Big Boy 30. Alice in Wonderland 33. San Francisco Docks 41. Mrs Miniver 42. The Lodger 44. Moss Rose 47. The Fan 49. Abbott and Costello Meet the Keystone Kops 55. The Lost World 60. My Fair Lady 64.

Campbell, Colin (1937–).
Young British proletarian actor of the 60s.
Saturday Night Out 63. The Leather Boys 63. The High Bright Sun 65.

Campbell, Eric (1878–1917).
Scottish actor who played the bearded heavy in some of Chaplin's most famous two-reelers 1916–17: *Easy Street, The Cure, The Adventurer*, etc.

Campbell, Glen (1935–).
American pop singer, venturing into films.
True Grit 69. Norwood 69. Uphill All the Way 85. Rock-a-Doodle (voice) 90, etc.

Campbell, Judy (1916–) (Judy Gamble).
British leading lady of stage and TV; film appearances infrequent. She is the mother of actress Jane Birkin.
Saloon Bar 40. Breach of Promise 41. The World Owes Me a Living 44. Green for Danger 46. Bonnie Prince Charlie 48. There's a Girl in My Soup 70. Forbush and the Penguins 71. Dust to Dust (TV) 85, etc.

Campbell, Martin.
New Zealand-born director, who made his name working for British television.
Reilly – Ace of Spies (TV) 81. Charlie (TV) 83. Edge of Darkness (TV) 85. Frankie and Johnnie (TV) 85. Criminal Law 88. Defenseless 91. No Escape 94. GoldenEye 95, etc.

Campbell, Naomi (1971–).
English model and occasional actress, who has also appeared in many music videos. A ghosted novel, *Swan*, was published under her name in 1994.
Autobiography: 1996, *Naomi*.
The Night We Never Met 93. Prêt-à-Porter/Ready to Wear 94. Miami Rhapsody 95. Girl 6 96, etc.

Campbell, Neve (1973–).
Canadian leading actress. Born in Guelph, Ontario, she grew up in Toronto and trained as a dancer with the National Ballet School of Canada, later working as a model before beginning her acting career in commercials and the theatre. Formerly married (1995–98) to actor Jeff Colt.
The Canterville Ghost (TV) 96. The Craft 96. Scream 96. Scream 2 97. Wild Things 98. The Lion King II: Simba's Pride (voice) 98. 54 98. Hair Shirt 98, etc.
TV series: Party of Five 94– .

Campbell, Mrs Patrick (1865–1940) (Beatrice Tanner).
Leading British stage actress, the original Eliza in *Pygmalion*, who spent her last years playing supporting roles in Hollywood. A wayward talent – she once upstaged an actor by flicking chocolates against a backdrop of a starry sky, where they fell with an audible 'plop' throughout his big scene – she moved to America, where she had frequently toured, when she could no longer find employment in Britain. By that time she had lost her looks and grown fat, though retaining her acid wit. She was the model for the character of Hesione in Shaw's *Heartbreak House* and Orinthia in his *The Apple Cart*, and was caricatured by Marie Dressler as Carlotta Vance in *Dinner at Eight*. The love letters between her and George Bernard Shaw were turned into a successful play, *Dear Liar*, by Jerome Kilty. She wrote an unpublished memoir, *Chance Medley*, dealing with her experiences in Hollywood.
Autobiography: 1922, *My Life and Some Letters*.
Biographies: 1961, *Mrs Patrick Campbell* by Alan Dent; 1984, *Mrs Pat* by Margot Peters.
■ The Dancers 30. Riptide 34. One More River 34. Outcast Lady 34. Crime and Punishment 35.
❝ She was as beautiful among women as Venice is among cities, and all her beauty was at the service of a genius as remarkable. – *Rebecca West*
She has an ego like a raging tooth. – *W. B. Yeats*
She was not a great actress; but she was a great enchantress, how or why I don't know; but if she wanted to capture you you might as well go quietly; for she was irresistible. – *George Bernard Shaw*
What enchanted me was her unwavering and ingenious rudeness to everyone there [Hollywood] who could possibly have been of assistance to her. She would encounter Harold Lloyd or Ruth Chatterton at a party, and murmur, 'Now tell me, what do you do? Are you connected with the cinema?' Her failure to be politic took on the proportions of a magnificent gesture. She was like a sinking ship firing on the rescuers. – *Alexander Woollcott*
Oh, Mr Thalberg, I've just met that extraordinary wife of yours with the teensy-weensy little eyes! – *Mrs P.C. to Irving Thalberg, on Norma Shearer*
Wedlock: the deep, deep peace of the double bed after the hurly-burly of the chaise-longue. – *Mrs. P.C.*
It doesn't matter what you do in the bedroom as long as you don't do it in the street and frighten the horses. – *Mrs. P.C.*
I was under the impression that the great battle of life was fought in our youth – not a bit of it – it's when we are old, and our work not wanted, that it rages and goes on – and on – and on. – *Mrs P.C.*
(Reported conversation) 'You are handsome enough to be in pictures.' – 'But Mrs Campbell, my name is Joseph Schildkraut.' – 'Never mind, you can change it.'
Famous line (when offered the role of the pawnbroker in *Crime and Punishment*): 'I could not possibly become a tradesperson.'

Campbell, Patrick (1913–1980).
British humorist and screenplay writer, the latter usually with Vivienne Knight.
Captain Boycott 47. Helter Skelter 50. The Oracle 54. Lucky Jim 57. Go to Blazes 62. Girl in the Headlines 63, etc.

Campbell, William (1926–).
American actor, often seen as personable villain or friend of the hero.
The Breaking Point 50. The People against O'Hara 52. Escape from Fort Bravo 53. The High and the Mighty 54. Man without a Star 55. Cell 2455 Death Row (as Caryl Chessman) 55. Backlash

56. Eighteen and Anxious 57. The Naked and the Dead 58. The Young Racers 63. The Secret Invasion 64. Hush Hush Sweet Charlotte 64. Dementia 13 65. Blood Bath 66. Black Gunn 72. Dirty Mary Crazy Larry 74, etc.

TV series: Cannonball 58–59. Dynasty 84–85. Crime Story 86–88.

Campion, Jane (1955–).
New Zealand director and screenwriter. She studied at the Australian Film and Television School.

Sweetie 89. An Angel at My Table 90. The Piano (AAw, AANd) 93. The Portrait of a Lady 96.

Campos, Rafael (1936–1985).
Dominican actor best remembered for *The Blackboard Jungle* 55. Died of cancer.

The Blackboard Jungle 55. The Shark Fighters 56. This Could Be the Night 57. Dino 57. Tonka 58. Savage Sam 63. The Tenderfoot 64. Lady in a Cage 64. Mister Buddwing 65. The Appaloosa 66. Girl in Gold Boots 68. The Astro-Zombies 69. The Doll Squad 73. Hangup 73. Oklahoma Crude 73. The Hanged Man (TV) 74. Slumber Party '57 76. Where the Buffalo Roam 80. V (TV) 83. A Streetcar Named Desire (TV) 84. Fever Pitch 85. The Return of Josey Wales 86, etc.

TV series: Rhoda 77–78. Centennial 78–79.

Camus, Marcel (1912–1982).
French director, a former art teacher, who worked as an assistant to Henri Decoin, Alexandre Astruc, and others. He made his first short in 1950 and achieved international success with *Black Orpheus*, one of several films he made in Brazil and which starred his wife, Marpessa Dawn.

Mort en Fraude 56. Black Orpheus/Orfeu Negro (AA) 58. Os Bandeirantes 60. Le Chant du Monde 65. Vivre la Nuit 68. Le Mur de l'Atlantique 70. Otalia de Bahia 77, etc.

Canale, Gianna Maria (1927–).
Italian leading lady, occasionally seen in international films.

Rigoletto 49. Go For Broke 51. The Man from Cairo 53. Theodora Slave Empress 54. The Silent Enemy 58. The Whole Truth 58. Queen of the Pirates 60. Scaramouche 63. The Marauder 65, etc.

Canary, David (1938–).
American western actor who played for a while in both *Wagon Train* and *Bonanza* before concentrating on daytime soap operas.

Hombre 67. Sharks' Treasure 74. Posse 75. The Dain Curse (TV) 78, etc.

Candy, John (1950–1994).
Bulky Canadian actor and writer in Hollywood, often as a good-natured slob.

The Silent Partner 78. Lost and Found 79. Stripes 81. Brewster's Millions 84. Splash! 84. Summer Rental 84. Volunteers 85. Little Shop of Horrors 87. Planes, Trains and Automobiles 87. Spaceballs 87. The Great Outdoors 88. Hot to Trot 88. Uncle Buck 89. Who's Harry Crumb? 89. The Rescuers Down Under (voice) 90. Only the Lonely 91. Delirious 91. Career Opportunities 91. Nothing but Trouble 91. JFK 91. Once Upon a Crime 92. Cool Runnings 93. Rookie of the Year (uncredited) 93. Hostage for a Day (TV) (& d) 94. Wagons East! 94. Canadian Bacon 95, etc.

TV series: Second City TV 77–79. SCTV Network 90 81–83.

Canning, Victor (1911–1986).
British detective novelist whose works have often been filmed.

Spy Hunt 50. The Golden Salamander 51. Venetian Bird 53. The House of the Seven Hawks 59. Masquerade 63. Family Plot 76.

Cannom, Greg.
American make-up and special effects expert. He began working for Rick BAKER before setting up his own company, Cannom Creations.

The Howling 80. The Sword and the Sorcerer 82. Greystoke: The Legend of Tarzan, Lord of the Apes 84. Cocoon 85. The Lost Boys 87. A Nightmare on Elm Street 3: Dream Warriors 87. Cocoon: The Return 88. Big Top Pee-Wee 88. Back to the Future Part II 89. Postcards from the Edge 90. Exorcist III 90. Highlander II: The Quickening 91. Hook (AAN) 92. Forever Young 92. Hoffa (AAN) 92. Alien^3 92. Batman Returns 92. Bram Stoker's Dracula (AA) 93. The Man without a Face 93. The Shadow 94. The Puppet Masters 94. Mrs Doubtfire (AA) 94. Roommates (AAN) 95. Stephen King's Thinner 96. Star Truckers 97. Titanic 97. Steel 97. Kull the Conqueror 97. House of Frankenstein (TV) 97. From the Earth to the Moon (TV) 98. Blade 98, etc.

Cannon and Ball (Tommy Derbyshire, 1938– ; Robert Harper, 1944–).
British comedians from the working-men's club circuit. First film, *The Boys in Blue* 83.

Cannon, Danny (1968–).
English director and screenwriter who went to work for Hollywood after his first film.

Young Americans (co-w, d) 93. Judge Dredd (d) 95. Phoenix 98. I Still Know What You Did Last Summer 98, etc.

Cannon, Dyan (1937–) (Samile Diane Friesen).
American leading actress who tends to play floozies. She was married to Cary Grant (1965–68).

The Rise and Fall of Legs Diamond 59. *Bob and Carol and Ted and Alice* (AAN) 69. Doctors' Wives 70. The Anderson Tapes 71. The Love Machine 71. *Such Good Friends* 72. Shamus 72. The Last of Sheila 73. Child Under a Leaf 75. Revenge of the Pink Panther 77. *Heaven Can Wait* (AAN) 78. Lady of the House (TV) 79. Coast to Coast 80. Honeysuckle Rose 80. Deathtrap 82. Author! Author! 82, etc. Master of the Game (TV) 83. Jenny's War (TV) 84. Caddyshack II 88. The End of Innocence (& wd) 90. Jailbirds (TV) 90. The Pickle 93. That Darn Cat 96. 8 Heads in a Duffel Bag 96. Out to Sea 97. The Sender 98, etc.

❝ Lately I've been so satisfied just realizing my own wholeness, my own completeness. Thank you, God, you know? – *D.C., 1997*

Cannon, Esma (1896–1972).
Diminutive British character actress often seen in bit parts. Notable in *Sailor Beware* 56.

Cannon, J. D. (1922–).
Cold-eyed American character actor.

An American Dream 66. Cool Hand Luke 67. Cotton Comes to Harlem 70. Lawman 71. Testimony of Two Men (TV) 77. Killing Stone (TV) 78. Ike (TV) 79. Raise the Titanic 80. Walking through the Fire (TV) 80. Death Wish 2 81. Street Justice 89, etc.

TV series: McCloud 71–76. Call to Glory 84–85.

Cannon, Robert (1901–1964).
American animator, a leading figure at UPA during the formative period and the designer of simplified, witty cartoons like *Gerald McBoing Boing* and *Christopher Crumpet*.

Canonero, Milena.
Italian costume designer, in Hollywood.

A Clockwork Orange 71. Barry Lyndon (AA) 75. Midnight Express 78. The Shining 80. Chariots of Fire (AA) 81. The Hunger 83. The Cotton Club 84. Give My Regards to Broad Street 84. Out of Africa (AAN) 85. Barfly 87. Haunted Summer 88. Tucker: The Man and His Dream (AAN) 88. Dick Tracy (AAN) 90. Godfather III 90. Single White Female 92. Only You 94. Love Affair 94. Camilla 94. Death and the Maiden 94. Bulworth 98, etc.

Canova, Diana (1953–).
American light actress, daughter of Judy Canova.

The First Nudie Musical 76. Love Boat II (TV) 77. With This Ring (TV) 78. Night Partners 93, etc.

TV series: Soap 77–80. But I'm a Big Girl Now 81. Foot in the Door 83. Throb 86.

Canova, Judy (1916–1983) (Juliet Canova).
American hillbilly comedienne whose strident yodelling and cornfed humour enlivened a number of forties programmers.

■ In Caliente 35. Broadway Gondolier 35. Going Highbrow 35. Artists and Models 37. Thrill of a Lifetime 37. Scatterbrain 40. Sis Hopkins 41. Puddin'head 41. Sleepytime Gal 42. True to the Army 42. Joan of Ozark 42. Chatterbox 43. Sleepy Lagoon 43. Louisiana Hayride 44. Hit the Hay 45. Singin' in the Corn 45. Honeychile 51. Oklahoma Annie 52. The WAC from Walla Walla 52. Untamed Heiress 54. Carolina Cannonball 55. Lay That Rifle Down 55. The Adventures of Huckleberry Finn 60.

Cantinflas (1911–1993) (Mario Moreno).
Mexican clown, acrobat and bullfighter who made unambitious local comedies for years and was briefly beckoned by Hollywood in the 50s. Immensely popular in Spanish-speaking countries. In Mexican films from 1936. He appeared as a ghost, played by Herbert Siguenza, in Miguel Arteta's *Star Maps* 97.

Neither Blood Nor Sand 41. Romeo and Juliet 44. *Around the World in 80 Days* 56. *Pepe* 59, many others.

Cantor, Eddie (1892–1964) (Edward Israel Itskowitz).
Rolling-eyed American vaudeville entertainer whose inimitable high-toned voice and sprightly movement made him a big Hollywood star of the 30s. He appeared briefly in a 1953 biopic, *The Eddie Cantor Story*, in which he was played by Keefe Brasselle, and in 1956 received an Academy Award 'for distinguished service to the film industry'.

Autobiographies: 1957, *Take My Life*; 1959, *The Way I See It*; 1962, *As I Remember Them*.

Biography: 1998, *Banjo Eyes: Eddie Cantor and the Birth of Modern Stardom* by Herbert G. Goldman.

■ Kid Boots 26. Special Delivery 27. Glorifying the American Girl 29. *Whoopee* 30. Palmy Days 31. *The Kid from Spain* 32. *Roman Scandals* 33. Kid Millions 34. Strike Me Pink 35. Ali Baba Goes to Town 37. Forty Little Mothers 40. *Thank Your Lucky Stars* 43. *Show Business* 44. If You Knew Susie 48. The Story of Will Rogers (guest) 52.

❝ Another bride; another groom;
Another sunny honeymoon;
Another season; another reason
For makin' whoopee . . .
– *Cantor's most famous song*

Canty, Marietta (1906–1986).
American character actress.

The Searching Wind 46. Home Sweet Homicide 47. My Foolish Heart 49. Father of the Bride 50. The I Don't Care Girl 53, etc.

Canutt, Yakima (1895–1986) (Enos Edward Canutt).
American stuntman and second unit director specializing in action. A former rodeo rider, who won world championships in 1917, 19, 20, and 23, he began in movies as an actor in 1919. He turned to stunts with the coming of sound, performing them in innumerable westerns, including many of John Wayne's early films. He then used his expertise as a second unit director in epic films and was awarded an Oscar in 1966.

Autobiography: 1980, *Stunt Man*.

Lightning Bryce (serial) 19. 'Scar' Hanan 25. Lonesome Trail 30. Westward Bound 31. Two-Fisted Justice 32. Fighting Texans 33. West of the Divide 34. The Last Days of Pompeii 35. San Francisco 36. Riders of the Dawn 37. Stage Coach (including as the Indian who jumps on the lead horse of the coach and is shot by Wayne) 39. Man of Conquest 39. Gone with the Wind (including doubling Gable driving a one-horse hack through the burning streets of Atlanta) 39. Dark Command 40. They Died with Their Boots On 41. Gentleman Jim 42. The Devil's Doorway 50. Only the Valiant 51. Ivanhoe 53. Mogambo 53. Knights of the Round Table 53. Westward Ho, the Wagons 55. Old Yeller 57. Ben Hur 59. Spartacus 60. El Cid 61. The Fall of the Roman Empire 64. Cat Ballou 65. Khartoum 66. Where Eagles Dare 67. A Man Called Horse 69. Rio Lobo 70. Equus 76, etc.

❝ It doesn't matter how great the stunt is, what matters is what gets on film. – Y.C.

You don't have to be crazy in the picture business, but it sure helps. – Y.C.

Capaldi, Peter.
Scottish leading actor and screenwriter.

Local Hero 83. The Love Child 87. Lair of the White Worm 88. Dangerous Liaisons 88. Soft Top, Hard Shoulder (& w) 92. Prime Suspect 3 (TV) 93. Captives 94. Franz Kafka's It's a Wonderful Life (AA short) 94. The Crow Road (TV) 96. Smilla's Sense of Snow/Smilla's Feeling for Snow 97. Bean 97. Tom Jones (TV) 97. Shooting Fish 98, etc.

❝ People should be more pretentious. I go up to people and say, 'Be pretentious, it's the only chance you've got.' – P.C.

Capellani, Albert (1870–1931).
French director of silent films, in Hollywood from 1915.

Camille 15. La Vie de Bohème 16. Daybreak 17. The Red Lantern 19. The Fortune Teller 20. The Young Diana 22. Sisters 22, etc.

Capone, Al (1899–1947).
Italian–American gangster, the king of Chicago during the roaring 20s. Has been impersonated many times on screen, notably by Paul Muni (*Scarface*), Edward G. Robinson (*Little Caesar*), Rod Steiger (*Al Capone*), Neville Brand (*The Scarface Mob*), Jason Robards (*The St Valentine's Day Massacre*), Robert De Niro (*The Untouchables*).

❝ It was ironic that he, who was guilty of committing countless murders, had to be punished merely for failing to pay taxes on the money he had made by murder. – *Herbert Hoover*

Capote, Truman (1924–1984) (Truman Persons).
Diminutive, boyish American Southern short-story writer, novelist, playwright and screenwriter, who achieved literary fame at the age of 21 with his first book, *Other Voices, Other Rooms*. Late in life, when corpulent and alcoholic though retaining his curiously high-pitched voice, he starred in *Murder by Death* 76. His lovers are said to have included Errol Flynn and John Garfield.

Biographies: 1988, *Capote* by Gerald Clarke; 1998, *Truman Capote* by George Plimpton.

Beat the Devil (co-w) 53. Breakfast at Tiffany's (oa) 61. The Innocents (co-w) 61. In Cold Blood (oa) 67. The Grass Harp (oa) 95. Other Voices, Other Rooms (oa) 95. In Cold Blood (oa) (TV) 96.

❝ I'd rather be a friend of mine than an enemy. – T.C.

The trouble with most actors (*and* actresses) is that they are dumb. And, in many instances, the dumbest are the most gifted. – T.C.

A work of art is the one mystery, the one extreme magic; everything else is either arithmetic or biology. – T.C.

The most perfect writer of a generation. – *Norman Mailer*

Capra, Frank (1897–1991).
Italian-American director who is justly celebrated for a stylish handful of 30s and 40s comedies demonstrating a whimsical attachment to the common man and to the belief that even the nastiest of us can be human if given a chance. His best films are masterpieces of timing and organization, but his career ended with sentimental and flabby remakes of his own successes.

Autobiography: 1971, *The Name Above the Title*.

Biography: 1992, *Frank Capra: The Catastrophe of Success* by Joseph McBride.

■ The Strong Man 26. Tramp Tramp Tramp 26. Long Pants 27. For the Love of Mike 27. That Certain Feeling 28. So This is Love 28. The Matinée Idol 28. The Way of the Strong 28. Say it with Sables 28. Submarine 28. Power of the Press 28. The Younger Generation 29. The Donovan Affair 29. Flight 29. Ladies of Leisure 30. Rain or Shine 30. Dirigible 31. The Miracle Woman 31. Forbidden 31. *Platinum Blonde* 32. *American Madness* 32. The Bitter Tea of General Yen 32. *Lady for a Day* (AAN) 33. *It Happened One Night* (AA) 34. Broadway Bill 34. *Mr Deeds Goes to Town* (AA) 36. *Lost Horizon* 37. *You Can't Take It With You* (AA) 38. *Mr Smith Goes to Washington* (AAN) 39. *Meet John Doe* 41. *Why We Fight* (war documentaries) 42–44. Arsenic and Old Lace 44. *It's A Wonderful Life* (AAN) 46. State of the Union 48. Riding High 50. Here Comes the Groom 51. A Hole in the Head 59. Pocketful of Miracles 61.

✪ For presenting an amiable if mythical picture of Mr Joe Smith American, and for doing so with great style. *It's a Wonderful Life*.

❝ He has achieved his effects mainly through a brilliantly fluid editing style, a command of masses of people, and a constantly moving camera. – *Charles Higham*

I made some mistakes in drama. I thought drama was when the actors cried. But drama is when the audience cries. – F.C.

The obligatory scene in most Capra films is the confession of folly in the most public manner possible. – *Andrew Sarris*

Capshaw, Kate (1953–) (Katherine Nail).
American leading actress, a former teacher. Married to Steven Spielberg.

A Little Sex 82. Best Defence 84. Dreamscape 84. *Indiana Jones and the Temple of Doom* 84.

Windy City 84. Power 86. SpaceCamp 86. The Quick and the Dead (TV) 87. Internal Affairs (TV) 88. Black Rain 89. Love at Large 90. Love Affair 94. Next Door (TV) 94. Love Affair 94. Just Cause 95. How to Make an American Quilt 95. The Locusts 97. The Alarmist 98, etc.
TV series: Black Tie Affair 93.

Capucine (1933–1990) (Germaine Lefebvre).
Lean and beautiful French model who was leading lady of a number of international films. Committed suicide.
Song without End 60. North to Alaska 60. A Walk on the Wild Side 62. *The Pink Panther* 63. The Seventh Dawn 64. What's New Pussycat? 65. The Honey Pot 67. The Queens 67. Fräulein Doktor 68. Satyricon 69. Red Sun 72. Jaguar Lives 78. Arabian Adventure 79. Martin Eden (TV) 79. Trail of the Pink Panther 82. Curse of the Pink Panther 83.
❝ I'm weary, always weary these days. I'd like to work, but the enthusiasm is gone. But then, so are the opportunities. – C. *in 1989*

Cara, Irene (1957–).
American actress and singer.
Aaron Loves Angela 75. Sparkle 76. Fame 80. City Heat 84. D.C. Cab 84. Certain Fury 85. Killing Them Softly 85. Busted Up 86. For Us, the Living 88, etc.

Carax, Leos (1962–).
French director and screenwriter, a former critic.
Boy Meets Girl 84. Bad Blood/Mauvais Sang 86. Les Amants du Pont-Neuf 91. Pola X 99, etc.

Cardiff, Jack (1914–).
Superb British colour cinematographer who became an indifferent director of routine films.
Autobiography: 1996, *Magic Hour – The Life of a Cameraman*.
AS CINEMATOGRAPHER: *Wings of the Morning* 37. *The Four Feathers* 39. *Western Approaches* 44. Caesar and Cleopatra 45. *A Matter of Life and Death* 46. *Black Narcissus* (AA) 46. *The Red Shoes* 48. Pandora and the Flying Dutchman 51. The Barefoot Contessa 54. *War and Peace* (AAN) 56. The Vikings 58. Fanny (AAN) 61. The Prince and the Pauper 77. The Fifth Musketeer 78. Death on the Nile 78. Avalanche Express 79. The Awakening 80. Ghost Story 81. The Dogs of War 81. The Far Pavilions (TV) 83. Conan the Destroyer 84. The Last Days of Pompeii (TV) 85. Taipan 86. Million Dollar Mystery 87. Call from Space 89, etc.
■ AS DIRECTOR: Intent to Kill 58. Beyond This Place 59. Scent of Mystery 60. *Sons and Lovers* (AAN) 60. My Geisha 62. The Lion 62. The Long Ships 64. Young Cassidy 65. The Liquidator 65. Dark of the Sun 67. Girl on a Motorcycle (& p, ph) 69. Penny Gold 73. The Mutations 74. Ride a Wild Pony 76.

Cardinal, Tantoo.
Canadian character actress, of European and Indian descent, born in Fort McMurray, Alberta. In her early films, she was sometimes credited as Tantoo Martin.
Marie Ann 78. Running Brave 83. Loyalties 86. Candy Mountain 87. War Party 89. Dances with Wolves 90. The Lightning Incident (TV) 91. Black Robe 91. Where the Rivers Flow North 93. Silent Tongue 93. Spirit Rider 93. Legends of the Fall 94. Tecumseh: The Last Warrior (TV) 95. Silence 97. The Education of Little Tree 97. Smoke Signals 98, etc.

Cardinale, Claudia (1939–).
Italian leading lady who was given the international star build-up but did not quite manage the front rank.
Persons Unknown 58. Upstairs and Downstairs (GB) 58. Il Bell' Antonio 59. Rocco and his Brothers 60. Cartouche 61. The Leopard 62. Eight and a Half 63. *The Pink Panther* 63. Circus World 64. Vaghe Stelle dell'Orsa 65. Blindfold 65. Lost Command 66. The Professionals 66. Don't Make Waves 67. The Queens 67. Day of the Owl 68. The Hell with Heroes 68. Once Upon a Time in the West 69. A Fine Pair 69. Adventures of Brigadier Gerard 70. Popsy Pop 70. The Red Tent 71. Papal Audience 71. Days of Fury 73. Conversation Piece 76. Midnight Pleasures 76. Escape to Athena 78. The Salamander 80. Burden of Dreams 82. Princess Daisy (TV) 83. Henry IV 84. Woman of Wonders 85. History 86. A Man in Love/Un Homme Amoureux 87. Blu Elettrico 88. Mother/Mayrig 91. Act of Contrition/Atto di dolore 91. 588 rue Paradis 92. Son of the Pink Panther 93. Elles ne Pensent qu'à ça 94, etc.

Carère, Christine (1930–) (Christine de Borde).
French leading lady who had a brief Hollywood career.
Olivia 50. Les Collégiennes 57. *A Certain Smile* 57. Mardi Gras 58. A Private's Affair 59. I Deal in Danger 66, etc.

Carette (1897–1966) (Julien Carette).
Dapper French character actor.
L'Affaire est dans le Sac 32. La Grande Illusion 37. La Bête Humaine 38. La Marseillaise 38. *La Règle du Jeu* 39. Adieu Léonard 43. Sylvie et le Fantôme 45. Les Portes de la Nuit 46. *Occupe-Toi d'Amélie* 49. *The Red Inn* 51. Éléna et les Hommes 55. Archimède le Clochard 59. The Green Mare's Nest 61, many others.

Carew, Arthur Edmund (1894–1937) (aka Arthur Carewe).
Tall, dark, Armenian-born leading actor of silent films, usually in villainous roles, and a notable Svengali. Born in Trebeizond, he trained as an artist, and began on stage. Shot himself following a stroke.
Bonnie Bonnie Lassie 19. Rio Grande 20. The Ghost Breaker 22. *Trilby* 23. Phantom of the Opera 25. The Torrent 26. Uncle Tom's Cabin 27. The Claw 27. The Matrimonial Bed 30. The Gay Diplomat 31. Doctor X 32. The Mystery of the Wax Museum 33. Thunder in the Night 35. Charlie Chan's Secret 36, etc.

Carew, James (1876–1938) (James Usselman).
American actor, on stage from 1897. He moved to England, where he made his stage debut in 1905 and was in films from 1913, often as the villain. The third husband of actress Dame Ellen Terry, he also partnered comedian Billy Bennett in Alexander and Mose, a black-face act on radio and music hall in the early 30s.
The Fool 13. The Rajah's Tiara 14. Justice 17. The Kinsman 19. Alf's Button 20. Mr Justice Raffles 22. High Treason 29. Guilt 31. Royal Cavalcade 35. The Improper Duchess 36. Wings over Africa 36. Jericho/Dark Sands 37. Glamour Girl 38, etc.

Carewe, Edwin (1883–1940) (Jay Fox).
American director of silent films noted for their pictorial beauty, a former hobo.
The Final Judgment 15. The Trail to Yesterday 18. Shadow of Suspicion 19. Rio Grande 20. Son of the Sahara 24. Resurrection 27. Ramona 28. Evangeline 29. The Spoilers 30. Are We Civilized? 34, etc.

Carey, Harry (1878–1947).
American leading man of silent westerns who later became a character actor in quiet dependable roles.
Riding the Trail 11. Travellin' On 14. Two Guns 17. The Outcasts of Poker Flat 19. Desperate Trails 20. Man to Man 22. Roaring Rails 24. The Texas Trail 25. Trail of 98 27. *Trader Horn* 30. Law and Order 32. Barbary Coast 35. Sutter's Gold 36. Kid Galahad 37. King of Alcatraz 38. *Mr Smith Goes to Washington* (AAN) 39. They Knew What They Wanted 40. The Spoilers 42. Happy Land 43. The Great Moment 44. Duel in the Sun 46, many others.

Carey, Harry, Jnr (1921–).
American light actor, son of Harry Carey; followed his father's example and was seen mostly in westerns.
Autobiography: 1994, *Company of Heroes: My Life as an Actor in the John Ford Stock Company*.
Pursued 47. Red River 48. So Dear to My Heart 49. Wagonmaster 50. Rio Grande 50. Island in the Sky 53. The Long Gray Line 55. The Searchers 56. The River's Edge 57. Rio Bravo 59. The Great Imposter 61. Alvarez Kelly 66. Bandolero 68. One More Time 71. A Man from the East 74. Nickelodeon 76. The Long Riders 80. Endangered Species 82. Princess Daisy (TV) 83. The Whales of August 87. Illegally Yours 88. Breaking In 89. Back to the Future III 90. Tombstone 94. Sunchaser 96. Last Stand at Saber River (TV) 96, many others.

Carey, Joyce (1898–1993) (Joyce Lawrence).
British stage actress, daughter of Lilian Braithwaite; made a few silent films then appeared more regularly as upper-class ladies in the 40s and 50s.
God and the Man 21. The Newcomers 25. *In Which We Serve* 42. Blithe Spirit 45. *The Way to the Stars* 45. *Brief Encounter* 45. The October Man 48. London Belongs to Me 48. The Chiltern Hundreds 49. The Astonished Heart 50. Happy Go Lovely 51. Cry the Beloved Country 52. The End of the Affair 55. The Eyes of Annie Jones 63. A Nice Girl Like Me 69. The Black Windmill 74, etc.

Carey, Leonard (1893–1977).
British character actor in Hollywood in the forties, best remembered as old Ben in *Rebecca* 40.

Carey, Macdonald (1913–1994).
American leading man, usually the sympathetic good guy in routine romantic comedy-dramas.
Autobiography: 1991, *The Days of My Life*.
Dr Broadway 42. Wake Island 42. Shadow of a Doubt 43. Suddenly It's Spring 46. Dream Girl 47. East of Java 49. Streets of Laredo 49. The Lawless 50. Copper Canyon 50. Let's Make It Legal 51. My Wife's Best Friend 52. Stranger at My Door 56. Blue Denim 59. The Damned (GB) 62. Tammy and the Doctor 63. Broken Sabre 65. End of the World 77. It's Alive III 87, etc.
TV series: Dr Christian 56. Lock Up 59–65. Days of Our Lives 73–94.

Carey, Michele.
American actress, probably at her best as a sharp-shooter in leather jeans in *El Dorado* 67.
The Sweet Ride 68. Change 69. Live a Little, Love a Little 68. Dirty Dingus Magee 70. The Animals 70. Scandalous John 71. The Norliss Tapes (TV) 73. The Choirboys 77. Delta County USA (TV) 77. The Legend of the Golden Gun (TV) 79. In the Shadow of Kilimanjaro 86, etc.
TV series: A Man Called Sloane (as Effie, the voice of a super-computer) 79–80.

Carey, Olive (1896–1988) (Olive Fuller Golden).
American actress who had leading roles in silent films, retired soon after her marriage to Harry Carey in 1920 and returned later as a character actress, often in the films of John Ford.
Storm Country 14. Trader Horn 30. The Searchers 56. Run of the Arrow 56. Gunfight at the O.K. Corral 57. Two Rode Together 61, etc.

Carey, Phil (Philip) (1925–).
American leading man of the rugged but good-humoured type, in routine films of the 50s and 60s; latterly in senior officer roles.
Operation Pacific 51. *Pushover* 54. Mister Roberts 55. Port Afrique 56. *Wicked As They Come* 56. Screaming Mimi 58. Tonka 59. The Time Travellers 64. The Great Sioux Massacre (as Custer) 65. The Seven Minutes 71. Fighting Mad 76, many others.
TV series: 77th Bengal Lancers 56. Philip Marlowe 59. Laredo 66–67.

Carey, Timothy (1929–1994).
Heavy-eyed American character actor, often a loathsome villain.
Hellgate 52. Alaska Seas 54. The Killing 56. Paths of Glory 57. One-Eyed Jacks 61. Reprieve 62. The World's Greatest Sinner (& wd) 62. Bikini Beach 64. Waterhole 3 67. Head 68. Minnie and Moskowitz 71. The Conversation 73. The Killing of a Chinese Bookie 75. Speedtrap 77. Fast Walking 82. D.C. Cab 85. Echo Park 86, etc.

Carfagno, Edward C. (1907–1996).
American art director.
Best Foot Forward 43. The Secret Heart 46. Neptune's Daughter 49. Quo Vadis 51. The Story of Three Loves 52. The Bad and the Beautiful (AA) 53. Julius Caesar (AA) 53. Ben Hur (AA) 59. Ada 61. The Cincinnati Kid 65. The Shoes of the Fisherman 69. Skyjacked 73. The Man Who Loved Cat Dancing 73. The Hindenburg 75. The Last Hard Men 76. Gable and Lombard 76. Demon Seed 77. Looking for Mr Goodbar 77. Meteor 79. Time After Time 79. Little Miss Marker 80. Beulah Land (TV) 81. Wrong is Right 83. Sudden Impact 83. All of Me 84. Tightrope 84. City Heat 84. Pale Rider 85. Ratboy 86. Heartbreak Ridge 86. Bird 88. The Dead Pool 88. Pink Cadillac 89, etc.

Cargill, Patrick (1918–1996).
Impeccable British farce actor with long stage experience. He was co-author of the play *Ring for Catty*, which was the basis of the film *Carry On Nurse*. A bachelor, he had as pets a monkey named Josephine and a parrot called Pavement-Kerbstone, because he thought it deserved an aristocratic-sounding name.
The Cracksman 63. This is my Street 63. A Stitch in Time 64. *A Countess from Hong Kong* 66. Inspector Clouseau 68. Every Home Should Have One 70. Up Pompeii 71. Father Dear Father 73. The Picture Show Man (Austr.) 77, etc.
TV series: *Father Dear Father* 68–73, 77. The Many Wives of Patrick 77–78.

Carides, Gia. (1964–).
Australian leading actress.
Love Letters from Terabla Road 77. Midnight Spares 83. Bliss 85. The Coca-Cola Kid 85. Backlash 86. Strictly Ballroom 92. Lucky Break 94. *Brilliant Lies* 96. Lifebreath 97. Paperback Romance 97. Primary Colors (US) 98. Be the Man (US) 98. Letters from a Killer 98, etc.

Cariou, Len (1939–).
Canadian leading actor.
A Little Night Music 77. The Four Seasons 81. Who'll Save Our Children? (TV) 82. Killer in the Mirror (TV) 86. Louisiana (TV) 87. Lady in White 88. The Sea Wolf (TV) 93. Witness to the Execution (TV) 94. Never Talk to Strangers 95. Executive Decision 96, etc.

Carle, Gilles (1929–).
Canadian director.
Red 69. Bernadette 72. La Tête de Normande St Onge 75. Fantastica 80. Les Plouffe 81. Maria Chapdelaine 83. The Crime of Ovide Plouffe (co-d) 85. Scalp 85. La Guêpe 86, etc.

Carle, Richard (1871–1941) (Charles Carleton).
American character actor.
Zander The Great 25. Eve's Leaves 26. The Understanding Heart 27. Madame X 29. Brothers 30. One Hour With You 32. Morning Glory 33. Caravan 34. The Ghost Walks 35. Anything Goes 36. One Rainy Afternoon 36. True Confession 37. Persons in Hiding 39. The Great McGinty 40. The Uncertain Feeling 41, many others.

Carlei, Carlo (1962–).
Italian director who went to Hollywood after his first feature.
Captain Cosmos (short) 90. Flight of the Innocent/La Corsa dell'Innocente 92. Fluke (US) 95, etc.

Carleton, Claire (1913–1966).
American character actress of the 40s and 50s, usually as a wisecracking blonde.
The Crooked Road 40. Petticoat Politics 40. Crime Doctor's Man Hunt 46. A Close Call for Boston Blackie 46. A Double Life 47. Bal Tabarin 52. Death of a Salesman 52. The Fighter 52. Witness to Murder 54. The Buster Keaton Story 56. Accused of Murder 56. Devil's Partner 59, etc.

Carlin, George (1937–).
American comedian in occasional films.
With Six You Get Egg Roll 68. Car Wash 76. Outrageous Fortune 87. Bill & Ted's Excellent Adventure 89. Bill & Ted's Bogus Journey 91. The Prince of Tides 91, etc.
TV series: That Girl 66–67.

Carlin, Lynn (1930–).
American character actress.
Faces (AAN) 68. Tick Tick Tick 70. *Taking Off* 71. Wild Rovers 71. Battle Beyond the Stars 80. Forbidden Love (TV) 82. Superstition 82, etc.
TV series: James at 15 77–78.

Carlino, Lewis John (1932–).
American screenwriter.
The Brotherhood 68. Reflection of Fear 71. The Mechanic 72. Crazy Joe 74. The Sailor Who Fell from Grace with the Sea (& d, p) 76. I Never Promised You a Rose Garden (AAN) 77. Resurrection 80. The Great Santini (& d) 80. Class (d only) 83. Haunted Summer 88, etc.

Carlisle, Kitty (1915–) (Catherine Conn).
American singer and actress, in occasional films. Born in New Orleans, she was brought up in Europe and studied acting at RADA in London, before

beginning her career on the New York stage. Married writer Moss HART in 1946.

Autobiography: 1988, *Kitty*.

■ Murder at the Vanities 34. She Loves Me Not 34. Here is my Heart 34. *A Night at the Opera* 35. Hollywood Canteen 43. Radio Days 87. Six Degrees of Separation 93.

Carlisle, Mary (1912–).
American leading lady of the 30s.

Justice for Sale 32. College Humor 33. One Frightened Night 35. Love in Exile 36. Dr Rhythm 38. Call a Messenger 40. Baby Face Morgan 42. Dead Men Walk 43, etc.

Carlo-Rim (1905–1989) (Jean-Marius Richard).
French writer-director, mainly of Fernandel comedies.

L'Armoire Volante 47. Les Truands/Lock Up the Spoons 56. Le Petit Prof 59, etc.

Carlos, Wendy (1941–).
American composer, a former engineer, born Walter Carlos, and a pioneer in the use of synthesizers.

A Clockwork Orange 71. The Shining 80. Tron 82. Woundings 98, etc.

Carlsen, Henning (1927–).
Danish director and screenwriter, a former documentary film-maker and cinema manager.

Dilemma 62. The Cats/Kattorna 64. Hunger/Sult 66. We Are All Demons/Klabautermanden 69. Oh, to Be on the Bandwagon!/Man sku' Vaere Noget ved Musikken 72. A Happy Divorce/En Lykkelig Skilsmisse 75. Did Somebody Laugh?/Hör, Var der Ikke en, Som Lo? 78. Your Money or Your Life/Pengene eller Livet 82. The Wolf at the Door/Oviri 86. Two Green Feathers 95, etc.

Carlson, Richard (1912–1977).
American leading man of the 40s, mainly in routine films; played the diffident juvenile so long that he had nothing to give to mature roles.

The Young in Heart 38. Winter Carnival 39. The Ghost Breakers 40. No No Nanette 40. Back Street 41. Hold That Ghost 41. *The Little Foxes* 41. White Cargo 42. Presenting Lily Mars 43. So Well Remembered 47. Behind Closed Doors 48. King Solomon's Mines 50. The Blue Veil 51. Valentino 51. Whispering Smith Hits London 52. The Magnetic Monster 53. It Came from Outer Space 53. All I Desire 53. Riders to the Stars (& d) 54. The Creature from the Black Lagoon 54. Four Guns to the Border (d only) 54. Three for Jamie Dawn 56. The Helen Morgan Story 57. Appointment with a Shadow (d only) 59. Kid Rodelo (& d) 66. The Power 68. The Valley of Gwangi 69, many others.

TV series: I Led Three Lives 52. Mackenzie's Raiders 58.

Carlson, Veronica (1944–).
British leading lady, mainly in screamies.

Dracula has Risen from the Grave 68. Frankenstein must be Destroyed 69. The Horror of Frankenstein 70. Pussycat Pussycat I Love You 70. The Ghoul 75, etc.

Carlyle, Robert (1962–).
Scottish actor, best known as TV policeman Hamish Macbeth.

Riff-Raff 90. Being Human 94. Priest 94. Go Now (TV) 95. *Trainspotting* (as Begbie) 96. The Full Monty 96. Face 97. Looking After Jo Jo (TV) 98. Plunkett and Macleane 98. Angela's Ashes 98, etc.

TV series: Hamish Macbeth 95–97.

Carmel, Roger C. (1929–1986).
Rotund American character actor. Died of a drug overdose.

Goodbye Charlie 64. The Silencers 66. Gambit 66. The Venetian Affair 66. Skullduggery 69. Thunder and Lightning 77.

TV series: Fitz and Bones 81.

Carmet, Jean (1921–1994).
French character actor, usually in ordinary roles. He appeared in some 200 movies. He won two Césars as best actor and was awarded a César for lifetime achievement in 1993.

Les Enfants du Paradis 45. The Little Theatre of Jean Renoir 71. The Tall Blond Man with One Black Shoe/Le Grand Blond avec une Chaussure Noire 72. Return of the Tall Blond Man with One Black Shoe 74. Black and White in Colour/La Victoire en Chantant 76. Violette 78. Buffet Froid/Cold Cuts 79. Les Misérables 82. Secret Sorceress 87. Obsession 88. Merci la Vie 92. La Nuit des Cerfs-Volants 95, etc.

❝ In my imagination, I have been recasting my old films and casting all the films I never made, and the male star is always Jean Carmet. –*Jean Renoir*

Carmichael, Hoagy (1899–1981) (Hoaglund Howard Carmichael).
American song composer and lyricist, best known for 'Stardust' and 'In the Cool, Cool, Cool of the Evening' (AA 1951). Also a slow-speaking actor of light supporting roles, usually involving his singing at the piano. He was played by Romano Luccio Orzari in the biopic *Bix*, about Bix BEIDERBECKE.

Autobiographies: 1946, *The Stardust Road*. 1965, *Sometimes I Wonder*.

AS ACTOR/PERFORMER: To Have and Have Not 44. Canyon Passage 46. *The Best Years of Our Lives* 46. Young Man with a Horn 50. Belles on Their Toes 52. Timberjack 55, etc.

TV series: Laramie 59–62.

Carmichael, Ian (1920–).
British light leading man, adept at nervous novices; long experience in revue. Trained at RADA, he was on stage from 1939 and in films from 1947.

Autobiography: 1979, *Will the Real Ian Carmichael . . .*

Meet Mr Lucifer 54. The Colditz Story 54. Storm over the Nile 55. *Simon and Laura* 55. *Private's Progress* 55. *Brothers in Law* 57. *Lucky Jim* 57. Happy is the Bride 57. The Big Money 57. Left, Right and Centre 59. *I'm All Right, Jack* 59. School for Scoundrels 60. Light Up the Sky 60. Double Bunk 61. The Amorous Prawn 62. Hide and Seek 63. Heavens Above 63. Smashing Time 67. The Magnificent Seven Deadly Sins 71. From Beyond the Grave 75. The Lady Vanishes 79. Diamond Skulls/Dark Obsession 89, etc.

TV series: The World of Wooster 65. Bachelor Father 70–71.

Carminati, Tullio (1894–1971) (Count Tullio Carminati de Brambilla).
Italian romantic actor who had a modest career in British and American as well as European films.

The Bat 26. Three Sinners 28. Moulin Rouge 33. *One Night of Love* 34. *The Three Maxims* 35. Safari 40. The Golden Madonna 49. La Beauté du Diable 51. Roman Holiday 53. Saint Joan 57. El Cid 61. The Cardinal 63, many others.

Carne, Judy (1939–) (Joyce Botterill).
Pert British actress who found fame as the 'sock it to me' girl in Hollywood's *Laugh-In* TV series. She was married to actor Burt REYNOLDS (1966–69).

A Pair of Briefs 63. The Americanization of Emily 64. All the Right Noises 69. Only with Married Men 74, etc.

TV series: Fair Exchange 62. The Baileys of Balboa 64. Love on a Rooftop 66. Laugh-In 67–72.

Carné, Marcel (1909–1996).
Certainly the most brilliant of French directors 1937–45; his career later suffered a semi-eclipse.

■ Jenny 36. *Drôle de Drame* 37. *Quai des Brumes* 38. Hôtel du Nord 38. *Le Jour Se Lève* 39. *Les Visiteurs du Soir* 42. *Les Enfants du Paradis* 44. Les Portes de la Nuit 46. La Marie du Port 48. Juliette Ou La Clef des Songes 51. Thérèse Raquin 53. L'Air de Paris 54. Le Pays d'Où Je Viens 56. Les Tricheurs 58. Terrain Vague 60. Du Mouron pour les Petits Oiseaux 62. Three Rooms in Manhattan 65. The Young Wolves 68. Les Assassins de l'Ordre 71. La Vie à Belles Dents (w only) 80. La Bible (wd) 84.

✪ For creating, almost single-handedly, the images of French *film noir* in the 30s. *Les Enfants du Paradis*.

❝ The precise mood of the period – a sense of fatalism enveloping a pair of doomed lovers, drably poetic urban settings – is to be found in his work. – *Roy Armes*

Carney, Alan (1911–1973).
American comedy supporting actor who in the mid-40s made some second features with Wally BROWN. His solo appearances were sparse.

Mr Lucky 43. The Pretender 47. Lil Abner 59. It's a Mad Mad Mad Mad World 63. The Love Bug Rides Again 73, etc.

Carney, Art (1918–).
American comedy actor, popular on TV, especially from 1955 in *The Honeymooners*.

Pot O'Gold 41. The Yellow Rolls Royce 64. A Guide for the Married Man 67. *Harry and Tonto* (AA) 74. Won Ton Ton 76. Lanigan's Rabbi (TV) 76. *The Late Show* 77. Movie Movie 78. Sunburn 79. Roadie 80. Steel 80. St Helens 81. Take This Job and Shove It 81. Firestarter 84. The Naked Face 84. Izzy and Moe (TV) 85. Night Friend 88. The Last Action Hero 93, etc.

Carney, George (1887–1947).
British character actor of stage and screen, on screen from 1916.

Say It With Flowers 34. Father Steps Out (title role) 37. The Stars Look Down 39. Convoy 40. *Love on the Dole* 41. The Common Touch 41. Tawny Pipit 44. I Know Where I'm Going 45. Good Time Girl 47, etc.

❝ The embodiment of the commonplace civilian turned warrior. – *James Agate*

Carnovsky, Morris (1897–1992).
Distinguished American stage actor, with long experience in Jewish theatre. Films regrettably few.

■ The Life of Emile Zola 37. Tovarich 37. Edge of Darkness 43. Address Unknown 44. The Master Race 44. Our Vines Have Tender Grapes 45, *Rhapsody in Blue* 45. Cornered 45. Miss Susie Slagle's 45. *Dead Reckoning* 47. Dishonored Lady 47. Joe Palooka in The Knockout 47. Saigon 48. Maneater of Kumaon 48. Siren of Atlantis 48. Gun Crazy 49. Thieves' Highway 49. Western Pacific Agent 50. Cyrano de Bergerac 50. The Second Woman 51. A View from the Bridge 62. The Gambler 74.

Carol, Martine (1922–1967) (Maryse Mourer).
French leading lady popular in undressed roles in the early 50s.

Voyage Surprise 48. *Caroline Chérie* 50. A Night with Caroline 52. *Lucrezia Borgia* 52. The Bed 53. The Beach 54. Nana 55. *Lola Montes* 55. Action of the Tiger 57. Ten Seconds to Hell 59. Le Cave Se Rebiffe 61. Hell is Empty 66, etc.

Carol, Sue (1906–1982) (Evelyn Lederer).
American leading lady of the early 30s. Widow of Alan Ladd.

Is Zat So? 27. Girls Gone Wild 29. Dancing Sweeties 30. Her Golden Calf 30. Graft 31. Secret Sinners 34. A Doctor's Diary 37, etc.

Caron, Glenn Gordon.
American director and screenwriter, from television and advertising. He created the TV series *Moonlighting* 85–89 that first brought Bruce Willis to fame.

Moonlighting (TV) 85. Clean and Sober 88. Wilder Napalm 92. Love Affair 94. Picture Perfect 97, etc.

Caron, Leslie (1931–).
French leading lady and dancer who after being discovered by Gene Kelly followed a successful English-speaking career in light drama and comedy. She was married to director Peter Hall (1957–65).

An American In Paris 51. Man with a Cloak 51. Glory Alley 52. The Story of Three Loves 53. *Lili* (BFA, AAN) 53. The Glass Slipper 54. Daddy Longlegs 55. Gaby 56. *Gigi* 58. The Doctor's Dilemma 58. The Man Who Understood Women 59. The Subterraneans 60. Austerlitz 60. *Fanny* 61. Guns of Darkness 62. *The L-Shaped Room* (BFA, AAN) 62. Three Fables of Love 63. Father Goose 64. A Very Special Favour 65. Promise Her Anything 66. Is Paris Burning? 66. Head of the Family 68. Madron 69. Purple Night 71. Chandler 72. QB VII (TV) 74. The Man Who Loved Women 77. Valentino 77. Sérail 77. Goldengirl 79. Tous Vedettes 80. The Contract 80. Imperatives 82. Master of the Game (TV) 84. Dangerous Moves 85. The Genius 85. Courage Mountain 89. Guerriers et Captives 89. Damage 92. That's Entertainment! III 94. Funny Bones 95, etc.

Carp, Jean-Philippe.
French production designer.

Delicatessen 92. Johnny Mnemonic (US) 95. French Exit 95. Barb Wire (US) 96, etc.

Carpenter, Carleton (1926–).
American light leading man groomed by MGM in the early 50s.

Lost Boundaries 48. Father of the Bride 50. Summer Stock 51. Fearless Fagan 53. Sky Full of Moon 53. Take the High Ground 53. Up Periscope 59. Some of My Best Friends Are 71. The Prowler 81, etc.

Carpenter, John (1948–).
American director, screenwriter and composer who, in the late 70s, swiftly carved a niche for himself with scary but derivative horror movies. Married to actress Adrienne BARBEAU (1979–84).

The Resurrection of Broncho Billy (short) (AA) 70. *Dark Star* 74. *Assault on Precinct 13* 76. Someone's Watching Me (TV) 77. Halloween 78. Eyes of Laura Mars (w only) 78. Elvis (TV) 79. The Fog 79. Escape from New York (& co-w) 81. Halloween II (co-w, co-p only) 81. The Thing 82. Halloween III (co-p only) 83. Christine 83. Starman 84. Big Trouble in Little China 86. Something Wild (a only) 86. Black Moon Rising (w) 86. Prince of Darkness (d, m) 87. The House on Carroll Street (a) 88. They Live (wd, m) 88. Memoirs of an Invisible Man 92. In the Mouth of Madness 95. Village of the Damned 95. Escape from LA 96. John Carpenter's Vampires 98, etc.

TV series: John Carpenter's Body Bags 93.

❝ Movies are pieces of film stuck together in a certain rhythm, an absolute beat, like a musical composition. The rhythm you create affects the audience. – J.C.

Real life is scarier than any movie these days. – J.C.

Carpenter, Paul (1921–1964).
Canadian leading man long in Britain as hero of scores of second features.

School for Secrets 46. Albert RN 53. Night People 54. The Sea Shall Not Have Them 55. Fire Maidens from Outer Space 56. The Iron Petticoat 56. Jet Storm 59. Murder Reported 60. Call Me Bwana 63, etc.

Carpenter, Russell.
American cinematographer.

Sole Survivor 84. The Wizard of Speed and Time 88. Critters 2: The Main Course 88. Lady in White 88. Cameron's Closet 89. Death Warrant 90. The Perfect Weapon 91. The Lawnmower Man 92. Hard Target 93. True Lies 94. The Indian in the Cupboard 95. *Titanic* (AA) 97. Money Talks 97. The Negotiator 98, etc.

Carpi, Fiorenzo (1918–1997).
Italian composer.

Zazie/Zazie dans le Métro (Fr.) 60. A Very Private Affair 62. Italian Secret Service 68. Equinozio 71. La Vacanza 72. La Chair de l'Orchidée (Fr.) 74. Salon Kitty 76. Piso Pisello 82. La Storia 85. Il Prete Bello 89. Marcellino 91. Abyssinia 93, etc.

Carr, Allan (1941–).
Chubby American impresario associated with *Grease*, *La Cage aux Folles* and the unsuccessful *Can't Stop the Music*.

Carr, Darleen (1950–).
American leading lady mainly familiar in TV series: *The John Forsythe Show*, *The Smith Family*, *The Oregon Trail*, etc.

Monkeys Go Home 66. The Impossible Years 68. The Beguiled 70. Runaway (TV) 73. Young Joe the Forgotten Kennedy (TV) 77, etc.

Carr, Jane (1909–1957) (Rita Brunstrom).
British leading lady, in occasional films.

Taxi to Paradise 33. Lord Edgware Dies 37. Lilac Domino 37. The Lady from Lisbon 37. It's Not Cricket 48. 36 Hours 54, etc.

Carr, John Dickson (1905–1977).
American detective story writer, curiously few of whose many novels have been adapted for the screen.

Man with a Cloak 51. That Woman Upstairs 52. Dangerous Crossing 52, etc.

Carr, Mary (1874–1973) (Mary Kennevan).
Leading American character actress of the 20s; the archetypal white-haired old mother. Married actor-producer William Carr; their children included silent film actors Thomas, Stephen, Rosemary and Maybeth Carr, who all appeared with their mother in *Over the Hill to the Poorhouse*.

Mrs Wiggs of the Cabbage Patch 19. *Over the Hill to the Poorhouse* 20. Silver Wings 22. Why Men Leave Home 24. The Wizard of Oz 25. Jesse

James 27. Lights of New York 28.Beyond Victory 31. Change of Heart 34. East Side of Heaven 36. Friendly Persuasion 56, many others.

Carr, Thomas (1907–1997).
American director, mainly of second-feature westerns. Born in Philadelphia, the son of actress Mary CARR, he was a child star in silents, on screen from the age of two. He continued acting until 1937, when he was first a dialogue clerk with Republic before becoming a director in the mid-40s. From the mid-60s he worked in television.
Bandits of the Badlands 45. Red River Renegades 46. Code of the Saddle 47. Colorado Ranger 50. Wyoming Roundup 52. Captain Scarlett 53. The Bowery Boys Meet the Monsters 54. Bobby Ware Is Missing 55. Three for Jamie Dawn 56. The Tall Stranger 57. Gunsmoke in Tucson 58. Cast a Long Shadow 59. Sullivan's Empire 67, many others.

Carradine, David (1936–) (John Arthur Carradine).
Lanky sad-eyed American character actor, son of John Carradine.
The Violent Ones 67. Young Billy Young 69. The McMasters 70. Macho Callahan 71. Boxcar Bertha 72. You and Me (& d) 73. Mean Streets 73. Death Race 2000 75. Cannonball 76. *Bound for Glory* 76. Carquake 77. Thunder and Lightning 77. The Silent Flute 78. Cloud Dancer 80. The Long Riders 80. Safari 3000 82. The Winged Serpent 82. Mr Horn 82. Lone Wolf McQuade 82. Armed Response 86. North and South (TV) 86. Wheels of Terror 87. The Misfit Brigade 87. Warlords 88. Crime Zone 88. Future Force 89. Wizards of the Lost Kingdom II 89. Bird on a Wire 90. Future Zone 90. Think Big 90. Evil Toons 91. Deadly Surveillance 91. You and Me (d) 91. Roadside Prophets 92. Animal Instincts 92. Night Rhythms 92. Karate Cop 93. Last Stand at Saber River (TV) 96. Capital Punishment 96, many others.
TV series: *Shane* 66. *Kung Fu* 72–75. Kung Fu: The Legend Continues 93.
❝ David Carradine is about as good a martial artist as I am an actor. – *Chuck Norris*

Carradine, John (1906–1988) (Richmond Reed Carradine).
Gaunt American actor who scored a fine run of character roles in the 30s and 40s but later sank to mad doctors in cheap horror movies, touring meanwhile with one-man Shakespeare readings. Played 1930–35 under the name John Peter Richmond.
Tol'able David 30. The Sign of the Cross 32. Cleopatra 34. Bride of Frankenstein 35. Dimples 36. The Prisoner of Shark Island 36. The Garden of Allah 36. Winterset 36. Captains Courageous 36. The Last Gangster 37. The Hurricane 37. Alexander's Ragtime Band 38. Jesse James 39. Drums along the Mohawk 39. *Five Came Back* 39. *Stagecoach* 39. Brigham Young 40. *The Grapes of Wrath* 40. Blood and Sand 41. Man Hunt 41. Son of Fury 42. Hitler's Madman (as Heydrich) 43. Gangway for Tomorrow 43. *Bluebeard* (title role) 44. The Invisible Man's Revenge 44. It's In the Bag 45. *House of Frankenstein* (as Dracula) 45. Fallen Angel 45. House of Dracula 45. The Face of Marble 46. The Private Affairs of Bel Ami 47. C – Man 49. Casanova's Big Night 54. The Egyptian 54. The Kentuckian 55. The Black Sleep 56. The Ten Commandments 56. Hell Ship Mutiny 57. The Last Hurrah 58. The Cosmic Man 59. Sex Kittens go to College 60. Invasion of the Animal People 62. *The Man Who Shot Liberty Valance* 62. Cheyenne Autumn 64. Billy the Kid vs Dracula 66. Hillbillies in a Haunted House 67. The Fiend with the Electronic Brain 67. The Astro-Zombies 68. The Good Guys and the Bad Guys 69. Bigfoot 69. The McMasters 70. The Seven Minutes 71. Boxcar Bertha 72. The House of the Seven Corpses 73. Silent Night Bloody Night 74. The Shootist 76. The Sentinel 77. The Bees 78. The Boogey Man 80. The Scarecrow 82. The House of Long Shadows 83. Evils of the Night 85. Peggy Sue Got Married 86. The Tomb 87, many others.

Carradine, Keith (1950–).
American leading man of the 70s, half brother of David Carradine. He is the father of actress Martha Plimpton.
A Gunfight 71. McCabe and Mrs Miller 71. Hex 73. Emperor of the North 73. The Godchild (TV) 74. Thieves Like Us 74. Nashville (AA song) 75. Lumiere 76. Welcome to L.A. 77. Pretty Baby 78. An Almost Perfect Affair 79. Old Boyfriends 79. The Long Riders 80. Southern Comfort 81. Maria's Lovers 83. Choose Me 85. Chiefs (TV) 85. Scorned and Swindled (TV) 85. Blackout 86. Half a Lifetime 86. Backfire 87. The Inquiry/L'Inchiesta 87. The Moderns 88. Sans Espoir de Retour 88. Cold Feet 89. My Dear Doctor Grasler/Mio Caro Dottor Gräsler 89. Daddy's Dyin', Who's Got the Will? 90. The Ballad of the Sad Café 91. The Bachelor 91. Payoff 91. You and Me 91. Crisscross 92. Andre 94. Mrs Parker and the Vicious Circle 94. The Tie that Binds 95. Wild Bill 95. 2 Days in the Valley 96. Last Stand at Saber River (TV) 96. Larry McMurtry's Dead Man's Walk (TV) 96. A Thousand Acres 97, etc.

Carradine, Robert (1954–).
American leading man, youngest son of John Carradine (brother of Keith, half-brother of David).
The Cowboys 72. Mean Streets 73. Aloha Bobby and Rose 75. You and Me 75. Jackson County Jail 76. Cannonball 76. Orca 77. Coming Home 78. The Big Red One 80. Heartaches 82. Wavelength 83. Revenge of the Nerds 84. Number One with a Bullet 87. Revenge of the Nerds II 87. All's Fair 89. Buy and Cell 89. Revenge of the Nerds IV: Nerds in Love (TV) 94. Bird of Prey 95. Humanoids from the Deep 96, etc.
TV series: The Cowboys 74.

Carré, Ben (1883–1978).
French-born art director and scenic painter, in America from 1912. In the mid-30s he returned to scenic painting, including backgrounds for *The Wizard of Oz* 39, *Meet Me in St Louis* 44, and *An American in Paris* 51. Retired in the mid-60s.
The Blue Bird 18. *Phantom of the Opera* 25. Mare Nostrum 25. *Don Juan* 26. The Jazz Singer 27. *Dante's Inferno* 35, many others.

Carrera, Barbara (1947–).
Nicaraguan leading lady of smouldering personality.
Puzzle of a Downfall Child 70. The Master Gunfighter 75. Embryo 76. The Island of Dr Moreau 78. Never Say Never Again 83. Wild Geese II 84. Love at Stake 87. The Underachievers 88. Loverboy 89. Wicked Stepmother 89. Love Is All There Is 96, etc.
TV series: Dallas 85–86.

Carrera, Carlos (1962–).
Mexican director and screenwriter.
Benjamin's Wife/La Mujer de Benjamin (co-w, d) 91. A Conjugal Life/La Vida Conyugal (co-w, d) 92.

Carreras, Sir James (1909–1990).
British production executive, former exhibitor; chairman of Hammer Films.
❝ All Roman Catholic countries are wonderful for business. In Hammer films the crucifix wins every time. In Spain and Italy, when the monster is defeated by the sign of the cross, the audience stands up and cheers. – *J.C.*

Carreras, Michael (1927–1994).
British producer-director for Hammer Films. Son of James Carreras.
Blackout (p) 54. The Snorkel (p) 57. Ten Seconds to Hell (p) 58. Passport to China 61. The Two Faces of Dr Jekyll (d) 61. Maniac (d) 62. What a Crazy World (d) 63. The Curse of the Mummy's Tomb (d) 64. She (p) 65. One Million Years BC (p) 67. The Lost Continent (pd) 68, etc.

Carrere, Tia (1967–) (Althea Janairo).
American actress and singer, born in Honolulu.
Nightmare 87. Aloha Summer 88. Showdown in Little Tokyo 91. Harley Davidson and the Marlboro Man 91. Wayne's World 92. Rising Sun 93. Wayne's World 2 93. True Lies 94. Jury Duty 95. High School High 96. Hollow Point 96. Kull the Conqueror 97, etc.
TV series: General Hospital 82–83.

Carrey, Jim (1962–) (aka James Carrey).
Canadian comic actor in Hollywood, best known for appearing in the 90s television series *In Living Color* until *Ace Ventura, Pet Detective* was a surprise hit. Overnight his fee for a film role increased from $450,000 to a reported $7m. He was paid $20m to star in *The Cable Guy*. Married actress Lauren HOLLY, his second wife, in 1996. She filed for divorce in 1997.
Club Med 83. Finders Keepers 84. Once Bitten 85. Peggy Sue Got Married 86. Earth Girls Are Easy 89. Pink Cadillac 89. Ace Ventura, Pet Detective 94. *The Mask* 94. Dumb and Dumber 95. Batman Forever 95. Ace Ventura: When Nature Calls 95. The Cable Guy 96. Liar, Liar 97. The Truman Show 98. Simon Birch 98, etc.
TV series: The Duck Factory 84.
❝ I tend to stay up late, not because I'm partying but because it's the only time of day when I'm alone and don't have to be on, performing. – *J.C.*

Carrick, Edward (1905–1998) (Edward Anthony Craig).
British art director, son of Edward Gordon Craig. Author of *Designing for Moving Pictures*, 1941, and *Art and Design in the British Film*, 1948.
Autumn Crocus 34. Jump for Glory 36. Captain Boycott 47. The Divided Heart 54. Tiger Bay 59. What a Crazy World 63. The Nanny 65, many others.

Carrière, Jean-Claude (1931–).
French screen writer who began by collaborating with Tati and Etaix.
Book: 1994, *The Secret Language of Film*.
Belle de Jour 66. Hotel Paradiso 66. Le Voleur 67. Borsalino 67. The Milky Way/La Voie Lactée 69. Taking Off 70. *The Discreet Charm of the Bourgeoisie* (AAN) 72. The Phantom of Liberty/Le Fantôme de la Liberté 74. Le Gang 76. That Obscure Object of Desire 77. The Tin Drum 79. Circle of Deceit/Die Flaschung 81. Danton 82. The Return of Martin Guerre/Le Retour de Martin Guerre 82. Swann in Love/Un Amour de Swann 83. The Tragedy of Carmen 83. Max, My Love 86. The Mahabharata 89. Valmont 89. At Play in the Fields of the Lord 91. The Horseman on the Roof 95, etc. (Usually in collaboration.)

Carriere, Mathieu (1950–).
German leading actor in international films.
Young Torless/Der Junge Törless 66. Bluebeard 72. India Song (Fr.) 75. Coup de Grace 78. La Passante 83. Benvenuta (Bel.) 83. A Woman in Flames/Die Flambierte Frau 84. The Bay Boy (Can.) 85. Shining Through (US) 92. Dieu que les Femmes Sont Amoureuses (Fr.) 94, etc.

Carrillo, Leo (1880–1961).
American light character actor. A Spanish Californian from a wealthy landowning family, he enjoyed many years in Hollywood as an assortment of amiably talkative fellows, usually in fractured English.
Mr Antonio 29. Hell Bound 31. Girl of the Rio 31. The Broken Wing 32. Moonlight and Pretzels 33. Manhattan Melodrama 34. In Caliente 35. *The Gay Desperado* 36. *History Is Made at Night* 37. Blockade 38. Rio 39. Lillian Russell 40. Horror Island 41. Riders of Death Valley 41. Sin Town 42. Top Sergeant 43. Ghost Catchers 44. Mexicana 45. The Fugitive 47. The Gay Amigo 48. Pancho Villa Returns 50, many others.
TV series: The Cisco Kid 51–55.
❝ Ze female of ze species she is a-deadlier zan ze male. – L. C. *in History Is Made at Night*

Carroll, Diahann (1935–) (Carol Diahann Johnson).
American entertainer and actress. She is married to singer Vic Damone.
Carmen Jones 54. Porgy and Bess 59. Goodbye Again 60. Paris Blues 61. Hurry Sundown 67. The Split 68. Claudine (AAN) 74. The Five Heartbeats 91, etc.
TV series: *Julia* 68–70. Dynasty 84–87.

Carroll, Joan (1932–) (Joan Felt).
American child star of the 40s.
Primrose Path 40. Laddie 41. Petticoat Larceny 43. Meet Me in St Louis 44. Tomorrow the World 45. The Bells of St Mary's 46. Jack of Diamonds 49. The Feminine Touch 57, etc.

Carroll, John (1906–1979) (Julian La Faye).
Latin-American leading man with a decent singing voice but not much personality.
■ Marianne 29. Devil May Care 29. Hearts in Exile 29. Rogue Song 30. Dough Boys 30. Monte Carlo 30. New Moon 30. Reaching for the Moon 30. Go into Your Dance 35. Hi Gaucho 35. The Accusing Finger 36. Murder on the Bridle Path 36. Muss 'Em Up 36. We Who Are About to Die 37. Zorro (serial) 37. Death in the Air 37. Rose of the Rio Grande 38. I am a Criminal 38. Only Angels Have Wings 39. Wolf Call 39. Congo Maisie 40. Phantom Raiders 40. Susan and God 40. Hired Wife 40. Go West 40. Sunny 41. This Woman is Mine 41. Lady be Good 41. *Rio Rita* 42. Pierre of the Plains 42. Flying Tigers 42. Hit Parade of 1943 42. The Youngest Profession 43. Bedside Manner 45. A Letter for Evie 45. Fiesta 47. Wyoming 47. The Fabulous Texan 47. The Flame 47. Old Los Angeles 48. I Jane Doe 48. Angel in Exile 48. The Avengers 50. Surrender 50. Hit Parade of 1951 50. Belle Le Grand 51. The Farmer Takes a Wife 53. Geraldine 53. The Reluctant Bride 55. Decision at Showdown 57. Plunderers of Painted Flats 59.

Carroll, Leo G. (1892–1972).
Distinguished, dry-faced British character actor long based in Hollywood; usually played doctors, judges or academics.
■ What Every Woman Knows 34. Sadie McKee 34. Outcast Lady 34. Stamboul Quest 34. The Barretts of Wimpole Street 34. Murder on a Honeymoon 35. The Right to Live 35. Clive of India 35. The Casino Murder Case 35. London by Night 37. Captains Courageous 37. A Christmas Carol 38. The Private Lives of Elizabeth and Essex 39. *Wuthering Heights* 39. Bulldog Drummond's Secret Police 39. Charlie Chan in the City of Darkness 39. Tower of London 39. *Rebecca* 40. Charlie Chan's Murder Cruise 40. Waterloo Bridge 40. Scotland Yard 41. Bahama Passage 41. This Woman is Mine 41. Suspicion 41. *The House on 92nd Street* 45. *Spellbound* 45. Forever Amber 47. Time Out of Mind 47. Song of Love 47. The Paradine Case 48. So Evil My Love 48. Enchantment 48. The Happy Years 50. Father of the Bride 50. The First Legion 51. Strangers on a Train 51. The Desert Fox 51. The Snows of Kilimanjaro 52. The Bad and the Beautiful 52. Rogues' March 52. Treasure of the Golden Condor 52. Young Bess 53. We're No Angels 55. Tarantula 55. The Swan 56. *North by Northwest* 59. The Parent Trap 61. One Plus One 61. *The Prize* 63. That Funny Feeling 65. The Spy with My Face 66. One of Our Spies Is Missing 66. One Spy Too Many 66.
TV series: *Topper* 53–54. *Going My Way* 62. *The Man from U.N.C.L.E.* (as Mr Waverly) 64–67.

Carroll, Lewis (1832–1898) (Charles Lutwidge Dodgson)
British writer, an Oxford lecturer in mathematics who wrote *Alice in Wonderland*. His poem *Jabberwocky* from *Through the Looking Glass* inspired the film of the same name.

Carroll, Madeleine (1906–1987) (Marie Madeleine Bernadette O'Carroll).
British leading lady of the 30s and 40s; her gentle, well-bred air made her popular in Hollywood for a while.
■ *The Guns of Loos* 28. The First Born 28. What Money Can't Buy 29. The American Prisoner 29. Atlantic 30. *Young Woodley* 30. Escape 30. The W Plan 30. Madame Guillotine 31. Kissing Cup's Race 31. French Leave 31. The Written Law 31. Fascination 32. School for Scandal 33. Sleeping Car 33. *I Was a Spy* 33. The World Moves On 34. Loves of a Dictator 35. *The 39 Steps* 35. The Case Against Mrs Ames 36. Secret Agent 36. *The General Died at Dawn* 36. Lloyds of London 36. *On the Avenue* 37. *The Prisoner of Zenda* 37. It's All Yours 38. Blockade 38. Honeymoon in Bali 39. Café Society 39. My Son My Son 40. Safari 40. Northwest Mounted Police 40. Virginia 41. One Night in Lisbon 41. Bahama Passage 42. My *Favourite Blonde* 42. White Cradle Inn 46. Don't Trust Your Husband 48. *The Fan* 49.

Carroll, Nancy (1906–1965) (Ann La Hiff).
Warmly-remembered American leading lady of early talkie musicals and light dramas.
Biography: 1969, *The Films of Nancy Carroll* by Paul L. Nemcek.
■ Ladies Must Dress 27. Abie's Irish Rose 28. Easy Come Easy Go 28. Chicken à la King 28. The Water Hole 28. Manhattan Cocktail 28. *The Shopworn Angel* 29. The Wolf of Wall Street 29. Sin Sister 29. Close Harmony 29. The Dance of Life 29. Illusion 29. Sweetie 29. Dangerous Paradise 30. Honey 30. Paramount on Parade 30. The Devil's Holiday (AAN) 30. Follow Through 30. *Laughter* 30. Stolen Heaven 31. The Night Angel 31. Personal Maid 31. Broken Lullaby 32. Wayward 32. Scarlet Dawn 32. Hot Saturday 32. Undercover Man 32. Child of Manhattan 33. The Woman Accused 33. The Kiss Before the Mirror 33. I Love that Man 33. Springtime for Henry 34.

Transatlantic Merry-go-round 34. Jealousy 34. I'll Love You Always 35. After the Dance 35. Atlantic Adventure 35. There Goes My Heart 38. That Certain Age 38.

Carroll, Willard.
American producer, director and screenwriter. He has also been involved, as executive producer and writer, in animated versions of stories by Frank L. Baum released direct to video.
Nutcracker: The Motion Picture (p) 86. The Brave Little Toaster (p) 87. The Runestone (wd) 90. Rover Dangerfield (p) 91. Bebe's Kids (p) 92. Tom's Midnight Garden (wd) 98. Playing by Heart (p, wd) 98, etc.

Carson, Charles (1885–1977).
British character actor of stage and screen, seen latterly as distinguished old gentleman. Born in London, and educated in Heidelberg and Boston, he was a civil engineer before beginning his career on stage in 1919; he was in films from 1930.
Leap Year 32. Sanders of the River 35. Victoria the Great 37. Dark Journey 37. Quiet Wedding 40. Pink String and Sealing Wax 45. Cry the Beloved Country 52. Reach for the Sky 56. The Trials of Oscar Wilde 60, many others.

Carson, Jack (1910–1963).
Beefy Canadian comedy actor; a former vaudevillian, he usually played 'smart guys' who were really dumber than the suckers they tried to take. Formerly married to actress Lola Albright. Died of cancer.
■ You Only Live Once 37. Stage Door 37. Stand In 37. Too Many Wives 37. It Could Happen To You 37. Music for Madame 37. The Toast of New York 37. Reported Missing 37. The Saint in New York 37. Vivacious Lady 37. Mr Doodle Kicks Off 38. Crashing Hollywood 38. She's Got Everything 38. Night Spot 38. Law of the Underworld 38. This Marriage Business 38. Having Wonderful Time 38. Maids Night Out 38. Everybody's Doing It 38. Quick Money 38. Bringing Up Baby 38. Go Chase Yourself 38. Carefree 38. Destry Rides Again 39. The Kid from Texas 39. Mr Smith Goes to Washington 39. Legion of Lost Flyers 39. The Escape 39. The Honeymoon's Over 39. The Girl in 313 40. Shooting High 40. Young As You Feel 40. Enemy Agent 40. Parole Fixer 40. Alias the Deacon 40. Queen of the Mob 40. Sandy Gets His Man 40. Love Thy Neighbour 40. Lucky Partners 40. I Take this Woman 40. Typhoon 40. *The Strawberry Blonde* 41. Mr and Mrs Smith 41. Love Crazy 41. The Bride Came COD 41. Navy Blues 41. Blues in the Night 41. The Male Animal 42. Gentleman Jim 42. Larceny Inc. 42. Wings for the Eagle 42. The Hard Way 42. Princess O'Rourke 43. Thank Your Lucky Stars 43. Shine On Harvest Moon 44. Arsenic and Old Lace 44. The Doughgirls 44. *Make Your Own Bed* (leading role) 44. *Roughly Speaking* 45. *Mildred Pierce* 45. One More Tomorrow 46. The Time The Place and The Girl 46. Two Guys from Milwaukee 46. Love and Learn 47. April Showers 48. Romance on the High Seas 48. Two Guys from Texas 48. John Loves Mary 49. My Dream is Yours 49. It's a Great Feeling 49. Bright Leaf 50. Mr Universe 51. The Groom Wore Spurs 51. The Good Humor Man 51. Dangerous When Wet 53. Phffft! 54. *Red Garters* 54. *A Star is Born* 54. Ain't Misbehavin' 54. The Bottom of the Bottle 56. The Magnificent Roughnecks 56. The Tattered Dress 57. *Cat on a Hot Tin Roof* 58. Rally Round the Flag Boys 58. The Tarnished Angels 58. The Bramble Bush 60. King of the Roaring Twenties 61. Sammy the Way Out Seal (TV) 62.
Famous line (*Mildred Pierce*): 'Oh boy! I'm so smart it's a disease!'

Carson, Jeannie (1928–) (Jean Shufflebottom).
Vivacious British entertainer who became popular in America and then surprisingly retired.
Love in Pawn 51. As Long as They're Happy 54. An Alligator Named Daisy 56. Rockets Galore 57. Seven Keys 62, etc.
TV series: *Hey Jeannie!* 56.

Carson, John (1927–).
British character actor with a James Mason-like voice. Much on TV, especially heard on commercials.
The Plague of the Zombies 67. The Man Who Haunted Himself 70. Taste the Blood of Dracula 70. Captain Kronos Vampire Hunter 72, etc.

Carson, Johnny (1925–).
American comedian and late-night talk show host. He retired in 1992.
“ He's an anaesthetist. Prince Valium. – *Mort Sahl*

Carson, Kit (1809–1868).
American western frontiersman and guide who became a legendary figure and has been portrayed in several films, notably *Kit Carson* 40, in which he was played by Jon Hall (also on TV by Bill Williams).

Carson, L. M. 'Kit'.
American screenwriter, occasional actor and director. He is divorced from actress Karen Black.
David Holzman's Diary 67. The Lexington Experience 70. The American Dreamer (wd) 71. The Last Word 79. Breathless 83. Chinese Boxes 84. Paris, Texas 84. The Texas Chainsaw Massacre Part 2 86. Running on Empty 88 (a). Hurricane (a) 97, etc.

Carstairs, John Paddy (1912–1970) (John Keys).
British director, usually of light-hearted subjects; also comic novelist and painter. Son of Nelson Keys.
Autobiographies: 1942, *Honest Injun*. 1945, *Hadn't We the Gaiety*. 1946, *Kaleidoscope and a Jaundiced Eye*.
The Saint in London 39. Spare a Copper 40. He Found a Star 40. Dancing with Crime 46. *Sleeping Car to Trieste* 48. *The Chiltern Hundreds* 49. Made in Heaven 52. Trouble in Store 53. Up to His Neck 54. Up in the World 56. Just My Luck 57. The Square Peg 58. Tommy the Toreador 59. Sands of the Desert 60. Weekend with Lulu 61, many others.

Carsten, Peter (1929–) (Pieter Ransenthaler).
German character actor in international films.
Zeppelin 71. Tutti Fratelli nel West . . . Per Parte di Padre 72. Partizan 74. The Squeeze 78. The Serbian Girl/Das Serbische Mädchen 91, etc.

Carter, Ann (1936–).
American child star of the 40s.
I Married a Witch 42. North Star 43. *Curse of the Cat People* 44. The Two Mrs Carrolls 46. Song of Love 47. A Connecticut Yankee in King Arthur's Court 49, etc.

Carter, Ben (1911–1947).
American character actor.
Gone with the Wind 39. *Maryland* 40. Tin Pan Alley 40. Chad Hanna 40. Reap the Wild Wind 42. The Harvey Girls 46, etc.

Carter, Benny (1907–).
American composer, arranger and multi-instrumentalist, one of the finest jazz alto saxophonists.
A Man Called Adam 66. Buck and the Preacher 72. Manhunter (TV) 74. Louis Armstrong – Chicago Style (TV) 76, etc.

Carter, Helena (1923–) (Helen Rickerts).
American leading lady of second features in the 40s: former model.
Time Out of Mind 46. River Lady 48. Double Crossbones 51. The Golden Hawk 52. Invaders from Mars 53, etc.

Carter, Jack (1922–) (John Chakrin).
American nightclub and TV comic of the 50s.
The Horizontal Lieutenant 62. Viva Las Vegas 63. The Extraordinary Seaman 64. Hustle 75. The Amazing Dobermans 76. Rainbow (TV) 78. Alligator 80. Ecstasy 84. Hambone and Hillie 84. Death Blow 87. Red Nights 87. Deadly Embrace 88. Sexpot 88. Robo-Chic 89. Satan's Princess 90. In the Heat of Passion 91. Neil Simon's Broadway Bound (TV) 91, etc.
TV series: American Minstrels of 1949 49. Cavalcade of Stars 49–50. The Jack Carter Show 50–51. Make Me Laugh 97.

Carter, Janis (1921–1994) (J. Dremann).
American leading lady of minor films in the 40s; former radio experience.
Cadet Girl 41. The Fighting Guardsmen 45. The Notorious Lone Wolf 46. I Love Trouble 47. Framed/Paula 47. The Woman on Pier 13 49. My Forbidden Past 51. Flying Leathernecks 51. The Half-Breed 52, etc.

Carter, Mrs Leslie (1862–1937) (Caroline Louise Dudley).
American stage actress, a protégée of David Belasco; a 1940 biopic, *Lady with Red Hair*, starred Miriam Hopkins. Film appearances rare.
■ Du Barry 15. The Heart of Maryland 15. The Vanishing Pioneer 34. Rocky Mountain Mystery 34.

Carter, Nell (1948–).
American comedy actress and singer.
Hair 79. Back Roads 81. Modern Problems 81. The Grass Harp 95, etc.
TV series: Lobo 80–81. Gimme a Break 81–87. You Take the Kids 90–91.

Carter, Rick.
American production designer.
Back to the Future II 89. Back to the Future III 90. Death Becomes Her 92. Jurassic Park 93. Forrest Gump 94. Forrest Gump (AAN) 94. The Lost World: Jurassic Park 97. Amistad 97, etc.

Cartlidge, Katrin (c. 1961–).
English actress, from the stage, where she has acted notably with the Royal Court Theatre, the Royal National Theatre, and with Steven Berkoff's company.
Sacred Hearts (TV) 85. Naked 93. Before the Rain 95. 3 Steps to Heaven (TV) 95. *Breaking the Waves* (Den./Swe.) 96. Seasick (Fin./Swe.) 96. Saint-Ex 97. Career Girls 97. Claire Dolan 98. Hi-Life (US) 98, etc.
TV series: Brookside 80–81.

Cartwright, Angela (1953–).
English-born actress, in Hollywood from childhood, the sister of Veronica Cartwright.
Lad: A Dog 61. The Sound of Music 65. Beyond the Poseidon Adventure 79. High School USA (TV) 83, etc.
TV series: The Danny Thomas Show 57–64. Lost in Space (as Penny) 65–68. Make Room for Granddaddy 70–71.

Cartwright, Veronica (1949–).
English-born actress in Hollywood from childhood, the sister of Angela Cartwright.
In Love and War 58. The Children's Hour 62. The Birds 63. Inserts 77. Going South 78. Invasion of the Body Snatchers 78. Alien 79. Guyana Tragedy (TV) 80. Prime Suspect (TV) 81. The Right Stuff 83. My Man Adam 85. Flight of the Navigator 86. Wisdom 86. The Witches of Eastwick 87. Valentino Returns 88. False Identity 90. Dead in the Water 91. Man Trouble 92. Candyman 2: Farewell to the Flesh 94. Money Talks 97, etc.
TV series: Daniel Boone 64–66.

Caruso, Anthony (1913–).
American character actor, usually seen as menace.
Johnny Apollo 40. Sunday Punch 42. Objective Burma 45. Wild Harvest 47. Bride of Vengeance 49. Tarzan and the Slave Girl 50. The Iron Mistress 52. Phantom of the Rue Morgue 54. Hell on Frisco Bay 56. The Badlanders 58. The Most Dangerous Man Alive 61. Young Dillinger 65. Flap 70. Zebra Force 76. Claws 77, many others.

Caruso, David (1955–).
Red-haired American leading actor, best known so far as Detective John Kelly in *NYPD Blue*. His salary per film is currently reportedly $1m.
Without Warning 80. An Officer and a Gentleman 82. First Blood 82. Thief of Hearts 84. Blue City 86. China Girl 87. Twins 88. King of New York 90. Hudson Hawk 91. Mad Dog and Glory 93. Kiss of Death 95. Jade 95. Elmore Leonard's Gold Coast (TV) 97. Cold around the Heart 97. Body Count 97, etc.
TV series: NYPD Blue 93–94. Michael Hayes 97–98.

Caruso, Enrico (1873–1921).
Celebrated Italian operatic tenor who appeared in a few silent films, for which he was paid $100,000 a time, and was played by Mario Lanza in *The Great Caruso* 51.
My Cousin 18. A Splendid Romance 18, etc.

Carver, Louise (1869–1956) (Louise Spilger Murray).
American character actress, a famous silent comedienne.
The Extra Girl 23. Shameful Behaviour 26. The Fortune Hunter 27. The Man from Blankley's 30. The Big Trail 30. Side Show 31. Hallelujah I'm a Bum 33. Every Night at Eight 35, etc.

Carver, Lynne (1909–1955) (Virginia Reid Sampson).
American general-purpose actress.
Roberta 35. Maytime 37. A Christmas Carol 38. Calling Dr Kildare 39. Charley's Aunt 41. Tennessee Johnson 42. Law of the Valley 44. Crossed Trails 48, etc.

Carvey, Dana (1955–).
American actor and writer, best known for his performance as Garth in *Wayne's World* on the TV show *Saturday Night Live*, which became a successful film series.
Halloween II 81. This Is Spinal Tap 84. Racing with the Moon 84. Tough Guys 86. Moving 88. Opportunity Knocks 90. Wayne's World (& co-w) 92. Wayne's World 2 (& co-w) 93. Clean Slate 94. The Road to Wellville 94. Trapped in Paradise 94. The Shot 96, etc.
TV series: One of the Boys 82. Blue Thunder 84. The Dana Carvey Show 96.

Carwithen, Doreen (1922–).
British composer of the 50s, who started working as an assistant to musical director Muir Mathieson; married composer William Alwyn.
Boys in Brown 49. Break in the Circle 55. On the Twelfth Day 55. Three Cases of Murder 55, etc.

Cary, Joyce (1888–1957).
British writer of novels about the necessity of individual freedom. He studied art in Edinburgh and Paris before working in Africa, becoming a full-time writer from the 20s. He is the father of composer Tristram Cary.
The Horse's Mouth (oa) 58. Mr Johnson (oa) 90.

Cary, Tristram (1925–).
British composer, the third son of novelist Joyce Cary, many of whose scores incorporate electronic music. Educated at Oxford and Trinity College of Music, London, he founded the electronic music studio at the Royal College of Music in the mid-60s and set up his own electronic music facility in England before moving to Australia, where he became Dean of Music at Adelaide University in the 80s. He now runs Tristram Cary Creative Music Services. Author of the *Illustrated Compendium of Musical Technology*, 1992. Apart from features, he has scored many documentaries.
The Ladykillers 55. Time without Pity 55. Town on Trial 56. The Flesh Is Weak 57. Tread Softly Stranger 58. She Didn't Say No 58. The Little Island (cartoon) 58. The Boy Who Stole a Million 61. The Prince and the Pauper 62. Sammy Going South 63. The Silent Playground 63. Daylight Robbery 64. Quatermass and the Pit 67. A Twist of Sand 67. Blood from the Mummy's Tomb 72. The Fourth Wish 76, etc.

Casanova, Giovanni (1725–1798).
The celebrated Italian lover, whose career was much romanticized during his lifetime and afterwards, was a popular cinema figure although until the 70s his exploits had to be bowdlerized. Principal films are as follows:

France 1946	*Les Aventures de Casanova*, Georges Guetary
US 1948	*The Adventures of Casanova*, Arturo de Cordova
Italy 1955	*Casanova*, Gabriele Ferzetti
Italy 1965	*Casanova 70*, Marcello Mastroianni
Italy 1969	*Casanova the Venetian*, Leonard Whiting
Italy/West Germany/ France 1977	*The Rise and Rise of Casanova*, Tony Curtis
UK 1971	*Casanova* (TV serial by Dennis Potter), Frank Finlay
Italy 1977	*Fellini's Casanova*, Donald Sutherland
Italy 1978	*The Return of Casanova*, Giulio Boseti

And in 1954 Vincent Price played Casanova in a Bob Hope spoof, *Casanova's Big Night*.

Casarès, Maria (1922–1996) (Maria Casares Quiroga).
Dark-eyed, solemn-looking French-Spanish character actress. Her lovers included writer Albert Camus, with whom she had a 16-year relationship.
Les Dames du Bois de Boulogne 44. Les Enfants du Paradis 45. La Chartreuse de Parme 47. Bagarres 48. *Orphée* (as Death) 49. Le Testament d'Orphée 59. The Rebel Nun 74. Flavia 76. Blanche et Marie 85. De Sable et de Sang 88. La Lectrice 88. Les Chevaliers de la Table Ronde 90, etc.

Caselotti, Adriana (1916–1997).
American singer who was the voice of Snow White in Walt Disney's animated feature in 1937.
The Bride Wore Red 37. The Wizard of Oz 39.

Caserini, Mario (1874–1920).
Italian director of silent epics, a former actor and artist.
Othello 07. Romeo and Juliet 08. Beatrice Cenci 09. Hamlet 10. Lucrezia Borgia 10. Dante e Beatrice 12. The Last Days of Pompeii/Gli Ultimi Giorni di Pompei 13. Resurrection 17. Il Miracolo 19. La Modella 20, etc.

Casey, Bernie (1939–).
American character actor, a former professional football player.
Tick Tick Tick 69. Black Gunn 72. Cornbread Earl and Me 75. Brothers 77. Sharky's Machine 81. Revenge of the Nerds 84. Spies Like Us 85. Steele Justice 87. Backfire 88. Rent-A-Cop 88. Bill & Ted's Excellent Adventure 89. Another 48 Hrs 90. The Cemetery Club 93. The Glass Shield 94. In the Mouth of Madness 95, etc.
TV series: Harris and Company 79. Bay City Blues 83.

Cash, Jim.
American screenwriter, often in collaboration with Jim Epps Jnr.
Top Gun (co-w) 86. Legal Eagles (co-w) 86. The Secret of My Success (co-w) 86. Turner & Hooch (co-w) 89. Dick Tracy (co-w) 90. Anaconda (co-w) 97, etc.

Cash, Johnny (1932–).
American country singer.
Five Minutes to Live 62. A *Gunfight* 70. The Pride of Jesse Hallam (TV) 80. Murder in Coweta County 83. The Baron and the Kid 84. Stagecoach (TV) 86. Last Days of Frank and Jesse James (TV) 86, etc.

Cash, Rosalind (1938–1995).
American leading lady. Died of cancer.
■ Klute 71. The Omega Man 71. The All-American Boy 71. The New Centurions 72. Hickey and Boggs 72. Melinda 72. Uptown Saturday Night 74. Amazing Grace 74. Hit the Open Man 75. Dr Black, Mr Hyde 76. The Monkey Hustle 76. The Class of Miss McMichael 78. Flashpoint (TV) 79. Guyana Tragedy (TV) 80. Wrong is Right 82. Death Drug 83. The Adventures of Buckaroo Banzai across the Eighth Dimension 84. The Offspring/From a Whisper to a Scream 86.

Casini, Stefania (1949–).
Italian leading actress and occasional director. She has a degree in architecture, studied acting at the Accademia Filodrammatica in Milan, and was on-stage from 1969.
Till Divorce Do You Part/Le Castagne Sono Buone 70. Andy Warhol's Dracula 74. Suspiria 76. 1900 76. Andy Warhol's Bad 76. Bye Bye Monkey/Ciao Maschio 77. The Bloodstained Shadow/Solamente Nero 78. Cocktail Molotov 79. Morra 79. Lontano da Dove (co-d) 83. The Belly of an Architect (GB) 87, etc.

Caspary, Vera (1899–1987).
American romantic crime novelist.
The Night of June 13th (oa) 32. I'll Love You Always (w) 35. Scandal Street (oa) 38. Lady from Louisiana (w) 41. *Laura* (oa) 44. Claudia and David (w) 46. Bedelia (oaw) 46. A Letter to Three Wives (w) 48. Three Husbands (oaw) 51. The Blue Gardenia (oa) 53. Bachelor in Paradise (oa) 61, etc.

Cass, Henry (1902–1989).
British director. Born in London, he began work at the age of 14, becoming involved in theatre in 1923, and later working as a producer at the Old Vic Theatre in the 30s. During the Second World War he directed documentary films.
Lancashire Luck 37. 29 Acacia Avenue 45. The Glass Mountain 48. No Place for Jennifer 49. Last Holiday 50. Young Wives' Tale 51. Windfall 55. Blood of the Vampire 59. The Hand 60. Give a Dog a Bone 66, etc.

Cass, Maurice (1884–1954).
American character actor of Russian origin; often played old men.
Two for Tonight 35. Charlie Chan at the Opera 37. Son of Monte Cristo 40. Blood and Sand 41. Charley's Aunt 41. Up in Arms 44. Angel on My Shoulder 46. Spoilers of the North 47. We're Not Married 52, many others.

Cass, Peggy (1925–).
American comedy actress, mainly on Broadway: films few.
The Marrying Kind 52. *Auntie Mame* (AAN) 58. Gidget Goes Hawaiian 62. If It's Tuesday This Must be Belgium 69. Age of Consent 69. Paddy 70. Cheaters 84. Tales from the Darkside 85. Zoya (TV) 95, etc.
TV series: The Hathaways 61–62. Women in Prison 87–88.

Cassavetes, John (1929–1989).
Slight, intense American actor who played a variety of parts and later became an experimental director. He was married to actress Gena Rowlands.
■ Taxi 54. The Night Holds Terror 55. Crime in the Streets 56. Edge of the City 57. Saddle the Wind 58. Virgin Island 58. The Webster Boy 61. *Shadows* (d only) 61. Too Late Blues (d only) 62. A Child is Waiting (d only) 62. The Killers 64. The Dirty Dozen (AAN) 67. Affair in Havana 67. The Devil's Angels 67. Rosemary's Baby 68. *Faces* (w, d only) (AANw) 68. Bandits in Rome (It.) 69. If It's Tuesday This Must be Belgium 69. Husbands (& w, d) 70. Machine Gun McCain 70. *Minnie and Moskowitz* (& w, d) 71. A Woman Under the Influence (w, d only) (AAN) 74. Capone 75. Two Minute Warning 76. Mikey and Nicky 76. Opening Night (& w, d) 78. The Killing of a Chinese Bookie (w, d only) 78. Brass Target 78. The Fury 78. Flesh and Blood (TV) 80. Gloria (w, p, d only) 80. Whose Life is it Anyway? 81. Tempest 82. The Incubus 82. Love Streams (w, p, d) 83. Marvin and Tige 83. Big Trouble 84. She's So Lovely (oa) 97.
TV series: *Johnny Staccato* 59.
❝ People have forgotten how to relate or respond . . . what I'm trying to do with my movies is build something audiences can respond to. – J.C.
When I started making films, I wanted to make Frank Capra pictures. But I've never been able to make anything but these crazy, tough pictures. You are what you are. – J.C.
As a director, too much of the time he is groping when he should be gripping. – *Andrew Sarris, 1968*
One of the most garrulous noncomformists in show business. – *Anon*

Cassavetes, Nick (1959–).
American actor turned director, the son of John Cassavetes and Gena Rowlands. He began to direct in the mid-90s and made *She's So Lovely* from one of his father's scripts; he also remade his father's *The Killing of a Chinese Bookie*.
Reunion (TV) 80. Mask 85. The Wraith 86. Quiet Cool 86. Black Moon Rising 86. Assault of the Killer Bimbos 88. Under the Gun 88. Backstreet Dreams 90. Blind Fury 90. Delta Force 3: The Killing Game 91. Broken Trust 92. Sins of Desire 92. Sins of the Night 93. Class of 1999 II: The Substitute 93. Body of Influence 93. Twogether 94. Mrs Parker and the Vicious Circle 94. Black Rose of Harlem/Machine Gun Blues 95. Unhook the Stars (d) 96. Face/Off 97. She's So Lovely (d) 97. The Killing of a Chinese Bookie (wd) 97, etc.

Cassel, Jean-Pierre (1932–) (Jean-Pierre Crochon).
French leading man.
Les Jeux de l'Amour 60. L'Amant de Cinq Jours 61. The Vanishing Corporal 62. La Ronde 64. Those Magnificent Men in Their Flying Machines 65. Les Fêtes Galantes 65. Is Paris Burning? 66. Jeu de Massacre 67. Baxter 71. The Discreet Charm of the Bourgeoisie 72. The Three Musketeers 74. Murder on the Orient Express 74. That Lucky Touch 75. The Four Musketeers 75. Grandison 78. Who Is Killing the Great Chefs of Europe 78. La Vie Continue 81. The Trout/La Truite 82. Tranches de Vie 84. Mangeclous 88. Mister Frost 90. The Favour, The Watch and The Very Big Fish/Rue Saint-Sulpice 91. The Maid 91. In Heaven as on Earth/Sur la Terre, comme au Ciel 92. Pétain 93. Prêt-à-Porter/Ready to Wear 94. Hell/L'Enfer 94. A Judgment in Stone/La Cérémonie 95. Love Kills/Amores Que Matan 96. Incognito (US) 97, etc.

Cassel, Seymour (1935–).
American character actor associated with the films of John Cassavetes.
Too Late Blues 61. The Killers 64. The Sweet Ride 68. Faces (AAN) 68. The Revolutionary 70. *Minnie and Moskowitz* 71. The Last Tycoon 76. The Killing of a Chinese Bookie 78. Convoy 78. California Dreaming 79. The Mountain Men 80. Love Streams 84. Eye of the Tiger 86. Tin Men 87. Colors 88. Plain Clothes 88. Wicked Stepmother 89. Cold Dog Soup 90. Dick Tracy 90. White Fang 91. In the Soup 92. Diary of a Hit Man 92. Indecent Proposal 93. Boiling Point 93. When Pigs Fly 93. Handgun 94. Chasers 94. It Could Happen to You 94. Dark Side of Genius 94. There Goes My Baby 94. Imaginary Crimes 94. Handgun 94. Tollbooth 94. Chameleon (Fr.) 96. Obsession 97. Slaughter of the Cock (Gr.) 97. This World, Then the Fireworks 97. Rushmore 98, etc.
TV series: Good Company 96.

Cassel, Vincent (1967–).
French leading actor, the son of Jean-Pierre Cassel. He has been romantically linked with actress Monica Bellucci.
Keys to Paradise/Les Clés du Paradis 91. Amour et Chocolat 92. Metisse 93. Jefferson in Paris (US) 95. Adultery, A User's Manual/Adultère, Mode d'Emploi 95. La Haine 95. L'Éleve 96. As You Want Me/Come Mi Vuoi (It./Fr.) 96. The Appartment/L'Appartement 96. Dobermann 97. Pleasure/Le Plaisir 98. Elizabeth (GB) 98. Joan of Arc/Jeanne d'Arc 99, etc.

Cassidy, David (1950–).
American actor who enjoyed fame on the television series *The Partridge Family* 70–74, together with his step-mother Shirley Jones, and was the teeny-boppers' favourite singer in the early 70s. He retired for three years in the mid-70s, began recording again in the 80s but has so far not regained his early success. He is the son of Jack Cassidy and actress Evelyn Ward.
The Spirit of '76 90.
TV series: David Cassidy – Man Undercover 78–79.

Cassidy, Jack (1926–1976).
American light actor, mostly on TV; husband of Shirley Jones and father of David Cassidy. Died in a fire at his Hollywood apartment.
Look in any Window 62. FBI Code 98 64. Guide for the Married Man 67. Your Money or Your Wife (TV) 72. Phantom of Hollywood (TV) 74. The Eiger Sanction 75. W. C. Fields and Me (as John Barrymore) 76, etc.
TV series: He and She 67.

Cassidy, Joanna (1944–) (Joanna Caskey).
American leading lady.
The Laughing Policeman 73. The Outfit 73. Bank Shot 74. Stunts 77. Blade Runner 82. Under Fire 83. Hollywood Wives (TV) 85. Club Paradise 86. The Fourth Protocol 87. Who Framed Roger Rabbit 88. 1969 89. The Package 89. May Wine 90. Where the Heart Is 90. All-American Murder 91. Lonely Hearts 91. The Tommyknockers (TV) 93. Vampire in Brooklyn 95. Chain Reaction 96. Loved 96. The Second Civil War 97. Dangerous Beauty 98, etc.
TV series: The Roller Girls 78. 240-Robert 79–80. The Family Tree 83. Buffalo Bill 83–84. Codename Foxfire 85. Hotel Malibu 94.

Cassidy, Ted (1932–1979).
Giant-size American character actor who became popular in 1964 as Lurch the butler in TV's *The Addams Family*.
Mackenna's Gold 68. Harry and Walter Go to New York 76. The Last Remake of Beau Geste 77, etc.

Casson, Ann (1915–1990).
English leading actress, mainly on the stage, the daughter of Sir Lewis Casson and Dame Sybil Thorndike. On stage from 1921 (as Tiny Tim in *A Christmas Carol*), and in a few films from 1930.
Escape 30. Dance Pretty Lady/Carnival 32. Bachelor's Baby 32. George and Margaret 40, etc.

Casson, Sir Lewis (1875–1969).
Leading English actor, on stage from 1900, who made a few films. Husband of Sybil Thorndike.
Crime on the Hill 33. Midshipman Easy 35. Rhodes of Africa 36. Victoria the Great 37. Sixty Glorious Years 38. The Winslow Boy 48. Shake Hands with the Devil 59, etc.

Castel, Lou.
Italian leading actor, in European films.
Fists in the Pocket/I Pugni in Tasca 65. A Bullet for the General/El Chucho, Quién Sabe? 66. Paranoia/A Beautiful Place to Kill 69. In the Name of the Father/In Nome del Padre 71. The Scarlet Letter/Der Scharlachrote Buchstabe (Ger.) 73. The Cassandra Crossing 76. The American Friend (Ger.) 77. The Eyes, the Mouth/Gli Occhi, la Bocca 82. Trauma (Ger.) 83. Rorret 87. Treasure Island/L'Île au Trésor (Fr.) 91. Year of the Gun (US) 91. La Naissance de l'Amour (Fr.) 93. Manila Paloma Blanca 93. Irma Vep 96. Three Lives and Only One Death 96, etc.

Castellani, Renato (1913–1985).
Italian director.
Un Colpo di Pistola 41. My Son the Professor 46. E Primavera 50. Due Soldi di Speranza 51. Romeo and Juliet (GB) 54. Nella Città l'Inferno 59. Il Brigante 61. Mare Matto 62. Three Nights of Love 64. Sotto il Cielo Stellato 66. Ghosts Italian Style 67. Una Breva Stagione 69. Leonardo da Vinci (TV) 72, etc.

Castellano, Richard (1931–1988).
Fat Italian-American character actor who came to fame in *Lovers and Other Strangers* (AAN) 69.
A Fine Madness 66. The Godfather 72. Honor Thy Father (TV) 73. Night of the Juggler 80.
TV series: The Super 72. Joe and Sons 75–76. Gangster Chronicles 81.

Castelnuovo, Nino (1937–).
Italian leading man.
La Garçonnière 60. Escapade in Florence 62. Les Parapluies de Cherbourg 64. Camille 2000 69. Love and Anger/Amore e Rabbia 69. Loving in the Rain/Un Amour de Pluie 73. Nude per l'Assassino 75. L'Emmerdeur 75. Metallica/Sette Uomini d'Oro nello Spazio 78. The English Patient (US) 96, etc.

Castelnuovo-Tedesco, Mario (1895–1968).
Italian composer in America.
The Return of the Vampire 44. The Black Parachute 44. *And Then There Were None* 45. Night Editor 46. Time out of Mind 47. Mark of the Avenger 51, etc.

Castle, Don (1919–1966).
American leading man of 40s second features.
Love Finds Andy Hardy 38. I Take this Woman 40. Power Dive 41. Tombstone 42. The Guilty 47. The Invisible Wall 47, etc.

Castle, Irene, Vernon (Irene Foote, Vernon Blythe).
A dancing team who were highly popular in American cabaret 1912–17. Irene (1893–1969) was American, Vernon (1893–1918) was British. Apart from some 1914 shorts, their only feature together was *The Whirl of Life* 15; but Irene alone made a number of dramatic films, especially after Vernon's death in an air crash: *Patria* 17, *The Hillcrest Mystery* 18, *The Invisible Bond* 19, *The Broadway Bride* 21, *No Trespassing* 22, etc. In 1939 Fred Astaire and Ginger Rogers appeared in *The Story of Vernon and Irene Castle*; in 1958 Irene published an autobiography, *Castles in the Air*.

Castle, John (1940–).
British character actor.
The Lion in Winter 68. The Promise 69. Antony and Cleopatra 71. Man of La Mancha 72. The Incredible Sarah 77. The Three Hostages (TV) 78. Eagle's Wing 79. Night Shift 80. Second Star to the Right 80. King David 85. Lost Empires (TV) 86, etc.

Castle, Mary (1931–).
American leading lady of the 60s.
Criminal Lawyer 51. Eight Iron Men 52. The Lawless Breed 53. The Jailbreakers 61, etc.

Castle, Nick (1910–1968).
American dance director.
Swanee River 39. Hellzapoppin 42. Royal Wedding 47. Red Garters 54, many others.

Castle, Nick (1947–).
American screenwriter and director, the son of choreographer Nick Castle.
Skatetown U.S.A. (w) 79. Pray TV (w) 80. Escape from New York (co-w) 81. The Last Starfighter (d) 84. The Boy Who Could Fly (wd) 86. Tap (wd) 89. Dennis the Menace/Dennis 93. Major Payne 95. Mr Wrong 96, etc.

Castle, Peggie (1927–1973).
American leading lady of 50s second features.
Mr Belvedere Goes to College 49. Buccaneer's Girl 50. Air Cadet 51. I the Jury 53. The Long Wait 54. Jesse James' Women 54. Target Zero 55. Bury Me Dead 57. Seven Hills of Rome 58, etc.
TV series: Lawman 58–61.

Castle, Roy (1932–1994).
British light entertainer, in occasional films.
Autobiography: 1994, *Now and Then*.
Dr Terror's House of Horrors 66. Dr Who and the Daleks 66. Carry On Up the Khyber 71. Legend of the Werewolf 75, etc.

Castle, William (1914–1977) (William Schloss).
American director of second features (1941–57) who became a cheerful purveyor of gimmicky horror films involving give-away insurance policies, mobile skeletons, tingling seats, etc; these he not only produced and directed but introduced in the Hitchcock manner.
Autobiography: 1976, *Step Right Up! . . .* I'm Gonna Scare the Pants off America.
■ The Chance of a Lifetime 43. Klondike Kate 43. *The Whistler* 44. *When Strangers Marry* 44. She's a Soldier Too 44. The Mark of the Whistler 44. Voice of the Whistler 46. Just Before Dawn 46. Mysterious Intruder 46. The Return of Rusty 46. The Crime Doctor's Manhunt 46. The Crime Doctor's Gamble 47. Texas Brooklyn and Heaven 48. The Gentleman from Nowhere 48. Johnny Stool Pigeon 49. Undertow 49. It's a Small World 50. The Fat Man 51. Hollywood Story 51. Cave of Outlaws 51. Serpent of the Nile 53. Fort Ti 53. Conquest of Cochise 53. Slaves of Babylon 53. Charge of the Lancers 54. Drums of Tahiti 54. Jesse James vs the Daltons 54. Battle of Rogue River 54. The Iron Glove 54. The Saracen Blade 54. The Law vs Billy the Kid 54. Masterson of Kansas 54. The Americano 55. New Orleans Uncensored 55. The Gun that Won the West 55. Duel on the Mississippi 55. The Houston Story 56. Uranium Boom 56. *Macabre* 58. *House on Haunted Hill* 59. The Tingler 59. Thirteen Ghosts 60. *Homicidal* 61. Sardonicus 61. Zotz! 62. Thirteen Frightened Girls 63. The Old Dark House 63. Strait Jacket 64. *The Night Walker* 64. I Saw What You Did 65. Let's Kill Uncle 66. The Busy Body 67. The Spirit is Willing 67. Rosemary's Baby (p only) 68. Project X 68. The Sex Symbol (TV) (a) 74. Shanks (& p) 74. Shampoo (a) 75. Bug (p only) 75. Day of the Locust (a) 75.
TV series: Ghost Story 72.

Cates, Georgina (1975–) (Clare Woodgate).
English actress, from television. Married actor Skeet Ulrich.
Au Pair 94. An Awfully Big Adventure 95. Frankie Starlight 95. Loving (TV) 96. Stiff Upper Lips 97. Clay Pigeons (US) 98, etc.

Cates, Gilbert (1934–) (Gilbert Katz).
American director with Broadway and TV experience.
■ *I Never Sang for My Father* 69. To All My Friends on Shore (TV) 71. Summer Wishes, Winter Dreams 73. The Affair (TV) 73. Johnny We Hardly Knew Ye (TV) 77. The Promise 79. Oh God Book Two 80. The Last Married Couple in America 80. Backfire 87. Fatal Judgement (TV) 88. My First Love (TV) 88. Confessions: Two Faces of Evil (TV) 93. Innocent Victims (TV) 96.

Cates, Phoebe (1963–).
American leading lady who after modelling experience became an instant star in 1984 as the heroine of the TV mini-series *Lace*. She married actor Kevin Kline in 1990.
Fast Times at Ridgemont High 82. Paradise 82. Private School 83. Gremlins 84. Date with an Angel 87. Bright Lights, Big City 88. Shag 88. Heart of Dixie 89. Gremlins 2: The New Batch 90. Drop Dead Fred 91. Bodies, Rest and Motion 93. Princess Caraboo 94. My Life's in Turnaround (as herself) 94, etc.

Cathcart, Dick (1924–1993).
American jazz musician, born in Michigan City, Indiana, who dubbed the trumpet playing for Jack Webb in *Pete Kelly's Blues* 55, and for Billy May in *Nightmare* 56. He also dubbed the cornet playing of William Reynolds in the TV series *Pete Kelly's Blues* 59.
Dragnet 54. The Five Pennies (soundtrack musician) 59, etc.

Cather, Willa (1876–1947).
American novelist of the Middle West, whose *A Lost Lady* was filmed in 1923. She was so horrified by the result that she resolved that no more of her writings would be filmed or dramatized in any form or in any medium, leaving instructions in her will to that effect.

Catherine the Great (1729–1798).
'mother of all the Russias', has appeared in the following screen personifications:

Pola Negri	*Forbidden Paradise* 24
Marlene Dietrich	*The Scarlet Empress* 34
Elisabeth Bergner	*Catherine the Great* 34
Tallulah Bankhead	*A Royal Scandal* 45
Viveca Lindfors	*Tempest* 58
Bette Davis	*John Paul Jones* 59
Hildegarde Neff	*Catherine of Russia* 62
Jeanne Moreau	*Great Catherine* 68
Catherine Zeta Jones	*Catherine the Great* (TV) 95

What a pity that Mae West's play *Catherine Was Great* never reached the screen . . .

Cathey, Reg E.
American actor, from the stage. He studied at the Yale School of Drama.
Funny Farm 88. Crossing Delancey 88. Born on the Fourth of July 89. Quick Change 90. Loose Cannons 90. What about Bob? 91. Clean Slate 94. Airheads 94. The Mask 94. Clear and Present Danger 94. Tank Girl 95. Seven 95, etc.

Catlett, Walter (1889–1960).
Bespectacled American comedian with long vaudeville experience; his flustered gestures often characterized inept crooks, commercial travellers, or Justices of the Peace.
Second Youth 24. Summer Bachelors 29. Why Leave Home? 29. Palmy Days 31. Rain 32. Mama Loves Papa 33. The Captain Hates the Sea 34. Mr Deeds Goes to Town 36. On the Avenue 37. *Bringing Up Baby* 38. Pop Always Pays 40. Horror Island 41. Yankee Doodle Dandy 42. They Got Me Covered 43. Ghost Catchers 44. I'll Be Yours 47. *Look for the Silver Lining* 49. Here Comes the Groom 51. Father Takes the Air 51. Friendly Persuasion 56, many others.

Caton-Jones, Michael (1958–).
Scottish-born director, now working in Hollywood.
Scandal 89. Memphis Belle 90. Doc Hollywood 91. This Boy's Life 92. Rob Roy 95. The Jackal 97. Trinity (TV) 98, etc.
❝ When I'm shooting I become a monstrous exhibitionist egomaniac. It's quite weird, because you have to play the role of being a director. It's not necessarily because that's what you believe in, but it's what other people want out of you. I kind of debunk the whole thing by mincing around with a riding crop and whacking people with it and barking orders. – M.C-J.
Hollywood really is an industry about making money, not making films. – M.C-J.

Cattaneo, Peter (c. 1964–).
English director, from television. *The Full Monty* is the most commercially successful film so far shown in the UK, taking more than $167.2m at the box-office worldwide.
Dear Rosie (short) (AAN) 90. Loved Up (TV) 95. *The Full Monty* 97, etc.

Catto, Max (1907–1992).
Popular British adventure novelist.
Daughter of Darkness (oa) 48. A Prize of Gold (oa) 54. West of Zanzibar (w) 54. Trapeze (oa) 56. Seven Thieves (oa) 60. The Devil at Four o'Clock (oa) 61. Mister Moses (oa) 65. Murphy's War 71, etc.

Cattrall, Kim (1956–).
British-born actress, on stage and screen in Canada and America as well as England. Married actor Daniel Benzali in 1997.
Rosebud 75. Porky's 81. Police Academy 84. City Limits 84. Big Trouble in Little China 86. Mannequin 87. Masquerade 88. Return of the Musketeers 89. Brown Bread Sandwiches 89. Bonfire of the Vanities 90. Star Trek VI: The Undiscovered Country 91. Split Second 92. Tom Clancy's Op Center (TV) 95. The Heidi Chronicles (TV) 95. Unforgettable 96. Where Truth Lies 97, etc.

Caulfield, Joan (1922–1991).
Demure American leading lady of the 40s.
■ Miss Susie Slagle's 46. *Monsieur Beaucaire* 46. *Blue Skies* 46. *Dear Ruth* 47. Welcome Stranger 47. The Unsuspected 47. The Sainted Sisters 48. Larceny 48. Dear Wife 50. The Petty Girl 50. The Lady Says No 51. The Rains of Ranchipur 55. Cattle King 63. Red Tomahawk 66. Buckskin 68.
TV series: My Favorite Husband 53. Sally 57.

Caulfield, Maxwell (1959–).
British leading actor in Hollywood. Married actress Juliet Mills.
Grease 2 82. Electric Dreams 84. The Boys Next Door 85. The Supernaturals 86. Sundown 88. Mind Games 89. Fatal Sky 90. Exiled 91. Animal Instincts 92. Alien Intruder 93. Gettysburg 93. Inevitable Grace 94. Empire Records 95. Prey of the Jaguar 96. The Real Blonde 97, etc.

Cavalcanti, Alberto (1897–1982).
Brazilian director who made interesting films in several countries but never quite achieved a masterpiece.
Rien que les Heures 26. En Rade 27. Sea Fever 29. North Sea 38. Men of the Lightship 41. *Went the Day Well?* 42. Champagne Charlie 45. Dead of Night (part) 45. *Nicholas Nickleby* 47. They Made Me a Fugitive 47. The First Gentleman 48. For Them that Trespass 49. O Canto do Mar (Braz.) 53. Herr Puntila (Ger.) 55. La Prima Notte (It.) 58. Yerma (It.) 62, etc.

Cavanagh, Paul (1895–1964).
Suave British actor who went to Hollywood in the 20s and spent the rest of his career playing elegant villains, understanding husbands, and murder victims. Born in Chislehurst, Kent, he was educated at Cambridge University and was a barrister before turning to the stage, making his debut in 1924.
The Runaway Princess 29. Grumpy 30. The Devil to Pay 30. The Squaw Man 31. The Devil's Lottery 32. A Bill of Divorcement 32. The Kennel Murder Case 33. Tarzan and his Mate 34. *The Notorious Sophie Lang* 34. *Goin' to Town* (opposite Mae West) 35. Champagne Charlie 36. Romance in Flanders 37. Crime over London 38. Reno 39. The Case of the Black Parrot 40. Maisie was a Lady 41. The Strange Case of Dr RX 42. The Hard Way 43. The Scarlet Claw 44. The Man in Half Moon Street 44. House of Fear 45. The Verdict 46. Humoresque 46. Ivy 47. You Gotta Stay Happy 48. The Iroquois Trail 50. House of Wax 53. Casanova's Big Night 54. The Purple Mask 55. Francis in the Haunted House 56. Diane 57. The Four Skulls of Jonathan Drake 59, many others.

Cavanaugh, Hobart (1886–1950).
Mild-mannered, bald and bespectacled American character actor usually seen as clerk, nervous husband or frightened caretaker.
San Francisco Nights 27. I Cover the Waterfront 33. Convention City 33. Housewife 34. I Sell Anything 34. Don't Bet on Blondes 35. A Midsummer Night's Dream 35. Stage Struck 36. Cain and Mabel 36. Reported Missing 37. *Rose of Washington Square* (as a double act with Al Jolson) 39. An Angel from Texas 40. Meet the Chump 41. Horror Island (as the villain) 41. The Magnificent Dope 42. Sweet Rosie O'Grady 43. Kismet 44. Black Angel 46. You Gotta Stay Happy 48. Stella 50, many others.

Cavani, Liliana (1937–).
Italian director.
■ Night Encounter 61. Philip Pétain 64. Francis of Assisi 66. Galileo 68. The Cannibals 69. The Hospital 71. The Night Porter 74. Beyond Evil 77. The Berlin Affair 85. St Francis of Assisi 89. Dove Sietea? Io Sono Qui 93.

Cave, Nick (1960–).
Australian composer, musician, singer and actor. He also wrote and has performed at London's National Film Theatre a score to accompany Dreyer's silent *The Passion of Joan of Arc*.
Wings of Desire (co-m) 87. Ghosts . . . of the Civil Dead (a, co-w, co-m) 89. Johnny Suede (a) 92. Batman Forever (m) 95. To Have and to Hold (m) 96, etc.

Cawthorn, Joseph (1868–1949).
American character actor of the 30s.
Very Confidential 27. Silk Legs 28. Jazz Heaven 29. The Taming of the Shrew 29. Dixiana 30. Kiki 31. White Zombie 32. Love me Tonight 32. Whistling in the Dark 33. Housewife 34. The Last Gentleman 34. Go into Your Dance 35. Naughty Marietta 35. The Great Ziegfeld 36. Lillian Russell 40. The Postman Didn't Ring 42, many others.

Cayatte, André (1909–1989).
French lawyer who became writer-director of films with something to say.
Justice Est Faite 50. *Nous Sommes Tous des Assassins* 52. An Eye for an Eye 56. The Mirror Has Two Faces 57. The Crossing of the Rhine 60. La Vie Conjugale 63. A Trap for Cinderella 65. Die of Loving 70, etc.

Cazale, John (1936–1978).
American character actor. Died of cancer.
The Godfather 72. The Conversation 74. The Godfather Part II 74. *Dog Day Afternoon* 75. *The Deer Hunter* 78, etc.

Cazenove, Christopher (1945–).
British leading man, mostly on TV.
Royal Flash 74. East of Elephant Rock 75. Zulu Dawn 79. From a Far Country 80. Eye of the Needle 81. The Letter (TV) 81. Heat and Dust 82. Jenny's War (TV) 84. Mata Hari 85. Lace II (TV) 85. The Fantasist 87. Souvenir 88. Three Men and a Little Lady 90. Hold My Hand, I'm Dying 90. Aces: Iron Eagle 3 92. The Proprietor 96, etc.
TV series: Dynasty 86–88. A Fine Romance 89.

Cecchi d'Amico, Suso (1914–) (Giovanna Cecchi d'Amico).
Italian screenwriter.
Vivere in Pace 46. Bicycle Thieves 49. Miracle in Milan 51. Bellissima 51. Le Amiche 55. Rocco and His Brothers 60. Salvatore Giuliano 61. The Leopard 63. Casanova 70 65. The Stranger 67. Brother Sun, Sister Moon 72. Ludwig 73. La Storia 86. Stradivari 89. The Dark Illness/Il Male Oscuro 89. Parenti e Serpenti 92. La Fine E'Nota 93. Cari Fottutissimi Amici 94. Looking for Paradise 95. Scirocco (co-w) 98, many others.

Cecil, Henry (1902–1976).
British novelist, a county court judge who poked fun at the vagaries of the British legal system in a series of amusing but rather overstretched books, of which *Brothers in Law* was successfully filmed.

Cecil, Jonathan (1939–).
British light comic actor usually seen as gangling ineffective types.
The Yellow Rolls-Royce 64. Otley 68. The Private Life of Sherlock Holmes 70. Barry Lyndon 75. Rising Damp 80. History of the World Part One 81. Dead Man's Folly (TV) 85. Second Victory 86. Murder in Three Acts (TV) 86. Little Dorrit 87. Tchin-Tchin 91, etc.

Cedrón, Jorge (1946–1980).
Argentinian director and occasional actor who studied film at the University of La Plata and worked in Brazil. After the military coup in Argentina in 1976, he went into exile in Paris, leaving a film unfinished. His *Operación Masacre*, written by Rodolfo Walsh from his book on the execution of Peronist officers in 1956, had terrible consequences: Julio Troxler, one of its cast, was killed by a right-wing paramilitary group and Walsh 'disappeared' and was never heard of again; Cedrón died of a gunshot wound, murdered by

agents of the military junta according to his associates, though the police decided he had committed suicide.
El Habilitado 71. Por los Senderos del Libertador 71. *Operación Masacre* 72, etc.

Celi, Adolfo (1922–1986).
Solidly-built Italian character actor who followed a Brazilian stage career by playing villains in international films.
Escape into Dreams 50. *That Man from Rio* 64. Von Ryan's Express 65. *Thunderball* 65. El Greco 66. Grand Prix 67. The Honey Pot 67. The Bobo 67. Grand Slam 68. Fragment of Fear 70. Murders in the Rue Morgue 71. Hitler – The Last Ten Days 73. And Then There Were None 75. The Next Man 76. Sandokan 77. Cafe Express 79. The Borgias (TV) 82, etc.

Cellier, Frank (1884–1948).
British stage actor who seemed to frown a lot and usually played unsympathetic types.
Soldiers of the King 33. The 39 Steps 35. Rhodes of Africa 36. Tudor Rose 36. Non Stop New York 37. Sixty Glorious Years 38. The Ware Case 39. Quiet Wedding 40. Love on the Dole 41. Give Us the Moon 44. Quiet Weekend 46. The Blind Goddess 48, etc.

Cervantes, Miguel de (1547–1616).
Spanish novelist whose *Don Quixote* has been much filmed.

Cervi, Gino (1901–1974).
Stocky Italian character actor.
Frontier 34. An Ideal Marriage 39. Four Steps in the Clouds 42. Fabiola 47. Furia 48. *The Little World of Don Camillo* (as the mayor) 51. OK Nero 52. Three Forbidden Stories 53. Indiscretion 53. Maddalena 53. The Return of Don Camillo 54. Wife for a Night 55. The Naked Maja 59. Wild Love 60. The Revolt of the Slaves 61. Becket 64, many others.

Chabrol, Claude (1930–).
Variable but generally distinguished French director, credited with starting the *nouvelle vague*. His second wife was Stephane Audran.
■ *Le Beau Serge* 58. Les Cousins 59. A Double Tour 59. Les Bonnes Femmes 60. Les Godelureaux 60. The Third Lover 61. The Seven Deadly Sins (part) 61. Les Plus Belles Escroqueries du Monde (part) 61. Ophelia 62. Landru 62. Paris vu Par (part) 64. Le Tigre se Parfume à la Dynamite 64. Le Tigre Aime la Chair Fraîche 65. Marie Chantal 65. Line of Demarcation 66. The Champagne Murders 67. The Road to Corinth 68. *Les Biches* 68. La Femme Infidèle 69. *The Beast Must Die* 69. La Rupture 70. *The Butcher* 70. Just Before Nightfall 71. La Décade Prodigieuse 71. Blood Wedding 71. Ten Days' Wonder 72. The Wolf Trap 72. Scoundrel in White 72. Ophelia 73. Nada 73. Innocents with Dirty Hands 73. Une Partie de Plaisir 73. Les Magiciens 73. Le Banc de la Désolation 74. Folies Bourgeoises 77. Alice 77. Violette Nozière 78. Il Etait Un Musicien 78. Fantomas I (TV) 78. Fantomas IV (TV) 78. Monsieur Prokoviev (TV) 78. La Bouche à l'Oreille 78. Les Menteurs 79. Blood Relatives 79. Le Cheval d'Orgueil 80. Les Fantômes du Chapelier 81. Le Sang des Autres 83. Cop au Vin 84. Inspector Lavardin 86. Le Cri du Hibou 87. Masques 87. Story of Women/Une Affaire de Femmes 88. Docteur M. 89. Quiet Days in Clichy/Jours Tranquilles à Clichy 90. Madame Bovary 91. Sam Suffit (a) 91. Betty 92. Hell/L'Enfer 94. A Judgement in Stone/ La Cérémonie 95. Rien Ne Vas Plus (wd) 97.

Chaffey, Don (1917–1990).
British director; started in art department at Gainsborough in the early 40s.
Time is My Enemy 53. The Girl in the Picture 56. The Flesh is Weak 57. A Question of Adultery 58. *The Man Upstairs* 59. Danger Within 59. Dentist in the Chair 60. Nearly a Nasty Accident 60. Greyfriars Bobby 61. A Matter of Who 61. The Prince and the Pauper 62. *Jason and the Argonauts* 63. A Jolly Bad Fellow 64. One Million Years BC 66. The Viking Queen 67. A Twist of Sand 68. Creatures the World Forgot 71. Persecution 73. Pete's Dragon 77. The Gift of Love (TV) 78. The Magic of Lassie 78. C.H.O.M.P.S. 79. Lassie; the New Beginning (TV) 79. Strike Force (TV) 79. Hollywood Beat (TV) 84. International Airport (TV) 85, etc.

Chagrin, Francis (1905–1972).
Russian-born composer in films (mostly British) from 1934; composed over 200 scores.
Behind the Guns 40. Helter Skelter 49. Last Holiday 50. Castle in the Air 52. The Happy Family 52. The Intruder 53. The Beachcomber 54. An Inspector Calls 54. The Colditz Story 54. Simba 55. Charley Moon 56. No Time for Tears 57. The Scamp 57. Danger Within 58. The Snorkel 58. Clue of the Twisted Candle 60. The Man Who Was Nobody 60. Marriage of Convenience 60. Greyfriars Bobby 61. In the Cool of the Day 62, etc.

Chahine, Youssef (1926–).
Egyptian director. He studied acting in America and gave Omar Sharif his start in movies. Following a heart attack in the 70s, he turned to directing an autobiographical trilogy that began with *Alexandria . . . Why?*
Father Amine/Baba Amine 50. The Nile's Son/ Ibn el Nil 51. Struggle in the Valley/Sera'a fil Wadi 53. Struggle on the Pier/Sera'a fil Mina 55. Cairo Station/Bab el Haded 58. Saladin/El Naser Salah el Dine 64. The Land/El Ard 69. The Sparrow/Al Asfour 73. Alexandria . . . Why?/ Iskendria . . . Leh? 78. An Egyptian Story/Hadota Misreya 82. Alexandria, More and More/Iskendria Kaman Wakaman 89. Alexandria Now and Forever/Alexandrie Encore et Toujours 90. The Emigrant/Al Mohager 94. Destiny/Al Massir (AAN) 97, etc.

Chakiris, George (1933–).
American dancer (from the chorus) and leading man; his star blazed for a while in the early 60s.
Brigadoon 54. Two and Two Make Six (GB) 60. *West Side Story* (AA) 61. Diamond Head 63. Kings of the Sun 63. Flight from Ashiya 64. 633 Squadron 64. The High Bright Sun (GB) 65. Is Paris Burning? 66. The Young Girls of Rochefort 67. The Big Cube 69. Return to Fantasy Island (TV) 78. Why Not Stay for Breakfast (GB) 80. Pale Blood 91, etc.

Chaliapin, Feodor (1873–1938).
Russian opera singer who appeared in two films and was played by Ezio Pinza in *Tonight We Sing*.
■ Pskovityanka 15. *Don Quixote* 33.

Challis, Christopher (1919–).
Distinguished British cinematographer.
■ Theirs is the Glory 46. End of the River 47. *The Small Back Room* 48. Tales of Hoffman 50. Gone to Earth 50. The Elusive Pimpernel 52. *Genevieve* 53. Angels One Five 53. 24 Hours in a Woman's Life 53. Saadia 54. The Story of Gilbert and Sullivan 54. Twice Upon a Time 54. Malaga 54. The Flame and the Flesh 54. Oh Rosalinda 55. Quentin Durward 55. Raising a Riot 55. The Battle of the River Plate 56. Footsteps in the Fog 56. Ill Met By Moonlight 56. The Spanish Gardener 56. Miracle in Soho 56. Windom's Way 56. Floods of Fear 57. Rooney 57. Sink the Bismarck 60. The Grass is Greener 61. Surprise Package 61. The Captain's Table 62. Never Let Go 62. Blind Date 62. Flame in the Streets 63. HMS Defiant 64. Five Golden Hours 64. The Long Ships 64. Those Magnificent Men in Their Flying Machines 64. The Americanization of Emily 64. *The Victors* 65. A Shot in the Dark 65. Return from the Ashes 65. *Arabesque* 66. Two for the Road 67. Kaleidoscope 67. A Dandy in Aspic 68. Chitty Chitty Bang Bang 69. Staircase 69. The Private Life of Sherlock Holmes 71. Villain 71. Catch Me a Spy 71. Mary Queen of Scots 72. Follow Me 72. The Boy Who Turned Yellow 72. The Little Prince 74. Mister Quilp 75. The Incredible Sarah 76. The Deep 77. Force Ten From Navarone 78. The Riddle of the Sands 79. The Mirror Crack'd 80. Evil Under the Sun 81. Top Secret 84. Secrets 84. Steaming 84.

Chamberlain, Cyril (1909–1974).
British small-part player often seen as average man, policeman or dull husband.
This Man in Paris 39. Old Mother Riley in Business 40. The Black Sheep of Whitehall 41. The Upturned Glass 47. Quartet 48. The Chiltern Hundreds/The Amazing Mr Beecham 49. Stage Fright 50. The Lavender Hill Mob 51. Hell below Zero 53. Trouble in Store 53. Doctor in the House 54. Simon and Laura 55. Above Us the Waves 55. Doctor at Sea 55. The Green Man 56. Doctor at Large 57. The Duke Wore Jeans 58. A Night to Remember 58. Blue Murder at St Trinian's 58. Carry On Sergeant 58. Carry On Nurse 59. Carry On Teacher 59. The Bulldog Breed 60. Carry On Constable 60. Two-Way Stretch 60. Doctor in Love 60. Pure Hell of St Trinian's 61. Carry On Regardless 61. Dentist on the Job 61. Carry On Cruising 62. The Iron Maiden 62. Carry On Cabby 63. Two Left Feet 63. Carry On Spying 64. The Yellow Hat 66. The Great St Trinian's Train Robbery 66, many others.

Chamberlain, Richard (1935–).
Boyish-looking American leading man who used his success in a TV series to establish himself as a serious international actor.
■ The Secret of the Purple Reef 60. A Thunder of Drums 62. Twilight of Honor 63. Joy in the Morning 65. Petulia 68. The Madwoman of Chaillot 69. Julius Caesar 70. *The Music Lovers* (as Tchaikovsky) 70. *Lady Caroline Lamb* (as Byron) 72. The Last of the Belles (TV) 74. The Three Musketeers 74. The Towering Inferno 75. *The Slipper and the Rose* 76. The Count of Monte Cristo (TV) 76. The Man in the Iron Mask (TV) 77. The Last Wave 78. Swarm 78. Shogun (TV) 80. Murder by Phone 82. *The Thorn Birds* (TV) 83. King Solomon's Mines 85. Raoul Wallenberg. Lost Hero (TV) 85. Allan Quatermain and the Lost City of Gold 86. The Bourne Identity (TV) 88. The Return of the Musketeers 89. Night of the Hunter (TV) 91. Aftermath 91. Bird of Prey 95. The Thorn Birds: The Missing Years (TV) 96.
TV series: *Dr Kildare* 61–66.

Champion.
The name given to Gene Autry's steed, known as the 'World's Wonder Horse'. There were three of them: the first Champion was in films in the 30s; the second and third, who were father and son, were in films of the 40s and early 50s. They also appeared on the TV series *The Gene Autry Show* 47–54, and in the children's TV series Autry produced, *The Adventures of Champion/Champion the Wonder Horse*, 55–56.

Champion, Gower (1919–1980).
American dancer who appeared with his then wife Marge in several musicals of the early 50s; later turned director.
Till the Clouds Roll By (solo) 46. Mr Music 50. *Show Boat* 51. Lovely to Look At 52. Give a Girl a Break 53. Jupiter's Darling 55. Three for the Show 55. My Six Loves (d) 63. Bank Shot (d) 74, etc.

Champion, Gregg.
American director.
Short Time 90. The Cowboy Way 94.

Champion, Marge (1923–) (Marjorie Belcher).
American dancer who teamed with her then husband Gower Champion. Solo appearances include *The Story of Vernon and Irene Castle* 39; later appeared as character actress. She was the model for Snow White in Disney's animated feature, and for the Blue Fairy in Disney's *Pinocchio*.
The Swimmer 67. The Party 68.

Chan, Jackie (1954–) (Chan Kwong Sang).
Hong Kong actor, director and writer of martial arts movies who has appeared in more than 100 films. Trained in classical Chinese theatre, he first worked as a stuntman and still does his own stunts, suffering many injuries as a result.
Autobiography: 1998, *I Am Jackie Chan: My Life in Action* (with Jeff Yang).
Biography: 1998, *Jackie Chan: Inside the Dragon* by Clyde Gentry III.
Eagle Shadow Fist 71. Fists of Fury (& d) 73. Dragon Fist 78. Fantasy Mission Force 78. Half a Loaf of King-Fu 78. The Fearless Hyena (& d) 79. Young Master (& d) 79. Dragon Lord 82. Project A 83. Police Story (& d) 85. The Fearless Hyena Part II (& d) 86. The Armour of God (& d) 86. Project A Part II 87. The Brothers 87. Police Story – Part II 88. Miracle/Keitsik 89. Police Story 3: Supercop 93. Drunken Master II/Tsui Kun II 94. Rumble in the Bronx 95. Thunderbolt 96. First Strike 96. Mr Nice Guy 98. *Rush Hour* (US) 98, many others.
❝ The story is very simple in every Jackie Chan movie. I'm the good guy; then there's the bad guy. – J.C.
What is a bad movie? Nobody sees it, that's a bad movie. – J.C.
The Buster Keaton of Hong Kong. – *Movieline magazine*

Chan, Michael Paul.
American character actor.
Thief 81. The Goonies 85. Thousand Pieces of Gold 90. Rapid Fire 92. Falling Down 93. Heaven and Earth 93. Maverick 94, etc.

Chan, Patrick.
Hong Kong film director.
He's a Woman, She's a Man 96. Who's the Woman, Who's the Man? 96.

Chance, Naomi (1930–).
Stylish British leading lady who appeared sporadically in the 50s.
Dangerous Voyage 53. The Saint's Return 54. Operation Bullshine 59. The Trials of Oscar Wilde 60, etc.

Chancellor, Anna (1964–).
English actress.
Four Weddings and a Funeral 94. Princess Caraboo 94. Tom and Viv 94. Staggered 94. Pride and Prejudice (TV) 95. Karaoke (TV) 96. The Man Who Knew Too Little 97, etc.
TV series: Kavanagh QC 95– .

Chandler, Chick (1905–1988).
Wiry American hero or second lead of many a second feature in the 30s and 40s.
Melody Cruise 33. Murder on a Honeymoon 35. Woman Wise 36. Born Reckless 37. Alexander's Ragtime Band 38. Time Out for Murder 38. Hotel for Women 39. Hollywood Cavalcade 39. Honeymoon Deferred 40. Cadet Girl 41. Hot Spot 41. The Big Shot 42. He Hired the Boss 43. Irish Eyes are Smiling 44. Seven Doors to Death 44. The Chicago Kid 45. Do You Love Me? 46. Lost Continent 47. Family Honeymoon 49. The Great Rupert 50. Aaron Slick from Punkin Crick 52. Battle Cry 55. The Naked Gun 58. It's a Mad Mad Mad Mad World 63, many others.
TV series: Soldiers of Fortune 55.

Chandler, George (1899–1985).
American character actor, an ex-vaudevillian who specialized in sly or comically nervous roles.
The Light of Western Stars 30. Blessed Event 32. Hi Nellie 34. Fury 36. Three Men on a Horse 36. Nothing Sacred 37. Jesse James 39. Arizona 41. *Roxie Hart* 42. It Happened Tomorrow 44. This Man's Navy 45. Dead Reckoning 47. Kansas Raiders 50. Hans Christian Andersen 52. The High and the Mighty 54. Spring Reunion 57. Dead Ringer 64. One More Time 71, many others.

Chandler, Helen (1906–1965).
American leading lady of the 30s: her early retirement through personal problems robbed Hollywood of an interesting personality. Her husbands included screenwriter and novelist Cyril Hume and actor Bramwell Fletcher.
■ The Music Master 27. Joy Girl 27. Mother's Boy 29. Salute 29. The Sky Hawk 29. A Rough Romance 30. Outward Bound 30. Mother's Cry 30. *Dracula* 31. Daybreak 31. *The Last Flight* 31. Salvation Nell 31. Fanny Foley Herself 31. A House Divided 32. Vanity Street 32. Behind Jury Doors 32. Christopher Strong 33. Alimony Madness 33. Dance Hall Hostess 33. Goodbye Again 33. The Worst Woman in Paris 33. Long Lost Father 34. Midnight Alibi 34. Unfinished Symphony (GB) 35. It's a Bet (GB) 35. Radio Parade (GB) 35. Mr Boggs Steps Out (GB) 37.

Chandler, Jeff (1918–1961) (Ira Grossel).
American leading man with the unusual attraction of prematurely grey hair; carved a solid niche for himself by playing an Indian, but his films seldom rose above co-feature level. Died of blood poisoning following surgery.
■ Johnny O'Clock 47. Invisible Wall 47. Roses are Red 47. Mr Belvedere Goes to College 49. Sword in the Desert 49. Abandoned 49. *Broken Arrow* (as Cochise) (AAN) 50. Two Flags West 50. Deported 50. Bird of Paradise 51. Smuggler's Island 51. Iron Man 51. Flame of Araby 51. The Battle at Apache Pass 52. Yankee Buccaneer 52. Red Ball Express 52. Because of You 52. The Great Sioux Uprising 53. East of Sumatra 53. Yankee Pasha 54. War Arrow 54. Sign of the Pagan 54. Foxfire 55. The Female on the Beach 55. The Spoilers 55. Toy Tiger 55. Away all Boats 56. Pillars of the Sky 56. Drango 57. The Tattered Dress 57. *Jeanne Eagels* 57. Man in the Shadow 57. The Lady Takes a Flyer 58. Raw Wind in Eden 58. Stranger in my Arms 59. Thunder in the Sun

59. Ten Seconds to Hell 59. The Jayhawkers 59. The Plunderers 60. A Story of David (TV) 60. Return to Peyton Place 61. Merrill's Marauders 61.

Chandler, Joan (1923–1979).
American leading lady, briefly featured in the 40s.
Humoresque 47. The Street with No Name 48. Rope 48, etc.

Chandler, John Davis (1937–).
American character actor, in tough roles.
Mad Dog Coll (title role) 60. The Young Savages 61. Ride the High Country 62. Major Dundee 64. Once a Thief 64. Return of the Gunfighter 66. Barquero 70. Pat Garrett and Billy the Kid 73. The Outlaw Josey Wales 76. Adventures in Babysitting 87. Body of Evidence 92, etc.

Chandler, Lane (1899–1972) (Robert Oakes).
American western character actor.
Open Range 27. Texas Tornado 34. Two Gun Justice 38. Sundown Jim 42. Northwest Stampede 48. Montana 50. Requiem for a Gunfighter 65, many others.

Chandler, Raymond (1888–1959).
American crime novelist to whom literary acclaim came late in life. Several films and a TV series were based on the exploits of his cynical but incorruptible private eye Philip Marlowe. Born in Chicago, he was educated in England and worked in various occupations, turning to writing after being sacked for alcoholism from well-paid employment in the oil industry. He went to Hollywood in 1943.
Biographies: 1976, *The Life of Raymond Chandler* by Frank McShane; 1982 (revised ed. 1998), *Raymond Chandler in Hollywood* by Al Clark; 1997, *Raymond Chandler* by Tom Hiney.
The Falcon Takes Over (oa) 42. Time to Kill (oa) 42. *Double Indemnity* (co-w, AAN) 44. And Now Tomorrow 44. The Unseen 45. *Murder My Sweet* (oa) 45. *The Big Sleep* (oa) 46. *The Lady in the Lake* (oa) 46. The Blue Dahlia (AANw) 46. The Brasher Doubloon (oa) 47. *Strangers on a Train* (w) 51. Marlowe (oa) 69. The Long Goodbye (oa) 72. Farewell my Lovely (oa) 76. The Big Sleep (oa) 79.
TV series: Philip Marlowe 59.
❝ The making of a motion picture is an endless contention of tawdry egos, almost none of them capable of anything more creative than credit stealing and self promotion. – *R.C.*
Like every writer, or almost every writer who goes to Hollywood, I was convinced in the beginning that there must be some discoverable method of working in pictures, which would not be completely stultifying to whatever creative talent one might happen to possess. But like others before me, I discovered that this was a dream. – *R.C.*
He looked as inconspicuous as a tarantula on a slice of angel food. – *Farewell my Lovely*
The edges of the folded handkerchief in her breast pocket looked sharp enough to slice bread. – *The Lady in the Lake*
She had a lot of face and chin. She had pewter-coloured hair set in a ruthless permanent, a hard beak and large moist eyes with the sympathetic expression of wet stones. There was lace at her throat, but it was the kind of throat that would have looked better in a football sweater. – *The High Window*

Chanel, Coco (1883–1971).
French fashion designer, who also designed costumes for a few films.
Tonight or Never 31. La Marseillaise 38. Rules of the Game/La Règle du Jeu 39. Last Year at Marienbad/L'Année Dernière à Marienbad 61.

Chaney, Lon (1883–1930) (Alonzo Chaney).
American star character actor, known as 'the man of a thousand faces' because of his elaborate disguises in macabre roles; hence the joke, 'Don't step on that spider, it might be Lon Chaney.' Born in Colorado Springs, Colorado, he was on stage from 1901 with his brother's stock company, and in films from 1912, becoming a regular in Universal's films from 1915. He went freelance in 1918 and became a star with *The Miracle Man*. His best-remembered performances were in films directed by Tod Browning. Married twice. Died from throat cancer. He was played by James Cagney in the biopic *Man of a Thousand Faces* 57.
■ Where the Forest Ends 14. The Chimney Sweep 15. The Oyster Dredger 15. The Stool Pigeon 15. Fires of Rebellion 17. Triumph 17. That Devil Bateese 18. Riddle Gawne 18. The Kaiser, Beast of Berlin 18. Paid in Advance 19. The Rap 19. The Unholy Three 19. *The Miracle Man* 19. False Faces 19. Victory 19. The Wolf Breed 19. The Wicked Darling 19. Nomads of the North 19. Treasure Island 20. Daredevil Jack 20. *The Penalty* 21. Outside the Law 21. The Ace of Hearts 21. Bit o' Life 21. For Those We Love 21. The Night Rose 21. The Trap 22. Quincy Adams Sawyer 22. Shadows 22. *A Blind Bargain* 22. Flesh and Blood 22. Voices of the City 22. The Light in the Dark 22. Oliver Twist 22. *The Hunchback of Notre Dame* 23. The Shock 23. All the Brothers were Valiant 23. While Paris Sleeps 23. He Who Gets Slapped 24. The Next Corner 24. *The Phantom of the Opera* 25. The Tower of Lies 25. The Monster 25. *The Unholy Three* 25. The Black Bird 26. The Road to Mandalay 26. Tell it to the Marines 26. Mr Wu 27. The Unknown 27. Mockery 27. *London After Midnight* 27. The Big City 28. Laugh Clown Laugh 28. While the City Sleeps 28. West of Zanzibar 28. The Thunder 29. Where East is East 29. The Unholy Three 30.
✪ For becoming an international household word through his ability to distort his own body and hide it under layers of disguise. *The Phantom of the Opera.*
❝ My whole career has been devoted to keeping people from knowing me. – *L.C.*

Chaney, Lon, Jnr (1906–1973) (Creighton Chaney).
Massive American character actor, who largely followed his father's type of role in progressively inferior films, with many bit parts. In *Man of a Thousand Faces* he was played by Roger Smith.
Bird of Paradise 32. Lucky Devils 33. Sixteen Fathoms Deep 34. The Life of Vergie Winters 35. Accent on Youth 35. Wife, Doctor and Nurse 37. Love and Hisses 37. Charlie Chan on Broadway 37. Road Demon 38. Mr Moto's Gamble 38. Jesse James 39. Frontier Marshal 39. *Of Mice and Men* (his best performance, as Lennie) 39. One Million BC 40. Northwest Mounted Police 40. Man Made Monster 41. *The Wolf Man* 41. North to the Klondike 42. *The Ghost of Frankenstein* (as the monster) 42. The Mummy's Tomb 42. Frankenstein Meets the Wolf Man 43. Son of Dracula 43. Ghost Catchers 44. Weird Woman 44. Dead Man's Eyes 44. House of Frankenstein 45. Strange Confession 45. My Favourite Brunette 47. Sixteen Fathoms Deep 48. *Abbott and Costello Meet Frankenstein* 48. Captain China 49. Once a Thief 50. Behave Yourself 51. High Noon 52. A Lion is in the Streets 53. Casanova's Big Night 54. Not as a Stranger 55. Manfish 56. The Black Sleep 56. Cyclops 57. The Defiant Ones 58. The Alligator People 59. The Haunted Palace 63. Witchcraft 64. Apache Uprising 66. Hillbillies in a Haunted House 67. Buckskin 68, many others.
TV series: *The Last of the Mohicans* (as Chingachgook) 56.

Chaney, Norman 'Chubby' (1918–1936).
American child actor who replaced Joe Cobb as the plump boy in the Our Gang comedies of the mid-20s and early 30s. Died of glandular problems.

Chang-Ho, Bae (1953–).
South Korean director, often causing local controversy.
People in the Slums/Kkobang Dongne Saramdul 82. Whale Hunter/Gorae Sanyan 84. Deep Blue Day/Gipgo Purun Bam 85. Hwang Jin-I 86. Our Sweet Days of Youth 87, etc.

Changwei, Gu (1957–).
Chinese cinematographer. He studied at the Beijing Film Academy and went to work at the Xi'an studios. He has worked on three of director Chen Kaige's films.
The Beach 84. The Magic Braid 86. The King of Children 87. *Red Sorghum* 88. Ju Dou 90. Life on a String 91. *Farewell My Concubine* (AAN) 93, etc.

Channing, Carol (1921–).
Vivacious American cabaret comedienne whose films have been few.
■ Paid in Full 50. The First Travelling Saleslady 56. *Thoroughly Modern Millie* (AAN) 67. Skidoo 69. Shinbone Alley (voice) 71. Thumbelina (voice) 94.
❝ I am terribly shy, but of course no one believes me. Come to think of it, neither would I. – C.C.
She never just enters a room. Even when she comes out of the bathroom, her husband applauds. – *George Burns*

Channing, Stockard (1944–) (Susan Stockard).
Tomboy-type American leading lady, mainly on television.
The Girl Most Likely To (TV) 73. The Fortune 75. Sweet Revenge 76. The Big Bus 76. Lucan 77. The Cheap Detective 78. Grease 78. Silent Victory (TV) 79. The Fish That Saved Pittsburgh 79. Safari 3000 82. Without a Trace 83. Heartburn 86. The Men's Club 86. A Time of Destiny 88. Staying Together 89. Meet the Applegates 90. Married to It 93. Six Degrees of Separation (AAN) 93. David's Mother (TV) 94. Bitter Moon 94. Up Close and Personal 96. Moll Flanders 96. Edie & Penn 96. The First Wives Club 96. An Unexpected Family (TV) 96. The Baby Dance (TV) 98. Practical Magic 98. Twilight 98, etc.

Chapin, Billy (1943–).
American child actor of the 50s.
Cluny Brown 48. Tobor the Great 53. Naked Alibi 54. There's No Business Like Show Business 54. A Man Called Peter 55. Violent Saturday 55. *Night of the Hunter* 55. Tension at Table Rock 56, etc.

Chaplin, Ben (1970–).
British actor, in Hollywood. Raised in Windsor, Berkshire, he studied at the Guildhall School of Drama and first came to notice as Matthew Malone in the TV series *Game On*. Now resident in the USA, he is romantically involved with actress Embeth Davidtz.
Bye Bye Baby (TV) 91. Feast of July 95. The Truth about Cats and Dogs 96. Washington Square 97. The Thin Red Line (US) 98, etc.
TV series: Game On 96.

Chaplin, Sir Charles (1889–1977).
A legendary figure in his own lifetime despite a comparatively limited output, this British pantomimist went to the US in 1910 with Fred Karno's troupe and was invited to join the Keystone company; later also worked for Essanay and Mutual, and these early two-reelers are held by many to be superior to the later, more pretentious features which he produced himself. Honorary AA 1971. A biopic, *Chaplin*, appeared in 1992, directed by Richard Attenborough with Robert Downey Jnr in the title role.
Autobiographical books: 1922, *My Trip Abroad*. 1930, *My Wonderful Visit*. 1964, *My Autobiography*. 1974, *My Life in Pictures*.
Other books: 1951, *The Little Fellow* by Peter Cotes and Thelma Nicklaus. 1952, *The Great Charlie* by Robert Payne. 1961, *Charlie Chaplin* by Theodore Huff. 1966, *My Life with Chaplin* by Lita Grey Chaplin. 1974, *Charlie Chaplin. His Life and Art* by William Dodgson Bowman. 1977, *Sir Charlie* by Edwin P. Hoyt. The best biography is 1985, *Chaplin* by David Robinson. 1997, *Charlie Chaplin and His Times* by Kenneth S. Lynn. 1997, *Tramp: The Life of Charlie Chaplin* by Joyce Milton. 1997, *The Chaplin Encyclopedia* by Glenn Mitchell.
■ SHORTS: Making a Living 14. Kid Auto Races at Venice (in which he first wore the improvised tramp costume in which he later became famous) 14. Mabel's Strange Predicament 14. Between Showers 14. A Film Johnnie 14. Tango Tangle 14. His Favorite Pastime 14. Cruel Cruel Love 14. The Star Boarder 14. Mabel at the Wheel 14. Twenty Minutes of Love 14. The Knockout 14. Tillie's Punctured Romance 14. Caught in a Cabaret 14. Caught in the Rain 14. A Busy Day 14. The Fatal Mallet 14. Her Friend the Bandit 14. Mabel's Busy Day 14. Mabel's Married Life 14. Laughing Gas 14. The Property Man 14. The Face on the Barroom Floor 14. Recreation 14. The Masquerader 14. His New Profession 14. The Rounders 14. The New Janitor 14. These Love Pangs 14. Dough and Dynamite 14. Gentlemen of Nerve 14. His Musical Career 14. His Trysting Place 14. Getting Acquainted 14. His Prehistoric Past 14. His New Job 15. A Night Out 15. The Champion 15. In the Park 15. A Jitney Elopement 15. *The Tramp* 15. By the Sea 15. Work 15. A Woman 15. The Bank 15. Shanghaied 15. A Night in the Show 15. Carmen 16. Police 16. The Floorwalker 16. The Fireman 16. The Vagabond 16. One a.m. 16. The Count 16. *The Pawnshop* 16. Behind the Screen 16. *The Rink* 16. *Easy Street* 17. *The Cure* 17. *The Immigrant* 17. *The Adventurer* 17. Triple Trouble 18. *A Dog's Life* 18. The Bond 18. *Shoulder Arms* (& m) 18. Sunnyside 19. A Day's Pleasure 19. *The Idle Class* 21. Pay Day 22.
■ FEATURES: *The Kid* (& m) 20. The Pilgrim (& m) 23. A Woman of Paris (d only) 23. *The Gold Rush* (& m) 24. *The Circus* (& m) (AA) 28. *City Lights* (& m) 31. *Modern Times* (& m) 36. *The Great Dictator* (AANa, w, score) 40. *Monsieur Verdoux* (& m) 47. *Limelight* (AA score) 52. A King in New York (& m) (GB) 57. A Countess from Hong Kong (& m) (GB) 66.
✪ For combining precision of comedy technique with a sentimental view of the common man which pleased the millions of oppressed and disarmed sophisticated criticism. *Easy Street.*
❝ The son of a bitch is a ballet dancer!
So pronounced W.C. Fields, having been urged to sit through and enjoy a Chaplin movie. Fields promptly realized that the Chaplin brand of comic art was not only more popular than his own, but one which it was impossible for him to emulate. He continued:
He's the best ballet dancer that ever lived, and if I get a good chance I'll strangle him with my bare hands . . .
Many people have been jealous of Chaplin's success, partly because he was never modest about it. His poverty-stricken childhood made him mercenary, and once at the top he displayed a private personality it was difficult to like. Even his friend Mary Pickford called him:
That obstinate, suspicious, egocentric, maddening and lovable genius of a problem child.
And Chaplin had never found a way of making friends with his public. Even in his autobiography he seemed at pains to present himself unsympathetically, as when he recalled telling Mack Sennett:
The public doesn't line up outside the box office when your name appears as they do for mine.
His memories of his manifold romantic activities are tastelessly presented:
Like everyone else's, my sex-life went in cycles. Sometimes I was potent, other times disappointing.
In the more intimate details his phrasing is curious to say the least:
[She was] a big handsome woman of twenty-two, well built, with upper regional domes immensely expansive and made alluring by an extremely low décolleté summer dress which, on the drive home, evoked my libidinous curiosity . . .
His willingness to prognosticate on matters of which he plainly knows little, such as the true authorship of the Shakespeare plays, is often foolhardy:
I can hardly think it was the Stratford boy. Whoever wrote them had an aristocratic personality.
His philosophy is usually naïve, as in his much-attacked defence of murder in *Monsieur Verdoux*:
Wars, conflict, it's all business. One murder makes a villain. Millions, a hero. Numbers sanctify . . .
Determined to make his clown a tragic hero, he is frequently guilty of relentless sentimentality. The opening title of *The Kid* runs:
A picture with a smile and perhaps a tear.
As Hannen Swaffer once said:
His gospel is like Mary Pickford's: the hope of a little child.
Billy Wilder was more caustic:
When he found a voice to say what was on his mind, he was like a child of eight writing lyrics for Beethoven's Ninth.
He frequently over-estimated himself. Of *The Great Dictator* he declared:
I made this picture for the Jews of the world.
He was a poor loser. Having been forced to leave the United States, which made him rich and to which he owed a large amount in back taxes, he stated:
I have no further use for America. I wouldn't go back there if Jesus Christ was President.
Over the years he had alternately denied and proclaimed his Jewishness. This was a typical announcement of the late 40s:
I am not a Jew! I am a citizen of the world! I am not a communist! I am a peacemonger!
A rather limited attitude is struck in his remark about Negroes:
They have suffered too much ever to be funny to me.
(Yet Chaplin's own comedy derives from poverty and deprivation.) He took credit for every aspect

of his films, and frequently denied it to those who helped him most. Yet he was not an inventive director:

I am the unusual and do not need camera angles.

Cinematographer Karl Struss said of him:

He has no knowledge of camera direction. His films are completely theatre.

Yet there is no denying that Chaplin managed very well by feeding his own self-importance. He used to say:

You have to believe in yourself, that's the secret.

And as late as 1960:

I remain one thing and one thing only, and that is a clown. It places me on a far higher plane than any politician.

In a sense he was right. Despite all Chaplin's failings, his tramp is an archetypal creation which strikes a chord in everybody and will live as long as films can be preserved. Chaplin always knew the virtue of simplicity:

All I need to make a comedy is a park, a policeman and a pretty girl.

That was in 1916, and ambition soon overtook him. Colleen Moore in her autobiography *Silent Star* tells that in 1922 a producer was contemplating a life of Christ, and Chaplin demanded audience and became very excited:

I want to play the role of Jesus. I'm a logical choice. I look the part. I'm a Jew. And I'm a comedian . . . And I'm an atheist, so I'd be able to look at the character objectively . . .

The funny thing is, he was very likely right. But Andrew Sarris saw the other side of his psyche:

He will die as he has lived, an unregenerate classicist who believes in making movies he can feel in his frayed lace valentine heart.

While nobody denied his business acumen, least of all Sam Goldwyn:

Chaplin is no business man – all he knows is that he can't take anything less.

And Douglas Fairbanks in 1925 saw the emotional force of his screen personality:

He shows one inadequate man struggling against all the forces of nature.

Chaplin's essential trouble was that he could never take advice. That he needed it was shown by his remark during pre-production of the truly awful *A Countess from Hong Kong*:

A millionaire falling in love with a prostitute. What better story could they want than that?

Chaplin, Geraldine (1944–).
Actress daughter of Charles CHAPLIN.
Doctor Zhivago 65. A Countess from Hong Kong 66. Stranger in the House 67. Peppermint Frappé (Sp.) 67. I Killed Rasputin 68. Honeycomb (Sp.) 69. The Hawaiians 70. Zero Population Growth 72. Innocent Bystanders 72. The Three Musketeers 74. *Nashville* 75. Buffalo Bill and the Indians 76. Roseland 77. Welcome to L.A. 77. Cria! 77. The Word (TV) 78. Remember My Name 78. The Mirror Crack'd 80. Les Uns et les Autres 80. Voyage en Douce 81. Life is a Novel 81. Bolero 82. Love on the Ground 83. Buried Alive 84. Gentille Alouette 85. White Mischief 87. The Moderns 88. Je Veux Rentrer à la Maison 89. Return of the Musketeers 89. The Children 90. Buster's Bedroom 91. The Milky Way/La Via Lactea 92. Chaplin 92. A Foreign Field (TV) 93. The Age of Innocence 93. Words upon the Window Pane 94. Home for the Holidays 95. Gulliver's Travels (TV) 96. Jane Eyre 96. The Odyssey (TV) 97. To Walk with Lions 98, etc.

Chaplin, Saul (1912–1997) (Saul Kaplan).
American song-writer, arranger and producer.
Rookies on Parade (c) 41. Time Out for Rhythm (c) 41. *An American in Paris* (arr) (AA) 51. *Seven Brides for Seven Brothers* (arr) (AA) 54. Can Can (p) 59. *West Side Story* (p) (AA) 61. *The Sound of Music* (p) 65. Star! (p) 68. That's Entertainment, Part Two (p) 76, etc.

Chaplin, Syd (1885–1965).
British comedian, elder brother of Charles CHAPLIN; popular internationally in the 20s.
A Submarine Pirate 15. Shoulder Arms 18. King Queen Joker 21. Her Temporary Husband 23. The Perfect Flapper 24. Charley's Aunt 25. Oh What a Nurse 26. The Better 'Ole 27. The Missing Link 27. A Little Bit of Fluff 28, etc.

Chaplin, Sydney (1926–).
Actor son of Charles CHAPLIN; has not achieved the distinction of which he seems capable.
Limelight 52. Confession 55. Land of the Pharaohs 55. Four Girls in Town 56. Quantez 57. Follow that Man 61. A Countess from Hong Kong 66. The Sicilian Clan 70, etc.

Chapman, Constance (1912–).
English character actress, much on radio and television. Born in Weston-super-Mare, she trained as a broadcaster and was on-stage from 1938.
The Raging Moon 70. Say Hello to Yesterday 70. A Day in the Death of Joe Egg 72. In Celebration 74. Hedda 75. The Three Hostages 77. Our Winnie (TV) 82. Clockwise 85. Run for the Lifeboat (TV) 88. Cider with Rosie (TV) 98, etc.
TV series: Born and Bred 78–80. Never Say Die 87. News at Twelve 88.

Chapman, Eddie (1914–1997).
English secret agent and professional criminal. He was played by Christopher PLUMMER in the film *Triple Cross*, based on the biography *The Eddie Chapman Story*, about his life as a spy for both England and Germany during the Second World War. After the war he returned for a time to his old occupation as an expert safe-breaker.

Chapman, Edward (1901–1977).
British character actor of solid dependable types, corrupt aldermen and northern millowners.
Juno and the Paycock 29. Murder 30. The Skin Game 31. *Things to Come* 36. Rembrandt 36. The Man Who Could Work Miracles 37. The Citadel 38. The Proud Valley 39. The Briggs Family 40. They Flew Alone 42. Ships with Wings 42. *The October Man* 47. *It Always Rains on Sunday* 47. Mr Perrin and Mr Traill 49. *The Card* 52. Folly to be Wise 53. A Day to Remember 54. His Excellency 55. School for Scoundrels 60. Oscar Wilde (as Queensberry) 60. A Stitch in Time 63. Joey Boy 64, many others.

Chapman, Graham (1941–1989).
British character comedian, a member of the Monty Python group who also had a go on his own. Died of cancer.
The Odd Job 78. Yellowbeard 83.

Chapman, Lonny (1920–).
American character actor.
Young at Heart 54. Baby Doll 57. The Birds 63. The Reivers 69. The Cowboys 71. Where the Red Fern Grows 74. Moving Violation 76. Norma Rae 79. Running Scared 80. When Time Ran Out 80. The Border 82. 52 Pick-Up 86. The China Lake Murders (TV) 90. The Rape of Doctor Willis (TV) 91. Nightwatch 98, etc.

Chapman, Marguerite (1916–).
Dependable American heroine of many 40s co-features.
Charlie Chan at the Wax Museum 40. The Body Disappears 41. Parachute Nurse 42. Destroyer 43. My Kingdom for a Cook 43. Pardon My Past 45. The Walls Came Tumbling Down 46. Mr District Attorney 47. Coroner Creek 48. Kansas Raiders 50. Man Bait 51. Flight to Mars 51. The Seven Year Itch 55. The Amazing Transparent Man 61, etc.

Chapman, Matthew (1950–).
American screenwriter and director.
Hussy (wd) 80. Stranger's Kiss (wd) 84. Slow Burn (wd) (TV) 86. Heart of Midnight (wd) 89. Consenting Adults (w) 92. Color of Night (co-w) 94, etc.

Chapman, Michael (1935–).
American cinematographer. Married writer-director Amy HOLDEN-JONES.
The Last Detail 73. The White Dawn 73. Taxi Driver 76. The Front 76. Fingers 78. Invasion of the Body Snatchers 78. The Last Waltz 78. Hardcore 79. The Wanderers 79. *Raging Bull* (AAN) 80. Personal Best 82. Dead Men Don't Wear Plaid 82. The Lost Boys 87. Shoot to Kill 88. Scrooged 88. Ghostbusters II 89. Quick Change 90. Kindergarten Cop 90. Rising Sun 93. The Fugitive (AAN) 93. Primal Fear 96. Space Jam 96. Six Days, Seven Nights 98, etc.

Chappele, David (1973–).
American actor and comedian.
Undercover Blues 93. Robin Hood: Men in Tights 93. The Nutty Professor 96. Joe's Apartment 96. The Real Blonde 97. Damn Whitey 97. Con Air 97, etc.
TV series: Buddies 96.

Charisse, Cyd (1922–) (Tula Ellice Finklea).
Stylish, long-legged American dancer and heroine of MGM musical dramas of the 50s.
Autobiography: 1976, *The Two of Us* (with Tony Martin, her husband).
■ Mission to Moscow 43. Something to Shout About 43. Ziegfeld Follies 45. The Harvey Girls 46. Three Wise Fools 46. Till the Clouds Roll By 46. Fiesta 47. *The Unfinished Dance* 47. On an Island with You 48. Words and Music 48. The Kissing Bandit 49. East Side West Side 49. Tension 49. Mark of the Renegade 51. The Wild North 52. *Singin' in the Rain* 52. Sombrero 53. Easy to Love 53. *The Band Wagon* 53. Brigadoon 54. Deep in My Heart 54. *It's Always Fair Weather* 55. Meet Me in Las Vegas 56. *Invitation to the Dance* 57. Silk Stockings 57. Twilight for the Gods 58. Party Girl 58. Black Tights 60. Five Golden Hours 61. *Two Weeks in Another Town* 62. The Silencers 67. Maroc 7 67. Assassination in Rome 67. Call Her Mom (TV) 72. Warlords of Atlantis 78. Portrait of an Escort (TV) 80. Swimsuit (TV) 89. Visioni Privati 90. That's Entertainment! III 94.

Charles I
of England (1600–1649) (reigned 1625–1649) has not been a popular screen figure. Alec Guinness in *Cromwell* provided the nearest to a full-length portrait; cameos were given by Hugh Miller in *The Vicar of Bray* and Robert Rietty in *The Scarlet Blade*.

Charles II
of England (1630–1685) (reigned 1660–1685) has been a popular screen figure, attracting the talents of Cedric Hardwicke in *Nell Gwyn*, Vincent Price in *Hudson's Bay*, George Sanders in *Forever Amber*, Douglas Fairbanks Jnr in *The Exile*, and Sam Neill in *Restoration*.

Charles, Maria (1929–) (Maria Zena Schneider).
Diminutive British redhead, familiar as Jewish matron in TV's *Agony*.
■ Folly to Be Wise 52. The Deadly Affair 66. Eye of the Devil 67. The Return of the Pink Panther 74. Great Expectations (TV) 75. Cuba 79. Victor Victoria 82.

Charleson, Ian (1954–1990).
British leading actor. He died of AIDS.
Chariots of Fire 81. Gandhi 82. Greystoke 84. The Sun Also Rises (TV) 84. Car Trouble 85.

Charlesworth, John (1934–1960).
British teenage actor of the 50s. Committed suicide.
Tom Brown's Schooldays 51. Scrooge 51. John of the Fair 54. Yangtse Incident 57. The Angry Silence 59, etc.

Charlot, André (1882–1956).
French producer of intimate star revues in London and New York in the 20s. Later played small parts in Hollywood films.

Charpin, Fernand (1887–1944).
Plump French character actor, from the stage. He is best known for his role as the rich widower who marries the pregnant Fanny in Marcel Pagnol's trilogy of films set in Marseilles, his birthplace.
Marius 31. *Fanny* 32. César 36. They Were Five/La Belle Équipe 36. Pépé Le Moko 36. The Baker's Wife/La Femme du Boulanger 38. The Well-Digger's Daughter/La Fille du Puisatier 41, etc.

Charrel, Erik (1894–1974).
German producer best known abroad for *Congress Dances* 31, which he also directed.

Charteris, Leslie (1907–1993) (Leslie Charles Bowyer Yin).
Chinese-English crime novelist, creator of 'the SAINT'. Born in Singapore, he was educated in England, spending a year at Cambridge University before leaving to become a writer. He wrote his first book featuring the Saint in 1928, then went to Hollywood as a screenwriter in the early 30s. RKO made the first Saint movie, starring Louis HAYWARD, in 1938; its success led the studio to buy all the stories featuring the suave detective, who was subsequently played by George SANDERS in five films. Charteris later sued the studio when, in 1941, it launched its Falcon series, featuring a suave detective played by Sanders. He became an American citizen in the 30s and presided over a growing empire of writers to ghost his stories. Married four times.
Midnight Club (co-w) 33. Two Smart People (co-w) 46, etc.

Charters, Spencer (1878–1943).
American character actor. He frequently played rural fellows who may have been deaf, but were not too dumb to outsmart city slickers. Born in Duncannon, Pennsylvania, he was on stage for 37 years before repeating his role in the Broadway musical comedy *Whoopee* in Hollywood, where he stayed. Most often in comic roles, he made some 200 screen appearances. Committed suicide.
Little Old New York 23. Janice Meredith 24. Whoopee 30. The Bat Whispers 30. The Front Page 31. The Match King 32. Female 33. Wake up and Dream 34. It's a Gift 34. The Ghost Walks 34. The Raven 35. Colleen 36. Banjo on my Knee 36. Mountain Music 37. In Old Chicago 38. Professor Beware 38. Topper Takes a Trip 38. Jesse James 39. Drums Along the Mohawk 39. Alias the Deacon 40. Our Town 40. Tobacco Road 41. The Remarkable Andrew 42. Juke Girl 42, many others.

Chartoff, Robert (1933–).
American producer, usually with Irwin Winkler.
The Split 68. Leo the Last 69. They Shoot Horses Don't They? 69. The Mechanic 72. Up the Sandbox 72. The Gambler 74. Nickelodeon 76. Rocky (AA) 76. New York New York 77. Comes a Horseman 78. Rocky II 79. Raging Bull (AAN) 80. True Confessions 81. Rocky III 82. The Right Stuff (AAN) 83. Rocky IV 85. Rocky V 90, etc.

Chase, Borden (1900–1971).
American screenwriter.
Under Pressure 35. Blue White and Perfect 41. Destroyer 43. Flame of the Barbary Coast 45. Tycoon 47. Montana 48. Red River (AAN) 48. The Great Jewel Robber 50. Lone Star 51. Bend of the River 52. The World in his Arms 52. Man without a Star 55. Backlash 56. Night Passage 57. Gunfighters of Casa Grande 65, many others.

Chase, Charley (1893–1940) (Charles Parrott).
Toothbrush-moustached American comedian who made many two-reel comedies from 1924, usually as henpecked husband. Brother of James Parrott.
■ COMPLETE TALKIE SHORTS: The Big Squawk 29. Leaping Love 29. Snappy Sneezer 29. Crazy Feet 29. Stepping Out 29. Great Gobs 29. The Real McCoy 30. Whispering Whoopee 30. All Teed Up 30. Fifty Million Husbands 30. Fast Work 30. Girl Shock 30. Dollar Dizzy 30. Looser than Loose 30. High Cs 30. Thundering Tenors 31. *The Pip from Pittsburgh* 31. Rough Seas 31. One of the Smiths 31. The Panic Is On 31. Skip the Maloo 31. What a Bozo 31. The Hasty Marriage 31. The Tabasco Kid 32. The Nickel Nurser 32. In Walked Charley 32. First in War 32. Young Ironsides 32. Good Grief 32. Now We'll Tell One 32. Mr Bride 32. *Fallen Arches* 32. Nature in the Wrong 33. His Silent Racket 33. Arabian Tights 33. Sherman Said It 33. Midsummer Mush 33. *Luncheon at Twelve* 33. The Cracked Iceman 34. Four Parts 34. I'll Take Vanilla 34. Another Wild Idea 34. It Happened One Day 34. Something Simple 34. You Said a Hatful 34. Fate's Fathead 34. *The Chases of Pimple Street* 34. Okay Toots 35. Poker at Eight 35. Southern Exposure 35. The Four Star Boarder 35. Nurse to You 35. Manhattan Monkey Business 35. Public Ghost Number One 35. Life Hesitates at 40 36. The Count Takes the Count 36. Vamp Till Ready 36. *On the Wrong Trek* 36. *Neighborhood House* 36. The Grand Hooter 37. From Bad to Worse 37. The Wrong Miss Wright 37. Calling All Doctors 37. The Big Squirt 37. Man Bites Lovebug 37. Time Out for Trouble 38. The Mind Needer 38. Many Sappy Returns 38. The Nightshirt Bandit 38. Pie à la Maid 38. The Sap Takes a Rap 39. The Chump Takes a Bump 39. *Rattling Romeo* 39. Skinny the Moocher 39. Teacher's Pest 39. The Awful Good 39. *The Heckler* 40. South of the Boudoir 40.
~Feature appearance: *Sons of the Desert* 33.

Chase, Chaz (1902–1983).
American comedian who appeared in a few films with his act of eating peculiar objects, including lighted cigarettes and matches, boxes and corks.
Start Cheering 38. The Man on the Eiffel Tower 49. I Love, You Love (It.) 61, etc.

Chase, Chevy (1943–) (Cornelius Crane Chase).
American light leading man. He hosted an unsuccessful late-night TV chat show for Fox in 1993.
Tunnelvision 76. *Foul Play* 78. O Heavenly Dog 80. Seems Like Old Times 80. Under the Rainbow 81. Modern Problems 81. National Lampoon's Vacation 83. Deal of the Century 83. Fletch 85. National Lampoon's European Vacation 85. Spies Like Us 85. Three Amigos 86. Caddyshack II 88. The Couch Trip 88. Funny Farm 88. Fletch Lives 89. National Lampoon's Christmas Vacation 89. Nothing but Trouble 91. Memoirs of an Invisible Man 92. Cops and Robbersons 94. Man of the House 95. Vegas Vacation 96, etc.
❝ I guess I look so straight and normal nobody expects me to pick my nose and fall. – C.C.
We're basically very shy, have a very low self-esteem and we're like children who need a quick fix, or else we wouldn't be performing. – C.C.

Chase, Courtney (1988–).
American child actress.
Roommates 95. Reunion (TV) 95. Nick of Time 95, etc.

Chase, Ilka (1900–1978).
American columnist who occasionally brightened films.
Autobiographies: 1945, *Past Imperfect*. 1948, *Free Admission*.
Why Leave Home? 29. South Sea Rose 29. Free Love 30. The Animal Kingdom 32. Soak the Rich 36. Stronger than Desire 39. *Now Voyager* 42. No Time for Love 43. Miss Tatlock's Millions 48. Johnny Dark 54. The Big Knife 55. Ocean's Eleven 60, etc.
TV series: The Trials of O'Brien 65.

Chase, James Hadley (1906–1985) (René Raymond).
British author of violent crime stories, set in the United States via a slang dictionary and a vivid imagination. His most famous, *No Orchids for Miss Blandish*, was filmed in 1948 and again, as *The Grissom Gang*, in 1971. Other films: *I'll Get You for This* 49, *The Man in the Raincoat* 56, *Young Girls Beware* 58, *What Price Murder* 58, *Eve* 63, *Rough Magic* (from *Miss Shumway Waves a Wand*) 95.

Chase, Mary (1907–1981).
American playwright best known for her whimsical comedy *Harvey*, filmed with James Stewart.

Chater, Geoffrey (1921–) (Geoffrey Robinson).
English character actor of stage, screen and television, often playing mild-mannered men. Born in Barnet, Hertfordshire, he was on-stage from 1946.
The Strange World of Planet X 58. The Day the Earth Caught Fire 61. Sammy Going South 63. If . . . 68. 10 Rillington Place 71. Endless Night 72. O Lucky Man! 73. Barry Lyndon 75. Brideshead Revisited (TV) 81. Othello (TV) 81. Gandhi 82. In the Secret State (TV) 85. Blunt (TV) 86. Bethune: The Making of a Hero (Can.) 90. The Secret Life of Ian Fleming (TV) 90, etc.
TV series: Devenish 77–78. Agony 79. The New Statesman 90–93.

Chattaway, Jay (1946–).
American composer, mainly for action and horror movies.
Maniac 81. The Big Score 83. Vigilante 83. Missing in Action 84. Invasion U.S.A. 85. Maniac Cop 87. Red Scorpion 89. Relentless 89. Bar Sinister 90. Maniac Cop II 90. Rich Girl 91, etc.

Chatterton, Ruth (1893–1961).
Dignified American leading lady, popular in 20s and 30s after stage success; later had success as novelist.
■ Sins of the Fathers 28. The Doctor's Secret 29. The Dummy 29. *Madame X* (AAN) 29. Charming Sinners 29. The Laughing Lady 29. Sarah and Son (AAN) 30. Paramount on Parade 30. The Lady of Scandal 30. Anybody's Woman 30. The Right to Love 30. Unfaithful 31. The Magnificent Lie 31. Once a Lady 31. Tomorrow and Tomorrow 32. The Rich are Always with Us 32. The Crash 32. Frisco Jenny 33. Lilly Turner 33. Female 33. Journal of a Crime 33. Lady of Secrets 36. Girls' Dormitory 36. *Dodsworth* 36. The Rat (GB) 38. A Royal Divorce (GB) 38.
Rough Magic (from Miss Shumway Waves a Wand) 95.

Chaumette, François (1923–1996).
French leading actor, mainly on the stage, who worked at the Comédie Française from the late 50s to the late 80s, and also gained a popular success on television in the 60s.
Les Visiteurs du Soir 43. Le Bossu 60. Galia 66. Caroline Chérie 67. L'Héritier 72. Les Maîtres du Soleil 84. Mes Nuits Sont Plus Belles que Vos Jours 89, etc.

Chauvel, Charles (1897–1959).
Australian writer-producer-director.
In the Wake of the Bounty 33. Forty Thousand Horsemen 42. The Rats of Tobruk 48. The Rugged O'Riordans 48. Jedda 53, many others.

Chayefsky, Paddy (1923–1981) (Sidney Stuchevsky).
Distinguished but latterly somewhat hysterical American writer whose greatest success was in TV.
Autobiography: 1978, *Altered States*.
Biography: 1994, *Mad as Hell: The Life and Work of Paddy Chayefsky* by Shaun Considine.
■ As Young as You Feel (oa) 51. *Marty* (AA) 55. The Catered Affair (oa) 56. *The Bachelor Party* 57. The Goddess (AANw) 58. Middle of the Night (oa) 59. The Americanization of Emily (w) 64. *The Hospital* (w) (AA) 71. *Network* (w) 76. Altered States 80 (as Sidney Aaron).

Chaykin, Maury (1949–).
Canadian character actor.
The Kidnapping of the President 80. Death Hunt 81. Soup for One 82. Of Unknown Origins 83. Mrs Soffel 84. Harry and Son 84. Highpoint 84. Wild Thing 87. Twins 88. Caribe 88. Iron Eagle II 88. Stars and Bars 88. Breaking In 89. Dances with Wolves 90. Mr Destiny 90. Where the Heart Is 90. The Adjuster 91. George's Island 91. My Cousin Vinny 92. Hero/Accidental Hero 92. Sommersby 93. Camilla 93. Josh and S.A.M. 93. Money for Nothing 93. Whale Music 94. Camilla 94. Unstrung Heroes 95. Devil in a Blue Dress 95. CutThroat Island 95. The Sweet Hereafter 97. Mouse Hunt 97. Love and Death on Long Island 97. A Life Less Ordinary 97. The Mask of Zorro 98, etc.

Cheadle, Don (1964–).
American actor, from television.
Hamburger Hill 87. Colors 88. Roadside Prophets 92. The Meteor Man 93. *Devil in a Blue Dress* (as Mouse) 95, etc.
TV series: The Golden Palace 92–93. Picket Fences 93–95.

Chechik, Jeremiah.
Canadian-born director, in Hollywood.
National Lampoon's Christmas Vacation 89. Benny and Joon 93. Tall Tale: The Unbelievable Adventures of Pecos Bill 95. Diabolique 96. The Avengers 98, etc.

Checker, Chubby (1941–) (Ernest Evans).
Endlessly gyrating American pop singer-dancer, briefly popular in the early 60s.
Twist Around the Clock 62. Don't Knock the Twist 62. Calendar Girl 93, etc.

Chee-Ak.
Eskimo cinematographer, writer and actor. Born in Alaska, he was cameraman for Danish explorer Knud Rasmussen's film *Teddy Bear* 23. He went to Hollywood to work as cameraman on *Iceberg* and *Frozen Justice* 30, and co-wrote and starred in *Igloo* 32, set in the Arctic, for Universal, but it failed at the box-office.

Cheech and Chong:
see CHONG, Thomas, MARIN, Richard 'Cheech'.

Chekhov, Anton (1860–1904).
Introspective Russian writer whose plays about the melancholies of the upper classes have been frequently filmed, though never very commercially. Sidney Lumet's version of *The Seagull*, with Simone Signoret and James Mason, was a valiant try. Sir Laurence Olivier filmed his National Theatre production of *The Three Sisters* in 1970, with a cast that included himself, Joan Plowright, Alan Bates, Derek Jacobi and Ronald Pickup. *Uncle Vanya* attracted attention in the 90s, although there had been a TV version directed by Olivier in 1963. Michael Blakemore transferred it to an Australian setting in *Country Life* 95; Anthony Hopkins made his directorial debut with *August* 96, a version set in Wales; best of all, in *Vanya on 42nd Street* 94, Louis Malle directed Wallace Shawn, Julianne Moore and others in a rehearsal of the play.

Chekhov, Michael (1891–1955).
Russian character actor who set up drama schools in London and New York; films sparse.
■ Song of Russia 44. In Our Time 44. *Spellbound* (AAN) 45. *Spectre of the Rose* 46. Cross My Heart 46. Abie's Irish Rose 46. Arch of Triumph 47. Invitation 51. Holiday for Sinners 52. Rhapsody 54.

Chelsom, Peter (1956–).
English actor, director and screenwriter. Studied at the Central School of Speech and Drama and was on stage from 1978.
The Ringer (a) 78. An Englishman Abroad (a) (TV) 83. Indian Summer (a) 87. *Hear My Song* (co-w, d) 91. Funny Bones (co-w, d) 95. The Mighty (US) 98, etc.

Chen, Joan (1961–) (Chen Chong).
Chinese actress, who began her career at the age of 14 and studied at the Shanghai Film Studio. She moved to America in 1981, and majored in film production at California State University before resuming her career, first on television.
Dim Sum: A Little Bit of Heart 85. James Clavell's Tai-Pan 86. The Night Stalker 87. The Last Emperor 87. Salute of the Jugger/The Blood of Heroes 90. Wedlock 90. Hollywood Zen 92. Turtle Beach 92. The Joy Luck Club 93. You Seng (HK) 93. Heaven and Earth 93. On Deadly Ground 94. Golden Gate 94. Judge Dredd 95. Red Rose, White Rose 95. The Hunted 95. Precious Find 96. Xiu Xiu: The Sent Down Girl (p, d, co-w) 98, etc.
TV series: Twin Peaks 90.

Chenal, Pierre (1903–1990) (Pierre Cohen).
French director.
Crime and Punishment 35. The Late Mathias Pascal 36. *Alibi* 37. Le Dernier Tournant 39. Sirocco 45. Clochemerle 48. Native Son (US) 51. Sinners of Paris 59, etc.

Cher (1946–) (Cher Bono, formerly Cherilyn Sarkisian).
American pop singer, once of Sonny and Cher, now turned actress. She has a daughter, Chastity, by Sonny BONO, and a son, Elijah Blue, by Gregg Allman.
Biography: 1991, *Totally Uninhibited: The Life and Wild Times of Cher* by Lawrence J. Quirk.
Good Times 68. Come Back to the Five and Dime, Jimmy Dean, Jimmy Dean 83. Silkwood (AAN) 83. Mask 85. The Witches of Eastwick 87. Moonstruck (AA) 87. Suspect 87. Mermaids 90. The Player 92. Prêt-à-Porter/Ready to Wear 94. Faithful 96. If These Walls Could Talk (& co-d) 96. Tea with Mussolini 99, etc.
❝ I'm scared to death of being poor. It's like a fat girl who loses 500 pounds but is always fat inside. I grew up poor and will always feel poor inside. It's my pet paranoia. – C.
Men are luxuries, not necessities. – C.
I love aliens – I've dated a few. – C.
When you take away those wild wings, there's an honest, complex screen presence underneath. – *New York Times*
She's not a brilliant talent. Not a great actress or a great singer. The best thing about Cher is the package, the persona. But you can't stay – especially if you're a woman, because unfortunately that's not the way nature is – you can't stay on glamour all your life. – *Sonny Bono*, 1995

Chéreau, Patrice (1944–).
French director, screenwriter and occasional actor. A notable theatre and opera director, he was co-director of Lyon's Théâtre National Populaire in the 70s and director of the Théâtre des Amandiers in Nanterre in the early 80s.
Le Chair de l'Orchidée (d) 74. Judith Therpauve (d) 78. Danton (a) 82. L'Homme Blessé (d) 83. Hôtel de France (d) 87. Le Temps et la Chambre (d) 92. The Last of the Mohicans (a) 92. *Queen Margot*/La Reine Margot (co-w, d) 94. Ceux Qui m'Aiment Prendront le Train 98, etc.

Cherkassov, Nicolai (1903–1966).
Russian leading actor of epic hero stature.
Autobiography: 1957, *Notes of a Soviet Actor*.
■ Baltic Deputy 37. *Peter the Great* 37. Ski Battalion 38. The Man with the Gun 38. *Alexander Nevsky* 38. Friends 39. Captain Grant's Children 39. Lenin in October 39. General Suvorov 41. *Ivan the Terrible Part One* 42. In the Name of Life 42. Ivan the Terrible Part Two 44. Spring 48. The First Front 49. Ivan Pavlov 50. Mussorgsky 51. Rimsky Korsakov 54. *Don Quixote* 53.

Cherrill, Virginia (1908–1996).
American leading lady, a society girl who had a brief film career in the early 30s. She was formerly married to Cary Grant (1934–35).
■ *City Lights* (as the blind girl) 31. Girls Demand Excitement 31. The Brat 31. Delicious 31. Fast Workers 33. The Nuisance 33. Charlie Chan's Greatest Case 32. White Heat 34. What Price Crime 35. Troubled Waters 35.

Cherry, Helen (1915–).
Cool and gracious British actress, mostly on stage; married Trevor HOWARD.
The Courtneys of Curzon Street 48. Adam and Evelyn 49. Morning Departure 50. Young Wives' Tale 51. Castle in the Air 53. Three Cases of Murder 55. High Flight 57. The Naked Edge 61. Flipper's New Adventure 64. Hard Contract 69. 11 Harrowhouse 74. No Longer Alone 78. Time after Time 85. The Girl in a Swing 89. A Ghost in Monte Carlo (TV) 90, etc.

Chesebro, George (1888–1959).
American star of silent westerns who became a sidekick to Ken Maynard, Gene Autry and Tex Ritter in cowboy movies of the 30s and 40s.
Hands Up (serial) 18. Rustler's Ranch 26. Tex Takes a Holiday 32. In Old Santa Fe 34. Laramie Kid 35. Tumbling Tumbleweeds 35. Red River Valley 36. Roamin' Wild 36. Starlight over Texas 38. Gun Code 40. The Renegade 43. Boss of Rawhide 44. Return of the Lash 47. Cheyenne Takes Over 47. Stage to Mesa City 48. Gunslingers 50. The Kid from Amarillo 51. Last of the Comanches 53, many others.

Chester, Hal E. (1921–).
American teenage actor who, as Hally Chester, was one of the 'Little Tough Guys' in 1938–40. Later became producer and settled in Europe.
Joe Palooka Champ 46. The Underworld Story 50. The Highwayman 53. Crashout 55. The Bold and the Brave 56. Night of the Demon 57. School for Scoundrels 60. Hide and Seek 64. The Secret War of Harry Frigg 67. The Double Man 67, etc.

Chesterton, G. K. (1874–1936).
English novelist and journalist, an irrepressible wit whose chief bequest to the cinema is the clerical detective Father Brown, played in movies by Walter Connolly and Alec Guinness and on TV by Heinz Ruhmann and Kenneth More.

Cheung, Jacky (1960–).
Hong Kong actor and pop singer.
Where's Officer Tuba 86. As Tears Go By 88. Curry and Pepper 90. Bullet in the Head 90. A Chinese Ghost Story II 90. Once upon a Time in China 91. A Chinese Ghost Story III 91. Days of Being Wild 91. A Chinese Legend 92. The Wicked City 92. Ashes of Time 94. The Private Eye Blues 94, etc.

Cheung, Leslie (c. 1956–) (Zhang Guorong).
Hong Kong leading actor, a former pop singer. Born in Hong Kong, he went to school in England and studied textile design at Leeds University. He began by winning a singing contest and appearing on television. In the 90s he settled in Canada and began working as a singer once more.
A Chinese Ghost Story 88. Rouge 88. A Chinese Ghost Story II 89. Once a Thief 90. Days of Being Wild 90. *Farewell My Concubine*/Bawang Bie Ji 93. The Bride with White Hair/Jiang-Hu: Between Love and Glory 93. The Eagle Shooting Heroes: Dong Cheng Xi Jiu 93. He's a Woman, She's a Man 95. The Chinese Feast/Gamyuk Muntong 95. Temptress Moon 96. Happy Together 96, etc.

Cheung, Maggie (1964–).
Hong Kong leading actress, a former model, who has so far made more than 80 films. She lived in England as a child and won a best actress award at the Berlin Film Festival in 1992 for her performance in *Actress*.
Prince Charming 84. Police Story 85. Rose 86. Project A Part Two 87. As Tears Go By 88. Police Story 2 88. Full Moon in New York 90. Farewell China 90. Days of Being Wild 90. The Perfect Match 91. Twin Dragons 92. *Actress* 92. Police Story 3 92. Moon Warriors 92. Too Happy for Words 93. The Mad Monk 93. Green Snake 93. Irma Vep (Fr.) 96. Chinese Box 97, many others.

Chevalier, Albert (1861–1923).
British actor and songwriter who found fame in the music halls from the 1890s as 'The Coster Laureate' singing Cockney songs. His best-known, 'My Old Dutch', was the basis of a silent film, in which he starred, and a movie made in 1934 with Gordon Harker and Betty Balfour.
The Middleman 15. The Bottle 15. My Old Dutch 15. A Fallen Star 16, etc.
❝ He and his songs are as immortal as the cliffs of Dover. – *W. Macqueen-Pope*

Chevalier, Maurice (1888–1972).
Inimitable French singing entertainer. Born into poverty in Paris, he began as a 12-year-old in café and musical-hall entertainments before becoming the protégé and lover of Mistinguett. He appeared in French silent films from 1908, but his international stardom dates from his contract with Paramount in Hollwyood in the 30s and his later films with Jeanette MacDonald for MGM. His film career faltered when he left Hollywood and returned to France in the late 30s. He re-emerged as an international star after surviving accusations of collaborating with the Nazis during the Second World War. Retired in his 80s and suffered from depression, attempting suicide. Special Academy Award 1958 'for his contributions to the world of entertainment for more than half a century'.
Autobiographies: 1949, *The Man in the Straw Hat*; 1960, *With Love*; 1968, *Bravo Maurice* (translated by Mary Fitton, a compilation from his nine volumes of autobiographical writings); 1972, *I Remember It Well*.
Biography: 1993, *Thank Heaven For Little Girls* by Edward Behr.
■ Sound films: Innocents in Paris 29. *The Love Parade* (AAN) 30. Paramount on Parade 30. The Big Pond (AAN) 30. Playboy of Paris 30. The Smiling Lieutenant 31. *One Hour With You* 32. *Love Me Tonight* 32. Bedtime Story 33. The Way to Love 33. The Merry Widow 34. *Folies Bergère* 35. L'Homme du Jour 36. Avec Le Sourire 36. Break the News 36. The Beloved Vagabond 37. Pièges 39. *Le Silence est d'Or* 47. Le Roi 49. Ma Pomme 50. J'Avais Sept Filles 55. Love in the Afternoon 57. *Gigi* 58. Count Your Blessings 59. Can Can 59. Black Tights 60. A Breath of Scandal 60. Pepe 60. *Fanny* 61. Jessica 62. *In Search of the Castaways* 62. A New Kind of Love 63. Panic Button 64. I'd Rather be Rich 64. Monkeys Go Home 67.
✪ For his incomparable technique as a singing entertainer; and for cheering up two widely separate generations of the international audience. *Love Me Tonight*.
❝ Love the public the way you love your mother. – M.C.
The 70-odd years young Maurice Chevalier takes his place beside children and animals as one of the great scene stealers of all times. – *Mike Connolly*
The biggest bottom pincher I have ever come across. – *Jeanette MacDonald*

Chevallier, Gabriel (1895–1969).
French novelist whose chief gift to the film world was *Clochemerle*, about the furore caused by the building of a public lavatory in a French village.

Chew, Richard.
American editor.
The Conversation 74. One Flew over the Cuckoo's Nest (AAN) 76. Star Wars (AA) 77. Goin' South 78. My Favorite Year 82. Real Genius 85. Where the River Runs Black 86. Clean and Sober 88. Men Don't Leave 90. Late for Dinner 91. Singles (& co-p) 92. My Life 93. Tall Tale: The Unbelievable Adventures of Pecos Bill 94. Waiting to Exhale 95. That Thing You Do! 96. Hope Floats 98, etc.

Cheyney, Peter (1896–1951).
British mystery writer who created Lemmy Caution and Slim Callaghan, some of whose adventures were filmed.
Deputy Drummer (w) 32. Uneasy Terms (w) 48. Meet Mr Callaghan (w) 50. Diplomatic Courier 52. Alphaville 65.

Chiari, Mario (1909–1989).
Italian production designer.
Miracle in Milan 51. The Golden Coach 54. Neapolitan Fantasy 54. I Vitelloni 54. The Sea Wall 56. War and Peace 57. White Nights/Le Notti Bianche 57. Barabbas 62. The Bible 66. Doctor Dolittle (US) (AAN) 67. A Man Called Sledge 70. Ludwig 73. King Kong (US) 76. The White Buffalo (US) 77, etc.

Chiari, Walter (1924–1991) (Walter Annichiarico).
Italian comic actor, occasionally in international films.
Bellissima 51. OK Nero 51. The Moment of Truth 53. Nana 56. The Little Hut 57. Bonjour Tristesse 58. Pepote 58. Chimes at Midnight 66. *They're a Weird Mob* 66. Squeeze a Flower 69. The Valachi Papers 72. Tracce di Vita Amorosa 91, etc.

Chiau, Stephen (Stephen Chiau Shing-Chi, aka Stephen Chow and Steven Chow).
Chinese leading comic actor, in Hong Kong films. He began as a television presenter on children's programmes. His comedy, sending up action movie genres, depends greatly on his verbal dexterity in Cantonese, so that his following in the West remains small.
Dragon Fight 88. The Defector 89. Legend of the Dragon 90. *All for the Winner* 90. Fist of Fury '91 91. God of Gamblers II 91. God of Gamblers III: Back to Shanghai 91. Justice My Foot 92. Royal Tramp 92. King of Beggars 93. *The Flirting Scholar* 93. The Mad Monk 93. Love on Delivery 95. A Chinese Odyssey/Xi You Ji 96. *Forbidden City Cop* 96, etc.

Chiba, Sonny (1939–) (Shinichi Chiba).
Japanese actor, star of violent martial arts movies, in films from 1961. He formed his own martial arts school to train stuntmen and fight choreographers for film work.
Terror beneath the Sea 70. The Bodyguard 70. Street Fighter 75. Return of the Street Fighter 76. The Killing Machine 76. Kowloon Assignment 77. The Street Fighter's Last Revenge 77. Champion of Death 78. Sister Streetfighter 78. Hunter in the Dark 80. Virus 82. Shogun's Ninja 83. Legend of the Eight Samurai 84. Aces: Iron Eagle III 92. Resort to Kill 93. The Storm Riders (HK) 98, etc.

Chief Thundercloud (1899–1955) (Victor Daniels).
American Indian actor who began in films as a stuntman.
Ramona 36. Union Pacific 38. Western Union 41. The Falcon Out West 44. Unconquered 47. The Half Breed 51, many others.

Chief Thundercloud (1901–1967) (Scott Williams).
American actor of Indian descent who appeared in many second feature westerns and played Tonto on radio.

Chihara, Paul (1938–).
American composer, also scoring many television movies.
Death Race 2000 75. Sweet Revenge 76. I Never Promised You a Rose Garden 77. The Bad News Bears Go to Japan 77. Prince of the City 81. The Legend of Walks Far Woman 82. The Survivors 83. Manimal (TV) 83. Impulse 84. The Morning After 86. Jackals 86. A Walk on the Moon 87. The Killing Time 87. Crossing Delancey 88. Penn and Teller Get Killed 89, etc.

Child, Jeremy (1944–).
English character actor, usually in upper-class roles. Born in Woking, he studied at the Bristol Old Vic Theatre School.
Privilege 67. Decline and Fall 68. Oh What a Lovely War 69. The Breaking of Bumbo 70. Jane Eyre 70. Quest for Love 71. Young Winston 72. Quadrophenia 78. The Stud 79. High Road to China 83. Give My Regards to Broad Street 84. The Jewel in the Crown (TV) 84. The Madness of King George 94, etc.
TV series: Father, Dear Father 72. The Happy Apple 83. Fairly Secret Army 84. Is It Legal? 96.

Childress, Alvin (1907–1986).
American character actor who made occasional films, best known for playing Amos in the TV series *Amos 'n' Andy* 51–53.
Anna Lucasta 58. The Man in the Net 59. The Bingo Long Traveling All-Stars and Motor Kings 76. Sister, Sister (TV) 82, etc.

Chiles, Linden (1934–).
American character actor who usually plays well-educated types.
Sanctuary 61. A Rage to Live 64. Texas across the River 67. Death Be Not Proud (TV) 75. Who Is the Black Dahlia? (TV) 75. Deadline Assault/Act of Violence 79. Red Flag: The Ultimate Game (TV) 81. Forbidden World/Mutant 82. To Heal a Nation (TV) 88. Deadline Assault 90, etc.
TV series: Convoy 65. James at 15 77–78.

Chiles, Lois (1950–).
American leading lady of the late 70s.
The Way We Were 73. The Great Gatsby 74. Death on the Nile 78. Coma 78. Moonraker 79. Courage 84. Sweet Liberty 85. Creepshow 2 87. Broadcast News 87. Twister 88. Until the End of the World/Bis ans Ende der Welt 91. Diary of a Hit Man 92. Lush Life 93. The Babysitter 95. Bliss 96. Speed 2: Cruise Control 97, etc.
TV series: Dallas 82–83.

Chin, Tsai (c. 1938–).
Chinese leading lady in international films.
Autobiography: 1990, *Daughter of Shanghai*.
The Face of Fu Manchu 65. Invasion 66. The Brides of Fu Manchu 66. You Only Live Twice 67. Rentadick 72. The Joy Luck Club 93. The West Side Waltz (TV) 95, etc.

Ching, William (1912–1989).
American general-purpose actor of the 40s.
Something in the Wind 47. D.O.A. 50. Belle le Grand 51. Pat and Mike 52. Scared Stiff 53, etc.
TV series: Our Miss Brooks 55–56.

Chionglo, Mel (1946–).
Filipino director who studied in New York with Lee Strasberg and Stella Adler, and began in films as a production designer.
You Are Mine (p, d) 78. Eagle (p, d) 80. Playgirl (d) 80. Sinner or Saint (d) 82. Santa Mahalin Ako (d) 87. *Midnight Dancers*/Sibak (d) 94, etc.

Chirgwin, G. H. (1855–1922) (George Chirgwin).
English black-faced comedian and one-string fiddle-player who performed in music halls as a child with his brothers. In the 1870s he went solo as 'The White-Eyed Kaffir', so-called because he painted a diamond shape around his right eye white when he made up. He twice filmed *The Blind Boy*, based on his most popular song and intended to be shown synchronized to his recording.
■ Chirgwin in his Humorous Business 1896. Chirgwin Plays a Scotch Reel 1896. The Blind Boy 1900. The Blind Boy 1917.

Chitty, Erik (1906–1977).
British character actor who spent many years playing crotchety little men, notably in the TV series *Please Sir*.
Contraband 40. Raising a Riot 55. Doctor Zhivago 65. The Railway Children 70. Great Expectations 75. A Bridge Too Far 77, many others.

Chlumsky, Anna (1980–).
American child actress, a former model.
My Girl 91. My Girl 2 94. Trading Mom 94. Gold Diggers: The Secret of Bear Mountain 95.

Chodorov, Edward (1904–1988).
American screenwriter and dramatist. He was blacklisted in 1953 for refusing to co-operate with the House Un-American Activities Committee.
The World Changes 33. Kind Lady 35. The Story of Louis Pasteur (co-w) 35. Yellow Jack 38. Undercurrent 46. The Hucksters 47. Roadhouse 48, etc.

Chodorov, Jerome (1911–).
American writer, usually with Joseph Fields.
Louisiana Purchase 41. My Sister Eileen 42. Junior Miss 45. Happy Anniversary 59 (all from their plays), etc.

Chomsky, Marvin (1929–).
American director of efficient but nondescript style.
■ Assault on the Wayne (TV) 70. *Family Flight* (TV) 71. Evel Knievel 71. Mongo's Back in Town (TV) 71. Fireball Forward (TV) 72. Female Artillery (TV) 73. The FBI vs Alvin Karpis (TV) 74. Mrs Sundance (TV) 74. Attack on Terror (TV) 74. Kate McShane (TV) 75. A Matter of Wife and Death (TV) 75. Murph the Surf 75. Brinks: the Great Robbery (TV) 76. Law and Order (TV) 76. *Roots* (co-d) (TV) 76. Danger in Paradise (TV) 77. Little Ladies of the Night (TV) 77. MacKintosh and TJ 77. Good Luck Miss Wyckoff 78. *Holocaust* 78. Hollow Image 79. King Crab 80. Dr Franken 80. Attica (TV) 80. Evita Peron (TV) 81. My Body My Child (TV) 82. Inside the Third Reich (TV) 82. Nairobi Affair (TV) 84. Tank 84. Robert Kennedy and his Times (TV) 85. Catherine the Great (TV) 95.

Chong, Rae Dawn (1962–).
Canadian-born actress. She is the daughter of Thomas Chong.
Quest for Fire 79. Commando 85. The Color Purple 85. Choose Me 86. Soul Man 86. The Principal 87. The Squeeze 87. Walking After Midnight 88. The Borrower 89. Far Out, Man! 90. Amazon 90. Tales from the Darkside: The Movie 91. Time Runner 92. Amberwaves 93. Boulevard (& w) 94. Boca 94. Hideaway 95. Crying Freeman 95. Starlight 96. Mask of Death 97, etc.

Chong, Thomas (1938–).
Canadian guitarist, actor, director and screenwriter who formed a coarse comic double-act with Richard 'Cheech' Marin, which split up in 1985. He is the father of actress Rae Dawn Chong.
Up in Smoke (a) 79. Cheech & Chong's Next Movie (a, wd) 80. Cheech & Chong's Nice Dreams (a, wd) 81. Things Are Tough All Over (a, wd) 82. Cheech & Chong: Still Smokin' (a, wd) 83. Yellowbeard (a) 83. Cheech & Chong's The Corsican Brothers (a, wd) 84. After Hours (a) 85. Tripwire (a) 89. Far Out, Man! (a, wd) 90. Life after Sex (a) 91. Ferngully . . . the Last Rainforest (voice) 92. National Lampoon's Senior Trip 95. McHale's Navy 97, etc.

Chopin, Frédéric (1810–1849).
Polish pianist and composer most famous in film circles for his love affair with the eccentric George Sand. ('Frederic, stop composing that Polonaise jangle!' said Merle Oberon to Cornel Wilde in *A Song to Remember*.) His chief cinematic interpreters have been as follows:

1935	*Un Amour de Frédéric Chopin*	Jean Servais
1945	*A Song to Remember*	Cornel Wilde
1951	*The Young Chopin*	Czeslaw Wollejko
1960	*Song Without End*	Alex Davion
1975	*Lisztomania*	Ken Colley
1991	*Impromptu*	Hugh Grant
1991	*La Note Bleue*	Janusz Olejniczak

Chopra, Joyce (1938–).
American director.
Smooth Talk 86. The Lemon Sisters 89. Danger of Love (TV) 95. My Very Best Friend (TV) 96, etc.

Chouraqui, Elie (1950–).
French director.
Mon Premier Amour 78. Love Songs/Paroles et Musique 84. Man on Fire 87. Miss Missouri 90. Les Marmottes 94. The Liars 96, etc.

Choureau, Etchika (1923–).
French leading lady.
Children of Love 53. The Fruits of Summer 55. Lafayette Escadrille (US) 57. Darby's Rangers (US) 58, etc.

Chow, Raymond (1929–).
Chinese producer who in the early 80s expanded his interests from kung fu action films, through his Golden Harvest group, to international vehicles such as *The Cannonball Run*, *The Return of the Soldier* and *Teenage Mutant Ninja Turtles*.

Chow, Stephen, aka Steven Chow:
see CHIAU, Stephen.

Chrétien, Henri (1879–1956).
French inventor of the anamorphic lens subsequently used in CinemaScope and allied processes.

Christensen, Benjamin (1879–1959).
Danish director whose career faded after a sojourn in Hollywood.
The Mysterious X 13. The Night of Revenge 15. Häxan/Witchcraft through the Ages 21. Seine Frau Die Unbekannte 23. The Devil's Circus 25. Mockery 27. The Hawk's Nest 28. Seven Footprints to Satan 29, many others.

Christian, Linda (1923–) (Blanca Rosa Welter).
Mexican-born leading lady who appeared in a few international films. She was Tyrone Power's second wife, then married into European nobility.
Holiday in Mexico 46. Green Dolphin Street 47. Tarzan and the Mermaids 48. The Happy Time 52. Athena 54. Thunderstorm 56. The House of Seven Hawks 59. The VIPs 63. How to Seduce a Playboy 66, etc.

Christian, Paul:
see HUBSCHMID, Paul.

Christian, Roger.
English director, in Hollywood from the mid-90s.
The Dollar Bottom (short) 81. The Sender 83. Lorca and the Outlaws/Starship 85. Nostradamus (& co-w) 94. The Final Cut (US) 96. Masterminds (US) 97. Underworld (US) 97, etc.

Christian-Jaque (1904–1994) (Christian Maudet).
French writer-director, former journalist.
Les Disparus de Saint-Agil 38. La Symphonie Fantastique 42. Sortilèges 44. *Un Revenant* 46. D'Homme à Hommes 48. Souvenirs Perdus 50. Bluebeard 51. *Fanfan la Tulipe* 51. Lucrezia Borgia 52. Adorables Créatures 52. Nana 54. Si Tous les Gars du Monde/Race for Life 55. Babette Goes to War 59. Madame Sans Gêne 61. The Black Tulip 63. The Secret Agents/The Dirty Game (co-d) 66. The Saint Versus . . . 66. Two Tickets to Mexico/Dead Run 67. La Ville a Belles Dents 80. Carné, l'Homme à la Caméra 85, etc.

Christians, Mady (1900–1951) (Margarethe Marie Christians).
Austrian-born stage actress in occasional Hollywood films.
The Waltz Dream (GB) 26. Slums of Berlin 27. The Runaway Princess (GB) 29. A Wicked Woman 35. Escapade 36. Seventh Heaven 37. Heidi 37. Address Unknown 44. All My Sons 48. Letter from an Unknown Woman 48, etc.

Christie, Dame Agatha (1890–1976) (Mary Clarissa Miller).
Best-selling British mystery novelist and playwright whose innumerable puzzle plots have furnished film-makers with relatively few, and usually forgettable, movies. In *Agatha* 79, a fiction based on a mysterious episode in her real life, she was played by Vanessa Redgrave. Her work has also been turned into television films and series, most notably featuring her two eccentric detectives, Miss MARPLE and Hercule POIROT.
Autobiography: 1977, *An Autobiography*.
Biography: 1984, *Agatha Christie* by Janet Morgan.
Book: 1993, *The Films of Agatha Christie* by Scott Palmer.
■ Die Abenteuer GmbH (from The Secret Adversary) 28. The Passing of Mr Quinn 28. Alibi 31. Black Coffee 31. Lord Edgware Dies 34. Love from a Stranger 37 and 47. And Then There Were None 45 and, as Ten Little Indians, 65, 75, 89. Witness for the Prosecution 57. The Spider's Web 60. Murder She Said 62. Murder at the Gallop 63. Murder Most Foul 64. The Alphabet Murders 66. Endless Night 72. Murder on the Orient Express 74. Death on the Nile 78. The Mirror Crack'd 80. Evil under the Sun 82. Ordeal by Innocence 85.
❝ I'm a sausage machine, a perfect sausage machine. – A.C.
An archaeologist is the best husband a woman can have. The older she gets, the more interested he is in her. – A.C.
~A mysterious episode in her own life was fictitiously cleared up in *Agatha* 79.

Christie, Al (1886–1951).
American comedy producer, mainly of two-reelers, in Hollywood from 1914 and a rival of Mack Sennett.
Features include *Tillie's Punctured Romance* 17, *Up in Mabel's Room* 26; produced and directed *Charley's Aunt* 25.

Christie, Audrey (1912–1989).
American supporting actress.
Deadline 52. Carousel 56. Splendor in the Grass 61. The Unsinkable Molly Brown 64. The Ballad of Josie 68. Mame 73, etc.

Christie, Howard (1912–1992).
American producer.
Lady on a Train 44. Abbott and Costello Meet the Invisible Man 50. The Purple Mask 55. Away All Boats 56. Gunfight at Abilene 60. Nobody's Perfect 68, etc.

Christie, Julie (1940–).
Striking British leading actress whose choice of roles has not always been fortunate.
Crooks Anonymous 62. The Fast Lady 63. *Billy Liar* 63. Young Cassidy 64. *Darling* (AA, BFA) 65. *Doctor Zhivago* 65. Fahrenheit 451 66. Far From the Madding Crowd 67. Petulia 68. In Search of Gregory 69. The Go-Between 71. McCabe and Mrs Miller (AAN) 71. *Don't Look Now* 74. Shampoo 75. Nashville 75. Demon Seed 77. Heaven Can Wait 78. Memoirs of a Survivor 82. The Return of the Soldier 82. The Gold Diggers 83. Heat and Dust 83. Power 86. Miss Mary 86. Secret Obsession 88. Fools of Fortune 90. The Railway Station Man 92. Karaoke (TV) 96. Dragonheart 96. Afterglow (AAN) 97, etc.

Christine, Virginia (1917–1996).
American character actress, best known in the States for appearing as the Swedish-sounding Mrs Olsen in TV adverts for Folger's coffee for 20 years. Married actor Fritz FELD.
Edge of Darkness 42. The Mummy's Curse 45. The Killers 46. Cyrano de Bergerac 50. Never Wave at a WAC 53. Not as a Stranger 55. Nightmare 56. Invasion of the Body Snatchers 56. The Careless Years 58. Judgment at Nuremberg 61. The Prize 63. Guess Who's Coming to Dinner 67. Hail, Hero! 69, etc.
TV series: Tales of Wells Fargo 61.

Christopher, Dennis (1955–) (Dennis Carelli).
American leading man.
The Boys in Company C 77. A Wedding 78. Breaking Away 79. California Dreaming 80. Fade to Black 80. Chariots of Fire 81. Don't Cry It's Only Thunder 82. Flight of the Spruce Goose 86. Jake Speed 86. Alien Predator 87. A Sinful Life 89. Doppelganger 92. Plughead Rewired: Circuitry Man II 94. Boys Life 94. The Silencers 95. It's My Party 95, etc.

Christopher, Jordan (1942–).
American leading actor of the 60s. He was also leader of a rock group, The Wild Ones.
The Return of the Seven 66. Angel, Angel, Down We Go/Cult of the Damned 69. The Tree 69. Pigeons/Sidelong Glances of a Pigeon Kicker 70. Brainstorm 83. Star 80 83. That's Life 86, etc.
TV series: Secrets of Midland Heights 80–81.

Chrystall, Belle (1911–).
British leading lady of the 30s.
Hindle Wakes 31. Friday the Thirteenth 33. Edge of the World 38, etc.

Chu, Emily (Bo Yi).
Taiwanese-born leading actress, in Hong Kong films.
A Better Tomorrow 86. Shanghai Express 87. A Better Tomorrow II 87. Rouge 87. Big Brother 89. Ghostly Love 90. Magic Sword 93, etc.

Chukrai, Grigori (1920–).
Russian director.
The Forty First 56. Ballad of a Soldier 59. Clear Sky 61. There Was an Old Man and an Old Woman 65. People! 66. Pamyat 71. La Vita è Bella 82, etc.

Church, Thomas Haden (1960–).
American actor. Born in Texas, he studied at North Texas State University and began in commercials.
Tombstone 93. Tales from the Crypt Presents Demon Knight 95. One Night Stand 97. George of the Jungle 97. Free Money 98, etc.
TV series: Wings 90–95. Ned & Stacey 95– .

Churchill, Berton (1876–1940).
Forceful Canadian stage actor who in later years settled in Hollywood and played stern bosses and fathers.
Tongues of Flame 24. Nothing but the Truth 29. Secrets of a Secretary 31. The Rich are Always with Us 32. American Madness 32. Master of Men 33. Hi Nellie 34. Dames 34. Babbitt 34. Page Miss Glory 35. Parole 36. Parnell 37. The Singing Marine 37. Sweethearts 38. *Stagecoach* (as the absconding banker) 39. The Way of All Flesh 40. Turnabout 40, many others.

Churchill, Diana (1913–1994).
British leading lady, mostly on stage. Multiple sclerosis brought her career to an end. Married to actors Barry K. Barnes and Mervyn Johns.
School for Husbands 36. Housemaster 38. House of the Arrow 40. Eagle Squadron (US) 44. Scott of the Antarctic 48. The History of Mr Polly 49, etc.

Churchill, Donald (1930–1991).
British light actor who developed from callow young men to eccentric middle-aged creations. Also wrote many TV scripts.
Victim 60. The Wild Affair 63, etc.
TV series (a, w) include Bulldog Breed 62. Never a Cross Word 68. Moody and Pegg 63. Spooner's Patch 80.

Churchill, Frank (1901–1942).
American composer, always with Disney and the author of several hit songs.
Three Little Pigs ('Who's Afraid of the Big Bad Wolf?') 33. *Snow White and the Seven Dwarfs* 37. *Dumbo* 41. *Bambi* 42, etc.

Churchill, Marguerite (1910–).
Pert American leading lady of the 30s, now retired and living in Europe. She was married to actor George O'Brien (1933–48).
The Valiant 29. Seven Faces 29. Born Reckless 30. The Big Trail 30. Charlie Chan Carries On 31. Quick Millions 31. Forgotten Commandments 32. Girl without a Room 33. The Walking Dead 36. Dracula's Daughter 36. Legion of Terror 36, etc.

Churchill, Sarah (1914–1982).
British actress, daughter of Sir Winston Churchill.
He Found a Star 40. All Over the Town 47. *Royal Wedding* (US) 51. Serious Charge 58, etc.

Churchill, Sir Winston (1874–1965).
British statesman and author who has been the subject of a major documentary, *The Finest Hours* 64, and a TV series, *The Valiant Years* 60. He was impersonated by Dudley Field Malone in *Mission to Moscow* 43, by Patrick Wymark in *Operation Crossbow* 65, by a number of Russian actors in various propaganda pieces, by Simon Ward in *Young Winston* 72, by Nigel Stock in *A Man Called Intrepid* 79 and by Wensley Pithey in *Ike* 79.
❝ He would rather make love to a word than to a woman. – *Ingrid Bergman*

Churikova, Inna (1943–).
Russian leading actress, frequently in the films of her husband, director Gleb PANFILOV. Her best role was probably Pasha, the simple worker who plays the role of Joan of Arc in a film, in *The Debut*.
Jack Frost/Morozko 65. No Ford in the Fire/V Ognye Broda Nyet 68. *The Debut*/Nachalo 70. Elizaveta Uvarova 74. May I Have the Floor/Proshu Slova 75. The Theme/Tema 79. Valentina, Valentine 81. Vassa 83. Wartime Romance/Voienno-Polevoi Roman 83. *Mother*/Mat 88. God Sobaki 93. Ryaba My Chicken/Kurochka Ryaba 93. The Delegation/Il Delegazione 92. Shily Myrly 95, etc.

Chytilova, Vera (1929–).
Czech director. A former model, she studied at the Prague Film School. Always controversial, she was forbidden to make films in the early 70s.
Another Way of Life 63. Pearls at the Bottom (co-d) 66. Daisies/Sedmikrásky 66. The Apple Game/Hra o Jablko 76. Panel Story 79. Calamity/Kalamita 80. The Very Late Afternoon of a Faun 84. Wolf's Lair/Vlcíbouda 86. The Jester and the Queen/Sasek a Kralovna 88. Dedictvi Aneb Kurvahosigutntag 93. Traps/Pasti, Pasti, Pasticky (& co-w) 98, etc.

Ciampi, Yves (1921–1982).
French director.
Suzanne et Ses Brigands 50. Un Grand Patron 51. L'Esclave 53. Les Héros Sont Fatigués 55. Typhoon over Nagasaki 57. Qui Etes-vous Monsieur Sorge 60. Le Ciel sur la Tête 62. A Quelques Jours 69, etc.

Ciannelli, Eduardo (1887–1969).
Italian character actor, long in Hollywood; his finely-etched features and incisive speech were usually employed in villainous roles, but he could also strike sympathetic chords.
Reunion in Vienna 33. The Scoundrel 35. *Winterset* 36. Marked Woman 37. Law of the Underworld 38. Gunga Din 39. Foreign Correspondent 40. The Mummy's Hand 40. They Met in Bombay 41. Cairo 42. They Got Me Covered 43. *The Mask of Dimitrios* 44. The Conspirators 44. Dillinger 45. Wife of Monte Cristo 46. Perilous Holiday 47. The Creeper 48. Rapture 50. The People Against O'Hara 51. Volcano 53. Mambo 55. Helen of Troy 55. Houseboat 58. The Visit 64. Mackenna's Gold 68. The Brotherhood 68. The Secret of Santa Vittoria 69, many others.
TV series: *Johnny Staccato* 59.

Cicognini, Alessandro (1905–1995).
Italian composer.
Four Steps in the Clouds 42. Shoeshine 46. Bicycle Thieves 48. I Miserabili 48. Tomorrow is Too Late 50. Miracle in Milan 51. Don Camillo 52. Umberto D 52. Due Soldi di Speranza 52. Gold of Naples 54. Ulysses 54. Summer Madness 55. The Black Orchid 58. It Started in Naples (US) 60. A Breath of Scandal (US) 60. Don Camillo Monsignore Ma Non Troppo 61. The Pigeon that Took Rome (US) 62. Compagno Don Camillo 65, etc.

Cilento, Diane (1933–).
Versatile Australian leading actress whose talent has not been fully tested in movies. She was married to Sean Connery (1962–73) and is the mother of actor Jason Connery.
Wings of Danger 52. The Angel who Pawned Her Harp 54. The Passing Stranger 54. Passage Home 55. The Woman for Joe 56. *The Admirable Crichton* 57. Jet Storm 59. The Full Treatment 60. The Naked Edge 61. I Thank a Fool 62. *Tom Jones* (AAN) 63. The Third Secret 64. *Rattle of a Simple Man* 64. The Agony and the Ecstasy 65. *Hombre* 67. Negatives 68. Zero Population Growth 72. The Wicker Man 73. Hitler: the Last Ten Days 74. For the Term of His Natural Life (TV) 82. The Boy Who Had Everything 84. Winner Takes All 86, etc.

Cimino, Michael (c. 1940–).
American director and screenwriter who, after the success of *The Deer Hunter*, helped to ruin United Artists with the financial disaster of *Heaven's Gate*, from which his career has taken a long time to recover. Raised in New York City and Old Westbury, Long Island, he studied at Yale University before going on to study ballet and acting, and to work for a New York company producing industrial films and commercials. He moved to Los Angeles in the early 70s to work as a screenwriter and, through the influence of Clint EASTWOOD, directed the star in his script of *Thunderbolt and Lightfoot*.
Books: 1985, *Final Cut: Dreams and Disaster in the Making of Heaven's Gate* by Steven Bach; 1985, *Martin Scorsese and Michael Cimino* by Michael Bliss.
■ Silent Running (co-w) 72. Magnum Force (co-w) 73. Thunderbolt and Lightfoot (wd) 74. *The Deer Hunter* (wd) (AAd, AANw) 78. Heaven's Gate (wd) 80. The Year of the Dragon 85. The Sicilian 87. Desperate Hours 90. The Sunchaser 96.
❝ Films are home movies of your past. – M.C.

Cioffi, Charles (1935–).
American character actor.
Klute 71. The Don is Dead 73. The Thief who Came to Dinner 73. Crazy Joe 74. The Next Man 76. The Other Side of Midnight 77. Dog and Cat (TV) 77. Time after Time 79. Missing 82. All the Right Moves 83. Remo Williams: The Adventure Begins 85. Newsies/News Boys 92. The Shadow Conspiracy 96, etc.
TV series: Assignment Vienna 72. Get Christy Love 74. Kojak 89–90.

Cipriani, Stelvio.
Italian composer.
The Stranger Returns/El Precio de un Hombre 66. La Belva 70. La Polizia Ringrazia 72. Blondy 75. Frankenstein – Italian Style 76. Vudu Baby 79. City of the Walking Dead 80. Sweet Sins 81. La Voce 82. Piranha II: The Spawning (US) 83. La Classe 84. Rage 84. Rage of Honor (US) 87, etc.

Cissé, Souleymane Oumar (1940–).
Malian director. He studied cinema in Moscow from 1963–69 before returning to his homeland to make documentaries for the Ministry of Information.
The Young Girl/Den Moussa 74. Work/Baara 78. The Wind/Finye 82. The Light/Yeleen 87. Waati 95.

Clair, René (1898–1981) (René Chomette).
Distinguished French director of light comedy; he brought to the screen a nimble command of technique, an optimistic outlook, and a total lack of malice or message.
Novel: 1925, *Star Turn*.
■ Paris Qui Dort 23. Entr'acte 24. Le Fantôme du Moulin Rouge 24. Le Voyage Imaginaire 25. La Proie du Vent 26. Les Deux Timides 28. *An Italian Straw Hat* 28. *Sous les Toits de Paris* 30. *Le Million* 31. *A Nous la Liberté* 31. Le Quatorze Juillet 33. Le Dernier Milliardaire 34. The Ghost Goes West 35. Break the News 36. The Flame of New Orleans 41. *I Married a Witch* 42. Forever and a Day (part) 43. *It Happened Tomorrow* 44. *And Then There Were None* 45. Le Silence est d'Or 47. La Beauté du Diable 49. *Les Belles de Nuit* 52. Les Grandes Manoeuvres 55. Porte des Lilas 56. Tout l'Or du Monde 60. Love and the Frenchwoman (part) 60. Les Quatre Vérités (part) 62. Les Fêtes Galantes 65.
✪ For creating films in which, by a dextrous combination of sound and picture, the feet of the characters appeared never to touch the ground. *Le Million*.
❝ Once too good to be called even the French Lubitsch, he now seems more like the French Mamoulian. – *Andrew Sarris, 1968*
A film-maker who would sooner raise a soufflé than roast an ox. – *Alexander Walker*

Claire, Ina (1892–1985) (Ina Fagan).
American stage actress, noted for her comic style, in occasional films. Born in Washington, D.C., she began in vaudeville in 1905. The second of her three husbands was actor John GILBERT (1929–31). When, after the wedding, a reporter asked her how it felt marrying a great star, she replied, 'I don't know. You better ask Mr Gilbert.'
The Puppet Crown 15. Wild Goose Chase 15. Polly with a Past 20. The Awful Truth 29. The Royal Family of Broadway 31. Rebound 31. The Greeks Had a Word for Them 32. Ninotchka 39. Claudia 43, etc.

Clampett, Bob (1913–1984).
American animator, in at or near the birth of Bugs Bunny, Porky Pig, Daffy Duck and Tweety, who went on to work in television, creating *Time for Beany* (1949–59) and *Beany and Cecil* (1959–67).
Lady Play Your Mandolin 31. The Lone Stranger and Porky 38. Jeepers Creepers 39. Falling Hare 43, etc.

Clancy, Tom (1947–).
Best-selling American writer of technological thrillers featuring CIA agent Jack Ryan. Alec Baldwin starred as Ryan in the first film; subsequently the role has been played by Harrison Ford.
The Hunt for Red October 90. Patriot Games 92. Clear and Present Danger 94. Tom Clancy's Op Center (TV) 95.
❝ Giving your book to Hollywood is like turning your daughter over to a pimp. – *T.C.*

Clapton, Eric (1945–).
British rock guitarist, singer and composer. He was a member of the 60s groups The Yardbirds and Cream. In 1997, *Business Age* estimated his personal fortune at £120m.
Biography: 1986, *Clapton* by Ray Coleman.
AS PERFORMER: Tommy 75. The Last Waltz 78. Eric Clapton and Friends (concert) 86, etc.
AS COMPOSER: The Hit 84. Edge of Darkness (TV) 86. Lethal Weapon 87. Homeboy 88. Lethal Weapon 2 89. Communion 89. Rush 91. Lethal Weapon 3 92. The Van 96, etc.

Clare, Mary (1894–1970).
British character actress, latterly in formidable matron roles.
Becket 24. Hindle Wakes 31. The Constant Nymph 33. The Clairvoyant 34. The Passing of the Third Floor Back 35. Young and Innocent 37. The Lady Vanishes 38. A Girl Must Live 39. Old Bill and Son 40. *Mrs Pym of Scotland Yard* (title role) 40. Next of Kin 42. *The Night Has Eyes* 42. The Hundred-Pound Window 44. The Three Weird Sisters 48. *Oliver Twist* 48. Moulin Rouge 53. Mambo 55. The Price of Silence 59, many others.

Clarence, O. B. (1870–1955).
British stage actor who played benevolent doddering roles in a number of films.
Liberty Hall 14. Perfect Understanding 32. Friday the Thirteenth 33. The Scarlet Pimpernel 34. Seven Sinners 36. Pygmalion 38. Inspector Hornleigh Goes To It 41. Penn of Pennsylvania 42. On Approval 43. A Place of One's Own 44. Great Expectations (as the aged P) 46. Uncle Silas 47, many others.

Clark, Bob (1941–).
American director.
Children Shouldn't Play with Dead Things 72. Black Christmas 72. Breaking Point 76. Murder by Decree 78. Tribute 80. Porky's 82. Porky's II 83. A Christmas Story 83. Rhinestone 84. Turk 182 85. From the Hip 87. Loose Cannons 89. It Runs in the Family 94. Stolen Memories: Secrets from the Rose Garden (TV) 96. I'll Remember April 99, etc.

Clark, Bobby (1888–1960).
Bouncy American vaudeville comedian who with Paul McCullough made thirty-six two-reel comedies for RKO between 1928 and 1936, when McCullough died. Clark made only one solo film appearance, in *The Goldwyn Follies* 38.

Clark, Candy (1947–).
American leading lady of the 70s.
Fat City 72. American Graffiti (AAN) 73. The Man Who Fell to Earth 76. I Will, I Will, For Now 76. Citizen's Band 77. When You Comin' Back, Red Ryder? 79. More American Graffiti 79. Blue Thunder 83. Amityville 3-D 83. Hambone and Hillie 84. Stephen King's Cat's Eye 85. At Close Range 86. The Blob 88. Cool as Ice 91. Buffy the Vampire Slayer 92. Radioland Murders 94, etc.

Clark, Carroll.
American art director. He worked for Pathé and David SELZNICK before joining RKO in the 30s, where he worked under Van Nest POLGLASE on most of the studio's biggest films, including the Fred ASTAIRE-Ginger ROGERS musicals. In the 50s he became supervising art director of DISNEY's live-action films.
Hell's Angels 30. The Most Dangerous Game 32. King Kong 33. Flying Down to Rio 33. The Gay Divorcee (AAN) 34. Of Human Bondage 34. Roberta 35. Top Hat (AAN) 35. Mary of Scotland 36. Swing Time 36. Follow the Fleet 36. A Damsel in Distress (AAN) 37. Shall We Dance 37. Carefree 38. Bachelor Mother 39. Suspicion 41. Joan of Paris 42. Flight for Freedom (AAN) 43. Days of Glory 44. Step Lively (AAN) 44. Notorious 46. Sinbad the Sailor 47. Mr Blandings Builds His Dream House 48. The Blue Veil 51. Clash by Night 52. Second Chance 53. While the City Sleeps 56. Old Yeller 57. Darby O'Gill and the Little People 59. Pollyana 60. The Absent Minded Professor (AAN) 61. The Parent Trap 61. Son of Flubber 63. The Incredible Journey 63. Mary Poppins (AAN) 64. That Darn Cat 65. Follow Me Boys! 66. The Gnome-mobile 67. Blackbeard's Ghost 68. The Love Bug 68, etc.

Clark, Cliff (1893–1953).
Short, stocky American character actor who played tough sheriffs and police inspectors in 40s co-features.
Mr Moto's Gamble 38. Kentucky 39. Honolulu 39. The Grapes of Wrath 40. Double Alibi 40. Manpower 41. Kid Glove Killer 42. The Falcon's Brother 42. The Falcon in Danger 43. The Falcon out West 44. Bury Me Dead 47. Deep Waters 48. The Men 50. Cavalry Scout 51. The Sniper 52, many others.

Clark, Curtis.
American cinematographer, in Britain for much of his career.
British Hustle (doc, & d) 78. Blue Suede Shoes (doc, & d) 80. *The Draughtsman's Contract* 82. Alamo Bay 85. Dominick and Eugene 88. Triumph of the Spirit 89. A Talent for the Game 91, etc.

Clark, Dane (1913–1998) (Bernard Zanville).
Pint-sized American tough guy of the 40s, a poor man's John GARFIELD. Born in Brooklyn, New York, he studied at Cornell University and took a law degree at St John's University, New York; he tried unsuccessfully to become a baseball player and a boxer before working in labouring jobs and as a writer for radio. He was on stage from 1934 and worked with the Group Theatre before going to Hollywood. There his career suffered when he quarrelled with Jack WARNER over a renewal of his contract: Warner called him 'a ham', and Clark hit him. As a result, Warner refused to lend him to Columbia to star in *The Jolson Story*, or to United Artists for the role of the boxer in *Champion*, which made Kirk DOUGLAS a star. Warner also warned other studios against him, and he was forced to go to Europe to make a few uninteresting movies. Married twice. His lovers included Ida LUPINO, his co-star in *Deep Valley*.
Tennessee Johnson 43. Destination Tokyo 43. The Very Thought of You 44. God is My Co-Pilot 45. A Stolen Life 46. Her Kind of Man 46. That Way with Women 47. Deep Valley 47. Whiplash 48. *Moonrise* 49. Barricade 50. Without Honour 50. Highly Dangerous (GB) 50. Go Man Go (& co-p) 53. Port of Hell 54. The Toughest Man Alive 55. Murder by Proxy (GB) 55. This Man is Armed 56. The Outlaw's Son 57. The McMasters 70. Say Goodbye, Maggie Cole (TV) 72. Murder on Flight 502 (TV) 75. James Dean (TV) 76. The Woman Inside 81. Blood Song 82. Last Rites 88, etc.
TV series: Justice 52. Bold Venture 54. Wire Service 56–57. Bold Venture 59. The New Perry Mason 73–74.

Clark, Ernest (1912–1994).
British character actor of all media, usually in cold, tight-lipped roles.
Private Angelo 49. Doctor in the House 53. Beau Brummell 54. The Dam Busters 55. Time without Pity 57. A Tale of Two Cities 58. Sink the Bismarck 60. Nothing but the Best 64. Arabesque 66. Salt and Pepper 68. Gandhi 82, many others.

Clark, Fred (1914–1968).
Bald-domed American character comedian, usually in explosive roles.
■ The Unsuspected 47. Ride the Pink Horse 47. Hazard 48. Cry of the City 48. Two Guys from Texas 48. Fury at Furnace Creek 48. Alias Nick Beal 49. Flamingo Road 49. The Younger Brothers 49. Task Force 49. White Heat 49. The Lady Takes a Sailor 49. *Sunset Boulevard* 50. The Eagle and the Hawk 50. Return of the Frontiersman 50. The Jackpot 50. Mrs O'Malley and Mr Malone 50. The Lemon Drop Kid 51. Hollywood Story 51. A Place in the Sun 51. Meet Me After the Show 51. Three for Bedroom C 52. Dreamboat 52. The Stars are Singing 53. The Caddy 53. How to Marry a Millionaire 53. Here Come the Girls 53. Living It Up 54. Abbott and Costello Meet the Keystone Kops 54. Daddy Longlegs 55. How to be Very Very Popular 55. The Court Martial of Billy Mitchell 55. Miracle in the Rain 56. The Birds and the Bees 56. *The Solid Gold Cadillac* 56. Back from Eternity 56. Joe Butterfly 57. The Fuzzy Pink Nightgown 57. *Don't Go Near the Water* 57. Mardi Gras 58. Auntie Mame 58. The Mating Game 59. It Started with a Kiss 59. Visit to a Small Planet 60. Bells are Ringing 60. Zotz 62. Boys' Night Out 62. Hemingway's Adventures of a Young Man 62. Move Over Darling 63. John Goldfarb Please Come Home 64. The Curse of the Mummy's Tomb (GB) 65. Sergeant Deadhead 65. Dr Goldfoot and the Bikini Machine 65. When the Boys meet the Girls 65. War Italian Style 67. The Horse in the Grey Flannel Suit 68. Skidoo 68. I Sailed to Tahiti with an All-Girl Crew 68.
TV series: *The Double Life of Henry Phyfe* 65. Also with Burns and Allen for several seasons.

Clark, Harvey (1886–1936).
American character actor, usually in comic roles, from the stage and vaudeville.
The Innocence of Lizette 16. The Kiss 21. Alias Julius Caesar 22. The Roughnecks 24. Black Paradise 26. Camille 27. The Olympic Hero 28. Seven Keys to Baldpate 29. Man Trouble 30. Cracked Nuts 31. The Big Shot 32. Red-Headed Woman 32. West of Singapore 33. Alice in Wonderland 33. Countess of Monte Cristo 34. Three Godfathers 36. The Singing Cowboy 36. History Is Made at Night 37. Spawn of the North 38, etc.

Clark, James B. (1908–).
American director, former editor.
Under Fire 57. Sierra Baron 58. The Sad Horse 59. A Dog of Flanders 60. One Foot in Hell 60. The Big Show 60. Misty 61. Flipper 63. Island of the Blue Dolphins 64. And Now Miguel 66. My Side of the Mountain 68. The Little Ark 71, etc.

Clark, Jim (1931–).
British editor.
The Grass is Greener 61. The Innocents 61. Charade 63. The Pumpkin Eater 64. Darling 65. Zee and Co. 72. The Day of the Locust 75. Marathon Man 76. Yanks 79. Agatha 79. Honky Tonk Freeway 81. The Killing Fields (AA) 84. The Frog Prince 84. The Mission 86. Meeting Venus 90. This Boy's Life 93. A Good Man in Africa 94. Radio Inside 94. Copycat 95. I Love You, I Love You Not 97. The Jackal 97, etc.
ALSO DIRECTOR: ■ The Christmas Tree 68. Every Home Should Have One 70. Rentadick 72. Madhouse 74.

Clark, Ken. (1932–).
American supporting actor, usually in tough roles. In the 60s, he moved to Italy and appeared in films there.
Between Heaven and Hell 56. The Proud Ones 56. Love Me Tender 56. On the Threshold of Space 56. South Pacific 58. Attack of the Giant Leeches 59. Twelve to the Moon 60. Hercules the Invincible/Ercole l'Invincibile 63. Secret Agent FX 18 (It./Fr./Sp.) 64. Hercules against the Mongols/ Maciste contro i Mongoli 64. From the Orient with Fury/Agente 077 dall'Oriente con Furore (It./Fr./ Sp.) 65. Agente 077 Missione Bloody Mary (It./ Fr./Sp.) 65. Nebraska il Pistolero (It./Sp.) 66. Savage Gringo/Ringo nel Nebraska (It./Sp.) 66. Tiffany Memorandum (It./Fr.) 67. A Man Called Sledge (It.) 70, etc.

Clark, Larry (1943–).
American director, photographer and artist. Born in Tulsa, Oklahoma, he first attracted attention with his photographic studies *Tulsa* 71, picturing young amphetamine addicts, and *Teenage Lust* 83.
Kids 95. Another Day in Paradise 98.
❝ When I was 16 I started shooting amphetamine. I shot with my friends every day for three years and then left town but I've gone back through the years. Once the needle goes in, it never comes out. – *L.C.*

Clark, Marguerite (1883–1940).
American heroine of the silent screen, a rival for Mary Pickford in waif-like and innocent roles. Retired 1921.
Wildflower 14. The Goose Girl 15. Molly Make-Believe 16. Snow White 17. Prunella 18. Mrs Wiggs of the Cabbage Patch 18. Girls 19. All-of-a-Sudden Peggy 20. Scrambled Wives 21.

Clark, Matt. (1936–).
American character actor, mostly as western villain.
Will Penny 67. Monte Walsh 70. Emperor of the North 73. Hearts of the West 75. Kid Vengeance 77. Brubaker 80. The Legend of the Lone Ranger 81. Honkytonk Man 82. Love Letters 82. Country 84. Return to Oz 84. Tuff Turf 84. Out of the Darkness (TV) 85. The Quick and the Dead (TV) 87. The Horror Show 89. Back to the Future III 90. Class Action 90. Frozen Assets 92. Barbarians at the Gate (TV) 93. Homegrown 97, etc.

Clark, Petula (1932–).
British child actress who later made it big as a singer and settled in France. She played the role of Norma Desmond in the London version of the musical *Sunset Boulevard* in 1996.
■ Medal for the General 44. Murder in Reverse 45. I Know Where I'm Going 45. London Town 46. Strawberry Roan 47. *Here Come the Huggetts* 48. Vice Versa 48. Easy Money 48. Don't Ever Leave Me 49. Vote for Huggett 49. The Huggetts Abroad 50. Dance Hall 50. The Romantic Age 50. White Corridors 51. Madame Louise 51. Made in Heaven 52. *The Card* 52. The Runaway Bus 54. The Gay Dog 54. The Happiness of Three Women 55. Track the Man Down 56. That Woman Opposite 57. Daggers Drawn 64. Finian's Rainbow 68. *Goodbye Mr Chips* 69. Never Never Land 81.

Clark, Robert (1905–1984).
British executive, longtime director (resigned 1969) of Associated British Picture Corporation. Former lawyer; producer of many ABPC films including *The Hasty Heart*, *The Dam Busters*, etc.

Clark, Susan (1940–).
Canadian leading lady in Hollywood.
Banning 67. Madigan 68. Coogan's Bluff 68. Something for a Lonely Man (TV) 68. The Challengers (TV) 68. The Forbin Project 69. Tell Them Willie Boy Is Here 69. Skullduggery 69. Valdez Is Coming 70. The Skin Game 71. The Astronaut (TV) 71. Showdown 73. Trapped (TV) 73. Airport 75 74. The Midnight Man 74. The Apple Dumpling Gang 75. *Babe* (TV) 75. Night Moves 75. *Amelia Earhart* (TV) 76. Murder by Decree 78. Promises in the Dark 79. City on Fire 79. The North Avenue Irregulars 80. Double Negative 80. Nobody's Perfekt 81. Porky's 82. Maid in America (TV) 82. Butterbox Babies 95, etc.
TV series: Webster 83–88. Emily of New Moon 98.

Clarke, Alan (1935–1990).
British director, from television, noted for his films of tough working-class life.
Book: 1998, *Alan Clarke*, ed. Richard Kelly.
Scum 79. Contact (TV) 85. Made in Britain (TV) 83. Billy the Kid and the Green Baize Vampire 85. Rita, Sue and Bob, Too 87. The Firm (TV) 90, etc.
❝ I wouldn't make a film with the edge written out. – A.C.

Clarke, Sir Arthur C. (1917–).
British science fiction writer who provided the basis for *2001: A Space Odyssey* (AAN). Non-fiction interests include the popular science TV series of 1981, *Arthur C. Clarke's Mysterious World*.

Clarke, Charles G. (1899–1983).
American cinematographer.
The Light That Failed 23. Friendly Enemies 25. Whispering Smith 26. Upstream 27. The Exalted Flapper 29. So This Is London 30. The Cat and the Fiddle 34. Tarzan and His Mate 34. The Return of the Cisco Kid 39. *Moontide* 42. Guadalcanal Diary 43. *Margie* 46. Miracle on 34th Street 47. The Iron Curtain 48. Sand 49. The Big Lift 50. Destination Gobi 53. Prince of Players 55. Carousel 56. The Barbarian and the Geisha 58. The Sound and the Fury 59. Return to Peyton Place 59. Madison Avenue 62, many others.

Clarke, Mae (1907–1992) (Mary Klotz).
Pert American leading lady at her peak in the early 30s; from musical comedy. She may be best remembered for having a grapefruit ground into her face by James Cagney in *Public Enemy*. She was also the inspiration for Lorelei Lee in Anita Loos's *Gentlemen Prefer Blondes*.
Big Time 29. Fall Guy 30. *The Front Page* 31. *Public Enemy* 31. *Waterloo Bridge* 31. Frankenstein 31. Night World 32. The Penguin Pool Murder 32. Parole Girl 33. Penthouse 33. Lady Killer 33. Nana 34. The Silk Hat Kid 35. Wild Brian Kent 36. Trouble in Morocco 37. Women in War 40. Sailors on Leave 41. Flying Tigers 42. Here Come the Waves 44. Kitty 45. Daredevils of the Clouds 48. Annie Get Your Gun 50. The Great Caruso 51. Because of You 52. Women's Prison 55. Mohawk 56. Ask Any Girl 59. Big Hand for a Little Lady 66. Thoroughly Modern Millie 67, many others.

Clarke, Margi (1954–).
British actress, a former TV presenter.
Letter to Brezhnev 85. Helsinki Napoli All Night Long 87. I Hired a Contract Killer 90. Blonde Fist 91, etc.
TV series: Making Out 89–91. The Good Sex Guide 93–94.

Clarke, Shirley (1919–1997) (Shirley Brimberg).
American director of the New York *cinema vérité* school. Born in New York, she was a dancer with Martha Graham before turning to film. With Jonas Mekas, she founded the Film-Makers Co-operative to distribute independent films, and was one of the signatories to the *Statement for a New American Cinema*, with its manifesto: 'We don't want rose-coloured films any more, but films the colour of blood'. She taught film and video production at the University of California, Los Angeles, in the 70s and 80s before succumbing to Alzheimer's disease.
Skyscraper (short) (AAN) 59. The Connection 60. Robert Frost: A Lover's Quarrel with the World (doc) 63. Cool World 63. Portrait of Jason 67. Lions Love (a) 69. Ornette: Made in America (doc) 86, etc.

Clarke, Stanley (1951–).
American composer and bassist, a founding member of the 70s jazz group Return to Forever, and the Clark/Duke Project and Animal Logic.
Book of Love 91. Boyz N The Hood 91. Cool as Ice 91. The Five Heartbeats 91. Watch It 93. What's Love Got to Do with It? 93. Little Big League 94. Higher Learning 95. Panther 95. Eddie 96. Dangerous Ground 96. The Cherokee Kid (TV) 96. B.A.P.S. 97. On the Line (TV) 98. Down in the Delta 98, etc.

Clarke, T. E. B. (1907–1989).
British screenwriter, former journalist; associated with the heyday of Ealing comedy.
Autobiography: 1974, *This Is Where I Came In*.
Johnny Frenchman 45. *Against the Wind* 46. *Hue and Cry* 46. *Passport to Pimlico* (AAN) 48. The Blue Lamp 50. *The Lavender Hill Mob* (AA) 51. *The Titfield Thunderbolt* 53. Barnacle Bill 57. Law and Disorder 58. Gideon's Day 58. Sons and Lovers (AAN) 60. The Horse Without a Head 63. A Man Could Get Killed 66, etc.

Clarke, Warren.
Burly English character actor, much on television.
A Clockwork Orange 71. Antony and Cleopatra 72. O Lucky Man 73. Hawk the Slayer 80. Firefox 82. Enigma 82. Top Secret (US) 83. The Jewel in the Crown (TV) 84. Cold Room 84. Lassiter 84. Gulag (TV) 85. Mandela 87. Crusoe 88. Joseph (TV) 95. i.d. 95. A Respectable Trade (TV) 98, etc.
TV series: The Onedin Line 71–80. Shelley 79–82. The Manageress 89–90. All Good Things 91. Gone to the Dogs 91. Gone to Seed 92. House of Windsor 94. Moving Story 94. Dalziel and Pascoe 96. The Locksmith 97.

Clarke-Smith, D. A. (1888–1959).
British character actor, mainly on stage.
Atlantic 30. The Ghoul 33. Warn London 34. Sabotage 36. The Flying Fifty-Five 39. Frieda 47. Quo Vadis 51. The Baby and the Battleship 56, etc.

Clavell, James (1922–1994).
Australian writer of Anglo-Irish descent.
The Fly 58. Five Gates to Hell (& pd) 58. Walk Like a Dragon (& pd) 60. The Sweet and the Bitter (wpd) (Can.) 62. The Great Escape 63. The Satan Bug 65. King Rat (oa) 65. To Sir With Love (& pd) 66. Where's Jack? (& pd) 69. Shogun (TV) 80.
❝ I'm not a novelist, but a storyteller. I'm not a literary figure at all. – J.C.

Claxton, William F. (1914–1996).
American director.
Fangs of the Wild 55. The Quiet Gun 57. Desire in the Dust 60. Law of the Lawless 64. Night of the Lepus 72. Bonanza: The Next Generation (TV) 88, etc.

Clay, Andrew Dice (1958–) (Andrew Clay Silverstein).
Controversial American comedian.
Making the Grade 84. Pretty in Pink 86. Amazon Women on the Moon 86. Casual Sex? 88. The Adventures of Ford Fairlane 90. Dice Rules 91. Brain Smasher 93. The Good Life 97. Foolish 98, etc.
TV series: Bless This House 95. Hitz 97.

Clay, Nicholas (1946–).
British leading man.
The Night Digger 71. The Darwin Adventure 75. Tristan and Isolde 76. Zulu Dawn 78. Excalibur 81. Lady Chatterley's Lover 81. Evil under the Sun 82. Hound of the Baskervilles (TV) 83. Lionheart 87. Sleeping Beauty 89. The Odyssey (TV) 97. Merlin (TV) 98, etc.

Clayburgh, Jill (1944–).
American leading lady of the 70s. She married dramatist and screenwriter David Rabe in 1979.
■ The Wedding Party 69. The Telephone Book 71. Portnoy's Complaint 72. The Thief Who Came to Dinner 73. The Terminal Man 74. The Art of Crime (TV) 74. *Hustling* (TV) 74. Griffin and Phoenix (TV) 76. *Gable and Lombard* (as Lombard) 76. Silver Streak 76. Semi-Tough 77. *An Unmarried Woman* (AAN) 78. La Luna 79. Starting Over (AAN) 79. It's My Turn 80. First Monday in October 81. I'm Dancing as Fast as I Can 82. Hannah K 83. Where Are The Children? 85. Shy People 87. Beyond the Ocean 90. Day of Atonement/Le Grand Pardon 2 92. Whispers in the Dark 92. Naked in New York 93. Firestorm: 72 Hours in Oakland (TV) 93. Day of Atonement 93. Honor Thy Father and Mother (TV) 94. The Face on the Milk (TV) 95. Sins of the Mind (TV) 97. When Innocence Is Lost (TV) 97. Crowned and Dangerous (TV) 97. Fools Rush In 97. Going All the Way 97.
TV series: Trinity 98– .

Clayton, Ethel (1884–1966).
American silent star actress.
Her Own Money 12. The College Widow 15. Pettigrew's Girl 19. Sham 21. If I Were Queen 22. The Remittance Woman 23. Wings of Youth 25. Mother Machree 28. Hit the Deck 30. Continental 32. Secrets 33. Artists and Models 37. The Buccaneer 38. Ambush 39, many others.

Clayton, Jack (1921–1995).
British producer-director who worked his way up through the industry.
■ The Bespoke Overcoat £ 55. Three Men in a Boat (p) 56. *Room at the Top* (AANd) 58. *The Innocents* (d) 61. *The Pumpkin Eater* (d) 64. Our Mother's House (d) 67. The Great Gatsby (d) 74. Something Wicked This Way Comes 83. The Lonely Passion of Judith Hearne 87. Memento Mori (TV) 92.
❝ I don't believe in being fashionable. Try to be, and you're usually out of date before you start. – J.C.

Cleese, John (1939–).
Lanky English actor, writer and producer, adept at playing aggressive or obsessive middle-class middle managers, the type promoted beyond their abilities. Educated at Cambridge University and a former schoolmaster, he began in television comedy, notably as one of Monty Python's Flying Circus. His finest moments so far were writing (with his then-wife Connie Booth) the TV sitcom *Fawlty Towers*, and acting as its manic hotel-owner Basil Fawlty. He is also the co-author, with psychoanalyst Dr Robin Skynner, of the books *Families and How to Survive Them* and *Life and How to Survive It*.
Interlude 68. The Best House in London 68. The Rise and Rise of Michael Rimmer 70. And Now for Something Completely Different 71. The Love Ban 72. *Monty Python and the Holy Grail* 74. The Life of Brian 79. The Secret Policeman's Ball 80. *Time Bandits* 82. Privates on Parade 82. Monty Python and the Meaning of Life 83. Yellowbeard 83. *Clockwise* 85. A Fish Called Wanda (& p, w) (AAN) 88. The Big Picture 89. Erik the Viking 89. Bullseye! 90. An American Tail: Fievel Goes West (voice) 91. Splitting Heirs 93. Mary Shelley's Frankenstein 94. The Jungle Book 94. The Swan Princess (voice) 94. Fierce Creatures 96. Parting Shots 98, etc.
TV series: *Fawlty Towers* 75, 79.
❝ Filming is like a long air journey: there's so much hanging around and boredom that they keep giving you food. – J.C.
I auditioned a young actor last week who had scenes with Stallone in a film and he never spoke to him, except on camera. I don't know why people behave like that. It's infantile. Even the nice stars go mad. People I like very much have quite clearly gone barmy. – J.C.

Clemens, Brian (1931–).
British screenwriter especially associated with *The Avengers;* author of many TV thrillers.
Station Six Sahara 64. The Corrupt Ones 64. And Soon the Darkness 70. See No Evil 71. Dr Jekyll and Sister Hyde 71. Captain Kronos Vampire Hunter (& d) 72. The Golden Voyage of Sinbad 73. The Watcher in the Woods 80, etc.

Clemens, William (1905–).
American director of second features.
■ Man Hunt 36. The Law in Her Hands 36. The Case of the Velvet Claws 36. Down the Stretch 36. Here Comes Carter 36. Once a Doctor 37. The Case of the Stuttering Bishop 37. Talent Scout 37. The Footloose Heiress 37. Missing Witnesses 37. Torchy Blane in Panama 38. Accidents Will Happen 38. Mr Chump 38. Nancy Drew Detective 38. Nancy Drew Reporter 39. Nancy Drew Trouble Shooter 39. Nancy Drew and the Hidden Staircase 39. The Dead End Kids on Dress Parade 39. Calling Philo Vance 40. King of the Lumberjacks 40. Devil's Island 40. She Couldn't Say No 41. Knockout 41. The Night of January 16th 41. A Night in New Orleans 42. Sweater Girl 42. Lady Bodyguard 43. The Falcon in Danger 43. The Falcon and the Co-Eds 43. The Falcon Out West 44. Crime by Night 44. The Thirteenth Hour 47.

Clément, Aurore.
French leading actress.
Lacombe Lucien 73. Caro Michele 76. Apocalypse Now 79. Lovers and Liars 79. Paris, Texas 84. Le Livre de Marie. Stan the Flasher 90. Eline Vere 91. Pas d'Amour sans Amour 92. Looking for Paradise 95, etc.

Clement, Dick (1937–).
British writer-director.
The Jokers (co-w) 67. *Otley* (co-w, d) 69. A Severed Head (d) 70. Villain (w) 71. Catch Me a Spy (co-w, d) 71. The Likely Lads 76. The Prisoner of Zenda (w) 79. Porridge (wd) 79. Bullshot (d) 83. Water (d) 84. Vice Versa (co-w) 88. The Commitments (co-w) 91. Excess Baggage (co-w) 97. Still Crazy (co-w) 98, etc.

Clément, René (1913–1996).
Distinguished French director whose later films have disappointed.
■ *La Bataille du Rail* 43. Les Maudits 46. Le Père Tranquille 46. Au-Delà des Grilles 49. Le Château de Verre 50. *Les Jeux Interdits* 51. Knave of Hearts (GB) 53. *Gervaise* 55. The Sea Wall 56. Plein Soleil 59. Quelle Joie de Vivre 61. The Day and the Hour 63. The Love Cage 65. Is Paris Burning? 66. Rider on the Rain 69. The House under the Trees 71. And Hope to Die 72. Wanted: Babysitter 75.

Clementi, Pierre (1941–).
French leading actor.
The Leopard 63. *Belle de Jour* 67. Benjamin 68. The Milky Way 68. Pigsty 70. The Conformist 71. Steppenwolf 74. Les Apprentis Sorciers 77. La Chanson de Roland 78. Zoo-Zero 78. L'Amour des Femmes 81. Le Pont du Nord 81. Quartet 81. Exposed 83. Canicule 84. Clash 84. A L'ombre de la Canaille Bleue (& wd) 86. Hard to Be a God 89. Hideous Kinky (GB) 98, etc.

Clements, Sir John (1910–1988).
Distinguished British actor-manager, on stage from 1930. He married actress Kay Hammond in 1946.
Ticket of Leave 35. Things to Come 36. Rembrandt 36. Knight Without Armour 36. South Riding 38. The Housemaster 39. *The Four Feathers* 39. Convoy 40. This England 41. Ships with Wings 41. Tomorrow We Live 42. Undercover 42. They Came to a City 45. Call of the Blood (& wpd) 47. The Silent Enemy 57. *The Mind Benders* 63. Oh What a Lovely War 69. Gandhi 82, etc.

Clements, Stanley (1926–1981).
American actor familiar in the 40s as tough teenager.
Tall Dark and Handsome 41. Going My Way 44. Salty O'Rourke 45. Bad Boy 49. Jet Job 52. Robbers' Roost 55. Up in Smoke 59. Saintly Sinners 61. Tammy and the Doctor 63, many others.

Cleopatra (69–30 BC).
The sultry Egyptian queen has been portrayed in many films, notably in a Méliès trick film of 1899; by unspecified American actresses in 1908 and 1909; by Helen Gardner in 1911; by Theda Bara in 1917; by Claudette Colbert in the de Mille version of 1934; by Vivien Leigh in Pascal's 1945 *Caesar and Cleopatra;* by Rhonda Fleming in *Serpent of the Nile* 1953; by Hedy Lamarr in *The Story of Mankind* 1957; by Elizabeth Taylor in the well-publicized 1962 version; and by Amanda Barrie in a spoof, *Carry On Cleo*, in 1963. There seems to be something about the lady that encourages waste, for the Leigh version was Britain's most expensive film and the Taylor version the world's; in neither case did the money show on the screen.

Cleveland, George (1886–1957).
American character actor, typically cast as grizzled old prospector.
Keeper of the Bees 35. Revolt of the Zombies

36. Goldtown Ghost Riders 38. Port of Missing Girls 38. Mutiny in the Big House 39. Call Out the Marines 41. The Spoilers 42. Woman of the Town 44. Can't Help Singing 44. Dakota 45. The Runaround 46. The Wistful Widow of Wagon Gap 47. Please Believe Me 50. Trigger Jnr 52. Untamed Heiress 54, many others.

TV series: *Lassie* 55–57.

Cliff, Laddie (1891–1937) (Clifford Perry).
British light comedian and composer.

The Co-Optimists 29. Sleeping Car 33. Happy 33, etc.

Clifford, Graeme.
Australian director and screenwriter, a former film editor.

AS EDITOR: Don't Look Now 74. The Rocky Horror Picture Show 76. The Man Who Fell to Earth 76. F.I.S.T. 78. Convoy 78. The Postman Always Rings Twice 81, etc.

AS DIRECTOR: Frances 82. Burke & Wills (& w) 85. Gleaming the Cube 88. Turn of the Screw (TV) 89. Ruby Cairo 93. Past Tense (TV) 94. Loss of Innocence (TV) 96. The Last Don (TV) 97. The Last Don II (TV) 98, etc.

Clifford, Hubert (1904–1954).
Australian composer and conductor. Born in Bairnsdale, Victoria, he came to England to study at the Royal College of Music, and in the late 40s became musical director of Alexander KORDA's London Film Productions.

Steel (doc) 45. An Ideal Husband (conductor) 47. Pandora and the Flying Dutchman 50. Seven Days to Noon (md) 50. The Bridge 50. Cry the Beloved Country 52. House of Secrets 56. The One that Got Away (md) 57. Hell Drivers 57. Bachelor of Hearts 58, etc.

Clift, Montgomery (1920–1966).
Romantic American leading actor of stage and screen, usually in introspective roles; his career was jeopardized in 1956 by a car accident which somewhat disfigured him.

Biographies: 1977, *Monty* by Robert La Guardia; 1978, *Montgomery Clift* by Patricia Bosworth; 1997, *Montgomery Clift* by Maurice Leonard.

■ *The Search* (AAN) 48. *Red River* 48. The Heiress 49. The Big Lift 50. *A Place in the Sun* (AAN) 51. I Confess 53. *From Here to Eternity* (AAN) 53. Indiscretion of an American Wife 54. Raintree County 57. The Young Lions 58. Lonelyhearts 59. Suddenly Last Summer 59. Wild River 60. The Misfits 60. Judgment at Nuremberg (AAN) 61. *Freud* 63. The Defector 66.

Clifton, Elmer (1890–1949).
American director, mainly of second features; started as an actor with Griffith.

Boots 19. Nugget Nell 19. Mary Ellen Comes to Town 21. Down to the Sea in Ships 22. The Wreck of the Hesperus 27. Virgin Lips 28. Six Cylinder Love 31. Crusade against Rackets 37. Isle of Destiny 40. Swamp Woman 41. Seven Doors to Death 44. Not Wanted 49, many others.

Cline, Edward (1892–1961).
American comedy director who began with the Sennett bathing beauties.

Summer Girls 18. Three Ages 23. Captain January 24. Old Clothes 25. *Sherlock Junior* 26. Let it Rain 27. Soft Cushions 27. Ladies Night in a Turkish Bath 27, etc.

■ SOUND FILMS COMPLETE: Broadway Fever 29. His Lucky Day 29. The Forward Pass 29. In the Next Room 30. Sweet Mama 30. Leathernecking 30. Hook Line and Sinker 30. The Widow from Chicago 30. Cracked Nuts 31. The Naughty Flirt 31. The Girl Habit 31. *Million Dollar Legs* 32. Parole Girl 33. So This is Africa 33. Peck's Bad Boy 34. The Dude Ranger 34. When a Man's a Man 35. The Cowboy Millionaire 35. It's a Great Life 36. F Man 36. On Again Off Again 37. Forty Naughty Girls 37. High Flyers 37. Hawaii Calls 38. Go Chase Yourself 38. Breaking the Ice 38. Peck's Bad Boy with the Circus 38. My *Little Chickadee* 40. The Villain Still Pursued Her 40. *The Bank Dick* 40. Meet the Chump 41. Cracked Nuts 41. Hello Sucker 41. *Never Give a Sucker an Even Break* 41. Snuffy Smith 32. What's Cookin' 42. Private Buckaroo 42. Give Out Sisters 42. Behind the Eight Ball 42. He's My Guy 43. Crazy House 43. Swingtime Johnny 44. Ghost Catchers 44. Slightly Terrific 44. Moonlight and Cactus 44. Night Club Girl 44. See My Lawyer 45. Penthouse Rhythm 45. Bringing Up Father 46. Jiggs and Maggie in Society 48. Jiggs and Maggie in Court 48.

Clitheroe, Jimmy (1916–1973).
Diminutive (4 ft 2 ins tall) English comedian, who spent a lifetime playing a naughty schoolboy, mainly on his long-running radio show *The Clitheroe Kid* 58–72, and occasionally in films.

Old Mother Riley in Business 40. Much Too Shy 42. Rhythm Serenade 43. Somewhere in Politics 49. School for Randle 49. Stars in Your Eyes 56. Rocket to the Moon 67, etc.

Clive, Colin (1898–1937) (Clive Greig).
British leading man who looked older than his years; in Hollywood from 1930, playing fraught, serious roles. Died of TB complicated by alcoholism. Married actress Jeanne DE CASALIS.

■ *Journey's End* 30. *Frankenstein* (title role) 31. The Stronger Sex (GB) 31. Lily Christine (GB) 32. Christopher Strong 33. Looking Forward 33. The Key 34. *Jane Eyre* (as Rochester) 34. One More River 34. Clive of India 35. The Right to Live 35. *The Bride of Frankenstein* 35. The Girl from Tenth Avenue 35. *Mad Love* 35. The Man who Broke the Bank at Monte Carlo 35. *History is Made at Night* 37. The Woman I Love 37.

❝ He was the handsomest man I ever saw – and also the saddest. – *Mae Clarke*

Clive, E. E. (1879–1940).
British character actor who came late in life to Hollywood and played a succession of sour-faced but often amiable butlers, burgomasters and statesmen, with a sprinkling of lower orders.

■ The Invisible Man 33. The Poor Rich 34. The Gay Divorcee 34. Long Lost Father 34. One More River 34. Riptide 34. Bulldog Drummond Strikes Back 34. Charlie Chan in London 34. The Mystery of Edwin Drood 35. *The Bride of Frankenstein* 35. Remember Last Night 35. We're in the Money 35. Gold Diggers of 1935 35. Stars Over Broadway 35. A Tale of Two Cities 35. Captain Blood 35. Atlantic Adventure 35. Father Brown Detective 35. Sylvia Scarlett 35. The Widow from Monte Carlo 35. The King Steps Out 36. Little Lord Fauntleroy 36. Love Before Breakfast 36. Dracula's Daughter 36. The Unguarded Hour 36. Trouble for Two 36. Piccadilly Jim 36. All American Champ 36. Libeled Lady 36. Tarzan Escapes 36. Isle of Fury 36. *The Charge of the Light Brigade* 36. Cain and Mabel 36. Palm Springs 36. Ticket to Paradise 36. Lloyds of London 36. The Dark Hour 36. Live, Love and Learn 36. They Wanted to Marry 37. Maid of Salem 37. Bulldog Drummond Escapes 37. *Bulldog Drummond Comes Back* 37. Bulldog Drummond's Revenge 37. Ready Willing and Able 37. It's Love I'm After 37. On the Avenue 37. Love Under Fire 37. Danger Love at Work 37. *Personal Property* 37. Night Must Fall 37. The Emperor's Candlesticks 37. Beg Borrow or Steal 37. Arsène Lupin Returns 38. The First Hundred Years 38. The Last Warning 38. Kidnapped 38. Gateway 38. Submarine Patrol 38. Bulldog Drummond's Peril 38. Bulldog Drummond in Africa 38. Arrest Bulldog Drummond 39. I'm from Missouri 39. The Little Princess 39. Bulldog Drummond's Secret Police 39. Man About Town 39. Bulldog Drummond's Bride 39. The Hound of the Baskervilles 39. Rose of Washington Square 39. The Adventures of Sherlock Holmes 39. The Honeymoon's Over 39. Raffles 39. Bachelor Mother 39. The Earl of Chicago 40. Congo Maisie 40. Pride and Prejudice 40. Foreign Correspondent 40.

Cloche, Maurice (1907–1990).
French director, in films (as documentarist) from 1933.

La Vie est Magnifique 38. Monsieur Vincent 47. Cage aux Filles 48. Né de Père Inconnu 50. Les Filles de la Nuit 57. Coplan, Secret Agent 64. Mais Toi, Tu Es Pierre 71. Hommes de Rose (TV) 77, etc.

Cloerec, René (1911–).
French composer.

Douce 43. Le Diable au Corps 46. The Red Inn 51. Occupe-Toi d'Amélie 51. La Blé en Herbe 53. En Cas de Malheur 57, many others.

Clooney, George (1961–).
American leading actor, best known for his role as Dr Doug Ross in the TV series *ER*; he also took over the role of Batman from Val KILMER, for a fee of $10m. Born in Maysville, Kentucky, he studied journalism at Northern Kentucky University before heading for Los Angeles. Formerly married to actress Talia Balsam, he was romantically involved with actresses Kelly PRESTON, Dedee PFEIFFER and Denise CROSBY. The son of former TV news anchorman Nick Clooney, he is the nephew of singer Rosemary CLOONEY.

Biography: 1997, *George Clooney* by Andy Dougan.

Combat High/Combat Academy (TV) 86. Return of the Killer Tomatoes 88. Red Surf 90. Without Warning: Terror in the Towers (TV) 93. From Dusk till Dawn 96. One Fine Day 96. Batman and Robin 97. The Peacemaker 97. Out of Sight 98. The Thin Red Line 98. Wild, Wild West 98, etc.

TV series: E/R 84–85. The Facts of Life 85–86. Roseanne 88–89. Sunset Beat 90. Baby Talk 91. Sisters 92–93. Bodies of Evidence 92–93. Sisters 93–94. ER 94–99.

Clooney, Rosemary (1928–).
Breezy American singer who made a few film appearances. Born in Maysville, Kentucky, she performed from her early teens, making many hit records in the early 50s. Married actor José FERRER (1952–67), with whom she had five children, including actor Miguel FERRER. Addiction to prescription drugs brought a breakdown in the mid-60s and admission to a psychiatric hospital before her recovery, detailed in her autobiography and the subsequent TV movie *Rosie: The Rosemary Clooney Story* 82, in which she was played by Sondra LOCKE. Since the 80s, she has re-emerged as a jazz singer. Married Dante DiPaolo in 1997.

Autobiography: 1977, *This for Remembrance*.

■ The Stars are Singing 53. Here Come the Girls 53. *Red Garters* 54. *White Christmas* 54. Deep in My Heart 54. Radioland Murders 94.

❝ I think acting is the most thankless profession in the world. – R.C.

Cloquet, Ghislain (1924–1981).
Belgian cinematographer.

Night and Fog/Nuit et Brouillard 55. The Fire Within/Le Feu Follet 63. Mickey One 65. Au Hasard, Balthazar 66. The Young Girls of Rochefort 67. Une Femme Douche 69. Donkey Skin/Peau d'âne 70. Pouce 71. Rendez-vous à Bray 71. Belle 73. Love and Death 75. Monsieur Albert 75. Tess (AA) 79. I Sent a Letter to My Love/ Chère Inconnue 80. Four Friends 81, etc.

Close, Glenn (1947–).
American leading actress. She played the role of Norma Desmond in Los Angeles and on Broadway in Andrew Lloyd Webber's musical version of *Sunset Boulevard*.

The World According to Garp (AAN) 82. The Big Chill (AAN) 84. Something about Amelia (TV) 84. The Natural (AAN) 84. Maxie 85. *Jagged Edge* 85. *Fatal Attraction* (AAN) 87. Dangerous Liaisons (AAN) 88. Light Years (voice) 88. Immediate Family 89. Hamlet 90. Reversal of Fortune 90. Meeting Venus 90. The House of the Spirits 94. The Paper 94. Mary Reilly 96. Mars Attacks! 96. 101 Dalmatians (as Cruella de Vil) 96. Serving in Silence: The Marguerite Cammermeyer Story (TV) 95. 101 Dalmatians (as Cruella DeVil) 96. Mars Attacks! 96. In the Gloaming (TV) 97, etc.

❝ Mine is not a face that can take care of itself. If I want to look beautiful in movies I have to have help with lighting and camera angles. – G.C.

Clothier, William H. (1903–1996).
American cinematographer.

Sofia 48. Confidence Girl 52. Track of the Cat 54. Blood Alley 55. The Man in the Vault 56. The Horse Soldiers 59. The Alamo 60. The Deadly Companions 61. The Man Who Shot Liberty Valance 62. A Distant Trumpet 64. Cheyenne Autumn 64. Shenandoah 65. The Way West 67. The War Wagon 67. Firecreek 67. The Devil's Brigade 68. Hellfighters 68. The Cheyenne Social Club 70. Big Jake 71. The Train Robbers 73, etc.

Clouse, Robert. (1928–1997).
American director.

Happy Mothers Day, Love George (w only) 73. Enter the Dragon 73. Golden Needles 74. Black Belt Jones 74. The Ultimate Warrior (wd) 74. The Pack 77. The Amsterdam Kill 78. The Big Brawl 80. Force Five 81. Night Eyes 83. Dark Warrior 84. Gymkata 85. China O'Brien 89, etc.

Cloutier, Suzanne (1927–).
French-Canadian leading lady. She was married to Peter Ustinov (1954–71).

Temptation (US) 46. Au Royaume des Cieux 47. Juliette ou la Clef des Songes 50. Othello 51. Derby Day (GB) 51. Moulin Rouge 53. Romanoff and Juliet (US) 61, etc.

Clouzot, Henri-Georges (1907–1977).
French writer-director, noted for suspense melodramas.

Un Soir de Rafle (w) 31. Le Dernier des Six (w) 41. Les Inconnus dans la Maison (w) 42. L'Assassin Habite au 21 (wd) 42. *Le Corbeau* (wd) 43. *Quai des Orfèvres* (wd) 47. Manon (wd) 49. Retour à la Vie (wd) 49. *The Wages of Fear* (wd) 53. *Les Diaboliques* (wd) 54. The Picasso Mystery (wd) 56. Les Espions (wd) 57. The Truth (wd) (AA) 60. La Prisonnière (wd) 70. L'Enfer (co-w) 94, etc.

Clouzot, Vera (1921–1960).
Portuguese actress, wife of H. G. Clouzot.

The Wages of Fear 53. Les Diaboliques 54. Les Espions 57, etc.

Clunes, Alec (1912–1970).
British stage actor who made occasional film appearances.

Convoy 40. Saloon Bar 40. Melba 53. Quentin Durward 56. *Richard III* 56. Tomorrow at Ten 62, etc.

Clunes, Martin (1963–).
English comic actor and director. Son of actor Alec CLUNES.

Staggered (a, d) 94. An Evening with Gary Lineker (TV) 94. Over Here (TV) 96. The Acid House 98. Touch and Go (TV) 98, etc.

TV series: Men Behaving Badly 92–95. Demob 93.

Clurman, Harold (1901–1980).
American stage director chiefly associated with New York's Group Theatre of the 30s. Directed one very pretentious film: *Deadline at Dawn* 46. He was portrayed by actor Jordan Charney in the biopic *Frances* 82.

Autobiography: 1974, *All People Are Famous*.

Clute, Chester (1891–1956).
American character comedian. His startled look, small stature, tiny moustache and bald pate made him an inimitable henpecked husband or harassed clerk in scores of films.

Dance Charlie Dance 37. Rascals 38. Annabel Takes a Tour 38. Dancing Co-Ed 39. Hired Wife 40. She Couldn't Say No 41. Yankee Doodle Dandy 42. Chatterbox 43. Arsenic and Old Lace 44. Guest Wife 45. Angel on my Shoulder 46. Something in the Wind 47. Mary Ryan Detective 50, many others.

Clyde, Andy (1892–1967).
Scottish acrobatic comedian, long in Hollywood as western side-kick and hero of innumerable two-reelers, often as grizzled, toothless old fool.

The Goodbye Kiss 28. Million Dollar Legs 32. The Little Minister 34. McFadden's Flats 35. Two in a Crowd 36. Abe Lincoln in Illinois 40. The Green Years 46, many others.

TV series: The Real McCoys 57–60. Lassie 63. No Time for Sergeants 64–65.

Clyde, David (1887–1945).
Scottish character actor, in Hollywood. He was the brother of Andy CLYDE. Married actress Fay HOLDEN.

Bonnie Scotland 35. The Girl from Mandalay 36. Suzy 36. Lost Horizon 37. Bulldog Drummond's Secret Police 39. The Philadelphia Story 40. Smilin' Through 41. H. M. Pulham Esq. 41. Mrs Miniver 42. Nightmare 42. Jane Eyre 44. Frenchman's Creek 44. The Lodger 44. The Scarlet Claw 44. The House of Fear 45. The Lost Weekend 45. Two Years before the Mast 46, etc.

Clyde, June (1909–1987).
American musical comedy actress who played leading roles in the 30s and character parts thereafter. She was working in vaudeville, billed as Baby Tetrazzini, from the age of eight and was in Britain from the mid-30s. Married to director Thornton Freedland.

Tanned Legs 29. Hit the Deck 30. Arizona/The Virtuous Wife 31. Back Street 32. Steady Company 32. Cohens and Kellys in Hollywood 32. Radio Patrol 32. Only Yesterday 33. A Study in Scarlet 33. Dance Band (GB) 35. Charing Cross Road (GB) 35. She Shall Have Music (GB) 35. School for Husbands (GB) 37. Unfinished Business 41. Sealed Lips 41. Hi Ya, Chum/Everything Happens to Us 43. Treasure Hunt (GB) 52. The Love Lottery (GB) 53. After the Ball (GB) 57. The Story of Esther Costello 57, etc.

Coates, Anne V. (1925–).
British editor. She married director Douglas Hickox, and is the mother of director Anthony Hickox.
Grand National Night 53. Lost 56. The Horse's Mouth 59. Tunes of Glory 60. Lawrence of Arabia (AA) 63. Becket (AAN) 64. The Bofors Gun 68. The Adventurers 70. Bequest to the Nation 73. Murder on the Orient Express 74. The Eagle Has Landed 76. The Legacy 79. The Elephant Man (AAN) 80. Ragtime 81. The Bushido Blade 81. Greystoke: The Legend of Tarzan, Lord of the Apes 84. Lady Jane 86. Farewell to the King 89. What About Bob? 91. Chaplin 92. In the Line of Fire (AAN) 93. Pontiac Moon 94. Striptease 96. Out to Sea 97. Out of Sight 98, etc.

Coates, Eric (1886–1957).
British composer.
■ The Old Curiosity Shop 35. Nine Men 43. The Dam Busters 55. High Flight 57.

Coates, Phyllis (1925–) (Gipsy Ann Stell).
American leading actress of the 50s, a former dancer. Her first husband was director Richard Bare.
Blues Busters 50. Superman and the Mole Men 51. El Paso Stampede 53. Jungle Drums of Africa 53. Marshal of Cedar Rock 53. Panther Girl of the Congo (serial) 55. The Incredible Petrified World 58. I Was a Teenage Frankenstein 58. Chicago Confidential 57. The Babymaker 70. Goodnight, Sweet Marilyn 89, etc.
TV series: The Adventures of Superman (as Lois Lane) 51. The Duke 54. Professional Father 55. This is Alice 58–59.

Cobb, Edmund (1892–1974).
Stocky American actor, on screen for more than 55 years from 1910. Born in Alberquerque, New Mexico, he begin on stage and in vaudeville, starred in silent westerns, was a character actor in later westerns, frequently as a villain, and appeared in 'B' features in the 50s and 60s. Died of a heart attack.
A Pueblo Legend 12. Tish's Spy 15. Wolves of the Street 20. The Law Rustlers 23. Riders of the Range 24. General Custer at Little Big Horn 26. Beyond the Rio Grande 30. Law of the Rio Grande 31. Wild Horse 31. Gun Law 33. The Westerner 34. Wild Horse Rodeo 38. Stranger from Texas 39. Citizen Kane 41. Down Rio Grande Way 42. The Glass Key 42. Texas Kid 43. House of Frankenstein 44. Double Indemnity 44. Rio Grande Riders 46. The Falcon's Alibi 46. Buffalo Bill Rides Again 47. Red Canyon 49. Winchester 73 50. Carson City 52. River of No Return 54. The Girl in the Red Velvet Swing 55. The True Story of Jesse James 56. The Oklahoma Woman 56. The Amazing Colossal Man 57. Motorcycle Gang 57. Tales of Terror 62. Requiem for a Gunfighter 65. Johnny Reno 66, many others.

Cobb, Irvin S. (1876–1944).
American humorous writer who appeared in a few films and was touted as another Will Rogers after that actor's death.
■ Pardon My French 21. Peck's Bad Boy 21. The Five Dollar Baby 22. The Great White Way 24. Turkish Delight 27. *Steamboat Round the Bend* 34. Everybody's Old Man 36. Pepper 36. Hawaii Calls 38. The Arkansas Traveller 38. The Young in Heart 38.

Cobb, Joe (1917–).
American child actor, the original fat boy in the Our Gang comedy shorts in the 20s and early 30s.

Cobb, Lee J. (1911–1976) (Leo Jacoby).
Powerful American character actor who forsook stage for screen.
■ North of the Rio Grande 37. Ali Baba Goes to Town 37. Rustler's Valley 37. Danger on the Air 38. The Phantom Creeps 39. *Golden Boy* 39. Men of Boys' Town 41. This Thing Called Love 41. Paris Calling 42. Tonight We Raid Calais 43. Buckskin Frontier 43. *The Moon is Down* 43. The Song of Bernadette 43. Winged Victory 44. *Anna and the King of Siam* 46. Boomerang 47. Johnny O'Clock 47. Captain from Castile 47. Call Northside 777 48. The Miracle of the Bells 48. The Luck of the Irish 48. *The Dark Past* 48. Thieves' Highway 49. The Man Who Cheated Himself 50. Sirocco 51. The Family Secret 51. The Fighter 52. The Tall Texan 53. Yankee Pasha 54. Gorilla at Large 54. *On the Waterfront* (AAN) 54. Day of Triumph 54. The Racers 55. The Road to Denver 55. The Left Hand of God 55. *The Man in the Grey Flannel Suit* 56. Miami Exposé 56. *Twelve Angry Men* 57. The Garment Jungle 57. The Three Faces of Eve 57. The Brothers Karamazov (AAN) 58. Man of the West 58. Party Girl 58. The Trap 59. Green Mansions 59. But Not for Me 59. Exodus 60. The Four Horsemen of the Apocalypse 62. How the West Was Won 62. *Come Blow Your Horn* 63. Our Man Flint 66. In Like Flint 67. Il Giorno della Civetta (It.) 67. Mackenna's Gold 68. Coogan's Bluff 68. They Came to Rob Las Vegas 68. The Liberation of L. B. Jones 70. Macho Callahan 70. Lawman 70. Heat of Anger (TV) 71. Double Indemnity (TV) 73. The Exorcist 73. The Man Who Loved Cat Dancing 73. Dr Max (TV) 74. The Great Ice Rip-Off (TV) 74. Trapped Beneath the Sea (TV) 74. That Lucky Touch 75. Blood, Sweat and Fear (It.) 75.
TV series: *The Virginian* 62–66. The Young Lawyers 70.

Cobb, Randall 'Tex' (1954–).
Burly American character actor, a former boxer.
The Champ 79. Uncommon Valor 83. The Golden Child 86. Critical Condition 87. Police Academy 4: Citizens on Patrol 87. Raising Arizona 87. Buy and Cell 89. Blind Fury 89. Ernest Goes to Jail 90. Raw Nerve 91. Naked Gun 33 : The Final Insult 94. Ace Ventura: Pet Detective 94. Liar, Liar 96, etc.

Cobb, Ty (1886–1961) (Tyrus Raymond Cobb).
Legendary American baseball player and occasional actor in baseball movies. A biopic of his life was made in 1994 by Ron Shelton starring Tommy Lee Jones.
Somewhere in Georgia in 16 16. The Ninth Innings 42. Angels in the Outfield 51.

Cobert, Bob (1926–).
American composer who has also scored television movies.
Ladybug, Ladybug 63. House of Dark Shadows 70. Night of Dark Shadows 71. Dracula (TV) 74. Burnt Offerings 76. Scalpel 76. The Scarlet Pimpernel (TV) 82. The Winds of War (TV) 83. War and Remembrance (TV) 89. Me and the Kid 93. The Love Letter (TV) 98, etc.
TV series: Dark Shadows 91.

Coborn, Charles (1852–1945) (Colin McCallum).
British music-hall artiste famous for his longevity and his rendering of 'The Man Who Broke the Bank at Monte Carlo'.
Say it with Flowers 34. Music Hall 35. Variety Jubilee 41, etc.

Coburn, Charles (1877–1961).
Distinguished American actor. A stage star for many years, he came late in life to Hollywood and delighted audiences for another twenty years in roles of crusty benevolence.
■ Boss Tweed 33. The People's Enemy 35. Of Human Hearts 38. Vivacious Lady 38. Yellow Jack 38. Lord Jeff 38. Idiot's Delight 39. The Story of Alexander Graham Bell 39. Made for Each Other 39. *Bachelor Mother* 39. Stanley and Livingstone 39. In Name Only 39. Road to Singapore 40. Florian 40. Edison the Man 40. Three Faces West 40. The Captain is a Lady 40. *The Lady Eve* 41. *The Devil and Miss Jones* (AAN) 41. Our Wife 41. Unexpected Uncle 41. H. M. Pulham Esq. 41. Kings Row 41. In This Our Life 42. George Washington Slept Here 42. *The More the Merrier* (AA) 43. The Constant Nymph 43. *Heaven Can Wait* 43. Princess O'Rourke 43. My Kingdom for a Cook 43. *Knickerbocker Holiday* 44. Wilson 44. The Impatient Years 44. Together Again 44. A Royal Scandal 45. Rhapsody in Blue 45. Over 21 45. Colonel Effingham's Raid 45. Shady Lady 45. *The Green Years* (AAN) 46. Lured 47. BF's Daughter 48. The Paradine Case 48. Green Grass of Wyoming 48. Impact 49. Yes Sir That's My Baby 49. Everybody Does It 49. The Doctor and the Girl 49. The Gal who Took the West 49. Louisa 50. Peggy 50. Mr Music 50. The Highwayman 51. *Monkey Business* 52. *Has Anybody Seen My Gal?* 52. Gentlemen Prefer Blondes 53. Trouble along the Way 53. The Long Wait 54. The Rocket Man 54. How to Be Very Very Popular 55. The Power and the Prize 56. Around the World in Eighty Days 56. Town on Trial 57. The Story of Mankind 57. How to Murder a Rich Uncle 57. Stranger in My Arms 59. The Remarkable Mr Pennypacker 59. John Paul Jones (as Benjamin Franklin) 59. Pepe 60.
✪ For becoming a beloved international star after the age of sixty. *The More the Merrier*.
Famous line (to Marilyn Monroe, playing his secretary in *Monkey Business*): 'Find someone to type this.'
Famous line (to Barbara Stanwyck in *The Lady Eve*): 'We must be crooked but never common.'

Coburn, James (1928–).
American leading man of lithe movement and easy grin; career has been patchy.
Ride Lonesome 59. Face of a Fugitive 59. *The Magnificent Seven* 60. Hell is for Heroes 62. The Great Escape 63. *Charade* 63. The Man from Galveston 64. The Americanization of Emily 64. Major Dundee 65. A High Wind in Jamaica 65. The Loved One 65. *Our Man Flint* 66. What Did You Do in the War, Daddy? 66. Dead Heat on a Merry-Go-Round 66. In Like Flint 67. Waterhole #3 67. The President's Analyst 67. Duffy 68. Candy 68. Hard Contract 68. Blood Kin 69. *A Fistful of Dynamite* 71. The Carey Treatment 72. The Honkers 72. A Reason to Live, A Reason to Die 72. Pat Garrett and Billy the Kid 73. The Last of Sheila 73. Harry in Your Pocket 73. The Internecine Project (GB) 74. Bite the Bullet 75. Hard Times 75. The Last Hard Men 75. Midway 76. Sky Riders 76. Cross of Iron 77. The Dain Curse (TV) 78. California Suite 78. Firepower 79. The Muppet Movie 79. Goldengirl (TV) 79. Loving Couples 80. The Baltimore Bullet 80. Mr Patman 80. Looker 81. High Risk 81. Malibu (TV) 83. Digital Dreams 83. Draw! 84. Sins of the Father (TV) 85. Martin's Day 85. The Lions Roar 85. The Leonski Incident 85. Death of a Soldier 86. Walking after Midnight 88. Call from Space 89. Train to Heaven/Tag Till Himlen 89. Young Guns II 90. Hudson Hawk 91. Deadfall 93. Sister Act 2: Back in the Habit 93. Ray Alexander: A Taste for Justice (TV) 94. Maverick 94. Eraser 96. The Nutty Professor 96. Affliction 98, etc.
TV series: Klondike 60. Acapulco 61. Darkroom 81–82.

Coca, Imogene (1908–).
American TV and revue comedienne. Rare film appearances.
Under the Yum Yum Tree 64. Rabbit Test 78. The Return of the Beverly Hillbillies (TV) 81. National Lampoon's Vacation 83. Nothing Lasts Forever 84. Buy and Cell 89, etc.
TV series: *Grindl* 63. It's About Time 66.

Cochise (c. 1818–1874).
Peace-loving Apache Indian chief who became a prominent cinema character after Jeff Chandler played him in *Broken Arrow* 50, and later in *Battle at Apache Pass* 52 and *Taza Son of Cochise* 53. John Hodiak took over for *Conquest of Cochise* 53. Previously, Antonio Moreno had played him in *Valley of the Sun* and Miguel Inclan in *Fort Apache*. Michael Ansara took over in the TV series *Broken Arrow*.

Cochran, Steve (1917–1965) (Robert Cochran).
American leading man, usually a good-looking heavy, in mainly poor films.
Wonder Man 45. The Best Years of Our Lives 46. The Chase 46. The Kid from Brooklyn 47. A Song is Born 48. White Heat 49. The Damned Don't Cry 50. *Storm Warning* 50. The Tanks are Coming 51. Operation Secret 52. The Desert Song 53. Carnival Story 54. *Come Next Spring* 56. The Weapon (GB) 56. I, Mobster 58. The Beat Generation 59. The Deadly Companions 61. Of Love and Desire 63. Mozambique 65, etc.

Coco, James (1928–1987).
Chubby American comic actor.
■ Ensign Pulver 64. Generation 69. End of the Road 70. The Strawberry Statement 70. Tell Me That You Love Me Junie Moon 70. A New Leaf 71. Such Good Friends 71. Man of La Mancha 72. *The Wild Party* 75. Murder by Death 76. Bye Bye Monkey 78. The Cheap Detective 78. Charleston 78. Scavenger Hunt 79. Wholly Moses 80. Only When I Laugh (AAN) 81. The Muppets Take Manhattan 84. Hunk 87. The Chair/Hot Seat 89. That's Adequate 90.
TV series: Calucci's Department 73. The Dumplings 76.

Cocteau, Jean (1889–1963).
Fanciful French poet and writer who occasionally dabbled in cinema with effective if slightly obscure results.
■ *Le Sang d'un Poète* (wd) 30. La Comédie du Bonheur (w) 40. Le Baron Fantôme (w) 43. L'Eternel Retour (w) 43. Les Dames du Bois de Boulogne (co-w) 44. *La Belle et la Bête* (w, co-d) 46. Ruy Blas (w) 47. L'Aigle á Deux Têtes (d) 48. Les Parents Terribles (wd) 48. Les Enfants Terribles (w) 50. *Orphée* (wd) 50 *Le Testament d'Orphée* (wd) 59. La Princesse de Clèves (w) 60. Thomas l'Imposteur (w) 65.
✪ For bringing a unique visual imagination to the cinema. *Orphée*.
❝ A film is a petrified fountain of thought. –*J.C.*

Codee, Ann (1890–1961).
Belgian-born character actress in Hollywood who played a variety of middle-aged roles for many years.
Hi Gaucho 35. Captain Caution 40. Old Acquaintance 44. The Other Love 47. On the Riviera 51. Kiss Me Kate 53. Daddy Long Legs 55. Can Can 59, etc.

Cody, Iron Eyes (1907–1999).
American Indian actor.
The Iron Horse 24. Ride 'Em Cowboy 42. The Paleface 48. Broken Arrow 50. Sitting Bull 54. The Great Sioux Massacre 67. El Condor 70, many others.

Cody, Lew (1884–1934) (Louis Coté).
Smartly-dressed American leading man of the silent screen; his French accent affected his sound career. He was married to actresses Mabel Normand and Dorothy Dalton.
Comrade John 15. The Demon 18. *Don't Change Your Husband* 19. The Sign on the Door 21. Secrets of Paris 22. Within the Law 23. *Rupert of Hentzau* (title role) 23. The Shooting of Dan McGrew 24. Exchange of Wives 25. Adam and Evil 27. On Ze Boulevard 27. Beau Broadway 28. What a Widow 30. Dishonoured 31. Sporting Blood 31. The Tenderfoot 32. Sitting Pretty 33. Shoot the Works 34, many others.

Cody, William Frederick (Buffalo Bill) (1846–1917).
American guide, Indian scout and buffalo hunter, who discovered he could make an easier living playing himself on-stage and in 'Buffalo Bill's Wild West', a show which toured America and, later, Europe. Famous for having killed and scalped Chief Yellow Hand in single combat, he did much to create the myths that formed the basis of western movies. He is said to have invented the Indian war whoop, with the hand flapping over the mouth, to add excitement to his shows and so that it could be heard over the sound of gunfire. He featured sharp-shooting cowboys and battles between marauding Indians and western immigrants with their wagons drawn in a circle (in real life, attacks on wagon trains usually came when they were spread out across the plains). He gave employment to Wild Bill Hickok, Annie Oakley and Sitting Bull, and can claim to have been one of the first film-makers of faction – fiction based on fact. In 1913, he formed the W. F. Cody Historical Pictures Company to re-create major events in the history of the American West, using, where possible, the actual participants. His first and only film, of which a few minutes survive, was based on the massacre of the Sioux at Wounded Knee, and was distributed by Essanay, the company formed by 'Bronco Billy' Anderson. He has been played in movies by James Ellison in *The Plainsman* 36, Joel McCrea in *Buffalo Bill* 42, Louis Calhern in *Annie Get Your Gun* 50, Charlton Heston in *Pony Express* 52, Clayton Moore in *Buffalo Bill in Tomahawk Territory* 53, Gordon Scott in *Buffalo Bill* (Ger.) 64, Guy Stockwell in *The Plainsman* 66, Paul Newman in *Buffalo Bill and the Indians* 76, Peter Coyote in *Buffalo Girls* (TV) 95, and Keith Carradine in *Wild Bill* 95. He was a favourite hero of silent movies.
Biography: 1973, *Buffalo Bill: The Noblest Whiteskin* by John Burke.

“ Making a film is harder to organize and run than three circuses. – *W.C.*

The doc says I've got thirty-six hours. Let's forget about it and play some cards. – *W.C. on his deathbed*

Perhaps the handsomest American of all time. – *Gene Fowler*

Coe, Barry (1934–).
American juvenile actor of the 50s.
On The Threshold of Space 56. Peyton Place 57. The Bravados 58. One Foot in Hell 60. The 300 Spartans 62, etc.
TV series: Follow the Sun 61.

Coe, Fred (1914–1979).
American producer-director from stage and TV.
The Left-handed Gun (p) 58. The Miracle Worker (p) 62. A Thousand Clowns (pd) 65. Me Natalie (d) 69, etc.

Coe, Peter (1929–1987).
British director with stage experience.
Lock Up Your Daughters 69.

Coen, Ethan (1958–).
American screenwriter and producer who works in collaboration with his brother Joel.
Blood Simple 84. Crimewave 85. Raising Arizona 87. Miller's Crossing 90. Barton Fink 91. The Hudsucker Proxy (p, co-w) 94. *Fargo* (AAw, AANp, ed) 96. The Big Lebowski 97, etc.

Coen, Franklin (1912–).
American screenwriter.
This Island Earth (co-w) 55. The Train (co-w) 64. Alvarez Kelly 66. Black Gunn 72. The Take 74. Deadly Family Secrets (oa) (TV) 95, etc.

Coen, Joel (1955–).
American director and screenwriter who works in partnership with his brother Ethan. Married actress Frances McDormand.
Blood Simple 84. Crimewave (co-w only) 85. Raising Arizona 87. Miller's Crossing 90. Barton Fink 91. The Hudsucker Proxy (co-w, d) 94. *Fargo* (AAw, AANd, ed) 96. The Big Lebowski 97, etc.

Coffee, Lenore (1900–1984).
American screenwriter, in films from 1919.
Autobiography: 1973, *Storyline*.
Ladyfingers 21. East Lynne 25. Chicago 28. Arsène Lupin 32. Suzy 36. Four Daughters (AAN) 38. The Way of All Flesh 40. The Gay Sisters 42. Tomorrow Is Forever 46. Beyond the Forest 49. Lightning Strikes Twice 51. Sudden Fear 52. Young at Heart 55. The End of the Affair 55. Cash McCall 60, etc.

Coffey, Scott (1967–).
American actor.
Reuben Reuben 82. Once upon a Time in America 84. Girls Just Want to Have Fun 85. Some Kind of Wonderful 87. Satisfaction 88. The Big Picture 88. Shag 89. Wild at Heart 90. Shout 91. Wayne's World II 93. The Temp 93. Dream Lover 94. Jade 95, etc.

Coffin, Tristram (1912–1990).
American actor, a villain in many a 'B' western.
No Greater Sin 41. Blackmail 47. Outrage 50. Undercover Girl 50, etc.
TV series: 26 Men 56.

Coghlan, Junior (1916–) (Frank Coghlan).
American boy star of the 20s; previously played baby roles.
Autobiography: 1992, *They Still Call Me Junior*.
Slide, Kelly, Slide 26. The Country Doctor 27. River's End 31. Penrod and Sam 32. Boys' Reformatory 39. The Adventures of Captain Marvel (serial) 40. Henry Aldrich for President 41. The Sand Pebbles 66.

Cohan, George M. (1878–1942).
Dapper American actor-dancer-author-composer of the Broadway stage. Songs include: 'Mary's a Grand Old Name', 'Give My Regards to Broadway', 'Over There', 'Yankee Doodle Dandy'; plays include the much-filmed *Seven Keys to Baldpate*.
FILM APPEARANCES: *Broadway Jones* 16. *Hit-the-Trail Holiday* 18. *The Phantom President* 32. *Gambling* 34, etc. Was impersonated by James Cagney in a biopic, *Yankee Doodle Dandy* 42, and in *The Seven Little Foys* 55.

“ Whatever you do, kid, always serve it with a little dressing. – *G.M.C. to Spencer Tracy*

I don't care what you say about me so long as you spell my name right. – G.M.C.

Cohen, Herman (1928–).
American producer and director of low-budget horror films.
I Was a Teenage Werewolf 57. Konga 61. Black Zoo 63. Berserk 68. Crooks and Coronets 69. Trog 70. Craze 73, etc.

Cohen, Larry (1938–).
American creator of 'realist' horror films.
Book: 1998, *Larry Cohen: The Radical Allegories of an Independent Film-maker* by Tony Williams.
Bone 72. It's Alive (wpd) 76. Demon (wpd) 77. The Private Files of J. Edgar Hoover 77. Dial Rat for Terror/Housewife (wpd) 80. It Lives Again (wpd) 80. The Winged Serpent 81. Perfect Strangers (wd) 83. Scandalous (story) 84. Special Effects (wd) 85. The Stuff (wd) 85. Best Seller (w) 87. Deadly Illusion (wd) 87. It's Alive III: Island of the Alive (wd) 87. Return to Salem's Lot (wd) 87. Maniac Cop (w) 88. Wicked Stepmother (wd) 89. Maniac Cop 2 (w) 90. The Ambulance (wd) 90. Brute Force (wd) 92. Guilty as Sin 93. Bodysnatchers (co-story) 94. Original Gangstas (d) 96. Invasion of Privacy (w) 96. The Ex (co-w) 96, etc.

Cohen, Norman (1936–).
Irish director.
■ Brendan Behan's Dublin 67. The London Nobody Knows 68. Till Death Us Do Part 68. Dad's Army 70. Adolf Hitler, My Part in His Downfall 72. Stand Up Virgin Soldiers 77.

Cohen, Rob (1949–).
American producer and director, mainly of episodes of such TV series as *Miami Vice* and *thirtysomething*. He began producing for the Motown Corporation before setting up the Badham-Cohen Group with director John Badham.
AS PRODUCER: Mahogany 75. The Bingo Long Traveling All-Stars and Motor Kings 76. Scott Joplin 76. Almost Summer 77. Thank God It's Friday 77. The Wiz 78. The Razor's Edge 84. Light of Day 86. The Witches of Eastwick 87. Ironweed 87. Disorganized Crime 89. The Hard Way 90, etc.
AS DIRECTOR: A Small Circle of Friends 80. Scandalous 84. Dragon: The Bruce Lee Story (co-w, d) 93. Dragonheart 96. Daylight 96. The Rat Pack (TV) 98, etc.

Cohl, Emile (1857–1938) (Emile Courte).
Pioneer French cartoonist of the 1908–18 period.
Fantasmagorie 08. Les Allumettes Animées 09. Don Quichotte 09. Aventures d'un Bout de Papier 11. Monsieur Stop 13. Snookums (series) (US) 13–15. Les Pieds Nickelés 18, many others.

Cohn, Arthur (1928–).
Swiss producer.
The Sky Above the Mud Below 63. Woman Times Seven 67. Sunflower 70. *The Garden of the Finzi-Continis* (AA) 71. Wolf of the Seven Seas 74. Black and White in Colour (co-p, AA) 76. Dangerous Moves (AA) 84. American Dream 90, etc.

Cohn, Harry (1891–1958).
American executive, chief of Columbia Pictures for many years; a former song-plugger and vaudevillian who built the company in 1924, reputedly from his sales of a film called *Traffic in Souls*. He was the model for the character of producer Marcus Hoff in Clifford Odets's *The Big Knife*, filmed by Robert Aldrich in 1955.
Biography: 1967, *King Cohn* by Bob Thomas.
❂ For enjoying his career as an ogre and for bringing a Poverty Row studio up to the big time. *Gilda*.

“ When the big boss of Columbia Studios died in 1958, you could take your pick of brickbats and bouquets. The most famous tasteless comment came from Red Skelton on hearing of the huge crowds at Cohn's funeral:

It proves what they always say: give the public what they want to see, and they'll come out for it.

Then there was Hedda Hopper:

You had to stand in line to hate him.

And George Jessel:

He was a great showman, and he was a son of a bitch.

And Elia Kazan:

He liked to be the biggest bug in the manure pile.

And Samuel Goldwyn:

He never learned how to live.

And Budd Schulberg:

He was the meanest man I ever knew – an unreconstructed dinosaur.

But Cohn had a few defenders. There was Artie Shaw:

He was a lovable old pirate.

And, surprisingly, Ethel Barrymore:

He knew the score.

One thing was sure, Cohn thoroughly enjoyed his long tyranny. He said once:

Gower Street is paved with the bones of my executive producers.

And again:

I don't get ulcers: I give them.

Despite his frequent ill-treatment of actors and other creative people, he always averred:

I kiss the feet of talent.

He was disappointed in the treatment he got back from the stars he had created:

I have never met a grateful performer in the movies.

He maintained his confidence in his own ability:

Great pictures make great stars. This girl (Novak) has had five hit pictures. Send me your mother or your aunt and we will do the same for them.

He certainly knew what he wanted, and he had a long record of success. One of his mottoes was:

Let Rembrandt make character studies, not Columbia.

He once said to Daniel Taradash:

Promise me you'll never make a picture where the characters walk out of the room backward.

He claimed:

All I need to make pictures is an office.

In a more self-knowing mood, he admitted:

If I wasn't head of a studio, who would talk to me?

But he concluded:

It's better than being a pimp.

He once expounded his entire philosophy to Robert Parrish, who had asked to be allowed to direct good pictures:

I make fifty-two pictures a year here. Every Friday the front door opens on Gower Street and I spit a picture out. A truck picks it up and takes it away to the theatres, and that's the ball game. Now, if that door opens and I spit and nothing comes out, you and everybody else around here is out of work. So let's cut this crap about only good pictures . . . I run this place on the basis of making *one* good picture a year. I'll lay everything on the line for that one. I don't care if it's Capra, or Ford, or Riskin, or Milestone – that's the good one. The rest of the time I just have to keep spitting out.

As Frank Sinatra said:

He had a sense of humour like an open grave.

~Columbia was once known as the Pine Tree Studio (because it has so many Cohns).

Colbert, Claudette (1903–1996) (Lily Claudette Chauchoin).
French leading lady who went to America as a child and became one of Hollywood's most durable and versatile light actresses of the golden age, most typically cast in smart emancipated roles. Born in Paris, she moved with her family to New York and began on stage at the age of 16. She first gained notoriety as Nero's wife Poppaea, bathing in ass's milk in Cecil B. DE MILLE's *The Sign of the Cross*. By 1938 she was the highest-paid actor in Hollywood. She preferred to be photographed from her left side, which she regarded as her best profile. After her screen career declined, she returned to the stage in the late 50s and continued to act in the theatre until the mid-80s. The first of her two marriages was to actor Norman FOSTER (1928–35); her lovers included Clark GABLE, her co-star in *It Happened One Night*.
■ For the Love of Mike 28. The Hole in the Wall 29. The Lady Lies 29. The Big Pond 30. Young Man of Manhattan 30. Manslaughter 30. Honour among Lovers 31. The Smiling Lieutenant 31. Secrets of a Secretary 31. His Woman 31. The Wiser Sex 32. Misleading Lady 32. The Man from Yesterday 32. The Phantom President 32. *The Sign of the Cross* (as Poppaea) 32. Tonight is Ours 33. I Cover the Waterfront 33. *Three-Cornered Moon* 33. The Torch Singer 33. Four Frightened People 34. *It Happened One Night* (AA) 34. Cleopatra 34. *Imitation of Life* 34. The Gilded Lily 35. Private Worlds (AAN) 35. She Married Her Boss 35. The Bride Comes Home 35. Under Two Flags 36. Maid of Salem 37. *I Met Him in Paris* 37. Tovarich 37. Bluebeard's Eighth Wife 38. Zaza 39. *Midnight* 39. It's a Wonderful World 39. Drums along the Mohawk 39. Boom Town 40. *Arise My Love* 40. Skylark 41. Remember the Day 41. *The Palm Beach Story* 42. So Proudly We Hail 43. No Time for Love 43. *Since You Went Away* (AAN) 44. Practically Yours 45. Guest Wife 45. Tomorrow is Forever 46. Without Reservations 46. The Secret Heart 46. *The Egg and I* 47. Sleep My Love 48. Family Honeymoon 49. Bride for Sale 49. *Three Came Home* 50. The Secret Fury 50. Thunder on the Hill 51. Let's Make it Legal 51. The Planter's Wife (GB) 52. Love and the Frenchwoman 54. Si Versailles M'était Conté 55. Texas Lady 55. Parrish 60. The Two Mrs Grenvilles (TV) 86.
❂ For being more than a match for her male stars through twenty years of romantic comedy. *Midnight*.
Famous line (*Midnight*): 'The moment I saw you, I had an idea you had an idea.'

Cole, Dennis (1940–).
American general purpose actor who plays almost entirely on television.
Powderkeg (TV) 70. The Connection (TV) 73. Barbary Coast (TV) 74. Cave-In (TV) 79. Amateur Night 85. Pretty Smart 87. Dead End City 88, etc.
TV series: *The Felony Squad* 66–68. Lancer 68–69. Bearcats 71.

Cole, Gary (1956–).
American leading actor, from the stage.
Fatal Vision (TV) 84. Echoes in the Darkness (TV) 87. Son of the Morning Star (TV) 91. In the Line of Fire 93. The Brady Bunch Movie 95. A Very Brady Sequel 96. Gang Related 96. Santa Fe 97, etc.
TV series: Midnight Caller 88–91. American Gothic 95.

Cole, George (1925–).
British comedy actor who made his film debut as a cockney child evacuee; usually plays the befuddled innocent. Best known, though, as a bumbling con-man in the TV series *Minder*.
Cottage to Let 41. Henry V 44. *Quartet* 48. Morning Departure 50. Laughter in Paradise 50. Lady Godiva Rides Again 51. Scrooge 51. *Top Secret* 51. Will Any Gentleman? 52. Happy Ever After 53. Our Girl Friday 53. The Belles of St Trinian's 54. A Prize of Gold 55. The Weapon 56. It's a Wonderful World 56. The Green Man 57. Blue Murder at St Trinian's 58. Too Many Crooks 58. The Bridal Path 59. The Pure Hell of St Trinian's 60. Cleopatra 62. Dr Syn 63. One-Way Pendulum 64. The Legend of Young Dick Turpin 65. The Great St Trinian's Train Robbery 66. The Vampire Lovers 70. Fright 71. Take Me High 73. The Bluebird 76. Blott on the Landscape (TV) 85. Mary Reilly 96, etc.
TV series: Don't Forget to Write 77–79. Minder 79–94. The Bounder 82–83. Heggerty Haggerty 84–85. Comrade Dad 86. Root into Europe 92. An Independent Man 96. Dad 97.

Cole, Jack (1914–1974).
American dancer and choreographer.
Moon Over Miami (d) 41. Kismet (d) 44. Tonight and Every Night (ch) 45. The Jolson Story (ch) 46. On the Riviera (ch) 51. Designing Woman (dch) 55. Let's Make Love (ch) 61, etc.

Cole, Lester (1904–1985).
American screenwriter. One of the blacklisted Hollywood Ten.
If I Had a Million 32. The President's Mystery 34. The Crime of Dr Hallet 36. The Invisible Man Returns 39. Hostages 42. None Shall Escape 44. Objective Burma 45. Blood on the Sun 45. The Romance of Rosy Ridge 47. High Wall 48. Operation Eichmann (as Lewis Copley) 61. Born Free (as Gerald L. C. Copley) 66, etc.

Cole, Michael (1945–).
American leading man, mostly on television.
The Last Child (TV) 71. Beg Borrow or Steal (TV) 73. Evening in Byzantium (TV) 78. Nickel Mountain 85, etc.

TV series: *The Mod Squad* 68–72.

Cole, Nat King (1919–1965) (Nathaniel Coles).
American pianist and singer who made occasional film appearances.
The Blue Gardenia 53. St Louis Blues (as W. C. Handy) 58. The Night of the Quarter Moon 59. *Cat Ballou* 65, etc.

Cole, Sidney (1908–1998).
British producer, a former editor who worked at Ealing through its finest hours. Subsequently produced Black Beauty (72) and Dick Turpin (78) for TV.

Cole, Stephanie (1941–).
English leading actress, mostly on television. Born in Solihull, Warwickshire, she studied at the Bristol Old Vic Theatre School and began on stage. She gave up acting for much of the 70s.
Autobiography: 1998, *A Passionate Life*.
That Summer! 79. Memento Mori (TV) 92. In the Cold Light of Day (TV) 94, etc.
TV series: Open All Hours 81–82, 85. Tenko 81–84. A Bit of a Do 89. Waiting for God 90–94. Keeping Mum 98.

Coleman, Charles (1885–1951).
Australian character actor in Hollywood; almost always played the perfect portly butler.
That's my Daddy 28. Bachelor Apartment 31. Gallant Lady 33. Down to Their Last Yacht 34. Poor Little Rich Girl 36. That Certain Age 38. Mexican Spitfire 39. It Started with Eve 41. Twin Beds 42. The Whistler 44. The Runaround 46. The Imperfect Lady 47, many others.

Coleman, Charlotte (1968–).
English actress who began as a child on the television series *Educating Marmalade* and *Worzel Gummidge*, the daughter of actress Anne Beach.
Oranges Are Not the Only Fruit (TV) 90. Four Weddings and a Funeral 94. Different for Girls 96.
TV series: How Do You Want Me? 98.

Coleman, Cy (1929–).
American song composer, usually with lyricist *Carolyn Leigh* (1926–83).
Spartacus 60. Father Goose 64. The Troublemaker 64. The Art of Love 65. Sweet Charity (from his stage musical) (AAN) 69. The Heartbreak Kid (s) 72. Garbo Talks 84. Blame It on Rio (s) 84. Power 86. Family Business 89, etc.

Coleman, Dabney (1932–).
American comic actor, usually the heavy.
This Property Is Condemned 66. I Love My Wife 70. The Brotherhood of the Bell (TV) 70. Bad Ronald (TV) 74. Returning Home (TV) 75. Maneaters Are Loose (TV) 78. North Dallas Forty 79. How to Beat the High Cost of Living 80. Melvin and Howard 80. *Nine to Five* 80. Nothing Personal 80. On Golden Pond 81. Young Doctors in Love 82. Tootsie 82. War Games 83. The Muppets Take Manhattan 84. Cloak and Dagger 85. The Man with One Red Shoe 85. Dragnet 87. Hot to Trot 88. Short Time 90. Where the Heart Is 90. Meet the Applegates 90. Clifford 91. Amos & Andrew 93. The Beverly Hillbillies 93. Clifford 94, etc.
TV series: That Girl 66–70. Mary Hartman, Mary Hartman 76. Forever Fernwood 77. Buffalo Bill 83. Drexell's Class 91.

Coleman, Gary (1968–).
American juvenile actor, star of TV's *Diff'rent Strokes*. In 1998, he was working as a security guard.
On the Right Track 81. Jimmy the Kid 82. The Kid with the Broken Halo (TV) 82. The Kid with the 200 IQ (TV) 82. Jimmy the Kid 82. The Fantastic World of D. C. Collins (TV) 83. Playing with Fire (TV) 84.

Coleman, Nancy (1917–).
American leading lady of the 40s, usually in timid roles.
Kings Row 42. Dangerously They Live 42. The Gay Sisters 42. Desperate Journey 42. Edge of Darkness 43. In Our Time 44. *Devotion* (as Anne Brontë) 45. Her Sister's Secret 46. Mourning Becomes Electra 47. That Man from Tangier 53. Slaves 68, etc.

Colette (1873–1954) (Sidonie-Gabrielle Colette).
French writer, usually on sex themes.
Claudine á l'Ecole 38. Gigi 48 and 58. Julie de Carneilhan 50. L'Ingénue Libertine 51. Ripening Seed 54.

Colicos, John (1928–).
Canadian character actor in occasional films.
Anne of the Thousand Days 70. Raid on Rommel 71. Red Sky at Morning 71. Doctors' Wives 71. The Wrath of God 72. Scorpio 73. Drum 76. Breaking Point 76. Phobia 80. The Changeling 80. The Postman Always Rings Twice 81, etc.
TV series: Battlestar Galactica 78.

Colin, Jean (1905–1989).
British leading lady of the 30s; appearances sporadic.
The Hate Ship 30. Compromising Daphne 30. *The Mikado* 39. Bob's Your Uncle 41. Laxdale Hall 54, etc.

Colin, Sid (1920–1989).
British TV comedy scriptwriter.
I Only Arsked 58. The Ugly Duckling 59. Up Pompeii 70. Up the Chastity Belt 71. Up the Front 72. Percy's Progress 74, etc.

Colla, Richard A. (1918–).
American director.
Zigzag 70. *Fuzz* 72. Live Again, Die Again (TV) 74. The Tribe (TV) 74. The UFO Incident (TV) 75. Olly Olly Oxen Free 78. Battlestar Galactica 79. Stingray (TV) 85. That Secret Sunday (TV) 86. Something Is Out There (TV) 88. Web of Deception 93. Roseanne and Tom: Behind the Scenes (TV) 94. Dazzle (TV) 95. Ultimate Betrayal (TV) 98, etc.

Colleano, Bonar (1924–1958) (Bonar Sullivan).
Wisecracking American actor, from family of acrobats; worked chiefly in Britain. Died in a car crash. Married actress Susan SHAW: their son Mark Colleano (1955–) appeared in a few films of the late 60s and early 70s.
The Way to the Stars 45. A Matter of Life and Death 46. While the Sun Shines 46. Good Time Girl 47. One Night With You 48. Sleeping Car to Trieste 48. Pool of London 50. A Tale of Five Cities 52. Eight Iron Men (US) 52. The Sea Shall Not Have Them 55. Interpol 57. No Time To Die 58, etc.

Collette, Toni (1973–).
Australian leading actress, in international films. Born in Sydney, she studied acting at the city's National Institute of Dramatic Art.
Spotswood 91. Muriel's Wedding 94. Arabian Knight (voice) (US) 95. Lilian's Story 95. Cosi 96. The Pallbearer (US) 96. Emma (US) 96. Clockwatchers 97. Diana & Me 97. The Boys 98. The James Gang (GB) 98. Velvet Goldmine (US) 98, etc.

Collier, Constance (1878–1955) (Laura Constance Hardie).
Distinguished British stage actress who spent her later years in Hollywood playing great ladies with caustic tongues and eccentric habits.
Autobiography: 1929, *Harlequinade*.
■ Intolerance 16. The Code of Marcia Gray 16. Macbeth 16. Bleak House 20. The Bohemian Girl 22. *Our Betters* 33. Dinner at Eight 33. Peter Ibbetson 34. Shadow of Doubt 35. Anna Karenina 35. Girls' Dormitory 36. Professional Soldier 36. Little Lord Fauntleroy 36. Thunder in the City 37. Wee Willie Winkie 37. *Stage Door* 37. She Got What She Wanted 37. A Damsel in Distress 37. Zaza 39. Susan and God 40. Half a Sinner 40. Weekend at the Waldorf 45. *Kitty* 45. Monsieur Beaucaire 46. The Dark Corner 46. The Perils of Pauline 47. *An Ideal Husband* 48. Rope 48. The Girl from Manhattan 48. Whirlpool 50.

Collier, John (1901–1980).
British writer of polished macabre stories; his screen work was sporadic. He moved to Hollywood in the mid-30s and later lived in Mexico.
Sylvia Scarlett 35. Her Cardboard Lover 42. Deception 46. Roseanna McCoy 49. The Story of Three Loves 53. I Am a Camera 55. The War Lord 65, etc.

Collier, Lois (1919–) (Madelyn Jones).
American leading lady of 40s 'B' pictures.
A Desperate Adventure 38. The Phantom Plainsman 42. Cobra Woman 44. Weird Woman 44. Ladies Courageous 44. The Naughty Nineties 45. The Crimson Canary 45. The Cat Creeps 46. A Night in Casablanca 46. Slave Girl 47. Out of the Storm 48. Miss Mink of 1949 49. Flying Disc Man from Mars 51. Missile Monsters 58, etc.
TV series: Boston Blackie 51–53.

Collier, William (1866–1944) (William Senior).
American stage actor, usually of comedy character roles; moved to Hollywood in 1929.
Six Cylinder Love 31. The Cheater 34. Josette 38. Thanks for the Memory 38. Invitation to Happiness 39. There's Magic in Music 41, many others.

Collier, William 'Buster' Jnr (1902–1987).
Handsome American leading man of silents who retired in the 30s to become an agent. His father was actor William Collier.
The Bugle Call 16. The Sea Hawk 24. The Wanderer 25. The Lion and the Mouse 28. New Orleans 29. Little Caesar 31. Cimarron 31. The Story of Temple Drake 33. The People's Enemy 35, etc.

Collin, John (1931–).
British character actor.
Star! 68. Before Winter Comes 69. Innocent Bystanders 72. Tess 79, etc.

Collinge, Patricia (1892–1974).
Irish-American stage actress who made occasional film appearances.
The Little Foxes (AAN) 41. Shadow of a Doubt 43. Casanova Brown 44. Teresa 51. The Nun's Story 58, etc.

Collings, David (1940–).
British character actor, much on TV.
Scrooge (as Bob Cratchit) 70. Elizabeth R (TV) 71. Mahler 74. Hennessy 75. The 39 Steps 78. Julius Caesar (TV) 79. A Murder Is Announced 84. Persuasion 95, etc.

Collins, Alfred.
English comic actor, from music hall, and pioneer director, specializing in chase films. His approach was in advance of most of his contemporaries, using a mobile camera and close-ups to good effect.
The Runaway Match 03. Welshed – A Derby Day Incident 03. Rip Van Winkle 03. Two Little Vagabonds 03. Mutiny on a Russian Battleship 05. This Little Girl and That Little Girl 07. The Coster's Phantom Fortune 10. Algie's Expensive Stick 12, etc.

Collins, Anthony (1893–1963).
English composer and musical director, associated with the films of producer-director Herbert WILCOX. Born in Hastings, he began in films as composer and conductor on Wilcox's *Victoria the Great*, and went to Hollywood with Wilcox and his star, Anna NEAGLE, in 1939, to score the films they made there, returning to work in Britain in 1945.
Victoria the Great 37. The Rat 38. Sixty Glorious Years 38. A Royal Divorce 38. *Nurse Edith Cavell* (AAN) 39. Allegheny Rising (US) 39. Swiss Family Robinson (US) 40. *Irene* (US) (AAN) 40. Tom Brown's Schooldays (US) 40. No, No, Nanette (US) 40. Sunny (US) (AAN) 41. Forever and a Day (US) 43. Destroyer (US) 43. I Live in Grosvenor Square/A Yank in London 46. Piccadilly Incident 46. The Fabulous Texan 47. The Courtneys of Curzon Street 47. Odette 50. *The Lady with the Lamp* 51. Macao 52. Trent's Last Case 52. The Adventures of Robinson Crusoe 52. Laughing Annie 53, etc.

Collins, Cora Sue (1927–).
American child star of the 30s.
They Just Had to Get Married 33. Queen Christina 33. Torch Singer 34. The Scarlet Letter 35. Anna Karenina 35. Magnificent Obsession 36. The Adventures of Tom Sawyer 38, etc.

Collins, Eddie (1884–1940).
American character comedian from Vaudeville; crowded a few films into his last years.
In Old Chicago 38. Kentucky Moonshine 38. Charlie Chan in Honolulu 38. Young Mr Lincoln 39. Hollywood Cavalcade 39. *The Bluebird* 39. The Return of Frank James 40.

Collins, Gary (1938–).
Easy-going American leading man, familiar on television in the 70s: the lead in *Born Free* (series).
The Pigeon that Took Rome 62. Airport 69. Killer Fish 77. Hangar 18 80, etc.
Other TV series: The Wackiest Ship in the Army 65. The Iron Horse 66. The Sixth Sense 72.

Collins, Jackie (1939–).
British light novelist, sister of Joan COLLINS. Works filmed include *The World Is Full of Married Men*, *The Stud*, *The Bitch*.

Collins, Joan (1933–).
British leading lady whose sultry charms won her parts in an assortment of international films. Her husbands include actors Maxwell Reed (1954–57) and Anthony Newley (1963–71). In 1996, she won a court case brought against her by publisher Random House in which they claimed a novel she had written for a $1.3m advance was unpublishable.
Autobiographies: 1978, *Past Imperfect*; 1996, *Second Act*.
I Believe in You 52. Cosh Boy 53. Our Girl Friday 53. Turn the Key Softly 53. The Good Die Young 54. Land of the Pharaohs 55. The Virgin Queen 55. The Girl in the Red Velvet Swing 55. The Opposite Sex 56. The Wayward Bus 57. Island in the Sun 57. Sea Wife 57. The Bravados 58. Rally Round the Flag Boys 58. Seven Thieves 60. Road to Hong Kong 62. Warning Shot 66. Heironymus Merkin 69. The Executioner 69. Subterfuge 69. Up in the Cellar 70. Drive Hard, Drive Fast (TV) 70. Quest for Love 71. Revenge 71. Tales That Witness Madness 73. Alfie Darling 74. I Don't Want to Be Born 75. The Moneychangers (TV) 76. Empire of the Ants 77. The Stud 78. The Bitch 79. Game for Vultures 79. Sunburn 79. Nutcracker 82. The Wild Women of Chastity Gulch (TV) 82. The Making of a Male Model (TV) 83. Her Life as a Man (TV) 84. The Cartier Affair (TV) 85. Sins (TV) 85. Monte Carlo (TV) 86. Decadence 93. In the Bleak Midwinter 95. Clandestine Marriage 99. Sweet Deception 99, etc.
TV series: *Dynasty* 81–89.
❝ Dynasty was the opportunity to take charge of my career rather than walking around like a library book waiting to be loaned out. –*J.C.*
She appears to have the world by the balls, but underneath she's trying to solve the problem of loneliness, which I think is the universal problem of all rich people. –*J.C.* (of her character in *The Bitch*)
Even when you win the rat race, you're still a rat. –*J.C.*
The secret of having a personal life is not answering too many questions about it. –*J.C.*
I was thinking, who of the English actresses in the last 30 or 40 years have achieved as much as I have? –*J.C., 1995*

Collins, Lewis (1946–).
British leading man familiar from TV's *The Professionals* 78–80.
Who Dares Wins 82. Jack the Ripper (TV) 88, etc.

Collins, Pauline (1940–).
English leading actress, from the stage and television. She is married to actor John Alderton, with whom she starred in three TV series.
Shirley Valentine (AAN) 89. City of Joy 92. My Mother's Courage 95. Flowers of the Forest (TV) 96. Paradise Road 97, etc.
TV series: Upstairs Downstairs 71–73. No, Honestly 74. Thomas and Sarah 78. Forever Green 89–91. Ambassador 98.

Collins, Phil (1951–).
British singer, songwriter, drummer and actor. A member of the rock band Genesis, he began as a child actor, playing the Artful Dodger in the stage musical *Oliver!* In 1998, the *Sunday Times* estimated his wealth at £105m.
A Hard Day's Night 64. Chitty Chitty Bang Bang 69. Against All Odds (AAN for s) 84. Eric Clapton and Friends (concert) 86. The Return of Bruno 87. Buster (& s) (AAN) 88. Hook 91. Frauds 93. And the Band Played On (TV) 93. Balto (voice) 95, etc.

Collins, Ray (1890–1965).
American stage actor who came to Hollywood with Orson Welles, stayed to play kindly uncles and political bosses.
■ The Grapes of Wrath 40. *Citizen Kane* (as Boss Jim Geddes) 41. The Big Street 42. Highways by Night 42. The Navy Comes Through 42. The Commandos Strike at Dawn 42. *The Magnificent Ambersons* 42. The Human Comedy 43. Slightly Dangerous 43. Crime Doctor 43. Salute to the Marines 43. Whistling in Brooklyn 43. See Here Private Hargrove 43. The Hitler Gang 44. The Eve of St Mark 44. The Seventh Cross 44. Barbary Coast Gent 44. Can't Help Singing 44. Roughly Speaking 45. The Hidden Eye 45. Miss Susie Slagle's 45. Leave Her to Heaven 45. Up Goes Maisie 46. A Night in Paradise 46. Badman's Territory 46. Boys' Ranch 46. Crack-Up 46. Three Wise Fools 46. Two Years Before the Mast 46. The Return of Monte Cristo 46. The Best Years of Our Lives 46. *The Bachelor and the Bobbysoxer* 47. Red Stallion 47. The Swordsman 47. The Senator Was Indiscreet 47. Homecoming 48. A Double Life 48. Good Sam 48. For the Love of Mary 48. The Man from Colorado 48. Command Decision 48. Red Stallion in the Rockies 48. Hideout 49. It Happens Every Spring 49. The Fountainhead 49. The Heiress 49. Free for All 49. Francis 49. Paid in Full 50. Kill the Umpire 50. The Reformer and the Redhead 50. Summer Stock 50. You're in the Navy Now 51. Ma and Pa Kettle Back on the Farm 51. Vengeance Valley 51. Reunion in Reno 51. I Want You 51. The Racket 51. Invitation 52. Dreamboat 52. Young Man with Ideas 52. The Desert Song 53. Ma and Pa Kettle at the Fair 53. Column South 53. Ma and Pa Kettle on Vacation 53. The Kid from Left Field 53. Bad for Each Other 53. Rose Marie 54. Athena 54. The Desperate Hours 55. Texas Lady 55. Never Say Goodbye 56. The Solid Gold Cadillac 56. Spoilers of the Forest 57. Touch of Evil 58. I'll Give My Life 61.
TV series: Halls of Ivy 54. Perry Mason 57–65.

Collins, Russell (1897–1965).
Hardened-looking American character actor.
Shockproof 49. Niagara 53. Miss Sadie Thompson 53. Bad Day at Black Rock 55. Soldier of Fortune 56. The Enemy Below 57. The Matchmaker 58. Fail Safe 64, etc.
TV series: The Detectives 59–61. Many Happy Returns 64.

Collins, Wilkie (1824–1889).
British novelist, credited with being the inventor of the detective story via *The Moonstone*, whose complications have resisted filming. *The Woman in White* however was filmed with some fidelity in 1947.

Collinson, Peter (1938–1980).
British director who quickly slumped from arty pretentiousness to routine thrillers.
■ The Penthouse 67. Up the Junction 68. The Long Day's Dying 68. *The Italian Job* 69. You Can't Win 'em All 70. Fright 71. Straight on till Morning 72. Innocent Bystanders 72. The Man Called Noon 73. Open Season 74. And Then There Were None 74. The Spiral Staircase 75. The Sell Out 75. Tomorrow Never Comes 77. Tigers Don't Cry 77. The House on Garibaldi Street (TV) 79. The Earthling 80.

Collyer, June (1907–1968) (Dorothy Heermance).
American leading lady in a few light films of the early 30s; married Stuart Erwin.
Woman Wise 27. East Side West Side 28. Charley's Aunt 31. Alexander Hamilton 31. The Ghost Walks 35, etc.
TV series: The Stuart Erwin Show 53.

Colman, Edward (1905–).
American cinematographer who began work as an assistant cameraman in 1924 and worked almost exclusively for Disney after he became a director of photography.
The DI 57. Black Patch 57. Shaggy Dog 59. –30–/Deadline Midnight 59. The Absent-Minded Professor (AAN) 60. Big Red 61. Babes in Toyland 61. Son of Flubber 62. Savage Sam 62. Mary Poppins (AAN) 64. Those Calloways 64. The Monkey's Uncle 64. That Darn Cat 65. The Ugly Dachshund 65. The Adventures of Bullwhip Griffin 65. The Gnome-Mobile 66. The Happiest Millionaire 67. The Love Bug 68, etc.

Colman, Ronald (1891–1958).
Distinguished British romantic actor whose gentle manners, intelligence and good looks thrilled two generations. Turned to acting after World War I wounds, and went to Hollywood in 1920.
Biography: 1975, *A Very Private Person* by Juliet Benita Colman.
■ The Toilers 19. A Son of David 19. The Snow in the Desert 19. The Black Spider 20. Anna The Adventuress 20. Handcuffs or Kisses 21. The Eternal City 23. *The White Sister* 23. Twenty Dollars a Week 24. Tarnish 24. Romola 24. Her Night of Romance 24. A Thief in Paradise 24. His Supreme Moment 25. The Sporting Venus 25. Her Sister from Paris 25. *The Dark Angel* 25. Stella Dallas 25. Lady Windermere's Fan 25. Kiki 26. *Beau Geste* 26. The Winning of Barbara Worth 26. The Night of Love 27. The Magic Flame 27. The Lovers 28. The Rescue 29. *Bulldog Drummond* (AAN) 29. Condemned (AAN) 29. *Raffles* 30. The Devil to Pay 30. The Unholy Garden 31. *Arrowsmith* 31. Cynara 32. The Masquerader 33. Bulldog Drummond Strikes Back 34. Clive of India 35. The Man who Broke the Bank at Monte Carlo 35. *A Tale of Two Cities* 35. Under Two Flags 36. *Lost Horizon* 37. *The Prisoner of Zenda* 37. If I were King 38. The Light that Failed 39. Lucky Partners 40. My Life with Caroline 41. *The Talk of the Town* 42. *Random Harvest* (AAN) 42. Kismet 44. The Late George Apley 47. *A Double Life* (AA) 48. Champagne for Caesar 50. Around the World in Eighty Days 56. The Story of Mankind 57.
TV series: *Halls of Ivy* 54.
✪ For conquering world audiences by steadfastly playing the old-fashioned British gentleman adventurer in a number of elegant guises. *The Prisoner of Zenda*.
❝ He is as ingratiating when he talks as when he was silent. – *New York Times, 1929*
He led the perfect colonial life in Hollywood. The longer he stayed there the more English he got–but he never wanted to go home. – *Douglas Fairbanks Jnr*
Before God I'm worth 35 dollars a week. Before the motion picture industry I'm worth anything you can get. – *R.C.* (to his agent)
He is an excellent director's dummy. He has no personality of his own, only an appearance.
– *Alleged screen test report*
When Colman looks at the camera, the whole world knows what he is thinking. – *New Yorker, 1937*

Colombier, Michel (1939–).
French composer, mainly for American films.
L'Arme à Gauche 65. Dirty Money/Un Flic 72. Paul and Michelle 74. Steel 80. Against All Odds 84. Purple Rain 84. White Nights 85. The Money Pit 86. Ruthless People 86. The Golden Child 86. Surrender 87. The Couch Trip 88. Satisfaction 88. Loverboy 89. Who's Harry Crumb? 89. Impulse 90. New Jack City 91. Strictly Business 91. Diary of a Hit Man 92. Deep Cover 92. Folks! 92. Posse 93. The Program 93. Major League II 94. Foxfire 96. Meet Wally Sparks 97. Woo 98. Claudine's Return 98. How Stella Got Her Groove Back 98, etc.

Colonna, Jerry (1903–1986).
American comic actor with strong, high-pitched voice, walrus moustache and bulging eyes.
College Swing 38. Little Miss Broadway 38. Road to Singapore 40. Sis Hopkins 41. True to the Army 42. Star-Spangled Rhythm 42. Ice Capades 42. Atlantic City 44. It's in the Bag 45. Road to Rio 47. Kentucky Jubilee 51. Meet Me in Las Vegas 56. Andy Hardy Comes Home 58, etc.

Colpi, Henri (1921–).
French editor.
Night and Fog 55. The Picasso Mystery 56. Hiroshima Mon Amour 59. Last Year in Marienbad 61. Les Fruits de la Passion 81. Le Grand Frère 83, many others.
■ ALSO DIRECTOR: Une Aussi Longue Absence 61. Codine 63. Mona 66. Heureux Qui Comme Ulysse 70. Mysterious Island 73. Bilitis 76. Rue des Archives 87.

Coltrane, Robbie (1950–) (Robbie McMillan).
Portly Scottish actor, at first in comic roles, then gaining a wider fame, and several awards, as a criminal psychologist in the TV series *Cracker*.
Flash Gordon 80. Subway Riders 81. Britannia Hospital 82. Scrubbers 82. Ghost Dance 83. Krull 83. Loose Connections 83. Chinese Boxes 84. Defence of the Realm 85. Revolution 85. Supergrass (TV) 85. Absolute Beginners 86. Caravaggio 86. Mona Lisa 86. Eat the Rich (TV) 87. The Fruit Machine 88. Midnight Breaks 88. Slipstream 89. Bert Rigby, You're a Fool 89. Henry V (as Falstaff) 90. Nuns on the Run 90. Perfectly Normal 90. The Pope Must Die/The Pope Must Diet 91. Alive and Kicking (TV) 91. Oh, What a Night 92. The Adventures of Huck Finn 93. Boswell and Johnson's Tour of the Western Isles (TV) 93. GoldenEye 95. Alive and Kicking (TV) 96. Buddy 97. Ebb-Tide (TV) 97. Frogs for Snakes 98, etc.
TV series: Tutti Frutti 87. Coltrane in a Cadillac 93. *Cracker* 93– . Coltrane's Planes and Automobiles 97.

Columbo, Russ (1908–1934) (Ruggerio de Rudolpho Columbo).
American violinist, vocalist, songwriter and bandleader who appeared in a few films. Died in a shooting accident.
Wolf Song 29. The Street Girl 29. Hellbound 31. Broadway through a Keyhole 33. Wake Up and Dream 34, etc.

Columbus, Chris (1959–).
American director who began as a screenwriter on films produced by Steven Spielberg. *Home Alone* is one of the most successful films so far made, having grossed more than $500 million worldwide.
Gremlins (w) 84. Reckless (w) 84. The Goonies (w) 85. Young Sherlock Holmes (w) 85. Adventures in Babysitting (d) 87. Heartbreak Hotel (wd) 88. Home Alone (d) 90. Only the Lonely (wd) 91. Home Alone 2: Lost in New York 92. Mrs Doubtfire (co-w, d) 93. Nine Months (wd) 95. Jingle All the Way (p) 96. Stepmom (d) 98, etc.

Columbus, Christopher (1451–1506).
The explorer, born in Genoa, enjoyed a brief burst of screen fame 500 years after his epic voyage to America with three films: *1492: Discovery of Paradise*, in which he was played by a French actor, Gérard Depardieu, *Christopher Columbus: The Discovery*, in which he was played by a Franco-Greek actor, George Corraface, and *Carry On Columbus*, in which he was played by an English actor, Jim Dale. In 1949, in *Christopher Columbus*, he was played by Fredric March.

Colvig, Vance (1892–1967) (aka Pinto Colvig).
American actor who spent most of his career at the Disney studio and became the voice for Pluto and Goofy. He was also co-author of the song 'Who's Afraid of the Big Bad Wolf?'

Combs, Jeffrey.
American leading actor in horror movies.
Honky Tonk Freeway 81. Whose Life Is It Anyway? 81. The Man with Two Brains 83. Re-Animator 85. From Beyond 86. Cellar Dweller 87. Cyclone 87. Dead Man Walking 88. Phantom Empire 89. The Guyver 91. The Pit and the Pendulum 91. Bride of the Re-Animator 91. Dr Modrid 92. Fortress 92. Necronomicon 93. Love and a 45 94. Lurking Fear 94. The Frighteners 96. I Still Know What You Did Last Summer 98, etc.
TV series: Star Trek: Deep Space Nine 96– .

Comden, Betty (1918–) (Elizabeth Cohen).
American screenwriter who has collaborated with Adolph Green on books and lyrics of many Broadway shows and films.
Good News 47. The Barkleys of Broadway 49. On the Town 49. Singin' in the Rain 52. Band Wagon (AAN) 54. It's Always Fair Weather (AAN) 55. Auntie Mame 58. What a Way to Go 64, etc.

Comencini, Luigi (1916–).
Italian director.
Bambini in Città 46. Proibito Rubare 48. The Mill on the Po (co-w only) 49. La Città Si Difende (co-w only) 51. Persiane Chiuse 51. Bread, Love and Dreams (& w) 53. Bread, Love and Jealousy 54. Mariti in Città 58. Bebo's Girl 63. Le Bambole (part) 65. Misunderstood 67. Casanova 69. Le Avventure di Pinocchio 72. Sunday Woman 76. Till Marriage Us Do Part 77. Il Gatto 78. Traffic Jam/L'Ingorgo 79. They All Loved Him 80. Cercasi Gesu 82. The Boy from Calabria 87. La Bohème 88. Merry Christmas, Happy New Year/Buon Natale, Buon Anno (& co-w) 89. Bread and Wine/Pane e Vino 92, etc.

Comer, Anjanette (1942–).
American leading lady.
Quick Before It Melts 65. The Loved One 65. The Appaloosa 66. Banning 66. Guns for San Sebastian 68. Rabbit, Run 70. The Firechasers (TV) 70. The Baby 73. Lepke 74. Fire Sale 77. Netherworld 91. The Underneath 95, etc.

Comerford, Joe (1949–).
Irish director and screenwriter.
Traveller 81. Reefer and the Model 88. High Boot Benny 94.

Comfort, Lance (1908–1966).
British director, formerly cameraman.
Penn of Pennsylvania 41. Hatter's Castle 41. When We Are Married 42. Old Mother Riley, Detective 42. Daughter of Darkness (& p) 45. Great Day 45. Silent Dust 48. Portrait of Clare 50. Eight o'Clock Walk 54. At the Stroke of Nine 57. Make Mine a Million 58. The Ugly Duckling 59. Touch of Death 62. Tomorrow at Ten 62. Devils of Darkness 65, many others.
Directed many episodes of TV series, especially *Douglas Fairbanks Presents* which he also co-produced.

Comingore, Dorothy (1913–1971).
American actress who made few films but will always be remembered as the second Mrs Kane. Formerly known as Kay Winters and Linda Winters. Committed suicide.
■ Campus Cinderella 38. Comet over Broadway 38. Prison Train 38. Trade Winds 38. Blondie Meets the Boss 39. North of the Yukon 39. Scandal Sheet 39. Mr Smith Goes to Washington 39. Café Hostess 39. Pioneers of the Frontier 40. *Citizen Kane* 41. The Hairy Ape 44. Any Number Can Play 49. The Big Night 51.

Como, Perry (1912–) (Pierino Como).
American popular singer of Italian ancestry and barber apprenticeship. His deceptively relaxed manner made him immensely popular on television in the 60s and 70s.
■ Something for the Boys 44. Doll Face 45. If I'm Lucky 46. Words and Music 48.
❝ The audience knows I'm not going to do anything after all these years to upset them. – P.C.
I'm convinced that his voice comes out of his eyelids. – *Oscar Levant*

Compson, Betty (1897–1974).
American leading lady of the 20s, in Christie comedies from 1915. The first of her three husbands was director James Cruze.
The Miracle Man 19. Kick In 22. Woman to Woman (GB) 23 and 29. The Enemy Sex 24. The Fast Set 26. The Barker (AAN) 28. Docks of New York 28. The Great Gabbo 29. On with the Show 30. The Gay Diplomat 31. Destination Unknown 33. Laughing Irish Eyes (GB) 36. A Slight Case of Murder 38. Strange Cargo 40. Mr and Mrs Smith 41. Claudia and David 46. Hard-Boiled Mahoney 47. Here Comes Trouble 48, many others.

Compton, Fay (1894–1978).
British stage actress who made occasional film appearances.
She Stoops to Conquer 14. One Summer's Day 17. The Labour Leader 17. A Woman of No Importance 21. The Old Wives' Tale 21. Mary Queen of Scots 22. This Freedom 23. Robinson Crusoe 27. Fashions in Love (US) 29. Tell England 31. Autumn Crocus 34. The Mill on the Floss 35. The Prime Minister 41. Odd Man Out 46. London Belongs to Me 48. Laughter in Paradise 50. Othello 52. Aunt Clara 54. The Story of Esther Costello 57. The Haunting 63. The Virgin and the Gypsy 70, many others.

Compton, Joyce (1907–1997) (Eleanor Hunt).
American light second lead of the 30s.
Syncopating Sue 26. Dangerous Curves 29. Three Rogues 31. Only Yesterday 33. Magnificent Obsession 35. The Toast of New York 37. Balalaika 39. City for Conquest 40. Blues in the Night 42. Pillow to Post 45. Grand Canyon 51, etc.

Compton, Juliette (1899–1989).
American actress, a performer in Ziegfeld's Follies who came to England to appear in Cochran's revues and starred in local films before returning to America in 1929.
The Wine of Life (GB) 24. Bulldog Drummond's Third Round (GB) 25. Nell Gwyn (GB) 26. The

Intruder (GB) 28. Anybody's Woman 30. Strangers in Love 32. Westward Passage 32. Peg o' My Heart 33. Berkeley Square 33. The Count of Monte Cristo 34. Irene 40. That Hamilton Woman/Lady Hamilton 41, etc.

Conaway, Jeff (1950–).
American general-purpose actor.
Jennifer on My Mind 71. The Eagle Has Landed 76. Grease 78. Breaking Up Is Hard to Do (TV) 79. For the Love of It (TV) 80. Covergirl 83. The Patriot 86. Elvira, Mistress of the Dark 88. Ghost Writer 89. The Banker 89. The Sleeping Car 90. A Time to Die 91. Sunset Strip 91. Mirror Images 91. LA Goddess 92. Bounty Hunter 2002 94, etc.
TV series: Taxi 78–82.

Condon, Jackie (1913–1977).
American child actor, one of the original members of the Our Gang comedies of the 20s.

Condon, Richard (1915–1996).
American screenwriter and novelist of paranoid thrillers that have become successful movies. He is a former publicist for Walt Disney.
The Oldest Confession (from novel *The Happy Thieves*) 62. The Manchurian Candidate (oa) 62. Winter Kills (oa) 79. Prizzi's Honor (co-w, AAN) 85, etc.

Coninx, Stijn (1957–).
Belgian director.
Hector 87. Koko Flanel 89. Daens (AAN) 92, etc.

Conklin, Chester (1888–1971) (Jules Cowles).
American silent slapstick comedian, in innumerable short comedies for Keystone and Sennett; features rarer.
Greed 24. Rubber Heels 27. Gentlemen Prefer Blondes 28. Her Majesty Love 31. Hallelujah I'm a Bum 33. *Modern Times* 36. Hollywood Cavalcade 39. The Great Dictator 40. Hail the Conquering Hero 44. The Perils of Pauline 47. Big Hand for a Little Lady 66, etc.

Conklin, Heinie (1880–1959) (Charles Conklin).
American character comedian, one of the original Keystone Kops.

Conlin, Jimmy (1884–1962).
Birdlike little American character comedian, in many films, notably those of Preston Sturges.
College Rhythm 33. And Sudden Death 36. Sullivan's Travels 41. The Palm Beach Story 42. Ali Baba and the Forty Thieves 44. Mad Wednesday 47. The Great Rupert 50. Anatomy of a Murder 59, many others.

Connaughton, Shane.
Irish dramatist, screenwriter and occasional actor.
My Left Foot (co-w, AAN) 89. The Miracle (a) 91. The Playboys (co-w) 92. O Mary This London (TV) 94. The Run of the Country (w, oa) 95, etc.

Connell, Richard (1893–1949).
American writer whose chief bequest to Hollywood was his short story 'The Most Dangerous Game', filmed in 1932 (aka *The Hounds of Zaroff*) and remade several times. He also provided the original story for other films: *Seven Faces* 29. *F Man* 36. *Brother Orchid* 40. Meet John Doe (AAN) 41. Two Girls and a Sailor (co-w, AAN) 44.

Connelly, Christopher (1944–1988).
American light leading man, mostly on television.
Corky 72. Benji 74. Hawmps 76. The Norsemen 78, etc.
TV series: Peyton Place 64–69. Paper Moon 74.

Connelly, Jennifer (1970–).
American actress, in films from her early teens.
Once upon a Time in America 84. Creepers 85. Labyrinth 86. Seven Minutes in Heaven 86. Some Girls 88. The Hot Spot 90. The Rocketeer 91. Career Opportunities/One Wild Night 91. Of Love and Shadows 94. Higher Learning 95. Mulholland Falls 96. Inventing the Abbotts 97. Dark City 97, etc.

Connelly, Marc (1890–1980).
American playwright whose *The Green Pastures* was influentially filmed in 1936. He occasionally contributed to screenplays, e.g. *I Married a Witch*; and other movies based on his work are *Merton of the Movies*, *Make Me a Star*, *Dulcy* and *Beggar on Horseback*, all from the late 20s and early 30s.

Connery, Jason (1962–).
British actor, the son of actors Sean Connery and Diane Cilento.
Lords of Discipline 82. Dream One 83. The Boy Who Had Everything 83. Winner Takes All 86. Tank Malling 88. Bye Bye Baby 88. Casablanca Express 89. The Secret Life of Ian Fleming (TV) 90. Jamila 94. Urban Ghost Story 98, etc.
TV series: Robin of Sherwood 88–89.

Connery, Neil (1938–).
British leading man who made a brief appearance; Sean Connery's brother.
Operation Kid Brother 66. The Body Stealers 70, etc.

Connery, Sean (1930–) (Thomas Connery).
Virile Scots leading man who shot to fame as James Bond and has since cornered the market in gruffly indomitable characters. In 1998, the *Sunday Times* estimated his wealth at £60m. His production company, Fountainbridge Films, has a multi-film deal with Columbia Pictures, and he has announced plans to set up a film studio in Scotland.
Biographies: 1993, *Sean Connery* by John Parker. 1993, *Sean Connery: Neither Shaken nor Stirred* by Andrew Yule.
No Road Back 55. Time Lock 56. Hell Drivers 57. Action of the Tiger 57. Another Time Another Place 58. Darby O'Gill and the Little People 59. Tarzan's Greatest Adventure 59. Frightened City 60. On the Fiddle 61. The Longest Day 62. *Doctor No* 62. *From Russia With Love* 63. Woman of Straw 64. Marnie 64. *Goldfinger* 64. *The Hill* 65. Thunderball 65. A Fine Madness 66. You Only Live Twice 67. Shalako 68. The Molly Maguires 69. The Red Tent 69. The Anderson Tapes 71. Diamonds are Forever 71. The Offence 72. Zardoz 74. Ransom 74. Murder on the Orient Express 74. The Wind and the Lion 75. The Man Who Would Be King 76. Robin and Marian 76. The Next Man 76. A Bridge Too Far 77. The First Great Train Robbery 78. Meteor 79. Cuba 79. Outland 81. Time Bandits 81. Five Days One Summer 82. Wrong is Right 82. Never Say Never Again 83. Sword of the Valiant 83. Highlander 85. The Name of the Rose 86. The Untouchables (AA) 87. Memories of Me 88. The Presidio 88. Indiana Jones and the Last Crusade 89. The Hunt for Red October 90. The Russia House 90. Highlander II – the Quickening 90. Robin Hood: Prince of Thieves 91. Medicine Man 92. Rising Sun 93. A Good Man in Africa 94. Just Cause 94. First Knight 95. Dragonheart 96. The Rock 96. The Avengers 98. Playing by Heart 98, etc.
❝ I have always hated that damn James Bond. I'd like to kill him. – S.C.
With the exception of Lassie, he's the only person I know who's never been spoiled by success. – *Terence Young*

Connick, Harry, Jnr (1967–).
American singer, songwriter, pianist and actor.
When Harry Met Sally (s) 89. Memphis Belle (a, s) 90. The Godfather Part III (s) 90. Little Man Tate (a) 91. Copycat (a) 95. Independence Day (a) 96. Excess Baggage (a) 96. Hope Floats (a) 98, etc.

Connolly, Billy (1942–).
Scatological Scottish comedian, often hard to understand for Sassenachs, now in America.
Biography: 1995, *Big Yin: The Life and Times of Billy Connolly* by Jonathan Margolis.
Big Banana Feet 77. Absolution 78. Water 84. Blue Money (TV) 84. Crossing the Line 92. Indecent Proposal 93. Down among the Big Boys (TV) 93. Deacon Brodie (TV) 96. Muppet Treasure Island 96. *Mrs Brown* 97. The Imposters 98. Still Crazy 98, etc.
TV series: Head of the Class 90–92. Billy 92. Billy Connolly's World Tour of Australia 96.
❝ I set out to be a cross between Lenny Bruce and Robert the Bruce – my main thrust was the body and its functions and malfunctions – the absurdity of the thing. – B.C.

Connolly, Walter (1887–1940).
Chubby American character actor who spent his last years in films playing rasping millionaires and choleric editors.
■ No More Orchids 32. Washington Merry Go Round 32. Man Against Woman 32. Lady for a Day 33. East of Fifth Avenue 33. The Bitter Tea of General Yen 33. Paddy the Next Best Thing 33. Master of Men 33. Man's Castle 33. *It Happened One Night* 34. Once to Every Woman 34. Eight Girls in a Boat 34. Twentieth Century 34. Whom the Gods Destroy 34. Servants Entrance 34. Lady by Choice 34. Broadway Bill 34. The Captain Hates the Sea 34. White Lies 34. *Father Brown Detective* 35. She Couldn't Take It 35. So Red the Rose 35. One Way Ticket 35. The Music Goes Round 36. *Soak the Rich* 36. The King Steps Out 36. Libeled Lady 36. The Good Earth 37. Nancy Steele is Missing 37. Let's Get Married 37. The League of Frightened Men 37. First Lady 37. *Nothing Sacred* 37. Penitentiary 38. Start Cheering 38. Four's a Crowd 38. Too Hot to Handle 38. The Girl Downstairs 39. The Adventures of Huckleberry Finn 39. Bridal Suite 39. Good Girls Go to Paris 39. Coast Guard 39. Those High Gray Walls 39. *Fifth Avenue Girl* 39. *The Great Victor Herbert* 39.
❝ I am sitting here, Mr Cook, toying with the idea of cutting out your heart and stuffing it – like an olive! – *W.C. in Nothing Sacred*

Connor, Edric (1915–1968).
British West Indian actor and singer.
Cry the Beloved Country 52. Moby Dick 56. Fire Down Below 57. Four for Texas 63. Nobody Runs Forever 68, many others.

Connor, Kenneth (1918–1993).
British radio and TV comedian adept at nervous or shy roles. A mainstay of the 'Carry On' film series.
There Was a Young Lady 53. The Black Rider 55. Davy 57. Carry On Sergeant 58. Carry On Nurse 59. Dentist in the Chair 60. Carry On Constable 60. What a Carve-up 61. Gonks Go Beat 65. Carry On England 76. Carry On Emmanuelle 78, etc.

Connor, Kevin (1937–).
British director, former editor.
The Land That Time Forgot 75. From Beyond the Grave 75. At the Earth's Core 76. Dirty Knights' Work 76. The People That Time Forgot 77. Warlords of Atlantis 78. Arabian Adventure 79. Motel Hell 80. The House Where Evil Dwells 82. Master of the Game (TV) 84. The Return of Sherlock Holmes (TV) 87. What Price Victory (TV) 88. Dirty Dozen: Danko's Dozen (TV) 88. Great Expectations (TV) 89. The Hollywood Detective (TV) 89. The Old Curiosity Shop (TV) 95, etc.

Connors, Chuck (1921–1992) (Kevin Connors).
Tough guy American hero/villain, his thin smile being adaptable to friendship or menace.
Pat and Mike 52. South Sea Woman 53. Naked Alibi 54. Target Zero 55. Three Stripes in the Sun 55. Designing Woman 57. Geronimo 62. Move Over Darling 63. Synanon 65. Broken Sabre 65. Ride Beyond Vengeance 66. Captain Nemo and the Underwater City 69. Kill 'Em All and Come Back Alone 70. The Deserter 70. Pancho Villa 71. Embassy 72. Soylent Green 72. The Mad Bomber 72. 99 44/100% Dead 74. Banjo Hackett (TV) 76. Nightmare in Badham County (TV) 76. Roots (TV) 77. The Night They Took Miss Beautiful (TV) 77. Standing Tall (TV) 78. The Tourist Trap 79. Airplane 2: The Sequel 82. Summer Camp Nightmare 85. Terror Squad 87. Kill and Enjoy 88. Skinheads 88. Trained to Kill 88. Taxi Killer 88. Once Upon a Texas Train/Texas Guns (TV) 88. Jump 89. Critical Action 90. High Desert Kill 90. Salmonberries 91. Three Days to a Kill 92, etc.
TV series: *Rifleman* 57–61. Arrest and Trial 63. Branded 64–65. Cowboy in Africa 67. The Thrillseekers 72. The Yellow Rose 83.

Connors, Mike (1925–) (Kreker Ohanian).
American action hero of films and TV. Formerly known as Touch Connors.
Sudden Fear 52. The Ten Commandments 56. Where Love has Gone 64. Good Neighbour Sam 64. Situation Hopeless but not Serious 65. Harlow 65. *Stagecoach* 66. Kiss the Girls and Make them Die 67. The Killer who Wouldn't Die (TV) 76. S.S. Casino (TV) 79. Avalanche Express 79. Too Scared to Scream 85. Fist Fighter 88, etc.
TV series: *Tightrope* 57. *Mannix* 67–74. Today's FBI 81.

Conrad, Con (1891–1938) (Conrad K. Dober).
American song composer whose 'The Continental' in 1934 won the first song Oscar.
Broadway 29. Happy Days 30. Palmy Days 31. *The Gay Divorcee* 34. Reckless 35. The Great Ziegfeld 36. The Story of Vernon and Irene Castle 39, etc.

Conrad, Jess (1940–).
British pop singer and lightweight actor.
Too Young to Love 59. Konga 61. The Boys 62. The Golden Head 65. Hell is Empty 67. The Assassination Bureau 69. Absolute Beginners 86, etc.

Conrad, Joseph (1857–1924) (Teodor Josef Konrad Korzeniowski).
Polish-Ukrainian novelist, former seaman, who settled in Britain.
Lord Jim 26 and 65. Sabotage 37. Victory 30 and 40. An Outcast of the Islands 52. Laughing Anne 53. The Duellists 77. Apocalypse Now (from The Heart of Darkness) 79. Heart of Darkness (TV) 94. Amy Foster/Swept from the Sea 97. Victory 98, etc.

Conrad, Michael (1925–1983).
Giant-sized American character actor.
The War Lord 65. Sol Madrid 67. The Todd Killings 70. The Longest Yard 74. Baby Blue Marine 76, etc.
TV series: Delvecchio 76. *Hill Street Blues* 81–84.

Conrad, Robert (1935–) (Conrad Robert Falk).
Short but personable American leading man who never carried his TV popularity over to the big screen.
Palm Springs Weekend 63. Young Dillinger 65. The DA: Murder One (TV) 69. Weekend of Terror (TV) 70. The DA: Conspiracy to Kill (TV) 71. Five Desperate Women (TV) 71. The Adventures of Nick Carter (TV) 72. The Last Day (TV) 75. Live a Little Steal a Lot 75. Smash-up on Interstate Five (TV) 77. Sudden Death 77. Centennial (TV) 78. The Wild Wild West Revisited (TV) 79. Breaking Up Is Hard to Do (TV) 80. Wrong Is Right 82. Will (TV) 82. Confessions of a Married Man (TV) 84. Falling for the Stars 85. Two Fathers' Justice (TV) 85. Assassin (TV) 86. Samurai Cowboy 93. Jingle All the Way 96, etc.
TV series: Hawaiian Eye 59–62. *The Wild Wild West* 65–68. Assignment Vienna 72. Ba Ba Black Sheep 76–78. The Duke 79. A Man Called Sloan 79. Jesse Hawkes 89.

Conrad, William (1920–1994).
Heavily-built American radio writer and actor who came to Hollywood to play unpleasant villains, but later became a producer-director.
The Killers (a) 46. Arch of Triumph (a) 48. One Way Street (a) 50. Cry Danger (a) 51. Lone Star (a) 52. The Naked Jungle (a) 54. *Johnny Concho* (a) 56. The Ride Back (a) 57. Two on a Guillotine (pd) 64. Brainstorm (pd) 65. Chamber of Horrors (p) 66. An American Dream (p) 67. Covenant with Death (p) 67. Countdown (p) 68. The Brotherhood of the Bell (a) (TV) 70. O'Hara US Treasury (a) (TV) 71. Night Cries (a) (TV) 78. Keefer (a) (TV) 79. The Mikado (a) (TV) 82. Side Show (d) 84, etc.
TV series (as actor): The Fugitive (narrator) 63–67. Cannon 71–76. The Wild, Wild World of Animals (narrator) 73–78. Buck Rogers in the 25th Century (narrator) 79–80. Nero Wolfe 81. Jake and the Fat Man 87–92.

Conried, Hans (1917–1982).
Tall, weedy American comic actor with precise diction and a richly variable voice.
Dramatic School 37. Crazy House 43. Mrs Parkington 44. The Senator Was Indiscreet 47. My Friend Irma 49. The Twonky 53. *The Five Thousand Fingers of Doctor T* 53. Bus Stop 56. Rockabye Baby 58. The Patsy 64. The Brothers O'Toole 73. Oh God Book Two 80, many others.
TV series: The Danny Thomas Show 58–64. The Bullwinkle Show (voice) 61–62. Make Room for Granddaddy 70–71. The Tony Randall Show 77–78. American Dream 81.

Conroy, Frank (1890–1964).
British stage actor who went to Hollywood in the early 30s, generally played domestic tyrants.
The Royal Family of Broadway 30. Grand Hotel

32. Call of the Wild 35. Wells Fargo 37. *The Ox-Bow Incident* 43. Naked City 48. Lightning Strikes Twice 51. The Last Mile 59, etc.

Conroy, Pat (1945–).
American novelist.
The Water Is Wide (from Conrack) 74. The Great Santini 81. The Lords of Discipline 82. Prince of Tides (AANco-w, oa) 91.

Conroy, Ruaidhri (1979–).
Irish teenage actor.
Hear My Song 91. Into the West 92. Moondance 94. *Clockwork Mice* 95. Nothing Personal 95. The Van 96, etc.

Constanduros, Mabel (1880–1957).
English character actress, screenwriter and dramatist, best known for creating the cockney Buggins family on radio and records. In films from silents and radio from 1925.
Hello Radio 32. Radio Parade 33. Where's George? 35. Rose of Tralee 42. Variety Jubilee (co-w) 43. My Ain Folk 44. A Medal for the General 44. 29 Acacia Avenue (oa) 45. Caravan 46. This Man Is Mine (co-w) 46. Holiday Camp (co-w) 47. Easy Money 48, etc.

Constantine, Eddie (1917–1993).
Tough American actor popular in France where he plays Peter Cheyney heroes in crime films.
SOS Pacific 59. Treasure of San Teresa 60. Riff Raff Girls 62. Alphaville 65. Beware of a Holy Whore 77. The Long Good Friday 80. Box Office 83. Soap Bubbles 85. Macaroni Blues 86. Helsinki, Napoli All Night Long 88. The Return of Lemmy Caution 88. Europa 91. Germany Nine Zero/Allemagne Neuf Zero 91, many others.

Constantine, Michael (1927–) (Constantine Joanides).
Greek-American character actor, mostly on TV.
The Last Mile 59. The Hustler 61. Island of Love 63. Beau Geste 66. Hawaii 66. Skidoo 68. If it's Tuesday This Must Be Belgium 69. The Reivers 69. Peeper 74. Voyage of the Damned 76. Raid on Entebbe (TV) 77. The North Avenue Irregulars 79. Evita Peron (TV) 81. Pray for Death 85. In the Mood 87. Leap of Faith 88. Prancer 89. My Life 93. Deadfall 93. The Juror 96. Stephen King's Thinner 96, etc.
TV series: Hey Landlord 66–67. *Room 222* 69–74. Sirota's Court 76–77. Amanda's 83.

Conte, Richard (1911–1975) (Nicholas Conte).
Amiable Italian-American action hero in films of varying merit; often seen as oppressed hero or sympathetic gangster.
■ Heaven with a Barbed Wire Fence 39. *Guadalcanal Diary* 43. The Purple Heart 44. *A Walk in the Sun* 45. A Bell for Adano 45. Captain Eddie 45. The Spider 45. Somewhere in the Night 46. 13 Rue Madeleine 46. The Other Love 47. Call Northside 777 48. Cry of the City 48. Appointment with Murder 48. Thieves' Highway 49. Big Jack 49. *House of Strangers* 49. Whirlpool 49. The Sleeping City 50. Under the Gun 50. Hollywood Story 51. The Raging Tide 51. Thief of Damascus 52. The Fighter 52. The Raiders 52. Desert Legion 53. The Blue Gardenia 53. Slaves of Babylon 53. Highway Dragnet 54. A Race for Life 54. Target Zero 55. The Big Combo 55. Bengazi 55. New York Confidential 55. The Big Tip-Off 55. I'll Cry Tomorrow 55. Full of Life 56. The Brothers Rico 57. Little Red Monkey 57. This Angry Age 58. They Came to Cordura 59. Ocean's Eleven 60. Pepe 60. Who's Been Sleeping in My Bed? 63. The Eyes of Annie Jones 63. Circus World 64. Synanon 65. Stay Tuned for Terror 65. The Greatest Story Ever Told 65. Assault on a Queen 65. Tony Rome 66. Hotel 67. Lady in Cement 68. Operation Cross Eagle 69. Explosion 70. The Godfather 72.
TV series: The Four Just Men 59. The Jean Arthur Show 66.

Conti, Albert (1887–1967) (Albert de Conti Cedassamare).
Austrian actor in American films. He began as assistant director to Eric von Stroheim on *The Merry-Go-Round.*
The Eagle 25. The Merry Widow 25. Show People 28. Madam Satan 30. Morocco 30. Freaks 32. Suez 38. Gateway 38, etc.

Conti, Bill (1943–).
American composer.
Blume in Love 73. Harry and Tonto 74. Next Stop Greenwich Village 76. *Rocky* 76. Citizen's Band 77. F.I.S.T. 78. An Unmarried Woman 78. Paradise Alley 78. The Big Fix 78. Hurricane 79. Rocky II 79. Gloria 80. Private Benjamin 80. For Your Eyes Only 81. Victory 81. I the Jury 82. Rocky III 82. Split Image 82. The Right Stuff (AA) 83. Unfaithfully Yours 84. The Karate Kid 84. Mass Appeal 85. Nomads 85. Rocky IV 85. The Boss's Wife 86. F/X 86. The Next Karate Kid Part II 86. Broadcast News 87. Happy New Year 87. Cohen and Tate 88. A Night in the Life of Jimmy Reardon 88. The Karate Kid Part III 89. Lean on Me 89. Lock Up 89. The Fourth War 90. Rocky V 90. Year of the Gun 91. Necessary Roughness 91. Nails 92. The Adventures of Huck Finn 93. Blood In Blood Out 93. Rookie of the Year 93. 8 Seconds 94. The Next Karate Kid 94. The Scout 94. Bushwhacked 95. Spy Hard 96. Wrongfully Accused 98. Winchell (TV) 98, etc.

Conti, Tom (1941–).
Saturnine British actor, mostly on stage and TV.
Flame 74. Galileo 74. Eclipse 76. Full Circle 76. The Glittering Prizes (TV) 76. The Duellists 77. Blade on the Feather (TV) 80. The Wall (TV) 80. Merry Christmas Mr Lawrence 83. *Reuben Reuben* (AAN) 83. American Dreamer 84. Saving Grace 84. Miracles 85. Heavenly Pursuits 85. Nazi Hunter (TV) 86. Beyond Therapy 87. Shirley Valentine 89. That Summer of White Roses 89. Two Brothers Running 89. Shattered 90. Someone Else's America 95. Don't Go Breaking My Heart 98, etc.
❝ A film set is just a never-ending hell. – *T.C.*

Converse, Frank (1938–).
American general-purpose actor.
Hurry Sundown 67. Hour of the Gun 67. A Tattered Web (TV) 70. Dr Cook's Garden (TV) 73. The Rowdyman 73. Cruise into Terror (TV) 78. The Bushido Blade 79. Mystery at Fire Island 81. The Pilot 82. Spring Fever 83. Anne of Avonlea (TV) 87. Everybody Wins 90. Primary Motive 92, etc.
TV series: Coronet Blue 67. NYPD 67–68. *Movin' On* 74–75. The Family Tree 83.

Convertino, Michael.
American composer and songwriter. Educated at Yale University and the Paris Conservatoire, he was also a singer with the rock group The Innocents.
Children of a Lesser God 86. The Hidden 87. Bull Durham 88. Queen of Hearts 89. The End of Innocence 90. Aspen Extreme 93. Bodies, Rest & Motion 93. Wrestling Ernest Hemingway 93. Guarding Tess 94. Milk Money 94. The Santa Clause 94. Things to Do in Denver When You're Dead 95. Bed of Roses 96. Mother Night 96. Jungle 2 Jungle 96. Pie in the Sky 96. The Last of the High Kings 96. Critical Care 97. Where's Marlowe 98, etc.

Conway, Gary (1936–) (Gareth Carmody).
American light leading man.
I was a Teenage Frankenstein (as the monster) 57. How to Make a Monster (as Frankenstein's Monster) 58. Young Guns of Texas 62. Black Gunn 72. Once is not Enough 75. The Farmer (& p) 77. American Ninja II (& co-w) 86. Liberty and Bash 90, etc.
TV series: *Burke's Law* 63–65. Land of the Giants 68–69.

Conway, Jack (1887–1952).
American action director, launched as acting member of D. W. Griffith's stock company; long with MGM.
■ The Old Armchair 12. Bond of Fear 18. Because of a Woman 18. Little Red Decides 18. Her Decision 18. You Can't Believe Everything 18. Diplomatic Mission 19. Desert Law 19. Riders of the Dawn 20. Lombardi Limited 20. Dwelling Place of Light 21. The Money Changers 21. The Spenders 21. The Kiss 21. A Daughter of the Law 21. Step On It 22. A Parisian Scandal 22. The Millionaire 22. Across the Deadline 22. Another Man's Shoes 22. Don't Shoot 22. The Long Chance 22. The Prisoner 23. Sawdust 23. Quicksands 23. What Wives Want 23. Trimmed in Scarlet 23. Lucretia Lombard 23. The Trouble Shooter 24. The Heart Buster 24. The Roughneck 25. The Hunted Woman 25. The Only Thing 25. Brown of Harvard 26. Soul Mates 26. The Understanding Heart 27. Twelve Miles Out 27. The Smart Set 28. Bringing Up Father 28. While the City Sleeps 28. Alias Jimmy Valentine 29. *Our Modern Maidens* 29. Untamed 29. They Learned about Women 30. *The Unholy Three* 30. New Moon 30. The Easiest Way 31. Just a Gigolo 31. *Arsène Lupin* 32. But the Flesh is Weak 32. Red-headed Woman 32. Hell Below 33. The Nuisance 33. The Solitaire Man 33. *Viva Villa* 34. The Girl from Missouri 34. The Gay Bride 34. One New York Night 35. *A Tale of Two Cities* 35. *Libeled Lady* 36. Saratoga 37. *A Yank at Oxford* 38. Too Hot to Handle 38. Let Freedom Ring 39. Lady of the Tropics 39. *Boom Town* 40. Love Crazy 40. Honky Tonk 40. Crossroads 42. Assignment in Brittany 43. Dragon Seed 44. High Barbaree 47. *The Hucksters* 47. Julia Misbehaves 48.

Conway, Morgan (1900–1981).
Tough-guy American actor of 40s 'B' pictures, chiefly notable as the screen's first Dick Tracy.
Looking for Trouble 34. Crime Ring 38. Blackwell's Island 39. Brother Orchid 40. Sing Your Worries Away 42. Jack London 44. *Dick Tracy* 45. Badman's Territory 46. Dick Tracy vs Cueball 46, many others.

Conway, Tim (1933–).
American television comic who found a niche in Disney films.
McHale's Navy 64. The World's Greatest Athlete 73. The Apple Dumpling Gang 75. Gus 76. The Billion Dollar Hobo 77. The Apple Dumpling Gang Rides Again 79. The Prize Fighter 79. The Private Eyes 80. The Long Shot 85. Dorf and the First Games of Mount Olympus 87. Dear God 96. Air Bud: Golden Receiver 98, etc.
TV series: McHale's Navy 62–65. The Tim Conway Show 70. Later with Carol Burnett. Ace Crawford 83.

Conway, Tom (1904–1967) (Thomas Sanders).
British light leading man, brother of George Sanders; well-liked as 'the Falcon' in the 40s, but his career declined very suddenly. He began drinking heavily and died in poverty.
Sky Murder 40. The Trial of Mary Dugan 41. Grand Central Murder 42. *The Falcon's Brother* 42. *Cat People* 42. I Walked with a Zombie 43. The Falcon Strikes Back 43. The Seventh Victim 43. The Falcon Out West 44 (and five other Falcon adventures ending in 1946). Criminal Court 46. Repeat Performance 47. One Touch of Venus 48. Confidence Girl 52. Park Plaza 505 (GB) 53. Barbados Quest (GB) 55. The Last Man to Hang (GB) 56. The She-Creature 56. Twelve to the Moon 60. What a Way to Go (unbilled) 64, many others.
TV series: Mark Saber 52–54. The Betty Hutton Show 59.

Conyers, Darcy (1919–1973).
British director, former actor.
Ha'penny Breeze (& p) 52. The Devil's Pass (& w, p) 56. The Night We Dropped a Clanger 60. Nothing Barred 61. In the Doghouse 62, etc.

Cooder, Ry (1947–).
American guitarist, singer and composer of blues-tinged scores.
Goin' South (s) 78. The Long Riders 80. Southern Comfort 81. The Border 81. Streets of Fire 84. Paris, Texas 84. Alamo Bay 85. Brewster's Millions 85. Crossroads 86. Blue City 86. Extreme Prejudice (md) 87. Johnny Handsome 90. Geronimo: An American Legend 93. Last Man Standing 96. The End of Violence 97. Primary Colors 98, etc.

Coogan, Jackie (1914–1984).
American child actor of the 20s who achieved outstanding star status but later reappeared as a less appealing adult in minor roles. Louis B. Mayer of MGM kept him out of films for six years after he refused to drop a law suit against his mother and stepfather who had squandered his earnings. He was married to actress Betty Grable (1937–39).
The Kid 20. *Peck's Bad Boy* 21. *Oliver Twist* 21. My Boy 22. Trouble 22. Daddy 23. Circus Days 23. Long Live the King 24. A Boy of Flanders 24. The Rag Man 24. Little Robinson Crusoe 25. Johnny Get Your Gun 25. Old Clothes 25. Johnny Get Your Hair Cut 26. The Bugle Call 27. Buttons 27. Tom Sawyer 30. Huckleberry Finn 31. Home on the Range 35. College Swing 38. Kilroy Was Here 47. Outlaw Women 52. Lost Women 56. High School Confidential 58. A Fine Madness 66. The Shakiest Gun in the West 68. Marlowe 69. Cahill 73. The Escape Artist 82, many others.
TV series: Cowboy G-Men 52. McKeever and the Colonel 62. *The Addams Family* (as Uncle Fester) 64–66, 73–74.

Coogan, Keith (1970–) (Keith Franklin).
Young American actor. He is the grandson of Jackie Coogan.
Adventures in Babysitting 87. Hiding Out 87. Cheetah 89. Under the Boardwalk 89. Cousins 89. Book of Love 90. Toy Soldiers 91. Don't Tell Mom the Babysitter's Dead 91. In the Army Now 94. The Power Within 95. Downhill Willie 96, etc.

Cook, Clyde (1891–1984).
Australian clown and dancer who played in many Mack Sennett comedies and settled in California. Subsequently played character roles.
Soldiers of Fortune 19. Skirts 21. The Eskimo 22. He Who Gets Slapped 24. The Winning of Barbara Worth 26. Good Time Charley 27. The Spieler 28. The Taming of the Shrew 29. Sunny 30. Blondie of the Follies 32. Oliver Twist 33. Barbary Coast 35. Kidnapped 38. The Little Princess 39. The Sea Hawk 40. White Cargo 42. To Each His Own 46. Pride of Maryland 51, many others.

Cook, Donald (1900–1961).
American stage leading man who never quite made it in Hollywood.
The Public 31. The Mad Genius 31. The Man Who Played God 32. Frisco Jenny 33. Long Lost Father 34. Gigolette 35. Show Boat 36. Two Wise Maids 37. Bowery to Broadway 44. Patrick the Great 45. Our Very Own 50, etc.
TV series: Too Young to Go Steady 59.

Cook, Elisha, Jnr (1903–1995).
American character actor adept at cowards and neurotics.
Her Unborn Child 30. Two in a Crowd 36. Pigskin Parade 36. Love Is News 37. Breezing Home 37. Wife, Doctor and Nurse 37. Danger Love at Work 37. Life Begins in College 37. They Won't Forget 37. The Devil Is Driving 37. My Lucky Star 38. Submarine Patrol 38. Three Blind Mice 38. Grand Jury Secrets 39. Newsboy's Home 39. He Married His Wife 40. Stranger on the Third Floor 40. Public Deb Number One 40. Love Crazy 40. Tin Pan Alley 40. Man at Large 41. Sergeant York 41. Ball of Fire 41. *The Maltese Falcon* (as Wilmer the gunsel) 41. *I Wake Up Screaming* 41. A Gentleman at Heart 42. In This Our Life 42. Sleepytime Gal 42. A-Haunting We Will Go 42. Manila Calling 42. Hellzapoppin 42. Wildcat 42. Casanova Brown 44. *Phantom Lady* 44. Up in Arms 44. Dark Mountain 44. *Dark Waters* 44. Dillinger 44. Why Girls Leave Home 44. *The Big Sleep* 46. Blonde Alibi 46. Cinderella Jones 46. The Falcon's Alibi 46. Joe Palooka Champ 46. Two Smart People 46. Born to Kill 47. The Fall Guy 47. The Long Night 47. The Gangster 47. Flaxy Martin 49. The Great Gatsby 49. Behave Yourself 51. Don't Bother to Knock 51. I the Jury 53. Thunder over the Plains 53. *Shane* 53. The Outlaw's Daughter 54. Drum Beat 54. Timberjack 55. The Indian Fighter 55. Trial 55. *The Killing* 56. Accused of Murder 56. The Lonely Man 57. Voodoo Island 57. Baby Face Nelson 57. Plunder Road 57. Chicago Confidential 57. House on Haunted Hill 58. Day of the Outlaw 59. Platinum High School 60. College Confidential 60. One-Eyed Jacks 61. Papa's Delicate Condition 63. The Haunted Palace 63. Black Zoo 63. Johnny Cool 63. Blood on the Arrow 64. The Glass Cage 64. Welcome to Hard Times 67. Rosemary's Baby 68. The Great Bank Robbery 69. El Condor 70. The Movie Murderer (TV) 70. Night Chase (TV) 70. The Great Northfield Minnesota Raid 72. Blacula 72. The Night Stalker (TV) 72. Emperor of the North Pole 73. Electra Glide in Blue 73. The Outfit 73. The Black Bird 75. Messiah of Evil 75. Winterhawk 75. St Ives 76. Mad Bull (TV) 77. 1941 79. The Champ 79. Leave 'Em Laughing (TV) 80. Carny 80. Tom Horn 80. Harry's War 80. Salem's Lot 80. Hammett 82. This Girl for Hire 84. National Lampoon Goes to the Movies 84, etc.
❝ As he has grown older, the vulnerable look has congealed in his face so that his very presence has become an open invitation to destroy him. – *Ian Cameron*

Cook, Fielder (1923–).
American TV director who makes occasional films.
Patterns of Power 56. Home is the Hero (Eire) 59. *Big Hand for a Little Lady* 66. How to Save a Marriage 67. Prudence and the Pill 68. Teacher Teacher (TV) 69. Who Killed the Mysterious Mr Foster? (TV) 70. Goodbye Raggedy Ann (TV) 71. Eagle in a Cage 71. The Hands of Cormac Joyce (TV) 72. Miracle on 34th Street (TV) 73. From the Mixed Up Files of Mrs Basil E. Frankenweiler 73. This Is the West that Was (TV) 74. Judge Horton and the Scottsboro Boys (TV) 76. Beauty and the Beast (TV) 77. Too Far to Go (TV) 79. I Know Why the Caged Bird Sings (TV) 79. Family Reunion (TV) 81. Evergreen (TV) 85. A Special Friendship (TV) 87. The Member of the Wedding (TV) 97, etc.

Cook, Joe (1890–1959) (Joseph Lopez).
American comic in Broadway musicals and revues of the 20s, 30s and 40s, and star of the movie version of his 1928 stage success *Rain and Shine*, which was directed in 1930 by Frank Capra, who turned it into a drama without music. A comedian with a broad grin and an original line in nonsense patter, he was also a multi-instrumentalist, knife-thrower, expert shot, rope-spinner, juggler, slack-wire walker and acrobat, skills which he demonstrated in the film.

Cook, Peter (1937–1995).
English comic actor, writer and revue artist. Born in Torquay, Devon, and educated at Cambridge University, he found success early as a revue writer, and as a performer with Alan Bennett, Jonathan Miller and Dudley Moore in the revue *Beyond the Fringe*. He founded the briefly fashionable nightclub The Establishment in the 60s and was the principal owner of the satirical magazine *Private Eye*. He formed a successful double-act with Dudley Moore, but boredom and heavy drinking hampered his later life. The second of his three wives was actress Judy Huxtable.
Biography: 1997, *Peter Cook* by Harry Thompson.
■ The Wrong Box 66. Bedazzled 67. A Dandy in Aspic 68. Monte Carlo or Bust 69. The Bed Sitting Room 69. The Rise and Rise of Michael Rimmer 70. The Adventures of Barry Mackenzie 72. The Hound of the Baskervilles 77. Yellowbeard 83. Supergirl 84. Whoops Apocalypse 86. Mr Jolly Lives Next Door 87. The Princess Bride 87. Without a Clue 88. Getting It Right 89. Great Balls of Fire 89. Black Beauty 94.
TV series: Not Only . . . but Also 65–66. Goodbye Again 68–69. Not Only . . . but Also 71.
❝ In him, morality is discovered far from its official haunts, the message of a character like Peter's being that a life of complete self-indulgence, if *led* with the whole heart, may also bring wisdom. – *Alan Bennett*

Cook, Tommy (1930–).
American actor, in films from childhood; later became a tennis professional, concert promoter and producer.
The Tuttles from Tahiti 42. Tarzan and the Leopard Woman 45. Michael O'Halloran 48. American Guerilla in the Philippines 50. Panic in the Streets 50. Teen Age Crime Wave 55. Mohawk 56. Missile to the Moon 58. Roller Coaster (p) 77. Players (p) 79, etc.

Cool J, LL
see *LL Cool J*.

Coolidge, Martha (1946–).
American director and screenwriter. She trained as an actress and began as a documentary film-maker.
Not a Pretty Picture (& w) 76. Valley Girl 83. Joy of Sex 84. City Girl (& w) 84. Real Genius 85. Plain Clothes 88. That's Adequate (a) 90. Rambling Rose 91. Crazy in Love 92. Lost in Yonkers 93. Angie 94. Three Wishes 95. Out to Sea 97, etc.

Coombe, Carol (1911–1966).
Blonde Australian leading actress who came to Britain in 1930 and starred in several films of the decade.
P.C. Josser 31. The Sport of Kings 31. Sally in Our Alley 31. The Ringer 31. Tilly of Bloomsbury 31. The Ghost Train 31. The Strangler 32. Double Bluff 33. The Man without a Face 35. Woman to Woman 46, etc.

Cooney, Ray (1932–).
English dramatist, screenwriter, director, producer and actor, mainly of farces, in occasional films. Born in London, he was on stage from the age of 14. A Hungarian version of his farce *Out of Order* became one of the most successful releases in that country in the late 90s.
The Hand (co-w, a) 60. The Night We Got the Bird (co-w) 60. Prize of Arms (a) 61. What a Carve Up! (co-w) 61. Not Now, Darling (co-d, a, oa) 72. Not Now, Comrade (w, co-d, a) 76. There Goes the Bride (p, co-w) 79. Why Not Stay for Breakfast? (ex p, co-w) 79. Whose Life Is It, Anyway? (ex p) 81, etc.
TV series: My Sister and I (a) 56. They Met in a City (a) 60–62. Norman (co-w) 70.

Coop, Denys (1920–1981).
British cameraman.
A Kind of Loving 61. Billy Liar 63. This Sporting Life 63. One Way Pendulum 64. King and Country 65. Bunny Lake Is Missing 65. The Double Man 67. My Side of the Mountain 68. 10 Rillington Place 70. Superman (AA visual effects) 78, etc.

Cooper, Ben (1930–).
American light juvenile lead, mainly in westerns.
The Woman They almost Lynched 52. Perilous Journey 53. Johnny Guitar 54. Jubilee Trail 54. The Eternal Sea 55. The Last Command 56. *The Rose Tattoo* 57. Chartroose Caboose 60. Gunfight at Comanche Creek 64. Arizona Raiders 65. Red Tomahawk 67. Support Your Local Gunfighter 71. One More Train to Rob 71. The Sky's the Limit 75. Lightning Jack 94, many others.

Cooper, Chris (1957–).
American character actor, often seen in the films of John Sayles.
Bad Timing 80. Matewan 87. Lonesome Dove (TV) 89. Guilty by Suspicion 90. City of Hope 91. Return to Lonesome Dove (TV) 93. This Boy's Life 93. Pharaoh's Army 95. Money Train 95. Lone Star 96, etc.

Cooper, Frederick (1890–1945).
Ferrety-looking British character actor who managed a few choice roles.
Thunder Rock 42. The Great Mr Handel 42. Henry V (as Nym) 44, etc.

Cooper, Gary (1901–1961) (Frank J. Cooper).
Slow-speaking, deep-thinking American leading man, a long-enduring Hollywood star who always projected honest determination. Born in Helena, Montana, of successful English immigrant parents, he was educated partly in England, before working unenthusiastically as an illustrator and cartoonist. Determined to break into films, he went to Hollywood, where he used his horse-riding skills, learned on the family ranch, as an extra and bit player in westerns, progressing to two-reelers before becoming a star in his first feature, *The Winning of Barbara Worth* 26. Thereafter, he remained one for 30 years, as an embodiment of a strong, silent man of integrity and honour. Special Academy Award 1960 'for his many memorable screen performances and for the international recognition he, as an individual, has gained for the film industry'. Married Veronica Balfe, who had a brief Hollywood career under the name of Sandra Shaw. His lovers included Clara Bow, Evelyn Brent, Lupe Velez, Ingrid Bergman and Patricia Neal; Cecil Beaton also claimed to have had an affair with him. His defining roles were as The Virginian, in the film of the same name; Tom Brown, in *Morocco*; Lieutenant McGregor, in *The Lives of a Bengal Lancer*; Longfellow Deeds in *Mr Deeds Goes to Town*; Beau Geste, in the film of the same name; Long John Willoughby, in *Meet John Doe*; Alvin C. York, in *Sergeant York*; Lou Gehrig, in *Pride of the Yankees*; Robert Jordan, in *For Whom the Bell Tolls*; Howard Roark, in *The Fountainhead*; and Will Kane, in *High Noon*.
Biographies: 1979, *Gary Cooper: An Intimate Biography* by Hector Arce; 1981, *The Last Hero* by Larry Swindell.
■ The Thundering Herd 25. Wild Horse Mesa 25. The Lucky Horseshoe 25. The Vanishing American 25. The Eagle 25. The Enchanted Hill 26. Watch Your Wife 26. The Winning of Barbara Worth 26. It 27. Children of Divorce 27. Arizona Bound 27. Wings 27. Nevada 27. The Last Outlaw 27. Beau Sabreur 28. Legion of the Condemned 28. Doomsday 28. Half a Bride 28. *Lilac Time* 28. The First Kiss 28. Shopworn Angel 28. Wolf Song 29. The Betrayal 29. The Virginian 29. Only the Brave 29. The Texan 29. Seven Days' Leave 30. A Man from Wyoming 30. Paramount on Parade 30. The Spoilers 30. Morocco 30. Fighting Caravans 31. I Take This Woman 31. His Woman 31. The Devil and the Deep 32. *A Farewell to Arms* 32. *City Streets* 32. If I Had a Million 32. One Sunday Afternoon 33. Alice in Wonderland (as the White Knight) 33. Today We Live 33. Design for Living 34. Peter Ibbetson 34. Operator Thirteen 34. The Wedding Night 35. *Lives of a Bengal Lancer* 35. Now and Forever 35. Desire 36. *Mr Deeds Goes to Town* (AAN) 36. The General Died at Dawn 36. *The Plainsman* 36. Souls at Sea 37. The Adventures of Marco Polo 38. Bluebeard's Eighth Wife 38. The Cowboy and the Lady 39. *Beau Geste* 39. The Real Glory 39. *The Westerner* 40. Northwest Mounted Police 40. *Meet John Doe* 41. *Sergeant York* (AA) 41. Ball of Fire 41. Pride of the Yankees (AAN) 42. *For Whom the Bell Tolls* (AAN) 43. The Story of Dr Wassell 44. Saratoga Trunk 44. Casanova Brown 44. Along Came Jones (& p) 45. Cloak and Dagger 46. Unconquered 47. Variety Girl 47 (cameo). Good Sam 48. The Fountainhead 49. Task Force 49. It's a Great Feeling 49 (cameo). Bright Leaf 50. Dallas 50. You're in the Navy Now 51. Distant Drums 51. Springfield Rifle 52. *High Noon* (AA) 52. Return to Paradise 52. Blowing Wild 53. Garden of Evil 54. *Vera Cruz* 54. The Court Martial of Billy Mitchell 55. Alias Jesse James 55 (cameo). Friendly Persuasion 56. Love in the Afternoon 56. *Ten North Frederick* 58. Man of the West 58. They Came to Cordura 59. The Hanging Tree 59. The Wreck of the Mary Deare 59. The Naked Edge (GB) 61.
✪ For his sheer domination of the Hollywood scene for the first twenty years of the talkies. *Mr Deeds Goes to Town.*
❝ The most underrated actor I ever worked with said Henry Hathaway.
Fred Zinnemann put it another way:
He had magic. The only time he was in trouble was when he tried to act.
He was a poet of the real
said Clifford Odets. Whatever that means, it would have embarrassed Cooper. Perhaps Carl Sandburg put it another way:
One of the most beloved illiterates this country has ever known.
Cooper had no very high estimate of his own talent.
People ask me how come you been around so long. Well, it's through playing the part of Mr Average Joe American.
He had Mr Average Joe's reputed insularity:
From what I hear about communism, I don't like it because it isn't on the level.
He distrusted the socialism of plays like *Death of a Salesman:*
Sure there are fellows like Willy Loman, but you don't have to write plays about them.
He enjoyed his niche:
Until I came along, all the leading men were handsome, but luckily they wrote a lot of stories about the fellow next door.
For a man without acting training, he managed very well. King Vidor thought that:
He got a reputation as a great actor just by thinking hard about the next line.
Coop's own explanation was simpler:
To get folks to like you, I figured you sort of had to be their ideal. I don't mean a handsome knight riding a white horse, but a fellow who answered the description of a right guy.
Richard Arlen summed up:
Coop just likes people, it's as simple as that.
But Richard Zanuck latched on to another Cooper essential: he was part of the great outdoors:
You could never put Coop in a small hat and get your money back.
Famous line (*Sergeant York*): 'Folks back home used to say I could shoot a rifle before I was weaned. They was exaggerating some.'
Famous line (*The Virginian*): 'If you want to call me that, smile.'
Famous line (*For Whom the Bell Tolls*): 'A man fights for what he believes in, Fernando.'

Cooper, George A. (1916–).
British character actor of vengeful types.
Miracle in Soho 56. Violent Playground 58. Tom Jones 63. Nightmare 64. Life at the Top 65. The Strange Affair 68. Dracula Has Risen from the Grave 68. Start the Revolution without Me 70. Bless This House 72. The Black Windmill 74, etc.
TV series: Nice Work 89.

Cooper, Dame Gladys (1888–1971).
Distinguished, gracious British stage actress who essentially began her film career in Hollywood at the age of 52, subsequently airing her warm aristocratic personality in many unworthy roles and a few good ones.
Autobiography: 1931, *Gladys Cooper*.
Biography: 1953, *Without Veils* by Sewell Stokes.
■ Masks and Faces 17. The Sorrows of Satan 17. My Lady's Dress 18. The Bohemian Girl 22. Bonnie Prince Charles 23. Dandy Donovan 31. The Iron Duke 35. *Rebecca* 40. Kitty Foyle 40. That Hamilton Woman 41. The Black Cat 41. The Gay Falcon 41. This Above All 42. Eagle Squadron 42. *Now Voyager* (AAN) 42. Forever and a Day 43. Mr Lucky 43. Princess O'Rourke 43. The Song of Bernadette (AAN) 43. The White Cliffs of Dover 44. Mrs Parkington 44. The Valley of Decision 45. Love Letters 45. The Green Years 46. The Cockeyed Miracle 46. Green Dolphin Street 47. Beware of Pity 47. The Bishop's Wife 47. Homecoming 48. The Pirate 48. The Secret Garden 49. Madame Bovary 49. Thunder on the Hill 51. At Sword's Point 52. The Man Who Loved Redheads 54. *Separate Tables* 58. The List of Adrian Messenger 63. *My Fair Lady* (AAN) 64. The Happiest Millionaire 67. A Nice Girl Like Me 69.
TV series: *The Rogues* 64.

Cooper, Jackie (1921–).
'Little tough guy' American child actor who in adult life found roles getting rarer and became a powerful TV executive.
Autobiography: 1981, *Please Don't Shoot My Dog*.
■ *Our Gang* shorts 27–28. Movietone Follies 28. Sunny Side Up 29. *Skippy* (AAN) 31. Young Donovan's Kid 31. *The Champ* 31. Sooky 31. When a Feller Needs a Friend 32. Divorce in the Family 32. Broadway to Hollywood 33. *The Bowery* 33. *Treasure Island* 34. Peck's Bad Boy 34. Lone Cowboy 34. Dinky 35. O'Shaughnessy's Boy 35. Tough Guy 36. The Devil is a Sissy 36. Boy of the Streets 37. White Banners 38. That Certain Age 38. Gangster's Boy 38. Newsboys' Home 39. Scouts to the Rescue 39. Spirit of Culver 39. Streets of New York 39. Two Bright Boys 39. What a Life 39. The Big Guy 39. Seventeen 40. The Return of Frank James 40. Gallant Sons 40. Life with Henry 41. Ziegfeld Girl 41. Her First Beau 41. Glamour Boy 41. Syncopation 42. Men of Texas 42. The Navy Comes Through 42. Where are your Children? 44. Stork Bites Man 47. Kilroy Was Here 47. French Leave 48. Everything's Ducky 61. Shadow on the Land (TV) 68. The Astronaut (TV) 71. The Love Machine 71. Maybe I'll Come Home in the Spring (TV) 71. Stand Up and Be Counted (d only) 72. Chosen Survivors 74. The Day the Earth Moved (TV) 74. The Invisible Man (TV) 75. Mobile Two (TV) 75. Superman 78. Superman II 80. Superman III 83. Superman IV 87.
TV series: The People's Choice 56–58. Hennessey 59–71. Mobile One 75.

Cooper, James Fenimore (1789–1851).
American adventure novelist whose 'westerns' include *The Last of the Mohicans*, *The Pathfinder* and *The Deerslayer*, all frequently filmed.

Cooper, Melville (1896–1973).
British comedy character actor, long in Hollywood playing pompous upper-class idiots.
■ The Calendar 31. Black Coffee 31. Two White Arms 32. Forgin' Ahead 33. Leave It To Me 33. To Brighton with Gladys 33. The Private Life of Don Juan 34. The Scarlet Pimpernel 34. The Bishop Misbehaves (US from now on) 35. The Gorgeous Hussy 36. The Last of Mrs Cheyney 37. Thin Ice 37. The Great Garrick 37. Tovarich 37. Women Are Like That 37. *The Adventures of Robin Hood* (as Sheriff of Nottingham) 38. Gold Diggers in Paris 38. Four's a Crowd 38. Hard to Get 38. The Dawn Patrol 38. Comet over Broadway 38. Dramatic School 38. Garden of the Moon 38. I'm from Missouri 39. Blind Alley 39. The Sun Never Sets 39. Two Bright Boys 39. Rebecca 40. Too Many Husbands 40. *Pride and Prejudice* (his best role, as the pompous Mr Collins)

40. Murder over New York 40. Submarine Zone 40. The Flame of New Orleans 41. The Lady Eve 41. Scotland Yard 41. You Belong to Me 41. This Above All 42. The Affairs of Martha 42. Random Harvest 42. Life Begins at 8.30 42. The Immortal Sergeant 43. Hit Parade of 1943 43. Holy Matrimony 43. My Kingdom for a Cook 43. Heartbeat 46. 13 Rue Madeleine 46. The Imperfect Lady 47. Enchantment 48. The Red Danube 49. Love Happy 49. And Baby Makes Three 49. The Underworld Story 50. Father of the Bride 50. Let's Dance 50. The Petty Girl 50. It Should Happen to You 53. Moonfleet 55. The King's Thief 55. Diane 55. Bundle of Joy 56. Around the World in 80 Days 56. The Story of Mankind 57. From the Earth to the Moon 58.

Cooper, Merian C. (1893–1973).
American executive producer associated with many adventurous films. Special Academy Award 1952 'for his many innovations and contributions to the art of the motion picture'.
Grass 25. *Chang* 27. The Four Feathers 29. *King Kong* 33. The Last Days of Pompeii 35. The Toy Wife 38. Fort Apache 48. Mighty Joe Young 49. Rio Grande 50. The Quiet Man 52. *This is Cinerama* 52. The Searchers 56, etc.

Cooper, Miriam (1892–1976).
American silent screen actress who married Raoul Walsh.
Autobiography: 1978, *Dark Lady of the Silents*.
A Blot on the Scutcheon 11. When Fate Frowned 14. The Birth of a Nation 15. His Return 15. The Woman and the Law 18. Kindred of the Dust 22. Her Accidental Husband 23, many others.

Cooper, Richard (1893–1947).
English character actor, on stage from 1913 and notable in the title role of *Charley's Aunt*. In films from 1929, usually in muddle-headed roles.
At the Villa Rose 29. Enter the Queen 30. Black Coffee 31. The First Mrs Fraser 32. Home Sweet Home 33. Lord Edgware Dies 34. The Black Abbot 34. That's My Uncle 35. Shipyard Sally 39. Inspector Hornleigh Goes to It 41, etc.

Cooper, Stuart (1942–).
American director who got his first breaks in Britain.
Little Malcolm and his Struggle against the Eunuchs 74. Overlord 75. The Disappearance 77. A.D. (TV) 84. The Long Hot Summer (TV) 85. Christmas Eve (TV) 86. The Fortunate Pilgrim (TV) 88, etc.

Cooper, Violet Kemble (1886–1961).
British stage actress who appeared in a few Hollywood films in the 30s.
Our Betters 33. Vanessa 34. David Copperfield (as Miss Murdstone) 35. The Invisible Ray 36. Romeo and Juliet 36, etc.

Cooper, Wilkie (1911–).
British cinematographer, once a child actor.
The Rake's Progress 45. Green for Danger 46. Captain Boycott 47. London Belongs to Me 48. Stage Fright 50. The Admirable Crichton 57. Jason and the Argonauts 63. One Million Years BC 66, etc.

Coote, Robert (1909–1982).
British stage character actor who filmed mainly in Hollywood; familiar in amiable silly-ass roles.
Sally in Our Alley 31. *A Yank at Oxford* 38. Gunga Din (US) 39. You Can't Fool Your Wife 40. The Commandos Strike at Dawn 43. A Matter of Life and Death 46. The Ghost and Mrs Muir 47. Forever Amber 47. Bonnie Prince Charlie 48. The Three Musketeers 48. The Elusive Pimpernel 50. Rommel, Desert Fox 51. *The Prisoner of Zenda* 52. The Constant Husband 55. Othello (as Roderigo) 55. The Swan 56. Merry Andrew 58. The League of Gentlemen 59. The Golden Head 65. A Man Could Get Killed 66. The Swinger 66. Prudence and the Pill 68. Up the Front 72. Theatre of Blood 73. Institute for Revenge (TV) 79, etc.
TV series: *The Rogues* 64.

Cope, Kenneth (1931–).
British TV actor, usually of Liverpudlian types.
The Criminal 60. The Damned 62. Genghis Khan 65. Dateline Diamonds 65. She'll Follow You Anywhere 71, etc.
TV series: Coronation Street. Randall and Hopkirk (Deceased).

Copeland, Stewart (1952–).
American drummer and composer, in England as a child, and a founder of the rock band Police.
Rumble Fish 83. Out of Bounds 86. Wall Street 87. Talk Radio 88. She's Having a Baby 88. See No Evil, Hear No Evil 88. Hidden Agenda 90. The First Power 90. Highlander 2 90. Wide Sargasso Sea 93. Airborne 93. Bank Robber 93. Rapa Nui 94. Fresh 94. Surviving the Game 94. Silent Fall 94. The Pallbearer 96. Gridlock'd 96. Good Burger 97. Four Days in September 97. Pecker 98. Very Bad Things 98, etc.

Copland, Aaron (1900–1990).
American composer.
■ *The City* 39. *Of Mice and Men* (AAN) 39. *Our Town* (AAN) 40. North Star (AAN) 43. Fiesta 47. *The Red Pony* 49. The Heiress (AA) 49. Something Wild 61. He Got Game 98.

Copley, Peter (1915–).
British stage actor who makes occasional film appearances, usually in quiet, downtrodden or slightly sinister roles. Born in Bushey, Hertfordshire, he studied acting at the Old Vic School, and was on stage from 1932. The first of his three wives was actress Pamela Brown.
The Golden Salamander 49. The Card 52. The Sword and the Rose 53. Foreign Intrigue 56. Victim 61. King and Country 64. Help! 65. The Knack 65. Quatermass and the Pit 67. The Shoes of the Fishermen 68. Frankenstein Must Be Destroyed 69. Jane Eyre 70. Hennessy 75. Shout at the Devil 76. Empire of the Sun 87. Second Best 94, etc.

Coppel, Alec (1910–1972).
Australian playwright, screenwriter and novelist.
Over the Moon (w) 39. Obsession (oa) 46. Mr Denning Drives North (w) 51. The Captain's Paradise (AANw) 53. The Gazebo (oa) 59. Moment to Moment (w) 66. The Bliss of Mrs Blossom (w) 69.

Coppola, Carmine (1910–1991).
American composer, musician and conductor, the father of Francis Ford Coppola and Talia Shire, and the grandfather of actor Nicolas Cage.
Tonight for Sure 61. Finian's Rainbow 68. The Godfather Part II (co-m) (AA) 74. Apocalypse Now 79. The Black Stallion 79. The Outsiders 83. Blood Red 86. Gardens of Stone 87. Tucker: The Man and His Dream 88. New York Stories 89. The Godfather Part III (AAN for s) 90, etc.
❝ My father had a slogan he always used to tell us – and it's a good slogan: Steal from the best. – *Francis Ford Coppola*

Coppola, Francis Ford (1939–).
American writer-director of overweening ambition, who began working for Roger Corman. After the deserved success of *The Godfather* he set up his own studio, American Zoetrope, but later ran into financial difficulties as the filming of *Apocalypse Now* went out of control. In the 90s, he reverted to being a director for hire.
Biographies: 1989, *Coppola* by Peter Cowie; 1995, *Whom God Wishes to Destroy: Coppola and the New Hollywood* by Jon Lewis.
Book: 1988, *Hollywood Auteur – Francis Coppola* by Jeffrey Chown.
■ Dementia 63. This Property Is Condemned (w) 65. Is Paris Burning? (w) 66. *You're a Big Boy Now* (wd) 67. Finian's Rainbow (d) 68. The Rain People (wd) 69. Patton (w only) (AA) 69. *The Godfather* (co-w) (AAN) 72. American Graffiti (p only) 73. The Great Gatsby (w only) 74. *The Conversation* (wd, p) (AANw) 74. The Godfather Part Two (wd, p) (AA) 74. Apocalypse Now (BFA, AAN) 79. One from the Heart (wd, p) 82. Hammett (p) 82. The Escape Artist (p) 82. The Outsiders 83. Rumble Fish 83. The Cotton Club (& co-2) 84. Peggy Sue Got Married 86. Gardens of Stone 87. Lionheart (p) 87. Tough Guys Don't Dance (p) 87. Powaqqatsi (p) 88. Tucker: The Man and His Dream (d) 88. New York Stories (co-d, co-w) 89. The Godfather Part III (wd, p) (AAN) 90. Bram Stoker's Dracula 92. The Secret Garden (p) 93. Mary Shelley's Frankenstein (p) 94. Jack (p, d) 96. John Grisham's The Rainmaker (wd) 97.
❝ I bring to my life a certain amount of mess. – F.F.C.
If you don't bet, you don't have a chance to win. – F.F.C.
Basically, both the Mafia and America feel they are benevolent organizations. And both the Mafia and America have their hands stained with blood from what it is necessary to do to protect their power and interests. – F.F.C.
I probably have genius. But no talent. – F.F.C.
Wall Street got interested in film and communications, and these are the people who brought you the Big Mac. In the past 12 years, I can't think of one classic they've made. – F.F.C., *1996*
He is his own worst enemy. If he directs a little romance, it has to be the biggest, most overdone little romance in movie history. – *Kenneth Turan*

Coquillon, John.
British cinematographer.
Witchfinder General 68. Scream and Scream Again 69. The Oblong Box 69. Triple Echo 72. Cross of Iron 77. The Four Feathers (TV) 78. The Thirty-Nine Steps 78. Final Assignment 80. The Changeling 80. The Amateur 82. The Osterman Weekend 83. Master of the Game (TV) 83. The Last Place on Earth (TV) 84. Clockwise 85. Absolution 88, etc.

Corbett, Glenn (1929–1993) (Glenn Rothenburg).
American second lead.
The Fireball 50. Man on a String 60. The Mountain Road 60. All the Young Men 60. Homicidal 61. Pirates of Blood River (GB) 61. Shenandoah 65. Big Jake 71. Dead Pigeon on Beethoven Street (Ger.) 72. The Stranger 73. Ride in a Pink Car 74. Nashville Girl 76, etc.
TV series: It's a Man's World 62–63. Route 66 63–64. The Road West 66–67. Dallas 83–84.

Corbett, Gretchen (1947–).
American character actress, mostly on TV.
Out of It 70. Let's Scare Jessica to Death 71. The Savage Bees (TV) 76. The Other Side of the Mountain Part Two 78. Secrets of Three Hungry Wives (TV) 78. Jaws of Satan 81, etc.
TV series: The Rockford Files 74–80.

Corbett, Harry H. (1925–1982).
British stage actor who played tough guys, regional types and maniacs in an assortment of films before gaining great TV popularity in *Steptoe and Son*; subsequently starred in a number of unsatisfactory comedy vehicles.
Floods of Fear 57. Nowhere to Go 58. Cover Girl Killer 60. Sammy Going South 62. What a Crazy World 63. Ladies Who Do 63. The Bargee 64. Rattle of a Simple Man 64. Joey Boy 65. The Sandwich Man 66. Carry On Screaming 66. Crooks and Coronets 69. The Magnificent Seven Deadly Sins 71. Steptoe and Son 72, etc.

Corbett, Leonora (1907–1960).
British stage actress who made few films.
Heart's Delight 32. The Constant Nymph 33. Friday the Thirteenth 33. Farewell Again 36. Anything to Declare 38. Under Your Hat 40, etc.

Corbett, Ronnie (1930–).
Pint-sized British TV comedian, one of the Two Ronnies.
Rockets Galore 58. Casino Royale 67. Some Will Some Won't 70. The Rise and Rise of Michael Rimmer 70. No Sex Please We're British 73, etc.

Corbiau, Gérard (1941–).
Belgian director, from television, particularly of musical programmes.
The Music Teacher (AAN) 88. L'Année de l'Éveil 91. Farinelli il Castrato (AAN) 95, etc.

Corbin, Barry (1941–).
American character actor in hearty, expansive roles. Born in Texas, he is best known as Maurice Minnifield in the TV sitcom *Northern Exposure* 90–95.
Urban Cowboy 80. Bitter Harvest (TV) 81. Prime Suspect (TV) 82. The Thorn Birds (TV) 83. My Science Project 85. Under Cover 87. Permanent Record 88. It Takes Two 88. Who's Harry Crumb? 89. Ghost Dad 90. Short Time 90. Career Opportunities 91. The Chase (TV) 91, etc.
TV series: Boone 83–84. Spies 87.

Corbucci, Sergio (1927–1990).
Italian director.
Duel of the Titans 61. Son of Spartacus 62. The Slave 63. Minnesota Clay 64. Django 65. The Hellbenders 66. The Campanieros 71. Il Bestione 74. La Mazzetta 78. I Don't Understand You Anymore 80. I'm Getting Myself a Yacht 81. Super Fuzz 81. My Darling, My Dearest 82. Sing Sing 83. Sono un Fenomeno Paranormale 86. Rimini Rimini 87. Grazie Commissario 88, etc.

Corby, Ellen (1913–) (Ellen Hansen).
American character actress specializing in nosy neighbours and prim spinsters. She is best known for her early 70s role as Grandma in the TV series *The Waltons*, for which she won three Emmy awards as best supporting actress. Born in Racine, Wisconsin, and raised in Philadelphia, Pennsylvania, she first worked in Hollywood as a script girl from the early 30s, before becoming an actress in the 40s.
The Dark Corner 46. The Spiral Staircase 46. *I Remember Mama* (AAN) 48. Fighting Father Dunne 48. Madame Bovary 49. On Moonlight Bay 51. About Mrs Leslie 54. The Seventh Sin 57. Macabre 58. Visit to a Small Planet 60. The Strangler 64. The Gnome-Mobile 67. Support Your Local Gunfighter 71. Napoleon and Samantha 72. The Story of Pretty Boy Floyd (TV) 74. A Wedding on Waltons Mountain (TV) 82. A Walton Thanksgiving Reunion (TV) 93. A Walton Easter (TV) 97, many others.
TV series: Please Don't Eat the Daisies 65. *The Waltons* 72–81.

Corcoran, Donna (1942–).
American child actress of the 50s, the sister of Kevin Corcoran.
Angels in the Outfield 51. Don't Bother to Knock 52. Scandal at Scourie 53. Dangerous when Wet 53. Gypsy Colt 54. Violent Saturday 55, etc.

Corcoran, Kevin (1949–).
American child actor of the 50s and 60s who turned producer in the 70s.
Untamed 55. Old Yeller 59. The Shaggy Dog 59. Toby Tyler 60. The Swiss Family Robinson 61. Babes in Toyland 62. Bon Voyage 63. Savage Sam 64. A Tiger Walks 65, etc.

Cord, Alex (1931–) (Alexander Viespi).
Italian-American leading man.
Synanon 65. Stagecoach 66. The Brotherhood 68. Stiletto 69. Dead or Alive 69. The Last Grenade 69. The Dead Are Alive 72. Genesis II (TV) 73. Chosen Survivors 74. Sidewinder One 77. Greyeagle 77. Beggarman, Thief (TV) 79. Goliath Awaits (TV) 81. Jungle Warriors 84. A Girl to Kill For 90. Street Asylum 90. To Be the Best 93, etc.
TV series: W.E.B. 78. Cassie and Company 82. Airwolf 84–86.

Corda, Maria (1902–c. 1965) (Maria Farcas).
Hungarian actress, in films from 1921. She began as a dancer with the Royal Opera, Budapest, and was the first wife of producer and director Alexander Korda.
Dance Fever (Ger.) 21. A Modern Dubarry (Ger.) 21. The Last Days of Pompeii (It.) 26. The Guardsman (US) 27. The Private Life of Helen of Troy (US) 27. Tesha (GB) 28. Love and the Devil (US) 29, etc.

Corday, Mara (1932–) (Marilyn Watts).
American leading lady of the 50s, most notably when threatened by creatures from outer space or by giant insects mutated through atomic radiation. A former chorus girl and pin-up, she retired in the 60s after marrying actor Richard Long, returning to the screen in the late 70s in films starring Clint Eastwood.
Ready to Die 48. Sea Tiger 52. So This Is Paris 54. Drums across the River 54. Foxfire 55. Man without a Star 55. Tarantula 55. The Quiet Gun 56. The Giant Claw 57. Undersea Girl 57. The Black Scorpion 57. Girls on the Loose 58. The Gauntlet 77. Sudden Impact 83. Pink Cadillac 89. The Rookie 90, etc.

Corday, Paula (1924–1992) (aka Paule Croset and Rita Corday).
Anglo-Swiss leading lady who went to Hollywood in the 40s.
The Falcon Strikes Back 43. The Body Snatcher 45. The Exile 47. Sword of Monte Cristo 51. Because You're Mine 52. The French Line 54, etc.

Cordell, Frank (1918–1980).
British composer.
The Voice of Merrill 52. The Captain's Table 58. The Rebel 60. Flight from Ashiya (US) 63.

Never Put It in Writing 63. The Bargee 64. Khartoum 66. Project Z 68. Mosquito Squadron 68. Hell Boats 69. Ring of Bright Water 69. *Cromwell* (AAN) 70. Trial by Combat/A Choice of Weapons 76. God Told Me To (US) 76, etc.

Cording, Harry (1891–1954).
British supporting actor in Hollywood, usually as tough, blunt types.
The Knockout 25. Captain of the Guard 30. Forgotten Commandments 33. The Crusades 35. Mutiny on the Bounty 35. Sutter's Gold 36. The Prince and the Pauper 37. The Adventures of Robin Hood 38. The Hound of the Baskervilles 39. The Wolf Man 41. Arabian Nights 42. Lost in a Harem 44. The House of Fear 45. Terror by Night 46. A Woman's Vengeance 48. Samson and Delilah 49. Mask of the Avenger 51. Road to Bali 52. Titanic 53. Demetrius and the Gladiators 54. East of Eden 55, many others.

Cordy, Raymond (1898–1956) (R. Cordiaux).
French comedy actor, especially seen in René Clair's films.
Le Million 31. À Nous la Liberté 31. Le Quatorze Juillet 33. Le Dernier Milliardaire 34. Ignace 37. Les Inconnus dans la Maison 42. Le Silence est d'Or 46. La Beauté du Diable 49. Les Belles de Nuit 52. Les Grandes Manoeuvres 55, etc.

Corenblith, Michael.
American production designer.
Zandalee 91. He Said, She Said 91. Cool World 92. The Gun in Betty Lou's Handbag 92. Apollo 13 (AAN) 95. Down Periscope 96. Ransom 96, etc.

Corey, Jeff (1914–).
Gaunt American supporting actor seen as farmer, gangster, junkie, wino, convict, cop, and even Wild Bill Hickok.
All that Money Can Buy 41. My Friend Flicka 43. The Killers 46. Brute Force 47. Home of the Brave 49. Bright Leaf 50. Rawhide 51. Red Mountain 52. The Balcony 63. Lady in a Cage 64. Mickey One 65. The Cincinnati Kid 65. *Seconds* 66. In Cold Blood 67. True Grit 69. *Little Big Man* 71. Catlow 72. Paper Tiger 75. Oh God 77. Butch and Sundance: The Early Days 79. Battle Beyond the Stars 80. The Sword and the Sorcerer 82. Conan the Destroyer 84. Creator 85. Bird on a Wire 90. Pay Off 91. Ruby Cairo 93. Surviving the Game 94. Color of Night 94, many others.
TV series: Hell Town 85.

Corey, Wendell (1914–1968).
American leading actor who usually played solid dependable types.
■ Desert Fury 47. I Walk Alone 47. The Search 48. Maneater of Kumaon 48. Sorry Wrong Number 48. The Accused 48. Any Number Can Play 49. The File on Thelma Jordon 49. Holiday Affair 49. No Sad Songs for Me 50. The Furies 50. Harriet Craig 50. The Great Missouri Raid 50. Rich Young and Pretty 51. The Wild Blue Yonder 51. The Wild North 52. Carbine Williams 52. My Man and I 52. Laughing Anne (GB) 53. Jamaica Run 53. Hell's Half Acre 54. Rear Window 54. The Big Knife 55. The Bold and the Brave 56. The Killer is Loose 56. The Rack 56. The Rainmaker 56. Loving You 57. The Light in the Forest 58. Alias Jesse James 59. Blood on the Arrow 64. Agent for Harm 66. Waco 66. Women of the Prehistoric Planet 66. Picture Mommy Dead 66. Red Tomahawk 67. Cyborg 2087 67. The Astro Zombies 68. Buckskin 68.
TV series: Harbor Command 57. Peck's Bad Girl 59. The Eleventh Hour 62.

Corfield, John (1893–).
British producer in films from 1929; co-founder of British National Films with Lady Yule and J. Arthur Rank.
Turn of the Tide 35. Laugh It Off 40. Gaslight 40. Headline 42. Bedelia 46. The White Unicorn 47. My Sister and I 48, etc.

Corman, Gene (1927–).
American producer, brother of Roger Corman.
Tower of London 62. The Secret Invasion 64. Tobruk 66. You Can't Win 'Em All 70, etc.

Corman, Roger (1926–).
American producer and director who during the 50s made a record number of grade Z horror films, then presented an interesting series of Poe adaptations; when he seemed poised for better things his career as a director slowed and he turned to producing low-budget exploitation movies and distributing foreign films. Among those who began their careers working for him are Martin Scorsese, Francis Ford Coppola, Peter Bogdanovich, Jack Nicholson, Monte Hellman, Jonathan Demme, Joe Dante, Jonathan Sayles, Ron Howard, Gale Anne Hurd and James Cameron. In 1994, he set up an Irish-based production company, New Concorde, which he sold three years later, as Concorde-New Horizons, to producer Elliott Kastner for a reported $100m.
Autobiography: 1990, *How I Made a Hundred Movies in Hollywood and Never Lost a Dime*.
Biography: 1998, *Roger Corman: Best of the Cheap Acts* by Mark Thomas McGee.
■ Five Guns West 55. Apache Woman 55. The Day the World Ended 56. Swamp Woman 56. The Gunslinger 56. Oklahoma Woman 56. It Conquered the World 56. Naked Paradise 57. Attack of the Crab Monsters 57. *Not of this Earth* 57. The Undead 57. Rock all Night 57. Carnival Rock 57. Teenage Doll 57. Sorority Girl 57. The Viking Women and the Sea Serpent 57. War of the Satellites 57. Machine Gun Kelly 58. Teenage Caveman 58. She-Gods of Shark Reef 58. I Mobster 59. Wasp Woman 59. *A Bucket of Blood* 59. Ski Troop Attack 60. *House of Usher* 60. The Little Shop of Horrors 60. The Last Woman on Earth 60. Creature from the Haunted Sea 60. Atlas 60. The Pit and the Pendulum 61. The Premature Burial 62. *The Intruder* 62. Tales of Terror 62. Tower of London 62. *The Raven* 63. The Young Racers 63. The Haunted Palace 63. The Terror 63. X – The Man with X-ray Eyes 63. *The Masque of the Red Death* 64. Secret Invasion 64. *The Tomb of Ligeia* 65. The Wild Angels 66. The St Valentine's Day Massacre 67. The Trip 67. Bloody Mama 70. Gas-s-s! 70. Von Richthofen and Brown 71. Boxcar Bertha (p only) 72. I Escaped from Devil's Island (co-p only) 73. Big Bad Mama (p only) 74. Cockfighter (p only) 74. Grand Theft Auto (p only) 77. Thunder and Lightning (p only) 77. Piranha (p only) 78. St Jack (p only) 78. Battle Beyond the Stars (p only) 80. Humanoids from the Deep (p only) 80. Smokey Bites the Dust (p only) 81. Forbidden World (p only) 82. Love Letters (p) 83. Space Raiders (p) 83. Suburbia (p) 83. The Warrior and the Sorceress (p) 83. Deathstalker (p) 84. Streetwalkin' (p) 85. Amazons (p) 87. Big Bad Mama II (p) 88. Daddy's Boys (p) 88. Dangerous Love (p) 88. The Drifter (p) 88. Nightfall (p) 88. Not of This Earth (p) 88. Watchers (p) 88. Andy Colby's Incredibly Awesome Adventure (p) 89. The Lawless Land (p) 89. The Masque of the Red Death (p) 89. Stripped to Kill II (p) 89. The Terror Within (p) 89. Time Trackers (p) 89. Two to Tango (p) 89. Wizards of the Lost Kingdom II (p) 89. Back to Back (p) 90. Bloodfist II (p) 90. A Cry in the Wild (p) 90. Full Fathom Five (p) 90. The Haunting of Morella (p) 90. Overexposed (p) 90. Primary Target (p) 90. Frankenstein Unbound (co-w, d) 90. Silk 2 (p) 90. Streets (p) 90. Transylvania Twist (p) 90. Watchers II (p) 90. Welcome to Oblivion (p) 90. Hollywood Boulevard II (p) 91. The Terror Within II (p) 91. Dracula Rising (p) 92. In the Heat of Passion (p) 92. Reflections on a Crime (p) 94. Cheyenne Warrior (p) 94.
❝ I've never made the film I wanted to make. No matter what happens, it never turns out exactly as I hoped. – R.C.
Poe writes the first reel or the last reel. Roger does the rest. – *James H. Nicholson*
All my films have been concerned simply with man as a social animal. – R.C., *1970*
I think there is always a political undercurrent in my films. With the exception of *The Intruder*, I tried not to put it on the surface. – R.C.
To one degree or another, almost all films finally adhere to the Corman policy. So many of them do have an enormous amount of action; the sex is there; the laughs are there; and, sometimes, to some degree, the social statement is there as well. *The Godfather* films are the most expensive Roger Corman films ever made, and I think that everyone's trying to exploit that formula, one way or another. But most people are less candid about it than Roger is. – *Jonathan Demme*
He once said, 'Martin, what you have to get is a very good first reel because people want to know what's going on. Then you need a very good last reel because people want to hear how it all turns out. Everything else doesn't really matter.' Probably the best sense I have ever heard in the movies. – *Martin Scorsese*

Corneau, Alain (1943–).
French director and screenwriter, usually of thrillers. He trained at the national film school, IDHEC, before going to America to collaborate on a script with novelist Jim Thompson. He also worked as an assistant to Roger Corman, Marcel Camus and Costa-Gavras.
France S.A. 74. La Menace 77. Série Noire 79. Choice of Arms/Le Choix des Armes 81. Fort Saganne 84. Nocturne Indien 89. The New World 95, etc.

Cornelius, Henry (1913–1958).
British director with a subtle comedy touch.
■ It Always Rains on Sunday (co-w only) 47. *Passport to Pimlico* 48. The Galloping Major (& w) 51. *Genevieve* 53. I Am a Camera 55. Next to No Time 57. Law and Disorder 58.

Cornell, John (1941–).
Australian producer and director. A former journalist, he went on to work in television and discovered and managed comedian Paul Hogan.
Crocodile Dundee (p) 86. Crocodile Dundee II (p, d) 88. Almost an Angel (p) 90, etc.

Cornfield, Hubert (1929–).
American director.
■ Sudden Danger 56. Lure of the Swamp 57. Plunder Road 59. *The Third Voice* 59. Angel Baby (co-d) 61. Pressure Point 62. Night of the Following Day 68. Les Grands Moyens 76.

Corraface, Georges (1953–).
French-born leading actor, of Greek parents. He studied law in Paris before becoming an actor.
Mahabharata 89. Impromptu 90. Not without My Daughter 91. Columbus: The Discovery 92. Pasiones Turcas 94. Muere Mi Vida (Sp.) 95. Escape from LA 96. Slaughter of the Cock 97. Preference (Fr./It./Sp.) 98. Algiers-Beirut: A Souvenir (Fr./Leb.) 98, etc.

Corri, Adrienne (1930–) (Adrienne Riccoboni).
Tempestuous red-headed British leading lady of Italian descent.
The River 51. The Kidnappers 53. Devil Girl from Mars 54. *Lease of Life* 54. Make Me an Offer 54. The Feminine Touch 55. Three Men in a Boat 56. Corridors of Blood 58. The Rough and the Smooth 59. The Hellfire Club 61. The Tell-Tale Heart 61. A Study in Terror 65. Bunny Lake is Missing 65. The Viking Queen 67. Moon Zero Two 69. A Clockwork Orange 71. Vampire Circus 72. Madhouse 74, etc.
TV series: Sword of Freedom 57.

Corrigan, Douglas 'Wrong Way' (1907–1995).
American aviator who in 1939 left New York for Los Angeles and landed in Ireland, thus deserving the title Wrong Way Corrigan. In the same year he played himself in the film *The Flying Irishman*.

Corrigan, Lloyd (1900–1969).
Chubby American character actor, usually in jovial roles; also directed some films in the 30s.
The Splendid Crime 25. Daughter of the Dragon (d) 31. The Broken Wing (d) 32. Murder on a Honeymoon (d) 35. The Dancing Pirate (d) 36. Night Key (d) 37. Young Tom Edison 40. *The Ghost Breakers* 40. The Great Man's Lady 42. Since You Went Away 44. The Bandit of Sherwood Forest 45. Stallion Road 47. Cyrano de Bergerac 50. Son of Paleface 52. The Bowery Boys Meet the Monsters 54. Hidden Guns 57. The Manchurian Candidate 62, many others.
TV series: Willy 54–55. Happy 60–61. Hank 65–66.

Corrigan, Ray 'Crash' (1903–1976) (Ray Benard).
American leading man, hero of innumerable second-feature westerns, first for Republic as one of the Three Mesquiteers and then, for Monogram, as one of the three Range Busters. He also appeared in jungle films as a gorilla and was the creature in *It! The Terror from beyond Space* 58. Retired to run Corriganville, a Californian location for western movies, which he later sold for several million dollars, becoming a property developer in Oregon.
The Three Mesquiteers 36. Wild Horse Rodeo 38. The Purple Vigilantes 38. Three Texas Steers 39. West of the Pinto Basin 40. Wrangler's Roost 41. Rock River Renegades 42. Bullets and Saddles 43. Arizona Stage Coach 46. The White Gorilla 46. Texas Trouble Shooters 47. Thunder River Feud 47. Zamba the Gorilla 49, many more.
TV series: Crash Corrigan's Ranch 50.

Cort, Bud (1950–) (Walter Edward Cox).
American actor with a tendency to play demented youths.
M*A*S*H 70. The Travelling Executioner 70. Brewster McCloud 70. *Harold and Maude* 72. Why Shoot the Teacher 77. Hitler's Son 78. Die Laughing 80. She Dances Alone 82. Love Letters 83. Electric Dreams 84. Maria's Lovers 84. Invaders from Mars 86. Love at Stake 87. Out of the Dark 88. Brain Dead 89. Ted and Venus (& d) 92. Girl in the Cadillac 95. Theodore Rex 96, etc.

Cortese, Valentina (1924–).
Italian leading lady in international films. She was married to Richard Basehart.
The Glass Mountain 48. Thieves' Highway 49. Malaya 50. The House on Telegraph Hill 51. Les Misérables 52. The Barefoot Contessa 54. Le Amiche 55. Magic Fire 56. Calabuch 58. Barabbas 62. The Visit 64. Juliet of the Spirits 65. The Legend of Lylah Clare 68. Day for Night/La Nuit Américaine (AAN) 73. When Time Ran Out 80. The Adventures of Baron Munchhausen 89. Buster's Bedroom 91. Sparrow/Storia di una Capinera 93, etc.

Cortez, Ricardo (1899–1977) (Jake Kranz).
American leading man, groomed in the 20s as a Latin lover in the Valentino mould. Later developed outside interests and quit movies after a sojourn in routine roles.
Sixty Cents an Hour 23. Pony Express 24. *The Torrent* 26. *The Sorrows of Satan* 27. The Private Life of Helen of Troy 27. Behind Office Doors 28. Ten Cents a Dance 31. Melody of Life 32. The Phantom of Crestwood 33. *Wonder Bar* 34. Special Agent 35. The Walking Dead 36. Talk of the Devil (GB) 36. Mr Moto's Last Warning 38. City Girl (d only) 38. Free, Blonde and Twenty One (d only) 40. World Première 40. I Killed That Man 42. Make Your Own Bed 44. The Locket 46. Blackmail 47. The Last Hurrah 58, many others.

Cortez, Stanley (1908–1997) (Stanley Kranz).
American cinematographer, brother of Ricardo Cortez; in Hollywood from silent days.
■ Four Days Wonder 37. The Wildcatter 37. Armored Car 37. The Black Doll 38. Lady in the Morgue 38. Danger on the Air 38. Personal Secretary 38. The Last Express 38. For Love or Money 38. The Forgotten Woman 39. They Asked for It 39. Hawaiian Nights 39. Risky Business 39. Laugh It Off 39. Alias the Deacon 39. The Leatherpushers 40. Meet the Wildcat 40. Love Honor and Oh Baby 40. The Black Cat 40. A Dangerous Game 41. San Antonio Rose 41. Moonlight in Hawaii 41. Badlands of Dakota 41. Bombay Clipper 42. Eagle Squadron 42. *The Magnificent Ambersons* 42. Flesh and Fantasy 43. The Powers Girl 43. Since You Went Away (co-ph) 44. Smash-Up 47. The Secret Beyond the Door 48. Smart Woman 48. The Man on the Eiffel Tower 49. Underworld Story 50. The Admiral was a Lady 50. The Basketball Fix 51. Fort Defiance 51. Models Inc 52. Abbott and Costello Meet Captain Kidd 52. The Diamond Queen 53. Dragon's Gold 53. Shark River 53. Riders to the Stars 54. Black Tuesday 54. *The Night of the Hunter* 55. Man from Del Rio 56. Top Secret Affair 57. The Three Faces of Eve 57. Thunder in the Sun 59. Vice Raid 60. The Angry Red Planet 60. Dinosaurus 60. Back Street 61. Shock Corridor 63. The Candidate 64. Nightmare in the Sun 64. The Naked Kiss 65. The Navy vs the Night Monsters 66. The Ghost in the Invisible Bikini 66. Blue 68. The Bridge at Remagen 69. The Date 71. Do Not Fold, Spindle or Mutilate (TV) 72. Another Man, Another Chance (co-ph) 77.

Corti, Alex (1933–1993).
French-born director and screenwriter of Austrian descent, in international films.
The Refusal/Der Verweigerung 72. The Condemned/Totstellen 75. A Woman's Pale Blue Handwriting (& w) 84. God Does Not Believe in Us Anymore/An Uns Glaubt Gott Nicht Mehr 85. Sante Fe 85. Welcome in Vienna (& w) 86. The King's Whore (& w) 90, etc.

Cosby, Bill (1937–).
American leading man and TV personality.
To All My Friends on Shore (& p) (TV) 71. Hickey and Boggs 72. Uptown Saturday Night 74. Let's Do It Again 76. Mother, Jugs and Speed 76. A Piece of the Action 77. Top Secret (TV) 78. California Suite 79. Leonard Part 6 87. Ghost Dad 90. The Meteor Man 93. I Spy Returns (TV) 94. Jack 96, etc.
TV series: *I Spy* 66–68. The Bill Cosby Show 69–71, 72–73, 84–92. Fat Albert and the Cosby Kids 72. Cos 76. The Cosby Mysteries 94–95. Cosby 96– .

Coslow, Sam (1905–1982).
American producer, lyricist and composer. In collaboration with Arthur JOHNSTON, he wrote many songs for Paramount movies, including *Cocktails for Two, Just One More Chance*, My *Old Flame, Sing You Sinners*. Married actress Esther Muir.
Autobiography: 1977, *Cocktails for Two*.
AS PRODUCER: Dreaming Out Loud 40. Heavenly Music (short) (AA) 43. Out of This World 45. Copacabana 47, etc.
AS SONGWRITER: Dance of Life 29. Blonde Venus 32. College Coach 32. Too Much Harmony 33. Belle of the Nineties 34. Murder at the Vanities 34. All the King's Horses 35. Goin' to Town 35. It's Love Again 36. Mountain Music 37. This Way Please 37. You and Me 38. Out of This World 45. Copacabana 47, etc.

Cosma, Vladimir (1940–).
Romanian-born composer who has worked in France since the 60s.
Alexander 68. Maldonne 68. Le Distrait 70. The Tall Blond Man with One Black Shoe 72. Pleure pas la Bouche Pleine 73. Salut l'Artiste 73. The Mad Adventures of Rabbi Jacob 74. Lucky Pierre/La Moutarde me Monte au Nez 74. The Return of the Tall Blond Man with One Black Shoe 74. The Pink Telephone/Le Téléphone Rose 75. Dracula and Son 76. Pardon Mon Affaire/Un Éléphant ça Trompe Enormément 76. Pardon Mon Affaire Too!/Nous Irons Tous au Paradis 77. Anne 78. The Getaway/La Déborade 79. La Boum 80. Diva 82. La Boum II 83. Just the Way You Are 84. Asterix vs Caesar 85. Judith Krantz's Till We Meet Again (TV) 89. The Jackpot/La Totale! 91. Cuisine et Dépendances 93. Le Mari de Léon 93. Cache Cash 94, etc.

Cosmatos, George Pan (1941–).
Greek director of international adventures.
Massacre in Rome 74. The Cassandra Crossing 77. Escape to Athena 79. Rambo: First Blood II 84. Cobra 85. Leviathan 89. Tombstone 94. Shadow Conspiracy 97, etc.
❝ My pictures appeal all round the world. I do slick American pictures with a European sensitivity. – G.P.C.

Cossart, Ernest (1876–1951).
Portly British actor, inevitably cast by Hollywood in butler roles. Born in Cheltenham, Gloucestershire, he was a former clerk and was on stage from 1896, going to America in 1908. He was on screen from 1935, but continued to act in the theatre in a wider variety of roles than Hollywood offered him. His daughter, Valerie Cossart, was a stage actress in America from the 30s.
The Scoundrel 35. Desire 36. The Great Ziegfeld 36. Angel 37. Zaza 39. The Light That Failed 39. Tom Brown's Schooldays 40. *Charley's Aunt* 41. Casanova Brown 44. Cluny Brown 46. John Loves Mary 49, many others.

Cossins, James (1933–1997).
British character actor, usually of pompous, flustered type.
The Anniversary 68. Lost Continent 68. Melody 70. Villain 71. Blood from the Mummy's Tomb 72. Deathline 72. The Man with the Golden Gun 74. The First Great Train Robbery 79. Gandhi 82. Sherlock Holmes and the Masks of Death (TV) 84. Grand Larceny 87. Immaculate Conception 92, etc.

Costa-Gavras (1933–) (Constantin Costa-Gavras).
Russo-Greek director, in France from childhood.
The Sleeping Car Murders 65. Un Homme de Trop 67. 'Z' (AAN) 68. L'Aveu 70. State of Siege 72. Special Section 75. *Missing* (AA co-w) 82. Hannah K 83. Conseil de Femme 86. Betrayed 88. Music Box 89. La Petite Apocalypse 93. A Propos de Nice, la Suite (Fr., co-d) 95. Mad City 97, etc.

Costello, Dolores (1905–1979).
Gentle American silent screen heroine, in films from 1911; married John Barrymore. Her lovers included Darryl ZANUCK and Conrad NAGEL.
Lawful Larceny 23. *The Sea Beast* 25. Bride of the Storm 26. When a Man Loves 27. Old San Francisco 27. Glorious Betsy 28. The Redeeming Sin 29. *Noah's Ark* 29. Show of Shows 29. Second Choice 30. Expensive Women 31. Little Lord Fauntleroy 36. King of the Turf 39. *The Magnificent Ambersons* 42. This is the Army 43, many others.

Costello, Helene (1903–1957).
American silent screen leading lady, sister of Dolores Costello, in films from 1912. Her first husband was actor Lowell Sherman.
The Man on the Box 25. Bobbed Hair 25. Don Juan 26. In Old Kentucky 27. *Lights of New York* 28. Midnight Taxi 28. The Circus Kid 28. Show of Shows 29. Riffraff 35, etc.

Costello, Lou (1906–1959) (Louis Cristillo).
Dumpy American comedian, the zanier half of Abbott and Costello. For films, see *Bud Abbott*. Costello finally made one on his own, *The Thirty-Foot Bride of Candy Rock* 59.

Costello, Maurice (1877–1950).
American matinée idol, the father of Dolores and Helena Costello, in films from 1907.
A Tale of Two Cities 11. The Night Before Christmas 12. Human Collateral 20. Conceit 21. Glimpses of the Moon 23. The Mad Marriage 25. Camille 27. Hollywood Boulevard 36. Lady from Louisiana 41, many others.

Costner, Kevin (1955–).
American leading actor who scored a big hit with his first attempt at directing.
Biographies: 1991, *Kevin Costner* by Todd Keith. 1993, *Kevin Costner – A Life on Film* by Adrian Wright.
Night Shift 82. Table For Five 83. Testament 83. American Flyers 84. Fandango 84. Silverado 85. Sizzle Beach 86. The Untouchables 87. No Way Out 87. Bull Durham 88. Field of Dreams 89. Dances with Wolves (& d) (AAd, AANa) 90. Revenge 90. Robin Hood: Prince of Thieves 91. JFK 91. The Bodyguard 92. A Perfect World 93. Rapa Nui (p) 94. Wyatt Earp (& p) 94. Waterworld (& p) 95. Tin Cup 96. The Postman (& p, d) 97, etc.

Cottafavi, Vittorio (1914–1998).
Italian director, mainly of cut-rate spectaculars. Has won critical approval for stylish handling of some of them.
Revolt of the Gladiators 58. The Legions of Cleopatra 59. The Vengeance of Hercules 60. Hercules Conquers Atlantis 61, etc.

Cotten, Joseph (1905–1994).
Tall, quiet American leading man, former drama critic and Broadway stage star. His second wife was actress Patricia Medina.
Autobiography: 1987, *Vanity Will Get You Somewhere*.
■ *Citizen Kane* 41. Lydia 41. *The Magnificent Ambersons* 42. *Journey into Fear* 42. *Shadow of a Doubt* 43. Hers to Hold 43. Gaslight 44. Since You Went Away 44. Love Letters 45. *I'll Be Seeing You* 45. Duel in the Sun 46. The Farmer's Daughter 47. *Portrait of Jennie* 48. Under Capricorn 49. Beyond the Forest 49. *The Third Man* 49. Two Flags West 50. Walk Softly Stranger 50. September Affair 50. Half Angel 51. Man with a Cloak 51. Peking Express 52. Untamed Frontier 52. The Steel Trap 52. Niagara 52. Blueprint for Murder 53. Special Delivery 54. The Bottom of the Bottle 55. The Killer is Loose 56. The Halliday Brand 56. From the Earth to the Moon 58. Touch of Evil (uncredited cameo) 58. The Angel Wore Red 60. The Last Sunset 61. Hush Hush Sweet Charlotte 64. The Money Trap 65. The Great Sioux Massacre 65. The Tramplers 66. The Oscar 66. The Hellbenders 67. Jack of Diamonds 67. Brighty 67. Some May Live (TV) 67. Petulia 68. Days of Fire (It.) 68. Keene 69. Cutter's Trail (TV) 69. The Lonely Profession (TV) 69. Latitude Zero 69. The Grasshopper 70. Do You Take This Stranger (TV) 70. The Abominable Dr Phibes 71. City Beneath the Sea (TV) 71. Doomsday Voyage 71. Tora! Tora! Tora! 71. White Comanche 71. Lady Frankenstein 71. Baron Blood 72. Assault on the Wayne (TV) 72. The Screaming Woman (TV) 72. The Devil's Daughter (TV) 72. The Scientific Cardplayer 72. Soylent Green 73. A Delicate Balance 73. The Lindbergh Kidnapping Case (TV) 76. Twilight's Last Gleaming 76. Airport 77 77. Caravans 78. Churchill and the Generals (TV) 79. Island of Mutations 79. Guyana, Crime of the Century 79. The Survivor 80. Heaven's Gate 80. The Hearse 80. Delusion 81. The House Where Evil Dwells 82.
TV series: The 20th Century Fox Hour (as host) 55–56. The Joseph Cotten Show 56–57. Hollywood and the Stars 63–64.
❝ I didn't care about the movies, really. I was tall. I could talk. It was easy to do. – J.C.
I'm afraid you'll never make it as an actor. But as a star, I think you might well hit the jackpot. – *Orson Welles*

Cotton, Carolina (1926–1997) (Helen Hagstom).
Singing leading lady of westerns of the 40s and early 50s, opposite Ken Curtis and Gene Autry; she later worked as a school teacher.
Song of the Prairie 45. Singing on the Trail 46. Cowboy Blues/Beneath the Starry Skies 46. Blue Canadian Rockies 52. Apache Country 52, etc.

Cotton, Oliver (1944–).
Darkly brooding English character actor, mainly on stage, from 1965, and TV.
Here We Go round the Mulberry Bush 67. Firefox 82. Eleni 85. The Sicilian 87. Hiding Out 87. Columbus: The Discovery 92. Beowulf (US) 98, etc.
TV series: Robin of Sherwood 85–86. Westbeach 93.

Couffer, Jack (1922–).
American director with a penchant for natural history.
■ Nikki, Wild Dog of the North (co-d) 61. Ring of Bright Water 69. The Darwin Adventure 72. Jonathan Livingston Seagull (ph) 73. The Last Giraffe 79.

Coulouris, George (1903–1989).
British character actor, in America 1930–50; usually in explosive roles.
Christopher Bean 33. All This and Heaven Too 40. The Lady in Question 40. *Citizen Kane* 41. This Land is Mine 43. *Watch on the Rhine* 43. Between Two Worlds 44. The Master Race 44. Hotel Berlin 45. Confidential Agent 45. The Verdict 46. Sleep My Love 47. A Southern Yankee 48. *An Outcast of the Islands* 51. Doctor in the House 53. The Runaway Bus 54. I Accuse 57. Womaneater 59. Conspiracy of Hearts 60. King of Kings 61. The Skull 65. Arabesque 66. The Assassination Bureau 69. Blood from the Mummy's Tomb 71. Papillon 73. Mahler 74. Murder on the Orient Express 74. The Antichrist 75. The Ritz 76. The Long Good Friday 80, many others.

Coulter, Michael.
English cinematographer, closely associated with director Bill Forsyth.
That Sinking Feeling 79. Gregory's Girl 82. The Good Father 87. Housekeeping 87. The Dressmaker 88. Breaking In 89. Diamond Skulls/Dark Obsession 89. Bearskin: An Urban Fairytale 89. Monster in a Box 92. Being Human 94. The Neon Bible 95. Sense and Sensibility (AAN) 95. Fairytale: A True Story 97, etc.

Courant, Curt (1899–1968).
German cinematographer who did his best work elsewhere.
Quo Vadis 24. Woman in the Moon 29. Perfect Understanding (GB) 33. Amok 34. The Man Who Knew Too Much (GB) 34. The Iron Duke (GB) 35. Broken Blossoms (GB) 36. La Bête Humaine 38. Louise 39. Le Jour Se Lève 39. De Mayerling à Sarajevo 40. Monsieur Verdoux (US) 47. It Happened in Athens 61, etc.

Courcel, Nicole (1930–) (Nicole Andrieux).
French leading lady of warm personality.
La Marie du Port 49. Versailles 53. La Sorcière 55. The Case of Dr Laurent 56. Sundays and Cybele 62, etc.

Court, Hazel (1926–).
Red-headed British leading lady; moved into horror films and went to live in Hollywood.
Champagne Charlie 44. Dear Murderer 46. My Sister and I 48. It's Not Cricket 48. Bond Street 50. The Curse of Frankenstein 56. The Man Who Could Cheat Death 59. Doctor Blood's Coffin 60. The Premature Burial 62. The Masque of the Red Death 64, etc.
TV series: Dick and the Duchess 57.

Courtenay, Margaret (1923–1996).
British character actress, adept at playing grande dames. Born in Cardiff, she acted mainly on the stage, at the Old Vic and elsewhere, ranging from Shakespeare to musicals.
Hot Millions 68. Isadora 68. Under Milk Wood 71. Ooh . . . You Are Awful 72. Royal Flash 75. The Incredible Sarah 76. The Mirror Crack'd 80. Duet for One 86, etc.

Courtenay, Syd.
British comic actor and screenwriter. A sketch writer from 1919 for Leslie Fuller, with whom he worked in revue, he began in films in 1930, writing, and appearing in, Fuller's low-budget comedies.
Not So Quiet on the Western Front (a, w) 30. Why Sailors Leave Home (a, story) 30. Kiss Me Sergeant (co-w) 30. Bill's Legacy (co-w) 31. Tonight's the Night (a, co-w) 31. What a Night (a, story) 31. Poor Old Bill (a, story) 31. Hawleys of High Street (co-w) 33. Pride of the Force (a, co-w) 33. Lost in the Legion (a, co-w) 34. Doctor's Orders (story) 34. Cotton Queen (a, co-w) 35. Captain Bill (co-w) 35. Everything Is Rhythm (co-w) 36. The Man behind the Mask 36. Boys Will Be Girls (a, co-w) 37. Darby and Joan (w) 37. Sing as You Swing (w) 37. The Reverse Be My Lot (w) 38, etc.

Courtenay, Tom (1937–).
Lean British actor specializing in under-privileged roles.
Billy Liar 63. Private Potter 62. *The Loneliness of the Long Distance Runner* 63. King and Country 64. Operation Crossbow 65. King Rat 65. Doctor Zhivago (AAN) 65. The Night of the Generals 66. The Day the Fish Came Out 67. A Dandy in Aspic 68. *Otley* 69. One Day in the Life of Ivan Denisovich 71. Catch Me a Spy 71. *The Dresser* (AAN) 83. Happy New Year 87. Leonard Part 6 87. The Last Butterfly 90. Let Him Have It 91. The Old Curiosity Shop (as Quilp, TV) 95. The Boy from Mercury 96. A Rather English Marriage 98, etc.
❝ There just doesn't seem to be a market for something with aspiration any more. – T.C.
The film business is absurd. Stars don't last very long. It's much more interesting to be a proper actor. – T.C.
I don't want to peak too early. The worry is that you never know until it's all over whether you peaked at all – and then you're finished and it's too late. – T.C.

Courtland, Jerome (1926–).
Gangling young American lead of 40s comedies, now working as a producer.
Kiss and Tell 45. Man from Colorado 48. Battleground 49. The Barefoot Mailman 52. The Bamboo Prison 55. Tonka 59. O Sole Mio (It.) 60. Mary Read, Pirate (It.) 61. Thanis, Son of Attila (It.) 61. Black Spurs 65. Diamonds on Wheels (d only) 73. Pete's Dragon (co-p only) 77, etc.
TV series: Tales of the Vikings 60.

Courtneidge, Dame Cicely (1893–1980).
British comedienne; wife of Jack Hulbert. On stage from 1901; her great vitality made her a musical comedy favourite.
Autobiography: 1953, *Cicely*.
■ Elstree Calling 30. *The Ghost Train* 31. *Jack's the Boy* 32. Happy Ever After 32. Aunt Sally 33. *Soldiers of the King* 33. Falling for You 33. Things are Looking Up 34. Me and Marlborough 35. Everybody Dance 36. Take my Tip 37. *Under Your Hat* 40. Miss Tulip Stays the Night 56. The Spider's Web 60. *The L-Shaped Room* 62. Those Magnificent Men in their Flying Machines 65. The Wrong Box 66. Not Now Darling 72.
❝ When I was in Delhi,
I lay on my — hm, hm,
In a flat-bottomed canoe.
They all called me barmy,
But I know the army!
The nation depends on you!
– *sung by C.C. in Under Your Hat*

Courtney, Inez (1908–1967).
American actress, singer and dancer, often seen as the waspish friend of the female star; retired in the early 40s when she married.

Suzy 26. Bright Lights 30. Big City Blues 31. Let's Sing Again 36. The Reckless Way 36. The Thirteenth Man 37. The Shop around the Corner 40. Turnabout 40. The Farmer's Daughter 40, etc.

Cousteau, Jacques-Yves (1910–1997).
French underwater explorer and documentarist.
The Silent World (AA) 56. *World without Sun* (AA) 64, etc.

Coutard, Raoul (1924–).
French cinematographer.
Ranuntcho 50. A Bout de Souffle 59. Shoot the Pianist 60. *Lola* 60. *Jules et Jim* 61. Vivre Sa Vie 61. Bay of Angels 62. Les Carabiniers 63. Silken Skin 63. Pierrot le Fou 65. Made in USA 66. Sailor from Gibraltar 66. The Bride Wore Black 67. 'Z' 68. L'Aveu 70. L'Explosion 70. Embassy 72. The Jerusalem File 72. A Pain in the A . . . 73. Le Crabe-Tambour 77. Le Légion Saute sur Kolwezi (d only) 80. Passion 82. SAS à San Salvador (d) 82. First Name: Carmen/Prénom Carmen 83. La Garce 84. Max, Mon Amour 86. Fuegos 87. Burning Beds/Brennende Betten 88. Bethune: The Making of a Hero 90. La Femme Fardée 90. Dien Bien Phu 91. La Naissance de l'Amour 93. Faut Pas Rire du Bonheur 94, etc.

Cowan, Jerome (1897–1972).
American character actor with an easy manner. In films from 1936 (*Beloved Enemy:* out of character as a fanatical Irishman). He played hundreds of supporting roles, typically in *The Maltese Falcon* 41 as the detective killed while searching for the mysterious Floyd Thursby; played the lead in *Crime by Night* 43, *Find The Blackmailer* 44. Latterly graduated from jealous rivals to executives, from lawyers to judges.
Claudia and David 46. The Unfaithful 47. Miracle on 34th Street 47. June Bride 48. The Fountainhead 49. Young Man with a Horn 50. Dallas 51. The System 53. Visit to a Small Planet 60. Frankie and Johnny 65. The Gnome-Mobile 67. The Comic 69, many others.
TV series: The Tab Hunter Show 60. Tycoon 64.

Cowan, Lester (1907–1990).
American producer from 1934.
My Little Chickadee 39. Ladies in Retirement 41. The Story of G.I. Joe 45. Love Happy 50. Main Street to Broadway 52, etc.

Cowan, Maurice (1891–1974).
British producer of mainly routine films.
Derby Day 52. Turn the Key Softly 55. The Gypsy and the Gentleman 57, etc.

Coward, Sir Noël (1899–1973).
British actor-writer-composer-director, the bright, sophisticated young man of international showbusiness in the 20s and 30s. On stage as a boy from 1911, he came to public attention by starring in his play *The Vortex* in 1924 and remained in the spotlight for the rest of his career. His best work dates from the 30s and 40s; from the 50s onwards, his performances, in occasional films and in cabaret, outshone his new plays and musicals. He was the model for Beverly Carlton in George Kaufman and Moss Hart's play *The Man Who Came to Dinner* (played by Reginald Gardiner in the 1941 film version), and was portrayed by Daniel Massey, his godson, in *Star!* 65, about the life of Gertrude LAWRENCE. His lovers included actors Louis HAYWARD and Alan WEBB.
Autobiographies: 1937, *Present Indicative*; 1944, *Middle East Diary*; 1954, *Future Indefinite*; 1986, *Past Conditional*; 1982, *The Noël Coward Diaries*.
Biographies: 1969, *A Talent to Amuse* by Sheridan Morley; 1972, *Noël* by Charles Castle; 1976, *The Life of Noël Coward/Remembered Laughter* by Cole Lesley; 1995, *Noël Coward* by Philip Hoare.
Book: 1982, *Noël Coward the Playwright* by John Lahr.
■ Hearts of the World (a) 18. Private Lives (oa) 31. Cavalcade (oa) 33. Tonight is Ours (oa) 33. Bitter Sweet (oa) 33 and 40. Design for Living (oa) 34. *The Scoundrel* (a) 35. *In Which We Serve* (awpd) (AA special award, AANp, AANw) 41. We Were Dancing (oa) 42. *Blithe Spirit* (oa) 45. This Happy Breed (oa) 45. *Brief Encounter* (oa) 46. The Astonished Heart (a) 49. Meet Me Tonight (oa) 50. Around the World in Eighty Days (a) 56. *Our Man in Havana* (a) 59. Surprise Package (a) 60. Paris When it Sizzles (a) 64. Bunny Lake is Missing (a) 65. Boom (a) 66. The Italian Job (a) 69.
✪ For displaying, if only intermittently, a wholly professional talent to amuse. *In Which We Serve*.
❝ I don't think pornography is harmful, but it is terribly, terribly boring. – N.C.
There is nothing more old-fashioned than being up-to-date. – N.C.
Death seems to me as natural a process as birth; inevitable, absolute and final. If, when it happens to me, I find myself in a sort of Odeon ante-room queuing up for an interview with Our Lord, I shall be very surprised indeed. – N.C.
Destiny's tot. – *Alexander Woollcott*
He is simply a phenomenon, and one that is unlikely to occur ever again in theatre history. – *Terence Rattigan*
Coward invented the concept of cool, and may have had emotional reasons for doing so. – *Kenneth Tynan*
He wrote as he talked. I thought he was a lousy actor, personally. He was so mannered and unmanly. He was much better in cabaret, singing his own songs. But as an actor, he was a joke. – *Rex Harrison*

Cowen, William J. (1883–1964).
American director.
■ Kongo 32. Oliver Twist 33. Woman Unafraid 34.

Cowl, Jane (1884–1950).
American leading stage actress who made very few film appearances.
■ The Garden of Lies 15. The Spreading Dawn 17. Once More My Darling 49. No Man of Her Own 49. The Secret Fury 50. Payment on Demand 50.

Cox, Alex (1954–).
British director and screenwriter with a cult reputation. He studied law at Oxford and film at Bristol University before going to America for further film studies. He now lives and works in Mexico.
Repo Man (wd) 84. Sid and Nancy (wd) 86. Straight to Hell (wd) 87. Walker (d) 87. Highway Patrolman/El Patrullero (d) 92. Dead Beat (a) 94. The Queen of the Night 94. The Winner (d) 97. Fear and Loathing in Las Vegas (co-w) 98. Three Businessman (a, d) 98, etc.
❝ If you're a fascist in Hollywood, you work with great regularity. If you're not, you don't – so I don't. – A.C.
There is no place in Hollywood for certain directors. It has to do with the big corporations owning the studios and being tied into the military-industrial complex, or the Mafia. – A.C.
The movie business feels it must support war and encourage white yuppies to have babies. If you don't buy into that, you are ultimately excluded. – A.C.

Cox, Brian (1946–).
Scottish classical theatre actor and director, in occasional films.
Autobiographies: 1989, *From Salem to Moscow: An Actor's Odyssey*. 1992, *The Lear Diaries*.
Nicholas and Alexandra 71. In Celebration 75. Manhunter 86. Shoot for the Sun 86. Hidden Agenda 90. The Lost Language of Cranes (TV) 91. Sharpe's Rifles (TV) 93. Sharpe's Eagle (TV) 93. Iron Will 94. Rob Roy 95. Chain Reaction 96. The Long Kiss Goodnight 96. The Glimmer Man 96. Food for Ravens (as Aneurin Bevan) (TV) 97. Desperate Measures 98. The Boxer 98. Rushmore 98, etc.
❝ Big audiences in Britain are mind-dead. The best British audience I ever played to was in Broadmoor asylum. – B.C.

Cox, Courteney (1964–).
American actress. She became engaged to actor David ARQUETTE in 1998.
Misfits of Science (TV) 85. Masters of the Universe 87. Cocoon: The Return 88. Down Twisted 89. The Prize Pulitzer (TV) 89. Curiosity Kills (TV) 90. Mr Destiny 90. Shaking the Tree 92. The Opposite Sex and How to Live with Them 93. Ace Ventura: Pet Detective 94. Sketch Artist II: Hands that See (TV) 95. Commandments 96. Scream 96. Scream 2 98, etc.
TV series: Family Ties 82–89. Misfits of Science 85–86. The Trouble with Larry 93. Friends 94– .

Cox, Jack (1896–1960) (John Jaffray Cox).
Distinguished British cinematographer who became a director of photography in 1920. His career ranged from being Alfred Hitchcock's cameraman on his early movies to photographing the popular comedies of Norman Wisdom in the late 50s.
A Romance of Wastdale 20. The Four Feathers 21. Guy Fawkes 23. The Ring 27. The Farmer's Wife 28. Champagne 28. The Manxman 29. Blackmail 29. Almost a Honeymoon 30. Juno and the Paycock 30. Murder! 30. The Skin Game 31. Number Seventeen 32. Arms and the Man 32. Rich and Strange/East of Shanghai 32. The Man Who Changed His Mind 36. Dr Syn 37. The Lady Vanishes 38. They Came by Night 39. The Ghost Train 41. We Dive at Dawn 43. Madonna of the Seven Moons 44. The Wicked Lady 45. Idol of Paris 48. The Cure for Love 49. Mr Drake's Duck 50. Jumping for Joy 55. Up in the World 56. The Big Money 56. Just My Luck 57. The Square Peg 58, etc.

Cox, Joel.
American editor, associated with the films of Clint Eastwood.
Farewell My Lovely 75. The Enforcer (co-ed) 76. The Gauntlet (co-ed) 77. Every Which Way but Loose (co-ed) 78. Bronco Billy (co-ed) 80. Death Valley 82. Honkytonk Man (co-ed) 82. Sudden Impact 83. Tightrope 84. Pale Rider 85. Heartbreak Ridge 86. Ratboy 86. Bird 88. Pink Cadillac 89. White Hunter, Black Heart 90. The Rookie 90. Unforgiven 92. A Perfect World 93. The Bridges of Madison County 95. Absolute Power 97. Midnight in the Garden of Good and Evil 97, etc.

Cox, Paul (1940–).
Dutch-born director and screenwriter, a former photographer who settled in Australia in 1965. A *Journey with Paul Cox*, a Belgian documentary on his life, directed by Gerrit Messiaen and Robert Visser, was released in 1997.
Illuminations 76. Inside Looking Out 77. Kostas 79. Lonely Hearts 82. Man of Flowers 84. My First Wife 84. Death and Destiny 85. Cactus 86. Vincent: The Life and Death of Vincent van Gogh 87. Island 89. The Golden Braid 90. A Woman's Tale 91. Exile (wd, e) 94. Erotic Tales (co-d) 94. Lust and Revenge 96. Molokai 98, etc.

Cox, Ronny (1938–).
American character actor with stage background.
The Happiness Cage 72. *Deliverance* 72. Bound for Glory 76. The Car 77. The Onion Field 79. Taps 81. The Beast Within 82. Robocop 87. Steele Justice 87. Loose Cannons 89. One Man Force 89. Captain America 90. Total Recall 90. Pride/Unmei No Toki (Jap.) 98, etc.
TV series: Apple's Way 74. Spencer 84–85. Cop Rock 90.

Cox, Vivian (1915–).
British producer.
Father Brown 54. The Prisoner 55. Bachelor of Hearts 58, etc.

Cox, Wally (1924–1973).
American comic actor, usually seen as the bespectacled, weedy character he played in the TV series *Mr Peepers*.
■ State Fair 62. Spencer's Mountain 63. Fate Is the Hunter 64. The Bedford Incident 65. Morituri 65. The Yellow Rolls-Royce 65. A Guide for the Married Man 67. The One and Only Genuine Original Family Band 68. The Boatniks 70. The Cockeyed Cowboys of Calico County 70. Up Your Teddy Bear 70.
TV series: Mr Peepers 52–55. The Adventures of Hirman Holiday 56–57. Underdog (voice) 64–73.

Coyote, Peter (1942–) (Peter Cohon).
American leading actor with stage experience.
Tell Me a Riddle 80. Die Laughing 80. Southern Comfort 81. The Pursuit of D. B. Cooper 81. E.T. – the Extraterrestrial 82. Endangered Species 82. Out 82. Cross Creek 83. Slayground 84. The Legend of Billie Jean 85. Jagged Edge 85. Outrageous Fortune 87. Season of Dreams/Stacking 87. Baja Oklahoma 88. Heart of Midnight 88. The Man Inside 90. Keeper of the City 91. Crooked Hearts 91. Exposure 91. Blind Judgement 91. Living a Lie 91. Bitter Moon 92. Kika 93. That Eye, the Sky 94. Buffalo Girls (TV) 95. Unforgettable 96. Two for Texas (TV) 98. Route 9 98, etc.

Crabbe, Buster (1907–1983) (Clarence Linden Crabbe).
American Olympic athlete who became leading man of 'B' pictures.
King of the Jungle 33. Tarzan the Fearless 33. Nevada 36. *Flash Gordon's Trip to Mars* 38. Buck Rogers 39. Queen of Broadway 43. Caged Fury 48. Gunfighters of Abilene 59. Arizona Raiders 65, many others.
TV series: Captain Gallant 55–57.

Crabe, James (c. 1931–1989).
American cinematographer.
Zigzag 70. Save the Tiger 72. W.W. and the Dixie Dancekings 72. Rocky 76. Players 79. The China Syndrome 79. How to Beat the High Cost of Living 80. The Baltimore Bullet 80. The Formula (AAN) 80, etc.

Crabtree, Arthur (1900–1975).
British director, former cameraman.
Madonna of the Seven Moons 44. They Were Sisters 45. Dear Murderer 46. Caravan 46. The Calendar 48. Lili Marlene 50. Hindle Wakes 52. The Wedding of Lili Marlene 53. West of Suez 57. Morning Call 58. Horrors of the Black Museum 59, etc.

Craig, Alec (1878–1945).
Scottish character actor in Hollywood; often played misers, moneylenders and downtrodden roles.
Mutiny on the Bounty 35. Mary of Scotland 36. Winterset 36. Vivacious Lady 38. Tom Brown's Schooldays 40. Cat People 42. Holy Matrimony 43. Lassie Come Home 43. Spider Woman 44. Kitty 46, many others.

Craig, Edward Gordon (1872–1966) (Henry Edward Wardell).
British stage designer, a former actor, the son of Ellen TERRY and father of Edward CARRICK. Although not directly employed in films, his theories, which stressed the visual aspect of theatre, and his designs, with their dramatic use of light and shade, influenced art directors such as William Cameron MENZIES and Anton GROT. His lovers included dancer Isadora DUNCAN.
Autobiography: 1957, *Index to the Story of My Days 1872–1907*.
Books: 1911, *On the Art of Theatre*; 1913, *Towards a New Theatre*.

Craig, H(arold) A. L. (1925–1978).
British scriptwriter, on historical themes.
Anzio (w) 68. Fräulein Doktor (co-w) (It./Yug.) 68. The Adventures of Gerard (w) 70. Waterloo (co-w) (It./USSR) 70. Mohammed, Messenger of God (w) (Leb.) 76. Foxtrot (co-w) (Mex.) 77. Lion of the Desert (w) (US) 80, etc.

Craig, James (1912–1985) (John Meador).
American leading man, usually the good-natured but tough outdoor type.
Thunder Trail 37. The Buccaneer 38. The Man They Could Not Hang 39. Zanzibar 40. Kitty Foyle 40. *All that Money Can Buy* (the 'Faust' role, and his best) 41. Valley of the Sun 41. The Omaha Trail 42. The Human Comedy 43. Lost Angel 43. Kismet 44. Our Vines Have Tender Grapes 45. Boys Ranch 45. Little Mister Jim 46. Northwest Stampede 48. Side Street 50. Drums in the Deep South 51. Hurricane Smith 52. Fort Vengeance 53. While the City Sleeps 56. Four Fast Guns 59. The Hired Gun 67, many others.
❝ I was out there in Hollywood on vacation, and I saw a lot of people making movies. If they could do it, why couldn't I? – J.C.

Craig, Michael (1929–) (Michael Gregson).
British light leading man, a former crowd artist groomed by the Rank Organization; later attempted more ambitious roles before settling in Australia.
Malta Story 53. The Love Lottery 54. Yield to the Night 56. House of Secrets 56. High Tide at Noon 57. Campbell's Kingdom 58. The Silent Enemy 58. Nor the Moon by Night 58. Sea of Sand 59. Sapphire 59. Upstairs and Downstairs 59. *The Angry Silence* (& w) 59. Cone of Silence 60. Doctor in Love 60. Mysterious Island 61. *Payroll* 61. A Pair of Briefs 62. Life for Ruth 62. The Iron Maiden 62. Stolen Hours 63. Of a Thousand

Delights/Vaghe Stella dell'Orsa 65. Life at the Top 65. Modesty Blaise 66. Sandra (It.) 66. *Star!* 68. The Royal Hunt of the Sun 69. Twinky 69. Brotherly Love 70. A Town Called Bastard 71. Vault of Horror 73. The Emigrants (TV) 77. The Timeless Land (TV) 77. Turkey Shoot 82. Stanley 83, etc.

Craig, Stuart.
English production designer.
Saturn 3 80. The Elephant Man (AAN) 80. Gandhi (AA) 82. Greystoke: The Legend of Tarzan, Lord of the Apes 84. Cal 84. The Mission (AAN) 86. Cry Freedom 87. Stars and Bars (co-pd) 88. Dangerous Liaisons (AA) 88. Chaplin (AAN) 92. The Secret Garden 93. Shadowlands 93. The English Patient (US) (AA) 96. In Love and War 97. The Avengers (US) 98, etc.

Craig, Wendy (1934–).
British comedy actress, especially on TV in *Not in Front of the Children, And Mother Makes Three, Nanny*, etc.
The Mind Benders 63. The Servant 63. The Nanny 65. Just Like a Woman 66. I'll Never Forget What's 'Is Name 67. Joseph Andrews 77, etc.
TV series: Brighton Belles 93.

Craig, Yvonne (1941–).
American leading lady, now retired.
The Young Land 60. By Love Possessed 61. Seven Women from Hell 62. Kissin' Cousins 64. One Spy Too Many 66. In Like Flint 67, etc.
TV series: Batman (as Batgirl) 67–68.

Craigie, Jill (1914–).
British documentary director.
The Way We Live 46. Blue Scar 48. The Million Pound Note (w only) 51. Windom's Way (w only) 57, etc.

Crain, Jeanne (1925–).
American leading lady of the 40s; usually the personification of sweetness and light.
■ The Gang's All Here 43. Home in Indiana 44. In the Meantime Darling 44. Winged Victory 44. *State Fair* 45. Leave Her to Heaven 45. Centennial Summer 46. *Margie* 46. Apartment for Peggy 48. You Were Meant for Me 48. A Letter to Three Wives 49. The Fan 49. *Pinky* (AAN) 49. Cheaper by the Dozen 50. Take Care of My Little Girl 51. People Will Talk 51. The Model and the Marriage Broker 52. Belles on Their Toes 52. O'Henry's Full House 52. Dangerous Crossing 53. City of Bad Men 53. Vicki 53. Duel in the Jungle (GB) 54. Man Without a Star 55. Gentlemen Marry Brunettes 55. The Second Greatest Sex 55. The Fastest Gun Alive 56. The Tattered Dress 57. The Joker is Wild 58. Guns of the Timberland 60. Twenty Plus Two 61. Queen of the Nile (It.) 61. With Fire and Sword (It.) 61. Pontius Pilate (It.) 61. Madison Avenue 62. 52 Miles to Terror 64. The Night God Screamed 71. Skyjacked 72.

Cramer, Joey (1974–).
Canadian child actor of the 80s.
Runaway 84. I-Man (TV) 86. *Flight of the Navigator* 86. Clan of the Cave Bear 84. Stone Fox (TV) 87, etc.

Cramer, Rychard (1889–1960).
Malevolent-looking American character actor, a memorable foil for Laurel and Hardy in *Scram, Saps at Sea*, etc. He later played heavies in 'B' westerns.

Crane, Bob (1929–1978).
American light comic actor, popular in TV series *Hogan's Heroes*. He was murdered.
■ Return to Peyton Place 61. Mantrap 61. The Wicked Dreams of Paula Schultz 68. Superdad 74. Gus 76.

Crane, Richard (1919–1969).
American juvenile lead of the 40s.
Susan and God 40. This Time for Keeps 42. Happy Land 43. None Shall Escape 44. Captain Eddie 45. Behind Green Lights 46. Triple Threat 48. Dynamite 49. The Last Outpost 51. The Neanderthal Man 53. The Eternal Sea 55. The Deep Six 58. The Alligator People 59. House of the Damned 63. Surf Party 64, etc.
TV series: Surfside Six 61–62.

Crane, Stephen (1871–1900).
American novelist who crystallized aspects of the Civil War in *The Red Badge of Courage*.

Cranham, Kenneth (1944–).
British leading actor, mainly on stage and television.
Oliver! 68. All the Way Up 70. Brother Sun, Sister Moon 73. Joseph Andrews 77. Reilly, Ace of Spies (TV) 83. Hellbound: Hellraiser II 88. Oranges Are Not the Only Fruit (TV) 90. Prospero's Books 91. Chimera (TV) 93. The Tenant of Wildfell Hall (TV) 96. Our Mutual Friend (TV) 98, etc.
TV series: Shine on Harvey Moon 85–87.

Cravat, Nick (1911–1994).
Small, agile American actor, once Burt Lancaster's circus partner.
The Flame and the Arrow 50. The Crimson Pirate 52. King Richard and the Crusaders 54. Three-Ring Circus 55. Kiss Me Deadly 55. Davy Crockett 56. Run Silent, Run Deep 59. The Scalphunters 68. Ulzana's Raid 72. The Island of Dr Moreau 77, etc.

Craven, Frank (1875–1945).
American stage character actor who spent his later years in Hollywood; typically cast as kindly pipe-smoking philosopher.
■ We Americans 28. The Very Idea 29. State Fair 33. That's Gratitude 34. He Was Her Man 34. Let's Talk It Over 34. City Limits 34. Funny Thing Called Love 34. *Barbary Coast* 35. Car 99 35. Vagabond Lady 35. Small Town Girl 36. The Harvester 36. Penrod and Sam 37. Blossoms on Broadway 37. You're Only Young Once 37. Penrod and his Twin Brother 38. Our Neighbours the Carters 39. Miracles for Sale 39. Dreaming Out Loud 40. City for Conquest 40. *Our Town* (his stage role) 40. The Lady from Cheyenne 41. The Richest Man in Town 41. In This Our Life 41. *Thru Different Eyes* 42. Pittsburgh 42. Girl Trouble 42. Son of Dracula 43. Harrigan's Kid 43. Jack London 43. The Human Comedy 43. Keeper of the Flame 43. Destiny 44. My Best Gal 44. They Shall Have Faith 44. The Right to Live 45. Colonel Effingham's Raid 45.

Craven, Gemma (1950–).
Irish-born leading lady of the 70s.
■ *The Slipper and the Rose* 76. Why Not Stay for Breakfast 79. Wagner 83. Double X 92. The Mystery of Edwin Drood 93.
TV series: Pennies from Heaven 77.

Craven, Wes (1939–).
American director of horror movies, a former academic.
Book: 1998, *Screams and Nightmares: The Films of Wes Craven* by Brian J. Robb.
Summer of Fear 78. The Hills Have Eyes 79. Deadly Blessing 81. A Nightmare on Elm Street 84. Deadly Friend 86. Flowers in the Attic (w) 87. A Nightmare on Elm Street III: Dream Warriors (p, story) 87. The Serpent and the Rainbow (d) 88. Shocker (wd, a) 89. The People under the Stairs (wd) 91. Wes Craven's New Nightmare (wd, a) 94. The Fear (a) 95. Vampire in Brooklyn 95. Scream 96. Scream 2 97, etc.

Crawford, Andrew (1917–).
Scottish character actor.
The Brothers 46. Dear Murderer 47. London Belongs to Me 48. Morning Departure 50. Shadow of the Cat 61, etc.

Crawford, Anne (1920–1956) (Imelda Crawford).
British leading lady with gentle, humorous personality.
They Flew Alone (debut) 42. The Peterville Diamond 42. The Dark Tower 42. The Hundred-Pound Window 43. Millions Like Us 43. Two Thousand Women 44. They Were Sisters 45. Caravan 46. Bedelia 46. Master of Bankdam 47. Daughter of Darkness 48. The Blind Goddess 48. It's Hard To Be Good 49. Tony Draws a Horse 49. Thunder on the Hill (US) 50. Street Corner 52. Knights of the Round Table 53. Mad about Men 55, etc.

Crawford, Broderick (1911–1986).
Beefy American character actor, son of Helen Broderick; began by playing comic stooges and gangsters, with acting performances coming later; after a long spell in TV his popularity waned.
Woman Chases Man 37. The Real Glory 39. Eternally Yours 39. Beau Geste 39. Slightly Honorable 40. When the Daltons Rode 40. The Black Cat 41. Butch Minds the Baby 42. Broadway 42. Sin Town 42. *The Runaround* 46. Slave Girl 47. The Flame 47. The Time of Your Life 48. Anna Lucasta 49. *All the King's Men* (AA) 49. *Born Yesterday* 51. The Mob 51. Lone Star 52. Scandal Sheet 52. Last of the Comanches 52. Stop You're Killing Me 52. Night People 54. Human Desire 54. Down Three Dark Streets 54. New York Confidential 55. Il Bidone/The Swindlers 55. Not as a Stranger 55. The Fastest Gun Alive 56. The Decks Ran Red 58. Up from the Beach 65. The Oscar 66. The Texican 66. Red Tomahawk 66. The Vulture 67. Embassy 72. Terror in the Wax Museum 73. Smashing the Crime Syndicate 73. Mayday at 40,000 Feet (TV) 77. *The Private Files of J. Edgar Hoover* 78. A Little Romance 79. There Goes the Bride 80. Liar's Moon 82, etc.
TV series: *Highway Patrol* 55–58. King of Diamonds 61. The Interns 70.
❝ My trademarks are a hoarse, grating voice and the face of a retired pugilist: small narrowed eyes set in puffy features which look as though they might, years ago, have lost on points. – B.C.
A huge man with unlimited desire for trouble, he would often get into fights. The reason we didn't get hurt I can only attribute to the fact that Brod fought as a pro. Yet he could talk on most subjects as an erudite man. – *Don Siegel*

Crawford, Cindy (1966–).
American model and occasional actress, formerly married to Richard Gere.
Fair Game 95.

Crawford, Howard Marion:
see MARION CRAWFORD, Howard.

Crawford, Joan (1904–1977) (Lucille le Sueur; known for a time as Billie Cassin).
American leading lady; one of Hollywood's most durable stars, first as a flapper of the jazz age and later as the personification of the career girl and the repressed older woman. Few of her films have been momentous, but she has always been 'box office', especially with women fans, who liked to watch her suffering in mink.
Autobiography: 1962, *A Portrait of Joan*.
In 1978 her adopted daughter Christine Crawford published *Mommie Dearest*, which painted her as a monster and caused a sensation. A film version of the book was released in 1981, with Faye Dunaway playing J.C.
■ Pretty Ladies 25. The Only Thing 25. Old Clothes 25. Sally, Irene and Mary 25. The Boob 25. Paris 25. Tramp Tramp Tramp 26. The Taxi Dancer 27. Winners of the Wilderness 27. The Understanding Heart 27. The Unknown 27. Twelve Miles Out 27. Spring Fever 27. West Point 28. Rose Marie 28. Across to Singapore 28. The Law of the Range 28. Four Walls 28. *Our Dancing Daughters* 28. Dream of Love 28. The Duke Steps Out 29. Our Modern Maidens 29. Hollywood Revue 29. Untamed 29. Montana Moon 30. Our Blushing Brides 30. Paid 30. Dance Fools Dance 31. Laughing Sinners 31. This Modern Age 31. Possessed 31. Letty Lynton 32. *Grand Hotel* 32. *Rain* 32. Today We Live 33. *Dancing Lady* 33. Sadie McKee 34. Chained 34. Forsaking All Others 34. No More Ladies 35. I Live My Life 35. *The Gorgeous Hussy* 36. Love on the Run 36. The Last of Mrs Cheyney 37. The Bride Wore Red 37. Mannequin 38. The Shining Hour 38. Ice Follies 39. *The Women* 39. Strange Cargo 40. Susan and God 40. *A Woman's Face* 41. When Ladies Meet 41. They All Kissed the Bride 42. Reunion in France 42. Above Suspicion 43. Hollywood Canteen 44. *Mildred Pierce* (AA) 45. *Humoresque* 46. *Possessed* (AAN) 47. Daisy Kenyon 47. Flamingo Road 49. The Damned Don't Cry 50. Harriet Craig 50. Goodbye My Fancy 51. This Woman is Dangerous 52. *Sudden Fear* (AAN) 52. Torch Song 53. Johnny Guitar 54. The Female on the Beach 55. Queen Bee 55. Autumn Leaves 56. The Story of Esther Costello (GB) 57. The Best of Everything 59. *Whatever Happened to Baby Jane?* 62. The Caretakers 63. Strait Jacket 64. Della (TV) 64. I Saw What You Did 65. The Karate Killers (TV) 67. Berserk (GB) 67. Night Gallery (TV pilot) 69. Trog 70.
✪ For sheer determination. *Mildred Pierce*.
❝ Everybody imitated my fuller mouth, my darker eyebrows. But I wouldn't copy anybody. If I can't be me, I don't want to be anybody. I was born that way. – *J.C.*
The most important thing a woman can have, next to her talent of course, is her hairdresser. – *J.C.*
Inactivity is one of the great indignities of life. The need to work is always there, bugging me. – *J.C.*
I never go out unless I look like Joan Crawford the movie star. If you want to see the girl next door, go next door. – *J.C.*
Whenever she came to the realisation that the men she loved simply didn't come back, she compensated by adopting children. – *Hedda Hopper*
The best time I ever had with her was when I pushed her downstairs in *Baby Jane*. – *Bette Davis*
With her emergence as a film star she dieted off her excess weight, lowered her voice range by several tones, was taught how to dress by Adrian and how to enter a room by Douglas Fairbanks Jnr. And she never let up in her quest for self-improvement. – *Radie Harris*
She was a mean, tipsy, powerful, rotten-egg lady. – *Mercedes McCambridge*
She's like that old joke about Philadelphia. First prize four years with Joan. Second, eight. – *Franchot Tone*
I tried to be a good listener. I decided that was what she wanted all along – not so much a friend as an audience. – *June Allyson*
Famous line (*The Female on the Beach*): 'I wouldn't have you if you were hung with diamonds – upside down!'

Crawford, John (1926–).
Forgettable American leading man.
Cyrano de Bergerac 50. Actors and Sin 52. Slaves of Babylon 53. Battle of Royne River 54. Orders to Kill 58. John Paul Jones 59. Floods of Fear 59. Hell is a City 60. The 300 Spartans 62. Captain Sinbad 63. The Americanization of Emily 64. The Greatest Story Ever Told 65. I Saw What You Did 65. J. W. Coop 71. Napoleon and Samantha 72. The Poseidon Adventure 72. The Towering Inferno 74. Night Moves 75. The Enforcer 76. Tilt 78. The Apple Dumpling Gang Rides Again 79. From Here to Eternity (TV) 79. The Boogens 81, etc.
TV series: The Waltons 72–81.

Crawford, Johnny (1946–).
American actor, mainly on television as a juvenile. He began as a child, was a Mickey Mouse Club Mousketeer in the mid-50s, and in the 60s made a few hit records during a spell of television fame, playing Chuck Connors' son in the series *The Rifleman* 58–63. From the mid-60s he worked in rodeos and now concentrates on his singing, leading his own big band and playing music from the 30s.
Courage of Black Beauty 57. Indian Paint 64. Village of the Giants 65. El Dorado 67. Outlaw Blues 77. The Great Texas Dynamite Chase 77. Kenny Rogers as The Gambler Part II: The Adventure Continues (TV) 83, etc.

Crawford, Kathryn (1908–1980) (Kathryn Crawford Moran).
American leading actress and singer, from the Broadway stage, who quit films in the early 30s. She was married to Wesley Ruggles.
The Kid's Clever 29. King of the Rodeo 29. The Climax 30. Red Hot Rhythm 30. Hide Out 30. Safety in Numbers 30. King of Jazz 30. Flying High 31. Grand Hotel 32. New Morals for Old 32, etc.

Crawford, Michael (1942–) (Michael Dumble-Smith).
Lively British comedy lead, former child actor, now best known for stage musicals. In 1998, the *Sunday Times* estimated his wealth at £20m.
Soap Box Derby 50. Blow Your Own Trumpet 54. Two Living One Dead 62. The War Lover 63. Two Left Feet 63. *The Knack* 65. A Funny Thing Happened on the Way to the Forum 66. *The Jokers* 66. How I Won the War 67. *Hello Dolly* 69. The Games 69. Hello Goodbye 70. Alice's Adventures in Wonderland 72. Condorman 81. Once Upon a Forest 93, etc.
TV series: Sir Francis Drake 62. *Some Mothers Do 'Ave 'Em* 74–79. Chalk and Cheese 79.

The Crazy Gang.
Three pairs of British music hall comedians made up this famous group which was enormously popular on stage from 1935 till 1962. Bud FLANAGAN and Chesney ALLEN; Jimmy Nervo

(James Holloway) and Teddy Knox; Charlie Naughton and Jimmy Gold. The group's success depended upon their spontaneity and ad-libbing, and their films failed to capture much of their appeal.
Book: 1986, *The Crazy Gang* by Maureen Owen.
■ OK for Sound 37. Alf's Button Afloat 38. The Frozen Limits 39. Gasbags 40. Life is a Circus 54.

Creasey, John (1908–1973).
British thriller writer, author under various pseudonyms of more than six hundred books. Creator of the Toff, the Baron and Gideon of Scotland Yard.

Creber, William J.
American production designer.
Rio Conchos 64. The Greatest Story Ever Told 65. Caprice 67. Planet of the Apes 68. The Detective 68. Three in the Attic 68. Justine 69. Superdad 72. The Poseidon Adventure (AAN) 72. Towering Inferno (AAN) 72. Islands in the Stream 77. Any Which Way You Can 80. Yes, Giorgio 82. Twice in a Lifetime 85. Flight of the Navigator 86. Hot Pursuit 87. Mannequin 2: On the Move 91. Folks! 92. Spy Hard 96. Without Limits 97, etc.

Cregar, Laird (1916–1944).
Heavyweight American character actor who had a tragically brief but impressive career in a rich variety of roles.
■ Granny Get Your Gun 40. Oh Johnny How You Can Love 40. Hudson's Bay 40. Blood and Sand 41. *Charley's Aunt* 41. *I Wake Up Screaming* 41. Joan of Paris 42. Rings on Her Fingers 42. This Gun for Hire 42. *Ten Gentlemen from West Point* 42. *The Black Swan* 42. Hello Frisco Hello 43. *Heaven Can Wait* 43. Holy Matrimony 43. *The Lodger* 44. Hangover Square 44.
✪ For providing such a memorable gallery of middle-aged characters while still in his early 20s. *The Black Swan*.

Crehan, Joseph (1884–1966) (Charles Wilson).
American character actor, often as sheriff or cop.
Stolen Heaven 31. Before Midnight 33. Identity Parade 34. Boulder Dam 36. Happy Landing 38. Stanley and Livingstone 39. The Roaring Twenties 39. Brother Orchid 40. Texas 42. Phantom Lady 44. Deadline at Dawn 46. The Foxes of Harrow 48. Red Desert 54, many others.

Creme, Lol (1947–).
British director and musician. He was guitarist and vocalist with the 70s rock band 10CC, and also produces music videos.
The Lunatic 92.

Cremer, Bruno (1929–).
French leading actor.
The 317th Platoon/La 317ème Section 65. Is Paris Burning?/Paris Brûle-t-il? 68. Sorcerer (US) 77. A Simple Story/Histoire Simple 79. Josepha 82. Hail Mary/Je Vous Salue Marie 83. Tenue de Soirée/Menage) 86. Taxi de Nuit (Fr.) 94, etc.

Crenna, Richard (1926–).
American leading man, formerly boy actor on radio and TV.
Red Skies of Montana 52. It Grows on Trees 52. Over Exposed 56. John Goldfarb Please Come Home 65. Made in Paris 65. The Sand Pebbles 66. Wait until Dark 67. Star! 68. Marooned 69. The Deserter 70. Thief (TV) 71. Doctors' Wives 71. Red Sky at Morning 71. Catlow 72. The Man Called Noon 73. Double Indemnity (TV) 73. Nightmare (TV) 75. Breakheart Pass 76. Dirty Money (Fr.) 77. Body Heat 81. *Table for Five* 83. Rambo: First Blood 2 86. The Flamingo Kid 86. Rambo III 88. Leviathan 89. And the Sea Will Tell (TV) 91. A Place to Be Loved (TV) 93. Hot Shots! Part Deux 93. A Pyromaniac's Love Story 95. Jade 95. Sabrina 95. Wrongfully Accused 98, etc.
TV series: Our Miss Brooks 52–56. The Real McCoys 57–62. Slattery's People 64–65. All's Fair 76. It Takes Two 83. Gabriel's Fire 91–92.

Crevenna, Alfredo B.
German-born director and screenwriter, in Mexico from the mid-30s and the most prolific of Mexican film-makers, directing more than 100 films of mainly escapist entertainment.
La Dama del Velo 48. Angelica 51. Rebellion of the Hanged 54. Invisible Man in Mexico 58. Red Blossoms 60. Aventura al Centro de la Tierra 64. Santo Faces Black Magic 74. El Centauro Negro 75. Five Nerds Take Las Vegas/5 Nacos Asaltan Las Vegas 86. Carrasco's Escape 87. Una Luz en la Escalera 94, many more.

Crews, Laura Hope (1880–1942).
American stage actress who played character parts in many films, usually as fluttery matron.
Charming Sinners 29. New Morals for Old 32. Escapade 35. *Camille* 36. Thanks for the Memory 38. *Gone with the Wind* (as Aunt Pittypat) 39. The Bluebird 40. The Flame of New Orleans 41. One Foot in Heaven 41, many others.

Crewson, Wendy (1956–).
Canadian actress, born in Hamilton, Ontario. Married actor Michael Murphy.
Skullduggery 83. Boat House 85. The Doctor 91. Folks! 92. The Good Son 93. Corrina, Corrina 94. The Santa Clause 95. To Gillian on Her 37th Birthday 96. Air Force One 97. Gang Related 97. The Eighteenth Angel 97. From the Earth to the Moon (TV) 98, etc.

Cribbins, Bernard (1928–).
British comedy character actor and recording star. Played light support roles in several films.
Two Way Stretch 60. The Girl on the Boat 62. The Wrong Arm of the Law 62. Carry On Jack 63. Crooks in Cloisters 64. She 65. The Sandwich Man 66. Daleks Invasion Earth 2150 A.D. 66. The Railway Children 70. Frenzy 72. The Water Babies 78. Dangerous Davies (TV) 81. Carry On Columbus 92, etc.

Crichton, Charles (1910–).
British director, former editor. Latterly directing TV episodes.
For Those in Peril 44. Dead of Night (part) 45. Painted Boats 45. *Hue and Cry* 46. Against the Wind 47. Another Shore 48. Train of Events 49. Dance Hall 50. *The Lavender Hill Mob* 51. Hunted 52. *The Titfield Thunderbolt* 53. The Love Lottery 54. The Divided Heart 54. The Man in the Sky 56. Law and Disorder 57. Floods of Fear (& w) 58. The Battle of the Sexes 59. The Boy Who Stole a Million 60. The Third Secret 63. He Who Rides a Tiger 65. A Fish Called Wanda (& story) (AAN) 88, etc.
TV series: Dick Turpin 78.

Crichton, Michael (1942–).
American novelist and screenwriter. He studied at Harvard and lectured in anthropology at Cambridge before qualifying as a doctor at the Harvard Medical School and then turning to writing. He was paid a record $10m for the screen rights to his novel *Airframe*.
The Andromeda Strain (oa) 71. The Carey Treatment (oa) 72. The Terminal Man (oa) 72. *Pursuit* (oa, d) (TV) 72. *Westworld* (wd) 73. Coma (d) 77. The Great Train Robbery (wd) 78. Looker (wd) 80. Runaway 84. Physical Evidence 88. Jurassic Park (co-w from his novel) 93. Rising Sun (co-w from his novel) 93. Disclosure (oa) 94. Congo (oa) 95. Twister (co-w) 96. The Lost World 97, etc.
❝ One of the definitions of intelligence is that you don't make the same mistake twice. – M.C.

Crisanti, Andrea.
Italian art director, often for the films of Francesco Rossi and Giuseppe Tornatore.
Duck! You Sucker/Giu La Tester 71. The Mattei Affair/Il Caso Mattei 72. The Heroes/Gli Eroi 72. Lucky Luciano 73. Illustrious Corpses/Cadaveri Eccellenti 75. Christ Stopped at Eboli 79. Three Brothers/Tre Fratelli 80. Identification of a Woman 82. Chronicle of a Death Foretold 87. Cinema Paradiso 89. Everybody's Fine/Stanno Tutti Bene 90. The Stolen Children/Il Ladro di Bambini 92. A Simple Formality/Una Pura Formalita 94, etc.

Crisp, Donald (1880–1974).
Distinguished British screen actor, in Hollywood from 1906; worked with D. W. Griffith and directed some silents, but from 1930 settled on acting and played mainly stern character roles.
Home Sweet Home 14. The Birth of a Nation 15. Broken Blossoms 19. Why Smith Left Home (d) 19. The Bonnie Brier Bush (d) 21. The Mark of Zorro (d) 22. Ponjola (d) 23. *Don Q Son of Zorro* (ad) 25. The Black Pirate 26. Man Bait (d) 27. Stand and Deliver (d) 28. The Return of Sherlock Holmes 29. Runaway Bride (d) 30. Svengali 31. Red Dust 32. Crime Doctor 34. The Little Minister 34. Mutiny on the Bounty 35. Mary of Scotland 36. Beloved Enemy 36. Parnell 37. Jezebel 38. The Sisters 38. *The Dawn Patrol* 38. Wuthering Heights 39. The Old Maid 39. *Brother Orchid* 40. The Sea Hawk 40. Dr Jekyll and Mr Hyde 41. *How Green Was My Valley* (AA) 41. The Gay Sisters 42. Lassie Come Home 43. *The Uninvited* 44. National Velvet 44. Valley of Decision 45. Ramrod 47. Whispering Smith 49. Bright Leaf 50. Prince Valiant 54. The Man from Laramie 55. Saddle the Wind 58. The Last Hurrah 58. Pollyanna 60. Greyfriars Bobby 61. Spencer's Mountain 63, many others.

Crisp, Quentin (1909–) (Denis Pratt).
English eccentric and wit, artist's model, writer, film critic and occasional actor. He is the author of a best-selling autobiography, *The Naked Civil Servant*, which detailed his homosexuality and was turned into a successful TV drama in 1975. It led to his performing one-man shows in Britain and America. He now lives in New York.
Autobiography: 1996, *Resident Alien*.
Book: 1989, *How to Go to the Movies: A Guide for the Perplexed*.
■ Hamlet (as Polonius) 77. An Evening with Quentin Crisp (TV) 83. The Bride 85. Orlando (as Queen Elizabeth I) 93. Naked in New York (as himself) 94. Desolation Angels 95.
❝ I took a friend to see *King Kong* (the first time around). During a dramatic episode in which a certain Miss Wray lay gibbering across Mr Kong's wrist, my friend, in a voice shrill with irritation, cried out, 'I can't think what he sees in her.' – Q.C.
What keeps a woman young and beautiful is not repeated surgery but perpetual praise. – Q.C.
If we go to the movies often enough and in a sufficiently reverent spirit, they will become more absorbing than the outer world, and the problems of reality will cease to burden us. – Q.C.
I believe it was Miss Cher who said that being in a film was like being asked to swallow broken glass, and I endorse that impression. – Q.C.
If Quentin Crisp had never existed, it is unlikely that anyone would have had the nerve to invent him. – *The Times*

Crispino, Armando (1925–).
Italian director and screenwriter of macabre thrillers. He began working in the early 50s as an assistant director and screenwriter, becoming a director in the mid-60s. In the mid-70s, he quit making films to work in television and commercials.
Le Piacevoli Notti 66. John, il Bastardo 67. Commandos 68. L'Etrusco Uccide Ancora 72. Autopsy/Macchie Solari 74. Frankenstein all'Italiana 75, etc.

Cristal, Linda (1934–) (Victoria Maya).
Argentinian leading lady, in Hollywood from 1956.
Comanche 56. The Fiend Who Walked the West 58. The Perfect Furlough 58. Cry Tough 59. The Alamo 60. Panic in the City 68. Mr Majestyk 74, etc.
TV series: The High Chaparral 67–71.

Cristaldi, Franco (1924–1992).
Italian producer of good reputation. He was formerly married to actress Claudia Cardinale.
La Pattuglia Sperduta 53. La Sfida 59. L'Assassino 60. Salvatore Giuliano 61. Divorce Italian Style 61. The Red Tent 69. In the Name of the Father/In Nome del Padre 71. Lady Caroline Lamb 72. Amarcord (AA) 73. Christ Stopped at Eboli/Cristo Si è Fermato a Eboli 79. Ratataplan 79. And the Ship Sails On/E la Nave Va 83. The Name of the Rose 86. Cinema Paradiso (AA) 88. Vanille Fraise 89. C'era un Castello con 40 Cani 90, etc.

Cristiani, Gabriella (1949–).
Italian film editor.
La Luna 79. The Tragedy of a Ridiculous Man 82. The Last Emperor (AA) 87. High Season 88. Francesco 89. The Sheltering Sky 90, etc.

Cristofer, Michael (1945–) (Michael Procaccino).
American playwright, screenwriter and actor.
Crime Club (a) 75. The Entertainer (TV) 76. An Enemy of the People (a) 77. Falling in Love (w) 84. The Little Drummer Girl (a) 84. The Witches of Eastwick (w) 87. The Bonfire of the Vanities (w) 90. Mr Jones (co-w) 93. Breaking Up 97. Gia (co-w, d) (TV) 98, etc.

Criswell (1907–1982) (Charles Criswell King).
Psychic of newspapers and television, best remembered for his portentous narration to Ed Wood's *Plan 9 from Outer Space* 58, intoning, 'My friends, can your hearts stand the shocking facts about grave robbers from outer space?'
Night of the Ghouls 59. Orgy of the Dead 65, etc.

Crocker, Barry.
Australian leading man.
Squeeze a Flower 69. The Adventures of Barry Mackenzie 72. Barry Mackenzie Holds His Own 74.

Crockett, Davy (1786–1836).
American trapper and Indian scout who became a legendary hero and a politician before dying at the Alamo. He has been portrayed on film by George Montgomery (*Indian Scout*), Fess Parker (*Davy Crockett*, *Davy Crockett and the River Pirates*), Arthur Hunnicutt (*The Last Command*) and John Wayne (*The Alamo*), among others.

Crogan, Emma Jane (1972–).
Australian director and screenwriter.
Love and Other Catastrophes 96.

Crombie, Donald (1942–).
Australian director.
Caddie 76. The Irishman 78. Cathy's Child 79. The Killing of Angel Street 81. Kitty and the Bagman 82. Robbery under Arms (co-d) (TV) 85. Playing Beatie Bow 86. The Heroes (TV) 88. The Saint in Australia (TV) 89. The River Kings (TV) 91. Rough Diamonds 94, etc.

Crompton, Richmal (1890–1969).
British writer for children, author of the 'William' books which have been filmed from time to time.

Cromwell, James.
Lean American character actor, born in Los Angeles. The son of director John Cromwell and actress Kay Johnson, he came to notice as Archie Bunker's friend Stretch Cunningham in the TV sitcom *All in the Family*.
Murder by Death 76. The Deadly Game (TV) 77. The Girl in the Empty Grave (TV) 77. The Cheap Detective 78. The House of God 79. A Christmas without Snow (TV) 80. The Man with Two Brains 83. Spraggue (TV) 84. Revenge of the Nerds 84. Tank 84. Oh, God! You Devil 84. Explorers 85. A Fine Mess 86. Revenge of the Nerds II: Nerds in Paradise 87. The Rescue 88. Pink Cadillac 89. The Runnin' Kind 89. Miracle Landing (TV) 90. The Babe 92. Romeo Is Bleeding 93. The Shaggy Dog (TV) 94. *Babe* (AAN) 95. Star Trek: First Contact 96. The People vs Larry Flynt 96. Eraser 96. *LA Confidential* 97. The Education of Little Tree 97. Deep Impact 98. Species 2 98. Babe: Pig in the City 98, etc.
TV series: All in the Family 74. Hot L Baltimore 75. The Nancy Walker Show 76. The Last Precinct 86. Easy Street 86–87.

Cromwell, John (1888–1979).
Distinguished American director with stage background. Formerly married to actresses Ruth Nelson and Kay Johnson. He and Johnson are the parents of actor James Cromwell.
■ The Dummy (a only) 29. The Mighty 29. The Dance of Life 29. Close Harmony 29. Street of Chance 30. Tom Sawyer 30. The Texan 30. For the Defense 30. Scandal Street 31. Rich Man's Folly 31. Vice Squad 31. Unfaithful 31. The World and the Flesh 31. Sweepings 33. The Silver Cord 33. Double Harness 33. Ann Vickers 33. Spitfire 34. This Man is Mine 34. *Of Human Bondage* 34. The Fountain 34. Jalna 35. Village Tale 35. I Dream Too Much 35. Little Lord Fauntleroy 36. To Mary With Love 36. Banjo on My Knee 36. *The Prisoner of Zenda* 37. *Algiers* 38. Made for Each Other 38. In Name Only 39. Abe Lincoln in Illinois 40. Victory 40. So Ends Our Night 41. Son of Fury 42. *Since You Went Away* 44. The Enchanted Cottage 45. *Anna and the King of Siam* 46. Dead Reckoning 47. Night Song 47. Caged 50. The Company She Keeps 51. The Racket 51. Top Secret Affair (a only) 57. The Goddess 58. The Scavengers 60. A Matter of Morals 61. *Three Women* (a only) 77. *A Wedding* (a only) 78.

Cromwell, Oliver (1599–1658).
The Puritan Protector of England during the Civil War has been shown on screen as a repressed rather than a heroic figure, as follows:

1937	*The Vicar of Bray*	George Merritt
1949	*Cardboard Cavalier*	Edmund Willard
1958	*The Moonraker*	John Le Mesurier
1968	*Witchfinder General*	Patrick Wymark
1970	*Cromwell*	Richard Harris

Cromwell, Richard (1910–1960) (Roy Radebaugh).
American leading man, gentle hero of early sound films. He was married to Angela Lansbury.
■ *Tol'able David* 30. Fifty Fathoms Deep 31. Shanghaied Love 31. Maker of Men 31. That's My Boy 32. Emma 32. The Strange Love of Molly Louvain 32. Age of Consent 32. Tom Brown of Culver 32. This Day and Age 33. Hoopla 33. Above the Clouds 34. Carolina 34. Among the Missing 34. Name the Woman 34. When Strangers Meet 34. Most Precious Thing in Life 34. *Lives of a Bengal Lancer* 35. McFadden's Flats 35. Life Begins at Forty 35. Men of the Hour 35. Unknown Woman 35. Annapolis Farewell 35. Poppy 36. Our Fighting Navy (GB) 37. The Road Back 37. The Wrong Road 37. Jezebel 38. Come On Leathernecks 38. Storm Over Bengal 38. Young Mr Lincoln 39. Enemy Agent 40. The Villain Still Pursued Her 40. Village Barn Dance 40. Parachute Battalion 41. Riot Squad 42. Baby Face Morgan 42. Bungalow 13 48.

Cronenberg, David (1943–).
Canadian director of outlandish and generally over-the-top horror films.
Autobiography: 1992, *Cronenberg on Cronenberg* (edited by Chris Radley).
Biography: 1994, *David Cronenberg: A Delicate Balance* by Peter Morris.
Crimes of the Future 70. Squirm 74. Shivers 75. Rabid 77. The Brood 80. Scanners 81. Videodrome 83. The Dead Zone 83. The Fly 86. Dead Ringers 88. Nightbreed (a only) 90. Naked Lunch 91. M. Butterfly 93. Blood & Donuts (a) 95. Crash (wd) 97. eXistenZ 98, etc.
❝ My dentist said to me the other day, I've enough problems in my life, so why should I see your films? – *D.C.*
A friend of mine saw *Videodrome*, said he really liked it, and added, you know someday they're going to lock you up. – *D.C.*
I don't have a moral plan. I'm a Canadian. – *D.C.*
Censorship is about control. It's not about morality at all. And it's about fear. I can't see how one adult citizen can control what another adult citizen can or cannot see. – *D.C.*
He works from his dreams. If he'd just dream a little more normally, I'd love to work with him again. – *James Woods*

Cronenweth, Jordan. (*–1996).
American cinematographer.
Brewster McCloud 70. Play it as it Lays 72. Zandy's Bride 74. The Front Page 74. Handle With Care 77. Rolling Thunder 77. Altered States 80. Cutter's Way 81. Blade Runner 82. Best Friends 82. Peggy Sue Got Married (AAN) 86. Gardens of Stone 87. State of Grace 90. Get Back 91. Final Analysis 92, etc.

Cronin, A. J. (1896–1981).
British novelist, former doctor.
Grand Canary 34. The Citadel 38, 83 (TV). The Stars Look Down 39. Shining Victory 41. Hatter's Castle 41. The Keys of the Kingdom 44. The Green Years 46. The Spanish Gardener 56.
TV series: Dr Finlay's Casebook 59–66.

Cronjager, Edward (1904–1960).
American cinematographer.
The Quarterback 26. The Virginian 30. Cimarron 31. Roberta 35. The Gorilla 39. *Hot Spot* 41. *Heaven Can Wait* 43. Canyon Passage 46. The House by the River 50. Treasure of the Golden Condor 53. Beneath the Twelve-Mile Reef 53, many others.

Cronyn, Hume (1911–) (Hume Blake).
Canadian character actor of stage and screen; married Jessica Tandy.
Autobiography: 1991, *A Terrible Liar*.
■ *Shadow of a Doubt* 43. Phantom of the Opera 43. The Cross of Lorraine 43. *The Seventh Cross* (AAN) 44. Main Street After Dark 44. *Lifeboat* 44. A Letter for Evie 45. The Sailor Takes a Wife 45. The Green Years 46. The Postman Always Rings Twice 46. Ziegfeld Follies 46. The Beginning or the End 47. *Brute Force* 47. The Bride Goes Wild 48. Top o' the Morning 49. People Will Talk 51. Crowded Paradise 56. *Sunrise at Campobello* 60. Cleopatra 63. Hamlet 64. Gaily Gaily 69. The Arrangement 70. There Was a Crooked Man 70. The Parallax View 74. Conrack 74. Rollover 80. Honky Tonk Freeway 81. The World According to Garp 82. Brewster's Millions 84. Impulse 84. Cocoon 85. The Thrill of Genius 85. Batteries Not Included 87. Cocoon: The Return 88. To Dance with the White Dog (TV) 93. The Pelican Brief 93. Camilla 94.
❝ To act you must have a sense of truth and some degree of dedication. – H.C.

Cropper, Anna (1938–).
English actress, much on stage and television.
All Neat in Black Stockings 69. Cromwell 70. The Jewel in the Crown (TV) 84. Anna of the Five Towns (TV) 85, etc.
TV series: The Castles 95.

Crosbie, Annette (1934–).
Scottish character actress whose best roles have been on television as Catherine of Aragon in *The Six Wives of Henry VIII* 70, and as Queen Victoria in *Edward VII* 75. She is also known for the part of Margaret Meldrew in the TV sitcom *One Foot in the Grave*. Born in Gorebridge, she trained at the Bristol Old Vic Theatre School.
Sky West and Crooked 65. The Public Eye 72. The Slipper and the Rose 76. Hawk the Slayer 80. Ordeal by Innocence 84. Summer's Lease (TV) 89. Chernobyl: The Final Warning (TV) 91. The Pope Must Die/The Pope Must Diet 91. Leon the Pig Farmer 92. Solitaire for Two 94. Nervous Energy 95. P. D. James's An Unsuitable Job for a Woman (TV) 97, etc.
TV series: One Foot in the Grave 90–95. Doctor Finlay 93–96. Underworld 96.

Crosby, Bing (1903–1977) (Harry Lillis Crosby).
Star American crooner of the 30s and 40s; former band singer, later an agreeable comedian, romantic lead and straight actor. His first wife was actress Dixie Lee and his sons Gary, Philip, Dennis and Lindsay Crosby had show business careers.
Autobiography: 1953, *Call Me Lucky*.
Biography: 1982, *The Hollow Man* by Robert F. Slatzer.
■ King of Jazz 30. Check and Double Check 30. Reaching for the Moon 31. Confessions of a Co-Ed 31. The Big Broadcast 32. College Humor 33. Too Much Harmony 33. Going Hollywood 33. We're Not Dressing 34. She Loves Me Not 34. Here is My Heart 34. *Mississippi* 35. Two for Tonight 35. The Big Broadcast of 1936 36. *Anything Goes* 36. Rhythm on the Range 36. Pennies from Heaven 36. Waikiki Wedding 37. Double or Nothing 37. Dr Rhythm 38. *Sing You Sinners* 38. Paris Honeymoon 39. East Side of Heaven 39. The Star Maker 39. *Road to Singapore* 40. If I Had My Way 40. Rhythm on the River 40. Road to Zanzibar 41. Birth of the Blues 41. *Holiday Inn* 42. Road to Morocco 42. Star Spangled Rhythm 43. Dixie 43. *Going My Way* (AA) 44. Here Come The Waves 45. Duffy's Tavern 45. Road to Utopia 45. The Bells of St Mary's (AAN) 45. Out of This World (voice) 45. Blue Skies 46. Variety Girl 47. Welcome Stranger 47. Road to Rio 47. The Emperor Waltz 48. A Connecticut Yankee in King Arthur's Court 49. Top o' the Morning 49. Ichabod and Mr Toad (voice) 49. Riding High 50. Mr Music 50. Here Comes the Groom 51. Just for You 52. Road to Bali 52. Little Boy Lost 53. White Christmas 54. *The Country Girl* (AAN) 54. Anything Goes 56. High Society 56. Man on Fire 57. Say One for Me 59. High Time 60. Pepe 60. Road to Hong Kong 62. Robin and the Seven Hoods 64. Stagecoach 66. Dr Cook's Garden (TV) 70.
TV series: The Bing Crosby Show 64.
✪ For his songs; and for his acceptance as a member of everybody's family over a fifty-year career. *Holiday Inn*.
❝ Honestly, I think I've stretched a talent which is so thin it's almost transparent over a quite unbelievable term of years. – B.C.
He was an average guy who could carry a tune. – *B.C.'s own epitaph*
Once or twice I've been described as a light comedian. I consider this the most accurate description of my abilities I've ever seen. – B.C.

Crosby, Bob (1913–1993).
American bandleader, brother of Bing.
Let's Make Music 40. Reveille with Beverly 43. See Here Private Hargrove 44. Two Tickets to Broadway 51. The Five Pennies 59, etc.

Crosby, Denise (1957–).
American actress, the daughter of Dennis Crosby.
48 Hrs 82. Curse of the Pink Panther 83. Desert Hearts 85. Eliminators 86. Arizona Heat 87. Miracle Mile 89. Pet Sematary 89. Skin Deep 89. Red Shoe Diaries II: Double Dare 92. Desperate Crimes 93. Black Water 94. Max (Can.) 94. Mutant Species 95. Deep Impact 98, etc.

Crosby, Dennis (1934–1991).
American actor, singer and disc jockey, the son of Bing Crosby and Dixie Lee, twin brother of Philip and father of actress Denise Crosby. Committed suicide.
Duffy's Tavern 45. Sergeants 3 61, etc.

Crosby, Floyd (1899–1985).
American cinematographer who worked on everything from documentary to horror thrillers.
■ *Tabu* (AA) 31. *The River* (co-ph) 37. The Fight for Life 40. My Father's House 47. Of Men and Music 50. The Brave Bulls 51. *High Noon* 52. Man in the Dark 53. The Steel Lady 53. Man Crazy 53. Stormy 54. The Snow Creature 54. The Monster from the Ocean Floor 54. The Fast and the Furious 54. Five Guns West 55. The Naked Street 55. Shack out on 101 55. Hell's Horizon 55. Apache Woman 55. Naked Paradise 56. She Gods of Shark Reef 56. Attack of the Crab Monsters 56. Rock All Night 56. Reform School 57. Teenage Doll 57. Ride out for Revenge 57. Hell Canyon Outlaws 57. Carnival Rock 57. War of the Satellites 57. Suicide Battalion 58. Cry Baby Killer 58. Machine Gun Kelly 58. The Old Man and the Sea (co-ph) 58. Wolf Larsen 58. Hot Rod Gang 58. Teenage Caveman 58. I Mobster 59. Crime and Punishment USA 59. The Miracle of the Hills 59. The Wonderful Country 59. Blood and Steel 59. The Rookie 60. Twelve Hours to Kill 60. *House of Usher* 60. The High Powered Rifle 60. Walk Tall 60. Freckles 60. Operation Bottleneck 61. The Pit and the Pendulum 61. A Cold Wind in August 61. The Purple Hills 61. The Little Shepherd of Kingdom Come 61. The Gambler Wore a Gun 61. Seven Women from Hell 62. The Explosive Generation 62. Woman Hunt 62. The Premature Burial 62. The Two Little Bears 62. Tales of Terror 62. The Firebrand 62. The Broken Land 62. Terror at Black Falls 62. *The Raven* 63. Black Zoo 63. Yellow Canary 63. The Young Racers 63. X – the Man with X-ray Eyes 63. The Comedy of Terrors 64. Bikini Beach 64. Pajama Party 64. The Haunted Palace 64. Raiders from beneath the Sea 65. Beach Blanket Bingo 65. How to Stuff a Wild Bikini 65. Sergeant Deadhead 65. Sallah 65. Fireball 500 66. The Cool Ones 67.

Crosby, Gary (1933–1995).
American actor and singer, the eldest son of Bing Crosby and Dixie Lee. He began with appearances in his father's films and made a hit record in 1950 duetting with Bing, with whom he had an uneasy relationship (detailed in his 1983 autobiography *Going My Own Way*, written with Ross Firestone). He also performed in a musical act with his brothers Dennis, Philip and Lindsay. His career was disrupted by alcoholism and drug abuse.
Star Spangled Rhythm 42. Duffy's Tavern 45. Out of This World 45. Mardi Gras 58. Holiday for Lovers 59. A Private's Affair 59. Battle at Bloody Beach 61. Two Tickets to Paris 62. Girl Happy 65. Which Way to the Front? 70. The Night Stalker 87. Chill Factor 90, etc.
TV series: The Bill Dana Show 63–64. Adam 12 68–75. Chase 73–74.
❝ The way I saw it I only had two choices: manual labor or showbusiness. The more I thought about putting in ten hours a day busting my butt on someone's ranch the better showbusiness began to look. – G.C.
I did not make a lot of friends for myself on the set, not where it counted . . . Nor did the way I showed up for work totally wasted and bedraggled from the night before. I'd be popping bennies and juicing all morning just to stay up there enough to hit the mark and say the lines. – G.C.

Crosby, Lindsay (1938–1989).
American actor and singer, the son of Bing Crosby and Dixie Lee. Committed suicide.
Duffy's Tavern 45. Sergeants 3 61. The Glory Stompers 67. The Mechanic 72. Santee 72. Murph the Surf/Live a Little, Steal a Lot 74. Codename: Zebra 84, etc.

Crosby, Philip (1934–).
American actor and singer, the son of Bing Crosby and Dixie Lee.
Duffy's Tavern 45. Sergeants 3 61. Robin and the Seven Hoods 64. None but the Brave 65, etc.

Croset, Paule:
see Corday, Paula.

Crosland, Alan (1894–1936).
Routine American director who happened to handle two innovative films. A former actor, he died of injuries sustained in a car crash. Married actress Natalie Moorhead.
Enemies of Women 23. Under the Red Robe 23. Three Weeks 24. Bobbed Hair 25. *Don Juan* (first film with synchronized music) 26. The Beloved Rogue 27. Old San Francisco 27. *The Jazz Singer* (first film with talking sequences) 27. Glorious Betsy 28. General Crack 29. Song of the Flame 30. Captain Thunder 31. Weekends Only 32. The Case of the Howling Dog 34. Lady Tubbs 35. The Great Impersonation 35, many others.

Crosman, Henrietta (1861–1944).
American actress, a grande dame who made a few films. Born in Wheeling, West Virginia, she made her theatrical debut in 1883, becoming a star as Nell Gwyn in 1900, and acting on stage and in vaudeville thereafter.
■ The Unwelcome Mrs Hatch 14. How Molly Made Good 15. Broadway Broke 23. Wandering Fires 25. *The Royal Family of Broadway* 30. Pilgrimage 33. Three on a Honeymoon 34. Carolina 34. Such Women Are Dangerous 34. Among the Missing 34. The Curtain Falls 34. Menace 34. Elinor Norton 35. The Right to Live 35. *The Dark Angel* 35. Hitch Hike to Heaven 36. Charlie Chan's Secret 36. The Moon's Our Home 36. Girl of the Ozarks 36. Follow Your Heart 37. Personal Property 37.

Cross, Ben (1947–).
British leading man of somewhat lugubrious countenance.
Chariots of Fire 81. The Citadel (TV) 83. The Far Pavilions (TV) 83. The Assisi Underground 85. The Unholy 88. Steal the Sky 88. Paperhouse 89. Nightlife (TV) 89. Live Wire 92. Cold Sweat 93. Symphony 93. The Ascent 94. First Knight 95, etc.
TV series: Dark Shadows 91.

Cross, Eric (1902–).
British cinematographer.
Make Up 37. Song of Freedom 38. The First of the Few 42. Don't Take It To Heart 44. The Chance of a Lifetime 49. Hunted 52. The Kidnappers 53. Private's Progress 55. The One That Got Away 57. Behind the Curtain 60, many others.

Crosse, Rupert (1927–1973).
American actor best remembered for *The Reivers* (AAN) 68, and for the TV series *Partners*.

Crossley, Syd (1885–1960).
British music-hall comedian who played comic supporting roles in many films. In US in 20s.
Keep Smiling 25. Fangs of the Wild 28. Atlantic 29. Tonight's the Night 31. Those were the Days 34. Dandy Dick 35. Music Hath Charms 36. The Ghost Goes West 36. Silver Blaze 37. Penny Paradise 38, many others.

Crothers, Rachel (1878–1958).
American playwright and occasional screenwriter. Born in Bloomington, Illinois, she began as an actress and also directed her own plays from 1903. In the late 20s to the late 30s, her comedies of manners, dealing with the problems of liberated women, proved attractive to film producers.
When Ladies Meet 33 and 41. As Husbands Go 34. Splendor (w, oa) 35. Susan and God/The Gay Mrs Trexel 40, etc.

Crothers, Scatman (1910–1986) (Sherman Crothers).
American character actor with a penchant for comedy.
Between Heaven and Hell 56. Lady in a Cage 64. Hello Dolly 69. The Great White Hope 70. Lady Sing the Blues 72. The Fortune 74. One Flew Over the Cuckoo's Nest 75. The Shootist 76. Silver Streak 77. Scavenger Hunt 79. Bronco Billy 80. The Shining 80. Twilight Zone 83. The Journey of Natty Gann 85, etc.
TV series: Chico and the Man 74–77. One of the Boys 82. Casablanca 83. Morning Star, Evening Star 86.

Crouse, Lindsay (1948–).
American leading lady, daughter of Russel Crouse. She was formerly married to director and writer David Mamet.
All the President's Men 76. Between the Lines 77. Slapshot 77. The Verdict 82. Iceman 82. Places in the Heart (AAN) 85. House of Games 87. Communion, a True Story 89. Desperate Hours 90. Chantilly Lace (TV) 93. Being Human 94. Parallel Lives (TV) 94. Bye Bye, Love 95. The Indian in the Cupboard 95. The Juror 96. The Arrival 96. Prefontaine 97, etc.

Crouse, Russel (1893–1966).
American librettist, usually with Howard Lindsay. Their musicals that have been filmed include *Anything Goes*, *Call Me Madam* and *The Sound of Music*. Non-musicals: *Life with Father*, *State of the Union*, etc.

Crowden, Graham (1922–).
Scottish character actor, often in querulous or eccentric roles. Born in Edinburgh, he first worked as a stage manager and in repertory and has been a member of the Royal National Theatre Company and the Royal Shakespeare Company.
Don't Bother to Knock 61. Nil Carborundum (TV) 62. One Way Pendulum 64. Morgan 66. If . . . 68. The Virgin Soldiers 69. Leo the Last 70. Up the Chastity Belt 71. The Ruling Class 72. O Lucky Man 73. Jabberwocky 77. For Your Eyes Only 81. Britannia Hospital 82. Company of Wolves 85. Out of Africa 85. Gulliver's Travels (TV) 96. I Want You 98, etc.
TV series: HMS Paradise 64. A Very Peculiar Practice 86–88. Waiting for God 90–93.

Crowe, Cameron (1957–).
American screenwriter and director, a former journalist.
Fast Times at Ridgemont High (w) 82. The Wild Life (w) 84. Say Anything (wd) 89. Singles (wd) 92. Sessions (wd) 92. Jerry Maguire (AANw), etc.

Crowe, Russell. (1964–).
New Zealand-born leading actor who has lived most his life in Australia, now in international films. He began by playing guitar and singing with his own rock group.
Blood Oath 90. The Crossing 90. Proof 91. Spotswood/The Efficiency Expert 91. *Romper Stomper* 92. Love in Limbo 92. Hammers over the Anvil 93. The Silver Brumby 93. For the Moment (Can.) 94. The Quick and the Dead (US) 95. Virtuosity (US) 95. The Sum of Us 95. Rough Magic (Fr.) 95. No Way Back 97, etc.

Crowe, Sarah (1966–).
British blonde comic actress, best known as the greedy, giggling girl in TV advertisements for Philadelphia cheese.
Carry on Columbus 92. The Steal 95. Caught in the Act 96, etc.
TV series: Haggard 90–92. Roy's Raiders 91. Sometime Never 96.

Crowley, Pat (1929–).
American leading lady of the 50s.
Forever Female 53. Money from Home 54. Red Garters 54. There's Always Tomorrow 55. Hollywood or Bust 56. Key Witness 60. To Trap a Spy 64. A Family Upside Down (TV) 78, etc.
TV series: Please Don't Eat the Daisies 65–66. Joe Forrester 75. Dynasty 86.

Crowther, Bosley (1905–1981).
American film critic. Long with the *New York Times*.

Crudup, Billy (1968–).
American leading actor, from the theatre. Born in Long Island, New York, he was raised in Florida and Texas. He studied at the University of North Carolina, New York University and New York's Tisch School of the Arts. He has been romantically linked with actress Mary-Louise Parker.
Sleepers 96. Everyone Says I Love You 96. Inventing the Abbots 97. Grind 97. Without Limits 98. The Hi-Lo Country 98. Waking the Dead 99, etc.

Cruickshank, Andrew (1907–1988).
Scottish stage actor who appeared in a number of films, usually as doctor or judge. A national figure on TV as Dr Cameron in *Dr Finlay's Casebook* 59–66.
Auld Lang Syne 37. The Mark of Cain 47. Paper Orchid 49. Your Witness 50. The Cruel Sea 53. Richard III 56. Innocent Sinners 58. Kidnapped 60. *There Was a Crooked Man* 60. El Cid 61. Murder Most Foul 64, etc.

Cruise, Tom (1962–) (Thomas Cruise Mapother IV).
Leading American actor, the biggest attraction of the late 80s and early 90s. Born in Syracuse, New York, he is a high-school dropout who began acting in his late teens. His performance as a cocky jet pilot in *Top Gun* brought him stardom, and he proved he could also act in *Born on the Fourth of July*. He now runs his own production company, which starred him in the box-office hit *Mission: Impossible*; he then disappeared from view for more than a year, working on Stanley Kubrick's *Eyes Wide Shut*, while other, younger actors replaced him as box-office sensations. Married actress Mimi Rogers (1987–90) and, in 1990, actress Nicole Kidman.
Biography: 1997, *Tom Cruise* by Robert Sellers.
Endless Love 81. Taps 81. Losin' It 83. All the Right Moves 83. The Outsiders 83. Risky Business 84. Legend 84. *Top Gun* 85. *The Color of Money* 86. Cocktail 88. Rain Man 88. *Born on the Fourth of July* (AAN) 89. Days of Thunder 90. Far and Away 92. A Few Good Men 92. The Firm 93. Interview with the Vampire 94. Mission: Impossible 96. *Jerry Maguire* (AAN) 96. Without Limits (p only) 98. Eyes Wide Shut 99, etc.
“ Hollywood didn't create Tom Cruise so that he could do *Rain Man* and *Born on the Fourth of July*. Hollywood created him to make twelve *Top Guns*, and it will replace him if he doesn't. – *Joe Queenan*
He's no more my Vampire Lestat than Edward G. Robinson is Rhett Butler. – *Anne Rice*
He has this light around him like he holds a little piece of the universe in his hands, and he has so much of it that he can afford to give a little bit to each person he encounters. – *Renee Zellweger*

Crumb, Robert (1943–).
American comic-book artist who emerged from underground publications of the 60s. He is the creator of Fritz the Cat, the randy hero of two animated features, *Fritz the Cat* 72, directed by Ralph Bakshi, and *The Nine Lives of Fritz the Cat* 74, directed by Robert Taylor. (Crumb disowned both movies.) A two-hour documentary on his life, *Crumb*, was released in 1994, directed by Terry Zwigoff.

Crutchley, Rosalie (1920–1997).
Striking, lean-featured British stage actress who makes occasional film appearances.
Take My Life 47. Give Us This Day 49. Quo Vadis 51. Make Me an Offer 55. The Spanish Gardener 56. *A Tale of Two Cities* (as Madame Lafarge) 58. Beyond This Place 59. Sons and Lovers 60. Freud 62. The Girl in the Headlines 63. Behold a Pale Horse 64. Jane Eyre (TV) 70. Blood from the Mummy's Tomb 71. Who Slew Auntie Roo? 71. Man of La Mancha 72. Mahler 74. Smiley's People (TV) 82. Eleni 85. Four Weddings and a Funeral 94, etc.

Cruttwell, Greg.
English actor, born in London, from the theatre.
Naked 93. 2 Days in the Valley (US) 96. George of the Jungle (US) 97, etc.

Cruz, Brandon (1962–).
American child actor of the 70s. Born in Bakersfield, California, he later fronted punk rock bands and worked as a film editor, including on the animated TV series *South Park* in the late 90s.
But I Don't Want to Get Married (TV) 70. The Going Up of David Lev (TV) 72. The Bad News Bears 76. The One and Only 78, etc.
TV series: *The Courtship of Eddie's Father* 69–72.

Cruz, Penélope (1974–) (Penélope Cruz Sanchez).
Smouldering Spanish leading actress, born in Madrid. She trained as a dancer.
El Laberinto Griego 91. Jamon, Jamon 92. Belle Epoque 92. For Love, Only for Love/Per Amore, Solo per Amore 93. La Ribelle (It.) 93. It's All Lies/Todo Es Mentira 94. Allegro Ma No Troppo 95. The Man with Rain in His Shoes 98. The Hi-Lo Country (US) 98. Talk of Angels (US) 98, etc.

Cruze, James (1884–1942) (Jens Cruz Bosen).
Danish-American silent screen actor who broke his leg and turned to direction.
AS ACTOR: A Boy of Revolution 11. She 11. The Star of Bethlehem 12. Joseph in the Land of Egypt 14. *The Million Dollar Mystery* (serial) 14. The Twenty Million Dollar Mystery (serial) 15. Nan of Music Mountain 17. Too Many Millions 18, etc.
AS DIRECTOR: Too Many Millions 18. The Dollar a Year Man 21. One Glorious Day 22. The Dictator 22. *The Covered Wagon* 23. *Hollywood* 23. Ruggles of Red Gap 23. To the Ladies 23. Merton of the Movies 24. The Goose Hangs High 25. *Beggar on Horseback* 25. Pony Express 25. *Old Ironsides* 26. The Mating Call 27. The Great Gabbo 29. Salvation Nell 31. *Washington Merry Go Round* 32. I Cover the Waterfront 33. David Harum 34. Helldorado 34. *Sutter's Gold* 36. Prison Nurse 38. Gangs of New York 38, many others.

Cryer, Jon (1965–).
American actor.
No Small Affair 84. O. C. and Stiggs 85. Pretty in Pink 86. Dudes 87. Hiding Out 87. Morgan Stewart's Coming Home 87. Superman IV: The Quest for Peace 87. Hot Shots! 91. Heads 94. I'll Do Anything 94. The Pompatus of Love (& co-p, co-w) 96. Went to Coney Island on a Mission from God . . . Be Back by Five (& p, co-w) 98. Holy Man 98, etc.

Crystal, Billy (1947–).
American stand-up comedian and writer turned light leading man. Born in Long Beach, New York, he went to Marshall University, West Virginia, on a baseball scholarship before switching to New York University, where he studied film and television direction. He worked as a teacher while honing his comic act. He first gained national attention in the role of the gay Jodie Dallas in the TV sitcom *Soap*. His movie career began inauspiciously as a pregnant man in *Rabbit Test*. He recovered with an Emmy-award-winning performance on *Saturday Night Live*, and star performances in *When Harry Met Sally* and *City Slickers*.
Rabbit Test 78. Enola Gay: The Men, the Mission, the Atomic Bomb (TV) 80. This Is Spinal Tap 83. Running Scared 86. The Princess Bride 87. Throw Momma from the Train 88. Memories of Me 88. When Harry Met Sally 89. City Slickers 91. Mr Saturday Night (& d) 92. City Slickers II: The Legend of Curly's Gold 94. Forget Paris (& co-w, d) 95. Father's Day 97, etc.
TV series: Soap 77–81.

Cuadrado, Luis (1934–1980) (Luis Cuadrado Encinar).
Spanish cinematographer, associated with the films of Carlos Saura, José Luis Borau and other directors of the New Spanish Cinema. Born in Toro, he studied at EOC (Escuela Oficial de Cinematografía). His career ended in 1975, when he went blind.
The Hunt/La Caza 65. Peppermint Frappé 67. Night Hair Child (GB) 71. Ana and the Wolves/Ana y los Lobos 72. *The Spirit of the Beehive* 73. B. Must Die/Hay Que Matar a B. 73. Cousin Angelica 74. Poachers/Furtivos 75. Pascual Duarte 76, etc.

Cuaron, Alfonso (1961–).
Mexican director.
Tale of Love and Hysteria/Solo con Tu Pareja 91. *A Little Princess* (US) 95.

Cucciolla, Ricardo (1932–).
Italian leading actor.
Italia Brava Gente 65. Grand Slam 67. Sacco and Vanzetti 71, etc.

Cucinotta, Maria Grazia.
Sultry Italian actress.
The Day of the Beast/Dia de la Bestia (Sp.) 95. I Laureati 95. The Postman/Il Postino 95. Italiani 96. The Second Wife/La Seconda Moglie 98. Ballad of the Nightingale (US) 98, etc.

Cugat, Xavier (1900–1990).
Chubby, beaming Spanish-American bandleader and caricaturist, a feature of many MGM musicals of the 40s.
Autobiography: 1948, *Rumba Is My Life*.
You Were Never Lovelier 42. Two Girls and a Sailor 44. Holiday in Mexico 46. This Time for Keeps 47. A Date with Judy 48. Neptune's Daughter 49. Chicago Syndicate 55, etc.

Cukor, George (1899–1983).
American director, from the Broadway stage; proved to be one of Hollywood's most reliable handlers of high comedy and other literate material.
Biography: 1991, *A Double Life: Director George Cukor* by Patrick McGilligan.
■ Grumpy (co-d) 30. Virtuous Sin (co-d) 30. The Royal Family of Broadway 30. Tarnished Lady 30. Girls About Town 31. *One Hour with You* (with Lubitsch) 32. *What Price Hollywood?* 32. A Bill of Divorcement 32. Rockabye 32. Our Betters 33. *Dinner at Eight* 33. *Little Women* (AAN) 33. *David Copperfield* 34. Sylvia Scarlett 35. Romeo and Juliet 36. *Camille* 36. *Holiday* 38. Zaza 39. *The Women* 39. Susan and God 40. *The Philadelphia Story* (AAN) 40. A Woman's Face 41. Two-faced Woman 41. Her Cardboard Lover 42. *Keeper of the Flame* 43. Gaslight 44. Winged Victory 44. Desire Me (co-d) 47. A Double Life (AAN) 47. *Adam's Rib* 49. Edward My Son (GB) 49. A Life of Her Own 50. Born Yesterday (AAN) 50. The Model and the Marriage Broker 52. The Marrying Kind 52. Pat and Mike 52. The Actress 53. It Should Happen to You 53. *A Star is Born* 54. Bhowani Junction 56. Les Girls 57. Wild is the Wind 57. Heller in Pink Tights 59. Song Without End (part) 60. Let's Make Love 61. The Chapman Report 62. *My Fair Lady* (AA) 64. Justine 69. Travels with My Aunt 73. Love Among the Ruins (TV) 75. The Bluebird 76. The Corn Is Green (TV) 79. Rich and Famous 81.
✪ For adding to Hollywood a sense of light culture; and for his discretion in handling a score of the film colony's more temperamental ladies. *The Philadelphia Story*.
“ His films vary drastically in their visual texture, their style reposing mainly in the theatrically accomplished handling of the actors. – *Charles Higham*
When a director has provided polished tasteful entertainments of a high order consistently over a period of thirty years, it is clear that said director is much more than a mere entertainer. – *Andrew Sarris*

Culkin, Kieran (1982–).
American juvenile actor, the brother of Macaulay Culkin.
Father of the Bride 91. Home Alone II: Lost in New York 92. Nowhere to Run 93. It Runs in the Family 94. The Mighty 98, etc.

Culkin, Macaulay (1980–).
American juvenile actor who became a star with *Home Alone*, the most successful movie comedy yet made. He was reportedly paid $5 million and 5 per cent of the gross to appear in the sequel. Married actress Rachel Miner in 1998.
Rocket Gibraltar 88. Uncle Buck 89. See You in the Morning 89. Home Alone 90. Jacob's Ladder (uncredited cameo) 90. My Girl 91. Only the Lonely 91. Home Alone 2: Lost in New York 92. The Good Son 93. George Balanchine's The Nutcracker 93. Getting Even with Dad 94. The Pagemaster 94. Richie Rich 94, etc.

Culp, Robert (1930–).
American leading man.
P.T. 109 62. The Raiders 63. Sunday in New York 64. Rhino! 64. *Bob and Carol and Ted and Alice* 69. Hannie Caulder 71. Hickey and Boggs (& d) 72. See the Man Run (TV) 72. The Castaway Cowboy 74. A Cry for Help (TV) 75. Inside Out

75. Sky Riders 76. The Great Scout and Cathouse Thursday 76. Breaking Point 76. Word Games (TV) 79. Goldengirl 79. Turk 182 84. The Blue Lightning (TV) 86. The Gladiator (TV) 86. Big Bad Mama II 87. Silent Night, Deadly Night 3: Better Watch Out! 89. Timebomb 91. The Pelican Brief 93. I Spy Returns (TV) 94, etc.

TV series: Trackdown 57. *I Spy* 65–67. *The Greatest American Hero* 81–82.

Culver, Roland (1900–1984).
British stage actor of impeccable English types, usually comic. Born in London, he worked for an optical company before studying at RADA, and was on stage from 1924. In the late 40s he worked in Hollywood, under contract for two years to Paramount before returning to England. Married twice.

Autobiography: 1979, *Not Quite a Gentleman*.

77 Park Lane 32. Nell Gwyn 34. Paradise for Two 37. *French without Tears* (his stage role) 39. *Quiet Wedding* 40. Night Train to Munich 40. Talk about Jacqueline 42. *On Approval* 43. Dear Octopus 43. *Dead of Night* 45. Wanted for Murder 46. To Each His Own (US) 47. Down to Earth (US) 47. The Emperor Waltz (US) 48. Isn't It Romantic? 48. *Trio* (as Somerset Maugham) 50. The Holly and the Ivy 54. The Man Who Loved Redheads 55. Touch and Go 57. Bonjour Tristesse 58. The Yellow Rolls-Royce 64. A Man Could Get Killed 65. Fragment of Fear 70. Bequest to the Nation 73. The Word (TV) 78, many others.

Cumming, Alan (1965–).
Scottish actor.

Passing Glory (short) 86. Prague 92. Second Best 94. Black Beauty (voice) 94. Circle of Friends 95. GoldenEye 95. Emma 96, etc.

Cummings, Constance (1910–) (Constance Halverstadt).
American stage actress, long resident in England.

The Criminal Code (US) 31. The Guilty Generation (US) 31. Movie Crazy (US) 32. Channel Crossing 32. Broadway thro' a Keyhole (US) 33. Glamour 34. Looking for Trouble 34. Remember Last Night? (US) 35. Seven Sinners 36. *Busman's Honeymoon* 40. This England 41. The Foreman Went to France 42. *Blithe Spirit* 45. John and Julie 55. The Intimate Stranger 56. The Battle of the Sexes 59. Sammy Going South 62. In the Cool of the Day 63, etc.

Cummings, Irving (1888–1959).
American director, former actor; in films from 1909.

SELECTED SILENT FILMS: As Man Desires 25. The Johnstown Flood 26. The Brute 27, etc.

■ In Old Arizona (AAN) 29. Behind That Curtain 29. Cameo Kirby 30. On the Level 30. A Devil with Women 30. A Holy Terror 31. *The Cisco Kid* 31. Attorney for the Defense 32. Night Club Lady 32. Man Against Woman 32. Man Hunt 33. The Woman I Stole 33. The Mad Game 33. I Believed in You 34. Grand Canary 34. The White Parade 34. It's a Small World 35. Curly Top 35. Nobody's Fool 36. Poor Little Rich Girl 36. Girls Dormitory 36. White Hunter 36. Vogues of 1938 37. Merry go Round of 1938 37. Little Miss Broadway 38. Just Around the Corner 38. *The Story of Alexander Graham Bell* 39. *Hollywood Cavalcade* 39. Everything Happens at Night 39. *Lillian Russell* 40. Down Argentine Way 40. *That Night in Rio* 41. Belle Starr 41. Louisiana Purchase 41. My Gal Sal 42. Springtime in the Rockies 42. Sweet Rosie O'Grady 43. What a Woman 44. The Impatient Years 44. *The Dolly Sisters* 45. Double Dynamite 51.

Cummings, Jack (1900–1989).
American producer, especially of musicals; long with MGM.

The Winning Ticket 35. Born to Dance 36. Go West 40. Ship Ahoy 42. Bathing Beauty 44. Neptune's Daughter 49. Three Little Words 50. Lovely to Look At 52. Kiss Me Kate 53. Seven Brides for Seven Brothers 54. Many Rivers to Cross 55. The Teahouse of the August Moon 56. The Blue Angel 59. Can Can 60. Bachelor Flat 62. Viva Las Vegas 64, many others.

Cummings, Quinn (1967–).
American actress, from television, born in Hollywood.

Night Terror (TV) 76. The Goodbye Girl (AAN) 77. The Babysitter (TV) 80. Listen to Me 89, etc.

TV series: Big Eddie 75. Family 78–80. Hail to the Chief 85.

Cummings, Robert (1908–1990).
American light leading man of the 40s.

The Virginia Judge 35. Forgotten Faces 36. Last Train from Madrid 37. Souls at Sea 37. Three Smart Girls Grow Up 38. Rio 39. Spring Parade 40. The Devil and Miss Jones 41. Moon over Miami 41. *It Started with Eve* 41. *Kings Row* 41. *Saboteur* 42. Princess O'Rourke 43. You Came Along 45. The Bride Wore Boots 46. The Chase 46. Heaven Only Knows 47. The Lost Moment 47. Sleep My Love 48. The Accused 48. Paid in Full 50. For Heaven's Sake 50. The Barefoot Mailman 51. Marry Me Again 53. Lucky Me 54. Dial M for Murder 54. How to be Very Very Popular 55. My Geisha 62. Beach Party 63. What a Way to Go 64. *The Carpetbaggers* 64. Promise Her Anything 66. Stagecoach 66. 5 Golden Dragons 67. Partners in Crime (TV) 73, many others.

TV series: My Hero 52. *The Bob Cummings Show* 54–61. My Living Doll 64.

Cummins, Peggy (1925–).
British leading lady, former teenage star.

Dr O'Dowd 39. The Late George Apley (US) 47. Moss Rose (US) 47. Green Grass of Wyoming (US) 48. Escape (US) 48. My Daughter Joy 50. Who Goes There? 52. To Dorothy a Son 54. The March Hare 55. Night of the Demon 57. Dentist in the Chair 60. In the Doghouse 62, etc.

Cunard, Grace (1893–1967) (Harriet Jeffries).
American silent serial queen.

The Broken Coin 13. The Purple Mask 15. Peg o' the Ring 18. The Last Man on Earth 24. Untamed 29. Resurrection 31. Ladies They Talk About 33, many others.

Cundey, Dean.
American cinematographer.

Bare Knuckles 78. Halloween 78. Roller Boogie 79. Rock 'n' Roll High School 79. The Fog 80. Galaxina 80. Without Warning 80. Halloween II 81. Escape from New York 81. Angels Brigade 81. The Thing 82. Halloween III: Season of the Witch 82. Separate Ways 83. Psycho II 83. Romancing the Stone 84. Back to the Future 85. Warning Sign 85. Big Trouble in Little China 86. Project X 87. Big Business 88. Who Framed Roger Rabbit (AAN) 88. Road House 89. Back to the Future Part II 89. Back to the Future Part III 90. Nothing but Trouble 91. Hook 91. Death Becomes Her 92. Jurassic Park 93. The Flintstones 94. Apollo 13 95. Casper 95. Flubber 97. The Parent Trap 98, etc.

Cundieff, Rusty.
American director, screenwriter and actor, a former stand-up comedian.

Hollywood Shuffle (a) 87. House Party 2 (co-w) 91. *Fear of a Black Hat* (a, wd) 93. Tales from the Hood (a, co-w, d) 95. Sprung (co-w, d) 97, etc.

Cunningham, Cecil (1888–1959).
American character actress, usually in hard or wisecracking roles.

Their Own Desire 29. Monkey Business 31. Mata Hari 31. The Impatient Maiden 32. Blonde Venus 32. Baby Face 33. The Life of Vergie Winters 34. Come and Get It 36. Artists and Models 37. College Swing 38. Lady of the Tropics 39. Lillian Russell 40. New Moon 40. Back Street 41. Blossoms in the Dust 41. I Married an Angel 42. Twin Beds 42. The Hidden Hand 42. Du Barry Was a Lady 43. Wonder Man 45. Saratoga Trunk 45. My Reputation 46. The Bride Goes Wild 48, many others.

Cunningham, Sean S. (1941–).
American horror film director and producer.

Together 71. Here Come the Tigers 78. Manny's Orphans 79. Friday the 13th 80. A Stranger Is Watching 82. Spring Break 83. The New Kids (& p) 85. House (p) 86. House II (p) 87. Deepstar Six 89. My Boyfriend's Back (p) 93.

Cuny, Alain (1908–1994).
Tall, imposing French actor, in occasional films. He directed his first film at the age of 83.

Les Visiteurs du Soir 42. Il Cristo Proibito 50. The Hunchback of Notre Dame 56. Les Amants 58. The Milky Way 68. Satyricon 69. Valparaiso Valparaiso 70. Emmanuelle 74. Il Contesto 75. Cadaveri Eccellenti 76. Christ Stopped at Eboli 79. Les Jeux de la Comtesse 80. Basileus Quartet 81. Camille Claudel 89. The Annunciation of Marie/L'Annonce Faîte à Marie (& d) 91. Farewell Sweet War/Uova di Garofano 92, etc.

Cupito, Suzanne:
see BRITTANY, Morgan.

Currie, Finlay (1878–1968) (Finlay Jefferson).
Veteran Scottish actor with stage and music-hall experience.

The Case of the Frightened Lady 32. Rome Express 32. Edge of the World 38. The Bells Go Down 42. *Great Expectations* (as Magwitch) 46. *Sleeping Car to Trieste* 48. *The History of Mr Polly* 49. Trio 50. Treasure Island 50. *The Mudlark* (as John Brown) 51. Quo Vadis 51. Kangaroo 51. *People Will Talk* (US) 52. Ivanhoe 52. Rob Roy 53. Treasure of the Golden Condor 53. Captain Lightfoot 54. Beau Brummell 54. The End of the Road (leading role) 54. Make Me an Offer 55. King's Rhapsody 56. Around the World in 80 Days 56. Saint Joan 57. Zarak 57. The Little Hut 57. Naked Earth 57. Dangerous Exile 57. Ben Hur (US) 59. Tempest 59. Solomon and Sheba 59. The Angel Wore Red 60. Huckleberry Finn 60. Kidnapped 60. Five Golden Hours 61. Francis of Assisi 61. The Inspector 62. Hand in Hand 62. The Amorous Prawn 62. Corridors of Blood 63. The Cracksman 63. West Eleven 63. The Three Lives of Thomasina 63. Billy Liar 63. The Fall of the Roman Empire 64. Who Was Maddox? (leading role) 64. The Battle of the Villa Fiorita 65. Bunny Lake is Missing 65, etc.

Curry, Tim (1946–).
British actor, hard to cast but with a wide range.

The Rocky Horror Picture Show 74. Will Shakespeare (TV) (title role) 76. The Shout 77. Times Square 80. Oliver Twist (TV) 81. Annie 82. The Ploughman's Lunch 83. Baby 83. Legend 85. Clue 86. Pass the Ammo 87. The Hunt for Red October 90. Stephen King's It (TV) 91. Oscar 91. Passed Away 92. Home Alone 2: Lost in New York 92. Ferngully . . . The Last Rainforest (voice) 92. National Lampoon's Loaded Weapon 1 93. The Three Musketeers 93. The Shadow 94. Congo 95. The Pebble and the Penguin (voice) 95. Lover's Knot 96. Muppet Treasure Island (as Long John Silver) 96. McHale's Navy 97. Titanic (TV) 96. McHale's Navy 97, etc.

TV series: Over the Top (& p) 97. The Net (voice) 98– . The Wild Thornberrys (voice) 98– .

Curtin, Valerie.
American actress and screenwriter, formerly married to director Barry Levinson, with whom she has collaborated on scripts. She also wrote for the TV series *The Mary Tyler Moore Show* and *Phyllis*.

AS ACTRESS: Alice Doesn't Live Here Anymore 74. Silver Streak 76. Mother, Jugs and Speed 76. Silent Movie 76. All the President's Men 76. Different Story 78. A Christmas without Snow (TV) 80. Down and Out in Beverly Hills 85. Maxie 85. Big Trouble 86, etc.

AS WRITER: . . . And Justice for All (AAN) 79. Inside Moves 80. Best Friends 82. Unfaithfully Yours 84. Toys 92.

TV series: 9 to 5 82–83, 86–88.

Curtis, Alan (1909–1953) (Harold Neberroth).
American leading man, and sometimes villain, of many 'B' pictures of the 40s.

Walking on Air 36. Winterset 36. Mannequin 38. Hollywood Cavalcade 39. Buck Privates 40. The Great Awakening 41. Two Tickets to London 43. Hitler's Madman 43. *Phantom Lady* 44. Destiny 44. The Invisible Man's Revenge 44. The Naughty Nineties 45. Philo Vance's Gamble 48. The Masked Pirate 50, etc.

Curtis, Dan (1928–).
American producer specializing in horror themes for TV.

Dark Shadows (serial) 66. The Night Strangler (TV) 72. *The Norliss Tapes* (TV) 73. Dracula (TV) (& d) 73. Kolchak, the Night Stalker (TV series) 74. Supertrain (TV) 79, etc.

AS DIRECTOR: House of Dark Shadows 70. Burnt Offerings 76. Melvin Purvis G-Man (TV) 77. The Raid on Coffeyville (TV) 79. *The Winds of War* (& p) 83. War and Remembrance (TV) 88–89. Me and the Kid 93.

Curtis, Dick (1902–1952) (Richard D. Dye).
Tall American character actor, often as a villain in 'B' westerns. Born in Newport, Kentucky, he began as an extra in silents in his teens.

The Unpardonable Sin 18. Shooting Straight 30. King Kong 33. Code of the Mounted 35. Racing Luck 35. Ghost Patrol 36. A Lawman Is Born 37. Rawhide 38. Valley of Terror 38. Mandrake the Magician (serial) 39. The Stranger from Texas 39. Trouble Finds Andy Clyde 39. Terry and the Pirates (serial) 40. Billy the Kid 41. Men of San Quentin 42. Pardon My Gun 43. Song of Prairie 45. Bandit of Sherwood Forest 46. Wymong 47. Covered Wagon Raid 50. The Red Badge of Courage 51. Lorna Doone 51. Rose of Cimmaron 52, many others.

Curtis, Jackie (1947–1985).
Transvestite actor, best known for roles in Andy Warhol's films. Born in New York, he was also a dramatist, providing Robert De Niro with a notable success in his off-Broadway play *Glamour, Glory and Gold* in 1968. Died of a drug overdose.

Flesh 68. WR: Mysteries of the Organism 71. Women in Revolt 72. Underground U.S.A. 80. Burroughs (doc) 84, etc.

❝ It's much easier to be a weird girl than a weird guy. – *J.C.*

Curtis, Jamie Lee (1958–) (Lady Haden-Guest).
American leading lady who seemed to get stuck in horrors. Daughter of Tony CURTIS and Janet LEIGH. She is married to Christopher GUEST, now Lord Haden-Guest.

Operation Petticoat (TV) 78. Halloween 79. Prom Night 80. Terror Train 80. The Fog 80. Halloween II 81. Road Games 81. Love Letters 83. Trading Places 83. Grandview USA 84. Perfect 85. Amazing Grace and Chuck 87. Un Homme Amoureux 87. Dominick and Eugene 88. A Fish Called Wanda 88. Blue Steel 89. Queen's Logic 91. My Girl 91. Forever Young 92. My Girl 2 94. Mother's Boys 94. True Lies 94. The Heidi Chronicles (TV) 95. House Arrest 96. Fierce Creatures 97. Halloween: H20 98, etc.

TV series: Operation Petticoat 78.

Curtis, Ken (1916–1991) (Curtis Gates).
American singing cowboy of the 40s and later a character actor, mainly in John Ford's westerns. He began as a singer with big bands, including those of Tommy Dorsey and Shep Fields.

Song of the Prairie 45. Lone Star Moonlight 46. Call of the Forest 49. Rio Grande 50. Mr Roberts 55. The Searchers 56. The Last Hurrah 58. Escort West 59. Two Rode Together 61. Cheyenne Autumn 64. Pony Express Rider 76, many others.

TV series: Ripcord 61–63. Gunsmoke (as Festus Haggen) 64–75. The Yellow Rose 83–84.

Curtis, Richard.
British comedy screenwriter, from television. He was co-writer of the *Blackadder* television series starring Rowan Atkinson and also wrote for *Not the Nine O'Clock News*.

The Tall Guy 89. *Four Weddings and a Funeral* (AAN) 94. Bean (co-w) 97, etc.

❝ Whatever your script is like, no matter how much rewriting you do, if the punters don't want to sleep with the star, you may never be asked to write another one. – *R.C.*

I'm a great campaigner for light-hearted cinema. *The Sound of Music* gets called sentimental because it's about people who love children and hate Nazis. Whereas a TV play about a single mother raped by a schizophrenic black soldier would be called searingly realistic. – *R.C.*

Curtis, Tony (1925–) (Bernard Schwartz).
Bouncy American leading man of 50s actioners who constantly sought a wider range. He was married to Janet LEIGH (1951–62); their daughter is Jamie Lee CURTIS. He married for the fifth time in 1998.

Novel: 1977, *Kid Andrew Cody and Julie Sparrow*. Autobiography: 1994, *Tony Curtis* (with Barry Paris).

■ Criss Cross 49. City Across the River 49. The Lady Gambles 49. Johnny Stool Pigeon 49. Francis 49. I was a Shoplifter 50. Sierra 50. Kansas Raiders 50. Winchester 73 50. *The Prince Who Was a Thief* 51. Flesh and Fury 52. No Room for the Groom 52. Son of Ali Baba 52. *Houdini* 53. The All American 53. Forbidden 53. Beachhead 54. The Black Shield of Falworth 54. Johnny Dark 54. So This is Paris 54. The Purple Mask 54. Six

Bridges to Cross 55. The Square Jungle 55. *Trapeze* 56. The Rawhide Years 56. Mister Cory 57. The Midnight Story 57. *Sweet Smell of Success* 57. *The Vikings* 58. Kings go Forth 58. *The Defiant Ones* (AAN) 58. The Perfect Furlough 58. *Some Like It Hot* 59. Operation Petticoat 59. Pepe 60. Who Was That Lady? 60. The Rat Race 60. *Spartacus* 60. The Great Imposter 60. The Outsider 61. Forty Pounds of Trouble 62. Taras Bulba 62. The List of Adrian Messenger 63. Captain Newman MD 63. Wild and Wonderful 64. Goodbye Charlie 64. Sex and the Single Girl 64. *The Great Race* 65. Boeing Boeing 65. Not With My Wife You Don't 66. Drop Dead Darling 67. Don't Make Waves 67. The Chastity Belt 68. *The Boston Strangler* 68. Those Daring Young Men in their Jaunty Jalopies 69. You Can't Win Them All 70. Suppose They Gave a War and Nobody Came 71. Third Girl from the Left (TV) 73. Lepke 75. Casanova 76. The Count of Monte Cristo (TV) 76. The Last Tycoon 76. The Manitou 78. Scarlett 78. The Bad News Bears Go to Japan 78. Little Miss Marker 80. The Mirror Crack'd 80. The Scarlett O'Hara Wars (TV) 81. Inmates (TV) 81. Portrait of a Showgirl (TV) 82. Brain Waves 83. Insignificance (TV) 85. King of the City 85. The Last of Philip Banter 86. Midnight 88. Welcome to Germany 88. Lobster Man from Mars 89. Walter and Carlo/Amerika 89. Prime Target 91. Center of the Web 92. Naked in New York 93. The Continued Adventures of Reptile Man (and His Faithful Sidekick Tadpole) 96.

TV series: *The Persuaders* 71. McCoy 75. Vegas 78.

❝ I had to be careful where I went because I was a Jew, because I was young and because I was handsome. It made me wiry and erratic and paranoid, which is what I still am. Always on guard. – T.C.

Curtiz, Michael (1888–1962) (Mihaly Kertesz). Hungarian director of more than 60 films in Europe before settling in Hollywood, where he made some of the smoothest spectacles and melodramas of the 30s and 40s and also became famous for his fractured English. Born in Budapest, and educated at Markoszy University and the city's Royal Academy of Art and Theatre, he began as an actor before directing Hungary's first feature film, leaving the country when the Communists nationalized the film industry in 1918. He moved to Hollywood in the mid-20s to work for Warner's, where he became noted for his on-set ruthlessness, enabling him to finish films on time and budget, and for his often acerbic working relationships with Bette Davis and Errol Flynn, who both did much of their best work under his direction. Married actress Lucy Dorraine (1915–23) and screenwriter Bess Meredyth.

Book: 1995, *The Casablanca Man: The Cinema of Michael Curtiz* by James C. Robertson.

■ ENGLISH-SPEAKING FILMS: The Third Degree 26. A Million Bid 27. The Desired Woman 27. Good Time Charley 27. Tenderloin 28. *Noah's Ark* 28. Hearts in Exile 29. Glad Rag Doll 29. The Madonna of Avenue A 29. The Gamblers 29. *Mammy* 30. Under a Texas Moon 30. The Matrimonial Bed 30. Bright Lights 30. A Soldier's Plaything 30. River's End 30. God's Gift to Women 31. The Mad Genius 31. The Woman from Monte Carlo 32. Alias the Doctor 32. The Strange Love of Molly Louvain 32. *Doctor X* 32. Cabin in the Cotton 32. Twenty Thousand Years in Sing Sing 33. *The Mystery of the Wax Museum* 33. The Keyhole 33. Private Detective 33. Goodbye Again 33. The Kennel Murder Case 33. Female 33. Mandalay 34. *British Agent* 34. Jimmy the Gent 34. The Key 34. *Black Fury* 35. The Case of the Curious Bride 35. *Front Page Woman* 35. Little Big Shot 35. *Captain Blood* 35. The Walking Dead 36. *The Charge of the Light Brigade* 36. Mountain Justice 37. Stolen Holiday 37. Kid Galahad 37. The Perfect Specimen 37. Gold is Where You Find It 38. *The Adventures of Robin Hood* 38. *Four Daughters* (AAN) 38. Four's a Crowd 38. *Angels with Dirty Faces* (AAN) 38. Dodge City 39. Daughters Courageous 39. Four Wives 39. Elizabeth and Essex 39. Virginia City 40. *The Sea Hawk* 40. Santa Fe Trail 41. Dive Bomber 41. *The Sea Wolf* 41. Captains of the Clouds 42. *Yankee Doodle Dandy* 42. *Casablanca* (AA) 42. Mission to Moscow 43. This is the Army 43. Passage to Marseilles 44. Janie 44. Roughly Speaking 45. *Mildred Pierce* 45. Night and Day 46. Life with Father 47. The Unsuspected 47. Romance on the High Seas 48. My Dream is Yours 49. Flamingo Road 49. The Lady Takes a Sailor 49. Young Man with a Horn 50. Bright Leaf 50. The Breaking Point 51. Jim Thorpe – All American 51. Force of Arms 51. I'll See You in My Dreams 52. The Story of Will Rogers 52. The Jazz Singer 53. Trouble Along the Way 53. The Boy from Oklahoma 54. The Egyptian 54. White Christmas 54. We're No Angels 55. The Scarlet Hour 56. The Vagabond King 56. The Best Things in Life are Free 56. The Helen Morgan Story 57. The Proud Rebel 58. King Creole 58. The Hangman 59. The Man in the Net 59. The Adventures of Huckleberry Finn 60. A Breath of Scandal 60. Francis of Assisi 61. The Comancheros 62.

✪ For the striking Teutonic influence which he brought to a score of 30s melodramas; and for the apparent ease with which he handled top action films in a language which did not come easily to him. *Casablanca*.

❝ The next time I send a dumb sonofabitch to do something, I go myself – M.C.

So many times I have a speech ready but no dice. Always a bridesmaid, never a mother. – M.C.'s Oscar acceptance speech for *Casablanca*

When one speaks of a typical Warners film in the 30s and 40s, one is generally speaking of a typical Curtiz film of those periods. – *Andrew Sarris, 1968*

The only thing Curtiz has to say is 'Don't do it the way I showed you. Do it the way I mean.' – *James Cagney*

Bring on the empty horses! – *instruction attributed to* M.C.

Curwood, James Oliver (1878–1927). American journalist and author of novels about the outdoor life.

River's End 40. The Gold Hunters (from Trail of the Yukon) 49. Kazan the Wolf Dog 49. The Wolf Hunters 49. Snow Dog 51. Back to God's Country 53. Northern Patrol 54. Nikki, Wild Dog of the North (from Nomads of the North) 62, etc.

Curzon, George (1896–1976). British stage actor, in occasional films from early 30s, usually in aristocratic or sinister roles. Born in Amersham, Buckinghamshire, the grandson of the 3rd Earl Howe, he retired from the Royal Navy as a lieutenant-commander, made his stage debut at the age of 25, and was in films from 1931.

The Impassive Footman 32. Lorna Doone 35. *Young and Innocent* 37. Sexton Blake and the Hooded Terror 38. Uncle Silas 47. Harry Black 58, etc.

Cusack, Cyril (1910–1993). Diminutive Irish actor with fourteen years' Abbey Theatre experience. Film debut as child in 1917.

Odd Man Out 47. The Blue Lagoon 48. The Elusive Pimpernel 50. The Blue Veil (US) 51. Soldiers Three (US) 51. The Man Who Never Was 56. *Jacqueline* 56. The Spanish Gardener 56. Ill Met by Moonlight 57. Floods of Fear 58. Shake Hands with the Devil 59. A Terrible Beauty 59. The Waltz of the Toreadors 62. Eighty Thousand Suspects 63. The Spy Who Came in from the Cold 65. I Was Happy Here 66. *Fahrenheit 451* 66. The Taming of the Shrew 67. Oedipus the King 67. Galileo (It.) 68. David Copperfield 69. King Lear 70. Harold and Maude (US) 71. The Day of the Jackal 73. The Homecoming 73. The Abdication 74. Execution Squad 76. An Eye for an Eye 78. Strumpet City (TV) 80. Tristam and Isolt 81. True Confessions 81. Little Dorrit 87. Menace Unseen (TV) 88. My Left Foot 89. The Fool 90. Memento Mori (TV) 92. Far and Away 92. As You Like It 92, many others.

Cusack, Joan (1962–). American actress, often in comic roles. She is the sister of actor John Cusack.

My Bodyguard 80. Class 83. Grandview USA 84. Sixteen Candles 84. The Allnighter 87. Broadcast News 87. Married to the Mob 88. Stars and Bars 88. Working Girl (AAN) 88. Men Don't Leave 90. My Blue Heaven 90. The Cabinet of Dr Ramirez 91. Toys 92. Bram Stoker's Dracula 92. Addams Family Values 93. Corrina, Corrina 94. Nine Months 95. Mr Wrong 96. Two Much 96. *In & Out* (AAN) 97. Grosse Pointe Blank 97. Arlington Road 98, etc.

Cusack, John (1966–). American leading actor. Born in Evanston, Illinois, he began as a child in theatre in Chicago and in commercials. He is co-founder of the production company New Crime.

Class 83. Grandview USA 84. Sixteen Candles 84. Stand by Me 86. Broadcast News 87. Eight Men Out 88. Fat Man and Little Boy/Shadow Makers 89. Say Anything 89. The Grifters 90. True Colors 91. Shadows and Fog 91. Roadside Prophets 92. Bob Roberts 92. Map of the Human Heart 92. Money for Nothing 93. Bullets over Broadway 94. Floundering 94. The Road to Wellville 94. City Hall 96. *Grosse Pointe Blank* (& co-w) 97. Con Air 97. Anastasia (voice) 98. The Thin Red Line 98, etc.

❝ I've been in Hollywood for ten years, and most of the dumb scripts that get made have passed my way. I haven't sold out so far, although I have made bad movies. By selling out, I mean crashing cars, pulling out guns, killing people – idiotic stories. – J.C.

Cusack, Sinead (1948–). Irish leading lady, daughter of Cyril Cusack. Married actor Jeremy Irons in 1977.

David Copperfield 69. Alfred the Great 69. Hoffman 70. Revenge 71. Tam Ling 71. The Last Remake of Beau Geste 77. Bad Behaviour 93. The Cement Garden 93. Sparrow/Storia di una Capinera 93. Uncovered 94. Stealing Beauty 96. Have Your Cake and Eat It (TV) 97. Food for Ravens (TV) 97. The Nephew 98, etc.

Cushing, Peter (1913–1994). British character actor of stage, TV and screen. His slightly fussy manner at first confined him to mild roles, but since allying himself with the Hammer horror school he has dealt firmly with monsters of all kinds.

Autobiographies: 1986, *An Autobiography*. 1988, *Past Forgetting*.

■ The Man in the Iron Mask (US) 39. A Chump at Oxford (US) 39. Vigil in the Night (US) 40. Laddie (US) 40. They Dare Not Love (US) 41. Women in War (US) 42. *Hamlet* (as Osric) 47. Moulin Rouge 53. The Black Night 54. The End of the Affair 55. Magic Fire (US) 56. Time Without Pity 56. Alexander the Great 56. *The Curse of Frankenstein* 57. Violent Playground 57. The Abominable Snowman 57. *Dracula* 58. The Revenge of Frankenstein 58. Suspect 59. The Hound of the Baskervilles 59. John Paul Jones (US) 59. The Mummy 59. Cone of Silence 60. Brides of Dracula 60. The Hellfire Club 61. Fury at Smugglers Bay 61. The Flesh and the Fiends 61. Sword of Sherwood Forest 61. The Naked Edge 61. Captain Clegg 62. *Cash on Demand* 63. The Man Who Finally Died 63. The Gorgon 64. The Evil of Frankenstein 64. Dr Terror's House of Horrors 65. She 65. Dr Who and the Daleks 65. Island of Terror 66. Daleks Invasion Earth 66. The Skull 66. Frankenstein Created Woman 67. The Blood Beast Terror 67. Some May Live (TV) 67. Night of the Big Heat 67. The Torture Garden 67. Corruption 68. Frankenstein Must Be Destroyed 69. Scream and Scream Again 69. The House that Dripped Blood 70. The Vampire Lovers 70. One More Time 70. I Monster 70. Twins of Evil 71. Incense for the Damned 71. Dracula AD 1972 72. Dr Phibes Rises Again 72. Nothing But the Night 72. *Tales from the Crypt* 72. The Creeping Flesh 73. Asylum 73. Fear in the Night 73. The Satanic Rites of Dracula 73. Frankenstein and the Monster from Hell 73. From Beyond the Grave 74. The Beast Must Die 74. Horror Express 74. Shatter 74. The Legend of the Seven Golden Vampires 74. And Now the Screaming Starts 74. Madhouse 74. The Ghoul 75. Legend of the Werewolf 75. La Grande Trouille 75. Shock Waves 75. Trial by Combat 76. The Uncanny 76. The Devil's Men 76. At the Earth's Core 76. Battle Flag 77. Star Wars 77. The Great Houdinis (TV) 77. Hitler's Son 78. Arabian Adventure 79. A Touch of the Sun 79. Monster Island 81. The House of Long Shadows 83. The Masks of Death (TV) (as Sherlock Holmes) 85. Biggles 86.

❝ If I played Hamlet, they'd call it a horror film. – P.C.

Custer, Bob (1898–1974) (Raymond Anthony Glenn). American leading actor in westerns, a former engineer and cowboy.

Trigger Finger 24. The Dude Cowboy 26. Cactus Trails 27. Arizona Days 29. Riders of the Rio Grande 29. Code of the West 30. Riders of the North 31. Under Texas Skies 31. Mark of the Spur 32. The Law of the Wild (serial) 34. Ambush Valley 36, many others.

Custer, George Armstrong (1839–1876). American major-general whose romantic eccentricities and foolish death at Little Big Horn have been favourite screen fodder. The screen Custers include Dustin Farnum in *Flaming Frontier* 26, Frank McGlynn in *Custer's Last Stand* 36, Ronald Reagan in *Santa Fe Trail* 40, Addison Richards in *Badlands of Dakota* 41, Errol Flynn in the large-scale Custer biopic *They Died with Their Boots On* 41, James Millican in *Warpath* 51, Sheb Wooley in *Bugles in the Afternoon* 52, Britt Lomond in *Tonka* 58, Phil Carey in *The Great Sioux Massacre* 65, Robert Shaw in *Custer of the West* 67, Leslie Nielsen in *The Plainsman* (TV) and Richard Mulligan in *Little Big Man* 70. There has also been a TV series, *The Legend of Custer*, with Wayne Maunder.

Cuthbertson, Allan (1920–1988). Australian actor in Britain, adept at supercilious roles.

Carrington VC 55. Law and Disorder 57. *Room at the Top* 58. Tunes of Glory 60. Term of Trial 62. The Informers 63. The Seventh Dawn 64. Life at the Top 65. Press for Time 66. The Winds of War (TV) 83, many others.

Cutts, Graham (1885–1958). British director, eminent in silent days.

Flames of Passion 24. Woman to Woman 26. The Rat 27. The Sign of Four 32. Aren't Men Beasts? 37. Just William 39, etc.

Cutts, Patricia (1926–1974). British child actress and leading lady. Daughter of Graham Cutts.

Self Made Lady 31. Just William's Luck 49. Your Witness 50. The Man Who Loved Redheads 55. Merry Andrew 58. The Tingler (US) 58. Private Road 71, etc.

Cybulski, Zbigniew (1927–1967). Polish leading actor.

■ *A Generation* 54. *Ashes and Diamonds* 58. The Eighth Day of the Week 59. Pociag 59. He, She or It 62. Love at Twenty 62. Silence 63. How to be Loved 63. To Love 64. Salto 65. *The Saragossa Manuscript* 65. Jowita 67.

∼ Wajda's *Everything for Sale* was inspired by his accidental death.

Czerny, Henry (1969–). Canadian leading actor, from stage and television.

Buried on Sunday 92. *The Boys of St Vincent* 93. A Man in Uniform 93. Clear and Present Danger 94. Cold Sweat 94. When Night Is Falling 95. Notes from the Underground 95. Mission: Impossible 96. The Ice Storm 97. The Girl Next Door 98, etc.

TV series: Secret Service 92–93.

Czinner, Paul (1890–1972). Hungarian producer-director, long in Britain: husband of Elisabeth Bergner. From 1955 he concentrated on films of opera and ballet, using multiple cameras.

Der Traumende Mund 32. Catherine the Great 33. Escape Me Never 35. As You Like It 36. Dreaming Lips 37. Stolen Life 39. The Bolshoi Ballet 55. The Royal Ballet 59. Der Rosenkavalier 61. Romeo and Juliet 66, etc.

D

Da Costa, Morton (1914–1989) (Morton Tecosky).
American director of stage musicals and three films.
■ Auntie Mame 58. *The Music Man* 62. Island of Love 64.

Da Silva, Howard (1909–1986) (Harold Silverblatt).
Tough, suspicious-looking American character actor with stage experience. Graduated from bit parts to a peak in the late 40s, then had McCarthy trouble.
Abe Lincoln in Illinois 40. The Sea Wolf 41. The Big Shot 43. *The Lost Weekend* 45. The Blue Dahlia 46. Blaze of Noon 47. Unconquered 47. They Live by Night 48. The Great Gatsby 49. Three Husbands 50. Fourteen Hours 51. M 51. David and Lisa 62. The Outrage 65. Nevada Smith 66. '1776' 72. The Great Gatsby 74. Mommie Dearest (as Louis B. Mayer) 81, etc.

D'Abo, Olivia (1968–).
English actress in Hollywood. Born in London, she trained as a ballet dancer and appeared in television commercials as a teenager.
Conan the Destroyer 84. Mission Kill 85. Bullies 86. Flying 86. Into the Fire 87. Personal Choice 88. Beyond the Stars 89. The Spirit of 76 91. Point of No Return 93. Wayne's World 2 93. Clean Slate 94. Greedy 94. The Last Good Time 94. The Big Green 95. Kicking and Screaming 95. The Velocity of Gary 98, etc.
TV series: The Wonder Years 88–92.

Dacascos, Mark (1964–).
Hawaiian-born karate expert and star of action movies.
American Samurai 92. Only the Strong 93. Double Dragon 94. Crying Freeman 95. Island of Dr Moreau 96. Redline 97. DNA 97. Boogie Boy 97. No Code of Conduct 98, etc.
TV series: The Crow: Stairway to Heaven 98– .

Dade, Frances (1910–1968).
Blonde American leading actress of the early 30s, on stage from the age of 16.
Grumpy 30. Dracula 31. Seed 31. Mother's Millions 31. Pleasure 31. The She-Wolf 31. Daughter of the Dragon 31, etc.

Dade, Stephen (1909–).
British cinematographer, in films from 1927.
We'll Meet Again 42. Caravan 46. The Brothers 47. Snowbound 49. A Question of Adultery 57. Bluebeard's Ten Honeymoons 60. Zulu 64. City under the Sea 65. The Viking Queen 66, many others.

Dafoe, Willem (1955–).
American leading actor with powerful presence. Born in Appleton, Wisconsin, he studied for a time at the University of Wisconsin before joining a theatre group in Milwaukee, later becoming a founder-member of the Wooster Group, an experimental theatre company.
Heaven's Gate 80. The Loveless 81. New York Nights 82. The Hunger 83. Streets of Fire 84. Roadhouse 66 84. To Live and Die in L.A. 85. Platoon (AAN) 86. The Hitchhiker I (TV) 87. Off Limits/Saigon 88. The Last Temptation of Christ 88. Mississippi Burning 88. Born on the Fourth of July 89. Triumph of the Spirit 89. Cry-Baby 90. Wild at Heart 90. Flight of the Intruder 91. Light Sleeper 91. White Sands 92. Faraway, So Close!/In Weiter Ferne, So Nah 93. Body of Evidence 93. Tom and Viv 94. Night and the Moment 94. Clear and Present Danger 94. The English Patient 96. Basquiat 96. Speed 2: Cruise Control 97. Lulu on the Bridge 98. New Rose Hotel 98. Affliction 98, etc.

D'Agostino, Albert S. (1893–1970).
American art director, in Hollywood from early silent days; with RKO 1936–58.
The Raven 35. The Werewolf of London 35. Dracula's Daughter 36. The Magnificent Brute (AAN) 36. The Magnificent Ambersons (AAN) 42. The 7th Victim 43. Flight for Freedom (AAN) 43. The Curse of the Cat People 44. Step Lively (AAN) 44. Experiment Perilous (AAN) 44. Isle of the Dead 45. Notorious 46. Bedlam 46. The Spiral Staircase 46. Mourning Becomes Electra 48. The Thing 51. Clash by Night 52. Androcles and the Lion 52. Run of the Arrow 57, many others.

Dagover, Lil (1897–1980) (Marta Maria Liletts).
Distinguished German actress.
The Cabinet of Dr Caligari 19. Destiny 21. Dr Mabuse Der Spieler 22. Chronicles of the Grey House 24. Tartuffe 26. Hungarian Rhapsody 27. The White Devil 30. Congress Dances 31. Kreutzer Sonata 35. Fredericus 39. Die Fussganger 73. Karl May 74, etc.

Daguerre, Louis (1787–1851).
French pioneer of photography; his original copper-plated prints were known as *daguerrotypes*.

Dahl, Arlene (1924–).
Red-haired American leading lady, former model; also beauty columnist.
■ Life with Father 47. *My Wild Irish Rose* 47. The Bride Goes Wild 48. A Southern Yankee 48. Reign of Terror 49. Scene of the Crime 49. Ambush 49. The Outriders 50. Three Little Words 50. Watch the Birdie 50. Inside Straight 51. No Questions Asked 51. Caribbean 52. Jamaica Run 53. Desert Legion 53. Sangaree 53. The Diamond Queen 53. Here Come the Girls 54. Woman's World 54. Bengal Brigade 54. Slightly Scarlet 56. Wicked as They Come (GB) 56. Fortune is a Woman (GB) 57. *Journey to the Centre of the Earth* 59. Kisses for My President 64. The Land Raiders 69. The Road to Khatmandu 69. Night of the Warrior 91.
TV series: One Life to Live 82. Night of the Warrior 91.
❝ With enthusiasm anything is possible. – *A.D.*
I considered the years in Hollywood nothing but an interim. What I always wanted was to be a musical comedy star. – *A.D.*

Dahl, John (1956–).
American director and screenwriter.
Kill Me Again (wd) 89. Red Rock West (wd) 93. *The Last Seduction* (d) 94. Unforgettable 96. Rounders 98.
❝ Film noir is endlessly fascinating to me. I'm a movie buff, and I like to make films that movie fans like. – *J.D.*
It's only in the last thirty years that we've had all these Hollywood movies where they desperately want you to fall in love with the main character. I mean, who in a Shakespearean play did you ever want to take home and have dinner with? They were brooding, upset, frustrated, twisted, neurotic people. – *J.D.*

Dahl, Roald (1916–1990).
Norwegian writer of British adoption; switched from children's books to macabre short stories. He was married to actress Patricia Neal (1953–83).
You Only Live Twice 67. Chitty Chitty Bang Bang 69. Willy Wonka and the Chocolate Factory 70. Danny the Champion of the World (oa) 89. The Witches (oa) 90, etc.
TV series (which he also introduced): *Roald Dahl's Tales of the Unexpected* 79.

Dahlbeck, Eva (1920–).
Swedish actress, often in Ingmar Bergman's films.
Waiting Women 52. The Village (GB) 53. Smiles of a Summer Night 55. So Close to Life 61. Now About These Women 64. Loving Couples 64. Les Creatures 65. The Red Mantle 67. People Meet 69, etc.

Dahlquist, Åke (1901–1991).
Swedish cinematographer who helped Ingrid Bergman on her way to stardom by photographing her sympathetically in six of her early films. He also photographed the screen test that took Greta Garbo to Hollywood.
Swedenheilms 35. The Count of the Old Town/Munkbrogreven 35. Intermezzo 37. Dollar 38. A Woman's Face/En Kvinnas Ansikte 38. June Night/Juninatten 40. Ride Tonight!/Rid i Natt! 42. The Talisman/Galgmannen 45. The Song of the Scarlet Flower/Sangen Om Den Eldroda Blömman 56. The Doll 62. Carmilla 68. The Man from the Other Side/Mannen Fran Andra Sidan 72, many others.

Dailey, Dan (1914–1978).
Tall, affable American actor-dancer with wide experience in vaudeville and cabaret. Born in New York City, he began in minstrel shows as a child and was on Broadway in the mid-30s. He was at his most successful and popular in musicals, particularly when teamed with Betty GRABLE. In the early 50s various problems – a marital break-up, heavy drinking and transvestism – led to a breakdown, and he spent four months in a psychiatric hospital. He later enjoyed some success on television and returned to perform in the theatre and nightclubs. After a fall from a stage in the mid-70s left him slightly crippled, he retired and became reclusive and once more drank heavily. He was married and divorced four times and had one son, who committed suicide in 1975 at the age of 28.
The Mortal Storm 40. Dulcy 40. Ziegfeld Girl 41. Moon over Her Shoulder 41. Lady Be Good 41. Panama Hattie 42. Give Out Sisters 42. *Mother Wore Tights* 47. *Give My Regards to Broadway* 48. You Were Meant for Me 48. When My Baby Smiles at Me (AAN) 48. Chicken Every Sunday 49. My Blue Heaven 50. *When Willie Comes Marching Home* 50. A Ticket to Tomahawk 50. I Can Get It for You Wholesale 51. Call Me Mister 51. Pride of St Louis 51. What Price Glory? 52. Meet Me at The Fair 53. There's No Business Like Show Business 54. *It's Always Fair Weather* 55. Meet Me in Las Vegas 56. *The Best Things in Life are Free* 56. The Wings of Eagles 56. Oh Men, Oh Women 57. The Wayward Bus 57. Pepe 60. Hemingway's Adventures of a Young Man 62. The Private Files of J. Edgar Hoover 77, many others.
TV series: The Four Just Men 59. The Governor and J.J. 69. Faraday and Company 73.

Dainton, Patricia (1930–).
British leading lady who started as a teenager.
Don't Ever Leave Me 49. The Dancing Years 50. Castle in the Air 52. Operation Diplomat 54. The Passing Stranger 57. Witness in the Dark 60, etc.

Dalby, Amy (1888–1969).
British character actress who normally on screen played ageing spinsters.
The Wicked Lady 45. The Man Upstairs 57. The Lamp in Assassin Mews 62. *The Secret of My Success* 65. Who Killed the Cat? 66. The Spy with a Cold Nose 67, etc.

Dale, Charles (1881–1971) (Charles Marks).
American vaudevillian who, with Joe Smith (c. 1884–1981), made up Smith and Dale, the inspiration for *The Sunshine Boys*.
■ Manhattan Parade 31. The Heart of New York 32. Two Tickets to Broadway 51.

Dale, Esther (1885–1961).
American character actress usually a motherly soul, nurse or grandma.
Crime without Passion 34. Curly Top 35. Fury 36. Dead End 37. Prison Farm 38. Tell No Tales 39. The Mortal Storm 40. Back Street 41. North Star 43. Margie 44. Stolen Life 46. The Egg and I 47. Ma and Pa Kettle 49. No Man of Her Own 50. Ma and Pa Kettle at the Fair 52. The Oklahoman 57, many others.

Dale, Jim (1935–) (James Smith).
Cheerful English singer and songwriter turned light comedian and a member of the Carry On team. Born in Rothwell, Northamptonshire, he trained as a dancer, began as a comedian in the early 50s, and first came to notice on TV rock shows as a performer and host, with several hit records in the late 50s. He turned to acting in the 60s, enjoying his greatest success in the theatre, both with the National Theatre Company and notably in the acrobatic title role of the musical *Barnum*. He is now resident in the USA. He was nominated for an Oscar for writing the lyrics to the title tune for *Georgy Girl* 64.
Raising the Wind 62. Carry On Spying 64. Carry On Cleo 65. The Big Job 65. Carry On Cowboy 66. Carry On Screaming 66. Lock Up Your Daughters 69. *The National Health* 73. Digby 73. Joseph Andrews 77. *Pete's Dragon* 77. Bloodshy 79. The Spaceman and King Arthur 79. Scandalous 84. Adventures of Huckleberry Finn 85. Carry On Columbus 92. The Hunchback of Notre Dame (TV) 97, etc.

Dalen, Zale (1947–).
Canadian director, born in the Philippines.
Skip Tracer 77. Hounds of Nôtre Dame 80. Hollywood North 87. Terminal City Ricochet 90. Expect No Mercy 95, etc.

Daley, Cass (1915–1975) (Catherine Dailey).
American comedienne whose shouted songs and acrobatic contortions were a feature of several light musicals of the 40s.
The Fleet's In 41. Star Spangled Rhythm 42. Crazy House 43. Out of This World 45. Ladies' Man 46. Here Comes the Groom 51. Red Garters 54. The Spirit Is Willing 67, etc.

Dali, Salvador (1904–1989).
Spanish surrealist painter who collaborated with Luis Buñuel in making two controversial films: *Un Chien Andalou* 29 and *L'Age d'Or* 30. Later designed the dream sequence for *Spellbound* 45.
❝ His contribution to Mediterranean culture is as great as Warhol's to Anglo-Saxon culture. – *Bigas Luna*

Dalio, Marcel (1900–1983) (Israel Mosche Blauschild).
Dapper French comedy actor, frequently in Hollywood.
La Grande Illusion 37. Pépé le Moko 37. *La Règle du Jeu* 39. Unholy Partners 41. Casablanca 42. The Song of Bernadette 43. Temptation Harbour (GB) 46. On the Riviera 51. *The Happy Time* 52. The Snows of Kilimanjaro 52. Lucky Me 54. Sabrina 54. Miracle in the Rain 56. Pillow Talk 59. Can Can 59. Jessica 62. Wild and Wonderful 63. Lady L 65. The 25th Hour 67. How Sweet It Is 68. Catch 22 70. The Mad Adventures of Rabbi Jacob 73. L'Ombre de Château 76. Brigade Mondaine 80, many others.

Dall, Evelyn (c. 1914–).
American nightclub singer who appeared in some British film extravaganzas of the 40s.
He Found a Star 41. King Arthur Was a Gentleman 42. Miss London Ltd 43. Time Flies 44, etc.

Dall, John (1918–1971).
American stage leading man; played in occasional films.
■ For the Love of Mary 45. *The Corn Is Green* (AAN). Something in the Wind 47. *Rope* 48. Another Part of the Forest 48. Gun Crazy 49. The Man Who Cheated Himself 50. Spartacus 60. Atlantis the Lost Continent 61.

Dalle, Béatrice (1965–).
French leading actress.
Betty Blue 86. Charlie Spencer 86. The Witches' Sabbath/La Visione del Sabba 88. Les Bois Noirs 89. Chimère 89. The Beautiful Story/La Belle Histoire 91. Night on Earth 91. La Fille de l'Air 92. I Can't Sleep/J'ai Pas Sommeil 94. Six Days Six Nights/A la Folie 94. Desire 96, etc.

Dallesandro, Joe (1948–).
American actor who gained fame as the object of desire in Andy Warhol's films.
The Loves of Ondine 67. Flesh 68. Lonesome Cowboys 68. Trash 70. Heat 72. Andy Warhol's Frankenstein 73. Blood for Dracula 74. The Gardener 74. Black Moon 75. Seeds of Evil 76. Merry Go Round 83. The Cotton Club 84. Critical Condition 87. Sunset 88. Private War 89. The Hollywood Detective (TV) 89. Cry-Baby 90. Double Revenge 90. Wild Orchid II: Two Shades of Blue 92. Sugar Hill 93. LA without a Map (GB/Fr./Fin.) 98, etc.
❝ I don't know whether I'll ever become a household name in America, but my big thing is to land that television series that goes 50 episodes and you sit at home and collect the cheques. – *J.D. in 1993*

D'Almeida, Neville (1941–).
Brazilian director who spent some time studying film in the United States.
Jardin de Guerra 70. Lady on the Bus/A Dama de Lotaçao 78. Rio Babilonia 82, etc.

Dalrymple, Ian (1903–1989).
British screenwriter, producer and director. He was educated at Cambridge University and worked as an editor and supervising editor at Gaumont-British and Gainsborough Pictures from the late 20s to the mid-30s before becoming a screenwriter. In the 40s, he was a producer for the Crown Film Unit, producing wartime documentaries, then worked for MGM-Korda productions before setting up his own company, Wessex Productions, as part of Independent Producers, working at Pinewood Studios. Married twice.
The Good Companions (co-w) 33. Jury's Evidence (w) 35. South Riding (co-w) 37. Storm in a Teacup (wd) 37. Action for Slander (co-w) 37. *Pygmalion* (co-w) (AA) 38. The Citadel (co-w) 38. The Divorce of Lady X (co-w) 38. A Window in London (co-w) 39. Q Planes (co-w) 39. French without Tears (co-w) 39. *London Can Take It* (p) 40. Old Bill and Son (co-w, d) 41. Pimpernel Smith (co-w) 41. *Target for Tonight* (p) 41. *Coastal Command* (p) 42. The Woman in the Hall (p, co-w) 47. Esther Waters (p, d) 47. Once a Jolly Swagman (p) 48. Dear Mr Prohack (p, co-w) 49. All Over the Town (p) 49. Family Portrait (p) 50. The Wooden Horse (p) 50. The Heart of the Matter (p, co-w) 53. Three Cases of Murder (p, co-w) 54. Raising a Riot (p, co-w) 55. A Hall in Korea (co-w) 56. The Admirable Crichton (p) 57. A Cry from the Streets (p) 58. Mix Me a Person (co-w) 61, etc.
❝ Ian is one of the great men of the British cinema. – *Michael Powell*

Dalton, Abby (1932–).
American actress, a former model who first appeared in low-budget teen movies in the late 50s.
Viking Woman and the Sea Serpent 57. Rock All Night 57. Stakeout on Dope Street 58. Cole Younger, Gunfighter 58. Girls on the Loose 58. The Plainsman 66. A Whale of a Tale 76. Roller Blade Warriors: Taken by Force 90. Cyber-Tracker 93. Buck and the Magic Bracelet 97, etc.
TV series: Hennesey 59–62. The Joey Bishop Show 62–65. Falcon Crest 81–86.

Dalton, Audrey (1934–).
British leading lady in Hollywood.
My Cousin Rachel 52. The Girls of Pleasure Island 53. Titanic 53. Casanova's Big Night 54. The Prodigal 55. Separate Tables 58. Mr Sardonicus 62. The Bounty Killer 65, etc.

Dalton, Dorothy (1894–1972).
American silent screen leading lady with stage experience.
The Disciple 14. Black is White 20. Moran of the Lady Letty 22. The Crimson Challenge 22. Fogbound 23. The Moral Sinner 24. The Lone Wolf 24, etc.

Dalton, Timothy (1946–).
Saturnine British stage actor in occasional films.
The Lion in Winter 68. *Wuthering Heights* 70. Mary Queen of Scots 71. Lady Caroline Lamb 72. Sextette 78. Agatha 79. Flash Gordon 80. Chanel Solitaire 81. Mistral's Daughter (TV) 84. Florence Nightingale (TV) 84. The Doctor and the Devils 85. Sins (TV) 85. *The Living Daylights* (as James Bond) 87. Hawks 88. Licence to Kill 89. Brenda Starr 90. The King's Whore 90. The Rocketeer 91. Naked in New York 93. Scarlett (TV) 94. The Beautician and the Beast 97, etc.

Daltrey, Roger (1944–).
British rock singer, composer, actor and producer. The lead singer with The Who, he was given dramatic roles by Ken Russell.
Tommy 74. Lisztomania 75. The Legacy 79. McVicar 80. Murder: Ultimate Grounds for Divorce 85. Mack the Knife 89. Buddy's Song (& p, m) 90. Teen Agent 91. Lightning Jack 94. Vampirella (TV) 96. Pirate Tales (TV) 97. Like It Is 98, etc.
❝ Of course, chicks keep popping up. When you're in a hotel, a pretty young lady makes life bearable. – *R.D.*

Daly, James (1918–1978).
American stage actor; film appearances rare.
■ The Court Martial of Billy Mitchell 55. The Young Stranger 57. I Aim at the Stars 60. Planet of the Apes 68. The Big Bounce 68. The Five Man Army 69. Wild in the Sky 72. The Resurrection of Zachary Wheeler 73.
TV series: Foreign Intrigue 53–54. *Medical Center* 69–76.

Daly, John (1937–).
British independent producer and distributor, who moved to America in the 80s. A former journalist and actor, and David Hemmings's manager, he founded Hemdale Film Corporation, of which he was chairman, in 1967 with Hemmings, who sold his interest four years later. Hemdale went bankrupt in 1992, with debts of more than $130m. He now heads Global Entertainment Assets Corp., a company incorporated in Antigua, specializing in the entertainment industry. In 1998 he co-founded Greenhills Films, a European-based production company.
Melody 71. Where Does It Hurt? 71. Triple Echo 72. Images 72. The Amazing Mr Blunden 72. Cattle Annie and Little Britches 80. Race for the Yankee Zephyr 81. Carbon Copy 81. Yellowbeard 83. Terminator 84. Return of the Living Dead 85. Platoon (AA) 86. At Close Range 86. Salvador 86. Hoosiers 86. The Last Emperor (AA) 87. Buster 88. Miracle Mile 89. Out Cold 89. Chattahoochee 90. Hidden Agenda 90. Bright Angel 91, etc.

Daly, Mark (1887–1957).
British character actor, on stage from 1906, in films from 1930, often as cheerful tramp.
The Private Life of Henry VIII 33. A Cuckoo in the Nest 33. The Ghost Goes West 36. Wings of the Morning 37. Next of Kin 42. Bonnie Prince Charlie 49. Lease of Life 54. The Shiralee 57, many others.

Daly, Timothy (1956–).
American actor, the son of James Daly and brother of Tyne Daly.
Diner 82. I'll Take Manhattan 87. Made in Heaven 87. Spellbinder 88. Ambush in Waco (TV) 93. Dr Jekyll and Ms Hyde 95. Denise Calls Up 95. The Associate 96. The Object of My Affection 98, etc.

Daly, Tyne (1946–).
American leading lady. She is the daughter of James Daly.
John and Mary 69. Angel Unchained 70. Heat of Anger (TV) 71. Play It as It Lays 72. The Entertainer (TV) 75. The Enforcer 76. Telefon 77. Speedtrap 77. The Women's Room (TV) 80. Zoot Suit 82. Your Place or Mine (TV) 83. Movers and Shakers 85. The Aviator 85. Tricks 97. The Student Affair 97, etc.
TV series: Cagney and Lacey 82. Christy 94–95.

D'Amato, Joe (1936–1999) (Aristide Massaccesi).
Prolific Italian director of quickie exploitation movies that reach international audiences on video-cassette. His output, made under such pseudonyms as Steve Benson, Michael Wotruba, David Hills and Kevin Mancuso, ranges from horror to fantasy and soft-core pornography, including a *Black Emanuelle* series in the 70s.
Heroes in Hell/Eroi all'Inferno 67. Kneel Bastard/Inginocchiate 72. Black Emanuelle/Emanuelle Nera 73. Emanuelle and the Last Cannibals/Emanuelle e gli Ultimi Cannibali/Trap Them and Kill Them 77. Beyond the Darkness/Buio Omega 79. Grim Reaper/Anthropophagus 81. Ator the Fighting Eagle/Ator l'Invincible 82. Ator the Invincible – the Return/Blade Master 83. 2020 Texas Gladiators/Texas 2000 84. Buried Alive 84. Quest for the Mighty Sword 90. Return from Death 91. Love Appurtenance 92, many others.
❝ I like to manipulate intestines, pieces of meat, vital organs. Is there a limit? Not at all! – *J. D'A.*
There's little doubt that sitting through one of Joe's efforts is as near to brain death as a film viewer can get. – *Stefan Jaworzyn, Shock Xpress*
His only fault, if you can call it that, is that he sees the cinema purely as a means of making money, and consequently he only puts so much effort into improving the quality of his products. – *Luigi Montefiori*

Damiani, Damiano (1922–).
Italian director.
The Empty Canvas 64. A Bullet for the General 66. Confessions of a Police Captain 71. The Tempter 74. The Genius 75. I Am Afraid 77. Goodbye and Amen 78. L'Ultimo Nome 79. Time of Jackals 80. Amityville II: The Possession 82. Attacco alla Piovra 85. The Inquiry/L'Inchiesta 87. Massacre Play/Gioco al Massacro (& co-w) 89. Angel of Death/L'Angelo con la Pistola 92, etc.

Damiano, Gerald.
American director of hard-core porn movies.
Deep Throat 73. The Devil in Miss Jones 73. The Story of Joanna 75. Let My Puppets Come 77. Throat – 12 Years After 84, etc.

Damita, Lili (1901–1994) (Lilliane Carré).
French leading lady who made a few American films and married Errol Flynn (1935–42). Her death certificate gave her age as 85.
The Rescue 28. The Bridge of San Luis Rey 29. The Cockeyed World 29. The Match King 31. This Is the Night 32. Goldie Gets Along 33. The Frisco Kid 35. L'Escadrille de la Chance (Fr.) 36, etc.

Damon, Cathryn (1933–1987).
American comedy actress who played the slightly more sensible sister in TV's *Soap*.
Friendships, Secrets and Lies (TV) 80. How to Beat The High Cost of Living 80.

Damon, Mark (1933–) (Alan Mark Harris).
American leading man in routine films, now a producer in Europe.
Between Heaven and Hell 56. The Fall of the House of Usher 60. The Young Racers 63. Anzio 68. There Is No Thirteen 77. The Choirboys (co-p only) 77, etc.

Damon, Matt (1970–) (Matthew Paige Damon).
American leading actor and screenwriter. Born in Cambridge, Massachusetts, he was educated at Harvard, leaving to pursue his career as an actor. He became a star with *Good Will Hunting*, which he wrote for himself with fellow actor Ben Affleck. He has been romantically linked with actresses Claire Danes and Minnie Driver.
Mystic Pizza 88. The Good Mother 88. Rising Son (TV) 90. School Ties 92. Geronimo: An American Legend 93. The Good Old Boys 95. Courage under Fire 96. John Grisham's The Rainmaker 97. Chasing Amy 97. *Good Will Hunting* (AAw, AANa) 97. Saving Private Ryan 98. Rounders 98, etc.
❝ For the most part, young actors in Hollywood are actors by default. They're morons. – *M.D., 1994*

Damone, Vic (1928–) (Vito Farinola).
American light leading man and singer. He was married to actress Pier Angeli (1955–59) and married singer Diahann Carroll in 1987.
Rich, Young and Pretty 51. The Strip 51. Athena 53. Deep in My Heart 55. Kismet 55. Hell to Eternity 60, etc.

Dampier, Claude (1879–1955) (Claude Cowan).
British comedian noted for nasal drawl and country yokel characterization. Long on stage and music hall.
Biography: 1978, *Claude Dampier, Mrs Gibson and Me* by Billie Carlyle (his wife and partner on the halls).
Boys Will Be Boys 35. Mr Stringfellow Says No 37. Riding High 39. Don't Take It to Heart 44. Meet Mr Malcolm 53, etc.

Damski, Mel (1946–).
American director, working mainly in television.
Yellowbeard 83. Mischief 85. Happy Together 90. Still Kicking: The Fabulous Palm Springs Follies (short) (AAN) 97, etc.

Dana, Bill (1924–).
American television comedian who used to play Mexicans.
Rossetti and Ryan (TV) 77. A Guide for the Married Woman 78. The Hungry Reunion 81. Lena's Holiday 91, etc.
TV series: The Bill Dana Show 62–65. No Soap Radio 82. Zorro and Son 83.

Dana, Leora (1923–1983).
American general-purpose actress.
3:10 to Yuma 57. Kings Go Forth 58. Some Came Running 58. Pollyanna 60. A Gathering of Eagles 63. Shoot the Moon 82, etc.

Dana, Viola (1897–1987) (Violet Flugrath).
American silent screen actress, usually in light comedy and fashionable drama.
Molly the Drummer Boy 14. Rosie O'Grady 17. A Chorus Girl's Romance 20. The Willow Tree 20. Open All Night 24. Merton of the Movies 24. Winds of Chance 25. Kosher Kitty Kelly 26. The Sisters 29, etc.

Dance, Charles (1946–).
British leading actor.
Saigon (TV) 83. *The Jewel in the Crown* (TV) 84. For Your Eyes Only 84. Plenty 86. Good Morning Babylon 86. Out on a Limb (TV) 87. The Golden Child 87. Hidden City 87. White Mischief 87. Pascali's Island 88. Alien 3 92. The Last Action Hero 93. Century 93. China Moon 94. Nanook/Kabloonak 94. Shortcut to Paradise (Sp.) 94. Michael Collins 96. Rebecca (TV) 97. In the Presence of Mine Enemies (TV) 97. Don't Go Breaking My Heart 98. Hilary and Jackie 98, etc.

Dandridge, Dorothy (1923–1965).
American leading actress and singer whose career was one of unrealized potential. Born in Cleveland, she began in films as a child, but, apart from two charismatic performances in the musicals *Carmen Jones* and *Porgy and Bess*, was to find few roles as an adult that gave her the opportunity to display her talents. She died in poverty, of an overdose of drugs. She was played by Halle Berry in the TV biopic *Dorothy Dandridge* 99. The first of her two husbands was Harold Nicholas of the Nicholas Brothers. Her lovers included director Otto Preminger and actors Curt Jurgens and Peter Lawford.
Autobiography: 1970, *Everything and Nothing*.
Biography: 1997, *Dorothy Dandridge* by Donald Bogle.
A Day at the Races 37. Lady from Louisiana 41. Drums of the Congo 42. Bright Road 52. *Carmen Jones* (AAN) 54. Island in the Sun 57. The Decks Ran Red 58. Porgy and Bess 59. Tamango 59. Moment of Danger 60, etc.

Dane, Karl (1886–1934) (Karl Daen).
Lanky Danish character actor who almost accidentally became a popular comedian at the end of the silent period, but could not survive sound. Committed suicide.
Lights of Old Broadway 25. *The Big Parade* 25.

The Scarlet Letter 26. The Red Mill 27. *Rookies* 27. Baby Mine 28. Circus Rookies 28. Alias Jimmy Valentine 28. Speedway 29. Montana Moon 30. The Big House 30. Billy the Kid 30, etc.

Daneman, Paul (1925–).
British light leading man, mainly on stage.
The Clue of the New Pin 61. Zulu 64. How I Won the War 67. Oh What a Lovely War 69, etc.
TV series: Spy Trap.

Danes, Claire (1979–).
American actress, from the stage. Born in New York, she enrolled at the Lee Strasberg Theater Institute at the age of 10 and also studied at the Professional Performing Arts School. She made her television debut at the age of 11, and first gained fame as the troubled teenager Angela Chase in the TV series My *So-Called Life*. She is currently studying at Yale University.
Little Women 94. Home for the Holidays 95. How to Make an American Quilt 95. Romeo and Juliet 96. I Love You, I Love You Not 96. To Gillian on Her 37th Birthday 96. U-Turn 97. John Grisham's The Rainmaker 97. Les Misérables 98. Polish Wedding 98. The Cherry Orchard 98. Monterey Pop 98. The Mod Squad 99. Brokedown Palace 99, etc.
TV series: My So-Called Life 94.

D'Angelo, Beverly (1953–).
American leading lady.
Every Which Way but Loose 78. Hair 79. Coal Miner's Daughter 80. Paternity 81. Honky Tonk Freeway 81. The Woo Woo Kid 87. Trading Hearts 88. High Spirits 88. Cold Front 89. National Lampoon's Christmas Vacation 89. Pacific Heights 90. Daddy's Dyin', Who's Got the Will? 90. The Miracle 90. The Pope Must Die/The Pope Must Diet 91. Lonely Hearts 91. Man Trouble 92. Lightning Jack 94. Menendez: A Killing in Beverly Hills (TV) 94. Eye for an Eye 95. Pterodactyl Woman from Beverly Hills 96. Merchants of Venus 98. American History X 98, etc.

Dangerfield, Rodney (1921–) (Jacob Cohen).
American comedian and screenwriter.
The Projectionist 71. Caddyshack 80. Easy Money (& w) 83. Back to School (& story) 86. Moving 88. Rover Dangerfield 91. Ladybugs 92. Natural Born Killers 94. Meet Wally Sparks (& co-w) 97, etc.

Daniel, Rod.
American director.
Teen Wolf 85. Stranded (TV) 86. Like Father Like Son 87. K-9 89. The Super 91. Ace Ventura: Pet Detective 92. Beethoven's 2nd 93, etc.

Daniell, Henry (1894–1963).
Incisive, cold-eyed British stage actor, a popular Hollywood villain of the 30s and 40s.
■ Jealousy 29. The Awful Truth 29. The Last of the Lone Wolf 30. Path of Glory 34. The Unguarded Hour 36. *Camille* 36. Under Cover of Night 37. The Thirteenth Chair 37. The Firefly 37. Madame X 37. Holiday 38. Marie Antoinette 38. The Private Lives of Elizabeth and Essex 39. We Are Not Alone 39. All This and Heaven Too 40. *The Sea Hawk* 40. The Great Dictator 40. *The Philadelphia Story* 40. A Woman's Face 41. Dressed to Kill 41. Four Jacks and a Jill 41. The Feminine Touch 41. Castle in the Desert 42. Random Harvest 42. Sherlock Holmes and the Voice of Terror 42. Reunion in France 42. The Great Impersonation 42. Nightmare 42. Mission to Moscow 43. *Sherlock Holmes in Washington* 43. Watch on the Rhine 43. Jane Eyre 43. *The Suspect* 44. The Chicago Kid 45. Hotel Berlin 45. The Woman in Green 45. *The Body Snatcher* 45. Captain Kidd 45. The Bandit of Sherwood Forest 46. Song of Love 47. The Exile 47. Siren of Atlantis 48. Wake of the Red Witch 48. The Secret of St Ives 49. Buccaneer's Girl 50. The Egyptian 54. The Prodigal 55. Diane 55. The Man in the Grey Flannel Suit 56. Lust for Life 56. Les Girls 57. The Story of Mankind 57. The Sun Also Rises 57. Witness for the Prosecution 57. Mr Cory 57. From the Earth to the Moon 58. The Four Skulls of Jonathan Drake 59. Voyage to the Bottom of the Sea 61. The Comancheros 61. Madison Avenue 62. The Notorious Landlady 62. Five Weeks in a Balloon 62. The Chapman Report 62. My Fair Lady 64.
Famous Line (*The Philadelphia Story*): 'I understand we understand each other.'

Daniels, Bebe (1901–1971) (Virginia Daniels).
American leading lady of the silent screen. Film debut at seven; played opposite Harold Lloyd and became a popular star; later married Ben Lyon, moved to Britain and appeared with their family on radio and TV.
Male and Female 19. Why Change Your Wife? 20. The Affairs of Anatol 21. Pink Gods 22. Unguarded Women 24. Monsieur Beaucaire 24. Campus Flirt 26. She's a Sheik 27. Rio Rita 29. Alias French Gertie 30. Reaching for the Moon 30. The Maltese Falcon 31. Forty-Second Street 33. Counsellor at Law 33. The Return of Carol Deane 35. Hi Gang (GB) 40. Life with the Lyons (GB) 53. The Lyons in Paris (GB) 55, etc.

Daniels, Gary.
British-born actor in action movies.
Ring of Fire 91. Firepower 93. Knights 93. White Tiger 96. Fist of the North Star 96. American Streetfighter 96. Bloodmoon 97. American Streetfighter 2: The Full Impact 97, etc.

Daniels, Jeff (1955–).
Clean-cut American leading actor.
Ragtime 81. Terms of Endearment 83. The Purple Rose of Cairo 85. Something Wild 86. Radio Days 87. The House on Carroll Street 88. Love Hurts 89. Arachnophobia 90. Welcome Home, Roxy Carmichael 91. The Butcher's Wife 91. There Goes the Neighborhood/Paydirt 92. Gettysburg 93. Speed 94. 101 Dalmatians 96. Fly Away Home 97. Pleasantville 98, etc.

Daniels, Mickey (1914–1970).
American actor, one of the original kids in the Our Gang comedies of the 20s. He retired in the early 40s to work as an engineer.
This Day and Age 33. Magnificent Obsession 35. The Great Ziegfeld 36, etc.

Daniels, Phil (1958–).

English character actor, best known for his role as a moody mod rebel in *Quadrophenia* 79.
The Class of Miss McMichael 78. Scum 79. Zulu Dawn 79. Breaking Glass 80. Meantime (TV) 81. Number One 84. Billy the Kid and the Green Baize Vampire 85. The Bride 85. Bad Behaviour 93. Sex and Chocolate (TV) 97. Still Crazy 98, etc.
TV series: The Molly Wopsies 76. Four Idle Hands 76. Sunnyside Farm 97. Holding On 97.

Daniels, William (1895–1970).
Distinguished American cinematographer, associated with the films of Greta Garbo.
■ Foolish Wives 21. Merry Go Round (co-ph) 23. Helen's Babies (co-ph) 24. *Greed* (co-ph) 25. Women and Gold 25. The Merry Widow (co-ph) 25. Bardelys the Magnificent 26. The Boob 26. Dance Madness (co-ph) 26. *Flesh and the Devil* 26. Money Talks 26. Monte Carlo 26. The Temptress (co-ph) 26. The Torrent 26. Altars of Desire 27. Captain Salvation 27. Love 27. On Ze Boulevard 27. Tillie the Toiler 27. The Actress 28. Bringing Up Father 28. Dream of Love 28. Lady of Chance 28. The Latest from Paris 28. The Mysterious Lady 28. Sally's Shoulders 28. A Woman of Affairs 28. *The Kiss* 29. The Last of Mrs Cheyney 29. Their Own Desire 29. The Trial of Mary Dugan 29. Wild Orchids 29. Wise Girls 29. Anna Christie 30. Montana Moon 30. Romance 30. Strictly Unconventional 30. Strangers May Kiss 31. The Great Meadow 31. Inspiration 31. A Free Soul 31. Susan Lenox 31. *Mata Hari* 32. Lovers Courageous 32. Grand Hotel 32. As You Desire Me 32. Skyscraper Souls 32. Rasputin and the Empress 33. The White Sister 33. Dinner at Eight 33. The Stranger's Return 33. Broadway to Hollywood 33. Christopher Bean 33. *Queen Christina* 33. The Barretts of Wimpole Street 34. The Painted Veil 34. Naughty Marietta 35. *Anna Karenina* 35. Rendezvous 35. Rose Marie 36. Romeo and Juliet 36. *Camille* 36. Personal Property 37. Broadway Melody of 1938 37. Double Wedding 37. The Last Gangster 37. Beg Borrow or Steal 37. Marie Antoinette 38. Three Loves Has Nancy 38. Dramatic School 38. Idiot's Delight 39. Stronger Than Desire 39. Ninotchka 39. Another Thin Man 39. The Shop Around the Corner 40. The Mortal Storm 40. New Moon 40. So Ends Our Night 41. Back Street 41. They Met in Bombay 41. Shadow of the Thin Man 41. Dr Kildare's Victory 41. *Keeper of the Flame* 42. Girl Crazy 42. Brute Force 47. Lured 47. *The Naked City* (AA) 48. For the Love of Mary 48. Family Honeymoon 48. The Life of Riley 49. Illegal Entry 49. Abandoned 49. The Gal who Took the West 49. Woman in Hiding 49. Winchester 73 50. Harvey 50. Deported 50. Thunder on the Hill 51. Bright Victory 51. The Lady Pays Off 51. When in Rome 52. Pat and Mike 52. Glory Alley 52. Plymouth Adventure 52. Never Wave at a WAC 53. Forbidden 53. Thunder Bay 53. *The Glenn Miller Story* 53. War Arrow 54. The Far Country 54. Six Bridges to Cross 55. Foxfire 55. The Shrike 55. Strategic Air Command 55. The Girl Rush 55. The Benny Goodman Story 55. Away All Boats (co-ph) 56. The Unguarded Moment 56. Istanbul 56. Night Passage 57. Interlude 57. My Man Godfrey 57. Voice in the Mirror 57. Cat on a Hot Tin Roof 58. Some Came Running 59. Stranger in My Arms 59. A Hole in the Head 60. Never So Few 60. Can Can 60. Ocean's Eleven 60. All the Fine Young Cannibals 60. Come September 61. Jumbo 62. How the West was Won (co-ph) 63. Come Blow Your Horn 63. The Prize 63. Robin and the Seven Hoods (& p) 64. Von Ryan's Express 65. Marriage on the Rocks 65. Assault on a Queen (& p) 66. In Like Flint 67. Valley of the Dolls 67. The Impossible Years 68. Marlowe 68. The Maltese Bippy 69. Move 70.
❝ We try to tell the story with light, and the director tells it with action. – *W.D.*

Daniels, William (1927–).
Dapper American actor, much on television. Born in Brooklyn, New York, he began working as a child with a family song-and-dance act and made his Broadway stage debut at the age of 16. He came to films and television in mid-career, where he was best known for his roles as heart surgeon Dr Mark Craig in *St Elsewhere*, for which he won two Emmys as best actor, and as the voice of the car in *Knight Rider*. Married actress Bonnie Bartlett.
Family Honeymoon 49. A Thousand Clowns 65. The President's Analyst 67. *The Graduate* 67. Two for the Road 67. Marlowe 69. *1776* (as John Adams) 72. The Parallax View 74. Black Sunday 77. The One and Only 78. Sunburn 79. The Blue Lagoon 80. All Night Long 81. Reds 81. Blind Date 87. Her Alibi 89. Magic Kid II 94. The Lottery (TV) 96, many others.
TV series: St Elsewhere 82–88. Knight Rider (voice of KITT) 82–86. Boy Meets World 93.

Daniely, Lisa (1930–).
Anglo-French leading lady.
Lili Marlene 50. Hindle Wakes 51. The Wedding of Lili Marlene 53. Tiger by the Tail 55. The Vicious Circle 57. An Honourable Murder 60. The Lamp in Assassin Mews 62. Goldeneye: The Secret Life of Ian Fleming (TV) 89, etc.

Danischewsky, Monja (1911–1994).
Russian writer-producer, in Britain since 20s. Publicist and writer for Ealing 1938–48. Produced *Whisky Galore* 48. *The Galloping Major* 50. *The Battle of the Sexes* 61, etc. Screenplays, *Topkapi* 64. *Mister Moses* 65.
Autobiography: 1966, *White Russian, Red Face*. 1972, *Out of My Mind*.

Dankworth, John (1927–).
British bandleader who has written scores. Married singer Dame Cleo Laine in 1958.
The Criminal 60. Saturday Night and Sunday Morning 60. The Servant 64. Return from the Ashes 65. Accident 67. The Last Grenade 69. Ten Rillington Place 70. Loser Take All 89, etc.

Danner, Blythe (1944–).
American young actress of the 70s.
Dr Cook's Garden (TV) 70. 1776 72. To Kill a Clown 72. Lovin' Molly 74. The Last of the Belles (TV) 74. Sidekicks (TV) 74. Hearts of the West 75. Futureworld 76. A Love Affair: The Eleanor and Lou Gehrig Story (TV) 78. Are You in the House Alone? (TV) 78. *Too Far to Go* (TV) 79. The Great Santini 80. Man, Woman and Child 83. Brighton Beach Memoirs 86. One Art 87. Another Woman 88. Alice 90. Mr & Mrs Bridge 90. The Prince of Tides 91. Husbands and Wives 92. Oldest Living Confederate Widow Tells All (TV) 94. Homage 95. The Myth of Fingerprints 97. Mad City 97. A Call to Remember (TV) 97. The X Files Movie 98. No Looking Back 98. The Proposition 98, etc.
TV series: Adam's Rib 73.

Danning, Sybil (1950–).
Blonde Austrian actress, in glamorous roles in forgettable films.
Swedish Love Games/Urlaubsreport 71. Bluebeard 72. The Three Musketeers 73. The Four Musketeers 74. The Prince and the Pauper 77. Meteor 79. Battle beyond the Stars 80. The Salamander 81. Jungle Warriors 84. The Seven Magnificent Gladiators 85. Howling II . . . Your Sister Is a Werewolf 86. Private Property/Young Lady Chatterley II 86. Reform School Girls 86. The Tomb 86. Warrior Queen 87. Amazon Women on the Moon 87, etc.
❝ What I am is the new dream girl – one who has both body and intelligence. – *S.D.*

Dano, Royal (1922–1994).
American general-purpose supporting actor.
■ Undercover Girl 49. Under the Gun 50. *The Red Badge of Courage* (as The Tattered Man) 51. Flame of Araby 51. Bend of the River 52. Johnny Guitar 54. The Far Country 55. The Trouble with Harry 55. Tribute to a Bad Man 55. Santiago 56. Moby Dick 56. Tension at Table Rock 56. Crime of Passion 57. Trooper Hook 57. All Mine to Give 57. Man in the Shadow 57. Saddle the Wind 57. Handle with Care 58. Man of the West 58. Never Steal Anything Small 59. These Thousand Hills 59. Hound Dog Man 59. Face of Fire 59. Huckleberry Finn 60. Cimarron 60. Posse from Hell 61. King of Kings 61. Savage Sam 61. Seven Faces of Dr Lao 64. Gunpoint 66. The Dangerous Days of Kiowa Jones (TV) 66. Welcome to Hard Times 67. The Last Challenge 67. Day of the Evil Gun 68. If He Hollers Let Him Go 68. The Undefeated 69. Backtrack (TV) 69. Run Simon Run (TV) 70. Moon of the Wolf (TV) 72. The Great Northfield Minnesota Raid 72. The Culpepper Cattle Company 72. Howzer 72. Ace Eli and Rodger of the Skies 73. Cahill 73. Electra Glide in Blue 73. Big Bad Mama 74. The Wild Party 75. Huckleberry Finn (TV) 75. Capone 75. Manhunter (TV) 76. Drum 76. Messiah of Evil 76. The Outlaw Josey Wales 76. The Killer Inside Me 76. Murder in Peyton Place (TV) 77. Donner Pass (TV) 78. Strangers (TV) 79. Take This Job and Shove It 81. Hammett 82. Something Wicked This Way Comes 83. The Right Stuff 83. Teachers 84. Red-Headed Stranger 86. Ghoulies II 88. Once Upon a Texas Train/Texas Guns 88. Cocaine Wars 89. Spaced Invaders 90. The Dark Half 93.

Danova, Cesare (1926–1992).
Italian leading man, often in Hollywood.
The Captain's Daughter 47. The Three Corsairs 52. Don Juan 55. The Man Who Understood Women 59. Cleopatra 63. Viva Las Vegas 64. Chamber of Horrors 66. Che 69. Tentacles 77, etc.
TV series: Garrison's Gorillas 67.

Danson, Ted (1947–).
Tall, craggy American leading man. Married actress Mary STEENBURGEN.
The Onion Field 79. Body Heat 81. Creepshow 82. Something about Amelia (TV) 84. Little Treasure 85. Just between Friends 85. A Fine Mess 86. Three Men and a Baby 87. Cousins 89. Dad 89. Three Men and a Little Lady 90. Made in America 93. Getting Even with Dad 94. Pontiac Moon 94. Gulliver's Travels (title role, TV) 96. Loch Ness 96. Saving Private Ryan 98, etc.
TV series: Somerset 74–76. *Cheers* 82–93. Ink 96–97. Becker 98– .

Dante, Joe (1946–).
American director, associated with Steven Spielberg. He is a former journalist who began his career cutting trailers for Roger Corman's movies.
Hollywood Boulevard (co-d) 76. Piranha 78. The Howling 80. Twilight Zone – the Movie (co-d) 83. *Gremlins* 84. Explorers 85. Amazon Women on the Moon (co-d) 87. Innerspace 87. The 'burbs 89. Gremlins II: The New Batch 90. Sleepwalkers (a) 92. *Matinee* 93. Picture Windows (TV) 95. The Second Civil War (TV) 97. Small Soldiers 98, etc.
❝ We did all kinds of things in trailers to help sell films. We had a famous exploding helicopter shot from one of those Filipino productions that we'd cut in every time a trailer was too dull because that was always exciting. – *J.D.*

Dante, Michael (1935–) (Ralph Vitti).
American 'second lead' with a screen tendency to villainy.
Fort Dobbs 58. Westbound 59. Seven Thieves

60. Kid Galahad 62. The Naked Kiss 64. Harlow 65. The Farmer 77. Cruise Missile 78. Beyond Evil 80. The Big Score 83. Cage 89. Crazy Horse and Custer – the Untold Story 90, etc.

Dantine, Helmut (1917–1982).
Lean good-looking Austrian actor, in US from 1938. Latterly an executive with the Joseph M. Schenck organization.
International Squadron 41. *Mrs Miniver* 41. Northern Pursuit 43. Passage to Marseilles 44. Hotel Berlin 45. Escape in the Desert 45. Shadow of a Woman 46. Whispering City 48. Call Me Madam 53. Stranger from Venus (GB) 54. War and Peace 56. Fraulein 57. Thundering Jets (d only) 58. Operation Crossbow 65. Garcia 74, etc.

Danton, Ray (1931–1992).
Tall, dark American leading man with radio experience.
Chief Crazy Horse 52. The Spoilers 55. I'll Cry Tomorrow 55. *Too Much Too Soon* 58. *The Rise and Fall of Legs Diamond* 59. Ice Palace 60. A Fever in the Blood 61. *The George Raft Story* 61. The Chapman Report 62. The Longest Day 62. Sandokan the Great (It.) 63. Tiger of Terror (It.) 64. The Spy Who Went into Hell (Ger.) 65. The Deathmaster (d only) 72. The Centrefold Girls 74, etc.
TV series: The Alaskans 59–60.

D'Antoni, Philip (1929–).
American producer for cinema and TV.
The French Connection (AA) 71. The Connection (TV) 73. Mr Inside Mr Outside (TV) 73. The Seven-Ups (& d) 74, etc.

Danvers-Walker, Bob (1907–1990).
A radio and television announcer, he was the distinctive voice of British Pathé newsreels from 1940–70.

The Danziger Brothers (Edward and Harry).
American producers who after making *Jigsaw* 46 and two or three other films came to England, set up New Elstree Studios and spent 15 years producing hundreds of second features and TV episodes, hardly any worth recalling. Their reputation in the industry was not high. When working on a film for the exploitation director-producer Harry Alan Towers, an actor was told to crouch down. Instructed to crouch lower, he protested that he was as low as he could get. Came the voice of the cameraman, 'You could be working for the Danzigers!'

Dapkunaité, Ingeborga.
Lithuanian leading actress, in international films.
Night Whispers/Nochnye shyopoty 86. Thirteenth Apostle/Trinadtsatyj Apostol 88. Cynics/Tsiniki 91. Burnt by the Sun 94. Katia Ismailova 94. On Dangerous Ground (TV) 95. Mission: Impossible (US) 96. Seven Years in Tibet (US) 97, etc.
TV series: Alaska Kid 93.

Darabont, Frank (1959–).
American screenwriter and director.
A Nightmare on Elm Street 3: Dream Warriors (co-w) 87. The Blob (co-w) 88. The Fly II (co-w) 89. Buried Alive (d) (TV) 90. *The Shawshank Redemption* (wd) 94. Mary Shelley's Frankenstein (w) 94, etc.

D'Arbanville, Patty (1951–).
American actress, a former model, who began her career in one of Andy Warhol's underground films.
Flesh 68. Rancho Deluxe 75. Bilitis 77. Big Wednesday 78. Time after Time 79. The Main Event 79. The Fifth Floor 80. Hog Wild 80. Modern Problems 81. Real Genius 85. The Boys Next Door 85. Fresh Horses 88. Call Me 88. Wired 89. Frame-Up II: The Cover-Up 92. The Fan 96. New York Undercover 97. Archibald the Rainbow Painter 98, etc.

Darby, Ken (1909–1992).
American composer and arranger.
Song of the South 46. So Dear to My Heart 48. Rancho Notorious 52. The Robe 53. The Egyptian 54. Bus Stop (AAN) 56. The King and I (AA) 56. South Pacific (AAN) 58. Hound Dog Man 59. Porgy and Bess (AA) 59. Flower Drum Song (AAN) 61. How the West Was Won (AAN) 62. The Greatest Story Ever Told 65. Camelot (AA) 67, many others.

Darby, Kim (1947–) (Deborah Zerby).
American leading lady.
Bus Riley's Back in Town 65. A Time for Giving 69. *True Grit* 69. Norwood 69. The Grissom Gang 71. Rich Man Poor Man (TV) 76. The One and Only 78. The Pink Telephone 78. The Last Convertible (TV) 79. Better Off Dead 85. Teen Wolf Too 87. Halloween: The Curse of Michael Myers 95, etc.

Darc, Mireille (1938–) (M. Aigroz).
French leading lady.
Tonton Flingueurs 64. Galia 65. Du Rififi à Paname 66. Weekend 67. Jeff 68. Blonde from Peking 68. There was Once a Cop 72. The Tall Blond Man With One Black Shoe 74. The Pink Telephone/Le Téléphone Rose 75. Les Passagers 76. Man in a Hurry/L'Homme Pressé 77. Whirlpool/Pour la Peau d'un Flic 81. Si Elle Dit Oui . . . Je Ne Dis Pas Non 83, etc.

Darcel, Denise (1925–) (Denise Billecard).
French leading lady, in Hollywood from 1947.
To the Victor 48. Battleground 49. Tarzan and the Slave Girl 50. Westward the Women 51. Dangerous When Wet 53. Flame of Calcutta 53. Vera Cruz 54. Seven Women from Hell 62, etc.

D'Arcy, Alex (1908–1996) (Alexander Sarruf).
Egyptian light actor who has appeared in films of many nations.
Champagne 28. A Nous la Liberté 31. La Kermesse Héroique 35. The Prisoner of Zenda 37. Fifth Avenue Girl 39. Marriage Is a Private Affair 44. How to Marry a Millionaire 53. Soldier of Fortune 56. Way Way Out 66. The St Valentine's Day Massacre 67. Blood of Dracula's Castle (as Dracula) 69. The Seven Minutes 71, etc.

D'Arcy, Roy (1894–1969) (Roy F. Guisti).
American actor who hovered on the edge of stardom during the 20s and was in second features in the 30s, usually as a villain. Born in San Francisco, he was educated at the University of Jena, Germany, and worked in South America before becoming an actor in New York.
The Merry Widow 25. La Bohème 26. Trelawney of the Wells 26. King of the Khyber Rifles 26. The Gay Deceiver 26. Adam and Evil 27. The Actress 28. A Woman of Affairs 29. Romance 30. Sherlock Holmes 32. Whispering Shadows (serial) 33. Flying Down to Rio 33. Orient Express 34. Outlawed Guns 35. Revolt of the Zombies 36. Captain Calamity 36. Chasing Danger 39, etc.

Darden, Severn (1929–1995).
American comedy character actor.
Dead Heat on a Merry-Go-Round 67. The President's Analyst 67. Luv 68. Pussycat Pussycat I Love You 70. Vanishing Point 71. The Hired Hand 71. Cisco Pike 71. The War Between Men and Women 72. Who Fears the Devil 74. In God We Trust 79. Why Would I Lie 80. Saturday the 14th 81. Real Genius 85. Back to School 86, etc.
TV series: Mary Hartman, Mary Hartman 77–78. Beyond Westworld 80. Take Five 87.

Darien, Frank (1876–1955).
American character actor often seen as meek or downtrodden little man.
Five Star Final 31. The Miracle Man 32. Professional Sweetheart 33. Marie Galante 34. Brides are Like That 36. Love Finds Andy Hardy 38. At the Circus 39. *The Grapes of Wrath* 40. Hellzapoppin 42. Tales of Manhattan 42. The Outlaw 43. Bowery to Broadway 44. Kiss and Tell 45. Claudia and David 46. You Gotta Stay Happy 46. Merton of the Movies 47. The Flying Saucer 50, many others.

Darin, Bobby (1936–1973) (Walden Robert Cassotto).
American pop singer who alternated lightweight appearances with more serious roles. He was married to Sandra Dee.
Come September 60. Pepe 60. Too Late Blues 61. *Pressure Point* 62. Captain Newman MD (AAN) 63. That Funny Feeling 65. Gunfight at Abilene 67. Stranger in the House 67. The Happy Ending 69, etc.

Daring, Mason (1949–).
American composer, often for the films of John Sayles.
Return of the Secaucus Seven 80. The Brother from Another Planet 84. Matewan 87. Eight Men Out 88. The Laserman 88. Little Vegas 90. City of Hope 91. Wild Hearts Can't Be Broken 91. Passion Fish 92. The Secret of Roan Inish 94. Lone Star 96. Hidden in America (TV) 96. Prefontaine 97. Cold around the Heart 97. The Opposite of Sex 98, etc.

Darling, Candy (1946–1974) (James Hope Slattery).
Transvestite star, best known for roles in Andy Warhol's movies. Born in Massapequa, Long Island, he also appeared in European films and on stage. Died of leukaemia. He was played by Stephen Dorff in *I Shot Andy Warhol* 96.
Autobiography: 1992, *Candy Darling*.
Flesh 68. Der Tod der Maria Malibran (TV) 71. Women in Revolt 72. Silent Night, Bloody Night 73, etc.
❝ Candy didn't want to be a perfect woman – that would be too simple, and besides it would give her away. What she wanted was to be a woman with all the little problems that a woman has to deal with – runs in her stocking, runny mascara, men that left her. – *Andy Warhol*

Darling, William (1882–1963) (Wilhelm Sandorhazi).
Hungarian-American art director, long with Twentieth Century-Fox.
A Question of Honor 22. Seven Faces 29. Renegades 30. *Cavalcade* (AA) 33. In Old Kentucky 35. The Littlest Rebel 35. Under Two Flags 36. Lloyds of London 36. On the Avenue 37. *The Rains Came* 39. The Song of Bernadette (AA) 43. The Keys of the Kingdom 44. Anna and the King of Siam (AA) 46, etc.

Darnborough, Anthony (1913–).
British producer.
The Calendar 47. Quartet 48. The Astonished Heart 50. The Net 52. To Paris with Love 55. The Baby and the Battleship 56, etc.

Darnell, Linda (1921–1965) (Monetta Eloisa Darnell).
Wide-eyed American leading lady of the 40s. Died in a fire.
■ Hotel for Women 39. Daytime Wife 39. Stardust 40. Brigham Young 40. The Mark of Zorro 40. Chad Hanna 40. Blood and Sand 41. Rise and Shine 41. The Loves of Edgar Allan Poe 42. The Song of Bernadette (as the Virgin Mary) 43. City Without Men 43. Buffalo Bill 44. *It Happened Tomorrow* 44. Summer Storm 44. Sweet and Lowdown 44. The Great John L 45. Fallen Angel 45. Hangover Square 45. Anna and the King of Siam 46. Centennial Summer 46. My Darling Clementine 46. Forever Amber 47. The Walls of Jericho 48. Unfaithfully Yours 48. A Letter to Three Wives 48. Slattery's Hurricane 49. Everybody Does It 49. No Way Out 50. Two Flags West 50. The Thirteenth Letter 51. The Lady Pays Off 51. The Guy who Came Back 51. Saturday Island 52. Night Without Sleep 52. Blackbeard the Pirate 52. Second Chance 53. This Is My Love 54. Forbidden Women (It.) 55. The Last Five Minutes (It.) 56. Dakota Incident 56. Zero Hour 57. Homeward Borne (TV) 57. Black Spurs 65.
❝ Linda Darnell, who you may remember as the star of Hollywood's 1947 romantic blockbuster *Forever Amber*, was a firm believer in moving her facial muscles as little as possible. It didn't do much for her acting, but when she died in her forties she had remarkably unlined skin. – *Joan Collins*

D'Arrast, Harry D'Abbabie (1893–1968).
American director of the 20s, with a reputation for style.
■ Service for Ladies 27. A Gentleman of Paris 27. Serenade 27. The Magnificent Flirt 28. Dry Martini 28. Raffles (part) 30. *Laughter* (AA co-story) 30. Topaze 33. It Happened in Spain 34.

Darren, James (1936–) (James Ercolani).
American leading man whose appeal seems to have waned with maturity although he is still seen occasionally on TV.
Rumble on the Docks 56. Operation Mad Ball 57. Gidget 59. Let No Man Write My Epitaph 60. *The Guns of Navarone* 61. Diamondhead 63. For Those Who Think Young 64. Venus in Furs 70. The Boss's Son 78, etc.
TV series: Time Tunnel 66. T. J. Hooker 83–86.

Darrieux, Danielle (1917–).
Vivacious French leading lady, in films since 1931.
Le Bal 32. *Mayerling* 36. *The Rage of Paris* (US) 38. *Battement de Coeur* 39. Premier Rendezvous 44. *Occupe-Toi d'Amélie* 49. La Ronde 50. Le Plaisir 51. Rich, Young and Pretty (US) 51. Five Fingers (US) 52. Adorables Créatures 52. *Madame De* 53. Alexander the Great (US) 56. Le Rouge et le Noir 57. Marie Octobre 58. Lady Chatterley's Lover 59. Murder at 45 RPM 61. The Greengage Summer (GB) 61. Landru 63. L'Or du Duc 65. Le Dimanche de la Vie 66. The Young Girls of Rochefort 67. L'Homme à la Buick 67. Birds in Peru 68. The Lonely Woman 75. L'Année Sainte 76. Le Cavaleur 79. At the Top of the Stairs 83. The Scene of the Crime 86. Bille en Tête 89. Le Jour de Rois 90, many others.

Darro, Frankie (1918–1976) (Frank Johnson).
Tough-looking little American actor, former child and teenage player; star of many second features.
So Big 24. The Cowboy Cop 26. Long Pants 27. The Circus Kid 28. The Mad Genius 31. Wild Boys of the Road 33. Broadway Bill 34. Charlie Chan at the Race Track 36. Racing Blood 37. Chasing Trouble 39. Laughing at Danger 40. Freddie Steps Out 45. Heart of Virginia 48. Across the Wide Missouri 51. Operation Petticoat 59. Hook, Line and Sinker 68, many others.

Darrow, Clarence (1857–1938).
Celebrated American defence lawyer, impersonated by Orson Welles in *Compulsion* 58, and by Spencer Tracy in *Inherit the Wind* 60. In the 70s Henry Fonda played him in a one-man stage and TV show. In the 90s, Leslie Nielsen also played him in a one-man show.

Darrow, John (1907–1980) (Harry Simpson).
American light leading man of the 20s and 30s, who later became an agent.
High School Hero 27. Girls Gone Wild 29. Hell's Angels 30. The Lady Refuses 31. Ten Nights in a Bar-Room 31. The All American 32. Midshipman Jack 33. Monte Carlo Nights 34. A Notorious Gentleman 35. Crime over London (GB) 36, etc.

Darvi, Bella (1927–1971) (Bayla Wegier).
Polish-French leading lady, in a few Hollywood films after being discovered by Darryl Zanuck. Committed suicide.
■ Hell and High Water 54. The Egyptian 54. The Racers 55. Je Suis Un Sentimental 55. Sinners of Paris 59. Lipstick 65.

Darwell, Jane (1880–1967) (Patti Woodward).
American character actress, usually in warm-hearted motherly roles.
Rose of the Rancho 14. Brewster's Millions 20. Tom Sawyer 30. Back Street 32. Design for Living 34. Life Begins at Forty 35. Captain January 36. Slave Ship 37. Three Blind Mice 38. Jesse James 39. The Rains Came 39. Gone with the Wind 39. *The Grapes of Wrath* (AA; as the indomitable Ma Joad) 40. *All That Money Can Buy* 41. Private Nurse 41. The Ox Bow Incident 43. The Impatient Years 44. *Captain Tugboat Annie* (title role) 46. My Darling Clementine 46. Three Godfathers 48. Wagonmaster 50. Caged 50. The Lemon Drop Kid 51. Fourteen Hours 51. We're Not Married 52. The Sun Shines Bright 52. Hit the Deck 55. The Last Hurrah 58. Mary Poppins 64, many others.
✪ For the sheer maternal strength of her characterizations. *The Grapes of Wrath*.
Famous line (*The Grapes of Wrath*): 'Can't nobody lick us, pa. We're the people.'

Dash, Stacey (1966–).
American actress who began in commercials as a child.
Enemy Territory 87. Moving 88. Tennessee Nights 89. Mo' Money 92. Renaissance Man 94. Clueless 95. Hoodlum 96. Cold around the Heart 97, etc.
TV series: TV 101 88–89.

Dassin, Jules (1911–).
American director, former radio writer and actor. Joined MGM 1941 to direct shorts (including a two-reel version of *The Tell-Tale Heart*); moved to features; left for Europe during the McCarthy witch hunt of the late 40s.
■ Nazi Agent 42. The Affairs of Martha 42. Reunion in France 42. Young Ideas 43. The Canterville Ghost 44. A Letter for Evie 44. Two Smart People 46. *Brute Force* 47. *Naked City* 48. *Thieves' Highway* (& a) 49. Night and the City (GB) 50. *Rififi* (also a, as Perlo Vita) 54. He Who Must Die 56. Where the Hot Wind Blows 58. *Never*

on Sunday (also a) (AAN) 60. Phaedra 62. Topkapi 64. 10.30 p.m. Summer 66. Survival 68. Uptight 68. Promise at Dawn 70. Dream of Passion 78. Circle of Two 80.

Daugherty, Herschel (1909–1993).
American director, from TV.
The Light in the Forest 58. The Raiders 63. Winchester 73 (TV) 67. The Victim (TV) 72. Twice in a Lifetime (TV) 74, etc.

Dauphin, Claude (1903–1978) (Claude Franc-Nohain).
Dapper French actor of stage and screen: in films from 1930.
Entrée des Artistes 38. Battement de Coeur 39. Les Deux Timides 42. English Without Tears (GB) 44. Deported (US) 50. Le Plaisir 51. Casque d'Or 52. Little Boy Lost (US) 53. Innocents in Paris (GB) 54. Phantom of the Rue Morgue (US) 54. The Quiet American (US) 58. The Full Treatment 60. Lady L 65. Two for the Road 67. Hard Contract 69. Rosebud 75. The Tenant 76, many others.
TV series: Paris Precinct.

Davenport, A. Bromley (1867–1946).
Eton-educated English character actor who made his stage debut in Siberia in 1892 and was in films from 1920.
The Great Gay Road 20. Bonnie Prince Charlie 23. What the Butler Saw 24. Roses of Picardy 27. Too Many Crooks 30. Glamour 31. Mischief 32. Mr Bill the Conqueror 32. The Return of Raffles 32. A Shot in the Dark 33. The Warren Case 34. The Scarlet Pimpernel 35. The Cardinal 36. Owd Bob 38. Jamaica Inn 39. Love on the Dole 41. Old Mother Riley's Ghosts 41. The Young Mr Pitt 42. When We Are Married 43. The Way Ahead 44, etc.

Davenport, Doris (1915–1980).
American leading lady, formerly a Goldwyn Girl. Played several bit parts, but was prominent only in *Kid Millions* 35, *The Westerner* 40, *Behind the News* 40. Her career ended after she was injured in a car crash that left her with a limp.

Davenport, Dorothy (1895–1977) (aka Dorothy Reid).
Silent screen actress, often opposite her husband Wallace Reid, who turned to directing, writing and producing after his death in 1923.
Her Indian Hero 09. The Intruder 13. Fruit of Evil 14. The Fighting Chance 20. Every Woman's Problem 21. Human Wreckage 23. Broken Laws (& p) 24. The Earth Woman (p) 26. Linda (pd) 29. Sucker Money (d) 33. Road to Ruin (co-w, d) 34. Prison Break (w) 38. The Haunted House (w) 40. Redhead 41. Who Killed Doc Robbin? 48. Footsteps in the Fog 55, etc.

Davenport, Harry (1866–1949).
American character actor; long stage career, then in Hollywood as chucklesome, benevolent old man.
■ Her Unborn Child 30. My Sin 31. His Woman 32. Get That Venus 33. Three Cheers for Love 34. The Scoundrel 35. Three Men on a Horse 36. The Case of the Black Cat 36. King of Hockey 36. Fly Away Baby 36. The Life of Emile Zola 37. Under Cover of Night 37. Her Husband's Secretary 37. White Bondage 37. They Won't Forget 37. Mr Dodd Takes the Air 37. First Lady 37. The Perfect Specimen 37. Paradise Express 37. As Good as Married 37. Armored Car 37. Wells Fargo 37. Fit for a King 37. Gold is Where You Find It 38. Saleslady 38. The Sisters 38. The Long Shot 38. The First Hundred Years 38. Marie Antoinette 38. The Cowboy and the Lady 38. Reckless Living 38. The Rage of Paris 38. Tailspin 38. Young Fugitives 38. *You Can't Take It With You* 38. The Higgins Family 38. Orphans of the Street 38. Made for Each Other 39. My Wife's Relatives 39. Should Husbands Work 39. The Covered Trailer 39. Money to Burn 39. Exile Express 39. Death of a Champion 39. The Story of Alexander Graham Bell 39. Juarez 39. Gone with the Wind 39. *The Hunchback of Notre Dame* 39. Dr Ehrlich's Magic Bullet 40. Granny Get Your Gun 40. Too Many Husbands 40. Grandpa Goes to Town 40. Lucky Partners 40. I Want a Divorce 40. All This and Heaven Too 40. Foreign Correspondent 40. That Uncertain Feeling 41. I Wanted Wings 41. Hurricane Smith 41. The Bride Came COD 41. One Foot in Heaven 41. Kings Row 41. *Son of Fury* 42. Larceny Inc 42. Ten Gentlemen from West Point 42. Tales of Manhattan 42. Heading for God's Country 43. We've Never Been Licked 43. Riding High 43. *The Ox Bow Incident* 43. The Amazing Mrs Holliday 43. Gangway for Tomorrow 43. Government Girl 43. Jack London 43. Princess O'Rourke 43. *Meet Me In St Louis* 44. The Impatient Years 44. The Thin Man Goes Home 44. Kismet 44. Music for Millions 45. *The Enchanted Forest* 45. Too Young to Know 45. This Love of Ours 45. She Wouldn't Say Yes 45. Courage of Lassie 46. Blue Sierra 46. A Boy a Girl and a Dog 46. Faithful in My Fashion 46. Three Wise Fools 46. War Brides 46. Lady Luck 46. Claudia and David 46. Pardon My Past 46. Adventure 46. The Farmer's Daughter 47. That Hagen Girl 47. Stallion Road 47. Keeper of the Bees 47. Sport of Kings 47. The Fabulous Texan 47. *The Bachelor and the Bobbysoxer* 47. Three Daring Daughters 48. The Man from Texas 48. For the Love of Mary 48. That Lady in Ermine 48. The Decision of Christopher Blake 48. Down to the Sea in Ships 49. Little Women 49. Tell It To the Judge 49. *That Forsyte Woman* 49. Riding High 50.
✪ For being everybody's cheerful grandpa. *The Hunchback of Notre Dame*.

Davenport, Nigel (1928–).
Breezy, virile British actor, much on TV. His second wife was actress Maria Aitken (1972–80).
Peeping Tom 59. In the Cool of the Day 63. A High Wind in Jamaica 65. Sands of the Kalahari 65. Where the Spies Are 66. *A Man for All Seasons* 67. Red and Blue 67. Play Dirty 68. Sinful Davey 69. *The Virgin Soldiers* 69. The Royal Hunt of the Sun 69. No Blade of Grass 71. Villain 71. *Living Free* 72. Mary Queen of Scots 72. Dracula (TV) (as Van Helsing) 73. Phase IV 73. The Island of Dr Moreau 77. An Eye for an Eye 78. Zulu Dawn 79. Nighthawks 81. Strata 82. Greystoke: The Legend of Tarzan, Lord of the Apes 84. Caravaggio 86. Without a Clue 88. The Return of El Coyote/La Vuelta de El Coyote (Sp.) 98, etc.
TV series: *Prince Regent* (as George III) 79.

Daves, Delmer (1904–1977).
American writer-producer-director with highly miscellaneous experience. Writer with MGM from 1933, writer-director with Warners from 1943.
Destination Tokyo (wd) 43. The Red House (wd) 47. *Dark Passage* (wd) 47. Broken Arrow (d) 50. Bird of Paradise (wd) 51. Never Let Me Go (d) 53. Demetrius and the Gladiators (d) 54. Jubal (wd) 56. The Last Wagon (wd) 56. *3.10 to Yuma* (d) 57. Cowboy (wd) 58. The Hanging Tree (d) 59. Parrish (wd) 61. Spencer's Mountain (wpd) 62. Youngblood Hawke (wd) 64. The Battle of the Villa Fiorita (wpd) 65, many others.
❝ He remains the property of those who can enjoy stylistic conviction in an intellectual vacuum. – *Andrew Sarris, 1968*

Davi, Robert (1953–).
Burly American actor, usually in menacing roles.
The Goonies 85. Wild Thing 87. Licence to Kill 89. Maniac Cop 2 90. Amazon 90. Predator 2 90. Legal Tender 90. Illicit Behaviour 91. The Taking of Beverly Hills 91. Center of the Web 92. Christopher Columbus: The Discovery 92. Wild Orchid 2: Two Shades of Blue 92. Maniac Cop 3 93. Night Trap/Mardi Gras for the Devil 93. Son of the Pink Panther 93. The November Men 93. Cops and Robbersons 94. Showgirls 95. An Occasional Hell 96. LA without a Map (GB/Fr./Fin.) (as himself) 98, etc.
TV series: The Gangster Chronicles 81.

Daviau, Allen. (1942–).
American cinematographer.
E.T. – the Extraterrestrial (AAN) 82. Twilight Zone – the Movie 83. Harry Tracy 83. The Falcon and the Snowman 85. The Color Purple (AAN) 86. Harry and the Hendersons 87. Empire of the Sun (AAN) 87. Avalon (AAN) 90. Defending Your Life 91. Bugsy 91. Fearless 93. Congo 95, etc.

David, Hal (1921–).
American lyricist and collaborator with Burt Bacharach (see entry for credits). He is the brother of Mack David.
Autobiography: 1968, *What The World Needs Now*.

David, Keith (1956–).
American actor. Born in New York, he studied at the High School for the Performing Arts and the Juilliard School, beginning in the theatre.
The Thing 82. Platoon 86. Bird 88. Stars and Bars 88. They Live 88. Always 89. Road House 89. Marked for Death 90. Article 99 92. The Last Outlaw 93. The Puppet Masters 94. Reality Bites 94. Blue in the Face 95. Clockers 95. Dead Presidents 95. The Quick and the Dead 95. Larger than Life 96. Johns 96. Loose Women 96, etc.

David, Mack (1912–1993).
American songwriter, in Hollywood from 1949, often in collaboration with Jerry Livingston. He is the brother of Hal David.
Cinderella (AAN) 49. At War with the Army 50. Sailor Beware 51. Jumping Jacks 52. Scared Stiff 53. The Hanging Tree (AAN) 59. Bachelor in Paradise (AAN) 61. Walk on the Wild Side (AAN) 62. It's a Mad, Mad, Mad, Mad World (AAN) 63. Hush, Hush Sweet Charlotte (AAN) 64. Cat Ballou (AAN) 65. Hawaii (AAN) 66, etc.

David, Saul (1921–1996).
American producer.
Autobiography: 1981, *The Industry*.
Von Ryan's Express 65. Our Man Flint 65. Fantastic Voyage 67. Skullduggery 69. The Black Bird 75. Logan's Run 76.

David, Thayer (1926–1978) (David Thayer Hersey).
American character actor.
A Time to Love and a Time to Die 58. *Journey to the Centre of the Earth* 59. The Story of Ruth 60. The Eiger Sanction 74. The Duchess and the Dirtwater Fox 76. Meet Nero Wolfe (TV) 77. House Calls 78, etc.

Davidovich, Lolita (1962–) (aka Lolita David).
Canadian actress of Yugoslavian descent.
Adventures in Babysitting 1987. The Big Town 1987. Blaze 89. Object of Beauty 91. The Inner Circle/El Proiezionista 91. Money Men 92. Raising Cain 92. Boiling Point 93. Younger and Younger 93. Intersection 94. Cobb 94. Now and Then 95. For Better or Worse (TV) 95. Touch 96. Jungle 2 Jungle 96. Dead Silence (TV) 96. Santa Fe 97. Gods & Monsters 98, etc.
❝ I'm Yugoslavian. They're passionate but not really ambitious. Life is eating and drinking and children. – *L.D.*

Davidson, Boaz (1943–).
Israeli director.
Azit the Paratrooper Dog 72. Lupo Goes to New York 77. Lemon Popsicle 81. Going Steady/Lemon Popsicle II 81. Hot Bubblegum/Lemon Popsicle III 82. The Last American Virgin 82. Private Popsicle/Lemon Popsicle IV 82. Dutch Treat 86. Going Bananas 87. Salsa 88. American Cyborg: Steel Warrior 94. Outside the Law 95, etc.

Davidson, Jaye (1968–).
American actor whose role as a transvestite surprised the hero, and the audience, of *The Crying Game*. Born in California, he moved to England as a small child, returning to the United States to star in a million-dollar role in *Stargate*.
The Crying Game (AAN) 93. Stargate 94.

Davidson, John (1886–1968).
American character actor, a piercing-eyed, white-haired villain of the 20s and 30s.
The Green Cloak 15. The Spurs of Sybil 18. The Bronze Bell 21. Under Two Flags 22. Monsieur Beaucaire 24. Kid Gloves 29. Arsène Lupin 32. Dinner at Eight 33. Hold That Girl 34. The Last Days of Pompeii 35. Mr Moto Takes a Vacation 38. Arrest Bulldog Drummond 38. Miracles for Sale 39. Captain Marvel 41. Captain America 44. The Purple Monster Strikes 45. Shock 46. Daisy Kenyon 47. A Letter to Three Wives 48. Oh You Beautiful Doll 49. A Gathering of Eagles 63, many others.

Davidson, John (1941–).
American light singer and leading man, mostly on television.
The Happiest Millionaire 67. The One and Only Genuine Original Family Band 68. Coffee, Tea or Me (TV) 73. The Mitera Targets (TV) 78. Shell Game (TV) 78. The Concorde – Airport '79 79. The Squeeze 87. Edward Scissorhands 90, etc.
TV series: The Entertainers 64–65. The Kraft Summer Music Hall 66. The John Davidson Show 69, 76. The Girl with Something Extra 73–74. That's Incredible 80–84.

Davidson, Max (1875–1950).
German-born slapstick comedian, in America from the 1890s and silents from 1913. Born in Berlin, he made a series of two-reelers for Hal Roach in the late 20s, often with Walter 'Spec' O'Donnell as his charmless son, which have been rediscovered and shown to acclaim in recent years. Later, he appeared as a character actor in small roles in the films of Cecil B. De Mille and others. He is featured in the compilation film *Laurel and Hardy's Laughing 20s* 65. He is also credited with suggesting to D. W. Griffith, a fellow-actor in the late 1890s, that he should seek work in films.
Love in Armor 15. Intolerance 16. The Idle Rich 21. The Light that Failed 22. Untamed Youth 24. Hats Off (short) 27. *Call of the Cuckoos* (short) 27. *Don't Tell Everything* (short) 28. *Pass the Gravy* (short) 28. Jewish Prudence (short) 28. The Boy Friend (short) 28. Docks of San Francisco 32. The Cohens and Kellys in Trouble 33. Roamin' Wild 36. The Girl Said No 37. Union Pacific 39. Reap the Wild Wind 42, etc.
❝ Davidson is definitely and defiantly politically incorrect. He resurrects the Jewish comic stereotype that was already disreputable in his own time – apologetically shrugged shoulders, hands raised in palms-up supplication, clutching his cheeks, or stroking his beard. – *David Robinson*

Davidson, William B. (1888–1947).
American character actor, in hundreds of small roles, usually as pompous, lecherous or overbearing businessman.
A Modern Cinderella 17. The Capitol 19. Partners of the Night 20. Adam and Eva 23. Women and Gold 25. The Gaucho 28. For the Defense 30. Sky Devils 32. Fog over Frisco 34. Dangerous 35. Earthworm Tractors 36. Easy Living 37. Love on Toast 38. Indianapolis Speedway 39. Maryland 40. My Little Chickadee 40. Juke Girl 42. Up in Arms 44. See My Lawyer 45. My Darling Clementine 46. The Farmer's Daughter 47, many others.

Davidtz, Embeth.
South African-born actress in America. She is romantically involved with actor Ben Chaplin.
Army of Darkness 92. Deadly Matrimony (TV) 92. Schindler's List 93. Murder in the First 94. Feast of July 95. Matilda 96. The Gingerbread Man 97. The Garden of Redemption 97. Fallen 97. Simon Magus 99, etc.

Davie, Cedric Thorpe (1913–1983).
British composer; he studied at the Royal College of Music under Ralph Vaughan Williams.
The Brothers 47. Snowbound 48. The Heart Is Highland (doc) 52. Rob Roy the Highland Rogue 53. The Dark Avenger/The Warriors 55. Jacqueline 56. The Green Man 56. The Kid from Canada 57. Rockets Galore/Mad Little Island 58. The Bridal Path 59. A Terrible Beauty/Night Fighters 60. Kidnapped 60, etc.

Davies, Betty Ann (1910–1955).
British stage actress, usually in tense roles; occasional films from early 30s.
Chick 34. Kipps 41. It Always Rains on Sunday 47. The History of Mr Polly 49. *Trio* 50. Cosh Boy 52. Grand National Night 53. The Belles of St Trinian's 54, etc.

Davies, Jack (1913–1994).
British comedy scriptwriter, busy since 1932 on Will Hay and Norman Wisdom comedies, 'Doctor' series, etc. Father of John Howard Davies.
Laughter in Paradise 51. Top Secret 52. An Alligator Named Daisy 56. *Very Important Person* 61. *The Fast Lady* 62. Those Magnificent Men in Their Flying Machines 65. Gambit 66. Monte Carlo 68. Doctor in Trouble 70. Paper Tiger 75, many others.

Davies, Jeremy (1971–).
American leading man in independent films, born in Rockford, Iowa.
Guncrazy 92. Spanking the Monkey 94. Nell 94. Twister 96. The Locusts 97. Going All the Way 97. Up at the Villa 98. Saving Private Ryan 98. The Billion Dollar Hotel 98. Ravenous 99, etc.
TV series: General Hospital 92.

Davies, John Howard (1939–).
British child actor, who became a BBC TV director.
Oliver Twist 48. The Rocking-Horse Winner 50. Tom Brown's Schooldays 51, etc.

Davies, Marion (1897–1961) (Marion Douras).
American leading lady famous less for her rather mediocre films than for being the protégée of William Randolph Hearst the newspaper magnate, who was determined to make a star out of her. She enjoyed moderate success 1917–36, then retired.
Pictorial autobiography: 1975, *The Times We Had*, collated by Pamela Pfau.
Biography: 1973, *Marion Davies* by Fred Lawrence Guiles.
■ Runaway Romany 17. Cecilia of the Pink Roses 18. The Burden of Proof 18. Getting Mary Married 19. The Cinema Murder 19. The Dark Star 19. The Belle of New York 19. The Restless Sex 20. April Folly 20. Enchantment 21. Buried Treasure 21. The Bride's Play 22. Beauty Worth 22. When Knighthood was in Flower 22. The Young Diana 22. Daughter of Luxury 22. Little Old New York 22. Adam and Eva 23. Janice Meredith 24. Yolanda 24. Lights of Old Broadway 25. Zander the Great 25. Beverly of Graustark 26. Quality Street 27. The Fair Co-ed 27. The Red Mill 27. Tillie the Toiler 27. The Cardboard Lover 28. The Patsy 28. *Show People* 28. Hollywood Revue 29. Marianne 29. The Gay Nineties 29. Not so Dumb 30. The Floradora Girl 30. It's a Wise Child 31. Five and Ten 31. Bachelor Father 31. Polly of the Circus 32. Blondie of the Follies 32. The Dark Horse 32. Peg O'My Heart 33. Operator 13 34. Going Hollywood 34. *Page Miss Glory* 35. Hearts Divided 36. Cain and Mabel 36. Ever Since Eve 37.
❝ Upon my honour
I saw a madonna
Sitting alone in a niche
Above the door
Of the glamorous whore
Of a prominent son-of-a-bitch.
– attributed to Dorothy Parker on seeing the elaborate dressing room built by W. R. Hearst for M.D. at MGM
With me it was 5 per cent talent and 95 per cent publicity. *– M.D.*
She was quite a comedian, and would have been a star in her own right without the cyclonic Hearst publicity. *– Charles Chaplin*
I have yet to encounter a single movie fan with the slightest respect for her ability – and yet the coal that has been used to keep her name flaming on the electric signs would probably run the city of Syracuse for a whole year. *– Robert Sherwood*

Davies, Rupert (1916–1976).
British character actor, formerly in small roles, then famous as TV's Maigret.
The Key 58. Sapphire 59. The Uncle 65. The Spy Who Came in from the Cold 65. Brides of Fu Manchu 66. House of a Thousand Dolls 67. Witchfinder General 68. Waterloo 70. Zeppelin 71, etc.
TV series: Sailor of Fortune 56.

Davies, Terence (1945–).
British director of autobiographical films of working-class life in the 50s. He left school at 15 and worked as a clerk for 12 years before raising the money to make his first short.
Terence Davies Trilogy (The Children 76; Madonna and Child 80; Death and Transfiguration 83). Distant Voices, Still Lives 88. The Long Day Closes 92. The Neon Bible 95, etc.
❝ Cinema is not valid for me if it's just people talking their way through a plot. I couldn't get interested in all that. I just get bored, because that's not real cinema at all. It's talking pictures. *– T.D.*
The great thing in life is to be very beautiful and very stupid. *– T.D.*
I believe Mr Davies went to film school – presumably not for long. *– Ken Russell*

Davies, Valentine (1905–1961).
American screenwriter.
Three Little Girls in Blue 46. *Miracle on 34th Street* (AA original story) 47. You Were Meant for Me 48. Chicken Every Sunday 48. It Happens Every Spring 49. On the Riviera 51. The Glenn Miller Story 53. *The Benny Goodman Story* (& d) 55. The Bridges at Toko-Ri 55. Strategic Air Command 55. Bachelor in Paradise 61, etc.

Davies, Windsor (1930–).
British comedy character actor who rather overdoes the blustering sergeant-major act.
The Alphabet Murders 65. Hammerhead 67. Sex Clinic 71. Mister Quilp 74. Carry on Behind 74. Not Now Comrade 76. Old Scores 91. Arabian Knight (voice) 95. Mosley (as Lloyd George) (TV) 98, etc.
TV series: It Ain't Half Hot, Mum 73–77. The New Statesman 85. Never the Twain 81–91.

Davion, Alexander (1929–).
Anglo-French leading man, mostly on stage and American TV.
Song without End (as Chopin) 60. Paranoiac 63. Valley of the Dolls 67. The Royal Hunt of the Sun 69. Incense for the Damned 71, etc.
TV series: Gideon's Way 64. The Man Who Never Was 66. Custer 67. Bloodsuckers 70, etc.

Davis, Andrew.
American director and screenwriter, a former cinematographer.
Over the Edge (ph) 79. Stony Island (wd) 80. The Final Terror 83. Code of Silence 85. Above the Law (wd) 88. The Package 89. Under Siege 92. *The Fugitive* 93. Steal Big, Steal Little 95. Chain Reaction 96. A Perfect Murder 98, etc.

Davis, Bette (1908–1989) (Ruth Elizabeth Davis).
Inimitably intense American dramatic actress; a box-office queen for ten years from 1937, she later played eccentric roles. Her fourth, and last, husband was actor Gary Merrill (1940–50).
Autobiographies: 1962, *The Lonely Life*. 1975, *Mother Goddam* (with Whitney Stine).
Biographies: 1991, *No Guts, No Glory: Conversations with Bette Davis* by Whitney Stine. 1992, *Bette Davis* by Barbara Leaming.
■ Bad Sister 31. Seed 31. Waterloo Bridge 31. Way Back Home 31. The Menace 31. *The Man Who Played God* 32. Hell's House 32. So Big 32. The Rich are Always with Us 32. The Dark Horse 32. *The Cabin in the Cotton* 32. Three on a Match 32. 20,000 Years in Sing Sing 32. Parachute Jumper 32. The Working Man 33. Ex Lady 33. Bureau of Missing Persons 33. Fashions of 1934 34. The Big Shakedown 34. Jimmy the Gent 34. Fog over Frisco 34. *Of Human Bondage* 34. Housewife 34. Bordertown 34. The Girl from Tenth Avenue 35. *Front Page Woman* 35. Special Agent 35. *Dangerous* (AA) 35. The Petrified Forest 36. The Golden Arrow 36. Satan Met a Lady 36. Marked Woman 37. Kid Galahad 37. That Certain Woman 37. It's Love I'm After 37. *Jezebel* (AA) 38. The Sisters 38. *Dark Victory* (AAN) 39. Juarez 39. *The Old Maid* 39. *The Private Lives of Elizabeth and Essex* 39. All This and Heaven Too 40. *The Letter* (AAN) 40. *The Great Lie* 41. The Bride Came COD 41. *The Little Foxes* (AAN) 41. *The Man Who Came to Dinner* 41. In This Our Life 42. *Now Voyager* (AAN) 42. Watch on the Rhine 43. Thank Your Lucky Stars 43. Old Acquaintance 43. Mr *Skeffington* (AAN) 44. Hollywood Canteen 44. *The Corn is Green* 45. A Stolen Life 46. Deception 46. Winter Meeting 48. June Bride 48. Beyond the Forest 49. *All About Eve* (AAN) 50. Payment on Demand 51. Another Man's Poison 51. Phone Call from a Stranger 52. The Star (AAN) 52. The Virgin Queen 55. The Catered Affair 56. Storm Center 56. John Paul Jones 59. The Scapegoat 59. A Pocketful of Miracles 61. *Whatever Happened to Baby Jane?* (AAN) 62. Dead Ringer 64. The Empty Canvas 64. Where Love Has Gone 64. *Hush Hush Sweet Charlotte* 64. *The Nanny* 65. *The Anniversary* 68. Connecting Rooms 69. Bunny O'Hare 71. Madame Sin (TV) 71. The Scientific Cardplayer 72. The Judge and Jake Wyler (TV) 73. Scream Pretty Peggy (TV) 74. Burnt Offerings 76. The Disappearance of Aimée (TV) 76. The Dark Secret of Harvest Home (TV) 78. Return from Witch Mountain 78. Death on the Nile 78. Strangers (TV) 79. White Mama (TV) 79. The Watcher in the Woods 80. Skyward (TV) 81. Family Reunion (TV) 81. *Little Gloria . . .* Happy at Last (TV) 82. *A Piano for Mrs Cimino* (TV) 82. Hotel (TV) 83. Right of Way (TV) 83. *The Whales of August* 87. Wicked Stepmother 89.
✪ For her ten-year domination of the 'woman's picture'. *The Great Lie*.
❝ For a girl with no looks, Bette Davis rose fast to the top and stayed there a long time. When she first arrived in Hollywood the official greeter missed her at the station, and his later excuse was:
No one faintly like an actress got off the train.
Carl Laemmle is credited with two waspish remarks about her:
I can't imagine any guy giving her a tumble.
And:
She has as much sex appeal as Slim Summerville.
She herself confesses:
When I saw my first film test I ran from the projection room screaming.
She finally settled for a career without glamour:
Nobody knew what I looked like because I never looked the same way twice.
Determination carried her through. As her later husband Gary Merrill said:
Whatever Bette had chosen to do in life, she would have had to be the top or she couldn't have endured it.
She admitted this herself:
If Hollywood didn't work out I was all prepared to be the best secretary in the world.
As David Zinman summarizes:
All she had going for her was her talent.
But by 1937 she was at the top of the tree, dishing out hell to those who had dished it out to her. Said her once co-star Brian Aherne:
Surely no one but a mother could have loved Bette Davis at the height of her career.
E. Arnot Robertson in 1935 had expressed a similar feeling in a different way:
She would probably have been burned as a witch if she had lived two or three hundred years ago. She gives the curious feeling of being charged with power which can find no ordinary outlet.
By the early 50s she was no longer a bankable star, and work was suddenly in short supply. She inserted a full-page ad in the Hollywood trade papers:
MOTHER OF THREE: divorcee; American. Twenty years experience as an actress in motion pictures. Mobile still and more affable than rumour would have it. Wants steady employment in Hollywood. (Has had Broadway.) References upon request.
She reflected bitterly on her career at the top:
I was the only star they allowed to come out of the water looking wet.
Jack L. Warner however remembered her with affection:
An explosive little broad with a straight left.
But despite all difficulties she persevered, and was still acting as she neared eighty. Vincent Canby said:
Her career has been recycled more often than the average rubber tyre.
Famous line (*The Cabin in the Cotton*): 'I'd like to kiss yuh, but I just washed my hair.'
Famous line (*All About Eve*): 'Fasten your seat belts, it's going to be a bumpy night.'
Famous line (*Old Acquaintance*): 'There comes a time in every woman's life when the only thing that helps is a glass of champagne.'
Famous line (*Now Voyager*): 'Oh, Jerry, don't let's ask for the moon: we have the stars.'
~One story has it that she named the awards statuette Oscar because its backside resembled that of her first husband, Ham Oscar Nelson.

Davis, Brad (1949–1991).
American leading actor. Died of AIDS.
Midnight Express 77. A Small Circle of Friends 80. Chariots of Fire 81. Querelle 84. Chiefs (TV) 84. Robert Kennedy and his Times (TV) 84. Blood Ties 86. Cold Steel 87. Rosalie Goes Shopping 89. Hangfire 90. Child of Light (TV) 91, etc.

Davis, Carl (1936–).
American composer in Britain, best known for his silent film scores: *Napoleon*, *The Crowd*, Hollywood TV series, etc.
The Bofors Gun 68. Up Pompeii 71. Rentadick 72. Man Friday 75. The Sailor's Return 77. The French Lieutenant's Woman (BFA) 81. The Far Pavilions (TV) 81. King David 85. Scandal 89. The Rainbow 89. Frankenstein Unbound 90. The Trial 94. Widow's Peak 94. Coming Home (TV) 98, etc.

Davis, Desmond (1927–).
British director, former cameraman.
■ *Girl with Green Eyes* 64. The Uncle 65. *I Was Happy Here* 66. Smashing Time 67. A Nice Girl Like Me 69. Clash of the Titans 81. The Sign of Four (TV) 83. The Country Girls (TV) 83. Ordeal by Innocence 84. Camille (TV) 84. Freedom Fighter (TV) 88. The Man Who Lived at the Ritz (TV) 88.

Davis, Gail (1925–1997) (Betty Jeanne Grayson).
American leading lady of westerns, opposite Gene Autry in 15 films and many episodes of his TV show; she also had her own TV series, produced by Autry, and appeared with his rodeo.
Cow Town 50. Valley of Fire 51. Blue Canadian Rockies 52. Goldtown Ghost Riders 52. The Old West 52. On Top of Old Smoky 53. Winning of the West 53, etc.
TV series: Annie Oakley 53–56.

Davis, Geena (1957–).
Tall American leading actress, usually in off-beat roles. Born in Wareham, Massachusetts, she studied at Boston University and began as a model. Her career, which reached its peak so far with *Thelma and Louise*, seemed to lose its impetus in the films directed by her then third husband Renny HARLIN (1992–97). Her second husband was actor Jeff GOLDBLUM (1987–90).
Tootsie 82. Fletch 84. Transylvania 6–5000 84. The Fly 86. Beetlejuice 88. The Accidental Tourist (AA) 88. Earth Girls Are Easy 89. Quick Change 90. Thelma and Louise (AAN) 91. Hero 92. A League of Their Own 92. Speechless 94. Angie 94. CutThroat Island 95. The Long Kiss Goodnight 96, etc.
TV series: Buffalo Bill 83–84. Sara 85.
❝ It seems that if a woman has a job in a movie now, she's cold and gets no sex – or if she does have sex, then she's either going to be punished for it or she's a psycho killer. *– G.D.*
A feminist spirit in the body of a goddess.
– Premiere

Davis, Hope (1967?–).
American actress. Born in Tenafly, New Jersey, she studied cognitive science at Vassar.
Flatliners 90. Home Alone 90. Kiss of Death 95. Daytrippers 96. Mr Wrong 96. The Myth of Fingerprints 97. Next Stop, Wonderland 98. Arlington Road 98. Mumford 98, etc.

Davis, James (Jim) (1915–1981).
Burly American actor who, despite star billing opposite Bette Davis, subsided quickly into second-feature westerns.
White Cargo 42. Swing Shift Maisie 43. Gallant Bess 46. The Fabulous Texan 47. *Winter Meeting* 48. Brimstone 49. Cavalry Scout 52. Woman of the North Country 52. The Fighting 7th 52. The Last Command 55. Timberjack 55. The Maverick Queen 56. Alias Jesse James 59. Fort Utah 66. Rio Lobo 70. Monte Walsh 70. Big Jake 71. The Honkers 72. Bad Company 72. The Deputies (TV) 76. The Choirboys 77. Comes a Horseman 78. The Day Time Ended 80, many others.
TV series: Stories of the Century. *Rescue* 8. *The Cowboys*. Dallas 78–80.

Davis, Joan (1907–1961).
Rubber-faced American comedienne, in show business from infancy, who enlivened many routine musicals of the 30s and 40s.
■ Millions in the Air 35. Bunker Bean 35. The Holy Terror 36. On the Avenue 37. Time Out for Romance 37. Wake Up and Live 37. Angel's Holiday 37. You Can't Have Everything 37. The Great Hospital Mystery 37. Sing and Be Happy 37. *Thin Ice* 37. Life Begins in College 37. Love and Kisses 37. Sally, Irene and Mary 38. Josette 38. My Lucky Star 38. *Hold that Coed* 38. Just Around the Corner 38. Tailspin 39. Daytime Wife 39. Too Busy to Work 39. Free, Blonde and Twenty One 40. Manhattan Heartbeat 40. Sailor's Lady 40. For Beauty's Sake 41. Sun Valley Serenade 41. *Hold that Ghost* 41. Two Latins from Manhattan 42. Yokel Boy 42. Sweetheart of the Fleet 42. He's My Guy 43. Two Señoritas from Chicago 43. Around the World 43. *Show Business* 44. Beautiful but Broke 44. Kansas City Kitty 44. She Gets Her Man 45. *George White's Scandals* 45. She Wrote the Book 46. If You Knew Susie 48. The Traveling Saleswoman 50. Love that Brute 50. The Groom Wore Spurs 51. Harem Girl 53.
TV series: I Married Joan 52–56.

Davis, Sir John (1906–1993).
British executive, a former accountant who became chairman of the Rank Organization. After the artistic extravagance of the mid-40s, he imposed financial stability; but subsequent film production was comparatively routine and in the late 60s

dwindled to nothing as the group was diversified into other fields.

Davis, Judy (1955–).
Australian leading lady, a former singer. Married actor Colin Friels.
My *Brilliant Career* (BFA) 79. Winter of Our Dreams 81. Hoodwink 81. Heatwave 82. Who Dares Wins 82. A Woman Called Golda (TV) 82. A Passage to India (AAN) 84. Kangaroo 86. High Tide 87. Georgia 88. Impromptu 89. Alice 90. Barton Fink 91. Where Angels Fear to Tread 91. Naked Lunch 91. *Husbands and Wives* (AAN) 92. The Ref 94. The New Age 94. Children of the Revolution 96. Blood & Wine 96. Deconstructing Harry 97. Absolute Power 97. Celebrity 98, etc.
❝ She's the patron saint of modern emotions. – *Michael Tolkin*

Davis, Lilian Hall (1896–1933) (aka Lillian Hall-Davis).
Blonde English leading actress of the silent era and star of two of Hitchcock's early movies. Born in London, she was in films from childhood, but failed to make the transition to sound and committed suicide.
The Admirable Crichton 18. The Better 'Ole 18. The Honey Pot 20. The Game of Life 22. Brown Sugar 22. The Faithful Heart 22. A Royal Divorce 23. The Knock Out 23. Pagliacci 23. Should a Doctor Tell 23. Quo Vadis? 24. Roses of Picardy 27. The Ring 27. Blighty 27. The Farmer's Wife 28. Many Waters 31. Volga Volga 33, etc.

Davis, Martin S. (1927–).
American production executive. He resigned as chairman and chief executive of Paramount in April 1994.

Davis, Miles (1926–1991).
Innovative American jazz trumpeter, composer and actor. He was married to actress Cicely Tyson (1981–89).
Lift to the Scaffold/Ascenseur pour l'Echafaud (m) 57. Jack Johnson (m) 71. Siesta (m) 87. Dingo – Dog of the Desert (a, m) 91.

Davis, Nancy (1921–) (Anne Frances Robbins).
American leading lady of a few 50s films; married Ronald Reagan.
Shadow on the Wall 50. The Doctor and the Girl 50. Night into Morning 51. It's a Big Country 53. Donovan's Brain 53. Crash Landing 57. Hellcats of the Navy 59, etc.

Davis, Ossie (1917–).
American actor of massive presence.
No Way Out 50. The Joe Louis Story 53. Gone Are the Days (& w) 63. *The Hill* 65. *The Scalphunters* 68. Sam Whiskey 69. Slaves 69. Cotton Comes to Harlem (d only) 70. Kongi's Harvest (d only) 71. Black Girl (d only) 72. Malcolm X 72. Gordon's War (d only) 73. Let's Do It Again 75. Hot Stuff 79. Harry and Son 83. Avenging Angel 84. School Daze 88. Do the Right Thing 89. Joe versus the Volcano 90. Jungle Fever 91. Gladiator 92. Queen (TV) 93. Grumpy Old Men 93. Ray Alexander: A Taste for Justice (TV) 94. The Stand (TV) 94. The Client 94. I'm Not Rapaport 96. Get on the Bus 96. Twelve Angry Men (TV) 97. Miss Evers' Boys (TV) 97, etc.

Davis, Philip (1953–).
English actor, director and writer, usually in working-class roles. He began with the National Youth Theatre.
AS ACTOR: Quilp 74. Quadrophenia 79. Pink Floyd: The Wall 82. The Bounty 84. The Doctor and the Devils 85. Comrades 86. *High Hopes* 88. Blue Ice 92. Still Crazy 98, etc.
TV series: Moving Story 94–95.
AS DIRECTOR: i.d. 95.

Davis, Sammi (1964–).
British actress.
Mona Lisa 86. Hope and Glory 87. Lionheart 87. A Prayer for the Dying 87. Consuming Passions 88. The Lair of the White Worm 88. The Rainbow 89. Chernobyl: The Final Warning (TV) 91. Shadow of China 91. Four Rooms (US) 95. Stand-Ins (US) 97. Woundings (US) 98, etc.

Davis, Sammy, Jnr (1925–1990).
American singer and entertainer, a bundle of vitality who described himself as 'a one-eyed Jewish Negro'. His second wife was actress Mai Britt (1960–67).
Autobiographies: 1966, *Yes I Can*. 1980, *Hollywood in a Suitcase*. 1989, *Why Me?*
Biography: 1996, *Sammy Davis Jnr, My Father* by Tracey Davis.
■ Rufus Jones for President (debut) 29. Season's Greetings 30. *Anna Lucasta* 58. *Porgy and Bess* 59. *Ocean's Eleven* 60. Pepe 60. A Raisin in the Sun 61. Sergeants Three 62. Convicts Four 62. Nightmare in the Sun 63. Johnny Cool 63. Robin and the Seven Hoods 64. The Threepenny Opera 65. A Man Called Adam 66. Salt and Pepper 68. Sweet Charity 68. Man without Mercy 69. Gone with the West 69. The Pigeon (TV) 70. One More Time 70. The Trackers (TV) 71. Diamonds Are Forever 71. Poor Devil (TV) 73. Cinderella at the Palace (TV) 78. Stop the World I Want to Get Off 78. Little Moon and Jud McGraw 78. The Cannonball Run 81. Heidi's Song 82. Cracking Up 83. Cannonball Run II 84. Moon over Parador 88. Tap 89.

Davis, Stringer (1896–1973).
Gentle-mannered British character actor who was usually to be found playing small roles in the films of his wife Margaret Rutherford.
The Happiest Days of Your Life 50. Curtain Up 53. Murder Most Foul 62. Murder Ahoy 64, etc.

Davis, Tamra (1962–).
American director, from rock videos.
Guncrazy 92. CB4 93. Billy Madison 95. Half-Baked 97, etc.
❝ Most of Hollywood's so-called women's movies are based on men's fantasies. – *T.D.*

Davison, Bruce (1946–).
Slightly-built young American character actor.
Last Summer 69. The Strawberry Statement 70. *Willard* 71. The Jerusalem File 71. Ulzana's Raid 72. Mame 73. The Affair (TV) 73. Mother, Jugs and Speed 76. Short Eyes 77. Brass Target 78. High Risk 81. Crimes of Passion 84. Spies Like Us 85. The Ladies Club 86. The Misfit Brigade 86. Longtime Companion (AAN) 90. Steel and Lace 91. Oscar 91. An Ambush of Ghosts 93. Short Cuts 93. Six Degrees of Separation 93. Far from Home: The Adventures of Yellow Dog 95. Homage 95. The Cure 95. The Crucible 96. Hidden in America (TV) 96. Lovelife 97. Paulie 98. Apt Pupil 98, etc.
TV series: Hunter 85–86. Harry and the Hendersons 90–92.

D'Avril, Yola (1907–1984).
French actress and dancer who went to North America in the 20s, arriving in Hollywood in the mid-20s, where she first worked as an extra.
Lady Be Good 28. *All Quiet on the Western Front* 30. The Bad One 30. The Man from Yesterday 32. I Met Him in Paris 37. Little Boy Lost 53, etc.

Daw, Evelyn (1912–1970).
American leading lady of the 30s.
Something to Sing About 37. Panamint's Bad Man 38, etc.

Dawson, Anthony (1916–1992).
Lean-faced British character actor.
The Way to the Stars 45. The Queen of Spades 48. The Long Dark Hall 51. Dial M for Murder (US) 54. Midnight Lace (US) 60. Seven Seas to Calais (US) 63, etc.

Dawson, Anthony M.:
see MARGHERITI, Antonio.

Dawson, Marion (1889–1975).
English actress who began as an opera singer and switched to comedy when her voice failed. Her screen career faltered after she lost an eye in an accident with fireworks in 1932.
The Last Coupon 32. His Wife's Mother 32. The Love Nest 33. A Political Party 34. Save a Little Sunshine 38, etc.

Dawson, Ralph (1897–1962).
American editor.
Lady of the Night 25. The Singing Fool 28. Outward Bound 30. Girl Missing 33. The Story of Louis Pasteur 35. A Midsummer Night's Dream 35. Anthony Adverse 36. The Adventures of Robin Hood 38. Ivy 47. All My Sons 48. Undertow 49. Harvey 50. Island in the Sky 53. The High and the Mighty 54, many others.

Day, Clarence (1874–1935).
American humorist whose light pieces about his family were the basis for the apparently immortal play *Life with Father*, which was successfully filmed in 1947.

Day, Dennis (1921–1988) (Eugene Patrick McNulty).
American singer and light actor of the 40s and 50s, most familiar from Jack Benny's radio and TV show.
Buck Benny Rides Again 40. Music in Manhattan 44. One Sunday Afternoon 48. I'll Get By 50. Golden Girl 51. The Girl Next Door 53, etc.

Day, Doris (1924–) (Doris Kappelhoff).
Vivacious American dance-band singer who achieved instant star status in 1948 and preserved her eminence by transferring to a brand of innocent sex comedy which was all her own and pleased the 60s.
Biographies: 1976, *Doris Day, Her Own Story* by A. E. Hotchner. 1992, *Doris Day* by Eric Braun.
■ *Romance on the High Seas* 48. My Dream is Yours 49. It's a Great Feeling 49. Young Man with a Horn 50. Tea for Two 50. West Point Story 50. *Storm Warning* 50. Lullaby of Broadway 51. *On Moonlight Bay* 51. I'll See You in My Dreams 51. Starlift 51. The Winning Team 52. April in Paris 52. By the Light of the Silvery Moon 53. *Calamity Jane* 53. Lucky Me 54. *Young at Heart* 55. Love Me or Leave Me 55. The Man Who Knew Too Much 56. Julie 56. *The Pajama Game* 57. Teacher's Pet 58. The Tunnel of Love 58. It Happened to Jane 59. *Pillow Talk* (AAN) 59. Please Don't Eat the Daisies 60. Midnight Lace 60. Lover Come Back 62. *That Touch of Mink* 62. Jumbo 62. The Thrill of It All 63. Move Over Darling 63. Send Me No Flowers 64. Do Not Disturb 65. The Glass Bottom Boat 66. Caprice 67. The Ballad of Josie 68. Where Were You When the Lights Went Out? 68. With Six You Get Egg Roll 68. That's Entertainment! III 94.
TV series: *The Doris Day Show* 68–72. Doris Day's Best Friends 85.
✪ For her box-office domination of 60s comedies by playing the perennial virgin. *That Touch of Mink*.
❝ I've been around so long I can remember Doris Day before she was a virgin. – *Groucho Marx*
She thinks she doesn't get old. She told me once it was her cameraman who was getting older. She was going to fire him. – *Joe Pasternak*
Just about the remotest person I know. – *Kirk Douglas*
No one guessed that under all those dirndls lurked one of the wildest asses in Hollywood. – *Ross Hunter*
My doctor won't let me watch Doris Day. I have a family history of diabetes. – *Marvin Kitman*
Underneath her wholesome exterior beat the heart of a true sex goddess and a very strong woman. – *Debbie Harry*

Day, Ernest (1927–).
British cinematographer and occasional director.
Running Scared 72. Visit to a Chief's Son 74. Ghost in a Noonday Sun 74. Made 75. The Song Remains the Same 76. The Revenge of the Pink Panther 78. Sphinx 80. Green Ice (co-d) 81. Waltz across Texas (d) 83. A Passage to India (AAN) 84. Superman IV: The Quest for Peace 87. Burning Secret 88. Parents 88, etc.

Day, Frances (1907–1984) (Frances Victoria Schenk).
American revue star, in London from 1925.
■ The Price of Divorce 27. OK Chief 30. Big Business 30. The First Mrs Frazer 32. Two Hearts in Waltztime 34. The Girl from Maxim's 34. Temptation 34. Oh Daddy 34. Public Nuisance No. 1 36. You Must Get Married 36. Dreams Come True 36. Who's Your Lady Friend? 37. The Girl in the Taxi 37. Kicking the Moon Around 38. Room for Two 40. *Fiddlers Three* (as Poppaea) 44. Tread Softly 52. There's Always a Thursday 57. Climb up the Wall 60.
❝ Little Day, you've had a busy man. – *Bud Flanagan, when F.D. turned up for rehearsals looking decidedly shaggy*

Day, Jill (1932–1990).
British pop singer and leading lady.
Always a Bride 54. All for Mary 56.

Day, Josette (1914–1978) (J. Dagory).
French leading lady.
Allo Berlin, Ici Paris 32. La Fille du Puisatier 40. *La Belle et la Bête* 46. Les Parents Terribles 48. Four Days' Leave 50, etc.

Day, Laraine (1917–) (Laraine Johnson).
American leading lady of the 40s, with stage experience.
Autobiographical book 1952: *Day With The Giants*.
Stella Dallas 37. Scandal Street 38. Border G-Men 38. *Young Dr Kildare* (and others in the series) 39. My Son, My Son 40. *Foreign Correspondent* 40. *The Trial of Mary Dugan* 41. Unholy Partners 41. Fingers at the Window 41. Journey for Margaret 42. Mr Lucky 43. The Story of Dr Wassell 43. Bride by Mistake 44. Those Endearing Young Charms 45. Keep Your Powder Dry 45. *The Locket* 46. Tycoon 47. My Dear Secretary 48. I Married a Communist 49. Without Honour 49. The High and the Mighty 54. Toy Tiger 56. Three for Jamie Dawn 57. The Third Voice 59. Murder on Flight 502 (TV) 75. Return to Fantasy Island (TV) 78, etc.

Day, Matt.
Australian actor, from the theatre.
Muriel's Wedding 94. Love and Other Catastrophes 96. Dating the Enemy 96. Kiss or Kill 97. Doing Time for Patsy Cline 97. Muggers 98, etc.
TV series: Water Rats 95–96.

Day, Richard (1896–1972).
Canadian-born production designer, in Hollywood from 1918.
Foolish Wives 22. Greed 24. The Merry Widow 25. The Student Prince 27. Queen Kelly 28. Whoopee (AAN) 30. The Front Page 31. Rain 32. Arrowsmith (AAN) 32. Moulin Rouge 34. The Affairs of Cellini (AAN) 34. *The Dark Angel* (AA) 35. *We Live Again* 35. Clive of India 35. *Dodsworth* (AA) 36. Dead End (AAN) 37. Goldwyn Follies (AAN) 38. Lillian Russell (AAN) 40. Down Argentine Way (AAN) 40. *How Green Was My Valley* (AA) 41. Tobacco Road 41. *The Little Foxes* 41. Blood and Sand (AAN) 41. This Above All (AA) 42. My Gal Sal (AA) 42. Orchestra Wives 42. The Razor's Edge (AAN) 46. Joan of Arc (AAN) 48. *A Streetcar Named Desire* (AA) 51. Hans Christian Andersen (AAN) 52. *On the Waterfront* (AA) 54. Solomon and Sheba 59. Exodus 60. The Chase 66. Valley of the Dolls 67. The Greatest Story Ever Told (AAN) 65. Tora! Tora! Tora! (AAN) 70, etc.

Day, Robert (1922–).
British director, former cameraman.
The Green Man 57. Grip of the Strangler 58. First Man into Space 58. Corridors of Blood 59. Bobbikins 59. Two-Way Stretch 60. The Rebel 61. Operation Snatch 62. Tarzan's Three Challenges 64. She 65. Tarzan and the Valley of Gold 66. Tarzan and the Great River 67. Ritual of Evil (TV) 69. The House on Greenapple Road (TV) 70. Banyon (TV) 71. In Broad Daylight (TV) 71. Mr and Mrs Bo Jo Jones (TV) 71. Death Stalk (TV) 75. Switch (TV) 75. Having Babies (TV) 76. Logan's Run (TV) 77. The Initiation of Sarah (TV) 77. The Grass Is Always Greener Over the Septic Tank (TV) 78. *Murder by Natural Causes* (TV) 79. Walking Through the Fire (TV) 79. The Man with Bogart's Face 80. Peter and Paul (TV) 81. Running Out (TV) 83. Hollywood Wives (TV) 85. Love, Mary (TV) 85. The Quick and the Dead (TV) 87. Higher Ground (TV) 88, etc.

Day, Vera (1939–).
Bubbly blonde British actress.
Dance Little Lady 52. A Kid for Two Farthings 55. It's a Great Day 56. Hell Drivers 57. Quatermass II 57. The Prince and the Showgirl 57. Up the Creek 58. I Was Monty's Double 58. Too Many Crooks 59. Watch It Sailor 61. Saturday Night Out 63, etc.

Day-Lewis, Daniel (1957–).
British leading actor. He is the son of Cecil Day-Lewis, poet laureate, and actress Jill BALCON.
Biography: 1995, *Daniel Day-Lewis* by Laura Jackson.
Gandhi 83. The Bounty 84. My Beautiful Laundrette 85. A Room with a View 85. Nanou 87. Stars and Bars 88. The Unbearable Lightness of Being 88. Eversmile, New Jersey 89. My Left Foot (AA) 89. The Last of the Mohicans 92. The Age of Innocence 93. *In the Name of the Father* (AAN) 93. The Crucible 96. The Boxer 97, etc.
❝ You always, in the end, believe you're a fraud. – *D.D-L.*

De Acosta, Mercedes (1893–1968).
American screenwriter and dramatist, the daughter of Spanish and Cuban parents, whose lasting claim to fame is that she was the lover of, among others, actresses Eva Le Gallienne, Ona Munson (Belle Watling in *Gone with the Wind*), Greta Garbo and Marlene Dietrich.
Autobiography: 1960, *Here Lies the Heart*.
Biography: 1994, *Loving Garbo* by Hugo Vickers.
❝ You can't dismiss Mercedes lightly. She has had two of the most important women in the United States – Garbo and Dietrich. – *Alice B. Toklas*

De Almeida, Joaquim (1957–).
Leading Portuguese actor, in international films.
The Honorary Consul/Beyond the Limit 83. Good Morning Babylon 87. Clear and Present Danger 94. Only You 94. According to Pereira 95. Desperado 95. Adam and Eve/Adao e Eva 96. Nostromo (TV) 96. Larry McMurtry's Dead Man's Walk (TV) 96, etc.

De Anda, Peter (1940–).
American leading man of the 70s. In the 90s, he was working in a bookshop in Manhattan.
Cutter (TV) 72. Come Back Charleston Blue 72. The New Centurions 72. Beulah Land (TV) 80, etc.
TV series: One Life to Live 68–70.

De Angelis, Guido.
Italian composer, in collaboration with Maurizio De Angelis.
They Call Me Trinity 70. Trinity Is Still My Name 71. All the Way Boys 73. Run Run Joe 74. Zorro 75. Keoma/The Violent Breed 76. Charleston 78. Killer Fish 79. Between Miracles 79. Safari Express 80. The Immortal Bachelor 80. Great White 82. Blue Paradise 82. Yor, the Hunter from the Future 83. Body Beat 89, etc.

De Angelis, Maurizio.
Italian composer, in collaboration with Guido DE ANGELIS (see entry for films).

De Antonio, Emile (1920–1989).
American experimental documentarist.
Point of Order 64. Rush to Judgment 67. America Is Hard to See 68. In the Year of the Pig 69. Milhouse 71. Painters Painting 73. Underground 76. In the King of Prussia 82. Mr Hoover and I 89, etc.

De Banzie, Brenda (1915–1981).
British character actress who got her big chance on the edge of middle age; later played flouncy matrons.
The Long Dark Hall 51. I Believe in You 52. *Hobson's Choice* 54. The Purple Plain 54. What Every Woman Wants 54. A Kid for Two Farthings 55. The Man Who Knew Too Much 56. The 39 Steps 59. *The Entertainer* 60. Flame in the Streets 61. The Mark 61. The Pink Panther 63. Pretty Polly 67, etc.

De Benning, Burr.
American character actor.
Beach Red 67. Sweet November 69. City Beneath the Sea (TV) 71. St Ives 76. The Incredible Melting Man 77. Hanging by a Thread (TV) 79. A Nightmare on Elm Street 5: The Dream Child 89, etc.

De Bont, Jan (1943–).
Dutch cinematographer turned director, in Hollywood from the mid-80s. *Speed*, his first feature, was a success, his asking price as director rising to $4m. He followed it with *Twister*, another hit. He is co-founder of the production company Blue Tulip.
Turkish Delight/Turks Fruit 73. Katie's Passion/Keetje Tippel 75. Max Havelaar 76. Private Lessons 81. I'm Dancing as Fast as I Can 82. Cujo 83. All the Right Moves 83. The Fourth Man/De Vierde Man 83. Flesh and Blood 85. The Jewel of the Nile 85. Ruthless People 86. The Clan of the Cave Bear 86. Who's That Girl? 87. Leonard Part 6 87. Die Hard 88. Black Rain 89. Bert Rigby, You're a Fool 89. The Hunt for Red October 90. Flatliners 90. Basic Instinct 92. Shining Through 92. Lethal Weapon 3 92. *Speed* (d) 94. Twister (d) 96. Speed 2: Cruise Control (& co-w) 97, etc.

De Borba, Dorothy (1925–).
American child actress, in the Our Gang comedies 1930–35.

De Bray, Yvonne (1889–1954).
French character actress, in films from 1943.
Gigi 48. *Les Parents Terribles* 49. Olivia 50. Caroline Chérie 50. Nous Sommes Tous des Assassins 52, etc.

De Broca, Philippe (1933–).
French director and screenwriter who first worked as an assistant to François Truffaut and Claude Chabrol.
Les Jeux de l'Amour 60. Le Farceur 60. The Seven Deadly Sins (part) 61. L'Amant de Cinq Jours 61. Cartouche 62. *Les Veinards* (part) 63. *That Man from Rio* 63. Un Monsieur de Compagnie 64. Les Tribulations d'un Chinois en Chine 65. The Oldest Profession 67. King of Hearts 67. Devil by the Tail 68. Give Her the Moon 70. La Poudre d'Escampette 71. Chère Louise 72. Le Magnifique 73. Dear Inspector 77. Psy 80. On a Volé la Cuisse de Jupiter 80. Louisiana 84. The Gypsy 85. Chouans! 88. The 1001 Nights/Sheherazade (wd) 90. The Keys of Paradise/Les Clés du Paradis 91. Tales from the Zoo 95. On Guard! (co-w, d) 97, etc.

De Brulier, Nigel (1878–1948).
British actor in Hollywood: career waned with sound.
Intolerance 16. The Four Horsemen of the Apocalypse 21. The Three Musketeers (as Richelieu) 21. Salome 23. The Hunchback of Notre Dame 23. Ben Hur 26. Wings 27. Noah's Ark 29. The Iron Mask 29. Moby Dick 31. Rasputin and the Empress 32. Mary of Scotland 36. The Garden of Allah 36. The Hound of the Baskervilles 39. One Million B.C. 40. The Adventures of Captain Marvel 41, many others.

De Camp, Rosemary (1913–).
American character actress specializing in active motherly types.
Cheers for Miss Bishop 41. Jungle Book 42. This is the Army 43. *The Merry Monahans* 44. *Rhapsody in Blue* 45. From this Day Forward 46. Nora Prentiss 47. Night unto Night 49. The Big Hangover 50. *On Moonlight Bay* 51. By the Light of the Silvery Moon 53. Many Rivers to Cross 55. Thirteen Ghosts 60. Blind Ambition (TV) 79. Saturday the 14th 81, etc.
TV series: The Life of Riley 49–50. *The Bob Cummings Show* 55–59. That Girl 66–70.
~ Miss De Camp was thirteen years James Cagney's junior – but in *Yankee Doodle Dandy* she played his mother.

De Carlo, Yvonne (1922–) (Peggy Middleton).
Canadian leading lady, a star in the 40s of Hollywood's most outrageous easterns and westerns.
Salome Where She Danced 45. Frontier Gal 45. Song of Scheherezade 47. Brute Force 47. Slave Girl 47. Black Bart (as Lola Montez) 48. Casbah 48. River Lady 48. *Criss Cross* 49. Calamity Jane and Sam Bass 49. The Desert Hawk 50. Tomahawk 51. Hotel Sahara 51. Scarlet Angel 52. Sea Devils 52. Sombrero 53. The Captain's Paradise 53. Passion 54. Magic Fire 56. The Ten Commandments 56. Death of a Scoundrel 56. Band of Angels 57. McLintock 63. Law of the Lawless 64. Munster Go Home 66. The Power 68. The Seven Minutes 71. Guyana Cult of the Damned 80. The Man with Bogart's Face 80. Liar's Moon 82. Flesh and Bullets 85. A Masterpiece of Murder (TV) 86. American Gothic 88. Oscar 91, etc.
TV series: *The Munsters* 64–65.

De Casalis, Jeanne (1897–1966).
British revue comedienne and character actress, best known as radio's 'Mrs Feather' in dithery telephone monologues. She was married to Colin Clive.
Autobiography: 1953, *Things I Don't Remember*.
Settled out of Court 25. The Arcadians 27. Nell Gwyn 34. Cottage to Let 41. Charley's Big Hearted Aunt 41. Those Kids from Town 42. Medal for the General 44. This Man Is Mine 46. Woman Hater 48, etc.

De Cordoba, Pedro (1881–1950).
American stage actor, lean and often sinister, in many silent and sound films.
Carmen 15. Maria Rosa 16. Runaway Romany 20. Young Diana 22. The Crusades 35. Anthony Adverse 36. The Light That Failed 39. The Ghost Breakers 40. The Mark of Zorro 40. Son of Fury 42. For Whom the Bell Tolls 43. The Beast with Five Fingers 47. When the Redskins Rode 50, etc.

De Cordova, Arturo (1908–1973) (Arturo Garcia).
Mexican leading man with flashing grin and impudent eyes. Popular in Mexico from 1935; made a few Hollywood films in the 40s.
For Whom the Bell Tolls 43. Hostages 43. *Frenchman's Creek* 44. Incendiary Blonde 44. A Medal for Benny 45. Masquerade in Mexico 45. The Flame 47. New Orleans 47. The Adventures of Casanova 48. *El* (Mex.) 51. Kill Him for Me 53, etc.

De Cordova, Frederick (1910–).
American director with stage and TV experience.
■ Too Young to Know 45. Her Kind of Man 46. That Way with Women 47. Love and Learn 47. Always Together 47. Wallflower 48. For the Love of Mary 48. The Countess of Monte Cristo 48. Illegal Entry 49. The Gal Who Took the West 49. Buccaneer's Girl 50. Peggy 50. The Desert Hawk 50. Bedtime for Bonzo 51. Katie Did It 51. Little Egypt 51. Finders Keepers 51. Here Come the Nelsons 52. Bonzo Goes to College 52. Yankee Buccaneer 53. Column South 53. I'll Take Sweden 65. Frankie and Johnny 66.

De Corsia, Ted (1904–1973).
American character actor with long vaudeville experience; usually played surly villains.
The Lady from Shanghai 47. *Naked City* 48. The Enforcer 51. Vengeance Valley 51. Man In the Dark 53. 20,000 Leagues under the Sea 54. The Big Combo 55. Slightly Scarlet 56. The Killing 56. Baby Face Nelson 57. Gunfight at the O.K. Corral 57. Blood on the Arrow 61. The Quick Gun 64. Nevada Smith 66. Five Card Stud 68, many others.
TV series: Steve Canyon 57–60.

De Courville, Albert (1887–1960).
British stage director who directed a few film comedies.
Wolves 30. The Midshipmaid 32. This is the Life 33. Things Are Looking Up 34. The Case of Gabriel Perry 35. Seven Sinners 36. Crackerjack 38. The Lambeth Walk 38. An Englishman's Home 39, etc.

DeCuir, John (1918–).
American production designer.
Naked City 48. The Snows of Kilimanjaro 51. Call Me Mister 52. The King and I 56. South Pacific 57. Cleopatra 63. The Agony and the Ecstasy 65. Hello Dolly 69. The Great White Hope 70. Once is not Enough 75. Raise the Titanic 80. Dead Men Don't Wear Plaid 82. Ghostbusters 84. Jo Jo Dancer, Your Life Is Calling 86. Legal Eagles 86, etc.

De Filippo, Eduardo (1900–1984) (Eduardo Passarelli).
Italian actor and director of many and varied talents.
Tre Uomini in Frac (a) 32. Il Capello a Tre Punte (a) 40. In Campagna e Caduta una Stella (w, d, a) 40. Il Sogno di Tutti (a) 40. La Vita Ricomincia (a) 45. Assunta Spina (w, a) 47. Napoli Milionaria (w, d, a) 50. Altri Tempi (a) 51. Filumena Marturano (w, d, a) 51. The Girls of the Spanish Steps (a) 52. Villa Borghese (a) 53. Napoletani a Milano (w, d, a) 53. Questi Fantasmi (w, d, a) 54. Fortunella (d, a) 58. Raw Wind in Eden (a) 58. Ghosts of Rome (a) 60. Shoot Loud, Louder, I Don't Understand (w, d, a) 66, many others.

De Forest, Lee (1873–1961).
American inventor, pioneer of many developments in wireless telegraphy, also the De Forest Phonofilm of the 20s, an early experiment in synchronized sound.

De Funès, Louis (1908–1983).
French character comedian.
Lock up the Spoons 56. Femmes de Paris 58. Taxi 59. A Pied à Cheval et en Spoutnik 61. The Sucker 65. Fantomas 66. Don't Look Now 67. Jo 71. The Mad Adventures of Rabbi Jacob 73. Up a Tree 75. What's Cooking in Paris 77. Les Charlots 79. L'Avare 80, many others.

De' Giorgi, Elsa (1915–1997).
Leading Italian actress of the 30s and 40s, who turned in the 50s to writing novels and running an acting school. Her lovers included novelist Italo Calvino.
Autobiography: 1955, *I Coetantei*.
I'll Always Love You/T'Amero Sempre 33. Nini Falpala 33. Porto 35. Ma Non e Una Cosa Seria 36. La Mazurka di Papa 38. Il Fornaretto di Venezia 39. La Sposa dei Re 39. Capitan Fracassa 40. Fra Diavolo 42. La Locandiera 44. Manu, il Contrabbandiere 48. Salo, the 120 Days of Sodom 75, etc.

De Govia, Jackson.
American production designer.
Boulevard Nights 79. Butch and Sundance, the Early Years 79. It's My Turn 80. My Bodyguard 80. Spacehunter: Adventures in the Forbidden Zone 83. Red Dawn 84. Remo Williams: The Adventure Begins 85. 'Night, Mother 86. Nobody's Fool 86. Roxanne 87. Punchline 88. Die Hard 88. In Country 89. Dad 89. Sister Act 92. Speed 94. Multiplicity 96. Volcano 97. My Giant 98, etc.

De Grasse, Robert (1900–1971).
American cinematographer, with RKO from 1934.
Three Pals 26. Fury of the Wild 29. Break of Hearts 35. *Stage Door* 37. The Story of Vernon and Irene Castle 39. Bachelor Mother 39. Kitty Foyle 40. Forever and a Day 43. Step Lively 44. *The Body Snatcher* 45. The Miracle of the Bells 48. Home of the Brave 49. The Men 50. Chicago Calling 52, many others.

De Grasse, Sam (1875–1953).
Canadian leading actor, often in villainous roles. In films from 1912.
Birth of a Nation 15. Intolerance 16. The Scarlet Car 17. Robin Hood (as Prince John) 22. The Spoilers 23. The Black Pirate 26. King of Kings 27. The Farmer's Daughter 28. Wall Street 29. Captain of the Guard 30, etc.

De Grunwald, Anatole (1910–1967).
British producer, in films since 1939.
French Without Tears (w) 39. Quiet Wedding (w) 40. The First of the Few (w) 42. The Demi-Paradise 42. The Way to the Stars 45. The Winslow Boy (& w) 48. The Holly and the Ivy (& w) 54. The Doctor's Dilemma 58. Libel (& w) 61. Come Fly with Me 62. The VIPs 63. The Yellow Rolls-Royce 64. Stranger in the House 67, many others.

De Grunwald, Dmitri (1914–1990).
British producer, brother of Anatole de Grunwald.
The Dock Brief 62. Perfect Friday 67. Connecting Rooms 69. The Last Grenade 69. Murphy's War 71. That Lucky Touch 75, etc.

De Haven, Carter (1887–1977).
American stage star who appeared in a few silent films. His son *Carter de Haven Jnr* (1910–1979) was a production manager, especially for Chaplin.

De Haven, Gloria (1924–).
American soubrette, films mostly light musicals of no enduring quality.
■ Modern Times 36. The Great Dictator 40. Susan and God 40. Keeping Company 41. Two Faced Woman 41. The Penalty 41. *Best Foot Forward* 43. Thousands Cheer 43. Broadway Rhythm 44. *Two Girls and a Sailor* 44. Step Lively 44. The Thin Man Goes Home 44. Between Two Women 45. Summer Holiday 48. Scene of the Crime 49. The Doctor and the Girl 49. Yes Sir That's My Baby 49. The Yellow Cab Man 50. Three Little Words 50. Summer Stock 50. I'll Get By 50. Two Tickets to Broadway 51. Down among the Sheltering Palms 53. So This Is Paris 55. The Girl Rush 55. Call Her Mom (TV) 72. Who Is the Black Dahlia? (TV) 75. Banjo Hackett (TV) 76. Sharon, Portrait of a Mistress 77. Evening in Byzantium (TV) 78. The Legend of O. B. Taggart 94. That's Entertainment! III 94.
TV series: Ryan's Hope 75. Nakia 79.

De Havilland, Olivia (1916–).
British-born leading lady, sister of Joan Fontaine. In Hollywood from teenage as leading lady of comedy, romance and costume drama; later proved herself an actress.

Semi-autobiography: 1960, *Every Frenchman Has One*.

■ *A Midsummer Night's Dream* 35. The Irish in Us 35. Alibi Ike 35. Captain Blood 35. Anthony Adverse 36. The Charge of the Light Brigade 36. Call It a Day 36. The Great Garrick 36. It's Love I'm After 37. Gold Is Where You Find It 37. Four's a Crowd 38. *The Adventures of Robin Hood* 38. Hard To Get 38. Wings of the Navy 39. Dodge City 39. *Gone with the Wind* (AAN) 39. Elizabeth and Essex 39. Raffles 40. My Love Came Back 40. Santa Fe Trail 40. Strawberry Blonde 41. Hold Back the Dawn (AAN) 41. They Died with Their Boots On 41. The Male Animal 42. In This Our Life 42. Government Girl 43. Thank Your Lucky Stars 43. Princess O'Rourke 43. The Well-Groomed Bride 45. *Devotion* (as Charlotte Brontë) 46. *The Dark Mirror* 46. *To Each His Own* (AA) 46. *The Snake Pit* (AAN) 47. *The Heiress* (AA) 49. My Cousin Rachel 52. That Lady 55. Not as a Stranger 55. The Ambassador's Daughter 56. The Proud Rebel 58. Libel (GB) 60. The Light in the Piazza 62. Lady in a Cage 64. *Hush Hush Sweet Charlotte* 64. The Adventurers 69. Pope Joan 72. The Screaming Woman (TV) 72. The Fifth Musketeer 77. Airport 77 77. The Swarm 78. Roots: The Next Generation (TV) 79. Murder Is Easy (TV) 82. Charles and Diana: A Royal Romance (TV) (as the Queen Mother) 82. The Woman He Loved (TV) 88.

☼ For her development from a charming leading lady to a star actress of some distinction. *The Dark Mirror*.

Famous line (*The Heiress*): 'Yes, I can be very cruel. I have been taught by masters.'

De Heer, Rolf (1957–).
Dutch-born screenwriter and director, in Australia. He worked for the Australian Broadcasting Commission in a variety of jobs before studying at the Australian Film and TV School.

Tail of a Tiger 84. Incident at Raven's Gate 88. Dingo 91. *Bad Boy Bubby* 93. The Quiet Room (p, wd) 96. Dance Me to My Song (p, co-w, d) 98.

De Jesus, Luchi (1923–1984).
American composer and arranger.

Slaughter 72. A Time for Love 74. Black Belt Jones 74. Thieves 77, etc.

De Keyzer, Bruno.
French cinematographer in international films.

A Sunday in the Country/Un Dimanche à la Campagne 84. 'Round Midnight 86. Little Dorrit 87. Beatrice 88. Reunion/L'Ami Retrouvé 89. Life and Nothing But/La Vie et Rien d'Autre 89. December Bride (GB) 91. Impromptu (GB) 91. War of the Buttons (GB) 94. The Queen of the Night 94. North Star 96. The Fifth Province 97. Mojo (GB) 97. The Commissioner 98, etc.

De La Iglesia, Alex (1965–).
Spanish director and screenwriter, born in Bilbao.

Acción Mutante (co-w, d) 93. The Day of the Beast (co-w, d) 95. Perdita Durango 97.

De La Motte, Marguerite (1902–1950).
American leading actress in silent films. Born in Deluth, Minnesota, she trained as a dancer, studying under Pavlova, and had her greatest successes playing opposite Douglas FAIRBANKS. Married actor John Bowers, with whom she also starred in several films.

The Mark of Zorro 20. The Three Musketeers 21. When a Man's a Man 24. The Beloved Brute 24. Red Dice 26. The Unknown Soldier 26. The Iron Mask 29. Woman's Man 34. Reg'lar Fellers 42, etc.

De La Patellière, Denys (1921–).
French director.

Le Défroqué (w only) 52. Les Aristocrates 56. Retour de Manivelle 57. Les Grandes Familles 59. Marco the Magnificent 65. Du Rififi à Paname 66. Black Sun 66. Le Tatoué 68. Prêtres Interdits 73. Diamond Swords 95, etc.

De La Tour, Frances (1945–).
Angular British character actress who plays both comedy and drama.

Country Dance 69. Every Home Should Have One 70. Our Miss Fred 72. To the Devil a Daughter 76. Wombling Free 77. Rising Damp 80. Genghis Cohen (TV) 93. Tom Jones (TV) 97, etc.

TV series: Rising Damp 74–78. Every Silver Lining 93. Downwardly Mobile 94.

De Lane Lea, William (1900–1964).
British executive, pioneer of sound dubbing processes.

De Laurentiis, Dino (1919–).
Italian producer who made a stab at Hollywood in the 70s.

Bitter Rice 48. Ulysses 52. La Strada 54. Barabbas 62. The Bible 65. Kiss the Girls and Make Them Die 67. Anzio 68. Barbarella 68. Waterloo 69. Wild Horses 73. Death Wish 74. King Kong 76. The White Buffalo 77. King of The Gypsies 78. Hurricane 79. The Brinks Job 79. Flash Gordon 80. Ragtime 81. Conan the Barbarian 82. Fighting Back 82. The Bounty 84. Dune 85. Cat's Eye 85. Manhunter 86. Desperate Hours 90. Once Upon a Crime 92. Body of Evidence 93. Assassins 95. Solomon and Sheba (TV) 95. Unforgettable 96. Breakdown 97, etc.

De Luise, Dom (1933–).
Rotund American comedy star who became one of the Mel Brooks repertory company. He is also the author of books, videos and a CD-ROM on the subject of cooking.

The Glass Bottom Boat 65. The Twelve Chairs 70. Blazing Saddles 73. Sherlock Holmes' Smarter Brother 75. Silent Movie 76. The World's Greatest Lover 78. The End 78. Hot Stuff (& d) 79. The Muppet Movie 79. Fatso 80. Smokey and the Bandit II 80. The Last Married Couple in America 80. Wholly Moses 80. The Cannonball Run 81. History of the World Part One 81. The Best Little Whorehouse in Texas 82. Happy (TV) 83. Johnny Dangerously 84. Haunted Honeymoon 86. Going Bananas 87. Spaceballs 87. Oliver and Company (voice) 88. All Dogs Go to Heaven (voice) 89. Loose Cannons 89. Happily Ever After 90. Driving Me Crazy 91. An American Tail: Fievel Goes West (voice) 91. Robin Hood: Men in Tights 93. Munchie Strikes Back 94. A Troll in Central Park (voice) 94. The Silence of the Hams (It.) 94. All Dogs Go to Heaven 2 (voice) 96, etc.

TV series: Lotsa Luck 73. Burke's Law 94.

❝ I'm actually a thin serious person but I play fat and funny, but only for the movies. – D. De L.

De Marney, Derrick (1906–1978).
Good-looking British actor with stage experience.

Music Hall 35. Things to Come 36. *Young and Innocent* 37. Victoria the Great (as Disraeli) 37. Blonde Cheat (US) 38. The Spider 39. The Lion Has Wings 40. Dangerous Moonlight 40. The First of the Few 42. Latin Quarter (& co-p) 46. Uncle Silas 47. Sleeping Car to Trieste 48. She Shall Have Murder (& p) 50. Meet Mr Callaghan (& p) 54. Private's Progress 55. Doomsday at Eleven 62. The Projected Man 66, etc.

De Marney, Terence (1909–1971).
British actor with stage experience, brother of Derrick de Marney. Died after falling under a train.

The Mystery of the Marie Celeste 36. I Killed the Count 38. Dual Alibi 46. No Way Back 49. Uneasy Terms 49. The Silver Chalice (US) 55. Death Is a Woman 66. All Neat in Black Stockings 69, etc.

De Masi, Francesco (1930–).
Italian composer. Born in Rome, he studied composition in Naples.

Maciste il Gladiatore Piu Forte del Mondo 62. Il Leone di Tebe 64. Arizona Colt 66. Sette Dollari Sul Rosso 66. Ostia 69. Bawdy Tales 73. The Arena (US) 74. Private Vices, Public Virtues 76. Lone Wolf McQuade (US) 83. Thunder Warrior 83. Rush 84. The Manhunt 85. Escape from the Bronx 85. Formula for Murder 86, etc.

De Maupassant, Guy (1850–1893).
French short storywriter. Work filmed includes *Diary of a Madman, Une Vie, Le Rosier de Madame Husson*, and many versions of *Boule de Suif*.

De Medeiros, Maria (1965–) (Maria de Almeida).
Portuguese leading actress, in international films from the 90s.

Henry and June 90. Meeting Venus 91. Tous les Jours Dimanche 94. Des Feux Mal Éteints 94. Two Brothers, My Sister/Tres Irmaos 94. Pulp Fiction 94. Adam and Eve/Adao e Eva 96. Limited Edition/Tire à Part 96. New from the Good Lord 96, etc.

De Mille, Cecil B. (1881–1959).
American producer-director, one of Hollywood's pioneers and autocrats. Notable in the 20s for sex comedies, in the 30s and 40s for action adventures, then for biblical epics; all now seem very stolid, but were enormously successful in their day.

Autobiography: 1959.

■ *The Squaw Man* 13. The Virginian 14. The Call of the North 14. What's His Name 14. The Man from Home 14. Rose of the Rancho 14. The Girl of the Golden West 15. The Warrens of Virginia 15. The Unafraid 15. The Captive 15. Wild Goose Chase 15. The Arab 15. Chimmie Fadden 15. Kindling 15. Maria Rosa 15. Carmen 15. Temptation 15. Chimmie Fadden Out West 15. *The Cheat* 15. The Golden Chance 16. The Trail of the Lonesome Pine 16. Joan the Woman 16. The Heart of Nora Flynn 16. The Dream Girl 16. A Romance of the Redwoods 17. The Little American 17. The Woman God Forgot 17. The Devil Stone 17. The Whispering Chorus 18. Old Wives for New 18. We Can't Have Everything 18. Till I Come Back to You 18. The Squaw Man 18. Don't Change Your Husband 19. For Better for Worse 19. Male and Female 19. Why Change your Wife? 20. Something to Think About 20. Forbidden Fruit 21. *The Affairs of Anatol* 21. Fool's Paradise 22. Saturday Night 22. Manslaughter 22. Adam's Rib 23. *The Ten Commandments* 23. Triumph 24. Feet of Clay 24. The Golden Bed 25. The Road to Yesterday 25. The Volga Boatmen 26. *King of Kings* 27. The Godless Girl 28. Dynamite 29. Madam Satan 30. The Squaw Man 31. *The Sign of the Cross* 32. This Day and Age 33. Four Frightened People 34. Cleopatra 34. *The Crusades* 35. *The Plainsman* 36. The Buccaneer 38. *Union Pacific* 39. Northwest Mounted Police 40. *Reap The Wild Wind* 42. The Story of Dr Wassell 44. Unconquered 47. Variety Girl (a) 47. Samson and Delilah 49. Sunset Boulevard (a) 50. The Greatest Show on Earth (AAp, AANd) 52. The Ten Commandments 56. The Buccaneer (p only) 59.

☼ For making himself an unseen star by imposing the personality of an autocratic schoolmaster on a variety of somewhat dubious material. *The Sign of the Cross*.

❝ Ready when you are, Mr De Mille. It's the tagline of a long shaggy dog story, the purpose of which is to establish de Mille as the producer of enormous, stagey biblical epics. Towards the end of his life he did submerge himself in this role, but his career embraced almost every kind of movie. Whatever the show, he made a success of it, and he was respected throughout Hollywood as a disciplinarian who always got his films out under budget. There was a joke during World War II:

Anyone who leaves de Mille for the armed forces is a slacker.

He is credited with sending back a writer's script and attaching a terrifying cover note:

What I have crossed out I didn't like.

What I haven't crossed out I am dissatisfied with.

He exercised supreme control over his stars, and once said to Paulette Goddard:

Remember you are a star. Never go across the alley even to dump garbage unless you are dressed to the teeth.

He told his staff:

You are here to please me. Nothing else on earth matters.

He went to extreme lengths to prove his authority. Arthur Miller thought:

I never met such an egotist in my life.

Even if he was wrong and knew it, once he said it it had to be.

His brother William was awed by his ambition and achievement:

The trouble with Cecil is that he always bites off more than he can chew – and then chews it.

The same William cast a wry eye on Cecil's first Bible picture in the 20s:

Having attended to the underclothes, bathrooms and matrimonial irregularities of his fellow citizens, he now began to consider their salvation.

Even when Cecil dealt with heavenly themes, he kept his feet on earth. He said to a scriptwriter:

It's just a damn good hot tale, so don't get a lot of thees, thous and thums on your mind.

His comparative ignorance of his favourite subject provoked a much-repeated clerihew:

Cecil B. De Mille
Much against his will
Was persuaded to keep Moses
Out of the Wars of the Roses.

He saw the Bible as a ready-made script factory:

Give me any couple of pages of the Bible and I'll give you a picture.

He took neither credit nor blame for his themes:

I didn't write the Bible and didn't invent sin.

He was also quite clear where his support lay:

I make my pictures for people, not for critics.

His approach to actresses was on similarly direct lines. In 1934, when he thought of Claudette Colbert as Cleopatra, he said to her:

How would you like to be the wickedest woman in history?

But he knew that what really mattered to a movie is not the star but the producer:

A picture is made a success not on a set but over the drawing board.

Action was another essential ingredient:

I will trade you forty gorgeously beautiful Hawaiian sunsets for one good sock in the jaw.

He chuckled at the result of his labours:

Every time I make a picture the critics' estimate of American public taste goes down ten per cent.

Typical reaction was Pauline Kael's:

He made small-minded pictures on a big scale.

But Graham Greene had a soft spot for him:

There has always been a touch of genius as well as absurdity in this warm-hearted sentimental salvationist.

He remained true to the literary tradition of Cooper's Leatherstocking tales and to the dramatic conventions of David Belasco. – *Andrew Sarris, 1968*

I learned an awful lot from him by doing the opposite. – *Howard Hawks*

He wore baldness like an expensive hat, as though it were out of the question for him to have hair like other men. – *Gloria Swanson*

He didn't make pictures for himself or for the critics. He made them for the public. – *Adolph Zukor*

De Mille, Katherine (1911–1995) (Katherine Lester).
American leading lady of the 30s. She was married to actor Anthony Quinn (1937–55).

Viva Villa 34. Call of the Wild 35. Ramona 36. Banjo on My Knee 37. Blockade 38. Reap the Wild Wind 42. The Story of Dr Wassell 44. Unconquered 47. The Gamblers 50, etc.

De Mille, William (1878–1955).
American director. Elder brother of Cecil B. De Mille, with theatrical background.

Nice People 22. Craig's Wife 28. Captain Fury (p only) 39, etc.

DeMornay, Rebecca (1962–).
American actress. She was educated in Austria and England (at Summerhill School). She had a daughter in 1997 by her partner Patrick O'NEAL.

One from the Heart 82. Testament 83. Risky Business 84. The Trip to Bountiful 85. Runaway Train 85. The Slugger's Wife 85. The Murders in the rue Morgue (TV) 86. Beauty and the Beast 87 . . . And God Created Woman 87. Feds 88. Dealers 89. By Dawn's Early Light (TV) 90. An Inconvenient Woman (TV) 91. Backdraft 91. The Hand that Rocks the Cradle 92. Guilty as Sin 93. The Three Musketeers 93. Getting Out (TV) 94. Never Talk to Strangers 95. The Winner 96, etc.

❝ My mother told me: 'If you do not find a way of earning a living, a man will pay for the roof over your head and he's going to tell you what to do.' I've never forgotten that. I do not want anyone telling me how to live or saying what I can do or can't do or who I can or cannot see. – *R. DeM.*

In the best of all worlds and on the best of all days the last thing I like to do at night is feel the physical embrace of someone I love. – *R. DeM.*

De Niro, Robert (1943–).
Intense, brooding American leading actor whose best roles have been in the films of Martin SCORSESE. Born in New York City, he studied

acting with Stella ADLER and Lee STRASBERG and began in off-Broadway theatre. He founded the production facility TriBeCa Film Center, which houses his own production company, Tribeca Films, in New York in the late 80s, and is an occasional director. He married former flight attendant Grace Hightower in 1997. His first wife was actress Diahnne ABBOTT (1976–78), with whom he had a son, and he has a daughter by singer Helena Springs and twin sons with a former model, Toukie Smith. His finest performances have been as Bruce Pearson in *Bang the Drum Slowly*, Johnny Boy in *Mean Streets*, Don Corleone in *The Godfather Part II*, Travis Bickle in *Taxi Driver*, Jake LaMotta in *Raging Bull*, and Al Capone in *The Untouchables*.

Biographies: 1986, *Robert DeNiro: The Man Behind the Mask* by Keith McKay; 1995, *De Niro* by John Parker; 1997, *Untouchable: Robert De Niro* by Andy Dougan.

Greetings 68. Sam's Song 69. The Wedding Party 69. Hi Mom 70. Bloody Mama 70. Born to Win 71. The Gang that couldn't Shoot Straight 71. Jennifer on my Mind 71. *Bang the Drum Slowly* 73. *Mean Streets* 73. The Godfather Part Two (AA) 74. Taxi Driver (AAN) 76. The Last Tycoon 76. 1900 76. New York New York 77. *The Deer Hunter* (AAN) 78. *Raging Bull* (for which he became fifty pounds overweight) (AA) 80. True Confessions 81. King of Comedy 83. Once Upon a Time in America 84. Falling in Love 85. Brazil 85. The Mission 86. Angel Heart 87. The Untouchables 87. Midnight Run 88. Jacknife 89. We're No Angels 89. Awakenings (AAN) 90. *GoodFellas* 90. Stanley and Iris 90. Guilty by Suspicion 91. Backdraft 91. *Cape Fear* (AAN) 91. Mistress 92. Night and the City 92. This Boy's Life 93. A Bronx Tale (& p, d) 93. Mad Dog and Glory 93. Mary Shelley's Frankenstein (as the creature) 94. Casino 95. Heat 95. Sleepers 96. The Fan 96. Copland 97. Great Expectations 98. Jackie Brown 98. Wag the Dog 98. Ronin 98. Flawless 99, etc.

✪ For becoming the best film actor of his generation. *Raging Bull*.

❝ There is a mixture of anarchy and discipline in the way I work. – *R. de N.*

After my first movies, I gave interviews. Then I thought, what's so important about where I went to school, and hobbies . . . what does any of that have to do with acting, with my own head? – *R. de N.*

It's ridiculous for an actor that good to keep playing Las Vegas hoods – *Charlton Heston*

De Oliveira, Manoel (1908–).
Portuguese director of features and documentaries, a former racing driver, trapeze artist and businessman.

Aniki-Bobo 42. The Passion of Jesus/Acto de Primavera 63. Amor de Perdição (TV) 78. Francisca 81. The Satin Slipper (Fr.) 85. Mon Cas 86. The Cannibals/Os Canibais 88. The Divine Comedy/La Divina Comedia 91. The Day of Despair/O Dia do Desespero 92. Vale Abraao 93. Blindman's Buff/A Caixa 94. The Convent 95, etc.

De Ossorio, Amando (1925–).
Spanish director of horror movies, best known for his movies about the blind dead – corpses of the Knights Templar who rise from their graves to attack the living.

Fangs of the Living Dead/Malenka, la Nipote del Vampiro 68. Tomb of the Blind Dead/La Noche del Terror Ciego 71. Return of the Blind Dead/El Ataque de los Muertos sin Ojos 72. When the Screaming Stops/Las Garras de Lorelei 72. Horror of the Zombies/El Buqué Maldito 73. Night of the Sorcerers/La Noche de los Brujos 73. Night of the Death Cult/La Noche de las Gaviotas 74, etc.

De Palma, Brian (1940–).
American director who began in the satirical underground school, then graduated to glossy shock/horrors, usually in clever imitation of somebody else's style.

■ Murder à la Mode (& w) 68. *Greetings* 68. The Wedding Party 69. Dionysus 70. Hi Mom 70. Get to Know Your Rabbit 72. Sisters 73. Phantom of the Paradise (& w) 74. Obsession 76. *Carrie* 76. The Fury 78. Home Movies 79. Dressed to Kill 80. Blow Out 81. Scarface 83. Body Double 84. Wise Guys 86. *The Untouchables* 87. Casualties of War 89. Bonfire of the Vanities 90. Father's Day 92. Raising Cain 92. Carlito's Way 93. Mission: Impossible 96. Snake Eyes (& p, story) 98.

❝ A superb cinematic talent unable to do more than play doctor with his toy implements. – *Sunday Times, 1981*

My films deal with a stylized, expressionistic world that has a kind of grotesque beauty about it. – *B. de P.*

I don't see scary films. I certainly wouldn't go see my films. – *B. de P.*

De Palma, Rossy (1965–) (Rosy Garcia).
Tall, angular Spanish actress, known internationally for her appearances in the films of Pedro Almodóvar.

Women on the Verge of a Nervous Breakdown/Mujeres al Borde de un Ataque de Nervios 88. Tie Me Up! Tie Me Down!/¡Atame! 89. Don Juan, My Darling Ghost/Don Juan, Mi Querido Fantasma 90. Sam Suffit (Fr.) 92. Kika 93. Prêt-à-Porter/Ready to Wear 94. The Next Worst Thing Is Death/Peggio di Cosi Si Muore 95. The Flower of My Secret/La Flor de Mi Secreto 95. Body in the Wood 96. Foul Play/Hors Jeu (Fr.) 98. Talk of Angels (US) 98, etc.

De Putti, Lya (1901–1931) (Amalia Putty).
Hungarian star of silents in Germany, Britain and Hollywood. Died of pneumonia after an operation to remove a chicken bone from her throat.

Othello (Ger.) 22. Variety (Ger.) 25. Manon Lescaut (Ger.) 26. The Sorrows of Satan (US) 26. The Prince of Tempters (US) 26. Buck Privates (US) 28. The Scarlet Lady (US) 28. The Informer (GB) 29, etc.

De Rochemont, Louis (1899–1978).
American producer, from the world of newsreel. Devised *The March of Time* 34; later produced semi-documentaries like *The House on 92nd Street* 46 and *Boomerang* 47; and was involved in many ventures including Cinerama and Cinemiracle.

DeSalvo, Albert (1931–1973).
Serial killer known as The Boston Strangler who was the subject of a biopic of the same name starring Tony Curtis and directed by Richard Fleischer in 1968. DeSalvo raped and murdered at least 13 women (he claimed to have raped many hundreds) in the early 60s. He was committed to a mental institution in 1967 and was stabbed to death in his cell.

De Santis, Giuseppe (1917–1997).
Italian director and screenwriter, one of the leading figures in the NEO-REALISM movement. Born in Fondi, he studied film at Rome's Centro Sperimentale di Cinematografia and began as a critic. He was one of the writers of VISCONTI's first film *Ossessione* 42, before becoming a director himself, usually writing his screenplays in collaboration with others.

Caccia Tragica 47. *Bitter Rice* (AANw) 49. *No Peace among the Olives* 50. Rome Eleven O'Clock 51. A Husband for Anna 53. Men and Wolves 56. La Garçonnière 60. Italiani Brava Gente 64. Un Apprezzato Professionista di Sicuro Avvenire 71, etc.

De Santis, Joe (1909–1989).
American character actor who often played Italianate gangsters.

Slattery's Hurricane 49. Man with a Cloak 51. The Last Hunt 56. Tension at Table Rock 57. And Now Miguel 66. The Professionals 66. Blue 68, etc.

De Santis, Pasqualino (1927–1996).
Italian cinematographer who has worked with such directors as Robert Bresson, Luchino Visconti and Francesco Rosi.

Romeo and Juliet (AA) 68. The Damned/Götterdämmerung (co-p) 69. *Death in Venice*/Morte a Venezia 71. The Assassination of Trotsky 72. Lancelot du Lac 74. Conversation Piece/Gruppo di Famiglia in un Interno 74. Illustrious Corpses/Cadaveri Eccellenti 75. L'Innocente 76. *Christ Stopped at Eboli* 79. Three Brothers 80. Bizet's Carmen 84. Sheena, Queen of the Jungle 84. Harem 85. Salome 86. *Chronicle of a Death Foretold*/Cronica di una Morte Annunciata 87. High Frequency 89. To Forget Palermo/Dimenticare Palermo 89. Music for Old Animals/Musica per Animali 90. A Month by the Lake 95, etc.

De Sarigny, Peter (1911–).
South African-born producer, in Britain from 1936.

The Malta Story 53. Simba 55. True as a Turtle 56. Never Let Go 61, etc.

De Seta, Vittorio (1923–).
Italian director, mainly of shorts until *Bandits at Orgosolo* 62.

Bandits at Orgosolo 62. Almost a Man/Uomo a Meta 66. The Uninvited/L'Invitata 69. Diary of a Teacher/Diario di un Maestro (TV) 73, etc.

De Sica, Vittorio (1901–1974).
Italian actor and director, in the latter respect an important and skilful realist. Well known in Italy in the 30s, but not elsewhere until after World War II.

Teresa Venerdi (d) 41. I Bambini ci Guardino (d) 42. *Shoeshine* (AA) (d) 46. *Bicycle Thieves* (AA) (d) 48. *Miracle in Milan* (d) 50. *Umberto D* (d) 52. *Madame De* (a) 52. Stazione Termini/Indiscretion (d) 52. Bread, Love and Dreams (a) 53. Gold of Naples (d) 54. A Farewell to Arms (a, AAN) 57. Il Generale della Rovere (a) 59. Two Women (d) 61. The Condemned of Altona (d) 63. Yesterday, Today and Tomorrow (d) (AA) 64. Marriage Italian Style (d) 64. A New World (d) 66. The Biggest Bundle of Them All (a) 66. After the Fox (d) 66. Woman Times Seven (d) 67. The Shoes of the Fisherman (a) 68. A Place for Lovers (d) 69. Sunflower (d) 70. *The Garden of the Finzi-Continis* (d, AA) 71. The Voyage (d) 73, etc.

TV series as actor: *The Four Just Men* (GB) 59.

✪ For a half-dozen splendid films dotting a very variable career. *Miracle in Milan*.

❝ A fine actor, a polished hack, and a flabby whore – not necessarily in that order. – *Stanley Kauffmann*

De Souza, Edward (1933–).
British leading man, mostly on stage.

The Roman Spring of Mrs Stone 61. The Phantom of the Opera 62. Kiss of the Vampire 63, etc.

De Souza, Steven E.
American screenwriter.

48 Hours 82. The Return of Captain Invincible 83. Commando 85. The Running Man 87. Seven Hours to Judgement 88. Die Hard 88. Bad Dreams 88. Die Hard 2 90. Hudson Hawk 91. Ricochet 92. The Flintstones (co-w) 94. Beverly Hills Cop III 94. Streetfighter (wd) 94. Judge Dredd 95. Knockoff 98, etc.

De Sylva, B. G. 'Buddy' (1895–1950) (George Gard De Sylva).
American lyricist, screenwriter and producer, notably in collaboration with Lew BROWN and Ray HENDERSON, though he also worked with Naçio Herb BROWN, George GERSHWIN, Jerome KERN and Vincent YOUMANS. Born in New York, he was in vaudeville from childhood and from the 20s was writing songs for Al JOLSON. He became a producer, first of his Broadway shows and then in films for Fox, producing musicals for Shirley TEMPLE, and, from 1939 to 1944, for Paramount, where he was production chief; later, he became an independent producer. He was also a co-founder of Capitol Records in the early 40s. In the biopic of De Sylva, Brown and Henderson, *The Best Things in Life Are Free* 56, he was played by Gordon MACRAE; in *Star Spangled Rhythm* 42 he was caricatured by Walter ABEL as G. B. de Soto. His best-known songs include 'April Showers', 'The Birth of the Blues', 'California Here I Come', 'If You Knew Susie', 'Look for the Silver Lining', and 'You're the Cream in My Coffee'.

The Singing Fool (s 'Sonny Boy') 28. Say It with Songs (s) 29. Sunny Side Up (co-w, s) 29. Good News (s) 30. Follow Thru (co-w, s) 30. Just Imagine (co-w, s) 30. Indiscreet (co-w, s) 31. My Weakness (s) 33. Take a Chance (co-w, s) 33. The Littlest Rebel (p) 35. The Birth of the Blues (p, s) 41. Caught in the Draft (p) 41. Louisiana Purchase (oa) 41. Lady in the Dark (p) 44. Frenchman's Creek (p) 44. The Stork Club (p, co-w) 45. Good News (s) 47. Jolson Sings Again (s) 49. The Eddie Cantor Story (s) 53, etc.

De Toth, André (1912–).
Hungarian-American director, mainly of routine actioners. Oddly enough, directed one of the first 3-D films; having only one eye, he could not see the effect.

Autobiography: 1994, *Fragments: Portraits from the Inside*.

Book: 1997, *De Toth on De Toth: Putting the Drama in Front of the Camera*, ed. Anthony Slide.

■ Ot Ora forty (Hung.) 38. Ketlany Azultean (Hung.) 38. Har Het Bologsag (Hung.) 38. Semmelweis (Hung.) 38. Balalaika (Hung.) 39. Toprini Nasz (Hung.) 39. Passport to Suez 43. None Shall Escape 44. *Dark Waters* 44. Ramrod 47. The Other Love 47. Pitfall 48. Slattery's Hurricane 49. Man in the Saddle 51. Carson City 52. Springfield Rifle 52. Last of the Comanches 52. *House of Wax* 53. The Stranger Wore a Gun 53. Thunder Over the Plains 53. Crime Wave 54. Riding Shotgun 54. Tanganyika 54. The Bounty Hunter 54. The Indian Fighter 55. Monkey on My Back 57. Hidden Fear 57. The Two Headed Spy (GB) 59. Day of the Outlaw 59. Man on a String 60. Morgan the Pirate 61. The Mongols 62. Gold for the Caesars 64. Play Dirty (GB) 69.

DeTreaux, Tamara (1959–1990).
Tiny (31 ins) American actress who played E.T. in some scenes of the film.

Ghoulies 85. Rockula 90. The Linguini Incident 92, etc.

De Vinna, Clyde (1892–1953).
American cinematographer.

SELECTED SILENTS: The Raiders 16. Madam Who 18. Leave it to Me 20. Yellow Men and Gold 22. The Victor 23. Ben Hur (co-ph) 26. California 27. White Shadows in the South Seas (co-ph) (AA) 28. The Pagan 29.

■ SOUND FILMS: *Trader Horn* 31. The Great Meadow (co-ph) 31. Shipmates 31. Politics 31. Tarzan the Ape Man (co-ph) 32. Bird of Paradise (co-ph) 32. Eskimo 33. Tarzan and His Mate (co-ph) 34. *Treasure Island* 34. West Point of the Air 35. The Last of the Pagans 35. Ah Wilderness 35. Old Hutch 36. Good Old Soak 36. Bad Man of Brimstone 38. Of Human Hearts 38. Fast Company 38. The Girl Downstairs 39. Bridal Suite 39. Blackmail 39. They All Come Out 39. 20 Mule Team 40. Phantom Raiders 40. Wyoming 40. The Bad Man 41. The People vs Dr Kildare 41. Barnacle Bill 41. Tarzan's Secret Treasure 41. The Bugle Sounds 41. Jackass Mail 41. Whistling in Dixie 42. The Immortal Sergeant 43. Within these Walls 45. The Caribbean Mystery 45. It's a Joke Son 47. Sword of the Avenger 48. The Jungle 52.

De Vito, Danny (1944–).
Diminutive and aggressive American character actor, often in venal roles, and producer, a former hairdresser. Born in Neptune, New Jersey, he studied acting at the American Academy of Dramatic Arts, and first came to public attention as Louie DiPalma in the TV series *Taxi*. He began directing in the late 80s. He also runs a production company, Jersey Films. Married actress Rhea PERLMAN.

Dreams of Glass 68. La Mortadella 72. Hurry Up, Or I'll Be 30 73. Scalawag 73. One Flew Over the Cuckoo's Nest 75. The Van 77. The World's Greatest Lover 77. Goin' South 78. Going Ape! 81. Terms of Endearment 83. Johnny Dangerously 84. The Ratings Game (& d) (TV) 84. Romancing the Stone 84. The Jewel of the Nile 85. Head Office 86. My Little Pony: The Movie 86. Ruthless People 86. Wise Guys 86. Throw Momma from the Train (& d) 87. Tin Men 87. Twins 88. Wars of the Roses (& d) 89. Other People's Money 91. Batman Returns 92. Hoffa (& d) 92. Jack the Bear 93. Look Who's Talking Now (voice) 93. Renaissance Man 94. Junior 94. Reality Bites (p) 94. Get Shorty (& p) 95. Sunset Park (p) 96. Matilda (& d) 96. Mars Attacks! (a) 96. Hercules (voice) 97. *John Grisham's The Rainmaker* (a) 97. *LA Confidential* (a) 97. Out of Sight (p) 98. Living Out Loud (a) 98, etc.

TV series: Taxi 78–83.

❝ If you're my height and look the way I do and you don't have an abundance of ego and self-esteem, you become a basket case, one of life's prime losers, because height and looks and suave and all those qualities are worshipped. – *D. de V.*

De Vol, Frank (1925–).
American composer.

The Big Knife 55. Kiss Me Deadly 55. Attack 56. Pillow Talk (AAN) 59. Whatever Happened to Baby Jane? 62. McLintock 63. Hush Hush Sweet Charlotte (AAN) 64. Send Me No Flowers 64. Cat Ballou 65. The Flight of the Phoenix 65. Guess Who's Coming to Dinner (AAN) 67. The Dirty Dozen 67. Krakatoa East of Java 68. Ulzana's Raid 71. The Longest Yard 74. Doc Savage 75. The Choirboys 77. The Frisco Kid 79. Herbie Goes Bananas 80 . . . All the Marbles 81, etc.

De Vorzon, Barry.
American composer.
The Warriors 79. The Ninth Configuration 80. Xanadu 80. Looker 81. Tattoo 81. Tarzan, the Ape Man 82. Jekyll and Hyde . . . Together Again 82. Stick 85. Night of the Creeps 86. Exorcist III 90, etc.

De Wilde, Brandon (1942–1972).
American child actor, later juvenile lead. Died in a car accident.
■ *The Member of the Wedding* 52. *Shane* (AAN) 53. Goodbye My Lady 56. Night Passage 57. The Missouri Traveller 58. Blue Denim 59. All Fall Down 62. *Hud* 63. In Harm's Way 65. Those Calloways 65. The Deserter 70. Wild in the Sky 72.
TV series: Jamie 54.

De Wolfe, Billy (1907–1974) (William Andrew Jones).
Toothy, moustachioed American comedy actor, formerly dancer, with vaudeville and night club experience. (Famous act: a lady taking a bath.)
Dixie 43. Blue Skies 46. *Dear Ruth* 47. Dear Wife 50. Tea for Two 50. Lullaby of Broadway 51. *Call Me Madam* 53. Billie 65. The World's Greatest Athlete 73, etc.
TV series: The Pruitts of Southampton 67. Good Morning World 67. The Queen and I 69. The Debbie Reynolds Show 69. The Doris Day Show 70–71.

De Wolff, Francis (1913–1984).
Bearded, burly British character actor.
Adam and Evelyne 48. Under Capricorn 49. Treasure Island 50. Scrooge 51. Ivanhoe 53. The Master of Ballantrae 55. Geordie 55, many others.

De Young, Cliff (1945–).
American general-purpose actor.
Sunshine (TV) 73. Harry and Tonto 74. The Night that Panicked America (TV) 75. The Lindbergh Kidnapping Case (TV) (title role) 76. Blue Collar 78. King (TV) (as Bobby Kennedy) 78. Shock Treatment 81. The Hunger 83. Protocol 84. F/X 85. Flight of the Navigator 87. Crackdown 90. Nails 92. Revenge of the Red Baron 94. Infinity 95. The Substitute 96. The Craft 96. The Last Don (TV) 97, etc.
TV series: Sunshine 75. Centennial 78–79. Master of the Game 84.

Deacon, Brian (1949–).
British general-purpose actor.
Triple Echo 73. Vampire 74. Lillie (TV) 78. A Zed and Two Noughts 86, etc.

Deacon, Richard (1922–1984).
Bald, bespectacled American character actor who usually played comic snoops.
Abbott and Costello Meet the Mummy 55. The Power and the Prize 56. The Remarkable Mr Pennypacker 58. Blackbeard's Ghost 68. Piranha 78, many others.
TV series: Leave It to Beaver 57–63. *Dick Van Dyke* 61–66. Mothers-in-law 67–68.

Deakins, Roger (1949–).
British cinematographer.
Before Hindsight 77. Blue Suede Shoes 80. Another Time, Another Place 83. 1984 84. Return to Waterloo 85. Defence of the Realm 85. Shadey 85. Sid and Nancy 86. Kitchen Toto 87. Personal Services 87. White Mischief 87. Pascali's Island 88. Stormy Monday 88. Air America 90. Mountains of the Moon 90. The Long Walk Home 90. Barton Fink 91. Homicide 91. Thunderheart 92. The Secret Garden 93. The Hudsucker Proxy 94. The Shawshank Redemption (AAN) 94. Rob Roy 95. Dead Man Walking 95. Fargo 96. Courage under Fire 96. *Fargo* (AAN) 96. *Kundun* (AAN) 97. The Big Lebowski 97, etc.

Dean, Basil (1888–1978).
British stage producer who also directed several important films for Associated Talking Pictures, which he founded. He was also responsible for the formation in wartime of the organization of travelling entertainers, ENSA, often known disrespectfully as Every Night Something Awful, but standing in fact for Entertainments National Service Association. Married actress Victoria Hopper.
Autobiography: 1973, *Mind's Eye*.
The Impassive Footman 32. The Constant Nymph (& co-w) 33. Java Head 34. Sing As We Go 34. Lorna Doone 35. 21 Days 39, etc.

Dean, Eddie (1907–) (Edgar D. Glossup).
American star of western second features in the 30s and 50s.
Renegade Trail 39. Sierra Sue 41. Romance of the West 47. Hawk of Powder River 50, many others.
TV series: The Marshal of Gunsight Pass 50.

Dean, Isabel (1918–1997) (Isabel Hodgkinson).
British stage actress, usually in upper-class roles: very occasional film appearances. She was at one time married to writer William Fairchild.
The Passionate Friends 47. 24 Hours of a Woman's Life 52. The Story of Gilbert and Sullivan 53. Out of the Clouds 55. Virgin Island 58. The Light in the Piazza 62. A High Wind in Jamaica 65. Inadmissible Evidence 68. Catch Me a Spy 71. Five Days One Summer 82. Weather in the Streets 84, etc.

Dean, James (1931–1955).
Moody young American actor who after a brief build-up in small roles was acclaimed as the image of the mid-50s; his tragic death in a car crash caused an astonishing world-wide outburst of emotional necrophilia. A biopic, *The James Dean Story*, was patched together in 1957.
Biographies: 1956, *James Dean* by William Bast. 1974, *James Dean: The Mutant King* by David Dalton. 1975, *James Dean* by John Howlett. 1982, *James Dean: A Portrait* by Roy Schatt. 1994, *James Dean: Boulevard of Broken Dreams* by Paul Alexander. 1996, *Rebel: The Life and Legend of James Dean* by Donald Spoto. 1996, *James Dean* by Val Holley. 1997, *James Dean* by John Howlett.
■ Has Anybody Seen My Gal? 51. Sailor Beware 51. Fixed Bayonets 52. Trouble Along the Way 53. *East of Eden* (AAN) 55. *Rebel Without A Cause* 55. *Giant* (AAN) 56.
❝ Another dirty shirt-tail actor from New York. – *Hedda Hopper*
He was sad and sulky. You kept expecting him to cry. – *Elia Kazan*

Dean, Julia (1878–1952).
American stage actress who made a few movies after she retired to California.
How Molly Made Good 15. Curse of the Cat People 44. O.S.S. 46. Nightmare Alley 48. People Will Talk 51. Elopement 51, etc.

Dean, Loren (1969–).
American juvenile actor.
Plain Clothes 88. Say Anything 89. Billy Bathgate (title role) 91. 1492: Conquest of Paradise 92. JFK: Restless Youth (TV) 93. The Passion of Darkly Noon 95. How to Make an American Quilt 95. Apollo 13 95. Mrs Winterbourne 96. Gattaca 97. The End of Violence 97. Enemy of the State 98, etc.

Dean, Man Mountain (1899–1963).
American wrestler who played comedy roles in a few films.
Reckless 35. The Gladiator 36. Surprise Package 60, etc.

Dean, Priscilla (1896–1987).
American star of silent films, on stage from the age of four and in films from the age of 12, notably for Universal.
Even as You and I 17. The Hand that Rocks the Cradle 17. She Hired a Husband 18. The Wicked Darling 19. The Exquisite Thief 19. Pretty Smooth 19. The Virgin of Stamboul 20. Outside the Law 21. Reputation 21. Under Two Flags 22. The Flame of Life 23. Drifting 23. The White Tiger 23. The Storm Daughter 24. Slipping Wives 26. Behind Stone Walls 32, etc.

Dear, William.
American director.
Time Rider 83. Harry and the Hendersons 87. If Looks Could Kill 91. Angels in the Outfield 94. Wild America 97, etc.

Dearden, Basil (1911–1971).
British director, former editor. Began by co-directing Will Hay's last films for Ealing, then formed a writer-producer-director partnership with Michael Relph. Killed in a car crash.
■ The Black Sheep of Whitehall (co-d) 41. The Goose Steps Out (co-d) 42. The Bells Go Down 43. My Learned Friend (co-d) 43. The Halfway House 44. They Came to a City 44. Dead of Night (part) 45. *The Captive Heart* 46. Frieda 47. Saraband for Dead Lovers 48. Train of Events (co-d) 49. *The Blue Lamp* 50. Cage of Gold 50. Pool of London 51. I Believe in You (co-d) 52. The Gentle Gunman 52. The Square Ring 53. The Rainbow Jacket 54. Out of the Clouds (co-d) 55. The Ship That Died of Shame (co-d) 55. Who Done It (co-d) 56. The Smallest Show on Earth 57. Violent Playground 58. *Sapphire* 59. *The League of Gentlemen* 60. Man in the Moon 60. The Secret Partner 61. *Victim* 61. All Night Long (co-d) 62. Life for Ruth 62. The Mind Benders 63. A Place to Go 63. Woman of Straw 64. Masquerade 65. Khartoum 66. Only When I Larf 68. The Assassination Bureau 69. The Man Who Haunted Himself 70.
❝ He was a master film-maker. If we'd have had the right atmosphere in which he could have worked, he would have been a top one. – *Dirk Bogarde*

Dearden, James (1949–).
British director and screenwriter. He is the son of Basil Dearden.
Fatal Attraction (w) (AAN) 87. Pascali's Island 88. A Kiss before Dying, 91. Rogue Trader 99, etc.

Dearing, Edgar (1893–1974).
American character actor, often seen as tough cop.
Thanks for Everything 35. Swing Time 37. Miss Annie Rooney 42, many others.

D'Eaubonne, Jean (1903–1971).
French art director who studied painting and sculpture before entering films in the 30s. He also worked in Britain and the US.
Blood of a Poet/Le Sang d'un Poète 32. The Girl in the Taxi (GB) 37. La Chartreuse de Parme 47. Orphée 49. Black Magic (US) 49. La Ronde 50. Casque d'Or 52. Touchez Pas au Grisbi 54. Lola Montès 55. The Reluctant Debutante (US) 58. Crack in the Mirror (US) 60. Charade 63. Paris When It Sizzles (US) 64. Custer of the West (US) 66. The Girl on a Motorcycle 68, etc.

Debucourt, Jean (1894–1958) (J. Pelisse).
French character actor with long stage experience.
Le Petit Chose 22. La Chute de la Maison Usher 28. Douce 43. Le Diable au Corps 46. Occupe-Toi d'Amélie 49, etc.

Decae, Henri (1915–1987).
Distinguished French cinematographer.
Le Silence de la Mer 49. Les Enfants Terribles 49. Crève-Coeur 52. Bob le Flambeur 55. Lift to the Scaffold 57. Le Beau Serge 58. A Double Tour 59. Les Quatre Cents Coups 59. Les Cousins 59. Plein Soleil 59. Les Bonnes Femmes 60. Léon Morin, Priest 61. Sundays and Cybele 62. Dragées au Poivre 63. Viva Maria 65. Weekend at Dunkirk 65. Night of the Generals 66. Le Voleur 67. The Comedians 67. Castle Keep 69. The Sicilian Clan 70. The Light at the Edge of the World 71. Bobby Deerfield 77. The Island 80. Exposed 83, etc.

Decker, Diana (1926–).
Bright, blonde, American leading lady, in Britain from 1939; became known through toothpaste commercials ('Irium, Miriam?').
Fiddlers Three 44. Meet Me at Dawn 48. Murder at the Windmill 49. Is Your Honeymoon Really Necessary? 53. Lolita 62. Devils of Darkness 65, etc.
TV series: Mark Saber 54

Deckers, Eugene (1917–1977).
French character actor who played Continental types in British films after 1946.
Sleeping Car to Trieste 48. The Elusive Pimpernel 50. The Lavender Hill Mob 51. Father Brown 54. Port Afrique 56. Northwest Frontier 59. Lady L 66. The Limbo Line 68, many others.

Decoin, Henri (1896–1969).
French director, in films since 1929.
Abus de Confiance 37. Les Inconnus dans la Maison 42. La Fille du Diable 46. Three Telegrams 50. The Truth about Bebe Donge 52. The Lovers of Toledo 53. Razzia sur la Chnouf 55. Charmants Garçons 57. The Face of the Cat 58. Outcasts of Glory 64, many others.

Dee, Frances (1907–) (Jean Dee).
American leading lady of the 30s, long married to Joel McCrea; a former extra, she was chosen by Chevalier to play opposite him in her first speaking role.
Playboy of Paris 30. An American Tragedy 31. Rich Man's Folly 32. King of the Jungle 33. Becky Sharp 35. If I Were King 38. So Ends Our Night 41. Meet the Stewarts 42. I Walked with a Zombie 43. Happy Land 43. Bel Ami 48. Four Faces West 48. Payment on Demand 51. Because of You 53. Mr Scoutmaster 53. Gypsy Colt 54, etc.

Dee, Ruby (1924–) (Ruby Ann Wallace).
American actress.
No Way Out 50. Tall Target 51. Go Man Go 53. Edge of the City 57. Take a Giant Step 59. *A Raisin in the Sun* 61. The Balcony 62. Buck and the Preacher 72. Black Girl 72. Cat People 82. Do the Right Thing 89. Jungle Fever 91. A Cop and a Half 93. The Stand (TV) 94. Just Cause 95. Mr & Mrs Loving 96. A Simple Wish 97. The Wall 98, etc.

Dee, Sandra (1942–) (Alexandra Zuck).
Petite American leading lady, former model.
Until They Sail 57. The Reluctant Debutante 58. Gidget 59. *Imitation of Life* 59. A Summer Place 59. Portrait in Black 60. Romanoff and Juliet 61. Come September 62. Tammy and the Doctor 63. Take Her She's Mine 64. That Funny Feeling 65. A Man Could Get Killed 66. Doctor, You've Got to be Kidding 67. Rosie 68. The Daughters of Joshua Cabe (TV) 72. Houston We've Got a Problem (TV) 74. Manhunter (TV) 76. Fantasy Island (TV) 77, etc.

Deed, André (1884–1938) (Andre Chapuis).
French actor and director who was probably cinema's first comedian. A music-hall acrobat and singer, he entered films in 1905, when he was discovered by Charles Pathé, to become one of the screen's first stars, though hardly any of his films survive. He was known by different names in different countries: Boireau in France, Foolshead in Britain, Cretinetti in Italy, and Toribio in Spain. His popularity ending with the coming of sound, he became night-watchman at the Pathé studios and died forgotten.
Boireau Déménage 05. Cretinetti al Cinema 11. Boireau Domestique 13. Graine au Vent 28, etc.

Deeley, Michael (1932–).
British producer, a former EMI executive.
The Case of the Mukkinese Battlehorn 61. One Way Pendulum 64. Robbery 67. The Italian Job 69. Murphy's War 70. The Man Who Fell to Earth 75. Nickelodeon 76. The Deer Hunter 78, etc.

Deems, Barrett (1914–1998).
American jazz drummer and bandleader with a hyperactive style, in a few films as himself. Born in Springfield, Illinois, he is best known for playing with the Louis Armstrong All Stars in the 50s.
Rhythm Inn 51. High Society 56. Satchmo the Great 56, etc.

Defoe, Daniel (1659–1731).
English writer whose work included the oft-filmed *Robinson Crusoe;* also *Moll Flanders*, which the 1965 film resembled but slightly. A 1996 version also wandered far from the original.

DeFore, Don (1917–1993).
American second lead, the good guy or dumb hearty westerner of dozens of forgettable films in the 40s and 50s.
You Can't Escape Forever 42. A Guy Named Joe 43. Thirty Seconds Over Tokyo 44. The Affairs of Susan 45. You Came Along 45. Ramrod 47. Romance on the High Seas 48. Too Late for Tears 48. My Friend Irma 49. Dark City 50. The Guy Who Came Back 51. She's Working Her Way Through College 52. Battle Hymn 57. The Facts of Life 61. A Rare Breed (TV) 81, etc.
TV series: Ozzie and Harriet 52–58. Hazel 61–65.

DeGeneres, Ellen (1958–).
American actress and stand-up comedian, best known for her title role in the TV sitcom *Ellen*. She caused a minor sensation in 1997 when she (as well as the character she plays in the sitcom) announced that she was a lesbian, and that her partner was actress Anne HECHE. Her sitcom was cancelled soon after the announcement.

Coneheads 93. Mr Wrong 96. Goodbye, Lover 98. Doctor Dolittle (voice) 98, etc.

TV series: Open House 89–90. Ellen 92–98.

Degermark, Pia (1949–).
Swedish leading lady in international films.

Elvira Madigan 67. The Looking Glass War 71, etc.

Degregorio, Eduardo (1942–).
Argentinian-born screenwriter and director who has lived in France since the mid-60s.

The Spider's Stratagem/La Strategia del Ragno (co-w) 70. Celine and Justine Go Boating/Celine et Justine Vont en Bateau (co-w) 74. Serail (d) 76, etc.

Dehlavi, Jamil.
Pakistani director.

The Blood of Hussain 80. Immaculate Conception (GB) 92.

Dehn, Paul (1912–1976).
British screenwriter, former film critic.

Seven Days to Noon (AA) 51. Orders to Kill 58. *Goldfinger* 64. The Spy Who Came in from the Cold 65. The Deadly Affair 66. The Taming of the Shrew 67. Beneath the Planet of the Apes (and two sequels) 67. Fragment of Fear (& p) 69. Murder on the Orient Express (AAN) 74, etc.

Dehner, John (1915–1992) (John Forkum).
American character actor, usually as sympathetic smart alec or dastardly villain, a former animator, from radio.

Captain Eddie 45. The Secret of St Ives 49. Last of the Buccaneers 50. Lorna Doone 51. Scaramouche 52. Apache 54. Carousel 56. The Left-handed Gun (as Pat Garrett) 58. Timbuktu 59. The Chapman Report 62. Critic's Choice 63. Youngblood Hawke 63. Stiletto 69. Support Your Local Gunfighter 71. Fun with Dick and Jane 77. The Boys from Brazil 78. The Right Stuff 83. Creator 84. Jagged Edge 85, etc.

TV series: The Westerner 60. The Roaring Twenties 60–62. The Baileys of Balboa 64–65. The Doris Day Show 71–73. Temperatures Rising 73–74. Big Hawaii 77. Young Maverick 79–80. Enos 80–81.

Deighton, Len (1929–).
British writer of convoluted spy thrillers.

The Ipcress File (oa) 65. Funeral in Berlin (oa) 66. Billion Dollar Brain (oa) 67. Only When I Larf (w) 68. Spy Story 76, etc.

Deitch, Donna (1945–).
American director who first attracted attention by making a lesbian affair a box-office success in *Desert Hearts*. She studied as an artist before attending film school and began by making documentaries. She appears in a documentary on women film-makers, *Calling the Shots* 88.

Woman to Woman (doc) 75. The Great Wall of Los Angeles (doc) 78. *Desert Hearts* 85. The Women of Brewster Place (TV) 89. Angel of Desire 94. Angel on My Shoulder (doc) 97, etc.

Dejczer, Maciej (1953–).
Polish director and screenwriter.

Dzieci-Smieci (wd) 86. Three Hundred Miles to Heaven/300 Mil Do Nieba (d) 89. The Brute/The Hoodlum (d) 96, etc.

Dekker, Albert (1905–1968).
Dutch-American stage actor of long experience; film career disappointing. Hanged himself.

■ The Great Garrick 37. Marie Antoinette 38. The Last Warning 38. She Married an Artist 38. The Lone Wolf in Paris 38. Extortion 38. Paris Honeymoon 39. Never Say Die 39. Hotel Imperial 39. Beau Geste 39. The Man in the Iron Mask 39. The Great Commandment 39. *Dr Cyclops* 40. Strange Cargo 40. Rangers of Fortune 40. Seven Sinners 40. You're the One 41. Blonde Inspiration 41. Reaching for the Sun 41. Buy Me That Town 41. Honky Tonk 41. *Among the Living* 41. Night in New Orleans 42. Wake Island 42. Once Upon a Honeymoon 42. Star Spangled Rhythm 42. The Lady Has Plans 42. In Old California 42. Yokel Boy 42. The Forest Rangers 42. Woman of the Town 43. War of the Wildcats 43. Buckskin Frontier 43. The Kansan 43. Experiment Perilous 44. Incendiary Blonde 45. Hold that Blonde 45. Salome Where She Danced 45. The French Key 46. *The Killers* 46. California 46. Suspense 46. The Pretender 47. Gentleman's Agreement 47. Wyoming 47. Cass Timberlane 47. Slave Girl 47. The Fabulous Texan 47. Fury at Furnace Creek 48. Lulu Belle 48. Search for Danger 49. Bride of Vengeance 49. Tarzan's Magic Fountain 49. The Kid from Texas 50. Destination Murder 50. The Furies 50. As Young as You Feel 51. Wait till the Sun Shines Nellie 52. The Silver Chalice 54. East of Eden 55. Kiss Me Deadly 55. Illegal 55. She Devil 57. These Thousand Hills 59. Middle of the Night 59. The Wonderful Country 59. Suddenly Last Summer 59. The Sound and the Fury 59. Come Spy with Me 67. The Wild Bunch 69.

Dekker, Fred (1959–).
American screenwriter and director.

Night of the Creeps 86. Monster Squad 87. Teen Agent (story) 91. Ricochet (story) 91. Robocop 3 (co-w, d) 93.

Del Carril, Hugo (1912–1989) (Piero Bruno Fontana).
Argentinian leading director and actor who first gained fame as a tango singer. The son of an Italian architect who spent his earliest years in France, he was in films from 1937, becoming a director in the late 40s. His greatest success came during the regime of Argentinian president Juan Perón, and his career declined with the president's departure in the mid-50s. When Perón returned to power in the early 70s, he became head of the National Film Institute, resigning on the death of the president in 1974.

Los Muchachos de Antes No Usaban Gomina (a only) 37. Madreselva (a only) 38. La Vida de Carlos Gardel (a only) 39. Historias del 900 49. *Dark River*/Las Aguas Bajan Turbias 52. La Quintrala 55. La Fille de Feu (Fr.) (a only) 58. Culpable 60. Amorina 61. Yo Maté a Facundo 75. The Tango Tells Its Story (a only) 78, etc.

Del Giudice, Filippo (1892–1961).
Exuberant Italian producer who settled in England and helped create some of the best British films of the 40s, persuading Noël Coward to write and star in *In Which We Serve* and Laurence Olivier to make *Henry V* (Olivier handed over the special Oscar he won for the film to Del Giudice in gratitude). Born in Trani, he became a lawyer, leaving Italy in the early 30s because of financial difficulties. In London, he first taught English to Italian waiters before finding financial backing to found Two Cities Films in 1937. After he lost control of the company to the Rank Organization in the mid-40s, when *Henry V* went over budget, he retired to a monastery and then founded Pilgrim Films, planning a series of religious epics. Later plans foundered for lack of finance, and he returned to Italy to die.

Book: 1997, *The Best of British* by Charles Drazin (contains a chapter on Del Giudice)

French without Tears 39. In Which We Serve 42. Henry V 44. The Way Ahead 44. Blithe Spirit 45. Odd Man Out 47. The Guinea Pig 48, many others.

❝ Everyman's image of the big-time movie producer – a cigar-chewing, language-fracturing executive, dumpy, pot-bellied and masked by the inevitable dark glasses. – *John Cottrell*

I know no one else in British films so kind, generous, imaginative and courageous. – *Laurence Olivier*

Del Prete, Duilio (c. 1937–1998).
Italian actor, singer and cabaret entertainer, from the stage.

I Sette Fratelli Cervi 68. Alfredo Alfredo 72. The Assassination of Trotsky 72. How Funny Can Sex Be? 73. Daisy Miller (US) 74. My Friends/Amici Miei 75. Divine Creature 75. At Long Last Love (US) 75. Nella Misura In Cui . . . 79. The Marseilles Connection 84. Carla 89. Voci dal Profundo 91, etc.

Del Rio, Dolores (1905–1983) (Dolores Asunsolo).
Mexican leading lady with aristocratic background; beautiful and popular star of the 20s and 30s. Her second husband was Cedric Gibbons.

Joanna (debut) 25. High Stepper 26. What Price Glory? 27. *The Loves of Carmen* 27. Resurrection 28. Evangeline 29. The Bad One 30. The Dove 31. Bird of Paradise 32. Flying Down to Rio 33. Wonder Bar 34. Madame Du Barry 34. Lancer Spy 37. *Journey into Fear* 42. Portrait of Maria 45. The Fugitive 47. *Cheyenne Autumn* 64. Once upon a Time 67, many others.

Del Ruth, Roy (1895–1961).
Very competent American director, former gag writer for Mack Sennett.

■ SOUND FILMS: Conquest 29. The Desert Song 29. The Hottentot 29. Gold Diggers of Broadway 29. The Aviator 29. Hold Everything 30. The Second Floor Mystery 30. Three Faces East 30. The Life of the Party 30. My Past 31. Divorce Among Friends 31. *The Maltese Falcon* 31. Side Show 31. Blonde Crazy 31. Taxi 32. Beauty and the Boss 32. Winner Take All 32. *Blessed Event* 32. Employees Entrance 33. The Mind Reader 33. The Little Giant 33. Captured 33. Bureau of Missing Persons 33. *Lady Killer* 33. Bulldog Drummond Strikes Back 34. Upperworld 34. Kid Millions 34. *Folies Bergere* 35. Broadway Melody of 1936 35. *Thanks a Million* 35. It Had to Happen 36. Private Number 36. Born to Dance 36. *On the Avenue* 37. Broadway Melody of 1938. Happy Landing 38. My Lucky Star 38. Tail Spin 39. The Star Maker 39. Here I Am A Stranger 39. He Married His Wife 40. *Topper Returns* 41. The Chocolate Soldier 41. Maisie Gets Her Man 42. Dubarry was a Lady 43. Broadway Rhythm 44. Barbary Coast Gent 44. It Happened on Fifth Avenue 47. The Babe Ruth Story 48. The Red Light 49. Always Leave Them Laughing 49. West Point Story 50. On Moonlight Bay 51. Starlift 51. About Face 52. Stop You're Killing Me 52. Three Sailors and a Girl 53. Phantom of the Rue Morgue 54. The Alligator People 59. Why Must I Die 60.

Del Toro, Benicio. (1967–).
American actor, from television. Born in Santurce, Puerto Rico, he was raised in Pennsylvania and studied at the University of California, planning to become a lawyer. Instead, he went on to study acting at New York's Circle in the Square Acting School, the Stella Adler Conservatory, and the Actors Circle Theater in Los Angeles.

Big Top Pee-wee 88. Licence to Kill 89. The Indian Runner 91. Christopher Columbus: The Discovery 92. Golden Balls/Huevos de Oro 93. Fearless 93. Money for Nothing 93. China Moon 94. Swimming with Sharks/The Buddy Factor 94. The Usual Suspects 95. Basquiat 96. The Fan 96. The Funeral 96. Cannes Man 97. Excess Baggage 97. Fear & Loathing in Las Vegas 98. Che Guevara: A Revolutionary Life 99, etc.

❝ It is possible for an actor to take his part too seriously. – *Terry Gilliam*

Del Toro, Guillermo (1965–).
Mexican director and screenwriter, from television, a former assistant to Jaime Humberto Hermosillo and a special effects and make-up expert, studying in the US under Dick Smith. He is also the author of a study of Alfred Hitchcock.

Invasion (TV) 90. Cronos 93. Mimic (co-w, d) 97, etc.

Delair, Suzy (1916–).
Vivacious French entertainer, in several films.

Quai des Orfèvres 47. Lady Paname 49. Robinson Crusoe Land 50. Gervaise 55. Rocco and his Brothers 60. Is Paris Burning? 66, etc.

Delaney, Shelagh (1939–).
British playwright whose chief contributions to the screen are *A Taste of Honey* and *Charlie Bubbles*.

The Railway Station Man 92.

Delannoy, Jean (1908–).
French director, formerly journalist and cutter.

La Symphonie Pastorale 40. *L'Eternel Retour* 43. Les Jeux Sont Faits 47. *Dieu a Besoin des Hommes* 49. Le Garçon Sauvage 51. The Moment of Truth 52. Marie Antoinette 56. Notre Dame de Paris 56. Maigret Sets a Trap 57. Le Soleil des Voyous 67. Only the Cool/La Peau de Torpedo 69. Bernadette 87, many others.

Delany, Dana (1956–).
American leading actress.

The Fan 81. Almost You 84. Where the River Runs Black 86. Moon over Parador 88. Patty Hearst 88. Light Sleeper 91. Housesitter 92. Tombstone 93. Batman: Mask of the Phantasm (voice) 94. *Exit to Eden* (as Mistress Lisa) 94. Fly Away Home 96, etc.

TV series: China Beach (as Nurse Colleen McMurphy) 88–91.

Delderfield, Ronald Frederick (1912–1972).
English playwright and novelist of provincial domestic life, a former journalist.

Autobiographies: 1951, *Nobody Shouted Author*. 1956, *Bird's Eye View*.

All over Town (oa) 48. Worm's Eye View (w) 50. Glad Tidings (oa) 52. Where There's a Will (w) 53. Now and Forever (w) 56. On the Fiddle (oa) 61, etc.

TV series: The Adventures of Ben Gunn 56.

Delerue, Georges (1925–1992).
French composer.

Hiroshima Mon Amour 58. Les Jeux de L'Amour 60. Une Aussi Longue Absence 61. Shoot the Pianist 61. Jules et Jim 61. Silken Skin 63. The Pumpkin Eater 64. Viva Maria 65. A Man for All Seasons 66. The 25th Hour 67. Interlude 68. Women in Love 69. Anne of the Thousand Days (AAN) 69. The Conformist 70. The Horseman 70. The Day of the Dolphin (AAN) 73. The Slap 74. Julia (AAN) 77. Tendre Poulet 77. Get Out Your Handkerchiefs 78. A Little Romance (AA) 79. Love on the Run 79. True Confessions 81. Partners 82. The Escape Artist 82. Exposed 83. Agnes of God 85. Salvador 86. Platoon 86. The Lonely Passion of Judith Hearne 87. The House on Carroll Street 88. Biloxi Blues 88. Twins 88. Beaches 88. Steel Magnolias 89. Show of Force 90. Curly Sue 91. Black Robe 91. Dien Bien Phu 92. Memento Mori (TV) 92, many others.

Delevanti, Cyril (1887–1975).
British-born stage actor who played aged gentlemen for many years.

Red Barry 38. Man Hunt 41. Son of Dracula 43. Ministry of Fear 45. Forever Amber 47. Land of the Pharaohs 55. Bye Bye Birdie 63. Mary Poppins 64. *Night of the Iguana* 64. The Greatest Story Ever Told 65. Counterpoint 67. The Killing of Sister George 68. Bedknobs and Broomsticks 71. Black Eye 73, many others.

Delfont, Bernard (1910–1994) (Lord Delfont, formerly Barnet Winogradsky).
British show business entrepreneur, brother of Lord Grade; mainly involved in live entertainment until the 70s when he came to head the EMI entertainment complex.

Delgado, Roger (1918–1973).
English character actor, of Spanish and French parents, in aristocratic and villainous roles, best known as The Master in the TV series *Dr Who*. Educated at the London School of Economics, he began acting in regional repertory. Died in a car crash.

The Captain's Paradise 53. Star 53. Storm over the Nile 56. Battle of the River Plate 56. Sea Fury 58. First Man in Space 59. The Stranglers of Bombay 60. The Terror of the Tongs 61. The Singer Not the Song 61. The Road to Hong Kong 62. The Running Man 63. Masquerade 65. Khartoum 66. The Mummy's Shroud 67. The Assassination Bureau 69. Anthony and Cleopatra 73, etc.

TV series: Sir Francis Drake 62.

Dell, Dorothy (1915–1934) (Dorothy Goff).
American beauty queen whose film career was cut short by a car crash.

■ Wharf Angel 34. Little Miss Marker 34. Shoot the Works 34.

Dell, Gabriel (1920–1988) (Gabriel del Vecchio).
American actor, one of the original Dead End Kids who in the 60s emerged as a TV character actor.

Dell, Jeffrey (1904–1985).
British comedy writer, author in the 30s of *Nobody Ordered Wolves*, a satirical novel of the film industry.

Sanders of the River (co-w) 35. The Saint's Vacation 41. Thunder Rock (co-w) 42. *Don't Take it to Heart* (& d) 44. It's Hard to Be Good (& d) 48. The Dark Man (& d) 50. Brothers-in-Law (co-w) 56. Lucky Jim (co-w) 58. Carlton-Browne of the F.O. (& co-d) 59. A French Mistress (co-w) 61. Rotten to the Core (co-w) 65. The Family Way (co-w) 66, etc.

Dell, Myrna (1924–) (Marilyn Dunlap).
American supporting actress, with RKO in the 40s.

The Falcon in San Francisco 45. Step by Step 46. Nocturne 46. Fighting Father Dunne 48. The Judge Steps Out 49. The Bushwhackers 52. Last of the Desperados 55. Naked Hills 55. The Toughest

Man Alive 55. Ma Barker's Killer Brood 60. Buddy Buddy 81, etc.

Delli Colli, Tonino (1923–).
Distinguished Italian cinematographer, noted for his work with Sergio Leone and Pier Paolo Pasolini.
Il Paese senza Pace 42. Toto a Colori 51. Le Rouge et le Noir 54. Accattone 61. Mama Roma 62. The Gospel According to St Matthew/Il Vangelo Secondo Matteo 64. The Hawks and the Sparrows/Uccellacci e Uccellini 66. The Good, the Bad and the Ugly 66. La Mandragola 66. Once Upon a Time in the West 68. Pigsty/Porcile 69. Pussycat, Pussycat I Love You 70. The Decameron 70. The Canterbury Tales 71. Lacombe, Lucien 73. Salo, or the 120 Days of Sodom 75. Seven Beauties 76. The Purple Taxi/Un Taxi Mauve 77. Viva Italia 78. Sunday Lovers 80. Tales of Ordinary Madness/Storie di Ordinaria Follia 81. Trenchcoat 83. Once Upon a Time in America 84. Ginger and Fred 86. The Name of the Rose 86. The Voice of the Moon/La Voce della Luna 90. The African/L'Africana 91. Bitter Moon 92. En Suivant la Comète 94. Death and the Maiden (GB/US/Fr.) 94. Life Is Beautiful 97, many others.

Delluc, Louis (1892–1924).
Pioneer French director of the 20s, associated with the impressionist school.
■ Fièvre 21. La Femme de Nulle Part 22. L'Inondation 24.

Delon, Alain (1935–).
Romantic-looking French leading man.
Plein Soleil 59. Rocco and his Brothers 60. The Eclipse 61. The Leopard 62. The Big Snatch 63. The Black Tulip 64. The Yellow Rolls-Royce 64. The Love Cage 65. Once a Thief 65. Lost Command 66. Is Paris Burning? 66. Texas Across the River 66. Les Aventuriers 66. Histoires Extraordinaires 67. Diabolically Yours 67. Samurai 67. Girl on a Motorcycle 67. La Piscine 67. Jeff 68. *Borsalino* 70. The Sicilian Clan 70. The Red Circle 70. Red Sun 71. The Assassination of Trotsky 72. Scorpio 72. Dirty Money 72. Borsalino and Co. 73. Shock 74. The Investigator 74. The Gypsy 75. Zorro 75. Mr Klein 76. Farewell Friend 77. The Concorde–Airport 79 79. Harmonie 79. Trois Hommes à Abattre 80. *Swann in Love* 84. Cop's Honour 85. The Passage 86. New Wave/Nouvelle Vague 89. Dancing Machine 90. Casanova 91. Dérapage 92. L'Ours en Peluche 94. The Day and the Night/Le Jour et la Nuit 97, etc.

Delon, Nathalie (1938–) (Francine Canovas).
French leading actress.
Le Samourai 67. La Sorelle 69. When Eight Bells Toll 71. Bluebeard 72. The Romantic Englishwoman 75. Sweet Lies (& d) 88, etc.

Delorme, Danièle (1926–) (Gabrielle Girard).
French leading lady.
Gigi 48. La Cage aux Filles 49. Sans Laisser d'Adresse 51. Tempi Nostri 54. Prisons de Femmes 58. La Guerre des Boutons (p only) 62. Pardon Mon Affaire 77. Novembermond 85. Sortez des Rangs 96, etc.

Delpy, Julie (1969–).
Young French leading actress.
Bad Blood/Mauvais Sang 86. Beatrice/La Passion Béatrice 86. Europa, Europa 91. Voyager 92. The Three Musketeers 93. Younger and Younger 93. Killing Zoe 94. Three Colours: White/Trois Couleurs: Blanc 94. Before Sunrise 95. An American Werewolf in Paris 97. LA without a Map 98, etc.

Delvaux, André (1926–).
Belgian director.
The Man Who Had His Hair Cut Short 67. Un Soir un Train 68. *Rendezvous at Bray* 73, etc.

Demarest, William (1892–1983).
American character actor, an 'old pro' with vast vaudeville experience before film debut in 1927.
The Jazz Singer 27. Fingerprints 27. The Murder Man 35. Wedding Present 36. Rosalie 38. Mr Smith Goes to Washington 39. Tin Pan Alley 40. The Great McGinty 40. *Sullivan's Travels* 41. The Palm Beach Story 42. *Hail the Conquering Hero* 43. *The Miracle of Morgan's Creek* (as Officer Kockenlocker) 43. Once upon a Time 44. Pardon My Past 45. Along Came Jones 45. *The Jolson Story* (AAN) 46. The Perils of Pauline 47. On Our Merry Way 49. Jolson Sings Again 50. *The First Legion* 51. Riding High 51. Dangerous When Wet 52. Escape from Fort Bravo 53. Jupiter's Darling 54. The Rawhide Years 56. Son of Flubber 63. It's a Mad Mad Mad Mad World 63. That Darn Cat 65. The McCullochs 75. Won Ton Ton 76, many others.
TV series: Wells Fargo 56–58. Love and Marriage 59. My Three Sons 67–71.
✪ For his reliability in a wide variety of roles, and for his ability to be instantly recognized and welcomed by people who didn't know his name. *Hail the Conquering Hero*.

Demick, Irina (1937–).
Franco-Russian leading lady in international films.
The Longest Day 62. Those Magnificent Men in Their Flying Machines 65. Up from the Beach 65. Cloportes 65. Prudence and the Pill 68, etc.

Deming, Peter.
American cinematographer.
Hollywood Shuffle 87. Evil Dead II 87. House Party 90. Drop Dead Fred 91. Scorchers 91. My Cousin Vinny 92. National Lampoon's Loaded Weapon 93. The Son in Law 93. SFW 94. Joe's Apartment 96. Lost Highway 96. Scream 96. Austin Powers: Man of Mystery 97, etc.

Demme, Jonathan (1944–).
American director. He is a former critic, film publicist for Joseph Levine and screenwriter and producer for Roger Corman's New World Productions.
Angels Hard As They Come (p, co-w) 71. The Hot Box (p, co-w) 72. Black Mama, White Mama (co-w) 72. Caged Heat (wd) 74. Crazy Mama 75. Fighting Mad (wd) 76. Citizens Band 77. Last Embrace 79. *Melvin and Howard* 80. Swing Shift 84. Stop Making Sense 84. Swimming to Cambodia 87. Something Wild 87. Married to the Mob 88. *The Silence of the Lambs* (AA) 91. Cousin Bobby 92. Philadelphia 93. Subway Stories (co-d) 97. Beloved 98. Storefront Hitchcock 98, etc.
❝ I don't care what I get remembered for – or don't get remembered for. That's no interest to me whatsoever. I just love making movies. *–J.D.*

Demme, Ted.
American director.
Who's the Man 93. The Ref 94. Beautiful Girls 96. Subway Stories (co-d) 97, etc.

Demongeot, Mylène (1936–).
Blonde French leading lady, briefly flaunted as sex symbol.
Les Enfants de L'Amour 54. It's a Wonderful World (GB) 56. *The Witches of Salem* 56. Bonjour Tristesse 57. Upstairs and Downstairs (GB) 59. The Giant of Marathon 60. Gold for the Caesars 62. Uncle Tom's Cabin (Ger.) 65. Fantomas 66. The Vengeance of Fantomas 67. The Private Navy of Sgt O'Farrell 68. By the Blood of Others 77. La Piste du Télégraphe/In the Wind's Eye 94. The Telegraph Route 94, etc.

Dempsey, Patrick (1966–).
American actor.
Heaven Help Us 85. Meatballs III 86. In the Mood/The Woo Woo Kid 87. Can't Buy Me Love 87. In a Shallow Grave 88. Some Girls 88. Lover Boy 89. Happy Together 90. Coupe de Ville 90. Run 91. Mobsters 91. Face the Music 92. JFK: Reckless Youth (TV) 93. Bank Robber 93. With Honors 94. Outbreak 95. Bloodknot (TV) 95. Hugo Pool 97. There's No Fish Food in Heaven 98, etc.
TV series: Fast Times 86.

Dempster, Austin.
British cinematographer, a former camera operator from the mid-40s.
Bedazzled 67. Otley 69. Loot 70. The Looking Glass War 70. A Severed Head 71. Tales of Beatrix Potter 71. A Touch of Class 73, etc.

Dempster, Carol (1901–1991).
American leading lady of the silent screen, especially for D. W. Griffith.
Scarlet Days 19. The Love Flower 20. Dream Street 21. *One Exciting Night* 22. America 24. Isn't Life Wonderful? 24. That Royle Girl 26. The Sorrows of Satan 26, etc.

Demy, Jacques (1931–1990).
French director. He was married to director Agnès Varda.
■ *Lola* 60. The Seven Deadly Sins (part) 61. La Baie des Anges 62. *Les Parapluies de Cherbourg* 64. The Young Girls of Rochefort 67. The Model Shop (US) 70. Peau d'Ane 71. The Pied Piper 72. The Slightly Pregnant Man 73. Lady Oscar 79.

Dench, Dame Judi (1934–).
British stage actress. She is married to actor Michael Williams.
Biography: 1985, *Judi Dench* by Gerald Jacobs.
The Third Secret 64. A Study in Terror 65. He Who Rides a Tiger 66. Four in the Morning (BFA) 66. A Midsummer Night's Dream 68. Luther 73. Dead Cert 74. Saigon – Year of the Cat (TV) 83. Wetherby 84. 84 Charing Cross Road 87. A Handful of Dust 88. Henry V 90. Jack & Sarah 95. GoldenEye 95. Hamlet 96. Tomorrow Never Dies 97. Mrs Brown (AAN) 97. *Shakespeare in Love* 98. Tea with Mussolini 99, etc.
TV series: A Fine Romance 81–84. As Time Goes By 92–98.

Dene, Terry (1938–) (Terence Williams).
English rock singer who had a few hits in the late 50s, then got religion and became an evangelist, returning to singing with less success in the 80s.
Biography: 1974, *I Thought Terry Dene Was Dead* by Dan Wooding.
The Golden Disc 58.

Deneuve, Catherine (1943–) (Catherine Dorléac).
French leading lady, sister of Françoise Dorleac.
Vice and Virtue 62. *Les Parapluies de Cherbourg* 64. *Repulsion* (GB) 65. Das Liebeskarussell/Who Wants to Sleep? 65. Les Créatures 66. The Young Girls of Rochefort 67. *Belle de Jour* 67. Benjamin 68. Manon 70 68. Mayerling 68. The April Fools (US) 69. The Mississippi Mermaid 69. *Tristana* 70. Peau d'Ane 71. The Lady in Red Boots 74. Hustle 76. Le Sauvage 76. L'Argent des Autres 78. Ils Sont Grands ces Petits 79. Le Dernier Métro 80. The Hunger 83. Abattre 80. The African 84. Fort Saganne 85. The Scene of the Crime 86. Indochine 92. La Reine Blanche 92. My Favourite Season/Ma Saison Préférée 93. Les Demoiselles Ont Eu 25 Ans (doc) 93. The Convent (Port.) 95. Thieves/Les Voleurs 96. Place Vendôme 98, etc.
❝ She is the man I would have liked to be. *– Gérard Depardieu*

Denham, Maurice (1909–).
British character actor with stage experience from 1934.
It's Not Cricket 48. London Belongs to Me 48. The Spider and the Fly 50. The Million Pound Note 54. Simon and Laura 55. *Animal Farm* (all voices) 55. Checkpoint 56. Night of the Demon 57. Our Man in Havana 59. Sink the Bismarck 60. HMS Defiant 62. The Seventh Dawn 64. Hysteria 65. The Alphabet Murders 65. After the Fox 66. The Midas Run 69. The Virgin and the Gypsy 70. Countess Dracula 70. Nicholas and Alexandra 71. Luther 73. Shout at the Devil 75. Julia 77. 84 Charing Cross Road 87. Memento Mori (TV) 92, many others.

Denham, Reginald (1894–1983).
British playwright (usually with Edward Percy) who also directed several films. Born in London, he studied at the Guildhall School of Music, and was on stage as an actor from 1913, becoming a producer in the 20s. He became an executive of Paramount British Pictures in the early 30s. The second of his three wives was actress Lilian Oldland. His daughter Isolde Denham, a stage actress, was the first wife of actor-writer-director Peter Ustinov.
Autobiography: 1958, *Stars in My Hair.*
Book: 1966, *Footlights and Feathers* (with Mary Orr).
Borrow a Million 34. Death at Broadcasting House 34. The Price of Wisdom 35. Lucky Days 35. The House of the Spaniard 36. Kate Plus Ten 38. Anna of Brooklyn 59, etc.

Denis, Claire (1946–).
French director whose films often explore colonial relationships. She spent her childhood in Africa and studied film at IDHEC.
Chocolat 87. S'en Fout la Mort 90. La Robe à Cerceaux (TV) 92. I Can't Sleep/J'ai Pas Sommeil 94. Nenette and Boni (co-w, d) 96, etc.

Denis, Prince (1900–1984).
Diminutive French-born actor and circus performer who played the Mayor of the Munchkins in *The Wizard of Oz* 39.
Three Wise Fools 46. The Greatest Show on Earth 52.

Denison, Michael (1915–1998).
British leading actor with firm but gentle manner. Born in Doncaster, he was educated at Harrow and Oxford University before studying acting at the Webber-Douglas School. He was on stage from 1938 and in films from 1940, frequently acting opposite his wife Dulcie Gray, whom he married in 1939.
Autobiographies (with Dulcie Gray): 1973, *Overture and Beginners*; 1985, *Double Act.*
Book: 1964, *The Actor and His World* (with Dulcie Gray).
Tilly of Bloomsbury 40. Hungry Hill 46. My *Brother Jonathan* 47. *The Glass Mountain* 47. The Blind Goddess 48. The Importance of Being Earnest 51. Angels One Five 51. The Franchise Affair 52. The Tall Headlines 52. Landfall 53. The Truth about Women 57. Faces in the Dark 61. Dark River 90. Shadowlands 93, etc.
TV series: Boyd QC 56–64.

Dennehy, Brian (1939–).
Heavily built American character actor, mostly on television.
Johnny We Hardly Knew Ye (TV) 77. It Happened at Lakewood Manor (TV) 77. Semi Tough 77. Foul Play 78. Ruby and Oswald (TV) 78. A Death in Canaan (TV) 78. A Real American Hero (as Buford Pusser) (TV) 78. Pearl (TV) 79. Silent Victor (TV) 79. '10' 79. Butch and Sundance 79. Little Miss Marker 80. A Rumour of War (TV) 80. Split Image 82. First Blood 82. Gorky Park 83. Never Cry Wolf 83. Cocoon 85. Silverado 85. Twice in a Lifetime 85. Legal Eagles 86. The Belly of an Architect 87. Best Seller 87. Dear America 87. Cocoon: The Return 88. Miles from Home 88. Return to Snowy River Part II 88. Indio 89. Perfect Witness (TV) 89. Last of the Finest 89. Seven Minutes 89. Presumed Innocent 90. Rising Sun 90. FX2 – the Deadly Art of Illusion 91. To Catch a Killer (TV) 91. Gladiator 92. Foreign Affairs (TV) 93. Murder in the Heartland (TV) 93. Tommy Boy 95. The Stars Fell on Henrietta 95. William Shakespeare's Romeo and Juliet 96. Nostromo (TV) 96. Larry McMurtry's Dead Man's Walk (TV) 96, etc.
TV series: *Big Shamus Little Shamus* 79. Star of the Family 82. Birdland 94.

Denner, Charles (1926–1995).
Polish-born leading actor in France, from the stage.
Landru 62. *Life Upside Down* 63. The Sleeping Car Murder 66. The Two of Us 68. The Bride Wore Black 68. A Gorgeous Bird Like Me 72. And Now My Love 75. *The Man Who Loved Women* 77. Le Coeur a L'Envers 80. Golden Eighties 86, etc.

Denning, Richard (1914–1998) (Louis A. Denninger).
American leading man who from 1937 played light romantic roles and manly athletes. Born in Poughkeepsie, New York, he studied business administration before deciding to become an actor, and was contracted to Paramount at the age of 23. Married actress Evelyn Ankers. In the early 60s he retired to Hawaii, afterwards making only a couple of films, and appearing in the TV series *Hawaii Five-O*.
Hold 'Em Navy 37. Persons in Hiding 38. Union Pacific 39. Golden Gloves 40. Adam Had Four Sons 41. Beyond the Blue Horizon 42. The Glass Key 42. Seven Were Saved 46. Black Beauty 46. Caged Fury 48. No Man of Her Own 48. Weekend with Father 50. Scarlet Angel 51. Hangman's Knot 53. The Creature from the Black Lagoon 54. Assignment Redhead (GB) 56. The Black Scorpion 57. Twice Told Tales 63. I Sailed to Tahiti with an All-Girl Crew 69. Mary Queen of Scots 71, many others, mainly second features.
TV series: Mr and Mrs North 53–54. The Flying Doctor 59. Michael Shayne 60. Karen 64. Hawaii Five-O (occasionally) 68–79.

Dennis, Sandy (1937–1992) (Sandra Dale Dennis).
American leading actress.
■ Splendour in the Grass 61. *Who's Afraid of Virginia Woolf?* (AA) 66. Up the Down Staircase 67. The Fox 68. Sweet November 68. That Cold Day in the Park 69. A Touch of Love 69. The Out-

of-Towners 69. The Only Way Out Is Dead 70. Something Evil (TV) 71. Mr Sycamore 75. Nasty Habits 76. God Told Me To 76. Three Sisters 77. Perfect Gentlemen (TV) 78. The Four Seasons 81. Come Back to the Five and Dime, Jimmy Dean, Jimmy Dean 82. The Execution (TV) 84. 976-EVIL 88. Another Woman 88. Parents 89. The Indian Runner 91.

❝ She has made an acting style out of post-nasal drip. – *Pauline Kael on S.D.*

When you finish an acting stint, there's nothing except money. You have to keep going, giving the best you've got, to get something intangible. – *S.D.*

Denny, Reginald (1891–1967) (Reginald Leigh Daymore).
British actor, on stage from childhood. From 1919 starred in many Hollywood action comedies and when sound came in began to play amiable stiff-upper-lip Britishers. More or less retired after 1950 to devote time to his aircraft company.

49 East 20. Footlights 21. *The Leather Pushers* 22. The Abysmal Brute 23. *Skinner's Dress Suit* 25. Oh Doctor 26. California Straight Ahead 27. Embarrassing Moments 29. Madame Satan 30. Private Lives 32. Of Human Bondage 34. Anna Karenina 35. Romeo and Juliet 36. Several Bulldog Drummond films 37–38 (as Algy). *Rebecca* (as Frank Crawley) 40. Sherlock Holmes and the Voice of Terror 42. Love Letters 45. The Macomber Affair 47. The Secret Life of Walter Mitty 47. *Mr Blandings Builds His Dream House* (as Mr Simms) 48. Abbott and Costello Meet Dr Jekyll and Mr Hyde 53. Around the World in Eighty Days 56. Fort Vengeance 59. Cat Ballou 65. Batman 66, many others.

Dent, Vernon (1894–1963).
American character actor, a pompous butt for the Three Stooges in many of their two-reelers.

Denver, Bob (1935–).
American TV comedian.

Take Her She's Mine 63. For Those Who Think Young 64. Who's Minding the Mint? 67. The Sweet Ride 67. Do You Know The One About the Travelling Saleslady 68, etc.

TV series: Dobie Gillis 59–62. Gilligan's Island 64–66. The Good Guys 68. Dusty's Trail 73. High School U.S.A. (TV) 83. Back to the Beach 87, etc.

Denver, John (1943–1997) (Henry John Deutschendorf, Jnr).
American country singer and composer, in occasional films. Born in New Mexico, he dropped out of architectural college to become a singer, joining the Chad Mitchel Trio in the mid-60s and performing as a solo artist with many hits in the early 70s. Died when the experimental rear-propelled plane he was flying crashed into Monterey Bay, California. A TV movie on his life is being planned.

Autobiography: 1994, *Take Me Home*.

Oh God! 77. The Christmas Gift (TV) 86. The Leftovers (TV) 86. Foxfire (TV) 87. Higher Ground (TV) 88, etc.

Deodato, Ruggero (1939–).
Italian director of exploitation movies, a former assistant director to Antonio Margheriti and Sergio Corbucci. Born in Potenza, he began as an actor in the mid-50s, and has also worked extensively in television, directing drama series.

Donne . . . Botte e Bersaglieri 68. Zenabel 69. Ultimo Mondo Cannibale 77. Concorde Affaire '79 79. Cannibal Holocaust 80. The House on the Edge of the Park/La Casa Sperduta nel Parco 80. The Barbarians 87. Casablanca Express 88. The Lone Runner 88. Phantom of Death 88. Dial: Help 88. Oceano 91. Mom I Can Do It 92. The Washing Machine 93, etc.

Depardieu, Gérard (1948–).
Burly, ubiquitous French leading actor who has made more than 70 films. He left home at 13 to work in a variety of menial jobs, was sometimes in trouble with the police, and turned to acting in his late teens.

Biography: 1994, *Depardieu* by Paul Chutkow.

Le Cri du Cormoran le Soir au-dessus des Jonques 71. Un Peau de Soleil dans l'Eau Froide 71. Le Viager 72. Le Tueur 72. La Scoumoune 72. Au Rendez-Vous de la Mort Joyeuse 73. Nathalie Granger 73. L'Affaire Dominici 73. Rude Journée pour la Reine 73. Deux Hommes dans la Ville 73. Les Gaspards 74. *Les Valseuses* 74. La Femme du Gange 74. Vincent, François, Paul et les Autres 74. Pas Si Méchant Que Ça 75. 1900/Novecento 76. Maîtresse 76. Sept Morts sur Ordonnance 75. The Last Woman/La Dernière Femme 76. Je t'Aime, Moi Non Plus 76. Barocco 76. Baxter, Vera Baxter 77. René La Canne 77. Le Camion 77. La Nuit, Tous les Chats Sont Gris 77. Dites-Lui que Je l'Aime 77. Violanta 78. *Get Out Your Handkerchiefs*/Préparez Vos Mouchoirs 78. La Femme Gauchère 78. Bye Bye Monkey/Ciao Maschio 78. Les Chiens 79. Buffet Froid 79. Loulou 80. Rosy la Bourrasque 80. Mon Oncle d'Amérique 80. *The Last Metro*/Le Dernier Métro 80. Je Vous Aime 80. Inspecteur La Bavure 80. Le Choix des Armes 81. La Femme d'à Côté 81. La Chèvre 81. *The Return of Martin Guerre*/Le Retour de Martin Guerre 82. Le Grand Frère 82. *Danton* 83. The Moon in the Gutter/La Lune dans le Caniveau 83. Les Compères 83. Fort Saganne 84. Tartuffe 84. Rive Droite, Rive Gauche 84. *Police* 85. Une Femme ou Deux 85. Jean de Florette 86. Ménage/Tenue de Soirée 86. Les Fugitifs 86. Sous le Soleil de Satan 87. *Camille Claudel* 88. Drôle d'Endroit pour une Rencontre 88. Deux 89. Too Beautiful for You/Trop Belle pour Toi 89. I Want to Go Home 89. *Cyrano de Bergerac* 90. Green Card (US) 90. Uranus 90. Merci la Vie 91. Mon Père, Ce Héros 91. Tous les Matins du Monde 91. 1492 (US) 92. *Germinal* 93. Hélas pour Moi 93. Une Pure Formalité 94. My Father, the Hero (US) 94. Colonel Chabert 94. Le Garcu 95. The Horseman on the Roof 95. Guardian Angels 95. Secret Agent (GB) 95. Unhook the Stars (US) 96. Hamlet (US) 96. Bogus (US) 96. Joseph Conrad's Secret Agent (GB) 96. The Word Love Exists (It.) 98. The Man in the Iron Mask (US) 98, etc.

❝ Having to confront policemen and judges is an excellent way to train your imagination. In a few seconds you have to improvise a role with talent and emotion. – *G.D.*

There appears to be nothing he cannot do well on the screen. – *New York Times*

I sometimes think I shall never view/A French film lacking Gérard Depardieu. – *John Updike*

Depp, Johnny (1963–).
American leading actor, often in fey or eccentric roles. Born in Owensboro, Kentucky, he played in a rock group, The Kids, before turning to acting in the mid-80s. Divorced, he has been engaged to actresses Sherilyn Fenn, Jennifer Grey and Winona Ryder, and romantically linked with model Kate Moss.

A Nightmare on Elm Street 84. Private Resort 85. Platoon 86. Cry-Baby 90. Edward Scissorhands 90. Arizona Dream 92. Benny & Joon 93. What's Eating Gilbert Grape? 93. *Ed Wood* 94. Don Juan DeMarco 95. Nick of Time 95. Dead Man 95. Donnie Brasco 96. The Brave (& d) 97. Fear and Loathing in Las Vegas 98. LA without a Map (GB/Fr./Fin.) (as himself) 98, etc.

TV series: 21 Jump Street 87–90.

❝ I don't pretend to be Captain Weird. I just do what I do. – *J.D.*

Feet are fascinating, don't you think? They tell you so much about people. – *J.D.*

Deray, Jacques (1927–).
French director.

Le Gigolo 60. Rififi in Tokyo 61. Symphony for a Massacre 63. Our Man in Marrakesh 66. The Swimming Pool 69. Borsalino 70. The Outside Man 72. Flic Story 75. Le Gang 77. A Butterfly on the Shoulder 78. Trois Hommes à Abattre 80. Le Marginal 83. On ne Meurt que Deux Fois 85. Réglements de Comptes 86. Maladie d'Amour 87. Le Solitaire 87. Les Bois Noirs 89. Netchaiev est de Retour 91. Dérapage 92. L'Ours en Peluche 94, etc.

Derek, Bo (1957–) (Mary Cathleen Collins).
American pin-up who rather curiously caused a press sensation in her first starring film. Wife of John Derek.

■ Orca Killer Whale 77. '10' 79. A Change of Seasons 80. Tarzan the Ape Man 81. Fantasies 81. Bolero 84. Hot Chocolate 92. Sognando La California (It.) 93. Woman of Desire 94. Tommy Boy 95.

TV series: Wind on Water 98.

Derek, John (1926–1998) (Derek Harris).
American light leading man who later turned to directing, cinematography, producing – and displaying his third wife Bo Derek in a series of banal films. Born in Los Angeles, the son of director Lawson Harris and actress Dolores Johnson, he was previously married to actresses Ursula Andress (1957–64) and Linda Evans.

AS ACTOR: I'll Be Seeing You 45. *Knock on Any Door* 49. *All the King's Men* 49. *Rogues of Sherwood Forest* 50. Saturday's Hero 51. The Family Secret 51. Mask of the Avenger 51. Thunderbirds 52. Scandal Sheet 52. Ambush at Tomahawk Gap 53. Sea of Lost Ships 53. An Annapolis Story 53. The Last Posse 53. Prince of Pirates 53. The Adventures of Hajji Baba 54. The Outcast 54. The Leather Saint 55. Run for Cover/Colorado 55. Prince of Players 55. The Ten Commandments 56. Fury at Showdown 57. The Flesh Is Weak 57. Omar Khayyam 58. High Hell 58. Prisoner of the Volga/I Battellieri del Volga (It.) 58. Exodus 60. Nightmare in the Sun 63. Once Before I Die 66. Flair (TV) 89, etc.

TV series: Frontier Circus 61–62.

AS DIRECTOR: Once Before I Die (& p) 65. A Boy . . . a Girl 69. Childish Things/Confessions of Tom Harris 69. Love You 80. Tarzan, the Ape Man (& co-ph) 81. Fantasies (& ph) 81. Bolero (& w, ph) 84. Ghosts Can't Do It 90, etc.

Dermithe, Edouard (1925–1995) (Antoine Dhermitte).
French actor and painter, associated with the films of Jean Cocteau. The son of a miner, he first sought employment as Cocteau's gardener and was offered a film role instead. After the death of Cocteau, he turned to painting.

Orphée 49. Les Enfants Terribles 50. Le Testament d'Orphée 59. Thomas l'Imposteur 64.

Dern, Bruce (1936–).
American general-purpose actor, usually seen as tough guy or psychotic. He is the father of actress Laura Dern.

Wild River 60. Marnie 64. The Wild Angels 66. The Trip 67. The War Wagon 67. Will Penny 68. Castle Keep 69. Number One 69. They Shoot Horses Don't They? 69. Bloody Mama 70. The Incredible Two-headed Transplant 70. Drive He Said 71. The Cowboys 72. *Silent Running* 72. The King of Marvin Gardens 72. The Laughing Policeman 73. The Great Gatsby 74. Posse 75. *Family Plot* 75. *Smile* 75. Black Sunday 76. Won Ton Ton 77. *Coming Home* (AAN) 78. The Driver 78. Middle Age Crazy 80. Tattoo 81. Harry Tracy 81. That Championship Season 82. On the Edge 84. The Big Town 87. 1969 88. World Gone Wild 88. The 'burbs 89. After Dark, My Sweet 91. Diggstown/Midnight Sting 92. Amelia Earhart: The Final Flight (TV) 94. Wild Bill 95. Mrs Munck 95. Mulholland Falls 96. Down Periscope 96. Last Man Standing 96, etc.

TV series: Stony Burke 62.

❝ I've played more psychotics and freaks and dopers than anyone. – *B.D.*

Dern, Laura (1966–).
American actress, the daugher of actor Bruce Dern. Born in Santa Monica, California, she studied acting at the Lee Strasberg Institute and RADA.

Teachers 84. Mask 85. Smooth Talk 86. Blue Velvet 86. Haunted Summer 88. Fat Man and Little Boy/The Shadowmakers 89. Wild at Heart 90. Rambling Rose (AAN) 91. Jurassic Park 93. A Perfect World 93. Down Came a Blackbird (TV) 95. Precious 96. Citizen Ruth 96. The Baby Dance (TV) 98, etc.

Derr, Richard (1917–1992).
American leading man, usually in minor films.

Ten Gentlemen from West Point 42. Tonight We Raid Calais 43. The Secret Heart 47. Joan of Arc 48. When Worlds Collide 51. Something to Live For 52. Terror Is a Man 59. Three in the Attic 68. The Drowning Pool 75, etc.

Deruddere, Dominique (1957–).
Belgian director, a former assistant cameraman.

Crazy Love/Love Is a Dog from Hell 87. Wait until Spring, Bandini 89. Suite 16 95.

Desailly, Jean (1920–).
French leading man.

Le Voyageur de la Toussaint 42. Sylvie et le Fantôme 45. *Occupe-Toi d'Amélie* 49. Les Grandes Manoeuvres 55. Maigret Sets a Trap 59. Le Doulos 62. *La Peau Douce* 64. The Twenty-Fifth Hour 66. Un Flic 72. The Assassination of Trotsky 72. Le Cavaleur 74. Pile ou Face 80. Le Professionel 81. Le Fou du Roi 84, etc.

Deschanel, Caleb (1944–).
American cinematographer.

The Black Stallion 79. More American Graffiti 79. Being There 79. The Escape Artist (d) 82. The Right Stuff (AAN) 83. The Natural (AAN) 84. The Slugger's Wife 85. It Could Happen to You 94. Fly Away Home (AAN) 96. Hope Floats 98, etc.

Desmond, Florence (1905–1993) (Florence Dawson).
British dancer and impersonator, seen in many stage revues but few films.

Autobiography: 1953, *Florence Desmond by Herself*.

The Road to Fortune 30. Sally in Our Alley 31. No Limit 35. *Keep Your Seats Please* 37. Hoots Mon 40. Three Came Home (US) 50. Charley Moon 56. Some Girls Do 68, etc.

Desmond, William (1878–1949) (William Mannion).
Irish leading man of the American silent screen, mostly in westerns.

The Sunset Trail 24. Blood and Steel 26. Tongues of Scandal 29. Hell Bent for Frisco 31. Flying Fury 33. Arizona Days 36, etc.

Desmonde, Jerry (1908–1967).
British character actor with long music-hall experience, a perfect foil for comedians from Sid Field to Norman Wisdom.

London Town 46. Cardboard Cavalier 48. Follow a Star 59. A Stitch in Time 63. The Early Bird 65, many others.

Desni, Tamara (1913–).
Russian-born, British-resident leading lady.

Jack Ahoy 34. Fire over England 36. The Squeaker 37. Traitor Spy 40. Send for Paul Temple 46. Dick Barton at Bay 50, etc.

Desny, Ivan (1922–).
Continental leading man, in films from 1948.

Madeleine (GB) 50. La Putain Respectueuse 52. Lola Montes 55. Anastasia 56. The Mirror Has Two Faces 58. The Magnificent Rebel 60. Das Liebeskarussel/Who Wants to Sleep? 65. The Mystery of Thug Island 66. I Killed Rasputin 68. Mayerling 68. The Adventures of Gerard 70. Paper Tiger 75. The Marriage of Maria Braun 78. Bloodline 79. The Lady without Camelias 80. Quicker than the Eye 88, etc.

Detmers, Maruschka (1961–).
Dutch actress, in international films.

First Name: Carmen/Prénom Carmen 83. Devil in the Flesh 86. Hanna's War 88. Le Brasier 90. The Mambo Kings 92. Love in the Strangest Way/Elle N'Oublient Jamais (Fr.) 94. The Shooter 95. Still Waters Run Deep (Fr.) 96, etc.

Deutch, Howard.
American director, from rock videos.

Pretty in Pink 86. Some Kind of Wonderful 87. The Great Outdoors/Big Country 88. Article 99 92. Getting Even with Dad 94. Grumpier Old Men 95. The Odd Couple II 98, etc.

Deutsch, Adolph (1897–1980).
London-born composer, conductor and arranger, in Hollywood, where he worked primarily for Warner's and MGM.

Mr Dodds Takes the Air 37. The Great Garrick 37. Broadway Musketeers 38. The Kid from Kokomo 39. Angels Wash Their Faces 39. Castle on the Hudson 40. Saturday's Children 40. They Drive by Night 40. *The Maltese Falcon* 41. High Sierra 41. Manpower 41. All through the Night 42. George Washington Slept Here 42. Action in the North Atlantic 43. Northern Pursuit 43. The Mask of Dimitrios 44. Julia Misbehaves 48. Take Me Out to the Ball Game 48. Little Women 48. The Big Hangover 49. Stars in My Crown 49. Intruder in the Dust 49. *Annie Get Your Gun* (AA) 50. Father of the Bride 50. Pagan Love Song 50. Soldiers Three 51. *Show Boat* (AAN) 51. The Belle of New York 51. The Band Wagon 53. Torch Song 53. Deep in My Heart 54. Seven Brides for Seven Brothers (AA) 54. Interrupted Melody 55. *Oklahoma!* (AA) 55. Tea and Sympathy 56. The Matchmaker 57. Funny Face 57. Les Girls 57. Some Like It Hot 59. The Apartment 60. Go Naked in the World 60, etc.

Deutsch, David (1926–1992).
British producer, in films from 1949. Son of Oscar Deutsch who founded the Odeon circuit.
Blind Date 59. Nothing But the Best 64. Catch Us If You Can 65. Lock Up Your Daughters 69, etc.

Deutsch, Ernst (1890–1969).
German character actor.
Die Rache der Toten (debut) 16. The Golem 20. Lady Godiva 21. The Marriage of Corbal (GB) 35. Nurse Edith Cavell (US) 39. The Man I Married (US) 40. So Ends Our Night (US) 41. The Third Man (GB) 49. Der Wasserdoktor 58, etc.

Deutsch, Helen (1907–1992).
American screenwriter and dramatist.
The Seventh Cross 44. National Velvet 45. Loves of Carmen 48. King Solomon's Mines 50. Kim 50. Lili (AAN) 53. I'll Cry Tomorrow 55. Forever Darling 56. The Unsinkable Molly Brown 64. Valley of the Dolls 67, etc.

Devane, William (1937–).
Craggy, toothy American leading actor who rode the crest for a while in the late 70s.
■ The Pursuit of Happiness 71. My Old Man's Place 71. McCabe and Mrs Miller 71. Mortadella 71. Irish Whiskey Rebellion 73. The Bait (TV) 73. Crime Club (TV) 73. *Missiles of October* (TV) (as John F. Kennedy) 73. Report to the Commissioner 75. *Fear on Trial* (TV) (as John Henry Faulk) 75. *Family Plot* 76. Marathon Man 76. Red Alert (TV) 77. Black Beauty (TV) 77. The Bad News Bears in Breaking Training 77. Rolling Thunder 77. *From Here to Eternity* (TV) 79. Yanks 79. The Dark 79. Honky Tonk Freeway 81. Testament 83. Jane Doe (TV) 84. Timestalkers 87. Vital Signs 90. Nightwatch 95. Forgotten Sins 96. Exception to the Rule 97. The Absolute Truth (TV) 97. Knots Landing: Back to the Cul-de-Sac (TV) 97. Doomsday Rock (TV) 97.
TV series: Knots Landing 84–88. The Monroes 95. Turks 98– .

Devereaux, Ed.
Australian character actor who in addition to starring in the *Skippy* TV series appeared in some international films.
Floods of Fear 58. Carry on Regardless 61. The Wrong Arm of the Law 63. They're a Weird Mob 66. The Nickel Queen 71. Barry Mackenzie Holds His Own 74. Pressure 75. Edward & Mrs Simpson (TV) 80. Robbery under Arms (TV) 85. Claudia 85. Goldeneye: The Secret Life of Ian Fleming (TV) 89. Buddy's Song 90. The Preventers (TV) 96, etc.

Devi, Phoolan.
Indian 'bandit queen', whose life was the basis of the film of the same name. In 1996, two years after her release from prison, she was elected to the Indian parliament.
Autobiography: 1996, *I, Phoolan Devi* (with Marie-Thérèse Cuny and Paul Rambali).

Deville, Michel (1931–).
French director.
Ce Soir ou Jamais 60. L'Appartement des Filles 63. Benjamin 67. Bye Bye Barbara 69. The Bear and the Doll 71. La Femme en Bleu 73. Love at the Top 74. L'Apprenti Salaud 77. Le Dossier 51 79. Le Voyage en douce 80. Eaux Profondes 81. La Petite Bande 83. Péril en la Demeure 84. Death in a French Garden 86. Le Paltoquet 86. The Reader/La Lectrice 88. Nuit d'Été en Ville 90. Toutes Peines Confondues 92. Aux Petits Bonheurs 93, etc.

Devine, Andy (1905–1977).
Fat, husky-voiced American character comedian, seen in innumerable westerns.
We Americans 28. Hot Stuff 29. Law and Order 32. Midnight Mary 33. Stingaree 34. Way Down East 35. Romeo and Juliet 36. A Star is Born 37. In Old Chicago 37. *Stagecoach* 39. When the Daltons Rode 40. Badlands of Dakota 41. Sin Town 42. Crazy House 43. Ghost Catchers 44. Frisco Sal 45. Canyon Passage 46. The Vigilantes Return 47. Old Los Angeles 48. *The Red Badge of Courage* 51. New Mexico 51. Montana Belle 52. Island in the Sky 53. Pete Kelly's Blues 55. The Adventures of Huckleberry Finn 60. Two Rode Together 61. The Man who Shot Liberty Valance 62. It's a Mad Mad Mad Mad World 63. Zebra in the Kitchen 65. The Ballad of Josie 68. A Whale of a Tale 77, many others.
TV series: *Wild Bill Hickok* 51–54. Andy's Gang 57. Flipper 64.

Devon, Laura (1940–).
American leading lady from TV.
Goodbye Charlie 65. Red Line 7000 66. Gunn 67, etc.

DeVore, Gary M. (1942–1997).
American screenwriter, mainly of action movies. Born in Los Angeles, he was a trucker for six years before beginning in television; he later worked as a script doctor on such films as *The Mean Season*, *The Relic* and *Passenger 57*. Died when his car ran off the road into an aqueduct, where his body lay undiscovered for a year. At the time of his death, he was planning to direct an updated remake of the 1949 movie *The Big Steal*. Married four times, including to Maria Cole, widow of Nat 'King' Cole, and actress Claudia Christian.
The Dogs of War (co-w) 80. Back Roads 81. Heart of Steel (TV) 83. Raw Deal (co-w) 86. Running Scared (co-w) 86. Traxx 88, etc.
❝ He radiated testosterone. He wrote great street cop. – *Peter Hyams*

Devry, Elaine (1935–).
American leading lady.
Mantrap 61. Diary of a Madman 63. Guide for the Married Man 67. The Boy Who Cried Werewolf 73, etc.

Dewaere, Patrick (1946–1982).
French leading man. Committed suicide.
Les Mariés de l'An II 70. Going Places 73. Get Out Your Handkerchiefs 78. Coup de Tête 78. Psy 80. Hotel of the Americas 81. Plein Sud 81. Paradise for All 83, etc.

Dewhurst, Colleen (1924–1991).
American general-purpose actress most notable for her stage performances, especially in the plays of Eugene O'Neill. She was twice married to actor George C. Scott (1960–65, 1967–72).
■ The Nun's Story 59. Man on a String 60. A Fine Madness 63. The Last Run 71. The Cowboys 72. McQ 74. The Story of Jacob and Joseph (TV) 74. Annie Hall 77. Ice Castles 78. Silent Victory (TV) 79. Studs Lonigan (TV) 79. When a Stranger Calls 79. Final Assignment 80. Tribute 80. Guyana Tragedy (TV) 80. A Perfect Match (TV) 81. The Dead Zone 83. The Boy Who Could Fly 86. Lantern Hill 89. Termini Station 89. Bed and Breakfast 90. Dying Young 91.

Dewolf, Patrick.
French screenwriter and director.
Moi Vouloir Toi (d) 85. Monsieur Hire (co-w) 89. Lapse of Memory (co-w, d) (Fr./Can.) 92. Halcyon Days (co-w, d) (GB) 94. Innocent Lies (Fr./GB) (co-w, d) 95, etc.

Dexter, Anthony (1919–) (Walter Fleischmann).
American leading man with stage experience. Cast as Rudolph Valentino, he never lived down the tag, and his subsequent roles have been in small-scale action dramas and science-fiction quickies.
Valentino 51. The Brigand 52. Captain John Smith and Pocahontas 53. Captain Kidd and the Slave Girl 54. Fire Maidens from Outer Space (GB) 54. He Laughed Last 56. The Parson and the Outlaw (as Billy the Kid) 57. Twelve to the Moon 59. Thoroughly Modern Millie 67, etc.

Dexter, Brad (1917–).
American character actor often seen as a tough hoodlum.
The Asphalt Jungle 50. Macao 52. Untamed 55. The Oklahoman 57. The Magnificent Seven 60. Taras Bulba 62. Bus Riley's Back in Town 64. Von Ryan's Express 65. Blindfold 66. The Naked Runner (p only) 67. The Lawyer (p only) 69. Winter Kills 79, etc.

Dexter, John (1925–1990).
British director, a former actor. He was also a theatre and opera director, notably with Britain's National Theatre.
Autobiography: 1993, *The Honourable Beast*.
■ The Virgin Soldiers 69. Sidelong Glances of a Pigeon Kicker 70. I Want What I Want 71.

Dexter, Maury (1927–).
American producer-director of second features.
The Third Voice (p) 60. Harbour Lights (pd) 63. The Day Mars Invaded Earth (pd) 63. House of the Damned (pd) 63. The Naked Brigade (d) 65. The Outlaw of Red River (pd) 65. Maryjane (pd) 68. Hell's Belles (pd) 70, etc.

Dey, Susan (1952–).
American juvenile actress of the 70s.
Skyjacked 72. Terror on the Beach (TV) 73. Cage without a Key (TV) 75. Mary Jane Harper Cried Last Night (TV) 77. First Love 77. The Comeback Kid 80. Looker 81. Sunset Limousine (TV) 83. Love Leads the Way (TV) 84. Echo Park 86. The Trouble with Dick 88. That's Adequate 90, etc.
TV series: The Partridge Family 70–74. Emerald Point 83. L.A. Law 86.

Dhery, Robert (1921–) (Robert Foulley).
Dapper French cabaret comedian and pantomimist.
Les Enfants du Paradis 44. Sylvie et le Fantôme 45. La Patronne (d only) 49. *Ah, Les Belles Bacchantes* (Femmes de Paris) (& w, p) 54. *La Belle Américaine* (& w, p) 61. Allez France (& w, p) 64. Le Petit Baigneur (& w, p) 67. A Time for Loving 71. Malevil 80, etc.

Dhiegh, Khigh (1910–1991).
Oriental American character actor familiar on TV as the evil villain of *Hawaii Five-O*.
The Manchurian Candidate 62. Judge Dec (TV) 77, etc.

DiCaprio, Leonardo (1974–).
Boyish American leading actor who rose to superstar status with his performance in James CAMERON's record-breaking *Titanic*, which brought him fan worship from millions of young girls. Born in Los Angeles, California, of a German mother and an Italian father, he began on television at the age of five, but did not act again until he was in his early teens, when he first worked in commercials and educational films. He was paid $20m to star in *The Beach*.
Critters 3 91. Incident at Oglala 92. This Boy's Life 93. What's Eating Gilbert Grape (AAN) 93. The Quick and the Dead 95. The Basketball Diaries 95. Total Eclipse 95. Romeo and Juliet 96. Marvin's Room 96. Titanic 97. The Man in the Iron Mask 98. The Beach 99, etc.
TV series: Growing Pains 91–92.
❝ The best thing about acting is that I get to lose myself in another character and actually get paid for it. As for myself, I'm not sure who I am. It seems that I change every day. – *L.DiC.*

Di Palma, Carlo (1925–).
Italian cinematographer and occasional director whose international reputation was made in the mid-60s. Recently he has worked in America for Woody Allen.
Ivan 54. The Lady Killer of Rome/L'Assassino 61. Omicron 63. Red Desert/Deserto Rosso 64. Blow-Up 66. The Appointment (US) 69. The Pacifist/La Pacifista 71. Teresa la Ladra (d) 73. Amo non Amo 79. The Black Stallion Returns (US) 83. Hannah and Her Sisters (US) 86. Off Beat (US) 86. Radio Days (US) 87. September 87. The Secret of My Success (US) 87. Alice (US) 90. Shadows and Fog 92. Husbands and Wives 92. Manhattan Murder Mystery 93. Bullets over Broadway 94. The Monster/Le Monstre 94. Mighty Aphrodite (US) 95. Everyone Says I Love You (US) 96. Deconstructing Harry (US) 97, etc.

Di Venanzo, Gianni (1920–1966).
Italian cinematographer, in films from 1941.
Amore in Città 53. Le Amiche 55. Il Grido 57. I Soliti Ignoti 58. Salvatore Giuliano 61. La Notte 61. L'Eclisse 62. Eva 62. *Eight and a Half* 63. *Juliet of the Spirits* 65, etc.

Diamond, I. A. L. (1920–1988) (Itek Dommnici, later Isadore Diamond).
Romanian-American screenwriter, his best work being in collaboration with Billy Wilder.
Murder in the Blue Room 44. Never Say Goodbye 46. Always Together 47. The Girl from Jones Beach 49. Something for the Birds 52. That Certain Feeling 56. Love in the Afternoon 57. Merry Andrew 58. *Some Like It Hot* 59. *The Apartment* (AA) 60. *One Two Three* 61. Irma la Douce 63. Kiss Me Stupid 64. *The Fortune Cookie* (AAN) 66. Cactus Flower 69. *The Private Life of Sherlock Holmes* 70. Avanti 72. The Front Page 74. Fedora 78, etc.

Diamond, Jack 'Legs'.
New York gangster and bootlegger. Murdered while sleeping by rival hoodlums, he was played by Ray Danton in two films: the factually inaccurate *The Rise and Fall of Legs Diamond* 60, directed by Budd Boetticher, and *Portrait of a Mobster* 61, directed by Joseph Pevney.
❝ That clay-pigeon sneak-thief who got his nickname because he could outrun the cops after robbing a pushcart. Today he is solemnly presented by the motion pictures as having won the name 'Legs' because of his great ability to *dance!* – *Gene Fowler*

Diamond, Neil (1941–).
American pop singer who failed to break into the movies in 1981 with *The Jazz Singer*.
❝ I'm not there to entertain people. We're there to do something together. – *N.D.*

Diaz, Arturo Sotto.
Cuban screenwriter and director.
Think of Me 96. Vertical Love/Amor Vertical (AAN) 97.

Diaz, Cameron (1973–).
American actress. Born in Long Beach, California, she began working as a model at 16, making her movie debut, with no acting experience, in *The Mask*. She has been romantically linked with actor Matt DILLON.
The Mask 94. The Last Supper 95. Feeling Minnesota 96. She's the One 96. Head above Water 96. A Life Less Ordinary 97. Fear and Loathing in Las Vegas 98. *There's Something about Mary* 98. Very Bad Things 98, etc.
❝ She may be a Jean Harlow for the '90s – a tough-talking bombshell who isn't afraid to be the butt of the joke. – *People*
A lucky model who's been given a lot of opportunities I just wish she would have done more with. – *Jennifer Lopez*
Cameron's like Grace Kelly – but with gas. – *Bobby Farrelly*

DiCillo, Tom.
American director and screenwriter of independent films, a former cinematographer working with director Jim Jarmusch.
Johnny Suede 91. *Living in Oblivion* 95. Box of Moonlight 96. The Real Blonde (wd) 97, etc.

Dick, Douglas (1920–).
Innocent-looking American 'second lead', now a psychologist.
The Searching Wind 46. Saigon 47. The Accused 48. Home of the Brave 49. The Red Badge of Courage 51. The Gambler from Natchez 55. The Oklahoman 57. North to Alaska 60, etc.

Dick, Philip K. (1928–1982).
American science-fiction writer of dark fables whose stories have been the basis of some memorable movies.
Biography: 1991, *Divine Invasions: A Life of Philip K. Dick* by Lawrence Sutin.
Blade Runner (from Do Androids Dream of Electric Sheep?) 82. Total Recall (from We Can Remember It for You Wholesale) 90.. Barjo (from Confessions of a Crap Artist) 93. Screamers (from Second Variety) 95.
❝ The SF writer sees not just possibilities but *wild* possibilities. It's not just 'What if . . .' It's 'My God, what if . . .' The Martians are always coming. – *P.K.D.*

Dickens, Charles (1812–1870).
Prolific British novelist whose gusto in characterization and plot-weaving made his books ideal cinema material until the last decade when producers seem to have thought them old-fashioned. Most filmed has perhaps been *A Christmas Carol*, usually personified as *Scrooge*; but *Oliver Twist* runs it a close second. There had been several early silent versions of *David Copperfield* before Cukor's splendid 1934 version, and *The Old Curiosity Shop* was popular as the basis of one-reelers before the talkie versions with Hay Petrie (1935) and Anthony Newley (1975). *A Tale of Two Cities* had been a popular stage play under the title *The Only Way*; after many early versions it was directed as a spectacular by Frank Lloyd in 1917, with William Farnum; as a British silent in 1926, with Martin Harvey; as a vehicle for Ronald Colman in 1935; and in a rather uninspired British version of 1958 starring Dirk Bogarde. A 1969 all-star version of

David Copperfield was primarily intended for American TV.

Other Dickens novels less frequently filmed include *The Mystery of Edwin Drood*, once as an early British silent, again in Hollywood in 1935, with Claude Rains as John Jasper, and again in Britain in 1993 with Robert Powell; *Great Expectations*, which had two silent versions, a rather dull Hollywood remake of 1934 and the magnificent David Lean version of 1946; *Dombey and Son*, under the title *Rich Man's Folly*, starring George Bancroft in 1931; *Nicholas Nickleby*, the only picturization of which was the patchy Ealing version of 1947, though the Royal Shakespeare Company's epic stage production has been released on video; and *The Pickwick Papers*, seen in various potted versions in silent days and in Noel Langley's superficial version of 1952.

Dickens' novels which were filmed in the silent period but not since sound include *The Cricket on the Hearth*, *Martin Chuzzlewit*, *Our Mutual Friend* and *Barnaby Rudge*. *Little Dorrit* was made in Germany in 1933 with Anny Ondra, and in 1987 by the Richard Brabourne group at a 6-hour length with a cast headed by Alec Guinness.

Dickerson, Ernest (1952–).
American cinematographer closely associated with director Spike Lee. He studied as an architect and worked as a photographer before entering films. He began writing and directing in the 90s.

The Brother from Another Planet 84. Krush Groove/Rap Attack 85. She's Gotta Have It 86. Enemy Territory 87. Eddie Murphy 'Raw' 87. School Daze 88. Do the Right Thing 89. Ava and Gabriel 89. Mo' Better Blues 90. Def by Temptation 90. The Laserman 90. Jungle Fever 91. Sex, Drugs, Rock & Roll 91. Juice (wd) 92. Cousin Bobby 92. Malcolm X 92. The Untouchables (TV) (d) 93. Surviving the Game (d) 94. Bulletproof (d) 96. Blind Faith (d) 98, etc.

Dickinson, Angie (1932–) (Angeline Brown).
Capable American leading lady, former beauty contest winner, in films from 1954.

Lucky Me 54. Man with the Gun 55. Tennessee's Partner 55. The Return of Jack Slade 55. Gun the Man Down 56. Hidden Guns 56. The Black Whip 56. Tension at Table Rock 56. Shootout at Medicine Bend 57. Calypso Joe 57. China Gate 57. I Married a Woman 58. Cry Terror 58. Rio Bravo 59. The Bramble Bush 60. Ocean's Eleven 60. A Fever in the Blood 61. The Sins of Rachel Cade 62. Rome Adventure 62. Jessica 62. Captain Newman MD 63. The Killers (TV) 64. The Art of Love 65. The Chase 66. Cast a Giant Shadow 66. Point Blank 67. The Last Challenge 67. Sam Whiskey 69. Young Billy Young 69. Some Kind of a Nut 69. The Love War (TV) 70. Thief (TV) 71. Pretty Maids All in a Row 71. The Resurrection of Zachary Wheeler 71. See the Man Run (TV) 71. The Norliss Tapes (TV) 73. The Outside Man 73. Pray for the Wildcats (TV) 74. Big Bad Mama 74. Labyrinth 79. Pearl (TV) 79. Dressed to Kill 80. Klondike Fever 80. Charlie Chan and the Curse of the Dragon Queen 81. Death Hunt 81. Big Bad Mama II 88. Once Upon a Texas Train/Texas Guns 88. Even Cowgirls Get the Blues 93. The Maddening 95. Sabrina 95. National Lampoon's The Don's Analyst 97, etc.

TV series: Police Woman 75–78. Cassie and Co. 81.

❝ I dress for women, and undress for men. – *A.D.*

Dickinson, Desmond (1902–1986).
British cinematographer.

Detective Lloyd (serial) 31. Men of Two Worlds 45. Fame is the Spur 46. *Hamlet* 47. The History of Mr Polly 49. Morning Departure 50. The Browning Version 52. The Importance of Being Earnest 52. Carrington VC 55. Orders to Kill 58. City of the Dead 60. Sparrows Can't Sing 63. A Study in Terror 65. Circus of Blood 67. Decline and Fall 68. Who Slew Auntie Roo? 71. The Fiend 71, etc.

Dickinson, Thorold (1903–1984).
British director, in films from 1925. Retired to teach film theory at Slade School, London.

Books: 1971, *A Discovery of Cinema*; 1998, *Thorold Dickinson and the British Cinema* by Jeffrey Richards.

■ The High Command 36. The Arsenal Stadium Mystery 39. *Gaslight* 39. The Prime Minister 41. *Next of Kin* 41. Men of Two Worlds 45. *The Queen of Spades* 48. The Secret People 52. Hill 24 Doesn't Answer 55.

Dickson, Dorothy (1893–1995).
American musical comedy star who spent most of her career in Britain. Mother of actress Dorothy Hyson.

Money Mad 17. Channel Crossing 32. Danny Boy 34. Sword of Honour 39, etc.

Dickson, Gloria (1916–1945) (Thais Dickerson).
American leading lady of the 30s. Died of asphyxiation from a fire.

They Won't Forget 37. Racket Busters 38. No Place to Go 39. They Made Me a Criminal 39. I Want a Divorce 40. The Big Boss 41. Affairs of Jimmy Valentine 42. Lady of Burlesque 43, etc.

Dickson, Paul (1920–).
British director, hailed for documentaries: *The Undefeated* 49, *David* 51. His feature films have been less distinguished: *Satellite in the Sky* 56. *The Depraved* 57, many second features and TV episodes.

Didion, Joan (1934–).
American screenwriter, novelist and essayist. She is married to writer John Gregory Dunne, with whom she has collaborated on film scripts.

Panic in Needle Park (co-w) 71. Play It as It Lays (oa, co-w) 71. A Star Is Born (co-w) 76. True Confessions (co-w) 81. Broken Trust (co-w, TV) 95. Up Close and Personal (co-w) 96.

Diegues, Carlos (1940–).
Brazilian director, screenwriter and poet, a former film critic.

Ganga Zumba 64. Xica da Silva 76. Bye Bye Brazil 79. Quilombo 84. Subway to the Stars/Um Trem para as Estrelas 86. Dias Melhores Virao 91, etc.

Dierkes, John (1905–1975).
Gaunt American supporting actor.

Macbeth 48. *The Red Badge of Courage* 51. Shane 53. The Naked Jungle 54. Jubal 56. The Alamo 60. The Comancheros 61. The Haunted Palace 63, many others.

Dieterle, William (1893–1972) (Wilhelm Dieterle).
Distinguished German director, long in Hollywood; at his best, an incomparable master of crowd scenes and pictorial composition. Formerly an actor in Germany, e.g. in Leni's *Waxworks*.

■ Die Heilige und ihr Narr 26. The Weavers 29. Behind the Altar 29. The Dance Goes On 31. *The Last Flight* 31. Her Majesty Love 31. Man Wanted 32. Jewel Robbery 32. The Crash 32. Six Hours to Live 32. Scarlet Dawn 32. Lawyer Man 32. Grand Slam 33. Adorable 33. Devils in Love 33. Female 33. From Headquarters 33. Fashions of 1934 34. Fog Over Frisco 34. Madame du Barry 34. The Firebird 34. The Secret Bride 35. Dr Socrates 35. *A Midsummer Night's Dream* 35. *The Story of Louis Pasteur* 35. Concealment 35. Men on Her Mind 36. The White Angel 36. Satan Met a Lady 36. The Great O'Malley 37. Another Dawn 37. *The Life of Emile Zola* (AAN) 37. Blockade 38. *Juarez* 39. *The Hunchback of Notre Dame* 39. *Dr Ehrlich's Magic Bullet* 40. A Dispatch from Reuters 40. *All That Money Can Buy* 41. Syncopation 42. Tennessee Johnson 42. Kismet 44. *I'll Be Seeing You* 44. Love Letters 45. This Love of Ours 45. The Searching Wind 47. The Accused 48. *Portrait of Jennie* 48. Rope of Sand 49. Paid in Full 50. Dark City 50. September Affair 50. Volcano 50. Peking Express 51. Red Mountain 51. Boots Malone 52. The Turning Point 52. Salome 53. Elephant Walk 54. Magic Fire 56. Omar Khayyam 57. Dubrowsky (Yug.) 58. Mistress of the World (Ger.) 60. The Confession 66.

✪ For marshalling the tricks of his trade with spectacular professionalism. *Portrait of Jennie.*

❝ One day I walked on to his set, he was directing some young children. He wasn't getting what he wanted. He grabbed a child by her arms, swung her in the air and, screaming in German, forcibly placed her in a new position. He took his hands off the child and she fainted dead away. I left wondering what directing was about. – *Don Siegel*

Dietrich, Marlene (1901–1992) (Maria Magdalena von Losch).
German singer-actress long in America, a legend of glamour despite many poor films and her domination in the 30s by the heavy style of Josef Von Sternberg.

Biographies: 1955, *Blonde Venus* by Leslie Frewin. 1984, *Dietrich* by Alexander Walker. 1992, *Marlene Dietrich* by Maria Riva (her daughter). 1992, *Marlene Dietrich* by Stephen Bach. 1992, *Blue Angel: The Life of Marlene Dietrich* by Donald Spoto.

■ Der Mensch am Wege 23. The Tragedy of Love 24. Der Sprung ins Leben 24. Joyless Street 25. Manon Lescaut 26. Cafe Electric 26. A Modern Dubarry 27. Sein Groesster Bluff 27. Der Jux Baron 27. Princess Olala 28. I Kiss Your Hand Madame 28. Die Frau nach der Man Sich Sehnt 28. Das Schiff der Verlorenen Menschen 29. Gefahren der Brautzeit 30. *The Blue Angel* 30. Morocco (AAN) 30. Dishonoured 31. *Shanghai Express* 32. Blonde Venus 32. Song of Songs 33. *The Scarlet Empress* 34. The Devil Is a Woman 35. *Desire* 36. The Garden of Allah 36. Knight Without Armour (GB) 37. Angel 37. *Destry Rides Again* 39. Seven Sinners 40. The Flame of New Orleans 41. Manpower 41. The Lady Is Willing 42. The Spoilers 42. Pittsburgh 42. Follow the Boys 44. Kismet 44. Martin Roumagnac (Fr.) 46. Golden Earrings 47. *A Foreign Affair* 48. Stage Fright (GB) 50. No Highway (GB) 51. Rancho Notorious 52. The Monte Carlo Story 53. Around the World in Eighty Days 56. Witness for the Prosecution 57. Touch of Evil 58. Judgement at Nuremberg 61. Paris When It Sizzles 64. Just a Gigolo 78.

✪ For enjoying being a legend. *Destry Rides Again.*

❝ If she had nothing but her voice, she could break your heart with it. But she also has that beautiful body and the timeless loveliness of her face. – *Ernest Hemingway*

Age cannot wither her, nor custom stale her infinite sameness – *David Shipman*

I have a child and I have made a few people happy. That is all. – *M.D.*

The relationship between the make-up man and the film actor is that of accomplices in crime – *M.D.*

There is a lack of dignity to film stardom. – *M.D.*

She has sex but no positive gender. Her masculinity appeals to women and her sexuality to men. – *Ken Tynan*

The legs aren't so beautiful, I just know what to do with them. – *M.D.*

I never ever took my career seriously. – *M.D.*

I was an actress. I made my films. Finish. – *M.D.*

You should be afraid of life, yes, but not of death. Then you know nothing more. It's all over. – *M.D.*

It took more than one man to change my name to Shanghai Lily. – *M.D. in Shanghai Express*

See what the boys in the back room will have
And tell them I'm having the same.
See what the boys in the back room will have
And give me the poison they name.
And if I die, don't bring a preacher
To witness all my follies and my shame;
Just see what the boys in the back room will have
And tell them I sighed –
And tell them I cried –
And tell them I died of the same! – *M.D. in Destry Rides Again*

Dietz, Howard (1896–1983).
American librettist and writer, with MGM from its inception. Best film score: *The Band Wagon* 53.

Autobiography: 1974, *Dancing in the Dark*.

Diffring, Anton (1918–1989).
German actor, in British films from 1951; often the villainous Nazi or the protagonist of a horror film.

State Secret 50. *Albert RN* 53. The Sea Shall Not Have Them 55. The Colditz Story 55. *I Am a Camera* 56. *The Man Who Could Cheat Death* 59. Circus of Horrors 60. Incident at Midnight 63. The Heroes of Telemark 65. Fahrenheit 451 66. The Double Man 67. Counterpoint (US) 67. Where Eagles Dare 68. Zeppelin 71. The Swiss Conspiracy 75. Operation Daybreak 76. Vanessa 76. Valentino 77, etc.

Digges, Dudley (1879–1947).
Versatile Irish character actor, with Abbey Theatre experience; played a variety of good roles in Hollywood in the 30s.

■ *Condemned* 29. Outward Bound 30. Upper Underworld 30. *The Maltese Falcon* 31. The Ruling Voice 31. Alexander Hamilton 31. Devotion 31. The Hatchet Man 32. The Strange Case of Clara Deane 32. Roar of the Dragon 32. The First Year 32. Tess of the Storm Country 32. The King's Vacation 33. Mayor of Hell 33. Silk Express 33. The Narrow Corner 33. The Invisible Man 33. The Emperor Jones 33. Before Dawn 33. Fury of the Jungle 34. Caravan 34. The World Moves On 34. Massacre 34. What Every Woman Knows 34. I am a Thief 34. Notorious Gentleman 35. Kind Lady 35. *Mutiny on the Bounty* 35. China Seas 35. The Bishop Misbehaves 35. Three Live Ghosts 36. The Voice of Bugle Ann 36. The Unguarded Hour 36. *The General Died at Dawn* 36. Valiant is the Word for Carrie 36. Love is News 37. *The Light that Failed* 39. The Fight for Life 40. *Raffles* 40. Son of Fury 42. The Searching Wind 46.

Dighton, John (1909–).
British writer, in films from 1935.

Let George Do It 40. Nicholas Nickleby 47. Saraband for Dead Lovers 48. *Kind Hearts and Coronets* 49. *The Happiest Days of Your Life* (from his own play) 49. The Man in the White Suit (co-w, AAN) 51. Roman Holiday (co-w, AAN) 53. Summer of the Seventeenth Doll 60, many others.

Dignam, Basil (1905–1979).
British character actor, in innumerable small parts, often as barrister or other professional man.

His Excellency 53. Brothers in Law 57. Room at the Top 58. The Silent Partner 61. Life for Ruth 63. Victim 62, etc.

Dignam, Mark (1909–1989).
British character actor, brother of Basil Dignam. Also played professional men.

Murder in the Cathedral 52. The Maggie 54. The Prisoner 55. Sink the Bismarck 60. No Love for Johnnie 62. Hamlet 69, etc.

Diller, Phyllis (1917–).
Zany, grotesque American comedienne who has had trouble adapting her TV style to movies.

Splendor in the Grass 60. Boy Did I Get a Wrong Number 66. Eight on the Lam 67. The Private Navy of Sergeant O'Farrell 68. Did You Hear the One about the Travelling Saleslady? 68. The Adding Machine (GB) 69. Pink Motel 82. The Bone Yard 90. Wisecracks (doc) 92. The Perfect Man 93. The Silence of the Hams (It.) 94. A Bug's Life (voice) 98, etc.

TV series: The Pruitts of Southampton 66. The Beautiful Phyllis Diller Show 68. The Bold and the Beautiful 95– .

❝ It's a good thing that beauty is only skin deep, or I'd be rotten to the core. – *P.D.*

I have an agreement with Bob Hope. I don't make fun of his nose and he doesn't ridicule my body. – *P.D.*

My house used to be haunted, but the ghosts haven't been back since the night I tried on all my wigs. – *P.D.*

Dilley, Leslie.
British production designer, from TV.

The Last Remake of Beau Geste 77. Star Wars (AA) 77. Superman 78. Alien (AAN) 79. The Empire Strikes Back (AA) 80. An American Werewolf in London 81. Raiders of the Lost Ark (AA) 81. Eureka 83. Never Say Never Again 83. Invaders from Mars 86. Legend 86. Stars and Bars 88. The Abyss (AAN) 89. Guilty by Suspicion 91. What About Bob? 91. Honey, I Blew Up the Kid 93. Monkey Trouble 94. Casper 95. How to Make an American Quilt 95. Diabolique 96. Deep Impact 98, etc.

Dillinger, John (1903–1934).
American gangster of the 30s, public enemy number one; he was shot after leaving a cinema (where he had seen *Manhattan Melodrama*). He has been played in *Dillinger* 45 by Lawrence Tierney, in *Young Dillinger* 64 by Nick Adams, and in *Dillinger* 73 by Warren Oates.

Dillman, Bradford (1930–).
Lean American actor, a staple of TV movies and series.

A Certain Smile 58. *Compulsion* 59. Circle of Deception 61. Francis of Assisi 61. A Rage to Live 65. The Helicopter Spies 67. The Bridge at Remagen 69. Suppose They Gave a War and Nobody Came 71. Brother John 71. Escape from the Planet of the Apes 71. The Way We Were 73.

The Iceman Cometh 73. Mastermind 77. The Lincoln Conspiracy (as John Wilkes Booth) 77. The Swarm 78. Piranha 78. Guyana Cult of the Damned 80. Sudden Impact 83. The Treasure of the Amazon 85, etc.
TV series: Court Martial (GB) 65, many guest appearances; King's Crossing 82. Falcon Crest 82–83.

Dillon, Carmen (1908–1995).
British art designer.
Melody Express 37. The Five Pound Man 37. Quiet Wedding 41. The Demi Paradise 43. *Henry V* (AAN) 44. The Way to the Stars 45. *Hamlet* (AA) 48. Cardboard Cavalier 49. The Rocking Horse Winner 49. The Browning Version 51. The Story of Robin Hood and His Merrie Men 52. The Importance of Being Earnest 52. Doctor in the House 54. Doctor at Sea 55. *Richard III* 56. The Prince and the Showgirl 57. A Tale of Two Cities 58. Sapphire 59. Carry On Constable 60. Watch Your Stern 60. Kidnapped 60. The Naked Edge 61. Carry On Cruising 62. The Iron Maiden 63. The Chalk Garden 64. The Battle of the Villa Fiorita 65. Accident 67. Otley 68. The Rise and Rise of Michael Rimmer 70. *The Go-Between* 71. Lady Caroline Lamb 72. Bequest to the Nation 73. Butley 73. The Omen (US) 76. Julia (US) 77. The Corn Is Green (TV) 79, etc.

Dillon, John Francis (1887–1934).
American director.
Children of the Ritz 29. Sally 29. Kismet 30. The Finger Points 31. The Cohens and Kellys in Hollywood 32. Call Her Savage 32. Humanity 33. The Big Shakedown 34, etc.

Dillon, Kevin (1965–).
American actor, the brother of Matt Dillon.
Heaven Help Us/Catholic Boys 85. Platoon 86. The Rescue 88. The Blob 88. War Party 89. Immediate Family 89. The Doors 91. A Midnight Clear 91. No Escape 94. True Crime 95. Criminal Hearts 95. Stag 97. Misbegotten 98, etc.

Dillon, Matt (1964–).
American leading actor who became a star in his teens but has found adult roles less rewarding. Born in New Rochelle, New York, he was plucked from high school to appear in *Over the Edge* 78; subsequent roles as moody teenagers won him a dedicated following. In the 90s, though, he has struggled to find such defining roles. He has been romantically linked with actress Cameron DIAZ.
Liar's Moon 82. Tex 82. The Outsiders 84. Rumble Fish 84. The Flamingo Kid 85. Target 85. Rebel 85. Native Son 86. The Big Town/The Arm 87. Dear America 87. Kansas 88. Bloodhounds of Broadway 89. Drugstore Cowboy 89. A Kiss before Dying 91. Singles 92. Golden Gate 92. The Saint of Fort Washington 93. Mr Wonderful 93. Golden Gate 94. To Die For 95. Frankie Starlight 95. Beautiful Girls 96. Grace of My Heart 96. Albino Alligator 96. In and Out 97. Wild Things 98. There's Something about Mary 98, etc.
❝ He's a natural who takes to the camera with the baffling ease of a puppy. – *Pauline Kael*

Dillon, Melinda (1939–).
American leading actress.
The April Fools 69. Slapshot 77. Close Encounters of the Third Kind 77. Bound for Glory 78. The Critical List (TV) 78. F.I.S.T. 78. Reunion (TV) 80. Absence of Malice 81. Harry and the Hendersons 87. Spontaneous Combustion 89. Nightbreak (TV) 89. Staying Together 89. Captain America 90, etc.
❝ She gives off a lovely light. – *Steven Spielberg*

Dillon, Robert.
American screenwriter.
Prime Cut 72. 99 and 44/100 per cent Dead 74. French Connection II 75. The River 84. Revolution 85. The Survivalist 86. Flight of the Intruder 90. Ruby Cairo 93, etc.

Dinehart, Alan (1886–1944).
American supporting actor who played many bluff-businessman roles.
The Brat 31. Street of Women 32. Rackety Rax 32. Supernatural 33. Cross Country Cruise 34. Jimmy the Gent 34. The Cat's Paw 34. Dante's Inferno 35. Your Uncle Dudley 35. Thanks a Million 35. Charlie Chan at the Race Track 36. Step Lively Jeeves 37. Ali Baba Goes to Town 37. Rebecca of Sunnybrook Farm 38. Second Fiddle 39. Slightly Honorable 39. Girl Trouble 42. Fired Wife 43. Moon over Las Vegas 44. The Whistler 44. Oh What a Night 44, many others.

Dinelli, Mel (1912–1991).
American screenwriter.
The Spiral Staircase 46. House by the River 50. Beware My Lovely 52. Jeopardy 53. Lizzie 57, etc.

Dingle, Charles (1887–1956).
American stage actor who made occasional screen appearances, usually in cheerfully wicked roles.
■ One Third of a Nation 39. *The Little Foxes* 41. Unholy Partners 41. Johnny Eager 42. Calling Dr Gillespie 42. Are Husbands Necessary 42. The Talk of the Town 42. George Washington Slept Here 42. Tennessee Johnson 42. Somewhere I'll Find You 42. Edge of Darkness 43. Someone to Remember 43. She's for Me 43. The Song of Bernadette 43. Home in Indiana 44. National Barn Dance 44. Together Again 44. A Medal for Benny 45. Here Come the Co-eds 45. Guest Wife 45. Cinderella Jones 46. Wife of Monte Cristo 46. Centennial Summer 46. Three Wise Fools 46. Sister Kenny 46. The Beast with Five Fingers 46. Duel in the Sun 46. My Favorite Brunette 47. Welcome Stranger 47. The Romance of Rosy Ridge 47. *State of the Union* 48. If You Knew Susie 48. A Southern Yankee 48. Big Jack 49. Never Wave at a WAC 52. Call Me Madam 53. The President's Lady 53. Half a Hero 53. The Court Martial of Billy Mitchell 55.

Dingwall, John (1940–).
Australian screenwriter turned director, from television.
Sunday Too Far Away (w) 75. Buddies (p, w) 84. Phobia (wd) 90. The Custodian (wd) 93, etc.

Dinner, Michael (1953–).
American director, a former songwriter and musician, most recently working in television.
Miss Lonelyhearts (TV) 83. Heaven Help Us/Catholic Boys 85. Off Beat 86. Hot to Trot 88.

Dinsdale, Reece (1959–).
English leading actor, best known for his role as Detective Inspector Charlie Scott in the TV series *Thief Takers* 96.
Winter Flight 84. A Private Function 84. Glamour Night (TV) 85. Threads (TV) 85. Young Catherine (TV) 91. i.d. 95, etc.
TV series: Home to Roost 85–89. Haggard 88–89. Bliss 95.

The Dionne Quins,
Born in 1934, were Cecile, Annette, Emilie (d. 1954), Marie (d. 1970), and Yvonne. Born in North Bay, Ontario, they became a tourist attraction, being first exhibited by their father, and then by the government of Ontario, which built for them Quintland, which at its height was visited by 6,000 people a day. Their parents regained custody of them in 1943, as their popularity waned. They appeared in three films: *The Country Doctor* 36, a fictionalization of their birth; *Reunion* 36; *Five of a Kind* 38.
❝ Multiple births should not be confused with entertainment, nor should they be an opportunity to sell products. Our lives have been ruined by the exploitation we suffered. – *C., A., Y.D.*

Dior, Christian (1905–1957).
French fashion designer who worked occasionally in films.
Autobiography: 1956, *Dior and I*.
Biography: 1998, *Christian Dior: The Man Who Made the World Look New* by Marie-France Pochna.
Stage Fright 50. The Indiscretion of an American Wife (AAN) 54. The Ambassador's Daughter 54, etc.
❝ All I required to be happy was friendship and people I could admire. – *C.D.*

Dishy, Bob.
American character actor.
The Tiger Makes Out 67. Lovers and Other Strangers 70. The Big Bus 76. The First Family 80. The Last Married Couple in America 80. Author! Author! 82. Brighton Beach Memoirs 86. Don Juan DeMarco 95, etc.

Diskant, George E. (1907–1965).
American cinematographer.
Riff Raff 47. The Narrow Margin 50. On Dangerous Ground 51. The Bigamist 53, many others.

Disney, Walt (1901–1966).
American animator and executive whose name is a household word all over the world. Formerly a commercial artist, he produced his first Mickey Mouse cartoon in 1928, using his own voice; also Silly Symphonies, one of which (*Flowers and Trees* 33) was the first film in full Technicolor. Donald Duck first appeared in 1936. First full-length cartoon: *Snow White and the Seven Dwarfs* 37, followed by *Pinocchio* 39, *Fantasia* 40, *Dumbo* 41, *Bambi* 42, *The Three Caballeros* (combining cartoon and live action) 44, *Cinderella* 50, *Alice in Wonderland* 51, *Peter Pan* 53, *Lady and the Tramp* 56, *The Sleeping Beauty* 59, *One Hundred and One Dalmatians* 61, *The Sword in the Stone* 63, *Winnie the Pooh and the Honey Tree* 66, *The Jungle Book* 67, *The Aristocats* 70, *Robin Hood* 73, *The Rescuers* 77, The Black Cauldron 85, The Great Mouse Detective 86, Little Mermaid 89, The Rescuers Down Under 90, *Beauty and the Beast* (AAN) 91, *Aladdin* 92, *The Lion King* 94, Pocahontas 95. First live-action feature *Treasure Island* 50, followed by a plentiful supply including westerns (*Westward Ho the Wagons*, *The Nine Lives of Elfego Baca*), adventure classics (*Kidnapped*, *Dr Syn*), animal yarns (*Greyfriars Bobby*, *Old Yeller*, *The Incredible Journey*), cosy fantasies with music (*In Search of the Castaways*, *Mary Poppins*), trick comedies (*The Absent-Minded Professor*, *Son of Flubber*) and plain old-fashioned family fun (*Bon Voyage*, *The Ugly Dachshund*). The patchiness of these films has meant that although the Disney label is still a sure sign of suitability for children, it no longer necessarily indicates quality of any other kind. In 1948 began the irresistible series of 'True-Life Adventures' (cleverly jazzed-up animal documentaries containing much rare footage) and in 1953 came the first feature of this kind, *The Living Desert*; the series has unfortunately died out. In 1994, *The Lion King* became the company's top-grossing animated film, and one of the all-time top ten box-office successes in America, taking more than $220m at the box-office. Disney's other recent animated films have also been successes, with *Aladdin* grossing $217.4m and *Beauty and the Beast* $145.8m, although Disney's first, *Snow White and the Seven Dwarfs*, remains among its top hits, having taken $175.3m over the years. In August 1995, Disney paid $19 billion to take over Capital Cities/ABC, companies with interests in broadcasting, satellite and cable TV, including the ABC television network.
Disney's long list of Academy Awards are all for shorts, apart from 'special awards' for *Snow White*, *Fantasia*, *The Living Desert* and *The Vanishing Prairie*. They include a special award for creating Mickey Mouse 32. *Three Little Pigs* 33. *The Tortoise and the Hare* 34. *Three Orphan Kittens* 35. *The Old Mill* 37. *Ferdinand the Bull* 38. *The Ugly Duckling* 39. *Lend a Paw* 41. *Der Fuhrer's Face* 42. *Seal Island* 48. *Beaver Valley* 50. *Nature's Half Acre* 51. *Water Birds* 52. *Toot Whistle Plunk and Boom* 53. *Bear Country* 53. *The Alaskan Eskimo* 53. *Men against the Arctic* 55. *The Wetback Hound* 57. *White Wilderness* 58. *Ama Girls* 58. *The Horse with the Flying Tail* 60. *Winnie the Pooh and the Blustery Day* 68, etc.
A biography, *Walt Disney*, was published in 1958 by his daughter Diane, and in 1968 came Richard Schickel's iconoclastic *The Disney Version*, with Marc Elliot's even more iconoclastic *Walt Disney: Hollywood's Dark Prince* being published in 1993. A massive informational tome is Christopher Finch's *The Art of Walt Disney* 73. Further information was contained in 1973 in *Disney Animation: The Illusion of Life*, by Frank Thomas and Ollie Johnston. In 1998, thriller writer Carl Hiassen wrote a biting polemic, attacking Walt Disney's worldview, as enshrined in Disneyland, in *Team Rodent: How Disney Devours the World*.
✪ For creating a whole new world of magic as a corrective to the real one. *Pinocchio*.
❝ I love Mickey Mouse more than any woman I've ever known. – *W.D.*
Disney has the best casting. If he doesn't like an actor, he just tears him up. – *Alfred Hitchcock*
At the bottom line he was a down-to-earth farmer's son who happened to be a genius. – *Ward Kimball*
He had no knowledge of draughtsmanship, no knowledge of music, no knowledge of literature, no knowledge of anything really, except he was a great editor. – *Art Babbitt*

Disraeli, Benjamin (1804–1881).
Novelist and prime minister; has been notably portrayed on screen by George Arliss in 1921 and 1930 (in each case his wife Florence Arliss played Mrs Disraeli), by Derrick de Marney in *Victoria the Great* 37 and *Sixty Glorious Years* 38, by John Gielgud in *The Prime Minister* 40; and by Alec Guinness in *The Mudlark* 50. In a rather dismal 1978 TV series he was played by Ian McShane.

Divine (1945–1988) (Harris Glenn Milstead).
Obese American transvestite who became notorious for eating dog's droppings in *Pink Flamingos* and was a regular in the films of John Waters.
Biography: 1993, *Not Simply Divine* by Bernard Jay.
Mondo Trasho 69. Multiple Maniacs 70. Pink Flamingos 72. Female Trouble 74. Polyester 81. Trouble in Mind 85. Lust in the Dust 85. Out of the Dark 88. Hairspray 88, etc.
❝ Of course, the last thing my parents wanted was a son who wears a cocktail dress that glitters, but they've come around to it. – *D.*

Dix, Richard (1894–1949) (Ernest Brimmer).
Stalwart American leading man of the 20s and 30s, after which his vehicles declined.
Dangerous Curve Ahead 21. Fools First 22. The Sin Flood 22. The Christian (GB) 23. Souls for Sale 23. Icebound 24. Unguarded Women 24. Too Many Kisses 25. The Lady Who Lied 25. *The Vanishing American* 25. The Quarterback 26. Shanghai Bound 27. Sporting Goods 28. Moran of the Marines 28. Nothing but the Truth 29. *Seven Keys to Baldpate* 29. Shooting Straight 30. *Cimarron* (AAN) 31. The Public Defender 31. The Lost Squadron 32. Roar of the Dragon 32. The Great Jasper 33. Ace of Aces 33. Stingaree 34. West of the Pecos 34. The Arizonian 35. The Tunnel (GB) 35. Special Investigator 36. The Devil's Playground 37. The Devil is Driving 37. Sky Giant 38. Man of Conquest 39. Here I am a Stranger 39. Cherokee Strip 40. Badlands of Dakota 41. Tombstone 42. Eyes of the Underworld 42. The Kansan 43. Top Man 43. The Ghost Ship 43. The Whistler 44. Mark of the Whistler 44. The Thirteen Hour 47, many others.

Dix, William (1956–).
British child actor of the 60s.
The Nanny 65. Doctor Dolittle 67.

Dixon, Adele (1908–1992).
British musical comedy actress and singer, rarely in films.
Uneasy Virtue 31. The Happy Husband 32. Calling the Tune 36. Banana Ridge 41. Woman to Woman 47, etc.

Dixon, Denver (1901–1972) (Victor Adamson).
New Zealand-born actor, writer, producer and director in 20s and 30s Hollywood. A star of silent westerns, he also worked under the names of Art James and Art Mix. (Art Mix was a name later adopted by two other western actors, George Kesterson and Bob Roberts.) He was the father of director Al ADAMSON.
Circle Canyon (d) 33. Fighting Cowboy (d) 33. Lightning Range (d) 34. Rawhide Romance (d) 34. Boss Cowboy (d) 35. Range Riders (d) 35. Arizona Trails (a) 35. Lightning Bill (d) 35. Mormon Conquest (d) 38, etc.

Dixon, Donna (1957–).
American actress. Married Dan Aykroyd.
Margin for Murder (TV) 81. Doctor Detroit 83. Spies Like Us 85. The Couch Trip 87. Lucky Stiff 88. Speed Zone 88. It Had to Be You 89. Wayne's World 92, etc.
TV series: Bosom Buddies 80–82. Berrengers 85.

Dixon, Jean (1896–1981).
American stage actress, in a few films.
The Lady Lies 29. The Kiss Before the Mirror 33. Sadie McKee 34. She Married Her Boss 35. My Man Godfrey 36. You Only Live Once 37. Joy of Living 38. *Holiday* 38, etc.

Dixon, Thomas (1864–1946).
American Baptist minister who wrote the anti-Negro novel *The Clansman*, on which Griffith's *The Birth of a Nation* was based.

Djola, Badja.
American actor, a former dancer, usually in villainous roles.
Penitentiary 79. The Main Event 79. The Lightship 86. The Serpent and the Rainbow 88. Mississippi Burning 88. A Rage in Harlem 91. The Last Boy Scout 91. The Waterdance 92. Who's the Man 93. Heaven's Prisoners 95. Rosewood 96. The Players Club 97, etc.

Dmytryk, Edward (1908–).
American director, in films from 1923. After years of second features he gained a reputation as a stylist with some tough adult thrillers of the 40s; but after years of exile due to the McCarthy witch-hunt his more ambitious recent films have seemed impersonal.
Autobiography: 1979, *It's a Hell of a Life but Not a Bad Living*.
■ The Hawk 35. Television Spy 39. Emergency Squad 40. Golden Gloves 40. Mystery Sea Raider 40. Her First Romance 40. The Devil Commands 41. Under Age 41. Sweetheart of the Campus 41. Blonde from Singapore 41. Confessions of Boston Blackie 41. Secrets of the Lone Wolf 41. Counter Espionage 42. Seven Miles from Alcatraz 42. Hitler's Children 43. The Falcon Strikes Back 43. Behind the Rising Sun 43. Captive Wild Woman 43. Tender Comrade 44. *Murder My Sweet* 44. Back to Bataan 45. Cornered 46. Till the End of Time 46. *Crossfire* (AAN) 47. So Well Remembered (GB) 47. Obsession (GB) 48. Give Us This Day (GB) 49. Mutiny (Fr.) 52. The Sniper 52. Eight Iron Men 52. The Juggler 53. *The Caine Mutiny* 54. Broken Lance 54. The End of the Affair (GB) 54. Soldier of Fortune 55. The Left Hand of God 55. The Mountain (& p) 56. Raintree County 57. The Young Lions 58. Warlock 59. The Blue Angel 59. The Reluctant Saint (It.) 61. A Walk on the Wild Side 62. The Carpetbaggers 63. Where Love Has Gone 64. *Mirage* 65. Alvarez Kelly 66. Anzio 68. Shalako 68. Bluebeard 72. The Human Factor 75. He Is My Brother 76.
❝ My lifelong ambition has been to spend my money as soon as I can get it. – *E.D.*

Dobbs, Lem (1961–).
American screenwriter who took his pseudonym from the character played by Humphrey Bogart in *The Treasure of the Sierra Madre*. He is the son of artist R. B. Kitaj.
Hider in the House 89. The Hard Way 91. Kafka 91, etc.
❝ I think the phrase 'ignorant talentless scum' is best to characterize the people involved in *Hider in the House* at every level. – *L.D.*
The age of the superstar director is over. I think that's bad for us; it's one reason movies aren't good any more. Directors aren't as powerful or as famous. – *L.D.*

Dobie, Alan (1932–).
British leading actor, usually in astringent roles on stage or TV.
Seven Keys 62. The Comedy Man 64. The Long Day's Dying 68. Alfred the Great 69. The Chairman 69, etc.

Dobson, Peter (1964–).
American actor.
Plain Clothes 88. Last Exit to Brooklyn 89. Sing 89. The Marrying Man/Too Hot to Handle 91. Where the Day Takes You 91. Forrest Gump 94. The Frighteners 96. Dead Cold 96. The Big Squeeze 96, etc.

Dobson, Tamara (1947–).
American leading lady.
Cleopatra Jones 73. Cleopatra Jones and the Casino of Gold 75. Norman Is That You? 76. Murder at the World Series (TV) 77. Chained Hat 83. Amazons (TV) 84, etc.

Dobtcheff, Vernon (1934–).
French character actor, in international films.
The Taming of the Shrew (US) 67. Baby Love (GB) 68. The Beast in the Cellar (GB) 70. Darling Lili (US) 70. The Horsemen (US) 71. The Day of the Jackal (GB/US) 73. India Song 75. Le Sauvage 75. March or Die (GB) 77. Nijinsky (US) 80. Condorman (GB) 81. Enigma (GB/Fr.) 82. Testimony (GB) 88. Pascali's Island (GB) 88. Berlin Jerusalem (Fr./Isr.) 89. The Hour of the Pig (GB) 93. M. Butterfly (US) 93. Hilary and Jackie (GB) 98, etc.

Doctorow, E. L. (1931–).
American novelist whose *Ragtime* created an original, almost cinematic, method of prose storytelling which simply could not be afforded in the disappointing film version. There was an earlier film of his *Welcome to Hard Times*. His *Billy Bathgate* was filmed in 91.

Dodd, Claire (1908–1973).
Pert supporting actress or second lead of the 30s.
Our Blushing Brides 30. An American Tragedy 31. The Match King 32. *Hard to Handle* 33. Footlight Parade 33. Babbitt 34. *The Case of the Curious Bride* 35. The Glass Key 35. The Case of the Velvet Claws 36. Three Loves Has Nancy 38. Charlie Chan in Honolulu 38. The Black Cat 41. The Mad Doctor of Market Street 42, many others.

Doherty, Shannen (1971–).
American leading actress, on television as a child and best known for her role as Brenda Walsh in the series *Beverly Hills 90210*.
Night Shift 82. Girls Just Want to Have Fun 85. Heathers 89. Freeze Frame 89. Blindfold: Acts of Obsession (TV) 94. Mallrats 95. The Ticket (TV) 97, etc.
TV series: Little House on the Prairie 82–83. Our House 86–88. Charmed 98– .

Doillon, Jacques (1944–).
French director and screenwriter, often of films dealing with the problems of youth, a former film editor.
L'An 01 (co-d) 72. Les Doigts dans la Tête (co-w, d) 74. Un Sac de Billes (co-w, d) 75. La Drôlesse (wd) 79. La Fille Prodigue (wd) 81. La Pirate (wd) 84. La Vie de Famille (co-w, d) 85. Comédie (co-w, d) 87. La Vengeance d'une Femme (wd) 90. Le Petit Criminel (wd) 90. Amoureuse (wd) 91. Le Jeune Werther (wd) 92. Germaine and Benjamin/Du Fond du Coeur – Germaine et Benjamin (wd) 94. Ponette/Arrow (wd) 96, etc.

Dolan, Robert Emmett (1906–1972).
American composer, in Hollywood from 1941.
Scores include: Birth of the Blues 41. Going My Way 44. The Bells of St Mary's 45. My Son John 51, etc. Produced White Christmas 54. Anything Goes 56, etc.

Doldinger, Klaus.
German composer.
The Boat/Das Boot 81. Die Wilden Fuenziger 83. The Neverending Story (co-m) 84. Me and Him 89, etc.

Doleman, Guy (1923–1996).
Australian character actor, in British films.
Phantom Stockade 53. The Shiralee 57. The Ipcress File 65. Thunderball 65. The Idol 66. Funeral in Berlin 66. The Deadly Bees 67. Billion Dollar Brain 67. A Dangerous Summer 81. The Shiralee (TV) 88. Taggert (TV) 91, etc.
TV series: General Hospital 86–87.

Dolenz, George (1908–1963).
Dullish Trieste-born leading man who played leads in some Hollywood films from 1941.
Unexpected Uncle 41. Enter Arsène Lupin 45. Vendetta 50. My Cousin Rachel 53. The Purple Mask 55. The Four Horsemen of the Apocalypse 62, many others.
TV series: The Count of Monte Cristo 55.

Dolenz, Mickey (1945–).
American child actor, the son of George Dolenz, who became a member of the pop group The Monkees. He provided voices for TV cartoons in the 70s and later became a TV producer in Britain. In 1996, he was working on the score for a musical based on the TV sitcom *Happy Days*.
Head 69.
TV series: Circus Boy 56–58. The Monkees 66–68.

Dolly, Jenny (1893–1941), and **Rosie**(1893–1970) (Janszieka and Roszika Deutsch).
European-American twins who became a world famous singing act and in 1918 starred in *The Million Dollar Dollies*. Jenny committed suicide. In 1946 Betty Grable and June Haver portrayed them in *The Dolly Sisters*.

Domergue, Faith (1925–).
American leading lady, launched in 1950 with a publicity campaign which misfired. However, she played competently in a number of films.
Vendetta 50. Where Danger Lives 50. This Island Earth 55. California 63. Prehistoric Planet Women 66. One on Top of the Other 70. Legacy of Blood 71. The House of the Seven Corpses 73, etc.

Domingo, Placido (1941–).
Spanish operatic tenor, who makes occasional films.
Autobiography: 1984, My *First Forty Years*.
La Traviata 82. Carmen 84. Otello 86.

Dommartin, Solveig (1961–).
French leading actress, often in the films of Wim Wenders.
Wings of Desire 88. Until the End of the World 91. Faraway, So Close!/In Weiter Ferne, So Nah 93, etc.

Donaggio, Pino (1941–) (Giuseppe Donaggio).
Italian composer.
Don't Look Now 73. Carrie 76. Piranha 78. The Black Cat 80. Dressed to Kill 80. The Howling 81. The Fan 81. Hercules 83. Body Double 84. Hercules II 85. Déjà Vu 85. The Berlin Affair 85. Crawlspace 86. Dancers 87. The Barbarians 87. Hotel Colonial 87. Zelly and Me 88. Appointment with Death 88. Phantom of Death 89. Night Game 89. Meridian – Kiss of the Beast 90. Tchin Tchin 91. Trauma 93. Dove Siete? Io Sono Qui 93. Giovanni Falcone 93. Oblivion 94. State Secret 95. Never Talk to Strangers 95. Call Girl/Squillo 96, etc.

Donahue, Troy (1937–) (Merle Johnson).
American beefcake hero of the 60s.
Tarnished Angels 57. This Happy Feeling 58. The Perfect Furlough 59. Imitation of Life 59. A Summer Place 59. The Crowded Sky 61. *Parrish* 61. Susan Slade 61. Rome Adventure 62. Palm Springs Weekend 63. A Distant Trumpet 64. My Blood Runs Cold 65. Rocket to the Moon 67. Sweet Saviour 71. Godfather Part II 74. The Legend of Frank Woods 77. Malibu (TV) 83. Cyclone 87. Deadly Prey 87. Hawkeye 87. Hollywood Cop 87. A Woman Obsessed 88. Sexpot 88. Dr Alien 88. Assault of the Party Nerds 89. Bad Blood 89. The Chilling 89. Cry-Baby 90. Omega Cop 90. Terminal Force 90. Shock 'em Dead 91. The Pamela Principle 92, etc.
TV series: Hawaiian Eye 59–60. Surfside Six 60–62.

Donald, James (1917–1993).
British stage actor who has been in occasional films since 1941; usually plays a man of conscience rather than action.
The Missing Million 41. In Which We Serve 42. The Way Ahead 44. Broken Journey 47. *The Small Voice* 47. Trottie True 49. *White Corridors* 51. Brandy for the Parson 51. The Gift Horse 52. The Pickwick Papers 52. The Net 53. Beau Brummell 54. Lust for Life 56. *The Bridge on the River Kwai* 57. The Vikings 58. The Great Escape 63. King Rat 65. Cast a Giant Shadow 66. *The Jokers* 67. Hannibal Brooks 69. David Copperfield 69. The Royal Hunt of the Sun 69. The Big Sleep 78, etc.

Donaldson, Roger (1945–).
Australian director who made films in New Zealand before going to work in Hollywood.
Sleeping Dogs 77. Smash Palace 81. The Bounty 84. Marie 85. Deceit 86. No Way Out 87. Cocktail 88. Cadillac Man 90. White Sands 92. The Getaway 94. Species 95. Dante's Peak 97, etc.

Donaldson, Ted (1933–).
American child star of the 40s.
Once upon a Time 44. *A Tree Grows in Brooklyn* 45. For the Love of Rusty 47 (and others in this series). The Decision of Christopher Blake 48. Phone Call from a Stranger 52, etc.

Donaldson, Walter (1893–1947).
American composer who wrote the music for *Whoopee!*, a Broadway musical starring Eddie Cantor that Samuel Goldwyn turned into a movie with virtually the same cast in 1930. The film version retained only three of the original 16 songs, dropping, among others, 'Love Me or Leave Me'. His Hollywood output includes 'You' and 'You Never Looked So Beautiful Before' for *The Great Ziegfeld* 30, and 'Did I Remember' for *Suzy* 36.

Donat, Peter (1928–).
Canadian character actor.
My Old Man's Place 71. The Godfather Part II 74. Russian Roulette 75. The Hindenburg 75. F.I.S.T. 78. A Different Story 78. The China Syndrome 79. Mazes and Monsters 82. The Bay Boy 84. Honeymoon 87. Tucker: The Man and His Dream 88. The War of the Roses 89. School Ties 92. The Babe 92. The Game 97. Red Corner 97, etc.

Donat, Robert (1905–1958).
Distinguished British stage actor (of Polish descent) with an inimitably melodious voice; he made some impressive films despite asthma, which blighted his career. Meticulous in his approach, he used to draw a graph of the emotional pitch of a role, and for a part that covered a considerable amount of time, as in *Goodbye Mr Chips*, a graph showing the changes in his age and appearance. His second wife was actress Renée ASHERSON (1953–56). He was romantically involved with actresses Merle OBERON, Pearl Argyle, Elissa LANDI, Madeleine CARROLL, and Rosamund JOHN.
Biography: 1985, *Mr Chips: The Life of Robert Donat* by Kenneth Barrow.
■ Men of Tomorrow 32. That Night in London 32. Cash 32. The Private Life of Henry VIII 33. *The Count of Monte Cristo* 34. *The Thirty-Nine Steps* 35. *The Ghost Goes West* 36. Knight without Armour 37. *The Citadel* (AAN) 38. *Goodbye Mr Chips* (AA) 39. *The Young Mr Pitt* 42. The Adventures of Tartu 43. Perfect Strangers 45. Captain Boycott (guest appearance) 47. *The Winslow Boy* 48. The Cure for Love (& d) 50. The Magic Box 50. Lease of Life 55. Inn of the Sixth Happiness 58.
✪ For the ethereal quality, partly caused by illness, of a few of his greatest performances. *Goodbye Mr Chips*.
❝ I never had any real security in my life until I found the false security of stardom. – *R.D.*

Donath, Ludwig (1900–1967).
Austrian character actor busy in America from the 30s.
The Strange Death of Adolf Hitler 43. *The Jolson Story* 46. Cigarette Girl 47. Jolson Sings Again 50. The Great Caruso 51. Sins of Jezebel 53. Torn Curtain 66, many others.

Donati, Danilo (1926–).
Italian costume and production designer, from television and the theatre.
The Mandrake/La Mandragola (cos) 65. The Gospel according to St Matthew (cos) 64. The Taming of the Shrew (cos) 67. Oedipus Rex (cos) 67. Romeo and Juliet (AAcos) 68. Medea (cos) 69. The Decameron (cos) 71. Brother Sun, Sister Moon (cos) 72. Amarcord (cos) 73. Casanova (AAcos) 76. Hurricane (pd) 79. Flash Gordon (pd) 80. Red Sonja (cos, pd) 85. Ginger and Fred (cos) 86. Intervista (co-ad) 87. Francesco (pd) 89. En Suivant la Comète £ 94, etc.

Donehue, Vincent J. (1916–1966).
American stage director who came to Hollywood to make *Lonelyhearts* 59. *Sunrise at Campobello* 60.

Donen, Stanley (1924–).
American director, former dancer; later branched out from musicals to sophisticated comedies and thrillers.
Biography: 1996, *Dancing on the Ceiling: Stanley Donen and His Movies* by Stephen M. Silverman.
■ *On The Town* (co-d) 49. Royal Wedding 51. Fearless Fagan 51. Give a Girl a Break 51. Love is Better than Ever 52. *Singin' in the Rain* (co-d) 52. *Seven Brides for Seven Brothers* 54. Deep in My Heart 54. It's Always Fair Weather (co-d) 55. *Funny Face* 57. *The Pajama Game* (& co-p) 57. Kiss Them for Me 57. *Indiscreet* (& p) 58. Damn Yankees (& co-p) 58. Once More with Feeling (& p) 60. Surprise Package (& p) 60. The Grass is Greener (& p) 61. *Charade* (& p) 63. Arabesque (& p) 66. Two for the Road (& p) 67. Bedazzled (& p) 67. Staircase (& p) 69. The Little Prince (& p) 73. Lucky Lady (& p) 76. Movie Movie 78. Saturn Three 80. Blame It on Rio 85.

Donfeld.
American costume designer.
Days of Wine and Roses (AAN) 62. They Shoot Horses, Don't They? (AAN) 69. Tom Sawyer (AAN) 73. The China Syndrome 79. Prizzi's

Honor (AAN) 85. Next of Kin 89. Gladiator 92, etc.

Doniger, Walter (1917–).
American writer.
Mob Town 41. Red Sundown 49. Cease Fire 52. The Steel Jungle (& d) 56. Madonna Red 78, etc.

Donlan, Yolande (1920–).
American leading lady who had great success on the British stage as the dumb blonde in *Born Yesterday*; settled in England and married Val Guest.
Autobiography: 1976, *Shake the Stars Down*.
Turnabout 41. Miss Pilgrim's Progress 50. Mr Drake's Duck 50. Penny Princess 51. They Can't Hang Me 55. Expresso Bongo 59. Jigsaw 62. Eighty Thousand Suspects 63. Seven Nights in Japan 76, etc.

Donlevy, Brian (1899–1972).
Irish-American leading man, later character actor, in Hollywood after stage experience; characteristically in fast-talking tough roles with soft centres.
Mother's Boy 28. Barbary Coast 35. In Old Chicago 38. We're Going To Be Rich (GB) 38. Jesse James 39. *Beau Geste* (as the evil sergeant) (AAN) 39. Destry Rides Again 39. *The Great McGinty* (leading role) 40. Brigham Young 40. The Great Man's Lady 40. A Gentleman after Dark 41. Billy the Kid 41. The Remarkable Andrew 41. Wake Island 42. *The Glass Key* 42. Nightmare 42. Hangmen Also Die 43. The Miracle of Morgan's Creek 43. An American Romance 44. Two Years Before the Mast 44. The Virginian 45. The Trouble with Women 46. The Beginning or the End 47. Kiss of Death 47. The Lucky Stiff 48. Shakedown 50. Hoodlum Empire 52. The Woman They Almost Lynched 53. The Big Combo 55. The Quatermass Experiment (GB) 55. A Cry in the Night 56. Quatermass II (GB) 56. Cowboy 58. Never So Few 59. The Errand Boy 61. Curse of the Fly (GB) 65. How to Stuff a Wild Bikini 65. The Fat Spy 66. Waco 66. Rogues' Gallery 67, etc.
TV series: Dangerous Assignment 52.

Donnell, Jeff (1921–1988) (Jean Marie Donnell).
Pert American actress who played the heroine's friend in many routine comedies of the 40s, and later played mothers.
A Night to Remember 43. He's My Guy 45. In a Lonely Place 50. Thief of Damascus 52. Sweet Smell of Success 57. Gidget Goes Hawaiian 61. The Iron Maiden (GB) 62. Stand Up and Be Counted 72. The Amazing Spiderman (TV) 77, etc.
TV series: The George Gobel Show 56. Matt Helm 75.

Donnelly, Donal (1931–).
Irish stage actor, in occasional films.
The Rising of the Moon 57. Shake Hands with the Devil 59. Young Cassidy 65. The Knack 65. Up Jumped a Swagman 65. Waterloo 70. The Dead 87. The Godfather Part III 90. Squanto: A Warrior's Tale 94, etc.

Donnelly, Dorothy (1880–1928).
American stage actress who became lyricist and librettist for Sigmund Romberg, and was played by Merle Oberon in *Deep in My Heart* 54.

Donnelly, Ruth (1896–1982).
American character actress, a wisecracking girlfriend in the 30s, latterly in maternal roles.
Rubber Heels 27. Transatlantic 31. Ladies They Talk About 33. Footlight Parade 33. Convention City 33. Wonder Bar 34. Alibi Ike 35. Mr Deeds Goes to Town 36. More than a Secretary 36. A Slight Case of Murder 38. Holiday 38. Mr Smith Goes to Washington 39. My Little Chickadee 39. Rise and Shine 41. Pillow to Post 45. Cinderella Jones 46. The Snake Pit 48. I'd Climb the Highest Mountain 51. The Spoilers 55. Autumn Leaves 56. The Way to the Gold 57, many others.

Donner, Clive (1926–).
British director, former editor, in films since 1942, directing since the mid-50s.
■ The Secret Place 56. Heart of a Child 57. A Marriage of Convenience 59. The Sinister Man 60. Some People 62. The Caretaker 63. Nothing But the Best 63. What's New Pussycat? 65. Luv 67. Here We Go Round the Mulberry Bush 67. Alfred

the Great 69. Vampira 74. Spectre (TV) 76. Rogue Male (TV) 76. The Three Hostages (TV) 77. She Fell Among Thieves (TV) 78. The Thief of Baghdad (TV) 78. The Nude Bomb 80. Charlie Chan and the Curse of the Dragon Queen 81. Oliver Twist (TV) 82. The Scarlet Pimpernel (TV) 82. Arthur the King (TV) 83. Agatha Christie's Dead Man's Folly (TV) 86. Babes in Toyland (TV) 86. Stealing Heaven 88.

Donner, Jörn (1933–).
Finnish writer-director, producer and novelist, who worked in Sweden as a film critic and also directed four features there in the mid-60s before returning to his homeland.
Sunday in September 63. To Love 65. Black on White 67. Portraits of Women 69. Anna 70. Fuck Off! Images of Finland (doc) 71. Tenderness 72. Man Cannot Be Raped 78. Dirty Story 85, etc.

Donner, Richard (1939–).
American director.
X-15 62. Salt and Pepper (GB) 68. Twinky (GB) 69. *The Omen* 76. Superman 78. Superman II (uncredited) 80. Inside Moves 80. The Final Conflict 81. The Toy 82. Ladyhawke 84. Lethal Weapon 87. Scrooged 88. Lethal Weapon 2 89. Lethal Weapon 3 92. Radio Flyer 92. Dave (p) 93. Maverick 94. Assassins 95. Conspiracy Theory 97. Lethal Weapon 4 98, etc.

D'Onofrio, Vincent (1959–).
American leading actor. Born in Brooklyn, New York, he studied acting at New York's American Stanislavski Theatre and the Actors' Studio. He has a daughter by actress Greta SCACCHI.
Full Metal Jacket 87. Adventures in Babysitting 87. Mystic Pizza 88. Signs of Life 89. Salute of the Jugger/The Blood of Heroes 90. Naked Tango 90. Crooked Hearts 91. Dying Young 91. JFK 91. The Player 92. Salt on Our Skin 93. Household Saints 93. Mr Wonderful 93. Being Human 94. Ed Wood (as Orson Welles) 94. Imaginary Crimes 94. Strange Days 95. Stuart Saves His Family 95. The Whole Wide World 95. Feeling Minnesota 96. Good Luck 96. Men in Black 97. The Newton Boys 97. Claire Dolan 98. The Velocity of Gary 98, etc.

Donohoe, Amanda (1962–).
British leading actress.
Castaway 86. Foreign Body 86. The Lair of the White Worm 88. Diamond Skulls 89. The Rainbow 89. Tank Malling 89. Paper Mask 90. It's Nothing Personal (TV) 93. A Woman's Guide to Adultery (TV) 93. The Madness of King George 95. The Thorn Birds: The Missing Years (TV) 96. One Night Stand 97. Liar Liar 97. I'm Losing You 98. A Knight in Camelot (TV) 98. The Real Howard Spitz 98, etc.
TV series: L.A. Law 90–92.

Donohue, Jack (1908–1984).
American director, former Ziegfeld Follies dancer. Worked on many MGM musicals.
The Yellow Cab Man 50. Watch the Birdie 51. Calamity Jane (dances only) 53. Lucky Me 54. Babes in Toyland 61. Marriage on the Rocks 65. Assault on a Queen 66, etc.

Donovan, Jason (1969–).
Australian leading actor and singer, on television from the age of 11. Best known for playing Scott in the television soap opera *Neighbours*, he is the son of actor Terence Donovan.
Blood Oath 90. Shadows of the Heart (TV) 90. Rough Diamonds 94.

Donovan, King (1919–1987).
American general-purpose actor, usually in support roles; a frequent TV guest star.
Cargo to Capetown 50. The Beast from Twenty Thousand Fathoms 53. Invasion of the Body Snatchers 56. The Hanging Tree 59, many others.
TV series: The Bob Cummings Show 54. Please Don't Eat the Daisies 66.

Donovan, Martin (1957–).
American actor, a regular in the films of Hal HARTLEY.
Trust 90. Julia Has Two Lovers 90. Simple Men 92. Flirt 93. Scam (TV) 93. Quick 93. Amateur 94. Nadja 94. The Rook 94. The Portrait of a Lady 96. Hollow Reed 96. Living Out Loud 98. The Opposite of Sex 98. Heaven (NZ) 98. Spanish Fly 99. Onegin 99, etc.

Donovan, Tate (1964–).
American actor, born in New York City. He studied at the University of Southern California. He is also a musician, playing traditional Irish music with his group The McGuffins. He has been romantically linked with actresses Sandra BULLOCK and Jennifer ANISTON.
Into Thin Air (TV) 85. Space Camp 86. Dangerous Curves 88. Clean and Sober 88. Dead-Bang 89. Memphis Belle 89. Equinox 92. Love Potion No. 9 92. Ethan Frome (TV) 93. Inside Monkey Zetterland 93. Holy Matrimony 94. Murder at 1600 97. Hercules (voice) 97, etc.
TV series: Partners 95. Trinity 98.

Donovan, Terence.
Australian actor, much on television, including roles in the two best-known Australian soaps, *Home and Away* and *Neighbours*. He is the father of actor Jason Donovan.
The Getting of Wisdom 77. Money Movers 79. Breaker Morant 80. The Man from Snowy River 82. Death of a Soldier 85. Emma's War 85. Running from the Guns 87. Jigsaw 90, etc.

Donskoi, Mark (1901–1981).
Russian director celebrated for his 'Maxim Gorki trilogy'.
The Pigeon 29. Alien Shore 30. Fire 31. *The Childhood of Maxim Gorki* 38. My Apprenticeship 39. My Universities 40. How the Steel Was Tempered 42. The Rainbow 44. The Village Teacher 47. Mother 56. The Gordeyev Family 59. A Mother's Heart 66. A Mother's Devotion 67. Nadyezhda 73, many others.

Doohan, James (1920–).
Canadian-born character actor best known for playing Scotty, the chief engineer of Starship *Enterprise*, in *Star Trek*.
The Wheeler Dealers 63. The Satan Bug 65. Bus Riley's Back in Town 65. Pretty Maids All in a Row 71. Star Trek: The Motion Picture 79. Star Trek II: The Wrath of Khan 82. Star Trek III: The Search for Spock 84. Star Trek IV: The Voyage Home 86. Star Trek V: The Final Frontier 89. Star Trek VI: The Undiscovered Country 91. Double Trouble 92. Story Book 94. Star Trek: Generations 94. Bug Buster 98, etc.
TV series: Star Trek 66–68. Jason of Star Command 78–79.

Dooley, Paul (1928–).
American character actor associated chiefly with the films of Robert Altman.
Slapshot 77. A Wedding 78. A Perfect Couple 79. Breaking Away 79. Rich Kids 79. Health 80. Popeye 80. Paternity 81. Endangered Species 82. Kiss Me Goodbye 82. Going Berserk 83. Big Trouble 84. Sixteen Candles 85. O.C. and Stiggs 87. Last Rites 88. Flashback 90. Shakes the Clown 91. My Boyfriend's Back 93. The Underneath 95. Telling Lies in America 96. Loved 97. Clockwatchers 97. Angels in the Endzone (TV) 98, etc.

Doonan, Patric (1925–1958).
British stage and screen actor, usually in honest, put-upon roles. Son of comedian George Doonan. Committed suicide.
Once a Jolly Swagman 48. The Blue Lamp 50. The Gentle Gunman 52. The Net 53. Seagulls over Sorrento 54. Cockleshell Heroes 55, many second features.

Dor, Karin (1938–).
German leading lady.
Treasure of Silver Lake 62. Winnetou II 64. The Face of Fu Manchu 65. You Only Live Twice 67. Topaz 69. Live and Let Die 73, etc.

Doran, Ann (1914–).
American character actress, often a friend of the heroine.
Penitentiary 38. Blondie 38. Blue, White and Perfect 42. The More the Merrier 43. Fear in the Night 46. The Snake Pit 48. Rebel without a Cause 55. The Man Who Turned to Stone 58. The Rawhide Trail 60. Rosie 67. First Monday in October 81, many others.
TV series: Longstreet 71. Shirley 79.

Dorff, Stephen (1973–).
American actor.
The Gate 87. I Know My First Name Is Steven (TV) 89. A Son's Promise (TV) 90. An Ambush

of Ghosts 93. Judgment Night 93. Backbeat 94. S.F.W. 94. Innocent Lies 95. Reckless 95. I Shot Andy Warhol (as Candy Darling) 96. Blood and Wine 96. City of Industry 97. Blade 98. Earthly Possessions 99, etc.
TV series: What a Dummy 90–91.

Dorff, Steve.
American composer. He also wrote the theme for the TV series *Uncle Buck* 90–91. He is the father of Stephen DORFF.
Every Which Way but Loose 78. Bronco Billy 80. Honky Tonk Freeway 81. Honkytonk Man 82. Cannonball Run II 84. Stick 85. Ratboy 86. Back to the Beach 87. My Best Friend Is a Vampire 88. Pink Cadillac 89. Pure Country 92, etc.

Dorfmann, Robert (1912–).
French producer.
Jeux Interdits 52. Road to Salina 69. The Red Circle 70. Red Sun 71. Papillon 73, etc.

Dorléac, Françoise (1941–1967).
French leading lady, killed in car crash. Sister of Catherine Deneuve.
That Man from Rio 64. Genghis Khan 65. Where the Spies Are 65. Cul de Sac (GB) 66. The Young Girls of Rochefort 67. Billion Dollar Brain 67, etc.

Dorn, Dolores (1935–) (D. Dorn-Heft).
American stage actress briefly in Hollywood.
Phantom of the Rue Morgue 54. Uncle Vanya 58. Underworld USA 60. 13 West Street 62. Tell Me a Riddle 80, etc.

Dorn, Philip (1905–1975) (Frits van Dongen).
Dutch stage actor who went to Hollywood in 1940 and was used mainly in sincere refugee or thoughtfully professional roles: returned to Holland in the 50s, later settled in California.
Ski Patrol 40. Escape 40. Ziegfeld Girl 41. Tarzan's Secret Treasure 41. Calling Dr Gillespie 41. Random Harvest 42. Reunion in France 42. Chetniks 43. Passage to Marseilles 44. Blonde Fever 44. Escape in the Desert 45. I've Always Loved You 46. I Remember Mama 48. Panther's Moon 49. Sealed Cargo 51, etc.

Dorne, Sandra (1925–1992).
British 'platinum blonde', often in tawdry roles. Married actor Patrick Holt.
Eyes That Kill 45. Once a Jolly Swagman 48. The Beggars' Opera 51. Roadhouse Girl 54. The Gelignite Gang 56. The Iron Petticoat 57. Orders to Kill 58. The Devil Doll 64. All Coppers Are ... 72. Eat the Rich 87, etc.

Doro, Marie (1882–1956) (Marie Steward).
American leading lady of the silent screen, one of Zukor's 'Famous Players'.
The Morals of Marcus 15. The White Pearl 15. Oliver Twist (title role) 16. The Heart of Nora Flynn 16. The Wood Nymph 16. The Mysterious Princess 19. Twelve Ten 19. Maid of Mystery 20, etc.

Dörrie, Doris (1955–).
German director and screenwriter.
Straight through the Heart/Mitten ins Herz 83. In the Belly of the Whale/Im Innern des Wals 84. Men .../Manner ... 85. Paradise /Paradies 86. Me and Him (US) 88. Money/Geld 89. Happy Birthday, Türke! 91. Nobody Loves Me/Keiner Liebt Mich 95. Am I Beautiful?/Bin Ich Schoen! (co-w, d) 98, etc.

Dors, Diana (1931–1984) (Diana Fluck).
British 'blonde bombshell' who played good-time girls from the mid-40s.
Wrote several catchpenny memoirs.
The Shop at Sly Corner 46. Holiday Camp 47. Dancing with Crime 47. My Sister and I 48. Peggy and the Pownall Case 48. Oliver Twist 48. Good Time Girl 48. The Calendar 49. Here Come the Huggetts 49. Vote for Huggett 49. It's Not Cricket 49. A Boy a Girl and a Bike 49. Diamond Lily 49. Dance Hall 50. Lady Godiva Rides Again 51. Worm's Eye View 51. The Last Page 52. My Wife's Lodger 52. The Weak and the Wicked 52. Is Your Honeymoon Really Necessary? 52. It's a Grand Life 53. The Great Game 53. The Saint's Return 54. Value for Money 55. A Kid for Two Farthings 55. Miss Tulip Stays the Night 55. As Long as They're Happy 55. Yield to the Night 56. I Married a Woman (US) 56. The Unholy Wife (US) 56. The Long Haul 57. The Love Specialist (It.) 57. Tread

Softly, Stranger 58. Passport to Shame 59. On the Double (US) 60. Scent of Mystery (US) 60. The Big Bankroll (US) 61. Mrs Gibbons' Boys 62. West Eleven 63. Allez France 64. The Sandwich Man 66. Berserk 67. Danger Route 67. Hammerhead 68. Baby Love 69. There's a Girl in My Soup 70. Deep End 71. Hannie Caulder 71. The Pied Piper 71. Every Afternoon 72. Nothing but the Night 72. The Amazing Mr Blunden 72. The Amorous Milkman 72. Theatre of Blood 73. Steptoe and Son Ride Again 73. Craze 73. Rosie 74. Steaming 85, etc.

D'Orsay, Fifi (1904–1983) (Yvonne Lussier).
Vivacious Canadian leading lady of Hollywood films in the early 30s.
Hot for Paris 30. *Just Imagine* 31. Silk Stockings 32. Wonder Bar 34. Accent on Youth 45. Wild and Wonderful 63. The Art of Love 65, many others.

Dorsey, Jimmy (1904–1957) and **Tommy** (1905–1956).
American bandleaders and brothers; individually they decorated many musicals of the 40s, and came together in a biopic, *The Fabulous Dorseys* 46.

Dorziat, Gabrielle (1880–1979) (G. Sigrist).
French character actress, in films from 1922.
Mayerling 36. La Fin du Jour 39. Premier Rendezvous 41. *Les Parents Terribles* 48. Manon 49. Little Boy Lost 53. Act of Love 54. Les Espions 57. Germinal 63, etc.

Dos Santos, Nelson Pereira (1928–).
Brazilian screenwriter, producer, editor and director. Born in Sao Paulo, he studied law and worked as a journalist and critic before working as an assistant director and studying film at IDHEC in Paris. He was influenced by the Italian neo-realist movement.
Rio 40. Graus 55. Rio, Zona Norte 57. Boca de Ouro 62. Barravento (ed only) 62. Vidas Secas 63. Como Era Gostoso o Meu Frances 71. O Amuleto de Ogum 74. Memorias do Cárcere 84. Jubiabá 86, etc.

Dostoievsky, Fyodor (1821–1881).
Russian writer, chiefly of doom-laden novels, of which the most frequently-filmed is *Crime and Punishment;* there have also been attempts at *The Idiot*, *The Brothers Karamazov*, *White Nights*, *The Great Sinner*, *Pyriev* and others.

Dotrice, Karen (1955–).
British child actress who matured gracefully. Daughter of Roy Dotrice.
The Three Lives of Thomasina 63. Mary Poppins 64. The Gnome-Mobile 67. Joseph Andrews 77. The Thirty-Nine Steps 79, etc.

Dotrice, Michele (1947–).
British leading actress, mostly on TV. Daughter of Roy Dotrice.
And Soon the Darkness 70. Jane Eyre (TV) 73. Not Now Comrade 76, etc.
TV series: Bramwell 95.

Dotrice, Roy (1923–).
British stage actor with a strong line in senile impersonation.
The Heroes of Telemark 65. A Twist of Sand 68. Lock Up Your Daughters 69. One of Those Things 71. Nicholas and Alexandra 71. Family Reunion (TV) 82. Amadeus 84. Eliminators 85. Young Harry Houdini (TV) 87. Carmilla (TV) 89. Suburban Commando 91. The Cutting Edge 92. The Scarlet Letter 95, etc.
TV series: Space 1999 75–77.

Doucet, Catherine (1875–1958) (Catherine Green).
American stage actress of imposing presence; played dowagers in a few films.
As Husbands Go 33. Little Man What Now 34. Accent on Youth 35. Millions in the Air 35. *These Three* 36. Poppy 36. When You're in Love 37. It Started with Eve 41. Nothing But the Truth 41. Family Honeymoon 49, etc.

Doug E. Doug (1970–) (Douglas Bourne).
American actor and rap performer.
Jungle Fever 91. Hangin' with the Homeboys 91. Class Act 91. Dr Giggles 92. Cool Runnings 93. Operation Dumbo Drop 95. That Darn Cat 97, etc.
TV series: Where I Live 93. Cosby 96.

Douglas, Lord Alfred 'Bosie' (1870–1945).
Litigious English minor poet, whose involvement with Oscar WILDE resulted in Wilde's libel action against his father, Lord Queensberry, which eventually led to Wilde's imprisonment, exile and early death. He was played by John NEVILLE in *Oscar Wilde* 60, John FRASER in *The Trials of Oscar Wilde* 60, Douglas HODGE in *Salome's Last Dance* 87, and Jude LAW in *Wilde* 97.
Autobiography: 1929, *Autobiography*.
Biography: 1963, *Bosie: The Story of Lord Alfred Douglas* by Rupert Croft-Cooke.
❝ Your slim gilt soul walks between passion and poetry. I know Hyacinthus, whom Apollo loved so madly, was you in Greek days. – *Oscar Wilde on Bosie*
Obviously mad (like all his family, I believe). – *Max Beerbohm on Bosie*

Douglas, Angela (1940–).
British general-purpose actress.
Shakedown 59. Some People 61. The Comedy Man 63. Carry On Cowboy 64. Carry On Follow That Camel 66. Carry On up the Khyber 67. Maroc 7 68. Digby 74.

Douglas, Bill (1937–1991).
Scottish director and screenwriter. A former miner, and an astringent chronicler of working-class life, he devoted his first three films to an autobiographical account of his tough early years. He also taught at Britain's National Film and Television School.
Book: 1993, *Bill Douglas, A Lanternist's Account*, edited by Eddie Dick, Andrew Noble and Duncan Petrie.
Childhood 72. *My Ain Folk* 73. *My Way Home* 78. *Comrades* 86, etc.
❝ Never show the audience something they can imagine better than you can show it. – *B.D.*

Douglas, Donald (1905–1945) (Douglas Kinleyside).
Quiet-spoken American actor, usually seen as smooth villain or 'good loser'.
Men in White 34. Alexander's Ragtime Band 38. Whistling in the Dark 41. The Crystal Ball 43. Show Business 44. Farewell My Lovely 44. Club Havana 45. Gilda 46, etc.

Douglas, Donna (1933–) (Doris Smith).
Chirpy American blonde supporting player who found fame and fortune 1962–71 as Ellie Mae in TV's *The Beverly Hillbillies*.
Career 62. Lover Come Back 62. Frankie and Johnny 66, etc.

Douglas, Gordon (1909–1993).
American director, former comedy writer for Hal Roach. Jobs grew in importance but talent remained routine.
Saps at Sea 40. Broadway Limited 41. The Devil with Hitler 43. Zombies on Broadway 45. If You Knew Susie 48. The Doolins of Oklahoma 49. Kiss Tomorrow Goodbye 50. Only the Valiant 51. I Was a Communist for the FBI 51. Come Fill the Cup 51. Mara Maru 52. The Iron Mistress 53. So This is Love 53. The Charge at Feather River 53. *Them* 54. Young at Heart 54. Sincerely Yours 55. The Big Land 56. Bombers B-52 58. Yellowstone Kelly 59. The Sins of Rachel Cade 60. Gold of the Seven Saints 61. Follow That Dream 62. Call Me Bwana 63. Robin and the Seven Hoods 64. Rio Conchos 64. Sylvia 65. Harlow 65. Stagecoach 66. Way Way Out 66. In Like Flint 67. Chuka 67. Tony Rome 67. *The Detective* 68. Lady in Cement 68. Skullduggery 69. Viva Knievel 77, etc.

Douglas, Jack (1927–).
British comedian who has appeared exclusively in *Carry Ons*. Much on TV.

Douglas, Kirk (1916–) (Issur Daniclovitch Demsky).
American leading actor with stage experience; started playing weaklings and gangsters but graduated to tense, virile, intelligent heroes in films of many kinds.
■ *The Strange Love of Martha Ivers* 46. *Out of the Past* 47. I Walk Alone 47. My Dear Secretary 47. Mourning Becomes Electra 47. The Walls of Jericho 48. A Letter to Three Wives 48. *Champion* (AAN) 49. Young Man with a Horn 50. The Glass Menagerie 51. *Ace in the Hole* 51. Along the Great Divide 51. *Detective Story* 51. The Big Trees 52. The Big Sky 52. The Bad and the Beautiful (AAN) 52. The Story of Three Loves 53. The Juggler 53. Act of Love 54. Ulysses (It.) 54. Twenty Thousand Leagues under the Sea 54. Man without a Star 55. The Racers 55. The Indian Fighter 55. *Lust for Life* (as Van Gogh) (AAN) 56. Top Secret Affair 57. *Gunfight at the OK Corral* (as Doc Holiday) 57. *Paths of Glory* 57. The Vikings 58. Last Train from Gun Hill 58. The Devil's Disciple 59. *Spartacus* 60. Town Without Pity 61. The Last Sunset 61. Strangers When We Meet 61. *Lonely Are the Brave* 62. Two Weeks in Another Town 62. *The List of Adrian Messenger* 63. For Love or Money 63. The Hook 63. *Seven Days in May* 64. In Harm's Way 65. The Heroes of Telemark 65. *Cast a Giant Shadow* 66. Is Paris Burning? 66. The Way West 67. The War Wagon 67. A Lovely Way to Die 68. The Brotherhood 68. The Arrangement 69. There Was a Crooked Man 70. A Gunfight 71. The Light at the Edge of the World 71. Catch Me a Spy 71. A Man to Respect 72. Scalawag (& d) 73. Mousey (TV) 73. Posse (& d) 75. Once is not Enough 75. The Moneychangers (TV) 76. Victory at Entebbe (TV) 76. Holocaust 2000 77. The Fury 78. Saturn Three 79. Home Movies 79. The Villain 79. The Final Countdown 80. The Man from Snowy River 82. Remembrance of Love (TV) 82. Eddie Macon's Run 83. Tough Guys 86. Oscar 91. Vézaz 91. Greedy/Greed 94.
✪ For determination and intelligence above the call of duty. *Ace in the Hole*.
❝ My kids never had the advantage I had. I was born poor. – *K.D.*
I want my sons to surpass me, because that's a form of immortality. – *K.D.*
I've made a career of playing sons of bitches. – *K.D.*
He's wanted to be Burt Lancaster all his life. – *John Frankenheimer*
Champion established the essential Kirk Douglas persona – a ruthless, selfish, fiercely driven upstart. – *Stephen Farb and Marc Green, Hollywood Royalties*
Kirk never makes an effort towards people. He's pretty much wrapped up in himself. – *Doris Day*
Famous line (*Ace in the Hole*): 'I'm a thousand a day man, Mr Boot. You can have me for nothing.'

Douglas, Lloyd C. (1877–1951).
American best-selling novelist: a Lutheran minister who did not begin writing till in his 50s. Films of his books include *The Green Light*, *Magnificent Obsession*, *The Robe*, *White Banners*, *Disputed Passage*, *The Big Fisherman*.

Douglas, Melvyn (1901–1981) (Melvyn Hesselberg).
Suave, polished American leading man of the 30s and 40s, most at home in a dinner jacket with an elegant lady on his arm; later spent some years on Broadway and emerged as a fine character actor.
■ Tonight or Never 31. Prestige 32. The Wiser Sex 32. Broken Wing 32. As You Desire Me 32. *The Old Dark House* 32. Nagana 33. The Vampire Bat 33. Counsellor at Law 33. Woman in the Dark 34. *Dangerous Corner* 34. People's Enemy 35. She Married Her Boss 35. Mary Burns Fugitive 35. Annie Oakley 35. *The Lone Wolf Returns* 35. And So They Were Married 36. The Gorgeous Hussy 36. Theodora Goes Wild 36. Women of Glamour 37. Captains Courageous 37. *I Met Him In Paris* 37. Angel 37. I'll Take Romance 37. There's Always a Woman 38. Arsène Lupin Returns 38. The Toy Wife 38. Fast Company 38. *That Certain Age* 38. The Shining Hour 38. There's That Woman Again 38. Tell No Tales 38. Good Girls Go to Paris 39. The Amazing Mr Williams 39. *Ninotchka* 39. Too Many Husbands 40. He Stayed for Breakfast 40. Third Finger Left Hand 40. This Thing Called Love 41. That Uncertain Feeling 41. A Woman's Face 41. Our Wife 41. Two Faced Woman 41. They All Kissed the Bride 42. Three Hearts for Julia 43. Sea of Grass 47. The Guilt of Janet Ames 47. *Mr Blandings Builds His Dream House* 48. My Own True Love 48. A Woman's Secret 49. The Great Sinner 49. My Forbidden Past 51. On the Loose 51. Billy Budd 62. *Hud* (AA) 63. Advance to the Rear 64. The Americanization of Emily 64. Rapture 65. Hotel 67. Companions in Nightmare (TV) 67. *I Never Sang for My Father* (AAN) 69. Hunters are for Killing (TV) 70. Death Takes a Holiday (TV) 71. The Going Up of David Lev (TV) 71. One is a Lonely Number 72. The Candidate 72. Death Squad (TV) 73. Murder or Mercy? (TV) 74. The Tenant 76. Twilight's Last Gleaming 76. The Seduction of Joe Tynan 79. Tell Me a Riddle 79. Being There (AA) 79. The Changeling 81. Ghost Story 81.
TV series: Steve Randall 52. Hollywood Confidential 54.
✪ For perfecting the image of the smart-spoken 30s playboy. *Ninotchka*.
❝ The Hollywood roles I did were boring: I was soon fed up with them. It's true they gave me a world-wide reputation I could trade on, but they also typed me as a one-dimensional non-serious actor. – *M.D.*

Douglas, Michael (1944–).
American leading actor and producer, the son of Kirk DOUGLAS. Born in New Brunswick, New Jersey, he studied at the University of California and began by working as an assistant director on some of his father's films in the 60s. He first came to notice as Steve Keller in the TV series *The Streets of San Francisco*, and then produced *One Flew over the Cuckoo's Nest*, a project his father had once planned to star in. Since then, his roles have successfully ranged from the romantic to the ruthless, and he has revealed a great ability to choose parts that plug into contemporary concerns. His success has not been without some personal difficulties: in 1990 he attended a clinic for alcohol and substance abuse.
Biographies: 1993, *Michael Douglas* by Alan Lawson. 1994, *Acting on Instinct* by John Parker.
Hail Hero 70. Adam at 6 a.m. 70. Summertree 71. When Michael Calls (TV) 72. Napoleon and Samantha 72. One Flew Over the Cuckoo's Nest (co-p only) (AA) 75. Coma 78. Running 79. The China Syndrome 80. It's My Turn 80. The Star Chamber 83. Romancing the Stone 84. A Chorus Line 85. Jewel of the Nile 86. Fatal Attraction 87. Wall Street (AA) 87. Black Rain 89. The War of the Roses 89. Flatliners (p) 90. Shining Through 92. Basic Instinct 92. *Falling Down* 93. Made in America (co-p) 93. Disclosure 94. The American President 95. The Ghost and the Darkness 96. The Game 97. A Perfect Murder 98, etc.
TV series: *The Streets of San Francisco* 72–75.
❝ The exciting thing about making movies today is that everything is up for grabs. And you had better grab. – *M.D., 1980*
Revenge is a very good motivation if you can direct it. It's healthy. Very healthy. – *M.D.*
Unlike me, he never had to worry about making a living, but he has worked hard, never forgetting to help others. – *Kirk Douglas*
Michael has madness in him. – *Kirk Douglas*

Douglas, Paul (1907–1959).
Burly American actor with unexpected comedy sense.
■ *A Letter to Three Wives* 48. It Happens Every Spring 49. Everybody Does It 49. The Big Lift 50. Love that Brute 50. Panic in the Streets 50. *Fourteen Hours* 51. The Guy who Came Back 51. Angels in the Outfield 51. When in Rome 52. Clash by Night 52. We're Not Married 52. Never Wave at a WAC 52. Forever Female 53. *Executive Suite* 54. The Maggie 54. Green Fire 54. *Joe Macbeth* 55. The Leather Saint 56. *The Solid Gold Cadillac* 56. The Gamma People 56. This Could Be the Night 57. Beau James 57. Fortunella (It.) 58. The Mating Game 59.

Douglas, Robert (1909–1999) (Robert Douglas Finlayson).
British stage leading man who made some home-grown films during the 30s; moved to Hollywood after the war and played mainly suave villains in routine melodramas, then went into TV direction.
P.C. Josser 31. The Blarney Stone 34. The Street Singer 36. The Challenge 38. Over the Moon 39, etc; war service: The End of the River 47. The Decision of Christopher Blake 48. The New Adventures of Don Juan 48. Sons of the Musketeers 51. Ivanhoe 52. The Prisoner of Zenda 52. Fair Wind to Java 53. King Richard and the Crusaders 54. The Virgin Queen 55. The Scarlet Coat (as Benedict Arnold) 55. Night Train to Paris (GB) (d only) 64, etc.

Douglas Home, William (1912–1992).
Scottish playwright and screenwriter. Born in Edinburgh, the son of the 13th Earl of Home, he was educated at Eton and Oxford. He began as an actor, after studying at RADA, and was on-stage from 1937. He was court-martialled and jailed for a year in 1944 for refusing, on grounds of conscience, to take part in the bombardment of Le Havre after the Germans refused to evacuate the French civilian population.
Autobiographies: 1954, *Half Term Report*; 1991, *Old Men Remember*.
Now Barabbas (oa) 49. *The Chiltern Hundreds*

(oa, co-w) 49. Your Witness (co-w) 50. Made in Heaven (co-w) 52. The Colditz Story (co-w) 54. The Reluctant Debutante (oa, w) (US) 58. Follow That Horse! (co-w) 60. Under Ten Flags (co-w) (US) 60, etc.

Dourif, Brad (1950–).
American character actor.
One Flew Over the Cuckoo's Nest (AAN) 75. Gruppenbild mit Dame 77. The Eyes of Laura Mars 78. Wise Blood 79. Studs Lonigan 79. Guyana Tragedy (TV) 80. Heaven's Gate 80. Ragtime 81. Dune 84. Blue Velvet 86. Impure Thoughts 86. Fatal Beauty 87. Mississippi Burning 88. Medium Rare 89. Grim Prairie Tales 90. Hidden Agenda 90. Graveyard Shift 90. London Kills Me 91. Jungle Fever 91. Scream of Stone 91. Body Parts 91. Amos & Andrew 93. Trauma 93. Color of Night 94. Murder in the First 95. Nightwatch 96. Black Out 96. Alien: Resurrection 97. Senseless 98. Bride of Chucky (voice) 98, etc.

Douy, Max (1914–).
French production designer, often for the films of Claude Autant-Lara.
Falbalas 45. Ladies of the Park/Les Dames du Bois de Boulogne 46. Devil in the Flesh/Le Diable au Corps 47. Keep an Eye on Amelia/Oh, Amelia!/Occupe-Toi d'Amélie 49. The Red Inn/L'Auberge Rouge 51. The Ripening Seed/The Game of Love/Le Blé en Herbe 53. Scarlet and Black/Le Rouge et le Noir 54. A Pig across Paris/Four Bags Full/La Traversée de Paris 56. Love Is My Profession/En Cas de Malheur 58. The Gambler/Le Joueur 58. The Green Mare's Nest/La Jument Verte 59. Thou Shalt Not Kill/Non Uccidere 61. Topkapi 64. Woman in White/Le Journal d'une Femme en Blanc 65. Castle Keep (US) 69. L'Insolent 72. Moonraker 79, etc.

Dove, Billie (1904–1997) (Lilian Bohny).
American leading lady of the 20s; could not adapt to sound.
Beyond the Rainbow 22. Polly of the Follies 22. Wanderer of the Wasteland 24. The Black Pirate 26. One Night at Susie's 28. Painted Angel 30. Blondie of the Follies 32. Diamond Head 62, etc.

Dovzhenko, Alexander (1894–1956).
Russian writer-director, former teacher; in films since 1925.
Arsenal 29. *Earth* 30. Ivan 32. *Aerograd* 35. Life in Blossom 47, etc.

Dow, Peggy (1928–) (Peggy Varnadow).
American leading lady who before retiring to marry made a strong impression in several films of the early 50s.
■ Undertow 49. Woman in Hiding 50. Showdown 50. The Sleeping City 50. *Harvey* 50. Reunion in Reno 51. You Never Can Tell 51. *Bright Victory* 51. I Want You 51.

Dowd, Nancy (1944–).
American screenwriter.
Slapshot 77. Coming Home 78. Swing Shift 83. Happy New Year 87. Let It Ride 89.

Dowling, Constance (1923–1969).
American leading lady who flowered briefly in the 40s. She was married to producer Ivan Tors.
Knickerbocker Holiday 44. Up in Arms 44. The Flame 47. Gog 54, etc.

Dowling, Doris (1921–).
American leading lady, sister of Constance Dowling. Briefly in Hollywood character roles, then moved to Italy.
The Lost Weekend 45. The Blue Dahlia 46. Bitter Rice 48. Othello 51. Running Target 58. The Party Crashers 58. The Car 77. Scruples (TV) 80. Separate Ways 81, etc.
TV series: My Living Doll 64.

Dowling, Eddie (1894–1976) (Joseph Nelson Goucher).
American singer, comedian and director of the Broadway stage; appeared only in silent films.

Dowling, Joan (1929–1954).
British teenage actress who failed to get mature roles. She was found dead in a gas-filled room. Married actor Harry Fowler.
Hue and Cry 46. *No Room at the Inn* 48. Landfall 49. Pool of London 51. Woman of Twilight 52, etc.

Down, Lesley-Anne (1955–).
British leading lady of the late 70s; made her name on TV in *Upstairs, Downstairs*. Her first husband was director William Friedkin (1982–85).
All the Right Noises 69. Assault 70. Scalawag 74. The Pink Panther Strikes Again 76. A Little Night Music 77. The Betsy 78. *The One and Only Original Phyllis Dixey* (TV) 78. The Great Train Robbery 79. Hanover Street 79. Rough Cut 80. Sphinx 81. Murder Is Easy (TV) 81. The Hunchback of Notre Dame (TV) 82. Nomads 84. The Last Days of Pompeii (TV) 84. Arch of Triumph (TV) 85. *North and South* (TV) 86. Night Trap/Mardi Gras for the Devil 93. Death Wish V: The Face of Death 94. Munchie Strikes Back 94. Family of Cops (TV) 95. Beastmaster3: The Eye of Braxus 95. The Secret Agent Club 96, etc.

Downey, Robert (1936–).
American independent director and screenwriter of small, quirky films.
Putney Swope (wd) 69. Greaser's Palace (wd) 72. Up the Academy (d) 80. America (wd) 82. Rented Lips (d) 88. Hugo Pool (d) 97, etc.

Downey, Robert, Jnr (1965–).
American leading actor, the son of director Robert Downey. Born in New York City, he acted in his father's films as a child, and first gained fame by appearing on TV's *Saturday Night Live* in the mid-80s. His career in the 90s has suffered from his drug-related problems: in 1996 he was ordered to attend a rehabilitation centre after three court appearances; in 1997 he was jailed for 180 days for violating his probation, and ordered to take part in a residential drugs programme.
Pound 70. Greaser's Palace 72. America 82. Baby It's You 82. Firstborn 84. Tuff Turf 85. Weird Science 85. Back to School 86. Less than Zero 87. The Pick-Up Artist 87. 1969 88. Johnny Be Good 88. Rented Lips 88. True Believer 89. Chances Are 89. Air America 90. That's Adequate 90. Soapdish 91. *Chaplin* (AAN) 92. Heart and Souls 93. Short Cuts 93. Natural Born Killers 94. Only You 94. Home for the Holidays 95. Richard III 95. Danger Zone 95. One Night Stand 97. Hugo Pool 97. The Gingerbread Man 97. US Marshals 98. Two Girls and a Guy 98. Friends and Lovers 98, etc.

Downs, Cathy (1924–1976).
American leading lady of a few 40s films.
Diamond Horseshoe 45. My Darling Clementine 46. The Noose Hangs High 48. Short Grass 50. Gobs and Gals 52. Missile to the Moon 59, etc.
TV series: Joe Palooka 54.

Downs, Johnny (1913–1994).
American light leading man and dancer, former member of 'Our Gang'. He later became a presenter of children's TV programmes.
The Clock Strikes Eight 35. Melody Girl 40. All-American Co-Ed 41. Harvest Melody 44. The Right to Love 45. Cruising Down the River 53, many others.

Doyle, Sir Arthur Conan (1859–1930).
British novelist and creator of Sherlock Holmes. His other chief bequest to the screen is the twice-filmed *The Lost World*.

Doyle, Christopher.
Australian-born cinematographer, in Hong Kong, associated with the films of Wong Kar-Wai. He studied art history at the University of Maryland.
Noir et Blanc 86. Days of Being Wild 91. Mary from Beijing 93. Beijing Bastards 93. *Ashes of Time* 93. *Chungking Express* 94. Red Rose, White Rose 95. Fallen Angels 95. Temptress Moon 96. Happy Together 97, etc.

Doyle, David (1925–1997).
American character actor, in avuncular roles. Born in Omaha, Nebraska, he trained as a lawyer before beginning in the theatre. He was best known for his role as John Bosley in the TV series *Charlie's Angels* 76–81.
Paper Lion 68. Loving 70. Pigeons/The Sidelong Glances of a Pigeon Kicker 70. Parades 72. Lady Liberty 72. The Comeback 78. The Blue and the Gray (TV) 82. Love or Money 88. Ghost Writer 89, etc.
TV series: Bridget Loves Bernie 72–73. The New Dick Van Dyke Show 72–73.

Doyle, Laird (1907–1936).
American screenwriter.
Oil for the Lamps of China 35. The Prince and the Pauper 36. Another Dawn 37. Strangers on Honeymoon (GB) 37, etc.

Doyle, Patrick (1953–).
Scottish composer and occasional actor, who often scores Kenneth Branagh's films. After studying at the Royal Scottish Academy of Music and Drama, he became a teacher and then wrote music for the stage, including work for Branagh's Renaissance Theatre Company. He played the role of the court singer Balthazar in *Much Ado about Nothing*.
Henry V 89. Shipwrecked 90. Dead Again 91. Into the West 92. Much Ado about Nothing 93. Indochine 93. Needful Things 93. Carlito's Way 93. Mary Shelley's Frankenstein 94. Exit to Eden 94. Une Femme Française 94. A Little Princess 95. Sense and Sensibility (AAN) 95. Mrs Winterbourne 96. *Hamlet* (AAN) 96. Donnie Brasco 96. Great Expectations 97. Quest for Camelot 98, etc.

Doyle, Roddy (1958–).
Irish novelist and screenwriter of Dublin working-class life. He won the Booker Prize in 1993 for his novel *Paddy Clarke Ha Ha Ha*.
The Commitments (oa) 91. The Snapper (w) 93. The Family (w) (TV) 94. The Van (w, oa) 96.

Dozier, William (1908–1991).
American producer, former talent agent. With RKO, Columbia and Goldwyn in 40s; independently made *Two of a Kind* 51. *Harriet Craig* 53; then into TV.

Drach, Michel (1930–1990).
French director.
Amélie ou le Temps d'Aimer 60. Diamond Safari 65. Elise ou la Vraie Vie 69. Les Violons du Bal 73. Parlez-moi d'Amour 75. Le Passé Simple 77, etc.

Drago, Billy.
American actor, usually in exploitation movies.
Invasion USA 85. The Untouchables 87. Freeway 88. Hero and the Terror 88. Prime Suspect 88. Dark before Dawn 89. Delta Force 2: Operation Stranglehold 90. Martial Law 2: Undercover 91. Guncrazy 92. The Outfit 93. In Self Defense 93. Cyborg 2 93. Solar Force 94. Never Say Die 94. Phoenix 95. Sci-Fighters 96. Deadly Heroes 96, etc.

Dragon, Carmen (1914–1984).
American composer, arranger and conductor.
Cover Girl (AA) 44. Mr Winkle Goes to War 44. Dishonored Lady 47. The Time of Your Life 48. Kiss Tomorrow Goodbye 50. When in Rome 52. Invasion of the Body Snatchers 56, etc.

Dragoti, Stan (1932–).
American director.
Dirty Little Billy 73. Love at First Bite 78. Mr Mom 83. The Man with One Red Shoe 85. She's Out of Control 89. Necessary Roughness 91, etc.

Drake, Alfred (1914–1992) (Alfredo Capurro).
Italian-American singer-dancer popular in Broadway shows.
Tars and Bars 46. Trading Places 83. The Life and Adventures of Santa Claus (voice) 85.

Drake, Betsy (1923–).
American leading lady, formerly on stage; married for a time to Cary Grant (1949–62).
Every Girl Should Be Married 48. Pretty Baby 50. The Second Woman 51. Room for One More 52. Clarence the Cross-Eyed Lion 65. Players 79, etc.

Drake, Charles (1914–1994) (Charles Ruppert).
American actor usually found in dullish, good-natured 'second leads'.
Dive Bomber 41. The Man Who Came to Dinner 41. Yankee Doodle Dandy 42. Air Force 43. You Came Along 44. Conflict 45. A Night in Casablanca 45. Whistle Stop 46. Tarzan's Magic Fountain 49. Harvey 50. Gunsmoke 52. It Came from Outer Space 53. The Glenn Miller Story 53. All That Heaven Allows 55. The Price of Fear 56. The Third Day 65. Valley of the Dolls 67. The Swimmer 68. The Arrangement 69. The Seven Minutes 71, many others.
TV series: Rendezvous (GB) 61.

Drake, Charlie (1925–) (Charles Springall).
Diminutive British TV comedian with high-pitched voice and tendency to acrobatic slapstick.
Sands of the Desert 60. Petticoat Pirates 61. The Cracksman 63. Mister Ten Per Cent 66. Filipina Dreamgirls (TV) 91, etc.

Drake, Dona (1914–1989) (Rita Novella).
Mexican singer, dancer and general livewire, former band vocalist as Rita Rio.
Aloma of the South Seas 41. Road to Morocco 42. Salute for Three 43. The House of Tao Ling 47. So This Is New York 48. Beyond the Forest 49. Valentino 51. Princess of the Nile 54, etc.

Drake, Fabia (1904–1990) (F. D. McGlinchy).
British stage and screen character actress: usually played battleaxes.
Autobiography: 1978, *Blind Fortune*.
Meet Mr Penny 38. All over the Town 48. Young Wives' Tales 51. Fast and Loose 54. The Good Companions 57. Valmont 89, many others.

Drake, Frances (1908–).
American leading lady of the 30s.
The Jewel 33. Bolero 34. Ladies Should Listen 34. Forsaking All Others 34. *Les Misérables* 35. Mad Love 35. The Invisible Ray 36. And Sudden Death 36. Love Under Fire 37. There's Always a Woman 38. It's a Wonderful World 39. I Take This Woman 40, etc.

Drake, Tom (1918–1982) (Alfred Alderdice).
American actor, the 'boy next door' of many a 40s film.
Two Girls and a Sailor 44. Meet Me in St Louis 44. *The Green Years* 46. I'll Be Yours 47. Master of Lassie 48. Never Trust a Gambler 51. Sudden Danger 55. The Sandpiper 65. Red Tomahawk 67. The Spectre of Edgar Allan Poe 72. The Return of Joe Forrester (TV) 75, etc.

Draper, Peter (1925–).
British playwright and screenwriter.
The System 64. I'll Never Forget What's 'Is Name 67. The Buttercup Chain 70, etc.

Dravic, Milena (1940–).
Serbian (formerly Yugoslavian) leading actress, born in Belgrade and a star of some 70 films. She is best known internationally as the witty, passionate exponent of sexual freedom in *W.R. – Mysteries of the Organism* 71.
The Door Remains Open/Vrata Ostaju Otvorena 59. Better Wise than Rich/Bolje Je Umeti 60. Chasing Michael/Prekobrojna 62. The Girl/Devojka 65. Morning/Jutro 67. Horoskop 69. Deps 74. Round Trip/Aller Retour 78. Sunday Lunch/Nedeljni Rucak 82. AntiCasanova 85. Blackbird/Cavka 88, many others.

Drayton, Alfred (1881–1949) (Alfred Varick).
Bald British actor who in later life often played comedy villains in stage farces co-starring Robertson Hare. Born in Brighton, he was on stage from 1908.
Iron Justice 15. A Little Bit of Fluff 19. Honeypot 20. A Scandal in Bohemia 25. The Squeaker 30. The W Plan 31. The Calendar 31. Friday the Thirteenth 33. Jack Ahoy 34. The Crimson Circle 36. So This Is London 38. A Spot of Bother 40. The Big Blockade 42. They Knew Mr Knight 44. The Halfway House 44. *Nicholas Nickleby* (as Squeers) 47. Things Happen at Night 48, etc.
❝ I understood his success in cruel parts when I took in a bullying corpulence surmounted by a bullet head completely bald, cold eyes and rapped-out sergeant-major syllables. – *Emlyn Williams*

Dreier, Alex (1916–).
Rotund American character actor, former news presenter.
Chandler 72. The Carey Treatment 72. Murdock's Gang (TV) 74.

Dreier, Hans (1884–1966).
German art director, primarily associated with Lubitsch and, like him, long in Hollywood. Born in Bremen, he trained as an architect and began as a designer in Germany, working on more than 30 films in four years before joining Paramount in the early 20s. In 1932 he became the studio's supervising art director, and remained there until he retired in 1950.

Peter the Great 23. The Hunchback of Notre Dame 23. *Forbidden Paradise* 24. Underworld 27. The Patriot (AAN) 28. The Love Parade (AAN) 29. The Vagabond King (AAN) 29. *Morocco* (AAN) 30. *Dr Jekyll and Mr Hyde* 31. *A Farewell to Arms* (AAN) 32. *Trouble in Paradise* 32. Duck Soup 33. The Lives of a Bengal Lancer (AAN) 34. *Cleopatra* 34. Ruggles of Red Gap 35. Souls at Sea (AAN) 37. *If I Were King* (AAN) 38. Dr Cyclops 39. Beau Geste 39. Arise My Love (AAN) 40. Hold Back the Dawn (AAN) 41. Take a Letter, Darling (AAN) 42. Reap the Wild Wind (AAN) 42. Five Graves to Cairo (AAN) 43. *For Whom the Bell Tolls* (AAN) 43. No Time for Love (AAN) 44. *Lady in the Dark* (AAN) 44. Frenchman's Creek (AA) 44. Love Letters (AAN) 45. Lost Weekend 45. Kitty (AAN) 45. Blue Dahlia 46. The Emperor Waltz 48. The Great Gatsby 49. *Samson and Delilah* (AA) 49. *Sunset Boulevard* (AA) 50. A Place in the Sun 51, many others.

Dreifuss, Arthur (1908–1993).
German-born American director of second features, former child conductor and choreographer.
Mystery in Swing 40. Reg'lar Fellers 41. Baby Face Morgan 42. Boss of Big Town 42. The Payoff 42. Sarong Girl 43. Melody Parade 43. Campus Rhythm 43. Nearly Eighteen 43. The Sultan's Daughter 43. Ever Since Venus 44. Eadie was a Lady 45. Booked on Suspicion 45. Boston Blackie's Rendezvous 45. The Gay Señorita 45. Prison Ship 45. Junior Prom 46. Freddie Steps Out 46. High School Hero 46. Vacation Days 47. Betty Co-Ed 47. Little Miss Broadway 47. Two Blondes and a Redhead 47. Sweet Genevieve 47. Glamor Girl 48. Mary Lou 48. I Surrender Dear 48. An Old Fashioned Girl 49. Manhattan Angel 49. Shamrock Hill 49. There's a Girl in My Heart 49. Life Begins at 17 58. The Last Blitzkrieg 58. Juke Box Rhythm 58. *The Quare Fellow* 62. Riot on Sunset Strip 67. The Love Ins 67. For Singles Only 68. A Time to Sing 68. The Young Runaways 68, etc.

Dreiser, Theodore (1871–1945).
Serious American novelist, a social realist who was popular in the early part of the century. Films of his books include *An American Tragedy* (remade as *A Place in the Sun*), *Jennie Gerhardt* and *Carrie*.

Drescher, Fran (1957–).
American leading actress, born in Flushing, Queens, New York. She is best known for her role as Fran Fine in the TV series *The Nanny*, which she co-created. She is also a partner in a company producing gourmet food products.
Autobiography: 1996, *Enter Whining*.
Saturday Night Fever 77. American Hot Wax 77. Stranger in Our House (TV) 78. Ragtime 81. Doctor Detroit 83. This Is Spinal Tap 83. The Rosebud Beach Hotel 84. UHF 89. The Big Picture 89. It Had to Be You 89. Wedding Band (TV) 90. Cadillac Man 90. Car 54, Where Are You 94. Jack 96. The Beautician and the Beast 97, etc.
TV series: The Nanny 93– .

Dresdel, Sonia (1909–1976) (Lois Obee).
British stage actress usually cast in masterful roles.
The World Owes Me a Living 42. While I Live 47. This Was a Woman 47. The Fallen Idol 48. The Clouded Yellow 50. The Third Visitor 51. Now and Forever 54. The Trials of Oscar Wilde 60. Lady Caroline Lamb 72, etc.

Dresser, Louise (1881–1965) (Louise Kerlin).
American character actress of the 30s, former vaudevillian.
Prodigal Daughters 23. The Eagle 25. Not Quite Decent 27. A Ship Comes In (AAN) 27. Mammy 30. State Fair 33. The Scarlet Empress 34. Maid of Salem 37, etc.

Dressler, Marie (1869–1934) (Leila Von Koerber).
Canadian-born comedy character actress, the heavyweight heroine of silent comedy and star of MGM comedy-dramas of the early 30s.
Autobiographical books: 1924, *The Life Story of an Ugly Duckling*. 1934, My Own Story.
■ *Tillie's Punctured Romance* 14. Tillie's Tomato Surprise 15. Tillie's Nightmare 15. The Scrublady 17. The Agonies of Agnes 18. The Red Cross Nurse 18. The Callahans and the Murphys 27. Breakfast at Sunrise 27. The Joy Girl 27. Bringing Up Father 28. The Patsy 28. The Divine Lady 29. The Vagabond Lovers 29. Hollywood Revue of 1929. Road Show 29. Chasing Rainbows 30. One Romantic Night 30. Let Us Be Gay 30. Derelict 30. *Anna Christie* 30. Caught Short 30. The Swan 30. The March of Time 30. Call of the Flesh 30. The Girl Said No 30. *Min and Bill* (AA) 30. Reducing 31. Politics 31. *Emma* (AAN) 32. *Prosperity* 32. *Tugboat Annie* 33. *Dinner at Eight* 33. Christopher Bean 33.
✪ For turning her unlikely personality into true star quality at an advanced age. *Dinner at Eight*.
❝ I'm too homely for a prima donna and too ugly for a soubrette. – *M.D.*
You're only as good as your last picture. – *M.D.*
I have been known to grande dame it, at times. – *M.D.*

Dréville, Jean (1906–1997).
French director.
Cage aux Rossignols 43. La Ferme du Pendu 46. Le Visiteur 47. Operation Swallow/The Battle for Heavy Water 47. Les Casse-Pieds 48. Horizons Sans Fin 53. A Pied à Cheval et en Spoutnik 58. Normandie-Niemen 60. Lafayette 61. The Sleeping Sentry 66, etc.

Drew, Ellen (1915–) (Terry Ray).
American light leading lady of the 40s.
College Holiday 36. Hollywood Boulevard 36. Night of Mystery 37. Murder Goes to College 37. The Buccaneer 38. You and Me 38. Sing you Sinners 38. If I Were King 38. Geronimo 39. French Without Tears 39. *Christmas In July* 40. The Mad Doctor 41. Our Wife 41. The Remarkable Andrew 42. The Impostor 44. China Sky 45. Isle of the Dead 46. Johnny O'Clock 47. The Swordsman 47. The Crooked Way 49. Davy Crockett Indian Scout 50. The Great Missouri Raid 50. The Outlaw's Son 57, many others.

Drew, Mr and Mrs Sidney (1864–1919 and 1868–1925) (Sidney White and Lucille McVey).
American stage actors who appeared in a number of very popular middle-class domestic film comedies.
Duplicity 16. Hypochondriacs 17. Henry's Ancestors 17. Her First Love 17. His Deadly Calm 17. His First Love 18. A Youthful Affair 18. Romance and Rings 19. Once a Mason 19. Harold the Last of the Saxons 19. The Charming Mrs Chase 20, etc.

Dreyer, Carl (1889–1968).
Celebrated Danish director whose later works were few but notable.
■ Praesidenten 20. *Leaves from Satan's Book* 20. Praesteenken 21. Elsker Hverandre 22. Once Upon a Time 22. Michael 24. Du Skal Aere Din Hustru 25. Glomsdal Bruden 26. *The Passion of Joan of Arc* 28. *Vampyr* 32. *Day of Wrath* 43. Tva Manniskor 45. Ordet 55. Gertrud 64.

Dreyfus, Alfred (1859–1935).
The French officer unjustly sentenced to Devil's Island in 1885 for selling secrets, but reprieved by Zola's advocacy, has been played on screen by Cedric Hardwicke in *Dreyfus* (GB 1930) (Fritz Kortner in the German version), by Joseph Schildkraut in *The Life of Emile Zola* (US 1937) and by Jose Ferrer in *I Accuse* (GB 1957).

Dreyfuss, Richard (1947–).
American leading man in Hollywood. Over-indulgence in drink and drugs brought a break in his career in the early 80s.
The Graduate 67. Hello Down There 68. The Young Runaways 69. Dillinger 73. The Second Coming of Suzanne 73. *American Graffiti* 73. *The Apprenticeship of Duddy Kravitz* 74. *Jaws* 75. Inserts 75. Victory at Entebbe (TV) 76. Close Encounters of the Third Kind 77. The Goodbye Girl (AA, BFA) 77. The Big Fix 78. The Competition 80. Whose Life is It Anyway? 81. Down and Out in Beverly Hills 85. Stand By Me 86. Stakeout 87. Tin Men 87. Nuts 87. Moon over Parador 88. Always 89. Let It Ride 89. Postcards from the Edge 90. Once Around 90. Rosencrantz and Guildenstern Are Dead 90. What about Bob? 91. Prisoner of Honor 92. Lost in Yonkers 93. Another Stakeout 93. Silent Fall 94. The American President 95. Mr Holland's Opus (AAN) 95. Mad Dog Time 96. James and the Giant Peach (voice) 96. Mad Dog Time/Trigger Happy 96. Night Falls on Manhattan 97. Oliver Twist 97. Krippendorf's Tribe 98, etc.
❝ Behind all art is ego, and I am an artist and I am unique. – *R.D.*
I enjoyed the journey to the top but then found myself disappointed. – *R.D.*
The motion picture business is run by corporate thieves. – *R.D.*
Working is better than snorting. – *R.D.*

Driscoll, Bobby (1937–1968).
American boy actor of the 40s and 50s; AA 1949 as best child actor. He died in poverty, a drug addict.
Lost Angel 43. The Sullivans 44. From This Day Forward 46. So Goes My Love 46. Song of the South 46. If You Knew Susie 48. So Dear to My Heart 48. *The Window* 49. *Treasure Island* 50. *The Happy Time* 52. Peter Pan (voice) 53. The Scarlet Coat 55, etc.
❝ I was carried on a satin cushion and then dropped in a garbage can. – *B.D.*

Drivas, Robert (1938–1986).
American leading man, mainly on TV.
Where It's At 69. Janice 73. Road Movie 74. God Told Me To 76. Demon 77, etc.
TV series: Our Private World 65.

Driver, Minnie (1972–) (Amelia Driver).
British leading actress. She studied at the Webber-Douglas Academy of Dramatic Art. She has been romantically involved with actors John Cusack and Matt Damon.
God on the Rocks (TV) 92. The Politician's Wife (TV) 95. *Circle of Friends* 95. Sleepers 96. Big Night 96. Hard Rain (US) 97. Grosse Point Blanke (US) 97. *Good Will Hunting* (US) (AAN) 97. The Governess (US) 98. At Sachem Farm (US) 98, etc.
TV series: My Good Friend 95.

Dru, Joanne (1923–1996) (Joanne la Coque).
American leading lady of the 40s, formerly model.
Abie's Irish Rose 46. *Red River* 48. *All the King's Men* 49. She Wore a Yellow Ribbon 49. Wagonmaster 50. Vengeance Valley 51. Return of the Texan 52. Thunder Bay 53. Three Ring Circus 54. Sincerely Yours 55. The Light in the Forest 58. September Storm 60. Sylvia 65. Supersnooper 80, etc.
TV series: Guestward Ho 61.

Drury, Allen (1918–1998).
American novelist, whose *Advise and Consent* became one of the better film exposés of Washington.

Drury, James (1934–).
American second lead and TV western star.
Forbidden Planet 56. Love Me Tender 56. Bernardine 57. Pollyanna 60. Ride the High Country 62. The Young Warriors 65. The Meanest Man in the West 76. Walker, Texas Ranger: One Riot, One Ranger (TV) 93. The Gambler Returns: The Luck of the Draw (TV) 93, etc.
TV series: *The Virginian* 62–69. Firehouse 74.

Dryburgh, Stuart (1953–).
New Zealand cinematographer, associated with the films of Jane Campion.
An Angel at My Table 90. The Piano (AAN) 93. The Perez Family 95. Lone Star 96. The Portrait of a Lady 96. Poodle Springs (TV) 98, etc.

Dryhurst, Edward (1904–1989) (Edward Roberts).
British producer, former writer, in films from 1920.
Autobiographies: 1987, *Gilt off the Gingerbread*. 1987, *Who Needs Enemies?*
So Well Remembered 47. Master of Bankdam 48. Noose 48. While I Live 49. Castle in the Air 52, etc.

Du Barry, Madame (1741–1793).
The French courtesan and mistress of Louis XV whose life was ended on the guillotine was a favourite role for many actresses, though Lubitsch's 1919 German film starring Pola Negri is probably still the best. Other actress who have played the role include Mrs Leslie Carter in *Du Barry* 15; Theda Bara in *Du Barry* 17; Norma Talmadge in *Du Barry, Woman of Passion* 30; Dolores del Rio in *Madame Du Barry* 34; Lucille Ball in *Du Barry Was a Lady* 43; and Martine Carol in *Mistress Du Barry* 54.

Du Maurier, Daphne (1907–1989).
Best-selling English novelist, the daughter of Sir Gerald Du Maurier. Born in London, she was a published author from her early twenties. Married athlete and army officer Frederick 'Boy' Browning, who was knighted in 1946; she also had an earlier affair with director Carol Reed and a later passion for Gertrude Lawrence. She was unhappy with most of the movie adaptations of her novels, apart from *Rebecca* and *Don't Look Now*, particularly disliking the films of *Jamaica Inn* – 'a wretched affair' – and *The Birds*. She set up her own production company with Alec Guinness to make *The Scapegoat*, as she thought him perfect for the central role, but hated the result: 'not one word of mine in the screenplay and the whole story changed'. She also objected to the portrayal of her husband, as played by Dirk Bogarde, in Richard Attenborough's *A Bridge Too Far*.
Autobiography: 1977, *Growing Pains*.
Biography: 1993, *Daphne du Maurier* by Margaret Forster.
Jamaica Inn 39. *Rebecca* (US) 40. Frenchman's Creek (US) 44. The Years Between 46. Hungry Hill 47. My Cousin Rachel (US) 52. The Scapegoat 58. The Birds (US) 63. *Don't Look Now* 73. Birds II: Land's End (TV) (US) 94, etc.
❝ To my mind, drinking and making love are the two most lonely pastimes on earth. – *D. du M.*
No one ever imagined more than Daphne. – *Norman Collins*

Du Maurier, George (1834–1896).
English artist and novelist, whose main gift to the screen has been the character of the hypnotic Svengali in his best-known novel, *Trilby*. Born in Paris, he studied chemistry at University College, London, and art in Paris and Antwerp before working in London as an illustrator (the 1931 production of *Trilby* was based on his illustrations). He was the father of actor Sir Gerald du Maurier.
Biography: 1937, *The Du Mauriers* by Daphne du Maurier.
Peter Ibbetson 14. Trilby 14. Forever (from Peter Ibbetson) 21. Svengali (from Trilby) 31. Peter Ibbetson 35. Svengali 54. Svengali (TV) 83.

Du Maurier, Sir Gerald (1873–1934).
Elegant English actor-manager, in occasional films. The son of artist and novelist Gerald Du Maurier and father of novelist Daphne Du Maurier, he was the most popular stage actor of his day, notable as one of the leaders of a new 'natural' style of acting. On stage from 1894, he created the roles of Captain Hook and Mr Darling in *Peter Pan*, as well as those of Raffles and Bulldog Drummond. At the invitation of Basil Dean, he became chairman of Dean's company Associated Talking Pictures towards the end of his career. He loathed filming, resorting to it only after his stage productions had failed and he needed money. He was knighted in 1922. Died of cancer.
Biographies: 1934, *Gerald. A Portrait* by Daphne du Maurier; 1989, *Gerald du Maurier* by James Harding.
Masks and Faces 16. Escape 30. Lord Camber's Ladies 32. I Was a Spy 33. Catherine the Great 34. The Scotland Yard Mystery 34. Jew Suss 34, etc.
❝ Making films is a heart-breaking business even in the most up-to-date studio, worked with every conceivable gadget; and when a scene, consisting of two lines and a movement to a door, has been played for the fortieth time, and is still not right, and it's hours over time and you've a headache like a load of bricks and an empty stomach, there was nothing, according to Gerald, which bore a greater similarity to unadultered hell. – *Daphne du Maurier*
We really thought, looking at him, that it was easy; and for the first ten years of our life in the theatre, nobody could hear a word we said. We thought he was being really natural; of course, he was a genius of a technician giving that appearance, that's all. – *Sir Laurence Olivier*

Du Pré, Jacqueline (1945–1987).
English cellist, whose career was brought to an end in 1973 by multiple sclerosis. Married conductor Daniel Barenboim. She was played by Emily Watson in the biopic *Hilary and Jackie* 98.
Biographies: 1997, *A Genius in the Family* by Hilary and Piers du Pré; 1998, *Jacqueline du Pré* by Elizabeth Wilson.

Du Prez, John (1946–).
British composer.
Bullshot! 83. Monty Python's The Meaning of Life 83. A Private Function 84. She'll Be Wearing

Pink Pajamas 84. Once Bitten 85. Personal Services 87. A Fish Called Wanda 88. A Chorus of Disapproval 89. Teenage Mutant Ninja Turtles 90. Teenage Mutant Ninja Turtles II: The Secret of the Ooze 91. Teenage Mutant Ninja Turtles III: The Turtles Are Back . . . in Time 92, etc.

Dubbins, Don (1929–1991).
American second lead of the 50s.
From Here to Eternity 53. Tribute to a Bad Man 56. These Wilder Years 57. From the Earth to the Moon 58. The Enchanted Island 58. The Prize 63. The Illustrated Man 69, etc.

Dubov, Paul (c. 1917–1979).
American character actor and, with his wife Gwen Bagni, novelist and screenwriter; his best roles were in the films of Samuel FULLER.
Little Tough Guy 38. The Boss of Big Town 42. Bombay Clipper 42. Strange Holiday 45. Triple Trouble 50. High Noon 52. I, the Jury 53. Abbott and Costello Meet the Keystone Kops 55. The Day the World Ended 56. Shake, Rattle & Rock! 56. China Gate 57. Forty Guns 57. The Crimson Kimono 59. Verboten! 59. The Purple Gang 60. Underworld USA 61. Irma la Douce 63. Shock Corridor 63. With Six You Get Egg Roll (oa, co-w) 68, etc.

Duchin, Eddy (1909–1951).
American pianist and bandleader, best remembered for being impersonated by Tyrone Power in *The Eddy Duchin Story*.
■ Mr Broadway 32. Coronado 35. Hit Parade 37.

Duchovny, David (1960–).
American leading actor, best known for playing FBI agent Fox Mulder in the TV series *The X Files*. Born in New York, he studied at Princeton and Yale, where he began acting to help pay for his studies. Married actress Tea LEONI in 1997.
Working Girl 88. New Year's Day 89. Julia Has Two Lovers 90. Bad Influence 90. The Rapture 91. Don't Tell Mom the Babysitter's Dead 91. Red Shoe Diaries (TV) 92. Ruby 92. Chaplin 92. Beethoven 92. Venice, Venice (It.) 92. Kalifornia 93. Playing God 97. Red Shoe Diaries 8: Night of Abandon 97. The X Files Movie 98, etc.
TV series: Twin Peaks 90.
❝ I am the conduit through which America views the soft underbelly of women's erotic desires. – *D.D.*

Dudgeon, Elspeth (1871–1955).
British stage actress who made her first appearance on screen disguised as an old man.
The Old Dark House (as John Dudgeon) 32. The Moonstone 34. Becky Sharp 35. Camille 36. The Great Garrick 37. Mystery House 38. Pride and Prejudice 40. Random Harvest 42. The Canterville Ghost 44. If Winter Comes 47. The Paradine Case 48. The Great Sinner 49, etc.

Dudikoff, Michael (1954–).
American leading actor in action movies.
The Black Marble 77. Bloody Birthday 80. I Ought to Be in Pictures 82. Tron 82. Making Love 82. Bachelor Party 84. American Ninja 85. Avenging Force 86. Radioactive Dreams 86. American Ninja 2: The Confrontation 87. Platoon Leader 87. River of Death 90. American Ninja 4: The Annihilation 91. The Human Shield 92. Cyberjack/Virtual Assassin 95. Soldier Boyz 95. Chain of Command 95. Moving Target 96. Crash Drive 96. Bounty Hunters 96. Black Thunder 97. Freedom Strike 97. Hardball 97. Ringmaster 98, etc.
TV series: Cobra 93.

Dudley, Anne (1956–).
British composer and keyboard player, born in Chatham, Kent.
Hiding Out (US) 87. Buster 88. Wilt 89. The Mighty Quinn (US) 89. Say Anything (US) 89. The Pope Must Die/The Pope Must Diet 91. The Crying Game 92. Knight Moves (US/Ger.) 92. Felidae 94. When Saturday Comes 96. The Grotesque/Gentlemen Don't Eat Poets 95. Hollow Reed 96. The Full Monty (AA) 97. American History X (US) 98, etc.

Dudley-Ward, Penelope (1919–1982).
British leading lady of the 40s.
The Case of the Frightened Lady 39. The Demi-Paradise 43. The Way Ahead 44, etc.

Duel, Pete (1940–1972) (Peter Deuel).
American leading man. Died of a gunshot wound, an apparent suicide.
A Time for Giving 69. Cannon for Cordoba 70. The Young Country (TV) 71, etc.
TV series: Gidget 65–66. Love on a Rooftop 66–67. *Alias Smith and Jones* 71–72.

Duff, Howard (1917–1990).
American actor with stage experience; usually played good-looking but shifty types.
Brute Force 47. *Naked City* 48. All My Sons 48. Calamity Jane and Sam Bass 50. Woman in Hiding 50. Shakedown 50. Steel Town 52. Women's Prison 54. While the City Sleeps 56. Boys' Night Out 62. Sardanapalus the Great (It.) 63. The Late Show 77. In the Glitter Palace (TV) 78. A Wedding 78. Kramer vs Kramer 79. Double Negative 80. Oh God Book Two 80. No Way Out 87, etc.
TV series: Mr Adams and Eve 56–57. Dante 60. The Felony Squad 66–68. Flamingo Road 80–81.

Duffell, Peter (1924–).
British director.
The House that Dripped Blood 71. England Made Me 72. Inside Out 75. The Far Pavilions (TV) 84. Letters to an Unknown Lover (TV) 85. Inspector Morse 88. Genghis Khan 92, etc.

Dugan, Dennis (1948–).
American director of lowbrow comedies, a former leading actor, usually in rather clumsy comic roles. He began acting while still at school and appeared in off-Broadway productions in the early 70s. Married actress Joyce Van Patten.
AS ACTOR: The Day of the Locust 74. Smile 74. Norman . . . Is That You? 76. Harry and Walter Go to New York 76. The Spaceman and King Arthur 79. The Howling 80. Water 85. Can't Buy Me Love 87. Parenthood 89, etc.
AS DIRECTOR: Problem Child 90. Brain Donors 92. Happy Gilmore 96. Beverly Hills Ninja 97, etc.
TV series: Rich Man, Poor Man – Book 1 76. Richie Brockelman, Private Eye 78. Empire 84. Shadow Chasers 85–86.

Dugan, Tom (1889–1955).
American supporting comic actor, often seen as Irish cop or minor criminal.
Sharp Shooters 27. Lights of New York 28. Sonny Boy 29. Bright Lights 31. Doctor X 32. Grand Slam 33. Palooka 34. Princess O'Hara 35. Pick a Star 37. Four Daughters 38. The Housekeeper's Daughter 39. The Ghost Breakers 40. The Monster and the Girl 41. *To Be Or Not To Be* 42. Bataan 43. Up in Arms 44. Bringing Up Father 46. Good News 47. Take Me Out to the Ball Game 49. The Lemon Drop Kid 51, many others.

Duggan, Andrew (1923–1988).
American character actor of stalwart types.
Patterns 56. The Bravados 58. The Chapman Report 62. FBI Code 98 66. The Secret War of Harry Frigg 67. The Skin Game 71. Jigsaw (TV) 72. The Bears and I 74. It's Alive 77. The Private Files of J. Edgar Hoover 78, etc.
TV series: Bourbon Street Beat 59. Room for One More 61. Twelve O'Clock High 65–67. Lancer 68–69.

Duggan, Pat (1910–).
American producer, former performer and writer.
Red Garters 54. The Vagabond King 56. The Search for Bridey Murphy 57. The Young Savages 61, etc.

Duhamel, Antoine (1925–).
French composer.
Gala 62. Un Amour de Guerre 64. Pierrot le Fou 65. Fugue 66. Weekend 68. Stolen Kisses/Baisers Volés 68. Mississippi Mermaid/La Sirène du Mississippi 69. The Wild Child/L'Enfant Sauvage 69. Bed and Board/Domicile Conjugal 71. L'Acrobate 75. Twisted Obsession 90. These Foolish Things/Daddy Nostalgie 90. Age of Beauty/Belle Époque 92. Belmonte 95. Ridicule 96. The Good Life/La Buena Vida 96, etc.

Duigan, John (1949–).
English-born director and screenwriter, in Australia from the early 60s.
The Firm Man 75. The Trespassers 76. Mouth to Mouth 78. Dimboola 79. Winter of Our Dreams 81. Far East 82. One Night Stand 84. The Year My Voice Broke 87. Romero 89. Flirting 91. Wide Sargasso Sea 93. Sirens 94. The Journey of the August King 95. The Leading Man 96, etc.

Dukakis, Olympia (1931–).
American actress, mainly on the stage.
Lilith 64. Twice a Man 64. John and Mary 69. Death Wish 74. Rich Kids 79. The Wanderers 79. The Idolmaker 80. Flanagan 85. Moonstruck (AA) 87. Working Girl 88. Dad 89. Look Who's Talking 90. Steel Magnolias 90. In the Spirit 90. Look Who's Talking Too 91. Fire in the Dark 91. Over the Hill 92. The Cemetery Club 93. Look Who's Talking Now 93. Digger 93. I Love Trouble 94. Jeffrey 95. Mighty Aphrodite 95. Mr Holland's Opus 95. Jerusalem 96. Picture Perfect 96. Milk & Money 96. Mafia!/Jane Austen's Mafia 98. Armistead Maupin's More Tales of the City (TV) 98. Better Living 98, etc.
TV series: Tales from the City 93.

Duke, Bill (1943–).
American director and actor, usually as a heavy, from television, where he also directed episodes of *Falcon Crest*, *Hill Street Blues* and *Miami Vice*.
An American Gigolo (a) 80. The Killing Floor (d) 84. Commando (a) 85. Predator (a) 87. No Man's Land (a) 87. Action Jackson (a) 88. Bird on a Wire (a) 91. A Rage in Harlem (d) 91. Deep Cover (d) 92. The Cemetery Club (d) 93. Menace II Society (a) 93. Sister Act 2 (d) 93. Hoods (d) 96. Hoodlum (d) 97. Susan's Plan (d) 98, etc.
TV series: Palmerstown, USA 80–81.

Duke, Daryl.
Canadian director in Hollywood.
The Psychiatrist (TV) 70. Happiness Is a Warm Clue (TV) 73. The President's Plane Is Missing (TV) 73. I Heard the Owl Call My Name (TV) 73. Payday 73. A Cry for Help (TV) 75. *Griffin and Phoenix* (TV) 76. The Silent Partner 78. Hard Feelings 82. *The Thorn Birds* (TV) 83. Florence Nightingale (TV) 84. Tai-pan 86. Fatal Memories (TV) 92, etc.

Duke, Ivy (1895–).
Star of British silent screen; married to Guy Newall.
The Garden of Resurrection 18. The Lure of Crooning Water 20. The Persistent Lover 22. The Starlit Garden 23. The Great Prince Shan 24. A Knight in London 29, etc.

Duke, Patty (1946–).
American child actress who found difficulty in graceful adaptation to adult roles. Former wife of John Astin.
I'll Cry Tomorrow 55. Somebody Up There Likes Me 56. Country Music Holiday 57. The Goddess 58. Happy Anniversary 59. 4-D Man 59. The Power and the Glory (TV) 62. *The Miracle Worker* (AA) 62. Billie 65. Valley of the Dolls 67. Me Natalie 69. My Sweet Charlie (TV) 70. Two on a Bench (TV) 71. If Tomorrow Comes (TV) 71. She Waits (TV) 71. You'll Like My Mother 72. Deadly Harvest (TV) 72. Nightmare (TV) 73. Captains and the Kings (TV) 76. A Family Upside Down (TV) 78. The Swarm 78. Hanging by a Thread (TV) 79. The Miracle Worker (TV) 79. Before and After (TV) 80. Best Kept Secrets (TV) 84. Prelude to a Kiss 92. Harvest of Fire (TV) 95, etc.
TV series: *The Patty Duke Show* 63–65. It Takes Two 82. Hail to the Chief 85. Amazing Grace 95– .

Duke, Vernon (1903–1969) (Vladimir Dubelsky).
Russian-American song composer. Shows filmed include *Cabin in the Sky*, but he wrote mostly for revue.

Dukes, David (1945–).
American leading man.
A Fire in the Sky (TV) 77. A Little Romance 79. The First Deadly Sin 80. Only when I Laugh 81. Without a Trace 83. The Winds of War (TV) 83. Space (TV) 85. The Men's Club 86. Catch the Heat 87. Date with an Angel 87. See You in the Morning 89. Snow Kill 90. She Woke Up 92. Me and the Kid 93. Norma Jean and Marilyn (TV) 95. Last Stand at Saber River (TV) 96, etc.

Dulac, Germaine (1882–1942) (G. Saisset-Schneider).
French director with an interest in surrealism and the avant-garde. She began as a journalist, forming her own production company in 1915, becoming a member of the Impressionist school that also included Louis DELLUC. Many of her films no longer exist.
Ames de Fous 18. Le Diable dans la Ville 24. The Seashell and the Clergyman 26. Theme and Variations 30, etc.

Dullea, Keir (1936–).
American leading man, usually in roles of nervous tension.
The Hoodlum Priest 61. *David and Lisa* 62. Mail Order Bride 64. The Thin Red Line 64. Bunny Lake is Missing 65. Madame X 66. The Fox 68. De Sade 69. 2001: A Space Odyssey 69. Last of the Big Guns 73. Paperback Hero 73. Paul and Michelle 74. Black Christmas 75. Full Circle 77. Leopard in the Snow 78. Brave New World (TV) 79. Brain Waves 83. 2010 84. The Next One 85. Oh, What a Night 92, etc.

Dumas, Alexandre, père (1802–1870).
Highly industrious French novelist, mainly of swashbuckling adventures. Films resulting include several versions of *The Count of Monte Cristo* and *The Three Musketeers*, *The Man in the Iron Mask*, *The Fighting Guardsman* and *The Black Tulip*.

Dumas, Alexandre, fils (1824–1895).
French novelist best known for *Camille*, which has been filmed several times.

Dumbrille, Douglass (1890–1974).
Canadian character actor, long in Hollywood and typecast as smooth, suave villain of many a 'B' picture and an admirable foil for many great comedians.
His Woman 31. That's My Boy 32. Elmer the Great 33. Voltaire 33. Lady Killer 34. Broadway Bill 34. Naughty Marietta 35. Crime and Punishment 35. Lives of a Bengal Lancer 35. *Mr Deeds Goes to Town* 36. *A Day at the Races* 37. The Firefly 37. Ali Baba Goes to Town 37. Mr Moto on Danger Island 38. The Three Musketeers 39. Charlie Chan at Treasure Island 39. *The Big Store* 41. Ride 'Em Cowboy 42. Lost in a Harem 44. The Frozen Ghost 45. *Road to Utopia* 45. The Cat Creeps 46. Christmas Eve 47. Alimony 49. Riding High 50. Son of Paleface 52. Jupiter's Darling 55. The Ten Commandments 56. The Buccaneer 58. Shock Treatment 63, many others.
TV series: China Smith 52–55. The Life of Riley 53–58. The Phil Silvers Show 63. Petticoat Junction 64–65.

Dumke, Ralph (1900–1964).
Heavily-built American supporting actor.
All the King's Men 49. Mystery Street 50. The Mob 51. Lili 53. Rails into Laramie 54. The Solid Gold Cadillac 56. The Buster Keaton Story 57, etc.

Dumont, Margaret (1889–1965) (Margaret Baker).
American character comedienne, the stately butt of many a comedian, notably Groucho Marx ('Ah, Mrs Rittenhouse, won't you . . . lie down?).
■ *The Coconuts* 29. *Animal Crackers* 30. The Girl Habit 30. *Duck Soup* 33. The Gridiron Flash 34. Fifteen Wives 34. Kentucky Kernels 34. *A Night at the Opera* 35. Orchids to You 35. Rendezvous 35. The Song and Dance Man 36. Anything Goes 36. *A Day at the Races* 37. The Life of the Party 37. High Flyers 37. Youth on Parole 37. Wise Girl 37. Dramatic School 39. *At the Circus* 39. *The Big Store* 41. Never Give a Sucker an Even Break 41. For Beauty's Sake 41. Born to Sing 41. Sing Your Worries Away 42. Rhythm Parade 42. About Face 42. The Dancing Masters 43. Bathing Beauty 44. Seven Days Ashore 44. Up in Arms 44. The Horn Blows at Midnight 45. Diamond Horseshoe 45. Sunset in El Dorado 45. The Little Giant 46. Susie Steps Out 46. Three for Bedroom C 52. Stop You're Killing Me 53. Shake Rattle and Rock 56. Auntie Mame 58. Zotz! 62. What a Way to Go 64.
TV series: My Friend Irma 52–54.
✪ For suffering beyond the call of comic duty. *A Day at the Races*.

Duna, Steffi (1913–1992) (Stephanie Berindey).
Hungarian dancer who appeared in some dramatic roles in the 30s.
The Indiscretions of Eve 31. La Cucaracha 35. The Dancing Pirate 36. Anthony Adverse 36. Pagliacci 37. Waterloo Bridge 40. River's End 41, etc.

Dunaway, Faye (1941–).
Blonde American leading actress. Born in Bascom, Florida, she studied drama at the University of Florida and at Boston University's School of Fine and Applied Arts, after which she made her debut on the New York stage, was soon contracted to producer Sam SPIEGEL and director Otto PREMINGER, and rapidly became a star with *Bonnie and Clyde*. Her best performances so far have been as Evelyn Mulwray in *Chinatown* and Diana Christensen in *Network*, though her performance as Joan Crawford in *Mommie Dearest* has become a camp classic. She was romantically involved with comedian Lenny BRUCE, director Jerry SCHATZBERG and actors Marcello MASTROIANNI and Harris YULIN. Married rock singer Peter Wolf (1974–77) and photographer Terry O'Neill (divorced).

Autobiography: 1995, *Looking for Gatsby: My Life* (with Betsy Sharkey).

Biography: 1986, *Faye Dunaway* by Allan Hunter.

Hurry Sundown 67. The Happening 67. *Bonnie and Clyde* (AAN) 67. The Thomas Crown Affair 68. The Extraordinary Seaman 69. A Place for Lovers 69. The Arrangement 69. Little Big Man 70. Puzzle of a Downfall Child 71. Doc 71. The Deadly Trap 71. Oklahoma Crude 73. The Three Musketeers 73. Chinatown (AAN) 74. The Four Musketeers 74. The Towering Inferno 74. 3 Days of the Condor 75. Voyage of the Dammed 76. *Network* (AA) 76. The Disappearance of Aimée (TV) 76. The Eyes of Laura Mars 78. The Champ 79. The First Deadly Sin 80. Mommie Dearest 81. Evita Peron (TV) 82. The Wicked Lady 83. Christopher Columbus (TV) 84. Supergirl 84. Ordeal by Innocence 85. Barfly 87. Burning Secret 88. Midnight Crossing 88. The Gamble/La Partita 88. The Handmaid's Tale 89. Crystal or Ash, Fire or Wind, as Long as It's Love/In una Notte di Chiaro di Luna 89. Wait until Spring, Bandini 89. Silhouette 90. Christopher Columbus 91. Scorchers 91. Arizona Dream 92. The Temp 93. Don Juan DeMarco 95. Drunks 95. Dunston Checks In 96. Albino Alligator 96. Rebecca (TV) 97. The Twilight of the Golds (TV) 97. Gia (TV) 98, etc.

TV series: It Had to Be You 93.

❝ A star today has to take charge of every aspect of her career. There are no studios left to do it for you. – *F.D.*

You could stand in the middle of the dirt road that ran in front of the house I was born in and look hard either way and see nothing but the long rows of peanuts snaking their way up to a stand of trees in the distance. – *F.D.*

Dunbar, Adrian (1958–).
Irish actor and screenwriter.

A World Apart 87. The Dawning 88. My Left Foot 89. *Hear My Song* (& w) 91. Force of Duty (TV) 92. The Crying Game 92. A Woman's Guide to Adultery (TV) 93. Widow's Peak 94. Innocent Lies 95. The Near Room 95. Richard III 95. Melissa (TV) 97. The Jump (TV) 98. The General 98, etc.

Dunbar, Dixie (1915–1991) (Christina Dunbar).
American dancer and light lead, in films of the 30s.

George White's Scandals 34. King of Burlesque 36. Sing Baby Sing 36. Rebecca of Sunnybrook Farm 38. Alexander's Ragtime Band 38, etc.

Duncan, Archie (1914–1979).
Burly Scottish actor, the 'Little John' of TV's Robin Hood series.

Operation Diamond 47. The Bad Lord Byron 48. The Gorbals Story 51. Robin Hood 53. The Maggie 53. Laxdale Hall 54. Johnny on the Run 56. Harry Black 58. Lancelot and Guinevere 63. Ring of Bright Water 69, etc.

Duncan, Arletta (1914–1938).
American actress and singer, on the stage as a child, who was given a seven-year contract by Universal after winning a trip to Hollywood in a photographic contest. Committed suicide by jumping from the 'Hollywoodland' sign.

Frankenstein 31. Law and Order 32. Back Street 32. The Unexpected Father 32. Night World 32. Fast Companions 32, etc.

Duncan, David (1913–).
American screenwriter.

Sangaree 53. The Black Scorpion 57. The Thing that Couldn't Die 58. Monster on the Campus 58. The Leech Woman 60. The Time Machine 60.

Duncan, Isadora (1878–1927).
Flamboyant American dancer. Died when her scarf caught in the wheel of a car. She was the subject of a biopic, *Isadora/The Loves of Isadora* 58, directed by Karel Reisz and starring Vanessa Redgrave.

Duncan, Patrick (Patrick Sheane Duncan).
American screenwriter, director and producer.

The Beach Girls (co-w) 82. Charlie Mopic (wd) 89. A Home of Our Own (p, w) 93. The Pornographer (wd) 94. Nick of Time (w) 95. Mr Holland's Opus (w) 95. Courage under Fire (w) 96. The Wall (w) 98, etc.

Duncan, Rosetta (1900–1959).
American vaudeville performer with her sister Vivian as the Duncan Sisters, who made only two films: an unsuccessful silent from their long-running stage show, based on *Uncle Tom's Cabin* (with Rosetta blacked up as Topsy), which they were still performing in the 40s, and one successful talkie.

Topsy and Eva 27. It's a Great Life 29.

Duncan, Sandy (1946–).
Tomboyish American leading lady.

■ Million Dollar Duck 71. *Star Spangled Girl* 71. Roots (TV) 77. The Cat from Outer Space 78. Rock-a-Doodle (voice) 90. The Swan Princess (voice) 94.

TV series: *Funny Face* 71.

Duncan, Todd (1903–1998).
American opera singer and actor, in occasional films. Born in Danville, Kentucky, he was educated at Butler University and Columbia University Teachers College, and also taught at Howard University and the Curtis Institute of Music in Philadelphia. A baritone, he was picked by GERSHWIN to originate the role of Porgy in *Porgy and Bess*.

Syncopation 42. Unchained 55.

Duncan, Vivian (1902–1986).
American vaudeville performer with her sister Rosetta DUNCAN. She was married to Nils Asther.

Dundas, David.
English composer.

Withnail and I 87. How to Get Ahead in Advertising 89, etc.

Dunham, Duwayne.
American editor turned director.

AS EDITOR: Return of the Jedi 83. The Mean Season 85. Blue Velvet 86. Mad House 90. Wild at Heart 90. Twin Peaks (TV) 90, etc.

AS DIRECTOR: Homeward Journey: The Incredible Journey 93.

Duning, George (1919–).
American music director and composer.

The Corpse Came COD 46. To the Ends of the Earth 48. The Dark Past 49. No Sad Songs for Me 50. The Mob 51. Paula 52. Salome 53. The Man from Laramie 55. Bell Book and Candle 58. Houseboat 58. The Last Angry Man 59. The World of Suzie Wong 61. Toys in the Attic 63. Dear Brigitte 65. Any Wednesday 66. Terror in the Wax Museum 73. The Man with Bogart's Face 80. Goliath Awaits (TV) 81, many others.

Dunlap, Paul (1919–).
American composer, mainly for low-budget movies.

The Baron of Arizona 50. The Steel Helmet 50. Little Big Horn 51. Park Row 52. Loophole 54. Fort Yuma 55. The Broken Star 56. Dance with Me, Henry 56. Apache Warrior 57. I Was a Teenage Werewolf 57. I Was a Teenage Frankenstein 57. Blood of Dracula 57. Frankenstein – 1970 58. The Four Skulls of Jonathan Drake 59. The Rookie 59. The Angry Red Planet 60. Shock Corridor 63. The Naked Kiss 64. Castle of Evil 66. The Money Jungle 68, many others.

Dunn, Emma (1875–1966).
British character actress, long in Hollywood, typically as housekeeper.

Old Lady 31 20. Pied Piper Malone 23. Side Street 29. Bad Sister 31. Hard to Handle 33. The Glass Key 35. Mr Deeds Goes to Town 36. Thanks for the Memory 38. Son of Frankenstein 39. The Great Dictator 40. Ladies in Retirement 41. I Married a Witch 42. It Happened Tomorrow 44. Life with Father 47. The Woman in White 48, many others.

Dunn, James (1905–1967).
Genial American leading man of the 30s; later seized one good acting chance but slipped into low-budget westerns.

Bad Girl 31. Over the Hill 31. Sailor's Luck 33. Hold Me Tight 33. Stand Up and Cheer 34. Baby Take a Bow 34. Bright Eyes 34. The Daring Young Man 35. Don't Get Personal 36. Mysterious Crossing 37. Shadows over Shanghai 38. Government Girl 43. *A Tree Grows in Brooklyn* (AA) 45. That Brennan Girl 46. Killer McCoy 48. The Golden Gloves Story 50. The Bramble Bush 60. The Nine Lives of Elfego Baca 62. Hemingway's Adventures of a Young Man 62. The Oscar 66, etc.

TV series: It's A Great Life 54.

Dunn, Linwood Gale (1904–1998).
American visual effects cinematographer and photographic equipment designer. Born in Brooklyn, he was a projectionist and assistant cameraman before working for RKO as a visual effects cinematographer from 1929 to 1957. He was awarded an Oscar in 1944, together with associate Cecil Love, for designing the Acme-Dunn Special Effects Optical Printer, and received the Academy's Outstanding Service and Dedication Award in 1979.

Cimarron 30. King Kong 33. Bringing Up Baby 38. Citizen Kane 41. The Thing 51. China Gate 57. West Side Story 61. It's a Mad, Mad, Mad, Mad World 63. My Fair Lady 64. Darling Lili 70. The Devil's Rain 75, etc.

Dunn, Michael (1935–1973) (Gary Neil Miller).
American dwarf actor. Found dead, a possible suicide, while filming *The Abdication*.

Ship of Fools 65. You're a Big Boy Now 67. No Way to Treat a Lady 68. Madigan 68. Boom 68. Justine 69. Murders in the Rue Morgue 71. Goodnight My Love (TV) 72. The Mutations 74, etc.

Dunne, Dominique (1959–1982).
American actress, the sister of Griffin Dunne. Killed by a former boyfriend.

Magic on Love Island 80. Poltergeist 82. The Shadow Riders (TV) 82. Haunting of Harrington House (TV) 82, etc.

Dunne, Griffin (1955–).
American leading actor who also produces and directs, the son of novelist and former TV and film producer Dominick Dunne.

AS PRODUCER: Chilly Scenes of Winter 79. Head over Heels 80. Baby, It's You 82. After Hours 85. Running on Empty 88. White Palace 90. Once Around 91, etc.

AS DIRECTOR: The Duke of Groove (short) (AAN) 95. Addicted to Love 97. Practical Magic 98, etc.

Dunne, Irene (1898–1990).
Gracious American leading lady of the 30s and 40s, usually in sensible well-bred roles.

■ Leathernecking 30. *Cimarron* (AAN) 31. The Great Lover 31. Consolation Marriage 31. Bachelor Apartment 31. *Back Street* 32. *Symphony of Six Million* 33. Thirteen Women 32. No Other Women 33. The Secret of Madame Blanche 33. The Silver Cord 33. *Ann Vickers* 33. If I Were Free 34. This Man is Mine 34. Stingaree 34. The Age of Innocence 34. Sweet Adeline 35. *Roberta* 35. *Magnificent Obsession* 35. *Show Boat* 36. *Theodora Goes Wild* (AAN) 36. *The Awful Truth* (AAN) 37. High Wide and Handsome 37. Joy of Living 38. *Love Affair* (AAN) 39. Invitation to Happiness 39. When Tomorrow Comes 39. *My Favourite Wife* 40. Penny Serenade 41. Unfinished Business 41. Lady in a Jam 42. A Guy Named Joe 43. The White Cliffs of Dover 44. Together Again 45. Over Twenty One 45. *Anna and the King of Siam* 46. *Life with Father* 47. *I Remember Mama* (AAN) 48. Never a Dull Moment 50. *The Mudlark* (as Queen Victoria) 51. It Grows on Trees 52.

✪ For epitomizing the American lady of a gentler, more romantic age than ours. *Love Affair*.

Dunne, John Gregory (1932–).
American screenwriter, novelist and essayist. He is also the author of *The Studio* (1970), a study of Twentieth Century Fox during the year it was making *Dr Dolittle* and *Star!* He is married to Joan DIDION, with whom he has collaborated on his film scripts.

Autobiography: 1997, *Monster: Up Close with a Screenplay*.

Panic in Needle Park (co-w) 71. Play It as It Lays (co-w) 71. A Star Is Born (co-w) 76. True Confessions (oa, co-w) 81. Broken Trust (co-w, TV) 95. Up Close and Personal (co-w) 96, etc.

❝ The truly absorbing aspect of the motion picture ethic, of course, is that it affects not only motion picture people but almost everyone alive in the United States today. By adolescence, children have been programmed with a set of responses and life lessons learned almost totally from motion pictures, television and the recording industry. – *J.G.D.*

Dunne, Philip (1908–1992).
American screenwriter and director.

Student Tour 34. The Last of the Mohicans 36. Lancer Spy 37. Suez 38. Stanley and Livingstone 39. The Rains Came 39. Swanee River 39. How Green was My Valley (AAN) 41. The Late George Apley 47. Forever Amber 47. The Luck of the Irish 48. Pinky 49. David and Bathsheba (AAN) 51. The Robe 53. Prince of Players (& pd) 55. Hilda Crane (& d) 56. Ten North Frederick (& d) 58. Blue Denim (& d) 59. Lisa (d only) 62. The Agony and the Ecstasy 65. Blindfold (& d) 66, many others.

Dunning, George (1920–1979).
Canadian animator whose main feature work was *The Yellow Submarine*.

Dunning, Ruth (1911–1983).
British character actress, mainly on TV.

Dunnock, Mildred (1904–1991).
American character actress specializing in motherly types.

The Corn is Green 45. Kiss of Death 47. *Death of a Salesman* (AAN) 51. Viva Zapata 52. The Jazz Singer 53. Love Me Tender 56. Baby Doll (AAN) 56. Peyton Place 57. The Nun's Story 57. Cat on a Hot Tin Roof 58. Butterfield 8 60. Something Wild 61. Sweet Bird of Youth 62. Behold a Pale Horse 64. Seven Women 66. Whatever Happened to Aunt Alice? 69. Murder or Mercy (TV) 74. The Spiral Staircase (GB) 75. The Pickup Artist 87, etc.

Dunst, Kirsten (1982–).
American child actress.

Bonfire of the Vanities 90. Greedy/Greed 94. Interview with the Vampire 94. Little Women 94. Jumanji 95. Mother Night 96. Wag the Dog 97. Small Soldiers 98. The Virgin Suicides 98. Strike 98, etc.

Dupont, E. A. (1891–1956) (Ewald André).
German director who moved with unhappy results to Britain and Hollywood.

Baruh 23. *Variety* 26. Love Me and the World Is Mine 27. Moulin Rouge 28. *Piccadilly* 29. Atlantic 30. Ladies Must Love 33. The Bishop Misbehaves 35. Forgotten Faces 36. Hell's Kitchen 39. The Scarf (& w) 50. The Neanderthal Man 53. Return to Treasure Island 54. Magic Fire (co-w only) 56, etc.

Dupree, Minnie (1873–1947).
American character actress seen infrequently as sweet old lady.

Night Club 29. *The Young in Heart* 38. Anne of Windy Poplars 40, etc.

Duprez, June (1918–1984).
British leading lady who moved to Hollywood in the 40s.

The Crimson Circle 36. The Spy in Black 38. The Four Feathers 39. The Thief of Baghdad 41. None But the Lonely Heart (US) 44. *And Then There Were None* (US) 45. Calcutta (US) 46. That Brennan Girl (US) 47. The Kinsey Report (US) 61, etc.

Dupuis, Paul (1916–1976).
French-Canadian leading man popular in British films in the late 40s.

Johnny Frenchman 45. The White Unicorn 47. Sleeping Car to Trieste 48. Passport to Pimlico 49. The Reluctant Widow 50, etc.

Durante, Jimmy 'Schnozzle' (1893–1980).
Long-nosed, well-loved American comedian with long career in vaudeville and nightclubs. Film appearances spasmodic, and most successful when involving his old routines: 'Umbriago', 'Ink-a-dink', etc.

Biographies: 1951, *Schnozzola* by Gene Fowler. 1963, *Goodnight Mrs Calabash* by William Cahn.

■ Roadhouse Nights 30. The New Adventures of Get-Rich-Quick Wallingford 31. Cuban Love Song 31. The Passionate Plumber 32. The Wet Parade 32. Speak Easily 32. The Phantom President 33. Blondie of the Follies 33. Meet the Baron 33. What No Beer 33. Hell Below 33. Broadway to Hollywood 33. George White's Scandals 34. Hollywood Party 34. Joe Palooka 34. She Learned About Sailors 34. Strictly Dynamite 34. Student Tour 34. Carnival 35. Land without Music (GB) 36. Sally, Irene and Mary 38. Start Cheering 38. Little Miss Broadway 38. Melody Ranch 40. *You're in the Army Now* 40. *The Man who Came to Dinner* 41. Two Girls and a Sailor 44. Music for Millions 45. *Two Sisters from Boston* 46. It Happened in Brooklyn 47. This Time for Keeps 47. On an Island with You 48. The Great Rupert 50. The Milkman 50. Beau James 57. Pepe 60. The Last Judgment 61. *Jumbo* 62. It's a Mad Mad Mad Mad World (cameo) 63. That's Entertainment! III 94.

TV series: The Jimmy Durante Show 54–56.

❝ Everybody wants to get into de act! – *J.D., catchphrase*

Dere's a million good-looking guys in the world, but I'm a novelty. – *J.D.*

Goodnight, Mrs Calabash, wherever you are. – *J.D., closing words of music-hall act* (Mrs Calabash was his pet name for his late wife)

I don't split infinitives. When I go to work on 'em, I break 'em up into little pieces. – *J.D.*

Duras, Marguerite (1914–1996) (Marguerite Donnadieu).
French director, screenwriter, novelist and dramatist, born in French Indochina. Her award-winning autobiographical novel *L'Amant/The Lover* was turned into a hit movie in France in 1991.

The Sea Wall/Barrage contre le Pacifique (oa) 57. *Hiroshima Mon Amour* (w) 59. Moderato Cantabile (w) 60. The Long Absence/Une Aussi Longue Absence 61. 10.30 p.m. Summer (w) 66. La Musica (w, co-d) 66. The Sailor from Gibraltar (oa) 67. Destroy, She Said/Détruire, Dit-elle (wd) 69. Jaune de Soleil (wd) 71. Nathalie Granger (wd) 73. La Femmes du Gange (wd) 74. *India Song* (a, wd) 75. Entire Days in the Trees/Des Journées Entières dans les Arbres (wd) 77. Baxter, Vera Baxter (wd) 77. Le Navire Night (wd) 79. Aurelia Steiner (wd) 79. Les Enfants (w, co-d) 85, etc.

Durbin, Deanna (1921–) (Edna Mae Durbin).
Canadian girl-singer who won instant world-wide success as a teenage star; her career faltered after ten years when weight problems added to a change in musical fashion brought about her premature retirement. Special Academy Award 1938 'for bringing to the screen the spirit and personification of youth'. Long retired and living in France.

■ Every Sunday 36. *Three Smart Girls* 36. *One Hundred Men and a Girl* 37. *Mad about Music* 38. *That Certain Age* 38. Three Smart Girls Grow Up 38. First Love 39. It's a Date 39. Spring Parade 40. Nice Girl 40. *It Started with Eve* 41. The Amazing Mrs Holliday 42. Hers to Hold 43. His Butler's Sister 43. Christmas Holiday 44. *Can't Help Singing* 44. Lady on a Train 45. Because of Him 45. I'll Be Yours 46. Something in the Wind 47. Up in Central Park 47. For the Love of Mary 48.

❂ For pleasing world audiences by being the character she despised: 'Little Miss Fixit who bursts into song.' *That Certain Age*.

❝ Just as a Hollywood pin-up represents sex to dissatisfied erotics, so I represented the ideal daughter millions of fathers and mothers wished they had. – *D.D. in 1959*

She is one of those personalities whom the world will insist on regarding as its private property. – *Joe Pasternak, her producer*

Durfee, Minta (1897–1975).
American leading lady of knockabout comedies 1914–16, including some with Chaplin. Married Roscoe Arbuckle and retired, but much later played bit parts.

Durkin, Junior (1915–1935) (Trent Durkin).
American juvenile player who was Huck Finn in *Tom Sawyer* 30 and *Huckleberry Finn* 31. On stage from the age of two, he died in a car crash.

Durning, Charles (1933–).
Burly American TV actor who slowly gained a star footing in movies.

Harvey Middleman Fireman 65. I Walk the Line 70. Hi Mom 70. Deadhead Miles 72. Dealing 72. Sisters 72. The Connection (TV) 73. The Sting 73. The Front Page 74. Dog Day Afternoon 75. The Hindenburg 75. The Trial of Chaplin Jensen (TV) 75. Queen of the Stardust Ballroom (TV) 75. Switch (TV) 75. Captains and the Kings (TV) 76. Breakheart Pass 76. Harry and Walter Go to New York 76. Twilight's Last Gleaming 77. Special Olympics (TV) 78. *The Choirboys* 78. The Greek Tycoon 78. An Enemy of the People 78. The Fury 78. F.I.S.T. 79. Studs Lonigan (TV) 79. The Muppet Movie 79. North Dallas Forty 79. Tilt 79. Starting Over 79. When a Stranger Calls 79. Die Laughing 80. The Final Countdown 80. True Confessions 81. Sharky's Machine 81. *The Best Little Whorehouse in Texas* (AAN) 82. Tootsie 82. To Be or Not to Be (AAN) 83. Two of a Kind 83. Side by Side 83. Mass Appeal 84. Stick 85. The Man with One Red Shoe 85. Stand Alone 85. Private Conversations 85. Tough Guys 86. Happy New Year 87. A Tiger's Tale 87. The Rosary Murders 87. Cop 88. Far North 88. Brenda Starr 89. Cat Chaser 89. Etoile 89. Dick Tracy 90. Fatal Sky 90. Project: Alien 90. V.I. Warshawski 91. Brenda Starr 92. The Music of Chance 93. The Hudsucker Proxy 94. I.Q. 94. Home for the Holidays 95. Spy Hard 96. Mrs Santa Claus (TV) 96. One Fine Day 96. Shelter 98. Hi-Life 98, etc.

TV series: Another World 64. The Cop and The Kid 75–76. Eye to Eye 85. Evening Shade 91–94.

Durrell, Lawrence (1912–1990).
English poet, novelist and occasional screenwriter. Born in India, he lived in England in his late teens before moving to France and several Mediterranean islands. The first part of *The Alexandria Quartet*, his celebrated sequence of novels on modern love, was filmed as *Justine* 69, directed by George Cukor and starring Anouk Aimée, Michael York, Dirk Bogarde and Anna Karina.

Biographies: 1996, *Through the Dark Labyrinth: A Biography of Lawrence Durrell* by Gordon Bowker; 1998, *Lawrence Durrell: A Biography* by Ian MacNiven.

Cleopatra 63. Judith (story) 65, etc.

Dury, Ian (1942–).
British actor, singer and composer. He was leader of the rock bands Kilburn & The High Roads and The Blockheads in the 70s and 80s.

As actor: Radio On 79. Number One 84. Pirates 86. Rocinante 86. Hearts of Fire 87. Red Ants 87. The Raggedy Rawney 88. The Cook, the Thief, His Wife and Her Lover 89. Bearskin 89. Split Second 92.

As songwriter: Take It or Leave It 81. Real Genius 85. Brennende Betten 88.

Duryea, Dan (1907–1968).
Laconic, long-faced American character actor often typecast as whining villain.

■ *The Little Foxes* 41. Ball of Fire 41. Pride of the Yankees 42. That Other Woman 42. Sahara 43. Man from Frisco 44. Ministry of Fear 44. None but the Lonely Heart 44. *The Woman in the Window* 44. Main Street After Dark 44. Mrs Parkington 45. The Great Flamarion 45. Lady on a Train 45. Scarlet Street 45. Along Came Jones 45. The Valley of Decision 45. *Black Angel* 46. White Tie and Tails 46. Black Bart 48. River Lady 48. *Another Part of the Forest* 48. Larceny 48. *Criss Cross* 49. Manhandled 49. Too Late for Tears 49. Johnny Stoolpigeon 50. One Way Street 50. The Underworld Story 50. Winchester 73 50. Al Jennings of Oklahoma 50. *Chicago Calling* 51. Sky Commando 53. Thunder Bay 53. 36 Hours 53. World for Ransom 54. Ride Clear of Diablo 54. Silver Lode 54. This is My Love 54. Rails Into Laramie 54. The Marauders 55. Foxfire 55. Storm Fear 56. Battle Hymn 57. The Burglar 57. Night Passage 57. Slaughter on Tenth Avenue 57. Kathy O 58. Platinum High School 60. Six Black Horses 62. He Rides Tall 64. Taggart 64. Walk a Tightrope 64. Do You Know This Voice? 64. The Bounty Killer 65. Incident at Phantom Hill 65. *The Flight of the Phoenix* 65. The Hills Run Red 67. Stranger on the Run (TV) 67. Five Golden Dragons 67. The Bamboo Saucer 68.

TV series: China Smith 58. Peyton Place 68.

❝ The crime movie equivalent of an absolute bounder. – *Ian Cameron*

Duse, Eleonora (1858–1924).
Eminent Italian tragedienne whose one film appearance was in *Cenere* 16.

❝ Something quite different is needed. I'm too old for it. Isn't it a pity. – *E.D. after making her film*

Dussollier, André (1946–).
French leading actor.

And Now My Love 74. Perceval le Gallois 78. A Gorgeous Bird Like Me/Such a Gorgeous Kid Like Me/Une Belle Fille comme Moi 72. Le Beau Mariage 82. Three Men and a Cradle/Trois Hommes et un Couffin 85. De Sable et de Sang/Blood and Sand 87. Un Coeur en Hiver 92. Les Marmottes 93. Montparnasse-Pondichery 94. Aux Petits Bonheurs 94. Le Colonel Chabert 94. The Story of a Poor Young Man (It.) 95. Same Old Song/On Connaît la Chanson 97, etc.

Dutta, Dulal (1925–).
Indian editor, who worked on all of Satyajit Ray's films.

Pather Panchali 55. Aparajito 56. The Music Room/Jalsaghar 58. The World of Apu 59. Three Daughters/Teen Kanya 61. Kanchenjungha 62. Mahanagar 63. Nayak 66. Days and Nights in the Forest 69. Company Limited 71. Distant Thunder 73. The Middle Man 75. The Chess Players 77. Deliverance 81. The Home and the World 84. An Enemy of the People/Ganasatru 89. Target 95, etc.

Dutton, Charles S. (1951–).
American character actor.

No Mercy 86. Crocodile Dundee II 88. Runaway (TV) 89. An Unremarkable Life 89. Jacknife 89. Q & A 90. Alien³ 92. Mississippi Masala 92. Rudy 93. Surviving the Game 94. A Lowdown Dirty Shame 94. Foreign Student 94. Cry the Beloved Country 95. Nick of Time 95. A Time to Kill 96. Get on the Bus 95. Mimic 97. Blind Faith 98. Black Dog 98, etc.

TV series: Roc 91–92.

Duvall, Robert (1930–).
American character actor, often as a nervy outsider in early roles, later as an efficient, no-nonsense fixer. Born in San Diego, California, he studied under Sanford Meisner at the Neighborhood Playhouse in New York. After 13 years of trying to raise $5m for *The Apostle*, he decided to finance it himself.

Biography: 1985, *Robert Duvall: Hollywood Maverick* by Judith Slawson.

Captain Newman MD 63. To Kill a Mockingbird 63. The Chase 65. Bullitt 68. The Rain People 69. True Grit 69. M*A*S*H 70. Lawman 71. *The Godfather* (AAN) 72. The Great Northfield Minnesota Raid 72. Joe Kidd 72. The Godfather Part Two 74. The Outfit 74. Breakout 75. Killer Elite 76. Network 76. The Seven Per Cent Solution (as Dr Watson) 76. The Greatest 77. The Eagle Has Landed 77. The Betsy 78. Ike (TV) 79. Apocalypse Now (BFA, AAN) 79. The Great Santini (AAN) 80. True Confessions 81. The Pursuit of D. B. Cooper 81. Tender Mercies (AA) 83. The Stone Boy 84. The Natural 84. The Lightship 85. Hotel Colonial 87. Let's Get Harry 87. Colors 88. The Handmaid's Tale 89. Days of Thunder 90. A Show of Force 90. Rambling Rose 91. Newsies/The News Boys 92. *Falling Down* 93. Geronimo: An American Legend 93. Wrestling Ernest Hemingway 93. The Paper 94. The Stars Fell on Henrietta 95. Something to Talk About 95. The Scarlet Letter 95. A Family Thing 96. Phenomenon 96. The Man Who Captured Eichmann (TV) 96. The Gingerbread Man 97. *The Apostle* (& wd) (AANa) 97. Deep Impact 98. A Civil Action 98, etc.

❝ Being a star is an agent's dream, not an actor's. – *R.D.*

There are only two actors in America. One is Brando, who's done his best work, and the other is Robert Duvall. – *Sanford Meisner*

Famous line (as Lieutenant-Colonel Kilgore in *Apocalypse Now*): 'I love the smell of napalm in the morning . . . It smells like victory.'

Duvall, Shelley (1949–).
American actress in off-centre roles. In the 80s, she became a producer for cable television.

Brewster McCloud 70. McCabe and Mrs Miller 71. Thieves Like Us 74. Nashville 75. Three Women 77. Annie Hall 77. The Shining 80. Popeye 80. Time Bandits 81. Roxanne 87. Suburban Commando 91. The Underneath 95. The Portrait of a Lady 96. Changing Habits 97. Home Fries 98. Teen Monster 99, etc.

Duvivier, Julien (1896–1967).
Celebrated French director of the 30s whose touch seemed to falter after a wartime sojourn in Hollywood. Born in Lille, he abandoned acting to become an assistant to directors Louis Feuillade and Marcel L'Herbier before making his first feature in 1919. Among his regular collaborators were screenwriters Charles Spaak and Henri Jeanson.

Hacadelma 19. Poil de Carotte 25 and 32. David Golder 30. Maria Chapdelaine 33. Le Golem 35. La Belle Equipe 36. *Pépé Le Moko* 37. *Un Carnet de Bal* 37. The Great Waltz (US) 38. *La Fin du Jour* 39. La Charrette Fantôme 39. Lydia (US) 41. Tales of Manhattan (US) 42. Flesh and Fantasy (US) 43. The Imposter (US) 44. *Panique* 46. Anna Karenina (GB) 48. Au Royaume des Cieux 49. Sous le Ciel de Paris 51. *Don Camillo* 52. La Fête à Henriette 54. L'Affaire Maurizius 54. Voici le Temps des Assassins 55. The Man in the Raincoat 57. Pot-Bouille 57. Marie Octobre 59. La Femme et le Pantin 59. La Grande Vie 61. La Chambre Ardente 62. Chair de Poule 63, etc.

❝ He was a loner, too rich for his own good, who shot too many films, like others drink too much. The cinema was his drug. – *Charles Spaak*

If I were an architect and I had to build a monument to the cinema, I would place a statue of Duvivier over the entrance. – *Jean Renoir*

Dvorak, Ann (1912–1979) (Ann McKim).
Smart but sensitive American leading lady of the 30s.

Hollywood Revue 29. Way out West 30. The Guardsman 31. This Modern Age 31. The Crowd Roars 32. *Scarface* 32. The Strange Love of Molly Louvain 32. Three on a Match 32. The Way to Love 33. Heat Lightning 34. Housewife 34. I Sell Anything 34. G Men 35. Folies Bergère 35. *Dr Socrates* 35. We Who Are About to Die 36. Racing Lady 37. The Case of the Stuttering Bishop 37. Merrily We Live 38. Blind Alley 39. Café Hostess 40. Girls of the Road 40. Squadron Leader X (GB) 41. This Was Paris (GB) 42. Escape to Danger 44. Flame of the Barbary Coast 45. Abilene Town 46. The Long Night 47. The Walls of Jericho 48. A Life of Her Own 50. I Was an American Spy 51. The Secret of Convict Lake 51, etc.

Dwan, Allan (1885–1981).
Veteran American director, former writer; he competently handled commercial movies of every type.

Wildflower 14. The Good Bad Man 15. Manhattan Madness 16. A Modern Musketeer 18. Luck of the Irish 20. *Robin Hood* 22. Big Brother 23. Zaza 23. Manhandled 24. Stage Struck 25. *The Iron Mask* 29. Man to Man 31. Mayor of Hell 33. Human Cargo 36. Heidi 37. Suez 38. The Three Musketeers (Ritz Brothers version) 39. Trail of the Vigilantes 40. Rise and Shine 41. Abroad with Two Yanks 44. Up in Mabel's Room 44. Brewster's Millions 45. Getting Gertie's Garter 46. Angel in Exile 48. *Sands of Iwo Jima* 49. The Wild Blue Yonder 51. Montana Belle 52. The Woman They Almost Lynched 53. Silver Lode 54. Tennessee's Partner 55. Hold Back the Night 56. Slightly Scarlet 56. The River's Edge 56. The Most Dangerous Man Alive 61, many others.

❝ If you get your head up above the mob, they try to knock it off. If you stay down, you last forever. – *A.D.*

Dwyer, Leslie (1906–1986).
Plump cockney character actor, in films from childhood.

The Fifth Form at St Dominic's 21. The Flag Lieutenant 31. The Goose Steps Out 41. The Way Ahead 44. Night Boat to Dublin 46. When the Bough Breaks 48. The Calendar 48. Midnight Episode 50. Laughter in Paradise 51. Hindle Wakes 52. Where There's a Will 53. Act of Love 54. Left, Right and Centre 59. I've Gotta Horse 64. Monster of Terror 65. Lionheart 68. Dominique 78, many others.

Dyall, Franklin (1874–1950).
British stage actor from 1894, in films from 1930.
He was the father of Valentine Dyall.
  Atlantic 30. The Ringer 32. The Private Life of
Henry VIII 33. The Iron Duke 35. Fire Over
England 36. Bonnie Prince Charlie 49, etc.

Dyall, Valentine (1908–1985).
Gaunt British actor with resounding voice, famous
as radio's wartime 'Man in Black'. Son of stage actor
Franklin Dyall. Film debut *The Life and Death of
Colonel Blimp* 43; later in many supporting roles,
notably Henry V 44. Caesar and Cleopatra 45.
Brief Encounter 45. Vengeance Is Mine 48. City of
the Dead 60. The Haunting 63. The Horror of It
All 65, etc.

Dyer, Anson (1876–1962).
Pioneer British cartoonist: many
entertainment shorts, also work for government
departments.

Dykstra, John (1947–).
Special effects expert. After working as an assistant
to Douglas Trumbull, he founded Industrial Light
and Magic with George Lucas before leaving to set
up his own company, Apogee.
  Silent Running 71. Star Wars (AA) 77.
Avalanche Express 78. Star Trek: The Motion
Picture (AAN) 79. Caddyshack 80. Firefox 82.
Lifeforce 86. Invaders from Mars 87. My Stepmother
Is an Alien 88. Spontaneous Combustion 89.
Batman Forever 95. Batman & Robin 97, etc.

Dylan, Bob (1941–) (Robert Allen Zimmerman).
American singer in occasional films.
  Don't Look Back 66. Pat Garrett and Billy the
Kid 73. Renaldo and Clara 78. Hearts of Fire 87,
etc.

Dyneley, Peter (1921–1977).
British character actor.
  Beau Brummell 54. The Young Lovers 55. The
Split 60. Call Me Bwana 63. Chato's Land 72,
etc.

Dysart, Richard (1929–).
American character actor.
  Petulia 68. The Terminal Man 74. The
Hindenburg 75. Being There 79. Bitter Harvest
81. The Thing 82. The Falcon and the Snowman
85. Mask 85. Pale Rider 85. Wall Street 87. Back
to the Future Part III 90. Panther 95. Hard Rain
97, etc.
  TV series: L.A. Law 86–93.

Dzundza, George (1945–)
Burly American character actor.
  The Deer Hunter 78. Brubaker 80. A Long Way
Home 81. Honky Tonk Freeway 81. Streamers 83.
Act of Passion 83. Best Defence 84. Brotherly Love
(TV) 85. No Mercy 86. Glory Years (TV) 87. No
Way Out 87. The Beast 88. White Hunter, Black
Heart 89. Impulse 89. The Butcher's Wife 91.
Basic Instinct 92. Crimson Tide 95. Dangerous
Minds 95. That Darn Cat 96. Trading Favors 97.
Species 2 98, etc.
  TV series: Jesse 98– .

E

Eady, David (1924–).
British director who turned to making mainly children's films in the 70s.
The Bridge of Time (doc) 52. Three Cases of Murder (one story) 55. In the Wake of a Stranger 58. Faces in the Dark 60. The Verdict 64. Operation Third Form 66. Anoop and the Elephant 72. Hide and Seek 72. The Laughing Girl Murder 73. The Hostages 75. Night Ferry 76. Deep Waters 78. Danger on Dartmoor 80, etc.

Eagels, Jeanne (1894–1929).
American leading lady of the 20s; her private life was highly publicized and Kim Novak played her in a 1957 biopic.
Biography: 1930, *The Rain Girl* by Edward Doherty.
■ The World and the Woman 16. Fires of Youth 17. Under False Colours 17. The Cross Bearer 18. Man, Woman and Sin 27. The Letter (AAN) 29. Jealousy 29.

Earle, Merie (1889–1984).
American character actress who began her career in her mid-70s.
Cat Ballou 65. Fitzwilly 67. Gaily, Gaily 69. Norwood 70. Crazy Mama 75. Fatso 80. Going Ape! 81, etc.
TV series: The Jerry Reed When You're Hot You're Hot Hour 72. The Waltons 73–79.

Earles, Harry (1902–1985).
German-American midget who appeared in *The Unholy Three* 25 and 30, Baby Mine 26, Do It Again 27, *Freaks* 32, *The Wizard of Oz* 39.

Earp, Wyatt (1848–1929).
American frontier marshal, the most famous lawman of the wild west. Screen impersonations of him include Walter Huston in *Law and Order* 31, George O'Brien in *Frontier Marshal* 35, Randolph Scott in *Frontier Marshal* 39, Richard Dix in *Tombstone* 42, Henry Fonda in *My Darling Clementine* 46, Joel McCrea in *Wichita* 55, Burt Lancaster in *Gunfight at the OK Corral* 57, James Stewart in *Cheyenne Autumn* 64, James Garner in *Hour of the Gun* 67, Harris Yulin in *Doc* 70, Kurt Russell in *Tombstone* 94, Kevin Costner in *Wyatt Earp* 94. There was also a long-running TV series starring Hugh O'Brian.
Biography: 1997, *Wyatt Earp: The Life behind the Legend* by Casey Tefertiller.
❝ Suppose, suppose . . . – *W.E.'s last words*

Easdale, Brian (1909–1995).
English composer, associated with the films of Michael Powell and Emeric Pressburger. He studied at the Royal College of Music and began working on documentary films. After the failure of Powell's *Peeping Tom*, he wrote little for the screen. In the 90s, shortly before his death, his *Red Shoes Suite* was performed to acclaim.
GPO Film Unit shorts 34–38. Ferry Pilot 42. Black Narcissus 46. The Red Shoes (AA) 48. Gone to Earth 50. An Outcast of the Islands 51. The Battle of the River Plate 56. Peeping Tom 60, etc.

Eason, B. Reeves (1886–1956).
American action director, mostly of second features.
SELECTED SILENT FILMS: Moon Rider 20. *Ben Hur* (chariot race) 26.
■ SOUND FILMS: The Lariat Kid 29. Winged Horseman 29. Troopers Three 30. The Roaring Ranch 30. Trigger Tricks 30. Spurs 30. The Galloping Ghost 31. The Sunset Trail 32. Honor of the Press 32. The Heart Punch 32. Cornered 33. Behind Jury Doors 33. Alimony Madness 33. Revenge at Monte Carlo 33. Her Resale Value 33. Dance Hall Hostess 33. Red River Valley 36. Land Beyond the Law 37. Empty Holsters 37. Prairie Thunder 37. Sergeant Murphy 38. The Kid Comes Back 38. Daredevil Drivers 38. Call of the Yukon 38. Blue Montana Skies 39. Mountain Rhythm 39. Men with Steel Faces 40. Murder in the Big House 42. Spy Ship 42. Truck Busters 43. Rimfire 49.
Also directed action scenes in major films, notably *The Charge of the Light Brigade* 36.

Eastman, Carole.
American screenwriter, a former dancer, who also used the pseudonym of Adrien Joyce. Born in Los Angeles, she became friendly with actor Jack NICHOLSON, for whom she wrote four films, when they attended the same acting classes. She stopped writing for a time after the failure of *The Fortune*; *Man Trouble* was originally written in the early 70s and gained a reputation as one of the best unproduced scripts in Hollywood – it, too, received a poor critical and commercial reception.
■ The Shooting 66. The Model Shop 69. Puzzle of a Downfall Child 70. Five Easy Pieces (AAN) 70. The Fortune 75. Man Trouble (& p) 92.

Eastman, George (1854–1932).
American pioneer of cinematography: invented the roll film, which made him a millionaire.

Eastwood, Clint (1930–).
American leading man who after TV success made his big screen name in Italian westerns, then returned to Hollywood and became one of the big action stars of the late 60s. From the 70s he also began to produce and direct. Married television reporter Dina Ruiz in 1996.
Biographies: 1977, *Clint Eastwood, the Man behind the Myth* by Patrick Agan. 1983, *Clint Eastwood* by Gerald Cole and Peter Williams. 1992, *Clint Eastwood: Sexual Cowboy* by Douglas Thompson. Book: 1993, *Clint Eastwood, A Cultural Production* by Paul Smith.
Revenge of the Creature 55. Francis in the Navy 55. Lady Godiva 55. Tarantula 55. Never Say Goodbye 56. The First Travelling Saleslady 56. Star in the Dust 56. Escapade in Japan 57. Ambush at Cimarron Pass 58. Lafayette Escadrille 58. *A Fistful of Dollars* 64. *For a Few Dollars More* 65. *The Good the Bad and the Ugly* 66. The Witches 67. Hang 'em High 68. *Coogan's Bluff* 68. Where Eagles Dare 69. Paint Your Wagon 69. Kelly's Heroes 70. Two Mules for Sister Sara 70. The Beguiled 71. *Play Misty for Me* (& d) 71. *Dirty Harry* 71. Joe Kidd 72. Breezy (d only) 73. High Plains Drifter (& d) 73. Magnum Force 73. Thunderbolt and Lightfoot 74. The Eiger Sanction (& d) 75. The Outlaw Josey Wales (& d) 76. The Enforcer 76. The Gauntlet (& d) 77. Every Which Way but Loose 78. Escape from Alcatraz 79. Any Which Way You Can 80. Bronco Billy (& d) 80. Firefox 82. Honky Tonk Man 82. Sudden Impact 83. Tightrope 84. City Heat 84. Pale Rider 85. Heartbreak Ridge (& d) 86. Bird (p, d) 88. The Dead Pool (& p) 88. Thelonius Monk: Straight No Chaser (p) 88. Pink Cadillac 89. The Rookie (& d) 90. White Hunter, Black Heart (& p, d) 90. *Unforgiven* (& p, d) (AAp, d, AANa) 92. In the Line of Fire 93. A Perfect World (& d) 93. The Bridges of Madison County (a, d) 95. Absolute Power (a, p, d) 97. Absolute Power (a, p, d) 97. Midnight in the Garden of Good and Evil (p, d) 97, etc.
TV series: *Rawhide* 58–65.
✪ For being the cynical tough guy the 70s seemed to want. *Dirty Harry*.
❝ I like to play the line and not wander too far to either side. If a guy has just had a bad day in the mines and wants to see a good shoot-'em-up, that's great. – *C.E.*
My involvement goes deeper than acting or directing. I love every aspect of the creation of motion pictures and I guess I'm committed to it for life. – *C.E.*
Whatever success I've had is due to a lot of instinct and a little luck. – *C.E.*
I've always had the ability to say to the audience, watch this if you like, and if you don't, take a hike. – *C.E.*
I try to approach film intellectually – how it moves me. If you start below the intellectual level, I think you're starting without the nucleus. – *C.E.*
I always cry when I watch myself on screen. – *C.E.*
I've actually had people come up to me and ask me to autograph their guns. – *C.E.*
I've never worked with a guy who was less conscious of his good image. – *Don Siegel of C.E.*

Eaton, Mary (1901–1948).
American leading lady whose brief teaming with Ziegfeld and the Marx Brothers makes her career a footnote at least to film history.
■ His Children's Children 23. Broadway after Dark 24. *Glorifying the American Girl* 29. *The Coconuts* 29.

Eaton, Shirley (1936–).
Pneumatic blonde British leading lady.
Doctor at Large 56. Sailor Beware 57. Carry on Sergeant 58. Carry on Nurse 59. What a Carve Up 62. The Girl Hunters 63. Goldfinger 64. Rhino 65. Ten Little Indians 65. Around the World Under the Sea 66. Eight on the Lam 67. Sumuru 68, many others.

Eatwell, Brian (1939–).
British art director and production designer.
Just Like a Woman 66. Here We Go round the Mulberry Bush 67. The Strange Affair 68. Walkabout (Aus.) 70. *The Abominable Dr Phibes* 71. Dr Phibes Rises Again 72. Godspell (US) 73. The Three Musketeers 73. The Four Musketeers 74. The Man Who Fell to Earth 76. Sgt Pepper's Lonely Hearts Club Band (US) 78. Butch and Sundance: The Early Days (US) 79. White Dog (US) 82. Exposed (US) 83. American Dreamer (US) 84. Morons from Outer Space 85. Wired (US) 89, etc.

Eberhardt, Thom.
American director.
Sole Survivor 84. Night of the Comet 84. Without a Clue 88. Gross Anatomy 89. Captain Ron 92.

Eberhart, Mignon G. (1899–1996).
American detective novelist, several of whose works were filmed.
The White Cockatoo 35. While the Patient Slept 35. Murder by an Aristocrat 36. The Murder of Dr Harrigan 36. The Great Hospital Mystery 37. The Dark Stairway 38. Mystery House 38. The Patient in Room 18 38. Three's a Crowd 45, etc.

Ebsen, Buddy (1908–) (Christian Rudolf Ebsen).
American actor-dancer of the 30s, usually in 'countrified' parts; later emerged as a character actor and achieved his greatest success in a long-running TV series.
Autobiography: 1993, *The Other Side of Oz*.
Broadway Melody 1936. Captain January 36. Born to Dance 36. Banjo on My Knee 36. The Girl of the Golden West 38. Four Girls in White 39. Parachute Battalion 41. Sing Your Worries Away 42. Thunder in God's Country 51. Night People 54. Red Garters 54. Davy Crockett 55. Attack 56. Breakfast at Tiffany's 61. The Interns 62. Mail Order Bride 64. The One and Only Genuine Original Family Band 68. The Daughters of Joshua Cabe (TV) 72. Horror at 37,000 Feet (TV) 72. The President's Plane is Missing (TV) 74. Smash-up on Interstate Five (TV) 77. Leave Yesterday Behind (TV) 78. The Bastard (TV) 78. *The Critical List* (TV) 81. The Return of the Beverly Hillbillies (TV) 81. The Beverly Hillbillies 93. That's Entertainment! III 94, etc.
TV series: Northwest Passage 57. *The Beverly Hillbillies* 62–70. Barnaby Jones 72–80. Matt Houston 85.
~ Ebsen was to have played the Tin Man in *The Wizard of Oz*, but was badly affected by the aluminium dust in the make-up.

Eburne, Maude (1875–1960).
Diminutive American character actress who usually played frowning matrons and nosey neighbours.
The Bat Whispers 30. The Guardsman 31. The Vampire Bat 33. Lazy River 34. *Ruggles of Red Gap* 35. Champagne Waltz 37. Meet Doctor Christian 39. West Point Widow 41. Bowery to Broadway 44. The Suspect 45. Mother Wore Tights 47. Arson Inc. 50, many others.

Eccleston, Christopher (c. 1964–).
British leading actor. Born in Salford, he studied at the Central School of Speech and Drama.
Let Him Have It 91. Anchoress 93. *Shallow Grave* (as David Stephen) 94. Jude 96. A Price above Rubies 98. Elizabeth 98. Heart 98, etc.
TV series: Cracker 93–94. Hearts and Minds 95. Our Friends in the North 96.
❝ The last of a dying breed within British acting: the committed working-class thirtysomething raised on a strain of homegrown, indigenous drama that is fast fading out. – *Xan Brooks*

Echevarria, Nicolas (1947–).
Mexican director and composer. Born in Tepic, he studied film in New York in the early 70s, and began by making documentaries.
Poetas Campesinos (doc) 80. Nino Fidencio, el Taumaturgo de Espinazo (doc) 81. Cabeza de Vaca 90, etc.

Eck, Johnnie (1909–1991).
American actor, born with a body that ended at the waist, and one of the stars of Tod Browning's *Freaks* 32. He also appeared in *Tarzan, the Ape Man* 32.

Ecoffey, Jean-Philippe.
French leading actor.
L'Effrontée 85. No Man's Land (Swiss) 85. Nanou 87. L'Enfant de L'Hiver 88. The Possessed/Les Possedés 88. La Femme de Rose Hill 89. Henry and June (US) 90. Mina Tannenbaum 93. Sandra, C'est la Vie 94. Fiesta 95. L'Appartement 96, etc.

Eddy, Helen Jerome (1897–1990).
American character actress who retired early. Always in high class films.
Rebecca of Sunnybrook Farm 16. The March Hare 21. The Country Kid 23. The Dark Angel 25. Camille 27. The Divine Lady 29. Skippy 31. Mata Hari 31. Madame Butterfly 32. The Bitter Tea of General Yen 33. Riptide 34. Keeper of the Bees 35. Stowaway 36. Winterset 36. The Garden of Allah 36. Outside the Law 38. Strike Up the Band 40, many others.

Eddy, Nelson (1901–1967).
Romantic American actor-singer with opera background; famous on screen for series of operettas with Jeanette MacDonald.
■ Broadway to Hollywood 31. Dancing Lady 33. Student Tour 34. *Naughty Marietta* 35. *Rose Marie*

36. *Maytime* 37. Rosalie 37. The Girl of the Golden West 38. *Sweethearts* 38. Let Freedom Ring 39. Balalaika 39. *New Moon* 40. Bitter Sweet 40. The Chocolate Soldier 41. I Married an Angel 43. Phantom of the Opera 43. Knickerbocker Holiday 44. Make Mine Music (voice only) 46. Northwest Outpost 47.

~Eddy and MacDonald were rudely known in some quarters as The Singing Capon and The Iron Butterfly.

Edel, Uli (1947–) (Ulrich Edel).
German director.
The Little Soldier 70. Tommi Kehrt Zurúck 72. Oisthalter 75. Christiane F. 81. *Last Exit to Brooklyn* 89. Body of Evidence 92. Tyson (TV) 95. Rasputin (TV) 96, etc.

Edelman, Herb (1930–1996).
Bald, lanky American character actor, usually in comic roles.
In Like Flint 67. Barefoot in the Park 67. The Odd Couple 68. The Front Page 74. The Yakuza 75. Charge of the Model-Ts 77. Smorgasbord 83, etc.
TV series: The Good Guys 68–70. Ladies' Man 80–81. Strike Force 81–82. 9 to 5 82–83.

Edelman, Louis F. (1901–1976).
American producer.
Once upon a Time 44. White Heat 48. I'll See You in My Dreams 52, etc.
TV series include *Wyatt Earp* and *The Big Valley*.

Edelman, Randy (1947–).
American composer.
Outside In 72. Executive Action 73. Feds 88. Twins 88. Troop Beverly Hills 89. Ghostbusters II 89. Quick Change 90. Come See the Paradise 90. V.I. Warshawski 92. Shout 92. Drop Dead Fred 92. Dragon: The Bruce Lee Story 93. Gettysburg 93. Beethoven's 2nd 93. Angels in the Outfield (p) 94. The Mask 94. Billy Madison 95. While You Were Sleeping 95. The Indian in the Cupboard 95. Down Periscope 96. Diabolique 96. The Quest 96. Dragonheart 96. Anaconda 96. Daylight 96. Leave It to Beaver 97. Gone Fishin' 97. For Richer or Poorer 97. Six Days, Seven Night 97, etc.

Eden, Barbara (1934–) (Barbara Huffman).
American leading lady, former chorine.
Back from Eternity 56. Twelve Hours to Kill 60. Flaming Star 60. Voyage to the Bottom of the Sea 61. Five Weeks in a Balloon 62. The Wonderful World of the Brothers Grimm 63. The Brass Bottle 64. Seven Faces of Dr Lao 64. The Feminist and the Fuzz (TV) 71. The Woman Hunter (TV) 72. A Howling in the Woods (TV) 72. The Amazing Dobermans 76. Harper Valley PTA 78. Chattanooga Choo Choo 84. The Stepford Children (TV) 87. Her Wicked Ways (TV) 90, etc.
TV series: How to Marry a Millionaire 58. I Dream of Jeannie 65–70. Harper Valley PTA 81.

Edens, Roger (1905–1970).
American musical supervisor who moulded many MGM musicals, often as associate to producer Arthur Freed. Academy Awards for Easter Parade 48. On the Town 49. Annie Get Your Gun 50. Produced Deep in My Heart 55. Funny Face 56. Hello Dolly 69, etc.

Edeson, Arthur (1891–1970).
American cinematographer.
Wild and Woolly 17. *Robin Hood* 23. *The Thief of Baghdad* 24. *The Lost World* 25. The Bat 26. The Patent Leather Kid 27. In Old Arizona 28. *All Quiet on the Western Front* 30. *Frankenstein* 31. The Old Dark House 32. *The Invisible Man* 33. Mutiny on the Bounty 35. They Won't Forget 37. Each Dawn I Die 39. They Drive by Night 40. Sergeant York 41. *The Maltese Falcon* 41. *Casablanca* 42. Thank Your Lucky Stars 43. The Mask of Dimitrios 44. The Fighting O'Flynn 48, many others.

Edgar, Marriott (1880–1951).
British comedy scenarist, in films from 1935. Worked on many of the best vehicles of Will Hay and the Crazy Gang.
Good Morning Boys 36. Oh Mr Porter 38. Alf's Button Afloat 38. The Frozen Limits 39. The Ghost Train 41, many others; later on children's films. Also author of the 'Sam Small' and 'Albert' monologues made famous by Stanley Holloway.

Edgren, Gustav (1895–1954).
Swedish director, a former journalist; his early silent films tended towards slapstick comedy, while his later work dealt more with social problems.
Skeppargatan 25. The Ghost Baron 27. Tired Teodor 31. People of Värmland 32. Karl Fredrik Reigns 34. *Walpurgis Night* 35. *Katrin* 43. If Dew Falls Rain Follows (& co-w) 46, etc.

Edison, Thomas Alva (1847–1931).
American inventor of the phonograph and the incandescent lamp, among over a thousand other devices including the kinetoscope (a combined movie camera and projector), edge perforations and 35 mm gauge.
Biopics: *Young Tom Edison* 39 with Mickey Rooney; *Edison the Man* 40 with Spencer Tracy.

Edouart, Farciot (1895–1980).
American special effects man, with Paramount for many years.
Alice in Wonderland 33. Lives of a Bengal Lancer 35. Sullivan's Travels 41. Reap the Wild Wind 42. Unconquered 47. Ace in the Hole 51. The Mountain 56, many others.

Edwards, Anthony (1962–).
American leading actor. Born in Santa Barbara, California, he studied at the University of Southern California.
Fast Times at Ridgemont High 82. Heart Like a Wheel 82. Revenge of the Nerds 84. Gotcha! 85. The Sure Thing 85. Top Gun 86. Revenge of the Nerds II 87. Summer Heat 87. Mr North 88. Miracle Mile 89. How I Got into College 89. Hawks 89. Downtown 90. Landslide 92. Pet Sematary II 92. The Client 94. In Cold Blood (TV) 96. Don't Go Breaking My Heart 98. Playing by Heart 98, etc.
TV series: It Takes Two 82–83. Northern Exposure 92–93. ER 94– .

Edwards, Blake (1922–) (William Blake McEdwards).
American writer-producer-director with a leaning for all kinds of comedy. Married to Julie Andrews, who now appears mainly in his films, not always to her own advantage.
■ Panhandle (a, w) 47. All Ashore (w) 53. Cruising down the River (w) 53. Drive a Crooked Road (w) 54. Sound Off (w) 54. Bring Your Smile Along (wd) 55. My Sister Eileen (w) 55. He Laughed Last (wd) 55. Mr Cory (wd) 56. Operation Mad Ball (w) 57. This Happy Feeling (wd) 58. The Perfect Furlough (wd) 58. Operation Petticoat (d) 59. High Time (d) 60. Breakfast at Tiffany's (d) 61. Experiment in Terror (d) 62. Notorious Landlady (w) 62. *Days of Wine and Roses* (d) 62. The Pink Panther (wd) 63. A Shot in the Dark (wd, p) 64. *The Great Race* (wd, p) 64. Soldier in the Rain (w) 64. What Did You Do in the War, Daddy? (wd, p) 66. Waterhole 3 (p) 67. Gunn (d, p) 67. The Party (wd, p) 68. Darling Lili (wd, p) 69. Wild Rovers (wd, p) 71. The Carey Treatment (wd, p) 72. The Tamarind Seed (wd) 74. The Return of the Pink Panther (wd, p) 74. The Pink Panther Strikes Again (wd, p) 76. Revenge of the Pink Panther (wd, p) 78. '10' (wd, p) 79. S.O.B. (wd, p) 81. Trail of the Pink Panther (wd, p) 82. Victor/Victoria (wd, p) (AANw) 82. Curse of the Pink Panther (wd, p) 83. The Man Who Loved Women (wd) 83. Micki and Maude (d) 84. A Fine Mess (d) 86. That's Life! (d) 87. Blind Date (d) 87. Sunset (wd) 88. Skin Deep (wd) 89. Switch (wd) 91. Son of the Pink Panther (wd) 93.
TV series: Richard Diamond. Dante. Peter Gunn (all as creator).
❝ Make 'em redecorate your office. That's primary, to let them know where you stand. Then, when you're shooting interior sequences, use your own interior decorator and set dresser. That way, everything on the set will fit your house when you're finished. – *B.E.*

Edwards, Cliff (1895–1971).
Diminutive American entertainer known as 'Ukelele Ike'. Born in Hannibal, Missouri, he played Charles STARRETT's sidekick in many westerns. A recording star in the 20s, he is best known for providing the voice of Jiminy Cricket in Disney's *Pinocchio*.
Hollywood Revue 29. Parlour Bedroom and Bath 31. Hell Divers 31. Flying Devils 33. Red Salute 35. Bad Guy 39. Pinocchio 40. The Monster and the Girl 41. The Falcon Strikes Back 43. She Couldn't Say No 45. The Avenging Rider 53, many others.

Edwards, Henry (1882–1952).
Gentlemanly British romantic lead of the 20s; later directed some films and came back to acting as amiable elderly man.
Broken Threads 18. The Amazing Quest of Ernest Bliss 22. A Lunatic at Large 23. *The Flag Lieutenant* 26. Fear 27. Three Kings 28. Call of the Sea 31. The Flag Lieutenant (talkie) 31. The Barton Mystery (d) 32. General John Regan 33. Discord Driven (d) 33. Scrooge (d) 35. Juggernaut (d) 37. Spring Meeting (d) 41. Green for Danger 46. Oliver Twist 48. London Belongs to Me 48. Madeleine 50. The Long Memory 52, many others.

Edwards, Hilton (1903–1982).
English stage actor, director and producer, in occasional films. With his partner Michael MACLIAMMOIR, he founded the influential Gate Theatre, devoted to international drama, in Dublin in 1928, and gave Orson Welles his first engagement there as an actor in 1931.
Biography: 1994, *The Boys* by Christopher Fitz-Simon.
Return to Glennascaul (AAN, wd, short) 51. Othello 52. Cat & Mouse 58. She Didn't Say No 58. This Other Eden 59. A Terrible Beauty 60. Victim 61. The Quare Fellow 62. The Wrong Box 66, etc.

Edwards, J. Gordon (1867–1925).
American director of silent epics, especially for Theda Bara.
Anna Karenina 15. Under Two Flags 16. Cleopatra 17. Salome 18. The Queen of Sheba 21. Nero 22. The Shepherd King 23, many others.

Edwards, James (1922–1970).
American actor, on stage from 1945.
The Set-Up 49. *Home of the Brave* 49. The Member of the Wedding 52. The Caine Mutiny 54. The Phenix City Story 55. Men in War 57. The Sandpiper 65, etc.

Edwards, Jimmy (1920–1988).
Moustachioed British comedian of stage, radio and TV.
Autobiography: 1953, *Take It from Me*.
Murder at the Windmill 48. Treasure Hunt 52. Three Men in a Boat 55. Bottoms Up 60. Nearly a Nasty Accident 61. Rhubarb 70, etc.
TV series: *Whack-O!* 56–60. Seven Faces of Jim 61. Six More Faces of Jim 62. More Faces of Jim 63. Bold as Brass 64. Mr John Jorrocks 66. Blandings Castle 67. The Fossett Saga 69. Sir Yellow 73. The Glums 79.

Edwards, Meredith (1917–1999).
Balding Welsh character actor with stage experience.
A Run for Your Money 50. The Blue Lamp 50. Girdle of Gold 53. The Cruel Sea 53. The Long Arm 56. The Trials of Oscar Wilde 60. Only Two Can Play 61. This Is My Street 64. The Great St Trinian's Train Robbery 66. Fame Is the Spur (TV) 82, etc.

Edwards, Penny (1928–1998) (Millicent Edwards).
American light leading lady of the 40s.
Let's Face It 43. That Hagen Girl 47. Two Guys from Texas 48. The Wild Blue Yonder 51. Street Bandits 52. Powder River 53. Lady Beware 87, etc.

Edwards, Percy (1908–1996).
English animal impersonator who could imitate 600 species and provided many bird and animal sounds for films. A former plough-maker, he began in music hall in the 20s and was best known for his Psyche the dog in the long-running BBC radio sitcom *A Life of Bliss* in the 50s and 60s. His film work was not always credited.
The Rise and Rise of Michael Rimmer (bird impersonations) 70. The Belstone Fox 73. Orca – Killer Whale (title role) 77. The Dark Crystal (the voice of Fizzgig) 82. The Plague Dogs 82. The Labyrinth (the voice of Ambrosius) 86, etc.
TV series: Pet Pals 65. Hilary (as a myna bird) 84.

Edwards, Vince (1928–1996) (Vincento Eduardo Zoino).
American leading man of the tough/sincere kind; also a singer and director of TV series.
Mr Universe 51. Hiawatha 52. The Killing 56. City of Fear 58. *Murder by Contract* 59. The Victors 63. The Devil's Brigade 68. Hammerhead 68. The Desperadoes 69. The Mad Bomber 72. The Power and the Passion (TV) 79. Space Raiders 83. Cellar Dweller 87. The Gumshoe Kid 89. The Fear 95, etc.
TV series: *Ben Casey* 61–66. Matt Lincoln 70–71.

Edzard, Christine (1945–).
British director of meticulously researched historical films.
Stories from a Flying Trunk 79. Biddy 83. *Little Dorrit* (AANw) 87. The Fool 90. As You Like It 92, etc.

Egan, Eddie (1930–1995).
Burly American policeman whose exploits were the basis of *The French Connection*. He subsequently left the force and played small parts in films.
TV series: Joe Forrester 75. Eischied 79.

Egan, Peter (1946–).
British TV leading man who has sporadically appeared on stage and in films.
The Hireling 73. Callan 74. Hennessy 75. Chariots of Fire 81. A Woman of Substance (TV) 84. A Perfect Spy (TV) 87. Bean 97, etc.
TV series: Lillie (as Oscar Wilde) 78. Prince Regent 79. Ever Decreasing Circles 85–88.

Egan, Richard (1921–1987).
Virile American leading man once thought likely successor to Clark Gable but who was mainly confined to westerns and action dramas.
The Damned Don't Cry 49. Undercover Girl 50. Split Second 52. Demetrius and the Gladiators 54. Wicked Woman 54. Gog 54. Underwater 55. Untamed 55. Violent Saturday 55. The View from Pompey's Head 55. Seven Cities of Gold 55. Love Me Tender 56. Tension at Table Rock 56. These Thousand Hills 58. A Summer Place 59. Pollyanna 60. Esther and the King 60. The 300 Spartans 62. The Destructors 66. Chubasco 68. The Big Cube 69. The Day of the Wolves (TV) 72. The Sweet Creek County War 79, etc.
TV series: Empire 62. Redigo 64.

Ege, Julie (1943–).
Decorative Norwegian leading lady in British films of the 70s.
Every Home Should Have One 70. Up Pompeii 70. Creatures the World Forgot 71. The Magnificent Seven Deadly Sins 71. Rentadick 72. The Garnett Saga 72. Not Now Darling 73. Craze 73. The Mutations 74, etc.

Eggar, Samantha (1939–).
British leading lady, in international films.
The Wild and the Willing 62. Dr Crippen 63. Doctor in Distress 63. Psyche 59 63. *The Collector* (AAN) 65. Return from the Ashes 65. Walk Don't Run 66. Doctor Dolittle 67. The Molly Maguires 69. The Walking Stick 69. The Lady in the Car 70. The Light at the Edge of the World 71. The Dead Are Alive 72. A Name for Evil 72. Double Indemnity (TV) 73. All the Kind Strangers (TV) 74. The Seven Per Cent Solution 76. The Killer Who Wouldn't Die (TV) 76. Why Shoot the Teacher? 77. The Uncanny 77. Welcome to Blood City 77. Ziegfeld: The Man and His Women (TV) 78. Hagen (TV pilot) 79. The Brood 79. The Exterminator 80. Demonoid 81. Hot Touch 82. For the Term of His Natural Life 85. Ragin' Cajun 90. Dark Horse 92. Round Numbers 92. A Case for Murder (TV) 93. Inevitable Grace 94. The Phantom 96, etc.
TV series: *Anna and the King* 72.

Eggby, David.
Australian cinematographer.
Mad Max 79. Kansas 88. The Salute of the Jugger 90. Quigley Down Under 90. Warlock 91. Harley Davidson and the Marlboro Man 91. The Paper 94. Dragonheart 96. Daylight 96, etc.

Eggleston, Colin.
Australian director of adventure and horror movies.
Long Weekend 79. Bellamy 80. Sky Pirates 86. Cassandra 87. Innocent Prey 88. The Wicked 89, etc.

Egoyan, Atom (1960–).
Armenian director and screenwriter, in Canada.
Next of Kin 85. Family Viewing 87. Speaking Parts 89. Montreal Sextet (co-d) 91. The Adjuster 91. Calendar 93. Exotica 94. Sweet Hereafter (AAN) 97, etc.
❝ The difference between a Hollywood film and what I do is this: in mainstream films, you're encouraged to forget that you're watching a movie, whereas in my films, you're always encouraged to remember that you're watching a collection of designed images. – *A.E.*

Ehle, Jennifer (c. 1970–).
Leading English actress, the daughter of Rosemary Harris and novelist John Ehle. Born in North Carolina, she studied at London's Central School of Speech and Drama.
The Camomile Lawn (TV) 91. Backbeat 93. Pride and Prejudice (TV) 95. Melissa (TV) 97. Paradise Road 97. Wilde 97. Bedrooms & Hallways 98. This Year's Love 99, etc.

Eichhorn, Lisa (1952–).
American actress who studied drama in Britain and works in both countries.
The Europeans 79. Yanks 79. Who Would I Lie? 80. Cutter's Way 81. The Weather in the Streets 83. Wildrose 84. Opposing Force 86. Grim Prairie Tales 90. Moon 44 90. The Vanishing 93. King of the Hill 93. A Modern Affair 95. First Kid 96. Spitfire Grill 96. Sticks and Stones 96. Judas Kiss 98, etc.

Eidelman, Cliff (1964–).
American composer and conductor.
Silent Night 88. To Die For 89. Triumph of the Spirit 89. Strike It Rich (co-w) 90. Crazy People 90. The Meteor Man 93. Untamed Heart 93. My Girl 2 94. Picture Bride 94. A Simple Twist of Fate 94. If These Walls Could Talk (TV) 96. The Beautician and the Beast 97. Free Willy 3: The Rescue 97. One True Thing 98, etc.

Eikenberry, Jill (1947–).
American leading lady of the early 80s.
The Deadliest Season (TV) 77. A Night Full of Rain 77. Butch and Sundance 79. Hide in Plain Sight 80. Arthur 81. Sessions 83. Manhattan Project 86. Cast the First Stone (TV) 89. Chantilly Lace (TV) 93. Parallel Lives (TV) 94. My Very Best Friend (TV) 97, etc.
TV series: Nurse 82. LA Law 86–94.

Eilbacher, Lisa (1947–).
American leading lady.
The War between Men and Women 72. Wheels (TV) 78. The Winds of War (TV) 83. Beverly Hills Cop 84. Monte Carlo (TV) 86. Leviathan 89. Living a Lie 91. Live Wire (TV) 92, etc.
TV series: The Texas Wheelers 74–75. The Hardy Boys Mysteries 77. Ryan's Four 83. Me and Mom 85.

Eilers, Sally (1908–1978).
Quiet-spoken American leading lady of the 30s. She was briefly married to cowboy star Hoot Gibson (1930–33).
The Goodbye Kiss 28. She Couldn't Say No 30. Quick Millions 31. The Black Camel 31. Over the Hill 31. State Fair 33. She Made Her Bed 34. Alias Mary Dow 34. Strike Me Pink 35. Talk of the Devil 36. Danger Patrol 37. Nurse from Brooklyn 38. They Made Her a Spy 39. Full Confession 39. I Was a Prisoner on Devil's Island 41. A Wave a WAC and a Marine 44. Coroner Creek 48. Stage to Tucson 50, many others.

Eisenmann, Ike (1962–).
American child actor of the 70s.
Escape to Witch Mountain 74. Banjo Hackett (TV) 76. Return from Witch Mountain 78. The Hound of Hell (TV) 79, etc.
TV series: Fantastic Journey 77.

Eisenstein, Sergei (1898–1948).
Russian director, one of the cinema giants.
Biographies: 1952, *Sergei Eisenstein* by Marie Seton; 1966, *Eisenstein* by Yon Barna; 1998, *Eisenstein: A Life in Conflict* by Ronald Bergan.
Books published include: 1942, *The Film Sense*. 1948, *Notes of a Film Director*. 1949, *Film Form*.
■ *Strike* 24. *The Battleship Potemkin* 25. *October*/Ten Days That Shook the World 27. *The General Line* 28. *Que Viva Mexico* (unfinished: sections later released under this title and as *Time in the Sun*) 32. *Alexander Nevsky* 38. *Ivan the Terrible* 42–46.
✪ For virtually inventing montage, and for using the grammar of film-making more vividly and purposefully than almost anyone else. *Alexander Nevsky*.

Eisinger, Jo.
American screenwriter.
The Spider 45. Gilda 46. The Sleeping City 50. Night and the City 51. The System 53. Bedevilled 55. The Poppy is Also a Flower/Danger Grows Wild 66. The Jigsaw Man 84, many others.

Eisler, Hanns (1898–1962).
Austrian composer, who also collaborated with Brecht on plays and songs. Born in Leipzig, he studied music in Vienna under Arnold Schoenberg and left Germany in 1933, moving to the United States in the late 30s to lecture, teach, and to work in Hollywood. He fell foul of the Un-American Activities Committee in the late 40s and was deported, going to live and work in East Germany, where he wrote that country's national anthem.
Book: 1947, *Composing for Films*.
Kuhle Wampe (Ger.) 32. Song of Heroes (USSR) 32. New Earth (Netherlands) 34. Le Grand Jeu (Fr.) 34. Our Russian Front (co-m) 41. Hangmen Also Die 43. None but the Lonely Heart 43. Jealousy 45. The Spanish Main 45. Deadline at Dawn 46. A Scandal in Paris/Thieves' Holiday 46. Monsieur Verdoux 47. The Woman on the Beach 47. So Well Remembered 47. Herr Puntila and His Servant Matti/Herr Puntila und Sein Knecht Matti (Aus.) 55. Night and Fog/Nuit et Brouillard (Fr.) 55. Les Arrivistes (Fr.) 60, many others.
❝ Once or twice a year I write a motion picture. It interests me and I need the money – *H.E.*
Hanns Eisler is the Karl Marx of Communism in the musical field. – *Robert E. Stripling, chief investigator of the Un-American Activities Committee*

Eisley, Anthony (1925–).
American general-purpose actor.
The Naked Kiss 64. Frankie and Johnny 65. Journey to the Centre of Time 67. Star! 68. Blood of Frankenstein 70. The Doll Squad 73. Secrets (TV) 77, etc.
TV series: Hawaiian Eye 59–73. Capitol 82–84.

Eisner, Lotte H. (1896–1983).
German film historian.
Most noted book: *The Haunted Screen*.

Eisner, Michael (1942–).
American production executive. He is chairman and chief executive officer of the Walt Disney Company.
Autobiography: 1998, *Work in Progress*.

Ekberg, Anita (1931–).
Statuesque Swedish blonde who decorated a number of films in various countries.
The Golden Blade 53. Blood Alley 55. Artists and Models 55. Back from Eternity 56. War and Peace 56. Zarak 56. Interpol 57. Sign of the Gladiator 58. La Dolce Vita 59. The Mongols 60. Boccaccio 70 61. Summer is Short (Sw.) 62. Il Comandante (It.) 63. Call Me Bwana 63. Four for Texas 63. The Alphabet Murders 65. Who Wants to Sleep/Das Liebeskarussel 65. Way Way Out 66. The Glass Sphinx 67. If It's Tuesday, This Must Be Belgium 69. The Divorcee 70. The Clowns 70. Fangs of the Living Dead 73. Gold of the Amazon Women (TV) 79, etc.

Ekk, Nikolai (1902–1976).
Russian director.
The Road to Life 31. The Nightingale 36. A Night in May 41, etc.

Ekland, Britt (1942–) (Britt-Marie Eklund).
Swedish leading lady in international films. She was formerly married to Peter Sellers.
Too Many Thieves (TV) 66. After the Fox 66. The Bobo 67. The Double Man 68. The Night They Raided Minsky's 68. Stiletto 69. Percy 71. Get Carter 71. A Time for Loving 71. Night Hair Child 71. Baxter 72. Endless Night 72. Asylum 72. The Wicker Man 73. The Man with the Golden Gun 73. Royal Flash 74. The Ultimate Thrill 74. Casanova 77. High Velocity 77. King Solomon's Treasure 77. The Great Wallendas (TV) 77. Ring of Passion (TV) 79. Satan's Mistress 82. Moon in Scorpio 88. Scandal 89. The Children 90, etc.
❝ The ideal man doesn't exist. A husband is easier to find. – *B.E.*
I said I don't sleep with married men, but what I meant was I don't sleep with happily married men. – *B.E.*

Ekman, Gosta (1890–1948).
Swedish leading actor.
Charles XII 24. Faust 26. Intermezzo 36, etc.

Elam, Jack (1916–).
Laconic, swarthy American character actor, often seen as western villain or sinister comic relief.
Rawhide 50. Kansas City Confidential 52. The Moonlighter 53. Vera Cruz 54. Moonfleet 55. Kiss Me Deadly 55. *Gunfight at the OK Corral* 57. Baby Face Nelson 57. Edge of Eternity 59. The Comancheros 61. The Rare Breed 66. The Way West 67. Firecreek 67. Once Upon a Time in the West 69. Support Your Local Sheriff 69. Rio Lobo 70. Support Your Local Gunfighter 71. A Knife for the Ladies 74. Creature from Black Lake 76. Grayeagle 77. Lacy and the Mississippi Queen (TV) 78. The Villain 79. The Sacketts (TV) 79. The Cannonball Run 80. Jinxed! 82. Cannonball Run II 83. The Aurora Encounter 86. Hawken's Breed 89. Big Bad John 90. Suburban Commando 91. The Giant of Thunder Mountain 91. Uninvited 93. Shadow Force 93. Bonanza: The Return (TV) 93. Bonanza: Under Attack (TV) 95, etc.
TV series: *The Dakotas* 62. Temple Houston 63. The Texas Wheelers 77. Struck by Lightning (as the Frankenstein monster) 79.

Eldredge, John (1917–1960).
Mild-looking American actor usually cast as weakling brother or bland schemer.
The Man with Two Faces 34. Persons in Hiding 38. Blossoms in the Dust 41. The French Key 47. Champagne for Caesar 50. Lonely Hearts Bandits 52. The First Travelling Saleslady 56, many others.

Eldridge, Florence (1901–1988) (Florence McKechnie).
Distinguished American stage actress, wife of Fredric March. Film appearances occasional.
Six Cylinder Love 23. The Studio Murder Mystery 29. The Matrimonial Bed 30. The Story of Temple Drake 33. Les Misérables 35. Mary of Scotland (as Elizabeth I) 36. *An Act of Murder* 48. *Another Part of the Forest* 48. Christopher Columbus 49. Inherit the Wind 60, etc.

Eldridge, John (1904–1961).
British documentary and feature director.
Waverley Steps 47. Three Dawns to Sydney 49. Brandy for the Parson 51. Laxdale Hall 53. Conflict of Wings 54, etc.

Eles, Sandor (1936–).
Hungarian leading man in Britain.
The Naked Edge 61. The Evil of Frankenstein 64. And Soon the Darkness 70. Countess Dracula 70. The Greek Tycoon 78, etc.

Elfand, Martin (1937–).
American producer.
Serpico 73. Dog Day Afternoon 75. It's My Turn 80. An Officer and a Gentleman 82. King David 85. Clara's Heart 86. A Talent for the Game 90, etc.

Elfman, Danny (1949–).
American musician, composer and singer with the rock band Oingo Boingo, who has scored the movies so far made by director Tim Burton. He also composed the theme music for the TV series *The Simpsons*.
Forbidden Zone 80. Pee-Wee's Big Adventure 85. Back to School 86. Wisdom 86. Summer School 87. Hot to Trot 88. Beetlejuice 88. Midnight Run 88. Big Top Pee-Wee 88. Scrooged 88. Batman 89. Nightbreed 90. Dick Tracy 90. Darkman 90. Edward Scissorhands 90. Article 99 92. Batman Returns 92. Sommersby 93. Tim Burton's The Nightmare before Christmas (& voice) 93. Black Beauty 94. To Die For 94. Dolores Claiborne 95. Dead Presidents 95. Freeway 96. The Frighteners 96. Mission: Impossible 96. Mars Attacks! 96. Extreme Measures 96. Mission: Impossible 96. *Men in Black* (AAN) 97. Flubber 97. *Good Will Hunting* (AAN) 97. A Simple Plan 98, etc.

Elg, Taina (1931–).
Finnish leading lady in international films.
The Prodigal 55. Diane 56. Gaby 56. Les Girls 57. Imitation General 57. Watusi 58. The Thirty-Nine Steps 59, etc.

Elias, Michael (1940–).
American director and screenwriter, a former actor and comedian. He worked in television as a writer and producer on such shows as *The Mary Tyler Moore Show*, *All in the Family*, and *Head of the Class*.
The Jerk (co-w) 79. The Frisco Kid (co-w) 79. Serial (co-w) 80. Young Doctors in Love (co-w) 82. Lush Life (wd) 93.

Eliot, T. S. (1888–1965).
American poet who lived mainly in England. His play *Murder in the Cathedral* was his only work adapted for the cinema. A biopic about his first unhappy marriage, *Tom and Viv*, was released in 1994, with Willem Dafoe and Miranda Richardson in the title roles.

Eliscu, Edward (1902–1998).
American lyricist and screenwriter, a former actor. Born in New York, he studied science at the City College and made his Broadway stage debut in 1924 before turning to lyric writing, collaborating with such composers as Vincent Youmans, Gus Kahn and Vernon Duke. In the early 30s he worked as a writer and dialogue director for RKO. From the 50s, when he was blacklisted, he concentrated on television and the stage.
Professional Sweetheart (s) 33. Diplomaniacs (s) 33. *Flying Down to Rio* (s) 33. Silk Hat Kid (co-w) 35. Music Is Magic (co-w) 35. Paddy O'Day (co-w, s) 35. Every Saturday Night (w) 36. High Tension (co-w) 36. Little Miss Nobody (co-w) 36. Little Tough Guys in Society (w) 38. His Exciting Night (w) 38. Sis Hopkins (co-w) 41. Something to Shout About (co-w) 43. The Heat's On (s) 43. Hey, Rookie (co-w, s) 44. The Gay Senorita (w) 45, etc.

Elizabeth I,
Queen of England (1533–1603), has been notably played by Sarah Bernhardt in *Queen Elizabeth* 12; by Flora Robson in *Fire Over England* 36 and *The Sea Hawk* 40; by Florence Eldridge in *Mary of Scotland* 36; by Bette Davis in *Elizabeth and Essex* 39 and *The Virgin Queen* 55; by Agnes Moorehead in *The Story of Mankind* 57; by Irene Worth in *Seven Seas to Calais* 63; by Catherine Lacey in *The Fighting Prince of Donegal* 65, and by Glenda Jackson in a 1971 TV series followed by *Mary Queen of Scots* 72; Jean Simmons played the young queen in *Young Bess* 53; Jean Kent had the role in the TV series *Sir Francis Drake*; Quentin Crisp played it in *Orlando* 92; Cate Blanchett played her as a far from virginal queen in *Elizabeth* 98.

Elizondo, Hector (1936–).
American character actor, mainly on stage.
Pocket Money 71, Stand Up and Be Counted 72. The Taking of Pelham One Two Three 74. Report to the Commissioner 75. Thieves 77. Cuba 79. American Gigolo 80. The Fan 81. Young Doctors in Love 82. The Flamingo Kid 84. Courage (TV) 86. Nothing in Common 86. Leviathan 89. Frankie and Johnny 91. Necessary Roughness 91. Lunatics: A Love Story 91. Final Approach 92. There Goes the Neighborhood/Paydirt 92. Samantha 92. Being Human 94. Exit to Eden 94. Beverly Hills Cop III 94. Getting Even with Dad 94. Dear God 96. Turbulence 96, etc.
TV series: Freebie and the Bean 80. Casablanca 83. The Flamingo Kid/Pablo 84. Private Resort 85. Nothing in Common 86. Chicago Hope 94.

Ellenshaw, Peter (c. 1914–).
British special effects artist and production designer, with Disney from 1950.
Things to Come 36. Victoria the Great 37. The Drum 38. A Matter of Life and Death 45. The Red Shoes 48. Treasure Island 50. *20,000 Leagues Under the Sea* 54. Johnny Tremain 57. Darby O'Gill and the Little People 59. In Search of the Castaways 61. *Mary Poppins* 64. The Island at the Top of the World 74. *The Black Hole* 79, etc.

Ellington, Duke (1899–1974) (Edward Kennedy Ellington).
Celebrated American jazz bandleader, composer and pianist.
Hit Parade 37. New Faces 37. Reveille with

Beverly 43. Anatomy of a Murder 59. Paris Blues 61. Change of Mind (m only) 69, etc.

Elliot, Laura (1929–).
American supporting actress.
Special Agent 49. Paid in Full 50. *Strangers on a Train* 51. When Worlds Collide 52. Jamaica Run 53. About Mrs Leslie 54, etc.

Elliott, Alison (1969–).
American actress. Raised in San Francisco, she worked as a model until gaining a role in the TV sitcom *Living Dolls*.
Wyatt Earp 94. Monkey Trouble 94. The Underneath 95. The Buccaneers (TV) 95. The Spitfire Grill 97, etc.
TV series: Living Dolls 89.

Elliott, Denholm (1922–1992).
Incisive British actor of stage, screen and television, often of well-mannered, ineffectual types, latterly in more sophisticated roles. He trained briefly at RADA, then began acting in a German POW camp during the Second World War. The first of his two wives was actress Virginia McKenna (1954–57). Died of AIDS.
Biography; 1994, *Denholm Elliott – Quest for Love* by Susan Elliott with Barry Turner.
Dear Mr Prohack 49. The Sound Barrier 52. The Cruel Sea 53. The Heart of the Matter 53. They Who Dare 54. The Night My Number Came Up 55. Pacific Destiny 56. Scent of Mystery/Holiday in Spain 59. Station Six Sahara 63. *Nothing But the Best* 64. The High Bright Sun 65. You Must Be Joking 65. King Rat 65. Alfie 66. The Spy with a Cold Nose 67. Maroc 7 67. *Here We Go Round the Mulberry Bush* 67. The Night They Raided Minsky's 68. Too Late the Hero 69. The Rise and Rise of Michael Rimmer 70. Percy 70. Quest for Love 71. A Doll's House 73. Madame Sin 73. The Apprenticeship of Duddy Kravitz 75. Robin and Marian 75. Russian Roulette 76. A Bridge Too Far 77. The Boys from Brazil 78. Saint Jack 79. Cuba 79. Bad Timing 80. Sunday Lovers 80. Raiders of the Lost Ark 81. The Missionary 82. Brimstone and Treacle 82. Trading Places 83. The Razor's Edge 84. A Private Function (BFA) 84. A Room With a View (AAN) 85. Defence of the Realm (BFA) 85. Maurice 87. The Happy Valley (TV) 87. September 87. The Bourne Identity (TV) 88. Stealing Heaven 88. Indiana Jones and the Last Crusade 89. Killing Dad 89. Return to the River Kwai 89. Toy Soldiers 91. Scorchers 91. Noises Off 92, etc.
❝ I like actors – such as Margaret Rutherford and Peter Lorre – who aren't afraid to over-act like real people. When I take a job I can always come up with ten different ways of doing the part. But I'll always choose the flashiest one. You've got to dress the window a bit. – *D.E.*
He has a manner which suggests that he is about to preside with great dignity at a court martial, yet also to be cashiered in cringing disgrace at one and the same time, and that either pose is for him a matter both of raging disgust and total indifference. – *Dennis Potter*

Elliott, Robert (1879–1951).
Irish leading man of American silents.
Spirit of Lafayette 17. Resurrection 18. A Woman There Was 19. A Virgin Paradise 21. Man and Wife 23. Romance of the Underworld 28. Thunderbolt 29. The Divorcee 30. Five Star Final 31. Phantom of Crestwood 32. Crime of the Century 33. Girl of the Limberlost 34. Circumstantial Evidence 35. Trade Winds 38. Gone with the Wind 39. Captain Tugboat Annie 45, many others.

Elliott, Sam (1944–).
American leading man of the 70s.
■ The Games 70. Frogs 72. Molly and Lawless John 72. The Blue Knight (TV) 73. I Will Fight No More Forever (TV) 75. Evel Knievel (TV) 75. Lifeguard 76. Once an Eagle (TV) 77. The Last Convertible (TV) 79. Aspen (TV) 79. The Sacketts (TV) 79. The Legacy 79. Wild Times (TV) 80. Murder in Texas (TV) 81. The Shadow Riders (TV) 82. Travis McGee (TV) 82. Mask 85. Fatal Beauty 87. Shakedown/Blue Jean Cop 88. Prancer 89. Road House 89. Sibling Rivalry 90. Rush 91. Gettysburg 93. Tombstone 94. The Desperate Trail (TV) 94. Woman Undone 94. Hole in the Sky (TV) 95. Buffalo Girls (TV) 95. Blue River (TV) 95. The Final Cut 96. Rough Riders (TV) 97. Dogwatch (TV) 97. The Big Lebowksi 97. The Hi-Lo Country 98.

Elliott, Stephan (1964–).
Australian director and screenwriter.
Frauds 93. *The Adventures of Priscilla, Queen of the Desert* 94. Welcome to Woop Woop 97, etc.

Elliott, Ted.
American scriptwriter, usually in collaboration with Terry Rossio.
Little Monsters 89. Aladdin (& co-d) 92. Puppet Masters 94. Godzilla (story) 98. Small Soldiers 98. The Mask of Zorro (story) 98. Antz (story consultant) 98, etc.

Elliott, 'Wild Bill' (1904–1965) (Gordon Elliott).
Burly American leading man of the 20s who later appeared in many second feature westerns and mysteries.
The Private Life of Helen of Troy 27. Broadway Scandals 28. The Great Divide 31. Wonder Bar 34. False Evidence 40. Blue Clay 42. The Plainsman and the Lady 46. The Fabulous Texan 48. Hellfire 49. The Longhorn 51. Dial Red O 55. Chain of Evidence 57, etc.

Ellis, Don (1933–1978).
American composer, former jazz trumpeter.
Moon Zero Two 69. The French Connection 71. The Seven Ups 73. French Connection II 75. Ruby 77, etc.

Ellis, Edward (1872–1952).
American stage character actor who made a number of films in the 30s, usually as stern father or judge.
I Am a Fugitive from a Chain Gang 32. From Headquarters 33. The President Vanishes 34. The Return of Peter Grimm 35. Fury 36. Maid of Salem 37. *A Man to Remember* 38. Three Sons 39. A Man Betrayed 41. The Omaha Trail 42, etc.

Ellis, Mary (1900–) (Mary Elsas).
American leading lady and singer famous in British stage musicals, especially those of Ivor Novello.
Bella Donna 34. Paris Love Song 35. All the King's Horses 35. Glamorous Night 36. The Three Worlds of Gulliver 61, etc.

Ellis, Patricia (1916–1970) (Patricia Gene O'Brien).
American leading lady of the 30s.
Three on a Match 32. 42nd Street 33. Picture Snatcher 33. The St Louis Kid 34. The Case of the Lucky Legs 34. Boulder Dam 36. Melody for Two 37. Blockheads 38. Back Door to Heaven 39. Fugitive at Large 39, etc.

Ellis, Robert (1892–1974) (Robert Ellis Reel).
American leading actor, director of silents, and screenwriter. Born in Brooklyn, he worked in musical comedy and as a stuntman before entering films in 1913, working as an actor-director, and then acting in early talkies. In the mid-30s, he switched to screenwriting at Twentieth Century-Fox. Married actresses May ALLISON and Vera Reynolds, and screenwriter Helen Logan, with whom he wrote thrillers and musicals.
A Modern Jekyll and Hyde 13. The Apaches of Paris (& d) 15. Almost a Heroine (& d) 16. The Lurking Peril (& d) 16. The Lifted Veil 17. Louisiana 19. The Daughter Pays (& d) 20. Handcuffs or Kisses 21. A Divorce of Convenience (d only) 21. Chivalrous Charley (d only) 21. Anna Ascends 22. Wild Honey 22. Mark of the Beast 23. For Sale 24. Lady Robinhood 25. Ragtime 27. Restless Youth 28. Night Parade 29. The Deadline 31. The Good Bad Girl 31. The Fighting Fool 32. Reform Girl 33. A Girl of the Limberlost 34. Madame Spy 34, many others.
AS WRITER, IN COLLABORATION WITH HELEN LOGAN: Charlie Chan in Egypt 35. Charlie Chan in Shanghai 35. Charlie Chan's Secret 36. Charlie Chan at the Race Track 36. Charlie Chan on Broadway 37. Charlie Chan in the City of Darkness 39. Tin Pan Alley 40. Sun Valley Serenade 41. Iceland 42. Song of the Islands 42. Hello Frisco Hello 43. Pin Up Girl 44. Four Jills in a Jeep 44. Something for the Boys 44. Do You Love Me? 46. I'll Get By (story) 50, etc.

Ellis, Robert (1933–1973).
American actor who began in films at the age of five; he was known as Bobby Ellis in his juvenile roles. Died of kidney failure.
April Showers 48. The Green Promise 49. Walk Softly, Stranger 50. Call Me Mister 51. Retreat Hell! 52. The McConnell Story 55. Space Master X-7 58. Gidget 59, many others.
TV series: Meet Corliss Archer 51–52, 54–55. The Aldrich Family 52–53.

Ellis, Ruth (1927–1955).
The last woman to be hanged for murder in Britain has been the subject of two films: *Yield to the Night/Blonde Sinner* 56, starring Diana Dors, and *Dance with a Stranger* 85, starring Miranda Richardson.

Ellis, Vivian (1904–1996).
English composer and lyricist, a former concert pianist, who began writing for theatrical revues in 1922. 'Spread a Little Happiness' and 'This Is My Lovely Day' are his best-known songs, but most of his tinkly tunes were aired only on the London stage. He was also a novelist and wrote a series of humorous books (*How to Enjoy Your Operation*, *How to Bury Yourself in the Country*, etc.).
Autobiographies: *Ellis in Wonderland*; 1953, *I'm on a See-Saw*.
Elstree Calling 30. Out of the Blue 31. Brother Alfred 32. Lord Babs 32. Jack's the Boy 32. The Water Gipsies 32. Falling for You 33. Mr Cinders 34. Over the Garden Wall 34. Public Nuisance No. 1 36. Who's Your Lady Friend 37. Under Your Hat 40, etc.

Ellis, Walter (1874–*).
English playwright, mainly of farces. Born in London, he was educated at Cambridge University; his plays were a mainstay of the London stage from 1911 until the mid-40s.
A Little Bit of Fluff 28. Almost a Honeymoon 30. Let Me Explain, Dear (from his play A Little Bit of Fluff) 32. Hawleys of High Street 33. Her Last Affaire 35. Almost a Honeymoon 38. Bedtime Story 38, etc.

Ellison, James (1910–1993) (James Ellison Smith).
Genial American leading man, mainly seen in routine westerns.
The Play Girl 32. Hopalong Cassidy 35. The Plainsman (as Buffalo Bill) 36. Vivacious Lady 38. Fifth Avenue Girl 39. Ice Capades 41. Charley's Aunt 41. The Undying Monster 42. I Walked with a Zombie 43. The Ghost Goes Wild 46. Calendar Girl 47. Last of the Wild Horses 48. Lone Star Lawman 50. Dead Man's Trail 52, etc.

Elmes, Frederick (1947–).
American cinematographer.
The Killing of a Chinese Bookie 76. Eraserhead 78. Opening Night 79. Valley Girl 83. Blue Velvet 86. Allan Quatermain and the Lost City of Gold 87. Heaven 87. River's Edge 87. Permanent Record 88. Moonwalker 89. Wild at Heart 90. Night on Earth 92. The Saint of Fort Washington 93. Trial by Jury 94. Reckless 95. The Empty Mirror 96. The Ice Storm 97, etc.

Elmes, Guy (1920–).
British writer.
The Planter's Wife (co-w) 51. The Stranger's Hand 53. Across the Bridge (co-w) 57. Swordsman of Siena 62. A Face in the Rain 63. El Greco 66. The Night Visitor 71, etc.

Elphick, Michael (1946–).
Heavy-set British character actor of all media.
Fraulein Doktor 67. Cry of the Banshee 69. Blind Terror 70. O Lucky Man 73. The Elephant Man 80. Privates on Parade 83. Gorky Park 83. Masada (TV) 83. Hitler's SS (TV) 84. Ordeal by Innocence 85. Supergrass 85. Little Dorrit 87. Buddy's Song 90. Let Him Have It 91. Ken Russell's Treasure Island (TV) 95, etc.
TV series: Boon 85–90. Three Up Two Down 85–87. Harry 93–95.

Elsom, Isobel (1893–1981) (Isobel Reed).
British stage actress who starred in over 60 early British romantic films; went to Hollywood in the late 30s and played innumerable great ladies.
A Debt of Honour 19. Dick Turpin's Ride to York 22. The Sign of Four 23. The Wandering Jew 23. The Love Story of Aliette Brunon 24. Stranglehold 30. Illegal 31. *Ladies in Retirement* 41. You Were Never Lovelier 42. Between Two Worlds 44. The Unseen 45. Of Human Bondage 46. Ivy 47. Love from a Stranger 47. Monsieur Verdoux 47. Desiree 54. 23 Paces to Baker Street 57. The Miracle 59. Who's Minding the Store? 63. My Fair Lady 64, many others.

Eltinge, Julian (1882–1941) (William J. Dalton).
American female impersonator who appeared in a few silent films.
The Countess Charming 17. Over the Rhine 18. Madame Behave 24, etc.

Elton, Sir Arthur (1906–1973).
British producer especially associated with documentary; GPO Film Unit 34–37, Ministry of Information 37–45, Shell Film Unit 45 on. Founder Film Centre, governor BFI, etc.

Elton, Ben (1959–).
English stand-up comedian, actor, writer, novelist and playwright. He studied drama at Manchester University and gained fame performing at London's Comedy Store, on television in *The Ben Elton Show*, and as co-writer of the popular TV series *The Young Ones* (1982–84) and *Blackadder* (1983–89), and writer of *Filthy Rich and Catflap* 87.
Stark (a, w from his novel) (TV) 93. Much Ado about Nothing (a) 93.
❝ I do feel sorry for my mum. For years she thought she had a fairly reasonable, moderately pleasant child, and it turns out she had a hypocritical, foul-mouthed, self-righteous wanker. – *B.E.*
His anxiety levels make Woody Allen look like a Zen Master. – *Guardian*

Elvey, Maurice (1887–1967) (William Folkard).
Veteran British director of over 300 features.
Maria Marten 12. Comradeship 18. Nelson 19. At the Villa Rose 20. The Elusive Pimpernel 20. The Hound of the Baskervilles 21. Dick Turpin's Ride to York 22. The Love Story of Aliette Brunon 24. The Flag Lieutenant 26. Hindle Wakes 27. Balaclava 28. High Treason 30. The School for Scandal 30. Sally in Our Alley 31. In a Monastery Garden 31. The Water Gypsies 32. The Lodger 32. The Wandering Jew 33. The Clairvoyant 34. *The Tunnel* 34. Heat Wave 35. The Return of the Frog 37. For Freedom 39. Room for Two 39. Under Your Hat 40. The Lamp Still Burns 43. The Gentle Sex (co-d) 43. Medal for the General 44. Salute John Citizen 44. *Beware of Pity* 46. The Third Visitor 51. My Wife's Lodger 52. Fun at St Fanny's 55. Dry Rot 56, many others.

Elwes, Cary (1962–).
British actor.
Another Country 84. The Bride 85. Lady Jane 86. The Princess Bride 87. Glory 89. Days of Thunder 90. Hot Shots! 91. Bram Stoker's Dracula 92. The Crush 93. Robin Hood: Men in Tights 93. The Chase 94. Rudyard Kipling's The Jungle Book 94. CutThroat Island 95. Twister 96. Liar Liar 96. Kiss the Girls 97. The Pentagon Wars (TV) 98. Quest for Camelot (voice) 98, etc.

Ely, Ron (1938–) (Ronald Pierce).
American athlete who was television's Tarzan 1966–68.
The Fiend Who Walked the West 58. South Pacific 58. Night of the Grizzly 59. The Remarkable Mr Pennypacker 59. Once Before I Die 65. Mountains of the Moon 67. Doc Savage (title role) 75. Slavers 78, etc.
TV series: The Aquanauts 61.

Emerson, Eric (1946–1975).
Boyish American dancer, a star of Andy Warhol's films. He was found dead in a New York street, apparently the victim of a hit-and-run accident, though Warhol thought that he probably died of a drug overdose.
The Chelsea Girls 66. Lonesome Cowboys 68. Heat 72, etc.

Emerson, Faye (1917–1983).
American socialite leading lady popular for a time in the 40s following her marriage to Elliot Roosevelt, son of the President (1944–50). Retired to Majorca in the 60s.
Between Two Worlds 44. The Mask of Dimitrios 44. Hotel Berlin 45. Danger Signal 45. Nobody Lives Forever 46. Guilty Bystander 50. A Face in the Crowd 57, etc.
TV series: Faye Emerson Show 50. Faye Emerson's Wonderful Town 51–52.

Emerson, Hope (1897–1960).
Brawny 6 foot 2 inch American character actress, in films from early 30s.
Smiling Faces 32. Cry of the City 48. Adam's Rib 49. Caged (AAN) 50. Casanova's Big Night

54. The Day They Gave Babies Away 56. Rock a Bye Baby 58, many others.
TV series: Doc Corkle 52. Peter Gunn 58–60.

Emerson, Keith (1944–).
English composer and keyboard player, a former member of the rock groups Nice and Emerson, Lake and Palmer.
Inferno (US) 80. Nighthawks (US) 81. Best Revenge (Can.) 83. Murderock, Uccide a Passo di Danza (It.) 84, etc.

Emerton, Roy (1892–1944).
Long-nosed British character actor: an eminently hissable villain.
The Sign of Four 32. Java Head 34. Lorna Doone (as Carver) 35. Doctor Syn 38. The Drum 38. Busman's Honeymoon 40. The Thief of Baghdad 40. The Man in Grey 43. Henry V 44, etc.

Emery, Dick (1918–1983).
Chubby British TV comedian with a flair for disguise.
Autobiography: 1974, *In Character*.
Light Up the Sky 60. A Taste of Money 62. The Wrong Arm of the Law 63. Baby Love 69. *Ooh You Are Awful* 72, etc.

Emery, Gilbert (1875–1945) (Gilbert Emery Bensley Pottle).
British character actor long in Hollywood as police commissioners, lords of the manor, etc.
Behind that Curtain 29. The Royal Bed 30. A Farewell to Arms 32. The House of Rothschild 34. One More River 34. Clive of India 35. Magnificent Obsession 35. Dracula's Daughter 36. A Man to Remember 38. Nurse Edith Cavell 39. Raffles 39. Rage in Heaven 41. That Hamilton Woman 41. The Loves of Edgar Allan Poe 42. Between Two Worlds 44. The Brighton Strangler 45, many others.

Emery, John (1905–1964).
American stage and screen actor of suave and sometimes Mephistophelean types. Married actress Tallulah Bankhead (1937–41).
Here Comes Mr Jordan 41. Spellbound 45. Blood on the Sun 45. The Woman in White 48. The Gay Intruders 48. Let's Live Again 49. The Mad Magician 54. Ten North Frederick 57. Youngblood Hawke 64, many others.

Emhardt, Robert (1914–1994).
American character actor, short and tubby; once understudied Sydney Greenstreet.
The Iron Mistress 52. 3.10 to Yuma 57. Underworld USA 60. The Stranger 61. Kid Galahad 62. *The Group* 66. Where Were You When the Lights Went Out? 68. Lawman 71. Alex and the Gypsy 76, etc.

Emilfork, Daniel.
Thin, beaky French character actor, usually in sinister roles.
The Hunchback of Notre Dame 57. What's New Pussycat? 65. Lady L 65. The Liquidator 66. Trans-Europ-Express 66. The Devil's Nightmare/Succubus 71. Travels with My Aunt 72. Kill 72. Who Is Killing the Great Chefs of Europe? 78. Pirates 86. The City of Lost Children/La Cité des Enfants Perdus 95, etc.

Emlyn, Endaf (1945–).
Welsh director and screenwriter, from television.
One Full Moon 91. Leaving Lenin 93.

Emmer, Luciano (1918–).
Italian director.
Domenica d'Agosto 50. The Girls of the Spanish Steps 52. The Bigamist 56, etc.

Emmerich, Roland (1955–).
German-born director of action and science-fiction films, in Hollywood. His special-effects-filled *Independence Day* was the surprise hit of 1996, breaking many box-office records.
Making Contact 85. Hollywood Monster 87. Moon 44 89. Universal Soldier 92. Stargate 94. *Independence Day* 96. Godzilla (US) 98, etc.
TV series: The Visitor (p, w) 97–98.

Emmett, E. V. H. (1902–1971).
Urgent-voiced commentator, film editor, screenwriter and producer, a former journalist. He was the voice of Gaumont-British News in the 30s until the mid-40s and Universal News in the 50s, and can also be heard as narrator in *Carry On Cleo* 64. He also produced features at Ealing from 1946–50.
Sabotage (co-w) 36. Young Man's Fancy (co-w) 39, etc.

Emney, Fred (1900–1980).
Heavyweight British comedian, characterized by a growl, a cigar, and a top hat.
Brewster's Millions 35. Yes Madam 39. Just William 40. Let the People Sing 42. Fun at St Fanny's 56. San Ferry Ann 65. The Sandwich Man 66. Lock Up Your Daughters 69, etc.

Ende, Michael (1929–1995).
German children's novelist, a former actor, whose bestseller *The Neverending Story*, about the power and importance of fantasy, was filmed by Wolfgang Petersen. He disliked the result, describing it as 'a gigantic melodrama of kitsch, commerce, plush and plastic'. Two lacklustre sequels followed.
The Neverending Story 84. Momo 85. The Neverending Story II 90. The Neverending Story III 94.
❝ In a world in which not just our own lives but nature itself is explained to us in terms of its usefulness, I think it is wonderful that there are creatures which have no use whatsoever. – *M.E.*

Endfield, Cy (1914–1995).
American director, in films since 1942. Made second features until 1951; thereafter resident in Britain.
Gentleman Joe Palooka 47. Stork Bites Man (& w) 47. The Argyle Secrets (& w) 48. Underworld Story 50. *The Sound of Fury* 51. Tarzan's Savage Fury 52. The Search 55. Child in the House 56. *Hell Drivers* 57. Sea Fury 58. Jet Storm 59. Mysterious Island 61. *Zulu* 63. Sands of the Kalahari 65. De Sade 69. Universal Soldier 71. Zulu Dawn (co-w) 79, etc.

Endore, Guy (1900–1970).
American screenwriter and novelist.
Mark of the Vampire 35. Mad Love 35. The Raven 35. The Devil Doll 36. The League of Frightened Men 37. Carefree 38. The Story of G.I. Joe (AAN) 45. Whirlpool (oa) 49. He Ran All the Way 51. Curse of the Werewolf (oa) 61. Captain Sinbad 63, etc.

Engel, Morris (1918–).
American producer-director of off-beat semi-professional features.
The Little Fugitive 53. Lovers and Lollipops 55. Weddings and Babies 58.

Engel, Samuel G. (1904–1984).
American producer, a former screenwriter.
Earthbound (w) 40. Scotland Yard (w) 41. My Darling Clementine 46. Sitting Pretty 48. Rawhide 50. Belles on Their Toes 52. Daddy Long Legs 55. Boy on a Dolphin 57. The Story of Ruth 60. The Lion 62, many others.

English, Arthur (1919–1995).
English stand-up comedian who became a sympathetic character actor, mainly on TV, from the 60s. A former painter and decorator, he began his career as a comic in 1949, when he was best known for his fast-talking (300 words a minute at its climax) act as a spiv in floor-length overcoat and wide, garish tie.
Autobiography: *Through the Mill and Beyond*.
The Hi-Jackers 63. Percy 71. For the Love of Ada 72. Love Thy Neighbour 73. Barry McKenzie Holds His Own 74. Are You Being Served? 77. The Boys in Blue 83, etc.
TV series: Are You Being Served? 73–85. How's Your Father? 74–75. The Ghosts of Motley Hall 76–78. In Sickness and in Health 86–91. Never Say Die 87.
~Catchphrase: Start the music – open the cage!

English, John (1903–1969).
British director of second features, long in America; a specialist in serials.
Arizona Days 37. Drums of Fu Manchu 40. Captain Marvel 41. King of the Texas Rangers 41. Captain America 44. Don't Fence Me In 45. The Phantom Speaks 45. Murder in the Music Hall 46. Loaded Pistols 48. Riders in the Sky 49. Valley of Fire 51, many others.

Englund, George H. (1926–).
American producer-director.
The World, the Flesh and the Devil (p) 59. The Ugly American £ 62. Signpost to Murder (d) 64. Dark of the Sun (p) 67. Zachariah (d) 70. Snowjob (d) 71. A Christmas to Remember (d) (TV) 78. Dixie: Changing Habits (d) (TV) 83. The Vegas Strip War (d) (TV) 84, etc.

Englund, Ken (1914–1993).
American writer, in films from 1938.
Good Sam 47. The Secret Life of Walter Mitty 48. The Caddy 53. The Vagabond King 56, etc.

Englund, Robert (1949–).
American character actor who became a mild cult after playing the demoniacal Freddy in *Nightmare on Elm Street* and its sequels.
Buster and Billie 74. The Great Smokey Roadblock 76. St Ives 76. A Star Is Born 76. Blood Brothers 78. Galaxy of Terror 81. 976-EVIL (d) 88. The Phantom of the Opera 89. The Adventures of Ford Fairlane 90. Dance Macabre 91. Wes Craven's New Nightmare 94. Killer Tongue 96. Wishmaster 97. Perfect Target 98. Meet the Deedles 98. Urban Legend 98. Dee Snider's Strangeland 98, etc.
TV series: V 84–85. Downtown 86–87. Freddy's Nightmares (host) 88–90.

Engstead, John (1909–1983).
American portrait photographer in Hollywood. Born in Los Angeles and a graduate of Hollywood High School, he first worked at Paramount and, later, as a freelance, taking portraits of such stars as Humphrey Bogart, Lauren Bacall, Joan Crawford, James Stewart and Marlon Brando.

Ennis, Skinnay (1907–1963).
American bandleader and vocalist who appeared in such 30s films as *College Swing*, *Sleepytime Gal* and *Follow the Band*.

Eno, Brian (1948–).
English composer and keyboard player, a founder-member of Roxy Music.
Land of the Minotaur (co-m) 76. Dune (co-m) 84. For All Mankind (doc) 89, etc.

Enrico, Robert (1931–).
French director.
Incident at Owl Creek 64. Au Coeur de la Vie 65. La Belle Vie 65. Les Aventuriers 67. Zita 67. Ho! 68. Rum Runner 76. The Old Gun 76. L'Empreinte des Géants 80. For Those I Loved 83. Zone Rouge 86. The French Revolution (co-d) 89. Zone Rouge 90. East Wind/Vent d'Est 93, etc.

Enright, Nick.
Australian dramatist and screenwriter.
Lorenzo's Oil (co-w) (AAN) 92. Blackrock (oa, w) 97, etc.

Enright, Ray (1896–1965).
American director, former editor and Sennett gagman. Films mostly routine.
Tracked by the Police 27. Dancing Sweeties 30. Havana Widows 33. Twenty Million Sweethearts 34. Dames 34. Alibi Ike 35. Miss Pacific Fleet 35. Earthworm Tractors 36. Slim 37. *Swing Your Lady* 37. Gold Diggers in Paris 38. Angels Wash Their Faces 39. On Your Toes 39.

Enyedi, Ildikó (1955–).
Hungarian director and screenwriter.
My Twentieth Century 90. Magic Hunter/Buvos Vadas (co-w, d) 94. Tamás és Juli 97, etc.

Ephron, Henry (1912–1992).
American screenwriter who invariably worked as a team with his wife Phoebe Ephron (1914–71). He also produced a few films.
Bride by Mistake 44. Always Together 46. John Loves Mary 49. *The Jackpot* 50. On the Riviera 51. Belles on Their Toes 52. There's No Business Like Show Business 54. Daddy Long Legs 55. Carousel (& p) 56. The Best Things in Life Are Free (p only) 56. *Desk Set* 57. Take Her, She's Mine 63. Captain Newman MD (AAN) 63, etc.

Ephron, Nora (1941–).
American screenwriter and novelist, particularly witty on the traumas of marriage, who has now turned to directing. She is the daughter of screenwriters Phoebe and Henry Ephron, who wrote the plays *Three's a Family* about her childhood and *Take Her, She's Mine* about her life at college.
Silkwood (AAN) 83. Heartburn 86. Cookie 89. When Harry Met Sally (AAN) 89. My Blue Heaven 90. This Is My Life (wd) 92. Sleepless in Seattle (co-w, d) (AANw) 93. Mixed Nuts (co-w, d) 94. Michael (p, co-w, d) 96. You've Got Mail (wd) 98, etc.
❝ I know that people are afraid of me . . . Sometimes it's helpful. The opposite of it is something I'm not interested in, which is that people think they can walk all over you – and when you're a screenwriter, people think that anyway. – *N.E.*
When you're a director, everyone wants a piece of you; they want to know what you think of the tablecloth. I loved nothing more than being asked 10,000 questions in one day. – *N.E.*

Epps, Jack, Jnr.
American screenwriter, often in collaboration with Jim Cash.
Top Gun (co-w) 86. Legal Eagles (co-w) 86. The Secret of My Success (co-w) 86. Turner & Hooch (co-w) 89, etc.

Epstein, Jean (1897–1953).
French director since 1922; also wrote books on film theory.
Cocur Fidèle 23. The Fall of the House of Usher 28. Finis Terrae 28. Mor Vran 30. His sister *Marie Epstein* (1899–) often worked with him, and herself directed La Maternelle 33. La Mort du Cygne 38, etc.

Epstein, Julius J. (1909–) and **Philip G.**(1909–1952).
American twin screenwriters.
Four Daughters (AAN) 38. Four Wives 39. No Time for Comedy 40. Strawberry Blonde 41. The Man Who Came to Dinner 41. *Casablanca* (AA) 42. Mr Skeffington (& p) 44. Romance on the High Seas 48. My Foolish Heart 49. Forever Female 53. The Last Time I Saw Paris 54.
JULIUS ALONE: The Tender Trap 55. Tall Story 60. Take a Giant Step (& p) 61. Fanny 61. Send Me No Flowers 64. Any Wednesday (& p) 66. Pete 'n Tillie (& p) (AAN) 72. Reuben Reuben (AAN) 83, etc.

Erbe, Kathryn.
American actress.
What about Bob? 91. Rich in Love 92. D2: The Mighty Ducks 94. The Addiction 95. Kiss of Death 95. Dream with the Fishes 97, etc.

Erdman, Richard (1925–).
American actor who began playing callow youths, later taking rather crustier roles; now a director for TV.
Thunder across the Pacific 44. Objective Burma 45. The Men 50. The Happy Time 52. Benghazi 55. Bernardine 57. Saddle the Wind 58. Namu the Killer Whale 66. The Brothers O'Toole (d only) 73. Heidi's Song 82. Tomboy 85. Trancers 85. Stewardess School 87. Valet Girls 87. The Pagemaster (voice) 94, etc.
TV series: The Tab Hunter Show 60.

Erice, Victor (1940–).
Spanish director.
Los Desafios 69. Spirit of the Beehive 73. El Sur 83. El Sol del Membrillo 92. The Promise of Shanghai 99, etc.

Erickson, Leif (1911–1986) (William Anderson).
American 'second lead', former singer. In unspectacular roles from 1935.
Wanderer of the Wasteland 35. College Holiday 36. Ride a Crooked Mile 38. Nothing But the Truth 41. Eagle Squadron 42. Sorry, Wrong Number 48. Fort Algiers 50. Carbine Williams 52. On the Waterfront 54. The Fastest Gun Alive 56. Tea and Sympathy 57. Straitjacket 63. Mirage 65. Twilight's Last Gleaming 76, many others.
TV series: High Chaparral 67–71.

Ericson, John (1926–) (Joseph Meibes).
German-born leading man, long in America.
Teresa (debut) 51. Rhapsody 54. Green Fire 54. Bad Day at Black Rock 54. The Return of Jack Slade 55. Forty Guns 57. Pretty Boy Floyd 59. Under Ten Flags 60. The Seven Faces of Dr Lao 64. The Destructors 66. Operation Bluebook 67. Bedknobs and Broomsticks 71. Hustler Squad 76.

Crash 77. Zone of the Dead 78. Primary Target 89, etc.

TV series: Honey West 65.

Ermey, R(onald) Lee (1944–).
American character actor.

The Boys in Company C 78. Full Metal Jacket 87. Mississippi Burning 88. Fletch Lives 89. The Rift/La Grieta 89. I'm Dangerous Tonight (TV) 90. Kid 90. Toy Soldiers 91. Bodysnatchers 93. Sommersby 93. On Deadly Ground 94. Dead Man Walking 95. Leaving Las Vegas 95. Seven 95. Prefontaine 97, etc.

Errol, Leon (1881–1951).
Australian comedian who in 1910 left medicine for Broadway musical comedy and vaudeville, lately becoming familiar to filmgoers as twitchy, bald-pated, henpecked little man in innumerable 30s two-reelers and a number of features, mainly unworthy of his talents.

Paramount on Parade 30. Only Saps Work 30. One Heavenly Night 30. Alice in Wonderland 33. We're Not Dressing 34. Princess O'Hara 35. Make a Wish 37. Mexican Spitfire (first of a series with Lupe Velez in which Errol appeared as the drunken Lord Epping) 39. Pop Always Pays 40. Six Lessons from Madame la Zonga 41. Never Give a Sucker an Even Break 41. Higher and Higher 43. Hat Check Honey 44. The Invisible Man's Revenge 44. What a Blonde 45. Mama Loves Papa 45. Joe Palooka Champ (first of another series) 46. The Noose Hangs High 48, etc.

☼ For bringing a breath of inspired vaudeville to some pretty tired Hollywood formats, and for inventing Lord Epping. Mexican Spitfire.

Erskine, Chester (1905–1986).
American writer-producer-director.

Call it Murder £ 34. The Egg and I (wpd) 47. All My Sons (wp) 48. Take One False Step (co-wpd) 49. Androcles and the Lion (wd) 53. Witness to Murder (wp) 57. The Wonderful Country (p) 59, etc.

Erwin, Stuart (1903–1967).
American character comedian, who usually played Mr Average or the hero's faithful but slow-thinking friend.

Mother Knows Best 28. The Trespasser 29. Sweetie 29. Men Without Women 30. Dude Ranch 31. Misleading Lady 32. International House 33. Palooka 34. After Office Hours 35. All American Chump 36. Pigskin Parade (AAN) 36. Slim 37. Three Blind Mice 38. Hollywood Cavalcade 39. Our Town 40. Cracked Nuts 41. Blondie for Victory 42. He Hired the Boss 43. The Great Mike 44. Pillow to Post 45. Killer Dill 47. Strike It Rich 48. Father Is a Bachelor 50. For the Love of Mike 60. Son of Flubber 64. The Misadventures of Merlin Jones 64, many others.

TV series: The Trouble with Father 53. The Greatest Show on Earth 63. The Bing Crosby Show 65.

Escamilla, Teo (1940–1997).
Spanish cinematographer and occasional director, associated with the films of Carlos Saura, with whom he worked in the late 70s and the 80s. He began as a camera operator to Luis Cuadrado. Died of a heart attack.

Raise Ravens 75. Mama Turns a Hundred 79. Blood Wedding 81. Carmen 83. You Alone/Tu Solo (d) 84. A Love Bewitched 86. Things I Left in Havana 97, etc.

Escoffier, Jean Yves.
French cinematographer, a fixture on Leos Carax's early films; he studied at the Louis Lumière Film School.

Trois Hommes et un Couffin 85. Bad Blood/Mauvais Sang 86. Les Amants du Pont Neuf 91. Charlie and the Doctor 93. Dream Lover (US) 94. Grace of My Heart (US) 96. The Crow: City of Angels (US) 96, etc.

Esmond, Carl (1906–) (Willy Eichberger).
Good-looking Austrian actor usually in haughty or arrogant roles, first in Britain and later in Hollywood.

Evensong 33. Invitation to the Waltz 37. Dawn Patrol 38. Thunder Afloat 39. Pacific Rendezvous 42. The Story of Dr Wassell 43. Ministry of Fear 44. Address Unknown 44. Without Love 45. This Love of Ours 45. Catman of Paris 46. Smash-Up 47. Walk a Crooked Mile 48. The Desert Hawk

50. Mystery Submarine 51. The World in His Arms 52. From the Earth to the Moon 58. Thunder in the Sun 59. Agent for H.A.R.M. 66. Morituri 66, etc.

Esmond, Jill (1908–1990).
British leading lady of the 30s, later in Hollywood. She was married to Laurence Olivier (1930–40).

The Skin Game 31. Ladies of the Jury 32. No Funny Business 32. This Above All 42. Random Harvest 42. The White Cliffs of Dover 44. The Bandit of Sherwood Forest 46. Escape 48. Night People 54. A Man Called Peter 55, etc.

Esposito, Giancarlo (1958–).
American actor.

Sweet Lorraine 87. School Daze 88. Do the Right Thing 89. King of New York 90. Mo' Better Blues 90. Night on Earth 91. Bob Roberts 92. Amos & Andrew 93. Fresh 94. Smoke 95. Blue in the Face 95. The Keeper 96. Loose Women 96. Twilight 98, etc.

Esquivel, Laura (1950–).
Mexican screenwriter and novelist. She is married to actor and director Alfonso Arau.

Like Water for Chocolate/Como Agua para Chocolate (oa, w) 92. Estrellita Marinera 94.

Essex, David (1947–).
British pop singer.

■ Assault 70. Carry on Henry 71. All Coppers Are . . . 71. That'll Be the Day 73. Stardust 74. Silver Dream Racer 80.

Essex, Harry (1910–1997).
American screenwriter and occasional director, often for television.

Boston Blackie and the Law 43. Desperate 47. Dragnet 47. He Walked by Night 48. The Killer that Stalked New York 50. The Fat Man 50. Undercover Girl 50. The Las Vegas Story 52. Kansas City Confidential 52. It Came from Outer Space 53. The Forty-Ninth Man 53. I the Jury (& d) 53. The Creature from the Black Lagoon 54. Raw Edge 56. The Lonely Man 57. The Sons of Katie Elder 65. Octaman (& d) 71. The Cremators (d only) 72, etc.

Estabrook, Howard (1884–1978).
American screenwriter.

The Four Feathers 28. Hell's Angels 30. Cimarron (AA) 31. A Bill of Divorcement 32. The Masquerader 33. David Copperfield 34. International Lady 39. The Bridge of San Luis Rey 44. The Human Comedy 45. The Girl from Manhattan 48. Lone Star 51. The Big Fisherman 59, many others.

Estevez, Emilio (1962–).
American leading man, son of Martin Sheen.

Tex 82. Repo Man 84. The Breakfast Club 84. St Elmo's Fire 84. That was Then . . . This is Now 85. Maximum Overdrive 86. Wisdom 86. Stakeout 87. Young Guns 88. Never on Tuesday 89. Men at Work (& wd) 90. Young Guns II 90. Freejack 92. The Mighty Ducks 92. National Lampoon's Loaded Weapon 1 93. Another Stakeout 93. Judgment Night 93. D2: The Mighty Ducks 94. Mission: Impossible 96. The War at Home (& p, d) 96. D3: The Mighty Ducks 96. The War at Home (& d) 97. Late Last Night 98. A Dollar for the Dead 99, etc.

Estrada, Erik (1949–).
American leading man of Puerto Rican descent.

The New Centurions 74. Trackdown 76. Fire! (TV) 77. Hour of the Assassin 87. Caged Fury 90. The Last Riders 90. Do or Die 91. The Divine Enforcer 91. National Lampoon's Loaded Weapon 1 93. Final Goal 94, etc.

TV series: Chips 77–82.

Estridge, Robin (1920–).
British screenwriter.

Above Us the Waves 54. The Young Lovers 54. Campbell's Kingdom 57. Northwest Frontier 59. Escape from Zahrain 62. Eye of the Devil 67, etc.

Eszterhas, Joe (1944–).
Hungarian-born American screenwriter. A former journalist, he writes scripts that tend to reflect current social concerns. He received a reported $3 million for his script for Basic Instinct.

F.I.S.T. 78. Flashdance 83. Jagged Edge 85. Big Shots 87. Hearts of Fire 87. Betrayed 88. Checking

Out 89. Music Box 89. Basic Instinct 92. Crossing the Line 92. Nowhere to Run (co-w) 93. Sliver 93. Showgirls 95. Jade 95. An Alan Smithee Film: Burn, Hollywood, Burn 97. Telling Lies in America 97, etc.

❝ I've always loved the notion of doing movies that provoke people, either move them in their hearts or disturb them, but when they leave the theater it sticks with them. – J.E.

He writes with a cattle prod. – Janet Maslin

Etaix, Pierre (1928–).
French mime comedian, former circus clown and assistant to Tati.

Rupture (short) 61. Happy Anniversary (short) 61. The Suitor 62. Yo Yo 65. As Long As You Have Your Health 67. Le Grand Amour 69. Henry and June 90, etc.

Etting, Ruth (1896–1978).
American popular singer of the 20s, a version of whose life was told in 1955 in Love Me or Leave Me. Very briefly on screen.

■ Roman Scandals 33. Hips Hips Hooray 33. Gift of Gab 34.

Eustache, Jean (1938–1981).
French director and screenwriter. A former film editor, he also acted in Godard's Weekend and Wender's The American Friend. He committed suicide.

Les Mauvaises Fréquentations 63. Le Père Noel a les Yeux Bleus 66. Le Cochon 70. Numéro Zéro 71. The Mother and the Whore/La Maman et la Putain 73. Mes Petites Amoureuses 74. Une Sale Histoire 77. Le Jardin des Délices de Jerome Bosch 79. Offre d'Emploi 80, etc.

Eustrel, Anthony (1903–1979).
British character actor.

The Silver Fleet 43. Caesar and Cleopatra 45. The Robe 53, etc.

Evans, Barry (1945–1997).
Youthful-looking English light leading man of the 70s, from the stage. He won a Gielgud scholarship to study at the Central School of Speech and Drama and found brief stardom with his first feature and TV sitcom. His career faltered in the 80s and at the time of his death he was working as a taxi driver. An 18-year-old man was charged with his attempted murder, but the prosecution offered no evidence at the trial and a verdict of not guilty was recorded.

Here We Go Round the Mulberry Bush 67. Alfred the Great 69. Die Screaming Marianne 70. Adventures of a Taxi Driver 75. Under the Doctor 76. Legacy of Murder (TV) 82. The Mystery of Edwin Drood 93, etc.

TV series: Doctor in the House 69–70. Doctor at Large 71. Mind Your Language 77–79, 86.

Evans, Clifford (1912–1985).
Welsh actor with stage experience. In films from 1936, at first as leading man and latterly as character actor.

Ourselves Alone 36. The Mutiny on the Elsinore 37. The Luck of the Navy 39. The Proud Valley 39. His Brother's Keeper 39. The Saint Meets the Tiger 40. Love on the Dole 41. Penn of Pennsylvania 41. Suspected Person 42. The Foreman Went to France 42; war service; The Silver Darlings 47. While I Live 48. Valley of Song 52. The Gilded Cage 55. Passport to Treason 56. Violent Playground 58. SOS Pacific 60. Curse of the Werewolf 62. Kiss of the Vampire 63. The Long Ships 64. Twist of Sand 69. One Brief Summer 70, etc.

TV series: Stryker of the Yard. The Power Game 65–67, etc.

Evans, Dale (1912–) (Frances Octavia Smith).
American leading lady of the 40s, former band singer; appeared frequently with Roy Rogers, and in 1947 married him.

Orchestra Wives 42. Swing Your Partner 43. Casanova in Burlesque 44. The Yellow Rose of Texas 44. Utah 45. Belles of Rosarita 45. My Pal Trigger 46. Apache Rose 47. Slippy McGee 48. Susanna Pass 49. Twilight in the Sierras 50. Trigger Jnr 51. Pals of the Golden West 51. Roy Rogers: King of the Cowboys (doc) 91, many others.

TV series: The Roy Rogers Show 51–56.

Evans, David Mickey.
American screenwriter and director.

Radio Flyer (w) 92. Hocus Pocus (co-w) 93. Ed (w) 96. First Kid (d) 96, etc.

Evans, Dame Edith (1888–1976).
Distinguished British stage actress who made occasional films.

Biographies 1977: Ned's Girl by Bryan Forbes. Edith Evans: A Personal Memoir by Jean Batters.
■ A Welsh Singer 15. East is East 15. The Queen of Spades 48. The Last Days of Dolwyn 48. The Importance of Being Earnest 51. Look Back in Anger 59. The Nun's Story 59. Tom Jones (AAN) 63. The Chalk Garden (AAN) 64. Young Cassidy 65. The Whisperers (BFA, AAN) 67. Fitzwilly (US) 68. Prudence and the Pill 68. Crooks and Coronets 69. The Madwoman of Chaillot 69. David Copperfield 69. Scrooge 70. A Doll's House 73. Craze 73. QB VII (TV) 74. The Slipper and the Rose 76. Nasty Habits 76.

❝ As a young actress I always had a rule. If I didn't understand a line I always said it as though it were improper. – E.E.

Comedy, dear, is just like blowing powder puffs out of a cannon. – E.E.

Acting with her was heaven. It was like being in your mother's arms. – Sir Michael Redgrave

The dame, great actress though she was, resembled a gifted amateur. She didn't really know what she was doing. What she had was an infallible ear for the turn of a speech, or a line, and what she did was entirely instinctive, and executed without much thought, imagination, or guile. – Robert Stephens

Evans, Edward (1914–).
Welsh character actor, best known as Bob Grove in The Grove Family, Britain's first TV soap opera, 1954–57.

The Small Voice 48. Deadly Nightshade 53. Valley of Song 53. It's a Great Day! 56. Blind Corner 63. One More Time 70. Out of Season 75, etc.

Evans, Fred (1889–1951).
English comic actor and director, from music hall, who was one of the earliest stars of British cinema, notably in the character of 'Pimple' (renamed 'Flivver' in America). In films from 1910, he made his first Pimple short in 1912 and turned out between 10 and 30 a year until his last, Pimple's Three Musketeers, in 1922. In the 30s and 40s, he worked as an extra in films. He was the nephew of Will Evans and was a member of a famous family of music-hall performers and clowns.

Evans, Gene (1922–1998).
Stocky American actor in demand for heavy roles. Born in Holbrook, Arizona, and raised in Colton, California, he began acting as a GI in Europe in the late 40s. Retired in the 80s to farm in Tennessee.

Berlin Express 48. Park Row 52. Donovan's Brain 53. The Golden Blade 53. Hell and High Water 54. The Sad Sack 57. Operation Petticoat 59. Apache Uprising 65. Support Your Local Sheriff 69. The Ballad of Cable Hogue 70. Walking Tall 73. Devil Times Five 82, etc.

TV series: My Friend Flicka 57. Matt Helm 75. Spencer's Pilots 76.

Evans, Joan (1934–) (Joan Eunson).
American actress who played teenage roles in the early 50s, now working in education.

Our Very Own 50. On the Loose 51. Roseanna McCoy 51. Skirts Ahoy 52. Edge of Doom 54. The Fortune Hunter 54. No Name on the Bullet 59. The Flying Fontaines 60, etc.

Evans, Joe (1891–1967).
English music-hall performer who starred in many comedy shorts from 1912–18 and also appeared in the films of his brother Fred 'Pimple' Evans.

Evans, Josh (1971–).
American actor, director and writer, the son of Robert Evans and Ali McGraw.

Dream a Little Dream 89. Born on the Fourth of July 89. Ricochet 90. The Doors 90. Inside the Goldmine (& co-w, d) 94, etc.

Evans, Lee (1965–).
English stand-up comedian and actor, in a style that owes something to Jerry Lewis and much to Norman Wisdom. He also runs a production company, Little Mo Films.

Funny Bones 95. The Fifth Element 97. *Mouse Hunt* 97, etc.

TV series: The World of Lee Evans 95.

66 I don't think comedians are born. You have to find a way of surviving in this strange world and that tends to be with an exaggeration of your own personality. – *L.E.*

Evans, Linda (1943–) (Linda Evanstad).
Blonde American leading lady. Her first husband was actor-director John DEREK.

Twilight of Honor 63. Those Calloways 64. Female Artillery (TV) 73. The Klansman 74. Mitchell 75. Nowhere to Run (TV) 78. Avalanche Express 79. The Gambler Part Two (TV) 83. *The Last Frontier* (TV) 86. She'll Take Romance 90. The Gambler Returns: The Luck of the Draw (TV) 93. The Stepsister (TV) 97, etc.

TV series: Bachelor Father 60. The Big Valley 65–69. Hunter 77. *Dynasty* 81–89.

Evans, Madge (1909–1981).
American actress, a child star of silent days, pretty heroine of mainly unremarkable films in the 30s.

The Sign of the Cross 14. The Burglar 16. Classmates 24. Son of India 29. Lovers Courageous 30. The Greeks Had a Word for Them 32. Hallelujah I'm a Bum 33. Dinner at Eight 33. Grand Canary 34. David Copperfield 34. The Tunnel (GB) 35. Piccadilly Jim 37. The Thirteenth Chair 37, etc.

Evans, Maurice (1901–1989).
Eloquent Welsh actor who, long in America, distinguished himself on the Broadway stage.

White Cargo 30. Raise the Roof 30. Wedding Rehearsal 32. Scrooge (GB) 35. Kind Lady 51. The Story of Gilbert and Sullivan (as Sullivan) 53. Androcles and the Lion (as Caesar) 53. Macbeth (title role) 59. The War Lord 65. Jack of Diamonds 67. Planet of the Apes 67. Rosemary's Baby 68. Terror in the Wax Museum 73, etc.

TV series: Bewitched 68–71.

Evans, Norman (1901–1962).
British north-country music hall comedian famous for toothless characterization and female impersonation.

Demobbed 45. Under New Management 46. Over the Garden Wall 50, etc.

Evans, Ray (1915–).
American songwriter, in Hollywood from 1945 in partnership with Jay LIVINGSTON. He wrote the theme to the TV series *Bonanza*.

Why Girls Leave Home (AANs 'The Cat and the Canary') 45. Smooth Sailing 47. Paleface (AAs 'Buttons and Bows') 48. The Great Lover 49. Captain Carey, USA (AAs 'Mona Lisa') 50. The Lemon Drop Kid 51. Aaron Slick from Punkin Crick 52. The Man Who Knew Too Much (AAs 'Whatever Will Be, Will Be') 56. Tammy and the Bachelor (AANs 'Tammy') 57. Houseboat (AANs 'Almost in Your Arms') 58. Dear Heart (AAN title s) 64, etc.

Evans, Rex (1903–1969).
British character actor in Hollywood. Often played

stately butlers, as in The Philadelphia Story 40. Other appearances include Camille 36, It Should Happen to You 53, The Matchmaker 58. Ran an art gallery in his spare time.

Evans, Robert (1930–).
Bland-faced American juvenile of the 50s; gave up acting to become a Paramount production executive, then went independent. He was formerly married to Ali MCGRAW. Married actress Catherine Oxenberg in July 1998; the couple agreed to annul their marriage the next month.

Autobiography: 1994, *The Kid Stays in the Picture*.

Lydia Bailey 52. The Man of a Thousand Faces (as Irving Thalberg) 57. The Sun Also Rises 57. The Fiend Who Walked the West (title role) 58. The Best of Everything 59. Desperate Hours 90, etc.

AS PRODUCER: Chinatown 74. The Great Gatsby 74. Marathon Man 76. Black Sunday 77. Players 79. Popeye 80. Urban Cowboy 80. The Cotton Club 84. The Two Jakes 90. Sliver 93. Jade 95. The Phantom 96. The Saint 97, etc.

Evans, Will (1867–1931).
English comic actor, notable pantomime dame at Drury Lane, and playwright, who filmed many of his classic music-hall slapstick sketches and appeared in the silent shorts of his nephew Fred Evans. He was the co-author of Tons of Money, the long-running and influential farce of the 20s which was filmed in 1930.

They Do Such Things at Brighton 1899. Will Evans the Living Catherine Wheel 1899. The Jockey 07. Harnessing a Horse 13. Whitewashing the Ceiling 14. Building a Chicken House 14. Moving a Piano 14. A Study in Skarlit 15, etc.

Eve, Trevor (1951–).
Slightly built British leading man who became popular from 1979 as TV's radio station detective *Shoestring*.

Dracula 79. Jamaica Inn (TV) 82. Lace (TV) 84. The Corsican Brothers (TV) 84. Scandal 88. In the Name of the Father 93. The Tribe (TV) 98.

TV series: Shadow Chasers 85. Heat of the Sun 98.

Evein, Bernard (1929–).
French art director.

Les Amants 57. Les Jeux de L'Amour 60. Zazie dans le Métro 61. Lola 61. Cléo de 5 à 7 62. La Baie des Anges 62. Le Feu Follet 63. The Umbrellas of Cherbourg 64. Do You Like Women? 64. Viva Maria 65. The Young Girls of Rochefort 67. Woman Times Seven 67. The Confession/L'Aveu 70. The Toy/Le Jouet 76. A Room in Town/Une Chambre en Ville 82. Separate Rooms/Notre Histoire 84. Thérèse 86, etc.

Evelyn, Judith (1913–1967) (J. E. Allen).
American stage actress; often played neurotic women.

The Egyptian 54. Rear Window 54. Hilda Crane 56. The Tingler 59, etc.

Everest, Barbara (1890–1968).
British stage actress who appeared in many films, latterly in motherly roles.

Lily Christine 31. The Wandering Jew 33. The Passing of the Third Floor Back 35. He Found a Star 40. Mission to Moscow (US) 43. Jane Eyre (US) 43. The Uninvited (US) 44. The Valley of Decision (US) 45. Wanted for Murder 46. Frieda 47. Madeleine 49. Tony Draws a Horse 51. The Man Who Finally Died 62, etc.

Everett, Chad (1936–) (Raymond Cramton).
Handsome American leading man of the 60s; films unremarkable.

Claudelle Inglish 61. The Chapman Report 62. Get Yourself a College Girl 65. The Singing Nun 66. First to Fight 67. The Last Challenge 67. The Firechasers (TV) 70. The French Atlantic Affair (TV) 79. Airplane 2: The Sequel 82. Fever Pitch 85. Heroes Stand Alone 89. Jigsaw Murders 89. The Rousters (TV) 90. Official Denial (TV) 93. When Time Expires 97, etc.

TV series: Medical Center 69–75. Hagen 79. The Rousters 83. McKenna 94–95.

Everett, Rupert (1959–).
English leading actor, often in aristocratic or effete roles, and occasional singer. Born in Norfolk, he studied briefly at the Central School of Speech and Drama before working at Glasgow's Citizens' Theatre. He became a star with his first film, *Another Country*, but the roles that followed were less successful until his scene-stealing performance in My Friend's Wedding; his subsequent revelations about working as a male prostitute when young and penniless in London may not have helped his long-term career prospects. He has also modelled for Yves St Laurent's perfume advertisements and written two novels: Hello Darling, Are You Working? 93 and The Hairdressers of St Tropez 95.

Princess Daisy (TV) 83. *Another Country* 84. Dance with a Stranger 85. The Right Hand Man 86. Duet for One 86. Hearts of Fire 87. Gli Occhiali d'Oro 87. Tolerance 89. The Comfort of Strangers 90. Dellamorte Dellamore (It.) 94. The Madness of King George 95. Dunston Checks In 96. My Friend's Wedding 97. B Monkey 98, etc.

66 English actors are like immigrants – they're a gypsy race. They go where the work is and there's never been much work in England. They're treated very badly. – *R.E.*

One of the great things about getting older is that unemployment becomes more and more fun. – *R.E.*

He's clever, self-destructive, bright and brash at the same time. I must admit that I really like that mix. – *Rupert Graves*

What's most important about Rupert Everett is that aside from being talented, he's one of the first gay leading men who is sexy. – *Paul Rudnick*

Evers, Jason (1922–) (Herbert Evers).
American general-purpose actor.

The Brain that Wouldn't Die 62. Tarzan's Jungle Rebellion 65. The Green Berets 68. A Man Called Gannon 69. The Illustrated Man 69. Escape from the Planet of the Apes 71. Claws 77. A Piece of the Action 77. Barracuda 78. Basket Case 2 90, etc.

TV series: Wrangler 60. Channing 63–64.

Ewell, Tom (1909–1994) (S. Yewell Tompkins).
American comic actor with wide stage experience.

Adam's Rib 49. A Life of Her Own 50. An American Guerilla in the Philippines 50. Mr Music 50. Finders Keepers 51. Up Front 51. Back at the Front 52. Abbott and Costello Lost in Alaska 52. *The Seven Year Itch* 55. The Lieutenant Wore Skirts 55. The Great American Pastime 56. The Girl Can't Help It 57. A Nice Little Bank that Should be Robbed 58. Tender is the Night 61. State Fair 62. Suppose They Gave a War and Nobody Came 70. To Find A Man 72. They Only Kill Their Masters 72. The Great Gatsby 74. Promise Him Anything (TV) 75, etc.

TV series: The Tom Ewell Show 60–61. Baretta 75–78. Best of the West 81–82.

Exton, Clive (1930–).
British dramatist who wrote notable television plays in the 60s and turned to screenwriting with less happy results.

No Fixed Abode (TV) 59. The Big Eat (TV) 62. A Place to Go 63. The Trial of Dr Fancy (TV) 64. Night Must Fall 64. Isadora (co-w) 68. Entertaining Mr Sloane 69. 10 Rillington Place 70. Running Scared (co-w) 72. The House in Nightmare Park (co-w) 73. Doomwatch (made 71) 76. The Awakening (co-w) 80. Red Sonja (co-w) 85, etc.

TV series: The Crezz 77. Dick Barton – Special Agent 79. Jeeves and Wooster 92–93.

Eyre, Peter (1942–).
English actor, of stage, screen and television.

Alice in Wonderland (TV) 67. The Pied Piper 72. Mahler 74. Hedda 75. La Luna (It./US) 75. Dragonslayer 81. The Two Mrs Grenvilles (TV) (US) 87. Maurice 87. Just Ask for Diamond/ Diamond's Edge 88. Mountains of the Moon 90. Memento Mori (TV) 92. Orlando 92. The Remains of the Day 93. Princess Caraboo 94. Scarlett (TV) (US) 94. Joseph (TV) 95. Surviving Picasso 96. The Tango Lesson 97. Dangerous Beauty 98, etc.

Eyre, Sir Richard (1943–).
English theatre and film director, director of the Royal National Theatre from 1988 to 1997. He was knighted in the 1996 New Year's Honours.

Autobiography: 1993, *Utopia and Other Places*.

The Ploughman's Lunch 83. Loose Connections 83. Tumbledown (TV) 88. Suddenly Last Summer 92, etc.

Eythe, William (1918–1957).
American leading man of the 40s.

The Ox-Bow Incident 42. The Song of Bernadette 43. The Eve of St Mark 44. A Royal Scandal 45. The House on 92nd Street 45. Meet Me at Dawn 47. Customs Agent 50, etc.

Eziashi, Maynard.
British leading actor.

Mr Johnson 90. Twenty-One 91. Bopha! 93. A Good Man in Africa 94. Ace Ventura: When Nature Calls 95. Bad Boy Blues 96, etc.

F

Fabares, Shelley (1944–).
American juvenile leading lady of the early 60s. Niece of Nanette Fabray.
Never Say Goodbye 56. Summer Love 58. Ride the Wild Surf 64. Girl Happy 65. Hold On 66. Spinout 66. Clambake 67. The Great American Traffic Jam 80. Love or Money 88. A Dream Is a Wish Your Heart Makes: The Annette Funicello Story (TV) 95, etc.
TV series: The Donna Reed Show 58–63. The Brian Keith Show 72–74. The Practice 76–77. Mary Hartman, Mary Hartman 77–78. Highcliffe Manor 79. One Day at a Time 81–84. Coach 89.

Faber, Matthew (1973–).
American actor in independent films.
Dollhouse 96. Stonewall 96, etc.

Fabian (1942–) (Fabian Forte Bonaparte).
American teenage idol, singer and guitarist.
The Hound Dog Man (debut) 59. North to Alaska 60. Mr Hobbs Takes a Vacation 62. Dear Brigitte 65. Ten Little Indians 65. Fireball 500 66. The Devil's Eight 68. A Bullet for Pretty Boy 70. Lovin' Man 72, Little Laura and Big John 73. Kiss Daddy Goodbye 81, etc.

Fabian, Françoise (1932–) (Michele Cortes de Leone y Fabianera).
French leading actress who has made several forays into international films.
Mamzelle Pigalle 56. Fernandel the Dressmaker 56. The Fanatics 57. Maigret Sees Red 63. Le Voleur 67. *Belle de Jour* 67. *Ma Nuit Chez Maud* 70. La Bonne Année 73. Down the Ancient Stairs 75. Salut l'Artiste 76. Madame Claude 77. Reflections in a Dark Sky/Riflessi in un Cielo Scuro 91, etc.

Fabray, Nanette (1920–) (Nanette Fabares).
American comedy actress and singer, former child star of 'Our Gang' comedies.
Adult films: Elizabeth and Essex 39. Band Wagon 53. The Happy Ending 69. Amy 81. Personal Exemptions 88. That's Entertainment! III 94, etc.
TV series: Peck's Bad Girl 59. Caesar's Hour 64.

Fabre, Saturnin (1884–1961).
French character actor.
Pépé le Moko 37. Ils étaient Neuf Célibataires 42. Un Ami Viendra Ce Soir 46. Les Portes de la Nuit 46. Clochemerle 52. La Fête à Henriette 54, etc.

Fabri, Zoltan (1917–1994).
Hungarian director.
The Storm 52. Merry-Go-Round 55. Professor Hannibal 56. The Brute 59. The Last Goal 61. Twenty Hours 65. The Paul Street Boys 68. One Day More One Day Less 73. Hungarians 77. Balint Fabian Meets God 80. Requiem 82, etc.

Fabrizi, Aldo (1905–1990).
Italian character actor, known abroad.
Open City 45. Vivere in Pace 47. First Communion 50. Cops and Robbers, 54. Altri Tempi 55. The Angel Wore Red 60. The Birds the Bees and the Italians 65. Made in Italy 68.

Factor, Max, Jnr (1904–1996) (Francis Factor).
Cosmetics manufacturer who began by providing make-up for Hollywood's performers. He went on to produce it on a vast commercial scale from the 40s, using film stars such as Hedy Lamarr and Rita Hayworth to promote his products. His Polish-born father, a wigmaker for the Imperial Theatre of Tsar Nicholas II, emigrated to America in the early 1900s and set up the family business in Los Angeles, making wigs for film actors and importing theatrical make-up. The firm was sold for $480m in the early 70s.

Fahey, Jeff (1956–).
American leading actor.
Silverado 85. Psycho III 86. Backfire 87. Split Decisions 88. True Blood 89. The Last of the Finest 90. Impulse 90. White Hunter, Black Heart 90. Body Parts 91. Iron Maze 91. The Lawnmower Man 92. Sketch Artist 92. Freefall 94. Woman of Desire 94. Wyatt Earp 94. Sketch Artist II: Hands that See (TV) 95. Serpent's Lair 95. Northern Passage 95. Eye of the Wolf 95. Virtual Seduction 96. Lethal Tender 96. The Underground 97. Operation: Delta Force 97. On the Line (TV) 98, etc.

Fain, Sammy (1902–1989) (Samuel Feinberg).
American composer, a former vaudeville performer, whose songs featured in many Hollywood films.
Young Man of Manhattan 30. Footlight Parade 33. Sweet Music 35. Meet the People 44. Call Me Mister 51. Alice in Wonderland 51. The Jazz Singer 53. Peter Pan 53. Calamity Jane (AAs) 53. Love Is a Many Splendored Thing (AA title s) 55. Hollywood or Bust 56. April Love (AANs) 57. The Big Circus 59. Marjorie Morningstar (AANs) 58. A Certain Smile (AANs) 58. Tender Is the Night (AANs) 62. The Stepmother (AANs) 72. Half a House (AANs) 76. The Rescuers (AANs) 77, etc.

Fairbanks, Douglas (1883–1939) (Douglas Ullman).
Swashbuckling American star of the silent screen, the acrobatic, zestful, ever-smiling hero of many comedies and costume adventures, almost all of which he produced himself. Despite long stage experience, sound did not suit him, and his 30s films showed a marked decline. He had a famous marriage with Mary Pickford, and in 1919, with Chaplin and Griffith, they were co-founders of United Artists Film Corporation. Posthumous AA 1939 'for his unique and outstanding contribution to the international development of the motion picture'.
Biographies: 1953, *The Fourth Musketeer* by Elton Thomas. 1976, *The Fairbanks Album* by Richard Schickel. 1977, *His Majesty the American* by John C. Tibbetts and James M. Welsh.
■ The Lamb 15. Double Trouble 15. His Picture in the Papers 16. The Habit of Happiness 16. The Good Bad Man 16. Reggie Mixes In 16. Flirting with Fate 16. The Mystery of the Leaping Fish 16. The Half Breed 16. Manhattan Madness 16. American Aristocracy 16. The Matrimaniac 16. The Americano 16. In Again Out Again 17. Wild and Woolly 17. Down to Earth 17. The Man from Painted Post 17. Reaching for the Moon 17. A Modern Musketeer 18. Headin' South 18. Mr Fix-It 18. Say Young Fellow 18. Bound in Morocco 18. He Comes Up Smiling 18. Arizona (& wd) 18. Knickerbocker Buckaroo 19. His Majesty the American 19. When the Clouds Roll By 20. The Mollycoddle 20. *The Mark of Zorro* (& w) 20. The Nut (& w) 21. *The Three Musketeers* 21. *Robin Hood* (& w) 21. *The Thief of Baghdad* (& w) 23. *Don Q Son of Zorro* 25. *The Black Pirate* 26. The Gaucho (& w) 27. The Iron Mask (& w) 29. The Taming of the Shrew 29. Reaching for the Moon 30. Around the World in Eighty Minutes (& w) 31. Mr Robinson Crusoe 32. The Private Life of Don Juan 34.
✪ For giving his high spirits to a world which needed them. *The Black Pirate*.
❝ Quotes about the elder Fairbanks all point the same way; despite his comparatively short stature, he was much larger than life.
He has such verve. We can use his body,
said D. W. Griffith.
From that day Fairbanks kept himself in rigorous training, believing that:
The man that's out to do something has to keep in high gear all the time.
He managed. An anonymous critic in 1920 put his finger on the Fairbanks magic:
He smiles, and you feel relieved.
Alistair Cooke called him:
A sort of Ariel,
and added:
At a difficult period in American history, Douglas Fairbanks appeared to know all the answers.
Director Allan Dwan commented:
Stunt men have had to imitate him and it always looked like a stunt when they did it. With him it always looked right.
But Mary Pickford, who should know, had a minority view:
In his private life Douglas always faced a situation in the only way he knew, by running away from it.

Fairbanks, Douglas, Jnr (1909–).
American leading man who has spent much time in Britain; of more conventional debonair mould than his father, he spent as much time in drawing rooms as on castle battlements, but was at home in any surroundings. During the early 50s, produced and sometimes played in innumerable TV half-hours under the title *Douglas Fairbanks Presents*.
Biography: 1955, *Knight Errant* by Brian Connell.
■ Party Girl 20. Stephen Steps Out 23. Air Mail 25. Wild Horse Mesa 25. Stella Dallas 25. The American Venus 25. Padlocked 26. Manbait 26. Is Zat So? 27. A Texas Steer 27. The Barker 28. A Woman of Affairs 28. *The Jazz Age* 29. Fast Life 29. Our Modern Maidens 29. The Careless Age 29. The Forward Pass 29. Show of Shows 29. Loose Ankles 30. *The Dawn Patrol* 30. Little Accident 30. The Way of All Men 30. *Outward Bound* 30. Little Caesar 30. One Night at Susie's 30. Chances 31. I Like Your Nerve 31. Union Depot 32. It's Tough to be Famous 32. Love is a Racket 32. Parachute Jumper 32. The Narrow Corner 33. *Morning Glory* 33. Captured 33. The Life of Jimmy Dolan 33. *Catherine the Great* 34. Success at any Price 34. Mimi 35. The Amateur Gentleman 35. Accused 36. Jump for Glory 36. *The Prisoner of Zenda* (as Rupert of Hentzau) 37. Joy of Living 38. The Rage of Paris 38. Having Wonderful Time 38. *The Young in Heart* 38. *Gunga Din* 39. The Sun Never Sets 39. Rulers of the Sea 39. Green Hell 40. Safari 40. Angels over Broadway 40. The Corsican Brothers 41. *Sinbad the Sailor* 47. The Exile 47. That Lady in Ermine 48. The Fighting O'Flynn 49. *State Secret* 50. Mr Drake's Duck 51. The Crooked Hearts (TV) 72. Ghost Story 81. The Hostage Tower (TV) 81.

Fairbrass, Craig.
British leading actor, frequently in tough-guy roles.
For Queen and Country 89. Prime Suspect (TV) 90. Prime Suspect II (TV) 92. Beyond Bedlam 93. Cliffhanger 93. Terminal Force 95. Proteus 95. Darklands 97. Killing Time 98, etc.
TV series: Duck Patrol 98– .

Fairbrother, Sydney (1873–1941) (S. Tapping).
British character actress, in films occasionally from 1916.
Iron Justice 16. The Third String 31. Chu Chin Chow 33. The Crucifix 34. The Last Journey 36. King Solomon's Mines (as Gagool) 37. Little Dolly Daydream 38, etc.

Fairchild, Morgan (1950–) (Patsy McClenny).
American leading lady.
The Initiation of Sarah (TV) 78. Murder in Music City (TV) 79. The Dream Merchants (TV) 80. The Seduction 82. Campus Man 87. Midnight Cop 88. The Haunting of Sarah Hardy (TV) 89. Mob Boss 90. Sherlock Holmes and the Leading Lady (TV) 91. Writer's Block 91. Test Tube Teens from the Year 2000 93. Freaked 93. Gospa 94. Venus Rising 95. Criminal Hearts 95. Holy Man (as herself) 98, etc.
TV series: Flamingo Road 80–81. Paper Dolls 84. Falcon Crest 85–86.

Fairchild, William (1918–).
British screenwriter.
Morning Departure 50. An Outcast of the Islands 51. The Gift Horse 52. The Net 53. The Malta Story 53. Front Page Story 54. John and Julie (& d) 54. Value for Money 57. The Silent Enemy (& d) 58. Star! 68. Embassy 72. Invitation to the Wedding 85, etc.

Fairhurst, Lyn (1920–).
British writer.
Band of Thieves 62. Touch of Death 63. Be My Guest 64. Devils of Darkness 65, etc.

Fairlie, Gerard (1899–1983).
British novelist and screenwriter. A former Guards officer, army heavyweight boxing champion and rugby player, he was a model for Bulldog Drummond, who was created by his friend 'Sapper' (Lt-Col. H. C. McNeile). Fairlie wrote seven Drummond novels after McNeile's death and ran a commando training school during the Second World War.
Autobiography: 1952, *With Prejudice*.
Shot in the Dark (oa) 33. Bulldog Jack (co-w) 34. Jack Ahoy! (co-w) 34. Open All Night 34. The Ace of Spades 35. Forever England (co-w) 35. The Lad 35. Lazybones 35. The Big Noise 36. The Lonely Road (co-w) 36. Troubled Waters 36. Calling Bulldog Drummond (oa, co-w) 51, etc.

Faison, Frankie.
American actor.
Permanent Vacation 81. Ragtime 81. Cat People 82. The Exterminator II 84. Maximum Overdrive 86. Manhunter 86. Coming to America 88. Mississippi Burning 88. Do the Right Thing 89. City of Hope 91. Silence of the Lambs 91. Freejack 92. Sommersby 93. The Stupids 95. Roommates 95. Stephen King's The Langoliers (TV) 95. Mother Night 96, etc.

Faith, Adam (1940–) (Terence Nelhams).
British pop singer turned actor, popular as the cheerful cockney crook in the TV series *Budgie* in 1971.
Never Let Go 60. Beat Girl 61. Mix Me a Person 62. Stardust 74. Yesterday's Hero 79. McVicar 80. Murder on the Orient Express (TV) 85, etc.
TV series: Love Hurts 91–92.

Faith, Percy (1908–1976).
American orchestral conductor and composer.
Love Me or Leave Me 55, *I'd Rather Be Rich* 64, *The Oscar* 66.

Faithfull, Geoffrey (1893–1979).
British cinematographer and occasional director, with Hepworth from 1908.
For You Alone (d) 44. The Lavender Hill Mob 51. Corridors of Blood 59. Village of the Damned 60. On the Beat 62, etc.

Faithfull, Marianne (1947–).
British leading lady and singer.
Autobiography: 1994, *Faithfull*.
I'll Never Forget What's 'Is Name 67. Girl on a Motorcycle 68. Hamlet 69. Ghost Story 74. When Pigs Fly 93. Shopping 94. Moondance 95, etc.

❝ I was never an actress. That's a waste of my time, and exploitative. – M.F.

Falconetti (1901–1946) (Marie Falconetti).
French stage actress, unforgettable in her only film, *The Passion of Joan of Arc* 28.

Falk, Peter (1927–).
Fast-talking, cast-eyed American actor from the off-Broadway stage.
Wind Across the Everglades 58. The Bloody Brood 59. Pretty Boy Floyd 59. The Secret of the Purple Reef 60. Murder Inc. (AAN) 60. Pocketful of Miracles (AAN) 61. Pressure Point 62. The Balcony 63. It's a Mad Mad Mad Mad World 63. Robin and the Seven Hoods 64. *The Great Race* 65. Italiano Brava Gente 65. Too Many Thieves (TV) 66. Penelope 66. Luv 67. Prescription Murder (TV) (his first appearance as Columbo) 67. Anzio 68. Castle Keep 69. Machine Gun McCain 70. A Step Out of Line (TV) 70. Husbands 70. Operation Snafu 70. Ransom for a Dead Man (start of Columbo series) (TV) 71. A Woman Under the Influence 76. Murder by Death 76. Griffin and Phoenix (TV) 76. Mikey and Nicky 76. The Brinks Job 78. The Cheap Detective 78. The In-Laws 79. All the Marbles 81. Big Trouble 84. Happy New Year 87. The Princess Bride 87. Vibes 88. Cookie 89. In the Spirit 89. Columbo Goes to the Guillotine (TV) 89. Tune in Tomorrow/Aunt Julia and the Scriptwriter 90. Motion and Emotion. Columbo Goes to College (TV). Columbo: Grand Deception (TV) 90. Faraway, So Close!/In Weiter Ferne, So Nah 93. Roommates 95. Pronto (TV) 97, etc.
TV series: *The Trials of O'Brien* 65. *Columbo* 71–78.

Falkenburg, Jinx (1919–) (Eugenia Falkenburg).
Tall, good-looking American model who made a few light comedies and musicals in the 40s. From 1946, she hosted a radio talk show with her husband Tex McCrary.
Autobiography: 1951, *Jinx*.
Nothing Sacred 37. The Lone Ranger Rides Again 39. Sweetheart of the Fleet 42. Two Latins from Manhattan 42. Sing for Your Supper 42. Lucky Legs 43. Tahiti Nights 44. Talk about a Lady 46, etc.

Faltermeyer, Harold. (1952–).
American composer.
Thief of Hearts 84. Beverly Hills Cop 84. Fletch 85. Top Gun 86. Fire and Ice 87. Fatal Beauty 87. Beverly Hills Cop II (AANs) 87. The Running Man 87. Fletch Lives 89. Tango & Cash 89. Kuffs 92. White Magic 94, etc.

Fanck, Arnold (1889–1974).
German director, renowned for mountaineering films.
■ Wunder des Schneeschuhs 19. Kampf mit dem Berge 21. Der Heilige Berg 25. Der Grosse Sprung 27. The White Hell of Pitz Palu (co-d) 29. Storm over Mont Blanc 30. Der Weisse Rausch 31. SOS Iceberg 33. Der Ewige Traum 34. Die Tochter des Samurai 37. Ein Robinson 40.

Fantoni, Sergio (1930–).
Italian leading man in international films.
Esther and the King 60. The Prize 63. Kali-Yug Goddess of Vengeance 63. Von Ryan's Express 65. Do Not Disturb 65. What Did You Do in the War, Daddy? 66. Hornet's Nest 70. Bad Man's River 71. The Belly of an Architect 87, etc.

Fapp, Daniel (1921–).
American cinematographer.
Kitty 45. Golden Earrings 47. Bride of Vengeance 49. Union Station 50. Knock on Wood 54. Living It Up 54. Desire under the Elms 58. One, Two, Three 61. West Side Story (AA) 61. I'll Take Sweden 65. Our Man Flint 66. Lord Love a Duck 66. Sweet November 67. Ice Station Zebra (AAN) 68. Marooned (AAN) 69, many others.

Faragoh, Francis Edwards (1898–1966).
American screenwriter, often in collaboration.
Her Private Affair 29. *Little Caesar* (AAN) 31. *Frankenstein* 31. The Last Man 32. Becky Sharp 35. The Return of Peter Grimm 35. The Dancing Pirate 36. My Friend Flicka 43. Renegades 46. Easy Come Easy Go 47, etc.

Farentino, James (1938–).
American leading man, mostly on TV.
Psychomania 64. Ensign Pulver 64. The War Lord 65. The Pad 66. Banning 67. Rosie 68. Me Natalie 69. The Story of a Woman 70. Jesus of Nazareth (TV) 77. Son-Rise (TV) 79. The Final Countdown 80. Dead and Buried 81. Evita Peron (TV) 81. License to Kill 84. Family Sins (TV) 87. Her Alibi 88. Bulletproof 96, etc.
TV series: The Bold Ones 69–71. *Cool Million* 71. Dynasty 81–82.

Fargas, Antonio (1943–).
Puerto Rican actor who became popular as Huggy Bear in TV's *Starsky and Hutch*.
Putney Swope 69. Shaft 71. Cleopatra Jones 73. The Gambler 74. Car Wash 76. Next Stop Greenwich Village 76. Pretty Baby 78. The Ambush Murders (TV) 82. Florida Straits (TV) 86. I'm Gonna Git You, Sucka 88. Night of the Sharks 89. The Borrower 89. Howling 6: The Freaks 90. Whore 91. Don't Be a Menace to South Central While Drinking Your Juice in the Hood 96, etc.

Fargo, James (1938–).
American director.
The Enforcer 86. Every Which Way But Loose 78. Caravans 79. Game for Vultures (UK) 80. Forced Vengeance 82. Voyage of the Rock Aliens/When the Rain Begins to Fall 84. Born to Race 88. Riding the Edge 89, etc.

Farina, Dennis (1944–).
American character actor, a former detective who spent 18 years in the Chicago police.
Thief 81. Code of Silence 85. Manhunter/Red Dragon 86. Midnight Run 88. The Hillside Strangler (TV) 89. Men of Respect 91. Street Crimes 92. Another Stakeout 93. Striking Distance 93. Romeo Is Bleeding 94. Little Big League 94. *Get Shorty* 95. Eddie 96. Out of Sight 98, etc.
TV series: Crime Story 86–88. Buddy Faro 98– .

Farley, Chris (1960–1997).
Bulky, 290-pound American comic actor, whose appeal was limited to his homeland. The star of broad comedies, and able to command fees of $6m a movie, he was born in Madison, Wisconsin, studied theatre and communication at Marquette University, and began in the late 80s working with Chicago's Second City comedy troupe, gaining national fame on the TV series *Saturday Night Live*. Given to overeating and alcohol and drug abuse, he was found dead from an accidental overdose of cocaine and morphine. He had planned to star in a movie about Fatty ARBUCKLE, written for him by David MAMET.
Wayne's World 92. Wayne's World II 93. Coneheads 93. Airheads 94. Tommy Boy 95. Billy Madison 95. Black Sheep 96. Beverly Hills Ninja 97. Edwards and Hunt 98, etc.
TV series: Saturday Night Live 90–95.
❝ I have a tendency towards pleasures of the flesh. It's a battle for me, as far as weight and things like that. But I'm curbing them because I want to continue to do comedy, and the two don't mix. – C.F.

Farmer, Frances (1914–1970).
American leading lady of the 30s who trained in New York's Group Theatre, found Hollywood distasteful and retired prematurely through ill-health and family pressures.
In 1972 a posthumous autobiography, *Will There Ever Be a Morning*, was published. This was also the title of a TV movie in 1983, in which she was portrayed by Susan Blakely. In the same year Jessica Lange played her in a theatrical film, *Frances*.
■ Too Many Parents 36. Border flight 36. Rhythm on the Range 36. *Come and Get It* 36. The Toast of New York 37. Exclusive 37. Ebb Tide 37. Ride a Crooked Mile 38. South of Pago Pago 40. Flowing Gold 40. World Première 41. Badlands of Dakota 41. Among the Living 41. Son of Fury 42. The Party Crashers 58.
❝ The nicest thing I can say about Frances Farmer is that she is unbearable. – *William Wyler*
Cinderella goes back to the ashes on a liquor-slicked highway. – *Louella Parsons*

Farmer, Mimsy (1945–).
American leading actress who went to Europe in the 60s and worked in Italy, often in horror movies, and in French films and television. Born in Chicago, Illinois, she was on screen from the early 60s. Formerly married to Italian screenwriter Vincenzo Cerami.
Spencer's Mountain 63. Bus Riley's Back in Town 65. Riot on Sunset Strip 66. Hot Road to Hell 67. Devil's Angels 67. The Wild Racers 68. More 69. The Road to Salina/Quando il Sola Scotta (Fr./It.) 71. Four Flies on Gray Velvet/4 Mosche di Velluto Grigio (It.) 71. Allonsanfan (It.) 74. Autopsy/Macchie Solarie 74. Bye Bye Monkey/Ciao Maschio 77. Concorde Affaire '79 (It.) 79. The Black Cat/Il Gatto Nero (It.) 81. The Death of Mario Ricci (Swe.) 83. Codename Wild Geese (It.) 84. Wild Rainbow (It.) 85. Evil Senses/Sensi (It.) 86. Safari (TV) 89, etc.
❝ I suppose I got picked for horror films because of my angelic face, which surprised people when I turned nasty. – M.F.

Farnon, Robert (1917–).
Canadian composer.
Spring in Park Lane 48. Captain Horatio Hornblower 51. Gentlemen Marry Brunettes 55. All for Mary 56. The Little Hut 57. Road to Hong Kong 62. The Truth About Spring 65. Shalako 68. Bear Island 79, etc.

Farnsworth, Richard (1919–).
American character actor, a former stuntman.
The Duchess and the Dirtwater Fox 76. Comes a Horseman (AAN) 78. Tom Horn 80. Resurrection 80. *The Grey Fox* 82. Waltz Across Texas 83. The Natural 84. Rhinestone 84. Sylvester 85. Space Rage 87. Havana 90. The Two Jakes 90. Misery 90. Highway to Hell 92. The Fire Next Time (TV) 93. The Getaway 94. Lassie 94, etc.

Farnum, Dustin (1870–1929).
American cowboy star of silent days. Brother of William Farnum.
The Squaw Man 13. The Virginian 14. The Scarlet Pimpernel 17. The Corsican Brothers 19. Flaming Frontier 26, etc.

Farnum, Franklyn (1876–1961).
American leading man of the silent screen, especially westerns; appeared in more than a thousand films.

Farnum, William (1876–1953).
American leading man of the silent screen.
The Spoilers 14. Les Misérables 17. The Lone Star Ranger 19. If I Were King 20. A Stage Romance 22. The Man Who Fights Alone 24. The Painted Desert 31. Supernatural 33. The Crusades 35. The Spoilers 42. Captain Kidd 45. Samson and Delilah 49. Jack and the Beanstalk 52, many others.

Farr, Derek (1912–1986).
British leading man of stage and screen, married to Muriel Pavlow; former schoolmaster.
The Outsider 40. Spellbound 40. Quiet Wedding 40. Quiet Weekend 46. Wanted for Murder 46. Teheran 47. Bond Street 48. Noose 48. Silent Dust 49. Man on the Run 49. Young Wives' Tale 51. Reluctant Heroes 52. The Dam Busters 55. Town on Trial 56. Doctor at Large 57. The Truth About Women 58. Attempt to Kill 61. The Projected Man 66. Thirty is a Dangerous Age Cynthia 68, etc.

Farr, Felicia (1932–).
American leading lady. She married actor Jack Lemmon in 1962.
Timetable 56. Jubal 56. 3.10 to Yuma 57. The Last Wagon 57. Hell Bent for Leather 60. Kiss Me Stupid 64. The Venetian Affair 67. Charley Varrick 73, etc.

Farr, Jamie (1936–) (Jamiel Farah).
Long-nosed American character actor who reached his greatest comic heights in TV's *M*A*S*H* and *Aftermash*.
Ride beyond Vengeance 65. Who's Minding the Mint? 67. With Six You Get Egg Roll 68. The Blue Knight (TV) 73. The Cannonball Run 81. Cannonball Run II 84. Happy Hour 87. Curse II: The Bite 88. Scrooged 88. Speed Zone! 89. Fearless Tiger 94, etc.

Farrar, David (1908–1995).
Tall, virile-looking British leading man whose career faltered when he went to Hollywood and played villains.
Autobiography: 1948, *No Royal Road*.
Return of a Stranger 38. The Sheepdog of the Hills 41. Suspected Person 41. Danny Boy 42. The Night Invader 42. The Dark Tower 43. They Met in the Dark 44. The World Owes Me a Living 44. Meet Sexton Blake (title role) 44. The Echo Murders 45. The Lisbon Story 46. The Trojan Brothers 46. *Black Narcissus* 46. Frieda 47. *Mr Perrin and Mr Traill* 48. *The Small Back Room* 48. Diamond City 49. Night Without Stars 51. The Golden Horde (US) 51. Gone to Earth 52. Duel in the Jungle 54. The Black Shield of Falworth (US) 54. Lilacs in the Spring 55. The Sea Chase (US) 55. Lost 56. I Accuse 57. Solomon and Sheba (US) 59. John Paul Jones (US) 59. Beat Girl 60. The 300 Spartans 62, etc.
❝ When they started offering me the parts of the fathers of the heroes, I decided to pack it in. – *D.F. on his retirement in the early 60s*

Farrar, Geraldine (1882–1967).
American operatic star who, unexpectedly, appeared for Samuel Goldwyn as heroine of silent films.
Carmen 15. Maria Rosa 16. The Devil Stone 17. Joan the Woman 17. Flame of the Desert 19. The Riddle Woman 20, etc.

Farrell, Charles (1901–1990).
Gentle-mannered American leading man of the 20s; formed a well-liked romantic team with Janet Gaynor. Retired in middle age to become Mayor of Palm Springs.
The Ten Commandments 23. Wings of Youth 25. Old Ironsides 26. *Seventh Heaven* 27. Street Angel 28. Lucky Star 29. Sunny Side Up 29. High Society Blues 30. Liliom 30. Merely Mary Ann 31. Tess of the Storm Country 32. Aggie Appleby, Maker of Men 33. Change of Heart 34. Fighting Youth 35. Moonlight Sonata (GB) 37. Tailspin 39. The Deadly Game 42, etc.
TV series: My Little Margie 52–54. The Charlie Farrell Show 56, 60.

Farrell, Charles (1901–1988).
Irish character actor who played bit parts in British films from childhood.
Creeping Shadows 31. Meet Mr Penny 38. Meet Sexton Blake 44. Night and the City 50. The Sheriff of Fractured Jaw 58. Oh! What a Lovely War 69. The Abominable Dr Phibes 71, etc.

Farrell, Glenda (1904–1971).
American leading lady and comedienne of the 30s, often seen as wisecracking reporter; made a comeback in the 50s as character actress.
Little Caesar (debut) 30. Three on a Match 31. I Am a Fugitive from a Chain Gang 32. *The Mystery of the Wax Museum* 32. Hi Nellie 33. Gold Diggers of 1935 35. In Caliente 36. *Torchy Blane in Chinatown* (and ensuing series) 39. Johnny Eager 41. A Night for Crime 42. Heading for Heaven 47. I Love Trouble 48. Apache War Smoke 52. Girls in the Night 52. Susan Slept Here 54. The Girl in the Red Velvet Swing 55. The Middle of the Night 59. Kissing Cousins 64. The Disorderly Orderly 64. Tiger by the Tail 68, many others.

Farrell, James T. (1904–1979).
Irish-American novelist best known for his twice-filmed Studs Lonigan trilogy.

Farrell, Sharon (1946–).
American general-purpose actress.
Kiss Her Goodbye 59. Forty Pounds of Trouble 63. A Lovely Way to Die 68. Marlowe 69. The Reivers 69. Quarantined (TV) 70. The Love Machine 71. The Eyes of Charles Sand (TV) 72. It's Alive 76. The Last Ride of the Dalton Gang (TV) 79. The Stunt Man 80. One Man Force 89, etc.

Farrelly, Bob.
American screenwriter and director who works in collaboration with his brother Peter FARRELLY.
Dumb and Dumber (co-w) 94. Kingpin (co-w, co-d) 96. *There's Something about Mary* 98. Outside Providence 99, etc.
❝ What's offensive to us, what we won't do, is any gay-bashing or racism. But who gets hurt by a guy sitting on a dumper letting a huge one rip? – B.F.

As my brother says, in what form of society is lighting your farts *not* funny? – *Peter Farrelly*

Farrelly, Peter.
American director, screenwriter and novelist, who works in collaboration with his brother, Bobby FARRELLY. He studied at Columbia University.
Dumb and Dumber (co-w, d) 94. Kingpin (co-w, co-d) 96. *There's Something about Mary* 98. Outside Providence 99, etc.
❝ We've got one rule: DON'T BE A F***ING PUSSY. For some reason people are just afraid to go for it; they think about their grandmothers too much. Oh no, he nearly stepped in the dog shit . . . Why not have his f***ing face fall in the dog shit? – P.F.

Farrow, John (1904–1963).
Stylish Australian director, former research scientist; in Hollywood from the mid-30s. Also wrote many of his own scripts.
■ Men in Exile 37. West of Shanghai 37. She Loved a Fireman 38. Little Miss Thoroughbred 38. My Bill 38. Broadway Musketeers 38. Women in the Wind 39. The Saint Strikes Back 39. Sorority House 39. *Five Came Back* 39. Full Confession 39. Reno 39. Married and in Love 40. A Bill of Divorcement 40. Wake Island (AAN) 42. The Commandos Strike at Dawn (& w) 43. China 43. *The Hitler Gang* (& w) 44. You Came Along 45. Two Years Before the Mast (& w) 46. California 46. Easy Come Easy Go 47. Blaze of Noon 47. Calcutta 47. *The Big Clock* 48. Night Has a Thousand Eyes 48. Beyond Glory 48. *Alias Nick Beal* 49. Red Hot and Blue 49. Where Danger Lives 50. Copper Canyon 50. *His Kind of Woman* (& w) 51. Submarine Command 51. Ride Vaquero 53. *Plunder of the Sun* 53. Botany Bay 53. Hondo 54. A Bullet is Waiting 54. The Sea Chase (& w) 55. Back from Eternity 56. Around the World in Eighty Days (co-w) (AA) 56. The Unholy Wife 57. John Paul Jones (& w) 59.

Farrow, Mia (1945–) (Maria Farrow).
American leading lady, daughter of John Farrow and Maureen O'Sullivan. She married Frank Sinatra (1966–68) and André Previn (1970–79) and has a son by Woody Allen. Patsy Kensit played her in the TV biopic *Love and Betrayal: The Mia Farrow Story* 95.
Autobiography: 1997, *What Falls Away*.
Biography: 1990, *Mia Farrow* by Sam Rubin and Richard Taylor.
Guns at Batasi 64. A Dandy in Aspic 67. Rosemary's Baby 68. Secret Ceremony 68. John and Mary 69. See No Evil 71. Follow Me 72. Goodbye Raggedy Ann (TV) 72. Scoundrel in White 72. The Great Gatsby 73. Full Circle 77. *Death on the Nile* 78. A Wedding 78. Avalanche 78. The Hurricane 79. A Midsummer Night's Sex Comedy 82. Zelig 83. Broadway Danny Rose 84. Supergirl 84. The Purple Rose of Cairo 85. Hannah and Her Sisters 86. Radio Days 87. September 87. Another Woman 88. Crimes and Misdemeanors 89. New York Stories 89. Alice 90. Shadows and Fog 92. Widows' Peak 94. Miami Rhapsody 95. Reckless 95, etc.
TV series: Peyton Place 64–67.
❝ If I seem to be running, it's because I'm pursued. – M.F.

Fasano, John.
American director of low-budget features and writer of big-budget action movies.
Black Roses (d) 88. The Jitters (d) 89. Another 48 Hrs (co-w) 90, etc.

Fassbinder, Rainer Werner (1946–1982).
Fashionable German director of the 70s, usually with something despairing to say about the current state of society.
Biography: 1987, *Love Is Colder than Death* by Robert Katz and Peter Berling; 1997, *Fassbinder: The Life and Work of a Provocative Genius* by Christian Thomsen.
Gods of the Plague 69. Katzelmacher 69. The Pedlar of Four Seasons 71. The Bitter Tears of Petra Von Kant 72. Wild Game 73. Martha 73. Effi Briest 74. Fear Eats the Soul 74. Fox 75. Fear 75. Mother Kusters Goes to Heaven 75. Tenderness of the Wolves 75. Chinese Roulette 76. Satan's Brew 76. Despair 77. The Marriage of Maria Braun 78. In a Year with 13 Moons 78. Berlin Alexanderplatz 79, etc.
❝ I hope to build a house with my films. Some of them are the cellar, some are the walls, and some are the windows. But I hope in time there will be a house. – *R.W.F.*
He was a genius. And geniuses are notoriously loony, because it's a very fine line between madness and genius. – *Dirk Bogarde*

Fast, Howard (1914–).
American historical novelist, Works filmed include *Freedom Road, The Last Frontier, Spartacus, The Immigrants*.

Faulds, Andrew (1923–).
British character actor and MP.
The Card 52. The One That Got Away 56. Payroll 61. Jason and the Argonauts 64. The Prince and the Pauper 65. The Devils 70. The Music Lovers 71. Mahler 74. Lisztomania 76, etc.

Faulkner, W. G. (1864–*).
English journalist, a former teacher, with claims to being the first regular newspaper film critic in Britain. He reviewed films for the London *Evening News* from 1910–21.

Faulkner, William (1897–1962).
Distinguished American novelist of the South who spent time in Hollywood. Born in Oxford, Mississippi, he set the majority of his novels, including those that were filmed, in the mythical county of Yoknapatawpha. He went to Hollywood in the early 30s to work first at MGM with director Howard HAWKS, with whom he became friendly; he also began an affair with Hawks's secretary. He later worked for Fox and MGM again, though his reputation for heavy drinking and his lack of interest in movies was a hindrance. He sold the screen rights to *The Unvanquished* to MGM for $25,000, but the film was never made. He returned to Warner's in the 40s, when he was in debt and all his novels were out of print, on a junior writer's pay of $300 a week. There, he worked on 17 screenplays, of which 11 were produced, and two gained him on-screen credits. As a favour to Hawks in the 50s he wrote a script of the religious novel *The Left Hand of God*, which was never filmed, and worked briefly on Hawks's Egyptian epic, *The Land of the Pharaohs*, asking the director if it was all right to write the pharaoh 'like a Kentucky colonel'. He later turned down offers to write the screenplays for some of his own novels. He was awarded the Nobel Prize for Literature in 1949. The character of the writer in the COEN Brothers' 1991 film *Barton Fink* is partly based on him.
Biography: 1974, *Faulkner* by Joseph Blotner.
Books: 1976, *Sometime in the Sun* by Tom Dardis; 1982, *Faulkner's MGM Screenplays*, ed. Bruce F. Kawin; 1990, *Writers in Hollywood 1915–1951* by Ian Hamilton.
The Story of Temple Drake (from Sanctuary) 33. Today We Live (co-w, from his story Turn About) 33. The Road to Glory (co-w) 36. Slave Ship (co-w) 37. Gunga Din (uncredited) 39. Air Force (uncredited) 43. The Southerner (uncredited) 45. *To Have and to Have Not* (co-w) 45. *The Big Sleep* (co-w) 46. Intruder in the Dust (oa) 49. The Land of the Pharaohs (co-w) 55. The Tarnished Angels (from his novel Pylon) 58. The Sound and the Fury (oa) 59. Sanctuary (oa) 60. William Faulkner's Old Man (oa) (TV) 97, etc.
❝ I don't like the climate, the people, their way of life. Nothing ever happens and then one morning you wake up and find that you are sixty-five. – *W.F. on Hollywood*
I feel that I have made a bust at moving picture writing and therefore have mis-spent and will continue to mis-spend time which at my age I cannot afford. – *W.F. to Jack Warner, 1945*
Artists in America don't have to have privacy because they don't need to be artists as far as America is concerned. America doesn't need artists because they don't count in America; artists have no more place in American life than the employers of the weekly pictorial magazines have in the private life of a Mississippi novelist. – *W.F.*
My ambition is to put everything into one sentence – not only the present but the whole past on which it depends and which keeps overtaking the present, second by second. – *W.F.*

Faust, Johann (1488–1541).
These at least are the approximate dates of a German conjurer, the scanty details of whose wandering life were the basis of plays by Marlowe (1593) and later Goethe (1808) which turned into classics. The theme of the man who sells his soul to the Devil in exchange for a rich full life has been seen in innumerable film versions, including many musical ones based on Gounod's opera, and a puppet one from Czechoslovakia. The first straight version was made in France in 1905; the most famous silent version is Murnau's of 1926, with Emil Jannings and Gosta Ekman. 1941 brought Dieterle's *All That Money Can Buy*, from Stephen Vincent Benet's *The Devil and Daniel Webster*; René Clair's version, *La Beauté du Diable*, followed in 1949, *Alias Nick Beal* in the same year, Autant-Lara's *Marguerite de la Nuit* in 1955, *Damn Yankees* in 1958 and Richard Burton's *Dr Faustus* in 1967. There were modernized versions in France 63, USA 64 and Rumania 66, and a Spanish version of 1957, *Faustina*, in which the hero becomes a heroine. The latest variations on the theme are *Bedazzled* 67, a comic extravaganza with Peter Cook as the tempter and Dudley Moore as the tempted and *Hammersmith Is Out* 72 with Richard Burton and Peter Ustinov.

Favio, Leonardo (1938–).
Argentinian director, a former actor, singer and circus performer. Born in Mendoza, he began in films in 1958 and became a leading actor in the films of Leopoldo Torre-Nilsson, who encouraged him to start directing. His career was interrupted from 1976–83 when the military government prevented him from working.
El Ángel de España (a) 58. El Secuestrador (a) 58. Fin de Fiesta (a) 60. La Terraza (a) 63. Crónica de un Niño Solo 65. El Dependiente 69. Juan Moreira 73. Nazareno Cruz y El Lobo 75. Soñar, Soñar 76, etc.

Favreau, Jon (1966–).
American actor and screenwriter. Born in Queens, New York, he worked in the theatre in Chicago before moving to Los Angeles.
Folks! 92. Rudy 93. PCU 94. Mrs Parker and the Vicious Circle 94. Notes from the Underground 95. Just Your Luck 96. *Swingers* (& co-p, w) 96. Deep Impact 98. Very Bad Things 98, etc.

Fawcett, Farrah (1947–) (formerly Farrah Fawcett-Majors).
American pin-up who enjoyed brief success as one of the original 1976 *Charlie's Angels*.
■ A Man I Like 67. Myra Breckinridge 70. The Feminist and the Fuzz (TV) 71. The Great American Beauty Contest (TV) 73. Murder on Flight 502 (TV) 75. Logan's Run 76. Somebody Killed Her Husband 78. Sunburn 78. Strictly Business 79. The Helper 79. Saturn Three 79. The Cannonball Run 80. Extremities 86. Unfinished Business (TV) 86. Between Two Women (TV) 86. Nazi Hunter: The Beate Klarsfeld Story 86. Poor Little Rich Girl (TV) 87. See You in the Morning 88. Margaret Bourke-White (TV) 88. Small Sacrifices (TV) 89. The Substitute Wife (TV) 94. Man of the House 95. Dalva (TV) 95. A Good Day to Die (TV) 95. The Apostle 97.
TV series: Good Sports 91.
❝ Marriages that last are with people who do not live in Los Angeles. – *F.F.*
I was always serious. But nobody would take me seriously. – *F.F.*
She is uniquely suited to play a woman of limited intelligence. – *Harry and Michael Medved*

Fay, Frank (1897–1961) (Francis Anthony Donner).
American comedian, a star of vaudeville and Broadway, who made a few undistinguished films. Born in San Francisco, he was on stage from the age of four. His later career was hampered by his heavy drinking, and he spent the 30s in obscurity until unexpectedly scoring his biggest success in the mid-40s as the alcoholic Elwood P. Dowd, whose friend is a giant, invisible rabbit, in the play *Harvey*. He was noted for his self-confident wit. Once, after a court appearance, his lawyer complained, 'I told you to answer simply. The other lawyer asked, "What is your profession?" How could you answer, "I'm the greatest comedian in the world"?' Fay replied, 'I was under oath, wasn't I?' His third wife was actress Barbara STANWYCK (1928–35).
Show of Shows 29. God's Gift to Women 31. Stars over Broadway 35. They Knew What They Wanted 40. Spotlight Scandals 43. Love Nest 51, etc.
❝ The 32 model lover – built for speed, style and endurance. – *Warner's publicity*

Fay's friends could be counted on the missing arm of a one-armed man. – *Milton Berle*

Fay, W. G. (1872–1947) (William George Fay).
Irish leading actor, director and screenwriter, a member of the Abbey Theatre from its start, in occasional films. Born in Dublin, he founded a touring company with his brother Frank (1870–1931) in the late 1890s, and was also a director at the Abbey, helping to set its particular style. In the early 1900s, he went to America and then worked in Britain from 1914.
Autobiographies: 1932, *Merely Players*; 1935, *The Fays of the Abbey Theatre* (with Catherine Carswell).
The Dangerous Moment 21. The Blarney Stone 33. General John Regan 33. The Last Curtain 37. My Irish Molly (co-w) 38. Spellbound 41. Spring Meeting 41. *Odd Man Out* 47, etc.

Faye, Alice (1912–1998) (Ann Leppert).
American leading lady of the 30s and 40s, once a singer with Rudy Vallee's band. Her wry expression tended to limit her roles, but she was a key star of her time and commanded a loyal following. Born in New York City, she began in her teens as a dancer and, after a succession of forgettable movies for Twentieth Century-Fox, made her mark in musicals and became a star with *In Old Chicago*. Her movie career came to an end in the mid-40s (apart from a couple of unsuccessful later appearances) after a series of disputes with Darryl ZANUCK, who promoted the career of Betty GRABLE instead. Married twice, first to singer Tony MARTIN (1937–40), and, in 1941, to bandleader Phil HARRIS.
■ George White's Scandals 34. Now I'll Tell 34. She Learned about Sailors 34. 365 Nights in Hollywood 34. George White's 1935 Scandals 35. Every Night at Eight 35. Music Is Magic 35. King of Burlesque 36. Poor Little Rich Girl 36. Sing Baby Sing 36. Stowaway 36. On the Avenue 37. Wake Up and Live 37. You Can't Have Everything 37. You're a Sweetheart 37. Sally Irene and Mary 38. *In Old Chicago* 38. *Alexander's Ragtime Band* 38. Tailspin 39. *Rose of Washington Square* 39. *Hollywood Cavalcade* 39. Barricade 39. Little Old New York 40. *Lillian Russell* 40. Tin Pan Alley 40. That Night in Rio 41. The Great American Broadcast 41. Weekend in Havana 41. *Hello Frisco Hello* 43. The Gang's All Here 43. Fallen Angel 45. State Fair 62. The Magic of Lassie 78.

Faye, Julia (1896–1966).
American actress. A former Max Sennett Bathing Beauty, she played important roles in De Mille's early pictures.
As in Days of Old 15. The Squaw Man 18. Male and Female 19. The Ten Commandments 23. The King of Kings 27. The Squaw Man 31. Only Yesterday 33. Union Pacific 39. North West Mounted Police 40. Reap the Wild Wind 42. Samson and Delilah 49. The Greatest Show on Earth 52. The Ten Commandments 56. The Buccaneer 58, etc.

Faylen, Frank (1907–1985) (Frank Ruf).
American character actor with stage experience. Played scores of bartenders, gangsters, sheriffs, cops, etc., from 1936.
Bullets or Ballots 36. The Grapes of Wrath 40. Top Sergeant Mulligan 42. *The Lost Weekend* (his best role, as the male nurse) 45. Blue Skies 46. Road to Rio 47. Detective Story 51. Riot in Cell Block Eleven 54. Killer Dino 58. The Monkey's Uncle 65. Funny Girl 68, many others.
TV series: Dobie Gillis 59–62.

Fazan, Adrienne.
American editor.
The Bride Wore Red 37. Barbary Coast Gent 44. The Kissing Bandit 48. *An American in Paris* 51. *Singin' in the Rain* 52. Deep in My Heart 54. Invitation to the Dance 56. *Gigi* (AA) 58. The Gazebo 59. Two Weeks in Another Town 62. This Property is Condemned 66. The Comic 69, many others.

Fazenda, Louise (1895–1962).
American leading lady of the Mack Sennett era: bathing beauty, slapstick comedienne, later a character actress.
The Beautiful and Damned 22. Main Street 23. Cheaper to Marry 25. Bobbed Hair 25. The Bat 26. The Red Mill 27. The Terror 28. Riley the Cop 28. Noah's Ark 29. The Desert Song 29. No

No Nanette 30. Leathernecking 30. Cuban Love Song 31. Alice in Wonderland 33. Wonder Bar 34. Colleen 36. The Road Back 37. Swing Your Lady 38. The Old Maid 39, many others.

Fearing, Kenneth (1902–1961).
American novelist of urban cynicism: *The Big Clock* is his chief contribution to the screen.

Fearless Nadia (1908–1996) (Mary Evans).
Blonde Australian-born actress of Anglo-Greek parents who became a star of Indian cinema, in singing, whip-cracking and horse-riding roles, in which she was famous for doing her own acrobatic stunts. She moved with her family to Bombay at the age of 10 and was a circus and variety performer before becoming a star in 1935 in *The Lady with the Whip*/Hunterwali. Retired in the late 50s to breed racehorses and married her producer, Homi Wadia. A documentary on her life, *Fearless Nadia – The Hunterwali Story*, was made in 1993.

Fegté, Ernst (1900–1976).
German production designer, in Hollywood from the early 30s. Born in Hamburg, he began in films in Germany in 1919.
The General Died at Dawn 36. The Palm Beach Story 42. I Married a Witch 42. Five Graves to Cairo (AAN) 43. Frenchman's Creek (AA) 44. *The Princess and the Pirate* (AAN) 44. Concerto 47. Destination Moon (AAN) 50. Beyond the Time Barrier 60, etc.

Fehmiu, Bekim (1932–).
Stalwart Slav leading man in international films.
The Happy Gypsies 66. *The Adventurers* 70. The Deserter 71. Permission to Kill 75. Black Sunday 76. Madam Kitty 77. La Voce (It.) 82. The Red and the Black (Yug.) 85. Genghis Khan 92, etc.

Fehr, Rudi (1911–).
German-American editor.
Invisible Enemies (GB) 35. Honeymoon for Three 41. Desperate Journey 42. Watch on the Rhine 43. The Conspirators 44. Humoresque 46. Possessed 47. Key Largo 48. The Inspector General 49. House of Wax 53. Dial M for Murder 54, many others.

Feiffer, Jules (1929–).
American satirical strip cartoonist, venturing into screenwriting.
Little Murders 71. Carnal Knowledge 71. Popeye 80. I Want to Go Home 89, etc.

Feist, Felix E. (1906–1965).
American director, at first of short subjects including Pete Smith Specialities; in Hollywood from 1928.
■ Stepping Sisters 32. The Deluge 33. All By Myself 43. You're a Lucky Fellow Mr Smith 43. This is the Life 44. Pardon My Rhythm 44. Reckless Age 44. George White's Scandals 45. The Devil Thumbs a Ride (& w) 47. The Winner's Circle 47. The Threat 49. Treason 49. The Golden Gloves Story 50. The Man Who Cheated Himself 50. Tomorrow is Another Day 51. The Basketball Fix 51. This Woman is Dangerous 52. The Big Trees 52. The Man Behind the Gun 52. Donovan's Brain 53. Pirates of Tripoli 55.

Fejos, Paul (1893–1963).
Hungarian director, in America from 1923.
The Last Moment 27. Lonesome 28. Erik the Great 29. Broadway 29. The Big House (co-d) 30. Maria (Hung.) 32. The Golden Smile (Dan.) 35. A Handful of Rice (Swe.) 38.

Feld, Fritz (1900–1993).
Dapper German character comedian, once stage director for Max Reinhardt; long in Hollywood playing temperamental head waiters and clerks in more than 400 films.
Broadway 29. I Met Him in Paris 37. Bringing Up Baby 38. Idiot's Delight 39. *At the Circus* (as Jardinet) 39. Sandy is a Lady 40. *World Première* 41. Iceland 42. Phantom of the Opera 43. The Great John L 45. Catman of Paris 46. The Secret Life of Walter Mitty 47. My Girl Tisa 48. Mexican Hayride 49. The Jackpot 50. Full House 52. The Patsy 64. Barefoot in the Park 67. Hello Dolly 69. The Love Bug Rides Again 73. Silent Movie 76. The World's Greatest Lover 77. History of the World Part One 81, many others.

Feldman, Andrea (1948–1972).
American actress in Andy Warhol's films. She committed suicide, leaving a note that read, 'I am going for the big time. Heaven.'
The Imitation of Christ 67. Trash 69. Heat 70.

Feldman, Charles K. (1904–1968) (Charles Gould).
American producer, former lawyer and talent agent.
Pittsburgh 42. Follow the Boys 44. To Have and Have Not 44. The Big Sleep 46. Red River 48. The Red Pony 49. A Streetcar Named Desire 51. The Seven Year Itch 54. A Walk on the Wild Side 62. The Seventh Dawn 64. What's New Pussycat? 65. The Group 66. Casino Royale 67, etc.

Feldman, Corey (1971–).
American actor, performing in commercials from the age of three.
Time after Time 79. Friday the 13th – the Final Chapter 83. Gremlins 84. Friday the 13th Part V: A New Beginning 85. The Goonies 85. Stand by Me 86. The Lost Boys 87. License to Drive 88. The 'burbs 89. Dream a Little Dream 89. Teenage Mutant Ninja Turtles 90. Edge of Honor 91. Meatballs IV 92. Round Trip to Heaven 92. Blown Away 93. Lipstick Camera 94. National Lampoon's Last Resort 94. Maverick 94. Lipstick Camera 94. Tales from the Crypt Presents Bordello of Blood 96. Red Line 96. South Beach Academy 96. Evil Obsession 96. Legion 98, etc.
TV series: The Bad News Bears 79–80. Madame's Place 82.

Feldman, Marty (1933–1982).
Pop-eyed British TV comic who from writing TV comedy scripts became a limited but well-known international star in his own right.
Every Home Should Have One 69. Young Frankenstein 73. The Adventures of Sherlock Holmes' Smarter Brother 75. Silent Movie 76. The Last Remake of Beau Geste 77. High Anxiety 78. Sex with a Smile 79. In God We Trust 80. Yellowbeard 83, etc.

Feldon, Barbara (1939–).
American leading lady of the 70s who came to notice on TV.
Fitzwilly 67. Playmates (TV) 72. Smile 74. Let's Switch (TV) 75. No Deposit No Return 76. A Vacation in Hell (TV) 79. Get Smart: The Movie (TV) 89, etc.
TV series: *Get Smart* 65–69.

Feldshuh, Tovah (1952–).
American leading lady who came to the fore in *Holocaust* (TV) 78 but then failed to justify her promise.
Scream Pretty Peggy (TV) 73. The Amazing Howard Hughes (TV) 77. Terror out of the Sky (TV) 78. The Triangle Factory Fire Scandal (TV) 79. Cheaper to Keep Her 80. The Women's Room (TV) 80. The Idolmaker 80. Daniel 83. Brewster's Millions 85. The Blue Iguana 88. A Day in October/ En Dag Oktober 91. Love and Betrayal: The Mia Farrow Story (TV) 95, etc.

Felix, Maria (1915–).
Mexican actress of strong personality. Born in Alamos, and brought up in Guadalajara, she was in films from 1942.
The Kneeling Goddess 47. Dona Diabla 49. Mare Nostrum 50. Messalina 52. The Kidnapping 52. French Can Can 53. Les Héros Sont Fatigués 55, many Mexican films.

Felix, Seymour (1892–1961).
American dance director, in films since 1929.
The Great Ziegfeld (AA) 36. Alexander's Ragtime Band 38. Cover Girl 44. The I Don't Care Girl 52, many others.

Fell, Norman (1924–1998).
Sad-looking American character actor.
Ocean's Eleven 61. Pork Chop Hill 59. Bullitt 68. If It's Tuesday This Must Be Belgium 69. The Stone Killer 73. Guardian of the Wilderness 76. On the Right Track 81. Paternity 81. Transylvania 6–5000 85. Stripped to Kill 87. The Bone Yard 90. For the Boys 91. Hexed 93. The Destiny of Marty Fine 96, etc.
TV series: 87th Precinct 61–64. The Man from UNCLE 68. Dan August 71. Needles and Pins 74. *Three's Company* 77–78. The Ropers 79–80, etc.

Fellini, Federico (1920–1993).
Fashionable and influential Italian director, formerly cartoonist. Film actor and writer from 1941. He was married to actress Giulietta Masina. Awarded an honorary Oscar for lifetime achievement in 1993.
Biographies: 1977, *Fellini the Artist* by Edward Murray. 1986, *Fellini: A Life* by Hollis Alpert. 1992, *The Cinema of Federico Fellini* by Peter Bondanella. 1993, *Fellini* by John Baxter. 1996, *I Fellini* by Charlotte Chandler.
■ AS DIRECTOR: Lights of Variety 50. The White Sheik 50. I Vitelloni 53. *La Strada* (AA, AANw) 54. Il Bidone 55. Notti di Cabiria (AA) 57. *La Dolce Vita* (AAN) 59. Boccaccio 70 (part) 62. *Eight and a Half* (AAN) 63. Juliet of the Spirits 65. Histoires Extraordinaires (part) 68. *Satyricon* (AAN) 69. The Clowns 70. Fellini Roma 72. Amarcord (AAN) 74. Casanova 77. City of Women 81. And the Ship Sails On 83. *Ginger and Fred* 85. Federico Fellini's Intervista 87. Voices of the Moon/La Voce della Luna 90.
❝ I always direct the same film. I can't distinguish one from another. – *F.F.*
Our dreams are our real life. – *F.F.*
Although my father wanted me to become an engineer and my mother a bishop, I myself am quite content to have succeeded in becoming an adjective. – *F.F.*

Fellner, Eric (1960–).
British producer, co-founder with Tim Bevan of Working Title films.

Fellowes, Rockliffe (1885–1950).
Canadian general-purpose actor in Hollywood films of silent days.
The Easiest Way 17. In Search of a Sinner 20. The Spoilers 23. The Garden of Weeds 24. East of Suez 25. Syncopating Sue 26. The Taxi Dancer 27. The Third Degree 27. The Charlatan 29. Outside the Law 30. Monkey Business 31. Lawyer Man 32. The Phantom Broadcast 33. The Black Page 34, many others.

Fellows, Edith (1923–).
American teenage star of the 30s.
Riders of Death Valley 32. Jane Eyre 34. Pennies from Heaven 36. Five Little Peppers 38. Five Little Peppers in Trouble 41. Girls' Town 42. Her First Romance 47, etc.

Fellows, Robert (1903–1969).
American producer.
Virginia City 39. They Died with Their Boots On 41. The Spanish Main 45. A Yankee in King Arthur's Court 49. Hondo 54. The High and the Mighty 54, etc.

Felmy, Hansjoerg (1931–).
German leading man.
Der Stern von Afrika (debut) 56. Wir Wunderkinder 58. Buddenbrooks 59. Station Six Sahara 63. Torn Curtain 66.

Felton, Felix (1912–1972).
English character actor, from radio.
Lady Godiva Rides Again 51. The Pickwick Papers 52. Doctor in the House 54. Doctor at Sea 55. Around the World in Eighty Days 56. Pacific Destiny 56. Just My Luck 57. The Two Faces of Dr Jekyll 60. Licensed to Kill 65. Chitty Chitty Bang Bang 68, etc.

Felton, Verna (1890–1966).
American character actress, often seen as neighbour or busybody.
The Gunfighter 50. New Mexico 52. Picnic 55. Little Egypt 55. The Oklahoman 57, etc.
TV series: December Bride 54–59. Pete and Gladys 60.

Fenn, Sherilyn (1964–).
American leading actress.
Out of Control 85. Just One of the Guys 85. Thrashin' 86. The Wraith 86. Zombie High 87. Two Moon Junction 88. Crime Zone 88. True Blood 89. Wild at Heart 90. Meridian/Kiss of the Beast 90. Backstreet Dreams 90. Of Mice and Men 92. Ruby 92. Diary of a Hit Man 92. Desire and Hell at Sunset Motel 92. Boxing Helena 93. Three of Hearts 93. Fatal Instinct 93. The Assassination File 96. Lovelife 97. National Lampoon's The Don's Analyst 97. Darkness Falls 98. Just Write 98, etc.
TV series: Twin Peaks 90. Rude Awakening 98– .

Fennell, Albert (1920–1988).
British producer best known for TV's *The Avengers* and *The Professionals*.
The Green Scarf 54. Next to No Time 57. Tunes of Glory 59. The Innocents 61. Night of the Eagle 62. And Soon the Darkness 71. Dr Jekyll and Sister Hyde 71. The Legend of Hell House 73, etc.

Fenton, Frank (1906–1957) (Frank Fenton-Morgan).
American general-purpose supporting actor.
Lady of Burlesque 42. Buffalo Bill 44. Magic Town 46. Red River 48. Island in the Sky 53. Emergency Hospital 56. Hellbound 58, many others.

Fenton, George (1950–).
British composer, from TV.
Hitting Town (TV) 76. Gandhi (AAN) 82. Company of Wolves 84. 84 Charing Cross Road 87. Cry Freedom (AAN) 87. High Spirits 88. The Dressmaker 88. White Mischief 87. Dangerous Liaisons (AAN) 88. We're No Angels 89. Memphis Belle 90. White Palace 90. The Fisher King (AAN) 91. Final Analysis 92. Hero/ Accidental Hero 92. Groundhog Day 93. Born Yesterday 93. Shadowlands 93. China Moon 94. Interview with a Vampire 95. Land and Freedom 95. Mary Reilly 96. Heaven's Prisoners 96. Multiplicity 96. The Crucible 96. Carla's Song 96. In Love and War 97. The Woodlanders 97. My Name Is Joe 98. The Object of My Affection 98. Dangerous Beauty 98. Ever After 98. Living Out Loud 98. You've Got Mail 98, etc.

Fenton, Leslie (1902–1978).
British-born director of Hollywood 'B' pictures. (Former actor in many silent films and early talkies including *What Price Glory?, The Man I Love, Broadway, Public Enemy, F.P.I*, etc.)
■ *Tell No Tales* 39. Stronger than Desire 39. The Man from Dakota 40. The Golden Fleecing 40. The Saint's Vacation 41. Tomorrow the World 46. Pardon my Past 46. On Our Merry Way (co-d) 48. Saigon 48. Lulu Belle 48. Whispering Smith 48. Streets of Laredo 49. The Redhead and the Cowboy 50.

Feore, Colm.
Canadian leading actor.
Blades of Courage (TV) 88. Personals (TV) 90. Beautiful Dreamers 90. *Thirty-Two Short Films about Glenn Gould* 93. The Spider and the Fly (TV) 94. Truman (TV) 95. Night Falls on Manhattan 96. Hostile Waters (TV) 97. Face/Off 97. Critical Care 97. City of Angels 98. The Lesser Evil 98, etc.

Ferber, Edna (1887–1968).
American novelist and dramatist. Born in Kalamazoo, Michigan, she began as a journalist, though she had hoped to be an actress. She became a Broadway playwright and best-selling novelist, winning a Pulitzer Prize in 1924. She had an acerbic wit: when the *New Yorker* gave a bad review to a film based on one of her stories and blamed her for it, she wrote to the editor, 'Will you kindly inform the moron who runs your motion picture department that I did not write the movie? Also inform him that Moses did not write the motion picture entitled *The Ten Commandments*.'
Biography: 1978, *Ferber* by Julia Goldsmith Gilbert.
Our Mrs McChesney 18. Welcome Home (from Minick) 25. Mother Knows Best 28. Showboat 29, 35 and 51. The Royal Family of Broadway 31. Cimarron 31 and 61. So Big 32 and 53. Dinner at Eight 33. Come and Get It 36. Stage Door (with George S. Kaufman) 38. No Place to Go (from Minick) 39. Saratoga Trunk 43. Giant 56. Ice Palace 59.
❝ Life can't ever really defeat a writer who is in love with writing, for life itself is the writer's lover until death – fascinating, cruel, lavish, warm, cold, treacherous, constant; the more varied the moods the richer the experience. – *E.F.*
Being an old maid is like death by drowning. It's a really delightful sensation after you cease to struggle. – *E.F.*
Edna reminds me of a Confederate general. And I'm from Pittsburgh. – *George S. Kaufman*, a frequent collaborator

Ferguson, Elsie (1883–1961).
American leading lady of silent melodramas about the upper classes. Popular 1918–27, then retired.
Barbary Sheep 17. The Lie 18. Song of Songs

18. A Society Exile 19. His House in Order 20. Sacred and Profane Love 21. Outcast 22, etc.

Ferguson, Frank (1899–1978).
Toothy American character actor, often in comic bit parts.
This Gun for Hire 42. The Miracle of the Bells 48. Abbott and Costello Meet Frankenstein 49. Elopement 51. Johnny Guitar 54. Andy Hardy Comes Home 58. Raymie 60, many others.
TV series: My Friend Flicka 56. Peyton Place 64–68.

Ferguson, Larry.
American screenwriter and director.
St Helens 81. Highlander 86. Beverly Hills Cop II 87. The Presidio 88. The Hunt for Red October 90. Nails 92. Alien 3 92. Fixing the Shadow (wd) 92. Maximum Risk 96. Gunfighter's Moon (& d) 96, etc.

Ferguson, Perry (1901–*).
American art director. Born in Fort Worth, Texas, he worked for RKO in the 30s and 40s.
A Bill of Divorcement 32. Kentucky Kernels 34. The Silver Streak 34. Alice Adams 35. The Ex-Mrs Bradford 36. Winterset (AAN) 36. New Faces of 1937 37. Bringing Up Baby 38. The Saint in New York 38. Gunga Din 39. In Name Only 39. Swiss Family Robinson 40. Ball of Fire 41. Citizen Kane 41. They Got Me Covered 42. The Pride of the Yankees (AAN) 42. The North Star (AAN) 42. The Outlaw 43. Up in Arms 44. Casanova Brown (AAN) 44. The Best Years of Our Lives 46. The Stranger 46. Song of the South 46. The Secret Life of Walter Mitty 47. The Bishop's Wife 47. Rope 48. A Song Is Born 48. Without Honor 49. The Sound of Fury 50. Queen for a Day 51. The Lady Says No 51. The Big Sky 52. Main Street to Broadway 53. Dead Ringer 64. Coffy 73. The Shaggy D.A. 76. Herbie Goes to Monte Carlo 77, etc.

Ferman, James (1930–).
British executive, a former television director, who was secretary of the British Board of Film Classification 1975–98. He caused controversy in his final year by advocating a relaxation of official attitudes to pornography, and regretting not cutting more from Quentin TARANTINO's *Pulp Fiction*.
❝ The instinctive good taste of the artist usually prevents him from indulging in unnecessarily explicit detail. But we are faced too rarely with the work of first-class artists. – *J.F.*

Fernandel (1903–1971) (Fernand Contandin).
Rubber-faced French comedian with toothy grin and music-hall background. Films usually 'naughty but nice.'
Regain/Harvest 37. Un Carnet de Bal 37. *Fric Frac* 39. *La Fille du Puisatier* 40. *The Red Inn* 51. Forbidden Fruit 52. The *Don Camillo* series from 1952. *The Sheep Has Five Legs* 54. Paris Holiday 57. The Cow and I 59. Croesus 60. La Cuisine au Beurre 63. Le Voyage du Père 66. L'Homme à la Buick 67, Heureux qui comme Ulysse 69, etc.

Fernández, Emilio (1904–1986).
Prolific Mexican director and actor, few of whose films have been seen abroad. Born in El Hondo, he began as a bit actor in the USA in the 20s, became a leading man of Mexican films in the mid-30s, and began directing in the early 40s. He made 16 films with cinematographer Gabriel FIGUEROA and these, often featuring Dolores DEL RIO and Pedro ARMENDARIZ, enjoyed great local popularity.
Isle of Passion 41. Maria Candelaria 44. The Pearl 45. Rio Escondido 47. Maclovia 48. The Torch 50. Bring Me the Head of Alfredo Garcia (a) 74. Breakout 75. México Norte 77. Erótica 78, etc.

Ferrara, Abel (1952–).
American director of action films and, under the name of Jimmy Laine, occasional actor. He has directed episodes of *Miami Vice* for TV.
The Driller Killer (& a) 79. Ms 45 (& a) 81. Fear City 84. China Girl 87. Cat Chaser 89. King of New York 90. Bad Lieutenant 92. Body Snatchers 93. Snake Eyes 93. The Addiction 95. The Funeral 96. Subway Stories (co-d) 97. New Rose Hotel 98, etc.

Ferrell, Conchata (1943–).
American character actress.
A Death in Canaan (TV) 78. *Heartland* 80. The Girl Called Hatter Fox (TV) 80. The Seduction of Miss Leona (TV) 81. Rape and Marriage (TV) 81. Where the River Runs Black 86. Deadly Intentions . . . Again (TV) 91. Heaven and Earth 93. The Buccaneers (TV) 95. Touch 96. My Fellow Americans 96, etc.
TV series: Hot L Baltimore 75. B.J. and the Bear 79–80. McClain's Law 81–82. E/R 84–85. A Peaceable Kingdom 89. L.A. Law 92.

Ferréol, Andréa. (1947–).
French leading actress, in international films.
Blow-Out/La Grande Bouffe 73. The Day of the Jackal 73. The Tin Drum 79. The Last Metro 80. Three Brothers/Tre Fratelli 81. The Night of Varennes/La Nuit de Varennes 82. The Two Lives of Mattia Pascal/Le Due Vite di Mattia Pascal 84. A Zed and Two Noughts 85. The Sleazy Uncle/Lo Zio Indegno 89. Stroke of Midnight (US) 91. A Linha do Horizonte 93. Domenica 94. The Boxing Promoter/Le Montreur de Boxe 96, many others.

Ferrer, José (1912–1992) (José Vincente Ferrer y Centron).
Distinguished American stage actor of Puerto Rican origin; film career spotty but interesting. His third wife was singer Rosemary Clooney (1953–67). Their son Miguel is an actor.
■ *Joan of Arc* (as the Dauphin) (AAN) 48. Whirlpool 49. Crisis 50. *Cyrano de Bergerac* (AA) 50. Anything Can Happen 52. *Moulin Rouge* (as Toulouse Lautrec) (AAN) 53. Miss Sadie Thompson 53. The Caine Mutiny 54. Deep in My Heart 54. The Shrike (& d) 55. Cockleshell Heroes (& d) (GB) 56. The Great Man (& wd) 56. I Accuse (& d) 58. The High Cost of Loving (d) 58. Return to Peyton Place (d only) 61. State Fair (d only) 62. Lawrence of Arabia 62. Nine Hours to Rama 63. Stop Train 349 64. Cyrano contre d'Artagnan (Fr.) 64. The Greatest Story Ever Told 65. *Ship of Fools* 65. Enter Laughing 67. Cervantes 67. The Aquarians (TV) 70. Banyon (TV) 71. Cross Current (TV) 71. The Missing Are Deadly (TV) 73. The Marcus Nelson Murders (TV) 73. Order to Kill 75. Medical Story (TV) 75. Roman Grey (TV) 75. E Lollipop 75. The Big Bus 76. Voyage of the Damned 76. The Sentinel 77. Crash 77. The Private Files of J. Edgar Hoover 78. Dracula's Dog 78. The Swarm 78. Natural Enemies 79. The Big Brawl 80. The French Atlantic Affair (TV) 79. Gideon's Trumpet (TV) 80. The Dream Merchants (TV) 80. Bloody Birthday 80. Evita Peron (TV) 81. Blood Feud (TV) 82. A Midsummer Night's Sex Comedy 82. Blood Tide 82. To Be or Not to Be 83. Dune 84. The Evil That Men Do 84. Ingrid (TV) 85. Blood and Orchids (TV) 85.
TV series: Bridges to Cross 85.

Ferrer, Mel (1917–).
Sensitive-looking American leading man, former radio producer and writer.
Girl of the Limberlost (d only) 45. *Lost Boundaries* 49. The Secret Fury (d only) 50. Vendetta (d only) 50. Born to Be Bad 50. The Brave Bulls 51. *Scaramouche* 52. Rancho Notorious 52. Lili 53. Knights of the Round Table (GB) 54. Saadia 54. Oh! Rosalinda (GB) 55. War and Peace 56. The Vintage 57. The Sun Also Rises 57. Fräulein 58. The World, the Flesh and the Devil 59. Green Mansions (d only) 59. Blood and Roses 61. The Fall of the Roman Empire 64. Sex and the Single Girl 64. El Greco 65. Wait until Dark (p only) 67. Every Day's a Holiday (& wd, p) (Sp.) 67. A Time for Loving (& p) 71. Embassy (p only) 72. W (p only) 73. Brannigan 75. Eaten Alive 77. The Norseman 78. The Fifth Floor 80. The Top of the Hill (TV) 80. The Memory of Eva Ryker (TV) 81. Fugitive Family (TV) 81. Lili Marlene 81. Eye of the Widow 91. Catherine the Great (TV) 95, etc.
TV series: Behind the Screen 81–82. Falcon Crest 81–84.

Ferrer, Miguel (1955–).
American character actor, the son of José Ferrer and Rosemary Clooney.
The Last Horror Film 81. . . . And They're Off 82. The Evil that Men Do 83. Heartbreaker 83. Star Trek III: The Search for Spock 84. Flashpoint 84. Robocop 87. Deepstar Six 88. The Guardian 90. Broken Badges (TV) 90. Innocent Blood 91. Twin Peaks: Fire Walk with Me 92. The Harvest 92. Scam 93. Point of No Return 93. Hot Shots! Part Deux 93. Another Stakeout 93. Blank Check 94. The Stand (TV) 94. Incident at Deception Ridge (TV) 94. Stephen King's The Nightflier (TV) 96. The Disappearance of Garcia Lorca 96. Mr Magoo 97. Where's Marlowe? 98. Mulan (voice) 98, etc.

Ferreri, Marco (1928–1997).
Italian director and screenwriter, a maker of blackly humorous satires on middle-class life and attitudes. Born in Milan, he studied medicine before working in advertising and creating a magazine-style newsreel that failed. In the late 50s, he moved to Spain to work with director Rafael Azcona and made three features there before returning to Italy.
El Pisto (Sp.) 56. The Wheelchair (Sp.) 60. Queen Bee 63. The Bearded Lady 64. Wedding March 65. *Dillinger Is Dead* 68. Liza 72. *Blowout* 73. The Last Woman 76. The Future Is Woman 84. I Love You 86. Y'a Bon les Blancs 87. House of Smiles/La Casa del Sorriso 91. The Flesh/La Carne 91. Diario di un Vizio 93. Do What Thou Wilt (Fr.) 95. Silver Nitrate 96, etc.
❝ The master of bad taste – *Sunday Times*

Ferrero, Anna Maria (1931–) (Anna Maria Guetra).
Italian leading lady of the 50s, now retired.
The Sky Is Red/Il Cielo è Rosso 49. Giuseppe Verdi 53. The Golden Falcon/Il Falco d'Oro 55. War and Peace (US) 56. Bad Girls Don't Cry/La Notte Brava 59. The Hunchback of Rome/Il Gobbo 60. Controsesso 64, etc.

Ferretti, Dante (1943–).
Italian production designer, frequently on the films of Pier Paolo PASOLINI and Federico FELLINI.
Medea 69. The Decameron 71. The Canterbury Tales 72. The Arabian Nights 74. The Night Porter 74. Salo or the 120 Days of Sodom 75. Orchestra Rehearsal/Prova d'Orchestra 78. City of Women/Città delle Donne 80. Tales of Ordinary Madness/Storie di Ordinaria Follia 81. Ginger and Fred 86. The Name of the Rose 86. The Adventures of Baron Munchausen (AAN) 88. The Voice of the Moon/La Voce della Luna 90. Hamlet (AAN) 90. The Age of Innocence (AAN) 93. Interview with the Vampire (AAN) 94. Casino 95. *Kundun* (AANpd, cos) 97. Meet Joe Black 98, many others.

Ferretti, Robert A.
American editor.
Gymkata 85. Out of Control 85. Tango & Cash (co-ed) 89. Die Hard 2 (co-ed) 91. Out for Justice (co-ed) 91. Showdown in Little Tokyo (co-ed) 91. Under Siege 92. On Deadly Ground 94. The Hunted 95. Shadow Conspiracy 97. Fire Down Below 97, etc.

Ferreyra, Jose Agustin (1889–1943).
Argentinian director, one of the leading talents in the days of silent movies, who continued working after the coming of sound. He was also an artist, set designer, composer and occasional actor and screenwriter, in films from 1915. He is said to have worked without a script and to have refused to watch films made by other directors. His lyrics to a tango for *The Girl from Arrabal* 22 provided the first live musical accompaniment in Argentinian cinema. He also directed the country's first sound feature, *Port Dolls* 31, which used discs.
El Tango de la Muerte 17. La Guacha 21. La Maleva 23. La Canción del Gaucho 30. Rapsodia Gaucha 32. Calles de Buenos Aires 33. Puente Alsina 35. Chimbela 39. La Mujer y la Selva 41, etc.

Ferrigno, Lou (1952–).
Muscular American actor, a former Mr Universe and footballer, who gained fame on TV as the green Incredible Hulk 78–82.
Pumping Iron (doc) 77. Hercules 83. Hercules II 85. Desert Warrior 88. The Cage 88. All's Fair 89. Sinbad of the Seven Seas 89. Liberty & Bash 90. The Making of 'And God Spoke' 94, etc.

Ferrini, Franco (1944–).
Italian screenwriter, a former film critic. Born in La Spezia, he studied at the University of Pisa, and is best known internationally for his work with horror directors Lamberto BAVA and Dario ARGENTO.
Poliziotti Violenti 76. Enigma Rosso 78. Sing Sing 83. Once Upon a Time in America 84. Phenomena 84. Creepers 84. Demons/Demoni 85. Demons 2/Demoni 2 87. Opera 87. Two Evil Eyes/Due Occhi Diabolici 89. The Church/La Chiesa 91. Trauma 93. The Stendahl Syndrome (uncredited) 96, etc.

Ferrio, Gianni (1924–).
Italian composer, particularly in westerns. Born in Vicenza, where he studied music, he collaborated with Ennio Morricone on the score for *Fort Yuma Gold* 67.
Latin Lovers/Le Italiane e L'Amore 61. I Fidanzati 63. One Silver Dollar 65. Wanted 66. El Hombre Que Mató Billy El Niño 67. Fort Yuma Gold/Per Pochi Dollari Ancora 67. Death Sentence/Sentenza di Morte 67. The Sweet Sins of Sexy Susan 67. House of Pleasure 68. Sexy Susan Sins Again 68. Wanted 68. A Few Bullets More 68. Io Emmanuelle 69. Vengeance Is Mine 69. A Man Called Sledge 70. La Morte Risale a Ieri Sera 70. A Bullet for Sandoval 70. A Man Called Sledge 71. The Mysterious Island 73. Vices in the Family/Il Vizio di Famiglia 75. One Silver Dollar/Un Dollaro Bucato 75. Tex Willer and the Lord of the Deep 85, etc.

Ferris, Barbara (1940–).
British leading lady.
Catch Us If You Can 66. Interlude 68. A Nice Girl Like Me 69. A Chorus of Disapproval 89, etc.

Ferris, Pam.
Plump British character actress, best known as Ma Larkin in the TV series *The Darling Buds of May*.
Meantime 83. Mr Wakefield's Crusade (TV) 92. Roald Dahl's Matilda 96, etc.
TV series: The Darling Buds of May 91–93. Where the Heart Is 97.

Ferzetti, Gabriele (1925–) (Pasquale Ferzetti).
Italian leading man.
William Tell 48. Cuore Ingrato 51. Three Forbidden Stories 52. Puccini 54. Le Amiche 55. Donatello 56. L'Avventura 59. Torpedo Bay 64. Once Upon a Time in the West 69. On Her Majesty's Secret Service 69. Hitler – The Last Ten Days 73. The Night Porter 74. A Matter of Time 76. End of the Game 76. Julia and Julia 87, etc.

Fetchit, Stepin (1892–1985) (Lincoln Perry).
Gangly, slow-moving American comedian, popular in films of the 30s.
In Old Kentucky 29. Stand Up and Cheer 33. Steamboat Round the Bend 35. Charlie Chan in Egypt 35. Dimples 36. On the Avenue 37. Zenobia 39. Bend of the River 52. The Sun Shines Bright 53, many others.

Feuillade, Louis (1873–1925).
Much-fêted French director who made marathon silent serials about master criminals.
Fantômas 13. Les Vampires 15. Judex (remade by Franju 63) 16–17. Tih Minh 18. Parisette 21, etc.

Feuillère, Edwige (1907–1998) (Edwige Cunati).
Distinguished French actress, a leading member of the Comédie Française.
Le Cordon Bleu 30. Topaze 32. I Was An Adventuress 38. Sans Lendemain 40. La Duchesse de Langeais 42. *L'Idiot* 46. L'Aigle à Deux Têtes 47. Woman Hater (GB) 48. *Olivia* 50. Adorable Creatures 52. *Le Blé en Herbe* 53. The Fruits of Summer 54. En Cas de Malheur/Love Is My Profession 57. Crime Doesn't Pay 62. Do You Like Women? 64, etc.

Feydeau, Georges (1862–1921).
French writer of stage farces, many of which have become classics and are often filmed, the best cinematic examples being *Occupe Toi d'Amélie* 49 and *Hotel Paradiso* 66.

Feyder, Jacques (1885–1948) (Jacques Frederix).
French director, former actor; married Françoise Rosay.
L'Atlantide 21. Crainquebille 22. Thérèse Raquin 28. *Les Nouveaux Messieurs* 29. The Kiss (US) 29. Le Grand Jeu 34. *La Kermesse Héroique* 35. Knight without Armour (GB) 37. Les Gens du Voyage 38. La Loi du Nord 39. Une Femme Disparaît 41, Macadam (supervised only) 45, etc.

Fiander, Lewis (1938–).
Australian-born stage and TV actor in Britain.
Dr Jekyll and Sister Hyde 71. The Abdication 73. Death is Child's Play 75. Sweeney 2 78. The Doctor and the Devils 86, etc.

Fiedel, Brad (1951–).
American composer.
The Calendar Girl Murders (TV) 83. The Terminator 84. Compromising Positions 85. Fright Night 85. Desert Bloom 86. Popeye Doyle (TV) 86. Let's Get Harry 86. The Big Easy 87. Nowhere to Hide 87. The Serpent and the Rainbow 88. The Accused 88. Fright Night Part 2 89. True Believer 89. Immediate Family 89. Blue Steel 90. Gladiator 92. The Real McCoy 93. Blink 94. True Lies 94. Johnny Mnemonic 95. Eden 96. Rasputin (TV) 96, etc.

Fiedler, John (1925–).
Mild, bespectacled American character actor.
Twelve Angry Men 57. Stage Struck 58. That Touch of Mink 62. The World of Henry Orient 64. Kiss Me Stupid 64. Fitzwilly 67. The Odd Couple 68. True Grit 69. Making It 71. The Shaggy D.A. 76. The Cannonball Run 81. Savannah Smiles 82, etc.
TV series: The Bob Newhart Show 73–78. Kolchak: The Night Stalker 74–75. Buffalo Bill 83–84.

Field, Alexander (1892–1971).
English character actor, usually in cockney roles. Born in London, he was on stage from 1912, and in films from 1926.
The Woman Juror 26. The Crooked Billet 29. All Quiet on the Western Front 30. When London Sleeps 32. Dick Turpin 33. Invitation to the Waltz 35. Limelight 36. Dark Eyes of London 39. Let the People Sing 42. Loyal Heart 46. London Belongs to Me 48. Poet's Pub 49. Undercover Girl 58. Naked Fury 59, etc.

Field, Ben (1878–1939).
Short English character actor, often in cockney roles, on stage from 1897 and in films from 1918.
The Face at the Window 18. The Happy Prisoner 24. Caste 30. Sally in our Alley 31. Jack's the Boy 32. When London Sleeps 32. The Good Companions 33. Say It with Flowers 34. Music Hall 34. Sing as We Go 34. On Top of the World 36. Secret Lives 37. The Girl in the Taxi 37, etc.

Field, Betty (1918–1973).
American character actress who played a variety of roles from neurotic girls to slatternly mums.
■ What a Life 39. *Of Mice and Men* 39. Seventeen 40. Victory 40. The Shepherd of the Hills 41. Blues in the Night 41. *Kings Row* 42. Are Husbands Necessary? 42. Flesh and Fantasy 43. The Great Moment 44. Tomorrow the World 44. *The Southerner* 45. The Great Gatsby 49. Picnic 55. Bus Stop 56. Peyton Place 57. The Hound Dog Man 59. Butterfield 8 60. Bird Man of Alcatraz 62. Seven Women 65. How to Save a Marriage 68. Coogan's Bluff 68.

Field, Chelsea (1957–) (Kim Botfield).
American actress.
Prison 88. Skin Deep 89. Harley Davidson & the Marlboro Man 91. Last Boy Scout 91. Hotel Room (TV) 93. The Dark Half 93. Andre 94. A Passion to Kill 94. Birds II: Land's End (TV) 94. Flipper 96. Wicked 98, etc.
TV series: The Bronx Zoo 88. Nightingales 89. Capital News 90.

Field, Mary (1896–1968).
British executive long associated with films specially made for children. From 1926 worked as continuity girl, editor, etc., also directed some instructional films, including the *Secrets of Nature* series. Well-known writer and lecturer on social aspects of film.

Field, Mary (c. 1905–1963).
American character comedienne, usually as prissy spinster.
Wild Geese Calling 41. *Ball of Fire* 41. The Affairs of Susan 45. A Song Is Born 48. Sitting Pretty 48, etc.

Field, Rachel (1894–1942).
American novelist.
■ All This and Heaven Too 40. And Now Tomorrow 44. Time Out of Mind 47.

Field, Sally (1946–) (S. F. Mahoney).
Feisty, diminutive American leading actress, usually in combative, down-to-earth roles; in the 90s, she has appeared in more maternal parts. The daughter of actress Margaret Field (aka Maggie Mahoney following her marriage to actor Jock Mahoney in the mid-50s), she first gained fame on television, in the teen comedy *Gidget* and as Sister Bertrille, the Flying Nun. She has her own production company and plans to direct films.
The Way West 67. Home for the Holidays (TV) 72. Maybe I'll Come Home in the Spring (TV) 72. Marriage Year One (TV) 72. Stay Hungry 76. Sybil/Emmy 76. Smokey and the Bandit 77. Heroes 77. Hooper 78. The End 78. *Norma Rae* (AA) 79. Smokey and the Bandit II 80. Back Roads 81. Absence of Malice 81. Kiss Me Goodbye 82. *Places in the Heart* (AA) 84. Murphy's Romance 85. Surrender 87. Punchline 88. Steel Magnolias 89. Not Without My Daughter 91. Soapdish 91. Mrs Doubtfire 93. Forrest Gump 94. A Woman of Independent Means (TV) 95. Eye for an Eye 95. Homeward Bound II: Lost in San Francisco (voice) 96, etc.
TV series: Gidget 65–66. The Flying Nun 67–70. Alias Smith and Jones 71–73. Girl with Something Extra 73–74.
❝ My country is still so repressed. Our idea of what is sexual is blonde hair, long legs, 22 years old. It has nothing to do with humour, intelligence, warmth, everything to do with teeth and cleavage. – *S.F.*

Field, Shirley Anne (1938–) (Shirley Broomfield).
British leading lady with stage experience; career waned after a promising start.
Autobiography: 1991, *A Time for Love.*
Dry Rot 56. Once More with Feeling 59. The Entertainer 59. *Saturday Night and Sunday Morning* 60. The Man in the Moon 60. The Damned 61. The War Lover 62. Lunch Hour 63. Kings of the Sun (US) 63. Doctor in Clover 66. *Alfie* 66. My Beautiful Laundrette 85. Shag 88. Getting It Right 89. The Rachel Papers 89. Hear My Song 91. Lady Chatterley (TV) 93. UFO: The Movie 93. At Risk 94, etc.

Field, Sid (1904–1950).
British comedian who after years in music-hall became West End star in 1943. First film, *London Town* 46, valuable as record of his sketches; second and last, *Cardboard Cavalier* 48, a patchy historical farce.
Biography: 1975, *What a Performance!* by John Fisher.
❝ It took me thirty years to become an overnight star. – *S.F.*
He has the pathos of all great comics and his grandeur is inspired. – *Noël Coward*
~Catchphrase: What a performance!

Field, Virginia (1917–1992) (Margaret Cynthia Field).
British-born second lead of Hollywood films in the 40s.
The Primrose Path (GB) 35. Lloyds of London 37. Lancer Spy 38. Waterloo Bridge 40. Hudson's Bay 41. The Perfect Marriage 46. Dial 1119 50. The Big Story 58. The Earth Dies Screaming 65, many others.

Fielding, Fenella (1930–).
Anglo-Rumanian leading lady, usually in outrageously exaggerated roles on stage and TV.
In the Doghouse 62. The Old Dark House 63. Doctor in Clover 66. Carry on Screaming 66. Arrivederci Baby 66. Lock Up Your Daughters 69, etc.

Fielding, Henry (1707–1754).
Influential English novelist whose chief bequests to films have been *Tom Jones*, *Lock Up Your Daughters* (indirectly) and *Joseph Andrews*.

Fielding, Jerry (1922–1980).
American composer.
Advise and Consent 62. The Wild Bunch (AAN) 69. Johnny Got His Gun 71. Lawman 71. The Nightcomers 71. Straw Dogs 71. Chato's Land 72. Bring Me the Head of Alfredo Garcia 74. The Outlaw Josey Wales 76. Demon Seed 77. Semi-Tough 77. The Big Sleep 78. Beyond the Poseidon Adventure 79. Escape from Alcatraz 80. High Midnight (TV) 80, etc. Much TV, including *Hogan's Heroes*, *McMillan and Wife*, The Bionic Woman.

Fielding, Marjorie (1892–1956).
British stage actress who usually played strict but kindly gentlewomen. Repeated her stage role in *Quiet Wedding* 40 and was subsequently in many films.
The Demi-Paradise 43. Quiet Weekend 46. Spring in Park Lane 47. The Conspirator 49. The Chiltern Hundreds 49. The Franchise Affair 50. The Lavender Hill Mob 51. Mandy 52. Rob Roy 53, etc.

Fields, Benny (1894–1959) (Benjamin Geisenfeld).
American vaudevillian whose career was linked with Blossom Seeley. Their story was told (more or less) in *Somebody Loves Me*.
■ Mr Broadway 33. The Big Broadcast of 1937 36. Minstrel Man 44.

Fields, Freddie (1923–).
American agent and producer.
Lipstick 76. Looking for Mr Goodbar 77. American Gigolo 80. Wholly Moses 80. Victory 81. The Fever 85. Crimes of the Heart 86. Glory 89, etc.

Fields, Dame Gracie (1898–1979) (Grace Stansfield).
British singer and comedienne whose Lancashire humour and high spirits helped working-class audiences through the 30s Depression. An inimitable voice and personality.
Autobiography: 1960, *Sing As We Go.*
■ *Sally in our Alley* 31. Looking on the Bright Side 32. This Week of Grace 33. Love Life and Laughter 33. *Sing As We Go* 34. Look Up and Laugh 35. Queen of Hearts 36. The Show Goes On 37. We're Going to Be Rich 38. Keep Smiling 38. Shipyard Sally 39. Stage Door Canteen 43. *Holy Matrimony* 43. Molly and Me 45. Paris Underground 45.
✪ For keeping a nation cheerful. *Sing As We Go.*

Fields, Stanley (1884–1941) (Walter L. Agnew).
American character actor, former prizefighter and vaudevillian.
Mammy 30. Little Caesar 30. Island of Lost Souls 32. Kid Millions 35. Way Out West 37. Algiers 38. New Moon 40, many others.

Fields, Tommy (1908–1988) (Thomas Stansfield).
English light actor and dancer, the brother of Gracie FIELDS, in a few films of the 30s.
This Week of Grace 33. Look Up and Laugh 35. The Penny Pool 37. Keep Smiling 38, etc.

Fields, Verna (1918–1982).
American editor.
The Savage Eye 60. Studs Lonigan 60. Medium Cool 69. What's Up Doc? 72. American Graffiti 73. Paper Moon 73. *Jaws* (AA) 75, etc.

Fields, W. C. (1879–1946) (William Claude Dukinfield).
Red-nosed, gravel-voiced, bottle-hitting, misogynist American comedian around whose intolerance and eccentric habits many legends have been built. After a hard life as a tramp juggler, his off-beat personality found a niche in silent films, though sound was necessary to his full flowering as a screen personality. Many of his routines were made up as he went along; once he sold for $25,000 a storyline written on the back of an envelope.
Books on him include: 1949, *W. C. Fields, His Follies and Fortunes* by Robert Lewis Taylor; 1960, *The Films of W. C. Fields* by Donald Deschner; 1997, *Man on the Flying Trapeze: The Life and Times of W. C. Fields* by Simon Louvish. Rod Steiger impersonated him in an inaccurate 1976 film of his life, *W. C. Fields and Me*, from a book by his mistress Carlotta Monti.
■ *Pool Sharks* 15. Janice Meredith 24. Sally of the Sawdust 25. That Royle Girl 26. It's the Old Army Game 26. So's Your Old Man 26. The Potters 27. Running Wild 27. Two Flaming Youths 27. Tillie's Punctured Romance 27. Fools for Luck 28. The Golf Specialist 30. Her Majesty Love 31. Million Dollar Legs 32. If I Had a Million 32. The Dentist 32. The Fatal Glass of Beer 32. The Pharmacist 33. The Barber Shop 33. International House 33. Tillie and Gus 33. Alice in Wonderland (as Humpty Dumpty) 33. Six of a Kind 34. You're Telling Me 34. The Old-Fashioned Way 34. Mrs Wiggs of the Cabbage Patch 34. *It's a Gift* 34. *David Copperfield* (as Micawber) 34. Mississippi 35. The Man on the Flying Trapeze 35. Poppy 36. The Big Broadcast of 1938 37. You Can't Cheat an Honest Man 39. *My Little Chickadee* 40. *The Bank Dick* 40. *Never Give a Sucker an Even Break* 41. Follow the Boys 44. Song of the Open Road 44. Sensations of 1945 44.
✪ For making a disreputable character almost entirely sympathetic; and for moments of inspired surrealism. *It's a Gift.*
❝ Today the centre of a cult which would have astonished him, W. C. Fields was one of life's genuine oddballs, able to see the funny side of his own misanthropy and to turn it to commercial use. In most of his films he was strait-jacketed, but the few he controlled personally are uniquely Fieldsian, anarchic and paceless, fantasticated versions of his unyielding private life with a few in-jokes for good measure. They feature such characters as:

J. Frothingham Waterbury
Ogg Ogilvie
Filthy McNasty
Ouliotta Haemoglobin
F. Snoopington Pinkerton
Elmer Prettywillie
T. Frothingwell Bellows
A. Pismo Clam
Ambrose Wolfinger
Egbert Souse
Cuthbert J. Twillie
Larson E. Whipsnade

Fields' own pseudonyms, either for professional use on his screenplays or merely to conceal a new bank account, include:

Primrose Magoo
Mahatma Kane Jeeves
Otis Criblecoblis
Ampico J. Steinway
Charles Bogle
Felton J. Satchelstern

He had a splendid command of the English language which effectively silenced criticisms when he was cast as Micawber in *David Copperfield*. His nasal delivery and orotund phrasing were imitated the world over, and they are essential to the effectiveness of such oft-quoted lines as:
I must have a drink of breakfast.
or:
Somebody left the cork out of my lunch.
or (of an elderly lady dressed to kill):
She's all done up like a well-kept grave.
or:
I exercise extreme self control. I never drink anything stronger than gin before breakfast.
or:
If at first you don't succeed, try again. Then quit. No use being a damn fool about it.
or:
There's an Ethiopian in the fuel supply.
or:
I never vote for anyone. I always vote against.
His oaths were splendid, consisting of such watered-down versions of profanity as 'Godfrey Daniel!' or 'Great Mother of Pearl!' He was indeed a profane and outlandish man. When his lady neighbour in Beverly Hills came out to remonstrate with him for standing in the middle of his new green lawn and shooting the singing birds with a rifle, he is alleged to have growled:
I'll go on shooting the bastards till they learn to shit green . . .
When another lady, an inquiring journalist this time, asked why he never drank water, he gave the simple reason:
Fish fuck in it.
He occasionally mentioned to acquaintances that he was involved in charity work, and when asked what charity he would murmur: 'The F.E.B.F.' When an explanation of the initials was requested, it was given as:
Fuck Everyone but Fields.
As his biographer Robert Lewis Taylor said:
His main purpose seemed to be to break as many rules as possible and cause the maximum amount of trouble for everybody.
He hated children and animals, and once said of a churlish friend:
Anyone who hates small dogs and children can't be all bad.
It is of course alleged that when co-starring with Baby Le Roy he spiked the infant's milk with gin, and when Le Roy proved unfit for further work that day stalked around yelling:
The kid's no trouper!
He hated women too:
Women are like elephants. I like to look at them but I wouldn't want to own one.
and:

A woman drove me to drink. I never had the courtesy to thank her for it.

But he was essentially impartial:

I am free of all prejudices. I hate everybody equally.

Fiennes, Joseph (1970–).
English actor, the brother of Ralph Fiennes, from the stage. Born in Salisbury, Wiltshire, he studied acting at the Young Vic Theatre School and the Guildhall School of Music and Drama, and came to notice acting with the Royal Shakespeare Company.

Stealing Beauty 96. Martha, Meet Frank, Daniel & Laurence 98. Elizabeth 98. Shakespeare in Love 98, etc.

Fiennes, Ralph (1962–).
British leading actor, from the theatre. Formerly married to actress Alex Kingston (divorced 1997), he has been romantically linked with actress Francesca Annis.

A Dangerous Man – Lawrence after Arabia (TV) 91. Wuthering Heights 92. The Baby of Macon 93. Schindler's List (AAN) 93. Quiz Show 94. Strange Days 95. The English Patient (AAN) 96. Oscar and Lucinda 97. The Avengers 98. Prince of Egypt (voice) 98. Onegin (& ex p) 99, etc.

❝ I am sure acting is a deeply neurotic thing to do. I veer away from trying to understand why I do it. – *R.F.*

Fierstein, Harvey (1954–).
American actor and screenwriter, from the theatre.

Garbo Talks (a) 84. Apology (a) 86. Torch Song Trilogy (a, w) 88. Tidy Endings (a, oa) 88. The Harvest 93. Mrs Doubtfire (a) 93. Dr Jekyll and Ms Hyde 95. Independence Day 96. Kull the Conqueror 97. Mulan (voice) 98, etc.

Figgis, Mike (1950–).
British director, screenwriter and musician, now in Hollywood. He first worked in experimental theatre in Britain.

The House (TV) 85. Stormy Monday (wd, m) 88. Internal Affairs (d, m) 89. Liebestraum 91 (wd, m). Mr Jones 93. The Browning Version 94. *Leaving Las Vegas* (& m) (AANd) 95. One Night Stand (p, wd) 97. The Loss of Sexual Innocence 99, etc.

❝ If you're trying to raise money to make your script, almost by definition you have to write something that the people with the money will understand. When I handed in the early draft of *Short Stories*, which is a feature length script, an executive weighed it in his hand and said, 'How long is this?' I said an hour and a half, two hours. He said: 'Feels more like 45.' The executives go on the basis that a page of script is a minute of screen time. – M.F.

Figueroa, Gabriel (1907–1997).
Mexican cinematographer who worked on more than 200 films. After beginning as a still photographer in the early 30s, he trained with Gregg Toland in Hollywood. He had a notable collaboration with director Emilio Fernández, worked on Luis Buñuel's Mexican films and also with US directors, including John Ford and John Huston.

The Fugitive 47. Tarzan and the Mermaids (US) 48. Maclovia 48. The Bandit General (US) 49. Young and the Damned/Los Olvidados 50. He/El 52. Nazarin 58. La Fievre Monte a El Pao 59. Macario 60. The *Exterminating Angel/El Angel Exterminador* 62. *The Night of the Iguana* (US) 64. Simon of the Desert/Simon del Desierto 65. Kelly's Heroes (US) 70. Under the Volcano (US) 84, etc.

Finch, Flora (1869–1940).
British-born actress, formerly on stage; famous as John Bunny's partner in early film comedies. After his death in 1915 she formed her own production company and was in many silent films of the 20s.

Finch, Jon (1941–).
British leading man.

The Vampire Lovers 70. Horror of Frankenstein 71. Macbeth 71. Sunday Bloody Sunday 71. Frenzy 72. Lady Caroline Lamb 72. The Final Programme 73. Diagnosis: Murder 74. A Faithful Wife (Fr.) 75. The Man with the Green Cross (Sp.) 76. Battleflag (Sp.) 76. Death on the Nile 78. El Barracho (Sp.) 78. Breaking Glass 80. Peter and Paul (TV) 81. Riviera (TV) 82. Giro City (TV) 85. La Più Bella del Reame 89, etc.

Finch, Peter (1916–1977) (William Mitchell).
British leading actor in British and US films. Born in London, he was brought up in France and Australia. In films in Australia from 1937, he made his stage debut in 1939, as a stooge to a comedian, and was on the British stage from 1949. Married three times, he had much-publicized affairs with actresses Kay Kendall, Vivien Leigh and Mai Zetterling, among others. His off-stage and -screen antics, as a hard-drinking womanizer, sometimes obscured his abilities as one of the best film actors of his time.

Biographies: 1979, *Peter Finch* by Trader Faulkner. 1980, *Finchy: My Life* by Peter Finch with Yolande Finch. 1980, *Finch, Bloody Finch* by Elaine Dundy.

■ The Magic Shoes 35. Dad and Dave Come to Town 37. Red Sky at Morning 37. Mr Chedworth Steps Out 38. Rats of Tobruk 44. The Power and the Glory 45. A Son Is Born 46. Eureka Stockade 47. Train of Events 49. The Wooden Horse 50. The Miniver Story 50. *Robin Hood* (as Sheriff) 51. The Heart of the Matter 53. The Story of Gilbert and Sullivan 53. Elephant Walk 54. *Father Brown* (as Flambeau) 54. Make Me an Offer 54. The Dark Avenger 55. Passage Home 55. Josephine and Men 55. *Simon and Laura* 55. *The Battle of the River Plate* (as Langsdorff) 56. *A Town Like Alice* (BFA) 56. The Shiralee 56. Robbery Under Arms 57. Windom's Way 57. Operation Amsterdam 58. Kidnapped 59. *The Nun's Story* 59. The Sins of Rachel Cade 60. *The Trials of Oscar Wilde* (BFA) 60. *No Love for Johnnie* (BFA) 61. I Thank a Fool 62. In the Cool of the Day 63. Girl with Green Eyes 64. The Pumpkin Eater 64. Judith 65. The Flight of the Phoenix 65. 10.30 pm Summer 67. *Far from the Madding Crowd* 67. The Legend of Lylah Clare 68. The Red Tent 69. *Sunday Bloody Sunday* (BFA, AAN) 71. Something to Hide 72. England Made Me 72. *Lost Horizon* 73. A Bequest to the Nation 73. The Abdication 73. *Network* (AA, BFA) 76. Raid on Entebbe (TV) 77.

❝ Good acting should teach people to understand rather than judge. – *P.F.*

An Australian outlaw character, wild and unruly, who despised himself for having become an actor – *Mai Zetterling*

He was a piss-pot and a hell-raiser, but he was also a happy drunk, a gigglebum and very, very good company. – *Yolande Finch*

My first and lasting impression of Finchie was of a withdrawn man with a quiet assurance in his own ability as a remarkable actor which belied his vulnerability. – *Trader Faulkner*

He was a deeply complex man. Film acting is not just acting, it's catching something about the essence of a personality very often, and I think that's what makes someone extraordinary in movies, and it was Peter's complexity that was inescapable. I remember sometimes he'd suddenly stop and say, 'I've lost it! I've lost it! Please don't let's do any more!' – *John Schlesinger*

Famous line (*Network*): 'I want you to get up right now and go to the window, open it and stick your head out and yell "I'm mad as hell, and I'm not going to take this any more!"'

Fincher, David (1965–).
American director, from TV commercials and music videos, who made his debut as director with a movie costing more than $50 million. Co-founder in the mid-80s of the production company Propaganda Films.

Alien³ 92. *Seven* 95. The Game 97.

Fine, Larry (1911–1975) (Laurence Feinberg).
American comedian, one of the Three Stooges.

Finklehoffe, Fred F. (1911–1977).
American writer-producer.

Brother Rat (co-w & co-w original stage play) 39. For Me and My Gal (co-w) 42. Meet Me in St Louis (co-w, AAN) 44. The Egg and I (co-wp) 47. At War with the Army (co-wp) 50, etc.

Finlay, Frank (1926–).
British stage and TV actor who has made tentative screen appearances.

Life for Ruth 62. The Informers 63. Othello (as Iago) (AAN) 65. Robbery 67. Inspector Clouseau 68. Twisted Nerve 68. Cromwell 69. Assault 71. Gumshoe 71. Danny Jones 71. Sitting Target 72. Shaft in Africa 73. The Three Musketeers 74. The Four Musketeers 75. Murder by Decree 79. Enigma 82. The Ploughman's Lunch 83. Arch of Triumph (TV) 84. The Key 85. Sakharov 85. Life Force 85. In the Secret State (TV) 86. The Return of the Musketeers 89. King of the Wind 89. Cthulhu Mansion 92. An Exchange of Fire (TV) 93. Sparrow/Storia di una Capinera 93, etc.

TV series: Common as Muck 97. How Do You Want Me? 98. Other TV successes include The Last Days of Hitler (title role), Casanova (title role) and Bouquet of Barbed Wire.

Finlayson, James (1877–1953).
Scottish comic actor who went to Hollywood in early silent days and became an indispensable comic villain, known for the exaggerated reaction known as a 'double take and fade away'. A memorable opponent for Laurel and Hardy.

Small Town Idol 21. Ladies Night in a Turkish Bath 28. Lady Be Good 28. The Dawn Patrol 30. *Big Business* 30. Pardon Us 31. Fra Diavolo 33. Our Relations 36. *Way Out West* 37. Blockheads 38. The Flying Deuces 39. The Perils of Pauline 47. Grand Canyon Trail 48. Royal Wedding 51, many others.

Finnerman, Gerald Perry (1931–).
American photographer, mostly in television.

Night Gallery (TV) 69. The Lost Man 69. Brother John 70. They Call Me Mr Tibbs 70. Joe Forrester (TV) 76. Salvage (TV) 78. Ziegfeld the Man and His Women (TV) 78. That Man Bolt 78. The Dream Merchants (TV) 80. Smorgasbord 83, etc.

Finney, Albert (1936–).
Leading British actor whose comparatively few films have tended to be controversial.

Biography: 1992, *Albert Finney in Character* by Quentin Falk.

The Entertainer 59. *Saturday Night and Sunday Morning* 60. *Tom Jones* (AAN) 63. The Victors 63. Night Must Fall (& p) 63. Two for the Road 67. *Charlie Bubbles* (& p, d) 68. The Picasso Summer 69. Scrooge 70. Gumshoe (& p) 71. Alpha Beta 73. Murder on the Orient Express (as Hercule Poirot) (AAN) 74. The Duellists 77. Wolfen 80. Looker 80. Loophole 80. Annie 82. Shoot the Moon 82. The Dresser (AAN) 83. Under the Volcano (AAN) 84. The Biko Inquest (TV) 85. Orphans 87. Miller's Crossing 90. The Playboys 92. Rich in Love 93. A Man of No Importance 94. The Browning Version 94. The Run of the Country 95. Karaoke (TV) 96. Cold Lazarus (TV) 96. Washington Square 97. Nostromo (TV) 97. A Rather English Marriage 98, etc.

Finney, Jack (1911–1995) (Walter Braden Finney).
American science-fiction author whose *The Body Snatchers* has been filmed three times, notably by Don Siegel in 1956. The catch-penny title obscured the most subtle film in the 50s science-fiction cycle, with no visual horror whatever, about a small town whose population is taken over by duplicates from outer space.

Five against the House (oa) 55. Invasion of the Body Snatchers (oa) 56, 74, 92. House of Numbers (oa) 57. Good Neighbour Sam (oa) 65. Assault on a Queen (oa) 66. Maxie (oa) 85. Body Snatchers (oa) 94.

Fiorentino, Linda (1958–).
American leading actress.

After Hours 85. Gotcha! 85. Vision Quest 85. Wildfire 88. The Moderns 88. Neon Empire (TV) 89. Queen's Logic 91. Shout 91. Strangers 91. All Shook Up 91. Acting on Impulse 93. *The Last Seduction* 94. Bodily Harm 95. Jade 95. Unforgettable 96. Men in Black 97. Kicked in the Head 97. Body Count 97, etc.

Firbank, Ann.
British actress, usually in refined roles.

Behind the Mask 58. Nothing Barred 61. The Servant 65. Darling 65. Accident 67. A Severed Head 70. Sunday Bloody Sunday 71. Asylum 74. Stories from a Flying Trunk 79. Nelly's Version 83. Foreign Body 86. Hotel du Lac 86. Lionheart 87, etc.

Firstenberg, Sam (1950–).
Israeli director of action and martial arts movies.

One More Chance 81. Revenge of the Ninja 83. Ninja III: The Domination 84. Breakin' 2: Electric Boogaloo 84. American Ninja 85. Avenging Force 86. American Ninja 2: The Confrontation 87. Night of the Eagles 89. One More Chance 90. Delta Force 3: The Killing Game 91. American Samurai 92. Cyborg Cop 2 94. Operation: Delta Force 97, etc.

Firth, Colin (1960–).
English leading actor, from the stage. He spent his early childhood in Africa, and went from drama college to star in the West End production of *Another Country*. He has a son by actress Meg Tilly.

Another Country 84. Camille (TV) 84. Dutch Girls (TV) 85. Lost Empires (TV) 86. Apartment Zero 88. Valmont 89. Wings of Fame 90. Femme Fatale 91. Hostages (TV) 93. The Hour of the Pig 93. Circle of Friends 95. *Pride and Prejudice* (TV, as Mr Darcy) 95. The English Patient 96. A Thousand Acres 97. Nostromo (TV) 97. My Life So Far 98. Shakespeare in Love 98, etc.

❝ I'm constantly asking myself, is acting putting on frocks and chasing one's ego or is it something more? – C.F.

Firth, Peter (1953–).
English actor who began as a juvenile lead in the late 70s. Born in Bradford, Yorkshire, he began acting as a child and came to notice with the National Theatre company, as Alan Strang in *Equus*, a role he repeated on film.

■ Brother Sun, Sister Moon 71. Diamonds on Wheels 73. Aces High 76. Equus (AAN) 77. Joseph Andrews 77. When You Coming Back, Red Ryder? 79. Tess 80. The Aerodrome (TV) 83. Life Force 85. Letter to Brezhnev 85. Lifeforce 85. A State of Emergency 86. Born of Fire 87. Prisoner of Rio 88. Deadly Triangle 89. Tree of Hands 89. Burndown 90. The Hunt for Red October 90. The Rescuers Down Under (voice) 90. The Pleasure Principle 91. Prisoner of Honor 92. Shadowlands 93. White Angel 93. *An Awfully Big Adventure* 95. Seasick (Swe.) 96. The Garden of Redemption 97.

TV series: The Flaxton Boys 71–72. Heartbeat 94.

Fishburne, Lawrence (1961–).
American leading actor. Born in Augusta, Georgia, he was raised in Brooklyn, and began as an actor as an 11-year-old on the TV soap opera *One Life to Live*.

Fast Break 79. Apocalypse Now 79. Willy and Phil 80. Rumble Fish 83. The Cotton Club 84. The Color Purple 85. Quicksilver 86. Band of the Hand 86. Gardens of Stone 87. A Nightmare on Elm Street 3: Dream Warriors 87. School Daze 88. Red Heat 88. King of New York 90. Boyz N the Hood 91. Deep Cover 92. *What's Love Got to Do with It* (AAN) 93. Searching for Bobby Fischer/Innocent Moves 93. Higher Learning 95. Bad Company 95. Just Cause 95. The Tuskegee Airmen (TV) 95. Othello (title role) 95. Fled 96. Hoodlum 96. Miss Evers' Boys (TV) 97. Event Horizon 97. Always Outnumbered 98. The Matrix 99, etc.

TV series: The Six O'Clock Follies 90. Pee Wee's Playhouse 86., etc.

Fischbeck, Harry. (*–1968).
American cinematographer.

Wives of Men 18. The Devil 21. The Green Goddess 23. Monsieur Beaucaire 24. A Sainted Devil 24. Cobra 25. Sally of the Sawdust 25. That Royle Girl 25. The Sorrows of Satan 26. Serenade 27. Manhattan Cocktail 28. The Canary Murder Case 29. The Mysterious Dr Fu Manchu 29. Ladies Love Brutes 30. The Spoilers 30. Working Girls 31. Lady and Gent 32. Terror Aboard 33. Search for Beauty 34. Double Door 34. Millions in the Air 35. The Jungle Princess 36. John Meade's Woman 37. Bulldog Drummond's Revenge 37. Prison Farm 38. Persons in Hiding 39. Parole Fixer 40, many others.

Fischer, Gunnar (1911–).
Swedish cinematographer who has worked on most of Ingmar Bergman's films.

Smiles of a Summer Night 55. The Seventh Seal 56. Wild Strawberries 57. The Face 58. The Devil's Eye 60. Siska 62. Min Kara Ar En Ros 63. Adamson i Sverige 66. Made in Sweden 68. Miss and Mrs Sweden 69. Parade 74, etc.

Fischer, O. W. (1915–).
Leading Austrian actor, in films since 1936 but hardly known outside Germany.

Sommerliebe 42. Seven Letters 44. Heidelberger Romanze 51. Der Traumende Mund 52. The Heart Plays False 53. Ludwig II (title role) 54. El Hakim 57. Arms and the Man 58. Uncle Tom's Cabin 65, many others.

Fischinger, Oskar (1900–1967).
Innovative German animator, from the early 20s; moved to Hollywood in 1936. Noted for films featuring ballets of abstract shapes synchronized to music, he worked on the 'Toccata and Fugue' sequence of DISNEY's *Fantasia*, but left before it was completed. He later made commercials while continuing to experiment. Also worked on special effects for *The Woman in the Moon* 28 and *The Big Broadcast of 1937* 38.
Dein Schicksal 28. Study No. 1 29. Composition in Blue/Komposition in Blau 35. Allegretto 36. Optical Poem 38. American March 41. Organic Fragment 45. Motion Painting Number 1 47, etc.

Fisher, Carrie (1956–).
American leading lady of routine talent, daughter of Debbie REYNOLDS and Eddie FISHER. She is also a screenwriter and novelist. Her first husband was singer Paul SIMON (1983–84). She worked as a script doctor on *Lethal Weapon 3*, *Sister Act* and *Hook*. In 1997 she signed a contract giving her $3m over two years to create TV shows for Universal.
■ Shampoo 75. Star Wars 77. Mr Mike's Mondo Video 78. The Empire Strikes Back 80. The Blues Brothers 80. Under the Rainbow 81. Return of the Jedi 83. Garbo Talks 84. The Man with One Red Shoe 85. Hannah and Her Sisters 86. Hollywood Vice Squad 86. Amazon Women on the Moon 87. The Time Guardian 87. Appointment with Death 88. The 'burbs 89. Loverboy 89. She's Back 89. When Harry Met Sally 89. Postcards from the Edge (w) 90. Sibling Rivalry 90. Drop Dead Fred 91. Soapdish 91. Sweet Revenge 91. This Is My Life 92. Austin Powers: International Man of Mystery 97.
❝ I always wanted to do what my mother did – get all dressed up, shoot people, fall in the mud. I never considered anything else. – C.F.

Fisher, Eddie (1927–).
American nightclub singer and actor. He was married to Debbie Reynolds and Elizabeth Taylor.
Bundle of Joy 56. Butterfield 8 60, etc.

Fisher, Gerry (1926–).
British cinematographer.
AS OPERATOR: The Devil's Disciple 59. Suddenly Last Summer 60. Night Must Fall 63. Guns at Batasi 64. Modesty Blaise 66.
AS CINEMATOGRAPHER: Accident 67. Sebastian 68. Interlude 68. The Go-Between 70. Macho Callahan 71. See No Evil 71. The Amazing Mr Blunden 72. A Bequest to the Nation 73. S.P.Y.S. 74. Juggernaut 74. The Romantic Englishwoman 74. Aces High 76. Mr Klein 77. The Last Remake of Beau Geste 77. The Island of Dr Moreau 77. Fedora 78. Don Giovanni 79. Wise Blood 79. The Ninth Configuration 80. Wolfen 81. Victory 81. Yellowbeard 82. The Holcroft Covenant 84. Highlander 85. Man on Fire 87. Running on Empty 88. Dead Bang 89. Black Rainbow 89. The Fourth War 90. The Exorcist III 90. Company Business 91. Diggstown/Midnight Sting 92. The Positively True Adventures of the Alleged Texas Cheerleader-Murdering Mom (TV) 93. Cops and Robbersons 94. When Saturday Comes 96, etc.

Fisher, Joely.
American actress and singer, the daughter of Connie Stevens and Eddie Fisher.
I'll Do Anything 94. Pretty Smart 86. Mixed Nuts 94. I'll Do Anything 94. The Mask 95, etc.
TV series: Ellen 94–98. In the Loop 98.

Fisher, Terence (1904–1980).
British director, former editor, in films from 1933. Work mainly routine; latterly associated with Hammer horror. Also worked for TV, especially *Douglas Fairbanks Presents*.
Biography: 1991, *The Charm of Evil: The Life and Films of Terence Fisher* by Wheeler Winston Dixon.
To the Public Danger 47. Portrait from Life 48. Marry Me 49. The Astonished Heart 49. So Long at the Fair 50. Home to Danger 51. Kill Me Tomorrow 55. The Curse of Frankenstein 56. Dracula 57. The Hound of the Baskervilles 58. Brides of Dracula 59. The Two Faces of Dr Jekyll 60. The Phantom of the Opera 62. The Gorgon 64. Dracula, Prince of Darkness 65. Island of Terror 66. The Devil Rides Out 68. Frankenstein and the Monster from Hell 73, etc.

Fishman, Jack (1920–1997).
British journalist, writer, songwriter and producer. After a career as a journalist that included editing a national Sunday newspaper, he worked as a writer of books on current affairs, and as a film musical supervisor and songwriter.
Something to Hide (co-m) 71. Steptoe and Son (co-m) 72. Steptoe and Son Ride Again (co-m) 73. Diamonds (co-w title s) (US) 75. Lemon Popsicle (Isr.) 77. Making the Grade (US) 84. Lifeforce 85. Dancers (US) 87. Superman IV: The Quest for Peace 87. Salsa (US) 88, etc.

Fisk, Jack (1945–).
American production designer who has turned to directing. He married actress Sissy Spacek in 1974.
Badlands 73 (pd). Phantom of the Paradise (pd) 74. Carrie (pd) 76. Days of Heaven (pd) 78. Movie Movie (pd) 78. Raggedy Man (d) 81. Violets Are Blue (d) 86. Daddy's Dyin', Who's Got the Will? (d) 90. Final Verdict (d) 91, etc.

Fiske, Minnie Maddern (1866–1932).
American stage actress who made two silent films.
■ Tess of the D'Urbervilles 13. Vanity Fair 15.

Fisz, Benjamin (1922–1989).
Polish-born independent producer, long in England.
Hell Drivers 57. Sea Fury 58. On the Fiddle 61. Heroes of Telemark (co-p) 65. The Battle of Britain (co-p) 69. A Town Called Bastard 71, etc.

Fitzgerald, Barry (1888–1961) (William Shields).
Diminutive Irish character actor who found his way to Hollywood and eventually achieved star status, usually in irascible or whimsical 'Oirish' roles. Born in Dublin, he worked for 20 years in the Civil Service before becoming an actor with the Abbey Theatre, where his most famous role was as Captain Jack Boyle in the first production of Sean O'CASEY's *Juno and the Paycock*. His brother was actor Arthur SHIELDS.
■ Juno and the Paycock 30. When Knights were Bold 36. *The Plough and the Stars* 36. *Ebb Tide* 37. Bringing Up Baby 38. Marie Antoinette 38. Four Men and a Prayer 38. The Dawn Patrol 38. The Saint Strikes Back 39. Pacific Liner 39. Full Confession 39. *The Long Voyage Home* 40. San Francisco Docks 41. The Sea Wolf 41. How Green Was My Valley 41. Tarzan's Secret Treasure 41. The Amazing Mrs Holliday 43. Two Tickets to London 43. Corvette K225 43. *Going My Way* (AAN) 44. I Love a Soldier 44. None but the Lonely Heart 44. Incendiary Blonde 45. *And Then There Were None* 45. Duffy's Tavern 45. The Stork Club 45. Two Years Before the Mast 46. California 46. Easy Come Easy Go 47. Welcome Stranger 47. Variety Girl 47. The Sainted Sisters 48. *The Naked City* 48. Miss Tatlock's Millions 48. Top o' the Morning 49. The Story of Seabiscuit 49. *Union Station* 50. Silver City 51. *The Quiet Man* 52. Happy Ever After 54. The Catered Affair 56. *Rooney* 57. Broth of a Boy 59.

Fitzgerald, Ella (1917–1996).
Mellifluous American jazz singer and occasional actress, one of the greatest interpreters of popular song. She began her career by winning a talent contest at the age of 16, and later sang with Chick Webb's band in the 30s, taking over as leader for two years after his death before becoming a solo performer from the early 40s; her greatest achievement came in the 50s with a series of 'Songbooks', albums devoted to the works of George Gershwin, Cole Porter, Rodgers and Hart and others.
Ride 'Em Cowboy 41. Pete Kelly's Blues 55. St Louis Blues 56. Let No Man Write My Epitaph 60. Listen Up: The Lives of Quincy Jones 90, etc.

Fitzgerald, F. Scott (1896–1940).
American novelist and chronicler of 'the jazz age' who made several disastrous forays into working in Hollywood, even taking a screen test in the late 20s at the urging of actress Lois MORAN: the verdict was that he was too old to act in films. He first went there in 1927 to work unsuccessfully for United Artists, returning in 1931 under a weekly contract to MGM to adapt *The Red-Headed Woman* for Jean HARLOW; but he was drinking heavily, behaving badly, and was sacked after a few weeks. He turned down offers to return in the early 30s, but went back in 1937, when he was in debt, to work for MGM at $1,000 a week for six months, with an option on an additional year at $1,250 a week. The offer came from story editor Edwin KNOPF, who had earlier written *The Wedding Night* for GOLDWYN, starring Gary COOPER and Anna STEN in roles based on Fitzgerald and his wife, Zelda. He stayed for 18 months, receiving his only screen credit, as co-writer on *Three Comrades* 38. He also began an affair with columnist Sheilah GRAHAM. (*Beloved Infidel*, her story of their affair, in which he was played by Gregory Peck, was filmed in 1959.) Walter WANGER then hired him, at $1,500 a week, to write a film, *Winter Carnival*, about a college love affair. He went with co-writer Budd SCHULBERG to Dartmouth on a disastrously drunken research trip and was sacked. (Schulberg wrote a novel, *The Disenchanted*, about the experience.) He tinkered with a few scripts after that, and wrote a novel, *The Last Tycoon*, with its character of Monroe Stahr based on MGM producer Irving THALBERG. His novels and stories have fared better in Hollywood than his screenplays.
Biographies: 1983, *F. Scott Fitzgerald, A Biography* by Andre Le Vot; 1995, *Intimate Lies: F. Scott Fitzgerald & Sheilah Graham* by Robert Westbrook.
Books: 1976, *Sometime in the Sun* by Tom Dardis; 1990, *Writers in Hollywood 1915–1951* by Ian Hamilton; 1993, *West of Eden: Writers in Hollywood 1928–1940* by Richard Fine.
The Chorus Girl's Romance (from Head and Shoulders) 20. The Offshore Pirate 21. The Great Gatsby 26, 49, 74. The Last Time I Saw Paris (from Babylon Revisted) 54. Tender Is the Night 62.
❝ As long past as 1930, I had a hunch that the talkies would make even the best-selling novelist as archaic as silent pictures. – F.S.F.
Isn't Hollywood a dump, in the human sense of the word. A hideous town, pointed up by the insulting gardens of its rich, full of the human spirit at a new low of debasement. – F.S.F.
For nineteen years, with two years out for sickness, I've written best-selling entertainment, and my dialogue is supposedly right at the top. But I learn from the script that you've suddenly decided that it isn't good dialogue and you can take a few hours off and do better. – F.S.F. *to Joseph Mankiewicz*
Scott Fitzgerald wrote very bad spoken dialogue. – *Joseph Mankiewicz*

Fitzgerald, Geraldine (1914–).
Irish leading lady who played in British films from 1935; went to Hollywood in 1939 but had rather disappointing roles. In her 60s made a stage comeback as a folk singer.
Turn of the Tide 35. The Mill on the Floss 36. Dark Victory 39. *Wuthering Heights* (AAN) 39. Till We Meet Again 40. Flight from Destiny 41. The Gay Sisters 42. Watch on the Rhine 43. Ladies Courageous 44. *Wilson* 44. Uncle Harry 45. Three Strangers 46. O.S.S. 46. Nobody Lives Forever 47. So Evil My Love (GB) 48. Ten North Frederick 58. The Fiercest Heart 61. The Pawnbroker 65. Rachel Rachel 69. The Last American Hero 73. Harry and Tonto 74. Echoes of a Summer 76. Yesterday's Child (TV) 77. The Quinns (TV) 77. Arthur 81. The Mango Tree 82. Easy Money 83. Kennedy (TV) 83. The Link 85. Poltergeist II: The Other Side 86, etc.

Fitzgerald, Tara (1967–).
English leading actress of stage and screen.
Hear My Song 91. The Camomile Lawn (TV) 92. Sirens 94. A Man of No Importance 94. The Englishman Who Went up a Hill but Came down a Mountain 95. Brassed Off 96. The Tenant of Wildfell Hall (TV) 96. Conquest 98, etc.

Fitzgerald, Walter (1896–1976) (Walter Bond).
British character actor, on stage from 1922, films from 1930.
Murder at Covent Garden 30. This England 40. Squadron Leader X 41. Strawberry Roan 45. Mine Own Executioner 47. Treasure Island 50. Pickwick Papers 52. Personal Affair 53. Lease of Life 54. Cockleshell Heroes 55. Something of Value 57. Third Man on the Mountain 59. HMS Defiant 62, many others.

Fitzmaurice, George (1885–1940).
American director of French origin, noted in the 20s for visual style.
A Society Exile 19. On with the Dance 20. Experience 21. *Belladonna* 23. Cytherea 24. *The Dark Angel* 25. *Son of the Sheik* 26. Rose of the Golden West 27. *Lilac Time* 28. His Captive Woman 29. Tiger Rose 29. The Devil to Pay 30. One Heavenly Night 30. The Unholy Garden 31. Mata Hari 32. As You Desire Me 32. Petticoat Fever 36. The Emperor's Candlesticks 37. Arsène Lupin Returns 38. Adventure in Diamonds 40, many others.

Fitzpatrick, James A. (1902–1980).
American documentarist, who from 1925 produced and narrated innumerable travel shorts ('Fitzpatrick Traveltalks'), invariably concluding 'And so we leave . . .' Wrote, produced and directed one feature, *Song of Mexico* 45.

Fix, Paul (1901–1983) (Paul Fix Morrison).
American general-purpose actor who played hundreds of sheriffs, ranchers, doctors, etc., from the 20s.
The First Kiss 28. Ladies Love Brutes 30. The Last Mile 32. Zoo in Budapest 33. Little Man What Now? 34. Prisoner of Shark Island 36. Souls at Sea 37. News Is Made at Night 39. The Ghost Breakers 40. In Old Oklahoma 43. Dakota 45. Tycoon 47. California Passage 50. Hondo 53. The High and the Mighty 54. Blood Alley 55. Giant 56. To Kill a Mockingbird 63. Shenandoah 65. Nevada Smith 66. El Dorado 67. The Day of the Evil Gun 68. Something Big 71. Grayeagle 77. Wanda Nevada 80, many others.
TV series: The Rifleman 57–61.

Flagg, Cash:
see STECKLER, Ray Dennis.

Flagg, Fannie (1941–).
American TV comedienne, notably in *The New Dick Van Dyke Show*.
Five Easy Pieces 70. Some of My Best Friends Are 71. Stay Hungry 76. Sex and the Married Woman (TV) 77. Rabbit Test 78. Grease 78. My Best Friend Is a Vampire 88. Fried Green Tomatoes at the Whistle Stop Café (w) (AAN) 91, etc.

Flagstad, Kirsten (1895–1962).
Norwegian operatic soprano whose only film appearance was, surprisingly, in *The Big Broadcast of 1938*.
❝ She walks meaninglessly round the stage, like a wardrobe at a seance. – *Mrs Patrick Campbell*

Flaherty, Robert (1884–1951).
Very influential American documentary pioneer, originally an explorer; noted for superb visual sense. Claude Massot's *Nanook/Kabloonak* in 1994 recreated Flaherty's expedition to the Arctic, and starred Charles Dance as Flaherty.
Biographies: 1953, *The World of Robert Flaherty* by Richard Griffith. 1963, *The Innocent Eye* by Arthur Calder-Marshall.
■ *Nanook of the North* 20. The Pottery Maker 25. Moana (co-d) 26. 24-Dollar Island 27. *White Shadows in the South Seas* (co-d) 28. Tabu (co-d) 31. Industrial Britain (co-d) 33. *Man of Aran* 34. *Elephant Boy* (co-d) 37. The Land 42. Louisiana Story (AANw) 48.
❝ I took it to the biggest of the distributors first – Paramount. When the film was over, they all pulled themselves together and got up in a rather dull way, I thought, and silently left the room. The manager came up to me and very kindly put his arm around my shoulders and told me that he was terribly sorry, but it was a film that just couldn't be shown to the public – *R.F. on Nanook of the North*
His films slip so easily into the stream of fictional cinema that they hardly seem like documentaries at all. – *Andrew Sarris*
World-famous and world-loved, his standing in his own profession was nil. You might suppose that a master film director who would work for a salary normally paid an assistant would be in great demand, but that is not the way of things in the film world. – *Richard Griffith*

Flanagan, Bud (1896–1968) (Reuben Weinthrop).
Genial English comedian, singer and composer of sentimental songs. Born in London, he began as 'Fargo the Boy Wizard' before emigrating at the age of 14 to America; he worked as a blackface act, and appeared with many partners (Harlem and Bronx, Flanagan and Roy, Flanagan and Hunter, etc.), only becoming successful when he joined singer Florrie FORDE's company and she teamed him with Chesney ALLEN. The pair were part of The CRAZY GANG from 1931. After Allen retired in the 40s, he continued as a solo act. He wrote the song 'Underneath the Arches', and popularized

such songs as 'Strolling' and 'Maybe Because I'm a Londoner'.

Autobiography: 1961, *My Crazy Life*.

Flanagan, Fionnula (Fionnuala) (1941–).
Irish-American character actress, mostly in TV.
Ulysses 67. *Rich Man Poor Man* (TV) 76. Nightmare in Badham County (TV) 76. Mary White (TV) 77. Young Love First Love (TV) 79. Mr Patman 80. Through Naked Eyes (TV) 83. Scorned and Swindled (TV) 84. Youngblood 86. Mad at the Moon 92. Money for Nothing 93. White Mile (TV) 94. Sons and Warriors 95. Some Mother's Son 96. Waking Ned Devine 98, etc.
TV series: How the West Was Won 79. To Have and to Hold 98– .

Flanders, Ed (1934–1995).
American character actor and Truman impersonator.
Goodbye Raggedy Ann (TV) 71. Indict and Convict (TV) 74. The Legend of Lizzie Borden (TV) 75. Eleanor and Franklin (TV) 76. *The Amazing Howard Hughes* (TV) 77. MacArthur 77. Collision Course (TV) 77. Backstairs at the White House (TV) 79. The Ninth Configuration 80. Salem's Lot (TV) 80. True Confessions 81. The Pursuit of D. B. Cooper 81. Special Bulletin (TV) 83. Exorcist III 90. Bye Bye Love 95, many others.
TV series: St Elsewhere 82–88.

Flanery, Sean Patrick.
American leading actor.
Powder 95. The Grass Harp 95. Raging Angels 95. Eden 96. Girl 98, etc.
TV series: The Young Indiana Jones Chronicles (title role) 92–93. Just Your Luck 96. The Method 97.

Flannery, Susan (1943–).
American general-purpose actress, from TV soap opera *Days of Our Lives*.
The Towering Inferno 74. The Moneychangers (TV) 76. The Gumball Rally 76. Anatomy of a Seduction (TV) 79. Women in White (TV) 79, etc.

Flaubert, Gustave (1821–1880).
French novelist whose *Madame Bovary*, written in 1856–57, has been filmed several times. When Vincente MINNELLI ran into censorship difficulties while planning to film the novel in Hollywood in 1949, screenwriter Robert ARDREY added a prologue and an epilogue dealing with Flaubert's trial and acquittal on the charge of writing an immoral book, in which the novelist was played by James MASON.

Flavin, James (1906–1976).
Irish-American supporting actor, usually as genial or bewildered cop.
King Kong 33. The Grapes of Wrath 40. Cloak and Dagger 46. Desert Fury 47. Mighty Joe Young 50. Fighter Attack 53. Mister Roberts 55. The Last Hurrah 58. It's a Mad Mad Mad Mad World 63. Cheyenne Autumn 64. Bullwhip Griffin 67, many others.

Fleet, James.
English character actor, often in diffident, upper-class roles.
Electric Moon 90. Common Pursuit (TV) 91. Blue Black Permanent 92. Four Weddings and a Funeral 94. The Grotesque/Gentlemen Don't Eat Poets/Grave Indiscretions 95. Sense and Sensibility 95. Three Steps to Heaven 95. The Butterfly Effect (Sp.) 95. Moll Flanders (TV) 96. A Dance to the Music of Time (TV) 97, etc.
TV series: The Vicar of Dibley 96–98. Underworld 97. Spark 97– .

Fleetwood, Susan (1944–1995).
Scottish leading actress, mainly on stage and TV. Died of cancer.
Clash of the Titans 81. The Sacrifice 86. White Mischief 87. Dream Demon 88. The Krays 90. A Few Short Journeys of the Heart (TV) 94. Jane Austen's Persuasion (TV) 95, etc.
TV series: Chandler and Co. 95.

Fleischer, Max (1889–1972).
Austrian-born cartoonist and producer, long in Hollywood. Created Betty Boop, Koko, Out of the Inkwell series, Popeye the Sailor, etc. His brother *Dave Fleischer* (1894–1979) worked as his administrative head.
Biography: 1988, *The Fleischer Story* by Louis Cabarca.
Gulliver's Travels 39. Mr Bug Goes to Town 41.

Fleischer, Richard (1916–).
American director, son of Max Fleischer; former shorts producer. His films usually sound more interesting than they prove to be.
Autobiography: 1994, *Just Tell Me When to Cry: A Memoir*.
■ Child of Divorce 46. Banjo 47. Bodyguard 48. So This Is New York 49. Make Mine Laughs 49. Trapped 49. Follow Me Quietly 49. The Clay Pigeon 49. The Armored Car Robbery 50. *The Narrow Margin* 51. *The Happy Time* 52. Arena 53. *Twenty Thousand Leagues under the Sea* 54. Violent Saturday 55. The Girl in the Red Velvet Swing 55. Bandido 56. Between Heaven and Hell 56. *The Vikings* 57. These Thousand Hills 58. Compulsion 59. Crack in the Mirror 60. The Big Gamble 61. Barabbas 62. *Fantastic Voyage* 66. Doctor Dolittle 67. *The Boston Strangler* 68. Che! 69. Tora! Tora! Tora! 70. The Last Run 70. Blind Terror 70. The New Centurions 71. 10 Rillington Place 71. Soylent Green 72. The Don is Dead 73. Mr Majestyk 74. The Spikes Gang 74. Mandingo 75. The Incredible Sarah 76. The Prince and the Pauper 77. Ashanti 78. The Jazz Singer 80. Tough Enough 82. Amityville 3-D 83. Conan, King of Thieves 84. Conan the Destroyer 85. Red Sonja 86. Million Dollar Mystery 87.

Fleiss, Noah (1984–).
American child actor, from television and the stage, a former model.
Josh and S.A.M. 93. A Mother's Prayer (TV) 95. Roommates 95. An Unexpected Family (TV) 96. An Unexpected Life (TV) 98, etc.

Fleming, Eric (1924–1966).
Taciturn American general-purpose actor. Died by drowning.
Conquest of Space 55. Fright 57. Curse of the Undead 59. The Glass Bottom Boat 66, etc.
TV series: *Rawhide* (as Gil Favor, trail boss) 58–65.

Fleming, Ian (1888–1969).
Australian-born character actor, long in British films as doctors, civil servants, solicitors, etc. A memorable Dr Watson in the 30s series with Arthur Wontner as Sherlock Holmes.
Second to None 26. The School for Scandal 30. The Sleeping Cardinal 31. The Missing Rembrandt 32. The Triumph of Sherlock Holmes 35. The Crouching Beast 35. Jump for Glory 37. The Nursemaid who Disappeared 39. The Butler's Dilemma 43. George in Civvy Street 45. Quartet 48. The Woman in Question 50. The Voice of Merrill 52. The Seekers 54. High Flight 57. Bluebeard's Ten Honeymoons 60. No My Darling Daughter 61. The Boys 63. The Return of Mr Moto 65, many others.

Fleming, Ian (1908–1964).
Creator of James Bond, whose exploits have been so successfully filmed from the novels. Jason Connery played him in a TV film, *The Secret Life of Ian Fleming* 90.
❝ Fleming relies on sex, sadism and snobbery.
– *Alistair MacLean*

Fleming, Rhonda (1922–) (Marilyn Louis).
Red-haired American leading lady of the 40s and 50s.
When Strangers Marry 43. Spellbound 45. The Spiral Staircase 45. Adventure Island 46. Out of the Past/Build My Gallows High 47. A Connecticut Yankee in King Arthur's Court 49. Cry Danger 50. The Redhead and the Cowboy 51. The Great Lover 51. Little Egypt 52. The Golden Hawk 52. Serpent of the Nile 53. Inferno 53. Yankee Pasha 54. The Killer Is Loose 56. Slightly Scarlet 56. Gunfight at the OK Corral 57. Gun Glory 57. Home Before Dark 58. Alias Jesse James 59. The Big Circus 59. Run For Your Wife 66. The Nude Bomb 80, etc.

Fleming, Victor (1883–1949).
American director, long with MGM: he was in charge of a few outstanding films, but they seemed to succeed for other reasons.
■ When the Clouds Roll By 20. The Mollycoddle 20. Mamma's Affair 21. Woman's Place 22. Red Hot Romance 22. The Lane That Had No Turning 22. Anna Ascends 22. Dark Secrets 23. Law of the Lawless 23. To the Last Man 23. Call of the Canyon 23. Empty Hands 24. The Code of the Sea 24. A Son of His Father 25. Adventure 25. The Devil's Cargo 25. Lord Jim 25. The Blind Goddess 26. *Mantrap* 26. Rough Riders 27. The Way of all Flesh 27. Hula 27. Abie's Irish Rose 28. The Awakening 28. Wolf Song 29. *The Virginian* 29. Common Clay 30. Renegades 30. Around the World in Eighty Minutes 31. *The Wet Parade* 32. *Red Dust* 32. The White Sister 33. Bombshell 33. *Treasure Island* 34. Reckless 35. The Farmer Takes a Wife 35. Captains Courageous 37. *Test Pilot* 38. *The Wizard of Oz* 39. *Gone with the Wind* (AA) (with assistance) 39. *Dr Jekyll and Mr Hyde* 41. Tortilla Flat 42. A Guy Named Joe 43. Adventure 45. Joan of Arc 48.

Flemyng, Gordon (1933–1995).
British director, from TV.
Solo for Sparrow 62. Five to One 63. Dr Who and the Daleks 65. Great Catherine 68. The Split 68. The Last Grenade 69. A Good Human Story (TV) 77. Mirage (TV) 78. Cloud Waltzer (TV) 87, etc.

Flemyng, Jason.
British leading actor.
Rudyard Kipling's The Jungle Book 94. Hollow Reed 95. Stealing Beauty 96. Spiceworld the Movie 97. Deep Rising 97. The James Gang 97. The Life of Stuff 97. Lock, Stock and Two Smoking Barrels 98. The Red Violin 98, etc.

Flemyng, Robert (1912–1995).
British actor who usually played attractive professional men. On stage from 1931, films from 1936 (*Head Over Heels*).
The Guinea Pig 49. The Blue Lamp 50. The Holly and the Ivy 52. The Man Who Never Was 55. Funny Face (US) 56. Windom's Way 57. A Touch of Larceny 59. The Terror of Dr Hichcock (It.) 63. The Deadly Affair 66. The Spy with a Cold Nose 67. The Blood Beast Terror 67. Young Winston 72. Travels with my Aunt 73. The Medusa Touch 77. The 39 Steps 78. Kafka 91. Shadowlands 94, etc.

Fletcher, Bramwell (1904–1988).
British light leading man of the 30s.
Chick 30. To What Red Hell 30. Raffles (US) 31. Svengali (US) 31. The Mummy (US) 32. The Scarlet Pimpernel 34. Random Harvest (US) 42. White Cargo (US) 42. The Immortal Sergeant (US) 42, etc.

Fletcher, Cyril (1913–).
British comedian and entertainer who has made appearances in a few films.
Yellow Canary 43. Nicholas Nickleby 47. A Piece of Cake 48, etc.

Fletcher, Dexter (1966–).
British actor, in films from 1972.
Bugsy Malone 76. Les Misérables (TV) 78. The Long Good Friday 80. The Elephant Man 80. The Bounty 84. Revolution 85. Caravaggio 86. Lionheart 87. Gothic 86. The Raggedy Rawney 87. When the Whales Came 89. The Rachel Papers 89. Exit Genua 89. The Mad Monkey 90. All Out 91. Lock, Stock and Two Smoking Barrels 98, etc.

Fletcher, Louise (1934–).
American character actress.
Thieves Like Us 74. Russian Roulette 75. *One Flew Over the Cuckoo's Nest* (AA) 75. Exorcist II: The Heretic 77. *The Cheap Detective* 78. Thou Shalt Not Commit Adultery (TV) 78. The Lady in Red 79. Natural Enemies 79. The Magician of Lublin 79. The Lucky Star 80. Mama Dracula (Fr.) 80. Strange Behaviour 81. *Brainstorm* 83. Firestarter 84. The Boy Who Could Fly 85. Invaders from Mars 86. Best of the Best 89. In a Child's Name 92. Tryst 94. Tollbooth 94. Virtuosity 95. Frankenstein and Me 96. High School High 96. Sins of the Mind (TV) 97. Breast Men 97. Love to Kill 97, etc.

Flicker, Theodore J. (1930–).
American director, former Greenwich Village satirist.
The Troublemaker 64. The President's Analyst 68. Up in the Cellar (& w) 70. Playmates (TV) 72. Guess Who's Sleeping in My Bed (TV) 73. Just a Little Inconvenience (TV) 77. Last of the Good Guys (& w) 78. Where the Ladies Go (TV) 80. Soggy Bottom USA 82, etc.

Flippen, Jay C. (1898–1971).
Bulky American character actor with vaudeville background; often seen as cop, sergeant or sheriff.
Marie Galante 34. Intrigue 48. Love that Brute 50. Flying Leathernecks 51. Bend of the River 52. The Wild One 53. The Far Country 55. Oklahoma 55. *The Killing* 56. Night Passage 57. From Hell to Texas 58. Studs Lonigan 60. Cat Ballou 65. Firecreek 67. Hellfighters 68. The Seven Minutes 71, many others.
TV series: Ensign O'Toole 62.

Flon, Suzanne (1923–).
French leading actress.
La Cage aux Filles 49. La Belle Image 51. Moulin Rouge 53. Mr Arkadin 55. *Thou Shalt Not Kill* 61. A Monkey in Winter 62. The Trial 62. The Train 64. Le Soleil des Voyous 67. Le Silencieux 73. Mr Klein 76. Blackout 77. Comme un Boomerang 77. L'Eté Meurtrier 83. En Toute Innocence 87. Gaspard et Robinson 90. Voyage à Rome 92, etc.

Florance, Sheila (1916–1991).
Australian character actress. She died shortly after receiving an award as best actress for her performance in her last film, *A Woman's Tale*, portraying an 80-year-old woman dying of cancer, from which she also suffered.
The Devil's Playground 76. Cactus 86. The Tale of Ruby Rose 87. Hungry Heart 88. Golden Braid 90. Nirvana Street Murders 90. A Woman's Tale 91, etc.

Florey, Robert (1900–1979).
French-born director, in Hollywood since 1921.
The Romantic Age 27. The Coconuts 29. *The Murders in the Rue Morgue* 32. Ex Lady 33. The Woman in Red 34. Hollywood Boulevard 36. Hotel Imperial 38. The Face Behind the Mask 40. Lady Gangster 42. Dangerously They Live 43. God Is My Co-Pilot 44. *The Beast with Five Fingers* 46. Monsieur Verdoux (co-d) 47. Rogues' Regiment 48. Outpost in Morocco 48. Johnny One Eye 49. The Gangster We Made 50, many second features; latterly directed hundreds of TV films. Also wrote several scripts, including work on *Frankenstein* 31.

Flowers, Bess (1900–1984).
American bit-part player, 'queen of the Hollywood extras', who appeared in literally hundreds of films between 1922 and 1962.

Fluegel, Darlanne (1956–).
American actress.
Eyes of Laura Mars 78. Battle beyond the Stars 80. Once Upon a Time in America 84. To Live and Die in LA 85. Running Scared 86. Tough Guys 86. Crime Story 86. Bulletproof 88. Freeway 88. Pet Sematary 2 92. Relative Fear 93. Breaking Point 93. Scanner Cop 93. Darkman 3: Die, Darkman, Die 95, etc.

Fluellen, Joel (1907–1990).
American character actor.
White Pongo 45. The Jackie Robinson Story 50. White Goddess 53. Jungle Gents 54. Sitting Bull 54. Friendly Persuasion 56. The Monster from Green Hell 58. A Raisin in the Sun 61. He Rides Tall 64. The Learning Tree 69. The Great White Hope 70. The Autobiography of Miss Jane Pittman (TV) 74. Man Friday 75. The Bingo Long Travelling All-Stars and Motor Kings 76. Casey's Shadow 78. Freedom Road (TV) 79, etc.

Flynn, Errol (1909–1959).
Swashbuckling Australian-born leading man in Hollywood, who by his handsome impudence maintained a worldwide following for nearly 20 years before hard living got the better of him. Born in Hobart, Tasmania, the son of an academic, he was educated briefly at the University of Tasmania, and after various dubious enterprises and escapades, he began his acting career proper in the English repertory theatre before gaining a contract with Warner's. He became an American citizen in 1942. His definitive appearances were the title roles in *Captain Blood* and *The Adventures of Robin Hood*, as Major Geoffrey Vickers in *The Charge of the Light Brigade*, Captain Richard Courtney in *The Dawn Patrol*, Captain Geoffrey Thorpe in *The Sea Hawk*, General Custer in *They Died with Their Boots On*, James Corbett in *Gentleman Jim*, Soames Forsyte in *That Forsyte Woman*, and as his idol and fellow-drunk John Barrymore in *Too Much, Too Soon*. He wrote a novel, *Showdown* 46, which in its original, unpublished version included savage

caricatures of Jack WARNER and director Michael CURTIZ. According to biographer Charles Higham, Flynn was also a Nazi sympathizer and a bisexual whose lovers included Tyrone POWER, Howard HUGHES and Truman CAPOTE. Married three times: his first wife was actress Lili DAMITA (1935–42) and his third actress Patrice WYMORE. He was played by Guy PEARCE in a biopic, *My Forgotten Man* 93.

Autobiographies: 1937, *Beam Ends*; 1959, *My Wicked Wicked Ways*.

Biographies: 1960, *Errol and Me* by Nora Eddington (his second wife); 1977, *The Life and Crimes of Errol Flynn* by Lionel Godfrey; 1980, *Errol Flynn: The Untold Story* by Charles Higham.

Books: 1969, *The Films of Errol Flynn* by Tony Thomas, Rudy Behlmer, Clifford McCarty; 1998, *Errol Flynn: The Movie Posters* by Lawrence Bassoff.

■ In the Wake of the Bounty (as Fletcher Christian) 33. I Adore You 33. Murder at Monte Carlo (GB) 34. The Case of the Curious Bride 34. Don't Bet on Blondes 35. *Captain Blood* 35. *The Charge of the Light Brigade* 36. The Green Light 36. The Prince and the Pauper 37. Another Dawn 37. The Perfect Specimen 37. *The Adventures of Robin Hood* 38. Four's a Crowd 38. The Sisters 38. *The Dawn Patrol* 38. Dodge City 39. Elizabeth and Essex 39. Virginia City 39. *The Sea Hawk* 40. Santa Fe Trail 40. Footsteps in the Dark 41. Dive Bomber 41. *They Died with Their Boots On* 41. Desperate Journey 42. *Gentleman Jim* 42. Edge of Darkness 43. Northern Pursuit 43. Thank Your Lucky Stars 43. Uncertain Glory 44. Objective Burma! 45. San Antonio 45. Never Say Goodbye 45. Cry Wolf 46. Escape Me Never 47. Silver River 47. Always Together (uncredited) 47. The New Adventures of Don Juan 48. *That Forsyte Woman* (as Soames) 49. It's a Great Feeling 49. Montana 50. Rocky Mountain 50. Kim 51. The Adventures of Captain Fabian (& w) 51. Mara Maru 52. Against All Flags 52. The Master of Ballantrae (GB) 53. Crossed Swords (It.) 53. Lilacs in the Spring (GB) 55. The Dark Avenger (GB) 55. King's Rhapsody (GB) 56. The Big Boodle 56. Istanbul 57. The Sun Also Rises 57. *Too Much Too Soon* 58. Roots of Heaven 58. Cuban Rebel Girls 59.

TV series: Errol Flynn Theatre 57.

✪ For living several lives in half of one, and almost getting away with it. *The Adventures of Robin Hood*.

❝ He was one of the wild characters of the world, said Ann Sheridan. His wicked wicked ways were well known, but nobody ever admitted to disliking him for them; perhaps because, as Jack L. Warner said:

To the Walter Mittys of the world he was all the heroes in one magnificent, sexy, animal package.

Yakima Canutt added:

I think any man who had his appeal for women would have played it just the way he did – a bit wild.

Henry King's view was that

He loved to talk about how much he could drink and the women he'd made love to, but most of it was just the rationalizations of a disappointed moralist.

Bette Davis said:

Basically a nice man, and very honest about the fact that he knew he didn't have much talent.

Old drinking cronies like David Niven (who shared with him a house called Cirrhosis-by-the-sea) and Peter Finch later talked of him with affection. Lewis Milestone perhaps exaggerated slightly when he said:

His faults harmed no one but himself.

But even the people he did jar against seem to have borne him little ill-will, with the possible exception of the Australian creditors from whom he escaped before going to Hollywood. In a later broadcast to the people down under, he said jovially:

If there's anyone listening to whom I owe money, I'm prepared to forget it if you are.

Gene Autry said:

He spent more time on a bar stool, or in court, or in the headlines, or in bed, than anyone I knew.

And David Niven summed up his own experience:

The great thing about Errol was that you knew precisely where you were with him – because he *always* let you down.

A lot of people certainly looked at him and tut-tutted. Herbert Wilcox thought that:

His love of life defeated his ability as an artist.

And Leslie Mallory described his life as:

A fifty-year trespass against good taste.

There were other ways of looking at his behaviour. One of his wives, Nora Eddington, said rather proudly:

He wasn't afraid of anything, particularly if there was a challenge to it.

Some of the things he did were a reaction against being under-employed:

I felt like an impostor, taking all that money for reciting ten or twelve lines of nonsense a day.

He defended himself blithely:

The public has always expected me to be a playboy, and a decent chap never lets his public down.

And:

Women won't let me stay single, and I won't let myself stay married.

He exaggerated cheerfully in the cause of publicity:

I allow myself to be understood as a colourful fragment in a drab world.

But he was determined to have a good time:

I'll live this half of my life, I don't care about the other half.

He gleefully acknowledged his troubles:

My difficulty is trying to reconcile my gross habits with my net income.

And at the end he could say:

I've had a hell of a lot of fun, and I've enjoyed every minute of it.

At his passing, Tony Britton cabled Trevor Howard:

Old Errol died laughing. Can you beat that?

As Patric Knowles said:

He didn't give a damn for picture making: he thought it was ridiculous.

Famous line (*The Adventures of Robin Hood*): 'It's injustice I hate, not the Normans.'

Famous line (*Desperate Journey*): 'Now for Australia and a crack at those Japs!'

Flynn, Joe (1925–1974).

American character comedian, much on TV.

Did You Hear the One about the Travelling Saleslady? 68. Million Dollar Duck 71. Superdad 74, etc.

TV series: McHale's Navy 62–65.

Flynn, John (1931–).

American director.

■ The Sergeant 68. The Jerusalem File 72. The Outfit 73. Rolling Thunder 77. Defiance 80. Marilyn, the Untold Story (TV) 80. Touched 83. Best Seller 87. Lock Up 89. Out for Justice 91. Nails (TV) 92. Scam 93. Brainscan 94.

Flynn, Sean (1941–1970).

Athletic American leading man, son of Errol FLYNN.

Son of Captain Blood 62. Duel at Rio Grande 62. Five Ashore in Singapore/Singapore, Singapore 68, etc.

Flynt, Larry (1942–).

American founder and publisher of the porn magazine *Hustler*, who was shot and paralysed from the waist down in 1978. He was the subject of the biopic *The People vs Larry Flynt* 97, directed by Milos FORMAN and dealing with his legal battles, in which he was played by Woody HARRELSON. He also played a small part in the film, as a judge. Born in Kentucky, he ran strip clubs before beginning his magazine in the 70s.

❝ The Goebbels in the war against women – *Gloria Steinem*

Foch, Nina (1924–) (Nina Fock).

Cool, blonde, Dutch-born actress, long in America. Also associate director of George Stevens' *The Diary of Anne Frank*.

■ The Return of the Vampire 43. Nine Girls 43. Cry of the Werewolf 44. Shadows in the Night 44. A Song to Remember 44. I Love a Mystery 44. Escape in the Fog 45. Prison Ship 45. *My Name Is Julia Ross* 45. Johnny o'Clock 46. The Guilt of Janet Ames 48. The Dark Past 49. Undercover Man 50. *An American in Paris* 51. Young Man with Ideas 51. Scaramouche 52. Fast Company 53. Sombrero 53. *Executive Suite* (AAN) 54. Four Guns to the Border 54. You're Never Too Young 55. Illegal 55. The Ten Commandments 56. Three Brave Men 57. Spartacus 60. Cash McCall 60. Prescription Murder (TV) 67. Gidget Grows Up (TV) 69. Such Good Friends 71. Female Artillery (TV) 73. Salty 73. The Great Houdinis (TV) 76. Mahogany 76. Jennifer 78. Child of Glass (TV) 78. Ebony, Ivory and Jade (TV) 78. Rich and Famous 81. Shadow Chasers (TV) 85. Dixie Lanes 87. Skin Deep 89. Sliver 93. Morning Glory 93.

Foley, James.

American director and screenwriter.

Reckless 84. At Close Range 86. Who's That Girl 87. After Dark, My Sweet 90. Glengarry Glen Ross 92. Two Bits 95. Fear 96. The Chamber 96, etc.

Folsey, George J. (1898–1988).

American cinematographer who was nominated 13 times for Academy Awards for cinematography.

The Fear Market 20. Born Rich 24. *Applause* 29. The Smiling Lieutenant 31. Reckless 35. *The Great Ziegfeld* 36. The Shining Hour 38. Lady Be Good 41. Meet Me in St Louis 44. A Guy Named Joe 44. Under the Clock 45. The Green Years (AAN) 46. Green Dolphin Street (AAN) 47. State of the Union 48. Take Me Out to the Ball Game 48. The Great Sinner 49. *Adam's Rib* 49. Man with a Cloak 51. Million Dollar Mermaid 53. Executive Suite (AAN) 54. Seven Brides for Seven Brothers (AAN) 55. The Fastest Gun Alive 56. Imitation General 58. I Passed for White 60. The Balcony (AAN) 63, etc.

Fonda, Bridget (1964–).

American actress, the daughter of Peter FONDA.

You Can't Hurry Love 88. Aria 88. Shag 88. Scandal 89. Strapless 89. The Godfather Part III 90. Roger Corman's Frankenstein Unbound 90. Drop Dead Fred 91. Leather Jackets 91. Iron Maze 91. Out of the Rain 91. Doc Hollywood 91. Single White Female 92. Singles 92. Bodies, Rest & Motion 93. Point of No Return 93. Little Buddha 93. It Could Happen to You 94. Camilla 94. The Road to Wellville 94. Rough Magic 95. Balto (voice) 95. City Hall 96. Grace of My Heart 96. Rough Magic 97. In the Gloaming (TV) 97. Touch 97. Jackie Brown 97. Finding Graceland 98. A Simple Plan 98, etc.

Fonda, Henry (1905–1982).

Tall, lean American leading actor, the father of Jane and Peter FONDA. He began playing gauche young fellows (cartoonist Al Capp modelled his L'il Abner on Fonda in *The Trail of the Lonesome Pine*) and graduated to roles of determined integrity and amiable wisdom. Only occasionally did he play against type, notably as a killer in *Once Upon a Time in the West*. Born in Grand Island, Nebraska, he dropped out of the University of Minnesota to join a local drama company (run by Marlon BRANDO's mother Dorothy), which he first combined with temporary jobs, before working for small companies and reaching Broadway in *The Farmer Takes a Wife*, a role he then repeated for Hollywood. He signed a seven-year contract with Twentieth Century-Fox in order to star in *The Grapes of Wrath*, but disliked most of the roles Darryl ZANUCK found for him. In the late 40s and early 50s, he returned to the Broadway stage, appearing with success in *Mister Roberts* and *The Caine Mutiny Court Martial*, before recreating his stage role in the film of *Mister Roberts*, which brought to an end his friendly collaborations with director John FORD. His later films tended to be routine at best, though he had a popular and sentimental success with his last, *On Golden Pond*, playing opposite his daughter Jane. In 1981, he was given an honorary Oscar 'in recognition of his brilliant achievements'. Married actress Margaret SULLAVAN (1931–33); Frances Brokaw, mother of Jane and Peter Fonda, who committed suicide in 1950; actress Susan Blanchard (1950–56), the step-daughter of Oscar Hammerstein II; Baroness Afdera Franchetti (1957–61); and Shirlee Adams (1965–82). His defining performances, at first in films directed by John Ford, were in the title role of *The Young Mr Lincoln*, as Tom Joad in *The Grapes of Wrath*, Gil Carter in *The Ox-Bow Incident*, Wyatt Earp in *My Darling Clementine*, and Juror No. 8 in *Twelve Angry Men*.

Autobiography: 1981, *Fonda: My Life* (as told to Howard Teichmann).

Biographies: 1982, *Henry Fonda: His Life and Work* by Norm Goldstein; 1984, *The Fondas* by Gerald Cole and Wes Farrell; 1991, *The Fondas: A Hollywood Dynasty* by Peter Collier.

■ The Farmer Takes a Wife 35. Way Down East 35. I Dream Too Much 36. The Trail of the Lonesome Pine 36. *The Moon's Our Home* 36. Spendthrift 36. Wings of the Morning (GB) 37. You Only Live Once 37. Slim 37. That Certain Woman 37. I Met My Love Again 37. Jezebel 38. Blockade 38. Spawn of the North 38. The Mad Miss Manton 38. Jesse James 39. Let Us Live 39. The Story of Alexander Graham Bell 39. *Young Mr Lincoln* 39. Drums Along the Mohawk 39. *The Grapes of Wrath* (AAN) 40. Lillian Russell 40. The Return of Frank James 40. Chad Hanna 40. *The Lady Eve* 41. Wild Geese Calling 41. You Belong to Me 41. The Male Animal 42. Rings on Her Fingers 42. The Big Street 42. Tales of Manhattan 42. The Magnificent Dope 42. The Immortal Sergeant 42; *The Ox Bow Incident* 43; war service; *My Darling Clementine* (as Wyatt Earp) 46. The Long Night 47. The Fugitive 47. Daisy Kenyon 47. On Our Merry Way 48. Fort Apache 48; long absence on stage; Mister Roberts 55. The Wrong Man 56. War and Peace 56. *Twelve Angry Men* (BFA) (& p) 57. *Stage Struck* 57. The Tin Star 57. Warlock 59. The Man Who Understood Women 59. Advise and Consent 61. The Longest Day 62. How the West Was Won 62. Spencer's Mountain 63. The Best Man 64. *Fail Safe* 64. The Dirty Game 64. Sex and the Single Girl 64. The Battle of the Bulge 65. The Rounders 65. In Harm's Way 65. Big Hand for a Little Lady 66. Welcome to Hard Times 67. Firecreek 67. Stranger on the Run (TV) 67. Madigan 68. Yours, Mine and Ours 68. The Boston Strangler 68. Once upon a Time in the West 69. Too Late the Hero 69. There Was a Crooked Man 70. The Cheyenne Social Club 70. Sometimes a Great Notion 71. The Red Pony (TV) 72. The Serpent 72. The Alpha Caper (TV) 73. Ash Wednesday 73. My Name Is Nobody (It.) 73. Inside Job 75. Midway 76. Captains and the Kings (TV) 76. Tentacles 77. Rollercoaster 77. The Great Smokey Roadblock 78. The Swarm 78. Home to Stay (TV) 78. Fedora 78. Roots: The Next Generations (TV) 79. Wanda Nevada 79. Gideon's Trumpet (TV) 79. City on Fire 79. Meteor 79. *On Golden Pond* (AA) 81.

TV series: The Deputy 59–60. The Smith Family 70–71.

✪ For being a 40-year paradox: a self-effacing star. *Twelve Angry Men*.

❝ I ain't really Henry Fonda. Nobody could have that much integrity. – *H.F.*

A lean, stringy, dark-faced piece of electricity walked out on the screen and he had me. I believed my own story again. – *John Steinbeck on watching The Grapes of Wrath*

I look at Henry Fonda and I see the face of America. – *Orson Welles*

Famous speech (from *The Grapes of Wrath*): 'I'll be around in the dark. I'll be everywhere, wherever you can look. Wherever there's a fight, so hungry people can eat, I'll be there. Wherever there's a cop beatin' up a guy, I'll be there. I'll be there in the way guys yell when they're mad. I'll be there in the way kids laugh when they're hungry an' they know supper's ready. And when people are eatin' the stuff they raised, and livin' in the houses they built, I'll be there, too.'

Fonda, Jane (1937–).

American leading lady, daughter of Henry FONDA. Stage and modelling experience. She was married to director Roger VADIM (1965–73), and subsequently married Ted TURNER. She has published more than a dozen exercise videos following the success of her first, *Jane Fonda's Workout* 82, and half a dozen books on similar themes.

Biography: 1991, *Citizen Jane: The Turbulent Life of Jane Fonda* by Christopher Andersen.

■ Tall Story (debut) 60. Walk on the Wild Side 61. The Chapman Report 62. Period of Adjustment 62. In the Cool of the Day 63. Sunday in New York 63. La Ronde 64. Joy House 65. Cat Ballou 65. The Chase 66. Any Wednesday 66. The Game is Over (Fr.) 66. Hurry Sundown 67. Barefoot in the Park 67. Histoires Extraordinaires 67. Barbarella 68. They Shoot Horses Don't They? (AAN) 69. *Klute* (AA) 71. F.T.A. (& p) 72. Tout va Bien 72. Steelyard Blues 73. A Doll's House 74. The Bluebird 76. Fun with Dick and Jane 77. Julia (BFA, AAN) 77. Coming Home (AA) 78. California Suite 78. Comes a Horseman 79. The China Syndrome (BFA, AAN) 80. The Electric Horseman 80. Nine to Five 81. On Golden Pond (AAN) 81. Rollover 81. The Dollmaker (TV) 84. Agnes of God 85. The Morning After (AAN) 86.

Leonard, Part 6 87. Old Gringo (& p) 89. Stanley and Iris 90.
TV series: Nine to Five 82–83.
❝ Being a movie star is not a purpose. – *J.F.*
I'm hard-working. Honest. – *J.F.*

Fonda, Peter (1939–).
American actor, son of Henry FONDA.
Autobiography: 1998, *Don't Tell Dad: A Memoir*.
Biographies: 1984, *The Fondas* by Gerald Cole and Wes Farrell; 1991, *The Fondas: A Hollywood Dynasty* by Peter Collier.
Tammy and the Doctor 63. The Victors 63. Lilith 64. The Wild Angels 66. The Trip 67. *Easy Rider* (& co-w, p) (AANw) 69. The Last Movie 71. The Hired Hand (& d) 71. Two People 73. Dirty Mary Crazy Larry 74. Open Season 74. Race with the Devil 75. Killer Force 75. Fighting Mad 76. 92 in the Shade 76. Futureworld 76. Outlaw Blues 77. High Ballin' 78. Wanda Nevada (& d) 79. The Hostage Tower (TV) 80. Cannonball Run 81. Split Image 82. Peppermint Freedom 84. Certain Fury 85. Come the Day 85. Hawker 86. The Long Voyage 88. The Rose Garden 89. Fatal Mission 90. South Beach 92. Deadfall 93. Molly & Gina 94. Nadja 94. Love and a.45 94. Escape from LA 96. *Ulee's Gold* (as Ulee Jackson) (AAN) 97, etc.
❝ Civilization has always been a bust. – *P.F.*

Fonseca, Gregg.
American production designer.
Eyes of Fire 84. A Nightmare on Elm Street 84. Critters 85. Johnny Be Good 88. Honey, I Shrunk the Kids 89. The Guardian 89. Shattered 91. Wayne's World 92. Coneheads 93. Wayne's World 2 93.

Fontaine, Joan (1917–) (Joan de Havilland; sister of Olivia).
British-born leading actress, in America from childhood. Became typed as a shy English rose; later made efforts to play sophisticated roles.
Autobiography: 1978, *No Bed of Roses*.
■ No More Ladies 35. Quality Street 37. You Can't Beat Love 37. Music for Madame 37. Maid's Night Out 38. A Damsel in Distress 38. Blonde Cheat 38. The Man Who Found Himself 38. The Duke of West Point 38. Sky Giant 38. Gunga Din 39. Man of Conquest 39. The Women 39. *Rebecca* (AAN) 40. *Suspicion* (AA) 41. This Above All 42. The Constant Nymph (AAN) 43. *Jane Eyre* 43. *Frenchman's Creek* 44. The Affairs of Susan 45. *From This Day Forward* 46. Ivy 47. The Emperor Waltz 48. Kiss the Blood off My Hands 48. *Letter from an Unknown Woman* 48. You Gotta Stay Happy 48. Born To Be Bad 50. September Affair 50. Darling How Could You? 51. Something To Live For 52. Ivanhoe 52. Decameron Nights (GB) 53. Flight to Tangier 53. The Bigamist 53. Casanova's Big Night 54. Serenade 56. Beyond a Reasonable Doubt 56. Island in the Sun 56. Until They Sail 57. A Certain Smile 58. Tender Is the Night 61. Voyage to the Bottom of the Sea 61. The Devil's Own/The Witches (GB) 66. The Users (TV) 79.
✪ For successfully playing several variations on what was clearly a limited theme. *Rebecca*.
❝ If you keep marrying as I do, you learn everybody's hobby. – *J.F.*
Famous line (*Rebecca*): 'Last night I dreamed I went to Manderley again.'

Fontanne, Lynn (1887–1983).
Celebrated British-born stage actress, long in America and the wife of Alfred Lunt. Never really took to the screen.
■ The Man Who Found Himself 25. Second Youth 26. The Guardsman (AAN) 32. Stage Door Canteen 43.

Foote, Horton (1916–).
American screenwriter and dramatist.
To Kill a Mockingbird (AA) 62. Baby, the Rain Must Fall 65. The Chase 66. Hurry, Sundown 67. Fools Parade 71. Tomorrow 72. Tender Mercies (AA) 83. 1918 84. On Valentine's Day 86. The Trip to Bountiful (AAN) 85. Convicts 91. Of Mice and Men 92. Alone (TV) 97. Old Man (TV) 97, etc.

Foran, Dick (1910–1979) (Nicholas Foran).
Burly American leading man of light comedies and westerns in the early 40s; often played the good guy who didn't get the girl. Born in Flemington, New Jersey, the son of a senator, he was educated at Princeton, and began as a singer and bandleader.
Stand Up and Cheer 34. Shipmates Forever 35. The Petrified Forest 36. The Perfect Specimen 37. Four Daughters 38. Daughters Courageous 39. The Mummy's Hand 40. Horror Island 41. Butch Minds the Baby 42. He's My Guy 43. Guest Wife 45. Fort Apache 48. El Paso 49. Al Jennings of Oklahoma 51. Chicago Confidential 57. Atomic Submarine 60. Taggart 64, many others.
TV series: OK Crackerby 65.

Forbes, Bryan (1926–) (John Clarke).
Lively British small-part actor who became a useful scriptwriter, director and production executive. He is also a novelist. Married actress Nanette Newman.
Autobiographies: 1976, *Notes for a Life*. 1992, *A Divided Life*.
■ AS ACTOR: The Small Back Room 48. All Over the Town 48. Dear Mr Prohack 49. The Wooden Horse 50. Green Grow the Rushes 51. Appointment in London 52. Sea Devils 53. Wheel of Fate 53. The Million Pound Note 54. *An Inspector Calls* 54. Up to his Neck 54. The Colditz Story 54. Passage Home 55. Now and Forever 55. The Quatermass Experiment 55. The Last Man to Hang 55. The Extra Day 56. It's Great to be Young 56. The Baby and the Battleship 56. Satellite in the Sky 56. Quatermass II 57. The Key 58. I Was Monty's Double 58. Yesterday's Enemy 59. *The League of Gentlemen* 59. The Guns of Navarone 61. A Shot in the Dark 64. The Slipper and the Rose 76. International Velvet 78.
■ AS WRITER/PRODUCER/DIRECTOR: Cockleshell Heroes (w) 56. The Baby and the Battleship (w) 56. The Black Tent (w) 56. House of Secrets (w) 56. *I Was Monty's Double* (w) 58. The Captain's Table (w) 59. The Angry Silence (w) 59. *The League of Gentlemen* (w) 60. Man in the Moon (w) 60. *Whistle down the Wind* (d) 61. *Only Two Can Play* (w) 62. Station Six Sahara (w) 62. *The L-Shaped Room* (wd) 62. Of Human Bondage (w) 64. The High Bright Sun (w) 64. Seance on a Wet Afternoon (wd) 64. King Rat (wd) 65. The Wrong Box £ 66. *The Whisperers* (wd) 67. Deadfall (wd) 67. The Madwoman of Chaillot (d) 69. The Raging Moon (wd) 70. The Stepford Wives (d) 74. The Slipper and the Rose (wd) 76. International Velvet (wd) 78. Sunday Lovers (d part) 80. Jessie (TV) (d) 80. Better Late Than Never 82. The Naked Face (d) 85. The Endless Game (d) 89. Chaplin (co-w) 92.
❝ I may not have come up the hard way, but I have come up the whole way. – *B.F.*
An actor must have arrogance, conceit . . . I would never have made it as an actor, but I still have that conceit. – *B.F.*
If you treat the production of films like the production of shoes, you end up with Hush Puppies. – *B.F.*
I wish Bernie Delfont had had the courage of my convictions more often. – *B.F., of his period as production controller at EMI*
I knew I was there at Elstree to be shot at, but I never found time to be fitted for a bullet-proof vest. – *B.F.*
He perpetually pursues the anticliché only to arrive at anticlimax. – *Andrew Sarris, 1968*

Forbes, Mary (1882–1974).
British character actress in Hollywood, usually as haughty society lady.
Sunny Side Up 29. A Farewell to Arms 32. Blonde Bombshell 33. Les Misérables 35. Wee Willie Winkie 37. The Awful Truth 37. Always Goodbye 38. You Can't Take It With You 38. The Adventures of Sherlock Holmes 40. This Above All 42. The Picture of Dorian Gray 44. Ivy 47. You Gotta Stay Happy 48. The Ten Commandments 56, many others.

Forbes, Meriel (1913–) (M. Forbes-Robertson).
British stage actress, wife of Sir Ralph Richardson.
Borrow a Million 35. Young Man's Fancy 39. Come on George 39. The Gentle Sex 43. The Captive Heart 46. Home at Seven 52. Oh What a Lovely War 69.

Forbes, Ralph (1902–1951) (Ralph Taylor).
British leading man who became a Hollywood star in the late 20s.
The Fifth Form at St Dominics (GB) 21. Beau Geste 26. Mr Wu 29. The Trail of '98 30. Bachelor Father 31. Smilin' Through 32. The Barretts of Wimpole Street 34. The Three Musketeers 36. Romeo and Juliet 36. If I Were King 39. Elizabeth and Essex 39. Frenchman's Creek 44, etc.

Forbes, Scott (1921–1997).
Minor American leading man of the 50s.
Rocky Mountain 50. Raton Pass 51. Operation Pacific 51. Subterfuge 68. The Mind of Mr Soames 70, many others.

Forbstein, Leo F. (1892–1948).
American musical director, credited on all Warner sound films up to 1948.

Ford, Alexander (1908–1980).
Polish director who made films from 1930. Best known abroad: *The Young Chopin* 51. *Five Boys from Barska Street* 53. *Knights of the Teutonic Order* 60.

Ford, Cecil (1911–1980).
Former Irish actor who turned production manager on some notable films: *Moby Dick* 56. *Around the World in Eighty Days* 56. *The Bridge on the River Kwai* 57. *The Inn of the Sixth Happiness* 58.
Produced: *The Guns of Navarone* 61. *633 Squadron* 64, others.

Ford, Constance (1929–1993).
American general-purpose actress of the 50s.
The Last Hunt 56. A Summer Place 59. Home from the Hill 60. Claudelle Inglish 61. All Fall Down 62. The Cabinet of Caligari 62. The Caretaker 63, etc.

Ford, Dorothy (1923–).
Tall American leading lady of the 40s and 50s.
An American Romance 44. Here Come the Coeds 45. Love Laughs at Andy Hardy 47. Three Godfathers 49. One Sunday Afternoon 49. Jack and the Beanstalk 52. The High and the Mighty 54, etc.

Ford, Faith (1964–).
Perky American actress, best known for her role as Corky Sherwood Forrest in the television sitcom *Murphy Brown*.
'You Talkin' To Me?' 87. North 94. A Weekend in the Country (TV) 96, etc.
TV series: The Popcorn Kid 87.

Ford, Francis (1883–1953) (Francis O'Fearna).
American character actor, often seen as grizzled, cheery westerner; formerly star of early silents and serials. Brother of John Ford.
The Deserter 12. The Invader 13. The Broken Coin 15. Charlie Chan's Greatest Case 33. The Informer 35. Prisoner of Shark Island 36. In Old Chicago 38. Drums Along the Mohawk 39. Lucky Cisco Kid 40. The Ox-Bow Incident 42. The Big Noise 44. My Darling Clementine 46. Wagonmaster 50. The Sun Shines Bright 52, many others.

Ford, Glenn (1916–) (Gwyllyn Ford).
Stocky Canadian-born star of Hollywood dramas; from the early 40s he radiated integrity and determination, and continued his stardom into tortured middle-aged roles.
■ Heaven with a Barbed Wire Fence 39. My Son is Guilty 39. Convicted Woman 40. Men Without Souls 40. Babies for Sale 40. Blondie Plays Cupid 40. The Lady in Question 40. So Ends Our Night 41. Texas 41. Go West Young Lady 41. The Adventures of Martin Eden 42. Flight Lieutenant 42. The Desperadoes 43. Destroyer 43. *Gilda* 46. A Stolen Life 46. Framed 47. The Mating of Millie 48. The Loves of Carmen 48. The Return of October 48. The Man from Colorado 48. The Undercover Man 49. Mr Soft Touch 49. Lust for Gold 49. The Doctor and the Girl 49. The White Tower 50. Convicted 50. The Redhead and the Cowboy 50. The Flying Missile 50. Follow the Sun 51. The Secret of Convict Lake 51. The Green Glove 52. Affair in Trinidad 52. Young Man with Ideas 52. Time Bomb 53. The Man from the Alamo 53. Plunder of the Sun 53. *The Big Heat* 53. Appointment in Honduras 53. Human Desire 54. The Americano 55. The Violent Men 55. *The Blackboard Jungle* 55. Interrupted Melody 55. Trial 55. Ransom 56. Jubal 56. *The Fastest Gun Alive* 56. The Teahouse of the August Moon 56. *3.10 to Yuma* 57. Don't Go Near the Water 57. Cowboy 58. *The Sheepman* 58. Imitation General 58. Torpedo Run 58. It Started with a Kiss 59. The Gazebo 59. Cimarron 60. Cry for Happy 61. Pocketful of Miracles 61. The Four Horsemen of the Apocalypse 62. Experiment in Terror 62. Love is a Ball 63. The Courtship of Eddie's Father 63. Advance to the Rear 64. Fate is the Hunter 64. Dear Heart 64. The Rounders 65. The Money Trap 66. Is Paris Burning? 66. Rage 67. The Last Challenge 67. A Time for Killing 67. Day of the Evil Gun 68. Heaven with a Gun 69. Smith! 69. Brotherhood of the Bell (TV) 70. Santee 73. Jarrett (TV) 73. The Disappearance of Flight 412 (TV) 74. Punch and Jody (TV) 74. The Greatest Gift (TV) 75. Midway 76. Once an Eagle (TV) 76. Evening in Byzantium (TV) 78. Superman 78. The Sacketts (TV) 79. Beggarman Thief (TV) 80. Happy Birthday to Me 81. Virus 82. Casablanca Express 89. Border Shootout 90. Raw Nerve 91.
TV series: *Cade's County* 71. Holvak 75.
❝ If they tried to rush me, I'd always say I've only got one other speed, and it's slower. – *G.F.*
I've never played anyone but myself on screen. – *G.F.*

Ford, Harrison (1892–1957).
American leading man of the silent screen. Born in Kansas City, he was in films from 1916 and was one of the most commercially successful actors of his time, while being noted for reclusiveness, shunning personal publicity and Hollywood itself. He retired in the early 30s.
The Mysterious Mrs M. 17. Food for Scandal 20. Foolish Wives 22. Janice Meredith 24. That Royle Girl 25. Up in Mabel's Room 26. The Girl in the Pullman 27. Three Weekends 28. Love in High Gear 32, many others.

Ford, Harrison (1942–).
American leading actor, the thinking man's action hero, at his best playing tough roles that allow room for a few moral scruples. Born in Chicago, he began acting at Ripon College, Wisconsin, and briefly in the theatre before going to Hollywood, where he was put under contract by Columbia, a studio that provided him with lacklustre roles; after his contract ended, he went to work for Universal, playing bit parts in various television series, such as *Gunsmoke* and *The Partridge Family*. In the early to mid-70s, he worked as a self-taught carpenter, while appearing in a few supporting roles; but it was not until *Star Wars* that he became a star, a status he confirmed by his role as Indiana Jones in *Raiders of the Lost Ark* and its sequels. Married screenwriter Melissa MATHISON, his second wife, in 1983. Publicity-shy, he lives with his family on an 800-acre ranch in Wyoming. His best roles so far have been as Hans Solo in the *Star Wars* trilogy, as Indiana Jones, as John Book in *Witness*, and in the title role in *The Fugitive*.
Biographies: 1993, *Harrison Ford* by Robert Sellers; 1997, *Harrison Ford: Imperfect Hero* by Garry Jenkins.
■ Dead Heat on a Merry Go Round 66. A Time for Killing 67. Luv 67. Journey to Shiloh 68. Getting Straight 70. The Intruders (TV) 70. Zabriskie Point 70. American Graffiti 73. The Conversation 74. Dynasty (TV) 76. The Possessed (TV) 77. Heroes 77. *Star Wars* 77. Force Ten from Navarone 78. Apocalypse Now (bit) 79. Hanover Street 79. The Frisco Kid 79. The Empire Strikes Back 80. *Raiders of the Lost Ark* 81. Blade Runner 82. Return of the Jedi 83. Indiana Jones and the Temple of Doom 84. Witness (AAN) 85. The Mosquito Coast 87. Frantic 87. Working Girl 88. Indiana Jones and the Last Crusade 89. Presumed Innocent 90. Regarding Henry 91. Patriot Games 92. The Fugitive 93. Clear and Present Danger 94. Jimmy Hollywood (as himself) 94. Devil's Own 97. Air Force One 97. Six Days, Seven Nights 98.
❝ Before, I was grateful for a job, almost any job. Now, I'm apprehensive, but I know I have other options, and when I ask for the money, they pay it. It's that simple. – *H.F.*
I don't use any particular method. I'm from the let's pretend school of acting. – *H.F.*
All I would tell people is to hold on to what is individual about themselves. Not to allow their ambition for success to cause them to try and imitate the success of others. You've got to find it on your own terms. – *H.F.*
I don't want to be a movie star. I want to be in movies that are stars. – *H.F.*
Harrison, more I think than any other actor on world screens, embodies the Everyman. – *Philip Noyce*
You look at Harrison and you listen; he looks like he's carrying a gun, even if he isn't. – *Carrie Fisher*

Ford, John (1895–1973) (Sean O'Fearna).
Distinguished Irish-American director who from 1917 made over 125 features, many of them silent westerns. In the 30s he built up to a handful of incomparable human dramas; in the 40s he turned towards roving, brawling, good-natured outdoor action films using a repertory of his favourite actors. His best films are milestones, but he disclaimed any artistic pretensions.

Biography: 1982, *The Unquiet Man* by Dan Ford (grandson).

SELECTED SILENT FILMS: The Tornado 17. A Woman's Fool 18. Bare Fists 19. The Wallop 21. Silver Wings 22. The Face on the Bar Room Floor 23. *The Iron Horse* 24. Lightnin' 25. Three Bad Men 26. Four Sons 28. Mother Machree 28. Riley the Cop 28. Strong Boy 29.

■ SOUND FILMS: Black Watch 29. Salute 29. *Men Without Women* 30. Born Reckless 30. Up the River 30. The Seas Beneath 30. The Brat 31. *Arrowsmith* 31. Air Mail 32. Flesh 32. Pilgrimage 33. Doctor Bull 33. *The Lost Patrol* 34. The World Moves On 34. *Judge Priest* 34. *The Whole Town's Talking* 35. *The Informer* (AA) 35. *Steamboat Round the Bend* 35. Prisoner of Shark Island 36. Mary of Scotland 36. The Plough and the Stars 36. Wee Willie Winkie 37. *The Hurricane* 37. Four Men and a Prayer 38. Submarine Patrol 38. *Stagecoach* (AAN) 39. *Young Mr Lincoln* 39. *Drums Along the Mohawk* 39. *The Grapes of Wrath* (AA) 40. The Long Voyage Home 40. *Tobacco Road* 41. *How Green Was My Valley* (AA) 41. Why We Fight and other war documentaries 42–45. They Were Expendable 45. *My Darling Clementine* 46. The Fugitive 47. Fort Apache 48. Three Godfathers 48. *She Wore A Yellow Ribbon* 49. When Willie Comes Marching Home 50. Wagonmaster 50. Rio Grande 50. This is Korea 51. *The Quiet Man* (AA) 52. What Price Glory? 52. Mogambo 53. *The Sun Shines Bright* 54. The Long Gray Line 55. Mister Roberts (co-d) 55. *The Searchers* 56. The Wings of Eagles 57. The Rising of the Moon 57. *The Last Hurrah* 58. Gideon's Day 59. The Horse Soldiers 59. Sergeant Rutledge 60. Two Rode Together 61. The Man Who Shot Liberty Valance 62. How the West Was Won (part) 63. Donovan's Reef 63. Cheyenne Autumn 64. Young Cassidy (part) 64. Seven Women 66.

✪ For half-a-dozen simply marvellous films. *The Grapes of Wrath*.

❝ Anybody can direct a picture once they know the fundamentals. Directing is not a mystery, it's not an art. The main thing about directing is: photograph the people's eyes. – *J.F.*

It's no good asking me to talk about art. – *J.F.*

He developed his craft in the 20s, achieved dramatic force in the 30s, epic sweep in the 40s, and symbolic evocation in the 50s. – *Andrew Sarris, 1968*

He never once looked in the camera when we worked together. You see, the man had bad eyes, as long as I knew him, but he was a man whose veins ran with the business. – *Arthur Miller, photographer*

Knockabout comedy and tragedy co-exist with perfect ease in his work, which throughout a long career shows a clear development and progression. – *John M. Smith*

He had instinctively a beautiful eye for the camera. But he was also an egomaniac. – *Henry Fonda*

His films look entirely different one from another, the style emerging rather from a personal response to people: affectionate, warm, with a rural decency and intimacy. – *Charles Higham*

Ford, Paul (1901–1976) (Paul Ford Weaver).
American character actor best known on TV as the harassed colonel in the Bilko series and star of *The Baileys of Balboa*.

The House on 92nd Street 45. Lust for Gold 49. Perfect Strangers 50. *The Teahouse of the August Moon* 56. The Matchmaker 58. Advise and Consent 61. *The Music Man* 62. *Never Too Late* 65. Big Hand for a Little Lady 66. The Russians Are Coming, The Russians Are Coming 66. The Spy with a Cold Nose (GB) 67. The Comedians 67, etc.

Ford, Wallace (1898–1966) (Sam Grundy).
British general-purpose actor who went to Hollywood in the early 30s and after a few semi-leads settled into character roles.

Freaks 32. Lost Patrol 34. *The Informer* 35. OHMS (GB) 36. The Mummy's Hand 40. Inside the Law 42. Shadow of a Doubt 43. The Green Years 46. Embraceable You 48. *Harvey* 50. The Nebraskan 53. Destry 55. Johnny Concho 56. The Last Hurrah 58. A Patch of Blue 66, etc.

TV series: The Deputy 59.

Forde, Eugene (1898–1986).
American director of second features, former silent-screen actor.

Charlie Chan in London 33. Buy Me That Town 41. Berlin Correspondent 42. Jewels of Brandenberg 46. Invisible Wall 47, many others.

Forde, Florrie (1876–1940).
Australian actress and singer who became a top music-hall performer in Britain from the late 1890s with songs that featured a catchy chorus, including 'Down at the Old Bull and Bush' and 'It's a Long Way to Tipperary'.

Say It with Flowers 34. My Old Dutch 34. Royal Cavalcade 35, etc.

Forde, Walter (1897–1984) (Thomas Seymour).
British director, formerly a popular slapstick comedian of the silents: *Wait and See*, *Would You Believe It*, many shorts, one of which was featured in *Helter Skelter* 49. Directed some high-speed farces and several thrillers and melodramas.

The Silent House 28. Lord Richard in the Pantry 30. *The Ghost Train* 31. Jack's the Boy 32. *Rome Express* 32. Orders Is Orders 33. Jack Ahoy 34. Chu Chin Chow 34. *Bulldog Jack* 35. King of the Damned 35. Land Without Music 36. The Gaunt Stranger 38. The Four Just Men 39. Inspector Hornleigh on Holiday 39. *Saloon Bar* 40. Sailors Three 40. The Ghost Train 41. Atlantic Ferry 41. Charley's Big-Hearted Aunt 41. *It's That Man Again* 42. Time Flies 44. Master of Bankdam 47. Cardboard Cavalier 48, many others.

Foreman, Carl (1914–1984).
American writer-producer-director, latterly resident in Britain after being blacklisted.

So This Is New York (w) 48. The Clay Pigeon (w) 49. Home of the Brave (w) 49. *Champion* (AANw) 49. The Men (AANw) 50. Cyrano de Bergerac (w) 50. *High Noon* (w) 52. *The Bridge on the River Kwai* (AAw) 57. The Key (wp) 58. *The Guns of Navarone* (wp) (AAN) 61. The Victors (wpd) 63. Born Free (p) 65. Mackenna's Gold (p) 68. The Virgin Soldiers (p) 69. Young Winston (wp) (AAN) 72. Force Ten from Navarone (p) 78. When Time Ran Out (co-w) 80.

❝ I think I was the only director who ever made a second film for Foreman. He was an excellent producer and an excellent, if lazy, writer but he did interfere with directors as well as being obsessive about credits. – *J. Lee-Thompson*

Foreman, John (1925–1992).
American producer, former agent.

WUSA 70. They Might Be Giants 71. The Effect of Gamma Rays on Man in the Moon Marigolds 72. The Life and Times of Judge Roy Bean 72. The Man Who Would Be King 75. The First Great Train Robbery 78. Prizzi's Honor 85, etc.

Forest, Mark (1933–) (Lou Degni).
American athlete and gymnast who appeared in many Italian muscle-man epics.

■ Goliath and the Dragon 60. Maciste the Mighty/Son of Samson 60. The Strongest Man in the World 61. Death in the Arena 62. Goliath and the Sins of Babylon 63. The Terror of Rome Against the Son of Hercules 63. Hercules Against the Sons of the Sun 64. The Lion of Thebes 64. Hercules Against the Barbarians 64. Hercules Against the Mongols 64. Kindar the Invulnerable 64.

Forester, C. S. (1899–1966).
British adventure novelist. Works filmed include *Captain Horatio Hornblower*, *The African Queen*, *Payment Deferred*, *The Pride and the Passion* ('The Gun').

Forman, Milos (1932–).
Czech director of realistic comedies.

Autobiography: 1994, *Turnaround – A Memoir* with Jan Novak.

Peter and Pavla 64. *A Blonde in Love* 65. The Fireman's Ball 68. *Taking Off* (US) 71. *One Flew Over the Cuckoo's Nest* (AA) 75. *Hair* 79. Ragtime 81. Amadeus (AA) 83. Valmont 89. The People vs Larry Flynt (AAN) 96, etc.

❝ One of the criteria of casting was that we couldn't afford to have a prick in the company. – *M.F., on One Flew Over the Cuckoo's Nest*

Formby, George (1904–1961) (George Booth).
British north-country comedian with a toothy grin and a ukelele, long popular in music halls.

Biography: 1974, *George Formby* by Alan Randal and Ray Seaton.

■ Boots Boots (debut) 33. Off the Dole 34. *No Limit* 35. *Keep Your Seats Please* 36. Feather Your Nest 37. *Keep Fit* 37. I See Ice 38. *It's in the Air* 38. Trouble Brewing 39. Come On, George 39. *Let George Do It* 40. Spare a Copper 41. Turned Out Nice Again 41. South American George (dual role) 42. Much Too Shy 42. Get Cracking 43. Bell-Bottom George 43. He Snoops To Conquer 44. I Didn't Do It 45. George in Civvy Street 46.

Forrest, Frederic (1936–).
American leading man of the 70s.

■ Where the Legends Die 72. The Don Is Dead 74. The Conversation 74. The Gravy Train 74. Larry (TV) 74. Promise Him Anything (TV) 75. Permission to Kill 75. The Missouri Breaks 77. It Lives Again 79. Apocalypse Now 79. The Rose (AAN) 79. One from the Heart 82. Hammett 82. Saigon – Year of the Cat (TV) 83. Valley Girl 83. The Stone Boy 84. Best Kept Secrets (TV) 84. Return 85. Where are the Children? 85. Stacking 87. Valentino Returns 87. Quo Vadis 88. Tucker: The Man and His Dream 88. Cat Chaser 89. Music Box 89. The Two Jakes 90. Falling Down 93. Trauma 93. Against the Wall (TV) 94. Chasers 94. Hidden Fears 94. Before the Night 94. Lassie 94. One Night Stand 95. Andersonville (TV) 95. Crash Dive 96.

Forrest, Sally (1928–) (Katharine Scully Feeney).
American leading lady of the early 50s.

Not Wanted 49. Mystery Street 50. Never Fear 50. Hard Fast and Beautiful 51. Excuse My Dust 51. The Strange Door 51. The Strip 51. Son of Sinbad 55. Ride the High Iron 56. While the City Sleeps 56, etc.

Forrest, Steve (1924–) (William Forrest Andrews).
American leading man, brother of Dana Andrews.

The Bad and the Beautiful 52. Phantom of the Rue Morgue 54. Prisoner of War 54. Bedevilled 55. The Living Idol 57. Heller in Pink Tights 60. The Yellow Canary 63. Rascal 69. The Wild Country 71. Wanted the Sundance Woman (TV) 76. North Dallas Forty 79. The Manions of America (TV) 81. Malibu (TV) 83. Hollywood Wives (TV) 84. Spies Like Us 85. Amazon Women on the Moon 87. Killer: A Journal of Murder 95, etc.

TV series: The Baron 65. S.W.A.T. 75–76. Dallas 86.

Forst, Willi (1903–1980) (Wilhelm Frohs).
Austrian director and actor.

Maskerade (wd) 34. Bel Ami (a, wd) 39. Operette (a, wd) 40. Wiener Maedelin (a, w) 45. The Sinner (wd) 50. Vienna, City of My Dreams (d) 57, etc.

Forster, E. M. (1879–1970).
British novelist who stopped writing fiction in 1924. His novels, with the exception of *The Longest Journey*, have all been filmed in a mood of nostalgic Edwardiana.

A Passage to India (d David Lean) 84. A Room with a View (d James Ivory) 85. Maurice (d James Ivory) 87. Where Angels Fear to Tread (d Charles Sturridge) 91. Howards End (d James Ivory) 92.

Forster, Robert (1941–).
Sardonic-looking American leading man with echoes of John Garfield.

Reflections in a Golden Eye 67. The Stalking Moon 68. Justine 69. Medium Cool 69. Pieces of Dreams 70. Cover Me Babe 72. Death Squad (TV) 73. The Don Is Dead 73. Nakia (TV) 74. Stunts 77. Avalanche 78. Standing Tall 78. The Black Hole 79. Alligator 80. Vigilante 83. Goliath Awaits (TV) 84. Hollywood Harry (& pd) 85. Once a Hero 88. The Banker 89. Peacemaker 90. Satan's Princess 90. Jackie Brown (AAN) 97. Rear Window (TV) 98. Supernova 99, etc.

TV series: *Banyon* 71.

❝ Where have I been? I've had a five-year first act and a 25-year second act. I've been sliding quite a long time. – *R.F., 1998*

Forster, Rudolph (1884–1968).
German leading actor of heavy personality, seen abroad chiefly in *Die Dreigroschenoper/The Threepenny Opera* (as Macheath) 32.

Forsyth, Bill (1947–).
Scottish writer-director who met with instant success for his small local comedies. He moved to Hollywood in the late 80s, but failed to find a receptive audience for his pawky sense of humour. *Being Human*, made at a cost of $20m, was a box-office flop.

■ That Sinking Feeling 80. *Gregory's Girl* 81. Local Hero 83. Comfort and Joy 84. Housekeeping (US) 87. Breaking In (US) 89. Being Human (US) 94.

❝ The thing about Hollywood is the mind-set that prevails. It works from the assumption that if you're in the movie business, you want all those people to like your film, you want to win an Oscar and you want to have a $100 million gross. That's what having a career in the industry means. – *B.F.*

The only ambitions I have for the films I make is that they're appreciated as poetical works. Either film is too crude a medium to handle that or else I can't make it do these things. If something doesn't work over a period of time you tend not to be so interested in it. In a way my perception of film has been reduced. – *B.F.*

My problem is that 40 per cent of me wants to make an entertaining film and 60 per cent of me wants to subvert the idea of movies. It's actually not a very happy way to work. – *B.F.*

Forsyth, Bruce (1927–) (Bruce Forsyth Johnson).
Bouncy, beaming, British TV comedian whose film appearances have been scant.

■ Star! 68. Hieronymus Merkin 69. The Magnificent Seven Deadly Sins 71. Bedknobs and Broomsticks 71.

❝ A tall, lean figure of inexhaustible energy, he wears down his audience by an aggressive humility, like Uriah Heep on speed. – *International Herald Tribune*

Forsyth, Frederick (1938–).
British writer of adventure thrillers, most of which have been picked up as screen material: *The Day of the Jackal*, *The Odessa File*, *The Dogs of War*, *The Fourth Protocol*.

❝ I've yet to be convinced that the film business is a profession for adults. – *F.F.*

Forsyth, Rosemary (1944–).
American leading actress.

Shenandoah (debut) 65. The War Lord 65. Texas Across the River 66. Where It's At 69. Whatever Happened to Aunt Alice? 69. How Do I Love Thee? 70. City Beneath the Sea (TV) 71. One Little Indian 73. Black Eye 74. Gray Lady Down 78. The Gladiator (TV) 86. A Friendship in Vienna (TV) 88. Disclosure 94. Daylight 96, etc.

Forsythe, John (1918–) (John Freund).
Smooth American leading man with Broadway experience.

Destination Tokyo 43. Captive City 52. Escape from Fort Bravo 53. The Trouble with Harry 56. *The Ambassador's Daughter* 56. See How They Run (TV) 64. Kitten with a Whip 65. Madame X 66. In Cold Blood 67. Topaz 69. The Happy Ending 69. Murder Once Removed (TV) 71. The Healers (TV) 75. The Feather and Father Gang (TV) 77. The Users (TV) 79. And Justice for All 79. Sizzle (TV) 81. Scrooged 88, etc.

TV series: Bachelor Father 57–61. The John Forsythe Show 65. To Rome with Love 69–70. Charlie's Angels (voice only) 76–80. *Dynasty* 81–86.

❝ I can't afford to bulge. Being a 64-year-old sex symbol is a hell of a weight to carry. – *J.F.*

Forsythe, William (1950–).
Burly American actor, often as a villain.

Cloak and Dagger 84. Once upon a Time in America 84. Savage Dawn 84. The Lightship 85. The Long Hot Summer (TV) 87. Raising Arizona 87. Extreme Prejudice 87. Weeds 87. Patty Hearst 88. Dead-Bang 89. Torrents of Spring (It./Fr.) 89. Dick Tracy 90. Career Opportunities 91. Out for Justice 91. Stone Cold 91. The Waterdance 91. The Gun in Betty Lou's Handbag 92. Things to Do in Denver When You're Dead 95. Virtuosity 95. The Substitute 96. The Rock 96. Gotti (TV) 96. Palookaville 96. First Time Felon 97. Firestorm 98. Hell's Kitchen 98. Ambushed 98, etc.

TV series: The Untouchables (as Al Capone) 92–93.

Fosse, Bob (1927–1987).
American dancer who became a Broadway director.
Biography: 1989, *Razzle Dazzle: The Life and Work of Bob Fosse* by Kevin Boyd Grubb.
■ Give a Girl a Break 52. The Affairs of Dobie Gillis 52. Kiss Me Kate 53. My Sister Eileen (& ch) 55. *The Pajama Game* (ch only) 57. Damn Yankees (ch only) 58. *Sweet Charity* (d, ch) 68. *Cabaret* (d, ch) (AA) 72. Lenny (AANd) 74. The Little Prince (a only) 75. *All That Jazz* (allegedly based on his life) (d, ch) (AAN) 79. Star 80 (wd) 83.

Fossey, Brigitte (1945–).
French actress.
Jeux Interdits 52. Le Grand Meaulnes 67. Adieu l'Ami 68. M comme Mathieu 71. Un Mauvais Fils 80. Enigma 82. The Last Butterfly 90. Les Enfants du Naufrageur 92, etc.

Foster, Barry (1931–).
British light actor, usually figuring as comic relief, but popular on TV as the Dutch detective Van der Valk.
Sea of Sand 56. Yesterday's Enemy 59. King and Country 64. The Family Way 66. Robbery 67. Twisted Nerve 68. Ryan's Daughter 70. Frenzy 72. Divorce His Divorce Hers (TV) 73. The Sweeney 77. The Three Hostages (TV) 78. The Wild Geese 78. Smiley's People (TV) 81. A Woman Called Golda (TV) 82. Heat and Dust 83, To Kill a King 84. The Whistle Blower 86, etc.

Foster, David (1929–).
American producer, a former publicist. He is the father of producers Gary Foster, Greg Foster and Tim Foster.
McCabe and Mrs Miller 71. The Getaway 72. The Drowning Pool 75. The Thing 82. Mass Appeal 84. The Mean Season 85. Short Circuit 86. Running Scared 86. Short Circuit II 88. Full Moon in Blue Water 88. The Getaway 93. The Mask of Zorro 98, etc.

Foster, Dianne (1928–) (D. Laruska).
Canadian leading lady who has made British and American films.
The Quiet Woman (GB) 51. Isn't Life Wonderful? (GB) 53. Drive a Crooked Road (US) 54. The Kentuckian (US) 55. The Brothers Rico (US) 57. Gideon's Day (GB) 58. The Last Hurrah (US) 58. King of the Roaring Twenties (US) 61. Who's Been Sleeping in My Bed (US) 63, etc.

Foster, Jodie (1962–).
Child actress in precocious roles who has matured successfully and become a director. She was in adverts from the age of three, including some as the Coppertone Girl for suntan lotion.
Biographies: 1997, *Foster Child* by Buddy Foster; 1997, *Jodie* by Louis Chunovic.
Napoleon and Samantha 72. Kansas City Bomber 72. One Little Indian 73. Tom Sawyer 73. One Little Indian 73. *Alice Doesn't Live Here Any More* 74. *Bugsy Malone* 76. *Taxi Driver* (AAN) 76. The Little Girl Who Lives Down the Lane 76. Candleshoe 77. Freaky Friday 77. Carny 80. Foxes 80. O'Hara's Wife 81. Svengali (TV) 82. The Blood of Others 84. Hotel New Hampshire 84. Five Corners 87. Siesta 87. The Accused (AA) 88. Stealing Home 88. Catchfire/Backtrack 89. *Silence of the Lambs* (AA) 91. Little Man Tate (& d) 91. Shadows and Fog 91. Sommersby 93. Maverick 94. Nell (AAN) 94. Home for the Holidays (d) 95. Contact 97, etc.
TV series: Mayberry 69. Bob & Carol & Ted & Alice 73. Paper Moon 74–75.
❝ I believe women should be sexual. And why not? What a great thing to be: a sexual woman, coming of age and discovering sensuality and the intoxification of it. I've seen so many movies about women who don't like sex and really don't want to have sex, or have that posey stuff in Calvin Klein ads. Well, that's just not true and I'm sick of that myth being out there. What I'd like to do is develop movies that better reflect my generation of women. – J.F.
I don't talk about my private life, and that's probably why I'm sane. – J.F.

Foster, Julia (1941–).
British leading lady.
The Small World of Sammy Lee 63. Two Left Feet 63. The System 64. The Bargee 64. One-Way Pendulum 64. Alfie 66. Half a Sixpence 67. All Coppers Are 72. The Great McGonagall 74. F. Scott Fitzgerald in Hollywood (TV) 76. The Thirteenth Reunion 81, etc.

Foster, Lewis (1899–1974).
American director, former Hal Roach gag writer; won an Oscar in 1939 for the original story of Mr *Smith Goes to Washington*.
The Lucky Stiff (& w) 48. Manhandled (& w) 49. Captain China 49. The Eagle and the Hawk (& w) 49. Crosswinds 51. Those Redheads from Seattle (& w) 53. Top of the World 55. The Bold and the Brave 56. Tonka (& w) 58, etc.

Foster, Meg (1948–).
American leading lady with striking blue eyes.
The Death of Me Yet (TV) 71. Sunshine (TV) 73. Things in Their Season (TV) 74. James Dean (TV) 76. A Different Story 79. The Legend of Sleepy Hollow 79. Carny 80. Guyana Tragedy (TV) 81. Ticket to Heaven 81. The Osterman Weekend 83. The Emerald Forest 85. The Wind 87. Masters of the Universe 87. They Live 88. Tripwire 89. Blind Fury 89. Relentless 89. Stepfather II 89. Backstab 90. To Catch a Killer (TV) 92. Hidden Fears 94. Oblivion 94. Space Marines 96. The Man in the Iron Mask 97, etc.
TV series: Sunshine 73. Cagney and Lacey 82–84.

Foster, Norman (1900–1976) (Norman Hoeffer).
American leading man of the early 30s; became a director and had a rather patchy career. Married Claudette COLBERT and Sally BLANE.
Gentlemen of the Press 29. It Pays to Advertise 31. Reckless Living 31. Alias the Doctor 32. Skyscraper Souls 32. State Fair 33. Professional Sweetheart 33. Orient Express 34. Behind the Green Lights 35. High Tension 36. I Cover Chinatown (& d) 36.
■ DIRECTED ONLY: Fair Warning 37. Think Fast Mr Moto 37. Thank You Mr Moto 37. Walking Down Broadway 38. Mysterious Mr Moto 38. Mr Moto Takes a Chance 38. Mr Moto's Last Warning 39. Charlie Chan in Reno 39. Mr Moto Takes a Vacation 39. *Charlie Chan at Treasure Island* 39. Charlie Chan in Panama 40. Viva Cisco Kid 40. Ride Kelly Ride 41. Scotland Yard 41. *Journey Into Fear* 42. Rachel and the Stranger 48. Kiss the Blood off My Hands 48. Tell It to the Judge 49. Father is a Bachelor 50. Woman on the Run 50. Navajo 52. Sky Full of Moon 52. Sombrero 53. Davy Crockett 55. Davy Crockett and the River Pirates 56. The Nine Lives of Elfego Baga 58. The Sign of Zorro 60. Indian Paint 66. Brighty 67.

Foster, Preston (1901–1970).
Handsome American leading man of the 30s, former clerk and singer.
Nothing But the Truth (debut) 30. Life Begins 31. *The Last Mile* 31. Wharf Angel 34. The Informer 35. The Last Days of Pompeii 35. Annie Oakley 36. The Plough and the Stars 37. First Lady 38. News Is Made at Night 38. Geronimo 39. Moon over Burma 40. Northwest Mounted Police 40. Unfinished Business 41. Secret Agent of Japan 42. My Friend Flicka 43. The Bermuda Mystery 44. The Valley of Decision 45. The Last Gangster 45. The Harvey Girls 46. Ramrod 47. Green Grass of Wyoming 48. Tomahawk 49. The Tougher They Come 51. The Big Night 52. Kansas City Confidential 53. I the Jury 55. Destination 60,000 58. Advance to the Rear 64. The Time Travellers 65. Chubasco 68, many others.
TV series: Waterfront 54–55. Gunslinger 60.

Foster, Stephen (1826–1864).
American songwriter of popular sentimental ballads: 'Old Folks at Home', 'Beautiful Dreamer', etc. Impersonated on screen by Douglass Montgomery in *Harmony Lane* 35, Don Ameche in *Swanee River* 39, and Bill Shirley in *I Dream of Jeannie* 52.

Foster, Susanna (1924–) (Suzan Larsen).
American operatic singer and heroine of several 40s films. She angered producers by turning down roles in order to study opera, and quit Hollywood to sing in operettas in the late 40s and early 50s with her husband, tenor Wilbur Evans (1948–56). After her divorce, she worked in a variety of low-paid office jobs.
The Great Victor Herbert 40. *There's Magic in Music* 41. The Hard Boiled Canary 42. Top Man 43. *Phantom of the Opera* 43. The Climax 44. Bowery to Broadway 44. This Is the Life 44. Frisco Sal 45. That Night with You 45, etc.

Fotopoulos, Vassilis (1934–).
Greek production designer, from the stage.
America America/The Anatolian Smile 63. Zorba the Greek (AA) 64. You're a Big Boy Now 67, etc.

Foulger, Byron (1900–1970).
American small-part actor, the prototype of the worried, bespectacled clerk.
The Prisoner of Zenda 37. Edison the Man 40. Sullivan's Travels 41. Since You Went Away 44. Champagne for Caesar 49. The Magnetic Monster 53. The Long Hot Summer 59. The Gnome-Mobile 67, many others.
TV series: Captain Nice 67. Petticoat Junction 68–70.

Fowlds, Derek (1937–).
British comedy character actor, usually in unassuming roles.
The Smashing Bird I Used to Know 69. Hotel Paradiso 66. Tower of Evil 71. Over the Hill 92, etc.
TV series: The Basil Brush Show 69–73. Yes Minister 80–85. Yes Prime Minister 86–90. Heartbeat 92– .

Fowler, Gene (1890–1960).
American journalist, author and screenwriter. Born in Denver, Colorado, he studied at the University of Colorado and worked as a reporter, sports editor and managing editor of New York newspapers while becoming a best-selling author. He went to Hollywood in the 30s, and was a biographer of Jimmy DURANTE, and chronicler and close friend of actor John BARRYMORE, who used to enjoy reciting his poem 'Testament of a Dying Ham'.
Autobiographies: 1958, *Timberline*; 1961, *Skyline*.
The Roadhouse Murder 32. What Price Hollywood? 32. State's Attorney 32. The Way to Love 33. The Mighty Barnum 34. The Call of the Wild 35. Career Woman (story) 36. Professional Soldier 36. A Message to Garcia 36. Love under Fire 37. Nancy Steele Is Missing 37. Billy the Kid 41. Big Jack 49. Beau James (oa) 56, etc.
❝ What is success? It is a toy balloon among children armed with pins. – G.F.
You do not waste time; time wastes you. – G.F.

Fowler, Gene, Jnr. (1918–1988).
American editor and director, the son of Gene FOWLER. He was also responsible for the technical direction of George S. KAUFMAN's one attempt at film direction, *The Senator Was Indiscreet* 48.
AS EDITOR: *The Oxbow Incident* 43. Philo Vance Returns 47. Captain Scarface 53. Main Street to Broadway 53. Naked Hills 55. Beyond a Reasonable Doubt 56. While the City Sleeps 56. China Gate 57. Forty Guns 57. Run of the Arrow 57. A Child Is Waiting 62. *It's a Mad, Mad, Mad World* (AAN) 63. Hang 'em High 68. A Death of Innocence 71. Smorgasbord 81, etc.
AS WRITER: My Outlaw Brother 51. The Oregon Trail 59.

Fowler, Harry (1926–).
British cockney actor on screen since the early 40s, often in cameo roles.
Those Kids from Town 42. Champagne Charlie 44. Hue and Cry 46. For Them That Trespass 48. I Believe in You 52. Pickwick Papers 53. Home and Away 56. Idol on Parade 59. Ladies Who Do 63. Doctor in Clover 66. The Prince and the Pauper 77. Chicago Joe and the Showgirl 89, many others.
TV series: The Army Game, Our Man at St Mark's.

Fowler, Hugh (c. 1904–1975).
American editor.
Les Misérables 52. Gentlemen Prefer Blondes 53. The Last Wagon 56. Say One for Me 59. The Lost World 60. The List of Adrian Messenger 63. Stagecoach 66. Planet of the Apes 67. Patton (AA) 70. The Life and Times of Judge Roy Bean 72, many others.

Fowles, John (1926–).
British novelist whose slightly mystic themes have generally attracted film-makers, though not always with satisfactory results: *The Collector*, *The Magus*, *The French Lieutenant's Woman*.

Fowley, Douglas (1911–1998).
American character actor often seen as nervous or comic gangster.
Let's Talk it Over 34. Crash Donovan 36. Charlie Chan on Broadway 37. Mr Moto's Gamble 38. Dodge City 39. Ellery Queen Master Detective 40. Tanks a Million 41. Jitterbugs 42. The Kansan 43. One Body Too Many 44. The Hucksters 47. If You Knew Susie 48. Battleground 49. Edge of Doom 50. Criminal Lawyer 51. *Singin' in The Rain* (as the hysterical director) 52. The High and the Mighty 54. Macumba Love (p and d only) 59. Desire in the Dust 60. Barabbas 62. From Noon till Three 76. The White Buffalo 77, many others.
TV series: The Life and Legend of Wyatt Earp (as Doc Holliday) 56–61. Pistols and Petticoats 66. Gunsmoke 68–74.

Fox, Bernard.
British character actor in Hollywood: plays a rather stiff gent of the old school.
Soho Incident 56. The Safecracker 58. Honeymoon Hotel 64. Star 68. Big Jake 71. The Hound of the Baskervilles (TV) (as Dr Watson) 72. Herbie Goes to Monte Carlo 77. Alien Zone 78. The Private Eyes 80. Yellow Beard 83. Haunted Honeymoon 86. 18 Again 87. The Rescuers Down Under (voice) 90. Titanic 97, etc.
TV series: Bewitched 67–72.

Fox, Charles (1940–).
American composer.
Barbarella (co-m) 67. Goodbye Columbus 69. Star Spangled Girl 71. The Laughing Policeman 73. The Other Side of the Mountain 75. Foul Play 78. Nine to Five 80. Why Would I Lie 80. Zapped! 82. Love Child 82. Strange Brew 83. National Lampoon's European Vacation 85. Longshot 86. Parent Trap 87. Love at Stake 88. Short Circuit II 88. The Gods Must Be Crazy II 89. It Had to Be You 89, etc.
Much TV including Happy Days, The Love Boat.

Fox, Edward (1937–).
Diffident British leading man of the 70s.
The Naked Runner 67. The Long Duel 67. Oh What a Lovely War 69. Skullduggery 69. The Breaking of Bumbo 70. The Go-Between 71. *The Day of the Jackal* 73. Doll's House 73. Galileo 74. The Squeeze 77. A Bridge Too Far 77. The Cat and the Canary 78. Force Ten From Navarone 78. *Edward and Mrs Simpson* (TV) 78. The Mirror Crack'd 80. Gandhi 82. Never Say Never Again 83. The Dresser 83. The Shooting Party 84. The Bounty 84. Wild Geese 2 85. Return to the River Kwai 89. They Never Slept 90. Robin Hood 90. Gulliver's Travels (TV) 96. A Dance to the Music of Time (TV) 97, etc.

Fox, James (1939–).
British leading man, who usually plays a weakling. Once a child actor, notable in *The Magnet* 50 (as William Fox). Returned to acting 1982 after a ten-year break in good works. Brother of Edward Fox, and very similar in style.
Autobiography: 1983, *Comeback*.
The Loneliness of the Long Distance Runner 62. The Servant 63. Tamahine 64. Those Magnificent Men in Their Flying Machines 65. King Rat 65. The Chase 65. Thoroughly Modern Millie 67. Duffy 68. Isadora 68. Arabella 69. Performance 70. Runners 83. A Passage to India 84. Greystoke 84. Absolute Beginners 85. The Whistle Blower 86. High Season 87. Boys in the Island 89. Farewell to the King 89. She's Been Away 89. Russia House 90. A Question of Attribution (TV) 91. Afraid of the Dark 91. As You Like It 92. Hostage 92. Patriot Games 92. The Remains of the Day 93. Heart of Darkness (TV) 94. The Dwelling Place (TV) 94. Doomsday Gun (TV) 94. Clockwork Mice 95. The Old Curiosity Shop (TV) 95. A Month by the Lake 95. Gulliver's Travels (TV) 96. Jinnah (Pak.) 98, etc.
TV series: The Choir 95.

Fox, Kerry.
New Zealand leading actress.
An Angel at My Table 90. The Last Days of Chez Nous 91. Friends 92. Taking Liberties 93. Country Life 94. The Last Tattoo 94. Shallow Grave 94. Black Tuesday (TV) 95. The Affair (TV) 95. Saigon Baby (TV) 96. Welcome to Sarajevo 97. The Hanging Garden 98, etc.

Fox, Michael J. (1961–).
Canadian leading man in Hollywood who plays younger than his years. Married actress Tracy Pollan. In 1998 he revealed that he had been suffering from Parkinson's disease for seven years.
Midnight Madness 80. Class of 84 83. *Back to the Future* 85. Teen Wolf 85. Poison Ivy (TV) 85. The Secret of my Success 87. Light of Day 87. Bright Lights, Big City 88. Back to the Future II 89. Casualties of War 89. Back to the Future III 90. Doc Hollywood 91. The Hard Way 91. The Concierge 92. Where the Rivers Flow North 93. Life with Mikey 93. Greedy/Greed 94. Coldblooded 95. Blue in the Face 95. The American President 95. Homeward Bound II: Lost in San Francisco (voice) 96. The Frighteners 96. Mars Attacks! 96, etc.
TV series: Palmerstown USA 80–81. *Family Ties* 82–89. Spin City 96– .

Fox, Sidney (1910–1942).
American leading lady of the early 30s.
Bad Sister 31. The Mouthpiece 32. Once In a Lifetime 32. Murders in the Rue Morgue 32. Midnight 34, etc.

Fox, Vivica A. (1964–).
American actress, a former model, from television. She was born in South Bend, Indiana, and raised in Indianapolis. According to her publicity, she was discovered by a producer while having lunch at a restaurant on Sunset Boulevard in the mid-80s.
Independence Day 96. Set It Off 96. Booty Call 96. Batman and Robin 97. Soul Food 97. Why Do Fools Fall in Love 98, etc.
TV series: Getting Personal 98– .

Fox, Wallace (1898–1958).
American director.
The Amazing Vagabond 29. Cannonball Express 32. Powdersmoke Range 35. The Last of the Mohicans (co-d) 36. Racing Lady 37. Pride of the Plains 40. Bowery Blitzkrieg 41. Kid Dynamite 43. Riders of the Santa Fe 44. Mr Muggs Rides Again 45. Gunman's Code 46. Docks of New York 48. Six Gun Mesa 50. Montana Desperado 51, many others.

Fox, William (1879–1952) (Wilhelm Fried).
Hungarian-American pioneer and executive, the Fox of Twentieth Century-Fox. Moved from the garment industry into exhibition, production and distribution.
Biography: 1933, *Upton Sinclair Presents William Fox*.
❝ I always bragged of the fact that no second of those contained in the twenty-four hours ever passed but that the name of William Fox was on the screen, being exhibited in some theatre in some part of the world. – *W.F.*

Foxwell, Ivan (1914–).
British producer, in films since 1933.
No Room at the Inn 47. The Intruder 51. The Colditz Story 54. Manuela 56. A Touch of Larceny 59. Tiara Tahiti 62. The Quiller Memorandum 66. Decline and Fall (& w) 68, etc.

Foxworth, Robert (1941–).
American general-purpose actor.
The New Healers (TV) 72. Frankenstein (TV) 73. The Devil's Daughter (TV) 73. The Questor Tapes (TV) 74. Mrs Sundance (TV) 74. James Dean (TV) 76. Treasure of Matecumbe 76. It Happened at Lake Wood Manor (TV) 77. Death Moon (TV) 78. Damien: Omen II 78. Prophecy 79. The Black Marble 80. Double Standard (TV) 88. Beyond the Stars 89, etc.
TV series: Storefront Lawyers 70–71. Falcon Crest 81–89.

Foxx, Redd (1922–1991) (John Elroy Sanford).
American vaudevillian who became a 70s star in the long-running *Sanford and Son*.
Norman, Is That You? 76. Harlem Nights 89.
TV series: Sanford and Son 72–77. Redd Foxx 77–78. Sanford 80–81. The Redd Foxx Show 86.

Foy, Bryan (1895–1977).
American producer, mostly of low budgeters at Warner. Wrote song, 'Mr Gallagher & Mr Shean'; and was the oldest of the 'seven little Foys'.
The Home Towners (d) 28. Little Old New York (d) 28. The Gorilla (d) 31. Berlin Correspondent 42. Guadalcanal Diary 43. Doll Face 46. Trapped 49. Breakthrough 50. Inside the Walls of Folsom Prison 51. The Miracle of Fatima 52. *House of Wax* 53. The Mad Magician 54. Women's Prison 55. Blueprint for Robbery 61. PT 109 63, many others.

Foy, Eddie, Snr (1854–1928) (Edward Fitzgerald).
Famous American vaudeville comedian who made few film appearances but was several times impersonated by Eddie Foy Jnr: in *Yankee Doodle Dandy, Wilson, Bowery to Broadway*, etc. Bob Hope played him in *The Seven Little Foys*. Films include A Favourite Fool 15.

Foy, Eddie, Jnr (1905–1983).
American vaudeville entertainer, son of another and one of the 'seven little Foys'.
Fugitive from Justice 40. The Farmer Takes a Wife 53. Lucky Me 54. *The Pajama Game* 57. Bells Are Ringing 60. Thirty Is a Dangerous Age, Cynthia 67, etc.
TV series: Fair Exchange 63.

Fraker, William A. (1923–).
American cinematographer.
Games 67. The Fox 67. The President's Analyst 67. *Bullitt* 68. Rosemary's Baby 68. Paint Your Wagon 69. *Monte Walsh* (& d) 70. Day of the Dolphin 73. Lipstick 76. Exorcist II: The Heretic 77. Looking for Mr Goodbar (AAN) 77. American Hot Wax 78. Heaven Can Wait (AAN) 78. Hard Contract 78. 1941 (AAN) 79. Old Boyfriends 79. Hollywood Knights 80. Sharkey's Machine 81. The Legend of the Lone Ranger (d only) 81. The Best Little Whorehouse in Texas 82. War Games (AAN) 83. Protocol 84. Murphy's Romance (AAN) 85. Burglar 87. Baby Boom 87. Chances Are 89. An Innocent Man 89. The Freshman 90. Memoirs of an Invisible Man 92. There Goes My Baby 94. Street Fighter 94. Father of the Bride Part II 95. The Island of Dr Moreau 96. Vegas Vacation 97, etc.

Frakes, Jonathan (1952–).
American actor and director, born in Bethlehem, Pennsylvania, best known for his role as Commander William Riker in the TV series *Star Trek: The Next Generation*.
Beach Patrol (TV) 79. Nutcracker: Money, Madness and Murder (TV) 87. Star Trek: Generations 94. *Star Trek: First Contact* (& d) 96.
TV series: North and South Book 1 85.

France, C. V. (1868–1949).
British stage character actor, most typically seen in films as dry lawyer or ageing head of household.
Lord Edgware Dies 35. Scrooge 35. Victoria the Great 37. A Yank at Oxford 38. If I Were King (US) 39. Night Train to Munich 40. Breach of Promise 41. The Halfway House 44, etc.

Francen, Victor (1888–1977).
Belgian stage actor, occasionally in French films from 1921, but most familiar in Hollywood spy dramas during World War II.
Crépuscule d'Epouvante 21. Après l'Amour 31. Nuits de Feu 36. Le Roi 36. J'Accuse 38. Sacrifice d'Honneur 38. La Fin du Jour 39. Tales of Manhattan 42. Mission to Moscow 43. Devotion 43. The Mask of Dimitrios 44. The Conspirators 44. Passage to Marseilles 44. Confidential Agent 45. The Beast with Five Fingers 46. La Nuit s'achève 49. The Adventures of Captain Fabian 51. Hell and High Water 54. Bedevilled 55. A Farewell to Arms 58. Fanny 61. Top-Crack 66, many others.

Franciosa, Anthony (Tony) (1928–) (Anthony Papaleo).
Italian-American leading actor with lithe movement and ready grin. He was married to actress Shelley Winters (1957–60).
A Face in the Crowd (debut) 57. This Could Be the Night 57. *A Hatful of Rain* (his stage role) (AAN) 57. Wild Is the Wind 58. *The Long Hot Summer* 58. The Naked Maja 59. Career 59. The Story on Page One 59. Go Naked in the World 60. Period of Adjustment 62. Rio Conchos 64. The Pleasure Seekers 65. A Man Could Get Killed 65. Assault on a Queen 66. The Swinger 66. Fathom (GB) 67. The Sweet Ride 68. In Enemy Country 68. A Man Called Gannon 68. Across 110th Street 72. The Drowning Pool 75. The World Is Full of Married Men (GB) 79. Firepower 79. Death Wish II 82. Unsane/Tenebrae 82. Stagecoach (TV) 86. Death House 88. Ghostwriter 89. Backstreet Dreams 90. Double Threat 92. City Hall 96, etc.
TV series: Valentine's Day 64. *The Name of the Game* 68–70. Search 72. Matt Helm 75.

Franciosa, Massimo (1924–1998).
Italian screenwriter, director and novelist. Many of his 60 or so screenplays were written in collaboration with Pasquale Festa Campanile, often for the films of Dino Risi. He turned to directing in the 60s, and later wrote mainly for television.
Wild Love 55. Poor but Beautiful 56. Beautiful but Poor 57. La Nonna Sabella 57. Venice, the Moon and You 58. Young Husbands 58. The Love Nakers 61. The Lady Killer of Rome 61. The Conjugal Bed 63. The Four Days of Naples (AAN) 63. Un Tentativo Sentimentale (& co-d) 63. White Voices/Le Voci Bianche (& co-d) 64. Extra Coniugale (co-d) 65. The Dreamer/Il Morbidone (d) 66. The Girl and the General 67. Pronto . . . C'e una Certa Giuliana per Te (d) 67. Quella Chiara Notte d'Ottobre (d) 70. The Voyage 74. Sono Fotogenico 80, etc.

Francis, Alec B. (1869–1934).
British-born character actor in Hollywood films as elderly gentleman.
Flame of the Desert 19. Smiling Through 22. Three Wise Fools 23. Charley's Aunt 25. Tramp Tramp Tramp 26. The Terror 28. Outward Bound 30. Arrowsmith 31. The Last Mile 32. Oliver Twist 33. Outcast Lady 34, many others.

Francis, Anne (1930–).
American leading lady of several 50s films: formerly model, with radio and TV experience.
Summer Holiday (debut) 48. So Young So Bad 50. Elopement 52. Lydia Bailey 52. Susan Slept Here 54. Bad Day at Black Rock 54. The Blackboard Jungle 55. Forbidden Planet 56. Don't Go Near the Water 57. Girl of the Night 60. The Satan Bug 65. Funny Girl 68. The Love God 69. More Dead than Alive 70. Pancho Villa 71. Haunts of the Very Rich (TV) 72. A Masterpiece of Murder (TV) 86. Little Vegas 92. The Double O Kid 93, etc.
TV series: Honey West 65. My Three Sons 71.

Francis, Arlene (1908–) (Arlene Kazanjian).
American TV personality who has appeared in a few films. Married actor Martin Gabel.
Stage Door Canteen 43. All My Sons 48. One Two Three 61. The Thrill of it All 63. Fedora 78, etc.

Francis, Connie (1938–) (Concetta Franconero).
American pop singer who had some light films built around her. She dubbed the singing voice of Freda Holloway in *Jamboree* 57, and Tuesday Weld in *Rock, Rock, Rock* 57.
Where the Boys Are 63. Follow the Boys 64. Looking for Love 65, etc.

Francis, Derek (1923–1984).
Portly British character actor, often in self-important roles.
Bitter Harvest 63. Ring of Spies 64. The Comedy Man 64. Carry on Camping 69. To the Devil a Daughter 75. Jabberwocky 77, etc.

Francis, Freddie (1917–).
British cinematographer who turned to direction with less distinguished results.
Mine Own Executioner 47. Time without Pity 57. Room at the Top 59. *Sons and Lovers* (AA) 60. The Innocents 61. The French Lieutenant's Woman 80. The Elephant Man 81. Dune 85. Code Name: Emerald 85. Dark Tower 87. Clara's Heart 88. Her Alibi 89. Brenda Starr 89. Glory (AA) 89. The Plot to Kill Hitler (TV) 90. Cape Fear 91. The Man in the Moon 91. School Ties 92. A Life in the Theatre 93. Princess Caraboo 94, etc.
AS DIRECTOR ONLY: Two and Two make Six 61. Vengeance 62. Paranoiac 63. Nightmare 63. The Evil of Frankenstein 64. Traitor's Gate 65. The Skull 65. The Deadly Bees 66. They Came from Beyond Space 66. The Torture Garden 67. Dracula has Risen from the Grave 68. Mumsy Nanny Sonny and Girlie 69. Tales from the Crypt 71. Asylum 72. Tales that Witness Madness 73. Legend of the Werewolf 74. The Doctor and the Devils 86. Dark Tower 87. Rainbow 95, etc.

Francis, Ivor (c. 1911–1986).
American character actor who played self-important or bumbling types.
I Love My Wife 70. The Late Liz 71. The World's Greatest Athlete 73. Superdad 74. The Prisoner of Second Avenue 75. The North Avenue Irregulars 78, etc.
TV series: Gilligan's Island 64–67. Dusty's Trail 73.

Francis, Karl (1943–).
Welsh director.
The Mouse and the Woman 81. Giro City 82. The Happy Alcoholic 84. Boy Soldier (TV) 86. Angry Earth (TV) 90. Rebecca's Daughters 91, etc.
TV series: Judas and the Gimp (p, wd) 93.

Francis, Kay (1899–1968) (Katherine Gibbs).
Ladylike, serious-faced American star of women's films in the 30s.
■ Gentlemen of the Press 29. The Coconuts 29. Dangerous Curves 29. Illusion 29. The Marriage Playground 29. Behind the Makeup 30. *Street of Chance* 30. Paramount on Parade 30. A Notorious Affair 30. Raffles 30. For the Defence 30. Let's Go Native 30. The Virtuous Sin 30. Passion Flower 30. Scandal Sheet 31. Ladies' Man 31. The Vice Squad 31. Transgression 31. Guilty Hands 31. Twenty-Four Hours 31. Girls about Town 31. The False Madonna 32. Strangers in Love 32. Man Wanted 32. Street of Women 32. Jewel Robbery 32. *One Way Passage* 32. *Trouble in Paradise* 32. *Cynara* 32. The Keyhole 33. Storm at Daybreak 33. Mary Stevens MD 33. I Loved a Woman 33. The House on 56th Street 33. Mandalay 34. Wonder Bar 34. Doctor Monica 34. British Agent 34. Stranded 34. The Goose and the Gander 35. Living on Velvet 35. I Found Stella Parish 35. *The White Angel* (as Florence Nightingale) 36. Give Me Your Heart 36. Stolen Holiday 37. Confession 37. Another Dawn 37. *First Lady* 37. Women Are Like That 38. My Bill 38. Secrets of an Actress 38. Comet over Broadway 38. King of the Underworld 39. Women in the Wind 39. In Name Only 39. It's a Date 40. Little Men 40. When the Daltons Rode 40. Play Girl 40. The Man Who Lost Himself 40. *Charley's Aunt* 41. The Feminine Touch 41. Always in My Heart 42. Between Us Girls 42. Four Jills in a Jeep 44. Divorce 45. Allotment Wives 45. Wife Wanted 46.

Francis, Raymond (1909–1987).
English character actor, best known for playing the precise, snuff-taking infallible detective Tom Lockhart in several TV crime series of the 50s and 60s. Born in Finchley, London, he began as a conjuror in his teens and worked in repertory for many years before succeeding on TV. He was the father of actor Clive Francis (1946–).
Mr Denning Drives North 51. Carrington VC 54. Storm over the Nile 55. Above Us the Waves 55. Reach for the Sky 56. Doublecross 56. Carve Her Name with Pride 58. It Shouldn't Happen to a Vet 76. The Case of Marcel Duchamp 83, etc.
TV series: Sherlock Holmes (as Dr Watson) 51. Murder Bag 57–59. Crime Sheet 59. No Hiding Place 59–67.

Francis, Robert (1930–1955).
American leading man whose budding career was cut short by an air crash.
The Caine Mutiny 54. The Long Gray Line 55, etc.

Franciscus, James (1933–1991).
American leading man.
Four Boys and a Gun 56. I Passed for White 60. The Outsider 61. The Miracle of the White Stallions 63. Youngblood Hawke 64. The Valley of Gwangi 69. Marooned 69. Beneath the Planet of the Apes 69. Cat O'Nine Tails 71. The Dream Makers (TV) 75. The Amazing Dobermans 76. The Greek Tycoon 78. When Time Ran Out 80. Jacqueline Bouvier Kennedy (TV) 81. Butterfly 81. The Great White 82. The Courageous 82. Secret Weapons (TV) 85, etc.
TV series: Naked City 58. Mr Novak 63–64. Longstreet 71. Hunter 77.

Francks, Don (1932–).
Canadian singer whose first notable film role was in *Finian's Rainbow* 68.
My Bloody Valentine 81. Terminal Choice 85. The Christmas Wife (TV) 88. Madonna: Innocence Lost 95. First Degree 95. Johnny Mnemonic 95.

Harriet the Spy 96. Bogus 96. Summer of the Monkeys 98. Dinner at Fred's 98, etc.
TV series: La Femme Nikita 97.

Franco, Jess (Jesús).
Prolific Spanish director, mainly of exploitation and horror movies of extremely variable quality, usually ranging from bad to abysmal. He has made as many as eight features a year under several pseudonyms, including Jess Frank, Clifford Brown, and Frank Hollman, and was an assistant to Orson Welles on his unfinished *Don Quixote*.
Dr Orloff's Monster 64. The Diabolical Dr Z/Miss Muerte 65. Attack of the Robots 66. Succubus/Necronomicon 67. The Castle of Fu Manchu/El Castillo de Fu Manchu 68. Deadly Sanctuary 68. Kiss and Kill 68. 99 Women 69. Venus in Furs 69. Mrs Hyde/Sie Toetete in Extase 70. Lesbian Vampires/Vampyros Lesbos 70. De Sade 70 70. Bram Stoker's Count Dracula/Count Dracula/El Conde Dracula 70. Virgin among the Living Dead 71. Dracula Prisoner of Frankenstein/The Screaming Dead/Dracula contra Frankenstein 72. Jack the Ripper 76. Ilsa the Wicked Warden (& a) 78. Revenge in the House of Usher/El Hundimiento de la Casa Usher 83. Faceless 88, many others.

Franco, Ricardo (1949–1998).
Spanish director, the nephew of director Jesús Franco. Died of heart failure. He was part of Madrid's Independent Cinema, making films about life's dispossessed.
El Desastre de Anual (& a) 70. Pascal Duarte 75. The Remains from the Shipwreck/Los Restos del Naufragio (& a) 78. La Paloma Azul (a only) 80. In 'N' Out (US/Mex.) 84. The Dream of Tangiers/El Sueño de Tanger (d) 86. Berlin Blues 88. Blood and Sand (co-w) 89. Lucky Star 97, etc.

Franju, Georges (1912–1987).
French director, former set designer. Co-founder of Cinémathèque Française. Best-known documentaries: *Le Sang des Bêtes* 49. *Hôtel des Invalides* 51. *Le Grand Méliès* 51. Features: *La Tête contre les Murs/The Keepers* 58. *Eyes without a Face* 59. Spotlight on a Murderer 61. Thérèse Desqueyroux 62. Judex 63. Thomas the Impostor 64. Les Rideaux Blancs 65.

Frank, A. Scott.
American screenwriter.
Plain Clothes 88. Little Man Tate 91. Dead Again 91. Fallen Angels 2 (co-w) (TV) 93. Malice (co-w) 93. Get Shorty 95. Heaven's Prisoners (co-w) 95. Out of Sight 98, etc.

Frank, Charles (1910–).
British director, former dubbing expert.
Uncle Silas 47. Intimate Relations 53, etc.

Frank, Christopher (1943–1993).
British-born director and screenwriter, based in France.
Josepha 81. The Year of the Jellyfish 84. Love in the Strangest Way/Elles N'Oublient Pas 94, etc.

Frank, Fredric M. (1911–1977).
American scriptwriter.
The Greatest Show on Earth (co-w, AA) 52. The Ten Commandments (co-w) 56. El Cid (co-w) 61, etc.

Frank, Gerold (1907–1998).
American 'ghost writer' who co-authored the autobiographies of such luminaries as Sheilah Graham, Lillian Roth and Diana Barrymore.

Frank, Harriet:
see Ravetch, Irving.

Frank, Melvin (1913–1988).
American comedy scriptwriter and latterly producer/director.
WITH NORMAN PANAMA: My *Favourite Blonde* 42. Thank Your Lucky Stars 43. Road to Utopia (AAN) 45. Monsieur Beaucaire 46. *Mr Blanding Builds His Dream House* 48. The Reformer and the Redhead 50. Above and Beyond 52. Knock on Wood (AAN) 54. White Christmas 56. That Certain Feeling 56. Li'l Abner 59. *The Facts of Life* 61. Road to Hong Kong 62. Strange Bedfellows 65, etc.
SOLO: A Funny Thing Happened on the Way to the Forum (wp) 66. Buona Sera Mrs Campbell (wpd) 68. A Touch of Class (wpd) (AANw) 72. The Prisoner of Second Avenue £ 75. The Duchess and the Dirtwater Fox (wpd) 76. Lost and Found (wpd) 79.

Frankau, Ronald (1894–1951).
British stage and radio comedian with an 'idle rich' characterization.
The Calendar 31. His Brother's Keeper 39. Double Alibi 46. The Ghosts of Berkeley Square 47, etc.
❝ To the pure *nothing* is pure. – *R.F.*

Frankel, Benjamin (1906–1973).
British composer. Born in London, he studied at the Guildhall School of Music and began as a nightclub violinist and a musical director in the theatre. Scores include:
The Years Between 46. The Seventh Veil 46. Mine Own Executioner 47. Sleeping Car to Trieste 48. Appointment with Venus 51. The Importance of Being Earnest 52. A Kid For Two Farthings 55. Simon and Laura 55. Happy is the Bride 58. Libel 59. Guns of Darkness 62. Night of the Iguana 64. Battle of the Bulge 65, etc.

Frankel, Cyril (1921–).
British director, former documentarist with Crown Film Unit.
Devil on Horseback 54. Make Me an Offer 55. It's Great To Be Young 56. No Time for Tears 57. She Didn't Say No 58. Alive and Kicking 58. Never Take Sweets from a Stranger 61. Don't Bother To Knock 61. On the Fiddle 61. The Very Edge 63. The Witches/The Devil's Own 66. The Trygon Factor 67. Permission to Kill 75, etc.

Frankel, Mark (1962–1996).
English leading actor.
Leon the Pig Farmer 92. Solitaire for 2 95. The Ruth Rendell Mysteries: Vanity Dies Hard (TV) 95. Clare de Lune 95. Roseanna's Grave 97, etc.
TV series: Sisters 92–93. Fortune Hunter 94. Kindred: The Embraced 96.

Frankenheimer, John (1930–).
Ebullient American director, formerly in TV.
The Young Stranger 57. The Young Savages 61. All Fall Down 61. *The Manchurian Candidate* 62. *Birdman of Alcatraz* 62. *Seven Days in May* 64. The Train 64. *Seconds* 66. Grand Prix 67. The Extraordinary Seaman 68. The Fixer 68. The Gypsy Moths 69. I Walk the Line 70. The Horsemen 71. Impossible Object 73. The Iceman Cometh 73. 99 44/100 Dead 74. French Connection II 75. Black Sunday 76. Prophecy 79. The Challenge 82. The Holcroft Covenant 85. 52 Pick-Up 86. Dead Bang 89. The Fourth War 90. Year of the Gun 91. Against the Wall (TV) 94. The Burning Season (TV) 94. The Island of Dr Moreau 96. The Long Rains 97. George Wallace (TV) 97. Ronin 98, etc.

Franklin, Carl (1941–).
American director, a former actor on stage and television.
Nowhere to Run (d) 88. Eye of the Eagle II: Inside the Enemy (d) 89. Full Fathom Five (d) 90. Eye of the Eagle III (a) 91. *One False Move* (d) 91. Laurel Avenue (TV) 93. Devil in a Blue Dress (wd) 95. One True Thing (d) 98, etc.
TV series (as actor): Caribe 75. Fantastic Journey 77. McClain's Law 81–82.

Franklin, Howard.
American director.
Quick Change 90. The Public Eye 92. Larger than Life 96, etc.

Franklin, Pamela (1949–).
British juvenile actress of the 60s.
The Innocents 61. The Lion 62. The Third Secret 64. The Nanny 65. Our Mother's House 67. The Night of the Following Day 68. *The Prime of Miss Jean Brodie* 69. Sinful Davey 69. David Copperfield 69. And Soon the Darkness 70. Necromancy 72. The Legend of Hell House 73. Food for the Gods 76, etc.

Franklin, Richard (1948–).
Australian director.
■ Belinda 72. Loveland 73. The True Story of Eskimo Nell/Dick Down Under 75. Fantasm 77. Patrick 78. Road Games 81. *Psycho II* 83. Cloak and Dagger 84. Link 86. FX/2: The Deadly Art of Illusion 91. Hotel Sorrento 95. Brilliant Lies 96.

Franklin, Sidney (1893–1972).
American producer-director, in Hollywood since leaving school. Academy Award 1942 'for consistent high achievement'.
Martha's Vindication (d) 16. Heart o' the Hills (d) 19. Dulcy (d) 23. Beverly of Graustark (d) 26. The Last of Mrs Cheyney (d) 29. Private Lives (d) 31. The Guardsman (d) 32. Smiling Through (d) 32. Reunion in Vienna (d) 33. The Barretts of Wimpole Street (d) 33. The Dark Angel (d) 35. The Good Earth (AANd) 37. On Borrowed Time (p) 39. Waterloo Bridge (p) 40. Mrs Miniver (p) 42. Random Harvest (p) 42. The White Cliffs of Dover (p) 44. The Yearling (p) 46. The Miniver Story (p) 50. Young Bess (p) 54. The Barretts of Wimpole Street (d) 57, many others.

Franklyn, Leo (1897–1975).
English character actor, mainly on the stage in musical comedy, revue and farce. In films from the early 30s in Australia. Father of actor William Franklyn.
Two Minutes Silence 34. I've Got a Horse 38. The Same to You 59. The Night We Dropped a Clanger 59. The Night We Got the Bird 60, etc.

Franklyn, William (1926–).
Smooth British character actor, popular on TV.
Quatermass II 57. Fury at Smugglers' Bay 58. Pit of Darkness 62. The Legend of Young Dick Turpin 64. The Intelligence Men 65. The Satanic Rites of Dracula 73. Splitting Heirs 93, etc.

Frankovich, Mike (1910–1992).
American producer, a former sports commentator and screenwriter. During the 50s he ran Columbia's British organization, and in the 60s became their head of world production, then turned independent again. He was the adopted son of Joe E. Brown and married to Binnie Barnes.
Fugitive Lady 51. Decameron Nights 53. Footsteps in the Fog 55. Joe Macbeth 56. Marooned 69. Bob and Carol and Ted and Alice 69. Cactus Flower 69. Butterflies are Free 72. Forty Carats 73. The Shootist 76, etc.

Franz, Arthur (1920–).
American leading man, latterly character actor; radio, stage and TV experience.
Jungle Patrol (debut) 48. Sands of Iwo Jima 49. Abbott and Costello Meet the Invisible Man 51. The Sniper 52. Eight Iron Men 52. The Caine Mutiny 54. The Unholy Wife 57. Running Target 58. Hellcats of the Navy 59. Alvarez Kelly 66. Anzio 68. Sisters of Death 77. That Championship Season 82, etc.

Franz, Dennis (1944–) (D. Schlachta).
American character actor, best known for his TV roles as a tough cop, from the stage.
The Fury 78. Remember My Name 78. Dressed to Kill 80. Blow Out 81. Psycho 2 83. Body Double 84. Kiss Shot 89. The Package 89. Die Hard 2 90. The Player 92. American Buffalo 96. City of Angels 98, etc.
TV series: Chicago Story 82. Bay City Blues 83. Hill Street Blues 85–87. NYPD Blue 93–95.

Franz, Eduard (1902–1983).
American character actor, often seen as foreign dignitary, Jewish elder, or psychiatrist.
The Iron Curtain 48. Francis 50. The Thing 51. The Jazz Singer 52. Dream Wife 53. Broken Lance 54. The Ten Commandments 56. Man Afraid 57. A Certain Smile 58. The Story of Ruth 60. Hatari 62. The President's Analyst 67, many others.
TV series: The Breaking Point 63. Zorro 78.

Fraser, Bill (1908–1987).
Burly Scottish comic character actor, with wide experience on stage and in revue, who found fame on television as the preening Sergeant Snudge in *The Army Game* and *Bootsie and Snudge*. He was in films from 1938, usually in small roles until the 50s. Born in Perth, he first worked as a bank clerk, and was on stage from the early 30s. Married actress Pamela Cundell.
Meet Me Tonight 52. The Americanization of Emily 65. Joey Boy 65. Masquerade 65. I've Gotta Horse 65. Up the Chastity Belt 71. That's Your Funeral 72, etc.
TV series: *The Army Game* (as Sgt Snudge) 57–59. Bootsie and Snudge 60–64, 74. Barney Is My Darling 65. Vacant Lot 67. That's Your Funeral 71. The Train Now Standing 72. Doctor's Daughters 80. The Secret Diary of Adrian Mole Aged 13¾ 85. The Growing Pains of Adrian Mole 87.
❝ What I do is play stuffy, pot-bellied, pompous old sods. Thank God England is full of them. – *B.F.*

Fraser, Brendan (1967–).
American leading actor. The son of Canadian parents, he studied theatre at the Cornish College of the Arts in Seattle.
Dogfight 91. Encino Man/California Man 92. School Ties 92. Twenty Bucks 93. With Honors 94. Airheads 94. The Scout 94. The Passion of Darkly Noon 95. Now and Then 95. Mrs Winterbourne 96. The Twilight of the Golds 97. George of the Jungle 97. Gods & Monsters 98. Blast from the Past 98, etc.

Fraser, John (1931–).
British leading man with stage experience, sporadically in films.
The Good Beginning 53. Touch and Go 55. The Good Companions 57. Tunes of Glory 59. *The Trials of Oscar Wilde* (as Lord Alfred Douglas) 60. El Cid 61. Fury at Smugglers' Bay 61. The Waltz of the Toreadors 62. Repulsion 65. Operation Crossbow 65. Isadora 68. Schizo 77, etc.

Fraser, Liz (1933–).
British character actress, specializing in dumb cockney blondes.
Wonderful Things 58. I'm All Right, Jack 59. Two-Way Stretch 60. The Rebel 61. Double Bunk 61. Carry On Regardless 61. The Painted Smile (leading role) 61. Raising the Wind 62. Live Now Pay Later 63. The Americanization of Emily 64. The Family Way 66. Up the Junction 68. Dad's Army 70. Confessions of a Driving Instructor 76. Confessions from a Holiday Camp 77. Chicago Joe and the Showgirl 88, etc.

Fraser, Moyra (1923–).
Australian comedienne in British stage and TV.
Here We Go Round the Mulberry Bush 67. Prudence and the Pill 68. The Boy Friend 71, etc.

Fraser, Richard (1913–1971).
Scottish-born leading man of some American second features in the 40s.
How Green Was My Valley 41. The Picture of Dorian Gray 44. Fatal Witness 46. The Cobra Strikes 48. Alaska Patrol 51, etc.

Fraser, Ronald (1930–1997).
Stocky British character actor, in films and TV since 1954. Born in Ashton-under-Lyme, Lancashire, he studied at RADA and began on stage with Sir Donald Wolfit.
The Sundowners 59. The Pot Carriers 62. The Punch and Judy Man 63. Crooks in Cloisters 64. The Beauty Jungle 64. The Flight of the Phoenix 65. The Whisperers 67. The Killing of Sister George 68. Sinful Davey 69. Too Late the Hero 69. The Rise and Rise of Michael Rimmer 70. The Magnificent Seven Deadly Sins 71. Rentadick 72. Ooh You Are Awful 72. Swallows and Amazons 74. Paper Tiger 75. The Wild Geese 78. Trail of the Pink Panther 82. Absolute Beginners 86. Let Him Have It 91. The Mystery of Edwin Drood 93. P. G. Wodehouse's Heavy Weather (TV) 95, etc.
TV series: The Misfit 70–71. Spooner's Patch 79.

Frawley, James (1937–).
American director.
The Christian Licorice Store 70. Kid Blue 73. Delancey Street (TV) 75. The Eddie Capra Mysteries (pilot) (TV) 76. The Big Bus 76. The Muppet Movie 79. The Great American Traffic Jam (TV) 80. Fraternity Vacation 85. Assault and Matrimony (TV) 87. Spies, Lies and Naked Thighs 91. Sins of the Mind (TV) 97, etc.

Frawley, William (1887–1966).
Stocky, cigar-chewing American comedy character actor from vaudeville, in innumerable films as taxi driver, comic gangster, private detective or incompetent cop.
Moonlight and Pretzels 33. Crime Doctor 34. Alibi Ike 35. Desire 36. High Wide and Handsome 37. Professor Beware 38. Persons in Hiding 39. One Night in the Tropics 40. Footsteps in the Dark 42. *Roxie Hart* 42. Whistling in Brooklyn 43. Going My Way 44. Lady on a Train 45. The Crime Doctor's Manhunt 46. Miracle on 34th Street 47. The Babe Ruth Story 48. East Side West Side 49.

Kill the Umpire 50. The Lemon Drop Kid 51. Rancho Notorious 52. Safe at Home 62, etc.
TV series: *I Love Lucy* 51–60. My Three Sons 60–63.

Frayn, Michael (1933–).
British dramatist, novelist and occasional screenwriter, a former journalist.
Clockwise 86. Noises Off (oa) 92.

Frazee, Jane (1918–1985) (Mary Jane Frehse).
Vivacious American singer and leading lady of minor musicals in the 40s.
Buck Privates 41. Moonlight in Havana 42. When Johnny Comes Marching Home 42. Practically Yours 44. Swing and Sway 44. Kansas City Kitty 45. Incident 48. Rhythm Inn (last appearance) 51, etc.
TV series: Beulah 52.

Frears, Stephen (1931–).
British director. Born in Leicester, he studied law at Cambridge University, worked at the Royal Court Theatre as assistant to Lindsay ANDERSON, and then joined the BBC, directing documentaries and drama before making his first feature in 1971.
Gumshoe 71. Saigon–Year of the Cat (TV) 83. The Hit 84. *My Beautiful Laundrette* 85. Prick Up Your Ears 87. Sammy and Rosie Get Laid 87. Dangerous Liaisons 88. *The Grifters* (AAN) 90. Hero (GB Accidental Hero) 92. *The Snapper* (TV) 93. Mary Reilly 96. The Van 96. The Hi-Lo Country 98, etc.
❝ Being English drives you barmy. – *S.F.*
What happened to self-doubt? That was the basis of my generation – doubt mixed with confidence. – *S.F.*

Frechette, Mark (1947–1975).
American leading man of *Zabriskie Point*; subsequently died in prison.

Freda, Riccardo (1909–) (aka Robert Hampton, George Lincoln, Willy Pareto).
Egyptian-Italian director who brings some style to exploitation pictures; former art critic.
Les Misérables 46. Theodora, Slave Express 54. I Vampiri 57. The Giant of Thessaly 61. The Terror of Dr Hitchcock 62. The Spectre 63. Le Due Orfanelle 66. Coplan FX18/Coplan, Secret Agent FX18 66. La Morte non Conta i Dollari 67. A Doppia Faccia 69. L'Iguana della Lingua di Fuoco 70. L'Ossessione che Uccide/Murder Obsession 80, etc.

Frederick, Lynne (1953–1994).
British leading lady, widow of Peter Sellers. She was briefly married to David Frost.
No Blade of Grass 70. Vampire Circus 71. Henry VIII and His Six Wives 72. Schizo 76. Voyage of the Damned 76. The Prisoner of Zenda 79, etc.

Frederick, Pauline (1885–1938) (Pauline Libbey).
American leading lady of silent days.
Bella Donna 15. The Slave Island 16. Sleeping Fires 17. Her Final Reckoning 18. The Peace of Roaring River 19. *Madame X* 20. La Tosca 21. Married Flirts 24. Her Honour the Governor 26. Mumsie (GB) 27. On Trial 28. The Sacred Flame 29. This Modern Age 31. The Phantom of Crestwood 32. My Marriage 36. Thank You Mr Moto 38, etc.

Fredericks, Ellsworth.
American cinematographer.
Invasion of the Body Snatchers 56. The Friendly Persuasion 56. Sayonara 57. High Time 60. Seven Days in May 64. Pistolero 66. The Power 67. Mister Buddwing 67, etc.

Freed, Alan (1922–1965).
American disc-jockey, the self-styled 'King of Rock 'n' Roll', which is a term he claimed to have coined. A tireless promoter of the music, he appeared as himself in several 50s films. His career was ruined at the end of that decade following accusations that he had accepted bribes to play records. Two movies have been made about his life: *Mister Rock and Roll*, in which he starred, and *American Hot Wax* 78, in which he was played by Tim McIntire.
■ Rock around the Clock 56. Don't Knock the Rock 56. Mister Rock and Roll 57. Rock Rock Rock 57. Go Johnny Go (& p) 58.

Freed, Arthur (1894–1973) (Arthur Grossman).
American producer, mainly of musicals for MGM, many of them featuring his own lyrics. He collaborated with Nacio Herb Brown on many songs, including 'All I Do Is Dream of You', 'I've Got a Feelin' You're Foolin'', 'Make 'Em Laugh', 'Pagan Love Song', 'Singin' in the Rain', 'You Are My Lucky Star' and 'You Were Meant for Me'.
Book: 1984, *The Movies' Greatest Musicals Produced in Hollywood USA by the Freed Unit* by Hugh Fordin.
Hold Your Man (ly only) 33. Hollywood Party (ly only) 34. Broadway Melody of 1936 (ly only). Broadway Melody of 1938 (ly only). *Babes In Arms* (& ly) 39. Strike Up the Band 40. Lady Be Good (& ly) 41. Cabin in the Sky 43. Meet Me in St Louis 44. Ziegfeld Follies 46. The Pirate 48. *On the Town* 49. Annie Get Your Gun 50. Showboat 51. *An American in Paris* 51. *Singin' in The Rain* (& ly) 52. *Band Wagon* 53. Kismet 55. Invitation to the Dance 56. *Gigi* 58. Bells are Ringing 60. The Light in the Piazza 62, many others.
❝ Frequently he would begin a sentence on, let us say, Wednesday and complete it on Friday. Yet this same man could look at me and say: 'Stop trying to be different. You don't have to be different to be good. To be good is different enough.' – *Alan Jay Lerner*

Freed, Bert (1919–1994).
Burly American character actor.
The Company She Keeps 50. Detective Story 51. Paths of Glory 57. The Goddess 58. The Gazebo 60. Invitation to a Gunfighter 64. Nevada Smith 65. Madigan 67. Hang 'Em High 68. Wild in the Streets 68. There Was a Crooked Man 70. Billy Jack 71. Norma Rae 79, etc.

Freed, Ralph (1907–1973).
American lyricist, the brother of Arthur FREED. His collaborators included Burton LANE, Sammy FAIN and Jimmy McHUGH.
She Married a Cop 39. Babes on Broadway (AANs, 'How About You') 41. Two Girls and a Sailor 44. No Leave, No Love 45. Holiday in Mexico 46. This Time for Keeps 47, etc.

Freedman, Jerrold (1919–).
American director.
Kansas City Bomber 72. Borderline 80. Native Son 86. The Comeback (TV) 89, etc.

Freeland, Thornton (1898–1987).
American director, former cameraman.
Three Live Ghosts 29. Whoopee 30. *Flying Down to Rio* 33. Brewster's Millions (GB) 35. The Amateur Gentleman (GB) 36. Jericho (GB) 37. The Gang's All Here (GB) 39. Over the Moon (GB) 39. Too Many Blondes 41. Meet Me at Dawn 47. The Brass Monkey/Lucky Mascot (GB) 48. Dear Mr Prohack (GB) 49, etc.

Freeman, Al, Jnr (1934–).
American leading man, a regular on the daytime soap opera *One Life to Live*.
Black Like Me 64. Dutchman 67. The Detective 68. Finian's Rainbow 68. Castle Keep 69. The Lost Man 70. A Fable (& d) 71. Seven Hours to Judgment 88. The Defense Never Rests (TV) 90. Malcolm X 92. Once Upon a Time . . . When We Were Colored 96. Down in the Delta 98, etc.
TV series: Hot L Baltimore 75. Roots 79.

Freeman, Everett (1911–1991).
American writer, usually in collaboration.
Larceny Inc. 42. Thank Your Lucky Stars 43. The Secret Life of Walter Mitty 47. Million Dollar Mermaid 52. My Man Godfrey 57. The Glass Bottom Boat 66. Where Were You When the Lights Went Out? (& co-p) 68. Zigzag 70, many others.

Freeman, Howard (1899–1967).
American character actor, usually in comic roles as businessman on the make.
Pilot Number Five 43. Once Upon a Time 44. Take One False Step 49. Scaramouche 52. Remains To Be Seen 53. Dear Brigitte 65, many others.

Freeman, Joan (1941–).
American general-purpose actress.
The Remarkable Mr Pennypacker 58. Come September 61. The Rounders 65. The Fastest Guitar Alive 66. The Reluctant Astronaut 67, etc.

Freeman, Kathleen (1919–).
American character actress.
Naked City 47. Lonely Heart Bandits 52. Bonzo Goes To College 52. Full House 52. Athena 54. The Fly 58. The Ladies' Man 61. The Disorderly Orderly 65. Three on a Couch 66. Support Your Local Gunfighter 71. Stand Up and Be Counted 72. The Blues Brothers 80. Innerspace 87. Gremlins 2: The New Batch 90. Dutch 91. FernGully: The Last Rainforest (voice) 92. Reckless Kelly 93. Hocus Pocus 93. Naked Gun 33 : The Final Insult 94. At First Sight 95. Carpool 96. Hercules (voice) 97. Blues Brothers 2000 98, etc.
TV series: Topper 53. Mayor of the Town 54–55. It's about Time 66–67. The Beverly Hillbillies 69–71. Funny Face 71. Lotsa Luck 73–74.

Freeman, Leonard (1921–1974).
American TV producer best known for *Hawaii Five-O*.

Freeman, Mona (1926–) (Monica Freeman).
American leading lady, at her peak as a troublesome teenager in the 40s.
■ National Velvet 44. Our Hearts Were Young and Gay 44. Till We Meet Again 44. Here Come the Waves 44. Together Again 44. Roughly Speaking 45. Junior Miss 45. Danger Signal 45. Black Beauty 46. That Brennan Girl 46. Our Hearts Were Growing Up 46. Variety Girl 47. *Dear Ruth* 47. Mother Wore Tights 47. Isn't It Romantic? 48. Streets of Laredo 49. The Heiress 49. Dear Wife 49. Branded 50. Copper Canyon 50. I Was a Shoplifter 50. Dear Brat 51. Darling How Could You? 51. The Lady from Texas 51. Flesh and Fury 52. Jumping Jacks 52. Angel Face 52. Thunderbirds 52. Battle Cry 55. The Road to Denver 55. The Way Out (GB) 56. Before I Wake (GB) 56. Hold Back the Night 56. Huk 56. Dragoon Wells Massacre 57. The World Was His Jury 58.

Freeman, Morgan (1937–).
American star character actor. Born in Memphis, Tennessee, he spent five years in the air force before studying acting in Los Angeles; he was on stage from 1968.
Brubaker 80. Eyewitness 80. Harry and Son 84. Teachers 84. That Was Then . . . This Is Now 85. Street Smart (AAN) 87. Clean and Sober 88. Driving Miss Daisy (AAN) 89. Glory 89. Johnny Handsome 89. Lean on Me 89. Bonfire of the Vanities 90. Robin Hood: Prince of Thieves 91. The Power of One 92. Unforgiven 92. The Positively True Adventures of the Alleged Texas Cheerleader-Murdering Mom (TV) 93. Bopha! (d) 93. The Shawshank Redemption (AAN) 94. Outbreak 95. The American President 95. *Seven* 95. Chain Reaction 96. Moll Flanders 96. Kiss the Girls 97. Hard Rain 97. Amistad 97. Deep Impact 98. Desert Blue (wd) 98, etc.

Freeman, Paul (1943–).
British character actor, often as a villain.
The Long Good Friday 80. The Dogs of War 81. Raiders of the Lost Ark 81. The Sender 82. An Unsuitable Job for a Woman 82. Shanghai Surprise 86. A World Apart 88. Prisoner of Rio 89. Aces: Iron Eagle III 92. Pretty Princess (It.) 93. Mighty Morphin Power Rangers: The Movie 95. Samson and Delilah (TV) 96. Call Girl/Squillo 96, etc.

Freeman, Robert (c. 1935–).
British director, former fashion director and title artist (*A Hard Day's Night*, *Help*).
The Touchables 68. World of Fashion (short) 68. L'Echelle Blanche 69. The Erotic Adventures of Zorro 72. Alexandra – Queen of Sex 83, etc.

Fregonese, Hugo (1908–1987).
Argentine-born director, former journalist, in Hollywood from 1945.
One-Way Street 50. Saddle Tramp 51. Apache Drums 51. Mark of the Renegade 52. My Six Convicts 52. The Raid 53. Decameron Nights 53. Blowing Wild 54. The Man in the Attic 54. Black Tuesday 54. Seven Thunders (GB) 57. Harry Black and the Tiger 58. Marco Polo 61. Apaches Last Battle/Old Shatterhand (Ger.) 64. Savage Pampas (Sp.) 66, etc.

Fréhel (1891–1951) (Marguérite Boulc'h).
French music-hall star who appeared in occasional films, usually playing a singer who has seen better days. Self-destructive and noted for her abandoned behaviour, she began performing in cafés at the age of five and was top of the bill in her teens, but died in alcoholic poverty. She was Maurice Chevalier's lover at the start of his career.
Coeur de Lilas 31. La Rue sans Nom 34. *Pépé le Moko* (as Tania) 37. La Rue sans Joie 38. L'Enfer des Anges 39. L'Homme Traque 46. Maya 49, etc.
❝ By the time she was forty, Fréhel had become so coarse and overweight, with hideous gaps in her blackened teeth, that it was difficult to imagine her earlier radiance. Her septum was so damaged by cocaine that she could do a frightening parlor trick, inserting a silk scarf up one nostril and exhaling it down the other. – *Edward Behr, Thank Heaven for Little Girls*

Freleng, Friz (1906–1995) (Isidore Freleng).
American director of cartoons whose creations include Speedy Gonzales, Yosemite Sam, and the Pink Panther. Born in Kansas City, he began working in animated films in 1924 and was among the first animators to work for Walt Disney, although the association was a brief one. In the 30s he became head animator and later a director at Warner, where he remained until the early 60s, apart from two unhappy years at MGM in the late 30s. With David De Patie, he set up his own cartoon production company, De Patie-Freleng Enterprises, before returning to Warner in 1980.
Wicked West 29. Bosko in Person 33. Bing Crosbyana 36. Sweet Sioux 37. A Star Is Hatched 38. Poultry Pirates 38. You Ought to Be in Pictures 40. Hiawatha's Rabbit Hunt (AAN) 41. Rhapsody in Rivets (AAN) 41. Pigs in a Polka (AAN) 42. Greetings Bait (AAN) 43. Life with Feathers (AAN) 45. Hare Trigger 45. Tweetie Pie (AA) 47. Sandy Claws (AAN) 54. Speedy Gonzales (AA) 55. Birds Anonymous (AA) 57. Show Biz Bugs 57. Knighty Knight Bugs (AA) 58. Mexicali Shmoes (AAN) 59. Mouse and Garden (AAN) 60. Pied Piper of Guadelupe (AANp) 61. The Pink Phink (AA) 64. The Pink Blueprint (AANp) 66. Friz Freleng's Looney Looney Bugs Bunny Movie (compilation) 81. Bugs Bunny's 3rd Movie: 1001 Rabbit Tales (compilation) 82. Daffy Duck's Movie: Fantastic Island (compilation) 83. Porky Pig in Hollywood (compilation, co-d) 86, many others.

French, Harold (1897–1997).
British stage actor and producer, in films since 1931.
Biographies: 1970, *I Swore I Never Would*. 1972, *I Thought I Never Could*.
AS DIRECTOR: The House of the Arrow 39. Jeannie 41. Unpublished Story 42. The Day Will Dawn 42. Secret Mission 42. *Dear Octopus* 43. English Without Tears 44. Mr Emmanuel 44. Quiet Weekend 46. My Brother Jonathan 47. The Blind Goddess 48. Quartet (part) 48. The Dancing Years 49. Trio (part) 50. Encore (part) 51. The Hour of 13 52. Isn't Life Wonderful 53. Rob Roy 53. Forbidden Cargo 54. The Man Who Loved Redheads 55, etc.

French, Leslie (1899–).
Diminutive British character player.
This England 41. *Orders to Kill* 58. The Leopard 63. More than a Miracle 67. Death in Venice 70. The Singing Detective (TV) 86. The Living Daylights 87, etc.

French, Valerie (1931–1990).
British actress, in occasional Hollywood films. Married screenwriter Michael Pertwee.
Jubal 56. Garment Center 57. Decision at Sundown 57. The Four Skulls of Jonathan Drake 59. Shalako 68, etc.

Frend, Charles (1909–1977).
British director.
AS EDITOR: Waltzes from Vienna 33. Secret Agent 36. Sabotage 37. Young and Innocent 37. The Citadel 38. Goodbye Mr Chips 39. Major Barbara 40, etc.
■ AS DIRECTOR: The Big Blockade 42. The Foreman Went to France 42. *San Demetrio London* (& w) 43. Johnny Frenchman 45. Return of the Vikings 45. The Loves of Joanna Godden 47. Scott of the Antarctic 48. A Run for Your Money 49. The Magnet 49. *The Cruel Sea* 53. Lease of Life 54. The Long Arm 56. Barnacle Bill 58. Cone of Silence 60. Girl on Approval 62. Torpedo Bay 62. The Shy Bike 67.

Fresnay, Pierre (1897–1975) (Pierre Laudenbach).
Distinguished French stage actor who made many films.
Marius (debut) 31. Fanny 32. César 34. The Man Who Knew Too Much (GB) 34. *La Grande Illusion* 37. Le Corbeau 43. *Monsieur Vincent* 47. *God Needs Men* 50. The Fanatics 57, many others.

Freud, Sigmund (1856–1939).
Viennese physician who became the virtual inventor of psychoanalysis and the discoverer of sexual inhibition as a mainspring of human behaviour; a gentleman, therefore, to whom Hollywood has every reason to be grateful. A biopic *Freud* 62 was directed by John Huston starring Montgomery Clift.

Freund, Karl (1890–1969).
Czech-born cinematographer, famous for his work in German silents like The Last Laugh 24. Metropolis 26. Variety 26. Berlin 27, etc.
SINCE IN USA: *The Mummy* (& d) 33. Moonlight and Pretzels (d only) 33. Madame Spy (d only) 33. Mad Love (d only) 35. Camille 36. *The Good Earth* (AA) 37. Marie Walewska 38. Pride and Prejudice 40. The Seventh Cross 44. Key Largo 48. Bright Leaf 50, many others.

Frewer, Matt (1958–).
American actor, best known for his role as Max Headroom on television.
Max Headroom (TV) 84. Supergirl 84. Speed Zone 88. Far from Home 89. Honey, I Shrunk the Kids 89. Short Time 90. The Taking of Beverly Hills 91. National Lampoon's Senior Trip 95. Lawnmower Man 2: Beyond Cyberspace 96. Kissinger and Nixon (TV) 97. Breast Men 98, etc.
TV series: Max Headroom 87.

Frey, Leonard (1938–1988).
American character actor. He died of AIDS.
The Magic Christian 70. Tell Me That You Love Me Junie Moon 70. *The Boys in the Band* 70. Fiddler on the Roof (AAN) 71. Shirts/Skins (TV) 73. Where the Buffalo Roam 80.
TV series: Best of the West 81.

Frey, Sami (1937–) (Samuel Frei).
French leading actor, in films from a teenager.
Cleo from 5 to 7 61. The Outsiders/Band of Outsiders/Bande à Part 64. César and Rosalie 72. Sweet Movie 75. Nea 78. The Little Drummer Girl 84. Blood and Sand/Sand and Blood/De Sable et de Sang 87. La Fille de D'Artagnan 94. Conjugal Duty 95, etc.

Fricker, Brenda (1944–).
Irish character actress.
My Left Foot (AA) 89. The Field 90. Utz (TV) 91. Home Alone 2: Lost in New York 92. So I Married an Axe Murderer 93. Seekers (TV) 93. Angels in the Outfield 94. Deadly Advice 94. A Man of No Importance 94. A Time to Kill 96. Moll Flanders 96. Swann 96, etc.
TV series: Casualty 86–90.

Friderici, Blanche (1870/78–1933).
American character actress of stark, dour presence.
Trespassing 22. Sadie Thompson 28. Jazz Heaven 29. Billy the Kid 30. Kismet 30. Night Nurse 31. Murder by the Clock 31. Mata Hari 31. Love Me Tonight 32. A Farewell to Arms 32. If I Had a Million 32. Flying down to Rio 33. It Happened One Night 34, many others.

Fridriksson, Fridrick Thor (1954–).
Icelandic director and screenwriter, a former critic who founded and edited the country's first film magazine. He began as a documentary film-maker.
White Whales/Skytturnar 87. Sky without Limit/Flugthrá 89. Children of Nature (AAN) 91. Movie Days/Bíódagar 94. Cold Fever 95. Angel of the Universe 99, etc.

Fried, Gerald (1928–).
American composer, mainly for TV.
Killer's Kiss 55. Terror in a Texas Town 58. A Cold Wind in August 60. The Cabinet of Caligari 62. One Potato Two Potato 64. The Killing of Sister George 68. Too Late the Hero 69. The Grissom Gang 71. Soylent Green 73. Roots (TV) 76. Testimony of Two Men (TV) 77. Foul Play 78. Little Darlings 80. Nine to Five 80, many others.

Friedhofer, Hugo (1902–1981).
American composer.
The Adventures of Marco Polo 38. China Girl 42. The Lodger 44. The Woman in the Window 45. *The Best Years of Our Lives* (AA) 46. The Bishop's Wife 47. Joan of Arc 48. Broken Arrow 50. Ace in the Hole 51. Above and Beyond 52. Vera Cruz 54. The Rains of Ranchipur 55. The Harder They Fall 56. One-Eyed Jacks 59. The Secret Invasion 64. The Red Baron 71. Die Sister Die 78, etc.

Friedkin, William (1939–).
American director and screenwriter, from TV. Formerly married to actresses Jeanne Moreau and Lesley-Anne Down, subsequently to production executive Sherry Lansing.
Biography: 1990, *Hurricane Billy* by Nat Segaloff.
Good Times 67. The Birthday Party 68. The Night They Raided Minsky's 68. The Boys in the Band 70. *The French Connection* (AA) 71. *The Exorcist* (AAN) 73. Sorcerer 77. The Brinks Job 79. Cruising 80. Deal of the Century 84. To Live and Die in L.A. 85. Rampage 87. The Guardian 90. Blue Chips 94. Jade 95, etc.
❝ By the time a film of mine makes it into the theatres, I have a love-hate relationship with it. There is always something I could have done to make it better. – *W.F.*

Friedman, Seymour (1917–).
American second feature director.
Trapped by Boston Blackie 48. Prison Warden 49. Customs Agent 50. Criminal Lawyer 51. Son of Dr Jekyll 51. Escape Route (co-d) (GB) 53. Secret of Treasure Mountain 56, etc.

Friedman, Stephen (1937–1996).
American producer.
Loving Molly (& w) 73. Little Darlings 80. Hero at Large 80. Eye of the Needle 81. All of Me 84. Creator 85. Enemy Mine 85. The Big Easy 87. Miss Firecracker 89. There Goes the Neighborhood 92. Mother 96, etc.

Friel, Anna (1976–).
English actress, from television. Born in Rochdale, Lancashire, she began as a 13-year-old and was best known in the role of Beth Jordache on the TV soap opera *Brookside*.
GBH (TV) 91. Our Mutual Friend (TV) 98. The Tribe (TV) 98. The Land Girls 98. The Stringer 98. Rogue Trader 99, etc.
TV series: Brookside 93–95.

Friel, Brian (1929–).
Irish playwright. Born in Omagh, County Tyrone, he studied at St Patrick's College, Maynooth, and St Joseph's Training College, Belfast; he was a teacher for 10 years before becoming a writer in 1960.
Philadelphia, Here I Come (w, oa) 75. Dancing at Lughnasa (oa) 98.

Friels, Colin (1954–).
Scottish-born leading man, in Australia. He is married to actress Judy Davis.
Hoodwink 81. Monkey Grip 82. Buddies 83. Malcolm 86. Kangaroo 86. High Tide 87. Ground Zero 87. Warm Nights on a Slow Moving Train 87. Grievous Bodily Harm 88. Darkman 90. Dingo 90. Weekend with Kate 90. Class Action 91. The Nostradamus Kid 93. Stark (TV) 93. A Good Man in Africa 94. Angel Baby 95. Back of Beyond 95. Cosi 96. Mr Reliable: A True Story 96. Dark City 97, etc.

Friend, Philip (1915–1987).
British leading man with stage experience.
Pimpernel Smith 41. Next of Kin 42. The Flemish Farm 43. Great Day 45. My Own True Love (US) 48. Panthers' Moon (US) 50. The Highwayman (US) 51. Background 53. Son of Robin Hood 59. Strangehold 62, etc.

Friese-Greene, William (1855–1921).
Pioneer British inventor who built the first practical movie camera in 1889. Died penniless; his life was the subject of *The Magic Box* 51.
Biography: 1948, *Friese-Greene, Close-Up of an Inventor* by Ray Allister.

Friml, Rudolf (1879–1972).
Czech-American composer of operettas which were frequently filmed: *The Firefly, Rose Marie, The Vagabond King*, etc.

Frings, Ketti (1909–1981) (Catherine Frings).
American scenarist.
Hold Back the Dawn (& oa) 41. Guest in the House 44. The Accused 48. Dark City 50. Because of You 52. Come Back Little Sheba 53. Foxfire 55, etc.

Frinton, Freddie (1911–1968).
English comedian of stage, TV and films, best known for playing opposite Thora Hird in the 60s TV series *Meet the Wife*.
Trouble in the Air 48. Force's Sweetheart 53. Stars in Your Eyes 56. Make Mine Mink 60. What a Whopper 61!, etc.

Fritsch, Willy (1901–1973).
Popular German leading man, in films since 1921.
The Spy 28. Congress Dances 31. Drei Von Der Tankstelle 31 (and 55). Amphitryon 35. Film Ohne Titel 47, many others.

Frobe, Gert (1913–1988).
German character actor first seen abroad as the downtrodden little man of *Berliner Ballade* 48; later put on weight and emerged in the 60s as an international semi-star, usually as villain.
Ewiger Walzer 54. Double Destin 54. The Heroes Are Tired 55. He Who Must Die 56. The Girl Rosemarie 58. Menschen im Hotel 59. The Thousand Eyes of Dr Mabuse 60. The Longest Day 62. Die Dreigroschenoper 63. The Testament of Dr Mabuse 64. *Goldfinger* 64. Those Magnificent Men in Their Flying Machines 65. Is Paris Burning? 66. Du Rififi à Paname 67. I Killed Rasputin 67. Rocket to the Moon 67. Monte Carlo or Bust 69. Dollars 71. Ludwig 72. And Then There Were None 75. The Serpent's Egg 77. Bloodline 79. Le Coup de Parapluie 80, etc.

Froeschel, George (1891–1979).
Viennese-American scriptwriter, long in Hollywood; often one of a team.
Waterloo Bridge 40. The Mortal Storm 40. Mrs Miniver (co-w, AA) 42. Random Harvest (AAN) 42. The White Cliffs of Dover 44. Command Decision 48. The Miniver Story 50. Scaramouche 52. Never Let Me Go 53. Betrayed 54. Quentin Durward 55. Me and the Colonel 58, many others.

Frohlich, Gustav (1902–1987).
German actor (from *Metropolis* 26) and director (*The Sinner* 51, etc.). Few of his films have been exported.
Asphalt 29. Stadt Anatol 36. Der Grosse König 41, etc.

Froman, Jane (1907–1980).
American band-singer, whose heroic resumption of her career following an air crash was portrayed in *With a Song in My Heart*, in which she was played by Susan Hayward.
Stars over Broadway 35. Radio City Revels 38.

Frome, Milton (1911–1989).
American comedy character actor, often in bad-tempered bits.
You're Never Too Young 55. Short Cut to Hell 59. I'd Rather Be Rich 64. The St Valentine's Day Massacre 67. The Strongest Man in the World 75, etc.

Frontière, Dominic (1931–).
American composer.
The Marriage Go Round 60. Hero's Island 62. The Outer Limits (TV) 63. Billie 65. The Invaders (TV) 67. Hang 'Em High 68. Popi 69. Chisum 70. Cancel My Reservation 72. Hammersmith is Out 72. Freebie and the Bean 74. Brannigan 75. The Gumball Rally 76. Washington Behind Closed Doors (TV) 77. The Stunt Man 80. Modern Problems 81. Roar 81. The Aviator 87. Color of Night 94, etc.

Frost, Sir David (1939–).
Britain's Mr Television of the 60s, later exported to America; mixes entertainment shows with hard-hitting political interviews, and financed a number of rather indifferent movies.
The Rise and Rise of Michael Rimmer 70. The Slipper and the Rose 76.
❝ He has risen without trace. – *Kitty Muggeridge*
Hello, good evening, and welcome. – *catchphrase*

Frost, Sadie.
English actress. Formerly married to actor-songwriter Gary KEMP, she married actor Jude LAW in 1997.
Diamond Skulls 91. Bram Stoker's Dracula 92. Splitting Heirs 93. The Cisco Kid (TV) 94. Shopping 94. Magic Hunter/Buvos Vadas 94. A Pyromaniac's Love Story 95. Crimetime 96. Final Cut 97. Captain Jack 98, etc.

Fruet, William (1933–).
Canadian director.
Death Weekend 76. Search and Destroy 79. Funeral Home 81. Baker County U.S.A. 82. Spasms 83. Bedroom Eyes 84. Killer Party 86. Blue Monkey 87, etc.

Fry, Stephen (1957–).
English actor, writer, comedian and novelist. Born in Hampstead, London, he was educated at Cambridge University and began working in TV in 1980 and films from 1985. He often collaborates with Hugh LAURIE, a partnership that began with the Cambridge Footlights revue of 1981. He also scripted the revival of the long-running stage musical *Me and My Girl*. He walked out of a starring role in a West End play and disappeared for a time in 1995.
Autobiography: 1997, *Moab Is My Washpot*.
The Good Father 85. A Fish Called Wanda 88. The Secret Policeman's Other Ball 88. A Handful of Dust 88. The Common Pursuit (TV) 92. Peter's Friends 92. I.Q. 94. Wilde (as Oscar Wilde) 97. Spice World: The Movie 97. The Tichborne Claimant 98, etc.
TV series: Blackadder 84–91. This Is David Lander 88. A Bit of Fry and Laurie 89–92. Jeeves and Wooster 90–93. Stalag Luft 93.
❝ I cannot deny that, as a flushed adolescent in a dusty library, much of the thrill I got from reading of the world of the aesthete came from the notion of a place where one could swan about in costly raiment with houseboys and ephebes in tow – and not a rugby player in sight. – *S.F.*

Frye, Dwight (1899–1943).
American character actor who made a corner in crazed hunchbacks.
■ The Night Bird 27. Doorway to Hell 30. Man to Man 31. The Maltese Falcon 31. *Dracula* 31. The Black Camel 31. *Frankenstein* 31. By Whose Hand 32. Attorney for the Defense 32. The Invisible Man 33. Strange Adventure 33. Western Code 33. The Vampire Bat 33. The Circus Queen Murder 33. King Solomon of Broadway 33. The Crime of Dr Crespi 33. The Great Impersonation 35. Atlantic Adventure 35. Bride of Frankenstein 35. Florida Special 36. Alibi for Murder 36. The Man who Found Himself 36. Something to Sing About 36. Beware of Ladies 37. The Shadow 37. Great Guy 37. Sea Devils 37. Renfrew of the Royal Mounted 37. Invisible Enemy 38. Fast Company 38. Adventure in Sahara 38. Who Killed Gail Preston 38. Sinners in Paradise 38. Conspiracy 39. Son of Frankenstein 39. The Man in the Iron Mask 39. I Take This Woman 39. Gangs of Chicago 40. Phantom Raiders 40. Drums of Fu Manchu 40. Sky Bandits 40. Mystery Ship 41. Son of Monte Cristo 41. The People vs Dr Kildare 41. Blonde from Singapore 41. The Devil Pays Off 41. Prisoner of Japan 42. The Ghost of Frankenstein 42. Sleepytime Gal 42. Danger in the Pacific 42. Frankenstein meets the Wolf Man 43. Dead Men Walk 43. Submarine Alert 43. Hangmen Also Die 43. Dangerous Blondes 43.

Fryer, Robert (1920–).
American producer, former casting director.
The Boston Strangler 68. The Prime of Miss Jean Brodie 69. Myra Breckinridge 69. The Salzburg Connection 71. Travels with My Aunt 73. The Abdication 73. Voyage of the Damned 76.

Fu Sheng, Alexander (1954–1983).
Hong Kong star of kung fu movies. Killed in a road accident.
Men from the Monastery 73. Temple of the Dragon 73. Disciples of Shaolin 75. Marco Polo 75. Shaolin Avengers 76. Chinatown Kid 77. Cold Blooded Avenging Angel 78. Heroes of Kwan Tung 80. Heroes Shed No Tears 81, etc.

Fuchs, Daniel (1909–1993).
American screenwriter and novelist, a former teacher. Born in Brooklyn, he went to Hollywood after his early novels, based on his childhood, failed to find a big enough readership.
The Big Shot (co-w) 42. The Hard Way 42. Between Two Worlds (w) 44. Love Me or Leave Me (AA) 55. Jeanne Eagels 57, etc.

Fuest, Robert (1927–).
British director, from TV.
■ Just Like a Woman 66. And Soon the Darkness 70. *Wuthering Heights* 70. The Abominable Dr Phibes 71. Dr Phibes Rises Again 72. The Final Programme (& w) 73. The Devil's Rain (US) 76. The Revenge of the Stepford Wives (TV) 80. Aphrodite 82.

Fujimoto, Tak.
Japanese-American cinematographer.
Remember My Name 78. Last Embrace 79. Borderline 80. Melvin and Howard 80. Where the Buffalo Roam 80. Heart Like a Wheel 83. Swing Shift 84. Ferris Bueller's Day Off 86. Pretty in Pink 86. Something Wild 86. Backfire 87. Cocoon: The Return 88. Married to the Mob 88. Sweethearts Dance 88. Miami Blues 90. The Silence of the Lambs 91. Philadelphia 93. Devil in a Blue Dress 95. That Thing You Do! 96. A Thousand Acres 97. Beloved 98, etc.

Fukasaku, Kinji (1930–).
Japanese director, best known internationally for his exuberant fantasy films; in 1990 Japanese critics voted his violent gangster movie *Battles without Honour and Humanity* one of the 20 best Japanese films of all time.
League of Gangsters/Gyangu Domei 63. Black Lizard 68. Green Slime 68. Tora! Tora! Tora! (co-d) 70. Battles without Honour and Humanity/Jinginaki Tatakai 73. Graveyard of Honour and Humanity/Jingi No Hakaba 75. Message from Space/Uchu Karano Message 78. Virus/Fukkatsu No Hi 80. Jingsei Gekijo 83. Hana No Ran 88. Chushingura Gaiden Yotsuya Kaidan 94, etc.

Fukuda, Jun (1923–).
Japanese director, best known internationally for his monster movies.
Secret of the Telegian/Denso Ningen 60. White Rose of Hong Kong/Honkon No Shiroibara 65. Ebirah, Horror of the Deep/Nankai No Dai Ketto 66. Godzilla on Monster Island/Gojira Tai Gaigan 72. Son of Godzilla/Gojira No Musuko 67. Godzilla vs Mechagodzilla/Gojira Tai Mekagojira 72. Godzilla vs Megalon/Gojira Tai Megalon 73. War in Space/Wakusei Daisenso 77, etc.

Fulci, Lucio (1927–1996).
Italian general-purpose director who gained some international attention with horror films in the 80s. Born in Rome, he began as a journalist, then worked as a documentarist. In the 50s, he was as an assistant director and screenwriter on comedies, turning to directing horror movies in the mid-60s.
I Ladri 59. Le Massaggiatrici 62. I Maniaci 64. Beatrice Cenci 69. La Pretora 76. Zombi 2/Zombie Flesh Eaters 79. City of the Living Dead/Paura nella Città dei Morti Viventi 80. The Black Cat/Il Gatto Nero di Park Lane 80. Manhattan Baby 82. House of Doom (co-d) (TV) 89. Nightmare Concert 90. Voices from the Deep 90, many others.
❝ I find much of what I film very repugnant. But it has to be done. – *L.F.*
Italy's last great sleaze merchant. – *The Dark Side*

Fuller, Leland (1899–*).
American art director, a former architect, in films from the early 40s with Twentieth Century-Fox.
Laura (AAN) 44. Fallen Angel 46. The Fan 49. Fourteen Hours (AAN) 51. On the Riviera (AAN) 51. Viva Zapata! (AAN) 52. The President's Lady (AAN) 53. Hell and High Water 54. The Girl Can't Help It 56. Will Success Spoil Rock Hunter? 57. Bachelor Flat 61, etc.

Fuller, Leslie (1889–1948).
Beefy British concert-party comedian who was popular in broad comedy films of the 30s.
■ Not So Quiet on the Western Front 30. Kiss Me Sergeant 30. Why Sailors Leave Home 30. Old Soldiers Never Die 31. Poor Old Bill 31. What a Night 31. The Last Coupon 32. Old Spanish Customers 32. Tonight's the Night 32. Hawleys of the High Street 33. The Pride of the Force 33. A Political Party 34. The Outcast 34. Lost in the Legion 34. Doctor's Orders 34. Strictly Illegal 35. Captain Bill 35. The Stoker 35. One Good Turn 36. Boys Will Be Girls 37. The Middle Watch 39. Two Smart Men 40. My Wife's Family 41. Front Line Kids 42. What Do We Do Now 45.

Fuller, Mary (1887–1973).
Popular American star of silent films who disappeared from view in 1917 and was forgotten until her death in a Washington mental hospital.
Frankenstein 10. What Happened to Mary (serial) 12. Under Southern Skies 15. The Strength of the Week 16. Public Be Damned 17. The Long Trail 17, etc.

Fuller, Robert (1934–).
American leading man, mostly on TV.
Return of the Seven 66. Incident at Phantom Hill 67. The Hard Ride 70. The Gatling Gun 72. Mustang Country 76. Donner Pass: The Road to Survival (TV) 78. Maverick 94, etc.
TV series: *Laramie* 59–62. Wagon Train 62–63. Emergency 72–77.

Fuller, Samuel (1912–1997).
American writer-director who has also produced most of his own pictures, which have normally been violent melodramas on topical subjects. Born in Worcester, Massachusetts, he began as a copy boy on the *New York Journal*, and by the age of 17 was a crime reporter. After working as a reporter and cartoonist on various newspapers, in the mid-30s he became a crime novelist, and began, with the aid of Gene FOWLER, to work as a screenwriter and script doctor. His wartime experiences serving in the Ist Infantry, fighting through Europe, formed the basis of his film *The Big Red One*. In the late 60s he moved to live in France, where he appeared as himself in Jean-Luc GODARD's *Pierrot le Fou*, before returning in his later years to the United States. His second wife was actress Christa Lang.
Books: 1969, *Samuel Fuller*, ed. David Will and Peter Wollen; 1970, *Samuel Fuller* by Phil Hardy.
■ I Shot Jesse James 49. The Baron of Arizona 50. Fixed Bayonets 51. The Steel Helmet 51. Park Row 52. Pickup on South Street 52. Hell and High Water 54. House of Bamboo 55. Run of the Arrow 55. China Gate 56. Forty Guns 57. Verboten 58. The Crimson Kimono 59. Underworld USA 60. Merrill's Marauders 62. Shock Corridor 64. The Naked Kiss 66. Shark 67. Dead Pigeon on Beethoven Street 72 (Ger.). The American Friend (a only) 77. The Big Red One 80. White Dog 82. Thieves after Dark/Les Voleurs de la Nuit 84. Let's Get Harry (story) 87. A Return to Salem's Lot (a) 87. Helsinki Napoli All Night Long (a) 88. Street of No Return/Sans Espoir de Retour 89. Tell Me Sam (a) 89. Bohemian Life/La Vie de Bohème (a) 92. Petrified Garden (a) 93. Somebody to Love (a) 94. Tigrero: A Film that Was Never Made (as himself, doc) 94. Words/Milim (a) 96. The End of Violence (a) 97.
❝ Film is a battleground. Love, hate, violence, action, death ... In a word, emotion. – S.F.

Fullerton, Fiona (1955–).
British juvenile actress of the 70s.
Run Wild Run Free 69. Nicholas and Alexandra 71. Alice's Adventures in Wonderland 72. Gauguin the Savage (TV) 80. A View to a Kill 85. Shaka Zulu (TV) 87. Hold the Dream (TV) 87. The Secret Life of Ian Fleming (TV) 90, etc.

Fulton, John P. (1902–1965).
American special effects photographer, responsible for the tricks in most of the *Invisible Man* series and other fantasy movies.

Funicello, Annette (1942–).
American leading lady, former juvenile actress; was host of Disney's TV Mickey Mouse Club, and in his films is known simply as 'Annette'. She was played by Eva LaRue in the made-for-TV biopic *A Dream Is a Wish Your Heart Makes: The Annette Funicello Story* 95, in which she also appeared. She has been suffering from multiple sclerosis since 1987.
Johnny Tremain 57. The Shaggy Dog 61. Babes in Toyland 61. The Misadventures of Merlin Jones 63. Bikini Beach 64. The Monkey's Uncle 65. Fireball 500 66. Back to the Beach 87, etc.

Funt, Allen (1914–).
American TV trickster who appeared for years on *Candid Camera* and in 1970 produced and starred in a film version, *What Do You Say to a Naked Lady?*
Money Talks (d) 71.

Furie, Sidney J. (1933–).
Canadian director with a restless camera; came to Britain 1959, Hollywood 1966.
■ A Dangerous Age 57. A Cool Sound from Hell 58. The Snake Woman 60. Doctor Blood's Coffin 61. During One Night 61. Three on a Spree 61. The Young Ones 61. The Boys 62. The Leather Boys 63. Wonderful Life 64. *The Ipcress File* 65. Day of the Arrow 65. The Appaloosa 66. The Naked Runner 67. The Lawyer 69. Little Fauss and Big Halsy 70. Lady Sings the Blues 72. Hit 73. Sheila Levine Is Dead and Living in New York 75. Gable and Lombard 76. The Boys in Company C 77. The Entity 82. Purple Hearts 84. Iron Eagle 85. Superman IV 87. Iron Eagle II 88. The Taking of Beverly Hills 91. Ladybugs 92. Iron Eagle IV 95. Hollow Point 96.
TV series: Hudson's Bay 59.

Furlong, Edward (1977–).
American teenage actor.
Terminator 2: Judgment Day 91. American Heart 93. A Home of Our Own 94. Brainscan 94. Little Odessa 94. The Grass Harp 95. Before and After 96. Pecker 98. American History X 98, etc.

Furneaux, Yvonne (1928–).
French leading lady in British films.
Meet Me Tonight 52. The Dark Avenger 55. Lisbon 56. The Mummy 59. La Dolce Vita 59. Enough Rope (Fr.) 63. *Repulsion* 64. The Scandal (Fr.) 66, etc.

Furrer, Urs (1934–1975).
Swiss-born American cinematographer.
Pigeons 70. Desperate Characters 71. Shaft 71. Shaft's Big Score 72. Dr Cook's Garden (TV) 72. The Seven Ups 73, etc.

Furse, Judith (1912–1974).
British character actress who often played district nurses, matrons, heavy schoolmistresses, etc.
Goodbye Mr Chips 39. English Without Tears 44. Black Narcissus 46. The Man in the White Suit 51. Doctor at Large 57. Serious Charge 59. Carry On Regardless 61. Carry On Spying 64. Sinful Davy 69. The Adventures of Barry McKenzie 72, etc.

Furse, Margaret (1911–1974).
British costume designer.
Oliver Twist 48. The Mudlark 50. The Inn of the Sixth Happiness 58. Sons and Lovers 60. Young Cassidy 64. Anne of the Thousand Days 70. Mary Queen of Scots 72. Love Among the Ruins (TV) 75, etc.

Furse, Roger (1903–1972).
British stage designer.
Henry V (costumes only) 44. The True Glory 45. Odd Man Out 47. Hamlet 47. Ivanhoe 52. Richard III 56. The Prince and the Showgirl 57. Saint Joan 57. Bonjour Tristesse 58. The Roman Spring of Mrs Stone 61. Road to Hong Kong 62, etc.

Furst, Anton (1944–1991) (Anthony Francis Furst).
British production designer who trained as an architect and first worked on elaborate laser-light shows for rock concerts. He left Britain to work in Hollywood in the late 80s and committed suicide there.
Lady Chatterley's Lover 81. An Unsuitable Job for a Woman 81. The Company of Wolves 85. The Frog Prince 85. Full Metal Jacket 87. High Spirits 88. Batman (AA) 89. Awakenings 90, etc.

Furst, Stephen (1954–).
Plump American character actor who has also turned to writing and directing.
National Lampoon's Animal House 78. Swim Team 79. Getting Wasted 80. Midnight Madness 80. The Unseen 80. Up the Creek 84. The Dream Team 89. Magic Kid 2 (& co-w, d) 93, etc.

Furthman, Jules (1888–1966).
Seminal American writer, usually in collaboration. Born in Chicago, Illinois, he studied at Northwestern University and began as a journalist. He was in cinema from 1917, writing many silent films. He also directed a few during his time with Fox in the early 20s, writing some early scripts as Stephen Fox. He formed close working relationships with directors Josef VON STERNBERG, for whom he worked on around nine films, and Howard HAWKS, for whom he wrote five, also working uncredited on the screenplay of Hawks's *Red River*. His brother, Charles Furthman, was also a screenwriter.
Steady Company 15. When a Man Rides Along 18. Victory 19. Treasure Island 20. The Texan 20. The Roof Tree 21. Pawn Ticket 210 22. Condemned 23. Try and Get It 24. Sackcloth and Scarlet 25. Any Woman 25. Hotel Imperial 27. The Way of All Flesh 27. Barbed Wire 27. Docks of New York 28. The Dragnet 28. Thunderbolt 29. New York Nights 29. Common Clay 30. Renegades 30. *Morocco* 30. Over the Hill 31. The Yellow Ticket 31. Merely Mary Ann 31. Body and Soul 31. *Shanghai Express* 32. Blonde Venus 32. Bombshell 33. *Mutiny on the Bounty* (AAN) 35. China Seas 35. Fatal Lady 36. Come and Get It 36. Spawn of the North 38. Only Angels Have Wings 39. The Shanghai Gesture 41. The Outlaw 43. To Have and Have Not 45. *The Big Sleep* 46. Moss Rose 47. Nightmare Alley 47. Jet Pilot 57. *Rio Bravo* 59, etc.
❝ Furthman ... has written about half of the most entertaining movies to come out of Hollywood. – *Pauline Kael*
Furthman wasn't hard for me to get along with ... He's just such a mean guy that we thought he was great. – *Howard Hawks*

Fury, Billy (1941–1983) (Ronald Wycherly).
British pop singer.
■ Play it Cool 62. I've Gotta Horse 65. That'll Be the Day 73.

Fusco, Giovanni (1906–1968).
Italian composer, especially associated with Antonioni.
Cronaca di un Amore 50. Le Amiche 51. Il Grido 57. Hiroshima Mon Amour 59. L'Avventura 59. The Eclipse 62. The Red Desert 64. The War is Over 66, etc.

Fyffe, Will (1884–1947).
Pawky Scots comedian, famous in the halls for his song 'I Belong to Glasgow'.
Happy 34. Annie Laurie 36. Cotton Queen 37. Owd Bob 38. The Mind of Mr Reeder 39. Rulers of the Sea (US) 39. For Freedom 40. Neutral Port 40. Heaven Is Round the Corner 44. The Brothers 47, etc.

G

Gaal, Franceska (1904–1972) (Fanny Zilveritch).
Hungarian leading lady who made three American films: The Buccaneer 38. Paris Honeymoon 39. The Girl Downstairs 39.

Gabel, Martin (1912–1986).
Balding, rotund American character actor, mostly on stage. Born in Philadelphia, he studied acting at the American Academy of Dramatic Art, beginning his stage career in 1933. He was also the author of a novel, *I Got a Country* 44. Married actress Arlene Francis.
The Lost Moment (d only) 47. Fourteen Hours 51. M 51. The Thief 52. Tip on a Dead Jockey 57. Marnie 64. Lord Love a Duck 66. Divorce American Style 67. Lady in Cement 68. There was a Crooked Man 70. The Front Page 75. The First Deadly Sin 80, etc.

Gabel, Scilla (1937–).
Buxom Italian leading lady, a regular in the sword-and-sandal epics of the 60s, and in international films.
Tarzan's Greatest Adventure (GB) 59. The Fruit Is Ripe 60. Village of Daughters (GB) 62. Colossus of the Arena/Maciste, il Gladiotore Piu Forte del Mondo 62. Sodom and Gomorrah 62. The Revenge of the Gladiators/The Revenge of Spartacus 64. Romulus and the Sabines/Il Ratto delle Sabine 64. Seven Slaves against Rome 64. Son of Cleopatra/Il Figlio di Cleopatra 65. Modesty Blaise (GB) 66, etc.

Gabin, Jean (1904–1976) (Alexis Moncorgé).
Distinguished French actor, former Folies Bergères extra, cabaret entertainer, etc. His stocky virility and world-weary features kept him a star from the early 30s.
■ Chacun sa Chance 30. Mephisto 31. Paris Béguin 31. Gloria 31. Tout ça ne vaut pas l'Amour 31. Coeur de Lilas 32. La Belle Marinière 32. Les Gaités de l'Escadron 32. La Foule Hurle 33. L'Etoile de Valencia 33. Adieu les Beaux Jours 33. Le Tunnel 33. De Haut en Bas 33. Au Bout du Monde 34. Zouzou 34. *Maria Chapdelaine* 34. Passage Interdit 35. Variétés 35. Golgotha 35. La Bandera 36. *La Belle Equipe* 36. Les Bas-Fonds 36. *Pépé le Moko* 37. *La Grande Illusion* 37. Le Messager 37. Gueule d'Amour 37. *Quai des Brumes* 38. *La Bête Humaine* 38. Le Récif de Corail 38. *Le Jour se Lève* 39. Remorques 41. Moontide (US) 42. The Imposter (US) 42. Martin Roumagnac 46. Miroir 47. Au-delà des Grilles 49. La Marie du Port 50. It's Easier for a Camel (It.) 51. Victor 51. Night is my Kingdom 51. Le Plaisir 52. The Truth about Bébé Donge 52. Bufere 53. La Vierge du Rhin 53. Leur Dernière Nuit 53. *Touchez Pas au Grisbi* 54. L'Air de Paris 54. Napoleon 55. French Can Can 55. Razzia sur la Chnouff 55. Port of Desire 55. Lost Dogs 56. Important People 56. Gas-Oil 56. Voici le Temps des Assassins 56. Pig Across Paris 56. Le Sang à la Tête 56. Crime and Punishment 56. Le Rouge est Mis 57. Les Misérables 57. The Case of Dr Laurent 58. Le Désordre et la Nuit 58. *Maigret Sets a Trap* 58. En Cas de Malheur 58. Les Grandes Familles 58. The Tramp 59. Maigret et l'Affaire Saint-Fiacre 59. Rue des Prairies 59. Le Baron de l'Ecluse 60. Les Vieux de la Vieille 61. Le Président 61. Le Cave se Rebiffe 61. *A Monkey in Winter* 62. Le Gentleman d'Epsom 62. Mélodie en Sous-sol 63. Maigret Sees Red 63. Monsieur 64. The Ungrateful Age 65. God's Thunder 65. Rififi in Paname 66. Le Jardinier d'Argenteuil 67. Le Soleil des Voyous 67. Le Pacha 67. The Tattooed Man 68. Fin de Journée 69. The Sign of the Bull 69. The Sicilian Clan 70. La Horse 70. Le Drapeau Noir Flotte sur la Marmite 71. Le Tueur 72. *Le Chat* 72. L'affaire Dominici 73. Deux Hommes dans la Ville 74. Verdict 74. L'Année Sainte 76.
✪ For forcing such a wide range of roles, without ever losing sympathy, to fit his own dominant personality. *Quai des Brumes*.

Gable, Christopher (1940–1998).
British actor, ex-ballet dancer.
Women in Love 69. The Music Lovers 70. The Boy Friend 71. The Slipper and the Rose 76. The Lair of the White Worm 88. The Rainbow 88, etc.

Gable, Clark (1901–1960).
American leading man who kept his popularity for nearly thirty years, and was known as the 'king' of Hollywood. His big ears were popular with caricaturists; his impudent grin won most female hearts. Born in Cadiz, Ohio, he began acting in his teens, marrying his first teacher, Josephine Dillon, and, after failing to find work in Hollywood, making it to the Broadway stage. He married Ria Langham, a wealthy Texan woman, in 1931, a year after his divorce, as his screen career began at MGM. Before long, he was important enough for Louis B. Mayer to find somebody else to take the blame for a manslaughter charge, following a drink-driving accident. His career at the studio began to decline in the late 40s and was over by the mid-50s. His defining roles were as Dennis Carson in *Red Dust*, Peter Warne in *It Happened One Night*, Fletcher Christian in *Mutiny on the Bounty*, Blackie Norton in *San Francisco*, Rhett Butler in *Gone with the Wind*, Vic Norton in *The Hucksters*, and Gay Langland in *The Misfits*. Also married actress Carole Lombard (1939–42), Lady Sylvia Ashley, the widow of Douglas Fairbanks (1949–52), and, in 1955, Kay Spreckels, dying of a heart attack before their son, John Clark Gable, was born, just after he completed *The Misfits*. His lovers included Joan Crawford, Jean Harlow, Elizabeth Allan and Grace Kelly.
Biographies: 1961, *Clark Gable* by George Carpozi; 1973, *Clark Gable* by René Jordan; 1974, *Gable and Lombard* by Warren G. Hastings; 1976, *Long Live the King* by Lyn Tornabere.
Book: 1967, *Gable, A Complete Gallery of His Screen Portraits* by Gabe Essoe and Ray Lee.
■ Forbidden Paradise 24. The Merry Widow 25. The Pacemakers 25. The Plastic Age 25. North Star 26. The Painted Desert 30. The Easiest Way 31. Dance Fools Dance 31. A Free Soul 31. The Finger Points 31. The Secret Six 31. Laughing Sinners 31. Night Nurse 31. Sporting Blood 31. Susan Lenox 32. Possessed 32. Hell's Divers 32. Polly of the Circus 32. *Red Dust* 32. Strange Interlude 32. No Man of Her Own 32. The White Sister 32. Dancing Lady 33. Hold Your Man 33. Night Flight 33. *It Happened One Night* (AA) 34. Men in White 34. Manhattan Melodrama 34. Chained 34. After Office Hours 35. Forsaking All Others 35. *Mutiny on the Bounty* 35. China Seas 35. Call of the Wild 35. Wife Versus Secretary 36. *San Francisco* 36. Cain and Mabel 36. Love on the Run 37. Parnell 37. Saratoga 37. Test Pilot 38. Too Hot to Handle 38. Idiot's Delight 39. *Gone with the Wind* (AAN) 39. Strange Cargo 40. Boom Town 40. Comrade X 40. They Met in Bombay 41. Honky Tonk 41. Somewhere I'll Find You 41; war service; Adventure 45. *The Hucksters* 47. Homecoming 48. Command Decision 48. Any Number Can Play 49. Key to the City 50. To Please a Lady 50. Across the Wide Missouri 51. Lone Star 52. Never Let Me Go (GB) 53. Mogambo 53. Betrayed 54. The Tall Men 55. Soldier of Fortune 55. The King and Four Queens 56. Band of Angels 57. Teacher's Pet 58. Run Silent Run Deep 58. But Not for Me 59. It Started in Naples 59. *The Misfits* 61.
✪ For effortlessly maintaining a Hollywood legend, and for doing so with cheerful impudence. *Gone with the Wind*.
❝ The King of Hollywood? He modestly disclaimed the title, but there was sense to it: he always seemed to be in charge. As the *New York Times* said:
Gable was as certain as the sunrise. He was consistently and stubbornly all man.
He said himself:
The only reason they come to see me is that I know life is great – and they know I know it.
And again:
I'm no actor and I never have been. What people see on the screen is me.
What they saw, they liked. Publicity man Ralph Wainwright said:
All of his life people turned around to stare at him.
This was remarkable considering his famous physical drawback, well phrased by Howard Hughes:
His ears made him look like a taxicab with both doors open.
Milton Berle called him:
The best ears of our lives.
It didn't stop him from influencing the world, and not only the female half of it. Historian Frederick Lewis Allen recalled that:
When Clark Gable in *It Happened One Night* disclosed that he wore no undershirt, the knitwear manufacturers rocked from the shock to their sales.
But Gable disclaimed his sexual reputation:
Hell, if I'd jumped on all the dames I'm supposed to have jumped on – I'd have had no time to go fishing.
Eve Arden remembered:
He used to claim that he was very dull in bed.
Carole Lombard confirmed this:
Listen, he's no Clark Gable at home.
And her husband nodded ruefully:
I can't emote worth a damn.
David Selznick knew the secret:
Gable has enemies all right, but they all like him.
Gable himself summed up:
This King stuff is pure bull. I eat and drink and go to the bathroom just like anybody else. I'm just a lucky slob from Ohio who happened to be in the right place at the right time.
And seven years after his death, Joan Crawford could say:
He was king of an empire called Hollywood. The empire is not what it was – but the king has not been dethroned, even after death.
Famous line (*It Happened One Night*): 'Behold the walls of Jericho!'
Famous line (*Gone with the Wind*): 'Frankly, my dear, I don't give a damn.'

Gabor, Eva (1919–1995).
Hungarian leading lady, sister of Zsa Zsa Gabor. Married five times.
Autobiography: 1954, *Orchids and Salami*.
Pacific Blackout 41. Forced Landing 41. A Royal Scandal 45. Wife of Monte Cristo 46. Song of Surrender 49. The Mad Magician 54. Tarzan and the Slave Girl 54. The Truth about Women 56. Gigi 58. A New Kind of Love 63. Youngblood Hawke 63. The Princess Academy 87. The Rescuers Down Under (voice) 90, etc.
TV series: *Green Acres* 65–70. Bridges to Cross 86.

Gábor, Pál (1932–1987).
Hungarian director, one of the first students at the Béla Balázs Studio in the early 60s and among the best film-makers of his generation. His anti-totalitarian *Angi Vera* brought him international recognition. Married actress Juli Básti who starred in his *Wasted Lives*. Died of heart disease.
Forbidden Ground 68. Horizont (& co-w) 71. Journey with Jacob/Utazas Jakabbal 72. Epidemic 78. *The Education of Vera*/Angi Vera 79. Wasted Lives/Kettevalt Mennyezet 82. Brady's Escape/The Long Run/Hosszu Vagta (US/Hung.) 83. The Bride Was Radiant/La Sposa Era Bellissima (It./Hung.) 87, etc.

Gabor, Zsa Zsa (1919–) (Sari Gabor).
Exotic international leading lady, Miss Hungary of 1936, who has decorated films of many nations. The third of her eight husbands was actor George Sanders (1949–54).
Autobiographies: 1961, My *Story*. 1991, *One Lifetime Is Not Enough*.
Lovely To Look At (US) 52. Lili (US) 53. Moulin Rouge (GB) 53. Public Enemy Number One (Fr.) 54. Diary of a Scoundrel (US) 56. The Man Who Wouldn't Talk (GB) 57. Touch of Evil (US) 58. Queen of Outer Space (US) 59. Arrivederci Baby 66. Picture Mommy Dead (US) 66. Up the Front (GB) 72. Won Ton Ton, the Dog Who Saved Hollywood 75. Frankenstein's Great Aunt Tillie 85. Smart Alec/Movie Maker 86. A Nightmare on Elm Street 3: Dream Warriors 87. Happily Ever After (voice) 90. The Naked Gun 2½: The Smell of Fear 91. A Very Brady Sequel 96, etc.
❝ I believe in large families: every woman should have at least three husbands. – Z.Z.G.
I never hated a man enough to give him his diamonds back. – Z.Z.G.
Husbands are like fires: they go out if unattended. – Z.Z.G.
She's an expert housekeeper. Every time she gets divorced, she keeps the house. – *Henny Youngman*
Her face is inscrutable, but I can't vouch for the rest of her. – *Oscar Levant*

Gabriel, Peter (1950–).
British composer and singer, a co-founder of the rock band Genesis.
Birdy (m) 84. The Last Temptation of Christ (m) 88.

Gabrilovich, Yevgeny (1898–1993).
Russian screenwriter and founder of the national screenwriting school.
The Last Night/Poslednaya Noch (co-w) 37. Girl No. 217/Chelovek No. 217 (co-w) 44. In the Name of Life/Vo Imya Zhizni (co-w) 47. The Return of Vasili Bortnikov (co-w) 53. The Communist/Kommunist 58. Stories about Lenin/Rasskazi o Lenine (co-w) 58. Lenin in Poland 66. Your Contemporary/Tvoi Sovremyonnik 67. The Beginning/Nachalo (co-w) 70. Strange Woman/Strannaya Zhenshchina 78. Declaration of Love/Obyasneniye v Liubvi (oa) 79, etc.

Gahagan, Helen (1900–1980).
American actress who limited herself to just one film: the title role in the 1935 version of *She*. Married Melvyn Douglas.

Gaillard, Bulee 'Slim' (1916–1991).
American jazz vocalist, multi-instrumentalist and dancer, born in Cuba. An eccentric performer of his own hit nonsense songs, often using an invented language called 'Vout', he appeared as himself in occasional films and on British TV in the 80s.
Star Spangled Rhythm 42. Hellzapoppin 42. Almost Married 42. Go, Man, Go 54. Too Late Blues 62. Absolute Beginners 86, etc.

Gainsbourg, Charlotte (1971–).
Young French leading actress, the daughter of actors Serge Gainsbourg and Jane Birkin.
Words and Music/Paroles et Musique 84. L'Effrontée 86. Charlotte Forever 86. The Little

Thief/La Petite Voleuse 88. Night Sun/Il Sole Anche di Notte 90. Merci la Vie 91. Autobus/Aux Yeux du Monde 91. L'Amoureuse 92. The Cement Garden 93. Jane Eyre (title role) 96, etc.

Gainsbourg, Serge (1929–1991) (Lucien Ginzburg).
French singer, composer, director and actor whose songs, full of a direct sexuality, often caused controversy. His daughter Charlotte, by actress Jane Birkin, is a leading French actress.

Game for Six Lovers/L'Eau à la Bouche (m) 60. Revolt of the Slaves (a) 61. Strip-Tease (m) 63. Comment Trouvez-vous Ma Soeur? (m) 64. The Defector/L'Espion (m) 66. Manon 70 (m) 66. L'Horizon (m) 67. Le Jardinier d'Argenteuil (m) 67. Le Pacha (m) 68. Paris n'Existe pas (m) 68. The Marriage Came Tumbling Down/Ce Sacré Grand-père (a, m) 68. Mr Freedom (a, m) 69. Cannabis (m) 70. The Romance of a Horse Thief (m) 71. Le Sex Shop (m) 73. Je t'Aime Moi non plus (wd, m) 75. Goodbye Emmanuelle (m) 77. The French Woman/Madame Claude (m) 79. Je Vous Aime (a) 80. Equator/Equateur (d, m) 83. Evening Dress/Tenue de Soirée (m) 86. Charlotte Forever (d) 86. Stan the Flasher (d) 90, etc.

Galabru, Michel (1924–).
French leading actor who appeared in more than 140 films, including a series of police comedies in partnership with Louis DE FUNES.

La Croix et la Bannière 60. War of the Buttons 62. La Cuisine au Beurre 63. La Bourse et la Vie 65. Le Corniaud 65. Le Gendarme à New York 65. Le Gendarme de Saint-Tropez 65. Le Gendarme en Balade 70. *The Judge and the Assassin* 76. *La Cage aux Folles* 78. Le Gendarme et Les Extra-Terrestres 79. Une Semaine de Vacances 80. La Cage aux Folles II 80. The Gendarme Wore Skirts/Le Gendarme et les Gendarmettes 82. Separate Rooms/Nôtre Histoire 84. Subway 85. La Cage aux Folles III: The Wedding 86. Uranus 90. Room Service 92. Belle Époque 92. Mon Homme 96. Foul Play/Hors Jeu 98. Astérix et Obélix 98, many more.

Gale, Bob (1952–).
American screenwriter, in collaboration with director Robert Zemeckis.

I Wanna Hold Your Hand 78. 1941 79. Used Cars 80. Back to the Future (AAN) 85. Back to the Future II 89. Back to the Future III 90. Trespass 93, etc.

Galeen, Henrik (1881–1949).
Dutch writer-director, a leading figure of German silent cinema.

The Student of Prague (wd) 12. *The Golem* (wd) 14. *The Golem* (w) 20. Nosferatu (w) 22. Waxworks (w) 25. The Student of Prague 26. Alraune 27. After the Verdict 30. Salon Dora Greene 36, many others.

Gallagher, Peter (1955–).
American leading actor, in films from 1980.

The Idolmaker 80. Summer Lovers 82. Dreamchild 85. My Little Girl 87. High Spirits 88. sex, lies and videotape 89. Tune In Tomorrow/Aunt Julia and the Scriptwriter 90. An Inconvenient Woman (TV) 91. Late for Dinner 91. Watch It 93. Short Cuts 93. Malice 93. The Hudsucker Proxy 94. Mother's Boys 94. Mrs Parker and the Vicious Circle 94. White Mile (TV) 94. The Underneath 95. While You Were Sleeping 95. Last Dance 96. To Gillian on Her 37th Birthday 96. Titanic (TV) 96. Path to Paradise (TV) 97. The Man Who Knew Too Little 97. Cafe Society 97, etc.

TV series: Skag 80. The Secret Lives of Men 98– .

Gallagher, Skeets (1891–1955).
Cheerful American vaudevillian, in some films of the early talkie period.

The Racket 28. It Pays to Advertise 31. Merrily We Go to Hell 32. Riptide 34. Polo Joe 37. Idiot's Delight 39. Zis Boom Bah 42. The Duke of Chicago 50, etc.

Gallian, Ketti (1913–1959).
French leading lady in America; films few.

■ Marie Galante 34. Under the Pampas Moon 35. Espionage 37. Shall We Dance 37.

Gallico, Paul (1897–1976).
American novelist whose work has been much adapted.

Wedding Present 36. Joe Smith American 42. Pride of the Yankees (AAN) 42. The Clock 45. Never Take No for an Answer 52. Lili 53. Merry Andrew 58. Next to No Time 58. The Three Lives of Thomasina 63. The Snow Goose (TV) 71. The Poseidon Adventure 72, etc.

Galligan, Zach (1963–.).
American leading actor.

Nothing Lasts Forever 84. Gremlins 84. Waxwork 88. Rebel Storm 90. Mortal Passions 90. Gremlins 2: The New Batch 90. Psychic 91. Waxwork II: Lost in Time 92. Warlock: The Armageddon 93. Ice 94. Cyborg 3: The Recycler 95. Cupid 96. Prince Valiant 97, etc.

Gallo, George.
American screenwriter and director.

Wise Guys (w) 86. Midnight Run (w) 88. Relentless (a) 89. 29th Street (co-w, d) 91. Trapped in Paradise (p, wd) 94. Bad Boys (story) 95, etc.

Gallo, Mario (1878–1945).
Italian-born musician who became one of the pioneers of Argentinian cinema, making *El Fusilamiento de Dorrego*, the country's first feature film using professional actors, in 1908. He continued making films, most of which are now lost, until 1919.

Gallo, Vincent (c. 1962–).
American actor, director, writer, composer and painter. Born in Buffalo, New York, he has also worked as a musician and model and raced motorcycles professionally.

AS ACTOR: Doc's Kingdom 89. Goodfellas 90. Arizona Dream 93. US Go Home (Fr.) 94. The House of the Spirits 94. Angela 95. The Funeral 96. Truth or Consequences, NM 97. Palookaville 97. LA without a Map (GB/Fr./Fin.) 98, etc.

AS DIRECTOR: Buffalo 66 (& co-w, a, m) 98.

❝ I crave an incredible amount of love and attention and approval. – V.G.

I'm the only creative person on the planet who's an extreme, right-wing Republican. – V.G.

Gallone, Carmine (1886–1973).
Veteran Italian director who ranged from opera to action epics.

Pawns of Passion 28. Un Soir de Rafle 30. My Heart Is Calling 34. Madame Butterfly 39. Manon Lescaut 40. La Traviata 47. Faust and the Devil 49. La Forza del Destino 51. Tosca 56. Michael Strogoff 59. Carthage in Flames 59, many others.

Galloway, Don (1937–).
American TV leading man, familiar in *Ironside*.

The Rare Breed 66. Rough Night in Jericho 67. The Ride to Hangman's Tree 67. Lt Schuster's Wife (TV) 72. The Big Chill 83. Two Moon Junction 88. Clifford 96, etc.

Gallu, Samuel (1918–1991).
American director, former opera singer.

Theatre of Death 66. The Man Outside 67. The Limbo Line 68.

Galsworthy, John (1867–1933).
British novelist who wrote about the upper middle class. Works filmed include *Escape* 30 and 48. *The Skin Game* 31. *Loyalties* 34. *Twenty-one Days* 39. *That Forsyte Woman* 49, etc.

Galton, Ray (1930–).
British comedy writer; with Alan Simpson, co-author of successful TV series, e.g. *Hancock's Half-Hour*, *Steptoe and Son*; films include *The Rebel* 61. *The Wrong Arm of the Law* 62. *The Bargee* 64. *The Spy with a Cold Nose* 67, etc.

Galvani, Dino (1890–1960).
Distinguished-looking Italian actor, in films (mainly British) from 1908.

Atalantic 30. In a Monastery Garden 32. Midnight Menace 35. Mr Satan 38. It's That Man Again (as Signor So-So) 42. Sleeping Car to Trieste 49. Father Brown 54. Checkpoint 57. Bluebeard's Ten Honeymoons 60, many others.

Gam, Rita (1928–) (Rita Mackay).
American leading actress, of French and Romanian descent, born in Pittsburg, Pennsylvania. She was on stage from the late 40s, and found few worthwhile roles in Hollywood. Formerly married to director Sidney LUMET.

The Thief 52. Sign of the Pagan 54. Night People 54. Magic Fire 55. Mohawk 56. King of Kings 61. Klute 71. Such Good Friends 71. Noah – the Deluge (TV) 79. Distortions 87. Midnight 89. Rowing Through 96, etc.

Gambon, Sir Michael (1940–).
British leading actor, of stage and screen. Born in Dublin, Ireland, he was educated in London and was an engineer before becoming an actor. He was on stage from the early 60s, notably with the Royal Shakespeare and National Theatre companies. Few film roles have offered the opportunities provided by the theatre; his best screen performance remains that of the sardonic protagonist of the TV drama *The Singing Detective*. Knighted in 1997.

The Beast Must Die 74. Turtle Diary 85. The Singing Detective (TV) 88. Paris by Night 88. The Cook, the Thief, His Wife and Her Lover 89. A Dry White Season 89. The Rachel Papers 89. Mobsters 91. Toys 92. Clean Slate 94. The Browning Version 94. A Man of No Importance 94. Squanto: A Warrior's Tale 94. Nothing Personal 95. Two Deaths 95. The Wind in the Willows (voice, as Badger) 96. Mary Reilly 96. The Gambler 97. Midnight in St Petersburg 97. The Wings of the Dove 97. Plunkett and Macleane 98. Dancing at Lughnasa 98, etc.

TV series: Maigret 92.

Gamley, Douglas (1924–).
Australian composer in Britain.

The Admirable Crichton 57. Gideon's Day 59. Watch It Sailor 61. The Horror of It All 64. Spring and Port Wine 70. Tales from the Crypt 72. Asylum 72. The Vault of Horror 73. And Now the Screaming Starts 73. From Beyond the Grave 73. Madhouse 74. The Beast Must Die 74. The Land that Time Forgot 75. The Monster Club 81, etc.

Gance, Abel (1889–1981).
French producer-director, in films since 1910. Pioneer of wide-screen techniques.

Barberousse 16. *J'Accuse* 19 and 37. La Roue 21. *Napoleon* 27. La Fin du Monde 31. Lucrezia Borgia 35. Un Grand Amour de Beethoven 36. Paradis Perdu 39. La Tour de Nesle 54. The Battle of Austerlitz 60, etc.

~Gance's *Napoleon* had sterling qualities which were never properly noted because of its length, its wide-screen reels, and the fact that silents were overwhelmed by sound soon after its release. In the late 70s, however, film scholar Kevin Brownlow assembled a five-hour version to which Thames TV added a newly commissioned musical score; in this version it was shown again triumphantly in the early 80s, in all the capitals of the world.

Gandhi, Mahatma (1869–1948).
Indian nationalist leader who carried out a policy of non-violent civil disobedience against the British to achieve Indian independence. A biopic, *Gandhi*, with Ben Kingsley in the role, directed by Richard Attenborough, appeared in 1982, and *The Making of the Mahatma*, about his early life, with Rajit Kapur in the role, directed by Shyam Benegal, in 1996.

Gandolfini, James.
American actor, from the stage.

A Stranger among Us 92. True Romance 93. Money for Nothing 93. Angie 94. Terminal Velocity 94. Crimson Tide 95. Le Nouveau Monde (Fr.) 95. Get Shorty 95. The Juror 96. Night Falls on Manhattan 97. 12 Angry Men (TV) 97. Perdita Durango 97. She's So Lovely 97. Fallen 98. A Civil Action 98. The Mighty 98, etc.

Gann, Ernest K. (1910–1991).
American adventure novelist. Films of his work include *The High and the Mighty*, *Blaze of Noon*, *Fate Is the Hunter*.

Ganz, Bruno (1941–).
Swiss leading actor, in international films, from German experimental theatre.

Rece Do Gory 67. Lumière 75. The Marquise of O 76. The American Friend/Der Amerikanische Freund 77. The Boys from Brazil 78. Nosferatu 78. Der Erfinder 80. A Girl from Lorraine/La Provinciale 80. Circle of Deceit/Die Falschung 81. In the White City/Dans la Ville Blanche 82. Wings of Desire/Der Himmel über Berlin 87. Strapless 89. Especially on Sunday/La Domenica Specialmente 91. The Last Days of Chez Nous 91. Success/Erfolg 91. Night on Fire 92. Prague 92. Faraway, So Close!/In Weiter Ferne, So Nah 93. A Judge in Anxiety/Ein Richter in Angst 96. Saint-Ex (GB) 96. Eternity and a Day (Gr.) 98, etc.

Ganz, Lowell (1948–).
American comedy screenwriter, in collaboration with Babaloo Mandel.

Nightshift 82. Splash 84. Spies Like Us 85. Gung Ho 86. Vibes 88. Parenthood 89. City Slickers 91. Mr Saturday Night 92. A League of Their Own 92. City Slickers II: The Legend of Curly's Gold 94. Greedy/Greed 94. Forget Paris 95. Multiplicity 96. Fathers' Day 98, etc.

Ganzer, Alvin.
American second-feature director.

The Girls of Pleasure Island (co-d) 53. The Leather Saint 56. When the Boys Meet the Girls 65. Three Bites of the Apple 67. Nightmare 68, etc.

Garas, Kaz (1940–).
American leading man.

The Last Safari 68. Ben 72. Final Mission 84. Naked Vengeance 85. Fast Gun 93. Puppet Master 5: The Final Chapter 94, etc.

Garber, Matthew (1956–1977).
British child actor.

The Three Lives of Thomasina 63. Mary Poppins 64. The Gnome-Mobile 67.

Garbo, Greta (1905–1990) (Greta Gustafson).
Swedish leading actress who was taken to Hollywood by her director Mauritz Stiller and became a goddess of the screen, her aloof beauty carefully nurtured by MGM through the late 20s and early 30s. Her early retirement enhanced the air of mystery which has always surrounded her. Special Academy Award 1954 'for her unforgettable screen performances'. Her lovers included actor John GILBERT, conductor Leopold STOKOWSKI, writer Mercedes DE ACOSTA and photographer Cecil BEATON.

Biographies: 1954, *Garbo* by John Bainbridge; 1970, *Garbo* by Norman Zierold; 1992, *Conversations with Greta Garbo* by Sven Broman; 1994, *Loving Garbo* by Hugo Vickers; 1994, *Greta and Cecil* by Diana Souhami; 1997, *Greta Garbo: A Life Apart* by Karen Swenson.

■ Peter the Tramp 22. The Atonement of Gösta Berling 24. Joyless Street 25. The Torrent 26. The Temptress 26. *Flesh and the Devil* 27. Love 27. The Mysterious Lady 27. The Divine Woman 28. The Kiss 29. A Woman of Affairs 29. Wild Orchids 29. The Single Standard 29. *Anna Christie* (AAN) 30. Romance (AAN) 30. Inspiration 31. Susan Lenox 31. Mata Hari 31. *Grand Hotel* 32. As You Desire Me 32. *Queen Christina* 33. The Painted Veil 34. *Anna Karenina* 35. *Camille* (AAN) 36. Conquest 37. *Ninotchka* (AAN) 39. Two Faced Woman 41.

✪ For stretching a mystery over twelve splendid years and for knowing when to quit. *Queen Christina*.

❝ Boiled down to essentials, she is a plain mortal girl with large feet.

So wrote Herbert Kretzmer, sick of the 'sphinx' image, which in the early 30s was overpowering. Alistair Cooke called her:

Every man's harmless fantasy mistress. She gave you the impression that, if your imagination had to sin, it could at least congratulate itself on its impeccable taste.

Life in 1928 hailed her thus:

She is the dream princess of eternity, the knockout of the ages.

Richard Watts Jnr called her:

That fascinating, inscrutable, almost legendary personage . . .

The *New York Mirror* said:

Her alluring mouth and volcanic, slumbrous eyes stimulate men to such passion that friendships collapse.

Graham Greene in his review of *Conquest* defined her:

A great actress? Oh, undoubtedly, one wearily assents, but what dull pompous films they make for her, hardly movies at all so retarded are they by her haggard equine renunciations, the slow consummation of her noble adulteries!

To Clare Boothe Luce she was:

A deer in the body of a woman, living resentfully in the Hollywood zoo.

A 1929 critic said:

She is a woman who marches to some unstruck music, unheard by the rest of us.

Rouben Mamoulian thought her:

A wonderful instrument.

Even the sensible Lilian Gish considered that:

Garbo's temperament reflected the rain and gloom of the long dark Swedish winters.

More recently Ken Tynan remarked:

What when drunk one sees in other women, one sees in Garbo sober.

Remoteness was part of her charm. To Fredric March:

Co-starring with Garbo hardly constituted an introduction.

To James Wong Howe, the famous cameraman:

She was like a horse on the track. Nothing, and then the bell goes, and something happens.

But the image always had its knockers, including the lady herself:

I never said, I want to be alone. I only said I want to be let alone.

(She did say it actually, but in *Grand Hotel*.) She added:

My talent falls within definite limits. I'm not a versatile actress.

She also said with a smile:

I'm a woman who's unfaithful to a million men.

But the fact is, men were not her fans. It was women who queued to see her suffer. J. Robert Rubin of MGM noted in wonder:

Garbo was the only one we could kill off. The Shearer and Crawford pictures had to end in a church, but the public seemed to enjoy watching Garbo die.

George Cukor, who directed her several times, thought:

She is a fascinating actress but she is limited. She must never create situations. She must be thrust into them. The drama comes in how she rides them out.

When she suddenly retired in 1941, her reason, given much later, was:

I had made enough faces.

And:

Being in the newspapers is awfully silly to me. I have nothing to contribute.

David Niven commented:

The longer she stayed away, the stronger and stranger the Garbo myth grew.

In the 70s, thirty years after her retirement, her movies were still making money all over the world and the lady herself was front-page news. You can't kill a legend. And it wasn't the movies that kept the interest; as Richard Whitehall remarked:

Subtract Garbo from most of her films, and you are left with nothing.

Isobel Quigley remained undecided:

I can't make up my mind whether Garbo was a remarkable actress or simply a person so extraordinary that she made everything she did, including acting, seem remarkable.

C. Aubrey Smith's appraisal was the oddest of all:

She's a rippin' gel.

Christopher Isherwood pondered her appeal:

I suppose everybody who meets Garbo dreams of saving her – either from herself, or from Metro-Goldwyn-Mayer, or from some friend or lover. And she always eludes them by going into an act. That is what has made her a universal figure. She is the woman whose life everyone wants to interfere with.

If you're going to die on screen, you've got to be strong and in good health. – G.G.

Famous line (*Ninotchka*): 'Don't make an issue of my womanhood.'

Famous line (*Anna Christie*): 'Gimme visky, ginger ale on the side. And don't be stingy, baby.'

Famous line (*Queen Christina*): 'I have been memorizing this room. In the future, in my memory, I shall live a great deal in this room.'

Garbuglia, Mario (1927–).
Italian production designer, often for the films of Visconti.

The White Nights/Le Notti Bianche 57. A Farewell to Arms 57. Rocco and his Brothers 60. Boccaccio '70 62. *The Leopard/Il Gattopardo* 63. The Stranger/Lo Straniero 67. Barbarella 67. Waterloo 70. Valdez 73. *Conversation Piece*/Gruppo di Famiglia in un Interno 75. The Intruder/L'Innocente 76. Orca 77. La Cage aux Folles 78. Lion of the Desert 80. La Cage aux Folles III: The Wedding 86. Dark Eyes/Oci Ciornie 87. The Night before Christmas 94. The Troublemakers 95, etc.

Garci, José Luis (1944–) (José Luis Garci Monoz).
Spanish director and screenwriter, a former film critic, born in Madrid.

Unfinished Business/Asignatura Pendiente 77. The Crack/El Crack 80. *To Live Again/Volver a Empezar* (AA) 82. Double Feature/Sesión Continua 84. The Grandfather/El Abuelo 98, etc.

Garcia, Andy (1956–) (Andrés Arturo García-Menéndez).
Cuban-born American leading actor. Born in Havana, he moved to the USA at the age of five. He studied at Florida International University and spent several years performing in regional theatre before moving to Los Angeles to pursue a film career in the late 70s.

Blue Skies Again 83. A Night in Heaven 83. The Lonely Guy 84. The Mean Season 85. 8 Million Ways to Die 86. Stand and Deliver 87. The Untouchables 87. American Roulette 88. Black Rain 89. A Show of Force 90. Internal Affairs 90. The Godfather, Part III (AAN) 90. Dead Again 91. Hero 92. Jennifer 8 92. Cachao . . . Como Su Ritmo No Hay Dos (doc) (p, d) 93. When a Man Loves a Woman 94. Things to Do in Denver When You're Dead 95. Steal Big, Steal Little 95. Night Falls on Manhattan 97. Hoodlum 97. Desperate Measures 98. The Scalper 98, etc.

❝ I spent seven years without working, so if they're making cop movies, I'll play cops. I got two kids to bring up. – A.G.

Garcia Márquez, Gabriel (1928–).
Colombian novelist and screenwriter. Born in Aracataca, he worked as a journalist, and began writing novels after he came to Europe in the 50s. A leading exponent of Magic Realism, he won the Nobel Prize for literature in 1982.

In This Town There Are No Thieves/En Este Pueblo No Hay Ladrones (oa) 65. The Year of the Plague/El Año de la Peste (co-w) 79. La Viuda de Montiel (oa) 80. El Mar del Tiempo Perdido (oa) 81. My Dearest Maria/María de Mi Corazón (oa, co-w) 82. Erendira (oa, w) 82. Time to Die/Tiempo de Morir (w) 85. Chronicle of a Death Foretold/Cronaca di una Morte Annunciata (oa) 87. Letters from the Park/Cartas del Parque (oa) 88, etc.

Gardel, Carlos (1890–1935) (Charles Romuald Gardes).
French-born tango singer who was a popular Argentinian star. He made 10 shorts with optical sound in 1931, before leaving to work in France and in Hollywood on Spanish-language versions of US films. Died in a plane crash on his way back to Argentina to make a feature. A biopic, *La Vida de Carlos Gardel*, was made in 1939, starring Hugo DEL CARRIL. He appears in film clips in Fernando Solanas's film *Tangos: Gardel's Exile*, made in France in 1985.

Luces de Buenos Aires (Fr.) 31. Espérame (Fr.) 32. El Día que Me Quieras 35. Tango Bar 35, etc.

Gardenia, Vincent (1922–1992) (Vincent Scognamiglio).
American comic character actor.

Mad Dog Coll 61. A View from the Bridge 61. The Pursuit of Happiness 71. Cold Turkey 71. Hickey and Boggs 72. Bang the Drum Slowly (AAN) 73. *Death Wish* 74. The Front Page 74. Greased Lightning 77. Fire Sale 77. Heaven Can Wait 78. Home Movies 79. The Dream Merchants (TV) 80. Death Wish II 81. *Kennedy* (as J. Edgar Hoover) (TV) 83. Little Shop of Horrors 86. Moonstruck (AAN) 87. Cavalli Si Nasce 89. Age-Old Friends (TV) 89. Skin Deep 89, etc.

Gardiner, Reginald (1903–1980).
British actor who perfected the amiable silly ass type, in Hollywood from 1936.

The Lovelorn Lady 32. Borrow a Million 34. *Born to Dance* 36. Everybody Sing 37. Marie Antoinette 38. Sweethearts 39. *The Great Dictator* 40. My Life with Caroline 41. *The Man Who Came to Dinner* 41. Captains of the Clouds 42. The Immortal Sergeant 43. Molly and Me 44. Christmas in Connecticut 45. Cluny Brown 46. Fury at Furnace Creek 48. Wabash Avenue 50. Halls of Montezuma 51. The Black Widow 54. Ain't Misbehavin' 55. The Birds and the Bees 56. Mr Hobbs Takes a Vacation 62. Do Not Disturb 65. Sergeant Deadhead 66, many others.

TV series: The Pruitts of Southampton 66.

Famous line (*The Man Who Came to Dinner*): 'I've very little time, and so the conversation will be entirely about me, and I shall love it.'

Gardner, Arthur (1910–) (Arthur Goldberg).
American independent producer, of Levy-Gardner-Laven, a former actor.

Without Warning 52. Down Three Dark Streets 54. Geronimo 62. The Glory Guys 65. The Scalphunters 68. The McKenzie Break 70. The Hunting Party 71. Kansas City Bomber 72. Brannigan 75. Gator 76, etc.

TV series include: Rifleman, The Detectives, Law of the Plainsman, The Big Valley.

Gardner, Ava (1922–1990).
American leading actress of the 40s and 50s, once voted the world's most beautiful woman. Born in Grabtown, North Carolina, she intended to become a secretary, but began her film career after a talent scout spotted her photograph in her brother-in-law's shop window, and she was put under contract to MGM. It was not until she made *The Killers* that her potential was noted, though she continued to star in unmemorable films. The few roles that allowed her to be more than a beautiful woman were as Julie in *Show Boat*, though her singing voice was, to her annoyance, dubbed; as Pandora Reynolds in *Pandora and the Flying Dutchman*; as Eloise Kelly in *Mogambo*; as Maria Vargas in *The Barefoot Contessa*; and as Maxine Falk in *The Night of the Iguana*. Her performances improved as her looks faded, owing to some heavy drinking and a growing dislike of the restraints of film-making. She retired to live in London. Married actor Mickey ROONEY (1942–43), bandleader Artie SHAW (1945–47), and singer Frank SINATRA (1951–57). Her lovers included producer Howard HUGHES, matador Luis Miguel Dominguin, and actors Howard DUFF and Walter CHIARI.

Autobiography: 1991, *Ava: My Story*.

Biographies: 1960, *Ava* by David Hanna. 1984, *Ava Gardner* by John Daniell.

■ We Were Dancing 42. Joe Smith American 42. Sunday Punch 42. This Time for Keeps 42. Calling Dr Gillespie 42. Kid Glove Killer 42. Pilot No. 5 43. Hitler's Madman 43. Ghosts on the Loose 43. Reunion in France 43. Dubarry was a Lady 43. Young Ideas 43. Lost Angel 43. Swing Fever 44. Music for Millions 44. Three Men in White 44. Blonde Fever 44. Maisie Goes to Reno 44. Two Girls and a Sailor 44. She Went to the Races 45. Whistle Stop 46. *The Killers* 46. *The Hucksters* 47. Singapore 47. One Touch of Venus 48. The Great Sinner 49. East Side West Side 49. The Bribe 49. My Forbidden Past 51. *Show Boat* 51. *Pandora and the Flying Dutchman* 51. Lone Star 52. The Snows of Kilimanjaro 52. Ride Vaquero 53. *Mogambo* (AAN) 53. Knights of the Round Table 53. *The Barefoot Contessa* 54. Bhowani Junction 56. The Little Hut 57. *The Sun Also Rises* 57. The Naked Maja 59. On the Beach 59. The Angel Wore Red 60. 55 Days at Peking 63. Seven Days in May 64. *The Night of the Iguana* 64. The Bible 66. Mayerling 68. Tam Lin 70. Judge Roy Bean 72. Earthquake 74. Permission to Kill 75. The Bluebird 76. The Cassandra Crossing 77. The Sentinel 77. City on Fire 79. The Kidnapping of the President 80. Priest of Love 81.

TV series: Knots Landing 85.

❝ Although no one believes me, I have always been a country girl, and still have a country girl's values. – A.G.

No one ever thanked me during all those years when I was the good girl on the lot. I felt like I was in slavery. They may have found me, but I came to feel I owed them, and the business they represented, nothing at all. – A.G.

I'll never forget seeing Bette Davis at the Hilton in Madrid. I went up to her and said, 'Miss Davis, I'm Ava Gardner and I'm a great fan of yours.' And do you know, she behaved exactly as I wanted her to behave. 'Of course you are, my dear,' she said. 'Of course you are.' And she swept on. Now that's a star. – A.G.

Because she looks the way she does, everyone assumes Ava is sophisticated, intelligent and mature. In fact she is none of those things. She is a simple farm girl and she has the mind and mentality of a simple farm girl. – *Stanley Kramer*

A lady of strong passions, one of them rage. – *Mickey Rooney (former husband)*

Gardner, Ed (1901–1963).
American radio comic who starred in the 1945 film version of his series *Duffy's Tavern*.

Gardner, Erle Stanley (1889–1970).
American best-selling crime novelist, the creator of PERRY MASON.

Gardner, Herb (1934–).
American director and dramatist, from television.

A Thousand Clowns (oa, w) 65. Who Is Harry Kellerman and Why Is He Saying Those Terrible Things about Me? (w) 71. Thieves (oa, w) 77. The Goodbye People (d) 84. Ishtar (a) 87. I'm Not Rappaport (oa, wd) 96, etc.

Gardner, Joan (1914–).
British leading lady of the 30s who married Zoltan Korda.

Men of Tomorrow 32. Catherine the Great 34. The Scarlet Pimpernel 35. The Man Who Could Work Miracles 36. Dark Journey 39. The Rebel Son (last to date) 39, etc.

Garfein, Jack (1930–).
American stage and screen director, married to Carroll Baker (1955–69).

The Strange One 57. Something Wild 62. Magic 98, etc.

Garfield, Allen (1939–) (aka Allen Goorwitz).
Heavy-set American character actor.

Get to Know Your Rabbit 72. Slither 73. Busting 74. The Long Goodbye 74. The Conversation 74. The Front Page 74. Nashville 76. Mother Jugs and Speed 76. Gable and Lombard (as Louis B. Mayer) 76. The Brinks Job 78. One Trick Pony 80. The Stunt Man 80. Continental Divide 81. One from the Heart 82. The Black Stallion Returns 83. Get Crazy 83. The Cotton Club 84. Desert Bloom 86. Beverly Hills Cop II 87. Let It Ride 89. Night Visitor 90. Dick Tracy 90. Club Fed 91. Until the End of the World/Bis ans Ende der Welt 91. Family Prayers 93. Les Patriotes (Fr.) 94. Destiny Turns on the Radio 95. Crime of the Century 96. Diabolique 96, etc.

Garfield, Brian. (1921–).
American screenwriter and novelist. *Death Wish*, his novel of a lone vigilante, was filmed by Michael Winner and so far has spawned four sequels. He is the author of *Western Films, A Complete Guide* (1982).

Death Wish (oa) 74. The Last Hard Men 76. Hopscotch (co-w) 80. The Stepfather (co-story) 87.

Garfield, John (1913–1952) (Julius Garfinkle).
American leading actor, usually in aggressive or embittered roles; formerly a star of New York's leftish Group Theatre. Born in poverty in New York, he studied acting at the city's Ouspenskaya Drama School. In the late 40s he formed his own production company, but was blacklisted soon after. Died from a heart attack, probably brought on by the stress and anger he felt following his blacklisting, and his refusal to name names to HUAC.

Biography: 1978, *John Garfield* by James Beaver.

Book: 1975, *The Films of John Garfield* by Howard Gelman.

■ *Four Daughters* (AAN) 38. Blackwell's Island 38. *They Made Me a Criminal* 39. Juarez 39. Daughters Courageous 39. Dust Be My Destiny 39. Four Wives (cameo) 39. Saturday's Children 40. East of the River 40. Castle on the Hudson 40. Flowing Gold 40. *The Sea Wolf* 41. Out of the Fog 41. Tortilla Flat 42. Dangerously They Live 42. Air Force 43. The Fallen Sparrow 43. Thank Your Lucky Stars 43. Between Two Worlds 44. Hollywood Canteen (cameo) 44. Destination Tokyo 44. Pride of the Marines 45. Nobody Lives Forever 46. *The Postman Always Rings Twice* 46. *Humoresque* 46. *Body and Soul* (AAN) 47. *Gentleman's Agreement* 47. We Were Strangers 48. *Force of Evil* 49. Jigsaw (cameo) 49. Under My Skin 50. The Breaking Point 50. He Ran All the Way 51.

❝ Projected on the screens of the world, he was the Eternal Outsider, obliged to glimpse Paradise but not to dwell there. – *Larry Swindell*

His feeling never changed that he was mandated by the American public to go in there and keep punching for them. – *Clifford Odets*

Garfunkel, Arthur (1941–).
American pop singer, half of Simon and Garfunkel; occasional actor.

Biography: 1996, *Simon and Garfunkel* by Victoria Kingston.

■ Catch 22 70. Carnal Knowledge 71. Bad Timing 79. Good to Go 86. Short Fuse 88. Boxing Helena 93.

Gargan, Ed (1902–1964).
American character actor, brother of William Gargan; often seen as comedy cop or prizefighter's manager.

Gambling Ship 33. Belle of the Nineties 34. Miss Pacific Fleet 35. My Man Godfrey 36. Big City 37. Gateway 38. Another Thin Man 39. Road to Singapore 40. A Date with the Falcon 41. Over My Dead Body 42. Hit the Ice 43. The Falcon Out West 44. The Bullfighters 45. Wonder Man 45. Gallant Bess 46. Little Miss Broadway 47. You Gotta Stay Happy 48. Red Light 49. Belle of Old Mexico 50. Bedtime for Bonzo 51, many others, often in one-line or one-shot roles.

Gargan, William (1905–1979).
American light leading man of the 30s and 40s, usually in 'good guy' roles; retired when left voiceless after operation. Brother of Ed Gargan.

Autobiography: 1969, *Why Me?*

The Misleading Lady 32. Rain 32. The Story of Temple Drake 33. Four Frightened People 34. Black Fury 35. The Milky Way 36. You Only Live Once 37. The Crowd Roars 38. *The Housekeeper's Daughter* 39. Turnabout 40. *They Knew What They Wanted* (AAN) 40. Bombay Clipper 41. Miss Annie Rooney 42. The Canterville Ghost 44. The Bells of St Mary's 45. Till the End of Time 46. Night Editor 46. The Argyle Secrets 48. Miracle in the Rain 56, many others.

TV series: *Martin Kane* 57.

Garland, Beverly (1926–) (Beverly Fessenden).
Pert and pretty leading lady of some 50s Hollywood films; more successful on TV.

DOA 49. The Glass Web 53. The Miami Story 54. The Desperate Hours 55. It Conquered the World 56. Not of this Earth 56. The Joker is Wild 57. The Alligator People 59. Twice Told Tales 63. Pretty Poison 68. The Mad Room 69. Airport 75 74. Roller Boogie 79. It's My Turn 80. The World's Oldest Living Bridesmaid (TV) 92. Haunted Symphony (TV) 94, etc.

TV series: Mama Rosa 50. *Decoy* 57. The Bing Crosby Show 64. My Three Sons 69–72. Scarecrow and Mrs King 87.

Garland, Judy (1922–1969) (Frances Gumm).
American entertainer and leading lady who for many years radiated the soul of show business. The child of vaudeville performers, on stage from five years old, she later seemed unable to stand the pace of her own success; but her resultant personal difficulties only accentuated the loyalty of her admirers. Special Academy Award 1939 'for her outstanding performance as a screen juvenile'. Died from an overdose of sleeping pills. Married composer David Rose (1941–45), director Vincente MINNELLI (1945–51), producer Sid Luft (1952–65), actor Mark Herron (1965–67), and, in 1969, nightclub manager Mickey Dean. She is the mother of actress and singer Liza MINNELLI and singer Lorna Luft.

Biographies: 1971, *The Other Side of the Rainbow* by Mel Tormé; 1993, *Judy Garland* by David Shipman; 1993, *Judy Garland – World's Greatest Entertainer* by John Fricke; 1998, *Me and My Shadows: Living with the Legacy of Judy Garland* by Lorna Luft.

■ Every Sunday (short) 36. Pigskin Parade 36. Broadway Melody of 1938 37. Thoroughbreds Don't Cry 38. Everybody Sing 38. Listen Darling 38. Love Finds Andy Hardy 38. *The Wizard of Oz* 39. *Babes in Arms* 39. Andy Hardy Meets a Debutante 39. Strike Up the Band 40. Little Nellie Kelly 40. Ziegfeld Girl 41. Life Begins for Andy Hardy 41. Babes on Broadway 41. *For Me and My Gal* 42. Presenting Lily Mars 42. Girl Crazy 42. Thousands Cheer (guest) 43. Meet Me in St Louis 44. Ziegfeld Follies 45. *The Clock* 45. The Harvey Girls 46. Till the Clouds Roll By (guest) 46. The Pirate 47. *Easter Parade* 48. Words and Music (guest) 48. In the Good Old Summertime 49. Summer Stock 50. *A Star Is Born* (AAN) 54. Judgment at Nuremberg (AAN) 60. A Child Is Waiting 62. I Could Go On Singing (GB) 63.

✪ For her incredible voice; and for drawing cathartic tears as much by her own life as by her performances. *The Wizard of Oz*.

❝ If I'm such a legend, why am I so lonely? – J.G.
I had the stage mother of all time. If I wasn't well, and didn't want to go on, she'd yell 'Get out on that stage or I'll tie you to the bedpost.' – J.G.
I didn't know her well, but after watching her in action I didn't want to know her well. – Joan Crawford
An angel with spurs. – Joe Pasternak, producer
You see that girl? She used to be a hunchback. You see what I've made her into? – Louis B. Mayer
Her mental attitude may have been pathetic but it turned her into a great bore. – Anita Loos
Famous line (*The Wizard of Oz*): 'If I ever go looking for my heart's desire again, I won't look any further than my own backyard, because if it isn't there, I never really lost it to begin with.'

Garmes, Lee (1897–1978).
Distinguished American cinematographer, in Hollywood from 1916.

The Grand Duchess and the Waiter 26. The Private Life of Helen of Troy 27. Disraeli 29. Lilies of the Field 30. Whoopee 30. Morocco 30. Dishonoured 31. City Streets 31. An American Tragedy 31. *Shanghai Express* (AA) 32. *Scarface* 32. Smilin' Through 32. Zoo in Budapest 33. Crime without Passion 34. The Scoundrel 34. Dreaming Lips (GB) 37. Gone with the Wind (co-ph) (uncredited) 39. Angels over Broadway 40. *Lydia* 41. Jungle Book 42. Guest in the House 44. Since You Went Away 44. Love Letters 45. *Duel in the Sun* 46. The Spectre of the Rose (& co-p) 46. The Secret Life of Walter Mitty 47. The Paradine Case 48. Our Very Own 50. Detective Story 51. Actors and Sin (& co-d) 52. The Desperate Hours 55. Land of the Pharaohs 55. The Big Fisherman 59. Hemingway's Adventures of a Young Man 62. Lady in a Cage 64. Big Hand for a Little Lady 66. How to Save a Marriage 68, etc.

✪ For his contributions to black-and-white photography, and especially for the effects he created with 'north light'. Zoo in Budapest.

❝ A cameraman is often the saviour of a film. His lighting can be the main factor in its success. – L.G.

Garner, James (1928–) (James Baumgarner).
Amiable, good-looking American leading man of the 60s; showed a sense of humour among the action and romance, but did not quite measure up as a substitute for Clark Gable.

Toward the Unknown 56. The Girl He Left Behind 56. Shoot out at Medicine Bend 57. Sayonara 57. Darby's Rangers 58. Up Periscope 59. Cash McCall 59. The Children's Hour 62. Boys' Night Out 62. *The Great Escape* 63. *The Thrill of It All* 63. The Wheeler Dealers 63. Move Over Darling 63. *The Americanization of Emily* 64. 36 Hours 64. The Art of Love 65. Duel at Diablo 66. A Man Could Get Killed 66. Mister Buddwing 66. Grand Prix 66. Hour of the Gun (as Wyatt Earp) 67. The Pink Jungle 68. How Sweet It Is 68. *Support Your Local Sheriff* 69. Marlowe 69. A Man Called Sledge 70. *The Skin Game* 71. Support Your Local Gunfighter 71. They Only Kill Their Masters 72. One Little Indian 73. The Castaway Cowboy 74. The New Maverick (TV) 78. Health 80. The Fan 81. Victor/Victoria 82. The Long Summer of George Adams (TV) 82. Tank 84. Murphy's Romance (AAN) 85. Space (TV) 85. Sunset 88. My Name Is Bill W (TV) 89. Decoration Day (TV) 90. Barbarians at the Gate (TV) 93. Fire in the Sky 93. Breathing Lessons (TV) 94. Maverick 94. My Fellow Americans 97. Legalese (TV) 98. Twilight 98, etc.

TV series: *Maverick* 57–71. Nichols 71. The Rockford Files 74–80. Bret Maverick 81.

❝ I became an actor by accident; I'm a businessman by design. – J.G.
I am an actor. I hire out. I am not afraid of hurting my image. – J.G.
He is a master at playing dumb while maintaining a sense of shrewdness and dignity. He always throws us off guard. He is the macho stud who makes fun of himself; he is the scaredy-cat we know will not let us down in the end. – Esquire

Garner, Peggy Ann (1931–1984).
American child star of the 40s; Academy Award 1945 as 'outstanding child actress'. Did not make it as adult star.

■ Little Miss Thoroughbred 38. Blondie Brings Up Baby 39. In Name Only 39. Abe Lincoln in Illinois 40. The Pied Piper 42. Eagle Squadron 42. Jane Eyre 44. A Tree Grows in Brooklyn 45. The Keys of the Kingdom 45. Nob Hill 45. Junior Miss 45. Home Sweet Homicide 46. Daisy Kenyon 47. Thunder in the Valley 47. The Sign of the Ram 48. The Lovable Cheat 49. Bomba the Jungle Boy 49. The Big Cat 49. Teresa 51. The Black Widow 54. Eight Witnesses 54. The Black Forest 54. The Cat 67. A Wedding 78.

Garnett, Tay (1894–1977).
American director, a light professional talent.

Autobiography: 1974, *Light Up Your Torches and Pull on Your Tights*.

● Celebrity 28. The Spieler 28. Flying Fools 29. Oh Yeah 29. Officer O'Brien 30. *Her Man* (& w) 30. Bad Company 31. *One Way Passage* (& w) 32. Prestige 32. Okay America 32. Destination Unknown 33. SOS Iceberg 33. China Seas (& w) 35. She Couldn't Take It 35. Professional Soldier 35. Love is News (& w) 37. *Slave Ship* (& w) 37. Stand In 37. Joy of Living 38. Trade Winds (& w) 38. Eternally Yours (& p) 39. Slightly Honorable (& wp) 40. Seven Sinners 40. Cheers for Miss Bishop (& w) 41. My Favorite Spy 42. Bataan 43. The Cross of Lorraine 43. Mrs Parkington 44. The Valley of Decision 45. *The Postman Always Rings Twice* 46. Wild Harvest 47. A Connecticut Yankee in King Arthur's Court 49. The Fireball (& w) 50. Soldiers Three 51. Cause for Alarm 51. One Minute to Zero 52. Main Street to Broadway 53. The Black Knight 54. Seven Wonders of the World 56. A Terrible Beauty 60. Cattle King 63. The Delta Factor 70. The Timber Tramps 73.

Garnett, Tony (1936–).
British producer.

■ Kes 69. The Body 70. *Family Life* 71. Prostitute 80. Handgun (& d) 82.

Garofalo, Janeane (1964–).
American actress.

Reality Bites 94. Coldblooded 95. Bye Bye, Love 95. Now and Then 95. The Truth about Cats and Dogs 96. The Cable Guy 96. Larger than Life 96. Cop Land 97. The Matchmaker 97. Romy and Michele's High School Reunion 97. Touch 97. Dog Park 98. Permanent Midnight 98. Clay Pigeons 98. The Bumblebee Flies Anyway 98, etc.

TV series: Saturday Night Live 94–95.

Garr, Teri (1949–).
American leading lady.

Oh God 77. Close Encounters of the Third Kind 77. Mr Mike's Mondo Video 78. The Black Stallion 79. Honky Tonk Freeway 81. Wrong Is Right 82. One from the Heart 82. Tootsie (AAN) 82. The Sting II 82. The Black Stallion Returns 83. Mr Mom 83. Firstborn 84. After Hours 85. Full Moon in Blue Water 88. Out Cold 88. Let It Ride 89. Short Time 90. Waiting for the Light 90. Mom and Dad Save the World 92. The Whole Shebang (TV) 93. Dumb and Dumber 94. Prêt-à-Porter/Ready to Wear 94. Michael 96. Changing Habits 97. A Simple Wish 97, etc.

TV series: Girl with Something Extra 73–74. The Sonny and Cher Comedy Hour 73–74. The Sonny Comedy Revue 74. Good and Evil 91. Women of the House 95.

Garrett, Betty (1919–).
Peppy American singer and actress with musical comedy experience. Married actor Larry PARKS, and quit films when she was blacklisted in the early 50s after he admitted to HUAC that he had once been a communist, which brought his film career to an end. She appeared with him in a nightclub act and in the theatre, and later acted mostly on television.

Big City (debut) 46. Words and Music 48. Take Me Out to the Ball Game 48. Neptune's Daughter 49. On the Town 49. My Sister Eileen 55. The Shadow on the Window 57. That's Entertainment! III 94. The Long Way Home (TV) 98, etc.

TV series: All in the Family 73–75. Laverne and Shirley 76.

Garrett, Oliver H. P. (1897–1952).
American screenwriter.

Forgotten Faces 28. Street of Chance 30. She Couldn't Take It 35. One Third of a Nation 39. The Man I Married 40. Flight for Freedom 43. Duel in the Sun 46. Dead Reckoning 47. Sealed Cargo 51, etc.

Garrett, Otis (c. 1895–1941).
American director.

■ The Black Doll 37. The Last Express 38. Personal Secretary 38. Danger on the Air 38. *Lady in the Morgue* 38. The Witness Vanishes 39. The Mystery of the White Room 39. Exile Express 39. Margie 40. Sandy Gets Her Man 41.

Garrett, Pat (1850–1908).
American western adventurer who allegedly, as sheriff, shot BILLY THE KID. Actors who have played him include Wallace Beery in *Billy the Kid* 30, Thomas Mitchell in *The Outlaw* 43, Charles Bickford in *Four Faces West* 48, Frank Wilcox in *The Kid from Texas* 50, John Dehner in *The Left-Handed Gun* 58, Glenn Corbett in *Chisum* 70, James Coburn in *Pat Garrett and Billy the Kid* 73.

On TV, Barry Sullivan was Garrett in *The Tall Men*.

Garrick, David (1717–1779).
Famous English actor who has been impersonated on screen by Cedric Hardwicke in *Peg of Old Drury* 34 and Brian Aherne in *The Great Garrick* 37.

Garrick, John (1902–1966) (Reginald Dandy).
English actor and singer, from the stage. Born in Brighton, Sussex, he was a bank clerk before beginning his career in variety. He was on stage from 1924, usually in musical comedies and operetta, and in films in the USA from the late 20s, returning to England in the early 30s. He was often cast as 'the other man'.

The Sky Hawk (US) 29. Song o' My Heart (US) 30. Just Imagine (US) 30. The Lottery Bride (US) 30. Charlie Chan Carries On (US) 31. Always Goodbye (US) 31. Bad Company 31. Chu Chin Chow 34. Too Many Millions 34. D'Ye Ken John Peel? 35. Turn of the Tide 35. Street Song 35. Royal Eagle 36. A Woman Alone 36. Sunset in Vienna 37. The Bells of St Mary's 37. Riding High 37. Special Edition 38. The Great Victor Herbert 39. Suicide Legion 40, etc.

Garrison, Sean (1937–).
American leading man of the 60s.

Moment to Moment 66. Banning 67. Breakout 68. Cover Girls (TV) 77, etc.

TV series: Dundee and the Culhane 67.

Garson, Greer (1903–1996).
Red-haired Anglo-Irish leading lady who after stage experience was cast as Mrs Chipping in *Goodbye Mr Chips* (AAN) 39 and promptly went to Hollywood, where her gentle aristocratic good looks enabled her to reign as a star for ten years. Born in Essex rather than, as she claimed, County Down, she studied at London University and made her London stage debut in 1934. The first of her two husbands was actor Richard Ney, who played her son in *Mrs Miniver*.

■ Remember 39. Pride and Prejudice 40. *Blossoms in the Dust* (AAN) 41. When Ladies Meet 41. *Mrs Miniver* (AA) 42. Random Harvest 42. *Madame Curie* (AAN) 43. Mrs Parkington (AAN) 44. The Valley of Decision (AAN) 45. Adventure 45. Desire Me 47. Julia Misbehaves 48. *That Forsyte Woman* 49. The Miniver Story 50. The Law and the Lady 51. Scandal at Scourie 52. Julius Caesar 53. Her Twelve Men 53. Strange Lady in Town 54. Sunrise at Campobello (as Eleanor Roosevelt) (AAN) 60. Pepe 60. The Singing Nun 66. The Happiest Millionaire 67. Little Women (TV) 78.

❝ If you're going to be typed, there are worse moulds in which you can be cast. – G.G.
One of the most richly syllabled queenly horrors of Hollywood. – Pauline Kael
Metro's Glorified Mother. – Anon
The mixture of Irish charm, natural red-haired beauty and her unceasing capacity to project the shopgirl's vision of the great lady made her an incontestable star in a decade that required a staunch, wholesome ideal. – New Yorker
After Greer Garson they stopped trying to make English stars out here. – Anna Lee, 1983

Garvin, Anita (1907–1994).
American actress, a charming foil to Laurel and Hardy and Charley Chase in many comedy shorts from 1918. She was a Mack Sennett Bathing Beauty at the age of 12 and became a Ziegfeld girl a year later. She also made a few features before retiring in the early 40s.

The Snow Hawk 25. Why Girls Love Sailors 27. With Love and Hisses 27. The Battle of the Century 27. From Soup to Nuts 28. A Pair of Tights

28. Red Hot Rhythm 29. Trent's Last Case 29. Dynamite 29. Blotto 30. Be Big 31. A Chump at Oxford 40, etc.

Garwood, Norman.
British production designer.
The Missionary 81. Time Bandits 81. Brimstone and Treacle 82. Bullshot 83. Red Monarch 83. Water 84. Brazil (AAN) 85. Shadey 85. Link 86. The Princess Bride 87. Glory (AAN) 89. Misery 90. Hook (AAN) 91. Being Human 94. CutThroat Island 95. Dangerous Beauty 98. Lost in Space 98, etc.

Gary, Lorraine (1937–).
American general-purpose actress.
Jaws 75. I Never Promised You a Rose Garden 77. Jaws II 78. 1941 79. Just You and Me Kid 79. Jaws – the Revenge 87.

Gary, Romain (1914–1980) (Romain Kassevgari).
French novelist and occasional screenwriter and director. Born in Tiflis, Georgia, he lived in Poland when young, becoming a French citizen in 1935 and a member of the French Foreign Service; for a time he was French consul in Los Angeles. Married author Lesley Blanch and actress Jean SEBERG.
Roots of Heaven (co-w, oa) 58. Lady L (oa) 65. Birds in Peru (& d) 68. Promise at Dawn (oa) 70. Kill (wd) 71, etc.

Gasnier, Louis J. (1882–1963).
American director: mostly of foreign language versions.
Darkened Rooms 29. The Lawyer's Secret 31. Forgotten Commandments 32. Gambling Ship 33. The Last Outpost 35. Bank Alarm 37. Murder on the Yukon 40. Fight On Marines 42, etc.

Gassman, Vittorio (1922–).
Italian actor and matinée idol, in occasional films since 1946.
Bitter Rice 48. Sombrero (US) 53. Rhapsody (US) 54. War and Peace 56. Tempest 57. The Love Specialist 60. Barabbas 62. The Devil in Love 66. Woman Times Seven 67. Lucky Thirteen 70. We All Loved Each Other So Much 73. Scent of a Woman 75. The Prophet 76. A Wedding 78. Quintet 79. The Nude Bomb 80. La Terrazza 80. Il Turno 81. Sharky's Machine 81. Tempest 82. La Vie est un Roman 83. The Family/La Famiglia 87. To Forget Palermo/Dimenticare Palermo 89. The Sleazy Uncle/Lo Zio Indegno 89. The 1001 Nights/Sheherazade 90. I Divertimenti della Vita Privata 91. I Won't Disturb You/Tolgo il Disturbo 91. The Long Winter/El Largo Invierno 92. When We Were Repressed/Quando eravamo Repressi 92. The Bible: Abraham (TV) 93. Sleepers 96, etc.

Gassner, Dennis (1948–).
American production designer.
The Hitcher 86. Wisdom 86. In the Mood 87. Like Father Like Son 87. Field of Dreams 88. Earth Girls Are Easy 88. Miller's Crossing 90. Barton Fink (AAN) 91. Bugsy (AA) 91. Hero/Accidental Hero 92. The Hudsucker Proxy 94. Waterworld 95. The Truman Show 98, etc.

Gastoni, Lisa (1935–).
Italian leading lady in British films of the 50s.
The Runaway Bus 54. Man of the Moment 55. The Baby and the Battleship 56. Intent to Kill 58. Hello London 59. Passport to China 64. Maddalena 72. The Last Days of Mussolini 74, etc.

Gates, Larry (1915–1997).
American character actor, often seen as small-town merchant or middle-aged good guy.
Has Anybody Seen My Gal? 52. The Girl Rush 54. Invasion of the Body Snatchers 56. Jeanne Eagels 57. Cat on a Hot Tin Roof 58. One Foot in Hell 60. The Hoodlum Priest 62. Toys in the Attic 63. The Sand Pebbles 67. Airport 69. Funny Lady 75, etc.

Gates, Nancy (1926–).
American leading lady of the 40s and 50s.
The Great Gildersleeve 42. The Spanish Main 45. The Atomic City 52. The Member of the Wedding 53. Suddenly 54. The Search for Bridey Murphy 56. The Brass Legend 56. Death of a Scoundrel 56. Some Came Running 59. Comanche Station 60, etc.

Gateson, Marjorie (1891–1977).
American character actress of dignified mien.
The Beloved Bachelor 31. Silver Dollar 32. Cocktail Hour 33. Lady Killer 33. Big Hearted Herbert 34. Your Uncle Dudley 35. The Milky Way 36. Wife versus Secretary 36. First Lady 37. Stablemates 38. Geronimo 39. Pop Always Pays 40. Submarine Zone 41. Rings on Her Fingers 42. The Youngest Profession 43. Ever Since Venus 44. One More Tomorrow 46. Passage West 51. The Caddy 53, many others.

Gaudio, Tony (1885–1951) (Gaetano Gaudio).
Italian cinematographer, long in Hollywood.
The Mark of Zorro 20. Secrets 24. The Temptress 25. Two Arabian Knights 27. *Hell's Angels* 30. Sky Devils 32. Bordertown 35. The Story of Louis Pasteur 35. *Anthony Adverse* (AA) 36. *The Life of Emile Zola* 37. *The Adventures of Robin Hood* 38. Juarez 39. *The Letter* 40. The Great Lie 41. The Constant Nymph 43. A Song to Remember 45. Love From a Stranger 47. The Red Pony 49, many others.

Gauge, Alexander (1914–1960).
Heavyweight British actor, Friar Tuck in TV's *Robin Hood* series.
The Interrupted Journey (debut) 49. Murder in the Cathedral 51. Pickwick Papers 52. Fast and Loose 54. Martin Luther 55. The Iron Petticoat 56. The Passing Stranger 57, etc.

Gaultier, Jean-Paul (1952–).
French fashion designer and television presenter who has designed outrageous costumes for several films.
The Cook, the Thief, His Wife and Her Lover 89. Kika 93. Prêt-à-Porter/Ready to Wear 94. The City of Lost Children/La Cité des Enfants Perdus 95. The Fifth Element 97, etc.

Gaumont, Léon (1863–1946).
Pioneer French inventor, producer and exhibitor. Founder of Gaumont Studios at Shepherds Bush, also Gaumont circuit, both later sold to Rank. Invented sound on disc in 1902.

Gaup, Nils (1955–).
Lapp director and screenwriter, a former actor in Norway.
Pathfinder/Ofelas (AAN) 1987. Shipwrecked/ Hakon Hakonsen 91. Head above Water 93. North Star 96. Misery Harbour 99, etc.

Gautier, Dick (1939–).
American leading man of the 70s.
Wild in the Sky 72. Fun with Dick and Jane 77. Billy Jack Goes to Washington 78. Marathon 80. Glitch! 88, etc.
TV series: *Here We Go Again* 71.

Gavin, John (1928–) (John Golenor).
Stolid, handsome American leading man. Born in Los Angeles, he studied at Stanford University and was set on a diplomatic career before being offered a screen test at Universal, where he was at first seen as a successor to Rock HUDSON. During the Reagan administration, he became US Ambassador to Mexico, and later pursued a business career. Married actress Constance TOWERS.
A Time to Live and a Time to Die 58. Imitation of Life 59. Spartacus 60. Psycho 60. A Breath of Scandal 61. Back Street 61. Romanoff and Juliet 61. Thoroughly Modern Millie 67. The Madwoman of Chaillot 69. Pussycat Pussycat I Love You 70. Rich Man Poor Man (TV) 76. Jennifer 78. Sophia Loren: Her Own Story (TV) 80, etc.
TV series: Destry 64. Convoy 65.

Gawthorne, Peter (1884–1962).
Splendidly pompous-looking British stage actor, often seen as general, admiral or chief constable in comedies of the 30s.
Sunny Side Up (US) 29. Charlie Chan Carries On (US) 31. Jack's the Boy 32. The Iron Duke 35. Wolf's Clothing 36. Alf's Button Afloat 38. *Ask a Policeman* 40. Much Too Shy 42. The Case of Charles Peace 49. Five Days 54, many others.

Gaxton, William (1893–1963) (Arturo Gaxiola).
American entertainer who made a few film appearances.
Fifty Million Frenchmen 31. Something to Shout About 42. Best Foot Forward 43. Tropicana 44. Diamond Horseshoe 45, etc.

Gay, John (1924–).
American writer.
Run Silent Run Deep 58. The Four Horsemen of the Apocalypse (co-w) 62. The Hallelujah Trail 65. No Way to Treat a Lady 68. Soldier Blue 70. Sometimes a Great Notion 71. Hennessy 75. A Matter of Time 76. Golden Rendezous 77. The Bunker (TV) 80. Windmills of the Gods (TV) 88. Ship Hunters (It.) 92, etc.

Gay, Noel (1898–1954) (Richard Moxon Armitage).
British composer of musicals and songs for stage and screen. His song 'Tondelayo', featured in *White Cargo*, was the first to be synchronized with the action in a British talking picture.
White Cargo (s) 28. The Camels Are Coming (s) 34. Me and Marlborough (s) 35. Okay for Sound (s) 37. Father Knew Best (s) 37. Sailors Three/ Three Cockeyed Sailors (s) 40, etc.

Gaye, Gregory (1900–1993).
American character actor.
Dodsworth 36. Hollywood Boulevard 36. Ninotchka 39. Cash 42. The Bachelor and the Bobbysoxer 47. The Eddy Duchin Story 56. Auntie Mame 58, etc.

Gaynes, George (1917–) (George Jongejans).
Finnish-born character actor, in America, a former opera singer; best known for playing the senile police chief in the *Police Academy* series.
The Group 65. Doctors' Wives 70. The Way We Were 73. Nickelodeon 76. Washington: Behind Closed Doors (TV) 79. Dead Men Don't Wear Plaid 79. Altered States 80. Tootsie 82. To Be or Not to Be 83. It Came upon the Midnight Clear 84. Micki & Maude 84. Police Academy 84. Police Academy 2: Their First Assignment 85. Police Academy 3: Back in Training 86. Police Academy 4: Citizens on Patrol 88. Police Academy 5: Assignment Miami Beach 88. Police Academy 6: City under Siege 89. Stepmonster 92. Vanya on 42nd Street 94. Police Academy: Mission to Moscow 94. The Crucible 96, etc.
TV series: Rich Man, Poor Man – Book II 76–77. Punky Brewster 84–86. The Days and Nights of Molly Dodd 89–91.

Gaynor, Janet (1906–1984) (Laura Gainer).
American leading lady of the 20s and 30s, immensely popular in simple sentimental films, especially when teamed with Charles Farrell. Played in many short comedies and westerns before achieving star status. She was married to costume designer Adrian and producer Paul Gregory.
■ The Johnstown Flood 26. The Shamrock Handicap 26. The Midnight Kiss 26. The Blue Eagle 26. The Return of Peter Grimm 26. *Seventh Heaven* (AA) 27. *Sunrise* (AA) 27. Two Girls Wanted 27. Street Angel (AA) 28. Four Devils 29. Christina 29. Lucky Star 29. Sunny Side Up 29. Happy Days 30. High Society Blues 30. The Man Who Came Back 30. *Daddy Longlegs* 31. Merely Mary Ann 31. Delicious 31. The First Year 32. Tess of the Storm Country 32. *State Fair* 33. Adorable 33. Paddy the Next Best Thing 33. Carolina 34. Change of Heart 34. Servants' Entrance 34. One More Spring 35. The Farmer Takes a Wife 35. Small Town Girl 36. Ladies in Love 36. *A Star Is Born* (AAN) 37. Three Loves Has Nancy 38. *The Young in Heart* 38. Bernardine 57.
Famous line (*A Star Is Born*): 'Hello, everybody. This is Mrs Norman Maine.'

Gaynor, Mitzi (1930–) (Francesca Mitzi von Gerber).
American light leading lady with singing and dancing talents.
■ My Blue Heaven 50. Take Care of My Little Girl 51. *Golden Girl* 51. We're Not Married 51. Bloodhounds of Broadway 51. The I Don't Care Girl 53. Down Among the Sheltering Palms 53. Three Young Texans 54. There's No Business Like Show Business 54. Anything Goes 56. The Birds and the Bees 56. The Joker is Wild 57. Les Girls 57. *South Pacific* 58. Happy Anniversary 59. Surprise Package 60. For Love or Money 63. For the First Time 69.

Gayson, Eunice (1931–).
British leading lady, also on stage.
Melody in the Dark 48. Dance Hall 50. Street Corner 53. Out of the Clouds 54. Zarak 57. The Revenge of Frankenstein 58. Dr No 62. From Russia with Love 63.

Gazzara, Ben (1930–) (Biagio Gazzara).
American actor, usually of rebellious types.
The Strange One 57. *Anatomy of a Murder* 59. The Young Doctors 61. Convicts Four 62. The Captured City 62. A Rage to Live 65. If It's Tuesday This Must Be Belgium 69. The Bridge at Remagen 69. Husbands 70. When Michael Calls (TV) 71. The Passionate Thief 71. Pursuit (TV) 72. Fireball Forward (TV) 72. The Family Rico (TV) 72. Indict and Convict (TV) 73. The Neptune Factor 73. Maneater (TV) 73. *QB VII* (TV) 74. Capone 75. High Velocity 76. The Sicilian Connection 76. Voyage of the Damned 76. The Killing of a Chinese Bookie 76. The Death of Richie (TV) 77. The Trial of Lee Harvey Oswald (TV) 77. Opening Night 77. Saint Jack 79. Bloodline 79. They all Laughed 81. Inchon 81. Tales of Ordinary Madness 83. The Girl From Trieste 83. An Early Frost (TV) 85. The Professor 86. Il Giorno Prima 87. Secret Obsession/La Mémoire Tatouée 88. Quicker than the Eye 88. Road House 89. Beyond the Ocean/Oltre l'oceano (& co-w, d) 90. Forever 91. Els de Davant (Sp.) 94. Parallel Lives (TV) 94. Swallows Never Die in Jerusalem 94. Farmer and Chase 95. Shadow Conspiracy 97. Buffalo '66 97. Happiness 98. Illuminata 98, etc.
TV series: *Arrest and Trial* 63. *Run for Your Life* 65–67.

Gazzo, Michael V. (1923–1995).
American character actor, screenwriter and playwright.
A Hatful of Rain (co-w, from his play) 57. King Creole (co-w) 58. Godfather Part II (AAN) 74. Black Sunday 77. King of the Gypsies 78. Love and Bullets 79. The Fish that Saved Pittsburg 79. Kill Castro 80. Alligator 80. Fear City 84. Cookie 89, etc.

Geer, Will (1902–1978) (William Ghere).
American character actor with a penchant for sinister old men.
The Misleading Lady 32. Deep Waters 48. Intruder in the Dust 49. Broken Arrow 50. The Tall Target 51. Salt of the Earth 53. Advise and Consent 61. *Seconds* 66. In Cold Blood 67. Bandolero 68. The Reivers 70. Brother John 70. Napoleon and Samantha 72. Executive Action 73. Jeremiah Johnson 73. Moving Violation 76. Billion Dollar Hobo 78, etc.
TV series: *The Waltons* 72–78.

Geesink, Joop (1913–1984).
Dutch puppeteer who in the late 30s made several shorts under the general heading of 'Dollywood'.

Geeson, Judy (1948–).
British leading lady who started with sexy teenage roles.
Berserk 67. To Sir With Love 67. Here We Go Round the Mulberry Bush 67. Prudence and the Pill 68. Hammerhead 68. Three into Two Won't Go 69. The Executioner 69. 10 Rillington Place 70. One of Those Things 71. Who Killed the Mysterious Mr Foster? (TV) 71. Doomwatch 72. Fear in the Night 72. Brannigan 75. The Eagle Has Landed 76. Dominique 78. Inseminoid/Horror Planet 80. The Plague Dogs (voice) 82. Young Goodman Brown 93. Young Goodman Brown 93. To Sir with Love 2 96. Houdini (TV) 98, etc.
TV series: Danger UXB 79. Mad about You 92.

Geeson, Sally (1950–).
British juvenile actress of the 60s, sister of Judy Geeson.
■ What's Good for the Goose 68. Cry of the Banshee 70. The Oblong Box 70. Forbush and the Penguins 71. Carry on Abroad 72. Bless This House 73 (and TV series). Carry on Girls 74.

Geffen, David (1943–).
American producer and record company head, a former agent. Born in Brooklyn, he founded the Asylum record label in 1970 before becoming a top executive at Warner in the mid-70s. He then taught music at Yale, started another record company, and became an independent producer. He set up his own studio in 1994 with partners Jeffrey Katzenberg and Steven Spielberg.
Personal Best 82. Lost in America 85. Little Shop of Horrors 86. Beetlejuice 88. Interview with the Vampire 94, etc.
❝ David is holographic, his advantages multidimensional. He is holding more or better information than his adversary and he is fearless –

having owned his own soul all of his career. – *Linda Obst*

David Geffen is too rich to be anything but cordial with. – *Robert Towne*

Gégauff, Paul (1922–1983).
French screenwriter, actor and novelist, associated with the work of Claude Chabrol and best known for writing and starring with his first wife Danielle in Chabrol's *Une Partie de Plaisir* (in which he also played the soundtrack piano), about a disintegrating marriage. He was stabbed to death by his second wife.

Web of Passion/Á Grand Tour (w) 59. The Girls/ Les Bonnes Femmes (w) 60. Purple Noon/Plein Soleil (co-w) 60. Le Reflux (d) 61. Vice and Virtue/ Le Vice et le Vertu (a) 63. The Champagne Murders/Le Scandale (co-w) 67. Les Biches (co-w) 68. Weekend (a) 68. Killer!/This Man Must Die/ Que Le Bête Meure (w) 69. Love Match/A Piece of Pleasure/Une Partie de Plaisir (a, w) 75, etc.

Gein, Ed (1906–1984).
American murderer who was the model for the character of Norman Bates in *Psycho*, Robert Bloch's novel filmed by Alfred Hitchcock and followed by three sequels from other directors, all starring Anthony Perkins. His characteristics were used for the character of James 'Buffalo Bill' Gumb, played by Ted Levine in *Silence of the Lambs*, filmed by Jonathan Demme from Thomas Harris's novel. He was also the inspiration for *The Texas Chainsaw Massacre* 74, directed by Tobe Hooper, and its sequels, and *Deranged* 74, directed by Alan Ormsby and Jeff Gillen and starring Roberts Blossom. Gein was a solitary mother-dominated farmer who wanted to change sex. He killed two women, dressed in female clothing and wore the skins of dead women, taken from corpses he dug up. Following his trial in 1957 he was committed to an asylum.

Gelbart, Larry (1928–).
American comic screenwriter and playwright. Born in Chicago, he worked in radio and wrote for the TV shows of Bob Hope, Sid Caesar, Red Buttons and other comedians. He was creator of the TV series M*A*S*H 72–83, which he also co-produced, and *Roll Out* 73–74.

Autobiography: 1998, *Laughing Matters: On Writing M*A*S*H, Tootsie, Oh God!, and a Few Other Funny Things*.

The Notorious Landlady (co-w) 62. Not with My Wife You Don't (co-w) 66. The Wrong Box (co-w) (GB) 66. A Funny Thing Happened on the Way to the Forum (oa) (GB) 66. The Chastity Belt (co-w) (It.) 67. A Fine Pair/Ruba al Prossimo Tua (co-w) (It.) 68. Oh God! (w) (AAN) 77. Movie Movie (co-w) 78. Neighbors (w) 81. Tootsie (co-w) (AAN) 82. Blame It on Rio (co-w, ex p) 83. Weapons of Mass Distraction (TV) 97, etc.

TV series: United States 80.

Gélin, Daniel (1921–).
French leading man with stage experience. In films since 1941.

Rendezvous de Juillet 49. *Edouard et Caroline* 50. *La Ronde* 50. Les Mains Sales 51. Rue de l'Estrapade 53. Les Amants du Tage/The Lovers of Lisbon 54. The Man Who Knew Too Much (US) 55. Charmants Garçons 57. There's Always a Price Tag 58. Carthage in Flames 60. The Season for Love 65. Black Sun 66. Le Souffle au Coeur 71. Far from Dallas 72. Trop c'est Trop 74. Nous Irons Tous au Paradis 77. Mister Frost 90. Un Type Bien 91. Les Marmottes 93. Runaways 95. Les Bidochon 96. Hommes, Femmes, Mode d'Emploi 96. Obsession 97, etc.

Gemma, Giuliano (1940–).
Italian leading man of spaghetti westerns.

The Titans 62. Goliath and the Sins of Babylon 63. Adios Gringo 65. A Pistol for Ringo 65. Day of Anger 67. A Man to Respect 72. The Great Battle 78. Corleone 85. Avatar 86. There Are No Men Left (Arg.) 91, etc.

Gemora, Charlie (1903–1961).
American character actor with an unusual speciality: playing gorillas. He also played aliens.

The Gorilla 39. At the Circus 39. The War of the Worlds 53. Phantom of the Rue Morgue 54. I Married a Monster from Outer Space 58. Jack the Giant Killer 62, etc.

Genina, Augusto (1892–1957).
Italian pioneer director.

La Gloria 13. Prix de Beauté 30. The White Squadron 35. Bengasi 42. Heaven Over the Marshes 49. Three Forbidden Stories 52. Maddalena 54. Frou Frou 55, many others.

Genn, Leo (1905–1978).
Bland British character actor, formerly a practising barrister.

Immortal Gentleman 35. Dream Doctor 36. Jump for Glory 37. Kate Plus Ten 38. Contraband 40. The Way Ahead 44. *Henry V* 44. Caesar and Cleopatra 45. *Green for Danger* 46. Mourning Becomes Electra (US) 48. The Velvet Touch (US) 48. *The Snake Pit* (US) 48. The Wooden Horse 50. The Miniver Story 50. *Quo Vadis* (AAN) 51. Plymouth Adventure (US) 52. Personal Affair 53. The Green Scarf 55. Beyond Mombasa 56. Lady Chatterley's Lover (Fr.) 56. Moby Dick 56. I Accuse 57. No Time to Die 58. Too Hot to Handle 60. The Longest Day 62. 55 Days at Peking 62. Ten Little Indians 65. Circus of Fear 67. Connecting Rooms 69. Die Screaming Marianne 70. The Mackintosh Man 73. The Martyr 76, etc.

George, Chief Dan (1899–1981) (Geswanouth Slaholt).
Canadian Indian actor.

■ Smith! 69. *Little Big Man* (AAN) 70. Alien Thunder 73. Harry and Tonto 74. The Bears and I 74. The Outlaw Josey Wales 76. Shadow of the Hawk 76. Americathon 79. Spirit of the Wind 80.

George, Christopher (1931–1983).
American TV leading man.

El Dorado 68. Tiger by the Tail 69. Escape (TV) 69. The Immortal (TV) 69. Man on a String (TV) 72. I Escaped from Devil's Island 73. Grizzly 76. Day of the Animals 77. Whiskey Mountain 77. Mortuary 83, etc.

TV series: The Rat Patrol 66. The Immortal 69, etc.

George, Gladys (1900–1954) (Gladys Clare).
American leading actress with stage experience.

■ Red Hot Dollars 20. Home Spun Folks 20. The Easy Road 21. Chickens 21. The House that Jazz Built 21. Straight is the Way 34. *Valiant Is the World for Carrie* (AAN) 36. They Gave Him a Gun 37. *Madame X* 37. Love is a Headache 38. Marie Antoinette 38. *The Roaring Twenties* 39. Here I Am a Stranger 39. I'm from Missouri 39. A Child is Born 40. The Way of all Flesh 40. The House Across the Bay 40. *The Maltese Falcon* 41. The Lady from Cheyenne 41. Hit the Road 41. The Hard Way 42. Nobody's Darling 43. The Crystal Ball 43. Minstrel Man 44. Christmas Holiday 44. Steppin In Society 45. The Best Years of Our Lives 46. Millie's Daughter 47. Alias a Gentleman 48. Flamingo Road 49. Undercover Girl 50. Bright Leaf 50. He Ran all the Way 51. Detective Story 51. Lullaby of Broadway 51. Dark City 51. Silver City 53. It Happens Every Thursday 54.

George, Götz.
German leading actor.

As Long as the Heart Beats/So Lange das Herz Schlagt 58. Jacqueline 59. Kirmes 60. The Flight/ Die Flucht 63. Kiss and Kill/Der Todekuss des Dr Fu Manchu 68. Wind from the East/Le Vent d'Est 69. Death Is My Trade/Aus Einem Deutschen Leben 77. The Beautiful End of This World 83. Out of Order/Abwarts 84. Dopplespiel 85. Zabou 86. Schtonk! 92. The Deathmaker/Der Totmacher 95. The Sandman/Der Sandman 96. Solo Fuer Klarinette 98, etc.

George, Grace (1879–1961).
American stage actress whose one film, in 1943, was *Johnny Come Lately*.

George, Heinrich (1893–1946).
German leading man of the 20s.

Kean 21. Lady Hamilton 21. Lucretia Borgia 22. Metropolis 26. Dreyfus 30. Jew Suss 40. The Postmaster 40. Kolberg 45.

George, Lynda Day (1944–) (formerly Lynda Day).
American leading lady of the 70s. Started in TV's *Petticoat Junction*; wife of Christopher George.

The Sound of Anger (TV) 68. The House on Greenapple Road (TV) 70. Chisum 71. Set This Town on Fire (TV) 71. She Cried Murder (TV) 73. The Trial of Chaplain Jensen (TV) 75. Murder at the World Series (TV) 77. Cruise into Terror (TV) 78. Casino (TV) 80. The Junkman 82. Mortuary 83, many others.

George, Muriel (1883–1965).
Plump, motherly British character actress who often played charladies or landladies. Music-hall background.

His Lordship (debut) 32. Yes Mr Brown 33. Dr Syn 37. A Sister to Assist 'Er (leading role) 38. Quiet Wedding 40. Dear Octopus 43. The Dancing Years 49. Simon and Laura 55, many others.

George, Screaming Mad (1956–) (Joji Tani).
Japanese-born director and special effects make-up expert in horror movies.

A Nightmare on Elm Street 4: The Dream Master (sfx) 88. The Guyver (co-d) 91. Bride of Re-Animator (sfx) 91. Society (sfx) 92. Necronomicon (sfx) 93. Children of the Corn III 94. Star Kid 97, etc.

George, Susan (1950–).
British leading lady, former child actress; usually typed as sexpot. Also now involved in production.

Billion Dollar Brain 67. The Strange Affair 68. Twinky 68. All Neat in Black Stockings 69. Spring and Port Wine 69. The Looking Glass War 69. Die Screaming Marianne 70. Eye Witness 70. Fright 71. The Straw Dogs 71. Dirty Mary Crazy Larry 73. Sonny and Jed 74. Mandingo 75. Out of Season 75. A Small Town in Texas 76. Tintorea 77. Tomorrow Never Comes 78. Enter the Ninja 81. Venom 82. The Jigsaw Man 84. Lightning 86. Stealing Heaven (p) 88. The Lifeguard 88. That Summer of White Roses (& p) 89, etc.

TV series: Stay Lucky 93.

George, Terry.
British director and screenwriter.

In the Name of the Father (co-w) 93. Some Mother's Son (co-w, d) 96. The Boxer (co-w) 97. A Bright Shining Lie (wd) (TV) 98.

Gérald, Jim (1889–1958) (Jacques Guenod).
French actor, in occasional films from 1911.

An Italian Straw Hat 27. Le Chant du Marin 31. French Without Tears (as le professeur) 39. Boule de Suif 45. The Crimson Curtain 52. Father Brown 54. Fric Frac en Dentelles 57, etc.

Gerard, Gil (1940–).
American leading man who generates a little wisdom amid the derring-do.

Airport 77 76. Ransom for Alice (TV) 77. Killing Stone (TV) 78. Buck Rogers in the Twentieth Century (TV) 79. Hear No Evil (TV) 83, etc.

TV series: Buck Rogers 80–81.

Gerasimov, Sergei (1906–1985).
Russian director, best known abroad for *And Quietly Flows the Don* 57. Formerly an actor.

Geray, Steve (1904–1973) (Stefan Gyergyay).
Hungarian character actor of stage and screen, usually seen as mild-mannered little fellow. In London from 1934, Hollywood from 1941.

Dance Band 34. Inspector Hornleigh 39. Man at Large 41. *The Moon and Sixpence* (as Dirk Stroeve) 42. Night Train from Chungking 43. The Mask of Dimitrios 44. *So Dark the Night* (leading role) 46. *Gilda* 46. I Love Trouble 48. The Big Sky 52. Call Me Madam 53. The Birds and the Bees 56. Count Your Blessings 59. Dime with a Halo 63, many others.

Gere, Richard (1949–).
American leading man, usually in arrogant roles, formerly married to model Cindy Crawford. (Shortly before they separated the couple took out a full-page advertisement in *The Times* to announce, 'We are heterosexual and monogamous and take our commitment to each other very seriously.') A Buddhist, he set up a lobby group, the International Campaign for Tibet, in the early 90s, and in 1997 brought out *Pilgrim*, a book of photographs he had taken in Tibet and the surrounding countries over a 15-year period.

Biography: 1995, *Richard Gere* by John Parker.

Report to the Commissioner 75. Strike Force (TV) 75. Baby Blue Marine 76. Looking for Mr Goodbar 77. Days of Heaven 78. Bloodbrothers 78. *Yanks* 79. American Gigolo 79. An Officer and a Gentleman 82. The Honorary Consul 83. Breathless 83. The Cotton Club 84. King David 85. Power 85. No Mercy 86. Miles from Home 88. Internal Affairs 90. Pretty Woman 90. Rhapsody in August/Hachigatsu-no Kyoshikyoku 91. Final Analysis 92. Mr Jones 93. Sommersby 93. And the Band Played On (TV) 93. Intersection 94. First Knight 95. Primal Fear 96. Red Corner 97. The Jackal 97, etc.

❝ I'm still like this guy who, like, washed his dad's car. I don't feel like I'm some sort of rarefied species of creature. – R.G.

Gering, Marion (1901–1977).
Polish-Russian director with long stage experience; in America from 1925.

The Devil and the Deep 32. Madame Butterfly 33. Jennie Gerhardt 33. Thirty Day Princess 34. Rumba 35. Lady of Secrets 36. Thunder in the City (GB) 37. She Married an Artist 38. Sarumba (& co-p) 50, etc.

Germaine, Mary (1933–).
British leading lady of the 50s.

Laughter in Paradise 51. Where's Charley? 52. Women of Twilight 53. The Green Buddha (last to date) 54, etc.

Germi, Pietro (1914–1974).
Italian director, in films since 1945.

In the Name of the Law 49. The Road to Hope 50. Man of Iron 56. Maledetto Imbroglio/A Sordid Affair 59. Divorce Italian Style (AAw) 61. Seduced and Abandoned 63. The Birds, the Bees and the Italians 65. Alfredo Alfredo 73, many others.

Geronimo (1829–1909).
Apache Indian chief who dealt destruction to the whites.

Memorably impersonated by Chief Thundercloud in *Geronimo* 38, Jay Silverheels in *The Battle at Apache Pass* 52, Chuck Connors in *Geronimo* 62, Wes Studi in *Geronimo: An American Legend* 93.

Gerrard, Gene (1892–1971) (Eugene O'Sullivan).
British music-hall comedian with engaging light style: starred in several comedy musicals of the 30s.

Let's Love and Laugh 31. *My Wife's Family* 31. *Out of the Blue* (& d) 31. Let Me Explain Dear (& d) 32. The Love Nest 33. It's a Bet 35. No Monkey Business 35. Where's Sally? 36. Glamour Girl 37, etc.

Gershenson, Joseph (1904–).
Russian musician, long in US. In films from 1920; head of Universal music department from 1941. Not himself a composer.

House of Dracula 45. Abbott and Costello Meet the Invisible Man 51. Meet Me at the Fair 52. Scarlet Angel 52. It Came from Outer Space 53. Walking My Baby Back Home 53. *The Glenn Miller Story* (AAN) 53. Destry 54. Creature from the Black Lagoon 54. Magnificent Obsession 54. Naked Alibi 54. Ain't Misbehavin' 55. Captain Lightfoot 55. Francis in the Navy 55. *The Benny Goodman Story* 55. The Rawhide Years 55. Revenge of the Creature 55. The Square Jungle 55. The Mole People 56. The Incredible Shrinking Man 56. A Day of Fury 56. Francis in the Haunted House 56. Tammy and the Bachelor 57. The Big Beat 57. Live Fast, Die Young 58. The Thing that Couldn't Die 58. Pillow Talk 59. Imitation of Life 59. Seven Ways from Sundown 60. Spartacus 60. Back Street 61. Posse from Hell 61. The Ugly American 62. Captain Newman, MD 63. The List of Adrian Messenger 63. Island of the Blue Dolphins 64. Shenandoah 65. The War Lord 65. The Rare Breed 65. The Appaloosa 66. Beau Geste 66. The Pad 66. Texas across the River 66. Tobruk 66. Counterpoint 67. Madigan 67. The King's Pirate 67. The Secret War of Harry Frigg 67. *Thoroughly Modern Millie* (AAN) 67. The Hell with Heroes 68. Hellfighters 68. Sweet Charity 68, many others.

Gershon, Gina (1962–).
American actress.

Pretty in Pink 86. Red Heat 88. Cocktail 88. Voodoo Dawn 89. City of Hope 91. Out for Justice 91. Sinatra (TV) 92. The Player 92. Joey Breaker 93. Love Matters 93. Showgirls 95. Bound 96. This World, Then the Fireworks 97. Face/Off 97. Touch 97. Lulu on the Bridge 98. I'm Losing You 98. Legalese (TV) 98. One Tough Cop 98, etc.

❝ I don't consider myself a movie star. I'm not like John Travolta and Nic Cage. I think I will be, though. – G.G.

Gershwin, George (1898–1937) (Jacob Gershowitz).
American popular composer of scores of songs and concert pieces.
Contributed to many films. His biography was told in *Rhapsody in Blue* 45, and his music was used exclusively in *An American in Paris* 51. Three hitherto unpublished songs were even used in *Kiss Me Stupid* 64.
❝ His was a modernity that reflected the civilization we live in as excitingly as the headline in today's newspaper. – *Ira Gershwin*
He was a child of his age who never became old enough to outlive his usefulness. – *Charles Schwartz*

Gershwin, Ira (1896–1983) (Israel Gershowitz).
American lyricist, brother of George GERSHWIN. He wrote for stage from 1918, films from 1931.
Autobiography: 1997, *Lyrics on Several Occasions*.
Book: 1996: *Ira Gershwin: The Art of the Lyricist* by Philip Furia.
Delicious 31. Goldwyn Follies 39. Cover Girl 44. An American in Paris 51. Kiss Me Stupid 64, many others.

Gertsman, Maury (c. 1910–).
American cinematographer.
Strange Confession 45. Terror by Night 46. Singapore 47. Rachel and the Stranger 48. One Way Street 50. Meet Danny Wilson 52. The World in My Corner 55. Kelly and Me 57. Gunfight in Abilene 66, many others.

Gertz, Jami (1965–).
American leading actress. Born in Chicago, she studied at New York University Drama School.
Endless Love 81. Alphabet City 84. Sixteen Candles 84. Mischief 85. Crossroads 86. Quicksilver 86. Solarbabies 86. Less than Zero 87. The Lost Boys 87. Listen to Me 89. Renegades 89. Silence Like Glass/Zwei Frauen 89. Don't Tell Her It's Me 90. Sibling Rivalry 90. Twister 96, etc.
TV series: Square Pegs 82–83. Dreams 84. Sibs 91.

Gessner, Nicolas (1931–).
Hungarian-born director who has worked in France, Germany, Canada and Hollywood.
Diamonds Are Brittle/Un Milliard dans un Billard (Fr.) 65. The Peking Blonde (Fr.) 67. Twelve Plus One (Fr.) 69. The Little Girl Who Lives down the Lane 76. It Rained All Night the Day I Left (Can.) 79. Quicker than the Eye (Fr.) 89. Tennessee Nights 89. Twist of Fate 91, etc.

Getchell, Robert.
American screenwriter.
■ Alice Doesn't Live Here Any More (AAN) 74. Bound for Glory (AAN) 76. Mommie Dearest (co-w) 81. Sweet Dreams 85. Stella 90. This Boy's Life (co-w) 93. Point of No Return (co-w) 93. The Client (co-w) 94.

Getino, Octavio (1935–).
Spanish-born director, cinematographer and film theorist. In Argentina from the early 50s, he co-founded with Fernando SOLANAS the influential radical collective CINE LIBERACIÓN, and worked with Solanas on the clandestine political documentary *The Hour of the Furnaces* 68. Following the return of Perón as president in the mid-70s, he was briefly Argentina's film censor, relaxing the harsh regime, though he was soon displaced by a harsher incumbent. He left Argentina in 1976 and settled in Peru to work as a teacher, resisting attempts to extradite him by Argentina's military rulers, and moving to Mexico in the 80s.
El Familiar 73, etc.

Getty, Balthazar (1975–).
American teenage actor.
Lord of the Flies 90. Young Guns II 90. My Heroes Have Always Been Cowboys 91. The Pope Must Die/The Pope Must Diet 91. Red Hot 92. Where the Day Takes You 92. Dead Beat 94. Don't Do It 94. Natural Born Killers 94. Judge Dredd 95. Lost Highway 97, etc.

Getty, Estelle (1923–) (E. Scher).
American character actress and comedian, best known for playing Sophie Petrillo in a trio of TV sitcoms.
Tootsie 82. The Chosen 82. Protocol 84. Mask 84. Mannequin 87. Stop! Or My Mom Will Shoot 92, etc.
TV series: *The Golden Girls* 85–92. The Golden Palace 92–93. Empty Nest 93–95.

Geva, Tamara (1906–1997).
Russian-born ballet dancer, in America from the late 20s. Born in St Petersburg, she appeared in Broadway musicals before making a few film appearances in the 30s. She claimed her movie career had been cut short by the plastic surgeons who took too much off her nose. Her three husbands included choreographer George BALANCHINE and actor John EMERY.
The Girl Habit 31. Their Big Moment 34. Manhattan Merry-Go-Round 37. Orchestra Wives 42. Night Plane from Chungking 43. The Gay Intruders 48. The Specter of the Rose (ch only) 46, etc.

Ghatak, Ritwik (1925–1976).
Indian director, screenwriter and author, from the theatre. A Communist, he was hospitalized for schizophrenia in the 70s and died from alcoholic poisoning.
The Citizen/Nagarik 53. Pathetic Fallacy/Ajantrik 58. The Runaway/Bari Theke Paliye 59. The Cloud Capped Star/Meghe Dhaka Tara 60. E Flat/Komal Gandhar 61. Subarnarekha 65. A River Called Titah/Titash Ekti Nadir Naam 73. Reason, Argument and Story/Jukti Takko Ar Gappo 74, etc.

Gherardi, Piero (1909–1971).
Italian production and costume designer.
Daniele Cortis 46. Her Favourite Husband 50. Nights of Cabiria/Le Notti di Cabiria 56. Big Deal on Madonna Street 58. La Dolce Vita (AAN) 59. 8½ (AAN) 63. Juliet of the Spirits (AAN) 65. The Appointment 69. Quemada! 69, many others.

Gherman, Alexei:
see GUERMAN, Alexei.

Ghose, Goutam (1950–).
Indian director and screenwriter, a former maker of documentaries.
Our Land/Ma Bhoomi 79. The Occupation/Dakhai 82. The Crossing/Paar 84. The Voyage Beyond/Antarjali Yatra 88. Boatman of the River Padma/Padma Nadir Majhi 93. The Kite/Patang 94, etc.

Ghostley, Alice (1926–).
American revue comedienne and character actress.
New Faces 54. To Kill a Mockingbird 62. My Six Loves 63. The Flim Flam Man 67. Viva Max 68. Ace Eli and Rodger of the Skies 72. Not for Publication 84. The Wrong Guys 88. Perry Mason: The Case of the Silenced Singer (TV) 90. The Odd Couple II 98, etc.
TV series: The Jackie Gleason Show 62–64. Captain Nice 67. The Jonathan Winters Show 68–69. Bewitched 69–72. Mayberry, RFD 70–71. Nichols 71–72. The Julie Andrews Show 72–73. Temperature Rising 74. Designing Woman 87–93. Small Wonder 88–89.

Giallelis, Stathis (1939–).
Greek actor who went to Hollywood.
America America 63. Cast a Giant Shadow 66. The Eavesdropper 67. The Blue 68. Requiem (Yug.) 70. Panagulis Lives (It.) 80, etc.

Giannetti, Alfredo (1924–1995).
Italian screenwriter and director, often associated with the films of Pietro Germi; worked mainly in television from the mid-70s.
A Husband for Anna/Un Marito per Anna Zaccheo (co-w) 53. The Railroad Man (co-w) 56. The Straw Man/L'Uomo di Paglia (co-w) 57. The Facts of Murder/Un Maledetto Imbroglio (co-w) 59. Giorno per Giorno Disperatamente (wd) 61. Divorce, Italian Style (co-w) (AA) 62. Regazza in Prestita (wd) 64. Serafino (story) 68. La Sciantosa (wd) 70. L'Automobile (d) 71. Il Bandito dagli Occhi Azzurri (d) 80. Legati da Tenera Amicizia (d) 83, etc.

Giannini, Giancarlo (1942–).
Italian leading actor.
Rita the Mosquito 66. Anzio 68. The Secret of Santa Vittoria 69. The Pizza Triangle 70. The Seduction of Mimi 72. The Sensual Man 73. Swept Away 74. *Seven Beauties* (AAN) 76. The Innocent 76. A Night Full of Rain 77. Travels with Anita 79. Suffer or Die 79. American Dreamer 84. Fever Pitch 85. Saving Grace 86. Ternosecco (& d) 86. Snack Bar Budapest 88. Blood Red 89. Brown Bread Sandwiches 89. New York Stories 89. The Sleazy Uncle/Lo Zio Indegno 89. Le Raccourci 91. Black Heart/Nero come il Cuore 91. Once Upon a Crime 92. Colpo di Coda 92. Giovanni Falcone 93. Come Due Coccodrilli 94. A Walk in the Clouds (US) 95. Palermo – Milan No Return 95. The She Wolf/La Lupa 96. Scirocco 98, etc.

Gibbons, Cedric (1893–1960).
Elegant and influential American art director. Born in Dublin and educated privately in Europe, he worked in his father's architect's office in New York before becoming an assistant to Hugo BALLIN at Edison, 1915–17, where he insisted on the use of three-dimensional sets rather than painted backdrops, then going on to work for GOLDWYN, 1918–23, and MGM, which he joined at its inception in 1924. His contract specified that his name appear on all films produced by the studio in the USA, which numbered more than 1,000 by the time of his retirement in 1956. He also designed the Oscar statuette, and his art department went on to win 11 of them. He directed one film, *Tarzan and His Mate* 34. (In MGM's first Tarzan film, one of the savage tribes is named the Gibbonies in his honour.) The first of his two wives was actress Dolores COSTELLO (1930–41).
Thais 17. The Return of Tarzan 20. Madame X 20. Ben Hur 25. The Big Parade 25. The Student Prince 27. The Crowd 28. The Bridge of the San Luis Rey (AA) 28. When Ladies Meet (AAN) 32. The Merry Widow (AA) 34. The Great Ziegfeld (AAN) 36. Romeo and Juliet (AAN) 36. Conquest (AAN) 37. Marie Antoinette 38. The Wizard of Oz (AAN) 39. Pride and Prejudice (AA) 40. Bitter Sweet (AAN) 40. When Ladies Meet (AAN) 41. Blossoms in the Dust (AA) 41. Random Harvest (AAN) 42. Madame Curie (AAN) 43. Thousands Cheer (AAN) 43. Gaslight (AA) 44. Kismet (AAN) 44. The Picture of Dorian Gray (AAN) 45. National Velvet (AAN) 45. The Yearling (AA) 46. Madame Bovary (AAN) 49. Little Women (AA) 49. The Red Danube (AAN) 50. Annie Get Your Gun (AAN) 50. Too Young to Kiss (AAN) 51. An American in Paris (AA) 51. Quo Vadis (AAN) 51. The Bad and the Beautiful (AA) 52. The Merry Widow (AAN) 52. Lili (AAN) 53. The Story of Three Loves (AAN) 53. Young Bess (AAN) 53. Julius Caesar (AA) 53. Executive Suite (AAN) 54. Brigadoon (AAN) 54. Blackboard Jungle (AAN) 55. I'll Cry Tomorrow (AAN) 55. Somebody Up There Likes Me (AA) 56. Lust for Life (AAN) 56, many others.
❝ When I find things I like, I see no reason to change them. Except women. – C.G.

Gibbs, Anthony (1925–).
British editor.
Oscar Wilde 60. A Taste of Honey 61. Tom Jones 63. The Knack 64. Petulia 68. Performance 70. Fiddler on the Roof 71. Jesus Christ Superstar 74. Juggernaut 75. Rollerball 75. A Bridge Too Far 77. F.I.S.T. 78. The Dogs of War 81. Ragtime 81. Dune 84. Tai-Pan 86. Stealing Home 88. In Country 89. The Taking of Beverly Hills 91. Devlin 92. The Man without a Face 93, etc.

Gibbs, Gerald (1907–1990).
British cinematographer. He joined Stoll Pictures at its Cricklewood Studios as a camera assistant in 1928, staying until the studio closed in 1938. In the early 40s, he worked for Ealing, and was later with British National.
Cod – A Mellow Drama (co-d) 28. No Orchids for Miss Blandish 48. Whisky Galore 49. Alice in Wonderland 49. The Accused 53. X the Unknown 56. Blue Murder at St Trinian's 57. Quatermass 2/Enemy from Outer Space 57. The Man Upstairs 58. The Pure Hell of St Trinian's 60. A Prize of Arms 61. Station Six Sahara 62. The Leather Boys 63. The Curse of Simba 64. Mister Ten Per Cent 67, etc.

Gibbs, Michael (1937–) (Michael Irving).
South African-born composer, arranger, jazz trombonist, pianist and bandleader, in America from the mid-70s and since busy there and in Europe.
Heat 87. Housekeeping 87. American Roulette 88. Riding the Edge 89. Breaking In 89. Iron & Silk 91. Whore 91. Close My Eyes 91. Century 93. Being Human 94, etc.

Gibney, Sheridan (1903–1988).
American screenwriter.
I Am a Fugitive from a Chain Gang 32. The World Changes 33. The Story of Louis Pasteur (AA) 36. Green Pastures 36. Letter of Introduction 38. Disputed Passage 39. Cheers for Miss Bishop 41. Once Upon a Honeymoon 42. Our Hearts Were Young and Gay 44. The Locket 47, etc.

Gibson, Alan (1938–1987).
Canadian director in Britain.
■ Crescendo 69. Goodbye Gemini 70. Dracula AD 1972 72. The Satanic Rites of Dracula 73. Crash 77. Churchill and the Generals (TV) 79. A Woman Called Golda (TV) 82. Witness for the Prosecution (TV) 82. Martin's Day 84.

Gibson, Brian (1944–).
British director, from TV.
Breaking Glass 80. Poltergeist II: The Other Side 86. The Josephine Baker Story (TV) 90. What's Love Got to Do with It? 93. The Juror 96. Wilde 97. Still Crazy 98, etc.

Gibson, Helen (1892–1977) (Rose August Wenger).
American leading lady of the silent screen; of Swiss descent; married to Hoot Gibson. Former stuntgirl. Appeared in *Hollywood Story* 51.
The Hazards of Helen (serial) 15. No Man's Woman 20. The Wolverine 21, etc.

Gibson, Henry (1935–).
Diminutive American comedy character actor who came to the fore in TV's *Laugh-In*.
Kiss Me Stupid 64. Evil Roy Slade (TV) 72. Nashville 75. The Last Remake of Beau Geste 78. Amateur Night at the Dixie Bar and Grill (TV) 79. A Perfect Couple 79. Health 80. The Blues Brothers 80. The Incredible Shrinking Woman 81. Monster in the Closet 86. Innerspace 87. Long Gone (TV) 87. Switching Channels 88. Tune in Tomorrow/Aunt Julia and the Scriptwriter 90. Bio-Dome 96. Color of a Brisk and Leaping Day 96. A Stranger in the Kingdom 98, etc.

Gibson, Hoot (1892–1962) (Edward Richard).
American cowboy hero of silent films; in Hollywood from 1911 after real cowpunching experience. Films good-humoured but not memorable. He ended his career as a greeter at a Los Angeles night-club. His third wife was actress Sally Eilers.
The Hazards of Helen 15. The Cactus Kid 19. The Denver Dude 22. Surefire 24. Galloping Fury 27. Points West 29. Spirit of the West 32. Powdersmoke Range 35. Sunset Range 35. The Marshal's Daughter 53. The Horse Soldiers 59. Ocean's Eleven 61, many others.
~Allegedly, his name became Hoot because he loved to go owl-hunting.

Gibson, Mel (1956–).
American-born leading actor, in Australia from childhood. After graduating from the National Institute of Dramatic Arts in 1977, he began in the theatre before the Mad Max movies catapulted him to stardom. His asking price: around $15m a movie.
Biography: 1993, *Lethal Hero* by Roland Perry; 1997, *Mel Gibson* by Brian Pendreigh.
Book: 1998, *The Films of Mel Gibson* by John McCarty.
■ Summer City 77. Tim 79. Mad Max 79. Gallipoli 81. Mad Max II/The Road Warrior 81. Attack Force Z 82. The Year of Living Dangerously 83. The Bounty 84. The River 84. Mrs Soffel 84. Mad Max Beyond Thunderdome 85. Lethal Weapon 87. Tequila Sunrise 88. Lethal Weapon 2 89. Air America 90. Bird on a Wire 90. Hamlet 90. Lethal Weapon 3 92. The Man without a Face (& d) 93. Maverick 94. *Braveheart* (AAd, AANp) 95. Pocahontas (voice) 95. Ransom 96. Fairytale: A True Story (uncredited) 97. Father's Day (uncredited) 97. Conspiracy Theory 97. Lethal Weapon 4 98.
❝ He seems to think he's Lee Marvin. Except he's two feet shorter. And about one third the talent. – *John Boorman*

Gibson, Thomas (1962–).
American actor.
Far and Away 92. The Age of Innocence 93. Love and Human Remains 93. Barcelona 94. Sleep

with Me 94. Men of War 94. The Next Step 95. The Devil's Child (TV) 97. More Tales of the City (TV) 98, etc.
TV series: Chicago Hope 96–97. Dharma & Gregg 97.

Gibson, Wynne (1899–1987).
American leading lady, from the chorus.
Nothing But the Truth 30. Ladies of the Big House 32. I Give My Love 34. The Captain Hates the Sea 34. Gangs of New York 38. Café Hostess 40. The Falcon Strikes Back 43, many others.

Gidding, Nelson (1915–).
American screenwriter.
I Want to Live (AAN) 58. Odds against Tomorrow 59. Nine Hours to Rama 61. The Inspector 62. The Haunting 64. Lost Command 66. The Andromeda Strain 70. The Hindenburg 75. Beyond the Poseidon Adventure 79. Wheels of Terror 87. Shogun Mayeda 92. The Mummy Lives 93, etc.

Giehse, Therese (1898–1975).
German stage actress whose occasional films included *Kinder, Mutter und Ein General* 58 and *Black Moon* 75.

Gielgud, Sir John (1904–).
Distinguished British stage actor and director, for whom cinema has been a secondary matter. On stage from the early 20s, he made his reputation playing Shakespeare at the Old Vic in the 30s, establishing himself as a pre-eminent speaker of verse, particularly in the roles of Romeo and Hamlet and, later, Prospero. In the 70s, he formed a notable partnership with Ralph Richardson in modern plays by Pinter and David Storey, but his greatness has been captured rarely on film.
Autobiographies: 1953, *Early Stages*. 1972, *Distinguished Company*. 1979, *An Actor in His Time*.
Who Is the Man? 24. The Clue of the New Pin 29. Insult 32. The Good Companions 32. Secret Agent 36. The Prime Minister (as Disraeli) 40. *Julius Caesar* (as Cassius) 53. Richard III 56. The Barretts of Wimpole Street 57. Saint Joan 57. Becket (AAN) 64. The Loved One 65. Chimes at Midnight 66. Around the World in 80 Days 66. Sebastian 67. *The Charge of the Light Brigade* 68. Assignment to Kill 68. The Shoes of the Fisherman 68. Oh What a Lovely War 69. Julius Caesar 70. Eagle in a Cage 71. Probe (TV) 72. Lost Horizon 73. Frankenstein, the True Story (TV) 73. QB VII (TV) 74. 11 Harrowhouse 74. Luther 74. Gold 74. *Murder on the Orient Express* 74. Galileo 75. Aces High 76. Joseph Andrews 77. *Providence* 77. Murder by Decree 79. Les Misérables (TV) 79. A Portrait of the Artist as a Young Man 79. Caligula 79. The Human Factor 79. The Elephant Man 80. The Formula 80. The Seven Dials Mystery (TV) 80. Marco Polo (TV) 80. *Arthur* (AA) 81. Sphinx 81. Lion of the Desert 81. Chariots of Fire 81. Priest of Love 81. *Brideshead Revisited* (TV) 81. Gandhi 82. Wagner (TV) 82. The Conductor 82. The Scarlet and the Black (TV) 82. Inside the Third Reich (TV) 82. The Wicked Lady 83. Invitation to a Wedding 83. Wagner 83. The Shooting Party 84. Scandalous 84. The Far Pavilions (TV) 84. The Master of Ballantrae (TV) 84. Camille (TV) 85. Romance on the Orient Express (TV) 86. The Whistle Blower 86. Plenty 86. War and Remembrance (TV) 88. Barbablu Barbablu 88. Appointment with Death 88. Arthur 2: On the Rocks 88. Getting It Right 89. Strike It Rich 89. Prospero's Books 91. Shining Through 92. The Power of One 92. First Knight 95. Haunted 95. Gulliver's Travels (TV) 96. Shine 96. The Leopard Son (narrator) 96. The Portrait of a Lady 96. A Dance to the Music of Time (TV) 97. Merlin (TV) 98. Quest for Camelot 98. Elizabeth 98. The Tichborne Claimant 98, etc.
❝ John has a dignity, a majesty which suggests that he was born with a crown on his head. – *Sir Laurence Olivier*
The finest actor on earth from the neck up. – *Kenneth Tynan*
When Gielgud speaks the verse, I can hear Shakespeare *thinking*. – *Lee Strasberg*

Gifford, Alan (1905–1989).
American character actor in British films.
It Started in Paradise 52. Lilacs in the Spring 54. The Iron Petticoat 56. A King in New York 57. Too Young to Love 60. Carry On Cowboy 66. Arrivederci Baby 66. Phase IV 73, etc.

Gifford, Frances (1922–1994).
American leading lady of the 40s, trained as lawyer. Career subsequently halted by ill-health.
Hold That Woman 40. Jungle Girl 41. My Son Alone 42. Tarzan Triumphs 43. She Went to the Races 45. Little Mister Jim 46. Luxury Liner 48. Riding High 49. Sky Commando 53, etc.

Giger, Hans.
Influential Swiss artist whose creations have enlivened science-fiction films of the 80s and 90s.
Alien 79. Poltergeist II 85. Aliens 86. The Mirror 88. Alien³ 92. Species 95, etc.

Gigli, Beniamino (1890–1957).
Famous Italian tenor who starred in several films.
Forget Me Not 35. Ave Maria 37. Pagliacci 42. Night Taxi 50, etc.

Gilbert, Billy (1893–1971).
American character comedian usually seen as a fat, excitable Italian. In films since 1929, after vaudeville experience; a memorable stooge for Laurel and Hardy, the Three Stooges and the Marx Brothers.
Noisy Neighbours (debut) 29. The Music Box 32. Sutter's Gold 37. Snow White and the Seven Dwarfs (as the voice of Sneezy) 37. Blockheads 38. Destry Rides Again 39. *The Great Dictator* (as Goering) 40. *His Girl Friday* 40. Tin Pan Alley 41. Anchors Aweigh 45. Down among the Sheltering Palms 52. Five Weeks in a Balloon 62, many others.

Gilbert, Brian.
British director, from television.
Sharma and Beyond (TV) 84. The Frog Prince/French Lesson 84. Vice Versa 88. Not without My Daughter 91. Tom and Viv 94, etc.

Gilbert, Herschel Burke (1918–).
American composer and conductor.
Mr District Attorney 47. Shamrock Hill 49. There's a Girl in My Heart 49. Three Husbands 50. The Scarf 51. Without Warning 52. The Ring 52. The Thief (AAN) 52. No Time for Flowers 52. Sabre Jet 53. Vice Squad 53. Riot in Cell Block 11 54. Carmen Jones (AAN) 54. While the City Sleeps 56. Beyond a Reasonable Doubt 56. The Naked Hills 56. No Place to Hide 56. Slaughter on Tenth Avenue 57. Crime and Punishment USA 59. Sam Whiskey 69. I Dismember Mama 72, etc.

Gilbert, John (1895–1936) (John Pringle).
American leading man of the 20s. From a theatrical family, he worked his way from bit parts to romantic leads, but sound revealed his voice to be less dashing than his looks. The character of the alcoholic Norman Maine in *A Star Is Born* was based on him.
Biography: 1985, *Dark Star* by Leatrice Gilbert Fountain with John R. Maxim.
■ Hell's Hinges 16. Bullets and Brown Eyes 16. The Apostle of Vengeance 16. The Phantom 16. The Eye of the Night 16. Shell 43 16. The Princess of the Dark 16. Happiness 16. The Millionaire Vagrant 16. Golden Rule Kate 16. Hater of Men 17. The Devil Dodger 17. Nancy Comes Home 18. More Trouble 18. Shackled 18. Three X Gordon 18. Wedlock 18. The Mask 18. The Dawn of Understanding 18. White Heather 19. The Busher 19. Heart o' the Hills 19. The Red Viper 19. Should Women Tell? 19. Widow By Proxy 19. The Servant in the House 20. The Great Redeemer 20. The White Circle 20. Deep Waters 21. Ladies Must Live 21. Gleam o' Dawn 22. Monte Cristo 22. Arabian Love 22. The Yellow Stain 22. Honor First 22. Calvert's Valley 22. The Love Gambler 22. While Paris Sleeps 22. Truxten King 23. The Madness of Youth 23. Saint Elmo 23. *Cameo Kirby* 23. A California Romance 23. Just Off Broadway 24. The Wolf Man 24. A Man's Mate 24. The Lone Ranch 24. Romance Ranch 24. His Hour 24. He Who Gets Slapped 24. The Snob 24. The Wife of the Centaur 25. *The Merry Widow* 25. *The Big Parade* 25. La Boheme 26. Bardelys the Magnificent 26. *Flesh and the Devil* 27. The Show 27. Twelve Miles Out 27. *Love* 27. Man, Woman and Sin 28. The Cossacks 28. Four Walls 28. Marks of the Devil 28. A Woman of Affairs 29. Desert Nights 29. Hollywood Revue 29. His Glorious Night (the talkie which killed his romantic image) 29. Redemption 30. Way for a Sailor 30. Gentleman's Fate 30. The Phantom of Paris 31. West of Broadway 32. Downstairs 32. Fast Workers 33. Queen Christina 33. The Captain Hates the Sea 35.

Gilbert, Lewis (1920–).
British director, former actor and documentarist.
■ The Little Ballerina 47. Marry Me (w only) 49. Once a Sinner 50. There Is Another Sun 50. The Scarlet Thread 51. Emergency Call 52. Time Gentlemen Please 52. Cosh Boy 53. Johnny on the Run 53. *Albert RN* 53. The Sea Shall Not Have Them 54. *The Good Die Young* 54. Cast a Dark Shadow 55. *Reach for the Sky* 56. The Admirable Crichton 57. Carve Her Name with Pride 57. A Cry from the Streets 58. Ferry to Hong Kong 59. *Sink The Bismarck* 60. Light Up the Sky 60. The Greengage Summer 61. HMS Defiant 62. The Seventh Dawn 64. Alfie 66. You Only Live Twice 67. The Adventurers 70. Friends (& w) 71. Paul and Michelle 73. Operation Daybreak 75. Seven Nights in Japan 76. The Spy Who Loved Me 77. Moonraker 79. Educating Rita 83. Not Quite Jerusalem 84. Shirley Valentine 89. Stepping Out 91. Haunted 95.
❝ Paramount backed *Alfie* because it was going to be made for £500,000, normally the sort of money spent on executives' cigar bills. – *L.G.*

Gilbert, Olive (1898–1981).
Welsh contralto, in opera and musical comedy.
■ Glamorous Night 37. The Dancing Years 50. King's Rhapsody (voice only) 55.

Gilbert, Paul (1917–1976) (Paul MacMahon).
American comedy dancer, former trapezist.
So This Is Paris 55. The Second Greatest Sex 55. You Can't Run Away from It 56. Women of the Prehistoric Planet 66, etc.
TV series: The Duke 54.

Gilbert, W. S. (1836–1911) (William Schwenck).

Sullivan, Sir Arthur (1842–1900).
Celebrated British composers (words and music respectively) of the Savoy operas of the 80s, most cherished for their comic aspects and still performed all over the world by the D'Oyly Carte Company. Many film versions have been made, notably of *The Mikado*. In 1954 came a moderate biopic, *The Story of Gilbert and Sullivan*, with Robert Morley and Maurice Evans.

Gilbreth, Elizabeth (1908–).
American author of *Cheaper by the Dozen* and *Belles on Their Toes*, two books of reminiscences which centre on her father, who tried to apply his time-and-motion-study techniques to bringing up his large family.

Gilchrist, Connie (1901–1985) (Rose Gilchrist).
American character actress of stage and screen.
Billy the Kid 41. The Hucksters 47. A Letter to Three Wives 49. The Man in the Grey Flannel Suit 56. Some Came Running 58. Auntie Mame 59. Say One For Me 59. A House Is Not a Home 64. Sylvia 65. Tickle Me 65. Fuzz 70, etc.
TV series: Long John Silver 55.

Giler, David.
American screenwriter with many TV credits.
Myra Breckinridge (co-w) 70. The Parallax View (co-w) 74. The Black Bird (& d) 75. Fun with Dick and Jane (co-w) 77. Alien (co-w) 79. Southern Comfort (co-w) 81. The Money Pit 86. Aliens (co-story) 86. Alien³ (co-w, p) 92. Tales from the Crypt Presents the Demon Knight (p) 95, etc.

Gilford, Jack (1907–1990) (Jacob Gellman).
American comic actor with long stage career.
Hey Rookie 53. Main Street to Broadway 53. A Funny Thing Happened on the Way to the Forum 66. Mister Buddwing 66. Enter Laughing 67. The Happening 67. Who's Minding the Mint? 67. They Might Be Giants 71. Catch 22 71. *Save the Tiger* (AAN) 73. Harry and Walter Go to New York 76. Wholly Moses 80. Caveman 81. Hotel (TV) 82. Cocoon 85. Cocoon: The Return 88. Arthur 2 On the Rocks 88, etc.
TV series: Paul Sand in Friends and Lovers 74–75. Apple Pie 78. The Duck Factory 84.

Gill, Basil (1877–1955).
British leading actor in silent films, from the stage.
Henry VIII 11. The Admirable Crichton 18. God's Good Man 19. The Worldlings 20. High Treason 29. The School for Scandal 30. The Wandering Jew 33. The Immortal Gentleman 35. Rembrandt 36. Knight without Armour 37. St Martin's Lane/Sidewalks of London 38. The Citadel 38. Dangerous Medicine 38, etc.

Gill, Maude.
English character actress, from the stage, best known for playing the role of Thirza Tapper in the long-running *The Farmer's Wife*, which she repeated on (silent) film for Hitchcock.
Autobiography: 1938, *See the Players*.
The Farmer's Wife 28. Glorious Youth 28. The Price of Divorce 28. Under the Greenwood Tree 29. A Sister to Assist 'Er 30. Excess Baggage 33. Lilies of the Field 34. Look Up and Laugh 35. Love at Sea 36. Keep Your Seats Please 36, etc.
❝ I have met with a certain amount of recognition. For years I was well known to the army of fierce little boys who guard the outer offices of theatrical agents as a woman to whom they had to say at once: 'Sorry! Nothing doing.' – M.G.
Once an uncomplimentary friend asked me if I preferred the Films to acting! – M.G.

Gilles, Geneviève (1946–) (Genevieve Gillaizeau).
French leading lady, protégée of Darryl Zanuck.
■ World of Fashion (short) 67. Hello – Goodbye 69.

Gillespie, A. Arnold (1899–1978).
American art director, at MGM and, from the mid-30s, in charge of the studio's special effects department, responsible for the earthquake in *San Francisco* 36, the tornado in *The Wizard of Oz* (AAN) 39, and similar effects.
AS ART DIRECTOR: Ben-Hur 25. The Crowd 28. Eskimo 33. Tarzan and His Mate 34. Mutiny on the Bounty 35. Captains Courageous 37, etc.
AS FX DIRECTOR: Boom Town (AAN) 40. Flight Command (AAN) 40. Mrs Miniver (AAN) 42. Stand By for Action (AAN) 43. Thirty Seconds over Tokyo (AA) 44. They Were Expendable (AAN) 45. Green Dolphin Street (AA) 47. Plymouth Adventure (AA) 52. Forbidden Planet (AAN) 56. Ben-Hur (AA) 59. Mutiny on the Bounty (AAN) 62, etc.

Gillespie, John Birks 'Dizzy' (1917–1993).
Distinguished and innovative American jazz trumpeter, composer, singer and actor.
Jazz Is Our Religion (doc) 72. A Night in Havana: Dizzy Gillespie in Cuba (doc) 90. The Winter in Lisbon (a, m) 92.

Gillette, William (1855–1937).
American stage actor famous for his personification of *Sherlock Holmes*, which he played on film in 1916.

Gilliam, Terry (1940–).
American director, writer and artist, in Britain from the mid-60s. He was first noticed for his animated cartoons for Monty Python's Flying Circus, and co-directed the group's first film. Some of his later films have been marked by controversy: *Baron Munchausen* became a casualty of studio in-fighting when it went over budget, and he had difficulty getting his cut of *Brazil* shown in the US.
AS DIRECTOR: Jabberwocky 76. Time Bandits 81. Brazil 85. The Adventures of Baron Munchhausen 88. The Fisher King 91. Twelve Monkeys 95. Fear and Loathing in Las Vegas (US) 98.
❝ When I'm making a film, my biggest problem is keeping myself from getting so depressed that I can't function. – *T.G.*
The success of the Hollywood marketing machine is to limit what we see. Not just to limit what we can see, but also to limit our expectations – to limit what we want to see. – *T.G.*
Terry will never grow up. He had his chance about 20 years ago and he bungled it. – *Michael Palin*

Gilliat, Leslie (1917–).
British producer, most often in collaboration with his brother, Sidney GILLIAT. Born in New Malden, Surrey, he began as an assistant director for Gainsborough.

Gilliat, Sidney (1908–1994).
British comedy screenwriter usually in collaboration with Frank LAUNDER; they also produced most of their films since the 40s.
Rome Express 33. *Friday the Thirteenth* 33. Jack Ahoy 34. Chu Chin Chow 34. Bulldog Jack 35. Where There's a Will 36. Seven Sinners 36. Take My Tip 37. *A Yank at Oxford* 38. *The Lady Vanishes* 38. The Gaunt Stranger 38. Jamaica Inn 39. *Ask*

a Policeman 39. They Came by Night 40. *Night Train to Munich* 40. Kipps 41. *The Young Mr Pitt* 42. Millions Like Us (& d) 43. *Waterloo Road* (& d) 44. *The Rake's Progress* (& d) 45. *Green for Danger* (& d) 46. London Belongs to Me (& d) 48. *State Secret* (& d) 50. The Story of Gilbert and Sullivan (& d) 53. The Constant Husband (& d) 55. Fortune is a Woman (& d) 57. Left Right and Centre (& d) 59. *Only Two Can Play* (& d) 62. The Great St Trinian's Train Robbery (& d) 65. Endless Night 72, etc.

Gilliatt, Penelope (1933–1993).
British critic and screenwriter. She was the third wife of playwright John Osborne.
Sunday Bloody Sunday (AAN) 72.

Gillie, Jean (1915–1949).
British leading lady, former chorine.
School for Stars 35. Brewster's Millions 35. While Parents Sleep 36. Sweet Devil 38. Tilly of Bloomsbury 40. Sailors Don't Care 40. The Gentle Sex 43. *Tawny Pipit* 44. Decoy (US) 47. The Macomber Affair (US) 47, etc.

Gillin, William (1868–1942).
English showman who became one of the first travelling cinema operators in the north of England in the 1900s. From the 1910s he turned to performing as a ventriloquist, using a dummy that walked off the stage on its own at the end of his act.

Gilling, John (1910–1984).
British writer-director who turned out dozens of crime and adventure pot-boilers after the war.
The Greed of William Hart (w) 48. The Man from Yesterday (wd) 49. No Trace (wd) 50. Mother Riley Meets the Vampire (wd) 52. The Voice of Merrill (d) 52. The Gamma People (wd) 55. Odongo (wd) 56. Interpol (wd) 57. High Flight (d) 57. The Man Inside (wd) 58. Idol on Parade (d) 59. The Flesh and the Fiends (wd) 59. The Challenge (wd) 60. Fury at Smuggler's Bay (wd) 61. Shadow of the Cat (wd) 62. Pirates of Blood River (wd) 62. The Scarlet Blade (wd) 63. The Brigand of Kandahar (wd) 64. The Plague of the Zombies (wd) 65. The Mummy's Shroud (wd) 67, many others.

Gillingwater, Claude (1870–1939).
Lofty American character actor who came to films in middle age to play irascible old men. Born in Lauseanna, Missouri, he ran away from home to join a touring repertory company, and also worked on the New York stage. He shot himself, leaving a note that read: 'I am ending my life because, in my advanced age, in my physical condition, there is no chance of ever being well again and I will not permit myself to become a helpless lingering invalid.'
Little Lord Fauntleroy 21. Dulcy 23. Daddies 24. Daddy Long Legs 31. The Captain Hates the Sea 34. A Tale of Two Cities 36. Prisoner of Shark Island 36. Conquest 37. Café Society 39, etc.

Gillis, Ann (1927–) (Alma O'Connor).
American child star of the 30s; adult roles routine. Now retired and living in Belgium.
The Garden of Allah 37. Off to the Races 37. *The Adventures of Tom Sawyer* 38. The Underpup 39. Little Men 40. Nice Girl 41. In Society 44. Since You Went Away 44. Janie Gets Married 46. 2001: A Space Odyssey 68, etc.

Gillmore, Margalo (1897–1986).
American stage actress in occasional films.
Wayward 32. Perfect Strangers 50. The Law and the Lady 51. Skirts Ahoy 52. Woman's World 54. Gaby 56. High Society 56, etc.

Gilmore, Lowell (1907–1960).
American general-purpose actor.
The Picture of Dorian Gray 44. Calcutta 47. Dream Girl 48. Tripoli 50. Lone Star 52. Plymouth Adventure 52. Saskatchewan 54, etc.

Gilmore, Peter (1931–).
British light actor, familiar on TV as the hero of *The Onedin Line* 71–80.
Bomb in the High Street 61. Carry on Jack 64. Doctor in Clover 66. My Lover My Son 69. The Abominable Dr Phibes 71. Warlords of Atlantis 78. The Lonely Passion of Judith Hearne 87, etc.

Gilmore, Stuart (1913–1971).
American editor.
Arrest Bulldog Drummond 38. The Lady Eve 41. Sullivan's Travels 41. The Palm Beach Story 42. The Miracle of Morgan's Creek 43. Hail the Conquering Hero 44. Road to Utopia 45. Vendetta 50. The French Line 54. Underwater 55. Journey to the Center of the Earth 59. The Alamo 60. Hatari 62. A Rage To Live 65. Hawaii 66. Thoroughly Modern Millie 67. Sweet Charity 69. Airport 70. The Andromeda Strain 71, many others.
■ AS DIRECTOR: The Virginian 46. Hot Lead 51. Captive Women 52. The Half Breed 52. Target 52.

Gilmore, Virginia (1919–1986) (Sherman Poole).
American leading lady of the 40s; films routine.
Winter Carnival 39. Laddie 40. Swamp Water 41. The Loves of Edgar Allan Poe 42. Orchestra Wives 42. Chetniks 43. Wonder Man 45. Close Up 48. Walk East on Beacon 52, etc.

Gilroy, Frank D. (1925–).
American playwright, screenwriter and director.
Autobiography: 1993, *I Wake Up Screening!*
The Fastest Gun Alive 56. The Gallant Hours 60. The Subject Was Roses 68. The Only Game in Town 69. Desperate Characters (& d) 71. From Noon till Three (& d) 74. Once in Paris (& d) 78. Jinxed 82. The Gig (& d) 85. The Luckiest Man in the World (& d) 89. Money Plays (& d) (TV) 97, etc.

Gilson, René (1931–).
French director.
■ L'Escadron Volapuk 70. On n'Arrête pas le Printemps 71. La Brigade 73. Juliette et l'Air du Temps 76. Ma Blonde Entends-tu dans la Ville 80. Un Été à Paris 87.

Ging, Jack (1931–).
American actor who seemed to be destined for romantic leads and then was seen in lesser roles. Born in Alva, Oklahoma, and a former marine, he appeared in many television dramas and series.
The Ghost of Dragstrip Hollow 59. *Tess of the Storm Country* 60. Desire in the Dust 60. Sniper's Ridge 61. Intimacy 65. Mosby's Marauders 66. Play Misty for Me 71. That Man Bolt 73. Where the Red Fern Grows 74. Die Sister, Die 74. Un Autre Homme une Autre Chance (Fr.) 77. The Winds of War (TV) 83, etc.
TV series: Tales of Wells Fargo 61–62. The Eleventh Hour 62–64. Dear Detective 79. Riptide 84–85. P.S. I Luv U 91–92.

Gingold, Hermione (1897–1987).
British revue comedienne and writer who delighted in grotesque characters. Born in London, she began on stage at the age of 10 and was in films from the mid-30s, moving to America in 1951. Her second husband was the screenwriter and lyricist Eric Maschwitz.
Autobiographies: 1958, *The World Is Square.* 1988, *How to Grow Old Disgracefully.*
Someone at the Door 36. Meet Mr Penny 39. The Butler's Dilemma 43. Cosh Boy 52. *Pickwick Papers* 52. Our Girl Friday 53. Around the World in 80 Days 56. *Bell, Book and Candle* (US) 58. *Gigi* (US) 58. *The Music Man* (US) 61. I'd Rather Be Rich (US) 64. Harvey Middleman, Fireman (US) 65. Munster Go Home (US) 66. Banyon (TV) 71. *A Little Night Music* 76. Garbo Talks 84, etc.
❝ I had all the schooling any actress needs. I learned enough to sign contracts. – H.G.
The trouble with men is that there aren't enough of them. – *H.G.*
The nearest my mother ever came to telling me the facts of life was the day she called me to her room and said she had something important to tell me. After a good deal of embarrassed coughing, she spluttered, 'Don't ever sit down on a strange lavatory seat'. – H.G.
I believe in trying everything once – except country dancing and incest. – H.G.
An amalgam of Groucho Marx and Tallulah Bankhead. – *S. J. Perelman*

Giovannini, Giorgio.
Italian art director.
The Naked Maja 58. Esther and the King 60. *Revenge of the Vampire*/La Maschera del Demonio 60. The Invaders/Gli Invasori 61. The Evil Eye/La Ragazza che Sapeva Troppo 62. Black Sabbath/I Tre Volti della Paura 63. The Last Man on Earth 64. Planet of the Vampires/Terrore nello Spazio 65. Fellini Satyricon 69. Hercules against Kung Fu/ Ming, Ragazzi 73. Fellini's Casanova 76, etc.

Girard, Bernard (1930–).
American director.
Ride Out for Revenge 57. Green Eyed Blonde 57. The Party Crashers 58. As Young as we Are 58. A Public Affair 62. Dead Heat on a Merry Go Round 68. The Mad Room 69. The Happiness Cage 72. Gone with the West 75.

Girard, François (1963–).
Canadian film director.
32 Short Films about Glenn Gould 93. The Red Violin 98, etc.

Girard, Rémy.
Canadian leading actor.
The Decline of the American Empire 86. Jesus of Montreal 89. La Florida 93. Million Dollar Babies 94. Lilies 96. Fish Tale Soup 96. L'Homme Idéal 96. Les Boys 97. Les Boys II 98, etc.

Girardot, Annie (1931–).
French leading lady.
Thirteen at Table 56. Maigret Sets a Trap 58. Vice and Virtue 63. Vivre pour Vivre 67. Les Gauloises Bleues 68. Dillinger Is Dead 69. A Man I Like 69. The Novices 70. Traitement de Choc 73. The Slap 76. Une Robe Noire pour un Tueur 80. Le Coeur à l'Envers 80. La Vie Continue 81, All Night Long 81. Memories, Memories 84. Departure, Return 85. L'Autre Enigma 86. Cinq Jours en Juin 89. Comédie d'Amour 89. Merci la Vie 91. Toujours Seuls 91. Les Braqueuses 94. When I Will Be Gone (Can.) 98. Preference 98, etc.

Girardot, Etienne (1856–1939).
Dapper Anglo-French character actor, in many American plays and films.
The Violin of Monsieur 12. The Kennel Murder Case 33. *Twentieth Century* 34. Clive of India 35. Metropolitan 35. Go West Young Man 36. *The Great Garrick* 37. Professor Beware 38. The Hunchback of Notre Dame 39. Isle of Destiny 40, many others.

Girotti, Massimo (1918–).
Italian leading man.
Obsession 42. Caccia Tragica 47. Fabiola 47. Bellissima 51. Aphrodite 57. Theorem 68. Mr Klein 76. Cagliostro 76. An Outcast of the Islands 79. The Art of Love 83. Il Mostro 94, etc.

Gish, Annabeth (1970–) (Anne Elizabeth Gish).
American actress.
Desert Bloom 86. Hiding Out 87. Mystic Pizza 88. Shag: The Movie 89. When He's Not a Stranger (TV) 89. Coupe de Ville 90. Silent Cries (TV) 93. Wyatt Earp 94. Beautiful Girls 96. True Women (TV) 97. Steel 97, etc.

Gish, Dorothy (1898–1968) (Dorothy de Guiche).
Famous American silent star, in films for D. W. Griffith from 1912: *Hearts of the World*, *Orphans of the Storm*, etc. On stage between 1928 and 1944. Our Hearts Were Young and Gay 44. The Whistle at Eaton Falls 51. The Cardinal 63, etc.

Gish, Lillian (1893–1993) (Lillian de Guiche).
Famous American silent star, sister of Dorothy Gish, and also a D. W. Griffith discovery, on stage as a child and in films from 1912. From mid-20s spent much time on stage, but filmed occasionally. Directed one film, Remodelling Her Husband 21. She was given a special Academy Award in 1970.
Autobiography: 1969, *The Movies, Mr Griffith, and Me.*
Birth of a Nation 14. *Intolerance* 16. *Broken Blossoms* 18. *Way Down East* 20. Orphans of the Storm 22. The Scarlet Letter 26. Annie Laurie 27. His Double Life 34. The Commandos Strike at Dawn 43. Miss Susie Slagle's 46. *Duel in the Sun* (AAN) 46. Portrait of Jennie 48. *Night of the Hunter* 55. Orders to Kill 58. The Unforgiven 59. Follow Me Boys 66. Warning Shot 66. The Comedians 67. Twin Detectives (TV) 76. Hambone and Hillie 85. Sweet Liberty 85. The Whales of August 87, etc.
✪ For her early stardom and her later graciousness; and for achieving the longest acting career in show business. *Way Down East.*
❝ You know, when I first went into the movies Lionel Barrymore played my grandfather. Later he played my father and finally he played my husband. If he had lived, I'm sure I would have played his mother. That's the way it is in Hollywood. The men get younger and the women get older. – *L.G.*
Fans always write asking why I didn't smile more in films. I did in *Annie Laurie*, but I can't recall that it helped much. – *L.G.*
I can't remember a time when I wasn't acting, so I can't imagine what I would do if I stopped now. – *L.G.*
I don't care for modern films – all crashing cars and close-ups of people's feet. – *L.G.*
I've never been in style, so I can't go out of style. – *L.G.*

Gist, Robert (1924–).
American general-purpose actor; turned director once, then went into TV.
Jigsaw 49. I Was a Shoplifter 50. The Band Wagon 53. D Day Sixth of June 56. Operation Petticoat 59. Blueprint for Robbery 61. An American Dream (d only) 66, etc.

Givenchy, Hubert de (1927–).
French fashion designer who worked on occasional movies.
Funny Face (AAN) 57. Breakfast at Tiffany's 61. The VIPs 63, etc.

Givens, Robin (1964–).
Sultry American actress who studied medicine before being tempted by TV roles. She was married briefly to heavyweight boxer Mike Tyson.
The Wiz 78. Fort Apache, The Bronx 81. A Rage in Harlem 91. Boomerang 92. Foreign Student 94. Blankman 94, etc.
TV series: Head of the Class 86. Angel Street 92.

Givney, Kathryn (1897–1978).
American general-purpose character actress.
Isn't It Romantic? 48. Operation Pacific 51. Three Coins in the Fountain 54. Guys and Dolls 55. The Wayward Bus 57. The Man in the Net 59, etc.

Givot, George (1903–1984).
American character actor, usually in hearty roles. Born in Omaha, Nebraska, he studied at Chicago University and worked in vaudeville and radio as a comedian, beginning his stage career with the Ziegfeld Follies.
The Chief 33. Hollywood Party 34. Beg, Borrow or Steal 37. When's Your Birthday 37. Wake Up and Live 37. Marie Waleska 38. Hollywood Cavalcade 39. As Young as You Feel 40. Road to Morocco 42. Dubarry Was a Lady 43. The Falcon and the Co-Eds 43. Riff Raff 46. Fiesta 47. Captain Pirate/Captain Blood, Fugitive 52. April in Paris 52. Three Sailors and a Girl 53. The Lady and the Tramp (voice) 55. Miracle in the Rain 56. China Gate 57, etc.

Glaser, Paul Michael (1943–).
American leading man who leaped to fame as Starsky in TV's *Starsky and Hutch* (1975–79), but subsequently found roles scarce. He began directing in the 80s.
Fiddler on the Roof 71. Butterflies Are Free 72. Trapped Beneath the Sea (TV) 74. The Great Houdinis (TV) 77. Phobia 80. Wait till Your Mother Gets Home (TV) 81. Princess Daisy (TV) 82. Single Bars, Single Women (TV) 84. Amazons (TV) (d) 84. Band of the Hand (d) 86. The Running Man (d) 87. The Cutting Edge (d) 92. The Air Up There (d) 94. Kazaam (d) 96, etc.
TV series: Love Is a Many Splendoured Thing 69–70. Love of Life 71–72.

Glass, Ned (1905–1984).
Crusty American character actor.
Storm Warning 50. Back from the Dead 57. Experiment in Terror 62. Blackbeard's Ghost 68. Save the Tiger 72, etc.
TV series: Bridget Loves Bernie 73.

Glass, Philip (1937–).
American composer.
Koyaanisqatsi 82. Mishima: A Life in Four Chapters 85. Hamburger Hill 87. Powaqqatsi 88. The Thin Blue Line 88. The Church (s) 90. A Brief History of Time (TV) 91. Joseph Conrad's Secret Agent 96. *Kundun* (AAN) 97. *The Truman Show* 98, etc.

Glasser, Albert (1916–).
American composer.
Call of the Jungle 44. The Cisco Kid in Old Mexico 45. Law of the Lash 47. The Gay Amigo 49. I Shot Jesse James 49. The Treasure of Monte Cristo 49. I Shot Billy the Kid 50. The Neanderthal Man 52. Top Banana 54. Huk 56. The Amazing Colossal Man 57. Monster from Green Hell 57. When Hell Broke Loose 58. Teenage Caveman 58. The Boy and the Pirates 60. The Unbelievable 66. The Cremators 72, many others.

Glazer, Mitch.
American screenwriter.
Off and Running 92. Three of Hearts 93. Great Expectations 97. Beat 97, etc.

Gleason, Jackie (1916–1987).
Heavyweight American TV comedian who as a young man played small movie roles, then returned as a star but never found his niche.
Biographies: 1956, *The Golden Ham* by Jim Bishop. 1992, *The Great One: The Life and Legend of Jackie Gleason* by William A. Henry III.
Navy Blues 41. Orchestra Wives 42. Springtime in the Rockies 42. The Desert Hawk 50. *The Hustler* (as Minnesota Fats) (AAN) 61. Gigot (& w) 62. Requiem for a Heavyweight 62. Papa's Delicate Condition 63. Soldier in the Rain 63. Skidoo 68. How to Commit Marriage 69. Don't Drink the Water 69. How Do I Love Thee? 70. Mr Billion 77. Smokey and the Bandit 77. Smokey and the Bandit II 80. The Sting II 82. Smokey and the Bandit III 83. The Toy 83. Izzy and Moe (TV) 85, etc.
TV series: The Life of Riley 49. *The Honeymooners* 49–54. The Jackie Gleason Show 64–70.
❝ I'm no alcoholic, I'm a drunkard. The difference is, drunkards don't go to meetings. –*J.G.*
I have no use for humility, I am a fellow with an exceptional talent. –*J.G.*
Jackie's consistent: he's got a fat mouth and a fat belly. –*Joe Namath*

Gleason, James (1886–1959).
American character actor, noted for hard-boiled comedy roles, usually in Brooklynese. Born in New York City, to parents who were actors, he was on stage from infancy; he also wrote several Broadway plays and worked as a screenwriter and dialogue writer in Hollywood.
AS ACTOR: A Free Soul 30. Her Man 30. Oh Yeah (& oa) 30. Orders Is Orders (GB) 33. Murder on the Bridle Path 36. The Higgins Family 38. On Your Toes 39. Meet John Doe 41. *Here Comes Mr Jordan* (AAN) 41. A Guy Named Joe 43. Arsenic and Old Lace 44. *Once Upon a Time* 44. A Tree Grows in Brooklyn 44. This Man's Navy 45. Captain Eddie 45. Down to Earth 47. The Bishop's Wife 48. The Life of Riley 49. Come Fill the Cup 51. *Suddenly* 54. The Last Hurrah 58, many others.
AS WRITER: Broadway Melody 29. The Flying Fool 29. Dumbbells in Ermine 30. The Fall Guy (oa) 30. Beyond Victory 31. The Bowery 33. Orders Is Orders (GB) 33. Change of Heart 34, etc.
TV series: The Life of Riley 54–57 (as postman).
✪ For adding a little comic acid to any number of routine comedies. *Here Comes Mr Jordan*.

Gleason, Joanna (1950–) (Joanna Hall).
Canadian actress in Hollywood films.
Hannah and Her Sisters 86. Heartburn 86. Crimes and Misdemeanours 89. FX/2 91. For Richer, for Poorer (TV) 92, etc.

Gleason, Lucille (1886–1947).
American character actress, wife of James Gleason, with whom she often appeared.
The Shannons of Broadway 29. Nice Women 32. Beloved 33. Klondike Annie 36. First Lady 37. *The Higgins Family* (& four subsequent episodes) 38. Lucky Partners 40. The Clock 45, etc.

Gleason, Russell (1908–1945).
American juvenile actor, son of James and Lucille Gleason. Died following a fall from a hotel window.
Strange Cargo 29. All Quiet on the Western Front 30. Nice Women 32. Private Jones 33. Off to the Races 37. Big Business (as Jones Family member) 37. *The Higgins Family* (& four subsequent episodes) 38. News Is Made at Night 39. Unexpected Uncle 41. Salute to the Marines 43. The Adventures of Mark Twain 44, etc.

Gleeson, Brendan.
Irish leading actor.
Into the West 92. Braveheart 95. I Went Down 97. The General 98. Sweety Barrett 98, etc.

Glen, Iain (1961–).
Scottish leading actor.
Paris by Night 88. Mountains of the Moon 89. Silent Scream 89. Rosencrantz and Guildenstern Are Dead 90. Fools of Fortune 90. Adam Bede (TV) 91. Young Americans 93. Painted Lady (TV) 97, etc.

Glen, John (1932–).
British director, a former editor.
For Your Eyes Only 81. Octopussy 83. A View to a Kill 85. The Living Daylights 87. Licence to Kill 89. Aces: Iron Eagle III 92. Christopher Columbus: The Discovery 92, etc.

Glenn, Pierre-William (1943–).
French cinematographer, particularly associated with the films of Bertrand Tavernier, and director.
AS CINEMATOGRAPHER: Day for Night/La Nuit Américaine 72. The Watchmaker of St Paul 74. Let Joy Reign Supreme/Que La Fête Supreme 75. M. Klein 75. The Judge and the Assassin/Le Juge et l'Assassin 76. Clean Slate/Coup de Torchon 81. Loulou 79. Street of No Return 88. A Dry White Season 89. Luck or Coincidence/Hasards ou Coincidences 98, etc.
AS DIRECTOR: Le Cheval de Fer 74. Les Enragés 84. Terminus 87. 23 Heures 58 93, etc.

Glenn, Roy, Snr (1905–1971).
American character actor.
Bomba and the Jungle Girl 52. The Golden Idol 54. Written on the Wind 56. A Raisin in the Sun 61. Dead Heat on a Merry Go Round 67. *Guess Who's Coming to Dinner?* 67. Escape from the Planet of the Apes 71, many others.

Glenn, Scott (1942–).
American leading man.
Hex 73. Fighting Mad 76. Apocalypse Now 79. Urban Cowboy 80. Personal Best 82. The Challenge 82. The Right Stuff 83. Wild Geese 84. The River 84. Silverado 85. Wild Geese II 85. Gangland 87. Man on Fire 87. Off Limits 88. Miss Firecracker 89. The Hunt for Red October 90. The Silence of the Lambs 91. Backdraft 91. My Heroes Have Always Been Cowboys 91. The Player 92. Shadowhunter 93. Slaughter of the Innocents 93. Tall Tale: The Unbelievable Adventures of Pecos Bill 95. Reckless 95. Edie & Penn 96. Courage under Fire 96. Firestorm 97. Absolute Power 97. The Virgin Suicides 98, etc.

Glennon, Bert (1893–1967).
Distinguished American cinematographer.
Ramona 16. The Torrent 20. *The Ten Commandments* 23. Woman of the World 26. The Patriot 28. Java Head 34. *The Hurricane* 37. *Drums along the Mohawk* 39. *Stagecoach* 39. They Died with Their Boots On 41. Dive Bomber 42. Destination Tokyo 44. The Red House 47. *Wagonmaster* 50. Operation Pacific 50. The Big Trees 52. *House of Wax* 53. The Mad Magician 54. Sergeant Rutledge 60, many others.

Glenville, Peter (1913–1996).
British stage director who has made occasional films, usually of theatrical successes.
■ The Prisoner 54. Me and the Colonel 58. Summer and Smoke 60. Term of Trial 61. *Becket* (AAN) 64. Hotel Paradiso 66. The Comedians 67.

Glickenhaus, James (1950–).
American screenwriter, producer and director. In 1987 he founded with Lenny Shapiro the production and distribution company Shapiro Glickenhaus Entertainment.
The Astrologer/The Suicide Cult 77. The Exterminator 80. The Soldier 82. The Protector 85. Shakedown/Blue Jean Cop 88. McBain 91. Slaughter of the Innocents (wd) 93. Time Master 93, etc.
❝ Home video is a blessing, but it's also a terrible liability. We can't just become people that make films for video, because then no more big films will get made. –*J.G.*

Globus, Yoram (1941–).
Israeli film producer in partnership with Menahem GOLAN until 1989. He now runs his own production company. He formed a new production company with Menahem Golan in 1993.

Glover, Brian (1934–1997).
Bluff English character actor. Born in Barnsley, he worked as a teacher and professional wrestler (under the name 'Leon Arras – from Paris, France') until given the part of a games master in *Kes*, written by a fellow teacher, Barry Hines. Later, after being offered a role in the West End, he became a full-time actor, working on stage, notably at the National Theatre, and in film and television, for which he also wrote plays. Died from a brain tumour.
Kes 69. Mister Quilp 75. Jabberwocky 75. Trial by Combat 76. The First Great Train Robbery 78. An American Werewolf in London 81. Britannia Hospital 82. Laughterhouse (w) 84. Company of Wolves 84. Kafka 91. Alien^3 92. Leon the Pig Farmer 93. Stiff Upper Lips 98, etc.
TV series: Porridge 74–77. South of the Border 85. Rumble 95.

Glover, Crispin (1964–).
American juvenile actor.
My Tutor 82. Friday the 13th – the Final Chapter 83. Racing with the Moon 84. Teachers 84. Back to the Future 85. At Close Range 86. River's Edge 87. Twister 89. Where the Heart Is 90. Wild at Heart 90. Ruben and Ed 91. Little Noises 91. Hotel Room (TV) 93. Even Cowgirls Get the Blues 93. What's Eating Gilbert Grape 93. Chasers 94. Dead Man 95. The People vs Larry Flynt 96, etc.

Glover, Danny (1947–).
American actor.
Escape from Alcatraz 79. Chu Chu and the Philly Flash 81. Out 82. Iceman 84. Place in the Heart 84. The Stand-In 84. The Color Purple 85. Silverado 85. Witness 85. Lethal Weapon 87. BAT 21 88. Lethal Weapon 2 89. Predator 2 90. To Sleep with Anger 90. Flight of the Intruder 91. A Rage in Harlem 91. Pure Luck 91. Grand Canyon 92. Lethal Weapon 3 92. The Saint of Fort Washington 93. Queen (TV) 93. Bopha! 93. Angels in the Outfield 94. Maverick (cameo) 94. Operation Dumbo Drop 95. Switchback/Going West in America 97. John Grisham's The Rainmaker 97. Gone Fishin' 97. Buffalo Soldiers 97. Lethal Weapon 4 98. Antz (voice) 98. Beloved 98. Prince of Egypt (voice) 98, etc.

Glover, John (1944–).
American character actor, often as a heavy.
Shamus 72. Annie Hall 77. Last Embrace 79. Brubaker 80. Melvin and Howard 80. The Evil that Men Do 84. White Nights 84. 52 Pick-Up 86. The Chocolate War 88. Scrooged 88. Traveling Man (TV) 89. Gremlins 2: The New Batch 90. Robocop 2 90. Ed and His Dead Mother 93. Assault at West Point (TV) 94. Dead on the Money (TV) 95. In the Mouth of Madness 95. Love! Valor! Compassion! 96. Batman and Robin 97, etc.

Glover, Julian (1935–).
British general-purpose actor chiefly on stage and TV.
Tom Jones 63. Girl with Green Eyes 64. I Was Happy Here 66. Alfred the Great 69. The Adding Machine 69. Wuthering Heights 70. Nicholas and Alexandra 71. Dead Cert 74. Juggernaut 75. The Brute 77. For Your Eyes Only 81. Heat and Dust 83. Cry Freedom 87. The Fourth Protocol 87. Hearts of Fire 87. Indiana Jones and the Last Crusade 89. Tusks 90. King Ralph 91, etc.

Glyn, Elinor (1864–1943).
Extravagant British romantic novelist whose 'daring' *Three Weeks* was filmed in Hollywood in 1924 and proved both sensational and influential. Her grandson Anthony Glyn wrote her biography in 1968. She invented the catchword 'It' for sex appeal, and this in 1926 was made the basis of a movie which brought fame to Clara Bow and in which Miss Glyn consented to appear.

Glynne, Mary (1898–1954).
British stage actress of the well-bred school.
The Cry of Justice 19. The Hundredth Chance 20. The Good Companions (as Miss Trant) 32. Emil and the Detectives 34. Scrooge 35. The Heirloom Mystery (last film) 37, etc.

Gobel, George (1919–1991).
American TV comedian of 'little man' appeal.
■ The Birds and the Bees 56. I Married a Woman 57. The Invisible Woman (TV) 83. The Fantastic World of D. C. Collins (TV) 84.
TV series: The George Gobel Show 54–60. Harper Valley PTA 80.

Goblin.
Italian rock group whose music has featured in horror movies.
Deep Red/Profondo Rosso 76. Suspiria 77. Dawn of the Dead 79. Patrick 79. Alien Contamination 80. Night of the Zombies 80. Buried Alive 81. Creepers/Phenomena 85, etc.

Godard, Jean-Luc (1930–).
Semi-surrealist French writer-director of the 'new wave', his talent often muffled by incoherent narrative.
A *Bout de Souffle*/Breathless (d only) 60. Une Femme Est Une Femme 61. Vivre Sa Vie 62. Le Petit Soldat 63. Les Carabiniers 63. Bande à Part 64. Une Femme Mariée 64. Alphaville 65. Pierrot Le Fou 66. Made in USA 66. Weekend 67. One Plus One 69. Numéro Deux 75. Comment Ça Va 76. Ici et Ailleurs 77. Sauve Qui Peut 80. Passion 82. First Name: Carmen/Prénom Carmen 83. Detective 85. Hail Mary/Je Vous Salue, Marie 85. Aria (co-d) 87. King Lear 87. Soigne Ta Droite 87. Nouvelle Vague 89. Germany Nine Zero/Allemagne Neuf Zéro 91. Hélas pour Moi 93. JLG/JLG – Self-Portrait in December 94. The Kids Play Russian (doc) 95. For Ever Mozart (Swiss) 97, etc.
❝ My aesthetic is that of the sniper on the roof. –*J-L.G.*
The cinema is truth 24 times a second. –*J-L.G.*
You don't make a movie, the movie makes you. –*J-L.G.*
I pity the French cinema because it has no money. I pity the American cinema because it has no ideas. –*J-L.G.*
Since Godard's films have nothing to say, perhaps we could have 90 minutes' silence instead of each of them. –*John Simon*

Goddard, Alf (1897–1981).
English character actor in cockney roles, often comic, from the stage. Born in London, he was a former boxer and began in films as a stuntman.
The Sign of Four 23. White Heat 26. Hindle Wakes 27. Sailors Don't Care 28. You Know What Sailors Are 28. Alf's Button 30. East Lynne on the Western Front 31. Lost in the Legion 34. Strictly Illegal 35. The Scarlet Pimpernel 37. King Solomon's Mines 37. The Squeaker 37. Bank Holiday 38. St Martin's Lane 38. Murder in Soho 39. The Young Mr Pitt 42. The Way Ahead 44. The Way to the Stars 45. Innocents in Paris 53, many others.

Goddard, Paulette (1911–1990) (Marion Levy).
Pert, pretty American leading lady of the early 40s; started as a Goldwyn girl, married Charlie Chaplin and Burgess Meredith, and when her not inconsiderable career petered out married Erich Maria Remarque.
Biography: 1986, *Paulette* by Joe Morella and Edward Epstein.
■ The Girl Habit 31. The Mouthpiece 32. The Kid from Spain 32. *Modern Times* 36. The Young in Heart 38. Dramatic School 38. The Women 39. *The Cat and the Canary* 39. *The Ghost Breakers* 40. The Great Dictator 40. Northwest Mounted Police 40. Second Chorus 40. Pot o' Gold 41. Nothing But the Truth 41. Hold Back the Dawn 41. The Lady Has Plans 42. *Reap The Wild Wind* 42. The Forest Rangers 42. Star Spangled Rhythm 43. The Crystal Ball 43. So Proudly We Hail (AAN) 43. Standing Room Only 44. I Love a Soldier 44. Duffy's Tavern 45. *Kitty* 45. *The Diary of a Chambermaid* 46. Suddenly It's Spring 47. Variety Girl 47. Unconquered 47. An Ideal Husband (GB) 47. On Our Merry Way 48. Hazard 48. Bride of Vengeance 49. Anna Lucasta 49. The Torch 50. Babes in Baghdad 52. Vice Squad 53. Paris Model 53. Sins of Jezebel 53. Charge of the Lancers 54. The Stranger Came Home (GB) 54. Time of Indifference 66. The Snoop Sisters (TV) 72.

Goddard, Willoughby (1932–).
Heavyweight British character actor, mostly on TV.
In the Wake of a Stranger 59. The Wrong Box

66. The Charge of the Light Brigade 68. Young Sherlock Holmes 85, etc.
TV series: *William Tell* 57.

Godden, Rumer (1907–1998).
Much-filmed British novelist.
Black Narcissus 46. Enchantment 48. The River 51. The Greengage Summer 61. Battle of the Villa Fiorita 65, etc.

Godfrey, Bob (1921–).
British animator: shorts include *Polygamous Polonius, The Do-It-Yourself Cartoon Kit, The Plain Man's Guide to Advertising, Great,* etc.

Godfrey, Peter (1899–1970).
English director, actor and playwright, in Hollywood. Born in Chislehurst, Kent, he began in music hall in 1915, and his early experience included working in a circus. He directed two quota quickies for Gaumont-British (*Thread o' Scarlet* 30; *Down River* 31) and subsequently went to Hollywood, where he remained to direct routine films. He was one of the many writers who contributed to *Forever and a Day* 46. Married twice.
AS ACTOR: Third Time Lucky (GB) 31. Leave It to Me (GB) 33. Heads We Go (GB) 33. Good Morning Boys (GB) 37. Blockade 38. Raffles 39. The Earl of Chicago 40. Dr Jekyll and Mr Hyde 41. The Two Mrs Carrolls 47, etc.
AS DIRECTOR: ■ The Lone Wolf Spy Hunt 39. Unexpected Uncle 41. Highways by Night 42. Make Your Own Bed 44. Hotel Berlin 45. Christmas in Connecticut 45. One More Tomorrow 46. The Two Mrs Carrolls 47. Cry Wolf 47. That Hagen Girl 47. Escape Me Never 47. *The Woman in White* 48. The Decision of Christopher Blake 48. The Girl from Jones Beach 49. One Last Fling 49. Barricade 49. The Great Jewel Robber 50. He's a Cockeyed Wonder 50. One Big Affair 52. Please Murder Me 56.

Godreche, Judith.
French actress.
La Fille de 15 Ans 88. Ferdydurke 91. Grande Petite 93. Une Nouvelle Vie 93. Tango 93. Ridicule 96, etc.

Godsell, Vanda (1918–1990).
British character actress, usually in blowsy roles.
The Large Rope 54. Hour of Decision 57. Hell Is a City 60. This Sporting Life 63. The Earth Dies Screaming 64. Who Killed the Cat? 66. The Pink Panther Strikes Again 76. Trail of the Pink Panther 82, etc.

Godunov, Alexander (1949–1995).
Russian ballet dancer who defected and turned actor in the occasional film.
Witness 85. The Money Pit 86. Die Hard 88. Waxwork 2: Lost in Time 91. The Runestone 91. North 94, etc.

Goehr, Walter (1903–1960).
German-born composer and conductor in Britain. Born in Berlin, he began working in British films in the mid-30s. He also used the pseudonym Walter George.
Amateur Gentleman (co-m) 36. Spellbound/The Spell of Amy Nugent 40. For Freedom 40. The Ghost Train 41. Great Expectations 46. Stop Press Girl 49. I'll Get You for This/Lucky Nick Cain 50. Betrayed (US) 54, etc.

Goetz, Ben (1891–1979).
American executive, long with MGM and in charge of their British studios in the 40s.

Goetz, William (1903–1969).
American producer, in films since 1923, chiefly with Fox and Universal. As independent, he latterly produced the following:
The Man from Laramie 55. Sayonara 57. They Came to Cordura 58. Me and the Colonel 58. Song without End 60, etc.

Goff, Ivan (1910–).
Australian-born screenwriter; usually in collaboration with Ben ROBERTS.
My Love Came Back 40. *White Heat* 49. Captain Horatio Hornblower 51. Come Fill the Cup 51. Full House 52. King of the Khyber Rifles 53. Green Fire 54. Serenade 56. Man of a Thousand Faces 57. Shake Hands with the Devil 59. Portrait in Black 60. The Second Sin 66. The Legend of the Lone Ranger 81, etc.
TV series: The Rogues 64. Charlie's Angels 75. Time Express 79.

Golan, Gila (c. 1940–).
Hollywood leading lady of indeterminate background, being a European war orphan of probably Polish-Jewish parentage.
Ship of Fools 65. Our Man Flint 66. Three on a Couch 66. The Valley of Gwangi 69, etc.

Golan, Menahem (1929–) (Menahem Globus).
Flamboyant Israeli producer, director and screenwriter noted for quantity rather than quality. He trained in stage-management in London, became a theatre director in Israel, and began his film career working for Roger Corman. With his cousin Yoram Globus he ran Noah Films in Israel and then, from 1979–89, the international Cannon Group. The partnership foundered and he now heads a new production company, the 21st Century Film Corporation, with plans to produce programmes for 'erotic TV'. He formed a new production company with Yoram Globus in 1993.
Biography: 1986, *Hollywood a Go-go* by Andrew Yule.
AS PRODUCER: Sallah (AAN) 64. The House on Chelouche Street (AAN) 73. Lemon Popsicle 77. Going Steady – Lemon Popsicle II 78. Hot Bubblegum 81. Death Wish 2 81. Lady Chatterley's Lover 81. Body and Soul 81. The Last American Virgin 82. That Championship Season 82. The Wicked Lady 83. Revenge of the Ninja 83. Breakin' 84. Sahara 84. Hot Chili 85. Hot Resort 85. The Ambassador 85. Maria's Lovers 85. Missing in Action 2 85. Invasion U.S.A. 85. Death Wish 3 85. King Solomon's Mines 85. Fool for Love 85. Runaway Train 85. Ordeal by Innocence 85. The Assisi Underground 85. Delta Force 86. Murphy's Law 86. Otello 86. 52 Pickup 86. Firewalker 86. The Naked Cage 86. P.O.W.: The Escape 86. Avenging Force 86. Assassination 87. Allan Quatermain and the Lost City of Gold 87. Number One with a Bullet 87. Street Smart 87. Superman IV: The Quest for Peace 87. Masters of the Universe 87. Dancers 87. Barfly 87. Shy People 87. Tough Guys Don't Dance 87. Hero and The Terror 88. Messenger of Death 88. King Lear 88. Going Bananas 88. Apppointment with Death 88. Kinjite/Forbidden Subjects 89. The Phantom of the Opera 89. Cyborg 89. Manifesto 89. The Forbidden Dance 90. Night of the Living Dead 90. The Fifth Monkey 90. Crazy Joe 92. Mad Dog Coll 92. Invader 92. The Finest Hour 92. Emmanuelle 7 92, etc.
AS DIRECTOR: El Dorado 63. Trunk to Cairo 67. Tevye and His Seven Daughters 68. What's Good for the Goose 69. Margo 70. Lupo! 70. Kazablan 73. Diamonds 75. Lepke 75. Entebbe: Operation Thunderbolt (AAN) 77. The Magician of Lublin 79. The Apple 80. Enter the Ninja 81. Delta Force 86. Over the Top 87. Hanna's War 88. Mack the Knife 89. Hit the Dutchman 92, etc.
❝ If you make an American film with a beginning, a middle and an end, with a budget of less than five million dollars, you must be an idiot to lose money. – M.G.
We have some good news. We didn't buy anything today. – M.G. *(Cannes 1986)*

Gold, Ernest (1921–).
Viennese-American composer.
Girl of the Limberlost 45. The Falcon's Alibi 46. Unknown World 51. Jennifer 53. The Naked Street 55. Too Much Too Soon 57. On the Beach 59. Exodus (AA) 60. Inherit the Wind 60. Judgment at Nuremberg 60. A Child Is Waiting 62. Pressure Point 62. It's a Mad Mad Mad Mad World 63. Ship of Fools 65. The Secret of Santa Vittoria 69. Small Miracle (TV) 73. Betrayal (TV) 74. Cross of Iron 77. Fun with Dick and Jane 77. The Runner Stumbles 79. Tom Horn 80. Safari 3000 82. Dreams of Gold (TV) 86. Gore Vidal's Lincoln (TV) 88, etc.

Gold, Jack (1930–).
British TV director who moved into films.
The Bofors Gun 68. The Reckoning 69. The National Health 73. *Catholics* (TV) 73. Who? 74. Man Friday 75. *The Naked Civil Servant* (TV) 75. Aces High 76. The Medusa Touch 77. Charlie Muffin (TV) 79. The Sailor's Return (TV) 79. Praying Mantis (TV) 82. Sakharov 84. The Chain 85. Escape from Sobibor (TV) 86. Ball-Trap on the Côte Sauvage 89. The Last Romantics (TV) 90. P. G. Wodehouse's Heavy Weather (TV) 95, etc.

Gold, Jimmy (1886–1967).
Scottish slapstick comedian, a former painter and decorator. Born in Glasgow, he formed a double act with Charlie NAUGHTON that lasted for 53 years, and the pair became part of The CRAZY GANG from the early 30s.
■ Highland Fling 36. Wise Guys 37. O-Kay for Sound 37. Alf's Button Afloat 38. The Frozen Limits 39. Gasbags 40. Down Melody Lane 43. Life Is a Circus 58.

Goldbeck, Willis (1899–1979).
American director, former writer (co-author of *Freaks*).
Dr Gillespie's New Assistant 42. Between Two Women 44. She Went to the Races 45. Love Laughs at Andy Hardy 46. Johnny Holiday 50. Ten Tall Men 51, etc.

Goldberg, Whoopi (1949–) (Caryn Johnson).
American actress, often in comic roles. In 1996, she was paid a reported $6m advance by an American publisher for her autobiography.
Autobiography: 1998, *Book*.
The Color Purple (AAN) 85. Jumpin' Jack Flash 87. Fatal Beauty 87. Burglar 87. Clara's Heart 87. The Telephone 88. Beverly Hills Brats 89. Homer and Eddie 89. Ghost (AA) 90. The Long Walk Home 90. Soapdish 91. Kiss Shot 91. Change of Heart 92. The Player 92. Sarafina! 92. Sister Act 92. Made in America 93. National Lampoon's Loaded Weapon 1 93. Naked in New York 93. Sister Act 2: Back in the Habit 93. The Lion King (voice) 94. The Little Rascals 94. Corrina, Corrina 94. The Pagemaster (voice) 94. Star Trek: Generations 94. Boys on the Side 95. Moonlight and Valentino 95. Eddie 96. Bogus 96. The Associate 96. Theodore Rex 96. In the Gloaming (TV) 97. How Stella Got Her Groove Back 98. Rudolph the Red-Nosed Reindeer: The Movie (voice) 98. A Knight in Camelot (TV) 98. The Rugrats Movie (voice) 98, etc.
❝ I worked in strip joints – but I never got my clothes off. People were screaming: 'Don't do it!' – W.G.
I'm really glad we do what we do, man. We are amazing! – W.G. *at the Oscars, 1994*

Goldblatt, Mark.
American editor and occasional director, frequently of action movies.
Piranha (co-ed) 78. Humanoids of the Deep 80. Halloween II 80. The Howling 80. Enter the Ninja 81. The Terminator 84. Rambo: First Blood Part II 85. Commando 85. Jumping Jack Flash 86. Robocop (second unit d) 87. Nightbreed 89. Predator 2 90. Terminator 2: Judgment Day (AAN) 91. The Last Boy Scout (co-ed) 91. Super Mario Brothers 93. True Lies 94. Showgirls (co-ed) 95. Starship Troopers (co-ed) 97, etc.
AS DIRECTOR: Dead Heat 88. The Punisher 89.

Goldblatt, Stephen.
British cinematographer, now working in Hollywood.
Breaking Glass 80. Outland 81. The Return of the Soldier 82. The Hunger 83. The Cotton Club 84. Young Sherlock Holmes 85. Lethal Weapon 87. Everybody's All American 88. Lethal Weapon 2 89. Joe versus the Volcano 90. For the Boys 91. The Prince of Tides (AAN) 91. Consenting Adults 92. The Pelican Brief 93. Batman Forever (AAN) 95. Striptease 96. Batman and Robin 97, etc.

Goldblum, Jeff (1952–).
Lanky American leading man, frequently as an eccentric scientist in science-fiction films. Born in Pittsburgh, the son of a doctor, he studied acting in New York with Sanford MEISNER and began in the theatre. Formerly married to actresses Patricia Gaul and Geena DAVIS, he was engaged for a time to actress Laura DERN.
Death Wish 74. California Split 74. Nashville 75. Next Stop Greenwich Village 76. Between the Lines 77. Invasion of the Body Snatchers 78. Remember My Name 78. Thank God It's Friday 78. Escape from Athena 79. The Big Chill 83. Buckaroo Banzai 84. Silverado 85. Into the Night 85. Transylvania 6–5000 85. *The Fly* 86. Beyond Therapy 87. Life Story (TV) 87. Vibes 88. Earth Girls Are Easy 89. The Mad Monkey (El Mono Loco) 89. The Tall Guy 89. Mister Frost 90. The Favour, the Watch and the Very Big Fish (Rue Saint-Sulpice) 91. Deep Cover 92. Shooting Elizabeth 92. *Jurassic Park* 93. Lush Life 93. Hideaway 95. Nine Months 95. Powder 95. *Independence Day* 95. The Great White Hype 96. Mad Dog Time 96. The Lost World: Jurassic Park 97. Holy Man 98, etc.
TV series: Tenspeed and Brown Shoe 80.

Golden, Michael (1913–).
British character actor.
Send for Paul Temple 46. Hungry Hill 47. Escape 48. The Blue Lamp 50. The Green Scarf 55. Murder She Said 62, etc.

Goldenberg, Billy (1936–).
American composer, mainly for TV films.
The Grasshopper 69. Red Sky at Morning 70. Duel (TV) 71. The Marcus Nelson Murders (TV) 72. The Last of Sheila 73. Reflections of Murder (TV) 73. The Domino Principle 76. Scavenger Hunt 78. King (TV) 78. Haywire (TV) 81. The Diary of Anne Frank (TV) 82. Reuben Reuben 83. Rage of Angels (TV) 83. The Sun Also Rises (TV) 84. Kane and Abel (TV) 85. Rage of Angels: The Story Continues (TV) 86. 18 Again 88. People Like Us (TV) 90. Message from 'Nam (TV) 93, many others.
Several TV series include Kojak, Columbo, McCloud, Harry O, Executive Suite.
❝ Movies are a group endeavour, and people don't want to know that. They want to know that Clint Eastwood is really Superman and Richard Attenborough is Plato reincarnated. – *B.G.*

Goldenberg, Michael.
American screenwriter, director and dramatist. He has a degree from Carnegie-Mellon University.
Bed of Roses (wd) 96. Contact (w) 97, etc.

Goldenthal, Elliot.
American composer.
Pet Sematary 89. Drugstore Cowboy 89. Alien^3 92. Demolition Man 93. Golden Gate 94. Interview with the Vampire 94. Batman Forever 95. Heat 95. A Time to Kill 96. Michael Collins (AAN) 96. Butcher Boy 97. Batman and Robin 97. Sphere 98, etc.

Golding, Louis (1896–1958).
English novelist and screenwriter. Born in Manchester, he was educated at Oxford University.
Cotton Queen (co-w) 37. Proud Valley (co-w) 38. Freedom Radio (w) 40. Mr Emmanuel (co-w, oa) 45. Five Silver Daughters (co-w) 44. The Silver Cat (co-w) 47. Theirs Is the Glory (co-w) 47. The Call of the Blood (co-w) 47, etc.

Goldman, Bo (1932–).
American screenwriter. He first worked in TV as a producer and writer.
One Flew over the Cuckoo's Nest (AA) 76. The Rose 79. Melvin and Howard (AA) 80. Shoot the Moon 82. Swing Shift 83. Little Nikita 88. Dick Tracy 90. Scent of a Woman 92. City Hall (co-w) 96. Meet Joe Black (co-w) 98, etc.

Goldman, James (1927–1998).
American playwright and screenwriter.
The Lion in Winter (oa & w) (AA) 68. *They Might Be Giants* 71. Nicholas and Alexandra 72. Robin and Marian 75. White Nights (co-w) 85, etc.

Goldman, William (1931–).
American screenwriter and novelist.
Autobiographies: 1985, *Adventures in the Screen Trade*. 1990, *Hype and Glory*.
Soldier in the Rain (oa) 63. Masquerade 65. Harper 66. No Way to Treat a Lady (oa) 67. *Butch Cassidy and the Sundance Kid* (AA) 69. The Hot Rock 71. The Great Waldo Pepper 75. *All the President's Men* (AA) 76. Marathon Man (& oa) 77. A Bridge Too Far 77. Magic (& oa) 78. Heat (& oa) 87. The Princess Bride (& oa) 87. Misery 90. Year of the Comet 92. Chaplin (co-w) 92. Memoirs of an Invisible Man 92. Maverick 94. Absolute Power 97, etc.
❝ Nobody knows anything. – *W.G. on the film business*

Goldner, Charles (1900–1955).
Austrian character actor, in Britain from the 30s.
Room for Two 40. Brighton Rock 47. One Night With You 48. Third Time Lucky 48. Give Us This Day 49. Black Magic 49. Shadow of the Eagle 50. *The Captain's Paradise* 54, etc.

Goldoni, Lelia (c. 1938–).
American actress.

Shadows 59. Hysteria 64. The Italian Job 69. Alice Doesn't Live Here Any More 74. The Day of the Locust 75. Baby Blue Marine 76. Bloodbrothers 78. Invasion of the Body Snatchers 78. The Disappearance of Sister Aimee (TV) 79. Scruples (TV) 81. Anatomy of an Illness (TV) 83, etc.

Goldsman, Akiva.
American screenwriter.

The Client 94. Silent Fall 94. Batman Forever 95. A Time to Kill 96. Batman and Robin 97. Practical Magic 98, etc.

Goldsmith, Jerry (1929–) (Jerrald Goldsmith).
American composer.

Black Patch 57. City of Fear 59. Lonely Are the Brave 62. Freud (AAN) 63. The Prize 63. Seven Days in May 64. Lilies of the Field 64. In Harm's Way 65. A Patch of Blue (AAN) 65. The Trouble with Angels 66. Stagecoach 66. The Blue Max 66. Seconds 66. The Sand Pebbles (AAN) 66. In Like Flint 67. Planet of the Apes (AAN) 68. Patton (AAN) 70. Tora! Tora! Tora! 71. The Mephisto Waltz 71. Papillon (AAN) 73. The Reincarnation of Peter Proud 75. Chinatown (AAN) 75. The Wind and the Lion (AAN) 75. The Omen (AA) 76. Islands in the Stream 77. MacArthur 77. Capricorn One 78. The Boys from Brazil (AAN) 78. Coma 78. Magic 78. Alien 79. Star Trek: the Motion Picture (AAN) 79. The First Great Train Robbery 80. The Final Conflict 81. Outland 81. Raggedy Man 81. Poltergeist (AAN) 82. Psycho II 83. Under Fire (AAN) 83. Gremlins 84. King Solomon's Mines 85. Poltergeist 2 85. Hoosiers (AAN) 86. Extreme Prejudice 86. Innerspace 87. Lionheart 87. Criminal Law 88. Rambo III 88. The 'burbs 89. Leviathan 89. Star Trek V: The Final Frontier 89. Warlock 89. Gremlins 2: The New Batch 90. The Russia House 90. Total Recall 90. Sleeping with the Enemy 90. Not without My Daughter 91. Medicine Man 92. Basic Instinct 92. Matinee 93. The Vanishing 93. Dennis the Menace/Dennis 93. Rudy 93. Malice 93. Six Degrees of Separation 93. Angie 94. Bad Girls 94. The River Wild 94. The Shadow 94. I.Q. 94. Powder 95. City Hall 96. Executive Decision 96. Chain Reaction 96. Star Trek: First Contact 96. The Ghost and the Darkness 96. Fierce Creatures 96. Air Force One 97. LA Confidential (AAN) 97. The Edge 97. Deep Rising 98. US Marshals 98. Mulan 98, etc.

TV series: Twilight Zone. Dr Kildare. The Man from UNCLE. The Waltons, etc.

Goldstein, Robert (1903–1974).
American producer, with Twentieth Century-Fox for many years.

Goldstone, James (1931–).
American director, from TV.
■ The Inheritors (TV) 64. Scalplock (TV) 66. Ironside (TV pilot) 67. Jigsaw (TV) 68. Shadow Over Elveron (TV) 68. A Clear and Present Danger (TV) 69. A Man Called Gannon 69. Winning 69. Brother John 70. Red Sky at Morning 71. The Gang that Couldn't Shoot Straight 72. They Only Kill Their Masters 72. Cry Panic (TV) 74. Dr Max (TV) 74. Things in Their Season (TV) 74. Eric (TV) 75. Journey from Darkness (TV) 75. Swashbuckler 76. Rollercoaster 77. When Time Ran Out 80. The Sun Also Rises (TV) 84.

Goldstone, Richard (1912–).
American producer.

The Outriders 50. Inside Straight 51. The Tall Target 51. The Devil Makes Three 52. Cinerama's South Seas Adventure 58. No Man Is an Island (& wd) 62. The Sergeant 68. The Baby Maker 70, etc.

Goldthwait, Bobcat (1962–).
Manic American comedian and actor.

Police Academy 2: Their First Assignment 85. Police Academy 3: Back in Training 86. One Crazy Summer 86. Burglar 87. An Evening with Bob Goldthwait: Share the Warmth (concert) 87. Police Academy 4: Citizens on Patrol 87. Hot to Trot 88. Scrooged 88. Little Vegas 90. Shakes the Clown (& wd) 92. Radioland Murders 94. Destiny Turns on the Radio 95. Out There (TV) 95. Back to Back 96, etc.

Goldwyn, Samuel (1882–1974) (Samuel Goldfish).
Polish-American producer, in Hollywood from 1910. Co-produced *The Squaw Man* (1913); a top producer ever after, with a high reputation for star-making; he always refused to make any but family films.

Biographies: 1937, *The Great Goldwyn* by Alva Johnston. 1976, *Samuel Goldwyn Presents* by Alvin H. Marill. 1976, *Goldwyn* by Arthur Marx.

■ FILMS SINCE SOUND: Bulldog Drummond 29. Condemned 29. Raffles 30. Whoopee 30. One Heavenly Night 30. The Devil To Pay 30. Street Scene 31. The Unholy Garden 31. Tonight or Never 31. Arrowsmith 31. The Greeks Had a Word for Them 32. Cynara 32. The Kid from Spain 32. The Masquerader 33. Roman Scandals 33. Nana 34. We Live Again 34. Kid Millions 34. The Wedding Night 35. The Dark Angel 35. Barbary Coast 35. Splendor 35. Strike Me Pink 36. These Three 36. *Dodsworth* 36. Come and Get It 36. Beloved Enemy 36. Woman Chases Man 37. *Hurricane* 37. Stella Dallas 37. *Dead End* 37. The Adventures of Marco Polo 38. The Goldwyn Follies 38. The Cowboy and the Lady 38. The Real Glory 39. *Wuthering Heights* 39. They Shall Have Music 39. Raffles 40. *The Westerner* 40. *The Little Foxes* 41. Ball of Fire 41. The Pride of the Yankees 41. They Got Me Covered 43. North Star 43. Up in Arms 44. The Princess and the Pirate 44. Wonder Man 45. The Kid from Brooklyn 46. *The Best Years of Our Lives* 46. The Secret Life of Walter Mitty 47. The Bishop's Wife 47. A Song Is Born 48. Enchantment 48. Roseanna McCoy 49. My Foolish Heart 49. Our Very Own 50. Edge of Doom 50. I Want You 51. Hans Christian Andersen 52. Guys and Dolls 55. Porgy and Bess 59.

☻ For giving the appearance of culture and refinement while keeping his standards modest though irreproachable. *Wuthering Heights*.

❝ He was the archetypal movie mogul: the glove salesman from Minsk who became more American than apple pie and founded his credo on the family audience. His maxims included:

Motion pictures should never embarrass a man when he brings his wife to the theatre, and:

I seriously object to seeing on the screen what belongs in the bedroom.

He was proud of his art:

The picture makers will inherit the earth.

As an executive, he certainly knew his own mind:

A producer shouldn't get ulcers: he should give them, and:

I was always an independent, even when I had partners, and:

In this business it's dog eat dog, and nobody's going to eat me.

He was a great showman:

What we want is a story that starts with an earthquake and works its way up to a climax . . .

But his logic was all his own:

I don't care if it doesn't make a nickel. I just want every man, woman and child in America to see it!

That was about *The Best Years of Our Lives*. He disdained subtlety. When a harassed publicist devised a campaign that began:

The directing skill of Rouben Mamoulian, the radiance of Anna Sten and the genius of Samuel Goldwyn have combined to bring you the world's greatest entertainment . . .

Goldwyn nodded approval:

That's the kind of advertising I like. Just the facts. No exaggeration . . .

He is said to have telegraphed Eisenstein as follows:

Have seen your picture (*The Battleship Potemkin*) and enjoyed it very much. Should like you to do something of the same kind, but cheaper, for Ronald Colman.

With this kind of gall, it is not surprising that intellectuals like Robert Sherwood continued to relish his company:

I find I can live with Sam just as one lives with high blood pressure.

Did he really coin all the famous Goldwynisms which have filled so many books? Not all of them, perhaps. One doubts the authenticity of:

Directors are always biting the hand that lays the golden egg, and:

In two words: im-possible, and:

Tell me, how did you love the picture? and:

We have all passed a lot of water since then. But I imagine Goldwyn probably did say, rather wittily:

Gentlemen, kindly include me out, and:

Let's bring it up to date with some snappy nineteenth-century dialogue, and:

Anyone who goes to a psychiatrist should have his head examined, and:

I had a great idea this morning, but I didn't like it, and:

A verbal contract isn't worth the paper it's written on.

His film appreciation was untutored but vivid, like his speaking style:

When everybody's happy with the rushes, the picture's always a stinker,

he once said; and he can't have been alone among Hollywood producers in vowing:

I'd hire the devil himself if he'd write me a good story.

Lindsay Anderson summed him up in 1974:

There are lucky ones whose great hearts, shallow and commonplace as bedpans, beat in instinctive tune with the great heart of the public, who laugh as it likes to laugh, weep the sweet and easy tears it likes to weep . . . Goldwyn is blessed with that divine confidence in the rightness (moral, aesthetic, commercial) of his own intuition – and that I suppose is the chief reason for his success.

Goldwyn had in fact summed up himself rather nicely:

I am a rebel. I make a picture to please me. If it pleases me, there is a chance it will please others. But it has to please me first.

And his son Samuel Goldwyn Jnr was taught the value of his legacy:

With every picture he made, my father raised the money, paid back the bank, and kept control of the negative. He said, you be careful of these films: some people will tell you they're not worth anything, but don't you believe it.

Goldwyn, Samuel, Jnr (1926–).
American producer, son of Samuel Goldwyn.

The Man with the Gun 55. Sharkfighters 56. The Proud Rebel 58. Huckleberry Finn 60. The Young Lovers (& d) 65. Cotton Comes to Harlem 70. Come Back Charleston Blue 72. The Golden Seal 83. A Prayer for the Dying 87. Mystic Pizza 88, etc.

Goldwyn, Tony (1960–).
American actor, the son of producer Samuel Goldwyn Jnr.

Gaby – a True Story 87. Ghost 90. Traces of Red 92. The Pelican Brief 93. Doomsday Gun (TV) 94. A Woman of Independent Means (TV) 95. Reckless 95. The Substance of Fire 96. The Boys Next Door (TV) 96. Kiss the Girls 97. Kiss the Sky (d only) 98. Trouble on the Corner 98. The Lesser Evil 98. A Walk on the Moon (p, d) 99, etc.

Golino, Valeria (1966–).
Italian leading actress, also in international films.

Blind Date 84. My Dearest Son/Figlio Mio Infinamente Caro 85. Dumb Dicks/Asilo di Polizia 86. Love Story/Storia d'Amore 86. Big Top Pee-Wee 88. Rain Man 88. Torrents of Spring 89. The King's Whore 90. Three Sisters/Paura e Amore 90. Hot Shots! 91. The Indian Runner 91. Year of the Gun 91. Tracce di Vita Amorosa 91. Hot Shots! Part Deux 93. Clean Slate 94. Come Due Coccodrilli 94. Immortal Beloved 94. Leaving Las Vegas 95. Four Rooms 95. Escape from LA 96. The Acrobats (It.) 97. Side Streets (US) 98. Shooting the Moon/L'Albero delle Pere (It.) 98, etc.

Golitzen, Alexander (1907–).
Russian-born production designer, in Hollywood from the mid-30s, who spent most of his career at Universal Studios.

The Call of the Wild 35. Foreign Correspondent (AAN) 40. Sundown (AAN) 41. Arabian Nights (AAN) 42. The Phantom of the Opera (AA) 43. The Climax (AAN) 44. Letter from an Unknown Woman 48. Seminole 53. The Glenn Miller Story 54. The Far Country 55. The Incredible Shrinking Man 57. A Time to Love and a Time to Die 58.

Imitation of Life 59. Spartacus (AA) 60. Flower Drum Song (AAN) 61. That Touch of Mink (AAN) 62. To Kill a Mockingbird (AA) 62. Gambit (AAN) 66. Coogan's Bluff 68. Sweet Charity (AAN) 69. Airport (AAN) 70. Play Misty for Me 71. Earthquake (AAN) 74, many others.

Gombell, Minna (1900–1973) (aka Winifred Lee and Nancy Carter).
American character actress of the 30s and 40s, usually in hard-boiled roles.

Doctors' Wives (debut) 31. The Thin Man 34. Babbitt 35. Banjo on My Knee 37. The Great Waltz 38. The Hunchback of Notre Dame 39. Boom Town 40. A Chip Off the Old Block 44. Man Alive 46. Pagan Love Song 51. I'll See You in My Dreams 52, etc.

Gomez, Nick (1963–).
American director, a former editor and musician.

Trust (e) 90. Laws of Gravity (d) 92. New Jersey Drive 95. Illtown 96, etc.

Gomez, Thomas (1905–1971).
Bulky American stage character actor who became a familiar villain or detective in Hollywood films.
■ Sherlock Holmes and the Voice of Terror 42. Arabian Nights 42. Pittsburgh 42. Who Done It 42. White Savage 43. Corvette K 225 43. Frontier Badmen 43. Crazy House 43. The Climax 44. Phantom Lady 44. Dead Man's Eyes 44. Follow the Boys 44. In Society 44. Bowery to Broadway 44. Can't Help Singing 45. Patrick the Great 45. I'll Tell the World 45. The Daltons Ride Again 45. Frisco Sal 45. A Night in Paradise 45. Swell Guy 46. *The Dark Mirror* 46. Singapore 47. *Ride the Pink Horse* (AAN) 47. Captain from Castile 47. Johnny O'Clock 47. Casbah 48. Angel in Exile 48. Key Largo 48. Force of Evil 48. Come to the Stable 49. Sorrowful Jones 49. That Midnight Kiss 49. The Woman on Pier 13 49. Kim 50. The Toast of New Orleans 50. The Eagle and the Hawk 50. The Furies 50. Anne of the Indies 51. The Harlem Globetrotters 51. The Sellout 51. The Merry Widow 52. Macao 52. Pony Soldier 52. Sombrero 53. The Gambler from Natchez 54. The Adventures of Hajji Baba 54. The Looters 55. The Magnificent Matador 55. Las Vegas Shakedown 55. Night Freight 55. Trapeze 56. The Conqueror 56. John Paul Jones 59. But Not for Me 59. Summer and Smoke 61. Stay Away Joe 68. Beneath the Planet of the Apes 70.

TV series: Life with Luigi 52.

Gonzalez, Myrtle (1891–1918).
American star of Vitagraph silents. Died of pneumonia.

The Spell 13. The Ebony Casket 15. The Secret of the Swamp 16. The End of the Rainbow 16. Captain Alvarez 17. Mutiny 17, etc.

Gooding, Cuba, Jnr (1968–).
American actor who made a breakthrough with his role in *Jerry Maguire*. Born in the Bronx, New York, and brought up in Los Angeles, he began in commercials. Current asking price: around $2m.

Boyz N The Hood 91. Gladiator 92. Judgment Night 93. Lightning Jack 94. Outbreak 95. Losing Isaiah 95. The Tuskegee Airmen (TV) 95. Outbreak 95. Jerry Maguire (AA) 96. As Good as It Gets 97. What Dreams May Come 98, etc.

Goodliffe, Michael (1914–1976).
British stage actor often cast as officer, professional man or diplomat.

The Small Back Room (debut) 48. The Wooden Horse 50. Rob Roy 53. The Adventures of Quentin Durward 55. The Battle of the River Plate 56. A Night To Remember 58. Sink the Bismarck 60. The Trials of Oscar Wilde 60. Jigsaw 62. The Seventh Dawn 64. The Man with the Golden Gun 73, many others.

TV series: Sam 73–75.

Goodman, Benny (1909–1986).
American clarinettist and bandleader, the 'King of Swing'.

Hollywood Hotel 38. Hello Beautiful 42. The Gang's All Here 44. Sweet and Lowdown 44. A Song Is Born 48, etc.

Provided the music for The Benny Goodman Story 55, in which he was portrayed by Steve Allen.

Goodman, David Zelag.
American screenwriter.
Lovers and Other Strangers (AAN) 69. Monte Walsh 70. Straw Dogs 71. Man on a Swing 73. Farewell My Lovely 74. Logan's Run 76. March or Die 77. The Eyes of Laura Mars 78. Freedom Road (TV) 79. Fighting Back 82. Man, Woman and Child 83. Sheena 84, etc.

Goodman, John (1952–).
Heavyweight American actor, often in comic roles, from the stage.
Eddie Macon's Run 83. The Survivors 83. C. H. U. D. 84. Revenge of the Nerds 84. Maria's Lovers 85. Sweet Dreams 85. The Big Easy 86. True Stories 86. Burglar 87. Raising Arizona 87. Punchline 88. Everybody's All-American 88. The Wrong Guys 88. Sea of Love 89. Always 89. Arachnophobia 90. Stella 90. King Ralph 91. Barton Fink 91. The Babe 92. Born Yesterday 92. *Matinee* 93. Born Yesterday 93. We're Back! A Dinosaur's Story (voice) 93. The Flintstones 94. Kingfish (as Huey Long, TV) 95. Pie in the Sky 95. A Streetcar Named Desire (TV) 95. Mother Night 96. Fallen 97. The Borrowers 97. The Big Lebowski 97. Blues Brothers 2000 98. Rudolph the Red-Nosed Reindeer: The Movie (voice) 98, etc.
TV series: Roseanne 88–97.
❝ I'm not a major player. I just turn up and do my job. – J.G.

Goodman, Miles (1949–1996).
American composer. Died of a heart attack.
Skatetown USA 79. The Man Who Wasn't There 83. Table for Five (co-w) 83. Footloose 84. Teen Wolf 85. La Bamba (co-m) 86. Real Men 87. Like Father Like Son 87. Dirty Rotten Scoundrels 88. Vital Signs 90. Opportunity Knocks 90. Funny about Love 90. Problem Child 90. The Super 91. What about Bob? 91. He Said, She Said 91. Housesitter 92. Blankman 94. Getting Even with Dad 94. Dunston Checks In 95. Larger than Life 96, etc.

Goodrich, Frances (1891–1984).
American screenwriter, almost always in collaboration with her husband Albert Hackett.
The Secret of Madame Blanche 33. *The Thin Man* (AAN) 34. Ah Wilderness 35. Naughty Marietta 35. After the Thin Man (AAN) 36. Another Thin Man 39. The Hitler Gang 44. Lady in the Dark 44. *It's a Wonderful Life* 46. The Pirate 48. Summer Holiday 48. Easter Parade 49. *Father of the Bride* (AAN) 50. Father's Little Dividend 51. The Long Long Trailer 54. Seven Brides for Seven Brothers (AAN) 55. The Diary of Anne Frank 60. Five Finger Exercise 62, etc.

Goodwin, Bill (1910–1958).
American character actor, usually of genial type in routine films.
Wake Island 42. So Proudly We Hail 43. Bathing Beauty 44. Spellbound 45. House of Horrors 46. *The Jolson Story* 46. Heaven Only Knows 47. Jolson Sings Again 49. Tea for Two 50. The Atomic Kid 54. The Big Heat 54. The Opposite Sex 56, etc.

Goodwin, Harold (1917–).
British character actor usually seen as cockney serviceman or small-time crook.
Dance Hall 50. The Card 52. The Cruel Sea 53. The Dam Busters 55. Sea of Sand 58. The Mummy 59. The Bulldog Breed 61. The Comedy Man 63. The Curse of the Mummy's Tomb 64. Frankenstein Must Be Destroyed 69, many others.

Goodwin, Ron (1929–).
English composer, arranger and orchestra leader. Born in Plymouth, Devon, he studied at the Guildhall School of Music.
I'm All Right Jack 59. The Trials of Oscar Wilde 60. Postman's Knock 62. Murder She Said 62. Lancelot and Guinevere 63. 633 Squadron 64. Operation Crossbow 65. Those Magnificent Men in Their Flying Machines 65. The Alphabet Murders 65. Where Eagles Dare 68. Battle of Britain 70. Frenzy 72. The Happy Prince 74. One of Our Dinosaurs Is Missing 75. Candleshoe 77. Force Ten from Navarone 78. Unidentified Flying Oddball 79. Clash of Loyalties 83. Valhalla 85, etc.

Goodwins, Leslie (1899–1969).
British-born director, in Hollywood for many years. Films mainly routine second features.
'Mexican Spitfire' series 39–44. Glamour Boy 39. Pop Always Pays 40. Silver Skates 43. Murder in the Blue Room 44. What a Blonde 45. The Mummy's Curse 46. Gold Fever 52. Fireman Save My Child 54. Paris Follies of 1956 56.

Goolden, Richard (1895–1981).
British character actor, on stage and screen for many years, usually in henpecked or bewildered roles; created the radio character of Old Ebenezer the night watchman.
Whom the Gods Love 38. Meet Mr Penny 38. Mistaken Identity 43, etc.

Goorney, Howard (1921–).
English character actor, mainly on the stage. Born in Manchester, he left school at 14 and worked as a clerk before becoming a founder member of Theatre Workshop, later joining the National Theatre Company. He is the author of *The Theatre Workshop Story* 81.
Marriage of Convenience 60. The Evil of Frankenstein 64. The Hill 65. Bedazzled 67. Circus of Blood 67. Where's Jack? 69. Blood on Satan's Claw 70. Fiddler on the Roof (US) 71. The Offence 72. To the Devil a Daughter 76. Fanny Hill 83. Little Dorrit 87, etc.

Goorwitz, Allen:
see GARFIELD, Allen.

Goosson, Stephen (1889–1973).
American art director, a former architect. In films from the early 20s, he worked for Mary Pickford and de Mille before going to Columbia in the 30s, where he became supervising art director.
Little Lord Fauntleroy 21. *The Hunchback of Notre Dame* 23. Skyscraper 28. Just Imagine (AAN) 30. American Madness 32. One Night of Love 34. It Happened One Night 34. The Black Room 35. *Lost Horizon* (AA) 37. Holiday (AAN) 38. The Little Foxes (AAN) 41. A Thousand and One Nights (AAN) 45. Gilda 46. The Lady from Shanghai 48, etc.

Gora, Claudio (1913–1998) (Emilio Giordana).
Italian actor, screenwriter and director. Born in Genoa, he was on-stage from 1937 and in films from 1939, appearing in 130 during his career, as well as continuing his acting on stage and television. Married actress Marina Berti.
AS ACTOR: Trappola d'Amore 39. Amami, Alfredo 40. Amore Imperiale 41. Mater Dolorosa 43. Signorinette 43. Preludio d'Amore 46. La Poupée 58. Un Amore a Roma 60. Everybody Go Home! 60. A Difficult Life 61. An Easy Life 62. Gidget Goes to Rome (US) 63. Le Voci Bianche 64. Made in Italy 65. Diabolik 67. Confessions of a Police Captain 71. The Sunday Woman 75. Section Speciale 75. Amok 82. L'Amore che Non Sai 93, etc.
AS DIRECTOR: The Sky Is Red/Il Cielo e Rosso 50. *Eager to Live*/Febbre di Vivere 53. The Enchanting Enemy/L'Incantevole Nemica 53. La Grande Ombra 58. La Contessa Azzurra 60. Hate Is My God/L'Odio e il Mio Dio (& a) 69, etc.

Gorcey, Bernard (1888–1955).
American character actor and ex-vaudevillian, father of Leo Gorcey, with whom he often appeared in the Bowery Boys series.
Abie's Irish Rose 28. The Great Dictator 40. Out of the Fog 41. No Minor Vices 49. Pick-Up 51, many others.

Gorcey, Leo (1915–1969).
Pint-sized American second feature star, one of the original Dead End Kids; his screen personality was that of a tough, fast-talking, basically kindly Brooklyn layabout, and he developed this in scores of routine films, mostly under the Bowery Boys banner.
Dead End 37. Mannequin 38. Crime School 38. *Angels With Dirty Faces* 38. Hell's Kitchen 39. Angels Wash Their Faces 39. Invisible Stripes 40. Pride of the Bowery 40. Spooks Run Wild 41. Mr Wise Guy 42. Destroyer 43. Midnight Manhunt 45. Bowery Bombshell 46. Spook Busters 46. Hard Boiled Mahoney 47. Jinx Money 48. Angels in Disguise 49. Lucky Losers 50. Crazy over Horses 51. No Holds Barred 52. Loose in London 52. The Bowery Boys Meet the Monsters 54. Bowery to Bagdad 55. Crashing Las Vegas 56. The Phynx 69, many others.

Gordon, Bert (1898–1974).
American radio comedian. Known as The Mad Russian, he made a few films in the 40s.

Gordon, Bert I. (1922–).
American producer-director of small independent horror exploitation films.
The Beginning of the End 57. The Amazing Colossal Man 57. Cyclops 57. The Boy and the Pirates 60. The Magic Sword 62. Picture Mommy Dead 66. How to Succeed with Sex (wd only) 69. Necromancy (pd) 73. The Mad Bomber 75. Food of the Gods 76. Empire of the Ants 77. The Coming 81. Doing It 84. The Big Bet 86. Malediction 89. Satan's Princess 90, etc.

Gordon, Bruce (1919–).
American character actor, invariably a heavy.
Love Happy 50. The Buccaneer 58. Rider on a Dead Horse 61. Slow Run 68. Machismo 70. Piranha 78. Timerider 82, etc.
TV series: *The Untouchables* (as Frank Nitti) 59–62. Run Buddy Run 66.

Gordon, C. Henry (1882–1940).
American character actor, often seen as maniacally evil villain or Indian rajah.
Charlie Chan Carries On 31. Rasputin and the Empress 32. Mata Hari 32. Lives of a Bengal Lancer 35. *The Charge of the Light Brigade* 36. The Return of the Cisco Kid 38. Kit Carson 40. Charlie Chan at the Wax Museum 40, etc.

Gordon, Colin (1911–1972).
British light comedy actor, on stage from 1931; often seen as mildly cynical civil servant or schoolmaster.
Bond Street 47. The Winslow Boy 48. The Man in the White Suit 51. *Folly to Be Wise* 52. Escapade 55. The Safecracker 58. Please Turn Over 59. Night of the Eagle 62. The Pink Panther 63. The Family Way 66. Casino Royale 67, many others.

Gordon, Dexter (1923–1990).
Hard-blowing jazz tenor saxophonist and occasional actor. He played a musician somewhat like himself (though actually based on pianist Bud Powell) in *Round Midnight*. In *Unchained*, his music was dubbed by saxophonist Georgie Auld. Born in Los Angeles, he played with Lionel HAMPTON's band and led his own groups before moving to live in Europe in the 60s and most of the 70s, returning to the US in the late 70s. Alcoholism and heroin addiction bedevilled his career from the 50s. Died of kidney failure.
Unchained 55 (a). Round Midnight (AAN) (a, m) 86. Awakenings (a) 91.

Gordon, Gale (1905–1995) (Gaylord Aldrich).
Plump, fussy American comedy actor, best known on TV.
Here We Go Again 42. A Woman of Distinction 50. Don't Give Up the Ship 59. Visit to a Small Planet 60. Sergeant Deadhead 65. Speedway 68. The 'burbs 89, etc.
TV series: My Favorite Husband 53–54. Our Miss Brooks 52–56. The Brothers 57. Dennis the Menace 59–63. *The Lucy Show* 62–68. Life with Lucy 86.

Gordon, Gavin (1906–1970).
American general-purpose actor.
Romance (lead) 30. The Bitter Tea of General Yen 32. The Scarlet Empress 34. Bride of Frankenstein 35. Windjammer 38. Paper Bullets 41. Centennial Summer 46. Knock on Wood 54. The Bat 59, etc.

Gordon, Hal (1894–1946).
Hearty British comedy actor, often seen as good-natured foil to star comedian.
Adam's Apple 31. Happy 34. Captain Bill 36. Keep Fit 37. It's in the Air 38. Old Mother Riley, Detective 43. Give Me the Stars 45 (last appearance), etc.

Gordon, Irving (1915–1996).
American songwriter, best known for putting lyrics to the instrumental compositions of Duke ELLINGTON and for writing 'Unforgettable'. He also wrote vaudeville sketches, including ABBOTT AND COSTELLO's 'Who's on first' routine which was featured in *Buck Privates*/*Rookies*.

Gordon, Keith (1961–).
American actor, screenwriter, producer and director.
AS ACTOR: Home Movies 79. All That Jazz 79. Dressed to Kill 80. Kent State (TV) 81. Silent Rebellion 82. Single Bars, Single Women (TV) 84. Static (& co-w, p) 89. Christine 84. Legend of Billie Jean 85. Combat Academy 86. Back to School 86.
AS DIRECTOR: The Chocolate War (wd) 88. A Midnight Clear (wd) 92. Wild Palms (TV) (co-d) 93. Mother Night 96, etc.

Gordon, Lawrence (1934–).
American producer who veers between films and television (where he was the original producer of *Burke's Law*).
Dillinger 73. Hard Times 75. Rolling Thunder 77. Hooper 78. The Driver 78. The End 78. The Warriors 79. Xanadu 80. Paternity 81. 48 Hours 82. Streets of Fire 84. Brewster's Millions 85. Predator 87. Die Hard 88. Field of Dreams 89. Die Hard II 90. Predator 2 90. The Rocketeer 91, etc.

Gordon, Leo (1922–).
Thick-set American character actor, usually in tough-guy roles.
China Venture 53. Riot in Cell Block 11 53. Seven Angry Men 55. The Conqueror 55. The Man Who Knew Too Much 56. Cry Baby Killer (& w) 57. The Big Operator 59. The Stranger 62. The Terror (& w) 63. The Haunted Palace 64. Beau Geste 66. Tobruk (& w) 66. The St Valentine's Day Massacre 67. You Can't Win 'Em All 71. Rage 80. Bog 84. Maverick 94, etc.
TV series: Enos 81.

Gordon, Mack (1904–1959).
American lyricist.
Tin Pan Alley 40. Lillian Russell 40. Sun Valley Serenade ('Chattanooga Choo Choo') 41. Orchestra Wives ('Kalamazoo') 42. Mother Wore Tights 47. Wabash Avenue 50, etc.

Gordon, Mary (1882–1963).
Tiny Scottish character actress in Hollywood; best remembered as the perfect Mrs Hudson in many a Sherlock Holmes film.
The Home Maker 25. The Black Camel 31. The Little Minister 34. The Bride of Frankenstein 35. The Plough and the Stars 36. Kidnapped 38. The Hound of the Baskervilles 39. Tear Gas Squad 40. Appointment for Love 41. The Mummy's Tomb 42. Sherlock Holmes Faces Death 43. The Woman in Green 45. Little Giant 46. The Invisible Wall 47, many others.

Gordon, Michael (1909–1993).
American director with stage experience.
■ Boston Blackie Goes to Hollywood 42. Underground Agent 42. One Dangerous Night 43. Crime Doctor 43. *The Web* 47. Another Part of the Forest 48. An Act of Murder 48. The Lady Gambles 49. Woman in Hiding 49. Cyrano de Bergerac 50. I Can Get It for You Wholesale 51. The Secret of Convict Lake 51. Wherever She Goes 53. *Pillow Talk* 59. Portrait in Black 60. Boys' Night Out 62. For Love of Money 63. Move Over Darling 63. A Very Special Favor 65. Texas across the River 66. The Impossible Years 68. How Do I Love Thee? 70.

Gordon, Richard (1921–) (Gordon Ostlere).
British comic novelist whose accounts of hospital life were a staple of British comedy in the 50s and 60s and gave rise to the TV series *Doctor in the House* 70–73. The films were all directed by Ralph Thomas and the first established Dirk Bogarde as Britain's most popular actor.
Doctor in the House 54. Doctor at Sea 55. Doctor at Large 57. Doctor in Love 60. Doctor in Distress 63. Doctor in Clover 66. Doctor in Trouble 70.

Gordon, Ruth (1896–1985) (Ruth Gordon Jones).
Distinguished American stage actress who wrote several screenplays with her husband Garson Kanin, saw two of her own plays filmed, and had a long, sporadic career as film actress.
■ AS WRITER: Over 21 (oa/solo) 45. *A Double Life* 48. *Adam's Rib* (AAN) 49. The Marrying Kind 52. Pat and Mike (AAN) 52. The Actress (oa/solo) 53. Rosie (oa/solo) 58.
■ AS ACTRESS: Camille 15. The Wheel of Life 16. Abe Lincoln in Illinois 40. Dr Ehrlich's Magic Bullet 40. Two Faced Woman 41. Edge of Darkness 43. Action in the North Atlantic 43. Inside Daisy Clover (AAN) 66. Lord Love a Duck 66.

Rosemary's Baby (AA) 68. Whatever Happened to Aunt Alice? 69. Where's Poppa? 70. *Harold and Maude* 72. Isn't It Shocking? (TV) 73. Panic 75. The Big Bus 76. The Great Houdinis (TV) 76. Look What Happened to Rosemary's Baby (TV) 76. Prince of Central Park (TV) 77. Boardwalk 78. Perfect Gentlemen (TV) 78. *Every Which Way but Loose* 78. My Bodyguard 80. Any Which Way You Can 80. Don't Go to Sleep (TV) 83. Jimmy the Kid 83. Maxie 85. Delta Pi 85.

Gordon, Steve (1938–1982).
American writer-director. Died of a heart attack.
The One and Only (co-p, w) 78. *Arthur* (wd) (AANw) 81.

Gordon, Stuart (1947–).
American director and screenwriter of horror films, from the theatre.
Re-Animator 85. From Beyond 86. Dolls 87. Daughter of Darkness (TV) 89. Robojox/Robot Jox 89. Honey, I Shrunk the Kids (co-w) 89. The Pit and the Pendulum 90. Chicago Cops 92. Honey, I Blew Up the Kid (p) 92. Fortress 93. Body Snatchers (co-w) 93. Castle Freak 95. The Wonderful Ice-Cream Suit 98, etc.
“ One of the great things about genre movies is that as long as you follow the rules of the genre you can do anything you want and say anything you want. There's a tremendous amount of freedom. – S.G.
Horror films are really the subconscious of the movies. – S.G.

Gordon-Sinclair, John (1962–).
Scottish actor, a former electrician, who starred in Bill Forsyth's comedy *Gregory's Girl*.
That Sinking Feeling 79. *Gregory's Girl* 80. Britannia Hospital 82. Local Hero 83. The Girl in the Picture 86. Erik the Viking 89. The Brylcreem Boys (TV) 96, etc.
TV series: Hot Metal 86–88. Nelson's Column 94. Loved by You 97– .

Gore, Michael (1951–).
American composer.
Fame (AA) 80. Terms of Endearment (AAN) 83. Pretty in Pink 86. Don't Tell Her It's Me 90. The Butcher's Wife 91. Defending Your Life 91. Mr Wonderful 93, etc.

Goretta, Claude (1929–).
Swiss director.
The Invitation 73. *The Lacemaker* 77. La Provinciale/A Girl from Lorraine 80. La Mort de Mario Ricci 82. Si le Soleil ne Revenait pas 87. Le Rapport du Gendarme (TV) 87. Guillaume T – la Fouine 92, etc.

Goring, Marius (1912–1998).
British stage and screen actor adept at neurotic or fey roles.
Consider Your Verdict (debut) 36. Rembrandt 37. *The Case of the Frightened Lady* 38. *A Matter of Life and Death* 45. The Red Shoes 48. Mr Perrin and Mr Traill 49. So Little Time 52. *Ill Met by Moonlight* 57. Exodus 60. The Inspector/Lisa 62. Up From the Beach 65. Girl on a Motorcycle 68. Subterfuge 69. First Love 70. Zeppelin 71. Holocaust (TV) 78. Strike It Rich 89, etc.
TV series: The Scarlet Pimpernel 54. The Expert 68–70, 74.

Gorky, Maxim (1868–1936) (Alexei Maximovitch Peshkov).
Russian writer whose autobiography was filmed by Donskoi as *The Childhood of Maxim Gorky, Out in the World* and My *Universities*. Other filmed works include *The Lower Depths* (many times) and *The Mother*.

Gorman, Cliff (1936–).
American leading man of the 70s.
Justine 69. The Boys in the Band 70. Cops and Robbers 73. Rosebud 75. An Unmarried Woman 78. All That Jazz 79. Night of the Juggler 80. Angel 84. Internal Affairs 88. Murder Times Seven (TV) 90. Night and the City 92. Down Came a Blackbird (TV) 95, etc.

Gorney, Karen Lynn (1945–).
American leading lady who was top-billed with Travolta in *Saturday Night Fever* 77.
The Hard Way 91. Ripe 97, etc.

Gorris, Marleen (1948–).
Dutch director and screenwriter of features with a feminist slant.
A Question of Silence/De Stilte Rond Christine M 81. Broken Mirrors/Gebrokene Spiegels 84. The Last Island 91. Antonia's Line (AA) 95. Mrs Dalloway 97, etc.

Gorshin, Frank (1933–).
Wiry American impressionist and character actor, popular as 'The Riddler' in TV's *Batman* series.
The True Story of Jesse James 57. Warlock 59. Studs Lonigan 60. Ring of Fire 61. The George Raft Story 61. Batman 65. Sky Heist (TV) 75. Underground Aces 81. Hot Resort 85. Hollywood Vice Squad 86. Upper Crust 88. Midnight 89. Sweet Justice 92. The Meteor Man 93. Amore! 93. Hail Caesar 94. Twelve Monkeys 95. Bloodmoon 97, etc.

Gortner, Marjoe (1944–).
American evangelist turned actor (following a 1972 documentary on his life called *Marjoe*).
■ The Marcus Nelson Murders (TV) 73. Earthquake 74. The Gun and the Pulpit (TV) 74. Food of the Gods 76. Bobbie Joe and the Outlaw 76. Sidewinder One 77. Viva Knievel 77. Acapulco Gold 78. Starcrash 79. When You Comin' Back Red Ryder 79. Hellhole 85. American Ninja III 89. Fire, Ice and Dynamite 91. Wild Bill 95.
TV series: Falcon Crest 86–87.

Gorton, Assheton.
British production designer.
The Knack . . . and How to Get It 65. Blow Up 66. The Bed Sitting Room 69. Get Carter 71. The French Lieutenant's Woman (AAN) 81. Legend 85. Lost Angels 89. For the Boys 91. Rob Roy 95. 101 Dalmatians 96, etc.

Gosho, Heinosuke (1902–1981).
Japanese director and screenwriter who began as an assistant director and made his first film in 1925. He directed Japan's first talkie, *The Neighbour's Wife and Mine*, in 1931.
The Village Bride 28. Caress/Aibu 33. *Four Chimneys*/Entotsu No Mieru Basho 53. *Adolescence* 55. Yellow Crow/Kiiroi Karasu 57. The Fireflies/Hotarubi 58. When a Woman Loves/Waga Ai 60. Four Seasons of the Meiji Period/Meiji Haru Aki 68, etc.

Gossett, Lou (1936–) (aka Louis Gossett Jnr).
American character actor of striking presence.
Companions in Nightmare (TV) 68. The Landlord 70. The River Niger 72. It's Good to Be Alive (TV) 74. Sidekicks (TV) 74. Delancey Street (TV) 75. Roots (TV) 77. The Choirboys (TV) 77. The Deep (TV) 77. Little Ladies of the Night (TV) 78. To Kill a Cop (TV) 78. The Critical List (TV) 78. *The Lazarus Syndrome* (TV) (and series) 79. Backstairs at the White House (TV) 79. This Man Stands Alone (TV) 79. Don't Look Back (TV) 81. *An Officer and a Gentleman* (AA) 82. Sadat (TV) 83. Jaws 3-D 83. Finders Keepers 84. Enemy Mine 85. Iron Eagle 85. Firewalker 86. The Principal 87. Iron Eagle II 88. The Punisher 89. Cover Up 90. Toy Soldiers 91. Keeper of the City 91. Diggstown/Midnight Sting 92. Monolith 93. Blue Chips 94. Flashfire 94. Ray Alexander: A Taste for Justice (& p) (TV) 94. A Good Man in Africa 94. Curse of the Starving Class 94. Iron Eagle IV 95. Inside 96. Managua 97. In His Father's Shoes (TV) 97. Bram Stoker's The Mummy 97, etc.
TV series: The Powers of Matthew Starr 82.

Gotell, Walter (1924–).
British character actor, often as Nazi or KGB menace.
Treasure of San Teresa 59. The Guns of Navarone 61. The Damned 61. Our Miss Fred 72. The Spy Who Loved Me 77. The Boys from Brazil 78. For Your Eyes Only 80. Basic Training 86. The Living Daylights 87. Puppet Master III (US) 90. Wings of Fame 90, etc.

Gottlieb, Carl (1938–).
American screenwriter, with TV comedy experience.
Jaws 75. Which Way Is Up 77. Jaws 2 78. The Jerk 79. Caveman (& d) 81. Doctor Detroit 83. Jaws 3-D 83. Amazon Women on the Moon (co-d) 87, etc.

Gottschalk, Ferdinand (1869–1944).
Bald-domed English character actor in Hollywood.
Zaza 26. Grand Hotel 32. The Sign of the Cross 32. Les Misérables 35. The Garden of Allah 36, many others.

Goudal, Jetta (1898–1985).
French leading lady of American silent films.
The Bright Shawl 24. Open All Night 24. Spanish Love 25. Road to Yesterday 25. The Coming of Amos 25. 3 Faces East 26. White Gold 27. Forbidden Woman 28. Her Cardboard Lover 28. Lady of the Pavements 30. Business and Pleasure 32, etc.

Gough, Michael (1917–).
Tall British stage (since 1936) and screen (since 1946) actor; has recently gone in for homicidal roles.
Blanche Fury (debut) 46. The Small Back Room 48. The Man in the White Suit 51. Richard III 56. Dracula 57. Horrors of the Black Museum 58. The Horse's Mouth 59. Konga 61. Black Zoo 63. Dr Terror's House of Horrors 65. Circus of Blood 67. Trog 70. The Corpse 70. The Go-Between 70. Henry VIII and His Six Wives 72. Horror Hospital 73. The Boys from Brazil 78. Suez 1956 (TV) (as Anthony Eden) 79. The Dresser 83. Memed My Hawk 83. Out of Africa 85. Let Him Have It 91. Batman Returns 92. Wittgenstein 93. The Age of Innocence 93. The Hour of the Pig 93. Nostradamus 94. Uncovered 94. Batman Forever 95. All for Love 98. The Cherry Orchard (Gr.) 98, many others.

Gould, Elliott (1938–) (Elliot Goldstein).
American actor whose very unhandsomeness made him the man for the early 70s. Formerly married to Barbra Streisand (1963–66).
The Confession 66. The Night They Raided Minsky's 68. *Bob and Carol and Ted and Alice* (AAN) 69. M*A*S*H 70. Getting Straight 70. Move 70. I Love My Wife 70. The Touch 70. Little Murders 71. The Long Goodbye 72. Busting 73. S.P.Y.S. 74. California Split 74. Who? 74. Nashville 74. Whiffs 76. I Will . . . I Will . . . for Now 76. Harry and Walter Go to New York 76. Mean Johnny Barrows 76. A Bridge Too Far 77. Matilda 78. The Silent Partner 78. Capricorn One 78. Escape to Athena 79. The Lady Vanishes 79. The Muppet Movie 79. Falling in Love Again 80. The Last Flight of Noah's Ark 80. Dirty Tricks 81. The Devil and Max Devlin 81. Rites of Marriage (TV) 82. The Muppets Take Manhattan 84. The Naked Face 84. Inside Out 86. I Miei Primi Quarant'Anni 87. Der Joker 87. Dangerous Love 88. The Telephone 88. The Lemon Sisters 89. Night Visitor 89. Scandalo Segreto 89. Massacre Play/Gioco al Massacro 89. Dead Men Don't Die 90. I Won't Disturb You/Tolgo il Disturbo 91. Bugsy 91. Exchange Lifeguards (Aus.) 93. The Glass Shield 94. White Man's Burden 94. A Boy Called Hate 95. Kicking and Screaming 95. Johns 96. The Feminine Touch 96. The Big Hit 98. American History X 98, etc.
TV series: E. R. 84. Together We Stand 86.
“ Success didn't change me. I was distorted *before* I became a star. – E.G.

Gould, Harold (1923–).
American light character actor, a former drama teacher.
He and She 69. Where Does It Hurt? 71. Love and Death 75. Silent Movie 76. The Big Bus 76. *Washington: Behind Closed Doors* (TV) 77. The Feather and Father Gang 77. Seems Like Old Times 80. The Man in the Santa Claus Suit (TV) 80. Moviola (TV) 80. The Dream Chasers 84. The Fourth Wise Man 85. Romero 89. Killer: A Journal of Murder 95. My Giant 98, etc.
TV series: He & She 67–68. Rhoda 74–78. The Feather and Father Gang 77. Park Place 81. Foot in the Door 83. Under One Roof 85. Singer & Sons 90.

Gould, Heywood.
American screenwriter and director.
Rolling Thunder (co-w) 77. The Boys from Brazil (w) 78. Fort Apache, the Bronx (w) 81. Streets of Gold (co-w) 86. Cocktail (w, oa) 88. One Good Cop (wd) 91. Trial by Jury (co-w, d) 94. Mistrial (wd) (TV) 96, etc.

Gould, Jason (1966–).
American actor, the son of Barbra Streisand and Elliott Gould.
The Big Picture 88. Listen to Me 89. The Prince of Tides 91, etc.

Gould, Morton (1913–1996).
American composer (and conductor).
Delightfully Dangerous 42. Cinerama Holiday 55. Holocaust (TV) 77.

Goulding, Alfred J. (1896–1972).
American director; active with Harold Lloyd in the 20s and later with Laurel and Hardy (*A Chump at Oxford*).

Goulding, Edmund (1891–1959).
English-born director, screenwriter, composer, playwright and novelist, in Hollywood, where he was a safe handler of female stars of the 30s and 40s. Born in London, he was on stage from 1904, emigrating to the US in 1915, where he began writing for the movies from the early 20s. In 1925, as a writer and director, he joined MGM, where he was protected from the consequences of several sexual scandals until Mayer fired him in 1936. He then worked for Warner's and Twentieth Century-Fox. He directed four of Bette Davis's films, but he is said to have faked a heart attack while arguing with her on the set of *Old Acquaintance* in order not to work with her again. Apart from his qualities as a director, he was noted for his ability to invent scenarios, design costumes and compose melodies, which he managed by whistling tunes to an arranger. 'Mam'selle', a ballad based on one of the themes he wrote for *The Razor's Edge*, was a hit in 1947.
■ Sun Up 25. Sally, Irene and Mary 25. Paris 26. Women Love Diamonds 26. Love 27. *The Trespasser* (& w) 29. The Devil's Holiday (& w) 30. Paramount on Parade (part) 30. Reaching for the Moon (& w) 30. The Night Angel (& w) 31. *Grand Hotel* 32. Blondie of the Follies 32. Riptide 34. The Flame Within (& wp) 35. That Certain Woman (& w) 37. White Banners 38. The Dawn Patrol 38. *Dark Victory* 39. *The Old Maid* 39. We Are Not Alone 39. Till We Meet Again 40. *The Great Lie* 41. Forever and a Day (co-d) 43. The Constant Nymph 43. *Claudia* 43. Of Human Bondage 46. *The Razor's Edge* 46. *Nightmare Alley* 47. Everybody Does It 49. Mister 880 50. We're Not Married 52. Down Among the Sheltering Palms 53. Teenage Rebel 56. Mardi Gras 58.
“ Eddie was terribly inventive and full of ideas, but one of his peculiarities was that he could tell a story in the morning and forget everything about it by afternoon. – *Larry Weingarten*

Goulet, Robert (1933–) (Stanley Applebaum).
Canadian singer and leading man, with experience mainly on TV.
Honeymoon Hotel 63. I'd Rather Be Rich 64. Underground 70. Atlantic City USA 80. Scrooged 88. The Naked Gun 2½: The Smell of Fear 91. Mr Wrong 96, etc.
TV series: The Blue Light 64.

Gowers, Patrick (1936–).
English composer.
The Virgin and the Gypsy 70. A Bigger Splash 75. Stevie 78. Smiley's People (TV) 82. Sorrel and Son (TV) 86. Whoops Apocalypse 86. The Hound of the Baskervilles (TV) 88, etc.

Gowland, Gibson (1872–1951).
English character actor in mainly American films.
The Promise 17. Blind Husbands 19. Ladies Must Love 21. Shifting Sands 23. *Greed* 24. The Phantom of the Opera 25. Don Juan 26. Topsy and Eva 27. Rose Marie 28. The Mysterious Island 29. The Sea Bat 30. Doomed Battalion 32. SOS Iceberg 33. The Secret of the Loch 34. The Mystery of the Marie Celeste 36. Cotton Queen 37, many others.

Goyer, David.
American screenwriter. He graduated from the University of Southern California in 1988 with a degree in screenwriting.
Death Warrant 90. The Puppet Masters 94. The Crow: City of Angels 96. Ghost Rider 97. Venom 97. Dark City 97.

Gozzi, Patricia (1950–).
French juvenile actress of the 60s.
Sundays and Cybele 62. Rapture 65. Hung Up 68, etc.

Grable, Betty (1916–1973).
American leading lady who personified the peaches-and-cream appeal which was required in the 40s but which later seemed excessively bland.

She performed efficiently in a series of light musicals and dramas, and was the most famous pin-up of World War II. Born in St Louis, she worked in vaudeville from childhood, encouraged by her mother, and began in films in blackface in the chorus line at the age of 13, also singing in her teens with the Ted Fio Rita orchestra. Her success began when Darryl ZANUCK signed her for Twentieth Century-Fox after Paramount had dropped her contract; she made an impact in the Broadway musical *Du Barry Was a Lady* and then replaced Alice FAYE in the film *Down Argentina Way*. By the mid-40s she was the highest-paid star in Hollywood and America's highest-paid woman, forming a successful musical partnership with Dan DAILEY. By the early 50s, Zanuck wanted to get rid of her, and she tore up her contract with the studio. In the mid-60s, she performed in theatres, returning to Broadway to replace Martha RAYE in *Hello Dolly*. Died from cancer. Married actor Jackie COOGAN (1937–40) and bandleader Harry JAMES (1943–65); she was romantically involved with bandleader Artie SHAW, singer Desi ARNAZ, and actor George RAFT.

Biography: 1982, *Betty Grable: The Reluctant Movie Queen* by Doug Warren.

■ Let's Go Places 30. New Movietone Follies of 1930 30. Whoopee 30. Kiki 31. Palmy Days 31. The Greeks had a Word for Them 32. The Kid from Spain 32. Child of Manhattan 32. Probation 32. Hold 'Em Jail 32. Cavalcade 33. What Price Innocence 33. Sweetheart of Sigma Chi 33. Melody Cruise 33. By Your Leave 34. Student Tour 34. *The Gay Divorcee* 34. The Nitwits 35. Old Man Rhythm 35. Collegiate 35. Follow the Fleet 36. Pigskin Parade 36. Don't Turn 'Em Loose 36. This Way Please 37. Thrill of a Lifetime 37. College Swing 38. Give Me a Sailor 38. Campus Confessions 38. Man About Town 39. Million Dollar Legs 39. The Day the Bookies Wept 39. *Down Argentine Way* 40. *Tin Pan Alley* 40. *Moon Over Miami* 41. A Yank in the RAF 41. *I Wake Up Screaming* 41. Footlight Serenade 42. Song of the Islands 42. Springtime in the Rockies 42. *Coney Island* 43. Sweet Rosie O'Grady 43. Four Jills in a Jeep 44. Pin Up Girl 44. Diamond Horseshoe 45. The Dolly Sisters 45. Do You Love Me (cameo) 46. The Shocking Miss Pilgrim 47. *Mother Wore Tights* 47. That Lady in Ermine 48. When My Baby Smiles at Me 48. The Beautiful Blonde from Bashful Bend 49. Wabash Avenue 50. My Blue Heaven 50. Call Me Mister 51. Meet Me After the Show 51. The Farmer Takes a Wife 53. *How To Marry A Millionaire* 53. Three for the Show 54. How to be Very Very Popular 55.

❝ There are two reasons why I'm in show business, and I'm standing on both of them. – B.G.

I'm strictly an enlisted man's girl. – B.G.

There's nothing mysterious about me. – B.G.

I don't think Betty would want an Oscar on her mantelpiece. She has every Tom, Dick and Harry at her feet. – *Nunnally Johnson*

Grace, Nickolas (1949–).
English character actor, mainly on stage. In films from 1974.

Sleepwalker 75. City of the Dead 78. Europe after the Rain 80. Heat and Dust 83. Salome's Last Dance 87. Just Ask for Diamond/Diamond's Edge 88. Dream Demon 88. Tom and Viv 94. Two Deaths 95. Shooting Fish 97, etc.

Grade, Lew (Lord Grade) (c. 1906–1998) (Lewis Winogradsky).
British impresario, brother of Lord Delfont, long in charge of Associated Television, latterly producing feature films for family audiences.

Autobiography: 1987, *Still Dancing*.

Biographies: 1982, *My Fabulous Brothers* by Rita Grade Freeman. 1984, *The Grades* by Hunter Davies. 1987, *Last of a Kind: The Sinking of Lew Grade* by Quentin Falk and Dominic Prince.

Voyage of the Damned 76. March or Die 77. The Cassandra Crossing 77. The Boys from Brazil 78. Movie Movie 78. Firepower 79. Raise the Titanic 80. *On Golden Pond* 81. The Great Muppet Caper 81. Green Ice 81. The Legend of the Lone Ranger 81. Barbarosa 81. The Salamander 82. Sophie's Choice 82. The Dark Crystal 82, etc.

❝ All my shows are great. Some of them are bad, but they're all great. – L.G.

I intend to produce more feature films than any major studio in the world. I am only 68 and just beginning. By the time I am 70, British films will rule the world. – L.G.

It would have been cheaper to lower the Atlantic. – L.G. on *Raise the Titanic*

Lew Grade only did what everyone else did before him, which was to lose money on British films. People may not have liked the films he made. But he went out and slogged away and got money for hundreds and thousands of British actors, directors and technicians. I think the man should be applauded for that. – *Michael Winner*

Graetz, Paul (1901–1966).
Franco-Austrian independent producer.

Le Diable au Corps 46. Monsieur Ripois/Knave of Hearts 53. Is Paris Burning? 66, etc.

Graham, Heather (1970–).
American actress. Born in Milwaukee, Wisconsin, and brought up in California.

License to Drive 87. Drugstore Cowboy 89. Shout 91. Diggstown/Midnight Sting 92. Twin Peaks: Firewalk with Me 92. Guilty as Charged 92. The Ballad of Little Jo 93. Six Degrees of Separation 94. Toughguy 94. Don't Do It 94. Desert Winds 95. Nowhere 96. Swingers 96. *Boogie Nights* 97. Two Girls and a Guy 98. Lost in Space 98, etc.

Graham, Morland (1891–1949).
Stocky Scottish character actor, on stage and screen from 20s.

The Scarlet Pimpernel 35. Jamaica Inn 39. Old Bill and Son (as Old Bill) 40. The Ghost Train 41. The Shipbuilders 44. The Brothers 47. Bonnie Prince Charlie 48. Whisky Galore 48, etc.

Graham, Ronny (1919–).
American comic actor and screenwriter.

New Faces (& w) 54. Dirty Little Billy 72. The World's Greatest Lover 77. To Be or Not to Be 83. The Ratings Game (TV) 84. The Substance of Fire 96.

Graham, Sheilah (1904–1988) (Lilly Shiel).
British gossip columnist in America, companion of F. Scott Fitzgerald. Author of *Beloved Infidel*, *The Garden of Allah*, etc.

Graham, William (c. 1930–).
American director, from TV. (Sometimes billed as William A. Graham.)

The Doomsday Flight (TV) 66. Waterhole 3 67. Then Came Bronson (TV) 68. Submarine X1 68. Change of Habit 69. Thief (TV) 71. *Birds of Prey* (TV) 73. Get Christie Love (TV) 74. Trapped Beneath the Sea (TV) 74. 21 Hours at Munich (TV) 76. *Minstrel Man* (TV) 77. *The Amazing Howard Hughes* (TV) 77. Contract on Cherry Street (TV) 77. And I Alone Survived (TV) 78. Transplant (TV) 79. Guyana Tragedy (TV) 81. Harry Tracy 81. Mothers Against Drunk Drivers (TV) 82. Mussolini: The Untold Story (TV) 85. The Last Days of Frank and Jesse James (TV) 86. Proud Men 87. Street of Dreams 88. Return to the Blue Lagoon 91, etc.

Grahame, Gloria (1924–1981) (Gloria Hallward).
Blonde American leading lady, usually in off-beat roles.

■ Blonde Fever (debut) 44. Without Love 45. It's a Wonderful Life 46. It Happened in Brooklyn 47. Merton of the Movies 47. Song of the Thin Man 47. *Crossfire* (AAN) 47. Roughshod 48. A Woman's Secret 48. *In a Lonely Place* 50. *The Bad and the Beautiful* (AA) 52. Macao 52. Sudden Fear 52. The Glass Wall 53. Man on a Tightrope 53. Prisoners of the Casbah 53. The Greatest Show on Earth 53. Naked Alibi 54. *The Big Heat* 54. The Good Die Young (GB) 54. Human Desire 55. The Man Who Never Was (GB) 55. Not as a Stranger 55. The Cobweb 55. Oklahoma 56. Ride Out for Revenge 57. Odds Against Tomorrow 59. Ride Beyond Vengeance 66. The Todd Killings 70. Black Noon (TV) 71. Chandler 72. The Loners 72. Blood and Lace 72. Tarot 73. Mama's Dirty Girls 74. The Girl on the Late Late Show (TV) 75. Rich Man Poor Man (TV) 76. Mansion of the Doomed 76. Seventh Avenue (TV) 77. Head Over Heels 79. Melvin and Howard 80. A Nightingale Sang in Berkeley Square 80.

Grahame, Margot (1911–1982).
British leading lady of the 30s, with stage experience.

The Love Habit 30. Rookery Nook 30. Sorrell and Son 34. The Informer (US) 35. The Three Musketeers (US) 36. Michael Strogoff (US) 37. The Shipbuilders 44. Broken Journey 48. The Romantic Age 49. Venetian Bird 52. Orders Are Orders 55. Saint Joan 57, etc.

Grainer, Ron (1922–1981).
Australian composer in Britain.

A Kind of Loving 62. Nothing But the Best 64. To Sir with Love 67. Lock Up Your Daughters 68. In Search of Oregon 70. The Omega Man 71. Yellow Dog 73. I Don't Want to Be Born 75, many others.

Grainger, Edmund (1906–1981).
American producer and executive, long with RKO. Specialized in quality action pictures.

Diamond Jim 35. Sutter's Gold 36. International Squadron 41. Wake of the Red Witch 48. Sands of Iwo Jima 49. Flying Leathernecks 50. One Minute to Zero 52. Treasure of Pancho Villa 55. Green Mansions 59. Home from the Hill 60. Cimarron 61, many others.

Grammer, Kelsey (1955–).
American actor, best known for his role as Dr Frasier Crane in the 80s and 90s TV sitcoms *Cheers* and *Frasier*. Married his third wife, model Camille Donatucci, in 1997.

Autobiography: 1995, *So Far*.

Biography: 1995, *Kelsey Grammer* by Jeff Rovin.

Beyond Suspicion 93. Down Periscope 96. Anastasia (voice) 97. The Pentagon Wars (TV) 98. The Real Howard Spitz 98, etc.

TV series: Cheers 82–93. Frasier 94– .

Granach, Alexander (1890–1945).
Polish character actor who went to Hollywood in the late 30s.

Biography: 1945, *There Goes an Actor*.

Warning Shadows 23. Kameradschaft 31. *Ninotchka* 39. Hangmen Also Die 43. For Whom the Bell Tolls 43. The Hitler Gang 44. A Voice in the Wind 44. The Seventh Cross 44, etc.

Granger, Dorothy (1912–1995).
American actress, a foil to Laurel and Hardy, Charley Chase, and W. C. Fields, and Leon Errol's wife in a series of comedy shorts.

Hog Wild 30. The Laurel-Hardy Murder Case 30. One Good Turn 31. The Dentist 32. Crime Rave 39. When the Daltons Rode 40. Twin Husbands 46. Killer Dill 47. New York Confidential 55. Raintree Country 57, etc.

Granger, Farley (1925–).
American leading man who began his film career straight from school.

North Star (debut) 43. They Live By Night 47. *Rope* 48. *Strangers on a Train* 51. Hans Christian Andersen 52. Senso (It.) 53. The Girl in the Red Velvet Swing 55. Rogues' Gallery 68. Something Creeping in the Dark (It.) 71. The Serpent 72. Confessions of a Sex Maniac (It.) 72. They Call Me Trinity (It.) 72. The Man Called Noon 73. Arnold 75. Black Beauty (TV) 78. The Imagemaker 85. The Whoopee Boys 86, etc.

Granger, Stewart (1913–1993) (James Lablanche Stewart).
Darkly handsome English-born leading actor who gained fame in romantic melodramas of the 40s. Born in London, he studied acting at the Webber-Douglas School and started his career on the stage, beginning in films as an extra. He went to Hollywood, under contract to MGM, in 1950, and appeared in a series of swashbuckling roles. As his appeal declined, he returned to make films in Europe. He became an American citizen in 1956. The first two of his three wives were actresses Elspeth March (1938–48) and Jean SIMMONS (1950–60).

Autobiography: 1981, *Sparks Fly Upward*.

■ A Southern Maid 33. Give Her a Ring 34. So This Is London 38. Convoy 40. Secret Mission 42. Thursday's Child 43. *The Man in Grey* 43. The Lamp Still Burns 43. Fanny by Gaslight 43. *Waterloo Road* 44. *Love Story* 44. Madonna of the Seven Moons 44. *Caesar and Cleopatra* 45. Caravan 45. The Magic Bow (as Paganini) 46. *Captain Boycott* 47. Blanche Fury 48. Saraband for Dead Lovers (as Koenigsmark) 48. Woman Hater 49. Adam and Evelyne 49. *King Solomon's Mines* (US) 50. The Light Touch (US) 51. Soldiers Three 51. The Wild North 52. *Scaramouche* (US) 52. The Prisoner of Zenda (US) 52. Young Bess (US) 53. Salome (US) 53. All the Brothers Were Valiant (US) 54. *Beau Brummell* (US) 54. Green Fire (US) 55. Moonfleet (US) 55. Footsteps in the Fog 55. Bhowani Junction 56. The Last Hunt (US) 56. Gun Glory 57. The Little Hut 57. The Whole Truth 58. Harry Black and the Tiger 58. North to Alaska (US) 60. The Secret Partner 61. Sodom and Gomorrah 62. Swordsman of Siena (It.) 62. The Legion's Last Patrol (It.) 63. Among Vultures (Ger.) 64. The Secret Invasion 64. The Crooked Road 65. Der Oelprinz (Ger.) 65. Mission Hong Kong 65. Requiem for a Secret Agent 66. Glory City 66. Where Are You Taking that Woman? 66. The Trygon Factor 67. The Last Safari 67. The Flaming Frontier 68. The Hound of the Baskervilles (TV) (as Holmes) 71. The Wild Geese 77. The Royal Romance of Charles & Diana (TV) 82. Hell Hunters 88.

TV series: The Men from Shiloh 70.

❝ I've never done a film I'm proud of. – S.G.

The cinema world is not easy. It is full of envy from little people – heads of studios, for example, who hate people for their attractiveness. – S.G.

I was a good costume actor, but I shortened my career because I made the wrong choices. – S.G.

Grangier, Gilles (1911–1996).
French director. Born in Paris, he began as an extra and a stuntman, becoming an assistant director and emerging in the 50s as a commercially successful director, particularly with films starring Jean GABIN. He later worked in television.

Ademai Bandit d'Honneur 43. L'Aventure de Cabassou 46. L'Amant de Paille 51. L'Amour Madame 52. Gas-Oil 55. Le Sang à la Tête 56. Speaking of Murder/Le Rouge est Mis 57. Le Désordre et la Nuit 58. *The Magnificent Tramp*/Archimide le Clochard 59. The Old Guard/Les Vieux de la Ville 60. The Counterfeiters/Le Cave Se Rebiffe 61. *The Awkward Age*/L'Age Ingrat 61. Le Gentleman d'Epsom 62. La Cusine au Beurre 63. Maigret Viot Rouge 63. Les Bons Vivants (co-d) 66. L'Homme à la Buick 67. Sous le Signe du Taureau 69. Un Cave 72. Le Locataire d'en Haut (TV) 84, etc.

Grant, Arthur (1915–1972).
British cinematographer.

Hell Is a City 60. Jigsaw 62. Eighty Thousand Suspects 63. The Tomb of Ligeia 64. Blood from the Mummy's Tomb 71, etc.

Grant, Cary (1904–1986) (Archibald Leach).
Debonair British-born leading man with a personality and accent all his own; varied theatrical experience before settling in Hollywood. Married five times, including to actresses Virginia CHERRILL (1934–35), Betsy DRAKE (1949–62) and Dyan CANNON (1965–68).

Biographies: 1989, *Cary Grant: The Lonely Heart* by Charles Higham and Roy Moseley; 1991, *Evenings with Cary Grant* by Nancy Nelson; 1997, *Cary Grant: A Class Apart* by Graham McCann.

■ This Is the Night 32. Sinners in the Sun 32. Hot Saturday 32. Merrily We Go to Hell 32. The Devil and the Deep 32. Madame Butterfly 33. Blonde Venus 33. *She Done Him Wrong* 33. Alice in Wonderland (as the Mock Turtle) 33. The Eagle and the Hawk 33. Woman Accused 33. Gambling Ship 33. I'm No Angel 33. Thirty Day Princess 34. Born To Be Bad 34. Kiss and Make Up 34. Enter Madame 34. Ladies Should Listen 34. Wings in the Dark 35. The Last Outpost 35. Sylvia Scarlett 35. Big Brown Eyes 35. Suzy 36. Wedding Present 36. The Amazing Quest of Mr Ernest Bliss (GB) 36. When You're in Love 36. *The Awful Truth* 37. The Toast of New York 37. *Topper* 37. *Bringing Up Baby* 38. Holiday 38. *Gunga Din* 39. Only Angels Have Wings 39. In Name Only 39. *My Favorite Wife* 40. The Howards of Virginia 40. *His Girl Friday* 40. *The Philadelphia Story* 40. Penny Serenade (AAN) 41. Suspicion 41. Talk of the Town 42. Once upon a Honeymoon 42. Destination Tokyo 43. Mr Lucky 43. Once upon a Time 44. None But the Lonely Heart (AAN) 44. *Arsenic and Old Lace* 44. Night and Day (as Cole Porter) 45. Notorious 46. *The Bachelor and the Bobbysoxer* 47. The Bishop's Wife (as an angel) 48. Every Girl Should Be Married 48. *Mr Blandings Builds His Dream House* 48. I Was a Male War Bride 49. Crisis 50. People Will Talk 51. Room for One More 52. Monkey Business 52. Dream Wife 53. To Catch a Thief 55. The Pride and the Passion 57. *An Affair to Remember* 57. Kiss Them for Me 57. *Indiscreet* (GB) 58. Houseboat 58. *North by Northwest* 59. Operation Petticoat 59. The Grass Is Greener 60. That Touch of Mink 62. Charade 63. Father Goose 64. Walk Don't Run 66.

✪ For being the world's most admired sophisticated man for twenty-five years. *Mr Blandings Builds His Dream House*.

❝ When a journalist wired his agent 'How old Cary Grant?', Grant himself replied: 'Old Cary Grant fine. How you?'

Everyone tells me I've had such an interesting life, but sometimes I think it's been nothing but stomach disturbances and self-concern. – C.G.

I improve on misquotation. – C.G.

I think making love is the best form of exercise. – C.G.

I'd like to have made one of those big splashy Technicolor musicals with Rita Hayworth. – C.G.

Everyone wants to be Cary Grant, even I want to be Cary Grant. – C.G.

The drama in a Cary Grant movie is always seeing whether the star can be made to lose his wry, elegant and habitual aplomb. – *Richard Schickel*

A completely private person, totally reserved, and there is no way into him. – *Doris Day*

Cary's enthusiasm made him search for perfection in all things, particularly the three that meant most to him – film-making, physical fitness and women. – *David Niven*

Grant, Hugh (1960–).

Diffident-seeming English leading actor, often in foppish roles. Born in London and educated at Oxford University, he became a star with *Four Weddings and a Funeral*, and through his high-profile romance with actress Elizabeth HURLEY, who is also his partner in a production company. (Public interest in the couple was so strong that, in 1996, the mattress from their holiday home fetched £550 at auction.) In 1995, his career was threatened when he was arrested for committing a lewd act in a car on Sunset Boulevard with Divine Brown, a prostitute who subsequently appeared in a direct-to-video movie, *Taken for Granted*, featuring a Hugh Grant lookalike.

Biography: 1996, *Hugh Grant* by Jody Tresidder.

Maurice 87. White Mischief 87. The Dawning 88. The Lair of the White Worm 88. La Nuit Bengali 88. Impromptu 89. The Big Man 90. Bitter Moon 92. Night Train to Munich 92. The Remains of the Day 93. *Four Weddings and a Funeral* 94. *Sirens* 94. An Awfully Big Adventure 95. The Englishman Who Went up a Hill but Came Down a Mountain 95. Nine Months 95. Sense and Sensibility 95. Restoration 95. Extreme Measures 96, etc.

❝ He is a very bright man. He will not suffer fools gladly. – *Mike Newell*

He's found something that's gone from the movies: the intelligent comic leading man. – *Duncan Kenworthy*

From my personal experience, I think he is a self-important, boring, flash-in-the-pan Brit. – *Robert Downey Jnr*

Grant, James Edward (1902–1966).

American writer.

Whipsaw 35. We're Going to Be Rich 38. Belle of the Yukon 44. The Great John L. 45. Angel and the Bad Man (& d) 46. Sands of Iwo Jima 49. Big Jim McLain 52. Hondo 54. Ring of Fear (co-w, d) 54. The Sheepman (AAN) 58. The Alamo 60. McLintock 63, etc.

Grant, Jennifer (1966?–).

American actress, the daughter of Cary GRANT and Dyan CANNON, from television.

The Evening Star 96, etc.

Grant, Kathryn (1933–) (Olive Grandstaff).

American leading lady who retired to marry Bing Crosby.

Arrowhead 53. Living it Up 54. The Phenix City Story 55. Mister Cory 56. Gunman's Walk 58. Operation Mad Ball 58. The Seventh Voyage of Sinbad 58. The Big Circus 60, etc.

Grant, Kirby (1914–1985) (K. G. Horn).

Dutch-Scottish-American leading man, former bandleader.

Red River Range 39. Ghost Catchers 44. The Lawless Breed 47. Trail of the Yukon 50. Snow Dog 51. Yukon Gold 52. The Court Martial of Billy Mitchell 55. Yukon Vengeance 55, etc.

TV series: Sky King 53–54.

Grant, Lawrence (1870–1952).

British character actor in American films.

The Great Impersonation 21. His Hour 24. The Grand Duchess and the Waiter 26. Doomsday 28. The Canary Murder Case 29. *Bulldog Drummond* 29. The Cat Creeps 30. Daughter of the Dragon 31. The Unholy Garden 31. Jewel Robbery 32. The Mask of Fu Manchu 32. Grand Hotel 32. Shanghai Express 32. Queen Christina 33. By Candlelight 34. Nana 34. Werewolf of London 34. The Devil is a Woman 35. Little Lord Fauntleroy 36. The Prisoner of Zenda 37. Bluebeard's Eighth Wife 38. Son of Frankenstein 39. Women in War 40. Dr Jekyll and Mr Hyde 41. Confidential Agent 45, many others.

Grant, Lee (1927–) (Lyova Rosenthal).

Dynamic American stage actress, sporadically seen in films. She turned to directing in the 80s. She is the mother of Dinah Manoff.

■ AS ACTRESS: *Detective Story* (AAN) 51. Storm Fear 55. Middle of the Night 59. The Balcony 63. An Affair of the Skin 63. Terror in the City 66. Divorce American Style 67. In the Heat of the Night 67. Valley of the Dolls 67. Buona Sera Mrs Campbell 68. The Big Bounce 69. Perilous Voyage (TV) 69. Marooned 69. There Was a Crooked Man 70. *The Landlord* (AAN) 70. Night Slaves (TV) 70. Plaza Suite 71. *The Neon Ceiling* (TV) 71. Ransom for a Dead Man (TV) 71. Lt Schuster's Wife (TV) 72. Portnoy's Complaint 72. Partners in Crime (TV) 73. What Are Best Friends For (TV) 73. The Internecine Project 74. *Shampoo* (AA) 75. Voyage of the Damned (AAN) 76. Airport 77 77. The Spell (TV) 77. The Mafu Cage 77. The Swarm 78. Damien: Omen II 78. Backstairs at the White House (TV) 79. When You Comin' Back Red Ryder 79. You Can't Go Home Again (TV) 79. Tell Me a Riddle (d only) 80. Little Miss Marker 80. Charlie Chan and the Curse of the Dragon Queen 81. Visiting Hours 82. Will There Really Be a Morning? (TV) 83. Teachers 84. The Big Town 87. Calling the Shots 88. Staying Together (d) 89. Defending Your Life 91. Citizen Cohn (TV) 92. It's My Party 95. The Substance of Fire 96.

AS DIRECTOR: Tell Me a Riddle 80. A Matter of Sex (TV) 84. Nobody's Child (TV) 86. Staying Together 89. Women on Trial (TV) 92, etc.

Grant, Richard E. (1957–) (Richard Grant Esterhuysen).

Lanky British leading actor and novelist. Born in Mbabane, Swaziland, he studied English and drama at the University of Cape Town, moving to London in the early 80s.

Autobiography: 1996, *With Nails – The Film Diaries of Richard E. Grant*.

Honest, Decent and True 85. Withnail and I 87. Hidden City 87. How to Get Ahead in Advertising 88. Killing Dad 89. Warlock 89. Henry and June 90. Mountains of the Moon 90. Hudson Hawk 91. L.A. Story 91. The Player 92. Bram Stoker's Dracula 92. Suddenly Last Summer (TV) 93. The Age of Innocence 93. Prêt-à-Porter/Ready to Wear 94. Jack and Sarah 95. Karaoke (TV) 96. A Royal Scandal (TV) 96. The Portrait of a Lady 96. The Serpent's Kiss 97. Food of Love 97. Spice World: The Movie 97. Keep the Aspidistra Flying 97. All for Love 98. Cash in Hand 98. The Scarlet Pimpernel (TV) 98, etc.

❝ I defy anyone not to have their head turned by megastardom because it is a completely abnormal existence. You live a life of extreme fantasy: you're wonderful, you're paid millions, everyone thinks you're beautiful, brilliant, everyone's gagging to hear your every word, capture your every expression, and then the next day you learn you're ugly, you speak all wrong, you're not talented after all, your last three movies were shit, and you're gone. It's so fast and ruthless. – *R.E.G.*

Granville, Bonita (1923–1988).

American child actress of the 30s; adult career gradually petered out but she became a producer.

Westward Passage 32. Cradle Song 33. Ah Wilderness 35. *These Three* (AAN) 36. Maid of Salem 37. Call It a Day 37. Merrily We Live 38. Nancy Drew Detective (and subsequent series) 38. Angels Wash Their Faces 39. Escape 40. H.M. Pulham Esq. 41. The Glass Key 42. Now Voyager 42. *Hitler's Children* 43. Youth Runs Wild 44. Love Laughs at Andy Hardy 46. The Guilty 47. Treason 50. The Lone Ranger 56. Lassie's Greatest Adventure (p) 63, etc.

TV series: Lassie (p) 55–67.

Grapewin, Charley (1869–1956).

American character actor best remembered in movies for his range of grizzled old gentlemen.

Only Saps Work 30. The Night of June 13th 32. Heroes for Sale 33. Judge Priest 34. Ah Wilderness 35. Alice Adams 35. Libelled Lady 36. The Good Earth 37. Captains Courageous 37. Big City 37. Three Comrades 38. The Wizard of Oz 39. *The Grapes of Wrath* 40. Ellery Queen Master Detective 40. *Tobacco Road* (as Jeeter Lester) 41. They Died with Their Boots On 41. Crash Dive 42. The Impatient Years 44. Gunfighters 47. Sand 49. When I Grow Up 51, many others.

Grauman, Sid (1879–1950).

Flamboyant American showman and movie exhibitor. His family ran tent shows and movie houses in San Francisco, and he managed cinemas in various parts of the United States before opening in Los Angeles the Million Dollar Theater, the 3,600-seater Metropolitan, the Egyptian and, most famously, the Chinese Theater on Hollywood Boulevard in 1927. A notorious practical joker, he once gave a slight heart attack to director Ernst LUBITSCH, who was frightened of flying, by having two stuntmen dressed as pilots run down the aisle and parachute from the plane on which Lubitsch was travelling. He was given a special Oscar in 1948 for raising the standard of exhibition of motion pictures.

Grauman, Walter (1922–).

American director, from TV.

Lady in a Cage 63. 633 Squadron 64. A Rage to Live 65. I Deal in Danger 66. The Last Escape 69. Force Five (TV) 75. Most Wanted (TV) 76. Are You in the House Alone? (TV) 78. Pleasure Palace (TV) 80. Scene of the Crime (TV) 85. Shakedown on the Sunset Strip (TV) 88. Nightmare on the 13th Floor (TV) 90, etc.

TV series include The Untouchables, Naked City, Route 66, The Felony Squad.

Graves, George (1876–1949).

English comic actor, in films of the 30s as an elderly bumbler. Born in London, he made his stage debut in 1896 and thereafter alternated between dramas, operetta, pantomime (often as a dame) and music hall.

Autobiography: 1931, *Gaieties and Gravities*.

The Crooked Lady 32. A Sister to Assist 'er 33. Those Were the Days 34. Royal Cavalcade 35. Wolf's Clothing 36. The Robber Symphony 36. A Star Fell from Heaven 36, etc.

❝ Nor must George Graves' dressing room be overlooked. Visitors going there found themselves in a sort of crazy chamber. Chairs collapsed when sat upon, cigarettes thrust upon them exploded, pencils refused to write and turned on those wielding them, coat hangers proffered for their coats shut up and threw the garments on the ground, and when the thoroughly startled visitor was offered a drink, he found the liquor pouring all over his waistcoat from cleverly concealed small holes in the chasing on the glass. Royal personages came, saw, even suffered, and laughed good naturedly. – *W. J. Macqueen-Pope, Theatre Royal, Drury Lane*

Graves, Peter (1926–) (Peter Aurness).

American leading man, usually in 'B' action pictures: brother of James Arness.

Rogue River (debut) 50. Fort Defiance 52. Red Planet Mars 52. Stalag 17 53. Beneath the Twelve-Mile Reef 53. Black Tuesday 55. It Conquered the World 56. Wolf Larsen 59. A Rage to Live 65. The Ballad of Josie 67. The Five Man Army 68. Call to Danger (TV) 73. The President's Plane Is Missing (TV) 73. Scream of the Wolf (TV) 74. The Underground Man (TV) 74. Where Have All the People Gone (TV) 74. Dead Man on the Run (TV) 75. Disaster in the Sky (TV) 77. The Rebels (TV) 79. Airplane 80. Death Car on the Freeway (TV) 80. The Memory of Eva Ryker (TV) 81. Airplane 2: the Sequel 82. Savannah Smiles 82. The Winds of War (TV) 83. Number One with a Bullet 87, etc.

TV series: Fury 55–59. Whiplash 60. Court Martial/Counsellors at War 66. Mission Impossible 66–72.

Graves, Peter (1911–1994).

British light leading man, tall and suave, usually in musical comedy.

Kipps (debut) 41. King Arthur Was a Gentleman 42. Bees in Paradise 44. I'll Be Your Sweetheart 44. Waltz Time 45. The Laughing Lady 46. Spring Song 47. Mrs Fitzherbert (as the Prince Regent) 47. Spring in Park Lane 48. Maytime in Mayfair 49. Derby Day 52. Lilacs in the Spring 54, etc. Latterly in cameo roles, e.g. The Wrong Box 66, The Slipper and the Rose 76.

Graves, Ralph (1901–1977).

American silent star of heroic roles. Later became writer and producer of minor films.

Talkies include: Submarine 28. Dirigible 30. Ladies of Leisure 30.

Graves, Rupert (1963–).

British actor usually in upper-class roles.

A Room with a View 86. Maurice 87. A Handful of Dust 88. The Children 90. Where Angels Fear to Tread 91. Damage 92. The Madness of King George 94. Different for Girls 96. Intimate Relations 96. The Tenant of Wildfell Hall (TV) 96. Mrs Dalloway 97. Different for Girls 97. The Revenger's Comedies 97. Bent 97, etc.

Graves, Teresa (1944–).

American leading lady.

Black Eye 73. That Man Bolt 73. Vampira 74.

TV series: Rowan and Martin's Laugh-In 69–70. Get Christie Love 74–75.

Gravey, Fernand (1904–1970) (Fernand Martens).

Debonair French leading man with some Hollywood experience.

Bitter Sweet 33. The Great Waltz 38. Fools for Scandal 38. Le Dernier Tournant 38. La Ronde 50. Short Head 53. How to Steal a Million 66. The Madwoman of Chaillot 69, etc.

Gray, Allan (1904–*).

Polish-born composer in Britain.

Emil and the Detectives (Ger.) 36. The Life and Death of Colonel Blimp 43. *A Matter of Life and Death* 45. Mr Perrin and Mr Traill 48. *The African Queen* 51. The Planter's Wife 52. Destination Milan 54. The Big Hunt 58, etc.

Gray, Billy (1938–).

American juvenile actor of the 50s, latterly working as a motorcycle racer.

Specter of the Rose 46. Fighting Father Dunne 49. *On Moonlight Bay* 52. The Day the Earth Stood Still 52. The Seven Little Foys 55. Two for the Seesaw 62. Werewolves on Wheels 71, etc.

TV series: Father Knows Best 54–60.

Gray, Carole (1940–).

South African leading lady in British films of the 60s.

The Young Ones 61. Curse of the Fly 64. Rattle of a Simple Man 64. Island of Terror 66, etc.

Gray, Charles (1928–) (Donald M. Gray).

British stage and TV actor usually seen in smooth, unsympathetic roles.

The Entertainer 60. The Man in the Moon 61. Masquerade 65. The Night of the Generals 66. The Secret War of Harry Frigg (US) 67. *The Devil Rides Out* 68. The File of the Golden Goose 69. Cromwell 69. *Diamonds Are Forever* 71. The Beast Must Die 74. Seven Nights in Japan 76. The Seven Per Cent Solution (as Mycroft Holmes) 76. Silver Bears 77. The Legacy 78. The Mirror Crack'd 80. The Jigsaw Man 84. An Englishman Abroad (TV) 84. Dreams Lost, Dreams Found (TV) 87. The Tichborne Claimant 98, etc.

Gray, Coleen (1922–) (Doris Jensen).

American leading lady of the 40s.

Kiss of Death 47. Nightmare Alley 47. Fury at Furnace Creek 48. *Red River* 48. Sand 49. Riding High 50. The Sleeping City 51. Kansas City Confidential 52. Sabre Jet 53. Arrow in the Dust 54. The Killing 56. Hell's Five Hours 57. The Leech Woman 60. Town Tamer 65. PJ 68. The Late Liz 71. Cry from the Mountain 86, etc.

TV series: Window on Main Street 61.

Gray, David Barry.

American actor.

Blind Faith (TV) 90. Mr Wonderful 92. Cops and Robbersons 94. SFW 94. Soldier Boyz 95. Dead Presidents 95. John Grisham's The Client (TV) 95. Lawn Dogs 97, etc.

TV series: Dream Street 89.

Gray, Dolores (1924–).
Statuesque American singer-dancer, on stage in musical comedy (played *Annie Get Your Gun* in London).
■ It's Always Fair Weather 54. Kismet 55. The Opposite Sex 56. Designing Woman 57.

Gray, Donald (1914–1978) (Eldred Tidbury).
One-armed British leading man, former radio actor and announcer; best known as TV's Mark Saber.
Strange Experiment 37. The Four Feathers 39. Idol of Paris 48. Saturday Island/Island of Desire 52. Timeslip 55. Satellite in the Sky 56, etc.

Gray, Dulcie (1919–) (Dulcie Bailey).
Gentle-mannered British leading lady, married to Michael Denison.
A Place of One's Own 44. They Were Sisters 45. Mine Own Executioner 47. The Glass Mountain 48. Angels One Five 51. A Man Could Get Killed 65, etc.

Gray, Eddie (1898–1969) (Edward Earl Gray).
English comedian, eccentric juggler and conjuror, usually billed in theatres as 'Monsewer' Eddie Gray, because of the fractured French of his comic patter. Born in London, he was a performer from the age of nine and, later, was a frequent member of The Crazy Gang. *European Nights* preserves part of his juggling act.
First a Girl 35. Skylarks 36. Keep Smiling 38. Don Chicago 45. Life Is a Circus 58. European Nights (It.) 59, etc.
❝ Je suis now is goin' to parlez Francais, and moi's goin' to do quelque-chose for vous that you 'ave never seen on any stage. As a matter of fact I goin' to take this 'ere pack of cards, and I'm goin' to ask Madame, or Mainsewer, to extract un card. Not deux. But un. – *E.G., on stage*

Gray, F. Gary (1969–).
American director, from music videos.
Friday 95. Set It Off 96, etc.

Gray, Gary (1936–).
American boy actor of the 40s.
A Woman's Face 41. Address Unknown 44. The Great Lover 47. Rachel and the Stranger 48. Father Is a Bachelor 49. The Next Voice You Hear 50. The Painted Hills 51. The Party Crashers 58, many others.

Gray, Gilda (1901–1959) (Marianna Michalska).
Polish dancer who went to America and is credited with inventing the shimmy.
Aloma of the South Seas 26. The Devil Dancer 28. Rose Marie 36, etc.

Gray, Nadia (1923–1994) (Nadia Kujnir-Herescu).
Russian-Rumanian leading lady, in European and British films.
The Spider and the Fly 49. Night Without Stars 51. Valley of Eagles 51. Neapolitan Fantasy 54. Folies Bergères 56. The Captain's Table 58. Parisienne 59. La Dolce Vita 59. Maniac 63. Two for the Road 67. The Naked Runner 67, etc.

Gray, Sally (1916–) (Constance Stevens).
Popular British screen heroine of the 30s and 40s, with stage experience from 1925.
School for Scandal 30. Radio Pirates 35. Cheer Up! 36. The Saint in London 38. The Lambeth Walk 38. Dangerous Moonlight 40. Carnival 46. *Green for Danger* 46. They Made Me a Fugitive 47. The Mark of Cain 48. Silent Dust 49. Obsession 49. Escape Route 52, etc.

Gray, Simon (1936–).
British dramatist, novelist and screenwriter. He is also a university lecturer in English.
Butley 74. A Month in the Country 87. Common Pursuit (TV) 91. Running Late (TV) 93. Femme Fatale (TV) 93, etc.

Gray, Spalding (1941–).
American character actor and writer who turned a small part in *The Killing Fields* into a witty one-man show, *Swimming to Cambodia*, filmed by Jonathan Demme.
Heavy Petting 83. The Killing Fields 84. True Stories 86. Hard Choices 86. Swimming to Cambodia (& w) 87. Beaches 88. Clara's Heart 88. Stars and Bars 88. Monster in a Box (& w) 91. Straight Talk 92. Twenty Bucks 93. The Pickle 93. King of the Hill 93. The Paper 94. Bad Company 95. Beyond Rangoon 95. Drunks 95. Diabolique 96. Gray's Anatomy (& w) 97, etc.

Graysmark, John.
British production designer.
Young Winston (AAN) 72. The Big Sleep 78. Flash Gordon 80. Ragtime (AAN) 81. The Lords of Discipline 83. The Bounty 84. Duet for One 87. Superman IV: The Quest for Peace 87. Gorillas in the Mist 88. White Hunter, Black Heart 90. Robin Hood: Prince of Thieves 91. White Sands 92. So I Married an Axe Murderer 93. Blown Away 94. Courage under Fire 96, etc.

Grayson, Godfrey.
British second-feature director, especially for the Danzigers.
Room to Let 50. To Have and to Hold 51. The Fake 53. Black Ice 57. High Jump 59. Spider's Web 60. So Evil So Young 61. She Always Gets Their Man 62, etc.

Grayson, Kathryn (1922–) (Zelma Hedrick).
American singing star in Hollywood from 1941 (as one of Andy Hardy's dates).
■ Andy Hardy's Private Secretary 40. Andy Hardy's Spring Fever 41. The Vanishing Virginian 41. Rio Rita 42. Seven Sweethearts 42. Thousands Cheer 43. Anchors Aweigh 45. Two Sisters from Boston 46. Ziegfeld Follies 46. Till the Clouds Roll By 46. It Happened in Brooklyn 47. The Kissing Bandit 48. The Midnight Kiss 49. The Toast of New Orleans 50. Grounds for Marriage 50. *Show Boat* 51. Lovely to Look At 52. The Desert Song 53. So This Is Love (as Grace Moore) 53. *Kiss Me Kate* 53. The Vagabond King 55. That's Entertainment Two 76.

Grazer, Brian (1951–).
American producer, a former agent, now in partnership with director Ron Howard.
Night Shift 82. Splash 83. Real Genius 84. Spies Like Us 85. Armed and Dangerous (& story) 86. Like Father, Like Son 87. Parenthood 89. The Dream Team 89. Kindergarten Cop 90. Problem Child 90. Cry-Baby 90. Backdraft 91. Closet Land 91. My Girl 91. The Doors 91. Far and Away 91. Housesitter 92. Boomerang 92. For Love or Money 93. My Girl 2 94. The Cowboy Way 94. Greedy/Greed 94. The Paper 94. Apollo 13 95. Sgt Bilko 96. The Chamber 96. Fear 96. Ransom 96. The Nutty Professor 96. Liar Liar 97. Inventing the Abbotts 97. From the Earth to the Moon (TV) 98. Psycho 98, etc.

Graziano, Rocky (1921–1990) (Thomas Rocco Barbella).
World middleweight boxing champion whose 1955 autobiography, *Somebody Up There Likes Me*, was filmed in 1956 starring Paul Newman. He became a TV actor and a regular on variety shows in the 50s and 60s, and wrote another volume of autobiography, *Somebody Down Here Likes Me Too*, in 1981.
Mr Rock and Roll 57. Teenage Millionaire 61. Tony Rome 67, etc.
❝ I get a real belt out of this racket where I get paid because people laugh instead of stand up and scream for me to belt somebody. – *R.G.*

Gréco, Juliette (1927–).
French singer who acted in several films both at home and abroad.
Au Royaume des Cieux 49. The Green Glove 52. *The Sun Also Rises* 57. Naked Earth 58. Roots of Heaven 59. Whirlpool 59. Crack in the Mirror 60. The Big Gamble (US) 61. Uncle Tom's Cabin 65. The Night of the Generals 66. Lily Aime-Moi 75, etc.

Green, Adolph (1915–).
American writer of books and lyrics for many Broadway shows and musical films, usually with Betty Comden.

Green, Alfred E. (1889–1960).
American director of mainly routine but generally competent films; in Hollywood from 1912.
Little Lord Fauntleroy 20. Ella Cinders 23. Through the Back Door 26. The Green Goddess 30. Old English 31. Smart Money 31. Disraeli 31. The Rich Are Always with Us 32. Parachute 33. Dangerous 35. Duke of West Point 38. South of Pago Pago 40. Badlands of Dakota 41. Meet the Stewarts 42. A Thousand and One Nights 44. *The Jolson Story* 46. The Fabulous Dorseys 47. They Passed This Way 48. Cover Up 49. Invasion USA 52. The Eddie Cantor Story 53, many others.

Green, Danny (1903–1973).
Heavyweight British character actor usually in cheerful – or sometimes menacing – cockney roles. Appeared in some American silents.
Crime over London 37. Fiddlers Three 44. The Man Within 47. No Orchids for Miss Blandish 48. Little Big Shot 52. A Kid for Two Farthings 55. The Lady Killers 55. Beyond This Place 59. The Old Dark House 62. A Stitch in Time 63. Smashing Time 67. The Fixer 68, etc.

Green, David (1948–).
British director, from television.
Car Trouble 86. Buster 88. Fire Birds 90.

Green, Guy (1913–).
British cinematographer who became a useful director.
as cinematographer: In Which We Serve 42. The Way Ahead 44. *Great Expectations* (AA) 46. Take My Life 47. *Oliver Twist* 48. Captain Horatio Hornblower 51. The Beggar's Opera 52. Rob Roy 53, etc.
■ as director: River Beat 54. Portrait of Alison 55. Lost 56. House of Secrets 56. The Snorkel 58. Sea of Sand 58. SOS Pacific 59. *The Mark* 60. *The Angry Silence* 60. The Light in the Piazza 62. Diamond Head 63. A Patch of Blue 65. Pretty Polly 67. The Magus 68. A Walk in the Spring Rain 70. Luther 73. Once Is Not Enough 75. The Devil's Advocate 77. Strong Medicine (TV) 85.

Green, Harry (1892–1958).
American comedian, primarily on stage; former lawyer.
Close Harmony 31. Bottoms Up 34. The Cisco Kid and the Lady 37. Star Dust 40. Joe MacBeth (GB) 55. A King in New York (GB) 57, etc.

Green, Hughie (1920–1997).
Canadian actor in Britain, former juvenile, then popular TV quizmaster and talent scout.
Little Friend 34. Midshipman Easy 36. Tom Brown's Schooldays (US) 39. If Winter Comes (US) 48. Paper Orchid 49. What's Up Superdoc 78, etc.

Green, Jack N.
American cinematographer, mainly for Clint Eastwood's movies.
Heartbreak Ridge 86. Like Father, Like Son 87. The Dead Pool 88. Bird 88. Pink Cadillac 89. Race for Glory 89. White Hunter, Black Heart 90. The Rookie 90. Love Crimes 92. Rookie of the Year 93. A Perfect World 93. Trapped in Paradise 94. Bad Company 95. The Bridges of Madison County 95. The Net 95. The Amazing Panda Adventure 95. Twister 96. Absolute Power 97. Midnight in the Garden of Good and Evil 97. Speed 2: Cruise Control 97. Traveller (& d) 97, etc.

Green, Janet (1908–1993).
English screenwriter and playwright, a former actress. Born in London, she wrote her first play in 1945 and began working in films two years later, turning her story *The Clouded Yellow* into a screenplay. Her later scripts were written in collaboration with her husband, John McCormick.
The Clouded Yellow 50. The Good Beginning 53. Lost 55. Cast a Dark Shadow 55. The Long Arm 56. Eye Witness 56. Affair in Havana (US) 57. *Sapphire* 59. Midnight Lace (oa) (US) 60. *Victim* 61. Life for Ruth 62. 7 Women (US) 66, etc.

Green, Johnny (1908–1989).
American composer, songwriter, musical director and bandleader. Born in New York City, he studied at Harvard University and began as a rehearsal pianist and accompanist to Ethel Merman and Gertrude Lawrence. He worked for MGM in the early 40s, and then went to Warner before returning to MGM as general musical director in 1949, where he remained until 1958. He also produced some short films, winning an Oscar for *The Merry Wives of Windsor Overture* 53. His best-known songs include 'Body and Soul' and 'I Cover the Waterfront', which were both later used as the title themes for films. Married actresses Betty Furness and Bunny Waters.
Lost in a Harem 44. Bathing Beauty 44. Fiesta 47. *Easter Parade* (AA) 48. Up in Central Park 48. The Inspector General 49. Grounds for Marriage 50. Summer Stock 50. The Great Caruso 51. Royal Wedding/Wedding Bells 51. *An American in Paris* (AA) 51. Too Young to Kiss 51. Because You're Mine 52. Rhapsody 53. Brigadoon 54. I'll Cry Tomorrow 55. High Society 56. Meet Me in Las Vegas/Viva Las Vegas! 56. Raintree County 57. Pepe 60. West Side Story 61. This Rugged Land 62. Bye Bye Birdie 63. Twilight of Honor 63. Alvarez Kelly 66. *Oliver!* (GB) (AA) 68. *They Shoot Horses, Don't They?* (AAN) 69, etc.

Green, Joseph (1900–1996) (Joseph Greenberg).
American producer and director of Yiddish films, a former actor. Born in Poland, he went to America in the 20s, working as an extra in Hollywood, and began making films in Poland in the 30s for Yiddish-speaking audiences, a group that no longer existed by the end of the Second World War. His best-known *Yiddle with His Fiddle* starred Molly Picon.
■ Yiddle with His Fiddle 36. A Letter to Mama/A Brivele der Mamen 38. Mamele: Little Mothers 38. The Jester/Der Purimspieler 46.

Green, Martyn (1899–1975).
British light opera singer, with the D'Oyly Carte Company for many years; settled in America.
Autobiography: 1952, *Here's a How De Do.*
■ *The Mikado* 39. The Story of Gilbert and Sullivan 53. A Lovely Way to Die 68.

Green, Mitzi (1920–1969) (Elizabeth Keno).
American child performer of the 30s.
Honey 30. Tom Sawyer 30. Little Orphan Annie 32. Transatlantic Merry-Go-Round 34, etc.: later appeared in Lost in Alaska 52. Bloodhounds of Broadway 52.
TV series: So This is Hollywood 54.

Green, Nigel (1924–1972).
Dominant British character actor with stage experience.
Reach for the Sky 56. Bitter Victory 58. The Criminal 60. Jason and the Argonauts 63. *Zulu* 64. *The Ipcress File* 65. *The Face of Fu Manchu* 65. The Skull 66. Let's Kill Uncle (US) 66. *Deadlier than the Male* 66. *Tobruk* (US) 67. Africa Texas Style 67. Play Dirty 68. Wrecking Crew (US) 69. The Kremlin Letter 69. Countess Dracula 70. The Ruling Class 71, etc.
TV series: William Tell 57.

Green, Pamela.
British actress and nude model, best known for her appearance in her then lover George Harrison Marks's film *Naked as Nature Intended* 61, which led to a long cycle of British films mixing sex and comedy in the 60s and 70s.
The Chimney Sweeps 63. The Naked World of Harrison Marks 67, etc.
❝ While the British film industry is brilliant at parochial comedy, drama and historical subjects, it has not so far produced one really good film featuring the nude. The naturist films were, in the main, made by people with very little imagination for titillating the raincoat brigade, in the hope of making a few bob at the end of it. – *P.G.*

Green, Philip (1911–1982).
Prolific English composer and musical director of the 50s and 60s. Born in London, he studied at the Trinity College of Music and first worked in the theatre as a conductor. At his busiest, he composed as many as 14 film scores a year.
Landfall 49. Murder without Crime 50. Elstree Story 52. Isn't Life Wonderful! 53. The March Hare 54. John and Julie 55. Man of the Moment 55. The Extra Day 56. Up in the World 56. The March Hare 56. Who Done It? 56. Carry On Admiral 57. Woman and the Hunter 57. The Violent Playground 57. Just My Luck 57. The Golden Disc 58. Rooney 58. Operation Amsterdam 58. Alive and Kicking 58. Innocent Sinners 58. Sea Fury 58. The Square Peg 58. Life Is a Circus 58. Life in Emergency Ward 10 58. Upstairs and Downstairs 59. Bobbikins 59. The Shakedown 59. Witness in the Dark 59. A Touch of Larceny 59. Sapphire 59. The League of Gentlemen 59. Operation Amsterdam 59. Follow a Star 59. Friends and Neighbours 59. Desert Mice 59. Don't Panic Chaps 59. The Bulldog Breed 60. Make Mine Mink 60. Piccadilly Third Stop 60. The Singer Not the Song 60. Your Money or Your Wife 60. Man in the Moon 60. And Women Shall Weep 60. All Night Long 61. Victim 61. The Secret Partner 61. Flame in the Streets 61. On the Beat 62. Victim 62. Tiara Tahiti 62. The Man Who Finally Died

62. The Devil's Agent 62. The Girl Hunters 63. Two Left Feet 63. A Stitch in Time 63. It's All Happening (& co-p) 63. The Intelligence Men 65. Joey Boy 65. Masquerade 65. The Yellow Hat 66, etc.

Green, S. C. (1928–) (aka Sid Green).
Prolific British comedy scriptwriter, mainly for television.
The Intelligence Men 65. That Riviera Touch 66. The Magnificent Two 67. The Boys in Blue 83, etc.

Green, Walon (1936–).
American screenwriter and director.
The Wild Bunch (AAN) 69. Sorcerer 77. The Brinks Job 78. The Secret Life of Plants (& d) 78. The Border 82. Solarbabies 86. Crusoe 88. Robocop 2 90. Eraser (co-w) 96, etc.

Greenaway, Peter (1942–).
British director and screenwriter who has moved from the experimental to the near-mainstream without altering his style.
Book: 1996, *Being Naked Playing Dead: The Art of Peter Greenaway* by Alan Woods.
The Falls 80. Act of God 81. The Draughtsman's Contract 83. A Zed and Two Noughts 85. Drowning by Numbers 88. *The Cook, the Thief, His Wife and Her Lover* 89. A TV Dante (TV) 90. *Prospero's Books* 91. The Baby of Macon 93. The Pillow Book 95, etc.
❝ I do feel for me that cinema has somehow ceased to be a spectator sport. I get tremendous excitement out of making it rather than watching it. – *P.G.*
We live in a time of excess – excess population, excess information – *P.G.*
If you want to tell stories, be a writer, not a filmmaker. – *P.G.*
What is it about Greenaway's films that makes the flesh crawl? I think it's his apparent loathing of the human race. – *Ken Russell*
If Gucci handbags were still in fashion Greenaway would carry his scripts in them. – *Derek Jarman*

Greenberg, Adam.
Polish cinematographer, working in Hollywood.
Diamonds 75. The Passover Plot 77. Operation Thunderbolt 77. The Big Red One 80. Lemon Popsicle 80. Teen Mothers/Seed of Innocence 80. Paradise 82. 10 to Midnight 83. The Terminator 84. The Ambassador 85. Once Bitten 85. Wisdom 86. Iron Eagle 86. La Bamba 87. Near Dark 87. Jocks 87. Three Men and a Baby 87. Spellbinder 88. Alien Nation 88. Turner & Hooch 89. Worth Winning 89. Love Hurts 90. Ghost 90. Three Men and a Little Lady 90. Terminator 2 91. Sister Act 92. Toys 92. Dave 93. Renaissance Man 94. North 94. First Knight 95. Eraser 96. Sphere 98. Rush Hour 98, etc.

Greenberg, Gerald (1936–).
American editor.
Bye Bye Braverman 68. The Boys in the Band 70. The French Connection (AA) 71. The Seven Ups 73. The Taking of Pelham One Two Three 75. The Missouri Breaks 76. Apocalypse Now (AAN) 79. Dressed to Kill 80. Heaven's Gate 80. Scarface 83. Body Double 84. Wise Guys 86. The Untouchables 87. The Accused 88. Awakenings 90. For the Boys 91. School Ties 92. Reach the Rock 98. American History X 98, etc.

Greenberg, Stanley R.
American screenwriter.
Welcome Home Johnny Bristol (TV) 72. Skyjacked 72. Soylent Green 73. The Missiles of October (TV) 73. The Silence (TV) 76. Blind Ambition (TV) 79. FDR, the Last Years (TV) 81, etc.

Greene, Clarence (1918–).
American writer-producer, usually in collaboration with Russel Rouse.
The Town Went Wild 45. D.O.A. 48. The Well (AAN) 51. New York Confidential 55. A House Is Not a Home 64. The Oscar 66. Caper of the Golden Bulls 67, etc.
TV series: Tightrope 57.

Greene, David (1921–).
British director, former small-part actor; became a TV director in Canada and the US.
The Shuttered Room 66. Sebastian 68. The Strange Affair 68. I Start Counting (& p) 69. The People Next Door 70. Madame Sin (TV) 72. *Godspell* 73. Ellery Queen (TV) 75. Rich Man Poor Man (TV) (co-d) 76. Roots (co-d) (TV) 77. Lucan (TV pilot) 77. The Man in the Iron Mask (TV) 77. Gray Lady Down 78. The Trial of Lee Harvey Oswald (TV) 78. Friendly Fire (TV) 79. A Vacation in Hell (TV) 80. Hard Country 81. World War III (TV) 81. Ghost Dancing (TV) 81. Prototype (TV) 83. The Guardian (TV) 84. Sweet Revenge (TV) 84. Fatal Vision (TV) 84. Guilty Conscience (TV) 85. Miles to Go (TV) 86. Vanishing Act (TV) 86. The Betty Ford Story (TV) 87. Night of the Hunter (TV) 91. Honor Thy Mother (TV) 92. Beyond Obsession (TV) 94, etc.

Greene, Graham (1904–1991).
Distinguished British novelist who provided material for many interesting films. His film criticisms have been collected in *The Pleasure Dome* (Oxford, 1980) and *Mornings in the Dark: The Graham Greene Film Reader* (Carcanet, 1993).
Book: 1990, *Travels in Greeneland: The Cinema of Graham Greene* by Quentin Falk.
Stamboul Train/Orient Express 34. This Gun for Hire 42. The Ministry of Fear 43. Confidential Agent 45. The Man Within 46. Brighton Rock 47. The Fugitive 48. The Fallen Idol (AAN) 48. The Third Man 49. The Heart of the Matter 53. The Stranger's Hand 54. The End of the Affair 55. The Quiet American 58. Our Man in Havana 59. The Comedians 67. Travels with My Aunt 73, etc.

Greene, Graham.
Native American actor.
Dances with Wolves (AAN) 90. Clearcut 91. Thunderheart 92. Medicine River 92. Benefit of the Doubt 93. Cooperstown (TV) 93. Camilla 93. Maverick 94. North 94. Die Hard with a Vengenace 95. The Education of Little Tree 97. Shattered Image 98. Heart of the Sun 98, etc.

Greene, Leon.
Stalwart British supporting actor, former opera singer.
A Funny Thing Happened on the Way to the Forum 67. The Ritz 76. The Seven Per Cent Solution 76. Adventures of a Private Eye 77. Adventures of a Plumber's Mate 78. The Thief of Baghdad 78. Flash Gordon 80. The Return of the Musketeers 89, etc.

Greene, Lorne (1915–1987).
Solidly-built Canadian character actor, best known for his role as Ben Cartwright in the TV series *Bonanza* 59–73, and his similar role as Commander Adama in *Battlestar Galactica* 78–80.
The Silver Chalice 54. Tight Spot 55. Autumn Leaves 56. Peyton Place 57. The Gift of Love 58. The Trap 58. Legacy of a Spy (TV) 68. The Harness (TV) 71. Earthquake 74, etc.
TV series: Sailor of Fortune 56. *Bonanza* 59–73. Griff 73–74. Battlestar Galactica 78–80. Code Red 81–82.

Greene, Max (1896–1968) (Mutz Greenbaum).
German cinematographer, long in Britain.
The Stars Look Down 39. Hatter's Castle 41. Spring in Park Lane 48. Maytime in Mayfair 49. Night and the City 50, etc.

Greene, Richard (1918–1985).
Good-looking, lightweight British leading man with brief stage experience before 1938 film debut resulted in Hollywood contract. Born in Plymouth, Devon, he returned to England at the beginning of the Second World War to serve in the Army. From the mid-40s, he alternated between England and Hollywood, before gaining a new fame in the mid-50s as Robin Hood in the long-running TV series. He retired to Ireland in the 70s to breed horses.
■ *Four Men and a Prayer* 38. My Lucky Star 38. Submarine Patrol 38. Kentucky 38. The Little Princess 38. *The Hound of the Baskervilles* 39. Stanley and Livingstone 39. Here I Am a Stranger 39. Little Old New York 40. I Was an Adventuress 40. Unpublished Story 42. Flying Fortress 42. Yellow Canary 43. Don't Take It to Heart 45. Gaiety George 46. Forever Amber 47. The Fighting O'Flynn 48. The Fan 48. That Dangerous Age 49. Now Barabbas 49. The Desert Hawk 50. My Daughter Joy 50. Shadow of the Eagle 50. Lorna Doone 51. Black Castle 51. Rogue's March 53. Captain Scarlet 53. Bandits of Corsica 54. Contraband Spain 55. Beyond the Curtain 60. Sword of Sherwood Forest 61. Dangerous Island 67. Blood of Fu Manchu 68. Kiss and Kill 69. Tales from the Crypt 72.
TV series: *Robin Hood* 55–59.

Greene, W. Howard (*–1956).
American colour cinematographer.
Trail of the Lonesome Pine 36. *The Garden of Allah* 36. *A Star is Born* 37. Nothing Sacred 37. *The Adventures of Robin Hood* 38. Jesse James 39. Elizabeth and Essex 39. Northwest Mounted Police 40. Blossoms in the Dust 41. The Jungle Book (AAN) 42. Arabian Nights 42. *Phantom of the Opera* (AA) 43. Ali Baba and the Forty Thieves 44. Can't Help Singing 44. Salome Where she Danced 45. A Night in Paradise 46. Tycoon 47. High Lonesome 50. Quebec 51. The Brigand 52. Gun Belt 53, etc.

Greene, Walter (1910–).
American composer and arranger, mainly of 'B' features and TV films.
Crime Inc 45. Why Girls Leave Home (AAN) 45. Return of the Lash 47. Mark of the Lash 48. The Dalton Gang 49. Hostile Country 50. Naked Gun 56. Jesse James' Women 54. Teenage Thunder 57. Teenage Monster 58. *The Brain from Planet Arous* 58. War of the Satellites 58. Carnival Rock 58. I Bombed Pearl Harbor 61. The Pique Poquette of Paris 66, etc.

Greenleaf, Raymond (1892–1963).
American character actor, usually seen as benevolent elderly man.
Storm Warning 51. Angel Face 53. Violent Saturday 54. *When Gangland Strikes* (leading role) 56. The Story on Page One 60, many others.

Greenstreet, Sydney (1879–1954).
Immense British stage actor long in America; a sensation in his first film, made at the age of 61, he became a major star of the 40s.
■ *The Maltese Falcon* (AAN) 41. They Died with Their Boots On 41. *Across the Pacific* 42. Casablanca 42. Background to Danger 42. Passage to Marseilles 44. *Between Two Worlds* 44. *The Mask of Dimitrios* 44. The Conspirators 44. Hollywood Canteen 44. Pillow to Post 45. Conflict 45. Christmas in Connecticut 45. *Three Strangers* 46. Devotion (as Thackeray) 46. The Verdict 46. That Way with Women 47. *The Hucksters* 47. *The Woman in White* 48. The Velvet Touch 48. Ruthless 48. Flamingo Road 49. It's a Great Feeling 49. Malaya 50.
✪ For his inimitable chuckle; and for the sheer improbability of his success. *The Maltese Falcon*.
❝ By gad, sir, you're a fellow worth knowing, a character. No telling what you'll say next, except that it'll be something astonishing. – *S.G. in The Maltese Falcon*
I distrust a man who says when. He's got to be careful not to drink too much, because he's not to be trusted when he does. Well, sir, here's to plain speaking and clear understanding. You're a close-mouthed man?
– No, I like to talk.
– Better and better. I distrust a close-mouthed man. He generally picks the wrong time to talk, and says the wrong things. Talking's something you can't do judiciously, unless you keep in practice.
– *Ibid.*

Greenwald, Maggie (1955–).
American director, a former editor and dancer.
Home Remedy 87. The Kill Off 89. The Ballad of Little Joe 93.

Greenwood, Charlotte (1890–1978).
Tall American comedienne and eccentric dancer, on stage from 1905.
Autobiography: 1947, *Never Too Tall*.
Jane 18. Baby Mine 27. So Long Letty 30. Palmy Days 32. Down Argentine Way 40. Springtime in the Rockies 43. Up in Mabel's Room 44. Home in Indiana 47. Peggy 50. Dangerous when Wet 52. Glory 55. Oklahoma 56. The Opposite Sex 56, etc.

Greenwood, Jack (1919–).
British producer, responsible for second-feature crime series: Edgar Wallace, Scales of Justice, Scotland Yard, etc.

Greenwood, Joan (1921–1987).
Plummy-voiced British leading lady of the 40s. She was married to André Morell.
■ John Smith Wakes Up 40. My Wife's Family 40. He Found a Star 41. *The Gentle Sex* 42. They Knew Mr Knight 44. Latin Quarter 44. A Girl in a Million 45. The Man Within 46. *The October Man* 47. The White Unicorn 47. *Saraband for Dead Lovers* 48. The Bad Lord Byron 48. Whisky Galore 49. *Kind Hearts and Coronets* 49. Flesh and Blood 50. The Man in the White Suit 50. Young Wives' Tale 51. Mr Peek-a-Boo 51. *The Importance of Being Earnest* 52. Knave of Hearts 54. *Father Brown* 54. Moonfleet (US) 55. Stage Struck (US) 57. Mysterious Island 62. The Amorous Prawn 62. Tom Jones 63. The Moon Spinners 64. Girl Stroke Boy 71. The Uncanny 77. The Hound of the Baskervilles 78. The Water Babies 78. Little Dorrit 87.
❝ She speaks her lines as though suspecting in them some hidden menace that she can't quite identify. – *Karel Reisz*

Greenwood, John (1889–1975).
English composer. Born in London, he studied at the Royal College of Music.
To What Red Hell? 30. The Constant Nymph 33. Elephant Boy 37. Pimpernel Smith 41. San Demetrio, London 44. Frieda 47. Quartet 48. The Last Days of Dolwyn 48. Trio 50. The Gentle Gunman 52, many others.

Greenwood, Walter (1903–1974).
British writer who chronicled industrial life, notably in *Love on the Dole*.

Greer, Dabs (1917–) (William Greer).
American character actor.
Affair with a Stranger 53. House of Wax 53. Riot in Cell Block 11 54. D-Day the Sixth of June 56. Baby Face Nelson 57. My Man Godfrey 57. It! The Terror from Beyond Space 58. The Lone Texan 59. The Cheyenne Social Club 70. White Lightning 73. Two-Moon Junction 88. Sundown 91. House 4: Home Deadly Home 92, etc.
TV series: Gunsmoke 55–60. Hank 65–66. Little House on the Prairie 74–83.

Greer, Howard (1886–1964).
American costume designer, in films from 1923 and chief designer at Paramount from 1924–27 before establishing his own salon in Hollywood.
Autobiography: 1949, *Designing Male*.
The Spanish Dancer 23. The Cheat 23. The Covered Wagon 23. The Ten Commandments 24. Coquette 29. Hell's Angels 30. The Animal Kingdom 32. Page Miss Glory 35. Bringing Up Baby 38. When Tomorrow Comes 39. Christmas Holiday 44. Spellbound 45. Holiday Affair 49. The French Line 54, etc.
❝ For every luscious bloom there's been a fat, sharp thorn. – H.G.

Greer, Jane (1924–) (Bettyjane Greer).
Cool American leading lady of the 40s; could play good-humoured dames, well-bred ladies or *femmes fatales*.
■ Pan Americana 45. Two o'Clock Courage 45. George White's Scandals 45. Dick Tracy 45. The Falcon's Alibi 46. Bamboo Blonde 46. Sunset Pass 46. Sinbad the Sailor 47. *They Won't Believe Me* 47. *Out of the Past* 47. Station West 48. *The Big Steal* 49. You're in the Navy Now 51. The Company She Keeps 51. The Prisoner of Zenda 52. Desperate Search 52. You for Me 52. The Clown 53. Down among the Sheltering Palms 53. *Run for the Sun* 56. *Man of a Thousand Faces* 57. Where Love Has Gone 64. Billie 65. The Outfit 74. The Shadow Riders (TV) 82. Against All Odds 84.

Gregg, Colin (1947–).
British director.
Remembrance 82. Lamb 85. We Think the World of You 88.

Gregg, Everley (1898–1959).
British character actress.
The Private Life of Henry VIII 32. The Ghost Goes West 36. Pygmalion 38. Brief Encounter 45, etc.

Gregg, Hubert (1914–).
British songwriter, screenwriter, and light actor, married to Pat Kirkwood. On stage from 1933, films from 1942.
In Which We Serve 42. 29 Acacia Avenue 45. Vote for Huggett 49. Robin Hood 52. The Maggie 54. Simon and Laura 55. Stars in My Eyes 57, etc.

Gregor, Nora (c. 1890–1949).
Austrian leading lady.
The Trial of Mary Dugan (US) 29. His Glorious Night (US) 30. *La Règle du Jeu* (Fr.) 39, etc.

Gregory, James (1911–).
American character actor with stage experience, a familiar Hollywood 'heavy' or senior cop.
Naked City 48. The Frogmen 51. The Scarlet Hour 56. The Young Stranger 57. Al Capone 59. Two Weeks in Another Town 62. *The Manchurian Candidate* 62. P.T. 109 63. A Distant Trumpet 64. The Sons of Katie Elder 65. A Rage To Live 65. *The Silencers* 66. Clambake 68. The Hawaiians 70. Million Dollar Duck 71. Shootout 71. The Main Event 79, etc.
TV series: The Lawless Years 59. Barney Miller 81.

Gregory, Paul (c. 1905–) (Jason Lenhart).
American impresario who teamed with Charles Laughton in the 40s to present dramatized readings: also produced *Night of the Hunter* 55, which Laughton directed, and *The Naked and the Dead* 58.

Gregson, John (1919–1975).
English leading man, a likeable and dependable star of British comedies and action dramas in the 50s.
■ Saraband for Dead Lovers 48. Scott of the Antarctic 48. Whisky Galore 49. The Hasty Heart 49. Train of Events 49. Treasure Island 50. Cairo Road 50. *The Lavender Hill Mob* 51. Angels One Five 51. *The Brave Don't Cry* 51. Venetian Bird 52. The Holly and the Ivy 52. The Titfield Thunderbolt 53. *Genevieve* 53. The Weak and the Wicked 53. Conflict of Wings 54. To Dorothy a Son 54. The Crowded Day 54. Above Us the Waves 55. Value for Money 55. Three Cases of Murder 55. *Jacqueline* 56. The Battle of the River Plate 56. True as a Turtle 56. Miracle in Soho 57. *Rooney* 57. Sea of Sand 58. *The Captain's Table* 58. SOS Pacific 59. Faces in the Dark 60. Hand in Hand 60. Treasure of Monte Cristo 61. Frightened City 61. *Live Now Pay Later* 62. Tomorrow at Ten 62. The Longest Day 62. The Night of the Generals 66. Fright 71.
TV series: Gideon's Way 64. Shirley's World 71.

Greig, Robert (1880–1958).
Australian character actor, long in Hollywood; the doyen of portly pompous butlers.
Animal Crackers 30. Tonight or Never 31. Love Me Tonight 32. Trouble in Paradise 32. Horse Feathers 32. Merrily We Go to Hell 33. Pleasure Cruise 33. Clive of India 35. Lloyds of London 36. Easy Living 37. Algiers 38. No Time for Comedy 40. The Lady Eve 41. Sullivan's Travels 42. *The Moon and Sixpence* 42. I Married a Witch 42. The Palm Beach Story 42. The Great Moment 44. The Picture of Dorian Gray 45. The Cheaters 45. Unfaithfully Yours 48, many others.

Greist, Kim (1958–).
American actress.
C.H.U.D. 84. Brazil 85. Manhunter 86. Throw Momma from the Train 87. Punchline 88. Why Me? 90. Payoff 91. Duplicates 92. Homeward Bound: The Incredible Journey 93. Homeward Bound II: Lost in San Francisco 96, etc.

Grémillon, Jean (1901–1959).
French director with limited but interesting output since 1929.
Remorques 39. Lumière d'Eté 42. Pattes Blanches 48, etc.

Grenfell, Joyce (1910–1979) (Joyce Phipps).
Angular British comedienne adept at refined gaucherie; a revue star and solo performer, on stage from 1939.
Autobiographies: 1976, *Joyce Grenfell Requests the Pleasure*; 1979, *In Pleasant Places*; 1997, *Joyce and Ginnie; The Letters of Joyce Grenfell and Virginia Graham*, ed. Janie Hampton.
The Demi-Paradise 42. The Lamp Still Burns 43. While the Sun Shines 46. *The Happiest Days of Your Life* 49. Stage Fright 50. *Laughter in Paradise* 51. Genevieve 53. The Million Pound Note 54. The Belles of St Trinian's 54. Happy Is the Bride 57. Blue Murder at St Trinian's 58. The Pure Hell of St Trinian's 60. The Old Dark House 63. The Americanization of Emily 64. The Yellow Rolls-Royce 64, etc.

Gréville, Edmond (1906–1966).
French director; assistant to Dupont on *Piccadilly* 29, to Clair on *Sous les Toits de Paris* 30.
Remous 34. Mademoiselle Docteur 37. L'Ile du Péché 39. Passionnelle 46. Noose (GB) 48. The Romantic Age (GB) 49. But Not in Vain (also w, p) (GB) 49. Port du Désir 56. Guilty (GB) 56. Beat Girl (GB) 60. The Hands of Orlac (GB) 61. Les Menteurs 61, etc.

Grey, Anne (1907–) (Aileen Ewing).
British leading actress of the late 20s and early 30s, a former journalist. Born in London, and educated at Lausanne and King's College, London, she moved to Hollywood in the mid-30s to make a few films there before retiring. Married actor Lester MATTHEWS.
The Constant Nymph 27. The Warning 28. The School for Scandal 30. The Squeaker 30. Arms and the Man 32. The Faithful Heart 32. Leap Year 32. The Blarney Stone 32. The Fire Raisers 33. Just Smith 33. Colonel Blood 34. Bonnie Scotland (US) 35. Break of Hearts (US) 35. Just My Luck (US) 36. Dr Sin Fang 37. Chinatown Nights 38, etc.

Grey, Denise (1896–1996).
Leading French actress, most often seen in films in grandmotherly roles. She began her career at the Folies Bergère in 1915.
Bolero 41. Adieu Leonard 43. Devil in the Flesh/Le Diable au Corps 47. Carve Her Name with Pride (GB) 58. Sputnik/A Dog, a Mouse and a Sputnik 58. La Bonne Soupe 63. Hello-Goodbye (US) 70. La Venus de Milo 73. La Boum 80. La Boum II 82. Le Gaffeur 85. The Seasons of Pleasure/Les Saisons du Plaisir 87, etc.

Grey, Jennifer (1960–).
American actress, the daughter of Joel Grey.
Red Dawn 84. The Cotton Club 84. American Flyers 85. Ferris Bueller's Day Off 86. Dirty Dancing 87. Light Years 88. Bloodhounds of Broadway 89. The Sixth Family 90. Stroke of Midnight 91. A Case for Murder (TV) 93. The West Side Waltz (TV) 95. Lover's Knot 96, etc.

Grey, Joel (1932–) (Joe Katz).
American singing entertainer who took a long time to hit stardom, managed it on the New York stage in *Cabaret*, but proved difficult to cast.
■ About Face 52. Come September 63. Man on a String (TV) 71. *Cabaret* (AA) 72. Man on a Swing 74. Buffalo Bill and the Indians 76. The Seven Per Cent Solution 76. Remo Williams . . . the Adventure Begins 85. Kafka 91. The Music of Chance 93. The Empty Mirror (as Josef Goebbels) 96. My Friend Joe 96.

Grey, Lita (1908–1995) (Lillita MacMurray).
American juvenile actress of the 20s who appeared with Chaplin, became his child bride in 1924, and was the mother of Charles Chaplin Jnr (1925–68) and of actor Sydney CHAPLIN.
Autobiography: 1966, My *Life with Chaplin*.

Grey, Nan (1918–1993) (Eschal Miller).
American leading lady of the late 30s; married to singer Frankie Laine.
Dracula's Daughter 36. Three Smart Girls 36. Three Smart Girls Grow Up 38. Tower of London 39. The Invisible Man Returns 40. Sandy Is a Lady 41, etc.

Grey Owl
was the identity of an American Indian, adopted by Englishman Archie Belaney, who was born in Hastings, Sussex. After emigrating to North America in 1906, he lived in a log cabin in Canada, where he claimed to be the offspring of a Scottish father and an Apache mother. Through books and lecture tours, he campaigned for the preservation of forests and wildlife, particularly the Canadian beaver. His true identity was revealed only after his sudden death, from pneumonia. He was played by Pierce BROSNAN in a biopic in 1998.

Grey, Virginia (1917–).
American leading lady of minor films in the 30s and 40s.
Uncle Tom's Cabin (debut) 27. Misbehaving Ladies 31. Secrets 33. Dames 34. The Firebird 34. The Great Ziegfeld 36. Rosalie 37. Test Pilot 38. The Hardys Ride High 39. Hullaballoo 40. Blonde Inspiration 41. The Big Store 41. Grand Central Murder 42. Idaho 43. Strangers in the Night 44. Blonde Ransom 45. House of Horrors 46. Unconquered 47. Who Killed Doc Robbin? 48. Jungle Jim 49. Slaughter Trail 51. Desert Pursuit 52. Target Earth 54. The Last Command 55. Crime of Passion 56. The Restless Years 58. Portrait in Black 60. Back Street 61. Black Zoo 63. Love Has Many Faces 65. Madame X 66. Rosie 68. Airport 69, many others.

Grey, Zane (1875–1939).
American novelist whose western yarns provided the basis of hundreds of silent and sound movies. He lacked sophistication, but as late as 1960 TV had its *Zane Grey Theatre*. In 1996, Ed Harris and Amy Madigan starred in a TV film of his *Riders of the Purple Sage*, directed by Charles Haid.

Greyson, John.
Canadian director and screenwriter, of films on homosexual themes. *Zero Patience* was a musical about AIDS.
Kipling Meets the Cowboys (short) 85. Urinal 88. Zero Patience 93. Lilies 96, etc.

Grieco, Richard (1964–).
American leading actor in teen-oriented movies, from television.
If Looks Could Kill 91. Mobsters 91. Tomcat: Dangerous Desires 93. Born to Run (TV) 93. A Vow to Kill (TV) 94. Suspicious Agenda 94. The Demolitionist 95. Circuit Breaker 96. When Time Expires 97. A Night at the Roxbury 98, etc.
TV series: 21 Jump Street 88–89. Booker 89–90. Marker 95.

Griem, Helmut (1940–).
German leading man in international films.
The Damned 69. The Mackenzie Break 70. *Cabaret* 72. Ludwig 73. Voyage of the Damned 76. Sergeant Steiner 79. Children of Rage 82. Malou 83, etc.

Grier, David Alan (1955–).
American actor.
Streamers 83. A Soldier's Story 84. From the Hip 87. Off Limits 87. Loose Cannons 90. Boomerang 92. In the Army Now 94. Blankman 94. Tales from the Hood 95. Jumanji 95. McHale's Navy 97, etc.

Grier, Pam (1949–).
American leading lady, best known for her tough roles in blaxploitation movies of the 70s.
Beyond the Valley of the Dolls 70. Twilight People 72. Blacula 72. Hit Man 72. Coffy 74. Black Mama White Mama 74. The Arena 74. Sheba Baby 75. Friday Foster 75. Drum 76. Greased Lightning 77. Fort Apache, the Bronx 81. Something Wicked This Way Comes 83. Badge of the Assassin 85. On the Edge 86. Tough Enough 87. Naked Warriors 87. Above the Law 88. The Package 89. Class of 1999 90. Bill & Ted's Bogus Journey 91. Posse 93. Original Gangstas 96. Escape from LA 96. Mars Attacks! 96. *Jackie Brown* 97, etc.
TV series: Linc's 98– .

Grier, Roosevelt (1932–).
American footballer, cousin of Pam Grier; makes occasional showbiz appearances.
The Thing with Two Heads 72. Skyjacked 72. Evil in the Deep 76.

Grierson, John (1898–1972).
Distinguished British documentarist. Founded Empire Marketing Board Film Unit 30. GPO Film Unit 33; Canadian Film Commissioner 39–45, etc. Produced *Drifters* 29. *Industrial Britain* 33. *Song of Ceylon* 34. *Night Mail* 36, etc. In 1957–63 he had his own weekly TV show *This Wonderful World* showing excerpts from the world's best non-fiction films.

Gries, Tom (1922–1977).
American director (also co-writer and producer) with varied Hollywood experience from 1946 and much TV.
■ Hell's Horizon 55. The Girl in the Woods 58. *Will Penny* (& w) 68. 100 Rifles 69. Number One 69. The Hawaiians 70. Fools 71. Earth II (TV) 71. Call to Danger (TV) 72. The Glass House (TV) 72. Journey through Rosebud 72. Migrants (TV) 73. Lady Ice 73. QB VII (TV) 74. Breakout 75. Breakheart Pass 76. Helter Skelter (TV) 76. The Greatest 77.

Grifasi, Joe (1944–).
American character actor.
The Deer Hunter 78. On the Yard 78. Honky Tonk Freeway 81. Still of the Night 82. The Pope of Greenwich Village 84. Splash 84. Iron Weed 87. F/X 85. Presumed Innocent 90. City of Hope 91. Household Saints 93. Benny and Joon 93. Natural Born Killers 94. The Hudsucker Proxy 94. Money Train 95. Two Bits 96. One Fine Day 96. Sunday 97, etc.

Griffies, Ethel (1878–1975) (Ethel Woods).
Angular British character actress, in Hollywood for many years.
Waterloo Bridge 31. Love Me Tonight 32. The Mystery of Edwin Drood 35. Kathleen 37. We are Not Alone 39. Irene 40. Great Guns 41. *Time to Kill* 42. Jane Eyre 44. The Horn Blows at Midnight 45. Devotion 46. The Homestretch 47. The Birds 63. *Billy Liar* (GB) 63, many others.

Griffin, Josephine (1928–).
British leading lady.
The Weak and the Wicked 54. The Purple Plain 54. The Man Who Never Was 56. The Spanish Gardener (last to date) 56, etc.

Griffith, Andy (1926–).
Tall, slow-speaking American comic actor, adept at wily country-boy roles.
A Face in the Crowd (debut) 57. No Time for Sergeants 58. Onionhead 58. Winter Kill (TV) 73. Hearts of the West 75. *Washington: Behind Closed Doors* (TV) 76. The Girl in the Empty Grave (TV) 77. Deadly Game (TV) 77. Centennial (TV) 78. From Here to Eternity (TV) 79. Roots: The Next Generations (TV) 79. Fatal Vision (TV) 85. Spy Hard 96, etc.
TV series: The Andy Griffith Show 60–68. The Headmaster 70. Salvage 78. Matlock 86–92.

Griffith, Corinne (1898–1979).
American leading lady of the 20s.
The Yellow Girl 22. Six Days 23. Lilies of the Field 24. Love's Wilderness 24. The Marriage Whirl 25. Infatuation 25. Syncopating Sue 26. Three Hours 27. The Garden of Eden 28. The Divine Lady 29. Saturday's Children 29. Back Pay 30. Lily Christine 30. Papa's Delicate Condition (oa only) 52, etc.

Griffith, D. W. (1875–1948) (David Wark).
American film pioneer, the industry's first major producer-director; he improved the cinema's prestige, developed many aspects of technique, created a score of stars, and was only flawed by his sentimental Victorian outlook, which in the materialistic 20s put him prematurely out of vogue and in the 30s out of business.
Best biographies: 1969, *The Movies, Mr Griffith, and Me* by Lillian Gish. 1984, *D. W. Griffith and the Birth of Film* by Richard Schickel.
SELECTED EARLY FILMS: For the Love of Gold 08. The Song of the Shirt 08. Edgar Allan Poe 09. The Medicine Bottle 09. The Drunkard's Reformation 09. The Cricket on the Hearth 09. What Drink Did 09. The Violin Maker of Cremona 09. Pippa Passes 09. In the Watches of the Night 09. Lines of White on a Sullen Sea 09. Nursing a Viper 09. The Red Man's View 09. In Old California 10. Ramona 10. In the Season of Buds 10. The Face at the Window 10. The House with Closed Shutters 10. The Usurer 10. The Chink at Golden Gulch 10. Muggsy's First Sweetheart 10. The Italian Barber 10. The Manicure Lady 11. What Shall We Do with Our Old? 11. *The Lonedale Operator* 11. The Spanish Gypsy 11. Paradise Lost 11. Enoch Arden 11. Through Darkened Vales 11. The Revenue Man and the Girl 11. A Mender of Nets 12. The Goddess of Sagebrush Gulch 12. The Old Actor 12. *Man's Genesis* 12. The Sands of Dee 12. *The Musketeers of Pig Alley* 12. My Baby 12. *The New York Hat* 12. The God Within 12. The One She Loved 12. The Mothering Heart 13. The Sheriff's Baby 13. The Battle at Elderbush Gulch 13. *Judith of Bethulia* 13. The Escape 14. The Avenging Conscience 14. The Mother and the Law 14. Home Sweet Home 14, many others.
■ FROM 1915: *The Birth of a Nation* 15. *Intolerance* 16. *Hearts of the World* 18. The Great Love 18. The Greatest Thing in Life 18. A Romance of Happy Valley 19. *Broken Blossoms* 19. The Girl Who Stayed at Home 19. True Heart Susie 19. Scarlet Days 19. The Greatest Question 19. The Idol Dancer 20. The Love Flower 20. *Way Down East* 20. Dream Street 21. *One Exciting Night* 22.

Orphans of the Storm 22. The White Rose 23. America 24. Isn't Life Wonderful 25. Sally of the Sawdust 26. That Royle Girl 26. *The Sorrows of Satan* 26. Drums of Love 28. The Battle of the Sexes 28. Lady of the Pavements 29. Abraham Lincoln 30. The Struggle 31. One Million Years BC (reputed contribution) 39.

✪ For enduring the fate of most monuments, and for deserving the tribute in the first place, despite being a personality with clearly unlikeable aspects. *Intolerance*.

❝ Remember how small the world was before I came along. I brought it all to life: I moved the whole world onto a 20-foot screen. – *D.W.G.*

He did what he did genuinely, and straight from the heart. His best films are passionate and tender, terrifying and pregnant, works of art certainly, and products too of an imagination far ahead of its time. – *Paul O'Dell*

It is time D. W. Griffith was rescued from the pedestal of an outmoded pioneer. The cinema of Griffith, after all, is no more outmoded than the drama of Aeschylus. – *Andrew Sarris, 1968*

Griffith's enormous success was due largely to the fact that his heroes and heroines firmly believed, and practised the belief, that babies are brought by the stork. The lowbrow who believed otherwise was always the Griffith villain. – *George Jean Nathan*

He was the first to photograph thought, said Cecil B. de Mille. It was quite a compliment. But Griffith was full of contradictions. His brain was progressive, his emotions Victorian. For a few years the two aspects were able to join in public favour, but he could not adapt himself to the brisker pace of the 20s, when he made many such blinkered and stubborn pronouncements as:

❝ We do not want now and we never shall want the human voice with our films.

When the inevitable happened in 1928 he declared:

We have taken beauty and exchanged it for stilted voices.

He could be tactless too, as when in 1918 he commented:

Viewed as drama, the war is somewhat disappointing.

Yet this was the man of whom Gene Fowler could say:

He articulated the mechanics of cinema and bent them to his flair.

Lilian Gish, a great admirer of Griffith, said:

He inspired in us his belief that we were working in a medium that was powerful enough to influence the whole world.

To Mack Sennett:

He was my day school, my adult education program, my university . . . (but) he was an extremely difficult man to know.

He said himself:

The task I'm trying to achieve above all is to make you see . . .

He knew his own value, as many an actor found when asking for a rise:

It's worth a lot more than money to be working for me!

This was true enough up to the time of *The Birth of a Nation*, which President Wilson described as:

Like writing history with lightning.

But it became less so after the box-office flop of *Intolerance*, which Gene Fowler called:

The greatest commercial anticlimax in film history.

He became an embarrassment to Hollywood because his ideas seemed outmoded; in the 30s he scarcely worked at all. When he died in 1948 Hedda Hopper, recalling the marks made by stars in the wet cement at Hollywood's Chinese Theater, said:

Griffith's footprints were never asked for, yet no one has ever filled his shoes . . .

And James Agee added:

There is not a man working in movies, nor a man who cares for them, who does not owe Griffith more than he owes anyone else.

Ezra Goodman commented:

At Griffith's funeral, the sacred cows of Hollywood gathered to pay him homage. A week before, he probably could not have gotten any of them on the telephone.

It is said indeed that death had to come before such tributes as Frank Capra's:

Since Griffith there has been no major improvement in the art of film direction.

And Carmel Myers':

He was the umbrella that shaded us all.

And John Simon's:

Griffith did for film what Sackville and Norton, the authors of *Gorboduc*, did for drama.

Griffith, Edward H. (1894–1975).
American director.
Scrambled Wives 21. Unseeing Eyes 23. Bad Company 25. Afraid to Love 27. Paris Bound 29. Holiday 30. Rebound 31. The Animal Kingdom 32. Another Language 33. Biography of a Bachelor Girl 35. No More Ladies 35. Ladies in Love 36. Café Metropole 37. Café Society 39. Safari 40. Virginia 40. One Night in Lisbon 41. Bahama Passage 42. The Sky's the Limit 43. Perilous Holiday 46, etc.

Griffith, Hugh (1912–1980).
Flamboyant Welsh actor, former bank clerk.
Neutral Port (debut) 40; war service; The Three Weird Sisters 48. London Belongs to Me 48. The Last Days of Dolwyn 48. A Run for Your Money 49. Laughter in Paradise 51. The Galloping Major 51. The Beggar's Opera 52. *The Titfield Thunderbolt* 53. The Sleeping Tiger 54. Passage Home 55. *Lucky Jim* 57. *Ben Hur* (AA) 59. The Day They Robbed the Bank of England 60. Exodus 61. The Counterfeit Traitor 62. *Tom Jones* (AAN) 63. The Bargee 64. Moll Flanders 65. Oh Dad, Poor Dad 66. Sailor from Gibraltar 66. How to Steal a Million 66. The Chastity Belt 67. Oliver 68. The Fixer 68. Start the Revolution Without Me 69. Cry of the Banshee 70. Wuthering Heights 70. The Abominable Dr Phibes 71. Who Slew Auntie Roo? 72. What 72. Craze 73. Take Me High 73. Luther 75. Loving Cousins 76. Joseph Andrews 77. The Last Remake of Beau Geste 77. The Passover Plot 77, many others.

Griffith, James (1916–1993).
American general-purpose actor.
Bright Leaf 50. Rhubarb 51. The Law vs Billy the Kid (as Pat Garrett) 54. Anything Goes 56. The Big Fisherman 59. The Amazing Transparent Man 61. Advance to the Rear 63. A Big Hand for the Little Lady 66. Day of the Evil Gun 68. Vanishing Point 71. The Tooth of Crime 75. Speedtrap 78, etc.

Griffith, Kenneth (1921–).
Sharp-eyed Welsh actor of stage and screen, often the envious 'little man'.
Autobiography: 1994, *The Fool's Paradise*.
Love on the Dole 41. The Shop at Sly Corner 45. Bond Street 48. High Treason 50. Lucky Jim 57. I'm All Right, Jack 59. Circus of Horrors 59. *Only Two Can Play* 61. Rotten to the Core 65. The Bobo 67. The Whisperers 67. Revenge 71. The House in Nightmare Park 73. Remembrance 82. The Englishman Who Went up a Hill but Came Down a Mountain 95, many others.

Griffith, Melanie (1957–).
American leading actress, the daughter of Tippi Hedren. She married actor Don Johnson (1976–77) and, following another divorce, remarried him in 1989. They were divorced again in 1995, and she subsequently married actor Antonio Banderas in 1996.
Night Moves 75. The Drowning Pool 76. Body Double 84. Fear City 85. Something Wild 86. The Milagro Beanfield War 88. Cherry 2000 88. Stormy Monday 88. Working Girl (AAN) 88. In the Spirit 90. The Bonfire of the Vanities 90. Pacific Heights 90. Paradise 91. Shining Through 92. Born Yesterday 93. Milk Money 94. Nobody's Fool 94. Buffalo Girls (TV) 95. Now and Then 96. Mulholland Falls 96. Lolita 97. Another Day in Paradise 98. Celebrity 98, etc.
TV series: Once an Eagle 76–77. Carter Country 78–79. Me and George 98– .

❝ There's a bit of a stripper in every woman. – M.G.

The instantly recognisable Griffith Girl: a trashy babe in black underpant and matching garter belt with a squeaky voice, a butt that is not to be trifled with, and a heart as wide as Asia. – *Joe Queenan*

Griffith, Raymond (1894–1937).
Dapper American comedian of the 20s.
Fools First 22. The Eternal Three 23. Changing Husbands 24. Poisoned Paradise 24. Open All Night 24. Miss Bluebeard 24. A Regular Fellow 25. *Fine Clothes* 25. *Hands Up* 25. *Wet Paint* 26. You'd Be Surprised 27. Time to Love 27. Wedding Bills 27. *All Quiet on the Western Front* (as the dying soldier) 30, etc.

Griffith, Richard (1912–1969).
American film critic and curator of New York's Museum of Modern Art.

Griffith, Thomas Ian (1960–).
American actor, screenwriter and producer. Married actress Mary Page Keller.
Karate Kid Part III (a) 89. Ulterior Motives (a) 91. Night of the Warrior (p, w) 91. Excessive Force (p, a, w) 93. Crackerjack (a) 94. Blood of the Innocent (a) 94. Hollow Point (a) 95. Behind Enemy Lines (a) 96. Kull the Conqueror (a) 97. John Carpenter's Vampires (a) 97, etc.

Griffiths, Jane (1929–1975).
British leading lady of the 50s.
The Million Pound Note 54. The Green Scarf 54. Dead Man's Evidence 62. The Traitors 63, etc.

Griffiths, Linda.
Canadian leading actress, dramatist and screenwriter.
Lianna 83. Overdrawn at the Memory Bank 83. Reno and the Doc 84. The Darling Family (& w) 94, etc.

Griffiths, Richard (1947–).
Sizeable British actor, best known for his role as a police inspector-cum-restaurateur in the TV series *Pie in the Sky*. The son of deaf mute parents, he was for ten years a member of the Royal Shakespeare Company, where he was a notable Bottom in *A Midsummer Night's Dream*.
Greystoke 84. Gorky Park 84. A Private Function 85. Shanghai Surprise 86. Withnail and I 87. King Ralph 91. The Naked Gun 2½: The Smell of Fear 91. Blame It on the Bellboy 92. Guarding Tess 94. Funny Bones 95, etc.
TV series: Bird of Prey 84. Nobody's Perfect 80–82. Ffizz 87–89. A Kind of Living 88–90. Pie in the Sky 94–95.

❝ I think of myself as the world's most intelligent ambulatory aubergine. – *R.G.*

No actor chooses to be in a film. In the real world you kick, scramble and stagger to get into the thing. I know actors who hold parties simply because they have an audition, which is tragic. – *R.G.*

Griggs, Loyal (1906–1978).
American cinematographer.
Shane (AA) 53. Elephant Walk 54. We're No Angels 55. The Ten Commandments 56. The Hangman 59. Walk Like a Dragon 60. The Slender Thread 66. Hurry Sundown 67. P. J. 68, many others.

Grimault, Paul (1905–1994).
French animator. *Le Petit Soldat* 47, many shorts.

Grimes, Gary (1955–).
American juvenile lead of the 70s.
■ *Summer of 42* 71. The Culpepper Cattle Co. 72. Class of 44 73. Cahill 73. The Spikes Gang 74. Once an Eagle (TV) 76. Gus 76.

Grimes, Stephen (1927–1988).
British production designer.
Reflections in a Golden Eye 67. Ryan's Daughter 71. Murder by Death 76. The Electric Horseman 79. Urban Cowboy 80. Out of Africa (AA) 85, etc.

Grimes, Tammy (1934–).
American comedy actress who never really made it in the movies. She is the mother of Amanda Plummer.
■ Three Bites of the Apple 67. Arthur Arthur 69. The Other Man (TV) 70. Play It As It Lays 72. The Borrowers (TV) 73. Horror at 37,000 Feet (TV) 73. Somebody Killed Her Husband 78. You Can't Go Home Again (TV) 79. The Runner Stumbles 79. Can't Stop the Music 80. America 86. Mr North 88. Mr 247 94.

Grimm, Jakob (1785–1863) and **Wilhelm** (1786–1859).
German writers of philology and – especially – fairy tales. The latter are familiar throughout the world and have been the basis of many children's films by Walt Disney and others. A thin biopic, *The Wonderful World of the Brothers Grimm*, was made in 1962.

Grimm, Oliver (1948–).
German child actor of the 50s.
My Name is Nicki 52. Father Needs a Wife 52. My Father the Actor 56. Kleiner Mann – ganz gross 57. The Magnificent Rebel 60. Reach for Glory 61, etc.

Grinde, Nick (1891–1979).
American director.
Excuse Me 25. Upstage 26. Beyond the Sierra 28. *The Bishop Murder Case* 30. Good News 30. This Modern Age 31. Vanity Street 32. Ladies Crave Excitement 35. Public Enemy's Wife 36. White Bondage 37. King of Chinatown 39. The Man They Could Not Hang 39. Behind the Door 40. Hitler Dead or Alive 43. Road to Alcatraz 45, etc.

Grisham, John (1955–).
American best-selling novelist, a former lawyer. He was paid $2.25m for the film rights to *The Client* and a record $3.75m for the film rights to *The Chamber* before it was written. Film rights in his 1989 novel *A Time to Kill* were sold for around $6m in 1994. Screen rights to his novel *The Runaway Jury* were sold for $8m. In 1996, after a friend was killed by two teenagers who claimed to have been imitating the protagonists of *Natural Born Killers*, he suggested that the film's director Oliver Stone should be held legally accountable for it and other deaths – 'The "artist" should be required to share the responsibility along with the nut who actually pulled the trigger,' he wrote.
The Firm 92. The Pelican Brief 93. The Client 94. A Time to Kill (oa) 96. The Chamber (oa) 96. John Grisham's The Rainmaker 97.

Grizzard, George (1928–).
American stage actor, usually in sneaky roles in films.
From the Terrace 60. *Advise and Consent* 62. Warning Shot 66. Happy Birthday Wanda June 71. Travis Logan DA (TV) 71. Indict and Convict (TV) 74. The Stranger Within (TV) 74. Attack on Terror (TV) 75. The Lives of Jenny Dolan (TV) 75. Comes a Horseman 78. The Night Rider (TV) 79. Firepower 79. Seems Like Old Times 80. Wrong Is Right 82. Bachelor Party 84. Robert Kennedy and His Times (TV) 85. An Enemy of the People (TV) 90. Queen (TV) 93. Scarlett (TV) 94, etc.
TV series: Studio 5-B 89.

Grock (1880–1959) (Adrien Wettach).
Swiss clown who made a few silent films in Britain, and later in Germany. A biopic, *Farewell Mr Grock*, was made in 1954.

Grodin, Charles (1935–).
American leading man. He also hosts a television talk show.
■ Rosemary's Baby 68. Sex and the College Girl 70. Catch 22 70. *The Heartbreak Kid* 72. 11 Harrowhouse 74. King Kong 76. Thieves 77. Heaven Can Wait 78. Just Me and You (TV) 78. The Grass Is Always Greener Over the Septic Tank (TV) 78. Sunburn 79. Real Life 79. It's My Turn 80. Seems Like Old Times 80. The Great Muppet Caper 81. The Incredible Shrinking Woman 81. The Lonely Guy 83. Movers and Shakers 84. The Woman in Red 84. The Last Resort 86. Ishtar 87. The Couch Trip 88. Midnight Run 88. You Can't Hurry Love 88. Taking Care of Business 90. Clifford 91. Beethoven 92. Dave 93. So I Married an Axe Murderer 93. Beethoven's 2nd 93. Heart and Souls 93. Clifford 94. It Runs in the Family 94.

❝ He keeps threatening to be funny but he rarely makes it. – *Pauline Kael*

Grosbard, Ulu (1929–).
Belgian-American director, former diamond-cutter and Broadway director.
■ The Subject Was Roses 68. Who Is Harry Kellerman and Why Is He Saying Those Terrible Things About Me? 71. Straight Time 78. True Confessions 81. Falling in Love 84. Georgia 95.

Gross, Charles.
American composer, mainly for TV movies.
The Group 65. Valdez Is Coming 71. Heartland 79. Sweet Dreams 85. Punchline 88. Turner & Hooch 89. Air America 90, etc.

Gross, Larry.
American screenwriter.
Headin' for Broadway (co-w) 80. 48 Hrs (co-w) 82. Streets of Fire (co-w) 84. Another 48 Hrs (co-

w) 90. Geronimo (co-w) 93. Rear Window (co-w) (TV) 98, etc.

Grossmith, George (1874–1935).
Elegant British musical comedy star who appeared in a few films. He was the son of author and actor George Grossmith (1847–1912), and brother of Lawrence Grossmith (1877–1944), who also appeared in some 30s films. He was the first chairman of Alexander KORDA's London Films.
■ Women Everywhere 30. Service for Ladies 32. Wedding Rehearsal 32. The Girl from Maxim's 33. Princess Charming 34.

Grot, Anton (1884–1974) (Antocz Franziszek Groszewski).
Polish-born director in Hollywood, the driving force of Warner's 30s dream machine. He studied at the Cracow Academy of Arts and in Germany, emigrating to the United States in 1909. His paintings brought an offer of work in films with LUBIN; he then designed for Vitagraph and Pathé, moving to Hollywood in the early 20s to work on Douglas FAIRBANKS's *Robin Hood*. He designed for Cecil B. DE MILLE before joining Warner's in 1927, where he stayed until he retired in 1948, designing 80 films, including many directed by Michael CURTIZ. He was awarded a Technical Oscar in 1940 for his invention of a ripple machine used in *The Sea Hawk*. After he retired, he returned to his painting.
The Mouse and the Lion 13. Arms and the Woman 16. Pirate Gold 20. Tess of the Storm Country 22. *The Thief of Bagdad* 24. Don Q Son of Zorro 25. The Country Doctor 27. The King of Kings 27. The Blue Danube 28. Noah's Ark 29. *Little Caesar* 30. Hatchet Man 31. *Svengali* (AAN) 31. 20,000 Years in Sing Sing 32. Doctor X 32. Baby Face 33. Footlight Parade 33. *The Mystery of the Wax Museum* 33. Gold Diggers of 1933 33. Gold Diggers of 1935 34. *A Midsummer Night's Dream* 35. Captain Blood 35. Dr Socrates 35. *Anthony Adverse* (AAN) 36. Tovarich 37. The Life of Emile Zola (AAN) 37. *The Private Lives of Elizabeth and Essex* (AAN) 39. They Made Me a Criminal 39. *Juarez* 39. *The Sea Hawk* (AAN) 40. *The Sea Wolf* 41. Thank Your Lucky Stars 43. The Conspirators 44. Rhapsody in Blue 45. Mildred Pierce 45. My Reputation 46. *The Unsuspected* 47. Possessed 47. One Sunday Afternoon 48, etc.

Grualt, Jean (1924–).
French screenwriter.
Jules et Jim 61. The Wild Child/L'Enfant Sauvage 70. The Story of Adele H. 75. Mon Oncle d'Amérique (AAN) 80. L'Amour à Mort 84. Life Is a Bed of Roses/La Vie Est un Roman 84. Les Années 80s (co-w) 85. The Mystery of Alexina (co-w) 85. Australia 89. Le Bateau de Mariage 93, etc.

Gruber, Frank (1904–1969).
American screenwriter.
Death of a Champion (oa) 39. The Kansan (oa) 43. *The Mask of Dimitrios* 44. Terror by Night 47. Fighting Man of the Plains 49. The Great Missouri Raid 51. Denver and Rio Grande 52. Hurricane Smith 52. Backlash (oa) 56. The Big Land (oa) 57. Town Tamer 65. Arizona Raiders (oa) 67, etc.
TV: created *Tales of Wells Fargo*.

Gruenberg, Louis (1884–1964).
Russian-American composer.
Stagecoach (co-m) 39. So Ends Our Night 40. Arch of Triumph 49. All the King's Men 49, etc.

Gruendgens, Gustav (1899–1963).
German stage actor and director; films occasional.
M (a) 31. Pygmalion (a) 35. Capriolen (d) 37. Friedemann Bach (a) 41. Faust (ad) 61.

Grune, Karl (1890–1962).
Czech-Austrian director in German films.
The Street 23. At the Edge of the World 27. Waterloo 28. Abdul the Damned (GB) 35. Pagliacci (GB) 37, etc.

Gruner, Olivier (1960–).
French star of American action movies, a former marine and kick-boxing champion. Born in Paris, he worked as a model in TV commercials before moving to the USA.
Angel Town 89. Nemesis 93. Zero Hour 94. The Fighter 95. Savage 96. Mercenary 96. Mars 96. TNT 97, etc.

Grusin, Dave (1934–).
American composer.
Divorce American Style 67. The Graduate 67. Candy 68. The Mad Room 69. Tell them Willie Boy is Here 69. The Pursuit of Happiness 71. The Great Northfield Minnesota Raid 72. Bobby Deerfield 77. The Goodbye Girl 77. The Cheap Detective 78. Heaven Can Wait (AAN) 78. The Champ (AAN) 79. And Justice for All 79. The Electric Horseman 79. My Bodyguard 80. On Golden Pond (AAN) 81. Absence of Malice 81. Reds 81. The Little Drummer Girl 84. Falling in Love 84. The Goonies 85. Lucas 86. Ishtar 87. The Milagro Beanfield War (AA) 88. Tequila Sunrise 88. A Dry White Season 89. The Fabulous Baker Boys (AAN) 89. Bonfire of the Vanities 90. Look Who's Talking Too 90. Havana 90. For the Boys 91. The Firm (AAN) 93. The Cure 95. Mulholland Falls 96. Selena 96. In the Gloaming (TV) 97. Hope Floats 98, etc.

Guard, Dominic (1956–).
British juvenile actor of the 70s.
The Go-Between 70. The Hands of Cormac Joyce (TV) 72. Bequest to the Nation 73. The Count of Monte Cristo (TV) 74. Picnic at Hanging Rock 75. Gandhi 82. A Woman of Substance (TV) 84. Absolution 88. The Man Who Lost His Shadow 91, etc.

Guardino, Harry (1925–1995).
Leading American TV actor, in occasional films.
Houseboat 58. Pork Chop Hill 59. The Five Pennies 59. King of Kings 61. Hell is for Heroes 62. Rhino 64. Bullwhip Griffin 67. Madigan 68. Lovers and Other Strangers 69. Red Sky at Morning 71. Dirty Harry 71. Capone 75. St Ives 76. The Enforcer 76. Street Killing (TV) 76. Rollercoaster 77. Goldengirl (TV) 79. Any Which Way You Can 80. The Neon Empire 89, etc.
TV series: The Reporter 64. Monty Nash 71.

Guare, John (1938–).
American dramatist and screenwriter. Born in New York, he studied at the Yale School of Drama.
Taking Off (co-w) 71. Atlantic City (AANw) 81. Six Degrees of Separation (w, from his play) 93.

Guareschi, Giovanni (1908–1968).
Italian author of the 'Don Camillo' stories about a parish priest's comic struggles with a communist mayor. Several were filmed with Fernandel and Gino Cervi.

Guber, Peter (1939–).
Producer whose Guber-Peters production company, formed in partnership with Jon Peters, enjoyed success in the 80s. Head of Columbia 1989–94, following its takeover by Sony; now an independent producer.
Book: 1996, *Hit and Run: How Jon Peters and Peter Guber Took Sony for a Ride in Hollywood* by Nancy Griffin & Kim Masters.
The Deep 77. Midnight Express 78. An American Werewolf in London 81. Six Weeks 82. The Color Purple 85. The Clan of the Cave Bear 86. Innerspace 87. The Witches of Eastwick 87. Gorillas in the Mist 88. Rain Man 88. Batman 89. The Bonfire of the Vanities 90. Batman Returns 92. This Boy's Life 93. With Honors 94, etc.

Guerman, Alexei (1938–) (aka Alexei Gherman).
Russian director and screenwriter, the son of writer Yuri Guerman, whose stories formed the basis of his film My *Friend Ivan Lapshin*. His career has been dogged by government censorship: *Trial on the Road*, about a Red Army sergeant who deserts from the German Army, was banned for 14 years, and his next film, dealing with the difference between the reality of the Battle of Stalingrad and a film director's recreation of it, was also withdrawn for several years.
The Seventh Satellite (co-d) 67. Trial on the Road/Proverka Na Dorogakh 71. Twenty Days without War/Dvadtsat Dnei Bez Voini 76. My *Friend Ivan Lapshin* 86. Happy Days 92. Khroustaliov, My Car! 98, etc.

Guerra, Ruy (1931–).
Brazilian director, playwright, actor and composer. Born in Mozambique and educated in France, he lived in Brazil from the late 50s to the mid-60s, leaving to settle in Mozambique, where he founded the National Institute of Cinema and made that country's first feature film in 1980.
Os Cafajestes 62. Os Fuzis 64. Sweet Hunters 69. Mueda, Memoria e Massacre 80. Erendira 82. Opera do Malandro 86. Kuarup 89, etc.

Guerra, Tonino (1920–).
Italian screenwriter and novelist who wrote five films for Antonioni.
La Notte 61. L'Avventura 61. Red Desert 65. Casanova '70 (AAN) 65. Blow-Up (AAN) 66. Zabriskie Point 70. Amarcord (AAN) 74. Un Papillon sur l'Epaule 78. The Night of the Shooting Stars/La Notte di San Lorenzo 82. And the Ship Sails On 83. Nostalgia 84. Henry IV 85. Ginger and Fred 86. Good Morning Babylon 86. The Beekeeper/O Melissokomos 86. Chronicle of a Death Foretold 87. To Forget Palermo/Dimenticare Palermo 89. The Dark Illness/Il Male Oscuro 89. Stanno Tutti Bene 90. Journey of Love/Viàggio d'Amore 91. Especially on Sundays/La Domenica Specialmente 91. The Petrified Garden 93. Beyond the Clouds 95, etc.

Guest, Christopher (1948–) (Lord Haden-Guest).
British actor and screenwriter turned director. He married actress Jamie Lee CURTIS in 1984.
The Hot Rock 72. Girlfriends 78. The Long Riders 80. Heartbeeps 81. *This Is Spinal Tap* (& w) 84. Little Shop of Horrors 86. The Princess Bride 87. Beyond Therapy 87. Sticky Fingers 88. The Big Picture (wd) 89. Attack of the 50 Ft Woman (TV) (d) 93. Waiting for Guffman (& co-w, d, a) 97, etc.

Guest, Val (1911–) (Valmond Guest).
British writer-producer-director, former journalist. Worked on screenplays of 30s comedies for Will Hay, Arthur Askey, the Crazy Gang, etc. Married to Yolande Donlan.
SCREENPLAYS, MOSTLY IN COLLABORATION: The Maid of the Mountains 32. Good Morning Boys 36. Okay for Sound 37. *Oh Mr Porter* 38. Convict 99 38. *Alf's Button Afloat* 38. Band Waggon 39. The Frozen Limits 39. Old Bones of the River 39. *Ask a Policeman* 40. Charley's Aunt 40. Gasbags 40. Inspector Hornleigh Goes to It 41. *The Ghost Train* 41. Back Room Boy 42. London Town 46. Paper Orchid 49 etc.
■ AS DIRECTOR (usually writer also): Miss London Ltd. 43. Bees in Paradise 44. Give Us the Moon 44. I'll Be Your Sweetheart 45. Just William's Luck 47. William Comes to Town 48. Murder at the Windmill 49. Miss Pilgrim's Progress 50. The Body Said No 50. *Mr Drake's Duck* 51. Penny Princess 52. *The Runaway Bus* 54. Life with the Lyons 54. Men of Sherwood Forest 54. Dance Little Lady 54. They Can't Hang Me 54. The Lyons in Paris 55. Break in the Circle 55. *The Quatermass Experiment* 55. It's A Wonderful World 55. The Weapon 56. Carry On Admiral 57. *Quatermass II* 57. The Abominable Snowman 57. Camp on Blood Island 58. Up the Creek 58. Life is a Circus 59. Yesterday's Enemy 59. *Expresso Bongo* 60. Further Up the Creek 60. Hell is a City 60. The Full Treatment 60. The Day the Earth Caught Fire 62. *Jigsaw* 63. 80,000 Suspects 63. The Beauty Jungle 64. Where the Spies are 65. Casino Royale (wd) 67. Assignment K 67. When Dinosaurs Ruled the World 68. Tomorrow 70. Au Pair Girls 72. Confessions of a Window Cleaner 74. The Diamond Mercenaries 76. Dangerous Davies (TV) 80. The Boys in Blue 83. Possession (TV) 84. The Scent of Fear (TV) 85.

Guétary, Georges (1915–1997) (Lambros Worloou).
Greek/Egyptian singer and actor in occasional films. Born in Alexandria, Egypt, he studied music in France and worked in music hall, first as a band guitarist from the mid-30s, and then becoming a protégé of MISTINGUETT. He became a star in London, in the musical *Bless the Bride*, appeared on Broadway and made his only American film, *An American in Paris* 51, before returning to France to star in many operettas. Among his stage successes was a musical, *La Polka des Lampions*, adapted from Billy WILDER's *Some Like It Hot*. He retired in the mid-80s.
Black Cavalier/Le Cavalier Noir 45. The Adventures of Casanova/Les Aventures de Casanova 46. *An American in Paris* 51. Une Fille sur la Route 52. Plume au Vent 53. The Road to Paradise/Le Chemin du Paradis 56. Une Nuit aux Baléares 57, etc.

Guevara, Che (1928–1967) (Ernesto Guevara).
Argentinian-born guerrilla leader who became a revolutionary icon in the 60s, after he had joined Fidel Castro to overthrow the regime of president Batista in Cuba. He was killed while attempting to lead a revolution in Bolivia. He was played by Francisco Rabal in the Italian biopic *El 'Che' Guevara* 68, Omar Sharif in *Che!* 69, and Antonio Banderas in the film version of the musical *Evita* 96.

Guffey, Burnett (1905–1983).
Distinguished American cinematographer.
Cover Girl 44. Johnny O'Clock 46. Gallant Journey 46. The Reckless Moment 48. *All the King's Men* 49. In a Lonely Place 50. The Sniper 52. *From Here to Eternity* (AA) 53. Human Desire 55. The Harder They Fall 56. Edge of Eternity 59. Birdman of Alcatraz 62. King Rat 65. *Bonnie and Clyde* (AA) 67. The Split 68. The Madwoman of Chaillot 69. The Great White Hope 70, etc.

Guffroy, Pierre (1926–).
French art director and production designer who worked on Buñuel's later films and also several by Roman Polanski. A documentary on his work, *Behind the Scenes: A Portrait of Pierre Guffroy*, was made in 1992.
Le Testament d'Orphée 59. Mouchette 67. The Bride Wore Black/La Mariée Était en Noir 67. The Milky Way 68. Rider on the Rain 69. The Discreet Charm of the Bourgeoisie 72. Cesar and Rosalie 72. The Phantom of Liberty 74. The Tenant 76. That Obscure Object of Desire 77. Tess 79. L'Argent 83. Pirates 86. The Unbearable Lightness of Being 87. Mayrig 91. Giorgino 94. Death and the Maiden 95, etc.

Gugino, Carla (c. 1972–).
American actress, a former model.
Son-in-Law 93. This Boy's Life 93. Miami Rhapsody 95. The Buccaneers (TV) 95. Wedding Bell Blues 97. Snake Eyes 98, etc.

Guild, Nancy (1925–).
American leading lady.
Somewhere in the Night 46. The High Window 47. Give My Regards to Broadway 49. Abbott and Costello Meet the Invisible Man 51. Francis Covers the Big Town 54. Such Good Friends 71, etc.

Guilfoyle, Paul (1902–1961).
American character actor usually in sly or sinister roles.
Special Agent 36. Blind Alibi 38. Time to Kill 42. Sweetheart of Sigma Chi 46. Miss Mink of 1949. Mighty Joe Young 50. Torch Song 52. Julius Caesar 53. Valley of Fury 55, many others.
AS DIRECTOR: Captain Scarface 53. A Life at Stake 54. Tess of the Storm Country 60.

Guillaume, Robert (1930–) (Robert Williams).
Handsome American leading man and comedian, former opera singer.
Seems Like Old Times 80. The Kid with the Broken Halo (TV) 82. The Kid with the 200 I.Q. (TV) 83. Prince Jack 84. They Still Call Me Bruce 86. Wanted: Dead or Alive 86. Fire and Rain 89. The Meteor Man 93. The Lion King (voice) 94. First Kid 96. The Lion King II: Simba's Pride (voice) 98, etc.
TV series: *Soap* 77–80. *Benson* 79–86. Sports Night 98– .

Guillermin, John (1925–).
English director and screenwriter. Born in London of French parents, he was educated at Cambridge University and produced and directed documentaries in Paris before returning to England in the late 40s, moving to Los Angeles in the early 60s, after the success of *Waltz of the Toreadors*.
■ Torment 49. Smart Alec 50. Never Let Go (w) 50. Two on the Tiles 51. Four Days 51. Song of Paris 52. Miss Robin Hood 52. Operation Diplomat 53. Adventure in the Hopfields 54. The Crowded Day 54. Thunderstorm 55. Double Jeopardy 55. *Town on Trial* 56. The Whole Truth 57. *I Was Monty's Double* 58. Tarzan's Greatest Adventure 59. The Day They Robbed The Bank of England 60. Never Let Go (& w) 60. Waltz of the Toreadors 62. Tarzan Goes to India 62. Guns at Batasi 64. Rapture 65. *The Blue Max* 66. P.J. 68. House of Cards 68. The Bridge at Remagen 69. El Condor 70. Skyjacked 72. Shaft in Africa 74. The Towering Inferno (co-d) 74. King Kong 76. Death on the Nile

78. Mr Patman 80. Crossover 83. Sheena Queen of the Jungle 84. King Kong Lives 86.

Guinan, Texas (1884–1933) (Mary Louise Guinan).
Canadian star entertainer of 20s speakeasies: her catchphrase was 'Hello, sucker!', and she was one of Broadway's most prominent attractions. Betty Hutton played her in *Incendiary Blonde* 45.
■ The Gun Woman 18. Little Miss Deputy 19. I am the Woman 21. The Stampede 21. Queen of the Night Clubs 29. Glorifying the American Girl 29. Broadway through a Keyhole 33.

Guinness, Sir Alec (1914–).
Distinguished British stage actor, who in the late 40s started a spectacular film career, first as a master of disguise, then as a young hero and later as any character from an Arab king to Hitler. Honorary Oscar 1979 'for advancing the art of screen acting'.
Autobiography: 1985, *Blessings in Disguise*. 1996, *My Name Escapes Me: The Diary of a Retiring Actor*.
Biography: 1994, *Master of Disguise* by Garry O'Connor.
■ Evensong 33. Great Expectations (as Herbert Pocket) 46. *Oliver Twist* (as Fagin) 48. *Kind Hearts and Coronets* (playing eight roles) 49. A Run for Your Money 49. Last Holiday 50. *The Mudlark* (as Disraeli) 50. *The Lavender Hill Mob* (AAN) 51. *The Man in the White Suit* 51. *The Card* 52. The Captain's Paradise 52. The Malta Story 53. *Father Brown* 54. To Paris with Love 54. The Prisoner 55. The Ladykillers 55. The Swan 56. Barnacle Bill 57. *The Bridge on the River Kwai* (AA, BFA) 57. The Scapegoat 58. The Horse's Mouth (& w) (AAN) 58. Our Man in Havana 59. *Tunes of Glory* 60. A Majority of One 61. HMS Defiant 62. Lawrence of Arabia 62. The Fall of the Roman Empire 64. Situation Hopeless but Not Serious 64. Doctor Zhivago 66. Hotel Paradiso 66. The Quiller Memorandum 66. The Comedians 67. Cromwell (as Charles I) 69. Scrooge 70. Hitler: The Last Ten Days (as Hitler) 73. Brother Sun and Sister Moon 73. Murder by Death 76. Star Wars (AAN) 77. Tinker Tailor Soldier Spy (TV) 79. The Empire Strikes Back 80. Raise the Titanic 80. Little Lord Fauntleroy (TV) 80. Smiley's People (TV) 82. Lovesick 83. A Passage to India 84. Monsignor Quixote (TV) 85. Little Dorrit (AAN) 87. A Handful of Dust 88. Kafka 91. A Foreign Field (TV) 93. Mute Witness 95. Eskimo Day (TV) 96.
✪ For a multitude of disguises in which he never allowed humanity to be swamped by dexterity. *Father Brown*.
❝ I gave my best performances, perhaps, during the war – trying to be an officer and a gentleman. – A.G.
I don't know what else I could do but pretend to be an actor. – A.G.
Once I've done a film, it's finished. I never look at it again. – A.G.

Guiol, Fred (1898–1964).
American director, mainly of second features; also worked as assistant on many of George Stevens's pictures.
Live and Learn 30. The Cohens and Kellys in Trouble 33. The Nitwits 35. Hayfoot 41. Here Comes Trouble 48. Giant (co-w, AAN) 56, many others.

Guitry, Sacha (1885–1957).
Distinguished French writer-director, in films occasionally over a long period.
Autobiography: 1956, *If Memory Serves*.
Biography: 1968, *The Last Boulevardier* by James Harding.
Ceux de Chez Nous 15. Les Deux Couverts 32. Bonne Chance 35. Le Roman d'un Tricheur 36. Quadrille 38. Ils Etaient Neuf Célibataires 39. Donne-moi tes yeux 43. Le Comédien 49. Deburau 51. Versailles 54. Napoleon 55. La Vie à Deux 57, etc.

Guizar, Tito (1908–*) (Frederick Guizar).
Popular Mexican singer, guitarist and actor, in Hollywood from the mid-30s to the late 40s. Born in Mexico City, of Italian and French ancestry, he studied singing in Italy and worked with the Chicago Grand Opera in the early 30s. He became a star in Mexico with *Allá en el Rancho Grande* 36, which combined music and a narrative set on a ranch and established a popular genre, and was the first Mexican actor to gain an international reputation.
Big Broadcast of 1938 37. Tropic Holiday 38. Mis Dos Amores 38. St Louis Blues 39. The Singing Charro 39. The Llano Kid 39. Blondie Goes Latin 41. Brazil 44. Mexicana 46. The Thrill of Brazil 46. On the Old Spanish Trail 47. The Gay Ranchero 48. Tropical Masquerade 48. Música y Dinero 56, etc.

Gulager, Clu (1928–).
American leading man, mostly on TV.
The Killers (TV) 64. Winning 69. The Last Picture Show 71. The Glass House (TV) 72. Footsteps (TV) 72. Call to Danger (TV) 73. McQ 74. The Killer Who Wouldn't Die (TV) 76. The Other Side of Midnight 77. A Force of One 79. Touched by Love 80. The Return of the Living Dead 85. Hunter's Blood 86. The Offspring 86. Eddie Presley 93, etc.
TV series: The Tall Man 60–61. The Virginian 64–68. The Survivors 69. San Francisco International 70.

Gulpilil, David (1954–).
Australian actor, memorable as the aborigine youth in Nicolas Roeg's *Walkabout*. He is also head of an aboriginal dance company.
Walkabout 71. Mad Dog Morgan 76. Storm Boy 76. The Last Wave 77. Blue Fin 78. Long Weekend 78. Crocodile Dundee 86. Dark Age 88. Until the End of the World/Bis ans Ende der Welt 91, etc.

Güney, Yilmaz (1937–1984).
Leading Turkish actor and screenwriter who turned to directing after serving terms of imprisonment for his left-wing political activities. He supervised films in the mid-70s from his prison cell, escaped in 1981, lost his Turkish citizenship as a result, and died from cancer shortly afterwards.
My Name Is Kerim 67. Bride of the Earth 68. An Ugly Man 69. Hope 70. Tomorrow Is the Final Day 71. Pain 71. The Father 71. Anxiety (co-d) 74. The Poor Ones (co-d) 75. Yol (supervised direction by Serif Goren) 82. The Wall 83, etc.

Gunn, Gilbert (c. 1912–).
Scottish director and screenwriter, a former documentarist. Born in Glasgow and educated at Glasgow University, he was a playwright and theatre producer before entering films in the mid-30s as a screenwriter. He directed more than 50 documentaries for the Ministry of Information and the Central Office of Information.
The Door with Seven Locks (co-w) 40. Landfall (co-w) 49. The Elstree Story (p, d) 52. Valley of Song/Men Are Children Twice (d) 53. Strange World of Planet X (d) 57. Girls at Sea (co-w, d) 58. Operation Bullshine (co-w, d) 59. What a Whopper (d) 62, etc.

Gunn, Moses (1929–1993).
American actor.
The Great White Hope 70. Carter's Army (TV) 70. The Wild Rovers 71. Shaft 72. The Hot Rock 72. Haunts of the Very Rich (TV) 73. Rollerball 75. Remember My Name 78. The Ninth Configuration 80. Ragtime 81. Amityville II 82. Firestarter 84. Heartbreak Ridge 86.
TV series: The Cowboys 74. Roots 77. Good Times 77. The Contender 80. Father Murphy 80–81. A Man Called Hawk 89.

Gurie, Sigrid (1911–1969) (S. G. Haukelid).
American/Norwegian leading lady of the late 30s.
The Adventures of Marco Polo 38. Algiers 38. Rio 40. Three Faces West 40. Dark Streets of Cairo 41. A Voice in the Wind 44. Sword of the Avenger 48, etc.

Guthrie, A. B. (1901–1991).
American Western novelist and screenwriter, a former journalist, three of whose novels were filmed.
The Big Sky (oa) 52. Shane (AAN) 53. The Kentuckian 55. These Thousand Hills (oa) 59. The Way West (oa) 67.

Guthrie, Arlo (1947–).
American ballad singer, son of another (Woody Guthrie, whose story was told in *Bound for Glory*).
Alice's Restaurant 69. Roadside Prophets 92, etc.

Gutowski, Gene (1925–).
Polish producer with US TV experience.
Four Boys and a Gun 56. Station Six Sahara (GB) 63. Repulsion (GB) 65. Cul-de-Sac (GB) 66. The Fearless Vampire Killers (GB) 66. The Adventures of Gerard 70. Romance of a Horse Thief 71, etc.

Guttenberg, Steve (1958–).
American leading actor.
The Chicken Chronicles 77. Players 79. Diner 81. Police Academy 84. Police Academy II 85. Cocoon 85. Bad Medicine 85. Short Circuit 86. The Bedroom Window 86. Police Academy 4: Citizens on Parade 87. Surrender 87. Three Men and a Baby 87. Cocoon: The Return 88. High Spirits 88. Don't Tell Her It's Me 90. Three Men and a Little Lady 90. It Takes Two 95. The Big Green 95. Home for the Holidays 95. Zeus and Roxanne 96. Airborne (Can.) 97, etc.
TV series: Billy 79. No Soap, Radio 82.
❝ I'm not bragging but my movies have grossed well over a billion dollars. – S.G.
If you have a sister, you'd want her to marry Steve Guttenberg. He cooks, he gardens, he's kind to young children. – *Martha Frankel, Movieline*

Guy-Blaché, Alice (1873–1968).
French film director with claims to have been the world's first female director and possibly the world's first director. A secretary to Léon Gaumont, she began by making demonstration films for the company. With her cameraman-husband, Herbert Blaché, she went to America in 1910, set up her own companies and continued directing there until she returned to France in 1922. *The Lost Garden*, a documentary on her life and work directed by Marquise Lepage, was released in 1996.
Autobiography: 1997, *The Memoirs of Alice Guy-Blaché*, ed. Anthony Slide.
The Cabbage Fairy/La Fée aux Choux 1896. La Vie du Christ 06. Fra Diavolo 12. In the Year 2000 12. Michael Strogoff 14. Tarnished Reputations 20, many others.

Guyler, Deryck (1914–).
Deep-voiced English character actor, usually in comic roles and frequently as a pompous minor official; he was often on radio and television. Born in Wallasey, Cheshire, he began on stage with the Liverpool Repertory Company and first gained fame with the radio comedy series *ITMA* in the 40s. He also played the washboard.
The Fast Lady 62. It's Trad, Dad 62. Nurse on Wheels 63. Smokescreen 64. Ferry Cross the Mersey 64. A Hard Day's Night 64. The Big Job 65. The Magnificent Six and a Half 67. Carry On Doctor 67. Please Sir! 71. No Sex Please – We're British 73. Barry MacKenzie Holds His Own 74. One of Our Dinosaurs Is Missing 75, etc.
TV series: The Charlie Chester Show 51, 55. Emney Enterprises 54–57. Here's Harry 60. *Sykes* 60–65, 71–79 (as Corky the neighbourhood policeman). Three Live Wires 61–62. Room at the Bottom 67. Please Sir! 68–72.

Guzman, Pato (1933–1991).
American production designer.
I Love You Alice B. Toklas 68. Bob and Carol and Ted and Alice 69. Alex in Wonderland 70. Blume in Love 73. An Unmarried Woman 78. The In-Laws 79. Hide in Plain Sight 80. Willie and Phil 80. Tempest 82. Moscow on the Hudson 84. Down and Out in Beverly Hills 86. Enemies, a Love Story 89. Scenes from a Mall 91, etc.

Gwenn, Edmund (1875–1959).
Stocky English stage actor who in middle age became a Hollywood film star and gave memorable comedy portrayals into his 80s. Born in London, he was on stage from 1895. His brother was the stage and film actor Arthur Chesney (1882–1949).
■ SILENT FILMS: The Real Thing at Last 16. Unmarried 20. The Skin Game 20.
■ SOUND FILMS: How He Lied to Her Husband 31. Money for Nothing 31. Condemned to Death 31. Frail Women 31. Hindle Wakes 31. Tell Me Tonight 32. The Admiral's Secret 32. Love on Wheels 32. *The Skin Game* 32. *The Good Companions* 33. I Was a Spy 33. Early to Bed 33. Cash 33. Smithy 33. *Friday the Thirteenth* 33. Marooned 33. Java Head 34. Spring in the Air 34. Channel Crossing 34. Passing Shadows 34. Waltzes from Vienna 34. Father and Son 34. Warn London 34. The Bishop Misbehaves 35. Sylvia Scarlett 35. The Walking Dead 36. Anthony Adverse 36. All American Chump 36. Mad Holiday 36. *Laburnum Grove* 36. Parnell 37. A Yank at Oxford 38. *South Riding* 38. Penny Paradise 38. An Englishman's Home 38. Cheer Boys Cheer 39. The Earl of Chicago 40. Madmen of Europe 40. The Doctor Takes a Wife 40. *Pride and Prejudice* 40. *Foreign Correspondent* (rare villainous role) 40. Scotland Yard 41. Cheers for Miss Bishop 41. The Devil and Miss Jones 41. *Charley's Aunt* 41. One Night in Lisbon 41. A Yank at Eton 42. The Meanest Man in the World 43. Forever and a Day 43. *Lassie Come Home* 43. *Between Two Worlds* (his original 'Outward Bound' stage role) 44. The Keys of the Kingdom 45. Bewitched 45. Dangerous Partners 45. She Went to the Races 45. Of Human Bondage 46. Undercurrent 46. *Miracle on 34th Street* (AA) 47. Thunder in the Valley 47. Life with Father 47. Green Dolphin Street 47. Apartment for Peggy 48. Hills of Home 48. Challenge to Lassie 49. A Woman of Distinction 50. Louisa 50. *Pretty Baby* 50. *Mister 880* (AAN) 50. For Heaven's Sake 50. Peking Express 51. Sally and St Anne 52. Bonzo Goes to College 52. Les Misérables 52. Something for the Birds 52. Mister Scoutmaster 52. The Bigamist 53. *Them* 54. The Student Prince 54. *The Trouble with Harry* 55. It's a Dog's Life 55. Calabuch 57.
✪ For having the talent for remaining a star into his 80s, and the discretion not always to insist on star billing. *Pride and Prejudice*.

Gwynn, Michael (1916–1976).
British stage actor in occasional films.
The Runaway Bus 54. The Secret Place 57. The Revenge of Frankenstein (as the monster) 58. Village of the Damned 60. The Virgin Soldiers 69, etc.

Gwynne, Anne (1918–) (Marguerite Gwynne Trice).
American leading lady of the 40s, former model.
Sandy Takes a Bow 39. Jailhouse Blues 41. The Strange Case of Doctor RX 42. Weird Woman 44. House of Frankenstein 45. Fear 46. The Ghost Goes Wild 46. Dick Tracy Meets Gruesome 48. Call of the Klondike 51. Breakdown 52. The Meteor Monster 57, etc.

Gwynne, Fred (1926–1993).
Lanky, lugubrious American comic actor who appeared in TV series: Car 54 Where Are You? 61–62 and The Munsters 64–65.
On the Waterfront 54. Munster Go Home 66. Captains Courageous (TV) 77. La Luna 78. Simon 80. The Cotton Club 84. Fatal Attraction 87. Ironweed 87. The Secret of My Success 87. Disorganized Crime 89. Pet Sematary 89. Shadows and Fog 91. My Cousin Vinny 92, etc.

Gyllenhaal, Stephen (1949–).
American director, from TV.
A Certain Fury 85. The Abduction of Kari Swenson (TV) 87. Paris Trout 91. Waterland 92. A Dangerous Woman 93. Losing Isaiah 95. Homegrown (co-w, d) 97, etc.

Gynt, Greta (1916–) (Greta Woxholt).
Norwegian leading lady, popular in British films of the 40s.
The Arsenal Stadium Mystery 39. Dark Eyes of London 39. The Common Touch 41. Tomorrow We Live 42. It's That Man Again 42. Mr Emmanuel 44. London Town 46. Dear Murderer 47. Take My Life 47. The Calendar 48. Mr Perrin and Mr Traill 48. Shadow of the Eagle 50. Soldiers Three (US) 51. Forbidden Cargo 54. Bluebeard's Ten Honeymoons 60. The Runaway 66, many others.

Gyöngyössy, Imre (1930–1994).
Hungarian director, screenwriter, playwright and poet. Imprisoned in the early 50s, he later studied at the Budapest Academy of Film and Television and collaborated on films with his wife, the writer Katalin Petényi, and Barna Kabay, who co-wrote and co-directed their later work. In the late 70s, they moved to work from Munich.
Palm Sunday (wd) 69. You Are Naked 72. Sons of Fire 73. A Quite Ordinary Life (doc) 77. The Revolt of Job (AAN) 82. Homeless 90. Freedom of the Death/Holtak Szabadsaga 93. Death in Shallow Water/Halal A Sekely Vizben 94, etc.

H

Haanstra, Bert (1916–1997).
Dutch documentarist. Born in Holton, he studied to be a teacher and was first employed as a press photographer. He worked for a time with director Jacques TATI on *Traffic*, but left because of differences over Tati's style of directing.
Mirror of Holland 50. The Rival World 55. Rembrandt Painter of Man 56. Glass (AA) 58. Fanfare (feature) 58. Zoo 62. The Human Dutch (AAN) 64. The Voice of the Water 66. Traffic (co-d) 71. Ape and Super-Ape (AAN) 72. Doctor Pulder Sows Poppies 75. Mr Slotter's Jubilee 79. The World of Simon Carmiggelt 83, etc.

Haarman, Fritz (1879–1925).
German serial killer who raped and murdered at least 24 boys, though the body count was probably higher, and sold their flesh on the black market as pork. His character informed Fritz Lang's portrait of a mass murderer, M 31, starring Peter Lorre; his life was the basis of *The Tenderness of Wolves*, produced in 1973 by Rainer Werner FASSBINDER, directed by Ulli LOMMEL and written by Kurt RAAB, who also starred, and *The Deathmaker* 95, directed by Romauld Karmakar and starring Götz George.

Haas, Charles (1918–).
American director.
Star in the Dust 56. Screaming Eagles 56. Showdown at Abilene 56. Summer Love 58. Wild Heritage 58. The Beat Generation 59. The Big Operator 59. Girls' Town 59. Platinum High School 60, etc.

Haas, Dolly (1910–1994).
German leading lady of the 30s, in a few international films.
Dolly's Way to Stardom 30. Liebes-commando 32. Der Page vom Dalmasse Hotel 34. *Broken Blossoms* (GB) 36. Spy of Napoleon (GB) 37. I Confess (US) 53, etc.

Haas, Hugo (1901–1968).
Czech character actor, in Hollywood from the late 30s; later took to writing and directing low-budget melodramas as vehicles for himself.
Skeleton on Horseback 39. Summer Storm 44. A Bell for Adano 45. Dakota 45. Holiday in Mexico 46. The Foxes of Harrow 47. My Girl Tisa 48. King Solomon's Mines 50. Vendetta 50. The Girl on the Bridge (& wd) 51. Pickup (& wd) 51. Strange Fascination (& wd) 52. Thy Neighbour's Wife (& wd) 53. Hold Back Tomorrow (& wd) 55. The Other Woman (& wd) 55. Edge of Hell (& wd) 56. *Lizzie* (& wd) 57. Born to be Loved (& wd) 59. Night of the Quarter Moon (& wd) 59. Paradise Alley (& wd) 61, etc.

Haas, Lukas (1976–).
American juvenile actor.
Testament 83. Witness 85. Solarbabies 86. Lady in White 88. The Wizard of Loneliness 88. Music Box 89. See You in the Morning 89.Rambling Rose 91. Alan & Naomi 92. Leap of Faith 92. Johns 96. Mars Attacks! 96. Everyone Says I Love You 96. David and Lisa (TV) 98. The Thin Red Line 98, etc.

Haas, Philip (1944–).
American director and screenwriter who began as a maker of documentaries about artists.
The Music of Chance 93. Angels and Insects 95, etc.

Haas, Robert (1887–1962).
American art director, a former architect. In films from the early 20s, working for Warner Brothers from 1929.
Dr Jekyll and Mr Hyde 20. Sentimental Tommy 21. Fury 22. White Sister 23. Romola 24. Hell Harbor 30. Bureau of Missing Persons 33. The Key 34. The Story of Louis Pasteur 36. The Prince and the Pauper 37. Jezebel 38. Angels with Dirty Faces 38. Dark Victory 39. The Maltese Falcon 41. Now, Voyager 42. Devotion 46. Life with Father (AAN) 47. Johnny Belinda (AAN) 48. The Damned Don't Cry 50. The Glass Menagerie 50, etc.

Hack, Shelley (1948–).
American actress, a former teenage model. In the 90s, she became a TV producer.
Annie Hall 77. If I Ever See You Again 78. King of Comedy 83. Single Bars, Single Women (TV) 85. Troll 85. The Stepfather 85. Blind Fear 89. A Casualty of War (TV) 90. The Finishing Touch 92, etc.
TV series: Charlie's Angels 79–80. Cutter to Houston 83. Jack and Mike 86–87.

Hackathorne, George (1895–1940).
American light actor of the later silents.
The Last of the Mohicans 20. The Little Minister 21. Merry Go Round 23. Magnificent Obsession 35. Gone with the Wind 39, many others.

Hackett, Albert (1900–1995).
American writer, usually with his wife Frances GOODRICH. He began as an actor in silent films, together with his brother, Raymond Hackett.

Hackett, Buddy (1924–) (Leonard Hacker).
Tubby American comedian with vaudeville experience.
Walking My Baby Back Home 53. God's Little Acre 58. *The Music Man* 62. *It's a Mad Mad Mad Mad World* 63. The Golden Head 65. The Love Bug 69. The Good Guys and the Bad Guys 69. Bud and Lou (TV) 78. Scrooged 88. The Little Mermaid (voice) 89. Paulie 98, etc.
TV series: Stanley 56.

Hackett, Joan (1934–1983).
American leading lady usually seen in unglamorous roles. Died of cancer.
■ *The Group* 66. Will Penny 67. Support Your Local Sheriff 69. Assignment to Kill 69. The Other Man (TV) 70. How Awful About Allan (TV) 70. The Young Country (TV) 71. Five Desperate Women (TV) 71. The Rivals 73. The Last of Sheila 73. Class of 63 (TV) 73. Reflections of Murder (TV) 74. The Terminal Man 74. Mackintosh and T.J. 75. Treasure of Matecumbe 76. Stonestreet (TV) 77. The Possessed (TV) 77. Pleasure Cove (TV) 79. Mr Mike's Mondo Video 79. The North Avenue Irregulars 79. One Trick Pony 80. The Long Days of Summer (TV) 80. Only When I Laugh (AAN) 81. The Long Summer of George Adams (TV) 82. The Escape Artist 82.
TV series: The Defenders 61–62. Another Day 78.

Hackett, Raymond (1902–1958).
American leading man who had brief popularity during the changeover from silent to sound. Married actress Blanche Sweet.
The Loves of Sunya 28. Madame X 29. Our Blushing Brides 29. The Trial of Mary Dugan 30. The Sea Wolf 30. The Cat Creeps 31. Seed 31, etc.

Hackett, Walter (1876–1944).
American-born theatre manager and playwright, mainly of farces and light comedies, in England. Born in California, he came to London on his honeymoon in 1914 and stayed. Married actress Marion LORNE, who featured in many of his plays.
77 Park Lane 31. The Barton Mystery 32. Life Goes On 32. Freedom of the Seas 34. Road House 34. Their Big Moment 34. Hyde Park Corner 35. The Gay Adventure 36. Thunder in the City 37, etc.

Hackford, Taylor (1945–).
American director and producer who runs his own production company, New Visions Entertainment.
The Idolmaker 80. An Officer and a Gentleman 82. Against All Odds 83. White Nights 85. Hail! Hail! Rock 'n' Roll 87. La Bamba (p) 87. Everybody's All-American 88. Rooftops (p) 89. The Long Walk Home (p) 90. Mortal Thoughts (p) 91. Queen's Logic (p) 91. Sweet Talker (p) 91. Blood In, Blood Out (pd) 93. Dolores Claiborne 95. The Devil's Advocate 97, etc.

Hackman, Gene (1931–).
Virile American character actor who unexpectedly became a star from the early 70s.
Biography: 1997, *Gene Hackman* by Michael Munn.
Mad Dog Coll 61. Lilith 64. Hawaii 66. First to Fight 67. A Covenant with Death 67. Banning 67. *Bonnie and Clyde* (AAN) 67. The Split 68. Shadow on the Land (TV) 68. Riot 69. Downhill Racer 69. *I Never Sang for My Father* (AAN) 69. The Gypsy Moths 69. Marooned 70. Doctors' Wives 71. The Hunting Party 71. *The French Connection* (AA) 71. Cisco Pike 72. Prime Cut 72. The Poseidon Adventure 72. The Conversation 73. Scarecrow 73. Zandy's Bride 74. Young Frankenstein 74. Bite the Bullet 75. French Connection II 75. Lucky Lady 75. Night Moves 76. The Domino Principle 77. A Bridge Too Far 77. March or Die 77. Superman 78. Superman II 80. All Night Long 81. Reds 81. Eureka 83. Two of a Kind 83. Uncommon Valor 83. Under Fire 83. Misunderstood 84. Target 85. Twice in a Lifetime 85. Hoosiers 86. No Way Out 87. Superman IV 87. Another Woman 88. BAT 21 88. Full Moon in Blue Water 88. Split Decisions 88. Mississippi Burning (AAN) 88. The Package 89. Narrow Margin 90. Postcards from the Edge 90. Loose Cannons 90. Company Business 91. Class Action 91. Unforgiven (AA) 92. Geronimo: An American Legend 93. The Firm 93. Wyatt Earp 94. Crimson Tide 95. The Quick and the Dead 95. Get Shorty 95. The Bird Cage 96. Extreme Measures 96. The Chamber 96. Absolute Power 97. Twilight 98. Antz (voice) 98. Enemy of the State 98, etc.
❝ People in the street still call me Popeye, and *The French Connection* was 15 years ago. I wish I could have another hit and a new nickname. – G.H.
Each scene, I look for something not written down. – G.H.
The last honest man in America. – *Film Comment*

Hackney, Alan (1924–).
British comedy writer.
Private's Progress 55. I'm All Right, Jack 59. Two-way Stretch (co-w) 60. Swordsman of Siena 62. You Must Be Joking 65. Decline and Fall 68, etc.

Haddon, Peter (1898–1962) (Peter Tildsley).
British light actor, usually in silly-ass roles. Born in Rawtenstall, Lancashire, the son of a vicar, he studied medicine at Cambridge University, where he became a member of Footlights, and was on stage from 1920.
Death at Broadcasting House 34. The Silent Passenger (as Lord Peter Wimsey) 35. Kate Plus Ten 38. Helter Skelter 49. The Second Mrs Tanqueray 54, etc.

Haden, Sara (1897–1981).
American actress of quiet, well-spoken parts, best remembered as the spinster aunt of the Hardy family.
Spitfire (debut) 34. Magnificent Obsession 35. First Lady 38. H. M. Pulham Esquire 41. Lost Angel 43. Mr Ace 45. Our Vines Have Tender Grapes 45. She-Wolf of London (as villainess) 46. The Bishop's Wife 48. A Life of her Own 50. A Lion is in the Streets 53. Andy Hardy Comes Home 58, many others.

Hadjidakis, Manos (1925–1994).
Greek composer.
Stella 55. A Matter of Dignity 57. *Never on Sunday* (AA) 59. America America 63. Blue 68. The Martlet's Tale 70. The Pedestrian 74. Sweet Movie 75. Honeymoon 79, etc.

Hadley, Reed (1911–1974) (Reed Herring).
American 'second lead'.
Fugitive Lady 38. The Bank Dick 41. Guadalcanal Diary 43. Leave Her to Heaven 46. The Iron Curtain 48. Captain from Castile 49. Dallas 51. Big House USA 55. The St Valentine's Day Massacre 68, etc.
TV series: Racket Squad 51–53. Public Defender 53–54.

Hageman, Richard (1882–1966).
Dutch-American composer.
If I Were King (AAN) 38. Stagecoach (co-m, AA) 39. The Howards of Virginia (AAN) 40. The Long Voyage Home (AAN) 40. This Woman Is Mine (AAN) 41. The Shanghai Gesture (AAN) 42. Fort Apache 48. Three Godfathers 48. She Wore a Yellow Ribbon 49. Wagon Master 50, etc.

Hagen, Jean (1924–1977) (Jean Verhagen).
American comedy character actress, usually of Brooklynesque dames; also minor leading lady. Forced to retire in the mid-60s because of illness.
■ Side Street 49. *Adam's Rib* 49. Ambush 50. The Asphalt Jungle 50. A Life of Her Own 50. Night into Morning 50. No Questions Asked 51. *Singin' in the Rain* (a splendid performance as the silent star with the ghastly voice) (AAN) 52. Shadow in the Sky 52. Carbine Williams 52. Latin Lovers 53. Arena 53. Half a Hero 53. The Big Knife 55. Spring Reunion 57. The Shaggy Dog 59. Sunrise at Campobello 60. Panic in Year Zero 62. Dead Ringer 64.
TV series: The Danny Thomas Show 53–56.
Famous line (*Singin' in the Rain*): 'If we bring a little joy into your humdrum lives, we feel all our hard work ain't been in vain for nothin'.'

Hagen, Julius (1884–1939).
British producer, a former actor, who founded Twickenhan Film Studios and Real Art Productions in 1929, in partnership with director Leslie Hiscott, to turn out 'quota quickies' to meet the legal requirement of the time for exhibitors to show British films. Directors and writers spent a fortnight writing a script and a fortnight shooting it. He persuaded many leading British actors and some Hollywood ones to appear in his films, including Sydney Howard, Leslie Fuller, Henry Kendall, Sir John Martin Harvey, Ivor Novello, Gracie Fields, Sir Seymour Hicks, Flanagan and Allen, Edward Everett Horton and Conrad Veidt. He hired D.W. Griffith to remake *Broken Blossoms* in sound, but Griffith walked out after a disagreement. He ran into trouble trying to make more expensive films and became bankrupt in 1938.
To What Red Hell 29. At the Villa Rose 30. Chin, Chin, Chinaman 31. Alibi 31. Bill's Legacy 31. The Lyons Mail 31. Condemned to Death 32.

The Crooked Lady 32. The Lodger 32. Excess Baggage 33. This Week of Grace 33. The Wandering Jew 33. I Lived with You 33. The Black Abbot 34. Blind Justice 34. The Admiral's Secret 34. Bella Donna 34. Department Store 35. The Ace of Spades 35. A Fire Has Been Arranged 35. Scrooge 35. She Shall Have Music 35. The Triumph of Sherlock Holmes 35. The Last Journey 35. The Private Secretary 35. Broken Blossoms 36. Eliza Comes to Stay 36. Spy of Napoleon 36. Juggernaut 36. Beauty and the Barge 37. Silver Blaze 37. Clothes and the Woman 37. Underneath the Arches 37, etc.

Hagerty, Julie (1955–).
American actress, a former model, usually in comic roles.
Airplane 80. Airplane II 82. A Midsummer Night's Sex Comedy 82. Bad Medicine 85. Goodbye New York 85. Lost in America 85. Aria 87. Beyond Therapy 87. Bloodhounds of Broadway 89. Rude Awakening 89. Reversal of Fortune 90. What About Bob? 91. Noises Off 92. The Wife 95. U-Turn 97. Boys Will Be Boys 97, etc.
TV series: Princesses 91. Reunited 98– .

Haggar, William (1851–1924).
British pioneer producer, a former fairground showman who made short sensational films featuring himself and his family.
The Maniac's Guillotine 02. The Wild Man of Borneo 02. Mirthful Mary 03. A Dash for Liberty 03. The Sign of the Cross 04. The Life of Charles Peace 05. Desperate Footpads 07. Maria Marten 08. The Dumb Man of Manchester 08, etc.

Haggard, Sir H. Rider (1856–1925).
British adventure novelist, whose most famous novel, *She*, has been filmed at least nine times. There have also been two versions of *King Solomon's Mines*, and two lightly disguised variants, *Watusi* and *King Solomon's Treasure*.

Haggard, Piers (1939–).
British director.
Wedding Night 69. Satan's Skin 70. Pennies from Heaven (TV) 78. The Fiendish Plot of Dr Fu Manchu 80. Venom 82. A Summer Story (TV) 88. I'll Take Romance (TV) 90. The Lifeforce Experiment (TV) 94. Conquest 98, etc.

Haggerty, Dan (1941–).
Hefty American leading man, notably on TV in *The Legend of Grizzly Adams*.
The Tender Warrior 70. Hex 73. When the North Wind Blows 74. Starbird and Sweet William 75. Frontier Freemont 76. Desperate Women (TV) 79. Condominium (TV) 80. Grizzly Adams: The Mark of the Bear 91. Ice Pawn 92. Cheyenne Warrior 94. Abducted 2: The Reunion 94. Grizzly Mountain 97, etc.

Hagman, Larry (1931–).
American comedy leading man, much on TV; son of Mary Martin.
Ensign Pulver 64. Fail Safe 64. In Harm's Way 65. The Group 65. Vanished (TV) 70. Up in the Cellar 70. Beware the Blob (TV) 71. A Howling in the Woods (TV) 72. The Alpha Caper (TV) 73. Stardust 74. Harry and Tonto 74. Mother Jugs and Speed 76. The Eagle Has Landed 76. Crash 77. The President's Mistress (TV) 78. Superman 78. SOB 81. Nixon 95. Primary Colors 98, etc.
TV series: *I Dream of Jeannie* 65–70. The Good Life 71. Here We Go Again 71. *Dallas* 78–88.
❝ People I meet really want me to be J.R., so it's hard to disappoint them. – *L.H.*
I was born with success. Lucky for me, I am able to handle it. Also, I damn well deserve it! – *L.H.*

Hagmann, Stuart (1939–).
American director who turned to making TV commercials after the failure of his second feature.
The Strawberry Statement 70. Believe in Me 71. Tarantulas: The Deadly Cargo 77, etc.

Hahn, Don.
American producer of animated features, a former Walt Disney animator, who has worked at the studio since 1976. He was an assistant director on *The Fox and the Hound* and *Mickey's Christmas Carol*. He is the author of *Disney's Animation Magic: A Behind the Scenes Look at How an Animated Film Is Made*, 1996.
Beauty and the Beast 91. The Lion King 94. The Hunchback of Notre Dame 96, etc.

Haid, Charles (1943–).
American actor, producer and director.
AS ACTOR: The Choirboys 77. Oliver's Story 78. Who'll Stop the Rain/Dog Soldiers 78. Altered States 80. Twirl (TV) 81. Cop 88. Fire and Rain (TV) 89. Night Breed 90. Storyville 92. The Fire Next Time (TV) 93. Cooperstown (TV) 93. Broken Trust (TV) 95, etc.
AS DIRECTOR: Iron Will 94. Riders of the Purple Sage (TV) 96. Buffalo Soldiers 97, etc.
TV series (as actor): Kate McShane 75. Delvecchio 76–77. Hill Street Blues 81–87.

Haigh, Kenneth (1929–).
British stage actor, the original lead of *Look Back in Anger*, has tended to remain in angry young man roles.
My Teenage Daughter 56. High Flight 56. Saint Joan 57. Cleopatra 63. A Hard Day's Night 64. The Deadly Affair 66. A Lovely Way to Die (US) 68. Eagle in a Cage 71. Man at the Top 73. The Bitch 79. Wild Geese II 85. A State of Emergency 86. Shuttlecock 91, etc.
TV series: *Man at the Top* 71–73.

Hailey, Arthur (1920–).
English novelist who rigorously researches specific milieux and weaves a plot through them. Films of his work include *Hotel*, *Airport*, *The Moneychangers*, *Wheels*, *Flight into Danger* (which became *Zero Hour* and was parodied as *Airplane*).

Haim, Corey (1972–).
Canadian-born juvenile lead, in commercials from the age of 11.
Firstborn 84. Murphy's Romance 85. Secret Admirer 85. Silver Bullet 85. Lucas 86. The Lost Boys 87. License to Drive 88. Watchers 88. Dream a Little Dream 89. Dream Machine 90. Fast Getaway 91. Prayer of the Rollerboys 91. Oh, What a Night 92. Double O Kid 92. Fast Getaway II 94. National Lampoon's Last Resort 94. Demolition High 96, etc.

Haines, Randa (1945–).
American director, from television.
Under This Sky (TV) 79. Something about Amelia (TV) 84. Children of a Lesser God 86. The Doctor 91. Wrestling Ernest Hemingway 93. Dance with Me 98, etc.

Haines, William (1900–1973).
American leading man of the silents.
Three Wise Fools 23. Tower of Lies 24. Brown of Harvard 25. Tell It to the Marines 27. Alias Jimmy Valentine 28. Navy Blues 30. The Adventures of Get-Rich-Quick Wallingford 31. The Fast Life 33. The Marines Are Coming 35, etc.

Hajos, Karl (1889–1950).
Hungarian-born composer, in America from the 20s.
Morocco 30. Werewolf of London 35. Hitler's Hangman 43. Summer Storm (AAN) 44. Dangerous Intruder 45. Stars over Texas 46. Appointment with Murder 48. The Lovable Cheat 49. It's a Small World 50, etc.

Hakim, André (1915–).
Egyptian-born producer, long in US.
Mr Belvedere Rings the Bell 52. The Man Who Never Was 56. Sea Wife 56. Patate 64. Hello-Goodbye 70, etc.,

Hakim, Robert (1907–) and **Raymond** (1909–1980).
Egyptian-born brothers who were in and out of film production from 1927.
Pépé Le Moko 36. La Bête Humaine 38. Le Jour Se Lève 39. The Southerner 44. Her Husband's Affairs 47. The Long Night 47. The Blue Veil 52. Belle de Jour 67. Isadora 68, many others.

Halas, John (1912–1995).
Hungarian-born animator, long in Britain producing in association with his wife Joy Batchelor (1914–1991) a stream of efficient short cartoons, many sponsored by official organizations.
FEATURES: *Animal Farm* 54. Ruddigore 67.

Hale, Alan (1892–1950) (Rufus Alan McKahan).
Jovial American actor, a hero of silent action films from 1911 and a familiar cheerful figure in scores of talkies.
The Cowboy and the Lady (debut) 11. The Four Horsemen of the Apocalypse 21. Robin Hood (as Little John) 22. The Covered Wagon 23. Main Street 24. She Got What She Wanted 27. The Rise of Helga 30. So Big 32. It Happened One Night 34. The Last Days of Pompeii 35. Jump for Glory (GB) 36. Stella Dallas 37. *The Adventures of Robin Hood* (as Little John) 38. Dodge City 39. The Man in the Iron Mask 40. The Sea Hawk 40. Tugboat Annie Sails Again 41. *Strawberry Blonde* 41. Manpower 41. *Desperate Journey* 42. Action in the North Atlantic 43. Destination Tokyo 44. Hotel Berlin 45. Escape in the Desert 45. Night and Day 45. My Wild Irish Rose 47. Pursued 48. The New Adventures of Don Juan 48. My *Girl Tisa* 49. Rogues of Sherwood Forest (as Little John) 50, many others.
✪ For innumerable stalwart performances, including three as Little John. *The Adventures of Robin Hood*.

Hale, Alan, Jnr (1918–1990).
American character actor who bid fair to be his father's double.
To the Shores of Tripoli 42. One Sunday Afternoon 48. The Gunfighter 50. The Big Trees 52. Rogue Cop 54. Young at Heart 54. The Indian Fighter 55. The Killer is Loose 56, many others.
TV series: Biff Baker 52–53. *Casey Jones* 58. *Gilligan's Island* 64–67. The Good Guys 69.

Hale, Barbara (1922–).
Pleasant American leading lady of the 40s.
Higher and Higher 43. The Falcon in Hollywood 44. First Yank into Tokyo 45. Lady Luck 46. The Boy with Green Hair 48. The Window 48. *Jolson Sings Again* 49. The Jackpot 50. Lorna Doone 51. A Lion is in the Streets 53. Unchained 54. The Far Horizons 55. The Oklahoman 57. Airport 69. The Defence Never Rests (TV) 90, many others.
TV series: *Perry Mason* (as Della Street) 57–65.

Hale, Binnie (1899–1984) (Beatrice Mary Hale-Monro).
British actress and singer, the sister of Sonnie Hale, in occasional films. Born in Liverpool, she was on stage from 1916, appearing in revues, musicals and pantomimes.
This is the Life 34. The Phantom Light 35. Hyde Park Corner 36. Love from a Stranger 37. Take a Chance 37.
❝ The greatest woman caricaturist of the British stage. – *Charles B. Cochran*

Hale, Creighton (1882–1965) (Patrick Fitzgerald).
American leading man of the 20s, sometimes in meek-and-mild comedy roles.
The Exploits of Elaine 15. The Thirteenth Chair 19. Way Down East 20. Trilby (as Little Billee) 23. *The Marriage Circle* 24. The Circle 25. Beverly of Graustark 26. Annie Laurie 27. *The Cat and the Canary* 27. Rose Marie 28. Holiday 30. The Masquerader 33. Hollywood Boulevard 36. The Return of Dr X 39. The Gorilla Man 42. Bullet Scars 45. The Perils of Pauline 47, many others.

Hale, Georgia (1903–1985).
American leading lady of the 20s.
The Gold Rush 24. The Salvation Hunters 25. The Great Gatsby 26. The Last Moment 48, etc.

Hale, Georgina (1943–).
Generally strident British actress.
Eagle in a Cage 70. The Devils 71. Mahler 74. Sweeney 2 78. The World Is Full of Married Men 78. McVicar 80. The Watcher in the Woods 80. Castaway 86. Beyond Bedlam 94. Ken Russell's Treasure Island (TV) 95, etc.

Hale, Jonathan (1891–1966) (J. Hatley).
Canadian character actor, former consular attaché, in films from 1934, usually as mildly exasperated businessman or hero's boss. Committed suicide.
Lightning Strikes Twice 34. Alice Adams 35. Fury 36. The 'Blondie' series (as Mr Dithers) 38–50. Her Jungle Love 39. Johnny Apollo 40. Call Northside 777 48. The Steel Trap 52. The Night Holds Terror 56. Jaguar 58, many others.

Hale, Louise Closser (1872–1933).
American character actress with long stage experience.
The Hole in the Wall 29. Dangerous Nan McGrew 30. Platinum Blonde 31. Shanghai Express 32. Rasputin and the Empress 33. Today We Live 33. Dinner at Eight 33, etc.

Hale, Monte (1919–).
American western star of the 40s. Mostly with Republic.
Home on the Range 47. South of Rio 48. Rainbow Valley 49. The Missourians 50. Giant 56. The Chase 66. The Drifter 73. Guns of a Stranger 73, many others.

Hale, Richard (1893–1981).
American supporting actor.
The Other Love 47. All the King's Men 50. Scaramouche 52. Julius Caesar 53. Moonfleet 55. Pillars of the Sky 56. Ben Hur 59. Sergeants Three 62, etc.

Hale, Sonnie (1902–1959) (John Robert Hale-Monro).
English leading light comedian, director and writer, the brother of Binnie Hale. Born in London, he was on stage from 1921, becoming a star in revues and musicals. In the mid-30s, he quit the stage for five years to act in, and direct, films for Gaumont British. He starred in several with Jessie Matthews, the second of his three wives, and directed her in her least successful, *Head over Heels*, and two others only marginally better, *Gangway* and *Sailing Along*. His film career faltered in 1938 when *Asking for Trouble*, a large-scale musical he had co-written for Matthews, was abandoned and Gaumont British did not renew his contract; instead Carol Reed was hired to make a non-musical version of the story, retitled *Climbing High*. His first wife was actress Evelyn Laye.
■ On with the Dance 27. The Parting of the Ways 27. Tell me Tonight 32. Happy Ever After 32. Friday the Thirteenth 33. Early to Bed 33. Evergreen 34. Wild Boy 34. My Song for You 34. My Heart is Calling 34. Are You a Mason? 34. Marry the Girl 35. First a Girl 35. It's Love Again 36. Head over Heels (d only) 37. Gangway (d only) 37. Sailing Along (wd only) 38. The Gaunt Stranger 38. Climbing High (co-w only) 38. Let's Be Famous 39. Fiddlers Three 44. London Town 46. A French Mistress (oa) 60.
❝ That excellent comedian. – *James Agate*
A gross, unfunny person offstage and someone, on the whole, to avoid. – *Robert Stephens*

Hale, William (1937–).
American director, from TV.
Gunfight in Abilene 66. Journey to Shiloh 67. Stalk the Wild Child (TV) 76. One Shoe Makes It Murder (TV) 82. Lace (TV) 84. Lace 2 (TV) 85. Liberace (TV) 88. Deadly Revenge 90. People Like Us 90, etc.

Haley, Bill (1926–1981).
American rock-and-roll musician and bandleader; Bill Haley and his Comets provided the title music for *The Blackboard Jungle* and starred in *Rock around the Clock*, which caused cinema riots in 1956. Also, *Don't Knock the Rock* 56.

Haley, Jack (1899–1979).
Diffident American light comedian, popular in the 30s and 40s.
Broadway Madness 27. Follow Thru 30. Sitting Pretty 33. The Girl Friend 35. *Poor Little Rich Girl* 36. Wake Up and Live 37. Pick a Star 37. Rebecca of Sunnybrook Farm 38. *Alexander's Ragtime Band* 38. Hold that Co-Ed 38. *The Wizard of Oz* (as the Tin Man) 39. Moon over Miami 41. Beyond the Blue Horizon 42. F Man 42. Higher and Higher 43. Scared Stiff 44. George White's Scandals 45. People are Funny 45. Vacation in Reno 47. Norwood 69, etc.

Haley, Jack, Jnr (1934–).
American executive, best known for marrying Liza Minnelli and assembling *That's Entertainment* and *That's Dancing* 85. Directed *Norwood* 69 and *The Love Machine* 71.

Haley, Jackie Earle (1961–).
American juvenile of the 70s.
The Day of the Locust 74. Damnation Alley 75. The Bad News Bears 76. The Bad News Bears in Breaking Training 77. Breaking Away 79. The Zoo

Gang 85. Maniac Cop 3: Badge of Silence 92, etc.
TV series: Wait Till Your Father Gets Home (voice) 72–74.

Hall, Alexander (1894–1968).
American director from 1932, previously on Broadway.
■ Sinners in the Sun 32. Madame Racketeer 32. The Girl in 419 33. Midnight Club 33. Torch Singer 33. Miss Fane's Baby is Stolen 34. Little Miss Marker 34. The Pursuit of Happiness 34. Limehouse Blues 34. Going to Town 35. Annapolis Farewell 35. Give Us This Night 36. Yours for the Asking 36. Exclusive 37. There's Always a Woman 38. I am the Law 38. There's That Woman Again 38. The Lady's From Kentucky 39. Good Girls Go to Paris 39. The Amazing Mr Williams 39. The Doctor Takes a Wife 40. He Stayed for Breakfast 40. This Thing Called Love 40. *Here Comes Mr Jordan* (AAN) 41. Bedtime Story 41. They All Kissed the Bride 42. My Sister Eileen 42. The Heavenly Body 43. Once Upon a Time 44. She Wouldn't Say Yes 45. Down to Earth 47. The Great Lover 49. Love that Brute 50. Louisa 50. Up Front 51. Because You're Mine 52. Let's Do it Again 53. Forever Darling 56.

Hall, Anthony Michael (1968–).
American young leading actor, a former child actor on stage and TV.
Sixteen Candles 84. The Breakfast Club 85. Weird Science 85. Out of Bounds 86. Johnny Be Good 88. Edward Scissorhands 90. Into the Sun 92. Six Degrees of Separation 93. The Grave 96. Exit in Red 96. Hijacked: Flight 285 (TV) 96. Trojan War 97, etc.

Hall, Charles (1899–1959).
Rotund English-born music-hall comic and character actor, a member of Fred Karno's troupe. In America from the early 20s, he appeared in more than 40 movies as an irascible foil to Laurel and Hardy.
Leave 'Em and Weep 27. College 27. Pardon Us 31. Sons of the Desert 34. Them Thar Hills 34. Tit for Tat 35. Swing Time 36. A Chump at Oxford 40. Saps at Sea 40. The Lodger 44. The Canterville Ghost 44. Hangover Square 45. Forever Amber 47. The Big Clock 48. The Vicious Years 51, many others.

Hall, Charles D. (1899–1968).
British-born production designer, long in Hollywood; a key craftsman of his time. Born in Norwich, he worked in an architect's office before designing stage sets for Fred KARNO. He emigrated to Canada, and then made his way to the United States and the film industry, working first as a scenic painter and finally becoming chief art director for Universal. In the late 30s he moved to the Hal ROACH studios, becoming a freelance from the mid-40s.
The Gold Rush 24. *The Phantom of the Opera* 25. The Cohens and the Kellys 26. *The Cat and the Canary* 27. The Man Who Laughs 28. The Circus 28. The Last Warning 29. *Broadway* 29. *All Quiet on the Western Front* 30. *Dracula* 30. *Frankenstein* 31. City Lights 32. *The Old Dark House* 32. *The Invisible Man* 33. By Candlelight 33. *The Bride of Frankenstein* 35. The Good Fairy 35. Showboat 36. *Modern Times* 36. My Man Godfrey 36. Captain Fury 39. Big House USA 55, etc.
✪ For bringing to Hollywood Gothic a mixture of English and German artistic sensibilities.

Hall, Conrad L. (1926–).
American cinematographer.
Morituri (AAN) 65. Harper 66. The Professionals (AAN) 66. *Cool Hand Luke* 67. In Cold Blood (AAN) 67. Hell in the Pacific 69. *Butch Cassidy and the Sundance Kid* (AA) 69. Tell Them Willie Boy is Here 69. The Happy Ending 70. Fat City 72. The Day of the Locust (AAN) 75. Smile 75. Marathon Man 76. Black Widow 87. Tequila Sunrise (AAN) 88. Class Action 91. Jennifer 8 92. Searching for Bobby Fischer/Innocent Moves (AAN) 93. Love Affair 94. Without Limits 97. A Civil Action 98, etc.

Hall-Davis, Lillian:
see DAVIS, Lilian Hall.

Hall, Grayson (1927–1985).
American stage actress remembered for one film performance, in *Night of the Iguana* (AAN) 64.

Hall, Henry (1898–1989).
British bandleader of the 30s, popular on radio. Appeared in a few films including *Music Hath Charms* 36.
Autobiography: 1955, *Here's to the Next Time*.

Hall, Huntz (1920–1999) (Henry Hall).
Long-faced American character actor, the 'dumbbell' second lead of the original Dead End Kids and later of the Bowery Boys.
Dead End 37. Crime School 38. Angels with Dirty Faces 38. The Return of Doctor X 39. Give Us Wings 40. Spooks Run Wild 41. Private Buckaroo 42. Wonder Man 45. Bowery Bombshell 46. Bowery Buckaroos 47. Jinx Money 48. Angels in Disguise 49. Lucky Losers 50. Ghost Chasers 51. No Holds Barred 52. Loose in London 53. Paris Playboys 54. High Society 55. Dig That Uranium 56. Spook Chasers 57. In the Money 58. The Gentle Giant 67. The Love Bug Rides Again 73. The Escape Artist 82. Auntie Lee's Meat Pies 92, many others.
TV series: Chicago Teddy Bears 71.

Hall, James (1900–1940) (James Brown).
American leading man of the early talkie period.
The Campus Flirt 26. Stranded in Paris 27. Rolled Stockings 27. Four Sons 28. Smiling Irish Eyes 29. The Canary Murder Case 29. The Saturday Night Kid 29. Dangerous Nan McGrew 30. *Hell's Angels* 30. Millie 31. The Good Bad Girl 31. Divorce Among Friends 31. Manhattan Tower 33, etc.

Hall, Jon (1913–1979) (Charles Locher).
Athletic American leading man who became a star in his first year as an actor but whose roles gradually diminished in stature; he retired to a photography business. Committed suicide.
Charlie Chan in Shanghai 36. Mind Your Own Business 36. The Girl from Scotland Yard 37. *The Hurricane* 37. Kit Carson 40. South of Pago Pago 40. Aloma of the South Seas 41. Eagle Squadron 42. Invisible Agent 42. Arabian Nights 42. White Savage 43. Ali Baba and the Forty Thieves 44. Cobra Woman 44. The Invisible Man's Revenge 44. San Diego I Love You 45. Sudan 45. The Michigan Kid 47. Last of the Redmen 47. Prince of Thieves 48. Deputy Marshal 49. Hurricane Island 50. When the Redskins Rode 51. Last Train from Bombay 52. The Beachgirls and the Monster (& d) 65. Five the Hard Way (co-p & ph only) 69, etc.
TV series: Ramar of the Jungle 52–53.

Hall, Juanita (1901–1968).
American character actress and singer, best remembered in the stage and screen versions of *South Pacific* (as Bloody Mary) and *Flower Drum Song*.

Hall, Ken G. (1901–1994).
Australian producer, director and screenwriter, head of Cinesound Productions, which was the busiest company of the 30s and 40s, turning out low-budget movies reflecting Australian life, four of them based on the exploits of the Rudd family. The company was later part-owned by J. Arthur Rank and thereafter concentrated on distribution and exhibition. Hall began as a journalist and a film publicist and went on to run Australia's first television station in 1956.
Autobiographies: 1977, *Directed by Ken G. Hall*. 1980, *Australian Film: The Inside Story*.
On Our Selection (co-w, d) 32. The Squatter's Daughter (p, d) 33. The Silence of Dean Maitland (p, d) 34. Grandad Rudd (p, d) 35. It Isn't Done (p, d) 37. Lovers and Luggers (p, d) 37. Tall Timbers (p, d) 37. Let George Do It/In the Nick of Time (p, d) 38. Dad and Dave Come to Town/The Rudd Family Goes to Town (p, story) 38. Gone to the Dogs (p, d) 39. Dad Rudd MP (p, d) 40. Kokoda Front Line (p) (AA doc) 42. Smithy/Southern Cross/Pacific Adventure (co-w, d) 46, etc.

Hall, Kevin Peter (1955–1991).
American actor and stand-up comedian, 7 feet 2 inches tall, who was best known for playing the role of a Bigfoot in the film *Harry and the Hendersons* 87, and in the first season of the subsequent TV series 90–91.
Predator (as the alien) 87. Highway to Hell 92.
TV series: Misfits of Science 85–86.

Hall, Sir Peter (1930–).
British theatrical producer who ventured into films. His first wife was actress Leslie Caron (1956–65). In 1996, he became artistic director at London's Old Vic Theatre, staging productions of classic plays.
Autobiographies: 1983, *Peter Hall's Diaries*. 1993, *Making an Exhibition of Myself*.
Biography: 1995, *Power Play – The Life and Times of Peter Hall* by Stephen Fay.
■ Work Is a Four-Letter Word 68. A Midsummer Night's Dream 68. Three Into Two Won't Go 69. Perfect Friday 70. The Homecoming 73. Akenfield 74. Never Talk to Strangers 95.

Hall, Porter (1888–1953).
Wry-faced American character actor with stage experience before settling in Hollywood.
■ *The Thin Man* 34. Murder in the Private Car 34. The Case of the Lucky Legs 35. The Story of Louis Pasteur 35. The Petrified Forest 36. Too Many Parents 36. The Princess Comes Across 36. And Sudden Death 36. *The General Died at Dawn* 36. Satan Met a Lady 36. The Plainsman 36. Snowed Under 36. Let's Make a Million 37. Bulldog Drummond Escapes 37. Souls at Sea 37. Make Way for Tomorrow 37. King of Gamblers 37. Hotel Haywire 37. This Way Please 37. True Confession 37. Wild Money 37. Wells Fargo 37. Scandal Street 38. Stolen Heaven 38. Dangerous to Know 38. Bulldog Drummond's Peril 38. Prison Farm 38. King of Alcatraz 38. The Arkansas Traveller 38. Men with Wings 38. Tom Sawyer Detective 38. Mr Smith Goes to Washington 39. Grand Jury Secrets 39. They Shall Have Music 39. His Girl Friday 40. Dark Command 40. Arizona 40. Trail of the Vigilantes 40. Sullivan's Travels 41. The Parson of Panamint 41. Mr and Mrs North 41. The Remarkable Andrew 42. Butch Minds the Baby 42. A Stranger in Town 43. The Desperadoes 43. Woman of the Town 43. Standing Room Only 44. The Miracle of Morgan's Creek 44. Going My Way 44. Double Indemnity 44. The Great Moment 44. Mark of the Whistler 44. Blood on the Sun 45. Bring on the Girls 45. Kiss and Tell 45. *Murder He Says* 45. Weekend at the Waldorf 45. Unconquered 47. Miracle on 34th Street 47. Singapore 47. You Gotta Stay Happy 48. That Wonderful Urge 48. The Beautiful Blonde from Bashful Bend 49. *Intruder in the Dust* 49. Chicken Every Sunday 49. *Ace in the Hole* 51. The Half Breed 52. Carbine Williams 52. Holiday for Sinners 52. Pony Express 53. Vice Squad 53. Return to Treasure Island 54.

Hall, Thurston (1883–1958).
American character actor adept at choleric executives. Long stage experience; ran his own touring companies.
Cleopatra (as Mark Antony) 18. Theodora Goes Wild 36. Professor Beware 38. The Great McGinty 40. He Hired the Boss 43. Brewster's Millions 45. The Secret Life of Walter Mitty 47. Affair in Reno 56, many others.
TV series: Topper 53–54.

Hall, Willis (1929–).
British playwright and screenwriter (in collaboration with Keith Waterhouse).
The Long and the Short and the Tall 61. Whistle Down the Wind 61. A Kind of Loving 62. Billy Liar 63. Lock Up Your Daughters! 69, etc.

Hallahan, Charles (1943–1997).
American character actor of stage and screen, best known for his role as Captain Charlie Devane in the TV police series *Hunter*. Born in Philadelphia, he graduated from Rutgers University and began his acting career in the mid-70s. Died of a heart attack.
Twilight Zone: The Movie 76. American Hot Wax 77. Going in Style 79. Nightwing 79. Hide in Plain Sight 80. Skag 80. Margin for Murder (TV) 81. The Thing 82. Silkwood 83. Pale Rider 85. Vision Quest 85. A Winner Never Quits (TV) 86. True Believer 89. Nails 92. Body of Evidence 92. Warlock: Armageddon 93. Wild Palms 93. Dave 93. The Pest 96. The Rich Man's Wife 96. Executive Decision 96. The Fan 96. Dante's Peak 97, etc.
TV series: The Paper Chase 78–79. Hunter 86–91.

Hallatt, May (1882–1969).
British character actress, mainly on stage.
No Funny Business 33. The Lambeth Walk 39. Painted Boats 45. *Black Narcissus* 46. The Pickwick Papers 52. *Separate Tables* 58. Make Mine Mink 60, etc.

Haller, Daniel (1928–).
American director, former art director on Roger Corman's Poe films, etc.
Die Monster Die 67. The Devil's Angels 68. The Wild Racers 68. Paddy 70. The Dunwich Horror 70. Pieces of Dreams 70. The Desperate Miles (TV) 75. Sword of Justice (TV pilot) 78. Little Women (TV) 78. Little Mo (TV) 78. Buck Rogers in the 25th Century 78. Follow That Car 81. Welcome to Paradise 84, etc.

Haller, Ernest (1896–1970).
Distinguished American cinematographer.
Neglected Wives 20. Outcast 22. Stella Dallas 25. Weary River 29. The Dawn Patrol 31. The Emperor Jones 33. Dangerous 35. Jezebel 38. *Gone with the Wind* (AA) 39. Dark Victory 39. All This and Heaven Too 40. Saratoga Trunk 43. Mr Skeffington 44. *Mildred Pierce* 45. Humoresque 46. My Girl Tisa 47. The Flame and the Arrow 50. Rebel without a Cause 55. Back from the Dead 57. God's Little Acre 58. Man of the West 58. The Third Voice 59. Whatever Happened to Baby Jane? 62. Lilies of the Field 64. Dead Ringer 64, many others.

Halliday, John (1880–1947).
Suave and dapper Scottish actor, long in Hollywood.
■ The Woman Gives 20. East Side Sadie 29. Father's Sons 30. Recaptured Love 30. Scarlet Pages 30. Smart Women 31. Consolation Marriage 31. The Ruling Voice 31. Millie 31. Once a Sinner 31. Captain Applejack 31. Fifty Million Frenchmen 31. The Spy 31. Transatlantic 31. Men of Chance 32. The Impatient Maiden 32. The Age of Consent 32. Weekends Only 32. Bird of Paradise 32. Perfect Understanding 33. Terror Aboard 33. Bed of Roses 33. The House on 56th Street 33. Woman Accused 33. Return of the Terror 34. Housewife 34. A Woman's Man 34. Happiness Ahead 34. Registered Nurse 34. The Witching Hour 34. Desirable 34. Finishing School 34. Mystery Woman 35. The Dark Angel 35. The Melody Lingers On 35. Peter Ibbetson 35. *Desire* 36. Fatal Lady 36. Three Cheers for Love 36. *Hollywood Boulevard* 36. Arsène Lupin Returns 38. Blockade 38. That Certain Age 39. The Light that Failed 39. Hotel for Women 39. Intermezzo 39. *The Philadelphia Story* 40. Lydia 41. Escape to Glory 41.
Famous line (*The Philadelphia Story*): 'What most wives fail to realize is that their husbands' philandering has nothing to do with them.'

Halliwell, Leslie (1929–1989).
British critic, author and creator of two of cinema's best-loved reference books, *Halliwell's Film Guide* (from 1977) and *Halliwell's Filmgoer's Companion* (from 1965). A former cinema manager and journalist, he was a film researcher for Britain's Granada TV, and went on to become programme buyer for the whole ITV network and, later, Channel 4. He wrote eleven other books, including *Halliwell's Hundred*, his choice of favourite films.
Autobiography: 1985, *Seats in All Parts*.
❝ It was an aroma compounded of soft plush and worn carpet and Devon violets and sweat. It was that scent, perhaps, which first made me a film fan; for it was to the Queen's in Bolton that I ventured on my first remembered visit to any cinema, one wet and windy afternoon in 1933, when I was four. – *L.H.*

Hallström, Lasse (1946–).
Swedish director.
Abba – the Movie 77. Father to Be 79. The Rooster 81. Happy We 83. My Life as a Dog/Mitt Liv Som Hund (AAN) 85. A Lover and His Lass 85. The Children of Bullerby Village/Alla Vi Barn i Bullerby 86. More about the Children of Bullerby Village/Mer Om Oss Barn i Bullerbyn 87. Once Around 90. What's Eating Gilbert Grape? 93. Something to Talk About 95, etc.

Halop, Billy (1920–1976).
American actor, the erstwhile leader of the Dead End Kids; stardom failed to materialize, and he descended to bit parts.
Dead End 37. Crime School 38. Little Tough Guy 38. Angels with Dirty Faces 38. You Can't Get Away with Murder 39. Angels Wash Their Faces 39. Call a Messenger 39. Tom Brown's Schooldays 40. Hit the Road 41. Mob Town 41. Junior Army 43. Dangerous Years 47. Mister Buddwing 66. Fitzwilly 66, many others.
TV series: All in the Family 72–76.

Halperin, Victor (1895–*).
American director.
Party Girl 29. Ex Flame 30. *White Zombie* 32. Supernatural 33. I Conquer the Sea 36. Revolt of the Zombies 36. Nation Aflame 37. Torture Ship 39. Buried Alive 40. Girls' Town 42.

Halsey, Brett (1933–).
American leading man.
The Glass Web 53. Ma and Pa Kettle at Home 54. Cry Baby Killer 58. The Best of Everything 59. Desire in the Dust 60. Return to Peyton Place 61. Twice Told Tales 63. Spy in Your Eye 65. Where Does It Hurt? 72. Ratboy 86. Demonia (It.) 90. Search for Diana 93. First Degree 95, etc.
TV series: Follow the Sun 61–62.

Halton, Charles (1876–1959).
American character actor, inimitable as a sour-faced bank clerk, professor or lawyer.
Come and Get It 36. Penrod and Sam 37. Dead End 37. The Prisoner of Zenda 37. The Saint in New York 38. Room Service 38. Jesse James 39. Swanee River 39. Dodge City 39. Juarez 39. The Shop around the Corner 40. *Dr Cyclops* 40. Foreign Correspondent 40. Stranger on the Third Floor 40. The Westerner 40. Tobacco Road 41. The Smiling Ghost 41. *To Be or Not to Be* 42. Across the Pacific 42. Jitterbugs 43. Wilson 44. Rhapsody in Blue 45. The Best Years of Our Lives 46. Three Godfathers 48. The Nevadan 50. Here Comes the Groom 51. Carrie 52. Friendly Persuasion 56, many others.

Hambling, Gerry (1926–).
British film editor, a regular on the films of director Alan Parker, and a former sound editor.
The Whole Truth 58. The Bulldog Breed 60. The Early Bird 65. That Riviera Touch 68. Moses (TV) 75. Bugsy Malone 76. Midnight Express (AAN) 78. Fame (AAN) 80. Heartaches 82. Shoot the Moon 82. Pink Floyd the Wall 82. Another Country 84. Birdy 84. Invitation to the Wedding 85. Absolute Beginners 86. Leonard Part 6 87. Angel Heart 87. Mississippi Burning (AAN) 88. Lenny: Live and Unleashed 89. Come See the Paradise 90. The Commitments (AAN) 91. City of Joy 92. In the Name of the Father (AAN) 93. The Road to Wellville 94. White Squall 96. *Evita* (AAN) 96. The Boxer 97, etc.

Hamer, Gerald (1886–1973).
British character actor in Hollywood.
Swing Time 36. Bulldog Drummond's Bride 39. Sherlock Holmes Faces Death 43. The Scarlet Claw 44. The Sign of the Ram 48, etc.

Hamer, Robert (1911–1963).
British director, erratic but at his best impeccably stylish. Born in Kidderminster, Worcestershire, he graduated from Cambridge University, where he was sent down for a year because of a homosexual affair, and began as a clapper-boy at Gaumont Studios, later working as an editor, before becoming a producer and writer at Ealing Studios. His career was hampered by problems in getting backing for the dark-toned films he wanted to make, and by the alcoholism that finally made him unemployable. Married actress Joan Holt.
Book: 1998, *The Finest Years: British Cinema of the 1940s* by Charles Drazin (includes a chapter on Hamer).
■ San Demetrio London (w only) 43. Dead of Night (mirror sequence & w) 45. Pink String and Sealing Wax 45. *It Always Rains on Sunday* (& w) 47. *Kind Hearts and Coronets* (& w) 49. The Spider and the Fly 49. His Excellency (& w) 52. The Long Memory (& w) 52. *Father Brown* 54. To Paris With Love 54. The Scapegoat 59. *School for Scoundrels* 60. A Jolly Bad Fellow (w only) 63.
❝ No one can be satisifed with one death. I'd like to die like Charles XII, drowned in a butt of brandy, but I'd also like to die like Stefan George, poisoned by a rose-thorn. Bits of me have already died in these ways. – *R.H.*
He was a perfectionist, and knew more about acting for films than any director I know. He could be maddening over tiny details – he once had fifteen takes of a scene between Googie [Withers] and me, because he wanted Googie to give less emphasis to the 'k' in the word 'back'! – *John McCallum*

Hamill, Mark (1951–).
American leading man.
Sarah T (TV) 75. Delancey Street (TV) 75. Eric (TV) 75. Mallory (TV) 76. The City (TV) 77. *Star Wars* 77. Corvette Summer 78. The Big Red One 79. The Empire Strikes Back 80. The Night the Lights Went Out in Georgia 81. Return of the Jedi 83. Slipstream 89. Black Magic Woman 91. Sleepwalkers 92. Time Runner 93. Batman: Mask of the Phantasm (voice) 94. Village of the Damned 95. When Time Expires 97. Watchers Reborn 98. Hamilton (Swe.) 98, etc.
❝ I'm waiting for my body to catch up with my age. – M.H.
Acting in *Star Wars* I felt like a raisin in a giant fruit salad, and I didn't even know who the cantaloupes were. – M.H.

Hamilton, Ashley (1977–).
American teen actor, the son of George Hamilton.
Lost in Africa 94.

Hamilton, Bernie (1929–).
Burly American actor.
Let No Man Write My Epitaph 60. 13 West Street 62. Captain Sinbad 63. The Swimmer 67. The Lost Man 69. The Organization 71. Scream Blacula Scream 73. Bucktown 75, etc.
TV series: *Starsky and Hutch* 75–79.

Hamilton, Donald (1913–).
American thriller writer, creator of Matt Helm. The resulting films and TV series were undistinguished to say the least.

Hamilton, George (1939–).
American leading man, usually in serious roles.
Crime and Punishment USA (debut) 58. Home from the Hill 60. All the Fine Young Cannibals 60. Angel Baby 61. By Love Possessed 61. A Thunder of Drums 61. The Light in the Piazza 62. The Victors 63. *Act One* (as Moss Hart) 63. Your Cheatin' Heart 64. Viva Maria 65. Doctor, You've Got To Be Kidding 67. The Long Ride Home 67. Jack of Diamonds 67. The Power 67. Evel Knievel 72. The Man Who Loved Cat Dancing 73. Once Is Not Enough 75. The Dead Don't Die (TV) 75. Roots (TV) 77. The Strange Possession of Mrs Oliver (TV) 77. Killer on Board (TV) 77. The Users (TV) 78. Institute for Revenge (TV) 79. *Love at First Bite* (as Dracula) 79. Zorro the Gay Blade 81. Love at Second Bite 90. The Godfather Part III 90. Doc Hollywood 91. Once Upon a Crime 92. Danielle Steel's Vanished (TV) 95. 8 Heads in a Duffel Bag 96. Rough Riders (TV) 97, etc.
TV series: The Survivors 69. Paris 7000 70. Dynasty 85. Spies 86.

Hamilton, Guy (1922–).
British director, former assistant to Carol Reed.
■ The Ringer 52. The Intruder 53. *An Inspector Calls* 54. The Colditz Story 54. Charley Moon 56. Manuela 57. The Devil's Disciple 58. A Touch of Larceny 59. The Best of Enemies 62. The Party's Over 63. The Man in the Middle 64. *Goldfinger* 64. Funeral in Berlin 66. The Battle of Britain 70. Diamonds are Forever 71. Live and Let Die 72. The Man with the Golden Gun 73. Force Ten from Navarone (also p) 78. The Mirror Crack'd 80. Evil under the Sun 82. Remo Williams . . . the Adventure Begins 85. Try This One On for Size (Fr.) 89.

Hamilton, John (1886–1958).
Chubby American character actor, in hundreds of small parts as judge, cop, lawyer.
Rainbow Riley 26. White Cargo 30. Legion of Terror 37. Rose of Washington Square 39. The Maltese Falcon (as district attorney) 41. Meet Miss Bobby Socks 44. Law of the Golden West 49. The Pace that Thrills 52. On the Waterfront 54, many others.
TV series: Superman 51–57.

Hamilton, Josh (1969–).
American actor, from the stage and TV. Born in New York, he was a co-founder, with others including Ethan HAWKE, of the Malaparte Theater Company in 1993.
First Born 84. Old Enough 84. The Exchange Student (TV) 85. Another Woman 88. Abby, My Love (TV) 91. O Pioneers (TV) 92. Alive 93. With Honors 94. Kicking and Screaming 95. The Proprietor 96, etc.

Hamilton, Linda (1955–).
American actress.
Rape and Marriage: The Rideout Case (TV) 80. T.A.G. – the Assassination Game 82. The Terminator 84. Children of the Corn 84. Secret Weapons (TV) 85. King Kong Lives 86. Black Moon Rising 86. Mr Destiny 90. Terminator 2: Judgment Day 91. Silent Fall 94. Separate Lives 95. Dante's Peak 97. Shadow Conspiracy 97. On the Line (TV) 98. The Color of Courage 98, etc.
TV series: Secrets of Midland Heights 81–82. King's Crossing 82. Beauty and the Beast 87–90.

Hamilton, Lloyd (1891–1935).
American silent slapstick comedian, in many two-reelers from 1914.

Hamilton, Margaret (1902–1985).
American character actress, a former kindergarten teacher who came to films via Broadway and usually played hatchet-faced spinsters or maids.
Another Language 33. These Three 36. Nothing Sacred 37. *The Wizard of Oz* 39. Invisible Woman 41. *Guest in the House* 44. Mad Wednesday 47. State of the Union 48. The Great Plane Robbery 50. Thirteen Ghosts 60. The Daydreamer 66. Rosie 67. The Anderson Tapes 71. Brewster McCloud 71, etc.

Hamilton, Murray (1923–1986).
American general-purpose actor.
Bright Victory 50. No Time for Sergeants 58. The FBI Story 59. Seconds 66. The Graduate 67. No Way to Treat a Lady 68. The Boston Strangler 68. If It's Tuesday This Must Be Belgium 69. The Way We Were 73. Jaws 75. Jaws 2 78. 1941 79. The Amityville Horror 79. Brubaker 80, etc.
TV series: Love and Marriage 59–60. The Man Who Never Was 66–67. Rich Man, Poor Man Book I 76. B.J. and the Bear 81. Hail to the Chief 85.

Hamilton, Neil (1899–1984).
Stalwart American leading man of silent days, a former model.
White Rose 23. America 24. Isn't Life Wonderful? 25. Beau Geste 26. The Great Gatsby 27. Why Be Good? 28. Keeper of the Bees 29. The Dawn Patrol 30. The Wet Parade 31. The Animal Kingdom 32. Tarzan the Ape Man 32. One Sunday Afternoon 33. Tarzan and His Mate 34. Federal Fugitives 41. The Little Shepherd of Kingdom Come 61. Madame X 66, many others.
TV series: Hollywood Screen Test 48–53. That Wonderful Guy 49–50. Batman 65–67.

Hamilton, Patrick (1904–1962).
British novelist and playwright whose work inspired a small but significant group of films.
■ *Gaslight* 39 and 44. Hangover Square 44. Rope 49.

Hamlin, Harry (1952–).
American light leading man. He has a son by Ursula Andress.
Movie Movie 78. Studs Lonigan (TV) 79. Clash of the Titans 81. King of the Mountain 81. Dragonslayer 81. Making Love 82. Blue Skies Again 83. Maxie 85. Space (TV) 85. Laguna Heat 88. Dinner at Eight 89. Deceptions (TV) 90. Deadly Intentions . . . Again (TV) 91. Tom Clancy's Op Center (TV) 95. Frogs for Snakes 98, etc.
TV series: L.A. Law 86–91.

Hamlisch, Marvin (1945–).
American composer and pianist.
The Swimmer 68. The April Fools 69. Flap 70. The Sting (AA) 73. The Way We Were (AAs, m) 73. The Prisoner of Second Avenue 75. The Spy Who Loved Me 77. Same Time Next Year 78. Ice Castles 79. Chapter Two 79. Starting Over 79. Ordinary People 80. Seems Like Old Times 80. Pennies from Heaven 81. The Fan 81. I Ought to Be in Pictures 82. Sophie's Choice (AAN) 82. Romantic Comedy 83. A Chorus Line 85. D.A.R.Y.L. 85. Three Men and a Baby 87. The January Man 88. Little Nikita 88. The Experts 89. Frankie and Johnny 91. The Mirror Has Two Faces (AANs 'I've Finally Found Someone') 96, etc.
❝ My whole life revolves around dessert. – M.H.
To put something on the earth that wasn't there yesterday, that's what I like. – M.H.

Hammer, Will (1887–*) (William Hinds).
British producer, one of the founders of Hammer Films.

Hammerstein II, Oscar (1895–1960).
Immensely successful American lyricist who wrote many stage musicals, usually with Richard RODGERS. The King and I, South Pacific, The Sound of Music, etc.

Hammett, Dashiell (1894–1961).
American writer of detective novels and occasional screenplays.
City Streets (& w) 31. The Maltese Falcon 31. The Thin Man 34. The Glass Key 35. The Maltese Falcon 41. The Glass Key 42. Watch on the Rhine (AANw) 43, etc.
~Wim Wenders' film *Hammett*, which appeared in 1982, was a pastiche in which the real Hammett became one of his own detective creations. In the vein of the Chandler movies, but less entertaining, it had minority appeal.

Hammid, Alexander (c. 1910–) (Alexander Hackenschmied).
Czech documentarist in America.
Hymn of the Nations 46. Of Men and Music 51. To the Fair 65, etc.

Hammond, Kay (1909–1980) (Dorothy Standing).
Plummy-voiced English leading lady, mostly on the stage, the daughter of actor Sir Guy STANDING. Born in London, she studied at RADA and was on stage from 1927. Her best role, on stage and screen, was as Elvira in *Blithe Spirit*. Her second husband was actor Sir John CLEMENTS, and she was the mother of actor John STANDING.
Children of Chance 30. A Night in Montmartre 31. Out of the Blue 31. Almost a Divorce 32. A Night Like This 32. Sally Bishop 32. Yes Madam 33. Sleeping Car 33. Bitter Sweet 33. Two on a Doorstep 36. Jeannie 41. *Blithe Spirit* 45. Call of the Blood 47. Five Golden Hours 61, etc.

Hammond, Peter (1923–).
British juvenile player of the 40s; became a TV and film director.
They Knew Mr Knight 46. Holiday Camp 47. Fly Away Peter 48. Morning Departure 50. Vote for Huggett 50. The Adventurers 51. Spring and Port Wine (d only) 69, etc.
TV series: The Buccaneers 56–57.

Hampden, Walter (1879–1955) (Walter Hampden Dougherty).
American stage actor with a long career behind him when he came to Hollywood. Born in Brooklyn, the son of an attorney, he studied at Harvard University and in Paris, and was on stage, playing Shakespeare in England, from 1901.
■ Warfare of the Flesh 17. The Hunchback of Notre Dame 39. All This and Heaven Too 40. North West Mounted Police 40. They Died with Their Boots On 41. Reap the Wild Wind 42. The Adventures of Mark Twain 44. All About Eve 50. The First Legion 51. Five Fingers 52. Treasure of the Golden Condor 52. Sombrero 53. The Silver Chalice 54. Sabrina 54. Strange Lady in Town 55. The Prodigal 55. The Vagabond King 56.

Hampshire, Susan (1938–).
Talented British leading lady, somewhat handicapped by her own demureness.
■ Upstairs and Downstairs 59. Expresso Bongo 59. During One Night 61. The Long Shadow 61. The Three Lives of Thomasina 63. Night Must Fall 64. Wonderful Life 64. The Fighting Prince of Donegal 66. The Trygon Factor 67. Paris in August 67. Violent Enemy 69. Monte Carlo or Bust 69. David Copperfield (TV) 69. A Time for Loving 72. Living Free 72. Neither the Sea nor the Sand 72. Baffled (TV) 72. Malpertius 72. The Lonely Woman 76.
TV series: *The Forsyte Saga* (as Fleur) 68. *The Pallisers* 75. The Grand 97.

Hampton, Christopher (1946–).
English dramatist and screenwriter.
A Doll's House 73. Tales from the Vienna Woods 81. Beyond the Limit 83. The Wolf at the Door 86. The Good Father 87. Dangerous Liaisons (AA) 88. Carrington (wd) 95. Total Eclipse (w) 95. Mary Reilly (w) 96. Joseph Conrad's Secret Agent (wd) 96, etc.

Hampton, Hope (1899–1982).
American leading lady of the silents.
The Bait 21. The Gold Diggers 23. Hollywood 23. The Truth about Women 24. Lover's Island 25. The Unfair Sex 26, etc.

Hampton, Lionel (1909–).
American jazz musician and bandleader, in films as himself. Born in Louisville, Kentucky, he was a drummer before first gaining fame playing vibraphone with Benny GOODMAN's trio and quartet in the mid-30s, later leading his own big band and small groups. He is caricatured in the Merrie Melodies cartoon *Hollywood Canine Canteen* 46.
Sing, Sinner, Sing 33. Pennies from Heaven 36. Hollywood Hotel 37. A Song Is Born 48. *The Benny Goodman Story* 55. Mister Rock and Roll 57. Force of Impulse 61. No Maps on My Taps (doc) 78. Cha Cha (doc) 80, etc.

Hampton, Louise (1881–1954).
British character actress.
Goodbye Mr Chips 39. Busman's Honeymoon 40. Bedelia 46, etc.

Hancock, Herbie (1940–) (Herbert Jeffrey Hancock).
American composer and musician, a leading jazz keyboard player who turned to electronic music in the 70s, soon after he began writing for films.
Blow-Up 66. The Spook Who Sat by the Door 73. Death Wish 74. A Soldier's Story 84. Jo Jo Dancer, Your Life Is Calling 86. Round Midnight (& a) (AAm) 86. Action Jackson 88. Colors 88. Harlem Nights 89. Livin' Large 91, etc.

Hancock, John (1939–).
American director.
■ Let's Scare Jessica to Death 73. Bang the Drum Slowly 74. Baby Blue Marine 76. California Dreaming 78. Weeds 87. Prancer 89.

Hancock, Sheila (1933–).
British comic actress of stage and TV.
Light Up the Sky 58. The Girl on the Boat 61. Night Must Fall 63. The Anniversary 67. Take a Girl Like You 70. Three Men and a Little Lady 90. A Business Affair 94. Close Relations (TV) 98, etc.
TV series: The Rag Trade 61–63. The Bed-Sit Girl 65–66. Now Take My Wife . . . 71. Gone to Seed 92. Brighton Belles 93.

Hancock, Tony (1924–1968).
Popular British radio and TV comedian. He committed suicide in Australia, leaving a note that said 'Things seemed to go wrong too many times'. He was the model for Lon Bracton, a self-destructive comedian, in J. B. Priestley's novel *London End*.
Biography: 1969, *Hancock* by Freddie Hancock and David Nathan. 1995, *Tony Hancock: When the Wind Changed* by Cliff Goodwin.
■ Orders are Orders 61. The Rebel 61. The Punch and Judy Man 62. Those Magnificent Men in their Flying Machines 65. The Wrong Box 66.
❝ A comedian with a touch of genius who had no enemy except himself. – *J. B. Priestley*
An indifferent performer saved by two of the most brilliant scriptwriters of the decade, Galton and Simpson, whom he rejected. Thereafter, it was all downhill. – *Kenneth Williams*

Hand, David (1900–1986).
American animator, formerly with Disney; came to Britain 1945 to found a cartoon unit for Rank with some pleasing results (*Musical Paintbox* series, etc.), but it was a financial failure and Hand returned to America in 1950.

Handke, Peter (1942–).
Austrian avant-garde dramatist, novelist, screenwriter and director.
The Goalkeeper's Fear of the Penalty Kick/Die Angst des Tormanns beim Elfmeter (w) 72. Wrong Move/Falsche Bewegung (w) 75. The Left-Handed Woman/Die Linkshändige Frau (wd) 77. Wings of Desire/Der Himmel über Berlin (w) 87, etc.

Handl, Irene (1902–1987).
Dumpy British character comedienne, frequently seen as maid or charlady; became a star in her later years. Born in London, the daughter of an Austrian banker and his aristocratic French wife, she studied at the Embassy School of Acting, and was on stage from 1937. She also wrote two novels, *The Sioux* 65 and *The Gold Tipped Phitzer* 66, noted for their originality and ornate literary style.
Missing Believed Married 37. The Girl in the News 41. Pimpernel Smith 41. Temptation Harbour 46. Silent Dust 48. One Wild Oat 51. The Belles of St Trinian's 54. A Kid for Two Farthings 56. Brothers in Law 57. *I'm All Right Jack* 59. Make Mine Mink 60. The Rebel 61. Heavens Above 63. Morgan 66. Smashing Time 67. On a Clear Day You Can See Forever 70. The Private Life of Sherlock Holmes 70. For the Love of Ada 72. Adventures of a Private Eye 76. Stand Up Virgin Soldiers 77, etc.
TV series: *For the Love of Ada* 70–72. Maggie and Her 78–79.

Handley, Tommy (1894–1949).
British radio comedian most famous for his long-running, morale-building *ITMA* series during World War II.
Elstree Calling 30. Two Men in a Box 38. *It's That Man Again* 42. Time Flies 43. Tom Tom Topia (short) 46.

Handy, W. C. (1873–1958) (William Christopher Handy).
Blind American blues pioneer; was impersonated by Nat King Cole in *St Louis Blues*.

Haneke, Michael (1942–).
German director and screenwriter. Born in Munich, he studied philosophy, psychology and theatre in Vienna before entering television as a scriptwriter, from 1967, and as a director, from 1974. He also works as a theatre director.
The Seventh Continent/Der Siebente Kontinent 88. Benny's Video 92. 71 Fragments of a Chronology of Chance/71 Fragmente Einer Chronologie des Zufalls 94. Age of the Wolves 95. The Castle 97. Funny Games 97, etc.

Haney, Carol (1928–1964).
American dancer, former assistant to Gene Kelly.
■ Kiss Me Kate 53. Invitation to the Dance 54. *The Pajama Game* 57.

Hanff, Helen (1916–1997).
American writer and journalist. She was played by Anne BANCROFT in her autobiographical *84 Charing Cross Road* 86, which was also turned into a TV, stage and radio play. Born in Philadelphia, she began by writing plays that were not performed and also read novels for Paramount, once adding $40 for 'mental torture' to her invoice after ploughing through J. R. R. Tolkien's *Lord of the Rings* trilogy.

Hani, Susumu (1926–).
Japanese 'new wave' director, a former journalist and maker of documentary shorts. Often uses non-professional actors. Married actress Sachiko Hidari.
Bad Boys/Furyo Shonen 60. He and She/Kanojo Ta Kare 63. Bwana Toshi 65. Bride of the Andes/Andesu No Hanayome 66. Nanami 68. Aido 69. Mio 72. Morning Schedule/Gozencho No Jikanwari 73. The Green Horizon/Afurika Monogatari 81, etc.

Hanks, Tom (1956–).
Versatile American leading actor, in sympathetic roles both in comedy and drama. Born in Concord, California, he studied at California State University and began his career on stage at the Great Lakes Shakespeare Festival in Ohio. A TV series followed in 1980 and gained him the beginnings of fame, though many of his subsequent films were second-rate at best, and not particularly successful until *Big* established his deftness in comedy. His second wife is actress Rita Wilson. His current asking price: around $20m.
He Knows You're Alone 80. Bachelor Party 83. Splash! 84. The Man with One Red Shoe 85. Volunteers 85. The Money Pit 85. Nothing in Common 86. Every Time We Say Goodbye 86. Dragnet 87. Big (AAN) 88. Punchline 88. The 'burbs 89. Turner & Hooch 89. Bonfire of the Vanities 90. Joe versus the Volcano 90. Radio Flyer 92. A League of Their Own 92. Sleepless in Seattle 93. *Philadelphia* (AA) 93. Forrest Gump (AA) 94. Toy Story (voice) 95. Apollo 13 95. That Thing You Do (a, co-w, d) 96. *Saving Private Ryan* 98. You've Got Mail 98, etc.
TV series: Bosom Buddies 80–82.
❝ If you have to have a job in this world, a high-priced movie star is a pretty damned good gig. – *T.H.*

Hanley, Jenny (1947–).
British light leading lady and television personality, daughter of Dinah Sheridan and Jimmy Hanley.
Joanna 68. On Her Majesty's Secret Service 69. Tam Lin 70. The Private Life of Sherlock Holmes 70. Scars of Dracula 72. Soft Beds Hard Battles 74. Alfie Darling 75, etc.

Hanley, Jimmy (1918–1970).
Former British child actor developed as 'the boy next door' type by Rank in the 40s. He was on stage from the age of 12 and a circus bareback rider at 14 before making his film debut when he was 16. In the mid-50s he was also presenter of a daily television programme, *Jolly Good Time*, and a consumer programme, *Jim's Inn*. The first of his two wives was actress Dinah Sheridan. Their daughter is actress Jenny HANLEY and their son, Jeremy Hanley, MP, was chairman of the Conservative party in 1994–95.
Little Friend 34. Boys Will Be Boys 35. Night Ride 37. There Ain't No Justice 39. Salute John Citizen 42. For You Alone 44. The Way Ahead 44. Henry V 44. 29 Acacia Avenue 45. The Captive Heart 46. Master of Bankdam 47. It Always Rains on Sunday 48. It's Hard To Be Good 49. Here Come the Huggetts (and ensuing series) 49–52. The Blue Lamp 50. The Black Rider 54. The Deep Blue Sea 56. Lost Continent 68, etc.

Hanna, William (1910–).
American animator who with his partner Joe Barbera created Tom and Jerry for MGM, later founding their own successful company creating innumerable semi-animated series for TV: Huckleberry Hound, Yogi Bear, The Flintstones, The Jetsons, Wait Till Your Father Gets Home, etc.

Hannah, Daryl (1960–).
American leading lady.
The Fury 78. Hard Country 81. Blade Runner 82. The Pope of Greenwich Village 84. *Splash!* 84. Clan of the Cave Bear 86. Legal Eagles 86. Roxanne 87. Wall Street 87. High Spirits 88. Crimes and Misdemeanors 89. Steel Magnolias 89. At Play in the Fields of the Lord 91. Memoirs of an Invisible Man 92. Attack of the 50 Ft Woman (TV) 93. Grumpy Old Men 93. The Little Rascals 94. The Tie that Binds 95. Grumpier Old Men 95. Two Much 96. The Last Days of Frankie the Fly 96. The Last Don (TV) 97. The Gingerbread Man 97. Hi-Life 98. Rear Window (TV) 98, etc.

Hannah, John (1962–).
Scottish leading actor. Born in Glasgow, he trained as an electrician before studying at the Royal Scottish Academy of Drama.
Harbour Beat (Aus.) 90. Four Weddings and a Funeral 94. McCallum (TV) 95. Madagascar Skin 95. Resurrection Man 98. *Sliding Doors* 98. The James Gang 98. The Mummy 99, etc.
TV series: Out of the Blue 95. McCallum 97–98.

Hannam, Ken (1929–).
Australian director who moved to England in the late 60s to work as a television director.
Sunday Too Far Away 74. Break of Day 76. Summerfield 77. Dawn! 78.

Hannan, Peter (1941–).
Australian cinematographer, now working in Britain.
Eskimo Nell 71. Flame 74. The Haunting of Julia 77. The Stud 78. The Missionary 81. Brimstone and Treacle 82. Monty Python's Meaning of Life 83. The Razor's Edge 83. Blame It on Rio 83. Dance with a Stranger 84. Turtle Diary 85. Insignificance 85. Half Moon Street 85. Club Paradise 85. Withnail and I 87. The Lonely Passion of Judith Hearne 87. A Handful of Dust 88. How to Get Ahead in Advertising 89. Not without My Daughter 91, etc.

Hanray, Lawrence (1874–1947).
British stage character actor of great dignity. Born in London, he was on stage from 1892.
The Private Life of Henry VIII 32. That Night in London 33. Lorna Doone 34. The Scarlet Pimpernel 34. The Man Who Could Work Miracles 36. Knight without Armour 37. It's Never Too Late to Mend 37. On Approval 43, etc.

Hansberry, Lorraine (1930–1965).
American playwright, whose *A Raisin in the Sun* was filmed.

Hansen, Gunnar (1947–).
American actor, best known for playing the role of Leatherface in *The Texas Chainsaw Massacre* 74.
Scream of the Demon Lover 71. The Demon Lover 77. Hollywood Chainsaw Hookers 88. Mosquito 95. Freakshow 95, etc.

Hansen, Juanita (1895–1961).
American leading lady of the silents, especially in serials.
His Pride and Shame 16. Secret of the Submarine 16. Dangers of a Bride 17. The Brass Bullet 18. The Lost City 20. The Yellow Arm 21. Broadway Madonna 22. The Jungle Princess 23, etc.

Hansen, Peter (1922–).
American general-purpose actor.
Branded 50. When Worlds Collide 51. Darling How Could You 53. Three Violent People 56. The Deep Six 58. Harlow 65, etc.
TV series: Mr Parkson 64–65. General Hospital 65– .

Hanson, Curtis.
American director and screenwriter.
AS WRITER: The Silent Partner 78. White Dog 81. Never Cry Wolf 83, etc.
AS DIRECTOR: The Arousers 76. The Little Dragons 80. Losin' It 83. The Bedroom Window 87. Bad Influence 90. The Hand that Rocks the Cradle 92. The River Wild 94. *LA Confidential* (AANp, AAw, AANd) 97, etc.

Hanson, Lars (1887–1965).
Swedish stage actor who made silent films abroad but after the coming of sound remained in Sweden.
Ingeborg Holm (debut) 13. Dolken 16. Erotikon 19. The Atonement of Gosta Berling 24. The Scarlet Letter (US) 26. The Divine Woman (US) 27. The Wind (US) 28. The Informer (GB) 28, etc.

Harareet, Haya (1931–) (Haya Hararit).
Israeli leading lady. She is married to director Jack Clayton.
Hill 24 Does Not Answer 55. Ben Hur 59. The Secret Partner 61. The Lost Kingdom 61. The Interns 62. Our Mother's House (co-w only) 67, etc.

Harasimowicz, Cazary (1955–).
Polish screenwriter.
Sezon Na Bazanty 85. 300 Miles to Heaven/300 Mil Do Nieba 89. Seszele 90. Black Lights 91. Lazarus 94. The Brute/The Hoodlum 96, etc.

Harbach, Otto (1873–1963) (Otto Hauerbach).
American playwright and lyricist. Born in Salt Lake City, Utah, he was educated at Knox College, Galesburg, and Columbia University, and was for six years Professor of English at Whitman College, Washington, before working in advertising and journalism. The Broadway shows for which he wrote lyrics included *No, No, Nanette* and *The Desert Song*. His best-known lyrics include 'I Won't Dance', 'Indian Love Call', and 'Smoke Gets in Your Eyes'.
The Cat and Fiddle 34. Roberta 35. Rose Marie 36. Lovely to Look At 52. Rose Marie 54, etc.

Harburg, E. Y. (1896–1981) (Edgar 'Yip' Harburg).
American lyricist chiefly noted for the songs in *The Wizard of Oz*; also wrote 'Brother Can You Spare a Dime', 'Happiness Is a Thing Called Joe', 'Can't Help Singing', 'Lydia the Tattooed Lady', 'Last Night When We Were Young', 'April in Paris', 'How Are Things in Glocca Morra', etc.

Harden, Marcia Gay (1959–).
American leading actress.
Miller's Crossing 90. Late for Dinner 91. Used People 92. Sinatra (TV) 92. Crush (NZ) 92. Safe

Passage 94. The Spitfire Grill 96. Spy Hard 96. The First Wives Club 96. The Daytrippers 96. Flubber 97. Path to Paradise (TV) 97. Desperate Measures 98. Meet Joe Black 98, etc.

Hardin, Ty (1930–) (Orton Hungerford).
Muscular leading man, mostly on TV.
I Married a Monster from Outer Space 58. The Chapman Report 62. PT 109 63. Battle of the Bulge 65. Berserk (GB) 67. Custer of the West 68. The Last Rebel 71. Drums of Vengeance 77. Bad Jim 89. Born Killer 90, etc.
TV series: *Bronco* 58–61. Riptide 69.
❝ I'm really a very humble man. Not a day passes that I don't thank God for my looks and my talent. – *T.H.*

Harding, Ann (1902–1981) (Dorothy Gatley).
Gentlewomanly American leading lady of 30s romances. Born in Fort Sam Houston, Texas, the daughter of an army officer who rose to be a general, she was briefly educated at Bryn Mawr and worked as a clerk and script-reader before beginning on stage in 1921. Married actor Harry Bannister (1926–32) and conductor and composer Werner Janssen (1937–62). She retired for a time after her second marriage before returning to the screen in the early 40s in more mature ladylike roles. Her best performances were as Linda Seton in *Holiday*, Daisy Sage in *The Animal Kingdom*, Marion in *Biography of a Bachelor Girl* and Carol Howard in *Love from a Stranger*.
■ Paris Bound 29. Her Private Affair 29. Condemned 29. *Holiday* (AAN) 30. Girl of the Golden West 30. East Lynne 31. Devotion 31. Prestige 31. Westward Passage 32. The Conquerors 32. *The Animal Kingdom* 32. When Ladies Meet 33. Double Harness 33. Right to Romance 33. Gallant Lady 33. The Life of Vergie Winters 34. The Fountain 34. *Biography of a Bachelor Girl* 35. Enchanted April 35. The Flame Within 35. Peter Ibbetson 35. The Lady Consents 36. The Witness Chair 36. *Love from a Stranger* (GB) 37. Eyes in the Night 42. Mission to Moscow 43. North Star 43. Janie 44. Nine Girls 44. Those Endearing Young Charms 45. Janie Gets Married 46. It Happened on Fifth Avenue 47. Christmas Eve 47. The Magnificent Yankee 50. Two Weeks with Love 50. The Unknown Man 51. The Man in the Grey Flannel Suit 56. I've Lived Before 56. Strange Intruder 56.

Harding, Gilbert (1907–1960).
Explosive British TV personality who appeared in a few films.
The Gentle Gunman 52. Meet Mr Lucifer 53. As Long as They're Happy 55. An Alligator Named Daisy 55. Expresso Bongo 60, etc.

Harding, Lyn (1867–1952) (David Llewellyn Harding).
British stage actor who made a splendid 'heavy' in some films of the 20s and 30s.
The Barton Mystery 20. When Knighthood Was in Flower (as Henry VIII) 21. The Speckled Band (as Moriarty) 31. *The Triumph of Sherlock Holmes* (as Moriarty) 35. Spy of Napoleon 36. Fire Over England 36. Knight without Armour 37. *Goodbye Mr Chips* (as Chips' first headmaster) 39. The Prime Minister 40, etc.

Hardison, Kadeem (1965–).
American actor.
Rappin' 85. School Daze 88. I'm Gonna Git You Sucka 88. Dream Date (TV) 89. Def by Temptation 90. White Men Can't Jump 92. Mixed Nuts 94. Renaissance Man 94. Gunmen 94. Panther 95. Drive 96. The Sixth Man 97. Blind Faith 98, etc.
TV series: A Different World 87–92. Between Brothers 97– .

Hardwicke, Sir Cedric (1893–1964).
Distinguished British stage actor who settled in Hollywood and too frequently allowed his talents to be squandered on inferior material.
Autobiography: 1961, *A Victorian in Orbit*.
■ Nelson 26. Dreyfus 31. Rome Express 32. Orders is Orders 32. The Ghoul 33. *Nell Gwyn* (as Charles II) 34. The Lady is Willing 34. Jew Süss 34. King of Paris 34. Bella Donna 34. Peg of Old Drury 35. Les Misérables 35. *Becky Sharp* 35. Things to Come 36. Tudor Rose 36. Laburnum Grove 36. The Green Light 37. *King Solomon's Mines* (as Allan Quartermain) 37. *On Borrowed Time* (as Death) 39. *Stanley and Livingstone* (as Livingstone) 39. The Hunchback of Notre Dame (as Frollo) 39. The Invisible Man Returns 40. *Tom Brown's Schooldays* (as Dr Arnold) 40. The Howards of Virginia 40. *Victory* 40. Suspicion 41. Sundown 41. The Ghost of Frankenstein 42. Valley of the Sun 42. Invisible Agent 42. The Commandos Strike at Dawn 42. Forever and a Day 43. *The Moon is Down* 43. The Cross of Lorraine 43. The Lodger 44. Wing and a Prayer 44. Wilson 44. The Keys of the Kingdom 45. Sentimental Journey 46. The Imperfect Lady 47. Ivy 47. Lured 47. Song of My Heart 47. A Woman's Vengeance 47. Beware of Pity 47. *Nicholas Nickleby* 47. Tycoon 47. *I Remember Mama* 48. *The Winslow Boy* 48. Rope 48. A Connecticut Yankee in King Arthur's Court 49. Now Barabbas 49. The White Tower 50. Mr Imperium 51. The Desert Fox 51. The Green Glove 52. Caribbean 52. Salome 53. Botany Bay 53. Bait 54. *Richard III* 55. Helen of Troy 55. Diane 56. Gaby 56. The Vagabond King 56. The Power and the Prize 56. The Ten Commandments 56. Around the World in Eighty Days 56. The Story of Mankind 57. Baby Face Nelson 57. Five Weeks in a Balloon 62. The Pumpkin Eater 64.
TV series: Mrs G Goes to College 61.
❝ I can't act. I have never acted. And I shall never act. What I can do is suspend my audience's power of judgment till I've finished. – *C.H.*

Hardwicke, Edward (1932–).
English actor in occasional films, the son of Sir Cedric Hardwicke. On stage from 1954, after training at RADA, he became a member of the National Theatre company in the 60s. On television, he has played Dr Watson to Jeremy Brett's Sherlock Holmes.
Hell below Zero 53. Othello 65. Otley 68. A Flea in Her Ear 68. The Day of the Jackal 73. Venom 81. Shadowlands 93. The Scarlet Letter 95. Elizabeth 98, etc.
TV series: My Old Man 74–75.

Hardy, Forsyth (1910–1994).
Influential Scottish critic and writer. He was the first film critic of the *Scotsman* newspaper in 1929, one of the founders of *Film Quarterly* magazine in the 30s, and became the first director of the Edinburgh Film Festival, writing its history in *Slightly Mad and Full of Dangers* (1992). His other books include *Scotland in Film* (1990), and *John Grierson, A Documentary Biography*, and he also edited collections of Grierson's writings.

Hardy, Oliver (1892–1957).
Ample-figured American comedian, the fat half of the screen's finest comedy team, noted for his genteel pomposity, tie twiddle and long-suffering look at the camera.
Biographies: 1961, *Mr Laurel and Mr Hardy* by John McCabe. 1989, *Babe – the Life of Oliver Hardy* by John McCabe.
SELECTED SOLO APPEARANCES: Outwitting Dad 13. Playmates 15. Lucky Dog 17. He Winked and Won 17. The Chief Cook 18. The Three Ages 23. Rex, King of the Wild Horses 24. The Wizard of Oz (as the Tin Man) 24. The Nicklehopper 25. Zenobia 39. The Fighting Kentuckian 49. Riding High 50, many others.
■ LAUREL AND HARDY FILMS: Slipping Wives 26. With Love and Hisses 27. Sailors Beware 27. Do Detectives Think? 27. Flying Elephants 27. Sugar Daddies 27. Call of the Cuckoo 27. The Rap 27. Duck Soup 27. Eve's Love Letters 27. Love 'em and Weep 27. Why Girls Love Sailors 27. Should Tall Men Marry? 27. Hats Off 27. Putting Pants on Philip 27. *The Battle of the Century* 27. Leave 'em Laughing 28. From Soup to Nuts 28. *The Finishing Touch* 28. *You're Darn Tootin'* 28. Their Purple Moment 28. Should Married Men Go Home? 28. Early to Bed 28. *Two Tars* 28. Habeas Corpus 28. We Faw Down 28. Liberty 28. Wrong Again 29. That's My Wife 29. *Big Business* 29. *Double Whoopee* 29. *Berth Marks* 29. *Men o'War* 29. *The Perfect Day* 29. They Go Boom 29. Bacon Grabbers 29. Angora Love 29. Unaccustomed as We Are 29. Hollywood Revue of 1929 29. The Hoosegow 29. Night Owls 30. Blotto 30. The Rogue Song (feature) 30. Brats 30. Be Big 30. Below Zero 30. The Laurel and Hardy Murder Case 30. *Hog Wild* 30. Another Fine Mess 30. Chickens Come Home 30. *Laughing Gravy* 31. Our Wife 31. *Come Clean* 31. Pardon Us (feature) 31. One Good Turn 31. Beau Hunks 31. *Helpmates* 31. Any Old Port 31. *The Music Box* (AA) 32. The Chimp 32. *County Hospital* 32. *Scram* 32. Pack Up Your Troubles (feature) 32. Their First Mistake 32. *Towed in a Hole* 33. Twice Two 33. Me and My Pal 33. *Fra Diavolo* (feature) 33. *The Midnight Patrol* 33. *Busy Bodies* 33. *Dirty Work* 33. *Sons of the Desert* (feature) 33. Oliver the Eighth 33. Hollywood Party (feature) 34. Going Bye Bye 34. *Them Thar Hills* 34. *Babes in Toyland* (feature) 34. The Live Ghost 34. *Tit for Tat* 35. The Fixer Uppers 35. Thicker than Water 35. Bonnie Scotland (feature) 35. The Bohemian Girl (feature) 36. *Our Relations* (feature) 36. *Way out West* (feature) 36. Pick a Star (feature) 37. Swiss Miss (feature) 38. *Blockheads* (feature) 38. *The Flying Deuces* (feature) 39. *A Chump at Oxford* (feature) 40. Saps at Sea (feature) 40. Great Guns (feature) 41. A Haunting We Will Go (feature) 42. Air Raid Wardens (feature) 43. Jitterbugs (feature) 43. The Dancing Masters (feature) 43. The Big Noise (feature) 44. Nothing but Trouble (feature) 44. The Bullfighters (feature) 45. Robinson Crusoeland/ Atoll K (feature) 52.
■ COMPILATION FEATURES: The Golden Age of Comedy 58. When Comedy was King 60. Days of Thrills and Laughter 61. Thirty Years of Fun 62. MGM's Big Parade of Comedy 65. Laurel and Hardy's Laughing Twenties 65. The Crazy World of Laurel and Hardy 66. The Further Perils of Laurel and Hardy 69. Four Clowns 69. The Best of Laurel and Hardy 74.
✪ For his many unique qualities, seen to best advantage in his partnership with Stan Laurel. *Blockheads*.

Hardy, Robert (1925–).
British character actor, mostly on TV. He is also an authority on the longbow.
The Spy Who Came in from the Cold 65. How I Won the War 67. 10 Rillington Place 70. The Far Pavilions (TV) 84. The Shooting Party (TV) 84. Jenny's War (TV) 84. Middlemarch (TV) 94. Mary Shelley's Frankenstein 94. A Feast at Midnight 94. Sense and Sensibility 95. Gulliver's Travels (TV) 96. Mrs Dalloway 97. The Tichborne Claimant 98, etc.
TV series: *Elizabeth R* 71. All Creatures Great and Small 77–79. *Churchill: the Wilderness Years* 81. Hot Metal 86–88. Bramwell 95.

Hardy, Robin (1929–).
British director.
The Wicker Man 75. The Fantasist 86.

Hardy, Thomas (1840–1928).
British novelist of dour country stories.
Far from the Madding Crowd 67. Tess 79. Day after the Fair 76. Jude 96.

Hare, Sir David (1947–).
British playwright, screenwriter and director.
Licking Hitler (wd) 77. Saigon – Year of the Cat (w) 83. Wetherby (wd) 85. Plenty (w) 85. Paris by Night (wd) 88. Strapless (wd) 89. Heading Home (wd) 91. Damage (w) 92. The Secret Rapture (wd) 93. Designated Mourner (d) 96.

Hare, Lumsden (1875–1964).
Irish character actor, long in Hollywood.
Charlie Chan Carries On 31. Clive of India 35. She 35. Gunga Din 39. Rebecca 40. The Lodger 44. Challenge to Lassie 49. Julius Caesar 53. The Four Skulls of Jonathan Drake 59, many others.

Hare, Robertson (1891–1979).
Bald-headed British comedian, the put-upon little man of the Aldwych farces of the 20s and 30s, transferred intact from stage to screen.
Autobiography: 1958, *Yours Indubitably*.
Rookery Nook 30. A Cuckoo in the Nest 33. Thark 33. Fishing Stock 35. Aren't Men Beasts? 38. Banana Ridge 41. He Snoops To Conquer 45. Things Happen at Night 48. *One Wild Oat* 51. Our Girl Friday 53. Three Men in a Boat 56. The Young Ones 61, etc.

Harewood, Dorian (1951–).
American actor.
Sparkle 75. Gray Lady Down 77. Looker 81. Against All Odds 83. The Falcon and the Snowman 84. Full Metal Jacket 87. Pacific Heights 90. Solar Crisis 90. Getting Up and Going Home 92. Shattered Image (TV) 93. Sudden Death 95. Twelve Angry Men (TV) 97, etc.
TV series: Roots: The Next Generation 79. Strike Force 81–82. Trauma Centre 83. Glitter 84–85. Trials of Rose O'Neill 91–92. Viper 93.

Hargreaves, John (1945–1996).
Australian leading actor, on screen from 1974. He won an Australian Film Institute award as best actor for *My First Wife*.
The Removalists 74. Don's Party 76. Mad Dog Morgan 76. Long Weekend 77. The Killing of Angel Street 81. *Careful He Might Hear You* 83. *My First Wife* 84. *Malcolm* 86. Sky Pirates 86. Comrades (GB) 86. Cry Freedom (GB) 87. Au Bout de l'Espoir (Fr.) 88. Sweet Revenge (US/Fr.) 90. Waiting 90. Rome Romeo (Fr.) 91. No Worries 93. The Lizard King (TV) 94. Country Life 94. Lust and Revenge 96, etc.

Hark, Tsui (1951–) (Xu Ke).
Vietnamese-born, Hong Kong-based director and producer.
The Butterfly Murders 79. We're Going to Eat You 80. Zu Warriors from the Magic Mountain 83. Shanghai Blues 84. Peking Opera Blues/Do Ma Dan 86. A Chinese Ghost Story/Qian Nu Youhun 87. A Better Tomorrow III 89. The Swordsman 90. A Chinese Ghost Story III 91. Once upon a Time in China/Wong Fei-hung 91. Swordsman II (co-w, p) 92. Once upon a Time in China II/Wong Fei-Hung II (wd) 92. Monkey King 93. The Iron Monkey (co-w, p) 93. Once Upon a Time in China III (wd) 93. Swordsman III (co-w, p) 93. The Lovers 95. The Blade 96. The Chinese Feast/ Gamyuk Muntong (co-w, d) 95. Double Team/The Colony (d) (US) 97. Knock Off (d) (US) 98, etc.
❝ The single most successful filmmaker in the history of Hong Kong cinema – Asia's answer to Howard Hawks, Irving Thalberg and Ben Hecht all rolled into one. – *Box Office*

Harker, Gordon (1885–1967).
British comic actor, the jutting-lipped cockney of many a 30s comedy.
The Ring (debut) 27. The Calendar 31. *Rome Express* 33. Friday the Thirteenth 33. Boys Will Be Boys 35. Millions 37. The Return of the Frog 38. *Inspector Hornleigh* 40. *Saloon Bar* 41. Warn That Man 43. 29 Acacia Avenue 45. Things Happen at Night 48. Her Favourite Husband 50. The Second Mate 50. Derby Day 52. Small Hotel 58. Left, Right and Centre 59, etc.

Harlan, Kenneth (1895–1967).
American leading man of the silent screen.
Cheerful Givers 17. The Hoodlum 19. The Beautiful and the Damned 22. The Broken Wing 23. Bobbed Hair 24. Twinkletoes 26. San Francisco 36. Paper Bullets 41. The Underdog 44, many others.

Harlan, Otis (1865–1940).
Tubby American character actor with long stage experience.
What Happened to Jones? 25. Lightnin' 26. Man to Man 31. The Hawk 32. Married in Haste 34. Diamond Jim 35. A Midsummer Night's Dream 35. Mr Boggs Steps Out 38, many others.

Harlan, Russell (1903–1974).
American cinematographer, former stuntman.
Hopalong Rides Again 37. Stagecoach War 40. The Kansan 43. *A Walk in the Sun* 45. *Red River* 48. The Big Sky 52. *Riot in Cell Block Eleven* 54. The Blackboard Jungle 55. This Could Be the Night 57. Witness for the Prosecution 57. Run Silent Run Deep 58. King Creole 58. The Spiral Road 62. Hatari 62. To Kill a Mockingbird 62. Quick Before It Melts 65. Tobruk 66. Darling Lili 70, etc.

Harlan, Veit (1899–1964).
German director of Nazi propaganda.
Kreutzer Sonata 36. Jew Süss 40. Der Grosse Konig 41. Opfergang 43. Die Blaue Stunde 52. The Third Sex 57, etc.

Harlin, Renny (1959–) (Lauri Harjula).
Finnish director, now in Hollywood. He married actress Geena Davis in 1993.
Born American (& w) 86. A Nightmare on Elm Street Part 4: The Dream Master 88. Prison 88. The Adventures of Ford Fairlane 90. Die Hard II 90. Cliffhanger (& p) 93. CutThroat Island 95. The Long Kiss Goodnight 96. Deep Blue Sea 99, etc.
❝ In Europe, film-making is perceived as an art form with marginal business possibilities, and in the US, film-making is a business with marginal artistic possibilities. – *R.H.*

Harline, Leigh (1907–1969).
American screen composer.
Snow White and the Seven Dwarfs (s) 37. Pinocchio (s) (AA) 39. His Girl Friday 40. The Pride of the Yankees (AAN) 42. You Were Never Lovelier (AAN) 42. The Sky's the Limit (AAN) 43. Johnny Come Lately (AAN) 43. The More the Merrier 43. Road to Utopia 45. The Farmer's Daughter 47. The Big Steal 49. Monkey Business 52. Broken Lance 54. The Wayward Bus 57. Ten North Frederick 58. Warlock 60. The Wonderful World of the Brothers Grimm (AAN) 62. Seven Faces of Dr Lao 63. Strange Bedfellows 64, etc.

Harling, Robert.
American director, screenwriter and playwright.
Steel Magnolias (w, oa) 89. Soapdish (co-w) 91. Evening Star (wd) 96.

Harling, W. Franke (1887–1958).
American composer.
One Hour with You 32. So Big 32. The Scarlet Empress 34. So Red the Rose 35. Souls at Sea 37. Stagecoach (co-m, AA) 39. Penny Serenade 41. The Lady Is Willing 42. Three Russian Girls (AAN) 44. The Bachelor's Daughter 46, etc.

Harlow, Jean (1911–1937) (Harlean Carpentier).
American leading lady and most sensational star of the early 30s, a wisecracking 'platinum blonde' with a private life to suit her public image. Her three husbands included MGM producer Paul Bern, who killed himself two months after their marriage in 1932, and cinematographer Hal Rosson (1933–35). Her lovers included actor William Powell.
Biographies: 1937, *Hollywood Comet* by Dentner Davies. 1964, *Harlow* by Irving Shulman.
■ Moran of the Marines 28. Double Whoopee (short) 29. The Unkissed Man 29. The Fugitive 29. Close Harmony 29. New York Nights 29. The Love Parade 29. Weak but Willing 29. Bacon Grabbers (short) 29. The Saturday Night Kid 29. The Love Parade 30. *Hell's Angels* 30. City Lights 31. The Secret Six 31. Iron Man 31. *Public Enemy* 31. Goldie 31. Platinum Blonde 31. Three Wise Girls 32. Beast of the City 32. *Red Headed Woman* 32. *Red Dust* 32. *Dinner at Eight* 33. Hold Your Man 33. *Bombshell* 33. The Girl from Missouri 34. Reckless 35. *China Seas* 35. Riffraff 35. Wife vs Secretary 35. Suzy 36. *Libelled Lady* 36. Personal Property 37. Saratoga 37.
✪ For combining a sophistication which she acted with an innocence which was her own. *Red Dust*.
❝ Would it shock you if I put on something more comfortable? – *Jean Harlow in Hell's Angels*
She didn't want to be famous. She wanted to be happy. – *Clark Gable*
A square shooter if ever there was one. – *Spencer Tracy*
She was not a good actress, not even by Hollywood standards, but she is delightful to watch today because the spirit of her era all but shines from her eyes. – *William Redfield*
Last lines of *Dinner at Eight*:
Jean Harlow: 'You know, the other day I read a book. It said that machinery is going to take the place of every profession.'
Marie Dressler: 'Oh, my dear: that's something you'll *never* have to worry about!'

Harlow, John (1896–).
British writer-director, former music-hall performer.
Spellbound (d) 40. Candles at Nine (d) 43. Meet Sexton Blake (d) 44. The Agitator (d) 45. Appointment with Crime (wd) 46. Green Fingers (wd) 47. *While I Live*/Dream of Olwen (wd) 48. Old Mother Riley's New Venture (d) 49. Those People Next Door (d) 52. Dangerous Cargo 54, etc.

Harman, Hugh (1903–1982).
American animator who in the early 30s, with Rudolph Ising, formed Harman-Ising and made some brilliantly inventive cartoons for MGM. Later originated Merrie Melodies and Looney Tunes, and was cited by the Nobel Peace jury for *Peace on Earth* (1940).

Harmon, Mark (1951–).
Competent American leading man, difficult to distinguish from several others.
Eleanor and Franklin: the White House Years (TV) 77. Centennial 78. Comes a Horseman 78. Beyond the Poseidon Adventure 79. *The Dream Merchants* (TV) 80. Summer School 87. The Presidio 88. Worth Winning 89. Fourth Story (TV) 90. Till There Was You 91. Cold Heaven 92. Wyatt Earp 94. Magic in the Water 95. Casualties 97. Fear and Loathing in Las Vegas 98. Teen Monster 99, etc.
TV series: Flamingo Road 81–82.

Harmon, Robert (1953–).
American director.
The Hitcher 86. Nowhere to Run 93. Gotti (TV) 96, etc.

Harolde, Ralf (1899–1974) (R. H. Wigger).
American supporting actor often seen as thin-lipped crook.
Night Nurse 32. A Tale of Two Cities 35. Horror Island 41. Baby Face Morgan 42. Farewell My Lovely (as the doctor) 44. Alaska Patrol (last film) 51, many others.

Harper, Gerald (1929–).
Aristocratic-looking British actor familiar on TV as *Adam Adamant* and *Hadleigh*.
The Admirable Crichton 57. A Night to Remember 58. The League of Gentlemen 59. The Punch and Judy Man 62. The Lady Vanishes 79, etc.

Harper, Jessica (1949–).
American leading lady.
Inserts 76. Suspiria 77. The Evictors 79. Shock Treatment 81. Pennies from Heaven 81. My Favorite Year 82. Big Man on Campus 89. Safe 95, etc.

Harper, Tess (1950–) (Tessie Jean Washam).
American actress.
Amityville: The Demon/Amityville 3-D 83. Tender Mercies 83. Flashpoint 84. Crimes of the Heart (AAN) 86. Ishtar 87. Far North 88. Her Alibi 89. Criminal Law 89. Daddy's Dying . . . Who's Got the Will? 90. My Heroes Have Always Been Cowboys 91. The Man in the Moon 91. My New Gun 92. Christy (TV) 94. Children of Fury (TV) 94. The Road to Galveston (TV) 96. The Jackal 97, etc.

Harper, Valerie (1940–).
American leading comedy actress, a star of TV, a former dancer.
The Ones in Between 72. Freebie and the Bean 74. Thursday's Game (TV) 74. Night Terror (TV) 77. The Last Married Couple in America 79. Blame It on Rio 84. Drop-out Mother (TV) 88, etc.
TV series: *The Mary Tyler Moore Show* 70–73. *Rhoda* 74–78. Valerie 86–87.

Harrelson, Woody (1961–).
American leading actor, best known for his role as Woody Boyd in the TV series *Cheers*. He has been romantically linked with Penelope Ann Miller, Brooke Shields and Glenn Close. Married Laura Louie, with whom he has two daughters, in 1998.
Wildcats 86. Casualties of War 89. Ted and Venus 91. White Men Can't Jump 92. Indecent Proposal 93. The Cowboy Way 94. *Natural Born Killers* 94. Money Train 95. The Sunchaser 96. Kingpin 96. *The People vs Larry Flynt* (AAN) 96. Welcome to Sarajevo 97. Wag the Dog 97. Palmetto 98. The Hi-Lo Country 98. The Thin Red Line 98, etc.
TV series: Cheers 85–92.

Harrer, Heinrich (1912–).
Austrian explorer and mountaineer, author of *Seven Years in Tibet*, telling how he escaped British internment to enter Tibet and reach the holy city of Lhasa in the late 40s. In the film of the book, directed by Jean-Jacques Annaud in 1997, he was played by Brad Pitt. Born in Hüttenberg, he was an Olympic skier, and later went on expeditions to the Amazon, the Himalayas and Africa. Revelations that he had also been a member of the Nazi Party came soon after the film's release.

Harrigan, William (1894–1966).
American general-purpose actor of the 30s and 40s.
On the Level 17. Cabaret 27. Nix on Dames 27. Born Reckless 30. Pick Up 33. The Invisible Man 33. G Men 35. The Silk Hat Kid 35. Federal Bullets 37. Hawaii Calls 38. Back Door to Heaven 39. The Farmer's Daughter 47. Flying Leathernecks 51. Street of Sinners 55, etc.

Harrington, Curtis (1928–).
American director who made experimental shorts before graduating to features.
■ Night Tide 63. Voyage to a Prehistoric Planet 64. Queen of Blood 66. Games 67. How Awful About Allan (TV) 70. What's the Matter with Helen? 71. Who Slew Auntie Roo? 73. The Cat Creature (TV) 73. Killer Bees (TV) 74. The Dead Don't Die (TV) 74. The Killing Kind 76. Ruby 77. Devil Dog (TV) 78. Mata Hari 85.

Harris, Barbara (1935–).
American leading lady.
A Thousand Clowns 65. Oh Dad . . . 66. Plaza Suite 71. Who Is Harry Kellerman . . . ? (AAN) 71. The War between Men and Women 72. Family Plot 76. Freaky Friday 77. Movie Movie 78. The Seduction of Joe Tynan 79. Second Hand Hearts 80. Night Magic 85. Peggy Sue Got Married 86. Dirty Rotten Scoundrels 88. Grosse Pointe Blanke 97, etc.

Harris, Damian (1960–).
British director and screenwriter, the son of actor Richard Harris.
Otley (a) 68. The Rachel Papers (wd) 89. Deceived (d) 91. Bad Company 95.

Harris, Danielle (1976–).
American actress.
Halloween Four: The Return of Michael Myers 88. Halloween Five: The Revenge of Michael Myers 89. Marked for Death 90. The Last Boy Scout 91. Don't Tell Mom the Babysitter's Dead 91. City Slickers 91. Free Willy 93. Daylight 96. Back to Back 96, etc.
TV series: Roseanne 92–93.

Harris, Ed (1950–).
Dour American leading actor, from the stage. Born in Tenafly, New Jersey, he studied briefly at Columbia University and the University of Oklahoma, leaving to act; he then studied at the California Institute of the Arts, continuing to act on stage and in some forgettable films until he broke through to wider acclaim with the role of John Glenn in *The Right Stuff*. Married actress Amy Madigan.
Coma 77. Zombies 80. Borderline 80. Knightriders 81. Dream On 81. Creepshow 82. The Right Stuff 83. Under Fire 83. Swing Shift 84. Places in the Heart 84. Sweet Dreams 85. Alamo Bay 85. A Flash of Green 85. The Last Innocent Man 87. Walker 87. To Kill a Priest 89. Jackknife 89. The Abyss 89. State of Grace 90. Paris Trout 91. Glengarry Glen Ross 92. The Firm 93. Needful Things 93. China Moon 94. Milk Money 94. Just Cause 95. Riders of the Purple Sage (TV) 96. Apollo 13 (AAN) 95. Nixon 95. Eye for an Eye 95. The Rock 96. Absolute Power 97. *The Truman Show* 98. Stepmom 98, etc.

Harris, Edna Mae (1910–1997).
American actress and singer, mainly in movies made for black audiences of the 40s. Born in Harlem, she appeared on Broadway, sang with the bands of Noble Sissle, Benny Carter and Lucky Millinder, was featured on some soundies, and was mistress of ceremonies at Harlem's Apollo Theater in the mid-40s.
The Green Pastures 36. Bullets or Ballots 36. The Garden of Allah 36. Spirit of Youth 38. Paradise in Harlem 39. The Notorious Elinor Lee 39. Murder on Lennox Avenue 41. Sunday Sinners 41. Tall, Tan and Terrific 46, etc.

Harris, Frank (1856–1931).
English journalist and writer, an influential editor of magazines and newspapers, but notorious for his boastful tales of his own life and many lovers. He was played by Jack Lemmon in *Cowboy*, a film based on *On the Trail*, an account of his time in America, where he lived in the 1870s.

Harris, Georgie (1898–1986).
Diminutive (4 ft 9 ins) English comic actor, from musical comedy and vaudeville. Born in Liverpool, he worked in America in the 20s, including a stint as a Keystone Kop, before returning to Britain, where he quit films in the late 30s to become a successful businessman.
Lights of Old Broadway (US) 25. The Shamrock Handicap (US) 26. Three Bad Men (US) 26. The Floating College (US) 28. Don't Be a Dummy 32. I Adore You 33. Radio Parade of 1935 34. Captain Bill 35. Happy Days Are Here Again 36. Boys Will Be Girls 37. Saturday Night Revue 37. The Reverse Be My Lot 38, etc.

Harris, Jack (1905–1971).
British editor.
The Sleeping Cardinal 31. The Wandering Jew 33. The Face at the Window 39. Let the People Sing 42. This Happy Breed 44. Blithe Spirit 45. Brief Encounter 45. Great Expectations 46. Oliver Twist 48. Where No Vultures Fly 51. The Crimson Pirate 53. Indiscreet 58. The Sundowners 60. Billy Budd 62. The Chalk Garden 64. Three Sisters 70, many others.

Harris, James B. (1928–).
American producer and director, associated with director Stanley Kubrick.
The Killing 56. Paths of Glory 57. Lolita 62. The Bedford Incident (& d) 65. Some Call It Loving (& d) 71. Telefon 77. Fast Walking (& wd) 82. Cop (& wd) 88. Boiling Point (wd) 93, etc.

Harris, Jared (1961–).
British actor, the son of Richard Harris.
The Rachel Papers 89. The Public Eye 92. The Last of the Mohicans 92. Far and Away 92. Nadja 94. Natural Born Killers 94. Tall Tale: The Unbelievable Adventures of Pecos Bill 95. I Shot Andy Warhol (as Warhol) 96. Father's Day 96. Sunday 97. Lost in Space 98. B. Monkey 98. Happiness 98. Lulu on the Bridge 98, etc.

Harris, Jed (1900–1979) (Jacob Horowitz).
American theatrical impresario of the 30s and 40s, notorious for toughness and rudeness; lampooned in films *Twentieth Century* and *The Saxon Charm*. He was the model for both Walt Disney's Big Bad Wolf and Laurence Olivier's Richard III. Joseph Losey began as his assistant.
❝ The most loathsome man I'd ever met. – *Laurence Olivier*
Fresh as poison ivy. – *Edna Ferber*
When I die, I want to be cremated and have my ashes thrown in Jed Harris's face. – *George S. Kaufman*

Harris, Joel Chandler (1848–1908).
American journalist and story writer who created the characters of Uncle Remus and Brer Rabbit, filmed by Disney in *Song of the South*.

Harris, Jonathan (1914–).
American character actor, popular in prissy roles in TV series *The Third Man* 59–61, *The Bill Dana Show* 63–64, *Lost in Space* 65–68.
Botany Bay 54. The Big Fisherman 59. Pinocchio and the Emperor of the Night (voice) 87. Happily Ever After 90, etc.

Harris, Julie (1925–).
American stage actress.
The Member of the Wedding (AAN) 53. East of Eden 55. I Am a Camera 56. The Truth about Women 56. Sally's Irish Rogue 60. Requiem for a Heavyweight 62. *The Haunting* 63. Harper 66. You're a Big Boy Now 66. *Reflections in a Golden Eye* 67. The Split 68. The House on Greenapple Road (TV) 69. How Awful about Allan (TV) 70. The People Next Door 70. Home for the Holidays (TV) 72. The Greatest Gift (TV) 74. The Hiding Place 75. Voyage of the Damned 76. The Bell Jar 79. Backstairs at the White House (TV) 79. Bronte 83. Leaving Home 86. Gorillas in the Mist 88. The Woman He Loved (TV) 88. Too Good to Be True (TV) 88. Single Women, Married Men (TV) 89. The Dark Half (TV) 91. Paris Trout 91. Housesitter 92. The Dark Half 93. When Love Kills (TV) 93. *Lucifer's Child* (TV) 95. Carried Away 96. Passaggio per il Paradiso 96, etc.
TV series: Thicker than Water 73. The Family Holvak 76. Knots Landing 81–87.

Harris, Julie.
British costume designer.
The Naked Edge 61. The Fast Lady 62. The Chalk Garden 64. Darling 65. The Wrong Box 65. Casino Royale 67. Goodbye Mr Chips 69. Live and Let Die 73. Rollerball 74. The Slipper and the Rose 76. Prostitute 80. The Hound of the Baskervilles 83, etc.

Harris, Julius W.
American character actor.
Slaves 69. Incident in San Francisco (TV) 71. Shaft's Big Score 73. A Cry for Help (TV) 75. King Kong 76. Rich Man Poor Man (TV) 76. Victory

at Entebbe (as Idi Amin) (TV) 76. Islands in the Stream 77. Looking for Mr Goodbar 77. Ring of Passion (TV) 78. The First Family 80. Missing Pieces (TV) 83. Crimewave 85. Prayer of the Rollerboys 91. Harley Davidson and the Marlboro Man 91. Maniac Cop 3: Badge of Silence 92. Shrunken Heads 94, etc.

Harris, Mildred (1901–1944).
American leading lady of the silent era, first wife of Charles Chaplin.
Intolerance 15. Borrowed Clothes 18. Fool's Paradise 21. Fog 23. Unmarried Wives 24. My Neighbour's Wife 25. The Mystery Club 26. The Show Girl 27. Sea Fury 29. No No Nanette 30. Lady Tubbs 35. Reap the Wild Wind 42. The Story of Dr Wassell 44, etc.

Harris, Neil Patrick (1974–).
American actor, in films from his early teens, best known for his role as Doogie Howser in the TV sitcom *Doogie Howser, M.D.* 89–93.
Clara's Heart 88. Purple People Eater 88. Home Fires Burning (TV) 89. The Cold Sassy Tree (TV) 89. Stranger in the Family (TV) 91. My Antonia (TV) 95. The Animal Room 95. Starship Troopers 97. The Proposition/Tempting Fate 98, etc.

Harris, Phil (1904–1995).
American bandleader and comic singer, best known for providing the voice of Baloo the bear in Disney's animated *The Jungle Book* 67. Married actress Alice Faye.
Melody Cruise 33. Man about Town 39. Buck Benny Rides Again 40. Here Comes the Groom 51. The Glenn Miller Story 54. The High and the Mighty 54. Anything Goes 56. The Wheeler Dealers 63. The Cool Ones 67. Robin Hood (voice) 73. Rock-a-Doodle (voice) 90, etc.

Harris, Richard (1932–).
Gaunt Irish leading actor. Usually cast as a rebel, he tries to match the part in real life.
Alive and Kicking 58. Shake Hands with the Devil 59. The Wreck of the Mary Deare 59. A Terrible Beauty 60. All Night Long 61. The Long the Short and the Tall 61. The Guns of Navarone 61. *Mutiny on the Bounty* 62. *This Sporting Life* (AAN) 63. The Red Desert 64. I Tre Volti 64. Major Dundee 65. The Heroes of Telemark 65. The Bible 66. Hawaii 66. Caprice 66. *Camelot* (as King Arthur) 67. The Molly Maguires 69. A Man Called Horse 69. Bloomfield (& d) 70. *Cromwell* (title role) 70. The Snow Goose (TV) 71. Man in the Wilderness 71. The Deadly Trackers 73. 99 44/100 Dead 74. Juggernaut 75. Robin and Marian 76. The Return of a Man Called Horse 76. Echoes of a Summer 76. Gulliver's Travels 76. The Cassandra Crossing 77. Orca – Killer Whale 77. Golden Rendezvous 77. The Wild Geese 78. Game for Vultures 79. The Last Word 79. The Revengers 79. Your Ticket Is No Longer Valid 79. Highpoint 80. Tarzan the Ape Man 81. Triumphs of a Man Called Horse 82. Martin's Day 84. The Return 88. Mack the Knife 89. King of the Wind 89. *The Field* (AAN) 90. Patriot Games 92. *Unforgiven* 92. Silent Tongue 93. The Bible: Abraham (TV) 93. Wrestling Ernest Hemingway 93. Cry the Beloved Country 95. Trojan Eddie 96. The Hunchback of Notre Dame (TV) 97. The Royal Way 97. The Barber of Siberia 98. To Walk with Lions 99, etc.
❝ He's something of a fuck-up, no question. – *Charlton Heston*
He hauls his surly carcass from movie to movie, being dismembered. I'd just as soon wait till he's finished. – *Pauline Kael*

Harris, Richard A.
American editor.
Downhill Racer 69. The Candidate (co-ed) 72. Catch My Soul 74. Smile 75. The Bad News Bears 76. Semi-Tough 77. The Bad News Bears Go to Japan 78. The Island 80. Mommie Dearest 81. The Chosen 81. The Survivors 83. Fletch 85. The Golden Child 86. The Couch Trip 88. Fletch Lives 89. My Boyfriend's Back (TV) 90. LA Story 91. The Bodyguard (co-ed) 92. True Lies 94. Titantic (AA) 97, etc.

Harris, Robert (1900–1995).
British classical actor who has played occasional film roles. Educated at Oxford University, he studied acting at RADA and was on stage from 1923.
How He Lied to Her Husband 31. The Life and Death of Colonel Blimp 43. The Bad Lord Byron 48. That Lady 55. Oscar Wilde 60. Decline and Fall 68, etc.

Harris, Robert H. (1911–1981).
American character actor, usually beaky, officious and unsympathetic.
Bundle of Joy 56. How to Make a Monster 58. America America 63. Mirage 65. Valley of the Dolls 67, etc.
TV series: The Goldbergs 56. Court of Last Resort 57–60.

Harris, Rosemary (1930–).
British leading lady, chiefly on stage.
Beau Brummell 54. The Shiralee 55. A Flea in Her Ear 68. Holocaust (TV) 77. The Boys from Brazil 78. The Chisholms (TV) 78. Crossing Delancey 88. The Bridge 91. Tom and Viv (AAN) 93. Hamlet 96, etc.

Harris, Theresa (1910–1985).
American actress.
Morocco 30. Blood Money 33. Morning Glory 33. Jezebel 38. Santa Fe Trail 40. Blossoms in the Dust 40. I Walked with a Zombie 43. Three Little Girls in Blue 46. Neptune's Daughter 49. And Baby Makes Three 50. The Company She Keeps 51, many others.

Harris, Vernon (c. 1910–).
British screenwriter. He also scripted the 1938 BBC radio series *Band Waggon* with Arthur Askey and Richard Murdoch.
Joy Ride (story) 35. Improper Duchess 36. Tropical Trouble 36. Albert RN (co-w) 53. The Sea Shall Not Have Them (co-w) 55. Reach for the Sky 56. Ferry to Hong Kong 57. The Admirable Crichton 57. Light up the Sky 61. Oliver! (AAN) 68. Paul and Michelle (co-w) 75, etc.

Harrison, Doane (c. 1894–1968).
American editor.
Youth and Adventure 25. Celebrity 28. The Spieler 29. Her Man 30. 13 Hours by Air 36. Midnight 39. Hold Back the Dawn 41. The Major and the Minor 42. Five Graves to Cairo 43. The Uninvited 44. The Lost Weekend 45. A Foreign Affair 48. Branded 50, etc.
Later associate producer for Billy Wilder.

Harrison, George (1943–).
English composer, musician and producer. Formerly guitarist for The Beatles, he runs the British production company HandMade Films with Denis O'Brien. In 1997, *Business Age* estimated his personal fortune at £105m.
AS COMPOSER: Shanghai Surprise 86.
AS PERFORMER: A Hard Day's Night 64. Help 65. Magical Mystery Tour 67. The Concert for Bangladesh (concert) 72. The Rutles (TV) 78. Life of Brian 79, etc.
AS PRODUCER: Life of Brian 79. Time Bandits 81. Privates on Parade 83. Water 86. Withnail and I 87. Track 29 88. Powwow Highway 89. How to Get Ahead in Advertising 89. Cold Dog Soup 90. Nuns on the Run 90. The Raggedy Rawney 90, etc.
❝ I don't really think the film business is all it's cracked up to be . . . It's still much better being a guitar player. – G.H.

Harrison, Gregory (1950–).
American actor.
Trilogy of Terror (TV) 75. The Gathering (TV) 77. For Ladies Only 81. Razorback (Aus.) 84. Seduced (TV) 85. Oceans of Fire 86. The Hasty Heart 86. North Shore 87. Dangerous Pursuit 89. Bare Essentials (TV) 91. Body Chemistry II: Voice of a Stranger 91. Duplicates 92. Cadillac Girl 93. Hard Evidence 94. It's My Party 95, etc.
TV series: Logan's Run 77–78. Centennial 78–79. Trapper John, M.D. 79–86. Falcon Crest 89–90. The Family Man 90–91. True Detectives 90–91.

Harrison, Jim.
American novelist, poet and screenwriter.
Revenge (oa, co-w) 89. Cold Feet 89. Legends of the Fall (oa) 94. Wolf (co-w) 94. Carried Away (from his novel *Farmer*) 95. Dalva (oa) (TV) 95, etc.

Harrison, Joan (1911–1994).
British writer-producer, assistant for many years to Alfred Hitchcock. She was married to author Eric Ambler.
Jamaica Inn (w) 39. Rebecca (co-w, AAN) 40. Foreign Correspondent (co-w, AAN) 40. Suspicion (w) 41. Saboteur (w) 42. Dark Waters (w) 44. Phantom Lady (p) 44. Uncle Harry (p) 45. Ride the Pink Horse (p) 47. Circle of Danger (p) 51, etc.
TV series: *Alfred Hitchcock Presents* (p) 55–63.

Harrison, Kathleen (1892–1995).
British character actress, usually seen as a cockney but born in Lancashire. On stage from 1926; films made her an amiable, slightly dithery but warm-hearted national figure.
Our Boys 15. Hobson's Choice 31. The Ghoul 33. Broken Blossoms 36. Night Must Fall (US) 37. *Bank Holiday* 38. The Outsider 39. *The Ghost Train* 41. Kipps 41. *In Which We Serve* 42. Dear Octopus 43. Great Day 45. *Holiday Camp* 47. *The Winslow Boy* 48. Bond Street 48. Oliver Twist 48. *Here Come the Huggetts* (and ensuing series) 49–52. Waterfront 50. Scrooge 51. Pickwick Papers 52. *Turn the Key Softly* 53. Cast a Dark Shadow 54. Where There's a Will 54. Lilacs in the Spring 54. *All for Mary* 55. Home and Away 56. A Cry from the Streets 58. Alive and Kicking 58. Mrs Gibbons' Boys 62. West Eleven 63. Lock Up Your Daughters 69, many others.

Harrison, Linda (1945–).
American leading lady, briefly evident at Twentieth Century-Fox: married Richard Zanuck.
Way Way Out 66. A Guide for the Married Man 67. Planet of the Apes 67. Airport 75 75.
TV series: Bracken's World 69–70.

Harrison, Philip.
English production designer in Hollywood, associated with the films of John BADHAM. He studied at the Royal College of Art.
How I Won the War 67. The Ritz 76. Blue Thunder 83. Never Say Never Again 83. The Razor's Edge 84. Short Circuit 86. White Nights 85. 52 Pick Up 86. Stakeout 87. Mississippi Burning 88. Bird on a Wire 90. The Hard Way 91. Point of No Return 93. Timecop 94. Nick of Time 95. Sudden Death 95. The Relic 97. Spawn 97, etc.

Harrison, Sir Rex (1908–1990) (Reginald Carey Harrison).
Debonair British leading actor of pleasant if limited range, on stage since 1924; films only occasionally gave him the right material. Born in Huyton, Lancashire, he joined the Liverpool Repertory Company at the age of 16, began in films in 1929, and made his London stage debut in 1930. In 1936, after an unsuccessful screen test for Warner's, he was signed to an exclusive contract with Alexander KORDA, following it with his stage performance in *French without Tears* which established him as a star and provided him with a type – elegant and charming – that he played for most of his career. In the mid-40s he went to Hollywood under contract to Twentieth Century-Fox, but his stay there came to a sudden end after a scandal resulting from his affair with actress Carole LANDIS, which ended with her suicide. His best screen performances were as Professor Henry Higgins in *My Fair Lady* (repeating his stage success), Adolphus Cusins in *Major Barbara*, Charles Condomine in *Blithe Spirit*, and Vivian Kenway in *The Rake's Progess*. His six wives included Lilli PALMER (1942–57), Kay KENDALL (1957–59), whom he married knowing that she was dying from leukaemia, a fact he kept from her, and Rachel ROBERTS (1962–71). He was knighted in 1989.
Autobiographies: 1974, *Rex*. 1991, *A Damned Serious Business: My Life in Comedy*.
Biographies: 1985, *Rex Harrison* by Allen Eyles; 1991, *Rex Harrison* by Nicholas Wapshott; 1992, *Rex Harrison* by Alexander Walker; 1998, *The Incomparable Rex* by Patrick Garland.
■ The Great Game 30. The School for Scandal 30. All at Sea 34. Get Your Man 34. Leave It to Blanche 35. Men Are Not Gods 36. *Storm in a Teacup* 37. School for Husbands 37. St Martin's Lane 38. The Citadel 38. Over the Moon 39. The Silent Battle 39. Ten Days in Paris 39. *Night Train to Munich* 40. *Major Barbara* 40. I Live in Grosvenor Square 45. *Blithe Spirit* 45. *The Rake's Progress* 46. Anna and the King of Siam (US) 46. The Ghost and Mrs Muir (US) 47. The Foxes of Harrow (US) 47. Unfaithfully Yours (US) 48. Escape 48. The Long Dark Hall 51. The Fourposter (US) 52. King Richard and the Crusaders (as Saladin) (US) 54. The Constant Husband 55. The Reluctant Debutante (US) 58. Midnight Lace (US) 60. The Happy Thieves (US) 62. Cleopatra (US) (AAN) 62. *My Fair Lady* (AA) (US) 64. The Yellow Rolls-Royce 64. The Agony and the Ecstasy (US) (as a medieval pope) 65. The Honey Pot (US) 67. Doctor Dolittle (US) 67. A Flea in Her Ear (US/Fr.) 68. Staircase 69. Don Quixote (TV) 72. The Prince and the Pauper 77. The Fifth Musketeer 77. Ashanti 78. Shalimar 78. Crossed Swords 78. A Time to Die 79.
❝ I'm now at the age where I've got to prove that I'm just as good as I never was. – *R.H., 1980*
It takes a long time to learn to treat the camera as a friend and confidant, which finally you have to do if you're to become a good film actor. – *R.H.*
He exudes that combination of the aggressor and the injured, the schoolmaster and the truant, which adds up in Britain (and elsewhere) to erotic infallibility. – *Kenneth Tynan*
What has he ever done for England, except live abroad, refuse to pay his taxes, and call everyone a shit? – *Harold French*
If you weren't the finest light-comedy actor in the world next to me, you'd be good for only one thing – selling cars in Great Portland Street – *Noel Coward to R.H.*
A limited man, rather reppy, whose youthful good looks and some luck with the parts ensured a profitable career. – *Kenneth Williams*
Famous line (*Blithe Spirit*): 'If you're trying to compile an inventory of my sex life, I feel it only fair to warn you that you've omitted several episodes. I shall consult my diary and give you a complete list after lunch.'

Harrison, Richard.
American strongman in Italian spectaculars.
Executioner on the High Seas 61. Invincible Gladiator 61. Perseus among the Monsters 63. Spy Killers 65. Adventures of the Bengal Lancers 65. Vengeance 68. Commando Attack 70. The Way of the Godfather 73. Thirty-Six Hours of Hell 77. Fireback 78. Blood Debts 83. His Name Was King 85. Ninja Commandments 87. Hands of Death 88. Ninja Strike Force 88. The Channeler 89. Ninja Powerforce 90. Rescue Force 90. The Alien Within 91. Highway to Hell 91. Angel Eyes 93, etc.

Harrison Marks, George (*–1997).
English director of soft porn and limited talent, who deserves a footnote in the history of British cinema because of the ground-breaking success of his film *Naked as Nature Intended*, ostensibly about nudism but made as an exercise in exploitation, which ran for two years in London. A former music-hall comedian, he first specialized in air-brushed glamour photography for men's magazines. His still and moving pictures owed much to his mentor and lover, actress and nude model Pamela GREEN. Apart from his listed features, he made comedy shorts for children as well as several hundred shorts and, later, videos for the sex film market. From the mid-80s he specialized in producing a magazine, *Kane*, and videos devoted to spanking.
Naked as Nature Intended 61. The Naked World of Harrison Marks 65. Pattern of Evil 67. The Nine Ages of Nakedness 69. Come Play with Me 77.
❝ Marks actually led the kind of life that many assume to be concomitant with 'smut peddling': he was twice prosecuted for sending obscene materials through the post; he was bankrupted; and he survived four relationships (three marriages and an eight-year affair with his model Pamela Green) and five years of alcoholism. – *David McGillivray, Doing Rude Things*

Harrold, Kathryn (1950–).
American leading lady.
Yes Giorgio 82. The Sender 82. Into the Night 84. Raw Deal 86. Someone to Love 87. Deadly Desire 91. The Companion 94, etc.
TV series: MacGruder and Loud 85. The Bronx Zoo 87–88.

Harron, Mary.
British screenwriter and director.
I Shot Andy Warhol (wd) 96.

Harron, Robert (Bobby) (1894–1920).
American juvenile lead who joined D. W. Griffith's company almost from school; died in shooting accident.
Dr Skinum 07. Bobby's Kodak 08. Man's Genesis

12. The Birth of a Nation 15. Intolerance 16. Hearts of the World 18. True Heart Susie 19. Darling Mine 21, many others.

Harrow, Lisa (1943–).
New Zealand leading actress.
The Devil Is a Woman (It.) 75. It Shouldn't Happen to a Vet (GB) 76. The Final Conflict (US) 81. Under Capricorn (Aus.) 82. Shaker Run 85. The Last Days of Chez Nous (Aus.) 92. That Eye, the Sky (Aus.) 94. Sunday 97, etc.
TV series: Kavanagh QC 95–96.

Harry, Debbie (1954–) (Deborah Harry).
American actress and singer. She was the lead singer of the 70s rock band Blondie.
Roadie 80. Union City 81. Videodrome 83. The Foreigner 84. Forever Lulu 87. Hairspray 88. Satisfaction 88. New York Stories 89. Tales from the Darkside: The Movie 90. Intimate Stranger 91. After Midnight 93. Heavy 95. Drop Dead Rock 96. Six Ways to Sunday 98, etc.
❝ I am now a shopaholic and I shop 'til I drop. It's more expensive than taking drugs but it's legal and fun. – *D.H.*

Harryhausen, Ray (1920–).
American trick film specialist and model-maker; invented 'Superdynamation'.
Book: 1972, *Film Fantasy Scrapbook*.
Mighty Joe Young 49. It Came from Beneath the Sea 52. Twenty Million Miles to Earth 57. The Three Worlds of Gulliver 60. *Jason and the Argonauts* 63. The First Men in the Moon 64. One Million Years BC 66. The Valley of Gwangi 69. The Golden Voyage of Sinbad 73. Sinbad and the Eye of the Tiger 77, etc.

Hart, Dolores (1938–) (D. Hicks).
American lady of a few films in the late 50s. Retired to become a nun.
Loving You 56. Wild is the Wind 57. Lonelyhearts 59. Sail a Crooked Ship 60. Lisa 62, etc.

Hart, Dorothy (1923–).
American second lead of the 50s.
Naked City 47. Take One False Step 49. Undertow 49. I Was a Communist for the FBI 51. Tarzan's Savage Fury 52, etc.

Hart, Harvey (1928–1989).
Canadian director, from TV, latterly in Hollywood.
■ Dark Intruder 65. Bus Riley's Back in Town 65. Sullivan's Empire 67. The Sweet Ride 68. The Young Lawyers (TV) 69. Fortune and Men's Eyes 71. The Pyx 73. Panic on the 5.22 (TV) 74. Can Ellen Be Saved? (TV) 74. Murder or Mercy? (TV) 74. Shoot 77. Goldenrod (TV) 77. Prince of Central Park (TV) 77. W.E.B. (TV) 78. Captains Courageous (TV) 78. Standing Tall (TV) 78. Like Normal People (TV) 79. The Aliens Are Coming (TV) 79. East of Eden (TV) 81. The High Country 81. Massarati and the Brain (TV) 82. Born Beautiful (TV) 82. Getting Even 83. Master of the Game (TV) 84. Reckless Disregard (TV) 85. Beverly Hills Madam (TV) 86. Stone Fox (TV) 87. Murder Sees the Light (TV) 87. Passion and Paradise (TV) 89.

Hart, Ian (1964–).
English leading actor.
No Surrender 85. Backbeat (as John Lennon) 94. The Englishman Who Went up a Hill but Came Down a Mountain 95. Clockwork Mice 95. *Land and Freedom* 95. Loved Up (TV) 95. Nothing Personal 95. The Englishman Who Went up a Hill but Came down a Mountain 95. Michael Collins 96. Mojo 97. The Butcher Boy 98. Frogs for Snakes 98. B. Monkey 98. Enemy of the State 98, etc.

Hart, Lorenz (1895–1943).
American lyricist, mostly with Richard Rodgers as composer. Shows filmed include *On Your Toes, Pal Joey, The Boys from Syracuse*. Played by Mickey Rooney in *Words and Music*.

Hart, Moss (1904–1961).
American playwright (usually in collaboration with George S. KAUFMAN) and theatrical producer. Wrote occasional screenplays. Married actress Kitty CARLISLE.
Autobiography: 1958, *Act One* (filmed 1963).
Once in a Lifetime (oa) 32. You Can't Take It With You (oa) 38. *The Man Who Came to Dinner* (oa) 41. George Washington Slept Here (oa) 42. Lady in the Dark (oa) 44. Winged Victory (w) 44. *Gentleman's Agreement* (AANw) 47. Hans Christian Andersen (w) 52. A Star Is Born (w) 54. Prince of Players (w) 55, etc.

Hart, Richard (1915–1951).
American leading man with a very brief Hollywood career.
■ Green Dolphin Street 47. Desire Me 47. B.F.'s Daughter 48. The Black Book 49.

Hart, William S. (1870–1946).
Mature, solemn-faced hero of innumerable silent westerns; one of the key performers of the 20s. The initial 'S' is variously reputed to have stood for 'Shakespeare' and 'Surrey'.
Autobiography: 1929, *My Life East and West*.
The Disciple 15. The Captive God 16. The Return of Draw Egan 16. Hell's Hinges 17. Truthful Tolliver 17. Blue Blazes Rawden 18. Selfish Yates 18. Riddle Gawne 18. The Border Wireless 18. Wagon Tracks 18. The Poppy Girl's Husband 19. The Toll Gate 20. Sand 20. Cradle of Courage 20. O'Malley of the Mounted 21. White Oak 21. Travellin' On 22. Hollywood 23. Wild Bill Hickok 23. Singer Jim McKee 24. *Tumbleweeds* 25, many others.
❝ His frequently austere look breathed dedication to the West as a subject suited for all the artistic possibilities of cinema. – *Allen Eyles*

Harte, Bret (1836–1902) (Francis Brett Harte).
American short-story writer who wandered the old west. Works filmed include *The Outcasts of Poker Flat, Tennessee's Partner*.

Hartford-Davis, Robert (1923–1977).
British producer-director, in films from 1939.
That Kind of Girl 62. The Yellow Teddybears 63. Saturday Night Out 63. Black Torment 64. Gonks Go Beat 65. The Sandwich Man 66. Corruption 68. The Smashing Bird I Used to Know 69. The Fiend 71. Black Gunn (US) 72. The Take (US) 74, etc.

Hartl, Karl (1899–1978).
Austrian director.
The Doomed Battalion 31. F.P.1 32. Gold 34. The Gypsy Baron 35. The Man Who Was Sherlock Holmes 37. Whom the Gods Love 42. The Angel with the Trumpet 48. The Wonder Kid 51. Journey into the Past 54. Mozart 55. Love Is Red 57, many others. Also scenarist for many of the above.

Hartley, Hal (1959–).
American director, screenwriter and producer of quirky low-budget movies.
The Unbelievable Truth 90. Trust 91. Surviving Desire (TV) 92. Simple Men 92. Amateur 94. Flirt 95. Henry Fool 97, etc.

Hartley, L. P. (1895–1972) (Leslie Poles Hartley).
English novelist and short story writer of middle-class emotional repression. Born in Whittlesey, Cambridgeshire, he studied modern history at Oxford, and was a literary journalist before turning to fiction.
Biography: 1996, *Foreign Country: The Life of L. P. Hartley* by Adrian Wright.
The Go-Between (oa) 71. The Hireling (oa) 73.
❝ The past is another country. They do things differently there. – *L.P.H.*
After 70, it seems to me, there is no further need for self-discipline (e.g. avoiding the gin-bottle), or any form of self-improvement. – *L.P.H.*

Hartley, Mariette (1940–).
Under-used leading lady who makes an occasional impression.
Ride the High Country 62. Drums of Africa 63. Marooned 67. Barquero 70. The Return of Count Yorga 71. Earth II (TV) 71. Sandcastles (TV) 72. Genesis II (TV) 73. The Killer Who Wouldn't Die (TV) 76. The Last Hurrah (TV) 77. Improper Channels 81. No Place to Hide (TV) 82. 1969 89. Encino Man/California Man 92, etc.
TV series: Peyton Place 65. The Hero 66–67. Goodnight Beantown 83–84. WIOU 90–91.

Hartley, Richard.
British composer.
Galileo 75. The Romantic Englishwoman 75. The Rocky Horror Picture Show 75. Aces High 75. The Lady Vanishes 79. Bad Timing 80. Shock Treatment 81. The Trout 82. Bad Blood 83. Sheena 84. Parker 85. Dance with a Stranger 85. The Good Father 86. Soursweet 88. Consuming Passions 88. The Tree of Hands 89. Dealers 89. She's Been Away 89. Afraid of the Dark 91. The Railway Station Man 92. Princess Caraboo 94. An Awfully Big Adventure 95. Rough Magic 95. Stealing Beauty 96. The Van 96, etc.

Hartman, David (1937–).
Tall, gangling American leading man who after a few years, mostly in television, gained a permanent niche as anchorman for ABC's *Good Morning America*.
The Ballad of Josie 68. Nobody's Perfect 69. Ice Station Zebra 69. San Francisco International (TV) 70. The Feminist and the Fuzz (TV) 71. I Love a Mystery (TV) 73. You'll Never See Me Again (TV) 73. Miracle on 34th Street (TV) 74. The Island at the Top of the World 75, etc.
TV series: The Bold Ones 69–71. Lucas Tanner 76.

Hartman, Don (1901–1958) (Samuel Hartman).
American comedy screenwriter.
The Gay Deception (AAN) 35. The Princess Comes Across 35. Waikiki Wedding 37. Tropic Holiday 38. Paris Honeymoon 39. The Star Maker 39. *Road to Singapore* 40. Life with Henry 41. *Road to Zanzibar* 41. Nothing but the Truth 41. *Road to Morocco* (AAN) 42. True to Life 42. Up in Arms 44. The Princess and the Pirate 44. Down to Earth (& p) 47. It Had to be You (& d) 47. Every Girl Should Be Married (& pd) 48. Mr Imperium (& d) 51. Desire Under the Elms (p) 57. The Matchmaker (p) 58, many others.

Hartman, Elizabeth (1941–1987).
American leading actress. Committed suicide.
A Patch of Blue (AAN) 66. The Group 66. You're a Big Boy Now 67. The Fixer 68. The Beguiled 71. Walking Tall 73.

Hartman, Phil (1948–1998).
Canadian-born comic actor and writer. Born in Branford, Ontario, he was raised in Connecticut and Los Angeles, and first worked as a graphic designer, responsible for designing the logo for the rock group Crosby, Stills and Nash, before joining a Los Angeles comedy group in the mid-70s. He was noted for the brilliance of his impressions on NBC's *Saturday Night Live*, and for supplying many of the voices (including 'B'-movie star Troy McClure and sleazy lawyer Lionel Hutz) for the TV series *The Simpsons*. He was shot to death while sleeping by his wife, who committed suicide shortly after.
Cheech and Chong's Next Movie 80. Weekend Pass 84. Pee-Wee's Big Adventure (co-w only) 85. Jumpin' Jack Flash 86. Three Amigos 86. Blind Date 87. The Brave Little Toaster (voice) 87. Fletch Lives 89. Quick Change 90. Coneheads 93. So I Married an Axe Murderer 93. Greedy 94. Sgt Bilko 94. Jingle All the Way 96. Small Soldiers 98, etc.
TV series: Saturday Night Live 86–94. NewsRadio 95–98.

Hartnell, Sir Norman (1901–1979).
English couturier who designed costumes for British films of the 30s. Born in Streatham, London, he attended Cambridge University briefly before opening his own fashion business in the early 20s. He became a dressmaker to the British Royal Family from the mid-30s, and was knighted in 1977.
Autobiography: 1955, *Silver and Gold*.
Such Is the Law 30. Aunt Sally 33. That's a Good Girl 33. A Southern Maid 33. Give Her a Ring 34. Princess Charming 34. The Return of Bulldog Drummond 34. Brewster's Millions 35. Calling the Tune 36. Non-Stop New York 37. Sailing Along 38. A Clean Sweep 38, etc.

Hartnell, William (1908–1975).
Thin-lipped British character actor who rose briefly to star status in the 40s after playing many small-time crooks and tough sergeants. Popular on TV in the 60s as the first Dr Who.
Biography: 1996, *Who's There? – The Life and Career of William Hartnell* by Jessica Carney.
Follow the Lady 33. While Parents Sleep 35. Midnight at Madame Tussaud's 36. Farewell Again 37. They Drive by Night 39. Flying Fortress 40. Suspected Person 41. The Peterville Diamond 42. The Bells Go Down 43. Headline 43. *The Way Ahead* 44. The Agitator 44. Murder in Reverse 45. Strawberry Roan 46. Appointment with Crime 46. Odd Man Out 46. Temptation Harbour 47. *Brighton Rock* 47. Now Barabbas 49. The Lost People 49. The Dark Man 50. The Magic Box 51. The Holly and the Ivy 52. The Ringer 52. Will any Gentleman? 53. Footsteps in the Fog 54. Private's Progress 55. Hell Drivers 57. Carry on Sergeant 58. Piccadilly Third Stop 60. This Sporting Life 62. Heaven's Above 63, many others.
TV series: The Army Game 57–58.

Harvey, Anthony (1931–).
British editor, later director.
AS EDITOR: Private's Progress 56. Happy is the Bride 58. The Angry Silence 60. Lolita 62. Dr Strangelove 63. The Whisperers 67, etc.
■ AS DIRECTOR: Dutchman (& e) 66. The Lion in Winter (AAN) 68. They Might Be Giants 71. The Glass Menagerie (TV) 73. The Abdication 74. The Disappearance of Aimee (TV) 76. Players 79. Eagle's Wing 79. Richard's Things (TV) 81. Svengali (TV) 83. The Ultimate Solution of Grace Quigley 85.

Harvey, Forrester (1880–1945).
Irish character actor, long in Hollywood.
The Lilac Sunbonnet 22. The Flag Lieutenant 26. The Ring 27. The White Sheik 28. Sky Devils 32. Tarzan the Ape Man 32. Red Dust 33. The Invisible Man 33. The Painted Veil 34. The Mystery of Edwin Drood 35. Jalna 35. Lloyds of London 36. Personal Property 37. Kidnapped 38. Mysterious Mr Moto 38. Let Us Live 39. Rebecca 40. A Chump at Oxford 40. Little Nellie Kelly 40. The Wolf Man 41. Random Harvest 42. Scotland Yard Investigator 45, many others.

Harvey, Frank (1912–1981).
British playwright and screenwriter.
Saloon Bar (oa) 40. Things Happen at Night (oa) 48. Seven Days to Noon (w) 50. High Treason (w) 52. Private's Progress (w) 55. I'm All Right Jack (w) 59. Heaven's Above (w) 63. No My Darling Daughter (w) 63, etc.

Harvey, Laurence (1928–1973) (Larushka Mischa Skikne).
Lithuanian-born leading man who worked his way slowly from British second features to top Hollywood productions, but was only briefly in fashion. He was brought up in Johannesburg, South Africa, and studied at RADA. He became a protégé of James WOOLF, of Romulus Films, who made him a star. Married actress Margaret LEIGHTON (1957–60), Joan Cohn (1968–72), widow of film mogul Harry COHN, and, in 1969, model Paulene Stone. His lovers included Hermione BADDELEY. Died of cancer.
Biographies: 1973, *The Prince* by Emmett and Des Hickey. 1975, *One Tear is Enough* by Paulene Stone.
House of Darkness 48. Man on the Run 48. The Dancing Years 48. The Man from Yesterday 49. Cairo Road 49. The Scarlet Thread 50. Landfall 50. The Black Rose 50. There is Another Sun 51. A Killer Walks 51. I Believe in You 52. Women of Twilight 52. Innocents in Paris 53. Romeo and Juliet 54. King Richard and the Crusaders 54. The Good Die Young 55. I Am a Camera 55. Storm over the Nile 56. Three Men in a Boat 57. After the Ball 57. The Truth About Women 58. The Silent Enemy 58. *Room at the Top* (AAN) 59. Expresso Bongo 59. The Alamo 60. Butterfield Eight 60. The Long and the Short and the Tall 61. Two Loves 61. Summer and Smoke 61. A Walk on the Wild Side 62. The Wonderful World of the Brothers Grimm 63. A Girl Named Tamiko 63. The Manchurian Candidate 63. The Running Man 63. The Ceremony (& pd) 64. Of Human Bondage 64. The Outrage 64. Darling 65. Life at the Top 65. The Spy with the Cold Nose 66. A Dandy in Aspic 67. The Winter's Tale 68. Rebus 68. Kampf um Rom 69. He and She 69. The Magic Christian 70. WUSA 71. Flight into the Sun 72. Night Watch 73. Welcome to Arrow Beach 73, etc.
❝ He demonstrated conclusively that it is possible to succeed without managing to evoke the least audience interest or sympathy and to go on succeeding despite unanimous critical antipathy and overwhelming public apathy. – *David Shipman*
Life with him was exciting and funny, but he was consumed with a hunger to have everything – fame, fortune, all the riches of life. It was as if he knew there was only so much time alloted to him. – *Hermione Baddeley*
Behind the public dandy, the pirouetting fop, hid a mature and sensitive artist. He simply believed it was slightly vulgar to let it be seen. – *Paulene Stone*

An appalling man and, even more unforgivably, an appalling actor. – *Robert Stephens*

Harvey, Lilian (1906–1968).
British leading lady who in the 30s became star of German films.
Biography: 1974, *The Lilian Harvey Story* by Hans Borgen.
Leidenschaft 25. Die Tolle Lola 227. Drei von der Tankstelle 30. *Congress Dances* 31. Happy Ever After 32. My Weakness (US) 33. I Am Suzanne (US) 34. Invitation to the Waltz (GB) 35. Capriccio 38. Serenade (Fr.) (last film) 39, etc.

Harvey, Paul (1884–1955).
American character actor who often played the choleric executive or kindly father.
Advice to the Lovelorn 34. Rebecca of Sunnybrook Farm 38. Algiers 38. Stanley and Livingstone 39. Maryland 40. Pillow to Post 45. The Late George Apley 47. Father of the Bride 50. The First Time 52. Three for the Show 55, many others.

Harwood, Ronald (1934–).
South African-born dramatist and screenwriter, in England since 1951. He was formerly an actor with Sir Donald Wolfit's company.
Private Potter 62. Eyewitness 70. One Day in the Life of Ivan Denisovich 71. Operation Daybreak 75. The Dresser (AAN) 83. The Doctor and the Devils 85. Tchin Tchin 91. The Browning Version 94. Cry the Beloved Country 95.

Has, Wojciech (1925–).
Polish director and screenwriter. Born in Cracow, he studied at that city's Film Institute and began in the late 40s making shorts and documentaries. He directed features from 1958, moving from narratives of individual lives to large-scale epics in his later films. He became director of the Lodz Film School in the early 80s.
The Noose (& co-w) 58. Goodbye to the Past 61. The Saragossa Manuscript 65. Lalka/The Doll (& w) 68. The Hourglass Sanatorium (& w) 73. Write and Flight 85. The Fabulous Journey of Balthazar Kober 88, etc.

Haskell, Jimmy.
American composer, mainly for television movies since the 80s.
Love in a Goldfish Bowl 61. Wild on the Beach 65. Red Tomahawk 67. Zachariah 71. Night of the Lepus 72. Dirty Mary Crazy Larry 74. Joyride 77. Hard Country (co-m) 81. She's Back 89, etc.

Haskell, Peter (1934–).
American leading man.
The Ballad of Andy Crocker (TV) 69. The Eyes of Charles Sand (TV) 72. Phantom of Hollywood (TV) 74. Christina 74. The Night They Took Miss Beautiful (TV) 77. The Cracker Factory (TV) 79. Legend of Earl Durand 90. Child's Play 3 91, etc.
TV series: Bracken's World 69. Rich Man, Poor Man Book II 76–77. Rituals 84–85. The Law and Harry McGraw 87.

Haskin, Byron (1899–1984).
American director with a penchant for science fiction; some interesting films among the routine.
Cameraman and special effects expert through the 30s.
■ Matinée Ladies 27. Ginsberg the Great 27. Irish Hearts 27. The Siren 28. *I Walk Alone* 47. Maneater of Kumaon 48. Too Late for Tears 49. Treasure Island 50. Tarzan's Peril 51. Warpath 51. Silver City 51. Denver and Rio Grande 52. *The War of the Worlds* 53. His Majesty O'Keefe 53. The Naked Jungle 54. Long John Silver 55. Conquest of Space 55. The First Texan 56. The Boss 56. From the Earth to the Moon 58. The Little Savage 59. Jet over the Atlantic 59. September Storm 60. Armored Command 61. *Captain Sinbad* 63. *Robinson Crusoe on Mars* 64. The Power 67.

Hassall, Imogen (1942–1980).
Voluptuous English actress, a former dancer. Died of a drug overdose.
The Early Bird 65. The Long Duel 67. Mumsy, Nanny, Sonny and Girly 69. El Condor 70. The Virgin and the Gypsy 70. Tomorrow 70. When Dinosaurs Ruled the Earth 70. Carry on Loving 70. White Cargo 73. Licensed to Love and Kill 79, etc.

Hasse, O. E. (1903–1978).
German character actor: dubbed the voices of Spencer Tracy and Paul Muni.
Peer Gynt 34. Rembrandt 42. Berliner Ballade 48. Epilog 50. Decision Before Dawn (US) 51. I Confess (US) 53. Canaris 54. Mrs Warren's Profession 59. State of Siege 72. Ice Age 75, etc.

Hasselhoff, David (1952–).
American leading man, mainly on television.
Revenge of the Cheerleaders 76. Star Crash/Stella Star 78. Pleasure Cove (TV) 79. Cartier Affair (TV) 84. Terror at London Bridge (TV) 85. Witchery 88. The Final Alliance 89. Fire and Rain (TV) 89. Bail Out 90, etc.
TV series: The Young and the Restless 75–82. Semi-Tough 80. Knight Rider 82–86. Bay Watch 89– . Baywatch Nights 95– .

Hassett, Marilyn (1947–).
American leading lady.
Quarantined (TV) 70. They Shoot Horses Don't They? 72. *The Other Side of the Mountain* 76. Two Minute Warning 76. The Other Side of the Mountain: Part Two 77. The Bell Jar 79. Body Count 87. Messenger of Death 88, etc.

Hasso, Signe (1910–).
Swedish leading lady of the 40s, in Hollywood. Also a writer.
Assignment in Brittany 43. The Seventh Cross 44. *The House on 92nd Street* 45. Johnny Angel 45. A Scandal in Paris 46. Where There's Life 47. *To the Ends of the Earth* 48. A Double Life 48. Outside the Wall 50. Crisis 50. Picture Mommy Dead 66. Reflection of Fear 71. The Black Bird 75. I Never Promised You a Rose Garden 77, etc.

Hatcher, Teri (1964–).
American actress. She married actor Jon Tenney in 1994.
The Big Picture 89. Tango and Cash 89. Soapdish 91. Dead in the Water 91. Straight Talk 92. Brain Smasher 93. Heaven's Prisoners 96. 2 Days in the Valley 96. Tomorrow Never Dies 97, etc.
TV series: Lois & Clark: The New Adventures of Superman 93– .

Hatfield, Hurd (1918–1998).
American leading man whose coldly handsome face proved to be his misfortune.
■ Dragon Seed 44. *The Picture of Dorian Gray* 45. The Diary of a Chambermaid 46. The Beginning or the End 47. The Unsuspected 47. The Checkered Coat 48. Joan of Arc 48. Chinatown at Midnight 48. Tarzan and the Slave Girl 50. Destination Murder 51. The Left Handed Gun 58. King of Kings 61. El Cid 61. Mickey One 65. The Boston Strangler 68. Thief (TV) 70. Von Richthofen and Brown 71. The Norliss Tapes (TV) 73. The Word (TV) 78. You Can't Go Home Again (TV) 79. Crimes of the Heart 86. Her Alibi 88.

Hathaway, Henry (1898–1985).
American director, in films (as child actor) from 1907. Acted till 1932, then directed westerns. Later became known as a capable handler of big action adventures and thrillers.
■ Wild Horse Mesa 32. Heritage of the Desert 33. Under the Tonto Rim 33. Sunset Pass 33. Man of the Forest 33. To the Last Man 33. Come On Marines 34. The Last Round-Up 34. Thundering Herds 34. The Witching Hour 34. Now and Forever 34. *Lives of a Bengal Lancer* (AAN) 35. Peter Ibbetson 35. Trail of the Lonesome Pine 36. Go West Young Man 36. Souls at Sea 37. Spawn of the North 38. The Real Glory 39. Johnny Apollo 40. Brigham Young 40. Shepherd of the Hills 41. Sundown 41. Ten Gentlemen from West Point 42. China Girl 43. Home in Indiana 44. A Wing and a Prayer 44. Nob Hill 45. *The House on 92nd Street* 45. The Dark Corner 46. 13 Rue Madeleine 46. *Kiss of Death* 47. Call Northside 777 48. Down to the Sea in Ships 49. The Black Rose 50. You're in the Navy Now 51. Rawhide 51. Fourteen Hours 51. *Rommel, Desert Fox* 51. Diplomatic Courier 52. *Niagara* 52. White Witch Doctor 53. Prince Valiant 54. Garden of Evil 54. The Racers 54. The Bottom of the Bottle 55. 23 Paces to Baker Street 56. Legend of the Lost 57. From Hell to Texas 58. A Woman Obsessed 59. Seven Thieves 60. *North to Alaska* 60. How the West Was Won (part) 62. Circus World 64. The Sons of Katie Elder 65. Nevada Smith 66. The Last Safari 67. Five Card Stud 68. True Grit 69. Raid on Rommel 71. Shootout 72.
✪ For long-standing professionalism in handling all types of subject. *The House on 92nd Street*.
❝ Being educated is making the pictures themselves, if you make it your business to pay attention. – *H.H.*
To be a good director you've got to be a bastard. I'm a bastard and I know it. – *H.H.*
His charm consists of minor virtues uncorrupted by major pretensions. – *Andrew Sarris*

Hatley, Thomas Marvin (1905–1986).
American composer who was musical director at the Hal Roach Studio 1930–39, scoring several Laurel and Hardy movies. In the 40s he quit films to play the piano in cocktail lounges.
Hog Wild 30. The Music Box 31. Sons of the Desert (s, 'Honolulu Baby') 33. Way Out West (AAN) 37. Pick a Star 37. Block-Heads (AAN) 38. There Goes My Heart (AAN) 38. Captain Fury 39. Topper Takes a Trip 39. A Chump at Oxford 40, etc.

Hattie, Hilo (1901–1979).
Hawaiian entertainer who in 1942 made her only Hollywood musical: *Song of the Islands*.

Hatton, Raymond (1887–1971).
American character actor, the comic sidekick of a hundred minor westerns. Born in Bed Oak, Iowa, he first worked in carnivals and vaudeville, and was in Hollywood from 1911. He appeared with Buck Jones in the Rough Riders series in the late 30s before becoming one of The Three Mesquiteers in their later incarnation. He was comic relief to Johnny Mack Brown in more than 40 westerns, and formed a comedy team with Wallace Beery, 1926–29.
Oliver Twist 16. Whispering Chorus 18. Male and Female 19. Jes' Call Me Jim 20. The Affairs of Anatol 21. Ebb Tide 22. The Hunchback of Notre Dame 23. The Fighting American 24. In the Name of Love 25. Born to the West 26. *Behind the Front* 26. *We're In the Navy Now* 26. Fireman Save My Child 27. The Woman God Forgot 27. We're in the Air Now 27. Partners in Crime 28. Hell's Heroes 29. Midnight Mystery 30. Woman Hungry 31. The Squaw Man 31. Polly of the Circus 32. Terror Trail 33. Wagon Wheels 34. Laughing Irish Eyes 36. Roaring Timber 37. Love Finds Andy Hardy 38. Kit Carson 40. Tall in the Saddle 44. Black Gold 47. Operation Haylift 50. Shake Rattle and Rock 56. In Cold Blood 67, many others.

Hatton, Richard (1891–1931).
American star of silent westerns. Killed in a traffic accident.
Fearless Dick 22. Blood Test 23. Come On, Cowboys 24. 'Scar' Hanan 25. He-Man's Country 26. Saddle Jumpers 27. The Boss of Rustler's Roost 28. The Vanishing Legion (serial) 31, etc.
❝ Hatton was strictly a city man and our nickname for him was 'Fearless Richard' since he was actually afraid to go out at night unless someone was with him. – *Yakima Canutt*

Hatton, Rondo (1894–1946).
American actor who suffered from facial and bodily deformity as a result of acromegaly; he was rather tastelessly cast as a monstrous killer in several low-budget mysteries of the early 40s.
■ Hell Harbor 30. In Old Chicago 38. Alexander's Ragtime Band 38. The Hunchback of Notre Dame 39. Captain Fury 39. Chad Hanna 40. Moon over Burma 40. The Big Guy 40. The Cyclone Kid 42. The Moon and Sixpence 42. Sleepy Lagoon 43. The Ox Bow Incident 43. *The Pearl of Death* 44. Raiders of Ghost City 44. The Princess and the Pirate 44. Johnny Doesn't Live Here Any More 44. The Royal Mounted Rides Again 45. Jungle Captive 45. Spider Woman Strikes Back 46. House of Horrors 46. The Brute Man 46.

Hauer, Rutger (1944–).
Dutch leading actor, now in international films.
Soldier of Orange 77. Blade Runner 82. Eureka 83. The Osterman Weekend 83. A Breed Apart 84. Ladyhawke 85. Flesh and Blood 85. The Hitcher 86. Wanted Dead or Alive 86. The Legend of the Holy Drinker/La Leggenda del Santo Bevitore 88. Bloodhounds of Broadway 89. Blind Fury 89. The Salute of the Jugger 89. In una Notte di Chiaro di Luna 89. The Blood of Heroes 90. Wedlock 91. Split Second 92. Buffy the Vampire Slayer 92. Beyond Justice 92. Past Midnight 92. Arctic Blue 93. Amelia Earhart: The Final Flight (TV) 94. Surviving the Game 94. Nostradamus 94. Fatherland (TV) 94. Forbidden Choices/The Beans of Egypt, Maine 94. Mr Stitch 95. Precious Find 96. Omega Doom 96. Blast 96. Redline 97. Hostile Waters 97. Merlin (TV) 98. Simon Magus 99, etc.
❝ He's both a genius and crazy at the same time. His entire approach to filmmaking is that he comes in, and he's like a gorilla, he comes in and his primary job, he feels, is to take everything out of focus. – *Roger Avary*

Hauser, Wings.
Powerful American leading man of low-budget action films, who turned to directing in the 90s. He began in TV soap operas.
Who'll Stop the Rain/Dog Soldiers 78. Vice Squad 82. Homework 82. Deadly Force 83. Mutant 83. A Soldier's Story 84. The Long Hot Summer 86. Hostage 87. Tough Guys Don't Dance 87. The Wind 87. Nightmare at Noon 87. No Safe Haven 87. Dead Men Walking 88. Marked for Murder 89. Street Asylum 90. Reason to Die 90. Exiled 91. Pale Blood 91. Coldfire (& d) 91. Living to Die (& d) 91. In Between 92. Mind, Body and Soul 92. Frame-Up II: The Cover-Up 92. Tales from the Hood 95. Original Gangstas 96. Gang Boys 97, etc.
TV series: The Last Precinct 86. Lightning Force 91.

Havelock-Allan, Sir Anthony (1904–).
British producer. Born in Darlington, he first worked as an A&R manager in the record business and was in films from the mid-30s. Together with David Lean and Ronald Neame, he set up the production company Cineguild in the early 40s, to film works by Noël Coward and, later, Charles Dickens. He was formerly married to actress Valerie Hobson.
This Man Is News 38. In Which We Serve (associate) 42. Blithe Spirit 45. Brief Encounter (co-w, AAN) 46. Great Expectations 46. Oliver Twist 48. The Small Voice 49. Never Take No for an Answer 51. The Young Lovers 54. Orders to Kill 58. The Quare Fellow 61. An Evening with the Royal Ballet 64. Othello 65. The Mikado 67. Up the Junction 67. Romeo and Juliet 68. Ryan's Daughter 70, etc.

Haver, June (1926–) (June Stovenour).
American leading lady of the 40s, mostly in musicals; married Fred McMurray. Now retired.
■ The Gang's All Here 43. Home in Indiana 44. Irish Eyes Are Smiling 44. Where Do We Go from Here? 45. *The Dolly Sisters* 45. Three Little Girls in Blue 46. Wake Up and Dream 46. I Wonder Who's Kissing Her Now 47. Scudda Hoo Scudda Hay 48. Oh You Beautiful Doll 49. *Look for the Silver Lining* (as Marilyn Miller) 49. The Daughter of Rosie O'Grady 50. I'll Get By 50. Love Nest 51. The Girl Next Door 53.

Haver, Phyllis (1899–1960) (Phyllis O'Haver).
American leading lady of the silent screen, a former Sennett bathing beauty. Committed suicide.
Small Town Idol 20. Temple of Venus 23. Fig Leaves 25. Up in Mabel's Room 26. The Way of All Flesh 28. Hard Boiled 29. Hell's Kitchen 29, many others.

Havers, Nigel (1949–).
Elegant British actor. Born in London, the son of a former Attorney-General, he trained at the Arts Educational School and worked in the wine trade and as a researcher on radio before gaining success as an actor on television.
Chariots of Fire 81. A Passage to India 84. Burke and Wills 86. The Whistle Blower 86. Empire of the Sun 87. Farewell to the King 89. Quiet Days in Clichy 90. The Burning Season (TV) 94, etc.
TV series: Don't Wait Up 83–85. The Charmer 87. The Good Guys 92–93. Dangerfield 98– .

Havlick, Gene (c. 1895–1959).
American editor.
Beauty and Bullets 28. Madonna of the Streets 30. Shopworn 32. Broadway Bill 34. Mr Deeds Goes to Town 36. *Lost Horizon* (AA) 37. You Can't Take It with You 38. Mr Smith Goes to Washington 39. His Girl Friday 40. The Wife takes a Flyer 42. A Song to Remember 45. Relentless 48. Son of Dr Jekyll 51. Jungle Maneaters 54. Screaming Mimi 58, many others.

Havoc, June (1916–) (June Hovick).
American leading lady, former child actress; sister of Gypsy Rose Lee.
Autobiography: 1960, *Early Havoc*.
Four Jacks and a Jill 42. Brewster's Millions 45. The Story of Molly X 49. Once a Thief 50. A Lady Possessed 51. Three for Jamie Dawn 57. The Private Files of J. Edgar Hoover 78. Can't Stop the Music 80. A Return to Salem's Lot 87, etc.
TV series: Willy 54.

Hawke, Ethan (1970–).
American actor. He is also a novelist (1996, *The Hottest State*). Married actress Uma THURMAN in 1998.
Explorers 85. Dead Poets Society 89. Dad 89. White Fang 90. A Midnight Clear 91. Mystery Date 91. Waterland 92. Alive 93. White Fang 2: Myth of the White Wolf 94. Reality Bites 94. Floundering 94. Before Sunrise 95. Search and Destroy 95. Great Expectations 98. Gattaca 98. The Velocity of Gary 98. The Newton Boys 98, etc.

Hawkins, Jack (1910–1973).
Dominant British actor; after long apprenticeship, became an international star in middle age, but in 1966 lost his voice after an operation; his subsequent minor appearances were dubbed. His first wife was Jessica Tandy.
Autobiography: 1974, *Anything for a Quiet Life*.
Birds of Prey 30. The Lodger 32. The Good Companions 32. The Lost Chord 33. I Lived with You 33. The Jewel 33. A Shot in the Dark 33. Autumn Crocus 34. Death at Broadcasting House 34. *Peg of Old Drury* 35. Beauty and the Barge 37. The Frog 37. Who Goes Next 38. A Royal Divorce 38. Murder Will Out 39. The Flying Squad 40. Next of Kin 42. *The Fallen Idol* 48. Bonnie Prince Charlie 48. The Small Back Room 48. *State Secret* 50. The Black Rose 50. The Elusive Pimpernel 50. The Adventurers 51. No Highway 51. Home at Seven 51. *Angels One Five* 52. The Planter's Wife 52. Mandy 52. *The Cruel Sea* 53. Twice Upon a Time 53. The Malta Story 53. The Intruder 53. Front Page Story 54. The Seekers 54. The Prisoner 55. Touch and Go 55. Land of the Pharaohs 55. The Long Arm 56. The Man in the Sky 56. Fortune is a Woman 57. *The Bridge on the River Kwai* 57. Gideon's Day 58. The Two-Headed Spy 58. *The League of Gentlemen* 59. *Ben Hur* (US) 59. Two Loves (US) 61. Five Finger Exercise (US) 62. *Lawrence of Arabia* 62. Lafayette 63. *Rampage* (US) 63. Zulu 63. The Third Secret 64. Guns at Batasi 64. Masquerade 65. Lord Jim 65. Judith 65. Great Catherine 67. Shalako 68. Oh What a Lovely War 69. Monte Carlo or Bust 69. Waterloo 70. The Adventures of Gerard 70. Nicholas and Alexandra 71. Kidnapped 72. Young Winston 72. Theatre of Blood 73. Tales that Witness Madness 73, etc.
TV series: *The Four Just Men* 59.
✪ For humorously perpetuating the image of the friendly World War II officer. *The League of Gentlemen*.

Hawkins, Screamin' Jay (1929–) (Jalacy Hawkins).
Exuberant and eccentric American rhythm and blues singer and actor. He is a former Golden Gloves middleweight boxing champion.
American Hot Wax 78. Mystery Train 89. A Rage in Harlem 91, etc.

Hawks, Howard (1896–1977).
American director, at his best an incomparable provider of professional comedies and action dramas. Born in Goshen, Indiana, he studied mechanical engineering at Cornell University; he taught pilots to fly during the First World War and built the racing car that won the Indianapolis 500 in 1936. He began in films in 1917 as a prop boy, became an assistant director and, in the early 20s, ran Famous Players' story department. He began directing in 1926 for Fox, but after the success of *The Dawn Patrol* was able to work without signing a long-term contract with any studio. Awarded an honorary Oscar in 1974 as 'a master American filmmaker'. Died after a fall at his home. Married three times.
Biography: 1997: *Howard Hawks: The Grey Fox of Hollywood* by Todd McCarthy.
Books include: 1962, *The Cinema of Howard Hawks* by Peter Bogdanovich; 1977, *Howard Hawks* by Robin Wood; 1982, *Hawks on Hawks* (devised by Joe McBride); 1982, *Howard Hawks, Storyteller* by Gerald Mast.
■ Tiger Love (w only) 24. The Road to Glory (& w) 26. Fig Leaves (& w) 26. The Cradle Snatchers 27. Paid to Love 27. A Girl in Every Port (& w) 28. Fazil 28. The Air Circus 28. Trent's Last Case (& w) 29. *The Dawn Patrol* 30. The Criminal Code 31. The Crowd Roars 32. *Scarface* 32. Tiger Shark 32. Today We Live 33. *Twentieth Century* 34. Viva Villa (part) 34. *Barbary Coast* 35. Ceiling Zero 36. Road to Glory 36. Come and Get It (co-d) 36. *Bringing Up Baby* 38. Only Angels Have Wings 39. *His Girl Friday* 40. Sergeant York (AAN) 41. Ball of Fire 41. Air Force 42. Corvette K 225 (p only) 44. *To Have and Have Not* 44. *The Big Sleep* 46. A Song Is Born 48. *Red River* 48. I Was a Male War Bride 49. The Thing from Another World (p only) 52. The Big Sky 52. Monkey Business 52. O. Henry's Full House (one episode) 52. Gentlemen Prefer Blondes 53. Land of the Pharaohs 55. *Rio Bravo* 58. Hatari 62. Man's Favourite Sport 64. Red Line 7000 65. El Dorado 66. Rio Lobo 70.
✪ For the remarkably consistent vigour with which he presented a man's world invaded by a woman. *His Girl Friday*.
❝ For me the best drama is one that deals with a man in danger. – *H.H.*
He stamped his remarkably bitter view of life on adventure, gangster and private eye melodramas, the kind of thing Americans do best and appreciate least. – *Andrew Sarris, 1968*

Hawn, Goldie (1945–).
American leading lady who scored as blonde dimwit on TV's *Laugh-In*.
■ The One and Only Genuine Original Family Band 68. *Cactus Flower* (AA) 69. *There's a Girl in My Soup* 70. Butterflies are Free 72. Dollars 72. The Sugarland Express 73. The Girl from Petrovka 74. Shampoo 75. The Duchess and the Dirtwater Fox 76. Foul Play 78. Travels with Anita 79. Private Benjamin (AAN) 80. Seems Like Old Times 80. Best Friends 82. Protocol 84. Swing Shift 84. Wildcats 85. Overboard 87. Bird on the Wire 90. Deceived 91. Crisscross 92. Housesitter 92. Death Becomes Her 92. First Wives Club 96. Everyone Says I Love You 96. Hope (TV) (d) 97.
TV series: Good Morning World 67.
❝ All I ever wanted to do was run a dance school and marry a Jewish dentist. – *G.H.*

Haworth, Jill (1945–).
British leading lady in Hollywood.
Exodus 60. In Harm's Way 65. It 66. Home for the Holidays (TV) 72. The Mutations 74.

Haworth, Ted (1917–1993).
American production designer.
Strangers on a Train 51. I Confess 53. Marty (AAN) 54. Invasion of the Body Snatchers 56. Friendly Persuasion 56. Sayonara (AA) 57. The Naked and the Dead 58. Some Like It Hot (AAN) 59. Pepe (AAN) 60. The Longest Day (AAN) 62. What a Way to Go (AAN) 64. Half a Sixpence 67. Villa Rides 68. The Kremlin Letter 70. The Getaway 72. Pat Garrett and Billy the Kid 73. Claudine 74. The Killer Elite 76. Cross of Iron 77. Bloodline 79. Rough Cut 80. Death Hunt 81. Blame It on the Night 84. Poltergeist II: The Other Side 86. Batteries Not Included 87, etc.

Hawthorne, Nathaniel (1804–1864).
American novelist and short-story writer, of oppressive Puritan attitudes in New England. His *The Scarlet Letter*, about a woman accused of adultery, has been filmed at least five times, notably in 1926 with Lillian Gish and 1934 with Colleen Moore. An updated version, starring Demi Moore, flopped at the box-office in 1995. *The House of Seven Gables* was transferred flatly to the screen in 1940, with a cast that included George Sanders, Margaret Lindsay and Vincent Price. His story 'Young Goodman Brown' was even less successfully filmed in 1993 by Peter George.

Hawthorne, Sir Nigel (1929–).
British star character actor.
A Tale of Two Cities (TV) 80. The Hunchback of Notre Dame (TV) 81. Firefox 82. Gandhi 82. Dream Child 84. Turtle Diary 84. Jenny's War (TV) 84. The Chain 86. A Handful of Time/En Handfull Tid 90. Demolition Man 93. *The Madness of King George* 95. Richard III 95. The Fragile Heart (TV) 96. Twelfth Night 96. Inside (TV) 96. Murder in Mind (US) 97. Amistad (US) 97. The Object of My Affection (US) 98. Madeline (US) 98. At Sachem Farm (US) 98. Clandestine Marriage 99, etc.
TV series: *Yes, Minister* (as Sir Humphrey) 81–87.

Hawtrey, Charles (1914–1988) (George Hartree).
Spindle-shanked English comic actor, long cast as an ageing schoolboy in Will HAY's comedies. In the 60s, he was a familiar member of the Carry On team. Born in Hounslow, Middlesex, he trained at the Italia Conti School and was a boy soprano, on stage from 1925. His alcoholism brought to an end his association with the Carry On series in the early 70s. He retired to live in a cottage on the Kent coast in Deal, where the visiting Kenneth WILLIAMS reported, 'as we walked along the front, fishermen eyed us warily. Charlie was in orange trousers, blue shirt and silk scarf at the neck. He was carrying his umbrella as a parasol. The day was quite fine. The rest of us were trying to look anonymous. "Hello lads!"he kept calling out to men painting their boats. "They all adore me here," he told us, "brings a bit of glamour into their dull lives."'
Good Morning Boys 37. Where's That Fire 40. The Goose Steps Out 42. A Canterbury Tale 44. The Galloping Major 50. Brandy for the Parson 52. *You're Only Young Twice* 53. Carry On Jack 54. Carry On Sergeant 58. Carry On Nurse 59. Carry On Cowboy 67. Carry On at Your Convenience 71. Carry On Abroad 72, many others.
TV series: The Army Game 57–61. Our House 60. Best of Friends 63.

Hay, Alexandra (1944–1993).
American leading lady.
Skidoo 68. The Model Shop 69. The Love Machine 71. 1000 Convicts and a Woman 71. How Come Nobody's on Our Side 73, etc.

Hay, Will (1888–1949).
British character comedian, one of the screen's greats; after many years in the music halls, starred in several incomparable farces playing variations on his favourite role of an incompetent, seedy schoolmaster. Born in Stockton-on-Tees, he worked as a book-keeper before beginning in the music halls in a schoolmaster sketch in 1909, later joining Fred Karno's troupe and becoming a star attraction from the mid-20s. In private life, he was an expert amateur astronomer who built his own observatory and wrote a book on the subject (1935, *Through My Telescope*), a pilot and a linguist.
Biography: 1978, *Good Morning Boys* by Ray Seaton and Roy Martin.
■ Those Were the Days 34. Dandy Dick 34. Radio Parade 35. Boys will be Boys 35. Where There's a Will 36. Windbag the Sailor 36. *Good Morning Boys* 37. Convict 99 38. Hey Hey USA 38. *Old Bones of the River* 38. *Oh Mr Porter* 38. *Ask a Policeman* 39. Where's that Fire? 39. *The Ghost of St Michael's* 41. The Black Sheep of Whitehall 41. The Big Blockade 42. The Goose Steps Out 42. My *Learned Friend* 44.
✪ For developing an unforgettable comic persona which lives in the memory independently of his films; and for persuading us to root for that character despite its basically unsympathetic nature. *Oh Mr Porter*.
❝ A good comedy scenario is very near pathos. The character I play is really a very pathetic fellow. – *W.H.*
I've always found something funny in the idea of a hopelessly inefficient man blundering through a job he knows nothing about. – *W.H.*
For each one of us there comes a moment when death takes us by the hand and says: 'It is time to rest; you are tired; lie down and sleep; sleep well.' The day is gone and stars shine in the canopy of eternity. – *The last words Will Hay read before he died, which were inscribed at the foot of his grave*

Hayakawa, Sessue (1889–1973).
Japanese actor, a popular star of American silents; more recently in occasional character roles.
The Typhoon 14. *The Cheat* 15. Forbidden Paths 17. The Tong Man 19. Daughter of the Dragon 29. Tokyo Joe 49. Three Came Home 50. *The Bridge on the River Kwai* (AAN) 57. The Geisha Boy 59. The Swiss Family Robinson 60. Hell to Eternity 61, etc.

Hayasaka, Fumio (1914–1955).
Japanese composer, often for the films of Akira Kurosawa and Kenji Mizoguchi.
Drunken Angel/Yoidore Tenshi 48. Rashomon 50. Meshi 51. Ikiru 52. Ugetsu 53. Sansho the Bailiff/Sansho Dayu 54. Seven Samurai/Shichinin no Samurai 54. A Story from Chikamatsu/ Chikamatsu Monogatari 54. I Live in Fear 55, etc.

Hayashi, Kaizo (1957–).
Japanese director and screenwriter.
Circus Boys/Ni Ju-Seiki Shonen Dokuhon 89. The Most Terrible Time in My Life/Waga Jinsei Saisuku no Toki 94. The Breath/Umihoozuki 95, etc.

Hayden, Harry (1884–1955).
Tubby American character actor who played scores of bankers, clergymen and unassuming family chaps.
I Married a Doctor 36. Black Legion 36. Ever Since Eve 37. Kentucky 38. Angels with Dirty Faces 38. Swanee River 39. Christmas in July 40. The Palm Beach Story 42. Up in Mabel's Room 44. The Killers 46. The Unfinished Dance 47. Intruder in the Dust 49. Double Dynamite 51. Army Bound 52, many others.

Hayden, Linda (1951–).
British leading lady; started by playing teenage sexpots.
Baby Love 69. Taste the Blood of Dracula 69. Satan's Skin 70. Something to Hide 72. Confessions of a Window Cleaner 74. Let's Get Laid 77. Confessions from a Holiday Camp 77. The Boys from Brazil 78, etc.

Hayden, Russell (1912–1981) (Pate Lucid).
American 'second string' leading man, for many years Hopalong Cassidy's faithful sidekick. Later produced TV westerns.
Hills of Old Wyoming (debut) 37. Range War 39. Lucky Legs 42. 'Neath Canadian Skies 46. Seven Were Saved 47. Silver City 49. Valley of Fire 51, many others.
TV series: Cowboy G-Men 52. Judge Roy Bean 55.

Hayden, Sterling (1916–1986) (Sterling Walter Relyea).
Rangy American leading man and part-time explorer.
Autobiographies: 1963, *Wanderer*. 1978, *Voyage*.
Virginia 40. Bahama Passage 41. Blaze of Noon 47. El Paso 49. Manhandled 49. *The Asphalt Jungle* 50. Denver and Rio Grande 52. The Golden Hawk 52. The Star 52. So Big 53. Prince Valiant 54. Arrow in the Dust 54. Johnny Guitar 54. Suddenly 54. Timberjack 55. The Eternal Sea 55. The Last Command 55. *The Killing* 56. Crime of Passion 56. Five Steps to Danger 56. Zero Hour 57. Terror in a Texas Town 58. Dr Strangelove 63. Hard Contract 69. Loving 70. The Godfather 72. The Long Goodbye 73. Cobra 73. Deadly Strangers 74. Is It Any Wonder 75. 1900 77. King of the Gypsies 78. The Outsider 79. Winter Kills 79. Nine to Five 80. Venom 82. Lighthouse of Chaos 83. Voyager 84, etc.
❝ If I had the dough, I'd buy up the negative of every film I ever made . . . and start one hell of a fire. – *S.H.*
I don't think there are many other businesses where you can be paid good money and not know what you're doing. – *S.H.*
I started at the top and worked my way down. – *S.H.*

Haydn, Richard (1905–1985).
British revue star of the 30s, in Hollywood from 1941, usually in adenoidal character cameos. He performed in revue and on radio from the 30s as Professor Edwin Carp, the world's only fish mimic.
Ball of Fire (debut) 41. Charley's Aunt 41. Forever and a Day 43. And Then There Were None 45. *Cluny Brown* 46. *Sitting Pretty* 47. Miss Tatlock's Millions (& d) 48. Mr Music (& d) 50. Dear Wife (d only) 50. Jupiter's Darling 54. Please Don't Eat the Daisies 60. *The Lost World* 60. Mutiny on the Bounty 62. Five Weeks in a Balloon 62. The Sound of Music 65. Clarence the Cross-Eyed Lion 65. The Adventures of Bullwhip Griffin 66. Young Frankenstein 74, many others.

Haye, Helen (1874–1957) (Helen Hay).
Distinguished British stage actress (debut 1898), in occasional films, usually as kindly dowager.
Tilly of Bloomsbury 21. Atlantic 30. Congress Dances 31. *The Spy in Black* 39. Kipps 41. *Dear Octopus* 43. Anna Karenina 48. Richard III 56, many others.

Hayek, Salma (1969–).
Mexican leading actress, from TV soap opera.
Midaq Alley/El Callejón de los Milagros 95. Desperado 95. Four Rooms 95. From Dusk till Dawn 95. Fair Game 95. Fled 96. Fools Rush In 97. The Hunchback of Notre Dame (TV) 97. The Velocity of Gary 98. 54 98. The Faculty 98, etc.

Hayers, Sidney (1921–).
British director, in films since 1942. Former editor and second unit director.
■ Violent Moment 58. The White Trap 59. Circus of Horrors 59. Echo of Barbara 60. The Malpas Mystery 60. *Payroll* 61. *Night of the Eagle* 62. This Is My Street 63. Three Hats for Lisa 65. The Trap 66. Finders Keepers 66. The Southern Star 69. Mr Jerico 69. The Firechasers 70. Assault 71. Revenge 71. All Coppers Are . . . 72. Deadly Strangers 74. What Changed Charley Farthing 74. Diagnosis Murder (TV) 74. One Way 76. The Seekers (TV) 78. The Last Convertible (TV) 79. Condominium (TV) 80.

Hayes, Alfred (c. 1911–1985).
American screenwriter.
Paisa 46. Clash by Night 51. Teresa (co-w, AAN) 51. Act of Love 54. The Left Hand of God 55. The Double Man 67, etc.

Hayes, Allison (1930–1977) (Mary Jane Hayes).
American leading lady of a few films in the 50s.
Francis Joins the WACs 54. The Purple Mask 55. The Blackboard Jungle 55. Mohawk 56. The Zombies of Mora Tau 57. Attack of the Fifty-Foot Woman (title role) 58. Who's Been Sleeping in My Bed? 63. Tickle Me 65.
TV series: Acapulco 60.

Hayes, George 'Gabby' (1885–1969).
Bewhiskered American character comedian, in minor westerns from silent days. Born in Wellsville, New York, he began in theatre and vaudeville, becoming best known in the mid to late 30s as Hopalong Cassidy's sidekick Windy Halliday, before teaming up with 'Wild Bill' Elliott, and with Roy Rogers for much of the 40s.
The Rainbow Man 29. Beggars in Ermine 34. The Lost City 35. Three on the Trail 36. Mountain Music 37. Hopalong Rides Again 38. Gold is Where You Find It 38. Man of Conquest 39. Wagons Westward 40. Melody Ranch 41. In Old Oklahoma 43. Tall in the Saddle 44. Utah 45. My Pal Trigger 46. Wyoming 47. Return of the Badmen 48. El Paso 49. The Cariboo Trail 50, many others.
TV series: The Gabby Hayes Show 50.

Hayes, Helen (1900–1993) (Helen Hayes Brown).
Distinguished American stage actress who made a number of film appearances. She was married to writer Charles MacArthur.
Autobiographies: 1965, *A Gift of Joy*. 1969, *On Reflection*. 1981, *Twice Over Lightly*.
Biography: 1985, *Helen Hayes – First Lady of the American Theatre* by Kenneth Barrow.
The Weavers of Life 17. *The Sin of Madelon Claudet* (AA) 31. Arrowsmith 31. *A Farewell to Arms* 32. The Son Daughter 33. The White Sister 33. Another Language 33. Night Flight 33. What Every Woman Knows 34. Crime without Passion (unbilled) 34. Vanessa 35. Stage Door Canteen 43. My Son John 51. Main Street to Broadway 53. *Anastasia* 56. Third Man on the Mountain (unbilled) 59. *Airport* (AA) 69. Do Not Fold Spindle or Mutilate (TV) 71. Herbie Rides Again 73. The Snoop Sisters (TV) 73 (and series). One of Our Dinosaurs Is Missing 75. Victory at Entebbe (TV) 76. Candleshoe 77. A Family Upside Down (TV) 78. The Moneychangers (TV) 79. Murder Is Easy (TV) 82. A Caribbean Mystery (TV) 83. Murder with Mirrors (TV) 84, etc.
TV series: The Snoop Sisters 73–74.
❝ An actor's life is so transitory. Suddenly you're a building. – *H.H. (on having a theatre named after her)*

Hayes, Isaac (1942–).
American composer, singer and actor.
Shaft (AAs, AANm) 71. Shaft's Big Score (co-m) 72. Wattstax (doc) 73. Save the Children (doc) 73. Three Tough Guys (a, m) 74. Truck Turner (a, m) 74. Escape from New York 81. I'm Gonna Git You Sucka 88. Guilty as Charged 91. Prime Target 91. Robin Hood: Men in Tights 93. Posse 93. Acting on Impulse 93. It Could Happen to You 94. Oblivion 94. Flipper 96. Six Ways to Sunday 98, etc.

Hayes, John Michael (1919–).
American screenwriter.
Rear Window (AAN) 54. To Catch a Thief 55. The Trouble with Harry 56. Peyton Place (AAN) 57. *The Carpetbaggers* 63. Where Love Has Gone 64. Harlow 65. Judith 66. Nevada Smith 66. Iron Will (co-w) 94, etc.

Hayes, Margaret (1915–1977).
American character actress, also in TV and public relations.
The Blackboard Jungle 55. Violent Saturday 55. Omar Khayyam 57. Fraulein 57. Damn Citizen 58, etc.

Hayes, Melvyn (1935–).
British comedy character actor, a former child star who was part of Cliff Richards' support in *The Young Ones*, *Summer Holiday*, etc; later became familiar on TV in *It Ain't Half Hot Mum*.
The Curse of Frankenstein 56. No Trees in the Street 58. The Young Ones 61. Summer Holiday 62. Wonderful Life 64. A Walk with Love and Death 69. Love Thy Neighbour 73. Carry on England 76. Santa Claus 85. King of the Wild 89, etc.
TV series: Here Come the Double Deckers 71. Sir Yellow 73. It Ain't Half Hot Mum (as Bombardier 'Gloria' Beaumont) 74–81. Potter's Picture Palace 76.

Hayes, Patricia (1909–1998).
British character actress, mainly in low-life comedy roles. Much on TV. She was the mother of actor Richard O'Callaghan (1945–).
Candles at Nine 44. Nicholas Nickleby 46. The Love Match 54. The Battle of the Sexes 59. Goodbye Mr Chips 69. Love Thy Neighbour 73. The Corn Is Green (TV) 79. The Never Ending Story 84. Little Dorrit 87. The Last Island 91. Blue Ice 92. The Steal 95, etc.
TV series: The Arthur Askey Show 61. Hugh and I 62–64. Till Death Us Do Part 81. Spooner's Patch 82. The Lady Is a Tramp 84. Marjorie and Men 85.

Hayes, Terry.
Australian screenwriter and producer.
Mad Max II/The Road Warrior (co-w) 81. Mad Max beyond Thunderdrome (co-p, co-w) 85. Dead Calm (p, co-w) 89. Flirting (p) 89. The Saint (w) 97, etc.

Haygarth, Tony (1945–).
Bearded English character actor. Born in Liverpool, he worked as a psychiatric nurse before becoming an actor in the mid-60s.
Percy 70. Unman, Wittering and Zigo 71. Let's Get Laid 77. Dracula 79. The Human Factor 79. SOS Titanic (TV) 79. McVicar 80. A Private Function 85. A Month in the Country 87. The Dressmaker 88. Tree of Hands 89. London Kills Me 91. The Trial 92. The Infiltrator (TV) 95, etc.
TV series: Rosie 75–81. Kinvig 81. Round and Round 84. Farrington of the FO 86–87. Hardwicke House 87. All Change 89–91. El CID 90–92. The Borrowers 93. Where the Heart Is 97– .

Hayles, Brian (1930–1978).
British scriptwriter, from TV.
Warlords of Atlantis 78. Arabian Adventure 79.

Hayman, David (1950–).
Scottish director, a former actor.
as actor: A Sense of Freedom (TV) 79. Sid and Nancy 86. Heavenly Pursuits 86. Hope and Glory 87. Venus Peter 89. Rob Roy 95. Regeneration 97. The Jackal 97. My Name Is Joe 98, etc.
as director: Silent Scream 90. Black and Blue (TV) 92. The Hawk 93. A Woman's Guide to Adultery (TV) 93. The Near Room (& a) 95, etc.

Haymes, Dick (1918–1980).
High-living, heavy-drinking Argentine-born singer and actor. Born in Buenos Aires, he was one of the best crooners of the 40s, singing with the bands of Harry James, Benny Goodman and Tommy Dorsey, and went on to make many hit recordings. Died of cancer. His seven wives included actress Joanne Dru (1941–49) and actress Rita Hayworth (1953–55).
Irish Eyes Are Smiling (debut) 44. Diamond Horseshoe 45. *State Fair* 45. Do You Love Me? 46. The Shocking Miss Pilgrim 47. Up in Central Park 48. One Touch of Venus 48. St Benny the Dip 51. All Ashore 53. Betrayal (TV) 74, etc.

Haynes, Todd (1961–).
American independent director and editor. He first attracted attention with *Superstar: The Karen Carpenter Story*, a short made in 1987 about the pop singer's life and anorexic death, in which he used Barbie dolls instead of live actors.
Poison 91. *Safe* 95. Office Killer (dialogue) 97. Velvet Goldmine 98, etc.

Hays, Robert (1947–).
American leading man of the early 80s.
The Young Pioneers (TV) 76. Delta County USA (TV) 78. The Initiation of Sarah (TV) 78. The Fall of the House of Usher (TV) 79. Airplane 80. Take This Job and Shove It 81. Airplane 2: The Sequel 82. Trenchcoat 82. Touched 83. Cat's Eye 85. Murder by the Book 87. Honeymoon Academy 90. Fifty/Fifty 91. Homeward Bound II: Lost in San Francisco 96, etc.

Hays, Will H. (1879–1954).
American executive, for many years (1922–45) president of the Motion Picture Producers and Distributors Association of America, and author of its high-toned Production Code (1930), which for many years put producers in fear of 'the Hays Office'.
Autobiography: 1955, *The Memoirs of Will Hays*.
❝ Good taste is good business. – *W.H. (1930)*

Haysbert, Dennis.
American actor,
K 9000 89. Major League 89. Navy SEALS 90. Mr Baseball 92. Love Field 92. Return to Lonesome Dove (TV) 93. Suture 93. Major League II 94. Heat 95. Waiting to Exhale 95. Absolute Power 97, etc.

Hayter, James (1907–1983).
Portly, jovial British character actor, on stage from 1925, films from 1936.
Sensation 36. Sailors Three 41. School for Secrets 46. *Nicholas Nickleby* (as the Cheeryble twins) 47. The Blue Lagoon 48. *Trio* 50. Tom Brown's Schooldays 51. Robin Hood (as Friar Tuck) 52. *Pickwick Papers* (title role) 53. The Great Game 53. A Day to Remember 54. Touch and Go 56. Port Afrique 58. The Thirty-Nine Steps 59. Stranger in the House 67. Oliver 68. David Copperfield 69. Song of Norway 70, many others.
TV series: Are You Being Served? 78.

Haythorne, Joan (1915–) (Joan Haythornthwaite).
British stage actress, usually in aristocratic roles.
School for Secrets 46. Jassy 47. Highly Dangerous 50. Svengali 54. The Weak and the Wicked 54. The Feminine Touch 56. Three Men in a Boat 56. Shakedown 59. So Evil So Young 61. The Battleaxe 62. Countess Dracula 70, etc.

Hayton, Lennie (1908–1971).
American composer.
The Bugle Sounds 41. Meet the People 43. Salute to the Marines 43. The Harvey Girls 45. Summer Holiday 46. The Hucksters 47. The Pirate 48. Battleground 49. On the Town (co-w) (AA) 49. Inside Straight 51. Singin' in the Rain 52. Battle Circus 53. Star! (AAN) 68. Hello Dolly (co-w) (AA) 69, etc.

Hayward, Leland (1902–1971).
American talent agent and stage producer. Also produced films. Born in Nebraska City, Nebraska, he began as a publicist for United Artists and a writer for First National before becoming a successful agent. His second wife was actress Margaret Sullavan (1936–48).
Mister Roberts 55. The Spirit of St Louis 57. The Old Man and the Sea 58, etc.
❝ Leland's disdain for movies earned him quickly the respect of the movie makers – particularly the front-office bosses who did the buying. They felt that a man so full of sneer for their product must be peddling a superior kind of wares. This wasn't true. All that Leland peddled was a superiority complex – and the same old plots. – *Ben Hecht*

Hayward, Louis (1909–1985) (Seafield Grant).
Mild-mannered, South African-born leading man with stage experience; in Hollywood from 1935. He was formerly married to Ida Lupino.
Chelsea Life (GB) 33. The Man Outside (GB) 33. I'll Stick to You (GB) 33. The Thirteenth Candle (GB) 33. The Love Test (GB) 34. *Sorrell and Son* (GB) 34. The Flame Within 35. Anthony Adverse 36. The Luckiest Girl in the World 36. Midnight Intruder 37. The Rage of Paris 38. *The Saint in New York* 38. *Duke of West Point* 39. *The Man in the Iron Mask* 39. My Son, My Son 40. Son of Monte Cristo 40. Ladies in Retirement 41. And Then There Were None 45. Monte Cristo's Revenge 47. Young Widow 47. Repeat Performance 47. The Black Arrow 48. Walk a Crooked Mile 48. Pirates of Capri 49. The Fortunes of Captain Blood 50. House by the River 50. Son of Dr Jekyll 51. The Lady and the Bandit 51. Lady in the Iron Mask 52. Captain Pirate 52. Royal African Rifles 53. The Saint's Return (GB) 53. Duffy of San Quentin 54. *The Search for Bridey Murphy* 56. Chuka 67. Terror in the Wax Museum 73, etc.
TV series: The Lone Wolf 53. The Pursuers 63. The Survivors 69.

Hayward, Susan (1918–1975) (Edythe Marrener).
Red-haired, vivacious American leading actress, often in aggressive roles. Born in Brooklyn, she began as a model before going to Hollywood to make a screen test for the role of Scarlett O'Hara in *Gone with the Wind*. She stayed to rid herself of her accent and to learn how to act, beginning with minor roles in Warner films. She was then signed to a seven-year contract by Paramount, whose executives found her difficult and retaliated by giving her poor parts to play. She tried Twentieth Century-Fox, who provided her mainly with a series of uninteresting roles. Her big breakthrough came with *I'll Cry Tomorrow*, about troubled singer Lillian Roth: during the making of the film she attempted suicide. The first of her two husbands was actor Jess Barker (1944–54); she was romantically involved with actors John Carroll and Don Barry.
Biographies: 1974, *Divine Bitch* by Doug McClelland; 1985, *Red: The Tempestuous Life of Susan Hayward* by Robert Laguardia and Gene Arceri.
■ Girls on Probation 38. Our Leading Citizen 39. $1000 A Touchdown 39. Beau Geste 39. Adam Had Four Sons 41. Sis Hopkins 41. Among the Living 41. Reap the Wild Wind 42. The Forest Rangers 42. I Married a Witch 42. Star Spangled Rhythm 42. Change of Heart 43. Jack London 43. Young and Willing 43. The Fighting Seabees 44. And Now Tomorrow 44. The Hairy Ape 44. Canyon Passage 45. Deadline at Dawn 46. Smash-Up (AAN) 47. They Won't Believe Me 47. The Lost Moment 47. Tap Roots 48. The Saxon Charm 48. *Tulsa* 49. *My Foolish Heart* (AAN) 49. House of Strangers 49. I'd Climb the Highest Mountain 50. *I Can Get It For You Wholesale* 51. Rawhide 51. David and Bathsheba 51. *With a Song in My Heart* (AAN) 52. The Lusty Men 52. The Snows of Kilimanjaro 52. The President's Lady 53. White Witch Doctor 53. Demetrius and the Gladiators 54. Garden of Evil 54. Untamed 55. Soldier of Fortune 55. The Conqueror 55. *I'll Cry Tomorrow* (as Lillian Roth) (AAN) 55. Top Secret Affair 57. *I Want to Live* (as Barbara Graham) (AA) 58. A Woman Obsessed 59. Thunder in the Sun 59. The Marriage-Go Round 60. Ada 61. Back Street 61. Stolen Hours (GB) 63. I Thank a Fool (GB) 63. Where Love Has Gone 64. The Honey Pot 67. Valley of the Dolls 67. Fitzgerald and Pride (TV) 71. Heat of Anger (TV) 71. The Revengers 72. Say Goodbye Maggie Cole (TV) 72.

Haywood, Chris (1949–).
English character actor, in Australia.
Newsfront 78. In Search of Anna 79. Kostas 79. The Clinic 82. Heatwave 82. The Return of Captain Invincible 82. Man of Flowers 83. Strikebound 84. Razorback 84. A Street to Die 85. Malcolm 85. Burke and Wills 85. Dogs in Space 87. Manifesto 88. The Tale of Ruby Rose 88. Emerald City 89. Island 89. Quigley Down Under 90. Golden Braid 91. Sweet Talker 91. A Woman's Tale 91. Alex 93. Exile 94. Erotic Tales 94. Muriel's Wedding 94. Shine 96. Lust and Revenge 96. Kiss or Kill 97. Blackrock 97. Molokai 98, etc.
TV series: The Boys from the Bush 91.

Hayworth, Rita (1918–1987) (Margarita Carmen Cansino).
Star American leading actress and dancer of the 40s, often in tempestuous roles, who became a sex symbol of the age with her performance in *Gilda*. Born in Brooklyn, New York, she was the daughter of an American mother and a Spanish gypsy father, whose dancing had topped the bill in vaudeville. She began as a 12-year-old, in a dance act with her sexually abusive father, before being briefly contracted to Fox as a replacement for Dolores Del Rio. Columbia then signed her, but her success came only after her exploitative first husband made her lose weight, lighten her hair and raise her hairline. Often insecure with dialogue, she was at her best in roles that exploited her dancer's expressive movement: as Judy McPherson in *Only Angels Have Wings*; as Natalie Roguin in *The Lady in Question*; as Virgina Brush in *The Strawberry Blonde*; as Gilda Munson in *Gilda*; as Elsa Bannister in Orson Welles's *The Lady from Shanghai*; and as Sadie Thompson in *Miss Sadie Thompson*. Surprisingly, despite her ability, she was an uneasy partner for Fred Astaire in the two films they made together: *You'll Never Get Rich* and *You Were Never Lovelier*. She suffered from Alzheimer's disease from the early 70s, looked after by her daughter with Prince Aly Khan, Princess Yasmin, and was played by Lynda Carter in the 1983 TV movie, *Rita Hayworth: The Love Goddess*. Married Orson Welles (1943–48), Aly Khan (1949–53), singer Dick Haymes (1953–55), and producer James Hill (1958–61); she was romantically involved with actors Victor Mature, David Niven and Gary Merrill, singer Tony Martin, and producers Howard Hughes and Charles Feldman.

Biographies: 1983: *Rita: The Life of Rita Hayworth* by Edward J. Epstein and Joseph Morella; 1983, *Rita Hayworth: A Memoir* by James Hill; 1989, *If This Was Happiness: Rita Hayworth* by Barbara Leaming.

■ Dante's Inferno 35. Under the Pampas Moon 35. Charlie Chan in Egypt 35. Paddy O'Day 35. Human Cargo 36. A Message to Garcia 36. Meet Nero Wolfe 36. Rebellion 36. Old Louisiana 37. Hit the Saddle 37. Trouble in Texas 37. Criminals of the Air 37. Girls Can Play 37. The Game that Kills 37. Paid to Dance 37. The Shadow 37. Who Killed Gail Preston? 38. There's Always a Woman 38. Convicted 38. Juvenile Court 38. Homicide Bureau 38. The Lone Wolf's Spy Hunt 39. Renegade Ranger 39. *Only Angels Have Wings* 39. Special Inspector 39. Music in My Heart 40. Blondie on a Budget 40. Susan and God 40. *The Lady in Question* 40. Angels over Broadway 40. *The Strawberry Blonde* 41. Affectionately Yours 41. Blood and Sand 41. *You'll Never Get Rich* 41. My Gal Sal 42. Tales of Manhattan 42. You Were Never Lovelier 42. *Cover Girl* 44. Tonight and Every Night 45. *Gilda* 46. Down to Earth 47. *The Lady from Shanghai* 48. The Loves of Carmen 48. Affair in Trinidad 52. Salome 53. *Miss Sadie Thompson* 53. Fire Down Below 57. *Pal Joey* 57. *Separate Tables* 58. They Came to Cordura 59. The Story on Page One 59. The Happy Thieves 62. Circus World 64. The Money Trap 66. The Poppy is also a Flower 66. The Rover 68. Sons of Satan 68. The Road to Salina 70. The Naked Zoo 71. The Wrath of God 72.

✪ For supplying the kind of glamour the 40s needed, and for doing it with the saving grace of humour. *Gilda*.

❝ Every man I knew had fallen in love with Gilda and wakened with me. – *R.H.*

A girl is . . . a girl. It's nice to be told you're successful at it. – *R.H.*

I haven't had everything from life. I've had too much. – *R.H.*

I never really thought of myself as a sex symbol – more as a comedienne who could dance. – *R.H.*

Hazell, Hy (1920–1970) (Hyacinth Hazel O'Higgins).
British revue and musical comedy artist.

Meet Me at Dawn 46. Paper Orchid 49. Celia 49. The Lady Craved Excitement 50. The Night Won't Talk 52. Up in the World 56. The Whole Truth 58, etc.

Hazlehurst, Noni.
Australian leading actress.

The Getting of Wisdom 77. Fatty Finn 80. *Monkey Grip* 82. Waterfront (TV) 83. Fran 85. Australian Dream 85. True Colours 87. Waiting 90. Clowning Around 92, etc.

Head, Edith (1907–1981).
American dress designer, in Hollywood from the 20s. First solo credit *She Done Him Wrong* 33; later won Academy Awards for The Heiress 49. Samson and Delilah 51. A Place in the Sun 52, etc; worked on Olly Olly Oxen Free 78. Appeared in *The Oscar* 66.

Autobiography: 1940, *The Dress Doctor*.

Book: 1983, *Edith Head's Hollywood* (with Paddy Calistro).

Head, Murray (1946–).
Young British actor of the 70s.

Romeo and Juliet 68. *Sunday Bloody Sunday* 71. Gawain and the Green Knight 73. Madame Claude (Fr.) 76. White Mischief 87. The Savage/La Barbare 89. Stormy Summer (Fr.) 89. Beaumarchais the Scoundrel (Fr.) 96, etc.

Headly, Glenne (1955–).
American leading actress, from the stage. She was formerly married to actor John Malkovich (1982–90).

Four Friends 81. Eleni 85. Fandango 85. Seize the Day 86. Making Mr Right 87. Nadine 87. Dirty Rotten Scoundrels 88. Paperhouse 88. Stars and Bars 88. Dick Tracy 90. Mortal Thoughts 91. Grand Isle 92. Ordinary Magic 93. Getting Even with Dad 94. Mr Holland's Opus 95. Sgt Bilko 96. Bastard Out of Carolina 96. Winchell (TV) 98, etc.

TV series: Encore! Encore! 98– .

Healey, Myron (1922–).
American general-purpose actor; Doc Holliday in the *Wyatt Earp* TV series.

I Dood It 43. The Man from Colorado 48. Salt Lake Raiders 50. Fort Osage 52. Rage at Dawn 55. Hell's Crossroads 57. Escape from Red Rock 58. Gunfight at Dodge City 59. Harlow 65. Mirage 65. True Grit 69. Which Way to the Front? 70. Devil Bear 75. The Incredible Melting Man 77. Ghost Fever 86. Pulse 87, many others.

Healy, Ted (1886–1937).
Tough-looking, cigar-chewing American vaudevillian who originated the Three Stooges and took them to Hollywood.

Soup to Nuts 30. Dancing Lady 33. The Band Plays On 34. Mad Love 35. San Francisco 36. Hollywood Hotel 37, etc.

Heard, John (1946–).
American general-purpose actor.

First Love 77. Between the Lines 79. Head over Heels 80. Heartbeat 80. Cutter's Way 81. Cat People 82. Best Revenge 83. C.H.U.D. 84. Too Scared to Scream 84. Heaven Help Us 85. After Hours 85. The Trip to Bountiful 85. Violated 86. The Telephone 87. Big 88. The Milagro Beanfield War 88. Betrayed 88. Beaches 88. The Package 89. Mindwalk 90. Rambling Rose 91. Deceived 91. Radio Flyer 92. Gladiator 92. There Was a Little Boy (TV) 93. In the Line of Fire 93. The Pelican Brief 93. Spoils of War (TV) 94. Before and After 96. My Fellow Americans 96. 187 97. Snake Eyes 98. Desert Blue 98, etc.

Hearne, Richard (1908–1979).
British acrobatic comedian, in music hall and circus practically from the cradle. Made occasional films, often in his character of 'Mr Pastry'.

Dance Band 35. Millions 37. Miss London Ltd 42. The Butler's Dilemma 43. One Night with You 48. Helter Skelter 49. Captain Horatio Hornblower 51. Madame Louise 51. Miss Robin Hood 52. Something in the City 53. Tons of Trouble 56, etc.

Hearst, William Randolph (1863–1951).
American newspaper magnate thought to have been the original of *Citizen Kane*. Also noted for pushing his protégée Marion Davies to film stardom by buying a production company solely for her vehicles.

Biography: 1961, *Citizen Hearst* by W. A. Swanberg.

❝ When W. R. was out of earshot, Marion [Davies], inspired by his elephantine garments, called him 'Droopy Drawers'. – *Anita Loos*

Heatherton, Joey (1944–).
American leading lady, former child stage performer.

Twilight of Honor 64. Where Love Has Gone 64. My Blood Runs Cold 64. Bluebeard 72. The Happy Hooker Goes to Washington 77. Cry-Baby 90, etc.

Heche, Anne.
American leading actress who began in theatre as a 12-year-old and first came to attention in the soap opera *Another World*, playing teenage twins. She caused a minor sensation in 1997 with the announcement that she was the lover of actress Ellen DeGeneres.

The Adventures of Huck Finn 93. Against the Wall (TV) 93. Milk Money 94. Kingfish: A Story of Huey P. Long (TV) 95. Pie in the Sky 95. Wild Side 96. Walking and Talking 96. The Juror 96. Donnie Brasco 97. Volcano 97. Six Days, Seven Nights 98. Return to Paradise 98, etc.

Hecht, Ben (1894–1964).
American writer and critic with screenplay credits going back to silent days. Often worked in collaboration with Charles MacArthur.

Autobiographies: 1954, *A Child of the Century*. 1963, *Gaily Gaily*.

Biographies: 1978, *The Five Lives of Ben Hecht* by Doug Fetherling; 1995, *Ben Hecht: A Biography* by William MacAdams.

Underworld (w) (AA) 29. The Great Gabbo (oa) 29. *The Front Page* (oa) 31. Topaze (w) 33. Twentieth Century (oa) 34. *Crime Without Passion* (wd) 34. *The Scoundrel* (wd) (AA) 35. *Soak the Rich* (wpd) 36. *Nothing Sacred* (w) 37. The Goldwyn Follies (w) 38. *Wuthering Heights* (co-w, AAN) 39. *Angels Over Broadway* (wpd) (AANw) 40. Lydia (w) 41. Tales of Manhattan (w) 42. The Black Swan (w) 42. *Spellbound* (w) 45. *Notorious* (AANw) 46. The Specter of the Rose (wpd) 46. Her Husband's Affairs (w) 47. The Miracle of the Bells (w) 48. Whirlpool (w) 49. Actors and Sin (wpd) 52. Monkey Business (w) 52. Miracle in the Rain (w) 56. Legend of the Lost (w) 58. Circus World (w) 64, etc.

✪ For being connected in some way with most of the enjoyable hard-boiled comedies and melodramas with which one associates Hollywood in the 30s and 40s. *Nothing Sacred*.

❝ Hollywood held the lure . . . tremendous sums of money for work that required no more effort than a game of pinochle. – *B.H.*

Movies are one of the bad habits that have corrupted our century. They have slipped into the American mind more misinformation in one evening than the Dark Ages could muster in a decade. – *B.H.*

A movie is never any better than the stupidest man connected with it. – *B.H.*

The movies are an eruption of trash that has lamed the American mind and retarded Americans from becoming cultured people. – *B.H.*

If you wrote a good movie it was because you were lucky enough to get on the payroll of a classy boss. Classy or not, the boss called the shots and you did as bid. You were a sort of literary errand boy with an oil magnate's income. – *B.H.*

Writing a good movie brings a writer about as much fame as steering a bicycle. – *B.H.*

Hecht, Harold (1903–1985).
American producer, formerly dance director and literary agent. From 1947 produced jointly with Burt Lancaster and later James Hill.

Vera Cruz 54. Marty 55. Trapeze 56. Separate Tables 58. Taras Bulba 63. Cat Ballou 65. The Way West 67, etc.

Heckart, Eileen (1919–).
American character actress, mainly on stage.

Miracle in the Rain 56. The Bad Seed (AAN) 56. Somebody Up There Likes Me 57. Hot Spell 57. Heller in Pink Tights 60. Up the Down Staircase 68. No Way to Treat a Lady 68. Butterflies Are Free (AA) 72. Zandy's Bride 74. The Hiding Place 75. Burnt Offerings 77. Sunshine Christmas (TV) 77. Suddenly Love (TV) 78. Backstairs at the White House (TV) 79. White Mama (TV) 81. FDR: The Last Year (TV) 81. Heartbreak Ridge 86. Annie McGuire 88. Breathing Lessons (TV) 94. The First Wives Club 96, etc.

Heckerling, Amy (1954–).
American director and screenwriter, concentrating on low-brow comedies.

Fast Times at Ridgemont High 82. Johnny Dangerously 84. National Lampoon's European Vacation 85. Look Who's Talking (wd) 89. Look Who's Talking Too (wd) 90. Look Who's Talking Now (co-p) 93. *Clueless* (wd) 95. A Night at the Roxbury (p) 98, etc.

Heckroth, Hein (1901–1970).
German art director who did work in Britain, mainly for Powell and Pressburger.

Caesar and Cleopatra 45. *A Matter of Life and Death* 46. *The Red Shoes* (AA) 48. Tales of Hoffman 51. The Story of Gilbert and Sullivan 53. The Battle of the River Plate 56. Torn Curtain (US) 66, etc.

Hedaya, Dan.
American actor, a former teacher, from the theatre, best known as Nick Tortelli in the TV sitcom *Cheers*.

The Seduction of Joe Tynan 79. Night of the Juggler 80. Endangered Species 82. The Hunger 83. Blood Simple 84. Running Scared 86. Wise Guys 86. Tune in Tomorrow/Aunt Julia and the Scriptwriter 90. Pacific Heights 90. Rookie of the Year 90. The Addams Family 91. Mr Wonderful 92. Boiling Point 93. Benny and Joon 93. Maverick 94. The Usual Suspects 95. Clueless 95. To Die For 95. Nixon 95. Fair Game 95. Freeway 96. Ransom 96. Marvin's Room 96. Daylight 96. The First Wives Club 96. A Life Less Ordinary 97. The Garden of Redemption 97. Alien: Resurrection 97. Be the Man 98. A Night at the Roxbury 98, etc.

Hedison, David (1926–) (Ara Heditsian, formerly known as Al Hedison).
American leading man, mostly on TV.

The Enemy Below 57. *The Fly* 58. Son of Robin Hood 59. The Lost World 60. Marines Let's Go 61. The Greatest Story Ever Told 65. Live and Let Die 73. The Cat Creature (TV) 73. Adventures of the Queen (TV) 75. The Lives of Jenny Dolan (TV) 75. Murder in Peyton Place (TV) 77. The Power Within (TV) 79. North Sea Hijack 80. The Naked Face 84. Smart Alec 85. Licence to Kill 89, etc.

TV series: *Five Fingers* 59–60. *Voyage to the Bottom of the Sea* 64–68. Dynasty II: The Colbys 85–87.

Hedley, Jack (1930–).
Amiable British leading man best remembered as TV's 'Tim Frazer'.

Room at the Top (debut) 59. Make Mine Mink 60. Lawrence of Arabia 62. In the French Style 63. The Scarlet Blade 63. *Of Human Bondage* 64. Witchcraft 65. The Anniversary 67. Goodbye Mr Chips 69. Brief Encounter (TV) 74. For Your Eyes Only 81. Sophia Loren (TV) 81. Three Kinds of Heat 87, etc.

TV series: Kate 70–71. Colditz 72–73. Who Pays the Ferryman 77. Hard Cases 88.

Hedren, Tippi (1935–) (Nathalie Hedren).
American leading lady, former TV model. She is the mother of actress Melanie Griffith.

The Birds 63. Marnie 64. A Countess from Hong Kong 66. The Man with the Albatross 69. Tiger by the Tail 69. Satan's Harvest 69. Mr Kingstreet's War 73. The Harrad Experiment 73. Roar 82. The Thrill of Genius 85. Foxfire Light 86. Deadly Spygames 89. Pacific Heights 90. In the Cold of the Night 91. Inevitable Grace 94. The Birds II: Land's End (TV) 94. Teresa's Tattoo 94. Precious 96. Citizen Ruth 96. I Woke Up Early the Day I Died 98, etc.

Heerman, Victor (1892–1977).
Anglo-American director, in US from boyhood.

■ Don't Ever Marry 20. The Poor Simp 20. A Divorce of Convenience 21. The Chicken in the Case 21. My Boy 22. John Smith 22. Love Is an Awful Thing 22. Rupert of Hentzau 23. Modern Matrimony 23. The Dangerous Maid 23. The Confidence Man 24. Old Home Week 25. Irish Luck 25. For Wives Only 26. Rubber Heels 26. Ladies Must Dress 27. Love Hungry 28. Personality 30. Paramount on Parade 30. *Animal Crackers* 30. Sea Legs 30.

Also screenwriter, usually in collaboration.

Heffron, Richard T. (1930–).
American director, from TV.

Newman's Law 73. Toma (TV pilot) 73. Outrage (TV) 73. The Rockford Files (TV pilot) 74. The Morning After (TV) 74. The California Kid (TV) 74. Locusts (TV) 74. I Will Fight No More Forever (TV) 75. Death Scream (TV) 75. Trackdown 76. Futureworld 76. Young Joe the Forgotten Kennedy

(TV) 77. Outlaw Blues 77. See How She Runs (TV) 78. True Grit (TV) 78. A Rumor of War (TV) 80. Foolin' Around 80. I the Jury 82. Anatomy of an Illness (TV) 82. The French Revolution 89, etc.

Heflin, Van (1910–1971) (Emmett Evan Heflin).
Purposeful American leading man of the 40s; craggy character actor of the 50s and 60s.
■ A Woman Rebels 36. The Outcasts of Poker Flat 37. Flight from Glory 37. Saturday's Heroes 37. Annapolis Salute 37. Back Door to Heaven 39. *Santa Fe Trail* 40. The Feminine Touch 41. H. M. Pulham Esq 41. *Johnny Eager* (AA) 41. *Kid Glove Killer* 42. Seven Sweethearts 42. Grand Central Murder 42. Tennessee Johnson 42. Presenting Lily Mars 43. *The Strange Love of Martha Ivers* 46. Till the Clouds Roll By 46. Possessed 47. Green Dolphin Street 47. Tap Roots 48. B.F.'s Daughter 48. The Three Musketeers 48. Act of Violence 48. Madame Bovary 48. East Side West Side 49. Tomahawk 51. *The Prowler* 51. Weekend with Father 51. My Son John 52. Wings of the Hawk 53. *Shane* 53. Tanganyika 54. South of Algiers (GB) 54. The Raid 54. Woman's World 54. The Black Widow 54. Count Three and Pray 55. Battle Cry 55. *Patterns* 56. *3.10 to Yuma* 57. Gunman's Walk 58. They Came to Cordura 59. Tempest 59. Five Branded Women 60. Under Ten Flags 60. Cry of Battle 63. The Wastrel 64. To Be a Man 64. The Greatest Story Ever Told 65. Once a Thief 65. Stagecoach 66. The Man Outside (GB) 67. Each Man for Himself 68. *Airport* 69. The Big Bounce 69. The Last Child (TV) 71.

Hefti, Neal (1922–).
American composer, a former big band musician and arranger for the bands of Woody Herman, Harry James and Count Basie. He also wrote the theme for the *Batman* TV series.
Sex and the Single Girl 65. How to Murder Your Wife 65. Boeing Boeing 65. Harlow 65. Synanon 65. Duel at Diablo 66. Lord Love a Duck 66. Barefoot in the Park 66. The Odd Couple 68. Last of the Red Hot Lovers 72. Won Ton Ton, the Dog Who Saved Hollywood 76, etc.

Heggie, O. P. (1879–1936).
Australian character actor of stage and, latterly, Hollywood screen.
The Mysterious Dr Fu Manchu 29. East Lynne 31. Smiling Through 32. Midnight 34. The Count of Monte Cristo 34. Bride of Frankenstein (as the blind hermit) 35. Prisoner of Shark Island 36, etc.

Heifits, Joseph (1904–1995).
Russian director, from 1928. Known in the 30s for *Baltic Deputy*, but did not come to Western notice again until *The Lady with the Little Dog* 59.
In the Town of S 65. Salute Marya 70. Asya 77. Shurochka 82. The Accused 85, etc.

Heim, Alan.
American film editor.
The Twelve Chairs 70. Doc 71. Godspell 73. Lenny 74. Network (AAN) 76. Hair 79. All That Jazz (AA) 79. The Fan 81. So Fine 81. Star 80 83. Goodbye New York 85. She's Having a Baby 88. Funny Farm 88. Valmont 89. Quick Change 90. Billy Bathgate 91. Dennis the Menace/Dennis 93. Copycat 95. Leave It to Beaver 97. American History X 98, etc.

Heindorf, Ray (1908–1980).
American musical director.
Hard to Get 38. Strawberry Blonde 41. Yankee Doodle Dandy (AA) 42. This Is the Army (AA) 43. Calamity Jane 53. A Star Is Born 54. The Music Man (AA) 62. Finian's Rainbow (AAN) 68, many others.

Heinlein, Robert A. (1907–1988).
American best-selling science-fiction novelist. Born in Missouri, he graduated from the US Naval Academy and, after postgraduate studies in mathematics and physics at UCLA, turned to writing in the late 30s, and was one of the first science-fiction writers to move from pulp magazines to mainstream publications. His novel *Space Cadet* was the basis of a children's TV series of the early 50s, *Tom Corbett, Space Cadet*. *Starship Troopers*, with its theme of the value of a military élite, was rejected by his usual publishers.
Destination Moon (co-w, from his novel *Rocketship Galileo*) 50. The Puppet Masters (oa) 94. Starship Troopers (oa) 97.

Heinz, Gerard (1903–1972).
German character actor, mainly in British movies.
Thunder Rock 42. Went the Day Well? 42. Caravan 46. His Excellency 51. The Man Inside 57. House of the Seven Hawks 59. The Guns of Navarone 61. The Cardinal 63. The Dirty Dozen 67, many others.

Heisler, Stuart (1894–1979).
Competent American director.
■ Straight from the Shoulder 36. Poppy 37. The Hurricane (co-d) 38. The Biscuit Eater 40. *The Monster and The Girl* 41. Among the Living 41. The Remarkable Andrew 42. *The Glass Key* 42. Along Came Jones 45. *Blue Skies* 46. Vendetta (co-d) 46. *Smash Up* 47. Tulsa 49. Tokyo Joe 49. Chain Lightning 50. Dallas 50. Storm Warning 50. Journey into Light 51. Saturday Island 52. *The Star* 53. Beachhead 54. This is My Love 54. I Died a Thousand Times 55. The Lone Ranger 56. The Burning Hills 56. Hitler 62.

Heiss, Carol (1940–).
German-Swiss skating star: she came to Hollywood for one movie, *Snow White and the Three Stooges* 61.

Held, Anna (1873–1918).
German singer-dancer who married Ziegfeld and starred in his early Follies. Luise Rainer portrayed her in *The Great Ziegfeld* and Barbara Parkins in *Ziegfeld, the Man and His Women*. She made one film appearance in 1916: *Madame La Présidente*.

Held, Edward (1894–1985).
American set designer.
Lost Horizon 37. The Hurricane 38. The Goldwyn Follies 38. Wuthering Heights 39. Kings Row 41. Across the Pacific 42. Them 54, etc.

Held, Martin (1908–1992).
German leading actor.
Black Eyes 51. Captain from Kopenick 56. Roses for the Prosecutor 59. The Oldest Profession 67. The Serpent 72. Night Flight from Moscow 77. The Pentecost Outing 78, etc.

Helgeland, Brian (c. 1961–).
American screenwriter and director.
976-Evil (co-w) 88. A Nightmare on Elm Street Part Four: The Dream Master (co-w) 88. Highway to Hell (w) 92. Assassins (co-w) 95. Conspiracy Theory (co-w) 97. LA Confidential (co-w) 97. The Postman (co-w) 97. Parker (wd) 98, etc.

Helgenberger, Marg (1958–).
American actress, best known as K. C. Koloski in the TV series *China Beach* 88–91. She also appears intermittently in the mid-90s series *ER*.
Always 89. After Midnight 89. Blind Vengeance (TV) 90. Crooked Hearts 91. Death Dreams (TV) 91. Desperate Motives/Distant Cousins 92. Fallen Angels 2 (TV) 93. Stephen King's The Tommyknockers (TV) 93. The Cowboy Way 94. Bad Boys 95. Species 95. Fire Down Below 97. The Last Time I Committed Suicide 97. Elmore Leonard's The Gold Coast (TV) 98. Species 2 98, etc.

Heller, Joseph (1923–).
American satirical novelist, whose *Catch 22* was rather unsatisfactorily filmed.
Autobiography: 1998, *Now and Then: From Coney Island to Here*.
Dirty Dingus Magee (co-w) 70.

Heller, Lukas (1930–1988).
German-born screenwriter, associated chiefly with Robert Aldrich.
Whatever Happened to Baby Jane? 62. Hush Hush Sweet Charlotte (co-w) 64. The Dirty Dozen (co-w) 67. The Killing of Sister George 68. The Deadly Trackers 73. Damnation Alley (co-w) 77, etc.

Heller, Otto (1896–1970).
Czech-born cinematographer, in Britain since early 30s. Had more than 300 features to his credit.
The High Command 36. Tomorrow We Live 42. Mr Emmanuel 44. I Live in Grosvenor Square 45. *The Queen of Spades* 48. The Winslow Boy 48. Never Take No for an Answer 51. The Divided Heart 54. Manuela 57. The Light in the Piazza 62. West Eleven 63. The Ipcress File 65. Alfie 66. Funeral in Berlin 66. Duffy 68. Bloomfield 70, etc.

Hellinger, Mark (1903–1947).
American screenwriter and producer, a former Broadway columnist, noted for his capacity for alcohol.
Biography: 1952, *The Mark Hellinger Story* by Jim Bishop.
The Killers 46. Brute Force 47. Naked City (also narrated) 48.
❝ I got Mark Hellinger so drunk last night that it took three bellboys to put me to bed. – *W. C. Fields*

Hellman, Jerome (1928–).
American producer, former agent.
■ The World of Henry Orient 64. A Fine Madness 66. *Midnight Cowboy* (AA) 69. The Day of the Locust 75. *Coming Home* (AAN) 78. Promises in the Dark (& d) 79. Mosquito Coast 86.

Hellman, Lillian (1907–1984).
American playwright who adapted much of her own work for the screen and also wrote other screenplays.
Autobiographies: 1969, *An Unfinished Woman*. 1974, *Pentimento*, which was filmed as *Julia*.
These Three 36. *The Little Foxes* (AAN) 41. Watch on the Rhine 43. North Star (AAN) 43. The Searching Wind 46. *Another Part of the Forest* 48. *The Children's Hour* 62. Toys in the Attic 63. The Chase 66. Julia 77, etc.
❝ I cannot and will not cut my conscience to fit this year's fashions. – *L.H.*

Hellman, Marcel (1898–1985).
Rumanian producer, long in Britain.
The Amateur Gentleman 36. Jeannie 41. Happy Go Lucky 51. Northwest Frontier 59. Moll Flanders 65, many others.

Hellman, Monte (1931–).
American director and producer whose career began promisingly and then petered out in a succession of abandoned projects. A former editor, he began in films working for Roger Corman.
■ The Beast from Haunted Cave 59. Flight to Fury 65. Back Door to Hell 65. The Shooting 65. Ride in the Whirlwind 66. Two Lane Blacktop 71. Cockfighter 74. China 9, Liberty 37 78. Iguana 88. Reservoir Dogs (p) 92. The Killing Box (ed) 93. LA without a Map (GB/Fr./Fin.) (as himself) 98.

Helm, Brigitte (1906–1996) (Gisele Eve Schittenhelm).
German star actress of the 20s.
Metropolis 26. *The Loves of Jeanne Ney* 27. Alraune 28. Countess of Monte Cristo 31. L'Atlantide 31. Gold 33. The Blue Danube 34, etc.

Helm, Fay (1913–).
American actress.
Racket Busters 38. Dark Victory 39. A Child Is Born 40. Night Monster 42. Phantom Lady (title role) 44. Sister Kenny 46. The Locket 47, etc.

Helmond, Katherine (1933–).
Saucer-eyed American comedy actress.
Baby Blue Marine 74. Dr Max (TV) 74. Locusts (TV) 74. The Legend of Lizzie Borden (TV) 75. Family Plot 76. Little Ladies of the Night (TV) 77. Getting Married (TV) 79. Pearl (TV) 79. Time Bandits 81. Brazil 84. Shadey 85. Lady in White 88. Inside Monkey Zetterland 92. Amore! 93. The Spy Within 94. Fear and Loathing in Las Vegas 98, etc.
TV series: *Soap* 77–80.

Helpmann, Sir Robert (1909–1986).
Australian ballet dancer and actor of stage and screen, in Britain from 1930.
One of Our Aircraft Is Missing 42. Henry V 44. The Red Shoes 48. Tales of Hoffman 50. 55 Days in Peking 62. The Quiller Memorandum 66. Chitty Chitty Bang Bang 68. Alice's Adventures in Wonderland 72. Don Quixote (& co-d) 73, others.

Helton, Percy (1894–1971).
Chubby little American comedy actor; his round face expressed surprise and dismay in innumerable small roles.
Silver Wings 22. Miracle on 34th Street 47. The Set Up 49. My Friend Irma 49. Call Me Madam 52: A Star is Born 54. Butch Cassidy and the Sundance Kid 69, many others.
TV series: The Beverly Hillbillies 68–71.

Hemingway, Ernest (1899–1961).
Distinguished American novelist. Works filmed include *A Farewell to Arms* 32 and 57. *Spanish Earth* (orig sp, p) 37. *For Whom the Bell Tolls* 43. *The Killers* 46 and 64. *The Macomber Affair* 47. *The Snows of Kilimanjaro* 53. *The Sun Also Rises* 57. *The Old Man and the Sea* 58. *Adventures of a Young Man* 62. *To Have and Have Not* was filmed three times (inaccurately): in 1944, 1951 (as *The Breaking Point*) and 1956 (as *The Gun Runner*).
Book: 1981, *Hemingway and the Movies* by Frank M. Laurence.

Hemingway, Margaux (1955–1996).
American fashion model and occasional leading lady, granddaughter of Ernest HEMINGWAY. Problems with alcoholism and bulimia dogged her later career. Committed suicide.
Lipstick 76. Killer Fish 80. They Call Me Bruce 82. Over the Brooklyn Bridge 83. The Killing Machine 85. La Messe en Si Mineur 90. Inner Sanctum 91. Deadly Rivals 92. Frame-Up II: The Cover-Up 92, etc.

Hemingway, Mariel (1961–).
American actress, sister of Margaux HEMINGWAY.
Lipstick 76. I Want to Keep My Baby (TV) 76. Manhattan (AAN) 79. Personal Best 82. Star 80 83. Creator 84. The Mean Season 84. Superman IV 87. The Suicide Club 87. Sunset 88. Fire, Ice and Dynamite 90. Midnight Spy 90. Delirious 91. Falling from Grace 92. Deceptions 2: Edge of Deception 92. The Crying Child (TV) 94. Bad Moon 96. Deconstructing Harry 97. Louisa May Alcott's Little Men 98, etc.
TV series: Central Park West 95.

Hemmings, David (1941–).
Slightly-built British leading man who after appearing in many second features suddenly seemed to have the acceptable image for the late 60s.
No Trees in the Street 59. The Wind of Change 60. Some People 62. Live It Up 63. Dateline Diamonds 65. Eye of the Devil 66. *Blow Up* 66. Camelot 67. *The Charge of the Light Brigade* 68. A Long Day's Dying 68. Only When I Larf 68. Barbarella 68. Alfred the Great 69. The Walking Stick 69. Fragment of Fear 69. Unman, Wittering and Zigo 70. The Love Machine 71. Running Scared (d only) 72. Mister Quilp 75. The Squeeze 77. Islands in the Stream 77. The Prince and the Pauper 77. Just a Gigolo (& d) 78. Murder by Decree 79. Charlie Muffin (TV) 79. Race for the Yankee Zephyr (d only) 81. The Survivor (d only) 81. Man, Woman and Child 82. Calamity Jane (TV) 84. The Rainbow 89. Dark Horse (d) 92, etc.

Hempel, Anouska (Lady Weinberg).
Australian-born leading lady in Britain. She is now a hotelier and fashion designer.
On Her Majesty's Secret Service 69. Scars of Dracula 70. The Magnificent Seven Deadly Sins 71. Go for a Take 72. Slaves 73. Double Exposure 76, etc.

Henabery, Joseph (1886–1976).
American silent actor who played Lincoln in *The Birth of a Nation* and later directed Gish and Fairbanks.
His Majesty the American 19. A Sainted Devil 24, etc.
❝ If you'd had two or three years of motion pictures you were a pioneer, a veteran. You'd really been through the mill. You might have made a hundred and some pictures in that time – a one-reeler could be made in a day. – *J.H.*

Henderson, Florence (1934–).
American singer and actress with theatrical experience.
Song of Norway 70. Shakes the Clown 91.
TV series: The Brady Bunch 69–73.

Henderson, Marcia (1930–1987).
American leading lady of the 50s.
Thunder Bay 53. The Glass Web 53. Naked Alibi 54. Back to God's Country 54, etc.

Henderson, Ray (1896–1970) (Raymond Brost).
American composer, notably in collaboration with lyricists 'Buddy' DE SYLVA and Lew BROWN. Born in Buffalo, New York, he trained at the Chicago Conservatory of Music and worked as a song plugger and accompanist in vaudeville before teaming up with Brown and, later, De Sylva.

When De Sylva became a film producer and the partnership ended, he collaborated with Brown before retiring in the late 40s. His best-known songs include 'Alabamy Bound', 'Animal Crackers in My Soup', 'Black Bottom', 'Bye Bye Blackbird', 'Five Foot Two, Eyes of Blue', 'I'm a Dreamer, Aren't We All', 'I'm Sitting on Top of the World', 'Life Is Just a Bowl of Cherries', and 'You're the Cream in My Coffee'. In the biopic of De Sylva, Brown and Henderson, *The Best Things in Life Are Free* 56, he was played by Dan DAILEY.

The Singing Fool (s 'Sonny Boy') 28. Say It with Songs (s) 29. Sunny Side Up (co-w, s) 29. Good News (s) 30. Follow Thru (co-w, s) 30. Just Imagine (co-w, s) 30. Indiscreet (co-w, s) 31. George White's Scandals (s) 34. Curly Top (s) 35. The Jolson Story (s) 46. Good News (s) 47. Jolson Sings Again (s) 49, etc.

Hendrix, Wanda (1928–1981).
American leading lady.

Confidential Agent 45. Ride the Pink Horse 47. Miss Tatlock's Millions 48. Prince of Foxes 49. Captain Carey USA 50. The Highwayman 52. The Last Posse 53. The Black Dakotas 54. Johnny Cool 63. Stage to Thunder Rock 65, etc.

Hendry, Ian (1931–1984).
Virile, aggressive British leading actor, mostly on TV.

In the Nick 60. *Live Now Pay Later* 62. The Girl in the Headlines 63. Children of the Damned 63. This Is My Street 63. *The Beauty Jungle* 64. Repulsion 65. The Hill 65. The Sandwich Man 66. Casino Royale 67. Doppelganger 69. The Southern Star 69. The Mackenzie Break 70. Get Carter 71. The Jerusalem File 72. All Coppers Are . . . 72. Tales from the Crypt 72. Theatre of Blood 73. Assassin 73. The Internecine Project 74. The Bitch 79. McVicar 80, etc.

Henenlotter, Frank.
American exploitation and horror film director and screenwriter.

Basket Case 82. Brain Damage 88. Basket Case 2 89. Frankenhooker 90. Basket Case 3 91, etc.

❝ Sleazy movies are my world. Give me $23 million and I'll give you 23 low-budget sex and horror films. – *F.H.*

Henie, Sonja (1912–1969).
Norwegian skating star who appeared in light Hollywood musicals of the 30s and 40s. Died of leukaemia.

Autobiography: 1940, *Wings on My Feet*.

■ *One in a Million* 36. Thin Ice 37. Happy Landing 38. My Lucky Star 38. Second Fiddle 39. Everything Happens at Night 39. Sun Valley Serenade 41. Iceland 42. Wintertime 43. It's a Pleasure 45. The Countess of Monte Cristo 48. Hello London (GB) 58.

❝ Sonja, you'll never go broke. All you have to do is hock your trophies. – *Radie Harris*

Henley, Beth (1952–).
American dramatist and screenwriter.

True Stories 86. Crimes of the Heart (AAN) 86. Nobody's Fool (& a) 86. Miss Firecracker 89.

Hennesy, Dale (1926–1981).
American art director and production designer, a former illustrator.

Under the Yum Yum Tree 63. *Fantastic Voyage* (AA) 66. In Like Flint 67. Dirty Harry 71. Everything You Always Wanted to Know about Sex 72. Battle for the Planet of the Apes 73. Slither 73. *Sleeper* 73. *Young Frankenstein* 74. Logan's Run (AAN) 76. King Kong 76. Who'll Stop the Rain/Dog Soldiers 78. Wholly Moses! 80. Annie (AAN) 81, etc.

Henning-Jensen, Astrid (1914–).
Danish woman director, a former actress.

Denmark Grows Up 47. Krane's Bakery Shop 51. Ballet Girl 54. Unfaithful 66. Me and You 68. Winter Children/Vinterboern (wd) 78. Street of My Childhood/Barndommens Gade 86. In Spite Of/Trods Alt 90, etc.

Henreid, Paul (1908–1992) (Paul von Hernreid).
Austrian leading man of the 30s; fled to Britain, then to Hollywood, where his immobile good looks made him a suitable leading man, in the absence at war of home-grown talent, for a number of strong-willed leading ladies. In later life he directed the occasional film and many TV shows.

Autobiography: 1984, *Ladies' Man*.

Goodbye Mr Chips 39. *Night Train to Munich* 40. Joan of Paris 41. *Now Voyager* 42. Casablanca 42. In Our Time 44. Between Two Worlds 44. The Conspirators 44. The Spanish Main 45. Devotion 46. Of Human Bondage 46. Deception 46. Song of Love 47. The Scar 48. Rope of Sand 49. So Young So Bad 50. Last of the Buccaneers 50. For Men Only (& pd) 51. Thief of Damascus 52. Siren of Baghdad 53. Deep in My Heart (as Ziegfeld) 54. Pirates of Tripoli 55. A Woman's Devotion (& d) 57. Holiday for Lovers 59. The Four Horsemen of the Apocalypse 62. Dead Ringer (d only) 64. Operation Crossbow 65. The Madwoman of Chaillot 69. The Failing of Raymond (TV) 71. Mrs R (TV) 75. Exorcist II: The Heretic 77, etc.

❝ He looks as though his idea of fun would be to find a nice cold damp grave and sit in it. – *Richard Winnington, 1946, of Henreid's performance in Of Human Bondage*

Henrey, Bobby (1939–).
British child actor, notable in *The Fallen Idol* 48. Retired after *The Wonder Kid* 50.

Henriksen, Lance (1943–).
Lean, intense American character actor, often as a villain, whose performances enliven many exploitation movies.

Dog Day Afternoon 75. Damien: Omen II 78. The Visitor 80. Prince of the City 81. Piranha 2: The Spawning 83. The Right Stuff 83. Savage Dawn 84. The Terminator 84. The Jagged Edge 85. Aliens 86. Near Dark 87. Pumpkinhead 88. Deadly Intent 88. The Hit List 88. The Horror Show 89. Johnny Handsome 89. Stone Cold 91. The Pit and the Pendulum (as Torquemada) 91. Alien^3 92. Super Mario Bros 93. Excessive Force 93. No Escape 94. Boulevard 94. Man's Best Friend 94. Color of Night 94. The Quick and the Dead 95. Dead Man 95. Powder 95. Felony 95. Baja 95. Profile for Murder (TV) 96. Gunfighter's Moon 86. Face the Evil 97, etc.

TV series: Millennium 96– .

Henriques, Julian (1955–).
English director and screenwriter, from television, where he produced documentaries on the arts. He has a PhD in social psychology.

Babymother 98.

Henry, Buck (1930–) (B. Zuckerman).
Mild-looking American actor-writer of abrasive comedy.

The Troublemaker (w) 64. The Graduate (AANw) 67. Candy (w) 68. *Catch 22* (w) 70. The Owl and the Pussycat (w) 70. *Taking Off* (a) 71. The Day of the Dolphin (w) 73. The Man Who Fell to Earth (w) 76. Heaven Can Wait (co-d, AAN) 78. Old Boyfriends (a) 79. The First Family (wd) 80. Gloria (a) 80. Eating Raoul (a) 82. Protocol (w) 84. Aria (a) 87. I Love N.Y. (w) 87. Dark Before Dawn (a) 88. Rude Awakening (a) 89. Tune in Tomorrow/Aunt Julia and the Scriptwriter (a) 90. Defending Your Life (a) 91. The Lounge People (a) 91. The Linguini Incident (a) 91. Short Cuts (a) 93. Grumpy Old Men (a) 93. To Die For (w) 95. 1999 (a) 98. I'm Losing You (a) 98, etc.

Henry, Charlotte (1913–1980).
American juvenile actress of the early 30s.

Rebecca of Sunnybrook Farm 32. Alice in Wonderland 33. Babes in Toyland 34. Charlie Chan at the Opera 37. Stand and Deliver 41, etc.

Henry, Justin (1971–).
American child star.

■ *Kramer vs Kramer* (AAN) 79. Tiger Town 84. Sixteen Candles 84. Martin's Day 85. Sweet Hearts Dance 88.

Henry, Lenny (1958–).
English stand-up comedian, successful on TV.

The Suicide Club 88. Lenny: Live and Unleashed (concert) 90. True Identity 91. Alive and Kicking (TV) 91, etc.

TV series: The Fosters 76. The Lenny Henry Show 87–89. Chef! 93–94, 96. Lenny Goes to Town 98.

Henry, Mike (1939–).
American ex-athlete who came to the screen briefly as Tarzan.

Tarzan and the Valley of Gold 65. Tarzan and the Great River 67. Tarzan and the Jungle Boy 68. Skyjacked 72. Adios Amigo 75. Smokey and the Bandit 77. Smokey and the Bandit II 80. Smokey and the Bandit III 83. Psycho III 86. Outrageous Fortune 87, etc.

Henry, O. (1862–1910) (William Sydney Porter).
American story writer who for the last ten years of his life wrote a weekly story for the *New York World*. A compendium of them was used in *O. Henry's Full House* 52, and there followed a TV series, *The O. Henry Playhouse* 56.

Henry, William (1918–).
American leading man, former child actor, later in callow roles.

Lord Jim 26. The Thin Man 34. Tarzan Escapes 36. Four Men and a Prayer 38. Blossoms in the Dust 41. Women in Bondage 44. Federal Man 49. Jungle Moonmen 54. Mister Roberts 55. The Lone Ranger and the Lost City of Gold 58. How the West Was Won 62. The Man Who Shot Liberty Valance 62. Donovan's Reef 63. Cheyenne Autumn 64. Taggart 64. Dear Brigitte . . . 65. El Dorado 67. Skin Game 71, etc.

Henson, Gladys (1897–1983) (Gladys Gunn).
Irish character actress often seen as plump, homely mum, or latterly grand-mum. On stage from 1910.

The Captive Heart 45. It Always Rains on Sunday 47. *London Belongs to Me* 48. *The Blue Lamp* 50. Lady Godiva Rides Again 51. Those People Next Door 52. Cockleshell Heroes 55. The Leather Boys 63, etc.

Henson, Jim (1936–1990).
American creator of the Muppets; actor, writer, director, and the voice of Kermit the Frog. The Muppets, created in 1954, featured on such TV series as *Sesame Street* from 1969, *The Muppet Show* 76–81, and *Fraggle Rock* 83–87. His Creature Shop also created animatronic creatures for films, including *Teenage Mutant Ninja Turtles* and *The Witches*.

Biography: 1994, *Jim Henson – The Works* by Christopher Finch.

Book: 1997, *No Strings Attached: The Inside Story of Jim Henson's Creature Shop* by Matt Bacon.

The Muppet Movie 79. The Great Muppet Caper (d) 81. The Dark Crystal (co-d) 82. The Muppets Take Manhattan 84. Labyrinth 86.

Henson, Leslie (1891–1957).
British stage comedian with bulging eyes; often in musical farces. Born in London, he worked in the City before making his debut as a concert artist in 1910 and became a star in *Tonight's the Night* in 1915. Married three times: his second wife was actress Gladys HENSON; he was the father of actor Nicky HENSON.

Autobiographies: 1926, *My Laugh Story*; 1948, *Yours Faithfully*.

The Sport of Kings 30. It's a Boy 33. A Warm Corner 34. Oh Daddy 35. The Demi-Paradise 43. Home and Away 56, etc.

❝ He will, in moments of ecstasy, look at you out of eyes bulging like those of a moth who has eaten too much tapestry. Or, in the matter of indignant denial, shoot his head with the scowl of a tortoise accused of being born yesterday. Or, thrown by the passions, expire like Mrs Leo Hunter's frog. – *James Agate*

Henson, Nicky (1945–).
British general-purpose actor. He is the son of Leslie Henson.

Witchfinder General 68. There's a Girl in My Soup 70. All Coppers Are 71. Penny Gold 73. Vampira 74. The Bawdy Adventures of Tom Jones 76. Number One of the Secret Service 77. The Golden Triangle 80, etc.

Henstridge, Natasha (1975–).
Canadian actress, a former model.

Species 95. The Exchange 96. Maximum Risk 96. Adrenalin: Fear the Rush 96. Standoff 97. Species 2 98. Bella Donna 98. Dangerous Species 98. Dog Park 98, etc.

Henze, Hans Werner (1926–).
Leading modern German composer who writes the occasional film score.

Muriel 63. Young Torless 66. The Lost Honour of Katherina Blum 75. Good for Nothing 78. Swann in Love 84. L'Amour à Mort 84. Comrades 86, etc.

Henzell, Perry.
Jamaican producer, director and screenwriter, a former director of commercials. He is now a novelist.

The Harder They Come 72.

Hepburn, Audrey (1929–1993) (Audrey Hepburn-Ruston).
Belgian-born star actress of Irish-Dutch parentage; after small parts in English films, rose rapidly to Hollywood stardom as elegant gamine. She was married to Mel FERRER (1954–68). A small museum celebrating her career and her work for the UN Children's Fund was opened at Tolochenaz, Switzerland, where she was buried.

Biographies: 1993, *Audrey Hepburn* by Sheridan Morley. 1993, *A Star Danced: The Life of Audrey Hepburn* by Robyn Karney. 1994, *Audrey: Her Real Story* by Alexander Walker.

■ One Wild Oat 51. Young Wives' Tale 51. Laughter in Paradise 51. The Lavender Hill Mob 51. Monte Carlo Baby 52. The Secret People 52. *Roman Holiday* (AA, BFA) 53. Sabrina (AAN) 54. *War and Peace* 56. *Funny Face* 57. Love in the Afternoon 57. *The Nun's Story* (BFA, AAN) 59. Green Mansions 59. The Unforgiven 60. Breakfast at Tiffany's (AAN) 61. The Children's Hour 62. Charade 63. Paris When It Sizzles 64. My Fair Lady 64. How to Steal a Million 66. Two for the Road 66. *Wait until Dark* (AAN) 67. Robin and Marian 76. Bloodline 79. They All Laughed 81. Love among Thieves (TV) 87. Always 89.

✪ For providing the 50s with a fashionable image between a tomboy and a lady (and oddly failing to combine the two in *My Fair Lady*). *Roman Holiday*.

Hepburn, Katharine (1907–).
Dominant American star actress with Bryn Mawr personality; one of the most durable, talented and likeable interpreters of emancipated feminine roles.

Autobiography: 1991, *Me*.

Biographies: 1973, *Tracy and Hepburn* by Garson Kanin. 1976, *Kate* by Charles Higham. 1995, *Katherine Hepburn* by Barbara Leaming.

■ *A Bill of Divorcement* 32. Christopher Strong 33. *Morning Glory* (AA) 33. *Little Women* 33. Spitfire 34. Break of Hearts 34. The Little Minister 34. Alice Adams (AAN) 35. Sylvia Scarlett 35. Mary of Scotland 36. A Woman Rebels 36. Quality Street 37. *Stage Door* 37. *Bringing Up Baby* 38. *Holiday* 38. *The Philadelphia Story* (AAN) 40. *Woman of the Year* (AAN) 42. Keeper of the Flame 42. Stage Door Canteen 43. Dragon Seed 44. Without Love 45. Undercurrent 46. Sea of Grass 47. Song of Love 47. State of the Union 48. *Adam's Rib* 49. *The African Queen* (AAN) 51. *Pat and Mike* 52. *Summertime*/Summer Madness (AAN) 55. The Rainmaker (AAN) 56. The Iron Petticoat (GB) 56. *Desk Set* 57. *Suddenly Last Summer* (AAN) 59. *Long Day's Journey Into Night* (AAN) 62. *Guess Who's Coming to Dinner* (AA) 67. *The Lion in Winter* (AA, BFA) 68. The Madwoman of Chaillot 69. The Trojan Women 71. The Glass Menagerie (TV) 73. A Delicate Balance 73. Love Among the Ruins (TV) 74. Rooster Cogburn 75. Olly Olly Oxen Free 78. The Corn Is Green (TV) 79. On Golden Pond (AA, BFA) 81. The Ultimate Solution of Grace Quigley 84. Mrs Delafield Wants to Marry (TV) 86. Laura Lansing Slept Here (TV) 88. The Man Upstairs (TV) 92. Love Affair 94.

✪ For her unique qualities of understanding, diction and movement; and for winning two Oscars thirty years after being declared box-office poison. *The Philadelphia Story*.

❝ The screen's first lady has never had a lot to say for herself. Her most thoughtful piece of self-analysis was:

I was fortunate to be born with a set of characteristics that were in the public vogue.

Cecil Beaton was more poetic than kind in his description:

She has a face that belongs to the sea and the wind, with large rocking-horse nostrils and teeth that you just know bite an apple every day.

Robert Hopkins said of her physical angularity:

You could throw a hat at her, and wherever it hit, it would stick.

Tennessee Williams thought her a dream actress:

She makes dialogue sound better than it is by a matchless clarity and beauty of diction, and by a fineness of intelligence and sensibility that illuminates every shade of meaning in every line she speaks.

One feels too that she brings similar high standards to every corner of her life. She said of herself:

When I started out, I didn't have any desire to be an actress or to learn how to act. I just wanted to be famous.

Perhaps only chance kept her from being the first woman president. She obviously has the charm, as Garson Kanin says:

As the years go by she does not lose her old admirers, she goes on gaining new ones.

Other self-musings:

I've had a fascinating life. I don't think I'm the least bit peculiar, but people tell me I am.

And:

Acting is the most minor of gifts. After all, Shirley Temple could do it when she was four.

And:

We used to laugh so much then. Now everything is so solemn, so joyless. One must laugh. One cannot moan everlastingly.

And:

My privacy is my own. I am the one to decide whether it will be invaded.

And:

I am revered rather like an old building. Yet I still seem to be master of my fate. The boat may be only a canoe, but I'm paddling it.

Three final opinions from other people: first, Humphrey Bogart:

She talks at you as though you were a microphone . . . she lectured the hell out of me on temperance and the evils of drink. She doesn't give a damn how she looks. I don't think she tries to be a character. I think she *is* one.

And James Agate:

She has a cheekbone like a death's head attached to a manner as sinister and aggressive as crossbones.

And our old friend anon:

A cross between Donald Duck and a Stradivarius.

Famous line (*Stage Door*): 'The calla lilies are in bloom again . . .'

Famous line (*The Philadelphia Story*): 'I'm going crazy. I'm standing here, on my own two hands, and going crazy.'

Famous line (*The African Queen*): 'Nature, Mr Allnut, is what we are put into this world to rise above.'

Hepton, Bernard (1925–).
Tall, serious-looking British character actor, mostly on TV (*Colditz*, *The Squirrels*, *Secret Army*).
Get Carter 71. Henry VIII and His Six Wives 71. Voyage of the Damned 76. Tinker Tailor Soldier Spy (TV) 79. Gandhi 82. Smiley's People (TV) 82. Mansfield Park (TV) 85. Eminent Domain 91. Jane Austen's Emma (TV) 96, etc.

Hepworth, Cecil (1874–1953).
Pioneer British film producer-director. For many years had his own stock company of stars and was financially successful, though his films were old-fashioned and sentimental.
Wrote first book on cinema: 1897, *Animated Photography*.
Autobiography: 1951, *Came the Dawn*.
The Quarrelsome Anglers 98. Two Cockneys in a Canoe 99. Wiping Something off the Slate 00. How it Feels to be Run Over 00. The Glutton's Nightmare 01. Alice in Wonderland 03. Firemen to the Rescue 03. Rescued by Rover 05. Blind Fate 12. His Country's Bidding 14. The Canker of Jealousy 14. The Man Who Stayed at Home 15. Trelawney of the Wells 16. Annie Laurie 16. Comin' Through the Rye 16. Nearer My God to Thee 17. The Touch of a Child 18. The Forest on the Hill 19. Alf's Button 20. Wild Heather 21. The Pipes of Pan 22. Strangling Threads 22. *Comin' Through the Rye* (remake) 24. The House of Marney 27, many others.

Herbert, F. Hugh (1897–1957).
American comedy screenwriter.
Adam and Evil 27. Hotel Continental 32. If You Could Only Cook (oa) 35. That Certain Age (oa) 38. Melody Ranch 40. West Point Widow 41. Together Again 44. *Kiss and Tell* (& oa) 45. Home Sweet Homicide 46. *Margie* 46. Scudda Hoo Scudda Hay (& d) 48. *Sitting Pretty* 48. Our Very Own 50. The Girls of Pleasure Island (& d) 53. *The Moon is Blue* (& oa) 53. The Little Hut 57, many others.

Herbert, Holmes (1882–1956) (Edward Sanger).
British stage actor, on the Hollywood screen from 1917, usually in quiet British roles – butler, lawyer or clerk.
Gentlemen Prefer Blondes 27. The Terror 28. Dr Jekyll and Mr Hyde 32. Mystery of the Wax Museum 33. Mark of the Vampire 35. Lloyds of London 37. Stanley and Livingstone 39. This Above All 42. The Uninvited 44. Sherlock Holmes and the Secret Code/Dressed to Kill 46. David and Bathsheba 51. The Brigand 52, etc.

Herbert, Hugh (1887–1952).
American eccentric comedian, remembered for nervous 'woo woo' exclamation.
Caught in the Fog 28. Laugh and Get Rich 31. The Lost Squadron 32. Strictly Personal 33. Convention City 33. Wonder Bar 34. Dames 34. A Midsummer Night's Dream 35. One Rainy Afternoon 36. Top of the Town 37. Gold Diggers in Paris 38. The Great Waltz 38. Eternally Yours 39. La Conga Nights 40. The Black Cat 41. *Hellzapoppin* 41. Cracked Nuts 42. Mrs Wiggs of the Cabbage Patch 42. There's One Born Every Minute 43. Kismet 44. Men in Her Diary 45. Carnegie Hall 46. A Song Is Born 48. The Beautiful Blonde from Bashful Bend 49. Havana Rose 51, many others.

Herbert, Percy (1925–1992).
British character actor, usually seen as cockney rating or private.
The Baby and the Battleship 56. The Bridge on the River Kwai 57. *Tunes of Glory* 61. Mysterious Island 62. Mutiny on the Bounty 63. One Million Years BC 66. Tobruk (US) 66. The Viking Queen 67. The Royal Hunt of the Sun 69. Man in the Wilderness 71. Captain Apache 71. Doomwatch 72. Craze 73. The Wild Geese 78. The Sea Wolves 80, etc.
TV series: Cimarron Strip 67.

Herbert, Victor (1859–1924).
Irish popular composer long dominant in New York; played by Walter Connolly in *The Great Victor Herbert* 39. Scores filmed include *The Red Mill* and *Naughty Marietta*.

Herczeg, Géza (1888–1954).
Hungarian-born screenwriter and playwright in Hollywood, a former journalist.
Dreyfus (oa) (GB) 31. Wonder Bar (oa) 34. *The Life of Emile Zola* (co-w) (AA) 37. Florian (co-w) 39. The Shanghai Gesture (co-w) 41. The Inside Story (co-w) 48. Rapture 49. Queen of Jhansi (story) 53, etc.

Herek, Stephen (1958–).
American director.
Critters 86. Bill and Ted's Excellent Adventure 87. Don't Tell Mom the Babysitter's Dead 91. Mighty Ducks 92. The Three Musketeers 93. Mr Holland's Opus 95. 101 Dalmatians 96. Holy Man 98, etc.

Herlie, Eileen (1919–) (Eileen Herlihy).
Scottish stage actress who has made occasional films.
Hungry Hill (debut) 47. Hamlet 48. The Angel with the Trumpet 49. The Story of Gilbert and Sullivan 53. Isn't Life Wonderful? 53. For Better For Worse 54. She Didn't Say No 58. Freud 62. The Seagull 68.

Herlihy, James Leo (1927–1993).
American novelist, whose *All Fall Down* and *Midnight Cowboy* were fairly memorably filmed. Also acted in Blue Denim (oa) 59, In the French Style 63, Friends 81. Committed suicide.

Herman, Jerry (1932–).
American composer of popular shows; those filmed include *Hello Dolly* and *Mame*.
Mrs Santa Claus (TV) 96.

Herman, Mark.
English director and screenwriter.
Blame It on the Bellboy 92. Brassed Off 96. Little Voice 98, etc.

Herman, Pee-Wee:
see Reubens, Paul.

Hermosillo, Jaime Humberto (1942–).
Mexican director. Born in Aguascalientes, he studied at CUEC (Centro Universitario de Estudios Cinematográficos), where he also teaches.
La Verdadera Vocación de Magdalena 71. Naufragio 78. Confidencias 82. Maria de Mi Corazón 83. Dona Herlinda and Her Two Sons 85. Clandestino Destino 87. La Tarea 90. Encuentro Inesperado 91, etc.

Hernandez, Juano (1896–1970).
American character actor with powerful presence.
Intruder in the Dust 48. The Breaking Point 50. *Young Man with a Horn* 50. Kiss Me Deadly 55. Trial 55. Ransom 56. Something of Value 57. The Pawnbroker 64. The Extraordinary Seaman 68, etc.

Herrington, Rowdy.
American screenwriter and director.
■ Jack's Back (wd) 88. Road House (d) 89. Gladiator (d) 92. Striking Distance (co-w, d) 93.

Herrmann, Bernard (1911–1975).
American composer and orchestral conductor.
Biography: 1991, *A Heart at Fire's Center* by Steven C. Smith.
■ *Citizen Kane* 41. *All that Money Can Buy* (AA) 41. *The Magnificent Ambersons* 42. Jane Eyre 43. Hangover Square 45. Anna and the King of Siam 46. The Ghost and Mrs Muir 47. The Day the Earth Stood Still 51. On Dangerous Ground 51. Five Fingers 52. The Snows of Kilimanjaro 52. White Witch Doctor 53. Beneath the 12-mile Reef 53. King of the Khyber Rifles 53. Garden of Evil 54. The Egyptian 54. Prince of Players 55. The Kentuckian 55. *The Trouble with Harry* 56. The Man in the Grey Flannel Suit 56. The Man who Knew Too Much 56. The Wrong Man 57. A Hatful of Rain 57. Vertigo 58. The Naked and the Dead 58. The Seventh Voyage of Sinbad 58. *North by Northwest* 59. Blue Denim 59. Journey to the Centre of the Earth 59. *Psycho* 60. The Three Worlds of Gulliver 60. Mysterious Island 61. Cape Fear 61. Tender Is the Night 62. Jason and the Argonauts 63. Marnie 64. Joy in the Morning 65. Fahrenheit 451 66. The Bride wore Black 67. Twisted Nerve 69. Obsessions 69. The Battle of Neretva 70. The Night Diggers 71. Endless Night 72. Sisters 73. It's Alive 74. *Taxi Driver* (AAN) 76. Obsession (AAN) 76. Cape Fear 91. Psycho 98.
✪ For musical backing second to none. *All that Money Can Buy*.

Herrmann, Edward (1943–).
American character actor.
Lady Liberty 71. The Paper Chase 72. The Day of the Dolphin 73. The Great Gatsby 74. The Great Waldo Pepper 75. *Eleanor and Franklin* (as Franklin Roosevelt) (TV) 76. Eleanor and Franklin: The White House Years (TV) 77. The Betsy 78. A Love Affair: The Eleanor and Lou Gehrig Story (TV) 79. Freedom Road (TV) 79. The North Avenue Irregulars 79. Reds 81. Harry's War 81. A Little Sex 82. Annie (as FDR) 82, Mrs Soffel 84. Compromising Positions 84. The Man with One Red Shoe 85. The Lost Boys 87. Overboard 87. Big Business 88. Sweet Poison 91. Hero/Accidental Hero 92. Born Yesterday 93. A Foreign Field (TV) 93. My Boyfriend's Back 93. Foreign Student 94. Richie Rich 94. Nixon 95. Soul of the Game 96. Critical Care 97. Better Living 98, etc.

Herschel (Herschel McCoy).
American costume designer who worked for Twentieth Century-Fox (1936–42) and then MGM.
Thank You, Jeeves 36. Fair Warning 37. Lancer Spy 37. Charlie Chan in Reno 39. Mr Moto in Danger Island 39. Frontier Marshal 39. Street of Memories 40. Murder among Friends 41. Castle in the Desert 42. Tulsa 49. *Quo Vadis?* (AAN) 51. *Dream Wife* (AAN) 53. Julius Caesar 53, etc.

Hersey, John (1914–1993).
American novelist, most famous for his pamphlet reportage, *Hiroshima*. Two novels were filmed: *A Bell for Adano* and *The War Lover*.

Hershey, Barbara (1948–).
American leading actress. From 1974–76 she was known as Barbara Hershey Seagull.
With Six You Get Eggroll 68. Heaven with a Gun 69. Last Summer 69. The Baby Maker 70. The Liberation of L.B. Jones 70. The Pursuit of Happiness 71. Boxcar Bertha 72. Dealing: Or the Berkeley-to-Boston Forty-Brick Lost-Bag Blues 72. Angela 73. The Crazy World of Julius Vrooder 74. Diamonds 75. You and Me 75. A Choice of Weapons 76. The Last Hard Man 76. The Stunt Man 80. Americana 81. Take this Job and Shove It 81. The Entity 82. The Right Stuff 83. The Natural 84. Hannah and Her Sisters 86. Hoosiers 86. Shy People 87. Tin Men 87. Beaches 88. The Last Temptation of Christ 88. A World Apart 88. Tune in Tomorrow/Aunt Julia and the Scriptwriter 90. Paris Trout 91. You and Me 91. Defenseless 91. The Public Eye 92. Swing Kids 93. Falling Down 93. A Dangerous Woman 93. Splitting Heirs 93. The Bible: Abraham (TV) 93. Last of the Dogmen 95. The Pallbearer 96. *The Portrait of a Lady* (AAN) 96. A Soldier's Daughter Never Cries 98. Frogs for Snakes 98. Passion 98, etc.
TV series: The Monroes 66–67.

Hershman, Joel (1961–).
American director.
Hold Me, Thrill Me, Kiss Me 93.

Hersholt, Jean (1886–1956).
Phlegmatic Danish character actor in Hollywood, in sub-Jannings roles.
Princess Virtue 16. The Four Horsemen of The Apocalypse 21. *Greed* 23. Stella Dallas 25. The Secret Hour 28. Abie's Irish Rose 28. The Rise of Helga 30. Transatlantic 31. *Grand Hotel* 32. The Mask of Fu Manchu 32. Christopher Bean 35. Mark of the Vampire 35. Seventh Heaven 35. The Country Doctor (as Dr Dafoe) 35. Crime of the Century 36. Heidi 37. Alexander's Ragtime Band 38. Meet Doctor Christian (and ensuing series) 38–40. They Meet Again 41. Stage Door Canteen 43. Dancing in the Dark 49. Run for Cover 55, others.
❝ Dr Christian is such a sweet sentimental fellow, I'd hate to be stuck with playing him for the rest of my life. *– J.H., 1954*
~ A much respected industry figure, he was largely responsible for the foundation of the Motion Picture Country Home and Hospital in Calabasas.

Hervey, Irene (1910–1998) (Irene Herwick).
American leading lady of light films in the 40s.
Three on a Honeymoon 34. East Side of Heaven 39. Destry Rides Again 39. Unseen Enemy 42. Half Way to Shanghai 43. My Guy 44. Mr Peabody and the Mermaid 49. Teenage Rebel 56. Going Steady 59. Cactus Flower 69. Play Misty for Me 71, etc.
TV series: Honey West 65.

Herz, Michael (1949–).
American director, writer and producer of low-budget exploitation movies, in collaboration with Lloyd Kaufman. He is vice-president of the production and distribution company Troma.
Squeeze Play! (co-d) 80. Waitress! (co-d) 82. The First Turn-On! 84. The Toxic Avenger (co-d) 84. The Toxic Avenger: Part II (co-d) 88. Troma's War (co-d) 88. Sgt Kabukiman N.Y.P.D. (co-d) 94, etc.

Herzfeld, John.
American director, screenwriter and actor.
Cannonball (a) 76. Voices (w) 79. Two of a Kind 83. Cobra (a) 86. Daddy (TV) 87. A Father's Revenge (TV) 88. The Preppie Murder (TV) 89. Casualties of Love: The 'Long Island Lolita' Story (TV) 93. Two Days in the Valley 96, etc.

Herzog, Werner (1942–).
German director and screenwriter.
■ Signs of Life 67. Even Dwarfs Started Small 70. Fata Morgana 71. Land of Silence and Darkness 72. Aguirre Land of Silence and Darkness 72. *Aguirre Wrath of God* 73. The Enigma of Kaspar Hauser 74. Heart of Glass 76. Stroszek 77. Nosferatu 79. Woyzeck 79. *Fitzcarraldo* 82. Ballad of the Little Soldier 84. The Dark Glow of the Mountains 84. Where the Green Ants Dream 85. Gasherbrum – der Leuchtende Berg 85. Slave Coast/Cobra Verde 88. Herdsmen of the Sun 88. Echos aus einem Düsteren Reich 90. Scream of Stone/Schrei aus Stein 91. Lessons in Darkness 92.
❝ I'm not out to win prizes – that's for dogs and horses. *– W.H.*

Heslop, Charles (1883–1966).
British comic actor, longtime star of stage farces.
Waltzes from Vienna 33. The Lambeth Walk 39. Flying Fortress 42. The Late Edwina Black 51. Follow a Star 59.

Hessler, Gordon (1930–).
German-born director in Britain and Hollywood.
The Last Shot You Hear 64. The Oblong Box (& p) 69. Scream and Scream Again 70. Cry of the Banshee (& p) 70. Murders in the Rue Morgue (& p) 71. Embassy 72. Sinbad's Golden Voyage 73. Scream Pretty Peggy (TV) 73. Skyway to Death (TV) 74. A Cry in the Wilderness (TV) 74. The Strange Possession of Mrs Oliver (TV) 77. The Secrets of Three Hungry Wives (TV) 78. Wheels of Terror 87. The Girl on a Swing 88. Out on Bail 89. Shogun Mayeda 92, etc.

Heston, Charlton (1924–) (John Charlton Carter).
Stalwart American leading actor with stage experience; seemed likely for a time to become typed in biblical and medieval epics.
Autobiography: 1978, *An Actor's Life*. 1995, *In the Arena*.
■ Dark City 50. The Greatest Show on Earth 52. The Savage 52. Ruby Gentry 52. The President's Lady (as Andrew Jackson) 52. Pony Express 53. Arrowhead 53. Bad for Each Other 54. The Naked Jungle 54. The Secret of the Incas 54. The Far Horizons 55. The Private War of Major Benson 55. Lucy Gallant 55. *The Ten Commandments* (as Moses) 56. Three Violent People 56. Touch of Evil 58. The Big Country 58. The Buccaneer 58. The Wreck of the Mary Deare 59. Ben Hur (AA) 59. El Cid 61. The Pigeon that Took Rome 62. Diamond Head 62. 55 Days at Peking 63. The Greatest Story Ever Told 65. Major Dundee 65. The Agony and the Ecstasy (as Michelangelo) 65. *The War Lord* 65. *Khartoum* (as General Gordon) 66. Counterpoint 67. *Planet of the Apes* 67. *Will Penny* 68. Number One 69. Beneath the Planet of the Apes 69. Julius Caesar 70. The Hawaiians 70. The Omega Man 71. Antony and Cleopatra (& d) 71. Skyjacked 72. Call of the Wild 72. Soylent Green 73. Earthquake 73. The Three Musketeers 73. The Four Musketeers 74. Airport 75 74. The Last Hard Men 76. Two Minute Warning 76. Midway 76. Gray Lady Down 77. The Prince and the Pauper 77. The Awakening 80. The Mountain Men 80. Mother Lode 82. Chiefs (TV) 83. Call from Space 89. Treasure Island (TV) 89. Almost an Angel 90. Solar Crisis (TV) 90. The Little Kidnappers (TV) 90. Crucifer of Blood (TV) 91. Starfire 92. Tombstone 94. True Lies 94. In the Mouth of Madness 95. Alaska 96.
TV series: The Colbys 85–86.
❝ A careful and successful actor, Heston has been blessed with the kind of impressive face and physique that inevitably got him cast as a succession of epic heroes. This was a mixed blessing to his career. On the one hand, as he said:
There's a special excitement in playing a man who made a hole in history large enough to be remembered centuries after he died.
Commercially, furthermore:
If you can't make a career out of two de Milles, you'll never do it.
On the other hand:
After spending all of last winter in armour it's a great relief to wear costume that bends.
Heston has continued to explore, without having to resort to character parts. He knows however that:
The minute you feel you have given a faultless performance is the time to get out.
And:
I have played three presidents, three saints and two geniuses. If that doesn't create an ego problem, nothing does.
Having played Antony (and lost) he still feels:
The great roles are always Shakespearean.
and has found:
It's hard living up to Moses.
He believes:
It is essential that gun owners unite in an active, growing force capable of flexing great muscle as the next millennium commences.

Heston, Fraser C.
American director, producer and screenwriter, the son of Charlton Heston.
Treasure Island (p, wd) 89. The Crucifer of Blood (d) (TV) 91. Needful Things (d) 93. Alaska (d) 96.

Hexum, Jon-Eric (1957–1984).
Handsome American leading man, a former model. Died after accidentally shooting himself on the set of his TV series.
The Making of a Male Model (TV) 83. The Bear 84.
TV series: Voyagers 82–83. Cover Up 84.

Heydt, Louis Jean (1905–1960).
American character actor, often seen as a man with something to hide.
Test Pilot 38. Each Dawn I Die 39. Gone with the Wind 39. Dive Bomber 41. Our Vines Have Tender Grapes 45. The Furies 50. The Eternal Sea 55, many others.

Heyer, John (1916–).
Australian documentarist, former cameraman; with the Shell Film Unit 1948–56.
The Back of Beyond 54. Playing with Water 54. The Forerunner 57. Tumult Pond 62, etc.

Heyes, Douglas (1923–1993).
American director, from TV.
Kitten with a Whip 65. Beau Geste 67. The Highwayman (TV) 87, etc.

Heyman, John (1933–).
British agent and producer who turned his attention to television production (*Between the Lines*, *Cardiac Arrest*, etc).
Privilege 66. Boom! 68. Secret Ceremony 69. Twinky 70. Bloomfield 71. The Go-Between 71. A Passage to India 84. D.A.R.Y.L. 85, etc.

Heymann, Werner (1896–1961).
German composer who went to Hollywood.
Spione 28. Congress Dances 31. Bluebeard's Eighth Wife 38. Ninotchka 39. One Million BC 40. The Shop Around the Corner 40. That Uncertain Feeling 41. To Be or Not to Be 42. Hail the Conquering Hero 44. Knickerbocker Holiday 44. Kiss and Tell 45. Mad Wednesday 47. Tell It to the Judge 49. Congress Dances (Ger.) 55, etc.

Heyward, Louis M. (Deke) (1920–).
American producer, especially associated with horror films made in Europe for AIP.
De Sade 69. Wuthering Heights 70. The Abominable Dr Phibes 71. Murders in the Rue Morgue 71, etc.

Heywood, Anne (1931–) (Violet Pretty).
British leading lady, former beauty contestant.
Find the Lady 55. Checkpoint 56. Dangerous Exile 56. The Depraved 57. Violent Playground 58. Floods of Fear 58. Upstairs and Downstairs 59. A Terrible Beauty 60. Petticoat Pirates 61. Stork Talk 62. Vengeance 62. The Very Edge 62. Ninety Degrees in the Shade 66. *The Fox* 68. The Chairman 69. The Awful Story of the Nun of Monza (It.) 69. The Midas Run 69. I Want What I Want 71. Trader Horn 73. The Nun and the Devil (It.) 73. Good Luck Miss Wyckoff 79. The Secrets of the Phantom Caverns 83, etc.

Heywood, Pat (1927–).
British character actress.
Romeo and Juliet 68. All the Way Up 69. 10 Rillington Place 71. Who Slew Auntie Roo? 72. Wish You Were Here 87. Sparrow/Storia di una Capinera 93, etc.

Hibbert, Geoffrey (1922–1969).
British actor who played callow youths around 1940 but turned rather quickly into a character man.
Love on the Dole 41. The Common Touch 42. Next of Kin 42. Orders to Kill 58. Crash Drive 59, etc.

Hibbs, Jesse (1906–1985).
American director, mainly of routine 'B' features.
■ The All American 53. Ride Clear of Diablo 54. Black Horse Canyon 54. Rails into Laramie 54. The Yellow Mountain 54. To Hell and Back 55. The Spoilers 55. World in My Corner 56. Walk the Proud Land 56. Joe Butterfly 57. Ride a Crooked Trail 58.

Hibler, Winston (1911–1976).
American producer, almost entirely of wild life material for Disney.

Hickenlooper, George (1963–).
American director who began by making documentaries.
Hearts of Darkness (doc) 91. The Killing Box 92. The Low Life 95. Persons Unknown 97, etc.
❝ People don't want to embrace basic emotions now. It's why so many films are terrible. – *G.H.*

Hickey, William (1928–1997).
American character actor from the stage.
A Hatful of Rain 57. The Producers 67. The Boston Strangler 68. Little Big Man 70. A New Leaf 71. The Sentinel 77. Wise Blood 79. Prizzi's Honor (AAN) 85. The Name of the Rose 86. Bright Lights, Big City 88. Da 88. Pink Cadillac 89. Sea of Love 89. Mob Boss 90. My Blue Heaven 90. Tales from the Darkside: The Movie 90. The Runestone 92. Tim Burton's The Nightmare before Christmas (voice) 93. Hey Stranger 94. Twisted 96. Love Is All There Is 96. Mouse Hunt 97, etc.

Hickman, Darryl (1931–).
American juvenile actor who was later seen in heavy roles.
The Grapes of Wrath 40. Hearts in Springtime 41. Boys' Ranch 45. Dangerous Years 46. Prisoner of War 53. Tea and Sympathy 54. The Tingler 59. Network 76. Sharky's Machine 81. Looker 81. GoBots: War of the Rock Lords 86, etc.
TV series: The Blue and the Gold 58.

Hickman, Dwayne (1934–).
American juvenile, former child actor.
Captain Eddie 45. The Return of Rusty 46. The Sun Comes Up 49. Rally Round the Flag Boys 59. Beach Party 64. Cat Ballou 65. High School U.S.A. 83. Bring Me the Head of Dobie Gillis (TV) 88. Cops n Roberts 95. A Night at the Roxbury 98, many others.
TV series: The Affairs of Dobie Gillis 59.

Hickman, Howard (1880–1949).
Chubby American supporting actor, often seen as conventioneer, suburban husband or judge.

Hickok, Wild Bill (1837–1876).
American frontier gunfighter of wild west days, frequently personified on screen. He was shot in the back of the head while playing poker. His hand is said to have consisted of aces and eights.
Wild Bill Hickok 21: William S. Hart. *The Plainsman* 36: Gary Cooper. *Badlands of Dakota* 41: Richard Dix. *Wild Bill Hickok Rides* 41: Bruce Cabot. *Dallas* 50: Reed Hadley. *Pony Express* 52: Forrest Tucker. *Calamity Jane* 53: Howard Keel. *The Raiders* 55: Robert Culp. *The Plainsman* 66: Don Murray. *Little Big Man* 70: Jeff Corey. *Buffalo Girls* (TV) 95: Sam Elliott. *Wild Bill* 96: Jeff Bridges.
Guy Madison starred as Hickok in a TV series (51–54).
❝ Tell that longhaired son of a gun that I have no more use for him and his damned show business. – *W.B.H. on quitting Buffalo Bill's Wild West*

Hickox, Anthony (1961–).
British director, working in America. He is the son of director Douglas Hickox.
Waxwork 88. Sundown: The Vampire in Retreat 90. Waxwork II: Lost in Time 91. Hellraiser III: Hell on Earth 92. Warlock II: The Armageddon 93. Full Eclipse 94. Invasion of Privacy 96. Prince Valiant 97, etc.

Hickox, Douglas (1929–1988).
British director.
■ The Giant Behemoth (co-d) 58. Four Hits and a Mister 62. It's All Over Town 64. Just for You 64. Les Bicyclettes de Belsize 69. Entertaining Mr Sloane 70. Sitting Target 72. Theatre of Blood 73. Brannigan 75. Sky Riders 76. Zulu Dawn 79. The Hound of the Baskervilles (TV) 83. Mistral's Daughter (TV) 84. Blackout 85. Sins (TV) 86. I'll Take Manhattan (TV) 87.

Hickox, Sid (1895–1982).
American cinematographer, long with Warners.
The Little Giant 26. The Private Life of Helen of Troy 27. Lilac Time 28. The Gorilla 31. A Bill of Divorcement 32. Frisco Jenny 33. Dames 34. Special Agent 35. San Quentin 37. A Slight Case of Murder 38. Flowing Gold 40. The Big Shot 42. Edge of Darkness 43. To Have and Have Not 44. The Horn Blows at Midnight 45. The Big Sleep 46. Dark Passage 47. White Heat 49. Along the Great Divide 51. Them 54. Battle Cry 55, many others.

Hicks, Catherine (1951–).
American actress.
Marilyn: The Untold Story (as Marilyn Monroe) (TV) 80. Death Valley 81. Better Late than Never 83. Garbo Talks 84. The Razor's Edge 84. Star Trek IV: The Voyage Home 86. Peggy Sue Got Married 86. Laguna Heat (TV) 87. Like Father, Like Son 87. Secret Ingredient 88. Souvenir 88. She's Out of Control 89. Spy (TV) 89. Liebestraum 91. Redwood Curtain (TV) 95. Dillinger and Capone 95. Turbulence 96, etc.
TV series: The Bad News Bears 79–80. Tucker's Witch 82–83.

Hicks, Russell (1895–1957).
American character actor who almost always played executive types. Actor and director from silent days; in hundreds of films.
Laughing Irish Eyes 36. In Old Chicago 38. The Three Musketeers 39. The Big Store 41. His Butler's Sister 43. Bandit of Sherwood Forest 46. Bowery Battalion 51. Seventh Cavalry 56, many others.

Hicks, Scott (1953–).
Australian director, screenwriter and maker of TV documentaries.
Call Me Mr Brown (TV) 86. Sebastian and the Sparrow (wd) 90. *Shine* (d) 96, etc.

Hicks, Sir Seymour (1871–1949).
British stage farceur, also writer and producer. Occasional film appearances. Married actress Ellaline Terriss, who appeared with him on stage and made occasional films in the 20s and 30s.
Autobiographies: 1930, *Between Ourselves*. 1939, *Me and My Missus*.
Always Tell Your Wife 22. Sleeping Partners 26. The Secret of the Loch 34. Vintage Wine 35. *Scrooge* 35. Pastor Hall 39. *Busman's Honeymoon* 40. Silent Dust 48, etc.

Hickson, Joan (1906–1998).
British character actress, in innumerable films as understanding mum or slightly dotty aunt. At the age of nearly 80, J.H. made a big hit on TV in adaptations of Agatha Christie's Miss Marple stories.
Widow's Might 34. Love from a Stranger 37. I See a Dark Stranger 45. The Guinea Pig 48. Seven Days to Noon 50. The Card 52. The Man Who Never Was 56. Happy is the Bride 57. The Thirty-Nine Steps 59. Murder She Said 61. A Day in the Death of Joe Egg 70. Theatre of Blood 73. Clockwise 86. Century 93, many others.

Hidari, Sachiko (1930–).
Japanese leading actress and occasional director, a former teacher. Married director Susumu Hani.
The Maid/Jochukko 55. The Insect Woman/Nippon Konchuki 63. He and She/Kanojo To Kare 63. Bride of the Andes/Andesu No Hanayome 66. Emmanuelle et Ses Soeurs (co-d) (Fr.) 69. The Far Road/Toi Ippon No Michi (a, d) 76. Double Suicide of Sonezaki/Sonezaki Shinju 78. Mishima: A Life in Four Chapters (US) 85. The Singing Bamboo/Tada Hito Tabi No Hito 93, etc.
❝ If you want to say something about Japan, you have to focus on women. – *S.H.*

Higgins, Colin (1941–1988).
American screenwriter and director. Died of AIDS.
Harold and Maude 71. Silver Streak 77. Foul Play (& d) 78. Nine to Five (& d) 80. The Best Little Whorehouse in Texas (co-w, d) 82.

Higgins, Jack (1929–).
British adventure novelist.
The Wrath of God 72. The Eagle Has Landed 76. To Catch a King 84. A Prayer for the Dying 87. Night of the Fox 90.

Higgins, Ken (1919–).
British cinematographer.
French Dressing 63. Darling 65. The Virgin Soldiers 69. You Can't Win 'Em All 70. Games that Lovers Play 70. Julius Caesar 70. I'm Not Feeling Myself Tonight 75. Golden Rendezvous 77, etc.

Highsmith, Patricia (1921–1995) (Mary Patricia Plangman).
American crime novelist whose novels have appealed to European film-makers. Born in Fort Worth, Texas, she lived for many years in Switzerland, becoming somewhat reclusive from the 70s onwards.
Strangers on a Train (d Alfred Hitchcock) 51. Purple Noon/Plein Soleil (d René Clément from The Talented Mr Ripley) 60. The American Friend (d Wim Wenders from Ripley's Game) 77. This Sweet Sickness/Dîtes-Lui que Je l'Aime (d Claude Miller) 77. Deep Water/Eaux

Profondes (d Michel DEVILLE) 81. Ediths Tagebuch (d Hans W. Geissendörfer from Edith's Diary) 83. Le Cri de Hibou (d Claude CHABROL from The Cry of the Owl) 87. The Talented Mr Ripley (d Anthony MINGHELLA) 99, etc.

❝ The French character is so badly flawed, it will fall into many pieces at a tiny blow – like the tap given to a chocolate orange. – *P.H.*

Most Americans act as if they were born yesterday. – *P.H.*

Hildyard, Jack (1908–1990).
British cinematographer.
School for Secrets 46. While the Sun Shines 46. Vice Versa 48. The Sound Barrier 52. Hobson's Choice 54. The Deep Blue Sea 55. Summertime 55. *The Bridge on the River Kwai* (AA) 57. The Journey 59. Suddenly Last Summer 59. The Millionairess 60. 55 Days at Peking 62. The VIPs 63. The Yellow Rolls Royce 64. Battle of the Bulge 66. Casino Royale 67. The Long Duel 67. Villa Rides 68. Topaz 70. Puppet on a Chain 71. The Beast Must Die 74. The Message 76. The Wild Geese 78. Lion of the Desert 80, etc.

Hill, Arthur (1922–).
Canadian actor, on British and American stage and screen.
Miss Pilgrim's Progress 49. I Was a Male War Bride 49. Salute the Toff 52. Life with the Lyons 54. The Deep Blue Sea 55. The Ugly American 63. In the Cool of the Day 63. Moment to Moment 65. *Harper* 66. Petulia 68. The Chairman 69. *The Andromeda Strain* 70. The Pursuit of Happiness 70. Futureworld 76. A Bridge Too Far 77. Hagen (TV) 79. Butch and Sundance 79. The Champ 79. A Little Romance 79. Dirty Tricks 81. Making Love 82. The Amateur 82. One Magic Christmas 85, etc.
TV series: *Owen Marshall Counsellor at Law* 71–73. Hagen 80.

Hill, Benny (1925–1992) (Alfred Hawthorne Hill).
British vaudeville comedian and mimic, star of an occasional TV variety show with the emphasis on smut. An astonishing success on late-night American TV in 1979 and thereafter.
■ Who Done It? 56. Light Up the Sky 59. Those Magnificent Men in Their Flying Machines 65. Chitty Chitty Bang Bang 68. The Italian Job 69. The Best of Benny Hill 74.

Hill, Bernard (1944–).
British actor.
It Could Happen to You 75. A Choice of Weapons 76. Gandhi 82. Runners 83. The Bounty 84. No Surrender 86. Bellman & True 87. Drowning by Numbers 88. Shirley Valentine 89. Mountains of the Moon 90. Double X 92. Olly's Prison (TV) 93. Telltale (TV) 93. Speaking in Tongues (TV) 94. Skallagrigg (TV) 94. Madagascar Skin 95. The Wind in the Willows 96. The Ghost and the Darkness 96. Titanic 97, etc.
TV series: Once upon a Time in the North 94.

Hill, Dana (1964–1996) (Dana Goetz).
American actress. Died from diabetes.
Fallen Angel (TV) 81. Shoot the Moon 81. Cross Creek 83. Silence of the Heart (TV) 84. National Lampoon's European Vacation 85. Tom & Jerry: The Movie (as Jerry's voice) 92, etc.
TV series: The Two of Us 81–82.

Hill, Debra.
American producer and screenwriter.
Halloween (& w) 78. The Fog (& co-w) 80. Escape from New York 81. Halloween II (& co-w) 81. Halloween III 82. The Dead Zone 83. Head Office 85. Clue 85. Adventures in Babysitting 87. Big Top Pee-Wee 88. Heartbreak Hotel 88. The Fisher King 91. Attack of the 50 Ft Woman (TV) 93, etc.

Hill, George (1888–1934).
American director. Married to screenwriter Frances Marion. Shot himself.
Through the Dark 23. The Midnight Express 24. Zander the Great 25. Tell It to the Marines 26. The Cossacks 28. The Flying Fleet 29. *The Big House* 30. *Min and Bill* 30. The Secret Six 31. Hell Divers 31. Clear All Wires 33, etc.

Hill, George Roy (1922–).
American director with New York stage background.
■ Period of Adjustment 63. Toys in the Attic 63. *The World of Henry Orient* 64. Hawaii 66. Thoroughly Modern Millie 67. *Butch Cassidy and the Sundance Kid* (AAN) 69. *Slaughterhouse Five* 72. The Sting (AA) 73. The Great Waldo Pepper 75. Slap Shot 77. A Little Romance 79. The World According to Garp 82. The Little Drummer Girl 84. Funny Farm 88.

❝ He is famous in the movie business for never picking up a check. His dress can best be described as nondescript, or perhaps janitorial. A producer who once worked on a project with him told me that George would brag that he bought his clothes at an army surplus store in Santa Monica, where he could get khaki pants for under ten dollars; in our brief contacts I never had any reason to doubt this. – *John Gregory Dunne*

Hill, Howard (1898–1975).
American archer who, besides making sports shorts in the 40s, 'doubled' for Errol Flynn in several films.

Hill, James (1919–1994).
British director, former documentarist.
Journey for Jeremy 47. The Stolen Plans (& w) 52. The Clue of the Missing Ape (& w) 53. *Giuseppina* (& w) (AA) 61. The Kitchen 62. The Dock Brief 62. Every Day's a Holiday 64. A Study in Terror 65. Born Free 66. Captain Nemo and the Underwater City 69. Black Beauty 71. The Belstone Fox 73. Christian the Lion (co-d) 74. The Young Visitors (TV) 84, etc.

Hill, James (1916–).
American producer. Born in Jefferson, Indiana, and educated at the University of Washington, he began as a page-boy at NBC and became a contract writer at MGM. A friend of actor Burt LANCASTER, he became a partner with him and former agent Harold HECHT in the production company Hecht-Hill-Lancaster, 1956–60. Married actress Rita HAYWORTH (1958–61).
AS WRITER: Keeping Company 40. The Hoodlum Saint 46. His Majesty O'Keefe 54, etc.
AS PRODUCER: Vera Cruz 54. Trapeze 56. Sweet Smell of Success 57. The Unforgiven 60, etc.

Hill, Sinclair (1894–1945).
British director most eminent in the 20s.
The Tidal Wave 20. Don Quixote 23. Indian Love Lyrics 23. Boadicea 25. Beyond the Veil 25. The Chinese Bungalow 26. The King's Highway 27. A Woman Redeemed 27. *The Guns of Loos* 28. *The Price of Divorce* 28. The First Mrs Fraser 30. The Man from Toronto 33. My Old Dutch 34. Follow Your Star 38, etc.

Hill, Steven (1922–) (Solomon Berg).
American stage actor.
A Lady without Passport 50. The Goddess 58. A Child is Waiting 62. The Slender Thread 67. It's My Turn 80. Yentl 83. Garbo Talks 84. Heartburn 86. Legal Eagles 86. Raw Deal 86. Between Two Women 86. Boost 88. Running on Empty 88. White Palace 90. Billy Bathgate 91. The Firm 93, etc.
TV series: Mission Impossible 66–67. Law and Order 90– .

Hill, Terence (1939–) (Mario Girotti).
Italian leading man of spaghetti westerns.
The Leopard 63. Seven Seas to Calais 63. Blood River 67. Boot Hill 69. They Call Me Trinity 70. Man of the East 72. My Name is Nobody 73. Watch Out, We're Mad 74. Mr Billion 77. March or Die 77. Deux Super Flics 78. Super Fuzz 80. Renegade Luke 87. Lucky Luke (& d) 91, etc.

Hill, Walter (1942–).
American director, producer and screenwriter of action films.
Hickey and Boggs 72. The Thief Who Came to Dinner 72. The Getaway 72. The Mackintosh Man 73. The Drowning Pool 74. Hard Times (& d) 75. The Driver (& d) 78. The Warriors (& d) 78. The Long Riders (& d) 80. Southern Comfort (& co-w) 81. 48 Hours (co-w, d) 82. Brewster's Millions 84. Streets of Fire 85. Crossroads 85. Aliens (p, story) 86. Blue City (p, w) 86. Extreme Prejudice (d) 86. Red Heat (wdp) 88. Johnny Handsome (d) 89. Another 48 Hrs (d) 90. Alien³ (p) 92. Trespass (d) 92. The Getaway (w) 93. Geronimo: An American Legend (p, d) 93. Wild Bill (wd) 95. Last Man Standing (wd) 96. Alien: Resurrection (p) 97. Supernova (d) 99, etc.

Hillcoat, John (1961–).
Australian director, also making rock videos.
Ghosts . . . of the Civil Dead 89. To Have and to Hold 96, etc.

Hiller, Arthur (1923–).
Canadian-American director, from TV.
Massacre at Sand Creek (TV) 56. Homeward Borne (TV) 57. The Careless Years 57. Miracle of the White Stallions 63. The Wheeler Dealers 63. The Americanization of Emily 64. Promise Her Anything 66. Penelope 66. Tobruk 67. The Tiger Makes Out 67. Popi 69. The Out-of-Towners 70. *Love Story* (AAN) 70. Plaza Suite 70. The Hospital 71. Man of La Mancha 72. The Crazy World of Julius Vrooder 74. The Man in the Glass Booth 75. W. C. Fields and Me 76. Silver Streak 76. Nightwing 79. The In-Laws 79. Making Love 82. Author! Author! 82. Romantic Comedy 83. The Lonely Guy 84. Teachers 84. Outrageous Fortune 87. See No Evil, Hear No Evil 89. Taking Care of Business/Filofax 90. Married to It 91. The Babe 92. Carpool 96. An Alan Smithee Film: Burn, Hollywood, Burn 97, etc.

Hiller, Dame Wendy (1912–).
Distinguished British stage actress with inimitable voice and clarity of diction; her films have been fewer than one would like.
■ Lancashire Luck 37. *Pygmalion* (AAN) 38. *Major Barbara* 40. *I Know Where I'm Going* 45. An Outcast of the Islands 51. Single Handed 52. Something of Value 57. How to Murder a Rich Uncle 57. *Separate Tables* (AA) 58. *Sons and Lovers* 60. Toys in the Attic 63. *A Man for All Seasons* (AAN) 66. David Copperfield 69. Murder on the Orient Express 74. Voyage of the Damned 76. The Cat and the Canary 77. The Elephant Man 80. The Curse of King Tut's Tomb (TV) 80. Making Love 82. The Death of the Heart 86. The Lonely Passion of Judith Hearne 87.
Famous line (*Pygmalion*): 'Walk? Not bloody likely. I'm going to take a taxi.'
Famous line (*Pygmalion*): 'I washed me face and hands before I came, I did.'

Hillerman, John (1932–).
Dapper American actor, mainly of comedy roles.
Paper Moon 73. At Long Last Love 76. The Day of the Locust 76. Lucky Lady 77. Sunburn 79. History of the World Part One 81. Street of Dreams 88. Real Men Don't Eat Gummi Bears 89, etc.
TV series: The Betty White Show 77. Magnum 80–88.

Hilliard, Harriet (1909–1994) (Peggy Lou Snyder).
American leading lady of 30s romantic comedies and musicals. Married Ozzie Nelson and for 14 years from 1952 appeared with him in their weekly TV show *Ozzie and Harriet*; they also appeared with their family in the film *Here Come the Nelsons* 51.
Follow the Fleet 36. Cocoanut Grove 38. Sweetheart of the Campus 41. Canal Zone 42. Smash-up on Interstate Five (TV) 76. Death on the Freeway 79, etc.
TV series: Ozzie's Girls 73.

Hillier, Erwin (1911–).
British cinematographer.
The Lady from Lisbon 41. The Silver Fleet 43. Great Day 45. *I Know Where I'm Going* 45. London Town 47. *The October Man* 48. Mr Perrin and Mr Traill 49. Where's Charley? 52. *The Dam Busters* 55. Shake Hands with the Devil 59. A Matter of Who 62. Sammy Going South 63. Operation Crossbow 65. Sands of the Kalahari 65. Eye of the Devil 66. The Quiller Memorandum 66. The Shoes of the Fisherman 68. The Valley of the Gwangi 68, etc.

Hills, David:
see D'AMATO, Joe.

Hills, R. M. (1926–1996) (Richard Michael Hills).
Prolific British comedy scriptwriter, mainly for television, a former teacher. He wrote, in collaboration with Sid Green, Morecambe and Wise's three films, after writing their TV series (1961–69).
■ The Intelligence Men 65. That Riviera Touch 66. The Magnificent Two 67.

Hillyer, Lambert (1889–1969).
American director of westerns which declined in stature after his days of writing and directing for William S. Hart.
The Toll Gate 20. *Travellin' On* 22. *White Oak* 23. *The Spoilers* 23. The Branded Sombrero 28. Beau Bandit 30. Master of Men 33. *Dracula's Daughter* 36. The Invisible Ray 37. Batman (serial) 41. Blue Clay 42. The Case of the Baby Sitter 47. Sunset Pass 49, many others.

Hilton, James (1900–1954).
British novelist whose work was turned by himself and others into several highly successful films. Also worked as scenarist on other films, including *Mrs Miniver* (AA) 42.
Knight without Armour 37. *Lost Horizon* 37. *Goodbye Mr Chips* 39, 69. We Are Not Alone 39. *Random Harvest* 42. The Story of Dr Wassell 43. So Well Remembered 47, etc.

❝ Tempted by Hollywood, a writer must decide whether he would rather say a little less exactly what he wants, to millions, or a little more exactly, to thousands. – *J.H.*

Himes, Chester (1909–1984).
Tough American thriller writer, a former convict, whose Harlem detectives Grave Digger Jones and Coffin Ed Johnson have featured in three films based on his novels.
Autobiographies: 1972, *The Quality of Hurt*. 1976, *My Life of Absurdity*.
Cotton Comes to Harlem 70. Come Back, Charleston Blue 72. A Rage in Harlem 91.

Hindle, Art (1948–).
Canadian leading man.
Black Christmas 75. A Small Town in Texas 76. Invasion of the Body Snatchers 78. The Clone Master (TV) 78. The Power Within (TV) 79. The Brood 79. Desperate Lives 82. The Man Who Wasn't There 83. The Surrogate 84. The Gunfighters (TV) 87. Into the Fire 87. Dixie Lanes 88, etc.

Hinds, Anthony (1922–).
British producer, in films since 1946, latterly associated with Hammer's horror films. Also writes screenplays under the name 'John Elder'.

Hinds, Ciaran.
British leading actor.
Excalibur 81. The Cook, the Thief, His wife and Her Lover 89. December Bride 90. Hostages (TV) 93. Jane Austen's Persuasion (TV) 95. Cold Lazarus (TV) 96. Mary Reilly 96. Some Mother's Son 96. Ivanhoe (TV) 97. Jane Eyre (TV) 97. Titanic Town 98. The Life of Stuff 98, etc.

Hinds, Samuel S. (1875–1948).
Dignified American character actor, formerly a lawyer for thirty-five years; specialized in kindly fathers and crooked lawyers.
Gabriel over the White House 33. She 35. Trail of the Lonesome Pine 36. Test Pilot 38. *You Can't Take It with You* 38. *Destry Rides Again* 39. The Strange Case of Doctor RX 41. The Spoilers 42. A Chip off the Old Block 44. The Boy with Green Hair 48, many others.

Hines, Gregory (1946–).
American actor/dancer.
Wolfen 81. The Cotton Club 84. White Nights 85. Running Scared 86. Off Limits 88. Tap 89. Eve of Destruction 90. A Rage in Harlem 91. Renaissance Man 94. White Man's Burden (d) 94. Waiting to Exhale 95. Mad Dog Time 96. Good Luck 96, etc.
TV series: The Gregory Hines Show 97– .

Hines, Johnny (1895–1970).
American star comedian of the 20s; roles declined as sound came in.
Little Johnny Jones 23. The Speed Spook 24. The Crackerjack 25. The Brown Derby 26. Home Made 27. The Runaround 31. Whistling in the Dark 32. Her Bodyguard 33. Society Doctor 35. Too Hot to Handle 38, etc.

Hingle, Pat (1923–).
Burly American character actor with stage and TV experience.
On the Waterfront 54. The Strange One 57. No Down Payment 57. Splendor in the Grass 61. The Ugly American 63. Invitation to a Gunfighter 64. Nevada Smith 66. Hang 'Em High 68. Bloody Mama

69. Norwood 69. W.U.S.A. 70. The Carey Treatment 72. One Little Indian 73. Running Wild 73. The Gauntlet 77. Norma Rae 79. Sudden Impact 83. Brewster's Millions 84. Maximum Overdrive 86. The Land Before Time (voice) 88. The Grifters 90. Not of This World 91. Batman Returns 92. Lightning Jack 94. Batman Forever 95. The Quick and the Dead 95. Bastard out of Carolina (TV) 96. Larger than Life 96. The Shining (TV) 97. Batman & Robin 97. A Thousand Acres 97, etc.

TV series: Stone 80. Blue Skies 88.

Hinwood, Peter.
English model who enjoyed a brief moment of fame as the muscular Rocky in *The Rocky Horror Picture Show*. He later became an antique dealer.

Tam Lin/The Devil's Widow, The Ballad of Tam Lin 71. The Rocky Horror Picture Show 75. Sebastiane 76.

Hird, Dame Thora (1913–).
British north-country character comedienne, mother of Janette Scott; often plays acidulous landladies, etc.

Autobiography: 1976, *Seen and Hird*.

The Black Sheep of Whitehall 41. Corridor of Mirrors 46. The Blind Goddess 48. Conspirator 50. The Long Memory 53. Simon and Laura 55. The Entertainer 60. *A Kind of Loving* 62. Rattle of a Simple Man 64. The Nightcomers 71. Memento Mori (TV) 92. The Wedding Gift (TV) 94. Waiting for the Telegram (TV) 98. Lost for Words (TV) 98, many others.

TV series: Meet the Wife. First Lady. Flesh and Blood. In Loving Memory. Hallelujah. Thora on the Straight and Narrow, etc.

❝ An extremely adroit and skilful actress – John Osborne's favourite actress, for what that's worth – with an extraordinary ability, rather like Maggie Smith, to twist on a sixpence from being terribly funny to terribly touching. She's a bit mawkish, sometimes, but a brilliant comedienne. The tops. – *Robert Stephens*

Hirsch, Judd (1935–).
American character actor who nearly became a star.

The Law (TV) 74. Fear on Trial (TV) 75. The Legend of Valentino (TV) 75. The Keegans (TV) 78. King of the Gypsies 78. Sooner or Later (TV) 79. Ordinary People (AAN) 80. Without a Trace 83. Teachers 84. Running on Empty 88. Independence Day 96, etc.

TV series: Delvecchio 76–77. *Taxi* 82–83. Detective in the House 85. Dear John 88–92. George & Leo 97– .

Hirsch, Paul.
American editor.

Phantom of the Paradise 74. Star Wars (AA) 77. Carrie 76. The Empire Strikes Back 80. Creepshow 82. Footloose 84. Ferris Bueller's Day Off 86. Planes, Trains and Automobiles 87. Steel Magnolias 89. Coup de Ville 90. Dutch/Driving Me Crazy 91. Raising Cain 92. Wrestling Ernest Hemingway 93. I Love Trouble 94. Mission: Impossible 96. Hard Rain 98, etc.

Hirsch, Robert (1926–).
French character actor of the Comédie Française.

No Questions on Saturday 64. Kiss Me General 66. Rivers of Fire and Ice 68. La Crime 83. Mon Homme 96, etc.

Hirschfeld, Gerald (1921–).
American cinematographer.

Goodbye Columbus 69. Last Summer 69. Diary of a Mad Housewife 71. Doc 71. Summer Wishes Winter Dreams 73. *Young Frankenstein* 74. The Car 77. The World's Greatest Lover 77. Americathon 79. The Bell Jar 79. Sunday Lovers 80. Neighbors 81. My Favorite Year 82. To Be or Not to Be 83. The House of God 84. Head Office 85. Malone 87. The Neon Empire 87. Child in the Night (TV) 90, etc.

Hirschfelder, David.
Australian composer and keyboard player, leader of the 80s jazz group Pyramid.

Shadows of the Heart (TV) 90. *Strictly Ballroom* 92. Dallas Doll 94. Life of Harry Dare 94. Tunnel Vision 95. Dating the Enemy 95. *Shine* 96. Sliding Doors 98. The Interview 98, etc.

Hiscott, Leslie (1894–1968).
British director, in films from 1919.

The Passing of Mr Quinn 28. Black Coffee 32. While London Sleeps 33. The Triumph of Sherlock Holmes 35. She Shall Have Music 35. Tilly of Bloomsbury 40. The Seventh Survivor 41. Welcome Mr Washington 44. The Time of His Life 52. Tons of Trouble 56, etc.

Hitchcock, Sir Alfred (1899–1980).
British director, in Hollywood more or less since 1940. His name, his profile, and his lugubrious voice are a trademark around the world for suspense thrillers with a touch of impudence, using techniques which are purely cinematic; though of course he frequently fell below his own high standards. Of innumerable books written about him, the most detailed and typical is probably *Le Cinéma Selon Hitchcock* by François Truffaut (1966, translated into English). Others include *Hitch* by John Russell Taylor (the 'official' biography); *Alfred Hitchcock* by George Perry; a Freudian analysis, *The Secret Life of Alfred Hitchcock* by Donald Spoto; *Alfred Hitchcock – The Hollywood Years* by Joel Finler; and *Hitchcock on Hitchcock*, edited by Sidney Gottlieb.

■ The Pleasure Garden 25. The Mountain Eagle 25. *The Lodger* 26. Downhill 27. Easy Virtue 27. *The Ring* 27. The Farmer's Wife 28. Champagne 28. The Manxman 29. *Blackmail* 29. Elstree Calling (sketches) 30. Juno and the Paycock 30. *Murder* 30. The Skin Game 31. Rich and Strange 31. *Number Seventeen* 32. Waltzes from Vienna 33. *The Man Who Knew Too Much* 34. *The Thirty-Nine Steps* 35. Secret Agent 36. Sabotage 37. Young and Innocent 37. *The Lady Vanishes* 38. Jamaica Inn 39. *Rebecca* (AAN) 40. *Foreign Correspondent* 40. Mr and Mrs Smith 41. Suspicion 41. Saboteur 42. *Shadow of a Doubt* 43. Lifeboat (AAN) 43. *Spellbound* (AAN) 45. *Notorious* 46. The Paradine Case 47. Rope 48. Under Capricorn 49. Stage Fright 50. *Strangers on a Train* 51. I Confess 53. Dial M For Murder 54. *Rear Window* (AAN) 54. To Catch a Thief 55. *The Trouble with Harry* 55. The Man Who Knew Too Much 56. The Wrong Man 57. Vertigo 58. *North by Northwest* 59. *Psycho* (AAN) 60. *The Birds* 63. Marnie 64. Torn Curtain 66. Topaz 69. Frenzy 72. Family Plot 76.

TV series: *Alfred Hitchcock Presents* 55–61.

✪ For his understanding of the craft of the cinema; and for his virtuosity in expressing it. *Foreign Correspondent*.

❝ Hitch did not even have to build up his own legend: eager critics like Truffaut did it for him. The suspense master did, however, oblige the press with a variety of *bon mots* about himself and his work. Personally I like best his story of how he caused consternation in a crowded elevator by muttering very audibly to a friend:

I didn't think the old man would bleed so much.

His little epigrams include:

Drama is life with the dull bits left out.

and:

Always make the audience suffer as much as possible.

and:

There is no terror in a bang, only in the anticipation of it.

and:

Terror is a matter of surprise; suspense, of forewarning.

and

I've become a body of films, not a man. I *am* all those films.

and:

A good film is when the price of the admission, the dinner and the babysitter was well worth it.

and:

The cinema is not a slice of life, it's a piece of cake.

and:

Sometimes you find that a film is liked only for its content, without any regard to the style or the manner in which the story is told. But that, after all, is the art of the cinema.

And his defence if the tricks don't work:

All things considered, I think I'm doing well if I get the sixty per cent of my original conception on the screen.

He despised long dialogue sequences:

A film-maker isn't supposed to say things. He's supposed to show them.

He despised actors too. One of his most widely publicized remarks was:

Actors are cattle.

His current star, Carole Lombard, promptly led a troop of oxen onto the shooting stage and herself headed for home. Hitch thought it discreet to tell the press:

I didn't say actors are cattle. What I said was, actors should be *treated* like cattle.

He clearly knew himself to be typecast as a mystery man:

If I made *Cinderella*, the audience would be looking out for a body in the coach.

Perhaps his most quoted admission is:

That was the ending I wanted for *Blackmail*, but I had to change it for commercial reasons.

Many tributes have been paid to him, but John Frankheimer's is all-embracing:

Any American director who says he hasn't been influenced by him is out of his mind.

Cary Grant was happy with Hitch:

He couldn't have been a nicer fellow. I whistled coming to work on his films.

Andrew Sarris saw Hitch's problem:

His reputation has suffered from the fact that he has given audiences more pleasure than is permissible in serious cinema.

Doggedly into his 70s he continued to invent mayhem:

When people say I'm 70 I say that's a confounded lie. I'm twice 35, that's all. Twice 35.

He had little reason for complaint:

Even my failures make money and become classics a year after I make them.

And he continued to be a realist:

The length of the film should be directly related to the endurance of the human bladder.

~In 1944 Hitch also directed two war documentaries for the Ministry of Information: *Bon Voyage* and *Aventure Malagache*.

Hitler, Adolf (1889–1945) (Adolf Schickelgruber).
German fascist dictator, subject of many screen documentaries, notably *Mein Kampf* 63 and *The Life of Adolf Hitler* 65. Actors who have impersonated him include Chaplin in *The Great Dictator* 40; Luther Adler in *The Magic Face* 51 and *The Desert Fox* 52; Tom Dugan in *To Be or Not To Be* 42 and *Star Spangled Rhythm* 42; Ludwig Donath in *The Strange Death of Adolf Hitler* 43; Albin Skoda in *The Last Act* 55; Kenneth Griffith in *The Two-Headed Spy* 58; Richard Basehart in *Hitler* 61; Billy Frick in *Is Paris Burning?* 65; Sidney Miller in *Which Way to the Front?* 69; Alec Guinness in *Hitler: The Last Ten Days* 73. Most frequent Hitler-player, however, is Robert Watson, who in the 40s seemed to do little else; apart from an excellent serious portrayal in *The Hitler Gang* 44, he supplied Hitler walk-ons in *The Devil with Hitler* 42, *That Nazty Nuisance* 43, *Hitler Dead or Alive* 43, *The Miracle of Morgan's Creek* 44, *The Story of Mankind* 57, and many others.

In the 80s television began to show renewed interest in fanciful presentations of Hitler. Anthony Hopkins played him in *The Bunker*; Derek Jacobi in *Inside the Third Reich*; and Gunther Meisner in *The Winds of War*.

❝ A psychopath who somehow found his way from a padded cell to Potsdam. – *Malcolm Muggeridge*

Hively, Jack (1910–1995).
American director.

■ They Made Her a Spy 39. Panama Lady 39. The Spellbinder 39. Three Sons 39. Two Thoroughbreds 39. The Saint's Double Trouble 40. The Saint Takes Over 40. Anne of Windy Poplars 40. Laddie 40. The Saint in Palm Springs 41. They Met in Argentina 41. Father Takes a Wife 41. Four Jacks and a Jill 41. Street of Chance 42. Are You With It? 48. Starbird and Sweet William 76. The Adventures of Huckleberry Finn (TV) 81. California Gold Rush (TV) 81.

Hobart, Rose (1906–) (Rose Keefer).
American actress, usually in character roles.

Liliom 30. Dr Jekyll and Mr Hyde 32. Tower of London 39. Nothing but the Truth 41. Ziegfeld Girl 41. The Soul of a Monster 44. The Farmer's Daughter 47. Mickey 48, etc.

Hobbes, Halliwell (1877–1962).
British character actor, long the impeccable butler, on stage from 1898, films from 1929 (after which he lived in Hollywood).

Charley's Aunt 30. Dr Jekyll and Mr Hyde 32. *The Masquerader* 33. Bulldog Drummond Strikes Back 35. Dracula's Daughter 36. *You Can't Take It with You* 38. Lady Hamilton 41. *Sherlock Holmes Faces Death* 43. If Winter Comes 47. That Forsyte Woman 49. Miracle in the Rain 56, many others.

Hobbs, Jack (1893–1968).
British actor on screen from silent days, usually in genial roles.

The Sin Game 30. Trouble in Store 34. No Limit 35. Millions 37. *It's in the Air* 38. Behind These Walls 48. *Worm's Eye View* 51, etc.

Hobson, Valerie (1917–1998).
British leading actress in dignified and disciplined ladylike roles. Born in Larne, Northern Ireland, and raised in Hampshire, she trained as a dancer and studied at RADA. At the age of 17, she signed a contract with Universal and spent two years in Hollywood before returning to England, where she was put under contract by Alexander KORDA. Married producer Anthony HAVELOCK-ALLAN, and, in 1954, MP and, later, Conservative Minister John Profumo, after which she retired from acting. After a sex scandal (detailed in the film *Scandal* 88) ended her husband's political career, she helped him with his charity work in the East End of London.

■ Eyes of Fate 33. Two Hearts in Waltztime 34. The Path of Glory 34. Badger's Green 34. Strange Wives (US) 34. Rendezvous at Midnight (US) 35. Werewolf of London (US) 35. Bride of Frankenstein (US) (arguably in title role) 35. The Mystery of Edwin Drood (US) 35. Chinatown Squad (US) 35. The Great Impersonation (US) 35. Oh What a Night 35. August Weekend (US) 36. Tugboat Princess (US) 36. The Secret of Stamboul 36. No Escape 36. Jump for Glory 37. The Drum 38. Q Planes 38. *This Man is News* 38. This Man in Paris 39. *The Spy in Black* 39. The Silent Battle 39. *Contraband* 40. Atlantic Ferry 41. Unpublished Story 42. The Adventures of Tartu 43. The Years Between 46. *Great Expectations* 46. Blanche Fury 47. The Small Voice 48. *Kind Hearts and Coronets* 49. Train of Events 49. The Interrupted Journey 49. The Rocking Horse Winner 49. *The Card* 51. Who Goes There 52. Meet Me Tonight 52. The Voice of Merrill 53. Background 53. Knave of Hearts 54.

❝ Valerie was a tall, strong, intelligent girl with glorious eyes and a quick wit (too quick a wit, some people thought, but I had suffered too many English ladies to complain about that). – *Michael Powell*

Hoch, Winton C. (1905–1979).
American cinematographer, former research physicist.

Dr Cyclops 40. Captains of the Clouds 42. So Dear to My Heart 48. Joan of Arc (co-ph) (AA) 48. *She Wore a Yellow Ribbon* (AA) 49. Tulsa 49. Halls of Montezuma 51. *The Quiet Man* (co-ph) (AA) 52. Mr Roberts 55. *The Searchers* 56. Darby O'Gill and the Little People 59. The Lost World 60. Five Weeks in a Balloon 62. *Robinson Crusoe on Mars* 64. The Green Berets 68, etc.

Hodge, Douglas (1960–).
English leading actor, born in Plymouth.

Salome's Last Dance (as Lord Alfred Douglas) 88. Dealers 89. Diamond Skulls 89. Buddy's Song 90. The Trial 92. It Might Be You (TV) 95. Saigon Baby (TV) 95. The Uninvited (TV) 97. The Scold's Bridle (TV) 98, etc.

TV series: Capital City 88–90.

Hodge, John (1964–).
British screenwriter who has so far worked in collaboration with director Danny Boyle and producer Andrew Macdonald. He is also a doctor.

Shallow Grave 95. *Trainspotting* (AAN) 96. A Life Less Ordinary 97. The Beach 99.

Hodge, Patricia (1946–).
British actress, in haughty roles, mainly on television.

The Disappearance 77. Rosie Dixon – Night Nurse 78. The Elephant Man 80. Riding High 80. Betrayal 82. Skin (Nor.) 86. The Life and Loves of a She-Devil (TV) 86. Hotel du Lac (TV) 86. Sunset (US) 88. The Shell Seekers (TV) 89. The Secret Life of Ian Fleming (TV) 90. The Leading Man 96, etc.

TV series: Holding the Fort 80–81. Jemima Shaw Investigates 83. The Other 'Arf 80–84. Rich Tea and Sympathy 91. The Legacy of Reginald Perrin 96.

Hodges, Ken (1922–1993).
British cinematographer.
Faces in the Dark 60. The Comedy Man 63. The Jokers 67. Negatives 68. Every Home Should Have One 70. A Day in the Death of Joe Egg 70. The Ruling Class 72. Bedevilled 73. The Spiral Staircase 75. Stand Up for Virgin Soldiers 77. Confessions from a Holiday Camp 77. The Odd Job 78, etc.

Hodges, Mike (1932–).
British director, from TV.
■ Suspect (TV) 69. Rumour (TV) 70. *Get Carter* 71. Pulp 72. The Terminal Man (US) (& p) 73. Flash Gordon 79. Morons from Outer Space 84. A Prayer for the Dying 87. Black Rainbow 89.

Hodiak, John (1914–1955).
Serious-looking American leading man of the 40s, of Ukrainian descent.
■ A Stranger in Town 43. I Dood It 43. Song of Russia 43. Swing Shift Maisie 43. *Lifeboat* 44. Marriage is a Private Affair 44. Maisie Goes to Reno 44. Sunday Dinner for a Soldier 44. You Can't Do That to Me 44. *A Bell for Adano* 45. Ziegfeld Follies 46. The Harvey Girls 46. Somewhere in the Night 46. Two Smart People 46. The Arnelo Affair 47. Love from a Stranger 47. Desert Fury 47. Homecoming 48. Command Decision 48. Ambush 49. The Bribe 49. A Lady Without Passport 50. Battleground 50. The Miniver Story 50. Night into Morning 51. The People Against O'Hara 51. Across the Wide Missouri 51. Battle Zone 52. The Sellout 52. Conquest of Cochise 53. Ambush at Tomahawk Gap 53. Mission over Korea 53. Dragonfly Squadron 54. Trial 55. On the Threshold of Space 56.

Hoellering, George (c. 1899–1980).
producer of *Hortobagy*, long in Britain as specialized distributor and exhibitor; also producer of *Murder in the Cathedral* 51.

Hoey, Dennis (1893–1960) (Samuel David Hyams).
British character actor, mostly in Hollywood; a memorably obtuse Lestrade to Basil Rathbone's Sherlock Holmes.
Tell England 30. The Good Companions 32. Chu Chin Chow 34. The Wandering Jew 34. Brewster's Millions 35. Maria Marten 36. This Above All 42. Sherlock Holmes and the Secret Weapon 42. Spider Woman 44. Pearl of Death 44. House of Fear 45. Kitty 46. Where There's Life 47. If Winter Comes 47. Wake of the Red Witch 48. David and Bathsheba 51, many others.

Hoey, Iris (1885–1979).
English actress, in occasional films. Born in London, she studied at RADA and was on-stage from 1903. Her second husband was actor Cyril Raymond.
East Lynne 22. Those Were the Days 34. A Star Fell from Heaven 36. The Tenth Man 36. Let's Make a Night of It 37. Pygmalion 38. The Terror 38. Just William 39. Poet's Pub 49. The Girl Who Couldn't Quite 50, etc.

Hoffe, Monckton (1880–1951) (Reaney Monckton Hoffe-Miles).
Irish playwright and screenwriter, a former actor, in England from the early 1900s. He went to Hollywood to write for MGM in the mid-30s, returning to Britain on the outbreak of the Second World War to work in propaganda.
The Faithful Heart (oa) 22 and 32. Man without Desire (idea) 23. The Hate Ship (co-w) 29. Under the Greenwood Tree (co-w) 29. High Seas (story) 30. The Flame of Love (co-w) 30. Many Waters (w, oa) 31. Michael and Mary (co-w) 31. Bitter Sweet (co-w) 33. Little Damozel (oa) 33. The Queen's Affair/The Runaway Queen (co-w) 34. The Mystery of Mr X (co-w) (US) 34. What Every Woman Knows (co-w) (US) 34. London Melody (w) 37. The Last of Mrs Cheyney (co-w) (US) 37. The Emperor's Candlesticks (co-w) (US) 37. Pagliacci (co-w) 36. Busman's Honeymoon/Haunted Honeymoon 40. The Lady Eve (story, AAN) (US) 41. Daybreak (oa) 48, etc.

Hoffenstein, Samuel (1890–1947).
Lithuanian-American screenwriter, always in collaboration.
An American Tragedy 31. *Dr Jekyll and Mr Hyde* 31. *Love Me Tonight* 32. Song of Songs 33. Marie Galante 34. Desire 36. Conquest 38. The Great Waltz 39. Lydia 41. Flesh and Fantasy (AAN) 43. Phantom of the Opera 43. Laura 44. Cluny Brown 46. Give My Regards to Broadway 48.

Hoffman, Basil (1941–).
American character actor.
Lady Liberty 72. At Long Last Love 75. All the President's Men 76. Close Encounters of the Third Kind 77. The Electric Horseman 79. Ordinary People 80. My Favorite Year 82. Lambada 89. Communion 89. The Double O Kid 92. The Ice Runner 93, etc.

Hoffman, Dustin (1937–).
Diffident American leading actor who suited the mood of the late 60s and made a big comeback in the early 80s.
The Tiger Makes Out 67. *The Graduate* (AAN) 67. *Midnight Cowboy* (AAN) 69. John and Mary 69. Little Big Man 70. Who is Harry Kellerman . . . ? 71. Alfredo Alfredo 72. Straw Dogs 72. Papillon 73. Lenny (AAN) 74. *All the President's Men* 76. Marathon Man 76. Straight Time 78. Agatha 79. *Kramer vs Kramer* (AA) 80. *Tootsie* (AAN) 83. Death of a Salesman 85. Private Conversations 85. Ishtar 87. Rain Man (AA) 88. Family Business 89. Dick Tracy 90. Billy Bathgate 91. Hook 91. Hero/Accidental Hero 92. Outbreak 95. American Buffalo 96. Sleepers 96. Sphere 97. *Wag the Dog* (AAN) 97. Mad City 97. A Walk on the Moon 99, etc.
❝ A good review from a critic is just another stay of execution. – *D.H.*
I don't like the fact that I have to get older so fast, but I like the fact that I'm ageing so well. – *D.H.*
Never argue with a man who is shorter than his Oscar. – *Larry Gelbart*
Famous line (*The Graduate*): 'Mrs Robinson, if you don't mind my saying so, this conversation is getting a little strange.'

Hoffman, Joseph (1909–1997).
American screenwriter. Born in New York City, he was a journalist, publicist and radio writer before joining Fox in the mid-30s, later working for Universal and other studios. From the mid-50s he worked in television.
Thank You Jeeves 36. City of Silent Men 42. My Kingdom for a Cook 43. Carolina Blues 44. China Sky 45. One Way to Love 45. Don't Trust Your Husband 48. Buccaneer's Girl 49. And Baby Makes Three 50. Weekend with Father 51. No Room for the Groom 52. Duel at Silver Creek 52. At Sword's Point 52. Against All Flags 52. Has Anybody Seen My Gal 52. The Lone Hand 53. Rails into Laramie 54. Yankee Pasha 54. Chicago Syndicate 55, etc.

Hoffman, Michael.
American-born director and screenwriter who began his career in Britain.
Privileged (GB) (co-w, d) 82. Restless Natives (GB) (wd) 85. Promised Land (wd) 88. Sisters/Some Girls (d) 88. Soapdish (d) 91. Restoration (d) 95. One Fine Day (d) 96, etc.

Hoffman, Philip Seymour (aka Philip Hoffman, Philip S. Hoffman).
American character actor.
Triple Bogey on a Par Five Hole 91. Scent of a Woman 92. My New Gun 92. Leap of Faith 92. My Boyfriend's Back 93. Nobody's Fool 94. The Getaway 94. The Yearling (TV) 94. When a Man Loves a Woman 94. Hard Eight 96. Twister 96. Boogie Nights 97. The Big Lebowski 98. Flawless 99. The Talented Mr Ripley 99, etc.

Hoffmann, Kurt (1912–).
German director, mainly of comedies.
Quax der Bruch pilot 41. I Think Often of Piroschka 55. The Confessions of Felix Krull 57. Wir Wunderkinder 58. Swedish Interlude 63. Rheinsberg 67. The Captain 71, etc.

Hofschneider, Marco.
Young German actor.
Europa Europa 91. Foreign Student 94. Immortal Beloved 94. The Island of Doctor Moreau 96, etc.

Hogan, James P. (1891–1943).
American director.
Last Train from Madrid 37. Ebb Tide 38. The Texans 39. Power Dive 41. The Mad Ghoul 43. The Strange Death of Adolf Hitler 44, etc.

Hogan, Paul (1939–).
Australian comedian and screenwriter whose second film made him an international star. A former construction worker and Australian TV star, he married actress Linda Kozlowski in 1990.
Anzacs 85. Crocodile Dundee (AAN) 86. Crocodile Dundee II 88. The Humpty Dumpty Man 89. Almost an Angel 90. Lightning Jack (& p, w) 94. Flipper 96, etc.

Hogan, Paul J. (1962–).
Australian director. He is married to producer and director Jocelyn Moorhouse.
Muriel's Wedding 94. My Best Friend's Wedding 97, etc.

Hogan, Terry 'Hulk' (1953–).
Beefy American wrestler turned actor, attempting to widen his range from tough-guy roles to comedies.
Rocky 3 82. No Holds Barred 89. Gremlins 2: The New Batch 90. Suburban Commando 91. Mr Nanny 93. The Secret Agent Club 96. Santa with Muscles 96. Three Ninjas: High Noon at Mega Mountain 97, etc.
❝ I'd like to be the John Wayne of the 90s. – *T.H.*

Hohl, Arthur (1889–1964).
Staring-eyed American character actor who often played rustic types.
The Cheat 31. Island of Lost Souls 32. Man's Castle 33. Cleopatra 34. Show Boat 36. The Road Back 37. Kidnapped 38. Blackmail 39. Moontide 42. The Scarlet Claw 44. The Yearling 46. The Vigilantes Return 47, many others.

Holbrook, Hal (1925–).
American general-purpose stage and TV actor, also Mark Twain impersonator.
The Group 66. Wild in the Streets 68. A Clear and Present Danger (TV) 69. The People Next Door 70. Suddenly Single (TV) 71. *That Certain Summer* (TV) 72. Magnum Force 73. All the President's Men 76. Midway 76. Julia 77. Murder by Natural Causes (TV) 79. Natural Enemies 79. Capricorn One 79. The Legend of the Golden Gun (TV) 79. Fog 80. The Killing of the President 80. Creepshow 82. The Star Chamber 82. Behind Enemy Lines 85. Wall Street 87. Fletch Lives 89. Bonds of Love (TV) 93. The Firm 93. Carried Away 96. Eye of God 97. Judas Kiss 98, etc.
TV series: *The Bold Ones* 70–71.

Holcomb, Rod.
American director, mainly for TV films.
The Red Light Sting 84. Stark 85. Chase 85. Blind Justice 86. China Beach 88. Chains of Gold (TV) 92. Royce 93. Convict Cowboy (TV) 95, etc.

Holden, Fay (1894–1973) (Dorothy Hammerton).
British stage actress who went to Hollywood in the 30s and found a niche as the mother of the Hardy family. Once known as Dorothy Clyde. Born in Birmingham, she was on stage under the name of Gaby Fay. Married actor David Clyde.
Wives Never Know 36. Exclusive 37. Judge Hardy's Children 38. Sweethearts 38. The Hardys Ride High 39. Bitter Sweet 40. Andy Hardy's Private Secretary 41. Ziegfeld Girl 41. Blossoms in the Dust 41. Andy Hardy's Double Life 43. Andy Hardy's Blonde Trouble 44. Canyon Passage 46. Love Laughs at Andy Hardy 46. Samson and Delilah 49. The Big Hangover 50. Andy Hardy Comes Home 58, many others.

Holden, Gloria (1908–1991).
London-born leading lady, long in Hollywood.
Dracula's Daughter (title role) 36. The Life of Émile Zola 37. Test Pilot 38. A Child Is Born 40. The Corsican Brothers 41. Behind the Rising Sun 43. The Hucksters 47. Dream Wife 53. The Eddy Duchin Story 57. This Happy Feeling 68, etc.

Holden, Joyce (1930–) (Jo Ann Heckert).
Blonde leading American actress and dancer, a former beauty queen. She worked first in Universal's pictures before moving to low-budget movies and retiring in the late 50s.
The Milkman 50. Iron Man 51. You Never Can Tell 51. Bronco Buster 52. Girls in the Night 53. The Werewolf 56. Terror from the Year 5000 58, etc.

Holden, William (1872–1932).
American general-purpose actor of the late silent period, usually in small roles; no relation to the later William Holden.
The First Kiss 28. Dynamite 30, etc.

Holden, William (1918–1981) (William Beedle).
Good-looking American leading man who hit his greatest popularity in the 50s.
■ *Golden Boy* 39. Invisible Stripes 40. Our Town 40. Those were the Days 40. Arizona 40. I Wanted Wings 41. Texas 41. The Fleet's In 42. The Remarkable Andrew 42. Meet the Stewarts 42. Young and Willing 43. Blaze of Noon 47. Dear Ruth 47. Variety Girl 47. *Rachel and the Stranger* 48. Apartment for Peggy 48. The Man from Colorado 48. The Dark Past 49. The Streets of Laredo 49. Miss Grant Takes Richmond 49. Dear Wife 49. Father is a Bachelor 50. *Sunset Boulevard* (AAN) 50. Union Station 50. *Born Yesterday* 50. Force of Arms 51. Submarine Command 51. Boots Malone 52. The Turning Point 52. *Stalag 17* (AA) 53. The Moon is Blue 53. Forever Female 53. Escape from Fort Bravo 53. Executive Suite 54. Sabrina 54. The Country Girl 54. The Bridges at Toko-Ri 54. *Love is a Many-Splendored Thing* 55. *Picnic* 55. The Proud and Profane 56. Toward the Unknown 56. *The Bridge on the River Kwai* 57. The Key 58. The Horse Soldiers 59. The World of Suzie Wong 60. Satan Never Sleeps 62. The Counterfeit Traitor 62. The Lion 62. Paris When it Sizzles 64. The Seventh Dawn 64. Alvarez Kelly 66. Casino Royale 67. The Devil's Brigade 68. The Christmas Tree 69. *The Wild Bunch* 69. Wild Rovers 71. The Revengers 72. The Blue Knight (TV) 72. Breezy 73. Open Season 74. The Towering Inferno 74. *Network* (AAN) 76. 21 Hours at Munich (TV) 77. Ashanti 78. Damien: Omen II 78. Fedora 78. Escape to Athena 79. The Earthling 80. When Time Ran Out 80. S.O.B. 81.
❝ I'm a whore, all actors are whores. We sell our bodies to the highest bidder. – *W.H.*
Take any picture you can. One out of four will be good, one out of ten will be very good, and one out of fifteen will get you an Academy Award. – *W.H.*
When you look at him, the map of the US is right there on his – face. – *Pete Martin*
Famous line (*Picnic*): 'I gotta get somewhere in this world. I just gotta.'

Holden-Jones, Amy (1953–).
American screenwriter and director, a former editor. Married cinematographer Michael Chapman.
AS EDITOR: Hollywood Boulevard 76. Corvette Summer 78, etc.
AS WRITER: Mystic Pizza 88. Beethoven 92. Indecent Proposal 93. The Getaway 94, etc.
AS WRITER-DIRECTOR: The Slumber Party Massacre (d only) 82. Love Letters 83. Maid to Order 87. The Rich Man's Wife 96, etc.

Holdridge, Lee (1944–).
American composer, also for television movies.
Jonathan Livingston Seagull (co-m) 73. Jeremy 73. Mahogany (co-m) 75. Goin' Home 76. The Greatest (co-m) 77. French Postcards 78. Tilt 79. Oliver's Story (co-m) 79. The Beastmaster 82. Mr Mom 83. Splash 84. Micki and Maude 84. Sylvester 85. Walk Like a Man 87. Big Business 88. Old Gringo 89. Pastime 91. Cyborg Agent 92. The Whipping Boy (TV) 95, etc.

Holender, Adam.
American cinematographer.
Midnight Cowboy 69. Puzzle of a Downfall Child 70. Panic in Needle Park 71. Promises in the Dark 79. The Seduction of Joe Tynan 79. Simon 80. The Idolmaker 80. Street Smart 87. To Kill a Priest 88. The Dream Team 89. Sea of Love 89. Fresh 94. Smoke 95. Blue in the Face 95. I'm Not Rappaport 97. 8 Heads in a Duffel Bag 97, etc.

Holiday, Billie (1915–1959) (Eleonora Harris).
American jazz singer, one of the great interpreters of popular song, who made one feature film, in the role of a maid. She worked as an extra in *The Emperor Jones* 33, and also made a short with Duke Ellington, *Symphony in Black* 35. In the biopic of her life, *Lady Sings the Blues* 75, she was played by Diana Ross. In the 50s, when the film was first mooted, it was reported that Lana Turner was being considered for the role.
Autobiography: 1956, *Lady Sings the Blues*, with William Dufty.

Biographies: 1975, *Billie's Blues* by John Chilton. 1987, *Billie Holiday* by John White. 1994, *Wishing on the Moon: The Life and Times of Billie Holiday* by Donald Clarke.
New Orleans 47.

Holland, Agnieszka (1948–).
Polish director and screenwriter, now based in France. After studying at the Prague Film School, she began as an assistant to director Krzysztof Zanussi and then worked with Andrzej Wajda.
Rough Treatment/Bez Znieczulenia (w) 78. Provincial Actors/Aktorzy Prowincjonalni (d) 80. The Fever/Goraczka (d) 81. Woman on Her Own/ Kobieta Samotna i Chromy (d) 82. Danton (w) 83. Angry Harvest/Bittere Ernte (wd) 85. To Kill a Priest (wd) 88. Korczak (w) 90. Europa, Europa (wd) (AANw) 91. Olivier, Olivier (co-w, d) 92. The Secret Garden (d) 93. Total Eclipse (d) 95. Washington Square 97, etc.

Holland, Tom (1943–).
American director and screenwriter.
The Beast Within (w) 82. Psycho II (w) 83. Class of '84 (co-w) 84. Cloak and Dagger (w) 84. Scream for Help (w) 84. Fright Night 85. Fatal Beauty 87. Child's Play 88. The Temp 93. Stephen King's The Langoliers (TV) 95. Stephen King's Thinner (& co-w) 96, etc.

Hollander, Frederick (1892–1976).
German song composer, long in America.
The Blue Angel 30. Desire 36. *Destry Rides Again* 39. The Man Who Came to Dinner 42. A Foreign Affair 48. The Five Thousand Fingers of Dr T 53, etc.

Holles, Antony (1901–1950).
British actor who often played excitable foreigners.
The Lodger 32. Brewster's Millions 35. Dark Journey 37. Neutral Port 41. Warn That Man 43. Carnival 46. Bonnie Prince Charlie 49. The Rocking-Horse Winner 50, many others.

Holliday, Doc (1849–1885).
American wild west character; a tubercular dentist and poker-player who oddly changed to the right side of the law when he teamed up with Wyatt Earp in *Tombstone*. Played inaccurately but picturesquely on screen by Cesar Romero in *Frontier Marshal* 39; Walter Huston in *The Outlaw* 41; Kent Taylor in *Tombstone* 42; Victor Mature in *My Darling Clementine* 46; James Griffith in *Masterson of Kansas* 55; Kirk Douglas in *Gunfight at the OK Corral* 56; Arthur Kennedy in *Cheyenne Autumn* 64; Jason Robards in *Hour of the Gun* 67; Stacy Keach in *Doc* 70; Val Kilmer in *Tombstone* 94; Dennis Quaid in *Wyatt Earp* 94; and Douglas Fowley in the TV series *Wyatt Earp*.

Holliday, Judy (1922–1965) (Judith Tuvim).
American revue star who shot to fame in the 50s as a slightly daffy blonde in a handful of well-scripted comedies.
Biography: 1982, *Judy Holliday* by Gary Carey.
■ Greenwich Village 44. Something for the Boys 44. Winged Victory 44. Adam's Rib 49. *Born Yesterday* (AA) 50. The Marrying Kind 52. *It Should Happen to You* 53. Phffft 54. *The Solid Gold Cadillac* 56. Full of Life 56. Bells are Ringing 60.

Holliman, Earl (1928–).
American general-purpose actor who can play innocent or villainous.
Destination Gobi 53. The Bridges at Toko-Ri 54. Broken Lance 54. The Big Combo 55. Forbidden Planet 56. Giant 56. The Rainmaker 56. Gunfight at OK Corral 57. Trooper Hook 57. Hot Spell 58. The Trap 59. Last Train from Gun Hill 59. Visit to a Small Planet 60. Summer and Smoke 61. Armored Command 61. The Sons of Katie Elder 65. Covenant with Death 67. Anzio 68. Smoke 69. Trapped (TV) 73. I Love You, Goodbye (TV) 74. Alexander: The Other Side of Dawn (TV) 77. Sharky's Machine 81. The Thorn Birds (TV) 82. Gunsmoke: Return to Dodge (TV) 87, etc.
TV series: Hotel de Paree 59. The Wide Country 62. Police Woman 74–78.

Hollingsworth, John (1916–1963).
British conductor for many film scores of the 40s.

Holloway, Stanley (1890–1982).
British comedian, entertainer, singer and character actor with a long list of international credits in revue, musical comedy and variety as well as films. Born in London, he became a star with the concert party the Co-Optimists and was famous for his monologues delivered in a Yorkshire accent.
Autobiography: 1969, *Wiv a Little Bit of Luck*.
■ The Rotters 21. *The Co-Optimists* 30. Sleeping Car 33. The Girl from Maxim's 33. Lily of Killarney 34. Love at Second Sight 34. Sing as We Go 34. Road House 34. D'Ye Ken John Peel? 35. In Town Tonight 35. *Squibs* 35. Play Up the Band 35. Song of the Forge 36. *The Vicar of Bray* 36. Cotton Queen 37. Sam Small Leaves Town 37. Our Island Nation 37. Major Barbara 41. *Salute John Citizen* 42. *The Way Ahead* 44. *Champagne Charlie* 44. *This Happy Breed* 44. *The Way to the Stars* 45. *Brief Encounter* 45. Caesar and Cleopatra 45. Wanted for Murder 46. Carnival 46. Meet Me at Dawn 46. *Nicholas Nickleby* (as Mr Crummles) 47. Snowbound 48. Saraband for Dead Lovers 48. One Night With You 48. Noose 48. The Winslow Boy 48. *Hamlet* (as the gravedigger) 48. Another Shore 48. Passport to Pimlico 49. The Perfect Woman 49. Midnight Episode 50. One Wild Oat 50. *The Lavender Hill Mob* 51. Lady Godiva Rides Again 51. The Magic Box 51. The Happy Family 52. Meet Me Tonight 52. *The Titfield Thunderbolt* 52. *The Beggar's Opera* 53. A Day to Remember 53. Meet *Mr Lucifer* 53. Fast and Loose 53. An Alligator Named Daisy 55. Jumping for Joy 55. Alive and Kicking 58. No Trees in the Street 58. Hello London 58. *No Love for Johnnie* 61. On the Fiddle 61. *My Fair Lady* (as Doolittle) (AAN) 64. In Harm's Way 64. Ten Little Indians 64. The Sandwich Man 66. Mrs Brown You've Got a Lovely Daughter 68. Run a Crooked Mile (TV) 69. The Private Life of Sherlock Holmes 70. The Flight of the Doves 71. Up the Front 72. Journey into Fear 76.
TV series: *Our Man Higgins* 62.

Holloway, Sterling (1905–1992).
Slow-speaking American comic actor, usually of yokels or hillbillies. Busiest in the 30s; latterly the voice of many Disney characters.
Casey at the Bat 27. Alice in Wonderland 33. Life Begins at Forty 35. Professor Beware 38. The Bluebird 40. A Walk in the Sun 46. The Beautiful Blonde from Bashful Bend 49. Shake, Rattle and Rock 56. Live a Little Love a Little 68. Thunder and Lightning 77, many others.
TV series: The Life of Riley 53–58. Willie 55. The Baileys of Balboa 64.

Holly, Buddy (1936–1959) (Charles Hardin Holley).
Influential American rock singer and songwriter, killed in a plane crash while on tour with singer Richie Valens. He was played by Gary Busey in the biopic *The Buddy Holly Story* 78.
Biographies: 1996, *Buddy Holly: The Real Story* by Ellis Amburn. 1996, *Buddy: The Biography* by Philip Norman.

Holly, Lauren.
American actress. Married actor Jim Carrey in 1996, and filed for divorce in 1997.
Band of the Hand 86. Seven Minutes in Heaven 86. The Adventures of Ford Fairlane 90. Fugitive among Us (TV) 92. Dragon: The Bruce Lee Story 93. Dumb and Dumber 94. Sabrina 95. Turbluence 96. Beautiful Girls 96. Down Periscope 96. No Looking Back 98, etc.
TV series: Picket Fences 92–96.

Holm, Celeste (1919–).
Cool, calm, American stage actress whose films have usually provided her with wisecracking roles.
■ Three Little Girls in Blue 46. Carnival in Costa Rica 47. *Gentleman's Agreement* (AA) 47. Road House 48. *The Snake Pit* 48. Chicken Every Sunday 48. Come to the Stable (AAN) 49. Everybody Does It 49. A Letter to Three Wives (narrator only) 49. *All About Eve* (AAN) 50. Champagne for Caesar 50. The Tender Trap 55. *High Society* 56. Bachelor Flat 61. Cosa Nostra, Arch Enemy of the FBI (TV) 66. Doctor You've Got to be Kidding 67. The Delphi Bureau (TV) 72. Tom Sawyer 73. The Underground Man (TV) 74. Death Cruise (TV) 74. Captains and the Kings (TV) 76. Bittersweet Love 76. Love Boat II (TV) 78. The Private Files of J. Edgar Hoover 78. Backstairs at the White House (TV) 79. Midnight Lace (TV) 80. This Girl for Hire (TV) 83. Jessie (TV) 85. Three Men and a Baby 87. Murder by the Book (TV) 87. Polly (TV) 89.
TV series: Honestly Celeste 54. Nancy 70–71. Jessie 84. Falcon Crest 85.

Holm, Sir Ian (1932–) (Ian Holm Cuthbert).
British leading actor, much on the stage with the Royal Shakespeare Company in the 60s. From the mid-70s to the mid-90s, he suffered from stage fright and avoided the theatre, until he acted an acclaimed King Lear at the Royal National Theatre in 1997. Married actress Penelope Wilton, his third wife, in 1991. Knighted in 1998.
The Bofors Gun (BFA) 68. A Midsummer Night's Dream 68. The Fixer 68. Oh What a Lovely War 69. A Severed Head 70. Nicholas and Alexandra 71. Mary Queen of Scots 72. Young Winston 72. The Homecoming 73. Juggernaut 75. Shout at the Devil 76. Robin and Marian 76. Jesus of Nazareth (TV) 77. The Man in the Iron Mask (TV) 77. March or Die 77. Holocaust (TV) 77. Alien 79. The Lost Boys (TV) 79. SOS Titanic (TV) 79. All Quiet on the Western Front (TV) 80. Time Bandits (TV) 81. Chariots of Fire (BFA, AAN) 81. Return of the Soldier 82. Greystoke 84. Dance with a Stranger 85. Wetherby 85. Brazil 85. Laughterhouse 85. Dreamchild 86. Another Woman 88. Henry V 89. Hamlet 90. Kafka 91. Naked Lunch 91. Blue Ice 92. The Hour of the Pig 93. The Madness of King George 95. Loch Ness 95. Big Night 95. The Fifth Element 97. *The Sweet Hereafter* 97. Night Falls on Manhattan 97. A Life Less Ordinary 97. Shergar 98. Simon Magus 99, etc.

Holm, Sonia (1922–1974).
English leading lady of the late 40s. Married actor Patrick Holt.
When the Bough Breaks 47. The Loves of Joanna Godden 47. Miranda 48. The Bad Lord Byron 49. The Crowded Day 54, etc.

Holmes, Helen (1892–1950).
Athletic American actress, a heroine of silent serials. Born in South Bend, Indiana, she began in films in 1912 with Mack Sennett and became famous as the star of the serial *The Hazards of Helen* 14–15, for Kalem. Later she appeared in many action movies directed by her husband, J. P. McGowan, retiring in the mid-20s, though she appeared later in a few minor roles.
The Operator at Black Rock 13. The Car of Death 13. Grouch the Engineer 14. The Girl and the Game (serial) 15–16. When Seconds Count 16. One Million in Jewels 22. 40-Horse Hawkins 24. Fighting Fury 24. Barriers of the Law 25. Blood and Steel 25. Mistaken Orders 26. Crossed Signals 26. Poppy 36. The Californian 37. Dude Cowboy 41, etc.

Holmes, John (1945–1988) (aka Johnny Wadd).
Well-endowed American star of pornographic films of the 70s and 80s. A graduate of UCLA, he appeared in more than 1,500 movies, though his career was hampered by accusations of murder and burglary in the early 80s. Died of AIDS. The character of Dirk Diggler in *Boogie Nights* 97, directed by Paul Anderson, is based partly on him. Also being planned is *Wonderland*, a film about his problems in the 80s, starring Michael Biehn. *Exhausted* 81, directed by Julia St Vincent, was a documentary on his life and films.
Flesh of the Lotus 72. The Life and Times of Xaviera Hollander 74. Blonde in Black Lace 75. Autobiography of a Flea 76. Hard Soap, Hard Soap 77. The Erotic Adventures of Candy 78. Dracula Sucks 78. Eruption 78. Sweet Captive 79. Blonde Fire 79. Prisoner of Paradise 80. Studio of Lust 84. The Good, the Bad and the Horny (& d) 85. Looking for Mr Goodsex 86. The Devil and Mr Holmes 88, many others.

Holmes, Phillips (1907–1942).
American juvenile lead who went straight from college to Hollywood; son of Taylor Holmes. His rather stiff personality soon lost its appeal. Died in a plane crash.
■ Varsity 28. His Private Life 28. Illusion 29. The Wild Party 29. Stairs of Sand 29. The Return of Sherlock Holmes 29. Pointed Heels 29. Only the Brave 30. Paramount on Parade 30. The Devil's Holiday 30. Grumpy 30. Her Man 30. Man to Man 30. The Dancers 30. The Criminal Code 31. Stolen Heaven 31. Confessions of a Co-Ed 31. *An American Tragedy* 31. The Man I Killed 32. Two Kinds of Women 32. Make Me a Star 32. 70,000 Witnesses 32. Night Court 33. The Secret of Madame Blanche 33. Men Must Fight 33. Looking Forward 33. Storm at Daybreak 33. The Big Brain 33. Dinner at Eight 33. Penthouse 33. Beauty for Sale 33. Stage Mother 33. Private Scandal 34. Nana 34. Caravan 34. Great Expectations 34. Million Dollar Ransom 34. The Divine Spark 34. No Ransom 35. Ten Minute Alibi (GB) 35. Chatterbox 36. House of a Thousand Candles 36. General Spanky 36. The Dominant Sex (GB) 37. The Housemaster (GB) 38.

Holmes, Stuart (1887–1971).
American leading actor of silents who became a character performer after the coming of sound.
How Mrs Murray Saved the Army 11. Life's Shop Window 14. The Scarlet Letter 17. The Four Horsemen of the Apocalypse 21. The Prisoner of Zenda 22. Tess of the D'Urbervilles 24. The Age of Innocence 24. Captain of the Guard 30. Sitting Pretty 33. The Case of the Velvet Claws 36. Dark Victory 39. The Adventures of Mark Twain 44. Shady Lady 45. The Ghost and Mrs Muir 47. A Letter to Three Wives 48. Copper Canyon 50. Singin' in the Rain 52. The Girl in the Red Velvet Swing 55. The Birds and the Bees 56. The Man Who Shot Liberty Valance 62, etc.

Holmes, Taylor (1872–1959).
Veteran American character actor with long stage experience; latterly seen as amiably crooked politician or confidence trickster.
Efficiency Edgar's Courtship 17. Ruggles of Red Gap (title role) 18. One Hour of Love 28. The First Baby 36. Boomerang 47. Nightmare Alley 47. Father of the Bride 50. The First Legion 51. Beware My Lovely 52. The Maverick Queen 56, many others.

Holt, Charlene (1939–).
American leading lady, former star of TV commercials (and *The Tom Ewell Show*).
Man's Favourite Sport? 64. Red Line 7000 66. El Dorado 67. Zigzag 70. Melvin and Howard 80, etc.

Holt, Jack (1888–1951) (Charles John Holt II).
Tough-looking American leading man of silent and sound action films. He was the father of actors Tim and Jennifer Holt.
A Cigarette – That's All 15. The Little American 16. The Woman Thou Gavest Me 18. Held by the Enemy 20. Bought and Paid For 22. Empty Hands 24. Wanderer of the Wasteland 25. Vengeance 28. Hell's Island 30. *Dirigible* 31. War Correspondent 32. Whirlpool 33. The Littlest Rebel 35. *San Francisco* 36. Passport to Alcatraz 40. Holt of the Secret Service 43. They Were Expendable 45. Flight to Nowhere 46. Brimstone 49. Task Force 49. Across the Wide Missouri 51, many others.

Holt, Jennifer (1920–1997) (Elizabeth Holt).
American leading lady of 'B' westerns; daughter of Jack Holt. Married five times. Her second husband was actor William Bakewell.
Stick to Your Guns 42. Cheyenne Round up 43. Oklahoma Raiders 44. Buffalo Bill Rides Again 47. Tornado Range 48. Range Renegades 48, etc.

Holt, Nat (1892–1971).
American independent producer.
Badman's Territory 46. Trail Street 47. Return of the Badmen 48. Fighting Man of the Plains 49. The Great Missouri Raid 51. Denver and Rio Grande 52. Pony Express 53. Flight to Tangier 53, etc.
TV series: Tales of Wells Fargo 57–61. Overland Trail 60.

Holt, Patrick (1912–1993) (Patrick Parsons).
Bland British leading man of the 40s, later in character roles. Married actresses Sonia Holm and Sandra Dorne.
The Return of the Frog 38. Sword of Honour 39. Convoy 41. Hungry Hill 47. Master of Bankdam 47. The Mark of Cain 48. Portrait from Life 49. Marry Me 49. Guilt is My Shadow 50. The Dark Avenger 55. Miss Tulip Stays the Night 56. Thunderball 65. Murderers' Row 66. Hammerhead 68. No Blade of Grass 71. Little (TV) 78. Playing Away 86. Loser Takes All 89, many others.

Holt, Seth (1923–1971).
British director, formerly editor and associate producer for Ealing.
■ Nowhere to Go 58. Taste of Fear 61. Station Six Sahara 63. *The Nanny* 65. Danger Route 67. Monsieur Lecoq 68. Blood from the Mummy's Tomb 71.
❝ I always have a movie going on in my head. I dream in shots. It's getting those dreams out from your head and on to the floor that's the most difficult thing. – *S.H.*
Film has much more in common with literature than, say, television. – *S.H.*
The most ruthless director I've ever worked with next to William Wyler. – *Bette Davis*

Holt, Tim (1919–1973) (Charles John Holt III).
American leading man, son of Jack Holt. In films from 1937, and was hero of many low-budget westerns.
History Is Made at Night 37. The Law West of Tombstone 38. Stagecoach 39. The Swiss Family Robinson 40. *The Magnificent Ambersons* 42. Hitler's Children 42. My Darling Clementine 46. *The Treasure of the Sierra Madre* 47. The Mysterious Desperado 49. His Kind of Woman 51. The Monster That Challenged the World 57, etc.

Homans, Robert E. (1874–1947).
Round-faced American character actor, in hundreds of movies, usually as country cop.
Legally Dead 23. The Bandit Buster 26. Princess from Hoboken 27. Obey Your Husband 28. Isle of Lost Ships 29. Trigger Tricks 30. The Black Camel 31. Young America 32. She Done Him Wrong 33. The Woman in Red 35. Black Legion 36. Easy Living 37. The Amazing Dr Clitterhouse 38. The Grapes of Wrath 40. Honky Tonk 41. Night Monster 42. It Ain't Hay 43. Pin Up Girl 44. Captain Eddie 45. Girl on the Spot 46, many others.

Homeier, Skip (1930–) (George Vincent Homeier).
American child actor of the 40s, later in a variety of supporting roles.
Tomorrow the World 44. Boys' Ranch 46. Mickey 48. The Gunfighter 50. Fixed Bayonets 51. Sailor Beware 52. Beachhead 54. At Gunpoint 56. Comanche Station 60. The Ghost and Mr Chicken 66. Starbird and Sweet William 76. The Greatest 77. Overboard (TV) 78. The Wild Wild West Revisited (TV) 79, etc.
TV series: *Dan Raven* 60.

Homoki-Nagy, Istvan (1914–1979).
Hungarian naturalist who has made many films of wild life including *From Blossom Time Till Autumn Frost*.

Homolka, Oscar (1899–1978).
Viennese-born character actor, a fine 'heavy'. On stage from 1918, international films from mid-30s.
■ Dreyfus (Ger.) 30. Hokuspokus (Ger.) 30. Der Weg Nach Rio (Ger.) 31. Im Geheimdienst (Ger.) 31. Nachtkolonne (Ger.) 31. 1914 (Ger.) 31. Zwischen Nacht und Morgen (Ger.) 31. Die Nachte von Port Said (Ger.) 32. Moral und Liebe (Ger.) 33. Spione am Werk (Ger.) 33. Unsichbara Gegner (Austria) 33. *Rhodes of Africa* 35. *Sabotage* 36. Everything Is Thunder 36. Ebb Tide 37. Hidden Power 37. Seven Sinners 40. Comrade X 40. The Invisible Woman 41. Rage in Heaven 41. Ball of Fire 41. Mission to Moscow 43. Hostages 43. Code of Scotland Yard 47. *The Shop at Sly Corner* 47. *I Remember Mama* (AAN) 48. Anna Lucasta 49. The White Tower 50. Top Secret 52. The House of the Arrow 53. Prisoner of War 54. The Seven Year Itch 55. War and Peace 56. A Farewell to Arms 57. The Key 58. Tempest 58. Mr Sardonicus 61. Boy's Night Out 62. The Wonderful World of the Brothers Grimm 63. The Long Ships 64. Joy in the Morning 65. *Funeral in Berlin* 66. The Happening 67. Billion Dollar Brain 67. The Madwoman of Chaillot 69. Assignment to Kill 69. The Executioner 70. Song of Norway 70. The Tamarind Seed 74.

Honda, Inoshiro (1911–1993).
Japanese director, best known for *Godzilla* and other monster movies. He began in the early 30s as an assistant director, forming a lifelong friendship with another tyro, Akira Kurosawa, and also worked as a documentary film-maker. In the 70s, after monster movies had lost their appeal, he worked in television and then with Kurosawa on that director's *Kagemusha* 80, *Ran* 85, *Dreams* 90, *Rhapsody in August* 90, and *Madadayo* 93.
Eagle of the Pacific 53. Godzilla/Gojira 55. Rodan 56. The Mysterians 57. The H-Man 58. Varan the Unbelievable 58. The Human Vapor 60. Mothra 61. Gorath 62. Attack of the Mushroom People 63. Godzilla vs Mothra 64. Dagora – the Space Monster 64. Ghidrah – the Three-Headed Monster 64. Frankenstein Conquers the World 65. Godzilla vs Monster Zero 65. Invasion of the Astro-Monsters 67. Destroy All Monsters 68. Godzilla's Revenge 69. Yog – the Monster from Space 70. Monsters from an Unknown Planet 75, etc.

Hondo, Med (1936–) (Abid Mohamed Medoun Hondo).
Mauritanian director, a former actor in France.
Everywhere or Perhaps Nowhere/Partout ou Peut-être Nulle Part 69. Soleil O 69. Your Neighbours the Niggers/Les Bicots-Nègres, Vos Voisins 73. We'll Have the Whole of Eternity for Sleeping/Nous Aurons Toute la Mort pour Dormir 77. West Indies 79. Sarraounia 86. 1871 (a) 89. Black Light (p, wd) 94, etc.

Honegger, Arthur (1892–1955).
Swiss composer who worked on French and British pictures.
La Roue 22. Napoleon 27. Les Misérables 34. L'Idée 34. Mayerling 36. *Pygmalion* 38. *Pacific 231* 46.

Hong, James.
American character actor, on screen from 1955.
Love Is a Many Splendored Thing 55. Flower Drum Song 61. The Sand Pebbles 66. Chinatown 74. Airplane! 80. Blade Runner 82. Breathless 83. Big Trouble in Little China 86. The Golden Child 86. Tango & Cash 89. Caged Fury 90. The Two Jakes 90. Wayne's World 2 93. Bad Company 94. South Beach Academy 96. The Secret Agent Club 96. Red Corner 97, etc.

Honkasalo, Pirjo (1947–).
Finnish director, a former photographer and cinematographer, who studied at the film department of the University of Philadelphia. She worked in collaboration with director Pekka Lehto.
Their Age (short, co-d) 76. Flame Top/Tulipää (co-d) 80. Da Capo (co-d) 85. Mysterion (doc, d) 91. Tanjuska and the 7 Devils (doc, ph, d) 93, etc.

Hood, Darla (1931–1979).
American actress and singer who played Darla in the Our Gang shorts of the mid-30s and early 40s.
The Bohemian Girl 36. Happy Land 43. The Helen Morgan Story 57. The Bat 59, etc.

Hoogersteijn, Solveig (1943–).
Swedish-born director who was brought up in Venezuela. She studied film in Germany before returning to work in Venezuela, where *Macu* was the biggest local box-office hit of the 80s.
Manoa 79. El Mar del Tiempo Perdido 81. Macu, the Policeman's Wife/Macu, la Mujer del Policia 86, etc.

Hook, Henry (1960–).
British director.
Sins of the Father 82. The Kitchen Toto 87. Lord of the Flies 89. All for Love 98, etc.

Hooks, Kevin (1958–).
American director and actor, the son of Robert Hooks.
as actor: Sounder 72. A Hero Ain't Nothin' but a Sandwich 78. Take Down 79. Innerspace 87, etc.
as director: Roots: The Gift (TV) 88. Heat Wave (TV) 90. Strictly Business 91. Passenger 57 92. Fled 96. Black Dog 98, etc.

Hooks, Robert (1937–).
American leading man.
Sweet Love Bitter 66. Hurry Sundown 67. Crosscurrent (TV) 71. Trapped (TV) 73. Aaron Loves Angela 75. The Killer Who Wouldn't Die (TV) 76. Just an Old Sweet Song (TV) 76. Airport 77 77. To Kill a Cop (TV) 78. A Woman Called Moses (TV) 78. Backstairs at the White House (TV) 79. Hollow Image (TV) 79. Fast Walking 82. Star Trek III: The Search for Spock 84. D.C. Cop 86. Heat Wave (TV) 90. Passenger 57 92, etc.
TV series: N.Y.P.D. 67.

Hooper, Tobe (1943–).
American horror director and screenwriter.
The Texas Chainsaw Massacre 74. Eaten Alive 76. Salem's Lot (TV) 79. The Funhouse 81. Poltergeist 82. Lifeforce 85. Invaders from Mars 86. Texas Chainsaw Massacre II 86. Spontaneous Combustion 89. Leatherface: The Texas Chainsaw Massacre III 90. I'm Dangerous Tonight 90. Sleepwalkers (a) 92. Night Terrors 94. The Mangler 95, etc.

Hoover, J. Edgar (1895–1972).
American executive, director of the Federal Bureau of Investigation from 1935. In 1939 Paramount made several low-budgeters drawn from his book *Persons in Hiding*; in 1959 he appeared briefly in *The FBI Story*. Subsequently he was impersonated by Erwin Fuller in *Lepke*, by Broderick Crawford in *The Private Files of J. Edgar Hoover*, by Sheldon Leonard in *The Brinks Job*, by Vincent Gardenia in *Kennedy* (TV) and by Ernest Borgnine in *Blood Feud* (TV).

Hope, Anthony (1863–1933) (Sir Anthony Hope Hawkins).
British adventure novelist whose *The Prisoner of Zenda* and its sequel *Rupert of Hentzau* have frequently been filmed.

Hope, Bob (1903–) (Leslie Townes Hope).
Wisecracking American star comedian, a major name in entertainment for nearly forty years. Born in Britain, he spent years in American vaudeville and musical comedy before establishing himself as a big star of the 40s, usually as a comic coward who makes good. Special Academy Awards in 1940, 1944 and 1952, mainly in appreciation of his troop shows and charitable ventures.
Autobiographical books: 1958, *Have Tux Will Travel*. 1963, *I Owe Russia $2000*. 1976, *The Last Christmas Show*. 1977, *The Road to Hollywood*.
■ The Big Broadcast of 1938. College Swing 38. Give Me a Sailor 38. *Thanks for the Memory* 38. Never Say Die 39. Some Like It Hot 39. *The Cat and the Canary* 39. *Road to Singapore* 40. *The Ghost Breakers* 40. *Road to Zanzibar* 41. Caught in the Draft 41. Nothing But the Truth 41. Louisiana Purchase 41. *My Favorite Blonde* 42. *Road to Morocco* 42. Star Spangled Rhythm 42. They Got Me Covered 42. Let's Face It 43. The Princess and the Pirate 44. Road to Utopia 45. Monsieur Beaucaire 46. My Favorite Brunette 47. Where There's Life 47. Variety Girl 47. Road to Rio 48. *The Paleface* 48. Sorrowful Jones 48. The Great Lover 49. *Fancy Pants* 50. The Lemon Drop Kid 51. My Favorite Spy 51. Son of Paleface 52. Road to Bali 52. Off Limits 53. Here Come the Girls 53. Casanova's Big Night 54. The Seven Little Foys 54. That Certain Feeling 56. The Iron Petticoat 56. Beau James 57. Paris Holiday 58. Alias Jesse James 59. *The Facts of Life* 60. Bachelor in Paradise 61. Road to Hong Kong 62. Critics Choice 63. Call Me Bwana 63. A Global Affair 64. I'll Take Sweden 65. Boy Did I Get a Wrong Number 66. The Oscar 66. Eight on the Lam 67. The Private Navy of Sgt O'Farrell 68. How to Commit Marriage 69. Cancel My Reservation 72. The Muppet Movie (guest) 79. Masterpiece of Murder (TV) 85. The Best Show in Town 89. Entertaining the Troops 89.
✪ For a string of bright comedies which perfectly suited the 40s. *The Cat and the Canary*.
❝ I was lucky, you know, I always had a beautiful girl and the money was good. Although I would have done the whole thing over for, oh, perhaps half. – *B.H.*
My wife raised the kids and I was the guest of honour. For years, they thought I was the meter man. – *B.H.*
Bob Hope is still about as funny as he ever was. I just never thought he was that funny in the first place. – *Chevy Chase (1980s)*
Famous line (*The Cat and the Canary*): 'I get goose pimples. Even my goose pimples get goose pimples.'
Famous line (*The Ghost Breakers*): 'The girls call me Pilgrim, because every time I dance with one I make a little progress.'

Hope, Nicholas.
Australian leading actor.
Bad Boy Bubby 92. The Life of Harry Dare 95. Water Easy Reach/En Dag Til I Solen (Nor.) 98.

Hope, Vida (1918–1963).
British character actress, usually in comic proletarian roles; also stage director.
English Without Tears 44. Nicholas Nickleby 47. It Always Rains on Sunday 48. *The Man in the White Suit* 51. Lease of Life 54. Family Doctor 58, etc.

Hopkins, Antony (1921–).
British composer.
Vice Versa 48. Decameron Nights 53. The Pickwick Papers 53. Cast a Dark Shadow 55. Billy Budd 62, etc.

Hopkins, Sir Anthony (1937–).
Welsh leading actor, now in Hollywood. Born in Port Talbot, Swansea, he studied at RADA and was on stage from 1960. From 1967 to 1971, he was a member of Britain's National Theatre before going to the US to make films. A gifted mimic, he dubbed Olivier's voice for extra scenes added to the 1990 re-release of *Spartacus*. Also an accomplished pianist, he composed the score for his directorial debut, *August*. In 1998, he gave £1m to the National Trust towards the £3m cost of purchasing land surrounding Snowdon, Wales; shortly thereafter he announced his retirement from acting. 'Acting is bad for mental health. I can't take it any more,' he said. 'To hell with this stupid business, this ridiculous showbusiness.' He was knighted in 1993.
Biography: 1989, *Anthony Hopkins – Too Good to Waste* by Quentin Falk.
The Lion in Winter 68. The Looking Glass War 70. *When Eight Bells Toll* 71. Young Winston (as Lloyd George) 72. A Doll's House 73. All Creatures Great and Small 74. QB VII (TV) 74. The Girl from Petrovka 74. Juggernaut 74. The Lindbergh Kidnapping Case (TV) 76. Dark Victory (TV) 76. Victory at Entebbe (TV) 76. Audrey Rose 77. A Bridge Too Far 77. International Velvet 78. *Magic* 78. Mayflower (TV) 80. A Change of Seasons 80. The Elephant Man 80. The Bunker (as Hitler) (TV) 81. Peter and Paul (TV) 81. The Hunchback of Notre Dame (TV) 82. A Married Man (TV) 82. The Bounty 83. Mussolini and I (TV) 84. Hollywood Wives (TV) 85. Guilty Conscience (TV) 85. 84 Charing Cross Road 87. Desperate Hours 90. Spotswood 91. *The Silence of the Lambs* (AA) 91. *Howards End* 91. Freejack 92. The Trial 92. Bram Stoker's Dracula 92. Chaplin 92. The Trial 93. The Innocent 93. The Remains of the Day (AAN) 93. Shadowlands 93. Mario und der Zauberer 93. The Road to Wellville 94. Legends of the Fall 94. *Nixon* (title role, AAN) 95. August (& d, m) 96. Surviving Picasso (title role) 96. Amistad (AAN) 97. The Edge 97. The Mask of Zorro 98. Meet Joe Black 98, etc.
❝ I was lousy in school. Real screwed-up. A moron. I was antisocial and didn't bother with the other kids. A really bad student. I didn't have any brains. I didn't know what I was doing there. That's why I became an actor. – *A.H.*
I like to be centre-stage, taking the big parts. I'm not interested in being worthy. – *A.H.*
I am able to play monsters well. I understand monsters. I understand madmen. I can understand what makes people tick in these darker levels. – *A.H.*
However gentle he is, you feel that there is a bomb waiting to explode, that if the moment came the screen would shatter in front of you. – *Sir Richard Attenborough*
He has all those stutters and scratches and coughs and mini-splutters; it's always the same and it's awful. He's a much better actor than that, but these days he always seems to be doing the same irritating, mannered thing. He's forever coughing and spitting and winking and blinking. – *Robert Stephens*

Hopkins, Bo (1942–).
American action hero.
The Wild Bunch 69. Monte Walsh 70. The Culpeper Cattle Company 72. The Getaway 72. American Graffiti 73. White Lightning 73. The Nickel Ride 74. The Day of the Locust 75. Tentacles 77. Aspen (TV) 77. Thaddeus Rose and Eddie (TV) 78. Midnight Express 78. More American Graffiti 79. The Fifth Floor 80. Plutonium Incident 82. Mutant 83. Nightmare at Noon 87. The Bounty Hunter 89. The Final Alliance 89. Trapper County War 89. Big Bad John 90. Center of the Web 92. Romeo Is Bleeding 92. The Ballad of Little Joe 93. Cheyenne Warrior 94. Tom Clancy's Op Center (TV) 95. Painted Hero 95. The Feminine Touch 96. U-Turn 97. Uncle Sam 98, etc.

TV series: Doc Elliott 73. Dynasty 80–81.

Hopkins, John (1931–1998).
English playwright and screenwriter. Born in London, he studied at Cambridge University and then worked in television, becoming one of the writers for the TV series *Z Cars* before gaining a reputation as one of the most admired television dramatists of the 60s. Married actress Shirley KNIGHT, his second wife, and settled in Los Angeles. Died in an accident at his home.
Two Left Feet (co-w) 63. Thunderball (co-w) 65. The Virgin Soldiers 69. The Offence (w, from his play) 72. Murder by Decree 78. The Holcroft Covenant (co-w) 85. Torment (co-w) 86. Hiroshima (co-w) 95. Dunston Checks In (co-w) 96, etc.

Hopkins, Kenyon (1932–).
American composer.
Baby Doll 56. Twelve Angry Men 57. The Fugitive Kind 57. Wild in the Country 61. The Yellow Canary 63. Mister Buddwing 66. A Lovely Way to Die 69. Downhill Racer 69. The Tree 69, etc.

Hopkins, Miriam (1902–1972).
American leading lady of the 30s; her rather brittle style has dated.
■ Fast and Loose 30. The Smiling Lieutenant 31. Twenty Four Hours 31. *Dr Jekyll and Mr Hyde* 32. Two Kinds of Women 32. Dancers in the Dark 32. The World and the Flesh 32. *Trouble in Paradise* 32. *The Story of Temple Drake* 33. Design for Living 33. The Stranger's Return 33. All of Me 34. She Loves Me Not 34. The Richest Girl in the World 34. *Becky Sharp* (AAN) 35. Barbary Coast 35. Splendor 35. *These Three* 36. Men Are Not Gods (GB) 37. The Woman I Love 37. Woman Chases Man 37. Wise Girl 37. The Old Maid 39. Virginia City 40. *Lady With Red Hair* 41. A Gentleman after Dark 42. *Old Acquaintance* 43. The Heiress 49. The Mating Season 51. Carrie 52. The Outcasts of Poker Flat 52. The Children's Hour 62. Fanny Hill 65. The Chase 66.

Hopkins, Robert.
American screenwriter, mainly for MGM, whose special talent it was to improve scripts by adding gags, and providing instant dialogue for actors during filming. Born in San Francisco, he worked in odd jobs and at a gambling casino before going to Hollywood. Anita LOOS recalled that he was once asked to add some lines in a scene where circus aerialists crash from a high platform to their deaths: '"Something dramatic!" the director ordered. Scorning the suggestions, Hoppy offered the following: "I saw Mabel back in Tulsa." "That so? How does she like being married?" "Not too much. She's homesick." At which point the rigging broke and, as the two crashed to the ground, Hoppy's unrelated dialogue gave the tragedy an extra shock.'
Spite Marriage (titles) 29. Caught Short (co-w) 30. Love in the Rough (co-w) 30. Chasing Rainbows (dialogue) 30. The Floradora Girl (dialogue) 30. Flying High (co-w) 31. Sidewalks of New York (dialogue) 31. Stepping Out (co-w) 31. The Chief (co-w) 33. *San Francisco* (story) 36. Saratoga (co-w) 37, etc.
❝ He roamed the lot with a cup of black coffee in hand. He stalked the producers, and spying one on the lot, Hoppy would block his path to propound his latest idea, using his free hand to punch his index finger into the man's chest, talking in clipped, rapid-fire fashion, accenting points that only he understood: 'All right, you're a lucky man . . . here it is, New Orleans! Gable, Shearer, Crawford and Garbo! Get it?' – *Samuel Marx*
During the early years of the Second World War, Hoppy walked up to Zanuck, stuck a finger into Zanuck's shoulder and said, 'Zanuck! Tyrone Power – A Yank in the RAF! Zanuck – I've made ya!' He walked away. Zanuck made it into one of his most successful pictures. – *Joseph L. Mankiewicz*

Hopkins, Shirley Knight:
see KNIGHT, Shirley.

Hopkins, Stephen (1959–).
Australian director working in Hollywood. He began as an art director and director of music videos in London.
Dangerous Game 88. A Nightmare on Elm Street 5: The Dream Child 89. Predator 2 90. Judgment Night 93. Blown Away 94. The Ghost and the Darkness 96, etc.

Hopper, Dennis (1935–).
American juvenile of the 50s who later blossomed into a fashionable actor and director.
I Died a Thousand Times 55. Rebel without a Cause 55. Giant 56. The Story of Mankind 57. Key Witness 60. Night Tide 63. The Sons of Katie Elder 65. The Trip 67. Cool Hand Luke 67. *Easy Rider* (& co-w, d) (AANw) 69. The Last Movie (& wd) 71. Kid Blue (& d) 72. Mad Dog Morgan 76. The American Friend 77. Tracks 77. Apocalypse Now 79. Out of the Blue (& d) 80. The Osterman Weekend 83. The Inside Man 84. My Science Project 85. Blue Velvet 86. Hoosiers (AAN) 86. The Texas Chainsaw Massacre 2 86. Black Widow 87. The Pick-Up Artist 87. River's Edge 87. Colors (d) 88. Blood Red 88. Catchfire/Backtrack (& d) 89. Chattahoochee 89. The Hot Spot (d) 90. The Indian Runner 91. Paris Trout 91. Doublecrossed (TV) 91. Eye of the Storm 91. Nails 92. Super Mario Bros 93. Boiling Point 93. Red Rock West 93. *True Romance* 93. Chasers (& d) 94. *Speed* 94. Waterworld 95. Search and Destroy 95. Carried Away 96. Basquiat 96. Samson and Delilah (TV) 96. Top of the World 97. Star Truckers 97. The Good Life 97. The Blackout 97, etc.
TV series: Medic 54–55.

Hopper, Hedda (1890–1966) (Elda Furry).
American general-purpose actress, mainly in silent days; in later life became a powerful Hollywood columnist.
Autobiographies: 1952, *From Under My Hat*. 1963, *The Whole Truth and Nothing But*.
Biography: 1972, *Hedda and Louella* by George Eels.
Virtuous Wives 19. Heedless Moths 21. Sherlock Holmes 22. Has the World Gone Mad? 23. Reno 24. The Teaser 25. Don Juan 26. Wings 27. Harold Teen 28. His Glorious Night 29. Holiday 30. The Common Law 31. Speak Easily 32. Beauty For Sale 33. Little Man What Now? 34. Alice Adams 35. Dracula's Daughter 36. Topper 37. Thanks for the Memory 38. The Women 39. Queen of the Mob 40. Reap the Wild Wind 42. Sunset Boulevard 50. Pepe 60. The Oscar 66, many others.
❝ Nobody's interested in sweetness and light. – *H.H.*

Hopper, Jerry (1907–1989).
American director of routine action films and TV series. Married actress Marsha Hunt (1938–45).
■ The Atomic City 52. Hurricane Smith 52. Pony Express 53. Alaska Seas 54. The Secret of the Incas 54. Naked Alibi 54. Smoke Signal 55. The Private War of Major Benson 55. One Desire 55. The Square Jungle 55. Never Say Goodbye 56. Toy Tiger 56. The Sharkfighters 56. Everything but the Truth 56. The Missouri Traveller 58. Blueprint for Robbery 61. Madron 70.

Hopper, Victoria (1909–).
Canadian leading lady of a few British films of the 30s. Married producer-director Basil DEAN.
■ *The Constant Nymph* 33. *Lorna Doone* 34. Whom the Gods Love 36. Laburnum Grove 36. The Lonely Road 36. The Mill on the Floss 37. Escape from Broadmoor 38.

Hopper, William (1915–1970) (William Furry).
American general-purpose supporting actor, son of Hedda Hopper.
Footloose Heiress 37. Torchy Blane 38. Track of the Cat 54. Rebel Without a Cause 55. The Bad Seed 56. Twenty Million Miles to Earth (lead) 57, etc.
TV series: *Perry Mason* (as Paul Drake) 57–65.

Hopton, Russell (1900–1945).
American light leading man.
Ella Cinders 26. Street Scene 31. Night World 32. Lady Killer 33. He Was Her Man 34. Death from a Distance 35. High Wide and Handsome 37. The Saint Strikes Back 39. A Night of Adventure 44. Zombies on Broadway 45, etc.

Hordern, Sir Michael (1911–1995).
British character actor, on stage from 1937; film appearances usually as carewom official.
Autobiography: 1993, *A World Elsewhere*.
The Girl in the News (debut) 39; war service; School for Secrets 46. Mine Own Executioner 47. Good Time Girl 48. Passport to Pimlico 48. The Hour of Thirteen 51. The Heart of the Matter 53. The Baby and the Battleship 55. *The Spanish Gardener* 56. Sink the Bismarck 60. El Cid 61. The VIPs 63. Dr Syn 63. Genghis Khan 65. The Spy Who Came In from the Cold 66. Khartoum 66. *A Funny Thing Happened on the Way to the Forum* 66. The Taming of the Shrew 67. Where Eagles Dare 68. *The Bed-Sitting Room* 69. Anne of the Thousand Days 70. Futtock's End 70. Girl Stroke Boy 71. England Made Me 72. Alice's Adventures in Wonderland (as the Mock Turtle) 72. Theatre of Blood 73. The Mackintosh Man 73. Mister Quilp 74. Royal Flash 74. Lucky Lady 75. *The Slipper and the Rose* 76. Joseph Andrews 76. The Medusa Touch 77. Shogun (TV) 80. Ivanhoe (TV) 81. Oliver Twist (TV) 81. Gandhi 82. *The Missionary* 82. Yellowbeard 83. Lady Jane 84. Paradise Postponed (TV) 85. Scoop (TV) 87. Comrades 87. The Trouble with Spies 87. Diamond Skulls 89. The Fool 90. Memento Mori (TV) 92. Middlemarch (TV) 94, etc.

Horn, Camilla (1906–1996).
German leading actress who had brief careers in Britain and Hollywood. With the advent of talkies, she returned to work in Germany, until her criticism of the Nazi Party brought a hiatus to her career. In the late 40s, she returned to the stage, screen and television in maternal roles. Born in Frankfurt, she was educated in Germany and Switzerland, and trained as a dancer and actress in Berlin. Married six times: her first husband was actor Gustav Diessl and her second actor Louis Graveure; her lovers included Hollywood producer Joseph SCHENCK.
Tartuffe 25. *Faust* 26. Tempest (US) 28. Eternal Love (US) 29. The Royal Box (US) 30. The Devil's Holiday 30. The Return of Raffles (GB) 31. Matinée Idol (GB) 32. Love Nest (GB) 32. Luck of a Sailor (GB) 34. The Last Waltz 34. Schloss Königswald 88, etc.

Horn, Leonard (1926–1975).
American director, from TV.
Rogues' Gallery 68. The Magic Garden of Stanley Sweetheart 70. Going All Out 71, etc.

Hornbeck, William W. (1901–1983).
American editor, with Mack Sennett until 1929, working mainly on two-reel comedies.
The Extra Girl 23. Roman Scandals 33. The Scarlet Pimpernel 34. *Things To Come* 36. The Four Feathers 39. Lady Hamilton 42. *Why We Fight* series 43–45. *It's a Wonderful Life* 46. State of the Union 48. *A Place in the Sun* (AA) 51. Shane 53. Giant 56. The Quiet American 58, many others.

Hornblow, Arthur, Jnr (1893–1976).
American producer, in Hollywood from 1926.
Bulldog Drummond 29. Ruggles of Red Gap 34. The Cat and the Canary 39. Gaslight 44. Weekend at the Waldorf 45. The Hucksters 47. The Asphalt Jungle 50. Oklahoma 56. Witness for the Prosecution 57. The War Lover 63, many others.

Horne, David (1898–1970).
Portly British character actor, mainly on stage; almost always in pompous roles.
General John Regan 33. The Mill on the Floss 36. The First of the Few 42. The Seventh Veil 45. The Rake's Progress 45. The Man Within 46. It's Hard To Be Good 49. Madeleine 50. Lust for Life 56. The Devil's Disciple 59, many others.

Horne, Geoffrey (1933–).
British general-purpose actor.
The Bridge on the River Kwai 57. Tempest 58. Bonjour Tristesse 58. Esterina 59. I Fratelli Corsi 61. The Magnificent Three 63. Two People (US) 73, etc.

Horne, James W. (1880–1942).
American director, in Hollywood from 1911. Made some of Laurel and Hardy's best two-reelers, and appeared as the villain in *Beau Hunks*.
The Third Eye 20. American Manner 24. *College* 27. Bonnie Scotland 35. The Bohemian Girl 36. *Way Out West* 37. Holt of the Secret Service 42, many others.

Horne, Lena (1917–).
Lithe and sultry American singer whose best appearances were in 40s musicals.
Autobiographies: 1950, *In Person*. 1966, *Lena* (with Richard Schickel).
■ The Duke is Tops 38. Panama Hattie 42. *Cabin in the Sky* 43. *Stormy Weather* 43. Thousands Cheer 43. I Dood It 43. Swing Fever 43. Broadway Rhythm 44. Two Girls and a Sailor 44. Ziegfeld Follies 46. Till the Clouds Roll By 46. Words and Music 48. Duchess of Idaho 50. Meet Me in Las Vegas 56. *Death of a Gunfighter* (dramatic role) 69. The Wiz 78.
❝ In my early days I was a sepia Hedy Lamarr. Now I'm black and a woman, singing my own way. – *L.H.*

Horne, Victoria (c. 1920–).
American comedienne. She was married to Jack Oakie.
The Scarlet Claw 44. The Ghost and Mrs Muir 47. The Snake Pit 48. Abbott and Costello Meet the Killer 49. *Harvey* 50. Affair with a Stranger 53, etc.

Horner, Harry (1910–1994).
Czech-born production designer with stage experience in Vienna and New York.
Our Town 40. *The Little Foxes* 41. A Double Life 47. *The Heiress* (AA) 49. Born Yesterday 50. *The Hustler* (AA) 61. They Shoot Horses, Don't They? (AAN) 69. Harry and Walter Go to New York 76. Audrey Rose 77. Moment to Moment 78. The Driver 78, etc.
AS DIRECTOR: Beware My Lovely 52. Red Planet Mars 52. New Faces 54. A Life in the Balance 55. The Wild Party 56. Man from Del Rio 56, etc.

Horner, James (1953–).
American composer. Born in Los Angeles, he was brought up in England and studied at the Royal College of Music before taking a master's degree in composition at the University of Southern California and a PhD at UCLA, where he also taught for a time.
Battle beyond the Stars 80. Humanoids from the Deep 80. Star Trek II: The Wrath of Khan 82. 48 Hours 82. Krull 83. Gorky Park 83. The Dresser 83. The Stone Boy 84. Star Trek III: The Search for Spock 84. Commando 85. Aliens (AAN) 86. The Name of the Rose 86. An American Tale 86. Batteries Not Included 87. Willow 88. Red Heat 88. Cocoon: The Return 88. Field of Dreams (AAN) 89. Honey, I Shrunk the Kids 89. In Country 89. Dad 89. Glory 89. I Love You to Death 90. Another 48 Hrs 90. Class Action 91. The Rocketeer 91. An American Tail: Fievel Goes West 91. Thunderheart 92. Patriot Games 92. House of Cards 93. Once upon a Forest 93. Searching for Bobby Fischer 93. The Man without a Face 93. Bopha! 93. Jack the Bear 93. Swing Kids 93. A Far Off Place 93. We're Back! A Dinosaur's Story 93. The Pelican Brief 93. Clear and Present Danger 94. Legends of the Fall 94. Apollo 13 (AAN) 95. Braveheart (AAN) 95. Casper 95. Jade 95. Jumanji 95. Care of the Spitfire Grill 96. Courage under Fire 96. To Gillian on Her 37th Birthday 96. *Titanic* (AAm, AAs 'My Heart Will Go On') 97. The Mask of Zorro 98. Deep Impact 98, etc.

Horniman, Roy. (1872–1930).
Edwardian novelist whose *Bellamy the Magnificent* has been filmed twice, as *A Gentleman of Paris* 27, starring Adolphe Menjou, and as *A Bedtime Story* 33, which was a vehicle for Maurice Chevalier and Baby LeRoy. His novel *Israel Rank* was the basis for Robert Hamer's classic Ealing comedy *Kind Hearts and Coronets* 49.

Hornung, E. W. (1866–1921).
British novelist, creator of the gentleman burglar A.J. Raffles, who was impersonated on screen by Ronald Colman and David Niven, and on television by Anthony Valentine.

Hornung, Richard (1950–1995).
American costume designer, associated with the films of the Coen brothers, from the theatre. Died of AIDS.
Raising Arizona 86. Less than Zero 87. Patty Hearst 88. Young Guns 88. Miller's Crossing 90. Sleeping with the Enemy 90. The Grifters 90. Light Sleeper 91. Hero/Accidental Hero 92. Barton Fink (AAN) 92. This Boy's Life 93. The Hudsucker Proxy 94. Natural Born Killers 94. Nixon 95. City Hall 96, etc.

Horrocks, Jane (1964–).
British character actress, best known for her role as an anorexic daughter in *Life Is Sweet*.
The Dressmaker 88. Witches 90. Memphis Belle

90. Life Is Sweet 91. Bad Girl (TV) 92. Suffer the Little Children (TV) 94. Deadly Advice 94. Second Best 94. Henry IV (as Doll Tearsheet, TV) 95. Some Kind of Life (TV) 95. Little Voice 98, etc.
TV series: Absolutely Fabulous 93–94.

Horsfall, Bernard (1930–).
British character actor.
On Her Majesty's Secret Service 69. Gold 74. Shout at the Devil 76. Gandhi 82. A Distant Scream 84. The Hound of the Baskervilles (TV) 88. Nice Town (TV) 92. Braveheart 95, etc.

Horsley, John (1920–).
British character actor, often seen as plain clothes man or executive.
Highly Dangerous 48. The Long Memory 51. The Runaway Bus 54. Father Brown 54. Above Us the Waves 55. Bond of Fear 56. The Comedy Man 64. The Fourth Protocol 87. Stanley's Dragon 94. Rebecca (TV) 97, etc.

Horton, Edward Everett (1886–1970).
American star comic actor with inimitable crooked smile and diffident manner; a favourite throughout the 20s, 30s and 40s.
Too Much Business 22. Ruggles of Red Gap (title role) 23. Marry Me 25. The Nutcracker 26. The Terror 28. Sonny Boy 29. The Hottentot 29. The Sap 29. Take the Heir 30. *Holiday* 30. Once a Gentleman 30. Kiss Me Again 31. The Front Page 31. Six Cylinder Love 31. *Trouble in Paradise* 32. A Bedtime Story 33. Soldiers of the King (GB) 33. *Alice in Wonderland* (as the Mad Hatter) 33. It's a Boy (GB) 34. The Merry Widow 34. *The Gay Divorcee* 35. The Devil is a Woman 35. In Caliente 35. *Top Hat* 35. Your Uncle Dudley 35. The Private Secretary (GB) 35. The Man in the Mirror (GB) 36. *Lost Horizon* 37. Shall We Dance? 37. Angel 37. The Great Garrick 37. Bluebeard's Eighth Wife 38. *Holiday* (repeat of 1930 role) 38. That's Right You're Wrong 39. Ziegfeld Girl 41. Sunny 41. *Here Comes Mr Jordan* 41. The Body Disappears 41. The Magnificent Dope 42. Forever and a Day 43. *Thank Your Lucky Stars* 43. The Gang's All Here 43. Her Primitive Man 44. *Summer Storm* 44. *San Diego I Love You* 44. Arsenic and Old Lace 44. Lady on a Train 45. Cinderella Jones 46. Down to Earth 47. Her Husband's Affairs 47. The Story of Mankind 57. *Pocketful of Miracles* 61. Sex and the Single Girl 64. The Perils of Pauline 67. 2000 Years Later 69. Cold Turkey 70, many others.
TV series: *F Troop* (as a Red Indian chief) 65.
✪ For redeeming many a dull comedy by his superior twittering and double takes. *Trouble in Paradise*.

Horton, Peter (1953–).
American actor and occasional director.
She's Dressed to Kill 79. Serial 80. Fade to Black 80. Captured 81. Freedom (TV) 81. Seven Brides for Seven Brothers (TV) 82. Children of the Corn 84. Where the River Runs Black 86. Amazon Women on the Moon (& co-d) 87. Side Out 90. The Cure (d only) 95. 2 Days in the Valley 96. The End of Violence 97. Death Benefit 97, etc.
TV series: Thirtysomething 87–91. Brimstone 98– .

Horton, Robert (1924–) (Mead Howard Horton).
Good-looking American leading man who made it big on TV in the late 50s but could not manage the transfer to the big screen.
The Tanks are Coming 51. Bright Road 53. Prisoner of War 54. This Man is Armed 56. The Dangerous Days of Kiowa Jones (TV) 66. The Green Slime 69, etc.
TV series: *Wagon Train* 57–61. *A Man Called Shenandoah* 65.

Hoskins, Allen 'Farina' (1920–1980).
American comic actor and vaudeville performer, on screen from the age of 14 months. He played Farina in the Our Gang shorts of the 20s and 30s. In later life, he worked as a psychiatric technician.
You Said a Mouthful 32. The Mayor of Hell 33. The Life of Jimmy Dolan 33. After the Thin Man 36, etc.

Hoskins, Bob (1942–).
Stocky, untutored British character actor who made a big critical hit in TV's *Pennies from Heaven*.
Zulu Dawn 79. *The Long Good Friday* 80. Pink Floyd the Wall 82. The Honorary Consul 83. Mussolini and I (TV) 84. The Dunera Boys (TV) 84. Lassiter 84. The Cotton Club 84. Brazil 85. Sweet Liberty 85. *Mona Lisa* (AAN) 85. A Prayer for the Dying 87. The Lonely Passion of Judith Hearne 87. The Raggedy Rawney (& d) 88. *Who Framed Roger Rabbit* 88. Major League 89. Heart Condition 90. Mermaids 90. Shattered 91. Hook 91. The Favour, the Watch and the Very Big Fish/ Rue Saint-Sulpice 91. The Inner Circle 91. Passed Away 92. Super Mario Bros 93. Nixon (as J. Edgar Hoover) 95. Balto (voice) 95. Rainbow (& d) 96. Secret Agent 96. Michael 96. TwentyfourSeven 97. Parting Shots 98. Captain Jack 98, etc.

Hossein, Robert (1927–).
French actor.
Rififi 55. The Wicked Go to Hell (& d) 55. Girls Disappear 58. La Musica 60. Enough Rope 63. Marco the Magnificent 65. I Killed Rasputin (& d) 68. The Burglars (& d) 71. Les Uns et les Autres 80. Les Misérables (d only) 82. Bolero 82. L'Affaire 94. Les Misérables 95. House of Wax/The Wax Mask (It.) 97, etc.

Houdini, Harry (1873–1926) (Ehrich Weiss).
American escapologist and magician extraordinary, in films from 1918. A biopic in 1953 starred Tony Curtis, and a 1976 TV movie, *The Great Houdinis*, Paul Michael Glaser. In 1997, Harvey Keitel played him in *Illuminations*, a film about Edwardian fake photographs of fairies.
Biographies: 1969, *Houdini, the Unknown Story* by Christopher Milbourne. 1993, *The Life and Many Deaths of Harry Houdini* by Ruth Brandon.
The Master Mystery (serial) 18. The Grim Game 19. Terror Island 20. The Man from Beyond 21. Haldane of the Secret Service 23, etc.

Hough, John (1941–).
British director in international films.
Wolfshead 69. Eye Witness 70. Twins of Evil 71. Treasure Island 72. The Legend of Hell House 73. Dirty Mary Crazy Larry 74. Escape to Witch Mountain 75. Brass Target 78. The Watcher in the Woods 80. Triumphs of a Man Called Horse 82. The Incubus 82. Biggles 85. American Gothic 87. A Hazard of Hearts (TV) 87. Howling IV: The Original Nightmare 88. Dangerous Love (TV) 88. The Lady and the Highwayman (TV) 89. Duel of Hearts (TV) 90, etc.

Houghton, Katharine (1945–).
American leading lady of *Guess Who's Coming to Dinner* 67; niece of Katharine Hepburn.
Seeds of Evil 76. Eyes of the Amaryllis 82. Mr North 88. Billy Bathgate 91. Ethan Frome 93, etc.

House, Billy (1890–1961).
Rotund American character actor, formerly trumpet player.
Smart Money 32. Merry Go Round 37. Bedlam 44. The Stranger 45. Trail Street 46. The Egg and I 47. Where Danger Lives 50. People Will Talk 51, etc.

Houseman, John (1902–1988) (Jacques Haussmann).
American producer. After varied experience, helped Orson Welles to found his Mercury Theatre in New York in 1937, later followed him to Hollywood; unexpectedly became a star actor in his 70s.
Autobiographies: 1972, *Runthrough*. 1980, *Front and Center*. 1983, *Final Dress*.
The Blue Dahlia 46. Letter from an Unknown Woman 48. They Live by Night 48. The Bad and the Beautiful 52. Julius Caesar 53. Executive Suite 54. Lust for Life 56. Two Weeks in Another Town 62. This Property is Condemned 66, etc.
AS ACTOR: Seven Days in May 64. *Paper Chase* (AA) 74. Three Days of the Condor 75. Rollerball 75. Meeting at Potsdam (TV) (as Churchill) 76. Fear on Trial (TV) 76. St Ives 76. Captains and the Kings (TV) 76. Washington Behind Closed Doors (TV) 77. Aspen (TV) 77. Tentacles 77. The Cheap Detective 78. Old Boyfriends 79. My Bodyguard 80. The Fog 80. Wholly Moses 80. Ghost Story 81. Murder by Phone 82. Another Woman 88, etc.
TV series: *The Paper Chase* 78 and 83. Silver Spoons 82.

Housman, Arthur (1888–1942).
American character actor, usually seen as incoherent but gentlemanly drunk in comedies of the early 30s.
Under the Red Robe 23. Manhandled 24. The Bat 26. Sunrise 27. Fools for Luck 28. The Singing Fool 28. Broadway 29. The Squealer 30. Five and Ten 31. *Scram* (Laurel and Hardy two-reeler) 32. She Done Him Wrong 33. Mrs Wiggs of the Cabbage Patch 34. Our Relations 36. Step Lively Jeeves 37. Go West 40. Billy the Kid 41, etc.

Houston, Donald (1923–1991).
Burly, capable Welsh leading man of the early 50s. Later a useful character actor.
■ *The Blue Lagoon* 48. A Run for Your Money 49. Dance Hall 50. My Death is a Mockery 51. Crow Hollow 52. The Red Beret 53. Small Town Story 53. The Large Rope 53. Devil's Point 54. The Happiness of Three Women 54. Doctor in the House 54. The Flaw 55. Double Cross 55. The Girl in the Picture 56. Find the Lady 56. Yangtse Incident 57. The Surgeon's Knife 57. A Question of Adultery 58. The Man Upstairs 58. Danger within 58. *Room at the Top* 58. The Mark 61. Twice Round the Daffodils 62. The Prince and the Pauper 62. Maniac 62. The Longest Day 62. The 300 Spartans 63. Doctor in Distress 63. Carry on Jack 63. 633 Squadron 64. A Study in Terror 65. The Viking Queen 66. Where Eagles Dare 68. My Lover My Son 70. Tales that Witness Madness 73. Voyage of the Damned 76. The Sea Wolves 80. Clash of the Titans 81. The Secret Adversary (TV) 82.

Houston, George (1898–1944).
American actor and singer, best known for starring in a series of 'B' westerns as 'The LONE RIDER'. Born in Hampton, New Jersey, he studied at Rutgers University and the Juilliard School of Music, and sang with the American Opera Company and on Broadway before beginning his screen career in musicals. Died of a heart attack.
The Melody Lingers On 35. Captain Calamity 36. Let's Sing Again 36. Wallaby Jim of the Islands 37. Frontier Scout (as Wild Bill Hickok) 38. Laughing at Danger 40. The Howards of Virginia 40. The Lone Rider Ambushed 41. The Lone Rider in Ghost Town 41. The Lone Rider in Texas Justice 41. The Lone Rider in Cheyenne 42. The Lone Rider in Border Roundup 43, etc.

Houston, Glyn (1926–).
Welsh character actor, brother of Donald Houston; much on TV.
The Blue Lamp 50. Payroll 60. Solo for Sparrow (lead role) 62. The Secret of Blood Island 65. Invasion 66. Are You Being Served? 77. The Sea Wolves 80. The Mystery of Edwin Drood 93, etc.

Houston, Penelope.
English film critic, one of the founders of the influential Oxford University Film Society magazine SEQUENCE in the mid-40s and later the editor of the British Film Institute's magazine *Sight and Sound* from 1956–90. Author of *The Contemporary Cinema* (1963).

Houston, Renée (1902–1980) (Katherina Houston Gribbin).
British vaudeville and revue artiste, once teamed with her sister Billie, then later with Donald Stewart; character actress of screen and TV.
Autobiography: 1974, *Don't Fence Me In*.
Mr Cinders 34. A Girl Must Live 38. Old Bill and Son 40. Two Thousand Women 44. The Belles of St Trinians 54. *A Town Like Alice* 56. *Time Without Pity* 57. The Horse's Mouth 59. The Flesh and the Friends 60. Three on a Spree 61. Repulsion 64. Carry On at Your Convenience 71. Legend of the Werewolf 71, etc.

Houston, Sam (1793–1863).
An American hero of the early days of Texas who commanded the army when Texas revolted against Mexican rule, a war that included the defeat at the ALAMO before victory at San Jacinto. He was the first president of the new Republic of Texas in 1836, and later became the state's governor until deposed after he opposed secession. He was played by Tom Wilson in *Martyrs of the Alamo* 15; William Farnum in *The Conqueror* 17; Ed Piel in *Heroes of the Alamo* 37; Richard Dix in *Man of Conquest* 39; William Farnum in *Men of Texas* 42; Moroni Olsen in *Lone Star* 52; Howard Negley in *The Man from the Alamo* 53; Hugh Sanders in *The Last Command* 55; Joel McCrea in *The First Texan* 56; and Richard Boone in *The Alamo* 60. Lorne Greene played him in a TV movie: *The Alamo: 13 Days to Glory* 87. *Temple Houston*, a TV series about Houston's son, a lawyer, ran from 1963 to 1964.

Houston, Whitney (1963–).
American singer and actress, the daughter of soul singer Cissy Houston (1932–). Her debut, playing a singer, was a massive box-office success, as was her soundtrack album.
Biography: 1994, *Diva* by Jeffrey Bowman.
The Bodyguard 93. Waiting to Exhale 95. The Preacher's Wife 96. Cinderella (TV) 97, etc.

Hovey, Tim (1945–1989).
American child actor of the mid-50s. Later on TV.
The Private War of Major Benson 55. Toy Tiger 56. Man Afraid 57, etc.

Howard, Alan (1937–).
British Shakespearean actor in occasional films; the son of actor Arthur HOWARD.
Victim 61. Work Is a Four-Letter Word 68. Little Big Man 70. Strapless 88. The Return of the Musketeers 89. The Cook, the Thief, His Wife and Her Lover 89. Dakota Road 91. The Secret Rapture 93. No Bananas 96, etc.

Howard, Arliss (1955–).
American leading actor.
Door to Door 84. Sylvester 85. The Lightship 85. Hands of a Stranger (TV) 87. Full Metal Jacket 87. Tequila Sunrise 88. Men Don't Leave 90. Somebody Has to Shoot the Picture (TV) 90. Crisscross 91. Ruby 92. Wilder Napalm 93. Natural Born Killers 94. To Wong Foo, Thanks for Everything, Julie Newmar 95. Johns 96. Beyond the Call (TV) 96. The Lost World: Jurassic Park 97, etc.

Howard, Arthur (1910–1995).
British character actor, brother of Leslie Howard, often seen as schoolmaster, clerk, etc.
Passport to Pimlico 48. *The Happiest Days of Your Life* 49. The Intruder 53. The Shoes of the Fisherman 68. Zeppelin 70. Steptoe and Son 72. One of Our Dinosaurs Is Missing 75. The Missionary 82. Curse of the Pink Panther 83. Another Country 84, etc.
TV series: Whacko! (as Mr Pettigrew) 56–60. The Whitehall Worrier 67.

Howard, Curly (1906–1952) (Jerome Horowitz).
American comedy actor: the fat, bald member of the THREE STOOGES.

Howard, Cy (1915–1993) (Seymour Horowitz).
American director. His second wife was actress Gloria GRAHAME, who went on to marry her former stepson, prompting him to remark, 'If Gloria hadn't divorced me, she might never have become her own daughter-in-law.'
Lovers and Other Strangers 69. Every Little Crook and Nanny 72. Won Ton Ton (co-w only) 76.

Howard, Esther (1892–1965).
American character actress, usually in blowsy roles.
Ladies of the Big House 31. Ready for Love 35. Serenade 39. Sullivan's Travels 41. Farewell My Lovely 44. The Lady Gambles 49, etc.

Howard, James Newton.
American composer.
Head Office 86. Wildcats 86. Never Too Young to Die 86. 8 Million Ways to Die 86. Nobody's Fool 86. Tough Guys 86. Campus Man 87. Five Corners 87. Russkies 87. Promised Land 87. Off Limits 88. Some Girls 88. Everybody's All-American 88. Tap 89. Major League 89. The Package 89. Coupe de Ville 90. Pretty Woman 90. Flatliners 90. King Ralph 90. My Girl 91. The Man in the Moon 91. The Prince of Tides 91. Grand Canyon 91. American Heart 92. Alive 93. Falling Down 93. Dave 93. The Saint of Fort Washington 93. The Fugitive (AAN) 93. Intersection 94. Wyatt Earp 94. Outbreak 95. French Kiss 95. Waterworld 95. Restoration 95. Eye for an Eye 95. Primal Fear 96. Space Jam 96. *One Fine Day* (AANs 'For the First Time') 96. The Juror 96. Father's Day 96. The Postman 97. My *Best Friend's Wedding* (AAN) 97. The Devil's Advocate 97. A Perfect Murder 98, etc.

Howard, John (1913–1995) (John Cox).
Good-looking, useful American leading man of the 30s and 40s, mainly in routine films.
Annapolis Farewell 35. Soak the Rich 36. *Lost Horizon* 37. *Bulldog Drummond Comes Back* (and

ensuing series) 37. Penitentiary 38. Prison Farm 38. Disputed Passage 39. Green Hell 40. *The Philadelphia Story* 40. The Invisible Woman 40. The Mad Doctor 41. Tight Shoes 41. The Undying Monster 42. Isle of Missing Men 43. Love from a Stranger 47. I Jane Doe 48. The Fighting Kentuckian 49. Experiment Alcatraz 51. The High and the Mighty 54. Unknown Terror 58, etc.

TV series: *Dr Hudson's Secret Journal* 55–56. Adventures of Seahawk 58.

Howard, Joyce (1922–).
British leading lady of the 40s.

Freedom Radio 40. Love on the Dole 41. The Gentle Sex 43. They Met in the Dark 43. Woman to Woman 46. Mrs Fitzherbert 47. Shadow of the Past 50, etc.

Howard, Kathleen (1879–1956).
Canadian character actress, former opera singer; memorable as W. C. Fields's frequent screen wife.

Death Takes a Holiday 34. You're Telling me 34. The Man on the Flying Trapeze 35. It's a Gift 35. Laura 44. The Late George Apley 47, etc.

Howard, Ken (1944–).
Hulking American leading man who came to the fore on TV.

Tell Me That You Love Me Junie Moon 70. Such Good Friends 71. The Strange Vengeance of Rosalie 72. *1776* 72. Superdome (TV) 78. The Critical List (TV) 78. A Great American Hero (TV) 80. The Victims (TV) 81. Second Thoughts 83. Always Ready (doc) 85. Anchors Aweigh (doc) 85. Citizen Soldiers (doc) 85. The Wild Blue Yonder (doc) 85. Pudd'nhead Wilson (TV) 87. Strange Interlude (TV) 90. Oscar 91. Ulterior Motives 92. The Net 95, etc.

TV series: Adam's Rib 73. Manhunter 74. The White Shadow 78–81. It's Not Easy 83. Dynasty 85–86. Dynasty II: The Colbys 85–86.

Howard, Leslie (1893–1943) (Leslie Stainer).
Distinguished British actor of Hungarian origin; his image was that of the romantic intellectual who had only to ignore women to be idolized. He was equally successful in American films. Died when his plane was shot down in the Second World War.

Biography: 1959, *A Very Remarkable Father* by his daughter Ruth Howard.

■ *Outward Bound* 30. Never the Twain Shall Meet 31. A Free Soul 31. Five and Ten 31. Devotion 31. Service for Ladies 32. Smilin' Through 32. The Animal Kingdom 32. Secrets 33. Captured 33. *Berkeley Square* (AAN) 33. The Lady is Willing 34. *Of Human Bondage* 34. British Agent 34. *The Scarlet Pimpernel* 35. *The Petrified Forest* 36. Romeo and Juliet 36. It's Love I'm After 36. Stand-In 37. *Pygmalion* (& co-d) (AAN) 38. *Gone with the Wind* 39. *Intermezzo* 39. Pimpernel Smith (& pd) 41. 49th Parallel 41. *The First of the Few* (& oa, d) 42. The Gentle Sex (pd only) 43. The Lamp Still Burns (p only) 43.

✪ For having more Englishness than any pure Englishman, and for conquering world audiences with it. *Pygmalion*.

❝ He had a passion for England and the English ideal that was almost Shakespearean. – *C. A. Lejeune*

Famous line (*The Petrified Forest*): 'Let there be killing. All the evening I've had a feeling of destiny closing in.'

Famous line (*Pygmalion*): 'Where the devil are my slippers, Eliza?'

Howard, Moe (1895–1975) (Moses Horowitz).
American comedy actor, the fringed and violent member of the THREE STOOGES.

Howard, Robert E. (1906–1936).
American writer for pulp magazines and creator of sword-and-sorcery stories featuring barbaric, muscular heroes. After his death by suicide, his heroes continued in stories and comic-books from other writers. He was played by Vincent D'ONOFRIO in *The Whole Wide World* 96, about his friendship with a schoolmistress.

Conan the Barbarian 81. Conan the Destroyer 84. Red Sonja 85. Kull the Conqueror 98. Conan the Adventurer 98, etc.

Howard, Ron (1954–).
American child actor of the 60s who matured into a director, screenwriter and producer.

The Journey 59. The Music Man 62. The Courtship of Eddie's Father 63. Smoke 69. The Wild Country 71. American Graffiti 73. The Spikes Gang 75. The Shootist 76. Grand Theft Auto (& d) 77. More American Graffiti 79. Night Shift (d only) 82. Splash! (d only) 84. Cocoon (d only) 85. Gung Ho (d only) 85. No Man's Land (p) 87. Clean and Sober (p) 88. Vibes (p) 88. Willow (d) 88. The 'burbs (p) 89. Parenthood (d, story) 89. Closet Land (p) 91. Backdraft (d) 91. Far and Away (d) 92. The Paper (d) 94. Apollo 13 95. Ransom 96, etc.

TV series: The Andy Griffith Show 60–68. The Smith Family 71–2. Happy Days 74–80.

Howard, Ronald (1918–).
British actor, son of Leslie Howard; formerly a reporter.

Biography: 1980, *In Search of My Father*.

While the Sun Shines (debut) 46. The Queen of Spades 48. Tom Brown's Schooldays 51. Drango (US) 56. Babette Goes to War 59. Spider's Web 60. The Curse of the Mummy's Tomb 64. Africa Texas Style 67. The Hunting Party 71. Persecution 74. Take a Hard Ride 75, many others.

TV series: *Sherlock Holmes* 55. Cowboy in Africa 67.

Howard, Shemp (1891–1955) (Samuel Horowitz).
American character comedian, brother of Moe Howard of the Three Stooges and occasional substitute for him; usually played tramps and bartenders.

Soup to Nuts 30. Headin' East 37. *The Bank Dick* 40. Buck Privates 41. *Hellzapoppin* 41. Pittsburgh 42. Crazy House 43. Blondie Knows Best 46. Africa Screams 49, many others.

Howard, Sidney (1891–1939).
American playwright and screenwriter. His Pulitzer Prize-winning play *They Knew What They Wanted* was filmed three times, and was also the basis of Frank LOESSER's Broadway musical *The Most Happy Fella* 56. Born in Oakland, California, he studied at the University of California and at Professor George Baker's 47 Workshop at the Harvard drama department, first working as a journalist. Married stage actress Clare Eames (1896–1930). Died in an accident on his cattle farm.

The Secret Hour (w, from his play They Knew What They Wanted) 28. Condemned (w) 29. Bulldog Drummond (w) 29. Raffles (w) 30. One Heavenly Night (w) 30. A Lady to Love (w, from his play They Knew What They Wanted) 30. Arrowsmith (w) (AAN) 31. The Greeks Had a Word for Them (w) 32. Christopher Bean/Her Sweetheart (oa) 33. Dodsworth (w) (AAN) 36. Yellow Jack (oa) 38. Gone with the Wind (w) (AA) 39. Raffles (co-w) 39. They Knew What They Wanted (oa) 40, etc.

❝ The precision of his manners went into his playwriting. He wrote out of a warm heart and with a cabinetmaker's attitude towards its contents. – *Ben Hecht*

It is to Howard's great credit that he seemed to appreciate what Hollywood, for all his desperate effort to beat its influence, had done to him. Asked if Hollywood had had any sinister effect upon him – I here quote the *New York Times* – he said that it had, that the lack of an audience and the low standard of taste had exerted an impact on his own playwriting integrity. 'It's the easy money, perhaps; I don't know,' he said. 'But it's true.' – *George Jean Nathan*

Howard, Sydney (1884–1946).
Plump British comedian famous for fluttering gestures. On stage from 1912, films from 1930.

■ Splinters 29. French Leave 30. Tilly of Bloomsbury 31. Almost a Divorce 31. *Up for the Cup* 31. Splinters in the Navy 31. The Mayor's Nest 32. It's a King 32. Up for the Derby 32. *Night of the Garter* 33. Trouble 33. It's a Cop 34. Transatlantic Merry Go Round (US) 34. Where's George? 35. *Fame* 36. Chick 36. Splinters in the Air 37. What a Man 37. Shipyard Sally 39. Tilly of Bloomsbury 40. Once a Crook 41. Mr Proudfoot Shows a Light 42. *When We Are Married* 43. Flight from Folly 45.

~Catchphrase: What's to do?

Howard, Trevor (1916–1988).
Distinguished English leading man, on stage from 1934. Born in Margate, Kent, he studied acting at RADA. His best roles were as Dr Alec Harvey in *Brief Encounter*, Dr Barnes in *Green for Danger*, Major Calloway in *The Third Man*, Scobie in *The Heart of the Matter*, Walter Morel in *Sons and Lovers*, Captain Bligh in *Mutiny on the Bounty*, Lord Cardigan in *The Charge of the Light Brigade*, and as the Inspector in *The Night Visitor*. Married for 44 years to actress Helen CHERRY.

Biography: 1988, *Trevor Howard: A Gentleman and a Player* by Vivienne Knight.

■ The Way Ahead (debut) 44. The Way to the Stars 45. *Brief Encounter* 46. I See a Dark Stranger 46. *Green for Danger* 46. So Well Remembered 47. They Made Me a Fugitive 47. The Passionate Friends 48. *The Third Man* 49. The Golden Salamander 49. Odette 50. The Clouded Yellow 51. An Outcast of the Islands 52. The Gift Horse 52. *The Heart of the Matter* 53. The Lovers of Lisbon (Fr.) 54. The Stranger's Hand 54. Cockleshell Heroes 55. Around the World in Eighty Days 56. Run for the Sun (US) 56. Interpol 57. Manuela 57. *The Key* (BFA) 58. Roots of Heaven 59. Moment of Danger 60. *Sons and Lovers* (AAN) 60. *Mutiny on the Bounty* (as Captain Bligh) 62. The Lion 62. The Man in the Middle 64. Father Goose 64. Von Ryan's Express 65. Operation Crossbow 65. Morituri 65. The Liquidator 65. The Poppy is Also a Flower 66. Triple Cross 66. The Long Duel 67. Pretty Polly 68. *The Charge of the Light Brigade* 68. The Battle of Britain 69. Twinky 69. *Ryan's Daughter* 70. *The Night Visitor* 71. Catch Me a Spy 71. Mary Queen of Scots 72. Kidnapped 72. Pope Joan 72. Ludwig 72. The Offence 72. *Catholics* (TV) 73. Craze 73. A Doll's House 73. Persecution 74. 11 Harrowhouse 74. Who? 74. Death in the Sun 75. Conduct Unbecoming 75. Hennessy 75. The Bawdy Adventures of Tom Jones 76. Eliza Fraser 76. Aces High 76. Slaves 77. The Last Remake of Beau Geste 77. Stevie 77. Superman 78. Night Flight (TV) 78. Hurricane 79. Meteor 79. The Sea Wolves 80. Windwalker 80. Staying On (TV) 80. Light Years Away 81. Inside the Third Reich (TV) 82. The Deadly Game (TV) 82. Gandhi 82. The Missionary 82. Sir Henry at Rawlinson End 82. Sword of the Valiant 84. Foreign Body 85. White Mischief 87. The Unholy 87. The Dawning 88.

❝ I've been number two in films for donkey's years. – *T.H.*

Howard, William K. (1899–1954).
American director who made some interesting films in the 30s.

East of Broadway 24. Code of the West 25. Gigolo 26. The Main Event 27. The River Pirate 28. Live Love and Laugh 29. Scotland Yard 30. Don't Bet on Women 31. Transatlantic 31. *Sherlock Holmes* 32. *The Power and the Glory* 33. The Cat and the Fiddle 34. Evelyn Prentice 34. Vanessa 35. *Mary Burns Fugitive* 35. The Princess Comes Across 36. *Fire Over England* (GB) 36. Back Door to Heaven 39. Bullets for O'Hara 41. Johnny Come Lately 43, etc.

Howe, James Wong (1899–1976) (Wong Tung Jim).
Distinguished Chinese cinematographer, in Hollywood from 1917.

■ Drums of Fate 23. The Woman with Four Faces 23. Call of the Canyon 23. The Spanish Dancer 23. To the Last Man 23. The Trail of the Lonesome Pine 23. The Alaskan 24. The Breaking Point 24. The Side Show of Life 24. The Best People 25. The Charmer 25. The King on Main Street 25. Not So Long Ago 25. Mantrap 26. Padlocked 26. Sea Horses 26. The Song and Dance Man 26. The Rough Riders 27. Sorrell and Son 27. Four Walls 28. The Perfect Crime 28. Laugh Clown Laugh 28. Desert Nights 29. Today 30. The Criminal Code 31. Transatlantic 31. The Spider 31. The Yellow Ticket 31. Surrender 31. Dance Team 32. After Tomorrow 32. Amateur Daddy 32. Man about Town 32. Chandu the Magician 32. Hello Sister 33. Beauty for Sale 33. The Power and the Glory 33. The Show Off 34. *The Thin Man* 34. Hollywood Party 34. Stamboul Quest 34. Have a Heart 34. Biography of a Bachelor Girl 34. The Night is Young 35. Mark of the Vampire 35. The Flame Within 35. O'Shaughnessy's Boy 35. Three Live Ghosts 35. Whipsaw 36. Fire Over England 36. Farewell Again 36. Under the Red Robe 37. *The Prisoner of Zenda* 37. The Adventures of Tom Sawyer 37. Algiers 38. Comet Over Broadway 38. They Made Me a Criminal 39. The Oklahoma Kid 39. Daughters Courageous 39. Dust Be My Destiny 39. On Your Toes 39. Abe Lincoln in Illinois 39. *Dr Ehrlich's Magic Bullet* 40. Saturday's Children 40. Torrid Zone 40. City for Conquest 40. A Dispatch from Reuter's 40. The Strawberry Blonde 41. Shining Victory 41. Navy Blues 41. Out of the Fog 41. *Kings Row* 42. Yankee Doodle Dandy 42. The Hard Way 42. Hangmen also Die 43. Air Force 43. North Star 43. Passage to Marseille 44. Objective Burma 45. Counterattack 45. Confidential Agent 45. Danger Signal 45. My Reputation 46. Nora Prentiss 47. Pursued 47. Body and Soul 47. Mr Blandings Builds His Dream House 48. The Time of Your Life 48. The Eagle and the Hawk 49. The Baron of Arizona 50. Tripoli 50. The Brave Bulls 51. He Ran All the Way 51. Behave Yourself 51. The Lady Says No 52. Main Street to Broadway 53. Come Back Little Sheba 54. The Rose Tattoo (AA) 55. *Picnic* 56. Death of a Scoundrel 56. Drango 56. *Sweet Smell of Success* 57. The Old Man and the Sea 58. Bell, Book and Candle 58. The Last Angry Man 59. The Story on Page One 60. Song without End 60. Tess of the Storm Country 61. *Hud* (AA) 63. The Outrage 64. The Glory Guys 65. This Property Is Condemned 66. *Seconds* (AAN) 67. Hombre 67. The Heart is a Lonely Hunter 69. The Molly Maguires 70. Last of the Mobile Hotshots 70. Funny Lady (AAN) 75.

Directed Go Man Go 52.

✪ For the visual sensitivity which is evident in every shot of every one of his films. *Kings Row*.

Howell, C. Thomas (1966–).
American young leading actor. He is married to actress Rae Dawn CHONG.

The Outsiders 83. Grandview USA 84. Red Dawn 84. Tank 84. Secret Admirer 85. The Hitcher 86. Soul Man 86. A Tiger's Tale 87. Il Giovane Toscanini 88. The Return of the Musketeers 89. Far Out, Man 90. The Kid 90. Side Out 90. That Night 92. Nickel & Dime 92. To Protect and Serve 92. Acting on Impulse 93. Gettysburg 93. Teresa's Tattoo 94. Mad Dogs and Englishmen 95. Hourglass (& d) 95. Pure Danger (& d) 96. The Big Fall (& d) 96. Baby Face Nelson 97, etc.

TV series: Two Marriages 83–84.

Howells, Ursula (1922–).
British actress, mainly on stage and TV. Film roles infrequent.

Flesh and Blood 51. The Constant Husband 55. They Can't Hang Me 55. The Long Arm 56. Dr Terror's House of Horrors 65. The Forsyte Saga (TV) 67. Mumsy Nanny Sonny and Girly 68. Crossplot 69. A Rather English Marriage 98. The Tichborne Claimant 98, etc.

Howerd, Frankie (1922–1992) (Francis Howard).
British eccentric comedian of stage and TV.

Autobiography: 1977, *On My Way I Lost It*.

■ *The Runaway Bus* 54. An Alligator Named Daisy 55. Jumping for Joy 55. The Ladykillers 55. A Touch of the Sun 56. Further Up the Creek 59. Watch It Sailor 61. The Cool Mikado 63. Mouse on the Moon 63. The Great St Trinian's Train Robbery 66. Carry On Doctor 68. Carry On Up the Jungle 69. *Up Pompeii* 70. Up the Chastity Belt 71. Up the Front 72. *The House in Nightmare Park* 73. Sergeant Pepper's Lonely Hearts Club Band 78.

TV series: The Howerd Crowd 52. The Frankie Howerd Show 69. *Up Pompeii!* 69–70. Whoops Baghdad! 73. The Howerd Confessions 76. Frankie Howerd Strikes Again 81. All Change 89–91.

Howes, Bobby (1895–1972).
Diffident, diminutive British leading man of stage musical comedies in the 30s.

■ The Guns of Loos 28. Third Time Lucky 31. Lord Babs 32. For the Love of Mike 32. Over the Garden Wall 34. Please Teacher 37. Sweet Devil 38. *Yes Madam* 38. Bob's Your Uncle 41. The Trojan Brothers 45. Happy Go Lovely 51. The Good Companions 57. Watch It Sailor 61.

Howes, Sally Ann (1930–).
British child actress of the 40s, later an occasional leading lady. Daughter of Bobby Howes.

■ *Thursday's Child* 43. Halfway House 44. *Dead of Night* 45. Pink String and Sealing Wax 45. Nicholas Nickleby 47. My Sister and I 48. Anna Karenina 48. *The History of Mr Polly* 48. Fools Rush In 49. Stop Press Girl 50. Honeymoon Deferred 51. The Admirable Crichton 57. Chitty Chitty Bang Bang 68. The Hound of the Baskervilles (TV) 72. Female Artillery (TV) 72. Death Ship 80.

Howlett, Noel (1901–1984).
British stage actor who appeared in small film roles from 1936, often as solicitor, auctioneer or civil servant.

A Yank at Oxford 46. Corridor of Mirrors 47.

The Blind Goddess 49. Father Brown 54. The Scapegoat 59. Some Will Some Won't 70, etc.

Howlin, Olin (1896–1959) (formerly known as Olin Howland).
American character actor, in innumerable small film roles since the early talkies.
So Big 32. Nothing Sacred 37. This Gun for Hire 42. The Wistful Widow 47. Them 54. The Blob 58, etc.

Hoxie, Jack (1890–1965) (Hartford Hoxie).
American star of early westerns who quit with the coming of sound. A cowboy, born in Oklahoma, he won the national riding championship in 1914 and went to Hollywood to work as a stuntman.
Lightning Bryce (serial) 19. Dead or Alive 21. Riders of the Law 22. Red Warning 22. Desert Rider 23. The Man from Wyoming 24. Flying Hoofs 25. The Last Frontier 26. The Western Whirlwind 27. Gold 32. Outlaw Justice 33, etc.

Hoyt, Arthur (1873–1953).
American character actor who played mild or henpecked husband in hundreds of silent and sound movies.
Love Never Dies 16. The Grim Game 19. Camille 21. Kissed 22. Souls for Sale 23. Sundown 24. The Lost World 25. Shanghai Bound 27. The Criminal Code 31. Call Her Savage 32. Only Yesterday 33. Wake Up and Dream 34. The Raven 35. Mr Deeds Goes to Town 36. A Star Is Born 37. The Black Doll 38. East Side of Heaven 39. The Great McGinty 40. The Lady Eve 41. The Palm Beach Story 42. The Miracle of Morgan's Creek 44. Hail the Conquering Hero 44. Mad Wednesday 47. Brute Force 47, many others.

Hoyt, John (1905–1991) (John Hoysradt).
Incisive American character actor, sometimes cast as German officer or stylish crook.
O.S.S. 46. *Rommel, Desert Fox* 51. New Mexico 52. When Worlds Collide 52. Androcles and the Lion 53. Julius Caesar 53. The Blackboard Jungle 55. Trial 55. The Conqueror 56. Six Inches Tall 58. Never So Few 60. Duel at Diablo 66. Flesh Gordon 74, many others.

Hsiao-Hsien, Hou (1947–).
Taiwanese director and screenwriter. Born in China, he was taken by his family to Taiwan as a small child and studied at the National Taiwan Arts Academy.
Green, Green Grass of Home 82. Growing Up 82. The Sandwich Man 83. The Boys from Fengkuei 83. A Summer at Grandpa's 85. A Time to Live and a Time to Die 85. Dust in the Wind 87. Daughter of the Nile 88. City of Sadness/Pei-ch'ing Ch'eng Shih 89. Sunless Days 90. The Puppetmaster/Hsimeng Jensheng 93. Good Men, Good Women 95. Goodbye South, Goodbye 96. The Flowers of Shanghai 98, etc.

Hu, King (1932–1997) (Hu-chin-chuan).
Chinese producer and director, working in Hong Kong. Born in Beijing, he moved to Hong Kong in the 50s, beginning in films as a set dresser and actor, becoming an assistant director in the late 50s and achieving success with his meticulously executed kung-fu movies.
The Love Eterne (co-d) 63. Sons of the Good Earth 64. Come Drink with Me 65. The Dragon Gate Inn 66. *A Touch of Zen* 69. *The Fate of Lee Khan* 73. The Valiant Ones 75. Raining in the Mountain 79. Legend of the Mountain 79. Painted Skin 92, etc.

Hubbard, John (1914–1988).
American light leading man who starred in several Hal Roach comedies.
The Housekeeper's Daughter 39. *Turnabout* 40. Road Show 41. Gunfight at Comanche Creek 63. Fate Is the Hunter 64. Duel at Diablo 66. Herbie Rides Again 73, etc.
TV series: The Mickey Rooney Show 54–55. Don't Call Me Charlie 62–63.

Hubbard, Lucien (1890–1972).
American screenwriter.
The Perils of Pauline 14. Wild Honey 22. The Vanishing American 25. Wings 27. Star Witness (AANw) 31. Smart Money (AANw) 31. Five Star Final 31. 42nd Street 33. The Casino Murder Case (& p) 35. A Family Affair (& p) 37. Ebb Tide (p) 37. Nick Carter Master Detective (p) 39, etc.

Huber, Harold (1904–1959).
American character actor, former lawyer; often seen as sly crook or dumb detective.
The Bowery 33. The Thin Man 34. G-Men 35. San Francisco 36. A Slight Case of Murder 38. Kit Carson 40. The Lady from Chungking 43. Let's Dance 50, many others.
TV series: I Cover Times Square 50.

Huber, Lotti (1912–1998) (Lotti Goldman).
Diminutive German dancer, actress and cabaret performer, who in old age became a familiar presence in the films of director Rosa VON PRAUNHEIM. Born in Kiel, she studied dance, worked in Berlin and, after a year in a concentration camp in 1937, was allowed to emigrate to Palestine. Later, she worked in Cyprus, ran a hotel in London and then returned to Berlin where, penniless and widowed for the second time in the mid-70s, she met von Praunheim after obtaining a bit part in *Just a Gigolo*. She starred in his *Affengeil*, based on her life, and became a successful cabaret artiste and TV chat show presenter.
Just a Gigolo 78. Affengeil 79 Our Corpses are Still Alive/Unsere Leichen Leben Noch (TV) 81, etc.

Hubert, Jean-Loup (1949–).
French director whose best films are semi-autobiographical.
L'Année Prochaine Si Tout Va Bien 81. La Smala 84. The Grand Highway/Le Grand Chemin 87. La Reine Blanche 91. À Cause d'Elle 93, etc.

Hubert, Roger (1903–1964).
French cinematographer.
Napoléon 27. Fanny 32. J'Accuse 37. Le Baron Fantôme 43. Les Enfants du Paradis 45. Thérèse Raquin 53. Paris Holiday 58. Lafayette 62. La Bonne Soupe 64, many others.

Hubley, John (1914–1977).
American animator, associated with the early days of UPA; a co-creator of Mr Magoo. Latterly worked on experimental documentary cartoons: *Of Stars and Men*, etc.

Hubley, Season (1951–).
American leading lady of the 70s. She was formerly married to actor Kurt Russell.
Lolly Madonna XXX 73. Catch My Soul 74. She Lives (TV) 74. Death Flight (TV) 77. Loose Change (TV) 78. Elvis (TV) 79. Hardcore 79. Escape from New York 81. Prettykill 87.
TV series: Kung Fu 74–75. Family 76–77. Blue Skies 88.

Hubschmid, Paul (1917–) (known in US as Paul Christian).
German-Swiss leading man, in international films; also on stage, especially as Higgins in *My Fair Lady*.
Maria Ilona 40. Baghdad 49. The Thief of Venice 52. The Beast from 20,000 Fathoms 53. Der Tiger von Eschnapur 59. Journey to the Lost City 60. Mozambique 66. *Funeral in Berlin* 66. Skullduggery 69. Temptation in the Summer Wind 73. Class Meeting 88. Linda 94, etc.

Hudd, Walter (1898–1963).
British character actor of stage and screen; usually played aloof characters and in 1936 was cast as T. E. Lawrence but the production was abandoned.
Rembrandt 36. Black Limelight 37. Elephant Boy 37. The Housemaster 38. Major Barbara 40. I Know Where I'm Going 45. Paper Orchid 49. Life For Ruth 62, etc.

Huddleston, David (1930–).
Oversized American actor, often found in westerns.
All the Way Home 63. A Lovely Way to Die 66. Slaves 69. Rio Lobo 70. Bad Company 72. Fools Parade 72. Brock's Last Case (TV) 73. The Gun and the Pulpit (TV) 74. The Oregon Trail (TV) 76. Blazing Saddles 76. Capricorn One 78. Kate Bliss and the Tickertape Kid (TV) 78. Smokey and the Bandit II 80. Santa Claus, the Movie 85. The Tracker 88. Life with Mikey 93. The Big Lebowski 97, etc.
TV series: Tenafly 73–74. Petrocelli 74–76. The Kallikaks 77. Hizzonner 79. Cultivating Charlie 94.

Hudis, Norman (1923–).
English screenwriter, a former journalist, who is best known for scripting the first six Carry On comedies. Originally a playwright, he first worked in films at Pinewood as a trainee screenwriter. In the mid-60s he emigrated to America to write for television, including *The Man from U.N.C.L.E.* series.
The Tommy Steele Story 57. The Duke Wore Jeans 58. Carry On Sergeant 58. Carry On Nurse 59. Carry On Teacher 59. Please Turn Over 59. Carry On Constable 60. Carry On Regardless 60. Beware of the Children 60. Carry On Cruising 62. Twice around the Daffodils 62. The Karate Killers 67. How to Steal the World 68. Hot Resort (co-w) 85, etc.

Hudlin, Reggie (1962–).
American screenwriter and director. Educated at Harvard University, he worked in advertising and then produced music videos with his brother Warrington.
House Party (wd) 90. Bebe's Kids (w) 92. Boomerang (d) 92. The Great White Hype 96. Joe's Apartment (voice) 96.

Hudlin, Warrington (1953–).
American producer and director, in partnership with his brother Reggie. Educated at Yale University, he co-founded the Black Filmmaker Foundation to distribute black independent films and videos.
House Party (p) 90. Bebe's Kids (p) 92. Boomerang (p) 92.

Hudson, Ernie.
American actor, frequently in action movies.
Penitentiary 2 82. Spacehunter: Adventures in the Forbidden Zone 83. Weeds 87. The Wrong Guys 88. Leviathan 89. Ghostbusters II 89. The Hand that Rocks the Cradle 91. Wild Palms 93. Speechless 94. Airheads 94. Sugar Hill 94. No Escape 94. The Cowboy Way 94. The Crow 94. The Basketball Diaries 95. Congo 95. Tornado! (TV) 96. The Cherokee Kid (TV) 96. The Substitute 96. Just Your Luck 96. Mr Magoo 97. A Stranger in the Kingdom 98, etc.

Hudson, Hugh (1936–).
British director, from TV commercials.
Chariots of Fire (AAN) 81. Greystoke 84. Revolution 86. Lost Angels/The Road Home 89. My Life So Far 98, etc.

Hudson, Rochelle (1914–1972).
American leading lady who played *ingénue* roles in the 30s.
Laugh and Get Rich 30. She Done Him Wrong 33. Les Misérables 35. Way Down East 36. Smuggled Cargo 39. Island of Doomed Men 40. Meet Boston Blackie 41. Rubber Racketeers 42. Queen of Broadway 43. Skyliner 49. Rebel without a Cause 55. The Night Walker 65. Broken Sabre 65, etc.

Hudson, Rock (1925–1985) (Roy Scherer).
Giant-sized American leading man who did very well in Hollywood despite lack of acting training, moving from westerns to sob stories to sophisticated comedies. Died of AIDS.
Autobiography: 1986, *Rock Hudson His Story* (with Sara Davidson).
■ Fighter Squadron 48. Double Crossbones 48. Undertow 49. I Was a Shoplifter 50. One Way Street 50. Winchester 73 50. Peggy 50. The Desert Hawk 50. Shakedown 50. The Fat Man 50. Air Cadet 51. Tomahawk 51. Iron Man 51. Bright Victory 51. Bend of the River 52. Here Come the Nelsons 52. Scarlet Angel 52. Has Anybody Seen My Gal? 52. Horizons West 52. The Lawless Breed 52. Gun Fury 53. Seminole 53. Sea Devils (GB) 53. The Golden Blade 53. Back to God's Country 53. Taza Son of Cochise 53. *Magnificent Obsession* 54. Bengal Brigade 54. Captain Lightfoot 55. One Desire 55. All That Heaven Allows 55. Never Say Goodbye 56. *Giant* (AAN) 56. Battle Hymn 56. *Written on the Wind* 56. Four Girls in Town 56. Something of Value 57. *The Tarnished Angels* 57. A Farewell to Arms 57. Twilight for the Gods 58. This Earth is Mine 59. *Pillow Talk* 59. The Last Sunset 61. Come September 61. Lover Come Back 61. The Spiral Road 62. A Gathering of Eagles 63. Marilyn (narrator) 63. Man's Favourite Sport? 64. Send Me No Flowers 64. Strange Bedfellows 64. A Very Special Favor 65. Blindfold 66. *Seconds* 66. Tobruk 67. Ice Station Zebra 68. A Fine Pair 69. The Undefeated 69. Darling Lili 69. Hornet's Nest 70. Pretty Maids all in a Row 71. Showdown 73. Embryo 76. Avalanche 78. Wheels (TV) 78. The Mirror Crack'd 80. The Martian Chronicles (TV) 80. The Ambassador 84. The Vegas Strip War (TV) 84.
TV series: *McMillan and Wife* 71–75. McMillan 76. The Devlin Connection 82. Dynasty 85.
❝ I can't play a loser: I don't look like one. – *R.H.*
I have no philosophy about acting or anything else. You just do it. And I mean that. You just do it. However, I can say that with ease after thirty-five years. – *R.H.*
That big, lumpy Rock Hudson. – *James Dean*
I call him Ernie because he's certainly no Rock. – *Doris Day*

Huerta, Rodolfo Guzmán (1920–1984).
Masked Mexican wrestler who was also the hero of a series of some 50 low-budget action films that enjoyed great popularity in his homeland for 21 years, from 1961, and occasionally reached international audiences in dubbed versions, usually when he battled against Frankenstein, Dracula, and other movie monsters. He was known as EL SANTO.
El Enmascarado de Plata 52. Santo contra el Cerebro Diabólico 61. Samson versus the Vampire Woman/Santo en las Mujeres Vampiro 61. Santo en la Venganza de las Mujeres Vampiro 69. Santo contra la Hija de Frankenstein 71. Santo y Blue Demon contra Dracula y el Hombre Loco 72. El Santo contra el Asesino de la Televisión 82, many others.

Huffaker, Clair (1927–1990).
American screenwriter.
Flaming Star 60. Seven Ways from Sundown 60. Rio Conchos 64. Tarzan and the Valley of Gold 65. The War Wagon 67. Hellfighters 69. The Deserter 71. Chino 76, etc.

Huffman, David (1945–1985).
American general-purpose actor. He was murdered.
F.I.S.T. 78. Ice Castles 78. The Onion Field 79. Blood Beach 81. Firefox 82.

Huggins, Roy (1914–).
American screenwriter, later TV producer, the creator of, among other TV series, *Maverick*, *Colt 45* and *77 Sunset Strip* in the 50s, and *The Fugitive*, *The Rockford Files* and *City of Angels* in the 60s and 70s. He set up his own production company, Public Arts. *The Fugitive* 93 and *Maverick* 94 were successful movies based on the TV originals.
I Love Trouble 48. The Lady Gambles 49. Sealed Cargo 51. Hangman's Knot (& d) 52. *Pushover* 54. A Fever in the Blood (& p) 61. The November Plan (story) 76, etc.

Hughes, Albert and Allen (1972–).
American twin directors.
Menace II Society 93. Dead Presidents 95, etc.

Hughes, Barnard (1915–).
American character actor familiar on TV as *Doc*.
Midnight Cowboy 69. Where's Poppa 71. The Hospital 72. Rage 72. Sisters 73. Oh God 77. Best Friends 82. Tron 82. Maxie 85. The Lost Boys 87. Da 88. Doc Hollywood 91. Sister Act 2: Back in the Habit 93. The Odd Couple II 98, etc.
TV series: Mr Merlin 81.

Hughes, Howard (1905–1976).
American businessman and celebrated recluse of eccentric habits; once an enthusiastic film-maker. Married Jean Peters (1957–71). His lovers are said to have included Bette Davis, Ava Gardner, Rita Hayworth, Jean Harlow, Katharine Hepburn, Ginger Rogers and Lana Turner. A character based on him was played by George Peppard in *The Carpetbaggers* 64. Tommy Lee Jones played him in a 1977 TV movie, *The Amazing Howard Hughes*, and Jason Robards Jnr in *Melvin and Howard* in 1981. Other Hughes-like figures were seen in *Caught* (Robert Ryan). *The Barefoot Contessa* (Warren Stevens). *Harlow* (Leslie Nielsen) and *Diamonds are Forever* (Jimmy Dean).
Biographies: 1967, *The Bashful Billionaire* by Albert Gerber. 1967, *Howard Hughes* by John Keats. 1993, *Howard Hughes – The Secret Life* by Charles Higham. 1995, *Howard Hughes, the Untold Story* by Peter Harry Brown, Pat H. Broeske.
Book: 1998, *The Money: The Battle for Howard Hughes's Billions* by James R. Phelan and Lewis Chester.
Two Arabian Knights (p) 27. *Hell's Angels* (pd)

30. The Front Page (p) 31. *Scarface* (p) 32. Sky Devils 32. *The Outlaw* (pd) 43. Jet Pilot (p) 56. The Conqueror (p) 56, etc.

❝ There are two good reasons why men go to see her. Those are enough. – *H.H. on Jane Russell*

This is a very simple engineering problem.
– *H.H., designing a bra for Jane Russell*

Hughes never fired anybody. If he wanted to get rid of somebody, he'd merely put somebody in over the guy. – *Sam Bischoff*

In his heyday he boasted of deflowering 200 virgins in Hollywood. He must have got them all. – *Jimmy the Greek*

Hughes, John (1950–).
American director, screenwriter and producer of films aimed primarily at a teenage audience. *Home Alone* is the most commercially successful of all film comedies and ranks third in the top box-office movies.

Sixteen Candles (wd) 84. The Breakfast Club (wd, p) 85. Weird Science (wd) 85. Ferris Bueller's Day Off (wd, p) 86. Pretty in Pink (w, p) 86. Planes, Trains and Automobiles (wd) 87. Some Kind of Wonderful (w, p) 87. The Great Outdoors (w, p) 88. She's Having a Baby (wd, p) 88. National Lampoon's Christmas Vacation (w, p) 89. Uncle Buck (wd, p) 89. Home Alone (w, p) 90. Career Opportunities (w, p) 91. Curly Sue (wd, p) 91. Home Alone 2: Lost in New York (w, p) 92. Dennis the Menace (w, p) 93. Baby's Day Out (w, p) 94. Miracle on 34th Street (w) 94. Flubber (p, co-w) 97. 101 Dalmatians (p, w) 96. Reach the Rock (p, w) 98, etc.

Hughes, Kathleen (1929–) (Betty von Gerlean).
Blonde American leading lady of the 50s.

Mother Is a Freshman 49. For Men Only 51. The Golden Blade 53. It Came from Outer Space 53. The Glass Web 53. Dawn at Socorro 54. Cult of the Cobra 55. Promise Her Anything 66. The President's Analyst 67, etc.

Hughes, Ken (1922–).
British director who has tackled a great variety of projects with variable success.

■ Wide Boy 52. Black Thirteen 53. The Brain Machine 53. Little Red Monkey (& w) 53. Confession (& w) 53. Timeslip (& w) 53. The House Across the Lake (& w) 54. *Joe Macbeth* (& w) 55. Wicked as They Come (& w) 56. The Long Haul 57. Jazzboat 60: In the Nick 60. *The Trials of Oscar Wilde* (& w) 60. The Small World of Sammy Lee (& w) 63. Of Human Bondage 64. Drop Dead Darling (& w) 66. Casino Royale (co-d) 67. Chitty Chitty Bang Bang (& w) 69. *Cromwell* (& w) 70. The Internecine Project 74. Alfie Darling 74. Sextette 77. Night School 80.

Hughes, Lloyd (1896–1958).
American leading man of the 20s.

The Turn in the Road 19. Hail the Woman 21. Tess of the Storm Country 22. *The Sea Hawk* 24. *The Lost World* 24. The Desert Flower 25. Ella Cinders 26. Loose Ankles 26. The Stolen Bride 27. The Mysterious Island 29. Moby Dick 30. Hell Bound 31. The Miracle Man 32. Harmony Lane 35. Romance of the Redwoods 39, many others.

Hughes, Mary Beth (1919–1995).
American leading lady of the 40s, mainly in second features.

These Glamour Girls 39. Lucky Cisco Kid 40. Orchestra Wives 42. *The Ox-Bow Incident* 43. I Accuse My Parents 44. Caged Fury 47. Gun Battle at Monterey 57. How's Your Love Life? 77, etc.

Hughes, Roddy (1891–1970).
Welsh character actor in films from 1934, often in roly-poly comedy roles.

The Stars Look Down 39. The Ghost of St Michael's 41. Hatter's Castle 41. Nicholas Nickleby 47. Scrooge 51. Sea Wife 57, etc.

Hughes, Wendy.
Australian leading actress.

■ Sidecar Racers 75. High Rolling 77. Newsfront 78. Kostas 78. My *Brilliant Career* 79. Touch and Go 80. Partners 81. A Dangerous Summer 81. Lonely Hearts 82. Careful, He Might Hear You 83. My First Wife 84. An Indecent Obsession 85. I Can't Get Started 85. Promises to Keep 86. Warm Nights on a Slow Moving Train 87. The Heist 89. Wild Orchid II: Two Shades of Blue 92. Princess Caraboo 94. Lust and Revenge 96.

Hugo, Ian (1898–1985) (Hugh Parker Guiler).
American director, cinematographer and editor of short, experimental films. Born in Boston, he was educated in Scotland and at Columbia University and from the mid-20s to the late 30s lived in Paris. By profession a successful banker and stockbroker, he was also an engraver and was married to writer Anaïs Nin. A retrospective of his work was shown at the Edinburgh Film Festival in 1970 and at the Museum of Modern Art, New York, in 1971. In *Henry and June* 90, a character based on him was played by Richard E. Grant.

Ai-Ye 50. Bells of Atlantis 52. Jazz of Lights 54. Melodic Inversion 58. Venice, Étude No. 1 62. The Gondola Eye 63 (revised 71). Through the Magiscope 69. Apertura 70, etc.

❝ The motion picture is potentially the greatest of all arts because it unites them all: sound, movement and a luminosity of colour that a painter could never achieve. – *I.H.*

Hugo, Victor (1802–1885).
French novelist, poet and playwright, two of whose romantic epics, *The Hunchback of Notre Dame* and *Les Misérables*, have provided seemingly inexhaustible material for the cinema.

Hulbert, Claude (1900–1963).
British 'silly ass' comedian, brother of Jack Hulbert.

Champagne 28. Naughty Husbands 30. A Night Like This 32. The Mayor's Nest 32. *Thark* 32. Radio Parade 33. A Cup of Kindness 34. *Bulldog Jack* 34. Wolf's Clothing 36. The Vulture 37. His Lordship Regrets 38. *Sailors Three* 40. *The Ghost of St Michael's* 41. The Dummy Talks 43. *My Learned Friend* 44. London Town 46. The Ghosts of Berkeley Square 47. Cardboard Cavalier 48. Fun at St Fanny's 55. Not a Hope in Hell 60, etc.

Hulbert, Jack (1892–1978).
Jaunty, long-chinned British light comedian, popular in films of the 30s. On stage from 1913, he was married to Cicely Courtneidge.

Autobiography: 1976, *The Little Woman's Always Right*.

■ Elstree Calling 30. *The Ghost Train* 31. Sunshine Susie 31. *Jack's the Boy* 32. Love on Wheels 32. Happy Ever After 32. Falling for You 33. Jack Ahoy 34. The Camels are Coming 34. *Bulldog Jack* 34. Jack of all Trades 36. Take My Tip 37. Paradise for Two 37. Kate Plus Ten 38. Under Your Hat 40. Into the Blue 51. The Magic Box 51. Miss Tulip Stays the Night 55. Spider's Web 60. The Cherry Picker 72. Not Now Darling 73.

Hulce, Tom (1953–).
American character actor of the 80s.

■ '9/30/55' 77. National Lampoon's Animal House 78. Those Lips, Those Eyes 80. Amadeus (AAN, as Mozart) 84. Echo Park 85. Slam Dance 87. Dominick and Eugene/Nicky and Gino 88. Shadowman 88. Black Rainbow 89. Parenthood 89. Murder in Mississippi (TV) 90. The Inner Circle 91. Fearless 93. Mary Shelley's Frankenstein 94. Wings of Courage 95. The Heidi Chronicles (TV) 95. The Hunchback of Notre Dame (voice) 96.

Hull, Henry (1890–1977).
Versatile American character actor.

The Volunteer 17. One Exciting Night 22. The Hoosier Schoolmaster 24. For Woman's Favour 24. Midnight 34. Great Expectations 34. *Werewolf of London* (leading role) 35. Yellow Jack 38. Boys Town 38. The Great Waltz 38. Jesse James 39. Miracles for Sale 39. Judge Hardy and Son 39. My Son My Son 40. High Sierra 41. Lifeboat 43. Woman of the Town 44. Objective Burma 45. Mourning Becomes Electra 47. The Walls of Jericho 48. The Great Gatsby 49. Hollywood Story 51. Inferno 53. The Man with the Gun 55. The Proud Rebel 58. The Sheriff of Fractured Jaw 58. Master of the World 61. The Chase 66. Covenant with Death 67, many others.

Hull, Josephine (1884–1957) (Josephine Sherwood).
Bubbly little American stage actress who gave two memorable film performances.

■ After Tomorrow 32. Careless Lady 32. *Arsenic and Old Lace* 44. *Harvey* (AA) 50. The Lady from Texas 51.

Famous line (*Harvey*): 'Myrtle Mae, you have a lot to learn, and I hope you never learn it.'

Hull, Warren (1903–1974).
American leading man of many second features: also radio hero of such serials as Mandrake the Magician and The Spider.

Miss Pacific Fleet 35. The Walking Dead 36. Night Key 37. Wagons Westward 40. Bowery Blitzkrieg 41, etc.

Hulme, Kathryn C. (1900–1981).
Author of *The Nun's Story*, which was filmed with Audrey Hepburn playing her.

Humberstone, H. Bruce (1903–1984).
American director, a competent craftsman of action films and musicals.

If I Had a Million (part) 32. The Crooked Circle 32. Charlie Chan in Honolulu 37. Pack Up Your Troubles 39. Lucky Cisco Kid 40. Tall, Dark and Handsome 41. *Sun Valley Serenade* 41. Hot Spot 41. To the Shores of Tripoli 42. *Hello, Frisco Hello* 43. *Wonder Man* 45. Three Little Girls in Blue 46. *Fury at Furnace Creek* 48. East of Java 49. Happy Go Lovely (GB) 51. She's Working Her Way Through College 52. The Desert Song 53. The Purple mask 55. Tarzan and the Lost Safari 57. Madison Avenue 61, etc.

❝ He was known as Lucky Humberstone, for the very good reason he somehow continued to find work in Hollywood despite the fact that he had so small a talent. – *Milton Sperling*

Hume, Alan (1924–).
British cinematographer.

The Legend of Hell House 72. Carry on Girls 73. The Land that Time Forgot 74. Trial by Combat 76. Bear Island 80. The Eye of the Needle 81. For Your Eyes Only 81. Return of the Jedi 83. Octopussy 83. Supergirl 84. A View to a Kill 85. Lifeforce 85. Runaway Train 85. The Second Victory 87. Hearts of Fire 87. A Fish Called Wanda 88. Without a Clue 88. Shirley Valentine 89. Eve of Destruction 91. Just Like a Woman 95, etc.

Hume, Benita (1906–1967).
British leading lady of the 30s; in Hollywood from 1935; retired to marry Ronald Colman.

The Constant Nymph 28. High Treason 29. Service for Ladies 32. The Flying Fool 32. Lord Camber's Ladies 33. Jew Süss 34. The Garden Murder Case 36. Tarzan Escapes 36. The Last of Mrs Cheyney 37. Peck's Bad Boy with the Circus 39, etc.

TV series: Halls of Ivy 55.

Hume, Cyril.
British screenwriter and novelist in Hollywood, formerly married to actress Helen Chandler.

Trader Horn 31. Tarzan the Ape Man 32. *Flying Down to Rio* 33. Tarzan Escapes 36. The Jungle Princess 36. Twenty Mule Team 40. The Great Gatsby 49. Branded 50. Tarzan's Savage Fury 52. Bigger than Life 56. The Invisible Boy 57. Killers of Kilimanjaro 59, etc.

Hume, Kenneth (1926–1967).
British producer, former editor.

Cheer the Brave (wpd) 50. Hot Ice (wd) 51. Sail into Danger (wd) 57. Mods and Rockers (d) 64. I've Gotta Horse (d) 65, etc.

Humphries, Barry (1934–).
Australian entertainer, aesthete and novelist, best known for his stage and television performances as his alter egos, Dame Edna Everage, Sir Les Patterson and Sandy Stone, characters that have not transferred happily to the big screen. His *Private Eye* comic strip, 'Barry McKenzie', was also the basis of a film.

Autobiography: 1992, *More Please*.

The Adventures of Barry McKenzie 72. Barry McKenzie Holds His Own 74. The Getting of Wisdom 77. Les Patterson Saves the World 87. The Leading Man 96, etc.

Hung, Samo (1950–) (Hong Jinbao).
Hong Kong director, screenwriter and plump but agile leading actor of martial arts and comedy movies. *Painted Faces* is an autobiographical film based on his life from the age of seven to 17, training as a member of a traditional Chinese theatre group, where a fellow pupil was his frequent co-star Jackie CHAN.

Education of Love 61. Father and Son 63. The Fast Sword 70. The Valiant Ones 74. Iron Fisted Monk (& d) 77. Warriors Two 77. Enter the Fat Dragon 78. Spooky Encounters (& d) 80. Ghost against Ghost/Gui da Gui (& co-w, d) 81. Carry On Pickpocket 82. Prodigal Son 83. Winners and Sinners (& d) 83. The Dead and the Deadly 83. Wheels on Meals (& d) 84. Project A 84. Twinkle, Twinkle, Lucky Stars (& d) 85. Eastern Condors 87. Painted Faces 89. Pantyhose Hero 91. The Prisoner 91. The Eagle Shooting Heroes: Dong Cheng Xi Jiu (action director) 93. A Nice Guy (d) 97, etc.

TV series: Martial Law 98– .

Hung, Tran Anh (1962–).
Vietnamese director, now resident in France.

Scent of Green Papaya (AAN) 93. Cyclo 95.

Hunnicutt, Arthur (1911–1979).
American actor of slow-speaking country characters.

Wildcat 42. Lust for Gold 49. Broken Arrow 50. The Red Badge of Courage 51. The Big Sky (AAN) 52. The French Line 54. The Last Command 56. The Kettles in the Ozarks 56. Apache Uprising 65. Cat Ballou 65. El Dorado 66. Million Dollar Duck 71. The Revengers 72. Harry and Tonto 74. The Spikes Gang 74. Moonrunners 75, etc.

Hunnicutt, Gayle (1942–).
American leading lady of the 60s.

■ The Wild Angels 66. P.J. 68. Marlowe 69. Eye of the Cat 69. Fragment of Fear 70. Freelance 70. Scorpio 72. The Legend of Hell House 72. Running Scared 72. Voices 73. Nuits Rouges 73. The Spiral Staircase 75. Blazing Magnum 76. The Sellout 76. Once In Paris 78. A Man Called Intrepid (TV) 79. The Martian Chronicles (TV) 79. Kiss of Gold (TV) 80. The Return of the Man from UNCLE (TV) 83. The First Modern Olympics (TV) 84. A Woman of Substance (TV) 85. Target 85. Strong Medicine (TV) 86. Dream West (TV) 86. Turnaround 87. Hard to Be a God 87. Silence Like Glass 89.

Hunt, Helen (1963–).
American leading actress who began on television as a child. In 1998 she earned $1m an episode for her TV series *Mad about You*, and also won her third consecutive Emmy as comedy actress.

Trancers/Future Cop 84. Girls Just Want to Have Fun 85. Peggy Sue Got Married 86. Project X 87. Next of Kin 89. Trancers II 91. Into the Badlands (TV) 91. The Waterdance 91. Miles from Nowhere (TV) 92. Mr Saturday Night 92. Trancers III 92. Twister 96. *As Good as It Gets* (AA) 97, etc.

TV series: Amy Prentiss 74–75. Swiss Family Robinson 75–76. The Fitzpatricks 77–78. It Takes Two 82–83. Mad about You 92–99.

Hunt, Linda (1945–).
Diminutive American character actress.

The Year of Living Dangerously (AA) (as a man) 83. The Bostonians 84. Silverado 85. Eleni 85. Dune 85. Waiting for the Moon (as Alice B. Toklas) 87. She-Devil 89. Kindergarten Cop 90. Teen Agent 91. Younger and Younger 93. Twenty Bucks 93. Prêt-à-Porter/Ready to Wear 94. The Relic 96. Pocahontas II: Journey to a New World (voice) 98, etc.

TV series: Space Rangers 93.

Hunt, Marsha (1917–) (Marcia Hunt).
American leading lady who usually plays gentle characters. Married director Jerry Hoppert (1938–45) and writer Robert Presnell Jnr.

Virginia Judge (debut) 35. Hollywood Boulevard 36. The Hardys Ride High 38. These Glamour Girls 39. *Pride and Prejudice* 40. Blossoms in the Dust 41. Kid Glove Killer 42. Seven Sweethearts 42. The Human Comedy 43. *Lost Angel* 43. None Shall Escape 43. Cry Havoc 44. The Valley of Decision 45. A Letter for Evie 45. Carnegie Hall 46. Take One False Step 49. Mary Ryan, Detective 50. The Happy Time 52. No Place to Hide 56. Blue Denim 59. The Plunderers 60. Johnny Got His Gun 71. Rich and Famous 81, etc.

TV series: Peck's Bad Girl 59.

Hunt, Martita (1900–1969).
British stage and screen actress who graduated from nosy spinsters to *grandes dames*.

I Was a Spy (debut) 33. Spare a Copper 39. The Man in Grey 43. The Wicked Lady 45. *Great Expectations* (as Miss Havisham) 46. The Ghosts of Berkeley Square 47. My Sister and I 48. The Fan 49. *Treasure Hunt* 52. Melba 53. Three Men in a Boat 56. Anastasia 56. *Brides of Dracula* 60. The Unsinkable Molly Brown 64. Bunny Lake Is Missing 65, many others.

Hunt, Peter (1928–).
British director, former editor.
■ On Her Majesty's Secret Service 69. Gulliver's Travels 73. Gold 74. Shout at the Devil 76. The Beasts are on the Streets (TV) 78. Flying High (TV) 79. Death Hunt 80. Rendezvous Hotel (TV) 81. The Last Days of Pompeii (TV) 83. Wild Geese II 85. Hyper Sapien 86. Assassination 87.

Hunte, Otto (1883–1847).
German art director, associated with Fritz Lang's films of the 20s. He later worked on Nazi propaganda films, including the notorious *Jew Suess/Jud Süss* 40, and also designed the anti-Nazi *The Murderers Are among Us/Die Mörder Sind unter Uns* 46.
The Slave Ship/Die Spinnen 20. Dr Mabuse the Gambler/Dr Mabuse der Spieler 22. Die Niebelungen 24. Metropolis 26. The Woman in the Moon/Frau im Mond 29. The Blue Angel/Der Blaue Engel 30. Early to Bed 33. Gold 34. Razzia 47, etc.

Hunter, Bill (1940–).
Australian leading actor.
The Man from Hong Kong 75. Eliza Fraser 76. Backroads 77. Newsfront 77. Hard Knocks 80. Gallipoli 80. Heatwave 82. Far East 82. The Return of Captain Invincible 82. The Hit (GB) 84. Street Hero 84. An Indecent Obsession 85. Rebel 85. Death of a Soldier 86. Fever 88. The Last Days of Chez Nous 92. Strictly Ballroom 92. Broken Highway 93. The Custodian 93. The Adventures of Priscilla, Queen of the Desert 94. Muriel's Wedding 94. Everynight . . . Everynight 94. Race the Sun 96. River Street 96, etc.
TV series: The Dismissal 83.

Hunter, Evan (1926–) (Salvadore Lombino).
American novelist and screenwriter who also writes as Ed McBain.
The Blackboard Jungle (oa) 55. Strangers When We Meet (w) 60. The Young Savages (w) 61. The Birds (w) 63. Mister Buddwing (oa) 66. Walk Proud 79, etc.
TV series: 87th Precinct 61. The Chisholms 78.

Hunter, Glenn (1897–1945).
American leading man of the 20s.
The Case of Becky 21. The Country Flapper 22. Smilin' Through 22. Puritan Passions 23. *Merton of the Movies* 24. West of the Water Tower 24. The Pinch Hitter 25. For Beauty's Sake 41, etc.

Hunter, Holly (1958–).
American leading actress.
The Burning 81. Svengali (TV) 83. Swing Shift 84. Urge to Kill (TV) 84. The End of the Line 87. Crimes of the Heart 87. Raising Arizona 87. A Gathering of Old Men/Murder on the Bayou (TV) 87. Broadcast News (AAN) 87. Animal Behavior 89. Always 89. Roe vs Wade (TV) 89. Miss Firecracker 89. Once Around 90. Crazy in Love 92. The Positively True Adventures of the Alleged Texas Cheerleader-Murdering Mom (TV) 93. The Firm (AAN) 93. *The Piano* (AA) 93. Copycat 95. Home for the Holidays 95. Crash 96. A Life Less Ordinary 97. Living Out Loud 98, etc.

Hunter, Ian (1900–1975).
British actor of dependable characters; on stage from 1919, films soon after.
Mr Oddy 22. Not for Sale 24. Confessions 25. The Ring 27. Something Always Happens 31. The Sign of Four (as Dr Watson) 32. Death at Broadcasting House 34. A Midsummer Night's Dream (US) 35. The White Angel (US) 36. Call It a Day (US) 37. *52nd Street* (US) 38. The Adventures of Robin Hood (as King Richard) (US) 38. Tower of London (US) 39. Strange Cargo (US) 40. Bitter Sweet (US) 40. Billy the Kid (US) 41. *Dr Jekyll and Mr Hyde* (as Lanyon) (US) 41. A Yank at Eton (US) 42. Bedelia 46. White Cradle Inn 47. The White Unicorn 48. *Edward My Son* 49. Appointment in London 52. Don't Blame the Stork 53. The Battle of the River Plate 56. Fortune Is a Woman 57. Northwest Frontier 59. The Bulldog Breed 60. Dr Blood's Coffin 61. Guns of Darkness 63, many others.

Hunter, Jeffrey (1925–1969) (Henry H. McKinnies).
American leading man, in films from 1951 after radio experience.
Fourteen Hours (debut) 51. Red Skies of Montana 52. Singlehanded 53. White Feather 55. The Searchers 56. A Kiss Before Dying 56. The True Story of Jesse James 57. No Down Payment 57. The Last Hurrah 57. Hell to Eternity 60. *King of Kings* (as Jesus) 61. The Longest Day 62. Vendetta 65. Brainstorm 65. Custer of the West 66. The Private Navy of Sgt O'Farrell 68, many others.
TV series: Temple Houston 63.

Hunter, Kim (1922–) (Janet Cole).
Pert, dependable American leading lady who after brief stage experience started a rather desultory film career, not helped by being blacklisted in the 50s.
The Seventh Victim 43. Tender Comrade 43. When Strangers Marry 44. You Came Along 45. *A Matter of Life and Death* (GB) 45. *A Streetcar Named Desire* (AA) 51. *Deadline USA* 52. Anything Can Happen 52. Storm Center 56. The Young Stranger 57. Bermuda Affair 58. Money Women and Guns 58. Lilith 64. Planet of the Apes 67. The Swimmer 68. Beneath the Planet of the Apes 70. Dial Hot Line (TV) 70. In Search of America (TV) 71. Escape from the Planet of the Apes 71. The Magician (TV) 73. Unwed Father (TV) 74. Born Innocent (TV) 74. Bad Ronald (TV) 74. Ellery Queen (TV) 75. The Dark Side of Innocence (TV) 76. Once an Eagle (TV) 76. Backstairs at the White House (TV) 79. The Kindred 86. Two Evil Eyes 89. A Price above Rubies 97. Midnight in the Garden of Good and Evil 97, etc.

Hunter, Ross (1921–1996) (Martin Fuss).
American producer; a former actor, he has specialized in remakes of glossy dramas from Hollywood's golden age, and has seldom failed to make hot commercial properties of them.
AS ACTOR: A Guy a Gal and a Pal 45. Sweetheart of Sigma Chi 47, The Bandit of Sherwood Forest 47. The Groom Wore Spurs 51, etc.
AS PRODUCER: Take Me to Town 53. *Magnificent Obsession* 54. One Desire 55. The Spoilers 55. All that Heaven Allows 56. Battle Hymn 57. My Man Godfrey 57. *Pillow Talk* 58. *Imitation of Life* 59. Portrait in Black 60. Tammy Tell Me True 61. Back Street 61. Flower Drum Song 61. The Thrill of it All 63. The Chalk Garden 64. Madame X 66. The Pad 66. *Thoroughly Modern Millie* 67. *Airport* (AAN) 69. Lost Horizon 73. The Lives of Jenny Dolan (TV) 76. A Family Upside Down (TV) 78. The Best Place to Be (TV) 78. Suddenly Love (TV) 79, etc.
❝ The way life looks in my pictures is the way I want life to be. I don't want to hold a mirror up to life as it is. I just want to show the part which is attractive. – *R.H.*

Hunter, T. Hayes (1881–1944).
American director, in Britain in the 30s.
Desert Gold 19. Earthbound 20. The Triumph of the Scarlet Pimpernel 29. The Silver King 29. The Frightened Lady 31. Sally Bishop 33. *The Ghoul* 33, etc.

Hunter, Tab (1931–) (Andrew Arthur Kelm).
Athletic American leading man, a teenage rave of the 50s.
The Lawless (debut) 48. Saturday Island 52. Gun Belt 53. Return to Treasure Island 53. *Track of the Cat* 54. Battle Cry 55. The Sea Chase 55. The Burning Hills 56. The Girl He Left Behind 57. Gunman's Walk 57. *Damn Yankees* 58. That Kind of Woman 59. The Pleasure of His Company 60. The Golden Arrow (It.) 62. City under the Sea 65. Birds Do It 66. Hostile Guns 67. Judge Roy Bean 72. The Timber Tramps 73. Grease II 82. Pandemonium 82. Polyester 82. Lust in the Dust 85. Cameron's Closet 87. Grotesque 88. Out of the Dark 88. Dark Horse 92, etc.
TV series: The Tab Hunter Show 60.

Hunter, Tim.
American director.
Tex 82. Sylvester 85. River's Edge 87. Paint It Black 89. The Saint of Fort Washington 93, etc.

Huntington, Lawrence (1900–1968).
British director, mainly of routine thrillers.
Suspected Person (& w) 41. Night Boat to Dublin 41. *Wanted for Murder* 46. *The Upturned Glass* 47. When the Bough Breaks 48. *Mr Perrin and Mr Traill* 48. Man on the Run (& w) 49. The Franchise Affair (& w) 51. There Was a Young Lady (& w) 53. Contraband Spain (& w) 55. Stranglehold 62. The Fur Collar (& w, p) 63, etc.

Huntley, Raymond (1904–1990).
British character actor, often of supercilious types or self-satisfied businessmen; on stage from 1922, screen from 1934.
Rembrandt 37. *Night Train to Munich* 40. *The Ghost of St Michael's* 41. School for Secrets 45. Mr Perrin and Mr Traill 48. *Trio* 50. Room at the Top 59. Only Two Can Play 62. Rotten to the Core 65. Hostile Witness 67. Destiny of a Spy (TV) 69. *That's Your Funeral* 73, many others.

Huppert, Isabelle (1955–).
French leading lady in international films. Born in Paris, to a French father and English mother, she studied dramatic arts at the Conservatoire National and Russian at Paris University, and began acting in the city's café-theatres.
Faustine 71. Cesar and Rosalie 72. Les Valseuses 74. Rosebud 75. The Judge and the Assassin 76. *The Lacemaker* 77. *Violette Nozière* 78. Heaven's Gate 80. Sauve Qui Peut 80. Coup de Torchon 81. The Trout 82. Entre Nous/Coup de Foudre 83. My Best Friend's Girl/La Femme de Mon Pote 83. La Garce 84. Cactus 86. The Bedroom Window 87. Migrations 88. Malina 90. Madame Bovary 91. After Love/Après l'Amour 92. Amateur 94. The Flood/L'Inondation 94. A Judgment in Stone/La Cérémonie 95. Elective Affinities 96. Rien Ne Va Plus 97. The School of Flesh/L'École de la Chair 98, etc.

Hurd, Gale Anne (1955–).
American producer and screenwriter. She was married to director James Cameron (1985–89).
The Terminator (& w) 84. Aliens 86. Alien Nation 88. Bad Dreams 88. The Abyss 89. Downtown 90. Tremors 90. Terminator 2: Judgement Day 91. The Waterdance 92. Raising Cain 92. No Escape 94. Safe Passage 94, etc.

Hurley, Elizabeth (1966–).
English leading actress, from television. She studied dance at the London Studio and formed her own dance troupe before beginning in the theatre in 1986. She is partner in a production company with her boyfriend, Hugh GRANT.
Rowing with the Wind 87. Aria 88. Passenger 57 92. Beyond Bedlam 94. Mad Dogs and Englishmen 95. Samson and Delilah (TV) 96. Extreme Measures (p) 96. Dangerous Ground 96. *Austin Powers: International Man of Mystery* 97. Permanent Midnight 98, etc.
❝ I would nationalise Elizabeth Hurley so each of us could claim our share. – *J. G. Ballard*

Hurndall, Richard (1910–1984).
Incisive British character actor.
Joanna 67. I Monster 71. Royal Flash 75. The Prince and the Pauper 77, etc.

Hurok, Sol (1889–1974).
Distinguished American impresario whose life in classical music was recounted in *Tonight We Sing* 53.

Hurrell, George.
Hollywood photographer whose flawless studio portraits of the stars of the 30s and 40s helped to create their images.
Book: 1997, *Hurrell's Hollywood Portraits – The Chapman Collection* by Mark Vieira.
❝ *Marlene Dietrich* (returning photographs to be retouched): You don't take pictures like you did fifteen years ago, George.
GH: But Marlene, I'm fifteen years older!

Hurst, Brandon (1866–1947).
British character actor in Hollywood; better roles in silents than sound films.
Legally Dead 23. *The Hunchback of Notre Dame* 23. He Who Gets Slapped 24. *The Thief of Baghdad* 24. The Grand Duchess and the Waiter 26. Love 27. Interference 29. A Connecticut Yankee 31. White Zombie 32. The Lost Patrol 34. The Charge of the Light Brigade 36. Mary of Scotland 36. If I Were King 38. Stanley and Livingstone 39. If I Had My Way 40. Dixie 43. Jane Eyre 44. House of Frankenstein 44. Devotion 46. Road to Rio 47, many others.

Hurst, Brian Desmond (1900–1986).
Irish director who made many kinds of film.
Sensation 36. Glamorous Night 37. Prison Without Bars 39. On the Night of the Fire 40. *Dangerous Moonlight* 41. Alibi 42. The Hundred Pound Window 43. Theirs Is the Glory 45. Hungry Hill 47. The Mark of Cain 48. Tom Brown's Schooldays (p only) 51. *Scrooge* 51. The Malta Story 53. Simba 55. The Black Tent 56. Dangerous Exile 57. Behind the Mask 58. His and Hers 60. The Playboy of the Western World 62, etc.

Hurst, David (1925–).
Austrian actor who played some comedy roles in British films.
The Perfect Woman 49. So Little Time 52. Mother Riley Meets the Vampire 52. As Long As They're Happy 53. The Intimate Stranger 56. After the Ball 57. Hello Dolly (US) 69. Kelly's Heroes (US) 70. The Boys from Brazil (US) 78, etc.

Hurst, Fannie (1889–1968).
American popular novelist, several of whose romantic novels, usually with a tragic finale, have been filmed more than once: *Humoresque*, *Imitation of Life*, *Back Street*, etc.

Hurst, Paul (1889–1953).
American character actor in hundreds of cameo roles from 1912, usually as gangster, bartender, outlaw or cop. Committed suicide.
The Red Raiders 27. Tugboat Annie 32. Riff Raff 34. Gone with the Wind 39. Caught in the Draft 41. Jack London 44. Yellow Sky 49. The Sun Shines Bright 53, many others.

Hurst, Veronica (1931–).
British light leading lady of the 50s.
Laughter in Paradise 51. Angels One Five 51. The Maze (US) 53. Will Any Gentleman? 53. The Yellow Balloon 54. Peeping Tom 59. Dead Man's Evidence 62. Licensed to Kill 64. The Boy Cried Murder 66, etc.

Hurt, John (1940–).
Off-beat British stage and film leading man.
The Wild and the Willing 62. This is my Street 63. *A Man for all Seasons* 66. The Sailor from Gibraltar 67. Before Winter Comes 69. Sinful Davey 69. In Search of Gregory 70. *10 Rillington Place* 71. Forbush and the Penguins 71. The Pied Piper 72. The Ghoul 74. Little Malcolm and His Struggle against the Eunuchs 74. *The Naked Civil Servant* (TV) 75. I Claudius (TV) 76. East of Elephant Rock 78. The Disappearance 78. The Shout 78. *Midnight Express* (AAN) 78. Spectre (TV) 78. Alien 79. Heaven's Gate 80. *The Elephant Man* (BFA, AAN) 80. Night Crossing 81. History of the World Part One 81. Partners 82. The Osterman Weekend 83. Champions 84. 1984 84. The Hit 84. Success is the Best Revenge 84. Sunset People 84. Jake Speed 86. Rocinante 86. From the Hip 87. Aria 87. Spaceballs 87. Vincent – the Life and Death of Vincent van Gogh 87. White Mischief 87. Little Sweetheart 88. La Nuit Bengali 88. Deadline 89. Scandal 89. Windprints 90. Frankenstein Unbound 90. The Field 90. Resident Alien 91. King Ralph 91. Lapse of Memory/Mémoire Traquée 91. I Dreamt I Woke Up 91. Dark at Noon/La Terreur de Midi 92. Even Cowgirls Get the Blues 93. Monolith 93. Thumbelina (voice) 94. Great Moments in Aviation 94. Second Best 94. Rob Roy 95. Wild Bill 95. Dead Man 95. Brute 96. Contact (US) 97. Love and Death on Long Island 98. All the Little Animals 98, etc.
TV series: The Storyteller 87–88.
❝ America only makes children's pictures. – *J.H.*
Hollywood is simply geared to cheat you left, right and bloody centre. – *J.H.*

Hurt, Mary Beth (1948–) (Mary Supinger).
American leading lady.
Head over Heels 82. The World According to Garp 82. Compromising Positions 85. D.A.R.Y.L. 85. Parents 89. Slaves of New York 89. Light Sleeper 91. Defenseless 91. My Boyfriend's Back 93. The Age of Innocence 93. Six Degrees of Separation 93. Shimmer 93. From the Journals of Jean Seberg (as Jean Seberg) 95, etc.

Hurt, William (1950–).
American leading actor. With three children from his two marriages, he also has a daughter from a relationship with actress Sandrine BONNAIRE.
Altered States 80. Eyewitness 81. Body Heat 81.

The Big Chill 83. Gorky Park 83. *Kiss of the Spider Woman* (AA, BFA) 85. Children of a Lesser God (AAN) 86. Broadcast News (AAN) 87. The Accidental Tourist 88. A Time of Destiny 88. Alice 90. I Love You to Death 90. The Doctor 91. Until the End of the World/Bis ans Ende der Welt 91. The Plague/La Peste 92. Mr Wonderful 93. Second Best 94. Trial by Jury 94. Confidences d'un Inconnu 95. Smoke 95. Secrets Shared with a Stranger 95. A Couch in New York (Fr.) 96. Jane Eyre (as Rochester) 96. Michael 96. Loved 96. Dark City 97. Lost in Space 98. The Proposition 98. One True Thing 98, etc.

❝ I think what's taking something away from acting is not the inclusion of special effects, but what the studios have done to actors, which is to take away any rehearsal time. – *W.H.*

Film is not the innate art, theatre is. If all the film in the world burnt down today, you'd still have acting. – *W.H.*

William approaches every movie as if the studios and producers are commerce and he's art. – *Jesse Beaton, producer*

Hussein, Waris (1938–).
Anglo-Indian director, mostly for TV.
■ A Touch of Love 68. Quackser Fortune 69. Melody 71. The Possession of Joel Delaney 72. The Six Wives of Henry VIII 72. Divorce His, Divorce Hers (TV) 73. *The Glittering Prizes* (TV) 75. *Edward and Mrs Simpson* (TV) 78. *Little Gloria . . .* Happy at Last (TV) 82. Winter of our Discontent (TV) 83. Arch of Triumph (TV) 84. Surviving (TV) 85. Copacabana (TV) 86. When the Bough Breaks (TV) 86. Intimate Contact (TV) 87. Downpayment on Murder (TV) 87. The Richest Man in the World: The Aristotle Onassis Story (TV) 88. Those She Left Behind (TV) 89. She Woke Up 92. The Clothes in the Wardrobe/The Summer House (TV) 93.

Hussey, Olivia (1951–).
British leading lady, born in Argentina. She was married to actor Dean Paul MARTIN.
The Battle of the Villa Fiorita 65. Cup Fever 65. *Romeo and Juliet* 68. All the Right Noises 69. Summertime Killer 72. *Lost Horizon* 73. Black Christmas 75. Jesus of Nazareth (TV) 77. The Cat and the Canary 77. Death on the Nile 78. The Pirate (TV) 79. The Man with Bogart's Face 80. Turkey Shoot 81. Escape 2000 81. Virus 82. The Last Days of Pompeii (TV) 84. The Corsican Brothers (TV) 84. Distortions 87. The Goldsmith's Shop 87. The Undeclared War 90. Psycho IV: The Beginning 90. Save Me 93. Quest of the Delta Knights 93. Ice Cream Man 95, etc.

Hussey, Ruth (1914–) (Ruth Carol O'Rourke).
Smart, competent, sometimes wisecracking American leading lady of the early 40s.
■ Madame X 37. Big City 37. Judge Hardy's Children 38. Man Proof 38. Marie Antoinette 38. Hold that Kiss 38. Rich Man Poor Girl 38. Time Out for Murder 38. Spring Madness 38. Honolulu 39. Within the Law 39. Maisie 39. The Women 39. Another Thin Man 39. Blackmail 39. *Fast and Furious* 39. Northwest Passage 40. Susan and God 40. *The Philadelphia Story* (AAN) 40. Flight Command 40. Free and Easy 41. Our Wife 41. Married Bachelor 41. H. M. *Pulham Esq* 41. Pierre of the Plains 42. Tennessee Johnson 42. Tender Comrade 43. *The Uninvited* 44. Marine Raiders 44. Bedside Manner 45. I Jane Doe 48. The Great Gatsby 49. Louisa 50. Mr Music 50. That's My Boy 51. Woman of the North Country 52. Stars and Stripes Forever 52. The Lady Wants Mink 53. The Facts of Life 60. My Darling Daughter's Anniversary (TV) 72.

Huston, Anjelica (1952–).
American leading lady, daughter of John HUSTON. She was the partner of actor Jack NICHOLSON from the early 70s to 1990. Married sculptor Robert Graham in 1992.
Biography: 1992, *Anjelica Huston – The Lady and Her Legacy* by Martha Harris.
Sinful Davey 69. A Walk with Love and Death 69. The Last Tycoon 76. Swashbuckler 76. Frances 82. The Ice Pirates 83. *Prizzi's Honor* (AA) 85. Good to Go 86. The Dead 87. Gardens of Stone 87. A Handful of Dust 88. The Witches 89. Enemies: A Love Story (AAN) 89. Crimes and Misdemeanors 89. The Grifters (AAN) 90. The Addams Family 91. The Player 92. Family Pictures (TV) 93. Manhattan Murder Mystery 93. Addams Family Values 93. The Perez Family 95. Buffalo Girls (as Calamity Jane) 95. The Crossing Guard 95. Bastard out of Carolina (d only) 96. Buffalo '66 97. Ever After 98. The Mammy (& d) 99, etc.

Huston, Danny (1962–).
American screenwriter and director, the son of John HUSTON.
Bigfoot (TV) 87. Mr North 88. Becoming Colette 92. The Maddening 95.

Huston, John (1906–1987).
Unpredictable but occasionally splendid American director, son of Walter HUSTON.
Autobiography: 1981, *An Open Book*.
Biography: 1965, *King Rebel* by W. F. Nolan. 1990, *The Hustons* by Lawrence Grobel.
AS SCREENWRITER ONLY: Murders in the Rue Morgue 32. The Amazing Dr Clitterhouse 38. Jezebel 38. High Sierra 40. Dr Ehrlich's Magic Bullet (co-w, AAN) 40. Sergeant York (AAN) 41. Three Strangers 46, etc.
■ AS DIRECTOR: *The Maltese Falcon* (& w) 41. In This Our Life 42. Across the Pacific 42. Report from the Aleutians 43. Battle of San Pietro 45. Let There Be Light 45 (four other official war documentaries 44–45). *The Treasure of the Sierra Madre* (& w) (AA) 47. *Key Largo* (& w) 48. We Were Strangers 49. *The Asphalt Jungle* (& w) (AANw, d) 50. The Red Badge of Courage (& w) 51. *The African Queen* (& w) (AAN) 52. Moulin Rouge (& w) (AAN) 53. Beat the Devil (& w) 54. Moby Dick (& w) 56. Heaven Knows Mr Allison (& w) (AANw) 57. The Barbarian and the Geisha 58. The Roots of Heaven (& w) 58. The Unforgiven 60. The Misfits 60. *Freud* 62. The List of Adrian Messenger 63. *The Night of the Iguana* (& w) 64. The Bible 66. Casino Royale (part) 67. Reflections in a Golden Eye 67. Sinful Davey 69. A Walk with Love and Death 69. The Kremlin Letter 70. *Fat City* 72. Judge Roy Bean 72. The Mackintosh Man 73. The Man Who Would Be King (AANw) 75. Wise Blood 79. Phobia 80. Victory 81. Annie 82. Under the Volcano 84. *Prizzi's Honor* (AAN) 85. The Dead 87.
■ AS ACTOR: The Treasure of the Sierra Madre (uncredited) 47. The List of Adrian Messenger (uncredited) 63. *The Cardinal* (AAN) 63. *The Bible* (as Noah) 66. Casino Royale 67. Candy 68. A Walk with Love and Death 68. De Sade 69. The Kremlin Letter 70. The Bridge and the Jungle 70. Myra Breckinridge 70. The Deserter 70. Man in the Wilderness 71. Judge Roy Bean 72. Battle for the Planet of the Apes 73. Chinatown 74. Breakout 75. The Wind and the Lion 75. Tentacles 77. Sherlock Holmes in New York (TV) 77. The Word (TV) 78. Winter Kills 79. The Visitor 79. Jaguar Lives 79. Head On 80. Love Sick 83. Young Giants 83.

❝ I don't try to guess what a million people will like. It's hard enough to know what I like. – *J.H.*

I fail to see any continuity in my work from picture to picture. – *J.H.*

I completely storyboarded *The Maltese Falcon* because I didn't want to lose face with the crew: I wanted to give the impression that I knew what I was doing. – *J.H.*

Most of us go through life searching for the unobtainable and if we do get it, we find it's unacceptable. – *J.H.*

There is nothing more fascinating – and more fun – than making movies. Besides, I think I'm finally getting the hang of it. – *J.H. (1984)*

Huston, Walter (1884–1950) (W. Houghston).
Distinguished American character actor of stage and screen: latterly projected roguery and eccentricity with great vigour. He also played bit parts in his son John's first two films, as Captain Jacoby in *The Maltese Falcon* 41, and a bartender in *In This Our Life* 42. After his death his stage recording of 'September Song', played in *September Affair* 50, became a big hit.
Biography: 1998, *September Song* by John Weld.
■ Gentlemen of the Press 28. The Lady Lies 29. *The Virginian* 30. The Bad Man 30. The Virtuous Sin 30. *Abraham Lincoln* 30. The Criminal Code 31. Star Witness 31. The Ruling Voice 31. A Woman from Monte Carlo 31. A House Divided 32. *Law and Order* (as Wyatt Earp) 32. Beast of the City 32. The Wet Parade 32. Night Court 32. *American Madness* 32. Kongo 32. *Rain* 32. Hell Below 32. Gabriel over the White House 33. The Prizefighter and the Lady 33. Storm at Daybreak 33. Ann Vickers 33. Keep 'Em Rolling 33. The Tunnel (GB) 34. Rhodes of Africa (GB) 36. *Dodsworth* (AAN) 36. Of Human Hearts 38. The Light That Failed 39. *All that Money Can Buy* (as the devil) (AAN) 41. Swamp Water 41. The Shanghai Gesture 42. Always in My Heart 42. Yankee Doodle Dandy (AAN) 42. Mission to Moscow 42. Edge of Darkness 42. North Star 43. *The Outlaw* (as Doc Holliday) 43. Dragon Seed 44. *And Then There Were None* 45. Dragonwyck 46. Duel in the Sun 46. *The Treasure of the Sierra Madre* (AA) 47. Summer Holiday 47. The Great Sinner 49. The Furies 50.
✪ For star quality combined with acting ability; whatever the proportions, no audience could look away when he was on screen. *Dodsworth*.

❝ Son, give 'em a good show, and always travel first class. – *W.H.*

Hell, I ain't paid to make good lines sound good. I'm paid to make bad lines sound good. – *W.H.*

Famous line (*All that Money Can Buy*): 'A soul – a soul is nothing. Can you see it, smell it, touch it, no?'

Hutchence, Michael (1960–1997).
Australian rock singer, leader of the the band INXS, and occasional actor. Born in Sydney, he formed the Farris Brothers group with a school-friend in 1979, changing the name to INXS in 1980. He was romantically involved with singer and actress Kylie MINOGUE, model Helena Christensen, and had a daughter by English TV presenter and journalist Paula Yates. Committed suicide by hanging himself in a hotel room.
Dogs in Space 86. Frankenstein Unbound (as Shelley) (US) 90.

Hutcheson, David (1905–1976).
British light comedian who often played monocled silly-asses, mainly on stage.
This'll Make You Whistle 35. Sabotage at Sea 41. Convoy 42. School for Secrets 46. *Vice Versa* 48. Sleeping Car to Trieste 48. The Elusive Pimpernel 50. The Evil of Frankenstein 64. The National Health 73, etc.

Hutchins, Bobby 'Wheezer' (1920–1945).
American child actor in the Our Gang comedies of the late 20s and early 30s. Died in an accident.

Hutchins, Will (1932–).
Bland-faced American leading man who came to fame in 57–60 as TV's *Sugarfoot*.
No Time for Sergeants 58. Merrill's Marauders 62. The Shooting 66. Clambake 67. Slumber Party '57 77. The Happy Hooker Goes to Washington 77. Roar 81. Maverick 94, etc.

Hutchinson, Josephine (1903–1998).
American actress who usually played sweet or maternal types. Born in Seattle, she was on stage as a dancer from the age of seven, and made her film debut as a child in 1917 before returning to the stage until the 30s. The first of her three husbands was director Robert Bell.
The Little Princess 17. Happiness Ahead 34. The Story of Louis Pasteur 36. Son of Frankenstein 39. Somewhere in the Night 46. Ruby Gentry 52. Miracle in the Rain 56. North By Northwest 59. Huckleberry Finn 60. Baby the Rain Must Fall 64. Nevada Smith 66. Rabbit Run 70, etc.

Huth, Harold (1892–1967).
British light leading man of silent days; later became producer-director.
One of the Best 27. Balaclava 28. The Silver King 29. Leave it to Me 30. The Outsider 31. Sally Bishop 32. Rome Express 32. The Ghoul 33. The Camels are Coming 34. Take My Tip 37. Hell's Cargo (d) 39. East of Piccadilly (d) 40. Busman's Honeymoon (p) 40. Breach of Promise (d) 42. Love Story (p) 44. They Were Sisters (p) 45. Caravan (p) 46. Night Beat £ 47. My Sister and I £ 48. Look Before You Love £ 48. One Wild Oat (p) 51. Police Dog (p) 55. The Hostage (d) 56. Idol on Parade (p) 59. The Trials of Oscar Wilde (p) 60. The Hellions (p) 61, etc.

Hutton, Betty (1921–) (Betty Thornberg).
Blonde and bouncy American leading lady of many singing/dancing light entertainments of the 40s.
■ *The Fleet's In* 42. *Star Spangled Rhythm* 42. Happy Go Lucky 43. Let's Face It 43. *The Miracle of Morgan's Creek* 44. And the Angels Sing 44. Here Come the Waves 44. *Incendiary Blonde* (as Texas Guinan) 45. Duffy's Tavern 45. The Stork Club 45. Cross My Heart 46. *The Perils of Pauline* 47. Dream Girl 48. Red Hot and Blue 49. *Annie Get Your Gun* 50. Let's Dance 50. Somebody Loves Me 52. The Greatest Show on Earth 52. Spring Reunion 57.

Hutton, Brian G. (1935–).
American director.
■ Fargo 65. The Pad 66. Sol Madrid 67. *Where Eagles Dare* 68. Kelly's Heroes 70. Zee and Co 71. Night Watch 73. The First Deadly Sin 80. High Road to China 83. Ryder 89.

Hutton, Jim (1934–1979).
American leading man who usually played gangly types.
A Time to Love and a Time to Die 58. Bachelor in Paradise 61. The Horizontal Lieutenant 62. The Honeymoon Machine 62. Period of Adjustment 63. The Hallelujah Trail 65. Never Too Late 65. *Walk Don't Run* 66. Who's Minding the Mint 67. The Green Berets 68. Hellfighters 69, etc.
TV series: Ellery Queen 74.

Hutton, Lauren (1943–) (Mary Hutton).
American leading lady, a former model.
Little Fauss and Big Halsy 71. The Gambler 74. Welcome to L.A. 77. Viva Knievel 77. Someone's Watching Me! (TV) 78. A Wedding 78. American Gigolo 80. Zorro the Gay Blade 81. Paternity 81. Lassiter 83. Once Bitten 85. Flagrant Desire 85. Marathon 87. Malone 87. Forbidden Sun 88. Fear 89. Guilty As Charged 91. Billions/Miliardi 91. Missing Pieces 92. My Father, the Hero 94. A Rat's Tale 98. 54 98, etc.
TV series: The Rhinemann Exchange 77. Paper Dolls 84. Central Park West 95– .

Hutton, Marion (1919–1987) (Marion Thornburg).
American singer, with the Glenn Miller band; appeared in a few 40s musicals. Sister of Betty Hutton.
Orchestra Wives 42. Crazy House 44. In Society 44. Babes on Swing Street 45. Love Happy 50, etc.

Hutton, Robert (1920–1994) (Robert Bruce Winne).
American leading man of the 40s.
Destination Tokyo 44. Janie 44. Too Young To Know 45. Time Out of Mind 47. Always Together 48. The Steel Helmet 51. Casanova's Big Night 54. Invisible Invaders 58. Cinderfella 60. The Slime People (& pd) 62. The Secret Man (GB) 64. Finders Keepers (GB) 66. They Came from Beyond Space (GB) 68. Can Hieronymus Merkin Ever Forget Mercy Humpe and Find True Happiness 68. Cry of the Banshee 70. Trog 70. Tales from the Crypt 72, etc.

Hutton, Timothy (1960–).
Leading young American actor of the early 80s, son of Jim HUTTON. He was married to actress Debra WINGER (1986–89).
Ordinary People (AA) 80. Taps 81. Daniel 83. Iceman 84. The Falcon and the Snowman 85. Turk 182 85. Made in Heaven 87. A Time of Destiny 87. Everybody's All American/When I Fall in Love 88. Torrents of Spring 89. Q & A 90. The Temp 93. The Dark Half 93. French Kiss 95. Beautiful Girls 96. The Substance of Fire 96. Digging to China (d) 97. Playing God 97, etc.

Huxley, Aldous (1894–1963).
Distinguished British novelist who spent some time in Hollywood and worked on the screenplays of *Pride and Prejudice* 40 and *Jane Eyre* 43.
Biography: 1989, *Huxley in Hollywood* by David King Dunaway.

❝ His erudition was staggering. I never discovered how many languages he knew, but one day I found him in his office at MGM reading Persian. – *Anita Loos*

Huyck, Willard.
American screenwriter and director. He began as a reader for AIP.
American Graffiti (co-w only) 73. Lucky Lady (co-w only) 75. Messiah of Evil 75. French Postcards 79. Best Defence 84. Indiana Jones and the Temple of Doom (co-w only) 84. Howard the Duck 86. Radioland Murders (co-w) 94, etc.

Hyams, Leila (1905–1977).
Vivacious, blonde American leading lady of the 20s.
Sandra 24. Summer Bachelors 26. The Brute 27. The Wizard 27. Alias Jimmy Valentine 28. Spite Marriage 29. The Idle Rich 29. The Bishop Murder

Case 30. The Big House 30. The Flirting Widow 30. Men Call It Love 31. The Phantom of Paris 31. Red Headed Woman 32. Freaks 32. Island of Lost Souls 32. Sing Sinner Sing 33. Affairs of a Gentleman 34. Ruggles of Red Gap 35. Yellow Dust 36, many others.

Hyams, Peter (1943–).
American director and cinematographer.
T.R. Baskin (w & p only) 71. The Rolling Man (TV) 72. *Goodnight My Love* (TV) 73. Busting (& w) 74. Our Time (& w) 74. Peeper 76. Telefon (co-w only) 77. Capricorn One (& w) 78. Hanover Street (& w) 79. The Hunter (& w) 80. Outland (& w) 81. The Star Chamber 83. 2010 84. Running Scared 86. The Presidio 88. Narrow Margin 90. Stay Tuned 92. Timecop 94. Sudden Death 95. The Relic 96, etc.

Hyde-White, Wilfrid (1903–1991).
Impeccably British character actor of stage and screen, mainly in comedy roles. Born in Bourton-on-the-Water, Gloucestershire, the son of a canon, he studied acting at RADA and was on stage from 1922. He moved to America in the 60s, at first to appear in *Let's Make Love*, a job that lasted eight months instead of the eight weeks planned because of its star, Marilyn MONROE. Married twice.
Murder by Rope 37. *The Third Man* 49. The Story of Gilbert and Sullivan 54. See How They Run 55. The Adventures of Quentin Durward 56. *North-West Frontier* 59. Carry On Nurse 59. Two-Way Stretch 61. *My Fair Lady* 64. John Goldfarb Please Come Home 64. You Must Be Joking 65. Ten Little Indians 65. The Liquidator 65. Our Man in Marrakesh 66. Chamber of Horrors 66. Skullduggery 69. Gaily Gaily 69. Fragment of Fear 70. A Brand New Life (TV) 73. The Great Houdinis 76. The Cat and the Canary 78. The Rebels (TV) 79. In God We Trust 80. Oh God Book Two 80. Damien: Leper Priest (TV) 80. The Toy 82, etc.
TV series: Peyton Place 67. The Associates 79–80. Buck Rogers in the 25th Century 81.

66 I've owned 12 horses, seven Rolls-Royces, and I've had mistresses in Paris, London and New York – and it never made me happy. – *W.H-W.*

Hyer, Martha (1924–).
American light leading lady of the 50s, in mainly routine films.
The Locket 46. The Woman on the Beach 47. The Velvet Touch 48. The Clay Pigeon 49. The Lawless 50. Salt Lake Raiders 50. Abbott and Costello Go to Mars 52. So Big 53. Riders to the Stars 54. Sabrina 54. Francis in the Navy 55. Red Sundown 56. Battle Hymn 57. Mister Cory 57. My Man Godfrey 57. Paris Holiday 58. Houseboat 58. Some Came Running (AAN) 59. The Best of Everything 59. Ice Palace 60. The Last Time I Saw Archie 61. A Girl Named Tamiko 62. Wives and Lovers 63. The Carpetbaggers 64. The First Men in the Moon 64. The Sons of Katie Elder 65. The Chase 66. The Happening 67. Massacre at Fort Grant 68. Crossplot 69. Once You Kiss a Stranger 70, many others.

Hyland, Diana (1936–1977) (Diana Gentner).
American stage and TV actress. At her death she had just begun to star in the TV series *Eight is Enough*.
One Man's Way 64. The Chase 66. The Boy in the Plastic Bubble (TV) 76.

Hylands, Scott (1943–).
Canadian leading man.
Daddy's Gone A-Hunting 68. Fools 70. Earth II (TV) 71. Earthquake 74. Bittersweet Love 76. The Boys in Company C 77. With This Ring (TV) 78. Winds of Kitty Hawk (TV) 78. Tales of the Klondike: In a Far Country (TV) 81. A Savage Hunger 84. Coming Out Alive 84. Decoy 95. Titanic (TV) 96. The Halfback of Notre Dame (TV) 96, etc.
TV series: Night Heat 85–91.

Hylton, Jack (1892–1965).
British bandleader who appeared in two films: *She Shall Have Music* 35 and *Band Wagon* 40. Born in Bolton, Lancashire, he began his career in music hall at the age of 13, billed as 'The Singing Mill Boy', becoming a bandleader in the 30s and, from the 40s, an impresario.

Hylton, Jane (1926–1979).
British actress, in films after 1945.
When the Bough Breaks 47. Here Come the Huggetts 49. *It Started in Paradise* 52. The Weak and the Wicked 53. House of Mystery 59, many others.

Hylton, Richard (1921–1962).
American actor with stage experience.
Lost Boundaries 48. The Secret of Convict Lake 51. Fixed Bayonets 51. The Pride of St Louis 52, etc.

Hyman, Dick (1927–).
American composer and jazz pianist who has scored three of Woody Allen's films.
Scott Joplin 77. Zelig 83. Broadway Danny Rose 83. Radio Days 87. Leader of the Band 87. Moonstruck 87. Alan & Naomi 92. Everyone Says I Love You 96, etc.

Hyman, Eliot (1905–1980).
American entrepreneur who made a fortune from buying up Hollywood libraries for sale to television, notably Monogram and Warner. Formed Seven Arts, film financers and distributors.

Hyman, Kenneth (1928–).
American executive producer; formerly with Allied Artists and Seven Arts in Britain, now independent. Son of Eliot Hyman.
The Hound of the Baskervilles 59. The Roman Spring of Mrs Stone 61. Gigot 62. The Small World of Sammy Lee 63. The Hill 65. The Dirty Dozen 66, etc.

Hymer, Warren (1906–1948).
American character actor with stage experience; usually seen as dim-witted gangster.
Up the River 30. Charlie Chan Carries On 31. Twenty Thousand Years in Sing Sing 32. Kid Millions 35. San Francisco 36. Tainted Money 37. Destry Rides Again 39. Meet John Doe 41. Baby Face Morgan 42. Joe Palooka Champ 46, many others.

Hyson, Dorothy (1914–1996).
American-born leading lady of the 30s, in Britain. Born in Chicago, the daughter of Dorothy Dickson, she moved to England at the age of eight with her mother and was a noted beauty, on the West End stage from the age of 12. Married actor Robert DOUGLAS (1935–45) and retired soon after her second marriage, to Sir Anthony QUAYLE, in 1947.
Soldiers of the King 33. The Ghoul 33. Turkey Time 33. Sing As We Go 34. A Cup of Kindness 34. Spare a Copper 40, etc.
66 The most beautiful girl in the world. – *Cary Grant*
Without her I could have been nothing, done nothing. – *Sir Anthony Quayle*

Hytner, Nicholas (1957–).
British director, from the theatre, where he has worked for the Royal Shakespeare Company and the Royal National Theatre.
The Madness of King George 94. The Crucible 96. The Object of My Affection (US) 98, etc.

Hytten, Olaf (1888–1955).
Scottish character actor in American films.
It Is The Law 24. The Salvation Hunters 27. Daughter of the Dragon 31. Berkeley Square 33. Becky Sharp 35. The Good Earth 37. The Adventures of Robin Hood 38. Our Neighbours The Carters 40. The Black Swan 42. The Lodger 44. Three Strangers 46. Perils of the Jungle 53, etc.

Ibbetson, Arthur (1922–).
British cinematographer.
The Horse's Mouth 58. The Angry Silence 59. The League of Gentlemen 60. *Tunes of Glory* 61. Whistle Down the Wind 61. The Inspector 62. Nine Hours to Rama 63. I Could Go On Singing 63. The Chalk Garden 64. Sky West and Crooked 65. A Countess from Hong Kong 66. Inspector Clouseau 68. Where Eagles Dare 68. The Walking Stick 69. Anne of the Thousand Days (AAN) 70. The Railway Children 70. Willie Wonka and the Chocolate Factory 71. A Doll's House 73. Frankenstein: The True Story (TV) 73. 11 Harrowhouse 74. It Shouldn't Happen to a Vet 76. A Little Night Music 77. The Medusa Touch 77. The Prisoner of Zenda 79. Hopscotch 80. Little Lord Fauntleroy (TV) 80. Witness for the Prosecution 83. Master of the Game (TV) 83. The Bounty 84. Santa Claus 84.

Ibert, Jacques (1890–1962).
French composer.
The Italian Straw Hat 28. Don Quixote 34. Golgotha 35. La Charrette Fantôme 38. Panique 47. Macbeth 48. Invitation to the Dance 56, etc.

Ibsen, Henrik (1828–1906)
Norwegian dramatist who against great opposition brought social problems to the stage. Works filmed include *A Doll's House*, *An Enemy of the People*.

Ibuse, Masuji (1898–1993).
Distinguished Japanese novelist and short-story writer whose masterpiece *Black Rain/Kuroi Ame* was filmed in 1988 by Shohei Imamura.

Ice Cube (1968–) (O'Shea Jackson).
American rap performer, lyricist and actor. Born in Los Angeles, he trained as an architectural draughtsman before becoming a member of the group NWA (Niggaz With Attitude) and went solo in 1990 with raps notorious for their misogyny and violence.
Boyz N The Hood 91. Trespass 93. The Glass Shield 94. Higher Learning 95. Friday (a, ex p, co-w) 95. Dangerous Ground 96. Anaconda 97. The Players Club (a, wd) 97. I Got the Hook-Up 98, etc.

Ice-T (1959–) (Tracey Marrow).
Controversial American rap performer, lyricist and actor, notorious for his record 'Cop Killer'. Born in New Jersey, he was involved in crime before turning to performing.
Autobiography: 1994, *The Ice Opinion*.
Breakin' 84. Listen Up: The Lives of Quincy Jones 90. New Jack City 91. Ricochet 91. Who's the Man 93. Trespass 93. Surviving the Game 94. Johnny Mnemonic 95. Tank Girl 95. Mean Guns 96. The Deli 97. Body Count 97. Jacob Two Two Meets the Hooded Fang (Can.) 98, etc.
TV series: Players 97– .

❝ Those criminal activities in my youth have got me where I am today, man. That's why people don't fuck with me. They know I'm real. – *I.T.*
America is a vicious killing machine based on rip-offs, lies, cheating and murder . . . The pilgrims were some corrupt mothafuckas. – *I.T.*

Ichikawa, Kon (1915–).
Distinguished Japanese director and screenwriter.
The Heart 54. The Punishment Room 55. *The Burmese Harp* 55. Odd Obsessions 58. *Fires on the Plain* 59. The Sin 61. An Actor's Revenge 63. *Alone on the Pacific* 66. To Love Again 71. The Wanderers 73. I Am a Cat 75. The Inugami Family 76. Matababi 77. Queen Bee 78. The Devil's Island 78. The Phoenix 79. Actress 87. Taketori Monogatari 87. Noh Mask Murders/Tenkawa Densetsu Satsujin Jiken 91. 47 Ronin/Shiju Shichinin No Shikaku 94, etc.

Ichikawa, Raizo (1931-1969).
Brooding Japanese leading actor, sometimes compared to James Dean. He starred as wandering Eurasian samurai Kyoshiro Nemuri in eight films of the 60s.
Tales of the Taira Clan/Shin Heike Monogatari 55. Ambush at Iga Pass/Iga No Suigetsu 58. Conflagration/Flame of Torment/Enjo 58. The Lord and the Gambler/Nuregami Sandogasa 59. Bonchi 60. The Outcast/Hakai 61. Destiny's Son/Kiru 62. The Adventures of Kyoshiro Nemuri, Swordsman/Nemuri Kyoshiro Shobu 62. Band of Assassins/Shinobi No Mono 63. Sword Devil/Ken Ki 65. Nakano Army School/Rikugun Nakano Gakku 66. A Certain Killer/Aru Koroshiya 67. Castle Menagerie/Nemuri Kysoshiro Akujo-gari 69, etc.

Idle, Eric (1943–).
Comic actor and screenwriter, one of the members of Monty Python.
And Now for Something Completely Different 71. Monty Python and the Holy Grail 75. The Rutles (TV) (& d) 78. Monty Python's Life of Brian 79. Monty Python's The Meaning of Life 83. Yellowbeard 83. National Lampoon's European Vacation 85. Transformers – the Movie 86. The Adventures of Baron Munchausen 88. Nuns on the Run 90. Missing Pieces 92. Heirs and Graces 92. Mom and Dad Save the World 92. Splitting Heirs (a, w) 93. Casper 95. The Wind in the Willows 96. An Alan Smithee Film: Burn, Hollywood, Burn 97. Quest for Camelot (voice) 98. Rudolph the Red-Nosed Reindeer: The Movie (voice) 98, etc.

Idziak, Slawomir (1945–).
Polish cinematographer, frequently working with Krzysztof Zanussi and Krzysztof Kiéslowski. He studied at the Lodz Film School.
The Balance Sheet 74. The Scar 76. The Constant Factor/Constans 80. The Contract/Kontrakt 80. Man from a Far Country 81. A Short Film about Killing 88. The Double Life of Veronique 91. Enak (wd) 92. Three Colours: Blue 93. The Journey of August King (US) 95. Gattaca (US) 97, etc.

Ifield, Frank (1937–).
British-born ballad singer who grew up in Australia.
Only film: *Up Jumped a Swagman* 65.

Ifukube, Akira (1914–).
Prolific Japanese composer, best known for scoring many of the Godzilla movies, and for creating the sound of the monster's roar and his footsteps. Born in Hokkaido, he was influenced by Japanese and Ainu folk music and taught at a music school before beginning to work in films. He was usually given less than a week to write his music for a film. His suite *Symphonic Fantasia* features many of the themes from his fantasy films.
The Quiet Duel 49. Children of Hiroshima 52. The Saga of Anatahan 53. Godzilla/Gojira 55. Rodan 56. The Burmese Harp 56. The Mysterians 57. Varan the Unbelievable 58. The Three Treasures 59. Battle in Outer Space 60. King Kong vs Godzilla 63. Godzilla vs Mothra 64. Frankenstein Conquers the World 65. Ghidrah, the Three Headed Monster 66. Return of Giant Majin 67. King Kong Escapes 68. Destroy All Monsters 68. Yog – the Monster from Space 70. Zatoichi Meets Yojimbo 70. Bokyo 75. Terror of Mechagodzilla 75. Love and Faith: Lady Ogin 79. Godzilla vs King Gidrah 91. Godzilla vs Mothra 92. Godzilla vs Mechagodzilla 93. Godzilla vs Destroyer 95, many others.

Ihnat, Steve (1934–1972).
Czech-born general-purpose actor in Hollywood, mostly in TV. Died of a heart attack.
The Chase 66. Countdown 67. The Hour of the Gun 67. Kona Coast 68. Madigan 69. Fuzz 72. *The Honkers* (wd only) 72, etc.

Ihnen, Wiard (1897–1979).
American art director, a former architect. In films from 1919, co-founding a short-lived production company in the late 20s, then at Paramount 1928–34, moving to Twentieth Century-Fox until the mid-40s. Married costume designer Edith Head.
Blonde Venus 32. Madame Butterfly 32. Duck Soup 33. Cradle Song 33. The Trumpet Blows 34. Becky Sharp 35. Go West Young Man 36. Every Day's a Holiday (AAN) 37. Hollywood Cavalcade 39. Jane Eyre 44. Wilson (AA) 44. Along Came Jones 45. Blood on the Sun (AA) 45. The Time of Your Life 48. I the Jury 53, etc.

Ikebe, Shinchiro.
Japanese composer.
Kagemusha 80. The Ballad of Narayama 83. Zegen 87. Akira Kurosawa's Dreams 90, etc.

Iles, Francis (1893–1970).
British crime novelist who also wrote as Anthony Berkeley. *Before the Fact* formed the basis for Hitchcock's *Suspicion; Malice Aforethought* was filmed for television with Hywel Bennett.

Illing, Peter (1899–1966).
Austrian-born character actor, in British films since the 40s.
The End of the River 46. Eureka Stockade 48. I'll Get You for This 51. The Young Lovers 54. Zarak 56. Whirlpool 59. Sands of the Desert 60. The Twenty-fifth Hour 66, many others.

Image, Jean (1911–1989).
French animator, best known abroad for his cartoon feature *Johnny Lionheart/Jeannot l'Intrépide* 50.

Imai, Tadashi (1912–1991).
Japanese director, a controversial figure for his attacks on social injustice from a communist viewpoint. The son of a priest, he began as a screenwriter in 1934 and became a director in 1939; his best films were made in the 50s and 60s.
The Blue Mountains/Aoi Sanmyaku 49. Till We Meet Again/Mata au hi Made 50. And Yet We Live/Dokkoi Ikiteru 51. Troubled Waters/Nigorie 53. Monument of Star Lilies/Himeyuri no To 53. Darkness at Noon/Mahiru no Ankoku 56. Rice/Kome 57. Yoru no Tsuzumi/Night Drum 58. Kiku to Isamu 59. The Old Women's Paradise/Nippon no Obachan 62. Bushido: Samurai Saga/Bushido Zankoku Monogatari 63. A Story from Echigo/Echigo Tsutsuishi Oyashiraczu 64. A Woman Called En/En to iu Onna 71. The Life of a Communist Writer/Takiji Kobayashi 74. His Younger Sister/Ani Imoto 77. War and Youth/Senso to Seishun 91, etc.

Imamura, Shohei (1926–).
Japanese director, a former assistant to Ozu. He began as an amateur actor and playwright. During the 70s he worked mainly in television. In the 80s he founded his own film school, the Japan Academy of Visual Arts (Nihon Eiga Gakko) in Tokyo.
Stolen Desire/Nusumareta Yokubo 58. Endless Desire/Hateshi Naki Yokubo 58. Pigs and Battleships/Buta to Gunkan 61. The Insect Woman/Nippon Konchuki 63. The Pornographers/Jinruigaku Nyumon 66. The Profound Desire of the Gods/Kamigami no Fukaki Yokubo 68. Vengeance Is Mine/Fukushu Suru wa Ware ni Ari 79. The Ballad of Narayama/Narayamabushi 83. Zegen 87. Black Rain 89. Kanzo Sensei 98, etc.

Imi, Tony (1937–).
British cinematographer.
The Raging Moon 69. Dulcima 70. The Slipper and the Rose 76. International Velvet 78. Brass Target 78. The Sea Wolves 80. Inside the Third Reich (TV) 82. Little Gloria . . . Happy at Last (TV) 82. Night Crossing 82. Nate and Hayes 83. Princess Daisy (TV) 83. Sakharov (TV) 84. A Christmas Carol (TV) 84. Reunion at Fairborough (TV) 85. Oceans of Fire 85. Enemy Mine 85. Not Quite Paradise 85. Queenie (TV) 87. Empire State 87. Buster 88. Wired 89. Options 89. Firebirds 90. Fourth Story (TV) 91. Shopping 94, etc.

Imrie, Celia (1952–).
British character actress. Born in Guildford, Surrey, she began on stage and is much on television.
House of Whipcord 74. Death on the Nile 78. The Wicked Lady 83. Highlander 86. Oranges Are Not the Only Fruit (TV) 90. Blue Black Permanent 92. Dark-Adapted Eye (TV) 94. Mary Shelley's Frankenstein 94. In the Bleak Midwinter/A Midwinter's Tale 95. Black Hearts in Battersea (TV) 96. Hilary and Jackie 98, etc.
TV series: Victoria Wood – As Seen on TV 85–86. Victoria Wood 89. Snakes and Ladders 89. The Riff Raff Element 93–94. Dinnerladies 98– .

Inagaki, Hiroshi (1905–1980).
Japanese director and screenwriter, a former actor, in films from the 1910s. He began as an assistant director and made his first film in 1928. His best-known work celebrates the way of the samurai, often starring Toshiro Mifune.
Peace on Earth 28. Travels under the Blue Sky/Tabi Wa Aozora 32. Miyamoto Musashi 40. The Last Days of Edo/Edo Saigo No Hi 41. Sword for Hire/Sengoku Burai 52. *Samurai* (a trilogy: Miyamoto Musashi (AA); Ichijoji No Ketto; Ketto Ganryujima) 54–55. The Rickshaw Man/Muhomatsu No Isso 58. Forty-Seven Ronin/Chushingura 62. Whirlwind/Dai Tatsumaki 64. Kojiro 67. Samurai Banners/Furin Kazan 69. The Ambush 70, etc.

Ince, John (1887–1947).
American lead in silent films and a supporting actor in the 30s and 40s. On stage as a child, he was in films from 1913. The brother of Thomas and Ralph Ince, he also directed and produced some silent movies.
The Price of Victory (& d) 13. The House of Fear (& d) 14. The Urchin (d) 15. The Planter (& d) 17. Madame Sphinx 18. Old Lady 31 (d) 20. Hate 22. If Marriage Fails (d) 25. The Great Jewel Robbery (p, d) 26. Moby Dick 30. Passport to Paradise 32. Texas Terror 35. Way out West 36. Mr Smith Goes to Washington 39. Pride of the Yankees 42. Wilson 44. The Best Years of Our Lives 46. The Paradine Case 48, etc.

Ince, Ralph (1881–1937).
American leading man of the 20s who rather oddly ended his career in Britain directing quota quickies. He was killed in a car crash.
AS ACTOR: One Flag at Last 11. The Lady of the Lake 12. The Land of Opportunity 20. The Sea Wolf 25. Bigger than Barnum's 26. Wall Street 29. Little Caesar 30. The Big Gamble 31. The Hatchet Man 32. The Tenderfoot 32. Havana Widows 33, etc.
AS DIRECTOR: A Man's Home 21. Homeward

Bound 23. A Moral Sinner 24. Smooth as Satin 25. Bigger than Barnum's 26. South Sea Love 28. Lucky Devils 33. What's in a Name? 34. Murder at Monte Carlo 34. Blue Smoke 35. It's You I Want 35. Hail and Farewell 36. The Vulture 36. The Man Who Made Diamonds 37, many others.

Ince, Thomas (1882–1924).
American director, a contemporary of D. W. Griffith and some say an equal innovator. On stage from the age of six, he began in films as an actor before becoming a director with Carl Laemmle's company. He systematized production methods, built his own studio and provided films of a high quality. Died suddenly at the end of a weekend aboard William Randolph Hearst's yacht, officially of a heart attack brought on by acute indigestion. There were rumours that he had been shot by Hearst, who suspected that Ince had seduced his mistress Marion Davies, that he died accidentally, hit by a shot intended for Charlie Chaplin, and that Louella Parsons owed her position as a columnist for Hearst's papers to not revealing the truth about the incident. He was the brother of John and Ralph INCE. Best remembered now for *Custer's Last Fight* 12. *Civilization* 15. *Human Wreckage* 23.

Inescort, Frieda (1900–1976) (Frieda Wightman).
Scottish-born actress of well bred roles, once secretary to Lady Astor; on stage from 1922. Went to Hollywood to begin film career.
If You Could Only Cook 35. Call it a Day 37. Beauty for the Asking 38. Woman Doctor 39. Pride and Prejudice 40. The Amazing Mrs Holliday 43. The Return of the Vampire 43. The Judge Steps Out 47. Foxfire 55. The Crowded Sky 60, etc.

Inge, William (1913–1973).
American playwright, most of whose work has been translated to the screen. Born in Independence, Kansas, and educated at the University of Kansas, he worked as a teacher, actor and drama critic before turning to writing in the late 40s. His early successes were followed in the late 50s and 60s by failures; a depressive and an alcoholic, he killed himself.
Biography: 1965, *William Inge* by Robert B. Shuman.
Come Back Little Sheba 52. Picnic 56. Bus Stop 56. The Dark at the Top of the Stairs 60. Splendor in the Grass (w) 61. The Stripper 63. Good Luck Miss Wycoff 79, etc.

Ingels, Marty (1936–).
American character comedian. He has been married to actress Shirley Jones since 1977.
Ladies' Man 60. Armored Command 61. The Horizontal Lieutenant 62. Wild and Wonderful 64. The Busy Body 67. For Singles Only 68. How to Seduce a Woman 74. Instant Karma 90. Round Numbers 92, etc.
TV series: *I'm Dickens He's Fenster* 62.

Ingham, Barrie (1934–).
British light leading man and general-purpose actor.
Tiara Tahiti 62. Invasion 66. Dr Who and the Daleks 66. A Challenge for Robin Hood (title role) 68. The Day of the Jackal 73. The Great Mouse Detective (voice) 86. Josh Kirby Timewarrior: Chapter 3, Trapped on Toyworld 95. Josh Kirby Timewarrior: Chapter 4, Eggs from 70 Million BC 95, etc.

Ingraham, Lloyd (1875–1956).
American director, screenwriter and leading actor of silent films, from 1912, who became a character actor in the sound era.
Aurora of the North (a) 14. The Missing Link (d) 15. Intolerance (a) 16. The Little Liar (d) 16. Wives and Other Wives (d) 18. The Girl in the Taxi 20. At the Sign of the Jack O'Lantern (wd) 21. A Front Page Story (a) 22. Going Up 23. Midnight Molly 25. Silver Comes Through (wd) 27. Jesse James (d) 27. Kit Carson (co-d) 28. Take the Heir (d) 30. Texas Gunfighter (a) 32. Sons of Steel (a) 35. Destry Rides Again (a) 39. Adventures of Red Ryder (a) (serial) 40. Never Give a Sucker an Even Break (a) 41. Blazing Guns (a) 43. Sudan (a) 45. Sister Kenny (a) 46. The Savage Horde (a) 50, etc.

Ingram, Jack (1902–1969).
American character actor, often as a villain in 'B' westerns and in more than 30 serials for Columbia. Born in Chicago, he studied law at the University of Texas, and began in a minstrel show. In the 40s and 50s, he ran a ranch used for movie and television locations, including many Roy ROGERS movies and episodes of the TV series *The Lone Ranger*, and later owned a yacht used for the TV series *Sea Hunt*. Died of a heart attack.
Rebellion 36. Whistling Bullets 36. Zorro Rides Again (serial) 37. Dick Tracy Returns (serial) 38. Outlaws of Sonora 38. Tumbleweeds 39. Terry and the Pirates (serial) 40. Young Bill Hickock 40. King of the Texas Rangers (serial) 41. The Lone Rider Ambushed 41. Billy the Kid Trapped 42. Lone Star Trail 43. Range Law 44. Devil Riders 45. Chick Carter, Detective (serial) 46. Ghost Town Renegades 47. Superman (serial) 48. Congo Bill (serial) 48. Whirlwind Riders 48. Son of a Badman 49. Bandit Queen 50. Fort Dodge Stampede 51. Fargo 52. Lost in Alaska 52. Cow Country 53. Five Guns West 55. Zorro Rides Again 59, many others.

Ingram, Rex (1892–1950) (Reginald Hitchcock).
Irishman who went to Hollywood and became first an actor and screenwriter, then a noted director of silent spectaculars. Married to Alice Terry.
Biography: 1980, *Rex Ingram* by Liam O'Leary.
AS ACTOR: The Great Problem 16. Reward of the Faithless 17. Under Crimson Skies 19. Trifling Women 22, etc.
AS DIRECTOR: *The Four Horsemen of the Apocalypse* 21. The Conquering Power 21. *The Prisoner of Zenda* 22. Where the Pavement Ends 23. *Scaramouche* 23. The Arab 24. *Mare Nostrum* 26. The Magician 26. The Garden of Allah 27. Baroud 31. Love in Morocco 33, etc.

Ingram, Rex (1895–1969).
Impressive actor, in films from 1929; former doctor.
■ Hearts in Dixie 29. The Sign of the Cross 32. King Kong 33. The Emperor Jones 33. Harlem After Midnight 34. Captain Blood 35. *The Green Pastures* (as De Lawd) 36. *Huckleberry Finn* 39. *The Thief of Bagdad* 40. The Talk of the Town 42. Sahara 43. Cabin in the Sky 43. Fired Wife 43. Dark Waters 44. A Thousand and One Nights 45. Moonrise 48. King Solomon's Mines 50. Tarzan's Hidden Jungle 55. The Ten Commandments 56. Congo Crossing 56. Hell on Devil's Island 57. God's Little Acre 58. Anna Lucasta 59. Escort West 59. Watusi 59. Desire in the Dust 60. Elmer Gantry 60. Your Cheating Heart 64. Hurry Sundown 67. Journey to Shiloh 67.

Ingster, Boris (c. 1913–).
American writer-director.
The Last Days of Pompeii (co-w) 35. Happy Landing (w) 38. Stranger on the Third Floor (d) 40. Paris Underground (w) 45. The Judge Steps Out (wd) 49. Forgery (d) 50. Something for the Birds (co-w) 52. Abdulla the Great (co-w) 54. The Karate Killers (p) 67, etc.

Innes, Hammond (1913–1998).
English thriller writer, a former journalist.
Snowbound (oa) 48. Hell below Zero (oa) 53. Campbell's Kingdom (oa) 57. The Wreck of the Mary Deare (oa) 59, etc.

Ireland, Jill (1936–1990).
British leading lady of the 50s. She married David McCallum and, in 1968, Charles Bronson. She wrote *Life Wish*, detailing her battle against cancer, in 1987, and a further volume of autobiography: 1989, *Life Lines*.
Oh Rosalinda 55. Three Men in a Boat 55. Hell Drivers 57. Robbery under Arms 57. Carry On Nurse 59. Raising the Wind 61. Twice Round the Daffodils 62. Villa Rides (US) 68. Rider on the Rain (US) 70. The Mechanic (US) 72. Wild Horses (US) 73. The Valachi Papers (It.) 73. The Streetfighter 75. Breakheart Pass (US) 76. From Noon Till Three (US) 76. Death Wish II 82. Assassination 86, etc.
TV series: Shane 66.
❝ I'm in so many Charles Bronson films because no other actress will work with him. – *J.I.*

Ireland, John (1879–1962).
British composer whose only film score was *The Overlanders* (47).

Ireland, John (1914–1992).
Canadian leading man in Hollywood; a popular tough-cynical hero of the early 50s, he declined with unaccountable rapidity to bit parts and second features.
A Walk in the Sun 45. Behind Green Lights 46. The Gangster 47. Raw Deal 48. Red River 48. I Shot Jesse James 49. Anna Lucasta 49. The Doolins of Oklahoma 49. *All the King's Men* (AAN) 49. Cargo to Capetown 50. The Scarf 51. Red Mountain 51. Hurricane Smith 52. Outlaw Territory 53. Security Risk 54. *The Good Die Young* (GB) 54. Queen Bee 55. Gunfight at the OK Corral 57. Party Girl 58. No Place to Land 59. Spartacus 60. Brushfire 62. The Ceremony 63. The Fall of the Roman Empire 64. I Saw What You Did 65. Fort Utah 67. Caxambu 67. Arizona Bushwackers 68. One on Top of the Other 70. The House of the Seven Corpses 73. Welcome to Arrow Beach 75. The Swiss Conspiracy 76. Love and the Midnight Auto Supply 77. Madam Kitty 77. The Shape of Things to Come 79. Guyana 80. The Incubus 82, many others.
TV series: The Protectors 61.

Irene (1901–1962) (Irene Lenz-Gibbons).
American costume designer. Born in Brookings, South Dakota, she worked as an extra in Hollywood in the mid-20s before studying fashion design and opening her own dress shop on the UCLA campus. She was an established designer by the mid-30s, joining MGM in 1942, where she stayed, and later regretted it, for seven years before designing for a chain of boutiques, as well as creating clothes for many stars. Personal problems, allied to heavy drinking, led her to commit suicide.
The Animal Kingdom 32. Flying down to Rio 33. Mrs Parkington 44. Weekend at the Waldorf 45. The Postman Always Rings Twice 46. State of the Union 48. B.F.'s Daughter (AAN) 48. Key to the City 50. Midnight Lace (AAN) 60. A Gathering of Eagles 63, etc.
❝ So quiet she was – and expensive, Miss Don't-Melt-Ice-Cube. – *L. B. Mayer*

Iribé, Paul.
Paris fashion designer and artist who was brought to Hollywood by De Mille to create the costumes for Gloria Swanson in *Male and Female* 19 and went on to design several other of De Mille's films.
The Affairs of Anatol 20. The Ten Commandments 23. The Road to Yesterday 25. Madam Satan 30.

Irons, Jeremy (1948–).
British leading man of the introspective type. Married actress Sinead CUSACK.
Nijinsky 80. *The French Lieutenant's Woman* 81. *Brideshead Revisited* (TV) 81. Moonlighting 82. The Captain's Doll (TV) 82. Betrayal 82. The Wild Duck 83. Swann in Love 84. The Mission 85. Dead Ringers 88. Australia 89. A Chorus of Disapproval 89. Reversal of Fortune (AA) 90. Kafka 91. Damage 92. Waterland 92. M. Butterfly 93. The House of the Spirits 94. *The Lion King* (voice) 94. Die Hard with a Vengeance 95. Stealing Beauty 96. Lolita 97. Chinese Box 97. The Man in the Iron Mask 98, etc.
❝ Actors often behave like children and so we're taken for children. I want to be grown-up. – *J.I.*
One of the things we have to do as artists is to stir things up. There is too little debate in our society. – *J.I.*
I have always believed that the afterlife is what you leave behind in other people. – *J.I.*

Ironside, Michael (1950–).
Canadian leading actor, in American movies from the mid-80s. Born in Toronto, he studied at the Ontario College of Art.
Scanners 80. Visiting Hours 81. Spacehunter: Adventures in the Forbidden Zone 83. The Falcon and the Snowman 85. Top Gun 86. Jo Jo Dancer, Your Life Is Calling 86. Nowhere to Hide 87. Extreme Prejudice 87. Watchers 88. Mindfield 89. Office Party 89. Total Recall 90. Highlander II – the Quickening 90. Deadly Surveillance 91. McBain 91. Neon City 91. Chaindance (& w, p) 91. Black Ice 92. Night Trap/Mardi Gras for the Devil 93. Forced to Kill 93. Sweet Killing 93. Free Willy 93. Father Hood 93. The Next Karate Kid 94. Red Scorpion 2 94. The Glass Shield 94. Major Payne 95. Kids of the Round Table 95. The Destiny of Marty Fine 96. Starship Troopers 97. Desert Blue 98, etc.
TV series: V 84–85.

Irvin, John (1940–).
British director, from TV.
Tinker Tailor Soldier Spy (TV) 80. The Dogs of War 80. Ghost Story 81. Champions 84. Raw Deal 86. Hamburger Hill 87. Next of Kin 89. Robin Hood 90. Eminent Domain 91. Widow's Peak 94. Freefall 94. A Month by the Lake 95. Crazy Horse (TV) 96. City of Industry 96, etc.

Irving, Amy (1953–).
American leading actress who trained in San Francisco and London. She is the former wife of director Steven SPIELBERG (1985–89) and is now married to director Bruno BARRETO.
Carrie 78. The Fury 79. Voices 79. Honeysuckle Rose 80. The Competition 81. Yentl (AAN) 83. Micki and Maude 84. Rumpelstiltskin 87. Crossing Delancey 88. Who Framed Roger Rabbit (voice) 88. A Show of Force 90. An American Tail: Fievel Goes West (voice) 91. Benefit of the Doubt 93. Kleptomania 93. Carried Away 95. I'm Not Rapaport 96. Deconstructing Harry 97. One Tough Cop 98, etc.

Irving, George (1874–1961).
American character actor, long on the Broadway stage, for some while a film director, and most memorable in middle-aged businessman roles.
The Jungle 14. Madonna of the Streets 24. Wild Horse Mesa 25. Craig's Wife 28. Thunderbolt 29. The Spoilers 30. Island of Lost Souls 32. Dangerous 35. Sutter's Gold 36. The Toast of New York 37. Bringing Up Baby 38. New Moon 40. Son of Dracula 43. Christmas Holiday 44. Magic Town 47, many others.

Irving, Sir Henry (1838–1905) (John Henry Broadribb).
Distinguished English actor-manager of Victorian theatre, the first actor to be knighted. He deserves a footnote to film history as the model for DRACULA, the character created by his secretary and aide Bram STOKER. His son H. B. Irving (1870–1919), who died by drowning, appeared in a few silent films.

Irving, John (1942–).
American novelist and screenwriter.
The World According to Garp (oa) 82. The Hotel New Hampshire (oa) 84. Simon Birch (oa) 98. Cider House Rules (w, oa) 99, etc.

Irving, Laurence (1897–1988).
English art director and artist, the grandson of actor Sir Henry Irving, from the stage. He went to Hollywood in the late 20s to work for Douglas Fairbanks.
The Iron Mask (US) 29. The Taming of the Shrew (US) 29. Diamond Cut Diamond 32. Captain Blood 33. Moonlight Sonata 37. Pygmalion 38, etc.

Irving, Washington (1783–1859).
American humorist and storyteller whose *Rip Van Winkle* and *The Legend of Sleepy Hollow* have been filmed at various times and in various ways.

Irwin, Mark.
Canadian cinematographer.
Starship Invasion 77. Blood and Guts 78. The Brood 79. Scanners 81. Night School 81. Videodrome 83. The Dead Zone 83. Spasms 83. The Protector 85. The Fly 86. Youngblood 86. The Blob 88. Love at Stake 88. I Come in Peace 90. Class of 1999 90. Paint It Black 90. Robocop 2 90. Passenger 57 92. Man's Best Friend 93. Slaughter of the Innocents 93. D2: The Mighty Ducks 94. Dumb and Dumber 94. Wes Craven's New Nightmare 94. The Net 95. Vampire in Brooklyn 95. Robin of Locksley 96. Kingpin 96. Scream 96. Steel 97. Misbegotten 97. Joe Torre: Curveballs along the Way (TV) 97. There's Something about Mary 98, etc.

Irwin, May (1862–1938).
American actress who appeared in one of the very first short films, *The Kiss* 96; her only other film was *Mrs Black Is Back* 14.

Isaak, Chris (1956–).
American singer, songwriter and actor.
Married to the Mob 88. The Silence of the Lambs 91. Twin Peaks: Fire Walk with Me 92. Little Buddha 93, etc.

Isham, Mark (1951–).
American composer and musician. Born in New York, he began by playing trumpet in the Oakland and San Francisco Symphony Orchestras and then joined the rock group Sons of Champlin, and also toured with singer Van Morrison before forming his own band, Group 87, in the late 70s.
Never Cry Wolf 83. Mrs Soffel 84. The Hitcher 86. Made in Heaven 87. The Moderns 88. Everybody Wins 90. Reversal of Fortune 90. Fire in the Sky 93. Short Cuts 93. Nowhere to Run 93. Made in America 93. Romeo Is Bleeding 93. The Getaway 94. Mrs Parker and the Vicious Circle 94. Quiz Show 94. Timecop 94. The Browning Version 94. Miami Rhapsody 95. Losing Isaiah 95. Home for the Holidays 95. Last Dance 96. Gotti (TV) 96. Fly Away Home 96. Kiss the Girls 97. Afterglow 97. Night Falls on Manhattan 97. The Education of Little Tree 97. The Gingerbread Man 98. From the Earth to the Moon (TV) 98. Blade 98, etc.

Isherwood, Christopher (1904–1986).
English novelist and screenwriter, mainly in Hollywood. Born in Cheshire and briefly educated at Cambridge University, he was a member of the group of 30s left-wing writers clustered around poet W. H. Auden. An inveterate cinema-goer, he attempted to find work in British studios and first worked with visiting Hollywood director Berthold VIERTEL, a friendship he resumed after he and Auden moved to America in 1939. He lived in California, where he worked intermittently for Hollywood studios. *Goodbye to Berlin*, his book of stories, was dramatized by John VAN DRUTEN as *I Am a Camera*, which was subsequently filmed and later became the stage and screen musical *Cabaret*.
Autobiographies: 1971, *Kathleen and Frank*; 1976, *Christopher and His Kind*; 1996, *Diaries, Volume One: 1939–1960*, ed. Katherine Bucknell.
Biographies: 1977, *Isherwood* by Jonathan Fryer; 1979, *Christopher Isherwood* by Brian Finney.

Little Friend (co-w) (GB) 34. Rage in Heaven (co-w) 41. Free and Easy (co-w) 41. Forever and a Day (co-w) 43. The Woman in White (uncredited) 48. Adventure in Baltimore (co-w, story) 49. The Great Sinner (co-w) 49. I Am a Camera (oa) (GB) 55. Diane (w) 55. The Wayfarer (w) 57. The Loved One (co-w, a) 65. The Sailor from Gibraltar (co-w) (GB) 67. Cabaret (oa) 72. Frankenstein: The True Story (co-w) (TV) 73. Rich and Famous (a) 81, etc.
66 Screenwriting, to me, is the most absorbing of all games. – C.I.
I don't think that I bring very much to films. I think that films bring a great deal to me. By working in this medium, which is a medium of visualization primarily, I learned a great, great deal, which I could use in my books. I never really saw things before. – C.I.
I seem to have put my bad luck into film-writing and all my good luck into the rest of my life! It would be a bore to complain; but, really, the films I wrote have nearly all ended in disaster, mitigated or unmitigated. – C.I.
A good – because psychologically true – Hollywood story. A maid boasts to her friend – also a maid – about the house she works at: wonderful people – they entertain every night – and always big celebrities, top stars. The friend is thrilled: 'And what do they talk about?' The maid: 'Us.' – C.I.

Ishii, Sogo (1957–).
Japanese director and screenwriter.
Gyakufunsha Kazoku 84. Angel Dust/Tenshi No Kuzu 94. August in the Water 96. Labyrinth of Dreams/Yume No Ginga 97, etc.

Itami, Juzo (1933–1997) (Yoshihiro Ikeuchi).
Japanese director and screenwriter, a former actor. He died in hospital after being found lying injured in the street outside his office, having fallen or jumped from the roof of the eight-floor building.
The Funeral 84. Tampopo 86. A Taxing Woman/Marusa no Onna 88. A Taxing Woman Too 89. The Gangster's Moll/Mimbo no Onna 92. Daibyonin 93. A Quiet Life/Shizukana Seikatsu 95. Supermarket Woman/Supa no Onna 96. Murutai no Onna 97, etc.

Ito, Daisuke (1898–1981).
Japanese director and screenwriter, one of the important early directors, usually of dramas in a period setting.
Jogoshima 24. *A Diary of Chuji's Travels*/Chuji Tabernikki 28. The Swordsman 38. King of Chess/Oosho 48. Lion's Dance 53. The Story of Shunkin/Shunkin Monogatari 54. The Conspirator/Hangyakuji 61. An Actor's Revenge/Yukinojo Henge (co-w only) 63, etc.

Iturbi, José (1895–1980).
Spanish pianist and conductor who made his American concert debut in 1929; in the 40s he appeared in a number of MGM musicals and helped to popularize classical music.
■ Thousands Cheer 43. Two Girls and a Sailor 44. Music for Millions 44. A Song to Remember (dubbed piano for Cornel Wilde; his recording of a Chopin Polonaise sold over one million copies) 44. Anchors Aweigh 45. Holiday in Mexico 46. Three Daring Daughters 48. That Midnight Kiss 49.

Ivan, Rosalind (1884–1959).
American character actress, mainly on stage.
The Suspect 44. The Corn Is Green 45. Three Strangers 46. Ivy 47. The Robe 53. Elephant Walk 54, etc.

Ivano, Paul (1900–1984).
American cinematographer.
The Dancers 25. No Other Woman 28. Atlantic Flight 37. *The Shanghai Gesture* 41. See My Lawyer 44. Spider Woman Strikes Back 46. Champagne for Caesar 50. For Men Only 52. Hold Back Tomorrow 55. Lizzie 57. Chubasco 68, many others, especially second unit shooting.

Ivens, Joris (1898–1989).
Dutch writer-director best known for documentaries.
Autobiography: 1969, *The Camera and I*.
Rain 29. Zuidersee 30. New Earth 34. Spanish Earth 37. The 400 Millions 39. The Power and the Land 40. Song of the Rivers 53. The Threatening Sky 66. Une Histoire de Vent 88, etc.

Ives, Burl (1909–1995) (Burl Icle Ivanhoe).
American actor and ballad-singer, once itinerant worker and professional footballer. His paunchy figure, beard and ready smile are equally adaptable to villainous or sympathetic parts.
Smoky (debut) 46. East of Eden 54. Cat on a Hot Tin Roof 57. Wind Across the Everglades 58. *The Big Country* (AA) 58. Our Man in Havana 59. The Brass Bottle 64. Rocket to the Moon 67. The McMasters 70. The Only Way Out is Dead 70. Baker's Hawk 76. Just You and Me, Kid 79. Earthbound (TV) 81. Uphill All the Way 84. Poor Little Rich Girl (TV) 88. Two Moon Junction 88, etc.
TV series: O.K. Crackerby 65. The Bold Ones 69.

Ivory, James (1928–).
American director who began by making films in India.
Book: 1992, *The Films of Merchant Ivory* by Robert Emmet Long.
■ The Householder 62. *Shakespeare Wallah* 64. The Guru 69. Bombay Talkie 70. Savages (US) 72. The Wild Party (US) 75. Autobiography of a Princess 75. Roseland 77. Hullaballoo over Bonnie and George's Pictures 78. The Europeans 79. Jane Austen in Manhattan 79. Quartet 81. *Heat and Dust* 83. The Bostonians 84. *A Room with a View* (AAN) 86. *Maurice* 87. Slaves of New York 89. Mr & Mrs Bridge 90. *Howards End* 91. The Remains of the Day (AAN) 93. Jefferson in Paris 95. Surviving Picasso 96. A Soldier's Daughter Never Cries 98.

Iwerks, Ub (1900–1971).
American animator, long associated with Disney (he drew the first Mickey Mouse cartoon, *Plane Crazy*). Formed own company in 1930 to create Flip the Frog; went back to Disney 1940 as director of technical research. AA 1959 for improvements in optical printing, 1965 for advancing techniques of travelling matte. Iwerks did much of the complex trick-work for Hitchcock's *The Birds* (AAN).

Izzard, Eddie.
English stand-up comedian and actor.
Joseph Conrad's Secret Agent 96. Lust for Glorious (& p, w) (TV) 97. The Avengers 98. Velvet Goldmine 98, etc.

Jabor, Arnaldo (1940-).
Brazilian director, dramatist, poet and journalist.
Pindorama 70. Toda Nudez Será Castigada 72.
Tudo Bem 78. I Love You/Eu Te Amo 81. Love
Me for Ever or Never/Eu Sei Que Vou Te Amar
86, etc.

Jackley, Nat (1909-1988).
Skinny, lisping-voiced, rubber-necked English
comedian in occasional films. He began as a clog
dancer with the Eight Lancashire Lads, an act that
had earlier included Charlie Chaplin, and was the
son of comedian George Jackley.
Demobbed 44. Stars in Your Eyes 57. Magical
Mystery Tour 67. Mrs Brown, You've Got a Lovely
Daughter 68. Yanks 79. The Ploughman's Lunch
83, etc.

Jacks, Robert L. (1922-1987).
American producer, long with Fox.
Man on a Tightrope 53. White Feather 55. A
Kiss Before Dying 56. Bandido 57. Roots of
Heaven 59. Man in the Middle 64. Zorba the Greek
65. Bandolero 68, many others.

Jackson, Anne (1926-).
American actress, wife of Eli Wallach; films rare.
■ So Young So Bad 50. The Journey 58. Tall Story
60. The Tiger Makes Out 67. How to Save a
Marriage 67. The Secret Life of an American Wife
68. Lovers and Other Strangers 70. Zigzag 70.
Dirty Dingus Magee 70. The Angel Levine 70.
Nasty Habits 76. The Bell Jar 79. The Shining
80. A Woman Called Golda (TV) 82. The Family
Man 82. Blinded by the Light (TV) 82. Leave 'em
Laughing (TV) 82. Sam's Son 84. Funny about
Love 90. Folks! 92.

Jackson, Freda (1909-1990).
British character actress with a penchant for
melodrama; on stage from 1934, films from 1942.
A Canterbury Tale 44. Henry V 44. Beware of
Pity 46. Great Expectations 46. No Room at the Inn
47. Women of Twilight 49. The Crowded Day 53.
Brides of Dracula 60. The Third Secret 64.
Monster of Terror 65, etc.

Jackson, Glenda (1936-).
British star actress. She announced her retirement
from acting after being elected Labour MP for
Hampstead and Highgate at the 1992 British
general election.
■ This Sporting Life 63. The Marat/Sade 66. Tell
Me Lies 67. Negatives 68. Women in Love (AA) 69.
The Music Lovers 70. Sunday Bloody Sunday
(AAN) 71. The Boy Friend (uncredited) 71. Mary
Queen of Scots (as Queen Elizabeth) 71. A Touch
of Class (AA) 72. The Triple Echo 72. A Bequest
to the Nation 73. The Maids 74. The Tempter 74.
The Romantic Englishwoman 75. Hedda (AAN)
76. The Incredible Sarah 76. Nasty Habits 76.
House Calls 77. The Class of Miss MacMichael
78. Stevie 78. Lost and Found 79. Health 80.
Hopscotch 80. The Patricia Neal Story (TV) 81.
Return of the Soldier 82. Giro City (TV) 83.
Sakharov (TV) 84. Turtle Diary 85. Business as
Usual 88. Salome's Last Dance 88. The Rainbow
89. Doombeach 90.
TV series: Elizabeth R 71.
66 I had no real ambition about acting, but I knew
there had to be something better than the bloody
chemist's shop. – G.J.
She's an absolute dreamboat, the epitome of
professionalism, a splendid actress, and she has all
the make-up of a fully rounded person. – Walter
Matthau
If she went into politics she'd be prime minister;
if she went into crime she'd be Jack the Ripper.
– Roy Hodge (her former husband)

Jackson, Gordon (1923-1990).
Scottish actor whose rueful expression got him
typecast as a weakling; maturity brought more
interesting roles. He was best known for playing
Hudson, the butler (a character he detested), in the
TV series Upstairs, Downstairs. Born in Glasgow,
he began as a draughtsman and apprentice
engineer, and was on stage from the early 40s.
The Foreman Went to France (debut) 42.
Millions Like Us 43. Nine Men 43. San Demetrio,
London 44. Pink String and Sealing Wax 45. The
Captive Heart 46. Against the Wind 47. Eureka
Stockade 48. Whisky Galore 48. The Lady with a
Lamp 51. Meet Mr Lucifer 54. Pacific Destiny 56.
Tunes of Glory 60. The Great Escape (US) 62. The
Ipcress File 65. Cast a Giant Shadow (US) 66. The
Fighting Prince of Donegal 66. The Prime of Miss
Jean Brodie 69. Run Wild Run Free 69. Kidnapped
72. Russian Roulette 75. Spectre (TV) 77. The
Medusa Touch 77. The Last Giraffe (TV) 79. A
Town Like Alice (TV) 80. The Shooting Party 84.
The Masks of Death 85. The Whistle Blower 86.
My Brother Tom (TV) 86. Beyond Therapy 87.
The Lady and the Highwayman (TV) 89, many
others.
TV series: Upstairs Downstairs 70–75. The
Professionals 77–81.

Jackson, Janet (1966-).
American actress and singer, the sister of Michael
Jackson, on stage with her family from the age of
six.
Poetic Justice 93.
TV series: The Jacksons 76–77. Good Times 77–
79. A New Kind of Family 79–80. Diff 'rent Strokes
81–82. Fame 84–85.

Jackson, Kate (1948-).
American leading lady.
The Seven Minutes 70. Night of Dark Shadows
71. Limbo 72. Satan's School for Girls (TV) 73.
Killer Bees (TV) 74. Death Cruise (TV) 74. Death
Scream (TV) 75. Death at Love House (TV) 76.
James at 15 (TV) 77. Thunder and Lightning 77.
Topper (TV) 79. Jacqueline Bouvier Kennedy (TV)
81. Thin Ice (TV) 81. Dirty Tricks 81. Making
Love 82. Listen to Your Heart (TV) 83. Rage of
Angels (TV) 83. Loverboy 89. Adrift (TV) 93.
Sweet Deception 99, etc.
TV series: Dark Shadows 67–71. The Rookies
71–74. Charlie's Angels 76–80. Scarecrow and Mrs
King 83–87.

Jackson, Mary Ann (1923-).
American child actress, in the Our Gang comedies
of the late 20s and early 30s.

Jackson, Michael (1958-).
Precocious American rock singer and songwriter,
first as a member of the Jackson Five and then as a
solo artist. Rich and reclusive, he has spent a
fortune re-making his appearance with the aid of
plastic surgeons. Promotional videos of his songs
directed by, among others, John Landis and John
Singleton have cost more than many feature films.
In 1994, he married Elvis Presley's daughter, Lisa
Marie Presley.
Biography: 1994, Michael Jackson Unauthorized by
Christopher Andersen.
Save the Children (concert) 73. The Wiz 78.
Moonwalker 88.

Jackson, Mick (1943-).
British director, from television, now working in
Hollywood.
Threads (TV) 85. Yuri Nosenk, KGB (TV) 86.
A Very British Coup (TV) 88. Chattahoochee
90. L.A. Story 91. The Bodyguard 92. Clean Slate

94. Indictment: The McMartin Trial (TV) 95.
Volcano 97, etc.

Jackson, Pat (1916-).
British director, a war documentarist whose later
output has been disappointing.
Ferry Pilot 41. Western Approaches 44. The
Shadow on the Wall (US) 48. White Corridors 50.
Something Money Can't Buy 52. The Feminine
Touch 55. Virgin Island 58. Snowball 60. What a
Carve Up 62. Seven Keys 62. Don't Talk to Strange
Men 62. Seventy Deadly Pills 64. Dead End Creek
65. On the Run 69, etc.

Jackson, Peter (1961-).
New Zealand director, screenwriter and producer
whose low-budget visceral horror films have
achieved cult status. In 1996 he was paid $6.5m
plus bonuses to produce, write and direct a remake
of King Kong.
Bad Taste 87. Meet the Feebles 89. Braindead
92. Heavenly Creatures 94. Forgotten Silver (a, co-
w, co-d) 96. The Frighteners (co-p, co-w, d) 96,
etc.

Jackson, Samuel L. (1948-).
Prolific American actor, from the stage. Born in
Chattanooga, Tennessee, he studied drama at
Morehouse College and began his career with the
Negro Ensemble Company and at the New York
Shakespeare Festival. Current asking price: around
$5m a movie.
Ragtime 81. School Daze 88. Sea of Love 89. Do
the Right Thing 89. GoodFellas 90. Jungle Fever
91. White Sands 92. Patriot Games 92. Juice 92.
Amos & Andrew 93. National Lampoon's Loaded
Weapon 1 93. Menace II Society 93. Jurassic Park
93. Against the Wall (TV) 94. Fresh 94. Pulp Fiction
(AAN) 94. The New Age 94. Die Hard with a
Vengeance 95. Losing Isaiah 95. Kiss of Death 95.
Sydney 96. The Great White Hype 96. A Time to
Kill 96. The Search for One-Eyed Jimmy (made
93) 96. The Long Kiss Goodnight 96. Hard Eight
96. Sphere 97. 187 97. Jackie Brown 97. Eve's Bayou
97. The Negotiator 98. The Red Violin 98. Star
Wars: The Phantom Menace 99, etc.

Jackson, Selmer (1888-1971).
American character actor who played hundreds of
unobtrusive fathers, doctors, scientists and
executives.
Dirigible 31. Doctor X 32. The Witching Hour
34. Front Page Woman 35. The Westland Case
37. Stand Up and Fight 39. The Grapes of Wrath
40. It Started with Eve 41. It Ain't Hay 43. The
Sullivans 44. The French Key 46. Mighty Joe
Young 49. Elopement 51. Autumn Leaves 56. The
Gallant Hours 60, many others.
~In 1940 alone Jackson appeared in 20 films.

Jackson, Thomas E. (1886-1967).
American character actor often seen as police
officer.
Little Caesar 30. Doctor X 32. Terror Aboard 33.
The Mystery of the Wax Museum 33. Call of the
Wild 35. Hollywood Boulevard 36. The Westland
Case 37. Torchy Gets Her Man 38. Golden
Gloves 40. Law of the Tropics 41. The Woman in
the Window 44. The Big Sleep 46. Dead Reckoning
47. Stars and Stripes Forever 52. Attack of the
Fifty Foot Woman 58. Synanon 65, many others.

Jacob, Irène (1966-).
Swiss actress in French and international films.
Born in Geneva, she moved to live in Paris in
the mid-80s.
Au Revoir les Enfants 87. La Bande des Quatre
89. The Double Life of Veronique 91. Claude 92. La
Passion Van Gogh 93. The Secret Garden 93.

Three Colours: Red/Trois Couleurs: Rouge 94. La
Prédiction 94. Le Moulin de Daudet 94. Beyond
the Clouds 95. Runaways 95. Othello (as
Desdemona) 95. Incognito 97. Victory 98.
American Cuisine/Cuisine Américaine 98, etc.

Jacobi, Sir Derek (1938-).
British classical actor, in occasional films. A
member of the National Youth Theatre, he made
his professional debut in 1961, and acted with both
the National Theatre and the Royal Shakespeare
Company. He played the title role in the TV
adaptation of Robert Graves's I, Claudius and also
the medieval detective in the mid-90s TV series
Cadfael.
The Day of the Jackal 73. Blue Blood 74. The
Odessa File 74. Philby, Burgess and Maclean (TV)
77. The Medusa Touch 77. The Human Factor 79.
The Hunchback of Notre Dame (TV) (as Frollo)
82. Inside the Third Reich (TV) (as Hitler) 82.
Enigma 82. Mr Pye (TV) 86. Little Dorrit 87.
Henry V 89. The Fool 90. Dead Again 91. The
Vision Thing (TV) 93. Hamlet 96. Breaking the
Code (TV) 97. Love Is the Devil 98. Molokai 98,
etc.

Jacobi, Lou (1913-).
Chubby Canadian character actor.
Song without End 60. Irma la Douce 62.
Everything you Always Wanted to Know about
Sex 72. Roseland 77. Arthur 81. The Lucky Star
81. My Favorite Year 82. The Boss's Wife 86.
Amazon Women on the Moon 87. Avalon 90. I.Q.
94, etc.
TV series: Ivan the Terrible 76. Melba 86.

Jacobs, Arthur P. (1918-1973).
American independent producer, former publicist.
■ What a Way to Go 64. Dr Dolittle (AAN) 67.
Planet of the Apes 68. The Chairman 69. Goodbye
Mr Chips 69. Beneath the Planet of the Apes 69.
Escape from the Planet of the Apes 71. Conquest
of the Planet of the Apes 72. Tom Sawyer 73.
Huckleberry Finn 73.

Jacobs, W. W. (1863-1943).
British short story writer: The Monkey's Paw has
been filmed many times.

Jacobsson, Ulla (1929-1982).
Leading Swedish actress.
One Summer of Happiness 51. Smiles of a
Summer Night 55. Love is a Ball 63. Zulu 64. The
Heroes of Telemark 65, etc.

Jacoby, Scott (1956-).
American juvenile lead.
Baxter 72. Rivals 73. Love and the Midnight
Auto Supply 77. The Little Girl Who Lives Down
the Lane 77. Our Winning Season 78. To Die For
89. To Die For II 91, etc.

Jacques, Hattie (1924-1980).
Oversized British comedienne, well known at the
Players' Theatre and on TV. In most of the 'Carry
On' films. Married John Le Mesurier.
Nicholas Nickleby 47. Oliver Twist 48. Trottie
True 49. The Pickwick Papers 52. Make Mine
Mink 61. In the Doghouse 62. The Bobo 67.
Crooks and Coronets 69, etc.

Jaeckel, Richard (1926-1997).
American actor, former Fox mail-boy, who made
a name playing frightened youths in war films.
Guadalcanal Diary 43. Jungle Patrol 48. Sands
of Iwo Jima 49. The Gunfighter 50. Come Back
Little Sheba 52. The Violent Men 55. Attack! 55.
3.10 to Yuma 57. The Gallant Hours 60. Town
without Pity 61. Four for Texas 63. Town Tamer

65. The Dirty Dozen 67. The Devil's Brigade 68. The Green Slime 69. Chisum 70. Sometimes a Great Notion (AAN) 71. Chosen Survivors 74. Grizzly 76. Day of the Animals 77. *The Dark* 79. Herbie Goes Bananas 80. All the Marbles 81. The Awakening of Candra (TV) 81. The Fix 84. Starman 84. Pacific Inferno (TV) 85. Black Moon Rising 86. Ghetto Blaster 89. Delta Force II 90. King of the Kickboxers 91. Martial Outlaw 93, etc.

TV series: Frontier Circus 61. Banyon 70. Firehouse 74. Salvage 77. At Ease 83. Spenser: for Hire 85–87. Baywatch 91–92.

Jaeckin, Just (1940–).
French director and screenwriter of erotic movies that promise more than they deliver.

Emmanuelle 74. The Story of O 75. Madame Claude 79. The Last Romantic Lover/Le Dernier Amant Romantique 80. Lady Chatterley's Lover 82. The Perils of Gwendoline 84, etc.

Jaeger, Frederick (1928–).
Anglo-German general-purpose actor.

The Black Tent 56. I Was Monty's Double 59. The Looking Glass War 69. Scorpio 72. The Seven Percent Solution 76. The Passage 78. Nijinsky 80. Situation 81. Selling Hitler (TV) 91. Cold Comfort Farm (TV) 95, etc.

Jaffe, Carl (1902–1974).
Aristocratic-looking German actor, long in England.

Over the Moon 39. The Lion Has Wings 40. The Life and Death of Colonel Blimp 43. Gaiety George 46. Appointment in London 53. Operation Crossbow 65. The Double Man 67, many others.

Jaffe, Sam (1891–1984).
American character actor of eccentric appearance and sharp talent. On stage from 1916, films from 1933.

We Live Again 34. *The Scarlet Empress* 34. *Lost Horizon* (as the High Lama) 37. Gunga Din 39. Stage Door Canteen 43. 13 Rue Madeleine 46. Gentleman's Agreement 47. The Accused 48. Rope of Sand 49. *The Asphalt Jungle* (AAN) 50. Under the Gun 50. I Can Get It for You Wholesale 51. The Day the Earth Stood Still 51. All Mine to Give 57. Les Espions 57. The Barbarian and the Geisha 58. Ben Hur 59. A Guide for the Married Man 67. Guns for San Sebastian 68. The Great Bank Robbery 69. Night Gallery (TV) 69. Quarantined (TV) 70. The Kremlin Letter 70. The Old Man Who Cried Wolf (TV) 70. The Dunwich Horror 70. Who Killed the Mysterious Mr Foster? (TV) 71. Bedknobs and Broomsticks 71. QB VII (TV) 74. Battle Beyond the Stars 80. The End 81. Nothing Lasts Forever 82. On the Line 83, etc.

TV series: Ben Casey 60–64.

Jaffe, Stanley R. (1940–).
American producer. He is President and Chief Operating Officer of Paramount Communications.

Goodbye Columbus 69. Bad Company 72. The Bad News Bears 76. *Kramer vs Kramer* 78. Taps 81. Without a Trace (& d) 83. Racing with the Moon 84. Firstborn 84. Fatal Attraction (AAN) 87. The Accused 88. Black Rain 89. School Ties 92, etc.

Jaffrey, Madhur (1933–).
Indian actress, best known now for her books and television series on Indian cooking. She was formerly married to Saeed JAFFREY.

Shakespeare Wallah 65. The Guru 69. Autobiography of a Princess 75. Heat and Dust 82. The Assam Garden 85. The Perfect Murder 88. Vanya on 42nd Street 94, etc.

TV series: Firm Friends 93–94.

Jaffrey, Saeed.
Exuberant Indian actor, in Britain. He studied at RADA, has acted with the National Theatre and also appeared in many Indian movies. He was formerly married to Madhur JAFFREY.

The Guru 69. The Man Who Would Be King 75. The Wilby Conspiracy 75. The Chess Players 77. Staying On (TV) 81. Gandhi 82. The Jewel in the Crown (TV) 83. The Razor's Edge 84. A Passage to India 84. My Beautiful Laundrette 85. The Deceivers 87. Masala 91, etc.

TV series: Tandoori Nights 85–87. Little Napoleons 94. Common as Muck 97.

Jagger, Dean (1903–1991) (Dean Jeffries).
American star character actor of the 40s, usually in sympathetic roles; later seen as colonels, fathers, town elders, etc.

Women from Hell 29. College Rhythm 34. Home on the Range 34. Men without Names 35. Revolt of the Zombies 36. Exiled to Shanghai 37. *Brigham Young* (title role) 40. Western Union 41. The Men in Her Life 41. The Omaha Trail 42. North Star 43. When Strangers Marry 44. I Live in Grosvenor Square (GB) 45. Sister Kenny 46. Pursued 47. *Twelve O'Clock High* (AA) 49. Dark City 50. Denver and Rio Grande 52. It Grows on Trees 52. The Robe 53. *Executive Suite* 54. Bad Day at Black Rock 55. The Great Man 56. X the Unknown (GB) 57. The Proud Rebel 58. The Nun's Story 59. Elmer Gantry 60. Parrish 61. The Honeymoon Machine 62. First to Fight 67. Firecreek 68. The Kremlin Letter 70. The Brotherhood of the Bell (TV) 70. Vanishing Point 71. The Glass House (TV) 72. God Bless Dr Shagetz 77. End of the World 77. Alligator 80. Evil Town 87, many others.

TV series: Mr Novak 63–65.

Jagger, Mick (1943–).
Heavy-faced British pop idol whose film career didn't get off the ground. He has his own production company, Jagged Films. In 1998, the *Sunday Times* estimated his fortune at £140m.

Ned Kelly 69. Performance 70. Gimme Shelter 70. Burden of Dreams (doc) 82. The Nightingale (TV) 84. Freejack 92. Bent (a) 97. Tania (p) 97, etc.

❝ He sees all women as tarts. – *Bianca Jagger*

Mick's approach to acting was, once he discovered what it was about, he wasn't interested. – *James Fox*

Though fire and energy snake out of Mick like electricity in concert, he can't produce them cold as an actor. It's a problem with many rock performers. – *Tony Richardson*

Jaglom, Henry (1941–).
American writer-director of eccentric films.

■ A Safe Place 71. Tracks 76. Other People 79. Sitting Ducks (& a) 80. Can She Bake a Cherry Pie 83. Someone to Love 87. New Year's Day 89. Eating 90. Venice/Venice 92. Babyfever (co-w, d, e) 94. Last Summer in the Hamptons 95. Déjà Vu (co-w, d) 98.

Jakubowska, Wanda (1907–1998).
Polish director.

Soldier of Victory 43. The Last Stop 48. An Atlantic Story 54. Farewell to the Devil 56. Encounters in the Dark 60. The Hot Line 65. 150 Na Godzine 71. Bialy Mazur 73. Ludwik Warynski 78. Invitation to Dance 85, etc.

James, Brion (1945–).
American character actor, usually in menacing roles.

Southern Comfort 81. Blade Runner 82. 48 Hours 82. A Breed Apart 84. Enemy Mine 85. Flesh and Blood 85. Crime Wave 86. Armed and Dangerous 86. Steel Dawn 87. Nightmare at Noon 87. Dead Men Walking 88. Horror Show 89. Tango and Cash 89. Red Scorpion 89. Another 48 Hrs 90. Street Asylum 90. Mom 91. The Player 92. Black Magic (TV) 92. Time Runner 92. Future Shock 93. The Dark 93. Striking Distance 93. Cabin Boy 94. F.T.W. 94. Art Deco Detective 94. Cyberjack/Virtual Assassin 95. Pterodactyl Woman from Beverly Hills 96. American Strays 96. Bombshell 97. In God's Hands 98, etc.

James, Clifton (1893–1963).
British character actor who so resembled Field Marshal Montgomery that during World War II he was hired to impersonate him and hoodwink the Germans, as told in the subsequent book and film, *I Was Monty's Double*.

James, Clifton (1921–).
Corpulent American character actor.

David and Lisa 64. Cool Hand Luke 67. Tick Tick Tick 70. Live and Let Die 72. The Man with the Golden Gun 73. The Bank Shot 74. Silver Streak 76. The Bad News Bears in Breaking Training 77. Superman II 80. Talk to Me 82. Where Are the Children? 85. Eight Men Out 88. The Bonfire of the Vanities 90. Carolina Skeletons (TV) 91. Lone Star 96. The Summer of Ben Tyler 96, etc.

TV series: City of Angels 76. Lewis & Clark 81–82. All My Children 96–97.

James, Geraldine (1950–).
English leading actress, often on television. Born in Maidenhead, Kent, she trained at the Drama Centre.

Sweet William 80. Gandhi 82. *The Jewel in the Crown* (TV) 84. The Tall Guy 88. Blott on the Landscape (TV) 88. She's Been Away (TV) 89. The Wolves of Willoughby Chase 89. The Bridge 90. Beltenebros (Sp.) 91. Stanley and the Women (TV) 91. If Looks Could Kill/Teen Agent 91. Losing Track (TV) 92. No Worries (Aus.) 92. Words upon the Window Pane (Ire.) 94. The Healer (TV) 94. Drover's Gold (TV) 97. Seesaw (TV) 98, etc.

TV series: Band of Gold 95–96. Gold 97.

James, Harry (1916–1983).
American band-leader and trumpeter who appeared in occasional films. He was married to Betty Grable (1943–65).

Springtime in the Rockies 42. Best Foot Forward 43. Bathing Beauty 44. Do You Love Me 46. Carnegie Hall 47. I'll Get By 50. The Benny Goodman Story 56, etc.

James, Henry (1843–1916).
American novelist and playwright who lived for most of his life in Europe. Film-makers have been attracted by his supernatural story *The Turn of the Screw* and his novels dealing with Americans caught up in the more sophisticated and sometimes decadent society of Europe. He became a British citizen in 1915.

Autobiographies: 1913, *A Small Boy and Others*. 1914, *Notes of a Son and Brother*. 1917, *The Middle Years*.

Berkeley Square (from *The Sense of the Past*) 33. The Lost Moment (from *The Aspern Papers*) 47. The Heiress (from *Washington Square*) 49. The Innocents (from *The Turn of the Screw*) 61. I'll Never Forget You (from *The Sense of the Past*) 51. The Nightcomers (a prequel to *The Turn of the Screw*) 72. Daisy Miller 74. The Green Room (Fr., from *The Altar of the Dead*) 78. The Europeans 79. Aspern (Port.) 81. The Bostonians 84. Los Papeles de Aspern (Sp.) 91. The Portrait of a Lady 96. The Pupil (Fr.) 96. Washington Square 97, etc.

❝ I've always been interested in people, but I've never liked them. – *H.J.*

Poor Henry James! He's spending eternity walking round and round a stately park and the fence is just too high for him to peep over and he's just too far away to hear what the countess is saying. – *Somerset Maugham*

One of the nicest old ladies I ever met. – *William Faulkner*

James, Jesse (1847–1882).
American wild west outlaw who has acquired the legend of a Robin Hood but in fact plundered ruthlessly as head of a gang which also included his sanctimonious elder brother *Frank James* (1843–1915). Among the many screen personifications of Jesse are Tyrone Power in *Jesse James* 39; Lawrence Tierney in *Badman's Territory* 46; Macdonald Carey in *The Great Missouri Raid* 52; Audie Murphy in *Kansas Raiders* 53; Willard Parker in *The Great Jesse James Raid* 53; Robert Wagner in *The True Story of Jesse James* 56; Dale Robertson in *Fighting Man of the Plains* 59; Ray Stricklyn in *Young Jesse James* 60; Chris Jones in a TV series *The Legend of Jesse James* 65; Robert Duvall in *The Great Northfield Minnesota Raid* 72; James Keach in *The Long Riders* 80 (brother Stacy was brother Frank); and Clayton Moore in several Republic serials. Henry Fonda was in *The Return of Frank James* 40.

James, M. R. (1862–1936).
English ghost-story writer, an academic with a splendid command of language. *The Night of the Demon* is a fairly satisfactory film version of *Casting the Runes*.

James, Peter (1946–).
Australian cinematographer, now resident in Canada.

Caddie 76. The Irishman 78. The Wild Duck 84. Rebel 85. The Right Hand Man 87. Echoes of Paradise 89. Driving Miss Daisy 89. Mr Johnson 90. Black Robe 91. My Life 93. Alive 93. Thing Called Love 93. Silent Fall 94. Last Dance 96. Diabolique 96. Paradise Road 97. Newton Boys 98, etc.

James, Sid (1913–1976) (Sidney James Cohen).
Crumple-faced South African comedy actor, a former hairdresser, in London from 1946. He was a familiar face on TV and in scores of movies, including most of the Carry On series from 1958. Married three times. His lovers included actress Barbara WINDSOR. Died of a heart attack during a stage performance.

Black Memory 46. Once a Jolly Swagman 48. The Man in Black 49. The Lavender Hill Mob 51. The Titfield Thunderbolt 53. Joe Macbeth 55. The Silent Enemy 57. Too Many Crooks 58. Tommy the Toreador 59. Double Bunk 60. What a Carve Up 62. The Big Job 65. Don't Lose Your Head 67. Bless This House 73, many others.

TV series: Hancock's Half Hour 56–59. East End, West End 58. Citizen James 60. Taxi 63–64. George and the Dragon 66–68. Two in Clover 69–70. Bless This House 71–76.

James, Steve (1955–1993).
American star of martial arts movies. Born in New York City, he began in films as a stuntman. Died from leukaemia.

The Exterminator 80. The Brother from Another Planet 84. American Ninja 85. To Live and Die in LA 85. CAT Squad (TV) 86. Avenging Force 86. POW. The Escape 86. American Ninja 2: The Confrontation 87. Hero and the Terror 88. Johnny Be Good 88. CAT Squad: Python Wolf (TV) 88. American Ninja 3: Bloodhunt 89. I'm Gonna Get You Sucka 89. Riverbend 90. Street Hunter 90. McBain 91. Bloodfist V: Human Target 93. Weekend at Bernie's II 94. MANTIS (TV) 94, etc.

Jameson, Jerry.
American director.

The Dirt Gang 72. The Bat People 74. The Elevator (TV) 74. The Secret Night Caller (TV) 74. *Heatwave* (TV) 74. Hurricane (TV) 74. Terror on the 40th Floor (TV) 75. The Deadly Tower (TV) 75. The Invasion of Johnson County (TV) 76. Airport 77 77. A Fire in the Sky (TV) 77. High Noon Part Two (TV) 78. Raise the Titanic 80. The Cowboy and the Ballerina (TV) 84. Fire and Rain (TV) 89. Gunsmoke: To the Last Man (TV) 92. Bonanza: The Return (TV) 93. Gunsmoke: One Man's Justice (TV) 94, etc.

Jamison, Bud (1894–1944).
American character actor, a stock Columbia player who played the heavy in most of the Three Stooges two-reelers.

Jancso, Miklos (1921–).
Hungarian director.

Cantata 63. My Way Home 64. The Round Up 65. The Red and the White 67. Silence and Cry 68. Winter Wind 70. The Pacifist 71. Agnus Dei 71. Red Psalm 72. Electra 74. Private Vice and Public Virtue 76. Masterwork 77. Hungarian Rhapsody 79. Heart of a Tyrant 81. Huzsika (TV) 84. Omega, Omega 85. Budapest (doc) 85. Dawn 86. Season of Monsters 87. Jezus Krisztus Horoszkopia 89. The Blue Danube Waltz/Kek Duna Keringo 92, etc.

Jandl, Ivan (1941–1987).
Czech child actor whose sole performance as a war orphan in the tear-jerking *The Search*, opposite Montgomery Clift, won him an Academy Award for 'the outstanding juvenile performance of 1948'.

Janis, Conrad (1928–).
American character actor; began as a teenage player of the 40s.

Snafu 45. Margie 46. The High Window 46. Beyond Glory 48. Keep it Cool 58. The Duchess and the Dirtwater Fox 76. Roseland 77. Oh God Book Two 80. Brewster's Millions 84. Nothing in Common 86. Sonny Boy 90. The Feminine Touch (& d) 96, etc.

TV series: Quark 76. Mork and Mindy 78–80.

Janis, Elsie (1889–1956) (Elsie Bierbauer).
American musical comedy star who made a few silent movies such as *Betty in Search of a Thrill* and *A Regular Girl*; only talkie, *Women in War* 42.

Jankel, Annabel.
British director who works in collaboration with Rocky Morton.

The Max Headroom Story (co-d) (TV) 85. D.O.A. (co-d) 88. Super Mario Bros (co-d) 93.

Janney, Leon (1917–1980).
American child actor, a member of the original Our Gang.
Doorway to Hell 30. Penrod and Sam 31. Should Ladies Behave 32, etc.

Janni, Joseph (1916–1994).
Italian producer, in England from 1939.
The Glass Mountain 48. Romeo and Juliet 53. *A Town Like Alice* 56. *A Kind of Loving* 62. Darling 65. Modesty Blaise 66. Far From the Madding Crowd 67. *Poor Cow* 68. *Sunday Bloody Sunday* (AAN) 71. Made 72. Yanks 79, etc.

Jannings, Emil (1882–1950) (Theodor Emil Janenz).
Distinguished German actor, on stage from ten years old. Entered films through his friend Ernst Lubitsch.
■ Im Banne der Leidenschaft 14. Passionels Tagebuch 14. Frau Eva 15. Vendetta 16. Wenn Vier Dasselbe Tun 17. Life Is a Dream 18. The Eyes of the Mummy 18. The Brothers Karamazov 18. Der Stier von Oliviera 18. Rose Bernd 18. *Madame Dubarry* 19. Anne Boleyn 20. Kohlhiesel's Daughter 21. Danton 21. The Wife of the Pharaoh 21. Tragedy of Love 22. Ratten 22. *Othello* 23. Peter the Great 24. All for Gold 24. *Quo Vadis* 24. Nju 24. *The Last Laugh* 24. Waxworks 24. Tartuffe 25. *Faust* 26. *Variety* 26. *The Way of All Flesh* (US) (AA) 27. *The Last Command* (US) (AA) 28. The Street of Sin (US) 28. The Patriot (US) 28. The Sins of the Fathers (US) 29. The Betrayal (US) 29. *The Blue Angel* 30. Darling of the Gods 31. The Tempest 31. Le Roi Pausaole 32. Der Schwarze Walfisch 34. *The Old and the Young King* 35. Traumulus 35. Der Herrscher 37. The Broken Jug 37. Robert Koch 39. Ohm Kruger 40. Die Entlassing 42. An Old Heart Becomes Young Again 42. Where Is Herr Belling 45.
✪ For being the last ham of the old school to become an international star. *The Blue Angel*.
❝ Nine people out of ten, if asked to say who is the greatest actor on the screen, would unhesitatingly reply Emil Jannings. – *Lionel Collier, Picturegoer, 1929*

Jansen, Pierre (1930–).
French composer who has scored many of the films of Claude Chabrol.
Les Bonnes Femmes 60. Les Sept Péchés Capitaux 62. Ophélia 62. Bluebeard/Landru 62. Les Plus Belles Escroqueries du Monde 64. Le Tigre Aime la Chair Fraîche 64. La 317 Section 65. La Ligne de Démarcation 66. The Champagne Murders/Le Scandale 67. La Route de Corinthe 67. Les Biches 68. The Unfaithful Wife/La Femme Infidèle 68. This Man Must Die/Que la Bête Meure 69. Le Boucher 69. La Rupture 70. Just before Nightfall/Juste avant la Nuit 71. High Heels/Docteur Popaul 72. Wedding in Blood/Les Noces Rouges 73. Nada 74. Les Innocents aux Mains Sales 75. Nuit d'Or 76. The Lacemaker/La Dentellière 77. Violette 78. L'Etat Sauvage 78. Le Cheval d'Orgueil 80, etc.

Janssen, David (1930–1980) (David Meyer).
American leading man, very successful on TV; film roles routine, persona doggedly glum.
Yankee Buccaneer 52. Chief Crazy Horse 54. The Square Jungle 55. Toy Tiger 56. The Girl He Left Behind 56. *Hell to Eternity* 60. Ring of Fire 60. Mantrap 61. *King of the Roaring Twenties* (as Arnold Rothstein) 61. My Six Loves 63. Warning Shot 67. The Green Berets 68. The Shoes of the Fisherman 68. Where It's At 69. A Time for Giving 69. Macho Callahan 70. Birds of Prey (TV) 73. Fer de Lance (TV) 74. Once Is Not Enough 75. Stalk the Wild Child (TV) 76. The Swiss Conspiracy 76. Two Minute Warning 76. Mayday at 40,000 Feet 77. Warhead 77. The Word (TV) 78. The Golden Gate Murders (TV) 79. High Ice (TV) 79. City in Fear (TV) 79, etc.
TV series: *Richard Diamond* 59. *The Fugitive* 63–66. O'Hara US Treasury 71. Harry O 73–75.

Janssen, Eilene (1937–).
American child actress of the 40s.
The Green Years 46. About Mrs Leslie 54. The Search for Bridie Murphy 56. Beginning of the End 57. The Space Children 58. Escape from Red Rock 58. Black Zoo 63, etc.

Janssen, Famke (1964–).
Dutch-born actress and model who moved to the US in the mid-80s. Married director and screenwriter Todd Williams.
Fathers and Sons 92. Lord of Illusions 95. GoldenEye 95. City of Industry 97. The Gingerbread Man 98. Deep Rising 98. Monument Avenue 98. Rounders 98. Celebrity 98. The Faculty 98, etc.

Janssen, Werner (1899–1990).
American composer. He was married to actress Ann Harding (1937–63).
The General Died at Dawn (AAN) 36. Blockade (AAN) 38. Eternally Yours (AAN) 39. Slightly Honorable 40. Guest in the House 44. The Southerner (AAN) 45. Captain Kidd (AAN) 45. A Night in Casablanca 46. Ruthless 48, etc.

Janus, Samantha (1974–).
Blonde English actress and singer, mainly on television. She trained at LAMDA and sang the British entry in the 1991 Eurovision Song Contest.
Jekyll and Hyde (TV) 90. A Murder of Quality (TV) 91. Up 'n' Under 98, etc.
TV series: Demob 93. Pie in the Sky 95–96. Game On 95–98. Liverpool One 98.

Jarman, Claude, Jnr (1934–).
American boy actor of the 40s.
The Yearling (special AA) 46. High Barbaree 47. Intruder in the Dust 49. Rio Grande 51. Fair Wind to Java 53. The Great Locomotive Chase 56, etc.

Jarman, Derek (1942–1994).
British independent director and screenwriter, often on homosexual themes. He went to the Slade School of Fine Art and began as a painter, becoming a set and costume designer for ballet and opera. He started making short films in the early 70s and also directed pop videos in the 80s. He continued to work outside the mainstream, making low-budget films: *The Tempest* cost £150,000. Died of AIDS.
Autobiography: 1984, *Dancing Ledge*. 1991, *Modern Nature, the Journals of Derek Jarman*.
Biography: 1996, *Derek Jarman: Dreams of England* by Michael O'Pray.
■ The Devils (ad) 70. Savage Messiah (ad) 72. *Sebastiane* 76. Jubilee 78. The Tempest 79. In the Shadow of the Sun 72–80. Imagining October 84. The Angelic Conversation 85. Aria (co-d) 85. *Caravaggio* 86. The Last of England 86. War Requiem 89. The Garden 90. *Edward II* 91. *Wittgenstein* 93. Blue 93. Glitterbug 94.
❝ Most of the cinema is an enormous irrelevance, a medium that has crossed the boundaries of intelligence in very few hands. – *D.J.*

Jarmusch, Jim (1953–).
Off-beat, independent American director, screenwriter, musician and occasional actor.
Permanent Vacation 82. Stranger than Paradise 84. Down by Law 86. Mystery Train 89. Leningrad Cowboys Go America (a) 90. Night on Earth 91. In the Soup (a) 92. Iron Horsemen (a) 94. Blue in the Face (a) 95. Dead Man 95. Sling Blade (a) 96. Year of the Horse (wd, co-ph) 97, etc.
❝ If I had to make a film with some suit guys telling me how to make the damn thing, I think I'd go off my head and kneecap some executive. – *J.J.*

Jarre, Kevin.
American screenwriter, the son of actress Laura Devon.
Rambo: First Blood Part II (story) 85. Glory 89. Tombstone 94. The Devil's Own 97, etc.

Jarre, Maurice (1924–).
French composer, conductor and timpanist whose best work has been for director David Lean. Born in Lyon, he studied at the Paris Conservatoire of Music and first worked in the theatre with Jean-Louis Barrault and as director of music for the French National Theatre.
Hôtel des Invalides 52. La Tête contre les Murs 59. Eyes without a Face 59. Crack in the Mirror 60. *The Longest Day* 62. *Lawrence of Arabia* (AA) 62. Sundays and Cybele (AAN) 62. Weekend at Dunkirk 65. *Dr Zhivago* (AA) 65. Is Paris Burning? 66. The Professionals 66. The 25th Hour 67. Five Card Stud 68. Isadora 68. The Damned 69. *Ryan's Daughter* 70. Ash Wednesday 74. Great Expectations (TV) 76. The Last Tycoon 76. Jesus of Nazareth (TV) 76. March or Die 77. Mohammed, Messenger of God (GB/Leb.) (AAN) 77. Winter Kills 79. Resurrection 80. The Black Marble 80. Taps 81. Lion of the Desert 81. Young Doctors in Love 82. Firefox 82. The Year of Living Dangerously 83. A Passage to India (AA) 84. The Bride 84. Mistress (AAN, BFA) 84. Enemy Mine 85. Witness (AAN) 85. Mosquito Coast 86. Solarbabies 86. Tai-Pan 86. Fatal Attraction 87. No Way Out 87. Buster 88. Gorillas in the Mist (AAN) 88. Moon over Parador 88. Wildfire 88. Dead Poets Society 89. Enemies: A Love Story 89. Prancer 89. After Dark, My Sweet 90. Almost an Angel 90. Ghost 90. Jacob's Ladder 90. Solar Crisis 90. Only the Lonely 91. School Ties 92. Shadow of the Wolf (co-m) 93. Fearless 93. Mr Jones 94. A Walk in the Clouds 95. The Sunchaser 96, etc.

Jarrico, Paul (1915–1997) (Israel Shapiro).
American screenwriter who was blacklisted in the 50s. Born in Los Angeles, he graduated from the University of Southern California and went to work for Columbia Pictures, later moving to RKO. A Communist Party member, he refused to name names to HUAC in the early 50s and sued Howard Hughes for refusing to give him a credit for writing *Las Vegas Story*. (He was later refused a credit on the remake of *Tom, Dick and Harry* as *The Girl Most Likely* 58.) After he was blacklisted, he moved to Europe for 20 years, writing under pseudonyms, and returning to Hollywood in the late 70s. Died in a car crash while returning from a ceremony marking the 50th anniversary of the beginning of blacklisting, at which the president of the Screen Writers' Guild had apologized for its past conniving in the denial of credits to blacklisted writers.
Little Adventuress (co-story) 38. No Time to Marry (co-w) 38. Beauty for the Asking (co-w) 39. *Tom, Dick and Harry* (AAN) 41. The Face behind the Mask (co-w) 41. Song of Russia (co-w) 44. Little Giant/On the Carpet (co-w) 46. The Search (co-w) 48. The White Tower 50. Las Vegas Story 52. *Salt of the Earth* (co-w) (Mex.) 53. Five Branded Women (It.) 60. All Night Long (co-w) (GB) 61. Treasure of the Aztecs (Ger.) 65. The Day the Hot Line Got Hot (Fr.) 68. The Day that Shook the World (Yug.) 76. Messenger of Death 88. Stalin (uncredited) (TV) 92, etc.

Jarrott, Charles (1927–).
British director, from TV.
■ Time to Remember 62. *Anne of the Thousand Days* 70. Mary Queen of Scots 72. Lost Horizon 73. The Dove 74. Escape from the Dark 76. The Other Side of Midnight 77. The Last Flight of Noah's Ark 79. Condorman 81. The Amateur 82. The Boy in Blue 85. Poor Little Rich Girl (TV) 87. The Women He Loved (TV) 88. Morning Glory (co-w) 93.

Jarvilaturi, Ilkka (1961–).
Finnish director, now in America.
Kotia Pänö 89. *Darkness in Tallinn*/Tallinnan Pimeys 93, etc.

Jarvis, Martin (1941–).
British leading man in all media.
The Last Escape 70. Taste the Blood of Dracula 70. Ike (TV) 79. The Bunker (TV) 81. Who Dares Wins/The Final Option 82. Buster 88, etc.
TV series: Rings on their Fingers 78–80.

Jasny, Vojtech (1925–).
Czechoslovakian director and screenwriter, one of the leaders of the Czech new wave of the 50s. Born in Kelc, Moravia, he studied film at FAMU in Prague and began by directing documentaries. He went into exile after the Czech government banned *All My Good Countrymen*, which won the best director prize at the Cannes Film Festival in 1969, returning in 1998 to make *Return to Paradise Lost*.
Everything Ends Tonight (co-d) 54. September Nights (& co-w) 57. Desire (& co-w) 58. I Survived Certain Death 60. Pilgrimage to the Virgin Mary 61. When the Cat Comes (& co-w) 63. Pipes 65. All My Good Countrymen (& w) 68. The Clown (Aus.) 75. Attempt to Escape (Aus.) 76. The Maiden (Yug.) 80. The Suicide (Fin.) 84. The Great Land of Small (Can.) 87. Return to Paradise Lost 99, etc.

Jason, David (1940–) (David White).
British comedy character actor, mostly on radio and TV.
Under Milk Wood 73. Royal Flash 75. The Water Babies 78. The Odd Job 78. Porterhouse Blue (TV) 87. The Bullion Boys (TV) 93.
TV series: Open All Hours 76–85. A Sharp Intake of Breath 78–81. Only Fools and Horses 81–93. A Bit of a Do 88–90. The Darling Buds of May 91–93. A Touch of Frost 93– .

Jason, Leigh (1904–1979).
American director, mainly of second features.
The Price of Fear 28. Wolves of the City 29. High Gear 33. The Mad Miss Manton 38. Lady for a Night 39. Model Wife 41. Three Girls About Town 41. Nine Girls 44. Lost Honeymoon 46. Out of the Blue 48. Okinawa 52, etc.

Jason, Rick (1926–).
American leading man of the 50s.
Sombrero 53. The Saracen Blade 54. The Lieutenant Wore Skirts 55. The Wayward Bus 57. The Witch Who Came from the Sea 76. Partners 82. Around the World in 80 Days (TV) 89, etc.
TV series: The Case of the Dangerous Robin 60. *Combat* 62–67.

Jason, Sybil (1929–).
South African child actress of the 30s.
Barnacle Bill (GB) 35. Little Big Shot (GB) 36. The Singing Kid (US) 36. The Little Princess (US) 39. The Bluebird (US) 40, etc.

Jason, Will (1899–1970)
American second feature director.
The Soul of a Monster 44. Thief of Damascus 52, many others.

Jaubert, Maurice (1900–1940).
French composer.
L'Affaire Est dans le Sac 32. Le Quatorze Juillet 33. Zéro de Conduite 33. L'Atalante 34. Drôle de Drame 37. *Un Carnet de Bal* 37. *Quai des Brumes* 38. *Le Jour Se Lève* 39. La Fin du Jour 39, etc.

Jay, Ernest (1894–1957).
British stage character actor.
Tiger Bay 34. Broken Blossoms 36. Don't Take It to Heart 44. Vice Versa 47. The History of Mr Polly 49. Edward My Son 49. I Believe in You 52. Who Done It? 55. The Curse of Frankenstein 56.

Jayne, Jennifer (1932–).
British leading lady.
Once a Jolly Swagman 48. The Blue Lamp 50. It's a Grand Life 53. The Man Who Wouldn't Talk 57. The Trollenberg Terror 58. Raising the Wind 61. On the Beat 63. The Liquidator 65. The Medusa Touch 78. The Jigsaw Man 83. The Doctor and the Devils 85, etc.
TV series: The Adventures of William Tell 58–59.

Jayston, Michael (1935–) (Michael James).
British stage actor commanding reputable film roles.
Cromwell 70. *Nicholas and Alexandra* 71. Follow Me 72. Alice's Adventures in Wonderland 72. A Bequest to the Nation 73. Tales that Witness Madness 73. The Homecoming 73. Craze 73. The Internecine Project 74. She Fell Among Thieves (TV) 78. Tinker Tailor Soldier Spy (TV) 80. Dominique 78. Zulu Dawn 79. Highlander III: The Sorcerer 94. Element of Doubt 96. 20,000 Leagues under the Sea (TV) 97, etc.

Jeakins, Dorothy (1914–1995).
American costume designer.
Joan of Arc (AA) 48. Samson and Delilah (AA) 49. South Pacific 58. Let's Make Love 60. The Night of the Iguana (AA) 64. The Sound of Music (AAN) 65. The Hindenburg 75. The Way We Were (AAN) 73. The Betsy 78. On Golden Pond 81. The Dead (AAN) 87, etc.

Jean, Gloria (1927–) (Gloria Jean Schoonover).
Former American child singer, on screen from 1939 as second-feature rival to Deanna Durbin.
■ The Underpup 39. If I Had My Way 40. A Little Bit of Heaven 40. Never Give a Sucker an Even Break 41. What's Cookin'? 42. Get Hep to Love 42. It Comes Up Love 42. When Johnny Comes Marching Home 42. Mister Big 43. Moonlight in Vermont 43. Follow the Boys 44. Pardon My Rhythm 44. The Ghost Catchers 44. Reckless Age 44. Destiny 44. I'll Remember April 44. Easy to Look At 45. River Gang 45. Copacabana 47. I Surrender Dear 48. An Old Fashioned Girl 49. Manhattan Angel 49. There's a Girl in My Heart 50. Air Strike 55. The Ladies' Man 61.

Jean Louis:
see Louis, Jean.

Jean, Vadim (1966–).
British screenwriter and director.
Leon the Pig Farmer (co-d) 92. Beyond Bedlam (co-w, d) 94. Clockwork Mice (d) 95. The Real Howard Spitz 98, etc.

Jean-Baptiste, Marianne (1967?–).
English leading actress and singer. Born in London, she trained at RADA.
Secrets and Lies (as Hortense) (AAN) 95. Mr Jealousy 97. The 24-Hour Woman 98, etc.
❝ The old men running the industry just have not got a clue. They've got to come to terms with the fact that Britain is no longer a totally white place where people wear long frocks and drink tea. The national dish is no longer fish and chips, it's curry. – *M.J-B.*

Jeanmaire, Zizi (Renée) (1924–).
Leading lady and ballet dancer, in occasional films. Married choreographer Roland Petit.
Hans Christian Andersen 52. Anything Goes 56. Folies Bergère 56. Charmants Garçons 57. Black Tights 60, etc.

Jeans, Isabel (1891–1985).
British stage actress, invariably in aristocratic roles.
Tilly of Bloomsbury 21. The Rat 25. Downhill 27. Easy Virtue 28. Sally Bishop 33. *Tovarich* (US) 38. Suspicion (US) 41. Banana Ridge 41. Great Day 45. It Happened in Rome 57. *Gigi* 58. A Breath of Scandal 60. *Heavens Above* 63, etc.

Jeans, Ursula (1906–1973) (Ursula McMinn).
British stage actress, long married to Roger Livesey; in occasional films.
The Gypsy Cavalier (debut) 31. Cavalcade 33. Dark Journey 37. Mr Emmanuel 44. The Woman in the Hall 46. The Weaker Sex 48. The Dam Busters 55. Northwest Frontier 59. The Queen's Guards 61. The Battle of the Villa Fiorita 65, etc.

Jeanson, Henri (1900–1970).
French writer, a former actor and critic.
Pepe Le Moko 36. Life Dances On/Un Carnet de Bal 37. Hotel du Nord 38. The Curtain Rises/Entrée des Artistes 38. The Damned/Les Maudits 47. Lady Paname (& d) 50. Fanfan la Tulipe 51. Holiday for Henrietta/La Fête à Henrietta 52. Nana 55. The Lovers of Montparnasse/Modigliani of Montparnasse/Les Amants de Montparnasse 58. The Cow and I/La Vache et le Prisonnier 59. Madame/Madame Sans-Gêne 62. Paris in the Month of August/Paris au Mois d'Août 66, etc.

Jeayes, Allan (1885–1963).
British stage actor of dignified heavy presence; played supporting roles in many films.
The Impassive Footman 32. The Scarlet Pimpernel 34. Rembrandt 37. Elephant Boy 37. The Four Feathers 39. The Thief of Bagdad 40. The Man Within 46. Saraband for Dead Lovers 48. Waterfront 50, many others.

Jefford, Barbara (1930–).
British stage actress, more recently in films.
Ulysses 67. The Bofors Gun 68. A Midsummer Night's Dream 68. The Shoes of the Fisherman 68. Lust for a Vampire 70. And the Ship Sails On 84. When the Whales Came 89. Where Angels Fear to Tread 91. The Saint 97. The Ruth Rendell Mysteries: Thornapple (TV) 97, etc.

Jeffrey, Peter (1929–).
British general-purpose actor.
Becket 64. If 67. The Abominable Dr Phibes 71. The Horsemen 71. Dr Phibes Rises Again 72. The Odessa File 74. Midnight Express 78. The Adventures of Baron Munchausen 89. Middlemarch (TV) 94. Rasputin 96, etc.

Jeffreys, Anne (1923–) (Anne Carmichael).
American leading lady of the 40s, formerly in opera. She married actor Robert Sterling, her second husband, in 1956.
I Married an Angel 42. Step Lively 44. Dillinger 45. Riff Raff 47. Return of the Badmen 49. Boys Night Out 62. Panic in the City 68. Clifford 94, etc.
TV series: Topper 53. Love That Jill 58.

Jeffries, Fran (1939–) (Frances Makris).
American singer and actress, born in California. She appeared as a singer on the TV variety show *Spotlight* in 1967.
The Buccaneer 58. The Pink Panther 63. Sex and the Single Girl 64. A Talent for Loving 69, etc.

Jeffries, Lionel (1926–).
Bald British character comedian, who rose to co-star status, then turned to direction.
Stage Fright 50. Windfall 54. The Baby and the Battleship 55. Law and Disorder 57. The Nun's Story 58. Idol on Parade 59. *Two-Way Stretch* 60. *The Trials of Oscar Wilde* 60. The Hellions 61. The Notorious Landlady 61. The Wrong Arm of the Law 63. Call Me Bwana 63. The Long Ships 64. *The First Men in the Moon* 64. The Truth about Spring 65. The Secret of My Success 65. You Must Be Joking 65. Arrivederci Baby 66. *The Spy with a Cold Nose* 67. Rocket to the Moon 67. *Camelot* 67. Chitty Chitty Bang Bang 68. Eyewitness 70. Who Slew Auntie Roo 71. Royal Flash 75. The Prisoner of Zenda 79. Cream in My Coffee (TV) 80. Better Late than Never 81. A Chorus of Disapproval 88, etc.
■ AS DIRECTOR: *The Railway Children* 70. The Amazing Mr Blunden 72. Baxter 72. The Water Babies 78. Wombling Free 78.

Jenkins, Allen (1900–1974) (Alfred McGonegal).
'Tough guy' American comic actor, a staple of Warners' repertory in the 30s.
The Girl Habit 31. Rackety Rax 32. I am a Fugitive from a Chain Gang 32. 42nd Street 33. Professional Sweetheart 33. Jimmy the Gent 34. The St Louis Kid 34. Page Miss Glory 35. Miss Pacific Fleet 35. The Singing Kid 36. Three Men on a Horse 36. The Perfect Specimen 37. Dead End 37. Swing Your Lady 37. *A Slight Case of Murder* 38. The Amazing Dr Clitterhouse 38. Five Came Back 39. *Destry Rides Again* 39. Tin Pan Alley 40. Footsteps in the Dark 41. Maisie Gets Her Man 42. *Wonder Man* 45. Wild Harvest 47. Bodyhold 49. Behave Yourself 51. Pillow Talk 59. Robin and the Seven Hoods 64. Doctor You've Got to be Kidding 67. The Front Page 74, many others.
TV series: *Hey Jeannie* 56.

Jenkins, Charles Francis (1868–1934).
American inventor of the Phantascope, a camera using continuously moving film, which he patented in January 1894. He collaborated with Thomas Armat to demonstrate a Phantascope projector at the Cotton States Exposition at Atlanta, Georgia in October 1895. Armat improved the mechanism and patented it in February 1896 as the Vitascope, which was promoted under the aegis of Thomas Edison.

Jenkins, George (1914–).
American production designer.
The Best Years of Our Lives 46. The Secret Life of Walter Mitty 47. Roseanna McCoy 49. The Miracle Worker 62. Mickey One 65. Wait until Dark 67. Me Natalie 69. The Angel Levine 70. The Paper Chase 73. Night Moves 75. *All the President's Men* (AA) 76. Comes a Horseman 78. The China Syndrome (AAN) 79. Starting Over 79. The Postman Always Rings Twice 81. Rollover 81. Sophie's Choice 82. Dream Lover 86. Orphans 87. See You in the Morning 89. Presumed Innocent 90, etc.

Jenkins, Jackie 'Butch' (1937–).
Buck-toothed American child star of the 40s, son of Doris Dudley; retired because he developed a stutter.
■ *The Human Comedy* 43. National Velvet 44. An American Romance 44. Abbott and Costello in Hollywood 45. Our Vines Have Tender Grapes 45. Boys' Ranch 46. Little Mister Jim 46. My Brother Talks to Horses 46. Big City 48. The Bride Goes Wild 48. Summer Holiday 48.

Jenkins, Megs (1917–1998).
Plump British actress of kindly or motherly roles, on stage from 1933.
The Silent Battle 39. *Green for Danger* 46. The Brothers 47. The Monkey's Paw 48. *The History of Mr Polly* 49. White Corridors 51. Ivanhoe 52. The Cruel Sea 53. The Gay Dog 54. John and Julie 55. The Man in the Sky 56. Conspiracy of Hearts 59. *The Innocents* 61. The Barber of Stamford Hill 62. Bunny Lake Is Missing 65. Stranger in the House 67. Oliver 68. David Copperfield 69. The Amorous Milkman 74, etc.

Jenks, Frank (1902–1962).
American character comedian, usually seen as Runyonesque stooge, cop or valet.
When's Your Birthday? 37. You Can't Cheat an Honest Man 39. Dancing on a Dime 40. Rogues' Gallery 45. Loonies on Broadway 46. The She-Creature 56, many others.
TV series: Colonel Flack 53.

Jenks, Si (1876–1970) (Howard Jenkins).
American character actor, frequently a whiskery, comic sidekick in innumerable westerns. He worked in vaudeville and the circus before beginning his screen career in 1920.
Two Fisted Justice 31. Riders of Destiny 33. Charlie Chan's Courage 34. Rawhide Romance 34. The Outlaw Deputy 35. Fighting Shadows 35. Pigskin Parade 36. Captain January 36. Outcasts of Poker Flat 37. Topper 37. Rawhide 38. Stagecoach 39. Gone with the Wind 39. The Great Train Robbery 41. Sergeant York 41. It's a Great Life 43. Eve Knew Her Apples 45. Duel in the Sun 46. The Dark Horse 46. Son of Zorro (serial) 47. Kentucky Jubilee 51. Oklahoma Annie 52, etc.

Jennings, Al (1864–1961).
American outlaw of the old west who among other pursuits became a silent screen actor.
The Lady of the Dugout 18. Fighting Fury 24. The Sea Hawk 24. The Demon 26. Loco Luck 27. Land of Missing Men 30, etc.

Jennings, De Witt (1879–1937).
American character actor, stern and bulky.
The Warrens of Virginia 15. Three Sevens 21. The Enemy Sex 24. Exit Smiling 26. Alibi 29. The Big Trail 30. Min and Bill 30. Caught Plastered 31. Movie Crazy 32. Mystery of the Wax Museum 33. Little Man What Now 34. Mutiny on the Bounty 35. Sins of Man 36. Slave Ship 37, many others.

Jennings, Humphrey (1907–1950).
Distinguished British documentarist, with the GPO Film Unit from 1934. Responsible for a fine World War II series of sensitive film records of the moods of the time.
The First Days (co-d) 39. *London Can Take It* (co-d) 40. *Listen to Britain* 41. The Silent Village 43. *Fires Were Started* 43. *A Diary for Timothy* 45, etc. Also: The Cumberland Story 47. *Dim Little Island* 49. Family Portrait 50, etc.
✪ For his unbroken series of poetic and cinematic images of Britain at war. *Listen to Britain.*

Jennings, Talbot (1896–1985).
American screenwriter and playwright, usually in collaboration with other writers. Born in Shoshone, Idaho, he studied at Harvard and the Yale Drama School.
Mutiny on the Bounty (AAN) 35. Romeo and Juliet 36. The Good Earth 37. Spawn of the North 38. Rulers of the Sea 39. Northwest Passage 40. Edison the Man 40. So Ends Our Night 41. Frenchman's Creek 44. Anna and the King of Siam (AAN) 46. Landfall 49. The Black Rose 50. Across the Wide Missouri 51. Knights of the Round Table 53. Escape to Burma 55. Untamed 55, etc.

Jens, Salome (1935–).
American leading lady, in very occasional films.
■ *Angel Baby* 61. The Fool Killer 65. Seconds 66. Me Natalie 69. In the Glitter Palace (TV) 77. Sharon: Portrait of a Mistress (TV) 77. From Here to Eternity (TV) 79. Cloud Dancer 80. Harry's War 81. Clan of the Cave Bear 85. Just Between Friends 85.

Jergens, Adele (1922–).
American leading lady, mainly in second features. She was married to actor Glenn Langan.
A Thousand and One Nights 44. Ladies of the Chorus 48. Blonde Dynamite 50. Somebody Loves Me 52. The Cobweb 55. Girls in Prison 56. The Lonesome Trail 58, etc.

Jerome, Jerome K. (1859–1927).
British humorist and essayist. His *Three Men in a Boat* and *The Passing of the Third Floor Back* were filmed several times.

Jerrold, Mary (1877–1955) (Mary Allen).
British character actress, mainly on stage; in films, played mainly sweet old ladies.
Alibi 31. Friday the Thirteenth 33. The Man at the Gate 41. *The Way Ahead* 44. *The Queen of Spades* 48. Mr Perrin and Mr Traill 49. Top of the Form 52, etc.

Jessel, George (1898–1981).
American entertainer, in vaudeville from childhood. After making the mistake of turning down *The Jazz Singer*, he had a very spasmodic film career, but in the 50s he produced a number of musicals for Fox.
Autobiographies: 1946, *So Help Me*. 1955, *This Way Miss*. 1975, *The World I Live In*.
AS ACTOR: The Other Man's Wife 19. Private Izzy Murphy 26. Lucky Boy/My Mother's Eyes 29. Love Live and Laugh 29. Stage Door Canteen 43. Four Jills in a Jeep 44. The I Don't Care Girl 53. The Busy Body 57. Hieronymus Merkin 69, etc.
AS PRODUCER: Do You Love Me 46. When My Baby Smiles at Me 48. Dancing in the Dark 49. Meet Me After the Show 51. Golden Girl 51. Wait Till the Sun Shines Nellie 52. The I Don't Care Girl 53. Tonight We Sing 53, etc.
❝ Did you ever catch him at a funeral? It's wonderful. All through the years he makes notes on his friends. He wants to be ready. – *Eddie Cantor*
That son of a bitch started his reminiscences when he was eight years old. – *Walter Winchell*

Jessel, Patricia (1920–1968).
British character actress, mostly on stage.
The Flesh Is Weak 57. The Man Upstairs 58. *City of the Dead* 61. A Jolly Bad Fellow 64. A Funny Thing Happened on the Way to the Forum 66, etc.

Jessua, Alain (1932–).
French writer-director of off-beat films.
Life Upside Down 63. Jeu de Massacre 67. Traitement de Choc 73. Armageddon 77. Les Chiens 79. Paradis pour Tous 82. Frankenstein 90 84. En Toute Innocence 88, etc.

Jeunet, Jean-Pierre (1955–).
French screenwriter and director, of a quirky style.
Delicatessen (co-w, co-d) 90. City of Lost Children (co-w, co-d) 95. Alien: Resurrection (d) (US) 97.

Jewell, Isabel (1913–1972).
Diminutive American leading lady of the 30s, a minor 'platinum blonde' who graduated to character parts.
Blessed Event 33. Counsellor at Law 33. Manhattan Melodrama 34. A Tale of Two Cities 35. The Man Who Lived Twice 37. Marked Woman 37. *Lost Horizon* 37. Gone with the Wind 39. The Leopard Man 43. The Bishop's Wife 48. The Story of Molly X 48. Bernardine 57, many others.

Jewison, Norman (1926–).
Canadian director and screenwriter, from TV.
■ Forty Pounds of Trouble 63. The Thrill of It All 63. Send Me No Flowers 64. The Art of Love 65. *The Cincinnati Kid* 65. *The Russians Are Coming, the Russians Are Coming* (& p) (AANp) 66. *In the Heat of the Night* (p, d) (AAp, AANd) 67. The Thomas Crown Affair (p, d) 68. The Landlord (p) 69. Gaily, Gaily (p, d) 69. Fiddler on the Roof (p, d) (AAN) 71. Jesus Christ Superstar (p, d) 73. Rollerball 75. And Justice for All (& co-p) 79. The Dogs of War (co-p only) 81. Best Friends (& p) 82. A Soldier's Story 84. Agnes of God 85. Moonstruck (AAN) 87. The January Man 88. In Country 89. Other People's Money 91. Only You 94. Bogus (p, d) 96.

Jhabvala, Ruth Prawer (1927–).
German-born screenwriter and novelist, mainly for the films of Merchant-Ivory.
The Householder/Gharbar 63. Shakespeare Wallah 65. The Guru 68. Bombay Talkie 70. Autobiography of a Princess 75. Roseland 77. Hullabaloo over Georgie and Bonnie's Pictures 78. The Europeans 79. Jane Austen in Manhattan 80. Quartet 81. Courtesans of Bombay 82. Heat and Dust 82. The Bostonians 84. *A Room with a View* (AAN) 85. Madame Sousatzka 88. Mr & Mrs Bridge 90. *Howards End* 92. Remains of the Day 93. Jefferson in Paris 95. Surviving Picasso 96, etc.

Jianxin, Huang (1954–).
Chinese director, a former photographer. He studied at the Beijing Film Academy, graduating in 1985.
The Black Cannon Incident/Haipao Shijan 85. The Stand-In/Cuowei 87. Samsara/Lunhui 88. The Wooden Man's Bridge/Wu Kui 93. Back to Back, Face to Face 94, etc.

Jimenez, Neal.
American scriptwriter and director.
Where the River Runs Black (co-w) 86. River's Edge (w) 87. The Waterdance (w, co-d) 92. Sleep with Me (co-w) 94. Hideaway (co-w) 95, etc.

Jires, Jaromil (1935–).
Czech director, a graduate of the Prague Film School.
The Cry/Krick 63. *Valerie and Her Week of Wonders*/Valerie A Týden Divu 70. Payment in Kind/Causa Kralik 80. Helimadoe 94, etc.

Joan of Arc (c. 1412–1431).
The French heroine, martyr and saint, who persuaded the Dauphin that she had a divine mission to lead the French resistance to English occupation, was captured and sold to her enemies, tried for heresy and burned at the stake, and has defeated most film actresses who have tried to portray her. Carl Dreyer's silent *The Passion of Joan of Arc* 28 starred the remarkable Maria Falconetti in her only screen role; Ingrid Bergman took the role in Victor Fleming's dull *Joan of Arc* 48; Jean Seberg endured torments when directed by Otto Preminger in *Saint Joan* 57, based on Bernard Shaw's play; Hedy Lamarr popped up in the role in Irwin Allen's unintentionally hilarious *The Story of Mankind* 57; Robert Bresson's *The Trial of Joan of Arc* 62 had Florence Carrez as Joan; Jacques Rivette's four-hour *Jean La Pucelle* 94 starred Sandrine Bonnaire in a performance that came near to matching her subject.

Joanou, Phil (1961–).
American director.
Three O'Clock High 87. U2 Rattle and Hum (doc) 88. State of Grace 90. Final Analysis 92. Heaven's Prisoners 96, etc.

Jobert, Marlène (1943–).
French leading lady.
Masculin Féminin 66. Le Voleur 66. L'Astragale 68. Rider on the Rain 69. Last Known Address 70. Catch Me a Spy 72. Ten Days' Wonder 72. Juliette et Juliette 73. The Secret 74. Julie Pot de Colle 77. A Filthy Business 80. Souvenirs, Souvenirs 84. Les Cigognes n'en Font qu'à Leur Tête 89, etc.

Jodorowsky, Alexandro (1930–).
Chilean director, actor, writer and artist with surrealist tendencies.
Fando and Lis 70. El Topo 71. The Holy Mountain 74. Tusk 80. Santa Sangre 89, etc.

Joffe, Charles H.
American producer almost exclusively associated with the films of Woody Allen.
Take the Money and Run 69. Bananas 70. Everything You Always Wanted to Know about Sex 72. Sleeper 73. Love and Death 73. The Front 76. Annie Hall 77. Stardust Memories 80. A Midsummer Night's Sex Comedy 82. Zelig 83. Broadway Danny Rose 84. Hannah and Her Sisters 86. Radio Days 87. Alice 90. Shadows and Fog 92. Manhattan Murder Mystery 93. Bullets over Broadway 94. Mighty Aphrodite 95. Everyone Says I Love You 96. Deconstructing Harry 97. Celebrity 98, etc.

Joffe, Mark.
Australian director.
Grievous Bodily Harm 88. Shadow of the Cobra (TV) 89. Spotswood/The Efficiency Expert 91. Cosi 96. The MatchMaker 97, etc.

Joffé, Roland (1945–).
British director and screenwriter with TV experience.
The Killing Fields (AAN) 84. The Mission (AAN) 85. Fat Man and Little Boy/The Shadowmakers 89. City of Joy 92. The Scarlet Letter 95. Goodbye, Lover (US) 98, etc.

Johann, Zita (1904–1993).
American leading lady of the early 30s.
The Struggle 31. Tiger Shark 32. *The Mummy* 32. Luxury Liner 33. Grand Canary 34. Raiders of the Living Dead 89, etc.

John, Elton (1947–) (Reginald Dwight).
British pop singer. In 1997, *Business Age* estimated his personal fortune at £200m.
Tommy 75. The Lion King (AAs) 94.

John, Gottfried (1942–).
German actor, associated with Rainer Werner Fassbinder on stage and screen, in international films and television.
Carlos 71. Mother Kuster's Trip to Heaven/ Mutter Kusters Fahrt zum Himmel 75. 1982: Gutenbach 78. In a Year with 13 Moons/In einem Jahr mit 13 Monden 78. Fedora 78. The Marriage of Maria Braun/Die Ehe der Maria Braun 78. Berlin Alexanderplatz (TV) 79. Lili Marleen 80. Super 83. Chinese Boxes 84. Mata-Hari (US) 85. Of Pure Blood (TV) 86. Wings of Fame (Hol.) 90. Abraham (TV) 94. Institute Benjamenta (GB) 95. GoldenEye (US) 95. Am I Beautiful?/Bin Ich Schon? 98. Asterix and Obelix vs. Caesar/Astérix et Obélix (Fr.) 98, etc.

John, Rosamund (1913–1998) (Nora Jones).
Gentle-mannered British leading lady who turned in several pleasing performances in the 40s.
■ The Secret of the Loch 34. The First of the Few 42. *The Gentle Sex* 43. The Lamp Still Burns 43. Tawny Pipit 44. *The Way to the Stars* 45. Green for Danger 46. The Upturned Glass 47. Fame is the Spur 47. When the Bough Breaks 47. No Place for Jennifer 49. She Shall Have Murder 50. Never Look Back 52. Street Corner 53. Operation Murder 56.

Johns, Glynis (1923–).
Husky-voiced British actress, daughter of Mervyn Johns; on stage (as child) from 1935.
South Riding (debut) 36. Prison without Bars 38. 49th Parallel 41. Halfway House 44. *Perfect Strangers* 45. This Man Is Mine 46. Frieda 47. *Miranda* (as a mermaid) 47. An Ideal Husband 47. State Secret 50. Appointment with Venus 51. *The Card* 52. The Sword and the Rose 53. Personal Affair 53. Rob Roy 53. The Weak and the Wicked 54. The Beachcomber 55. Mad about Men 55. *The Court Jester* (US) 56. The Day They Gave Babies Away (US) 56. Shake Hands with the Devil 59. The Sundowners (AAN) 60. The Spider's Web 61. *The Chapman Report* (US) 62. Mary Poppins (US) 64. Dear Brigitte (US) 65. Don't Just Stand There (US) 68. Lock Up Your Daughters 69. Under Milk Wood 71. Vault of Horror 73. Little Gloria, Happy at Last (TV) 83. Zelly and Me 88. Nukie 89. The Ref/Hostile Hostages 94. While You Were Sleeping 95, etc.
TV series: Glynis 63.

Johns, Mervyn (1899–1992).
Welsh character actor, on stage from 1923; usually plays mild-mannered roles.
Lady in Danger (debut) 34. Jamaica Inn 39. *Saloon Bar* 40. *Next of Kin* 41. Went the Day Well? 42. My Learned Friend 44. *Dead of Night* 45. *Pink String and Sealing Wax* 45. Scrooge 51. The Intimate Stranger 56. No Love for Johnnie 61. 80,000 Suspects 63. The Heroes of Telemark 65. Who Killed the Cat? 66. The House of Mortal Sin 77, many others.

Johnson, Arch (1924–).
Burly American character actor.
Somebody Up There Likes Me 56. G.I. Blues 58. Twilight of Honor 63. Sullivan's Empire 67. Walking Tall 73. The Buddy Holly Story 77, many others.

Johnson, Arte (1934–).
Small-scale American comic actor.
Miracle in the Rain 56. The Subterraneans 60. The President's Analyst 67. Charge of the Model Ts 77. Love at First Bite 79. Bunco 83. The Raven Red Kiss-Off 90. Tax Season 90. Evil Spirits 91. Evil Toons 91, etc.
TV series: It's Always Jan 55–56. Sally 58. Hennessey 59–62. Don't Call Me Charlie 62–63. Rowan & Martin's Laugh-In 68–71. Games People Play 81–82. Glitter 84–85.

Johnson, Ben (1918–1996).
Leathery American character actor, a former cowboy and stunt rider. Born in Foreacre, Oklahoma, he began in movies after driving a herd of horses to California, where they had been ordered by Howard Hughes for *The Outlaw*. John Ford took him from the anonymity of stunt riding by giving him roles in his westerns, usually as a gruff but sympathetic companion to the hero. He went on to appear in around 300 films, with his finest moment coming in *The Last Picture Show* as Sam the Lion, proprietor of a failing cinema. He won a World Champion Cowboy title in 1953.
Three Godfathers 49. Mighty Joe Young 49. She Wore a Yellow Ribbon 49. *Wagonmaster* 50. Rio Grande 50. Fort Defiance 51. Shane 53. Slim Carter 57. Fort Bowie 60. One Eyed Jacks 61. Major Dundee 65. The Rare Breed 66. Will Penny 67. The Wild Bunch 69. The Undefeated 69. *The Last Picture Show* (AA) 71. Corky 72. Junior Bonner 72. Dillinger 73. The Sugarland Express 73. Bite the Bullet 75. Hustle 76. Breakheart Pass 76. The Greatest 77. The Town that Dreaded Sundown 77. The Swarm 78. Terror Train 80. The Hunter 80. Red Dawn 84. Cherry 2000 86. Let's Get Harry 86. Trespasses 86. Dark before Dawn 88. Back to Back 89. My Heroes Have Always Been Cowboys 91. Radio Flyer 92. The Legend of O. B. Taggart 94. Angels in the Outfield 94. Evening Star 96, many others.
TV series: The Monroes 66–67.

Johnson, Bumpy (1906–1968) (Ellsworth Johnson).
Gangster who controlled much of Harlem in the 20s and 30s, and was the subject of the biopic *Hoodlum* starring Laurence Fishburne in 1997. Fishburne also played Bumpy Rhodes, a character based on him, in *The Cotton Club* 84.

Johnson, Dame Celia (1908–1982).
Distinguished British actress, on stage from 1928, usually in well-bred roles: films rare.
Biography: 1991, *Celia Johnson* by Kate Fleming.
■ *In Which We Serve* (debut) 42. *Dear Octopus* 42. This Happy Breed 44. *Brief Encounter* (AAN) 46. The Astonished Heart 49. I Believe In You 52. The Captain's Paradise 53. The Holly and the Ivy 54. A Kid for Two Farthings 56. The Good Companions 57. The Prime of Miss Jean Brodie 69. Les Misérables (TV) 78. Staying On (TV) 79. The Hostage Tower (TV) 80.
❝ The only actress who thought acting was of secondary importance to living. – *Ronald Neame*

Johnson, Chic (1891–1962).
Portly American vaudeville comedian (with partner Ole Olsen).
■ Oh Sailor Behave 30. Fifty Million Frenchmen 31. Gold Dust Gertie 31. Country Gentlemen 36. All over Town 37. Hellzapoppin 41. Crazy House 43. Ghost Catchers 44. See My Lawyer 45, etc.

Johnson, Don (1950–).
American leading man; formerly twice married to Melanie Griffith (1976–77, 1989–95).
Zachariah 70. The Harrad Experiment 73. Return to Macon County 75. Law of the Land (TV) 76. The City (TV) 77. Ski Lift to Death (TV) 78. Beulah Land (TV) 79. The Long Hot Summer (TV) 85. Sweet Hearts Dance 88. Dead Bang 89. The Hot Spot 90. Harley Davidson and the Marlboro Man 91. Paradise 91. Born Yesterday 93. Guilty as Sin 93. In Pursuit of Honor (TV) 95. Tin Cup 96. Goodbye, Lover 98, etc.
TV series: From Here to Eternity 79. *Miami Vice* 85–89. Nash Bridges 96– .

Johnson, Jack (1878–1946).
American heavyweight boxer, world champion from 1908–15, who made a few films in the 20s. *The Great White Hope*, starring James Earl Jones, is a slightly fictionalized account of his life.
As the World Rolls On 21. For His Mother's Sake 22. Black Thunderbolt 22.

Johnson, Katie (1878–1957).
British character actress who became a star in her old age.
Jeannie 41. The Years Between 46. I Believe in You 52. *The Ladykillers* 55. How to Murder a Rich Uncle 56, many others.

Johnson, Kay (1904–1975) (Catherine Townsend).
American leading lady of the 30s. She was married to director John CROMWELL; their son is actor James CROMWELL.

■ *Dynamite* 29. The Ship from Shanghai 30. This Mad World 30. Billy the Kid 30. The Spoilers 30. Madam Satan 30. Passion Flower 30. The Single Sin 31. The Spy 31. American Madness 32. Thirteen Women 32. Eight Girls in a Boat 34. This Man Is Mine 34. Of Human Bondage 34. Their Big Moment 34. Village Tale 35. Jalna 35. White Banners 38. The Real Glory 39. Son of Fury 42. Mr Lucky 43. The Adventures of Mark Twain 44.

Johnson, Kyle (1952–).
American actor, in leading juvenile roles of the 60s.
Living between Two Worlds 63. *The Learning Tree* 69. The Sheriff (TV) 70. Man on the Run 74, etc.

Johnson, Lamont (1920–).
American director, from TV, a former actor.
Covenant with Death 67. Kona Coast (TV) 68. Deadlock (TV) 69. My Sweet Charlie (TV) 70. The Mackenzie Break 70. A Gunfight 71. That Certain Summer (TV) 72. The Groundstar Conspiracy 72. You'll Like My Mother 72. The Last American Hero 73. The Execution of Private Slovik (TV) 74. Fear on Trial (TV) 75. Lipstick 76. One On One 77. Somebody Killed Her Husband 78. Sunny Side 79. Foxes 80. Crisis at Central High (TV) 80. Off the Minnesota Strip 80. Escape from Iran (TV) 81. Cattle Annie and Little Britches 81. Spacehunter 83. Ernie Kovacs: Between the Laughter (TV) 84. Wallenberg: A Hero's Story (TV) 85. Unnatural Causes (TV) 86. Gore Vidal's Lincoln (TV) 88. The Kennedys of Massachusetts (TV) 89. Crash Landing: The Rescue of Flight 232 (TV) 92. Broken Chain 93, etc.

Johnson, Laurie (1927–).
British composer, mainly notable for themes of television's *The Avengers* and *The Professionals*.
The Good Companions 57. Tiger Bay 59. I Aim at the Stars 60. Dr Strangelove 63. First Men in the Moon 63. The Beauty Jungle 64. And Soon the Darkness 70. The Belstone Fox 74. Captain Kronos: Vampire Hunter 74. The Maids 75. Hedda 75. It Shouldn't Happen to a Vet 76. It's Alive II: It Lives Again 78. A Hazard of Hearts (TV) 87. The Lady and the Highwayman (TV) 89. A Ghost in Monte Carlo (TV) 90, etc.

Johnson, Lynn-Holly (1959–).
American leading lady, a former ice-skater.
Ice Castles 78. For Your Eyes Only 81. The Watcher in the Woods 81. The Sisterhood 88, etc.

Johnson, Martin (1884–1937) and **Osa** (1894–1953).
American explorers who made several feature-length films. A Johnson Safari Museum is situated in Chanute, Kansas (Mrs Johnson's birthplace).
Jungle Adventure 21. Simba 28. Congorilla 32. Wings over Africa 34. Baboona 35. Borneo 38. I Married Adventure 40, etc.

Johnson, Noble (1881–1978).
American actor who played a multitude of fearsome native chiefs.
Robinson Crusoe (as Friday) 22. The Ten Commandments 23. The Navigator 24. Hands Up 26. Vanity 27. Redskin 28. The Four Feathers 29. Moby Dick 30. The Mummy 32. *King Kong* 33. She 35. Conquest 37. The Ghost Breakers 40. Jungle Book 42. A Game of Death 45. She Wore a Yellow Ribbon 49. North of the Great Divide 50, many others.

Johnson, Nunnally (1897–1977).
American screenwriter, producer and director.
■ AS WRITER: Rough House Rosie 27. A Bedtime Story (co-w) 33. Mama Loves Papa (co-w) 33. Moulin Rouge (co-w) 34. *The House of Rothschild* 34. *Bulldog Drummond Strikes Back* 34. Kid Millions (co-w) 35. Cardinal Richelieu (co-w) 35. Thanks a Million 35. The Man Who Broke the Bank at Monte Carlo (co-w) 35. *The Prisoner of Shark Island* (& p) 36. The Country Doctor (p only) 36. The Road to Glory (p only) 36. Dimples (p and original idea) 36. Banjo on My Knee (& p) 36. Nancy Steele Is Missing (p only) 37. Cafe Metropole (p only) 37. Slave Ship (p only) 37. Love under Fire (p only) 37. *Jesse James* (& p) 39. Wife, Husband and Friend (& p) 39. *Rose of Washington Square* (& p) 39. *The Grapes of Wrath* (& p) (AANw) 40. I Was an Adventuress (p only) 40. Chad Hanna (& p) 40. *Tobacco Road* 41. *Roxie Hart* (& p) 42. The

Pied Piper (& p) 42. Life Begins at 8.30 (& p) 42. The Moon Is Down (& p) 43. Holy Matrimony (& p) (AANw) 43. Casanova Brown (& p) 44. *The Woman in the Window* (& p) 44. The Keys of the Kingdom (co-w) 44. Along Came Jones 45. *The Dark Mirror* (& p) 46. The Senator Was Indiscreet (p only) 47. Mr Peabody and the Mermaid (& p) 48. Everybody Does It (& p) 49. Three Came Home (& p) 49. The Gunfighter (co-w, p) 50. *The Mudlark* (& p) 50. The Long Dark Hall 51. *The Desert Fox* (& p) 51. Phone Call from a Stranger (& p) 52. We're Not Married (& p) 52. My Cousin Rachel (& p) 52. How to Marry a Millionaire (& p) 53. Night People (& pd) 53. Black Widow (& pd) 54. How to Be Very Very Popular (& pd) 55. The Man in the Grey Flannel Suit (& d) 56. Oh Men Oh Women (& pd) 56. *The Three Faces of Eve* (& p,d) 57. The Man Who Understood Women (& pd) 57. The Angel Wore Red (& d) 60. Flaming Star (co-d) 60. Mr Hobbs Takes a Vacation 62. Take Her She's Mine 63. The World of Henry Orient (co-d) 64. Dear Brigitte 65. The Dirty Dozen (co-w) 67.

✪ For being involved in so many of Hollywood's most intelligent pictures. *The Grapes of Wrath*.

❝ Movie actors wear dark glasses to funerals to conceal the fact that their eyes are not red from weeping. – *N.J.*

Johnson had been known to tell his bosses that he didn't want any producer 'pecking around' his work. 'It could delay me a month and if you don't like what I've written, it could upset me.' – *Fred Lawrence Guiles*

Johnson, Rafer (1935–).
American actor, formerly Olympic athlete.
The Fiercest Heart 61. The Sins of Rachel Cade 61. Wild in the Country 61. The Lion 63. None but the Brave 65. The Red, White and Black 70, etc.

Johnson, Richard (1927–).
British leading man of stage and screen.
Captain Horatio Hornblower 51. Never So Few (US) 59. Cairo (US) 62. *The Haunting* 63. Eighty Thousand Suspects 63. The Pumpkin Eater 64. Operation Crossbow 65. Moll Flanders 65. Khartoum 66. *Deadlier than the Male* (as Bulldog Drummond) 66. Danger Route 67. La Strega in Amore (It.) 67. Oedipus the King 68. A Twist of Sand 68. Lady Hamilton (as Nelson) (Ger.) 68. Some Girls Do 68. Julius Caesar 70. Hennessy 75. Aces High 76. The Four Feathers (TV) 78. Haywire (TV) 81. The Aerodrome (TV) 83. Turtle Diary (also p) 85. Lady Jane 86. Diving In 90. Crucifer of Blood (TV) 91. The Foreign Student 94. P. G. Wodehouse's Heavy Weather (TV) 95. Breaking the Code (TV) 97, etc.

Johnson, Rita (1912–1965).
American actress who usually played 'the other woman'.
Serenade 39. Edison the Man 40. Here Comes Mr Jordan 41. Thunderhead, Son of Flicka 44. They Won't Believe Me 47. Family Honeymoon 49. Susan Slept Here 54. Emergency Hospital 56. The Day They Gave Babies Away 57, etc.

Johnson, Tor (1903–1971).
Bald, menacing American character actor.
Ghost Catchers 44. Road to Rio 47. The Lemon Drop Kid 51. Bride of the Monster 55. Carousel 56. Plan 9 from Outer Space 56. Night of the Ghouls 59, etc.

Johnson, Van (1916–) (Charles Van Johnson).
American light leading man, in films since 1941 after stage experience.
Murder in the Big House (debut) 41. *Dr Gillespie's New Assistant* 42. The Human Comedy 43. A Guy Named Joe 43. The White Cliffs of Dover 44. Two Girls and a Sailor 44. Thirty Seconds over Tokyo 44. Thrill of a Romance 45. Weekend at the Waldorf 45. Easy to Wed 45. No Leave, No Love 45. High Barbaree 46. The Romance of Rosy Ridge 47. State of the Union 48. The Bride Goes Wild 48. In the Good Old Summertime 49. *Battleground* 50. Go for Broke 51. When in Rome 52. Plymouth Adventure 52. *The Caine Mutiny* 54. Brigadoon 55. The Last Time I Saw Paris 55. The End of the Affair (GB) 55. *Miracle in the Rain* 56. Twenty-Three Paces to Baker Street 57. Kelly and Me 57. Beyond This Place (GB) 59. Subway in the Sky (GB) 60. Wives and Lovers 63. Divorce American Style 67. Where Angels Go Trouble Follows 68. Battle Squadron (It.) 69. Company of Killers (TV) 70. Rich Man Poor Man (TV) 76. The Kidnapping of the President 80. Absurd! 81. The Purple Rose of Cairo 85. Down There in the Jungle 87. Killer Crocodile 88. Taxi Killer 88. Three Days to a Kill 92, etc.
TV series: Glitter 84.

Johnston, Arthur James (1898–1954).
American composer who began as an orchestrator for Irving Berlin and went with him to Hollywood in 1929, where he wrote many songs for Bing Crosby, usually with lyricist Sam Coslow. His hits include 'Just One More Chance' from *College Coach*, 'Cocktails for Two' from *Murder at the Vanities*, and the title song from *Pennies from Heaven*.
College Coach 32. College Humour 33. Too Much Harmony 33. Hello Everybody 33. Many Happy Returns 34. Belle of the Nineties 34. Murder at the Vanities 34. Thanks a Million 35. The Girl Friend 35. Go West Young Man 36. Pennies from Heaven 36. Sailing Along (GB) 37. Song of the South 47, etc.

Johnston, Eric A. (1895–1963).
American executive, successor to Will H. Hays as President of the MPAA (Motion Picture Association of America) (1945–63).

Johnston, Joe.
American director, a former production designer.
Raiders of the Lost Ark (AA, visual effects) 81. Honey, I Shrunk the Kids 89. The Rocketeer 91. The Pagemaster (co-d) 94. Jumanji 95, etc.

Johnston, Margaret (1917–).
Australian actress who has made occasional British films, notably in mid-40s.
The Prime Minister (debut) 40. *The Rake's Progress* 45. A Man About the House 47. Portrait of Clare 50. The Magic Box 51. Knave of Hearts 53. Touch and Go 55. *Night of the Eagle* 62. Life at the Top 65. The Psychopath 66. Sebastian 67, etc.

Johnston, Oliver (1888–1966).
British character actor.
Room in the House 55. *A King in New York* 57. A Touch of Larceny 60. Dr Crippen 62. Cleopatra 63. A Countess from Hong Kong 67, etc.

Jolie, Angelina (1975–).
American model turned actress, the daughter of Jon VOIGHT. Married actor Jonny Lee MILLER.
Cyborg II 93. Hackers 95. Without Evidence 96. Foxfire 96. Mojave Moon 96. Love Is All There Is 96. Playing God 97. True Women (TV) 97. George Wallace (TV) 97. Gia 97. Playing by Heart 98, etc.

Jolley, I. Stanford (1900–1978).
American western character actor.
The Sombrero Kid 42. Frontier Fury 43. Lighting Raiders 45. Prairie Express 47. Waco 52. The Young Guns 56. 13 Fighting Men 60, many others.

Jolson, Al (1886–1950) (Asa Yoelson).
Celebrated Jewish-American singer and entertainer, of inimitable voice and electric presence. After years as a big Broadway attraction, he starred in the first talking picture and although his fortunes subsequently declined, a biopic using his voice made him a world celebrity again in his 60s.
Biographies: 1962, *The Immortal Jolson* by Pearl Sieben. 1972, *Al Jolson* by Michael Friedland. 1975, *Sonny Boy* by Barrie Anderton.
■ *The Jazz Singer* 27. *The Singing Fool* 28. Sonny Boy 29. Say It with Songs 29. Mammy 30. Big Boy 30. Hallelujah I'm a Bum 33. Wonder Bar 34. Go into Your Dance 35. The Singing Kid 36. *Rose of Washington Square* 39. Hollywood Cavalcade 39. Swanee River 39. Rhapsody in Blue 45. *The Jolson Story* (voice only) 46. *Jolson Sings Again* (voice only) 49.

✪ For heralding an era, and for being a star again 20 years later without even being seen. *Rose of Washington Square*.

❝ It was easy enough to make Jolson happy at home. You just had to cheer him for breakfast, applaud wildly for lunch, and give him a standing ovation for dinner. – *George Burns*

He was more than just a singer or an actor. He was an experience. – *Eddie Cantor*

I'll tell you when I'm going to play the Palace. That's when Eddie Cantor and George Burns and Groucho Marx and Jack Benny are on the bill. I'm going to buy out the whole house, and sit in the middle of the orchestra and say: Slaves, entertain the king! – *A.J.*

Famous line (*The Jazz Singer*): 'You ain't heard nothin' yet!'

Jones, Allan (1907–1992).
American (originally Welsh) singing star of the 30s.
■ Reckless 35. *A Night at the Opera* 35. Rose Marie 36. The Great Ziegfeld (voice only, dubbing for Dennis Morgan) 36. Showboat 36. A Day at the Races 37. *The Firefly* 37. Everybody Sing 38. Honeymoon in Bali 39. The Great Victor Herbert 39. The Boys from Syracuse 40. One Night in the Tropics 40. There's Magic in Music 42. True to the Army 42. Moonlight in Havana 42. Rhythm of the Islands 43. Larceny with Music 43. Crazy House 43. You're a Lucky Fellow Mr Smith 43. When Johnny Comes Marching Home 43. Sing a Jingle 44. The Singing Sheriff 44. Señorita from the West 45. Honeymoon Ahead 45. A Swinging Summer 65. Stage to Thunder Rock 67.

Jones, Amy.
See HOLDEN-JONES, Amy.

Jones, Barry (1893–1981).
British character actor, usually in diffident roles; a well-known stage actor from 1921.
Arms and the Man (as Bluntschli) 31. Squadron Leader X 42. Dancing with Crime 46. Frieda 47. The Calendar 48. *Seven Days to Noon* (leading role) 50. White Corridors 51. *The Clouded Yellow* 51. Appointment with Venus 52. Plymouth Adventure (US) 52. Return to Paradise 53. Demetrius and the Gladiators 54. Prince Valiant (US) 54. *Brigadoon* (US) 55. The Glass Slipper 55. Alexander the Great 56. War and Peace 56. Saint Joan 57. *The Safecracker* 58. The Thirty Nine Steps 59. The Heroes of Telemark 65. A Study in Terror 65, etc.

Jones, Buck (1889–1942) (Charles Gebhardt).
Popular American western star of the 20s and 30s, mainly in second features. Died from burns.
Straight from the Shoulder 20. Skid Proof 23. Hearts and Spurs 25. Riders of the Purple Sage 26. The Flying Horseman 27. The Lone Rider 30. Border Law 32. The California Trail 33. When a Man Sees Red 34. Boss Rider of Gun Creek 36. Unmarried 39. Riders of Death Valley 41, many others.

Jones, Carolyn (1929–1983).
Dark-eyed American leading lady, usually in off-beat roles.
Road to Bali 52. House of Wax 52. The Big Heat 53. Invasion of the Body Snatchers 55. The Opposite Sex 56. *The Bachelor Party* (AAN) 57. Marjorie Morningstar 58. Last Train from Gun Hill 58. A Hole in the Head 59. Ice Palace 60. A Ticklish Affair 63. Heaven with a Gun 68. Color Me Dead 70. Eaten Alive 77. Good Luck Miss Wyckoff 79. The French Atlantic Affair (TV) 80. The Dream Merchants (TV) 80, etc.
TV series: *The Addams Family* (as Morticia) 64–5. Capitol 82–83.

Jones, Christopher (1941–).
American leading man of the 60s. He was formerly married to Susan Strasberg. He had a son by actress Susan CABOT. He quit acting for 25 years after *Ryan's Daughter*, and says he spent them painting and sculpting and had 'seven or eight children' by 'four or five women'.
Chubasco 67. Wild in the Streets 68. The Looking Glass War 69. Three in the Attic 69. *Ryan's Daughter* 70. Trigger Happy 96, etc.
TV series: *The Legend of Jesse James* 65.

❝ My manhood *is* my soul. If they cut my balls off I wouldn't have a soul. – *C.J.*

My career passed me by, I swear to God. I was just living my life. – *C.J.*

Jones, Chuck (1912–) (Charles M. Jones).
American animator and director of cartoons, mainly for Warner, noted for his skill in creating slapstick situations. Born in Spokane, Washington, he moved with his family to Hollywood as a boy, where he watched Chaplin at work. He arrived at Warner in 1933 and created ROAD RUNNER, WILE E. COYOTE and PEPE LE PEW, as well as directing many Bugs Bunny and Daffy Duck cartoons. Now runs his own company, Chuck Jones Productions, which is under contract to Warner. He was presented with an honorary Oscar in 1996.
Autobiography: 1989, *Chuck Amuck*. 1996, *Chuck Reducks: Drawing from the Fun Side of Life*.
The Night Watchman 38. Daffy and the Dinosaur 39. Hare Tonic 45. Mouse Wreckers (AAN) 48. For Scent-Imental Reasons (AA) 49. So Much for So Little (AA, doc) 50. From A to Z-Z-Z-Z (AAN) 53. Zipping Along 53. One Froggy Evening 55. High Note (AAN) 60. Beep Prepared (AAN) 61. Nelly's Folly (AAN) 61. Gay Purree (feature, co-w only) 62. Now Hear This (co-d, AAN) 62. The Dot and the Line (AA) 65. The Phantom Tollbooth (feature, p, wd) 69. The Bugs Bunny/Road Runner Movie (compilation, p, wd) 79. Porky Pig in Hollywood (compilation, co-d) 86. Superior Duck 96, many others.

Jones, David (1934–).
British director.
Betrayal 84. 84 Charing Cross Road 87. The Christmas Wife (TV) 88. Jacknife 89. Fire in the Dark 91. The Trial 93. And Then There Was One (TV) 94. Time to Say Goodbye 97, etc.

Jones, Davy (1946–).
British actor and singer who became one of The MONKEES, on stage from 1963.
Head 73. Hot Channels 73. Illusions of a Lady 73. Not Just Another Woman 73. Devil's Due 73, etc.

Jones, Dean (1931–).
American leading man who usually plays well-behaved fellows.
Tea and Sympathy 56. Handle with Care 58. Never So Few 60. *Under the Yum Yum Tree* 64. The New Interns 64. Two on a Guillotine 64. That Darn Cat 65. The Ugly Dachshund 66. Any Wednesday 66. Monkeys Go Home 67. Blackbeard's Ghost 67. The Love Bug 69. Million Dollar Duck 71. Snowball Express 73. Mr Superinvisible 76. The Shaggy D.A. 76. Herbie Goes to Monte Carlo 77. Born Again 78. Fire and Rain 89. Other People's Money 91. Beethoven 92. Clear and Present Danger 94. That Darn Cat 94, etc.
TV series: Ensign O'Toole 62. Chicago Teddy Bears 71. Herbie the Love Bug 82.

Jones, Emrys (1915–1972).
British stage actor.
One of Our Aircraft Is Missing 42. The Rake's Progress 45. The Wicked Lady 46. Nicholas Nickleby 47. The Small Back Room 48. Three Cases of Murder 55. Oscar Wilde 60, etc.

Jones, Evan (1927–).
British screenwriter, born in Jamaica, who wrote four films for Joseph Losey.
The Damned 61. Eve 62. King and Country 64. Modesty Blaise 66. Two Gentlemen Sharing 66. Funeral in Berlin 67. Outback 71. Wake in Fright 71. Night Watch 73. Escape to Victory 81. The Killing of Angel Street 81. Champions 84. Kangaroo 87. Shadow of the Wolf (co-w) 93, etc.

Jones, Freddie (1927–).
Clever British character actor who has yet to control a tendency towards twitchy caricatures.
The Bliss of Mrs Blossom 68. Otley 69. Frankenstein Must be Destroyed 70. Goodbye Gemini 70. Antony and Cleopatra 72. Sitting Target 72. The Satanic Rites of Dracula 73. The Elephant Man 80. Firefox 82. Krull 83. Dune 85. Firestarter 85. Young Sherlock Holmes 85. Consuming Passions 88. The Last Butterfly 90. Adam Bede (TV) 91. Hotel Room (TV) 93. The Mystery of Edwin Drood 93. Cold Comfort Farm (TV) 95. Drover's Gold (TV) 97, etc.

Jones, Gemma (1942–).
English leading actress, mostly on the stage, the daughter of Griffith JONES. Born in London, she studied at RADA and was on stage from 1963.
The Spoils of Poynton (TV) 71. The Devils 71. The Fall of Eagles (TV) 74. Very Like a Whale 81. Paperhouse 88. Feast of July 95. Sense and Sensibility 95. Wilde 97. Jane Eyre (TV) 97. The Theory of Flight 98, etc.
TV series: *The Duchess of Duke Street* 76–80.

Jones, Gordon (1911–1963).
American second lead of the football player type.
They All Kissed the Bride 42. My Sister Eileen 43. Flying Tigers 44. The Secret Life of Walter Mitty 47, etc.
TV series: The Abbott and Costello Show.

Jones, Grace (1952–).
American performer.
Conan the Destroyer 84. A View to a Kill 85. Vamp 86. Straight to Hell 87. Siesta 87. Boomerang 92. Cyber Bandits 94, etc.

Jones, Griff Rhys (1953–).
British comic actor and writer, from TV and stage.
Morons from Outer Space 85. Wilt/The Misadventures of Mr Wilt 89. Staggered 94.
TV series: Not the Nine o'Clock News 79–81. Alas Smith and Jones 84–86. Demob (TV) 93. Smith and Jones 95, 97– .

Jones, Griffith (1910–).
British light leading man, on stage from 1930.
The Faithful Heart (debut) 32. Catherine the Great 34. The Mill on the Floss 36. A Yank at Oxford 38. *The Four Just Men* 39. Young Man's Fancy 39. Atlantic Ferry 40. This Was Paris 41. Henry V 44. The Wicked Lady 45. *The Rake's Progress* 45. *They Made Me a Fugitive* 47. Good Time Girl 48. Miranda 48. Look before You Love 49. Honeymoon Deferred 51. Star of My Night 53. The Sea Shall Not Have Them 55. Face in the Night 57. Kill Her Gently 59. Strangler's Web 63. Decline and Fall 68, many others.

Jones, Harmon (1911–1972).
Canadian director in Hollywood.
■ As Young As You Feel 51. The Pride of St Louis 52. Bloodhounds of Broadway 52. The Silver Whip 53. City of Bad Men 53. The Kid from Left Field 53. Gorilla at Large 54. Princess of the Nile 54. Target Zero 55. A Day of Fury 56. Canyon River 56. The Beast of Budapest 58. Bullwhip 58. Wolf Larsen 58. Don't Worry We'll Think of a Title 66.

Jones, Henry (1912–).
American character actor of stage, TV and occasional films; usually plays the guy next door or the worm who turns.
The Lady Says No 51. *The Bad Seed* 56. The Girl Can't Help It 57. Vertigo 58. The Bramble Bush 60. Angel Baby 60. Never Too Late 65. Project X 67. Stay Away Joe 68. Support Your Local Sheriff 69. The Skin Game 71. Pete 'n' Tillie 72. The Outfit 74. Nine to Five 80. Deathtrap 82. Codename: Foxfire (TV) 85. Balboa 86. Nowhere to Run 88. Dick Tracy 90. Arachnophobia 90. Breathing Lessons (TV) 94, etc.
TV series: Channing 63–64. The Girl with Something Extra 73–74. Phyllis 75–77. Gunshy 83. Codename: Foxfire 85. Falcon Crest 85–86. I Married Dora 87–88.

Jones, James (1921–1977).
American novelist, best known for his stories of army life. Born in Robinson, Illinois, he served in the US Army in the Pacific from 1939 to 1944. Kris Kristofferson plays a character based on him in *A Soldier's Daughter Never Cries* 98, written by Jones's daughter.
From Here to Eternity (oa) 53. Some Came Running (oa) 58. The Longest Day (co-w) 62. The Thin Red Line (oa) 64. From Here to Eternity (oa) (TV) 79. The Thin Red Line (oa) 99.
TV series: From Here to Eternity (oa) 79–80.

Jones, James Cellan (1930–).
British director, in several senior TV posts.
Bequest to the Nation 72. *Jennie* (TV) 74. The Day Christ Died (TV) 80. Oxbridge Blues (TV) 84. Fortunes of War (TV) 87. Harnessing Peacocks (TV) 93.

Jones, James Earl (1931–).
Impressive American leading actor, from the stage. He was the voice of Darth Vader in the *Star Wars* trilogy.
The Great White Hope (AAN) 70. The Man (TV) 73. Claudine 74. The Bingo Long Traveling All Stars and Motor Kings 76. Deadly Hero 76. Swashbuckler 76. The River Niger 76. The Last Remake of Beau Geste 77. Jesus of Nazareth (TV) 77. The Greatest 77. Exorcist II: The Heretic 77. Star Wars (voice) 77. A Piece of the Action 77. The Greatest Thing That Almost Happened (TV) 77. Roots II (TV) (as Alex Haley) 79. The Bushido Blade 80. Conan the Barbarian 82. Allan Quatermain and the Lost City of Gold 86. Gardens of Stone 87. Matewan 87. Pinocchio and the Emperor of Night (voice) 87. Coming to America 88. Best of the Best 89. Field of Dreams 89. Three Fugitives 89. The Ambulance 90. Ivory Hunters (TV) 90. Grim Prairie Tales 90. The Hunt for Red October 90. True Identity 91. Convicts 91. Scorchers 91. Patriot Games 92. Sneakers 92. The Sandlot/The Sandlot Kids 93. The Meteor Man 93. Excessive Force 93. Sommersby 93. Clean Slate 94. The Lion King (voice) 94. Clear and Present Danger 94. Jefferson in Paris 95. Cry the Beloved Country 95. A Family Thing 96. Looking for Richard 96. Gang Related 96. Rebound: The Legend of Earl 'The Goat' Manigault (TV) 96. Good Luck 96. The Second Civil War (TV) 97. Merlin (TV) 98. The Lion King II: Simba's Pride (voice) 98, etc.
TV series: Paris 79–80. Roots: The Next Generation 79–81. Me and Mom 85. Gabriel's Fire 90–92. Under One Roof 95.

Jones, Jennifer (1919–) (Phylis Isley).
Intense, variable American leading actress, in small film roles from 1939. Born in Tulsa, Oklahoma, to showbusiness parents, she studied at North Western University and the American Academy of Dramatic Art. After a couple of unsuccessful minor westerns at Republic, she was put under contract by David Selznick, who guided her to stardom in *The Song of Bernadette* and, around the same time, replaced Robert Walker as her husband. She acted little after Selznick's death in 1965, and was married again, to industrialist Norton Simon, in 1971.
Biography: 1995, *Portrait of Jennifer* by Edward Z. Epstein.
■ Dick Tracy's G Men 39. The New Frontier 39. *The Song of Bernadette* (AA) 43. Since You Went Away (AAN) 44. Love Letters (AAN) 45. Cluny Brown 46. Duel in the Sun (AAN) 46. *Portrait of Jennie* 48. We Were Strangers 49. Madame Bovary 49. *Carrie* 51. Gone to Earth (GB) 51. Ruby Gentry 52. Indiscretion 53. Beat the Devil 54. *Love Is a Many-Splendored Thing* (AAN) 55. Good Morning, Miss Dove 55. The Man in the Grey Flannel Suit 56. The Barretts of Wimpole Street 57. A Farewell to Arms 58. Tender Is the Night 61. The Idol (GB) 66. Angel Angel Down We Go 69. The Towering Inferno 74.

Jones, Kenneth V. (1924–).
British composer.
How to Murder a Rich Uncle 57. High Flight 58. The Horse's Mouth 58. Indiscreet 58. Intent to Kill 58. Room 43 58. Task Force 58. Tom Thumb 58. Ten Seconds to Hell 59. Jazz Boat 60. Oscar Wilde 60. Tarzan the Magnificent 60. Ferry to Hong Kong 61. The Green Helmet 61. Two Way Stretch 61. Nearly a Nasty Accident 62. Operation Snatch 62. Tarzan Goes to India 62. Cairo 63. Horror Hotel 63. Dr Crippen 64. Maroc 7 67. The Projected Man 67. Battle beneath the Earth 68. Who Slew Auntie Roo? 71, etc.

Jones, L. Q. (1927–) (J. E. McQueen).
American character actor who took his name from the character he played in his first film, *Battle Cry* 55.
Target Zero 55. Love Me Tender 56. Operation Mad Ball 57. The Naked and the Dead 58. The Young Lions 58. Cimarron 60. Flaming Star 60. Ride the High Country 62. Apache Rifles 64. Major Dundee 65. The Wild Bunch 69. The Ballad of Cable Hogue 70. The Hunting Party 71. The Brotherhood of Satan (& p) 71. *A Boy and His Dog* (d) 75. Mother, Jugs and Speed 76. Standing Tall 78. The Beast Within 82. Sacred Ground 83. Timerider 83. Lone Wolf McQuade 83. Bulletproof 88. River of Death 90. Grizzly Adams: The Legend Continues 90. Lightning Jack 94. In Cold Blood (TV) 96. The Edge 97. The Mask of Zorro 98, etc.
TV series: Cheyenne 55–56. The Virginian 64–67.
❝ Let's face it, motion pictures are sausages. But that doesn't mean you can't make artful sausage. – *L.Q.J.*

Jones, Laura.
Australian screenwriter.
An Angel at My Table 90. The Portrait of a Lady 96, etc.

Jones, Marcia Mae (1924–).
American child actress of the 30s.
King of Jazz 31. These Three 36. Heidi 37. The Little Princess 39. Tomboy 40. Nice Girl 41. Nine Girls 44. Arson Inc. 50. Chicago Calling (under the name of Marsha Jones) 52. Rogue's Gallery 68. The Way We Were 73, etc.

Jones, Paul (1901–1968).
American producer, long with Paramount.
The Great McGinty 40. Sullivan's Travels 41. Road to Morocco 42. The Virginian 46. Dear Ruth 47. Here Come the Girls 53. Living It Up 54. Pardners 56. The Disorderly Orderly 64, many others.

Jones, Paul (1942–) (Paul Pond).
British leading man, former pop singer.
Privilege 66. Demons of the Mind 71, etc.

Jones, Peter (1920–).
British character actor and writer, usually in understated comic roles. He was the voice of The Book in the radio and TV versions of *The Hitchhiker's Guide to the Galaxy* 78, 81.
Fanny by Gaslight 44. The Yellow Balloon 53. Albert R. N. 53. Danger Within 58. Never Let Go 61. Romanoff and Juliet 61. Press for Time 66. Just Like a Woman 66. The Return of the Pink Panther 75. Carry On England 76. Chariots of Fire 81, etc.
TV series: The Rag Trade 61–63, 77–78. Beggar My Neighbour 67. Kindly Leave the Kerb 71. From a Bird's Eye View 71. Mr Big (& co-w) 77. Whoops Apocalypse 82. I Thought You'd Gone (& co-w) 84.

Jones, Quincy (1933–).
American composer.
The Pawnbroker 65. The Deadly Affair 66. In Cold Blood (AAN) 67. In the Heat of the Night 67. MacKenna's Gold 69. Bob and Carol and Ted and Alice 70. Cactus Flower 71. The Anderson Tapes 72. The Getaway 72. The Hot Rock 72. The New Centurions 72. *Roots* (TV) 77. The Wiz (AAN) 78. The Color Purple (AAN) 85. Listen Up: The Lives of Quincy Jones 90, etc.

Jones, Robert C. (1930–).
American editor and screenwriter, son of director Harmon Jones.
as editor: Invitation to a Gunfighter 64. Ship of Fools 65. Tobruk 67. Guess Who's Coming to Dinner (AAN) 69. Love Story 70. Man of La Mancha 72. The Last Detail 73. Shampoo 75. Bound for Glory (AAN) 76. Heaven Can Wait 78. Twice in a Lifetime 85. See No Evil, Hear No Evil 89. Married to It 91. Beyond the Law 92. Love Affair 94. City Hall 96. Bulworth 98, etc.
as writer: Coming Home (co-w, AA) 78.

Jones, Sam (1954–).
American leading actor of action films.
Flash Gordon 80. My Chauffeur 86. Jane and the Lost City (GB) 87. Silent Assassins 88. Under the Gun 88. Driving Force 88. In Gold We Trust 91. Maximum Force 92. Fist of Honor 92. DaVinci's War 92. Vegas Vice 94. Ballistic 94. Texas Payback 95. Where Truth Lies 96. American Strays 96, etc.

Jones, Shirley (1934–).
American singer and leading lady who blossomed into a substantial actress.
Oklahoma 55. Carousel 56. April Love 57. Never Steal Anything Small 58. Bobbikins (GB) 59. Pepe 60. *Elmer Gantry* (AA) 60. Two Rode Together 61. *The Music Man* 62. A Ticklish Affair 63. The Courtship of Eddie's Father 63. Bedtime Story 64. Dark Purpose 64. Fluffy 65. The Secret of My Success 65. Silent Night Lonely Night (TV) 69. But I Don't Want to Get Married (TV) 70. The Cheyenne Social Club 70. The Happy Ending 70. The Girls of Huntington House (TV) 73. The Family Nobody Wanted (TV) 75. Winner Take All (TV) 75. The Lives of Jenny Doland (TV) 75. Yesterday's Child (TV) 77. Evening in Byzantium (TV) 78. Who'll Save Our Children? (TV) 78. A Last Cry for Help (TV) 79. Beyond the Poseidon Adventure 79. The Children of An Lac (TV) 80. Inmates (TV) 81. Hotel 82. Tank 84. There Were Times, Dear 85. Charlie (TV) 89. Cops n Roberts (as herself) 95. Dog's Best Friend (TV) 97. This Is My Father 98. Gideon's Webb 98, etc.
TV series: *The Partridge Family* 70–73. Shirley 79.

Jones, Spike (1911–1965) (Lindley Armstrong Jones).
Pint-sized American bandleader ('Spike Jones and his City Slickers'), popular in the 40s for crazy variations on well-known songs. Talents employed in his band included Billy Barty, Mel Blanc, and Doodles Weaver. Died of complications from emphysema.
Biography: 1993, *Spike Jones Off the Record* by Jordan Young.
Thank Your Lucky Stars 43. Bring on the Girls 45. Variety Girl 47. Fireman Save My Child 55, etc.
TV series: The Spike Jones Show 54, 57, 60–61. Club Oasis 57–58.

Jones, Terry (1942–).
British performer/director and screenwriter, one of the Monty Python group.
And Now for Something Completely Different (co-w) 72. *Monty Python and the Holy Grail* (co-w, co-d) 74. *Monty Python's Life of Brian* (co-w, d) 79. Monty Python's The Meaning of Life (co-w, d) 83. Labyrinth (w) 86. Personal Services (d) 87. Consuming Passions (oa) 88. Erik the Viking (wd) 89. The Wind in the Willows (a, wd) 96, etc.

Jones, Tommy Lee (1946–).
American leading man.
Love Story 70. Jackson County Jail 75. Charlie's Angels (pilot) (TV) 76. Smash Up on Interstate Five (TV) 76. *The Amazing Howard Hughes* (TV) 77. Rolling Thunder 77. Eyes of Laura Mars 78. The Betsy 78. Coal Miner's Daughter 80. Back Roads 81. The Executioner's Song (TV) 82. Nate and Hayes 83. The Big Town 87. Stormy Monday 88. The Package 89. Fire Birds 90. JFK 91. Under Siege 92. *The Fugitive* (AA) 93. House of Cards 93. *Heaven and Earth* 93. The Client 94. Blown Away 94. Natural Born Killers 94. Blue Sky (made 91) 94. Cobb 94. Batman Forever 95. The Good Old Boys (& co-w, d, TV) 95. Men in Black 97. US Marshals 98, etc.
❝ I'm in the cattle business, I raise Brangus cattle, I'm a polo player, I'm an actor, a family man, and I'm a bit of an intellectual. 'Intellectual' is a pretentious term – just as easily call me a bookworm. I'm not really obsessive about anything other than cinema. And polo. – *T.L.J.*

Jones, Trevor (1949–).
South African-born composer. He studied at the Royal Academy of Music and at the National Film School.
Brothers and Sisters 80. Excalibur 81. The Dark Crystal 82. The Sender 82. Those Glory Glory Days 83. Nate and Hayes 83. Runaway Train 85. Labyrinth 86. Angel Heart 87. Dominick and Eugene 88. Just Ask for Diamond 88. Sweet Lies 88. Mississippi Burning 88. Sea of Love 89. Defenceless 90. Arachnophobia 90. Bad Influence 90. Freejack 92. Blame It on the Bellboy 92. Cliffhanger 93. In the Name of the Father 93. The Hideaway 95. Kiss of Death 95. Richard III 95. Loch Ness 95. Gulliver's Travels 95. Roseanna's Grave/For Roseanna 96. Brassed Off 96. GI Jane 97. Dark City 97. Merlin (TV) 98. Desperate Measures 98. Talk of Angels 98, etc.

Jordan, Bert (1887–1983).
English editor, a former cameraman and actor, in Hollywood from 1915. He spent most of his career at the Hal Roach Studio, editing many of its films and later its television programmes, including much of Laurel and Hardy's output, although the on-screen credit was given to Richard Currier, head of Roach's editing department from 1920–32.
County Hospital 32. Twice Two 32. The Devil's Brother 33. Busy Bodies 33. Sons of the Desert 33. Babes in Toyland 34. Bonnie Scotland 35. The Bohemian Girl 36. Our Relations 36. Way out West 37. Swiss Miss 38. Block-Heads 38. Of Mice and Men (AAN) 39. A Chump at Oxford 40, etc.

Jordan, Bobby (1923–1965).
American actor, one of the original Dead End Kids.
Dead End 37. Angels with Dirty Faces 38. They Made Me a Criminal 39. That Gang of Mine 40. Pride of the Bowery 41. Let's Get Tough 42. Clancy Street Boys 43. Bowery Champs 44. Bowery Bombshell 46. Hard Boiled Mahoney 47. Treasure of Monte Cristo 49. This Man Is Armed 56, many others.

Jordan, Dorothy (1906–1988).
American leading actress, from the stage. Retired after marrying producer Merian C. Cooper, returning in the 50s to play supporting roles in three films by John Ford.
Black Magic 29. The Taming of the Shrew (as Bianca) 29. Devil May Care 29. Love in the Rough 30. Beloved Bachelor 31. Lost Squadron 32. The Sun Shines Bright 53. The Searchers 56. The Wings of Eagles 57, etc.

Jordan, Neil (1950–).
Irish director and screenwriter.
Angel (Ire.) 82. Company of Wolves 84. Mona Lisa 85. High Spirits (wd) 88. We're No Angels (d) 89. The Miracle (wd) 90. *The Crying Game* (wd) (AAw, AANd) 92. *Interview with the Vampire* (co-w, d) 94. Michael Collins 96. The Butcher Boy (co-w, d) 97. In Dreams 98, etc.

Jordan, Richard (1937–1993).
American leading actor, often as a cold-eyed villain, and theatre director. He also appeared in more than a hundred Broadway and off-Broadway productions. He was divorced from actress Kathleen Widdoes and had a son by actress Blair Brown. Died of a brain tumour.
Lawman 70. Valdez Is Coming 71. The Friends of Eddie Coyle 73. The Yakuza 75. Kamouraska 75. Rooster Cogburn 75. *Captains and the Kings* (TV) 76. Logan's Run 76. Les Misérables (TV) 78. Interiors 78. The Defection of Simas Kurdika (TV) 78. Old Boyfriends 79. Raise the Titanic 80. The French Atlantic Affair (TV) 80. Dune 84. The Mean Season 84. The Men's Club 86. Solarbabies 86. The Secret of My Success 87. Romero 89. The Hunt for Red October 90. Shout 91. Gettysburg 93, etc.

Jory, Victor (1902–1982).
Saturnine Canadian actor, on stage from mid-20s. Usually a villain on screen.
Sailor's Luck (debut) 32. A Midsummer Night's Dream (as Oberon) 35. *The Adventures of Tom Sawyer* (as Injun Joe) 38. Gone with the Wind 39. Unknown Guest 44. The Gallant Blade 48. Canadian Pacific 49. Cat Women of the Moon 53. Valley of the Kings 54. Diary of a Scoundrel 56. The Man Who Turned to Stone 58. The Fugitive Kind 60. *The Miracle Worker* 63. Cheyenne Autumn 64. Mackenna's Gold (narration only) 69. A Time for Dying 69. Flap 70. Papillon 73. Devil Dog, Hound of Hell (TV) 78. The Mountain Men 80, many others.
TV series: Manhunt 59–60.

Joseph, Robert L. (1913–1969).
American producer of stage, screen and television, screenwriter and dramatist.
The Third Secret (p, w) 64. Companions in Nightmare (p, w) (TV) 68. Echoes of a Summer (p, w) 75. Rage of Angels (w) (TV) 82. The Sun Also Rises (co-p, w) (TV) 84. World War III (w) (TV) 86. Rage of Angels: The Story Continues (co-p, w) (TV) 86. Sworn to Silence (w) (TV) 87, etc.

Josephs, Wilfred (1927–1997).
English composer. He trained to be a dentist before studying at the Guildhall School of Music.
Fanatic 65. The Deadly Bees 67. My Side of the Mountain (US) 69. All Creatures Great and Small (TV) 75. Callan 75. The Uncanny 77. Martin's Day (US) 85. Mata Hari (US) 85, etc.

Josephson, Erland (1923–).
Swedish character actor.
So Close to Life 58. Hour of the Wolf 68. A Passion 69. Cries and Whispers 72. Scenes from a Marriage 73. Face to Face 75. Beyond Evil 77. Autumn Sonata 78. Marmalade Revolution (& w, co-d) 79. Montenegro 80. Fanny and Alexander 82. After the Rehearsal 84. House of the Yellow Carpet 84. The Sacrifice 86. Saving Grace 86. The Unbearable Lightness of Being 88. Hanussen 89. The Ox/Oxen 91. Sofie 92. Dreamplay/Dromspel 94. Ulysses' Gaze 95. Kristin Lavransdatter 95. In the Presence of a Clown/Larmar Och Gor Sig Tag 98, etc.

Joslyn, Allyn (1905–1981).
American character comedian whose crumpled features admirably portrayed bewilderment.
They Won't Forget (debut) 37. Bedtime Story 41. A Yank in Dutch 42. *Heaven Can Wait* 43. Bride by Mistake 44. Junior Miss 45. *It Shouldn't Happen to a Dog* 47. If You Knew Susie 48. As Young As You Feel 51. Titanic 53. The Fastest Gun Alive 56. The Brothers O'Toole 73, many others.
TV series: The Ray Bolger Show 53. The Eve Arden Show 57. McKeever and the Colonel 62. Don't Call Me Charlie 62. The Addams Family 64.

Jost, Jon (1943–).
American director, screenwriter and editor of independent and experimental movies, currently living in Italy.
Angel City 77. Chameleon 78. State Fright 81. Slow Moves 83. Laughing Rembrandt 88. All the Vermeers in New York 91. Sure Fire 92. The Bed You Sleep In 93. Frameup 93. One for Me, One for You, and One for Raffaello 94. Albrecht's Wings/ Albrechts Flügel 94, etc.

Jourdan, Louis (1920–) (Louis Gendre).
Smooth French leading man who has also made films in Britain and Hollywood.
Le Corsaire (debut) 39. The Paradine Case 48. *Letter from an Unknown Woman* 48. Madame Bovary 49. Bird of Paradise 50. Anne of the Indies 51. *The Happy Time* 52. *Rue de l'Estrapade* 52. Decameron Nights 53. *Three Coins in the Fountain* 54. The Swan 56. Julie 56. *Gigi* 58. The Best of Everything 59. Can-Can 60. The Count of Monte Cristo 61. *The VIPs* 62. Made in Paris 65. Peau d'Espion 67. A Flea in Her Ear 68. Run a Crooked Mile (TV) 71. The Count of Monte Cristo (TV) 76. The Silver Bears 77. The Man in the Iron Mask (TV) 77. Swamp Thing 82. Octopussy 83. Bayou Romance 86. Beverly Hills Madam (TV) 86. Gamble on Love 86. For the Love of Angela 86. Image of Passion 86. Love at the Top 86. Counterforce 87. Return of the Swamp Thing 89. Year of the Comet 92, etc.
TV series: Paris Precinct 53.

Jouvet, Louis (1887–1951).
Distinguished French actor of stage and screen.
■ Topaze 33. Doctor Knock 33. *La Kermesse Héroïque* 35. Mister Flow 36. Les Bas-Fonds 36. Mademoiselle Docteur 36. Un Carnet de Bal 37. *Drôle de Drame* 37. Alibi 37. Forfaiture 37. La Marseillaise 38. Ramuntcho 38. La Maison du Maltais 38. Entrée des Artistes 38. L'Education du Prince 38. Le Drame de Shanghai 38. *Hôtel du Nord* 38. La Fin du Jour 39. La Charrette Fantôme 39. Serenade 40. *Volpone* 40. Untel Père et Fils 40. Un Revenant 46. Copie Conforme 46. *Quai des Orfèvres* 47. Les Amoureux Sont Seuls au Monde 48. Entre Onze Heures et Minuit 49. Retour à la Vie 49. Miquette et Sa Mère 49. Doctor Knock (remake) 50. Une Histoire d'Amour 50.

Jovovich, Milla (1975–).
Russian-born actress, singer and model, in international films. Born in Kiev, she is the daughter of actress Galina Loginova. She moved to Los Angeles with her family in the early 80s and began as a model at the age of 11. Married French director Luc Besson.
Night Train to Katmandu (TV) 88. Two Moon Junction (US) 88. Return to the Blue Lagoon (US) 91. Kuffs (US) 92. Chaplin (GB) 92. Dazed and Confused (US) 93. Fifth Element (Fr.) 97. He Got Game (US) 98. Joan of Arc (Fr.) 99, etc.

Joy, Leatrice (1894–1985) (Leatrice Joy Zeidler).
Vivacious, self-confident American leading lady of the 20s. The first of her three husbands was actor John Gilbert (1921–24).
Bunty Pulls the Strings 20. The Marriage Cheat 21. Manslaughter 22. You Can't Fool Your Wife 23. The Ten Commandments 23. Triumph 24. The Dressmaker from Paris 25. For Alimony Only 26. Angel of Broadway 27. The Blue Danube 28. A Most Immoral Lady 29. First Love 39. Red Stallion in the Rockies 49. Love Nest 52, etc.

Joy, Nicholas (1894–1964).
American small part actor often seen as beaming toff or benevolent father.
Daisy Kenyon 47. If Winter Comes 47. The Great Gatsby 49. And Baby Makes Three 50. Man with a Cloak 51. Affair with a Stranger 53. Desk Set 57, etc.

Joy, Robert (1951–).
Canadian leading actor.
Amityville 3-D/Amityville: The Demon 83. Desperately Seeking Susan 85. Big Shots 87. She's Back 88. The Suicide Club 88. Millennium 89. Longtime Companion 90. Shadows and Fog 92. Ballad of Little Jo 93. The Dark Half 93. Henry and Verlin 94. Death Wish V 94. Waterworld 95. Harriet the Spy 96, etc.

Joyce, Adrien:
see Eastman, Carole.

Joyce, Alice (1889–1955).
American leading lady of the silent screen.
Womanhood 17. The Lion and the Mouse 19. Cousin Kate 21. The Green Goddess 23. Daddy's Gone a-Hunting 25. The Squall 29. Song o' My Heart 38, etc.

Joyce, Brenda (1918–) (Betty Leabo).
American leading lady, former model. Played innocent types in the 40s, then retired.
The Rains Came (debut) 39. Little Old New York 40. Maryland 40. Marry the Boss's Daughter 41. Whispering Ghosts 42. The Postman Didn't Ring 42. Little Tokyo USA 43. Strange Confession 45. The Enchanted Forest 46. Tarzan and the Huntress 47. Shaggy 48. Tarzan's Magic Fountain 49, etc.

Joyce, James (1882–1941).
Irish writer and dramatist. In 1909, backed by Swiss businessmen, he opened Dublin's first cinema, Cinematograph Volta, which began with a showing of Caserini's *Beatrice Cenci*.
Finnegans Wake 65. Ulysses 67. A Portrait of the Artist as a Young Man 79. The Dead (from Dubliners) 87.

Joyce, Yootha (1927–1980).
Angular British character actress, popular in TV comedy series *A Man About the House* and *George and Mildred*.
Sparrows Can't Sing 62. The Pumpkin Eater 64. Stranger in the House 67. Burke and Hare 71. George and Mildred 80.

Judd, Ashley (1969–).
American actress, daughter of country singer Naomi Judd.
Kuffs 92. *Ruby in Paradise* 93. Natural Born Killers 94. Smoke 95. Heat 95. Norma Jean and Marilyn (TV) 96. A Time to Kill 96. *Normal Life* 96. Kiss the Girls 97. The Locusts 97. Simon Birch 98, etc.
TV series: Sisters 91–94.

Judd, Edward (1932–).
British general-purpose actor.
The Day the Earth Caught Fire 61. Stolen Hours 63. The Long Ships 63. *The First Men in the Moon* 64. Strange Bedfellows 65. Island of Terror 66. Invasion 66. The Vengeance of She 68. Living Free 71. Universal Soldier 71. Vault of Horror 73. Assassin 73, The Incredible Sarah 76. The Kitchen Toto 87, etc.

Judge, Arline (1912–1974).
American general-purpose leading lady.
Bachelor Apartment 31. Girl Crazy 32. Name This Woman 35. King of Burlesque 36. Valiant Is the Word for Carrie 36. The Lady Is Willing 42. From This Day Forward 45. Two Knights in Brooklyn 49, etc.

Judge, Mike.
American director and screenwriter, best known as the creator of the animated TV series *Beavis and Butthead* and *King of the Hill*. Born in Ecuador and brought up in Albuquerque, he studed physics at the University of California, and is based in Austin, Texas.
Beavis and Butthead Do America 96.

Juillard, Robert (1906–).
French cinematographer.
Germany Year Zero 48. Jeux Interdits 52. Les Belles de Nuit 52. Les Grandes Manoeuvres 55. Austerlitz 60, etc.

Julia, Raul (1940–1994).
Puerto Rican character actor in Hollywood.
Eyes of Laura Mars 78. One from the Heart 82. The Escape Artist 82. Tempest 82. Compromising Positions 85. Kiss of the Spider Woman 85. The Morning After 86. Florida Straits 87. La Gran Fiesta 87. Moon over Parador 88. The Penitent 88. Tango Bar 88. Tequila Sunrise 88. Trading Hearts 88. Romero 89. Mack the Knife 89. A Life of Sin 90. Presumed Innocent 90. Frankenstein Unbound 90. Havana 90. The Rookie 90. The Addams Family 91. The Plague/La Peste 92. Addams Family Values 93. The Burning Season (TV) 94. Down Came a Blackbird (TV) 95, etc.

Julian, Rupert (1889–1943).
American director of the 20s.
Merry Go Round 23. Love and Glory 24. Hell's Highroad 25. *The Phantom of the Opera* 25. Three Faces West 26. Yankee Clipper 27. The Leopard Lady 28. Love Comes Along 30. The Cat Creeps 30, etc.

Julien, Isaac (1960–).
British screenwriter and director.
Looking for Langston (short) 90. Young Soul Rebels 91. Darker Side of Black (doc) 94.
❝ One of the things I've been trying to champion is a black independent cinema which deals with questions of sexuality and gender and national identity. – *I.J.*

Julius Caesar (102–44 BC).
The Roman emperor has been memorably portrayed by Claude Rains in *Caesar and Cleopatra*, Warren William in the 1934 *Cleopatra*, and Rex Harrison in the 1962 remake. Shakespeare's play was filmed many times in silent days, but the only notable sound versions in English have been Joseph L. Mankiewicz's 1953 production with Louis Calhern as Caesar, James Mason as Brutus, John Gielgud as Cassius, and Marlon Brando as Mark Antony, and the 1970 version with Gielgud as Caesar, Richard Johnson as Cassius, and Charlton Heston as Mark Antony. A British second feature of 1959, *An Honourable Murder*, brought the story up to date as a melodrama of boardroom intrigue. In *Carry On Cleo* Kenneth Williams played Caesar, and may have started the decline and fall of the Roman empire.

Jump, Gordon (1932–).
Plump Canadian character actor, familiar as the boss in TV series *WKRP in Cincinnati*.
Conquest of the Planet of the Apes 72. House Calls 78. Four Days in Dallas (TV) 78. The Fury 78. Dirkham Detective Agency 83. Making the Grade 84. Moving 88. Honeymoon Academy 90. Bitter Vengeance (TV) 94, etc.
TV series: Growing Pains 86–91. Sister Kate 89. The New WKRP in Cincinnati 91.

June (1901–1985) (June Howard Tripp).
British musical comedy star of the 20s and 30s. Married Lord Inverclyde; divorced. Films few.
Autobiography: 1960, *The Glass Ladder*.
■ Auld Lang Syne 17. Tom Jones 17. *The Lodger* 26. Forever and a Day 43. The River (voice only) 51.

June, Ray (1898–1958).
American cinematographer.
Wandering Husbands 24. The Silent Avenger 27. Alibi 29. Arrowsmith 31. Horse Feathers 32. Riptide 34. I Cover the Waterfront 35. Night Must Fall 37. Test Pilot 38. The Hoodlum Saint 46. A Southern Yankee 48. Crisis 50. The Reformer and the Redhead 51. Sombrero 53. The Court Jester 55. Funny Face 56. Houseboat 58, many others.

Junge, Alfred (1886–1964).
German art director with long experience at UFA; in Britain from the 20s.
Piccadilly 28. The Good Companions 32. *The Man Who Knew Too Much* 34. Bulldog Jack 35. *King Solomon's Mines* 37. The Citadel 38. *Goodbye Mr Chips* 39. The Silver Fleet 42. *The Life and Death of Colonel Blimp* 43. I Know Where I'm Going 45. *A Matter of Life and Death* 45. *Black Narcissus* (AA) 46. Edward My Son 49. The Miniver Story 50. Ivanhoe 52. Mogambo 53. *Invitation to the Dance* 56. The Barretts of Wimpole Street 57. A Farewell to Arms 58, many others.

Junkin, John (1930–).
Tall, balding British comic character actor, a TV familiar.
The Break 63. A Hard Day's Night 64. The Pumpkin Eater 64. Kaleidoscope 67. How I Won the War 67. Brass Target 78. Chicago Joe and the Showgirl 89, etc.

Jurado, Katy (1927–) (Maria Jurado Garcia).
Spirited Mexican actress who has made Hollywood films. Born in Guadalajara, she began in films at the age of 15, concentrating on US films from the 50s, though she has continued to appear in a few Mexican movies. She was romantically involved with Marlon Brando; married actor Ernest Borgnine (1959–64).
The Bullfighter and the Lady 51. San Antone 52. El Bruto 52. High Noon 52. Arrowhead 53. Broken Lance (AAN) 54. The Racers 55. Trial 55. Man from Del Rio 56. Trapeze 56. The Badlanders 58. One-Eyed Jacks 61. Seduction of the South/I Briganti Italiani (It./Fr.) 61. Barabbas/Barabba (It.) 62. Smoky 66. A Covenant with Death 66. Stay Away, Joe 68. Any Second Now 69. Bridge in the Jungle 70. Once Upon a Scoundrel 73. Pat

Garrett and Billy the Kid 73. The Children of Sanchez 78. Evita Peron (TV) 82. Under the Volcano 84. The Fearmaker 89. Divine 98, etc.

Juran, Nathan (1907–).
Austrian art director, long in the US. Won Academy Award for *How Green Was My Valley* 41. Later became a director of action films.
■ The Black Castle 52. Gunsmoke 53. Law and Order 53. The Golden Blade 53. Tumbleweed 53. Highway Dragnet 54. Drums along the River 54. The Crooked Web 55. The Deadly Mantis 57. Hellcats of the Navy 57. Twenty Million Miles to Earth 57. The Seventh Voyage of Sinbad 58. Good Day for a Hanging 58. Flight of the Lost Balloon 61. *Jack the Giant Killer* 62. Siege of the Saxons 63. First Men in the Moon 64. East of Sudan 65. The Land Raiders 70. The Boy Who Cried Werewolf 73.

Jurgens, Curt (1912–1982).
German stage leading man, in films from 1935; after the war he played internationally.

Koenigswalzer (debut) 35. Der Engel mit der Posaune 48. Orientexpress 54. The Devil's General 54. Les Héros Sont Fatigués 55. *An Eye for an Eye* 56. Without You It Is Night (& d) 56. And Woman Was Created 57. *Me and the Colonel* 57. The Enemy Below 57. Inn of the Sixth Happiness 58. The Blue Angel 58. Ferry to Hong Kong 58. *I Aim at the Stars* (as Wernher von Braun) 59. Tamango 60. Chess Novel 60. The Threepenny Opera 63. Lord Jim 64. Das Liebeskarussel/Who Wants to Sleep 65. The Assassination Bureau 68. The Battle of Neretva 70. Nicholas and Alexandra 71. Vault of Horror 73. Soft Beds and Hard Battles 74. The Spy Who Loved Me 77. l, Cagliostro 77. Sergeant Steiner 79. Goldengirl (TV) 79. Just a Gigolo 80, etc.

Jurow, Martin (1914–).
American producer who retired in the mid-60s to practise law.

The Hanging Tree 58. The Fugitive Kind 60. Breakfast at Tiffany's 61. Soldier in the Rain 63.

The Great Race 65. Waltz across Texas 82. Sylvester 85. Papa Was a Preacher (TV) 85, etc.

Jusid, Juan José (1941–).
Argentinian director, also active as a producer and director of commercials.

Tute Cabrero 78. Los Gauchos Judios 74. Espérame Mucho 83. Made in Argentina 86, etc.

Justice, James Robertson (1905–1975).
Bearded Scottish actor and personality, former journalist and naturalist.

Fiddlers Three (debut) 44. *Scott of the Antarctic* 48. Christopher Columbus 49. *Whisky Galore* 49. David and Bathsheba 51. The Voice of Merrill 52. *Doctor in the House* 54. Storm over the Nile 55. Land of the Pharaohs 55. Moby Dick 56. Campbell's Kingdom 57. Seven Thunders 57. Doctor at Large 58. A French Mistress 60. *Very Important Person* 61. Das Feuerschiff 62. *The Fast Lady* 62. Crooks Anonymous 62. You Must Be Joking 65. Doctor in Clover 66. Hell is Empty 67.

Mayerling 68. Chitty Chitty Bang Bang 68, many others.

Justin, John (1917–).
British leading man, on stage from 1933.

The Thief of Baghdad (film debut) 40. The Gentle Sex 43. Journey Together 45. Call of the Blood 47. The Sound Barrier 51. Melba 53. Seagulls over Sorrento 54. The Man Who Loved Redheads 55. The Teckman Mystery 55. Safari 56. Island in the Sun 56. The Spider's Web 61. Candidate for Murder 64. Savage Messiah 72. Valentino 77. The Big Sleep 78. Trenchcoat 83, etc.

Jympson, John.
British editor.

A Hard Day's Night 64. *Zulu* 64. The Bedford Incident 65. Where Eagles Dare 69. Kelly's Heroes 70. Frenzy 72. *The Optimists of Nine Elms* 73. Mr Quilp 75. The Incredible Sarah 76. A Little Night Music 77. Meetings with Remarkable Men 79. Little Shop of Horrors 86. *A Fish Called Wanda* 88. King Ralph 91. Splitting Heirs 93. Circle of Friends 95. Haunted 95. In and Out 97, etc.

K

Kachyna, Karel (1924–).
Czechoslovakian director and screenwriter, a former cinematographer, who began as a maker of documentaries.

Hope/Nadeje 63. Long Live the Republic/At Zije Republika 65. *Coach to Vienna/Kocar do Vidne* 66. Night of the Bride/Noc Nevesty 67. *The Ear/Ucho* 69. I'm Jumping over Puddles Again/Uz Zase Skacu Pres Kaluze 70. Laska/Love 73. A House of Sugar/Cukrova Bouda 80. An Amateur Photographer/Dobre Svetlo 85. Bilitis, My Love (US/Switz.) (co-d) 91. The Last Butterfly (GB/Czech.) 91. The Cow/Krava 94. Fanny 96, etc.

Kaczender, George (1933–).
Hungarian director.

U-Turn 73. In Praise of Older Women 78. Agency 80. Chanel Solitaire 81. The Finishing Touch 83. Prettykill 87. Christmas on Division Street (TV) 91. Danielle Steel's Vanished (TV) 95. Devil's Food 96. Maternal Instincts 96, etc.

Kadar, Jan (1918–1979).
Czech director who worked with writer Elmer Klos (1910–93).

Kidnap 56. Death Is Called Engelchen 58. The Accused 64. *A Shop on Main Street* (AA) 64. The Angel Levine (US) 70. Adrift 71. Lies My Father Told Me 76. *The Other Side of Hell* (TV) 77. Freedom Road (TV) 80, etc.

Kael, Pauline (1919–).
American critic, most of whose reviews have been collected for publications.

❝ Movies are so rarely great that if we cannot appreciate great trash we have very little reason to be interested in them – P.K.

Kafka, Franz (1883–1924).
German/Czech novelist who wrote puzzling tales of guilt and innocence in a glum fantasy world. *The Trial* and *The Castle* have been filmed. In 1992 *Kafka*, a film based on his life, was made by Steven Soderbergh.

Kagan, Jeremy Paul (1945–).
American director.

■ Unwed Father (TV) 74. Judge Dee (TV) 75. Katherine (TV) 75. Scott Joplin 76. Heroes 77. The Big Fix 78. The Chosen 82. Sting II 83. The Journey of Natty Gann 85. Courage (TV) 86. Conspiracy: Trial of the Chicago 8 (TV) 87. Big Man on Campus 89. Descending Angel 91. By the Sword 91. Roswell (TV) 94.

Kagawa, Kyoko (1931–).
Japanese leading actress, usually in demure roles, and often in Akira Kurosawa's films.

Mother/Okasan 52. Tokyo Story/Tokyo Monogatari 53. Sansho the Bailiff/Sanso Dayu 54. The Story of Chikamatsu/Chikamatsu Monogatari 54. The Lower Depths/Donzoko 57. The Bad Sleep Well/Warui Yoku Nemuru 60. Mothra 61. High and Low 63. Red Beard 65. Tora-san's Dream of Spring 79. Madadayo 93, etc.

Kahn, Gus (1886–1941).
German-American lyricist who made a specialty of film scores, and was played by Danny Thomas in *I'll See You in My Dreams*.

The Jazz Singer 27. Whoopee 30. Flying Down to Rio 33. San Francisco 36. Go West 40, many others.

Kahn, Madeline (1942–).
American comic actress who tends to overplay her hand; the darling of the Mel Brooks clique.

What's Up Doc? 72. Paper Moon (AAN) 73. Blazing Saddles (AAN) 74. Young Frankenstein 74.

The Adventures of Sherlock Holmes' Smarter Brother 75. At Long Last Love 75. Won Ton Ton 76. High Anxiety 77. The Cheap Detective 78. The Muppet Movie 79. The First Family 80. Happy Birthday Gemini 80. Simon 80. Wholly Moses 80. History of the World Part One 81. Yellowbeard 83. City Heat 84. Clue 85. An American Tail (voice) 86. My Little Pony 86. Betsy's Wedding 90. Mixed Nuts 94. A Bug's Life (voice) 98, etc.

TV series: Oh Madeline 83. Mr President 87–88.

Kahn, Michael.
American editor, from TV.

Rage 72. Trouble Man 72. The Spook Who Sat by the Door 73. Truck Turner 74. Buster and Billie 74. The Devil's Rain 75. The Return of a Man Called Horse 76. Close Encounters of the Third Kind (AAN) 77. Eyes of Laura Mars 78. 1941 79. Raiders of the Lost Ark (AA) 81. Poltergeist 82. Table for Five 83. Indiana Jones and the Temple of Doom 84. The Color Purple 85. The Goonies 85. Wisdom 86. Empire of the Sun (AAN) 87. Fatal Attraction (AAN) 87. Always 89. Indiana Jones and the Last Crusade 89. Arachnophobia 90. Toy Soldiers 91. Hook 91. Jurassic Park 93. Schindler's List (AA) 93. Nixon 95. Casper 95. Twister 96. The Lost World: Jurassic Park 97. Amistad 97. Saving Private Ryan 98, etc.

Kaidanovsky, Alexander (1946–1995).
Russian leading actor and director, from the stage, best known for playing the title role in Andrei Tarkovsky's *Stalker*. Following that film, he studied directing under Tarkovsky at Moscow's Institute of Cinema. Died of a heart attack.

AS ACTOR: At Home among Strangers/Svoi Sredi Chuzhikh, Chuzhoi Sredi Svoikh 74. Gold River/Zolotaya Rechka 76. Povorot 78. *Stalker* 79. El Aliento del Diablo (Sp.) 93. Magic Hunter (Hung.) 94, etc.

AS DIRECTOR: A Simple Death/Prostaya Smert 87. *The Kerosene Seller's Wife*/Zhena Kerosinshchika 88. The Visitor/Gost 88. Maestro (doc on Sergei Paradjanov) 93, etc.

Kaige, Chen (1952–).
Chinese director and screenwriter.

Yellow Earth 84. Forced Take-Off (TV) 85. The Big Parade 86. King of the Children (wd) 88. Life on a String/Bian Zou Bian Chang 91. Farewell My Concubine/Bawang Bie Ji (AAN) 93. Temptress Moon 97. The Assassin 98, etc.

Kalatozov, Mikhail (1903–1973).
Russian director and executive.

Their Kingdom 28. Salt for Svenetia 30. A Nail in a Boot 32. The Conspiracy of the Doomed 50. *The Cranes are Flying* 57. The Unsent Letter 60. I Am Cuba 66. The Red Tent 69.

Kalin, Tom (1962–).
American director, a former painter and photographer.

Swoon 92. Go Fish (p only) 94. I Shot Andy Warhol (p only) 96. Office Killer (co-w) 97, etc.

Kalloch, Robert (1893–1943).
American fashion designer, at Columbia studios from the early 30s.

That's My Boy 32. The Wrecker 33. The Bitter Tea of General Yen 33. Lady for a Day 33. One Night of Love 34. It Happened One Night 34. Women of Glamour 37. The Shadow 37. I'll Take Romance 37. Women in Prison 38. Joy of Living 38. Little Miss Roughneck 38. Blind Alley 39. Coast Guard 39. Golden Boy 39. Mr Smith Goes to Washington 39. His Girl Friday 40. Angels over

Broadway 40. Honky Tonk 41. Babes on Broadway 41. I Married an Angel 42. Random Harvest 42. Mrs Miniver 42. White Cargo 42. For Me and My Gal 42. Tortilla Flat 42, etc.

Kalmar, Bert (1884–1947).
American vaudevillian, songwriter (with Harry Ruby) and music executive.

Check and Double Check (& w) 30. The Kid from Spain (& w) 32. *Horse Feathers* (& w) 32. *Duck Soup* (& w) 33. Kentucky Kernels (& w) 34. Everybody Sing 38. Wake Up and Dream 46. Carnival in Costa Rica 48, many others.

Kalmus, Herbert T. (1881–1963).
American pioneer photographic expert, later president of Technicolor. His wife Natalie Kalmus (1892–1965) was adviser on all Technicolor films from 1933.

Kamen, Michael (1948–).
American composer; he studied at the Juilliard School in New York and was a member of 60s group the New York Rock and Roll Ensemble.

The Next Man 76. Between the Lines 77. Polyester 81. Angelo, My Love 83. The Dead Zone 83. Brazil 85. Highlander 85. Mona Lisa 85. Lethal Weapon 87. Adventures in Babysitting 87. Someone to Watch Over Me 87. Die Hard 88. For Queen and Country 88. The Adventures of Baron Munchausen 89. Round House 89. Licence to Kill 89. Lethal Weapon 2 89. The Krays 90. Die Hard II 90. Let Him Have It 91. Nothing but Trouble 91. The Last Boy Scout 91. Company Business 91. Shining Through 92. Lethal Weapon 3 92. Splitting Heirs 93. The Last Action Hero 93. Wilder Napalm 93. The Three Musketeers 93. Circle of Friends 95. Don Juan DeMarco 95. Mr Holland's Opus 95. Jack 96. 101 Dalmatians 96. The Winter Guest 97. Inventing the Abbots 97. Event Horizon 97. What Dreams May Come 98, etc.

Kaminska, Ida (1899–1980).
Polish character actress.

Autobiography: 1973, *My Life, My Theater*.
The Shop on High Street (AAN) 66. The Angel Levine (US) 70, etc.

Kaminski, Janusz (1961–).
Polish-born cinematographer who emigrated to America in 1981.

The Rain Killer 90. The Terror Within II 91. Schindler's List (AA) 93. The Adventures of Huck Finn 93. Little Giants 94. Tall Tale: The Unbelievable Adventures of Pecos Bill 95. How to Make an American Quilt 95. The Lost World: Jurassic Park 97. Amistad (AAN) 97, etc.

Kandel, Aben (1896–1993).
American screenwriter and novelist who worked on several British horror movies of the 60s and 70s produced by Herman Cohen; he sometimes used the pseudonym Kenneth Langtry.

Sing and Like It (story) 34. They Won't Forget (co-w) 37. Thunder in the City (GB) (co-w) 37. City for Conquest (oa) 40. They Won't Forget (co-w) 47. The Iron Major (co-w) 43. High Conquest 47. The Horrors of the Black Museum (GB) (co-w) 59. Konga (GB) (co-w) 60. Circus of Blood (GB) (co-w) 67. Trog (GB) 70. Craze (GB) 73, etc.

Kander, John (1927–).
American composer, with Fred Ebb, of *Cabaret*.

Something for Everyone 70. Kramer vs Kramer 79. Still of the Night 82. Blue Skies Again 83. I Want to Go Home (Fr.) 89.

Kane, Carol (1952–).
American leading lady of the late 70s.

Hester Street (AAN) 74. Annie Hall 77. The World's Greatest Lover 77. Valentino 77. The Muppet Movie 79. When a Stranger Calls 79. Strong Medicine 81. Norman Loves Rose 82. Can She Bake a Cherry Pie? 83. Over the Brooklyn Bridge 83. Racing with the Moon 84. The Secret Diary of Sigmund Freud 84. Transylvania 6–5000 85. Jumpin' Jack Flash 86. Ishtar 87. The Princess Bride 87. License to Drive 88. Scrooged 88. Sticky Fingers 88. Flashback 90. Joe versus the Volcano 90. The Lemon Sisters 90. My Blue Heaven 90. Addams Family Values 93. Big Bully 96. American Strays 96. Theodore Rex 96. Trees Lounge 96. Office Killer 97. Gone Fishin' 97, etc.

Kane, Helen (1904–1966) (Helen Schroeder).
American singer of the 20s, the 'boop-boop-a-doop' girl. Played by Debbie Reynolds in *Three Little Words* (in which Miss Kane supplied her own voice).

Pointed Heels 29. Dangerous Nan McGrew 29. Heads Up 30, etc.

Kane, Joseph (1894–1975).
American director since 1935, mainly of competent but unambitious Republic westerns.

The Man from Music Mountain 38. The Man from Cheyenne 42. Flame of the Barbary Coast 44. The Cheaters 45. The Plainsman and the Lady 46. The Plunderers (& p) 48. California Passage (& p) 50. Hoodlum Empire (& p) 51. Jubilee Trail (& p) 53. Spoilers of the Forest (& p) 57, many others.

Kanevsky, Vitaly (1934–).
Russian director and screenwriter who made his first film, an autobiographical account of his deprived boyhood, at the age of 55.

Don't Move, Die, and Rise Again!/Zamri, Umri, Voskresni 90. An Independent Life 92. We, the Children of the Twentieth Century (doc) 94, etc.

Kanganis, Charles T.
American director of action films.

Deadly Breed 89. Sinners 89. Intent to Kill 90. A Time to Die 91. No Escape, No Return 93. 3 Ninjas Kick Back 94. Race the Sun 96. Dennis the Menace Strikes Again 98, etc.

Kanievska, Marek.
British director, from television, who keeps busy making commercials.

Shoestring (TV) 80. Another Country 84. Less than Zero 87.

Kanin, Garson (1912–).
American writer and raconteur who has spent time in Hollywood as director, also as screenwriter, especially in collaboration with his wife Ruth Gordon.

Autobiographical books: 1974, *Hollywood*. 1976, *It Takes a Long Time to Become Young*.

■ AS DIRECTOR: A Man to Remember 38. Next Time I Marry 38. *The Great Man Votes* 38. *Bachelor Mother* 39. My Favorite Wife 40. They Knew What They Wanted 40. Tom, Dick and Harry 41. The True Glory (w, co-d) (AA) 45. Where It's At (& w) 69. Some Kind of a Nut (& w) 70.

AS WRITER: From This Day Forward 46. A Double Life (AAN) 47. *Adam's Rib* (AAN) 49. *Born Yesterday* (oa) 50. The Marrying Kind 52. Pat and Mike (AAN) 52. It Should Happen to You 53. The Girl Can't Help It 56. The Rat Race 60. The Right Approach 61. Where It's At (d) 68. Some Kind of Nut 69. Born Yesterday (oa) 93, etc.

Kanin, Michael (1910–1993).
American writer brother of Garson Kanin; often worked with his wife Fay.
Anne of Windy Poplars 40. *Woman of the Year* (AA) 42. The Cross of Lorraine 44. Centennial Summer 46. Rhapsody 54. The Opposite Sex 56. Teacher's Pet (AAN) 58. The Outrage 64. How to Commit Marriage 69, etc.

Kann, Lily (1898–1978).
German character actress, long in England.
The Flemish Farm 43. Latin Quarter 45. Mrs Fitzherbert 47. A Tale of Five Cities 51. Betrayed (US) 54. A Kid for Two Farthings 55. No Trees in the Street 59, many others.

Kanner, Alexis (1942–).
British character actor.
Reach for Glory 63. Crossplot 69. Connecting Rooms 69. Goodbye Gemini 70. Kings and Desperate Men (a, wd) 84. Nightfall 88. Twinsanity 88, etc.

Kanter, Hal (1918–).
American writer-director with TV background.
I Married a Woman (d) 55. Loving You (wd) 56. Once Upon a Horse (wd) 58. Pocketful of Miracles (co-w) 61. Move Over Darling (w) 63. Dear Brigitte (w) 65. For the Love of It (TV) 80, etc.

Kantor, Mackinlay (1904–1977).
American writer full of sentiment and patriotism.
The Voice of Bugle Ann 37. Happy Land 43. The Best Years of Our Lives 46. The Romance of Rosy Ridge 47. Andersonville 59. Follow Me Boys 66.

Kaper, Bronislau (1902–1983).
Polish composer who lived in US.
The Chocolate Soldier 41. Two Faced Woman 41. Gaslight 44. Without Love 45. Green Dolphin Street 47. The Forsyte Saga 49. *The Red Badge of Courage* 51. *Lili* (AA) 53. *Them* 54. The Swan 56. The Brothers Karamazov 58. Green Mansions 59. Butterfield 8 61. Mutiny on the Bounty (AAN) 62. Kisses for My President 64. Lord Jim 64. Tobruk 66. The Way West 67. A Flea in Her Ear 68, etc.

Kaplan, Jonathan (1947–).
American director, the son of Sol KAPLAN.
Student Teachers 73. Night Call Nurses 74. White Line Fever (& w) 75. Mr Billion (& w) 77. Over the Edge 79. Heart like a Wheel 83. Project X 87. The Accused 88. Immediate Family 89. Love Field 92. Unlawful Entry 92. Bad Girls 94. In Cold Blood (TV) 96, etc.

Kaplan, Marvin (1924–).
Owlish little American comedy actor.
The Reformer and the Redhead 50. I Can Get It for You Wholesale 51. Angels in the Outfield 51. Behave Yourself 51. Wake Me When It's Over 60. A New Kind of Love 63. It's a Mad Mad Mad Mad World 63. The Great Race 65. Wild at Heart 90, etc.
TV series: Chicago Teddybears 71. Alice 81–82.

Kaplan, Nelly (1934–).
French director and screenwriter.
■ La Fiancée du Pirate/Dirty Mary 69. Papa les Petits Bateaux 71. Néa 76. Le Satellite de Vénus 77. Au Bonheur des Dames 79. Charles et Lucie 79. Abel Gance et Son (wd) 84. Plaisir d'Amour (wd) 91.

Kaplan, Sol (1913–1990).
American composer.
Tales of Manhattan 42. Port of New York 49. Rawhide 51. Niagara 53. Happy Anniversary 59. The Victors 63. The Spy Who Came in from the Cold 65. Explosion 69. Living Free 72. Lies My Father Told Me 75. Over the Edge 79, etc.

Kapoor, Shashi (1938–).
Indian leading actor and producer, in occasional international films.
Aag 48. Awaara 51. Householder 62. Shakespeare Wallah 65. Bombay Talkie 70. Siddharta 72. Heat and Dust 83. Sammy and Rosie Get Laid 87. The Deceivers 88. In Custody/Hifazaat 93. Gulliver's Travels (TV) 96. Side Streets (US) 98, etc.

Kaprisky, Valérie (1963–).
French leading actress.
Aphrodite 82. Breathless 83. The Public Woman/La Femme Publique 83. The Year of the Jellyfish/L'Année des Méduses 86. L'Amant 89. Milena 90. The End Is Known/La Fine è Nota 93. Mouvements du Désir 94. Say Yes/Dis-Moi Oui 95, etc.

Kapur, Shekhar (1945–).
Indian director and actor. Born in Bombay, he studied economics in New Delhi and worked in Britain as an accountant before becoming involved in films. Married singer Suchitra Krishnamurti.
AS DIRECTOR: Masoom . . . 'Innocent' 82. Mr India 87. Bandit Queen 94. Dushmani 95. Time Machine 95. Elizabeth (GB) 98, etc.

Karas, Anton (1906–1985).
Viennese composer whose zither music, played by himself, helped to turn *The Third Man* into a classic.

Karaszewski, Larry.
American screenwriter, usually in collaboration with Scott ALEXANDER. The pair worked uncredited on *Mars Attacks!* 96.
Problem Child 90. Problem Child 2 91. Ed Wood 94. The People vs Larry Flynt 96, etc.
❝ *Twister* started a whole new era where the story and characters were totally unimportant. I feel the screenwriter's job is now similar to being a theme park ride operator. – *L.K.*

Karina, Anna (1940–) (Hanne Karin Beyer).
Danish leading lady, mostly in French films, especially those of Jean-Luc Godard.
She'll Have To Go (GB) 61. *Une Femme Est une Femme* 61. *Vivre Sa Vie* 62. Le Petit Soldat 63. Bande à Part 64. Alphaville 65. Made in USA 66. The Magus 68. Before Winter Comes 68. Laughter in the Dark 69. Justine 69. The Salzburg Connection 72. Bread and Chocolate 73. Chinese Roulette 76. Chaussette Surprise 78. Laissez Parler les Adultes 80. L'Ami de Vincent 83. Ave Maria 84. Cayenne-Palace 87. Last Song (& w) 87. The Abyss/L'Oeuvre au Noir 88. The Man Who Would Be Guilty 89. Treasure Island 91. Up Down Fragile/Haut Bas Fragile 95, etc.

Karlin, Fred (1936–).
American composer, mainly for TV films.
Up the Down Staircase 67. Yours Mine and Ours 68. Lovers and Other Strangers 69. The Little Ark 71. Westworld 73. The Spikes Gang 74. Death Be Not Proud (TV) 75. Futureworld 76. Man from Atlantis (TV) 77. Cloud Dancer 80. Loving Couples 80. Jacqueline Susann's Valley of the Dolls (TV) 81. Calamity Jane (TV) 83. Vasectomy: A Delicate Matter 86. Lady Mobster (TV) 88. Bridge to Silence (TV) 89, many others.

Karlin, Miriam (1925–) (M. Samuels).
Rasping-voiced British revue comedienne and character actress.
The Deep Blue Sea 55. The Entertainer 59. On the Fiddle 61. The Small World of Sammy Lee 63. Heavens Above 63. The Bargee 64. Ladies Who Do 64. A Clockwork Orange 71. Mahler 74. Utz 92, etc.
TV series: East End, West End 58. The Rag Trade 61–63, 77–78. So Haunt Me 92–94.

Karloff, Boris (1887–1969) (William Henry Pratt).
Gaunt British character actor, on stage from 1910, films from 1919, mainly in US. Achieved world fame as the monster in *Frankenstein* 31, and became typed in horrific parts despite his gentle, cultured voice.
Biographies: 1972, *Horror Man* by Peter Underwood. 1973, *Karloff, the Man, the Monster, the Movies* by Denis Gifford. 1974, *The Films of Boris Karloff* by Richard Bojarski and Kenneth Beals.
SELECTED SILENTS: His Majesty the American 19. The Last of the Mohicans 20. The Man from Downing Street 22. A Woman Conquers 23. Parisian Nights 25. Never the Twain Shall Meet 25. The Bells 26. Valencia 26. Tarzan and the Golden Lion 27. Two Arabian Knights 27. Vultures of the Sea 28. Phantoms of the North 29, many others.
■ SOUND FILMS: Behind that Curtain 29. King of the Kongo 29. The Unholy Night 29. The Bad One 30. The Sea Bat 30. The Utah Kid 30. Mothers Cry 30. The Criminal Code 30. Cracked Nuts 31. Young Donovan's Kid 31. King of the Wild 31. Smart Money 31. The Public Defender 31. I Like Your Nerve 31. Graft 31. Five Star Final 31. The Mad Genius 31. The Yellow Ticket 31. Guilty Generation 31. *Frankenstein* 31. Tonight or Never 31. Behind the Mask 32. Business and Pleasure 32. Scarface 32. The Cohens and Kellys in Hollywood 32. The Miracle Man 32. Night World 32. *The Old Dark House* 32. *The Mask of Fu Manchu* 32. *The Mummy* 32. The Ghoul 33. The Lost Patrol 34. The House of Rothschild 34. The Black Cat 34. The Gift of Gab 34. *The Bride of Frankenstein* 35. *The Black Room* 35. *The Raven* 35. The Invisible Ray 36. The Walking Dead 36. The Man Who Changed His Mind 36. Juggernaut 36. *Charlie Chan at the Opera* 37. Night Key 37. West of Shanghai 37. The Invisible Menace 37. Mr Wong Detective 38. Son of Frankenstein 39. The Mystery of Mr Wong 39. Mr Wong in Chinatown 39. The Man They Could Not Hang 39. Tower of London 39. The Fatal Hour 40. British Intelligence 40. Black Friday 40. The Man with Nine Lives 40. Devil's Island 40. Doomed to Die 40. Before I Hang 40. The Ape 40. You'll Find Out 40. The Devil Commands 41. The Boogie Man will Get You 42. The Climax 44. *House of Frankenstein* 44. *The Body Snatcher* 45. Isle of the Dead 45. Bedlam 46. The Secret Life of Walter Mitty 47. Lured 47. Unconquered 47. Dick Tracy meets Gruesome 47. Tap Roots 48. Abbott and Costello Meet the Killer 49. The Strange Door 51. The Black Castle 52. Abbott and Costello Meet Dr Jekyll and Mr Hyde 53. Monster of the Island 53. The Hindu 53. Voodoo Island 58. Grip of the Strangler 58. Corridors of Blood 58. Frankenstein 70 58. *The Raven* 63. The Terror 63. Comedy of Terrors 63. Black Sabbath 64. Bikini Beach 64. Die Monster Die 65. Ghost in the Invisible Bikini 66. The Venetian Affair 67. The Sorcerers 67. *Targets* 68. Curse of the Crimson Altar 68. The Snake People 70. The Incredible Invasion 70. Cauldron of Blood 70. The Fear Chamber 70. House of Evil 70.
TV series: Colonel March of Scotland Yard 53. Thriller 60–61.
✪ For his sinister Englishness, his sepulchral tones and his unfailing eagerness to please. *Bride of Frankenstein*.
❝ When I was nine I played the demon king in Cinderella and it launched me on a long and happy life of being a monster.
Though Karloff fought against being typecast, he later admitted:
The monster was the best friend I ever had.
How did he get the part? Said producer Carl Laemmle Junr:
His eyes mirrored the suffering we needed.
Director James Whale amplified this:
His face fascinated me. I made drawings of his head, adding sharp bony ridges where I imagined the skull might have joined.
Karloff however insisted:
You could heave a brick out of the window and hit ten actors who could play my parts. I just happened to be on the right corner at the right time.
His daughter Sara revealed that he was far from a monster in real life:
He was very British. He was soft-spoken, articulate, kind and well educated. He loved playing cricket and gardening and had a pet pig named Violet.

Karlson, Phil (1908–1985) (Philip Karlstein).
American director, in Hollywood from 1932. Mainly low-budget actioners until he suddenly gained stature in the 50s.
■ A Wave a WAC and a Marine 44. GI Honeymoon 45. There Goes Kelly 45. Shanghai Cobra 45. Swing Parade 46. Live Wires 46. Dark Alibi 46. Behind the Mask 46. Bowery Bombshell 46. The Missing Lady 46. Wife Wanted 46. Black Gold 47. Kilroy Was Here 47. Louisiana 47. Rocky 48. Adventures in Silverado 48. Thunderhoof 48. Ladies of the Chorus 49. The Big Cat 49. Down Memory Lane 49. The Iroquois Trail 50. Lorna Doone 51. The Texas Rangers 51. Mask of the Avenger 51. *Scandal Sheet* 52. The Brigand 52. *Kansas City Confidential* 53. 99 River Street 53. They Rode West 54. Tight Spot 55. Hell's Island 55. Five Against the House 55. *The Phenix City Story* 55. The Brothers Rico 57. Gunman's Walk 58. Hell to Eternity 60. Key Witness 60. The Secret Ways 61. The Young Doctors 61. Kid Galahad 62. Rampage 63. *The Silencers* 66. A Time for Killing 67. Wrecking Crew 69. Hornet's Nest 70. Ben 72. Walking Tall 73. Framed 75.

Karno, Fred (1866–1941) (Frederick John Westcott).
English impresario who originated or refined many influential slapstick routines (including the custard pie in the face) with his teams of comedians, who included over the years Betty Balfour, Billy Bennett, Charlie Chaplin, Stan Laurel, Naughton and Gold, Will Hay, Syd Walker and Robb Wilton. Born in Exeter, he was a factory worker at the age of 14, a plumber and a circus acrobat. In the mid-1890s he performed a silent act in music halls, turning in the early 1900s to producing shows and plays from his South London 'Fun Factory'. In the late 20s, bankrupted by his Karsino, a lavish showplace on a Thames island, he went to Hollywood and briefly worked for Hal Roach. Back in London, he wrote the story for an unsuccessful film, *Bad Companions*, before overseeing comedies based on his music-hall sketches. He set up his own production company, which failed after its first film, *Don't Rush Me*, and ended up running a wine and beer shop in Lilliput, a Dorset village. In the 1992 biopic *Chaplin*, he was played by John Thaw. Chaplin's early short *A Night at the Show* 15, and his own *Oh, What a Duchess!*, are based on his long-running music-hall act 'The Mumming Birds', in which a drunk (played by Chaplin on-stage) and a boy become entangled in a succession of second-rate acts.
Biographies: 1939, *Remember Fred Karno* by Edwin Adeler and Con West. 1971, *Fred Karno, Master of Mirth and Tears* by J. P. Gallagher.
■ Bad Companions 32. The Bailiffs 32. Handy Men 32. They're Off 33. The Dentist 33. Post Haste 33. Sign Please 33. Oh, What A Duchess! 34. Don't Rush Me 36. Jailbirds 39.
❝ Keep it wistful, gentlemen, keep it *wistful* as well. That's hard to do, but we want sympathy with the laughter. Wistful! – *F.K. to his comics*
When in doubt, fall on your arse. – *F.K.*
During a performance of one of his comedies if he did not like a comedian he would stand in the wings and hold his nose and give an audible raspberry. – *Charlie Chaplin*
Fred Karno is not only a genius, he is the man who originated slapstick comedy. – *Hal Roach*
He had no equal. His name *was* box-office. – *Stan Laurel*
Famous catchphrase (from his sketch 'The Bailiffs'): 'Meredith, we're in!'
Famous saying: 'Leave 'em wanting.'

Karns, Roscoe (1893–1970).
American character actor, very active in the 30s, usually in hard-boiled comedy roles.
Beggars of Life 28. *The Front Page* 30. Undercover Man 32. *Night After Night* 32. *Twentieth Century* 34. *It Happened One Night* 34. Thanks for the Memory 38. They Drive by Night 40. *His Girl Friday* 40. His Butler's Sister 43. Will Tomorrow Ever Come? 47. Inside Story 48. Onionhead 58, many others.
TV series: Rocky King Detective 50. Hennessey 59–61.
Famous line (*It Happened One Night*): 'Shapeley's the name, and that's the way I like 'em.'

Karras, Alex (1935–).
Heavyweight American character actor, former footballer.
Paper Lion 68. Hardcase (TV) 72. The 500 Pound Jerk (TV) 73. Blazing Saddles 74. Babe (TV) 75. Mulligan Stew (TV) 77. Mad Bull (TV) 77. Centennial (TV) 78. When Time Ran Out 80. Nobody's Perfekt 81. Victor/Victoria 82. Against All Odds 84. Buffalo '66 97, etc.
TV series: Webster 83–87.

Karvan, Claudia (1973–).
Australian actress, in films as a child.
Molly 83. High Tide 87. The Big Steal 90. Broken Highway 93. The Heartbreak Kid 93. My Forgotten Man 93. Exile 94. Lust and Revenge 96. *Dating the Enemy* 96, etc.

Kar-Wai, Wong (1958–).
Chinese director and screenwriter. Born in Shanghai, he moved to Hong Kong as a child, trained as a graphic designer and worked in television before beginning his film career as a writer in the early 80s.
As Tears Go By 88. Days of Being Wild/Ahfei Zhenjuang 91. Ashes of Time 93. *Chungking Express* 94. Fallen Angels 95. Happy Together 97, etc.
❝ WKW's most famous quip about his reason for working in Hong Kong rather than Hollywood or anywhere else is: 'I'd rather work with first-class gangsters than bad accountants.' – *Chris Doyle*

Karyo, Tcheky (1953–).
Turkish-born actor in French and international films.
La Balance 82. Les Nuits de la Pleine Lune 85. The Bear/L'Ours 89. Nikita 90. Isabelle Eberhardt 91. Exposure 91. Australia 91. Sketch Artist 92. 1492: Conquest of Paradise 92. C'est Beau une Ville la Nuit 93. And the Band Played On (TV) 93. Le Bonheur (Fr.) 94. Nostradamus 94. Love and Shadows (US) 94. Black Angel/L'Ange Noir 94. Zadoc et le Bonheur 95. Moon Shadow 95. Bad Boys 95. Operation Dumbo Drop 95. Foreign Land 95. Crying Freeman 95. GoldenEye 95. Follow Your Heart 96. Passaggio per il Paradiso 96. To Have and to Hold (Aus.) 96. Addicted to Love (US) 97. Habitat (US) 97. Que la Lumière Soit (Fr.) 98. Joan of Arc (Fr.) 99, etc.

Kasdan, Lawrence (1949–).
American writer-director.
Continental Divide (w) 80. The Empire Strikes Back (co-w) 80. Raiders of the Lost Ark (w) 81. *Body Heat* (wd) 82. *The Big Chill* (wd) (AAN) 83. Return of the Jedi (w) 83. Silverado (wd) 85. *The Accidental Tourist* (wd) (AAN) 88. I Love You to Death (d) 90. Grand Canyon (co-w, d) (AANw) 91. The Bodyguard (w) 92. Jumpin' at the Boneyard (p) 92. Wyatt Earp (p, co-w, d) 94. French Kiss 95. Home Fries (co-p) 98, etc.

Kasket, Harold (1915–).
British character actor of mixed descent, originally stage impressionist.
Hotel Sahara 51. Moulin Rouge 53. Interpol 57. Sands of the Desert 60. Arabesque 66. Trail of the Pink Panther 82. Curse of the Pink Panther 83, etc.

Kassar, Mario.
American production executive, former head of Carolco. In 1998, he formed a new partnership with his former partner Andrew VAJNA.

Kassovitz, Mathieu (1967–).
French actor turned screenwriter and director.
Regardez les Hommes Tomber (a) 94. Metisse (a, wd) 94. *La Haine* (wd) 95. Pleasure/Le Plaisir (a) 98, etc.

Kastner, Elliott (1930–).
American producer, former literary agent. In 1997 he bought Roger CORMAN's film production company, Concorde-New Horizons, for a reported $100m.
Bus Riley's Back in Town 65. Harper 66. Kaleidoscope 66. The Night of the Following Day 68. Where Eagles Dare 68. The Walking Stick 69. A Severed Head 70. When Eight Bells Toll 71. Villain 71. Zee and Co. 72. The Nightcomers 72. The Long Goodbye 73. 11 Harrowhouse 74. Farewell My Lovely 75. The Missouri Breaks 76. The Big Sleep 78. North Sea Hijack 80. Absolution 80. The First Deadly Sin 80. Death Valley 82. Oxford Blues 84. Garbo Talks 85. Angel Heart 87. Heat 87. The Blob 88. Jack's Back 88. A Chorus of Disapproval 89. Never on Tuesday 89, etc.etc.

Kästner, Erich (1899–1974).
German novelist whose *Emil and the Detectives* has been much filmed. He also wrote the original of *The Parent Trap*.

Kastner, Peter (1944–).
Canadian actor who made a corner in frustrated adolescents.
Nobody Waved Goodbye (Can.) 65. *You're a Big Boy Now* (US) 66. B.S. I Love You 70. Frightmare 83. Unfinished Business (a sequel to Nobody Waved Goodbye) 84, etc.
TV series: The Ugliest Girl in Town 68.

Kasznar, Kurt (1913–1979).
Chubby Austrian character actor, in US from 1936.
The Light Touch (debut) 51. The Happy Time 52. Lili 53. Sombrero 53. My Sister Eileen 55. Anything Goes 56. A Farewell to Arms 58. For the First Time 59. Casino Royale 66. The King's Pirate 67. The Ambushers 67, etc.
TV series: Land of the Giants 68–69.

Katch, Kurt (1896–1958) (Isser Kac).
Bald Polish character actor, in Hollywood from 1942.
Ali Baba and the Forty Thieves 43. *The Mask of Dimitrios* 44. Salome Where She Danced 45. The Mummy's Curse 45. Song of Love 47. The Secret of the Incas 54. Abbott and Costello Meet the Mummy 55. Pharaoh's Curse 57, etc.

Katselas, Milton (1933–).
American director with Broadway experience.
■ Butterflies Are Free 72. Forty Carats 73. Report to the Commissioner 74. When You Comin' Back Red Ryder? 79. Strangers (TV) 79. The Rules of Marriage (TV) 82.

Katt, William (1955–).
American leading man of the late 70s, son of Bill Williams and Barbara Hale.
Carrie 76. First Love 78. Big Wednesday 79. Butch and Sundance 79. Baby, Secret of the Lost Legend 84. House 85. Swimsuit 89. Naked Obsession 91. Tollbooth 94. The Paperboy 94. American Cop 94. Piranha 95. Daddy's Girl 96. Rough Riders (TV) 97. Mother Teresa: In the Name of God's Poor (TV) 97, etc.
TV series: The Greatest American Hero 81–82. Good Sports 91.

Katz, Gloria.
American producer and screenwriter, a former editor, usually in collaboration with her husband Willard Huyck.
American Graffiti (AAN) 73. Messiah of Evil 75. Lucky Lady 75. French Postcards 79. Indiana Jones and the Temple of Doom 84. Best Defense 84. Howard the Duck 86. Radioland Murders 94, etc.

Katzenberg, Jeffrey (1951–).
Production executive, president of the Walt Disney company's film production from 1985–94. He set up his own studio in 1994 with partners Steven Spielberg and David Geffen.

Katzin, Lee H. (1935–).
American director.
Heaven with a Gun 69. Along Came a Spider (TV) 70. Whatever Happened to Aunt Alice? 70. The Phynx 70. Le Mans 71. The Salzburg Connection 72. The Voyage of the Yes (TV) 72. Savages (TV) 74. The Last Survivors (TV) 75. Sky Heist (TV) 75. Man from Atlantis (TV) 77. The Bastard (TV) 78. Terror out of the Sky (TV) 78. Samurai (TV) 79. Death Ray 2000 (TV) 81. Spenser: For Hire (TV) 85. World Gone Wild 88, etc.

Katzman, Sam (1901–1973).
American producer, chiefly of low-budget co-features including the *Jungle Jim* and *East Side Kids* series, mainly for Monogram. He tapped into teenage tastes, from horror to rock 'n' roll.
Straight Shooter 39. That Gang of Mine 40. Return of the Ape Man 44. Vacation Days 47. Superman 48. King of the Congo/The Mighty Thunda (serial) 52. Prince of Pirates 52. Killer Ape 53. Pirates of Tripoli 54. It Came from Beneath the Sea 55. The Man Who Turned to Stone 56. Rock around the Clock 56. The Giant Claw 57. Zombies of Mora Tau 57. Pirates of Tortuga 61. Twist around the Clock 61. Riot on Sunset Street 67. The Loners 72, many others.

Kaufman, Boris (1906–1980).
Polish photographer, in France from 1928, Hollywood from 1942. Brother of Dziga Vertov.
■ La Marche des Machines 28. A Propos de Nice (& co-d) 30. Les Halles 30. *Zéro de Conduite* 32. Seine 33. *L'Atalante* 34. Pere Lampion 36. Fort Delores 37. Serenade 38. Better Tomorrow 45. Capital Story 45. The Southwest 45. Journey into Medicine 47. The Tanglewood Story 50. The Garden of Eden 54. *On the Waterfront* (AA) 54. Crowded Paradise 56. *Baby Doll* 56. Patterns 56. *Twelve Angry Men* 57. That Kind of Woman 59. The Fugitive Kind 60. Splendor in the Grass 61. Long Day's Journey into Night 62. All the Way Home 63. Gone are the Days 63. *The World of Henry Orient* 64. The Pawnbroker 65. *The Group* 66. *Bye Bye Braverman* 67. Uptight 68. The Brotherhood 68. Tell Me That You Love Me Junie Moon 70.

Kaufman, George S. (1889–1961).
American comedy playwright, theatre director, critic, screenwriter and wit, many of whose works were filmed. Born in Pittsburgh, he was a New York journalist before turning to the theatre, first collaborating with Marc CONNELLY and later with Edna FERBER, Morrie RYSKIND (on the MARX BROTHERS' Broadway hits *Cocoanuts* and *Animal Crackers*), and, most frequently, Moss HART. A regular at the ALGONQUIN ROUND TABLE, he avoided Hollywood as much as possible: his contract with Samuel GOLDWYN to write Eddie CANTOR's *Roman Scandals* had as conditions that he worked from New York and didn't have to listen to Cantor; when Cantor came to New York to make suggestions, he quit. Once, when studio head Adolph ZUKOR offered him $30,000 for the movie rights to one of his plays, he replied by offering Zukor $40,000 for Paramount Pictures. He worked briefly in Hollywood in the mid-30s when, at Groucho MARX's suggestion, Irving THALBERG offered him $100,000 to write *A Night at the Opera*. Observing Louis B. MAYER at work led him to write a song entitled 'I'd Rather Have TB than LB'. He returned only once, in 1947, to direct *The Senator Was Indiscreet*; when that film was denounced as 'unAmerican' by Senator Joseph MCCARTHY, he vowed never to return. He was involved in a minor scandal in the mid-30s, when actress Mary ASTOR's diary, describing him as a great lover, was read out in court. His second wife was actress Leueen MacGrath.
Biographies: 1972, *George S. Kaufman: An Intimate Portrait* by Howard Teichmann; 1974, *George S. Kaufman and His Friends* by Scott Meredith; 1979, *George S. Kaufman: His Life, His Theater* by Malcolm Goldstein.
Dulcy 23. Beggar on Horseback 25. *Animal Crackers* 30. The Royal Family of Broadway 30. *Once in a Lifetime* 32. Dinner at Eight 33. Stage Door 37. *You Can't Take It with You* 38. *The Man Who Came to Dinner* 41. George Washington Slept Here 42. The Late George Apley 47. The Senator Was Indiscreet (wd) 49. The Solid Gold Cadillac 56, etc.
❝ Do you want it Wednesday, or do you want it good? – G.S.K. *to Irving Thalberg, who had asked him to write a treatment quickly*
He had great integrity. You never had to watch him when he was dealing. – *Harpo Marx*
He was renowned for marrying very high comedy with very high farce; and with his wit, it came out satire. – *Howard Teichmann*
He was the kind of man I'd go over a cliff for. – *Mary Astor*

Kaufman, Lloyd (1945–).
American director, writer and producer of low-budget exploitation movies for Troma under the psuedonym Samuel Weil, in collaboration with Michael Herz.
Autobiography: 1998, *All I Need to Know about Filmmaking I Learned from the Toxic Avenger* (with James Gunn).
Squeeze Play! (co-d). Waitress! (co-d) 82. The First Turn-On! 84. The Toxic Avenger (co-d) 84. The Toxic Avenger: Part II (co-d) 88. Troma's War (co-d) 88. Sgt Kabukiman N.Y.P.D. (co-d) 94. Tromeo and Juliet (d) 96, etc.
❝ When in doubt, vomit green foam. – *L.K.*

Kaufman, Millard (1917–).
American screenwriter; output sparse and patchy, but interesting.
Gun Crazy 50. Take the High Ground (AAN) 53. *Bad Day at Black Rock* (AAN) 55. Raintree County 57. Never So Few 59. Convicts Four (& d) 62. The War Lord 65. Living Free 72. The Klansman 76, etc.

Kaufman, Philip (1936–).
American director and screenwriter.
■ Goldstein (co-d) 63. Fearless Frank 69. The Great Minnesota Raid 72. The White Dawn 73. The Outlaw Josey Wales (co-w only) 75. Invasion of the Body Snatchers 78. The Wanderers 79. Raiders of the Lost Ark (co-w only) 81. *The Right Stuff* (wd) 83. The Unbearable Lightness of Being (wd) (AANw) 88. Henry and June (wd) 90. Rising Sun (co-w, d) 93.

Kaufman, Robert (1931–1991).
American screenwriter.
Dr Goldfoot and the Bikini Machine 65. Divorce American Style (AAN) 67. Getting Straight 70. I Love My Wife (& p) 70. Harry and Walter Go to New York 76. Love at First Bite (& p) 79. How to Beat the High Cost of Living (& p) 80. Split Image (co-w) 82. The Check Is in the Mail 86. Separate Vacation 88, etc.

Kaufmann, Christine (1944–).
German leading lady in international films. She was married to actor Tony Curtis (1963–68).
Town without Pity 61. Taras Bulba 62. Wild and Wonderful 64. Tunnel 28 64. Murders in the Rue Morgue 71. Bagdad Café 87, etc.

Kaufmann, Maurice (1928–).
British actor, formerly married to actress Honor Blackman (1962–75).
It's a Wonderful World 56. Behemoth the Sea Monster 58. Gorgo 60. A Shot in the Dark 64. Fanatic/Die! Die! My Darling 65. Circus of Fear 66. Bloomfield 69. Man of Violence 70. The Abominable Dr Phibes 71. Fright 71, etc.

Kaun, Bernhard (1899–1980).
German-born composer in Hollywood, where he made a speciality of scores for horror movies.
Frankenstein 31. Dr X 32. The Mystery of the Wax Museum 33. Return of the Terror 34. The Walking Dead 36. The Return of Dr X 39. The Smiling Ghost 41. Special Delivery 55, etc.

Kaurismäki, Aki (1957–).
Prolific Finnish director and producer. He is the brother of Mika Kaurismäki who partners him in a production company Villealfa (which derives its name from Jean-Luc Godard's film *Alphaville*).
The Liar/Valehtelija (a, w) 80. The Saimma Gesture/Saimma – Ilmiö (co-d) 83. Crime and Punishment/Rikos Ja Rangaistus 83. Calamari Union 84. Shadows in Paradise/Varjoja Paratiisissa 86. Hamlet Goes Business/Hamlet Liikemaailmassa 87. Ariel 88. The Match Girl/Tulitikkutehtaan 89. Leningrad Cowboys Go America 89. I Hired a Contract Killer 90. Bohemian Life/La Vie de Bohème 92. Total Balalaika Show 94. Leningrad Cowboys Meet Moses (p, wd, e) 94. Take Care of Your Scarf, Tatjana/Pidä Huivista Kiinni, Tatjana 94. Drifting Clouds 96, etc.
❝ My favourite last line from a movie is in Ozu's *Tokyo Story*: 'Isn't life a disappointment?'. – *A.K.*
I want to die. But it's not a problem. That's why I'm living. – *A.K.*

Kaurismäki, Mika (1955–).
Finnish director and producer, the brother of Aki Kaurismäki.
The Liar/Valehtelija 80. The Saimma Gesture/Saimma – Ilmiö (co-d) 83. Rosso 85. Helsinki Napoli All Night Long 88. Cha Cha Cha 89. The Paper Star/Paperitahit 90. Amazon 90. Zombie and the Ghost Train/Zombie ja Kummitusjuna 91. The Last Border 93. Condition Red 95. Sambolico 96. LA without a Map 98, etc.

Kautner, Helmut (1908–1980).
German director who had an unhappy experience in Hollywood in the 50s.
Kitty and the World Conference 39. Adieu Franciska 41. Romanze in Moll 43. Unter den Brücken 45. In Jenen Tagen 47. Der Apfel Ist Ab 48. Epilog 50. The Last Brigade 54. Ludwig II 54. The Devil's General 55. Himmel Ohne Sterne 55. The Captain from Koepenick 56. The Wonderful Years (US) 58. Stranger in My Arms (US) 59. The Rest Is Silence 59. Der Glas Wasser 60. Die Rote 62, etc.

Kavner, Julie (1951–).
American actress.
Katherine (TV) 75. Revenge of the Stepford Wives (TV) 80. Bad Medicine 85. Hannah and Her Sisters 86. Radio Days 87. Surrender 87. New York Stories 89. Alice 90. Awakenings 90. Shadows and Fog 91. This Is My Life 92. I'll Do Anything 94. Forget Paris 95. Deconstructing Harry 97, etc.
TV series: Rhoda 74–78. The Simpsons (voice, as Marge) 89– .

Kawalerowicz, Jerzy (1922–).
Polish director.
Gromada 51. Cien 54. The True End of the Great War 57. *Pociag*/Night Train 59. *Mother Jeanne of the Angels*/The Devil and the Nun 60. *The Pharaoh* 64. Maddalena 71. Death of the President 78. Austeria 83. Jeniec Europy 89. Bronstein's Children 91, etc.

Kaye, Danny (1913–1987) (David Daniel Kaminsky).
Ebullient, lanky, red-haired American star entertainer of stage, screen and television. Born in New York, of Ukrainian immigrant parents, he began entertaining at summer camps and made several unpromising two-reelers in the 30s (later

compiled as *The Danny Kaye Story*). After he scored a success in Broadway musicals, Samuel GOLDWYN signed him to a five-year contract, turned him into a blond, and gave him the big build-up. His first films reworked gibberish songs and tongue-twisting numbers from his cabaret and musical performances, and he gained enormous popularity. He was at his best in live performance, though, and scored an immense success with a season at the London Palladium in 1948. He moved to Warners and, later Paramount, where he started his own production company with Norman PANAMA and Melvin FRANK. But their first film together, *Court Jester*, cost $4m and grossed $2.2m, and his later movies were disappointing. Thereafter, he concentrated on television, conducting symphony orchestras for charity, working as 'Ambassador at large' for UNICEF, and cooking at his home, where he created a restaurant-grade Chinese kitchen, preparing meals for small groups of friends, though conversation was discouraged. He was given a Special Academy Award in 1954 'for his unique talents, his service to the industry and the American people'. Married Sylvia Fine, who wrote most of his material and songs, and managed his career. His lovers included actress Eve ARDEN.

Biographies: 1948, *The Danny Kaye Saga* by Kurt Singer; 1949, *The Life Story of Danny Kaye* by Dick Richards; 1985, *The Secret Life of Danny Kaye* by Michael Freedland; 1994, *Nobody's Fool: The Lives of Danny Kaye* by Martin Gottfried.

Up in Arms 44. *Wonder Man* 45. The Kid from Brooklyn 46. *The Secret Life of Walter Mitty* 47. A Song Is Born 48. The Inspector General 49. On the Riviera 51. *Hans Christian Andersen* 52. *Knock on Wood* 53. White Christmas 54. Assignment Children (UN short) 54. *The Court Jester* 56. Me and the Colonel 57. Merry Andrew 58. The Five Pennies 59. On the Double 62. The Man from the Diners' Club 63. The Madwoman of Chaillot 69. Peter Pan (TV) 75. Pinocchio (TV) 76, etc.

TV series: The Danny Kaye Show 63–67.

✪ For his perfectionist comedy techniques. *Wonder Man*.

❝ I am a wife-made man. – *D.K.* (his wife Sylvia Fine wrote most of his best lyrics)

I became an entertainer not because I wanted to but because I was meant to. – *D.K.*

I'm Anatole of Paris,
I shriek with chic;
My 'at of ze week
Caused six divorces, three runaway 'orses . . .
I'm Anatole of Paris, ze 'ats I sell
Make people yell
'Is zat a 'at or a two-room flat?' – *Kaye lyric*

I can't say what Danny Kaye is like in private life. There are too many of them. – *Sylvia Fine*

Kaye, Davy (1916–1998).
Diminutive English comedian and character actor. Born in London, he began as a performer in variety from the mid-30s. In the Second World War, he was turned down for military service because of his size and claimed that the medical officer told him, 'When we declare war on pygmies, we'll send for you.'

Everything in Rhythm 36. Fun at St Fanny's 55. The Pot Carriers 62. The World Ten Times Over 63. Crooks in Cloisters 64. Carry On Cowboy 65. Those Magnificent Men in Their Flying Machines 65. The Biggest Bundle of Them All (US) 67. Chitty Chitty Bang Bang 68. Satan's Harvest (SA) 70. Carry On at Your Convenience 71. Alice's Adventures in Wonderland 72, etc.

Kaye, Norman.
Australian character actor, musician and screenwriter, from the theatre, often playing mild middle-aged men.

Illuminations (a) 76. Inside Looking Out (a) 77. Lonely Hearts (a, m) 82. Buddies (a) 83. Man of Flowers (a) 84. Where the Green Ants Dream (a) 84. Cactus (a, co-w) 86. Frenchman's Farm (a) 87. Warm Nights on a Slow Moving Train (a) 87. Vincent: The Life and Death of Vincent van Gogh (m) 88. Golden Braid (co-m) 90. A Woman's Tale 91. Turtle Beach 92. Broken Highway 93. Exile 94. Erotic Tales 94. Lust and Revenge 96. Heaven's Burning 97, etc.

Kaye, Stubby (1918–1997) (Bernard Kotzin).
Rotund American comic actor. Born in New York, he began in radio and vaudeville, billed as 'Stubby Kaye: Extra Padded Attraction'. He repeated his two most famous Broadway roles on film: as Nicely-Nicely Johnson, singing the show-stopping 'Sit Down, You're Rockin' the Boat', in *Guys and Dolls*, and as Marryin' Sam in *L'il Abner*. Married Angela Bracewell, a British TV personality of the 50s.

Guys and Dolls 55. Li'l Abner 59. 40 Pounds of Trouble 62. Cat Ballou 65. Sweet Charity 68. The Cockeyed Cowboys of Calico County 70. The Dirtiest Girl I Ever Met 73. Six Pack Annie 75. Minskie's Follies 83. Who Framed Roger Rabbit 88, etc.

TV series: Love and Marriage 59. My Sister Eileen 60.

Kazan, Elia (1909–) (Elia Kazanjoglous).
Distinguished American stage and screen director of Greek/Turkish descent. Intermittently an actor; with New York's Group Theatre in the 30s.

Autobiography: 1988, *A Life*.

AS ACTOR: City for Conquest 40. Blues in the Night 41, etc.

AS DIRECTOR: *A Tree Grows in Brooklyn* 45. The Sea of Grass 47. *Boomerang* 47. *Gentleman's Agreement* (AA) 47. Pinky 49. Panic in the Streets 50. A Streetcar Named Desire (AAN) 51. *Viva Zapata* 52. Man on a Tightrope 53. *On the Waterfront* (AA) 54. East of Eden (AAN) 55. Baby Doll 56. *A Face in the Crowd* (& p) 57. Wild River (& p) 60. Splendor in the Grass (& p) 61. America America (& w, p) (AAN) 63. The Arrangement (& w, p) 69. The Visitors (& w) 72. The Last Tycoon 76.

Kazan, Nicholas.
American director, screenwriter and dramatist, the son of Elia Kazan.

Frances (co-w) 82. At Close Range (w) 86. Patty Hearst (w) 88. Reversal of Fortune (AAN w) 90. Dream Lover (wd) 94, etc.

Keach, James (1948–).
American actor and producer, brother of Stacy KEACH. Married actress Jane SEYMOUR.

Sunburst 75. Death Play 76. Cannonball 76. FM 78. Comes a Horseman 78. Lacy and the Mississippi Queen (TV) 78. Like Normal People (TV) 79. Hurricane 79. *The Long Riders* (as Jesse James) 80. Love Letters 83. The Razor's Edge 84. Wildcats 85. The Experts 89. False Identity (d) 90. The Stars Fell on Henrietta (d) 95, etc.

Keach, Stacy (1941–).
American general-purpose actor.

The Heart Is a Lonely Hunter 68. End of the Road 68. The Travelling Executioner 69. Brewster McCloud 70. Doc 70. Judge Roy Bean 72. The New Centurions 72. Fat City 72. The Dion Brothers (TV) 74. All the Kind Strangers (TV) 74. Conduct Unbecoming 75. James Michener's Dynasty (TV) 76. Luther 76. Street People 76. The Killer Inside Me 76. The Squeeze 77. Jesus of Nazareth (TV) 77. Slave of the Cannibal God 78. Two Solitudes 78. Gray Lady Down 78. Up in Smoke 78. The Long Riders (as Frank James) 80. The Ninth Configuration 80. Cheech & Chong's Nice Dreams 81. Road Games 81. Butterfly 82. That Championship Season 82. Princess Daisy (TV) 83. Mistral's Daughter (TV) 84. Intimate Strangers (TV) 86. The Return of Mickey Spillane's Mike Hammer (TV) 86. Class of 1999 89. Mickey Spillane's Mike Hammer: Murder Takes All (TV) 89. False Identity 90. Milena/Geliebte Milena 90. Mission of the Shark 91. Sunset Grill 92. Batman: Mask of the Phantasm (voice) 94. Prey of the Jaguar 96. Escape from LA 96. Legend of the Lost Tomb (TV) 97. Future Fear 97. American History X 98, etc.

TV series: Get Smart 66–67. Caribe 75. Mickey Spillane's Mike Hammer 84–87.

Keane, Robert Emmett (1883–1981).
Toothbrush-moustached American character actor who played travelling salesmen and fall guys in scores of light comedies and dramas.

Men Call It Love 31. Boys Town 38. We're in the Army Now 40. Tin Pan Alley 41. Jitterbugs 43. When My Baby Smiles at Me 50. When Gangland Strikes 56, etc.

Kearton, Cherry (1871–1940)
Pioneer British travel film producer whose success lasted from 1912 to the mid-30s.

Keating, Larry (1897–1963).
American character actor, often as executive or uppity neighbour.

Whirlpool 49. Three Secrets 50. Come Fill the Cup 51. About Face 52. Inferno 53. Daddy Longlegs 55. The Buster Keaton Story 57. Who Was that Lady? 60. Boys' Night Out 62, many others.

TV series: *The Burns and Allen Show* 56–58. *Mister Ed* 60–62.

Keaton, Buster (1895–1966) (Joseph Francis Keaton).
One of America's great silent clowns, the unsmiling but game little fellow who always came out on top whatever the odds. In two-reelers with Fatty Arbuckle from 1917, but soon began to shape his own material. Special Academy Award 1959 'for his unique talents which brought immortal comedies to the screen'. Trained in vaudeville with family act. Did not easily survive sound, but later came back in featured roles and was gaining a fresh popularity at the time of his death.

Autobiography: 1960, My *Wonderful World of Slapstick*.

Biographies: 1966, *Keaton* by Rudi Blesh. 1969, *Buster Keaton* by David Robinson. 1989, *Keaton: The Man Who Wouldn't Lie Down* by Tom Dardis. 1996, *Buster Keaton: Cut to the Chase* by Marion Meade.

Keaton was played by Donald O'Connor in a 1957 biopic, *The Buster Keaton Story*.

■ FROM 1920: The Saphead 20. *One Week* 20. The High Sign 20. Convict 13 20. The Scarecrow 20. Neighbours 20. The Haunted House 21. The Goat 21. *The Playhouse* 22. *The Boat* 22. *The Paleface* 22. *Cops* 22. My Wife's Relations 22. The Blacksmith 22. The Frozen North 22. The Electric House 22. Daydreams 22. *Balloonatic* 22. The Love Nest 22. The Three Ages 23. *Our Hospitality* 23. *Sherlock Junior* 24. *The Navigator* 24. Seven Chances 25. Go West 25. Battling Butler 26. *The General* 27. College 27. Steamboat Bill Junior 27. *The Cameraman* 28. Spite Marriage 29. Hollywood Revue 29. Free and Easy 30. Doughboys 30. Parlor Bedroom and Bath 31. Sidewalks of New York 32. The Passionate Plumber 32. Speak Easily 32. What No Beer 33. Le Roi des Champs Elysées (Fr.) 34. An Old Spanish Custom (GB) 35. 18 Educational shorts 35–37. Hollywood Cavalcade 39. The Jones Family in Hollywood 39. Quick Millions 39. The Villain Still Pursued Her 40. Li'l Abner 40. Eight Columbia shorts 40–41. Forever and a Day 43. *San Diego I Love You* 44. That's the Spirit 45. That Night With You 46. God's Country 46. El Moderno Barba Azul (Mex.) 46. Duel to the Death (Fr.) 48. You're My Everything 49. The Loveable Cheat 50. In the Good Old Summertime 50. Sunset Boulevard 50. Limelight 52. Around the World in Eighty Days 56. Huckleberry Finn 60. Ten Girls Ago 62. It's a Mad Mad Mad Mad World 63. The Triumph of Lester Snapwill 63. *Railrodder* 65. Keaton Rides Again 65. Film 65. Pajama Party 65. Beach Blanket Bingo 65. How to Stuff a Wild Bikini 65. Two Marines and a General (It.) 65. A Funny Thing Happened on the Way to the Forum 66. The Scribe 66. Sergeant Deadhead 66.

✪ For being the funniest and most inventive silent clown of them all. *The General*.

❝ Only things that one could imagine happening to real people, I guess, remain in a person's memory. – *B.K.*

He passes into the universal folk heritage as the supreme clown poet. – *David Robinson, 1968*

He can impress a weary world with the vitally important fact that life, after all, is a foolishly inconsequential affair. – *Robert Sherwood*

Keaton, Diane (1946–)
American leading lady of the 70s and 80s.

Biography: 1990, *Diane Keaton* by Jonathan Moor.

Lovers and Other Strangers 70. The Godfather 72. Play it Again Sam 72. Sleeper 74. Godfather Two 74. Love and Death 75. Harry and Walter Go to New York 76. I Will, I Will . . . for Now 76. *Annie Hall* (AA) 77. Looking for Mr Goodbar 77. Interiors 78. Manhattan 79. Reds (AAN) 81. Shoot the Moon 82. The Little Drummer Girl 84. Mrs Soffel 84. Crimes of the Heart 86. Baby Boom 87. Radio Days 87. The Good Mother 88. The Lemon Sisters 90. The Godfather Part III 90. Father of the Bride 91. Manhattan Murder Mystery 93. Look Who's Talking Now (voice) 93. Amelia Earhart: The Final Flight (TV) 94. Unstrung Heroes (d) 95. Father of the Bride Part II 95. The First Wives Club 96. Marvin's Room (AAN) 96, etc.

Keaton, Joseph (1878–1946).
American knockabout comedian who supported his son Buster in several of his best silents.

Keaton, Michael (1951–) (Michael Douglas).
American leading man. He played Batman in two big-budget films but declined to appear in a third.

Night Shift 82. Mr Mom 83. Johnny Dangerously 84. Gung Ho 85. Touch and Go 86. The Squeeze 87. Clean and Sober 88. Beetlejuice 88. Batman 89. The Dream Team 89. Pacific Heights 90. One Good Cop 91. Batman Returns 92. Much Ado about Nothing 93. My Life 93. The Paper 94. Speechless 94. Multiplicity 96. Jackie Brown 97. Desperate Measures 98. Jack Frost 98, etc.

TV series: All's Fair 76. Working Stiffs 79.

Keats, Steven (1945–1994).
American general-purpose actor. Committed suicide.

The Story of Pretty Boy Floyd (TV) 74. The Dream Makers (TV) 75. Promise Him Anything (TV) 75. Black Sunday 76. Seventh Avenue (TV) 77. The Last Dinosaur (TV) 77. The Awakening Land (TV) 78. Zuma Beach (TV) 78. Silent Rage 82. The Executioner's Song (TV) 82. Eternity 90. Shadows and Fog 92, etc.

Kedrova, Lila (1918–).
Russian-French character actress, known internationally.

Zorba the Greek (AA) 64. A High Wind in Jamaica 65. Torn Curtain 66. Penelope 67. The Kremlin Letter 69. Soft Beds, Hard Battles 74. The Tenant 76. March or Die 77. Tell Me a Riddle 80. Sunset People 84. Sword of the Valiant 84. The Thrill of Genius 85. La Prossima Volta Il Fuoco 93, etc.

Keel, Howard (1917–) (Harold Leek).
Stalwart American leading man and singer whose career faltered when musicals went out of fashion.

■ The Small Voice (GB) 48. *Annie Get Your Gun* 50. Pagan Love Song 50. Three Guys Named Mike 51. *Showboat* 51. Texas Carnival 51. Callaway Went Thataway 51. Lovely to Look At 52. Desperate Search 52. Fast Company 53. Ride Vaquero 53. *Calamity Jane* 53. *Kiss Me Kate* 53. Rose Marie 54. *Seven Brides for Seven Brothers* 54. Deep in My Heart 54. Jupiter's Darling 54. Kismet 55. Floods of Fear (GB) 58. The Big Fisherman 59. Armored Command 61. The Day of the Triffids 63. Waco 66. Red Tomahawk 67. The War Wagon 67. Arizona Bushwhackers 68.

TV series: Dallas 81–91.

❝ I was one of God's chosen people, doing what I wanted to do in life. – *H.K.*

Keeler, Ruby (1909–1993) (Ethel Keeler).
Petite American singer-dancer who made a small talent go a long way in musicals of the early 30s. She was married to Al Jolson (1928–40).

■ *42nd Street* 33. Gold Diggers of 1933. Footlight Parade 33. *Dames* 34. Flirtation Walk 35. Go Into Your Dance 35. Shipmates Forever 35. Colleen 36. Ready Willing and Able 37. Mother Carey's Chickens 38. Sweetheart of the Campus 41. The Phynx 70.

Keen, Bob.
American director, a former special effects designer and animatronics engineer. He formed his own company, Image Animation, in 1985 after working on *The Dark Crystal*, *The Empire Strikes Back* and *Return of the Jedi*.

SFX: Krull 83. Lifeforce 85. The Unholy 88. Hellraiser 87. Waxwork 88. Children of the Corn II: The Final Sacrifice 92. Candyman 92. Warlock – The Armageddon (make-up) 93. Andre 94. Lord of Illusions 95. SFX: Event Horizon 97, etc.

AS DIRECTOR: Proteus 95. Big Game (TV) 95. To Catch a Yeti (TV) 95. The Lost World 98, etc.

Keen, Geoffrey (1916–).
Incisive British character actor, son of Malcolm Keen.

His Excellency 50. Genevieve 53. The Long Arm 56. No Love for Johnnie 61. The Spiral Road 62.

Live Now Pay Later 63. The Heroes of Telemark 65. Dr Zhivago 65. Born Free 66. Taste the Blood of Dracula 70. Living Free 71. Doomwatch 72. The Spy Who Loved Me 77. Moonraker 79. For Your Eyes Only 81. A View to a Kill 84. The Living Daylights 87, many others.

Keen, Malcolm (1888–1970).
British character actor, mostly on stage; father of Geoffrey Keen.
The Manxman 29. Sixty Glorious Years 39. The Great Mr Handel 42. The Mating Season (US) 51. Francis of Assisi 60, etc.

Keene, Ralph (1902–1963).
British documentarist, in films from 1934. With Ministry of Information, British Transport, etc.: emphasis on animal studies. *Cyprus Is an Island, Crofters, Journey into Spring, Between the Tides, Winter Quarters, Under Night Streets*, etc.

Keene, Tom (1896–1963) (also known at times as George Duryea and Richard Powers).
American western star, mainly in second features of the 30s and 40s.
Godless Girl 28. The Dude Wrangler 30. Saddle Buster 32. Our Daily Bread 33. Where the Trails Divide 37. Dynamite Cargo 41. Up in Arms 44. If You Knew Susie 48. Red Planet Mars 52. Plan 9 from Outer Space 56, many others.

Keighley, William (1889–1984).
American director with stage experience; made many highly polished entertainments for Warners.
■ The Match King 32. Ladies They Talk About 33. Easy to Love 34. Journal of a Crime 34. Dr Monica 34. Kansas City Princess 34. Big Hearted Herbert 34. Babbitt 34. The Right to Live 35. Mary Jane's Pa 35. G Men 35. Special Agent 35. Stars over Broadway 35. The Singing Kid 36. Bullets or Ballots 36. *The Green Pastures* 36. God's Country and the Woman 37. The Prince and the Pauper 37. Varsity Show 37. The Adventures of Robin Hood (co-d) 38. Valley of the Giants 38. Secrets of an Actress 38. Brother Rat 38. Yes My Darling Daughter 39. Each Dawn I Die 39. The Fighting 69th 40. Torrid Zone 40. No Time for Comedy 40. Four Mothers 41. The Bride Came COD 41. *The Man Who Came to Dinner* 42. George Washington Slept Here 42. Honeymoon 47. The Street with No Name 48. Rocky Mountain 50. Close to My Heart 51. The Master of Ballantrae 53.

Keir, Andrew (1926–1997).
Scottish character actor, usually in stern roles.
The Lady Craved Excitement 50. The Brave Don't Cry 52. The Maggie 54. Heart of a Child 57. Pirates of Blood River 60. Dracula, Prince of Darkness 65. Daleks Invasion Earth 2500 AD 65. The Viking Queen 67. *Quatermass and the Pit* 67. The Royal Hunt of the Sun 69. Zeppelin 70. Blood from the Mummy's Tomb 71. The Thirty-Nine Steps 78. Absolution 80. Lion of the Desert 81. Marco Polo (TV) 82. First Among Equals (TV) 86. Rob Roy 95, etc.
TV series: Adam Smith 72. The Outsiders 77.

Keitel, Harvey (1939–).
American leading actor, associated with the films of Martin Scorsese, often in tough and intense roles. A former marine, he studied acting with Lee Strasberg and Stella Adler and began on the off-Broadway stage. Formerly married to actress Lorraine Bracco.
Biography: 1997, *Harvey Keitel: The Art of Darkness* by Marshall Fine.
Mean Streets 73. Alice Doesn't Live Here Any More 74. That's The Way of the World 75. Mother Jugs and Speed 76. Taxi Driver 76. Buffalo Bill and the Indians 76. The Duellists 77. Welcome to L.A. 77. Blue Collar 78. Fingers 78. Deathwatch 79. Eagle's Wing 79. Bad Timing 80. Saturn Three 80. The Border 82. Exposed 83. Order of Death 83. Falling in Love 84. Camorra 85. Off Beat 85. The Men's Club 86. Wise Guys 86. The Pick-Up Artist 87. The Last Temptation of Christ 88. The January Man 89. Two Evil Eyes/Due Occhi Diabolici 89. The Two Jakes 90. Mortal Thoughts 91. Thelma and Louise 91. *Bugsy* (AAN) 91. Reservoir Dogs 92. Bad Lieutenant 92. Sister Act 92. Point of No Return 93. The Young Americans 93. Rising Sun 93. Snake Eyes 93. *The Piano* 93. Monkey Trouble 94. Pulp Fiction 94. Somebody to Love 94. Imaginary Crimes 94. Clockers 95. Smoke 95. Blue in the Face 95. Get Shorty (cameo) 95. From Dusk till Dawn 96. Head above Water 96. City of Industry 96. Fairytale: A True Story 97. Cop Land 97. Lulu on the Bridge 98. Three Seasons 98. Shadrach 98. Finding Graceland 98, etc.
❝ Existence is a struggle. – *H.K.*

Keith, Brian (1921–1997) (Robert Keith Jnr).
American actor of easy-going types, understanding fathers and occasional villains. Born in Bayonne, New Jersey. Married actress Victoria Young in 1970. Shot himself at a time when he was suffering from emphysema and lung cancer, and mourning the suicide of his 27-year-old daughter.
Arrowhead (debut) 52. Alaska Seas 53. The Violent Men 54. Five against the House 55. Storm Centre 56. Run of the Arrow 57. Sierra Baron 58. The Young Philadelphians 59. The Deadly Companions 61. The Parent Trap 61. Moon Pilot 62. Savage Sam 63. Those Calloways 65. The Hallelujah Trail 65. *Nevada Smith* 66. The Russians Are Coming 66. *Reflections in a Golden Eye* 67. With Six You Get Eggroll 68. Krakatoa 68. Suppose They Gave a War and Nobody Came 69. The Mackenzie Break 70. Scandalous John 71. Something Big 72. The Yakuza 75. *The Wind and the Lion* (as Theodore Roosevelt) 76. The Quest (TV) 76. Nickelodeon 76. Hooper 78. Meteor 79. The Mountain Men 80. Charlie Chan and the Curse of the Dragon Queen 81. Sharkey's Machine 81. Death before Dishonor 87. Young Guns 88. Welcome Home 89. Escape 90. Picture Windows (TV) 95. Entertaining Angels: The Dorothy Day Story (TV) 96. Rough Riders (TV) 97, etc.
TV series: Crusader 56. The Westerner 60. *Family Affair* 66–71. The Little People 72–73. Archer 75. Hardcastle and McCormick 83–86.

Keith, David (1954–).
American actor and occasional director.
The Rose 79. The Great Santini 79. Brubaker 80. Take This Job and Shove It 81. Back Roads 81. An Officer and a Gentleman 82. Independence Day (TV) 83. The Lords of Discipline 83. Firestarter 84. Gulag 85. The Curse (d) 87. The Further Adventures of Tennessee Buck (& d) 88. The Sacrifice (d) 88. Heartbreak Hotel 88. White of the Eye 88. The Two Jakes 90. Off and Running 91. Caged Fear 92. Desperate Motives 92. Major League II 94. Invasion of Privacy 96, etc.
TV series: Flesh 'n' Blood 91.

Keith, Ian (1899–1960) (Keith Ross).
American actor, latterly in character roles.
Manhandled 24. The Divine Lady 27. Abraham Lincoln 31. The Sign of the Cross 32. Queen Christina 33. The Crusades 35. The Three Musketeers (as de Rochefort) 36. The Sea Hawk 40. The Chinese Cat 44. Nightmare Alley 48. The Black Shield of Falworth 54. Prince of Players 55. The Ten Commandments (as Rameses I) 56, many others.

Keith, Penelope (1940–).
British character comedienne of haughty mien, familiar from TV's *Kate, The Good Life* and *To the Manor Born*.
Every Home Should Have One 69. Penny Gold 73. Ghost Story 74. The Priest of Love 81. The Norman Conquests (TV) 77. Coming Home (TV) 98, etc.
TV series: The Good Life 75–78. To the Manor Born 79–81. Moving 85. Executive Stress 86–88. No Job for a Lady 90–92. Law and Disorder 94. Next of Kin 95–97.
❝ I was very tall and very plain – I wasn't going to get very far on looks – so I thought I'd better be the funny girl. – *P.K.*

Keith, Robert (1896–1966).
American character actor with concert and stage experience. Father of actor Brian Keith.
The Other Kind of Love 24. Just Imagine 30. Destry Rides Again 39. Boomerang 47. My Foolish Heart 49. Fourteen Hours 51. I Want You 51. *The Wild One* 53. *Young at Heart* 54. Guys and Dolls 55. My Man Godfrey 57. Tempest 58. Cimarron 61, etc.

Kelland, Clarence Buddington (1881–1964).
American light novelist and short-story writer whose work was the basis of comedies of the 30s and 40s. His stories of Scattergood Baines, a cunning but seemingly ingenuous Yankee, inspired four second features of the early 40s starring Guy Kibbee.
French Heels (from Knots and Windshakers) 22. Speak Easily (from Footlights) 32. Thirty-Day Princess 34. Mr Deeds Goes to Town (from Opera Hat) 36. The Cat's Paw 36. Strike Me Pink (from Dreamland) 36. Stand In 37. Mr Dodd Takes the Air (from The Great Crooner) 37. Arizona 40. For Beauty's Sake (from Skin Deep) 41. Valley of the Sun 42. Sugarfoot 51, etc.

Kellaway, Cecil (1891–1973).
British character actor born in South Africa, who spent many years acting in Australia; came to Hollywood in 1939 and became an endearing exponent of roguish benevolence.
Wuthering Heights 39. Intermezzo 39. *I Married a Witch* 42. My Heart Belongs to Daddy 42. The Good Fellows (leading role) 43. Practically Yours 44. *Frenchman's Creek* 44. Love Letters 45. *Kitty* (as Gainsborough) 45. Monsieur Beaucaire 46. The Postman Always Rings Twice 46. Unconquered 47. Portrait of Jennie 48. *The Luck of the Irish* (as a leprechaun) (AAN) 48. Joan of Arc 48. *Harvey* 50. The Beast from 20,000 Fathoms 53. The Female on the Beach 55. The Shaggy Dog 59. The Cardinal 63. *Hush Hush, Sweet Charlotte* 64. Spinout 66. Fitzwilly 67. Guess Who's Coming to Dinner (AAN) 67. Getting Straight 70, many others.
✪ For being content to remain a star supporting actor of unfailing roguish charm. *I Married a Witch*.

Keller, Harry (1913–1987).
American director.
Blonde Bandit 49. Rose of Cimarron 52. The Unguarded Moment 56. The Female Animal 57. Quantez 58. Voice in the Mirror 58. Six Black Horses 61. Tammy and the Doctor 63. Kitten with a Whip 65. In Enemy Country (& p) 68, etc.

Keller, Helen (1881–1968).
Blind and deaf American lady whose problems became the subject of *The Miracle Worker* 62. She appeared to tell her story in one film, *Deliverance* 19.

Keller, Marthe (1945–).
Swiss leading lady in international films.
Funeral in Berlin 66. And Now My Love/Toute une Vie 74. Marathon Man 76. Black Sunday 76. Bobby Deerfield 77. Fedora 78. The Formula 80. The Amateur 82. Lapse of Memory/Mémoire Traquée 91. Mon Amie Max 94. According to Pereira 95. Elles (Lux.) 97. L'École de la Chair 98, etc.

Kellerman, Annette (1888–1975).
Australian dancer and swimming star who pioneered the one-piece bathing suit. Esther Williams played her in a biopic, *Million Dollar Mermaid* 52.
Neptune's Daughter 14. Daughter of the Gods 16. Queen of the Sea 18. What Women Love 20, etc.

Kellerman, Sally (1938–).
American leading lady of the 70s.
The Third Day 65. The Boston Strangler 68. The April Fools 69. M*A*S*H (AAN) 69. Brewster McCloud 70. Last of the Red Hot Lovers 72. Lost Horizon 73. Slither 73. Rafferty and the Gold Dust Twins 75. The Big Bus 76. Welcome to L.A. 77. Magee and the Lady (TV) 77. A Little Romance 79. Foxes 80. Head On 80. Loving Couples 80. Serial 80. Moving Violations 84. Back to School 86. That's Life 86. Meatballs III 87. You Can't Hurry Love 89. Boris and Natasha 90. The Player 92. Younger and Younger 93. Prêt-à-Porter/Ready to Wear 94. Mirror Mirror 2: Raven Dance 94. The Student Affair 97, etc.

Kellett, Bob (1927–).
British director.
A Home of Your Own 64. San Ferry Ann 65. Girl Stroke Boy 71. Up the Chastity Belt 71. Up the Front 72. The Garnett Saga 72. Our Miss Fred 72. Spanish Fly 76. Are You Being Served? 77. Haunted (co-w) 95, etc.

Kelley, Barry (1908–1991).
Tough-looking Irish-American supporting actor, usually in gangster roles.
Boomerang 47. The Asphalt Jungle 50. The Killer That Stalked New York 51. 711 Ocean Drive 52. The Long Wait 54. The Buccaneer 59. The Manchurian Candidate 62. The Love Bug 69, many others.

Kelley, De Forrest (1920–).
American actor, best known for playing Dr Leonard McCoy in the TV series *Star Trek* and some subsequent films. Born in Atlanta, Georgia, he began in films in the late 40s, usually cast in villainous roles.
Fear in the Night (leading role) 47. Duke of Chicago 50. House of Bamboo 55. Gunfight 57. Warlock 59. Johnny Reno 66. Star Trek 79. Star Trek II: The Wrath of Khan 82. Star Trek III: The Search for Spock 84. Star Trek IV: The Journey Home 86. Star Trek V: The Final Frontier 89. Star Trek VI: The Undiscovered Country 91, etc.
TV series: *Star Trek* 66–68.

Kellin, Mike (1922–1983).
American actor; much TV.
At War with the Army 52. Lonelyhearts 57. The Great Imposter 60. Invitation to a Gunfighter 63. The Boston Strangler 68. Assignment Danger (TV) 72. Connection (TV) 73. Freebie and the Bean 74. Midnight Express 78. The Jazz Singer 80. FDR: The Last Year (TV) 80. So Fine 81, many others.

Kellino, Pamela (1916–1996) (Pamela Ostrer; aka Pamela Mason).
Forceful British actress and screenwriter, married first to Roy Kellino and then to James Mason (1941–64). The daughter of Isidore Ostrer, one of five brothers who controlled the Gaumont cinema chain and Gaumont-British Productions, she was also a novelist, columnist and (as Pamela Mason) US TV personality. She, Mason and Kellino set up a short-lived production company, Portland, in the 50s.
Jew Süss 34. I Met a Murderer (& co-w) 39. They Were Sisters 45. The Upturned Glass 47. Pandora and the Flying Dutchman 50. Lady Possessed (& oa, co-w) 51. Charade (& co-w) 53. The Child 54. The Navy vs the Night Monsters 65. Wild in the Streets (as herself) 68. Everything You Wanted to Know about Sex (But Were Afraid to Ask) (as herself) 72. My Wicked, Wicked Ways (TV) 85, etc.

Kellino, Roy (1912–1956).
English cinematographer and director, the son of Will P. Kellino. Born in London, he acted from childhood, and was in films from 1915. In the mid-20s, he went to work for Gainsborough as a camera assistant, becoming a cinematographer in 1929. He set up a short-lived production company, Gamma Films, in the mid-30s with actor James Mason and his first wife, actress Pamela Kellino.
AS CINEMATOGRAPHER: The Phantom Light 37. The Last Adventurers 38. Johnny Frenchman 35, etc.
AS DIRECTOR: Catch as Catch Can 38. *I Met a Murderer* (& ph) 39. Guilt is My Shadow 49. Lady Possessed (US) 51. Charade 53. The Silken Affair 55, etc.

Kellino, Will P. (1873–1958) (William P. Gislingham).
English director, circus clown and acrobat, the father of cinematographer and director Roy Kellino. Born in London, he began in films in 1910 and made many early shorts featuring Fred and Joe Evans. He spent a year in Hollywood in 1926, working on Lupino Lane's comedies, before returning to England to direct some features.
How Willy Joined Barnum Bill (& a) 13. Grand Christmas Harlequinade (& a) 14. Playing the Deuce (& a) 15. A Wife in a Hurry (& a) 16. The Missing Link (& a) 17. Alf's Carpet 29. Alf's Button 30. The Poisoned Diamond 34. Sometimes Good 34. Wishes 34. Lend Me Your Wife 35. Royal Cavalcade 35. Hot News 36. Pay-Box Adventure 36, etc.

Kelljan, Robert (1930–1982) (Robert Kelljchian).
American director.
Little Sister 69. Count Yorga Vampire 69. The Return of Count Yorga 71. Scream Blacula Scream 74. Went on to TV work.

Kelly, Emmett (1895–1979).
American circus clown, famous for his downcast, tramp-like character Weary Willie, in occasional films. Born in Sedan, Kansas, he began as a cartoonist before joining a circus in the early 20s as a trapeze artist. He concentrated on clowning from the early 30s, working in London with Bertram Mills Circus and becoming a star of the Ringling Brothers and Barnum & Bailey Circus from the early 40s. Married twice.

Autobiography: 1968, *Clown*.

The Fat Man 51. The Greatest Show on Earth 52. Wind Across the Everglades 58, etc.

❝ I am the hobo who found out the hard way that the deck is stacked, the dice 'frozen', the race fixed and the wheel crooked, but there is always present that one tiny, forlorn spark of hope still glimmering in his soul, which makes him keep trying. – *E.K. on Weary Willie*

Kelly, Gene (1912–1996) (Eugene Curran Kelly).
Breezy, bouncy American dancer who became one of Hollywood's great star personalities of the 40s and 50s, although his acting and singing abilities were minimal and his 'good guy' characterization wore a little thin. When musicals lamentably went out of fashion, he turned to direction. Special Academy Award 1951 'in appreciation of his versatility as an actor, singer, director and dancer, and specially for his brilliant achievements in the art of choreography on film'. The first of his three wives was actress Betsy Blair (1941–57).

Biography: 1974, *Gene Kelly* by Clive Hirschhorn.

■ *For Me and My Gal* 42. Pilot Number Five 42. Dubarry was a Lady 43. Thousands Cheer 43. The Cross of Lorraine 43. *Cover Girl* 44. Christmas Holiday 44. Anchors Aweigh (AAN) 45. Ziegfeld Follies 46. Living in a Big Way 47. *The Pirate* 48. *The Three Musketeers* 48. Words and Music 48. *Take Me Out to the Ball Game* 49. *On the Town* (& co-d) 49. Black Hand 50. Summer Stock 50. It's A Big Country 51. *An American in Paris* 51. *Singin' in the Rain* (& co-d) 52. The Devil Makes Three 52. Brigadoon 54. Seagulls over Sorrento (GB) 54. Deep in My Heart 54. It's Always Fair Weather 55. *Invitation to the Dance* (& d) 56. The Happy Road (& pd) 57. Les Girls 57. Marjorie Morningstar 58. The Tunnel of Love (d only) 58. Inherit the Wind 60. Let's Make Love (cameo) 60. Gigot (d only) 62. What a Way to Go 64. The Young Girls of Rochefort 67. A Guide for the Married Man (d only) 67. Hello Dolly (d only) 69. The Cheyenne Social Club (pd only) 70. Forty Carats 73. That's Entertainment 74. That's Entertainment Two 76. Women of the Year (TV) (d only) 76. Viva Knievel 77. Xanadu 80. That's Dancing! 85.

TV series: Going My Way 62.

✪ For terpsichorean delights performed with cheerful proletarian grace. *Singin' in the Rain*.

❝ The days at MGM were marvellous. Everyone was pitching in. We had real collaboration. It was fun. We didn't think it was work. – *G.K.*

Fred Astaire represents the aristocracy when he dances. I represent the proletariat. – *G.K.*

His grin could melt stone. – *New Yorker, 1978*

Famous line (to Nina Foch in *An American in Paris*): 'That's quite a dress you almost have on.'

Kelly, George (1890–1974).
American playwright, a former actor, whose Broadway successes of the 20s were filmed several times. He was the brother of actor Walter C. KELLY, and uncle of actress Grace KELLY. The third, 1950, version of his Pulitzer Prize-winning play *Craig's Wife* gave Joan CRAWFORD one of her most typical roles as a possessive and domineering woman.

Craig's Wife 28. Men Are Like That (from The Show-Off) 29. The Show-Off 34. Doubting Thomas (from The Torch Bearers) 35. Craig's Wife 36. Too Busy to Work (from The Torch Bearers) 39. The Show-Off 46. Harriet Craig 50.

Kelly, Grace (1928–1982).
American leading actress of the 50s; her cool, blonde beauty quickly made her a star, but she retired to marry Prince Rainier of Monaco. Born in Philadelphia, the daughter of a self-made millionaire and the niece of playwright George KELLY, she studied at the American Academy of Dramatic Arts in New York and made an almost immediate impact as the Quaker bride of Gary COOPER in *High Noon*. Died of injuries sustained in a car crash. She was played by Cheryl LADD in the TV biopic *Grace Kelly* 83. Her lovers included actors William HOLDEN, Ray MILLAND, Gary Cooper, Clark GABLE, Jean-Pierre AUMONT and David NIVEN.

Biography: 1997, *Rainier and Grace* (revised edition) by Jeffrey Robinson.

■ Fourteen Hours 51. High Noon 52. Mogambo (AAN) 53. Dial M for Murder 54. *Rear Window* 54. *The Country Girl* (AA) 54. Green Fire 54. The Bridges at Toko-Ri 54. To Catch a Thief 55. The Swan 56. *High Society* 56.

❝ I hated Hollywood. It's a town without pity. I know of no other place in the world where so many people suffer from nervous breakdowns, where there are so many alcoholics, neurotics, and so much unhappiness. – *G.K.*

Writing about her is like trying to wrap up 115 pounds of smoke. – *Pete Martin*

Kelly, Jack (1927–1992).
Irish-American actor who usually played wryly humorous roles; notably in TV series *Kings Row* and *Maverick*. Born in Astoria, New York, to parents who were actors, he was on stage and radio as a child, and in films from the late 40s. He was the brother of actress Nancy KELLY.

Where Danger Lives 51. Drive a Crooked Road 54. To Hell and Back 56. Hong Kong Affair 58. Love and Kisses 65. Young Billy Young 69. Commandos 73, etc.

TV series: Kings Row 55–56. Dr Hudson's Secret Journal 55–57. Maverick 57–62. NBC Comedy Playhouse 70. NBC Comedy Theater 71–72. Get Christie Love 75. The Hardy Boys Mysteries 78–79.

Kelly, James (1931–1978).
British screenwriter and director of suspense and horror movies. Born in London, he was in TV from the late 40s, writing comedy scripts and for series such as *Happily Ever After*, *No Hiding Place* and *Our Man at St Marks*.

Mary Had a Little (co-w) 61. Three on a Spree (co-w) 61. Dr Blood's Coffin (co-w) 61. Tomorrow at Ten (co-w) 62. The Beast in the Cellar (wd) 70. Night Hair Child (d) 71. W (co-w) (US) 73, etc.

Kelly, Judy (1913–).
Australian leading actress, on stage and screen in Britain. Born in Sydney, she was a former teacher who began on stage in 1930 and won a film-test competition that brought her to England two years later. She retired in the late 40s.

Lord Camber's Ladies 32. His Night Out 35. Make Up 37. At the Villa Rose 40. Tomorrow We Live 43. The Butler's Dilemma 43. Dead of Night 45. Warning to Wantons 48, etc.

Kelly, Moira (1969–).
American actress.

Billy Bathgate 91. The Cutting Edge 91. Twin Peaks: Fire Walk with Me 92. Chaplin 92. With Honors 94. Little Odessa 94. The Lion King (voice) 94. The Tie that Binds 95. Unhook the Stars 96. Changing Habits 97. Love Walked In 97. Dangerous Beauty 98. The Lion King II: Simba's Pride (voice) 98. Hi-Life 98, etc.

Kelly, Nancy (1921–1995).
American leading lady, former child model; in films 1938–47, then on Broadway stage. She was the sister of actor Jack KELLY.

Submarine Patrol 38. *Tailspin* 38. Jesse James 39. Stanley and Livingstone 39. Parachute Battalion 41. Tornado 43. Show Business 44. Woman in Bondage 45. Betrayal from the East 45. Friendly Enemies 47. *The Bad Seed* (AAN) 56. Crowded Paradise 56. The Impostor (TV) 73, etc.

Kelly, Patsy (1910–1981).
Dumpy American comedienne of the 30s, often a pert wisecracker or a frightened maid.

Going Hollywood 33. The Girl from Missouri 34. Go Into Your Dance 35. Page Miss Glory 35. Kelly the Second 36. Sing Baby Sing 36. Pigskin Parade 36. Wake and Live 37. Merrily We Live 38. The Gorilla 39. Road Show 41. Topper Returns 41. *Broadway Limited* 41. Sing Your Worries Away 42. My Son the Hero 43. Please Don't Eat the Daisies 60. The Naked Kiss 64. The Ghost in the Invisible Bikini 66. Rosemary's Baby 68. Freaky Friday 77. The North Avenue Irregulars 79, etc.

TV series: Valentine's Day 64. The Cop and the Kid 76.

Kelly, Paul (1899–1956).
Wiry American leading man of the 30s and 40s, almost always in 'B' pictures.

Uncle Sam of Freedom Ridge 20. The New Klondike 26. Slide Kelly Slide 27. The Girl from Calgary 32. Broadway Thro' a Keyhole 33. Side Streets 34. Public Hero Number One 35. The Silk Hat Kid 35. The Accusing Finger 36. Navy Blue and Gold 37. Island in the Sky 38. Within the Law 39. The Roaring Twenties 39. Invisible Stripes 40. Queen of the Mob 40. Mystery Ship 41. Tarzan's New York Adventure 42. Flying Tigers 42. The Man from Music Mountain 43. Dead Man's Eyes 44. China's Little Devils 45. The Cat Creeps 46. Spoilers of the North 47. Fear in the Night 47. *Crossfire* 47. The File on Thelma Jordon 49. The Secret Fury 50. The Painted Hills 51. Springfield Rifle 52. Split Second 53. The High and the Mighty 54. The Square Jungle 55. Storm Center 56. Bail Out at 43,000 57, many others.

Kelly, Paula (1939–).
Tall, elegant American actress and dancer.

Sweet Charity 69. The Andromeda Strain 70. Trouble Man 72. Soylent Green 73. Uptown Saturday Night 74. Drum 76. Jo Jo Dancer, Your Life Is Calling 86. Uncle Tom's Cabin 87. The Women of Brewster Place (TV) 89. Once Upon a Time . . . When We Were Colored 95, etc.

TV series: Chiefs 83. Night Court 84.

Kelly, Tommy (1928–).
American child actor of the 30s.

The Adventures of Tom Sawyer 38. Peck's Bad Boy with the Circus 38. Nice Girl 41. Mugtown 43, etc.

Kelly, Walter C. (1873–1939).
American comic actor, best known for his act as 'The Virginia Judge', which he began performing in vaudeville from the 1890s and put on film in 1935. He was the brother of playwright George KELLY and uncle of actress Grace KELLY.

Autobiography: 1935, *Of Me I Sing*.

Seas Beneath 31. McFadden's Flats 35. *The Virginia Judge* 35. Laughing Irish Eyes 36, etc.

Kelsall, Moultrie (1901–1980).
Scottish character actor of stage and screen.

Landfall 49. The Lavender Hill Mob 51. The Master of Ballantrae 53. The Maggie 54. The Man Who Never Was 56. Violent Playground 58. The Battle of the Sexes 60. Greyfriars Bobby 61. The Birthday Party 68. One More Time 70, etc.

Kelsey, Fred (1884–1961).
American small-part actor, often seen as lugubrious sheriff or cop on the beat.

The Four Horsemen of the Apocalypse 21. The Eleventh Hour 23. The Gorilla 27. The Last Warning 29. Guilty as Hell 32. One Frightened Night 35. The Lone Wolf Keeps a Date 40. The Adventures of Mark Twain 44. Bringing Up Father 46. Hans Christian Andersen 52. Racing Blood 54, many others.

Kelton, Pert (1907–1968).
American character comedienne, usually in hard-boiled roles. Born in Great Falls, Montana, to parents who worked in vaudeville, she was performing from the age of three, was on Broadway in her late teens, and in films from 1929. She played Jackie GLEASON's wife Alice in his early 'Honeymooners' sketches on *Cavalcade of Stars*, but was replaced by Audrey MEADOWS when the comedian moved to CBS as a result of her blacklisting for left-wing associations.

Sally 29. *The Bowery* 33. Mary Burns Fugitive 35. Annie Oakley 35. Kelly the Second 36. Cain and Mabel 36. The Hit Parade 37. *The Music Man* 62. Love and Kisses 65. The Comic 69, etc.

TV series: Cavalcade of Stars 50–52. Henry Morgan's Great Talent Hunt 51.

Kemp, Gary (1960–).
English leading actor, guitarist and songwriter, a founder of the late-70s and 80s rock group Spandau Ballet, which also included his brother, Martin KEMP.

The Krays 90. Bodyguard 92. Paper Marriage 93. Killing Zoe 94. Magic Hunter/Buvos Vadas 94, etc.

Kemp, Jeremy (1934–) (Edmund Walker).
British leading man who resigned from TV series *Z Cars* and has had some success in films.

Dr Terror's House of Horrors 65. Operation Crossbow 65. Cast a Giant Shadow 66. The Blue Max 66. Face of a Stranger 66. Assignment K 67. The Strange Affair 68. Darling Lili 70. The Games 70. Eyewitness 70. The Belstone Fox 73. The Seven Per Cent Solution 76. A Bridge Too Far 77. The Rhinemann Exchange (TV) 77. East of Elephant Rock 78. Leopard in the Snow 78. Caravans 78. The Prisoner of Zenda 79. Return of the Soldier 82. The Winds of War (TV) 83. Sadat (TV) 83. George Washington (TV) 84. Top Secret 84. Peter the Great (TV) 86. When the Whales Came 89. Prisoners of Honor (TV) 91. Angels and Insects 95, etc.

Kemp, Martin (1961–).
English leading actor and musician, a member of the late-70s and 80s rock group Spandau Ballet, together with his brother Gary KEMP.

The Krays 90. Daydream Believer 92. Waxwork II: Lost in Time 92. Fleshtone 94. Boca 94. Embrace of the Vampire 95. Desire 95, etc.

TV series: EastEnders 98– .

Kemper, Victor J. (1927–).
American cinematographer.

Last of the Red Hot Lovers 72. The Candidate 72. Shamus 73. The Gambler 74. The Reincarnation of Peter Proud 75. Dog Day Afternoon 75. The Last Tycoon 76. Slapshot 77. Coma 78. The Jerk 79. The Final Countdown 80. Xanadu 80. Chu Chu and the Philly Flash 81. The Four Seasons 81. Partners 82. Author! Author! 82. Mr Mom 83. National Lampoon's Vacation 83. Cloak and Dagger 84. The Lonely Guy 84. Clue 85. Pee-Wee's Big Adventure 85. Secret Admirer 85. Walk Like a Man 87. Cohen and Tate 88. See No Evil, Hear No Evil 89. Crazy People 90. F/X2 91. Married to It 91. Another You 91. Beethoven 92. Tommy Boy 95. Eddie 96, etc.

Kemplen, Ralph (1912–).
British editor. Born in London, he began work as an assistant editor in 1928.

The Ghost Train 31. The Ghoul 33. Scrooge 35. Broken Blossoms 36. The Saint Meets the Tiger 41. Carnival 46. Trottie True 49. Pandora and the Flying Dutchman 51. *The African Queen* 52. Moulin Rouge 52. Alexander the Great 56. *Room at the Top* 59. Freud 62. Night of the Iguana 64. A Man for All Seasons 66. Oliver! 68. The Day of the Jackal 73. The Omen 76. Escape to Athena 79. The Great Muppet Caper 81. Dark Crystal 82, etc.

■ AS DIRECTOR: The Spaniard's Curse 58.

Kempson, Rachel (1910–).
British actress, widow of Michael REDGRAVE and mother of Vanessa, Lynn and Corin REDGRAVE. Born in Dartmouth, Devon, and educated in London and Paris, she studied at RADA, and began in films as an extra.

The Captive Heart 46. A Woman's Vengeance (US) 48. Georgy Girl 66. The Jokers 66. Jennie (TV) 76. Out of Africa 85. Stealing Heaven 88. Déjà Vu (US) 98, etc.

Kemp-Welch, Joan (1906–).
British character actress who used to play shy girls and spinsters on stage and screen. During the 50s emerged as a TV director of distinction.

Once a Thief 35. The Girl in the Taxi 37. Busman's Honeymoon 40. Pimpernel Smith 41. Jeannie 41 (last film to date), etc.

Kendal, Felicity (1946–).
English leading stage actress, in occasional films, and best known for playing Barbara Good in the TV sitcom *The Good Life*. Born in Olton, Warwickshire, she began acting as a child with her parents' theatre company, touring India and the Far East, an existence captured in the film *Shakespeare Wallah*. She returned to England in the mid-60s and acted with the National Theatre Company.

Autobiography: 1998, *White Cargo*.

Shakespeare Wallah 65. Valentino 77. Clouds of Glory (TV) 78. The Camomile Lawn (TV) 91. Parting Shots 98, etc.

TV series: The Good Life 75–78. Solo 81–82. The Mistress 85–87. Honey for Tea 94.

Kendall, Cyrus W. (1898–1953).
American character actor, a splendid cigar-chewing 'heavy' of the 30s.

The Dancing Pirate 36. Hot Money 36. They Won't Forget 37. The Shadow Strikes 37. Hawaii Calls 38. Stand Up and Fight 38. Angels Wash Their Faces 39. Men without Souls 40. Billy the Kid 41. Johnny Eager 42. The Whistler 44. She Gets Her Man 45, many others.

Kendall, Henry (1897–1962).
British entertainer, immaculate star of London revues in the 30s and 40s. Born in London, he was on stage from childhood.

Autobiography: 1960, *I Remember Romano's*.

Tilly of Bloomsbury 21. French Leave 30. Rich

and Strange 32. King of the Ritz 33. Death at Broadcasting House 34. The Amazing Quest of Ernest Bliss 36. School for Husbands 37. The Butler's Dilemma 43. 29 Acacia Avenue 45. The Voice of Merrill 52. An Alligator Named Daisy 55, etc.

Kendall, Kay (1926–1959) (Justine McCarthy).
Vivacious, stylish English leading actress of the 50s. Born in London, she left school at the age of 12 to appear in revue, and from the age of 14 joined her sister Kim in a variety act; they appeared together in her first films. She was married to Rex HARRISON from 1957 until her death from leukaemia.
■ Fiddlers Three 44. Dreaming 44. Champagne Charlie 44. Waltz Time 45. *London Town* 46. Dance Hall 50. Night and the City 50. Happy Go Lovely 51. Lady Godiva Rides Again 51. Wings of Danger 52. Curtain Up 52. It Started in Paradise 52. Mantrap 52. Street of Shadows 53. The Square Ring 53. *Genevieve* 53. Meet Mr Lucifer 53. Fast and Loose 54. Abdullah the Great 54. Doctor in the House 54. The Constant Husband 55. *Simon and Laura* 55. Quentin Durward 56. Les Girls 57. *The Reluctant Debutante* 58. Once More with Feeling 60.

Kendall, Suzy (1944–) (Frieda Harrison).
British leading lady. Married actor Dudley MOORE (1968–70).
Circus of Fear 67. To Sir with Love 67. Penthouse 67. *Up the Junction* 68. Thirty Is a Dangerous Age, Cynthia 68. Fräulein Doktor 68. The Betrayal 69. Darker than Amber (US) 70. The Bird with the Crystal Plumage (It.) 70. Assault 71. Tales that Witness Madness 73. Craze 73. Fear Is the Key 73. The Demon Master 73. Torso 74. Adventures of a Private Eye 77, etc.

Kennaway, James (1928–1968).
British novelist and screenwriter.
Biography: 1983, *James and Jim: A Biography of James Kennaway* by Trevor Royle.
Violent Playground 58. Tunes of Glory (AAN) 61. The Mind Benders 63. The Shoes of the Fisherman (co-w) 68. The Battle of Britain (co-w) 69. Country Dance 70, etc.

Kennedy, Arthur (1914–1990).
American leading actor who, despite many intelligent performances, failed to achieve stardom.
■ City for Conquest 40. High Sierra 41. Strange Alibi 41. Knockout 41. Highway West 41. Bad Men of Missouri 41. They Died with Their Boots On 41. Desperate Journey 42. Air Force 43. *Devotion* (as Branwell Brontë) 46. Cheyenne 47. Boomerang 47. Too Late for Tears 49. *Champion* (AAN) 49. *The Window* 49. The Walking Hills 49. Chicago Deadline 49. *The Glass Menagerie* 50. *Bright Victory* (AAN) 51. Red Mountain 52. *Rancho Notorious* 52. The Girl in White 52. Bend of the River 52. The Lusty Men 52. Impulse (GB) 54. The Man from Laramie 55. The Naked Dawn 55. Trial (AAN) 55. The Desperate Hours 55. Crashout 55. The Rawhide Years 56. Peyton Place (AAN) 57. Twilight for the Gods 58. Some Came Running (AAN) 58. A Summer Place 59. Elmer Gantry 60. Home is the Hero 61. Claudelle Inglish 61. Murder She Said (GB) 62. Hemingway's Adventures of a Young Man 62. Barabbas 62. *Lawrence of Arabia* 62. Cheyenne Autumn 64. Joy in the Morning 65. Murieta 65. Italiano Brava Gente 65. Fantastic Voyage 66. Nevada Smith 66. Monday's Child (Arg.) 67. The Prodigal Gun 68. Anzio 68. The Day of the Evil Gun 68. Dead or Alive 68. Hail Hero 69. Shark 69. The Movie Murderer (TV) 70. Glory Boy 71. A Death of Innocence (TV) 71. The President's Plane Is Missing (TV) 71. Crawlspace (TV) 72. Nakia (TV) 74. The Living Dead at the Manchester Morgue 74. L'Anticristo 74. The Sentinel 77. Brutal Justice 78. Covert Action 78. The Humanoid 79. My Old Man's Place 88. Signs of Life 89. Grandpa 91.

Kennedy, Burt (1923–).
American director, originally radio writer (from 1947), later TV writer-director (*Combat* series, etc.).
The Canadians (wd) 61. Mail Order Bride (wd) 63. The Rounders (wd) 64. The Money Trap (d) 65. *Return of the Seven* 66. Welcome to Hard Times (wd) 67. *The War Wagon* 67. Monday's Child (Arg.) 67. *Support Your Local Sheriff* 69. Young Billy Young 69. The Good Guys and the Bad Guys 69. The Dubious Patriots 70. Support Your Local Gunfighter 71. The Deserter 71. Hannie Caulder 71. The Train Robbers (& w) 75. The Killer Inside Me 76. Wolf Lake (& w) 79. The Wild Wild West Revisited (TV) 79. The Trouble with Spies 87. Once upon a Texas Train/Texas Guns (TV) 88. Where the Hell's That Gold?!! (TV) 88. Suburban Commando 91. All the Kind Strangers 92, etc.etc.

Kennedy, Douglas (1915–1973) (formerly known as Keith Douglas).
American leading man of action features, later character actor.
The Way of All Flesh 40. Women without Names 41. Dark Passage 47. Chain Gang 50. I Was an American Spy 51. Ride the Man Down 53. Bomba and the Lion Hunters 54. The Amazing Transparent Man 59, many others.
TV series: Steve Donovan Western Marshal.

Kennedy, Edgar (1890–1948).
Bald, explosive American comedian with vaudeville experience. A former Keystone Kop, he continued in demand for supporting roles and also starred in innumerable domestic comedy two-reelers, his exasperated gestures being familiar the world over. His brother Tom Kennedy (1885–1965), also a Keystone Kop, became a professional wrestler, and later played bit parts in movies and TV right up to his death.
Tillie's Punctured Romance 15. The Leather Pushers 22. Midnight Patrol 31. *Duck Soup* 33. King Kelly of the USA 34. Captain Tugboat Annie 46. Unfaithfully Yours 48, many others.
✪ For being one of Hollywood's instantly recognizable faces and for never failing to make one laugh. *Duck Soup*.

Kennedy, George (1925–).
American character actor, usually seen as menace but graduating to sympathetic roles.
Little Shepherd of Kingdom Come (debut) 60. Lonely Are the Brave 62. The Man from the Diners Club 63. *Charade* 63. Straitjacket 64. Mirage 65. Shenandoah 65. *The Flight of the Phoenix* 65. Hurry Sundown 67. The Dirty Dozen 67. *Cool Hand Luke* (AA) 67. Bandolero 68. The Boston Strangler 68. The Pink Jungle 69. Guns of the Magnificent Seven 69. The Good Guys and the Bad Guys 69. Airport 69. Tick Tick Tick 70. Fool's Parade 71. A Great American Tragedy (TV) 72. Lost Horizon 73. Cahill 73. Airport 75 74. Thunderbolt and Lightfoot 74. Earthquake 74. The Human Factor 75. The Eiger Sanction 75. Airport 77 77. The Double McGuffin 79. The Concorde – Airport '79 79. Death on the Nile 79. Backstairs at the White House (TV) 79. Steel 80. Modern Romance 81. Bolero 84. Rare Breed 84. Delta Force 85. Savage Dawn 85. Radioactive Dreams 86. Creepshow 2 87. Born to Race 88. Demonwarp 88. Esmeralda Bay 88. The Naked Gun: From the Files of Police Squad 88. Nightmare at Noon 88. Private Roads/No Trespassing 88. Uninvited 88. Counterforce 89. Ministry of Vengeance 89. The Terror Within 89. Brain Dead 90. Hangfire 90. The Naked Gun 2½: The Smell of Fear 91. Naked Gun 33 : The Final Insult 94, etc.
TV series: *Sarge* 71. The Blue Knight 75–76.

Kennedy, John Fitzgerald (1917–1963).
The American president who was assassinated in Dallas has been the subject of several films and even more TV movies. His wartime experiences in the Pacific were turned into the dull *PT 109*, directed by Leslie H. Martinson and starring Cliff Robertson. Martin Sheen played him in a TV mini-series, *Kennedy* 83, which covered his presidential career; Paul Rudd in *Johnny We Hardly Knew Ye* 77, which dealt with his first political campaign in Boston; and James Franciscus in *Jacqueline Bouvier Kennedy* 81, a TV biopic of his wife's life. The confusions surrounding his death have also been aired, notably in Oliver Stone's paranoaic conspiracy account *JFK* 91, while *Ruby* 92 dealt with the fate of the night-club owner Jack Ruby, who shot Kennedy's killer, Lee Harvey Oswald.

Kennedy, Kathleen (1954–).
American producer, formerly president of Amblin Entertainment, a company she formed with Steven Spielberg and Frank Marshall. Now runs Kennedy/Marshall Productions.
E.T. – the Extraterrestrial 81. Poltergeist 82. Gremlins 84. Indiana Jones and the Temple of Doom 84. The Color Purple 85. Back to the Future 85. The Money Pit 86. Batteries Not Included 86. An American Tail 87. Empire of the Sun 87. Who Framed Roger Rabbit 88. The Land before Time 88. Back to the Future II 89. Hook 91. Alive 92. Jurassic Park 93. Milk Money 94. The Indian in the Cupboard 95. Twister 96, etc.

Kennedy, Madge (1892–1987).
American star of silent films, from the stage; retired in the mid-20s and then returned to the screen in the 50s as a character actress.
Baby Mine 17. A Perfect Lady 18. The Truth 20. Help Yourself 21. Scandal Sheet 25. Oh Baby! 26. The Marrying Kind 52. The Rains of Ranchipur 55. Three Bad Sisters 56. Lust for Life 56. Houseboat 58. Let's Make Love 60. They Shoot Horses, Don't They? 69. The Baby Maker 70. The Day of the Locust 75. Marathon Man 76, etc.

Kennedy, Margaret (1896–1967) (Lady Davies).
English best-selling sentimental novelist, playwright and screenwriter. Born in London, she was educated at Oxford University.
Autobiography: 1937, *Where Stands a Winged Sentry*.
The Constant Nymph (co-w, oa) 28, 33. Little Friend (co-w) 34. The Old Curiosity Shop (co-w) 34. Escape Me Never (co-w, oa) 35. Whom the Gods Love (co-w) 37. Dreaming Lips (co-w) 37. The Man in Grey (co-w) 43. Escape Me Never (oa) 47, etc.

Kennedy, Merna (1908–1944) (Maude Kahler).
American leading lady of the late 20s. Retired to marry Busby Berkeley.
The Circus 28. Broadway 30. Laughter in Hell 32. Arizona to Broadway 33. Police Call 33. I Like It That Way 34, etc.

Kennedy, Tom:
see KENNEDY, Edgar.

Kenney, James (1930–1982).
English leading actor, in films from 1941 and on stage from 1944, also a revue and cabaret performer. The son of vaudeville comedian and occasional actor Horace Kenney, he studied at the Italia Conti Stage School and first attracted notice as a juvenile psychopath in *Cosh Boy*, on stage 51, and screen.
Circus Boy 47. Captain Horatio Hornblower 51. The Gentle Gunman 52. *Cosh Boy* 53. The Sea Shall Not Have Them 54. The Gelignite Gang 56. Son of a Stranger 58. Hidden Homicide 59. Ambush in Leopard Street 66, etc.

Kensit, Patsy (1968–).
Baby-faced English actress and singer; in TV commercials, programmes and films as a child, now making the transition to adult stardom.
The Great Gatsby 74. Alfie Darling 75. The Bluebird 76. Hanover Street 79. Silas Marner (TV) 85. Absolute Beginners 86. A Chorus of Disapproval 89. Lethal Weapon 2 89. Chicago Joe and the Showgirl 90. Bullseye! 91. Twenty-One 91. Adam Bede (TV) 91. Timebomb 91. Blame It on the Bellboy 92. Prince of Shadows/Beltenebros 92. The Turn of the Screw 92. Kleptomania 93. Bitter Harvest 93. Angels and Insects 95. Love and Betrayal: The Mia Farrow Story (TV) 95. Tunnel Vision 95. Grace of My Heart 96. Human Bomb 97, etc.
❝ She's a very intelligent girl who has succeeded in displaying stupidity in a rather clever way.
– A. S. Byatt

Kent, Jean (1921–) (Joan Mildred Summerfield).
British leading lady of the 40s, on stage aged ten, formerly (as Jean Carr) in the Windmill chorus.
■ The Rocks of Valpre (debut) 35. Who's Your Father 35. Frozen Limits 39. Hallo Fame! 40. It's That Man Again 42. Miss London Ltd 43. Warn That Man 43. Bees in Paradise 43. Fanny by Gaslight 44. *Waterloo Road* 44. Soldier, Sailor 44. 2000 Women 44. Champagne Charlie 44. Madonna of the Seven Moons 44. The Wicked Lady 45. The Rake's Progress 45. Caravan 46. Carnival 46. The Magic Bow 46. The Man Within 47. The Loves of Joanna Godden 47. *Good Time Girl* 48. Bond Street 48. Sleeping Car to Trieste 48. *Trottie True* 49. The Reluctant Widow 50. The Woman in Question 50. Her Favourite Husband 50. The Browning Version 51. The Lost Hours/The Big Frame 52. Before I Wake 54. The Prince and the Showgirl 57. Bonjour Tristesse 58. Grip of the Strangler 58. Beyond This Place 59. Please Turn Over 60. Bluebeard's Ten Honeymoons 60. Shout at the Devil 76.
TV series: *Sir Francis Drake* (as Queen Elizabeth I) 62–63. *Tycoon* 78. Crossroads 81–82. Lovejoy 91. Shrinks 91.

Kent, Keneth (1882–1963).
Englsh actor and dramatist, in occasional films. Born in Liverpool, the son of stage actor Charles Kent, he studied at RADA, and was on stage from 1912.
Luck of the Navy 38. Queer Cargo 38. At the Villa Rose 39. Night Train to Munich 40. *The House of the Arrow* 40. Dangerous Moonlight 41. Idol of Paris 48. A Time to Kill 55, etc.

Kenton, Erle C. (1896–1980).
American director, from 1914.
Small Town Idol 20. The Leather Pushers 22. Street of Illusion 25. Father and Son 27. Isle of Lost Souls 32. Remedy for Riches 39. Petticoat Politics 41. North to the Klondike 41. Ghost of Frankenstein 42. Who Done It? 42. Frisco Lil 42. House of Frankenstein 45. *House of Dracula* 45. Should Parents Tell? 49. Killer with a Label 50, etc.

Kenyon, Doris (1897–1979).
American silent-screen leading lady who was married to Milton Sills.
The Pawn of Fate 16. A Girl's Folly 17. The Hidden Hand 18. The Ruling Passion 22. Monsieur Beaucaire 24. Blonde Saint 26. The Hawk's Nest 28. Alexander Hamilton 31. Voltaire 33. Counsellor at Law 33. The Man in the Iron Mask 39, etc.
TV series: Tycoon 64.

Kerima (1925–).
Algerian actress. Married director Guy Hamilton.
An Outcast of the Islands 51. La Lupa 52. The Quiet American 58. Jessica 61. The Love Box 72, etc.

Kern, James V. (1909–1966).
American director, and screenwriter in collaboration with others. Born in New York City, he studied law at Fordham University and began as a member of the singing group the Yacht Club Boys. He also worked as an editor.
That's Right, You're Wrong (w) 39. If I Had My Way (w) 40. You'll Find Out (w) 40. Playmates (w) 41. Look Who's Laughing (w) 41. *Thank Your Lucky Stars* (w) 43. The Doughgirls (wd) 44. Shine On Harvest Moon (w) 44. The Horn Blows at Midnight (w) 45. Never Say Goodbye (wd) 46. Stallion Road (d) 46. April Showers (d) 48. The Second Woman (d) 50. Two Tickets to Broadway (d) 51. Angels in the Outfield (ed) 51. Lum and Abner Abroad (d) 55, etc.

Kern, Jerome (1885–1945).
Celebrated American songwriter. His Academy Award songs are 'The Way You Look Tonight' and 'The Last Time I Saw Paris'.
Roberta 35. Showboat 35 and 51. Swing Time 36. Cover Girl 44. Can't Help Singing 44. Centennial Summer 46. Till the Clouds Roll By (in which he was played by Robert Walker) 46.

Kerouac, Jack (1922–1969).
American novelist of the Beat generation, a legend he helped to create before dying of drink. *Heart Beat* was a film about him; there was also an underground film of his autobiographical *On the Road*.

Kerr, Bill (1922–).
South African-born stand-up comedian and character actor, in Australia from childhood. He performed in Britain from the 50s in radio and TV comedy with Tony Hancock before returning to Australia in the 70s.
Harmony Row (as Willie Kerr) 33. The Silence of Dean Maitland 34. Appointment in London 52. The Dam Busters 55. The Shiralee 57. The Captain's Table 58. The Wrong Arm of the Law 63. Doctor in Distress 63. Doctor in Clover 66. A Funny Thing Happened on the Way to the Forum 66. Tiffany Jones 73. Deadline 81. Gallipoli 82. The Pirate Movie 82. The Year of Living Dangerously 83. Razorback 83. Dusty 84. Vigil 84. The Coca Cola Kid 84. The Lighthorsemen 87. Miracle Down Under 87. Sweet Talker 91. Over the Hill/Round the Bend 92, etc.

Kerr, Deborah (1921–) (Deborah Kerr-Trimmer).
British leading lady usually cast in well-bred roles. She received an honorary Oscar 'for career achievement' in 1994.

Biography: 1977, *Deborah Kerr* by Eric Braun.

■ Major Barbara (debut) 40. *Love on the Dole* 41. Penn of Pennsylvania 41. Hatter's Castle 41. The Day Will Dawn 42. *The Life and Death of Colonel Blimp* 43. *Perfect Strangers* 45. *I See a Dark Stranger* 45. *Black Narcissus* 46. The Hucksters 47. If Winter Comes 48. Edward My Son (AAN) 49. Please Believe Me 49. King Solomon's Mines 50. Quo Vadis 51. Thunder in the East 51. The Prisoner of Zenda 52. Dream Wife 52. Julius Caesar 53. *From Here to Eternity* (AAN) 53. Young Bess 53. The End of the Affair 55. *The King and I* (AAN) 56. The Proud and Profane 56. *Tea and Sympathy* 56. Heaven Knows Mr Allison (AAN) 56. *An Affair to Remember* 57. *Separate Tables* (AAN) 58. Bonjour Tristesse 58. Count Your Blessings 59. The Journey 59. Beloved Infidel 59. *The Sundowners* (AAN) 60. The Grass Is Greener 61. *The Innocents* 61. The Naked Edge 61. The Chalk Garden 63. *The Night of the Iguana* 64. Marriage on the Rocks 65. Eye of the Devil 66. Casino Royale 67. *Prudence and the Pill* 68. The Gypsy Moths 69. The Arrangement 69. Witness for the Prosecution (TV) 84. Reunion at Fairborough (TV) 85. The Assam Garden 85. A Woman of Substance (TV) 85.

❝ All the most successful people these days seem to be neurotic. Perhaps we should stop being sorry for them and start being sorry for me – for being so confounded normal. – *D.K.*

Kerr, Frederick (1858–1933) (Frederick Keen).
British character actor of stage and, latterly, American screen; delightful as slightly doddering old man.

The Honour of the Family 27. Raffles 29. *The Devil to Pay* 30. *Frankenstein* (as the old baron) 31. Waterloo Bridge 31. The Midshipman 32. The Man from Toronto 33, etc.

Kerr, Jean (1923–) (Jean Collins).
American humorist and playwright, wife of Walter Kerr the drama critic. Her contributions to film include *Mary Mary* and *Please Don't Eat the Daisies*; *Critic's Choice* was probably based on her.

Kerr, John (1931–).
American leading man, now a lawyer.

The Cobweb 55. Gaby 56. *Tea and Sympathy* 56. *South Pacific* 58. The Pit and the Pendulum 61. Seven Women from Hell 62. The Amateur 81, etc.

Kerrigan, J. M. (1885–1964).
Irish character actor who went with the Abbey players to Hollywood in 1935, and stayed there.

Little Old New York 23. Song of My Heart 30. The Informer 35. Laughing Irish Eyes 36. Little Orphan Annie 38. Captains of the Clouds 42. Black Beauty 46. The Wild North 52. The Fastest Gun Alive 56, many others.

Kerrigan, J. Warren (1880–1947).
American actor of the silent screen.

Samson 13. Landon's Legacy 16. A Man's Man 18. The Covered Wagon 23. Captain Blood 24, etc.

Kerry, Norman (1889–1956) (Arnold Kaiser).
American actor of the silent screen.

The Black Butterfly 16. Merry Go Round 23. The Hunchback of Notre Dame 23. Phantom of the Opera 26. The Unknown 28. Air Eagles 31, many others.

Kershner, Irvin (1923–).
American director.

■ Stakeout on Dope Street 58. The Young Captives 59. The Hoodlum Priest 61. Face in the Rain 63. The Luck of Ginger Coffey 64. A Fine Madness 66. The Flim Flam Man 67. Loving 70. Up The Sandbox 72. S.P.Y.S. 74. The Return of a Man Called Horse 76. Raid on Entebbe (TV) 76. The Eyes of Laura Mars 78. The Empire Strikes Back 80. Never Say Never Again 83. Wildfire (p) 88. Robocop 2 90.

Kessel, Joseph (1898–1979).
German novelist.

Works filmed: The Lion 62. Belle de Jour 67. The Horsemen 75.

Kestelman, Sara (1944–).
English stage actress, in occasional films. Born in London, she trained as a ballet dancer and studied at the Central School of Speech and Drama. After working in repertory theatres, she made her reputation with the Royal Shakespeare Company from the late 60s, and in the late 70s also acted at the National Theatre.

Zardoz 73. Lisztomania 75. Break of Day 77. Lady Jane 86. Brazen Hussies (TV) 96. Tom Jones (TV) 97. Invasion Earth (TV) 98, etc.

Keyes, Evelyn (1919–).
American leading lady of the 40s, originally a dancer. She was married to directors Charles Vidor (1943–45) and John Huston (1946–50), and married bandleader Artie Shaw, from whom she is now separated, in 1956.

Autobiographies: 1977, *Scarlett O'Hara's Younger Sister*. 1991, *I'll Think about That Tomorrow*.

The Buccaneer (debut) 38. Gone with the Wind 39. Before I Hang 40. The Face behind the Mask 41. Here Comes Mr Jordan 41. Ladies in Retirement 41. Flight Lieutenant 42. The Adventures of Martin Eden 42. The Desperadoes 43. Nine Girls 44. A Thousand and One Nights 44. *The Jolson Story* 46. Renegades 46. Johnny O'Clock 47. The Mating of Millie 48. Enchantment 48. Mrs Mike 49. House of Settlement 49. The Killer That Stalked New York 50. Smugglers' Island 51. *The Prowler* 51. Rough Shoot (GB) 52. The Seven Year Itch 54. Hell's Half Acre 54. Around the World in Eighty Days 56. Across 110th Street 72. Return to Salem's Lot 87. Wicked Stepmother 88, etc.

Keys, Anthony Nelson (1913–1985).
British producer, associated with Hammer horror. Son of actor/comedian Nelson Keys.

Pirates of Blood River 63. The Gorgon 63. Dracula Prince of Darkness 65. Quatermass and the Pit 68, etc.

Keys, Nelson (1886–1939).
Short English comic actor, on stage from 1906, who made his reputation in revue and musical comedy. He was the father of producer Anthony Nelson Keys and writer and director John Paddy Carstairs.

Drowsy Dick's Dream 10. Once upon a Time 18. Triumph of the Scarlet Pimpernel 28. Almost a Divorce 31. The Last Journey 35. In the Soup 36. Knights for a Day 37, etc.

❝ The dramatic profession in a nutshell. – *James Barrie*

Khambatta, Persis (1948–1998).
Indian actress and model, a former beauty queen. Born in Bombay, she became Miss India in 1965, then continued her modelling career in London and the United States. She was best known for playing the bald Lieutenant Ilia, a Deltan navigator, in *Star Trek: The Motion Picture*.

Bombay by Night/Bombay Rat Ki Bahoon Mein 67. Kama Sutra (Ger.) 69. The Wilby Conspiracy (US) 75. Conduct Unbecoming (GB) 75. The Man with the Power (TV) 77. Star Trek: The Motion Picture (US) 79. Nighthawks (US) 81. Megaforce (US) 82. Warrior of the Lost World (It.) 85. Deadly Intent (US) 88. Phoenix the Warrior (US) 88, etc.

Khan, Michelle:
see Yeoh, Michelle.

Khayyam, Omar (1048–1122) (Gheyas Od-Din Abu al-Fath).
Persian poet whose *Rubaiyat*, freely translated in 1859 by Edward Fitzgerald, became a bag of popular clichés and was heavily quoted in the artier Hollywood films, notably those of Albert Lewin. The film called *Omar Khayyam* was a sword-and-sandal epic having nothing to do with the known facts of Omar's life, which are scant.

Khondji, Darius.
French cinematographer

Land of the Dead 90. Delicatessen 91. Prague 92. A Shadow of Doubt 93. Before the Rain 94. The City of Lost Children 95. Seven (US) 95. *Stealing Beauty* 96. Evita (AAN) 96. Alien: Resurrection 97, etc.

Khouri, Callie.
American screenwriter.

Thelma and Louise (AA) 91. Something to Talk About 95.

Kiarostami, Abbas (1940–).
Leading Iranian director. Born in Teheran, he studied fine arts at Teheran University and first worked as a graphic designer and as a director of commercials. In the late 60s, he joined the Institute for the Intellectual Development of Young Adults, which produced the majority of his features and short films.

The Passenger 72. The Report 77. First Graders 85. Where Is My Friend's House 87. Life and Nothing More 92. Under the Olive Trees 94. The White Balloon (w only) 95. A Propos de Nice, la Suite (Fr., co-d) 95. Journey into the Dawn 96, etc.

Kibbee, Guy (1882–1956).
Bald-headed American character comedian, usually in flustered, shifty or genial roles.

Stolen Heaven (debut) 31. City Streets 32. Forty-second Street 33. *Dames* 34. *Babbitt* 34. Captain January 35. Mr Smith Goes to Washington 39. Chad Hanna 41. Scattergood Baines 41. The Power of the Press 43. The Horn Blows at Midnight 45. Gentleman Joe Palooka 47. Fort Apache 48. Three Godfathers 49.

Kibbee, Roland (1914–1984).
American radio, TV and screen writer.

A Night in Casablanca 45. Angel on My Shoulder 46. *Vera Cruz* 54. Top Secret Affair 57. The Appaloosa 66. Valdez is Coming (& p) 71. The Midnight Man (& co-w, co-d) 75, etc.

Kiberlain, Sandrine (1968–).
Blonde French leading actress, of stage and screen. Born in Paris, the daughter of playwright David Decca, she studied at the Paris Conservatoire. Married actor Vincent Lindon.

Cyrano de Bergerac 90. The Patriots/Les Patriotes 93. L'Irrésolu 94. En Avoir (ou Pas) 95. A Self-Made Hero/Un Héros Très Discret 95. Beaumarchais 96. L'Appartement 96. Quadrille 97. Le Septième Ciel 97. À Vendre 98, etc.

Kidd, Michael (1919–) (Milton Greenwald).
American dancer and dance director.

Where's Charley? (ch only) 52. Band Wagon 53. *Seven Brides for Seven Brothers* 54. *It's Always Fair Weather* 54. Guys and Dolls 55. Merry Andrew (& d) 58. Hello Dolly 69. Smile 75. Movie Movie 79, etc.

Kidder, Margot (1948–).
Canadian leading lady. Formerly married to novelist Thomas McGuane, and briefly to actor John Heard, and director Philippe de Broca. Her career declined after 1990, when an accident confined her to a wheelchair for some time. In 1996, she was found in a confused condition, dressed in rags in a Los Angeles garden, and hospitalized for a while.

Gaily Gaily 69. Quackser Fortune 70. Suddenly Single (TV) 71. The Bounty Man (TV) 72. Sisters 72. The Dion Brothers (TV) 74. Honky Tonk (TV) 74. The Great Waldo Pepper 75. Black Christmas 75. The Reincarnation of Peter Proud 75. 92 in the Shade 77. *Superman* 78. The Amityville Horror 79. Superman II 80. Willie and Phil 80. Some Kind of Hero 82. Heartaches 82. Trenchcoat 83. Superman III 83. Picking up the Pieces (TV) 85. Gobots: Battle of the Rock Lords (voice) 86. Vanishing Act (TV) 86. Superman IV: The Quest for Peace 87. Body of Evidence (TV) 88. Mob Story 89. To Catch a Killer (TV) 91. The Pornographer 94. Never Met Picasso 96. The Clown at Midnight (Can.) 98, etc.

TV series: Nichols 71–72. Shell Game 87.

❝ I suppose that if you want to be famous and suddenly it happens and you don't like it, it's nobody's fault but your own. – *M.K.*

Kidman, Nicole (1968–).
Tall Australian leading actress, now in America. She married actor Tom Cruise in 1990.

Prince and the Great Race 83. BMX Bandits 84. Windrider 87. Night Master 87. Dead Calm 89. Flirting 89. Days of Thunder 90. Billy Bathgate 91. Far and Away 92. My Life 93. Malice 93. To Die For 95. Batman Forever 95. The Portrait of a Lady 96. The Peacemaker 97. Practical Magic 98, etc.

Kidron, Beeban (1962–).
British director, from television. She worked as a photographer's assistant before studying at the National Film School.

Oranges Are Not the Only Fruit (TV) 90. Used People (US) 93. Great Moments in Aviation 94. To Wong Foo, Thanks for Everything, Julie Newmar (US) 95. Swept from the Sea/Amy Foster 97, etc.

Kiel, Richard (1939–).
American giant (seven-foot) actor who came into his own as an adversary for James Bond.

House of the Damned 62. The Magic Sword 62. The Human Duplicators 65. Silver Streak 66. *The Spy Who Loved Me* 77. Force Ten from Navarone 78. Humanoid 78. Moonraker 79. So Fine 81. Hysterical 83. Pale Rider 85. Think Big 90. The Giant of Thunder Mountain (& p, co-w) 91. Happy Gilmore 96, etc.

❝ My wife is 5″ 4# and everybody asks me how we do it. – *R.K.*

Kieling, Wolfgang (1924–1985).
German character actor.

Maria die Magd (debut) 36. Falstaff in Wien 40. Damsels in Paris 56. Torn Curtain (US) 66. Goya 71. Dollars (US) 72. Out of Order 84, etc.

Kiepura, Jan (1902–1966).
Polish operatic tenor.

Farewell to Love (GB) 30. My *Song for You* (GB) 31. Be Mine Tonight (GB) 32. Give Us This Night (US) 36. Her Wonderful Lie (It.) 50.

Kier, Udo (1944–).
German actor in international films.

Mark of the Devil 69. Blood for Dracula 74. Andy Warhol's Frankenstein 74. Suspiria 77. Lili Marleen 80. My Own Private Idaho 91. Europa/Zentropa 92. Josh and S.A.M. 93. Ace Ventura, Pet Detective 94. The Kingdom/Riget 94. To Hell with Rotwang! 95. Paradise Framed (Hol.) 95. Over My Dead Body 95. Johnny Mnemonic 95. Barb Wire 96. Breaking the Waves (Den.) 96. The Adventures of Pinocchio 96. Les Lumières de Berlin 96. The End of Violence 97. Prince Valiant 97. Tainted (Den.) 98. Blade 98. There's No Fish Food in Heaven 98, etc.

Kiéslowski, Krzysztof (1941–1996).
Polish director and screenwriter who worked extensively in television. He won the Golden Lion for best picture at the 1993 Venice Film Festival with *Three Colours: Blue*.

Autobiography: 1992, *Kiéslowski on Kiéslowski*.

The Scar/Blizna 76. Camera Buff/Amator 79. Blind Chance/Przypadek 82. Bez Konka/No End 84. Dekalog (TV) 88–89. *A Short Film about Killing* (AA) 88. A Short Film about Love 88. The Double Life of Veronique/Podwojne Zycie Weronki 91. *Three Colours: Blue*/Trois Couleurs: Bleu 93. *Three Colours: White*/Trois Couleurs: Blanc 94. *Three Colours: Red*/Trois Couleurs: Rouge (AANd, AANw) 94, etc.

❝ I've realised that basically I don't give a shit for society which, in the case of Poland, is forty million people. But what I really care about is the individual human being. – *K.K.*

I don't think people want to be equal. Each of us wants to be a little better. We all want to be better than our neighbours and a bit more loved. We all want to be a bit richer and have a better car or TV. We all want to be a bit healthier and suffer less than others. We all want to die a slightly quieter and more peaceful death. – *K.K.*

Kilar, Wojciech (1932–).
Polish composer, in international films.

The Doll 68. Family Life 70. David (Ger.) 79. The Contract 80. The Constant Factor 80. Korczak 90. Bram Stoker's Dracula (US) 92. The Silent Touch (Pol.) 93. Death and the Maiden 95. The Portrait of a Lady (US) 96, etc.

Kilbride, Percy (1888–1964).
American character actor of wily hayseed roles. Died from injuries received in a car crash.

White Woman 33. Soak the Rich 36. George Washington Slept Here 42. Knickerbocker Holiday 44. She Wouldn't Say Yes 45. The Well-Groomed Bride 45. The Egg and I 47. Ma and Pa Kettle (series) 47–55.

Kilburn, Terry (1926–).
British boy actor of the 30s; never quite made it as adult. Now a drama teacher in America.

A Christmas Carol 38. The Boy from Barnardo's 38. Sweethearts 39. Goodbye Mr Chips (as three generations of Colley) 39. The Swiss Family Robinson 40. A Yank at Eton 42. National Velvet

45. Bulldog Drummond at Bay 47. Only the Valiant 51. The Fiend without a Face 58. Lolita 62, etc.

Kiley, Richard (1922–).
American general-purpose actor with stage experience: has latterly become a Broadway musical star.
The Mob 51. The Sniper 52. Pick Up on South Street 52. The Blackboard Jungle 55. The Phenix City Story 56. Spanish Affair 58. Pendulum 69. AKA Cassius Clay 70. Murder Once Removed (TV) 71. The Little Prince 73. Friendly Persuasion (TV) 75. The Macahans (TV) 76. Looking for Mr Goodbar 77. Endless Love 81. Angel on My Shoulder (TV) 81. Howard the Duck 86. My First Love (TV) 88. Absolute Strangers (TV) 91. Phenomenon 96, etc.
TV series: The Great Defender 95.

Kilian, Victor (1897–1979).
American character actor, usually as suspicious or downright villainous characters. He was murdered by burglars.
The Wiser Sex 32. Air Hawks 35. Seventh Heaven 36. Dr Cyclops 39. Reap the Wild Wind 42. Spellbound 45. Gentleman's Agreement 47. The Flame and the Arrow 50. Tall Target 51, etc.
1976: on TV in *Mary Hartman, Mary Hartman*.

Killiam, Paul (1916–).
American collector of silent movies, clips from which he introduces on TV in various series.

Kilmer, Val (1959–).
Independently wealthy, he studied acting at the Julliard School in New York. Formerly married to actress Joanne Whalley (1988–96). He was paid $6m to play The Saint in 1996, giving up his Batman role, which he took over from Michael Keaton, in which he was succeeded by George Clooney.
Top Secret! 84. Real Genius 85. Top Gun 86. Willow 88. Kill Me Again 89. *The Doors* 91. Thunderheart 92. True Romance 93. The Real McCoy 93. Tombstone 94. Heat 95. Wings of Courage 95. The Ghost and the Darkness 96. The Island of Dr Moreau 96. The Saint 97. Prince of Egypt (voice) 98. At First Sight 98, etc.

Kilpatrick, Lincoln (1933–).
American actor.
Cool Breeze 72. Soul Soldier 72. Soylent Green 73. Chosen Survivors 74. Uptown Saturday Night 74. The Master Gunfighter 75. Just an Old Sweet Song 76. Dr Scorpion 78. Deadly Force 83. Flicks 87. Bulletproof 88. Prison 88. Fortress 92. Piranha 95, etc.

Kilpatrick, Patrick.
American actor, a former journalist; usually cast as a villain.
Insignificance 85. Remo Williams: The Adventure Begins 85. The Toxic Avenger 85. The Quick and the Dead 87. Class of 1999 89. Showdown 94. 3 Ninjas Knuckle Up 95. Under Siege 2: Dark Territory 95. Eraser 96. Last Man Standing 96. Free Willy 3: The Rescue 97. The Replacement Killers 98, etc.

Kimball, Ward.
American animator and musician, one of the 'Nine Old Men' of the Walt Disney studios, joining in 1934, and working on features from *Snow White* and *Pinocchio* to *Bedknobs and Broomsticks* 71. He was also trombonist and leader of a Dixieland band, the Firehouse Five Plus Two.
Babes in Toyland (co-w) 61. It's Tough to Be a Bird (AA) 69.

Kimiai, Massoud (1943–).
Iranian director, born in Teheran. Concerned with social issues, he has had problems with censorship of his films, which often glory rebels, both before and after the revolution of 1979.
Come, Stranger! 69. The Emperor/Qaisar 69. Reza the Motorcycle Rider 70. Dash Akol 71. Soil 73. Ghazal 76. Journey of the Stone 78. Snake Fang/Dandane Mar 90. The Sergeant 91. The Wolf's Trail 93, etc.

Kimmins, Anthony (1901–1964).
British actor-writer-producer-director, almost entirely of light comedy subjects.
The Golden Cage (a) 33. White Ensign (a) 34. While Parents Sleep (w) 35. Keep Your Seats Please (w) 36. Talk of the Devil (w) 36. *Keep Fit* (wd) 37. The Show Goes On (w) 37. I See Ice (wd) 38. It's In the Air (wd) 38. Trouble Brewing (wd) 39. Under Your Hat (wd) 40. *Mine Own Executioner* (pd) 47. Bonnie Prince Charlie (d) 48. Flesh and Blood (d) 50. Mr Denning Drives North (d) 51. Who Goes There? (d) 52. *The Captain's Paradise* (wpd) 53. Aunt Clara (d) 54. Smiley (pd) 56. *The Amorous Prawn* (wpd) 62, etc.

King, Alan (1927–) (Irwin Kniberg).
American cabaret comedian who has made a few film appearances.
Hit the Deck 55. Miracle in the Rain 56. The Helen Morgan Story 57. On the Fiddle (GB) 61. Bye Bye Braverman 68. The Anderson Tapes 71. Just Tell Me What You Want 80. Author! Author! 82. I the Jury 82. Lovesick 83. Cat's Eye 84. Memories of Me 88. Enemies, a Love Story 89. The Bonfire of the Vanities 90. Casino 95, etc.

King, Allan (1930–).
Canadian documentarist.
Skid Row 56. Morocco 58. Rickshaw 60. The Pursuit of Happiness 62. Warrendale 66. The New Woman 68. A Married Couple 69. Who Has Seen the Wind 77. One Night Stand 79. Silence of the North 81. Ready for Slaughter (TV) 83. The Last Season (TV) 86. Termini Station 89, etc.

King, Andrea (1915–) (Georgetta Barry).
French-American leading lady with experience on the New York stage.
The Very Thought of You 44. Hotel Berlin 45. The Man I Love 46. Shadow of a Woman 46. The Violent Hour 50. The Lemon Drop Kid 51. Red Planet Mars 53. Band of Angels 57. Darby's Rangers 58. Daddy's Gone A-Hunting 69. Blackenstein 73. The Linguini Incident 91. The Color of Evening 94, etc.

King, Anita (1889–1963).
American leading lady of the silent screen, who came to fame in *The Virginian* 14.
Carmen 15. Maria Rosa 16. Temptation 16. The Squaw Man's Son 17. Mistaken Identity 19. Stripped for a Million 19, etc.

King, Charles (1894–1944).
Dapper American song-and-dance man, who appeared in early musicals before returning to the stage. Born in New York City, he was performing in vaudeville in his teens. Apart from his feature films, he also made more than 400 shorts. Died of pneumonia.
Broadway Melody 28. Hollywood Revue 29. Chasing Rainbows 30, etc.

King, Charles (1889–1957).
American character actor, usually a western heavy.
Range Law 32. Mystery Ranch 34. O'Malley of the Mounted 36. The Mystery of the Hooded Horsemen 37. Son of the Navy 40. Gunman from Bodie 42. Ghost Rider 43, etc.
❝ Old Charlie King – I must have killed him at least 20 times. Usually it was behind the same rock. – *Tex Ritter*

King, Dave (1929–).
British TV comedian of the 60s; made a few film appearances.
Pirates of Tortuga 61. Go to Blazes 62. Strange Bedfellows 65. Cuba 79. The Long Good Friday 81. Reds 81, etc.

King, Dennis (1897–1971) (Dennis Pratt).
British-born opera singer who in the early 30s starred in Hollywood films.
The Vagabond King 30. Fra Diavolo 33.

King, George (1900–1966).
British producer-director, mainly of independent quota quickies and melodramas.
Too Many Crooks (d) 31. John Halifax Gentleman (p) 36. The Chinese Bungalow (pd) 39. The Case of the Frightened Lady (pd) 40. The Face at the Window (pd) 40. The First of the Few (p) 42. Tomorrow We Live (pd) 42. Candlelight in Algeria (pd) 44. Gaiety George (pd) 45. The Shop at Sly Corner (pd) 46. Forbidden (pd) 48. Eight O'Clock Walk (p) 54, etc.

King, Henry (1888–1982).
Veteran American director with experience in most branches of show business. In Hollywood, he became a skilful exponent of the well-made expensive family entertainment, usually with a sentimental streak.
SELECTED SILENTS: Who Pays? 16. A Sporting Chance 19. *Tol'able David* 21. *The White Sister* 23. Romola 24. *Stella Dallas* 25. The Winning of Barbara Worth 26. The Woman Disputed 28.
■ TALKIES: Hell Harbor 30. The Eyes of the World 30. Lightnin' 30. Merely Mary Ann 31. Over the Hill 31. The Woman in Room 13 32. State Fair 33. I Loved You Wednesday 33. Carolina 34. Marie Galante 34. One More Spring 35. Way Down East 35. The Country Doctor 36. Ramona 36. Lloyd's of London 36. Seventh Heaven 37. *In Old Chicago* 38. *Alexander's Ragtime Band* 38. Jesse James 39. *Stanley and Livingstone* 39. Little Old New York 40. *Maryland* 40. *Chad Hanna* 40. A Yank in the RAF 41. Remember the Day 41. *The Black Swan* 42. *The Song of Bernadette* (AAN) 43. *Wilson* (AAN) 44. A Bell for Adano 45. *Margie* 46. Captain from Castile 47. Deep Waters 48. Prince of Foxes 49. *Twelve O'Clock High* 49. *The Gunfighter* 50. I'd Climb the Highest Mountain 51. David and Bathsheba 51. Wait Till the Sun Shines Nellie 52. Full House (part) 52. *The Snows of Kilimanjaro* 52. King of the Khyber Rifles 53. Untamed 55. *Love is a Many Splendored Thing* 55. Carousel 56. *The Sun Also Rises* 57. The Bravados 58. This Earth is Mine 59. Beloved Infidel 59. *Tender is the Night* 61.
✪ For his sympathy, professionalism and visual sense. *In Old Chicago*.

King, John 'Dusty' (1909–1987).
American leading actor in 'B' features, a former big band singer. He appeared in the 40s Monogram series The Range Busters with Ray 'Crash' Corrigan, Max Terhune and David Sharpe, and also starred in two serials for Universal, *Ace Drummmond* 36 and *The Adventures of Frank Merrivale* 36.
Crash Donovan 36. Love before Breakfast 36. Merry-Go-Round of 1938 37. The Road Back 37. State Police 38. Charlie Chan in Honolulu 39. Mr Moto Takes a Vacation 39. Midnight Limited 40. Half a Sinner 40. Law of the Jungle 42, etc.

King, Louis (1898–1962).
American director in films from 1919; brother of Henry King.
Persons in Hiding 38. Typhoon 40. The Way of All Flesh 40. Moon over Burma 41. Thunderhead, Son of Flicka 44. Smoky 46. Bob, Son of Battle 47. Green Grass of Wyoming 48. Mrs Mike 49. The Lion and the Horse 52. Powder River 53. Dangerous Mission 54, etc.

King, Perry (1948–).
American leading man of the late 70s.
■ The Possession of Joel Delaney 71. Slaughterhouse Five 72. The Lords of Flatbush 74. Mandingo 75. The Wild Party 75. Lipstick 76. Captains and the Kings (TV) 76. Andy Warhol's Bad 77. The Choirboys 77. Aspen (TV) 77. A Different Story 78. The Cracker Factory (TV) 79. Love's Savage Fury (TV) 79. Search and Destroy 81. Striking Back 81. Class of 1984 82. Riptide (TV) 84. Stranded (TV) 86. I'll Take Manhattan 87. Perfect People (TV) 88. Shakedown on the Sunset Strip (TV) 88. Disaster at Silo 7 (TV) 88. Roxanne: The Prize Pulitzer (TV) 89. Switch 91. Ship Hunters (It.) 92.

King, Philip (1904–1979).
English comic playwright and stage actor. Born in Beverley, Yorkshire, he began as an actor and turned writer in the early 40s.
Curtain Up 52. See How They Run 55. Sailor Beware (co-w) 56. Serious Charge 59. Watch It, Sailor! (co-w) 61, etc.

King, Stephen (1946–).
Best-selling American author of supernatural stories.
Carrie (oa) 76. Salem's Lot: The Movie (oa) 79. The Shining (oa) 80. Creepshow (a, w) 82. The Dead Zone (oa) 83. Christine (oa) 83. Cujo (oa) 83. Firestarter 84. Children of the Corn (oa) 84. Stephen King's Cat's Eye (w) 85. Silver Bullet (w) 85. Maximum Overdrive (wd) 86. Stand by Me (oa) 86. The Running Man (oa) 87. Creepshow 2 (a, oa) 87. Pet Sematary (a, w) 89. Tales from the Darkside: The Movie (oa) 90. Misery (oa) 90. Stephen King's Graveyard Shift (oa) 90. Sleepwalkers (w) 92. The Lawnmower Man (oa) 92. The Dark Half 93. Needful Things (oa) 93. The Tommyknockers (oa) (TV) 93. The Stand (TV) 94. The Shawshank Redemption (oa) 94. Dolores Claiborne 95. The Langoliers (TV) 95. Stephen King's The Stand (& a, w) 94. Stephen King's Thinner (& a) 96. Apt Pupil 98, etc.
❝ I was sitting one day and thinking about cannibalism, because that's what guys like me do . . . and I thought, suppose a guy was washed up on a rocky island, how much of himself could he eat? – *S.K.*
Movies are not books and books are not movies. I don't understand writers who get all wound up in the film adaptations of their novels, as though somehow the novel itself could be tainted by a bad adaptation. – *S.K.*
Most movie adaptations that work are shit. And you know that going in, and you figure that if you're going to get plastered with shit, somebody ought to pay you to do it, they ought to pay you a lot of money. – *S.K.*

King, Walter Woolf (1899–1984).
American actor, Broadway singing star who went to Hollywood and was gradually relegated to villain roles.
A Night at the Opera 35. Call It a Day 37. Swiss Miss 38. Balalaika 39. Marx Brothers Go West 41. Today I Hang 42. Tonight We Sing 53. Kathy O' 58, etc.

King, Zalman (1941–) (Zalman Lefkowitz).
American producer, director and writer of erotic movies, a former actor. He was co-creator of the TV series *Wind on Water* 98.
The Ski Bum (a) 71. Some Call It Loving (a) 73. Blue Sunshine (a) 78. Galaxy of Terror (a) 81. Nine and a Half Weeks (p, co-w) 86. Wildfire (co-w, d) 87. Two Moon Junction (wd) 88. Wild Orchid (co-w, d) 90. Wild Orchid 2: Two Shades of Blue (co-w, d) 92. Red Shoe Diaries (d) (TV) 92. Red Shoe Diaries 2: Double Dare (co-d) (TV) 92. Boca (p) 94. Delta of Venus (d) 95. In God's Hands (ex p, d) 98, etc.
TV series: The Young Lawyers 70–71.

Kingsford, Walter (1882–1958).
British character actor, in Hollywood from the 30s after long stage experience; usually played kindly professional men. Was Dr Carew in the *Kildare* series.
The Mystery of Edwin Drood 35. Captains Courageous 37. Algiers 38. Kitty Foyle 40. My Favorite Blonde 42. The Velvet Touch 49. Loose in London 53. Merry Andrew 58, many others.

Kingsley, Ben (1943–) (Krishna Bahji).
Anglo-Indian leading character actor.
Gandhi (AA, BFA) 82. Betrayal 82. Harem 84. Turtle Diary 85. Camille (TV) 85. Testimony 87. The Sahara Secret 87. Maurice 87. The Sealed Train 87. Pascali's Island 88. Without a Clue 88. Slipstream 89. The Children 90. The Fifth Monkey 90. Bugsy (AAN) 91. Necessary Love/L'Amore Necessario 91. Sneakers 92. Dave 93. Searching for Bobby Fischer/Innocent Moves 93. *Schindler's List* 93. Joseph (TV) 95. Death and the Maiden 95. Species 95. Moses (title role, TV) 96. Twelfth Night 96. Weapons of Mass Distraction (TV) 97. The Assignment (US) 97. Parting Shots (US) 98, etc.

Kingsley, Dorothy (1909–1997).
American screenwriter, from radio, where she wrote for Bob Hope and ventriloquist Edgar Bergen. Born in New York, the daughter of silent film actress Alma Hanlon, she worked for MGM for 15 years from the early 40s, writing seven of Esther Williams's musicals; she also created the late 60s TV series *Bracken's World*, about the head of a movie studio.
Look Who's Laughing (co-w) 41. Here We Go Again (co-w) 42. Broadway Rhythm (co-w) 43. Bathing Beauty (co-w) 44. Easy to Wed (w) 46. On an Island with You (co-w) 48. A Date with Judy (co-w) 48. Neptune's Daughter (w) 49. The Skipper Surprised His Wife (w) 50. Two Weeks with Love (co-w) 50. Angels in the Outfield (co-w) 51. When in Rome (co-w) 52. *Kiss Me Kate* (w) 53. Dangerous When Wet (w) 53. *Seven Brides for Seven Brothers* (co-w) 54. Jupiter's Darling (w) 55. Don't Go Near the Water (co-w) 57. Pal Joey (w) 57. Green Mansions (w) 59. Can Can (co-w) 59. Pepe (co-w) 60. Half a Sixpence (co-w) 67. Valley of the Dolls (co-w) 67. Angels in the Outfield (co-w) 94, etc.
❝ I only wrote because I needed the money. I had

no desire to express myself or anything like that. – D.K.

Kingsley, Sidney (1907–1995) (Sidney Kieschner). American playwright.

Plays filmed include: Men in White 35. Dead End 37. Detective Story 51.

Kinison, Sam (1954–1992). American comic actor, in films from 1986. Died as the result of a car crash.

Back to School 86. Three Amigos 86.

Kinnear, Greg (1963–). American leading actor, from television.

Sabrina 95. Dear God 96. A Smile Like Yours 97. As Good As It Gets (AAN) 97. You've Got Mail 98, etc.

TV series: Later with Greg Kinnear 95– .

Kinnear, Roy (1934–1988). Bulbous British character comedian whose perspiring bluster was a quickly overplayed hand. Born in Wigan, he trained at RADA and was on stage from the mid-50s. Married actress Carmel Cryan. Died following a fall from a horse during filming.

Sparrows Can't Sing 62. Heavens Above 63. French Dressing 65. The Hill 65. Help! 66. A Funny Thing Happened on the Way to the Forum 67. How I Won the War 67. Lock Up Your Daughters 67. Willy Wonka and the Chocolate Factory 71. The Three Musketeers 74. Juggernaut 74. One of Our Dinosaurs Is Missing 75. Herbie Goes to Monte Carlo 77. The Last Remake of Beau Geste 77. Hawk the Slayer 80. The Boys in Blue 82. The Zany Adventures of Robin Hood (TV) 84. Pirates 85. A Man for All Seasons (TV) 88, etc.

TV series: That Was the Week that Was 62–63. A World of His Own 65. Inside George Webley 68–70. No Appointment Necessary 77. George and Mildred 78–79. Cowboys 80–81. The Incredible Mr Tanner 81. The Clairvoyant 86.

Kinnoch, Ronald (c. 1911–). British producer, former scenarist and production manager.

Escape Route 52. How to Murder a Rich Uncle 57. The Secret Man (& wd) 58. Village of the Damned 60. Invasion Quartet 61. Cairo 62. The Ipcress File (a, p) 65, etc.

Kinoshita, Keisuke (1912–1998). Prolific Japanese director and screenwriter, initially of comedies, averaging nearly two films a year, before switching primarily to television dramas in the mid-60s. He worked his way up from assistant to the cameraman and assistant director.

The Blossoming Port/Hanna Saku Minato 43. Army/Rikugun 44. Here's to the Girls/Ojosan Kampai 49. Broken Drum/Yabure-daiko 49. Carmen Comes Home/Karumen Kokyo ni Kaeru 51. A Japanese Tragedy/Nihon no Higeki 53. Clouds at Twilight/Yuyake-gumo 56. Times of Joy and Sorrow/Yorokobi mo Kanashimi mo Ikutoshitsuki 57. The Ballad of the Narayama/Narayamabushi-ko 58. Immortal Love/Eien ni Hito 61. The Scent of Incense/Koge 64. Lovely Flute and Drum/Natsukashiki Fue ya Taiko 67. Love and Separation in Sri Lanka/Sri Lanka no Ai to Wakare 76. The Impulse Murder of My Son/Shodo Satsujin Musko yo 79. Leaving These Children Behind/Kono Ko o Nokoshite 83, many others.

Kinoy, Ernest. American screenwriter.

Brother John 70. Buck and the Preacher 71. Leadbelly 75. White Water Summer 87. Gore Vidal's Lincoln (TV) 88. Rescuers: Stories of Courage – Two Women (TV) 97, etc.

Kinskey, Leonid (1903–1998). Lanky Russian character actor, long in America, playing intense but not over-bright revolutionaries. Born in St Petersburg, where he trained in mime, he left for the United States in the early 20s. In the late 40s he opened a restaurant on Sunset Strip and turned to directing and writing industrial films. Married three times.

The Great Depression 26. Trouble in Paradise 32. Duck Soup 33. Manhattan Melodrama 34. Lives of a Bengal Lancer 34. The Garden of Allah 36. The Road to Glory 36. Rhythm on the Range 36. Espionage 37. Cafe Metropole 37. Flirting with Fate 38. Three Blind Mice 38. Everything Happens at Night 39. Exile Express 39. Daytime Wife 39.

Down Argentine Way 40. He Stayed for Breakfast 40. Weekend in Havana 41. Ball of Fire 41. Broadway Limited/The Baby Vanishes 41. So Ends Our Night 41. That Night in Rio 41. Lady for a Night 42. Casablanca 42. The Fighting Seabees 44. Can't Help Singing 44. Honeychile 51. The Man with the Golden Arm 55, many others.

Kinski, Klaus (1926–1991) (Claus Gunther Nakszynski).
German character actor of intense roles.
Autobiography: 1996, Kinski Uncut: The Autobiography of Klaus Kinski.

Ludwig II 54. Kali Yug Goddess of Vengeance 63. For a Few Dollars More 65. Dr Zhivago 65. Circus of Fear 67. Aguirre Wrath of God 72. The Bloody Hands of the Law 73. Nosferatu 78. La Femme-Enfant 80. Android 82. Venom 82. Love and Money 82. Codename Wildgeese 84. The Little Drummer Girl 84. Commando Leopard 85. Crawlspace 86. Nosferatu a Venezia 87. Cobra Verde 88. Paganini (a, wd) 88, etc.

❝ I'm like a wild animal who's behind bars. I need air, I need space. – K.K.

Making movies is better than cleaning toilets. – K.K.

I would have been better than Adolf Hitler. I could have delivered his speeches a lot better. That's for sure. – K.K.

None of these cretins will believe that I've turned down Ken Russell, Federico Fellini, Luchino Visconti, Pier Paolo Pasolini, Liliana Cavani, Arthur Penn, Claude Lelouch, and all the other so-called world-famous directors and that I do flicks only to make money. – K.K.

I wish I'd never been an actor! I wish I'd never had success! I'd rather have been a streetwalker, selling my body, than selling my tears and my laughter, my grief and my joy. – K.K.

Kinski, Nastassia (Nastassja) (1960–). German leading lady, daughter of Klaus KINSKI. Formerly married to Egyptian producer Ibrahim Moussa, with whom she has two children, she has a daughter by musician Quincy JONES. She was romantically involved with Roman POLANSKI, Marcello MASTROIANNI and Milos FORMAN.

To the Devil a Daughter 76. Stay as You Are 79. Tess 80. Cat People 82. One from the Heart 82. Love and Money 82. Exposed 83. The Moon in the Gutter 83. The Little Drummer Girl 84. Unfaithfully Yours 84. Paris, Texas 84. Maria's Lovers 85. Symphony of Love 85. Harem 85. Revolution 85. Maladie d'Amour 87. Silent Night 88. In Una Notte di Chiaro di Luna 89. Torrents of Spring 89. The Secret/Il Segreto 89. Night Sun/Il Sole Anche di Notte 90. Faraway, So Close!/In Weiter Ferne, So Nah (Ger.) 93. The Blonde/La Bionda (It.) 94. Terminal Velocity 94. Father's Day 97. One Night Stand 97. Your Friends and Neighbors 98. The Lost Son 98. Susan's Plan 98, etc.

Kinsolving, Lee (1938–1974). American teenage lead of the 60s.

The Dark at the Top of the Stairs 60. All the Young Men 60. The Explosive Generation 61.

Kinugasa, Teinosuke (1896–1982). Japanese director and screenwriter, a former actor who played female roles. His early films displayed a European influence and his Gate of Hell was one of the first Japanese films to find success in the West. Married actress Isuzu YAMADA.

The Death of My Sister 21. A Page of Madness/Kurutta Ippeiji 26. Crossways/Jujiro 28. Yukinojo's Revenge/Yukinojo Henge 35. Actress/Joyu 47. Gate of Hell/Jigokumon (AA) 53. The White Heron 58. Okoto and Sasuke 61. An Actor's Revenge/Yukinojo Henge (co-w only) 63. The Little Runaway (co-d) 67, many more.

Kipling, Rudyard (1865–1936). British novelist who mainly concerned himself with the high days of the British in India.

Films from his works include Gunga Din, Soldiers Three, Elephant Boy, Wee Willie Winkie, Captains Courageous, The Light That Failed, The Jungle Book, Kim, The Man Who Would Be King (in which he was played by Christopher Plummer).

Kirby, Bruno (1949–). American character actor.

The Harrad Experiment 73. The Godfather Part II 74. Almost Summer 77. Where the Buffalo Roam 80. Borderline 80. Modern Romance 81. Kiss

My Grits 82. This Is Spinal Tap 84. Birdy 84. Flesh and Blood 85. Good Morning, Vietnam 87. Tin Men 87. We're No Angels 89. Bert Rigby, You're a Fool 89. When Harry Met Sally 89. The Freshman 90. City Slickers 91. The Basketball Diaries 95. Sleepers 96. Donnie Brasco 96, etc.

Kirk, Phyllis (1926–) (Phyllis Kirkegaard). American leading lady of the 50s, former model and dancer.

Our Very Own 50. The Iron Mistress 52. House of Wax 53. Canyon Crossroads 55. The Sad Sack 57. That Woman Opposite (GB) 58. City after Midnight 59, etc.

TV series: The Thin Man 57.

Kirk, Tommy (1941–). American juvenile lead, former Disney child actor.

Old Yeller 57. The Shaggy Dog 59. The Swiss Family Robinson 60. The Absent-Minded Professor 60. Babes in Toyland 61. Bon Voyage 62. Son of Flubber 63. The Misadventures of Merlin Jones 63. The Monkey's Uncle 65. How to Stuff a Wild Bikini 65. The Unkissed Bride 66. Blood of Ghastly Horror 72. Attack of the 60 Foot Centerfold 95. Little Miss Magic 97, etc.

Kirkland, Geoffrey (1939–). British production designer, often for the films of Alan Parker.

Midnight Express 78. Bugsy Malone (BFA) 78. Fame 80. Shoot the Moon 82. The Right Stuff (co-pd) (AAN) 83. Birdy 84. Leonard Part 6 87. Mississippi Burning (co-pd) 88. Wildfire 89. Come See the Paradise 90, etc.

Kirkland, Muriel (1903–1971). American stage actress, briefly in films in the 30s.

Fast Workers 33. Hold Your Man 33. The Secret of the Blue Room 33. Nana 34. Little Man What Now? 34, etc.

Kirkland, Sally (1944–). American actress.

Coming Apart 69. Futz 69. Going Home 71. Cinderella Liberty 73. The Sting 73. The Way We Were 73. Bite the Bullet 75. A Star Is Born 76. Private Benjamin 80. The Incredible Shrinking Woman 81. Love Letters 83. Anna (AAN) 87. Best of the Best 89. Paint It Black 90. JFK 91. In the Heat of Passion 91. Hit the Dutchman 92. Primary Motive 92. Double Threat 92. Paper Hearts 93. Gunmen 93. Eye of the Stranger 94. Excess Baggage 96. Amnesia 96, etc.

TV series: Valley of the Dolls 94.

Kirkop, Oreste (1926–). Maltese operatic tenor whose sole film appearance to date has been in The Vagabond King 55.

Kirkwood, James (1883–1963). American silent director.

The House of Discord 13. Classmates 13. Rags 15. Environment 17. Bill Apperson's Boy 19. The Heart of Jennifer 19, many others.

AS ACTOR: A Corner in Wheat 09. The Rocky Road 10. The Great Impersonation 21. Pink Gods 22. Human Wreckage 23. Circe the Enchantress 24. The Reckless Lady 26. The Spoilers 30. Cheaters at Play 32. The Woman They Almost Lynched 53, many others.

Kirkwood, Pat (1921–). British leading lady, on stage in variety at 14, billed as 'The Schoolgirl Songstress'. She was London's highest-paid musical star of the 40s and 50s. The third of her four husbands was actor and songwriter Hubert Gregg.
Autobiography: 1999, The Time of My Life.

Save a Little Sunshine 38. Me and My Pal 39. Band Waggon 39. Come on George 39. Flight from Folly 44. No Leave, No Love (US) 46. Once a Sinner 50. Stars in Your Eyes 56. After the Ball 57. To See Such Fun 77, etc.

TV series: Our Marie (as Marie Lloyd) 53. Pygmalion (as Eliza Dolittle) 55. The Great Little Tilley (as Vesta Tilley) 56.

❝ Miss Kirkwood's legs must rank as the eighth wonder of the world. – Kenneth Tynan

Kirsanov, Dmitri (1899–1957). Russian émigré film-maker, at the forefront of France's avant-garde movement of the 20s.

■ Autumn Mists 25. Menilmontant 26. Rapt 35.

Kirshner, Mia (1976–). Canadian actress; born in Toronto, she began on television as a teenager.

Cadillac Girls 93. Love and Human Remains 93. Exotica 94. Murder in the First 95. The Grass Harp 95. The Crow: City of Angels 96. Mad City 97, etc.

Kitano, Takeshi (1947–) (aka 'Beat' Takeshi). Japanese director, screenwriter, editor and actor, a former stand-up comedian and television performer. Born in Tokyo, he worked in a comedy act, The Two Beats, which gave him his nickname, and published books of short stories and jokes before beginning a career as an actor in the 80s and, from 1989, as a director.

Merry Christmas Mr Lawrence (a) 82. Laughter and Tears (a) 84. No More Damn Comics! (a) 86. Violent Cop/Sono Otoko Kyobo Ni Tsuki (a, d) 89. Boiling Point/3–4X Jugatsu (a, wd) 90. A Scene at the Sea/Ano Natsu Ichban Shizukana Umi (wd, e) 91. Sonatine (wd, e) 93. Many Happy Returns/Kyoso Tanjo (oa, a) 93. Getting Any?/Minna Yatteruka (wd, e) 94. Johnny Mnemonic (a) 95. Kids Return (wd, e) 96. Flower and Fire/Hana-Bi (a, wd) 97. Limousin (a) (Fr.) 98, etc.

Kitaro (1953–). Japanese composer and recording artist.

Catch Your Dreams (Ger.) 83. Samuel Lount (Can.) 85. Heaven and Earth (US) 93, etc.

Kitchen, Michael (1948–). British character actor, from the stage.

Unman Wittering and Zigo 71. Dracula AD 72 72. Breaking Glass 80. Brimstone and Treacle 82. Out of Africa 85. The Dive 89. The Russia House 90. Fools of Fortune 90. Enchanted April 91. Hostage 92. The Trial 93. Doomsday Gun (TV) 94. GoldenEye 95. Wilderness (TV) 96. Mrs Dalloway 97. The Last Contract (Swe.) 98, etc.

TV series: Reckless 97. Sunnyside Farm 97.

Kitt, Eartha (1928–). American cabaret singer whose essential vibrance was captured only in her first film.
Autobiography: 1956, Thursday's Child.

■ New Faces 54. St Louis Blues 57. Mark of the Hawk 58. Anna Lucasta 58. Saint of Devil's Island 61. Synanon 65. Uncle Tom's Cabin (Ger.) 65. Up the Chastity Belt (GB) 71. Lt Schuster's Wife (TV) 72. Friday Foster 75. To Kill a Cop (TV) 78. All by Myself 82. The Pink Chiquitas 86. The Serpent Warriors 86. Dragonard 88. Master of Dragonard Hill 89. Erik the Viking 89. Living Doll 89. Ernest Scared Stupid 91. Boomerang 92. Harriet the Spy 96. Ill Gotten Gains (voice) 98. I Woke Up Early the Day I Died 98.

Kitzmiller, John (1913–1965). American character actor, in Italy from 1945 (after army service).

Paisa 46. To Live In Peace 46. Senza Pieta 48. The Naked Earth 57. Doctor No 62. Uncle Tom's Cabin (title role) (Ger.) 65, etc.

Kjellin, Alf (1920–1988). Swedish actor who went to Hollywood and worked mostly in TV, turning his talents to direction.

Frenzy 44. My Six Convicts 52. The Iron Mistress 53. The Juggler 63. Ship of Fools 65. Assault on a Queen 66. The Midas Run (d) 69. The McMasters (d) 70, etc.

Klane, Robert. American screenwriter and director.

Where's Poppa? 70. Every Little Crook and Nanny 72. Fire Sale 77. Thank God It's Friday (wd) 78. Unfaithfully Yours 84. The Man with One Red Shoe 85. National Lampoon's European Vacation 85. Walk Like a Man 87. Weekend at Bernie's 89. Folks! 92. Weekend at Bernie's 2 (wd) 93, etc.

Klein, William (1929–). American director, in Paris.

■ Far from Vietnam (part) 66. Qui Etes-Vous Polly Magoo? 67. Mr Freedom 68. Float Like a Butterfly, Sting Like a Bee (doc) 69. Festival Panafricain (doc) 69. Eldridge Cleaver (doc) 70. Le Couple Témoin 77. The French (doc) 81. Mode in France (doc) 85.

Kleiner, Harry (1916–). American screenwriter.

Fallen Angel 46. The Street with No Name 48. Red Skies of Montana 51. Salome 53. Miss Sadie

Thompson 53. *Carmen Jones* 54. The Garment Jungle (& p) 56. Ice Palace 60. Fantastic Voyage 66. *Bullitt* 68. Le Mans 71. Extreme Prejudice 87. Red Heat 88, etc.

Klein-Rogge, Rudolf (1888–1955).
German actor who appeared in some of the most famous German films of the 20s.
Der Mude Tod 21. Dr Mabuse 22. Siegfried 24. Metropolis 26. Spione 28. The Testament of Dr Mabuse 33. Between Heaven and Earth 34. The Old and the Young King 35. Intermezzo 36. Madame Bovary 37. Hochzeit auf Barenhof 42, etc.

Kleiser, Randal (1946–).
American director.
■ All Together Now (TV) 75. Dawn: Portrait of a Teenage Runaway (TV) 76. The Boy in the Plastic Bubble (TV) 76. The Gathering (TV) 77. *Grease* 78. The Blue Lagoon 80. Summer Lovers (& w) 82. Grandview USA 84. Flight of the Navigator 86. Big Top Pee-Wee 88. Getting It Right 89. White Fang 90. Honey, I Blew Up the Kid 92. It's My Party (wd) 96.

Klemperer, Werner (1920–).
Bald-pated German-American character actor, often seen as comic or sinister Nazi.
Death of a Scoundrel 56. Five Steps to Danger 56. The Goddess 58. Operation Eichmann (title role) 61. Judgment at Nuremberg 61. Escape from East Berlin 62. Youngblood Hawke 64. Ship of Fools 65. The Wicked Dreams of Paula Schultz 67. Wake Me When the War Is Over (TV) 69. Assignment Munich (TV) 72. The Rhinemann Exchange (TV) 77. The Return of the Beverly Hillbillies (TV) 81.
TV series: *Hogan's Heroes* 65–70.

Klimov, Elem (1933–).
Russian director and screenwriter, noted for his exuberant approach and use of documentary techniques. Born in Volgograd, he worked as an aeronautical engineer before studying film in Moscow. He first worked in television and was married to director and screenwriter Larissa Shepitko, making a documentary about her life following her untimely death in a car crash. *Agony*, about Rasputin, was banned for 10 years by the authorities.
Welcome, or No Entry for Unauthorized Persons 64. Adventures of a Dentist 65. Sport, Sport, Sport 71. And Nonetheless I Believe (co-d) 74. *Agony*/Agonia/Rasputin 75. Larissa (doc) 80. Farewell/Proshchanie 81. *Come and See*/Idi i Smotri (& co-w) 85, etc.

Klimovsky, Leon (1900–1996).
Argentinian director and film critic, a former dentist who founded the country's first cinema club in the 20s. In the mid-50s he settled in Spain and took Spanish nationality, turning out films in many genres, including horror movies and spaghetti westerns.
El Jugador 47. Marihuana 50. Suburbio 51. El Túnel 52. Maleficio 54. Viaje de Novios 56. Dos Mil Dólares por un Coyote 65. Operación Rommel 68. Reverendo Colt 70. El Dr Jekyl y el Hombre Loco 72. La Orgia Nocturna de los Vampiros 72. The Devil's Possessed/El Mariscal del Infierno 74. El Transexual 77. Laverna 78. The Most Beautiful Night/La Noche Más Hermosa 84, etc.

Kline, Herbert (1909–).
American director, sometimes of documentaries.
Crisis 39. Lights out in Europe 40. The Forgotten Village (& p) 41. My Father's House (& p) 47. The Kid from Cleveland 49. The Fighter (& w, p) 52. Walls of Fire (doc) 74. Acting: Lee Strasberg and the Actors Studio (doc) 81. Great Theatres of the World (doc) 87, etc.

Kline, Kevin (1947–).
Adaptable American leading actor. Born in St Louis, Missouri, he studied at Indiana University and the Juilliard School and was on stage from 1970, first making his reputation in Broadway musicals, including an updated version of *The Pirates of Penzance*, which was filmed in 1982. Married actress Phoebe Cates in 1990.
Sophie's Choice 82. The Big Chill 83. Silverado 85. Cry Freedom 87. A Fish Called Wanda (AA) 88. The January Man 89. I Love You to Death 90. Soapdish 91. Grand Canyon 91. Chaplin 92. Consenting Adults 92. Death Becomes Her 92. Dave 93. Princess Caraboo 94. French Kiss 95. Fierce Creatures 96. The Hunchback of Notre Dame (voice) 96. The Ice Storm 97. In and Out 97. Wild, Wild West 99, etc.

Kline, Richard (1926–).
American cinematographer.
Camelot (AAN) 67. *The Boston Strangler* 69. A Dream of Kings 69. The Andromeda Strain 70. Kotch 71. Black Gunn 72. The Harrad Experiment 73. Mandingo 75. King Kong (AAN) 76. The Fury 78. Star Trek 79. The Competition 80. Body Heat 81. Death Wish II 82. Breathless 83. Hard to Hold 84. All of Me 84. The Man with One Red Shoe 85. Howard the Duck 85. Touch and Go 86. My Stepmother Is an Alien 88. Downtown 90. Meet Wally Sparks 97, etc.

Klinger, Michael (1921–1989).
British producer.
Repulsion 64. Cul de Sac 66. The Yellow Teddy Bears 66. A Study in Terror 67. Baby Love 69. Get Carter 71. Pulp 73. Gold 74. Shout at the Devil 76. Tomorrow Never Comes 78. Heavy Metal 80, etc.

Klos, Elmar:
see Kadar, Jan.

Kloves, Steve.
American screenwriter and director.
Racing with the Moon (w) 84. The Fabulous Baker Boys (wd) 89. Flesh and Bone (wd) 93.

Kluge, Alexander (1932–).
German director.
Abschied von Gestern 66. Artists at the Top of the Big Top 68. Willy Tobler 71. Occasional Work of a Female Slave 74. Strongman Ferdinand 76. Der Angriff der Gegenwart auf die Ubrige Zeit 85. Vermischte Nachrichten 86, etc.

Klugman, Jack (1922–).
Lean American actor who can be comically henpecked, tragically weak, or just sinister.
Timetable 56. *Twelve Angry Men* 57. Days of Wine and Roses 62. Act One 63. I Could Go on Singing 63. Yellow Canary 63. The Detective 68. The Split 68. Goodbye Columbus 69. Who Says I Can't Ride a Rainbow? 71. Two Minute Warning 76. Parallel Lives (TV) 94. Dear God 96. The Twilight of the Golds (TV) 97, etc.
TV series: Harris against the World 64. *The Odd Couple* 70–75. Quincy 76–83. You Again 86–87.

Knapp, Evalyn (1908–1981).
American leading lady.
Fifty Million Frenchmen 31. Night Mayor 32. Fireman Save My Child 32. Air Hostess 33. The Perils of Pauline (serial) 34. Laughing Irish Eyes 36. The Lone Wolf Takes a Chance 42. Two Weeks to Live 43, etc.

Kneale, Nigel (1922–).
Manx writer, best known for BBC TV serials about Professor Quatermass, all three of which were filmed.
Look Back in Anger 59. The Entertainer 60. The First Men in the Moon 64. The Devil's Own 66, etc.

Knef, Hildegard:
see Neff, Hildegard.

Knieper, Jurgen (1941–).
German composer.
The Scarlet Letter 73. The Wrong Move 75. The American Friend 77. The River's Edge (US) 86. Wings of Desire 87. End of the Night 90. Madregilda (Sp.) 93. The Blonde/La Bionda (It.) 94. The Promise 95. Lisbon Story 95, etc.

Knight, Castleton (1894–1972).
British newsreel producer (Gaumont British).
Directed some films in the 30s, including *Kissing Cup's Race* and *The Flying Scotsman*; also various compilations such as *Theirs Is the Glory* and *Fourteenth Olympiad*, and records of state occasions such as *A Queen Is Crowned*.

Knight, David (1927–) (David Mintz).
American leading man, on London stage in the 50s.
The Young Lovers (debut) 55. Lost 57. Across the Bridge 57. Battle of the V.1 58. Nightmare 63. Demons II – the Nightmare Returns 87. Who Shot Patango? 90, etc.

Knight, Eric (1897–1943).
British writer whose 1940 juvenile book *Lassie Come Home* started a doggy industry.

Knight, Esmond (1906–1987).
Welsh actor, on stage from 1925, screen from 1928. Partially blinded during World War II. Married to actress Norah Swinburne.
Autobiography: 1943, *Seeking the Bubble*.
The Silver Fleet 42. *Henry V* 44. End of the River 47. Hamlet 47. The Red Shoes 48. Richard III 56. Sink the Bismarck 60. Where's Jack? 69. Anne of the Thousand Days 70. Robin and Marian 76. I Claudius (TV) 77. Blott on the Landscape (TV) 85, etc.

Knight, Fuzzy (1901–1976) (J. Forrest Knight).
American nightclub musician who found himself a niche in Hollywood as comic relief in innumerable westerns. Born in Fairmount, West Virginia, he was a graduate of the University of West Virginia law school.
She Done Him Wrong 33. The Trail of the Lonesome Pine 36. Johnny Apollo 40. Trigger Trail 44. Down to the Sea in Ships 50. Topeka 54. These Thousand Hills 59. Waco 66, etc.
TV series: Captain Gallant 55.

Knight, Shirley (1937–).
American leading actress, also on stage and TV; married writer John Hopkins and latterly known as Shirley Knight Hopkins.
Five Gates to Hell 59. The Dark at the Top of the Stairs (AAN) 60. Sweet Bird of Youth (AAN) 62. *The Group* 66. Dutchman 67. *Petulia* 68. The Rain People 69. Secrets 71. Juggernaut 74. Beyond the Poseidon Adventure 79. Endless Love 81. The Sender 82. With Intent to Kill (TV) 84. Hard Promises 91. Color of Night 94. Stuart Saves His Family 95. Indictment: The McMartin Trial (TV) 95. Stolen Memories: Secrets from the Rose Garden (TV) 96. Diabolique 96. If These Walls Could Talk (TV) 96. As Good as It Gets 97, etc.
TV series: Maggie Winters 98– .

Knoblock, Edward (1874–1945).
British author of plays *Kismet*, *Chu Chin Chow*, *Milestones*, all frequently filmed; in the 20s became a production associate of Douglas Fairbanks Senior.

Knopf, Edwin H. (1899–1981).
American producer, sometimes writer and director.
Border Legion (d) 30. Bad Sister (w) 31. The Wedding Night (w) 35. Piccadilly Jim (w) 36. The Trial of Mary Dugan (p) 41. The Cross of Lorraine (p) 44. The Valley of Decision (p) 45. BF's Daughter (p) 48. Edward My Son (p) 49. The Law and the Lady (d) 51. Lili (p) 53. The Vintage (p) 57, many others.

Knopfler, Mark (1949–).
British composer, guitarist and singer. A former teacher and journalist, he is a founder-member of the rock band Dire Straits. In 1998, the *Sunday Times* estimated his wealth at £50m.
Local Hero (m) 83. Cal 84. Comfort and Joy (m) 84. The Princess Bride (m) 87. Last Exit to Brooklyn (m) 90. Wag the Dog 97, etc.

Knott, Andrew.
English juvenile actor.
The Secret Garden 93. Black Beauty 94.

Knotts, Don (1924–).
American 'hayseed' comedian, from TV.
Wake Me When It's Over 60. The Last Time I Saw Archie 61. The Incredible Mr Limpet 62. *The Ghost and Mr Chicken* 66. The Reluctant Astronaut 67. The Shakiest Gun in the West 68. The Love God 69. How to Frame a Figg 71. The Apple Dumpling Gang 75. Gus 76. No Deposit No Return 76. Herbie Goes to Monte Carlo 77. The Apple Dumpling Gang Rides Again 79. The Private Eyes 81. Return to Mayberry (TV) 86. Pinocchio and the Emperor of the Night 87. Big Bully 96. Pleasantville 98, etc.
TV series: *The Andy Griffith Show* 60–68. Three's Company 79–84.

Knowles, Bernard (1900–1975).
British cinematographer who became a competent director.
AS CINEMATOGRAPHER: Dawn 29. The Good Companions 32. Jew Süss 34. The Thirty-Nine Steps 35. Gaslight 39. Quiet Wedding 40, etc.
■ AS DIRECTOR: *A Place of One's Own* 45. The Magic Bow 46. The Man Within 47. The White Unicorn 47. Jassy 47. Easy Money 48. The Lost People 49. The Perfect Woman 49. The Reluctant Widow 50. Park Plaza 605 53. Barbados Quest 54. Frozen Alive 64. Spaceflight IC-1 65. Hell is Empty 68.

Knowles, Patric (1911–1995) (Reginald Knowles).
British light 'second lead' who went to Hollywood in 1936 and stayed.
Irish Hearts (GB) 34. Abdul the Damned (GB) 34. The Guvnor (GB) 35. The Charge of the Light Brigade 36. The Adventures of Robin Hood 38. Storm over Bengal 39. Anne of Windy Poplars 40. How Green Was My Valley 41. The Wolf Man 41. Lady in a Jam 42. Eyes of the Underworld 42. Frankenstein Meets the Wolf Man 43. Always a Bridesmaid 43. Pardon My Rhythm 44. Kitty 45. Of Human Bondage 46. Monsieur Beaucaire 46. Ivy 47. The Big Steal 49. Three Came Home 50. Mutiny 52. Flame of Calcutta 53. Band of Angels 57. Auntie Mame 59. The Devil's Brigade 68. In Enemy Country 68. Chisum 71. Terror in the Wax Museum 73, many others.

Knox, Alexander (1907–1995).
Quiet-spoken Canadian actor, on British stage from 1930, films from 1938; also in Hollywood.
The Gaunt Stranger 38. *The Sea Wolf* 40. This Above All 42. None Shall Escape 43. *Wilson* (title role) (AAN) 44. Over Twenty-One 45. Sister Kenny 46. *The Judge Steps Out* 47. The Sign of the Ram 48. I'd Climb the Highest Mountain 50. Paula 52. The Sleeping Tiger 53. The Divided Heart 54. Reach for the Sky 56. High Tide at Noon 57. The Vikings 58. Operation Amsterdam 59. The Wreck of the Mary Deare 59. The Trials of Oscar Wilde 60. The Damned 61. Crack in the Mirror 62. The Man in the Middle 64. Crack in the World 65. Mister Moses 65. The Psychopath 66. Accident 66. Modesty Blaise 66. Khartoum 66. How I Won the War 67. Villa Rides 68. Shalako 68. Skullduggery 69. Nicholas and Alexandra 71. Puppet on a Chain 71. Meeting at Potsdam (TV) 76. Holocaust 2000 78. Tinker Tailor Soldier Spy (TV) 79. Gorky Park 83. Joshua Then and Now 85, etc.

Knox, Elyse (1917–).
American leading lady of the 40s.
Lillian Russell 40. The Mummy's Tomb 42. Hit the Ice 43. Linda be Good 47. There's a Girl in My Heart 49, etc.

Knox, Teddy (1896–1974) (Albert Edward Knox).
English comedian. Born in Gateshead, he began as a music-hall acrobat and juggler in a family act, then formed the juggling turn of Chinko and Kaufman. Success came when he partnered Jimmy Nervo in a comedy act from 1919; the pair became part of The Crazy Gang from the early 30s. Married variety artiste Clarice Mayne. As a youth, one of his functions was to lock his brother-in-law Sax Rohmer in a room to encourage him to write his stories and novels.

Knudsen, Peggy (1925–1980).
American starlet of the 40s.
Stolen Life 46. Humoresque 47. Trouble Preferred 48. Copper Canyon 50. Unchained 53. Good Morning Miss Dove 54. Istanbul 57, etc.

Knudtson, Frederic L. (c. 1900–1964).
American editor.
Headline Shooter 33. Gun Law 38. Stage to Chino 40. This Land is Mine 43. The Bachelor and the Bobbysoxer 47. The Window 48. Angel Face 53. Not as a Stranger 55. The Pride and the Passion 57. The Defiant Ones 58. Inherit the Wind 60. Judgment at Nuremberg 61, many others.

Kobayashi, Masaki (1916–).
Japanese director.
Ningen no Joken 61. Hara Kiri 63. *Kwaidan* 64. Rebellion 67. Hymn to a Tired Man 68. Inn of Evil 71. Fossils 75. Glowing Autumn 79. Tokyo Saiban 85, etc.

Kober, Jeff.
American actor
Out of Bounds 86. Viper 88. Lucky Stiff 88. Alien Nation 88. The First Power 90. Baby Doll Murders 92. The Hit List 93. Tank Girl 95. One Man's Justice 95. Demolition High 95. The Big Fall 96. Elmore Leonard's The Gold Coast (TV) 97, etc.
TV series: Falcon Crest 86–87. China Beach 88–91.

Koch, Howard (1902–1995).
American screenwriter and playwright. He adapted H. G. Wells's *The War of the Worlds* for Orson Welles's Mercury Theatre broadcast, which panicked America in 1938, and was an uncredited writer on *The Best Years of Our Life* (AA) 46. Blacklisted in 1950, partly for scripting the laudatory *Mission to Moscow*, he moved to Europe for most of the decade. In 1994, his Oscar for *Casablanca* fetched $184,000 at auction to help pay for his granddaughter's studies.

Autobiography: 1979, *As Time Goes By*.

The Sea Hawk (co-w) 40. *The Letter* (co-w) 40. Sergeant York (co-w, AAN) 41. *Casablanca* (co-w) (AA) 42. Mission to Moscow (co-w) 43. *Letter from an Unknown Woman* 47. The Thirteenth Letter 51. The War Lover 63. The Fox (co-wp) 68, many others.

Koch, Howard, Jnr (1945–).
American producer, the son of Howard W. Koch, a former assistant director.

The Frisco Kid 79. Honky Tonk Freeway 81. The Keep 83. Gorky Park 83. Rooftops 89. The Long Walk Home 90. Necessary Roughness 91. Sliver 93. Wayne's World 2 93. Virtuosity 95. Losing Isaiah 95. Primal Fear 96. The Beautician and the Beast 97, etc.

Koch, Howard W. (1916–).
American executive, from 1965–66 Paramount's vice-president in charge of production. Former producer and director.

Big House USA (d) 54. Beachhead (p) 55. The Black Sleep (p) 56. Frankenstein 70 (d) 58. Sergeants Three (p) 62. The Manchurian Candidate (p) 62. Come Blow Your Horn (p) 63. None But the Brave (p) 65. The Odd Couple (p) 68. On a Clear Day You Can See Forever (p) 70. Badge 373 73. Once Is Not Enough 75. The Other Side of Midnight 77. Heaven Can Wait 78. The Pirate (TV) 78. The Frisco Kid 79. The Idolmaker 80. Some Kind of Hero 81. Dragonslayer 81. Airplane II 82. Ghost 90, etc.

Koechlin, Charles (1867–1950).
Prolific French composer who wrote film scores, and also concert pieces in praise of the stars, the best of which is probably his *Seven Stars Symphony*, op. 132, which dates from 1933 and has movements named after Douglas Fairbanks, Lilian Harvey, Greta Garbo, Clara Bow, Marlene Dietrich and Charlie Chaplin; it was recorded by conductor James Judd in 1995.

L'Andalouse dans Barcelone (doc) 33, etc.

Koenekamp, Fred (1922–).
American cinematographer.

Patton (AAN) 70. Kansas City Bomber 72. Papillon 73. The Towering Inferno (AA) 74. Uptown Saturday Night 74. Posse 75. Doc Savage 75. Islands in the Stream 77. Fun with Dick and Jane 77. The Other Side of Midnight 77. The Domino Principle 77. The Amityville Horror 79. The Champ 79. The First Family 80. When Time Ran Out 80. First Monday in October 81. Wrong Is Right 82. Yes Giorgio 82. Two of a Kind 83. The Adventures of Buckaroo Banzai 84. Stewardess School 87. Listen to Me 89. Welcome Home 89. Flight of the Intruder 91, etc.

Koenig, Walter (1936–).
American actor, best known for playing the role of Chekov in the *Star Trek* television series and films.

Columbo: Fade in to Murder (TV) 79. Star Trek: The Motion Picture 79. Star Trek: The Wrath of Khan 82. Star Trek III: The Search for Spock 84. Star Trek IV: The Voyage Home 86. Moontrap 89. Deadly Weapon 89. Star Trek V: The Final Frontier 89. Star Trek VI: The Undiscovered Country 91. Star Trek: Generations 94. Drawing Down the Moon 97, etc.

TV series: Star Trek 67–69. Babylon 5 94.

Koepp, David.
American screenwriter and director.

Apartment Zero (co-w) 89. Bad Influence (w) 90. Toy Soldiers (co-w) 91. Death Becomes Her (co-w) 92. Carlito's Way (w) 93. Jurassic Park (co-w) 93. The Paper (co-w) 94. The Shadow (w) 94. Mission: Impossible (co-w) 96. The Trigger Effect (wd) 96. The Lost World: Jurassic Park (co-w) 97. Snake Eyes 98, etc.

Kohler, Fred, Snr (1889–1938).
American character actor often seen as western badman.

Soldiers of Fortune 19. The Stampede 21. Anna Christie 23. Riders of the Purple Sage 25. The Way of All Flesh 27. Chinatown Charlie 28. The Dragnet 28. The Leatherneck 29. Thunderbolt 29. Hell's Heroes 29. Corsair 31. Call Her Savage 32. Wild Horse Mesa 32. Kid Millions 35. Hard Rock Harrigan 35. The Plainsman 36. Daughter of Shanghai 37. Billy the Kid Returns 38, many others.

Kohlmar, Fred (1905–1969).
American producer in Hollywood from the early 30s, at first with Goldwyn.

That Night in Rio 41. The Glass Key 42. Kiss of Death 47. When Willie Comes Marching Home 50. It Should Happen to You 53. Picnic 55. Pal Joey 57. The Last Angry Man 59. The Notorious Landlady 62. How To Steal a Million 66. A Flea in Her Ear 68. The Only Game in Town 69, many others.

Kohner, Susan (1936–).
American leading lady.

To Hell and Back 55. Imitation of Life (AAN) 58. All the Fine Young Cannibals 60. Freud 62, etc.

Kolb, Clarence (1874–1964).
Veteran character actor, usually of explosive executive types; formerly in vaudeville.

Carefree 38. Nothing but the Truth 41. Hellzapoppin 42. True to Life 43. The Kid from Brooklyn 46. Christmas Eve 47. Adam's Rib 49. The Rose Bowl Story 53. Man of a Thousand Faces 57, many others.

Kolker, Henry (1874–1947).
American stage actor who played lawyers and heavy fathers in many films.

The Bigger Man 15. Disraeli 21. West Point 26. The Valiant 29. East Is West 30. Corsair 31. The Devil and the Deep 32. Jewel Robbery 33. Imitation of Life 34. The Ghost Walks 34. The Case of the Curious Bride 34. Diamond Jim 35. Mad Love 35. The Last Days of Pompeii 35. The Black Room 35. Bullets or Ballots 36. Romeo and Juliet (as Friar Laurence) 36. Theodora Goes Wild 36. Conquest 37. Maid of Salem 37. The Cowboy and the Lady 38. *Holiday* 38. Union Pacific 39. The Real Glory 39. Grand Old Opry 40. A Woman's Face 41. Sarong Girl 43. Bluebeard 44. The Secret Life of Walter Mitty 47, many others.

Koller, Xavier (1944–).
Swiss director.

Black Tanner (AAN) 86. Journey of Hope/Reise der Hoffnung (AA) 90. Squanto: A Warrior's Tale (US) 94, etc.

Kolski, Jan Jakub (1956–).
Polish film director and screenwriter with a penchant for rural fantasy.

Burial of Potatoes/Pogrzeb Kartofla 91. Johnnie the Aquarius 93. Miraculous Place 94. The Man Who Reads Music from Plates 96, etc.

Koltai, Lajos (1946–).
Hungarian-born cinematographer, in America from the late 80s.

Mephisto 80. Angi Vera 81. Colonel Redl 85. Hanussen 88. Homer and Eddie 89. White Palace 90. Mobsters 91. Wrestling Ernest Hemingway 93. Born Yesterday 93. When a Man Loves a Woman 94. Just Cause 95. Home for the Holidays 95. Mother 96. Out to Sea 97. The Legend of the Pianist on the Ocean (It.) 98, etc.

Komai, Tetsu (1893–1970).
Japanese-American character actor.

Daughter of the Dragon 31. Island of Lost Souls 33. Tokyo Joe 49. Japanese War Bride 52. The Night Walker 64, etc.

Komeda, Krystof (1931–1969) (Krzysztof Trzcinski).
Polish composer and jazz musician, associated with the films of Roman Polanski.

Two Men and a Wardrobe/Dwaj Ludzie z Szafa 58. See You Tomorrow/Do Widzenia Do Jutra 60. Innocent Sorcerers/Niewinni Czarodzieje 60. The Glass Mountain/Szklana Gora 60. The Chain/Lancuch 60. Knife in the Water/Noz w Wodzie 60. Epilogue/Hvad Med Os? (Den.) 63. The Cats/Kattorna (Swe.) 64. The Penguin/Pingwin 64. The Barrier/Bariera 65. Cul-de-Sac (GB) 66. Le Départ (Bel.) 66. Hunger/Sult (Den./Swe./Nor.) 66. The Fearless Vampire Killers (GB) 67. Rosemary's Baby (US) 68, etc.

Konchalovsky, Andrei (1937–).
Russian director in the West.

Maria's Lovers 85. Runaway Train 85. Duet for One 86. Shy People 87. Homer and Eddie 89. Tango and Cash 89. The Inner Circle 91. Ryaba My Chicken/Riaba Ma Poule 93. The Odyssey (TV) 97, etc.

Konstam, Phyllis (1907–1976).
British stage actress who occasionally played film heroines.

Autobiography 1969: *A Mixed Double* (with her husband Bunny Austin).

■ Champagne 28. Blackmail 29. Murder 30. Escape 30. Compromising Daphne 30. The Skin Game 31. Tilly of Bloomsbury 31. A Gentleman of Paris 31. The Forgotten Factor 52. Jotham Valley 52. The Crowning Experience 59. Voice of the Hurricane 60.

Kopelson, Arnold (1935–).
American producer and lawyer.

The Legacy 79. Lost and Found 79. Foolin' Around 80. Dirty Tricks 80. Platoon (AA) 86. Warlock 88. Triumph of the Spirit 89. Falling Down 93. The Fugitive 93. Outbreak 95. The Devil's Advocate 97. US Marshals 98. A Perfect Murder 98, etc.

Kopple, Barbara.
American director, mainly of documentaries. Born in Scarsdale, New York, she studied clinical psychology and political science at Northeastern University and began by working for Albert and David Maysles.

Harlan County USA 76. Keeping On (TV) 82. American Dream 90. Beyond JFK: The Question of Conspiracy 92. Wild Man Blues 98, etc.

Korda, Sir Alexander (1893–1956) (Sandor Corda).
Hungarian producer-director who worked in Paris, Berlin and Hollywood before settling in London 1930. More than any other man the saviour of the British film industry. Formed London Films and sealed its success with *The Private Life of Henry VIII* 32; built Denham Studios. He was married to actresses Maria Corda and Merle Oberon (1939–45).

Biographies: 1956, *Alexander Korda* by Paul Tabori. 1975, *Alexander Korda* by Karol Kulik, 1980, *Charmed Lives* by Michael Korda.

■ The Duped Journalist (d) 14. Tutyu and Totyo (d) 14. Lea Lyon (d) 15. The Officer's Swordknot (d) 15. Fedora (d) 16. The Grandmother (d) 16. Tales of the Typewriter (d) 16. The Man with Two Hearts (d) 16. The Million Pound Note (d) 16. Cyclamen (d) 16. Struggling Hearts (d) 16. Laughing Saskia (d) 16. Miska the Magnate (d) 16. St Peter's Umbrella (d) 17. The Stork Caliph (d) 17. Magic (d) 17. Harrison and Barrison (d) 17. Faun (d) 18. The Man with the Golden Touch (d) 18. Mary Ann (d) 18. Hail Caesar (d) 19. White Rose (d) 19. Yamata (d) 19. Neither In Nor Out (d) 19. Number 111 (d) 19. The Prince and the Pauper (d) 20. Masters of the Sea (d) 22. A Vanished World (d) 22. Samson and Delilah (d) 22. The Unknown Tomorrow (d) 23. Everybody's Woman (d) 24. Mayerling (d) 24. Dancing Mad (d) 25. Madame Wants No Children (d) 26. A Modern Dubarry (d) 27. (All previous titles in Hungary, France and Germany; now Hollywood.) The Stolen Bride (d) 27. *The Private Life of Helen of Troy* (d) 27. Yellow Lily (d) 28. Night Watch (d) 28. Love and the Devil (d) 29. The Squall (d) 29. Her Private Life (d) 29. Lilies of the Field (d) 30. Women Everywhere (d) 30. The Princess and the Plumber (d) 31. (Now Paris.) Laughter (d) 31. *Marius* (d) 31. (Now London.) Service for Ladies (p, d) 32. Wedding Rehearsal (p, d) 32. That Night in London (p) 33. Strange Evidence (p) 33. Counsel's Opinion (p) 33. Cash (p) 33. Men of Tomorrow (p) 33. *The Private Life of Henry VIII* (p, d) 33. The Girl from Maxim's (p, d) 33. *The Rise of Catherine the Great* (p) 34. The Private Life of Don Juan (p, d) 34. *The Scarlet Pimpernel* (p, some d) 34. *Sanders of the River* (p) 35. *The Ghost Goes West* (p) 35. *Things to Come* (p) 36. Moscow Nights (ep) 36. Men Are Not Gods (p). 36. Forget Me Not (p) 36. *Rembrandt* (p, d) 36. *The Man Who Could Work Miracles* (p) 37. Fire over England (ep) 37. I Claudius (unfinished) (p) 37. Dark Journey (p) 37. Elephant Boy (p) 37. Farewell Again (ep) 37. Storm in a Teacup (ep) 37. Action for Slander (ep) 37. *Knight without Armour* (p) 37. The Squeaker (p) 37. The Return of the Scarlet Pimpernel (ep) 37. Paradise for Two (ep) 37. The Divorce of Lady X (p) 38. The Drum (p) 38. South Riding (ep) 38. The Challenge (ep) 38. Prison without Bars (ep) 38. Q Planes (ep) 39. *The Four Feathers* (p) 39. The Rebel Son (ep) 39. The Spy in Black (ep) 39. The Lion Has Wings (p) 39. Over the Moon (p) 40 (shot 1938). Twenty-one Days (p) 40 (shot 37). Conquest of the Air (p) 40. *The Thief of Baghdad* (p) 40. Old Bill and Son (ep) 41. *That Hamilton Woman* (in US) (p, d) 41. Lydia (in US) (p) 41. *To Be or Not to Be* (in US) (ep) 42. Jungle Book (in US) (p) 42. *Perfect Strangers* (p) 45. The Shop at Sly Corner (ep) 47. A Man about the House (ep) 47. Mine Own Executioner (ep) 47. An Ideal Husband (p, d) 47. Night Beat (ep) 48. *Anna Karenina* (p) 48. The Winslow Boy (ep) 48. The Fallen Idol (ep) 48. Bonnie Prince Charlie (ep) 48. The Small Back Room (ep) 49. That Dangerous Age (ep) 49. The Last Days of Dolwyn (ep) 49. Saints and Sinners (ep) 49. *The Third Man* (ep) 49. The Cure for Love (ep) 50. The Angel with the Trumpet (ep) 50. My Daughter Joy (ep) 50. State Secret (ep) 50. Seven Days to Noon (ep) 50. Gone to Earth (ep) 50. The Elusive Pimpernel (ep) 51. Tales of Hoffman (ep) 51. Lady Godiva Rides Again (ep) 51. The Wonder Kid (ep) 51. Mr Denning Drives North (ep) 52. An Outcast of the Islands (ep) 52. Home at Seven (ep) 52. Who Goes There? (ep) 52. Cry the Beloved Country (ep) 52. *The Sound Barrier* (ep) 52. The Holly and the Ivy (ep) 52. The Ringer (ep) 53. Folly to Be Wise (ep) 53. Twice Upon a Time (ep) 53. The Captain's Paradise (ep) 53. The Story of Gilbert and Sullivan (ep) 53. The Man Between (ep) 53. The Heart of the Matter (ep) 54. Hobson's Choice (ep) 54. The Belles of St Trinian's (ep) 54. The Teckman Mystery (ep) 54. The Man Who Loved Redheads (ep) 55. Three Cases of Murder (ep) 55. The Constant Husband (ep) 55. A Kid for Two Farthings (ep) 55. The Deep Blue Sea (ep) 55. Summer Madness (ep) 55. Storm over the Nile (ep) 55. *Richard III* (ep) 56. Smiley (ep) 56.

~In the above list the abbreviation ep (executive producer) is meant to imply a considerable distancing by Korda from the product, as sponsor, or financier, or head of London Films.

✪ For reviving Britain's flagging film industry and making half-a-dozen imperishable classics. *Rembrandt*.

❝ The art of film-making is to come to the brink of bankruptcy and stare it in the face. – *A.K.*

Anyone who gets a raw deal in a film studio is no more deserving of pity than someone who gets beaten up in a brothel. A gentleman has no business in either place. – *A.K.*

When my friends and I were young in Hungary, we all dreamed of being poets. And what did we become? We became politicians and advertisement men and film producers. – *A.K.*

He represented, and indeed virtually created, the tradition of quality in the British cinema. – *Andrew Sarris*

His engaging personality and charm of manner must be resisted. His promises, even when they are sincere, are worthless. A very dominant man and very dangerous to converse with owing to (among other things) his powers of persuasion. – *Internal memo of the Prudential Assurance Company, which backed Korda*

His human wisdom was always greater than his film wisdom. – *Graham Greene*

~Other projects announced at various times by Korda include The Field of the Cloth of Gold, Marco Polo, Nijinsky, Hamlet, Zorro, Joseph and His Brothers, Young Mr Disraeli, Marlborough, King of the Jews, Franz Liszt, Lawrence of Arabia, Nelson, Precious Bane, Cyrano de Bergerac, Charles II, War and Peace, Burmese Silver, Elizabeth of Austria, Pocahontas, Manon Lescaut, New Wine, The Hardy Family in England, Greenmantle, The Old Wives' Tale, Mr Chips' Boys, The Pickwick Papers, The Wrecker, Around the World in Eighty Days, Gibraltar, The Eternal City, The King's General, Carmen, Salome, Faust, Arms and the Man, Macbeth, The Iliad.

Korda, Vincent (1896–1979).
Hungarian art director who usually worked on the films of his brothers Alexander and Zoltan.

The Private Life of Henry VIII 32. Sanders of the River 35. *Things to Come* 36. The Four Feathers 39. *The Thief of Baghdad* (AA) 40. To Be or Not to Be 42. The Fallen Idol 48. The Third Man 49. The Sound Barrier 52. The Deep Blue Sea 55. Summer Madness 56, etc.

Korda, Zoltan (1895–1961).
Hungarian director, brother of Alexander Korda; spent most of his career in Britain and Hollywood.
Cash 32. Sanders of the River 35. The Drum 38. *The Four Feathers* 39. Jungle Book 42. Sahara 43. Counterattack 43. *The Macomber Affair* 47. A Woman's Vengeance 48. Cry the Beloved Country 51, etc.

Korine, Harmony (1974–).
American screenwriter, director and novelist.
Kids (w) 96. Gummo (wd) 97.

Korjus, Miliza (1900–1980).
Polish operatic soprano who settled in America but did not pursue what looked like being a popular film career.
■ *The Great Waltz* (AAN) 38. Imperial Cavalry (Mex.) 42.

Korman, Harvey (1927–).
American character comedian, often as loud-mouthed show-off. On TV with Danny Kaye and Carol Burnett.
Lord Love a Duck 66. Don't Just Stand There 67. The April Fools 68. Blazing Saddles 74. High Anxiety 78. First Family 80. Herbie Goes Bananas 80. History of the World Part One 81. Trail of the Pink Panther 82. The Long Shot 85. Crash Course (TV) 88. The Flintstones 94. The Radioland Murders 94. Dracula: Dead and Loving It 95. Jingle All the Way 96, etc.
TV series: The Danny Kaye Show 64–67. The Carol Burnett Show 67–77. The Tim Conway Show 80–81. Mama's Family 83–84. Leo & Liz in Beverly Hills 86.

Korngold, Erich Wolfgang (1897–1957).
Czech composer-conductor, a child prodigy. To Hollywood in 1935 with Warners.
Biography: 1997, *Erich Wolfgang Korngold* by Jessica Duchen.
■ Captain Blood 35. *Anthony Adverse* (AA) 36. The Green Pastures 36. A Midsummer Night's Dream 36. The Story of Louis Pasteur 36. Another Dawn 37. The Prince and the Pauper 37. *The Adventures of Robin Hood* (AA) 38. Juarez 39. Elizabeth and Essex (AAN) 39. *The Sea Hawk* (AAN) 40. The Sea Wolf 41. *Kings Row* 41. The Constant Nymph 43. Between Two Worlds 44. Devotion 44. Deception 46. Of Human Bondage 46. Escape Me Never 47. Magic Fire 56.
✪ For stirring romantic themes of a finer texture than anyone else in Hollywood could accomplish. *Kings Row*.

Kornman, Mary (1917–1973).
American actress, the only girl in the original Our Gang comedies of the 20s, on screen from the age of five. As a teenager she acted in Hal Roach's *The Boy Friends* series of shorts and later appeared in some features before retiring in 1940. The first of her two husbands was cinematographer Leo Tover.
Are These Our Children? 31. Flying Down to Rio 33. The Adventurous Knights 35. Desert Trail 35. Queen of the Jungle 35. Swing It Professor 37. On the Spot 40, etc.

Korris, Harry (1888–1971) (Henry Corris).
British music-hall comedian who became popular on radio as Mr Lovejoy in the 40s show *Happidrome* and made several slapdash film farces.
Somewhere in England 40. Somewhere in Camp 41. Happidrome 43, etc.

Korsmo, Charlie (1978–).
American juvenile actor.
Men Don't Leave 89. Dick Tracy 89. What about Bob? 91. Hook 91. The Doctor 91. Can't Hardly Wait 98, etc.

Kortner, Fritz (1892–1970) (Fritz Nathan Kohn).
Austrian character actor, in films of many nations, and director.
Autobiography: 1959, *The Evening of All Days*.
Police No. 1111 (debut) 16. Satanas 20. The Brothers Karamazov 20. The Hands of Orlac 24. Beethoven 26. Warning Shadows 27. Mata Hari 27. *Pandora's Box* 28. The Murder of Dimitri Karamazov 30. Dreyfus 30. Chu Chin Chow 34. Evensong 34. Abdul the Damned 35. The Crouching Beast 36. The Strange Death of Adolf Hitler 43. The Hitler Gang 44. Somewhere in the Night 46. The Brasher Doubloon 47. Berlin Express 48, many others.
■ AS DIRECTOR: Der Brave Suender 31. So Ein Maedel Vergisst Man Nicht 33. Der Ruf 49. Die Stadt ist Voller Geheimnisse 55. Sarajevo 55. Lysistrata 61.

Korty, John (1941–).
American director.
The Crazy Quilt 65. Funnyman 67. Riverrun 68. The People (TV) 72. Class of 63 (TV) 73. Go Ask Alice (TV) 73. The Autobiography of Miss Jane Pittman (TV) 73. Silence 74. Alex and the Gypsy 76. Farewell to Manzanar (TV) 76. Who Are the De Bolts 77. Forever (TV) 78. Oliver's Story (& w) 78. A Christmas without Snow (TV) 80. Twice upon a Time (co-d) 83. The Haunting Passion (TV) 83. Second Sight: A Love Story (TV) 84. The Ewok Adventure (TV) 84. A Deadly Business (TV) 86. Resting Place (TV) 86. Baby Girl Scott (TV) 87. Eye on the Sparrow (TV) 87. Winnie (TV) 88. Long Road Home (TV) 91. They (TV) 93. Getting Out (TV) 94. Redwood Curtain (TV) 95, etc.

Korvin, Charles (1907–1998) (Geza Korvin Karpathi).
Hungarian-born leading actor, in Hollywood. Born in Piestany, he studied at the Sorbonne in Paris, working as a photographer and director of documentaries before moving to America in the late 30s. There he worked as a radio and stage actor before being put under contract by Universal. He was blacklisted in the early 50s, working in Europe until the mid-60s. Married three times.
Enter Arsène Lupin 44. This Love of Ours 45. Temptation 47. The Killer That Stalked New York 50. Lydia Bailey 52. Sangaree 53. Zorro the Avenger 60. Ship of Fools 65. The Man Who Had Power over Women 70. Inside Out 75, etc.
TV series: Interpol Calling 59.

Koscina, Sylva (1933–1994).
Yugoslavian leading lady in international films.
Hercules Unchained 60. Jessica 62. Hot Enough for June (GB) 63. Juliet of the Spirits (It.) 65. Three Bites of the Apple (US) 66. Deadlier Than the Male (GB) 67. A Lovely Way to Die 68. The Battle for Neretva 70. Hornet's Nest 70. Crimes of the Black Cat 72. The Slasher 74. Dracula in Brianza 75. Casanova and Co./The Rise and Rise of Casanova 77. Sunday Lovers 80. Cinderella '80 84. Deadly Sanctuary 86. Rimini Rimini 87, etc.

Kosleck, Martin (1907–1994) (Nicolai Yoshkin).
Russian character actor with experience on the German stage; in America from mid-30s.
Confessions of a Nazi Spy (as Goebbels) 39. Nurse Edith Cavell 39. A Date with Destiny 40. Foreign Correspondent 40. North Star 43. *The Hitler Gang* (as Goebbels) 44. The Frozen Ghost 44. The Mummy's Curse 45. House of Horrors 46. Hitler (as Goebbels) 61. Something Wild 62. Thirty-Six Hours 64. Morituri 65. The Flesh Eaters 67. Which Way to the Front? 70, etc.

Kosma, Joseph (1905–1969).
Hungarian composer, in France from 1933.
La Grande Illusion 37. *La Bête Humaine* 38. *Partie de Campagne* 38. La Règle du Jeu 39. *Les Enfants du Paradis* 44. Les Portes de la Nuit 45. Les Amants de Vérone 48. The Green Glove 52. Huis Clos 54. Calle Mayor 56. The Doctor's Dilemma 59. Lunch on the Grass 59. La Poupée 62. In the French Style 64. The Little Theatre of Jean Renoir 69, etc.

Kossoff, David (1919–)
British character actor and stage monologuist.
The Good Beginning 50. The Young Lovers 55. *A Kid for Two Farthings* 56. *The Bespoke Overcoat* 57. The Journey 59. Freud 62. Ring of Spies 64. Three for All 74. The London Connection 79. Staggered 94, etc.
TV series: The Larkins. A Little Big Business.

Kostal, Irwin (1911–1994).
American musical supervisor.
West Side Story (AA) 61. Mary Poppins (AAN) 64. *The Sound of Music* (AA) 65. Bedknobs and Broomsticks (AAN) 71. The Blue Bird 76. Pete's Dragon (AAN) 77, etc.

Koster, Henry (1905–1988) (Hermann Kosterlitz).
German director, in Hollywood from mid-30s, adept at sentimental comedy.
■ Thea Roland (Ger.) 32. Peter (Ger.) 33. Little Mother (Ger.) 33. Peter (Hung.) 35. Marie Bashkirtzeff (Ger.) 36. *Three Smart Girls* 36. *One Hundred Men and a Girl* 37. The Rage of Paris 38. Three Smart Girls Grow Up 38. First Love 39. Spring Parade 40. *It Started with Eve* 41. Between Us Girls 42. Music for Millions 44. Two Sisters from Boston 45. The Unfinished Dance 47. *The Bishop's Wife* (AAN) 47. The Luck of the Irish 47. Come to the Stable 49. *The Inspector General* 49. Wabash Avenue 50. My Blue Heaven 50. *Harvey* 50. No Highway (GB) 51. Mr Belvedere Rings the Bell 52. Elopement 52. Stars and Stripes Forever 52. My Cousin Rachel 52. *The Robe* 53. Désirée 54. A Man Called Peter 55. The Virgin Queen 55. Good Morning, Miss Dove 55. D-Day the Sixth of June 56. The Power and the Prize 56. My Man Godfrey 57. Fraulein 58. The Naked Maja 59. The Story of Ruth 60. Flower Drum Song 60. Mr Hobbs Takes a Vacation 62. Take Her She's Mine 63. Dear Brigitte 65. The Singing Nun 66.

Kosugi, Sho (1947–).
Japanese star of Hong Kong and US martial arts movies, a former karate champion. Born in Tokyo, he was educated in America.
Shaolin Temple Strikes Back (HK) 72. Master Ninja 78. The Bad News Bears Go to Japan 78. Enter the Ninja 82. Eagle Claws Champion (HK) 82. Revenge of the Ninja 84. Ninja III: The Domination 84. Nine Deaths of the Ninja 85. Pray for Death 85. Hanauma Bay 85. Rage of Honor 86. Aloha Summer 88. Black Eagle 88. Blind Fury 90, etc.
TV series: The Master 84.

Kotcheff, Ted (1931–).
Canadian director.
■ Tiara Tahiti 62. *Life at the Top* 65. Two Gentlemen Sharing 70. Outback 71. Billy Two Hats 73. The Apprenticeship of Duddy Kravitz 74. Fun with Dick and Jane 77. Someone Is Killing the Great Chefs of Europe 78. North Dallas Forty 79. First Blood 82. Split Image 83. Uncommon Valor 83. Joshua Then and Now 85. Switching Channels 88. Weekend at Bernie's 89. The Winter People 89. Hot and Cold 89. Folks! 92. The Shooter 95. The Populist 97.

Koteas, Elias (1961–).
Canadian actor, working in Hollywood.
One Magic Christmas 85. Gardens of Stone 87. Some Kind of Wonderful 87. Full Moon in Blue Water 88. Tucker: The Man and His Dream 88. Friends, Lovers and Lunatics 89. Desperate Hours 90. Teenage Mutant Ninja Turtles 90. Backstreet Dreams 90. Almost an Angel 90. The Adjuster 91. Teenage Mutant Ninja Turtles III 93. God's Army 93. Camilla 93. Exotica 94. God's Army 95. Sugartime (TV) 96. Crash 96. Gattaca 97. Fallen 97. Apt Pupil 98. Living Out Loud 98. The Thin Red Line 98, etc.
❝ I would think I'd accomplished it all if I could get to play Quasimodo. – *E.K.*

Kotto, Yaphet (1937–).
American actor.
The Thomas Crown Affair 68. The Liberation of L. B. Jones 70. Across 110th Street 72. *Live and Let Die* 73. Truck Turner 74. Report to the Commissioner 74. Drum 76. Monkey Hustle 76. Blue Collar 78. Alien 79. Brubaker 80. The Star Chamber 83. Warning Sign 85. Prettykill 87. The Running Man 87. Midnight Run 88. Nightmares of the Devil (d only) 88. Ministry of Vengeance 89. After the Shock 90. Freddy's Dead: The Final Nightmare 91. Extreme Justice 93. Two If by Sea/ Stolen Hearts 96, etc.
TV series: For Love and Honor 83. Homicide: Life on the Street 93–.

Kovack, Nancy (1935–).
American leading lady with stage and TV experience. Married conductor Zubin Mehta.
Strangers When We Meet 60. Diary of a Madman 62. Jason and the Argonauts 63. The Outlaws Is Coming 65. Frankie and Johnny 66. The Silencers 66. Tarzan and the Valley of Gold 66. Marooned 69, etc.

Kovacs, Ernie (1919–1962).
Big, cigar-smoking American comedian and TV personality. Died in a car crash. Married to Edie Adams.
Biography: 1976, *Nothing in Moderation* by David G. Walley.
■ *Operation Mad Ball* 57. Bell, Book and Candle 58. It Happened to Jane 58. *Our Man in Havana* 59. Wake Me When It's Over 60. Strangers When We Meet 60. North to Alaska 60. Pepe 60. Five Golden Hours 61. Sail a Crooked Ship 62.

Kovacs, Laszlo (1932–).
American cinematographer given to experimentation which does not always please the eye.
Targets 68. The Savage Seven 68. Easy Rider 69. Getting Straight 70. Five Easy Pieces 70. Alex in Wonderland 70. The Last Movie 71. Marriage of a Young Stockbroker 71. Pocket Money 72. What's Up Doc? 72. Paper Moon 73. Freebie and the Bean 74. Shampoo 75. At Long Last Love 75. Nickelodeon 76. New York New York 77. Close Encounters of the Third Kind (co-ph) 77. The Last Waltz 78. Butch and Sundance 79. Heartbeat 79. The Legend of the Lone Ranger 81. The Toy 82. Frances 82. Crackers 84. Ghostbusters 84. Mask 85. Legal Eagles 86. Little Nikita 88. Say Anything 89. Shattered 91. Radio Flyer 92. Ruby Cairo 93. The Next Karate Kid 94. The Scout 94. Free Willy 2: The Adventure Begins 95. Multiplicity 96. My Best Friend's Wedding 97, etc.

Kove, Kenneth (1893–1965).
English character actor, in silly-ass roles, from Aldwych farces.
Murder 30. Fascination 31. Two White Arms 32. Pyjamas Preferred 32. Dora 33. Song of the Plough 33. Crazy People 34. Radio Pirates 35. Look Up and Laugh 35. Talking Feet 37. Asking for Trouble 42. Innocents in Paris 53. Dr Terror's House of Horrors 65, etc.

Kowalski, Bernard (1929–).
American director, from TV.
Hot Car Girl 58. Attack of the Giant Leeches 58. Night of the Blood Beast 58. Blood and Steel 59. Krakatoa East of Java 69. Stiletto 70. Macho Callahan 70. Ssss 73. The Nativity (TV) 78. B.A.D. Cats (TV) 80. Miracle at Beekman's Place (TV) 88. Nashville Beat 89, etc.

Kozak, Harley Jane (1953–) (Susan Jane Kozak).
Leading American actress.
Hair 79. The World according to Garp 82. When Harry Met Sally 89. Parenthood 89. Side Out 90. Arachnophobia 90. Necessary Roughness 91. All I Want for Christmas 91. The Taking of Beverly Hills 91. Beyond Control: The Amy Fisher Story (TV) 93. The Favor 94. Magic in the Water 95. Titanic (TV) 96. Dark Planet 97, etc.
TV series: The Secret Life of Men 98– .

Kozintsev, Grigori (1905–1973).
Russian director, in films from 1924.
The Youth of Maxim 35. *Don Quixote* 57. *Hamlet* 64. King Lear 69, etc.

Kozlowski, Linda (1958–).
American leading actress. She is married to actor Paul Hogan.
Crocodile Dundee 86. Pass the Ammo 88. Crocodile Dundee II 88. Almost an Angel 90. The Neighbor 93. Zorn (Swe.) 94. Village of the Damned 95, etc.

Krabbé, Jeroen (1944–).
Dutch leading actor in international films.
The Little Ark 72. Alicia 74. Soldier of Orange 79. Spetters 80. A Flight of Rainbirds 81. The Fourth Man 82. Turtle Diary 85. Jumpin' Jack Flash 86. No Mercy 86. The Living Daylights 87. Crossing Delancey 88. A World Apart 88. Scandal 89. The Punisher 89. Robin Hood 90. Till There Was You 90. Murder East/Murder West 90. The Prince of Tides 91. Kafka 91. For a Lost Soldier/Voor Een Verloren Soldaat 92. King of the Hill 93. Going Home/Oeroeg 93. The Fugitive 93. Immortal Beloved 94. Farinelli il Castrato (as Handel) 95. The Disappearance of Garcia Lorca 96. The Odyssey (TV) 97. Dangerous Beauty 98. Left Luggage (& d) 98. Ever After 98, etc.

Kraly, Hans (1885–1950).
German screenwriter, associated with the early films of director Ernst LUBITSCH, whom he followed to the United States.

The Blouse King/Der Blusenkonig 17. Carmen 18. Madame Dubarry 19. The Oyster Princess/Die Austernprinzessin 19. Romeo und Julia im Schnee 20. Forbidden Paradise (US) 24. The Duchess of Buffalo (US) 26. The Garden of Eden (US) 28. The Kiss (US) 29. Betrayal (US) 29. Devil-May-Care (US) 29. Eternal Love (US) 29. By Candlelight (US) 33. One Hundred Men and a Girl 37. It Started with Eve (US) 41. The Mad Ghoul (US) 43, etc.

Kramer, Larry (1935–).
American screenwriter and dramatist.

Women in Love (& p) (AANw) 69. Lost Horizon 72, etc.

❝ Writing movies is exceptionally boring, especially when you're good at it, and for some reason, it comes very easily to me. But if you're a serious writer, you shouldn't write movies; movies are simply not a first-rate art form. – *L.K.*

Kramer, Stanley (1913–).
American producer and director of clean-cut, well-intentioned films which sometimes fall short on inspiration.

Autobiography: 1998, *A Mad, Mad, Mad World – A Life in Hollywood* (with Thomas M. Coffey).

■ So Ends Our Night 41. *The Moon and Sixpence* 42. So This Is New York 48. Champion 49. Home of the Brave 49. *The Men* 50. Cyrano de Bergerac 50. *Death of a Salesman* 51. *High Noon* 52. The Sniper 52. The Happy Time 52. My Six Convicts 52. The Member of the Wedding 52. Eight Iron Men 52. The Fourposter 53. The Juggler 53. The 5000 Fingers of Dr T 53. The Wild One 54. *The Caine Mutiny* 54. Not as a Stranger (& d) 55. The Pride and the Passion (& d) 57. The Defiant Ones (& d) (AAN) 58. *On the Beach* (& d) 59. *Inherit the Wind* (& d) 60. Judgment at Nuremberg (& d) (AAN) 61. Pressure Point 62. A Child is Waiting 62. It's a Mad Mad Mad Mad World (& d) 63. Invitation to a Gunfighter 64. *Ship of Fools* (& d) 65. *Guess Who's Coming to Dinner* (& d) (AAN) 67. The Secret of Santa Vittoria (& d) 69 R.P.M. (& d) 71. Bless the Beasts and Children (& d) 71. *Oklahoma Crude* (& d) 73. The Domino Principle (& d) 77. The Runner Stumbles (& d) 79.

✪ For trying. *Inherit the Wind.*

❝ I'm always pursuing the next dream, hunting for the next truth. – *S.K.*

He will never be a natural, but time has proved that he is not a fake. – *Andrew Sarris, 1968*

He's the kind of man who invariably says he saves other people's films in the cutting room. – *Fred Zinnemann*

Krampf, Gunter (1899–1957*).
German cinematographer, in Britain from 1931.

The Student of Prague 24. The Hands of Orlac 24. *Pandora's Box* 28. Rome Express 32. Little Friend 34. Latin Quarter 45. Fame is the Spur 46. Portrait of Clare 50. The Franchise Affair 52, many others.

Krasker, Robert (1913–1981).
Australian cinematographer, long in Britain.

Dangerous Moonlight 40. *Henry V* 44. Caesar and Cleopatra 45. *Brief Encounter* 46. *Odd Man Out* 47. *The Third Man* (AA) 49. Romeo and Juliet 53. Trapeze 56. The Quiet American 58. The Criminal 60. El Cid 61. Billy Budd 62. The Running Man 63. The Fall of the Roman Empire 64. The Heroes of Telemark 65, many others.

Krasna, Norman (1909–1984).
American playwright who worked on many films from 1932, including adaptations of his own plays.

The Richest Girl in the World (AAN) 34. *Fury* (AAN) 36. *Bachelor Mother* 39. The Flame of New Orleans 41. The Devil and Miss Jones (AAN) 41. *Princess O'Rourke* (AA) (& d) 43. The Big Hangover (& pd) 50. The Ambassador's Daughter (& d) 56. *Indiscreet* 58. Who Was That Lady? (& d) 60. Let's Make Love 61. Sunday in New York 64, many others.

Krasner, Milton (1901–1988).
American cinematographer.

I Love That Man 33. The Crime of Dr Hallet 36. The House of the Seven Gables 40. *The Woman in the Window* 44. Scarlet Street 45. *The Dark Mirror* 46. The Farmer's Daughter 47. *The Set Up* 49. Rawhide 50. *All About Eve* 50. Monkey Business 51. *Three Coins in the Fountain* (AA) 54. The Rains of Ranchipur 55. Bus Stop 56. An Affair to Remember 57. The Four Horsemen of the Apocalypse 62. Two Weeks in Another Town 62. Love with the Proper Stranger 64. The Sandpiper 65. The Singing Nun 66. Hurry Sundown 67. The Epic of Josie 67. The St Valentine's Day Massacre 68. The Sterile Cuckoo 69. Beneath the Planet of the Apes 70, many others.

Kraushaar, Raoul (1908–).
American composer.

Melody Ranch 40. Stardust on the Sage 42. Stork Bites Man 47. Bride of the Gorilla 51. The Blue Gardenia 53. Mohawk 56. Mustang 59. Billy the Kid vs Dracula 65. Jesse James Meets Frankenstein's Daughter 65. An Eye for an Eye 66. Thriller – a Cruel Story (Swe.) 72, etc.

Krauss, Werner (1884–1959).
Distinguished German actor.

ETA Hoffman (debut) 16. *The Cabinet of Dr Caligari* 19. The Brothers Karamazov 20. Othello 22. Nathan the Wise 23. *Waxworks* 24. The Student of Prague 25. A Midsummer Night's Dream 25. Secrets of a Soul 26. Tartuffe 26. Jew Süss 40. John Ohne Heimat 55, etc.

Kress, Harold F. (1913–).
American editor.

Bitter Sweet 40. Dr Jekyll and Mr Hyde 41. Mrs Miniver 42. Dragon Seed 44. Command Decision 49. Green Fire 54. The Cobweb 55. Silk Stockings 57. King of Kings 61. How the West Was Won (AA) 63. Alvarez Kelly 66. I Walk the Line 70. The Poseidon Adventure 72. The Towering Inferno (AA) 74. Viva Knievel 77. The Swarm 78, etc.

■ AS DIRECTOR: Purity Squad 45. No Questions Asked 51. The Painted Hills 51. Apache War Smoke 52. Cromwell (2nd unit) 70.

Kreuger, Kurt (1917–).
Swiss actor, former ski instructor, who appeared in many Hollywood films as smooth continental heartthrob or menace.

Sahara 43. The Moon is Down 43. Mademoiselle Fifi 44. Madame Pimpernel 45. Unfaithfully Yours 48. The Enemy Below 58. What Did You Do in the War, Daddy? 66. The St Valentine's Day Massacre 67, etc.

Krige, Alice (1955–).
South African leading lady in international films.

Chariots of Fire 81. Ghost Story 81. A Tale of Two Cities (TV) 81. Ellis Island (TV) 84. King David 85. Dream West (TV) 85. Barfly 87. See You in the Morning 89. Sleepwalkers 92. Scarlet and Black (TV) 93. The Institute Benjamenta 95. Joseph (TV) 95. Star Trek: First Contact 96. Hidden in America (TV) 96. Habitat 97. Molokai 98. Close Relations (TV) 98, etc.

Krish, John (1923–).
British director who began in sponsored documentary field.

Unearthly Stranger 61. The Wild Affair 65. Decline and Fall 68. The Man Who Had Power over Women 70. Jesus (co-d) 79. Out of the Darkness 85, etc.

Krishnamma, Suri.
English director, from television.

O Mary This London (TV) 94. A Man of No Importance 94.

Kristel, Sylvia (1952–).
Dutch-born leading lady who became famous in the nude.

Emmanuelle 73. Alice or the Last Escapade 76. The Fifth Musketeer 77. The Concorde – Airport 79 79. The Nude Bomb 80. Private Lessons 81. Lady Chatterley's Lover 82. Casanova (TV) 87. Emmanuelle 7 92, etc.

Kristofferson, Kris (1936–).
American leading man of the 70s, former folk singer and musician.

The Last Movie 70. Cisco Pike 72. Blume in Love 73. Pat Garrett and Billy the Kid 73. Bring Me the Head of Alfredo Garcia 74. Alice Doesn't Live Here Any More 75. The Sailor who Fell from Grace with the Sea 76. A Star Is Born 76. Vigilante Force 76. Semi-Tough 78. Convoy 78. Heaven's Gate 80. Rollover 81. Flashpoint 84. Songwriter 84. Trouble in Mind 85. Blood and Orchids (TV) 86. The Last Days of Frank and Jesse James (TV) 86. Stagecoach (TV) 86. Amerika (TV) 87. Big Top Pee-Wee 88. Millennium 89. Welcome Home 89. Pair of Aces (TV) 90. Another Pair of Aces: Three of a Kind (TV) 91. Miracle in the Wilderness (TV) 91. Paper Hearts 93. Sodbusters (TV) 94. Pharaoh's Army 95. Lone Star 96. Fire Down Below 97. Dance with Me 98. Two for Texas (TV) 98. Blade 98. A Soldier's Daughter Never Cries 98. Girls' Night (GB) 98. Molokai 98. Father Damien 99, etc.

Kruger, Alma (1868–1960).
American stage actress who made many films in later life and is specially remembered as the head nurse in the Dr Kildare series.

These Three 36. One Hundred Men and a Girl 37. Marie Antoinette 38. Balalaika 39. Saboteur 42. A Royal Scandal 46. Forever Amber (last film) 47, etc.

Kruger, Hardy (1928–).
Blond German leading man who has filmed internationally.

Junge Adler (debut) 43. Insel Ohne Moral 50. Solange 53. Alibi 55. *The One That Got Away* 57. Bachelor of Hearts 58. Blind Date 59. The Rest Is Silence 59. Sundays and Cybèle 62. Hatari 62. The Flight of the Phoenix 65. The Defector 66. The Secret of Santa Vittoria 69. The Red Tent 70. Night Hair Child 71. Paper Tiger 75. Barry Lyndon 75. A Bridge Too Far 77. The Wild Geese 78. Blue Fin 79. Society Limited 81. Wrong Is Right 82. The Inside Man 84. L'Atlantide 92, etc.

Kruger, Otto (1885–1974).
Suave American actor with long stage experience.

When the Call Came 15. Under the Red Robe 23. Beauty for Sale 33. The Prizefigher and the Lady 33. *Chained* 34. Springtime for Henry 34. Treasure Island 35. *Dracula's Daughter* 36. They Won't Forget 37. *The Housemaster* (GB) 38. Thanks for the Memory 38. Dr Ehrlich's Magic Bullet 40. This Man Reuter 40. The Big Boss 41. *Saboteur* 42. *Murder My Sweet* 44. Escape in the Fog 45. Duel in the Sun 46. Smart Woman 48. Payment on Demand 51. High Noon 52. Magnificent Obsession 54. The Last Command 56. The Wonderful World of the Brothers Grimm 63. Sex and the Single Girl 64, many others.

Krupa, Gene (1909–1973).
American jazz drummer and bandleader who rose to fame with the Benny Goodman orchestra in the 30s to become the first star of his instrument. In films usually as himself. In the biopic *The Gene Krupa Story* 59, he was played by Sal Mineo, though the drumming was his own.

Big Broadcast of 1937 36. Some Like It Hot/Rhythm Romance 39. Ball of Fire 41. George White's Scandals 45. Beat the Band 46. Glamour Girl 48. Make Believe Ballroom 49. The Glenn Miller Story 54. The Benny Goodman Story 55, etc.

Kruschen, Jack (1922–).
American character comedian of stage and TV.

Red Hot and Blue 49. The Last Voyage 60. The Apartment (AAN) 60. Lover Come Back 62. The Unsinkable Molly Brown 64. Harlow (TV) (as Louis B. Mayer) 66. Million Dollar Duck 71. Freebie and the Bean 74. Sunburn 79. Under the Rainbow 81. Legend of the Wild 81. Penny Ante 90, etc.

Kubik, Gail (1914–1984).
American composer.

The World at War (doc) 42. The Memphis Belle (doc) 43. Thunderbolt (doc) 45. C-Man 45. Gerald McBoing Boing 50. The Desperate Hours 55. I Thank a Fool 62, etc.

Kubrick, Stanley (1928–1999).
American writer-producer-director, in whose psyche independence seems equated with excess. His latest film, *Eyes Wide Shut*, began shooting in 1996, and continued for some 18 months, with both Harvey KEITEL and Jennifer Jason LEIGH having to be replaced because of other commitments.

Biographies: 1971, *Stanley Kubrick Directs* by Alexander Walker; 1982, *Kubrick, Inside a Film Artist's Maze* by T. A. Nelson; 1997, *Stanley Kubrick: A Biography* by Vincent LoBrutto; 1997, *Stanley Kubrick* by John Baxter.

■ Fear and Desire (wdph) 53. Killer's Kiss (wd) 55. *The Killing* (wd) 56. *Paths of Glory* (wd) 58. Spartacus (d) 60. Lolita (d) 62. *Dr Strangelove* (wdp) (AAN) 63. *2001: A Space Odyssey* (wdp) (AAN) 69. A Clockwork Orange (wdp) (AAN) 71. Barry Lyndon (AANp, AANw, AANd) 75. The Shining 79. Full Metal Jacket 87. Eyes Wide Shut 99.

✪ For managing to sustain a career on his own terms. *Dr Strangelove.*

❝ Man in the twentieth century has been cast adrift in a rudderless boat on an uncharted sea. The very meaninglessness of life forces man to create his own meaning. If it can be written or thought, it can be filmed. – *S.K.*

He gives new meaning to the word meticulous. – *Jack Nicholson*

Stanley Kubrick is a talented shit. – *Kirk Douglas*

His tragedy may have been that he was hailed as a great artist before he had become a competent craftsman. However, it is more likely that he has chosen to exploit the giddiness of middlebrow audiences on the satiric level of *Mad* magazine. – *Andrew Sarris, 1968*

Kudrow, Lisa (1963–).
American actress who is best known for her role as the animal-loving, vegetarian folk singer Phoebe Buffay in the TV sitcom *Friends*, having played Phoebe's twin sister Ursula in the TV sitcom *Mad about You*. Born in Encino, California, she studied biology at Vassar, and began as a scientific researcher before switching to performing, first with the Los Angeles improvisational group The Groundlings.

The Unborn 91. In the Heat of Passion 92. In the Heat of Passion 2: Unfaithful 94. Mother 96. Hacks 97. Romy and Michele's High School Reunion 97. Clockwatchers 97. The Opposite of Sex 98, etc.

TV series: Bob 92–94.

Kuei, Yuen:
see YUEN, Corey.

Kuleshov, Lev (1899–1970).
Influential and precocious Russian director, screenwriter and theorist. Born in Tambov, he studied painting at the Fine Arts School in Moscow, worked as a set designer from 1916 and began publishing theoretical articles on film from his late teens. He demonstrated the possibilities of manipulating an audience's reaction through editing, by juxtaposing the same shot of an actor with different objects to suggest various emotions. This 'Kuleshov effect', and his theories of montage, influenced Eisenstein and other directors. He was involved in the establishment of the First National Film School in Moscow, where he also taught. After many controversies, he stopped directing for a time from the early 30s. In the mid-40s he was appointed director of the State Institute of Cinematography in Moscow. Married actress Alexandra Khokhlova. His books include *Art of the Cinema*, published in 1929, and *Fundamentals of Film Direction*, published in 1941.

Book: 1997, *Lev Kuleshov: Fifty Years in Film*, ed. Ekaterina Khokhlova.

The Project of Engineer Prite/Proyekt Inzhenera (& ad) 18. The Extraordinary Adventures of Mr West in the Land of the Bolsheviks 24. The Death Ray/Luch Smerti (& a) 25. 40 Hearts 31. Horizon (& co-w) 32. The Siberians 40. Incident in a Volcano (co-d) 41. Timur's Oath 42. We Are from the Urals (co-d) 44, etc.

❝ An actor's play reaches the spectator just as the editor requires it to, because the spectator himself completes the connected shots and sees in it what has been suggested to him by the montage. – *L.K.*

Kuleshov maintained that film art does not begin when the artists act and the various scenes are shot – this is only the preparation of the material. Film art begins from the moment when the director begins to combine and join together the various pieces of film. – *Vsevolod Pudovkin*

Kulik, Buzz (1923–1999) (Seymour Kulik).
American director, from TV.

The Explosive Generation 61. The Yellow Canary 63. Ready for the People 64. Warning Shot (& p) 66. Villa Rides 68. Riot 68. Vanished (TV) 71. Brian's Song (TV) 71. Owen Marshall (TV) 71. To Find a Man 72. Incident in a Dark Street (TV) 72. Shamus 73. Pioneer Woman (TV) 73. Remember When (TV) 74. Bad Ronald (TV) 74. Cage without a Key (TV) 75. Babe (TV) 75. Matt Helm (TV) 75. Feather and Father (TV) 76. The Lindbergh Kidnapping Case (TV) 76. Corey for the People (TV) 77. Kill Me If You Can (TV) 77. Ziegfeld: The Man and His Women (TV) 78. From Here to Eternity (TV) 79. The Pursuit of D. B. Cooper 81. Rage of Angels (TV) 83. George Washington (TV) 84. Kane & Abel (TV) 85. Women of Valor (TV) 86. Her Secret Life (TV) 87. Too Young the Hero (TV) 88. Around the World in 80 Days (TV) 89. Miles from Nowhere 92, etc.

Kulle, Jarl (1927–1997).
Distinguished Swedish leading actor and occasional director. Born in Angleholm, he spent much of his career on the stage and was best known to international audiences for his roles in five films for Ingmar Bergman. A notable performer at the Royal Dramatic Theatre of Stockholm from the 50s, he also played Professor Higgins in a Scandinavian version of *My Fair Lady*.
Waiting Women 52. Barabbas 53. Karin Mansdotter 54. Smiles of a Summer Night 55. The Devil's Eye 60. The Girl and the Press Photographer (& d) 62. Now about These Women 64. Wedding – Swedish Style 64. The Bookseller Who Gave Up Bathing (& d) 69. Ministern (& d) 71. Mats-Peter (d) 72. Fanny and Alexander 82. Babette's Feast 87. Herman 90. Zorn 94. Alfred 95, etc.

Kulp, Nancy (1921–1991).
American comedy actress, famous for TV portrayals.
The Model and the Marriage Broker 52. Shane 53. Five Gates to Hell 59. The Parent Trap 61. The Patsy 64. The Return of the Beverly Hillbillies (TV) 81, etc.
TV series: The Bob Cummings Show 55–59. *The Beverly Hillbillies* 62–71. The Brian Keith Show 73–74.

Kumashiro, Tatsumi.
Japanese director of ROMAN PORNO.
Front Row/Kaburitsukiu Jinsei 68. Following Desire/Nureto Yokujo 72. Paper Doors of a Secret Room/Yojohan Fusuma No Urabari 73. Kagi 74. Mr, Mrs and Miss Lonely 81. Appasionata 83. Koibumi 85. Like a Rolling Stone/Bo No Kanashimi 94, etc.

Kumel, Harry (1940–).
Belgian director and screenwriter.
Rag to a Red Rose (w) 59. Princess (w) 69. Daughters of Darkness 71. Malpertius 73. De Komst Van Joachim Stiller 76. Het Verloren Paradijs 78. The Secrets of Love 86. Eline Vere 91, etc.

Kureishi, Hanif (1954–).
British screenwriter, director and novelist, of Pakistani descent.
My Beautiful Laundrette (w) (AAN) 85. Sammy and Rosie Get Laid (w) 87. London Kills Me (wd) 91. The Buddha of Suburbia (co-w from novel) (TV) 93.

Kurnitz, Harry (1907–1968).
American screenwriter and novelist. Born in New York City and educated at the University of Philadelphia, he was a journalist before joining MGM in 1938 when the studio bought his detective novel *Fast Company*, written under the pseudonym Marco Page. Blacklisted in the 50s, he left Hollywood to work in Europe.
Fast and Furious 38. The Thin Man Goes Home 44. What Next, Corporal Hargrove (AAN) 45. The Web 47. A Kiss in the Dark (& p) 48. Pretty Baby 49. The Inspector General 49. Melba 53. The Man Between 53. Land of the Pharaohs 55. *Witness for the Prosecution* 57. Goodbye Charlie 64. How to Steal a Million 66, many others.

Kurosawa, Akira (1910–1998).
Distinguished Japanese film director and screenwriter who revealed the splendours of Japanese cinema to the West when his *Rashomon* was shown at the Cannes Film Festival. Born in Tokyo, he planned to be a painter before, in the mid-30s, joining as an assistant director what was to become Toho studios. There he also wrote scripts before getting the opportunity to direct in the early 40s. His postwar films were to make an international star of actor Toshiro MIFUNE and also featured notable collaborations with composer Fumio HAYASAKA and, later, Masura SATO. His samurai epics, especially *Yojimbo* and *The Seven Samurai*, were copied by Hollywood and the Italian directors of spaghetti westerns. Noted for his meticulous and painstaking approach to writing, production and rehearsals, he found it hard to get the necessary financial backing from the mid-60s and attempted suicide in 1971. His later films depended on finance from outside Japan.
Autobiography: 1982, *Something Like an Autobiography*
Book: 1985, *The Films of Akira Kurosawa* by Donald Richie.
■ Sanshiro Sugata (& w) 43. The Most Beautiful (& w) 44. Sanshiro Sugata II (& w) 44. Tora-no-o (& w) 45. Those Who Make Tomorrow (co-d) 46. No Regrets for Our Youth 46. Wonderful Sunday 47. Drunken Angel 48. A Quiet Duel 49. Stray Dog 49. Scandal 50. Rashomon 50. The Idiot 51. *Ikiru* 52. *The Seven Samurai* 54. I Live in Fear 55. *Throne of Blood* 56. *The Lower Depths* 57. *The Hidden Fortress* 58. The Bad Sleep Well 60. *Yojimbo* 61. Sanjuro 62. High and Low 63. Redbeard 65. Dodeska-den 70. Dersu Uzala (AA) 75. *The Shadow Warrior* 81. *Ran* (AAN) 85. Kurosawa's Dreams 90. Rhapsody in August/Hachigatsu-no Kyoshikyoku 91. Madadayo 93.
✪ For his brilliance as a maker of historical films with a universal appeal. *The Seven Samurai*.

Kurten, Peter (1883–1931).
German murderer who was the model for Fritz Lang's *M* 31 and its 1951 remake by Joseph Losey, and *The Vampire of Düsseldorf* 64.

Kurtz, Swoosie (1944–).
American leading actress with stage background.
First Love 77. Slap Shot 77. Oliver's Story 78. Marriage Is Alive and Well (TV) 80. Walking through the Fire 80. The Mating Season 81. The World According to Garp 82. Against All Odds 83. A Time to Live (TV) 85. True Stories 86. Wildcats 86. Baja Oklahoma (TV) 87. Bright Lights, Big

City 88. Dangerous Liaisons 88. Vice Versa 88. The Image (TV) 89. A Shock to the System 90. Stanley and Iris 90. The Positively True Adventures of the Alleged Texas Cheerleader-Murdering Mom (TV) 93. And the Band Played On (TV) 93. Reality Bites 94. Story Book 94. Precious 96. Liar Liar 96. Citizen Ruth 96. Armistead Maupin's More Tales of the City (TV) 98, etc.
TV series: Love, Sidney 81–83.

Kurys, Diane (1948–).
French director and screenwriter of films that have an autobiographical basis. She was formerly an actress, working in theatre and playing small parts in movies.
Peppermint Soda/Diablo Menthe 77. Cocktail Molotov 79. Entre Nous/Coup de Foudre (AAN) 83. A Man in Love/Un Homme Amoureux 87. C'est la Vie/La Baule-les-pins 90. After Love/Après l'Amour 92. Six Days, Six Nights/À la Folie 94, etc.

Kusturica, Emir (1955–).
Yugoslavian director and screenwriter, from TV. He is now a French citizen.
Do You Remember Dolly Bell? 81. When Father Was Away on Business/Otac Na Sluzbenom Putu (AAN) 85. Time of the Gypsies/Dom Za Vesanje 88. Arizona Dream 93. Underground 95. Black Cat, White Cat 98, etc.

Kutz, Kazimierz (1929–).
Polish director and screenwriter, born in Silesia, who began as an assistant to Andrzej Wajda on *A Generation* 55. His films reflect his experience of the region during times of war, particularly in his Silesian trilogy, 1969–79.
Cross of War/Krzyz Walecznych 59. The Silence/Milczenie 63. Whoever May Know/Ktokolwiek Wie 66. Salt of the Black Country/Sol Ziemi Czarnej 69. Pearl in the Crown/Perla w Koronie 72. The Beads from a Rosary/Paciorki Jednego Rozanca 79. I Shall Always Stand Guard/Na Strazy Swej Stac Bede 84. Death as a Slice of Bread/Smierc Jak Kromka Chleba 94. Colonel Kwiatkowski 96, etc.

Kwan, Nancy (1939–).
Chinese-English leading lady.
The World of Suzie Wong 60. Flower Drum Song 61. Tamahine 63. Fate Is the Hunter 64. The Wild Affair 65. Lt Robin Crusoe 65. Arrivederci Baby 66. Nobody's Perfect 67. The Wrecking Crew 68. The Girl Who Knew Too Much 69. The McMasters 70. Wonder Woman (TV) 73. Project: Kill 76. Night Creature 78. Streets of Hong Kong 79. Walking the Edge 83. Night Children 88. Cold Dog Soup 89. Dragon: The Bruce Lee Story 93, etc.

Kwan, Stanley (1957–) (Guan Jinpeng).
Hong Kong director, from television.
Love unto Waste 86. Rouge/Yanzhi Kou 88. Full Moon in New York/Yan Tsoi Nau Yeuk 89. Center Stage/Yun Ling-Yuk 92. Red Rose, White Rose 95.

Hold You Tight/Yue Kuai Le, Yue Duo Luo 98, etc.

Kwang-Su, Park (1955–).
South Korean director. He studied sculpture at the Nation University in Seoul, founded the Seoul Film Group, the focus of the country's independent film movement, and studied at the ESEC Film School in Paris.
Chilsu and Mansu 89. The Black Republic 91. Berlin Report 92. To the Starry Island 94. A Single Spark 95, etc.

Kwapis, Ken (1958–).
American director.
The Beniker Gang (TV) 83. Follow That Bird 85. Vibes 88. He Said, She Said (co-d) 91. *Dunston Checks In* 95. The Beautician and the Beast 97, etc.

Kwon-Taek, Im (1936–).
Leading South Korean film director with a growing reputation in the West.
Testimony/Jungon 74. The Family Tree Book/Jokbo 78. The Hidden Hero/Gitbal Obnun Gisu 79. *Mandala* 81. Village in the Mist/Angemaeul 83. Gilsodom 85. Ticket 86. Surrogate Woman 86. Diary of Yonsan/Yonsan Ilgi 87. Son of a General 91. Son of a General II 92. Taebaek Sanmaek 95, etc.

Kwouk, Burt (1930–).
Chinese-English character actor.
Goldfinger 64. You Only Live Twice 68. The Most Dangerous Man in the World 69. Deep End 71. The Return of the Pink Panther 75. The Last Remake of Beau Geste 77. The Fiendish Plot of Dr Fu Manchu 81. Trail of the Pink Panther 82. Plenty 85. Empire of the Sun 87. Air America 90. Son of the Pink Panther 93. Bullet to Beijing 95, etc.

Kydd, Sam (1917–1982).
British character comedian whose sharp features were seen in many films from 1945.
The Captive Heart 45. The Small Back Room 48. Treasure Island 50. The Cruel Sea 53. The Quatermass Experiment 55. I'm All Right Jack 59. Follow That Horse 60. Island of Terror 66, etc.

Kyo, Machiko (1924–) (Motoko Yamo).
Japanese actress.
Rashomon 50. Gate of Hell 52. The Teahouse of the August Moon 56. Ugetsu Monogatari 58. Floating Weeds 59. The Great Wall 62. Thousand Cranes 69. The Family 70. Kesho 85, etc.

Kyser, Kay (1897–1985).
Mild-mannered American bandleader who made a number of comedy films in the early 40s, then retired to become an active Christian Scientist.
■ That's Right You're Wrong 39. You'll Find Out 40. Playmates 41. My Favorite Spy 42. Around the World 43. Swing Fever 44. Carolina Blues 44.

L

La Bern, Arthur.
British novelist whose low-life novels brought some realism into films of the 40s, although they cannot now stand comparison with such films of the 60s as *Saturday Night and Sunday Morning*.
Good-Timer Girl (from *Night Darkens the Streets*) 47. It Always Rains on Sundays 47. Paper Orchid 49. Dead Man's Evidence (w) 62. Freedom to Die (w) 62. Incident at Midnight (w) 63. Frenzy (from *Goodbye Piccadilly, Farewell Leicester Square*) 71.

La Cava, Gregory (1892–1952).
American director, former cartoonist and writer; a delicate talent for comedy usually struggled against unsatisfactory vehicles. He was impersonated by Allan Arbus in *W. C. Fields and Me*.
His Nibs 22. The New Schoolteacher 24. Womanhandled 25. Running Wild 27. Feel My Pulse 28. Laugh and Get Rich 31. Symphony of Six Million 32. The Half-Naked Truth 32. Gabriel over the White House 32. Affairs of Cellini 34. What Every Woman Knows 34. Private Worlds 35. She Married Her Boss 35. *My Man Godfrey* (AAN) 36. *Stage Door* (AAN) 37. Fifth Avenue Girl 39. The Primrose Path 40. Unfinished Business 41. Lady in a Jam 42. Living in a Big Way 47. One Touch of Venus 48, etc.

La Frenais, Ian (c. 1938–).
British comedy writer who works in conjunction with Dick Clement.

La Marr, Barbara (1896–1926) (Reatha Watson).
La Marr, Barbara
Sultry American leading lady of silent movies, a former dancer. She married five times, once bigamously, and was romantically linked with producer Paul Bern, who helped her by writing *The Girl from Montmartre* for her after her career faltered in the mid-20s, following a nervous breakdown. Died from an overdose of sleeping pills.
The Prisoner of Zenda 22. The Eternal City 23. Thy Name Is Woman 24. The Shooting of Dan McGrew 24. The Girl from Montmartre 26, etc.

La Planche, Rosemary (1923–1979).
American leading lady of the 40s.
Mad about Music 38. The Falcon in Danger 43. Prairie Chickens 43. Devil Bat's Daughter 46, etc.

La Plante, Laura (1904–1996).
Blonde American leading lady of Universal pictures in the 20s.
Burning Words 23. The Ramblin' Kidd 23. Sporting Youth 24. The Dangerous Blonde 24. Smouldering Fires 25. Skinner's Dress Suit 26. The Beautiful Cheat 26. Silk Stockings 27. The Cat and the Canary 27. The Last Warning 28. Show Boat 29. The Love Trap 29. Captain of the Guard 30. Little Mister Jim 46. Spring Reunion 56, etc.

La Rocque, Rod (1896–1969) (Roderick la Rocque de la Rour).
Popular American leading man of the silent screen, in Hollywood from 1914 after circus experience. He was married to actress Vilma Banky.
The Snow Man 14. The Lightbearer 16. Efficiency Edgar's Courtship 17. The Venus Model 18. The Ten Commandments 23. Forbidden Paradise 25. Resurrection 26. Our Modern Maidens 28. Let Us Be Gay 29. One Romantic Night 30. SOS Iceberg 33. Till We Meet Again 36. The Hunchback of Notre Dame 40. Dr Christian Meets the Women 41. Meet John Doe 41, many others.

La Rue, Danny (1927–) (Daniel Patrick Carroll).
British revue star and female impersonator.
■ Our Miss Fred 72.

La Rue, Jack (1903–1984) (Gaspare Biondolillo).
Grim-faced American actor, typed as gangster from the early 30s.
Lady Killer 34. Captains Courageous 37. Paper Bullets 41. Gentleman from Dixie (a rare sympathetic part) 41. Machine Gun Mama 44. No Orchids for Miss Blandish (GB) (as the maniacal Slim Grisson) 48. Robin Hood of Monterey 49. Ride the Man Down 53. Robin and the Seven Hoods 64. Won Ton Ton 76, many others.

La Rue, Lash (c. 1915–1996) (Alfred La Rue).
American star of low-budget westerns of the 40s, noted for dressing in black and for his way with a 15-foot bullwhip. After the vogue for westerns passed, he worked in carnivals as the King of the Bullwhip, later became an evangelist, was arrested on charges of vagrancy and possessing marijuana, attempted suicide and died poor. He claimed to have been married 10 times.
Song of Old Wyoming 45. The Caravan Trail 46. Wild West 46. Return of the Lash 47. Law of the Lash 47. Ghost Town Renegades 47. Stage to Mesa City 48. Mark of the Lash 49. The Son of Billy the Kid 49. Dead Man's Gold 49. The Dalton's Women 50. King of the Bullwhip 50. Black Lash 51. The Dark Power 85. Stagecoach (TV) 86. Pair of Aces (TV) 90, etc.
TV series: Lash of the West 52–53.

La Shelle, Joseph (1903–1989).
American cinematographer.
Happy Land 43. *Laura* (AA) 44. *Hangover Square* 44. The Foxes of Harrow 47. Come to the Stable 49. Mister 880 50. Les Misérables 52. Marty 55. Storm Fear 55. *The Bachelor Party* 57. I Was a Teenage Werewolf 57. No Down Payment 57 The Naked and the Dead 58. The Apartment 60. Irma la Douce 63. The Fortune Cookie 66. The Chase 66. Barefoot in the Park 67. Kona Coast 68. Eighty Steps to Jonah 69, many others.

Laage, Barbara (1925–) (Claire Colombat).
French leading lady of several 50s films.
La Putain Respectueuse 52. L'Esclave Blanche 54. Act of Love 54. Un Homme à Vendre 58. Paris Blues 61. Domicile Conjugal 71. Private Projection 76, etc.

LaBruce, Bruce (1969–).
Canadian actor, director and writer of independent films, on homosexual themes. He studied at Ryerson University in Toronto.
No Skin off My Ass 92. Super 8½ 94. Hustler White 96.

LaBute, Neil (1963–).
American director, screenwriter and playwright, born in Detroit, Michigan. A Mormon, he studied at Brigham Young University, the University of Kansas and New York University, and is a former teacher of drama.
In the Company of Men 97. Your Friends & Neighbors 98.
❝ I tend to be one of those writers who taps the glass, gets the scorpions angry, but sits at a safe distance and watches. – *N.L.*

Lacey, Catherine (1904–1979).
British stage and screen actress, adept at sympathetic spinsters and eccentric types.
The Lady Vanishes (debut) 38. Cottage to Let 41. I Know Where I'm Going 45. *The October Man* 47. Whisky Galore 49. Rockets Galore 56. Crack in the Mirror 60. The Fighting Prince of Donegal (as Queen Elizabeth I) 66. The Sorcerers 67, etc.

Lacey, Ronald (1935–1991).
Solidly built British character actor.
The Likely Lads 76. Charleston (TV) 77. Zulu Dawn 79. Raiders of the Lost Ark 80. Firefox 82. Invitation to the Wedding 84. Sword of the Valiant 85. Red Sonja 85. Valmont 89, etc.

Lachman, Ed(ward) (1946–).
American cinematographer.
The Lords of Flatbush 74. Stroszek 77. Lightning over Water 80. Union City 80. Say Amen, Somebody 83. Desperately Seeking Susan 85. True Stories 86. Making Mr Right 87. Less than Zero 87. Catchfire 90. Mississippi Masala 91. London Kills Me 91. Light Sleeper 91. My New Gun 92. My Family/Mia Familia 95. Selena 97. Touch 97. Why Do Fools Fall in Love 98. The Virgin Suicides 98, etc.

Lachman, Harry (1886–1975).
Anglo-American director, at his best in the 30s.
Weekend Wives 28. Under the Greenwood Tree 29. The Yellow Mask 30. The Outsider 30. The Compulsory Husband 30. Aren't We All 32. Insult 32. Paddy the Next Best Thing 33. Baby Take a Bow 34. *Dante's Inferno* 35. Charlie Chan at the Circus 36. *Our Relations* 36. The Devil Is Driving 37. No Time to Marry 38. They Came by Night 40. Dead Men Talk 41. The Loves of Edgar Allan Poe 42, etc.

Lackteen, Frank (1894–1968).
American character actor of Russian origin; his sharp features were adaptable to many ethnic roles.
Less Than the Dust 16. The Avenging Arrow 21. The Virgin 24. Hawk of the Hills 27. Hell's Valley 31. Escape from Devil's Island 35. Anthony Adverse 36. Suez 38. Juarez 39. Moon over Burma 40. The Sea Wolf 41. Chetniks 43. Can't Help Singing 44. Frontier Gal 45. Maneater of Kumaon 48. Daughter of the Jungle 49. King of the Khyber Rifles 53. Bengal Brigade 54. Devil Goddess 55. Requiem for a Gunfighter 65, many others.

Ladd, Alan (1913–1964).
Unsmiling, pint-sized tough-guy American star who proved to be just the kind of hero the 40s wanted. Born in Hot Springs, Arkansas, he worked in a variety of jobs, including as a grip on the Warner lot, before beginning to get small roles on stage and in films. Handicapped by his size – he was 5 feet 5 inches tall – and his lack of expression, he nevertheless became a star with *This Gun for Hire*, in which he played, for the first of several times, opposite Veronica Lake; by 1947 he was among the top ten stars. He never displayed much interest in the techniques of acting. According to Robert Emmett Dolan, one of Ladd's friends met him and said that he'd noticed the star was about to start a new picture. Ladd replied that he'd yet to read the script. 'That must be kind of disturbing,' said his friend. 'Sure is,' said Ladd. 'I don't know what I'm going to wear.' His career declined from the early 50s, a slump exacerbated by his heavy drinking. He died as the result of an overdose of sleeping pills combined with a high level of alcohol, a probable suicide. His career owed much to his second wife, agent and former actress Sue Carol. He was the father of producer Alan Ladd, Jnr.
Biography: 1979, *Ladd* by Beverly Linet.
■ Once in a Lifetime 32. Pigskin Parade 36. Last Train from Madrid 37. Souls at Sea 37. Born to the West 37. Hold 'em Navy 37. The Goldwyn Follies 38. Come on Leathernecks 38. The Green Hornet 39. Rulers of the Sea 39. Beast of Berlin 39. Light of Western Stars 40. Gangs of Chicago 40. Her First Romance (reissued as The Right Man) 40. In Old Missouri 40. The Howards of Virginia 40. Those Were the Days 40. Captain Caution 40. Wildcat Bus 40. Meet the Missus 40. Great Guns 41. Citizen Kane 41. Cadet Girl 41. Petticoat Politics 41. The Black Cat 41. The Reluctant Dragon 41. Paper Bullets 41. Joan of Paris 42. *This Gun for Hire* 42. *The Glass Key* 42. Lucky Jordan 42. Star Spangled Rhythm 42. China 43. And Now Tomorrow 44. Salty O'Rourke 45. Duffy's Tavern 45. *The Blue Dahlia* 46. O.S.S. 46. Two Years Before the Mast 46. Calcutta 47. Variety Girl 47. Wild Harvest 47. My Favourite Brunette 47 (cameo). Saigon 48. Beyond Glory 48. Whispering Smith 48. *The Great Gatsby* 49. Chicago Deadline 49. Captain Carey USA 50. Branded 51. Appointment with Danger 51. Red Mountain 52. The Iron Mistress 53. Thunder in the East 53. Desert Legion 53. *Shane* 53. Botany Bay 53. The Red Beret (GB) 53. Saskatchewan 54. Hell Below Zero (GB) 54. The Black Knight (GB) 54. Drum Beat 54. The McConnell Story 55. Hell on Frisco Bay 55. Santiago 56. The Big Land 57. Boy on a Dolphin 57. The Deep Six 58. The Proud Rebel 58. The Badlanders 58. The Man in the Net 58. Guns of the Timberland 60. All the Young Men 60. One Foot in Hell 60. Duel of the Champions (It.) 61. 13 West Street 62. *The Carpetbaggers* 64.
❝ I have the face of an ageing choirboy and the build of an undernourished featherweight. If you can figure out my success on the screen you're a better man than I. – *A.L.*
A small boy's idea of a tough guy. – *Raymond Chandler*
That man had stature even if he was short. – *Stewart Granger*
He succeeded in reducing murder to an act as casual as crossing the street. – *Richard Schickel*
Nobody ever pretended he could act. He got to the top, therefore, by a combination of determination and luck. – *David Shipman*
∼Ladd is said to have turned down both the James Dean role in *Giant* and the Spencer Tracy role in *Bad Day at Black Rock*.

Ladd, Alan, Jnr (1937–).
American producer and production executive, a former agent, the son of actor Alan Ladd. He became president of Fox in the mid-70s before leaving to found The Ladd Company. From the mid-80s he had an on-and-off relationship in charge of the troubled MGM/UA, finally resigning from the companies in 1993 to join Paramount.
The Night Comes 71. Fear Is the Key 72. Divine Madness 80. Outland 81. Chariots of Fire 81. Blade Runner 82. Five Days One Summer 82. Lovesick 83. Twice upon a Time 83. Braveheart 95. A Very Brady Sequel 96. The Phantom 96. The Man in the Iron Mask 98, etc.

Ladd, Cheryl (1951–) (Cheryl Stoppelmoor).
American leading lady who became familiar on TV as one of *Charlie's Angels* 78–81.
Satan's School for Girls 73. Evil in the Deep 76. Now and Forever 82. Grace Kelly (TV) 83. Purple Hearts 84. Romance on the Orient Express (TV) 85. Millennium 89. Lisa 90. Poison Ivy 92. Dancing with Danger (TV) 94. Permanent Midnight 98, etc.
TV series: One West Waikiki 94.

Ladd, Diane (1932–) (Diane Ladner).
American character actress, born in Meridian, Mississippi. She was formerly married to actor Bruce Dern, and is the mother of actress Laura Dern.
White Lightning 73. Chinatown 74. *Alice Doesn't Live Here Any More* (AAN) 75. Thaddeus Rose and Eddie (TV) 78. Willa 79. Cattle Annie and Little Britches 80. Guyana Tragedy (TV) 80.

All Night Long 81. Grace Kelly (TV) 83. Something Wicked This Way Comes 83. Wild at Heart (AAN) 90. A Kiss before Dying 91. Rambling Rose (AAN) 91. The Cemetery Club 93. Carnosaur 93. Father Hood 93. Mrs Munck (& wd) 95. Raging Angels 95. Nixon 95. Precious 96. Citizen Ruth (uncredited) 96. Family of Cops II: Breach of Faith 97. Primary Colors 98, etc.
TV series: Alice 80–81.

Laemmle, Carl (1867–1939).
German-American pioneer, in films from 1906; produced *Hiawatha* 09, founded Universal Pictures 1912.
Biography: 1931, *The Life and Adventures of Carl Laemmle* by John Drinkwater.
❝ Uncle Carl Laemmle
Had a very large faemmle. – *Ogden Nash, satirizing the number of Laemmle relations who were found jobs at Universal Studios*
I hope I didn't make a mistake coming out here. – *C.L., Hollywood, 1915*
The prototype of the slightly mad movie mogul – impulsive, quixotic, intrepid, unorthodox, unpredictable. – *Norman Zierold*

Laemmle, Carl, Jnr (1908–1979).
Son of Carl Laemmle; executive producer at Universal for many years. Credited with the success of *Frankenstein*, *Dracula*, and *All Quiet on the Western Front*.

Laffan, Patricia (1919–).
British stage actress.
The Rake's Progress 45. Caravan 46. Quo Vadis (as Poppea) 51. Devil Girl from Mars 54. Twenty-Three Paces to Baker Street 56. Crooks in Cloisters 64, etc.

Lafont, Bernadette (1938–).
Busy French leading actress, a former dancer, who has made more than 90 films.
Le Beau Serge 58. Web of Passion 59. Les Bonnes Femmes 60. Compartiment Tueurs/The Sleeping Car Murder 65. Le Voleur/The Thief 67. Catch Me a Spy 71. Une Belle Fille Comme Moi 72. Tendre Dracula 74. La Tortue sur le Dos 78. Il Ladrone 79. Le Roi des Cons 81. Cap Canaille 83. Inspector Lavardin 86. Waiting for the Moon 87. L'Air de Rien 89. Le Bonheur 94. Personne Ne M'Aime 94. Nine Months/Neuf Mois 94. Zadoc et le Bonheur 95, etc.

LaGarde, Jocelyn (1922–1979).
Tahitian-born actress who was nominated for a Best Supporting Actress Oscar for her only film, *Hawaii* 66.

Lagercrantz, Marika (1954–).
Swedish leading actress, best known internationally for the role of a teacher who has an affair with a 15-year-old boy in *Love Lessons*.
The Dive/Dykket 89. Hotell Cansino 91. Grandpa's Journey/Morfars Resa 92. Black Harvest/Sort Host 93. Against the Odds/Alskar, Alskar Inte 95. Love Lessons/All Things Fair/Lust och Fägring Stor 95. Vendetta 95. Nu är pappa trött igen! 96. Lithivm 98, etc.

LaGravenese, Richard (1959–).
American screenwriter turned director.
Rude Awakening 89. The Fisher King (AAN) 91. The Ref/Hostile Hostages 94. *The Bridges of Madison County* 95. A Little Princess 95. The Mirror Has Two Faces (w) 96. The Horse Whisperer (co-w) 98. Beloved (co-w) 98. Living Out Loud (wd) 98, etc.

Lahr, Bert (1895–1967) (Irving Lahrheim).
Wry-faced American vaudeville comedian who made occasional film appearances.
Biography: 1969, *Notes on a Cowardly Lion* by John Lahr (his son).
Faint Heart 31. Flying High 31. Love and Hisses 37. Josette 38. Just around the Corner 38. Zaza 39. *The Wizard of Oz* 39. Ship Ahoy 42. Meet the People 44. Always Leave Them Laughing 49. Mr Universe 51. Rose Marie 54. The Second Greatest Sex 56. The Night They Raided Minsky's 68, etc.
❝ After *The Wizard of Oz* I was typecast as a lion, and there aren't all that many parts for lions. – *B.L.*
The last and the most marvellous of the American clowns cradled by burlesque. – *Alastair Cooke*

Lahti, Christine (1950–).
American character actress, often in off-beat roles. Married director Thomas Schlamme in 1984.
. . . And Justice for All 79. The Henderson Monster (TV) 80. Whose Life Is It, Anyway? 81. The Executioner's Song (TV) 82. Ladies and Gentlemen, the Fabulous Stains 82. Swing Shift (AAN) 84. Single Bars, Single Women (TV) 84. Love Lives On (TV) 85. Just between Friends 86. Stacking 87. Housekeeping 87. Running on Empty 88. Gross Anatomy 89. Miss Firecracker 89. No Place Like Home (TV) 89. Funny about Love 90. The Doctor 91. Leaving Normal 92. The Fear Inside 92. Hideaway 95. Pie in the Sky 95. Liberman in Love (co-d, short) (AA) 96. A Weekend in the Country (TV) 96. Hope (TV) 97, etc.
TV series: Chicago Hope 95– .

Lai, Francis (1932–).
French film composer.
Un Homme et une Femme 66. Mayerling 68. House of Cards 68. Rider on the Rain 70. *Love Story* (AA) 71. Le Petit Matin 71. Emmanuelle 75. Seven Suspects for Murder 77. International Velvet 78. Oliver's Story 78. Second Chance 80. Beyond the Reef 81. Edith and Marcel 83. My New Partner/Les Ripoux 84. Marie 85. A Man and a Woman: 20 Years Later 86. Dark Eyes/Ocie Ciornie 87. Keys to Freedom 89. Too Beautiful for You/Trop Belle pour Toi 89. My New Partner 2/Ripoux contre Ripoux 90. The Beautiful Story/La Belle Histoire 91. Stranger in the House/L'Inconnu dans la Maison 92. Tout Ça . . . Pour Ça . . . ! 93. Luck or Coincidence/Hasards ou Coincidences (co-m) 98, etc.

Laine, Frankie (1913–) (Frank Paul Lo Vecchio).
American pop singer who made several light musicals in the 50s. He also sang the title song in *Gunfight at the O.K. Corral* and for the TV series *Rawhide*.
When You're Smiling 50. Make Believe Ballroom 50. The Sunny Side of the Street 51. Rainbow round My Shoulder 52. Bring Your Smile Along 55. He Laughed Last 56. Meet Me in Las Vegas 56, etc.

Laine, Jimmy:
see Ferrara, Abel.

Laird, Jenny (1917–).
British character actress.
Just William 39. The Lamp Still Burns 43. Black Narcissus 46. *Painted Boats* 47. The Long Dark Hall 51. Conspiracy of Hearts 60. The Horse without a Head 63, etc.

Lake, Arthur (1905–1987) (Arthur Silverlake).
Harrassed, crumple-faced American light comedy actor, best remembered as Dagwood Bumstead in the 'Blondie' series of 28 films in twelve years.
Jack and the Beanstalk 17. Skinner's Dress Suit 26. The Irresistible Lover 27. *Harold Teen* 28. On with the Show 29. Indiscreet 31. Midshipman Jack 33. Orchids to You 35. Topper 37. *Blondie* (and subsequent series) 38. Three is a Family 44. Sixteen Fathoms Deep 48, many others.
TV series: Blondie 54.

Lake, Florence (1904–1980).
American character comedienne best remembered as Edgar Kennedy's bird-brained wife in many of his two-reelers.

Lake, Lew (1874–1939).
British actor, from the theatre, who appeared in some popular 30s concert party films. His successful melodrama *The Bloomsbury Burglars*, performed in music halls in the early 1900s, gave the English language the nickname 'Jerry' to describe Germans in both the First and Second World Wars.
The Bloomsbury Burglars 12. Splinters 29. The Great Game 30. Splinters in the Navy 31. Splinters in the Air 37.

Lake, Ricki (1968–).
American actress, often in John Waters' films, and a successful television chat show hostess.
Hairspray 88. Working Girl 88. Cookie 89. Babycakes (TV) 89. Cry-Baby 90. Last Exit to Brooklyn 90. Where the Day Takes You 92. Cabin Boy 94. Serial Mom 94. Mrs Winterbourne 96, etc.

Lake, Veronica (1919–1973) (Constance Ockleman).
Petite American leading lady who now, with her limited acting ability and her 'peek a boo bang' (long blonde hair obscuring one eye), seems an appropriately artificial image for the Hollywood of the early 40s. Her second husband was André de Toth (1944–52).
Autobiography: 1968, *Veronica*.
■ All Women Have Secrets 39. Sorority House 39. Forty Little Mothers 40. *I Wanted Wings* 41. *Sullivan's Travels* 41. *This Gun for Hire* 42. The Glass Key 42. *I Married a Witch* 42. Star Spangled Rhythm 42. So Proudly We Hail 43. The Hour before the Dawn 44. Bring on the Girls 45. Out of this World 45. Duffy's Tavern 45. Hold That Blonde 45. Miss Susie Slagle's 45. *The Blue Dahlia* 46. Ramrod 47. Variety Girl 47. The Sainted Sisters 48. Saigon 48. Isn't It Romantic? 48. Slattery's Hurricane 49. Stronghold 52. Footsteps in the Snow 66. Flesh Feast 70.
❝ You could put all the talent I had into your left eye and still not suffer from impaired vision. – *V.L.*

LaLoggia, Frank (1955–).
American independent director, screenwriter, composer and occasional actor.
Fear No Evil (wd, m) 81. The Wizard of Speed and Time (a) 88. Lady in White (wd, m) 88. Mother (d) 94, etc.

Lam, Ringo (1954–).
Hong Kong-born director, screenwriter and producer, from television. He moved to Canada in the late 70s to study and became a Canadian citizen before returning to Hong Kong to make films. *City on Fire* was an influence on Quentin Tarantino's *Reservoir Dogs*.
Cupid One 85. Aces Go Places IV 86. *City on Fire* 87. Prison on Fire 87. School on Fire 88. Wild Search 90. Twin Dragons (co-d) 93. Full Contact 93. The Exchange (US) 96. Full Alert 97, etc.

Lamarque, Libertad (1908–).
Argentinian actress and singer, one of the most popular stars in Latin America, on stage and screen from childhood. She went to work in Mexico in the 50s because of a feud with Evita Perón, the president's wife.
Tango 33. Magic Kisses/Besos Brujos 37. The Law They Forgot 38. Una Vez en la Vida 41. Gran Casino 46. Soledad (Mex.) 47. La Loca (Mex.) 51. Rostros Olvidados (Mex.) 53. La Sonrisa de Mama (Mex.) 71. Black Is a Beautiful Colour (Mex.) 74, etc.

Lamarr, Hedy (1913–) (Hedwig Kiesler).
Austrian leading lady of the 30s and 40s, in Hollywood from 1937 after creating a sensation by appearing nude in the Czech film *Extase* 33. She became a household word for glamour, but lacked the spark of personality. The third of her six husbands was actor John Loder (1943–47).
Autobiography: 1966, *Ecstasy and Me*.
■ American films: *Algiers* 38. Lady of the Tropics 39. I Take This Woman 40. Boom Town 40. Comrade X 40. Come Live with Me 41. Ziegfeld Girl 41. H.M. Pulham Esq. 41. Tortilla Flat 42. Crossroads 42. *White Cargo* (as Tondelayo) 42. The Heavenly Body 43. The Conspirators 44. Experiment Perilous 44. Her Highness and the Bellboy 45. The Strange Woman 46. Dishonoured Lady 47. Let's Live a Little 48. *Samson and Delilah* 49. A Lady without Passport 50. Copper Canyon 50. My Favorite Spy 51. The Face that Launched a Thousand Ships 54. The Story of Mankind 57. The Female Animal 57.
❝ Any girl can be glamorous: all you have to do is stand still and look stupid. – *H.L.*
When she spoke one did not listen, one just watched her mouth moving and marvelled at the exquisite shapes made by her lips. – *George Sanders*
She married a European multimillionaire, Fritz Mandl, and was terribly unhappy in the marriage. She went to the opera with him one night, loaded down with a fortune in jewels. He kept these in his safe and only gave them to her to wear on important occasions. Halfway through the performance she told him that she was sick. 'I don't want to spoil your evening,' she said. 'I'll go home, but you stay and see the rest.' She convinced him, went home alone, took the suitcases she had packed and her jewels and took off. Eventually she ended up in Hollywood – *Paul Henreid*

Lamas, Fernando (1915–1982).
Argentinian leading man, in Hollywood from 1950 in routine musicals and comedies. He was married to actresses Arlene Dahl (1954–60) and Esther Williams.
Rich, Young and Pretty 51. The Law and the Lady 51. The Merry Widow 52. The Girl Who Had Everything 53. Sangaree 53. Rose Marie 54. The Girl Rush 55. The Lost World 60. The Violent Ones (& d) 67. 100 Rifles 69. Powder Keg 71. The Cheap Detective 78, etc.

Lamas, Lorenzo (1958–).
American leading man of action films. He is the son of actors Fernando Lamas and Arlene Dahl, and is married to actress Kathleen Kinmont.
100 Rifles 69. Grease 78. Tilt 78. Take Down 79. Body Rock 84. SnakeEater 89. SnakeEater 2: The Drug Buster 89. Final Impact 91. Killing Streets 91. Night of the Warrior 91. SnakeEater 3: His Law 92. Bounty Tracker 93. CIA Codename: Alexa 93. CIA 2: Target Alexa 94. Gladiator Cop: The Swordsman II 95. Blood for Blood 95. The Rage 96. Mask of Death 97, etc.
TV series: California Fever 79. Secrets of Midland Heights 80–81. Falcon Crest 81–90. Renegade 92–94.

Lamb, Gil (1906–1995).
Rubber-boned American comic, seen in many 40s musicals.
The Fleet's In (debut) 42. Rainbow Island 44. Practically Yours 44. Humphrey Takes a Chance 50. Terror in a Texas Town 58. Blackbeard's Ghost 67. Day of the Animals 77, etc.

Lambert, Christopher (1957–) (aka Christophe Lambert).
Franco-American leading man. He is married to actress Diane Lane.
Le Bar du Téléphone 80. Legitimate Violence 80. Greystoke: The Legend of Tarzan, Lord of the Apes 84. Love Songs/Paroles et Musique 84. Subway 85. Highlander 86. I Love You 86. The Sicilian 87. Love Dream 88. To Kill a Priest 88. Un Plan d'Enfer 89. Highlander II – the Quickening 91. Knight Moves 91. Fortress 93. Gunmen 93. Highlander III: The Sorcerer 94. Nine Months (Fr.) 94. The Hunted 95. Don't Forget You're Going to Die 95. Mortal Kombat 95. Nirvana 97. Beowulf 98, etc.
❝ Christophe has a beguiling innocence, a lot of energy and great charm. His only weakness is that when he kisses you on the cheek I think he assumes that you will never wash your cheek again. – *Joss Ackland*

Lambert, Constant (1905–1951).
British conductor whose one film score was *Anna Karenina* 47.

Lambert, Gavin (1924–).
British critic and novelist, in Hollywood since 1956. Stories about Hollywood: *The Slide Area*.
As scriptwriter: Bitter Victory 57. Sons and Lovers (AAN) 60. The Roman Spring of Mrs Stone 61. Inside Daisy Clover 65. I Never Promised You a Rose Garden (AAN) 77, etc.

Lambert, Jack (1899–1976).
Scottish character actor.
The Ghost Goes West 36. Nine Men 43. Hue and Cry 46. Eureka Stockade 47. The Brothers 47. The Lost Hours 50. The Sea Shall Not Have Them 54. Storm over the Nile 56. Reach for the Sky 56. Greyfriars Bobby 60. Modesty Blaise 66. Neither the Sea Nor the Sand 72, many others.

Lambert, Jack (1920–).
American character actor, usually an evil-eyed heavy.
The Cross of Lorraine 43. The Killers 46. The Unsuspected 47. The Enforcer 51. Scared Stiff 53. Kiss Me Deadly 55. Machine Gun Kelly 57. The George Raft Story 61. Four for Texas 63, many others.

Lambert, Mary.
American director.
Siesta 87. Pet Sematary 89. Pet Sematary II 92. Grand Isle 92. The Last Mardi Gras 92, etc.

Lambert, Paul (1922–1997).
American character actor, much on TV; born in El Paso, Texas.
Spartacus 60. Planet of the Apes 68. All the

Loving Couples 69. A Gunfight 70. Where Does It Hurt 72. The Execution of Private Slovik 74. All the President's Men 76. Death Wish II 81. Blue Thunder 82. A Soldier's Revenge 84, etc.
TV series: Executive Suite 76–77.

Lamble, Lloyd (1914–).
Australian light actor who has been in many British films as detective, official, or other man.
The Story of Gilbert and Sullivan 53. The Belles of St Trinian's 54. The Man Who Never Was 56. Quatermass II 57. Blue Murder at St Trinian's 58. No Trees in the Street 59. The Trials of Oscar Wilde 60. Term of Trial 62. Joey Boy 65. No Sex Please – We're British 73. And Now the Screaming Starts! 73. Eskimo Nell 74, etc.

Lamont, Charles (1898–1993).
American director, in Hollywood from silent days. With Universal from mid-30s, making comedies featuring Abbott and Costello; the Kettles, etc.
Love, Honour and Oh Baby 41. The Merry Monahans 44. Bowery to Broadway 44. Frontier Gal 45. The Runaround 46. Slave Girl 47. Baghdad 49. Flame of Araby 51. Abbott and Costello Meet Dr Jekyll and Mr Hyde 53. Ma and Pa Kettle in Paris 53. Untamed Heiress 54. Abbott and Costello Meet the Mummy 55. Francis in the Haunted House 56. The Kettles in the Ozarks 56, many others.

Lamont, Duncan (1918–).
Scottish actor with stage experience, in films since World War II.
The Golden Coach 53. *The Adventures of Quentin Durward* 56. Ben Hur 59. Mutiny on the Bounty 62. Murder at the Gallop 63. The Brigand of Kandahar 65. Arabesque 65. Decline and Fall 68. Pope Joan 72. Escape from the Dark 76, many others.

Lamont, Peter.
British art director and production designer, associated with the James Bond films. He began as a draughtsman on *Goldfinger*, later working as a set decorator and art director on the films before becoming the production designer of *For Your Eyes Only* and subsequent Bonds.
Fiddler on the Roof (AAN) 71. The Dove (US) 74. Inside Out 75. The Spy Who Loved Me (AAN) 77. For Your Eyes Only 81. Octopussy 83. On the Third Day 83. A View to a Kill 85. Aliens (US) (AAN) 86. The Living Daylights 87. License to Kill 87. The Taking of Beverly Hills (US) 91. True Lies (US) 94. GoldenEye 95. Titanic (AA) 97, etc.

Lamorisse, Albert (1922–1970).
French director known for short fantasy films.
Bim 49. *Crin Blanc* 52. *The Red Balloon* (AAw) 55. Stowaway in the Sky 61. Fifi La Plume 64, etc.

Lamour, Dorothy (1914–1996) (Dorothy Kaumeyer).
Good-humoured American leading lady of the 30s and 40s: became typed in sarong roles, and happily guyed her own image.
Autobiography: 1981, *Dorothy Lamour*, with Dick McInnes.
■ *The Jungle Princess* 36. Thrill of a Lifetime 37. Swing High Swing Low 37. Last Train from Madrid 37. High Wide and Handsome 37. *The Hurricane* 37. The Big Broadcast of 1938. Her Jungle Love 38. Spawn of the North 38. Tropic Holiday 38. St Louis Blues 39. Man About Town 39. Disputed Passage 39. Johnny Apollo 40. Typhoon 40. *Road to Singapore* 40. Moon Over Burma 40. Chad Hanna 40. Road to Zanzibar 41. Caught in the Draft 41. Aloma of the South Seas 41. The Fleet's In 42. Beyond the Blue Horizon 42. Road to Morocco 42. Star Spangled Rhythm 42. They Got Me Covered 43. Dixie 43. Riding High 43. And the Angels Sing 43. Rainbow Island 44. Road to Utopia 45. A Medal for Benny 45. Duffy's Tavern 45. Masquerade in Mexico 45. My Favorite Brunette 47. Road to Rio 47. Wild Harvest 47. Variety Girl 47. On Our Merry Way 48. Lulu Belle 48. The Girl from Manhattan 48. Slightly French 48. Manhandled 48. The Lucky Stiff 49. Here Comes the Groom 51. The Greatest Show on Earth 52. Road to Bali 52. Road to Hong Kong 62. Donovan's Reef 63. Pajama Party 64. The Phynx 70. Won Ton Ton 75. Death of Love House (TV) 76. Creepshow 2 87. Entertaining the Troops (doc) 88.

L'Amour, Louis (1908–1988).
Best-selling American writer of western novels, many of which have been filmed.
Hondo 53. Four Guns to the Border 54. Stranger on Horseback 54. The Burning Hills 56. The Tall Stranger 57. Apache Territory 58. Guns of the Timberland 59. Heller in Pink Tights 60. Taggart 64. Shalako 68. Catlow 71. The Man Called Noon 73, etc.

Lampedusa, Giuseppe (1896–1957).
Italian novelist, a nobleman whose *The Leopard* was filmed and gave a picture of 19th-century Sicily.

Lampert, Zohra (1936–).
American TV actress.
Splendour in the Grass 60. Pay or Die 60. A Fine Madness 66. Opening Night 77. Alphabet City 84. Teachers 84. Stanley and Iris 89, etc.

Lancaster, Burt (1913–1994).
Athletic American leading man and latterly distinguished actor. Former circus acrobat; acted and danced in soldier shows during World War II.
Biography: 1995, *Against Type: The Biography of Burt Lancaster* by Larry Fishgall.
■ *The Killers* 46. Desert Fury 47. I Walk Alone 47. *Brute Force* 47. Variety Girl (cameo) 47. Sorry, Wrong Number 48. Kiss the Blood Off My Hands 48. All My Sons 48. Criss Cross 49. Rope of Sand 49. Mister 880 50. *The Flame and the Arrow* 50. Vengeance Valley 51. Ten Tall Men 51. Jim Thorpe All-American 51. The Crimson Pirate 52. *Come Back Little Sheba* 53. South Sea Woman 53. From Here to Eternity (AAN) 53. His Majesty O'Keefe 54. Apache 54. *Vera Cruz* 54. The Kentuckian (& d) 55. The Rose Tattoo 55. Trapeze 56. The Rainmaker 57. *Gunfight at the OK Corral* (as Wyatt Earp) 57. Sweet Smell of Success 57. Separate Tables 58. Run Silent Run Deep 58. The Devil's Disciple (GB) 59. The Unforgiven 59. *Elmer Gantry* (AA) 60. The Young Savages 61. Judgment at Nuremberg 61. *Birdman of Alcatraz* (AAN) 62. A Child is Waiting 62. The Leopard 63. The List of Adrian Messenger 63. Seven Days in May 64. The Train 64. The Hallelujah Trail 65. *The Professionals* 66. *The Swimmer* 67. The Scalphunters 68. Castle Keep 69. The Gypsy Moths 69. Airport 69. Lawman 70. Valdez is Coming 71. Ulzana's Raid 72. Scorpio 73. Executive Action 73. The Midnight Man (& co-p, co-d) 74. Conversation Piece 75. Moses (TV) 75. Buffalo Bill and the Indians 76. *1900* 76. Twilight's Last Gleaming 76. Victory at Entebbe (TV) 76. The Cassandra Crossing 77. The Island of Dr Moreau 77. Go Tell the Spartans 78. Zulu Dawn 79. Atlantic City USA (BFA, AAN) 80. Cattle Annie and Little Britches 80. Marco Polo (TV) 81. Local Hero 83. The Osterman Weekend 83. Scandal Sheet (TV) 85. Little Treasure 85. On Wings of Eagles (TV) 85. Tough Guys 86. Barnum (TV) 86. Rocket Gibraltar 88. Field of Dreams 89. Phantom of the Opera (TV) 90.
✪ For enthusiasm, shrewdness and agility. *The Flame and the Arrow*.
❝ Life is to be lived within the limits of your knowledge and within the concept of what you would like to see yourself to be. – *B.L.*
If I'm working with frightened people, I do tend to dominate them. I'm no doll, that's for sure. – *B.L.*
Most people seem to think I'm the kind of guy who shaves with a blowtorch. Actually I'm bookish and worrisome. – *B.L.*
Before he can pick up an ashtray he discusses his motivation for a couple of hours. You want to tell him to pick up the ashtray and shut up. – *Jeanne Moreau*

Lanchester, Elsa (1902–1986) (Elizabeth Sullivan).
British character actress married to Charles Laughton. On stage and screen in Britain before settling in Hollywood in 1940.
Autobiographies: 1968, *Charles Laughton and I*. 1983, *Elsa Lanchester Herself*.
Bluebottles 28. *The Private Life of Henry VIII* 32. David Copperfield 35. *The Bride of Frankenstein* 35. The Ghost Goes West 36. *Rembrandt* 37. Vessel of Wrath 38. Ladies in Retirement 41. Tales of Manhattan 42. The Spiral Staircase 45. End of the Rainbow 47. The Inspector-General 49. Come to the Stable (AAN) 49. Androcles and the Lion 53. Bell, Book and Candle 57. *Witness for the Prosecution* (AAN) 57. Mary Poppins 64. Blackbeard's Ghost 67. Me, Natalie 69. Willard 71. Terror in the Wax Museum 73. *Murder by Death* 76, many others.
TV series: The John Forsythe Show 65.

Landau, David (1878–1935).
American character actor, familiar in early talkies as crook or roughneck.
I Take This Woman 31. Street Scene 31. Taxi 32. Polly of the Circus 32. Horse Feathers 32. I Am a Fugitive from a Chain Gang 32. She Done Him Wrong 33. One Man's Journey 33. Wharf Angel 34. Judge Priest 34, etc.

Landau, Ely (1920–1993).
American producer, former distributor.
Long Day's Journey into Night 62. The Pawnbroker 64. All productions of the American Film Theatre 72–74. Hopscotch 80. The Holcroft Covenant 85, etc.

Landau, Martin (1928–).
Gaunt American actor often in sinister roles.
North by Northwest 59. The Gazebo 59. Cleopatra 62. The Hallelujah Trail 65. Nevada Smith 66. They Call Me Mr Tibbs 70. Savage (TV) 72. Black Gunn 72. Blazing Magnum 76. Meteor 79. Without Warning 80. Alone in the Dark 82. Sweet Revenge 87. W.A.R. Women Against Rape 87. Empire State 87. *Tucker: The Man and His Dream* (AAN) 88. *Crimes and Misdemeanors* (AAN) 89. Neon Empire 89. Paint It Black 90. Real Bullets 90. The Color of Evening 91. Ganglands 91. Treasure Island 91. Mistress 92. Sliver 93. Intersection 94. Time Is Money 94. Eye of the Stranger 94. *Ed Wood* (as Bela Lugosi) (AA) 94. City Hall 96. The Adventures of Pinocchio 96. BAPS 97. The X Files Movie 98, etc.
TV series: Mission Impossible 66–68. Space 1999 75–76.

Landen, Dinsdale (1931–).
British stage actor who makes occasional films.
Operation Snatch 62. Rasputin the Mad Monk 66. Every Home Should Have One 70. Digby 71. International Velvet 78. Morons from Outer Space 85. The Steal 95, etc.
TV series: Devenish 77–78. Pig in the Middle 80–83.

Landers, Lew (1901–1962) (Lewis Friedlander).
American director of 'B' pictures, especially westerns, from silent days.
The Raven 35. The Man Who Found Himself 37. Canal Zone 39. Pacific Liner 39. The Boogie Man Will Get You 42. Return of the Vampire 43. The Enchanted Forest 46. State Penitentiary 49. Man in the Dark (in 3-D) 53. Captain Kidd and the Slave Girl 53. Hot Rod Gang 58. Terrified 62, many others.

Landeta, Matilde (1910–).
Mexican director. Born in San Luis Posi, she began as a continuity girl in the 30s and turned to directing in the late 40s, but prejudice made it difficult for her to continue her career, and she turned to writing and making short films. She was the subject of a 30-minute TV documentary, *Matilde Landeta – My Film-making, My Life* (GB) 90, directed by Patricia Diaz.
Lola Casanova 48. La Negra Augustias 49. Trotacalles 51. Islas Revillagigedo (doc) 90. Nocturno a Rosario (p, wd) 92, etc.

Landi, Elissa (1904–1948) (Elizabeth Kuhnelt).
Austrian-Italian leading lady, in international films of the 30s.
Underground 29. Children of Chance 30. Always Goodbye 31. The Yellow Ticket 31. Passport to Hell 32. *The Sign of the Cross* 32. The Masquerader 33. The Warrior's Husband 33. By Candlelight 34. Sisters under the Skin 34. *The Count of Monte Cristo* 34. Without Regret 35. Enter Madame 35. The Amateur Gentleman 36. After the Thin Man 36. The Thirteenth Chair 37. Corregidor 43, etc.

Landi, Marla (c. 1937–).
Italian leading lady and model, in British films.
Across the Bridge 57. First Man into Space 58. The Hound of the Baskervilles 59. Pirates of Blood River 61. The Murder Game 65, etc.

Landis, Carole (1919–1948) (Frances Ridste).
Uninhibited blonde American leading actress. Born in Fairchild, Wisconsin, she was working as a singer and dancer in nightclubs in her mid-teens, and was in films from the age of 18, first attracting attention clad in animal skins in *One Million BC*. Her best role was as herself in *Four Jills in a Jeep*, about her tour with Martha Raye, Kay Francis and Mitzi Mayfair, entertaining troops during the Second World War. Married four times, the first at the age of 15, she committed suicide over a failing love affair with actor Rex Harrison, which coincided with a decline in her career, as her unconventional attitudes alienated studio heads. Her lovers included Busby Berkeley, Darryl Zanuck and Jacqueline Susann, who used her as the model for the character Jennifer in her novel *Valley of the Dolls*.
Man and His Mate/One Million BC 40. *Turnabout* 40. Road Show 41. Topper Returns 41. Hot Spot 41. Orchestra Wives 42. Wintertime 43. Having Wonderful Crime 44. Behind Green Lights 45. It Shouldn't Happen to a Dog 46. A Scandal in Paris 46. Out of the Blue 47. The Brass Monkey (GB) 48. Noose (GB) 48, etc.
❝ I think I've always been a sucker. By sucker I mean someone who is very vulnerable, who wears her heart on her sleeve, who is easily hurt, who, in fact, almost asks to be hurt. – *C.L.*
I don't say she was a talented actress, but she was a beautiful girl, and full of life, and could certainly have fitted into many parts. – *Rex Harrison*

Landis, Cullen (1896–1975).
American silent screen hero.
Who Is Number One 17. Beware of Blondes 18. Almost a Husband 19. Born Rich 24, many others.

Landis, Jessie Royce (1904–1972) (Jessie Royce Medbury).
American character actress of long stage experience; usually in fluttery comedy roles.
Autobiography: 1954, *You Won't Be So Pretty*.
■ Derelict 30. Mr Belvedere Goes to College 49. It Happens Every Spring 49. My Foolish Heart 49. Mother Didn't Tell Me 50. Meet Me Tonight (GB) 51. *To Catch a Thief* 55. The Swan 56. The Girl He Left Behind 56. My Man Godfrey 57. I Married a Woman 58. *North by Northwest* 59. A Private's Affair 59. Goodbye Again 61. Bon Voyage 62. Boys' Night Out 62. Critic's Choice 63. Gidget Goes To Rome 63. Airport 69. Mr and Mrs Bo Jo Jones (TV) 71.
Famous line (*North by Northwest*): 'You gentlemen are not really trying to murder my son, are you?'

Landis, John (1950–).
American director.
Schlock 76. Kentucky Fried Movie 77. National Lampoon's Animal House 78. The Blues Brothers 80. *An American Werewolf in London* 81. Twilight Zone 83. Trading Places 83. The Muppets Take Manhattan (cameo) 84. Into the Night 85. Spies Like Us 85. Three Amigos 86. Amazon Women on the Moon (co-d) 87. Coming to America 88. Darkman (a) 90. Oscar 91. Sleepwalkers (a) 92. Innocent Blood 92. Beverly Hills Cop III 94. The Stand (TV) (a) 94. The Stupids 96. Mad City (a) 97. Quicksilver Highway (a) (TV) 97. Blues Brothers 2000 (co-w, d) 98. Susan's Plan (wd) 98, etc.
❝ When *Animal House* turned out the way it did, they all rushed to me with barrels of money begging me to make them rich. – *J.L.*

Landon, Michael (1937–1991) (Eugene Orowitz).
American leading man best known as Little Joe in TV series *Bonanza* 59–73. He also wrote and directed many episodes of the series. Born in Long Island, New York, he went to the University of California on an athletic scholarship, but dropped out to work in various occupations and to study acting briefly before finding work in television. Married three times, he had nine children. Died of cancer.
I Was a Teenage Werewolf 57. God's Little Acre 58. The Legend of Tom Dooley 59, etc.
TV series: Little House on the Prairie 74–82. Highway to Heaven 84–89.
～A TV movie about Landon's young manhood, *Sam's Son*, was released in 1984.

Landone, Avice (1910–1976).
British stage actress, usually in cool, unruffled roles.
My Brother Jonathan 48. The Franchise Affair 51. An Alligator Named Daisy 55. Reach for the Sky 56. Carve Her Name with Pride 58. Operation Cupid 60, etc.

Landres, Paul (1912–).
American director, former editor.
Oregon Passage 57. The Vampire 57. The Miracle of the Hills 58. The Flame Barrier 58. The Return of Dracula 58. Son of a Gunfighter 65, etc.

Landru, Henri Désiré (1869–1922).
The story of the French murderer who killed 10 women for their money has been told several times on film, usually in a fictional guise and most notably by Charlie Chaplin in *Monsieur Verdoux* 47, and also in *Bluebeard's Ten Honeymoons* 60, starring George Sanders, and Claude Chabrol's *Landru* 62. Other films that draw on the story, and also on the folk-tale of Bluebeard, include Edward Dmytryk's *Bluebeard* 72, starring Richard Burton, and Sam Wood's *Bluebeard* 23, with Huntley Gordon and Gloria Swanson, which was remade by Ernst Lubitsch in 1938, starring Gary Cooper and Claudette Colbert.

Lane, Allan 'Rocky' (1900–1973) (Harry Albershart).
American cowboy star of the 30s, former athlete.
Night Nurse 32. Maid's Night Out 38. The Dancing Masters 44. Trail of Robin Hood 51. The Saga of Hemp Brown 58. Hell Bent for Leather 60, many second features.
TV series: Mister Ed (voice) 62–64.

Lane, Burton (1912–1997) (Burton Levy).
American composer and screenwriter. Born in New York, he began writing songs in his teens, then went to work for MGM in the 30s, where his lyricists included Harold ADAMSON, Frank LOESSER and Ralph FREED. His collaboration with E. Y. 'Yip' HARBURG led to the Broadway musical *Finian's Rainbow* 47, filmed in 1968. His other Broadway hit, *On a Clear Day You Can See Forever* 65, written with Alan Jay LERNER, was filmed in 1970. He also wrote the Broadway musical *Carmelina* 78, based on the film *Buona Sera Mrs Campbell*.
Dancing Lady 33. Cocoanut Grove 38. St Louis Blues 39. Babes on Broadway (AANs 'How About You') 41. Ship Ahoy 42. Rainbow Island 44. Royal Wedding (AANs 'Too Late Now') 51. Give a Girl a Break 53. Jupiter's Darling 54. Affair in Havana (co-w) 57. The Adventures of Huckleberry Finn 60. Heidi's Song 82, etc.

Lane, Charles (1905–) (Charles Levison).
American character actor seen since early 30s as comedy snoop, salesman or tax inspector; at the age of 80, he was vigorously playing a judge in *Soap*.
Mr Deeds Goes to Town 36. In Old Chicago 38. You Can't Take It with You 38. The Cat and the Canary 39. Hot Spot 41. Arsenic and Old Lace 44. Intrigue 49. The Juggler 53. Teacher's Pet 58. The Gnome-Mobile 67. What's So Bad about Feeling Good? 68. The Little Dragons 80. Strange Invaders 83. Murphy's Romance 85. When the Bough Breaks (TV) 86. Date with an Angel 87. War and Remembrance (TV) 89, etc.
TV series: Dear Phoebe 54–55. The Lucy Show 62–63. Petticoat Junction 63–68. The Pruitts of Southampton 66–67. Karen 75.

Lane, Diane (1965–).
American actress, in theatre as a child. She is married to actor Christopher LAMBERT.
A Little Romance 79. Touched by Love 79. Cattle Annie and Little Britches 81. Ladies and Gentlemen: The Fabulous Stains 81. Child Bride of Short Creek (TV) 81. National Lampoon Goes to the Movies 82. Miss All-American Beauty (TV) 82. Six Pack 82. The Outsiders 83. Rumblefish 83. Streets of Fire 84. The Cotton Club 84. The Big Town 87. Lady Beware 87. Love Dream 88. Vital Signs 90. Priceless Beauty 90. Descending Angel 91. Chaplin 92. Knight Moves 93. Indian Summer 93. Oldest Living Confederate Widow Tells All (TV) 94. Judge Dredd 95. Wild Bill 95. A Streetcar Named Desire (TV) 95. Jack 96. Mad Dog Time/Trigger Happy 96. Murder at 1600 97. The Blouse Man 98. Kiss the Sky 98. A Walk on the Moon 99, etc.

Lane, Lupino (1892–1959) (Henry George Lupino).
Diminutive, dapper British stage comedian and master of the pratfall, member of a family who had been clowns for generations. His American two-reelers of the 20s were little masterpieces of timing and hair-raising stunts, but he failed to develop a personality for sound. On his return to Britain from Hollywood, he directed one of the first British musicals, *No Lady*, and went to work at Elstree for British International Pictures as a director, before returning to his first love, the stage, climaxing in the long-running musical *Me and My Girl* featuring his singing of 'The Lambeth Walk'.
Biography: 1957, *Born to Star* by James Dillon White.
The Reporter 22. Isn't Life Wonderful? 24. The Love Parade 29. Bride of the Regiment 30. The Golden Mask 30.
GB FILMS: No Lady (& d) 31. The Love Race (d) 31. Love Lies (d) 31. Innocents of Chicago (d) 32. The Maid of the Mountains (d) 32. A Southern Maid (& d) 33. Letting in the Sunshine (d) 33. The Deputy Drummer 35. Hot News 36. Me and My Girl 39, etc.

Lane, Nathan (1956–).
American leading actor, mainly on Broadway and in occasional films in comic roles.
Ironweed 87. Frankie and Johnny 91. He Said, She Said 91. Addams Family Values 93. Life with Mikey 93. The Lion King (voice) 94. Jeffrey 95. *The Birdcage* 96. The Boys Next Door (TV) 96. Mousehunt 97. The Lion King II: Simba's Pride (voice) 98, etc.
TV series: Encore! Encore! 98.

Lane, Richard (1900–1982).
American supporting player, formerly and latterly sports announcer; frequently seen in the 40s as reporter, tough cop, or exasperated executive.
The Outcasts of Poker Flat 37. Union Pacific 39. Hellzapoppin 41. Meet Boston Blackie 41. What a Blonde 45. Gentleman Joe Palooka 46. Take Me Out to the Ball Game 48. I Can Get It For You Wholesale 51, etc.

The Lane Sisters.
American leading ladies, real name Mullican. Three of the five sisters (all actresses) had sizeable roles in Hollywood films: *Lola* (1909–1981), *Rosemary* (1913–1974) and *Priscilla* (1917–1995).
TOGETHER: Four Daughters 38. Daughters Courageous 39. Four Wives 39. Four Mothers 40.
OTHER APPEARANCES FOR LOLA: Speakeasy 29. Death from a Distance 35. Marked Woman 37. Zanzibar 40. Why Girls Leave Home 36.
ROSEMARY: Hollywood Hotel 38. The Oklahoma Kid 38. The Return of Dr X 40. Time Out for Rhythm 42. The Fortune Hunter 45.
PRISCILLA: Brother Rat 39. Dust Be My Destiny 39. Yes My Darling Daughter 39. The Roaring Twenties 40. Blues in the Night 41. Saboteur 42. Arsenic and Old Lace 44. Fun on a Weekend 46. Bodyguard 48, etc.

Lanfield, Sidney (1900–1972).
American director from 1932; former jazz musician. Married actress Shirley Mason.
Hat Check Girl 32. Moulin Rouge 34. Sing Baby Sing 36. *The Hound of the Baskervilles* 39. Swanee River 39. You'll Never Get Rich 41. The Lady Has Plans 41. *My Favorite Blonde* 42. The Meanest Man in the World 42. Let's Face It 43. Standing Room Only 44. Bring on the Girls 45. The Well-Groomed Bride 45. Stations West 47. The Lemon Drop Kid 50. Follow the Sun 51. Skirts Ahoy 52, etc.

Lang, Charles (1902–1998).
Distinguished American cinematographer.
Shopworn Angel 29. *A Farewell to Arms* (AA) 33. Death Takes a Holiday 34. Lives of a Bengal Lancer 35. *Desire* 36. *The Cat and the Canary* 39. Nothing but the Truth 41. Practically Yours 44. The Uninvited 44. The Ghost and Mrs Muir 47. A Foreign Affair 47. *Ace in the Hole* 51. Sudden Fear 52. The Big Heat 53. The Female on the Beach 55. The Man from Laramie 55. Autumn Leaves 56. The Solid Gold Cadillac 56. Gunfight at the OK Corral 57. Some Like It Hot (AAN) 59. One-Eyed Jacks 59. The Facts of Life 60. The Magnificent Seven 60. Blue Hawaii 61. A Girl Named Tamiko 62. *Charade* 63. Inside Daisy Clover 65. How to Steal a Million 66. Not with My Wife You Don't 66. Hotel 67. The Flim Flam Man 67. Wait Until Dark 67. A Flea in Her Ear 68. Cactus Flower 69. Bob and Carol and Ted and Alice (AAN) 70. The Love Machine 71. Butterflies Are Free (AAN) 72, many others.

Lang, Charles (1915–).
American writer.
Killer Shark 50. Call of the Klondike 50. Captain Scarface 53. The Magnificent Matador 55. Buchanan Rides Alone 58. Desire in the Dust 60. Tess of the Storm Country 60, etc.

Lang, Fritz (1890–1976).
German director of distinguished silent films. Went to Hollywood 1934 and tended thereafter to make commercial though rather heavy-handed thrillers.
Biography: 1974, *Fritz Lang* by Lotte Eisner; 1997, *Fritz Lang: The Nature of the Beast* by Patrick McGilligan.
■ Helbblut 19. Der Herr der Liebe 19. Die Spinnen 19. Hara Kiri 19. Vier um die Frau 20. Das Wandernde Bild 21. *Destiny* 21. Das Brillanten Schiff 21. Der Müde Tod 21. *Dr Mabuse der Spieler* 22. Inferno 22. *Siegfried* 23. Krimhild's Revenge 24. *Metropolis* 26. *The Spy* 27. Frau im Mond 28. M 31. The Testament of Dr Mabuse 32. Liliom 33. *Fury* 36. *You Only Live Once* 37. You and Me 38. The Return of Frank James 40. Western Union 41. Man Hunt 41. Confirm or Deny (part) 42. Hangmen Also Die 43. *The Woman in the Window* 44. Ministry of Fear 44. Scarlet Street 45. Cloak and Dagger 46. The Secret beyond the Door 48. House by the River 49. An American Guerrilla in the Philippines 51. Rancho Notorious 52. Clash by Night 52. The Blue Gardenia 52. *The Big Heat* 53. Human Desire 54. Moonfleet 55. While the City Sleeps 55. Beyond a Reasonable Doubt 56. Der Tiger von Ischnapur (Ger.) 58. Das Indische Grabmal (Ger.) 58. The Thousand Eyes of Dr Mabuse (Ger.) 60. Contempt (a only) 63.
✪ For spinning out his well-deserved German reputation through an American career of dwindling talent. *Fury*.
❝ His cinema is that of the nightmare, the fable, and the philosophical dissertation. – *Andrew Sarris, 1968*
Lang makes you want to puke. Nobody in the whole world is as important as he imagines himself to be. I completely understand why he is so hated everywhere. – *Kurt Weill*

Lang, Harold (1923–1971).
Blond English general-purpose actor and drama teacher, often in shady roles, from the stage. Born in London, he studied at RADA.
Floodtide 49. Cairo Road 50. The Franchise Affair 51. Wings of Danger 52. The Intruder 53. Dance Little Lady 54. The Quatermass Experiment 55. It's a Wonderful World 56. Carve Her Name with Pride 58. Ben Hur 59. Dr Terror's House of Horrors 64. The Nanny 65. Two Gentlemen Sharing 69, etc.

Lang, Jennings (1915–1996).
American executive, long near the top of MCA TV and latterly executive producer of many Universal films. A lawyer and former agent, he was involved in the development of many successful TV series of the 50s and 60s, including *The Virginian*, *McHale's Navy* and *Wagon Train*. He also developed Sensurround, a sound system that helped make *Earthquake* a hit in 1975. In 1951, when he was agent of actress Joan Bennett, he was shot in the groin by Bennett's husband, producer Walter Wanger.
AS PRODUCER OR EXECUTIVE PRODUCER: Coogan's Bluff 68. Winning 69. Tell Them Willie Boy Is Here 69. The Beguiled 71. Play Misty for Me 71. Pete 'n' Tillie 72. Airport 1975 75. The Front Page 75. Airport '77 77. The Concorde: Airport '79/aka Airport 80: The Concorde (& story) 79, etc.

Lang, June (1915–) (June Vlasek).
American leading lady, former dancer.
Chandu the Magician 32. Bonnie Scotland 35. Ali Baba Goes to Town 38. Redhead 41. Flesh and Fantasy 44. Lighthouse 48, etc.

Lang, Matheson (1879–1948).
Scottish-Canadian stage actor, a London matinée idol of the 20s who made occasional films.
Autobiography: 1940, *Mr Wu Looks Back*.
Mr Wu 21. Carnival 21 & 31. Dick Turpin's Ride to York 22. The Wandering Jew 23. The Chinese Bungalow 25 & 30. Beyond the Veil 25. Island of Despair 26. The Triumph of the Scarlet Pimpernel 29. Channel Crossing 32. Little Friend 34. Drake of England 35. The Cardinal 36, etc.

Lang, Otto (1908–).
Austrian-born producer and director in Hollywood, a former ski instructor to Darryl Zanuck.
Call Northside 777 (p) 48. Five Fingers (p) 52. White Witch Doctor (p) 53. Vesuvius Express (AANp, short) 53. Jet Carrier (AANp, short) 54. Tora! Tora! Tora! (p) 69, etc.

Lang, Robert (1934–).
British character actor, mainly on stage.
Othello 65. Dance of Death 69. The Mackintosh Man 73. Night Watch 73. Savage Messiah 73. Shout at the Devil 76. The First Great Train Robbery 79. Runners 83. Hawks 88. The Trial 93. Four Weddings and a Funeral 94. Some Mother's Son 96. Rasputin (TV) 96. Wilde 97. Our Mutual Friend (TV) 98, etc.
TV series: The Old Boy Network 91. Under the Hammer 94.

Lang, Walter (1898–1972).
American director of competent but seldom outstanding entertainments.
The Satin Woman 27. The College Hero 27. Brothers 30. Hell Bound 30. Women Go On for Ever 31. No More Orchids 32. The Warrior's Husband 33. Meet the Baron 33. Whom the Gods Destroy 34. The Mighty Barnum 34. Carnival 35. Hooray for Love 35. Love Before Breakfast 36. *Wife, Doctor and Nurse* 37. Second Honeymoon 37. The Baroness and the Butler 38. I'll Give a Million 38. The Little Princess 39. *The Bluebird* 40. Star Dust 40. The Great Profile 40. *Tin Pan Alley* 40. Moon over Miami 41. Weekend in Havana 41. Song of the Islands 42. The Magnificent Dope 42. Coney Island 43. Greenwich Village 44. *State Fair* 45. Sentimental Journey 46. Claudia and David 46. Mother Wore Tights 47. *Sitting Pretty* 48. When My Baby Smiles at Me 48. You're My Everything 49. Cheaper by the Dozen 50. The Jackpot 50. On the Riviera 51. *With a Song in My Heart* 51. *Call Me Madam* 53. There's No Business like Show Business 54. *The King and I* (AAN) 56. The Desk Set 57. But Not for Me 59. Can Can 60. The Marriage Go Round 61. Snow White and the Three Stooges 61, many others.

Langan, Glenn (1917–1991).
American light leading man, in films from the early 40s after stage experience.
Four Jills in a Jeep 44. *Margie* 46. Forever Amber 47. The Snake Pit 48. Treasure of Monte Cristo 49. Rapture (Swe.) 50. Hangman's Knot 52. 99 River Street 54. The Amazing Colossal Man 57, etc.

Langdon, Harry (1884–1944).
Baby-faced, melancholy American clown who was a great hit in the 20s but could not reconcile his unusual image with sound.
Picking Peaches 23. *Tramp Tramp Tramp* 26. *The Strong Man* 26. *Long Pants* 26. His First Flame 27. Three's a Crowd 27. The Chaser (& d) 28. See America Thirst 30. A Soldier's Plaything 31. Hallelujah I'm a Bum 33. My Weakness 33. There Goes My Heart 38. *Zenobia* 39. Misbehaving Husbands 40. House of Errors 42. Spotlight Scandals 44, etc.
❝ He was a quaint artist who had no business in business. – *Mack Sennett*

Langdon, Sue Ane (1936–).
American leading lady and comedienne.
The Outsider 61. The Rounders 65. A Fine Madness 66. A Guide for the Married Man 67. The Cheyenne Social Club 70. Without Warning 80. Zapped! 82, etc.
TV series: Bachelor Father 58–61. The Jackie Gleason Show 62–63. Arnie 70–72. Grandpa Goes to Washington 78–79. When the Whistle Blows 80.

Lange, Arthur (1889–1956).
American composer.
Hollywood Revue 29. Marie Galante 34. Banjo on My Knee 36. This Is My Affair 37. Kidnapped 38. Lady of Burlesque 43. The Woman in the Window 45. Woman on the Run 50. The Mad Magician 54, many others.

Lange, Hope (1931–).
American leading lady of the 50s who developed into a mature and pleasing comedienne. Born in Redding Ridge, Connecticut, she was on stage at the age of 12, and later was a dancer on *The Jackie Gleason Show*.
Bus Stop 56. The True Story of Jesse James 57. Peyton Place (AAN) 57. The Young Lions 58. In Love and War 58. The Best of Everything 59. Wild in the Country 61. Pocketful of Miracles 61. Love Is a Ball 63. Jigsaw (TV) 68. Crowhaven Farm (TV) 70. That Certain Summer (TV) 72. The 500

Pound Jerk (TV) 72. Death Wish 74. I Love You Goodbye (TV) 74. Fer de Lance (TV) 74. The Secret Night Caller (TV) 75. Like Normal People (TV) 79. The Day Christ Died (TV) 80. I Am The Cheese 83. The Prodigal 83. Nightmare on Elm Street II 85. Blue Velvet 86. Tune in Tomorrow/Aunt Julia and the Scriptwriter 90. Dead before Dawn (TV) 93. Message from 'Nam (TV) 93. Coopertown (TV) 93. Clear and Present Danger 94. Just Cause 95, etc.

TV series: The Ghost and Mrs Muir 68–70. The New Dick Van Dyke Show 71–74.

Lange, Jessica (1949–).
American leading lady who developed into an actress. She has a daughter by actor and dancer Mikhail Baryshnikov and a son and a daughter by actor and dramatist Sam Shepard.

King Kong 76. All That Jazz 79. How to Beat the High Cost of Living 80. The Postman Always Rings Twice 81. *Frances* (AAN) 82. Tootsie (AA) 82. Country (AAN) 84. Sweet Dreams (AAN) 85. Crimes of the Heart 86. Everybody's All-American 88. Far North 88. Music Box (AAN) 89. Men Don't Leave 90. Cape Fear 91. Night and the City 92. Blue Sky (made 91) (AA) 94. Rob Roy 95. Losing Isaiah 95. A Streetcar Named Desire (TV) 95. Cousin Bette 97. A Thousand Acres 97. Hush 98, etc.

Langella, Frank (1940–).
American leading man of the 70s.

The Twelve Chairs 70. Diary of a Mad Housewife 70. The Wrath of God 72. The Mark of Zorro (TV) 74. *Dracula* (title role) 79. Those Lips Those Eyes 80. Sphinx 81. The Men's Club 86. Masters of the Universe 87. And God Created Woman 88. True Identity 91. 1492: Conquest of Paradise 92. Dave 93. Body of Evidence 93. Doomsday Gun (TV) 94. Bad Company 94. Brainscan 94. Bad Company 95. CutThroat Island 95. Eddie 96. Lolita 97. I'm Losing You 98, etc.

Langenkamp, Heather (1964–).
American leading actress of horror movies.

The Outsiders 83. Rumble Fish 83. A Nightmare on Elm Street 84. Nickel Mountain 85. A Nightmare on Elm Street 3: Dream Warriors 87. Shocker 89. Wes Craven's New Nightmare 94. Tonya & Nancy: The Inside Story (TV) 94. The Demolitionist 95, etc.

Langford, Frances (1914–).
American band singer, popular in the 40s, mainly in guest spots. Appeared mainly in light musicals. Her first husband was actor Jon Hall (1938–55).

Every Night at Eight 35. Broadway Melody 36. Hollywood Hotel 37. Too Many Girls 40. Swing It, Soldier 41. The Girl Rush 44. The Bamboo Blonde 45. Beat the Band 46. No Time For Tears 52. The Glenn Miller Story 54, etc.

Langley, Noel (1911–1980).
South African playwright and screenwriter, in Britain and Hollywood.

Maytime (co-w) 38. The Wizard of Oz (co-w) 39. They Made Me a Fugitive 47. Tom Brown's Schooldays 51. Scrooge 52. The Pickwick Papers (& d) 53. Our Girl Friday (& d) 53. The Search for Bridey Murphy (& d) 56, many others.

Langlois, Henri (1914–1977).
Idiosyncratic French archivist, instigator of the Cinémathèque Française. His methods annoyed some, but his good intentions were never in question. Received Special Academy Award in 1974. A documentary on his life, *Citizen Langlois*, directed by Edgardo Cozarinsky, was released in 1995.

Biography: 1983, *A Passion for Films* by Richard Roud.

Langton, David (1912–1994).
English actor of stage and screen, best known for playing Richard Bellamy, the head of the household, in the TV series *Upstairs, Downstairs* (1970–75).

The Ship that Died of Shame 55. Saint Joan 57. Seven Waves Away 57. A Hard Day's Night 64. The Pumpkin Eater 64. The Incredible Sarah 76. The Whistle Blower 86, etc.

Langton, Simon (1941–).
British director, in TV from 1964.

The Whistle Blower 86. Laguna Heat 87. The Cinder Path (TV) 94. Pride and Prejudice (TV) 95, etc.

Langtry, Lillie (1853–1929) (Emilie Charlotte Le Breton).
British light actress who charmed, among others, Judge Roy Bean and Edward VII. Sole film appearance *His Neighbour's Wife* 13. Ava Gardner played her in *The Life and Times of Judge Roy Bean*.

Lanoux, Victor (1936–).
French leading actor. He left school at 14 and worked in cabaret before making his cinema debut in 1965.

La Vieille Dame Indigne 65. La Ville Normale 67. L'Affaire Dominici 73. Deux Hommes dans la Ville 73. Folle à Tuer 75. Cousin Cousine 75. Pardon Mon Affaire/Un Éléphant ça Trompe Enormément 76. Servant et Maîtresse 77. One Wild Moment/Un Moment d'Egarement 77. Pardon Mon Affaire Too!/We Will All Meet in Paradise 78. Un Si Joli Village 79. Retour en Force 80. Dog Day/Canicule 83. Un Dimanche de Flics 83. Louisiana 84. National Lampoon's European Vacation 85. Scene of the Crime/Le Lieu du Crime 87. L'Invité Surprise 89. Le Bal des Casse-Pieds 92, etc.

Lansbury, Angela (1925–).
British character actress who has always seemed older than her years. Evacuated to Hollywood during World War II, she played a long succession of unsympathetic parts, but in the 60s became a Broadway musical star. She is best known as amateur detective Jessica Fletcher in the long-running TV series *Murder She Wrote*. Her first husband was actor Richard Cromwell (1945–46).

■ Gaslight (AAN) 44. National Velvet 44. *The Picture of Dorian Gray* (AAN) 45. The Harvey Girls 46. The Hoodlum Saint 46. The Private Affairs of Bel Ami 47. Till the Clouds Roll By 47. If Winter Comes 47. Tenth Avenue Angel 48. State of the Union 48. The Three Musketeers 48. The Red Danube 49. Samson and Delilah 49. Kind Lady 51. Mutiny 52. Remains to Be Seen 53. A Lawless Street 55. A Life at Stake 55. The Purple Mask 55. Please Murder Me 56. The Court Jester 56. The Reluctant Debutante 58. The Long Hot Summer 58. *The Dark at the Top of the Stairs* 60. A Breath of Scandal 61. Blue Hawaii 61. Summer of the Seventeenth Doll 61. All Fall Down 62. *The Manchurian Candidate* (AAN) 62. In the Cool of the Day 63. The World of Henry Orient 64. Dear Heart 64. The Greatest Story Ever Told 65. Harlow 65. Moll Flanders 65. Mister Buddwing 66. Something for Everyone 70. *Bedknobs and Broomsticks* 71. Death on the Nile 78. The Lady Vanishes 79. The Mirror Crack'd 80. Little Gloria . . . Happy at Last (TV) 82. The Pirates of Penzance 83. Lace (TV) 84. Company of Wolves 84. Rage of Angels: The Story Continues (TV) 86. Shootdown (TV) 88. The Shell Seekers (TV) 90. The Love She Sought (TV) 90. Beauty and the Beast (voice) 92. Mrs 'Arris Goes to Paris (TV) 92. Mrs Santa Claus (TV) 96. Beauty and the Beast: The Enchanted Christmas (voice) 97. Murder, She Wrote: South by Southwest (TV) 97. Anastasia (voice) 97.

TV series: Murder She Wrote 84–96.

Lansing, Joi (1928–1972) (Joyce Wassmansdoff).
American leading lady who played a few sharp blondes and left a pleasant impression.

■ The Counterfeiters 48. The Girl from Jones Beach 49. Hot Cars 56. The Brave One 56. Hot Shots 56. A Hole in the Head 59. It Started with a Kiss 59. The Atomic Submarine 59. Who Was That Lady? 59. Marriage on the Rocks 65. Bigfoot 71.

TV series: Love That Bob 56–59. Klondike 60–61.

Lansing, Robert (1929–1994) (Robert H. Brown).
Cold-eyed, virile American leading man of the 60s.

The 4-D Man 59. A Gathering of Eagles 63. Under the Yum Yum Tree 64. The Grissom Gang 71. Wild in the Sky 72. Bittersweet Love 76. Empire of the Ants 77. False Face 77. Island Claws/Night of the Claw 80. The Equalizer (TV) 87. The Nest 88. Blind Vengeance (TV) 90, etc.

TV series: 87th Precinct 61. 12 O'Clock High 64. The Man Who Never Was 66. Automan 83–84. The Equaliser 85–89.

Lansing, Sherry (1944–).
American producer, a former actress and one-time president of Twentieth Century-Fox, 1980–83, who is now chairman of the Motion Picture Group of Paramount Pictures. Married director William Friedkin.

Racing with the Moon 84. Firstborn 84. Fatal Attraction (AAN) 87. The Accused 88. Black Rain 89. School Ties 91. Indecent Proposal 93, etc.

Lantz, Walter (1900–1994).
American animator, in charge of Universal cartoons since 1928 and the creator of Woody Woodpecker. Special AA 1978 'for bringing joy and laughter to every part of the world'. His wife Grace (1904–1992) supplied Woody's laugh.

Biography: 1985, *The Walter Lantz Story* by Joe Adamson.

Lanza, Mario (1921–1959) (Alfredo Cocozza).
American opera singer, popular in MGM musicals until overcome by weight problem.

Biography: 1991, *Mario Lanza – A Biography* by Derek Mannering.

■ That Midnight Kiss 49. The Toast of New Orleans 50. *The Great Caruso* 51. Because You're Mine 52. The Student Prince (voice only) 54. Serenade 56. Seven Hills of Rome 58. For the First Time 58.

❝ That idiot Lanza! He had the greatest opportunities in the world, but he just couldn't handle success. *– Joseph Ruttenberg*

Mario, you doll, you sing like a son of a bitch. *– M.L.*

LaPaglia, Anthony (1959–).
Australian-born actor, working in America.

Betsy's Wedding 90. Criminal Justice (TV) 90. Mortal Sins 90. Dangerous Obsession 90. One Good Cop 90. He Said, She Said 91. Keeper of the City 91. 29th Street 91. Innocent Blood 92. So I Married an Axe Murderer 93. The Custodian 93. The Client 94. Killer 94. Lucky Break (Aus.) 94. Empire Records 95. Never Give Up: The Jimmy V. Story (TV) 96. Brilliant Lies 96. Trees Lounge 96. Paperback Romance 96. Commandments 97. The Garden of Redemption 97. Phoenix 98, etc.

TV series: Murder One 96.

Lapotaire, Jane (1944–).
Anglo-French stage actress in occasional films.

Crescendo 69. Antony and Cleopatra 72. The Asphyx 72. One of Our Dinosaurs Is Missing 75. Eureka 83. Lady Jane 86, etc.

Lardner, Ring, Jnr (1915–).
American screenwriter who was one of the 'Hollywood Ten'.

Woman of the Year (AA) 42. The Cross of Lorraine 44. Forever Amber 47. Britannia Mews 48. Cloak and Dagger 48. The Cincinnati Kid 65. M*A*S*H (AA) 70. The Greatest 77, etc.

Larkin, Peter.
American production designer, from the Broadway stage.

Nighthawks 81. Neighbors 81. Tootsie 82. Reuben, Reuben 82. Compromising Positions 85. The Secret of My Success 87. Three Men and a Baby 87. Life Stinks 91. Night and the City 92. The Concierge/For Love or Money 93. House of Cards 93. Guarding Tess 94. Major Payne 95. Get Shorty 95. The First Wives Club 96. Bean 97, etc.

Larner, Jeremy (1937–).
American screenwriter and novelist. He is a former journalist and speechwriter to 60s presidential candidate Senator Eugene McCarthy. Since winning an Oscar, he has worked on films that are yet to be produced.

Drive He Said (co-w, from his novel) 71. The Candidate (AA) 72.

Laroche, Pierre (1902–1962).
French screenwriter, mainly for films directed by his wife, Jacqueline Audry.

Les Visiteurs du Soir (co-w) 42. Lumière d'Été (co-w) 43. Les Malheurs de Sophie 45. Gigi 49. Minne 50. Huis Clos 54. La Garçonne 57, etc.

Larraz, José Ramón (1928–).
Spanish director of horror and erotic movies, sometimes combining both themes in movies featuring lesbian vampires. Born in Barcelona, he worked in Paris as a comic-book illustrator and fashion photographer before making his first film in Britain, where he continued to work until the mid-70s, when he was known as Joseph Larraz. *Symptoms* was a British entry at the Cannes Film Festival in 1974. He then returned to direct films in Spain and also worked under the pseudonym of Joseph Braunstein for the US video market.

Whirlpool/She Died with Her Boots On 69. Scream . . . and Die! 73. Symptoms/The Blood Virgin; The House that Vanished 74. Vampyres – Daughters of Dracula 74. The Violation of the Bitch/La Visita del Vicio 78. Golden Lady 79. The National Mummy/La Momia Nacional 81. Estigma 81. Los Ritos Sexuales del Diábolo 82. Rest in Pieces (as Joseph Braunstein) 87. Edge of the Axe (as Joseph Braunstein) 89. Deadly Manor 90. Sevilla Connection 92, etc.

❝ I've never had a proper understanding producer, only philistine money-men telling me what to do. *– J.R.L.*

Larroquette, John (1947–).
American leading actor.

The Texas Chainsaw Massacre (uncredited narrator) 74. Heart Beat 80. Altered States 80. Stripes 81. Green Ice 81. Cat People 82. Meatballs 2 84. Star Trek III: The Search for Spock 84. Choose Me 84. Convicted (TV) 86. Blind Date 87. Second Sight 89. Madhouse 90. Tune in Tomorrow/Aunt Julia and the Scriptwriter 90. Richie Rich 94, etc.

TV series: Doctor's Hospital 75–76. Baa Baa Black Sheep 76. Night Court 84–92. The John Larroquette Show 93– .

Larsen, Keith (1925–).
American second-string leading man. He was married to Vera Miles (1960–73).

Flat Top 52. Hiawatha 52. Arrow in the Dust 54. Wichita 55. Dial Red O 56. Fury River 61. Caxambu 67. The Trap on Cougar Mountain 76. White-Water Sam (wd) 78, etc.

TV series: The Hunter 54. Brave Eagle 55. Northwest Passage 57. The Aquanaut 60.

Larsen, Tambi.
Danish-born art director and production designer. He studied at the Yale Drama School in the mid-30s and first worked on Broadway as a scenic artist, entering films at Paramount Studios in the mid-40s.

Artists and Models 55. The Rose Tattoo (AA) 55. The Five Pennies 59. The Rat Race 60. Hud (AAN) 63. The Spy Who Came in from the Cold (AAN) 65. Nevada Smith 66. *The Molly Maguires* (AAN) 70. Thunderbolt and Lightfoot 74. The Outlaw Josey Wales 76. The White Buffalo 77. Heaven's Gate (AAN) 80, etc.

Larson, Eric (1905–1988).
Pioneer animator with Walt Disney, who worked on every full-length Disney animated film from *Snow White and the Seven Dwarfs* 37 to *The Great Mouse Detective* 86.

LaRue:
See *La Rue*.

Lasker, Lawrence (1949–).
American producer and screenwriter, a former art director.

War Games (co-w, AAN) 83. Project X (p, story) 87. Awakenings (AANp) 90. Sneakers (p, co-w) 92, etc.

Lasky, Jesse (1880–1958).
American pioneer. Formed his first production company in 1914 and had a big hit with *The Squaw Man*; in 1916 gained control of Famous Players and later Paramount. Later produced for Fox, Warner, RKO.

Autobiography: 1958, *I Blow My Own Horn*.

Sergeant York 41. The Adventures of Mark Twain 44. Rhapsody in Blue 45. The Miracle of the Bells 49. The Great Caruso 51, many others.

Lasky, Jesse, Jnr (1910–1988).
American screenwriter, son of Jesse Lasky.

Autobiography: 1974, *Whatever Happened to Hollywood?*

Union Pacific (co-w) 39. Reap the Wild Wind (co-w) 42. Unconquered (co-w) 48. Samson and Delilah (co-w) 49. The Thief of Venice 50. The Brigand 52. The Ten Commandments (co-w) 56. Seven Women from Hell (co-w) 61. Land Raiders 69. An Ace up My Sleeve 75. Crime and Passion 76, etc.

Lassally, Walter (1926–).
German cinematographer, long in Britain.

Autobiography: 1987, *Itinerant Cameraman*.

We Are the Lambeth Boys 58. *A Taste of Honey*

61. The Loneliness of the Long-Distance Runner 62. *Tom Jones* 63. *Zorba the Greek* (AA) 65. The Day the Fish Came Out 67. Oedipus the King 67. Joanna 68. Turnkey 70. Something for Everyone 72. Malachi's Cove 74. Too Far to Go (TV) 77. Gauguin the Savage (TV) 80. Memoirs of a Survivor 82. Heat and Dust 83. Private School 83. The Bostonians 84. Indian Summer 87. The Deceivers 88. The Perfect Murder 88. Fragment of Isabella 89. The Ballad of the Sad Café 90, etc.

Lasser, Louise (1939–).
American TV actress popular in the serial *Mary Hartman, Mary Hartman* 76. She was married to Woody ALLEN (1966–71).
Bananas 71. Such Good Friends 71. Everything You Always Wanted to Know about Sex 72. Coffee, Tea or Me? (TV) 73. Isn't It Shocking? (TV) 73. Slither 73. Just Me and You (TV) 78. In God We Trust 80. Stardust Memories (uncredited) 80. Blood Rage 83. Crimewave 85. Surrender 87. Sing 89. Rude Awakening 89. Frankenhooker 90. Modern Love 90. Sudden Manhattan 96. Layin' Low 96. Happiness 98, etc.
TV series: Mary Hartman, Mary Hartman 76–77. It's a Living 81–82.

Lasseter, John (1957–).
American director of computer-generated animated films, a former animator with Walt Disney. He was awarded an Oscar for special achievement for *Toy Story*.
Tin Toy (AA, short) 88. *Toy Story* 95. A Bug's Life 98, etc.

Lastfogel, Abe (1898–1984).
American talent agent, head of the William Morris Organization, which he joined in 1912 as an office boy.

Laszlo, Andrew (1926–).
Hungarian-American cinematographer.
You're a Big Boy Now 67. The Night They Raided Minsky's 68. Popi 69. Teacher Teacher 70. The Out of Towners 70. Lovers and other Strangers 71. The Owl and the Pussycat 71. Class of 44 73. The Man without a Country (TV) 74. Countdown at Kusini 76. The Warriors 79. Shogun (TV) 80. Southern Comfort 81. First Blood 82. Thief of Hearts 84. Remo Williams, the Adventure Begins 85. Poltergeist II 86. Innerspace 87. Star Trek V: The Final Frontier 89. Ghost Dad 90. Newsies 92, etc.

Laszlo, Ernest (1905–1984).
Hungarian-American cinematographer.
The Hitler Gang 44. Two Years Before the Mast 44. The Girl from Manhattan 48. Dead on Arrival 49. The Steel Trap 52. The Star 52. Stalag 17 53. *Vera Cruz* 54. The Big Knife 55. Judgment at Nuremberg 60. *Inherit the Wind* (AAN) 60. *It's a Mad Mad Mad Mad World* (AAN) 63. *Ship of Fools* (AA) 65. Fantastic Voyage (AAN) 66. Star! (AAN) 68. The First Time 69. Daddy's Gone A-Hunting 69. *Airport* (AAN) 69. Showdown 73. Logan's Run (AAN) 76. The Domino Principle (co-ph) 77, many others.

Latell, Lyle (1905–1967) (Lyle Zeiem).
Beefy American character actor in comic parts, best known for his role as Pat Patton, Dick Tracy's sidekick in the 'B' features of the 40s. Married actress Mary Foy (1903–1987), of vaudeville act 'Eddie Foy and the Seven Little Foys'.
Texas 41. In the Navy 41. Happy Go Lucky 43. One Mysterious Night 44. Hold That Blonde 45. Dick Tracy vs Cueball 45. Dick Tracy's Dilemma 47. Dick Tracy and Gruesome 47. Buck Privates Come Home/Rookies Come Home 47. The Noose Hangs High 48. Sky Dragon 49. A Street Car Named Desire 51. The Girl Rush 55, etc.

Latham, Louise.
American actress.
Marnie 64. Firecreek 67. Adam at 6 AM 70. Making It 71. White Lightning 73. The Sugarland Express 74. 92 in the Shade 75. The Awakening Land (TV) 78. Pray TV (TV) 82. Mass Appeal 84. Love Lives On (TV) 85. Toughlove (TV) 85. Fresno (TV) 86. Crazy from the Heart 91. Paradise 91. Love Field 92. In Cold Blood (TV) 96. Mary & Tim 96, etc.
TV series: Sara 76. The Contender 80. Scruples 80.

Lathrop, Philip (1916–1995).
American cinematographer.
The Monster of Piedras Blancas 57. Experiment in Terror 62. *Lonely Are the Brave* 62. Days of Wine and Roses 63. The Pink Panther 63. The Americanization of Emily 64. Thirty-Six Hours 65. The Cincinnati Kid 65. What Did You Do in the War Daddy? 66. The Russians are Coming 66. The Happening 67. Point Blank 68. *Finian's Rainbow* 69. The Gypsy Moths 69. The Illustrated Man 69. They Shoot Horses Don't They? 69. Von Richthofen and Brown 71. Airport 77 77. The Driver 78. Little Miss Marker 80. Loving Couples 80. All Night Long 81. Jekyll and Hyde Together Again 82. Hammett 82. National Lampoon's Class Reunion 82. Deadly Friend 86, etc.

Latifah, Queen (1970–) (Dana Owens).
American actress and rap performer; her production company, Flavor Unit Entertainment, also embraces a music label and an artist management firm.
Set It Off 96. Living Out Loud 98, etc.
TV series: Living Single 93–98. Latifah 99– .

Latimer, Jonathan (1906–1983).
American thriller writer.
Topper Returns 41. They Won't Believe Me 47. Alias Nick Beal 49. Plunder of the Sun 51. Botany Bay 54. The Unholy Wife 57, etc.

Latimore, Frank (1925–) (Frank Kline).
American leading man with stage experience.
In the Meantime, Darling 44. Three Little Girls in Blue 46. Black Magic 49. Three Forbidden Stories (It.) 50. John Paul Jones 59. The Sergeant 68. All the President's Men 76, etc.

Lattuada, Alberto (1914–).
Italian director.
The Mill on the Po 48. Without Pity 48. Lights of Variety (co-d) 50. Il Capotto 52. The Wolf 53. The Beach 53. Guendalina 56. Tempest 58. The Adolescents 61. La Steppa 62. The Mandrake 65. The Betrayal 68. A Dog's Heart 75. Stay As You Are 78. A Thorn in the Heart 85. Christopher Columbus (TV) 85. Amori (co-d) 89, etc.

Lau, Andy (1961–) (Lau Tak Wah).
Leading Hong Kong actor, often in action films.
Boat People 82. Rich and Famous 87. As Tears Go By 88. Dragon Family 89. Moment of Romance 90. The Prisoner 90. God of Gamblers II 91. Days of Being Wild 91. Moon Warriors 92. Saviour of the Soul 92. Full Throttle 96, etc.

Lau, Jeffrey (1956–).
Hong Kong director and producer.
Haunted Cop Shop 87. Haunted Cop Shop II 88. Thunder Cops II 89. Mortuary Blues 90. Fury Fist 91. 92 *The Legendary La Rose Noire*/92 Hak Muigwai Dui Hak Mauigwai 92. Rose Rose I Love You 93. The Eagle Shooting Heroes: Dong Cheng Xi Jiu 93, etc.

Lauder, Sir Harry (1870–1950).
Scottish music-hall entertainer, a former miner who was knighted in 1919. He became a star in 1900 and made some silent shorts from 1907.
Autobiography: 1928, *Roamin' in the Gloamin'*.
Biography: 1968, *Great Scot!* by Gordon Irving.
■ Huntingtower 27. Happy Days 29. Auld Lang Syne 33. End of the Road 36. Song of the Road 40.
❝ He has the great artist's overweening conceit of himself. He emerges from the wings like a sun from base clouds. He irradiates his world, flattering stalls and gallery with sovereign eye. That a creature like ourselves should glow with such intensity of self-appreciation warms the cockles of the most sceptical heart. – *James Agate*

Laughlin, Tom (1938–).
American independent director, producer and actor who enjoyed a cult success as Billy Jack, a violent hero on the side of the disadvantaged, in the early 70s. His most recent film, *The Return of Billy Jack* 86, has never been completed. He sometimes used the pseudonym T.C. Frank as director.
■ Tea and Sympathy 56. South Pacific 58. Gidget (a) 59. Tall Story (a) 60. The Proper Time (a, d) 60. The Young Sinners (d) 65. Born Losers (a, p, d) 67. Billy Jack (a, p, wd) 73. The Trial of Billy Jack (a, p) 74. The Master Gunfighter (a, p) 75. Billy Jack Goes to Washington (a, p, d) 78.

Laughton, Charles (1899–1962).
Distinguished British character actor, whose plump wry face was one of the most popular on screen in the 30s. His later Hollywood roles showed a regrettable tendency to ham, but he was always worth watching.
Biographies: 1938, *Charles Laughton and I* by his wife Elsa Lanchester. 1952, *The Charles Laughton Story* by Kurt Singer. 1976, *Charles Laughton* by Charles Higham. 1987, *Charles Laughton – a Difficult Actor* by Simon Callow.
■ Wolves 27. Bluebottles 28. Daydreams 28. Piccadilly 29. Comets 30. Down River 30. *The Old Dark House* 32. The Devil and the Deep 32. Payment Deferred 32. *The Sign of the Cross* (as Nero) 32. If I Had a Million 32. Island of Lost Souls 32. *The Private Life of Henry VIII* (AA) 33. White Woman 33. *The Barretts of Wimpole Street* 34. *Ruggles of Red Gap* 35. *Les Misérables* 35. *Mutiny on the Bounty* (as Captain Bligh) (AAN) 35. *Rembrandt* 36. *I Claudius* (unfinished) 37. Vessel of Wrath 37. St Martin's Lane 38. Jamaica Inn 39. *The Hunchback of Notre Dame* 39. They Knew What They Wanted 40. It Started with Eve 41. The Tuttles of Tahiti 42. Tales of Manhattan 42. Stand by for Action 43. Forever and a Day 43. This Land is Mine 43. The Man from Down Under 43. The Canterville Ghost 44. *The Suspect* 44. Captain Kidd 45. Because of Him 46. The Paradine Case 48. The Big Clock 48. Arch of Triumph 48. The Girl from Manhattan 49. The Bribe 49. The Man on the Eiffel Tower (as Maigret) 49. The Blue Veil 51. The Strange Door 51. Full House 52. Abbott and Costello Meet Captain Kidd 52. Salome 53. Young Bess 53. *Hobson's Choice* 54. *Witness for the Prosecution* (AAN) 57. Under Ten Flags 60. Spartacus 60. *Advise and Consent* 62.
AS DIRECTOR: *Night of the Hunter* 55.
✪ For a dozen splendid performances, unassailable by the self-doubt which later turned him into a ham. *Rembrandt*.
❝ They can't censor the gleam in my eye. – *C.L., when told that his performance as Mr Moulton-Barrett must not indicate incestuous love*
I have a face like the behind of an elephant. – *C.L.*
It's got so that every time I walk into a restaurant I get not only soup but an impersonation of Captain Bligh. – *C.L.*
You can't direct a Laughton picture. The best you can hope for is to referee. – *Alfred Hitchcock*
With him acting was an act of childbirth. What he needed was not so much a director as a midwife. – *Alexander Korda*
A great man who only accidentally became an actor. – *Alva Johnson*
You can tell how good an actor is by looking at his script. If he's no good, the script will be neat as a pin. Charles Laughton's was so filthy it looked like a herring had been wrapped in it. – *Billy Wilder*
Everybody thought he was a genius. I didn't. I thought he was more of a show-off, really. – *Rex Harrison*
Famous line (*Mutiny on the Bounty*): 'I'll live to see you – all of you – hung from the highest yardarm in the British fleet!'
Famous line (*The Private Life of Henry VIII*): 'Am I a king or a breeding bull?'
Famous line (*The Private Life of Henry VIII*): 'There's no delicacy nowadays. No consideration for others. Refinement's a thing of the past!'

Launder, Frank (1907–1997).
English director and scriptwriter, often in a memorable partnership with Sidney GILLIAT. Born in Hitchin, Hertfordshire, he began as a title writer at Elstree in the late 20s, later working at Gaumont British and Gainsborough Pictures. He began his collaboration with Gilliat in the mid-30s: they first worked as writers, then, from the mid-40s with their own production company, as producers and directors; the pair were, in the late 50s, also directors of British Lion. Their comedies included the St Trinian's series, based on the books by Ronald Searle. His second wife was actress Bernadette O'FARRELL.
Biography: 1977, *Launder and Gilliat* by Geoff Brown.
Under the Greenwood Tree 29. The W Plan 30. Children of Chance 30. After Office Hours 31. Josser in the Army 31. Facing the Music 33. Those Were the Days 34. Emil and the Detectives 35. Seven Sinners 36. Educated Evans 36. *Oh Mr Porter* 38. *The Lady Vanishes* 38. A Girl Must Live 39. They Came by Night 40. *Night Train to Munich* 40. Kipps 41. The Young Mr Pitt 42. Millions Like Us (& d) 43. 2000 Women (& d) 43. *I See a Dark Stranger* (& d) 45. Captain Boycott (& d) 47. The Blue Lagoon (& d) 48. *The Happiest Days of Your Life* (& d) 50. Lady Godiva Rides Again (& d) 51. *The Belles of St Trinian's* (& d) 54. Geordie (& d) 55. The Bridal Path (& d) 59. Joey Boy (& d) 65. The Great St Trinian's Train Robbery (& d) 66. The Wildcats of St Trinian's (wd) 80, etc.

Launer, Dale (1953–).
American screenwriter turned director.
Ruthless People 86. Blind Date 87. Dirty Rotten Scoundrels 88. My Cousin Vinny 92. Love Potion 9 (wd) 92, etc.

Laurel, Stan (1890–1965) (Arthur Stanley Jefferson).
British-born comedian, the thin half and gag deviser of the Laurel and Hardy team. Went to USA with Fred Karno's troupe, was in short comedies from 1915, teamed with Hardy 1926. He had director credit on some of their films and virtually directed many others. Special Academy Award 1960 'for his creative pioneering in the field of cinema comedy'.
For list of films see *Oliver Hardy*.
✪ For his genius in the invention of comic gags, and for finding his perfect niche in partnership with Oliver Hardy. *Way Out West*.
❝ They were visual comedians, of course. But they successfully transferred to sound by the use of minimum sound, mainly in the form of carefully scattered catch phrases which arose naturally out of their characters as every child's foolish uncles. When disaster struck, as it inevitably did, who could resist the sight of Olly among the debris, gazing reprovingly at the unharmed Stan and saying:
Here's another nice mess you've gotten me into.
Or:
Why don't you do something to HELP me?
Or simply:
I have NOTHING to say.
Such results are Olly's reward for listening to Stan's suggestions earlier on. Stan's meaning is always unclear to begin with, so that Olly has to say:
Tell me that again.
But he finally gets the drift and agrees:
That's a *good* idea.
Olly of course was always shy, especially with women. When introduced, he was apt to twiddle his tie and observe:
A lot of weather we've been having lately.
His great asset was his courtly manner, preserved even when mistaking an open can of milk for the telephone receiver:
Pardon me for a moment, my ear is full of milk.
Stan, having no catch phrases, relied on lively non sequiturs. When asked:
You never met my wife, did you?
He would reply:
Yes, I never did.
His speciality was putting his foot in it, as when he visits Olly in hospital and announces:
I brought you some hard-boiled eggs and some nuts.
Not surprisingly, he eats them himself, having thoughtfully brought salt and pepper canisters in his pocket. Then there was the time in a bar when they could afford only one beer, ordered by Olly with his usual majesty. Stan did rather ruin the effect by calling after the waiter:
And two clean straws that haven't been used . . .
But he was capable of saying the right thing, as when Olly prepared a mundane repast of coffee and beans. Stan liked it:
Boy, you sure know how to plan a meal!
Behind the scenes, Stan was the producer. Olly was ready to admit:
I have never really worked hard in the creation department.
But he astutely saw the secret of their success:
Those two fellows we created, they were nice, very nice people. They never get anywhere because they are both so dumb, but they don't know they're dumb. One of the reasons why people like us, I guess, is because they feel superior to us.
That was put another way in the opening title to one of their silent films:
Neither Mr Laurel nor Mr Hardy had any

thoughts of getting married. In fact, they had no thoughts of any kind . . .
And the opening of *Come Clean* summed up their best comedy style very neatly:
Mr Hardy holds that a man should always tell his wife the whole truth. Mr Laurel is crazy too.
Mr Laurel had his own philosophy:
We were doing a very simple thing, giving some people some laughs, and that's all we were trying to do.

Lauren, S. K. (1892–1979).
American screenwriter.
An American Tragedy 32. Bond Venus 34. Crime and Punishment 35. One Night of Love 36. Mother Carey's Chickens 39. Flight for Freedom 43, etc.

Laurenson, James (1935–).
New Zealand actor in British and Australian TV, especially series *Boney*.
The Magic Christian 69. Assault 70. The Monster Club 80. Pink Floyd the Wall 82. Heartbreakers 84. The Man Who Fell to Earth (TV) 87. A House in the Hills 93. The Cold Light of Day 94. Prime Suspect 4: Inner Circles (TV) 95. Sharpe's Siege (TV) 96. Sharpe's Mission (TV) 96. Sharpe's Revenge (TV) 97. The Vanishing Man (TV) 98, etc.

Laurents, Arthur (1918–).
American playwright.
Caught (orig sp) 48. Home of the Brave 49. Summertime 55. West Side Story (co-w) 61. The Way We Were (orig sp) 73. The Turning Point (orig sp) (AAN) 77.

Laurie, Hugh (1959–).
English comic actor and writer, most frequently seen partnering Stephen Fry in TV series and advertisements. He was educated at Eton and Cambridge University, where he was a rowing Blue and was a member of the losing crew in the Oxford and Cambridge Boat Race in 1980. He first partnered Fry in a Cambridge Footlights revue in 1981.
Blackadder's Christmas Carol (TV) 88. Peter's Friends 92. A Pin for the Butterfly 94. *Sense and Sensibility* 95. 101 Dalmatians 96. Cousin Bette 97. The Borrowers 97. The Man in the Iron Mask 98, etc.
TV series: Blackadder 84. Blackadder II 86. Blackadder the Third 87. Blackadder Goes Forth 89. A Bit of Fry and Laurie 89–92. Jeeves and Wooster 90–93.

Laurie, John (1897–1980).
Scottish character actor, often in dour roles. On stage from 1921.
Juno and the Paycock 30. Red Ensign 34. *The Thirty-Nine Steps* 35. Tudor Rose 36. As You Like It 36. Farewell Again 37. Edge of the World 38. Q Planes 39. Sailors Three 40. *The Ghost of St Michael's* 41. Old Mother Riley's Ghosts 41. The Gentle Sex 43. Fanny by Gaslight 43. *The Way Ahead* 44. *Henry V* 44. I Know Where I'm Going 45. Caesar and Cleopatra 45. The Brothers 47. Uncle Silas 47. Bonnie Prince Charlie 48. Hamlet 48. Trio 50. Laughter in Paradise 51. The Fake 53. Hobson's Choice 54. The Black Knight 55. Campbell's Kingdom 57. Kidnapped 60. Siege of the Saxons 63. Mr Ten Per Cent 66. Dad's Army 71. The Prisoner of Zenda 79, etc.

Laurie, Piper (1932–) (Rosetta Jacobs).
Pert American leading lady of 50s costume charades; later a notable character actress.
■ Louisa 50. The Milkman 50. Francis Goes to the Races 51. The Prince Who Was a Thief 51. No Room for the Groom 52. Has Anybody Seen My Gal 52. Son of Ali Baba 52. Mississippi Gambler 53. The Golden Blade 53. Dangerous Mission 54. Johnny Dark 54. Dawn at Socorro 54. Smoke Signal 55. Ain't Misbehavin' 55. Kelly and Me 57. Until They Sail 59. *The Hustler* (AAN) 61. *Carrie* (AAN) 76. Ruby 78. Tim 79. Skag (TV) 80. The Bunker (TV) 81. Mae West (TV) 82. The Thorn Birds (TV) 82. Toughlove (TV) 85. Return to Oz 85. Tender Is the Night (TV) 85. Children of a Lesser God (AAN) 86. Distortions 87. Appointment with Death 88. Tiger Warsaw 88. Dream a Little Dream 89. Other People's Money 91. Storyville 92. Trauma 93. Wrestling Ernest Hemingway 93. The Crossing Guard 95. The Grass Harp 95. Fighting for My Daughter (TV) 95. In the Blink of an Eye (TV) 96. Road to Galveston (TV) 96. St Patrick's Day 97. Alone (TV) 97. A Christmas Memory (TV) 97. Intensity (TV) 97. The Faculty 98.
TV series: Twin Peaks 90.

Lauter, Ed (1940–).
American general-purpose actor.
The Last American Hero 73. Executive Action 73. Lolly Madonna XXX 74. The Longest Yard 75. Last Hours before Morning (TV) 75. King Kong 76. The Chicken Chronicles 77. Eureka 83. The Big Score 83. Cujo 83. Lassiter 83. Finders Keepers 84. Death Wish 3 85. Youngblood 85. Raw Deal 86. The Last Days of Patton (TV) 86. Tennessee Waltz 88. Gleaming the Cube 89. Tennessee Nights 89. The Rocketeer 91. School Ties 92. Wagons East! 94. Trial by Jury 94. Girl in the Cadillac 95. Mulholland Falls 96. A Bright Shining Lie (TV) 98, etc.
TV series: B.J. and the Bear 79–80.

Lauter, Harry (1920–1990).
American supporting actor.
The Gay Intruders 48. Tucson 49. Whirlwind 51. The Sea Tiger 52. Dragonfly Squadron 54. The Crooked Web 55. Hellcats of the Navy 57. Gunfight at Dodge City 59. Posse from Hell 61. Ambush Bay 66. More Dead than Alive 68, many others.

Lauzon, Jean-Claude (1953–1997).
French-Canadian director and screenwriter. Died in a plane crash.
Night Zoo/Un Zoo la Nuit 87. Léolo (wd) 92.

Laven, Arnold (1922–).
American director, former dialogue coach. From the 60s to the 80s, he directed episodes of such TV series as *Planet of the Apes*, *Fantasy Island* and *Hill Street Blues*.
Without Warning 52. Down Three Dark Streets 54. The Rack 56. The Monster that Challenged the World 57. Slaughter on Tenth Avenue 58. Anna Lucasta 58. Geronimo (& p) 62. The Glory Guys 66. Rough Night in Jericho 67. Sam Whiskey 68. The Scalphunters (p only) 68, etc.

Laverick, June (1932–).
British leading lady, groomed for stardom by the Rank charm school of the 50s.
Doctor at Large 56. The Gypsy and the Gentleman 57. Son of Robin Hood 58. Follow a Star 59, etc.

Lavery, Emmet (1902–1986).
American screenwriter.
Hitler's Children 43. Behind the Rising Sun 43. The First Legion (orig sp) 51. The Magnificent Yankee (orig sp) 52. The Court Martial of Billy Mitchell 55, etc.

Lavery, Emmet, Jnr (1927–).
American TV executive producer, mainly with Paramount.
Delaney Street 75. Serpico (and series) 76. Nero Wolfe 77, etc.

Lavi, Daliah (1940–) (D. Levenbuch).
Israeli leading lady in international films.
Il Demonio (It.) 63. Old Shatterhand (Ger.) 64. Lord Jim 65. Ten Little Indians 65. The Silencers 66. The Spy with a Cold Nose 67. Some Girls Do 67. Nobody Runs Forever 68. Catlow 72, etc.

Law, Clara.
Hong Kong film director. *Autumn Moon* was winner of the Golden Leopard at the Locarno Film Festival in 1992. She is now resident in Australia.
The Reincarnation of Golden Lotus 89. Farewell China 90. Fruit Punch 91. Autumn Moon 92. Erotique (co-d) 94. Floating Life (Aus.) 96, etc.

Law, John Phillip (1937–).
American leading man.
The Russians Are Coming, the Russians Are Coming 66. Hurry Sundown 67. Barbarella 68. Skidoo 68. The Sergeant 68. Danger: Diabolik 68. The Hawaiians 70. Von Richthofen and Brown 71. The Love Machine 71. The Last Movie 71. The Golden Voyage of Sinbad 73. Your Heaven, My Hell 76. The Cassandra Crossing 77. Tarzan the Ape Man 81. Going Straight 82. Night Train to Terror 84. L.A. Bad 85. American Commandos 85. Moon in Scorpio 86. Space Mutiny 88. Blood Delirium 88. Thunder Warrior III 88. Alienator 89. Cold Heat 90. Day of the Pig 92. Hindsight 97. Ghost Dog/My Magic Dog 97, etc.
TV series: The Young and the Restless 89–90.

Law, Jude (c. 1973–).
English actor, from the theatre. He joined the National Youth Music Theatre before playing in the Granada TV soap opera *Families* and working for the Royal Shakespeare Company and Royal National Theatre. Married actress Sadie Frost in 1997.
Shopping 94. I Love You, I Love You Not 96. Wilde (as Lord Alfred Douglas) 97. Gattaca (US) 97. Midnight in the Garden of Good and Evil (US) 97. The Wisdom of Crocodiles 98. Onegin 99, etc.

Law, Phyllida (1932–).
English actress, the mother of Emma Thompson.
Otley 68. Hitler: The Last Ten Days 73. Tree of Hands 88. Peter's Friends 92. Much Ado about Nothing 93. Emma 96. Winter Guest 96, etc.

Lawford, Peter (1923–1984).
British light leading man, former child actor, in Hollywood from 1938.
Biography: 1991, *Peter Lawford: The Man Who Kept Secrets* by James Spada.
Poor Old Bill 31. The Boy from Barnardo's 38. Mrs Miniver 42. The White Cliffs of Dover 44. Cluny Brown 46. It Happened in Brooklyn 47. Easter Parade 48. Little Women 49. Royal Wedding 52. Exodus 60. Advise and Consent 61. Sylvia 65. Harlow 65. Dead Run (Austria) 67. Salt and Pepper (GB) 68. Buona Sera Mrs Campbell 68. The April Fools 69. One More Time 70. Don't Look behind You (TV) 71. Phantom of Hollywood (TV) 74. Rosebud 75, etc.
TV series: Dear Phoebe 54. The Thin Man 58.

Lawrance, Jody (1930–1986) (Josephine Lawrence Goddard).
American leading lady.
Mask of the Avenger 51. Son of Dr Jekyll 51. The Brigand 52. Captain John Smith and Pocahontas 53. The Scarlet Hour 55. Stagecoach to Dancer's Rock 62.

Lawrence, Barbara (1928–).
American comedy actress, usually seen as wise-cracking friend of the heroine.
Biography: 1977, *Hollywood Starlet: The Career of Barbara Lawrence* by Jim Connor.
Margie 46. You Were Meant for Me 47. Thieves' Highway 49. Two Tickets to Broadway 51. Jesse James Versus the Daltons 54. *Oklahoma* 55. Joe Dakota 57, etc.

Lawrence, Bruno (1949–1995).
British-born actor and musician, in New Zealand from childhood, who became that country's leading film actor, later working in Australia. Died of cancer.
Wild Man 77. Goodbye Pork Pie 80. Smash Palace 81. Race to the Yankee Zephyr 81. Utu 82. Heart of the Stag 83. The Quiet Earth 84. Bridge to Nowhere 85. Rikky and Pete 88. The Delinquents 89. Grievous Bodily Harm 89. Spotswood 91. Jack Be Nimble 93. Gino 94, etc.

Lawrence, D. H. (1885–1930).
Introspective British novelist whose novels have been adapted with varying success for the screen.
The Rocking Horse Winner 49. Lady Chatterley's Lover 58. Sons and Lovers 60. The Fox 68. Women in Love 69. The Virgin and the Gypsy 70. The Rainbow 88, etc.
Lady Chatterley's Lover was filmed again in 1980 and on TV in 1993, and in 1981 Ian McKellen played Lawrence in *Priest of Love*.

Lawrence, Delphi (1926–).
Anglo-Hungarian actress, in British films.
Blood Orange 54. Barbados Quest 55. It's Never Too Late 56. Too Many Crooks 59. Cone of Silence 60. Farewell Performance 63. Pistolero (US) 67. Cops and Robbers 73, many others.

Lawrence, Florence (1886–1938).
American leading lady of the silent screen; one of the industry's chief stars, she was known at first as 'the Biograph Girl'. Retired in the early 20s. Committed suicide.
Miss Jones Entertains 09. Resurrection 10. A Singular Cynic 14. The Enfoldment 20, many others.

Lawrence, Gertrude (1898–1952) (Alexandra Dagmar Lawrence-Klasen).
Vivacious British revue star of the 20s, especially associated with Noel Coward. Despite sporadic attempts, her quality never came across on the screen. She was impersonated by Julie Andrews in *Star!* 68. She was also unflatteringly portrayed as self-centred actress Lorraine Sheldon in *The Man Who Came to Dinner*.
Autobiography: 1949, *A Star Danced*.
■ The Battle of Paris 29. No Funny Business 32. Aren't We All 32. Lord Camber's Ladies 32. No Funny Business 33. Mimi 35. Rembrandt 36. Men are Not Gods 36. Stage Door Canteen 43. *The Glass Menagerie* 50.

Lawrence, Jerome (1915–).
American dramatist and screenwriter, in collaboration with Robert E. Lee.
Auntie Mame (from their play) 58. Inherit the Wind 60. First Monday in October 81.

Lawrence, Marc (1910–) (Max Goldsmith).
American character actor, former opera singer; usually seen as Italian gangster.
Autobiography: 1994, *Long Time, No See*.
White Woman 33. Dr Socrates 35. Penitentiary 38. The Housekeeper's Daughter 39. Johnny Apollo 40. The Monster and the Girl 41. Hold That Ghost 42. Dillinger 45. I Walk Alone 47. The Asphalt Jungle 50. My Favorite Spy 51. Helen of Troy 55. Kill Her Gently 58. Johnny Cool 64. Nightmare in the Sun (wd only) 64. Savage Pampas 66. Custer of the West 67. Krakatoa East of Java 69. Marathon Man 76. The Big Easy 86. Ruby 92. Life with Mikey 93. Four Rooms 95. From Dusk till Dawn 96, etc.

Lawrence, Marjorie (1902–1979).
Australian opera star crippled by polio; portrayed in 1955 by Eleanor Parker in *Interrupted Melody*.

Lawrence, Martin (1965–).
American stand-up comedian, actor, writer and director. He has also released the comedy albums *Talkin' Shit* and *Funk It*.
Do the Right Thing 89. House Party 90. House Party II 91. Boomerang 92. Bad Boys 95. You So Crazy (concert) 95. A Thin Line between Love and Hate (a, co-w, d) 96. Nothing to Lose 97, etc.
TV series: What's Happening Now!! 87–88. The Martin Lawrence Show 92–97.

Lawrence, Peter Lee (1943–1973) (Karl Hirenbach).
Italian leading actor, frequently in spaghetti westerns.
For a Few Dollars More 65. Days of Violence 67. The Man Who Shot Billy the Kid 67. Killer Adios 68. A Pistol for a Hundred Coffins 68. They Paid with Bullets: Chicago 1929 68. Special Forces/Hell in Normandy 68. Garringo 69. Manos Torpes/When Satan Grips the Colt 69. Viva Sabata! 70. Black Beauty (GB) 71. Four Gunmen of the Holy Trinity 71. God in Heaven, Arizona on Earth 72. Il Bacio di una Morta 74, etc.

Lawrence, Quentin (c. 1920–1979).
British director, from TV.
The Trollenberg Terror 55. Cash on Demand 62. The Man Who Finally Died 63. The Secret of Blood Island 65, etc.

Lawrence, T. E. (1888–1935).
British adventurer and soldier whose book *Seven Pillars of Wisdom* made him a cult and remotely inspired the film *Lawrence of Arabia*.

Lawrence, Viola (1894–1973).
American editor, long with Columbia.
An Alabaster Box 17. Fighting the Flames 21. Bulldog Drummond 29. Man's Castle 33. Craig's Wife 36. Penitentiary 38. Here Comes Mr Jordan 41. My Sister Eileen 42. Cover Girl 44. Hit the Hay 46. The Dark Past 48. Tokyo Joe 49. Sirocco 51. Miss Sadie Thompson 53. Queen Bee 55. Pal Joey 57. Who Was That Lady 60, many others.

Lawson, John Howard (1886–1977).
American writer with Marxist affiliations.
Heart of Spain 37. Algiers 38. *Blockade* (AAN) 38. *Five Came Back* 39. *Sahara* 43. Counter-Attack 43. Smash-Up 47, etc.

Lawson, Leigh (1944–).
British light leading man of the 70s. Married actress and model TWIGGY.
Ghost Story 74. Percy's Progress 74. Love among the Ruins (TV) 75. Golden Rendezvous 77. The Devil's Advocate 78. Tess 80. Why Didn't They Ask Evans? (TV) 81. Murder Is Easy (TV) 81. Lace (TV) 84. Sword of the Valiant (TV) 85. Queenie (TV) 87. Madame Sousatzka 88. O Pioneers! (TV) 92. Battling for Baby (TV) 92, etc.
TV series: Kinsey 92.

Lawson, Sarah (1928–).
British leading lady of the 50s.
The Browning Version 50. Street Corner 52. Blue Peter 54. It's Never Too Late 55. Night of the Big Heat/Island of the Burning Doomed 67. Battle of Britain 69. The Stud 78, etc.

Lawson, Wilfrid (1900–1966) (Wilfrid Worsnop).
British character actor, on stage from 1916; revelled in eccentric parts.
■ East Lynne on the Western Front 31. Strike it Rich 33. Turn of the Tide 35. The Man Who Made Diamonds 37. Bank Holiday 38. The Terror 38. Yellow Sands 38. The Gaunt Stranger 38. *Pygmalion* 38. Stolen Life 39. Dead Man's Shoes 39. *Pastor Hall* 40. Gentleman of Venture 40. The Man at the Gate 41. Danny Boy 41. Jeannie 41. The Farmer's Wife 41. Tower of Terror 41. *Hard Steel* 42. The Night Has Eyes 42. *The Great Mr Handel* 42. Thursday's Child 43. Fanny by Gaslight 44. The Turners of Prospect Road 47. Make Me an Offer 55. The Prisoner 55. An Alligator Named Daisy 55. Now and Forever 56. The Naked Truth 57. Hell Drivers 57. Tread Softly Stranger 59. Room at the Top 59. Expresso Bongo 60. The Naked Edge 61. Nothing Barred 61. Over the Odds 61. Go to Blazes 62. Postman's Knock 62. Tom Jones 63. Becket 64. *The Wrong Box* 66. The Viking Queen 66.

Lawton, Charles, Jnr (1904–1965).
American cinematographer.
My Dear Miss Aldrich 36. Miracles for Sale 39. Gold Rush Maisie 41. Fingers at the Window 42. Abroad with Two Yanks 44. The Thrill of Brazil 46. *The Lady from Shanghai* 48. Shockproof 49. Rogues of Sherwood Forest 50. Mask of the Avenger 51. *The Happy Time* 52. Miss Sadie Thompson 53. Drive a Crooked Road 54. The Long Gray Line 55. Jubal 56. *3.10 to Yuma* 57. The Last Hurrah 58. It Happened to Jane 59. Two Rode Together 61. 13 West Street 62. Spencer's Mountain 63. Youngblood Hawke 64. A Rage to Live 65, many others.

Lawton, Frank (1904–1969).
Charming but undynamic British leading man of the 30s, husband of Evelyn Laye; in British and American films.
Young Woodley 28. Birds of Prey 30. The Skin Game 31. The Outsider 31. Michael and Mary 31. After Office Hours 32. Cavalcade 33. Heads We Go 33. Friday the Thirteenth 33. One More River 34. *David Copperfield* (title role) 34. The Invisible Ray 36. The Devil Doll 36. The Mill on the Floss 37. The Four Just Men 39. Went the Day Well? 42. The Winslow Boy 48. Rough Shoot 52. The Rising of the Moon 57. A Night to Remember 57. Gideon's Day 57, etc.

Lay, Beirne, Jnr (1909–1982).
American screenwriter.
I Wanted Wings 41. Twelve O'Clock High 49. Above and Beyond 50. Strategic Air Command 54. Toward the Unknown 56, etc.

Laydu, Claude (1927–).
Undernourished-looking French leading actor.
Diary of a Country Priest 50. Nous Sommes Tous des Assassins 52. Symphonie d'Amour 55. Le Dialogue des Carmélites 59, etc.

Laye, Evelyn (1900–1996) (Elsie Evelyn Lay).
British musical comedy star of the 20s and 30s; films rare. Married Frank Lawton.
Autobiography: 1958, *Boo to My Friends*.
■ Luck of the Navy 27. Queen of Scandal 30. One Heavenly Night (US) 31. Waltz Time 33. Princess Charming 33. *Evensong* 34. The Night is Young 34. I'll Turn to You 46. Make Mine a Million 59. Theatre of Death 66. Say Hello to Yesterday 70. Within and Without (It.) 70. Second Star to the Right 80.

Lazar, Irving (1907–1993).
Prominent American agent, nicknamed 'Swifty' by Humphrey Bogart for making five movie deals for him in a day. He was noted for his skill in deals and was in part responsible for the growing importance and power of the agent in movie-making in Hollywood.

Lazenby, George (1939–).
Australian leading man who made the big jump from TV commercials to playing James Bond – once. In the 70s and 80s he raced motorcycles and in the 90s backed a restaurant chain, the Spy House.
On Her Majesty's Secret Service 69. Universal Soldier 71. The Man from Hong Kong 75. Cover Girls (TV) 77. Evening in Byzantium (TV) 78. Saint Jack 79. Never Too Young to Die 86. Hell Hunters 87. Eyes of the Beholder 91. Fatally Yours 95. Twinsitters 95, etc.
TV series: Rituals 84–85.

Le Borg, Reginald (1902–1989).
Austrian-born director, in Hollywood from 1937, at first as shorts director. Output mainly routine with occasional flashes of talent.
Book: 1992, *The Films of Reginald Le Borg* by Wheeler Winston Dixon.
She's for Me 42. The Mummy's Ghost 44. Calling Dr Death 44. *San Diego I Love You* 45. Joe Palooka, Champ 46. Young Daniel Boone 47. Wyoming Trail 49. Bad Blonde 51. Sins of Jezebel 53. The Black Sleep 56. The Dalton Girls 57. The Flight that Disappeared 61. The Diary of a Madman 62, many others.

Le Breton, Auguste (1915–1991).
French writer.
Razzia sur la Chnouf 54. Rififi 55. Bob le Flambeur 56. Rafles sur la Ville 57. Riff Raff Girls 59. Rififi in Paris 66. The Sicilian Clan 68, etc.

Le Brock, Kelly (1960–).
American leading lady. Formerly married to actor Steven Seagal.
The Woman in Red 84. Weird Science 85. Hard to Kill 90. Betrayal of the Dove 92. Hard Bounty 94. Tracks of a Killer 95. Wrongfully Accused 98, etc.

Le Carré, John (1931–) (David John Moore Cornwell).
British spy novelist, whose works have been eagerly filmed, though they centre on the more depressing aspects of espionage.
The Spy Who Came in from the Cold 66. The Deadly Affair (Call for the Dead) 67. The Looking Glass War 70. Tinker Tailor Soldier Spy (TV) 79. Smiley's People 82. The Little Drummer Girl 84. A Perfect Spy (TV) 87.
❝ If you live in secrecy, you think in secrecy. It is the very nature of the life you lead as an intelligence officer in a secret room that the ordinary winds of common sense don't blow through it. You are constantly looking to relate to your enemy in intellectual, adversarial and conspiratorial terms. – *J.L.C.*
Where I kick myself is where I think I actually contributed to the myth of the intelligence services being very good. – *J.L.C.*

Le Chanois, Jean-Paul (1909–1985) (J.-P. Dreyfus).
French director.
L'École Buissonnière 48. La Belle Que Voilà 51. Papa, Mama, the Maid and I 54. The Case of Dr Laurent 56. Les Misérables 58. Monsieur 64. Le Jardinier d'Argenteuil 66, etc.

Le Fanu, J. Sheridan (1814–1873).
Irish novelist specializing in mystery and the occult. His story *Carmilla*, about lesbian vampires, has been filmed as *Blood and Roses* and *The Vampire Lovers; Uncle Silas* was filmed in 1949.

Le Gallienne, Eva (1899–1991).
Distinguished American stage actress.
■ Prince of Players 54. The Devil's Disciple 59. Resurrection (AAN) 80.

Le Mat, Paul (1945–).
American leading man.
American Graffiti 73. Firehouse (TV) 74. Aloha Bobby and Rose 75. Citizen's Band 77. More American Graffiti 79. Melvin and Howard 80. Death Valley 81. Jimmy the Kid 82. Strange Invaders 83. The Hanoi Hilton 87. Private Investigations 87. Easy Wheels 89. Blind Witness (TV) 89. Puppet Master 89. Deuce Coupe 92. Wishman 93. Caroline at Midnight 94. Deep Down 94. Sensation 94. American History X 98, etc.

Le May, Alan (1899–1964).
American writer.
Reap the Wild Wind 42. The Adventures of Mark Twain 44. Tap Roots 48. High Lonesome (& d) 50. Thunder in the Dust 51. I Dream of Jeannie 53. The Searchers (oa) 56, etc.

Le Mesurier, John (1912–1983).
British character actor. Usually played bewildered professional men; a favourite for cameo roles from 1946. Married Hattie Jacques.
Autobiography: 1983, *A Jobbing Actor*.
Death in the Hand 48. Beautiful Stranger 54. Private's Progress 55. *Happy Is the Bride* 57. I Was Monty's Double 58. *School for Scoundrels* 60. *Only Two Can Play* 61. Invasion Quartet 62. The Pink Panther 63. The Moonspinners 64. Masquerade 65. Where the Spies Are 65. The Wrong Box 66. The Midas Run 69. *The Magic Christian* 70. Dad's Army 71. The Garnett Saga 72. Confessions of a Window Cleaner 75. Stand Up Virgin Soldiers 77. The Spaceman and King Arthur 79. The Fiendish Plot of Dr Fu Manchu 80. A Married Man (TV) 83, many others.
TV series: *Dad's Army* 67–77.

Le Roy, Mervyn (1900–1987).
American director, former actor, in Hollywood from 1924.
Autobiography: 1975, *Take One*.
Hot Stuff 27. Top Speed 28. Broken Dishes 29. *Little Caesar* 30. Broadminded 31. *Five Star Final* 32. Three on a Match 32. *I Am a Fugitive from a Chain Gang* 32. Two Seconds 32. *Tugboat Annie* 32. Gold Diggers of 1933. Hi Nellie 33. Oil for the Lamps of China 33. Hot to Handle 33. Sweet Adeline 34. Page Miss Glory 34. I Found Stella Parish 35. Anthony Adverse 36. Three Men on a Horse 36. *They Won't Forget* 37. Fools for Scandal 38. Stand Up and Fight (p only) 38. The Wizard of Oz (p only) 39. At the Circus (p only) 39. *Waterloo Bridge* 40. Escape 40. Blossoms in the Dust 41. Unholy Partners 41. Johnny Eager 41. *Random Harvest* (AAN) 42. Madame Curie 43. Thirty Seconds over Tokyo 44; war service; Without Reservations 47. Homecoming 48. Little Women 49. Any Number Can Play 49. East Side West Side 50. Quo Vadis 51. Lovely To Look At 52. Million Dollar Mermaid 53. Rose Marie 54. Mister Roberts (co-d) 55. Strange Lady in Town (& p) 55. The Bad Seed (& p) 56. Toward the Unknown (& p) 56. No Time for Sergeants (& p) 58. Home Before Dark (& p) 59. The FBI Story (& p) 59. A Majority of One (& p) 60. The Devil at Four O'Clock 61. Gypsy (& p) 62. Mary Mary (& p) 63. Moment to Moment (& p) 65, etc.

Leach, Rosemary (1935–).
British character actress, mostly on TV.
Brief Encounter (TV) 74. That'll Be the Day 74. SOS Titanic 79. The Jewel in the Crown (TV) 82. The Bride 84. Turtle Diary 85. A Room with a View 85. The Children 90. The Mystery of Edwin Drood 93. The Hawk 93. The Buccaneers (TV) 95, etc.
TV series: Berkeley Square 98.

Leachman, Cloris (1926–).
American character actress, mostly on TV.
Kiss Me Deadly 54. The Rack 56. The Chapman Report 62. Butch Cassidy and the Sundance Kid 69. WUSA 70. *The Last Picture Show* (AA) 71. Haunts of the Very Rich (TV) 72. Dillinger 73. Charley and the Angel 74. Daisy Miller 74. Hitch Hike (TV) 74. Crazy Mama 75. A Girl Named Sooner (TV) 75. Death Sentence (TV) 75. Young Frankenstein 75. Run Stranger Run 76. High Anxiety 78. SOS Titanic (TV) 79. The North Avenue Irregulars 79. Backstairs at the White House (TV) 79. Willa (TV) 79. Herbie Goes Bananas 80. History of the World Part One 81. Hansel and Gretel 87. Walk Like a Man 87. The Victory 88. Love Hurts 89. Prancer 89. Texasville 90. Miracle Child (TV) 93. My Boyfriend's Back 93. The Beverly Hillbillies 93. A Troll in Central Park (voice) 94. Double Double Toil and Trouble (TV) 94. Now and Then 95, etc.
TV series: Lassie (50s). The Mary Tyler Moore Show 70–73. *Phyllis* 75–76. The Facts of Life 86–88.

Leacock, Philip (1917–1990).
British director, noted for his way with children; latterly worked in American television.
■ *The Brave Don't Cry* 52. Appointment in London 52. *The Kidnappers* 53. Escapade 55. The Spanish Gardener 56. High Tide at Noon 57. Innocent Sinners 58. The Rabbit Trap 58. Let No Man Write My Epitaph 59. Hand in Hand 60. Take a Giant Step 61. Reach for Glory 61. 13 West Street 62. The War Lover 63. Tamahine 63. Adam's Woman 70. The Birdmen (TV) 71. The Great Man's Whiskers (TV) 72. When Michael Calls (TV) 72. Key West (TV) 72. The Daughters of Joshua Cabe (TV) 72. Baffled (TV) 72. Dying Room Only (TV) 73. Killer on Board (TV) 77. Wild and Wooly (TV) 78. The Curse of King Tut's Tomb (TV) 80. Angel City (TV) 80.

Leacock, Richard (1921–).
British-born cameraman and director, brother of Philip Leacock. Worked with Flaherty and became associated with the 'cinema vérité' school.
Primary 60. The Chair 62. Quints 63. Chiefs 68. Maidstone 70. Tread (d) 72. Elliott Carter 80. Lulu in Berlin (d) 84. Dance Black America 85. Girltalk 88, etc.

Lean, Sir David (1908–1991).
Distinguished British director whose work gradually took on epic proportions. Born in Croydon to a Quaker family, after working as a clerk he began as a runner at Gaumont Studios, where he was employed in various capacities before becoming an editor, eventually gaining the reputation as the best in Britain. He worked as co-director with Noël Coward on *In Which We Serve* and then became co-founder of the production company Cineguild, which began by filming Coward's plays. His six wives included actresses Kay WALSH and Ann TODD. His lovers included costume designer Margaret FURSE.
Biographies: 1989, *David Lean* by Stephen M. Silverman. 1996, *David Lean* by Kevin Brownlow.
■ In Which We Serve (co-d) 42. This Happy Breed 44. *Blithe Spirit* 45. *Brief Encounter* (AAN) 46. *Great Expectations* (AAN) 46. *Oliver Twist* 48. The Passionate Friends 48. Madeleine 49. *The Sound Barrier* (& p) 51. *Hobson's Choice* (& p) 54. *Summertime*/Summer Madness (AAN) 55. *The Bridge on the River Kwai* (AA) 57. *Lawrence of Arabia* (AA) 62. *Dr Zhivago* (AAN) 65. *Ryan's Daughter* 70. A Passage to India (AANd, AANw, AANed) 84.
✪ For his understanding of the art of cinema, despite his final submergence of his sensitive talent in pretentious but empty spectaculars. *Great Expectations*.
❝ I hope the money men don't find out that I'd pay them to let me do this. – *D.L.*
I wouldn't take the advice of a lot of so-called critics on how to shoot a close-up of a teapot. – *D.L.*
Actors can be a terrible bore on the set, though I enjoy having dinner with them. – *D.L.*
Inside every Lean film there is a fat film screaming to get out. – *Anon*
There was a touch of the bully about him – he'd take it out on the people who were weakest and most dependent. – *Judy Davis*
He played cruel games with us actors, did David. Not respecting actors too much, finding their breaking point gave him a kick. – *Sarah Miles*
He thought about film as a Jesuit thinks about his vocation. – *Anthony Havelock-Allan*

Lear, Norman (1926–).
American producer, former comedy writer.
Divorce American Style 67. The Night They Raided Minsky's 68. Start the Revolution without Me 69. Cold Turkey 71. The Princess Bride 87, etc.
TV series: *All in the Family* 71. *Maude* 72. Sanford and Son 72–78. One Day at a Time 75–84. Mary Hartman, Mary Hartman 76, etc.

Learned, Michael (1939–).
Motherly American character actress who scored on TV in *The Waltons* 72–81 and briefly in *Nurse* 82.
Hurricane (TV) 74. It Couldn't Happen to a Nicer Guy (TV) 74. Widow (TV) 76. Little Mo (TV) 78. Touched by Love 80. Power 86. All My Sons (TV) 86. Deadly Business (TV) 86. Roots: The Gift (TV) 88. Murder in New Hampshire: The Pamela Smart Story (TV) 91. Dragon: The Bruce Lee Story 93, etc.

Leary, Denis (1957–).
Aggressive American stand-up comedian and actor. He is co-founder of the production company Apostle Pictures.
The Sandlot/The Sandlot Kids 93. Gunmen 93. National Lampoon's Loaded Weapon 93. Who's the Man 93. Demolition Man 93. Judgment Night 93. The Ref 94. The Neon Bible 95. Operation Dumbo Drop 95. Two If by Sea/Stolen Hearts (& co-w) 96. Underworld 96. Subway Stories: Tales from the Underground (TV) 97. The Second Civil War (TV) 97. The Matchmaker 97. Wag the Dog 97. The Real Blonde 97. Suicide Kings 98. Small Soldiers 98. A Bug's Life (voice) 98, etc.

Leasor, James (1923–).
British thriller writer whose Dr Jason Love was brought to the screen in 1964 in *Where the Spies Are*.

Léaud, Jean-Pierre (1944–).
French leading actor who began as a boy star.
Les Quatre Cents Coups 59. Love at Twenty 61. Masculin-Féminin 66. La Chinoise 67. Stolen Kisses 68. Pigsty 69. Last Tango in Paris 72. Day for Night 73. Love on the Run 79. Detective 84. Treasure Island 85. With All Hands 86. 36 Fillette 88. Bunker Palace Hotel 89. I Hired a Contract Killer 90. Zone 91. Bohemian Life/La Vie de Bohème 92. La Naissance de l'Amour 93. Personne Ne M'Aime 94. Nine Months/Neuf Mois 94. Irma Vep 96, etc.

Leavitt, Sam (1904–1984).
American cinematographer.
The Thief 52. *A Star is Born* 54. Carmen Jones 54. The Man with the Golden Arm 55. *The Defiant Ones* (AA) 58. Anatomy of a Murder (AAN) 59. Exodus (AAN) 60. Advise and Consent 62. Two on a Guillotine 64. Major Dundee 65. Brainstorm 65. An American Dream 66. Guess Who's Coming to Dinner 67. The Desperados 68. The Grasshopper 70. Star Spangled Girl 71. The Man in the Glass Booth 75, etc.

Lebedeff, Ivan (1899–1953).
Russian character actor, former diplomat, in US from 1925.
The Sorrows of Satan 27. Midnight Mystery 30. Blonde Bombshell 33. China Seas 35. History Is Made at Night 37. Hotel for Women 39. The Shanghai Gesture 41. They Are Guilty 45. The Snows of Kilimanjaro 52, many others.

LeBlanc, Matt (1967–).
American actor, best known for his role in the TV sitcom *Friends*.
Anything to Survive (TV) 90. Red Shoe Diaries 3: Another Woman's Lipstick 93. Ed 96. Lost in Space 98, etc.

Leclerc, Ginette (1912–1992).
Sulky-looking French stage and screen actress.
Prison sans Barreaux 38. *La Femme du Boulanger* 38. *Le Corbeau* 43. Le Plaisir 51. Les Amants du Tage 54. Gas-Oil 55. Le Cave Se Rebiffe 61. Goto, Island of Love 68. Tropic of Cancer 69, etc.

Leconte, Patrice (1947–).
French director and screenwriter, a former comic-book writer and artist, who switched from making local comedies to dramas with an international appeal.
Monsieur Hire 90. The Hairdresser's Husband/Le Mari de la Coiffeuse (co-w, d) 91. *Tango* 93. Le Parfum d'Yvonne 94. The Grand Dukes 95. Ridicule (AAN) 96, etc.

Ledebur, Friedrich (c. 1908–).
Austrian actor of eccentric roles.
Moby Dick 56. Roots of Heaven 58. The Blue Max 66. Alfred the Great 69. Juliet of the Spirits 69. Slaughterhouse Five 72. Ginger and Fred 86, etc.

Leder, Mimi (c. 1952–).
American director, from television, where she directed many of the episodes of *ER*, winning two Emmy awards, and was also nominated for directing episodes of *China Beach*, the medical drama set in Vietnam. So far, her features have been action movies. She graduated as a cinematographer from the American Film Institute's graduate film programme in the mid-70s and worked in television as a script supervisor. She is the daughter of independent director Paul Leder. Married actor and writer Gary Werntz.
A Little Piece of Heaven 91. House of Secrets (TV) 93. The Innocent (TV) 94. The Peacemaker 97. Deep Impact 98, etc.

Leder, Paul (1926–1996).
American director, writer and producer of independent low-budget movies, a former singer and dancer on the Broadway stage.
AS ACTOR: The Grass Eater 61. Five Minutes to Love 63. How to Succeed with Girls 64.
AS DIRECTOR: Marigold Man 70. I Dismember Mama 72. Ape 76. My Friends Need Killing 76. Sketches of a Strangler 78. I'm Going to Be Famous 83. Vultures 84. Body Count 88. Goin' to Chicago 90. The Abduction of Alison Tate 92. The Baby Doll Murders 93. Killing Obsession 94. The Wacky Adventures of Dr Boris and Nurse Shirley 95, etc.

Lederer, Charles (1906–1976).
High-spirited American screenwriter and, later, director, in Hollywood from 1931. The nephew of actress Marion Davies, he was born in New York City and was a former journalist. He worked for writers Ben Hecht and Charles MacArthur when they set up their own unsuccessful production company, and spent a short period in the mid-30s as assistant to Irving Thalberg at MGM. Frequently off-hand in his attitude to work, and often mocking of studio bosses, he was also producer and co-author of the Broadway musical *Kismet*, which he helped adapt for the screen.
The Front Page 31. Topaze 33. Comrade X 40. His Girl Friday 40. Ride the Pink Horse 47. *Kiss of Death* 47. The Thing 52. It Started with a Kiss 58. The Spirit of St Louis 58. Can Can 59. Ocean's Eleven 61. Mutiny on the Bounty 62, many others.
■ AS DIRECTOR: Fingers at the Window 42. On the Loose 51. Never Steal Anything Small (& w) 58, etc.

Lederer, Francis (1906–).
Czech-born leading man, in Hollywood from 1933, after European stage and film experience.
Pandora's Box (Ger.) 28. Atlantic (Ger.) 30. The Bracelet (Ger.) 32. The Pursuit of Happiness 34. It's All Yours 36. The Lone Wolf in Paris 37. Midnight 38. *Confessions of a Nazi Spy* 39. The Man I Married 40. The Bridge of San Luis Rey 44. A Voice in the Wind 45. The Diary of a Chambermaid 45. Million Dollar Weekend 48. Captain Carey USA 49. A Woman of Distinction 50. Stolen Identity 53. Lisbon 56. The Return of Dracula 58. Terror Is a Man 59, etc.

Lederman, D. Ross (1895–1972).
American director, former prop man for Mack Sennett.
Man Hunter 30. Riding Tornado 32. Glamour for Sale 40. The Body Disappears 41. Strange Alibi 41. Shadows on the Stairs 43. Key Witness 47, etc.

Ledoux, Fernand (1897–1993).
Belgian-born actor who had a long and distinguished stage and film career in France, working in more than 800 plays and movies. He was a member of the Comédie Française for more than 20 years.
Le Carnaval des Vérités 19. L'Homme à la Barbiche 32. Le Vagabond Bien-aimé 36. The Human Beast/La Bête Humaine 38. The Devil's Envoys/Les Visiteurs du Soir 42. Devil's Daughter/La Fille du Diable 46. An Act of Love/Un Acte d'Amour 54. Les Misérables 58. The Truth/La Verité 60. The Big Gamble (US) 61. The Longest Day (US) 62. The Trial 62. Up from the Beach (US) 65. Donkey Skin/Peau d'Ane 71. A Trillion Dollars/Mille Milliards de Dollars 82, etc.

Leduc, Paul (1942–).
Mexican director and a pioneer of the country's 'New Cinema' movement. He studied architecture and theatre before becoming a film critic and worked in French TV before returning to Mexico, where he first produced and directed documentaries.
Reed: Mexico Insurgente 73. Etnocido: Notas sobre el Mezquital 78. Historias Prohibidas de Pulgarcito 79. La Cabeza de la Hidra (TV) 81. Frida 86. Barocco 89. Latino Bar 91. Dollar Mambo 93, etc.

Lee, Ang (1954–).
US-based Taiwanese director who studied at the University of Illinois and New York University.
Pushing Hands 91. The Wedding Banquet (AAN) 93. Eat Drink Man Woman (AAN) 94. *Sense and Sensibility* 95. *The Ice Storm* 97. Ride with the Devil 98, etc.

Lee, Anna (1914–) (Joanna Winnifrith).
British leading lady, in US since 1939 and a regular on the soap opera *General Hospital*.
Ebb Tide 32. The Camels Are Coming 36. King Solomon's Mines 37. The Four Just Men 39. My Life with Caroline 41. Summer Storm 44. Fort Apache 48. Whatever Happened to Baby Jane? 62. The Sound of Music 65. Seven Women 65. In Like Flint 67. Scruples (TV) 80. Right Hand Man 87. Beverly Hills Brats 89. What Can I Do? 94, many others.

Lee, Belinda (1935–1961).
Blonde British starlet trained for stardom by Rank but given poor material: appeared in Continental semi-spectaculars and died in car crash.
The Runaway Bus 54. The Belles of St Trinian's 54. Man of the Moment 55. Who Done It? 55. The Feminine Touch 56. The Secret Place 56. The Big Money 56. Miracle in Soho 57. Dangerous Exile 57. Nor the Moon by Night 58. Les Drageurs 59. Nights of Lucretia Borgia 59. Carthage in Flames 61, etc.

Lee, Bernard (1908–1981).
British character actor with solid, friendly personality, on stage from 1926. In films, often a sergeant or a superintendent . . . or 'M' in the James Bond films.
The River House Mystery 35. The Terror 37. Spare a Copper 40. Once a Crook 41; war service; The Courtneys of Curzon Street 47. *The Fallen Idol* 48. Quartet 48. *The Third Man* 49. The Blue Lamp 50. Appointment with Venus 51. The Gift Horse 52. The Purple Plain 54. *Father Brown* 54. The Battle of the River Plate 56. Dunkirk 58. Danger Within 59. The Angry Silence 59. The Secret Partner 60. Whistle Down the Wind 61. *Dr No* 62. Two Left Feet 63. From Russia with Love 63. Ring of Spies 63. Goldfinger 64. The Legend of Young Dick Turpin 65. Thunderball 65. The Spy Who Came In from the Cold 65. You Only Live Twice 66. The Raging Moon 70. Dulcima 71. Frankenstein and the Monster from Hell 73. The Man with the Golden Gun 74. Beauty and the Beast 76. The Spy who Loved Me 77. Moonraker 79, many others.

Lee, Bill (1928–).
American composer and musician, for the films of his son, Spike Lee.
She's Gotta Have It 86. School Daze 88. Do the Right Thing 89. Mo' Better Blues (s) 90, etc.

Lee, Billy (1930–1989).
American child star of the 30s.
Wagon Wheels 34. Coconut Grove 38. *The Biscuit Eater* 40. Hold Back the Dawn 41. Mrs Wiggs of the Cabbage Patch 42, etc.

Lee, Brandon (1965–1993).
American action film star, the son of Bruce Lee. Born in Oakland, California, he was brought up in Hong Kong, where he was taught martial arts from an early age by his father. He died following a shooting accident while filming *The Crow*, a film about a rock musician who returns from the dead.
Kung Fu: The Next Generation (TV) 85. Legacy of Rage 86. Lazer Mission 87. Showdown in Little Tokyo 91. Rapid Fire 92. The Crow 94, etc.
❝ None of my friends would come over to the house when I was a kid because they were all scared to death. There would always be six or seven grown men in the backyard screaming and throwing each other around. – *B.L.*

Lee, Bruce (1940–1973) (Lee Yenn Kam).
Diminutive Chinese-American leading man and practitioner of the martial arts. After comparative failure in Hollywood (a bit part in *Marlowe* 69, a supporting role in a TV series *The Green Hornet* 68), he went to Hong Kong and became a sensation in 'chop socky' movies. A biopic of his life, *Dragon*, starring Jason Scott Lee, was released in 1993. He was the father of Brandon Lee.
Biography: 1997, *The Unseen Bruce Lee* by Louis Chunovic.
Fist of Fury 72. The Big Boss 72. Enter the Dragon 73. The Way of the Dragon 73. Game of Death (posthumously re-edited) 79, etc.
❝ Bruce Lee had bad eyesight and one leg that was shorter than the other. But he had a mental image of what he wanted, and he became the quintessential martial artist and the first Chinese superstar in American films. – *Chuck Norris*

Lee, Canada (1907–1952) (Lionel Canegata).
American actor.
■ Lifeboat 43. Body and Soul 47. Lost Boundaries 49. Cry the Beloved Country 52.

Lee, Christopher (1922–).
Gaunt British actor whose personality lends itself best to sinister or horrific parts. Seems to have made more films than any other living actor, and has certainly played most of the known monsters.
Autobiography: 1977, *Tall, Dark and Gruesome*.
Corridor of Mirrors 47. Hamlet 48. They Were Not Divided 49. Prelude to Fame 50. Valley of Eagles 51. The Crimson Pirate 52. Moulin Rouge 53. The Dark Avenger 54. Private's Progress 55. Alias John Preston 56. Moby Dick 56. *The Curse of Frankenstein* (as the monster) 56. Ill Met by Moonlight 57. The Traitor 57. A Tale of Two Cities 57. *Dracula* (title role) 58. Corridors of Blood 58. The Hound of the Baskervilles (as Sir Henry) 59. The Man Who Could Cheat Death 59. *The Mummy* (title role) 59. Beat Girl 60. City of the Dead 60. The Hands of Orlac 60. Taste of Fear 61. The Terror of the Tongs 61. The Devil's Daffodil 62. Pirates of Blood River 62. Sherlock Holmes and the Deadly Necklace (Ger.) 62. The Gorgon 63. Dr Terror's House of Horrors 63. She 65. The Face of Fu Manchu 65. The Skull 65. Dracula Prince of Darkness 65. Rasputin the Mad Monk 65. Theatre of Death 66. Night of the Big Heat 67. The Devil Rides Out 68. Curse of the Crimson Altar 68. Julius Caesar 70. I Monster 71. Dracula AD 1972 72. The Wicker Man 73. The Satanic Rites of Dracula 73. The Three Musketeers 74. The Man with the Golden Gun 74. Diagnosis Murder 75. To the Devil a Daughter 75. The Wicker Man 75. Killer Force 75. Airport 77 77. Return from Witch Mountain 78. The Silent Flute 78. The Pirate (TV) 78. Starship Invasions 78. The Passage 78. Arabian Adventure 79. Circle of Iron 79. 1941 79. Serial 80. The Salamander 80. An Eye for an Eye 81. Safari 3000 82. The House of Long Shadows 83. The Return of Captain Invincible 83. Howling II 85. The Rosebud Beach Hotel 85. Jocks 86. Dark Mission 88. Mask of Murder 89. The Return of the Musketeers 89. The Miser/L'Avaro 89. Panga 90. Gremlins 2: The New Batch 90. Honeymoon Academy 90. Sherlock Holmes and the Leading Lady (TV) 91. Curse III: Blood Sacrifice 91. Cybereden (It.) 93. Police Academy 7: Mission to Moscow 94. Funny Man 94. The Stupids 96. Ivanhoe (TV) 97. Jinnah (title role) (Pak.) 98, etc.
❝ I stopped appearing as Dracula in 1972 because in my opinion the presentation of the character had deteriorated to such an extent, particularly bringing him into the contemporary day and age, that it really no longer had any meaning. – C.L.
As Boris Karloff told me, 'You have to make your mark in something other actors cannot, or will not, do and if it's a success you'll not be forgotten. The name of the game is survival.' – *C.L.*

Lee, Davey (1925–).
American child actor of the early talkies.
The Singing Fool 28. Sonny Boy 29. The Squealer 30, etc.

Lee, Dixie (1911–1952) (Wilma Wyatt).
American leading lady, wife of Bing Crosby. She later had problems with alcoholism. Died of cancer. Dorothy Parker drew on her life for the story of *Smash-Up, the Story of a Woman* 47, which dealt with an alcoholic.
Not for Sale 24. Movietone Follies 29. The Big Party 30. No Limit 31. Manhattan Love Song 34. Love in Bloom 35, etc.
❝ Once I discovered that the old man wasn't the pillar of virtue he pretended to be, and that her insinuations weren't the half-crazed ramblings of a drunk, I stopped being afraid of her. She became more of a person to me, and I started to feel some sympathy for her drinking. – *Gary Crosby, her eldest son*

Lee, Dorothy (1911–) (Marjorie Millsap).
American leading lady of the 30s, especially associated with Wheeler and Wolsey.
Syncopation 29. Rio Rita 29. The Cuckoos 30. Half Shot at Sunrise 30. Cracked Nuts 31. Caught Plastered 31. Girl Crazy 32. Take a Chance 33.

Hips, Hips Hooray 34. The Rainmakers 35. Silly Billies 36. Twelve Crowded Hours 39, etc.

Lee, Eugene (1933–).
American child actor who played 'Porky' in many of the Our Gang comedies of the mid to late 30s. Born in Fort Worth, Texas, he later became a teacher.

Lee, Gypsy Rose (1913–1970) (Louise Hovick).
American burlesque artiste, on stage from six years old: her early life, glamorized, is recounted in *Gypsy* 62, based on her 1957 book. She was the sister of actress June Havoc. The second of her three husbands was actor Alexander Kirkland, and she had a son by director Otto Preminger.
■ You Can't Have Everything 37. Ali Baba Goes to Town 38. My Lucky Star 39. Belle of the Yukon 44. Babes in Baghdad 52. Screaming Mimi 57. Wind Across the Everglades 58. The Stripper 62. The Trouble with Angels 66.
TV series: The Pruitts of Southampton 66.
“ Royalties are all very well, but shaking the beads brings in the money quicker. – *G.R.L.*
God is love, but get it in writing. – *G.R.L.*

Lee, Jack (1913–).
British director, originally in documentaries. Moved to work in Australia in the mid-50s.
Close Quarters 44. Children on Trial 46. The Woman in the Hall 47. *The Wooden Horse* (co-d) 50. Turn the Key Softly 53. *A Town Like Alice* 56. Robbery under Arms 57. The Captain's Table 58. Circle of Deception 61. From the Tropics to the Snow (doc) 64, etc.

Lee, Jason (1971–).
American actor in independent films, a former professional skateboarder.
My Crazy Life/Mi Vida Loca 93. Mallrats 95. Drawing Flies 96. A Better Place 97. Chasing Amy 97. Weapons of Mass Distraction (TV) 97. Dogma 98. Mumford 98. Kissing a Fool 98. Enemy of the State 98. American Cuisine (Fr.) 98, etc.

Lee, Jason Scott (1966–).
American leading actor. Born in Los Angeles, to a third-generation Chinese-Hawaiian family, and raised on the Hawaiian island of Oahu, he returned to Los Angeles at the age of 19, beginning with bit parts on television and in films.
Dragon: The Bruce Lee Story 93. Map of the Human Heart 93. Rapa Nui 94. The Jungle Book 95. Murder in Mind 97. Soldier 98, etc.

Lee, Jet:
see Li, Jet.

Lee, Lila (1902–1973) (Augusta Apple).
Demure American leading lady of the 20s.
The Cruise of the Make Believes 18. Male and Female 19. Terror Island 20. Blood and Sand 22. Million Dollar Mystery 25. Queen of the Night Clubs 29, etc.

Lee, Margaret (1943–).
English leading actress in European films, usually in sexy roles.
Colossus of the Stone Age/Fire Monsters against the Son of Hercules (It.) 62. Casanova 70 65. Five Golden Dragons 65. Circus of Fear 66. Dick Smart 2007 (It.) 66. Our Man in Marrakesh 66. The Action Man (Fr.) 66. Djurado (Sp.) 66. Devil's Garden (It.) 67. Five Golden Dragons 67. The Violent Four (It.) 68. Sons of Satan (It.) 68. House of Pleasure (Ger.) 68. Venus in Furs 69. Viva America! (Sp.) 69. Dorian Gray (Ger.) 70. Cold Blooded Beast/La Bestia Uccide a Sangue Freddo (It.) 71. Stangata Napoletana (It.) 82, etc.

Lee, Michele (1942–) (Michele Dusiak).
American leading lady and singer, with stage experience.
How to Succeed in Business 67. The Love Bug 69. The Comic 69. Dark Victory (TV) 76. Bud and Lou (TV) 78. Single Women, Married Men (TV) 89, etc.
TV series: Knots Landing 79–86.

Lee, Norman (1898–*).
British director and screenwriter, often of low-budget comedies. A former actor and playwright, he directed silent films in South Africa in the 20s, including a version of *The Blue Lagoon*. He was a theatre director and writer of revues in Britain before beginning to direct films at Elstree in 1929. After 1943, he concentrated on writing screenplays and novels.
Autobiographies: 1945, *A Film Is Born*. 1947, *My Personal Log*. 1949, *Log of a Film Director*.
The Song of London 29. Lure of the Atlantic 29. Strip Strip Hooray! Dr Josser K.C. (& co-w) 31. Money Talks (& co-w) 32. The Strangler (& w) 32. Josser Joins the Navy 32. Josser on the River (& co-w) 32. Pride of the Force (& co-w) 32. Doctor's Orders 34. The Outcast 34. A Political Party 34. Royal Cavalcade (co-d) 35. Don't Rush Me 36. Kathleen Mavourneen 37. French Leave 37. Knights for a Day 37. Luck of the Navy 38. Mr Reeder in Room 13 38. Yes, Madam? 38. Murder in Soho 39. The Farmer's Wife (co-w, co-d) 40. This Man Is Mine (co-w) 46. The Monkey's Paw 48. Idol of Paris (co-w) 48. The Case of Charles Peace (& co-w) 49. The Girl Who Couldn't Quite 50, etc.
“ The director is still a Big Shot but he shares his authority with others. He is no longer the man he was. The money kings have now got him by the short hairs. – *N.L.*

Lee, Pamela Anderson.
Blonde and busty Canadian-born leading actress. Born in Vancouver, she began as a model, becoming the 'Blue Zone girl' in an advertising campaign for Labatt's beer and appearing in *Playboy* magazine. She appeared on television as Liza, The Tool Time Girl in the sitcom *Home Improvement* and as C. J. Parker in the series *Baywatch*. Married rock drummer Tommy Lee.
Snapdragon 94. Good Cop, Bad Cop 94. Barb Wire 96. Deader than Ever (TV) 96, etc.

Lee, Peggy (1920–) (Norma Egstrom).
American singer and songwriter, in occasional films. One of the great interpreters of popular song, she sang with the Benny Goodman orchestra in the early 40s and wrote many of the songs, and also sang them in Walt Disney's animated film *The Lady and the Tramp* 55.
Stage Door Canteen 43. Mr Music 50. The Jazz Singer 53. Johnny Guitar (title song) 54. Pete Kelly's Blues (AAN) 55. The Russians Are Coming! The Russians Are Coming! (s) 66, etc.

Lee, Robert E. (1918–1994).
American dramatist and screenwriter, in collaboration with Jerome Lawrence.
Auntie Mame (from their play) 58. Inherit the Wind 60. First Monday in October 81.

Lee, Rowland V. (1891–1975).
American director, in films from 1918.
Alice Adams 26. Barbed Wire 26. The Mysterious Dr Fu Manchu 29. *Zoo in Budapest* 33. *The Count of Monte Cristo* 34. Cardinal Richelieu 35. The Three Musketeers 35. Service de Luxe 38. *Son of Frankenstein* 39. Tower of London 39. Son of Monte Cristo 41. The Bridge of San Luis Rey 44. Captain Kidd 45. The Big Fisherman (p only) 59, etc.

Lee, Sheryl (1966–).
American actress who gained fame through the TV series *Twin Peaks* 90.
Wild at Heart 90. I Love You to Death 90. Twin Peaks: Fire Walk with Me 92. The Distinguished Gentleman 92. Backbeat 94. Don't Do It 94. Fall Time 95. Homage 95. Follow the River 95. Mother Night 96. Bliss 96. This World, Then the Fireworks 97. Angel's Dance 98. John Carpenter's Vampires 98, etc.
TV series: LA Doctors 98– .

Lee, Spike (1956–) (Shelton Jackson Lee).
American director, screenwriter and actor. He has his own production company, Forty Acres & A Mule Filmworks.
Autobiography: 1997, *Best Seat in the House* (with Ralph Wiley).
Biography: 1992, *Spike Lee* by Alex Patterson.
She's Gotta Have It 86. School Daze 88. Do the Right Thing (AANw) 89. Mo' Better Blues 90. Jungle Fever 91. Malcolm X 92. Crooklyn (co-w, a, d) 94. Clockers (co-w, d) 95. Girl 6 96. 4 Little Girls (TV, doc) (AAN) 97. He Got Game (co-p, wd) 98, etc.
“ I remember trying to join the boy scouts and they told me I couldn't join because I wasn't Catholic. You can't help growing up thinking something is amiss. – *S.L.*

Lee-Thompson, J. (1914–).
Scottish director, screenwriter and playwright, a former actor. He had his first play produced in London at the age of 18, and went to work as a screenwriter for British International Pictures in 1935, turning director with a screen version of his second play.
■ The Middle Watch (w) 36. For Them that Trespass (w) 48. Murder without Crime (wd) 50. *The Yellow Balloon* (wd) 52. The Weak and the Wicked (wd) 53. As Long as They're Happy (d) 54. For Better for Worse (d) 54. An Alligator Named Daisy (d) 55. Yield to the Night (d) 56. The Good Companions (co-p, co-d) 57. No Trees in the Street (d) 58. Woman in a Dressing Gown (d) 59. Tiger Bay (d) 59. Northwest Frontier (d) 59. Ice Cold in Alex (d) 60. I Aim at the Stars (d) (US) 60. *The Guns of Navarone* (AANd) 61. Cape Fear (d) (US) 61. Taras Bulba (d) (US) 62. Kings of the Sun (d) (US) 63. What a Way to Go (d) (US) 64. John Goldfarb Please Come Home (d) (US) 65. Return from the Ashes (p, d) 65. Eye of the Devil (d) 66. Mackenna's Gold (d) (US) 68. Before Winter Comes (d) 68. The Chairman (d) 69. Country Dance (d) 70. Conquest of the Planet of the Apes (d) (US) 72. A Great American Tragedy (TV) 72. Huckleberry Finn (d) (US) 74. The Reincarnation of Peter Proud (d) (US) 74. The Blue Knight (TV) (d) 75. St Ives (d) 75. Widow (TV) (d) 76. The White Buffalo (d) (US) 77. The Greek Tycoon 78. The Passage 78. Cabo Blanco 79. Happy Birthday to Me 81. Ten to Midnight 83. The Ambassador 84. King Solomon's Mines 85. Murphy's Law 86. Firewalker 86. Death Wish IV: The Crackdown 88. Messenger of Death 88. Kinjite/Forbidden Subjects 89.

Leech, Richard (1922–) (Richard McClelland).
British character actor, often as army or air force officer.
The Dam Busters 55. A Night to Remember 57. The Good Companions 57. Ice Cold in Alex 59. The Horse's Mouth 59. Tunes of Glory 60. The Wild and the Willing 62. I Thank a Fool 63. The Fighting Prince of Donegal 66. Young Winston 72. Gandhi 82. The Shooting Party 84. A Woman of Substance (TV) 85. A Handful of Dust 87, etc.

Leeds, Andrea (1914–1984) (Antoinette Lees).
American leading lady of the late 30s.
Come and Get It 36. *Stage Door* (AAN) 37. The Goldwyn Follies 39. Letter of Introduction 39. Swanee River 39, etc.

Leeds, Herbert I. (c. 1900–1954) (Herbert I. Levy).
American director of second features, former editor.
Mr Moto in Danger Island 38. Island in the Sky 38. The Cisco Kid and the Lady 39. Manila Calling 42. *Time to Kill* 43. It Shouldn't Happen to a Dog 46. Let's Live Again 48. Father's Wild Game 51, etc.

Leeves, Jane (1962–).
English actress, in Hollywood, best known for her role as Daphne Moon in the TV sitcom *Frasier*. Born in London, and brought up in East Grinstead, Sussex, she is a former model and dancer who began on television in the early 80s as one of 'Hill's Angels', the girls that featured in comedian Benny Hill's TV series. Married TV executive Marshall Cohen in 1996.
Monty Python's The Meaning of Life 83. The Hunger 83. To Live and Die in LA 85. Mr Write (US) 92. Miracle on 34th Street (US) 94. James and the Giant Peach (voice) 96. Pandora's Clock (TV) 96. Us Begins with You 98, etc.
TV series: Throb 86–88. Murphy Brown 89–93. Frasier 93– .

Legg, Stuart (1910–1988).
British documentarist and administrator. From 1932 with GPO Film Unit and Empire Marketing Board. 1939–45: National Film Board of Canada. 1953–88: director of Film Centre Ltd.

Leggatt, Alison (1904–1990).
British character actress, mainly on stage.
Nine Till Six 32. This Happy Breed 44. Waterloo Road 45. Marry Me 47. The Card 52. Touch and Go 55. Never Take Sweets from a Stranger 60. Nothing but the Best 64. The Seven Per Cent Solution 76, etc.

Legrand, Michel (1931–).
French composer.
Lola 61. Eva 62. Vivre sa Vie 62. La Baie des Anges 63. *The Umbrellas of Cherbourg* (AAN) 64. Bande à Part 64. Une Femme Mariée 65. Les Demoiselles de Rochefort 67. Ice Station Zebra 68. Peau d'Ane 70. *Summer of 42* (AA) 71. A Time for Loving (& a) 71. One is a Lonely Number 72. Portnoy's Complaint 72. Cops and Robbers 73. The Three Musketeers 74. Ode to Billy Joe 75. The Other Side of Midnight 77. Atlantic City USA 80. Falling in Love Again 80. The Hunter 80. The Mountain Men 80. Best Friends 82. Yentl (AA) 83. Palace 84. Secret Places 85. Switching Channels 88. Eternity 90. The Pickle 93. Prêt-à-Porter/Ready to Wear 94. Madeline 98, etc.

LeGros, James (1962–).
American leading actor.
Phantasm 79. Near Dark 87. Phantasm II 88. Drugstore Cowboy 89. Hollywood Heartbreak 89. The Rapture 91. Singles 92. Guncrazy 92. My New Gun 92. Where the Day Takes You 92. Bad Girls 94. Don't Do It 94. Mrs Parker and the Vicious Circle 94. Living in Oblivion 95. The Low Life 95. Destiny Turns on the Radio 95. Safe 95. The Destiny of Marty Fine 96. Marshal Law 96. Countdown 96. Boys 96. Wishful Thinking 97. The Myth of Fingerprints 97. Thursday 98. LA without a Map (GB/Fr./Fin.) 98. There's No Fish Food in Heaven 98. Enemy of the State 98, etc.

Leguizamo, John (1965–).
American actor and comedian. Born in Bogotá, Colombia, he studied drama at New York University.
Casualties of War 89. Mambo Mouth 90. Street Hunter 90. Hangin' with the Homeboys 91. Regarding Henry 91. Super Mario Bros 93. Night Owl 93. Carlito's Way 93. To Wong Foo, Thanks for Everything, Julie Newmar 95. A Pyromaniac's Love Story 95. Executive Decision 96. The Fan 96. Romeo and Juliet 96. The Pest 97. Spawn 97. Body Count 97. Dr Dolittle (voice) 98, etc.
TV series: House of Buggin' 95.

Lehman, Ernest (1920–).
American screenwriter.
Inside Story 48. Executive Suite 54. Sabrina (AAN) 54. *The Sweet Smell of Success* 57. *North by Northwest* (AAN) 59. *The Prize* 63. The Sound of Music 65. Who's Afraid of Virginia Woolf? (& p) (AAN) 66. Hello Dolly (& p) (AAN) 69. Portnoy's Complaint (& p, d) 72. Family Plot 76. Black Sunday 77, etc.

Lehmann, Beatrix (1898–1979).
British character actress, often of withdrawn eccentrics; film appearances few. On stage from 1924.
The Passing of the Third Floor Back 36. Black Limelight 38. The Rat 38. The Key 58. Psyche 59 64. The Spy Who Came in from the Cold 66. Staircase 69, etc.

Lehmann, Carla (1917–1990).
Canadian leading lady, in British films of the 40s.
So This Is London 39. Cottage to Let 41. Talk about Jacqueline 42. Candlelight in Algeria 44. 29 Acacia Avenue 45. Fame Is the Spur 47, etc.

Lehmann, Michael (1957–).
American director and screenwriter.
Heathers (d) 88. Meet the Applegates (co-w, d) 89. Hudson Hawk (d) 91. Airheads (d) 94. The Truth about Cats and Dogs 96. My Giant 98, etc.

Lehrman, Henry 'Pathé' (1883–1946).
Austrian-born director and actor of silents in Hollywood who made Charlie Chaplin's earliest films for Keystone; later a screenwriter. His nickname was given to him by D. W. Griffith and derived from the fact that he claimed to have worked for the Pathé company in France. Born in Vienna, he emigrated in his late teens, working first as a tram conductor, and began in films as an extra and bit-part player before joining Keystone as a director and actor. Chaplin disliked working with him, complaining that he ruined his best jokes. He later founded his own company, L-KO (for Lehrman-Knock Out), using a former Fred Karno performer, Scotsman Billy Ritchie (1874–1921), as a comic in the Chaplin style, and then turned out comedies for Fox. After the arrival of sound, he had a brief career as a screenwriter, but was bankrupt by the early 40s. He was the lover

of Virginia Rappe, the starlet for whose death Fatty ARBUCKLE was blamed, and was the chief prosecution witness at the subsequent trial that ended Arbuckle's career.

AS DIRECTOR: Between Showers 14. Kid Auto Races at Venice, California 14. Mabel's Strange Predicament 14. Making a Living 14. Double Dealing 23. Fighting Blood 23. For Ladies Only 27. Chicken à la King 28, etc.

AS WRITER: The Poor Millionaire (co-w) 30. Moulin Rouge (co-w) 34. Bulldog Drummond Strikes Back (co-w) 34. Show Them No Mercy (co-w) 35, etc.

❝ He used to say that he didn't need personalities, that he got all his laughs from mechanical effects and film-cutting. – *Charlie Chaplin*

Lehto, Pekka.
Finnish director and producer, a former sound engineer, who began by working in collaboration with director Pirjo Honkasalo.

Their Age (short, co-d) 76. Flame Top/Tulipää (co-d) 80. Da Capo (co-d) 85. The Well (d) 91, etc.

Leiber, Fritz (1883–1949).
American Shakespearean actor who played many supporting roles in films.

A Tale of Two Cities 35. Anthony Adverse 36. The Hunchback of Notre Dame 40. Phantom of the Opera 43. Humoresque 46. Another Part of the Forest 48, etc.

Leibman, Ron (1937–).
American character actor of the 70s.

The Hot Rock 72. Slaughterhouse Five 72. The Super Cops 73. Your Three Minutes Are Up 74. The Art of Crime (TV) 75. Won Ton Ton 76. A Question of Guilt (TV) 78. Norma Rae 79. Up the Academy 80. Rivkin, Bounty Hunter (TV) 81. Zorro the Gay Blade 81, Romantic Comedy 83. Rhinestone 84. Seven Hours to Judgement 88. Night Falls on Manhattan 96. Don King: Only in America (TV) 97, etc.

TV series: *Kaz* 78.

Leigh, Janet (1927–) (Jeanette Morrison).
Capable American leading lady of the 50s and 60s; began as a peaches-and-cream heroine but graduated to sharper roles. Her third husband was Tony CURTIS (1951–62). She is the mother of actress Jamie Lee CURTIS.

■ The Romance of Rosy Ridge 47. If Winter Comes 47. Hills of Home 47. Words and Music 48. Act of Violence 48. Little Women 49. *That Forsyte Woman* 49. The Doctor and the Girl 49. The Red Danube 49. Holiday Affair 49. Strictly Dishonourable 51. Angels in the Outfield 51. Two Tickets to Broadway 51. It's a Big Country 51. Just This Once 52. Scaramouche 52. Fearless Fagan 52. The Naked Spur 53. Confidentially Connie 53. *Houdini* 53. Walking My Baby Back Home 54. Prince Valiant 54. Living It Up 54. The Black Shield of Falworth 54. Rogue Cop 54. Pete Kelly's Blues 55. *My Sister Eileen* 55. Safari (GB) 56. Jet Pilot 57. Touch of Evil 58. The Vikings 58. The Perfect Furlough 58. Who Was That Lady? 60. *Psycho* (AAN) 60. Pepe 60. The Manchurian Candidate 62. Bye Bye Birdie 62. Wives and Lovers 63. Three on a Couch 66. Harper 66. Kid Rodelo 66. An American Dream 66. Hello Down There 68. The Spy in the Green Hat 68. Grand Slam 68. Honeymoon with a Stranger (TV) 69. The House on Greenapple Road (TV) 70. The Monk (TV) 70. The Deadly Dream (TV) 71. One Is a Lonely Number 72. Night of the Lepus 72. Murdock's Gang (TV) 73. Murder at the World Series (TV) 77. Telethon (TV) 77. Boardwalk 79. The Fog 80. The Thrill of Genius 85. Halloween: H20 98.

Leigh, Jennifer Jason (1962–).
American actress, the daughter of actor Vic MORROW.

Eyes of a Stranger 80. The Best Little Girl in the World (TV) 81. The Killing of Randy Webster 81. Fast Times at Ridgemont High 82. Wrong Is Right 82. Death Ride to Osaka (TV) 83. Easy Money 83. Just Like Us (TV) 83. Grandview USA 84. Flesh and Blood 85. The Hitcher 85. The Men's Club 86. Sister, Sister 87. Heart of Midnight 88. The Big Picture 89. Last Exit to Brooklyn 89. Miami Blues 90. Crooked Hearts 91. Backdraft 91. Rush 91. Single White Female 92. Short Cuts 93. The Hudsucker Proxy 94. Mrs Parker and the Vicious Circle (as Dorothy Parker) 94. Dolores Claiborne 95. Georgia 95. Kansas City 96. Bastard out of Carolina 96. Washington Square 97. A Thousand Acres 97. eXistenZ 98, etc.

Leigh, Mike (1943–).
British director and screenwriter, also active in theatre and TV as a writer-director noted for creating scripts out of sessions of improvisation with his actors. He trained at RADA and was an assistant director with the Royal Shakespeare Company 1967–68. Formerly married to Alison Steadman.

Bleak Moments 71. High Hopes 89. Life Is Sweet 90. Naked 93. *Secrets and Lies* (AANw, AANd) 96. Career Girls 97, etc.

❝ Given the choice of Hollywood or poking steel pins into my eyes, I'd prefer steel pins. – M.L.

Leigh, Suzanna (1945–).
British leading lady.

Boeing Boeing 66. Paradise Hawaiian Style 66. Deadlier Than the Male 67. Lost Continent 68. Lust for a Vampire 70. The Fiend 71, etc.

Leigh, Vivien (1913–1967) (Vivian Hartley).
Distinguished British leading lady whose stage and screen career was limited by delicate health; for many years the wife of Laurence Olivier.

Biographies: 1973, *Light of a Star* by Gwen Robyns. 1977, *Vivien Leigh* by Anne Edwards. 1987, *Vivien* by Alexander Walker.

■ Things Are Looking Up 34. The Village Squire 35. Gentleman's Agreement 35. Look Up and Laugh 35. Fire Over England 36. *Dark Journey* 37. Storm in a Teacup 37. St Martin's Lane 38. Twenty-One Days 38. *A Yank at Oxford* 38. *Gone with the Wind* (AA: as Scarlett O'Hara) (US) 39. Waterloo Bridge (US) 40. *Lady Hamilton* (US) 41. *Caesar and Cleopatra* 45. Anna Karenina 48. *A Streetcar Named Desire* (AA) (US) 51. The Deep Blue Sea 55. The Roman Spring of Mrs Stone 61. Ship of Fools (US) 65.

✪ For one performance which made each of her later ones an event to be savoured. *Gone with the Wind.*

Leigh-Hunt, Barbara (1935–).
British character actress.

Frenzy 72. Henry VIII and His Six Wives 72. A Bequest to the Nation 73. O Heavenly Dog 80. Paper Mask 90. Pride and Prejudice (TV) 95, etc.

Leigh-Hunt, Ronald (1916–).
Smooth British supporting actor.

Tiger by the Tail 53. Shadow of a Man 55. A Touch of Larceny 59. Sink the Bismarck 60. Piccadilly Third Stop 61. The Truth about Spring 65. Hostile Witness 67. Le Mans 71. The Omen 76. Frankenstein (TV) 93, many others.

TV series: Sir Lancelot (as King Arthur) 56.

Leighton, Margaret (1922–1976).
Elegant English leading actress, mainly in the theatre. Born in Barnt Green, Worcestershire, she was on stage from the age of 16 and first gained notice acting with the Old Vic Company in the late 40s. Married three times: her second husband was actor Laurence HARVEY (1957–60) and her third Michael WILDING, whom she married in 1960. Her lovers included actor Robert STEPHENS.

■ Bonnie Prince Charlie 47. *The Winslow Boy* 48. Under Capricorn 49. The Astonished Heart 50. The Elusive Pimpernel 50. Calling Bulldog Drummond 51. Home at Seven 52. The Holly and the Ivy 52. The Good Die Young 54. Carrington VC 54. The Teckman Mystery 54. The Constant Husband 55. The Passionate Stranger 57. The Sound and the Fury 58. The Second Man (TV) 59. The Waltz of the Toreadors 62. The Third Secret 63. The Best Man 64. Seven Women 65. The Loved One 65. The Madwoman of Chaillot 69. The Go-Between (AAN) 70. Zee and Co 71. Lady Caroline Lamb 72. Bequest to the Nation 73. Frankenstein: The True Story (TV) 73. From Beyond the Grave 73. Galileo 74. Great Expectations 75. Trial by Combat 76.

Leisen, Mitchell (1898–1972).
American director, former set designer; his films are mostly romantic trifles, but many have considerable pictorial values.

Biography: 1972, *Hollywood Director* by David Chierichetti.

■ *Cradle Song* 33. *Death Takes a Holiday* 34. Murder at the Vanities 34. Behold My Wife 35. Four Hours to Kill 35. Hands across the Table 35. Thirteen Hours by Air 36. The Big Broadcast of 1937. Swing High Swing Low 37. *Easy Living* 37. The Big Broadcast of 1938 37. Artists and Models Abroad 38. *Midnight* 39. Remember the Night 40. *Arise My Love* 40. I Wanted Wings 41. *Hold Back the Dawn* 41. The Lady Is Willing 42. Take a Letter Darling 42. No Time for Love (& p) 43. *Lady in the Dark* (also w) 44. *Frenchman's Creek* 44. Practically Yours (& p) 44. *Kitty* 45. Masquerade in Mexico 45. To Each His Own 46. Suddenly It's Spring 46. Golden Earrings 47. Dream Girl 48. Bride of Vengeance 49. Song of Surrender 49. Captain Carey USA 50. No Man of Her Own (& w) 50. The Mating Season 51. Darling How Could You? 51. Young Man with Ideas 52. Tonight We Sing 53. Bedevilled 55. The Girl Most Likely 57.

✪ For adding style to comedies and dramas that badly needed it. *Kitty.*

❝ He found himself in the unenviable position of a diamond cutter working with lumpy coal. – *Andrew Sarris, 1968*

Leiser, Erwin (1923–1996).
Swedish documentarist.

Mein Kampf/Blodige Tiden 59. Murder by Signature/Eichmann and the Third Reich 61. Choose Life 62. Germany Awake 66. Women of the Third World 75. Hans Richter: Artist and Filmmaker 79. Following the Fuhrer 85. Berenice Abbott: American Photographer 92. Everyone Was a 'Pimpf' 93, etc.

Leister, Frederick (1885–1970).
British character actor, on stage from 1906, screen from 20s. Usually played distinguished and kindly professional men.

Dreyfus 30. The Iron Duke 35. Goodbye Mr Chips 39. The Prime Minister 41. *Dear Octopus* 43. *The Hundred Pound Window* 43. The Captive Heart 46. Quartet 48. The End of the Affair 54. Left, Right and Centre 59. A French Mistress 63, many others.

Leitao, Joaquim (1956–).
Portuguese director and screenwriter whose comedy *Adam and Eve* was that country's most successful local film.

One Marginal S/Um S Marginal (a, w) 83. Play . . . Boy/Uma Vez por Todas (wd) 87. To the Bitter End (Ger./Port.) 89. L'Amour Extreme (Fr./Port.) (wd) 90. Adios Princesa (co-w) 92. *Adam and Eve*/Adao e Eva (wd) 96, etc.

Leith, Virginia (1932–).
American leading lady of the 50s.

Black Widow 54. Violent Saturday 55. White Feather 55. A Kiss Before Dying 56. On the Threshold of Space 56. The Beast That Wouldn't Die 63. First Love 77, etc.

Lejeune, C. A. (1897–1973).
British film critic whose work now tends to seem blithe but facetious. Collections of reviews were published in 1947 as *Chestnuts in My Lap* and in 1991 as *The C. A. Lejeune Film Reader*.

Leland, David (1947–).
British director and screenwriter, a former actor.

Mona Lisa (w) 86. Personal Services (w) 87. Wish You Were Here (wd) 87. Checking Out (d) 89. The Big Man (d) 90. When Saturday Comes (a) 96. The Land Girls (wd) 98, etc.

Lelouch, Claude (1937–).
French director and screenwriter with lush visual style; internationally fashionable in the mid-60s, but overreached himself.

Le Propre de l'Homme 60. Une Fille et des Fusils 63. Avec des Si 64. Secret Paris 64. *Un Homme et une Femme* (AAw, AANd) 66. *Vivre pour Vivre* 67. Challenge in the Snow 68. Far from Vietnam 69. A Man I Like 69. Life Love Death 69. Le Rose et le Noir 70. The Crook 71. Smic, Smac, Smoc 71. Adventure Is Adventure 72. *La Bonne Année* 73. And Now My Love (AANw) 75. Seven Suspects for Murder 77. Another Man, Another Chance 77. The Good and the Bad 77. A Nous Deux 79. Les Uns et les Autres 80. Edith and Marcel 83. Long Live Life 84. Departure, Return 85. A Man and a Woman: 20 Years Later 86. Attention Bandits 87. Itinéraire d'un Enfant Gâté 88. Il y a des Jours et des Lunes 90. The Beautiful Story/La Belle Histoire 92. Tout Ça . . . pour Ça 93. Les Misérables du XXème Siècle 95. Hommes, Femmes: Mode d'Emploi 96. Luck or Coincidence/Hasards ou Coincidences (p, wd) 98, etc.

❝ Film-making is like spermatozoa: only one in a million makes it. – C.L.

One day I'll make a film for the critics, when I have money to lose. – C.L.

Lelouch, Salomé (1984–).
French child actress, the daughter of director Claude LELOUCH and actress Evelyne Bouix.

When I Was Five I Killed Myself 94. Les Misérables 95, etc.

LeMaire, Charles (1897–1985).
American costume designer. Born in Chicago, Illinois, he worked in vaudeville as an actor before designing for the theatre and beginning his own couture business. In the early 40s he ran the wardrobe department at Twentieth Century-Fox, often working in collaboration with other designers, including Edith HEAD and Mary WILLS.

Boomerang! 47. The Ghost and Mrs Muir 47. All about Eve (AA) 50. The Model and the Marriage Broker (AAN) 51. David and Bathsheba (AAN) 51. My Cousin Rachel (AAN) 52. With a Song in My Heart (AAN) 52. The President's Lady (AAN) 53. The Robe (AA) 53. Gentlemen Prefer Blondes 53. How to Marry a Millionaire (AAN) 53. Desiree (AAN) 54. There's No Business Like Showbusiness (AAN) 54. Love Is a Many Splendored Thing (AA) 55. Teenage Rebel (AAN) 56. An Affair to Remember (AAN) 57. Forty Guns 57. A Certain Smile (AAN) 58. The Young Lions 58. The Diary of Anne Frank (AAN) 59. The Marriage-Go-Round 60. Walk on the Wild Side 62, etc.

Lembeck, Harvey (1925–1982).
American character actor, born in Brooklyn, New York, and best known for playing Corporal Rocco Barbella in *The Phil Silvers Show*. Died of a heart attack. His son Michael Lembeck (1948–) is also an actor.

The Frogmen 51. You're In the Navy Now 53. Back at the Front 53. Stalag 17 54. Life after Dark 55. Sail a Crooked Ship 62. Bikini Beach 65. There is No Thirteen 77, etc.

TV series: The Phil Silvers Show 55–59. The Hathaways 61–62. Ensign O'Toole 62–63.

Lemmon, Chris (1954–).
American actor, the son of Jack LEMMON.

Just before Dawn 80. C.O.D. 83. Swing Shift 84. Weekend Warriors 86. That's Life! 86. Going Undercover 88. Dad 89. Firehead 90. Lena's Holiday 90. Corporate Affairs 90. Lena's Holiday 91. Land of the Free 97. Wishmaster 97, etc.

TV series: Brothers and Sisters 79. Knots Landing 90. Thunder in Paradise 94.

Lemmon, Jack (1925–).
American light comedy leading actor with Broadway experience; sometimes typed in mildly lecherous or otherwise sex-fraught roles.

Biographies: 1975, *Lemmon* by Don Widener. 1977, *The Films of Jack Lemmon* by Joe Baltake.

It Should Happen to You 53. Three for the Show 53. Phffft 54. My Sister Eileen 55. *Mister Roberts* (AA) 55. You Can't Run Away from It 56. Cowboy 57. Fire Down Below 57. Operation Mad Ball 57. Bell, Book and Candle 58. It Happened to Jane 58. *Some Like It Hot* (AAN) 59. The Wackiest Ship in the Army 60. *The Apartment* (AAN) 60. The Notorious Landlady 62. Days of Wine and Roses (AAN) 62. *Irma la Douce* 63. Under the Yum Yum Tree 64. Good Neighbour Sam 64. How to Murder Your Wife 65. *The Great Race* 65. The Fortune Cookie 66. Luv 67. *The Odd Couple* 68. The April Fools 69. The Out-of-Towners 69. *Kotch* (d only) 71. The War between Men and Women 72. Avanti 72. Save the Tiger (AA) 73. The Front Page 74. The Prisoner of Second Avenue 75. The Entertainer 75. Alex and the Gypsy 76. Airport 77 77. *The China Syndrome* (AAN, BFA) 79. Tribute (AAN) 80. Buddy Buddy 81. *Missing* (AAN) 82. Mass Appeal 84. Macaroni 85. That's Life! 86. Dad 89. JFK 91. Glengarry Glen Ross 92. Short Cuts 93. A Life in the Theatre 93. Grumpy Old Men 93. The Grass Harp 95. Grumpier Old Men 95. Getting Away with Murder 96. My Fellow Americans 96. The Odd Couple II 98, etc.

TV series: That Wonderful Guy 49–50. Heaven for Betsy 52. Alcoa Theatre 57–58.

❝ The worst part about being me is when people want me to make them laugh. – J.L.

Every time when I said, 'Action', Jack would

mutter under his breath, 'Magic time', as a little mantra to himself. – *Kenneth Branagh*
Famous line (*Mister Roberts*): 'Now, what's all this crud about no movie tonight?'

Lemont, John (1914–).
British director.
The Green Buddha 54. And Women Shall Weep (& co-w) 59. The Shakedown (& co-w) 59. Konga 60. Frightened City (& co-w) 61. Deep Waters (p) 78. A Horse Called Jester (p) 79, etc.

Lemper, Ute (1963–).
German actress and singer, noted for her interpretations of the songs of Kurt Weill.
L'Autrichienne 89. Prospero's Books 91. Prêt-à-Porter/Ready to Wear 94. Bogus 96. Wild Games/Combat de Fauves 97, etc.

Leni, Paul (1885–1929).
German director, former set designer; died in Hollywood.
Waxworks 24. *The Cat and the Canary* 27. The Man Who Laughs 28. The Chinese Parrot 28. The Last Warning 29, etc.

Lenica, Jan (1928–).
Polish animator.
Dom 58. Monsieur Tete 59. Janko the Musician 60. Rhinoceros 63. A 64. Adam 2 70. Ubu et la Grande Gidouille 87, etc.

Lenin (1870–1924) (Vladimir Ilyich Ulyanov).
Russian statesman, the power behind the Revolution. Little footage of him exists, but he has been played by various actors in such politically-based semi-fictions as *Lenin in October*, *Lenin in 1918* and *Lenin in Poland*. Michael Bryant played him in *Nicholas and Alexandra*; Roger Sloman in *Reds*; while Ben Kingsley played him in the TV film *The Train*.

Lennart, Isobel (1915–1971).
American screenwriter.
Lost Angel 44. Anchors Aweigh 45. East Side West Side 49. Skirts Ahoy 52. Latin Lovers 54. Love Me or Leave Me (AAN) 55. Inn of the Sixth Happiness 58. The Sundowners (AAN) 60. Period of Adjustment 62. Funny Girl 68, many others.

Lenoir, Denis.
French cinematographer.
Monsieur Hire 89. Daddy Nostalgie 90. Decadence 93. Cold Water/L'Eau Froide 94. Carrington (GB) 95. Joseph Conrad's Secret Agent (GB) 96. Thursday (US) 98. Early September/Fin Août, Debut Septembre 98, etc.

Lenska, Rula (1947–).
Polish born, British leading lady, much on TV.
Soft Beds Hard Battles 73. Alfie Darling 75. The Deadly Females 76, etc.

Lenya, Lotte (1899–1981) (Caroline Blamauer).
Austrian character actress; also inimitable singer of her husband Kurt Weill's songs.
Die Dreigroschenoper 31. The Roman Spring of Mrs Stone (AAN) 61. *From Russia with Love* 63. The Appointment 69. Semi-Tough 77, etc.

Lenz, Kay (1953–).
American leading actress, born in Los Angeles, California. Married actor and singer David Cassidy (1977–81).
Breezy 73. Lisa Bright and Dark (TV) 73. White Line Fever 75. The Great Scout and Cathouse Thursday 76. Rich Man Poor Man (TV) 76. The Passage 79. House 86. Death Wish IV: The Crackdown 87. Stripped to Kill 87. Smoke 88. Physical Evidence 89. Headhunter 90. Souvenirs 91. Falling from Grace 92. Trapped in Space 94. Gunfighter's Moon 96. A Gun, a Car, a Blonde 97, etc.

Lenz, Rick (1939–).
American actor.
Cactus Flower 70. Where Does It Hurt? 72. The Shootist 76. Melvin and Howard 80. Little Dragons 80. Malice in Wonderland (TV) 85. Spooner (TV) 89. Perry Mason: The Case of the Telltale Talk Show Host (TV) 93, etc.
TV series: Hec Ramsey 72–74.

Lenzi, Umberto (1931–).
Italian director of exploitation movies, specializing in macabre thrillers; a former journalist and law graduate.
Pirates of the Seven Seas/Sandokan, la Tigre di Mompracem 63. Messalina vs the Son of Hercules/Gladiatore di Messalina 63. Kriminal 66. Paranoia/Orgasmo 68. Battle of the Commandos/La Brigada de los Condenados 69. A Quiet Place to Kill/Paranoia 70. Sacrifice/Il Paese del Sesso Selvaggio 72. Eyeball/Gatti Rossi in un Labirinto di Vetro 74. Battleforce/Il Grande Attacco 78. From Hell to Victory 79. City of the Walking Dead/Incubo sulla Citta Contaminata 80. Emerald Jungle/Cannibal Ferox 81. The Wild Team 85. Wartime/Tempo di Guerra 86. Ghosthouse/La Casa 3 87. Hell's Gate/Le Porte dell'Inferno (& w) 89. Cop Target 90. Black Demon/Demoni 3 90, etc.

Leon de Aranoa, Fernando (c. 1968–).
Spanish director and screenwriter.
Los Hombres Siempre Mienten (w) 94. ¡Por fin solos! (w) 94. Familia (wd) 97. Barrio (d) 98, etc.

Leon, Valerie (1945–).
British leading lady.
Smashing Time 67. Carry On up the Jungle 70. *Blood from the Mummy's Tomb* 71. Carry On Matron 72. The Spy Who Loved Me 77. Revenge of the Pink Panther 78, etc.

Leonard, Brett.
American director.
The Dead Pit (co-w, d) 89. The Lawnmower Man 92. Hideaway 95. Virtuosity 95, etc.

Leonard, Elmore (1925–).
American western and crime novelist and screenwriter, who also adapts his thrillers into movies.
Hombre 66. Big Bounce 68. The Moonshine War (w) 70. Valdez Is Coming 71. Mr Majestyk 74. Stick 85. 52 Pick-Up 86. The Rosary Murders 87. Cat Chaser 90. Get Shorty (oa) 95. Jackie Brown (from Rum Punch) 97. Pronto (TV) 97. Elmore Leonard's Gold Coast (TV) 97. Last Stand at Saber River (TV) 97. Touch 97. Out of Sight 98, etc.
❝ In my books characters are more important than the plot, but Hollywood movies are based on plot. So when they make movies about the books they become much too theatrical. And Hollywood wants heroes who are major stars. My hero isn't a major star, he's just a guy. The films lose the feeling of the books completely. – *E.L.*
Donald Westlake wrote me a letter and asked: 'Why do you keep hoping to see a good movie made? The books are ours, everything else is virgins thrown in the volcano. Be happy if the check is good.' – *E.L.*

Leonard, Herbert B. (1922–).
American independent TV producer; best-known series include *Rin Tin Tin*, *Circus Boy*, *Naked City*, *Route* 66.

Leonard, Hugh (1926–) (John Keyes Byrne).
Irish playwright and occasional screenwriter.
Broth of a Boy (oa) 58. Interlude (co-w) 68. Great Catherine 68. Percy 71. Our Miss Fred 72. Da (from his play) 88. Widow's Peak 94.

Leonard, Murray (1898–1970).
American burlesque comedian who played small parts in films, notably with Abbott and Costello, who worked up several of his old routines.
Lost in a Harem 44. A Thousand and One Nights 45. Bring Your Smile Along 55, etc.

Leonard, Robert Sean (1969–).
American leading actor.
Bluffing It (TV) 87. My Best Friend Is a Vampire 88. Dead Poets Society 89. Mr & Mrs Bridge 91. Much Ado about Nothing 93. Married to It 93. Swing Kids 93. The Age of Innocence 93. Safe Passage 94. Killer: A Journal of Murder 96. The Boys Next Door (TV) 96. Standoff 97. In the Gloaming (TV) 97. I Love You, I Love You Not 97. The Last Days of Disco 98, etc.

Leonard, Robert Z. (1889–1968).
American director (former actor), in Hollywood from 1915. Showed care but not much imagination.
The Waning Sex 27. The Demi-Bride 27. Adam and Evil 28. Tea for Three 29. The Divorcee (AAN) 30. Susan Lenox 31. *Strange Interval* 32. *Dancing Lady* 33. Peg O' My Heart 33. Outcast Lady 34. *The Great Ziegfeld* (AAN) 36. Piccadilly Jim 37. Escapade 37. *Maytime* 38. The Firefly 38. New Moon (& p) 40. *Pride and Prejudice* 40. Ziegfeld Girl 41. When Ladies Meet (& p) 41. We Were Dancing 42. Stand By for Action 42. The Man from Down Under 43. Marriage Is a Private Affair 44. Weekend at the Waldorf 45. The Secret Heart 46. B.F.'s Daughter 48. The Bride 48. In the Good Old Summertime 49. Nancy Goes to Rio 49. Duchess of Idaho 50. Everything I Have Is Yours 52. The Clown 53. The King's Thief 55. Kelly and Me 56. Beautiful But Dangerous (It.) 56, many others.

Leonard, Sheldon (1907–1997) (Sheldon Bershad).
American character actor who played Runyonesque gangsters for years; finally quit to produce TV series.
Another Thin Man 39. Buy Me That Town 41. Street of Chance 42. *Lucky Jordon* 42. To Have and Have Not 44. Zombies on Broadway 45. Somewhere in the Night 46. Violence 47. The Gangster 47. Take One False Step 49. Behave Yourself 51. *Stop You're Killing Me* 52. Money from Home 54. Guys and Dolls 55. Pocketful of Miracles 61. The Brink's Job 78, many others.
TV series: The Duke 54. Danny Thomas 59–61. Big Eddie 75.

Leone, Sergio (1922–1989).
Italian director who came to the fore internationally via his savage westerns on the American pattern, making a star of Clint Eastwood in the process.
Biography: 1997, *Sergio Leone: The Great Italian Dream of Legendary America* by Oreste de Fornari.
The Colossus of Rhodes 61. *A Fistful of Dollars* 64. For a Few Dollars More 65. The Good the Bad and the Ugly 67. *Once upon a Time in the West* 69. A Fistful of Dynamite 72. *Once upon a Time in America* 84, etc.

Leonetti, Matthew F.
American cinematographer.
Mr Billion 77. Breaking Away 79. Raise the Titanic 80. Eyewitness 81. Poltergeist 82. Fast Times at Ridgemont High 82. The Ice Pirates 84. Fast Forward 85. Weird Science 85. Jagged Edge 85. Commando 85. Jumpin' Jack Flash 86. Dragnet 87. Extreme Prejudice 87. Red Heat 88. Johnny Handsome 89. Hard to Kill 90. Another 48 Hrs 90. Dead Again 91. Angels in the Outfield 94. Low Down, Dirty Shame 94. Strange Days 95. Fled 96. Star Trek: First Contact 96. Mortal Kombat: Annihilation 97. Species 2 98. Star Trek: Insurrection 98, etc.

Leoni, Tea (1966–) (Tea Pantleoni).
American actress, best known for her role as photo-journalist Nora Wilde in the TV sitcom *The Naked Truth*. Born in New York, she studied anthropology and psychology at Sarah Lawrence College. Married actor David Duchovny, her second husband, in 1998.
A League of Their Own 92. The Counterfeit Contessa (TV) 94. Wyatt Earp 94. Bad Boys 95. Flirting with Disaster 96. Deep Impact 98. There's No Fish Food in Heaven 98, etc.
TV series: Flying Blind 92. The Naked Truth 95– .

Leontovich, Eugenie (1894–1993).
Russian stage actress in occasional American films. She was formerly married to actor and director Gregory Ratoff.
Four Sons 40. The Men in Her Life 41. Anything Can Happen 52. The World in His Arms 53. Homicidal 61, etc.

Lepage, Robert (1957–).
Canadian director and actor, from the theatre.
Le Confessional 95. The Polygraph 96. No (co-w, d) 98, etc.

Lerner, Alan Jay (1918–1986).
American lyricist, screenwriter and producer, at his best in collaboration with Frederick (Fritz) Loewe. Born in New York City, he was sent to school in England before studying at Harvard. He began as a writer for radio shows, then worked with Loewe for 18 years from 1942; their collaboration was renewed in the 70s. Their first hit came in 1947 with *Brigadoon*. His eight wives included actress Nancy Olsen.
Autobiography: 1978, *The Street Where I Live*.
An American in Paris (w) (AA) 51. Brigadoon (w, m in collaboration) 54. Gigi (m) (AA) 58. My Fair Lady (w, m in collaboration) (AA) 64. Camelot (w, m in collaboration) 67. Paint Your Wagon 69. On a Clear Day You Can See Forever (& p) 70. The Little Prince 74, many others.
❝ I have always made it a policy never to judge anyone by his behaviour with money and the opposite sex. – *A.J.L.*

Lerner, Carl (c. 1905–1975).
American editor.
Cry Murder 50. On the Bowery 56. *Twelve Angry Men* 57. The Fugitive Kind 59. Something Wild 61. All the Way Home 63. The Swimmer 68. The Angel Levine 70. Klute 72, etc.
DIRECTED: Black Like Me 64.

Lerner, Irving (1909–1976).
American director, former cameraman and documentarist.
■ Muscle Beach 46. Man Crazy 54. Edge of Fury 58. *Murder by Contract* 58. City of Fear 59. Studs Lonigan 60. Cry of Battle 63. The Royal Hunt of the Sun 69.

Lerner, Michael (1941–).
American character actor.
Alex in Wonderland 70. The Candidate 72. Busting 74. St Ives 76. Outlaw Blues 77. Borderline 80. Coast to Coast 80. The Baltimore Bullet 80. The Postman Always Rings Twice 81. National Lampoon's Class Reunion 82. Strange Invaders 83. Rita Hayworth: The Love Goddess (as Harry Cohn) 83. Movers and Shakers 84. Vibes 88. Eight Men Out 88. Harlem Nights 89. Maniac Cop 2 90. Omen IV: The Awakening 91. *Barton Fink* (AAN) 91. Newsies/The News Boys 92. Amos & Andrew 93. Blank Check 94. No Escape 94. The Road to Wellville 94. Radioland Murders 94. Girl in the Cadillac 95. A Pyromaniac's Love Story 95. No Way Back 96. For Richer or Poorer (TV) 97. The Beautician and the Beast 97. Godzilla 98. Celebrity 98, etc.
TV series: Love Story 73–74. Starsky and Hutch 75–79. Hart to Hart 79–84. Hollywood Beat 85.

Lesley, Carole (1935–1974) (Maureen Rippingdale).
British leading lady briefly groomed for stardom.
These Dangerous Years 57. Woman in a Dressing-Gown 57. No Trees in the Street 59. Doctor in Love 60. What a Whopper 62. The Pot Carriers 62, etc.

Leslie, Bethel (1929–).
American leading actress, mainly on TV.
The Rabbit Trap 58. Captain Newman 63. A Rage to Live 65. The Molly Maguires 69. Old Boyfriends 79. Ironweed 87. Terror on Track 9 (TV) 92. Kansas (TV) 95. In Cold Blood (TV) 96, etc.
TV series: The Girls 50. The Richard Boone Show 63. The Doctors 66.

Leslie, Joan (1925–) (Joan Brodel).
Pert, pretty American leading lady of the 40s; in vaudeville from childhood. Born in Detroit, Michigan, she began as a singer and dancer with her sisters as The Three Brodels and worked as a model before going to Hollywood.
Camille (debut) 36. Men with Wings 38. Foreign Correspondent 40. High Sierra 41. *Sergeant York* 41. The Male Animal 42. Yankee Doodle Dandy 42. The Hard Way 42. This Is the Army 43. Thank Your Lucky Stars 43. Hollywood Canteen 44. *Rhapsody in Blue* 45. Where Do We Go From Here? 45. Too Young to Know 45. Cinderella Jones 46. Royal Flush 46. Repeat Performance 47. Northwest Stampede 48. Born to Be Bad 51. The Toughest Man in Arizona 52. The Woman They Almost Lynched 53. Jubilee Trail 54. The Revolt of Mamie Stover 57. The Keegans (TV) 76. Charley Hannah (TV) 86. Fire in the Dark (TV) 91, etc.

Lesser, Sol (1890–1980).
American pioneer exhibitor of silent days, later producer: many Tarzan films.
Thunder Over Mexico 33. Our Town 40. Kon-Tiki 52, etc.

Lester, Bruce (1912–) (Bruce Lister).
South African leading man who made some British and American films; now plays support roles.
Death at Broadcasting House 34. Crime over

London 37. If I Were King 39. Pride and Prejudice 40. Above Suspicion 43. Golden Earrings 47. King Richard and the Crusaders 54, etc.

Lester, Dick (Richard) (1932–).
American director who found his spurt to fame in Britain doing zany comedies full of fast fragmented action. As soon as commercial backing was available his style went way over the top.
■ It's Trad Dad 61. The Mouse on the Moon 63. *A Hard Day's Night* 64. *The Knack* 65. Help 65. A Funny Thing Happened on the Way to the Forum 66. How I Won the War 67. Petulia 68. The Bed Sitting Room 69. The Three Musketeers 73. Juggernaut 74. The Four Musketeers 75. Royal Flash 75. Robin and Marian 76. The Ritz 76. Butch and Sundance: The Early Days 79. Cuba 79. Superman II 80. Superman III 83. Finders Keepers 84. Return of the Musketeers 89. Get Back (doc) 91.

Lester, Mark L. (1946–).
American director.
Tricia's Wedding 71. Truck Stop Women 74. Bobbie Jo and the Outlaw 75. Stunts 77. Gold of the Amazon Women 77. Roller Boogie 79. Class of 84 82. Firestarter 84. Commando 85. Armed and Dangerous 86. Class of 1999 89. Showdown in Little Tokyo 91. The Fraternity 94. The Ex 96. Double Take 97. Misbegotten 98, etc.

Lester, Mark (1958–).
Innocent-looking British child star of the 60s. Now an osteopath.
Allez France 64. Spaceflight IC/1 65. Our Mother's House 67. *Oliver* (title role) 68. Run Wild Run Free 69. Eye Witness 70. Melody 71. Black Beauty 71. Night Hair Child 71. Who Slew Auntie Roo? 72. Scalawag 73. Little Adventurer 75. The Prince and the Pauper/Crossed Swords 77, etc.

Leterrier, François (1929–).
French director.
Les Mauvais Coups 61. Un Roi sans Divertissement 63. La Chasse Royale 68. Projection Privée 73. Goodbye Emmanuelle 77. The Rat Race 80. The Bodyguard 84. Slice of Life 85. Le Fils du Mekong 91, etc.

Leto, Jared (1972–).
American leading actor, best known for his role as Jordan Catalano in the TV series *My So-Called Life*. Born in Louisiania, he studied painting at the University of Arts in Philadelphia and the School of Visual Arts in New York.
How to Make an American Quilt 95. Last of the High Kings 96. Switchback/Going West in America 97. Prefontaine (title role) 97. Summer Fling 98, etc.

Lettieri, Al (1927–1975).
American character actor. Died of alcoholism.
The Bobo 68. The Godfather 72. Getaway 73. Mr Majestyk 74. Deadly Trackers 75, etc.

Leung, Tony (Tony Leung Kar-fai).
Hong Kong leading actor who found an international audience from the late 80s.
The Last Emperor 88. The Laserman 90. *The Lover*/L'Amant 92. 92 The Legendary La Rose Noire/Hak Muigwai Dui Hak Mauigwai 92. Evening Liaison 95, etc.

Leung, Tony (1962–) (Tony Leung Chiu Wai).
Chinese leading actor, best known in the west for his performances in the films of Wong KAR-WAI.
People's Hero 87. Roboforce 89. City of Sadness/Beiqing Chengsi 89. Bullet in the Head 90. Days of Being Wild 91. Chung King Express 94. Cyclo/Xich Lo 95. War of the Underworld 96. Happy Together 97. Chinese Midnight Express 98, many others.

Levant, Brian (1952–).
American director.
Problem Child II 91. Beethoven 92. The Flintstones 94. Jingle All the Way 96.

Levant, Oscar (1906–1972).
American pianist and master of insult who appeared in several films as his grouchy, neurotic self.
Autobiographical books: 1944, *A Smattering of Ignorance*. 1965, *Memoirs of an Amnesiac*. 1968, *The Unimportance of Being Oscar*.
■ The Dance of Life 29. In Person 35. Rhythm on the River 40. Kiss the Boys Goodbye 41. *Rhapsody in Blue* 45. Humoresque 46. You Were Meant for Me 47. Romance on the High Seas 48. The Barkleys of Broadway 49. *An American in Paris* 51. *The Band Wagon* 53. The I Don't Care Girl 53. The Cobweb 55.
❝ In some situations I was difficult, in odd moments impossible, in rare moments loathsome, but at my best unapproachably great. – *O.L.*
Strip the phoney tinsel off Hollywood and you'll find the real tinsel underneath. – *O.L.*
I'm a controversial figure. My friends either dislike me or hate me. – *O.L.*
I hate cold showers. They stimulate me, and then I don't know what to do. – *O.L.*
I played an unsympathetic part – myself. – *O.L. on his role in Humoresque*
I envy people who drink. At least they have something to blame everything on. – *O.L. in Humoresque*
It's not a pretty face, but underneath this flabby exterior is an enormous lack of character. – *O.L. of himself in An American in Paris*
There is absolutely nothing wrong with Oscar Levant that a miracle can't fix. – *Alexander Woollcott*
A tortured man who sprayed his loathing on anyone within range. – *Shelley Winters*
Oscar has mellowed – like an old pistol. – *Billy Rose*

Leven, Boris (1900–1986).
Russian-born production designer, long in US. Born in Moscow, he studied architecture at the University of Southern California and began at Paramount as a sketch artist.
Alexander's Ragtime Band (AAN) 38. *The Shanghai Gesture* (AAN) 41. Mr Peabody and the Mermaid 48. Sudden Fear 52. *Giant* (AAN) 56. Anatomy of a Murder 59. *West Side Story* (AA) 61. The Sound of Music (AAN) 65. The Sand Pebbles (AAN) 67. Star! (AAN) 68. The Andromeda Strain (AAN) 70. Jonathan Livingston Seagull 73. Mandingo 75. New York, New York 77. The Last Waltz 78. The King of Comedy 82. Fletch 85. The Color of Money (AAN) 86, many others.

Levene, Sam (1905–1980).
American stage actor, often in Runyonesque film roles.
Three Men on a Horse (debut) 36. Golden Boy 39. The Purple Heart 44. *Crossfire* 47. Boomerang 47. Guilty Bystander 50. Three Sailors and a Girl 53. Sweet Smell of Success 57. Act One 63. A Dream of Kings 69. Such Good Friends 71. Demon 77. Last Embrace 79. And Justice for All 79.

LeVien, Jack (1918–).
American documentarist responsible for several distinguished compilation films.
Black Fox 62. The Finest Hours 64. A King's Story 67.
TV series on Churchill: *The Valiant Years* 60.

Levien, Sonya (1888–1960).
American writer, former lawyer. Story editor at various times for Fox, MGM, Paramount.
Cavalcade 33. *State Fair* (AAN) 33. *Berkeley Square* 33. In Old Chicago 38. *The Hunchback of Notre Dame* 40. Ziegfeld Girl 41. Rhapsody in Blue 45. Cass Timberlane 48. Quo Vadis 51. *Interrupted Melody* (AA) 55. *Jeanne Eagels* 58, etc.

Levin, Henry (1909–1980).
American director, in Hollywood from 1943 after stage experience.
Cry of the Werewolf 44. I Love a Mystery 45. The Guilt of Janet Ames 47. The Mating of Millie 48. Jolson Sings Again 49. The Petty Girl 50. Convicted 50. Belles on Their Toes 52. The President's Lady 52. Mister Scoutmaster 53. Gambler from Natchez 54. The Lonely Man 57. Bernardine 57. Let's Be Happy (GB) 57. The Remarkable Mr Pennypacker 58. Holidays for Lovers 59. *Journey to the Centre of the Earth* 59. Where the Boys Are 60. The Wonderful World of the Brothers Grimm 62. Come Fly with Me 63. Honeymoon Hotel 64. Genghis Khan 65. Kiss the Girls and Make Them Die 66. Murderers' Row 67. The Desperados 70. That Man Bolt 73. The Thoroughbreds 77, many others.

Levin, Ira (1929–).
American thriller writer with a sharp edge.
A Kiss before Dying 56. Rosemary's Baby 68. The Stepford Wives 75. The Boys from Brazil 78. Death Trap 82. A Kiss before Dying 91. Sliver 93.

Levin, Meyer (1905–1981).
American author, the original writer of *Compulsion*, which was filmed in 1959.

Levine, Joseph E. (1905–1987).
American production executive and showman, former theatre owner. Formed Embassy Pictures in late 50s, originally to exploit cheap European spectacles; also set up finance for films like *Eight and a Half*, *Divorce Italian Style*, *Boccaccio*.
AS PRODUCER: The Carpetbaggers 63. Where Love Has Gone 64. Harlow 65. A Bridge Too Far 77. Magic 78, etc.
❝ You can fool all the people all the time if the advice is right and the budget is big enough. – *J.E.L.*
When I grew up, we were so poor that you had to go down the hall to the bathroom for a breath of fresh air. – *J.E.L.*
Everyone told me to make family films. So I made eight of them. Even my own family didn't go see them. – *J.E.L.*

Levinson, Barry (1942–).
American director and screenwriter. He began as a comedy writer and stand-up comedian. His first wife was actress and screenwriter Valerie CURTIN.
Autobiography: 1993, *Levinson on Levinson*.
Catholics (TV) 73. First Love 77. And Justice for All (AAN) 80. Inside Moves 81. *Diner* (& d) (AANw) 82. Best Friends 82. The Natural (d only) 84. Young Sherlock Holmes (d only) 85. Tin Men (wd) 87. Good Morning Vietnam (d) 87. *Rain Man* (d) (AA) 88. Avalon (wd, AAN) 90. Bugsy (d) (AAN) 91. Toys (co-w, d) 92. Jimmy Hollywood (wd) 94. Quiz Show (a) 94. Disclosure 94. Sleepers 96. Wag the Dog 97. Home Fries (co-p) 98, etc.

Levy, Jefery (1958–).
American director.
Drive 92. Inside Monkey Zetterland 93. S.F.W. 94.

Levy, Jules (1923–1975).
American independent producer, of Levy-Gardner-Laven. See Arthur Gardner for credits.

Levy, Louis (1893–1957).
British musical director and composer, in films from 1916. Scored *Nanook of the North* 20. With Gaumont and Gainsborough 1928–47, supervising all musical productions.
Jack's the Boy 32. It's a Boy! 33. Falling for You 33. Friday the Thirteenth 33. The Good Companions 33. A Cuckoo in the Nest 33. Man of Aran 34. The Man Who Knew Too Much 34. The Camels Are Coming 34. Chu-Chin-Chow 34. Boys Will Be Boys 35. Bulldog Jack 35. The 39 Steps 35. Rhodes of Africa 36. King Solomon's Mines 37. Pygmalion 38. The Citadel 38. The Lambeth Walk 39. An Englishman's Home 39. The Young Mr Pitt 42. Dear Octopus 43. The Man in Grey 43. Madonna of the Seven Moons 44. Waterloo Road 44. The Wicked Lady 45. Under Capricorn 49. The Hasty Heart 49. Murder without Crime 50. Stage Fright 50. Where's Charley? 52. His Majesty O'Keefe 53. Woman in a Dressing Gown 57, many others.

Levy, Ralph (1919–).
American director, in TV from 1947.
Bedtime Story 64. Do Not Disturb 65.

Lévy, Raoul (1922–1966).
French producer.
Les Orgueilleux 53. And God Created Woman (& w) 56. Heaven Fell That Night 57. En Cas de Malheur 58. Babette Goes to War (& co-w) 59. Moderato Cantabile 60. The Truth 60. The Defector (& wd) 66, etc.

Lewin, Albert (1895–1968).
American writer-producer-director with something of an Omar Khayyam fixation. Production executive 1931–41.
■ *The Moon and Sixpence* (wd) 42. *The Picture of Dorian Gray* (wd) 44. The Private Affairs of Bel Ami (wd, p) 47. *Pandora and the Flying Dutchman* (wd, p) 51. Saadia (wd, p) 54. The Living Idol (wd, p) 57.
❝ A most intriguing little man. He completely checked out of his executive office at MGM every year or so when he wanted a year off to make one of his own pictures. – *James Mason*
Would that there were more room for accident in his clogged literary narrations and his naive conception of refinement in the cinema. – *Andrew Sarris, 1968*

Lewin, Ben (1946–).
Polish-born director, in Australia.
The Dunera Boys (TV) 85. Georgia 89. The Favour, the Watch and the Very Big Fish 91. Lucky Break 94. Paperback Romance (wd) 94, etc.

Lewis, Albert E. (1884–1978).
Polish-American producer and Broadway impresario who was associated with several films.
International House 32. Torch Singer 35. Mutiny on the Bounty 35. Cabin in the Sky 43, etc.

Lewis, Cecil (1898–1997).
English novelist, screenwriter, director and producer, activities that were almost sideshows in a varied, adventurous life. An aviator in the First World War, shooting down six enemy planes, he helped form the Chinese air force in the 1920s, and was also the first deputy director of the BBC, the author of a classic novel of war, *Sagittarius Rising*, a farmer and journalist. He began directing through the efforts of George Bernard Shaw, who stipulated it on the first films made from his plays. In the late 30s, he worked briefly for Paramount as a writer.
Autobiographies: 1974, *Never Look Back*; 1993, *All My Yesterdays*.
How He Lied to Her Husband (co-w, d) 30. Carmen/Gipsy Blood (co-w, d) 32. Indiscretions of Eve (wd) 32. Arms and the Man (co-w, d) 32. Leave It to Me (co-w) 33. Café Mascot (oa) 36. Pygmalion (co-w) (AA) 38. Aces High (oa) 77, etc.

Lewis, Charlotte (1967–).
London-born actress, in international and American movies.
Pirates (Fr.) 86. The Golden Child 86. Dial Help (It.) 88. Tripwire 90. Bare Essentials (TV) 91. Storyville 92. Sketch Artist 92. Excessive Force 93. Men of War 94. Red Shoe Diaries 6: How I Met My Husband 95. Embrace of the Vampire 95. Decoy 95. The Glass Cage 96. Navajo Blues 97, etc.
TV series: Broken Badges 90–91.

Lewis, David (1903–1987) (David Levy).
American producer and associate producer, a former theatre actor, story editor, and personal assistant to Irving THALBERG at MGM. He worked at Warner for Hal B. WALLIS before becoming a fully fledged producer. He was also the lover of director James WHALE. Born in Trinidad, Columbia, he was educated at the University of Washington.
Crossfire 33. Where Sinners Meet 34. Camille 36. All This and Heaven Too 40. Kings Row 41. The Sisters 42. Frenchman's Creek 44. The Other Love 47. Arch of Triumph 48. The Seventh Sin 57. Raintree Country 57, etc.

Lewis, Diana (1919–1997).
American leading lady of the late 30s; retired when she married William Powell.
It's a Gift 34. Forty Little Mothers 39. Bitter Sweet 40. Johnny Eager 41. Seven Sweethearts 42. Cry Havoc 43, etc.

Lewis, Fiona (1946–).
British leading lady.
The Fearless Vampire Killers 67. Where's Jack? 69. Villain 71. Dracula (TV) 73. Lisztomania 75. The Fury 78. Strange Invaders 83. Innerspace 87, etc.

Lewis, Gena (1888–1979).
American screenwriter.
Sin Town 42. The Climax 44. Cobra Woman 45. Trail Street 49. Lonely Heart Bandits 51, etc.

Lewis, Geoffrey (1935–).
American character actor, often in harassed roles. He is the father of Juliette Lewis.
Culpepper Cattle Company 72. The Great Waldo Pepper 75. Macon County Line 74. Thunderbolt and Lightning 74. Smile 75. Return of a Man Called Horse 76. Every Which Way but

Loose 78. Lust in the Dust 85. Fletch Lives 89. Double Impact 91. The Lawnmower Man 92. Point of No Return 93. The Man without a Face 93. Joshua Tree 93. White Fang 2: Myth of the White Wolf 94. Maverick 94. Kansas 95. Rough Riders (TV) 97. American Perfekt 97. Midnight in the Garden of Good and Evil 97, etc.

TV series: Flo 80–81. Gun Shy 83. Land's End 95.

Lewis, Herschell Gordon (1926–).
American director of exploitation films.

The Living Venus 61. Goldilocks and the Three Bares 63. Blood Feast 63. Monster a Go Go 65. The Gruesome Twosome 67. A Taste of Blood 67. The Ecstasies of Women 69. The Wizard of Gore 70. Stick It in Your Ear 72. Black Love 72. The Gore-Gore Girls 72, many others.

❝ In my movies I went for intensive rather than extensive gore, and the rationale is quite simple: I didn't have any budget. – *H.G.L.*

Lewis, Jay (1914–1969).
British producer, in films from 1933.

Morning Departure 50. The Gift Horse 52, etc.

AS DIRECTOR: The Baby and the Battleship 55. Invasion Quartet 61. Live Now Pay Later 62. A Home of Your Own 65, etc.

Lewis, Jerry (1926–) (Joseph Levitch).
Goonish American comedian whose style is a mixture of exaggerated mugging and sticky sentiment. Until 1956 he formed a popular partnership with Dean Martin, but his increasingly indulgent solo films since then have gradually reduced his once-fervent band of admirers.

Biography: 1996, *King of Comedy* by Shawn Levy.

My Friend Irma 49. My Friend Irma Goes West 50. At War with the Army 51. That's My Boy 51. Sailor Beware 52. Jumping Jacks 52. The Stooge 53. Scared Stiff 53. The Caddy 53. Money from Home 54. Living It Up 54. Three Ring Circus 54. You're Never Too Young 54. Artists and Models 55. Pardners 56. Hollywood or Bust 56. The Delicate Delinquent 57. The Sad Sack 58. Rock a Bye Baby 58. The Geisha Boy 58. Don't Give up the Ship 59. Visit to a Small Planet 60. *The Bellboy* 60. Cinderfella 60. Ladies' Man 61. The Errand Boy 61. It's Only Money 62. The Nutty Professor 63. Who's Minding the Store? 64. The Patsy 64. The Disorderly Orderly 64. The Family Jewels 65. Boeing-Boeing 65. Three on a Couch 66. Way Way Out 66. The Big Mouth 67. Don't Raise the Bridge, Lower the River 68. Hook Line and Sinker 69. Which Way to the Front? 70. One More Time (d only) 71. Hardly Working (& d) 79. Slapstick of the Fourth Kind 82. King of Comedy 83. Smorgasbord (& co-w, d) 83. Cookie 89. The Arrowtooth Waltz 92. Arizona Dream 92. Funny Bones 95, etc.

Gag appearance: It's a Mad Mad Mad Mad World 63.

❝ When the light goes on in the refrigerator, I do twenty minutes. – *J.L.*

At some point he said to himself, I'm extraordinary, like Chaplin. From then on nobody could tell him anything. He knew it all. – *Dean Martin*

Lewis, Jerry Lee (1935–).
American country-rock singer whose turbulent life was filmed as *Great Balls of Fire* 89, in which he was played by Dennis Quaid.

AS HIMSELF: Jamboree/Disc Jockey Jamboree 57. High School Confidential 58. American Hot Wax 76. Chuck Berry Hail! Hail! Rock 'n' Roll 87, etc.

Lewis, Joe E. (1901–1971) (Joseph Kleevan).
American night-club comedian, played by Frank Sinatra in *The Joker is Wild*

■ Too Many Husbands 31. Private Buckaroo 42. Lady in Cement 69.

Lewis, Joseph H. (1900–).
American director, mainly of second features, some of them well above average.

Two-Fisted Rangers 40. The Mad Doctor of Market Street 41. Bombs over Burma 42. Minstrel Man 44. *My Name Is Julia Ross* 45. *So Dark the Night* 46. *The Jolson Story* (musical numbers only) 46. The Swordsman 47. The Return of October 48. *The Undercover Man* 49. A Lady without Passport 50. Gun Crazy 50. Retreat Hell 52. Cry of the Hunted 53. The Big Combo 55. A Lawless Street 55. Seventh Cavalry 56. The Halliday Brand 56. *Terror in a Texas Town* 58, etc.

Lewis, Juliette (1975–).
American leading actress. She is the daughter of Geoffrey Lewis.

My Stepmother Is an Alien 88. Life on the Edge 89. National Lampoon's Christmas Vacation 89. Cape Fear (AAN) 91. Crooked Hearts 91. Husbands and Wives 92. That Night 93. Kalifornia 93. Romeo Is Bleeding 93. What's Eating Gilbert Grape 93. Natural Born Killers 94. Strange Days 95. The Basketball Diaries 95. From Dusk till Dawn 96. The Evening Star 96. Some Girls 98, etc.

TV series: Home Fires 87. I Married Dora 87–88. A Family for Joe 90.

Lewis, Michael J. (1939–).
British composer.

The Madwoman of Chaillot 69. The Man Who Haunted Himself 70. Unman Wittering and Zigo 72. Theatre of Blood 73. 11 Harrowhouse 74. Russian Roulette 75. The Medusa Touch 78. The Stick Up/Mud 78. The Passage 79. The Legacy 79. North Seas Hijack/ffolkes 80. The Unseen 81. Sphinx 81. Yes, Giorgio 82. The Naked Face 85. The Rose and the Jackal (TV) 90, etc.

Lewis, Ralph (1872–1937).
American character actor, often in villainous roles, in films from 1912. He played the abolitionist senator Austin Stoneman in *The Birth of a Nation* 15.

The Escape 14. Intolerance 16. Eyes of Youth 19. Flesh and Blood 22. Desire 23. Dante's Inferno 24. Casey Jones 27. The Girl in the Glass Cage 29. Abraham Lincoln 30. Riot Squad 33. Mystery Liner 34. Behind the Green Light 35, etc.

Lewis, Richard (1949–).
American stand-up comedian, and actor.

Diary of a Young Comic (& co-w) (TV) 79. The Wrong Guys 88. That's Adequate 90. Once upon a Crime 92. Robin Hood: Men in Tights 93. Wagons East 94. Leaving Las Vegas 95. Danger of Love (TV) 95. A Weekend in the Country (TV) 96. Drunks 96. Hugo Pool 97, etc.

TV series: Harry 87. Anything but Love 89–91. Rude Awakening 98– .

Lewis, Robert (1909–1997).
American theatre director, teacher and occasional actor. He was a founding member of the GROUP THEATER of the 30s, and co-founder of the ACTORS' STUDIO, leaving after a disagreement with Elia KAZAN in 1948 to continue his career elsewhere as a director and teacher. Born in Brooklyn, he was educated at the Juilliard School, working in Hollywood as an actor in the 40s.

AS ACTOR: Paris after Dark 43. Tonight We Raid Calais 43. Dragon Seed 44. The Hidden Eye 45. Son of Lassie 45. Ziegfeld Follies 46. Monsieur Verdoux 47. The Lost Volcano 50, etc.

Lewis, Ronald (1928–1982).
British leading man, in films from 1953. Committed suicide.

The Prisoner 55. Storm over the Nile 55. A Hill in Korea 56. Bachelor of Hearts 59. The Full Treatment 61. Twice Round the Daffodils 62. Mr Sardonicus 62. The Brigand of Kandahar 65. Friends 71. Paul and Michelle 74, etc.

Lewis, Sheldon (1868–1958).
American character actor of stage and screen.

The Exploits of Elaine 15. Dr Jekyll and Mr Hyde (title role) 16. Orphans of the Storm 21. The Red Kimono 26. Black Magic 29. The Monster Walks 32. The Cattle Thief (last film) 36, many others.

Lewis, Sinclair (1885–1951).
American novelist. Works filmed include:

Arrowsmith 31. Ann Vickers 33. Babbitt 34. Dodsworth 36. Untamed 40. Cass Timberlane 47. Elmer Gantry 60.

Lewis, Stephen (1936–).
Lugubrious English comic actor and writer, best known as the put-upon Inspector Blake in the TV sitcom *On the Buses*. He also had recurring, occasional roles in the TV sitcoms *Last of the Summer Wine, One Foot in the Grave* and *2Point4 Children*. Born in London and a former bricklayer, he began on stage with THEATRE WORKSHOP.

A Prize of Arms 61. Sparrows Can't Sing (& co-w, oa) 62. Negatives 68. Staircase 69. Some Will, Some Won't 70. On the Buses 71. Mutiny on the Buses 72. Holiday on the Buses 73. Adventures of a Taxi Driver 75. Adventures of a Plumber's Mate 78. Personal Services 87, etc.

TV series: On the Buses 69–73. Don't Drink the Water 74–75. Rep 82. The All New Alexei Sayle Show 95. Oh, Doctor Beeching! 95–97.

Lewis, Ted (1891–1971) (Theodore Friedman).
American bandleader and entertainer ('Me and My Shadow') who appeared in a few movies.

■ Is Everybody Happy? 28. Show of Shows 29. Here Comes the Band 35. Manhattan Merry Go Round 37. Hold That Ghost 42. Follow the Boys 44.

Lewton, Val (1904–1951) (Vladimir Leventon).
American producer, remembered for a group of low-budget, high quality horror films made for RKO in the 40s.

Biography: 1973, *The Reality of Terror* by Joel E. Siegel.

■ *Cat People* 42. I Walked with a Zombie 43. The Leopard Man 43. The Seventh Victim 43. The Ghost Ship 43. Mademoiselle Fifi 44. Curse of the Cat People 44. Youth Runs Wild 44. *The Body Snatcher* 45. Isle of the Dead 45. Bedlam 46. My Own True Love 49. Please Believe Me 50. Apache Drums 51.

~Under the pseudonym Carlos Keith, Lewton contributed to the screenplays of *The Body Snatchers* and *Bedlam*.

Lexy, Edward (1897–1970) (Edward Gerald Little).
British character actor in films from 1936, usually as sergeant-major, police inspector or irascible father.

Farewell Again 37. South Riding 38. Laugh It Off 40. Spare a Copper 40. Piccadilly Incident 46. It's Not Cricket 48. Miss Robin Hood 52. Orders Are Orders 55. The Man Who Wouldn't Talk 58, many others.

Leyton, John (1939–).
British pop singer who transferred to dramatic roles.

The Great Escape 63. Von Ryan's Express 65. Krakatoa 68. Schizo 77. Dangerous Davies – the Last Detective 80, etc.

TV series: Jericho 66.

L'Herbier, Marcel (1888–1979).
French director, an avant-garde leader in silent days.

Autobiography: 1979, *La Tête Qui Tourne*.

Rose France 19. Eldorado 22. The Late Mathias Pascal 25. L'Epervier 33. Nuits de Feu 37. La Nuit Fantastique 42. The Last Days of Pompeii 49. Le Père de Mademoiselle 53, etc.

Lhermitte, Thierry.
French leading actor.

L'An 01 72. Next Year If All Goes Well 83. My Best Friend's Girl/La Femme de Mon Pote 83. Les Ripoux 84. Until September (US) 84. Tango 93. L'Honneur de la Tribu 93. Elles N'Oublient Jamais 94. Seven Sundays 94. Un Indien dans la Ville (& co-w) 95. My Woman Is Leaving Me 96. Fallait Pas! 96. Comme des Rois 97. An American Werewolf in Paris 97. Marquise (as Louis XIV) 97, etc.

Lhomme, Pierre (1930–).
French cinematographer.

St Tropez Blues 60. A Matter of Resistance/La Vie de Château 66. King of Hearts/Le Roi de Coeur 66. La Chamade 68. Mister Freedom 69. Four Nights of a Dreamer/Quatre Nuits d'un Rêveur 71. Sweet Movie 74. The Savage State/L'Etat Sauvage 78. Quartet 81. My Little Girl 87. Maurice 87. Cyrano de Bergerac 90. Voyager 91. Premier Amour 92. Summer Strolls/Promenades d'Eté 92. Toxic Affair 93. Dieu que les Femmes Sont Amoureuses 94. Jefferson in Paris 95. My Man 96. Stolen Life/Voleur de Vie 98, etc.

Li, Bruce (Ho Chung Tao, aka Li Shaolung).
Taiwanese-born star of kung fu movies and occasional director, one of the many who attempted to take the place of Bruce Lee. Retired in the mid-80s to teach martial arts.

Return of the Tiger 73. Dragon Dies Hard 76. Exit the Dragon Enter the Tiger 76. Fists of Fury 2 76. Enter the Panther 79. Bruce Li the Invincible 80. Enter Three Dragons 81. Story of the Dragon/Bruce Lee's Secret 82. Iron Dragon Strikes Back 84. Counter Attack (& d) 84. Chinese Connection 2 84. Kung Fu Avengers 85, etc.

Li, Gong (1966–).
Leading Chinese actress and drama teacher, closely associated with the work of director Zhang Yimou. In 1994, the Chinese government told her that she could no longer attend festivals in the West or give interviews to foreign journalists.

Red Sorghum/Hong Gaoliang 87. Ju Dou 90. The Terra-Cotta Warrior 90. *Raise the Red Lantern/* Dahong Denglong Gaogao Gua 91. *The Story of Qui Ju* 92. Mary from Beijing/Mungsing Sifan 93. Farewell My Concubine/Bawang Bie Ji 93. To Live 94. The Great Conqueror's Concubine/Xi Chu Bawang 94. La Peintre/Hua Hun 94. Shanghai Triad 95. Temptress Moon 96, etc.

Li, Jet (1963–) (Li Lian Jie).
Chinese star of martial arts movies, and occasional director and producer. Born in Beijing, he was Chinese Wu Shu (a form of martial arts) champion from 1974 to 1979. He moved to America for a time before settling in Hong Kong in the early 90s.

Shaolin Temple 82. Shaolin Temple 2: Kids from Shaolin 84. Born to Defence (& d) 86. Martial Arts of Shaolin 86. *Once Upon a Time in China* 90. Once Upon a Time in China 2 91. The Master 92. Shaolin Cult Master 93. Once Upon a Time in China 3: Dance of the Lion King 93. Fong Sai Yuk 93. Fong Sai Yuk II 93. Last Hero in China/Wong Fei-Hung Tsi Titgai Dau Nggung 93. Fist of Legend 94. My Father Is a Hero 95. High Risk 95. The New Legend of Shaolin (& p) 95. Black Mask 96. Once Upon a Time in China & America 97. Lethal Weapon 4 (US) 98, etc.

Liberace (1919–1987) (Wladziu Valentino Liberace).
American pianist-showman of stage, nightclubs and TV. Starred in his only major appearance, *Sincerely Yours* 55; also seen as a pianist in *East of Java* 49 and as a coffin salesman in *The Loved One* 65. Died of AIDS.

Autobiography: 1977, *The Things I Love*.

❝ You know that bank I used to cry all the way to? I bought it. – *L.*

Of course, I couldn't go out in the street in clothes like this, I'd get picked up. Come to think of it, it might be fun. – *L.*

Gee, you've been such a wonderful audience that I don't like to take your money. But I will! – *L.*

Some day that boy may take my place.
– *Paderewski, on hearing the seven-year-old Liberace play*

This deadly, winking, sniggering, snuggling, chromium-plated, scent-impregnated, luminous, quivering, giggling, fruit-flavoured, mincing, ice-covered heap of mother-love. – *Cassandra (William Connor), Daily Mirror*

Licht, Daniel.
Composer.

Bad Moon 96.

Licudi, Gabriella (1943–).
Italian leading lady in international films.

The Liquidators 65. The Jokers 66. Casino Royale 66. The Last Safari 67. Soft Beds, Hard Battles 73, many others.

Lieven, Albert (1906–1971).
German actor in films from 1933, including many British productions.

Victoria the Great 37. Night Train to Munich 40. *Jeannie* 40. Yellow Canary 43. *The Seventh Veil* 45. *Beware of Pity* 46. Frieda 47. *Sleeping Car to Trieste* 48. Hotel Sahara 50. Conspiracy of Hearts 60. Foxhole in Cairo 61. The Victors 63. Traitor's Gate 65, many others.

Lightner, Winnie (1901–1971) (Winifred Hanson).
American vaudeville comedienne who appeared in several early talkies.

Gold Diggers of Broadway 30. Playgirl 32. Dancing Lady 32. I'll Fix It 34, etc.

Lillie, Beatrice (1898–1989) (Constance Sylvia Munston, later Lady Peel).
Sharp-faced, mischievous British revue star of the 20s and 30s who graced only a few films with her wit. Born in Toronto, she moved to England in her early teens and was appearing in musical hall from the age of 16.

Autobiography: 1973, *Every Other Inch a Lady*.

■ *Exit Smiling* 26. Show of Shows 29. Are You There? 30. Dr Rhythm 38. *On Approval* 43.

Around the World in Eighty Days 56. Thoroughly Modern Millie 67.

Lima, Walter, Jnr (1938–).
Brazilian director, a former journalist, who also worked as assistant to Glauber Rocha.
Menino do Engenho 65. Brasil, Anno 2000 69. Taim 77. Xico Rei 82. Dolphin 87. The Oyster and the Wind 97, etc.

Lincoln, Abbey (1930–) (Anna Marie Woolridge).
American character actress.
The Girl Can't Help It 56. Nothing but a Man 64. For Love of Ivy 68. Mo' Better Blues 90, etc.

Lincoln, Abraham (1809–1865).
Sixteenth American president, a familiar screen figure with his stovepipe hat, bushy whiskers, and his assassination during a performance of *Our American Cousin*. More or less full-length screen portraits include *Abraham Lincoln's Clemency* 10; *Lincoln the Lover* 13; Joseph Henabery in *Birth of a Nation* 14; Frank McGlynn in *The Life of Abraham Lincoln* 15; George A. Billings in *Abraham Lincoln* 25; Walter Huston in *Abraham Lincoln* 30; John Carradine in *Of Human Hearts* 38; Henry Fonda in *Young Mr Lincoln* 39; Raymond Massey in *Abe Lincoln in Illinois* 39.

Lincoln, Elmo (1889–1952) (Otto Elmo Linkenhelter).
American silent actor who became famous as the first *Tarzan of the Apes* 18, and played small roles up to his death.
Birth of a Nation 14. Elmo the Mighty 19, etc.

Linda, Boguslaw (1952–).
Polish leading actor, who also directed one film.
No Trespassing/Droga Powrotna 72. Wierne Blizny 81. Man of Iron/Czlowiek z Zelaza 81. Shivers/Dreszcze 81. Danton/L'Affaire Danton 82. The Mother of Kings/Matka Krolow 82 (released 87). Lost Illusions/Elveszett Illuziok 83. Funeral Ceremony/Ceremonia Pogrzebowa 84. Cheap Money/Tanie Pieniadze 85. The Right Man for a Delicate Job/Megfelelö Ember Kényes Feladatra 85. Maskarada 86. Blind Chance/Przypadek 87. Suspended/W Zawieszeniu 87. Zabij Kill Me, Cop/Mnie, Glino 87. The Road Home/Cienie 88. Potyautasok/Stowaways 89. En Verden Til Forskel/A World of Difference 89. Seszele/Seychelles (d) 90. Jancio Wodnik/Johnnie the Aquarius 93. All the Most Important/Wszystko, Co Najwazniejsze 93. The Stranger Must Fly/Obcy Musi Fruwac 94. A Time for Witches/Pora na Czarownice 94. Psy 2/Ostatnia Krew 94. Szamanka 96, etc.

Lindblom, Gunnel (1935–).
Leading Swedish actress who became a director and screenwriter from the 70s.
The Seventh Seal 56. Wild Strawberries 57. The Virgin Spring 60. Winter Light 62. *The Silence* 63. Rapture 65. Loving Couples 66. Sult 67. Flickorna 68. The Father 69. Brother Carl 71. Scenes from a Marriage 74. Summer Paradise/Paradistorg (wd) 77. Bomsalva 78. Sally Och Friheten (d) 81. Bakom Jalusin 84. Summer Nights/Sommarkvallar (wd) 87, etc.

Linden, Eric (1909–).
Swedish-American juvenile lead of the 30s. Disliked Hollywood and quit acting in the early 40s.
Are These Our Children? 32. The Silver Cord 33. Girl of the Limberlost 34. The Voice of Bugle Ann 36. Gone with the Wind 39. Criminals Within 41, etc.

Linden, Hal (1931–) (Harold Lipshitz).
American character actor, best known as TV's *Barney Miller*.
When You Comin' Back, Red Ryder? 79. Father Figure (TV) 80. My Wicked, Wicked Ways: The Legend of Errol Flynn (TV) 85. A New Life 88. The Colony 95. Out to Sea 97. Killers in the House (TV) 98, etc.
TV series: Jack's Place 92. The Boys Are Back 94.

Linden, Jennie (1939–).
British leading actress.
Nightmare 63. Dr Who and the Daleks 66. *Women in Love* 69. A Severed Head 70. Hedda 75. Valentino 77. Charlie Muffin 79, etc.
TV series: Lillie 77.

Linder, Cec (1921–1992).
Canadian character actor, long in British films.
Crack in the Mirror 59. Jetstorm 59. Too Young to Love 60. SOS Pacific 60. Goldfinger 64. Explosion 71. A Touch of Class 73. Sunday in the Country 74. Lost and Found 79. Atlantic City 80, many others.

Linder, Max (1883–1925) (Gabriel Leuvielle).
Dapper French silent comedian, a likely source for Chaplin. Between 1906 and 1925 he scripted and directed most of his own films, from 1917 in Hollywood. Committed suicide, together with his wife.
The Skater's Debut 07. Max Takes a Bath 07. Max and His Mother-in-Law's False Teeth 08. Max's New Landlord 08. Max in a Dilemma 10. Max Is Absent-Minded 10. How Max Went Around the World 11. Max, Victim of Quinquina 11. Max Teaches the Tango 11. Max Is Forced to Work 12. Max Toreador 12. Max Virtuoso 12. Who Killed Max? 13. Max's Hat 14. Max and Jane Make a Dessert 14. Max and the Clutching Hand 15. Max Comes Across 17. Max Wants a Divorce 17. Max and His Taxi 17. The Little Café 19. Seven Years Bad Luck* 20. Be My Wife* 20. The Three Must-Get-Theres* 22. Help! 24. King of the Circus 25, many others.
*These films formed the basis of a compilation, *Laugh with Max Linder*, which was issued in 1963.

Lindfors, Viveca (1920–1995) (Elsa Torstendotter).
Swedish actress, in films from 1941, Hollywood from 1946. She trained at Stockholm's Royal Theatre and gave her best performances on the stage. Married director Don Siegel (1948–53) and writer George Tabori.
Autobiography: 1981, *Viveka . . .* Viveca.
To the Victor 47. Night Unto Night 48. The New Adventures of Don Juan 48. No Sad Songs for Me 50. Dark City 50. The Flying Missile 51. Four in a Jeep 51. The Raiders 52. Run for Cover 55. Moonfleet 55. I Accuse 57. Tempest 58. King of Kings 61. Sylvia 65. Brainstorm 65. The Way We Were 73. Welcome to L.A. 77. Girlfriends 78. A Wedding 78. Natural Enemies 79. Voices 79. The Hand 82. Creepshow 82. Silent Madness 83. The Sure Thing 85. Frankenstein's Aunt 86. Unfinished Business (& wd) 87. Rachel River 88. The Ann Jillian Story (TV) 88. Forced March 89. Zandalee 90. Luba 90. Exorcist III 90. Exiled 91. The Linguini Incident 92. Stargate 94. Last Summer in the Hamptons 95, many others.

Lindgren, Lars Magnus (1922–).
Swedish director.
Do You Believe in Angels? 60. Dear John 64. The Coffin/The Sadist 66. The Black Palm Trees 68. The Lion and the Virgin 74, etc.

Lindley, Audra (1913–1997).
American character actress, best known for her role as the lovelorn landlady Helen Roper in *Three's Company* and the spin-off series *The Ropers*.
The Heartbreak Kid 72. Pearl (TV) 79. When You Comin' Back Red Ryder 79. Moviola (TV) 80. Cannery Row 82. Desert Hearts 85. Spellbinder 88. Troop Beverly Hills 89. The New Age 94. Sudden Death 95, etc.
TV series: Bridget Loves Bernie 72–73. Fay 75–76. Doc 76. Three's Company 77–79. The Ropers 79–80.

Lindley, John (1952–).
American cinematographer.
The Goodbye People 84. Lily in Love 85. Killer Party 86. Home of the Brave 86. The Stepfather 87. In the Mood 87. The Serpent and the Rainbow 87. Shakedown/Blue Jean Cop 87. True Believer 89. Field of Dreams 89. Immediate Family 89. Vital Signs 90. Sleeping with the Enemy 91. Sneakers 92. The Good Son 93. I Love Trouble 94. Money Train 95. Michael 96, etc.

Lindo, Delroy (1952–).
London-born actor, of Jamaican parents, in America. He trained at the American Conservatory Theatre in San Francisco.
More American Graffiti 79. The Salute of the Jugger 89. Mountains of the Moon 89. Bright Angel 90. The Hard Way 91. Malcolm X 92. Blood In, Blood Out 93. Mr Jones 94. Crooklyn 94. Clockers 95. Get Shorty 95. Broken Arrow 96. Feeling Minnesota 96. Ransom 96, etc.

Lindo, Olga (1898–1968).
Anglo-Norwegian character actress, on British stage and screen.
The Shadow Between 32. The Last Journey 35. *When We Are Married* 42. Bedelia 46. Train of Events 49. *An Inspector Calls* 54. Woman in a Dressing Gown 57. Sapphire 59, etc.

Lindon, Lionel (1905–1971).
American cinematographer.
Going My Way 44. A Medal for Benny 45. Road to Utopia 46. *Alias Nick Beal* 49. Destination Moon 50. Conquest of Space 55. *Around the World in Eighty Days* (AA) 56. The Lonely Man 57. The Black Scorpion 57. Too Late Blues 61. *The Manchurian Candidate* 62. The Trouble with Angels 66. Boy Did I Get a Wrong Number 66. *Grand Prix* 66. Generation 69, etc.

Lindsay, Howard (1889–1968).
American actor-playwright-stage director. With Russel Crouse wrote *Life with Father and State of the Union*, both filmed. Acted in and directed *Dulcy* 21, co-authored *She's My Weakness* 31.

Lindsay, Margaret (1910–1981) (Margaret Kies).
American leading lady of the 30s, with stage experience; in Hollywood from 1931.
West of Singapore 32. Lady Killer 34. Bordertown 35. G-Men 35. The Green Light 37. Jezebel 38. The House of Seven Gables 40. There's Magic in Music 41. A Close Call for Ellery Queen 42. No Place for a Lady 43. Crime Doctor 43. Alaska 44. Club Havana 45. Scarlet Street 45. Her Sister's Secret 47. Cass Timberlane 47. Emergency Hospital 56. Jet over the Atlantic 59. Tammy and the Doctor 63, many others.

Lindsay, Robert (1949–).
English leading actor, from the stage.
Adventures of a Taxi Driver 75. Bert Rigby, You're a Fool 89. Strike It Rich/Loser Takes All 90. Fierce Creatures 96. Hornblower (TV) 98. Divorcing Jack 98, etc.
TV series: Citizen Smith 73–77. Jake's Progess 95.

Lindsay-Hogg, Michael (1940–).
British director and screenwriter. He is the son of actress Geraldine Fitzgerald.
Let It Be 70. Nasty Habits 77. Brideshead Revisited (co-d) (TV) 81. Master Harold and the Boys 84. As Is 86. The Object of Beauty (wd) 91. Frankie Starlight 95. Guy 96. Alone (TV) 97, etc.

Lindtberg, Leopold (1902–1984).
Austrian director, a former actor, who was a theatre director in Germany before moving to Switzerland in the early 40s, after the rise of the Nazis, to become an influential director of film and theatre there.
Jasoo (co-d) 35. Die Missbrauchten Liebesbriefe 40. Marie-Louise 44. The Last Chance/Die Letzte Chance 45. Four in a Jeep/Die Vier im Jeep 51. Daughter of the Storm 54, etc.

Linklater, Richard (1962–).
American actor, director and producer of independent films.
Slacker (a, wd) 91. Dazed and Confused (a, p, co-w) 93. Before Sunrise (co-w, d) 95. SubUrbia 97, etc.
❝ You need age and maturity to make a good film. – *R.L.*

Linn-Baker, Mark (1954–).
American actor.
My Favorite Year 82. Ghostwriter 84. Me and Him/Ich und Er (Ger.) 89. Bare Essentials 91. Noises Off 92, etc.
TV series: Perfect Strangers 86–93.

Linney, Laura (1964–).
American actress, from the theatre. Born in New York, she studied at Brown University, the Juilliard School, and at Moscow's Arts Theater School.
Class of '61 (TV) 92. Lorenzo's Oil 92. Searching for Bobby Fischer/Innocent Moves 93. Tales of the City (TV) 93. Dave 93. A Simple Twist of Fate 94. Congo 95. Primal Fear 96. Absolute Power 97. More Tales of the City (TV) 98. The Truman Show 98, etc.

Linson, Art (1942–).
American producer and occasional director. He is the author of *A Pound of Flesh: Perilous Tales of How to Produce Movies in Hollywood*, published in 1994.
Rafferty and the Gold Dust Twins 75. American Hot Wax 78. Melvin and Harold 80. Where the Buffalo Roam (& d) 80. Fast Times at Ridgmount High 82. The Wild Life (& d) 84. The Untouchables 87. Scrooged 88. Casualties of War 89. We're No Angels 89. Dick Tracy 90. Singles 92. Point of No Return 93. This Boy's Life 93, etc.

Linz, Alex D. (1989–).
American child star, born in Santa Barbara, California.
The Cable Guy 96. One Fine Day 96. Home Alone 3 97. Tarzan (voice) 99, etc.

Liotta, Ray (1955–).
American actor from TV.
The Lonely Lady 83. Something Wild 86. Dominick and Eugene 88. Field of Dreams 89. GoodFellas 90. Article 99 92. Unlawful Entry 92. Judgment Night 93. No Escape 94. Corrina, Corrina 94. Operation Dumbo Drop 95. Unforgettable 96. Turbulence 96. Cop Land 97. The Rat Pack (TV) 98, etc.
TV series: Casablanca 83. Our Family Honor 85–86.

Lipman, Jerzy (1922–1983).
Polish cinematographer.
A Generation 54. Kanal 57. The Eighth Day of the Week 58. Lotna 59. Knife in the Water 62. No More Divorces 63. Ashes 65. Zozya 67. Colonel Wolodyjowski 69. Dead Pigeon on Beethoven Street 72. The Martyr 75, etc.

Lipman, Maureen (1946–).
English character actress, often in comic roles. Married to writer Jack Rosenthal.
The Smashing Bird I Used to Know 61. Up the Junction 67. Gumshoe 71. The Wildcats of St Trinian's 80. Educating Rita 83. Water 85. Carry On Columbus 92. Eskimo Day (TV) 96. Captain Jack 98, etc.
TV series: A Soft Touch 78. Agony 79–81. All at Number 20 86.

Lippert, Robert L. (1909–1976).
American exhibitor, latterly head of company making second features for Twentieth Century-Fox, many of them produced by his son Robert L. Lippert Jnr (1928–).

Lipscomb, W. P. (1887–1958).
British screenwriter who spent some years in Hollywood.
French Leave 27. The Good Companions 32. I Was a Spy 33. Clive of India (co-w) 34. A Tale of Two Cities 35. The Garden of Allah 36. Pygmalion (co-w) 38. A Town Like Alice 56. Dunkirk (co-w) 58, many others.

Lipstadt, Aaron (1952–).
American director.
■ Android 82. City Limits 85. Police Story: Monster Manor (TV) 88. Pair of Aces (TV) 90. The People 97.

Lisi, Virna (1937–) (Virna Pieralisi).
Voluptuous Italian leading lady who after starring in innumerable local spectaculars came on to the international market. She won the best actress award at the Cannes Film Festival for *La Reine Margot*.
The Black Tulip 63. Eva 63. How to Murder Your Wife (US) 65. Casanova 70 65. Signore e Signori 65. Assault on a Queen (US) 66. Not with My Wife You Don't (US) 66. The Girl and the General 67. The Twenty-fifth Hour 67. Arabella 68. The Secret of Santa Vittoria 69. Un Beau Monstre 70. The Statue 71. The Serpent 72. Bluebeard 72. White Fang 74. Challenge to White Fang 75. Cocktails for Three 78. Ernesto 78. La Cicala 80. Miss Right 81. I Love N.Y. 87. Merry Christmas, Happy New Year/Buon Natale, Buon Anno 89. Queen Margot/La Reine Margot 94. Follow Your Heart 96, etc.

Lister, Eve (1913–1997).
English actress and singer, from the musical theatre. Born in Brighton, Sussex, of a theatrical family, and on-stage from childhood, she appeared

mainly in musicals in the 30s before returning to the theatre, retiring in the 50s.
■ A Glimpse of Paradise 34. Hyde Park 34. The Girl in the Crowd 34. City of Beautiful Nonsense 35. Cock o' the North 35. Birds of a Feather 35. Sunshine Ahead 36. Sweeney Todd, the Demon Barber of Fleet Street 36. Here and There 36. Servants All 36. Men of Yesterday 36.

Lister, Francis (1899–1951).
Suave British character actor, mainly on stage.
Comin' Thro' the Rye 24. Atlantic 30. Jack's the Boy 32. Clive of India 35. The Return of the Scarlet Pimpernel 38. Henry V 44. The Wicked Lady 45. Home to Danger 51, etc.

Lister, Moira (1923–).
South African leading lady and character actress, in British films.
My Ain Folk 44. Uneasy Terms 48. Another Shore 48. *A Run for Your Money* 49. Grand National Night 53. John and Julie 55. Seven Waves Away 57. The Yellow Rolls-Royce 64. Stranger in the House 67. Ten Little Indians 89, etc.

Litel, John (1895–1972).
American character actor, in films from 1929; often seen as judge, lawyer or stern father.
Marked Woman 37. The Life of Emile Zola 37. Virginia City 40. Men Without Souls 40. They Died with Their Boots On 41. Sealed Lips 41. Boss of Big Town 43. Kiss Tomorrow Goodbye 50. Houseboat 58. A Pocketful of Miracles 61. The Sons of Katie Elder 65, many others.
TV series: My Hero 52.

Lithgow, John (1945–).
American character actor, a semi-star of the 80s. A graduate of Harvard University, he studied for the stage at LAMDA and is also a theatre director. He is best known for the role of Dick Solomons in the TV sitcom *3rd Rock from the Sun*.
Obsession 76. All that Jazz 79. Blow Out 81. The World According to Garp (AAN) 82. Twilight Zone: The Movie 83. Terms of Endearment (AAN) 83. Buckaroo Banzai 84. 2010 84. Santa Claus 84. Footloose 84. Mesmerized 84. The Manhattan Project 86. Bigfoot and the Hendersons 87. Distant Thunder 88. Out Cold 88. Traveling Man (TV) 89. Memphis Belle 90. Ivory Hunters (TV) 90. At Play in the Fields of the Lord 91. L.A. Story 91. Ricochet 91. Raising Cain 92. The Wrong Man 93. Cliffhanger 93. The Pelican Brief 93. A Good Man in Africa 94. Love, Cheat & Steal 94. Princess Caraboo 94. Silent Fall 94. My Brother's Keeper (TV) 95. The Tuskegee Airmen (TV) 95. Redwood Curtain (TV) 95. Hollow Point 96. Homegrown 97. Johnny Skidmarks 98. A Civil Action 98, etc.
TV series: 3rd Rock from the Sun 96– .

Littin, Miguel (1942–).
Chilean film director, a former actor and television director. He went into exile following the overthrow of President Allende to work mainly in Mexico.
El Chacal de Nahueltoro 70. Letters from Marusia/Actas de Marusia (AAN) 75. La Viuda de Montiel 80. Alsino and the Condor/Alsino y el Cóndor 82. Sandino 90. The Shipwrecked/Los Naufragos 94, etc.

Little, Cleavon (1939–1992).
American comedy actor.
What's So Bad About Feeling Good 68. Cotton Comes to Harlem 70. Vanishing Point 71. *Blazing Saddles* 74. Greased Lightning 77. Scavenger Hunt 79. High Risk 81. The Gig 85. Fletch Lives 89. Hearts of Fire 92, etc.
TV series: *Temperatures Rising* 72.

Little, Dwight H.
American director of action and horror movies. He also directed *Ground Zero Texas*, a computer game on CD-ROM which claims to be the first 'interactive movie'.
Lethal/KGB – The Secret War 86. Getting Even 86. Bloodstone 88. Halloween 4: The Return of Michael Myers 88. The Phantom of the Opera 89. Marked for Death 90. Rapid Fire 92. Free Willy 2: The Adventure Home 95. Murder at 1600 97, etc.

Little, Mark.
Australian actor and stand-up comedian, more recently working as a television presenter in Britain.
An Indecent Obsession 85. Willis and Burke 86. A Cry in the Dark 88. The Passion and the Glory 89. Golden Braid 90. Nirvana Street Murders 90. Greenkeeping 91. Amnesty International's Big 30 (TV) 91, etc.
TV series: Neighbours 88–91.

Littlefield, Lucien (1895–1960).
American character actor, in Hollywood from 1913 in supporting roles.
The Sheik 22. Miss Pinkerton 32. Ruggles of Red Gap 34. Rose Marie 36. The Great American Broadcast 40. Scared Stiff 44. Susanna Pass 51. Pop Girl 56, etc.

Littlewood, Joan (1914–).
British stage director whose only film to date is *Sparrows Can't Sing* 63. Created London's 'Theatre Workshop', where she staged *Oh, What a Lovely War!*, which was later filmed by Richard Attenborough.
Autobiography: 1994, *Joan's Book*.

Litvak, Anatole (1902–1974).
Russian-born director in Germany and France from 1927, Hollywood from 1937.
■ Dolly Gets Ahead (Ger.) 31. Nie Wieder Liebe (Ger.) 32. Coeur de Lilas (Fr.) 32. Be Mine Tonight (Ger.) 33. Sleeping Car (GB) 33. Cette Vieille Canaille (Fr.) 35. L'Equipage (Fr.) 36. *Mayerling* (Fr.) 36. *The Woman I Love* 37. Tovarich 38. The Amazing Dr Clitterhouse 38. The Sisters 38. Castle on the Hudson 39. *Confessions of a Nazi Spy* 39. All This and Heaven Too 40. *City for Conquest* 40. Out of the Fog 41. Blues in the Night 41. This Above All 42. The Long Night 47. Sorry Wrong Number 48. *The Snake Pit* (AAN) 48. Decision Before Dawn 52. Act of Love 53. The Deep Blue Sea 55. Anastasia 56. The Journey 59. Goodbye Again 61. Five Miles to Midnight 63. The Night of the Generals 67. The Lady in the Car 70.

Livesey, Jack (1901–1961).
British actor, brother of Roger Livesey.
The Wandering Jew 33. The Passing of the Third Floor Back 35. Old Bill and Son 40. The First Gentleman 47. Paul Temple's Triumph 51, etc.

Livesey, Roger (1906–1976).
Husky-voiced, often roguish British character star who divided his time between stage and screen.
■ The Old Curiosity Shop 20. Where the Rainbow Ends 21. The Four Feathers 21. Married Love 23. East Lynne on the Western Front 31. A Veteran of Waterloo 33. A Cuckoo in the Nest 33. Blind Justice 34. The Price of Wisdom 35. Lorna Doone 35. Midshipman Easy 35. *Rembrandt* 36. *The Drum* 38. Keep Smiling 38. Spies of the Air 39. The Rebel Son 39. The Girl in the News 40. 49th Parallel 41. *The Life and Death of Colonel Blimp* 43. *I Know Where I'm Going* 45. *A Matter of Life and Death* 46. *Vice Versa* 47. That Dangerous Age 49. Green Grow the Rushes 50. The Master of Ballantrae 53. The Intimate Stranger 56. The League of Gentlemen 59. The Entertainer 60. No My Darling Daughter 61. Of Human Bondage 64. Moll Flanders 65. Oedipus the King 68. Hamlet 69. Futtock's End 70.

Livesey, Sam (1873–1936).
British actor, father of Jack and Roger Livesey.
Young Woodley 30. The Flag Lieutenant 32. The Private Life of Henry VIII 32. Jew Süss 34. Turn of the Tide 36. Dark Journey 37, etc.

Livingston, Jay (1915–) (Jacob Harold Levison).
American composer who, with his partner Ray Evans, was under contract to Paramount 1945–55, turning out a succession of hit songs.
The Stork Club 45. The Cat and the Canary (AAN) 45. Golden Earrings 47. The Paleface (AA for 'Buttons and Bows') 48. My Friend Irma 49. My Friend Irma Goes West 50. Captain Carey (AA for 'Mona Lisa') 50. Fancy Pants 50. The Lemon Drop Kid 51. Aaron Slick from Punkin Crick 51. Son of Paleface 52. Here Come the Girls 53. Red Garters 54. The Man Who Knew Too Much (AA for 'Que Sera, Sera') 56. Tammy and the Bachelor (AAN) 57. Houseboat (AAN) 58. Dear Heart (AAN) 64, etc.
TV series: Bonanza. Mr Ed (themes).

Livingston, Jerry (1909–1987) (Jerome Levinson).
American composer and songwriter, usually in collaboration with lyricist Mack David. In Hollywood from 1949, moving to television in the late 50s. A former bandleader.
Cinderella (AAN) 49. At War with the Army 50. Sailor Beware 51. Jumping Jacks 52. Scared Stiff 53. The Hanging Tree (AAN) 59. Cat Ballou (AAN) 65, etc.

Livingston, Margaret (1895–1984).
American silent-screen leading lady.
Within the Cup 18. Lying Lips 21. Divorce 23. Butterfly 24. Havoc 25. A Trip to Chinatown 26. Married Alive 27. Streets of Shanghai 28. The Last Warning 29. Seven Keys to Baldpate 30. Kiki 31. Call Her Savage 32. Social Register 34, many others.

Livingston, Robert (1908–1988) (Robert Randall).
Tough star of westerns, best known for his role as Stony Brooke, one of the Three Mesquiteers, in the popular series of the 30s and 40s. He also played the title role in the serial *The Lone Ranger Rides Again* 38 and was Zorro in *The Bold Caballero* 36.
The Three Mesquiteers 36. The Mounties Are Coming 37. Arson Racket Squad 38. Orphans of the Street 39. Brazil 44. Lake Placid Serenade 44. The Big Bonanza 45. The Undercover Woman 46. Daredevils of the Clouds 48. Riders in the Sky 50. Winning of the West 52. The Naughty Stewardesses 73. Girls for Rent 74, etc.

Lizzani, Carlo (1917–).
Italian director.
Caccia Tragica (co-w only) 47. Bitter Rice (co-w only) 49. Achtung Banditi 51. Ai Margini della Metropoli 54. The Great Wall 58. Hunchback of Rome 60. The Hills Run Red 66. The Violent Four 68. Crazy Joe 73. The Last Days of Mussolini 74. Kleinhoff Hotel 77. Fontamara 80. Nucleo Zero 84. Mamma Ebe 85. Selina 89. Wicked 91. Il Caso Dozier 93. Celluloide 95, etc.

LL Cool J (1969–) (James Todd Smith).
American rap performer and actor. Born in Queens, New York, he made his first record at the age of 16. His professional name is an acronym for 'Ladies Love Cool James'.
The Hard Way 91. Toys 92. The Right to Remain Silent 95. Out of Sync 95. Woo 98. Caught Up 98. Halloween: H20 98, etc.
TV series: In the House 95.

Llewellyn, Richard (1906–1983).
Welsh best-selling novelist, famous for *How Green Was My Valley*. *Noose* and *None but the Lonely Heart* were also filmed.

Llewelyn, Desmond.
British character actor, best known for playing 'Q' in the James Bond films.
They Were Not Divided 50. The Lavender Hill Mob 51. A Night to Remember 55. The Pirates of Blood River 61. Cleopatra 62. Goldfinger 64. Thunderball 65. You Only Live Twice 67. Chitty Chitty Bang Bang 68. On Her Majesty's Secret Service 69. Diamonds Are Forever 71. Live and Let Die 73. The Man with the Golden Gun 74. The Spy Who Loved Me 77. Moonraker 79. The Golden Lady 79. Dr Jekyll and Mr Hyde 80. For Your Eyes Only 81. Octopussy 83. A View to a Kill 85. The Living Daylights 87. GoldenEye 95. Tomorrow Never Dies 97, etc.

Llosa, Luis.
Peruvian-born director in Hollywood.
Hour of the Assassin 87. Crime Zone 89. Eight Hundred Leagues down the Amazon 93. Sniper 93. The Specialist 94. Anaconda 97, etc.

Lloyd, Christopher (1938–).
American character actor, often in crazed or comic roles.
One Flew over the Cuckoo's Nest 75. Goin' South 78. The Onion Field 79. The Black Marble 79. The Lady in Red 79. Schizoid 80. The Legend of the Lone Ranger 81. Mr Mom 83. To Be or Not To Be 83. Star Trek III: The Search for Spock 84. The Adventures of Buckaroo Banzai across the Eighth Dimension 84. Miracles 84. Clue 85. Back to the Future 85. Eight Men Out 88. Who Framed Roger Rabbit? 88. Dream Team 89. Back to the Future II 89. Back to the Future III 90. The Addams Family 91. Suburban Commando 91. T Bone 'n' Weasel (TV) 92. Dennis the Menace/Dennis 93. Twenty Bucks 93. Addams Family Values 93. Angels in the Outfield 94. Camp Nowhere 94. The Radioland Murders 94. The Pagemaster 94. Things to Do in Denver When You're Dead 95. Cadillac Ranch 96. Changing Habits 97. The Real Blonde 97. Angels in the Endzone (TV) 98. Convergence 98, etc.
TV series: The Addams Chronicles 76. Taxi 79–83. Avonlea 90.

Lloyd, Doris (1899–1968).
British actress with repertory experience; in Hollywood from the 20s.
Charley's Aunt (as Donna Lucia) 30. Disraeli 30. Tarzan the Ape Man 32. Oliver Twist 33. Clive of India 35. Vigil in the Night 39. Phantom Lady 44. The Secret Life of Walter Mitty 47. A Man Called Peter 55. The Time Machine 60. The Notorious Landlady 62. Rosie 67, etc.

Lloyd, Emily (1971–).
British actress, now working in Hollywood. She is the daughter of actor Roger Lloyd-Pack and the granddaughter of Charles Lloyd-Pack.
Wish You Were Here 87. Cookie 89. In Country 89. Chicago Joe and the Showgirl 90. A River Runs Through It 92. Livers Ain't Cheap 96. When Saturday Comes 96. Welcome to Sarajevo 97. The Real Thing 97. Woundings 98, etc.

Lloyd, Euan (1923–).
British independent producer, former publicist.
Genghis Khan 65. Murderers' Row 66. Shalako 68. Catlow 71. The Man Called Noon 73. Paper Tiger 75. The Wild Geese 78. The Sea Wolves 80. Who Dares Wins 82. Wild Geese II 85, etc.

Lloyd, Frank (1889–1960).
Scottish-born director, in Hollywood from 1913 after acting experience.
Les Misérables 18. Madame X 20. Oliver Twist 22. The Eternal Flame 23. The Sea Hawk 24. Dark Streets 26. *The Divine Lady* (AA) 29. East Lynne 30. Sin Flood 31. Passport to Hell 32. *Cavalcade* (AA) 33. *Berkeley Square* 33. *Mutiny on the Bounty* (AAN) 35. Under Two Flags 36. Maid of Salem 37. Wells Fargo 37. If I Were King (& p) 38. Rulers of the Sea 39. The Tree of Liberty (& d) 40. The Lady from Cheyenne (& p) 41. This Woman Is Mine 41. *Blood on the Sun* 45. The Shanghai Story (& p) 54. The Last Command (& p) 55, many others.

Lloyd, Harold (1893–1971).
American silent comedian, famous for his timid bespectacled 'nice boy' character and for thrill-comedy situations involving dangerous stunts. In hundreds of two-reelers from 1916. He began as a stage actor before finding work first as a film extra and then as a Chaplin imitator in his Lucky Luke series of two-reelers. He first presented what was to become his world-famous quiet, bespectacled persona in *Over the Fence* in 1917. His career was interrupted in 1919 when a prop bomb turned out to be real and exploded in his face, removing a finger and thumb from his right hand. He recovered, signed a new contract with Hal Roach and by the beginning of the 20s was making big money: *Bumping into Broadway*, which cost $17,000 to make, took more than $150,000 in three years, bringing him a personal profit of more than $30,000. By 1922 his popularity rivalled Chaplin's. *Grandma's Boy*, his first feature, grossed nearly a million dollars and *Safety Last* more than $1.5m. He left Roach to run his own company in 1923. His career dwindled with the coming of sound and he spent time on his hobbies, which included stereoscopic photography. He married Mildred Davis, who starred with him in several of his films. A collection of his 3-D photographs, *Harold Lloyd's Hollywood*, was published in 1992. He was given a special Academy Award in 1952 as 'master comedian and good citizen'.
Autobiography: 1928, *An American Comedy*.
Biographies: 1976, *Harold Lloyd* by Richard Schickel. 1983, *Harold Lloyd: The Man on the Clock* by Tom Dardis.
■ A Sailor-Made Man 21. *Grandma's Boy* 22. Dr Jack 22. *Safety Last* 23. Why Worry? 23. Girl Shy 24. Hot Water 24. *The Freshman* 25. For Heaven's Sake 26. *The Kid Brother* 27. Speedy 28. Welcome Danger 29. *Feet First* 30. *Movie Crazy* 32. The Catspaw 34. The Milky Way 36. Professor Beware 38. Mad Wednesday/The Sins of Harold Diddlebock 47.

Later produced two compilations of his comedy highlights: *World of Comedy* and *Funny Side of Life*.
✪ For skill, daring and ingenuity. *The Kid Brother*.
❝ Comedy comes from inside. It comes from your face. It comes from your body. – *H.L.*

I do not believe the public will want spoken comedy. Motion pictures and the spoken arts are two distinct arts. – *H.L.*

Basically he had not a funny bone in his body, but he was such a good actor that if you gave him a good script, he could play it to the best advantages for laughs. – *Hal Roach*

Lloyd was outstanding even among the master craftsmen at setting up a gag clearly, culminating and getting out of it deftly, and linking it smoothly to the next. – *James Agee*

Lloyd, Hugh (1923–).
British comic character actor, usually as a put-upon little man; in films and TV since 1955, often as a foil to Tony HANCOCK and Terry SCOTT.

She'll Have to Go 61. The Punch and Judy Man 62. Go to Blazes 62. The Mouse on the Moon 63. Intimate Games 76. Quadrophenia 79. Venom 81. August 96, etc.

TV series: Hugh and I 62–66. Hugh and I Spy 68. Lollipop Loves Mr Mole 71. Lollipop 72. The Clairvoyant 86.

Lloyd, Jeremy (1932–).
Lanky British comic actor and scriptwriter, frequently as an upper-class ass. He was co-creator of the television sit-coms *Are You Being Served?* 74–85, *O Happy Band!* 80, and *'Allo 'Allo!* 84–92. He was formerly married to actress Joanna Lumley.

Man in the Moon 61. Two and Two Make Six 62. Death Drums along the River 63. Doctor in Clover 65. Those Magnificent Men in Their Flying Machines 65. The Wrong Box 66. Salt and Pepper 68. Goodbye Mr Chips 69. The Magic Christian 70. Murder on the Orient Express 74. Are You Being Served? (co-w) 77, etc.

Lloyd, Norman (1914–).
British character actor in Hollywood, usually in mean or weak roles; gave up acting to become TV producer, mainly for Alfred Hitchcock but made an acting comeback in his 60s.

Autobiography: 1990, *Stages*.

Saboteur (as the villain who fell from the statue of Liberty) 42. The Unseen 45. The Southerner 45. Spellbound 45. The Green Years 46. The Beginning or the End 47. Scene of the Crime 49. The Flame and the Arrow 50. He Ran All the Way 51. Limelight 52. Audrey Rose 77. The Nude Bomb 80. Dead Poets Society 89. The Age of Innocence 93, etc.

TV series: St Elsewhere 82. 7 Days 98.

Lloyd, Russell (1916–).
British editor.

The Squeaker 37. Over the Moon 39. School for Secrets 46. Anna Karenina 48. Decameron Nights 52. The Sea Shall Not Have Them 54. Moby Dick 56. Roots of Heaven 58. The Unforgiven 60. Of Human Bondage 64. Reflections in a Golden Eye 67. The Kremlin Letter 70. The Mackintosh Man 73. The Man Who Would Be King 75. The Lady Vanishes 79. The Fiendish Plot of Dr Fu Manchu 80. Absolute Beginners 86, etc.

Lloyd, Sue (1939–).
British leading lady of the 60s.

The Ipcress File 66. Where's Jack? 68. Percy 71. The Bitch 79. UFO: The Movie 93. Bullet to Beijing 95, etc.

TV series: *The Baron* 66–67.

Lloyd, Walt.
American cinematographer.

Dangerously Close 86. The Wash 88. sex, lies and videotape 89. To Sleep with Anger 90. Pump Up the Volume 90. Kakfa 91. There Goes the Neighborhood/Paydirt 92. Short Cuts 93. The Santa Clause 94. Empire Records 95. Feeling Minnesota 96. Private Parts 97. Dark Harbor 98, etc.

Lloyd-Pack, Charles (1902–1983).
British character actor of stage and screen, usually in self-effacing roles: butlers, etc.

High Treason 51. *The Importance of Being Earnest* 52. The Constant Husband 55. Night of the Demon 57. Dracula 58. *Victim* 62. If 68. Song of Norway 70. Madame Sin 72. The Mirror Crack'd 80, etc.

Lloyd-Pack, Roger (1944–).
Lugubrious British character actor, the son of Charles LLOYD-PACK and the father of Emily LLOYD. He had a recurring role in the long-running TV sitcom *Only Fools and Horses* as the dim-witted Trigger.

The Magus 68. The Virgin Soldiers 69. The Go-Between 70. Figures in a Landscape 70. Fiddler on the Roof 71. Fright 71. 1984 84. Prick Up Your Ears 87. The Cook, the Thief, His Wife and Her Lover 89. Wilt 89. Hamlet 91. The Object of Beauty 91. American Friends 91. The Trial 92. Princess Caraboo 94. The Young Poisoner's Handbook 95. Hollow Reed 96. Preaching to the Perverted 97. Tom Jones (TV) 97, etc.

TV series: Spyder's Web 72. Moving 85. Health and Efficiency 93–95. The Vicar of Dibley 94–98.

Lloyd Webber, Sir Andrew (1948–).
British composer, mainly of long-running stage musicals. He became Lord Lloyd Webber of Sydmonton in the New Year's Honours of 1996. In 1998, the *Sunday Times* estimated his fortune at £480m.

Gumshoe 71. Jesus Christ Superstar 73. The Odessa File 74. Evita (AAs 'You Must Love Me') 96.

Lo Bianco, Tony (1936–).
American character actor.

The Honeymoon Killers 70. The French Connection 72. The Seven Ups 73. Jesus of Nazareth (TV) 77. Demon 77. Magee and the Lady (TV) 78. Bloodbrothers 78. F.I.S.T. 78. Separate Ways 81. City Heat 84. The Ann Jillian Story (TV) 88. City of Hope 91. Too Scared to Scream (d) 85. Boiling Point 93. Ascent 95. Tyson (TV) 95. Nixon 95. The Juror 96. Jane Austen's Mafia!/Mafia! 98, etc.

TV series: Jessie 84.

Loach, Ken (1936–).
English director and screenwriter, noted for the realism of his films, frequently dealing with working-class life, which often use little-known or non-professional actors. Born in Nuneaton, he studied law at Oxford University and worked in BBC-TV where he formed a notable partnership with producer Tony Garnett on the series *The Wednesday Play* and later in films. His *Cathy Come Home* 66, written by Jeremy Sandford, was one of the most controversial and memorable TV plays of its time. In the 80s, he made *Questions of Leadership*, four TV documentaries on the role of the embattled trades unions which were banned, and turned to making commercials for a time. He is also a director of Bath City Football Club, following a takeover by its fans.

Up the Junction 67. *Poor Cow* 67. *Kes* 69. *Family Life* 72. Days of Hope (TV) 75. Black Jack 79. The Gamekeeper 80. Auditions (TV) 80. Looks and Smiles 81. Fatherland 86. Hidden Agenda 90. *Riff-Raff* 90. *Raining Stones* 93. *Ladybird, Ladybird* 94. *Land and Freedom* 95. Carla's Song 96. My Name Is Joe 98, etc.

❝ We wanted to make plays or films that got the same responses as when you saw the news. We wanted to be seen as almost a part of the news, as reports from the front line. – *K.L. on his TV work*

There are two sorts of acting: theatre acting and film acting, which can be something different; where somebody can be taken through a story and experience the story and put themselves in that position, and respond as they would respond, so that you're really experiencing that person in that story. – *K.L.*

He's totally round the bend. You don't rehearse. Everything is a take. – *Ricky Tomlinson*

He reminds you always that you shouldn't become a film maker unless you have something to say. – *Alan Parker*

Locane, Amy (1971–).
American actress, from television. Born in Trenton, New Jersey, she began acting as a teenager.

Lost Angels 89. The Road Home 89. Cry-Baby 90. No Secrets 91. Blue Sky 92 (released 94). School Ties 92. Airheads 94. Carried Away 95. Prefontaine 96. Going All the Way 97. Love to Kill 97. Bram Stoker's The Mummy 97. Route 9 98, etc.

TV series: Spencer 84–85. Melrose Place 92–93.

Locke, Sondra (1947–).
American leading actress and occasional director.

Autobiography: 1997, *The Good, the Bad and the Very Ugly: A Hollywood Journey*.

The Heart Is a Lonely Hunter (AAN) 68. Willard 71. A Reflection of Fear 73. The Outlaw Josey Wales 76. Death Game 76. The Gauntlet 77. Seducers 77. Shadow of Chikara 77. Every Which Way but Loose 78. Any Which Way You Can 80. Bronco Billy 80. Suzanne 80. Sudden Impact 83. Ratboy (& d) 86. Impulse (d) 90. Death in Small Doses (d) 92, etc.

Lockhart, Calvin (1934–).
West Indian leading man.

A Dandy in Aspic 68. Joanna 68. Nobody Runs Forever 68. Leo the Last 70. Myra Breckinridge 70. Cotton Comes to Harlem 71. Melinda 72. The Beast Must Die 74. Uptown Saturday Night 74. Let's Do It Again 75. Three Days in Beirut 83. Wild at Heart 90. Predator 2 90, etc.

Lockhart, Gene (1891–1957).
Canadian character actor at home in genial or shifty parts. Also writer: in films since 1922.

■ Smilin' Through 22. The Gay Bride 34. Ah Wilderness 35. I've Been Around 35. Captain Hurricane 35. Star of Midnight 35. Thunder in the Night 35. Storm over the Andes 35. Crime and Punishment 35. Brides Are Like That 35. Times Square Playboy 36. Earthworm Tractors 36. The First Baby 36. Career Woman 36. The Garden Murder Case 36. The Gorgeous Hussy 36. The Devil Is a Sissy 36. Wedding Present 36. Mind Your Own Business 36. Come Closer Folks 36. Mama Steps Out 37. Too Many Wives 37. Make Way for Tomorrow 37. The Sheik Steps Out 37. Something to Sing About 37. Of Human Hearts 38. Listen Darling 38. A Christmas Carol 38. Sweethearts 38. Penrod's Double Trouble 38. Men Are Such Fools 38. Blondie 38. *Algiers* (AAN) 38. Sinners in Paradise 38. Meet the Girls 38. I'm from Missouri 39. Hotel Imperial 39. Our Leading Citizen 39. Geronimo 39. Tell No Tales 39. Bridal Suite 39. Blackmail 39. The Story of Alexander Graham Bell 39. Edison the Man 40. Dr Kildare Goes Home 40. We Who Are Young 40. South of Pago Pago 40. A Dispatch from Reuters 40. *His Girl Friday* 40. Abe Lincoln in Illinois 40. Billy the Kid 41. Keeping Company 41. Meet John Doe 41. All That Money Can Buy 41. The Sea Wolf 41. One Foot in Heaven 41. Steel Against the Sky 41. International Lady 41. They Died with Their Boots On 41. Juke Girl 42. The Gay Sisters 42. You Can't Escape Forever 42. Forever and a Day 43. Mission to Moscow 43. Hangmen Also Die 43. Find the Blackmailer 43. The Desert Song 43. Madame Curie 43. Northern Pursuit 43. The White Cliffs of Dover 44. *Going My Way* 44. Action in Arabia 44. The Man from Frisco 44. *The House on 92nd Street* 45. Leave Her to Heaven 45. That's the Spirit 45. Meet Me on Broadway 46. A Scandal in Paris 46. She Wolf of London 46. The Strange Woman 46. The Shocking Miss Pilgrim 47. Miracle on 34th Street 47. The Foxes of Harrow 47. Cynthia 47. Honeymoon 47. Her Husband's Affairs 47. Joan of Arc 48. Inside Story 48. That Wonderful Urge 48. Apartment for Peggy 48. I Jane Doe 48. Down to the Sea in Ships 49. Madame Bovary 49. The Red Light 49. The Inspector General 49. Riding High 50. The Big Hangover 50. The Sickle and the Cross 51. I'd Climb the Highest Mountain 51. Rhubarb 51. The Lady from Texas 51. Hoodlum Empire 52. A Girl in Every Port 52. Face to Face 52. Bonzo Goes to College 52. Androcles and the Lion 52. Apache War Smoke 52. Francis Covers the Big Town 53. Down Among the Sheltering Palms 53. Confidentially Connie 53. The Lady Wants Mink 53. World for Ransom 54. The Vanishing American 55. Carousel 56. The Man in the Grey Flannel Suit 56. Jeanne Eagels 57.

Lockhart, June (1925–).
American supporting actress, daughter of Gene LOCKHART.

All This and Heaven Too 40. Meet Me in St Louis 44. Keep Your Powder Dry 45. Bury Me Dead 47. Time Limit 47. Lassie's Greatest Adventure 63. Death Valley Days (TV) 65. Lost in Space (TV) 65. Curse of the Black Widow (TV) 77. The Gift of Love (TV) 78. Walking through the Fire (TV) 79. Deadly Games 80. Strange Invaders 83. Troll 86. A Whisper Kills (TV) 88. Rented Lips 88. The Big Picture 89. Sleep with Me 92. Out There (TV) 95. The Colony 95. Lost in Space 98, etc.

TV series: Lassie 55–64. Lost in Space 65–68. Petticoat Junction 68–70.

Lockhart, Kathleen (1893–1978).
American character actress, widow of Gene Lockhart; known previously as Kathleen Arthur.

The Devil is a Sissy 36. Sweethearts 38. All This and Heaven Too 41. Gentleman's Agreement 47. Plymouth Adventure 52. The Glenn Miller Story 54, many others.

Lockwood, Gary (1937–) (John Gary Yusolfsky).
American leading man of the 60s, mostly on TV.

Splendour in the Grass 61. Wild in the Country 61. It Happened at the World's Fair 63. Firecreek 67. 2001: A Space Odyssey 68. The Model Shop 69. RPM 70. Stand Up and Be Counted 72. Bad Georgia Road 77. Survival Zone 84. The Wild Pair 87. Terror in Paradise 90. Night of the Scarecrow 95, etc.

TV series: *Follow the Sun* 61. *The Lieutenant* 63.

Lockwood, Harold (1887–1918).
American romantic lead of early silents, most often opposite May ALLISON. He made more than 100 films before his early death from pneumonia.

Lockwood, Julia (1941–).
British leading lady, daughter of Margaret Lockwood.

My Teenage Daughter 56. Please Turn Over 59. No Kidding 60, etc.

Lockwood, Margaret (1916–1990) (Margaret Day).
Durable, indomitable British leading lady who was an appealing ingénue in the 30s, a rather boring star villainess in the 40s, and later a likeable character actress of stage and TV.

Autobiography: 1955, *Lucky Star*.

Biography: 1989, *Once a Wicked Lady* by Hilton Tims.

■ Lorna Doone 35. The Case of Gabriel Perry 35. Some Day 35. Honours Easy 35. Man of the Moment 35. Midshipman Easy 35. Jury's Evidence 36. The Amateur Gentleman 36. The Beloved Vagabond 36. Irish for Luck 36. The Street Singer 37. Who's Your Lady Friend? 37. Dr Syn 37. Melody and Romance 37. Owd Bob 38. Bank Holiday 38. *The Lady Vanishes* 38. A Girl Must Live 39. The Stars Look Down 39. Susannah of the Mounties (US) 39. Rulers of the Sea (US) 39. *Night Train to Munich* 40. The Girl in the News 40. Quiet Wedding 41. Alibi 42. *The Man in Grey* 43. Dear Octopus 43. Give Us the Moon 44. Love Story 44. A Place of One's Own 45. I'll Be Your Sweetheart 45. *The Wicked Lady* 45. Bedelia 46. Hungry Hill 46. Jassy 47. The White Unicorn 47. Look Before You Love 48. Cardboard Cavalier 49. Madness of the Heart 49. Highly Dangerous 50. Trent's Last Case 52. Laughing Anne 53. Trouble in the Glen 54. *Cast a Dark Shadow* 57. The Slipper and the Rose 76.

Lockwood, Preston (1912–1996).
Lean English character actor, often as a lawyer or cleric; he was much featured in radio drama, and best known for his role as Dennis the Dachshund in Children's Hour's *Toytown*.

Julius Caesar 70. Lady Caroline Lamb 72. The Black Windmill 74. The Prince and the Pauper 77. Absolution 78. Time Bandits 81. The Pirates of Penzance 82. The Fool 90, etc.

Loden, Barbara (1932–1980).
American general-purpose actress. She was married to director Elia Kazan.

Wild River 60. Splendor in the Grass 60, etc.
AS DIRECTOR: Wanda 72.

Loder, John (1898–1988) (John Lowe).
Handsome British leading man, in international films from 1927 after varied experience. Educated at Eton and Sandhurst, he was first a cavalry officer. He started as an extra in German films before being invited to Hollywood by Jesse Lasky of Paramount Pictures. His third wife was actress Hedy Lamarr. In the late 50s he became a cattle-rancher in Argentina.

Autobiography: 1977, *Hollywood Hussar*.

The First Born 29. Java Head 34. Lorna Doone 35. Murder Will Out 38. Meet Maxwell Archer 39. How Green Was My Valley 41. *Now Voyager* 42. Gentleman Jim 42. The Gorilla Man 42. Old

Acquaintance 43. The Hairy Ape 44. The Brighton Strangler 45. A Game of Death 46. Wife of Monte Cristo 46. Dishonoured Lady 47. Woman and the Hunter 57. Gideon's Day 58, etc.

❝ Why is it that I'm not able
to get the roles they give Clark Gable?
They always say 'You have no name,
But when you have one, come again.'
By that time I'll be old and stiff,
A kind of poor man's Aubrey Smith. – *J.L., 1940s*

John Loder played the king as though he was afraid someone would play the ace at any moment. – *Hannen Swaffer on Sing As We Go*

Lodge, David (1921–).
British character actor, with music-hall and stage experience.

Autobiography: 1986, *Up the Ladder to Obscurity*.

Private's Progress 56. Two Way Stretch 60. The Dock Brief 61. Yesterday's Enemy 61. The Long Ships 63. Guns at Batasi 64. Catch Us If You Can 65. Press For Time 66. Corruption 69. Doctors Wear Scarlet 70. The Railway Children 71. Go For a Take 72. The Amazing Mr Blunden 72. The Return of the Pink Panther 74. The Revenge of the Pink Panther 78. Sahara 82. Edge of Sanity 88, etc.

TV series: Potter's Picture Palace 76. Lovely Couple 79.

Lodge, John (1903–1985).
American leading man of the 30s, mainly European films. Retired to take up politics.

A Woman Accused (debut) 32. Little Women 33. The Scarlet Empress 34. Koenigsmark 35. Sensation 36. The Tenth Man 36. Bulldog Drummond at Bay 37. Bank Holiday 38. L'Esclave Blanche 39.

❝ Mr John Lodge continues to suffer from a kind of lockjaw, an inability to move the tight muscles of his mouth, to do anything but glare with the dumbness and glossiness of an injured seal. – *Graham Greene reviewing The Tenth Man*

LoDuca, Joseph.
American composer.

The Evil Dead 83. Evil Dead 2 87. Army of Darkness 92. Necronomicon 93.

Loeb, Philip (1894–1955).
American character actor, usually of smart types. Committed suicide after he was blacklisted and was unable to find work.

Room Service 38. A Double Life 48. Molly 51, etc.

Loesser, Frank (1910–1969).
American songwriter, in films since 1930. He began as a lyricist; from 1947 he wrote both words and music.

College Swing 38. St Louis Blues 39. Destry Rides Again 39. Seven Sinners 40. Kiss the Boys Goodbye 41. Thank Your Lucky Stars 43. The Perils of Pauline 47. Neptune's Daughter 49. Let's Dance 50. Where's Charley? 52. Hans Christian Andersen 52. Guys and Dolls 55. How to Succeed in Business without Really Trying 66, etc.

Loew, Marcus (1870–1927).
Austrian-American exhibitor and distributor, co-founder and controller of MGM, which is still run by Loews Inc.

Loewe, Frederick (1901–1988).
Austrian composer, in America from the early 20s. Born in Berlin of Austrian parents, he was a concert pianist at the age of 14. His father, an actor and singer, died while rehearsing a show in New York, stranding the young Loewe and his mother. He then worked as a cowboy, boxer and pianist before becoming a composer, notably in collaboration with Alan Jay Lerner from 1942.

Brigadoon 54. Gigi 58. My Fair Lady 64. Camelot 67. Paint Your Wagon 69. The Little Prince 74.

Loft, Arthur (1897–1947).
American supporting actor with a slightly bewildered face, often seen as businessman.

Prisoner of Shark Island 36. The Woman in the Window 45. Blood on the Sun 46. Scarlet Street 47, many others.

Lofting, Hugh (1886–1947).
English children's author, creator of the Doctor Dolittle stories, filmed as a musical starring Rex Harrison in 1967. In 1998, Eddie Murphy starred as Dr Dolittle in a non-musical version, and a new stage musical based on the stories also ran in London.

Loftus, Cecilia (1876–1943).
British character actress who went to Hollywood with a Shakespearean company in 1895, and stayed.

East Lynne 31. The Old Maid 39. The Bluebird 40. Lucky Partners 40. The Black Cat 41, etc.

Logan, Joshua (1908–1988).
American stage director whose occasional films tended towards stodginess.

Autobiographies: 1976, *Josh, My Up and Down, In and Out Life*. 1978, *Movie Stars, Real People and Me*.

■ I Met My Love Again 38. *Picnic* (AAN) 56. *Bus Stop* 56. *Sayonara* (AAN) 57. South Pacific 58. Tall Story 60. Fanny 61. Ensign Pulver 64. *Camelot* 67. Paint Your Wagon 69.

Logan, Phyllis (1956–).
Scottish-born actress, probably best known for her role as Lady Jane in the TV series *Lovejoy*.

Another Time Another Place (BFA) 83. 1984 84. The Chain 85. The McGuffin 85. The Inquiry 87. The Kitchen Toto 87. Silent Cries (TV) 93. Love and Reason (TV) 93. Secrets and Lies 96, etc.

Logan, Robert F. (1941–).
Brawny hero of American family films.

The Bridge at Remagen 69. The Wilderness Family 75. Across the Great Divide 76. The Wilderness Family Part Two 77. Snowbeast (TV) 77. The Sea Gypsies 78. Death Ray 2000 81. Man Outside 88, etc.

Loggia, Robert (1930–).
American leading man.

Somebody Up There Likes Me 56. Cop Hater 58. The Nine Lives of Elfego Baca (TV) 59. Cattle King 63. Che! 69. The Moneychangers (TV) 75. First Love 77. The Ninth Configuration 80. S.O.B. 81. An Officer and a Gentleman 82. Trail of the Pink Panther 82. A Woman Called Golda (TV) 82. Curse of the Pink Panther 83. Scarface 83. Jagged Edge (AAN) 85. The Believers 87. Over the Top 87. Hot Pursuit 87. Big 88. Relentless 89. Triumph of the Spirit 89. Opportunity Knocks 90. The Marrying Man/Too Hot to Handle 91. Necessary Roughness 91. Innocent Blood 92. Gladiator 93. Bad Girls 94. White Mile (TV) 94. I Love Trouble 94. The Last Tattoo 94. Coldblooded 95. Man with a Gun 95. Independence Day 96. Mistrial (TV) 96. Wide Awake 97. National Lampoon's The Don's Analyst 97. Holy Man 98. The Proposition 98, etc.

TV series: T.H.E. Cat 66–67. Emerald Point N.A.S. 83–84. Mancuso F.B.I. 89. Wild Palms 93.

Lohmann, Dietrich (1943–1997).
German cinematographer, associated with the films of Rainer Werner Fassbinder and other leading directors of the New German Cinema. Born in Berlin, he studied at the Berlin Film School, moving to the USA in the mid-80s. Died from leukaemia.

Signs of Life (co-ph) 67. Last Words (co-ph) 68. Precautions against Fanatics (co-ph) 68. Love Is Colder than Death 69. Katzelmacher 69. Gods of the Plague 70. Why Does Herr R. Run Amok 70. Rio das Mortes 70. The Niklashausen Journey 70. The American Soldier 70. Recruits in Ingolstadt 70. The Merchant of Four Seasons 71. Wildwechsel 72. Eight Hours Are Not a Day 72. Ludwig – Requiem for a Virgin King 72. Bremen Freedom (& co-d) 72. Effi Briest 74. Karl May 74. Baker's Bread 76. Hitler: A Film from Germany 77. The Serpent's Egg 77. Germany in Autumn (co-ph) 78. Strawanzer 83. War and Remembrance (TV) (US) 88. Silence Like Glass (US) 90. The Serbian Girl 91. Ted and Venus (US) 91. Wedlock (US) 91. Knight Moves (US/Fr.) 92. Salt on Our Skin (Ger./Fr./Can.) 92. The Innocent (GB/Ger.) 93. Me and the Kid (US) 93. La Machine (Fr./Ger.) 94. Color of Night (US) 94. The Peacemaker (US) 97. Deep Impact (US) 98, etc.

Lohr, Marie (1890–1975).
Distinguished Australian stage actress, on London stage from 1901; since 1930 in dowager roles.

Aren't We All? (debut) 32. *Pygmalion* 38. *Major Barbara* 40. The Winslow Boy 48. A Town Like Alice 56, many others.

Lollobrigida, Gina (1927–).
Italian glamour girl and international leading lady, in films since 1947.

Pagliacci 47. Fanfan la Tulipe 51. *Belles de Nuit* 52. The Wayward Wife 52. *Bread, Love and Dreams* 53. Beat the Devil 54. Le Grand Jeu 54. Trapeze 56. Where the Hot Wind Blows 58. Solomon and Sheba 59. Come September 61. Woman of Straw 64. Strange Bedfellows 65. Four Kinds of Love/Bambole 65. Hotel Paradiso 66. Buona Sera, Mrs Campbell 68. Bad Man's River 71. King Queen Knave 72. The Lonely Woman 76. La Romana 88, many others.

TV series: Falcon Crest 84.

Lom, Herbert (1917–) (Herbert Charles Angelo Kuchacevich ze Schluderpacheru).
Czech actor whose personality adapts itself equally well to villainy or kindliness; in Britain from 1939.

Mein Kampf 40. The Young Mr Pitt (as Napoleon) 41. The Dark Tower 43. Hotel Reserve 44. *The Seventh Veil* 46. Night Boat to Dublin 46. *Dual Alibi* 47. Good Time Girl 48. The Golden Salamander 49. *State Secret* 50. The Black Rose 50. Hell Is Sold Out 51. The Ringer 52. The Net 53. The Love Lottery 54. *The Ladykillers* 55. War and Peace (as Napoleon) 56. Chase a Crooked Shadow 57. Hell Drivers 57. No Trees in the Street 58. Roots of Heaven 58. Northwest Frontier 59. I Aim at the Stars (US) 59. Mysterious Island 61. El Cid 61. Phantom of the Opera (title role) 62. A Shot in the Dark 64. Return from the Ashes 65. Uncle Tom's Cabin (Ger.) 65. Gambit 66. Assignment to Kill 67. Villa Rides 68. Doppelgänger 69. The Hot Death (Ger.) 69. Murders in the Rue Morgue 71. Asylum 72. And Now the Screaming Starts 73. The Return of the Pink Panther 74. And Then There Were None 75. The Pink Panther Strikes Again 77. Revenge of the Pink Panther 78. Charleston 78. The Lady Vanishes 79. Hopscotch 80. The Man with Bogart's Face 80. Trail of the Pink Panther 82. Curse of the Pink Panther 83. The Dead Zone 83. Memed My Hawk 84. King Solomon's Mines 85. Whoops Apocalypse 86. Scoop (TV) 87. The Crystal Eye 88. River of Death 89. Ten Little Indians 89. The Sect 91. The Pope Must Die/The Pope Must Diet 91. Son of the Pink Panther 93, etc.

TV series: *The Human Jungle*.

Lomas, Herbert (1887–1961).
Gaunt, hollow-voiced British stage actor.

The Sign of Four 32. Lorna Doone 35. Rembrandt 36. Jamaica Inn 39. Ask a Policeman 39. *The Ghost Train* 41. I Know Where I'm Going 45. Bonnie Prince Charlie 48. The Net 53, etc.

Lombard, Carole (1908–1942) (Jane Peters).
American leading lady of the 30s, a fine comedienne with an inimitable rangy style. Married Clark Gable. Died in a plane crash.

Biography: 1976, *Screwball* by Larry Swindell.

■ A Perfect Crime 21. Hearts and Spurs 25. Marriage in Transit 25. Me Gangster 28. Power 28. Show Folks 28. Ned McCobb's Daughter 29. High Voltage 29. Big News 29. The Racketeer 29. The Arizona Kid 30. Safety in Numbers 30. Fast and Loose 30. It Pays to Advertise 31. Man of the World 31. Ladies' Man 31. Up Pops the Devil 31. I Take This Woman 31. No One Man 32. Sinners in the Sun 32. Virtue 32. No More Orchids 32. *No Man of Her Own* 32. From Heaven to Hell 33. Supernatural 33. The Eagle and the Hawk 33. Brief Moment 33. White Woman 33. *Bolero* 34. We're Not Dressing 34. *Twentieth Century* 34. Now and Forever 34. Lady by Choice 34. The Gay Bride 34. *Rumba* 34. Hands across the Table 35. Love before Breakfast 36. *My Man Godfrey* (AAN) 36. The Princess Comes Across 36. Swing High Swing Low 37. True Confession 37. *Nothing Sacred* 37. Fools for Scandal 38. Made for Each Other 38. In Name Only 39. Vigil in the Night 40. *They Knew What They Wanted* 40. *Mr and Mrs Smith* 41. *To Be or Not To Be* 42.

✪ For daring to be wacky while glamorous. *Nothing Sacred*.

❝ I live by a man's code designed to fit a man's world, yet at the same time I never forget that a woman's first job is to choose the right shade of lipstick. – C.L.

Carole was the first woman I ever met who used four-letter words like a truck driver. – *Radie Harris*

Lombard, Karina (1969–).
Sultry American actress, of Lakota Indian and Russian descent.

Wide Sargasso Sea 92. The Firm 93. Legends of the Fall 94. Last Man Standing 96, etc.

Lombardi, Francisco José (1950–).
Leading Peruvian director, producer and screenwriter of films on social and political themes, a former movie critic.

Muerte al Amanecer 77. Maruja en el Infierno 83. *The City and the Dogs*/La Ciudad y los Perros 85. The Lion's Den/La Boca del Lobo 88. Fallen from the Sky/Caidos del Cielo (& co-w) 90. Traces from Paradise/Huellas del Paraiso (& co-w) 92. Sin Compasión 94. Don't Tell Anyone/No Se Lo Digas a Nadie 98, etc.

Lombardo, Louis (1933–).
American film editor and occasional director.

The Wild Bunch 69. The Ballad of Cable Hogue 69. Brewster McCloud 70. McCabe and Mrs Miller 71. Thieves Like Us 73. The Long Goodbye 73. California Split 74. The Black Bird 75. Russian Roulette (d) 75. All the President's Men 76. The Late Show 77. The Changeling 78. Just One of the Guys 85. P.K and the Kid (d) 87. Moonstruck 87. January Man 89. Uncle Buck 89. Defenceless 90. Other People's Money 91, etc.

Lommel, Ulli (1944–).
German-born director, screenwriter and cinematographer who began by working as an actor with Rainer Werner Fassbinder, remade Fritz Lang's M with Fassbinder producing, and then went to America to direct low-budget gore-filled horror movies.

Whity (a) 70. The American Soldier/Der Amerikanische Soldat (a) 70. The Tenderness of Wolves/Die Zartlickeit der Wolfe (d) 73. Fontane Effi Briest (a) 74. Chinesisches Roulette (a) 76. Satan's Brew/Satansbraten (a) 76. Adolf und Marlene (wd) 77. Cocaine Cowboys 79. The Boogey Man (a, d) 80. A Taste of Sin (co-w, d, ph) 83. Brainwaves (& ph) 83. The Demonsville Terror (co-w, d, ph) 83. Defense Play 86. Overkill 86. Warbirds (co-w, d) 88. Natural Instinct (p,d) 91. The Big Sweat 91, etc.

Loncraine, Richard (1946–).
British director.

Flame 74. Full Circle 76. Blade on the Feather (TV) 80. Brimstone and Treacle 82. The Missionary 84. Bellman and True 87. The Wedding Gift (TV) 94. *Richard III* 95, etc.

London, Jack (1876–1916).
American adventure novelist, whose most-filmed stories include *The Sea Wolf*, *Adventures of Martin Eden*, *Call of the Wild* and *White Fang*.

London, Julie (1926–) (Julie Peck).
American leading lady and singer. She was married to actor and director Jack Webb (1945–53).

Jungle Woman 44. The Red House 47. The Fat Man 51. The Great Man 56. Saddle the Wind 58. Man of the West 58. The Third Voice 60. The George Raft Story 62, etc.

TV series: *Emergency* 72–77.

London, Roy (1943–1993).
American director, screenwriter, playwright and actor who was also a noted acting coach.

Hardcore (a) 79. Jake Speed (a) 86. Rampage (a) 87. Tiger Warsaw (w) 88. Diary of a Hitman (d) 92, etc.

Lone, John (1952–).
Hong Kong-born leading actor, in America, who also makes pop records aimed at the Asian market.

Iceman 84. Year of the Dragon 85. Echoes of Paradise/Shadows of the Peacock 86. The Last Emperor 87. The Moderns 88. Shadow of China 91. M. Butterfly 93. The Shadow 94. The Hunted 95, etc.

❝ I don't want to stand behind someone and look important and inscrutable. I don't do Fu Manchu. – *J.L.*

Lonergan, Arthur (1906–1989).
American art director, a former architect, in films from 1938, first as an illustrator.

Intrigue 48. The Actress 53. *Forbidden Planet* 56. Robinson Crusoe on Mars 64. The Oscar (AAN) 66. Che! 69. M*A*S*H 70. Beyond the Valley of the Dolls 70. Plaza Suite 70, etc.

Long, Audrey (1924–).
American leading lady of the 40s.
A Night of Adventure 44. Pan Americana 45. Song of My Heart 47. The Petty Girl 50. Indian Uprising 52, etc.

Long, Howie (1960–).
American actor, a former professional footballer, born in Charlestown, Massachusetts.
Broken Arrow 96. Firestorm 97, etc.

Long, Huey (1893–1935).
American politician, governor of Louisiana and US senator with presidential ambitions, who was assassinated. He was the model for Willie Stark, the corrupt Southern protagonist of Robert Penn Warren's novel *All the King's Men*, which was filmed with Broderick Crawford in the leading role. *Kingfish*, a film of his life made for cable TV, starred John Goodman in 1995. He was the brother of Earl Long, governor of Louisiana in the 50s, whose affair with a stripper was commemorated in the movie *Blaze* 89, starring Paul Newman.

Long, Richard (1927–1974).
American leading man, mainly in second features. Married actress Mara Corday.
Tomorrow Is Forever 44. The Stranger 45. The Egg and I 47. Criss Cross 49. Saskatchewan 54. Cult of the Cobra 55. Home from the Hills 59. The Tenderfoot 64, etc.
TV series: *77 Sunset Strip* 58–60. *Bourbon Street Beat* 59. *The Big Valley* 65–68. *Nanny and the Professor* 69–71. Thicker Than Water 73.

Long, Shelley (1949–).
American leading lady.
Irreconcilable Differences 84. The Money Pit 85. Outrageous Fortune 87. Hello Again 87. Troop Beverly Hills 89. Don't Tell Her It's Me 90. Frozen Assets 92. The Brady Bunch Movie 95. Freaky Friday (TV) 95. A Very Brady Sequel 96, etc.
TV series: Cheers 82–87. Good Advice 93–94. Kelly Kelly 98.

Long, Walter (1879–1952).
Tough-looking American character actor, usually as a villain, in films from 1909. He was a regular in D. W. Griffith's films and blacked up to play the rapist who chases Mae Marsh to her death in *The Birth of a Nation*. He appeared in several Laurel and Hardy films, notably as a convict in *Pardon Us*, ending his career opposite Ken Maynard and William Boyd in westerns and, in *Man's Country*, playing twin baddies.
The Birth of a Nation 15. Intolerance 16. Joan the Woman 17. The Little American 17. Scarlet Days 18. The Sheik 21. Blood and Sand 22. Moran of the Lady Letty 22. The Call of the Wild 23. Little Church round the Corner 23. Raffles 25. Soul-Fire 25. Yankee Clipper 27. Me, Gangster 28. Moby Dick 30. The Maltese Falcon 31. Sea Devils 31. Pardon Us 31. Any Old Port 32. I Am a Fugitive from a Chain Gang 32. The Thin Man 34. The Live Ghost 34. Going Bye-Bye! 34. Naughty Marietta 35. North of the Rio Grande 37. The Painted Trail 38. Man's Country 38. Six Shootin' Sheriff 38. Union Pacific 39. Flaming Lead 39. Silver Stallion 41. Wabash Avenue 50, etc.

Longden, John (1900–1971).
British leading man of the early 30s; later graduated to character roles.
Blackmail 30. Atlantic 30. The Ringer 31. Born Lucky 33. French Leave 37. The Gaunt Stranger 38. The Lion Has Wings 39. The Common Touch 41. The Silver Fleet 43. Bonnie Prince Charlie 48. The Man with the Twisted Lip (as Sherlock Homes) 51. Quatermass II 56. An Honourable Murder 60, many others.

Longden, Terence (1922–).
British actor, in secondary roles.
Never Look Back 52. Simon and Laura 55. Doctor at Large 57. Carry On Sergeant 58. Ben Hur 59. The Return of Mr Moto 65. The Wild Geese 78. The Sea Wolves 80, etc.

Longo, Robert.
American director and artist.
Johnny Mnemonic 95.

Longstreet, Stephen (1907–).
American screenwriter.
The Jolson Story 46. The Greatest Show on Earth (co-w) 52. The First Traveling Saleslady 55. The Helen Morgan Story 57, etc.

Lonsdale, Frederick (1881–1954) (Lionel Frederick Leonard).
Fashionable English playwright and screenwriter of the 20s and early 30s. Born in Jersey, the son of a tobacconist, he wrote sophisticated comedies of life in high society, and attempted to live in a similar manner. He signed a contract to work for MGM in 1930 but soon tired of Hollywood and returned to England, going back in 1936 to write a film for Ernst Lubitsch, which he abandoned after three weeks; he spent much of the remainder of his life in the United States.
Biography: 1957, *Freddy Lonsdale* by Frances Donaldson.
The Fast Set (US) 24. The Fake (oa, co-w) 27. The Last of Mrs Cheyney (US) 29. Canaries Sometimes Sing (oa, co-w) 30. On Approval 30. Lady of Scandal (US) 30. The Devil to Pay (US) (w) 30. Aren't We All 32. The Maid of the Mountains 32. Women Who Play 32. Lovers Courageous (US) (w) 32. Just Smith 33. The Private Life of Don Juan (co-w) 34. The Last of Mrs Cheyney (US) 37. On Approval 44. The Law and the Lady (US) 51, etc.
❝ I could never live in a film city because there is no conversation. – *F.L.*

Lonsdale, Michel (1931–) (sometimes Michael).
Chubby French character actor, in some international roles.
La Main Chaude 60. The Trial 62. Behold a Pale Horse 64. The Bride Wore Black 68. Stolen Kisses 68. Souffle au Coeur 71. *The Day of the Jackal* 73. Stavisky 74. Caravan to Vaccares 74. The Phantom of Liberty 74. The Romantic Englishwoman 75. The Pink Telephone 75. Mr Klein 76. The Passage 78. Moonraker 79. Les Jeux de la Comtesse 80. Enigma 82. The Name of the Rose 86. Souvenir 88. The Remains of the Day 93. Jefferson in Paris (as Louis XVI) 95. Nelly and M. Arnaud 95. Ronin (US) 98, many others.

Loo, Richard (1903–1983).
Hawaiian-Chinese actor who turned to films after business depression. Played hundreds of oriental roles.
Dirigible 31. The Good Earth 37. The Keys of the Kingdom 44. Rogues' Regiment 48. Love is a Many-Splendored Thing 54. The Quiet American 58. The Sand Pebbles 66. One More Time 71, etc.

Loos, Anita (1891–1981).
Witty American writer who spent 18 years with MGM. A former actress, she began by writing scenarios for D. W. Griffiths, progressing to subtitles for Douglas Fairbanks's films under the influence of director John Emerson, whom she married in 1919, though the liaison was a mostly unhappy one. She remains best known for her novel *Gentlemen Prefer Blondes*, inspired by writer H. L. Mencken's flirtation with a dumb blonde, which was turned into a film, a play and two musicals, one of which was also filmed as a vehicle for Marilyn Monroe.
Autobiographies 1966, *A Girl Like I*. 1974, *Kiss Hollywood Goodbye*. 1977, *Cast of Thousands*. Also wrote *The Talmadge Girls* (1977).
Biography: 1988, *Anita Loos* by Gary Carey.
Intolerance (subtitles) 16. Let's Get a Divorce (w) 18. A Temperamental Wife (oa) 19. Mama's Affair (d) 20. In Search of a Sinner (p) 20. Red Hot Romance (w) 22. Learning to Love (w) 25. Gentlemen Prefer Blondes (oa) 28. Midnight Mary (oa) 33. *San Francisco* (w) 36. Saratoga (w) 37. The Women (w) 39. When Ladies Meet (oa) 41. *Gentlemen Prefer Blondes* (oa) 53, etc.
❝ Kissing your hand may make you feel very, very good but a diamond and sapphire bracelet lasts forever. – *A.L., Gentlemen Prefer Blondes*
Today, much as girls *look* like boys, they flunk out on the solicitude men are developing for each other. Less and less do men need women. More and more do gentlemen prefer gentlemen. – *A.L., 1974*

Lopez, Jennifer (1970–).
Sultry American actress and singer, a former dancer. Born in the Bronx, New York, to Puerto Rican parents, she began as one of the Fly Girls on the TV series *In Living Color*. She was briefly married (1997–98) to Cuban Ojani Noa. Current asking price: $2m.
Nurses on the Line (TV) 93. My Family/Mia Familia 95. Money Train 95. Jack 96. Blood & Wine 96. Selena 97. Anaconda 97. U-Turn 97. Out of Sight 98. Antz (voice) 98, etc.
TV series: Malibu Road 92. Second Chances 93–94. South Central 94.

Lopez, Trini (1937–).
American character actor, ex-bandleader.
Marriage on the Rocks 66. The Dirty Dozen 67. Antonio 73, etc.

Loquasto, Santo (1944–).
American production designer, from the stage, often on Woody Allen's films.
Rancho Deluxe 75. Stardust Memories 80. The Fan 81. So Fine 81. Falling in Love 84. Desperately Seeking Susan 85. Radio Days (AAN) 87. September 87. Big 88. Another Woman 88. Bright Lights, Big City 88. New York Stories 89. Crimes and Misdemeanors 89. She-Devil 89. Alice 90. Shadows and Fog 92. Manhattan Murder Mystery 93. Bullets over Broadway (AAN) 94. Everyone Says I Love You 96. Deconstructing Harry 97. Celebrity 98, etc.

Lord, Del (1895–1970)
American second-feature director who handled most of the THREE STOOGES shorts.
Barnum Was Right 29. Trapped by Television 36. It Always Happens 39. She's a Sweetheart 44. I Love a Bandleader 45. Hit the Hay 45. Blonde from Brooklyn 45. Rough, Tough and Ready 45. Singin' in the Corn 46. It's Great to Be Young 46. In Fast Company 46, etc.

Lord, Jack (1928–1998) (John Joseph Ryan).
Craggy-faced American leading man who found his greatest success in television. Born in Brooklyn, he trained as a merchant marine officer, held a second mate's licence, and became interested in acting through involvement in maritime training films. He was also an accomplished artist, with work in the permanent collections of more than 35 museums around the world.
Cry Murder 51. The Court Martial of Billy Mitchell 55. God's Little Acre 58. Walk Like a Dragon 60. Doctor No 62. The Road to Hangman's Tree 67. The Name of the Game Is Kill 68. M Station: Hawaii (d) (TV) 80, etc.
TV series: *Stoney Burke* 62–63. *Hawaii Five-O* 68–80.

Lord, Jean-Claude (1943–).
Canadian director.
■ Eclair au Chocolat 79. Visiting Hours 82. Dreamworld 83. Covergirl 84. The Vindicator/ Frankenstein '88 85. Toby McTeague 85. Tadpole and the Whale 88. Mindfield 89. Eddie and the Cruisers: Eddie Lives! 89. Landslide 92.

Lord, Marjorie (1922–).
American leading lady of minor films in the 40s, later on TV as Danny Thomas' wife in comedy series. She is the mother of Anne Archer.
Forty Naughty Girls 38. Timber 42. Sherlock Holmes in Washington 42. Flesh and Fantasy 44. The Argyle Secrets 48. New Orleans 49. Port of Hell 55. Boy Did I Get a Wrong Number 66. Side by Side (TV) 88, etc.
TV series: Make Room for Daddy 53–57. Make Room for Granddaddy 70.

Lord, Pauline (1890–1950).
American stage actress who made only two films.
■ Mrs Wiggs of the Cabbage Patch 35. A Feather in Her Hat 36.

Lord, Robert (1900–1976).
American writer and producer associated with Warner Brothers throughout the 30s and 40s; later joined Humphrey Bogart in Santana Productions.
AS WRITER: The Johnstown Flood 26. A Reno Divorce 27. My Man 28. Five and Ten Cent Annie 28. On with the Show 29. Gold Diggers of Broadway 29. Hold Everything 30. Fireman Save My Child 32. One Way Passage (AA) 32. 20,000 Years in Sing Sing 32. The Little Giant 33. Dames 34. Page Miss Glory 35, etc.
AS PRODUCER: Wonder Bar 34. Oil for the Lamps of China 35. Black Legion 37. Tovarich 37. Brother Rat 38. The Dawn Patrol 38. Dodge City 39. Confessions of a Nazi Spy 39. The Letter 40. Dive Bomber 41. High Wall 47. Tokyo Joe 49. In a Lonely Place 50. Sirocco 51, etc.

Lords, Traci (1968–) (Nora Louise Kuzma).
American actress, a former star of pornographic films who made the transition to low-budget features in the late 80s.
Not of This Earth 88. Fast Food 89. Shock 'Em Dead 90. Cry-Baby 90. Raw Nerve 91. A Time to Die 91. Laser Moon 92. Skinner 93. The Tommyknockers (TV) 93. Ice 94. Serial Mom 94. Plughead Rewired: Circuitry Man II 94. The Nutt House 95. As Good as Dead 95. Blade 98, etc.

Loren, Sophia (1934–) (Sofia Scicolone).
Statuesque Italian leading lady, latterly an accomplished international actress. In films from 1950 (as extra). Married producer Carlo Ponti.
Autobiography: 1979, *Sophia: Living and Loving* (with A. E. Hotchner).
Biography: 1975, *Sophia* by Donald Zec; 1998, *Sophia Loren* by Warren G. Harris.
Aida 53. The Sign of Venus 53. Tempi Nostri 54. Attila 54. The Gold of Naples 54. *Woman of the River* 55. Too Bad She's Bad 55. The Miller's Wife 55. Scandal in Sorrento 55. Lucky To Be a Woman 56. The Pride and the Passion 57. *Boy on a Dolphin* 57. Legend of the Lost 57. Desire under the Elms 58. *The Key* 58. Houseboat 58. Black Orchid 59. That Kind of Woman 59. Heller in Pink Tights 60. A Breath of Scandal 61. *Two Women* (AA, BFA) 61. *The Millionairess* 61. El Cid 61. Boccaccio 70 61. The Condemned of Altona 62. Madame Sans Gêne 62. Five Miles to Midnight 62. Yesterday, Today and Tomorrow 63. The Fall of the Roman Empire 64. Marriage Italian Style (AAN) 64. Operation Crossbow 65. Judith 65. Arabesque 66. Lady L 66. A Countess from Hong Kong 66. Ghosts Italian Style 68. More Than a Miracle 69. Sunflower 70. Man of La Mancha 72. Lady Liberty 74. Brief Encounter (TV) 74. The Voyage 75. The Cassandra Crossing 77. A Special Day 77. Brass Target 78. Firepower 79. Angela 80. Sophia Loren (TV) 80. Aurora (TV) 84. Courage (TV) 86. The Fortunate Pilgrim (TV) 88. Running Away 89. Saturday, Sunday and Monday/Sabato, Domenica e Lunedi 90. Prêt-à-Porter/Ready to Wear 94. Grumpier Old Men 95, etc.
❝ Everything you see, I owe to spaghetti. – *S.L.*
Sex appeal is fifty per cent what you've got and fifty per cent what people think you've got. – *S.L.*
I'm not ashamed of my bare-bottomed beginnings. – *S.L.*
In a restaurant or at a function I just walk straight in and it's an eternity. When I'm sitting, it's OK, but then I have to start thinking of a short cut out. – *S.L.*
All the natural mistakes of beauty fall together in her to create a magnificent accident. – *Rex Reed*
Working with her is like being bombed by watermelons. – *Alan Ladd*

Lorentz, Pare (1905–1992).
American documentarist and film critic.
The Plow that Broke the Plains 36. *The River* 37. The Fight for Life 40. The Nuremberg Trials 46.

Lorenz, Juliane (1957–).
German editor, associated with the films of Fassbinder from the mid-70s to the early 80s.
Chinese Roulette 76. Despair 78. The Third Generation/Die Dritte Generation 79. Berlin Alexanderplatz (TV) 80. The Marriage of Maria Braun 79. Querelle 82. The Rose King 86. The Night of the Mareten 87. Malina 90, etc.

Lorimer, Glennis (1913–).
English actress of the stage and screen in the 30s who impersonated Thomas Gainsborough's portrait of actress Sarah Siddons in the trademark of Gainsborough Pictures, a company co-owned by her father, Henry Ostrer.
The Ringer 31. There Goes the Bride 32. Britannia of Billingsgate 33. My Old Dutch 34. Rhodes of Africa 36. Alf's Button Afloat 38. Ask a Policeman 39, etc.

Lorne, Marion (1886–1968) (Marion Lorne MacDougal).
American character actress who came to films in older roles. Born in Wilkes Barre, Pennsylvania, she spent much of her career in England, appearing in

the farces and comedies of her husband, playwright and theatre manager Walter HACKETT. After his death in 1944, she returned to the United States, where she was best known for playing the dithery Aunt Clara in the TV sitcom *Bewitched*.

■ Strangers on a Train 51. The Girl Rush 55. The Graduate 67.

TV series: Mr Peepers 52–55. Sally 57–58. The Garry Moore Show 58–62. Bewitched 64–68.

Lorre, Peter (1904–1964) (Laszlo Loewenstein).
Highly individual Hungarian character actor who filmed in Germany and Britain before settling in Hollywood. His rolling eyes, timid manner and mysterious personality could adapt to either sympathetic or sinister roles; a weight problem restricted his later appearances.

■ Frühlings Erwachen 29. Der Weisse Teufel 30. Die Koffer des Herrn O.F. 30. M 30. Bomben auf Monte Carlo 31. Fünf von der Jazzband 32. Schuss im Morgengrauen 32. Der Weisse Dämon 32. F.P.I. 32. Was Frauen Träumen 33. Unsichtbare Gegner 33. De Haut en Bas 34. *The Man Who Knew Too Much* 34. *Mad Love* 35. *Crime and Punishment* (as Raskolnikov) 35. *The Secret Agent* 36. Crack Up 36. Nancy Steele is Missing 37. Lancer Spy 37. Think Fast Mr Moto 37. Thank You Mr Moto 37. Mr Moto's Gamble 38. I'll Give a Million 38. Mr Moto Takes a Chance 38. Mysterious Mr Moto 38. Mr Moto on Danger Island 39. Mr Moto Takes a Vacation 39. Mr Moto's Last Warning 39. Strange Cargo 40. I Was an Adventuress 40. Island of Doomed Men 40. Stranger on the Third Floor 40. You'll Find Out 40. Mr District Attorney 41. *The Face Behind the Mask* 41. They Met in Bombay 41. *The Maltese Falcon* 41. All through the Night 42. Invisible Agent 42. The Boogie Man Will Get You 42. Casablanca 42. Background to Danger 43. The Cross of Lorraine 43. The Constant Nymph 43. Passage to Marseilles 44. *The Mask of Dimitrios* 44. Arsenic and Old Lace 44. The Conspirators 44. Hollywood Canteen 44. Hotel Berlin 45. Confidential Agent 45. Three Strangers 46. Black Angel 46. The Chase 46. The Verdict 46. *The Beast with Five Fingers* 46. My Favorite Brunette 47. Casbah 48. Rope of Sand 49. Quicksand 50. Double Confession 50. Der Verlorene (& d) 50. Beat the Devil 53. 20,000 Leagues under the Sea 54. *Congo Crossing* 56. Around the World in Eighty Days 56. The Buster Keaton Story 56. Silk Stockings 57. The Story of Mankind (as Nero) 57. Hell Ship Mutiny 57. The Sad Sack 58. The Big Circus 59. Scent of Mystery 59. Voyage to the Bottom of the Sea 61. *Tales of Terror* 62. Five Weeks in a Balloon 62. *The Raven* 63. The Comedy of Terrors 63. The Patsy 64.

✪ For the diffidence of his dark deeds and for his inimitable voice, still enthusiastically parodied by cartoon villains. *The Mask of Dimitrios*.

❝ Those marbly pupils in the pasty spherical face are like the eye pieces of a microscope through which you can see laid flat on the slide the entangled mind of a man: love and lust, nobility and perversity, hatred of itself, and despair jumping up at you from the jelly. – *Graham Greene*

Lorring, Joan (1926–) (Magdalen Ellis).
English-Russian actress, evacuated to US in 1939; played some nasty teenagers.

Girls under Twenty-One 41. Song of Russia 44. The Bridge of San Luis Rey 44. The Corn Is Green (AAN) 45. The Verdict 46. The Lost Moment 47. Good Sam 49. Stranger on the Prowl 53. The Midnight Man 74, etc.

TV series: Norby 54.

Losch, Tilly (1901–1975).
Austrian exotic dancer, in Hollywood in the 30s and 40s.

■ The Garden of Allah 36. The Good Earth 37. Duel in the Sun 46.

Losey, Joseph (1909–1984).
American director of somewhat pretentious movies, in Britain from 1952 after the communist witch-hunt.

Biographies: 1991, *Joseph Losey* by Edith Rham. 1994, *Joseph Losey: A Revenge on Life* by David Caute.

■ The Boy with Green Hair 48. The Lawless 50. *The Prowler* 50. M 51. The Big Night 51. Stranger on the Prowl 53. The Sleeping Tiger 54. The Intimate Stranger 56. Time without Pity 57. The Gypsy and the Gentleman 57. Blind Date 59. The Criminal 60. *The Damned* 61. Eva 62. *The Servant* 63. King and Country 64. Modesty Blaise 66. *Accident* 67. Boom 68. Secret Ceremony 68. Figures in a Landscape 70. The Go-Between 71. The Assassination of Trotsky 72. A Doll's House 73. Galileo 74. The Romantic Englishwoman 75. Mr Klein 76. Don Giovanni 79. The Trout 82. Steaming 84.

❝ Films can illustrate our existence . . . they can distress, disturb and provoke people into thinking about themselves and certain problems. But NOT give the answers. – *J.L.*

Lotinga, Ernie (1876–1951)
British vaudeville comedian who began his career as a comic vocalist under the name of Dan Roe in 1898. During the early 1900s he was a member of the Six Brothers Luck in music hall before creating the slapstick character Jimmy Josser that made him a star until the mid-20s. He continued the character in some broadly comic movies that had their followers in the 30s. He was married to music-hall performer and male impersonator Hetty King.

Joining Up 28. Nap 28. The Raw Recruit 28. Dr Josser, K.C. (& co-w) 31. P.C. Josser 31. Josser Joins the Navy 32. Josser in the Army 32. Josser on the River 32. Josser on the Farm 34. Smith's Wives (& story) 35. Love up the Pole 36, etc.

Louis-Dreyfus, Julia (1960–).
American actress, from television's *Saturday Night Live*. Best known for her role as Elaine Benes in the TV sitcom *Seinfeld*, for which she was reportedly paid $600,000 an episode.

Soul Man 86. Hannah and Her Sisters 86. National Lampoon's Christmas Vacation 89. Jack the Bear 93. North 94. London Suite (TV) 96. Deconstructing Harry 97. Father's Day 97. A Bug's Life (voice) 98, etc.

TV series: Day by Day 88–89. Seinfeld 90–98.

Louis, Jean (1907–1997) (Jean-Louis Berthault).
Paris-born costume designer, in the US from the mid-30s and Hollywood from the mid-40s, working first at Columbia Pictures for 15 years as chief designer. In the 60s he worked at Universal and later opened his own couture house in Los Angeles. Among his best-known creations were the strapless black satin dress worn by Rita HAYWORTH as she sang 'Put the Blame on Mame' in *Gilda*, Marlene DIETRICH's elaborate, sculpted gowns for her cabaret performances, and the sequinned body-stocking Marilyn MONROE wore when she sang 'Happy Birthday' to President Kennedy at Madison Square Garden in 1962. Married actress Loretta YOUNG, his second wife, in 1993.

Strange Affair 44. *Gilda* 46. The Jolson Story 46. The Lady from Shanghai 48. Jolson Sings Again 49. Born Yesterday (AAN) 50. Affair in Trinidad (AAN) 52. *Salome* 53. From Here to Eternity (AAN) 53. It Should Happen to You (AAN) 54. A Star Is Born (AAN) 54. The Caine Mutiny 54. Queen Bee (AAN) 55. Picnic 55. *The Sold Gold Cadillac* (AA) 56. Pal Joey (AAN) 57. The Story of Esther Costello 57. Bell, Book and Candle (AAN) 58. Imitation of Life 59. Song without End 60. Back Street (AAN) 61. Judgment at Nuremberg (AAN) 61. Ship of Fools (AAN) 65. Gambit (AAN) 66. Thoroughly Modern Millie (AAN) 67. Guess Who's Coming to Dinner 67. Lost Horizon 73, etc.

❝ Jean Louis's creations metamorphosed me into a perfect, ethereal being, the most seductive that ever was. – *Marlene Dietrich*

Louise, Anita (1915–1970) (Anita Louise Fremault).
American leading lady, usually in gentle roles. Played child parts from 1924.

What a Man 30. A Midsummer Night's Dream 35. The Story of Louis Pasteur 35. Anthony Adverse 36. The Green Light 37. Marie Antoinette 38. The Sisters 39. Phantom Submarine 41. The Fighting Guardsman 45. The Bandit of Sherwood Forest 46. Retreat, Hell! 52.

TV series: My *Friend Flicka* 56.

❝ As cold as a stepmother's kiss. – *Hal Wallis*

Louise, Tina (1934–) (Tina Blacker).
Statuesque American leading lady of routine films.

God's Little Acre 58. Day of the Outlaw 59. Armored Command 61. For Those Who Think Young 64. Wrecking Crew 68. The Good Guys and the Bad Guys 69. How to Commit Marriage 70. The Stepford Wives 75. Mean Dog Blues 78. The Day the Women Got Even 80. Hellriders 84. Evils of the Night 85. O.C. & Stiggs 87. Dixie Lanes 88. Johnny Suede 91, etc.

TV series: *Gilligan's Island* 64–66. Dallas 78. Rituals 84–85.

Lourié, Eugène (1905–1991).
French designer.

Les Bas Fonds 36. *La Grande Illusion* 37. La Règle du Jeu 39. This Land Is Mine (US) 42. *The Southerner* (US) 44. The River 51. What's the Matter with Helen 71. Burnt Offerings 76. Bronco Billy 80, etc.

AS DIRECTOR: The Beast from Twenty Thousand Fathoms 53. The Colossus of New York 58. Gorgo (GB) 60, etc.

Love, Bessie (1898–1986) (Juanita Horton).
Vivacious, petite American leading lady of the 20s. In films from childhood; from the mid-30s resident in London, playing occasional cameo parts.

Autobiography: 1977, *From Hollywood with Love*.

Intolerance 15. The Aryan 16. A Sister of Six 17. The Dawn of Understanding 18. The Purple Dawn 20. The Vermilion Pencil 21. Human Wreckage 23. Dynamite Smith 24. The Lost World 25. Lovey Mary 26. Sally of the Scandals 27. Broadway Melody (AAN) 28. Chasing Rainbows 30. Morals for Women 31. Conspiracy 32. Atlantic Ferry 42. Journey Together 45. Touch and Go 55. The Wild Affair 64. Isadora 68. Sunday Bloody Sunday 71. Mousey (TV) 74. The Ritz 76, many others.

Love, Courtney (1965–).
American rock singer and occasional actress. Widow of rock singer Kurt Cobain.

Biography: 1997, *Courtney Love: The Real Story* by Poppy Z. Brite.

Sid and Nancy 86. Straight to Hell 86. Feeling Minnesota 96. Basquiat 96. The People vs Larry Flynt 96. 200 Cigarettes 98, etc.

Love, Darlene (1938–) (Darlene Wright).
American character actress and singer. Born in Los Angeles, she sang with The Blossoms and was lead vocalist on 'He's a Rebel' and other hit singles made by Phil Spector in the 60s. On film, she is familiar as Danny Glover's wife in the *Lethal Weapon* series.

Lethal Weapon 88. Lethal Weapon 2 89. Lethal Weapon 3 92. Lethal Weapon 4 98, etc.

Love, Montagu (1877–1943).
Heavily built British character actor, long in Hollywood, latterly as stern fathers.

Bought and Paid For 16. The Gilded Cage 19. The Case of Becky 21. A Son of the Sahara 24. Son of the Sheik 26. Don Juan 26. King of Kings 27. Jesse James 27. The Haunted House 28. The Divine Lady 29. Bulldog Drummond 29. Outward Bound 30. The Cat Creeps 30. Midnight Lady 32. Clive of India 35. The White Angel 36. The Prince and the Pauper (as Henry VIII) 37. The Adventures of Robin Hood 38. Gunga Din 39. All This and Heaven Too 40. Shining Victory 41. The Constant Nymph 43. Devotion 44, many others.

Lovecraft, H. P. (1890–1937).
American horror writer, most of whose books were published posthumously. His stories featuring his invented Cthulhu mythology of ancient demonic forces attempting to return to Earth have become increasingly influential among makers of low-budget horror movies. The following all show the Lovecraft influence, though it is not always acknowledged by their makers:

The Haunted Palace (from *The Case of Charles Dexter Ward*) 63. Monster of Terror (from *Colour out of Space*) 65. Dunwich Horror (from *The Shuttered Room*) 69. Re-Animator (from *Herbert West – Re-Animator*) 85. From Beyond 86. The Farm 87. The Gate 87. Re-Animator 2 89. Gate 2 92. Cthulhu Mansion 92. The Unnameable Returns (from *The Statement of Randolph Carter*) 92. The Resurrected (from *The Case of Charles Dexter Ward*) 92. Necronomicon 93, a movie compendium, featured two Lovecraft stories, *Cool Air* and *The Whisperer in the Darkness*, with Jeffrey Combs appearing in the role of Lovecraft. In the Mouth of Madness 94. Lurking Fear 94, etc.

Lovejoy, Frank (1912–1962).
American actor of tough roles, with stage and radio experience.

Black Bart 48. Home of the Brave 49. In a Lonely Place 50. *The Sound of Fury* 51. I Was a Communist for the FBI 51. Force of Arms 51. The Hitch Hiker 52. Retreat Hell 52. The System 53. House of Wax 53. The Charge at Feather River 54. Beachhead 54. The Americano 55. Top of the World 55. Strategic Air Command 55. The Crooked Web 56. Cole Younger Gunfighter 58, etc.

TV series: Man against Crime 54. *Meet McGraw* 57–58.

Lovejoy, Ray.
English film editor.

2001: A Space Odyssey 68. A Day in the Death of Joe Egg 72. The Ruling Class 72. The Shining 80. The Dresser 83. Aliens (AAN) 86. The House on Carroll Street 88. Batman 89. Mr Frost 90. Let Him Have It 91. The Year of the Comet 92. A Far Off Place 93. Monkey Trouble 94. Rainbow 95. Mrs Munck 95. The Last of the High Kings 96. Inventing the Abbotts 97. Lost in Space 98, etc.

Lovelace, Linda (1952–).
American female lead of *Deep Throat* and other porno films.

Lovell, Raymond (1900–1953).
Canadian stage actor long in Britain: often in pompous or sinister roles.

Warn London 34. Contraband 40. 49th Parallel 41. *Alibi* 42. Warn That Man 43. The Way Ahead 44. *Caesar and Cleopatra* 45. The Three Weird Sisters 48. Time Gentleman Please 52. The Steel Key 53, etc.

Lovett, Lyle (1958–).
American country singer and occasional actor. Briefly married to actress Julia ROBERTS.

The Player 92. Short Cuts 93. Prêt-à-Porter/ Ready to Wear 94. Bastard out of California 96. Fear and Loathing in Las Vegas 98. The Opposite of Sex 98, etc.

Lovitz, Jon (1957–).
American character actor.

Jumpin' Jack Flash 86. Three Amigos 86. Last Resort 86. Big 88. My Stepmother Was an Alien 88. Mr Destiny 90. An American Tail: Fievel Goes West 91. A League of Their Own 92. Mom and Dad Save the World 92. National Lampoon's Loaded Weapon 1 93. North 94. City Slickers II: The Legend of Curly's Gold 94. Trapped in Paradise 94. The Great White Hype 96. High School High 96. Matilda 96. The Wedding Singer 97. Happiness 98, etc.

TV series: Saturday Night Live 85–90. Foley Square 85–86. NewsRadio 98– .

Low, Warren (1905–1989).
American editor.

Dr Socrates 35. Anthony Adverse 36. The Great Garrick 37. The Life of Emile Zola 37. Juarez 39. *The Letter* 40. The Gay Sisters 42. Now Voyager 42. The Searching Wind 46. Sorry Wrong Number 48. September Affair 50. The Stooge 52. About Mrs Leslie 54. The Bad Seed 56. Gunfight at the OK Corral 57. Summer and Smoke 61. Boeing Boeing 65. Will Penny 68. True Grit 69. Willard 71, many others.

Lowe, Arthur (1915–1982).
Portly British character actor who achieved star status on television, and was best known for the role of the pompous Captain Mainwaring in the sitcom *Dad's Army*. In the 60s he played Leonard Swindley, the lay preacher and draper in the TV soap opera *Coronation Street*, and remains the only character so far to have had a spin-off series, *Pardon the Expression* 65–66. Born in Hayfield, Derbyshire, he worked in an aircraft factory and began in amateur drama during his service in the Second World War, making his first professional appearance at the age of 30. Married actress Joan Cooper. His best film roles were as Tucker, the anarchist butler in *The Ruling Class* 72, and as Duff, Johnson and Munda in O *Lucky Man!* 73.

Stormy Crossing 48. Kind Hearts and Coronets 49. This Sporting Life 63. The Rise and Rise of Michael Rimmer 70. *Dad's Army* 71. *The Ruling Class* 71. Theatre of Blood 73. O *Lucky Man* 73. *No Sex Please, We're British* 73. The Bawdy Adventures of Tom Jones 76. The Lady Vanishes 79. Britannia Hospital 82, etc.

TV series: Turn Out the Light 67. *Dad's Army* 68–77. Doctor at Large 71. Potter 79–80. Bless Me Father 78–81. A. J. Wentworth, BA 82.

Lowe, Chad (1968–).
American actor, the brother of Rob Lowe.
Silence of the Heart 84. Apprentice to Murder 88. True Blood 89. Nobody's Perfect 90. An Inconvenient Woman (TV) 91. Highway to Hell 92. Siringo 94. In the Presence of Mine Enemies (TV) 97, etc.

Lowe, Edmund (1890–1971).
Suave American leading man of the 20s and 30s who did not manage to age into a character actor.
The Spreading Dawn 17. The Devil 20. Peacock Alley 21. The Silent Command 23. The Fool 25. *What Price Glory?* 26. Is Zat So? 27. Dressed to Kill 28. In Old Arizona 29. The Cockeyed World 29. Scotland Yard 30. Transatlantic 31. *Chandu the Magician* 32. *Dinner at Eight* 33. Gift of Gab 34. Mr Dynamite 35. The Great Impersonation 35. Seven Sinners (GB) 36. The Squeaker (GB) 37. Secrets of a Nurse 38. Our Neighbours the Carters 39. Wolf of New York 40. Call out the Marines 41. Murder in Times Square 43. Dillinger 45. Good Sam 48. Around the World in Eighty Days 56. The Wings of Eagles 57. Heller in Pink Tights 60, etc.
TV series: *Front Page Detective* 52.

Lowe, Rob (1964–).
American leading actor, born in Charlottesville, Virginia, and raised in Dayton, Ohio. A child model, he began acting in his teens, reaching starring roles in the 80s. His career came momentarily unstuck in the late 80s, when a videotape of his sexual exploits was made public and caused a minor scandal. He is the brother of actor Chad LOWE.
The Outsiders 83. Class 83. Oxford Blues 84. The Hotel New Hampshire 84. St Elmo's Fire 85. Youngblood 85. About Last Night 86. Square Dance 86. Masquerade 88. Illegally Yours 88. Bad Influence 90. Desert Shield 91. Stroke of Midnight 91. The Dark Backward 91. Wayne's World 92. The Finest Hour 92. Suddenly Last Summer (TV) 93. The Stand (TV) 94. Eye of the Storm 95. Midnight Man (TV) 95. On Dangerous Ground (TV) 95. First Degree 95. Tommy Boy 95. Mulholland Falls (uncredited) 96. For Hire 97. Living in Peril 97. Contact 97. Hostile Intent 97. Atomic Train (TV) 98. Outrage (TV) 98. One Hell of a Guy 98, etc.
TV series: A New Kind of Family 79–80.

Löwensohn, Elina.
Romanian-born actress in America.
Schindler's List 93. Amateur 94. Nadja 95. Basquiat 96. I'm Not Rappaport 96. Six Ways to Sunday 98. The Wisdom of Crocodiles 98. Sombre (Fr.) 98, etc.

Lowenstein, Richard (1960–).
Australian director and writer, also a director of rock videos.
Strikebound 84. White City 85. Dogs in Space 86. Say a Little Prayer 93.

Lowery, Robert (1916–1971) (R. L. Hanks).
American leading man of the 40s, mainly in routine films.
Wake Up and Live 37. Young Mr Lincoln 39. Lure of the Islands 42. A Scream in the Dark 44. Prison Ship 45. The Mummy's Ghost 46. Death Valley 48. Batman and Robin (serial) (as Batman) 50. Crosswinds 51. Cow Country 53. The Rise and Fall of Legs Diamond 60. Johnny Reno 66, many others.
TV series: Circus Boy 56–57.

Lowry, Malcolm (1905–1957).
English novelist of works based on his own life, which was characterized by heavy drinking and travelling. His second wife was American actress Margerie BONNER. His masterpiece, *Under the Volcano*, in which the central character of the alcoholic ex-British consul is a self-portrait, was filmed by John Huston with Albert Finney in the role.
Biography: 1973, *Malcolm Lowry* by Douglas Day; 1993, *Pursued by Furies: A Life of Malcolm Lowry* by Gordon Bowker.

Lowry, Morton (1908–1987).
British character actor in Hollywood.
The Dawn Patrol 38. The Hound of the Baskervilles 39. Tarzan Finds a Son! 39. Hudson's Bay 40. Charley's Aunt/Charley's American Aunt 41. How Green Was My Valley 41. This Above All 42. The Loves of Edgar Allan Poe 42. Immortal Sergeant 43. No Time for Love 43. The Man in Half Moon Street 44. Pursuit to Algiers 45. The Picture of Dorian Gray 45. The Verdict 46. Calcutta 47. Too Hot to Handle 59, etc.

Loy, Myrna (1905–1993) (Myrna Williams).
Likeable American leading lady of the 30s; began her career in villainous oriental roles but later showed a great flair for sophisticated comedy and warm domestic drama. She was awarded an Oscar for lifetime achievements in 1991.
Autobiography: 1987, *Myrna Loy: Being and Becoming*.
SELECTED SILENT FILMS: The Cave Man 26. Don Juan 26. The Climbers 27. Beware of Married Men 28. State Street Sadie 28. The Midnight Taxi 28. Noah's Ark 29, etc.
■ SOUND FILMS: The Jazz Singer 27. The Desert Song 29. The Squall 29. Black Watch 29. Hard Boiled Rose 29. Evidence 29. Show of Shows 29. The Great Divide 30. The Jazz Cinderella 30. Cameo Kirby 30. Isle of Escape 30. Under a Texas Moon 30. Cock of the Walk 30. Bride of the Regiment 30. Last of the Duanes 30. The Truth about Youth 30. Renegades 30. Rogue of the Rio Grande 30. The Devil to Pay 30. The Naughty Flirt 31. Body and Soul 31. A Connecticut Yankee 31. Hush Money 31. Transatlantic 31. Rebound 31. Skyline 31. Consolation Marriage 31. Arrowsmith 31. Emma 32. The Wet Parade 32. Vanity Fair 32. The Woman in Room 13 32. New Morals for Old 32. *Love Me Tonight* 32. Thirteen Women 32. *The Mask of Fu Manchu* 32. The Animal Kingdom 32. Topaze 33. The Barbarian 33. The Prizefighter and the Lady 33. *When Ladies Meet* 33. Penthouse 33. Night Flight 33. Men in White 34. Manhattan Melodrama 34. *The Thin Man* 34. Stamboul Quest 34. Evelyn Prentice 34. *Broadway Bill* 34. Wings in the Dark 35. Whipsaw 35. Wife versus Secretary 36. Petticoat Fever 36. The Great Ziegfeld 36. To Mary with Love 36. Libeled Lady 36. After the Thin Man 36. Parnell 37. *Double Wedding* 37. Man Proof 38. Test Pilot 38. Too Hot to Handle 38. Lucky Night 39. *The Rains Came* 39. Third Finger Left Hand 39. Another Thin Man 39. I Love You Again 40. Love Crazy 41. Shadow of the Thin Man 41. The Thin Man Goes Home 44. So Goes My Love 46. *The Best Years of Our Lives* 46. *The Bachelor and the Bobby Soxer* 47. Song of the Thin Man 47. *Mr Blandings Builds His Dream House* 48. The Red Pony 49. That Dangerous Age 49. *Cheaper by the Dozen* 50. Belles on Their Toes 52. The Ambassador's Daughter 56. Lonelyhearts 58. From the Terrace 60. Midnight Lace 60. The April Fools 69. Death Takes a Holiday (TV) 70. Do Not Fold Spindle or Mutilate (TV) 71. The Couple Takes a Wife (TV) 72. Indict and Convict (TV) 73. The Elevator (TV) 73. Airport 75 74. It Happened at Lakewood Manor (TV) 77. The End 79. Just Tell Me What You Want 80. Summer Solstice (TV) 81.
Gag appearance: The Senator Was Indiscreet 49.
✪ For the wit and elegance with which she lived up to her 30s title of 'Queen of Hollywood'. *The Thin Man*.

Loy, Nanni (1925–1995).
Italian director of the neo-realist school, a former assistant to Luigi ZAMPA.
Parola di Ladra 56. The Four Days of Naples (AAN) 62. Made in Italy 65. Head of the Family 67. Why 71. Insieme 79. Café Express 80. Where's Picone?/Mi Manda Picone 84. Amici Miei III 85. Gioco di Società 88. Scugnizzi 89. Pacco, Doppio Pacc e Contropaccotto 93, etc.

Lualdi, Antonella (1931–) (Antoinetta de Pasquale).
Italian leading lady of the 50s and 60s.
Three Forbidden Stories 52. Le Rouge et le Noir 54. Wild Love 55. Young Girls Beware 57. Run with the Devil 60. The Mongols 61. My Son the Hero 62. Let's Talk about Women 64. How to Seduce a Playboy 66. Vincent Francois Paul and the Others 75. Cross Shot/La Legge Violenta della Squadra Anticrimine 76. Una Spina nel Cuore 86. Diritto di Vivere 89, etc.

Lubezki, Emmanuel.
Mexican cinematographer.
The Long Road to Tijuana/El Camino Larga a Tijuana 89. Bandits/Bandidos 91. Like Water for Chocolate/Como Agua para Chocolate 92. Miroslava 92. Twenty Bucks (US) 93. Reality Bites (US) 94. Ambar 94. A Little Princess (AAN) 95. A Walk in the Clouds (US) 95. The Birdcage (US) 96. Meet Joe Black 98. Great Expectations 98, etc.

Lubin, Arthur (1899–1995).
American director from 1934, mainly of light comedy, and with a penchant for eccentric animals.
■ A Successful Failure 34. The Great God Gold 35. Honeymoon Limited 35. Two Sinners 35. Frisco Waterfront 35. The House of a Thousand Candles 36. Yellowstone 37. Mysterious Crossing 37. *California Straight Ahead* 37. I Cover the War 37. Idol of the Crowds 37. Adventure's End 37. Midnight Intruder 38. Beloved Brat 38. Prison Break 38. Secrets of a Nurse 38. Risky Business 38. Big Town Czar 39. Mickey the Kid 39. Called a Messenger 39. The Big Guy 40. *Black Friday* 40. Gangs of Chicago 40. I'm Nobody's Sweetheart Now 40. Meet the Wildcat 40. Who Killed Aunt Maggie? 40. San Francisco Docks 41. Where Did You Get That Girl? 41. *Buck Privates* 41. In the Navy 41. Hold That Ghost 41. Keep 'Em Flying 41. Ride 'Em Cowboy 42. Eagle Squadron 42. White Savage 43. *Phantom of the Opera* 43. Ali Baba and the Forty Thieves 44. Delightfully Dangerous 45. Spider Woman Strikes Back 46. A Night in Paradise 46. New Orleans 47. Impact 49. *Francis* 50. Queen for a Day 51. Francis Goes to the Races 51. *Rhubarb* 51. Francis Goes to West Point 52. It Grows on Trees 52. South Sea Woman 53, Francis Covers Big Town 53. Francis Joins the WACs 54. Francis in the Navy 55. Footsteps in the Fog 55. Lady Godiva 55. Star of India 56. The First Travelling Saleslady 56. Escapade in Japan 57. Thief of Baghdad 61. The Incredible Mr Limpet 64. Hold On 66. Rain for a Dusty Summer 71.
TV series: *Mister Ed* 60–65.

Lubitsch, Ernst (1892–1947).
German director, once a comic actor, in a series of silent farces starring him as 'Meyer'. After a variety of subjects he settled for a kind of sophisticated sex comedy that became unmistakably his: the 'Lubitsch touch' was a form of visual innuendo, spicy without ever being vulgar. His greatest period came after 1922, when he settled in Hollywood and became Paramount's leading producer. Early films include many shorts. Awarded special Oscar 1946 'for his distinguished contributions to the art of the motion picture'.
Biographies: 1968, *The Lubitsch Touch* by Herman G. Weinberg. 1994, *Ernst Lubitsch, Laughter in Paradise* by Scott Eyman.
SELECTED EUROPEAN FILMS: Carmen 18. Madame du Barry 19. Sumurun 20. Anne Boleyn 20. Pharaoh's Wife 21. The Flame 21, etc.
■ AMERICAN FILMS: Rosita 23. *The Marriage Circle* 24. Three Women 24. *Forbidden Paradise* 24. Kiss Me Again 25. Lady Windermere's Fan 25. So This Is Paris 26. The Student Prince 27. The Patriot (AAN) 28. Eternal Love 29. *The Love Parade* (first sound film) (AAN) 29. Paramount on Parade (Chevalier sequences) 30. Monte Carlo 30. The Smiling Lieutenant 31. The Man I Killed 32. *One Hour With You* 32. *Trouble in Paradise* 32. If I Had a Million (Laughton sequence) 32. Design for Living 33. The Merry Widow 34. *Desire* (p only) 36. Angel 37. Bluebeard's Eighth Wife 38. *Ninotchka* 39. *The Shop Around the Corner* 40. That Uncertain Feeling 41. *To Be or Not To Be* 42. *Heaven Can Wait* (AAN) 43. A Royal Scandal (p only) 45. Cluny Brown 46. That Lady in Ermine (finished by Otto Preminger) 48.
✪ For extending the period of elegant comedy which is now a part of history. *Trouble in Paradise*.
❝ It's the Lubitsch touch that means so much,
piped the posters.
He was the only director in Hollywood who had his own signature,
said S. N. Behrman. These were two ways of saying that Lubitsch was a master of cinematic innuendo.
I let the audience use their imaginations. Can I help it if they misconstrue my suggestions?
he asked archly. In fact he delighted in naughtiness, and carried it off with great delicacy, though he admitted his lapses:
I sometimes make pictures which are not up to my standard, but then it can only be said of a mediocrity that all his work is up to his standard.
And he gave in finally to the American way:
I've been to Paris France and I've been to Paris Paramount. Paris Paramount is better.
Some people, Mary Pickford for instance, failed to perceive his talents:
I parted company with him as soon as I could. I thought him a very uninspired director. He was a director of doors.
According to Andrew Sarris (1968):
He was the last of the genuine Continentals let loose on the American continent, and we shall never see his like again because the world he celebrated had died – even before he did – everywhere except in his own memory.

Lucan, Arthur (1887–1954) (Arthur Towle).
British music-hall comedian famous for his impersonation of Old Mother Riley, a comic Irish washerwoman. Made fourteen films featuring her, usually with his wife Kitty McShane (1898–1964) playing his daughter.
■ Stars on Parade 35. Kathleen Mavourneen 36. Old Mother Riley 37. Old Mother Riley in Paris 38. Old Mother Riley MP 39. Old Mother Riley Joins Up 39. Old Mother Riley in Business 40. Old Mother Riley's Ghosts 41. Old Mother Riley's Circus 41. Old Mother Riley Detective 43. Old Mother Riley Overseas 44. Old Mother Riley at Home 45. Old Mother Riley's New Venture 49. Old Mother Riley Headmistress 50. Old Mother Riley's Jungle Treasure 51. Mother Riley Meets the Vampire 52.

Lucas, George (1944–).
American director and producer, one of the most commercially successful of contemporary film-makers. He also established Industrial Light and Magic, specializing in special effects, and, through his company Lucasfilm, is involved in the development of computer games software and interactive entertainment.
Biography: 1983, *Skywalking: The Life and Films of George Lucas* by Dale Pollock.
THX 1138 (wd, ed) 73. *American Graffiti* (wd, p) (AAN) 73. *Star Wars* (wd) (AAN) 77. More American Graffiti (p) 79. The Empire Strikes Back (w, p) 80. Raiders of the Lost Ark (p, story) 81. Return of the Jedi (w, p) 83. Twice upon a Time (p) 83. Indiana Jones and the Temple of Doom (p, story) 84. Mishima: A Life in Four Chapters (p) 85. Captain Eo (p) 86. Howard the Duck (p) 86. Labyrinth (p) 86. The Land before Time (p) 88. Powaqqatsi (p) 88. Tucker: The Man and His Dream (p) 88. Willow (p, story) 88. Indiana Jones and the Last Crusade (p, story) 89. Radioland Murders (p, story) 94. Star Wars: The Phantom Menace (p, wd) 99, etc.
❝ He reminded me a little of Walt Disney's version of a mad scientist. – *Steven Spielberg*
It's not what you say, or what people think of you, it's what you do that counts. – *G.L.*
Making movies is like the construction business. You are fighting all possible odds and everyone is seemingly against you. – *G.L.*

Lucas, Leighton. (1903–1982).
British composer and musical director; former ballet dancer.
Target for Tonight 41. Portrait of Clare 50. Stage Fright 50. Talk of a Million 51. The Third Visitor 51. The Weak and the Wicked 53. The Dam Busters 55. Yangtse Incident 56. A King in New York 57. Ice Cold in Alex 58. Son of Robin Hood 58. Serious Charge 59. The Millionairess 61, etc.

Lucas, Wilfred (1871–1940).
Canadian character actor in Hollywood, best remembered as a foil for Laurel and Hardy.
The Barbarian 08. The Spanish Gypsy 11. Cohen's Outing 13. Acquitted 16. The Westerners 18. The Barnstormer 22. The Fatal Mistake 24. Her Sacrifice 26. Just Imagine 30. *Pardon Us* 31. Fra Diavolo 33. The Count of Monte Cristo 34. Modern Times 36. The Baroness and the Butler 38. Zenobia 39. A Chump at Oxford 40. The Sea Wolf 41, many others.

Lucas, William (1926–).
British leading man of stage, TV and occasional films.
Timeslip 55. X the Unknown 56. Breakout 59. Sons and Lovers 60. The Devil's Daffodil 61. Calculated Risk 63. Night of the Big Heat/Isle of the Burning Doomed 67. Scramble 70. Tower of Evil 72. Operation Daybreak 75. The Plague Dogs (voice) 82, etc.
TV series: Eldorado 92–93.

Luchaire, Corinne (1921–1950).
French actress who was a big hit in *Prison Without Bars* 38. After World War II was convicted as a collaborator and died in poverty.

Luchini, Fabrice (1948–).
French leading actor of stage and screen. Born in Paris, he began as a hairdresser at the age of 14, a trade to which he had to return in the late 70s when he could not find work.
Don't Be Blue/Tout Peut Arriver 69. Claire's Knee/Le Genou de Claire 70. Immoral Tales/ Contes Immoraux 74. Violette Nozière 77. Perceval le Gallois 78. The Aviator's Wife/La Femme de l'Aviateur 80. Full Moon in Paris 84. Emmanuelle 4 84. 4 Aventures de Reinette et Mirabelle 86. Hotel du Paradis 86. The Colour of the Wind/La Couleur du Vent 88. Uranus 90. Casanova's Return/Le Retour de Casanova 92. Toxic Affair 93. Le Colonel Chabert 94. Beaumarchais 96. Un Air Si Pur 97. Le Bossu 97, etc.

Luckinbill, Laurence (1934–).
American leading man.
The Boys in the Band 70. Such Good Friends 71. The Delphi Bureau (TV) 72 (and short series). Death Sentence (TV) 74. Panic on the 5.22 (TV) 74. Winner Take All (TV) 75. The Lindbergh Kidnapping Case (TV) 76. Ike (TV) 79. The Promise (TV) 80. Messenger of Death 88. Star Trek V: The Final Frontier 89, etc.

Lucking, Bill.
Sturdy American supporting actor.
Hell's Babies 69. Wild Rovers 71. Oklahoma Crude 73. The Return of a Man Called Horse 76. Power (TV) 79. Coast to Coast 80. The Mountain Men 80. Stripes 81. Rescue Me 93. Extreme Justice 93. The River Wild 94. Sleepstalker 95. The Trigger Effect 96, etc.
TV series: Big Hawaii 77. Shannon 81–82. The Blue and the Grey 82. The A-Team 83–84. Jessie 84.

Ludlow, Patrick (1903–1996).
Elegant English actor, on stage as a child from 1915 and still acting in the late 80s.
Autobiography: *Bloody Ludlow*.
Afraid of Love 25. Love on the Spot 32. Bitter Sweet 33. The Private Life of Henry VIII 33. Evergreen 34. Jury's Evidence 36. Old Mother Riley 37. Old Mother Riley MP 39. Goodbye Mr Chips 39. We'll Smile Again 42. The Great St Trinian's Train Robbery 66. Modesty Blaise 66, etc.

Ludwig, Edward (1899–1982).
American director, from 1932.
They Just Had To Get Married 33. Friends of Mr Sweeney 34. *The Man Who Reclaimed His Head* 34. Age of Indiscretion 36. That Certain Age 38. The Last Gangster 39. The Swiss Family Robinson 40. The Man Who Lost Himself 41. They Came to Blow Up America 43. The Fighting Seabees 44. Three's a Family 45. The Fabulous Texan 47. *Wake of the Red Witch* 48. Smuggler's Island 51. Big Jim McLain 52. Sangaree 53. Flame of the Islands 56. The Black Scorpion 57. The Gun Hawk 63, etc.

Ludwig, William (1912–).
American writer.
The *Hardy Family* films 38–44. Challenge to Lassie 49. Shadow on the Wall 50. The Great Caruso 51. *Interrupted Melody* (AA) 55. Back Street 61, etc.

Lugosi, Bela (1882–1956) (Bela Ferenc Blasko; known professionally for a time as Ariztid Olt).
Hungarian stage actor of chilling presence and voice; became famous in films as Dracula, but his accent was a handicap for normal roles and he became typecast in inferior horror films. He was played by Martin Landau in the 1994 biopic *Ed Wood*.
Biographies: 1974, *The Count* by Arthur Lennig; 1976, *Lugosi, the Man behind the Cape* by Robert Cremer; 1997, *Lugosi* by Barry Don Rhodes.
The Silent Command 23. The Rejected Woman 24. The Thirteenth Chair 29. Renegades 30. Oh For a Man 30. *Dracula* 30. Broad Minded 31. The Black Camel 31. *The Murders in the Rue Morgue* 31. *White Zombie* 32. *Chandu the Magician* 32. Island of Lost Souls 33. The Death Kiss 33. *The Black Cat* 34. Mysterious Mr Wong 35. The Mystery of the Marie Celeste (GB) 35. Mark of the Vampire 35. The Raven 35. The Invisible Ray 35. Postal Inspector 36. Dark Eyes of London (GB) 38. The Phantom Creeps 39. *Son of Frankenstein* (as Igor) 39. The Saint's Double Trouble 40. Black Friday 40. The Wolf Man 41. Spooks Run Wild 41. Night Monster 42. The Ghost of Frankenstein 42. The Ape Man 43. Frankenstein Meets the Wolf Man (as the monster) 43. The Return of the Vampire 43. One Body Too Many 44. Zombies on Broadway 45. The Body Snatcher 45. Scared to Death 47. *Abbott and Costello Meet Frankenstein* (as Dracula) 48. Bela Lugosi Meets a Brooklyn Gorilla 52. Mother Riley Meets the Vampire (GB) 52. Bride of the Monster 56. Plan 9 from Outer Space 56, etc.
✪ For bringing a touch of European mystery to a succession of rudimentary melodramas. *Son of Frankenstein*.
❝ For some people he was the embodiment of all mysterious forces, a harbinger of evil from the world of shadow. For others he was merely a ham actor appearing in a type of film unsuitable for children and often unfit for adults. – *Arthur Lennig*
Famous line (*Dracula*): 'Listen to them – children of the night! What music they make!'

Luhrmann, Baz (1962–).
Australian director, a former actor, from the theatre.
Winter of Our Dreams (a) 81. Southern Cross (a) 82. Kids of the Cross (d) (TV) 92. *Strictly Ballroom* (d) 92. Romeo and Juliet (d) 96.

Lukas, Paul (1887–1971) (Pal Lukacs).
Suave Hungarian leading actor, in Hollywood from the late 20s, first as a romantic figure, then as a smooth villain, finally as a kindly old man.
Two Lovers 28. Three Sinners 28. Manhattan Cocktail 28. Half Way to Heaven 29. Slightly Scarlet 30. The Benson Murder Case 30. Slightly Dishonorable 31. City Streets 31. Thunder Below 32. Rockabye 32. The Kiss Before the Mirror 33. The Secret of the Blue Room 33. *Little Women* 33. By Candlelight 33. Affairs of a Gentleman 34. I Give My Love 34. The Fountain 34. The Casino Murder Case 34. The Three Musketeers 35. I Found Stella Parish 35. *Dodsworth* 36. Dinner at the Ritz (GB) 37. *The Lady Vanishes* (GB) 38. The Chinese Bungalow (GB) 38. *Confessions of a Nazi Spy* 39. Strange Cargo 40. The Ghost Breakers 40. They Dare Not Love 41. Lady in Distress 42. *Watch on the Rhine* (AA) 43. Hostages 43. Uncertain Glory 44. *Address Unknown* 44. *Experiment Perilous* 44. Deadline at Dawn 46. Berlin Express 48. Kim 50. 20,000 Leagues Under the Sea 54. Roots of Heaven 58. Tender is the Night 61. 55 Days at Peking 63. Lord Jim 65. Sol Madrid 68, etc.
✪ For being such a gentleman. *The Lady Vanishes*.

Luke, Keye (1904–1991).
Chinese-American actor who was popular in the 30s as Charlie Chan's number-two son.
Charlie Chan in Paris 34. Oil for the Lamps of China 35. King of Burlesque 36. Charlie Chan at the Opera 36. Charlie Chan on Broadway 37. International Settlement 38. Mr Moto's Gamble 38. Disputed Passage 39. Bowery Blitzkrieg 41. Invisible Agent 42. Salute to the Marines 43. Three Men in White 44. First Yank into Tokyo 45. Sleep My Love 47. Hell's Half Acre 54. Battle Hell 57. Yangtse Incident (GB) 57. Nobody's Perfect 67. The Chairman (GB) 69. The Amsterdam Kill 78. Gremlins 84. A Fine Mess 86, many others.
TV series: Kentucky Jones 64–65. *Anna and the King* 72. *Kung Fu* 72–74. Harry-O 76. Sidekicks 86–87.

Lulli, Folco (1912–1970).
Italian character actor.
The Bandit 47. Caccia Tragica 48. Without Pity 49. Flight into France 49. No Peace Under the Olives 50. Infidelity 52. *The Wages of Fear* 54. An Eye for an Eye 60. Lafayette 63. Marco the Magnificent 66, many others.

Lulu (1948–) (Marie Lawrie).
British pop singer.
■ Gonks Go Beat 65. To Sir With Love 68. The Cherry Picker 72.

Lum and Abner Chester Lauck (1902–1980) and Norris Goff (1906–1978).
American comedy actors of hillbilly characters.
Dreaming Out Loud 40. Bashful Bachelors 42, etc.

Lumet, Sidney (1924–).
American director, former child actor and TV producer.
Autobiography: 1995, *Making Movies*.
Twelve Angry Men (AAN) 57. Stage Struck 58. That Kind of Woman 59. The Fugitive Kind 60. A View from the Bridge 61. Long Day's Journey into Night 62. *Fail Safe* 64. *The Pawnbroker* 65. *The Hill* 65. *The Group* 65. The Deadly Affair 66. Bye Bye Braverman 68. The Seagull 68. The Appointment 69. Blood Kin 69. The Anderson Tapes 71. The Offence 72. Child's Play 72. Lovin' Molly 73. Serpico 74. Murder on the Orient Express 74. *Dog Day Afternoon* (AAN) 76. *Network* (AAN) 76. Equus 77. The Wiz 78. Just Tell Me What You Want 80. Prince of the City (AAN) 81. Deathtrap 82. The Verdict (AAN) 82. Daniel 83. Garbo Talks 84. Power 85. The Morning After 86. Running on Empty 88. Family Business 89. Q & A (& w) 90. A Stranger among Us 92. Close to Eden 92. Guilty as Sin 93. Night Falls on Manhattan (& w) 97. Critical Care 97, etc.
❝ He's the only guy who could double park in front of a whorehouse. He's that fast. – *Paul Newman*
Those who would be led, Lumet will guide. Those who would lead, Lumet will follow – *Andrew Sarris, 1968*

Lumière, Louis (1864–1948).
Pioneer French cinematographer, with brother Auguste Lumière (1862–1954). Gave first public demonstration 1895, including *Arrival of Train at Station* and other simple events; later made short comedies.

Lumley, Joanna (1946–).
British leading lady, a former model. She was formerly married to actor and scriptwriter Jeremy Lloyd.
Autobiography: 1989, *Stare Back and Smile*.
Some Girls Do 68. On Her Majesty's Secret Service 69. Tam Lin 70. The Breaking of Bumbo 70. Games That Lovers Play 70. Satanic Rites of Dracula 73. Don't Just Lie There, Say Something 73. Trail of the Pink Panther 82. Curse of the Pink Panther 83. Mistral's Daughter (TV) 84. Shirley Valentine 89. Innocent Lies 95. James and the Giant Peach 96. Parting Shots 98. A Rather English Marriage 98, etc.
TV series: *The New Avengers* 76–77. Sapphire and Steel 79. Absolutely Fabulous 92–94. Class Act 94–95.
❝ Playing a mindless lovely is depressing when you don't (in your opinion) look lovely at all. – *J.L.*

Lummis, Dayton (1903–1988).
American character actor of stage and radio, latterly in films.
Les Misérables 52. Ruby Gentry 53. The Court Martial of Billy Mitchell 55. The Cobweb 56, etc.

Luna, Barbara (1937–).
American actress who usually plays beautiful foreigners. Formerly married to actor Doug McClure.
The Devil at Four O'Clock 60. Five Weeks in a Balloon 62. Synanon 64. Ship of Fools 65. Firecreek 67. Che! 69. The Gatling Gun 73. Woman in the Rain 76. Brenda Starr (TV) 76. Pleasure Cove (TV) 79. The Concrete Jungle 82, etc.

Luna, Bigas:
see Bigas Luna.

Lund, John (1911–1992).
American leading man with Broadway experience; film roles mainly stodgy.
To Each His Own 46. The Perils of Pauline 47. A Foreign Affair 47. Night Has a Thousand Eyes 48. Miss Tatlock's Millions 48. My Friend Irma 49. Duchess of Idaho 50. Darling, How Could You? 51. Steel Town 52. Bronco Buster 52. The Woman They Almost Lynched 53. Chief Crazy Horse 54. White Feather 55. Battle Stations 56. High Society 56. Affair in Reno 57. The Wackiest Ship in the Army 60. If a Man Answers 62, etc.

Lundgren, Dolph (1959–).
Muscular Swedish leading man and karate expert in action films. He has a master's degree in chemical engineering.
A View to a Kill 85. Rocky IV 85. Masters of the Universe 87. The Punisher 89. Red Scorpion 89. Dark Angel/I Come in Peace 90. Cover Up 90. Universal Soldier 92. Pentathlon 94. Johnny Mnemonic 95. Meltdown 95. The Shooter 95. Silent Trigger 96. The Peacekeeper 97. Blackjack (TV) 98, etc.
❝ My problem is that people get intimidated by someone big and beautiful like me. They hate to think I can be smart as well. – *D.L.*

Lundgren, P. A. (1911–).
Swedish art director, a former commercial artist, associated with the films of Ingmar Bergman.
It Rains on Our Love 46. Summer with Monika 52. Smiles of a Summer Night 55. The Seventh Seal 57. The Face/The Magician 58. The Virgin Spring 60. Winter Light 63. The Silence 63. The Island 66. My Sister, My Love 66. The Emigrants 71. The Night Visitor 71. The Touch 71. Around the World with Fanny Hill 74. What Are You Doing after the Orgy? 77, etc.

Lundigan, William (1914–1975).
American leading man of routine features, formerly in radio.
Three Smart Girls Grow Up 38. The Old Maid 39. The Sea Hawk 40. Sunday Punch 42. What Next, Corporal Hargrove? 45. Pinky 49. *I'd Climb the Highest Mountain* 51. Down among the Sheltering Palms 52. *Inferno* 53. Serpent of the Nile 53. The White Orchid 54. The Underwater City 61. The Way West 67. Where Angels Go Trouble Follows 68, etc.
TV series: *Men into Space* 59.

Lunghi, Cherie (1953–).
Anglo-Italian leading lady. She has a daughter by director Roland Joffe.
Excalibur 81. Oliver Twist (TV) 82. Praying Mantis (TV) 82. King David 85. Parker 85. The Mission 85. Harem (TV) 86. To Kill a Priest 89. A Question of Guilt (TV) 93. Silent Cries (TV) 93. Mary Shelley's Frankenstein 94. Jack & Sarah 95. Hornblower (TV) 98, etc.
TV series: The Manageress 90–91. Covington Cross 92.

Lunt, Alfred (1892–1977).
Distinguished American stage actor, husband of Lynn Fontanne.
■ Backbone 23. The Ragged Edge 23. Second Youth 24. Lovers in Quarantine 25. Sally of the Sawdust 26. *The Guardsman* (AAN) 31. Stage Door Canteen 43.

Lupino, Ida (1914–1995).
British leading lady, daughter of Stanley Lupino, who went to Hollywood and played a variety of mainly fraught roles; later became a director. Married actor Louis Hayward (1938–45), producer Collier Young (1948–52), and actor Howard Duff (1952–84).
■ As actress: Her First Affaire 33. Money for Speed 33. High Finance 33. The Ghost Camera 33. I Lived with You 34. Prince of Arcadia 34. Search for Beauty 34. Come on Marines 34. Ready for Love 34. Paris in Spring 35. Smart Girl 35. Peter Ibbetson 35. Anything Goes 36. One Rainy Afternoon 36. Yours for the Asking 36. The Gay Desperado 36. Sea Devils 37. Let's Get Married 37. Artists and Models 37. Fight for your Lady 37. The Lone Wolf Spy Hunt 39. The Lady and the Mob 39. The Adventures of Sherlock Holmes 39. The Light That Failed 40. *They Drive by Night* 40. *High Sierra* 41. The Sea Wolf 41. Out of the Fog 41. *Ladies in Retirement* 41. Moontide 42. *The Hard Way* 42. Life Begins at 8.30 42. Forever and a Day 43. Thank your Lucky Stars 43. In Our Time 44. Hollywood Canteen 44. Pillow to Post 45. *Devotion* (as Emily Brontë) 46. The Man I Love 47. Deep Valley 47. Escape Me Never 47. *Roadhouse* 48. Lust for Gold 49. Woman in Hiding 50. On Dangerous Ground 51. Beware My Lovely 52. Jennifer 53. The Bigamist 53. Private Hell 36 54. Women's Prison 55. The Big Knife 55. While the City Sleeps 56. Strange Intruder 56. I Love a Mystery (TV) 67. Backtrack (TV) 69. Deadhead Miles 70. Women in Chains (TV) 71. Female Artillery (TV) 72. Junior Bonner 72. The Letters (TV) 72. The Strangers in 7A (TV) 73. The Devil's Rain 75. The Food of the Gods 76. My Boys Are Good Boys 78. Deadhead Miles 82.
TV series: *Mr Adams and Eve* 56.
As director: Not Wanted (wp only) 49. Outrage (& w) 50. Never Fear 51. Hard, Fast and Beautiful 51. The Hitch Hiker (& w) 53. The Bigamist 53. Private Hell 36 (w only) 54. The Trouble with Angels 66, plus many TV episodes.
❝ Her familiar expression of strained intensity would be less quickly relieved by a merciful death

than by Ex-Lax. – *James Agee on Ida Lupino's performance in The Hard Way*

Lupino, Stanley (1893–1942).
British comedian on stage from 1900, especially in musical comedy.
Autobiography: 1934, *From the Stocks to the Stars*.
■ Love Lies 31. The Love Race 31. *Sleepless Nights* 32. King of the Ritz 33. Facing the Music 33. You Made Me Love You 33. Happy 34. Honeymoon for Three 35. Cheer Up! 36. Sporting Love 36. *Over She Goes* 37. Hold My Hand 38. Lucky To Me 39.

LuPone, Patti (1949–).
American leading actress and singer, from the musical stage.
King of the Gypsies 78. 1941 79. Fighting Back 82. Witness 85. Wise Guys 86. Driving Miss Daisy 89. Family Prayers 93. Song Spinner 95. The 24-Hour Woman 98, etc.

Lupu-Pick (1886–1931).
German director of silent days.
Die Fremde 17. Der Letzte Augenblick 18. The Wild Duck 22. Gassenhauer 24. Eine Nacht in London 28, etc.

Lurie, John (1952–).
American character actor and musician, in independent movies. He was leader and saxophonist with the jazz group The Lounge Lizards.
Permanent Vacation (& m) 80. Stranger Than Paradise 84. Paris, Texas 84. Desperately Seeking Susan 85. Down by Law (& m) 86. The Last Temptation of Christ 88. Mystery Train (m) 89. Wild at Heart 90. Until the End of the World 92. Blue in the Face (m) 95. Get Shorty (m) 95. Manny & Lo (m) 96. Excess Baggage (m) 96. New Rose Hotel (a) 98. Clay Pigeons (m) 98. Lulu on the Bridge (m) 98, etc.

Lustgarten, Edgar (1907–1979).
British journalist who introduced the *Scotland Yard* three-reelers of the 50s; also wrote many books on famous crimes and trials.

Lustig, Jan (1902–1978) (Jan Lustic, aka Jean Lustig).
Czechoslovakian screenwriter in Hollywood. Born in Brno, and educated at the University of Prague, he worked in Berlin as a journalist and critic before becoming a writer for Pathé in Paris from the early 30s to 1940, when he moved to the United States.
Sous les Yeux d'Occident (Fr.) 36. Orage (Fr.) 37. Dancing on a Dime 40. Reunion in France 42. The White Cliffs of Dover 44. Homecoming 47. That Forsyte Woman 49. The Story of Three Loves 53. Torch Song 53. Young Bess 53. The Knights of the Round Table (GB) 54. Moonfleet 55. Town without Pity 61. Situation Hopeless – But Not Serious 65, etc.

Lustig, William (1955–).
American director of horror movies.
The Violation of Claudia 77. Maniac 81. Vigilante 83. Maniac Cop 87. Hit List 89. Relentless 89. Maniac Cop 2 90. Maniac Cop 3: Badge of Silence 92. Brute Force 94, etc.

Lutic, Bernard (1943–).
French cinematographer.
The Aviator's Wife 81. The Well-Made Marriage 82. Entre Nous 83. Heat of Desire 84. Revolution 85. The Return of the Musketeers 90. Time Is Money 94. Le Colonel Chabert 94. Fric Frac 95. Between the Devil and the Deep Blue Sea 95. Hanuman 97. The Quarry 98, etc.

Lutyens, Elisabeth (1906–1983).
Distinguished English composer of serial and atonal music who also wrote film scores. Much of her feature work, often percussive in style, was for horror movies, but she also composed for documentaries and TV plays. The third daughter of Edwardian architect Sir Edwin Lutyens, she studied at the Royal College of Music and began writing for films to supplement her often meagre income from her concert works.
Autobiography: 1972, *A Goldfish Bowl*.
Biography: 1989, *A Pilgrim Soul* by Meiron and Susie Harries.
Penny and the Pownall Case 48. The Boy Kumasenu 51. The Bermuda Affair 56. The Malpas Mystery 60. Never Take Sweets from a Stranger 60. Don't Bother to Knock 61. Paranoiac 62. The Earth Dies Screaming 64. The Skull 65. Spaceflight IC-1 65. The Psychopath 66. Theatre of Death 66. The Terrornauts 67. My Nights with Susan, Olga, Albert, Julie, Piet and Sandra 75, etc.
❝ One cannot rest one's heart or companionship or a little fun on people. They die; they go; they are the least firm of anchors. – *E.L.*

Lydon, James (Jimmy) (1923–).
American actor familiar in the early 40s as gangling adolescent.
Back Door to Heaven 39. *Tom Brown's Schooldays* (title role) 40. Little Men 40. Henry Aldrich for President (and subsequent series of ten) 41. Aerial Gunner 43. The Town Went Wild 45. Life with Father 47. Bad Boy 49. September Affair 51. Island in the Sky 53. Battle Stations 56. I Passed for White 60. The Last Time I Saw Archie 61. Brainstorm 65. Death of a Gunfighter 69. Scandalous John 71. Vigilante Force 76, etc.
TV series: So This Is Hollywood 54. The First Hundred Years 56. Love That Jill 58.

Lye, Len (1901–1980).
New Zealander animator, remembered for British GPO and other shorts of the 30s. Went to US and was associated for a while with *The March of Time*.
Tusalava 29. Colour Box 34. Birth of a Robot 36. Rainbow Dance 36. Kaleidoscope 36. Trade Tattoo 37. Swinging the Lambeth Walk 39. Colour Cry 52. Rhythm 53. Free Radicals 58. Particles in Space 66, etc.

Lyel, Viola (1900–1972) (Violet Watson).
British character actress, mainly on stage in comedy roles.
Hobson's Choice (leading role) 30. Channel Crossing 32. Quiet Wedding 40. Wanted for Murder 46. No Place for Jennifer 50. Isn't Life Wonderful? 53. See How They Run 56, etc.

Lyles, A. C. (1918–).
American producer, former publicist; noted for his second-feature westerns using veteran talent.
Short Cut to Hell 57. Raymie 60. The Young and the Brave 61. Law of the Lawless 64. Stagecoach to Hell 64. Young Fury 65. Black Spurs 65. Town Tamer 65. Apache Uprising 66. Johnny Reno 66. Waco 66. Red Tomahawk 67. Buckskin 68. Night of the Lepus 72, etc.

Lymon, Frankie (1942–1968).
American rock 'n' roll singer who had a hit at the age of 13 with 'Why Do Fools Fall in Love?', featured on the soundtracks of *That'll Be the Day* 73 and *American Graffiti* 73, and who appeared in a couple of 50s movies. Drug addiction bedevilled his later career. He was played by Larenz TATE in the biopic *Why Do Fools Fall in Love* 98, directed by Gregory NAVA.
Mister Rock and Roll 57. Rock Rock Rock 57.

Lynch, Alfred (1933–).
Raw-boned British actor, often as cockney private.
■ On the Fiddle 61. Two and Two Make Six 61. West Eleven 63. 55 Days at Peking 63. The Hill 65. The Taming of the Shrew 67. The Seagull 68. The Blockhouse 73. Joseph Andrews 76. Loophole 80. Bewitched (TV) 85. The Krays 90. Until the End of the World/Bis ans Ende der Welt 91. Second Best 93.

Lynch, David (1946–).
American director, screenwriter, producer and occasional actor.
Autobiography: 1997, *Lynch on Lynch*.
Biography: 1997, *Weirdsville USA* by Paul A. Woods.
Eraserhead 78. *The Elephant Man* (AAN) 80. Dune 85. Blue Velvet (AAN) 86. Zelly and Me (a) 88. Wild at Heart (wd) 90. Twin Peaks: Fire Walk with Me (p, co-w, d) 92. Nadja (a) 94. Lost Highway (wd) 97, etc.
TV series: Twin Peaks 90.

Lynch, Jennifer Chambers (1968–).
American director and screenwriter, the daughter of director David Lynch.
Boxing Helena (wd) 93.

Lynch, John (1961–).
British actor from Ulster, mainly on the stage, who played the title role in *Cal*, his first film. He won an Australian Film Institute best actor award for *Angel Baby*.
Cal 84. 1871 90. Hardware 90. Edward II 91. The Railway Station Man 92. The Secret Garden 93. The Secret of Roan Inish 93. Words upon the Window Pane 94. *Angel Baby* 95. Nothing Personal 95. Some Mother's Son 96. Moll Flanders 96. This Is the Sea 96. Sliding Doors 98. The Quarry 98, etc.

Lynch, Kelly (1959–).
American actress; a former model.
Osa 85. Bright Lights, Big City 88. Cocktail 88. Drugstore Cowboy 89. Road House 89. Warm Summer Rain 89. Desperate Hours 90. Curly Sue 91. R.S.V.P. 92. Three of Hearts 93. Imaginary Crimes 94. White Man's Burden 95. Virtuosity 95. Heaven's Prisoners 96, etc.

Lynch, Richard (1936–).
American actor whose scarred skin and haughty mien make him a natural for evil roles.
Scarecrow 73. Steel 80. Vampire (TV) 80. The Formula 80. Alcatraz (TV) 81. The Sword and the Sorcerer 82. The Barbarians 87. Aftershock 88. Bad Dreams 88. Little Nikita 88. One Man Force 89. High Stakes 89. The Forbidden Dance 90. Trancers 2: The Return of Jack Deth 91. Double Threat 92. Necronomicon 93. Scanner Cop 94. Werewolf 95. Midnight Confessions 95. Dragon Fury 95. Cyborg 3: The Recycler 95. Warrior of Justice 96. Terminal Virus 96. The Proposition 96, etc.

Lynde, Paul (1926–1982).
American TV comedian who usually played a flustered character with a funny voice.
New Faces 54. Son of Flubber 62. Bye Bye Birdie 63. Send Me No Flowers 64. The Glass Bottom Boat 66. How Sweet It Is 68. Rabbit Test 78. The Villain 79, etc.
TV series: Stanley 56. Hey Landlord 66. The Pruitts of Southampton 66. *The Paul Lynde Show* 72. Temperatures Rising 73.

Lyndon, Barre (1896–1972) (Alfred Edgar).
British playwright, long in Hollywood as scriptwriter.
The Amazing Dr Clitterhouse (oa) 38. Sundown 41. The Lodger 44. The Man in Half Moon Street (oa) 44. The House on 92nd Street 45. Night Has a Thousand Eyes 48. The Greatest Show on Earth 51. The War of the Worlds 53. Conquest of Space 54. Sign of the Pagan 55. Omar Khayyam 57. Dark Intruder 65, etc.

Lyne, Adrian (1941–).
British director, from TV commercials; now in America.
■ Foxes 80. Flashdance 82. 9½ Weeks 86. Fatal Attraction (AAN) 87. Jacob's Ladder 90. Indecent Proposal 93. Lolita 97.

Lynen, Robert (1921–1944).
French child actor later executed by Nazis.
Poil de Carotte 32. The Little King 33. La Belle Equipe 36. Carnet de Bal 37. Education du Prince 38, etc.

Lynley, Carol (1942–) (Carole Jones).
American leading actress.
The Light in the Forest 58. Holiday for Lovers 59. *Blue Denim* 59. The Hound Dog Man 60. Return to Peyton Place 61. The Last Sunset 61. The Stripper 63. Under the Yum Yum Tree 63. The Cardinal 63. Shock Treatment 64. The Pleasure Seekers 64. *Bunny Lake Is Missing* (GB) 65. *Harlow* (TV) 66. The Shuttered Room (GB) 68. Danger Route (GB) 68. The Smugglers (TV) 68. The Maltese Bippy 69. Norwood 69. Once You Kiss a Stranger 70. Weekend of Terror (TV) 70. Crosscurrent (TV) 71. The Night Stalker (TV) 72. The Poseidon Adventure 72. Cotter 73. The Elevator (TV) 74. Death Stalk (TV) 75. Flood (TV) 76. The Four Deuces 76. Out of Control 76. Bad Georgia Road 77. Fantasy Island (TV) 77. Having Babies II (TV) 77. The Cops and Robin (TV) 78. The Beasts Are on the Streets (TV) 78. The Cat and the Canary 78. The Shape of Things to Come (TV) 79. Vigilante 83. Spirits 91. The Howling VI: The Freaks 91, etc.

Lynn, Ann (c. 1934–).
British actress, mainly on TV; granddaughter of Ralph Lynn.
Piccadilly Third Stop 60. The Wind of Change 61. Strongroom 61. Flame in the Streets 62. Black Torment 64. Four in the Morning 65. Baby Love 69, etc.

Lynn, Diana (1926–1971) (Dolores Loehr).
Pert, witty American leading lady of the 40s, former child actress and pianist.
■ They Shall Have Music 39. There's Magic in Music 41. Star Spangled Rhythm 42. *The Major and the Minor* 43. Henry Aldrich Gets Glamour 43. *The Miracle of Morgan's Creek* 44. And the Angels Sing 44. Henry Aldrich Plays Cupid 44. *Our Hearts Were Young and Gay* 44. Out of this World 45. Duffy's Tavern 45. Our Hearts Were Growing Up 46. The Bride Wore Boots 46. Easy Come Easy Go 47. Variety Girl 47. Ruthless 48. Texas Brooklyn and Heaven 48. Every Girl Should Be Married 48. My Friend Irma 49. Paid in Full 50. My Friend Irma Goes West 50. Rogues of Sherwood Forest 50. Peggy 50. Bedtime for Bonzo 51. The People against O'Hara 51. Meet Me at the Fair 52. Plunder of the Sun 53. Track of the Cat 54. An Annapolis Story 55. The Kentuckian 55. You're Never Too Young 55. Company of Killers (TV) 71.

Lynn, Emmett (1897–1958).
American character actor, from vaudeville and the stage, often as a comic sidekick in westerns. In films from 1913.
Along the Rio Grande 41. The Law Rides Again 43. Bluebeard 44. The Cisco Kid Returns 45. Stagecoach to Denver 46. Code of the West 47. Ride, Ryder, Ride 49. The Dungeon 50. Best of the Badmen 51. Monkey Business 52. Pickup on South Street 53. The Robe 53. Ring of Fear 54. A Man Called Peter 55. The Ten Commandments 56, many others.

Lynn, Jeffrey (1906–1995) (Ragnar Lind).
American leading man with varied experience, in films from 1938.
Four Daughters 38. Yes, My Darling Daughter 39. Espionage Agent 39. The Roaring Twenties 40. A Child Is Born 40. All This and Heaven Too 40. Four Mothers 40. Million Dollar Baby 41. The Body Disappears 41. Whiplash 47. Black Bart 48. A Letter to Three Wives 49. Up Front 51. Captain China 52. Come Thursday 64. Tony Rome 67, many others.
TV series: My Son Jeep 53. Star Stage 55–56.

Lynn, Jonathan (1943–).
British comedy screenwriter and director, a former actor.
The Internecine Project (w) 74. Clue (wd) 85. Nuns on the Run (wd) 90. My Cousin Vinny (d) 92. The Distinguished Gentleman (d) 92. Greedy/Greed 94. Sgt Bilko 96. Trial and Error 97, etc.
TV series: Yes, Minister (co-w) 80–87.

Lynn, Leni (1925–).
American girl singer who after debut in *Babes in Arms* 39 came to England and starred in several low-budget musicals.
Heaven Is Round the Corner 43. Give Me the Stars 44. Spring Song 46. Happy Go Lovely 51, etc.

Lynn, Loretta (1935–).
American country singer and guitarist, phenomenally successful and proud of her hillbilly background which was celebrated in the book and film *Coal Miner's Daughter*.

Lynn, Ralph (1882–1964).
Incomparable British comedy actor of the silly ass school; his monocled face, limp hands and mastery of timing were essential ingredients of several films of the Aldwych farces of the 30s.
■ *Rookery Nook* 30. Tons of Money 31. Plunder 31. Chance of a Night-Time 31. Mischief 31. A Night Like This 32. Thark 32. Just My Luck 33. Summer Lightning 33. Up to the Neck 33. Turkey Time 33. *A Cuckoo in the Nest* 33. A Cup of Kindness 34. Dirty Work 34. Fighting Stock 35. Stormy Weather 35. Foreign Affairs 35. In the Soup 36. Pot Luck 36. All In 36. For Valour 37.
✪ For personifying the Bertie Wooster tradition. *Rookery Nook*.

Lynn, Robert (1918–1982).
British director, in films from 1936 as camera assistant. Son of Ralph Lynn.
Postman's Knock 61. Dr Crippen 62. Victim Five 65. Change Partners 66. The Railway Children (p only) 71, etc.

Lynn, Sharon (1910–1963).
American leading lady of the 30s.
Sunny Side Up 29. The Big Broadcast 32. Enter Madame 34. *Way Out West* (tickling Stan Laurel) 36. West Point Widow 41, etc.

Lynn, Dame Vera (1917–).
British singing star, the 'Forces' Sweetheart' of World War II.
Autobiography: 1976, *Vocal Refrain*.
We'll Meet Again 44. One Exciting Night 45, etc.

Lyon, Barbara (1931–1995).
American actress and singer of the 50s, resident in Britain. The daughter of Bebe Daniels and Ben Lyon, she studied at RADA and starred with her parents and brother Richard in the BBC radio and, later, TV sitcom *Life with the Lyons* 50–61. She enjoyed a brief success as a singer in the mid-50s with a couple of minor hits, which led to her own TV series, *Dreamtime with Barbara* 55, and *Be My Guest* 56. Retired in the 60s; at the time of her death, she lived in an actors' rest home. Died of a cerebral haemorrhage.

Life with the Lyons 53. The Lyons in Paris 54.
∼Catchphrase: I'll die . . . I'll just die.

Lyon, Ben (1901–1979).
Amiable American leading man of the 20s and 30s; came to Britain with his wife Bebe Daniels and stayed to become popular radio personality; later became casting director for Twentieth Century-Fox.
Biography: 1976, *Bebe and Ben* by Jill Allgood.
Open Your Eyes 19. Potash and Perlmutter 23. So Big 24. Bluebeard's Seven Wives 25. The Prince of Tempters 26. Dance Magic 27. The Air Legion 28. Alias French Gertie 30. *Hell's Angels* 30. The Hot Heiress 31. Her Majesty Love 31. Hat Check Girl 32. I Cover the Waterfront 33. Crimson Romance 34. Dancing Feet 36. I Killed the Count (GB) 38. Hi Gang (GB) 40. Life with the Lyons (GB) 54, etc.

Lyon, Francis D. (1905–1996).
American director, former editor.
■ Crazylegs 53. The Bob Mathias Story 54. Cult of the Cobra 55. The Great Locomotive Chase 56. The Oklahoman 56. Bale Out at 43,000 57. Gunsight Ridge 57. South Seas Adventure (co-d) 58. Escort West 59. The Tomboy and the Champ

61. The Young and the Brave 63. Destination Inner Space 66. Castle of Evil 67. The Destructors 68. The Money Jungle 68. The Girl Who Knew Too Much 69.

Lyon, Richard (1934–).
London-born actor who began in films as a child in Hollywood. The adopted son of Bebe Daniels and Ben Lyon, his greatest success came in the 50s, appearing with his parents and sister Barbara in the radio and TV sitcom *Life with the Lyons* 50–61, and the BBC radio sitcom *The Trouble with Toby* 57.
The Howards of Virginia 42. The Unseen 45. The Green Years 46. Anna and the King of Siam 46. The Tender Years 47. The Boy with Green Hair 48. The Great Lover 49. Life with the Lyons 53. The Lyons in Paris 54. The Headless Ghost 59, etc.

Lyon, Sue (1946–).
American juvenile actress.
Lolita 62. *Night of the Iguana* 64. Seven Women 65. The Flim Flam Man 67. Tony Rome 67. Evel Knievel 72. Crash 77. End of the World 77. The

Astral Factor 78. Towing 78. Alligator 80. Invisible Strangler (made 76) 84, etc.

Lypsinka (John Epperson).
American drag artiste in occasional films.
Wigstock: The Movie 95. Witchcraft (TV) 95. Red Ribbon Blues 95.

Lys, Lya (1908–1986).
French actress, in Hollywood from the early 30s.
L'Age d'Or 30. Buster Se Marie 31. Clear All Wires (US) 33. Jimmy and Sally (US) 33. Vagabond Lady (US) 35. The Great Gambini (US) 37. Confessions of a Nazi Spy (US) 39. The Return of Dr X (US) 39. Murder in the Air (US) 40, etc.

Lytell, Bert (1888–1954).
American leading man of silent films.
To Have and to Hold 17. The Lone Wolf 17. A Message from Mars 23. Rupert of Hentzau 23. Lady Windermere's Fan 25. Steele of the Royal Mounted 27. Blood Brothers 30. The Single Sin 31. Stage Door Canteen 43, etc.

McAlpine, Donald (1934–).
Australian cinematographer, now working in Hollywood.

The Adventures of Barry Mackenzie 72. Barry Mackenzie Holds His Own 74. Don's Party 76. The Getting of Wisdom 77. My Brilliant Career 79. Breaker Morant 80. The Club 80. The Man from Snowy River 82. Tempest 82. Puberty Blue 83. Blue Skies Again 83. Moscow on the Hudson 84. King David 85. Down and Out in Beverly Hills 86. Predator 87. Orphans 87. Moving 88. Moon over Parador 88. See You in the Morning 89. Parenthood 89. Stanley and Iris 90. Career Opportunities/One Wild Night 91. The Hard Way 91. Medicine Man 92. Patriot Games 92. The Man without a Face 93. Mrs Doubtfire 93. Clear and Present Danger 94. Nine Months 95. William Shakespeare's Romeo and Juliet 96. The Edge 97. Stepmom 98, etc.

McAnally, Ray (1926–1989).
Bluff Irish character actor who was a mainstay of Dublin's Abbey Theatre. He studied for the priesthood before becoming an actor.

Shake Hands with the Devil 59. Billy Budd 62. The Looking Glass War 70. Fear Is the Key 72. Angel 82. Cal 84. Danny Boy 84. No Surrender 85. The Mission (AA) 86. The Fourth Protocol 87. Empire State 87. The Sicilian 87. White Mischief 87. A Perfect Spy (TV) 87. High Spirits 88. Taffin 88. A Very British Coup (TV) 89. My Left Foot 89. We're No Angels 89. Venus Peter 89, etc.

McAndrew, Marianne (1938–).
American leading lady.
Hello Dolly 69. The Seven Minutes 71. Bat People 74, etc.

MacArthur, Charles (1895–1956).
American playwright and screenwriter, long married to Helen Hayes; often collaborated with Ben HECHT.

Biography: 1957, *Charlie* by Ben Hecht.

The Front Page (oa, w) 31. The Unholy Garden 31. Rasputin and the Empress (AAN) 32. 20th Century 34. Crime without Passion (wd, p) 35. Barbary Coast 35. Soak the Rich (wd, p) 36. Once in a Blue Moon (wd, p) 36. Gunga Din (w) 39. Wuthering Heights (co-w, AAN) 39. His Girl Friday 40. The Senator Was Indiscreet (w) 47. Perfect Strangers (oa) 50, etc.

66 I don't think God is interested in us after puberty. He is interested only in our births, for this requires His magic. Our dying requires only His indifference. – C.M.

When asked for his philosophy of life, Charley one day replied in the words of a condemned man whose hanging he had witnessed as a reporter. The doomed fellow paused at the steps of the gallows to inquire, 'Is this thing safe?' – *Gene Fowler*

MacArthur, Douglas (1880–1964).
American general made famous by the phrase 'I shall return' when he was forced to evacuate the Philippines in 1942. Later a potential president of the US, he had been played by Gregory Peck in *MacArthur* and by Laurence Olivier in *Inchon*. Robert Barrat, who looked more like him, played him in both *They Were Expendable* and *An American Guerrilla in the Philippines*.

MacArthur, James (1937–).
American leading man, former juvenile; adopted son of Charles MacArthur and Helen Hayes.

The Young Stranger 57. The Light in the Forest 58. The Third Man on the Mountain 59. Kidnapped 60. The Swiss Family Robinson 60. The Interns 62. Spencer's Mountain 63. The Truth about Spring 65. The Bedford Incident 65. Ride

Beyond Vengeance 66. The Love-Ins 67. Hang 'Em High 68. Man on Fire 76, etc.
TV series: *Hawaii Five-O* 68–79.

Macauley, Richard.
American screenwriter.
The Roaring Twenties (co-w) 39. They Drive By Night (co-w) 40. Torrid Zone (co-w) 40. *Across the Pacific* 42. Born to Kill 47. The Good Die Young (oa) 54, etc.

McAvoy, May (1901–1984).
American leading lady of the 20s, a casualty of sound.
Hate 17. Mrs Wiggs of the Cabbage Patch 19. Sentimental Tommy 21. Clarence 22. The Enchanted Cottage 24. Ben Hur 26. The Jazz Singer 27. The Lion and the Mouse 28. The Terror 28. No Defense 29, etc.

McBain, Diane (1941–).
American leading lady of the 60s.
Ice Palace 60. Claudelle Inglish 61. A Distant Trumpet 64. Spin-Out 66. Thunder Alley 67. The Miniskirt Mob 68. The Delta Factor 70. Wicked, Wicked 73. Deathhead Virgin 74. Donner Pass – the Road to Survival (TV) 78. Flying from the Hawk 86, etc.

McBain, Ed (1926–).
American novelist, author of the *87th Precinct* crime novels. Actually a pseudonym for Evan Hunter, formerly Salvatore Lombino.
Blackboard Jungle (oa) 55. Cop Hater (oa) 57. The Pusher (oa) 59. Strangers When We Meet (w, oa) 60. Young Savages (oa) 61. High and Low/ Tengoku To Jigoku (w) 63. *The Birds* (w) 63. Mister Buddwing (oa) 65. *Last Summer* (oa) 69. Every Little Crook and Nanny (oa) 72. Fuzz (w, oa) 72. Blood Relatives (oa) 77, etc.

McBride, Donald (1894–1957).
American character comedian adept at explosive editors, dumb policemen, etc. Made debut in his stage role as the harassed hotel manager in *Room Service* 38.
The Story of Vernon and Irene Castle 39. *Here Comes Mr Jordan* 41. *Topper Returns* 41. Invisible Woman 41. They Got Me Covered 42. The Glass Key 42. Two Yanks in Trinidad 42. Abbott and Costello in Hollywood 45. Good News 48. Bowery Battalion 51. The Seven Year Itch 55, many others.

McBride, Elizabeth (1954–1997).
American costume designer. Died of cancer.
Tender Mercies 83. True Stories 86. Square Dance 86. Driving Miss Daisy (AAN) 89. Fried Green Tomatoes 91. Thelma and Louise 91. The Shawshank Redemption 94. Michael 96, etc.

McBride, Jim (1941–).
American director.
David Holzman's Diary 67. My Girlfriend's Wedding 68. Glen and Randa 71. A Hard Day for Archie 73. Breathless 83. The Big Easy 87. Great Balls of Fire 89. The Wrong Man 93. Uncovered 94. Pronto (TV) 97. The Informant 97. Dead by Midnight (TV) 97, etc.

McCabe, Patrick.
Irish novelist and screenwriter, on macabre subjects.
The Grotesque/Gentlemen Don't Eat Poets (co-w, oa) 96. Butcher Boy (w, oa) 98.

McCallister, Lon (1923–) (Herbert Alonzo McCallister Jnr).
American leading man, usually in callow roles.
Souls at Sea 37. Babes in Arms 39. *Stage Door Canteen* 43. Home in Indiana 44. Winged Victory 44. The Red House 47. The Big Cat 50. Letter from Korea 50. Combat Squad 54, etc.

McCallum, David (1933–).
Slightly built Scottish juvenile lead of the 50s and 60s; became popular on American television as Ilya Kuriakin in the *UNCLE* series. He was married to actress Jill Ireland (1957–67).
The Secret Place 56. Robbery Under Arms 57. Violent Playground 58. The Long the Short and the Tall 61. Billy Budd 62. Freud 62. *The Great Escape* 63. The Greatest Story Ever Told 65. Around the World Under the Sea 66. Three Bites of the Apple 67. Sol Madrid 68. Mosquito Squadron 69. Frankenstein, The True Story (TV) 73. Diamond Hunters 75. Dogs 76. King Solomon's Treasure 78. The Watcher in the Woods 80. The Return of the Man from UNCLE (TV) 83. Terminal Choice 85. The Wind 87. The Haunting of Morella 90. Fatal Inheritance 91. Hear My Song 91. Dirty Weekend 93. Healer 94. Mortal Challenge 97, etc.
TV series: *The Man from UNCLE* 64–67 (plus eight feature films 'amplified' from TV material for cinema release). Colditz 72. Invisible Man 75. Sapphire and Steel 79.

McCallum, John (1917–).
Australian leading man of stage and screen. Born in Brisbane, he studied at RADA and worked in England from the mid-40s to the late 50s, returning to Australia to concentrate on theatre management and the production of TV series, including *Skippy*, *The Bush Kangaroo* 67–69, *Barrier Reef* and *Boney*. Married actress Googie WITHERS.
Joe Goes Back 44. The Root of All Evil 47. The Loves of Joanna Godden 47. The Woman in Question 50. Trent's Last Case 52. Trouble in the Glen 53. Port of Escape 55. The Nickel Queen (d only) 71. Southern Cross (ex p) 82, etc.

McCallum, Neil (1929–1976).
Beefy Canadian actor in British films.
The Inspector 62. The Longest Day 62. The War Lover 63. Witchcraft 64, etc.

McCambridge, Mercedes (1918–).
Intense, unpredictable American character actress, often in cynical or hard-bitten roles. She also voiced the demon in *The Exorcist*. Her second husband was director Fletcher Markle (1950–62).
Autobiographies: 1960, *The Two of Us*. 1981, *The Quality of Mercy*.
■ All the King's Men (AA) 49. Lightning Strikes Twice 51. The Scarf 51. Inside Straight 51. Johnny Guitar 54. Giant (AAN) 56. A Farewell to Arms 57. Suddenly Last Summer 59. Cimarron 60. Angel Baby 61. 99 Women 69. The Hot Death (Ger.) 69. The Counterfeit Killer (TV) 70. Killer by Night (TV) 72. Two for the Money (TV) 72. The Girls of Huntington House (TV) 73. The President's Plane Is Missing (TV) 73. The Exorcist (voice only) 73. Who Is the Black Dahlia? (TV) 75. Thieves 77. The Sacketts (TV) 79. Airport 79 – the Concorde 79. Echoes 83.
TV series: Wire Service 56.

McCamus, Tom.
Canadian leading actor.
Norman's Awesome Experience 88. I Love a Man in Uniform 93. The Circle Game 94. First Degree (TV) 95. Long Day's Journey into Night 96. The Sweet Hereafter 97, etc.

McCann, Chuck (1938–).
American character actor, from television.
The Heart Is a Lonely Hunter 68. The Projectionist 71. Play It as It Lays 72. Silent Movie 76. Foul Play 78. C.H.O.M.P.S. 79. If Things Were Different 79. Lunch Wagon 80. National Lampoon Goes to the Movies 83. The Rosebud Beach Hotel 84. Hamburger – the Motion Picture 86. Cameron's Closet 89. That's Adequate 90. Storyville 92. Ladybugs 92, etc.

McCann, Donal (1944–).
Irish leading actor, from the stage.
The Fighting Prince of Donegal 66. Sinful Davey 68. Philadelphia, Here I Come 70. Miss Julie 72. The Mackintosh Man 73. The Hard Way 79. Angel 82. Cal 84. Mr Love 85. Out of Africa 85. The Dead 87. December Bride 90. The Miracle 91. The Bishop's Story 93. Stealing Beauty 96. The Nephew 98, etc.

McCarey, Leo (1898–1969).
American director with above-average talent and a sentimental streak. Before graduating to features he directed many silent shorts, including Laurel and Hardy as *Two Tars*.
■ The Sophomore 29. Red Hot Rhythm 29. Let's Go Native 30. Wild Company 30. Part Time Wife 30. Indiscretion 31. *Duck Soup* 33. Six of a Kind 34. Belle of the Nineties 34. *Ruggles of Red Gap* 35. The Milky Way 36. *The Awful Truth* (& w) (AA) 37. Love Affair (co-story, AAN) (AA screenplay) 39. Once upon a Honeymoon 42. Going My Way (AA) (& p) 44. The Bells of St Mary's (& p) (AAN) 45. Good Sam (& p) 48. My Son John (& w, p) (AANw) 52. An Affair to Remember (& w, p) 57. Rally round the Flag Boys (& w, p) 58. Satan Never Sleeps (& w, p) 62.

McCarey, Ray (1904–1948).
American director of second features, formerly making Hal Roach shorts. Brother of Leo McCarey.
Pack Up Your Troubles 32. Millions in the Air 36. That Other Woman 42. Atlantic City 44. The Falcon's Alibi 46, etc.

McCarthy, Andrew (1962–).
American leading actor, usually in teenage-oriented films.
Class 83. Heaven Help Us 85. St Elmo's Fire 85. Pretty in Pink 86. Less Than Zero 87. Waiting for the Moon 87. Mannequin 87. Kansas 88. Weekend at Bernie's 89. Docteur M 90. Quiet Days in Clichy 90. Year of the Gun 91. Common Pursuit (TV) 91. Only You 92. Weekend at Bernie's 2 93. The Joy Luck Club 93. Mrs Parker and the Vicious Circle 94. Student Body 94. Dead Funny 95. Escape Clause (TV) 96. Things I Never Told You 96. Mulholland Falls 96. Escape Clause (TV) 96. Stag 97. The Heist (TV) 97. I'm Losing You 98. I Woke Up Early the Day I Died 98, etc.

McCarthy, Frank (1912–1986).
American producer.
Decision before Dawn 51. Sailor of the King 53. A Guide for the Married Man 67. *Patton* (AA) 70, etc.

McCarthy, Joseph (1905–1957).
American senator who conducted in the early 50s a witch hunt of alleged communists, and was censured by the Senate in 1954. A 1977 television biopic, *Tail Gunner Joe*, starred Peter Boyle.

McCarthy, Kevin (1914–).
American leading man and latterly character actor, with stage experience.
Winged Victory (debut) 44. *Death of a Salesman* (AAN) 52. Stranger on Horseback 55. *Invasion of the Body Snatchers* 56. The Misfits 61. *The Prize* 63. The Best Man 64. Mirage 65. A Big Hand for the Little Lady 66. Hotel 67. If He Hollers Let Him Go 68. Revenge in El Paso 69. Kansas City Bomber 72. Alien Thunder 73. Buffalo Bill and the Indians 76. Invasion of the Body Snatchers (cameo) 78. Piranha 78. Captain Avenger 79. Those Lips Those Eyes 80. The Howling 81. My Tutor 83. Twilight Zone 83. Innerspace 87. The Sleeping Car 88. UHF 89. Eve of Destruction 90. Fast Food 91. The Distinguished Gentleman 92. Matinee 93. Just Cause 95, etc.
TV series: The Survivors 69. Flamingo Road 80–81. Amanda's 83. The Colbys 86–87.

McCarthy, Michael (1917–1959).
British director, in films from 1934.
Assassin for Hire 51. Mystery Junction 51. Crow Hollow 52. Shadow of a Man 54. It's Never Too Late 56. Smoke Screen 57. The Traitor 57. Operation Amsterdam 58, etc.

McCarthy, Neil (1935–).
English character actor, usually in tough or menacing roles, a former teacher.
Breakout 59. The Criminal 60. Zulu 64. The Hill 65. Where Eagles Dare 68. Steptoe and Son Ride Again 73. Operation Daybreak 75. The Incredible Sarah 76. The Thief of Bagdad 79. The Monster Club 80. Clash of the Titans (as Calibos) 81. Time Bandits 81, etc.

McCarthy, Sheila (1956–).
Canadian leading actress.
I've Heard the Mermaids Singing 87. Friends, Lovers and Lunatics/Crazy Horse 89. White Room 90. Die Hard 2 90. Pacific Heights 90. Paradise 91. Stepping Out 91. Bright Angel 91. George's Island 91. Beautiful Dreamers 92. Beethoven Lives Upstairs 92. The Lotus Eaters 93. House Arrest 96, etc.

McCartney, Sir Paul (1942–).
British songwriter, musician and composer. A member of The Beatles, he wrote many of the group's songs in collaboration with John Lennon and later formed the band Wings. He was played by Gary Bakewell in the feature *Backbeat* 94, about the early days of the Beatles. Knighted in the New Year's Honours of 1996. In 1997, *Business Age* estimated his personal fortune at £520m.
Biography: 1996, *Paul McCartney: Many Years from Now* by Barry Miles; 1997, *Paul McCartney* by Barry Miles.
The Family Way (m) 67. Live and Let Die (title s) 73. The Honorary Consul/Beyond the Limit (theme) 83. Give My Regards to Broad Street (a, w, m) 84. Twice in a Lifetime (co-m) 85. Eat the Rich (a) 87. Get Back (doc) 91, etc.

McCay, Winsor (1886–1934).
American pioneer animator who invented Gertie the Dinosaur in 1909.

McCleary, Urie.
American art director, at MGM for much of his career.
Blossoms in the Dust 41. National Velvet (AAN) 44. Plymouth Adventure 52. Kiss Me Kate 53. Young Bess (AAN) 53. Seven Brides for Seven Brothers 54. Raintree Country (AAN) 57. Some Came Running 58. The Prize 63. A Patch of Blue (AAN) 65. Patton (AA) 70, etc.

McClanahan, Rue (1934–).
American character actress, best known for her role as the flirtatious Blanche Devereaux in the TV sitcom *Golden Girls*. Born in Healdton, Oklahoma, she was on stage and on TV from the 60s, and appeared in daytime soap operas in the early 70s.
The Rotten Apple 63. The People Next Door 70. They Might Be Giants 71. Rainbow (TV) 78. Topper (TV) 79. Word of Honor (TV) 81. Liberace (TV) 88. The Strange Case of Dr Jekyll and Mr Hyde 79. Modern Love 90. Baby of the Bride (TV) 91. Innocent Victims (TV) 96. Out to Sea 97. Starship Troopers 97, etc.
TV series: Maude 72–78. Apple Pie 78. Mama's Family 83–84. Golden Girls 85–89.

McClory, Kevin (1926–).
Irish production executive, former sound technician. Wrote, produced and directed *The Boy and the Bridge* 59; produced *Thunderball* 65.

McClory, Sean (1923–).
Irish actor with Abbey Theatre experience; long in Hollywood.
Beyond Glory 49. Rommel, Desert Fox 51. Les Misérables 52. Ring of Fear 54. Moonfleet 55. Diane 57. Bandolero 68. The Dead 87. Fools of Fortune 90, etc.

McClure, Doug (1935–1995).
American leading man, from TV. Formerly married to Barbara Luna.
Because They're Young 59. The Unforgiven 60. Shenandoah 65. Beau Geste 66. The King's Pirate 67. Nobody's Perfect 68. The Judge and Jake Wyler (TV) 71. The Land That Time Forgot 75. At the Earth's Core 76. The People That Time Forgot 77. Warlords of Atlantis 77. Rebels (TV) 79. Humanoids from the Deep 80. The House Where Evil Dwells 82. Cannonball Run II 83. 52 Pick-Up 86. Omega Syndrome 87. Tapeheads 87. Dark before Dawn 88. Prime Suspect 88. Maverick 94. Riders in the Storm 95, etc.
TV series: Checkmate 59–61. Overland Trail 60. *The Virginian* 64–69. Search 72. Barbary Coast 76.

McClure, Greg (1918–) (Dale Easton).
American leading man who starred in his first film but did little thereafter.
The Great John L 45. Bury Me Dead 47. Lulu Belle 48. Joe Palooka in the Squared Circle 50. Stop That Cab 51. Stage Fright 89, etc.

McConaughey, Matthew (1969–).
American leading actor, born in Uvalde, Texas.
Dazed and Confused 93. My Boyfriend's Back 93. Angels in the Outfield 94. Boys on the Side 95. The Return of the Texas Chainsaw Massacre 95. Lone Star 96. A Time to Kill 96. Larger than Life 96. Glory Daze 96. Scorpion Spring 97. Contact 97. The Newton Boys 97. Amistad 97, etc.
❝ Let's face it, Matthew's got those three things that make a star: you got to be smart, you got to have talent, and the girls have got to want to fuck you. – *Don Phillips, casting director*
Don't just flounder. If you've got a backbone, have some passion about something and do it. – M.McC

McCord, Ted (1898–1976).
American cinematographer.
So Big 24. We Moderns 25. Irene 26. Valley of the Giants 26. Phantom City 28. The Fighting Legion 30. The Big Stampede 32. The Rainmakers 35. Fugitive in the Sky 36. Secret Service of the Air 39. The Case of the Black Parrot 41. Murder in the Big House 42. Action in the North Atlantic 43. Deep Valley 47. The Treasure of the Sierra Madre 48. *Johnny Belinda* 48. Flamingo Road 49. The Damned Don't Cry 50. Young Man with a Horn 50. The Breaking Point 50. Force of Arms 51. Young at Heart 54. East of Eden 55. The Helen Morgan Story 57. The Proud Rebel 58. The Hanging Tree 59. Two for the Seesaw 62. *The Sound of Music* 65. A Fine Madness 66, many others.

MacCorkindale, Simon (1952–).
Budding British leading man of the late 70s, now also a producer. He is married to actress Susan George.
Jesus of Nazareth (TV) 77. Death on the Nile 78. The Riddle of the Sands 79. Quatermass (TV) 79. Cabo Blanco 79. The Manions of America (TV) 80. The Sword and the Sorcerer 82. Jaws 3-D 83. Stealing Heaven (p) 88. That Summer of White Roses (w, p) 89, etc.
TV series: Manimal 83. Falcon Crest 85–87.

McCormack, Catherine (1972–).
British leading actress, born in Alton, Hampshire. She studied at the Oxford School of Drama.
Loaded 94. North Star 95. Braveheart 95. This Year's Love 98. Dangerous Beauty 98. The Land Girls 98. Dancing at Lughnasa 98, etc.

McCormack, John (1884–1945).
Irish tenor.
Song o' My Heart 30. Wings of the Morning 37.

McCormack, Mary (1969–).
American actress and singer. Born in Plainfield, New Jersey, she began in regional theatres. She studied at Trinity College in Hartford, Connecticut.
Miracle on 34th Street 94. Murder One (TV) 95. Backfire 95. Private Parts 97. Murder One: Diary of a Serial Killer (TV) 97. Deep Impact 98. Harvest 98, etc.

McCormack, Patty (1945–).
American juvenile actress who went to Hollywood to repeat her stage role as the evil child of *The Bad Seed* (AAN) 56.
The Day They Gave Babies Away 57. Kathy O' 58. The Adventures of Huckleberry Finn 60. The Explosive Generation 61. The Young Runaways 68. Invitation to Hell (TV) 84. Saturday the 14th Strikes Back 88. Mommy 95. Mommy 2: Mommy's Day 96, etc.
TV series: Peck's Bad Girl 59.

McCormick, F. J. (1891–1947) (Peter Judge).
Irish character actor, long on the Abbey Theatre stage. Well remembered as Shell in *Odd Man Out* 46.
The Plough and the Stars 37. Hungry Hill 46.

McCormick, Myron (1908–1962).
Wry-faced American character actor, with stage experience.
Winterset 37. One Third of a Nation 39. Jigsaw 49. Jolson Sings Again 50. No Time for Sergeants 58. *The Hustler* 61, etc.

McCowan, George (1931–).
Canadian director, mainly of TV movies.
Frogs 72. The Magnificent Seven Ride! 72. Murder on Flight 502 (TV) 75. Return to Fantasy Island (TV) 78. The Shape of Things to Come 79. Sanity Clause (TV) 90, etc.

McCowen, Alec (1925–).
British stage actor, in occasional films.
Time Without Pity 57. Town on Trial 57. The Loneliness of the Long Distance Runner 62. In the Cool of the Day 63. The Agony and the Ecstasy 65. The Witches 66. The Hawaiians (US) 70. Frenzy 72. *Travels With My Aunt* 72. Stevie 78. Hanover Street 79. Never Say Never Again 83. The Assam Garden 85. Personal Services 86. Cry Freedom 87. Henry V 89. The Age of Innocence 93, etc.

McCoy, Tim (1891–1978).
American cowboy star, in films from 1923 when, an ex-army officer, he went to Hollywood as adviser on *The Covered Wagon*.
War Paint 26. The Indians Are Coming 30. The Fighting Fool 31. Texas Cyclone 32. Whirlwind 33. Hell Bent for Love 34. Square Shooter 35, many others. Later played bit parts: Around the World in Eighty Days 56. Run of the Arrow 57. Requiem for a Gunfighter 65, etc.
TV series: The Tim McCoy Show 52.

McCrea, Jody (1934–).
American leading man of the 60s, the son of actor Joel McCrea, often as a large, good-natured, dim-witted surfer in beach movies. Born in Hollywood, he retired from acting to become a rancher.
The Naked Gun 56. The Monster that Challenged the World 57. The Restless Years 58. Force of Impulse 60. The Broken Land 61. Young Guns of Texas 62. Beach Party 63. Operation Bikini 63. Bikini Beach 64. Muscle Beach Party 64. Pajama Party 64. Beach Blanket Bingo 65. The Glory Stompers 67. Cry Blood Apache 68. Lady Streetfighter 85, etc.

McCrea, Joel (1905–1990).
Athletic, good-humoured, dependable American hero of the 30s and 40s, who later starred in westerns. He was married for 57 years to actress Frances Dee.
Biography: 1992, *Joel McCrea: Riding the High Country* by Tony Thomas.
■ The Jazz Age 29. So This Is College 29. Dynamite 29. The Silver Horde 29. Lightnin' 30. Once a Sinner 30. Kept Husbands 31. The Common Law 31. Born to Love 31. Girls about Town 31. Business and Pleasure 32. The Lost Squadron 32. *Bird of Paradise* 32. *The Most Dangerous Game* 32. Rockabye 32. The Sport Parade 32. Scandal for Sale 32. Laughter in Hell 33. The Silver Cord 33. Bed of Roses 33. One Man's Journey 33. Chance at Heaven 33. Gambling Lady 34. Half a Sinner 34. The Richest Girl in the World 34. Private Worlds 35. Our Little Girl 35. Woman Wanted 35. Barbary Coast 35. Splendour 35. These Three 36. Two in a Crowd 36. Adventure in Manhattan 36. Come and Get It 36. Banjo on My Knee 36. Internes Can't Take Money 37. Wells Fargo 37. Woman Chases Man 37. *Dead End* 37. Three Blind Mice 38. Youth Takes a Fling 38. Union Pacific 39. They Shall Have Music 39. Espionage Agent 39. He Married His Wife 40. The Primrose Path 40. *Foreign Correspondent* 40. Reaching for the Sun 41. *Sullivan's Travels* 41. The Great Man's Lady 42. *The Palm Beach Story* 42. *The More the Merrier* 43. Buffalo Bill 44. The Great Moment 44. The Unseen 45. The Virginian 46. Ramrod 47. Four Faces West 48. South of St Louis 49. Colorado Territory 49. Stars in My Crown 50. The Outriders 50. Saddle Tramp 50. Frenchie 50. Cattle Drive 51. The San Francisco Story 52. Lone Hand 53. Rough Shoot (GB) 53. Black Horse Canyon 54. Border River 54. Stranger on Horseback 55. Wichita 55. The First Texan 56. The Oklahoman 57. Trooper Hook 57. Gunsight Ridge 57. The Tall Stranger 57. Cattle Empire 58. Fort Massacre 58. Gunfight at Dodge City 59. *Ride the High Country* 62. Cry Blood Apache 71. Mustang Country 76.
TV series: *Wichita Town* 59.
✪ For the amiable generosity of his playing which turned him from a second lead into the undoubted star of several of the most prized films of the early 40s. *Sullivan's Travels*.

McCullers, Carson (1917–1967).
American novelist, usually on themes pertaining to her homeland, the Deep South. *The Member of the Wedding*, *Reflections in a Golden Eye*, *The Heart Is a Lonely Hunter* and *The Ballad of the Sad Café* were filmed.
❝ An hour with a dentist without Novocaine was like a minute with Carson McCullers. – *Gore Vidal*

McCullough, Paul (1884–1936).
American farce comedian, with Bobby Clark in two-reelers 1928–35.

McDaniel, Hattie (1895–1952).
American character actress of cheerful and immense presence; once a radio vocalist.
The Story of Temple Drake 33. Judge Priest 35. *Showboat* 36. Nothing Sacred 37. *Gone with the Wind* (AA) 39. Zenobia 39. *The Great Lie* 41. Thank Your Lucky Stars 43. Margie 46. Song of the South 47. Family Honeymoon 49, many others.
TV series: *Beulah* 52.

McDermott, Dylan (1962–).
American leading actor. Born in Waterbury, Connecticut, he trained at New York's Neighborhood Playhouse and began on stage.
Hamburger Hill 87. The Blue Iguana 88. Steel Magnolias 89. Hardware (GB) 90. Where Sleeping Dogs Lie 91. Jersey Girl 92. In the Line of Fire 93. The Cowboy Way 94. Miracle on 34th Street 94. Home for the Holidays 95. Destiny Turns on the Radio 95. Kansas City 96, etc.

McDermott, Hugh (1908–1972).
Scottish-born character actor, in British films from mid-30s, specializing in hearty transatlantic types.
The Wife of General Ling 38. Pimpernel Smith 41. The Seventh Veil 45. No Orchids for Miss Blandish 48. Trent's Last Case 52. A King in New York 57. The First Men in the Moon 64. Captain Apache 71. Chato's Land 72, many others.

McDevitt, Ruth (1895–1976) (Ruth Shoecraft).
American character actress.
The Parent Trap 62. The Birds 63. The Out of Towners 69. Change of Habit 72, many others.
TV series: Pistols and Petticoats 66. Kolchak 74.

Macdonald, Andrew.
British producer, from television, the grandson (and biographer) of Emeric Pressburger.
Shallow Grave 95. *Trainspotting* 96. A Life Less Ordinary 97, etc.

McDonald, Bruce (1959–).
Canadian director and screenwriter, born in Kingston, Ontario.
Roadkill (d) 89. Highway 61 (d) 91. Dance Me Outside (co-w, d) 95. Hard Core Logo (d) 96, etc.

MacDonald, David (1904–1983).
British director who showed promise in the 30s and 40s but declined to second features.
Double Alibi 27. It's Never Too Late to Mend 37. Dead Men Tell No Tales 38. A Spot of Bother 38. *This Man is News* 38. This Man in Paris 39. Spies of the Air 39. Law and Disorder 40. Men of the Lightship 40. This England 40. *The Brothers* 47. Good Time Girl 48. Snowbound 48. Christopher Columbus 49. Diamond City 49. The Bad Lord Byron 49. Cairo Road 50. The Adventures 51. The Lost Hours 52. Tread Softly 53. Devil Girl from Mars 54. Alias John Preston 56. Small Hotel 57. *The Moonraker* 58. Petticoat Pirates 61, etc.

McDonald, Dwight (1906–1982).
American film critic of semi-revered status: On *Movies* 69, etc.

McDonald, Francis (1891–1968).
American actor, a handsome leading man in silents who later became a villain in many 'B' westerns. His first wife was actress Mae BUSCH.
The Gun Woman 18. The Call of the North 21. The Arizona Express 24. Morocco 30. Anna Karenina 35. Under Two Flags 36. The Plainsman 36. Union Pacific 39. Strange Cargo 40. The Sea Wolf 41. The Kansan 43. The Devil's Playground 46. Duel in the Sun 46. The Paleface 48. Samson and Delilah 49. Red Mountain 51. Rancho Notorious 52. The Ten Commandments 55. The Big Fisherman 59. The Great Race 65, many others.

McDonald, Frank (1899–1980).
American director of second features; former stage actor and author.
The Murder of Dr Harrigan 38. Carolina Moon 40. One Body Too Many 44. My Pal Trigger 46. Father Takes the Air 51. The Treasure of Ruby Hills 55. The Underwater City 61, etc.

McDonald, Grace (1921–).
American singing and dancing second lead of many a 40s 'B'.
Dancing on a Dime 40. What's Cooking/Wake Up and Dream 42. Give Out Sisters 42. Crazy House 43. Gung Ho 43. It Ain't Hay 43. Follow the Boys 44. My Gal Loves Music 44. See My Lawyer 45. Honeymoon Ahead 45, etc.

MacDonald, J. Farrell (1875–1952).
American minstrel singer who became a familiar Hollywood character actor.
The Maltese Falcon 31. The Thirteenth Guest 32. The Cat's Paw 34. The Irish in Us 36. Topper 37. Little Orphan Annie 39. Meet John Doe 41. My Darling Clementine 46. Mr Belvedere Rings the Bell 51, etc.

MacDonald, Jeanette (1906–1965).
American concert singer and leading lady of the 30s. Popular on her own account, she made a fondly remembered series of film operettas with Nelson Eddy, and these are noted (E) below. Married actor Gene Raymond.
Biography: 1976, *The Jeanette MacDonald Story* by James Robert Parish; 1997, *Hollywood Diva* by Edward Baron Turk.
■ *The Love Parade* 29. The Vagabond King 30. Monte Carlo 30. Let's Go Native 30. The Lottery Bride 30. Oh For a Man 30. Don't Bet on Women 31. Annabelle's Affairs 31. *One Hour With You* 32. *Love Me Tonight* 32. The Cat and the Fiddle 32. The Merry Widow 34. *Naughty Marietta* (E) 35. *Rose Marie* (E) 36. *San Francisco* 36. Maytime (E) 37. The Firefly 37. The Girl of the Golden West (E) 38. Sweethearts (E) 39. Broadway Serenade 39. New Moon (E) 40. Bitter Sweet (E) 40. Smilin' Through 41. I Married an Angel (E) 42. Cairo 42. Follow the Boys 44. Three Daring Daughters 48. The Sun Comes Up 49.

MacDonald, John D. (1916–1986).
American detective story writer, author of the Travis McGee novels. (For John Ross MacDonald see under ROSS.)
Mantrap 61. Cape Fear/The Executioners 62. Darker than Amber 70. Travis McGee (TV) 82. Cape Fear 91.

MacDonald, Joseph (1906–1968).
American cinematographer.
Charlie Chan in Rio 41. Sunday Dinner for a Soldier 44. *Yellow Sky* 48. Panic in the Streets 50. *Viva Zapata* 52. Niagara 53. Titanic 53. How to Marry a Millionaire 53. Broken Lance 54. A Hatful of Rain 57. Ten North Frederick 57. Pepe 60. Kings of the Sun 63. The Carpetbaggers 63. Rio Conchos 64. Invitation to a Gunfighter 64. Mirage 65. Blindfold 65. The Sand Pebbles (AAN) 66. Mackenna's Gold 68, many others.

MacDonald, Kelly.
Scottish actress.
Stella Does Tricks 96. Trainspotting 96. Dead Eye Dick 97. Cousin Bette 98. Elizabeth 98, etc.

McDonald, Marie (1923–1965) (Marie Frye).
American leading lady, publicized as 'The Body'; former model.
Pardon My Sarong 42. A Scream in the Dark 44. Getting Gertie's Garter 46. Living in a Big Way 47. Tell It to the Judge 49. Geisha Boy 59. Promises Promises 63, etc.

Macdonald, Peter.
English director, a former second unit director and camera operator.
Rambo III 88. Mo' Money 92. The Neverending Story III 94. Be the Man 98, etc.

MacDonald, Philip (1896–*).
British thriller writer who contributed much material to the screen.
Raise the Roof 30. The Mystery of Mr X 34. Mystery Woman 34. The Last Outpost 34. Menace 34. The Princess Comes Across 36. Mr Moto's Last Warning 39. Sahara 43. Action in Arabia 44. The Body Snatcher 45. Love from a Stranger 47. The Dark Past 48. The Man Who Cheated Himself 50. Circle of Danger 51. The Hour of 13 52. Ring of Fear 54. 23 Paces to Baker Street (oa) 56. The List of Adrian Messenger (oa) 63, etc.

McDonald, Ray (1923–1959).
American actor-dancer of lightweight 40s musicals.
Babes on Broadway 41. Presenting Lily Mars 43. Till the Clouds Roll By 46. Good News 47. All Ashore 53, etc.

Macdonald, Richard (1919–1993).
British production designer. He studied at the Royal College of Art and was head of painting at Leeds College of Art before becoming an art director in advertising. From the mid-60s he switched to films following a chance meeting with Joseph Losey which resulted in him working on *Sleeping Tiger* 54 and many of the director's subsequent films.
The Servant 63. Modesty Blaise 66. *Far from the Madding Crowd* 67. Boom 68. A Severed Head 71. Jesus Christ Superstar 73. *Day of the Locust* 75. Marathon Man 76. Swashbuckler 76. F.I.S.T. 78. And Justice for All 79. The Rose 79. Cannery Row 82. Something Wicked This Way Comes 83. Supergirl 84. Electric Dreams 84. Teachers 84. Plenty 85. Spacecamp 86. Coming to America 88. The Russia House 90. The Addams Family 91. The Firm 93, etc.

MacDonald, Ross (1915–1983) (Kenneth Millar).
American detective story writer whose mysteries are much in the vein of Raymond Chandler.
Harper 66. The Drowning Pool 75.
TV series: Archer 75.

McDonell, Fergus (1910–1984).
British director.
The Small Voice 48. Prelude to Fame 50. Private Information 52, etc.

McDonnell, Mary (1952–).
American leading actress.
Matewan 87. Tiger Warsaw 88. Dances with Wolves (AAN) 90. Grand Canyon 91. Passion Fish 92. Sneakers 92. Blue Chips 94. Woman Undone 95. Independence Day 96. Twelve Angry Men (TV) 97. You Can Thank Me Later 98, etc.
TV series: E/R 84–85.

McDormand, Frances (1957–).
American leading actress who studied at the Yale School of Drama. Married director Joel Coen.
Blood Simple 84. Raising Arizona 87. Mississippi Burning (AAN) 88. Chatahoochee 90. Darkman 90. Hidden Agenda 90. Short Cuts 93. The Good Old Boys (TV) 95. Beyond Rangoon 95. *Fargo* (AA) 96. Lone Star 96. Primal Fear 96. Hidden in America (TV) 96. Paradise Road 97. Madeline 98. Talk of Angels (US) 98, etc.
TV series: Leg Work 87.

MacDougall, Ranald (1915–1973).
American screenwriter.
Mildred Pierce (AAN) 45. Objective Burma 45. Possessed 47. The Unsuspected 47. June Bride 48. The Hasty Heart 49. Bright Leaf 50. I'll Never Forget You 51. The Naked Jungle 54. Queen Bee (& d) 55. The Mountain 56. Man on Fire (& d) 57. The World the Flesh and the Devil (& d) 59. Go Naked in the World (& d) 61. The Cockeyed Cowboys of Calico County (& d) 69, etc.

MacDougall, Roger (1910–1993).
British screenwriter and playwright.
This Man Is News (w) 38. The Foreman went to France (w) 42. *The Man in the White Suit* (oaw) (AAN) 51. To Dorothy a Son (oa) 54. *Escapade* (oa) 56. The Mouse That Roared (w) 59. A Touch of Larceny (w) 60, etc.

McDowall, Betty.
Australian actress who at one time played wives in scores of British films.
The Shiralee 57. Time Lock 57. She Didn't Say No 58. Jack the Ripper 59. Jackpot 60. Spare the Rod 61. Tomorrow at Ten 62. Echo of Diana 63. Ballad in Blue 64. The Liquidator 65. The Omen 76, etc.

McDowall, Roddy (1928–1998).
British child actor of the 40s, in Hollywood from 1940. Developed into an unpredictable adult performer, but made a reputation as a photographer.
Murder in the Family 36. Just William 39. This England 40. Man Hunt 41. *How Green Was My Valley* 41. Confirm or Deny 41. The Pied Piper 42. My Friend Flicka 43. Lassie Come Home 43. The White Cliffs of Dover 44. Thunderhead 45. Holiday in Mexico 46. Macbeth 50. Killer Shark 50. The Subterraneans 60. The Longest Day 62. Cleopatra 63. Shock Treatment 64. The Loved One 65. That Darn Cat 65. Lord Love a Duck 66. The Cool Ones 67. It 67. Planet of the Apes 67. Five Card Stud 68. Angel Angel Down You Go 69. Tam Lin (d only) 70. Escape from the Planet of the Apes 71. Bedknobs and Broomsticks 71. Pretty Maids All in a Row 71. Conquest of the Planet of the Apes 72. The Poseidon Adventure 72. The Legend of Hell House 73. Battle for the Planet of the Apes 73. Arnold 74. Funny Lady 75. Mean Johnny Barrows 76. Embryo 77. Rabbit Test 78. The Cat from Outer Space 78. Circle of Iron 79. Scavenger Hunt 79. Evil under the Sun 82. Class of 1984 82. Dead of Winter 87. Fright Night Part 2 89. Cutting Class 89. The Big Picture 89. Shakma 89. Disturbed 90. The Color of Evening 91. Deadly Game (TV) 91. Double Trouble 92. The Grass Harp 95. Fatally Yours 95. Last Summer in the Hamptons 96. Rudyard Kipling's The Second Jungle Book: Mowgli and Baloo 97. A Bug's Life (voice) 98, etc.
TV series: Planet of the Apes 74. Fantastic Journey 77. Tales of the Gold Monkey 82–83. Bridges to Cross 86.

MacDowell, Andie (1958–).
American leading actress, a former model.
Greystoke: The Legend of Tarzan, Lord of the Apes 84. St Elmo's Fire 85. sex, lies and videotape 89. Green Card 90. Hudson Hawk 91. Object of Beauty 91. Ground Hog Day 93. Ruby Cairo 93. Short Cuts 93. Four Weddings and a Funeral 94. Bad Girls 94. Unstrung Heroes 95. Multiplicity 96. Michael 96. The End of Violence 97. Shadrach 98. The Scalper 98. The Muse 99, etc.

McDowell, Malcolm (1943–).
Fashionable British leading actor of the early 70s. His second wife was actress Mary Steenburgen (1980–90).
Poor Cow 67. *If* 69. Figures in a Landscape 70. The Raging Moon 71. *A Clockwork Orange* 71. *O Lucky Man* 73. Royal Flash 75. Voyage of the Damned 76. Aces High 76. The Passage 79. Time after Time 79. Caligula 79. Cat People 82. Britannia Hospital 82. Arthur the King (TV) 83. Blue Thunder 83. Cross Creek 83. Get Crazy 83. Buy and Cell 89. Class of 1999 89. Moon 44 89. Jezebel's Kiss 90. Lambarene 91. The Tsar's Assassin 91. The Player 92. East Wind (Fr.) 93. Bopha! 93. Seasons of the Heart (TV) 94. Star Trek: Generations 94. Milk Money 94. Tank Girl 95. Kids of the Round Table 95. The Man Who Wouldn't Die (TV) 95. Where Truth Lies 96. Mr Magoo 97. Hugo Pool 97. Asylum 97, etc.
TV series: Our Friends in the North 96. Fantasy Island 98– .
❝ The best thing I did was abuse myself when younger – I dabbled in everything, cocaine, booze, women – because now I don't have to do it any more.' – *M.D., 1996*

McEachin, James (1931–).
American actor of the 70s, TV's *Tenafly* 73–74. He also plays the role of Lieutenant Ed Brock in the Perry Mason TV movies of the 80s and 90s.
Play Misty for Me 71. The Alpha Caper (TV) 73. Every Which Way but Loose 79. 2010 84. Double Exposure 93, etc.

McElhone, Natascha (1971–).
British actress, mainly in Hollywood films. She studied at the London Academy of Music and Drama and began on stage.
Surviving Picasso 96. The Devil's Own (US) 96. Mrs Dalloway 97. The Truman Show (US) 98. Ronin (US) 98, etc.

McEnery, John (1945–).
British light leading man of the 70s.
Romeo and Juliet 68. The Lady in a Car 70. *Bartleby* 71. Nicholas and Alexandra 71. Days of Fury 73. The Land that Time Forgot 74. Little Malcolm 74. The Duellists 78. Hamlet 90. The Fool 90. Prince of Shadows/Beltenebros 92. Black Beauty 94. When Saturday Comes 96. Merlin (TV) 98, etc.

McEnery, Peter (1940–).
British leading man with TV experience.
Tunes of Glory 60. Victim 62. The Moonspinners 64. The Fighting Prince of Donegal 66. The Game Is Over 66. I Killed Rasputin 68. Negatives 68. Entertaining Mr Sloane 70. The Adventures of Gerard 70. Tales that Witness Madness 73. The Cat and the Canary 78. Florence Nightingale (TV) 85. Safari (It.) 91. The Boxing Promoter/Le Montreur de Boxe (Fr.) 96, etc.

McEntire, Reba (1955–).
American actress and leading country singer.
Tremors 90. The Little Rascals 94. North 94. Buffalo Girls (TV) 95, etc.
TV series: Forever Love 98– .

McEveety, Bernard.
American director, from TV. He is the brother of Vincent MCEVEETY. He subsequently directed during the 80s episodes of TV series such as *Knight Rider*, *Airwolf*, *Misfits of Science* and *Outlaws*.
Broken Sabre 65. Ride Beyond Vengeance 66. The Brotherhood of Satan 70. Napoleon and Samantha 72. One Little Indian 73. The Bears and I 74. Roughnecks (TV) 80, etc.

McEveety, Joseph L. (1926–1976).
American producer, long with Disney.

McEveety, Vince (Vincent).
American director. In the 90s, he directed TV movies in the *Columbo* series.
Firecreek 68. Million Dollar Duck 71. The Strongest Man in the World 74. Gus 76. Herbie Goes to Monte Carlo 77. The Apple Dumpling Gang Rides Again 79. Herbie Goes Bananas 80. Amy 81. Gunsmoke: Return to Dodge (TV) 87, etc.

McEwan, Geraldine (1932–).
Leading British stage actress.
Escape from the Dark 76. The Bawdy Adventures of Tom Jones 76. Foreign Body 87. Henry V 89. Robin Hood: Prince of Thieves 91. Moses (TV) 96, etc.
TV series: Mulberry 93.

McEwan, Ian (1948–).
British screenwriter and novelist.
The Imitation Game (TV) 81. The Ploughman's Lunch 83. The Comfort of Strangers (oa) 90. The

Innocent 92. The Cement Garden (oa) 92. The Innocent (w from his novel) 93. The Good Son (w) 93.

❝ Film is a brutish and deeply unsophisticated medium. You cannot have that access to unfolding states of mind that the novel can give you. It's like walking with one leg, you just have to learn to limp. – *I.M.*

It's an opportunity to fly first class, be treated like a celebrity, sit around the pool and be betrayed. – *I.M. on Hollywood*

McFadden, Hamilton (1901–).
American director of 'B' features.
Harmony at Home 30. Charlie Chan Carries On 31. Second Hand Wife 33. Stand Up and Cheer 34. Elinor Norton 35. The Three Legionnaires 37. Sea Racketeers 39. Inside the Law 42, etc.

McFarland, Spanky (1928–1993) (George Emmett McFarland).
American child actor of the 30s, the fat boy of the 'Our Gang' one-reelers.
Day of Reckoning 33. Kentucky Kernels 35. O'Shaughnessy's Boy 35. Trail of the Lonesome Pine 36. Peck's Bad Boy with the Circus 39. Johnny Doughboy 43. Moonrunners 74, etc.

McGann, Mark (1961–).
Irish actor, the brother of Paul McGann, from the stage.
No Surrender 85. Business as Usual 87. Let Him Have It 91. Catherine the Great (TV) 95. Samson and Delilah (TV) 96, etc.
TV series: The Hanging Gale 95. The Grand 97.

McGann, Paul (1959–).
British leading actor, from the stage.
Withnail and I 86. Empire of the Sun 87. Dealers 89. Drowning in the Shallow End 89. The Rainbow 89. Streets of Yesterday 89. Tree of Hands 89. Paper Mask 90. The Monk 90. Afraid of the Dark 91. Alien^3 92. The Three Musketeers 93. Catherine the Great (TV) 95. Dr Who (TV) 96. Fairytale: A True Story 97. Our Mutual Friend (TV) 98, etc.

McGann, William (1895–1977).
American director of second features, a former cinematographer, in films from 1915. Also made Spanish-language versions of Warner Brothers' First National films, and directed seven films in Britain in the 30s at Warner's First National Studio.
I Like Your Nerve 31. Illegal 32. The Case of the Black Cat 36. Penrod and Sam 37. Blackwell's Island 39. The Parson of Panamint 41. Tombstone 42. Frontier Badmen 43, etc.

McGavin, Darren (1922–).
American 'character lead' who can play unpleasant villains or tough heroes.
Fear 46. Summer Madness 55. The Court Martial of Billy Mitchell 55. *The Man with the Golden Arm* 56. The Delicate Delinquent 57. Beau James 57. The Case Against Brooklyn 58. Bullet for a Badman 64. The Great Sioux Massacre 65. Mrs Pollifax – Spy 70. Happy Mother's Day Love George 73. The Night Stalker (TV) 74. The Night Strangler (TV) 74. No Deposit No Return 76. Airport 77 77. Hot Lead and Cold Feet 78. Zero to Sixty 78. Ike (TV) 79. Hangar 18 80. From the Hip 87. Sunset 88. Blood and Concrete 91. Perfect Harmony (TV) 91. Billy Madison 94, etc.
TV series: Crime Photographer 53. *Mike Hammer* 58. *Riverboat* 60. The Outsider 68. The Night Stalker 74.

McGee, Fibber (1896–1988) (James Jordan).
American radio comedian, always with his wife 'Molly' (Marion: 1898–1961).
This Way Please 38. Look Who's Laughing 40. Here We Go Again 41. Heavenly Days 44, etc.

McGee, Vonetta (1948–).
American actress.
The Lost Man 69. The Kremlin Letter 69. Blacula 72. Shaft in Africa 73. The Eiger Sanction 75. Brothers 77. Superdome (TV) 78. To Sleep with Anger 90, etc.

McGill, Barney (c. 1890–1941).
American cinematographer.
Breezy Jim 19. The Critical Age 23. Casey at the Bat 27. The Terror 28. Show of Shows 29. Doorway to Hell 30. Mammy 30. *Svengali* 31. The Mouthpiece 32. Cabin in the Cotton 32. Twenty Thousand Years in Sing Sing 33. Mayor of Hell 33. *The Bowery* 33. The President Vanishes 34. My Marriage 35. Thank You Jeeves 36. Lancer Spy 37. Sharpshooters 38. The Cisco Kid and the Lady 40, many others.

McGillis, Kelly (1957–).
American actress.
Reuben, Reuben 82. Witness 85. Top Gun 85. Made in Heaven 87. The House on Carroll Street 88. The Accused 88. Winter People 89. Cat Chaser 89. The Babe 92. Grand Isle 92. Bonds of Love (TV) 93. North 94. The Settlement 98, etc.

McGinn, Walter (1936–1977).
American character actor of the 70s.
The Parallax View 74. Farewell My Lovely 75. Three Days of the Condor 75. Bobby Deerfield 77. The Deadliest Season (TV) 77, etc.

MacGinnis, Niall (1913–1977).
Irish-born actor, in films from 1935.
Turn of the Tide 35. Edge of the World 38. 49th Parallel 41. We Dive at Dawn 43. Henry V 44. No Highway 51. *Martin Luther* (title role) 53. The Battle of the River Plate 55. *Night of the Demon* 57. The Nun's Story 58. Billy Budd 62. A Face in the Rain 62. Becket 64. Island of Terror 66. The Torture Garden 67. Sinful Davey 69. The Mackintosh Man 73, etc.

McGiver, John (1913–1975).
American character comedian with worried, owl-like features.
Love in the Afternoon 57. *Breakfast at Tiffany's* 61. Mr Hobbs Takes a Vacation 62. The Manchurian Candidate 62. Who's Minding the Store? 63. Man's Favourite Sport? 64. Marriage on the Rocks 65. The Spirit is Willing 67. Fitzwilly 67. Midnight Cowboy 69. Lawman 70. The Great Man's Whiskers (TV) 71. The Apple Dumpling Gang 75, etc.
TV series: *Many Happy Returns* 64. *The James Stewart Show* 71.

McGivern, William P. (1924–1983).
American mystery novelist.
The Big Heat 53. Rogue Cop 54. Hell on Frisco Bay 55. Odds Against Tomorrow 59. The Caper of the Golden Bulls 67.

McGlynn, Frank (1867–1951).
American character actor, adept at portraying Abraham Lincoln.
Min and Bill 31. Little Miss Marker 34. The Littlest Rebel 35. Trail of the Lonesome Pine 36. Prisoner of Shark Island 37. Wells Fargo 37. Union Pacific 39. Boom Town 40, many others.

McGoohan, Patrick (1928–).
American-born leading man with individual characteristics; in British films, after stage experience, from the mid-50s.
Passage Home 55. Zarak 55. *High Tide at Noon* 56. *Hell Drivers* 57. The Gypsy and the Gentleman 57. Nor the Moon by Night 58. Two Living One Dead 60. All Night Long 61. The Quare Fellow 62. *Life For Ruth* 62. Dr Syn 63. Ice Station Zebra 68. The Moonshine War 70. Mary Queen of Scots 72. Catch My Soul (d only) 73. The Genius (It.) 75. Silver Streak 76. Brass Target 78. Escape From Alcatraz 79. Scanners 81. Jamaica Inn (TV) 83. Finding Katie 83. Baby . . . Secret of the Lost Legend 84. Three Sovereigns for Sarah (TV) 85. Braveheart 95. The Phantom 96. A Time to Kill 96, etc.
TV series: *Danger Man* (Secret Agent) 59–62. *The Prisoner* 67. Rafferty 77.

McGovern, Elizabeth (1961–).
American leading lady.
Ordinary People 80. Heaven's Gate 80. Ragtime (AAN) 81. Lovesick 83. Racing with the Moon 84. Once upon a Time in America 84. Native Son 86. The Bedroom Window 87. She's Having a Baby 88. Johnny Handsome 89. The Handmaid's Tale 90. A Shock to the System 90. Tune in Tomorrow/Aunt Julia and the Scriptwriter 90. The Favor 91. King of the Hill 93. The Favor 94. Wings of Courage 95. Broken Trust (TV) 95. The Summer of Ben Tyler (TV) 96. Broken Glass (TV) 96. The Wings of the Dove 97. The Scarlet Pimpernel (TV) 98. The Misadventures of Margaret 98, etc.
TV series: If Not for You 95.

McGovern, Jimmy.
British screenwriter, mainly for TV, a former teacher. Born in Liverpool, he began writing for the TV soap opera *Brookside* and was creator of the TV series *Cracker*.
Hearts and Minds (TV) 95. Priest 94. Hillsborough (TV) 96. The Lakes (TV) 97, etc.
❝ Most of the writers I see on British television are bone-idle: take the money and run. – *J.M.*

McGowan, J(ohn) P(aterson) (1880–1952).
Australian-born director, actor, screenwriter and producer, in America. Born in Terowie, he began in the theatre. He emigrated in the early 1900s, joining the Kalem Motion Picture company in 1909 as an actor before becoming a director of the company's New York studio. He went on to produce and write many of his own films, concentrating on action movies and westerns, some starring his wife, Helen Holmes. He managed the transition to sound, both as director and actor.
AS DIRECTOR: Brought to Bay 13. Grouch the Engineer (& a) 14. When Seconds Count 16. The Lure of the Circus 18. King of the Circus 20. Do or Die 21. One Million in Jewels (& a) 22. Perils of the Yukon 22. Calibre 45 24. Crossed Trails 24. Barriers of the Law (& a) 25. Cold Nerve 25. Blood and Steel 25. Peggy of the Secret Service 25. The Fighting Sheriff 25. Fighting Luck 26. The Lost Express 26. The Iron Fist 26. Ace of Clubs 26. Cyclone Bob 26. Crossed Signals 26. Aflame in the Sky 27. Tarzan and the Golden Lion 27. Arizona Days (& a) 28. The Chinatown Mystery 28. The Wilderness 29. Beyond the Law 30. The Canyon of Missing Men 30. Covered Wagon Trails (& a) 30. Call of the Desert (GB) 31. Law of the Plains (& a) (GB) 31. Shotgun Pass 31. The Cyclone Kid 31. 'Neath Western Skies (GB) 31. The Man from Nevada (GB) 31. Pioneers of the West (& a) 31. Quick Trigger Lee 31. The Phantom Rider 31. The Lone Horseman (GB) 31. Man from New Mexico 32. The Forty-Niners 32. The Hurricane Express (serial) 32. Deadwood Pass 33. When Lightning Strikes 33. Drum Taps 33. The Lone Bandit 34. Roaring Six Guns 37. Rough Ridin' Rhythm 38. Where the West Begins 38, etc.
AS ACTOR: The Lad from Old Ireland 10. The Colleen Bawn 11. The Fiddler's Requiem 11. From the Manger to the Cross 13. The Railroad Raiders 17. Cold Steel 21. Crack O' Dawn 25. Arizona Nights 27. The Code of the Scarlet 28. Dugan of the Dugouts (& w) 28. Mississippi 35. Ride 'em Cowboy 36. Hit the Saddle 37. Slave Ship 37. The Great Adventures of Wild Bill Hickok 38. Kennedy's Castle 38. Stagecoach 39, etc.

MacGowan, Kenneth (1888–1963).
American film theorist and teacher (at UCLA) who was also a notable producer. Author of several film textbooks.
Little Women 33. Becky Sharp 35. Young Mr Lincoln 39. Man Hunt 41. Lifeboat 43. Jane Eyre 43, etc.

McGowan, Robert A. (1882–1955).
American producer who devised the original 'Our Gang' comedies.

McGowan, Rose (1975–).
American actress and model, daughter of a French mother and an Irish father. She was brought up in Italy, and later lived in Oregon and California.
Encino Man 92. The Doom Generation 95. Scream 96. Bio-Dome 96. Phantoms 97. Going All the Way 97. Lewis & Clark & George 97, etc.

MacGowran, Jack (1918–1973).
Irish character film actor, notably in the plays of Samuel Beckett.
Biography: 1988, *The Beckett Actor: Jack MacGowran, Beginning to End* by Jordan R. Young.
The Quiet Man 52. The Gentle Gunman 52. The Titfield Thunderbolt 53. The Rising of the Moon 57. Darby O'Gill and the Little People 59. Blind Date 60. Mix Me a Person 61. Lord Jim 65. Cul de Sac 66. The Fearless Vampire Killers 67. How I Won the War 67. Wonderwall 68. The Exorcist 73, etc.
TV series: Sailor of Fortune 56.

McGrath, Doug.
American director and screenwriter; he worked as a writer on the TV series *Saturday Night Live*.
Bullets over Broadway (co-w) (AAN) 94. Emma (wd) 96.

McGrath, Frank (1903–1967).
Grizzled American stunt-man who appeared in countless westerns but achieved his greatest popularity as the trail cook in TV's *Wagon Train* series.

McGrath, Joe (1930–).
Scottish director whose TV style of goonish comedy has adapted less successfully to film.
Casino Royale (part) 67. Thirty is a Dangerous Age Cynthia 68. The Bliss of Mrs Blossom 68. The Magic Christian 70. Digby 73. The Great McGonagall 74. I'm Not Feeling Myself Tonight 76. Rising Damp 80. Just Desserts (TV) 86, etc.

MacGraw, Ali (1938–) (Alice McGraw).
American leading lady. She was married to producer Robert Evans (1971–73) and actor Steve McQueen (1973–78).
Autobiography: 1991, *Moving Pictures*.
■ A Lovely Way to Die 68. *Goodbye Columbus* 69. *Love Story* (AAN) 71. Getaway 72. Convoy 79. Players 79. Just Tell Me What You Want 80. The Winds of War (TV) 83. China Girl (TV) 83. The Killer Elite (TV) 85. Survive the Savage Sea 91. Gunsmoke: The Long Ride (TV) 93. Natural Causes 94.
TV series: Dynasty 85.

McGraw, Charles (1914–1980).
American actor, invariably in tough roles.
The Moon Is Down 43. The Killers 46. The Armored Car Robbery 50. *The Narrow Margin* 50. His Kind of Woman 51. The Bridges at Toko-Ri 51. Away All Boats 56. Slaughter on Tenth Avenue 58. The Defiant Ones 58. The Wonderful Country 59. Spartacus 60. Cimarron 61. In Cold Blood 67. Pendulum 69. Johnny Got His Gun 71. Twilight's Last Gleaming 76, etc.
TV series: Casablanca 55. The Smith Family 72.

McGregor, Ewan (1971–).
Scottish leading actor, born in Crieff. He began acting at 16 with the Perth Repertory Theatre and then studied at the Guildhall School of Music and Drama, leaving to appear on television in Dennis Potter's drama series *Lipstick on Your Collar*. He first attracted attention in *Shallow Grave* and then reached stardom with *Trainspotting*, both directed by Danny Boyle. His roles so far have been notable for their full-frontal nudity; his fame can only grow with his performances as the young Obi-Wan Kenobi (the role played by Alec Guinness in the first Star Wars film) in George Lucas's new Star Wars movies. He is co-founder of the production company Natural Nylon, together with actors Sadie Frost, Jude Law, Jonny Lee Miller, and Sean Pertwee. Married French production designer Eve Mouvrakis.
Biographies: 1997, *Ewan McGregor: The Story So Far* by Jane Smith; 1998, *Choose Life: Ewan McGregor and the British Film Revival* by Xan Brooks.
Lipstick on Your Collar (TV) 93. Shallow Grave 94. Blue Juice 95. *Trainspotting* 96. The Pillow Book 96. Emma 96. Brassed Off 96. Nightwatch 97. The Serpent's Kiss 97. A Life Less Ordinary 97. Velvet Goldmine 98. Little Voice 98. Rogue Trader 99. Star Wars: The Phantom Menace 99, etc.

MacGregor, Scott (1914–1971).
Scottish art director, from the stage. In films from 1941, first as an assistant to Edward Carrick, and often for science-fiction or horror films.
The Master Plan 54. The Secret 55. Fire Maidens from Outer Space 56. Action of the Tiger 57. Oscar Wilde 60. Dr Blood's Coffin 60. Five to One 63. It/Curse of the Golem 66. Invasion 66. The Frozen Dead 66. Moon Zero Two 69. Taste the Blood of Dracula 70. The Vampire Lovers 70. The Horror of Frankenstein 70. On the Buses 70. Burke and Hare 71. *Vampire Circus* 71. Blood from the Mummy's Tomb 71. Mutiny on the Buses 72. Frankenstein and the Monster from Hell 73, etc.

McGuane, Thomas (1939–).
American screenwriter.
Rancho de Luxe 75. 92 in the Shade (& d) 75. The Missouri Breaks 76. Tom Horn 80. Cold Feet 89, etc.

McGuire, Biff (1926–).
American character actor.
The Phoenix City Story 55. Station Six Sahara 62. The Thomas Crown Affair 68. Serpico 73. Midway 76. Deadline Assault 90, etc.
TV series: Gibbsville 76.

McGuire, Don (1919–1979).
American writer-director, former press agent. Then to TV as producer-director of the *Hennessey* series.
Meet Danny Wilson (w) 51. Walking My Baby Back Home (w) 52. Three Ring Circus (w) 54. Bad Day at Black Rock (co-w) 54. Johnny Concho (wd) 56. The Delicate Delinquent (wd) 57.

McGuire, Dorothy (1918–).
American leading lady of the 40s, latterly playing mothers; always in gentle, sympathetic roles.
■ *Claudia* 43. *A Tree Grows in Brooklyn* 44. The Enchanted Cottage 44. *The Spiral Staircase* 45. Claudia and David 46. Till the End of Time 46. Gentleman's Agreement (AAN) 47. Mother Didn't Tell Me 50. Mister 880 50. Callaway Went Thataway 50. I Want You 51. Invitation 52. Make Haste to Live 53. *Three Coins in the Fountain* 54. Trial 55. Friendly Persuasion 56. Old Yeller 57. The Remarkable Mr Pennypacker 59. This Earth Is Mine 59. A Summer Place 60. *The Dark at the Top of the Stairs* 60. The Swiss Family Robinson 60. Susan Slade 61. Summer Magic 63. The Greatest Story Ever Told (as the Virgin Mary) 65. Flight of the Doves 71. She Waits (TV) 71. The Runaways (TV) 75. Rich Man Poor Man (TV) 76. Little Women (TV) 78. The Incredible Journey of Dr Meg Laurel (TV) 79. *Ghost Dancing* (TV) 83. Amos (TV) 85. American Geisha (TV) 86. I Never Sang for My Father (TV) 87. Caroline (TV) 90.

McHattie, Stephen.
Lean Canadian leading man, in American films.
The People Next Door 70. Von Richthofen and Brown 71. Search for the Gods (TV) 75. The Ultimate Warrior 75. Look What Happened to Rosemary's Baby (TV) 76. *James Dean* (TV) (title role) 76. Moving Violation 76. Gray Lady Down 77. Centennial (TV) 77. Roughnecks (TV) 80. Death Valley 82. Belizaire the Cajun 86. One Man Out 88. Bloodhounds of Broadway 89. The Dark 93. Geronimo: An American Legend 93. Beverly Hills Cop III 94. Art Deco Detective 94. My Friend Joe 96. Theodore Rex 96. My Friend Joe 96. The Climb 97, etc.
TV series: Centennial 78–79. Highcliffe Manor 79. Beauty and the Beast 89–90.

McHugh, Frank (1899–1981).
Amiable American character actor with surprised look, frequently in Irish-American roles.
If Men Played Cards as Women Do 28. Dawn Patrol 30. The Mystery of the Wax Museum 33. Footlight Parade 33. Havana Widows 34. A Midsummer Night's Dream 35. Three Men on a Horse 36. Swing Your Lady 38. Going My Way 44. State Fair 45. Mighty Joe Young 49. My Son John 52. There's No Business Like Show Business 54. Career 59. A Tiger Walks 64. Easy Come Easy Go 67, many others.
TV series: *The Bing Crosby Show* 64.

McHugh, Jimmy (1895–1969).
American songwriter: 'I Can't Give You Anything But Love, Baby', 'I Feel a Song Comin' On', 'On the Sunny Side of the Street', etc.
You'll Find Out 40. Seven Days Ashore 43. Do You Love Me? 46, etc.

McIntire, John (1907–1991).
Spare, laconic American character actor with radio and stage experience, in Hollywood from the mid-40s, often as sheriff, editor, politician, cop. He was married to Jeanette Nolan.
The Asphalt Jungle 50. Lawless Breed 52. A Lion Is in the Streets 53. Apache 54. The Far Country 54. The Kentuckian 55. Backlash 56. The Phenix City Story 56. The Tin Star 57. Flaming Star 60. Psycho 60. Summer and Smoke 62. Rough Night in Jericho 67. Herbie Rides Again 73. Rooster Cogburn 75. The Jordan Chance (TV) 78. The Fox and the Hound (voice only) 81. Honkytonk Man 82. Cloak and Dagger 84. As Summers Die (TV) 86, etc.
TV series: *Naked City* 59. *Wagon Train* 61–64. *The Virginian* 67–69.

McIntire, Tim (1943–1986).
American actor, the son of actors John McIntire and Jeanette Nolan. Died of a heart attack.
Shenandoah 65. The Sterile Cuckoo 69. The Deadly Hunt 71. Aloha, Bobby and Rose 75. The Gumball Rally 76. Rich Man, Poor Man – Book 1 (TV) 76. The Choirboys 77. American Hot Wax 78. Brubaker 79. Stand by Your Man (TV) 81. Sacred Ground 83, etc.
TV series: The Legend of Jesse James 65–66.

McIntyre, Christine (1916–1984).
American actress, playing leading roles in westerns, especially opposite Johnny Mack Brown, and also appearing in more than 20 shorts with The Three Stooges in the 40s and 50s.
Forbidden Trails 41. Riders of the West 42. The Stranger from Pecos 43. Partners of the Trail 44. Valley of Fear 47. Gun Talk 48, etc.

Mackaill, Dorothy (1903–1990).
British leading lady of the American silent screen, former Ziegfeld chorine.
The Face at the Window (GB) 21. Twenty-one 26. Dancer of Paris 27. Children of the Ritz 29. Once a Sinner 30. Kept Husbands 31. No Man of Her Own 32. Bulldog Drummond at Bay 37, etc.

Mackay, Barry (1906–).
British stage leading man and singer.
Evergreen 34. Oh Daddy 35. Forever England 35. Glamorous Night 37. Gangway 37. Sailing Along 38. Smuggled Cargo 40. Pickwick Papers 52. Orders Are Orders 55.

Mackay, Fulton (1922–1987).
Scottish character actor, best known as the prison guard in TV's comedy *Porridge*.
The Brave Don't Cry 51. Gumshoe 71. Nothing but the Night 73. Porridge 79. Britannia Hospital 82. Local Hero 83. Water 85, etc.

McKee, Gina (1964–).
English actress, from television.
Quest of Eagles (TV) 78. The Lair of the White Worm 89. The Rachel Papers 89. Wilt 89. He's Asking for Me (TV) 90. Smack and Thistle 90. Naked 93. Our Friends in the North (TV) 96. Beyond Fear (TV) 97. The Life of Stuff 98, etc.
TV series: The Lenny Henry Show 87. Brass Eye 97.

McKellar, Don (1964–)
Canadian actor and screenwriter, born in Toronto.
Roadkill (& w) 89. Highway 61 (& w) 91. The Adjuster 91. 32 Short Films about Glenn Gould (& co-w) 93. Exotica 94. Camilla 94. When Night Is Falling 95. Dance Me Outside (co-w only) 95. In the Presence of Mine Enemies (TV) 97. Last Night (a, wd) 98. The Red Violin (& w) 98. eXistenZ 98, etc.

McKellen, Sir Ian (1939–).
British stage actor, in occasional films.
Alfred the Great 69. A Touch of Love 69. The Promise 69. The Priest of Love (as D. H. Lawrence) 81. The Scarlet Pimpernel (TV) (as Chauvelin) 82. *Walter* (TV) 82. Walter and June (TV) 83. The Keep 83. Plenty 85. Zina 85. Scandal 89. It's Only a Movie 92. Last Action Hero 93. The Ballad of Little Joe 93. And the Band Played On (TV) 93. Romeo Is Bleeding 93. Six Degrees of Separation 93. The Shadow 94. Thin Ice 94. Jack & Sarah 95. Restoration 95. *Richard III* (title role) 95. Bent 97. Amy Foster/Swept from the Sea 97. Apt Pupil 98. Gods & Monsters 98, etc.

Mackendrick, Alexander (Sandy) (1912–1993).
American director, long in Britain; pursued an erratic career with a couple of brilliant spots.
Biography: 1991, *Lethal Innocence: The Cinema of Alexander Mackendrick* by Philip Kemp.
■ Midnight Menace (w only) 37. Saraband for Dead Lovers (w only) 48. *Whisky Galore* (& w) 49. Dance Hall (w only) 50. *The Man in the White Suit* (& w) (AANw) 51. *Mandy* 52. The Maggie 54. The Ladykillers 55. *Sweet Smell of Success* 56. Sammy Going South 62. A High Wind in Jamaica 65. Don't Make Waves 67.

MacKenna, Kenneth (1899–1962) (Leo Mielziner).
American general-purpose actor, from the New York stage, who turned to directing for Fox in the 30s. He was the fourth husband of actress Kay Francis (1931–34).
AS ACTOR: Miss Bluebeard 25. The Lunatic at Large 27. Crazy that Way 30. Those We Love 32. High Time 60. 13 West Street 62, etc.
AS DIRECTOR: Always Goodbye (co-d) 31. The Spider (co-d) 31. Careless Lady 32. Walls of Gold 33. Sleepers East 34, etc.

McKenna, Siobhan (1923–1986).
Fiery Irish actress, on stage from 1940, and in very occasional films.
Biography: 1994, *Memoir of an Actress* by Michael O'Haodha.
Hungry Hill 46. Daughter of Darkness 48. The Lost People 49. King of Kings 61. Playboy of the Western World 62. Of Human Bondage 64. Doctor Zhivago 65. Philadelphia, Here I Come 75, etc.

McKenna, T. P. (1929–).
Irish general-purpose actor.
Ulysses 67. Anne of a Thousand Days 70. The Beast in the Cellar 70. Perfect Friday 70. Villain 71. The Outsider 79. Pascali's Island 88. Red Scorpion 89. Valmont 89, etc.

McKenna, Virginia (1931–).
Demure-looking but spirited British leading lady with stage experience; married to actor Bill Travers. With Travers, she founded in 1984 the Born Free Foundation, which campaigns for wild animals that are suffering, imprisoned or in danger.
The Second Mrs Tanqueray 52. Father's Doing Fine 52. The Oracle 53. *The Cruel Sea* 53. Simba 55. The Ship That Died of Shame 55. *A Town Like Alice* (BFA) 56. The Smallest Show on Earth 57. The Barretts of Wimpole Street 57. *Carve Her Name with Pride* 58. The Passionate Summer 58. The Wreck of the Mary Deare 59. Two Living One Dead 62. *Born Free* 66. Ring of Bright Water 69. An Elephant Called Slowly 70. Waterloo 70. Swallows and Amazons 74. Holocaust 2000 77. The Disappearance 77. The Chosen 78. Blood Link 82. The First Olympics: Athens 1896 (TV) 84. Staggered 94. The Scold's Bridle (TV) 98. Sliding Doors 98, etc.

Mackenzie, Sir Compton (1883–1972).
Scottish novelist. His *Carnival* was twice filmed, but he became best known for *Whisky Galore*, in which he also played a part.

McKenzie, Jacqueline (1968–).
Australian actress. She won an Australian Film Institute best actress award for *Angel Baby*.
Romper Stomper 92. Decays of Our Lives 93. Traps 94. *Angel Baby* 95. Mr Reliable: A True Story 96, etc.

Mackenzie, John (1932–).
British director, ex TV.
One Brief Summer 69. Unman Wittering and Zigo 71. Made 72. *The Long Good Friday* 80. A Sense of Freedom 81. The Honorary Consul 83. Act of Vengeance (TV) 86. The Fourth Protocol 87. The Last of the Finest 90. Ruby 92. Voyage 93, etc.

McKern, Leo (1920–) (Reginald McKern).
Australian character actor with wide stage experience and usually explosive personality. On stage from 1942, in England from 1946.
All for Mary 55. X the Unknown 56. *Time without Pity* 57. The Mouse That Roared 59. Mr Topaze 61. The Day the Earth Caught Fire 62. *A Jolly Bad Fellow* 64. King and Country 64. Moll Flanders 65. Help! 65. *A Man for All Seasons* 66. Decline and Fall 68. Ryan's Daughter 71. The Adventure of Sherlock Holmes' Smarter Brother 76. The Omen 76. The House on Garibaldi Street (TV) 79. The Blue Lagoon 80. Rumpole's Return (TV) 80. The French Lieutenant's Woman 81. Ladyhawke 84. The Chain 85. Murder with Mirrors (TV) 85. Monsignor Quixote (TV) 86. Travelling North 86. A Foreign Field (TV) 93. Dave and Dad on Our Selection 95. Molokai 99, etc.
TV series: Rumpole of the Bailey 78–92.

Mackie, Philip (1918–1985).
British playwright whose filmscripts included several Edgar Wallace mysteries and his own *The Whole Truth*.

McKinney, Nina Mae (1909–1967).
American actress.
Hallelujah 29. Sanders of the River 35. Dark Waters 44. Pinky 49, etc.

MacKinnon, Gillies (1948–).
Scottish director, born in Glasgow, from television.
Conquest of the South Pole 89. Needle (TV) 90. The Glass Arena (TV) 90. The Playboys 92. A Simple Twist of Fate 94. Small Faces 96. Trojan Eddie 97. Hideous Kinky 98, etc.

Mackintosh, Steven (1967–)
British actor, born in Cambridge.
The Browning Version (TV) 85. Prick Up Your Ears 87. Memphis Belle 90. London Kills Me 91. The Muppet Christmas Carol 92. The Buddha of Suburbia (TV) 93. The Return of the Native (TV) 94. Princess Caraboo 94. Midnight Movie 94. Blue Juice 95. Twelfth Night 96. Prime Suspect 5 (TV) 96. The Grotesque/Gentlemen Don't Eat Poets 96. Different for Girls 96. House of America 97. Our Mutual Friend (TV) 98. The Land Girls 98. Lock, Stock and Two Smoking Barrels 98. Undercover Heart (TV) 98, etc.

McKuen, Rod (1933–).
American composer, actor and poet. Born in Oakland, California.
AS ACTOR: Rock, Pretty Baby 56. Wild Heritage 58. Summer Love 58, etc.
AS COMPOSER: Joanna (GB) 68. A Boy Named Charlie Brown 68. The Prime of Miss Jean Brodie (GB) (AANs) 69. Come to Your Senses 71. Scandalous John 71. The Borrowers (co-m) (TV) 73. Lisa, Bright and Dark (TV) 73. Emily (GB) 76, etc.

MacLachlan, Kyle (1959–).
Clean-cut American leading man, associated with the films of David Lynch.
Dune 84. Blue Velvet 86. The Hidden 87. The Doors 90. Don't Tell Her It's Me 90. Where the Day Takes You 92. The Trial 92. Twin Peaks: Fire Walk with Me 92. Rich in Love 93. The Trial 93. Against the Wall (TV) 94. The Flintstones 94. Roswell (TV) 94. Showgirls 95. The Trigger Effect 96. Mad Dog Time/Trigger Happy 96. Moonshine Highway (TV) 96. One Night Stand 97. Route 9 98, etc.
TV series: Twin Peaks 90.

McLaglen, Andrew V. (1925–).
American director, son of Victor McLaglen; has made several big-scale westerns in the manner of John Ford.
■ Gun the Man Down 56. *The Abductors* 56. The Man in the Vault 57. Freckles 60. The Little Shepherd of Kingdom Come 61. *McLintock* 63. *Shenandoah* 65. The Rare Breed 66. Monkeys Go Home 67. The Way West 67. The Ballad of Josie 68. The Devil's Brigade 68. Bandolero 68. The Undefeated 69. Hellfighters 69. Chisum 70. One More Train to Rob 71. Something Big (& p) 71. Fool's Parade (& p) 71. The Train Robbers 73. Cahill 73. Stowaway to the Moon (TV) 74. Log of the Black Pearl (TV) 74. Mitchell 76. The Last Hard Men 76. Banjo Hackett (TV) 77. Murder at the World Series (TV) 77. Fantastic Journey (TV pilot) 77. The Wild Geese 78. Breakthrough 78. North Sea Hijack 80. The Sea Wolves 80. Travis McGee (TV) 82. The Shadow Riders (TV) 82. The Blue and the Gray (TV) 82. Sahara 84. The Dirty Dozen: The Next Mission (TV) 85. On Wings of Eagles (TV) 86. Return from the River Kwai 89. Eye of the Widow 92.

McLaglen, Victor (1883–1959).
Burly, good-humoured star of British silent films; later became popular in Hollywood.
Autobiography: 1935, *Express to Hollywood*.
The Call of the Road 20. The Glorious Adventure 21. The Beloved Brute 23. Beau Geste 26. *What Price Glory?* 26. Captain Lash 27. Mother Macree 28. The Cockeyed World 29. *Dishonoured* 30. Wicked 31. Rackety Rax 32. Hot Pepper 33. *Dick Turpin* 33. *The Lost Patrol* 34. *The Informer* (AA) 35. Under Two Flags 36. The Magnificent Brute 37. *Gunga Din* 39. Broadway Limited 41. Call Out the Marines 42. Powder Town 42. The Princess and the Pirate 44. The Michigan Kid 47. Fort Apache 48. *She Wore a Yellow Ribbon* 49. Rio Grande 50. *The Quiet Man* (AAN) 52. Fair Wind to Java 53. Prince Valiant 54. Lady Godiva 55. Many Rivers to Cross 55. Bengazi 56. The Abductors 57. Sea Fury 58, many others.

MacLaine, Shirley (1934–) (Shirley Maclean Beaty). Impish American leading lady, sister of Warren Beatty. Was signed for films while dancing in a Broadway chorus, and through the 70s was seen in TV musical specials.

Autobiographies: 1970, *Don't Fall off the Mountain*. 1975, *You Can Get There from Here*. 1983, *Out on a Limb*. 1985, *Dancing in the Light*. 1987, *It's All in the Playing*. 1989, *Going Within: A Guide for Inner Transformation*. 1995, My *Lucky Stars*.

■ *The Trouble with Harry* 55. Artists and Models 56. Around the World in Eighty Days 56. Hot Spell 57. *The Matchmaker* 58. Some Came Running (AAN) 58. The Sheepman 58. *Ask Any Girl* (BFA) 59. Career 59. Can-Can 59. *The Apartment* (BFA, AAN) 60. All in a Night's Work 61. Two Loves 61. My Geisha 62. The Children's Hour 62. Two for the Seesaw 63. *Irma La Douce* (AAN) 63. What a Way To Go 64. The Yellow Rolls-Royce 64. John Goldfarb Please Come Home 64. Gambit 66. Woman Times Seven 67. *Sweet Charity* 68. The Bliss of Mrs Blossom (GB) 68. Two Mules for Sister Sara 69. Desperate Characters 71. The Possession of Joel Delaney 72. The Turning Point (AAN) 77. Being There 79. A Change of Seasons 80. Loving Couples 80. Terms of Endearment (AA) 83. Out on a Limb (TV) 86. Madame Sousatzka 88. Steel Magnolias 89. Postcards from the Edge 90. Waiting for the Light 90. Defending Your Life 91. Used People 92. Wrestling Ernest Hemingway 93. Guarding Tess 94. The West Side Waltz (TV) 95. The Evening Star 96. Mrs Winterbourne 96. A Smile Like Yours 97.

TV series: *Shirley's World* 71.

❝ I've always felt that I would develop into a really fine actress because I care more about life beyond the camera than the life in front of it. – S.M.

I've played so many hookers they don't pay me in the regular way any more. They leave it on the dresser. – S.M.

MacLane, Barton (1900–1969).
Tough-looking American character actor, often seen as crooked cop, sheriff or gangster. In hundreds of films since 1924 debut.

Tillie and Gus 33. Black Fury 34. Ceiling Zero 36. You Only Live Once 37. Gold Is Where You Find It 38. The Maltese Falcon 41. Bombardier 43. San Quentin 46. The Treasure of the Sierra Madre 47. Kiss Tomorrow Goodbye 51. Captain Scarface (leading role) 53. Backlash 56. Geisha Boy 58. Gunfighters of Abilene 59. Law of the Lawless 63. Town Tamer 65. Buckskin 68, many others.

TV series: Outlaws 60. I Dream of Jeannie 65–69.

McLaren, Norman (1914–1987).
British-born Canadian animator-director of notable shorts, especially for the National Film Board, mainly with sound as well as picture drawn directly onto the celluloid; occasionally used live action with stop motion, and a variety of other techniques.

Allegro 39. *Dots and Loops* 40. Boogie Doodle 41. Hoppity Pop 46. Fiddle-de-dee 47. *Begone Dull Care* 49. Around is Around 51. *Neighbours* 52. Blinkety Blank 54. Rhythmetic 56. A Chairy Tale 57. Blackbird 58. Parallels 60. *Pas de Deux* 62. Mosaic 65, etc.

McLaughlin, Gibb (1884–1960).
British character actor of stage and screen, once a stage monologuist and master of disguise; used his splendidly emaciated features to great advantage.

Carnival 21. Nell Gwyn 24. The Farmer's Wife 27. Kitty 29. Sally in Our Alley 31. The Private Life of Henry VIII 32. No Funny Business 33. The Scarlet Pimpernel 34. Where There's a Will 36. Mr Reeder in Room Thirteen (title role) 40. My Learned Friend 43. Caesar and Cleopatra 45. Oliver Twist 48. The Black Rose 51. The Card 52. Hobson's Choice 54. Sea Wife 57, many others.

MacLean, Alistair (1922–1987).
Best-selling Scottish adventure writer, and occasional screenwriter. Born in Shettleston, Glasgow, and educated at the University of Glasgow, he began his writing career when, as a schoolmaster, he won a short story competition. His second book, *The Guns of Navarone*, became an international success as a novel and a film; much of his work was acquired for filming or, in some instances, written as scripts and turned into novels later. In the 60s, he also became an unsuccessful hotelier, buying, among other properties, the Jamaica Inn made famous by Daphne Du Maurier. He set up his own production company, Trio Productions, which also involved director Geoffrey Reeve, but it never produced a film. Screen rights were sold to *HMS Ulysses*, his first novel, *South by Java Head* and *The Golden Gate*, but no films have resulted so far. A proposed TV series, about a top-secret force operating under the UN Security Council, got no further than a pilot, *The Hostage Tower*. But the outlines for the series were turned into novels by other writers after his death, as was *Golden Girl*, from a screenplay he wrote. Alcoholism hampered his later career. Married twice.

Biography: 1991, *Alistair MacLean: A Life* by Jack Webster.

The Limping Man (co-w) 53. *The Guns of Navarone* 61. The Secret Ways 61. The Satan Bug (as Ian Stuart) 65. Ice Station Zebra 68. *Where Eagles Dare* (& w) 68. Puppet on a Chain (& co-w) 70. When Eight Bells Toll (& w) 71. Fear Is the Key 72. Caravan to Vaccares 74. Breakheart Pass (& co-w) 75. Golden Rendezvous 77. Force Ten from Navarone 78. Bear Island 79. The Hostage Tower (TV) 80.

❝ I detest the film world. Why? I think it is meretricious, cheap. Apart from authors, they're the biggest band of rogues in the world. – A.M.

McLean, Barbara P. (1909–1996).
American editor. Born in New Jersey, she began as an assistant editor and was hired by Daryl Zanuck in the early 30s, becoming supervising chief of Twentieth Century-Fox's editing divison from the late 40s to the 60s. Married director Robert D. Webb and also produced two of his films, *Seven Cities of Gold* 55 and *On the Threshold of Space* 56.

The Bowery 33. Clive of India 35. Les Misérables (AAN) 35. Lloyds of London (AAN) 36. Alexander's Ragtime Band 38. In Old Chicago 38. Jesse James 39. The Rains Came (AAN) 39. Stanley and Livingstone 39. Tobacco Road 41. The Black Swan 42. The Song of Bernadette (AAN) 43. *Wilson* (AA) 44. Margie 46. Nightmare Alley 47. All About Eve (AAN) 50. Twelve O'Clock High 50. Viva Zapata 52. Niagara 53. The Egyptian 54, many others.

MacLean, Douglas (1890–1967).
American silent screen comedian. Later became writer/producer. Retired 1938.

As Ye Sow 19. Captain Kidd Jnr 19. 23½ Hours' Leave 21. The Hottentot 22. Never Say Die 24. Introduce Me 25. Seven Keys to Baldpate 25, etc.

McLeod, Catherine (1921–1997).
American leading lady of the 40s.

I've Always Loved You 46. Will Tomorrow Ever Come? 47. So Young So Bad 50. The Fortune Hunter 54. Ride the Wild Surf 64, etc.

McLeod, Norman Z. (1898–1964).
American director, in Hollywood from the early 20s. Originally an animator; later wrote screenplays (e.g. *Skippy* 31); then turned to direction.

Monkey Business 31. *Horse Feathers* 32. If I Had a Million (part) 33. Alice in Wonderland 33. *It's a Gift* 34. Pennies from Heaven 36. *Topper* 37. Merrily We Live 38. Panama Hattie 41. The Kid from Brooklyn 46. *The Secret Life of Walter Mitty* 47. *The Paleface* 47. My Favorite Spy 51. Never Wave at a WAC 53. Casanova's Big Night 54. Alias Jesse James 59, etc.

McLerie, Allyn (1926–) (Allyn Ann McLerie; now so known).
Canadian-born dancer and leading lady who made films amid stage work.

Words and Music 48. Where's Charley? 52. The Desert Song 53. Phantom of the Rue Morgue 54. Battle Cry 55. The Cowboys 72. Cinderella Liberty 74. All The President's Men 76. A Shining Season (TV) 79. And Baby Makes Six (TV) 79, etc.

TV series: The Tony Randall Show 76–78. The Days and Nights of Molly Dodd 87–88.

MacLiammoir, Michael (1899–1978) (Alfred Willmore).
English actor of the old school, playwright, artist and stage designer who transformed himself into a significant figure in Irish theatre. Born in Willesden, London, he was on stage as a successful boy actor from 1911, appearing in several silent films, including the Irish-made *Land of Her Fathers* 24, which is now lost. From 1918, he re-invented himself as Irish, learning to speak the language, changing his name and claiming to have been born in Cork. In partnership with Hilton Edwards, he founded the influential Gate Theatre in Dublin in 1928. His film roles were few, but one, as Iago in Orson Welles's *Othello*, resulted in a book of witty reminiscences, *Put Money in Thy Purse* (1952). In later life, he received international acclaim for his one-man show about Oscar Wilde, *The Importance of Being Oscar*, which was also televised.

Autobiographies: 1946, *All For Hecuba: An Irish Theatrical Autobiography*. 1961, *Each Actor on His Ass*. 1968, *An Oscar of No Importance*. 1977, *Enter a Goldfish: Memoirs of an Irish Actor Young and Old*.

Biography: 1990, *The Importance of Being Michael* by Michael O'Haodha; 1994, *The Boys* by Christopher Fitz-Simon.

Othello 52. Tom Jones (voice) 63. Thirty is a Dangerous Age, Cynthia 68. The Kremlin Letter 70. What's the Matter with Helen? 71, etc.

❝ Life is a long rehearsal for a play that is never produced. – M.M.

McLish, Rachel.
American actress, a former Ms Olympia and world women's body-building champion. She has also written books on exercise and starred in an exercise video.

Pumping Iron 2: The Women (doc) 84. Aces: Iron Eagle III 92. Ravenhawke 95, etc.

MacMahon, Aline (1899–1991).
Sad-faced, gentle-mannered American character actress, mostly in films of the 30s.

Five Star Final 31. The Mouthpiece 32. Life Begins 32. Once in a Lifetime 32. *Golddiggers of 1933* 33. Heroes for Sale 33. *Babbitt* 34. Kind Lady 35. I Live My Life 35. Ah Wilderness 35. When You're in Love 37. Back Door to Heaven 39. Out of the Fog 41. The Lady is Willing 42. Dragon Seed (AAN) 44. Guest in the House 44. The Mighty McGurk 46. The Search 48. Roseanna McCoy 49. The Flame and the Arrow 50. The Eddie Cantor Story 53. The Man From Laramie 55. Cimarron 60. I Could Go on Singing 63. All the Way Home 63, etc.

MacMahon, Horace (1907–1971).
American character actor, likely to be best remembered as the older cop in the TV series *Naked City*. In films from 1937, often as cop or gangster.

Navy Blues 37. King of the Newsboys 38. Rose of Washington Square 39. Lady Scarface 41. Lady Gangster 45. Waterfront at Midnight 48. *Detective Story* 51. Man in the Dark 53. Susan Slept Here 54. My Sister Eileen 55. Beau James 57. The Swinger 66. *The Detective* 68, many others.

TV series: Martin Kane 50. The Danny Thomas Show 53. *Naked City* 59–62. Mr Broadway 64.

McMillan, Kenneth (1933–1989).
Burly American character actor.

The Taking of Pelham 123 74. Oliver's Story 78. Blood Brothers 78. Hide in Plain Sight 80. Carny 80. True Confessions 81. Eyewitness 81. Ragtime 81. Partners 82. Protocol 84. Dune 84. Runaway Train 85. Armed and Dangerous 86. Three Fugitives 89, etc.

TV series: Rhoda 77–78. Suzanne Pleshette Is Maggie Briggs 84. Our Family Honor 85–86.

McMillan, Terry.
American novelist and screenwriter.

Waiting to Exhale (oa, co-w) 95. How Stella Got Her Groove Back (oa, co-w) 98, etc.

MacMurray, Fred (1908–1991).
Likeable, durable American leading man of the 30s and 40s; found a new lease of life in Walt Disney comedies of the early 60s. His second wife was June Haver.

■ Grand Old Girl 35. *The Gilded Lily* 35. Car 99 35. Men without Names 35. Alice Adams 35. Hands Across the Table 35. The Bride Comes Home 35. *The Trail of the Lonesome Pine* 36. 13 Hours by Air 36. The Princess Comes Across 36. The Texas Rangers 36. Maid of Salem 37. Champagne Waltz 37. Swing High Swing Low 37. Exclusive 37. True Confession 37. Coconut Grove 38. *Sing You Sinners* 38. Men With Wings 38. Café Society 39. Invitation to Happiness 39. Honeymoon in Bali 39. Little Old New York 40. Remember the Night 40. Too Many Husbands 40. Rangers of Fortune 40. Virginia 41. One Night in Lisbon 41. New York Town 41. Dive Bomber 41. The Lady Is Willing 42. Take a Letter Darling 42. The Forest Rangers 42. Star Spangled Rhythm 42. Flight for Freedom 43. Above Suspicion 43. No Time for Love 43. Standing Room Only 44. And the Angels Sing 44. *Double Indemnity* 44. Murder He Says 44. Practically Yours 45. Where Do We Go from Here? 45. Captain Eddie 45. Pardon My Past 46. Smoky 46. Suddenly It's Spring 47. The Egg and I 47. Singapore 47. The Miracle of the Bells 48. On Our Merry Way 48. Don't Trust Your Husband 48. Family Honeymoon 48. Father was a Fullback 48. Borderline 50. Never a Dull Moment 50. A Millionaire for Christy 51. Callaway went Thataway 51. Fair Wind to Java 53. The Moonlighter 53. *The Caine Mutiny* 54. *Pushover* 54. Woman's World 54. The Far Horizons 55. The Rains of Ranchipur 55. At Gunpoint 55. There's Always Tomorrow 56. Gun for a Coward 57. Quantez 57. Day of the Badman 57. Good Day for a Hanging 58. *The Shaggy Dog* 59. Face of a Fugitive 59. The Oregon Trail 59. *The Apartment* 60. *The Absent Minded Professor* 61. Bon Voyage 62. Son of Flubber 63. Kisses for My President 64. Follow Me Boys 66. The Happiest Millionaire 67. Charlie and the Angel 73. The Chadwick Family (TV) 75. Beyond the Bermuda Triangle (TV) 76. The Swarm 78.

TV series: My *Three Sons* 60–72.

McMurray, Mary (1949–).
British director.

The Assam Garden 85. The Veiled One (TV) 89. Kissing the Gunner's Daughter (TV) 92, etc.

McMurtry, Larry (1936–).
American screenwriter and novelist.

Hud 63. The Last Picture Show (co-w) (AA) 71. Lovin' Molly (from Leaving Cheyenne) 74. Terms of Endearment (oa) 83. Lonesome Dove (oa) (TV) 89. Montana (TV) 90. Texasville (co-w) 90. Falling from Grace 92. Buffalo Girls (TV) 95. Larry McMurtry's 'Streets of Laredo' (TV) 95. Larry McMurtry's 'Dead Man's Walk' (TV) 96. The Evening Star 96, etc.

McNair, Barbara (1939–).
American actress and singer.

If He Hollers Let Him Go 69. Stiletto 69. Change of Habit 69. They Call Me Mister Tibbs 70. The Organization 71. Dead Right 88, etc.

McNally, Stephen (1913–1994) (Horace McNally).
American leading man and sometimes 'heavy', in films from 1942. Former lawyer.

The Man from Down Under 43. The Harvey Girls 45. Johnny Belinda 48. Rogues' Regiment 48. No Way Out 50. Winchester 73 50. The Raging Tide 51. Devil's Canyon 53. Black Castle 53. Make Haste to Live 54. A Bullet Is Waiting 54. Tribute to a Bad Man 56. Hell's Five Hours 58. The Fiend Who Walked the West 58. Hell Bent for Leather 59. Requiem for a Gunfighter 65. Panic in the City 68. Black Gunn 72. Hi-Riders 78. Dear Detective (TV) 79, etc.

TV series: *Target the Corruptors* 61.

McNally, Terrence (1939–).
American dramatist and screenwriter, often on homosexual themes. Born in St Petersburg, Florida, he was educated at Columbia University.

The Ritz (w, oa) 76. Earth Girls Are Easy (co-w) 88. Frankie and Johnnie (w, oa) 91. Love! Valour! Compassion! (w, oa) 97, etc.

TV series: Mama Malone (p, w) 84.

McNamara, Edward (1884–1944).
Burly American character actor, usually cast as a cop, which had been his occupation before he became an Irish tenor and then an actor.

Lucky in Love 29. I Am a Fugitive from a Chain Gang 32. 20,000 Years in Sing Sing 33. Great Guy 37. Girl Overboard 37. The League of Frightened Men 37. Strawberry Blonde 41. The Devil and Miss Jones 41. Johnny Come Lately 43. Margin of Error 43. Arsenic and Old Lace 44, etc.

McNamara, Maggie (1928–1978).
Capable but short-staying American leading lady of the 50s. Committed suicide. At the time of her death she was working as a secretary.

■ *The Moon Is Blue* (AAN) 53. Three Coins in the Fountain 54. Prince of Players 55. The Cardinal 63.

McNamara, William (1965–).
American actor, born in Dallas, Texas.
The Beat 88. Stealing Home 88. Dream a Little Dream 89. Dead Bang 89. Texasville 90. Wildflower (TV) 91. Honor Thy Mother (TV) 92. Sworn to Vengeance (TV) 93. Chasers 94. Surviving the Game 94. Copycat 95. Natural Enemy (TV) 96. The Brylcreem Boys (TV) 96. Stag 97, etc.

McNaught, Bob (1915–1976).
British director, also associate producer on many films.
Grand National Night 53. Sea Wife 57. A Story of David 61, etc.

McNaughton, Gus (1884–1969) (Augustus Howard).
British comedy actor, once a Fred Karno singer, on stage from 1899.
Murder 30. The Thirty-Nine Steps 35. Keep Your Seats Please 37. The Divorce of Lady X 38. Trouble Brewing 39. Jeannie 41. Much Too Shy 42. Here Comes the Sun 46, etc.

McNaughton, John (1949–).
American director and screenwriter.
Henry: Portrait of a Serial Killer 86. The Borrower 89. Sex, Drugs, Rock & Roll 91. Mad Dog and Glory 93. Normal Life 96. Wild Things 98. Condo Painting 98, etc.

McNear, Howard (1905–1969).
American comedy actor, familiar on Burns and Allen's television series as the plumber. Later with Andy Griffith.
The Long Long Trailer 54. Bundle of Joy 56. Voyage to the Bottom of the Sea 61. Follow That Dream 62. Irma la Douce 63. Kiss Me Stupid 64. The Fortune Cookie 66, etc.

Macnee, Patrick (1922–).
Smooth British leading man, best known on TV.
Autobiography: 1993, *King B: A Life in the Movies*.
The Life and Death of Colonel Blimp 43. Hamlet 48. Flesh and Blood 51. Three Cases of Murder 55. The Battle of the River Plate 56. Les Girls 58. Mr Jericho (TV) 70. Incense for the Damned 70. King Solomon's Treasure 77. Billion Dollar Threat (TV) 79. The Sea Wolves 80. The Howling 80. Young Doctors in Love 82. For the Term of His Natural Life (TV) 82. The Return of the Man from UNCLE (TV) 83. A View to a Kill 85. Shadey 85. Down Under 86. Waxwork 88. Lobster Man from Mars 89. Masque of the Red Death 89. Sorry, Wrong Number (TV) 89. Sherlock Holmes and the Leading Lady (TV) 91. Waxwork II: Lost in Time 91. The Hound of London 93. The Gambler Returns: The Luck of the Draw (TV) 93. The Avengers (as Invisible Jones) 98, etc.
TV series: *The Avengers* 60–68. *The New Avengers* 76. Gavilan 82. Empire 84.

McNeice, Ian (1950–).
Chubby British character actor who can be comic or menacing, as the occasion requires.
Top Secret! 84. Edge of Darkness 85. 84 Charing Cross Road 86. Whoops Apocalypse 86. Personal Services 87. The Lonely Passion of Judith Hearne 87. The Raggedy Rawney 87. Valmont 89. The Russia House 90. Year of the Comet 92. No Escape 94. Funny Bones 95. The Englishman Who Went up a Hill but Came Down a Mountain 95. Ace Ventura: When Nature Calls 95. The Beautician and the Beast 97. A Life Less Ordinary 97. P. D. James's A Certain Justice (TV) 98, etc.

McNichol, Kristy (1962–).
American actress.
Black Sunday 76. Like Mom, Like Me (TV) 78. The End 79. Summer of My German Soldier (TV) 79. Little Darlings 80. The Night the Lights Went Out in Georgia 81. Only When I Laugh 81. The Pirate Movie 82. Just the Way You Are 84. Dream Lover 85. You Can't Hurry Love 88. Two Moon Junction 88. The Forgotten One 90. Baby of the Bride (TV) 91, etc.
TV series: Apple's Way 74–75. Family 76–80.

MaCowan, Norman (1877–1961).
Scottish character actor.
Whisky Galore 48. Laxdale Hall 53. X the Unknown 56. Tread Softly Stranger 58. The Boy and the Bridge 59. Kidnapped 60, etc.

MacPhail, Angus. (1903–1962).
British screenwriter and production executive who began in films as a title writer in 1926, becoming story supervisor at Gainsborough (1931–37), at Gaumont British (1939–48), and at Ealing Studios. Educated at Cambridge, where he wrote a book of limericks, he was also a founding member of the Film Society and a film critic. His career was brought to a premature end by his alcoholism, and he spent his last years living in a hotel in Eastbourne.
The Wrecker (co-w) 28. The Calendar (co-w) 31. The Ghost Train (co-w) 31. My Old China (co-w) 31. Went the Day Well? (co-w) 42. The Captive Heart (co-w) 46. Frieda (co-w) 47. *It Always Rains on Sunday* (co-w) 47. Train of Events (co-w) 49. *Whisky Galore!* (co-w) 49. The Man Who Knew Too Much (co-w) 55. The Wrong Man (co-w) 56, etc.
❝ There is in existence a large number of excellent text-books on the writing of films. The authors tell you exactly how to handle plot situations, continuity, characters and dialogue; they know so much about it, in fact, that you can't help wondering why they don't make their own fortunes by writing film stories themselves. – A.M.
He was a contradiction: a man who treasured Tolstoy and Chekhov, who had ambitions to translate his favourite works in French literature, but earned his living by making up jokes for Tommy Trinder. – *Charles Drazin, The Finest Years: British Cinema in the 1940s*

MacPhail, Douglas (1910–1944).
American singer.
Born to Dance 36. Maytime 37. Sweethearts 38. *Babes in Arms* 39. Little Nellie Kelly 40. Born to Sing 42, etc.

Macpherson, Elle (1964–).
Australian model and actress.
Sirens 93. If Lucky Fell 96. Jane Eyre 96. The Mirror Has Two Faces 96. Batman and Robin 97. The Edge 97, etc.

MacPherson, Jeanie (1897–1946).
American actress, dancer, screenwriter and director. As an actress, she was associated with D. W. Griffith before becoming a leading lady at Universal, where she also worked as a director and writer. From 1916 she worked for Cecil B. De Mille as screenwriter.
AS ACTRESS: The Vaquero's Vow 08. The Death Disc 09. Enoch Arden 10. Carmen 13. Hollywood 23.
AS WRITER: The Golden Chance 15. Joan the Woman 16. The Dream Girl 16. The Devil Stone 17. The Whispering Chorus 18. Male and Female 19. The Affairs of Anatol 21. Adam's Rib 23. The Ten Commandments 23. The Golden Bed 25. Young April 26. The King of Kings 27. Dynamite 29. Madam Satan 30. Fra Diavolo 33. Buccaneer 38, etc.

McQueen, Butterfly (1911–1995) (Thelma McQueen).
American character actress. She quit acting because of the roles offered to her. Died of burns sustained while trying to light a heater.
Gone with the Wind (as the weeping maid) 39. Cabin in the Sky 43. Flame of the Barbary Coast 45. Mildred Pierce 45. Duel in the Sun 46. The Phynx 70. Amazing Grace 74. The Mosquito Coast 86, etc.
TV series: Beulah 50–53.
Famous line (*Gone with the Wind*): 'I don't know nothin' about birthin' babies.'

McQueen, Chad (1960–) (Chadwick Steven McQueen).
American leading actor, in run-of-the-mill action movies. He is the son of Steve MCQUEEN.
Skateboard 77. The Karate Kid 84. Fever Pitch 85. Nightforce 86. Martial Law 90. Death Ring 93. Number One Fan 94. New York Cop 94. Money to Burn 94. Indecent Behavior 2 94. Red Line 96, etc.

McQueen, Steve (1930–1980).
Unconventional but fashionable American leading man of the 60s and 70s: usually played tough, sexy and determined. The second of his three wives was actress Ali MCGRAW (1973–78).
Biographies: 1974, *Steve McQueen* by Malachy McCoy. 1984, *McQueen* by William F. Nolan. 1995, *Steve McQueen: Portrait of an American Rebel* by Marshall Terrill.
■ Somebody Up There Likes Me 56. Never Love a Stranger 58. The Blob 58. Never So Few 59. The Great St Louis Bank Robbery 59. *The Magnificent Seven* 60. The Honeymoon Machine 61. Hell is for Heroes 61. The War Lover 62. *The Great Escape* 63. *Love with the Proper Stranger* 63. Soldier in the Rain 63. Baby the Rain Must Fall 65. *The Cincinnati Kid* 65. Nevada Smith 66. The Sand Pebbles (AAN) 66. The Thomas Crown Affair 68. *Bullitt* 68. The Reivers 70. Le Mans 71. Junior Bonner 72. Getaway 72. Papillon 73. The Towering Inferno 74. An Enemy of the People 76. Tom Horn 80. The Hunter 80.
TV series: Wanted Dead or Alive 58.
❝ In my own mind, I'm not sure that acting is something for a grown man to be doing. – S.M.
Stardom equals freedom. It's the only equation that matters. – S.M.
I can honestly say he's the most difficult actor I ever worked with. – *Norman Jewison*
One thing about Steve, he didn't like the women in his life to have balls. – *Ali MacGraw*
You've got to realize that a Steve McQueen performance lends itself to monotony. – *Robert Mitchum*

Macquitty, William (1905–).
British producer who came to feature films via wartime MoI shorts.
The Happy Family 52. The Beachcomber 54. Above Us the Waves 55. A Night to Remember 58. The Informers 64, etc.

Macrae, Duncan (1905–1967) (John Macrae).
Craggy-faced Scottish stage actor who made some impressive film appearances.
■ *The Brothers* 47. Whisky Galore 48. The Woman in Question 50. *The Kidnappers* 53. You're Only Young Twice 53. The Maggie 54. Geordie 55. Rockets Galore 56. The Bridal Path 58. Kidnapped 59. Our Man in Havana 59. Greyfriars Bobby 60. *Tunes of Glory* 60. The Best of Enemies 61. A Jolly Bad Fellow 64. Thirty is a Dangerous Age Cynthia 67. Casino Royale 67.

MacRae, Gordon (1921–1986).
American actor-singer, a former child performer who broke into films from radio.
■ The Big Punch 48. Look for the Silver Lining 49. Backfire 49. The Daughter of Rosie O'Grady 50. Return of the Frontiersman 50. Tea for Two 50. West Point Story 51. On Moonlight Bay 51. Starlift 51. About Face 52. By the Light of the Silvery Moon 53. Three Sailors and a Girl 53. The Desert Song 53. Oklahoma 55. Carousel 56. The Best Things in Life Are Free 56. The Pilot 79.

Macready, George (1909–1973).
American character actor, a descendant of Macready the tragedian. A splendid villain, neurotic or weakling, he ran an art gallery before coming to films in 1942.
■ The Commandos Strike at Dawn 42. The Seventh Cross 44. Wilson 44. The Story of Dr Wassell 44. The Conspirators 44. Follow the Boys 44. Soul of a Monster 44. The Missing Juror 45. Counterattack 45. Don Juan Quilligan 45. The Fighting Guardsman 45. *I Love a Mystery* 45. The Monster and the Ape 45. A Song to Remember 45. My Name Is Julia Ross 45. *Gilda* 46. The Man Who Dared 46. The Walls Came Tumbling Down 46. The Return of Monte Cristo 46. The Bandit of Sherwood Forest 46. The Swordsman 47. Down to Earth 47. The Big Clock 48. The Black Arrow 48. Coroner Creek 48. Beyond Glory 48. The Gallant Blade 48. *Alias Nick Beal* 49. Knock on Any Door 49. Johnny Allegro 49. The Doolins of Oklahoma 49. The Nevadan 50. A Lady without Passport 50. The Desert Hawk 50. Fortunes of Captain Blood 50. Rogues of Sherwood Forest 50. Tarzan's Peril 51. The Golden Horde 51. *Detective Story* 51. The Desert Fox 51. The Green Glove 52. Treasure of the Golden Condor 53. Julius Caesar 53. The Stranger Wore a Gun 53. The Golden Blade 53. Duffy of San Quentin 54. Vera Cruz 54. A Kiss Before Dying 56. Thunder Over Arizona 56. The Abductors 57. Gunfire at Indian Gap 57. *Paths of Glory* 57. The Alligator People 59. Plunderers of Painted Flats 59. Jet Over the Atlantic 59. Two Weeks in Another Town 62. Taras Bulba 62. *Seven Days in May* 64. Dead Ringer 64. Where Love Has Gone 64. The Great Race 65. The Human Duplicators 65. Fame Is the Name of the Game (TV) 66. The Young Lawyers (TV) 69. Night Gallery (TV) 69. Daughter of the Mind (TV) 69. Tora! Tora! Tora! 70. The Return of Count Yorga 71.
TV series: Peyton Place 66–68.

McShane, Ian (1942–).
British general-purpose leading man. He is best known for his role as the antique dealer Lovejoy in the TV series.
The Wild and the Willing 62. The Pleasure Girls 65. Sky West and Crooked 66. The Battle of Britain 68. If It's Tuesday This Must Be Belgium (US) 69. Freelance 70. Pussycat Pussycat I Love You (US) 70. Tam Lin 70. Villain 71. Sitting Target 72. The Last of Sheila 73. Ransom 74. Journey into Fear 75. Jesus of Nazareth (TV) 77. Roots (TV) 77. Dirty Money (TV) 79. Cheaper to Keep Her 80. Grace Kelly (TV) 83. Exposed 83. Too Scared to Scream 84. Ordeal by Innocence 85. The Murders in the Rue Morgue (TV) 86. Perry Mason: The Case of the Paris Paradox (TV) 90. Soul Survivors (TV) 95, etc.
TV series: Disraeli 78. Lovejoy 86, 90–95. Madson 96.

McShane, Kitty (1898–1964).
British actress, wife of music-hall comedian Arthur Lucan (Old Mother Riley), who partnered him on the halls and in their many films as his daughter. For a list of films, see LUCAN, Arthur.

McTaggart, James (1928–1974).
British TV director.
All the Way Up 69.

McTiernan, John (1951–).
American director and screenwriter who began as a director of TV commercials.
Nomads (wd) 85. Predator 87. Die Hard 88. The Hunt for Red October 90. Medicine Man 92. The Last Action Hero 93. Die Hard 3 95, etc.

McWade, Robert (1872–1938).
American character actor who after long stage career came to films as an elderly crotch.
Second Youth 24. The Home Towners 28. Sins of the Children 30. Cimarron 31. Grand Hotel 32. Two Seconds 32. Movie Crazy 32. Back Street 32. The Kennel Murder Case 33. The Prizefighter and the Lady 33. College Rhythm 34. The President Vanishes 34. Diamond Jim 35. The Frisco Kid 35. Society Doctor 35. Anything Goes 36. Bunker Bean 36. California Straight Ahead 37. This Is My Affair 37. Of Human Hearts 38, many others.

MacWilliams, Glen (1898–1984).
American cinematographer.
Ever Since Eve 21. Captain January 24. Ankles Preferred 27. Hearts in Dixie 29. The Sea Wolf 30. Hat Check Girl 32. Evergreen (GB) 34. Great Guns 41. He Hired the Boss 43. Lifeboat 44. Wing and a Prayer 44. If I'm Lucky 46, many others.

Ma, Wu (aka Ng Ma).
Hong Kong actor and director, best known for movies combining kung fu and ghosts or other horrors.
The Deaf and Mute Heroine (& d) 71. 7 Blows of the Dragon (d) 72. By Hook or by Crook 80. Close Encounters of the Spooky Kind 80. Beware of Pickpocket (& d) 81. Close Encounters of the Spooky Kind 2 81. The Dead and the Deadly/Ren Xia Ren (& d) 83. Project A 83. Wheels on Meals 84. Mr Boo Meets Pom Pom (d) 85. The First Mission (& p) 85. Peking Opera Blues 86. Shanghai Express 86. A Chinese Ghost Story 87. Magnificent Warriors 87. My Cousin the Ghost (& d) 87. City on Fire 87. Painted Faces 88. Portrait of a Nymph/Hua Zhong Xian 88. Magic Cop 89. Burning Sensation/Huazhua Gui (& d) 89. A Chinese Ghost Story Part II 90. Once Upon a Time in China 90. Swordsman 90. Heroic Brothers 91. Red and Black 91. Painted Skin 92. Legend of Fong Sai Yuk 92. Drug Tiger 93. Master of Zen 94. The Chinese Ghostbuster (& d) 94. Circus Kids (& d) 94. Iron Monkey II 96, many others.

Maas, Dick (1951–).
Dutch director, screenwriter, composer and producer, a former cartoonist. He runs his own production company, First Floor Features, in partnership with Laurens Geels.
Rigor Mortis (d) 81. The Lift (wd, m) 83. Abel (p) 85. Flodder (wd, m) 86. Amsterdamned (wd, m) 87. My Blue Heaven (p) 89. The Last Island (p) 89. Wings of Fame (p) 90. Oh Boy! (p) 91.

The Northerners (p) 92. Flodder Does Manhattan (wd, m) 92. Channel Fever (d) 93. Flodder 3: The Final Story 95, etc.

Macat, Julio.
American cinematographer.
Home Alone 90. Only the Lonely 91. Home Alone 2: Lost in New York 92. So I Married an Axe Murderer 93. Ace Ventura, Pet Detective 94. Miracle on 34th Street 94. Moonlight and Valentino 95. The Nutty Professor 96. My Fellow Americans 96. Home Alone 3 97, etc.

Macchio, Ralph (1962–).
American leading man.
Dangerous Company 82. The Outsiders 83. The Karate Kid 84. Karate Kid 2 85. Crossroads 85. Distant Thunder 88. The Karate Kid Part III 89. Too Much Sun 91. My Cousin Vinny 92. Naked in New York 93, etc.
TV series: Eight Is Enough 80–81.

Macedo, Rita (1928–1993) (María Concepción Macedo Guzman).
Mexican leading actress. Her first husband was novelist Carlos Fuentes.
The Five Nights of Adam/Las Cinco Noches de Adan 42. The Criminal Life of Archibaldo de la Cruz 55. Nazarin 58. The Curse of the Crying Woman 61. El Fugitivo 65. You, Me and Us/Yo y Nosotros 71, etc.

Machaty, Gustav (1898–1963).
Czech director best remembered for exposing Hedy Lamarr's naked charms in *Extase* 33.
The Kreutzer Sonata 26. Erotikon 29. From Saturday to Sunday 31. Nocturno 35. Within the Law (US) 39. Jealousy (US) 45, etc.

Macht, Stephen (1942–).
Heavy-featured American leading man.
Amelia Earhart (TV) 76. Raid on Entebbe (TV) 77. The Choirboys 77. Loose Change (TV) 78. Ring of Passion (TV) 78. Hunters of the Deep (TV) 78. The Immigrants (TV) 78. Enola Gay (TV) 80. Killjoy (TV) 81. A Caribbean Mystery (TV) 82. The Monster Squad 87. Stephen King's Graveyard Shift (TV) 91. Trancers III: Deth Lives 92. Trancers IV: Jack of Swords 93. Trancers V: Sudden Deth 94. Siringo 94. Galgameth 96. Watchers Reborn 98, etc.
TV series: American Dream 91. Knots Landing 82–83. Cagney & Lacey 85–88.

Mack, Helen (1913–1986).
American leading lady of the 30s, former child actress.
Zaza 24. Grit 28. The Silent Witness 31. Son of Kong 34. She 35. The Return of Peter Grimm 35. The Milky Way 36. Last Train from Madrid 37. Gambling Ship 39. His Girl Friday 40. Divorce 45, etc.

Mack, Marion (1902–1989) (Joanne Marion McCreery).
American actress, best known for starring with Buster Keaton in *The General* 26. Born in Mammoth, Utah, she began in films for Mack Sennett and later appeared in a few westerns. After she retired from acting, she wrote some short films for MGM together with her husband, producer Louis Lewyn.
Mary of the Movies 23. One of the Bravest 25. Carnival Girl 26, etc.

Mack, Russell (1892–1972).
American director of the 30s.
Second Wife 30. Heaven on Earth 31. Once in a Lifetime 32. Private Jones 33. The Band Plays On 34. The Meanest Girl in Town 35, etc.

Macy, Bill (1922–).
American character actor.
All Together Now (TV) 75. The Late Show 76. Death at Love House (TV) 76. Stunt Seven (TV) 79. The Jerk 79. My Favorite Year 82. Movers and Shakers 85. Bad Medicine 85. Sibling Rivalry 90. Murder in the First 95, etc.
TV series: Maude 72–77.

Macy, William H. (1950–).
American character actor. He is also a scriptwriter and Director in Residence at the Atlantic Theatre Company in New York City. In 1998, he set up a film production company, Films of Atlantic, with David Mamet.
Somewhere in Time 80. House of Games 87. Radio Days 87. Things Change 88. Homicide 91. Shadows and Fog 91. Benny and Joon 93. Being Human 94. The Client 94. Oleanna 94. Murder in the First 94. Mr Holland's Opus 95. *Fargo* (as Jerry Lundegaard) (AAN) 96. Down Periscope 96. Boogie Nights 97. Air Force One 97. Wag the Dog 97. Pleasantville 98. Psycho 98, etc.
TV series: ER 94– .

Madden, John.
American director, from British television.
Poppyland (TV) 84. Grown Ups (TV) 85. The Widowmaker (TV) 90. Ethan Frome (TV) 92. Golden Gate (TV) 93. Prime Suspect: The Lost Child (TV) 95. *Mrs Brown* (GB) 97. Shakespeare in Love 98, etc.

Madden, Peter (1905–1976).
Gaunt British character actor of TV and films.
Counterblast 48. Tom Brown's Schooldays 51. The Battle of the V.1 58. Hell Is a City 60. Saturday Night and Sunday Morning 60. The Loneliness of the Long Distance Runner 62. The Very Edge 63. Doctor Zhivago 66, etc.

Maddern, Victor (1926–1993).
Stocky cockney character actor, formerly on stage and radio.
Seven Days to Noon (debut) 49. Cockleshell Heroes 55. Private's Progress 56. Blood of the Vampire 58. I'm All Right Jack 59. HMS Defiant 61. Rotten to the Core 65. Circus of Fear 67. Death on the Nile 78, many others.
TV series: Fair Exchange (US) 62.

Maddow, Ben (1909–1992).
American screenwriter.
The Asphalt Jungle (co-w, AAN) 50. The Unforgiven 60. The Way West (co-w) 67. The Chairman 69. The Secret of Santa Vittoria (co-w) 69, etc.

Madigan, Amy (1951–).
American leading lady of the 80s. She is married to actor Ed Harris.
Love Child 82. Love Letters 82. Alamo Bay 84. Places in the Heart 84. Streets of Fire 84. Twice in a Lifetime (AAN) 85. Nowhere to Hide 87. The Prince of Pennsylvania 88. Field of Dreams 89. Roe vs Wade (TV) 89. Uncle Buck 89. The Dark Half 93. And Then There Was None (TV) 94. Riders of the Purple Sage (TV) 96. Female Perversions 96. Loved 97. A Bright Shining Lie (TV) 98, etc.

Madison, Guy (1922–) (Robert Moseley).
American leading man, in films since 1944 after naval career.
Since You Went Away (debut) 44. Till the End of Time 46. The Charge at Feather River 53. The Command 54. Five Against the House 55. On the Threshold of Space 55. The Last Frontier 56. Hilda Crane 57. Bullwhip 58. La Schiava di Roma 60. Gunmen of the Rio Grande 65. The Mystery of Thug Island 66. The Last Panzer Battalion 68. Where's Willie 78, etc.
TV series: *Wild Bill Hickok* 51–54.

Madison, Noel (1898–1975) (Nathaniel Moscovitch).
American actor of sinister roles, especially gangsters. Formerly known as Nat Madison; son of actor Maurice Moscovitch.
Sinners' Holiday 30. Manhattan Melodrama 34. G-Men 35. The Man Who Made Diamonds 37. Crackerjack (GB) 39. Footsteps in the Dark 41. Jitterbugs 43. Gentleman from Nowhere 49, etc.

Madonna (1958–) (Madonna Louise Veronica Ciccone).
Raucous and raunchy pop-singer who courts controversy. Her film roles so far have won her few new fans. In 1992 she signed a $60 million deal with Time Warner to form Maverick, a joint production company covering records, music publishing, films, television and books. She was played by Terumi Matthews in the TV biopic *Madonna: Innocence Lost* 95.
A Certain Sacrifice 79. Desperately Seeking Susan 85. Shanghai Surprise 86. Who's That Girl? 87. Bloodhounds of Broadway 89. Dick Tracy 90. Truth or Dare/In Bed with Madonna 91. Shadows and Fog 91. A League of Their Own 92. Body of Evidence 92. Snake Eyes 93. Blue in the Face 95. Four Rooms 95. Girl 6 96. Evita 96, etc.
❝ I lost my virginity as a career move. – M.
Every decade has its star and Madonna was it in the 80s. But the 80s are over. – *Courtney Love*

Madsen, Michael (1947–).
Burly American actor, often in tough-guy roles. He is the brother of Virginia Madsen.
War Games 83. Racing with the Moon 84. The Natural 84. The Killing Time 87. Shadows in the Storm 88. Blood Red 89. Kill Me Again 89. The End of Innocence 90. The Doors 91. Thelma & Louise 91. Fatal Instinct 92. Straight Talk 92. Reservoir Dogs 92. A House in the Hills 93. Free Willy 93. Money for Nothing 93. Trouble Bound 93. The Getaway 93. Season of Change 94. Wyatt Earp 94. Final Combination 94. Species 95. Free Willy 2: The Adventure Home 95. God's Army 95. Man with a Gun 95. Mulholland Falls 96. The Maker 97. Executive Target 97. Diary of a Serial Killer 97. Species 2 98. The Sender 98. Ballad of the Nightingale 98, etc.
TV series: Our Family Honor 85–86. Vengeance Unlimited 98– .

Madsen, Virginia (1963–).
American actress. She is married to director Danny Huston.
Class 83. Electric Dreams 84. Dune 84. Modern Girls 86. Slam Dance 87. Hot to Trot 88. Mr North 88. The Hot Spot 90. Highlander II: The Quickening 91. Candy Man 92. A Murderous Affair: The Carolyn Warmus Story (TV) 92. Blue Tiger 94. Bitter Vengeance (TV) 94. The Prophecy 95. Just Your Luck 96. Ghosts of Mississippi 96. John Grisham's The Rainmaker 97. Ballad of the Nightingale 98, etc.

Maeterlinck, Maurice (1862–1949).
Belgian writer whose fantasy play *The Blue Bird* was filmed several times, never with success.

Maffia, Roma.
American actress, from the stage.
Smithereens 82. Married to the Mob 88. American Blue Note 91. The Paper 94. Disclosure 94. The Heidi Chronicles (TV) 95. Nick of Time 95. Eraser 96. Kiss the Girls 97, etc.
TV series: Chicago Hope 94–95. Profiler 96.

Magee, Patrick (1924–1982).
British general-purpose actor, often in sinister roles.
The Criminal 60. The Servant 63. Zulu 64. Masque of the Red Death 64. The Skull 65. *The Marat/Sade* 67. *The Birthday Party* 68. King Lear 70. You Can't Win 'Em All 71. The Fiend 71. A Clockwork Orange 71. Demons of the Mind 72. Asylum 72. Rough Cut 80, etc.

Magnani, Anna (1907–1973).
Volatile Italian star actress (Egyptian-born).
The Blind Woman of Sorrento 34. Tempo Massimo 36. *Open City* 45. Angelina 47. *The Miracle* 50. Volcano 53. The Golden Coach 54. Bellissima 54. *The Rose Tattoo* (AA) 55. Wild is the Wind (AAN) 57. The Fugitive Kind 59. Mamma Roma 62. Made in Italy 67. The Secret of Santa Vittoria 69, etc.

Magne, Michel (1930–1984).
French composer and arranger.
Le Pain Vivant 54. Les Bricoleurs 61. Gigot (AAN) 62. Any Number Can Win 63. Germinal 63. La Ronde 64. Fantomas 64. The Sleeping Car Murders 66. Two Weeks in September 67. Belle de Jour 67. Manon 70 70. Le Complot 75. Emmanuelle 4 84, etc.

Maguire, Tobey (1975–) (Tobias Vincent Maguire).
American actor, from television, born in Santa Monica, California. He began in commercials from his early teens.
This Boy's Life 93. SFW 94. A Child's Cry for Help (TV) 94. Empire Records 95. Joyride 96. The Ice Storm 97. Deconstructing Harry 98. Fear and Loathing in Las Vegas 98. Ride with the Devil 98. Pleasantville 98. The Cider House Rules 99, etc.
TV series: Great Scott! 92.
❝ I think fame is a real test of what kind of person you are and if you can stay intact. – T.M.

Maharis, George (1928–).
Intense-looking American leading man who has been most successful on TV.
■ Exodus 60. Sylvia 65. Quick Before it Melts 65. The Satan Bug 65. Covenant with Death 67. The Happening 67. The Land Raiders 69. The Monk (TV) 69. The Desperadoes 69. The Last Day of the War 69. The Victim (TV) 72. Rich Man Poor Man (TV) 76. Look What Happened to Rosemary's Baby (TV) 76. Death Flight (TV) 77. Return to Fantasy Island (TV) 78. Crash (TV) 78. The Sword and the Sorcerer 82.
TV series: *Route* 66 60–63. The Most Deadly Game 70.

Mahin, John Lee (1902–1984).
American scriptwriter.
Scarface 32. *Red Dust* 32. *Bombshell* 33. Naughty Marietta 35. Captains Courageous (AAN) 37. Too Hot to Handle 38. Dr Jekyll and Mr Hyde 41. Tortilla Flat 42. Down to the Sea in Ships 49. Quo Vadis? 51. Elephant Walk 54. Heaven Knows Mr Allison (AAN) 57. The Horse Soldiers (& p) 59. The Spiral Road 62. Moment to Moment 66, many others.

Mahoney, Jock (1919–1989) (Jacques O'Mahoney).
Athletic American leading man who, apart from playing Tarzan, was confined to routine roles. Former stuntman for Gene Autry and Charles Starrett.
The Doolins of Oklahoma 49. A Day of Fury 55. Away All Boats 56. I've Lived Before 56. A Time to Love and a Time to Die 58. The Land Unknown 58. Tarzan the Magnificent 60. Tarzan Goes to India 62. Tarzan's Three Challenges 64. The Walls of Hell 66. The Bad Bunch 76. The End 78, etc.
TV series: The Range Rider 51–52. Yancey Derringer 58.

Mahoney, John (1940–).
English-born actor in America, best known for playing Martin Crane in the TV sitcom *Frasier*.
Code of Silence 85. The Manhattan Project 86. Trapped in Silence 86. Tin Men 87. Moonstruck 87. Frantic 88. The Image 89. Say Anything 89. The Russia House 90. Barton Fink 91. Love Hurts 91. Article 99 92. In the Line of Fire 93. Striking Distance 93. The Hudsucker Proxy 94. Reality Bites 94. The American President 95. She's the One 96. Primal Fear 96. Antz (voice) 98, etc.
TV series: H.E.L.P. 90. Frasier 94– .

Maibaum, Richard (1909–1991).
American scriptwriter who wrote 13 Bond movies.
They Gave Him a Gun 37. Ten Gentlemen from West Point 40. O.S.S. 46. *The Great Gatsby* 49. Cockleshell Heroes 55. Zarak 57. The Day They Robbed the Bank of England 60. Dr No 62. From Russia with Love 63. Goldfinger 64. Thunderball 65. On Her Majesty's Secret Service 69. Diamonds Are Forever 71. The Man with the Golden Gun 74. The Spy Who Loved Me 77. For Your Eyes Only 81. Octopussy 83. A View to a Kill 85. The Living Daylights 87. Licence to Kill 89, etc.

Mailer, Norman (1923–).
Combative American novelist and occasional, unsuccessful screenwriter, director and actor.
The Naked and the Dead (oa) 58. An American Dream (oa) 66. Beyond the Law (wd) 68. Wild 90 (wd) 69. Maidstone (wd) 70. Town Bloody Hall (a) 79. Ragtime (a) 81. Tough Guys Don't Dance (wd) 87. King Lear (a) 87, etc.

Main, Marjorie (1890–1975) (Mary Tomlinson).
American character actress, probably best remembered as Ma Kettle in the long-running hillbilly series.
Take a Chance (debut) 33. *Dead End* 37. Stella Dallas 37. Test Pilot 38. Angels Wash Their Faces 39. The Women 39. Turnabout 40. Bad Man of Wyoming 40. A Woman's Face 41. Honky Tonk 41. Jackass Mail 42. Tish 42. Heaven Can Wait 43. Rationing 43. *Meet Me in St Louis* 44. *Murder He Says* 44. The Harvey Girls 45. Bad Bascomb 45. Undercurrent 46. *The Egg and I* (AAN) 47. The Wistful Widow of Wagon Gap 47. *Ma and Pa Kettle* 49. Ma and Pa Kettle Go to Town 50 (then one Kettle film a year till 56). Mrs O'Malley and Mr Malone 50. The Belle of New York 52. Rose Marie 54. Friendly Persuasion 56, many others.

Mainwaring, Daniel (1902–1977) (aka Geoffrey Homes).
American screenwriter and novelist.
No Hands on the Clock 41. Dangerous Passage 44. Tokyo Rose 45. They Made Me a Killer 46. Out of the Past 47. The Big Steal 49. The Eagle and the Hawk 50. Bugles in the Afternoon 52. This Woman Is Dangerous 52. The Desperado 54. Invasion of the Body Snatchers 56. Baby Face

Nelson 57. The Gun Runners 58. Walk Like a Dragon 60. The George Raft Story 61. Convict Stage 65, etc.

Maitland, Marne (1920–1991).
Anglo-Indian actor in British films; adept at sinister orientals.
Cairo Road 50. Father Brown 54. Bhowani Junction 56. The Camp on Blood Island 58. The Stranglers of Bombay 59. Sands of the Desert 60. Nine Hours to Rama 62. Lord Jim 65. The Reptile 65. Khartoum 66. The Pink Panther Strikes Again 76. The Black Stallion 79. Memed My Hawk 87. And the Violins Stopped Playing 89. The King's Whore 90, etc.

Majorino, Tina (1985–).
American child actor.
When a Man Loves a Woman 94. Corrina, Corrina 94. André 94. Waterworld 95. True Women (TV) 97. Santa Fe 97, etc.

Majors, Lee (1940–) (Harvey Lee Yeary II).
American leading man. Formerly married to actress Farrah Fawcett.
Will Penny 67. The Ballad of Andy Crocker (TV) 68. The Liberation of L.B. Jones 70. Weekend of Terror (TV) 73. The Six Million Dollar Man (TV) 73. Gary Francis Powers (TV) 76. Just a Little Inconvenience (TV) 78. The Norseman 78. Killer Fish 78. Steel 80. The Naked Sun 80. Agency 80. Sharks 80. The Fall Guy (TV) 81. Starflight One (TV) 83. The Cowboy and the Ballerina (TV) 84. Return of the Six Million Dollar Man and the Bionic Woman (TV) 87. Danger Down Under (TV) 88. Scrooged 88. Bionic Showdown (TV) 89. Keaton's Cop 90. Fire! Trapped on the 37th Floor (TV) 91. The Cover Girl Murders 93, etc.
TV series: *The Big Valley* 65–68. The Men from Shiloh 70. Owen Marshall 71–72. *Six Million Dollar Man* 73–78. The Fall Guy 81–86.

Makavejev, Dusan (1932–).
Yugoslavian director.
■ *The Switchboard Operator* 67. Innocence Unprotected 68. *WR: Mysteries of the Organism* 71. Sweet Movie 74. Montenegro 80. The Coca Cola Kid 84. Manifesto 88. Gorilla Bathes at Noon 93. A Hole in the Soul (doc) 95.

Makeham, Eliot (1882–1956).
British character actor of stage and screen, former accountant. For years played bespectacled little bank clerks who sometimes surprised by standing up for themselves.
Rome Express 32. Orders Is Orders 32. Lorna Doone 35. Dark Journey 37. Farewell Again 37. Saloon Bar 40. *Night Train to Munich* 40. The Common Touch 42. The Halfway House 44. Jassy 47. Trio 50. Scrooge 51. Doctor in the House 53. Sailor Beware 56, etc.

Makhmalbaf, Mohsen (1952–).
Iranian director, screenwriter, editor, author and playwright. Born in Teheran, he was a member of an Islamic militant group and was imprisoned for several years for his political activities. After the revolution of 1979, he began writing plays and became head of the Bureau of Islamic Arts and Thought. Some of his more recent films have run into censorship problems in Iran. He is the father of director Samirah Makhmalbaf.
Dasforush 87. The Cyclist 89. Close Up (a only) 90. Once upon a Time, the Movies 93. The Actor (& ed) 93. Gabbeh (AAN) 95. Bread and Flower 96. The Silence/Le Silence 98, etc.

Makk, Károly (1925–).
Hungarian director and screenwriter. He studied at the Academy of Film and Theatre Art.
Liliomfi 54. The House under the Rocks/Haz a Sziklak Alatt 58. Bolondas Vakacio 67. Love/ Szerelem 71. A Very Moral Night/Egy Erkolcsos 78. Another Way/Olelkezo Tekintetek (wd) 82. Jatsani Kell 85. Hungarian Requiem/Magyar Rekviem 90. The Gambler 97, etc.

Mako (1933–) (Makoto Iwamatsu).
Japanese-American character actor.
The Sand Pebbles (AAN) 66. Hawaii 67. The Island at the Top of the World 74. The Big Brawl 80. The Bushido Blade 80. Under the Rainbow 81. Testament 83. Conan the Destroyer 84. Armed Response 86. Tucker: The Man and His Dream 88. The Wash 88. Fatal Mission 89. An Unremarkable Life 89. Pacific Heights 90. The Perfect Weapon 91. Rising Sun 93. Robocop 3 93. Cultivating Charlie 94. Highlander III: The Sorcerer 94. Crying Freeman 95. Blood for Blood 95. Riot in the Streets 96. Balance of Power 96. Seven Years in Tibet 97, etc.
TV series: Hawaiian Heat 84.

Mala (1906–1952) (Ray Wise).
Eskimo actor who was popular in a few American films of the 30s.
Igloo 32. Eskimo 33. Hawk of the Wilderness 35. The Tuttles of Tahiti 42. Red Snow 52, etc.

Malahide, Patrick (1945–).
Gaunt English leading actor, mainly on television and best known as Inspector Alleyn in the TV series. He began as a stage manager before working in repertory as an actor and is also a television playwright.
The Killing Fields 84. Comfort and Joy 87. The Singing Detective (TV) 87. A Month in the Country 87. December Bride 90. Smack and Thistle 90. *Middlemarch* (TV) 94. A Man of No Importance 94. Two Deaths 95. CutThroat Island 95. Deacon Brodie (TV) 96. 'Til There Was You 96. The Long Kiss Goodnight 96. The Beautician and the Beast 97. Heaven (NZ) 98, etc.
TV series: Minder 79–85. The Inspector Alleyn Mysteries 93–94.

Malandrinos, Andrea (1896–1970).
Greek-born character actor in British films, from music hall.
Raise the Roof 30. The Lodger 32. The Admiral's Secret 34. Midshipman Easy 35. Limelight 36. Tropical Trouble 37. Thunder Rock 42. Champagne Charlie 44. My Brother Jonathan 48. The Lavender Hill Mob 51. Cockleshell Heroes 55. The Prince and the Showgirl 57. Tommy the Toreador 59. The Yellow Rolls-Royce 64. The Mummy's Shroud 67. The Oblong Box 69. Hell Boats 70, many more.

Malden, Karl (1914–) (Mladen Sekulovich).
Respected American stage actor whose film career has been generally disappointing because Hollywood has not seemed to know what to do with him.
Autobiography: 1997, *When Do I Start?* (with Carla Malden).
■ They Knew What They Wanted 40. Winged Victory 44. 13 Rue Madeleine 46. Boomerang 47. Kiss of Death 47. The Gunfighter 50. Where the Sidewalk Ends 50. Halls of Montezuma 50. *A Streetcar Named Desire* (AA) 52. Decision Before Dawn 52. Diplomatic Courier 52. Operation Secret 52. Ruby Gentry 52. I Confess 53. Take the High Ground 53. Phantom of the Rue Morgue 54. *On the Waterfront* (AAN) 54. *Baby Doll* 56. Fear Strikes Out 57. Time Limit (d only) 57. Bombers B52 57. The Hanging Tree 59. Pollyanna 60. The Great Imposter 60. Parrish 61. One Eyed Jacks 61. All Fall Down 62. Bird Man of Alcatraz 62. Gypsy 62. How the West Was Won 63. Come Fly with Me 63. Dead Ringer 64. Cheyenne Autumn 64. The Cincinnati Kid 65. Nevada Smith 66. The Silencers 66. Murderers Row 66. *Hotel* 67. The Adventures of Bullwhip Griffin 67. Billion Dollar Brain 67. Blue 68. Hot Millions 68. Patton 69. Cat O'Nine Tails 69. Wild Rovers 71. Captains Courageous (TV) 78. Meteor 79. Beyond the Poseidon Adventure 79. *Word of Honor* (TV) 81. The Sting II 82. Summertime Killer 82. Twilight Time 83. *Fatal Vision* (TV) 84. Billy Galvin 86. Nuts 87.
TV series: *Streets of San Francisco* 72–76. Skag 80.

Malick, Terrence (1945–).
American director.
■ Pocket Money (w only) 72. *Badlands* (& w, p) 73. The Gravy Train (w only) 74. *Days of Heaven* (& w, p) 79. The Thin Red Line (w) 98.

Malik, Art (1953–).
Pakistani actor who grew up in Britain and made his reputation on TV.
Arabian Adventure 79. The Jewel in the Crown (TV) 84. A Passage to India 84. The Living Daylights 87. City of Joy 92. The Year of the Comet 92. Hostage 92. Turtle Beach 92. Uncovered 94. True Lies 94. A Kid in King Arthur's Court (US) 95. Booty Call (US) 96. Path to Paradise (TV) 97. Side Streets (US) 98, etc.
TV series: Hothouse 89.

Malinger, Ross (1984–).
American child actor.
Kindergarten Cop 90. Eve of Destruction 91. Sleepless in Seattle 93. Bye Bye, Love 95. Sudden Death 95. Little Bigfoot 96. Toothless 97, etc.
TV series: Good Advice 93–94.

Malkovich, John (1953–).
American leading actor of icy demeanour, from the stage. Born in Benton, Illinois, and educated at Illinois State University, he was a co-founder, with Gary Sinise, of the Steppenwolf Theatre Company in Chicago.
The Killing Fields 84. Places in the Heart (AAN) 84. Eleni 85. Private Conversations 85. Making Mr Right 87. The Glass Menagerie 87. Empire of the Sun 87. Miles from Home 88. Dangerous Liaisons 88. The Sheltering Sky 90. Object of Beauty 91. Shadows and Fog 91. Queen's Logic 91. Of Mice and Men 92. Jennifer 8 92. In the Line of Fire (AAN) 93. Heart of Darkness (TV) 93. Mary Reilly 96. Beyond the Clouds 95. The Convent (Port.) 95. Mulholland Falls 96. The Portrait of a Lady 96. The Ogre 96. Con Air 97. The Man in the Iron Mask 98. Rounders 98. Joan of Arc (Fr.) 99, etc.

Malle, Louis (1932–1995).
French 'new wave' director, former assistant to Robert Bresson. Married Candice Bergen.
Book: 1993, *Malle on Malle* by Philip French.
World of Silence (co-d) 56. Lift to the Scaffold 57. *The Lovers* 58. *Zazie dans le Métro* 61. *Le Feu Follet* 63. Viva Maria 65. Le Voleur 67. *Souffle au Coeur* (AANw) 71. Lacombe Lucien 75. Black Moon 75. Pretty Baby 78. Atlantic City (BFA, AAN) 80. My Dinner with André 81. Crackers 84. Alamo Bay 85. *Au Revoir, les Enfants* (AAN) 87. *May Fools*/Milou en Mai 90. Bohemian Life/La Vie de Bohème (a) 92. Damage 92. Vanya on 42nd Street 94, etc.
❝ You see the world much better through a camera. – *L.M.*

Malleson, Miles (1888–1969).
British playwright, screen writer and actor whose credits read like a potted history of the British cinema.
AS WRITER: *Nell Gwyn* 34. Peg of Old Drury 35. Rhodes of Africa 36. *Victoria the Great* 37. The Thief of Bagdad 40. The First of the Few 42. They Flew Alone 43. Mr Emmanuel 44, etc.
AS ACTOR: City of Song 31. The Sign of Four 32. Bitter Sweet 33. Nell Gwyn 34. Tudor Rose 36. Knight without Armour 37. The Thief of Bagdad (as the sultan) 40. Major Barbara 41. They Flew Alone 42. Dead of Night 45. While the Sun Shines 47. Saraband for Dead Lovers 48. *Kind Hearts and Coronets* (as the hangman) 49. The Perfect Woman 49. Stage Fright 50. The Man in the White Suit 51. The Magic Box 51. *The Importance of Being Earnest* (as Canon Chasuble) 52. Folly to Be Wise 52. The Captain's Paradise 53. Private's Progress 56. *Brothers in Law* 57. The Naked Truth 57. *Dracula* 58. The Captain's Table 58. The Hound of the Baskervilles 59. I'm All Right Jack 59. Brides of Dracula 60. The Hellfire Club 61. Heavens Above 63. First Men in the Moon 64. You Must Be Joking 65, many others.

Mallory, Boots (1913–1958) (Patricia Mallory).
American leading lady of the 30s; married William Cagney and Herbert Marshall.
Handle with Care 32. Hello Sister 33. Sing Sing Nights 35. Here's Flash Casey 37, etc.

Malo, Gina (1909–1963) (Janet Flynn).
Irish-German-American leading lady of the 30s, usually in tempestuous roles. Filmed in Britain; married Romney Brent.
In a Monastery Garden 32. Good Night Vienna 32. Waltz Time 33. The Private Life of Don Juan 34. Jack of All Trades 36. Over She Goes 38. The Door with Seven Locks 40, etc.

Malone, Dorothy (1925–) (Dorothy Maloney).
American leading lady of the 50s, often in sultry roles.
■ The Falcon and the Co-Eds 43. One Mysterious Night 44. Show Business 44. Seven Days Ashore 44. Hollywood Canteen 44. Too Young to Know 45. Janie Gets Married 46. *The Big Sleep* 46. Night and Day 48. To the Victor 48. Two Guys from Texas 48. One Sunday Afternoon 48. Flaxy Martin 49. South of St Louis 49. Colorado Territory 49. The Nevadan 50. Convicted 50. Mrs O'Malley and Mr Malone 50. The Killer that Stalked New York 50. Saddle Legion 51. The Bushwhackers 52. Scared Stiff 53. Torpedo Alley 53. Law and Order 54. Jack Slade 54. Loophole 54. Pushover 54. The Fast and Furious 54. Private Hell 36 54. Young at Heart 54. The Lone Gun 54. Five Guns West 55. Battle Cry 55. Tall Man Riding 55. Sincerely Yours 55. Artists and Models 55. At Gunpoint 55. Pillars of the Sky 56. Tension at Table Rock 56. *Written on the Wind* (AA) 56. Quantez 57. *Man of a Thousand Faces* 57. *The Tarnished Angels* 57. Tip on a Dead Jockey 57. *Too Much Too Soon* (as Diana Barrymore) 58. Warlock 59. The Last Voyage 60. The Last Sunset 61. Beach Party 63. Fate Is the Hunter 64. The Pigeon (TV) 69. Exzess (Ger.) 70. The Man Who Would Not Die 75. Rich Man Poor Man (TV) 76. Little Ladies of the Night (TV) 77. Murder in Peyton Place (TV) 77. Katie: Portrait of a Centerfold (TV) 78. Good Luck Miss Wyckoff 79. Winter Kills 79. Condominium (TV) 80. The Being 83. Peyton Place, the Next Generation (TV) 85. Basic Instinct 92.
TV series: *Peyton Place* 64–68.

Malone, Mark.
American screenwriter who turned to directing in the mid-90s.
Dead of Winter (co-w) 87. Signs of Life (w) 89. Killer/Bulletproof Heart (d) 94.

Maloney, Michael (1957–).
English actor, from the stage, including leading roles with the Royal Shakespeare Company.
Sharma and Beyond (TV) 84. Henry V 89. Hamlet 90. Truly Madly Deeply 91. Love on a Branch Line (TV) 93. In the Bleak Midwinter 95. Othello 95. Looking for Richard 96. Hamlet 96. Sex and Chocolate (TV) 97. Painted Lady (TV) 97, etc.

Malraux, André (1901–1976).
French author and politician, finally Minister of Culture; the leading spirit behind the 1937 documentary of the Spanish Civil War, *Days of Hope*.

Maltby, Henry Francis (1880–1963).
Prolific British comedy playwright and screenwriter, and actor of choleric characters. Born in Ceres, South Africa, he was first a bank clerk, and made his stage debut in 1899. He was the author of more than 50 plays from 1905 onwards.
Autobiography: 1950, *Ring Up the Curtain*.
AS WRITER: For the Love of Mike (oa) 32. Just My Luck (oa) 33. The Laughter of Fools (oa) 33. The Love Nest (co-w) 33. Over the Garden Wall (co-w) 34. The Right Age to Marry (co-w, oa) 35. Department Store (co-w) 35. Busman's Holiday (co-w) 36. The Howard Case (oa) 36. Queen of Hearts (co-w) 36. It's Never Too Late to Mend 37. His Lordship Regrets (co-w, oa) 38. His Lordship Goes to Press (co-w) 38. Blind Folly 39. Crimes at the Dark House (co-w) 39, etc.
AS ACTOR: The Rotters (& w) 21. Facing the Music 33. Home Sweet Home 33. Those Were the Days 34. Josser on the Farm 34. Emil and the Detectives 35. Sweeney Todd 36. The Crimes of Stephen Hawke 36. Boys Will Be Girls 37. The Ticket of Leave Man 37. Pygmalion 38. A Yank at Oxford 38. Old Mother Riley Joins Up 39. Under Your Hat 40. Gert and Daisy's Weekend 41. The Great Mr Handel 42. A Canterbury Tale 44. Caesar and Cleopatra 45. The Trojan Brothers 46, many others.

Maltz, Albert (1908–1985).
American screenwriter who suffered from the anti-communist witch-hunt as one of the 'Hollywood Ten'.
Afraid to Talk 32. This Gun for Hire 42. Destination Tokyo 43. The Man in Half Moon Street 44. Pride of the Marines (AAN) 45. Cloak and Dagger 46. *Naked City* 48. The Robe 53. Broken Arrow 60. Two Mules for Sister Sara 70. Scalawag 73, etc.

Malyon, Eily (1879–1961).
English character actress in Hollywood, a familiar supporting face from *His Greatest Gamble* 34 to *The Secret Heart* 46, typically as the acidulous aunt in *On Borrowed Time* 38.

Mambéty, Djibril Diop (1945–1998).
Senegalese director, screenwriter and actor. Born in Dakar, he studied drama at the Daniel Sorano Theatre, where he worked as an actor and director, going on to make his first film with a camera he borrowed from the local Institut Français. Died of cancer.
■ Contras' City (short) 69. Badou Boy 70. Hyena's Progress/Touki-Bouki 73. Parlons Grandmère (short) 89. Hyenas/Hyènes 92. Le Franc 95. La Petite Vendeuse de Soleil 99.

Mamet, David (1947–).
American dramatist, director and screenwriter. He set up a film production company, Films of Atlantic, in 1998, with William H. Macy.
The Postman Always Rings Twice (w) 81. *The Verdict* (AANw) 82. About Last Night (oa) 86. Black Widow (a, w) 87. *House of Games* (wd) 87. *The Untouchables* (w) 87. Things Change (wd) 88. We're No Angels (w) 89. Homicide (wd) 91. Hoffa (w) 92. *Glengarry Glen Ross* (w) 92. The Water Engine (w) (TV) 92. A Life in the Theatre (w) 93. Vanya on 42nd Street (w) 94. American Buffalo (w) 96. The Edge (co-w) 97. Wag the Dog (co-w) (AAN) 97. The Spanish Prisoner (wd) 98, etc.
❝ I've always been more comfortable sinking while clutching a good theory than swimming with an ugly fact. – *D.M.*
If Eisenstein would have lived longer and spent more time in Hollywood, he might have talked less about the Theory of Montage, and more about healthy eating, and what to have on the Craft Service Table. – *D.M.*
Working as a screenwriter-for-hire, one is in the employ *not* of the eventual consumers (the audience, whose interests the honest writer must have at heart), but of speculators, whose ambition, many times, is not to please the eventual consumer, but to extort from him as much money as possible as quickly as possible. – *D.M.*
The movies are a momentary and beautiful aberration of a technological society in the last stages of decay. – *D.M.*
I have always thought that in the motion picture business the real violence was not what people do on screen, but what we do to raise the money. – *D.M.*

Mamoulian, Rouben (1897–1987).
American stage director of Armenian origin. Over the years he made a number of films which vary in quality but at their best show a fluent command of the medium.
■ *Applause* 29. *City Streets* 31. *Dr Jekyll and Mr Hyde* 32. *Love Me Tonight* 32. Song of Songs 33. *Queen Christina* 33. We Live Again 34. *Becky Sharp* 35. *The Gay Desperado* 36. High, Wide and Handsome 37. Golden Boy 39. *The Mark of Zorro* 40. Blood and Sand 41. Rings on Her Fingers 42. Summer Holiday 48. Silk Stockings 57.
Began work on *Cleopatra* 62 but was replaced.
❝ His tragedy is that of the innovator who runs out of innovations. – *Andrew Sarris, 1968*

Mancina, Mark (1957–).
American composer.
Speed 94. Monkey Trouble 94. Man of the House 95. Bad Boys 95. Money Train 95. Assassins 95. Fair Game 95. Twister 96. Moll Flanders 96. Speed 2: Cruise Control 97. Con Air 97. Return to Paradise 98, etc.

Mancini, Henry (1924–1994) (Enrico Mancini).
American composer and songwriter. Educated at the Juilliard School of Music, he was an arranger and pianist with the post-war Glenn Miller orchestra before working at Universal, 1952–58. Apart from films, he also worked in television, notably for the *Peter Gunn* series 58. His best-known song was 'Moon River', written with lyricist Johnny Mercer, for *Breakfast at Tiffany's*.
AS ARRANGER: The Glenn Miller Story (AAN) 53. The Benny Goodman Story 56, etc.
AS COMPOSER: Touch of Evil 58. High Time 60. *Breakfast at Tiffany's* (AA) 61. Bachelor in Paradise 61. Days of Wine and Roses 62. *Hatari* 62. *The Pink Panther* (AAN) 63. Charade 63. A Shot in the Dark 64. Dear Heart 65. What Did You Do in the War, Daddy? 66. Two for the Road 67. Darling Lili 69. The White Dawn 73. The Return of the Pink Panther 75. Once is Not Enough 76. Silver Streak 76. W. C. Fields and Me 76. House Calls 78. Who is Killing the Great Chefs of Europe? 78. Nightwing 79. 10 (AAN) 79. Little Miss Marker 80. Back Roads 81. Mommie Dearest 81. Victor/Victoria (AA) 82. Harry and Son 84. Lifeforce 85. Santa Claus: The Movie 85. That's Dancing! 85. A Fine Mess 86. That's Life! (AAN) 86. Blind Date 87. The Glass Menagerie 87. Heavy Petting 88. Physical Evidence 88. Sunset 88. Without a Clue 88. Welcome Home 89. Ghost Dad 90. Switch 91. Married to It 91. Son of the Pink Panther 93, etc.
~Academy Award songs: 'Moon River', 'Days of Wine and Roses'.

Mancuso, Frank (1928–).
American production executive, appointed head of MGM/UA in 1993, and a former chairman and CEO of Paramount. He remained in charge of the studio following a management buyout in 1996, financed by Kirk Kerkorian and the Australian television company Seven Network.

Mancuso, Kevin:
see D'Amato, Joe.

Mancuso, Nick (1949–).
Italian-born leading man who moved to Canada as a child.
Dr Scorpion (TV) 78. The House on Garibaldi Street (TV) 79. Torn between Two Lovers (TV) 80. Nightwing 80. The Kidnapping of the President 80. Scruples (TV) 81. Ticket to Heaven 81. Mother Lode 82. The Legend of Walks Far Woman (TV) 83. Heartbreakers 84. Night Magic 85. Death of an Angel 85. King of Love (TV) 87. Lena's Holiday 91. Double Identity 91. Rapid Fire 92. Danielle Steel's Message from 'Nam (TV) 93. Flinch 94. Young Ivanhoe 95. A Young Connecticut Yankee in King Arthur's Court 95. The Invader 96. The Ex 96. Marquis de Sade 97. Past Perfect 98. Misbegotten 98, etc.

Mandel, Babaloo. (c. 1949–) (Mark Mandel).
American screenwriter and television producer, usually in collaboration with Lowell Ganz.
Night Shift 82. Splash 84. Spies Like Us 85. Gung Ho 86. Vibes 88. Parenthood 89. City Slickers (AAN) 91. Mr Saturday Night 92. A League of Their Own 92. City Slickers II: The Legend of Curly's Gold 94. Greedy/Greed 94. Forget Paris 95. Multiplicity 96. Fathers' Day 97, etc.
TV series: Hiller & Diller (p, co-w) 97.

Mandel, Johnny (1935–).
American composer, trumpeter and trombonist. His song 'The Shadow of Your Smile' (lyrics by Paul Francis Webster), the love theme from *The Sandpiper*, was an Oscar-winner in 1965.
I Want to Live 58. The Third Voice 59. The Americanization of Emily 64. The Sandpiper (AA s) 65. Point Blank 67. M*A*S*H 70. The Last Detail 73. Freaky Friday 76. Agatha 79. Being There 79. The Baltimore Bullet 80. Deathtrap 82. The Verdict 82. Staying Alive 83. Brenda Starr 89, etc.

Mandell, Daniel (1895–1987).
American editor.
The Turmoil 24. Showboat 29. Counsellor at Law 33. Diamond Jim 35. Dodsworth 36. Dead End 37. Wuthering Heights 39. The Little Foxes 41. Arsenic and Old Lace 44. Wonder Man 45. The Best Years of Our Lives (AA) 46. My Foolish Heart 49. Valentino 52. Guys and Dolls 55. Witness for the Prosecution 57. The Apartment (AA) 60. Irma la Douce 63. The Fortune Cookie 66, many others.

Mander, Miles (1888–1946) (Lionel Mander).
British character actor, a former theatre manager with long experience of all kinds of stage work. Later settled in Hollywood.
The Pleasure Garden 26. *The First Born* (& wd) 28. Loose Ends (wd only) 30. The Missing Rembrandt (wd only) 31. The Private Life of Henry VIII 32. Loyalties 33. The Morals of Marcus (d only) 35, etc.
In Hollywood as actor: *The Three Musketeers* (as Richelieu) 36. Lloyds of London 37. Slave Ship 37. Suez 38. The Three Musketeers (musical version; as Richelieu again) 39. *Wuthering Heights* 39. Tower of London 39. Lady Hamilton 41. *Five Graves to Cairo* 43. *Farewell My Lovely* 44. The Scarlet Claw 44. Pearl of Death 44. The Bandit of Sherwood Forest 46. The Walls Came Tumbling Down 46, many others.

Mandoki, Luis.
Mexican-born director in Hollywood.
Motel 83. Gaby – A True Story 87. White Palace 90. Born Yesterday 93. When a Man Loves a Woman 94, etc.

Manfredi, Nino (1921–).
Italian leading actor, screenwriter and occasional director, from the stage.
Torna a Napoli 49. Viva il Cinema! 53. Gli Inamorati 55. Camping (a, w) 57. I Ragazzi dei Parioli 58. L'Impiegato (a, w) 59. Crimen 60. Wayward Love/L'Amore Difficile (a, d) 62. The Dolls/Le Bambole 65. A Rose for Everyone/Una Rosa per Tutti 67. Per Grazia Ricevuta (a, wd) 71. Il Conte de Monte Cristo 77. La Mazzetta 78. Café Express (a, w) 80. I Picari 87. Alberto Express 90. Mima 91. The Flying Dutchman 94, etc.

Manfredini, Harry.
American composer, mainly for horror movies.
Here Come the Tigers 78. Friday the 13th 80. Friday the 13th Part 2 81. Friday the 13th Part 3 82. Swamp Thing 82. The Returning 83. Friday the 13th: The Final Chapter 84. The Hills Have Eyes Part II 84. Friday the 13th: A New Beginning 85. House 86. Friday the 13th Part VI: Jason Lives 86. House II: The Second Story 87. Friday the 13th Part VII: The New Blood (co-m) 88. Deep Star Six 89. Double Revenge 90. Aces: Iron Eagle III 92. My Boyfriend's Back 93. Jason Goes to Hell: The Final Friday 93. Dead on Sight 94. Wishmaster 97, etc.

Mangano, Silvana (1930–1989).
Italian actress, wife of producer Dino de Laurentiis. Former model.
L'Elisir d'Amore 49. Bitter Rice 51. Anna 51. Mambo 53. Ulysses 54. The Wolves 56. The Sea Wall 57. Tempest 59. Five Branded Women 61. Barabbas 62. Theorem 68. The Decameron 70. Death in Venice 71. Ludwig 72. Conversation Piece 76. Dune 84, etc.

Mangold, James (c. 1964–).
American screenwriter and director.
Heavy 96. Cop Land (wd) 97.

Mankiewicz, Don (1922–).
American scriptwriter and novelist, son of Herman Mankiewicz.
Trial 55. House of Numbers 57. I Want to Live (AAN) 58.

Mankiewicz, Francis (1944–1993).
Canadian film director. Born in Shanghai, he studied at the London School of Film Technique. *Good Riddance* is one of the most admired of Canadian films. Died of cancer.
Valentin (TV) 73. Le Temps d'une Chasse 73. *Good Riddance*/Les Bons Debarras 81. Les Beaux Souvenirs 82. And Then You Die (TV) 87. Les Portes Tournantes 88. Conspiracy of Silence (TV) 92, etc.

Mankiewicz, Herman (1897–1953).
American screenwriter, playwright and wit. Born in New York, the son of a Columbia University professor, he studied at Columbia University and the University of Berlin and began as a journalist, including a period as drama critic of the *New Yorker*. Self-destructive, and a compulsive gambler, he often wasted his considerable talents, eventually moving from one studio to another as he lost jobs through non-attendance or indiscretions. An alcoholic, he once threw up at a dinner given by producer Arthur Hornblow, Jnr, and remarked, 'It's all right. The white wine came up with the fish.' He lost his job at Columbia after the studio head, Harry Cohn, explained that he could tell if a film was good or bad according to whether his fanny squirmed or not. 'Imagine,' said Mankiewicz, 'the whole world wired to Harry Cohn's ass!' He died of uremic poisoning. He was the brother of Joseph L. Mankiewicz; his son, Don Mankiewicz, was a novelist and screenwriter.
Road to Mandalay (co-w) 26. Stranded in Paris (w) 26. Abie's Irish Rose (co-w) 28. The Dummy (w) 29. Thunderbolt (co-w) 29. Men Are Like That (co-w) 29. The Vagabond King (w) 30. True to the Navy (co-w) 30. Honey (w) 30. The Royal Family of Broadway (co-w) 30. Ladies Love Brutes (co-w) 30. Ladies' Man (w) 31. Man of the World (w) 31. Dancers in the Dark (co-w) 32. Girl Crazy (co-w) 32. The Lost Squadron (co-w) 32. Dinner at Eight (co-w) 33. Another Language (co-w) 33. Meet the Baron (co-w) 33. The Show-Off (w) 34. Stamboul Quest (w) 34. Escapade (w) 35. After Office Hours (w) 35. Love in Exile (co-w) 36. John Meade's Woman (co-w) 37. The Emperor's Candlesticks (co-w) 37. The Three Maxims (w) (GB) 37. My Dear Miss Aldrich (w) 37. It's a Wonderful World (co-w) 39. *Citizen Kane* (contribution disputed; some say he wrote most of it) (AA) 41. Rise and Shine (w) 41. Pride of the Yankees (co-w) (AAN) 42. Goodfellows (oa) 43. Stand By for Action (co-w) 43. Christmas Holiday (w) 44. The Spanish Main (co-w) 45. The Enchanted Cottage (co-w) 45. A Woman's Secret (w) 49. The Pride of St Louis (w) 52, etc.
❝ Will you accept 300 per week to work for Paramount Pictures? All expenses paid. 300 is peanuts. Millions are to be grabbed out here and your only competition is idiots. Don't let this get around. – *H.M.'s wire to Ben Hecht, 1926*
Tell me, do you know any 75-dollar-a-week writers? – *Anon*
I know lots of them, but they're all making 1500 dollars a week. – *H.M.*
In a novel the hero can lay ten girls and marry a virgin for the finish. In a movie this is not allowed. The villain can lay anybody he wants, have as much fun as he wants cheating and stealing, getting rich and whipping the servants. But you have to shoot him in the end. When he falls with a bullet in the forehead, it is advisable that he clutch at the Gobelin tapestry on the wall and bring it down over his head like a symbolic shroud. Also, covered by such a tapestry, the actor does not have to hold his breath while being photographed as a dead man. – *H.M.*
Barbara Stanwyck is my favorite. My God, I could just sit and dream of being married to her, having a little cottage out in the hills, vines around the door. I'd come home from the office tired and weary, and I'd be met by Barbara, walking through the door holding an apple pie she had cooked herself. And wearing no drawers. – *H.M.*
I don't know how it is that you start working at something you don't like, and before you know it you're an old man. – *H.M.*
A greater phenomenon than Herman's wit was the fact that his victims employed him, at large sums, to write movies he despised for bosses he ridiculed. – *Ben Hecht*
Famous line (*Citizen Kane*): 'If I hadn't been so rich, I might have been a really great man.'

Mankiewicz, Joseph L. (1909–1993).
American film creator of many talents.
Biography: 1977, *Pictures Will Talk* by Kenneth Geist.
AS WRITER: The Mysterious Dr Fu Manchu 29. Skippy (AAN) 31. Million Dollar Legs 32. Forsaking All Others 34. The Keys of the Kingdom 44, etc.
AS PRODUCER: Fury 36. The Bride Wore Red 37. Three Comrades 38. Huckleberry Finn 39. Strange Cargo 40. The Philadelphia Story 40. Woman of the Year 42. The Keys of the Kingdom 44, etc.
■ AS WRITER-DIRECTOR: Dragonwyck 46. Somewhere in the Night 46. The Late George Apley 47. The Ghost and Mrs Muir 47. Escape 48. *A Letter for Three Wives* (AA script, AAd) 49. House of Strangers (d only) 50. No Way Out (AAN) 50. *All About Eve* (AA script, AAd) 50. People Will Talk 51. Five Fingers (d only) (AAN) 52. Julius Caesar 53. *The Barefoot Contessa* (AANw) 54. Guys and Dolls 55. The Quiet American (& p) 57. Suddenly Last Summer (d only) 59. Cleopatra 63. The Honey Pot 67. There Was a Crooked Man 70. Sleuth (d only) (AAN) 72.
❝ I got a job at Metro and went in to see Louis Mayer, who told me he wanted me to be a producer. I said I wanted to write and direct. He said, 'No, you have to produce first, you have to crawl before you can walk.' Which is as good a definition of producing as I ever heard. – *J.L.M.*
I felt the urge to direct because I couldn't stomach what was being done with what I wrote. – *J.L.M*
Every screenwriter worthy of the name has already directed his film when he has written his script. – *J.L.M*
There were always financial crises. Someone would come out from the East and announce that the business was in deep trouble, and what would happen was that they'd reduce the number of matzo balls in Louie Mayer's chicken soup from three to two. Then they'd fire a couple of secretaries and feel virtuous. – *J.L.M.*

The toughest three pictures I ever made. It was shot in a state of emergency, shot in confusion, and wound up in blind panic. – *J.L.M. on Cleopatra*

A cinema of intelligence rather than inspiration. . . his wit scratches more than it bites. – *Andrew Sarris, 1968*

Mankiewicz, Tom (1942–).
American screenwriter, son of Joseph L. Mankiewicz.
Live and Let Die 72. The Man with the Golden Gun 73. Mother, Jugs and Speed 76. The Cassandra Crossing 77. The Eagle Has Landed 77. Ladyhawke 85. Dragnet (co-w, d) 87. Delirious (d) 91, etc.

Mankowitz, Wolf (1924–1998).
British novelist and screenwriter.
A Kid for Two Farthings 56. Expresso Bongo 59. Waltz of the Toreadors 62. The Day the Earth Caught Fire 63. Where the Spies Are 65. Casino Royale 66. Dr Faustus 67. The 25th Hour 67. Bloomfield 71. The Hireling 73.

Mann, Abby (1927–).
American playwright and screenwriter.
Judgment at Nuremberg (oa, w) (AA) 61. A Child Is Waiting (w) 63. The Condemned of Altona (w) 63. Ship of Fools (w) (AAN) 65. The Detective (w) 68. The Marcus Nelson Murders (TV) 73. King (TV) (& d) 80. Skag (TV) 80. The Atlanta Child Murders (& d) (TV) 85. Murderers among Us: The Simon Wiesenthal Story (TV) 89. Indictment: The McMartin Trial (TV) 95, etc.

Mann, Anthony (1906–1967) (Emil Bundesmann).
American director, usually of outdoor films; his best work was concerned with the use of violence by thoughtful men.
■ Dr Broadway 42. Moonlight in Havana 42. Nobody's Darling 43. My Best Gal 44. Strangers in the Night 44. The Great Flamarion 45. Two O'Clock Courage 45. Sing Your Way Home 45. Strange Impersonation 46. The Bamboo Blonde 46. Desperate 47. Railroaded 47. T-Men 47. Raw Deal 48. The Black Book 49. Border Incident 49. Side Street 49. Devil's Doorway 50. The Furies 50. *Winchester 73* 50. The Tall Target 51. *Bend of the River* 51. The Naked Spur 52. Thunder Bay 53. *The Glenn Miller Story* 54. The Far Country 55. Strategic Air Command 55. *The Man from Laramie* 55. The Last Frontier 56. Serenade 56. Men in War 57. The Tin Star 57. God's Little Acre 58. Man of the West 58. Cimarron 60. El Cid 61. The Fall of the Roman Empire 64. The Heroes of Telemark 65. A Dandy in Aspic (completed by Laurence Harvey) 68.

Mann, Barry (1942–).
American composer, singer and songwriter, often in collaboration with his wife Cynthia Weill, whose songs have featured in many films since a move from New York to Los Angeles in the 70s.
Wild in the Streets (s) 68. I Never Sang for My Father (co-m) 69. An American Tail (s) 86. Summer Heat (s) 87. Harry and the Hendersons (s) 87. Million Dollar Mystery (s) 87. Oliver and Company (s) 88. National Lampoon's Christmas Vacation 89. Sibling Rivalry 90. Muppet Treasure Island (s) 96. All Dogs Go to Heaven 2 (s) 96, etc.

Mann, Daniel (1912–1991) (Daniel Chugerman).
American director, ex stage and TV.
■ *Come Back Little Sheba* 52. About Mrs Leslie 54. The Rose Tattoo 55. I'll Cry Tomorrow 55. The Teahouse of the August Moon 56. Hot Spell 58. The Last Angry Man 59. The Mountain Road 60. Butterfield 8 60. Ada 61. Who's Got the Action? 62. Five Finger Exercise 62. Who's Been Sleeping in My Bed? 63. Judith 65. Our Man Flint 66. For Love of Ivy 68. A Dream of Kings 69. Willard 71. The Harness (TV) 71. The Revengers 72. Maurie 73. Interval 73. Lost in the Stars 73. Journey into Fear 75. Matilda 78. Playing for Time (TV) 80. The Incredible Mr Chadwick 80. The Day the Loving Stopped (TV) 81. The Man Who Broke 1,000 Chains (TV) 87.

Mann, Delbert (1920–).
American director, ex TV.
■ *Marty* (AA) 55. *The Bachelor Party* 57. Desire Under the Elms 58. Separate Tables 58. Middle of the Night 59. *The Dark at the Top of the Stairs* 60. Lover Come Back 61. The Outsider 62. That Touch of Mink 62. A Gathering of Eagles 63. Dear Heart 65. Quick Before it Melts 65. Mister Buddwing 66. Fitzwilly 67. The Pink Jungle 68. Heidi (TV) 68. David Copperfield (TV) 69. She Waits (TV) 71. No Place to Run (TV) 72. Kidnapped 72. Jane Eyre (TV) 72. Man Without a Country (TV) 73. A Girl Named Sooner (TV) 75. Birch Interval 76. Francis Gary Powers (TV) 76. Tell Me My Name (TV) 77. Breaking Up (TV) 78. Love's Dark Ride (TV) 78. Home to Stay (TV) 78. Thou Shalt Not Commit Adultery (TV) 78. Torn Between Two Lovers (TV) 79. All Quiet on the Western Front (TV) 80. To Find My Son (TV) 81. Night Crossing 81. Love Leads the Way (TV) 84. A Death in California (TV) 84. The Last Days of Patton (TV) 86. The Ted Kennedy Jnr Story (TV) 86. April Morning (TV) 88. Incident in a Small Town (p, d) (TV) 94. Lily in Winter 94.

Mann, Hank (1887–1971) (David Liebermann).
Gargantuan American supporting player of silent days, especially with Chaplin; one of the Keystone Kops.
Modern Times 36. Hollywood Cavalcade 39. The Great Dictator 40, etc.

Mann, Heinrich (1871–1950).
German novelist. His story 'Professor Unrath', published in 1905, was filmed as *The Blue Angel*. Brother of Thomas Mann.

Mann, Leslie (1972–).
American actress, from television, born in San Francisco.
The Cable Guy 96. She's the One 96. Last Man Standing 96. George of the Jungle 97, etc.
TV series: Birdland 94.

Mann, Michael (1943–).
American director and screenwriter, from TV, where he produced *Miami Vice* 84–89 and *Crime Story* 86–88. *Heat* was a remake of *L.A. Takedown* 89, the pilot for a TV series that never materialized.
The Jericho Mile (TV) 79. Thief 81. The Keep 83. Manhunter (& w) 86. Last of the Mohicans (co-w, d) 92. *Heat* 95, etc.

Mann, Ned (1893–1967).
American special-effects director, a one-time professional roller-skater who entered films in 1920 as an actor. Best remembered for his long association with Alexander Korda.
Dirigible 30. *The Man Who Could Work Miracles* 35. *The Ghost Goes West* 36. *Things to Come* 36. *The Thief of Baghdad* 40. Anna Karenina 47. Bonnie Prince Charlie 48. Around the World in Eighty Days 56.

Mann, Stanley (1928–).
American screenwriter.
The Mouse That Roared 59. The Mark 61. Woman of Straw 64. Rapture 65. A High Wind in Jamaica 65. The Collector (AAN) 65. The Naked Runner 67. The Strange Affair 68. Russian Roulette 75. Sky Riders 76. Breaking Point 76. The Silent Flute 78. Damien – Omen II 78. Meteor 79. Circle of Iron 79. Eye of the Needle 81. Firestarter 84. Conan the Destroyer 84. Tai-Pan 86. Hanna's War 88, etc.

Mann, Thomas (1875–1955).
German novelist who spent his latter years in California. Brother of Heinrich Mann. *Buddenbrooks* became a TV serial (Germany, 1982), as did *The Confessions of Felix Krull* (Germany, 1981); *Death in Venice* was filmed to general acclaim.

Manners, David (1901–1998) (Rauff de Ryther Duan Acklom).
Canadian leading man of Hollywood films in the 30s; claimed to be descended from William the Conqueror.
■ *Journey's End* 30. He Knew Women 30. Sweet Mama 30. Kismet 30. Mother's Cry 30. The Truth About Youth 30. The Right to Love 30. Dracula 30. The Millionaire 31. *The Last Flight* 31. The Miracle Woman 31. The Ruling Voice 31. The Greeks Had a Word for Them 31. Lady with a Past 32. Beauty and the Boss 32. Stranger in Town 32. Crooner 32. Man Wanted 32. A Bill of Divorcement 32. They Call It Sin 32. The Mummy 32. The Death Kiss 32. From Hell to Heaven 33. The Warrior's Husband 33. The Girl in 419 33. The Devil in Love 33. Torch Singer 33. Roman Scandals 33. The Black Cat 34. The Luck of a Sailor 34. The Great Flirtation 34. The Moonstone 34. The Perfect Clue 35. The Mystery of Edwin Drood 35. Jalna 35. Hearts in Bondage 36. A Woman Rebels 36.

Manners, J. Hartley (1870–1928).
English-born actor and dramatist in America who enjoyed his greatest success with his play *Peg o' My Heart*, which starred his wife Laurette Taylor, as did all his subsequent works. This sentimental drama opened in 1912 and ran for 603 performances on Broadway, then the longest run of a non-musical play, and for 710 performances in London from 1914. It has been filmed twice: as a silent in 1922, directed by King Vidor and starring Laurette Taylor, and in 1931, directed by Robert Z. Leonard and starring Marion Davies. Born in London, of somewhat mysterious origins, he began as an actor in the late 1890s, and moved to the US in the early 1900s. Died of cancer.
Happiness (oa) 24. One Night in Rome (oa) 24.
❝ Alas, poor Hartley! Only the audiences liked his plays. – *Ethel Barrymore*

Mannheim, Lucie (1895–1976).
German-born character actress, married to Marius Goring.
The Thirty-Nine Steps (as the mysterious victim) 35. The High Command 37. Yellow Canary 43. Hotel Reserve 44. So Little Time 52. Beyond the Curtain 60. Bunny Lake Is Missing 65, etc.

Manni, Ettori (1927–1979).
Italian actor.
Girls Marked Danger 52. La Lupa 53. Two Nights with Cleopatra 54. Ulysses 54. Attila the Hun 54. Le Amiche 55. Revolt of the Gladiators 58. Legions of the Nile 59. Revolt of the Slaves 60. Hercules and the Captive Women 61. The Valiant 62. Gold for the Caesars 63. The Battle of the Villa Fiorita 65. The Devil in Love 66. The Battle of El Alamein 69. Street People 76, many others.

Manning, Irene (1917–) (Inez Harvuot).
American leading lady of the 40s, former café singer.
Two Wise Maids 37. The Big Shot 42. Yankee Doodle Dandy 42. The Desert Song 44. Shine On, Harvest Moon 44. Escape in the Desert 45. Bonnie Prince Charlie (GB) 48, etc.

Manoff, Dinah (1958–).
American actress, the daughter of actress and director Lee Grant.
The Possessed (TV) 77. Ordinary People 80. For Ladies Only (TV) 81. I Ought to Be in Pictures 82. Backfire 88. Child's Play 88. Bloodhounds of Broadway 89. Welcome Home Roxy Carmichael 90, etc.
TV series: Soap 78–79.

Manone, Joseph 'Wingy' (1900–1982).
American jazz trumpeter, singer and bandleader, in occasional films. Born in New Orleans, Louisiana, as a child he lost his right arm in a streetcar accident and learned to play left-handed. He moved to Hollywood in the early 40s, staying there until the mid-50s, appearing on Bing Crosby's radio shows. Some performances feature his 'rhyming jive talk', which was novel at the time but now sounds merely dated.
Autobiography: 1948, *Trumpet on the Wing* (with Paul Vandervoort II).
Rhythm on the River 40. Juke Box Jenny 42. Hi-Ya Sailor 43. Sarge Goes to College 47. Rhythm Inn 51, etc.
❝ I figured while I ain't blowin' and singin' I might be able to snatch me a picture or two, doin' this sort of stuff. A hang-around guy to break it up between intervals, like Rags Ragland or Phil Silvers did. – *W.M.*

Mansfield, Duncan.
American editor and occasional director.
as editor: The Bond Boy 22. Fury 23. Embarrassing Moments 30. The Front Page 31. I'd Give My Life 36. So This Is Washington 43. A Walk in the Sun 45. Arch of Triumph 48, etc.
as director: Along Came Love 36. Girl Loves Boy 37. Sweetheart of the Navy 37, etc.

Mansfield, Jayne (1932–1967) (Vera Jane Palmer).
Amply proportioned American leading lady whose superstructure became the butt of many jokes. She began as a beauty queen, Miss Photoflash 1952, and became a star on Broadway, after Warner had dropped her contract, in *Will Success Spoil Rock Hunter?* Her second husband, Mickey Hargitay, was a former Mr Universe and occasional actor, and her third was director Matt Cimber (aka Matteo Ottaviano). Her stardom was short-lived and she was performing in a night-club act at the time of her death in a car crash. Loni Anderson played her in a TV movie, *The Jayne Mansfield Story* 80.
Biographies: 1973, *Jayne Mansfield* by May Mann. 1986, *Pink Goddess: The Jayne Mansfield Story* by Michael Feeney Callan.
The Female Jungle 55. Illegal 56. Pete Kelly's Blues 56. The Burglar 57. The Girl Can't Help It 57. The Wayward Bus 57. Will Success Spoil Rock Hunter? 57. Kiss Them For Me 57. The Sheriff of Fractured Jaw 59. Too Hot to Handle (GB) 60. The Challenge (GB) 60. It Happened in Athens 62. Panic Button 64. Country Music USA 65. The Fat Spy 66. A Guide for the Married Man 67, etc.
❝ Men are those creatures with two legs and eight hands. – *J.M.*
I always felt all my life that people who didn't grow up to be movie stars . . . well, there was something wrong with them. – *J.M.*
You gotta have a body. – *J.M.*
Dramatic art in her opinion is knowing how to fill a sweater. – *Bette Davis*
Miss United Dairies herself. – *David Niven*
She was not strictly an exhibitionist, but she liked an audience. – *May Mann*

Mansfield, Martha (1900–1923).
American leading actress of silent films, from Broadway musicals. She died from burns after her dress caught fire during the filming of *The Warrens of Virginia*.
Broadway Bill 18. Dr Jekyll and Mr Hyde 20. Fogbound 23. The Woman in Chains 23. The Warrens of Virginia 24, etc.

Mantee, Paul (1936–) (Paul Marianetti).
American general-purpose actor.
Robinson Crusoe on Mars (leading role) 64. An American Dream 66. They Shoot Horses Don't They 69. W. C. Fields and Me 76. The Day of the Animals 77. The Great Santini 80. First Strike 87. Lurking Fear 94, etc.

Mantegna, Joe (1947–).
American character actor, associated on stage and screen with the work of writer and director David Mamet.
Who Stole My Wheels?/Towing 78. Second Thoughts 83. Compromising Positions 85. The Money Pit 86. Offbeat 86. Three Amigos! 86. Critical Condition 87. House of Games 87. Weeds 87. Suspect 87. Things Change 88. Wait until Spring, Bandini 90. Alice 90. Queen's Logic 90. The Godfather Part III 90. Homicide 91. Bugsy (as George Raft) 91. Body of Evidence 93. Family Prayers 93. Searching for Bobby Fischer/Innocent Moves 93. State of Emergency (TV) 94. Baby's Day Out 94. Airheads 94. Forget Paris 95. Eye for an Eye 95. Up Close and Personal 96. Underworld 96. Albino Alligator 96. Stephen King's Thinner 96. The Last Don (TV) 96. Face Down 96. A Call to Remember (TV) 97. The Wonderful Ice Cream Suit 97. The Rat Pack (TV) 98. Celebrity 98. Boy Meets Girl 98, etc.

Mantell Joe (1920–).
American character actor.
Barbary Pirate 49. Marty (AAN) 55. Storm Centre 56. The Sad Sack 57. Beau James 57. Onionhead 58. The Crowded Sky 60. The Scarface Mob (TV) 62. The Birds 63. Mister Buddwing 66. Chinatown 74. They Only Come Out at Night (TV) 75. Blind Ambition (TV) 79. The Two Jakes 90, etc.

Mantz, Paul (1903–1965).
American stunt pilot who died in a crash during the filming of *The Flight of the Phoenix*.
Biography: 1967, *Hollywood Pilot* by Don D. Wiggins.

Manvell, Roger (1909–1987).
British film historian. Director of the British Film Academy from 1947 and author of many books on cinema, the most influential being the Penguin *Film* 44.

Manx, Kate (1930–1964).
American leading lady.
■ Private Property 60. Hero's Island 62.

Manz, Linda (1961–).
American leading lady.
Days of Heaven 78. King of the Gypsies 78. Boardwalk 79. Orphan Train (TV) 80. Out of the Blue 80. Gummo 97, etc.

Manzano, Lucas.
Venezuelan director who directed, with Enrique Zimmerman, that country's first feature film, *La Dama de las Cayenas* 13, a version of Alexander Dumas's *Camille*.

Mapplethorpe, Robert (1946–1989).
American artist and photographer whose elegant photographs of sado-masochistic homosexual acts excited much controversy. He was the star of a once-celebrated underground film, *Robert Having His Nipple Pierced*, made by Sandy Daley and given its premiere at New York's Museum of Modern Art in 1971. Died of AIDS.
Biography: 1995, *Mapplethorpe* by Patricia Morrisroe.
“ Sex is the only thing worth living for. – *R.M.*
My theory about creativity is that the more money one has, the more creative one can be. – *R.M.*

Mara, Adele (1923–) (Adelaida Delgado).
Spanish-American dancer who played leads in Hollywood co-features of the 40s.
Alias Boston Blackie 42. Bells of Rosarita 45. Tiger Woman 46. Diary of a Bride 48. The Sea Hornet 51. Back from Eternity 56. Curse of the Faceless Man 58. The Big Circus 59. Wheels (TV) 78, etc.
TV series: Cool Million 72–73.

Marais, Jean (1913–1998) (Jean Marais-Villain).
French romantic actor well remembered in several Cocteau films. Later films less notable; recently in cloak-and-sword epics, also playing 'The Saint', 'Fantomas' and various secret agents.
Autobiography: 1975, *Histoires de Ma Vie*.
L'Eternel Retour 43. La Belle et la Bête 45. L'Aigle à Deux Têtes 47. Les Parents Terribles 48. Orphée 49. Nez de Cuir 51. Les Amants de Minuit 53. Julietta 53. Le Comte de Monte Cristo 54. Napoléon 54. Paris Does Strange Things/Eléna et les Hommes 56. White Nights/Le Notti Bianche 57. *The Testament of Orpheus*/Le Testament d'Orphée 59. Austerlitz 60. Patate 64. Thomas l'Imposteur 65. Train d'Enfer 65. Le Paria 68. Peau d'Ane 70. Erimou 82. Parking 85. Les Misérables du XXème Siècle 95. Stealing Beauty 96, etc.

Marceau, Sophie (1967–) (Sophie Mapuis).
French leading actress, in films from the age of 13. She has a son by her partner, Polish director Andrzej ZULAWSKI.
La Boum 80. Police 85. Mes Nuits Sont Plus Belles que Vos Jours 89. Pacific Palisades 90. Fanfan 93. La Fille de D'Artagnan 94. Braveheart 95. Beyond the Clouds 95. Leo Tolstoy's Anna Karenina (US) 97. Firelight (GB/Fr.) 97. Marquise 97, etc.

Marcel, Terry (1942–).
British director and screenwriter.
Why Not Stay for Breakfast? 79. There Goes the Bride 80. Hawk the Slayer 80. Prisoners of the Lost Universe 83. Jane and the Lost City 87. Heartbeat (TV) 93, etc.

March, Alex (1920–1989).
American director and producer, a former stage actor and television script editor.
Paper Lion 68. The Big Bounce 68. Mastermind 69 (released 76). Firehouse (TV) 72. The Amazing Captain Nemo 78, etc.

March, Fredric (1897–1975) (Frederick McIntyre Bickel).
One of America's most respected stage and screen actors, who always projected intelligence and integrity and during the 30s and 40s was at times an agreeable light comedian. Long married to Florence Eldridge.
■ The Dummy 29. The Wild Party 29. The Studio Murder Mystery 29. Paris Bound 29. Jealousy 29. Footlights and Fools 29. The Marriage Playground 29. Sarah and Son 30. Ladies Love Brutes 30. Paramount on Parade 30. True to the Navy 30. Manslaughter 30. Laughter 30. *The Royal Family of Broadway* (AAN) 30. Honor among Lovers 30. Night Angel 31. My Sin 31. Merrily We Go to Hell 32. *Dr Jekyll and Mr Hyde* (AA) 32. Smiling Through 32. Make Me a Star 32. Strangers in Love 32. The Sign of the Cross 33. Tonight Is Ours 33. The Eagle and the Hawk 33. The Affairs of Cellini 34. All of Me 34. Good Dame 34. Design for Living 34. *Death takes a Holiday* 34. The Barretts of Wimpole Street (as Robert Browning) 34. We Live Again 34. *Les Misérables* 35. The Dark Angel 35. Anna Karenina 35. Mary of Scotland 36. Anthony Adverse 36. The Road to Glory 36. *A Star Is Born* (AAN) 37. *Nothing Sacred* 37. The Buccaneer 38. There Goes My Heart 38. Trade Winds 39. Susan and God 40. Victory 40. So Ends Our Night 41. *One Foot in Heaven* 41. Bedtime Story 42. *I Married a Witch* 42. Tomorrow the World 44. *The Adventures of Mark Twain* 44. *The Best Years of Our Lives* (AA) 46. Another Part of the Forest 48. An Act of Murder 48. Christopher Columbus (GB) 49. It's a Big Country 51. *Death of a Salesman* (AAN) 52. Man on a Tightrope 53. *Executive Suite* 54. The Bridges at Toko Ri 54. The Desperate Hours 55. Alexander the Great 55. The Man in the Grey Flannel Suit 56. Middle of the Night 59. *Inherit the Wind* 60. The Young Doctors 62. The Condemned of Altona 63. *Seven Days in May* 64. Hombre 67. Tick Tick Tick 70. The Iceman Cometh 73.
✪ For the diligence with which he undertook every role, and for the satisfying success of most of the results. *A Star Is Born*.
“ He was able to do a very emotional scene with tears in his eyes, and pinch my fanny at the same time. – *Shelley Winters*

March, Hal (1920–1970).
American comic actor who never quite made it.
Outrage 50. Yankee Pasha 54. My Sister Eileen 55. *Hear Me Good* 57. Send Me No Flowers 64, etc.

March, Jane (1975–).
British actress, a former model.
The Lover/L'Amant 91. Color of Night 94. Provocateur 96. Tarzan and the Lost City 98, etc.

Marchal, Georges (1920–1997) (Georges-Louis Lucot).
French leading actor, usually in heroic or swashbuckling roles. Born in Nancy, he was on-screen from his late teens. Married actress Dany ROBIN.
The French Way/Fausse Alerte 40. Première Rendez-Vous 41. Lumière d'Été 42. Blondine 43. Vautrin 43. Pamela 44. Torrents 46. Bethsabée 47. The Last Days of Pompeii 48. Au Grand Balcon 49. Robinson Crusoe 50. Messalina 51. La Castiglione 53. The Three Musketeers (as D'Artagnan) 53. Theodora, Slave Empress 54. Si Versailles M'était Conte 54. Gil Blas 55. When the Sun Rises/Celà S'Appelle l'Aurore 55. Evil Eden/La Mort en Ce Jardin 56. Filles de Nuit 58. Spartan Gladiators/La Rivolta dei Gladiatori 58. Austerlitz 59. Legions of the Nile (as Mark Antony) 60. The Colossus of Rhodes 61. The Dirty Game/Guerre Secrète 65. Belle de Jour 67. The Milky Way/La Voie Lactée 69. Faustine 71. The Closet Children/Les Enfants du Placard 77, etc.

Marchand, Colette.
French actress who was nominated for an Oscar as best supporting actress in *Moulin Rouge* 52, her only international film.

Marchand, Corinne (1937–).
French leading lady of the 60s.
Cléo de 5 à 7 62. Seven Deadly Sins 63. The Milky Way 69. Rider on the Rain 70. Borsalino 70. Travels with My Aunt 72. Crime and Punishment 83. Attention Bandits 87. Le Parfum d'Yvonne 94, etc.

Marchand, Henri (1889–1959).
French comedy actor.
A Nous la Liberté 31. Je Vous Aimerai Toujours 33. Volga en Flammes 35. Les Deux Combinards 38. L'Ennemi sans Visage 46. La Sorcière 50. Operation Magali 53. Till Eulenspiegel 56, many others.

Marcus, Lawrence B.
American screenwriter.
Petulia 68. Justine 69. Alex and the Gypsy 76. The Stunt Man (AAN) 80.

Marcus, Mike (1945–).
American production executive, a former agent, who became president of MGM in 1993.

Marcuse, Theodore (1920–1967).
Shaven-pated American character actor, usually in sinister roles.
The Glass Bottom Boat 65. The Cincinnati Kid 65. Last of the Secret Agents 66. The Wicked Dreams of Paula Schultz 67, etc.

Margetson, Arthur (1897–1951).
British stage actor, former stockbroker's clerk, who went to Hollywood in 1940 and played supporting roles.
Other People's Sins 31. His Grace Gives Notice 33. Little Friend 34. Broken Blossoms 36. Juggernaut 37. Action for Slander 38. Return to Yesterday 40. Random Harvest 43. Sherlock Holmes Faces Death 44, etc.

Margheriti, Antonio (1930–) (aka Anthony M. Dawson).
Italian director of horror and exploitation movies. Born in Rome, he studied engineering at university and worked in the 50s as an assistant editor and scriptwriter; he is also a special effects expert, specializing in model-making and optical effects.
Space-Men 60. The Golden Arrow 62. Lightning Bolt 65. Wild, Wild Planet 66. The Young, the Evil and the Savage 68. Decameron 3 73. Blood Money 74. The House of 1,000 Pleasures 77. Killer Fish 78. Cannibals in the Streets 80. Car Crash 81. Yor, the Hunter from the Future 83. Ark of the Sun God 84. Codename: Wildgeese 84. The Commander 88. Indio 89. Indio 2: The Revolt 91, many others.
“ Sometimes when I do pictures I really need the money, so I just read the agreement and not the script, before I say OK. You do it because you want the house in town, the house in the country, you want this, that, maybe a beautiful girl . . . – A.M.

Margo (1918–1985) (Maria Marguerita Guadelupe Boldao Castilla y O'Donnell).
Mexican actress and dancer, once with Xavier Cugat's band, long married to Eddie Albert, in occasional Hollywood films from 1933.
Crime without Passion 34. Winterset 36. Lost Horizon 37. The Leopard Man 43. Behind the Rising Sun 43. Gangway for Tomorrow 44. Viva Zapata 52. I'll Cry Tomorrow 57. Who's Got the Action? 63, etc.

Margolin, Janet (1943–1993).
American leading lady.
David and Lisa 62. Bus Riley's Back in Town 65. The Greatest Story Ever Told 65. The Saboteur 65. Nevada Smith 66. Enter Laughing 67. Buona Sera Mrs Campbell 68. Take the Money and Run 70. The Last Child (TV) 71. Family Flight (TV) 72. Pray for the Wildcats (TV) 74. Planet Earth (TV) 74. Lanigan's Rabbi (TV) 76. Annie Hall 77. Murder in Peyton Place (TV) 77. The Triangle Factory Fire Scandal (TV) 79. Last Embrace 79. Ghostbusters II 89, etc.

Margolin, Stuart (c. 1940–).
American character actor and occasional director, born in Davenport, Iowa.
Limbo 72. The Stone Killer 73. Death Wish 74. Lanigan's Rabbi (TV) 76. The Big Bus 76. Futureworld 76. S.O.B. 81. Class 83. A Fine Mess 86. Iron Eagle II 88. Bye Bye Blues 90. Guilty by Suspicion 91. To Grandmother's House We Go (TV) 94. The Student Affair 97, etc.
AS DIRECTOR: A Shining Season (TV) 79. The Glitter Dome (TV) 84. Paramedics (TV) 88. Vendetta (& w) 90. Medicine River 94. How the West Was Fun (TV) 95, etc.
TV series: Occasional Wife 66–67. Love, American Style 69–72. Nichols 71–72. The Rockford Files 74–80. Bret Maverick 81–82. Mr Smith 83.

Margolyes, Miriam (1941–).
Plump British character actress, often in fussy roles.
A Nice Girl Like Me 69. Stand Up Virgin Soldiers 77. The Awakening 80. Reds 81. Scrubbers 82. Yentl 83. Morons from Outer Space 85. Little Shop of Horrors 86. Little Dorrit 88. Pacific Heights 90. The Fool 91. Dead Again 91. The Butcher's Wife 91. Ed and His Dead Mother 93. The Age of Innocence 93. Immortal Beloved 94. Babe (voice) 95. Balto 95. Romeo and Juliet 96. James and the Giant Peach 96. William Shakespeare's Romeo and Juliet (as The Nurse) (US) 96. Left Luggage (Hol.) 98. Pi 98. Vanity Fair (TV) 98, etc.
TV series: Frannie's Turn 92.

Margulies, Julianna (1966–).
American actress, best known for her role as Nurse Hathaway in the TV series *ER*. Born in Spring Valley, New York, she was partly educated in France and England and studied at Sarah Lawrence College.
Out for Justice 91. Paradise Lost 97. The Newton Boys 98. A Price above Rubies 98, etc.
TV series: ER 94– .

Marie, Lisa.
American actress and model.
Dead and Buried 81. Alice 90. Ed Wood (as Vampira) 94. Mars Attacks! 96. Breast Men (TV) 97. Frogs for Snakes 98, etc.

Marielle, Jean-Pierre (1932–).
French leading actor.
Peau de Banane 63. Que la Fête Commence 75. Calmos 76. One Wild Moment 78. Coup de Torchon 81. Evening Dress/Tenue de Soirée 86. Uranus 91. The Smile/Le Sourire 94. Le Parfum d'Yvonne 94. Les Milles 95. The Grand Dukes 95, etc.

Marin, Edwin L. (1901–1951).
American director.
The Death Kiss 32. A Study in Scarlet 33. Paris Interlude 34. The Casino Murder Case 35. I'd Give My Life 36. Everybody Sing 38. A Christmas Carol 38. Fast and Loose 39. Maisie 39. Florian 40. A Gentleman After Dark 42. *Show Business* 44. Tall in the Saddle 44. Johnny Angel 45. The Young Widow 46. Nocturne 46. Christmas Eve 47. Race Street 48. Canadian Pacific 49. Fighting Man of the Plains 49. The Cariboo Trail 50. Fort Worth 51, etc.

Marin, Jacques (1919–).
French character actor.
The Enemy General 60. Tiara Tahiti 62. Charade 63. The Train 64. How to Steal a Million 66. Lost Command 66. The Girl on the Motorcycle 68. The Night of the Following Day 68. Darling Lili 69. The Madwoman of Chaillot 69. Shaft in Africa 73. The Island at the Top of the World 74. Marathon Man 76. Herbie Goes to Monte Carlo 77. Who Is Killing the Great Chefs of Europe? 78. Les Minipouss 86. A Star for Two 90, etc.

Marin, Richard 'Cheech' (1946–).
American actor, musician and screenwriter. One half of a coarse comic double-act with Thomas CHONG featuring two druggy hippies, which began on record albums and enjoyed a high popularity in the early 80s. The act split up in 1985.
Up in Smoke (a, w) 79. Cheech & Chong's Next Movie (a, w) 80. Cheech & Chong's Nice Dreams (a, w) 81. Things Are Tough All Over (a, w) 82. Cheech & Chong: Still Smokin' (a, w) 83. Yellowbeard (a) 83. Cheech & Chong's The Corsican Brothers (a, w) 84. After Hours (a) 85. Echo Park (a) 86. Born in East L.A. (a, d) 87. Rude Awakening (a) 89. Troop Beverly Hills (a) 89. Boyfriend from Hell/The Shrimp on the Barbie (a) 90. Ferngully . . . the Last Rainforest (voice) 92. The Cisco Kid (TV) 94. Desperado 95. From Dusk till Dawn 95. The Great White Hype 96. Tin Cup 96. Paulie 98, etc.
TV series: Nash Bridges 96– .

Marion, Frances (1888–1973) (Frances Marion Owens).
American screenwriter. Married actor Fred THOMSON and director George HILL.
Autobiography: 1972, *Off with Their Heads*.
Book: 1997, *Frances Marion and the Powerful Women of Early Hollywood* by Cari Beauchamp.
Daughter of the Sea 16. Humoresque 22. Stella Dallas 25. The Winning of Barbara Worth 26. The Scarlet Letter 27. *Love* 27. The Wind 28. *The Big House* (AA) 30. *The Champ* (AA) 32. The Prizefighter and the Lady (AAN) 33. *Dinner at Eight* 33. Riff Raff 36. *Knight without Armour* 37. Green Hell 40, etc.

Marion-Crawford, Howard (1914–1969).
British actor often seen in Watsonian roles or as jovial, beefy, sporting types.
Forever England 32. Freedom Radio 40. The Rake's Progress 45. The Hasty Heart 49. The Man

in the White Suit 51. Where's Charley? 52. Reach for the Sky 56. Virgin Island 58. The Brides of Fu Manchu 66, etc.
TV series: Sherlock Holmes 55.

Maris, Mona (1903–1991) (Maria Capdevielle).
Franco-Argentinian 'second lead' in Hollywood films.
Romance of the Rio Grande 29. Secrets 33. Law of the Tropics 41. Tampico 44. Heartbeat 46. The Avengers 50, etc.

Maritza, Sari (1910–1987) (Patricia Nathan).
Anglo-Austrian leading lady, a short-lived sensation of the early 30s.
Monte Carlo Madness 31. Forgotten Commandments 32. Evenings for Sale 32. International House 33. Crimson Romance 34, etc.

Marken, Jane (1895–1976) (J. Krab).
French character actress with long stage experience.
Fioritures 15. Camille 34. *Partie de Campagne* 37. Hôtel du Nord 38. *Lumière d'Été* 42. Les Enfants du Paradis 44. L'Idiot 46. Clochemerle 47. Une Si Jolie Petite Plage 48. Manèges 49. Ma Pomme 50. Les Compagnes de la Nuit 52. Marie Antoinette 55. And God Created Woman 56. Pot Bouille 57. The Mirror Has Two Faces 58, etc.

Marker, Chris (1921–) (Christian Bouche-Villeneuve).
French documentary director. Leader of the modernist 'left bank' school.
Olympia 52. Toute la Mémoire du Monde 56. Letter from Siberia 58. Description d'un Combat 60. Cuba Si 61. Le Joli Mai 62. *La Jetée* 63. If I Had Four Dromedaries 66. Le Fond de l'Air est Rouge 77. Sans Soleil 82. A.K. 85. L'Héritage de la Chouette 89. The Last Bolshevik 93, etc.

Markey, Enid (1896–1981).
American character actress. In 1918 she was the first screen Jane, to Elmo Lincoln's Tarzan.
Civilisation 16. Tarzan of the Apes 18. The Romance of Tarzan 18. Snafu 46. The Naked City 48. The Boston Strangler 68, etc.
TV series: Bringing Up Buddy 60–61.

Markey, Gene (1895–1980).
American screenwriter, producer, playwright and novelist. He was the second husband of Joan Bennett (1932–37), and of Hedy Lamarr (1939–40, the divorce court judge suggesting that in future she should not marry a man she had known for only four weeks), and the third of Myrna Loy (1946–51).
Stepping High (oa) 28. The Battle of Paris 29. The Florodora Girl 30. As You Desire Me 32. Midnight Mary 33. Fashions 34. A Modern Hero 34. Let's Live Tonight 35. King of Burlesque 36. Private Number 36. *On the Avenue* 37, etc.
AS PRODUCER ONLY: Wee Willie Winkie 37. The Little Princess 39. The Hound of the Baskervilles 39. The Blue Bird 40. Lillian Russell 40. Moss Rose 47.

Markham, Kika.
English leading actress. Married Corin Redgrave.
Bunny Lake Is Missing 65. Futtocks End 69. Anne and Muriel (Fr.) 71. Operation: Daybreak (US) 75. Noriot (Fr.) 76. Outland 81. The Innocent 84, etc.

Markham, Monte (1935–).
American leading man, mostly on TV.
Death Takes a Holiday (TV) 71. One is a Lonely Number 72. Midway 76. Airport 77 77. Hotline 82. Off the Wall 83. Defense Play (& d) 88. Neon City (d) 91. At First Sight 95. Piranha 95, etc.
TV series: The Second Hundred Years 67. Mr Deeds Goes to Town 69. The New Perry Mason 73. Dallas 81. Rituals 84–85. Baywatch 89– .

Markle, Fletcher (1921–1991).
Canadian director, briefly in Hollywood. Married to Mercedes McCambridge (1950–62).
■ Jigsaw 49. Night into Morning 51. The Man with a Cloak 51. The Incredible Journey 63.

Markle, Peter (1946–).
American director.
The Personals 82. Youngblood 86. Bat-21 88. El Diablo (TV) 90. Through the Eyes of a Killer (TV) 92. Wagons East 94. White Dwarf 95. The Last Days of Frankie the Fly 96, etc.

Marks, Alfred (1921–1996).
Bald-pated British comedian, in films from 1950 but more usually seen on TV and stage.
Desert Mice 59. There Was a Crooked Man 60. Frightened City 61. Weekend with Lulu 62. She'll Have to Go 63. Scream and Scream Again 70. Our Miss Fred 72. Valentino 77, etc.

Marks, Richard (1943–).
American film editor.
Little Big Man 70. Parades 72. Bang the Drum Slowly 73. Serpico 73. The Godfather Part II 74. Lies My Father Told Me 75. The Last Tycoon 76. Apocalypse Now (AAN) 79. The Hand 81. Pennies from Heaven 81. Terms of Endearment (AAN) 83. The Adventures of Buckaroo Banzai across the Eighth Dimension 84. St Elmo's Fire 85. Pretty in Pink 86. Firewalker 86. Broadcast News (AAN) 87. Say Anything 89. Dick Tracy 90. One Good Cop 91. I'll Do Anything 94. Assassins 95. Things to Do in Denver When You're Dead 95. 'Til There Was You 97. As Good as It Gets 97. You've Got Mail 98, etc.

Marky Mark:
see WAHLBERG, Mark.

Marley, J. Peverell (1899–1964).
American cinematographer who worked on de Mille's silent epics.
The Ten Commandments 23. The Volga Boatmen 25. *King of Kings* 27. House of Rothschild 34. Clive of India 35. *Alexander's Ragtime Band* 38. *The Hound of the Baskervilles* 39. Night and Day 46. Life with Father 47. The Greatest Show on Earth 52. House of Wax 53. Serenade 56. The Left-Handed Gun 58. A Fever in the Blood 61, many others.

Marley, John (1907–1984).
American character actor.
My Six Convicts 52. Timetable 56. I Want to Live 58. America America 65. Cat Ballou 65. Faces 68. *Love Story* (AAN) 70. A Man Called Sledge 70. The Godfather 72. Blade 73. W. C. Fields and Me 76. The Car 77. The Greatest 77. Hooper 78. Tribute 80, etc.

Marlowe, Hugh (1911–1982) (Hugh Hipple).
American actor, former radio announcer, in films from 1937. His wives included actresses Edith Atwater and K. T. STEVENS; he was romantically linked with Eva GABOR.
Mrs Parkington 44. Meet Me In St Louis 44. *Twelve O'Clock High* 50. *All about Eve* 50. The Day the Earth Stood Still 51. Monkey Business 52. Garden of Evil 54. Earth Versus the Flying Saucers 56. Thirteen Frightened Girls 64. Castle of Evil 66. The Last Shot You Hear 68, etc.
TV series: Ellery Queen 54.

Marlowe, June (1903–1984).
American actress who was mainly a leading lady to Rin-Tin-Tin and later became the schoolteacher Miss Crabtree in the Our Gang shorts of the 30s.
Find Your Man 24. Clash of the Wolves 25. Night Cry 26. Don Juan 26. Life of Riley 27. Code of the Air 28. Pardon Us/Jail Birds 31. The Lone Defender (serial) 32. Riddle Ranch 36, etc.

Marlowe, Scott.
American juvenile actor of the late 50s.
Men in War 57. Young Guns 57. The Subterraneans 60. *A Cold Wind in August* 61. No Place Like Home (TV) 89. Chasers 94, etc.
TV series: Valley of the Dolls 94.

Marly, Florence (1918–1978) (Hana Smekalova).
Franco-Czech leading lady, married to Pierre Chenal. Made a few films in Hollywood.
Sealed Verdict 48. Tokyo Joe 49. Tokyo File 212 51. Gobs and Gals 52. The Idol (Chilean) 52. Confession at Dawn (Chilean) 53. Undersea Girl 58. Queen of Blood 65. Games 67. Doctor Death 73, etc.

Marmont, Percy (1883–1977).
Veteran British romantic actor of silent era, in films since 1913.
SILENT FILMS: The Silver King (GB) 24. Lord Jim (US) 25. Mantrap (US) 26. Rich and Strange (GB) 27, etc.
SOUND FILMS: The Silver Greyhound 32. Secret Agent 36. Action for Slander 38. I'll Walk Beside You 41. Loyal Heart 45. No Orchids for Miss Blandish 48. Lisbon 56, many others.

Marquand, Christian (1927–).
French leading man, who turned director with *Candy* 68.
Lucretia Borgia 53. Senso 54. And God Created Woman 56. Sait-on Jamais? 57. Une Vie 58. Victory at Entebbe (TV) 76. The Other Side of Midnight 77. Je Vous Aime 80. Emmanuelle IV 84, etc.

Marquand, John P. (1893–1960).
American novelist who wrote solid popular books about middle-aged men regretting their lost youth; also the Mr Moto series (filmed in the late 30s with Peter Lorre).
H.M. Pulham Esquire 41. The Late George Apley 47. B. F.'s Daughter 49. Top Secret Affair/Melville Goodwin USA 56. Stopover Tokyo 57, etc.

Marquand, Richard (1938–1987).
British director.
The Search for the Nile (TV) 75. The Legacy 78. Eye of the Needle 81. Return of the Jedi 83. Until September 84. *Jagged Edge* 85. Hearts of Fire 87.

Marriott, Moore (1885–1949) (George Thomas Moore-Marriott).
British leading man of silents who became a character comedian specializing in hoary rustics, chiefly beloved as the ancient but resilient old Harbottle of the Will Hay comedies: *Convict* 99 36, *Oh Mr Porter* 38, *Ask a Policeman* 39, *Where's That Fire?* 40, etc. Also notable with the Crazy Gang in *The Frozen Limits* 39, and *Gasbags* 40. Made over 300 films in all.
Dick Turpin 08. Passion Island 26. The Lyons Mail 31. The Water Gypsies 32. As You Like It 36. Millions Like Us 43. Time Flies 44. Green for Danger 46. The History of Mr Polly 49. High Jinks in Society 49.

Mars, Kenneth (1936–).
American character comedian who is usually way over the top.
The Producers 67. Desperate Characters 71. What's Up Doc? 72. Paper Moon 73. The Parallax View 74. Young Frankenstein 74. Night Moves 75. The Apple Dumpling Gang Rides Again 79. Radio Days 87. For Keeps 88. Police Academy 6: City under Siege 89. The Little Mermaid (voice) 89. Shadows and Fog 91. We're Back! A Dinosaur's Story (voice) 93. Precious 96. Citizen Ruth 96, etc.

Marsh, Carol (1926–) (Norma Simpson).
British leading lady whose career faltered when she outgrew *ingénue* roles.
■ *Brighton Rock* 47. Marry Me 49. Helter Skelter 50. Alice in Wonderland (French puppet version) 50. The Romantic Age 50. Scrooge 51. Salute the Toff 51. Private Information 51. Dracula 58. Man Accused 59.

Marsh, Garry (1902–1981) (Leslie March Geraghty).
Robust, balding British character actor; in films from 1930, usually as harassed father, perplexed policeman or explosive officer.
Night Birds 30. Dreyfus 30. Number Seventeen 32. The Maid of the Mountains 32. Scrooge 35. When Knights Were Bold 36. Bank Holiday 38. It's in the Air 38. The Four Just Men 39. Hoots Mon 40. I'll Be Your Sweetheart 45. The Rake's Progress 45. Dancing with Crime 46. Just William's Luck 48. Murder at the Windmill 49. Worm's Eye View 51. Mr Drake's Duck 53. Who Done It? 55. Where the Bullets Fly 66, many others.

Marsh, Jean (1934–).
British character actress who became internationally known as the maid in TV's *Upstairs Downstairs*, which she created with actress Eileen ATKINS. Also co-creator of the 90s TV series *The House of Elliott*. Married to actor Jon PERTWEE (1955–60).
The Tales of Hoffman 51. Cleopatra 63. Face of a Stranger 64. Unearthly Stranger 64. Frenzy 72. Dark Places 74. The Eagle Has Landed 77. Master of the Game (TV) 84. Return to Oz 85. Willow 88. A Connecticut Yankee in King Arthur's Court (TV) 89. Adam Bede (TV) 91. Fatherland (TV) 94, etc.
TV series: 9 to 5 82–83.

Marsh, Joan (1913–) (Nancy Ann Rosher).
American leading actress of the 30s, the daughter of cinematographer Charles ROSHER. On screen as a child, under the name Dorothy Rosher, returning as a blonde in *The King of Jazz* 30. Retired in the 40s.
The Little Princess 17. Daddy Longlegs 19. Little Lord Fauntleroy 21. All Quiet on the Western Front 30. The Little Accident 30. Three Girls Lost 31. Three-Cornered Moon 33. We're Rich Again 34. Anna Karenina 35. Hot Water 37. Fast and Loose 39. Road to Zanzibar 41. Secret Service in Darkest Africa 43. Follow the Leader 44, etc.

Marsh, Mae (1895–1968) (Mary Warne Marsh).
American leading lady of the silent screen; later played small character roles.
Man's Genesis 12. The Birth of a Nation 15. Intolerance 16. Polly of the Circus 17. Spotlight Sadie 18. The Little 'Fraid Lady 20. Flames of Passion 22. The White Rose 23. Daddies 24. The Rat (GB) 25. Tides of Passion 26. Over the Hill 32. Little Man What Now 34. Jane Eyre 43. A Tree Grows in Brooklyn 44. The Robe 53. Sergeant Rutledge 60, many others.

Marsh, Marian (1913–) (Violet Krauth).
American leading lady of English, German, French and Irish descent. Began in Hollywood as an extra; chosen by John Barrymore to play Trilby to his *Svengali* 31.
The Mad Genius 32. Five Star Final 32. The Eleventh Commandment 33. Love at Second Sight (GB) 34. The Black Room 35. When's Your Birthday 37. Missing Daughters 40. House of Errors 42, etc.

Marsh, Oliver H. T. (1893–1941).
American cinematographer.
The Floor Below 18. Good References 19. Lessons in Love 21. Jazzmania 23. The Dove 27. The Divine Woman 28. Not So Dumb 30. The Sin of Madelon Claudet 31. Arsene Lupin 32. Today We Live 33. The Merry Widow 34. *David Copperfield* 35. *A Tale of Two Cities* 35. The Great Ziegfeld 36. His Brother's Wife 36. After the Thin Man 36. Maytime 37. The Firefly 37. Sweethearts 38. It's a Wonderful World 39. Bitter Sweet 40. Rage in Heaven 41. Lady Be Good 41, many others.

Marsh, Terence (1931–).
British production designer.
Dr Zhivago (AA) 65. A Man for All Seasons 66. Oliver (AA) 68. The Looking Glass War 70. Perfect Friday 70. Scrooge (AAN) 70. Mary, Queen of Scots (AAN) 71. A Touch of Class 73. The Mackintosh Man 73. Juggernaut 74. The Adventures of Sherlock Holmes' Smarter Brother 75. Royal Flash 76. A Bridge Too Far 77. Magic 78. The Frisco Kid 79. Absence of Malice 81. To Be or Not To Be 83. Haunted Honeymoon 86. Spaceballs 87. Bert Rigby, You're a Fool 89. The Hunt for Red October 90. Havana 90. Basic Instinct 92. Clear and Present Danger 94. The Shawshank Redemption 94. Forget Paris 95. Executive Decision 96, etc.

Marshal, Alan (1909–1961).
Australian-born actor of light romantic leads; came to films in 1936 after New York stage experience.
The Garden of Allah 36. Night Must Fall 38. The Hunchback of Notre Dame 40. Tom, Dick and Harry 40. *Lydia* 41. The White Cliffs of Dover 43. The Barkleys of Broadway 48. The Opposite Sex 56. The House on Haunted Hill 59, etc.

Marshall, Alan (1938–).
British producer associated with the films of Alan Parker.
Bugsy Malone 76. Midnight Express (AAN) 78. Fame 80. Shoot the Moon 81. Pink Floyd the Wall 82. Another Country 84. Birdy 84. Angel Heart 87. Leonard, Part 6 87. Homeboy 88. Jacob's Ladder 90. Basic Instinct 92. Cliffhanger 93, etc.

Marshall, Brenda (1915–1992) (Ardis Ankerson Gaines).
American leading lady who married William Holden and retired.
Espionage Agent 39. The Sea Hawk 40. Footsteps in the Dark 41. Singapore Woman 41. Background to Danger 43. The Constant Nymph 44. Strange Impersonation 45. Whispering Smith 49. The Tomahawk Trail 50, etc.

Marshall, Connie (1938–).
American child actress of the 40s.
Sunday Dinner for a Soldier 44. *Sentimental Journey* 45. Dragonwyck 46. Home Sweet Homicide 47. Mother Wore Tights 48. Kill the Umpire 50. Sagmaw Trail 53, etc.

Marshall, E(verett) G. (1910–).
American character actor, usually in authoritarian roles. Born in Owatonna, Minnesota, of Norwegian parents, he was educated at the University of Minnesota. He began acting in touring companies and later studied at the Actors' Studio in the 40s. He was much on the Broadway stage in the 40s and frequently on television from the 50s. Married twice.
■ The House on 92nd Street 45. 13 rue Madeleine 46. Untamed Fury 47. Call Northside 777 48. The Caine Mutiny 54. Pushover 54. The Bamboo Prison 54. Broken Lance 54. The Silver Chalice 54. The Left Hand of God 55. The Scarlet Hour 56. The Mountain 56. *Twelve Angry Men* 57. *The Bachelor Party* 57. Man on Fire 57. The Buccaneer 58. The Journey 59. Compulsion 59. Cash McCall 59. Town without Pity 61. The Chase 66. Is Paris Burning? 66. The Poppy Is Also a Flower (TV) 66. The Bridge at Remagen 69. A Clear and Present Danger (TV) 70. Tora! Tora! Tora! 70. The Pursuit of Happiness 71. Vanished (TV) 71. The City (TV) 71. Don't Look behind You (TV) 71. Pursuit (TV) 72. Money to Burn (TV) 73. The Abduction of St Anne (TV) 75. Collision Course (TV) 76. Interiors 78. The Private Files of J. Edgar Hoover 78. The Lazarus Syndrome (TV) 79. Superman II 80. Creepshow 82. Kennedy (as Joseph Kennedy) (TV) 83. Saigon – Year of the Cat (TV) 83. The Winter of our Discontent (TV) 84. Power 85. At Mother's Request (TV) 87. The Hijacking of the Achille Lauro (TV) 89. Consenting Adults 92. The Tommyknockers (TV) 93. Oldest Living Confederate Widow Tells All (TV) 94. Nixon 95.
TV series: The Defenders 61–65. The New Doctors 69–73. Chicago Hope 94.

Marshall, Frank (1947–).
American producer turned director. A former actor, he founded the production company Amblin Entertainment with Steven Spielberg and his wife Kathleen Kennedy. Now heads Kennedy/Marshall Productions.
AS PRODUCER: The Other Side of the Wind 75. The Warriors 78. Raiders of the Lost Ark (AAN) 81. Poltergeist 82. Indiana Jones and the Temple of Doom 84. Fandango 84. The Goonies 85. The Color Purple (AAN) 85. Back to the Future 85. The Money Pit 86. Innerspace 86. Who Framed Roger Rabbit? 88. The Land before Time 88. Back to the Future II 89. Indiana Jones and the Last Crusade 89. Hook 91. Swing Kids 93. The Indian in the Cupboard 95. Snow Falling on Cedars 98, etc.
AS DIRECTOR: Arachnophobia 89. Alive 93. Milk Money 94. Congo 95, etc.

Marshall, Garry (1934–) (Gary Masciarelli).
American film director, screenwriter, producer and occasional actor, who started his career writing and producing TV sitcoms (*The Dick Van Dyke Show, Happy Days*, etc.). He is the brother of actress and director Penny Marshall.
How Sweet It Is (w, p) 68. The Grasshopper (w, p) 70. Young Doctors in Love (p, d) 82. The Flamingo Kid (wd) 84. Lost in America (a) 85. Nothing in Common (d) 86. Overboard (d) 87. Beaches (d) 88. Pretty Woman (d) 90. Frankie and Johnny (d) 91. Soapdish (a) 91. A League of Their Own (a) 92. Exit to Eden (d) 94. Dear God 96. The Twilight of the Golds (a) 97, etc.

Marshall, George (1891–1975).
American director with over 400 features to his credit. Entered films 1912 as an extra; graduated to feature roles in early serials and comedies; began directing 1917 with a series of Harry Carey westerns.
Pack Up Your Troubles 32. A Message to Garcia 34. The Crime of Dr Forbes 37. In Old Kentucky 38. The Goldwyn Follies 38. You Can't Cheat an Honest Man 39. *Destry Rides Again* 39. *The Ghost Breakers* 40. When the Daltons Rode 40. The Forest Rangers 42. Star Spangled Rhythm 43. And the Angels Sing 43. *Murder He Says* 44. Incendiary Blonde 45. Hold That Blonde 45. The Blue Dahlia 46. The Perils of Pauline 47. Tap Roots 48. *Fancy Pants* 50. The Savage 52. Scared Stiff 53. *Red Garters* 54. The Second Greatest Sex 55. Beyond Mombasa (GB) 56. The Sad Sack 57. The Sheepman 58. Imitation General 58. The Gazebo 59. Cry for Happy 61. How the West Was Won (part) 62. Advance to the Rear 64. Boy, Did I Get a Wrong Number 66. Eight on the Lam 67. Hook Line and Sinker 69, many others.

Marshall, Herbert (1890–1966).
Urbane British actor who despite the loss of a leg in World War I invariably played smooth, sometimes diffident but always gentlemanly roles. In Hollywood from early 30s.
■ Mumsie 27. The Letter 29. Murder 30. The Calendar 31. Secrets of a Secretary 31. *Michael and Mary* 32. The Faithful Heart 32. Blonde Venus 32. *Trouble in Paradise* 32. Evenings for Sale 32. The Solitaire Man 33. I Was a Spy 33. Four Frightened People 34. Outcast Lady 34. The Painted Veil 34. Riptide 34. The Good Fairy 35. The Flame Within 35. Accent on Youth 35. *The Dark Angel* 35. If You Could Only Cook 35. The Lady Consents 36. Forgotten Faces 36. Till We Meet Again 36. Girls' Dormitory 36. A Woman Rebels 36. Make Way for a Lady 36. *Angel* 37. Breakfast for Two 37. Mad About Music 38. Always Goodbye 38. Woman against Woman 38. Zaza 39. A Bill of Divorcement 40. *Foreign Correspondent* 40. *The Letter* 40. When Ladies Meet 41. *The Little Foxes* 41. Kathleen 41. Adventure in Washington 41. *The Moon and Sixpence* (as Somerset Maugham) 42. Young Ideas 43. Forever and a Day 43. Flight for Freedom 43. Andy Hardy's Blonde Trouble 44. The Unseen 45. *The Enchanted Cottage* 45. Crack up 46. *The Razor's Edge* (as Somerset Maugham) 46. Duel in the Sun 46. High Wall 47. Ivy 47. The Secret Garden 49. The Underworld Story 50. Anne of the Indies 51. Black Jack 52. Angel Face 53. The Black Shield of Falworth 54. Gog 54. Riders to the Stars 54. The Virgin Queen 55. Wicked as They Come 56. The Weapon 56. *Stage Struck* 57. The Fly 58. A Fever in the Blood 60. Midnight Lace 60. Five Weeks in a Balloon 62. The List of Adrian Messenger 63. The Third Day 65.
✪ For his comforting upper class presence over thirty-five years of talkies. *Trouble in Paradise*.
❝ Fantasy droops before Mr Herbert Marshall, so intractably British in the American scene. He does, I suppose, represent some genuinely national characteristics, if not those one wishes to see exported: a kind of tobacco, a kind of tweed, a kind of pipe; or in terms of dog, something large, sentimental and moulting, something which confirms our preference for cats. – *Graham Greene, reviewing If You Could Only Cook*

Marshall, Herbert (1900–1991).
British documentarist, married to Fredda Brilliant. Associate of John Grierson; worked on English dubbing of Russian films. Produced and directed feature, *Tinker* 49.

Marshall, James (1967–).
American actor.
Twin Peaks: Fire Walk with Me 92. Gladiator 92. A Few Good Men 92. Don't Do It 94. Hits! 94. The Ticket (TV) 97, etc.
TV series: Twin Peaks 90.
❝ Hollywood is just full of people who want the quick buck and the quick fame, and they get burned out. – *J.M.*

Marshall, Penny (1942–) (Carole Penny Marsciarelli).
American director, a former comedy actress, known from TV. She is the sister of director Garry Marshall. Formerly married to actor and director Rob Reiner.
AS ACTRESS: How Sweet It Is 68. 1941 79. Movers and Shakers 84. Jumpin' Jack Flash 86. The Hard Way 91, etc.
TV series: The Odd Couple 71–75. The Bob Newhart Show 72–73. Paul Sand in Friends and Lovers 74–75. *Laverne and Shirley* 76–83.
AS DIRECTOR: Big 88. Awakenings 90. A League of Their Own 92. Renaissance Man 94. The Preacher's Wife 96, etc.

Marshall, Trudy (1922–).
American leading lady of minor films in the 40s.
Secret Agent of Japan 42. Girl Trouble 44. Sentimental Journey 46. Disaster 48. Mark of the Gorilla 50. The President's Lady 53. Once Is Not Enough 75, etc.

Marshall, Tully (1864–1943) (William Phillips).
American silent screen actor; stage experience from boyhood.
Intolerance 15. Oliver Twist (as Fagin) 16. Joan the Woman 16. The Slim Princess 20. The Hunchback of Notre Dame 23. The Merry Widow 25. The Red Mill 27. The Cat and the Canary 28. Trail of '98 29. Show of Shows 29. The Unholy Garden 31. Scarface 32. Grand Hotel 33. Diamond Jim 35. Souls at Sea 37. A Yank at Oxford 38. Brigham Young 40. Chad Hanna 41. This Gun for Hire 42, many others.

Marshall, William (1924–).
American character actor.
Lydia Bailey 52. Something of Value 57. The Boston Strangler 68. Blacula 72. Scream Blacula Scream 73. Twilight's Last Gleaming 77. Vasectomy – a Delicate Matter 86. Maverick 94, etc.

Marshall, Zena (1926–).
British leading lady with French ancestry; stage experience.
Caesar and Cleopatra (debut) 45. Good Time Girl 47. Miranda 48. Sleeping Car to Trieste 48. Marry Me 49. Hell Is Sold Out 51. The Embezzler 54. My Wife's Family 56. The Story of David 61. Dr No 62. Those Magnificent Men in Their Flying Machines 65. The Terronauts 67, etc.

Martelli, Carlo.
English composer, mainly for horror movies of the 60s.
The Curse of the Mummy's Tomb 64. Catacombs 64. Witchcraft 64. The Murder Game 66. Who Killed the Cat? 66. Slave Girls/Prehistoric Women 68, etc.

Martelli, Otello (1903–).
Italian cinematographer, especially associated with Fellini.
Paisa 46. Bitter Rice 49. La Dolce Vita 50. I Vitelloni 52. La Strada 54. Il Bidone 55. I Tre Volti 63, etc.

Martin, Chris-Pin (1894–1953).
Rotund Yaqui Indian actor who provided comic relief in many a western.
Four Frightened People 34. The Gay Desperado 36. The Return of the Cisco Kid 39 (and ensuing series). The Mark of Zorro 41. Weekend in Havana 42. Mexican Hayride 49. Ride the Man Down 53, etc.

Martin, Darnell (1965–).
American director and screenwriter, a former assistant camera operator.
I Like It Like That (wd) 94.

Martin, Dean (1917–1995) (Dino Crocetti).
Heavy-lidded, self-spoofing American leading man and singer. Teamed with Jerry Lewis until 1956, then enjoyed spectacular solo success in 60s.
Biography (of Martin and Lewis): 1976, *Everybody Loves Somebody Sometime* by Arthur Marx. 1992, *Dino: Living High in the Dirty Business of Dreams* by Nick Tosches.
■ My Friend Irma 49. My Friend Irma Goes West 50. At War with the Army 51. That's My Boy 51. Sailor Beware 51. Jumping Jacks 52. The Stooge 52. Scared Stiff 53. The Caddy 53. Money from Home 53. Living It Up 54. Three Ring Circus 54. You're Never Too Young 55. Artists and Models 55. Pardners 56. Hollywood or Bust 56. Ten Thousand Bedrooms 57. *The Young Lions* 58. Some Came Running 58. *Rio Bravo* 59. Career 59. Who Was That Lady? 60. Bells are Ringing 60. Ocean's Eleven 60. All in a Night's Work 61. Ada 61. Sergeants Three 62. Who's Got the Action? 62. Toys in the Attic 63. Who's Been Sleeping in My Bed? 63. Four For Texas 64. What a Way to Go 64. Robin and the Seven Hoods 64. *Kiss Me Stupid* 64. The Sons of Katie Elder 65. Marriage on the Rocks 65. *The Silencers* 66. Texas Across the River 66. Murderers' Row 67. Rough Night in Jericho 67. The Ambushers 67. Bandolero 68. How to Save a Marriage 68. Five Card Stud 68. Wrecking Crew 68. Airport 69. Something Big 71. Showdown 73. Mr Ricco 75. Angels in Vegas (TV) 78. The Cannonball Run 80. Cannonball Run II 83.
❝ I'd hate to be a teetotaller. Imagine getting up in the morning and knowing that's as good as you're going to feel all day. – *D.M.*
I can't stand an actor or actress who tells me acting is hard work. It's easy work. Anyone who says it isn't never had to stand on his feet all day dealing blackjack. – *D.M.*
Motivation is a lotta crap. – *D.M.*
Without any doubt the most conscientious actor I have ever worked with. – *Andrew V. McLaglen*
King Leer. – *Life magazine*

Martin, Dean Paul (1951–1987).
American actor, son of Dean Martin. He died when the aircraft he was piloting crashed. Married to actress Olivia Hussey.
Players 79. Heart Like a Wheel 82. Backfire 87.

Martin, Dewey (1923–).
American leading man.
Knock on Any Door (debut) 49. Kansas Raiders 50. The Thing 52. The Big Sky 52. Tennessee Champ 54. Prisoner of War 54. Land of the Pharaohs 55. The Desperate Hours 55. Ten Thousand Bedrooms 57. Wheeler and Murdoch (TV) 72. Seven Alone 75, etc.

Martin, Dick (1923–):
see ROWAN, Dan. Married actress Dolly Read.
The Glass Bottom Boat 66. Carbon Copy 81. Air Bud: Golden Receiver 98, etc.

Martin, D'Urville (1939–1984).
American character actor, often in blaxploitation movies.
A Time to Sing 68. Watermelon Man 70. Book of Numbers 72. Hammer 72. The Legend of Nigger Charley 73. Black Caesar 73. Hell up in Harlem 73. The Soul of Nigger Charley 73. Boss Nigger 74. Dolemite (& d) 75. Death Journey 76. The Big Score 83. The Bear 84, etc.

Martin, Edie (1880–1964).
The frail, tiny old lady of many British films. On stage from 1886, films from 1932.
■ Farewell Again 37. Under the Red Robe 37. The Demi-Paradise 42. A Place of One's Own 45. Oliver Twist 48. The History of Mr Polly 49. The Lavender Hill Mob 51. *The Man in the White Suit* 51. Time Gentlemen Please 52. The Titfield Thunderbolt 52. The End of the Road 54. Lease of Life 54. As Long as They're Happy 55. The Lady Killers 55. My Teenage Daughter 56. Too Many Crooks 59. Weekend with Lulu 61. Sparrows Can't Sing 63.

Martin, Hugh (1914–).
American composer and lyricist, generally in collaboration with Ralph Blane.
Best Foot Forward 41. Meet Me in St Louis 44. Athena 54. The Girl Rush 55. The Girl Most Likely 57. Hans Brinker (TV) 58, etc.

Martin, Marion (1916–1985).
American leading lady of 'B' pictures, a statuesque blonde who graduated from the Ziegfeld chorus.
Boom Town 40. Mexican Spitfire at Sea 41. The Big Store 41. They Got Me Covered 42. Abbot and Costello in Hollywood 45. Queen of Burlesque 47. Oh You Beautiful Doll 50. Thunder in the Pines 54, etc.

Martin, Mary (1913–1990).
American musical comedy star; her film career did not seem satisfactory. She was the mother of actor Larry Hagman.
Autobiography: 1976, *My Heart Belongs*.
■ The Rage of Paris 38. The Great Victor Herbert 39. Rhythm on the River 40. Love Thy Neighbour 40. Kiss the Boys Goodbye 41. New York Town 41. *Birth of the Blues* 41. Star Spangled Rhythm 42. Happy Go Lucky 42. True to Life 43. Night and Day 46. Main Street to Broadway 53. Valentine (TV) 79.
❝ She's OK, if you like talent. – *Ethel Merman*

Martin, Millicent (1934–).
British songstress of stage and TV.
The Horsemasters 60. The Girl on the Boat 62. Nothing But the Best 64. Those Magnificent Men in Their Flying Machines 65. Alfie 66. Stop the World I Want To Get Off 66, etc.
TV series: From a Bird's Eye View 69. Downtown 86–87.

Martin, Pamela Sue (1953–).
American leading lady who became familiar on TV (1977–78) as Nancy Drew the teenage detective.
To Find a Man 71. The Poseidon Adventure 72. Buster and Billie 73. The Girls of Huntington House (TV) 73. The Gun and the Pulpit (TV) 74.

The Lady in Red 79. Torchlight 84. Flicks 87. A Cry in the Wild 90, etc.

Martin, Richard (1917–1994).
Tall, dark American actor, best remembered as Chito Rafferty, the half-Mexican, half-Irish sidekick to Tim Holt in many of his RKO westerns. He quit movies in the early 50s to become an insurance salesman.
Bombardier 43. Tender Comrade 43. Marine Raiders 44. Arizona Ranger 48. Guns of Hate 48. Mysterious Desperado 49. Riders of the Range 49. Rider from Tucson 50. Storm over Wyoming 50. Gun Play 51. Hot Lead 51. Road Agent 52. Target 52. Desert Passage 53. Four Fast Guns 59, etc.

Martin, Ross (1920–1981) (Martin Rosenblatt).
Polish-American character actor: film appearances sporadic.
Conquest of Space 55. The Colossus of New York 58. Experiment in Terror 62. The Ceremony 64. The Great Race 65. Charlie Chan: Happiness is a Warm Clue (TV: title role) 70.
TV series: *The Wild Wild West* 65–68.

Martin, Skip.
English dwarf actor, mainly in horror movies.
The Hellfire Club 60. Masque of the Red Death 64. Whom the Gods Wish to Destroy/Die Nibelungen 66. Circus of Fear 66. The Sandwich Man 66. Where's Jack? 69. Vampire Circus 71. Horror Hospital 73, etc.

Martin, Steve (1945–).
American nightclub comic who turned comic actor and even goes straight occasionally. Formerly married to actress Victoria Tennant. His play *Picasso at the Lapin Agile* was staged in New York in 1996.
The Kids Are Alright 78. Sgt Pepper's Lonely Hearts Club Band 78. The Jerk 79. The Muppet Movie 79. Pennies from Heaven 81. Dead Men Don't Wear Plaid 82. The Man with Two Brains 83. The Lonely Guy 83. All of Me 84. Movers and Shakers 84. Three Amigos 86. The Little Shop of Horrors 86. Roxanne 87. Planes, Trains and Automobiles 87. Dirty Rotten Scoundrels 88. Parenthood 89. My Blue Heaven 90. L.A. Story 91. Father of the Bride 91. Grand Canyon 91. Housesitter 92. Leap of Faith 92. A Simple Twist of Fate (& w) 94. Mixed Nuts 94. Father of the Bride Part II 95. Sgt Bilko 96. The Spanish Prisoner 97. Bofinger 99, etc.
❝ As you get older, it's harder to be silly on the screen. – S.M.

Martin, Strother (1920–1980).
American character actor, often in grizzled western roles.
The Asphalt Jungle 50. Storm over Tibet 52. The Big Knife 55. The Shaggy Dog 59. The Deadly Companions 61. The Man Who Shot Liberty Valance 62. The Sons of Katie Elder 65. Harper 66. *Cool Hand Luke* 67. True Grit 69. Butch Cassidy and the Sundance Kid 69. The Wild Bunch 69. The Ballad of Cable Hogue 70. The Brotherhood of Satan 70. Fool's Parade 71. Pocket Money 72. Sssss 73. Rooster Cogburn 75. Hard Times 75. The Great Scout and Cathouse Thursday 76. Slap Shot 77. The End 78. Up in Smoke 78. The Villain 79, many others.
Famous line (*Cool Hand Luke*): 'What we've got here is a failure to communicate.'

Martin, Tony (1912–) (Alfred Norris).
American cabaret singer and leading man, in Hollywood from 1936 after years of touring with dance bands. He married actress Cyd Charisse in 1948.
Joint autobiography: 1976, *The Two of Us*.
Sing, Baby, Sing 36. Banjo on My Knee 37. Ali Baba Goes to Town 38. Music in My Heart 40. The Big Store 41. Ziegfeld Girl 41. Till the Clouds Roll By 46. Casbah 48. Two Tickets to Broadway 51. Here Come the Girls 53. Deep in My Heart 54. Hit the Deck 55. Let's Be Happy (GB) 57, etc.

Martin-Harvey, Sir John (1863–1944).
British actor manager of the old school who appeared in a film or two.
Scaramouche 12. A Tale of Two Cities 13. The Cigarette Maker's Romance 13. The Only Way/A Tale of Two Cities (as Sydney Carton, his greatest stage success) 26. The Lyons Mail 31, etc.

Martinelli, Elsa (1933–).
Italian leading lady, in films from 1950.
The Indian Fighter (US) 55. Manuela (GB) 57. The Boatmen 60. Hatari (US) 62. The Trial 63. Marco the Magnificent 65. De l'Amour 65. The Tenth Victim 65. Candy 68. Once Upon a Crime 92, etc.

Martini, Nino (1904–1976).
Italian actor-singer, who made a few English-speaking films.
Here's to Romance (US) 35. The Gay Desperado (US) 36. One Night With You (GB) 48, etc.

Martino, Sergio (1938–).
Italian director, mainly known for horror films.
Mondo Sex/Wages of Sin/Mille Peccati . . . Nessuna Virtù 69. The Strange Vice of Mrs Ward/Lo Strano Vizio della Signora Ward 70. They're Coming to Get You/Demons of the Dead/Tutti i Colori del Buio 72. Torso 73. Sex with a Smile 76. Slave of the Cannibal God/Prisoner of the Cannibal God/La Montagna del Dio Cannibale 76. Island of Mutations/Screamers/L'Isola degli Uomini Pesce 79. Caiman/The Great Alligator 79. Casablanca Express 89, etc.

Martins, Orlando (1899–1985).
West African actor in British films.
Sanders of the River 35. Jericho 37. The Man from Morocco 44. Men of Two Worlds (as the witch doctor) 46. End of the River 47. Where No Vultures Fly 52. Simba 55. Sapphire 59. Mister Moses 65, etc.

Martinson, Leslie H.
American director, from TV.
PT 109 62. For Those Who Think Young 64. Batman 66. Fathom 67. Mrs Pollifax – Spy 70. Escape from Angola 76. Cruise Missile 78. The Kid with the Broken Halo (TV) 82. The Kid with the 200 I.Q. (TV) 83. The Fantastic World of D.C. Collins (TV) 84, etc.

Marton, Andrew (1904–1992).
Hungarian-born director, in Hollywood from 1923; settled there after return visits to Europe. Co-directed *King Solomon's Mines* 50; directed the chariot race in *Ben Hur*.
Book: 1992, *Andrew Marton* interviewed by Joanne d'Antonio.
Two o'Clock in the Morning 29. SOS Iceberg 32. The Demon of the Himalayas 34. Wolf's Clothing (GB) 37. Secrets of Stamboul (GB) 37. Gentle Annie 45. The Wild North 52. Prisoner of War 54. Green Fire 55. The Thin Red Line 64. *Crack in the World* 65. Around the World under the Sea 65, etc.
AS SECOND-UNIT DIRECTOR: *The Red Badge of Courage* 51. A Farewell to Arms 57. *Ben Hur* 59. 55 Days at Peking 62. *The Longest Day* 62. Cleopatra 62, etc.

Marvin, Lee (1924–1987).
Ruthless-looking American actor who latterly switched from unpleasant villains to unsympathetic heroes.
Biography: 1997, *Lee: A Romance* by Pamela Marvin.
You're in the Navy Now 51. Duel at Silver Creek 52. The Big Heat 53. The Wild One 54. Gorilla at Large 54. The Caine Mutiny 54. Bad Day at Black Rock 54. Violent Saturday 55. Not as a Stranger 55. Pete Kelly's Blues 55. Shack Out on 101 55. I Died a Thousand Times 56. Seven Men from Now 57. *Attack* 57. Raintree County 57. The Missouri Traveller 58. The Comancheros 61. The Man Who Shot Liberty Valance 62. Donovan's Reef 63. *The Killers* 64. *Cat Ballou* (AA) 65. Ship of Fools 65. The Professionals 66. The Dirty Dozen 67. Point Blank 67. Hell in the Pacific 68. Paint Your Wagon 69. Monte Walsh 70. Prime Cut 72. Emperor of the North Pole 73. The Iceman Cometh 73. The Spikes Gang 73. The Klansman 75. Shout at the Devil 76. The Great Scout and Cathouse Thursday 76. The Big Red One 79. Avalanche Express 79. Death Hunt 81. Gorky Park 83. Dirty Dozen, the Next Mission (TV) 85. Delta Force 85, etc.
TV series: M Squad 57–59. Lawbreaker 63.

The Marx Brothers
A family of Jewish-American comics whose zany humour convulsed minority audiences in its time and influenced later comedy writing to an enormous extent. *Chico* (1886–1961) (Leonard Marx) played the piano eccentrically and spoke with an impossible Italian accent; *Harpo* (1888–1964) (Adolph Marx) was a child-like mute who also played the harp; *Groucho* (1890–1977) (Julius Marx) had a painted moustache, a cigar, a loping walk and the lion's share of the wisecracks. In vaudeville from childhood, they came to films after Broadway success. Originally there were two other brothers: *Gummo* (1893–1977) (Milton Marx), who left the act early on, and *Zeppo* (1901–79) (Herbert Marx), who didn't fit in with the craziness and left them after playing romantic relief in their first five films. These first five films contain much of their best work: later their concentrated anarchy was dissipated by musical and romantic relief.
Harpo published his autobiography 1961: *Harpo Speaks!* Among Groucho's semi-autobiographical works are *Groucho and Me* (1959), *Memoirs of a Mangy Lover* (1964) and *The Groucho Letters* (1967). His son Arthur published *Life with Groucho* (1952) and *Son of Groucho* (1972). In 1974 Richard Anobile and Groucho came up with *The Marx Brothers Scrapbook*. The films are examined in detail in *The Marx Brothers at the Movies* by Paul D. Zimmerman and Burt Goldblatt. In 1978 Charlotte Chandler came up with *Hello, I Must Be Going*, a rather depressing account of Groucho's last years.
■ The Cocoanuts 29. *Animal Crackers* 30. *Monkey Business* 31. *Horse Feathers* 32. *Duck Soup* 33. *A Night at the Opera* 35. *A Day at the Races* 37. Room Service 38. *At the Circus* 39. Go West 40. The Big Store 41. *A Night in Casablanca* 46. Love Happy (a curious and unhappy failure) 50. The Story of Mankind (guest appearances) 57.
GROUCHO ALONE: Copacabana 47. Mr Music 50. Double Dynamite 51. A Girl in Every Port 52. Will Success Spoil Rock Hunter? (gag appearance) 57. You Bet Your Life (TV series) 56–61. Skiddo 68.
✪ For shattering all our illusions, and making us love it. *Duck Soup*.
❝ The leader wore a large painted moustache and affected a cigar, and his three henchmen impersonated respectively a mute harpist afflicted with satyriasis, a larcenous Italian, and a jaunty coxcomb, who carried the love interest. – *S. J. Perelman*
Lines written by or for the Marx Brothers would fill a book in themselves. This is a selection of personal favourites, arranged chronologically and attributed to the authors of the films concerned.
~1929: *The Cocoanuts* (George S. Kaufman, Morrie Ryskind)
Ah, Mrs Rittenhouse, won't you . . . lie down?
I'll wrestle anybody in the crowd for five dollars.
Be free, my friends. One for all and all for me – me for you and three for five and six for a quarter.
Do you know that this is the biggest development since Sophie Tucker?
Your eyes shine like the pants of my blue serge suit.
~1930: *Animal Crackers* (George S. Kaufman and Morrie Ryskind)
You're the most beautiful woman I've ever seen, which doesn't say much for you.
What do you get an hour?
– For playing, we get ten dollars an hour.
What do you get for not playing?
– Twelve dollars an hour. Now for rehearsing, we make a special rate – fifteen dollars an hour.
And what do you get for not rehearsing?
– You couldn't afford it. You see, if we don't rehearse, we don't play. And if we don't play, that runs into money.
How much would you want to run into an open manhole?
– Just the cover charge.
Well, drop in some time.
– Sewer.
Well, I guess we cleaned that up.
You go Uruguay and I'll go mine.
One morning I shot an elephant in my pajamas. How he got into my pajamas I'll never know.
~1931: *Monkey Business* (S. J. Perelman, Will B. Johnstone, Arthur Sheekman)
Do you want your nails trimmed long?
– Oh, about an hour and a half. I got nothing to do.
Look at me: I worked my way up from nothing to a state of extreme poverty.
I want to register a complaint. Do you know who sneaked into my room at three o'clock this morning?
– Who?
– Nobody, and that's my complaint.
Do you suppose I could buy back my introduction to you?
Sir, you have the advantage of me.
– Not yet I haven't, but wait till I get you outside.
~1932: *Horse Feathers* (Bert Kalmar, Harry Ruby, S. J. Perelman, Will B. Johnstone)
Why don't you bore a hole in yourself and let the sap run out?
There's a man outside with a big black moustache.
– Tell him I've got one.
The dean is furious. He's waxing wroth.
– Is Roth out there too? Tell Roth to wax the dean for a while.
You're a disgrace to our family name of Wagstaff, if such a thing is possible.
You've got the brain of a four-year-old boy, and I bet he was glad to get rid of it.
What a day! Spring in the air!
– Who, me? I should spring in the air and fall in the lake?
~1933: *Duck Soup* (Bert Kalmar, Harry Ruby, Arthur Sheekman, Nat Perrin)
Take a card. You can keep it: I've got fifty-one left.
My husband is dead.
– I'll bet he's just using that as an excuse.
I was with him to the end.
– No wonder he passed away.
I held him in my arms and kissed him.
– So it was murder!
This is a gala day for you.
– That's plenty. I don't think I could manage more than one gal a day.
What is it that has four pairs of pants, lives in Philadelphia, and it never rains but it pours?
I could dance with you till the cows come home. On second thoughts I'll dance with the cows and you come home.
Excuse me while I brush the crumbs out of my bed. I'm expecting company.
~1935: *A Night at the Opera* (George S. Kaufman, Morrie Ryskind, Al Boasberg)
Do they allow tipping on the boat?
– Yes, sir.
Have you got two fives?
– Oh, yes, sir.
Then you won't need the ten cents I was going to give you.
Let joy be unconfined. Let there be dancing in the streets, drinking in the saloons, and necking in the park.
~1937: *A Day at the Races* (George Seaton, Robert Pirosh, George Oppenheimer)
She looks like the healthiest woman I ever met.
– You look like you never met a healthy woman.
Don't point that beard at me, it might go off.
Closer . . . hold me closer . . .
– If I hold you any closer I'll be in back of you!
Marry me and I'll never look at another horse.
Isn't that awfully large for a pill?
– Well, it was too small for a basketball and I didn't know what to do with it.
One dollar and you remember me all your life.
– That's the most nauseating proposition I've ever had.
~1939: *At the Circus* (Irving Brecher)
If you hadn't sent for me, I'd be at home now in a comfortable bed with a hot toddy.
– That's a drink!
I bet your father spent the first year of your life throwing rocks at the stork.
~1945: *A Night in Casablanca* (Joseph Fields, Roland Kibbee, Frank Tashlin)
The first thing we're going to do is change all the numbers on all the doors.
– But sir, think of the confusion . . .
Yeah, but think of the fun.
Hey boss, you got a woman in there?
– If I haven't, I've been wasting thirty minutes of valuable time.
I'm Beatrice Ryner. I stop at the hotel.
– I'm Ronald Kornblow. I stop at nothing.
Groucho himself later proved to be sometimes as funny as his scripts. He wrote to resign from a club:
I don't care to belong to any social

organization which would accept me as a member.

And he wrote a threatening letter to *Confidential* magazine:

Dear Sir: If you continue to publish slanderous pieces about me I shall feel compelled to cancel my subscription.

His wit did not fail him with age:

I've been around so long I can remember Doris Day before she was a virgin.

His influence was international; an example of Paris graffiti in 1968 read:

Je suis Marxiste, tendance Groucho.

But life with the Marxes was seldom peaceful. Herman Mankiewicz said:

I never knew what bicarbonate of soda was until I wrote a Marx Brothers picture.

Groucho once removed Greta Garbo's hat and said:

Excuse me, I thought you were a fellow I once knew in Pittsburgh.

George F. Kaufman had soon had enough of them:

Cocoanuts was a comedy; the Marx Brothers are comics; meeting them was a tragedy.

Groucho was perhaps too fearless a critic, as when giving his opinion of *Samson and Delilah*, starring Victor Mature and Hedy Lamarr:

First picture I've seen in which the male lead has bigger tits than the female.

And on the nudist musical *Hair:*

Why should I pay ten dollars for something I can see in the bathroom for nothing?

Harpo could be bitchy too. His appraisal of *Abie's Irish Rose* has lingered down the decades:

No worse than a bad cold.

And he was witty when refusing Alexander Woollcott's invitation to share a holiday on the French riviera:

I can think of forty better places to spend the summer, all of them on Long Island in a hammock.

Groucho even aspired to be a political thinker:

Military intelligence is a contradiction in terms . . .

A final thought from Groucho:

If you want to see a comic strip you should see me in a shower.

Well, one more from Groucho for luck:

They say a man is as old as the woman he feels.

Masamura, Yazuso (1924–1986).
Japanese director, an influence on the country's 'New Wave' directors of the late 50s. He studied film at the Centro Sperimentale in Rome and was influenced by NEO-REALISM.

Kisses/Kuchizuke 57. Warm Current/Donryu 57. Giants and Toys/The Build/Kyojin To Gangu 58. A Man Blown by the Wind/Karakkaze Yaro 60. All Mixed Up/Manji 62. The Black Test Car/Kuro No Tesuto Ka 62. The Hoodlum Soldier/Heitai Yakuza 65. Tatoo/Shishei 66. Red Angel/Akai Tenshi 66. Love for an Idiot/Chijin No Ai 67, etc.

Maschwitz, Eric (1901–1969).
English screenwriter, playwright and songwriter, whose lyrics include 'These Foolish Things' and 'A Nightingale Sang in Berkeley Square'. Born in Birmingham, he was educated at Cambridge University and worked for the BBC as a commentator, scriptwriter, editor of the *Radio Times*, and the first director of variety programmes from 1933–37. In 1937 he went to Hollywood under contract to MGM, returning to Britain at the outbreak of the Second World War, and becoming head of Light Entertainment for BBC-TV in the mid-50s. He was married briefly to Hermione GINGOLD.

Autobiography: 1957, *No Chip on My Shoulder*.

Goodnight Vienna/Magic Night (co-w, oa) 32. Death at Broadcasting House (co-w) 34. Royal Cavalcade (co-w) 35. Land without Music (co-story) 36. Café Colette (co-w from radio programme) 37. Goodbye Mr Chips (co-w) 39. Balalaika (oa) 39. Carnival (w) 46. Queen of Song (w) 47, etc.

Masina, Giulietta (1920–1994).
Italian gamin-like actress, married to Federico Fellini. In films since 1941.

Senza Pietà 47. *Lights of Variety* 48. *La Strada* 54. Il Bidone 55. *Nights of Cabiria* 57. Juliet of the Spirits 65. The Madwoman of Chaillot 69. Ginger and Fred 85. Aujourd'hui Peut-être 91. La Nonna 92, etc.

Maskell, Virginia (1936–1968).
British leading lady with attractively soulful eyes. Committed suicide.

■ Happy is the Bride 57. Our Virgin Island 58. The Man Upstairs 59. Jet Storm 59. Suspect 60. Doctor in Love 60. The Wild and the Willing 62. *Only Two Can Play* 62. Interlude 68.

Mason, A. E. W. (1865–1948).
British novelist whose *The House of the Arrow* and *The Four Feathers* have been filmed several times. *Fire Over England* and *At the Villa Rose* also came to the screen.

Mason, Elliott (1897–1949).
Scottish character actress with repertory experience. The Ghost Goes West 36. Owd Bob 38. The Ghost of St Michael's 41. The Gentle Sex 43. The Captive Heart 46, etc.

Mason, Herbert (1891–1960).
British director.

His Lordship 36. Strange Boarders 38. Back Room Boy 41. Flight from Folly 45, etc.

Mason, Jackie (1930–) (Yacov Moshe Maza).
Acerbic American comedian, in occasional films. Born in Sheboygan, Wisconsin, he was brought up in New York and studied at the City College, planning to become a rabbi before he discovered his talent as a comic.

Operation Delilah 67. The Stoolie 72. The Jerk 79. History of the World Part 1 81. Caddyshack 2 88. In the Aftermath 88, etc.

❝ I was nearly drafted. It's not that I mind fighting for my country, but they called me at a ridiculous time: in the middle of a war! –J.M.

Mason, James (1909–1984).
Leading British and international actor who became a star at home in saturnine roles during World War II, went to Hollywood and initially had a thin time but during the 50s became a respected interpreter of varied and interesting characters. Married Pamela KELLINO.

Autobiography: 1982, *Before I Forget*.

Biographies: 1989, *James Mason: Odd Man Out* by Sheridan Morley. 1989, *James Mason – a Personal Biography* by Diana de Rosso.

■ Late Extra 35. Twice Branded 36. Troubled Waters 36. Prison Breaker 36. Blind Man's Bluff 36. The Secret of Stamboul 36. Fire Over England 36. The Mill on the Floss 37. The High Command 37. Catch as Catch Can 37. The Return of the Scarlet Pimpernel 38. *I Met a Murderer* 39. This Man Is Dangerous/The Patient Vanishes 41. Hatter's Castle 42. *The Night Has Eyes* 42. Alibi 42. Secret Mission 42. Thunder Rock 43. The Bells Go Down 43. *The Man in Grey* (a key role as an 18th-century villain) 43. They Met in the Dark 43. Candlelight in Algeria 44. Fanny by Gaslight 44. Hotel Reserve 44. A Place of One's Own 45. They Were Sisters 45. *The Seventh Veil* 45. *The Wicked Lady* 46. *Odd Man Out* 46. The Upturned Glass 47. Caught 49. Madame Bovary 49. The Reckless Moment 49. East Side West Side 49. One Way Street 50. *Pandora and the Flying Dutchman* 51. *The Desert Fox* (as Rommel) 51. Lady Possessed 52. *Five Fingers* 52. The Prisoner of Zenda 52 (as Rupert) 52. Face to Face 52. The Desert Rats 53. *Julius Caesar* (as Brutus) 53. The Story of Three Loves 53. Botany Bay 53. The Man Between 53. Charade 53. Prince Valiant 54. *20,000 Leagues under the Sea* (as Captain Nemo) 54. *A Star Is Born* (AAN) 54. Forever Darling 56. Bigger Than Life (& p) 56. Island in the Sun 57. Cry Terror 58. The Decks Ran Red 58. North by Northwest 59. *Journey to the Center of the Earth* 59. A Touch of Larceny 60. The Trials of Oscar Wilde 60. The Marriage Go Round 61. The Land We Love/Hero's Island 62. Escape from Zahrain 62. Tiara Tahiti 62. *Lolita* (as Humbert) 62. The Fall of the Roman Empire 64. Torpedo Bay 64. *The Pumpkin Eater* 64. Lord Jim 65. The Player Pianos 65. Genghis Khan 65. *The Blue Max* 66. Georgy Girl (AAN) 66. *The Deadly Affair* 67. Stranger in the House 67. Duffy 68. Mayerling 68. Age of Consent 69. The Seagull 69. Spring and Port Wine 70. Kill! 70. Cold Sweat 70. Bad Man's River 71. A Dangerous Summer 72. Ivanhoe 72. Child's Play 72. The Last of Sheila 73. Frankenstein, the True Story (TV) 73. The Mackintosh Man 73. 11 Harrowhouse 74. The Marseilles Contract 74. Great Expectations (TV) 74. The Tempest 74. Nostro Nero in Casa Nichols 74. Centra di Respetto 75. La Città Sconvolta 75. Mandingo 75. Autobiography of a Princess 75. Voyage of the Damned 76. Inside Out 76. The Left Hand of the Law 76. Jesus of Nazareth (TV) 77. Cross of Iron 77. The Water Babies 78. Heaven Can Wait 78. The Boys from Brazil 78. *Murder by Decree* (as Dr Watson) 79. The Passage 79. Bloodline 79. North Sea Hijack 80. Evil Under the Sun 82. The Verdict (AAN) 82. Yellowbeard 83. The Shooting Party 84.

✪ For his incisive professionalism over a long period of gradually declining standards. *A Star Is Born*.

Mason, Marsha (1942–).
American leading actress, formerly married to Neil Simon (1973–83).

Hot Rod Hullaballoo 66. Blume in Love 73. Cinderella Liberty (AAN) 73. Audrey Rose 77. *The Goodbye Girl* (AAN) 77. The Cheap Detective 78. Promises in the Dark 79. Chapter Two (AAN) 79. Only When I Laugh (AAN) 81. Max Dugan Returns 83. Heartbreak Ridge 86. Trapped in Silence (TV) 86. Dinner at Eight (TV) 89. Stella 90. Drop Dead Fred 91. I Love Trouble 94. Nick of Time 95. Broken Trust (TV) 95. 2 Days in the Valley 96, etc.

Mason, Richard (1919–1997).
English novelist and screenwriter, of stories of inter-racial love affairs. Born in Hale, Cheshire, he used his own wartime experiences as the basis for his first novel, *The Wind Cannot Read* (1947), about a soldier falling in love with a Japanese woman who teaches him her language. He stopped writing in the early 60s and moved to Rome. Married three times.

■ A Town Like Alice (co-w) 56. Pacific Destiny (w) 56. The Wind Cannot Read (w, oa) 58. Passionate Summer (oa) 58. The World of Susie Wong (oa) 60.

Mason, Shirley (1900–1979) (Leona Flugrath).
American leading lady of the silent screen, sister of Viola Dana.

Vanity Fair 15. Goodbye Bill 18. Treasure Island 20. Merely Mary Ann 20. Lights of the Desert 22. What Fools Men 25. Don Juan's Three Nights 26. Sally in Our Alley 27. Show of Stars 29, etc.

Massaccesi, Aristide:
see D'AMATO, Joe.

Massari, Lea (1933–) (Anna Maria Massatani).
French-Italian leading lady.

L'Avventura 58. The Colossus of Rhodes 61. Four Days of Naples 62. Made in Italy 65. Les Choses de la Vie 69. Le Souffle au Coeur 71. Impossible Object 73. Violette et François 77. Christ Stopped at Eboli 79. Vengeance 86. A Woman Destroyed 88. Journey of Love 91, etc.

Massen, Osa (1916–).
Danish-born actress in Hollywood from the late 30s.

Honeymoon in Bali 39. The Devil Pays Off 41. The Master Race 44. Tokyo Rose 44. Cry of the Werewolf 44. Deadline at Dawn 47. Rocketship XM 50, etc.

Massey, Anna (1937–).
British character actress, daughter of Raymond Massey.

Gideon's Day 58. Bunny Lake Is Missing 65. De Sade 69. Frenzy 72. A Doll's House 73. Vault of Horror 73. The Chain 85. Foreign Body 87. Impromptu 89. The Grotesque 95. Angels and Insects 95. Haunted 95. The Grotesque/Grave Indiscretions 96. Déjà Vu (US) 98. A Respectable Trade (TV) 98. Captain Jack 98, etc.

TV series: Rebecca (as Mrs Danvers) 79. Nice Day at the Office 94.

Massey, Daniel (1933–1998).
British actor, son of Raymond MASSEY, usually seen on stage or TV.

Girls at Sea 57. Upstairs and Downstairs 59. The Queen's Guard 61. Go to Blazes 62. Moll Flanders 65. The Jokers 66. *Star!* (as Noël Coward) (AAN) 68. Fragment of Fear 70. Mary Queen of Scots 72. Vault of Horror 73. The Incredible Sarah 76. The Cat and the Canary 77. Bad Timing 80. Escape to Victory 81. Love with a Perfect Stranger (TV) 86. Intimate Contact 87. Scandal 88. In the Name of the Father 93. Samson and Delilah (TV) 96, etc.

Massey, Ilona (1912–1974) (Ilona Hajmassy).
Hungarian-born leading lady, in Hollywood from the mid-30s.

■ Knox und die Lustigen Vagabunden 35. Der Himmel auf Erden 35. *Rosalie* 37. Balalaika 39. New Wine 41. International Lady 41. Invisible Agent 42. Frankenstein Meets the Wolf Man (as 'Frankenstein') 42. Holiday in Mexico 46. Northwest Outpost 47. The Plunderers 48. Love Happy 50. Jet over the Atlantic 59.

Massey, Raymond (1896–1983).
Canadian-born actor, on stage (in Britain) from 1922.

In films, has played saturnine, benevolent or darkly villainous, with a penchant for impersonations of Abraham Lincoln.

Autobiographies: 1976, *When I Was Young*. 1979, *A Hundred Lives*.

■ The Speckled Band (as Sherlock Holmes) 31. The Face at the Window 31. *The Old Dark House* 32. *The Scarlet Pimpernel* 34. *Things to Come* 36. Fire over England 36. Under the Red Robe 37. *The Prisoner of Zenda* 37. Dreaming Lips 37. The Hurricane 37. The Drum 38. Black Limelight 39. *Abe Lincoln in Illinois* (AAN) 40. Santa Fe Trail (as John Brown) 40. 49th Parallel 41. Dangerously They Live 41. Desperate Journey 42. Reap the Wild Wind 42. Action in the North Atlantic 43. *Arsenic and Old Lace* 44. The Woman in the Window 44. Hotel Berlin 45. God Is My Co-Pilot 45. A Matter of Life and Death 46. Possessed 47. Mourning Becomes Electra 47. The Fountainhead 48. Roseanna McCoy 49. Chain Lightning 49. Barricade 50. Dallas 50. Sugarfoot 51. Come Fill the Cup 51. David and Bathsheba 51. Carson City 52. The Desert Song 53. Prince of Players 55. Battle Cry 55. *East of Eden* 55. Seven Angry Men 55. Omar Khayyam 57. The Naked and the Dead 58. The Great Impostor 60. The Fiercest Heart 61. The Queen's Guard 61. How the West Was Won 62. Mackenna's Gold 68. All My Darling Daughters (TV) 72. The President's Plane Is Missing (TV) 73.

TV series: I Spy 55. Dr Kildare (as Dr Gillespie) 61–66.

✪ For his leathery, reliable and highly intelligent presence during most of the cinema's most interesting years (though in few of its more interesting films). *Things to Come*.

Famous line (*Things to Come*): 'It is this, or that – all the universe, or nothing. Which shall it be, Passworthy? Which shall it be?'

Massie, Paul (1932–).
Canadian-born actor, on British stage and screen.

High Tide at Noon 57. *Orders to Kill* 58. Sapphire 59. Libel 60. The Two Faces of Dr Jekyll 60. The Rebel 60. Raising the Wind 61. The Pot Carriers 62, many others.

Massine, Leonid (1896–1979).
Russian-born choreographer of international renown, best displayed on film in *The Red Shoes* 48.

Massingham, Richard (1898–1953).
British actor-producer-director: a qualified doctor who abandoned his medical career to make numerous short propaganda films for government departments during World War II and after, infusing them with quiet wit and sympathy. Gratefully remembered as the stout party bewildered by government restrictions: bathing in five inches of water, collecting salvage, avoiding colds, preventing rumours, wearing a gasmask, etc.

Masters, Anthony (1919–1990).
English art director and production designer.

The Bespoke Overcoat 55. The Story of Esther Costello 57. Corridors of Blood 58. Expresso Bongo 59. The Day the Earth Caught Fire 61. The Heroes of Telemark 65. 2001: A Space Odyssey (AAN) 68. ZPG/Zero Population Growth 70. Papillon 73. The Deep 77. Dune 84. The Clan of the Cave Bear 85, etc.

Masters, Quentin (1946–).
Australian director of international films.

■ Thumb Tripping (& w) 73. The Stud 78. The Psi Factor 81. A Dangerous Summer 82. Midnite Spares 83.

Masterson, Mary Stuart (1966–).
American leading actress.

The Stepford Wives 75. Heaven Help Us 85. At Close Range 86. My Little Girl 86. Gardens of

Stone 87. Some Kind of Wonderful 87. Mr North 88. Chances Are 89. Immediate Family 89. Funny about Love 90. Fried Green Tomatoes at the Whistle Stop Café 91. Mad at the Moon 92. Married to It 92. Benny & Joon 93. Bad Girls 94. The Radioland Murders 94. Bed of Roses 96. Lily Dale (TV) 96, etc.

Masterson, Peter (1934–) (Carlos B. Masterson).
American actor and director, the father of Mary Stuart Masterson.
AS ACTOR: Ambush Bay 66. Counterpoint 68. Von Richthofen and Brown 71. The Exorcist 73. The Stepford Wives 75. A Question of Guilt (TV) 78. Gardens of Stone 87, etc.
AS DIRECTOR: The Trip to Bountiful 85. Blood Red 88. Full Moon in Blue Water 88. Night Game 89. Convicts 91. Arctic Blue 93. Lily Dale (TV) 96, etc.

Masterson, William Barclay 'Bat' (1855–1921).
American lawman, buffalo hunter, and friend and colleague of Wyatt EARP, who became sheriff of Dodge City at the age of 22. After he was voted out of office, he was involved with Earp and Doc HOLLIDAY in various dubious enterprises in Dodge City and Tombstone, was an army scout during the Apache uprising of 1886, a gambler, and, finally, a sports reporter and drama critic in New York. He was played by Albert DEKKER in *Woman of the Town* 43, Randolph SCOTT in *Trail Street* 47, Monte HALE in *Prince of the Plains* 49, Steve Darrell in *Winchester '73* 50, George MONTGOMERY in *Masterson of Kansas* 54, Keith LARSEN in *Wichita* 55, Kenneth TOBEY in *Gunfight at the O.K. Corral* 56, Gregory WALCOTT in *Badman's Country* 58, Joel MCCREA in *The Gunfight at Dodge City* 58, and Tom SIZEMORE in *Wyatt Earp* 94.
❝ There are many in this old world of ours who hold that things break about even for all of us. I have observed for example that we all get the same amount of ice. The rich get it in the summertime and the poor get it in the winter. – B.M. *(discovered in his typewriter when he died of heart failure at his desk)*
Masterson was a bad man to cross; he had killed several hearties 'in self-defense'. This tight-lipped fellow had never been known to smile. – *Gene Fowler*

Mastrantonio, Mary Elizabeth (1958–).
American leading actress, with stage experience.
Scarface 83. The Color of Money (AAN) 86. Slam Dance 87. The January Man 88. The Abyss 89. Fools of Fortune 90. Class Action 91. Robin Hood: Prince of Thieves 91. White Sands 92. Consenting Adults 92. Three Wishes 95. Two Bits 96. My Life So Far 98, etc.

Mastroianni, Chiara (1972–).
French leading actress, the daughter of Catherine DENEUVE and Marcello MASTROIANNI.
My Favorite Season/Ma Saison Préférée 93. Under the Stars/À la Belle Étoile) 93. Prêt-à-Porter 94. Don't Forget You're Going to Die/N'Oublie Pas que Tu Vas Mourir 95. Chameleon/Cameleone 96, etc.

Mastroianni, Marcello (1923–1996).
Italian leading man, a former clerk who broke into films with a bit part in *I Miserabili* 47. In his day Italy's most respected and sought-after lead.
Sunday in August 49. Girls of the Spanish Steps 51. The Bigamist 55. *White Nights* 57. I Soliti Ignoti 58. La Dolce Vita 59. *Il Bell'Antonio* 60. La Notte 61. *Divorce Italian Style* (AAN, BFA) 62. Family Diary 62. Eight and a Half 63. *Yesterday, Today and Tomorrow* (BFA) 63. The Organizer 63. Marriage Italian Style 64. Casanova 70 65. The Tenth Victim 65. Shoot Loud, Louder, I Don't Understand 66. The Stranger 67. Diamonds for Breakfast (GB) 68. A Place for Lovers 69. Sunflower 70. What? 72. Blowout 73. The Slightly Pregnant Man 73. Massacre in Rome 74. The Priest's Wife 74. Down the Ancient Stairs 75. The Sunday Woman 76. A Special Day (AAN) 77. Traffic Jam 78. City of Women 80. Revenge 80. General of the Dead Army 83. Henry IV 84. The Two Lives of Mattia Pascal 85. Big Deal on Madonna Street – 20 Years Later 85. Macaroni 85. *Ginger and Fred* 85. The Bee Keeper 86. Dark Eyes/Oci Ciornie (AAN) 87. Miss Arizona 88. Splendor 89. Everybody's Fine/Stanno Tutti Bene 90. Sometime Tonight/Verso Sera 90. Le Voleur d'Enfants 91. Tchin-Tchin 91. The Suspended Step of the Stork/To Meteoro Vima to Pelargou 91. La Nonna 92. Used People 92. Viva i Bambini 92. Consenting Adults 92. 1, 2, 3, Soleil 93. We Don't Want to Talk about It/De Eso No Se Habla 93. How Long Till Daylight (TV) 94. Prêt-à-Porter/Ready to Wear 94. According to Pereira 95. Beyond the Clouds 95. Three Lives and Only One Death 96. Journey to the Beginning of the World 97, etc.
❝ I only really exist when I am working on a film. – M.M.
I don't like that Method thing: what sufferance to go into a role! I'm not going to enter a monastery so I can play a priest. An actor is a buffoon – this is the miracle, being a chameleon. – M.M.
Life has been generous to me. I come from a very modest family – my father was a cabinet-maker – and I'm in a profession I like. – M.M.

Masur, Richard (1948–).
Plump American supporting actor.
W.H.I.F.F.S. 75. Semi Tough 77. Who'll Stop the Rain 78. Hanover Street 79. Scavenger Hunt 79. Walking through the Fire (TV) 79. Heaven's Gate 80. East of Eden (TV) 81. *Fallen Angel* (TV) 81. I'm Dancing as Fast as I Can 82. The Thing 82. Risky Business 83. Under Fire 83. The Mean Season 84. My Science Project 85. Heartburn 86. The Believers 86. Walker 87. License to Drive 88. Rent-a-Cop 88. Shoot to Kill 88. Far from Home 89. Flashback 90. My Girl 91. The Man without a Face 93. Six Degrees of Separation 93. My Girl 2 94. Les Patriotes (Fr.) 94. Forget Paris 95. Multiplicity 96. Fire Down Below 97, etc.
TV series: One Day at a Time 75–76. Hot L Baltimore 75. Empire 84.

Mata Hari (1876–1917) (Margaret Gertrude Zelle).
Four films have been made about the French spy executed during World War I: by Friedrich Feher in 1927 with Magda Sonia; by George Fitzmaurice in 1931 with Greta Garbo; by Jean-Louis Richard in 1964 with Jeanne Moreau; by Curtis Harrington in 1984 with Sylvia Kristel. She was caricatured by Zsa Zsa Gabor in *Up the Front* 72. Her pseudonym, in Dutch, means 'eye of the dawn'.

Matarazzo, Heather (1982–).
American actress.
Welcome to the Dollhouse 95. The Devil's Advocate 97. 54 98.
TV series: The Adventures of Pete and Pete 93. Roseanne 97.

Maté, Rudolph (1898–1964).
Austrian-born cameraman, later in Hollywood.
The Passion of Joan of Arc 28. *Vampyr* 31. Liliom 33. *Dante's Inferno* 35. Dodsworth 36. Love Affair 39. *Foreign Correspondent* 40. To Be or Not To Be 42. Cover Girl 44, etc.
■ LATER AS DIRECTOR: It Had to Be You (co-d) 47. The Dark Past 49. D.O.A. 50. No Sad Songs for Me 50. *Union Station* 50. Branded 50. The Prince Who Was a Thief 51. When Worlds Collide 51. The Green Glove 52. Paula 52. Sally and Saint Anne 52. Mississippi Gambler 53. Second Chance 53. Forbidden 53. The Siege At Red River 54. *The Black Shield of Falworth* 54. The Violent Men 55. The Far Horizons 55. Miracle in the Rain 56. The Rawhide Years 56. Port Afrique 56. Three Violent People 57. The Deep Six 58. For the First Time 59. The Immaculate Road 60. Revak the Rebel 60. The 300 Spartans 62. Aliki 63. Seven Seas to Calais 64.

Mather, Aubrey (1885–1958).
British character actor, on stage from 1905, films from 1931. Settled in Hollywood and became useful member of English contingent, playing butlers and beaming, bald-headed little men.
Young Woodley 31. As You Like It 36. When Knights Were Bold 36. Jane Eyre 44. The Keys of the Kingdom 44. The Forsyte Saga 49. The Importance of Being Earnest 52, many others.

Mathers, Jerry (1948–).
American actor whose career has been mainly confined to playing 'Beaver' Cleaver in the folksy US sitcom *Leave It to Beaver*. In television from the age of two, he was a child star of the 50s and enjoyed some later success playing Beaver as an adult.
This Is My Love 54. The Trouble with Harry 55. Bigger than Life 56. That Certain Feeling 56. Still the Beaver (TV) 83. Back to the Beach 87, etc.
TV series: Leave It to Beaver 57–63. Still the Beaver 85–86. The New Leave It to Beaver 86–89.

Matheson, Murray (1912–1985).
Soft-spoken Australian actor in Hollywood, mostly on TV.
Hurricane Smith 52. Botany Bay 53. Love Is a Many Splendored Thing 55. Assault On a Queen 66. How to Succeed in Business 67, etc.
TV series: Banacek 72–74.

Matheson, Richard (1926–).
American science-fiction novelist and screenwriter.
The Incredible Shrinking Man (oa, w) 57. The House of Usher (w) 60. The Pit and the Pendulum (w) 61. The Raven (w) 63. The Comedy of Terrors (w) 63. The Last Man on Earth (oa) 64. The Young Warriors (oaw) 68. The Devil Rides Out (w) 68. De Sade (w) 69. The Omega Man (oa) 71. The Legend of Hell House (w) 73. Dracula (TV) 73. Somewhere in Time 80. Jaws 3-D 83. Twilight Zone: The Movie 83. Loose Cannons 90. Trilogy of Terror 2 (co-w) (TV) 96. What Dreams May Come (oa) 98, etc.

Matheson, Tim (1947–).
American leading man, in TV from childhood.
Yours Mine and Ours 65. Divorce American Style 68. Magnum Force 73. National Lampoon's Animal House 78. The Apple Dumpling Gang Rides Again 79. Dreamer 79. A Little Sex 82. To Be or Not To Be 83. Impulse 84. Fletch 85. Drop Dead Fred 91. Mortal Passion 91. Stephen King's Sometimes They Come Back 91. Starfire 92. Black Sheep 96. A Very Brady Sequel 96. Twilight Man 96. Buried Alive 2 97, etc.
TV series: Window on Main Street 61–62. Johnny Quest (voice) 64–65. The Virginian 69–70. Bonanza 72–73. The Quest 76. Tucker's Witch 82–83. Just in Time 88. Forever Love 98– .

Mathews, Kerwin (1926–).
American leading man, former teacher.
Five Against the House 55. The Seventh Voyage of Sinbad 58. Man on a String 60. The Three Worlds of Gulliver 60. Jack the Giant Killer 61. Pirates of Blood River 62. Maniac (GB) 63. Battle Beneath the Earth (GB) 68. Barquero 69. The Boy Who Cried Werewolf 73. Nightmare in Blood 78, etc.

Mathieson, Muir (1911–1975).
Influential Scottish musical director. Born in Stirling, he studied at the Royal College of Music and was in films from 1931 as assistant musical director to Alexander KORDA, later becoming musical director of London Films and musical director for Rank. He persuaded such British composers as Arthur BLISS, William WALTON, Ralph VAUGHAN WILLIAMS and Benjamin BRITTEN to write for films. He worked on more than 400 movies, and can be seen on screen, conducting the London Symphony Orchestra, in *The Seventh Veil* and *A Girl in a Million*.
Things to Come 36. Dangerous Moonlight 40. In Which We Serve 42. Brief Encounter 46. The Sound Barrier 52. The Swiss Family Robinson 60. Becket 64, many others.

Mathis, June (1892–1927).
American screenwriter.
An Eye for an Eye 18. *The Four Horsemen of the Apocalypse* 21. Blood and Sand 22. Three Wise Fools 23. Greed 23. *Ben Hur* 27, etc.

Mathis, Samantha (1970–).
American actress, daughter of actress Bibi BESCH.
Pump Up the Volume 90. This Is My Life 92. Ferngully: The Last Rainforest (voice) 92. The Music of Chance 93. The Thing Called Love 93. Super Mario Bros 93. Little Women 94. Jack and Sarah 95. The American President 95. Making an American Quilt 95. Broken Arrow 96. Sweet Jane 97, etc.
TV series: Aaron's Way 88. Knightwatch 88–89.

Mathison, Melissa (1949–).
American screenwriter. She married actor Harrison Ford in 1983.
The Black Stallion 79. The Escape Artist 82. E.T. – the Extraterrestrial (AAN) 82. Son of the Morning Star (TV) 91. Kundun 97, etc.

Matlin, Marlee (1965–).
American actress. She is deaf.
Children of a Lesser God (AA) 86. Walker 87. Bridge to Silence (TV) 89. The Linguini Incident 91. The Player 92. Hear No Evil 93. It's My Party 96, etc.

Matlock, Matty (1907–1978).
American jazz clarinettist and arranger. Born in Paducah, Kentucky, he worked with Ben Pollack's band and the Bob CROSBY Orchestra and Bobcats, becoming a studio musician and arranger in Los Angeles from the early 40s. He led the band and arranged the music for the film *Pete Kelly's Blues* 55, and the subsequent TV series 59.
Sis Hopkins 41. When You're Smiling 50. Rhythm Inn 51. Dragnet 54, etc.

Matras, Christian (1903–1977).
French cinematographer, in films from 1928.
La Grande Illusion 37. Boule de Suif 45. Les Jeux Sont Faits 47. La Ronde 50. Madame De 53. *Lola Montès* 55. Les Espions 57. Paris Blues 61. Les Fêtes Galantes 65. The Milky Way 68, many others.

Mattes, Eva (1955–).
Leading German actress of that country's New Wave cinema, associated with the films of Fassbinder (whom she played in the biopic *A Man Like Eva*) and Werner Herzog.
Jailbait/Wildwechsel 72. The Bitter Tears of Petra von Kant/Die Bitteren Tränen der Petra von Kant 72. Supermarket/Supermarkt 74. Stroszek 77. Ravine Racer/Schluchtenflitzer 79. David 79. Germany Pale Mother/Deutschland Bleiche Mutter 79. Woyzeck 79. Celeste 81. Rita, Ritter 84. A Man Like Eva/Ein Mann Wie Eva 84. Felix 87. Herbstmilch 89. Der Kinoerzähler 93. The Promise 95, etc.

Matthau, Charles (c. 1965–).
American director, producer and actor, a graduate of the University of Southern California Film School; he is the son of actor Walter MATTHAU.
Charley Varrick (a) 73. The Bad News Bears (a) 76. House Calls (a) 78. Doin' Time on Planet Earth (a, d) 89. Number One Fan (a) 95. The Grass Harp (a, p, d) 95, etc.

Matthau, Walter (1920–) (Walter Matasschanskayasky).
American character actor with a penchant for wry comedy; his lugubrious features and sharp talent made him a star in the late 60s.
■ The Kentuckian 55. The Indian Fighter 55. Bigger Than Life 56. *A Face in the Crowd* 57. Slaughter on Tenth Avenue 57. King Creole 58. Ride a Crooked Trail 58. The Voice in the Mirror 58. Onionhead 58. Strangers When We Meet 60. Gangster Story (& d) 60. Lonely Are the Brave 62. Who's Got the Action? 62. Island of Love 63. *Charade* 63. Ensign Pulver 64. Fail Safe 64. Goodbye Charlie 64. *Mirage* 65. *The Fortune Cookie* (AA) 66. *A Guide for the Married Man* 67. *The Odd Couple* 68. The Secret Life of an American Wife 68. Candy 68. *Hello Dolly* 69. Cactus Flower 69. A New Leaf 71. Plaza Suite 71. *Kotch* (AAN) 71. Pete 'n' Tillie 72. Charley Varrick 73. The Laughing Policeman 73. Earthquake 74. The Taking of Pelham 123 74. The Front Page 75. The Sunshine Boys (AAN) 75. The Bad News Bears 76. Casey's Shadow 77. House Calls 78. California Suite 78. Funny Business (TV) 78. Little Miss Marker 80. *Hopscotch* 80. First Monday in October 81. Buddy Buddy 81. I Ought to Be in Pictures 82. The Survivors 83. Movers and Shakers 84. Pirates 85. The Couch Trip 88. The Incident (TV) 90. JFK 91. Dennis the Menace/Dennis 93. Grumpy Old Men 93. Incident in a Small Town (TV) 94. I.Q. 94. The Grass Harp 95. Grumpier Old Men 95. I'm Not Rappaport 96. My Fellow Americans 97. Out to Sea 97. The Odd Couple II 98.
TV series: Tallahassee 7000 59.
❝ Once seen, that antique-mapped face is never forgotten – a bloodhound with a head cold, a man who is simultaneously biting on a bad oyster and caught by the neck in lift-doors, a mad scientist's amalgam of Wallace Beery and Yogi Bear. – *Alan Brien, Sunday Times*
He's about as likely a candidate for stardom as the neighborhood delicatessen man. – *Time*
He looks like a half-melted rubber bulldog. – *John Simon*

Matthews, A. E. (1869–1960).
British actor, on stage from 1886, films from the mid-20s; in his youth a suave romantic lead, he was later famous for the crotchety cheerfulness of his extreme longevity.

Autobiography: 1953, *Matty*.

A Highwayman's Honour 14. The Lackey and the Lady 19. The Iron Duke 35. Men Are Not Gods 36. *Quiet Wedding* 40. The Life and Death of Colonel Blimp 43. Piccadilly Incident 46. Just William's Luck 48. *The Chiltern Hundreds* (in his stage role as Lord Lister) 49. The Galloping Major 51. Made in Heaven 52. The Million Pound Note 54. Three Men in a Boat 56. Inn for Trouble 60, many others.

❝ I always wait for *The Times* each morning. I look at the obituary column, and if I'm not in it, I go to work. – *A.E.M.*

Good God, doesn't he know I haven't got long to live? – *A.E.M., when he thought a long speech was ending, and it wasn't*

He bumbled through the play like a charming retriever who has buried a bone and can't quite remember where. – *Noël Coward*

Although he was always terribly funny, he never looked as if he thought what he said or did was even remotely amusing. He had become such a master at manipulating an audience that he had developed a habit of getting a good laugh with a line one night, then the next night, deliberately killing it, and trying for a different laugh. – *Rex Harrison*

He was hell to act with. He really could see no reason why anyone should get a laugh from an audience except himself. – *Roland Culver*

Matthews, Francis (1927–).
British leading man with TV and repertory experience.

Bhowani Junction 56. The Revenge of Frankenstein 58. The Lamp in Assassin Mews 62. Dracula, Prince of Darkness 65. That Riviera Touch 66. Just Like a Woman 66. Crossplot 69. The McGuffin (TV) 85. May We Borrow Your Husband? (TV) 86, etc.

TV series: Golden Girl 60. A Little Big Business 64. My Man Joe 67. Paul Temple 69–71. A Roof over My Head 77. Don't Forget to Write 77–79. Tears before Bedtime 83.

Matthews, Jessie (1907–1981).
Vivacious English singing and dancing star of light musicals in the 30s, on stage from 1917. Born in London, she first made her mark in the theatre in Charles B. Cochran's revues and the musical comedy *Evergreen*, which led to a contract with Gaumont-British to star in *The Good Companions* and, later, the screen version of *Evergreen*. For six years from the early 30s she quit the stage for films, becoming Britain's most popular musical star, under the careful direction of Victor Saville. She turned down Hollywood offers because she did not want to be separated from Sonnie Hale, the second of her three husbands. She starred with her in several films, but her popularity waned when he took over as director for three movies. Her youthful appeal was fading, and she was having weight problems. Hale co-wrote and was to direct *Asking for Trouble*, which he intended as a lavish screen musical, but Gaumont-British were unable to raise the finance, and shooting was abandoned. Carol Reed was brought in to direct a version with the musical numbers cut, retitled *Climbing High*; it also failed, though she and Reed briefly became lovers. She returned to the stage and variety performances before becoming a radio personality as Mrs Dale in the BBC soap opera *The Dales* 63–69.

Autobiography: 1974, *Over My Shoulder*.

Biography: 1974, *Jessie Matthews* by Michael Thornton.

■ The Beloved Vagabond 23. Straws in the Wind 24. Out of the Blue 31. There Goes the Bride 32. The Midshipmaid 32. The Man from Toronto 32. *The Good Companions* 32. Friday the Thirteenth 33. Waltzes from Vienna 33. *Evergreen* 34. First a Girl 35. It's Love Again 36. Head over Heels 37. Gangway 37. Sailing Along 38. Climbing High 39. Forever and a Day 43. Candles at Nine 44. Tom Thumb 58. The Hound of the Baskervilles 77. Edward and Mrs Simpson (TV) 79.

❝ Jessie had an engaging way with a song and, apart from her accent, which I guess they could have fixed, she was the equal of many Hollywood stars with the advantage of a big publicity machine behind them. And Jessie had something they did not have – a nymph-like sexuality. – *Ken Russell*

She had a heart. It photographed. – *Victor Saville*

Matthews, Lester (1900–1975).
Lofty English character actor, often in aristocratic roles, and in Hollywood from the mid-30s. Born in Nottingham, he was on stage from 1916. His second wife was actress Anne Grey.

Shivering Shocks 29. The Lame Duck 31. The Werewolf of London 35. The Raven 35. Thank You, Jeeves 36. Lloyd's of London 36. The Prince and the Pauper 37. The Adventures of Robin Hood 38. The Three Musketeers 39. The Sea Hawk 40. Northwest Passage 40. A Yank in the RAF 41. The Invisible Man's Revenge 44. Gaslight 44. Ministry of Fear 44. Bulldog Drummond at Bay 47. Rogues of Sherwood Forest 50. The Son of Dr Jekyll 51. Desert Fox 51. Lorna Doone 51. Les Misérables 52. Young Bess 53. King Richard and the Crusaders 54. The Seven Little Foys 55. Moonfleet 55. The Miracle 55. Song without End 60. Mary Poppins 64. Assault on a Queen 66. Star! 68, many others.

TV series: The Adventures of Fu Manchu (as Sir Dennis Nayland-Smith) 55–56.

Mattoli, Mario (1898–1980).
Italian producer and director, from the stage. Born in Tolentino, he began by running innovative and experimental theatrical companies, first working in cinema as a producer before turning to directing many commercial successes in various genres, but succeeding especially with comedies starring Totò.

Tempo Massimo 34. Gli Ultimi Giorni di Pompeii 37. La Dama Bianca 38. Abbandono 40. *Ore Nove, Lezione di Chimica* 41. Catene Invisibli 42. La Vita Ricominicia 45. Assunta Spina 47. Toto al Giro d'Italia 48. Adamo ed Eva 49. Tototarzan 50. Un Turco Napoletano 53. Toto Cerca Pace 54. Two Nights with Cleopatra/Due Notti con Cleopatra 54. L'Ultimo Amante 55. Peppino, le Modelle e Chella Llà 57. Toto, Peppino e le Fanatiche 58. Hercules in the Vale of Woe 62. For a Few Dollars Less/Per Qualche Dollaro in Meno 66, many others.

Mattsson, Arne (1919–1995).
Swedish director, in films from 1942.

She Only Danced One Summer 51. The Girl in Tails 56. Mannequin in Red 59. The Doll 62. Ann and Eve 69. Black Sun 78. Mask of Murder 85. The Girl 87. Sleep Well, My Love 87, etc.

Mature, Victor (1915–).
American leading man of the 40s; once known as 'the Hunk', but beneath the brawn lurked some style and a sense of humour.

■ The Housekeeper's Daughter 39. One Million BC 40. Captain Caution 40. No No Nanette 40. I Wake Up Screaming 41. The Shanghai Gesture 41. Song of the Islands 42. My Gal Sal 42. Footlight Serenade 42. Seven Days' Leave 42. *My Darling Clementine* (as Doc Holliday) 46. Moss Rose 47. *Kiss of Death* 47. Fury at Furnace Creek 48. Cry of the City 48. Red Hot and Blue 49. Easy Living 49. *Samson and Delilah* 49. Wabash Avenue 50. Stella 50. Gambling House 50. The Las Vegas Story 52. Androcles and the Lion 52. Something for the Birds 52. Million Dollar Mermaid 52. The Glory Brigade 53. Affair with a Stranger 53. *The Robe* 53. Veils of Baghdad 53. Dangerous Mission 54. Demetrius and the Gladiators 54. Betrayed 54. *The Egyptian* 54. Chief Crazy Horse 55. Violent Saturday 55. The Last Frontier 55. Safari (GB) 56. The Sharkfighters 56. Zarak (GB) 57. Interpol (GB) 57. The Long Haul (GB) 57. China Doll 57. No Time to Die (GB) 58. Escort West 59. The Bandit of Zhobe (GB) 59. The Big Circus 59. Timbuktu 59. Hannibal 60. The Tartars 60. The Mongols 60. *After the Fox* 66. Head 68. Every Little Crook and Nanny 72. Won Ton Ton 76. Firepower 79. Samson and Delilah (TV) 84.

❝ I'm no actor, and I've 64 pictures to prove it. – V.M.

I didn't care for *Samson and Delilah*. No picture can hold my interest when the leading man's bust is bigger than the leading lady's. – *Groucho Marx*

Matz, Peter (1928–).
American composer and conductor, mainly for TV.

Bye Bye Braverman 68. Marlowe 69. Rivals 72. Funny Lady (AAN) 75. The Prize Fighter 79. The Private Eyes 80. Lust in the Dust 85. Torch Song Trilogy 88. The Gumshoe Kid 89. Stepping Out 91, etc.

Mauch, Billy and Bobby (1925–).
American twins, boy actors who appeared in several films in the mid-30s, notably a 'Penrod' series and the Errol Flynn version of *The Prince and the Pauper* 37. Billy became a Hollywood sound editor, while Bob worked as a film editor.

Mauch, Thomas.
German cinematographer, associated with the films of Werner Herzog.

Signs of Life/Lebenszeichen 68. Even Dwarfs Started Small/Auch Zwerge Haben Klein Angefangen 70. *Aguirre, Wrath of God*/Aguirre, Der Zorn Gottes 72. Stroszek 77. Signs of Life 81. *Fitzcarraldo* 82. War and Peace (co-ph) 83. The Blind Director 86. Deadline 87. i.d. 95. Sweety Barrett (Ire.) 98, etc.

Maude, Joan (1908–1998).
English actress, the daughter of Nancy Price. Born in Rickmansworth, Hertfordshire, she began her career as a solo dancer on the London stage at the age of 13, and worked in the theatre until the mid-30s, after which she appeared only in films and on television until the 50s. Married twice.

This Freedom 23. Chamber of Horrors 29. Hobson's Choice 31. The Wandering Jew 33. The Lash 34. Sabotage 34. Turn of the Tide 35. They Knew Mr Knight 45. The Rake's Progress 45. Night Boat to Dublin 46. A Matter of Life and Death 46. Corridor of Mirrors 48. Badger's Green 49. The Temptress 49. Life in Her Hands 51, etc.

Maugham, Robin (1916–1980).
British popular novelist, nephew of Somerset Maugham. *The Servant* and *The Intruder* have been filmed.

Maugham, W. Somerset (1874–1965).
Distinguished British novelist, short-story writer and playwright whose works have often been filmed.

Smith 17. A Man of Honour 19. The Circle 25 and 30 (as *Strictly Unconventional*). Rain 28 (as *Sadie Thompson*), 32 and 53 (as *Miss Sadie Thompson*). Our Betters 33. The Painted Veil 34 and 57 (as *The Seventh Sin*). Of Human Bondage 34, 46 and 64. Ashenden (as *Secret Agent*) 36. Vessel of Wrath 37 and 54 (as *The Beachcomber*). The Letter 40 (also very freely adapted as *The Unfaithful* 47). The Moon and Sixpence 42. Christmas Holiday 44. The Razor's Edge 46. Theatre (as *Adorable Julia*) 63, etc.

He also introduced three omnibus films of his stories: *Quartet* 48, *Trio* 50 and *Encore* 51; a film of his rather unhappy life is constantly promised.

❝ I'm all against pauses and silences. If the actors cannot give significance to their lines without these, they're not worth their salaries. – S.M.

He reminds me of an old Gladstone bag, covered with labels. God only knows what is inside. – *Christopher Isherwood*

Maunder, Wayne (1942–).
Canadian-born leading man of the 60s, who has been little heard from since.

Casino on Wheels (TV) 73. Porky's 81, etc.

TV series: *Custer* 67. Lancer 68–69. Chase 73–74.

Maura, Carmen (1945–).
Spanish leading actress from the stage, who gained national fame as a TV hostess. She has starred in several of Pedro Almodóvar's films.

El Hombre Oculto 70. La Petición 76. Los Ojos Vendados 78. La Mano Negra 80. Dark Habits/ Entre Tinieblas 83. What Have I Done to Deserve This/Que He Hecho Yo para Merecer Esto? 84. Matador 86. Law of Desire/La Ley del Deseo 87. Women on the Verge of a Nervous Breakdown/ Mujeres al Borde de un Ataque de Nervios 89. ¡Ay, Carmela! 90. Soleil Levant 91. How to Be a Woman and Not Die in the Attempt/Como Ser Mujer y No Morir en el Intento 91. In Heaven As on Earth/Sur la Terre, Comme au Ciel 92. La Reina Anónima 92. Sombras en una Batalla 93. Louis, Enfant Roi (Fr.) 93. How to Be Miserable and Enjoy It 94. King of the River/El Rey del Rio 95. Pareja de Tres 95. The Lame Pigeon/El Palomo Cojo 95. Love Kills/Amores que Matan 96. Elles (Lux.) 97. Alice and Martin (Fr.) 98, etc.

Maureen, Mollie (1904–1987) (Elizabeth Mary Campfield).
Diminutive British stage actress, in a few films.

■ The Private Life of Sherlock Holmes (as Queen Victoria) 70. The Return of the Pink Panther 75. Jabberwocky 77. The Hound of the Baskervilles 78. The Wicked Lady 83. Little Dorrit 87.

Maurey, Nicole (1925–).
French leading lady.

Little Boy Lost (US) 51. The Secret of the Incas (US) 54. The Weapon (GB) 56. Me and the Colonel (US) 58. The House of the Seven Hawks (GB) 59. High Time (US) 60. The Day of the Triffids (GB) 62. Gloria 77. Chanel Solitaire 81, etc.

Maxwell, Edwin (1886–1948).
Stocky, balding American character actor, frequently cast as shady businessman.

The Jazz Singer 27. The Taming of the Shrew 29. Daddy Longlegs 31. Scarface 32. Cleopatra 34. Fury 36. Young Mr Lincoln 39. His Girl Friday 40. I Live on Danger 42. Holy Matrimony 43. Wilson 44. The Jolson Story 46. The Gangster 47, many others.

Maxwell, Elsa (1883–1963).
Dumpy, talkative American columnist and party-giver.

Autobiographies: 1943, *My Last Fifty Years*. 1955, *I Married the World*. 1961, *Celebrity Circus*.

FILM APPEARANCES: Hotel for Women 39. Public Deb Number One 40. Stage Door Canteen 43, etc.

❝ Elsa Maxwell? She's just another pretty face. – *Hermione Gingold*

Maxwell, James (1929–1995).
American-born character actor, in Britain, often in avuncular roles. A founder member of Manchester's Royal Exchange Theatre Company from the mid-70s, he was also a theatre director and playwright.

Private Potter (TV) 61. Private Potter 62. Girl on Approval 62. One Day in the Life of Ivan Denisovich 71. Ransom 74, etc.

Maxwell, John (1875–1940).
Scottish lawyer who turned distributor and became co-founder of Associated British productions and the ABC cinema chain.

Maxwell, Lois (1927–) (Lois Hooker).
Canadian leading lady who had a brief Hollywood career (1946–48) before settling in England. She is best known for playing Miss Moneypenny in the James Bond films until *A View to a Kill* 85.

The Decision of Christopher Blake 47. Corridor of Mirrors 48. Women of Twilight 49. Domani È Troppo Tardi (It.) 50. The Woman's Angle 52. Aida (It.) 53. Passport to Treason 55. The High Terrace 56. Kill Me Tomorrow 57. Operation Kid Brother 67. Endless Night 72. Age of Innocence 77. Lost and Found 79. The Blue Man 87, etc.

Maxwell, Marilyn (1921–1972) (Marvel Maxwell).
Blond American radio singer and actress, formerly child dancer.

Stand By For Action 42. Swing Fever 42. Thousands Cheer 43. Lost in a Harem 44. Summer Holiday 47. The Lemon Drop Kid 51. Off Limits 53. New York Confidential 55. Rock-a-bye-Baby 58. Critic's Choice 62. Stagecoach to Hell 64, etc.

May, Brian (1934–1997).
Australian composer.

The True Story of Eskimo Nell 75. Barnaby and Me 78. Patrick 79. Mad Max 79. Harlequin 80. *The Survivor* 81. Gallipoli 81. Dangerous Summer 82. *Mad Max II*/The Road Warrior 82. Cloak and Dagger 84. Missing in Action II: The Beginning 84. Sky Pirates 86. Death before Dishonor 87. Steel Dawn 87. Hurricane Smith 90. Dead Sleep 90. Freddy's Dead: The Final Nightmare 91, etc.

May, Elaine (1932–).
American cabaret star of the 50s (with Mike Nichols); also screenwriter.

■ Luv (a) 67. Enter Laughing (a) 67. A New Leaf (a, wd) 71. Such Good Friends (w) 72. The Heartbreak Kid (d) 72. California Suite (a) 78. Mikey and Nickey (& w) 78. Heaven Can Wait (w) (AAN) 78. Ishtar (d) 87. In the Spirit (a) 90. The Birdcage (w) 95. Primary Colors (w) 98.

May, Hans (1891–1959).
Viennese composer who settled in Britain in the early 30s.
The Stars Look Down 39. Thunder Rock 42. The Wicked Lady 45. Brighton Rock 46. The Gypsy and the Gentleman 57, etc.

May, Joe (1880–1954) (Joseph Mandel).
German director of early serials and thrillers.
Stuart Webb 15. Veritas Vincit 16. The Hindu Tomb 21, etc.
Best German film probably *Asphalt* 29.
IN HOLLYWOOD: Music in the Air 34. The Invisible Man Returns 40. The House of Seven Gables 40. Hit the Road 41. Johnny Doesn't Live Here Any More 44, etc.

May, Johdi (1975–).
English juvenile actress.
A World Apart 88. Max and Helen (TV) 90. Eminent Domain 91. The Last of the Mohicans 92. Sister, My Sister 94. The Gambler 97, etc.

May, Karl (1842–1912).
German novelist whose output of pulp fiction included some 20 westerns, many of which were filmed, notably those about Winnetou, an Apache, and Shatterhand, a gentlemanly German-born adventurer. Shatterhand was played on screen by Lex Barker in a series of films mostly directed by Harald Reinl.
Der Schatz im Silbersee 52. Winnetou 64. Winnetou II 64. Shatterhand 64. Winnetou III 65. Winnetou und das Halbblut Apanatschi 67. Winnetou und Shatterhand im Tal der Toten 68, etc.

May, Mathilda (1965–).
French leading actress in international films.
Letters to an Unknown Lover 85. Lifeforce/Space Vampires (GB) 85. The Cry of the Owl/Le Cri du Hibou 87. Trois Places pour le 26 88. Naked Tango (Arg./US) 90. Isabel Eberhardt 91. Scream of Stone (Ger.) 91. Becoming Colette (Ger./US) 92. The Tit and the Moon (Sp.) 94. Grosse Fatigue 94. The Jackal (US) 97, etc.

Mayall, Rik (1958–).
Anarchic British actor, comedian and writer. He began writing comedy while at Manchester University and was a stand-up comedian before becoming a TV star in the 80s.
Whoops Apocalypse 86. Little Noises 91. Drop Dead Fred 91. The Princess and the Goblin (voice) 92. The Wind in the Willows (voice, as Toad) 96. Remember Me? 97. Bring Me the Head of Mavis Davis 98, etc.
TV series: The Young Ones 82–84. A Kick up the Eighties 84. Filthy Rich and Catflap 87. The New Statesman 88–92. Bottom 90–92. Rick Mayall Presents 93.
❝ Just as long as I can do a bit of film, a bit of TV, a bit of live theatre, and a bit of sunbathing in Devon, that'll do me for as long as I've got. – *R.M.*

Maybury, John (1958–).
English director, mainly of experimental shorts. He made an appearance in the documentary *The Alternative Miss World* 80, as Miss Winscale Nuclear Reactor.
The Last of England (ed only) 87. Premonition of Absurd Perversion in Sexual Personae Part 1 (p, wd, ph, ed) 92. Man to Man (TV) 92. Remembrance of Things Fast: True Stories Visual Lies (wd) 94. *Love Is the Devil* (d) 98, etc.

Mayehoff, Eddie (1911–1992).
American comic actor, former dance bandleader.
That's My Boy 51. Off Limits 53. How to Murder Your Wife 65. Luv 67, etc.
TV series: Doc Corkle 52. That's My Boy 54.

Mayer, Arthur L. (1886–1981).
American author and commentator, a former cinema exhibitor who displayed his lively wit in *Merely Colossal* (1953) and as co-author of *The Movies*.

Mayer, Carl (1894–1944).
German screenwriter.
■ *The Cabinet of Dr Caligari* 19. Genuine 20. Die Hintertreppe 21. Scherben 21. Schloss Vogelod 21. Phantom 22. Vanina 22. Sylvester 23. Die Strasse 23. *The Last Laugh* 24. Tartuff 25. Berlin 27. *Sunrise* 27. Four Devils 28. Ariane 31. Träumende Mund 32. Dreaming Lips 37.

Mayer, Edwin Justus (1896–1960).
American screenwriter.
In Gay Madrid 30. Never the Twain Shall Meet 31. Merrily We Go to Hell 32. The Night Is Ours 33. I Am Suzanne 34. Thirty Day Princess 34. The Affairs of Cellini (original play) 34. So Red the Rose 35. Give Us This Night 36. *Desire* 36. Till We Meet Again 36. The Buccaneer 38. Rio 39. They Met in Bombay 41. *To Be or Not To Be* 42. A Royal Scandal 45. Masquerade in Mexico 45, etc.

Mayer, Gerald (1919–).
American director.
■ Dial 1119 50. Inside Straight 51. The Sellout 52. Holiday for Sinners 52. Bright Road 53. The Marauders 55. Diamond Safari 57.

Mayer, Louis B. (1885–1957).
American executive, former production head of MGM. Once a scrap merchant, he became a cinema manager and later switched to distribution. With Sam Goldwyn, formed Metro-Goldwyn-Mayer in 1924, and when Goldwyn bought himself out became one of Hollywood's most flamboyant and powerful tycoons until the 50s when he found himself less in touch and responsible to a board. Special Academy Award 1950 'for distinguished service to the motion picture industry'.
Biographies: 1954, *Hollywood Rajah* by Bosley Crowther. 1975, *Mayer and Thalberg* by Sam Marx. 1993, *The Merchant of Dreams: Louis B. Mayer, MGM and the Secret Hollywood* by Charles Higham.
❝ This 'Hollywood rajah' was perhaps the archetypal movie mogul: sentimental, commonsensical, businesslike, unaesthetic, arrogant, illogical, naive, amoral, tasteless and physically unappealing. For twenty years he ran MGM splendidly in his own image, and became a legend of autocracy. He did not stint on his surroundings; Sam Goldwyn said of his office:
You need an automobile to reach the desk.
No detail escaped him. B. P. Schulberg gave him the title:
Czar of all the rushes.
Though he kept it well hidden, he did have a basic sense of humility:
You know how I'm smart? I got people around me who know more than I do.
His arguments were often irritatingly unanswerable. Arthur Freed recalls:
If a writer complained of his work being changed, Mayer always said:
'The number one book of the ages was written by a committee, and it was called The Bible.'
To Gottfried Reinhardt, who wanted to make a non-commercial picture, Mayer snapped:
You want to be an artist, but you want other people to starve for your art.
Mayer's idea of a good commercial movie was simple, homespun, warm, happy . . . in a phrase, the Hardy Family. That series, cheap to make, kept the studio in profit for many a year. Their success did not delude Mayer into thinking they were great movies:
Don't make these pictures any better. Just keep them the way they are.
This did not mean that he despised the American public, only that he knew what they liked. He even created and acted out for the producer a prayer that the son of the fictional family might speak when his mother was ill:
Dear God, don't let my mom die, because she's the best mom in the world.
He was similarly quick to correct a plot point:
A boy may hate his father, but he will always respect him.
As early as 1922 his credo in this vein was fully formed:
I will only make pictures that I won't be ashamed to have my children see.
His cry in later years, when permissiveness was creeping in, was:
Don't show the natural functions!
In argument Mayer was a great and exhausting opponent, violent, wheedling and pleading by turns. Robert Taylor remembered going in for more money. When he emerged, a friend asked him:
Did you get the rise?
– No, but I gained a father.
Taylor later remembered Mayer in a respectful light:
He was kind, understanding, fatherly and protective, always there when I had problems.
As Mayer himself said:
Life without service isn't worth living.
But he saw the dangers of life at the top:
Look out for yourself or they'll pee on your grave.
Herman J. Mankiewicz saw Mayer himself as a danger:
He had the memory of an elephant and the hide of an elephant. The only difference is that elephants are vegetarians and Mayer's diet was his fellow man.
Mayer was very proud of MGM's army of stars and technicians:
We are the only kind of company whose assets all walk out of the gate at night.
He needed their goodwill:
I want to rule by love, not fear.
But when he died, the usual caustic comments were heard:
The only reason so many people attended his funeral was they wanted to make sure he was dead.
He had then been for some years at odds with the MGM hierarchy, an unwilling exile from the boardroom. Said someone at the funeral:
I see MGM got L.B. back at last.
– Yeah, but on its own terms.
For some years people had been heard to remark:
The old grey Mayer he ain't what he used to be.
But Bob Hope, as so often, made the aptest wisecrack:
Louis B. Mayer came out west with twenty-eight dollars, a box camera and an old lion. He built a monument to himself – the Bank of America.

Mayersberg, Paul (1941–).
British screenwriter and director, a former critic who also worked in Paris and London as an assistant director for Roger Corman, Jean-Pierre Melville and Joseph Losey.
The Man Who Fell to Earth 76. The Disappearance 77. Merry Christmas, Mr Lawrence 83. Eureka 84. Captive (d) 86. Nightfall (& d) 88. Last Samurai (d) 89, etc.

Mayes, Wendell (1918–1992).
American screenwriter.
Spirit of St Louis 57. The Enemy Below 58. Anatomy of a Murder (AAN) 59. Advise and Consent 62. In Harm's Way 64. Hotel 67. The Poseidon Adventure (co-w) 72. Bank Shot 74. Death Wish 74. Go Tell the Spartans 78. Love and Bullets (co-w) 79. Monsignor (co-w) 82, etc.

Mayhew, Peter.
Tall (7 feet 2 inches) English actor, a former hospital porter, who played Chewbacca in the *Star Wars* trilogy.
Sinbad and the Eye of the Golden Tiger 77, etc.

Maylam, Tony (1943–).
British director.
Riddle of the Sands 78. The Burning 82. The Sins of Dorian Gray (TV) 83. Across the Lake 89. Split Second 92, etc.

Maynard, Bill (1928–) (Walter Williams).
Massive British comic actor familiar on TV 1976–78 as the accident-prone hero of *Oh No! It's Selwyn Froggitt*.
Autobiographies: 1975, *The Yo-Yo Man*; 1997, *Stand Up and Be Counted*.
Till Death Us Do Part 69. The Magnificent Six and a Half 69. Carry On Henry 71. The Four Dimensions of Greta 71. Steptoe and Son Ride Again 74. Carry On Dick 74. Confessions of a Pop Performer 75. Robin and Marian 76. All Things Bright and Beautiful (TV) 78. The Plague Dogs (voice) 82, etc.
TV series: Great Scott – It's Maynard 55–56. Mostly Maynard 57. Trinity Tales 75. The Life of Riley 75. Oh No! It's Selwyn Froggitt 76–77. Paradise Island 77. Selwyn 78. The Gaffer 81–83. Langley Bottom 86. Heartbeat 93– .

Maynard, Ken (1895–1973).
American cowboy star, mainly seen in low-budget features. Once a rodeo rider; broke into films as a stuntman. Died of malnutrition.
Janice Meredith 24. Señor Daredevil 26. The Red Raiders 27. Branded Men 31. Texas Gunfighter 32. Come on, Tarzan 32. Wheels of Destiny 34. Heir to Trouble 34. Wild Horse Stampede 45, many others.

Maynard, Kermit (1898–1971).
American action player, brother of Ken Maynard. Once doubled for George O'Brien, Victor McLaglen, Warner Baxter and Edmund Lowe.
The Fighting Trooper 34. Sandy of the Mounted 34. Wild Bill Hickok 38. Golden Girl 51, many others.
TV series: Saturday Roundup 51.

Mayne, Ferdy (1916–1998) (Ferdinand Mayer-Boerckel).
German-born actor, long in Britain; often seen as smooth villain.
Meet Sexton Blake 44. You Know What Sailors Are 53. Storm over the Nile 55. Ben Hur 59. Freud 62. Operation Crossbow 65. The Bobo 67. *The Fearless Vampire Killers* 68. Where Eagles Dare 69. When Eight Bells Toll 71. Innocent Bystanders 72. The Eagle Has Landed 76. The Pirate (TV) 78. A Man Called Intrepid (TV) 79. The Black Stallion Returns 83. Conan the Destroyer 84. Howling II 85. River of Diamonds 90, many others.

Mayo, Archie (1891–1968).
American director of very variable output. He began in films as an extra, after stage experience in musicals in America, Australia and Europe, then worked as a gag-man and a director of comedy shorts.
Money Talks 26. The College Widow 27. Beware of Married Men 28. Sonny Boy 29. Is Everybody Happy? 29. The Sacred Flame 29. Doorway to Hell 30. *Svengali* 31. Under Eighteen 31. The Expert 32. Night after Night 32. Mayor of Hell 33. Convention City 33. Desirable 34. *Bordertown* 34. *Go Into Your Dance* 35. The Case of the Lucky Legs 35. *The Petrified Forest* 36. Give Me Your Heart 36. Black Legion 36. Call it a Day 37. It's Love I'm After 37. Youth Takes a Fling 38. They Shall Have Music 39. The House Across the Bay 40. Four Sons 40. The Great American Broadcast 41. Charley's Aunt 41. Confirm or Deny 41. Moontide 42. Orchestra Wives 42. Crash Dive 43. Sweet and Low Down 44. A Night in Casablanca 46. Angel on My Shoulder 46. The Beast of Budapest (p only) 57, etc.

Mayo, Virginia (1920–) (Virginia Jones).
American 'peaches and cream' leading lady of the 40s; played a few bit parts before being cast as decoration in colour extravaganzas.
The Adventures of Jack London 43. *Up In Arms* 44. *The Princess and the Pirate* 44. Wonder Man 45. The Best Years of Our Lives 46. Out of the Blue 47. *The Secret Life of Walter Mitty* 47. A Song Is Born 48. Smart Girls Don't Talk 48. The Girl from Jones Beach 49. White Heat 49. Backfire 50. The Flame and the Arrow 50. Along the Great Divide 51. Captain Horatio Hornblower 51. She's Working Her Way through College 52. South Sea Woman 53. King Richard and the Crusaders 54. Pearl of the South Pacific 55. Congo Crossing 56. The Story of Mankind 57. Fort Dobbs 58. Jet over the Atlantic 59. The Revolt of the Mercenaries (It.) 61. Young Fury 65. Castle of Evil 66. Fort Utah 67. Won Ton Ton 76. French Quarter 78. Evil Spirits 91. Midnight Witness 93, etc.

Maysles, David (1931–1987) and **Albert** (1933–).
American film-making brothers, semi-professional and semi-underground.
Youth of Poland 57. Kenya 61. Safari Ya Gari 61. *Showman* 63. What's Happening 64. Marlon Brando 65. Truman Capote 66. *Salesman* 69. Gimme Shelter 71. Grey Gardens 75. Running Fence 77. When We Were Kings 97, etc.

Mazar, Debi.
American actress.
Little Man Tate 91. Beethoven's 2nd 93. Money for Nothing 93. I Married an Axe Murderer 93. Girl 6 96. Empire Records 96. Trees Lounge 96. Nowhere 96. Meet Wally Sparks 97. She's So Lovely 97. Hush 98. Trouble on the Corner 98, etc.

Mazurki, Mike (1909–1990) (Mikhail Mazurwski).
Immense American character actor of Ukrainian descent; former heavyweight wrestler. Began in Hollywood as an extra.
The Shanghai Gesture (debut) 41. *Farewell My Lovely* 44. The French Key 46. Unconquered 47. Rope of Sand 49. Ten Tall Men 51. My Favorite Spy 52. Blood Alley 55. Davy Crockett 56. Donovan's Reef 63. Cheyenne Autumn 64. Seven

Women 66. The Wild McCulloughs 75, many others.
TV series: It's About Time 66. Chicago Teddy Bears 71.

Mazursky, Paul (1930–) (Irwin Mazursky).
American writer-director and occasional actor.
I Love you Alice B. Toklas (co-w) 68. *Bob and Carol and Ted and Alice* (co-w, d) (AAN) 70. Alex in Wonderland (co-w, d, a) 70. Blume in Love (wd) 73. *Harry and Tonto* (co-w, p, d) (AAN) 74. Next Stop Greenwich Village (wd, p) 76. *An Unmarried Woman* (wd, co-p, a) (AAN) 78. Willie and Phil 80. Tempest 82. Moscow on the Hudson 84. Down and Out in Beverly Hills 85. Moon over Parador (a, wd) 88. Punchline (a) 88. Enemies, a Love Story (a, wd) (AANw) 89. Scenes from the Class Struggle in Beverly Hills (a) 89. Scenes from a Mall (a, co-w, d) 90. The Pickle (wd) 93. Love Affair (a) 94. Faithful (a, d) 95. 2 Days in the Valley (a) 96. Touch (a) 97. Weapons of Mass Distraction (a) (TV) 97. Why Do Fools Fall in Love (a) 98. Winchell (d) (TV) 98. Antz (voice) 98, etc.

Mazzacurati, Carlo (1956–).
Italian director and screenwriter.
Vagabondi 79. Notte Italiana 87. Il Prete Bello 89. Marrakech Express (w only) 89. Il Richiamo della Notte 91. Un 'Altra Vita 92. The Bull/Il Toro 93. Dear Diary/Caro Diario (a only) 94. Vesna Va Veloce 96, etc.

Mazzello, Joseph (1984–).
American child actor, in showbusiness from the age of five.
Unspeakable Acts (TV) 90. Presumed Innocent 90. Radio Flyer 92. Jurassic Park 93. Shadowlands 93. River Wild 94. The Cure 95. Three Wishes 95. Star Kid 97. Simon Birch 98, etc.

Mc:
see MAC.

Meadows, Audrey (1926–1996).
American character actress, the sister of Jayne Meadows. Born in China to missionary parents, she began as a soprano before turning to acting, and is best known for playing Alice Kramden, wife to Jackie Gleason's bus driver Ralph, in the TV sitcom *The Honeymooners* 55–56.
That Touch of Mink 62. Take Her, She's Mine 63. Rosie 67, etc.
TV series: The Jackie Gleason Show 52–55, 56–57. Too Close for Comfort 82–83.

Meadows, Jayne (1920–) (Jayne Cotter).
American actress whose biggest role was in 1947 as the unsympathetic sister in *Enchantment*. She married Steve Allen in 1954.
Undercurrent 46. Song of the Thin Man 47. David and Bathsheba 51. Suspense 53. Hollywood Palace 68. The Ratings Game 84. Murder by Numbers 89. City Slickers 91, etc.
TV series: Medical Center 69–72. It's Not Easy 83.

Meadows, Shane (1973–).
British director, writer, actor and producer, so far of low-budget films. He was born in Nottingham, which has served as the setting for his films.
Small Time 96. 24/7 97, etc.

Meaney, Colm (1953–).
Irish character actor.
Nailed (TV) 81. The Dead 87. The Commitments 91. Far and Away 92. Into the West 92. Dr Quinn, Medicine Woman (TV) 92. *The Snapper* (TV) 93. The Road to Wellville 94. The War of the Buttons 94. The Englishman Who Went Up a Hill but Came Down a Mountain 95. The Van 96. The Last of the High Kings 96. Con Air 97. Claire Dolan 98, etc.
TV series: Star Trek: The Next Generation 87–93. Star Trek: Deep Space Nine 93– .

Meara, Anne (1929–).
American comedienne who turned straight actress in a 1975 TV series, *Kate McShane*. Married actor Jerry Stiller in 1954. Mother of Ben Stiller.
Lovers and Other Strangers 69. Kate MacShane (TV) 75. Nasty Habits 76. The Boys from Brazil 78. The Other Woman (TV) 82. The Longshot 86. My Little Girl 86. That's Adequate 90. Awakenings 90. Kiss of Death 94. Heavyweights 94. The Search for One-Eyed Jimmy 96. The Daytrippers 96, etc.
TV series: The Paul Lynde Show 72–73. The Corner Bar 73. Kate McShane 75. Rhoda 76–77. Archie Bunker's Place 79–82.

Meat Loaf (1947–) (Marvin Lee Aday).
Bulky American character actor and rock singer.
Rocky Horror Picture Show 75. Americathon 79. Scavenger Hunt 79. Roadie 80. Feel the Motion 86. Out of Bounds 86. The Squeeze 87. Stand by Me (concert) 88. Wayne's World 92. Motorama 92. Leap of Faith 92. To Catch a Yeti 95. Spice World: The Movie 97. Black Dog 98. Everything that Rises (TV) 98, etc.

Medak, Peter (1937–).
Hungarian-born director, first in Britain, and later in the United States. Born in Budapest, he was in films from the mid-50s.
Negatives 68. *A Day in the Death of Joe Egg* 70. The Ruling Class 71. Third Girl from the Left (TV) 74. Ghost in the Noonday Sun (unreleased) 74. The Odd Job 78. The Changeling 80. Zorro the Gay Blade 81. Mistress of Paradise (TV) 82. The Men's Club 86. The Krays 90. Let Him Have It 91. Romeo Is Bleeding 93. Pontiac Moon 94. The Hunchback of Notre Dame (TV) 97. Species 2 98, etc.

Medem, Julio (1958–).
Spanish director. He studied medicine, intending to work as a psychiatrist, and was a film critic for the Basque newspaper *La Voz de Euskadi* before becoming a director.
Cows/Vacas 92. The Red Squirrel/La Ardilla Roja 93. Earth/Tierra 95. The Lovers of the Arctic Circle/Los Amantes del Círculo Polar 98, etc.

Medford, Don (1917–).
American director.
To Trap a Spy 64. Cosa Nostra, Arch Enemy of the FBI (TV) 66. Incident in San Francisco (TV) 71. The Hunting Party 71. The Organization 71. The November Plan 76. Sizzle (TV) 81. Hell Town (TV) 85, etc.

Medford, Kay (1914–1980).
American character actress.
The War Against Mrs Hadley 42. The Rat Race 60. Butterfield 8 60. Bye Bye Birdie 63. Funny Girl (AAN) 68. But I Don't Want to Get Married (TV) 70. No Place to Run (TV) 72. More Than Friends (TV) 78, etc.

Medina, Patricia (1921–).
British-born leading lady of the 40s and 50s, in routine international films. She married actor Joseph Cotten in 1960.
The Day Will Dawn 42. They Met in the Dark 42. The First of the Few 42. Don't Take It To Heart 44. Hotel Reserve 44. Waltz Time 45. The Secret Heart 46. Moss Rose 47. The Three Musketeers 48. The Fighting O'Flynn 49. Abbott and Costello in the Foreign Legion 50. The Magic Carpet 51. Lady in the Iron Mask 52. Siren of Baghdad 53. Phantom of the Rue Morgue 54. Pirates of Tripoli 55. Uranium Boom 56. Buckskin Lady 57. Count Your Blessings 59. The Killing of Sister George 68. The Big Push/Timber Tramps 77, etc.

Medoff, Mark (1940–).
American dramatist and screenwriter. Born in Mount Carmel, Illinois, he was educated at the University of Miami and at Stanford.
Good Guys Wear Black (co-w) 77. When You Comin' Back, Red Ryder (oa, w) 79. Off Beat (w) 86. *Children of a Lesser God* (co-w, oa) (AAN) 86. City of Joy (w) 92. Homage (p, w, oa) 95. Sante Fe (w) 97. Mighty Joe Young (w) 98, etc.

Medwin, Michael (1923–).
British light character comedian, usually seen as a cockney.
Piccadilly Incident 46. Boys in Brown 49. Top Secret 52. Above Us the Waves 55. A Hill in Korea 56. I Only Arsked 58. Night Must Fall 63. Rattle of a Simple Man 64. I've Gotta Horse 65. The Sandwich Man 66. Scrooge 70. The Jigsaw Man 84. Staggered 94, many others.
AS PRODUCER: Charlie Bubbles 67. If 68. Spring and Port Wine 69. Gumshoe 71. Alpha Beta 73. O Lucky Man 73. Law and Disorder 73.
TV series: *The Army Game* 57–62. Shoestring 79.

Meehan, John (1890–*).
Canadian dramatist, screenwriter and actor. Born in Lindsay, Ontario, and educated at Harvard University, he began as an actor and worked as a director for George M. COHAN until his first play was produced in 1918. He went to Hollywood in 1929 to write the screen treatment of his play *Gentleman of the Press*.
The Lady Lies 29. The Divorcee (AAN) 30. A Lady's Morals 30. The Phantom of Paris 31. A Free Soul 31. Strangers May Kiss 31. The Miracle Woman 31. Washington Masquerade 32. Letty Lynton 32. Hell Below 33. Stage Mother 33. The Prizefighter and the Lady 33. When Ladies Meet 33. The Painted Veil 34. Sadie McKee 34. What Every Woman Knows 34. Peter Ibbetson 35. I've Been Around 35. His Brother's Wife 36. Stardust 37. Madame X 37. Boys Town (AA) 38. Seven Sinners 40. Kismet 44. The Valley of Decision 45. Three Daring Daughters 48, etc.

Meehan, John (1902–*).
American art director who spent much of his career, from 1935 to 1950, at Paramount Studios. He studied architecture at the University of Southern California.
Bring on the Girls 45. The Virginian 46. The Bride Wore Boots 46. The Strange Love of Martha Ivers 46. The Heiress (AA) 49. Sunset Boulevard (AA) 50. Tarzan's Peril 51. Assignment Paris 52. The Marrying Kind 52. It Should Happen to You 53. Salome 53. Man in the Dark 53. 20,000 Leagues under the Sea (AA) 54. Cult of the Cobra 55, etc.

Meek, Donald (1880–1946).
Scottish-born character actor, long in Hollywood; a bald, worried and timidly respectable little man was his invariable role.
The Hole in the Wall (debut) 28. Mrs Wiggs of the Cabbage Patch 34. Barbary Coast 35. Captain Blood 35. Pennies from Heaven 36. The Adventures of Tom Sawyer 38. *Stagecoach* 39. Tortilla Flat 42. They Got Me Covered 43. State Fair 45. Magic Town 46, many others.

Meeker, George (1904–1963).
American character actor, frequently in smoothly sinister roles. Born in Brooklyn, he studied at the American Academy of Dramatic Arts and began on stage.
Chicken a la King 28. Four Sons 28. The Escape 28. Emma 31. Only Yesterday 33. Night of Terror 33. Broadway Bill 34. Hips, Hips, Hooray! 34. Melody in Spring 34. The Richest Girl in the World 34. Little Man, What Now? 34. The Wedding Night 35. Murder by Television 35. Remember Last Night? 35. Career Woman 36. Tango 36. Danger on the Air 38. Slander House 38. Tarzan's Revenge 38. Everything's on Ice 39. High Sierra 41. Love Crazy 41. Casablanca 42. Murder in the Big House 42. Secret Enemies 43. Up in Arms 44. Dead Man's Eyes 44. Seven Doors to Death 44. Crime Inc. 45. Mr Muggs Rides Again 45. The Red Dragon 45. The People's Choice 46. Her Sister's Secret 46. Apache Rose 47. Case of the Baby Sitter 47. Road to Rio 47. Superman 48. Omoo, Omoo/The Shark God 49. The Invisible Monster (serial) 50. Twilight in the Sierras 50. Wells Fargo Gunmaster 51, many others.

Meeker, Ralph (1920–1988) (Ralph Rathgeber).
American leading man of the Brando type, with Broadway experience.
Teresa (debut) 51. Four in a Jeep 51. Shadow in the Sky 51. Glory Alley 52. The Naked Spur 53. Jeopardy 53. Code Two 53. Big House USA 54. *Kiss Me Deadly* (as Mike Hammer) 55. Desert Sands 56. *Paths of Glory* 58. Ada 61. Something Wild 62. The Dirty Dozen 67. The St Valentine's Day Massacre 67. Gentle Giant 67. The Detective 68. I Walk the Line 70. The Anderson Tapes 71. The Happiness Cage 73. The Food of the Gods 76. Hi-Riders 78. Winter Kills 79. Without Warning 80, etc.

Meerson, Lazare (1900–1938).
Russian-born production designer. He worked in France 1924–36, where he influenced not only his contemporaries but a later generation of art directors, some of whom had been his assistants, before being brought to Britain by Sir Alexander Korda.
Gribiche 25. Carmen 26. An Italian Straw Hat 28. Sous les Toits de Paris 29. *Le Million* 31. À Nous la Liberté 32. *La Kermesse Héroïque* 35. As You Like It 36. *Fire over England* 37. *Knight without Armour* 37. The Citadel 38, etc.

Mehboob (1907–1964) (Ramjankhan Mehboobkhan).
Prolific Indian director, few of whose films have been seen in the west.
Aan 49. Mother India 56. A Handful of Grain 59, etc.

Meheux, Phil.
English cinematographer.
Black Joy 77. The Music Machine 79. Scum 79. Those Glory Glory Days 81. The Final Conflict (co-ph) 81. The Long Good Friday 82. The Final Option 83. Experience Preferred but Not Essential 83. Morons from Outer Space 85. The Fourth Protocol 87. Criminal Law 89. Renegades 89. Defenseless 91. Highlander 2: The Quickening 91. The Trial 93. Ghost in the Machine 94. Ruby 92. No Escape 94. GoldenEye 95. The Saint 97, etc.

Mehrjui, Darius (1940–).
Iranian director. Born in Teheran, he went to the United States to study philosophy and film-making at UCLA. His early films brought social realism into the mainly escapist pre-revolutionary Iranian cinema.
Diamond 33 67. The Cow/Gava 69. The Postman/Posstchi 72. The Cycle/Dayereh Mina 75. The Tenants 87. Shirak 89. Hamoon 90. Banoo 92. Sara 93. The Fairy and the Green Book/Pari 94, etc.

Mehta, Deepa (1949–) (Deepa Mehta Saltzman).
Indian-born director, based in Canada, from television.
Martha, Ruth & Edie (co-d) 87. Sam & Me 91. Camilla 94. Earth 98, etc.

Meighan, Thomas (1879–1936).
American leading man of the silent screen.
The Trail of the Lonesome Pine 16. Male and Female 19. The Miracle Man 19. Conrad in Quest of His Youth 22. Manslaughter 23. The Alaskan 24. Tin Gods 26. The New Klondyke 26. The Racket 27. Young Sinners 31. Peck's Bad Boy 34, etc.

Meillon, John (1934–1989).
Australian character actor, in Britain from 1960.
On the Beach 59. The Sundowners 59. Offbeat 60. The Valiant 61. Billy Budd 62. The Running Man 63. They're a Weird Mob 66. The Cars that Ate Paris 74. Crocodile Dundee 86. Crocodile Dundee II 88, etc.

Meisner, Sanford (1905–1997).
American character actor in occasional films. A founder member of New York's Group Theatre, he became an influential teacher as head of the acting department at the Neighborhood Playhouse School of Theatre.
The Story on Page One 59. Tender Is the Night 61. Mikey and Nicky 76.

Mekas, Adolfas (1925–).
Lithuanian underground film-maker, in US.
Hallelujah the Hills (wd) 63. Guns of the Trees (a) 64. Windflowers (wd) 68, etc.

Mekas, Jonas (1922–).
Lithuanian underground film-maker in US, brother of Adolfas Mekas.
The Secret Passions of Salvador Dali 61. The Brig 64. Guns of the Trees 64. Hare Krishna 66. Report from Millbrook 66. Diaries, Notes & Sketches 75, etc.

Melcher, Martin (1915–1968).
American producer, married to Doris Day and from 1952 the co-producer of all her films.
Calamity Jane 53. Julie 56. Pillow Talk 59. Jumbo 62. Move Over, Darling 63. Send Me No Flowers 64. Where Were You When the Lights Went Out? 68, etc.

Melchior, Ib (1917–).
Danish-born writer-director, long in US; former actor and set designer. Son of Lauritz Melchior.
■ Angry Red Planet (wd) 59. Reptilicus (wd) 61. The Time Travellers (wd) 64. Robinson Crusoe on Mars (w) 65.

Melchior, Lauritz (1890–1973).
Danish operatic tenor, in a few Hollywood films.
■ Thrill of a Romance 45. Two Sisters from Boston 46. This Time for Keeps 47. Luxury Liner 48. The Stars Are Singing 53.

Melford, Austin (1884–1971).
English comic actor, playwright, screenwriter and director. Born in Alverstoke, he began his stage career at the age of two months and continued as a child actor with his father's company. He was on the London stage from 1904.
Royal England, a Story of an Empire's Throne (a) 11. The Terrible Twins (a) 14. Battling Butler (oa) (US) 26. Sport of Kings (a) 30. A Warm Corner (a) 30. Aunt Sally (co-w) 33. It's a Boy! (co-w) 33. Night of the Garter (a, co-w) 33. Jack Ahoy! (co-w) 34. Happy (co-w) 34. My Song for You (co-w) 34. Car of Dreams (w, co-d) 35. Oh, Daddy! (w, co-d) 35. The Phantom Light (co-w) 35. First Offence (co-w) 36. Jack of All Trades (co-w) 36. Radio Lover (co-d) 36. Keep Fit (co-w) 37. I See Ice! (co-w) 38. Old Mother Riley in Society (co-w) 40. We'll Smile Again (co-w) 42. Old Mother Riley, Detective (co-w) 43. When We Are Married (co-w) 43. Give Me the Stars (co-w) 44. Heaven Is round the Corner (w) 44, etc.

Melford, George (1889–1961).
American director and actor, from the stage, in films from 1909. His silent films were more distinguished than his talkies, and from the late 30s he worked as a character actor. It has been claimed that his Spanish version of *Dracula*, made in 1931 at the same time as the version directed by Tod Browning, is the better film.
AS DIRECTOR: Arizona Bill (w, co-d) 11. The Boer War 14. To Have and to Hold 16. The Call of the East 17. Everywoman 19. The Sea Wolf 20. The Sheik 21. Moran of the Lady Letty 22. Burning Sands 22. The Light that Failed 23. Tiger Love 24. Simon the Jester 25. Whispering Smith 26. Freedom of the Press 28. Sinners in Love 28. The Viking 32. East of Borneo 32. The Boiling Point 32. East of Java 35, many others.
AS ACTOR: Rulers of the Sea 39. My Little Chickadee 40. Dixie Dugan 43. A Tree Grows in Brooklyn 45. The Robe 53. The Egyptian 54. The Ten Commandments 56. Bluebeard's Ten Honeymoons 60, etc.

Melia, Joe.
British character comedian.
Follow a Star 59. Too Many Crooks 59. The Intelligence Men 65. Modesty Blaise 66. Oh! What a Lovely War 69. Antony and Cleopatra 72. The Wildcats of St Trinian's 80. Privates on Parade 82. Let Him Have It 91. Sorry about Last Night (TV) 95, etc.

Méliès, Georges (1861–1938).
French film pioneer, an ex-conjuror who produced the cinema's first trick films, most of them ambitious and still effective. Credited with being the first to use the dissolve, double exposure, and fades. After World War I he found his films out of date and his talents unwanted. In 1952 Georges Franju made a documentary tribute, *Le Grand Méliès*.
Biography: 1973, *Méliès Enchanteur* by Madeleine Méliès.
Une Partie de Cartes (debut) 96. The Artist's Dream 98. The Dreyfus Affair 99. Cinderella 00. Indiarubber Head 01. *Voyage to the Moon* 02. The Kingdom of the Fairies 03. The Impossible Voyage 04. Twenty Thousand Leagues under the Sea 07. Baron Munchausen 11. The Conquest of the Pole 12, many others.
✪ For demonstrating that cinema is a medium of magic; and for devising tricks so effective that eighty years later they are still viewed with delight. *Voyage to the Moon*.

Mell, Marisa (1929–1992) (Marlies Moitzi).
French leading lady.
French Dressing 64. What's New Pussycat? 65. Casanova '70 65. Anyone Can Play 66. Danger: Diabolik 67. Mahogany 77, etc.

Mellé, Gil (1935–).
American composer.
The Andromeda Strain 70. The Organization 71. Frankenstein: The True Story (TV) 73. Dynasty (TV) 75. The Sentinel 77. Starship Invasion 78. Borderline 81. Blood Beach 81. The Last Chase 81. Hot Target 85. Restless 86. The Case of the Hillside Strangler (TV) 90, many others, mainly for TV.

Mellor, William C. (1904–1963).
American cinematographer.
Wings in the Dark 35. Disputed Passage 39. The Great McGinty 40. Dixie 43. Abie's Irish Rose 46. Love Happy 49. *A Place in the Sun* (AA) 51. The Naked Spur 52. Give a Girl a Break 53. Bad Day at Black Rock 54. *Giant* 55. The Diary of Anne Frank (AA) 59. State Fair 62, etc.

Melton, James (1904–1961).
American operatic tenor, in a few Hollywood films.
Stars over Broadway 35. Sing Me a Love Song 36. Melody for Two 37. Ziegfeld Follies 45.

Melville, Herman (1819–1891).
American novelist of now-classic stature who died in obscurity. *Moby Dick*, which has been filmed three times, was in part inspired by tales of a fierce white whale known to sailors as Mocha Dick.
Biography: 1969, *The Melville Log* by Jay Leyda.
Moby Dick 26 (as The Sea Beasts), 30 and 54. Billy Budd 62. Typee (as The Enchanted Island) 64. Bartleby 70.
See also: MOBY DICK (Section 2).

Melville, Jean-Pierre (1917–1973) (J. P. Grumbach).
French director, with stage experience.
Le Silence de la Mer 47. Les Enfants Terribles 48. Quand Tu Liras Cette Lettre 52. Bob le Flambeur 55. *Leon Morin Priest* 61. Second Wind 66. *The Samurai* 67. The Red Circle 70. Dirty Money 72, etc.

Melvin, Murray (1932–).
British light character actor with stage experience in Theatre Workshop.
The Criminal (debut) 60. *A Taste of Honey* 61. HMS Defiant 62. Sparrows Can't Sing 63. The Ceremony 64. Alfie 66. A Day in the Death of Joe Egg 70. The Boy Friend 71. Ghost Story 74. Barry Lyndon 75. The Bawdy Adventures of Tom Jones 76. Tales from a Flying Trunk 79. Nutcracker 82. Let Him Have It 91, etc.

Mendelsohn, Ben.
Young Australian leading actor.
The Year My Voice Broke 87. Return Home 90. The Big Steal 90. Quigley Down Under 90. Spotswood/The Efficiency Expert 91. Nirvana Street Murder 91. Say a Little Prayer 93. Sirens 94. Metal Skin 94. Cosi 96. Idiot Box 96, etc.

Mendeluk, George (1948–).
German-born director, working in Canada.
Stone Cold Dead (& w, p) 79. The Kidnapping of the President 80. Doin' Time (US) 84. Meatballs III 86, etc.

Mendes, Lothar (1894–1974).
German director, in Hollywood from 1926. Born in Berlin, he worked as an actor with Max Reinhardt before turning to directing with UFA. Married actress Dorothy Mackaill.
A Night of Mystery 27. The Four Feathers 29. Payment Deferred 32. Jew Süss (GB) 34. *The Man Who Could Work Miracles* (GB) 36. Moonlight Sonata (GB) 38. International Squadron 41. Flight for Freedom 43. The Walls Came Tumbling Down 46, etc.

Menges, Chris (1940–).
British cinematographer.
Kes 70. Gumshoe 71. Black Jack 79. Babylon 80. Looks and Smiles 81. Angel 82. Local Hero 83. Comfort and Joy 84. The Killing Fields (AA) 84. A Sense of Freedom 85. The Mission (AA) 86. High Season 87. Shy People 87. A World Apart (d) 88. Crisscross (d) 92. Second Best (d) 94. *Michael Collins* (AAN) 96. The Boxer 97. The Lost Son (d) 98, etc.

Menjou, Adolphe (1890–1963).
Dapper French-American leading man of the 20s, later a polished, sharp-spoken character actor; had the reputation of being Hollywood's best-dressed man.
Autobiography: 1952, *It Took Nine Tailors*.
SELECTED SILENT FILMS: The Kiss 16. The Faith Healer 21. The Three Musketeers 21. Bella Donna 23. *A Woman of Paris* 23. *The Marriage Circle* 24. *Forbidden Paradise* 24. The Swan 25. The Grand Duchess and the Waiter 26. Service for Ladies 27. Serenade 27. His Private Life 28. Marquis Preferred 28.
■ SOUND FILMS: Fashions in Love 29. Morocco 30. New Moon 30. Men Call It Love 31. The Easiest Way 31. *The Front Page* (AAN) 31. The Great Lover 31. Friends and Lovers 31. Prestige 32. Forbidden 32. Two White Arms 32. The Man From Yesterday 32. Bachelor's Affairs 32. Night Club Lady 32. A Farewell to Arms 32. Diamond Cut Diamond 32. The Circus Queen Murder 33. *Morning Glory* 33. The Worst Woman in Paris 33. Convention City 33. Journal of a Crime 34. Easy to Love 34. The Trumpet Blows 34. *Little Miss Marker* 34. Flirtation 34. The Human Side 34. The Mighty Barnum 34. Gold Diggers of 1935. Broadway Gondolier 35. The Milky Way 36. Sing Baby Sing 36. Wives Never Know 36. One in a Million 36. *A Star is Born* 37. Café Metropole 37. *One Hundred Men and a Girl* 37. *Stage Door* 37. The Goldwyn Follies 38. Letter of Introduction 38. Thanks for Everything 38. King of the Turf 39. That's Right You're Wrong 39. Golden Boy 39. *The Housekeeper's Daughter* 39. *A Bill of Divorcement* 40. Turnabout 41. Road Show 41. Father Takes a Wife 41. *Roxie Hart* 42. Syncopation 42. You Were Never Lovelier 42. Hi Diddle Diddle 43. Sweet Rosie O'Grady 43. *Step Lively* 44. Man Alive 45. Heartbeat 46. The Bachelor's Daughters 46. I'll Be Yours 47. Mr District Attorney 47. The Hucksters 47. *State of the Union* 48. My Dream is Yours 49. Dancing in the Dark 49. To Please a Lady 50. Tall Target 51. Across the Wide Missouri 51. *The Sniper* 52. Man on a Tightrope 53. Timberjack 55. The Ambassador's Daughter 56. Bundle of Joy 56. The Fuzzy Pink Nightgown 57. *Paths of Glory* 57. I Married a Woman 58. Pollyanna 60.
TV series: Target 51. My Favourite Story 53.
✪ For his omnipresent sartorial elegance, and for a surprising number of highly enjoyable performances. *Roxie Hart*.

Menke, Sally.
American editor, a graduate of the NYU Film School.
Cold Feet 84. Teenage Mutant Ninja Turtles 90. The Search for Signs of Intelligent Life in the Universe 91. Reservoir Dogs 91. Heaven & Earth 93. *Pulp Fiction* 94. Four Rooms (co-d) 95. Mulholland Falls 96. Jackie Brown 97. Nightwatch 98, etc.

Menken, Alan (1949–).
American composer, in collaboration with lyricist Howard Ashman until 1991.
Little Shop of Horrors (AAN) 86. The Little Mermaid (AAm, AAs) 89. Rocky V (song) 90. Beauty and the Beast (AAm, AAs) 91. Newsies 92. Home Alone II (song) 92. Aladdin (AAm, AAs) 92. Life with Mikey 93. Pocahontas (AAm, AAs) 95. The Hunchback of Notre Dame (AANm) 96. Hercules (AANs 'Go the Distance') 97, etc.

Men'shikov, Oleg (1960–).
Leading Russian actor, born in Moscow.
Relatives/Rodnya 81. My Favourite Clown 86. The Stairway/Lestnitsa 89. The Pit/Yama 90. Burnt by the Sun 94. *Prisoner of the Mountains*/Kavkazskii Plennik 96. The Barber of Siberia 98, etc.

Menzel, Jiri (1938–).
Czech director.
Closely Observed Trains (AA) 66. Capricious Summer 68. Crime at the Nightclub 68. Seclusion Near a Forest 76. The Apple Game 77. Those Wonderful Men with a Crank 79. My Sweet Little Village (AAN) 85. The End of the Good Old Days/Konec Starych Casu 89. Martha and I/Martha und Ich 90. The Beggar's Opera 91. The Life and Extraordinary Adventures of Private Chonkin 94, etc.

Menzies, William Cameron (1896–1957).
American art director who did much memorable work, especially with louring, impressionistic skyscapes. Also directed a few rather disappointing low-budget films. He was awarded a special Oscar in 1939 'for outstanding achievement in the use of color for the enhancement of dramatic mood in the production of *Gone with the Wind*'.
AS ART DIRECTOR: Robin Hood 22. *The Thief of Baghdad* 24. Tempest (AA) 27. *The Dove* (AA) 28. Alibi (AA) 29. The Awakening (AA) 29. Bulldog Drummond (AAN) 29. Alice in Wonderland 33. *Things to Come* (& co-d) 36. *The Adventures of Tom Sawyer* 38. *Gone with the Wind* 39. *Our Town* 40. *Foreign Correspondent* 40. *Kings Row* 41. For Whom the Bells Tolls 43. Ivy 47. Arch of Triumph 48. Around the World in Eighty Days 56, etc.
■ AS DIRECTOR: Always Goodbye 31. The Spider 31. Almost Married 32. Chandu the Magician 32. Wharf Angel 34. *Things to Come* 36. The Green Cockatoo 40. Address Unknown 44. Drums in the Deep South 51. The Whip Hand 51. The Maze 53. Invaders from Mars 54.
✪ For styling so many of the cinema's most memorable images. *Things to Come*.

Merande, Doro (c. 1898–1975).
American character actress who specialized in acidulous, eccentric and whimsical spinsters.
Our Town 40. Sullivan's Travels 41. Mr Belvedere Rings the Bell 52. The Seven Year Itch 55. The Cardinal 63. Hurry Sundown 67, many others.

Mercanton, Louis (1879–1932).
Swiss-born director, a naturalized Frenchman, who worked in England, where he was educated, France and America. He began as an actor in South Africa, became stage manager for Sir Herbert Tree, and directed Sarah Bernhardt in the title role of the silent *Queen Elizabeth* in 1911. Also directed Betty Balfour's sound debut, *The Brat/The Nipper* 30, and Jack Buchanan's first British sound film, *Man of Mayfair* 31.
Jeanne Doré 15. Monte-Carlo 25. Croquette 27. These Charming People (GB) 31, etc.

Mercer, Beryl (1882–1939).
British character actress, of small stature, in Hollywood from 1923; played mothers, maids, landladies.
The Christian 23. Seven Days' Leave 29. *Outward Bound* 30. Merely Mary Ann 31. Supernatural 32. *Cavalcade* 33. Berkeley Square 33. The Little Minister 34. Night Must Fall 37. The Hound of the Baskervilles 39, etc.

Mercer, David (1928–1980).
Leading British TV dramatist, playwright and occasional screenwriter; a former teacher.
Morgan – a Suitable Case for Treatment 66. *Family Life* 70. A Doll's House 73. Providence 77.

Mercer, Johnny (1909–1976).
American lyricist and composer, active in Hollywood from the early 30s. Songs include 'Blues in the Night', 'Black Magic', 'Something's Got to Give', 'Accentuate the Positive', etc.
The Harvey Girls (AA) 46. Here Comes the Groom (AA) 51. Seven Brides for Seven Brothers (AA) 54. Li'l Abner 59. Kotch (AANs) 71, etc.

Merchant, Ismail (1936–).
Indian producer, exclusively associated with films directed by James IVORY.
In Custody/Hifazaat (d) 93.

Merchant, Vivien (1929–1983) (Ada Thompson).
British leading actress, mainly on TV: once married to Harold Pinter.
Alfie (AAN) 66. Accident 67. Under Milk Wood 71. Frenzy 72. The Offence 72. The Homecoming 73. The Man in the Iron Mask (TV) 77, etc.

Mercier, Michèle (1939–).
French leading lady.
Retour de Manivelle 57. Aimez-vous Brahms? 61. Call of the Wild 72. Jean's Tonic 84.

Mercouri, Melina (1923–1994).
Volatile Greek star actress with flashing smile and dominant personality; married Jules Dassin and appeared in international films. In the 80s she became Greece's Minister of Culture.
Autobiography: 1971, *I Was Born Greek*.
■ *Stella* 54. He Who Must Die 56. The Gypsy and the Gentleman 58. The Law 59. *Never on Sunday* (AAN) 60. Il Giudizio Universale 61. Phaedra 61. Vive Henri IV 61. The Victors 63. *Topkapi* 64. A Man Could Get Killed 65. The Player Pianos 65. 10.30 pm Summer 66. Gaily Gaily 69. Promise at Dawn 71. Once Is Not Enough 75. Nasty Habits 76. A Dream of Passion 78. Not by Coincidence 83.

Mercurio, Paul.
Australian leading actor and dancer.
Strictly Ballroom 92. Exit to Eden 94. Joseph (title role, TV) 95. Red Ribbon Blues 95. Back of Beyond 95. Cosi 96. Dark Planet 97, etc.

Meredith, Burgess (1908–1997) (George Burgess). American star character actor who was famous on Broadway in the 30s, but never seemed to find the right Hollywood outlet for his enthusiastic, eccentric portrayals. Born in Cleveland, Ohio, he was on stage from 1929. Married four times, including to actress Margaret Perry (1936–38); actress Paulette GODDARD (1944–48); and former ballerina Kaja Sundsten, whom he married in 1950.
■ *Winterset* 36. There Goes the Groom 37. Spring Madness 38. Idiot's Delight 39. *Of Mice and Men* 39. Castle on the Hudson 40. Second Chorus 40. San Francisco Docks 41. *That Uncertain Feeling* 41. Tom Dick and Harry 41. Street of Chance 42. *The Story of GI Joe* (as Ernie Pyle) 45. The Diary of a Chambermaid (& p, w) 46. Magnificent Doll 46. On Our Merry Way 48. *Mine Own Executioner* (GB) 48. The Man on the Eiffel Tower (& d) 49. The Gay Adventure 53. Joe Butterfly 57. Advise and Consent 62. The Cardinal 63. In Harm's Way 65. A Big Hand for the Little Lady 66. Madame X 66. Batman 66. The Kidnappers/Philipp 66. Hurry Sundown 67. The Torture Garden (GB) 67. Mackenna's Gold 68. Stay Away Joe 68. Hard Contract 69. Skidoo 69. There Was a Crooked Man 70. Probe (TV) 71. Such Good Friends 71. Beware the Blob 71. A Fan's Notes 72. The Yin and Yang of Mr Go (& d) 72. Clay Pigeon 72. Golden Needles 74. The Day of the Locust (AAN) 74. The Hindenburg 76. Burnt Offerings 76. *Rocky* (AAN) 76. The Sentinel 77. 92 in the Shade 77. Magic 78. Foul Play 78. The Manitou 78. The Great Georgia Bank Hoax 78. Rocky II 79. Final Assignment 80. When Time Ran Out 80. True Confessions 81. The Last Chase 81. Clash of the Titans 81. Rocky III 82. Santa Claus 85. Broken Rainbow 85. King Lear 87. Full Moon in Blue Water 88. Rocky V 90. State of Grace 90. Night of the Hunter (TV) 91. Grumpy Old Men 93. Across the Moon 94. Grumpier Old Men 95.
TV series: Mr Novak 64–65. Batman (as The Penguin) 66–68. Search 72–73. That's Incredible 80. Gloria 82.

Meredith, Iris (1916–1980). American leading actress in westerns. She made 19 films opposite Charles Starrett and also appeared with Johnny Mack Brown and Robert Allen before retiring in the mid-40s.
Roman Scandals 33. A Lawman Is Born 37. Mystery of the Hooded Horseman 37. Cattle Raiders 38. West of the Santa Fe 39. Riders of Black River 39. The Return of Wild Bill 40. Green Archer 40. The Son of Davy Crockett 41. The Rangers Take Over 43, etc.

Meredyth, Bess (1890–1969) (Helen McGlashan). American scriptwriter.
Strangers in the Night 23. Ben Hur 26. Wonder of Women (AAN) 28. A Woman of Affairs 28. Our Blushing Brides 30. Cuban Love Song 31. Strange Interlude 32. The Affairs of Cellini 34. Folies Bergère 35. Under Two Flags 36. The Unsuspected 47, etc.

Merivale, Philip (1886–1946). British stage actor who moved to Hollywood in the late 30s. Married actress Gladys COOPER; he was the father of actor John Merivale (1917–1990).
Trilby 14. The Passing of the Third Floor Back 35. Give Us This Night 36. Mr and Mrs Smith 41. Rage in Heaven 41. This Above All 42. Pacific Blackout 42. Lady for a Night 42. This Land Is Mine 43. Lost Angel 43. The Hour before Dawn 44. The Stranger 46. Sister Kenny 46, etc.

Meriwether, Lee (1935–). Long-legged American leading lady, mostly in 'B's; former beauty queen.
The 4D Man 59. Batman (as Catwoman) 65. Namu the Killer Whale 66. Angel in My Pocket 68. The Undefeated 69. The Brothers O'Toole 73, etc.
TV series: Barnaby Jones 72–80.

Merkel, Una (1903–1986). American character actress who started in the 30s as heroine's girlfriend type, later played mothers and aunts.
Abraham Lincoln 30. Daddy Longlegs 31. Whistling in the Dark 33. The Merry Widow 34. Saratoga 37. Destry Rides Again 39. Road to Zanzibar 41. This Is the Army 43. Twin Beds 44. With a Song in My Heart 52. The Kentuckian 55. The Mating Game 59. Summer and Smoke (AAN) 61. A Tiger Walks 63. Spinout 66, many others.

Merman, Ethel (1908–1984) (Ethel Zimmermann). Brassy, vibrant, much-loved American star entertainer who had an incomparable way with a song that could be belted across. Her style was too outsize for Hollywood. She married four times, including briefly (1964) to actor Ernest BORGNINE. Her lovers are said to have included novelist Jacqueline SUSANN.
Autobiographies: 1955, *Who Could Ask for Anything More?* (UK *Don't Call Me Madam*). 1978, *Merman*.
■ Follow the Leader 30. We're Not Dressing 34. Kid Millions 34. *Anything Goes* 36. The Big Broadcast of 1936. Strike Me Pink 36. Happy Landing 38. *Alexander's Ragtime Band* 38. Straight Place and Show 38. Stage Door Canteen 43. *Call Me Madam* 53. There's No Business Like Show Business 54. It's a Mad Mad Mad Mad World 63. The Art of Love 65. Won Ton Ton 76. Airplane! 80.
❝ Broadway has been very good to me – but then, I've been very good to Broadway. – *E.M.*
When I do a show, the whole show revolves around *me*. – *E.M.*

Merrall, Mary (1890–1976) (Mary Lloyd). British character actress, on stage from 1907; often in fey or absent-minded roles.
The Duke's Son 20. You Will Remember 39. *Love on the Dole* 41. Squadron Leader X 42. *Dead of Night* 45. Nicholas Nickleby 47. Badger's Green 48. The Late Edwina Black 51. The Pickwick Papers 52. *The Belles of St Trinian's* 54. It's Great To Be Young 56. The Camp on Blood Island 58. Spare the Rod 61. Who Killed the Cat? 66, many others.

Merrick, David (1911–) (David Margulies). American impresario, a Broadway legend who also produced a few films.
Biography: 1993, *David Merrick – The Abominable Showman* by Howard Kissel.
Child's Play 72. The Great Gatsby 74. Semi-Tough 77. Rough Cut 80, etc.
❝ He liked writers the way a snake likes live rabbits. – *John Osborne*

Merrill, Bob (1920–1998) (Henry Robert Merrill Lavan). American composer, lyricist and screenwriter. Born in Atlantic City and educated at Temple University, he began as a nightclub singer and comedian before working as a dialogue director at Columbia Pictures. He wrote the lyrics for several Broadway shows, and his best-known songs include 'How Much Is That Doggie in the Window?', 'If I Knew You Were Comin' I'd Have Baked a Cake', and 'My Truly, Truly Fair'. A suicide, he shot himself while suffering from depression and gastrointestinal illness.
The Wonderful World of the Brothers Grimm (s) 62. Dangerous Christmas of Red Riding Hood (lyrics) (TV) 65. *Funny Girl* (AANs) 68. W. C. Fields and Me (w) 76, etc.

Merrill, Dina (1928–) (Nedenia Hutton Rumbough). American leading lady of the 60s, and leading socialite. Married actor Cliff Robertson (1966–89).
The Desk Set 57. The Sundowners 59. The Courtship of Eddie's Father 63. The Pleasure Seekers 64. I'll Take Sweden 65. Running Wild 73. The Greatest 77. A Wedding 78. Just Tell Me What You Want 80. Anna to the Infinite Power 83. Hot Pursuit 87. Caddyshack II 88. True Colors 91. The Player 92. Suture 93. Open Season 95. Milk & Money 96, etc.
TV series: Hot Pursuit 84.

Merrill, Gary (1914–1990). Dependable, tough-looking American actor. Born in Hartford, Connecticut, he was on stage from 1937. He was married to actress Bette DAVIS (1950–60), his second wife, a romance that began when he played her boyfriend in *All about Eve*, and romantically involved with Rita HAYWORTH.
Autobiography: 1988, *Bette, Rita and the Rest of My Life*.
Winged Victory 44. Slattery's Hurricane 48. Twelve O'Clock High 49. *All about Eve* 50. Decision Before Dawn 51. Another Man's Poison (GB) 51. Phone Call from a Stranger 52. Night Without Sleep 52. Blueprint for Murder 53. The Human Jungle 54. The Black Dakotas 54. Bermuda Affair 56. The Pleasure of His Company 61. Around the World Under the Sea 66. Destination Inner Space 66. Catacombs (GB) 66. The Power 68. Huckleberry Finn 74. Thieves 77, others.
TV series: The Mash 54. Young Dr Kildare 73. Reporter 74.

Merrison, Clive (1945–). English actor.
Riddles of the Sphinx 77. Escape to Victory/Victory 81. Private Schultz (TV) 81. Henry VIII and His Six Wives 82. Firefox 82. The Sign of Four 83. Monsignor Quixote (TV) 85. A Very British Coup (TV) 88. Rebecca's Daughters 91. Stalin (TV) 92. Heavenly Creatures 94. An Awfully Big Adventure 94. The English Patient 96. McLibel! (TV) 97, etc.
TV series: Pinkerton's Progress 83. Mann's Best Friends 85. Double First 88. The Labours of Erica 89. How Do You Want Me? 98.

Merritt, George (1890–1977). British character actor of solid presence, usually seen as trades unionist, policeman, or gruff north-country type.
Dreyfus 30. The Lodger 32. I was a Spy 33. Dr Syn 37. Q Planes 39. He Found a Star 41. Hatter's Castle 41. Waterloo Road 45. I'll Be Your Sweetheart 45. I'll Turn to You 46. Nicholas Nickleby 47. Marry Me 49. The Green Scarf 54. Quatermass II 57. Tread Softly Stranger 58. I Monster 70, etc.

Merrow, Jane (1941–). British leading lady.
Don't Bother to Knock 61. The Wild and the Willing 62. The System 63. *The Lion in Winter* 68. Hands of the Ripper 70. Adam's Woman 70. The Horror at 37,000 Feet (TV) 73. Diagnosis Murder 75. The Patricia Neal Story (TV) 81, etc.

Merson, Billy (1879–1947) (William Thompson). British comic actor and singer, from music hall and revue. He began as an acrobat and clown called Ping Pong and made his name singing his own composition, 'The Spaniard that Blighted My Life'.
Billy's Spanish Love Spasm 15. The Tales of a Shirt 16. Billy the Truthful 17. Billy Merson in Russian Opera 27. Comets 30. Bill and Coo (& co-w) 31. The Show Goes On 37. Riding High 37. Chips 38. Scruffy 38, etc.

Mervyn, William (1912–1976) (William Pickwood). Portly, plummy-voiced British character actor, much on TV in high comedy roles.
The Blue Lamp 52. The Long Arm 56. Invasion Quartet 61. Murder Ahoy 64. The Jokers 67. The Railway Children 70. The Ruling Class 71. Up The Front 72. The Bawdy Adventures of Tom Jones 76, many others.

Mescall, John (1899–). American cinematographer.
Hold Your Horses 20. So This Is Paris 26. *The Black Cat* 34. *Bride of Frankenstein* 35. *Showboat* 36. The Road Back 37. Josette 38. Kit Carson 40. Dark Waters 44. Bedside Manner 45. The Desperadoes Are In Town 56. Not of This Earth 57, many others.

Messel, Oliver (1904–1978). British stage designer who occasionally worked in films.
The Scarlet Pimpernel 34. Romeo and Juliet 36. The Thief of Baghdad 40. Caesar and Cleopatra 45. The Queen of Spades 48, etc.

Messemer, Hannes (1924–). German general-purpose actor.
Rose Bernd 56. Babette Goes to War 59. The Great Escape 63. Is Paris Burning? 66. Congress Dances 66. The Odessa File 74. The Little Brother 83, etc.

Meszaros, Marta (1931–). Hungarian director and screenwriter, often of semi-autobiographical films. She studied at the Moscow Film School and began as a documentary film-maker. She was married to director Miklos Jancso (1962–81).
Book: 1994, *Screen Memories, the Hungarian Cinema of Marta Meszaros* by Catherine Portuges.
The Girl/Eltéavozott Nap 68. Don't Cry, Pretty Girls/Széep Léanyok, Ne Sirjatok 71. 9 Months/Kilenc Héonap 76. On the Move/Utkozben 79. Diary for My Children/Napló Gyermekeimnek 82. Diary for My Loves/Napló Szerelmeimnek 87. Diary for My Father and Mother/Napló Apamnak, Anyammnak 90. Foetus/A Magzat (co-w, d) 94, etc.

Metalious, Grace (1924–1964). American novelist who hit the best-seller list with *Peyton Place*.
❝ If I'm a lousy writer, then a lot of people have got lousy taste. – G.M.

Metaxas, George (1899–1950). Romanian character actor in occasional American films.
Swing Time 37. The Mask of Dimitrios 44. Scotland Yard Investigator 48, etc.

Metcalf, Laurie (1955–). American actress, best known for playing Roseanne's sister Jackie in the TV sitcom *Roseanne* 88–97. After studying at Illinois State University, she was a member of Chicago's Steppenwolf Theatre Company.
Desperately Seeking Susan 85. Miles from Home 85. Candy Mountain 87. Making Mr Right 87. Stars and Bars 88. Uncle Buck 89. Internal Affairs 89. Pacific Heights 90. JFK 91. Mistress 92. A Dangerous Woman 93. Blink 94. Leaving Las Vegas 95. Dear God 96, etc.

Metcalf, Mark. American actor, usually as a villain.
Julia 77. National Lampoon's Animal House 78. The Final Terror 83. One Crazy Summer 86. Mr North 88. Dead Ahead: The Exxon Valdez Disaster (TV) 92. The Stupids 95, etc.

Methot, Mayo (1904–1951). American actress who is best remembered for her stormy marriage with Humphrey Bogart.
Corsair 31. The Mind Reader 33. Jimmy the Gent 33. Side Streets 34. Dr Socrates 35. Mr Deeds Goes to Town 36. Marked Woman 37. The Sisters 38. Unexpected Father 39. Brother Rat and a Baby 40, etc.

Metrano, Art (1937–). Chubby American character actor.
Cheaper to Keep Her 80. How to Beat the High Cost of Living 80. Going Ape 81. Breathless 83. Teachers 84. Malibu Express 85. Police Academy 2: Their First Assignment 85. Police Academy 3: Back in Training 86. Norma 89. Beverly Hills Bodysnatchers 89, etc.
TV series: Chicago Teddy Bears 71.

Metty, Russell (1906–1978). American cinematographer.
Sylvia Scarlett 35. Bringing Up Baby 38. Music in Manhattan 44. The Story of G.I. Joe 45. *The Stranger* 45. *Ivy* 47. All My Sons 48. We Were Strangers 49. Magnificent Obsession 54. Man without a Star 55. *Miracle in the Rain* 56. Written on the Wind 56. Man with a Thousand Faces 57. A Time to Love and a Time to Die 58. Touch of Evil 58. The Misfits 60. *Spartacus* (AA) 61. The Art of Love 65. The War Lord 65. Madame X 66. The Appaloosa 66. The Secret War of Harry Frigg 67. Madigan 68. Eye of the Cat 69. The Omega Man 71. Ben 72, many others.

Metzger, Radley (1930–). American director.
Dark Odyssey 61. The Dirty Girls 64. Carmen Baby 67. Therese and Isabelle 68. Camille 2000 69. The Lickerish Quartet 70. Little Mother 72. Score 73. Naked Came the Stranger 75. The Opening of Misty Beethoven 76. The Cat and the Canary 78. The Tale of Tiffany Lust (d as Henry Paris) 81. The Princess and the Call Girl 84, etc.

Metzner, Erno (1892–1953). Hungarian art director in the silent German cinema.
Sumurun 20. The Loves of Pharaoh 21. Salome 22. Old Heidelberg 23. Secrets of a Soul 26. The White Hell of Pitz Palu 29. Diary of a Lost Girl 29. Westfront 1918 30. Kameradschaft 31. L'Atlantide 32. Chu Chin Chow (GB) 34. It Happened Tomorrow (US) 44, etc.

Meurisse, Paul (1912–1979). French general-purpose actor.
Montmartre sur Seine 41. Marie la Misère 45. Diabolique 54. La Tête contre les Murs 58. Lunch on the Grass 59. La Vérité 60, etc.

Meyer, Breckin.
American actor who began in commercials at the age of 11.
An American Tail (voice) 86. Freddy's Dead: The Final Nightmare 91. Clueless 95. The Craft 96. Escape from LA 96. Prefontaine 97. Touch 97. 54 98. Dancer, Texas, Pop. 81 98, etc.
TV series: The Jackie Thomas Show 92.

Meyer, Dina (1969–).
American actress, from television. Born in Queens, New York, she studied at New York's High School of Performing Arts.
Johnny Mnemonic 95. Dragonheart 96. Starship Troopers 97. Poodle Springs (TV) 98, etc.
TV series: Beverly Hills 90210 93–94.

Meyer, Emile (1910–1987).
American character actor typically cast as crooked cop or prizefight manager; but sometimes an honest Joe.
The People Against O'Hara 51. Shane 53. The Blackboard Jungle 55. *Riot in Cell Block 11* 55. The Man with the Golden Arm 56. *Sweet Smell of Success* 57. Baby Face Nelson 57. Paths of Glory 58. The Fiend Who Walked the West 59. Young Jesse James 60. Taggart 64. Young Dillinger 65. Hostile Guns 67. More Dead Than Alive 70, etc.

Meyer, Nicholas (1945–).
American novelist whose *The Seven-Per-Cent Solution* became a best-seller and took him from publicity to direction.
The Seven-Per-Cent Solution (AANw) 77. Time after Time (wd) 79. Star Trek II: The Wrath of Khan (d) 82. The Day After (d) (TV) 83. Volunteers (d) 85. The Deceivers 88. Star Trek VI: The Undiscovered Country (co-w, d) 91. Company Business (d) 91. Sommersby (co-w) 93. Voices (co-w) 95. The Informant (w) 97, etc.

Meyer, Ron (1945–).
American motion picture executive, a former agent and president of Creative Artists Agency. He became president and chief operating officer of MCA/Universal after Seagram bought control of the company in 1995.

Meyer, Russ (1923–).
American director of erotic films who broke briefly into the big time.
Biography: 1990, *Russ Meyer – the Life and Films* by David K. Frasier.
■ The Immoral Mr Teas 59. Eroticon 61. Eve and the Handyman 61. Naked Gals of the Golden West 62. Europe in the Raw 63. Heavenly Bodies 63. Laura 64. Mudhoney 65. Motor Psycho 65. Fanny Hill 65. Faster Pussycat Kill Kill 66. Mondo Topless 66. Good Morning and Goodbye 67. Common Law Cabin 67. Finders Keepers Lovers Weepers 68. *Vixen* 68. Cherry Harry and Raquel 69. Beyond the Valley of the Dolls 70. The Seven Minutes 71. Black Snake 73. The Supervixens 73. *Up* 76. Beneath the Valley of the Ultravixens 79. The Breast of Russ Meyer 82.
❝ I always had a tremendous interest in big tits. – R.M.
To him, nothing is obscene providing it is done in bad taste. – R.M.

Meyer, Torben (1884–1975).
German-American character actor who played many waiters, music teachers and petty officials, especially memorable in the films of Preston Sturges.
Roberta 35. The Prisoner of Zenda 37. Christmas in July 40. Edge of Darkness 42. The Miracle of Morgans Creek 43. Mad Wednesday 47, many others.

Meyers, Jonathan Rhys (1977–).
Irish leading actor. Born in Dublin and raised in Cork, he left school at 16 and began in commercials. He has been romantically linked with actress Toni COLLETTE.
A Man of No Importance 94. The Disappearance of Finbar 95. The Killer Tongue (Sp.) 96. Michael Collins 96. Samson and Delilah (TV) 96. The Maker (US) 97. Telling Lies in America (US) 97. Velvet Goldmine (US) 98. The Tribe (TV) 98. The Governess 98. B Monkey 98. Ride with the Devil (US) 99, etc.

Michael, Gertrude (1911–1964).
American actress usually seen in secondary roles.
I'm No Angel 33. The Notorious Sophie Lang (lead) 37. Women in Bondage 44. Caged 50. Women's Prison 55. Twist All Night 62, etc.

Michael, Ralph (1907–1994) (Ralph Champion Shotter).
British character actor of stage and screen, often in stiff-upper-lip roles. Actress Fay Compton was the first of his three wives.
John Halifax Gentleman 38. San Demetrio, London 43. For Those in Peril 44. *Dead of Night* 45. Johnny Frenchman 45. The Captive Heart 46. Eureka Stockade 48. The Astonished Heart 49. The Sound Barrier 52. King's Rhapsody 56. Seven Waves Away 57. A Night to Remember 58. A Jolly Bad Fellow 64. House of Cards 68. Diary of a Mad Old Man 87. Empire of the Sun 87, etc.

Michaels, Beverly (1927–).
American leading lady of sultry dramas in the early 50s.
East Side West Side 49. Pick Up 51. Wicked Woman 53. Crashout 55, etc.

Michaels, Dolores (1930–).
American leading lady of the late 50s; retired early.
The Wayward Bus 57. April Love 57. Fraulein 58. Warlock 59. Five Gates to Hell 59. One Foot in Hell 60. The Battle at Bloody Beach 61. Wizards of the Lost Kingdom 85, etc.

Micheaux, Oscar (1884–1951).
American independent producer, director and author. A pioneer of black cinema, working outside the system and aiming his films at a ghetto audience, he began in the silent era and continued to produce and direct more than 30 feature films until the beginning of the 40s. Few have survived.

Michelet, Michel (1899–*).
Russian-born French composer.
Voice in the Wind 44. The Hairy Ape 44. Diary of a Chambermaid 46. Siren of Atlantis 46. Outpost in Morocco 49. Fort Algiers 53. Captain Sinbad 63.

Michell, Keith (1926–).
Australian leading man, on British stage and screen from the mid-50s.
True as a Turtle 57. Dangerous Exile 57. The Gypsy and the Gentleman 58. *The Hellfire Club* 61. All Night Long 62. Seven Seas to Calais 63. Prudence and the Pill 68. House of Cards 68. The Executioner 70. *Henry VIII and His Six Wives* 72. Moments 73. The Story of Jacob and Joseph (TV) 74. The Story of David 76. The Day Christ Died (TV) 79. Grendel Grendel Grendel 82. My Brother Tom (TV) 87. The Deceivers 88. The Prince and the Pauper (as Henry VIII) (TV) 96, etc.

Michelson, Harold (1920–).
American production designer and art director. Born in New York City, he began at Columbia Pictures in the late 40s and also worked at other studios, including Warner, Paramount, MGM, Twentieth Century-Fox, and Universal.
Pretty Poison 68. Catch 22 70. Johnny Got His Gun 71. Mame 74. Star Trek – The Motion Picture (AAN) 79. Can't Stop the Music 80. Mommie Dearest 81. Terms of Endearment (AAN) 83. Spaceballs 87. Planes, Trains and Automobiles 87. Dick Tracy (AAN) 90. Intersection 94, etc.

Michener, James A. (1907–1997).
Best-selling American novelist of adventure epics and historical blockbusters. Born in New York City, he was an orphan adopted by Quakers and brought up in Doylestown, Pennsylvania. He was a teacher before turning to writing about his wartime experiences in *Tales of the South Pacific*, which won a Pulitzer Prize and was turned into a musical by Richard RODGERS and Oscar HAMMERSTEIN. Over the years, his books grew vaster in size and subject-matter. A noted philanthropist, he gave away many millions of dollars, $24m in 1996 alone. Died of kidney failure after discontinuing dialysis treatment. Married three times.
❝ I'm not a stylist. There are a whole lot of things I'm not good at. I'm not hard in dialogue; I don't have that wonderful crispness. I don't think I'm good at psychology. But what I can do is put a good narrative together and hold the reader's interest. – J.A.M.

Middlemass, Frank (1919–).
English character actor, on stage from 1948. He took over the role of Dan Archer in the long-running BBC Radio rural soap opera *The Archers*.
Otley 68. Frankenstein Must Be Destroyed 69. Say Hello to Yesterday 70. Madame Sin 72. The Gangster Show (TV) 72. Barry Lyndon 75. The Island 80. King Lear (as the Fool, TV) 82. The River 84. The Invisible Man (TV) 84, etc.
TV series: Heartbeat 92–95. As Time Goes By 92–95.

Middleton, Charles (1874–1949).
American character actor usually in villainous roles; especially remembered as Ming the Merciless in the Flash Gordon serials.
Mystery Ranch 32. Mrs Wiggs of the Cabbage Patch 34. Kentucky 39. The Grapes of Wrath 40. Our Vines Have Tender Grapes 45. The Black Arrow 49, many others.

Middleton, Guy (1906–1973) (Guy Middleton-Powell).
Hearty-type British light character actor, in films as amiable idiot or gay Lothario from the early 30s after Stock Exchange career.
A Woman Alone 32. Fame 34. *Keep Fit* 37. *French Without Tears* 39. Dangerous Moonlight 40. The Demi-Paradise 43. Champagne Charlie 44. The Rake's Progress 45. The Captive Heart 46. One Night with You 48. The Happiest Days of Your Life 49. Never Look Back 52. Albert RN 53. The Belles of St Trinian's 54. The Passionate Summer 58. The Waltz of the Toreadors 62. The Magic Christian 70, etc.

Middleton, Noelle (1926–).
British leading lady of the 50s.
Carrington V.C. 55. John and Julie 55. Three Men in a Boat 56. The Iron Petticoat 56. The Vicious Circle 57, etc.

Middleton, Ray (1908–1984).
American actor-singer.
Gangs of Chicago 40. Lady For A Night 41. The Girl From Alaska 42. I Dream of Jeannie 52. Jubilee Trail 54. The Road To Denver 55, etc.

Middleton, Robert (1911–1977) (Samuel G. Messer).
Weighty American character actor usually cast as villain.
The Silver Chalice 55. The Big Combo 55. The Desperate Hours 55. The Court Jester 55. The Friendly Persuasion 56. The Tarnished Angels 58. Career 59. Gold of the Seven Saints 61. For Those Who Think Young 64. Big Hand for a Little Lady 66. Which Way to the Front? 71, many others.
TV series: The Monroes 66–67.

Midkiff, Dale (1959–).
American leading actor.
Streetwalkin' 85. Nightmare Weekend 86. Elvis and Me (as Elvis Presley) (TV) 88. Pet Sematary 89. Blackmail (TV) 91. Love Potion 9 92. Toothless 97. Any Place but Home (TV) 97, etc.
TV series: Dream Street 89.

Midler, Bette (1945–).
Diminutive but brassy and very vulgar American entertainer.
Autobiography: 1980, *A View from a Broad*.
■ Hawaii 65. The Rose (AAN) 79. Divine Madness (concert) 80. Jinxed 82. Down and Out in Beverly Hills 85. Ruthless People 86. Outrageous Fortune 87. Big Business 88. Oliver & Company (voice) 88. Beaches 88. Stella 90. Scenes from a Mall 91. For the Boys (& p) (AAN) 91. Hocus Pocus 93. Gypsy (TV) 93. Get Shorty 95. First Wives Club 96. That Old Feeling 97.
❝ I wouldn't say I invented tack, but I definitely brought it to its present high popularity. – B.M.
Underneath all this drag I'm really a librarian, you know. – B.M.
In Hawaii I was the chief chunker in a pineapple canning factory. I used to come home smelling like a compote. – B.M.
I do have my standards. They're low, but I have them. – B.M.

Mifune, Toshiro (1920–1997).
Versatile Japanese actor with a ferocious style, seen in many films by Kurosawa and others.
The Drunken Angel 48. The Stray Dog 49. *Rashomon* 50. *Seven Samurai* 54. The Lower Depths 57. *Throne of Blood* 57. The Hidden Fortress 58. The Bad Sleep Well 59. *Yojimbo* 61. Red Beard 64. The Lost World of Sinbad 64. Grand Prix (US) 66. Rebellion 67. Hell in the Pacific (US) 68. Red Sun 71. Paper Tiger 75. Midway 76. 1941 79. Winter Kills 79. The Bushido Blade 80. Inchon 80. The Challenge 82. Inchon 82. Seiha 84. Taketori Monogatari 87. Shogun Mayeda 90. Shadow of the Wolf 93. Agaguk/Shadow of the Wolf 93. Picture Bride (US) 94, etc.
AS DIRECTOR: Legacy of the Five Hundred Thousand 63.

Mihalka, George (1952–).
Hungarian-born director, resident in Canada.
My Bloody Valentine 81. Pick-up Summer 81. Scandale 82. Eternal Evil 87. Office Party 88. La Florida 93. Relative Fear 94. L'Homme Idéal 96, etc.

Mikhalkov, Nikita (1945–) (Nikita Mikhalkov-Konchalovsky).
Russian director and screenwriter, a former actor. He is the brother of director Andrei KONCHALOVSKY. *Burnt by the Sun* shared the Grand Jury prize at the 1994 Cannes Film Festival.
The Red Tent (a) 71. A Slave of Love 76. An Unfinished Piece for Mechanical Piano 76. Oblomov 79. Family Relations/Rodnia 83. Station for Two/Vokzal Dla Dvoish 83. Without Witnesses/Bez Svidetelei 83. Dark Eyes/Oci Ciornie 87. Urga 90. Anna 6–18 94. Burnt by the Sun (a, wd) (AA) 94. The Barber of Siberia 98, etc.

Milano, Alyssa (1972–).
American actress, on screen from childhood.
Old Enough 83. Commando 85. Where the Day Takes You 91. Candles in the Dark (TV) 93. Double Dragon 94. Fear 96. Glory Daze 96. Hugo Pool 97. Body Count 97, etc.
TV series: Who's the Boss (as Samantha Micelli) 84–92. Charmed 98– .

Milchan, Arnon (1944–).
Israeli-born producer in Hollywood. Head of New Regency Productions, a company in which Twentieth Century-Fox, Australian media mogul Kerry Packer and Samsung have a financial interest. It also has a stake in Puma, the sporting goods company, records and television (the series *Michael Hayes*).
Black Joy 77. The Medusa Touch 78. The King of Comedy 83. Once upon a Time in America 84. Brazil 85. Man on Fire 86. Legend 86. Who's Harry Crumb? 89. The War of the Roses 89. The Adventures of Baron Munchausen 89. Pretty Woman 90. The Power of One 91. Memoirs of an Invisible Man 91. The Mambo Kings 92. Made in America 93. Second Best 93. The New Age 93. Striking Distance 93. Six Degrees of Separation 93. The Client 94. Copycat 95. A Time to Kill 96. The Sunchaser 96. The Mirror Has Two Faces 96. *LA Confidential* (AAN) 97. The Negotiator 98, etc.

Miles, Sir Bernard (1907–1991) (Lord Miles).
British actor specializing in slow-speaking country-folk and other ruminating types. An ex-schoolmaster, on stage from 1930. Founder of London's Mermaid Theatre (1959).
Channel Crossing 32. Quiet Wedding 40. *In Which We Serve* 42. Tawny Pipit (& co-w and d) 44. Carnival 46. *Great Expectations* 46. Nicholas Nickleby 47. The Guinea Pig 48. Chance of a Lifetime (& wd, p) 49. Never Let Me Go 53. The Man Who Knew Too Much 56. Moby Dick 56. *The Smallest Show on Earth* 57. Tom Thumb 58. Sapphire 59. *Heavens Above* 63. Run Wild Run Free 69, etc.

Miles, Christopher (1939–).
British director, brother of Sarah MILES.
Six-Sided Triangle 64. Up Jumped a Swagman 65. *The Virgin and the Gypsy* 70. Time for Loving 71. The Maids 74. That Lucky Touch 75. Alternative 3 (TV) 78. Priest of Love 81. Daley's Decathlon (TV) 82. The Marathon (TV) 83. Aphrodisiac (TV) 84. Lord Elgin and Some Stones of No Value (TV) 85. Clandestine Marriage 99, etc.

Miles, Joanna (1949–).
American leading lady of the 70s.
Butterfield 8 60. Born Innocent 74. Bug 75. The Ultimate Warrior 75. Cross Creek 83. Blackout 88. Right to Die (TV) 87. Rosencrantz and

Guildenstern Are Dead 91. Judge Dredd 95, etc.

Miles, Peter (1938–) (Gerald Perreau).
American child actor of the 40s, brother of Gigi Perreau. As Richard Miles, he later became a writer, notably of *That Cold Day in the Park* (1968) based on his own novel.
Passage to Marseilles 44. The Red Pony 48. Roseanna McCoy 50. Quo Vadis 51, etc.

Miles, Sarah (1941–).
Vivacious leading British actress, from the stage, who became a star with her film debut, playing a schoolgirl. Married writer and director Robert Bolt twice. Her lovers included actors Sir Laurence Olivier, James Fox, Nicol Williamson and Julian Glover.
Autobiographies: 1992, *A Right Royal Bastard*. 1994, *Serves Me Right*. 1996, *A Bolt from the Blue*.
■ *Term of Trial* 62. The Servant 63. The Ceremony 64. Those Magnificent Men in Their Flying Machines 65. I Was Happy Here 65. Blow Up 66. *Ryan's Daughter* (AAN) 70. *Lady Caroline Lamb* 72. The Hireling 73. The Man Who Loved Cat Dancing 73. Great Expectations (TV) 75. Dynasty (TV) 76. The Sailor Who Fell from Grace with the Sea 76. The Big Sleep 78. Priest of Love 81. Venom 82. Ordeal by Innocence 84. Steaming 84. Harem (TV) 86. Hope and Glory 87. White Mischief 87. The Touch 92.
❝ I have been mocked and ridiculed all my life. – S.M.
Filming is a frustrating unfulfilling process, only made bearable by those few minutes, five maybe, of genuine creativity between 'Action!' and 'Cut!' – S.M.

Miles, Sylvia (1926–).
American character actress.
Parrish 61. Midnight Cowboy (AAN) 69. *Heat* 72. Farewell My Lovely (AAN) 75. 92 in the Shade 75. The Great Scout and Cathouse Thursday 76. The Sentinel 77. Zero to Sixty 78. Evil Under the Sun 82. Critical Condition 87. Wall Street 87. Crossing Delancey 88. She-Devil 89. Superstar: The Life and Times of Andy Warhol (doc) 90. Denise Calls Up 95. Rose's 98, etc.

Miles, Vera (1929–) (Vera Ralston).
Dependable American leading lady who came from TV to films.
For Men Only (debut) 52. Charge at Feather River 54. 23 Paces to Baker Street 55. *The Searchers* 56. *The Wrong Man* 57. The FBI Story 59. *Psycho* 60. A Tiger Walks 63. Those Calloways 65. Follow Me, Boys 66. The Spirit is Willing 66. Hell-fighters 68. The Castaway Cowboy 74. One Little Indian 75. Twilight's Last Gleaming 76. The Thoroughbreds 77. Psycho II 83. Into the Night 84. The Hijacking of the Achille Lauro (TV) 89. Separate Lives 94, many others.

Milestone, Lewis (1895–1980) (Levis Milstein).
Veteran American director whose later films never quite matched up to his early achievements. Former editor, in Hollywood from 1918.
■ Seven Sinners 25. The Cave Man 26. The New Klondike 26. *Two Arabian Knights* (AA) 27. The Garden of Eden 28. The Racket 28. Betrayal 29. New York Nights 29. *All Quiet on the Western Front* (AA) 30. *The Front Page* (AAN) 31. Rain 32. *Hallelujah I'm a Bum* 33. The Captain Hates the Sea 34. Paris in Spring 35. Anything Goes 36. *The General Died at Dawn* 36. *Of Mice and Men* 39. Night of Nights 40. Lucky Partners 40. My Life with Caroline (& p) 41. Edge of Darkness 43. North Star 43. The Purple Heart 44. The Strange Love of Martha Ivers 46. *A Walk in the Sun* 46. No Minor Vices 47. Arch of Triumph 48. The Red Pony 48. Halls of Montezuma 51. Kangaroo 52. Les Misérables 52. Melba 53. They Who Dare (GB) 54. The Widow (It.) 55. Pork Chop Hill 59. Ocean's Eleven 61. Mutiny on the Bounty 62.
✪ For a handful of seminal films of the 30s and for devising a fast crabwise tracking shot which was much imitated. *All Quiet on the Western Front*.
❝ His professionalism is as unyielding as it is meaningless. – *Andrew Sarris, 1968*
Ingrid [Bergman] told an incredible story about Lewis Milestone and Joan Crawford, the former picking out a v. handsome extra and saying, 'Miss Crawford, here is your flatterer. This man will be engaged to tell you how wonderful you are in every scene we shoot . . .' – *Kenneth Williams*

Milford, Gene (1903–1992).
American editor.
Ladies Must Play 30. One Night of Love (AAN) 34. Lost Horizon (AA) 37. On the Waterfront (AA) 54. Inchon 82, many others.

Milford, Penelope (1949–).
American actress.
Man on a Swing 75. Valentino 77. Coming Home (AAN) 78. The Last Word 80. Endless Love 81. Take This Job and Shove It 81. The Golden Seal 83. Blood Link 86. Heathers 89. Cold Justice 89. Normal Life 96. Henry: Portrait of a Serial Killer 2: Mask of Sanity 96, etc.

Milhollin, James (1920–1993).
Crumple-faced American character comedian, mostly on TV.
No Time for Sergeants 58. Bon Voyage 62, etc.
TV series: *Grindl* 63.

Milian, Tomas (1937–).
Cuban leading man in Italian action movies, now in the US.
The Bounty Killer 66. Face to Face 67. The Big Gundown 67. Run Man Run 68. Django Kill 68. Apache 70. The Companeros 70. The Counsellor 74. La Luna 78. Winter Kills 79. The Day Christ Died (TV) 79. Salome 85. Cat Chaser 89. Havana 90. Nails 92. Marilyn and Bobby: Her Final Affair (TV) 94. The Burning Season (TV) 94. The Cowboy Way 94. Fools Rush In 97. Amistad 97, etc.
TV series: Frannie's Turn 92.

Milius, John (1944–).
American director.
The Devil's Eight (w only) 68. Evel Knievel (w only) 72. Jeremiah Johnson (w only) 72. Judge Roy Bean (w only) 73. Magnum Force (co-w only) 73. *Dillinger* (& w) 73. The Wind and the Lion (& w) 75. Big Wednesday (& w) 78. Apocalypse Now (co-w) (AAN) 79. Conan the Barbarian (co-w, d) 82. Red Dawn (& co-w) 84. Farewell to the King (wd) 89. Flight of the Intruder (wd) 91. Geronimo: An American Legend (co-w, story) 93. Clear and Present Danger (co-w) 94. Rough Riders (wd) (TV) 97, etc.
❝ It was always my ambition to be a barbarian when I grew up. – *J.M.*

Miljan, John (1893–1960).
American character actor with stage experience; often played the suave villain.
Love Letters 23. The Amateur Gentleman 26. The Painted Lady 29. The Ghost Walks 35. Double Cross 41. The Merry Monahans 44. The Killers 46. Samson and Delilah 50. Pirates of Tripoli 55, etc.

Milland, Ray (1905–1986) (Reginald Truscott-Jones).
Welsh-born light leading man of ready smile and equable disposition; carved a pleasant niche for himself in Hollywood in the 30s, and later surprised many by becoming an actor and director of some repute before stepping on the inevitable downhill slope.
Autobiography: 1976, *Wide-Eyed in Babylon*.
■ The Plaything (GB) 29. The Flying Scotsman (GB) 29. The Informer 30. Passion Flower 30. Goodwin Sands 30. Bachelor Father 31. Just a Gigolo 31. Bought 31. Ambassador Bill 31. Blonde Crazy 31. Polly of the Circus 31. The Man Who Played God 32. Payment Deferred 32. This is the Life (GB) 33. Orders is Orders (GB) 33. Bolero 34. We're Not Dressing 34. Many Happy Returns 34. Menace 34. Charlie Chan in London 34. The Gilded Lily 35. One Hour Late 35. Four Hours to Kill 35. The Glass Key 35. Alias Mary Dow 35. Next Time We Love 36. The Return of Sophie Lang 36. *The Jungle Princess* 36. The Big Broadcast of 1937. Three Smart Girls 37. Wings Over Honolulu 37. Easy Living 37. Ebb Tide 37. Wise Girl 37. Bulldog Drummond Escapes 37. Her Jungle Love 38. Tropic Holiday 38. Men with Wings 38. Say It In French 38. Hotel Imperial 39. *Beau Geste* 39. Everything Happens at Night 39. *French without Tears* (GB) 39. Irene 40. The Doctor Takes a Wife 40. Untamed 40. *Arise My Love* 41. I Wanted Wings 41. Skylark 41. The Lady Has Plans 42. Are Husbands Necessary 42. The Major and the Minor 42. Reap the Wild Wind 42. Star Spangled Rhythm 42. Forever and a Day 43. The Crystal Ball 43. *The Uninvited* 44. Lady in the Dark 44. Till We Meet Again 44. *Ministry of Fear* 44. *The Lost Weekend* (AA) 45. Kitty 45. The Well Groomed Bride 46. California 46. The Imperfect Lady 47. The Trouble with Women 47. Golden Earrings 47. Variety Girl 47. The Big Clock 48. So Evil My Love 48. Sealed Verdict 48. *Alias Nick Beal* 49. It Happens Every Spring 49. A Woman of Distinction 50. A Life of Her Own 50. Copper Canyon 50. Circle of Danger (GB) 51. Night into Morning 51. Rhubarb 51. Close to My Heart 51. Bugles in the Afternoon 52. Something to Live For 52. *The Thief* 52. Jamaica Run 53. Let's Do It Again 53. *Dial M for Murder* 54. A Man Alone (& d) 55. The Girl in the Red Velvet Swing 55. Lisbon (& d) 56. Three Brave Men 57. The River's Edge 57. The Safecracker (& d) (GB) 58. High Flight (GB) 58. The Premature Burial 62. Panic in Year Zero (& d) 62. The Man with X-Ray Eyes 63. The Confession 65. Hostile Witness (& d) (GB) 68. River of Gold (TV) 69. Daughter of the Mind (TV) 69. Love Story 70. Company of Killers (TV) 70. Black Noon (TV) 71. Embassy 72. The Thing with Two Heads 72. Frogs 72. Terror in the Wax Museum 73. The House in Nightmare Park (GB) 73. Gold 74. The Student Connection 74. The Swiss Conspiracy 75. The Dead Don't Die (TV) 75. Look What Happened to Rosemary's Baby (TV) 76. Oil 76. Ellery Queen (TV) 76. Escape to Witch Mountain 76. Rich Man Poor Man (TV) 76. The Last Tycoon 76. Aces High 76. Cruise into Terror (TV) 77. Mayday at 40,000 Feet (TV) 77. Slaves 77. Testimony of Two Men (TV) 77. The Uncanny 77. Blackout 78. The Darker Side of Terror (TV) 79. Oliver's Story 79. Game for Vultures 79. The Attic 79. Cave In (TV) 79. Survival Run 80. Our Family Business (TV) 81. The Royal Romance of Charles and Diana (TV) 82. Starflight One (TV) 82. The Masks of Death (TV) 84.
TV series: Meet Mr McNutley 53. Markham 59.
✪ For his imperturbable cheerfulness, and for briefly demonstrating that with a different start he might have been an actor or director of stature. *Arise My Love*.

Millar, Gavin (1938–).
British director and film buff.
Cream in My Coffee (TV) 80. Dreamchild 85. Scoop (TV) 87. Tidy Endings (TV) 88. The Most Dangerous Man in the World 88. Danny, the Champion of the World 89. The Dwelling Place (TV) 94. This Could Be the Last Time (TV) 98, etc.

Millar, Sir Ronald (1919–).
English playwright and screenwriter for Ealing Studios and MGM, a former actor who was also a speech writer for three Conservative Prime Ministers: Edward Heath, John Major and Margaret Thatcher, coining the phrase 'the lady's not for turning' for the latter. His MGM scripts were written in collaboration with George Froeschel.
Autobiography: 1993, *A View from the Wings*.
We Dive at Dawn (a) 43. Frieda (co-w from his play) 47. So Evil My Love (co-w) 48. Saraband for Dead Lovers (co-w) 48. Train of Events (co-w) 49. The Miniver Story (co-w) 50. The Unknown Man (co-w) 51. Scaramouche (co-w) 52. Never Let Me Go (co-w) 53. Rose Marie (co-w) 54. Betrayed (co-w) 54, etc.

Millar, Stuart (1929–).
American producer.
The Young Stranger 57. Stage Struck 58. The Young Doctors 61. I Could Go On Singing 63. The Best Man 64. Paper Lion 68. When the Legends Die (& d) 72. Rooster Cogburn (d only) 75. Vital Signs (d) (TV) 86. The O'Connors (d) (TV) 89, etc.

Miller, Alice Duer (1874–1942).
American writer who collaborated on several film scripts and whose poem 'The White Cliffs of Dover' was filmed in 1944.
Manslaughter 30. Honey 30. And One Was Beautiful 40. Gowns by Roberta (as Roberta) 35 and (as Lovely to Look At) 52.

Miller, Ann (1919–) (Lucy Ann Collier).
Long-legged American dancer, in films from mid-30s.
Autobiography: 1974, *Miller's High Life*.
New Faces of 1937. *You Can't Take It With You* 38. Go West, Young Lady 41. *Reveille with Beverly* 43. Jam Session 44. Eve Knew Her Apples 45. Easter Parade 48. *On the Town* 49. Two Tickets to Broadway 51. *Kiss Me Kate* 53. The Opposite Sex 56. That's Entertainment! III 94, etc.
❝ I have worked like a dog all my life, honey. Dancing, as Fred Astaire said, is next to ditch-digging. You sweat and you slave and the audience doesn't think you have a brain in your head. – A.M. *in 1979 interview*

Miller, Arthur (1915–).
American playwright whose work has been adapted for the cinema. Married to Marilyn MONROE 1956–61.
All My Sons 48. Death of a Salesman 52. The Witches of Salem 57. A View from the Bridge 62. After the Fall 69. The Price 69. An Enemy of the People 78. All My Sons (TV) 87. Clara (TV) 91, etc.
SCREENPLAYS: The Story of G.I. Joe 45. The Misfits 60. The Hook 75. Everybody Wins 90. Broken Glass (TV) 96. *The Crucible* (AAN) 96, etc.
❝ It can take a long time to accept that celebrity is a kind of loneliness. – A.M.

Miller, Arthur (1895–1970).
Distinguished American cinematographer.
SELECTED SILENT FILMS: At Bay 15. The Iron Heart 17. The Profiteers 19. His House in Order 20. Kick In 22. The Cheat 23. The Coming of Amos 24. The Clinging Vine 26. The Fighting Eagle 28. The Spieler 29, etc.
■ SOUND FILMS: Oh Yeah 30. Sailor's Holiday 30. Strange Cargo 30. The Lady of Scandal 30. Officer O'Brien 30. The Truth about Youth 30. Behind the Make Up 30. Father's Son 30. Bad Company 31. Panama Flo 32. Big Shot 32. The Young Bride 32. Breach of Promise 32. Me and My Gal 32. Okay America 32. Sailor's Luck 33. Hold Me Tight 33. The Man Who Dared 33. The Last Trail 33. The Mad Game 33. My Weakness 33. Bottoms Up 34. Ever Since Eve 34. Handy Andy 34. Love Time 34. The White Parade 34. Bright Eyes 34. The Little Colonel 35. It's a Small World 35. Black Sheep 35. Welcome Home 35. Paddy O'Day 35. White Fang 36. 36 Hours to Kill 36. Pigskin Parade 36. Stowaway 36. *Wee Willie Winkie* 37. Heidi 37. The Baroness and the Butler 38. Rebecca of Sunnybrook Farm 38. Little Miss Broadway 38. Submarine Patrol 38. *The Little Princess* 39. Susannah of the Mounties 39. Here I Am a Stranger 39. *The Rains Came* 39. *The Blue Bird* 40. Johnny Apollo 40. On Their Own 40. *The Mark of Zorro* 40. Brigham Young 40. *Tobacco Road* 41. The Men in Her Life 41. Man Hunt 41. *How Green was My Valley* (AA) 41. *This Above All* 42. Iceland 42. The Moon Is Down 43. The Immortal Sergeant 43. The Ox Bow Incident 43. *The Song of Bernadette* (AA) 43. The Purple Heart 44. The Keys of the Kingdom 45. A Royal Scandal 45. Dragonwyck 46. *Anna and the King of Siam* 46. The Razor's Edge 46. Gentleman's Agreement 47. The Walls of Jericho 48. A Letter to Three Wives 49. Whirlpool 49. *The Gunfighter* 50. The Prowler 51.
✪ For a long succession of Hollywood's most lustrous black-and-white images. *The Rains Came*.
❝ The basic principle I have had in making pictures was to make them look like real life, and then emphasise the visuals slightly. – A.M.
I was never a soft focus man – I liked crisp, sharp, solid images. – A.M.

Miller, Claude (1942–).
French director and screenwriter who also worked as a producer on many of François TRUFFAUT's films.
Juliet dans Paris 67. La Question Ordinaire 70. Camille ou la Comédie Catastrophique 71. La Meilleure Façon de Marcher 76. Dîtes-lui Que Je l'Aime 77. Garde à Vue 81. Mortelle Randonnée 83. L'Effrontée 85. La Petite Voleuse 88. L'Accompagnatrice 92. The Smile/Le Sourire 94. Class Trip/La Classe de Neige 98, etc.

Miller, Colleen (1932–).
American leading lady.
The Las Vegas Story 52. The Purple Mask 55. Man with a Shadow 57. Step Down to Terror 59. Gunfight at Comanche Creek 63, etc.

Miller, David (1909–1992).
American director, formerly editor, in Hollywood from 1930.
Billy the Kid 41. Sunday Punch 42. Flying Tigers 43. Top o' the Morning 49. Love Happy 50. Our Very Own 51. Saturday's Hero 52. *Sudden Fear* 53. Beautiful Stranger 54. Diane 55. The Opposite Sex 56. The Story of Esther Costello 57. Happy Anniversary 59. Midnight Lace 60. Back Street 61.

Lonely Are the Brave 62. Captain Newman 63. Hammerhead (GB) 68. Hail Hero 69. Executive Action 73. Bittersweet Love 76, etc.

Miller, Dennis (1953–).
American stand-up comedian and actor, also a TV chat show host; he came to notice on the TV series *Saturday Night Live*.
Madhouse 90. Disclosure 94. The Net 95. Tales from the Crypt Presents Bordello of Blood 96, etc.
TV series: Saturday Night Live 85–91. Dennis Miller Live 94.

Miller, Denny (1934–).
Athletic American actor who had a shot at playing Tarzan.
Tarzan the Ape Man 59. Love in a Goldfish Bowl 61. The Party 68. Buck and the Preacher 72. The Gravy Train 74. The Norsemen 78, etc.
TV series: Wagon Train 61–64. Mona McCluskey 65–66.

Miller, Dick (1928–).
American actor, a regular in the films of Roger Corman and in other low-budget horror movies.
Apache Woman 55. The Undead 56. Not of This Earth 57. Thunder over Hawaii 57. A Bucket of Blood 59. The Terror 63. Ski Party 65. The Dirty Dozen 67. The Grissom Gang 71. Ulzana's Raid 72. Big Bad Mama 74. Hustle 75. Cannonball 76. Piranha 78. Used Cars 80. Heartbeeps 81. The Howling 81. Heart Like a Wheel 83. Gremlins 84. After Hours 85. Explorers 85. Chopping Mall 86. Night of the Creeps 86. Project X 87. Innerspace 87. Far from Home 89. Gremlins 2: The New Batch 90. Evil Toons 91. The Stalker 92. Matinee 93. Batman: Mask of the Phantasm (voice) 94. Mona Must Die 94. Tales from the Crypt Presents Demon Knight 95, etc.

Miller, George (1943–).
Scottish-born director, in Australia as a child, from television.
The Man from Snowy River 81. The Aviator 84. Anzacs (TV) 85. Cool Change 86. Les Patterson Saves the World 87. The Far Country (TV) 87. The Christmas Visitor (TV) 87. Neverending Story II 90. Frozen Assets (US) 91. Gross Misconduct 93. Andre 94. Zeus and Roxanne 97, etc.

Miller, George (1945–).
Australian director, a former doctor.
Mad Max 79. Mad Max 2: The Road Warrior 81. Twilight Zone (part) 83. Mad Max Beyond Thunderdome 85. The Witches of Eastwick 87. Lorenzo's Oil 92. *Babe* (p, co-w) (AANp, AANw) 95. Babe: Pig in the City (p, co-w, d) 98, etc.

Miller, Glenn (1904–1944).
American bandleader and composer, whose 'new sound' was immensely popular during World War II.
Appeared in *Orchestra Wives* 42. *Sun Valley Serenade* 42. Was impersonated by James Stewart in *The Glenn Miller Story* 53.

Miller, Henry (1891–1980).
American novelist and writer whose autobiographical and sexually explicit novels were banned in the 30s. His life, and his triangular relationship with his wife June and writer Anais Nin, have been the subject of two films: *Henry and June* 89 and *The Room of Words* 90. Of his novels, *The Tropic of Cancer* was filmed in 1969 and *Quiet Days in Clichy* in 1974 and 1990.

Miller, Jason (1939–).
American playwright who turned actor.
The Exorcist (AAN) 74. The Nickel Ride 76. A Home of Our Own (TV) 76. F. Scott Fitzgerald in Hollywood (TV) 76. The Dain Curse (TV) 78. The Devil's Advocate 79. The Ninth Configuration 80. That Championship Season (oa, d) 82. A Touch of Scandal (TV) 84. The Exorcist III 90. Rudy 93. Murdered Innocence 94. Mommy 95, etc.

Miller, Jonathan (1934–).
English writer and director, a former comic performer. Born in London, he studied at Cambridge University and at University College Hospital, London, gaining fame as one of the writers and performers of the early 60s revue *Beyond the Fringe*. Since then, his work has been mainly in the theatre, as an associate director of the National Theatre, artistic director of the Old Vic in the late 80s, and as a director of opera.
■ One Way Pendulum (a only) 65. Alice in Wonderland (TV) 67. Take A Girl Like You 70.
TV series: The Body in Question 78. Reflection 98.

Miller, Jonny Lee (1974–) (Jonathan Lee).
English actor, the son of actor Bernard Lee. He is also a founder member of the production company Natural Nylon with actors Jude Law, Sadie Frost, Ewan McGregor and Sean Pertwee. Married actress Angelina Jolie.
Prime Suspect 3 (TV) 93. Meat (TV) 94. Hackers 95. Trainspotting 96. Larry McMurty's Dead Man's Walk (TV) 96. *Regeneration* 97. Afterglow 97. Plunkett and Macleane 98. Mansfield Park 99, etc.

Miller, Mandy (1944–).
British child star.
The Man in the White Suit 51. *Mandy* 52. Dance Little Lady 54. A Child in the House 56. The Secret 57. The Snorkel 58, etc.

Miller, Marilyn (1898–1936) (Mary Ellen Reynolds).
American dancing and singing star of Broadway musicals in the 20s. She was impersonated by June Haver in a biopic, *Look for the Silver Lining* 49, and by Judy Garland in *Till the Clouds Roll By* 46.
Sally 30. Sunny 31. Her Majesty Love 32.

Miller, Martin (1899–1969) (Rudolph Muller).
Czechoslovakian character actor active in Britain from the late 30s.
Squadron Leader X 40. The Huggetts Abroad 51. Front Page Story 53. Libel 60. 55 Days at Peking 62. Children of the Damned 64. Up Jumped a Swagman 65, many others.

Miller, Marvin (1913–1985) (M. Mueller).
American tough-guy supporting actor who represented menaces of various nations.
Johnny Angel 45. Intrigue 47. The High Window 47. Off Limits 53. The Shanghai Story 54, etc.
TV series: The Millionaire 55–60.

Miller, Max (1895–1963) (Harold Sargent).
Ribald British music-hall comedian ('the Cheeky Chappie'). Starred in several vehicles during the 30s but his style and material had to be considerably toned down for the screen.
■ *The Good Companions* 32. Channel Crossing 32. Friday the Thirteenth 33. Princess Charming 34. Things Are Looking Up 35. *Educated Evans* 36. Get Off My Foot 36. Take It From Me 37. Don't Get Me Wrong 37. Thank Evans 38. Everything Happens to Me 39. The Good Old Days 39. Hoots Mon 40. Asking for Trouble 43.
❝ He was a popular hero more than a comic. He was cheeky because he was a genius. All genius is a cheek. You get away with your nodding little vision and the world holds its breath or applauds. Max took your breath away altogether and we applauded. – *John Osborne*

Miller, Patsy Ruth (1904–1995).
American leading lady of the silent screen, former juvenile player. Retired with the coming of sound and wrote novels and short stories. Married director Tay Garnett and screenwriter John Lee Mahin.
Autobiography: 1988, *My Hollywood – When Both of Us Were Young*.
Judgment 18. Camille 21. The Hunchback of Notre Dame 23. Lorraine of the Lions 24. *So This Is Paris* 26. Why Girls Go Back Home 27. The Hottentot 28. Lonely Wives 31. Quebec 51, etc.

Miller, Penelope Ann (1964–).
American actress.
Adventures in Babysitting/A Night on the Town 87. Big Top Pee-Wee 88. Biloxi Blues 88. Miles from Home 88. Dead-Bang 89. Awakenings 90. Downtown 90. The Freshman 90. Kindergarten Cop 90. Other People's Money 91. Year of the Comet 92. The Gun in Betty Lou's Handbag 92. Chaplin 92. Carlito's Way 93. The Shadow 94. The Relic 96. The Last Don (TV) 97. Rhapsody in Bloom 98, etc.

Miller, Robert Ellis (1927–).
American director, from TV.
■ Any Wednesday 66. Sweet November 68. The Heart Is a Lonely Hunter 68. The Buttercup Chain 70. The Girl from Petrovka 74. The Baltimore Bullet 80. Reuben, Reuben 83. Hawks 88. Brenda Starr 89. Bed and Breakfast 90. Triangle 92.

Miller, Seton I. (1902–1974).
American silent actor (*Brown of Harvard* 26, etc.) who turned into one of Hollywood's most prolific screenwriters.
Dawn Patrol 30. The Criminal Code (AAN) 31. *Scarface* 32. G-Men 35. *The Adventures of Robin Hood* 38. The Sea Hawk 40. *Here Comes Mr Jordan* (AA) 41. The Black Swan 42. The Ministry of Fear 43. Two Years Before the Mast (& p) 46. Istanbul 57, etc.

Miller, Sidney (1916–).
American actor, composer and director who began in films as a child and also worked in vaudeville. He directed many TV sitcoms, such as *Get Smart*, and partnered Donald O'Connor in a nightclub act and on his TV show from 1954 to 1955.
Mayor of Hell (a) 33. Dinky (a) 35. Boys Town (a) 38. Men of Boys Town (a) 41. Chip off the Old Block (s) 44. Babes on Swing Street (s) 44. Moonlight and Cactus (s) 44. This Is the Life (s) 44. Patrick the Great (s) 45. On Stage, Everybody (s) 45. Are You with It? (s) 48. Walking My Baby Back Home (a) 53. Get Yourself a College Girl (d) 64. Which Way to the Front? (as Adolf Hitler) 70. Everything You Wanted to Know about Sex (But Were Afraid to Ask) (a) 72. Star 80 (a) 83, etc.

Miller, Walter C. (1892–1940).
American leading man of the D. W. Griffith company.
The Informer 12. A Beggar Prince of India 14. The Marble Heart 16. Thin Ice 19. The Tie That Binds 23. Manhattan Knights 28. Three Smart Girls 36. Johnny Apollo 40, many others.
~Not to be confused with W. Christie Miller (1843–1922) who played elderly roles for Griffith.

Millhauser, Bertram (1892–1958).
American screenwriter mainly engaged on second features, some of them better than average.
The Garden Murder Case 36. Sherlock Holmes in Washington 42 (and others in this series including Pearl of Death 44). The Invisible Man's Revenge 44. Patrick the Great 45. Walk a Crooked Mile 48. Tokyo Joe 48, etc.

Millican, James (1910–1955).
American general-purpose actor, often in low-budget westerns.
The Remarkable Andrew 42. Bring on the Girls 44. Hazard 47. Rogues' Regiment 48. Carson City 52. The Man from Laramie 55, etc.

Millichip, Roy (1930–).
British independent producer.
The Uncle 65. I Was Happy Here 66. A Nice Girl Like Me 69. Joseph Andrews 76, etc.

Milligan, Spike (1918–).
Irish comedian and arch-goon of stage, TV and radio.
The Case of the Mukkinese Battlehorn 56. Watch Your Stern 60. Suspect 60. Invasion Quartet 61. Postman's Knock 62. The Magic Christian 70. Rentadick 72. Alice's Adventures in Wonderland 72. Adolf Hitler, My Part in His Downfall (& oa) 72. Digby, the Biggest Dog in the World 73. The Three Musketeers 74. The Great McGonagall 74. A Man About the House 76. The Last Remake of Beau Geste 77. The Life of Brian 79. Yellowbeard 83, etc.
TV series: Idiot's Weekly 56. A Show Called Fred 56. Son of Fred 57. Milligan at Large 61. Q5 69. Curry and Chips 69. Oh in Colour 72. Q6-Q9 75–80.
❝ The fondest memory I have is not really of the Goons. It is of a girl called Julia with enormous breasts. – S.M.

Mills, Donna (1945–).
American leading lady, mostly on TV.
The Incident 67. Play Misty for Me 71. Haunts of the Very Rich (TV) 72. Night of Terror (TV) 72. The Bait (TV) 73. Live Again Die Again (TV) 74. Who Is the Black Dahlia? (TV) 75. Smash-Up on Interstate Five (TV) 76. Curse of the Black Widow (TV) 76. The Hunted Lady (TV) 77. Superdome (TV) 78. Bare Essence (TV) 83. He's Not Your Son (TV) 84. False Arrest (TV) 91, etc.

Mills, Hayley (1946–).
British actress who shot to fame as a tomboy child; daughter of John Mills. She was married to director Roy Boulting (1971–76) and has a son by actor Leigh Lawson. In recent years, she has concentrated on stage performance, including long tours of Australia and the USA in the musical *The King and I*.
■ *Tiger Bay* 59. *Pollyanna* (US) (special AA as best child actress) 60. *The Parent Trap* (US) 61. Whistle Down the Wind 61. Summer Magic (US) 62. In Search of the Castaways 63. The Chalk Garden 64. The Moonspinners 65. The Truth about Spring 65. That Darn Cat 65. Sky West and Crooked 66. The Trouble with Angels 66. The Family Way 66. Pretty Polly 67. Twisted Nerve 68. Take a Girl Like You 70. Forbush and the Penguins 71. Endless Night 72. Deadly Strangers 75. What Changed Charley Farthing? 75. The Kingfisher Caper 75. The Flame Trees of Thika (TV) 81. Parent Trap II (TV) 86. Appointment with Death 88. Back Home (TV) 90.

Mills, Hugh (c. 1913–1971).
British screenwriter.
Blanche Fury 47. Blackmailed (co-w) 50. Knave of Hearts 52. The House by the Lake 54. Prudence and the Pill 68, etc.

Mills, Sir John (1908–) (Lewis Ernest Mills).
Popular British leading actor with musical comedy experience; overcame short stature to become a useful stiff-upper-lip type in the 40s, and later a character actor of some versatility.
Autobiography: 1980, *Up in the Clouds, Gentlemen Please*.
■ The Midshipmaid 32. Britannia of Billingsgate 33. The Ghost Camera 33. River Wolves 34. A Political Party 34. *Those Were the Days* 34. The Lash 34. Blind Justice 34. Doctor's Orders 34. Royal Cavalcade 35. Forever England 35. Charing Cross Road 35. Car of Dreams 35. First Offence 36. Tudor Rose 36. OHMS 37. The Green Cockatoo 37. Goodbye Mr Chips 39. Old Bill and Son 40. *Cottage to Let* 41. The Black Sheep of Whitehall 41. The Big Blockade 42. The Young Mr Pitt 42. *In Which We Serve* 42. We Dive at Dawn 43. This Happy Breed 44. *Waterloo Road* 44. *The Way to the Stars* 45. *Great Expectations* 46. So Well Remembered 47. *The October Man* 47. *Scott of the Antarctic* 48. *The History of Mr Polly* (& p) 49. The Rocking Horse Winner 50. Morning Departure 50. Mr Denning Drives North 51. The Gentle Gunman 52. The Long Memory 52. *Hobson's Choice* 54. The Colditz Story 54. The End of the Affair 54. Above Us the Waves 55. Escapade 55. It's Great to Be Young 56. The Baby and the Battleship 56. War and Peace 56. Around the World in 80 Days 56. *Town On Trial* 57. Vicious Circle 57. Dunkirk 58. I Was Monty's Double 58. Ice Cold in Alex 58. *Tiger Bay* 59. Summer of the Seventeenth Doll 60. *Tunes of Glory* 60. *The Swiss Family Robinson* (US) 61. Flame in the Streets 61. The Singer Not the Song 61. The Valiant 62. Tiara Tahiti 62. The Chalk Garden 63. The Truth about Spring 64. Operation Crossbow 65. *Sky West and Crooked* (d only) 65. King Rat (US) 66. *The Wrong Box* 66. The Family Way 66. Africa Texas Style (US) 67. Chuka (US) 67. Oh What a Lovely War 69. Run Wild Run Free 69. Emma Hamilton (Ger.) 69. A Black Veil for Lisa 69. *Ryan's Daughter* (AA) 71. Dulcima 71. Young Winston 72. Lady Caroline Lamb 72. Oklahoma Crude 73. The Human Factor 76. Trial by Combat 76. The Devil's Advocate 77. The Big Sleep 78. The 39 Steps 78. Dr Strange (TV) 78. Zulu Dawn 79. Gandhi 82. Sahara 83. Masks of Death (TV) 84. A Woman of Substance (TV) 85. Murder with Mirrors (TV) 85. Who's That Girl? 87. Harnessing Peacocks (TV) 93. Deadly Advice 94. Martin Chuzzlewit (TV) 94. Hamlet 96.
TV series: Dundee and the Culhane 67. Zoo Gang 73. Quatermass 79. Young at Heart 80–81.
✪ For being so thoroughly reliable. *Great Expectations*.

Mills, Juliet (1941–).
British leading lady, daughter of John Mills and sister of Hayley. Married actor Maxwell Caulfield.
No My Darling Daughter 61. Twice Round the Daffodils 62. Nurse on Wheels 63. Carry on Jack 64. The Rare Breed (US) 66. Oh What a Lovely War 69. Avanti 72. QB VII (TV) 74. Beyond the Door 75. Barnaby and Me 77. Alexander: The

Other Side of Dawn (TV) 77. The Cracker Factory (TV) 79. Waxwork 2: Lost in Time 91, etc.
TV series: Nanny and the Professor 70–71.

Milne, A(lan) A(lexander) (1882–1956).
British playwright, novelist, humorous writer and author of *Winnie the Pooh* and *The House at Pooh Corner*. He was briefly associated with the British production company MINERVA FILMS.
Autobiography: 1939, *It's Too Late Now*.
Biography: 1990, *A. A. Milne* by Ann Thwaite.
£5 Reward (w) 20. Bookworms (w) 20. The Bump (w) 20. Twice Two (w) 20. Mr Pim Passes By (oa) 21. The Birds of Prey (from The Fourth Wall) (oa) 30. The Perfect Alibi (oa) 31. Michael and Mary (oa) 31. Where Sinners Meet (from Dover Road) (oa) 34. Four Day's Wonder (oa) 37. Winnie the Pooh and the Honey Tree (oa) 65, etc.
❝ At a cinema half a dozen sentences were put on the screen, and one had to wait for minutes before the crowd had assimilated them. Minutes! It seemed like hours sometimes. What were their brains doing all that time? They had to say things over and over again to themselves before any meaning emerged. How hellish to be born with a brain like that! – A.A.M.

Milner, Martin (1927–).
American general-purpose actor.
Life with Father (debut) 47. Our Very Own 50. I Want You 52. Pete Kelly's Blues 55. The Sweet Smell of Success 57. Marjorie Morningstar 58. Thirteen Ghosts 60. Sullivan's County 67. Valley of the Dolls 67. Columbo: Murder by the Book (TV) 71. Hurricane (TV) 74. Flood! (TV) 76. Nashville Beat 89, etc.
TV series: The Trouble With Father 53–55. The Life of Riley 56–57. Route 66 60–63. Adam 12 68–75. The Swiss Family Robinson 75.

Milner, Victor (1893–1972).
Distinguished American cinematographer, with Paramount for many years.
Hiawatha 14. The Velvet Hand 18. Haunting Shadows 20. The Cave Girl 22. Thy Name is Woman 24. Lady of the Harem 26. Rolled Stockings 27. Wolf of Wall Street 29. *The Love Parade* 29. Monte Carlo 30. Daughter of the Dragon 31. *Trouble in Paradise* 32. Song of Songs 33. Design for Living 33. *Cleopatra* (AA) 34. The Crusades 35. *The General Died at Dawn* 36. The Plainsman 36. Artists and Models 37. The Buccaneer (AAN) 39. Union Pacific 39. The Great Victor Herbert 39. Northwest Mounted Police 40. Christmas in July 40. The Lady Eve 41. The Monster and the Girl 41. The Palm Beach Story 42. Hostages 43. The Story of Dr Wassell 44. The Mummy's Curse 44. The Strange Love of Martha Ivers 46. The Other Love 47. Unfaithfully Yours 48. The Furies 50. September Affair 50. *Carrie* 51. Jeopardy 53, many others.

Milton, Billy (1905–1989).
British light actor of the 30s, latterly in small parts. Also singer, pianist and composer.
Autobiography: 1976, *Milton's Paradise Mislaid*.
Young Woodley 30. Three Men in a Boat 33. Someone at the Door 36. Aren't Men Beasts? 37. Yes Madam 39. Who Was Maddox 64. Hot Millions 68. Sweet William 80, etc.

Milton, David.
American art director, mainly for Monogram and Allied Artists (as Monogram became in 1953). At his peak, he was designing more than 25 films a year.
The Ape Man 43. Live Wires 46. Dark Alibi 46. Louisiana 47. The Feathered Serpent 49. Flight to Mars 51. Riot in Cell Block 11 54. The Adventures of Haiji Baba 54. Dino 57. House on Haunted Hill 58. The Bat 59. Hell to Eternity 60. The George Raft Story 61, many more.

Milton, Ernest (1890–1974).
American-born Shakespearean actor with long theatrical history on both sides of the Atlantic. Few film appearances, in small parts.
A Wisp in the Woods 17. The Scarlet Pimpernel 34. Fiddlers Three 44.

Milton, Harry (1900–1965).
British leading man of 30s stage and screen.
■ The King's Cup 33. To Brighton with Gladys 33. King of the Ritz 33. Adventure Limited 34. Pagliacci 36.

Mimieux, Yvette (1942–).
American leading lady signed up for films almost straight from college. She married director Stanley Donen in 1972.
The Time Machine (debut) 60. Where the Boys Are 61. The Four Horsemen of the Apocalypse 62. *The Light in the Piazza* 62. The Wonderful World of the Brothers Grimm 63. Diamondhead 63. Joy in the Morning 65. Monkeys Go Home 66. The Caper of the Golden Bulls 67. Dark of the Sun 67. Three in an Attic 68. Black Noon (TV) 71. Skyjacked 72. The Neptune Factor 73. Hit Lady (& w) (TV) 74. Journey into Fear 75. Jackson County Jail 76. The Black Hole 78. Outside Chance (TV) 78. Brainwash 82, etc.
TV series: The Most Deadly Game 70. Berrengers 85.

Minciotti, Esther (1883–1962).
Italian-American character actress, wife of Silvio Minciotti.
■ House of Strangers 49. Shockproof 49. The Undercover Man 50. Strictly Dishonorable 51. *Marty* 55. Full of Life 56. The Wrong Man 57.

Minciotti, Silvio (1883–1961).
Italian-American character actor.
House of Strangers 49. Deported 49. The Great Caruso 51. Clash by Night 52. Kiss Me Deadly 54. Marty 55, etc.

Mineo, Sal (1939–1976).
Diminutive American actor, on Broadway as a child before going to Hollywood. He was murdered as he returned home after rehearsals for a play.
Six Bridges to Cross (debut) 55. Rebel without a Cause (AAN) 55. Giant 56. Somebody Up There Likes Me 57. Tonka 58. The Gene Krupa Story 60. Exodus (AAN) 60. Escape from Zahrain 62. Cheyenne Autumn 64. The Greatest Story Ever Told 65. Who Killed Teddy Bear? 66. Krakatoa 68. Escape from the Planet of the Apes 71, etc.

Miner, Allen H.
American director.
Ghost Town 55. The Ride Back 57. Black Patch (& p) 57. Chubasco 67, etc.

Miner, Michael.
American screenwriter and director.
Robocop (co-w) 89. Deadly Weapon (wd) 89.

Miner, Steve (1951–).
American director.
Friday the 13th Part 2 81. Friday the 13th Part 3 82. House 86. Soul Man 86. Warlock 89. The Fugitive 90. Wild Hearts Can't Be Broken 91. The Rest of Daniel 92. My Father, the Hero 94. Big Bully 96. Halloween: H20 98, etc.

Minevitch, Borrah (1904–1955).
Russian-American harmonica player who with his Rascals enlivened a few 30s musicals.
One in a Million 36. Love under Fire 37. Rascals 38. Always in My Heart 42, etc.

Minghella, Anthony (1954–).
British director and screenwriter, from the theatre. Born of Italian parents on the Isle of Wight, he taught at the University of Hull before becoming a playwright.
Truly Madly Deeply 91. Mr Wonderful 93. *The English Patient* (wd) (AAd, AANw) 96. The Talented Mr Ripley (wd) 99, etc.
TV series: Storyteller (w) 87.

Ming-liang, Ts'ai.
Taiwanese director.
Rebels of the Neon God 93. Vive l'Amour 94. The Hole 98, etc.

Minnelli, Liza (1946–).
American singer, daughter of Judy Garland; her gamine looks and vibrant voice made her a fashionable figure of the early 70s.
Biography: 1974, *Liza* by James Robert Parish.
■ Charlie Bubbles 67. The Sterile Cuckoo (AAN) 69. Tell Me That You Love Me Junie Moon 70. *Cabaret* (AA) 72. Lucky Lady 76. A Matter of Time 76. New York New York 77. Arthur 81. The Muppets Take Manhattan 84. That's Dancing! 85. Arthur 2: On the Rocks 88. Rent-a-Cop 88. Stepping Out 91. Parallel Lives (TV) 94. The West Side Waltz (TV) 95.
❝ Reality is something you rise above. – L.M.
~She first appeared as a baby in her mother's film *In the Good Old Summertime*.

Minnelli, Vincente (1903–1986).
American director who earned a reputation as a stylist with MGM musicals but whose other output was very variable. Stage experience as art director and producer. The second of Judy Garland's husbands, and the father of Liza Minnelli.
Autobiography: 1974, *I Remember It Well*.
■ *Cabin in the Sky* 43. I Dood It 43. Ziegfeld Follies 44. *Meet Me in St Louis* 44. *The Clock* 44. Yolanda and the Thief 45. Undercurrent 46. The Pirate 47. Madame Bovary 49. *Father of the Bride* 50. Father's Little Dividend 51. *An American in Paris* (AAN) 51. The Bad and the Beautiful 52. The Story of Three Loves (part) 52. *The Band Wagon* 53. The Long, Long Trailer 54. Brigadoon 54. Kismet 55. The Cobweb 55. Lust for Life 56. Tea and Sympathy 56. Designing Woman 57. *Gigi* (AA) 58. The Reluctant Debutante 58. Some Came Running 58. Home from the Hill 59. Bells Are Ringing 60. The Four Horsemen of the Apocalypse 62. Two Weeks in Another Town 62. The Courtship of Eddie's Father 63. Goodbye Charlie 65. The Sandpiper 65. On a Clear Day You Can See Forever 70. A Matter of Time 76.
❝ He believes implicitly in the power of his camera to turn trash into art, and corn into caviar. – *Andrew Sarris, 1968*

Minney, R. J. (1895–1979).
British producer and screenwriter, former journalist, in films since 1934.
AS WRITER: Clive of India 35. Dear Octopus 42. Carve Her Name with Pride 58, many others.
AS PRODUCER: Madonna of the Seven Moons 44. The Wicked Lady 45. The Final Test 53. Carve Her Name with Pride 58, etc.

Minogue, Kylie (1968–).
Diminutive Australian leading actress and singer, in television from the age of 11 and gaining wider recognition as a rebellious teenager on the TV soap opera *Neighbours*; hit recordings followed from 1988. She was romantically linked with actor Jason DONOVAN and singer Michael HUTCHENCE.
The Delinquents 90. Street Fighter 95. Bio-Dome 96.

Minter, George (1911–1966).
British producer-distributor, in films from 1938. Made films for his company, Renown.
The Glass Mountain 48. Tom Brown's Schooldays 50. Pickwick Papers 52. The Rough and the Smooth 58, many others.

Minter, Mary Miles (1902–1984) (Juliet Reilly).
American silent-screen heroine.
The Nurse 12. Barbara Frietchie 15. Environment 16. Lovely Mary 16. Melissa of the Hills 17. The Ghost of Rosy Taylor 17. Anne of Green Gables 19. Nurse Marjorie 20. Moonlight and Honeysuckle 21. South of Suva 22. The Trail of the Lonesome Pine 23. The Drums of Fate 23, many others.

Miou-Miou (1950–) (Sylvette Hery).
French leading actress, from the theatre.
Themroc 72. The Mad Adventures of Rabbi Jacob/Les Aventures de Rabbi Jacob 73. Going Places/Les Valseuses 74. Jonah Who Will Be 25 in the Year 2000 76. Les Routes du Sud 78. Bye – See You Monday 79. Josepha 82. Coup de Foudre/Entre Nous 83. Evening Dress/Tenue de Soirée 86. *The Reader*/La Lectrice 88. Milou en Mai 90. Netchaiev Is Back/Netchaiev Est de Retour 91. The Jackpot/La Totale! 91. Le Bal des Casse-Pieds 91. *Germinal* 93. Tango 93. Montparnasse Pondichery 94. Un Indien dans la Ville 95. My Woman Is Leaving Me 96. Elles (Lux.) 97. Dry Cleaning/Nettoyage à Sec 97. Foul Play/Hors Jeu 98, etc.

Miranda, Carmen (1913–1955) (Maria de Carmo Miranda de Cunha).
Portuguese singer, the 'Brazilian Bombshell'; always fantastically over-dressed and harshly made-up, yet emitting a force of personality which was hard to resist. Died of a heart attack. *Carmen Miranda: Bananas Is My Business*, a documentary on her life, her failure to escape from being stereotyped, and her subsequent depression, was released in 1995.
■ Down Argentine Way (debut) 40. That Night in Rio 41. Weekend in Havana 41. Springtime in the Rockies 42. *The Gang's All Here* 43. Four Jills in a Jeep 44. Greenwich Village 44. Something for the Boys 44. Doll Face 46. If I'm Lucky 46. Copacabana 47. A Date with Judy 48. Nancy Goes to Rio 50. Scared Stiff 53.

Miranda, Isa (1905–1982) (Ines Isabella Sanpietro).
Italian star actress. Occasional films.
Adventure in Diamonds (US) 38. Hotel Imperial (US) 40. La Ronde (Fr.) 50. Summertime (GB) 55. The Yellow Rolls Royce (GB) 64. The Shoes of the Fisherman 68. The Night Porter 74. Bambina 75.

The Mirisch Brothers: *Harold* (1907–1968), *Marvin* (1918–), *Walter* (1921–).
American producers, founders in 1957 of the Mirisch company, one of the most successful independent production groups since the decline of the big studios. Formerly the two elder brothers had been exhibitors, the youngest a producer of cheap second features: the 'Bomba' series, etc.
Man of the West 58. The Magnificent Seven 60. West Side Story 61. Two for the See-Saw 62. The Great Escape 63. Toys in the Attic 63. The Satan Bug 65. The Russians Are Coming, the Russians Are Coming 66. What Did You Do in the War, Daddy? 66. Hawaii 66. The Fortune Cookie 66. In the Heat of the Night 68. The Organization 70. Midway 76. Same Time Next Year 78. Dracula 79. The Prisoner of Zenda 79. Romantic Comedy 83, etc.
~Walter Mirisch was given the Jean Hersholt Humanitarian Award by the Motion Picture Academy in 1983.

Miroslava (1926–1955) (Miroslava Stern).
Mexican actress, of Czechoslovakian descent, best known for her role as Lavinia in Luis Buñuel's *The Criminal Life of Archibaldo de la Cruz* 55. She committed suicide. *Miroslava*, a biopic about her life and her unhappy love affair with bullfighter Luis Miguel Dominguin, starring Arielle Dombasle, was made by Mexican director Alejandro Pelayo Rangel in 1992.
A Woman's Five Faces/Cinco Nostras de Mujer 46. Blood Wedding/Bodas de Sangre 46. Adventures of Casanova 48. Death Is in Love/La Muerte Enamorada 50. The Brave Bulls (US) 51. The Bullfighter and the Lady (US) 52. Dreams of Glory/Sueños de Gloria 53. Stranger on Horseback (US) 55, etc.

Mirren, Helen (1946–).
British leading actress from the stage, whose best role has been in the TV series *Prime Suspect*. Married director Taylor HACKFORD in 1998.
Herostratus 67. A Midsummer Night's Dream (TV) 68. Age of Consent 70. Savage Messiah 72. Miss Julie 73. O Lucky Man 73. Caligula 79. SOS Titanic 79. Hussy 80. The Fiendish Plot of Dr Fu Manchu 80. Excalibur 81. The Long Good Friday 81. Cal 84. White Nights 85. Heavenly Pursuits 86. The Mosquito Coast 86. Pascali's Island 88. The Cook, the Thief, His Wife and Her Lover 89. When the Whales Came 89. Bethune: The Making of a Hero 90. The Comfort of Strangers 90. *Prime Suspect* (TV) 91. Where Angels Fear to Tread 91. Prime Suspect 2 (TV) 92. Prime Suspect 3 (TV) 93. The Hawk 93. *The Madness of King George* (AAN) 95. Sons and Warriors 95. Losing Chase (TV) 96. Prime Suspect 4 (TV) 96. Some Mother's Son 96. Prime Suspect 5 (TV) 96. Losing Chase (TV) 96. Critical Care 97. Painted Lady (TV) 97. Prince of Egypt (voice) 98, etc.
❝ I'm a would-be rebel. The good girl who'd like to be a bad one. – *H.M.*
Actors are rogues and vagabonds. Or they ought to be. I can't stand it when they behave like solicitors from Penge. – H.M.

Mishima, Yukio (1925–1970).
Japanese novelist, dramatist and screenwriter who committed ritual suicide. His life was the subject of Paul Schrader's film *Mishima: A Life in Four Parts* 85. His novella *The Sailor Who Fell from Grace with the Sea* was filmed by Lewis John Carlino in 1976.
Conflagration/Enjo (story) 58. A Man Blown by the Wind/Karakkaze Yaro (a) 60.

Misraki, Paul (1908–1998) (Paul Misrachi).
French composer, pianist and author. Born in Constantinople, of French parents of Italian descent, he was an infant prodigy as a musician and composer, and went to France to study. There he joined the band of Ray Ventura, for which he wrote many songs. After Germany invaded France

in the Second World War, he fled to South America and also worked in the USA. He once calculated that he had composed more than 180 songs and the music for 145 films. In later life, he wrote novels and biographies.

Retour à l'Aube 38. Battement de Coeur 39. The Devil and the Angel/La Foire aux Chimères 46. Follow the Band/Mademoiselle S'Amuse 47. All Roads Lead to Rome/Tous les Chemins Menent à Rome 48. Manon 48. Docteur Louise 49. Wild Boy/Le Garçon Sauvage 51. Dirty Hand/Les Mains Sales 51. L'Homme de Ma Vie 52. Monte Carlo Baby 52. The Proud and the Beautiful/Les Orgueilleux 53. Ali Baba et les 40 Voleurs 54. Obsession 54. Confidential Report/Mr Arkadin (Sp.) 55. Oasis 55. Thunderstorm (GB) 55. Fernandel the Dressmaker/Le Couturier de Ces Dames 56. Port Afrique 56. Mam'selle Striptease/En Effeuillant la Marguerite 56. And God Created Woman/Et Dieu . . . Créa la Femme 56. La Chatelaine du Liban 56. Les Fanatiques 57. Maigret Tend un Piège 58. A Double Tour 59. Les Cousins 59. Les Bonnes Femmes 60. Clash of Steel/Le Chevalier de Pardaillan 62. Alphaville 65. A Murder Is . . ./Un Meurtre Est un Meurtre 72, many others.

Mr T (1952–) (Lawrence Tero).
Massive American performer whose gold chains and Mohawk hairstyle became familiar in the TV series *The A-Team*.

Rocky III 82. D.C. Cab 83. The Toughest Man in the World (TV) 84. Straight Line 88. Freaked 93.

Mistinguett (1875–1956) (Jeanne Florentine Bourgeois).
Enduring French music-hall performer, the idol of Paris for most of her long career. As the star of the Folies Bergère in 1911, she chose the young Maurice Chevalier to be her partner. She began her career at the age of 15, first gaining attention for her *dance des apaches*, and continued to perform, and to display her elaborate plumed and bespangled costumes and her legs, which were insured for 500,000 francs, until her mid-70s. She became a star of silent movies, but made few in the era of talkies. Her lovers included, apart from Chevalier, King Alfonso XIII of Spain and, probably, Edward VII when he was the Prince of Wales.

Autobiography: 1954, *Mistinguett, Queen of the Paris Night*.

Fleur de Pave 09. Les Misérables 11. Une Soirée Mondaine 17. L'Ile d'Amour 27. Rigolboche 36, etc.

❝ I do not like films very much. I do not know how to act for the camera, for a machine that will not let itself be won. It is no longer a matter of capturing an audience but of being captured oneself, by a lens. – M.

The veterans of the theatre would only condescend to film for very substantial salaries and could not see that the cinema was something other than photographed theatre. Film technique was as yet rudimentary and they were pained and indignant to find themselves disfigured on screen. When Sarah Bernhardt saw herself in *The Lady of the Camelias* she fainted. – M.

Misumi, Kenji (1921–1975).
Japanese director, mainly of period dramas. Born in Kyoto, he studied at Ritsumeikan University and began working in the early 40s. He directed the first movie in the successful Zaitoichi series of the 60s starring Shintaro Katsu.

Momotaro Samurai 57. Joyo 60. Buddha/Shaka 61. Life and Opinion of Masseur Ichi/Zatoichi Monogatari 62. The Return of Giant Majin 66. Zatoichi Challenged/Zatoichi Chikemuri Kaido 67. Zatoichi's Trip to Hell/Zatoichi Jigokutabi 68. The Blind Swordsman's Fire Festival/Zatoichi Abare Himatsuri 70. Goyoki 72, etc.

Mitchell, Cameron (1918–1994) (Cameron Mizell).
American actor, ex-radio commentator and Broadway player.

They Were Expendable 45. Command Decision 48. *Death of a Salesman* 52. How to Marry a Millionaire 53. Love Me or Leave Me 55. Monkey On My Back 57. The Last of the Vikings 61. Unstoppable Man 61. Blood and Black Lace 65. Minnesota Clay (It.) 66. Hombre 67. Monster of the Wax Museum 67. Ride the Whirlwind 68. Buck and the Preacher 71. The Midnight Man 74. Viva Knievel 77. Silent Scream 79. Without Warning 80. Texas Lightning 81. My Favorite Year 82. Murder Baby 83. Killpoint 84. Low Blow 85. The Tomb 85. Blood Link 86. Codename: Vengeance 87. Rage to Kill 87. Valley of Death 88. Action U.S.A. 89. Crossing the Line 90. Easy Kill 91. Memorial Day Valley Massacre 92, etc.

TV series: The Beachcomber 60. High Chaparral 67–71. The Swiss Family Robinson 75.

Mitchell, Grant (1874–1957).
American character actor, often seen as a worried father, lawyer or small-town politician.

Man to Man 31. Dinner at Eight 33. The Life of Emile Zola 37. New Moon 40. *The Grapes of Wrath* 40. Tobacco Road 41. *The Man Who Came to Dinner* 41. Orchestra Wives 42. Father is a Prince 43. Arsenic and Old Lace 44. Blondie's Anniversary 48, many others.

Mitchell, Guy (1925–) (Al Cernick).
Boyish, stocky American singer with a brief career in films.

■ Aaron Slick from Punkin Crick 52. Those Redheads from Seattle 53. Red Garters 54. The Wild Westerners 62.

TV series: Whispering Smith 58.

Mitchell, James (1920–).
American dancer and character actor.

Cobra Woman 44. Colorado Territory 49. Stars in My Crown 50. Deep in My Heart 54. Oklahoma 55. The Prodigal 55. The Peacemaker 56. The Spook Who Sat by the Door 73. The Turning Point 77. What Waits Below 84, etc.

TV series: Where the Heart Is 69–73. All My Children 79– .

Mitchell, Julien (1884–1954).
British stage character actor who made his film debut as a crazed train driver in *The Last Journey* 36.

It's in the Air 37. The Drum 38. The Sea Hawk (US) 40. Hotel Reserve 44. Bedelia 46. Bonnie Prince Charlie 48. The Galloping Major 51. Hobson's Choice 54, etc.

Mitchell, Leslie (1905–1985).
British commentator and broadcaster; the voice of British Movietone News from 1938; co-author of a 1946 book, *The March of the Movies*.

Grand National Night 53. Genevieve (as himself) 53. Heart of a Man 59.

Mitchell, Margaret (1900–1949).
American author of the novel on which Hollywood's most famous film, *Gone with the Wind*, was based. Died after being knocked down by a car.

Mitchell, Millard (1900–1953).
Nasal-voiced, rangy American character actor, in films from 1940.

Mr and Mrs Smith 40. Grand Central Murder 42. *A Double Life* 47. *A Foreign Affair* 48. Twelve O'Clock High 49. The Gunfighter 50. My Six Convicts 52. *Singin' in the Rain* 52. The Naked Spur 52. Here Come the Girls 53, etc.

Mitchell, Oswald (c. 1890–1949).
British director.

Old Mother Riley 37. Danny Boy 41. The Dummy Talks 43. Loyal Heart 46. Black Memory 47. The Greed of William Hart 47. The Man From Yesterday 49, etc.

Mitchell, Thomas (1892–1962).
Irish-American character actor of great versatility; could be tragic or comic, evil or humane. Former reporter, Broadway star and playwright; in Hollywood from the mid-30s.

■ Six Cylinder Love 23. Craig's Wife 36. Adventure in Manhattan 36. Theodora Goes Wild 36. Man of the People 37. When You're in Love 37. *Lost Horizon* 37. *The Hurricane* (AAN) 37. I Promise to Pay 37. Make Way for Tomorrow 37. Love Honor and Behave 38. Trade Winds 38. Only Angels Have Wings 38. *Stagecoach* (AA) 39. Mr Smith Goes to Washington 39. The Hunchback of Notre Dame 39. Gone with the Wind 39. The Swiss Family Robinson 40. Three Cheers for the Irish 40. *Our Town* 40. The Long Voyage Home 40. Angels over Broadway 40. Flight from Destiny 41. Out of the Fog 41. Joan of Paris 42. Song of the Islands 42. This Above All 42. Moontide 42. Tales of Manhattan 42. *The Black Swan* 42. The Immortal Sergeant 43. The Outlaw 43. Bataan 43. *Flesh and Fantasy* 43. *The Sullivans* 44. Wilson 44. Dark Waters 44. Buffalo Bill 44. The Keys of the Kingdom 44. Within These Walls 45. Captain Eddie 45. Adventure 45. It's a Wonderful Life 46. Three Wise Fools 46. The Dark Mirror 46. High Barbaree 47. The Romance of Rosy Ridge 47. Silver River 48. *Alias Nick Beal* 49. The Big Wheel 49. Journey into Light 51. High Noon 52. Tumbleweed 53. The Secret of the Incas 54. Destry 54. Swell Guy 56. While the City Sleeps 56. Handle with Care 58. Too Young for Love (GB) 59. By Love Possessed 61. Pocketful of Miracles 61.

TV series: O. Henry Playhouse 56. Glencannon 58.

✪ For adding solid worth to a number of pictures which without him might not have had it.

❝ A man looks bigger in the bathtub than he does in the ocean. – T.M.

Mitchell, Warren (1926–) (Warren Misell).
British comedy character actor, mainly on TV, especially in series *Till Death Us Do Part*. Born in Stoke Newington, London, he studied chemistry at Oxford University and acting at RADA.

Tommy the Toreador 60. Postman's Knock 62. Where Has Poor Mickey Gone? 63. The Intelligence Men 65. Arrivederci Baby 66. *Till Death Us Do Part* 68. The Assassination Bureau 68. The Best House in London 69. All the Way Up 70. Innocent Bystanders 72. The Alf Garnett Saga 72. Stand Up Virgin Soldiers 77. The Chain 85. Foreign Body 87. Wall of Silence (TV) 93. Crackers 98, many others.

Mitchell, Yvonne (1925–1979) (Yvonne Joseph).
British actress and playwright, on stage from 1940.

Autobiography: 1957, *Actress*.

The Queen of Spades (film debut) 48. Turn the Key Softly 53. *The Divided Heart* 54. Yield to the Night 56. *Woman in a Dressing Gown* 57. The Passionate Summer 58. Tiger Bay 59. Sapphire 59. The Trials of Oscar Wilde 61. The Main Attraction 63. Genghis Khan 65. The Corpse 70. The Great Waltz 72. The Incredible Sarah 76, etc.

Mitchum, Christopher (1943–).
American minor leading man, son of Robert Mitchum.

Rio Lobo 70. Big Jake 71. Summertime Killer 72. The Mean Machine 73. Ricco 74. No Time to Die 78. American Commandos 84. Angel of Death 86. Aftershock 88. Real Men Don't Eat Gummi Bears 89. Death Feud 89. Tombstone 93. Striking Point 94. Biohazard: The Alien Force 95. Fugitive X 96. Lethal Seduction 97, etc.

Mitchum, James (1938–).
American actor, son of Robert Mitchum.

Thunder Road (debut) 58. The Young Guns of Texas 62. The Victors 63. The Tramplers 66. Ambush Bay 67. Moonrunners 75. Trackdown 76. Blackout 78. Maniac 78. Codename: Zebra 84. Hollywood Cop 87. Marked for Murder 89. Genghis Khan 92, etc.

Mitchum, Robert (1917–1997).
Sleepy-eyed American leading man who has sometimes hidden his considerable talent behind a pretence of carelessness. Born in Bridgeport, Connecticut, he worked in various labouring jobs, including boxing, and claimed to have served on a chain-gang in Georgia, before landing a role as a villain in Hopalong Cassidy films. His best roles were as Bill Walker in *GI Joe*, Jeb Rand in *Pursued*, Jeff Bailey in *Out of the Past*, Duke Halliday in *The Big Steal*, Preacher Harry Powell in *The Night of the Hunter*, Paddy Carmody in *The Sundowners*, Charles Shaughnessy in *Ryan's Daughter*, and Philip Marlowe in *Farewell, My Lovely*. His career survived the six-month sentence he served in 1948 for possession of marijuana. Married his childhood sweetheart Dorothy Spence in 1940. Their three children included Christopher and James Mitchum who had lesser careers as actors.

Biographies: 1975, *It Sure Beats Working* by Mike Tomkies; 1984, *Robert Mitchum* by George Eells.

Hoppy Serves a Writ 43. The Leather Burners 43. Border Patrol 43. Follow the Band 43. Colt Comrades 43. The Human Comedy 43. We've Never Been Licked 43. Beyond the Last Frontier 43. Bar 20 43. Doughboys in Ireland 43. Corvette K-225 43. Aerial Gunner 43. The Lone Star Trail 43. False Colors 43. The Dancing Masters 43. Riders of the Deadline 43. Gung Ho 43. Johnny Doesn't Live Here Any More 44. When Strangers Marry 44. The Girl Rush 44. Thirty Seconds Over Tokyo 44. Nevada 44. West of the Pecos 45. *The Story of G.I. Joe* (AAN) 45. Till the End of Time 46. Undercurrent 46. The Locket 46. *Pursued* 47. *Crossfire* 47. Desire Me 47. *Out of the Past* 47. Rachel and the Stranger 48. Blood on the Moon 48. The Red Pony 49. *The Big Steal* 49. Holiday Affair 49. Where Danger Lives 50. My Forbidden Past 51. His Kind of Woman 51. The Racket 51. Macao 52. One Minute to Zero 52. The Lusty Men 52. Angel Face 53. White Witch Doctor 53. Second Chance 53. She Couldn't Say No 54. River of No Return 54. Track of the Cat 54. Not as a Stranger 55. *Night of the Hunter* 55. The Man with the Gun 55. Foreign Intrigue 56. Bandido 56. Heaven Knows Mr Allison 57. Fire Down Below 57. The Enemy Below 57. Thunder Road 58. The Hunters 58. The Angry Hills 59. The Wonderful Country 59. Home from the Hill 60. A Terrible Beauty 60. The Grass Is Greener 60. *The Sundowners* 60. The Last Time I Saw Archie 61. Cape Fear 62. The Longest Day 62. Two for the Seesaw 62. The List of Adrian Messenger 63. Rampage 63. Man in the Middle 64. What a Way to Go 64. Mr Moses 65. The Way West 67. El Dorado 67. Anzio 68. Villa Rides 68. Five Card Stud 68. Secret Ceremony 68. Young Billy Young 69. The Good Guys and the Bad Guys 69. *Ryan's Daughter* 71. Going Home 71. The Wrath of God 72. The Friends of Eddie Coyle 73. The Yakuza 75. *Farewell My Lovely* 75. Midway 76. The Last Tycoon 76. The Amsterdam Kill 77. The Big Sleep 78. Matilda 78. Breakthrough 78. Nightkill 79. One Shoe Makes It Murder (TV) 82. That Championship Season 82. *The Winds of War* (TV) 83. Killer in the Family (TV) 83. The Ambassador 84. Maria's Lovers 84. Promises to Keep (TV) 85. The Hearst and Davies Affair (TV) 85. Reunion at Fairborough (TV) 85. Thompson's Last Run (TV) 86. War and Remembrance (TV) 87. Mr North 88. Scrooged 88. Presumed Dangerous 90. Cape Fear 91. Midnight Ride 92. Les Sept Péchés Capitaux 92. Tombstone (narrator) 93. Dead Man 95. Waiting for Sunset 97, etc.

✪ For triumphing by sheer force of personality over scores of inferior films; and for enhancing a few good ones. *Farewell My Lovely*.

❝ Robert Mitchum and his sleepy eyes have hypnotized audiences for over thirty years, through bad pictures, bad notices and narcotics cases. Just now and then he has been allowed to prove himself an excellent actor; and he has always been a commanding personality, though his attitude to himself and his career is presumably exemplified by the title of his biography – *It Sure Beats Working*. He claims:

I've survived because I work cheap and don't take up too much time

And he adds:

Movies bore me, especially my own.

He is not even proud of his physique:

People think I have an interesting walk.
Hell, I'm just trying to hold my gut in.

Or his fans:

You know what the average Robert Mitchum fan is? He's full of warts and dandruff and he's probably got a hernia too, but he sees me up there on the screen and he thinks if that bum can make it, I can be president.

He disclaims ambition:

I started out to be a sex fiend but I couldn't pass the physical.

He hated his early films:

I kept the same suit for six years – and the same dialogue. We just changed the title of the picture and the leading lady.

Then he had a stroke of luck:

I came back from the war and ugly heroes were in.

Even so he thinks films are a joke:

I gave up being serious about making pictures around the time I made a film with Greer Garson and she took a hundred and twenty-five takes to say no.

He is unashamed of his lapses:

The only difference between me and my fellow actors is that I've spent more time in jail.

He does have an ambition, to spend every cent he's got:

When I drop dead and they rush to the drawer, there's going to be nothing in it but a note saying 'Later'.

And when asked why in his mid-60s he took on the arduous task of starring in an 18-hour mini-series, *The Winds of War*, he answered:

It promised a year of free lunches.

He is loved by the press, for he doesn't care what they write about him:

They're all true – booze, brawls, broads, all true. Make up some more if you want to.

And he remains self-deprecating to the last:
Young actors love me. They think if that big slob can make it, there's a chance for us.
And his final word of advice to the health-conscious:
How do I keep fit? I lay down a lot.

Mitra, Subatra (1931–).
Leading Indian cinematographer who photographed Satyajit Ray's early films.
Pather Panchali 55. Aparajito 56. The Music Room 58. The World of Apu 58. Kanchenjungha 62. Charulata 64. The Householder/Gharbar 64. Shakespeare Wallah 65. The Guru 69. Bombay Talkie 70. Mahatma and the Mad Boy 73, etc.

Mitry, Jean (1907–1988).
French director of experimental shorts; also critic.
Pacific 231 49. Images pour Debussy 51. Symphonie Mécanique 55, etc.

Mix, Tom (1880–1940).
A US Marshal (by his own unconfirmed account) who turned actor and starred in over 400 low-budget westerns. In the 30s he also toured with his own circus. He died in a car crash in Arizona, where a monument was erected to the memory of the man 'whose spirit left his body on this spot and whose characterizations and portrayals in life served to better fix memories of the Old West in the minds of living men.'
Biographies: 1957, *The Fabulous Tom Mix* by Olive Stokes. 1972, *The Life and Legend of Tom Mix* by Paul E. Mix.
The Ranch Life in the Great Southwest 10. Child of the Prairie 13. Cupid's Round-Up 18. Tom Mix in Arabia 22. North of Hudson Bay 24. The Last Trail 27. Destry Rides Again 27. Painted Post 28. My Pal the King 32. The Terror Trail 33. The Fourth Horseman 33, etc.
❝ They say he rides like part of the horse, but they don't say what part. – *Robert Sherwood*
He was as elegant on a horse as Fred Astaire on a dance floor, and that's the elegantest there is. – *Adela Rogers St Johns*
~Mix was noted for wearing his white suit and boots even to fashionable parties.

Miyagawa, Kazuo (1908–).
Japanese cinematographer, working with such leading directors as Ichikawa, Kurosawa, Mizoguchi, Ozu and Shinoda.
Rashomon 50. Miss Oyu/Oyu-sama 51. Ugetsu/Ugetsu Monogatari 53. The Bailiff/Sansho Dayu 54. Crucified Lovers/Chikamatsu Monogatari 54. Street of Shame/Akasen Chitai 56. Conflagration/Enjo 58. Floating Weeds/Ukigusa 59. The Key/Kagi 59. Bonchi 60. Yojimbo 61. The Outcast/Hakai 62. Money Talks/Zemni no Odoti 64. Tokyo Olympiad/Tokyo Orimpikku 65. Banished Orin/Hanare Goze Orin 77. Kagemusha 80. Island of the Evil Spirit/Akureito 81. The Inland Sea Boys' Baseball Team/Setouchi Shonen Yakyudan 84. MacArthur's Children 85, etc.

Miyazaki, Hayao (1941–).
Japanese director and screenwriter of animated films. In 1996, Walt Disney signed a deal to distribute his work throughout the world. *Porco Rosso* was the top Japanese box-office film of 1992.
The Castle of Cagliostro 79. *Warriors of the Wind*/Nausicäa of the Valley of the Wind 84. Laputa 86. *My Neighbour Totoro* 88. Kiki's Delivery Service 89. Porco Rosso/Kurenai No Buta 92. Princess/Ghost/Princess/Mononoke 97, etc.

Mizner, Wilson (1876–1933).
American wit, occasional dramatist and screenwriter, boxing manager, gambler, and restaurateur. Born in Bernicia, California, he collaborated on his first Broadway play in 1909 and, after addiction to drugs and alcohol, ended up in Hollywood in the 30s, working for Warners. He was co-owner of the Hollywood restaurant the Brown Derby, opening it, according to Anita Loos, because he could find 'no spot where a man of his inertia could loaf in comfort'. He was the model for the character of Blackie Norton, played by Clark Gable in *San Francisco*.
Biography: 1975, *Rogue's Progress* by John Burke.
The Dark Horse (co-w) 32. One Way Passage (co-w) 32. Hard to Handle (co-w) 33. The Mind Reader (co-w) 33. 20,000 Years in Sing Sing (co-w) 33. Heroes for Sale (co-w) 33, etc.
❝ Working for Warner Brothers is like fucking a porcupine – it's one hundred pricks against one. – W.M.
Be nice to those you meet going up the ladder. They're the same people you'll meet coming back down again. – W.M.
Always treat a lady like a whore and a whore like a lady. – W.M.
People beat scenery. – W.M.

Mizoguchi, Kenji (1898–1956).
Japanese director, former actor. Directed from 1923, though few of his films were seen in the West.
A Paper Doll's Whisper of Spring 25. The Gorge between Love and Hate 32. The Story of the Last Chrysanthemums 39. Woman of Osaka 40. The Forty-Nine Ronin 42. The Life of O'Haru 52. *Ugetsu Monogatari* 52. Street of Shame 56, many others.

Mizrahi, Moshe (1931–).
Egyptian director and screenwriter, working in Israel and France.
Les Stances à Sophie 71. I Love You Rosa 73. The House on Chelouche Street 74. Madame Rosa (AA) 77. I Sent a Letter to My Love/Chère Inconnue 80. La Vie Continue 82. Une Jeunesse 83. War and Love 85. Everytime We Say Goodbye 87. Mangeclous 89, etc.

Mobley, Mary Ann (1939–).
American leading lady, former 'Miss America'. Married actor Gary Collins.
Girl Happy 65. Three on a Couch 66. For Singles Only 68. My Dog, the Thief 69. Crazy Horse and Custer: The Untold Story (TV) 90, etc.
TV series: Diff'rent Strokes 85–86.

Mockridge, Cyril (1896–1979).
British-born composer, in America from 1921, films from 1932.
The Littlest Rebel 35. Johnny Apollo 40. Happy Land 43. The Sullivans 44. My Darling Clementine 46. How to Marry a Millionaire 53. Many Rivers to Cross 55. Flaming Star 60. Donovan's Reef 63, many others.

Mocky, Jean-Pierre (1929–) (Jean Mokiejeswki).
French director.
Un Couple 60. Snobs 62. Les Vierges 63. La Bourse et la Vie 65. Les Compagnons de la Marguerite 67. Solo 70. Chut! 72. L'Ibis Rouge 75. A Mort l'Arbitre 83. Le Miracle 86. Divine Enfant 89. City for Sale/Ville à Vendre 91. Le Mari de Léon 93. Black for Remembrance 96, etc.

Modine, Matthew (1959–).
American leading actor.
Baby It's You 82. Private School 83. Vision Quest 84. Hotel New Hampshire 84. *Birdy* 85. Mrs Soffel 85. Full Metal Jacket 87. Orphans 87. Married to the Mob 88. The Gamble/La Partita 88. Gross Anatomy 89. Memphis Belle 90. Pacific Heights 90. Equinox 92. And the Band Played On (TV) 93. Short Cuts 93. The Browning Version 94. Bye Bye, Love 95. CutThroat Island 95. The Maker 97. The Real Blonde 97, etc.

Modley, Albert (1891–1979).
British north-country comedian who appeared in a few films including the 1951 version of *Up for the Cup*.

Modot, Gaston (1887–1970).
French character actor.
Fièvre 21. L'Age d'Or 30. Sous Les Toits de Paris 30. La Grande Illusion 37. Pépé le Moko 37. La Règle du Jeu 39. Les Enfants du Paradis 44. French Can Can 55. Le Testament du Docteur Cordelier 59, many others.

Moffat, Ivan.
Anglo-American screenwriter, the son of English actress and poet Iris Tree. Born in Havana and educated at Harvard, he worked on a few documentary films in Britain in the early 40s, then as assistant to director George STEVENS in the mid-40s, before becoming a writer and producer. Married twice. He was the model for the character of Patrick in Christopher ISHERWOOD's novel *A Meeting by the River*.
Shane (asst p) 52. Bhowani Junction (co-w) 55. D Day the Sixth of June (co-w) 56. Boy on a Dolphin (co-w) 57. They Came to Cordura (co-w) 59. Tender Is the Night (w) 61. The Heroes of Telemark (co-w) 65. Hitler: The Last Ten Days (co-w) 73. Black Sunday 76 (co-w), etc.

Moffatt, Graham (1919–1965).
British actor, fondly remembered as the impertinent fat boy of the Will Hay comedies: *Oh Mr Porter* 38. *Ask a Policeman* 39. Where's That Fire 40, etc.
Other films include A Cup of Kindness (debut) 34. Dr Syn 38. I Thank You 41. I Know Where I'm Going 45, many others. Retired to keep a pub, but made very occasional appearances: The Second Mate 50. Inn for Trouble 59. Eighty Thousand Suspects 63.

Moffett, Sharyn (1936–).
American child actress of the 40s.
My Pal Wolf 44. The Body Snatcher 45. Child of Divorce 47. The Judge Steps Out 47. Mr Blandings Builds His Dream House 48. Girls Never Tell 51, etc.

Mogotlane, Thomas (1953–1993).
South African actor and writer, best known for playing the lead role in *Mapantsula*. He worked mainly in the theatre.
How Long? (a, co-w) 86. Mapantsula (a, co-w) 88.

Moguy, Leonide (1899–1976) (L. Maguilevsky).
Russian newsreel producer, later in France and US as director.
Prison without Bars 38. The Night Is Ending 43. Action in Arabia 44. Whistle Stop 46. Tomorrow Is Too Late 50. Les Enfants de l'Amour 54, etc.

Mohner, Carl (1921–).
Austrian actor in films from 1949.
Rififi 55. He Who Must Die 56. The Key 58. Camp on Blood Island 58. The Kitchen 61. Hell is Empty 67. Callan 74. Wanted: Babysitter 75, etc.

Mohr, Gerald (1914–1968).
Suave American actor, in films from 1941; played the 'Lone Wolf', a gentleman crook, in a mid-40s series.
The Monster and the Girl 41. Ten Tall Men 51. Detective Story 53. The Eddie Cantor Story 53. Angry Red Planet 59. Funny Girl 68, many others.
TV series: Foreign Intrigue 56.

Mohr, Hal (1894–1974).
American cinematographer, in Hollywood from 1915.
The Last Night of the Barbary Coast 13. Money 14. The Deceiver 21. Bag and Baggage 23. The Monster 24. The High Hand 26. The Jazz Singer 27. The Last Warning 28. Broadway 29. Big Boy 30. Woman of Experience 31. A Woman Commands 32. State Fair 33. David Harum 34. *A Midsummer Night's Dream* (AA) 35. *Captain Blood* 35. *Green Pastures* 36. The Walking Dead 36. I Met My Love Again 38. Rio 39. *Destry Rides Again* 39. When the Daltons Rode 40. International Lady 41. Twin Beds 42. Phantom of the Opera (AA) 43. Ladies Courageous 44. Salome Where She Danced 45. Because of Him 46. The Lost Moment 47. Another Part of the Forest 48. Johnny Holiday 49. Woman on the Run 50. The Big Night 51. The Fourposter 52. *The Wild One* 54. The Boss 56. Baby Face Nelson 57. The Gun Runners 58. The Last Voyage 60. The Man from the Diner's Club 63. Bamboo Saucer 68, many others.
~Mohr was interviewed in *Behind the Camera*.

Mokae, Zakes (1935–).
South African actor, from the stage, now working in America.
Darling 65. The Comedians 67. The Island 80. Roar 81. Cry Freedom 87. The Serpent and the Rainbow 88. Dad 89. A Dry White Season 89. Gross Anatomy 89. Body Parts 91. A Rage in Harlem 91. Dust Devil: The Final Cut 93. Outbreak 95. Waterworld 95. Vampire in Brooklyn 95. Krippendorf's Tribe 98, etc.

Mokri, Amir (1956–).
Iranian-born cinematographer, in America since the mid-70s.
House of the Rising Sun 85. Slamdance 87. Eat a Bowl of Tea 89. Life Is Cheap . . . But Toilet Paper Is Expensive 90. Blue Steel 90. Pacific Heights 90. Whore 91. Queen's Logic 91. Freejack 92. The Joy Luck Club 93. Eye for an Eye 95, etc.

Mol, Gretchen (c. 1973–).
American actress. Born in Deep River, Connecticut, she studied at New York's William Esper Studio and appeared in summer stock in the mid-90s, before being noticed by an agent while working checking coats at a fashionable Manhattan restaurant.
Calm at Sunset 96. Girl 96. The Funeral 96. Donnie Brasco 97. The Last Time I Committed Suicide 97. Rounders 98. Celebrity 98. New Rose Hotel 98. Finding Graceland 98, etc.

Molander, Gustaf (1888–1973).
Veteran Swedish director, former actor and writer (including *Sir Arne's Treasure* 19). Directing since 1922, but few of his films have been seen abroad.
Sin 28. Intermezzo 36. A Woman's Face 38. Woman without a Face 47. Sir Arne's Treasure (remake) 55, many others.

Molina, Alfred (1953–).
English character actor of Spanish and Italian ancestry, often in menacing roles, from the theatre.
Raiders of the Lost Ark 81. Meantime 83. Number One 84. Water 84. Eleni 85. Ladyhawke 85. A Letter to Brezhnev 85. Prick Up Your Ears 87. Manifesto 88. Drowning in the Shallow End 89. American Friends 91. Not without My Daughter 91. Hancock (TV) 91. Enchanted April 91. The Trial 93. White Fang 2: Myth of the White Wolf 94. Maverick 94. The Perez Family 95. Hideaway 95. Species 95. Scorpion Spring 95. Before and After 96. Mojave Moon 96. Leo Tolstoy's Anna Karenina 96. The Man Who Knew Too Little 97. Boogie Nights 97. The Imposters 98, etc.
❝ My father was very disparaging about acting. He was under the impression that it wasn't quite the sort of thing for a good, upstanding heterosexual man to do. – A.M.

Molina, Angela (1956–).
Spanish leading actress in international films.
That Obscure Object of Desire 77. Demons in the Garden/Demonios en el Jardín 82. The Eyes, the Mouth (It.) 83. Half of Heaven/La Mitad del Cielo 86. Streets of Gold (US) 86. 1492: Conquest of Paradise (US) 92. Coitado do Jorge (Port.) 93. Con gli Occhi Chiusi (It.) 94. With Closed Eyes 94. Gimlet 95. Live Flesh/Carne Tremula 97. Wind with the Gone/El Viento Se Llevó lo Que 98, etc.

Molinaro, Edouard (1928–).
French director.
Evidence in Concrete/Le Dos au Mur 57. Girls for the Summer 60. A Ravishing Idiot 63. The Gentle Art of Seduction 64. Pain in the A . . . 74. La Cage aux Folles (AAN) 78. La Cage aux Folles II 80. Sunday Lovers 80. Just the Way You Are 84. L'Amour en Douce 85. Palace 85. Enchanté 88. Le Souper 93. Beaumarchais the Scoundrel 96, etc.

Mollo, John.
English costume designer.
Star Wars (AA) 77. Alien 79. The Empire Strikes Back 80. Gandhi (AA) 82. Greystoke: The Legend of Tarzan, Lord of the Apes 84. Cry Freedom 87. Air America 90. White Hunter, Black Heart 90. Chaplin 92. Rudyard Kipling's The Jungle Book 94. Event Horizon 97, etc.

Molloy, Mike (1940–).
Australian-born cinematographer, in international films. He began in Sydney in documentaries and commercials, then moved to England in the late 60s to work as a camera operator for Nicolas ROEG on *Performance* and *Walkabout*, and with Stanley KUBRICK on *A Clockwork Orange* and *Barry Lyndon*. Returned to live in Australia in 1996.
Mad Dog 76. Summerfield 77. The Shout 79. The Human Factor 79. The Great Rock'n'Roll Swindle (co-ph) 79. The Kidnapping of the President 80. Shock Treatment 81. Dead Easy 82. The Return of Captain Invincible 83. Reflections (TV) 84. The Hit 85. Link 86. Scandal 89. Bethune (co-ph) 90. Bliss 97. Welcome to Woop-Woop 97. All the Little Animals 98, etc.

Molnar, Ferenc (1878–1952).
Hungarian dramatist whose comedies were the basis of many Hollywood films including *The Shop around the Corner*, *One Two Three*, *The Guardsman*, *The Swan*, *A Breath of Scandal*, *Double Wedding* and *Liliom*.

Monaco, James (1885–1945).
American composer and musician who wrote songs for seven Bing Crosby movies. His most frequent collaborator was lyricist Johnny Burke.
Dr Rhythm 38. Sing You Sinners 38. East Side of Heaven 39. The Star Maker 38. Road to Singapore 40. If I Had My Way 40. Rhythm on the River 40. Stage Door Canteen 43. Pin-Up Girl 44. Sweet and Low Down 44. Irish Eyes Are Smiling 44, etc.

Monash, Paul (1917–).
American producer, former TV writer.
Butch Cassidy and the Sundance Kid 69. Slaughterhouse Five 72. The Friends of Eddie Coyle (& w) 74. The Front Page 74. Carrie 76. Big Trouble in Little China 86. Stalin (w, TV) 92, etc.
TV series: Peyton Place 64–69.

Mondy, Pierre (1925–) (Pierre Cuq).
French actor.
Rendezvous de Juillet 49. Sans Laisser d'Adresse 50. Les Louves 57. Austerlitz (as Napoleon) 60. Bebert et l'Omnibus 63. Retour en Force 80. The Gift 82, etc.

Monette, Paul (1945–1995).
American screenwriter and novelist, a former teacher, best known for his book *Borrowed Time: An AIDS Memoir* (1998), about the death of his lover. A documentary on his life, *Paul Monette: The Brink of Summer's End*, written and directed by Monte Bramer, was released in 1997. Died of AIDS.
Autobiography: 1992, *Becoming a Man: Half a Life Story*.
Secret Witness (co-w) 88, etc.

Monger, Christopher (1950–).
Welsh-born director, working in America.
Enough Cuts for a Murder 79. Repeater 80. Voice Over 81. The Mabinogi (TV) 84. Crime Pays 86. Just Like a Woman 92. The Englishman Who Went up a Hill but Came down a Mountain 95, etc.

Monicelli, Mario (1915–).
Italian director.
Cops and Robbers (co-d) 51. Persons Unknown 58. Boccaccio 70 (part) 61. The Organizer 63. Casanova 70 66. Girl with a Pistol 69. Mortadella 71. Romanzo Popolare 75. Caro Michele 76. Travels with Anita 79. Sono Fotogenico 80. Bertoldo, Bertoldino e Cacasenno 84. The Two Lives of Mattia Pascal/Le Due Vite di Mattia Pascal 85. The Rogues/I Picari 87. The Dark Illness/Il Male Oscuro 89. Parenti e Serpenti 92. Viva i Bambini 92. Cari Fottutissimi Amici 94. Looking for Paradise 95. I Panni Sporchi 98, etc.

The Monkees
sprang to fame in an American TV series of that title 66–67. They were a pop quartet deliberately recruited by Screen Gems to emulate the Beatles in crazy comedy with music; their ensuing popularity surprised not only themselves but their sponsors, and in 1969 they made a movie called *Head*. Individually they were: Peter TORK; Mike NESMITH; Micky DOLENZ; Davy JONES.

Monkhouse, Bob (1928–).
British comedian of TV, radio and occasional films.
Autobiography: 1998, *Over the Limit: My Secret Diaries 1993–8*.
Carry On Sergeant 58. Dentist in the Chair 59. Weekend with Lulu 61. She'll Have to Go 61. The Bliss of Mrs Blossom 68, etc.
TV series: Mad Movies.

Monroe, Marilyn (1926–1962) (Norma Jean Baker or Mortenson).
American leading lady, a former model whose classic rags-to-riches story was built on a super-sexy image which quickly tarnished, leaving her a frustrated, neurotic and tragic victim of the Hollywood which created her. The pity was that she had real talent as well as sex appeal.
Marilyn, a compilation feature, was released after her death. In 1976 Misty Rowe played her in *Goodbye Norma Jean*. She was played by Melody Anderson in the TV movie *Marilyn and Bobby: Her Final Affair* 93.
Autobiography: 1974, My Story.
Biographies: 1961, *Marilyn Monroe* by Maurice Zolotow. 1966, *Who Killed Marilyn Monroe?* by Charles Hamblett. 1969, *Norma Jean: The Life of Marilyn Monroe* by Fred Lawrence Guiles. 1974, *Marilyn* by Norman Mailer. 1976, *Conversations with Marilyn* by W. J. Weatherby. 1985, *Legend: The Life and Death of Marilyn Monroe* by Fred Lawrence Guiles. 1985, *Goddess: The Secret Lives of Marilyn Monroe* by Anthony Summers. 1993, *Marilyn Monroe: The Biography* by Donald Spoto. 1996, *Marilyn: Her Life in Her Own Words* by George Barris. 1998, *Marilyn Monroe* by Barbara Leaming.
■ Scudda Hoo, Scudda Hay 48. Dangerous Years 48. Ladies of the Chorus 48. Love Happy 50. A Ticket to Tomahawk 50. *The Asphalt Jungle* 50. All About Eve 50. The Fireball 50. Right Cross 50. Home Town Story 51. As Young as You Feel 51. Love Nest 51. Let's Make It Legal 51. We're Not Married 52. Clash by Night 52. Full House 52. Monkey Business 52. Don't Bother to Knock 52. *Niagara* (here the build-up really started) 52. *Gentlemen Prefer Blondes* 53. *How to Marry a Millionaire* 53. River of No Return 54. There's No Business Like Show Business 54. *The Seven-Year Itch* 55. Bus Stop 56. The Prince and the Showgirl (GB) 57. *Some Like It Hot* 59. Let's Make Love 60. The Misfits 61.
✪ For personifying the Hollywood cliché, the star created and destroyed by the system. *How to Marry a Millionaire*.
❝ A sex symbol becomes a thing. I hate being a thing.
The tragedy of Marilyn Monroe was such that she has inspired more books of reminiscence and analysis than any other star. Her problem was, oddly enough, best expressed in an earlier decade by Clara Bow:
Being a sex symbol is a heavy load to carry, especially when one is tired, hurt and bewildered.
Monroe knew her own limitations:
To put it bluntly, I seem to be a whole superstructure with no foundation. But I'm working on the foundation.
What she meant by that was:
The best way for me to prove myself as a person is to prove myself as an actress.
She was uncertain whether she would ever achieve this aim. She said once:
I enjoy acting when you really hit it right.
But she seldom felt she did. In her search for meaning she married playwright Arthur Miller, and the headline was:
EGGHEAD WEDS HOURGLASS
It finally failed to work although he was kind to her with press comments such as:
Her beauty shines because the spirit is forever showing itself.
Not that she was lacking in moral supporters; even unlikely people such as Edith Sitwell acclaimed her:
She knows the world, but this knowledge has not lowered her great and benevolent dignity; its darkness has not dimmed her goodness.
She settled for a flip image as expressed in her lively encounters with the press:
Didn't you have anything on?
– I had the radio on.
Sex is part of nature, and I go along with nature.
Do you wear falsies?
– Those who know me better, know better.
The contradictions within herself finally killed her, and the obituaries were many and varied:
You don't have to hold an inquest to find out who killed Marilyn Monroe. Those bastards in the big executive chairs killed her. – *Henry Hathaway*
If she was simple it would have been easy to help her. She could have made it with a little luck. – *Arthur Miller*
A professional amateur. – *Laurence Olivier*
Directing her was like directing Lassie. You needed fourteen takes to get each one of them right. – *Otto Preminger*
Anyone can remember lines, but it takes a real artist to come on the set and not know her lines and give the performance she did. – *Billy Wilder*
I have never met anyone as utterly mean as Marilyn Monroe. Nor as utterly fabulous on the screen, and that includes Garbo. – *Billy Wilder*
She has breasts like granite and a brain like Swiss cheese, full of holes. Extracting a performance from her is like pulling teeth. – *Billy Wilder*
As near genius as any actress I ever knew. – *Joshua Logan*
She was born afraid. She never got over it. In the end fear killed her. – *Pete Martin*
There's a broad with her future behind her. – *Constance Bennett*
She had curves in places other women don't even have places. – *Cybill Shepherd*
She's the girl you'd like to double-cross your wife with. – *Jean Negulesco*
An arrogant little tail-twitcher who learned to throw sex in your face. – *Nunnally Johnson*
A vacuum with nipples. – *Otto Preminger*
Popular opinion, and all that goes to promote it, is a horrible unsteady conveyance for life, and she was exploited beyond anyone's means. – *Laurence Olivier*

Monroe, Vaughan (1911–1973).
American bandleader who unexpectedly appeared as hero of a few westerns.
Meet the People 44. Carnegie Hall 47. Singing Guns 50. The Toughest Man in Arizona 52, etc.

Monsarrat, Nicholas (1910–1979).
British adventure novelist whose naval adventures, *The Cruel Sea* and *The Ship That Died of Shame*, were filmed by Ealing, as was *The Story of Esther Costello*.

Montagu, Ivor (1904–1984).
British producer, director and film theorist. In films from 1925; was associate of Hitchcock on several of his mid-30s thrillers; produced *Behind the Spanish Lines* 38, *Spanish ABC* 38, etc; co-authored many screenplays including *Scott of the Antarctic* 48. Last publication *Film World* 64.
Autobiography: 1970, *The Youngest Son*.

Montague, Lee (1927–).
British actor, mainly seen on stage and TV.
Savage Innocents 59. The Secret Partner 60. Billy Budd 61. The Horse without a Head 62. You Must Be Joking 65. The Best Pair of Legs in the Business 72. Mahler 74. Jesus of Nazareth (TV) 77. Holocaust (TV) 78. The Legacy 78. The Brass Target 78. Sakharov (TV) 84. Madame Sousatzka 88, etc.

Montalban, Ricardo (1920–).
Mexican leading man in Hollywood.
Fiesta 47. The Kissing Bandit 49. Border Incident 49. *Battleground* 50. Right Cross 50. Across the Wide Missouri 51. My Man and I 52. Sombrero 53. Latin Lovers 54. A Life in the Balance 55. *Sayonara* 57. Adventures of a Young Man 62. Love Is a Ball 63. The Money Trap 65. Madame X 66. Sol Madrid 68. Blue 68. *Sweet Charity* 68. Conquest of the Planet of the Apes 72. Desperate Mission (TV) 72. Joe Panther 76. How the West Was Won (TV) 77. Joe Panther 78. *Star Trek: The Wrath of Khan* 82. Cannonball Run II 84. The Naked Gun: From the Files of Police Squad 88, etc.
TV series: Fantasy Island 78–84. The Colbys 85–87.

Montana, Bull (1887–1950) (Luigi Montagna).
Italian-American strong man who played ape men and heavies in the 20s.
Brass Buttons 19. Go and Get It 20. Painted People 23. The Lost World 24. Son of the Sheik 26. Good Morning Judge 28. Show of Shows 29. Tiger Rose 29. Big City 37. Good Morning Judge 43, etc.

Montand, Yves (1921–1991) (Ivo Levi).
French actor-singer in films from the mid-40s; he was married to Simone SIGNORET. His body was ordered to be exhumed in 1997, for genetic tests to settle a paternity lawsuit and claim against his estate.
Les Portes de la Nuit 46. Lost Property 50. *The Wages of Fear* 53. The Heroes Are Tired 55. The Witches of Salem 56. *Let's Make Love* (US) 60. Sanctuary (US) 61. My Geisha (US) 62. The Sleeping Car Murders 65. The War Is Over 66. Is Paris Burning? 66. Grand Prix 67. Vivre pour Vivre 67. 'Z' 68. On a Clear Day You Can See Forever 69. L'Aveu 70. The Red Circle 70. The Son 72. Le Sauvage 76. Clair de Femme 79. Garçon! 83. *Jean de Florette* 86. *Manon des Sources* 86. Nobody Listened/Nadie Escuchaba 88. Trois Places Pour Le 26 88. Netchaiev est de Retour 91. I.P.5.: L'Ile aux Pachydermes 92, etc.
❝ Of all the male stars I've known, he was probably the most vain. – *Tony Richardson*

Montefiori, Luigi (1942–).
Italian actor, screenwriter and director, a former artist and graphic designer. He has used various pseudonyms: George Eastman and Louis London as actor, John Cart, Alex Carver and Richard Franks as writer, and G. L. Eastman as director.
Il Cobra (a) 66. The Belle Starr Story (a) 68. Satyricon 69. Django (a) 71. Call of the Wild (a) 72. Scallawag (a) 73. Bordella (a) 75. Keoma (co-w) 76. American Fever (co-w) 78. Sesso Nero (& w) 80. The New Barbarians/Il Nuovi Barbari (a) 82. Anno 2020 (w) 80. Blastfighter (a) 84. Christmas Present/Regalo di Natale (a) 86. Polar (a) 87. Stage Fright (co-w) 87. Metamorphosis (wd) 89. Desert Law (co-w) 90, etc.

Monteiro, João César (1939–).
Portuguese director, producer and actor. He studied at the London International Film School in the early 60s.
Traditional Tales/Veredas (d) 77. Silvestre (d) 80. A Flor do Mar (p, d) 86. Recollections of the Yellow House (a, wd) 89. The Last Dive (a, wd) 92. God's Comedy 95, etc.

Montes, Lola (1818–1861) (Maria Dolores Eliza Gilbert).
Scottish-Creole dancer who became world-famous as the mistress of King Ludwig I of Bavaria. Max Ophuls made a film about her in 1955, with Martine Carol, and Yvonne de Carlo played her in *Black Bart* 48. There was also a Spanish biopic in 1944 with Conchita Montenegro and Florinda Bolkan played her in *Royal Flash*.

Montesi, Jorge (1950–).
Chilean-born director, based in Canada.
Birds of Prey (TV) 84. Omen IV: The Awakening (TV) 91. Stealth Force 93. Soft Deceit 95, etc.

Montez, Maria (1919–1951) (Maria de Santo Silas).
Exotic Hollywood leading lady mainly seen in hokum adventures.
The Invisible Woman (debut) 41. South of Tahiti 41. The Mystery of Marie Roget 42. *Arabian Nights* 42. White Savage 43. *Cobra Woman* 44. Ali Baba and the Forty Thieves 44. Gypsy Wildcat 44. Sudan 45. Tangier 46. Pirates of Monterey 47. The Exile 47. Siren of Atlantis 48. The Thief of Venice 51, etc.
❝ When I see myself on the screen, I am so beautiful I jump for joy. – M.M.

Montgomery, Belinda (1950–).
American leading lady.
The Todd Killings 70. Women in Chains (TV) 72. Letters from Three Lovers (TV) 73. The Other Side of the Mountain 75. Breaking Point 76. Blackout 77. The Other Side of the Mountain Part Two 78. Silent Madness 84, etc.
TV series: Man from Atlantis 77–78. Aaron's Way 88. Doogie Howser M.D. 89.

Montgomery, Bernard (1887–1976).
British Field Marshal who through his waspish personality became famous, especially when he commanded the victorious Eighth Army in North Africa in 1942. He has been best played on TV by Ian Richardson, especially in *Ike*. Trevor Reid played him in *The Longest Day* and Michael Bates in *Patton*. An exciting and amusing film of 1958, *I Was Monty's Double*, featured his wartime stand-in, Clifton James. His insistence on having a full English breakfast on the battlefield is one of the derivations of the expression 'the full Monty', given new life by the box-office success in 1997 of the British film about male strippers.

Montgomery, Bruce (1921–1978).
English composer, conductor, and organist, a former teacher, in films from 1948. Educated at Oxford University, where he was a close friend of poet Philip Larkin, he is possibly better known for writing detective novels (as Edmund Crispin) featuring literary critic Professor Gervase Fen, the first being published while he was still an undergraduate. His other compositions included a Coronation anthem, written with Kingsley Amis. Alcoholism and difficulty in finishing his scores on time curtailed his movie career.
The Kidnappers 53. Cartouche 54. Doctor in the House 54. Doctor at Sea 55. Escapade 55. Eye Witness 56. Checkpoint 56. Guilty 56. Doctor at Large 57. The Truth about Women 57. Carry On Sergeant 58. Carry On Nurse 59. Carry On

Teacher 59. Too Young to Love 59. Please Turn Over 59. Carry On Constable 60. Carry On Regardless 60. Raising the Wind (& w) 61. Carry On Cruising (co-m) 62, etc.

❝ He had two genuine and precocious talents which both dried up quite quickly when he was about thirty . . . How are you supposed to handle that, lots of money now and some fame and nothing to say? Drinking yourself to death is one solution. – *Kingsley Amis*

Montgomery, Doreen (1916–1992).
British screenwriter, latterly in television where she created the character of Emma Peel for the long-running series *The Avengers*.

Meet Mr Penny 38. Mr Reeder in Room 13 38. Lassie from Lancashire 38. Just William 39. At the Villa Rose 39. Poison Pen 39. House of the Arrow 39. The Flying Squad 40. The Second Mr Bush 40. The Man in Grey 43. Fanny by Gaslight 44. Love Story 44. This Man Is Mine 45. She Died Young 47. Bonnie Prince Charlie 48. Narrowing Circle 55, etc.

Montgomery, Douglass (1907–1966) (Robert Douglass Montgomery).
Canadian leading man with stage experience; once known as Kent Douglass.

■ Paid 30. Daybreak 31. Five and Ten 31. *Waterloo Bridge* 31. A House Divided 31. *Little Women* 33. Eight Girls in a Boat 34. Little Man What Now 34. Music in the Air 34. The Mystery of Edwin Drood 35. Lady Tubbs 35. Harmony Lane 35. Everything Is Thunder 36. Tropical Trouble 36. Counsel for Crime 37. Life Begins with Love 37. *The Cat and the Canary* 39. *The Way to the Stars* 45. Woman to Woman 46. When in Rome 47. Forbidden 48.

Montgomery, Elizabeth (1933–1995).
Pert American leading lady, daughter of Robert Montgomery; most familiar as the witch-wife of the TV series *Bewitched* 64–71.

The Court Martial of Billy Mitchell 55. Who's Been Sleeping in My Bed? 63. Johnny Cool 63. The Victim (TV) 72. A Case of Rape (TV) 74. The Legend of Lizzie Borden (TV) 75. Dark Victory (TV) 76. A Killing Affair (TV) 77. The Awakening Land (TV) 78. Jennifer: A Woman's Story (TV) 79. Act of Violence (TV) 80. Belle Starr (TV) 81. When the Circus Came to Town (TV) 82. The Rules of Marriage (TV) 83. Second Sight (TV) 85. Face to Face (TV) 90. Black Widow Murders: The Blanche Taylor Moore Story (TV) 93, etc.

Montgomery, George (1916–) (George M. Letz).
Genial American leading man, mostly in low-budgeters; former boxer and stuntman who later had ambitions to direct.

The Cisco Kid and the Lady 39. Young People 40. *Roxie Hart* 42. *Ten Gentlemen from West Point* 42. Orchestra Wives 42. Coney Island 43. Bomber's Moon 43. Three Little Girls in Blue 46. The Brasher Doubloon 47. Lulu Belle 48. Dakota Lil 50. Sword of Monte Cristo 51. The Texas Rangers 51. Fort Ti 53. Street of Sinners 55. Huk 56. Black Patch 57. Watusi 59. The Steel Claw (& d) 61. Samar (& d) 62. From Hell to Borneo (& d) 64. Battle of the Bulge 65. Hallucination Generation 66. Huntsville 67. Satan's Harvest (& d) 69. The Wild Wind 86, etc.

TV series: Cimarron City 58.

Montgomery, Lee Harcourt.
American child actor of the 70s.

Million Dollar Duck 71. The Harness (TV) 71. Ben 72. The Savage Is Loose 74. A Cry in the Wilderness (TV) 74. Burnt Offerings 76. Baker's Hawk 76. Dead of Night (TV) 77. True Grit: A Further Adventure (TV) 78. Girls Just Want to Have Fun 85. The Midnight Hour (TV) 85. Into the Fire 88, etc.

Montgomery, Robert (1904–1981) (Henry Montgomery).
Smooth, smart American leading man of the 30s; later became a director, then forsook show business for politics.

■ So This Is College 29. Untamed 29. Three Live Ghosts 29. The Single Standard 29. Their Own Desire 29. Free and Easy 30. The Divorcee 30. The Big House 30. Our Blushing Brides 30. Sins of the Children 30. Love in the Rough 30. War Nurse 30. The Easiest Way 31. Strangers May Kiss 31. Inspiration 31. Shipmates 31. The Man in Possession 31. Private Lives 31. Lovers Courageous 31. But the Flesh is Weak 32. Letty Lynton 32. Blondie of the Follies 32. Faithless 32. Hell Below 33. Made on Broadway 33. *When Ladies Meet* 33. Night Flight 33. Another Language 33. Fugitive Lovers 34. Riptide 34. The Mystery of Mr X 34. Hideout 34. Forsaking All Others 35. Vanessa, Her Love Story 35. Biography of a Bachelor Girl 35. No More Ladies 35. Petticoat Fever 36. Trouble for Two 36. Piccadilly Jim 36. The Last of Mrs Cheyney 37. *Night Must Fall* (AAN) 37. Ever Since Eve 37. Live Love and Learn 37. The First Hundred Years 37. *Yellow Jack* 38. Three Loves has Nancy 38. Fast and Loose 39. The Earl of Chicago 40. *Busman's Honeymoon* (GB) (as Lord Peter Wimsey) 40. Rage in Heaven 41. Mr and Mrs Smith 41. *Here Comes Mr Jordan* (AAN) 41. Unfinished Business 41. They Were Expendable 45. *The Lady in the Lake* (as Philip Marlowe) (& d) 46. Ride the Pink Horse (& d) 47. The Saxon Charm 48. June Bride 48. Once More My Darling (& d) 49. Your Witness (GB) 50. The Gallant Hours (d only) 60.

TV series: Robert Montgomery Presents 50–56.

❝ If you are lucky enough to be a success, by all means enjoy the applause and the adulation of the public. But never, never believe it. – *R.M.*

Monti, Felix (1938–).
Argentinian cinematographer, from commercials.

The Official Story 85. South (Sur) 87. Old Gringo 87. I, the Worst of All/Yo, la Peor de Todas 90. A Wall of Silence/Un Muro de Silencio 93. We Don't Want to Talk about It/De Eso No Se Habla 93. A Shadow You Soon Will Be/Una Sombra Ya Pronto Serás 94. Love and Shadows (US) 94, etc.

Montiel, Sarita (1928–) (Maria Antonia Abad).
Spanish leading lady in Mexican and American films. She was formerly married to director Anthony Mann.

Vera Cruz 54. Serenade 56. She Gods of Shark Reef 57. Run of the Arrow 57, etc.

Moody, Ron (1924–) (Ronald Moodnick).
British character comedian of stage and TV.

■ Make Mine Mink 59. Follow a Star 59. Five Golden Hours 60. A Pair of Briefs 62. Summer Holiday 63. The Mouse on the Moon 63. Ladies Who Do 63. Murder Most Foul 64. Every Day's a Holiday 64. San Ferry Ann 65. The Sandwich Man 65. *Oliver* (as Fagin) (AAN) 68. David Copperfield 69. The Twelve Chairs 70. Flight of the Doves 71. Dogpound Shuffle 74. Legend of the Werewolf 75. Dominique 78. The Word (TV) 79. The Spaceman and King Arthur 79. Dial M for Murder (TV) 81. Wrong Is Right 82. A Kid in King Arthur's Court 92.

TV series: Nobody's Perfect 79.

Moon, Keith (1947–1978).
Wild rock drummer with The Who, and occasional actor.

Monterey Pop (doc) 68. Woodstock (doc) 69. 200 Motels 71. That'll Be the Day 73. Stardust 74. *Tommy* (as Uncle Ernie) 75. Sextette (US) 78. The Kids Are Alright (doc) (US) 78. Quadrophenia (ex p) 79, etc.

Moorcroft, Judy (1933–1991).
British costume designer.

The Prince and the Pauper 77. Murder by Decree 79. The Europeans (AAN) 79. Silver Dream Racer 80. Yentl 83. A Passage to India (AAN) 84. The Killing Fields 84. Clockwise 86. Without a Clue 88. Fools of Fortune 90. City of Joy 92, etc.

Moore, Brian (1921–1999).
Belfast-born novelist and screenwriter, now a Canadian citizen, who has lived in North America for much of his life.

The Luck of Ginger Coffey (w, from his novel) 64. Torn Curtain (w) 66. The Blood of Others (w, TV) 84. Control (w, TV) 87. *The Lonely Passion of Judith Hearne* (oa) 87. Cold Heaven (oa) 89 (released 92). *Black Robe* 91 (w, from his novel).

Moore, Clayton (1908–).
Tall American leading man of 40s serials such as *The Crimson Ghost*, *G-Men Never Forget*, *The Ghost of Zorro*. Later famous on TV as *The Lone Ranger*.

Autobiography: 1997, *I Was That Masked Man* (with Frank Thompson).

Moore, Cleo (1928–1973).
American leading lady who appeared chiefly in Hugo Haas's low-budget emotional melodramas.

This Side of the Law 50. On Dangerous Ground 50. One Girl's Confession 53. Bait 54. Women's Prison 55. Over-Exposed 56, etc.

Moore, Colleen (1900–1988) (Kathleen Morrison).
American leading lady of the silent screen.

Autobiography: 1968, *Silent Star*.

■ Bad Boy 17. An Old Fashioned Young Man 17. Hands Up 17. The Savage 18. A Hoosier Romance 18. Little Orphan Annie 18. The Busher 19. Wilderness Trail 19. Man in the Moonlight 19. The Egg Crate Wallop 19. Common Property 19. The Cyclone 20. A Roman Scandal 20. Her Bridal Nightmare 20. The Devil's Claim 20. So Long Letty 20. When Dawn Came 20. Dinty 20. The Sky Pilot 21. The Lotus Eater 21. His Nibs 21. Broken Hearts of Broadway 21. Come on Over 22. The Wallflower 22. Affinities 22. Forsaking All Others 22. Broken Chains 22. The Ninety and Nine 22. Look Your Best 23. Slippy McGee 23. The Nth Commandment 23. April Showers 23. Through the Dark 23. The Huntress 23. Flaming Youth 23. Painted People 24. The Perfect Flapper 24. Flirting with Love 24. *So Big* 24. *Sally* 25. The Desert Flower 25. We Moderns 25. Irene 26. *Ella Cinders* 26. It Must Be Love 26. Twinkletoes 27. Orchids and Ermine 27. Naughty But Nice 27. Her Wild Oat 27. Happiness Ahead 28. Oh Kay! 28. *Lilac Time* 28. Synthetic Sin 28. Why Be Good? 29. Smiling Irish Eyes 29. Footlights and Fools 29. The Power and the Glory 33. Success at Any Price 34. Social Register 34. The Scarlet Letter 34.

❝ I was the spark that lit up Flaming Youth, Colleen Moore was its torch. – *F. Scott Fitzgerald*

Moore, Constance (1919–).
American leading lady and singer, mildly popular in the 40s; usually in 'sensible' roles.

Prison Break 38. You Can't Cheat an Honest Man 39. La Conga Nights 40. Ma, He's Making Eyes at Me 40. I Wanted Wings 41. Take a Letter, Darling 42. *Show Business* 43. *Atlantic City* 44. Delightfully Dangerous 45. Earl Carroll's Vanities 45. In Old Sacramento 46. Hit Parade of 1947 47. Hats off to Rhythm 47. The 13th Letter 51. Spree 67, etc.

TV series: Window on Main Street 61.

Moore, Demi (1962–) (Demi Guynes).
American leading actress. She married actor Bruce WILLIS in 1987. She became the highest-paid Hollywood actress with a $12m price for her role in the thriller *Striptease*.

Choices 81. Young Doctors in Love 82. Parasite 82. Blame It on Rio 84. No Small Affair 85. St Elmo's Fire 85. One Crazy Summer 86. About Last Night . . . 86. Wisdom 87. The Seventh Sign 88. We're No Angels 89. Ghost 90. Mortal Thoughts 91. The Butcher's Wife 91. Nothing but Trouble 91. Indecent Proposal 93. A Few Good Men 93. Disclosure 94. Scarlet Letter 95. Now and Then (& p) 95. The Juror 96. The Hunchback of Notre Dame (voice) 96. Striptease 96. GI Jane 97. Deconstructing Harry 97, etc.

Moore, Dickie (1925–).
American child actor of the 30s, first on screen when one year old. He became the fifth husband of actress Jane Powell in 1988. He is the author of a book on child stars: 1984, *Twinkle, Twinkle Little Star (But Don't Have Sex or Take the Car)*.

The Beloved Rogue 26. Passion Flower 30. Blonde Venus 32. Oliver Twist 33. Peter Ibbetson 34. Sergeant York 41. Miss Annie Rooney 42. Dangerous Years 47. Out of the Past/Build My Gallows High 48. Killer Shark 50. The Member of the Wedding (last to date) 52, etc.

Moore, Dudley (1935–).
English comic actor, writer, musician and composer, who unexpectedly became a Hollywood star in the late 70s. Born in London, he won an organ scholarship to Oxford University, and became resident composer at the Royal Court Theatre, as well as playing piano with jazz groups. Despite being self-conscious of his height – he is 5 feet 2 inches – and club-foot, he was a natural performer who found fame with Peter COOK, Alan BENNETT and Jonathan MILLER in the revue *Beyond the Fringe* in 1960. A hilarious partnership with Cook followed, embracing records, television and film, until Cook's heavy drinking brought it to an end. In Hollywood, he became a star with '*10*', in a role that George SEGAL had walked away from (in 1997, Segal replaced him when Barbra STREISAND fired him from *The Mirror Has Two Faces*), but a succession of poor films followed. He also had a career as a concert pianist. Married four times, including to actresses Suzy KENDALL and Tuesday WELD. He also had a long relationship with actress Susan ANTON.

Biography: 1997, *Dudley Moore: The Authorised Biography* by Barbara Paskin.

■ The Wrong Box 65. *Bedazzled* (& m) 67. 30 Is a Dangerous Age, Cynthia (& co-w, m) 67. Inadmissible Evidence (m only) 68. Monte Carlo or Bust/Those Daring Young Men in Their Jaunty Jalopies 69. The Bed Sitting Room 69. Staircase (m only) 69. Alice's Adventures in Wonderland (as the Dormouse) 72. Hound of the Baskervilles (& co-w, m) 77. Foul Play 78. *'10'* 79. Wholly Moses 80. *Arthur* 80. Six Weeks (& m) 82. Lovesick 83. Romantic Comedy 83. Unfaithfully Yours 83. Best Defense 83. Micki and Maude 84. Santa Claus 85. Like Father Like Son 87. Arthur 2: On the Rocks 88. Milo and Otis (narration) 88. Crazy People 89. Blame It on the Bellboy 92. Parallel Lives (TV) 92. The Disappearance of Kevin Johnson (TV) 95. Weekend in the Country (TV) 95.

TV series: *Not Only . . . but Also* 65–66, 70. Goodbye Again 68. Orchestra 91. Dudley 93. Concerto 93. Daddy's Girls 94.

❝ The ability to enjoy your sex life is central. I don't give a shit about anything else. My obsession is total. What else is there to live for? – *D.M.*

The confidence I now have is rooted in the discovery that who I am is okay. – *D.M.*

I think my own desire to be loved is what makes me sexually attractive. – *D.M.*

I have a very ribald sense of humour, which is conventionally known as obscene. – *D.M.*

I suppose I haven't made the dent in life that I hoped to. I think I've missed the boat a bit. Maybe I should have tried harder. I haven't become a full-out comedian or musician or composer. – *D.M.*

A grubby cherub. – *Jonathan Miller*

Moore, Eileen (1932–).
English leading lady of the 50s who studied at RADA and made her stage debut in 1956. Formerly married to actor George COLE.

Laughter in Paradise 51. Mr Denning Drives North 51. The Happy Family/Mr Lord Says No 52. The Girl on the Pier 53. An Inspector Calls 54. The Men of Sherwood Forest 54. Street of Angels 54. A Town Like Alice 56. The Green Man 56. Devil's Bait 59, etc.

Moore, Eva (1870–1955).
British stage actress who made a few films in the 30s.

Chu Chin Chow 22. Brown Sugar 31. *The Old Dark House* (splendid in her cries of 'No beds! They can't have beds!') (US) 32. I Was a Spy 33. A Cup of Kindness 34. Vintage Wine 35. Old Iron 39. The Bandit of Sherwood Forest (US) 46, etc.

Moore, Grace (1901–1947).
American operatic singer who appeared in occasional films; Kathryn Grayson played her in a 1953 biopic, *So This Is Love*. She was killed in a plane crash.

Autobiography: 1946, *You're Only Human Once*.

■ A Lady's Morals (as Jenny Lind) 30. New Moon 30. *One Night of Love* (AAN) 34. Love Me Forever 35. The King Steps Out 36. When You're In Love 37. I'll Take Romance 37. Louise 40.

Moore, Ida (1883–1964).
American character actress.

The Merry Widow 25. She's a Soldier Too 44. To Each His Own 46. The Egg and I 47. Manhattan Angel 49. Harvey 50. Honeychile 51. Scandal At Scourie 53. The Country Girl 54. Ma and Pa Kettle at Waikiki 55. The Desk Set 57. Rock a Bye Baby 58, etc.

Moore, Juanita (1922–).
American character actress.

Lydia Bailey 52. Affair in Trinidad 52. Witness to Murder 54. Women's Prison 55. Ransom 56. The Girl Can't Help It 56. Green Eyed Blonde 57. *Imitation of Life* (AAN) 59. Tammy Tell Me True 61. A Raisin in the Sun 61. Walk on the Wild Side 62. Papa's Delicate Condition 63. The Singing Nun 66. Rosie 68. Up Tight 68. Fox Style 73. Thomasine and Bushrod 74. Abby 74. Two Moon Junction 88, etc.

Moore, Julianne (1961–).
Red-haired American leading actress, a graduate of Boston University, from the theatre. She has a son, born 1997, by writer and director Bart Freundlich (1950–).
Money, Power, Murder (TV) 89. Tales from the Darkside: The Movie 90. Lovecraft (TV) 91. The Hand that Rocks the Cradle 92. The Gun in Betty Lou's Handbag 92. Body of Evidence 93. Benny and Joon 93. The Fugitive 93. *Short Cuts* 93. *Vanya on 42nd Street* 94. Roommates 95. Nine Months 95. Assassins 95. *Safe* 96. The Lost World: Jurassic Park 97. *Boogie Nights* (AAN) 97. The Myth of Fingerprints 97. The Big Lebowski 98. Psycho 98, etc.

Moore, Kieron (1925–) (Kieron O'Hanrahan).
Hangdog Irish leading man with stage experience.
The Voice Within 44. *A Man about the House* 46. *Mine Own Executioner* 47. Anna Karenina 48. Ten Tall Men 51. The Key 58. The Day They Robbed the Bank of England 60. Dr Blood's Coffin 61. The Day of the Triffids 63. The Thin Red Line 64. Crack in the World 65. Arabesque 66. Custer of the West 67, etc.

Moore, Mary Tyler (1936–).
Pert American leading lady who has been most successful on TV, and with her then husband Grant Tinker formed her own production company, known as MTM Productions, which was later sold to the British TV company TVS.
Autobiography: 1995, *After All*.
■ X15 61. Thoroughly Modern Millie 67. What's So Bad About Feeling Good? 68. Don't Just Stand There 68. Change of Habit 69. Run a Crooked Mile (TV) 69. *First You Cry* (TV) 78. *Ordinary People* (AAN) 80. Six Weeks 82. Finnegan Begin Again (TV) 84. Just between Friends 85. Lincoln (TV) 88. Thanksgiving Day (TV) 90. Stolen Babies (TV) 93. Stolen Memories: Secrets from the Rose Garden (TV) 96. Flirting with Disaster 96. Murder at 1600 97.
TV series: Steve Canyon 58. Richard Diamond 59–60. *The Dick Van Dyke Show* 61–65. *The Mary Tyler Moore Show* 70–74. Mary 86. Annie McGuire 89. New York News 95.
❝ I'm not an actress who can create a character. I play me. – M.T.M.

Moore, Matt (1888–1960).
American silent actor, youngest of four Irish acting brothers (Tom, Owen and Joe were the others).
Traffic in Souls 13. Pride of the Clan 16. The Bondage of Barbara 19. Fools in the Dark 24. Grounds for Divorce 25. Dry Martini 28. Coquette 29. Spellbound 45, many others.

Moore, Michael.
American documentary writer and director.
Roger and Me 89. Canadian Bacon 95.
TV series: TV Nation 94.

Moore, Owen (1887–1939).
(See MOORE, Matt.) Owen married Mary Pickford.
The Cricket on the Hearth 09. Battle of the Sexes 13. Mistress Nell 15. Piccadilly Jim 19. Torment 24. The Red Mill 27. What a Widow 30. She Done Him Wrong 33, many others.

Moore, Richard (1925–).
American cinematographer.
The Wild Angels 65. Wild in the Streets 68. Winning 69. The Reivers 69. Myra Breckinridge 70. WUSA 70. Judge Roy Bean 72. The Stone Killer 73. Circle of Iron (d) 79. Annie 82, etc.

Moore, Robert (1927–1984).
American director, from TV.
Murder by Death 76. The Cheap Detective 78. Chapter Two 79, etc.
AS ACTOR: Tell Me That You Love Me Junie Moon 70.

Moore, Roger (1927–).
British light leading man, best known for his long stint as James Bond, succeeding Sean CONNERY in the role. In 1998, the *Sunday Times* estimated his wealth at £25m.
Biography: 1985, *Roger Moore* by Roy Moseley with Philip and Martin Masheter.
The Last Time I Saw Paris 54. Interrupted Melody 55. The King's Thief 55. Diane 55. The Miracle 59. The Sins of Rachel Cade 61. Gold of the Seven Saints 61. Rape of the Sabines 61. No Man's Land 62. Crossplot 69. The Man Who Haunted Himself 70. Live and Let Die (as James Bond) 73. The Man with the Golden Gun 74. Gold 74. That Lucky Touch 75. Shout at the Devil 76. Street People 76. The Spy Who Loved Me 77. Sherlock Holmes in New York (TV) 77. The Wild Geese 78. Escape from Athena 79. Moonraker 79. North Sea Hijack 80. Sunday Lovers 80. The Sea Wolves 80. The Cannonball Run 81. For Your Eyes Only 81. Octopussy 83. The Naked Face 84. A View to a Kill 85. The Magic Snowman (voice) 87. Bed and Breakfast 89. Bullseye 90. Fire, Ice and Dynamite 90. The Man Who Wouldn't Die (TV) 95. The Quest 96. Spice World: The Movie 97, etc.
TV series: Ivanhoe 57. The Alaskans 59. Maverick 61. *The Saint* 63–68. *The Persuaders* 71.
❝ If I kept all my bad notices, I'd need two houses. – *R.M.*
My acting range? Left eyebrow raised, right eyebrow raised. – *R.M.*
You're not a star till they can spell your name in Vladivostok. – *R.M.*

Moore, Ted (1914–1987).
South African cinematographer, in British films.
The Black Knight 54. Cockleshell Heroes 56. Dr No 62. From Russia with Love 63. Goldfinger 64. Thunderball 65. *A Man for All Seasons* (AA) 66. Shalako 68. The Prime of Miss Jean Brodie 69. The Most Dangerous Man in the World 69. Country Dance 70. Diamonds are Forever 71. Live and Let Die 73. The Man with the Golden Gun 74. Sinbad and the Eye of the Tiger 77. Orca 77. Dominique 79. Clash of the Titans 81. Priest of Love 81, etc.

Moore, Terry (1929–) (Helen Koford).
American leading lady, former child model, in films from infancy.
Autobiography: 1984, *The Beauty and the Billionaire* (dealing with her relationship with Howard Hughes).
The Murder in Thornton Square 43. Mighty Joe Young 50. Come Back Little Sheba (AAN) 52. The Sunny Side of the Street 53. King of the Khyber Rifles 54. Bernardine 57. A Private's Affair 59. Why Must I Die? 60. Town Tamer 65. Death Dimension 78. Hellhole 85. Death Blow 87. Beverly Hill Brats (& p) 88. Jake Spanner – Private Eye 89, etc.
TV series: Empire 62.

Moore, Tom (1883–1955).
Irish-born silent actor in America, brother of Matt and Owen MOORE. His three wives included actresses Alice Joyce (1914–20) and Rene Adoree (1921–24).
The Strange Story of Elsie Mason 12. The Hunchback 13. Vampire's Trail 14. The Cinderella Man 17. Dangerous Money 21. The Cowboy and the Lady 22. Big Brother 23. One Night in Rome 24. The Song and Dance Man 26. Cabaret 27. Anybody Here Seen Kelly? 28. Cannonball Express 32. Mr Broadway 33. Trouble for Two 36. Behind Green Lights 46. Mother Wore Tights 47. Forever Amber 47. The Fighting O'Flynn 49. The Redhead and the Cowboy 50, etc.

Moore, Victor (1876–1962).
Veteran American vaudeville comedian with hesitant, bumbling manner.
■ Chimmie Fadden 15. Chimmie Fadden Out West 15. Snobs 15. The Clown 16. The Race 16. The Best Man 16. Invited Out 17. Oh! U-Boat 17. Faint Heart and Fair Lady 17. Bungalowing 17. Commuting 17. Flivvering 17. Home Defence 17. The Man Who Found Himself 25. Heads Up 30. Dangerous Nan McGrew 30. Romance in the Rain 34. The Gift of Gab 34. *Swing Time* 36. Gold Diggers of 1937 36. We're on the Jury 37. Meet the Missus 37. The Life of the Party 37. She's Got Everything 37. *Make Way for Tomorrow* 37. Radio City Revels 38. This Marriage Business 38. *Louisiana Purchase* 41. *Star Spangled Rhythm* 42. True to Life 43. Riding High 43. The Heat's On 43. Carolina Blues 44. Duffy's Tavern 45. *It's In the Bag* 45. *Ziegfeld Follies* 46. It Happened on Fifth Avenue 47. A Miracle Can Happen 48. A Kiss in the Dark 49. *We're Not Married* 52. The Seven-Year Itch 55.
Famous line (*Make Way for Tomorrow*): 'Two old-fashioneds, for two old-fashioned people.'

Moorehead, Agnes (1906–1974).
Sharp-featured American character actress, often seen in waspish or neurotic roles.
■ Citizen Kane 41. *The Magnificent Ambersons* (AAN) 42. Journey into Fear 42. The Big Street 42. The Youngest Profession 43. Government Girl 43. Jane Eyre 43. Since You Went Away 44. Dragon Seed 44. The Seventh Cross 44. Mrs Parkington (AAN) 44. Tomorrow the World 44. Keep Your Powder Dry 45. Our Vines Have Tender Grapes 45. Her Highness and the Bellboy 45. Dark Passage 47. *The Lost Moment* (as a centenarian) 47. Summer Holiday 48. *The Woman in White* 48. Station West 48. Johnny Belinda (AAN) 48. The Stratton Story 49. The Great Sinner 49. Without Honor 49. Caged 50. Fourteen Hours 51. Show Boat 51. The Blue Veil 51. The Adventures of Captain Fabian 51. Captain Blackjack 52. The Blazing Forest 52. The Story of Three Loves 53. Scandal at Scourie 53. Main Street to Broadway 53. Those Redheads from Seattle 53. Magnificent Obsession 54. Untamed 55. The Left Hand of God 55. All That Heaven Allows 56. Meet Me in Las Vegas 56. The Conqueror 56. The Revolt of Mamie Stover 56. The Swan 56. Pardners 56. The Opposite Sex 56. Raintree County 57. The True Story of Jesse James 57. Jeanne Eagels 57. The Story of Mankind 57. Night of the Quarter Moon 59. Tempest 59. *The Bat* 59. Pollyanna 60. Twenty Plus Two 61. Bachelor in Paradise 61. Jessica 62. How the West Was Won 63. Who's Minding the Store? 63. Hush Hush Sweet Charlotte (AAN) 64. The Singing Nun 66. What's the Matter with Helen? 71. Suddenly Single (TV) 71. Rolling Man (TV) 72. Night of Terror (TV) 72. Dear Dead Delilah 72. Frankenstein: The True Story (TV) 73.
TV series: *Bewitched* 64–71.

Moorhead, Natalie (1901–1992).
American actress of the 30s, usually as a tough blonde. The first of her three husbands was director Alan Crosland.
Hook, Line and Sinker 30. Illicit 31. Morals for Women 31. The King Murder Case 32. Murder on the High Seas 32. Dancing Man 33. The Thin Man 34. Beloved Brat 38. Lady of the Tropics 39, etc.

Moorhouse, Jocelyn.
Australian director and producer, married to director Paul J. Hogan. She studied at the Australian Film Television and Radio School in the early 80s and worked in television as a writer and director.
Secrets (TV) 88. Proof 91. Muriel's Wedding 94. How to Make an American Quilt 95. A Thousand Acres (US) 97, etc.

Mora, Philippe (1949–).
Australian director.
Mad Dog 76. The Beast Within 81. The Return of Captain Invincible 82. Howling II 85. Death of a Soldier 86. The Marsupials: Howling III 87. Communion 89. Art Deco Detective 94. Pterodactyl Woman from Beverly Hills 96, etc.

Morahan, Christopher (1924–).
British director with stage and TV experience.
■ Diamonds for Breakfast 68. All Neat in Black Stockings 69. The Jewel in the Crown (TV) 83. In the Secret State (TV) 85. Clockwise 86. After Pilkington 87. Troubles 88. The Heat of the Day (TV) 89. Paper Mask 90.

Morahan, Jim.
English art director, often for Ealing productions and the films of Alexander Mackendrick.
Frieda 47. Whisky Galore 49. The Blue Lamp 50. The Man in the White Suit 51. Mandy 52. The Cruel Sea 52. The Maggie 54. *The Ladykillers* 55. Dunkirk 58. Summer of the Seventeenth Doll 59. The Long and the Short and the Tall 60. Battle beneath the Earth 67. Witchfinder General 68, etc.

Morahan, Tom.
English art director, a former architect.
St Martin's Lane 38. Jamaica Inn 39. Went the Day Well? 42. The Paradine Case 47. Under Capricorn 49. Treasure Island 50. Captain Horatio Hornblower 51. Sons and Lovers 60. Those Magnificent Men in Their Flying Machines 65, etc.

Moran, Dolores (1924–1982).
American leading lady of the 40s.
Old Acquaintance 43. To Have and Have Not 43. The Man I Love 47, etc.

Moran, Jackie (1925–1990) (John E. Moran).
American child actor who played Huckleberry Finn in the 1938 version of *Tom Sawyer* and featured in the first Buck Rogers serials. He made his last film in 1947.
Valiant Is the Word for Carrie 36. The Adventures of Tom Sawyer 38. Gone with the Wind 39. Spirit of Culver 39. Tomboy 40. The Old Swimmin' Hole 40. Henry Aldrich Haunts a House 43. Song of the Open Road 44. Betty Co-Ed 47, etc.

Moran, Lois (1908–1990) (Lois Darlington Dowling).
American leading actress of silents. Born in Pittsburgh and educated in France, she was a dancer with the Paris National Opera and appeared in French films before making her American debut in the mid-20s, when she became a star at the age of 16 and, soon after, formed a friendship with F. Scott Fitzgerald. She was the model for Rosemary Hoyt in his novel *Tender Is the Night*. She left films in the early 30s to appear in Broadway musicals, retiring in the mid-30s when she married; in the 50s she taught drama and dance at Stanford University, and returned to acting for a while on television.
La Galerie des Monstres (Fr.) 24. Stella Dallas 25. The Road to Mandalay 26. The Music Master 27. The Whirlwind of Youth 27. The River Pirate 28. Blindfold 28. Behind That Curtain 29. Mammy 30. The Dancers 30. Transatlantic 31. The Spider 31. West of Broadway 32. Alice in the Cities/Alice in den Stadten 74, etc.
TV series: Waterfront 53–56.

Moran, Peggy (1918–).
American leading lady of the 40s, with radio experience; married Henry Koster and retired.
Girls' School 39. The Mummy's Hand 40. Horror Island 41. Drums of the Congo 42. Seven Sweethearts 42. King of the Cowboys 43, etc.

Moran, Percy (1886–1952).
English leading actor in silent movies, notably as the dashing Lieutenant Daring in numerous adventures – from 1911, *Lt Daring Saves HMS Medina*, to 1924, *Lt Daring and the Water Rats*.

Moran, Polly (1884–1952).
American vaudeville comedienne who was in silent shorts from 1913 and made some early sound films, notably in partnership with Marie Dressler.
Hollywood Revue 29. Caught Short 29. Reducing 30. Politics 31. The Passionate Plumber 32. Alice in Wonderland 33.
Later played smaller roles in: Two Wise Maids 37. Tom Brown's Schooldays 39. Petticoat Politics 41. Adam's Rib 49, etc.

Moranis, Rick (1954–).
Canadian comic actor in wimpish roles.
Strange Brew (wd) 83. Hockey Night 84. Ghost Busters 84. The Wild Life 84. Streets of Fire 84. Brewster's Millions 85. Club Paradise 86. Head Office 86. Little Shop of Horrors 86. Spaceballs 87. Honey I Shrunk the Kids 89. Ghostbusters II 89. Parenthood 89. My Blue Heaven 90. L.A. Story 91. Honey, I Blew Up the Kid 92. Splitting Heirs 93. The Flintstones 94. Little Giants 94. Big Bully 96. Honey, We Shrunk Ourselves 97, etc.
TV series: Second City TV 80–81. SCTV Network 90 81–82.

Morante, Laura.
Italian leading actress, in European films.
Golden Dreams/Sogni d'Oro 81. The Tragedy of a Ridiculous Man/La Tragedia di un Uomo Ridicolo 81. A Breath of Crime/L'Air du Crime (Fr.) 84. Bianca 84. The Two Lives of Mattia Pascal/Le Due Vite di Mattia Pascal 85. Man on Fire 87. Corps Perdu (Fr.) 89. To the Bitter End/Bis Zum Bitteren Ende (Ger.) 89. La Femme Fardée (Fr.) 90. Pink Palace, Paradise Beach (Aus.) 90. The Voice/La Voix (Fr.) 92. Faux-Pas Rire du Bonheur (Fr.) 94, etc.

Moravia, Alberto (1907–1990).
Italian novelist and screenwriter.
Last Meeting/Ultimo Incontro (w) 52. Sensualità (w) 52. The She-Wolf/La Lupa (w) 53. The Wayward Wife (oa) 53. Woman of Rome (oa) 54. Roman Tales (oa) 56. Love on the Riviera (oa) 58. La Giornata Balorda (w) 60. Two Women/La Ciociara (oa) 60. Contempt (oa) 63. The Empty Canvas (oa) 63. A Time of Indifference/Gli Indifferenti (oa) 64. The Conformist (oa) 70. The

Lie (oa) 85. Io & Lui (oa) 87. Husbands and Lovers (oa) 91. L'Ennui (oa) 98, etc.

More, Kenneth (1914–1982).
Breezy British leading actor, a recognizable World War II type who later gave compassionate interpretations of middle-aged dreamers; film-makers forsook him after his great 50s success, and he turned to stage and TV.

Autobiographies: 1959, *Happy Go Lucky*. 1978, *More or Less*.

■ Look Up and Laugh 35. Windmill Revels 38. Carry on London 38. Scott of the Antarctic 48. Man on the Run 49. Now Barabbas 49. Stop Press Girl 49. Morning Departure 50. Chance of a Lifetime 50. The Clouded Yellow 50. The Franchise Affair 50. No Highway 51. *Appointment With Venus* 51. Brandy for the Parson 52. The Yellow Balloon 52. Never Let Me Go 53. *Genevieve* 53. Our Girl Friday 53. *Doctor In the House* 54. Raising a Riot 54. *The Deep Blue Sea* 55. *Reach For the Sky* (as Douglas Bader) 56. The Admirable Crichton 57. A Night to Remember 58. Next to No Time 58. The Sheriff of Fractured Jaw 58. The Thirty-Nine Steps 59. Northwest Frontier 59. *Sink The Bismarck* 60. Man in the Moon 60. The Greengage Summer 61. The Longest Day 62. Some People 62. We Joined the Navy 62. The Comedy Man 63. The Mercenaries 67. Oh What a Lovely War 69. Fraulein Doktor 69. Battle of Britain 69. Scrooge 70. Where Time Began 76. The Slipper and the Rose 76. Leopard in the Snow 78. The Spaceman and King Arthur 79. A Tale of Two Cities 81.

TV series: The Forsyte Saga 68. Father Brown 73. An Englishman's Castle 78.

✪ For encapsulating for a nation all the carefree heroes of World War II. *Genevieve*.

More O'Ferrall, George (1907–1982).
British director who was mainly successful in TV.

AS ASSISTANT DIRECTOR: Midshipman Easy 34 No Highway 51.

■ AS DIRECTOR: Angels One Five 52. The Holly and the Ivy 53. The Heart of the Matter 53. The Green Scarf 53. A Woman for Joe 55. The March Hare 56. Three Cases of Murder/Lord Mountdrago 56.

Moreau, Jeanne (1928–).
French actress of stage and screen; the Bette Davis of her time. Married twice, including to director William FRIEDKIN. She was romantically involved with Louis MALLE, Lee MARVIN and fashion designer Pierre Cardin.

Biography: 1994, *La Moreau* by Marianne Gray.

The She-Wolves 55. Lift to the Scaffold 57. *The Lovers* 59. Le Dialogue des Carmelites 59. Les Liaisons Dangereuses 60. Moderato Cantabile 60. La Notte 61. *Jules et Jim* 61. Eva 62. The Trial 63. The Victors 63. Le Feu Follet 64. *Diary of a Chambermaid* 64. The Yellow Rolls-Royce 64. The Train 64. Mata Hari 65. *Viva Maria* 65. Mademoiselle 65. Chimes at Midnight 66. Sailor from Gibraltar 66. The Bride Wore Black 67. Great Catherine 68. Le Corps de Diane 68. Monte Walsh 70. Alex in Wonderland 70. Louise 72. Mr Klein 76. The Last Tycoon 76. French Provincial 76. A Lumière (& wd) 76. The Adolescent (w, d only) 79. Plein Sud 80. The Trout 82. Querelle 82. Sauve-toi Lola 86. Le Miraculé 87. Calling the Shots 88. Nikita 89. La Femme Fardée 90. Alberto Express 90. La Vieille qui Marchait dans la Mer 91. The Suspended Step of the Stork/To Meteoro Vima to Pelargou 91. Ville à Vendre 91. Until the End of the World/Bis ans Ende der Welt 91. A Foreign Field (TV) 93. The Clothes in the Wardrobe/The Summer House (TV) 93. Je M'Appelle Victor 93. Belle Epoque (TV) 93. Catherine the Great (TV) 95. Beyond the Clouds 95. I Love You, I Love You Not 97. Ever After 98, etc.

✪ For sheer strength of acting. *Louise*.

❝ When I'm doing a role I'm the part. I'm the person. But when I'm finished, I'm me. – *J.M.*

The life you had is nothing. It is the life you have that is important. – *J.M.*

Jeanne's heart is like an enormous room that is always cold: a man comes in, lights a fire, the flames swallow everything and then die down. When there are only ashes left, she shivers: she knows you cannot bring the cinders back to life, you have to light another fire, and she is always looking for a man who will not let the fire die down. – *William Friedkin*

Morecambe, Eric (1926–1984) (Eric Bartholomew) and **Wise, Ernie** (1925–) (Ernest Wiseman).
British comedy team with music-hall experience since 1943. In the 60s they became immensely popular on TV, but their films were rather less than satisfactory.

Biography: 1995, *Morecambe and Wise: Behind the Sunshine* by Gary Morecambe and Martin Sterling.

■ The Intelligence Men 64. That Riviera Touch 66. The Magnificent Two 67.

Moreland, Mantan (1902–1973).
Chubby American character actor, long cast as frightened valet.

Frontier Scout 38. Laughing at Danger 40. King of the Zombies 41. The Strange Case of Doctor RX 41. Charlie Chan in the Secret Service (and many others in this series) 44. Murder at Malibu Beach 47. The Feathered Serpent 49. Enter Laughing 68. Watermelon Man 70, etc.

Morell, André (1909–1978) (André Mesritz).
Dignified British character actor.

Thirteen Men and a Gun (debut) 38. No Place for Jennifer 49. Seven Days to Noon 50. High Treason 51. Summer Madness 55. The Bridge on the River Kwai 57. Ben Hur 59. The Hound of the Baskervilles 59. Cone of Silence 60. Shadow of the Cat 62. Cash on Demand 64. She 65. Plague of the Zombies 65. The Mummy's Shroud 67. 10 Rillington Place 70. Barry Lyndon 75. The Message 76, etc.

Moreno, Antonio (1886–1967).
Romantic Spanish star of Hollywood.

SILENT FILMS: Voice of the Million 12. House of Hate 18. The Trail of the Lonesome Pine 23. The Spanish Dancer 24. Mare Nostrum 25. Beverly of Graustark 26. The Temptress 26. It 27. Synthetic Sin 28, etc.

CHARACTER PARTS: One Mad Kiss 30. Storm over the Andes 35. Rose of the Rio Grande 38. Valley of the Giants 42. The Spanish Main 45. Captain from Castile 47. Thunder Bay 53. The Creature from the Black Lagoon 54. The Searchers 56, many others.

Moreno, Rita (1931–) (Rosita Dolores Alverio).
Puerto Rican actress-dancer, in films sporadically since 1950, between stage appearances. She took over the role of Norma Desmond in the London stage musical of *Sunset Boulevard* in 1996.

Pagan Love Song 50. Singin' in the Rain 52. Garden of Evil 54. The Vagabond King 55. The King and I 56. The Deerslayer 57. *West Side Story* (AA) 61. The Night of the Following Day 68. Popi 69. Carnal Knowledge 71. *The Ritz* 76. The Boss's Son 78. Happy Birthday Gemini 79. *The Four Seasons* 81. Life in the Food Chain 91. The Dark Angel 92. I Like It Like That 94. Angus 95. Slums of Beverly Hills 98, etc.

TV series: Nine to Five 82–83.

❝ Bigger than life is not difficult for me. I *am* bigger than life. – *R.M.*

Moretti, Nanni (1953–).
Italian director, screenwriter, producer and actor, who also runs his own production company and a Rome cinema. He won the award for best director at the 1994 Cannes Film Festival with *Dear Diary*.

Io Sono un Autarchico 76. Ecce Bombo 78. Sweet Dreams/Sogni d'Oro 81. Bianca 84. The Mass Is Over/La Messa è Finita 85. Notte Italiana (p) 87. Domani Accadrà (p) 88. Palombella Rossa 89. Il Portaborse (a, p) 91. *Dear Diary*/Caro Diario 93. The Second Time (a) 95. April/Aprile 98, etc.

Morgan, Dennis (1910–1994) (Stanley Morner).
American leading man, former opera singer.

Suzy (debut) 36. The Great Ziegfeld 36. Kitty Foyle 40. Captains of the Clouds 42. Thank Your Lucky Stars 43. Two Guys from Texas 46. My Wild Irish Rose 47. Painting the Clouds with Sunshine 51. The Gun That Won the West 55. Uranium Boom 56. Rogues' Gallery 68, etc.

TV series: 21 Beacon Street 59.

Morgan, Diana (1910–1996).
Welsh screenwriter, playwright and actress. Born in Cardiff, she studied at the Central School of Dramatic Art and was on-stage from 1931. From the mid-30s, she also wrote revues and plays with her husband, Robert MacDermot, before working as a contract writer at Ealing Studios. Later she wrote for television, including the 50s drama series *Emergency Ward 10*, and created that programme's spin-off series *Call Oxbridge 2000* 61–62.

AS WRITER: Ships with Wings (co-w) 41. The Foreman Went to France/Somewhere in France (co-w) 41. *Went the Day Well?* (co-w) 42. *Fiddlers Three* (co-w) 44. The Halfway House (co-w) 44. Pink String and Sealing Wax (co-w) 45. Poet's Pub (w) 49. Dance Hall (co-w) 50. Let's Be Happy (w) 57. Hand in Hand (w) 60, etc.

Morgan, Frank (1890–1949) (Francis Wupperman).
American character actor. In films from 1916, usually playing his endearing if slightly fuddled self, but his real popularity came with sound, when he was an MGM contract player for over twenty years.

■ The Suspect 17. The Daring of Diana 17. Light in the Darkness 17. A Modern Cinderella 17. The Girl Philippa 17. Who's Your Neighbour 17. A Child of the Wild 17. Baby Mine 17. Raffles 17. The Knife 18. At the Mercy of Men 18. Gray Towers of Mystery 19. The Golden Shower 19. Manhandled 24. Born Rich 24. The Man Who Found Himself 25. The Crowded Hour 25. The Scarlet Saint 25. Love's Greatest Mistake 27. Queen High 30. Dangerous Dan McGrew 30. Fast and Loose 30. Laughter 30. The Half Naked Truth 32. Secrets of the French Police 32. Luxury Liner 33. *Hallelujah I'm a Bum* 33. Reunion in Vienna 33. The Nuisance 33. When Ladies Meet 33. Broadway to Hollywood 33. *Bombshell* 33. The Best of Enemies 33. Billion Dollar Scandal 33. The Kiss Before the Mirror 33. The Cat and the Fiddle 34. *The Affairs of Cellini* (AAN) 34. By Your Leave 34. There's Always Tomorrow 34. Success at Any Price 34. Sisters under the Skin 34. A Lost Lady 34. The Good Fairy 35. Naughty Marietta 35. Escapade 35. I Live My Life 35. The Perfect Gentleman 35. Enchanted April 35. The Dancing Pirate 35. *The Great Ziegfeld* 36. *Trouble for Two* 36. *Piccadilly Jim* 36. *Dimples* 36. *The Last of Mrs Cheyney* 37. The Emperor's Candlesticks 37. Saratoga 37. Beg Borrow or Steal 37. Rosalie 37. Paradise for Three 38. Port of Seven Seas 38. The Crowd Roars 38. Sweethearts 38. Broadway Serenade 39. *The Wizard of Oz* 39. Balalaika 39. The Shop around the Corner 40. Henry Goes to Arizona 40. Broadway Melody of 1940. The Ghost Comes Home 40. The Mortal Storm 40. *Boom Town* 40. Hullabaloo 40. Keeping Company 41. Washington Melodrama 41. Wild Man of Borneo 41. Honky Tonk 41. *The Vanishing Virginian* 42. *Tortilla Flat* (AAN) 42. White Cargo 42. Stranger in Town 43. *The Human Comedy* 43. Thousands Cheer 43. The White Cliffs of Dover 43. Casanova Brown 44. Yolanda and the Thief 45. The Courage of Lassie 45. The Great Morgan 46. The Cockeyed Miracle 46. Lady Luck 46. Green Dolphin Street 47. Summer Holiday 48. The Three Musketeers 48. Any Number Can Play 49. The Great Sinner 49. The Stratton Story 49. Key to the City 50.

Morgan, Harry (1915–) (Harry Bratsburg).
Mild-looking American character actor with stage experience.

To the Shores of Tripoli (debut) 42. From This Day Forward 45. The Saxon Charm 49. Moonrise 50. The Well 51. High Noon 52. The Glenn Miller Story 53. Not as a Stranger 55. The Teahouse of the August Moon 56. Inherit the Wind 60. John Goldfarb Please Come Home 64. What Did You Do in the War, Daddy? 66. Support Your Local Sheriff 69. The Barefoot Executive 71. Snowball Express 73. The Apple Dumpling Gang 75. The Apple Dumpling Gang Rides Again 79. Incident in a Small Town (TV) 94, many others.

TV series: December Bride 54–58. Pete and Gladys 60–61. The Richard Boone Show 63. Kentucky Jones 64. Dragnet 69. The D.A. 71. M*A*S*H 76–83. Aftermash 83. Black Magic 86. Dragnet 87.

Morgan, Helen (1900–1941).
American café singer of the 30s; film appearances few. Biopic 1956 with Ann Blyth: *The Helen Morgan Story*.

Biography: 1974, *Helen Morgan, Her Life and Legend* by Gilbert Maxwell.

■ *Applause* 29. Roadhouse Nights 30. You Belong to Me 34. Marie Galante 34. Sweet Music 35. Go Into Your Dance 36. *Showboat* 36. Frankie and Johnnie 36.

Morgan, Joan (1905–).
English star of early silents who became a screenwriter in the sound era; also a playwright and novelist. She began acting as a child and appeared in silents directed by her father Sidney MORGAN.

AS ACTRESS: The Great Spy Raid 14. Frailty 16. Little Dorrit 20. A Lowland Cinderella 21. The Crimson Circle 22. The Shadow of Egypt 24. A Window in Piccadilly 28, etc.

AS WRITER (as Joan Wentworth Wood): Contraband Love 31. The Callbox Mystery 32. The Flag Lieutenant 32. Chelsea Life (co-w) 33. Mixed Doubles 33. Honeymoon Merry-go-round 36. The Minstrel Boy 37. Lily of Laguna (story) 38, etc.

Morgan, Michèle (1920–) (Simone Roussel).
French leading lady, in films from mid-30s.

Orage 36. *Quai des Brumes* 38. Remorques 39. La Loi du Nord 39. La Symphonie Pastorale 40. Joan of Paris (US) 41. Higher and Higher (US) 43. Passage to Marseilles (US) 44. *The Fallen Idol* (GB) 48. Les Orgueilleux 50. The Seven Deadly Sins 51. Les Grandes Manoeuvres 55. Marguerite de la Nuit 56. The Mirror Has Two Faces 60. Landru 63. Lost Command 66. Benjamin 68. Le Chat et la Souris 75. Everybody's Fine/Stanno Tutti Bene 90. Bulworth (US) 98, etc.

Morgan, Ralph (1882–1956) (Ralph Wupperman).
American character actor, brother of Frank Morgan. Former lawyer; went on stage, then to films in the 20s.

Charlie Chan's Chance 31. Rasputin and the Empress 32. Strange Interlude 32. *The Power and the Glory* 33. Anthony Adverse 36. The Life of Emile Zola 37. Forty Little Mothers 40. Black Market Babies 45. The Monster Maker 45. Sleep My Love 48. Gold Fever 52, many others.

Morgan, Sidney. (1873–1946).
English director, producer and screenwriter, mainly of silents, who continued to produce and direct quota quickies in the 30s. Many of his early films starred his daughter, Joan MORGAN.

The Brass Bottle 14. Iron Justice 15. Little Dorrit 20. Lady Noggs 20. The Lilac Sunbonnet 22. The Shadow of Egypt 24. Bulldog Drummond's Third Round 25. A Window in Piccadilly 28. Contraband Love (p, d) 31. Her Reputation (p, wd) 31. Chelsea Life 33. Honeymoon Merry-go-round (p) 36. The Minstrel Boy (p, d) 37. Almost a Gentleman (p, co-w) 38. Lily of Laguna (p) 38, etc.

Morgan, Terence (1921–).
British leading man.

Hamlet (debut) 48. Mandy 52. Turn the Key Softly 53. They Can't Hang Me 55. The Scamp 56. Shakedown 58. Piccadilly Third Stop 61. The Curse of the Mummy's Tomb 64. The Lifetaker 89, many others.

TV series: Sir Francis Drake 62.

Moriarty, Cathy (1961–).
American actress.

Raging Bull (AAN) 80. Neighbors 81. White of the Eye 87. Burndown 89. Kindergarten Cop 90. Soapdish 91. The Indian Runner 91. The Mambo Kings 92. Matinee 93. Another Stakeout 93. Me and the Kid 93. Pontiac Moon 94. Forget Paris 95. Casper 95. Foxfire 96. Hugo Pool 97. Dream with the Fishes 97. Cop Land 97. A Brother's Kiss 97, etc.

TV series: Bless This House 95.

Moriarty, Michael (1941–).
American leading actor of the 70s. He is also an accomplished jazz pianist and singer. In 1996, he starred in his own one-man play about Shakespeare, *A Special Providence*.

Hickey and Boggs 72. The Last Detail 73. Bang the Drum Slowly 73. Shoot It Black Shoot It Blue 74. Report to the Commissioner 74. *Holocaust* (TV) 77. Who'll Stop the Rain? 78. Too Far to Go (TV) 79. The Winged Serpent 82. Odd Birds 85. Pale Rider 85. The Stuff 85. Troll 85. The Hanoi Hilton 87. It's Alive III: Island of the Alive 87. My Old Man's Place 88. Dark Tower 89. Full Fathom Five 90. Courage under Fire 96. Calm at Sunset (TV) 96. Shiloh 97. Managua 97, etc.

TV series: Law and Order 90–94.

Morison, Patricia (1915–) (Eileen Morison).
Slightly sulky-looking American leading lady of the 40s; never quite made it but did well later on stage.

Persons in Hiding 39. I'm from Missouri 39. The Magnificent Fraud 39. Untamed 40. Rangers of Fortune 40. One Night in Lisbon 41. Romance of the Rio Grande 41. The Roundup 41. A Night in

New Orleans 42. Beyond the Blue Horizon 42. Are Husbands Necessary? 42. Silver Skates 43. Hitler's Madman 43. Calling Dr Death 43. The Fallen Sparrow 43. The Song of Bernadette 43. Where are Your Children? 44. Without Love 45. Lady on a Train 45. Dressed to Kill 46. Danger Woman 46. Queen of the Amazons 47. Tarzan and the Huntress 47. Song of the Thin Man 47. Prince of Thieves 47. Walls of Jericho 48. The Return of Wildfire 48. Sofia 48. Song without End 60. Won Ton Ton, the Dog Who Saved Hollywood 75, etc.

Morita, Pat (1930–) (Noriyuki Morita).
Japanese-American character actor.
Thoroughly Modern Millie 64. Midway 76. When Time Ran Out 80. *The Karate Kid* (AAN) 84. Karate Kid II 86. Captive Hearts (& co-w) 87. Collision Course 88. The Karate Kid Part III 89. Ice Runner 91. Lena's Holiday 91. Golden Chute . . . Wings of Grey 92. Honeymoon in Vegas 92. The Next Karate Kid 94. Even Cowgirls Get the Blues 94. Time Master 95. Bloodsport 2 95. Bloodsport 3 95, etc.
TV series: The Queen and I 69. Sanford and Son 74–75. Happy Days 75–76. Mr T and Tina 76. Blansky's Beauties 77. Happy Days 82–83.

Morita, Yoshimitsu (1950–).
Japanese director of comedies.
Something Like Yoshiwara/No Yo Na Mono 81. *The Family Game*/Kazoku Geemu 83. Sorekara 86. The Mercenaries 87, etc.

Morlay, Gaby (1897–1964) (Blanche Fumoleau).
French character actress.
La Sandale Rouge 13. Les Nouveaux Messieurs 28. Derrière la Façade 38. Le Voile Bleu 42. Gigi 48. Le Plaisir 51. Mitsou 55. Ramuntcho 58, many others.

Morley, Karen (1905–) (Mildred Linton).
American leading lady of the 30s.
Inspiration 31. *Scarface* 32. Dinner at Eight 33. Our Daily Bread 34. Beloved Enemy 36. Kentucky 39. Pride and Prejudice 40. Jealousy 45. The Unknown 46. 'M' 51, many others.

Morley, Robert (1908–1992).
Portly British character actor (and playwright), on stage from 1929, films from 1938.
Autobiography: 1966, *Robert Morley, Responsible Gentleman*. Biography: 1993, *Robert My Father* by Sheridan Morley.
Marie Antoinette (US) (AAN) 38. *Major Barbara* 40. *The Young Mr Pitt* 42. I Live in Grosvenor Square 45. An Outcast of the Islands 51. The African Queen 51. *Gilbert and Sullivan* 53. *Beat the Devil* 53. Around the World in Eighty Days 56. The Doctor's Dilemma 59. *Oscar Wilde* 60. The Young Ones 61. Murder at the Gallop 63. Those Magnificent Men in Their Flying Machines 65. The Alphabet Murders 65. Genghis Khan 65. A Study in Terror 65. Hotel Paradiso 66. Way Way Out (US) 66. The Trygon Factor 67. Sinful Davey 69. When Eight Bells Toll 71. Theatre of Blood 73. The Blue Bird 76. *Who Is Killing the Great Chefs of Europe?* 78. Scavenger Hunt 79. The Human Factor 79. O Heavenly Dog 80. The Great Muppet Caper 81. High Road to China 82, etc.
❝ Anyone who works is a fool. I don't work: I merely inflict myself on the public. – *R.M.*
I believe there are two things necessary for salvation: money and gunpowder. – *R.M.*
It is a great help for a man to be in love with himself. For an actor it is absolutely essential. – *R.M.*
Fortunately, I'm not an actor who has ever got into the habit of refusing film roles, holding that if one doesn't read the script in advance, or see the finished product, there is nothing to prevent one accepting the money, and then spending it. – *R.M.*

Moroder, Giorgio (1940–).
Italian composer in America.
Midnight Express (AA) 78. Foxes 80. American Gigolo 80. Cat People 82. Flashdance (AA song) 83. Superman III 83. Scarface 83. The Neverending Story (co-m) 84. Electric Dreams 84. Metropolis (new m) 85. Top Gun (AAs) 86. Over the Top 87. Fair Game 88. Let It Ride 89. Cybereden (It.) 93, etc.

Moross, Jerome (1913–1983).
American composer.
When I Grow Up 51. The Sharkfighters 56. The Big Country 58. The Proud Rebel 58. The Jayhawkers 59. The Cardinal 63. The War Lord 65. Rachel Rachel 68, etc.

Morricone, Ennio (1928–).
Prolific Italian composer and arranger.
A Fistful of Dollars 64. El Greco 64. Fists in the Pockets 65. For a Few Dollars More 65. *The Good the Bad and the Ugly* 66. The Big Gundown 66. Matchless 67. Theorem 69. *Once Upon a Time in the West* 69. Investigation of a Citizen 69. Fraulein Doktor 69. The Bird with the Crystal Plumage 70. The Sicilian Clan 70. Two Mules for Sister Sara 70. Cat O'Nine Tails 71. The Red Tent 71. Four Flies in Grey Velvet 71. The Decameron 71. The Burglars 71. The Black Belly of the Tarantula 72. Bluebeard 72. The Serpent 72. A Fistful of Dynamite 72. 1900 76. Exorcist II: The Heretic 77. Orca 77. Days of Heaven 78. Bloodline 79. The Island 80. La Cage aux Folles II 80. So Fine 81. Butterfly 82. White Dog 82. The Thing 82. Nana 83. Sahara 83. Once upon a Time in America 84. La Cage aux Folles III 85. *The Mission* (AAN) 86. *The Untouchables* (AAN) 87. A Time of Destiny 88. Frantic 88. Casualties of War 89. *Cinema Paradiso* 89. To Forget Palermo/Dimenticare Palermo 89. Everybody's Fine/Stanno Tutti Bene 90. Tie Me Up! Tie Me Down!/¡Atame! 90. State of Grace 90. Bugsy (AAN) 91. Husbands and Lovers 91. Especially on Sunday/La Domenica Specialmente 91. Jona che Visse nella Balena 93. La Scorta 93. In the Line of Fire 93. Il Lungo Silenzio 93. A Simple Formality/Una Pura Formalita 94. En Suivant la Comète 94. Love Affair 94. Wolf 94. Genesis: The Creation and the Flood/Genesi: La Creazione e il Diluvio 94. The Night and the Moment 94. According to Pereira 95. Pasolini, an Italian Crime/Pasolini, un Delitto Italiano 95. The Star Man/L'Uomo delle Stelle 95. The Stendhal Syndrome 96. La Lupa/The She-Wolf 96. Nostromo (TV) 97. Bulworth (US) 98, etc.

Morris, Chester (1901–1970).
Jut-jawed American leading man of the 30s, an agreeable 'B' picture lead who later became a considerable stage and TV actor. Born in New York City, the son of actors, he was in silent films as a child, studied at the New York School of Fine Arts, and made his Broadway debut in 1918. His most familiar role was as Boston Blackie, a crook turned good guy in 13 films from 1941 to 1949. Married actress Suzanne Kilborne (1927–38) and model Lillian Barker. Died from an overdose of barbiturates.
Alibi (AAN) 29. She Couldn't Say No 30. The Divorce 30. *The Big House* 30. The Bat Whispers 31. The Miracle Man 32. Red Headed Woman 32. Blondie Johnson 33. The Gift of Gab 34. I've Been Around 35. Society Doctor 35. Moonlight Murder 36. They Met in a Taxi 36. Flight from Glory 37. Law of the Underworld 38. Smashing the Rackets 38. Blind Alibi 39. *Five Came Back* 39. The Marines Fly High 40. No Hands on the Clock 41. Meet Boston Blackie 41 (and subsequent series of 12 films until 1949). I Live on Danger 42. Wrecking Crew 43. Secret Command 44. Double Exposure 45. Unchained 55. The Great White Hope 70, etc.

Morris, Ernest (1915–1987).
British director, mainly of second features for the Danzigers.
The Tell-Tale Heart 60. Echo of Diana 64. The Return of Mr Moto 65, etc.

Morris, Errol (1948–).
American director and screenwriter, usually of quirky documentaries. His *The Thin Blue Line* helped release a man wrongly convicted of murder. *The Dark Wind* was his first fictional film.
Gates of Heaven 78. Vernon, Florida 81. The Thin Blue Line 88. A Brief History of Time (TV) 91. The Dark Wind 92. Fast, Cheap and Out of Control 97, etc.

Morris, Greg (1934–1996).
American supporting actor.
The Lively Set 64. The Doomsday Flight (TV) 66. Countdown at Kusini 76, etc.
TV series: Mission Impossible 66–73. Vegas 78–80.

Morris, Howard (1919–).
American comedy director.
Boys Night Out (a only) 62. Who's Minding the Mint? 67. With Six You Get Egg Roll 68. Don't Drink the Water 69. Goin' Coconuts 78, etc.

Morris, John (1926–).
American composer who has scored many of Mel Brooks' films.
The Producers 67. The Gamblers 69. The Twelve Chairs 70. Blazing Saddles (AAN title s) 74. Young Frankenstein 74. The Bank Shot 74. The Adventures of Sherlock Holmes' Smarter Brother 75. Silent Movie 76. The Last Remake of Beau Geste 77. The World's Greatest Lover 77. High Anxiety 77. The In-Laws 79. The Elephant Man (AAN) 80. In God We Trust 80. History of the World Part I 81. Table for Five 83. Yellowbeard 83. To Be or Not To Be 83. The Woman in Red 84. Johnny Dangerously 84. Clue 85. The Doctor and the Devils 85. Haunted Honeymoon 86. Ironweed 87. Dirty Dancing 87. Spaceballs 87. The Wash 88. Second Sight 89. Stella 90. Life Stinks 91, etc.

Morris, Lana (1930–1998).
British leading lady of the 50s.
Spring in Park Lane 47. The Weaker Sex 48. Trottie True 49. The Chiltern Hundreds 49. The Woman in Question 50. Trouble in Store 53. Man of the Moment 55. Home and Away 56. I Start Counting 70, many others.

Morris, Mary (1895–1970).
American stage actress who played her stage role of the evil old lady in *Double Door* 34.

Morris, Mary (1915–1988).
British character actress with dominant personality, on stage from 1925.
Prison without Bars (film debut) 38. The Spy in Black 39. The Thief of Baghdad 40. *Pimpernel Smith* 41. Undercover 43. The Man from Morocco 45. Train of Events 49. High Treason 51, many others.

Morris, Oswald (1915–).
British cinematographer, in films from 1932.
Green for Danger 46. *Moulin Rouge* 53. Knave of Hearts 53. Beat the Devil 53. Beau Brummell 54. Moby Dick 56. A Farewell to Arms 57. The Key 58. Roots of Heaven 59. Look Back in Anger 59. Our Man in Havana 59. The Entertainer 60. Lolita 62. Of Human Bondage 64. *The Pumpkin Eater* (BFA) 64. The Hill (BFA) 65. Life at the Top 65. The Spy Who Came In from the Cold 65. Stop the World I Want To Get Off 66. *The Taming of the Shrew* 67. Oliver! (AAN) 68. Goodbye Mr Chips 69. Scrooge 70. Fiddler on the Roof (AA) 71. Lady Caroline Lamb 72. The Mackintosh Man 73. The Odessa File 74. The Man Who Would Be King 75. Equus 77. The Wiz 78. Just Tell Me What You Want 80. The Great Muppet Caper 81. Dark Crystal 82, etc.

Morris, Wayne (1914–1959) (Bert de Wayne Morris).
Brawny American leading man with stage experience.
China Clipper (debut) 36. *Kid Galahad* 37. Brother Rat and a Baby 39. Bad Men of Missouri 40. The Smiling Ghost 41. Deep Valley 47. The Time of Your Life 47. The Tougher They Come 50. The Master Plan 55. The Crooked Sky 57. Paths of Glory 58, etc.

Morris, William (1873–1932) (Zelman Moses).
American agent who founded the company that bears his name, which remains one of the leading international showbusiness agencies. Born in Schwarzenau, Silesia, he came to the USA at the age of nine, and worked as a clerk and successfully sold advertising for a magazine publisher before working as an agent. He ran his company from its foundation in 1898 in New York to his death, when he was succeeded by his son, William Morris, Jnr, who headed it until 1952. Many successful agents began work in its mail room, and its former employees include Michael Ovitz.
Biography: 1995, *The Agency: William Morris and the Hidden History of Show Business* by Frank Rose.

Morrison, Ernie 'Sunshine Sammy' (1912–1989).
American child actor and vaudeville performer, one of the original kids in the Our Gang comedies of the early 20s, on screen from the age of three. In the early 40s, he appeared in films featuring the East Side Kids.

Morrison, James (1888–1974).
American leading actor in Vitagraph movies. He retired early to become a drama teacher.
A Tale of Two Cities 11. Beau Brummel 12. A Tale of Two Cities 17. Sacred Silence 19. The Midnight Bride 20. Black Beauty 21. The Little Minister 22. Captain Blood 24. Wreckage 25. The Count of Luxembourg 26. Twin Flappers 27, etc.

Morrison, Temuera.
New Zealand leading actor, best known in his home country for his role as a doctor in the TV soap opera *Shortland Street*. He was an adviser on Jane Campion's *The Piano*.
Other Halves 84. Never Say Die 88. *Once Were Warriors* 94. Barb Wire 96. Speed 2: Cruise Control 97. Six Days, Seven Nights 98, etc.

Morriss, Frank.
American editor, from television, who has worked on many of John Badham's films.
Duel (TV) 71. Charley Varrick 73. Ode to Billy Joe 76. First Love 77. I Wanna Hold Your Hand 78. Inside Moves 80. Whose Life Is It, Anyway? 81. Blue Thunder (AAN) 83. Romancing the Stone (AAN) 84. American Flyers 85. Short Circuit 86. Hot to Trot 88. Disorganized Crime 89. Bird on a Wire 90. Short Time 90. The Hard Way 91. Point of No Return 93. Another Stakeout 93. Drop Zone 94. Nick of Time 95. Incognito 97, etc.

Morrissey, Paul (1939–).
American 'underground' director associated with Andy Warhol.
Flesh 68. Trash 70. *Heat* 72. Women in Revolt 72. Andy Warhol's Frankenstein 73. Andy Warhol's Dracula 74. The Hound of the Baskervilles 77. Madame Wang's 81. Forty-Deuce 82. Mixed Blood 84. Beethoven's Nephew 85. Spike of Bensonhurst 88, etc.
❝ When you direct films you lose a lot of the qualities that Hollywood gave us, which were stars. So we look for stars and let them do what they want. – *P.M.*

Morros, Boris (1891–1963) (Boris Milhailovitch).
Russian-born independent producer in America from the late 30s. Later revealed as an American agent via his 1957 book *Ten Years a Counterspy*, filmed in 1960 as *Man on a String*, with Ernest Borgnine as Morros.
The Flying Deuces 39. Second Chorus 41. Tales of Manhattan 42. Carnegie Hall 48.

Morrow, Doretta (1925–1968) (Doretta Marano).
American singing star who appeared in one film, *Because You're Mine* 52.

Morrow, Jeff (1913–1993).
Mature American leading man, former Broadway and TV actor, in Hollywood from 1953.
The Robe 53. Flight to Tangier 53. Siege of Red River 54. Tanganyika 54. Sign of the Pagan 54. *This Island Earth* 55. The Creature Walks Among Us 56. The Giant Claw 57. The Story of Ruth 60. Harbour Lights 63. Octaman 71, etc.
TV series: Union Pacific 58–59. Temperatures Rising 73–74.

Morrow, Jo (1940–).
American leading lady of the 60s.
Because They're Young 56. Brushfire 57. The Legend of Tom Dooley 59. Our Man in Havana 59. The Three Worlds of Gulliver 60. He Rides Tall 63. Sunday in New York 64. Doctor Death 73, etc.

Morrow, Rob (1962–)
American leading actor, best known for his role as Dr Joel Fleischman in the TV series *Northern Exposure* 90–95.
Private Resort 85. Quiz Show 94. Last Dance 96. Mother 96. Into My Heart 98, etc.

Morrow, Vic (1932–1982).
American actor formerly cast as a muttering juvenile delinquent. Stage experience. He died in an accident while filming *The Twilight Zone*. He is the father of actress Jennifer Jason Leigh.
The Blackboard Jungle (film debut) 55. Tribute to a Bad Man 56. Men in War 57. God's Little Acre 58. Cimarron 61. Portrait of a Mobster 61. Sledge (d only) 69. The Glass House (TV) 72. The Take 74. Captains and the Kings (TV) 76.

Treasure of Matecumbe 76. The Bad News Bears 76. Roots (TV) 77. Funeral for an Assassin 77. The Hostage Heart (TV) 77. Wild and Wooly (TV) 78. Humanoids from the Deep 80. The Twilight Zone 83, etc.
TV series: Combat 62–66. B.A.D. Cats 80.

Morse, Barry (1919–).
British leading man who moved to Canada and became a star of stage and TV there.
The Goose Steps Out 42. When We Are Married 42. There's a Future in It 43. Late at Night 46. Daughter of Darkness 48. No Trace 50; then after long gap – Kings of the Sun 63. Justine 69. Asylum 72. Power Play 75. The Shape of Things to Come (TV) 79. The Changeling 80. The Winds of War (TV) 83. Sadat (as Begin) (TV) 83. Whoops Apocalypse 83. A Woman of Substance (TV) 84. Glory! Glory! 90, etc.
TV series: *The Fugitive* (as Lt Gerard) 63–66. The Adventurer 72. Zoo Gang 73. Space 1999 75–76.

Morse, David (1953–).
American actor, from theatre and television; best known for his role as Dr Jack Morrison in *St Elsewhere*. Born in Beverly, Massachusetts, he worked for the Boston Repertory Theatre from the early to mid-70s, when he moved to New York's Circle Repertory Company. He is co-founder of the Left Coast Repertory in Los Angeles. Married actress Susan Wheeler Duff.
Inside Moves 80. Max Dugan Returns 83. Prototype (TV) 83. Personal Foul 87. The Desperate Hours 90. Cry in the Wild 91. The Indian Runner 91. The Good Son 93. The Getaway 94. The Crossing Guard 95. Stephen King's The Langoliers 95. Twelve Monkeys 95. Extreme Measures 96. The Long Kiss Goodnight 96. The Rock 96. Contact 97. The Negotiator 98, etc.
TV series: St Elsewhere 82–88.

Morse, Helen (1948–).
Australian leading actress.
Jock Petersen 75. *Caddie* 78. Picnic at Hanging Rock 79. Agatha 79. *A Town Like Alice* (TV) 81. Far East 82. Iris 89, etc.

Morse, Robert (1931–).
American comedy actor who usually plays the befuddled innocent.
The Matchmaker 58. Honeymoon Hotel 64. Quick before It Melts 65. *The Loved One* 65. Oh Dad, Poor Dad 66. *How to Succeed in Business without Really Trying* 67. Where Were You When the Lights Went Out? 68. The Boatniks 69. The Emperor's New Clothes 87, etc.
TV series: That's Life 68.

Morse, Susan E.
American film editor, mainly on Woody Allen's movies.
Manhattan 79. Stardust Memories 80. Arthur 81. A Midsummer Night's Sex Comedy 82. Zelig 83. Broadway Danny Rose 84. The Purple Rose of Cairo 85. Hannah and Her Sisters (AAN) 86. Radio Days 87. Another Woman 88. New York Stories 89. Crimes and Misdemeanors 89. Alice 90. Shadows and Fog 91. Manhattan Murder Mystery 93. Bullets over Broadway 94. Mighty Aphrodite 95. Everyone Says I Love You 96. Deconstructing Harry 97. Celebrity 98, etc.

Morse, Terry (1906–1984).
American second-feature director.
■ Jane Arden 39. On Trial 39. Waterfront 39. Smashing the Money Ring 39. No Place to Go 39. British Intelligence 40. Tear Gas Squad 40. Fog Island 45. Danny Boy 46. Shadows over Chinatown 46. Dangerous Money 46. Bells of San Fernando 47. Unknown World 51. Godzilla (US version) 56. Taffy and the Jungle Hunter 65. Young Dillinger 65.

Mortensen, Viggo.
American leading actor.
Salvation! 87. Prison 88. The Reflecting Skin 91. The Indian Runner 91. American Yazuka 93. Boiling Point 93. Ruby Cairo 93. Young Americans 93. Carlito's Way 93. The Passion of Darkly Noon 95. Gimlet (Sp.) 95. Crimson Tide 95. God's Army 95. The Portrait of a Lady 96. Albino Alligator 96. Daylight 96. GI Jane 97. Kiss the Sky 98. A Perfect Murder 98. Psycho 98, etc.
❝ A lot of people want to get into acting because they want to be famous. I don't think much of that, but that's my perspective. It doesn't mean you'll be a bad actor if you're a shallow person. In fact, maybe it helps. – V.M.

Mortimer, John (1923–).
British playwright, novelist and barrister, who has occasionally worked in films, best known for his creation of the TV series *Rumpole of the Bailey*. He was originally a scriptwriter for the Crown Film Unit. Formerly married to novelist Penelope Mortimer.
Autobiography: 1982, *Clinging to the Wreckage*.
The Innocents 61. Guns of Darkness 63. The Dock Brief 63. The Running Man 63. Bunny Lake Is Missing 65. John and Mary 70. Brideshead Revisited 81. Paradise Postponed 86, etc.

Morton, Clive (1904–1975).
Straight-faced British character actor on stage from 1926, films from 1932, usually in slightly pompous roles.
The Blarney Stone 32. Dead Men Tell No Tales 39. While the Sun Shines 46. Scott of the Antarctic 48. The Blue Lamp 49. His Excellency 51. Carrington VC 54. Richard III 56. Shake Hands with the Devil 59. Lawrence of Arabia 62. Stranger in the House 67, many others.

Morton, Rocky.
British director who works in collaboration with Annabel Jankel.
The Max Headroom Story (co-d) (TV) 85. D.O.A. (co-d) 88. Super Mario Bros (co-d) 93.

Morton, Samantha (1977–).
English actress, born in Nottingham, who began in television as a 13-year-old.
Under the Skin 97. Jane Eyre (TV) 97. Tom Jones (TV) 97. Emma (TV) 97. Dreaming of Joseph Lees 98, etc.
TV series: Band of Gold 95.

Moscovitch, Maurice (1871–1940) (Morris Maaskoff).
American character player, a Russian immigrant who spent many years starring in the Yiddish Theatre. Father of Noel Madison.
■ Winterset 36. Make Way for Tomorrow 37. Lancer Spy 37. Gateway 37. Suez 38. Love Affair 39. Susannah of the Mounties 39. In Name Only 39. Rio 39. The Great Commandment 39. Everything Happens at Night 39. South to Karanga 40. The Great Dictator 40. Dance Girl Dance 40.

Mosjoukine, Ivan (1889–1939).
Russian actor of the old school, who appeared in many international films.
The Defence of Sebastopol 11. Satan Triumphant 22. Tempest (Fr.) 22. Shadows That Mass (Fr.) 23. Casanova (Fr./It.) 27. Sergeant X (Fr.) 30. Nitchevo (Fr.) 36, etc.

Mosley, Roger E.
American character actor.
The New Centurions 72. Hit Man 72. Terminal Island 73. Leadbelly (title role) 76. The Greatest 77. Semi-Tough 77. Roots II (TV) 78. The Jericho Mile (TV) 79. Steel 80. Heart Condition 90. Unlawful Entry 92. Pentathlon 94. A Thin Line between Love and Hate 96. Letters from a Killer 98, etc.

Moss, Arnold (1910–1989).
American character actor often seen in sly or sinister roles.
Temptation 47. The Black Book (as Napoleon) 49. Kim 51. Viva Zapata 52. Casanova's Big Night 54. The Twenty-Seventh Day 57. The Fool Killer 64. Gambit 66. Caper of the Golden Bulls 67, many others.

Mostel, Zero (1915–1977).
Heavyweight American comedian principally seen on Broadway stage.
Panic in the Streets 50. *The Enforcer* 51. A Funny Thing Happened on the Way to the Forum 66. Great Catherine 68. *The Producers* 68. The Great Bank Robbery 69. The Angel Levine 69. The Hot Rock 72. Marco 73. Rhinoceros 73. Journey into Fear 75. The Front 76. Mastermind 76, etc.
Famous line (*The Producers*): 'Leo, he who hesitates is poor.'

Moulder Brown, John (1945–).
British actor, usually of intense roles.
Deep End 69. Vampire Circus 71. King Queen Knave 72. Ludwig 72. The Confessions of Felix Krull (TV) 82, Rumpelstiltskin 87, etc.

Moullet, Luc (1937–).
French director, screenwriter, producer and actor, usually of comic movies, a former film critic.
Brigitte et Brigitte 66. Une Aventure de Billy le Kid 71. La Comédie du Travail 87. Les Sièges de l'Alcazar 89. Cabale des Oursins 91. La Parpaillon 92. More and More/Toujours Plus 94. Foix 94, etc.

Mount, Peggy (1916–).
British character comedienne with long experience in repertory before starring as the termagant mother-in-law in *Sailor Beware*.
■ The Embezzler 54. *Sailor Beware* 56. Dry Rot 57. The Naked Truth 58. Inn for Trouble 59. Ladies Who Do 63. One Way Pendulum 64. Hotel Paradiso 65. Finders Keepers 66. Oliver! 68. The Princess and the Goblin (voice) 92.
TV series: The Larkins 58–60. George and the Dragon 66–67. Winning Widows. You're Only Young Twice 77.

Movita (1915–) (Movita Castenada).
Mexican leading lady, briefly in Hollywood. She was formerly married to Marlon Brando.
Mutiny on the Bounty 35. Paradise Isle 36. Wolf Call 39. Dream Wife 53. Apache Ambush 55. The Panic in Needle Park 71, etc.

Mowbray, Alan (1893–1969).
Imperious-mannered British character actor, in America from the early 1920s; appeared later in nearly 400 films, often as butler or pompous emissary.
Alexander Hamilton 31. Sherlock Holmes 32. Roman Scandals 33. Becky Sharp 35. Desire 36. *My Man Godfrey* 36. *Topper* 37. Stand In 37. *The Villain Still Pursued Her* 40. Lady Hamilton 41. That Uncertain Feeling 41. A Yank at Eton 42. His Butler's Sister 43. Holy Matrimony 43. Where Do We Go from Here? 45. *Terror by Night* 45. Merton of the Movies 46. *My Darling Clementine* 46. Prince of Thieves 47. The Jackpot 50. Wagonmaster 50. Dick Turpin's Ride 51. Androcles and the Lion 53. The King's Thief 55. The King and I 56, many others.
TV series: Colonel Flack 53. The Mickey Rooney Show 54. Dante 60.

Mowbray, Malcolm.
British director who went to Hollywood after his first success.
A Private Function 84. Out Cold 88. Don't Tell Her It's Me 90. Clothes in the Wardrobe 92. Crocodile Shoes (TV) 94, etc.

Mower, Patrick (1940–).
British leading man, mainly in TV series *Callan*, *Special Branch*, *Target*.
The Smashing Bird I Used to Know 69. Cry of the Banshee 70. Black Beauty 70. Catch Me a Spy 71. Carry On England 76. The Devil's Advocate 78. Marco Polo (TV) 81, etc.

Moxey, John (1920–).
British TV director who has made occasional films and many TV movies in America (as John Llewellyn Moxey).
City of the Dead 59. The £20,000 Kiss 63. Ricochet 63. Strangler's Web 65. Circus of Fear 67. San Francisco International (TV) 70. The House That Would Not Die (TV) 70. A Taste of Evil (TV) 71. The Night Stalker (TV) 72. The Death of Me Yet (TV) 72. The Bounty Man (TV) 72. The Strange and Deadly Occurrence (TV) 74. Where Have All the People Gone? (TV) 74. Charlie's Angels (TV) 76. Nightmare in Badham County (TV) 77. The President's Mistress (TV) 78. Sanctuary of Fear (TV) 79. The Power Within (TV) 79. The Children of An Lac (TV) 80. No Place to Hide (TV) 81. Killjoy (TV) 81. The Cradle Will Fall (TV) 83. Through Naked Eyes (TV) 83. Lady Mobster (TV) 88, etc.

Moyle, Allan (1947–).
Canadian screenwriter and director, a former actor, now in Hollywood.
Montreal Main (a, co-w, co-d) 78. The Rubber Gun (a, d) 78. Times Square (d) 80. Pump Up the Volume (wd) 90. Love Crimes (w) 91. The Gun in Betty Lou's Handbag (wd) 92. Empire Records (d) 95, etc.

Mudie, Leonard (1884–1965) (Leonard M. Cheetham).
British character actor in Hollywood.
The Mummy 32. The House of Rothschild 34. Clive of India 35. Lancer Spy 37. Dark Victory 39. Berlin Correspondent 42. My Name is Julia Ross 45. Song of My Heart 48. The Magnetic Monster 53. The Big Fisherman 59, many others.

Mueller, Elisabeth (1926–).
Swiss-German leading lady who made some Hollywood films.
The Power and the Prize 56. El Hakim 58. Confess Dr Corda 58. The Angry Hills 59, etc.

Mueller-Stahl, Armin (1930–).
German leading actor, from the theatre, now in international films. He was formerly a concert violinist.
The Secret Marriage/Heimliche Ehen 56. Königskinder 62. Naked among the Wolves/Nackt unter Wölfen 63. Wolf unter Wölfen 65. Der Dritte 72. Kit and Co. 74. Nelken in Aspik 76. Lola 81. Veronika Voss/Die Sehnsucht der Veronika 82. Glut 83. Love in Germany/Un Amour en Allemagne 83. Angry Harvest/Bittere Ernte 85. Forget Mozart 85. Colonel Redl 85. Momo 86. Midnight Cop 88. God Does Not Believe in Us Anymore 88. Music Box 89. Avalon 90. Utz 91. Kafka 91. The Power of One 92. Night on Earth 92. Red Hot 92. Der Kinoerzähler 93. The House of the Spirits 94. Holy Matrimony 94. Taxandria 94. A Pyromaniac's Love Story 95. *Shine* (AAN) 96. Conversation with the Beast (& d) 96. Theodore Rex 96. The Ogre 96. Twelve Angry Men (TV) 97. The Peacemaker 97. In the Presence of Mine Enemies 97. The Game 97. The X Files Movie 98, etc.

Muir, Esther (1895–1995).
American character actress usually seen as hard-faced blonde. Married Busby Berkeley and Sam Coslow. Her birthdate is also given as 1907.
A Dangerous Affair 31. So This is Africa 33. The Bowery 33. Fury 36. *A Day at the Races* (in which she suffered memorably at the hands of Groucho Marx) 37. The Law West of Tombstone 38. Stolen Paradise 41. X Marks the Spot 42, etc.

Muir, Gavin (1907–1972).
Quiet-spoken American actor with a British accent, usually a smooth villain.
Lloyds of London 36. Wee Willie Winkie 37. Eagle Squadron 41. *Nightmare* 42. The Master Race 44. Salome Where She Danced 45. California 46. Ivy 47. Abbott and Costello Meet the Invisible Man 51. King of the Khyber Rifles 54. The Sea Chase 55. The Abductors 57. Johnny Trouble 59, many others.
TV series: The Betty Hutton Show 59.

Muir, Jean (1911–1996) (J. M. Fullerton).
American leading lady of the 30s. Her refusal to conform to the studios' expectations hampered her career, which declined still further when she was blacklisted in the 50s, losing a role in the TV series *The Aldrich Family*; in the late 60s she became a drama teacher.
Female 34. A Midsummer Night's Dream 35. Jane Steps Out (GB) 37. And One Was Beautiful 40. The Lone Wolf Meets a Lady 40. The Constant Nymph 44, etc.

Mulcahy, Russell (1953–).
Australian director, now working in America.
Derek and Clive Get the Horn (TV) 81. Razorback 84. Highlander 86. Highlander II – the Quickening 90. Ricochet 91. Blue Ice 92. The Real McCoy 93. The Shadow 94. Silent Trigger 97, etc.

Mulcaster, G. H. (1891–1964).
British character actor, mainly on stage; played formal types.
The Dummy Talks 43. Bonnie Prince Charlie 47. Spring in Park Lane 48. Under Capricorn 50, etc.

Muldaur, Diana (1943–).
Sensitive-looking American leading lady, McCloud's girlfriend on TV; adept at nice sophisticated types; also on TV in 1974, played Joy Adamson in *Born Free*.

■ The Swimmer 68. Number One 69. The Lawyer 70. The Other 71. One More Train to Rob 72. McQ 73. The Chosen Survivors 74. Charlie's Angels (TV) 76. Pine Canyon Is Burning (TV) 77. Black Beauty (TV) 78. To Kill a Cop (TV) 78. Maneaters Are Loose (TV) 78. The Word (TV) 78. Beyond Reason 82. Master Ninja 3 83.
TV series: The Survivors 69–70. McCloud 70–77. Born Free 74. The Tony Randall Show 76–78. Hizzonner 79. Fitz and Bones 81.

Muldoon, Patrick (1969–).
American actor, a former model. He studied at the University of Southern California, and began on the TV soap opera *Days of Our Lives* 92–95.
Rage and Honor II: Hostile Takeover 93. Starship Troopers 97. Black Cat Run (TV) 98. The Second Arrival 98. Wicked 98, etc.
TV series: Days of Our Lives 92–95. Melrose Place 95–96.

Mulford, Clarence E. (1895–1970).
American western novelist, the creator of Hopalong Cassidy.

Mulhall, Jack (1888–1979).
American silent-screen leading man.
Sirens of the Sea 17. Mickey 18. All of a Sudden Peggy 20. Molly O' 21. The Bad Man 23. The Goldfish 24. Friendly Enemies 25. The Poor Nut 27. Just Another Blonde 28. Dark Streets 29, many others; appeared as an 'old-timer' in Hollywood Boulevard 36.

Mulhare, Edward (1923–1997).
Polished Irish leading actor. Born in Cork, he was on the British stage until he went to America to replace Rex Harrison in the musical *My Fair Lady*, after which he stayed there. Best known for his TV roles as Captain Daniel Gregg in *The Ghost and Mrs Muir* 69–70, and Devon Miles in *Knightrider* 82–86.
Hill Twenty-Four Does Not Answer 55. Signpost to Murder 64. Von Ryan's Express 65. Our Man Flint 65. Eye of the Devil 67. *Caprice* 67. Gidget Grows Up (TV) 72. Megaforce 82, etc.

Mullan, Peter.
Scottish actor, screenwriter and director.
Riff-Raff 90. The Big Man 90. Shallow Grave 94. Ruffian Hearts 95. Braveheart 95. Trainspotting 96. Fairytale: A True Story 97. My Name Is Joe (a) 98. Orphans (wd) 98, etc.

Mullaney, Jack (1932–1982).
Easy-going light American actor.
The Young Stranger 57. Kiss Them for Me 58. The Absent Minded Professor 61. Seven Days in May 64. When the Legends Die 72. Where Does it Hurt? 72.
TV series: The Ann Sothern Show 58–60. Ensign O'Toole 62–63. My Living Doll 64–65. It's About Time 66–67.

Mullard, Arthur (1913–1995).
Big, bluff cockney character comedian who became a British television star of the 70s.
Autobiography: 1977, *Oh Yus, It's Arthur Mullard*.
Oliver Twist 48. The Lavender Hill Mob 51. Pickwick Papers 52. The Belles of St Trinian's 54. The Ladykillers 55. Brothers in Law 57. Two Way Stretch 60. Loneliness of the Long Distance Runner 62. Crooks Anonymous 62. The Wrong Arm of the Law 62. Sparrows Can't Sing 63. Morgan – a Suitable Case for Treatment 66. The Great St Trinian's Train Robbery 66. Casino Royale 67. Chitty Chitty Bang Bang 68. Lock Up Your Daughters! 69. On the Buses 71. Vault of Horror 73, etc.
TV series: The Arthur Askey Show 67. Vacant Lot 67. On the Rocks 69. Romany Jones 72–74. Yus My Dear 76–77.

Mullen, Barbara (1914–1979).
Irish-American actress, former dancer, who came to films as star of *Jeannie* 42.
Thunder Rock 42. A Place of One's Own 44. The Trojan Brothers 45. Corridor of Mirrors 48. So Little Time 52. The Challenge 60, etc.
TV series: Dr Finlay's Casebook 59–66.

Muller, Renate (1907–1937).
German leading lady best known abroad for *Sunshine Susie* 31.
Biography: 1944, *Queen of America?* by R. E. Clements.
Liebling der Götter 30. Viktor und Viktoria 34. Allotria 36.

Müller, Robby (1940–).
Dutch cinematographer, now in international films, who made his reputation working in Germany with Wim Wenders.
Summer in the City 70. The Goalkeeper's Fear of the Penalty Kick/Die Angst des Tormanns Beim Elfmeter 71. The Scarlet Letter/Der Scharlachrote Buchstabe 72. Alice in the Cities/Alice in den Städten 74. Falsche Bewegung/Wrong Move 75. Kings of the Road/Im Lauf der Zeit 76. The American Friend/Der Amerikanische Freund 77. Mysteries 79. Saint Jack 79. Honeysuckle Rose 80. They All Laughed 81. Paris, Texas 84. Repo Man 84. To Live and Die in L.A. 85. Down by Law 86. The Longshot 86. Barfly 87. The Believers 87. Mystery Train 89. Korczak 90. Until the End of the World/Bis ans Ende der Welt 91. Mad Dog and Glory 93. Beyond the Clouds 95. Breaking the Waves 96. The Tango Lesson 97. Shattered Image (US) 98, etc.

Mulligan, Gerry (1927–1996).
American jazz musician, arranger, composer and occasional actor. He was an influential baritone saxophonist and bandleader from the 50s, one of the creators of the cool approach to jazz, typified by his arrangements for the *Birth of the Cool* album made by Miles Davis. His early piano-less quartet included trumpeter Chet Baker. Lover of actress Judy Holliday, with whom he wrote songs in the late 50s and early 60s. Married actress Sandy Dennis (1965–76).
I Want to Live (soundtrack saxophone) 58. Jazz on a Summer's Day (doc) 60. The Bells Are Ringing (a) 60. The Rat Race (a) 60. The Subterraneans (a) 60. Luv (m) 67. The Hot Rock (soundtrack saxophone) 72. The Final Programme (soundtrack saxophone) 73. I'm Not Rappaport (m) 96.
❝ I think I managed to not be an adult in just about every imaginable area. – G.M.

Mulligan, Richard (1932–).
Lanky American character actor.
The Group 66. The Undefeated 69. Little Big Man 70. The Big Bus 76. Scavenger Hunt 79. S.O.B. 81. Trail of the Pink Panther 82. Micki and Maude 84. Teachers 84. The Heavenly Kid 85. A Fine Mess 86, etc.
TV series: The Hero 66. Diana 73–74. *Soap* 77–80. Reggie 83. Empty Nest 88–92.

Mulligan, Robert (1925–).
American director, from TV.
■ Fear Strikes Out 57. The Rat Race 60. Come September 61. The Great Impostor 61. The Spiral Road 62. *To Kill a Mockingbird* (AAN) 62. Love with the Proper Stranger 64. Baby the Rain Must Fall 65. Inside Daisy Clover 65. Up the Down Staircase 67. The Stalking Moon 68. The Pursuit of Happiness 70. *Summer of '42* 71. The Other 73. The Nickel Ride 75. Bloodbrothers 78. Same Time Next Year 78. Kiss Me Goodbye 82. Clara's Heart 88. The Man in the Moon 91.

Mulock, Al (c. 1925–1970) (aka Al Mullach).
Canadian character actor, usually as a heavy, who worked in Britain in the mid-50s to mid-60s and then moved to Italy to appear in spaghetti westerns.
Joe Macbeth 55. Kill Me Tomorrow 57. The Depraved 57. The Sheriff of Fractured Jaw 58. Tarzan's Greatest Adventure 59. Tarzan the Magnificent 60. The Hellions 61. The Longest Day 62. The Small World of Sammy Lee 62. Dr Terror's House of Horrors 64. The Good, the Bad and the Ugly 66. Reflections in a Golden Eye 67. Battle beneath the Earth 68, etc.

Mulroney, Dermot (1963–).
American actor.
Sunset 88. Young Guns 88. Staying Together 89. Survival Quest 89. Longtime Companion 90. Career Opportunities 91. Bright Angel 91. Where the Day Takes You 92. Samantha 92. Silent Tongue 93. Point of No Return 93. The Thing Called Love 93. Bad Girls 94. There Goes My Baby 94. Living in Oblivion 95. How to Make an American Quilt 95. Copycat 95. Kansas City 96. Bastard out of Carolina 96. The Trigger Effect 96. Box of Moonlight 96. My Best Friend's Wedding 97. Goodbye, Lover 98, etc.

Mumy, Billy (1954–).
American child actor of the 60s.
Palm Springs Weekend 63. A Ticklish Affair 63. *Dear Brigitte* 65. Rascal 69. Bless the Beasts and Children 71. Papillon 73. Twilight Zone – the Movie 83. Hard to Hold 84, etc.
TV series: Lost in Space 65–68. Sunshine 75.

Mundin, Herbert (1898–1939).
Short English character actor with expressive eyebrows, usually as comic relief. Born in St Helens, Lancashire, he began as a comedian in concert parties and revues. After working in British films in the 20s, he went to the US in search of work and was put under contract by Fox, remaining in Hollywood for the rest of his career, frequently in servile roles: as steward, publican or manservant. Died in a car crash. His best roles were as Barkis in *David Copperfield*, Much the Miller in *The Adventures of Robin Hood*, and Wilkins in *Another Dawn*.
The Devil's Lottery 31. Sherlock Holmes 32. Cavalcade 33. *David Copperfield* 34. Mutiny on the Bounty 35. Another Dawn 37. *The Adventures of Robin Hood* 38. Society Lawyer 39, etc.

Mune, Ian (1941–).
New Zealand director and screenwriter, a former actor.
Sleeping Dogs (a, co-w) 77. Goodbye, Pork Pie (co-w) 80. Came a Hot Friday (co-w, d) 84. Bridge to Nowhere (d) 85. The End of the Golden Weather (co-w, d) 91. The Piano (a) 93. Fallout (a) 93. The Whole of the Moon (co-w, d) 96. What Becomes of the Broken-Hearted (d) 99, etc.

Muni, Paul (1896–1967) (Muni Weisenfreund).
Distinguished American actor of Austrian parentage. Long stage experience.
Biography: 1974, *Actor* by Jerome Lawrence.
■ The Valiant (film debut) (AAN) 28. Seven Faces 29. *Scarface* 32. *I Am a Fugitive from a Chain Gang* (AAN) 32. The World Changes 33. Hi Nellie 33. Bordertown 34. Black Fury 35. Dr Socrates 35. *The Story of Louis Pasteur* (AA) 36. *The Good Earth* 37. *The Life of Emile Zola* (AAN) 37. The Woman I Love 38. Juarez 39. We Are Not Alone 39. Hudson's Bay 40. The Commandos Strike at Dawn 42. Stage Door Canteen 43. *A Song to Remember* 44. Counter Attack 45. Angel on My Shoulder 46. Stranger on the Prowl 51. The Last Angry Man (AAN) 59.
✪ For convincing world audiences of his day that heavy disguise made a great actor; and for his powerful early performances. *Scarface*.
❝ Every time Paul Muni parts his beard and looks down a microscope, this company loses two million dollars. – *Hal B. Wallis, as Warner head of production in the late 30s*
His voice is rich and pleasant, his personality is strong and virile, and if he is not pretty, neither is Lon Chaney. – *Variety, 1929*
He seemed intent on submerging himself so completely that he disappeared. – *Bette Davis*

Munk, Andrzej (1921–1961).
Polish director.
Men of the Blue Cross 55. Eroica 57. Bad Luck 60. The Passenger (incomplete) 61, etc.

Munro, Caroline (1951–).
British leading lady.
The Abominable Dr Phibes 71. Captain Kronos 72. The Golden Voyage of Sinbad 73. The Devil Within Her 73. At the Earth's Core 76. The Spy Who Loved Me 77. Maniac 80. Don't Open till Christmas 84. Slaughter High 86. Night Owl (as herself) 93, etc.

Munro, Janet (1934–1972).
Scottish leading lady with brief stage experience before films in both GB and US. Choked to death.
The Trollenberg Terror 57. The Young and the Guilty 57. Darby O'Gill and the Little People 58. Third Man on the Mountain 59. The Swiss Family Robinson 60. The Day the Earth Caught Fire 62. Life for Ruth 62. Bitter Harvest 63. A Jolly Bad Fellow 64. Sebastian 67, etc.

Munsel, Patrice (1925–).
American operatic soprano who played the title role in *Melba* 53.

Munshin, Jules (1915–1970).
Lanky, rubber-limbed American comedian and dancer, in occasional films from the mid-40s. Born in New York City, he began in vaudeville and worked on Broadway before and after his brief stints in films. Died from a heart attack. He is at his best teamed with Gene Kelly and Frank Sinatra, as Nat Goldberg in *Take Me Out to the Ball Game* and as Ozzie in *On the Town*. Kelly tried to reunite the trio for a sequel to the latter, but Sinatra declined and the resulting film, *It's Always Fair Weather*, was rewritten for other stars.
Easter Parade 48. Take Me Out to the Ball Game 48. *On the Town* 49. Ten Thousand Bedrooms 56. Silk Stockings 57. Wild and Wonderful 64, etc.

Munson, Ona (1906–1955) (Ona Wolcott).
American character actress, former dancer. Born in Portland, Oregon, she trained as a ballet dancer, and was on stage from childhood as a dancer and singer, working in vaudeville as a teenager and becoming a Broadway success in *Hold Everything!* in the late 20s. Her film career faltered after a row with the studios, and she became depressed and put on weight. In the early 40s she became the first woman producer at CBS. Died from an overdose of sleeping pills, leaving a note that read, 'This is the only way I know to be free again.' She was married three times, including to actor and director Edward Buzzell (1926–30), and to Russian artist and designer Eugène Berman (1950–55). Among her lovers were director Ernst Lubitsch and Mercedes De Acosta.
Going Wild 30. Five Star Final 32. Gone with the Wind 39. Drums of the Congo 40. *The Shanghai Gesture* (as Mother Gin Sling) 41. The Cheaters 45. The Red House 47, etc.

Muraki, Yoshiro (1924–).
Japanese production designer, often for the films of Akira Kurosawa.
Throne of Blood 57. The Lower Depths 57. Yojimbo 61. Sanjuro 62. Red Beard/Akahige 65. Dodeska-den 70. Tora! Tora! Tora! 70. Tidal Wave/Nippon Shinbotsu 75. Kagemusha 80. *Ran* 85, etc.

Muratova, Kira G. (1934–).
Romanian-born film director and screenwriter, in Russia. Born in Soroca, she studied at VGIK, and began making short films in collaboration with her then husband, Alexander Muratov. Her feature films, often using experimental approaches, have run into censorship problems, having been rejected both for 'bourgeois realism' and for their bleak view of Russian society.
Brief Encounters/Korotkie Vstrechi (& a) 67. Long Goodbye/Dolgie Provody 71. Getting to Know the World/Poznavaya Belyi Svet 79. Among the Grey Stones/Sredi Serykh Kamnei (credited to 'Ivan Sidorov') 83. Change of Fate/Peremana Uchasti 87. *The Asthenic Syndrome*/Astenicheskij Sindrom 89. The Sensitive Policeman/Le Milicien Amoureux 92. Enthusiasms/Uvlechen'ia 94, etc.

Murch, Walter.
American film and sound editor, screenwriter and occasional director. He is a graduate of the University of Southern California film school.
THX 1138 (co-w) 70. American Graffiti 73. The Conversation (AAN) 74. Julia (AAN) 77. Apocalypse Now (AA) 79. Return to Oz (co-w, d) 85. The Unbearable Lightness of Being 88. The Godfather Part III (AAN) 90. Ghost (AAN) 90. House of Cards 93. First Knight 95. The English Patient (AA) 96, etc.

Murdoch, Richard (1907–1990).
British radio entertainer, long partnered with Arthur Askey and Kenneth Horne.
Band Wagon 39. *The Ghost Train* 41. It Happened in Soho 48. Golden Arrow 52. Not a Hope in Hell 59. Strictly Confidential 61. Whoops Apocalypse 86, etc.

Muren, Dennis.
American special effects supervisor.
Equinox 71. Flesh Gordon 72. Close Encounters of the Third Kind 77. Star Wars 77. The Empire Strikes Back (AA) 80. Dragonslayer (AAN) 81. E.T. The Extra-Terrestrial (AA) 82. Return of the Jedi (AA) 83. Indiana Jones and the Temple of

Doom (AA) 84. Young Sherlock Holmes (AAN) 85. Innerspace (AA) 87. Willow (AAN) 88. Ghostbusters II 89. The Abyss (AA) 89. Terminator 2: Judgment Day (AA) 91. Jurassic Park (AA) 93. Casper 95. Twister 96. The Lost World: Jurassic Park (AAN) 97. Deconstructing Harry 97. Star Wars: The Phantom Menace 99, etc.

Murer, Fredi M. (1940–).
Swiss director, screenwriter and novelist.
Swiss Made 69. The Grey Zones/Die Grauzone 78. Alpine Fire/Hohenfeuer 85. Green Mountain/Der Grune Berg (doc) 90. Full Moon/Vollmond 98, etc.

Muresan, Gheorghe (1971–).
Romanian-born athlete and occasional actor, best known as the lofty (7 ft 7 ins) centre with Washington Wizards basketball team.
My Giant 98. The Mask of Zorro 98, etc.

Murfin, Jane (1893–1955).
American screenwriter.
The Right to Lie 19. Flapper Wives 24. White Fang 25. Meet the Prince 26. Dance Hall 29. Leathernecking 30. Friends and Lovers 31. Our Betters 33. Ann Vickers 33. Spitfire 34. This Man Is Mine 34. Roberta 35. Alice Adams 35. Come and Get It 36. The Shining Hour 38. Stand Up and Fight 39. Pride and Prejudice 40. Andy Hardy's Private Secretary 41. Flight for Freedom 43. Dragon Seed 44, etc.
~Miss Murfin's plays as co-author, usually with Jane Cowl, include *Daybreak* and *Smilin' Through*, both of which were filmed.

Murnau, F. W. (Friedrich) (1888–1931) (F. W. Plumpe).
German director in films from 1919; Hollywood from 1927. Died in a car crash.
Satanas 19. Dr Jekyll and Mr Hyde 20. *Nosferatu/Dracula* 22. *The Last Laugh* 24. Tartuffe 24. *Faust* 26. *Sunrise* 27. Four Devils 28. Our Daily Bread/City Girl 30. Tabu (co-d) 31, etc.
✪ For unquestionable brilliance in showing what the camera can do. *The Last Laugh*.

Murphy, Audie (1924–1971).
Boyish American leading man of the 50s; came to films on the strength of his war record as America's most decorated soldier, but despite some talent was soon relegated to low-budget westerns. Killed in a plane crash.
■ Beyond Glory 48. Texas Brooklyn and Heaven 48. Bad Boy 49. Sierra 50. The Kid from Texas 50. Kansas Raiders 50. *The Red Badge of Courage* 51. The Cimarron Kid 51. The Duel at Silver Creek 52. Gunsmoke 52. Column South 53. Tumbleweed 53. Ride Clear of Diablo 54. Drums Across the River 54. *Destry* 55. *To Hell and Back* (based on his autobiography) 55. The World in My Corner 56. Walk the Proud Land 56. The Guns of Fort Petticoat 57. Joe Butterfly 57. Night Passage 57. *The Quiet American* 58. Ride a Crooked Trail 58. The Gun Runners 58. No Name on the Bullet 59. The Wild and the Innocent 59. Cast a Long Shadow 59. Hell Bent for Leather 60. The Unforgiven 60. Seven Ways from Sundown 60. Posse from Hell 61. The Battle at Bloody Beach 61. Six Black Horses 62. Showdown 63. Gunfight at Comanche Creek 63. The Quick Gun 64. Bullet for a Badman 64. Apache Rifles 64. Arizona Raiders 65. Gunpoint 66. Trunk to Cairo 66. The Texican 66. Forty Guns to Apache Pass 67. A Time for Dying (& p) 71.
TV series: Whispering Smith 58.
❝ I guess my face is still the same, and so is the dialogue. Only the horses have changed. – A.M. *at 40*
I am working with a handicap. I have no talent. – A.M.

Murphy, Ben (1941–).
Athletic American TV hero of *Alias Smith and Jones*, *Griff*, *Gemini Man*, *The Chisholms*, etc.
The Letters (TV) 73. Runaway (TV) 73. Heatwave (TV) 74. This Was the West That Was (TV) 75. Sidecar Racers 75. Bridger (TV) 76. Time Walker 82. The Winds of War (TV) 83, etc.

Murphy, Brian (1933–).
English comic actor of stage and screen, also much on television and best known as the hen-pecked husband in the TV sitcoms *Man about the House* and *George and Mildred*. Born in Ventnor, Isle of Wight, he trained at RADA and was a member of THEATRE WORKSHOP from the mid-50s.
Sparrows Can't Sing 62. The Activist 69. The Devils 71. The Boy Friend 71. The Ragman's Daughter 72. Man about the House 74. I'm Not Feeling Myself Tonight 76. Black Jack 80. George and Mildred 80, etc.
TV series: Man about the House 73–76. George and Mildred 76–79. The Incredible Mr Tanner 81. L for Lester 82. Lame Ducks 84–85. Brookside 95.

Murphy, Brittany (1977–).
American actress, from television.
Family Prayers 93. Reporting Home (TV) 95. Clueless 95. Drive 96. Double Jeopardy (TV) 96. Freeway 96. The Prophecy 2: Ashtown 97. David and Lisa (TV) 98, etc.
TV series: Drexells' Class 91–92. Sister, Sister 94–95. Almost Home 93. King of the Hill (voice) 97– .

Murphy, Dudley (1897–1968).
American journalist who was briefly in films as director in the 20s and 30s.
High Speed Lee 23. Alex the Great 28. The Sport Parade 32. *The Emperor Jones* 33. The Night Is Young 35. Don't Gamble with Love 36. One Third of a Nation 39. Main Street Lawyer 39. Alma del Bronce (Mex.) 44, etc.

Murphy, Eddie (1961–).
Aggressive American comedian and actor. His brash, fast-talking, guffawing style led to success with *48 Hours* and *Beverly Hills Cop*, but films that followed, in which he took greater control as producer and writer, and even director, were less profitable; he began remaking his earlier hits with diminishing returns until he found success again by refurbishing an old Jerry Lewis vehicle, *The Nutty Professor*, which took more than $100m at the US box-office.
48 Hours 82. Trading Places 83. Best Defense 84. *Beverly Hills Cop* 85. The Golden Child 86. Beverly Hills Cop II 87. Eddie Murphy Raw 87. Hollywood Shuffle 87. Coming to America 88. Harlem Nights (& wd) 89. Another 48 Hrs 90. Boomerang 92. The Distinguished Gentleman 92. Beverly Hills Cop III 94. Vampire in Brooklyn 95. The Nutty Professor 96. Metro 96. Dr Dolittle 98. Bofinger 98. Holy Man 98, etc.
TV series: Saturday Night Live 81–84.
❝ Wouldn't it be a helluva thing if this was burnt cork and you folk were being tolerant for nothing? – E.M.

Murphy, Geoff (1938–).
New Zealand director and musician, now working in America.
Wildman 77. Goodbye Pork Pie 80. Utu 82. The Quiet Earth 84. Never Say Die 88. Young Guns II 90. Freejack 92. The Last Outlaw (TV) 93. Blind Side (TV) 93. Under Siege 2: Dark Territory 95. Don't Look Back (TV) 96, etc.

Murphy, George (1902–1992).
Amiable Irish-American actor and dancer, a pleasant light talent who left the screen for politics and became senator for California. Special Academy Award 1951 'for interpreting the film industry to the nation at large'.
Autobiography: 1970, *Say, Didn't You Used to Be George Murphy?*
■ Kid Millions 34. Jealousy 34. Public Menace 35. I'll Love You Always 35. After the Dance 35. Woman Trap 36. Top of the Town 36. London by Night 37. You're a Sweetheart 37. Broadway Melody of 1938 38. Letter of Introduction 38. Little Miss Broadway 38. Hold that Co-Ed 38. Risky Business 39. Broadway Melody of 1940 40. *Little Nellie Kelly* 40. Public Deb. No. 1 40. A Girl a Guy and a Gob 40. Ringside Maisie 41. *Tom Dick and Harry* 41. Rise and Shine 41. The Mayor of 44th Street 41. For Me and My Gal 41. The Navy Comes Through 42. The Powers Girl 42. Bataan 43. This Is the Army 43. Broadway Rhythm 44. *Show Business* 44. *Step Lively* 44. Having a Wonderful Crime 44. Up Goes Maisie 46. The Arnelo Affair 47. Cynthia 47. Tenth Avenue Angel 48. Big City 48. Border Incident 49. Battleground 49. No Questions Asked 51. It's a Big Country 51. Walk East on Beacon 52. Talk about a Stranger 52.

Murphy, Mary (1931–).
American leading lady.
The Lemon Drop Kid (debut) 51. The Wild One 54. Beachhead 54. Hell's Island 55. The Desperate Hours 55. The Intimate Stranger (GB) 56. Crime and Punishment USA 59. Forty Pounds of Trouble 63. Junior Bonner 72, etc.

Murphy, Michael (1949–).
American general-purpose actor.
Countdown 67. The Arrangement 69. Brewster McCloud 70. What's Up Doc? 72. The Thief Who Came to Dinner 73. Nashville 75. An Unmarried Woman 77. Manhattan 79. The Year of Living Dangerously 82. Cloak and Dagger 84. Salvador 85. Shocker 89. Folks! 92. Batman Returns 92. Clean Slate 94. Kansas City 96. Private Parts 96, etc.

Murphy, Ralph (1895–1967).
American director, in Hollywood from silent days.
The Gay City 41. Hearts in Springtime 41. Mrs Wiggs of the Cabbage Patch 42. Rainbow Island 44. The Man in Half Moon Street 44. Red Stallion in the Rockies 49. Dick Turpin's Ride 51. Captain Blood, Fugitive 52. Desert Rats 53. The Lady in the Iron Mask 53. Three Stripes in the Sun (& w) 55, etc.

Murphy, Richard (1912–1993).
American writer, in Hollywood from 1937.
Boomerang (AAN) 47. Cry of the City 48. Panic in the Streets 50. Les Misérables 52. Desert Rats (AAN) 53. Broken Lance 54. Compulsion 58. The Wackiest Ship in the Army (& d) 60, etc.

Murphy, Rosemary (1925–).
American stage actress in occasional films.
That Night 57. The Young Doctors 61. To Kill a Mockingbird 62. Any Wednesday 66. Ben 72. You'll Like My Mother 72. Walking Tall 73. Forty Carats 73. Ace Eli and Rodger of the Skies 73. Julia (as Dorothy Parker) 77. September 87. For the Boys 91. The Tuskegee Airmen (TV) 95, etc.

Murray, Barbara (1929–).
British leading lady with stage experience.
Anna Karenina 48. Passport to Pimlico 48. Doctor at Large 56. Campbell's Kingdom 58. A Cry from the Streets 58. Girls in Arms 60. A Dandy in Aspic 68. Tales from the Crypt 72, many others.
TV series: The Power Game 66–68. The Bretts 87.

Murray, Bill (1950–).
Abrasive American leading actor, who first came to notice on TV's *Saturday Night Live*. Current asking price: around $10m a movie.
Meatballs 79. Caddyshack 80. Stripes 82. Tootsie (uncredited) 82. *Ghostbusters* 84. The Razor's Edge 84. Little Shop of Horrors 86. Scrooged 88. Ghostbusters II 89. Quick Change (& co-d) 90. What about Bob? 91. Mad Dog and Glory 93. *Groundhog Day* 93. Ed Wood 94. Kingpin 96. Larger than Life 96. Space Jam 96. The Man Who Knew Too Little 97. Wild Things 98. Rushmore 98, etc.

Murray, Charlie (1872–1941).
American vaudeville comedian long with Mack Sennett. In *Tillie's Punctured Romance* 15, and later played with George Sidney in a long series about the Cohens and Kellys.

Murray, Don (1929–).
Ambitious American actor who graduated from innocent to tough roles but does not seem to have received the attention he sought and merited.
■ *Bus Stop* (AAN) 56. *The Bachelor Party* 57. A Hatful of Rain 57. From Hell to Texas 58. These Thousand Hills 59. Shake Hands with the Devil 59. One Foot in Hell 60. *The Hoodlum Priest* (& co-p) 61. *Advise and Consent* 62. Escape from East Berlin 62. One Man's Way 64. Baby the Rain Must Fall 65. Kid Rodelo 66. The Plainsman 66. Sweet Love, Bitter 67. The Viking Queen 67. Tale of the Cock 67. The Borgia Stick (TV) 67. The Intruders (TV) 67. Daughter of the Mind (TV) 69. Childish Things (& wp) 70. Conquest of the Planet of the Apes 72. Happy Birthday Wanda June 72. Cotter 73. A Girl Named Sooner (TV) 74. The Sex Symbol (TV) 74. The Girl on the Late Late Show (TV) 75. Deadly Hero 76. Damien (w, d) 77. Rainbow (TV) 78. Crisis in Mid-air (TV) 79. The Far Turn (TV) 79. Endless Love 81. Peggy Sue Got Married 86. Scorpion 86. Made in Heaven 87. Stillwatch (TV) 87. Mistress (TV) 87. A Brand New Life: The Honeymoon (TV) 89. Ghosts Can't Do It 90. Kickboxer the Champion 91.
TV series: The Outcasts 68. Knots Landing 80–81. Sons and Daughters 91.

Murray, James (1901–1936).
American leading man, a former extra who was chosen by King Vidor to play the hero of *The Crowd* 28, but subsequently took to drink and died in obscurity.
The Big City 28. Thunder 29. Bright Lights 30. The Reckoning 32. Heroes for Sale 32. Skull and Crown 35, etc.

Murray, Jan (1917–) (Murray Janofsky).
American stand-up comedian and 50s TV game show host, in occasional films.
Who Killed Teddy Bear? 65. Thunder Alley 65. Tarzan and the Great River 67. The Angry Breed 68. Which Way to the Front? 70. Roll, Freddy, Roll (TV) 74. The Dream Merchants (TV) 80. Fear City 85, etc.
TV series: Songs for Sale 50–51. Sing It Again 51. Dollar a Second 53–57. Treasure Hunt 56–58.

Murray, Ken (1903–1988) (Don Court).
American comedy actor, radio and TV entertainer, especially as collector of old 'home movies' of the stars. Collected special Oscar for his 1947 bird fantasy *Bill and Coo*.
Autobiography: 1960, *Life on a Pogo Stick*.
Half Marriage 29. A Night at Earl Carroll's 41. The Man Who Shot Liberty Valance 62. Follow Me Boys 66. Power 68.

Murray, Lyn (1909–1989).
American composer.
Son of Paleface 52. The Bridges at Toko Ri 54. To Catch a Thief 55. Escape from Zahrain 61. Promise Her Anything 66. Rosie 67. The Magic Carpet (TV) 71, etc.

Murray, Mae (1889–1965) (Marie Adrienne Koenig).
American leading lady of the silent screen; former dancer; usually in flashy roles. Retired to marry.
Biography: 1959, *The Self-Enchanted* by Jane Ardmore.
Sweet Kitty Bellairs 17. Her Body in Bond 18. The Mormon Maid 20. Jazz Mania 21. Fashion Row 23. The Merry Widow 25. Circe the Enchantress 27. Peacock Alley 31, etc.

Murray, Ruby (1935–1996).
Irish pop singer of the 50s, in occasional films. Born in Belfast, she toured Ireland as a child singer, and gained a wider fame on the BBC TV show *Quite Contrary*, having five records simultaneously in the Top Twenty. Alcoholism contributed to her later decline.
A Touch of the Sun 56. It's Great to Be Young 56, etc.

Murray, Stephen (1912–1983).
Under-used British character actor, on stage from 1933.
Pygmalion 38. *The Prime Minister* 41. *Next of Kin* 42. Undercover 43. *Master of Bankdam* 46. My Brother Jonathan 47. Silent Dust 48. *London Belongs to Me* 48. For Them That Trespass 49. Now Barabbas 50. The Magnet 50. 24 Hours of a Woman's Life 52. Four-Sided Triangle 53. The Stranger's Hand 54. The End of the Affair 55. Guilty 55. The Door in the Wall 56. At the Stroke of Nine 57. A Tale of Two Cities 58. The Nun's Story 59. Master Spy 63, etc.

Murray-Hill, Peter (1908–1957).
British leading man of stage and screen; was married to Phyllis Calvert.
A Yank at Oxford 38. The Outsider 39. Jane Steps Out 40. The Ghost Train 41. Madonna of the Seven Moons 44. They Were Sisters (last film) 45, etc.

Murton, Lionel (1915–).
Canadian character actor resident in Britain.
Meet the Navy 46. The Long Dark Hall 51. The Runaway Bus 54. The Battle of the River Plate 55. Up the Creek 58. Northwest Frontier 59. Confessions of a Window Cleaner 74. Twilight's Last Gleaming 77, etc.

Murton, Peter.
English art director and production designer.
Billy Budd 62. The Ipcress File 65. Thunderball 65. Funeral in Berlin 66. *Half a Sixpence* 67. The Lion in Winter 68. The Ruling Class 72. The Man with the Golden Gun 74. The Eagle Has Landed

76. Death on the Nile 78. Dracula 79. Superman II 80. Superman III 83. Spies Like Us 85. King Kong Lives 86. Diamond's Edge 90. Popcorn 91. Stargate 94, etc.

Musante, Tony (1936–).
American character actor.
Once a Thief 65. The Detective 68. The Bird with the Crystal Plumage 70. The Grissom Gang 71, The Last Run 71. Eutanasia di un Amore 78. Rearview Mirror (TV) 84. Nutcracker: Money, Madness and Murder (TV) 87, etc.
TV series: Toma 72.

Muse, Clarence (1889–1979).
American character actor.
Hearts in Dixie 28. Cabin in the Cotton 32. Showboat 36. Tales of Manhattan 42. An Act of Murder 48. So Bright the Flame 52. Car Wash 77. The Black Stallion 79, many others.

Musidora (1889–1957) (Jeanne Roques).
French actress, director and screenwriter of silent movies, best known as the star of Louis Feuillade's serials.
Fille d'Eve 15. Judex (serial) 16. Les Vampires (serial) 16. Le Spectre 16. La Vagabonde (lt.) 17. Vicenta (& wd) 18. Pour Don Carlos 21. Soleil et Ombre 22. La Terre des Toros (& wd) 25. Le Berceau de Dieu 26, etc.

Mustin, Burt (1884–1977).
American comedy character actor who was 67 when he made his first film.
Detective Story 51. The Lusty Men 53. The Desperate Hours 55. The Big Country 57. Huckleberry Finn 61. The Thrill of It All 63. Cat Ballou 65. Speedway 68. Hail Hero 70. The Skin Game 71, etc.
TV series: A Date with the Angels 57. Ichabod

61–62. The Andy Griffith Show 61–66. All in the Family 73–76. Phyllis 76.

Musuraca, Nicholas (1895–1975).
American cinematographer.
Bride of the Storm 24. Lightning Lanats 25. Tyrant of Red Gulch 27. The Cuckoos 31. Cracked Nuts 33. Long Lost Father 34. Murder on a Bridle Path 36. Blind Alibi 38. Five Came Back 39. Golden Boy 39. The Swiss Family Robinson 40. Tom Brown's Schooldays 40. Cat People 42. The Seventh Victim 43. Curse of the Cat People 44. The Spiral Staircase 45. The Locket 46. The Bachelor and the Bobbysoxer 47. Out of the Past 47. Blood on the Moon 48. Where Danger Lives 51. Clash by Night 52. Devil's Canyon 53. The Story of Mankind 57. Too Much Too Soon 58, many others.

Muti, Ornella (1955–) (Francesca Romana Rivelli).
Sultry Italian leading actress who began her career at the age of 15.
Most Beautiful Wife/La Moglie Più Bella 70. Sensual Man/Paolo il Caldo 73. Italian Graffiti 74. First Love/Primo Amore 78. Flash Gordon 80. Tales of Ordinary Madness 82. Swann in Love/Un Amour de Swann 84. Chronicle of a Death Foretold/Cronaca di una Morte Annunciata 87. Wait until Spring, Bandini 89. Captain Fracassa's Journey/Il Viaggio di Capitan Fracassa 90. Oscar 91. Tonight at Alice's 91. Christmas Vacation '91/Vacanze di Natale '91 91. Especially on Sundays/La Domenica Specialmente 91. Once upon a Crime 92. El Amante Bilingüe 93. The Stranger from Strasbourg/L'Inconnu de Strasbourg (Fr.) 98, many others.

Mutrux, Floyd.
American screenwriter and director.
The Christian Liquorice Store (w) 71. Dusty and Sweets McGhee (wd) 71. Freebie and the Bean 74.

Aloha, Bobby and Rose (wd) 75. American Hot Wax (d) 78. The Hollywood Nights (wd) 80. Blood In Blood Out (co-w) 92. American Me (co-w) 93. There Goes My Baby (wd) 94, etc.

Muybridge, Eadweard (1830–1904) (Edward Muggeridge).
British photographer who, in America in 1877, succeeded in analysing motion with a camera by taking a series of pictures of a horse in motion. (He used 24 cameras attached to a tripwire.) Later he invented a form of projector which reassembled his pictures into the appearance of moving actuality, and called it the Zoopraxiscope; in 1877 he published an influential book of his findings, Animal Locomotion.

Mycroft, Walter (1891–1959).
British director. Chief scriptwriter and director of productions at Elstree in the 30s.
Spring Meeting 40. My Wife's Family 41. Banana Ridge 41. The Woman's Angle (p only) 52, etc.

Myers, Carmel (1899–1980).
American leading lady of the 20s, in the 'vamp' tradition.
Sirens of the Sea 16. Intolerance 16. The Haunted Pyjamas 17. Mad Marriage 21. The Famous Mrs Fair 23. Beau Brummell 24. Ben Hur 25. Sorrell and Son 27. Svengali 31. Lady for a Night 42. Whistle Stop 45, etc.

Myers, Harry (1886–1938).
American character actor, in Hollywood from 1908.
Housekeeping 16. A Connecticut Yankee 21. The Beautiful and the Damned 26. City Lights (as the drunken millionaire) 31. Dangerous Lives 37, etc.

Myers, Mike (1964–).
Canadian comedian, actor and screenwriter, who first came to notice on the TV show Saturday Night Live in 1989 and turned his sketch 'Wayne's World' with Dana Carvey into an international success on film. Born in Toronto, he performed in commercials as a child.
Wayne's World (a, co-w) 92. So I Married an Axe Murderer (a) 93. Wayne's World 2 (a, co-w) 93. Austin Powers: International Man of Mystery (& w) 97. 54 98, etc.
66 Marriage can be viewed as the waiting room for death. – M.M.

Myers, Stanley (1930–1993).
British composer, from the theatre. His best-known work was Cavatina, originally written for The Walking Stick 76, but made famous by its use in The Deerhunter.
Kaleidoscope 66. Otley 69. Age of Consent 70. Raging Moon 71. Zee & Co 72. The Apprenticeship of Dudley Kravitz 74. The Greek Tycoon 78. The Deer Hunter 78. The Watcher in the Woods 80. Moonlighting 82. The Honorary Consul 83. The Lightship 85. My Beautiful Laundrette 85. Castaway 86. Prick Up Your Ears 87. Sammie and Rosie Get Laid 87. Wish You Were Here 87. Stars and Bars 88. The Boost 88. Scenes from the Class Struggle in Beverly Hills 89. The Witches 89. Torrents of Spring 90. Iron Maze 91. Voyager 91. Claude 92. Serafina! 92. Cold Heaven 92, many others.

Myrtil, Odette (1898–1978).
French character actress in Hollywood.
Dodsworth 36. Kitty Foyle 40. Yankee Doodle Dandy 42. Forever and a Day 43. Devotion 46. Here Comes the Groom 50. Lady Possessed 52, many others.

N

Nabokov, Vladimir (1899–1977).
Russian novelist and poet. Born in St Petersburg, he studied at Cambridge University, then lived in Europe, moving to the United States in 1940. He became an American citizen in 1945 and, in the late 40s, was appointed professor of Russian literature at Cornell University. From the early 40s he began to write in English, and caused controversy by the publication of *Lolita* in the mid-50s, which later flared up again when it was filmed, first by Stanley KUBRICK and then by Adrian LYNE.
Autobiography: 1967, *Speak Memory: An Autobiography Revisited.*
Biography: 1967, *Nabokov: His Life in Art* by Andrew Field.
Lolita (& w) 62. Laughter in the Dark (oa) 69. King, Queen, Knave (oa) 72. Despair (oa) 78. Lolita (oa) 98, etc.

Nader, George (1921–).
American leading man who after TV experience starred in many Universal action films of the 50s but has lately been less active.
Monsoon (debut) 52. Four Guns to the Border 54. The Second Greatest Sex 55. Away All Boats 56. Congo Crossing 56. Four Girls in Town 57. Joe Butterfly 57. Nowhere to Go (GB) 58. The Human Duplicators 65. The Million Eyes of Su-Muru 66. Beyond Atlantis 73, etc.
TV series: Ellery Queen 54. The Man and the Challenge 59. Shannon 61.

Naderi, Amir (1945–).
Iranian director and screenwriter. Born in Abadan, and orphaned at the age of five, he survived by shining shoes and similar jobs before finding work as a messenger in a Teheran film studio; he became a still photographer and an assistant director before turning director. In the 90s, he moved to live in the USA. He is best known for his semi-autobiographical *The Runner*.
Goodbye My Friend 71. Elegy 75. Marsiyeh 79. The Search 81. The Runner/Dawandeh 85. Water, Wind, Dust/Ab, Bad, Khak 85. Manhattan by Numbers 93, etc.

Nagase, Masatoshi.
Japanese leading actor.
Mystery Train (US) 89. Autumn Moon (HK) 92. The Most Terrible Time of My Life/Waga Jinsei Saisaku No Toki 94. Cold Fever 95. The Stairway to the Distant Past 95, etc.

Nagel, Anne (1912–1966) (Anne Dolan).
American supporting actress, the heroine's friend in countless movies of the 40s. Born in Boston, she was on screen from the early 30s. Married actor Ross ALEXANDER.
I Loved You Wednesday 33. Stand Up and Cheer 34. Hot Money 36. The Case of the Stuttering Bishop 37. Hoosier Schoolboy 37. Call a Messenger 39. Black Friday 40. Man Made Monster 40. The Green Hornet 40. Never Give a Sucker an Even Break 41. The Mad Monster 42. The Secret Code 42. Women in Bondage 43. Spirit of West Point 47, etc.

Nagel, Conrad (1896–1970).
American leading man of the 20s who came to Hollywood after stage experience; latterly ran acting school. Born in Keokuk, Iowa, he was on stage from 1914, and began his film career in 1919. He was one of Louis B. MAYER's three dinner guests who first discussed the idea of forming an Academy of Motion Picture Arts and Sciences in January 1927. The second of his three wives was actress Lynn Merrick. His lovers included actress Dolores COSTELLO.

Little Women 19. Fighting Chance 20. Three Weeks 24. The Exquisite Sinner 26. Slightly Used 27. Quality Street 27. One Romantic Night 30. Bad Sister 31. East Lynne 31. Dangerous Corner 34. Navy Spy 37. I Want a Divorce 40. The Woman in Brown 48. All that Heaven Allows 55. Stranger in My Arms 58. The Man Who Understood Women 59, many others.

Nagy, Ivan (1938–).
Hungarian-born director working in America, mainly as a director of TV movies.
Bad Charleston Charlie 73. Money, Marbles and Chalk 73. Five Minutes of Freedom 73. Deadly Hero 76. Captain America II: Death Too Soon (TV) 79. A Gun in the House (TV) 81. Jane Doe (TV) 83, etc.

Naha, Ed.
American screenwriter.
Troll 86. Dolls 86. Honey, I Shrunk the Kids (co-w) 89. Chud II: Bud the Chud 89. Matinee (co-w) 92. Omega Doom 96, etc.

Nail, Jimmy (1954–) (James Bradford).
Lean English actor, singer, writer and songwriter, best known for his role as the violent, unpredictable Oz in the TV series *Auf Wiedersehen, Pet*. Born in Newcastle, he ran his own construction firm and was a rock singer before becoming an actor. His recording of 'Ain't No Doubt' topped the singles hit parade in the early 90s.
Morons from Outer Space 85. Blott on the Landscape (TV) 85. Howling II: Your Sister Is a Werewolf (US) 85. Dream Demon 88. Crocodile Shoes (& w) (TV) 94. Evita 96, etc.
TV series: Auf Wiedersehen, Pet 84. Spender (& co-w) 90.

Nair, Mira (1957–).
Indian director, producer and screenwriter who began as a documentary film-maker.
Salaam Bombay! 88 (p, d). Mississippi Masala (p, wd) 91. The Perez Family 95. Kama Sutra 96, etc.

Naish, J. Carrol (1900–1973).
American character actor with stage experience, in films from 1930. Born in New York City, he worked in Europe after the First World War, including a period on stage in Paris, and on his return to Hollywood established himself as an actor capable of portraying many nationalities, including Italians, Mexicans, Chinese, and American Indians.
The Hatchet Man 32. Lives of a Bengal Lancer 35. Anthony Adverse 36. King of Alcatraz 38. Persons in Hiding 39. *Beau Geste* 39. Birth of the Blues 41. Blood and Sand 41. The Corsican Brothers 41. The Pied Piper 42. Dr Renault's Secret 42. Batman (serial) 43. Behind the Rising Sun 43. Sahara (AAN) 43. Gung Ho! 44. *A Medal for Benny* (AAN) 45. House of Frankenstein 45. The Southerner 45. Enter Arsène Lupin 45. The Beast with Five Fingers 46. Joan of Arc 48. Black Hand 49. Annie Get Your Gun 50. Across the Wide Missouri 51. Sitting Bull 54. Violent Saturday 54. New York Confidential 54. The Young Don't Cry 57. The Hanged Man 64. Blood of Frankenstein 70, many others.
TV series: Life With Luigi 52. The New Adventures of Charlie Chan 57. Guestward Ho! 60.

Naismith, Laurence (1908–1992) (Lawrence Johnson).
Amiable British character actor with wide stage experience. Born in Thames Ditton, Surrey, he was on stage from 1927 after working as a merchant seaman, and in films from 1947.
Trouble in the Air 47. A Piece of Cake 48. I Believe in You 51. The Beggar's Opera 52. Mogambo 53. Carrington VC 55. *Richard III* 56. Boy on a Dolphin 57. Tempest 58. A Night to Remember 58. Sink the Bismarck 60. The Singer Not the Song 61. Jason and the Argonauts 63. The Three Lives of Thomasina 63. Sky West and Crooked 65. The Scorpio Letters 67. The Long Duel 67. Fitzwilly 67. Camelot 67. The Valley of Gwangi 68. Eye of the Cat 69. Scrooge 70. Diamonds Are Forever 71. *The Amazing Mr Blunden* 72, etc.
TV series: The Persuaders 71.

Najimy, Kathy (1957–).
American actress in comic roles. Married actor Dan Finnerty.
Soapdish 91. Sister Act 92. Hocus Pocus 93. Sister Act 2: Back in the Habit 93. It's Pat 94. Jeffrey 95. Bride of Chucky 98, etc.
TV series: Veronica's Closet 97– . King of the Hill (voice) 97– .

Nakadai, Tatsuya (1932–).
Japanese leading actor who was memorable in Kurosawa's *Yojimbo* and gained fame in Masaki Kobayashi's trilogy *The Human Condition*, appearing in many of the director's subsequent films.
Seven Samurai 54. Untamed/Arakure 57. Conflagration/Enjo 58. The Key/Kagi 59. The Human Condition Part I: No Greater Love/Ningen no Joken I-II 59. The Human Condition Part II: The Road to Eternity/Ningen no Joken III-IV 59. When a Woman Ascends the Stairs/Onna ga Kaidan o Agaru Toki 60. Yojimbo 61. The Other Woman/Tsuma Toshite Onna Toshite 61. The Human Condition Part III: A Soldier's Prayer/Ningen no Joken V-VI 61. The Inheritance/Karamiai 62. Sanjuro 62. Harakiri 62. High and Low/Tengoku to Jigoku 63. Kwaidan 64. A Woman's Story/Onna no Rekishi 63. Samurai Rebellion/Joiuchi 67. Inn of Evil/Inochi Bo ni Furo 71. I Am a Cat/Wagahai wa Neko de Aru 75. Kagemusha 80. Ran 85. Return to the River Kwai 89. Basara: The Princess Goh 92, etc.

Nakano, Desmond.
American screenwriter.
Boulevard Nights 79. Body Rock 84. Black Moon Rising (co-w) 86. Last Exit to Brooklyn 90. American Me (co-w) 92. White Man's Burden (d) 95, etc.

Naldi, Nita (1899–1961) (Anita Donna Dooley).
Italian-American leading lady of the 20s, formerly in the Ziegfeld Follies.
Dr Jekyll and Mr Hyde 20. The Unfair Sex 22. Blood and Sand 22. The Ten Commandments 23. Cobra 25. A Sainted Devil 25. The Marriage Whirl 26. The Lady Who Lied 27, etc.

Namath, Joe (1943–).
American professional sportsman who made a few films.
■ Norwood 69. C. C. and Company 70. The Last Rebel 71. Avalanche Express 78. Marriage Is Alive and Well (TV) 80. Chattanooga Choo Choo 84.

Nance, Jack (1943–1997) (John Nance).
American character actor, from the stage; associated with the films of David LYNCH and best known for playing the lead in that director's cult film *Eraserhead*. Died after a fight in a doughnut shop.
Fools 70. Eraserhead 76. Hammett 82. Ghoulies 85. Blue Velvet 86. Barfly 87. The Blob 88. Colors 88. Wild at Heart 90. The Hot Spot 90. Love and a.45 94. Voodoo 95. The Secret Agent Club 96, etc.
TV series: Twin Peaks 90–91.

Napier, Alan (1903–1988) (Alan Napier-Clavering).
Dignified British character actor, in Hollywood from 1940; usually played butlers or noble lords. Born in Harborne, Birmingham, he studied at RADA and was on stage from 1924, moving to Hollywood in the 40s. He was best known for playing Batman's manservant Alfred in the 60s TV series and feature film.
In a Monastery Garden 31. Loyalties 32. For Valour 37. The Four Just Men 39. The Invisible Man Returns 40. Random Harvest 42. Ministry of Fear 43. Lost Angel 44. *The Uninvited* 44. Forever Amber 47. Tarzan's Magic Fountain 50. Julius Caesar 53. The Court Jester 55. Journey to the Centre of the Earth 59. Marnie 64. Batman 66, many others.
TV series: Don't Call Me Charlie 62–63. Batman 66–68.

Napier, Charles (1936–).
American character actor, often in the films of Jonathan Demme.
Cherry, Harry and Raquel 69. Caged Heat 74. Beyond the Valley of the Dolls 70. Super Vixens 74. Citizens Band 77. The Last Emperor 79. The Blues Brothers 80. Swing Shift 84. Rambo: First Blood II 85. Something Wild 86. Deep Space 88. Married to the Mob 88. Future Zone 90. The Grifters 90. Miami Blues 90. The Silence of the Lambs 91. Soldier's Fortune 91. Center of the Web 92. Skeeter 93. Philadelphia 93. Jury Duty 95. Original Gangstas 96. Riot 96. The Cable Guy 96. Steel 97. Austin Powers: International Man of Mystery 97, etc.
❝ I keep waiting for Chuck Napier to become a really big movie actor, but it seems so far it's been slightly out of his reach . . . I think he's one of America's finest actors. – *Jonathan Demme*

Napier, Diana (1905–1982) (Molly Ellis).
English leading lady of the 30s. Born in Bath, Somerset, she began on stage and, after several bit parts in silent films, was given a five-year contract, at £20 a week, by Alexander KORDA, who chose her to fit a female stereotype that he described as 'a high-class bitch'. She retired in the mid-30s, making a brief return to the screen in the late 40s. Her second husband was opera singer Richard TAUBER.
The Rat 25. The Farmer's Wife 28. Strange Evidence 32. Wedding Rehearsal 33. The Private Life of Henry VIII 33. Catherine the Great 34. The Private Life of Don Juan 34. Royal Cavalcade 35. Mimi 35. Heart's Desire 35. Land without Music 36. Pagliacci 36. *I Was a Dancer* 48. Bait 50, etc.

Napier, Russell (1910–1975).
Australian-born actor, long in Britain. Appeared in numerous small parts, usually as officials; also played the chief inspector in many of the 3-reel 'Scotland Yard' series.
End of the River 47. The Time Machine (TV) 49. Black Orchid 53. The Stranger Came Home 54. Little Red Monkey 54. The Brain Machine 54. The Narrowing Circle 55. A Town Like Alice 56. The Shiralee 57. Robbery under Arms 57. A Night to Remember 58. Hell Is a City 59. Sink the Bismarck! 60. Blood Beast Terror 67. The Black Windmill 74, etc.

Napoleon, Art (1923–).
American director.
Man on the Prowl (& w) 57. Too Much Too Soon 58. Ride the Wild Surf (w only) 64. The Activist 69, etc.

Napoleon Bonaparte
has been impersonated on screen by Charles Boyer in *Marie Walewska/Conquest*, Esmé Percy in *Invitation to the Waltz*, Emile Drain in *Madame sans Gêne* and *Les Perles de la Couronne*, Rollo Lloyd in *Anthony Adverse*, Julien Bertheau in *Madame*, Marlon Brando in *Désirée*, Arnold Moss in *The Black Book*, Pierre Mondy in *Austerlitz*, Herbert Lom in several films including *The Young Mr Pitt* and *War and Peace*, Eli Wallach in *The Adventures of Gerard*, Rod Steiger in *Waterloo*, and Kenneth Haigh in *Eagle in a Cage*.
Abel Gance's 1925 film *Napoleon* (with Albert Dieudonne) is noted for the first use of a triptych screen corresponding very closely to Cinerama. It was revived with international success in 1980, in a version painstakingly reassembled by Kevin Brownlow, who in 1983 published a book about it.

Narcejac, Thomas (1908–1998) (Pierre Ayraud).
French thriller writer and screenwriter, in collaboration with Pierre Boileau. Born in Rochefort-sur-mer, he studied philosophy and literature at the Sorbonne, and worked as a teacher. After writing on his own, in 1951, he began working with Boileau, who devised the plots, while he wrote the stories, which, with their macabre suspense, appealed to many directors.
Autobiography: 1986, *Tandem* (with Pierre Boileau).
The Fiends/Les Diaboliques (from Celle Qui N'était Plus 55. The She-Wolves (from Les Louves) (& w) 57. *Vertigo* (from D'entre les Morts) 58. *Eyes without a Face*/Les Yeux sans Visage 60. Faces in the Dark (GB) 60. Frantic 60. Murder at 45 RPM 60. Where the Truth Lies 61. Crime Does Not Pay/Le Crime Ne Paie Pas (co-w only) 62. Letters to an Unknown Lover (GB/Fr.) 85. Body Parts (US) 91. Diabolique (oa) (US) 96, etc.

Nardini, Tom (1945–).
American character actor.
Cat Ballou 65. Africa Texas Style 67. The Young Animals 68. Siege/Self Defense 82, etc.
TV series: Cowboy in Africa 67.

Nares, Owen (1888–1943) (O. N. Ramsay).
British matinée idol and silent screen star. Born in Maiden Erleigh, Berkshire, he was on the London stage from 1908 and in films from 1913.
Autobiography: 1925, *Myself and Some Others; Pure Egotism*.
Dandy Donovan 14. The Sorrows of Satan 17. God Bless the Red, White and Blue 18. Indian Love Lyrics 23. Young Lochinvar 23. Milestones 28. The Middle Watch 30. Sunshine Susie 31. The Impassive Footman 32. The Private Life of Don Juan 34. The Show Goes On 37. The Prime Minister 41, etc.
❝ For an actor whose chief charm was his complete 'ease' and naturalness on the stage, almost in the du Maurier tradition, it was quite extraordinary to realize, when one played with Owen, how much he relied on sheer mechanics. Every gesture, every move was planned beforehand, and adhered to rigidly. – *Jean Webster-Brough*

Narizzano, Silvio (1927–).
Canadian-born director, of Italian-American parents, in British TV in the 50s and films from the 60s. Born in Montreal, he was educated at Bishop's University, Quebec. He began as an actor in Ottawa before working in Canadian television and, later, in Britain.
■ Under Ten Flags (co-d) 60. Fanatic 65. *Georgy Girl* 66. Blue (US) 68. Loot 70. Redneck 72. The Sky is Falling 76. *Why Shoot the Teacher* 78. The Class of Miss MacMichael 78. *Staying On* (TV) 80. Choices 81.

Naruse, Mikio (1905–1969).
Prolific Japanese director from 1930 onwards. His films often depicted drab working-class life. He began as a prop-man before becoming a scriptwriter and director's assistant. At least half of his films have been lost, including most of his earliest work.
Koshiben Gambare 31. Nasanu Naka 32. Kimi to Wakarete 33. Otomo-gokoro Sannin Shimai 35. Hataraku Ikka 39. Shanghai Moon/Shanhai no Tsuki 41. Uta Andon 41. Ginza Gesho 51. Meshi 51. Lightning/Inazuma 52. Fufu 53. Bangiku 54. Nagareru 56. Untamed/Arakure 57. Anzukko 58. The Other Woman/Tsuma Toshite Onna Toshite 61. Yearning/Midareru 64. Two in the Shadow/ Midaregumo 67, many others.
❝ He was the most difficult director I ever worked for. He never said a word. A real nihilist. – *Tatsuya Nakadai*

Naschy, Paul (1936–) (Jacinto Molina Alvarez).
Spanish leading actor, writer and occasional producer and director of horror movies. His most notable and oft-repeated role is as werewolf Waldemar Daninsky. Born in Bilbao, he was a weightlifter and an architect before entering films in the mid-60s. He sometimes uses the pseudonym Jack Moll for his screenwriting.
Frankenstein's Bloody Terror/Hell's Creatures/La Marca del Hombre Lobo (& w) 67. Dracula vs Frankenstein/El Hombre que Vivo de Ummo (& w) 69. The Werewolf vs the Vampire Woman/ Shadow of the Werewolf/La Noche de Walpurgis (& co-w) 70. Fury of the Wolfman/La Furia del Hombre Lobo (& w) 71. Dr Jekyll and the Wolfman/De Jeckill y el Hombre Lobo (& w) 71. Dracula's Great Love/aka Dracula's Virgin Lovers/ El Gran Amor del Conde Dracula (& co-w) 72. Vengeance of the Zombies/La Rebellión de las Muertas (& w) 72. Horror Rises from the Tomb/ El Espanto Surge de la Tumba (& w) 72. The Rue Morgue Massacres/Hunchback of the Morgue/El Jorobado de la Morgue (& co-w) 73. The Mummy's Revenge/La Vengenzia de la Momia (& w) 73. House of Psychotic Women/The Blue Eyes of the Broken Doll/Los Ojos Azules de la Muñeca Rota (& w) 73. Curse of the Devil/El Retorno de Walpurgis (& w) 74. Exorcism/Exorcismo (& co-w) 74. Night of the Howling Beast/The Werewolf and the Yeti/La Maldición de la Bestia (& w) 75. People Who Own the Dark 75. Inquisition/ Inquisición (& wd) 76. The Craving/El Retorno del Hombre Lobo (& wd) 80. Human Beasts/El Carnaval de la Bestias (& p, wd) 80. Monster Island 81. The Beast and the Magic Sword (& p, wd) 83. Aqui Huele Muerto 90, etc.

Nascimbene, Mario (1916–).
Italian composer.
OK Nero 51. The Barefoot Contessa 54. Alexander the Great 55. A Farewell to Arms 57. *The Vikings* 58. Room at the Top 58. Solomon and Sheba 59. Sons and Lovers 60. Barabbas 61. Jessica 62. One Million Years BC 66. Dr Faustus 67. When Dinosaurs Ruled the Earth 70. Creatures the World Forgot 71. Year One/Anno Uno 74. The Messiah 78, many others.

Nash, Clarence (1904–1985).
American voice performer, the inimitable sound of Donald Duck for 40 years.

Nash, Marilyn (c. 1924–).
American leading lady selected by Chaplin to play in *Monsieur Verdoux* 47. Married writer-producer Philip Yordan.
Unknown World 51.

Nash, Mary (1885–1976) (Mary Ryan).
American stage actress in occasional films. Born in Troy, New York, she studied at the American Academy of Dramatic Art and was on stage from 1904.
■ Uncertain Lady 34. College Scandal 35. Come and Get It 36. The King and the Chorus Girl 37. Easy Living 37. Heidi 37. Wells Fargo 37. The Little Princess 39. The Rains Came 39. Charlie Chan in Panama 40. Sailor's Lady 40. Gold Rush Maisie 40. *The Philadelphia Story* 40. Men of Boys Town 41. Calling Dr Gillespie 42. The Human Comedy 43. In the Meantime Darling 44. Cobra Woman 44. The Lady and the Monster 44. Yolanda and the Thief 45. Monsieur Beaucaire 46. Swell Guy 46. Till the Clouds Roll By 46.

Nathan, Robert (1894–1985).
American novelist and screenwriter.
The Clock/Under the Clock (co-w) 45. The Bishop's Wife (oa) 47. Portrait of Jennie (oa) 48. Pagan Love Song (co-w) 50. One More Spring (oa) 50, etc.

Nation, Terry (1930–1997).
Welsh screenwriter, best known as the creator of the Daleks, the tinpot power-crazed villains of the *Dr Who* TV series and films. Born in Cardiff, he began as a stand-up comedian and comedy scriptwriter. He also created the science fiction TV series *Survivors* 75–77, and *Blake's Seven* 78–81. Moved to work in Hollywood in the late 70s.
What a Whopper! (w) 61. Dr Who and the Daleks (oa) 65. Daleks: Invasion Earth 2150 AD (oa) 66. And Soon the Darkness (co-w) 70. The House in Nightmare Park (co-w, p) 73, etc.

Natwick, Grim (1890–1990) (Myron Natwick).
Cartoonist and animator who created Betty Boop while working for Max Fleischer in 1930. He later worked for Disney on *Snow White and the Seven Dwarfs* 37, and animated the Sorcerer's Apprentice sequence in *Fantasia* 40.

Natwick, Mildred (1905–1994).
American character actress, at her best in eccentric roles. Born in Baltimore, Maryland, and educated at Bryn Mawr, she was on stage from 1932. Her best role, which she played first on Broadway, was as the harassed mother Mrs Banks in *Barefoot in the Park*.
■ The Long Voyage Home 40. The Enchanted Cottage 45. Yolanda and the Thief 45. The Late George Apley 47. A Woman's Vengeance 48. Three Godfathers 48. The Kissing Bandit 48. She Wore a Yellow Ribbon 49. Cheaper by the Dozen 50. The Quiet Man 52. Against All Flags 52. *The Trouble with Harry* 55. *The Court Jester* 55. Teenage Rebel 56. Tammy and the Bachelor 57. *Barefoot in the Park* (AAN) 67. If It's Tuesday This Must Be Belgium 69. The Maltese Bippy 69. Do Not Fold Spindle or Mutilate (TV) 71. The Snoop Sisters (TV) 72. Daisy Miller 74. At Long Last Love 75. Kiss Me Goodbye 82. Dangerous Liaisons 88.

Naughton, Bill (1910–1992).
Irish novelist, dramatist and screenwriter, a former lorry driver.
Autobiography: 1988, *Saintly Billy: A Catholic Boyhood*.
Alfie (AAN) 66. The Family Way 66. Spring and Port Wine 70. Alfie Darling (oa) 75.

Naughton, Charlie (1887–1976).
Chubby Scottish slapstick comedian, a former painter and decorator. Born in Glasgow, he formed a double act with Jimmy Gold, and was a member of the CRAZY GANG in the 30s.
Highland Fling 36. Wise Guys 37. O-Kay for Sound 37. Alf's Button Afloat 38. The Frozen Limits 39. Gasbags 40. Down Melody Lane 43. Life Is a Circus 58.

Naughton, David (1951–).
American leading actor. Brother of James NAUGHTON.
Separate Ways 79. Midnight Madness 80. An American Werewolf in London 81. Hot Dog – the Movie! 83. Not for Publication 84. Getting Physical (TV) 84. Separate Vacations 86. The Boy in Blue 86. Kidnapped 87. Private Affairs 89. Overexposed 90. The Sleeping Car 90. Wild Cactus 92. Body Bags (TV) 93. Desert Steel 94. Beanstalk 94. Ice Cream Man 95. Mirror, Mirror 3: The Voyeur 96, etc.
TV series: Making It 79. At Ease 83. My Sister Sam 86–88.

Naughton, James (1945–).
American leading man, mostly on television.
The Paper Chase 74. The Bunker (TV) 80. A Stranger Is Watching 82. The Glass Menagerie 87. The Good Mother 88. Second Wind 90. Birds II: Land's End (TV) 94. The First Wives Club 96. First Kid 96, etc.
TV series: Faraday and Company 72. Planet of the Apes 74. Making the Grade 82. Trauma Centre 83.

Nava, Gregory (1949–).
American director and screenwriter.
The Confessions of Amans (wd) 76. The End of August (co-w) 82. El Norte (wd) (AAN) 84. A Time of Destiny (wd) 88. My Family/Mi Familia (co-w, d) 95. Selena (wd) 97. Why Do Fools Fall in Love 98, etc.

Navarro, Guillermo.
Mexican cinematographer.
Cabeza de Vaca 90. Cronos 92. Desperado 95. Four Rooms (co-ph) 95. From Dusk till Dawn 96. The Long Kiss Goodnight 96. Spawn 97. Jackie Brown 97, etc.

Nazarro, Ray (1902–1986).
American director and screenwriter of second features. Born in Boston, he worked mainly for Columbia, later moving into TV and making films in Europe.
Song of the Prairie 45. Cowboy Blues 46. Last Days of Boot Hill 47. Six-Gun Law 48. Quick on the Trigger 49. The Tougher They Come 50. Al Jennings of Oklahoma 50. China Corsair 51. Bandits of Corsica 51. Cripple Creek 52. Kansas Pacific 53. The Lone Gun 54. Top Gun 55. The Hired Gun 57. Apache Territory 58. Dog Eat Dog (Ger./It.) 64. Arrivederci Cowboy (It.) 67, etc.

Nazimova, Alla (1879–1945) (Alla Nazimoff).
Russian-born stage actress who made a number of films in America. Born in Yalta, she studied at the Moscow Academy and joined the Moscow Art Theatre under Stanislavsky. After appearing on the Broadway stage in the early 1900s she decided to remain in the United States. She was in films from 1916; in the mid-20s she went back to the stage, returning to Hollywood for a few appearances in the 40s. Married Russian actor Paul Orleneff and director Charles Bryant, who directed her in some of her early silents.
Biography: 1997, *Nazimova* by Gavin Lambert.
■ War Brides 16. Revelation 18. Toys of Fate 18. An Eye for an Eye 19. The Red Lantern 19. The Brat 19. Stronger than Death 20. Heart of a Child 20. Madame Peacock 20. Billions 20. Camille 21. A Doll's House 22. *Salome* 23. Madonna of the Streets 24. The Redeeming Sin 24. My Son 25. *Escape* 40. Blood and Sand 41. The Bridge of San Luis Rey 44. In Our Time 44. Since You Went Away 45.

Nazzari, Amedeo (1907–1979) (Salvatore Amedeo Buffa).
Italian leading actor, usually in dashing roles. Born in Cagliari, he was Italy's biggest male star in the late 30s, though his popularity had waned by the late 50s; he played character parts thereafter.
Ginevra degli Almieri 35. Cavalleria 36. Luciano Serra Pilota 38. Centomila Dollari 40. Scarpe Grosse 40. Caravaggio 41. L'Ultimo Ballo 41. Fedora 42. Harlem 43. Il Bandito 46. Malacarne 47. Don Juan de Serrallonga 48. Il Brigante Musolino 50. Bellissima 51. Il Tradimento 51. Altri Tempi 52. Il Brigante di Tacca del Lupo 52. We Are All Murderers/Nous Sommes Tous des Assassins 52. Angelo Bianco 55. Cabiria/Le Notti di Cabiria 57. Anna di Brooklyn 58. Labyrinth 59. The Naked Maja (US/It.) 59. The Best of Enemies (GB/It.) 62. Il Gaucho 64. The Column/Columna 68. The Sicilian Clan/Le Clan des Siciliens (Fr.) 69. The Valachi Papers/Cosa Nostra 72. A Matter of Time (US/GB/It.) 76, many others.

Neagle, Dame Anna (1904–1986) (Florence Marjorie Robertson).
British leading lady, a former chorus dancer who, in partnership with producer and, later, her husband Herbert Wilcox, built up a formidable film gallery of historical heroines. Born in Forest Gate, London, she was on stage from 1925, and also worked in cabaret as a dancer in the late 20s. Her success dated from the film of *Goodnight Vienna*, starring Jack Buchanan. After Evelyn Laye turned down the role opposite Buchanan, Wilcox went to call on him, saw Neagle performing with him on stage, and signed her for the film. When film roles grew hard to find, she returned successfully to the stage. She was made a Dame of the British Empire in 1969.
Autobiographies: 1949, *It's Been Fun*. 1974, *There's Always Tomorrow*.
■ Those Who Love (as Marjorie Robertson) 29. The School for Scandal 30. Should a Doctor Tell? 30. The Chinese Bungalow 31. Goodnight Vienna 32. The Flag Lieutenant 32. The Little Damozel 33. *Bitter Sweet* 33. The Queen's Affair 33. *Nell Gwyn* 34. Peg of Old Drury 35. Limelight 36. The Three Maxims 36. London Melody 37. *Victoria the Great* 37. Sixty Glorious Years 38. *Nurse Edith Cavell* 39. Irene (US) 40. No No Nanette (US) 40. Sunny (US) 41. They Flew Alone (as Amy Johnson) 42. Forever and a Day 43. Yellow Canary 43. The Volunteer 43. I Live in Grosvenor Square 45. *Piccadilly Incident* 46. The Courtneys of Curzon Street 47. Royal Wedding (voice) 47. *Spring in Park Lane* 48. Elizabeth of Ladymead 49. Maytime in Mayfair 49. *Odette* 50. *The Lady with a Lamp* 51. Derby Day 52. Lilacs in the Spring 55. King's Rhapsody 56. My Teenage Daughter 56. No Time for Tears 57. The Man Who Wouldn't Talk 58. The Lady is a Square 58.

Produced three Frankie Vaughan films 58–61; returned to stage.
✪ For providing her faithful British admirers with the heroines they wanted her to be; and for her eagerness to please. *Victoria the Great*.

Neal, Patricia (1926–).
American leading actress who handled some interesting roles before illness caused her semi-retirement. Born in Packard, Kentucky, she studied drama at Northwestern University and first worked as a model, making her Broadway debut in the mid-40s. A massive stroke in 1965 left her unable to speak or walk for a time; after three years of therapy, she resumed her career in *The Subject Was Roses*. She was married to writer Roald DAHL (1953–83) and romantically linked with actor Gary COOPER. She was played by Glenda JACKSON in the TV biopic *The Patricia Neal Story* 81.
Autobiography: *As I Am*.
■ John Loves Mary 49. *The Fountainhead* 49. It's a Great Feeling 49. *The Hasty Heart* (GB) 50. Bright Leaf 50. Three Secrets 50. The Breaking Point 50. Operation Pacific 51. Raton Pass 51. Diplomatic Courier 51. The Day the Earth Stood Still 51. Weekend with Father 51. Washington Story 52. Something for the Birds 52. Stranger from Venus (GB) 54. *A Face in the Crowd* 57. Breakfast at Tiffany's 61. *Hud* (AA, BFA) 63. Psyche 59 (GB) 64. In Harm's Way (BFA) 64. The Subject was Roses (AAN) 68. The Homecoming (TV) 71. The Night Digger 71. Baxter 72. Happy Mother's Day Love George 73. Run Stranger Run (TV) 74. Things in Their Season (TV) 75. Eric (TV) 77. Tail Gunner Joe (TV) 77. The Bastard (TV) 78. The Passage 79. All Quiet on the Western Front (TV) 80. Ghost Story 81. Glitter (TV) 84. Love Leads the Way (TV) 85. An Unremarkable Life 89. Caroline? 90. Heidi (TV) 93. A Mother's Right: The Elizabeth Morgan Story (TV) 93.

Neal, Tom (1914–1972).
American leading man, mainly in second features; former athlete. Born in Evanston, Illinois, he studied at Northwestern University and was on stage from the mid-30s. He quit to take a law degree at Harvard and began making films in 1938. His career came to a spectacular end after he beat up actor Franchot TONE in a quarrel over actress Barbara Peyton, who then married Tone, divorced him within two months and returned to marry Neal. No studio would employ him thereafter and he worked as a landscape gardener. In 1965, he was charged with shooting his third wife and spent seven years in jail for her involuntary manslaughter. Shortly after his release he died from heart failure. His son, Tom Neal, Jnr (1957–) made his screen debut in 1990 in a remake of his father's *Detour*.
Four Girls in White 38. Within the Law 39. Another Thin Man 39. Jungle Girl 41. Bowery at Midnight 42. There's Something About a Soldier 43. She Has What It Takes 43. Detour 45. First Yank into Tokyo 45. Club Havana 46. The Brute Man 46. Bruce Gentry – Daredevil of the Skies 49. The Great Jesse James Raid 53, many others.

Neame, Ronald (1911–).
Outstanding British cinematographer who became a rather disappointing director. Born in London, the son of silent film actress Ivy Close, he began as an assistant cameraman on Hitchcock's *Blackmail* 29. In the 40s he became a producer at Cineguild, the independent company set up by Noël COWARD, David LEAN and Anthony HAVELOCK-ALLAN, and was cinematographer on some of Lean's best films.
SELECTED FILMS AS CINEMATOGRAPHER: Drake of England 34. The Gaunt Stranger 37. The Crimes of Stephen Hawke 39. Major Barbara 40. In Which We Serve 42. Blithe Spirit 45.
■ AS DIRECTOR: Take My Life 47. The Golden Salamander 50. *The Card* (& p) 52. The Million Pound Note 53. The Man Who Never Was 56. The Seventh Sin 57. Windom's Way 58. The Horse's Mouth 59. *Tunes of Glory* 60. Escape from Zahrain 61. I Could Go On Singing 62. The Chalk Garden 64. Mister Moses 65. A Man Could Get Killed (co-d) 66. Gambit 66. The Prime of Miss Jean Brodie 68. Scrooge 70. The Poseidon Adventure 72. The Odessa File 75. Meteor 79. Hopscotch 80. First Monday in October 81. Foreign Body 86.

Nebenzal, Seymour (1899–1961).
Distinguished German producer who had a disappointing career after going to Hollywood in the late 30s.
Westfront 30. M 31. Kameradschaft 32. The Testament of Dr Mabuse 33. Mayerling 36. We Who are Young 40. Summer Storm 44. Whistle Stop 46. Heaven Only Knows 47. Siren of Atlantis 48. M (remake) 51, etc.

Nedell, Bernard (1897–1972).
American character actor, often in villainous roles. Born in New York City, to parents in the theatre, and educated at Western Reserve University, Cleveland, he was on stage as a child. He trained as a violinist before deciding to become an actor, beginning in repertory and starting his film career as an extra. From the mid-20s to the late 30s he was on the London stage and appeared in British films. Married actress Olive Blakeney.
The Serpent 16. The Return of the Rat (GB) 29. Shadows (GB) 31. Lazybones (GB) 35. The Man Who could Work Miracles (GB) 36. Mr Moto's Gamble 38. Angels Wash Their Faces 39. Strange Cargo 40. The Desperadoes 43. One Body Too Many 44. Monsieur Verdoux 47. The Loves of Carmen 48. Heller in Pink Tights 60. Hickey and Boggs 72, many others.

Needham, Hal (1931–).
American director and screenwriter, associated with the films of Burt REYNOLDS. Born in Memphis, Tennessee, he worked in fairgrounds before going to Hollywood in the mid-50s as a stuntman and second-unit director. There he became friendly with Reynolds and directed the actor in movies that concentrated on high-spirited car chases.
■ *Smokey and the Bandit* 77. Hooper 78. The Villain 79. Death Car on the Freeway (TV) 79. Smokey and the Bandit II 80. The Cannonball Run 80. Stunts (TV) 81. Megaforce 82. Stroker Ace 83. Cannonball Run II 83. RAD 86. Body Slam 87.

Neeson, Liam (1952–).
Tall Irish leading actor, often in tough-guy roles. Born in Ballymena, Northern Ireland, he began acting on stage in 1976 and later joined the Abbey Theatre in Dublin, where he was spotted by director John BOORMAN, who cast him as Sir Gawain in *Excalibur*. His best performance so far has been as Oskar Schindler in *Schindler's List*. Married actress Natasha RICHARDSON in 1994.
Excalibur 81. The Bounty 84. The Innocent 84. Lamb 85. Duet for One 86. The Mission 86. A Prayer for the Dying 87. Suspect 87. The Dead Pool 88. The Good Mother 88. High Spirits 88. Satisfaction 88. Next of Kin 89. The Big Man 90. Darkman 90. Under Suspicion 91. Shining Through 92. Ethan Frome 93. Ruby Cairo 93. *Schindler's List* (AAN) 93. Nell 94. Rob Roy 95. Before and After 96. Michael Collins 96. Les Misérables 98, etc.

Neff, Hildegard (1925–) (Hildegard Knef).
German leading actress and cabaret artiste who spent some time in Hollywood. Born in Ulm, she studied art in Berlin and became a cartoonist for UFA before beginning her acting career in the theatre. After appearing in several German films, she was brought to Hollywood in the late 40s by David SELZNICK, but returned to Germany without making a film. In the early 50s she made a few American movies before returning to act in Europe. In the 60s she began a new career as a singer.
Autobiographies: 1971, *The Gift Horse*; 1975, *The Verdict*.
The Murderers Are amongst Us 46. *Film without Title* 47. The Sinner 50. Decision before Dawn 51. *The Snows of Kilimanjaro* 52. Diplomatic Courier 52. Henriette 52. The Man Between 53. The Girl from Hamburg 57. And So to Bed 63. Landru 63. Mozambique 65. The Lost Continent (GB) 68. Fedora 78. Witchery 88, etc.

Negri, Pola (1897–1987) (Appolonia Chalupek).
Polish-born leading lady with experience on German stage and screen; went to Hollywood in the 20s and was popular until sound came in. Born in Janowa, she worked as a dancer and violinist before beginning on stage in Warsaw in 1913. After making films for director Ernst LUBITSCH in Germany, she went to the US in the early 20s. Married three times; her lovers included Charlie CHAPLIN and Rudolph VALENTINO, whose funeral she attended dressed in black, accompanied by a nurse and a doctor, all in white. In the 30s she moved back to Europe, made films in England, and was later allegedly romantically linked with Adolf Hitler. From the early 40s, she settled in the United States.
Autobiography: 1970, *Memoirs of a Star*.
Die Bestie 15. Madame du Barry 18. The Flame 20. Bella Donna (US) 23. *Forbidden Paradise* 24. Hotel Imperial 26. Three Sinners 28. A Woman Commands 31. Madame Bovary 35. Hi Diddle Diddle 43. The Moonspinners 64, etc.

Negulesco, Jean (1900–1993).
Rumanian-born director, in US from 1927. Born in Craiova and educated at Lyceul Carol University, he was first an artist and stage director. He went to America in the mid-20s and began to work in Hollywood as a technical director, assistant producer and second-unit director.
Autobiography: 1984, *Things I Did . . . and Things I Think I Did*.
■ Kiss and Make Up 34. Singapore Woman 41. *The Mask of Dimitrios* 44. The Conspirators 44. Three Strangers 46. Nobody Lives Forever 46. *Humoresque* 46. Deep Valley 47. *Roadhouse* 48. *Johnny Belinda* (AAN) 48. Britannia Mews 49. Under My Skin 50. *Three Came Home* 50. *The Mudlark* 51. Take Care of My Little Girl 51. Phone Call from a Stranger 52. Lydia Bailey 52. Lure of the Wilderness 52. Full House (part) 52. Scandal at Scourie 53. Titanic 53. *How to Marry a Millionaire* 53. *Three Coins in the Fountain* 54. *Woman's World* 54. Daddy Longlegs 55. The Rains of Ranchipur 55. Boy on a Dolphin 57. A Certain Smile 58. The Gift of Love 58. Count Your Blessings 59. The Best of Everything 59. Jessica 62. The Pleasure Seekers 65. The Invincible Six 68. Hello Goodbye 70. The Heroes 79.
❝ A director I had not expected to praise is Jean Negulesco, who has always reminded me of Michael Curtiz on toast. Mr Curtiz, in turn, has always seemed like Franz Murnau under onions. – *James Agee*
He had been an artist back in Rumania, and he had an artist's eye for excellent shots, but as far as people went he was hopeless. – *Paul Henreid*

Neil, Hildegarde (1939–).
South African leading lady.
The Man Who Haunted Himself 70. Antony and Cleopatra 71. England Made Me 72. A Touch of Class 73. The Legacy 78. The Mirror Crack'd 80. Seaview Knights 94, etc.
TV series: Diamonds 80.

Neilan, Marshall 'Mickey' (1891–1958).
Leading American director of silents who had a meteoric rise in the 20s. Born in San Bernardino, California, he acted from childhood and began in films after becoming chauffeur to D. W. GRIFFITH. He became a leading actor and occasional writer of silents, but from 1916 concentrated on directing. He was frequently Mary PICKFORD's leading man and directed some of her best films, but their collaboration came to an end in 1929 when she hired him to direct her in *Forever Yours*, and abandoned the film when it was two-thirds made. From the late 20s, his efficacy began to suffer as his alcoholism interfered with his directing; he was virtually unemployable by the late 30s. He later worked as a taxi driver and an extra, and in the mid-40s was hired as a writer by Twentieth Century-Fox. He left instructions that, on his death, no one should accompany his body to the cemetery; instead, 15 of his closest friends held a wake at a Hollywood hotel, where, on the chair he was accustomed to sit in, was a sign saying 'Reserved for Mickey Neilan' and, set beside it, an empty glass and an open bottle of beer. Died of cancer. His second wife was actress Blanche SWEET (1922–29).
AS ACTOR: The Reward of Valor 12. A Busy Day in the Jungle 13. The Wall of Money (& w) 13. The Tattered Duke 14. Rags 15. A Girl of Yesterday 15. Madam Butterfly 15. The House of Discord 16. Calamity Anne 16. Daddy Long Legs 19. Broadway Gold 23. Souls for Sale 23. A Face in the Crowd 57, many others.
❝ Those were the days . . . We had fun, loved to go to the studio, and hated to go home. Today they hate to go to the studio, they have no laughs and are tickled to duck home. – *M.N., on his deathbed, to Mary Pickford*
Mickey was one of the most delightful, aggravating, gifted and charming human beings I have ever known. There were times when I could cheerfully have throttled him – especially at his frequent failures to make an appearance on the set until after luncheon, keeping a large company waiting at considerable expense. – *Mary Pickford*

Neill, Noel (1920–).
American actress, a former dancer, best known for playing Lois Lane in the 50s TV series *The Adventures of Superman*, after which she retired. She made a brief appearance as Lois Lane's mother in the *Superman* movie in 1978.
Henry Aldrich for President 41. Henry and Dizzy 42. Let's Face It 43. The Big Clock 47. Are You With It? 48. The Stork Club 48. Superman (serial) 48. The Adventures of Frank and Jesse James (serial) 48. Atom Man vs Superman (serial) 50. The James Brothers of Missouri (serial) 50, etc.
TV series: The Adventures of Superman 53–57.

Neill, Roy William (1890–1946) (Roland de Gostrie).
Irish-born director, long in Hollywood; never rose above low-budget thrillers but often did them well.
Love Letters 17. Good References 21. Toilers of the Sea 23. The Good Bad Girl 31. The Black Room 34. The Good Old Days (GB) 35. Dr Syn (GB) 37. Eyes of the Underworld 41. *Frankenstein Meets the Wolf Man* 43. Gypsy Wildcat 44. Black Angel 46, etc.; also produced and directed most of the *Sherlock Holmes* series starring Basil Rathbone 42–46.

Neill, Sam (1948–).
New Zealand leading actor in international films.
My Brilliant Career 80. Ivanhoe (TV) 82. The Final Conflict 82. From a Far Country 82. The Blood of Others (TV) 84. Robbery Under Arms 85. Plenty 85. For Love Alone 86. The Good Wife 86. Evil Angels 88. A Cry in the Dark 88. Dead Calm 89. The Hunt for Red October 90. Death in Brunswick 90. Until the End of the World/Bis ans Ende der Welt 91. Memoirs of an Invisible Man 92. Family Pictures (TV) 93. *The Piano* 93. Jurassic Park 93. Sirens 94. Country Life 94. In the Mouth of Madness 95. The Jungle Book 95. Restoration (as Charles II) 95. Children of the Revolution 96. In Cold Blood (TV) 96. Forgotten Silver 96. Show White: A Tale of Terror 97. Event Horizon 97. The Horse Whisperer 97. Victory 98. Merlin (TV) 98. Molokai 98, etc.
TV series: Reilly Ace of Spies 83.

Neilson, James (1909–1979).
American director, former war photographer, who worked mostly for Walt Disney.
■ The Blackwell Story (TV) 57. Night Passage 57. The Country Husband (TV) 58. Moon Pilot 62. Bon Voyage 62. Summer Magic 63. Dr Syn 63. The Moon Spinners 63. Return of the Gunfighter (TV) 66. The Adventures of Bullwhip Griffin 67. The Gentle Giant 67. Where Angels Go 68. The First Time 69. Flare Up 69. Tom Sawyer (TV) 75.

Nell Gwyn.
Charles II's orange-seller has appeared briefly in many films, but the two devoted to her story were both made in Britain by Herbert Wilcox: in 1927 with Dorothy Gish and in 1934 with Anna Neagle. Both caused censorship problems, the latter because of the lady's cleavage.

Nelligan, Kate (1951–).
Canadian actress first in Britain, now in Hollywood.
The Romantic Englishwoman 75. The Count of Monte Cristo (TV) 78. Dracula 79. Eye of the Needle 80. Without a Trace 83. Bethune: The Making of a Hero 84. Eleni 85. Kojak: The Price of Justice (TV) 87. Control (TV) 87. Il Giorno Prima 87. Love and Hate: A Marriage Made in Hell (TV) 90. The White Room 90. Frankie & Johnny 91. The Prince of Tides (AAN) 91. Shadows and Fog 92. Fatal Instinct 93. Spoils of War (TV) 94. Wolf 94. How to Make an American Quilt 95. Up Close and Personal 96. Romeo and Juliet 96. Calm at Sunset (TV) 96. US Marshals 98. Boy Meets Girl 98, etc.

Nelson, Barry (1920–) (Robert Neilson).
Stocky American leading man who makes films between stage shows.
China Caravan 42. A Guy Named Joe 43. Winged Victory 44. The Beginning of the End 45. The Man with My Face 51. The First Travelling Saleslady 56. Mary Mary 63. The Borgia Stick

(TV) 68. Airport 69. Pete 'n' Tillie 72. The Shining 80, many others.
TV series: My Favorite Husband 53–54. Hudson's Bay 59.

Nelson, Billy (1904–1979).
Diminutive English music-hall comedian and character actor, who began in films as one of Duggie WAKEFIELD's knockabout stooges; moved to the United States in the early 40s.
I'll Be Suing You 34. Look Up and Laugh 35. The Penny Pool 37. Calling All Crooks 38. I Live on Danger (US) 42. Wrecking Crew (US) 42. False Faces (US) 43. Minesweeper (US) 43. Hers to Hold (US) 43. Gambler's Choice (US) 44. Waterfront (US) 44. High-Powered (US) 45, etc.

Nelson, Craig T. (1946–).
Brawny American leading man.
And Justice for All 79. The Formula 80. Private Benjamin 80. Stir Crazy 80. Poltergeist 82. The Chicago Story (TV) 82. The Osterman Weekend 83. Silkwood 83. The Killing Fields 84. Call to Glory (TV) 84. Poltergeist II 86. Action Jackson 88. Troop Beverly Hills 89. Turner & Hooch 89. Me and Him 89. The Josephine Baker Story (TV) 91. The Fire Next Time (TV) 93. Probable Cause 95. I'm Not Rappaport 96. If These Walls Could Talk (TV) 96. Ghosts of Mississippi 96. The Devil's Advocate 97, etc.
TV series: Air Force 84. Coach 89–94.

Nelson, Ed (1928–).
American actor who played gangsters, brothers-in-law and boyfriends in innumerable 50s second features, then went into TV and found himself a secure niche as Dr Rossi in *Peyton Place* 64–68, and in *The Silent Force* 70.
Midway 76. Shining Star 77. Police Academy 3 85. The Boneyard 91. Cries of Silence 93, etc.

Nelson, Gary (1916–).
American director.
The Girl on the Late Late Show (TV) 74. Medical Story (TV) 75. Panache (TV) 76. *Washington: Behind Closed Doors* (TV) 77. To Kill a Cop (TV) 78. The Black Hole 79. Jimmy the Kid 82. Enigma 82. Allan Quatermain and the Lost City of Gold 86. Shooter (TV) 88. Get Smart, Again! (TV) 89. Ray Alexander: A Taste for Justice (TV) 94. Melanie Darrow (TV) 97, etc.

Nelson, Gene (1920–1996) (Leander Berg).
American actor-dancer, on stage from 1938, films from mid-40s. He began directing, mainly for TV, from the 60s.
I Wonder Who's Kissing Her Now 47. Gentleman's Agreement 48. The Daughter of Rosie O'Grady 50. Tea for Two 51. Lullaby of Broadway 52. She's Working Her Way through College 52. So This Is Paris 55. Oklahoma 55. 20,000 Eyes 62. The Purple Hills 63, etc.
AS DIRECTOR: Hand of Death 62. Hootenanny Hoot 63. Kissin' Cousins 64. Your Cheatin' Heart 64. Harum Scarum 65. The Cool Ones 67. Wake Me When the War Is Over (TV) 69. The Letters (TV) 73. The Baron and the Kid (TV) 84, etc.
TV series as director: *Washington behind Closed Doors* 77.

Nelson, Judd (1959–).
American leading actor.
Making the Grade 84. The Breakfast Club 85. Fandango 85. St Elmo's Fire 85. Blue City 86. Transformers – the Movie 86. Dear America 87. From the Hip 87. Never on Tuesday 89. Relentless 89. Far Out Man 90. The Dark Backward 91. New Jack City 91. Primary Motive 92. Every Breath 93. Blackwater Trail 95. Steel 97, etc.

Nelson, Lord Horatio (1758–1805),
the hero of Trafalgar, was portrayed in *Nelson* 19 by Donald Calthrop; in *Nelson* 26 by Cedric Hardwicke; in *The Divine Lady* 29 by Victor Varconi; in *Lady Hamilton* 42 by Laurence Olivier; in *Lady Hamilton* (Ger.) 68 by Richard Johnson; and in *Bequest to the Nation* 73 by Peter Finch.

Nelson, Lori (1933–).
American light leading lady of the 50s.
Ma and Pa Kettle at the Fair 52. Bend of the River 52. Walking My Baby Back Home 53. Destry 55. Mohawk 56. Hot Rod Girl 56. The Day the World Ended 56. Untamed Youth 57, etc.
TV series: How to Marry a Millionaire 58.

Nelson, Oliver (1932–1975).
American composer, arranger, jazz saxophonist, and bandleader. Died of a heart attack.
Death of a Gunfighter 67. Skullduggery 70. Zigzag 70. Last Tango in Paris 73. Inside Job 73.

Nelson, Ozzie (1906–1975).
American bandleader whose genial, diffident personality became familiar in long-running domestic comedy series on TV.
Sweetheart of the Campus 41. Hi Good Lookin' 44. People are Funny 45. Here Come the Nelsons 52. Love and Kisses (& wpd) 65. The Impossible Years 68, etc.
TV series: *The Adventures of Ozzie and Harriet* 52–65. Ozzie's Girls 73.

Nelson, Ralph (1916–1987).
American director.
■ Requiem for a Heavyweight 62. *Lilies of the Field* 63. Soldier in the Rain 64. Fate is the Hunter 64. Father Goose 64. Once a Thief 65. Duel at Diablo 66. Counterpoint 67. Charly 68. Tick Tick Tick 70. Soldier Blue 70. Flight of the Doves 71. The Wrath of God 72. The Wilby Conspiracy 75. Embryo 76. A Hero Ain't Nothing But a Sandwich 77. Because He's My Friend (Aust.) 78. Lady of the House (TV) 78. You Can't Go Home Again (TV) 79. Christmas Lilies of the Field (TV) 79.

Nelson, Rick (1940–1985).
American singer and light actor, son of bandleader Ozzie Nelson and his wife Harriet (formerly Harriet HILLIARD) with whom he appeared in the long-running TV series *The Adventures of Ozzie and Harriet* 52–65. He died in a plane crash.
Biography: 1992, *Teenage Idol, Travelin' Man* by Philip Bashe.
Here Come the Nelsons 52. Rio Bravo 59. The Wackiest Ship in the Army 60. Love and Kisses 65. The Over the Hill Gang (TV) 69, etc.

Nelson, Ruth (1905–1992).
American character actress, usually seen as sympathetic mother. She was married to actor-director John Cromwell.
Abe Lincoln in Illinois 40. Humoresque 46. The Late Show 77. 3 Women 77. The Haunting Passion (TV) 83. Awakenings 90, etc.

Nelson, Willie (1933–).
American singer and character actor.
The Electric Horseman 79. Honeysuckle Rose 80. Thief 81. Barbarosa 81. Hells Angels Forever 83. Red Headed Stranger 84. Songwriter 85. Amazons 87. Once upon a Texas Train/Texas Guns (TV) 88. Pair of Aces (TV) 90. Wild Texas Wind 91. Starlight 96. Wag the Dog 97. Gone Fishin' 97. Half-Baked 97, etc.

Nemec, Jan (1936–).
Czech director.
Diamonds of the Night 64. The Party and the Guests 66. The Martyrs of Love 67. The Unbearable Lightness of Being (a) 88. In the Light of the King's Love (d) 91, etc.

Nero, Franco (1941–) (F. Spartanero).
Italian leading man in international films. He has a son by actress Vanessa Redgrave.
The Tramplers 66. The Bible 66. *Camelot* 67. The Day of the Owl 68. A Quiet Place in the Country 68. Tristana 70. The Virgin and the Gypsy 70. The Battle of Neretva 70. Pope Joan 72. The Monk 72. White Fang 74. Challenge to White Fang 75. Force Ten from Navarone 78. The Man with Bogart's Face 80. The Salamander 80. Enter the Ninja 81. The Last Days of Pompeii (TV) 84. Ten Days that Shook the World 84. Garibaldi 86. The Girl 86. Kamikaze 87. Silent Night 88. Die Hard 2 90. Di Ceria dell'Untore/The Plague Sower 92. Jonathan of the Bears 94. The King and Me 95. The Innocent Sleep 95. Painted Lady (TV) 97. David 97. Talk of Angels (US) 98, etc.

Nervig, Conrad A. (1895–).
American editor.
Bardelys the Magnificent 26. The Divine Woman 28. The Guardsman 31. Eskimo (AA) 34. A Tale of Two Cities 36. The Crowd Roars 38. Northwest Passage 40. The Human Comedy 43. High Barbaree 47. Side Street 49. King Solomon's Mines (AA) 50. The Bad and the Beautiful 52. Gypsy Colt 54, many others.

Nervo, Jimmy (1890–1975) (James Holloway).
Short, stocky English comedian and acrobat. A member of a circus family, he was a high-wire performer from childhood as one of the Four Holloways, then worked for Fred KARNO, teaming up with Teddy KNOX in a comedy act in 1919 and becoming part of the CRAZY GANG in the 30s. The pair worked together for 44 years.
■ Nervo and Knox (short) 26. It's in the Bag 36. Skylarks 36. O-Kay for Sound 37. Alf's Button Afloat 38. Cavalcade of the Stars (short) 38. The Frozen Limits 39. Gasbags 40. Life Is a Circus 58.

Nesbit, Evelyn (1886–1967).
Notorious American beauty involved in a murder case of 1912; portrayed by Joan Collins in *The Girl in the Red Velvet Swing* and by Elizabeth McGivern in *Ragtime*.
■ Threads of Destiny 14. Redemption 17. The Hidden Woman 22.

Nesbitt, Cathleen (1888–1982).
British character actress, on stage from 1910; very occasional films, but active on stage and television into her nineties.
Autobiography: 1973, *A Little Love and Good Companions*.
The Case of the Frightened Lady 32. The Passing of the Third Floor Back 36. Fanny by Gaslight 43. Nicholas Nickleby 47. Three Coins in the Fountain 54. Désirée 54. *An Affair to Remember* 57. Promise Her Anything 66. The Trygon Factor 67. Staircase 69. Villain 71. Family Plot 76. Julia 77, etc.
TV series: *The Farmer's Daughter* 65.

Nesbitt, Derren (c. 1932–).
British character actor, usually a smiling villain.
The Man in the Back Seat 60. *Victim* 62. Strongroom 62. *The Naked Runner* 67. Nobody Runs Forever 68. Where Eagles Dare 68. Innocent Bystanders 72. Ooh You Are Awful 72. The Amorous Milkman (wd) 74. Bullseye! 91. Double X 92, etc.

Nesbitt, John (1911–1960).
American producer of MGM's long-running *Passing Parade* series of informational one-reelers.

Nesmith, Michael (1942–).
American guitarist and songwriter who was a member of The Monkees pop group in the 60s. He became an influential director of rock videos and a producer of independent movies in the 70s and 80s.
Head 68. Elephant Parts (& wd) 81. An Evening with Sir William Martin 81. Timerider (& co-w) 83. Repo Man (p) 84. Square Dance (p) 87. Tapeheads (& p) 87. The Monkees: Heart and Soul (concert doc) 87, etc.
TV series: The Monkees 66–68. Television Parts 85.

Nettleton, John (1929–).
British character actor.
A Man for All Seasons 67. Some Will Some Won't 69. And Soon the Darkness 69. Black Beauty 70, etc.

Nettleton, Lois (1930–).
American character actress.
Period of Adjustment 62. Come Fly with Me 63. Mail Order Bride 64. Valley of Mystery 66. Bamboo Saucer 68. The Good Guys and the Bad Guys 69. Dirty Dingus Magee 70. Sidelong Glances of a Pigeon Kicker 71. The Forgotten Man (TV) 71. The Honkers 72. Echoes of a Summer 75. Fear on Trial (TV) 75. Washington: Behind Closed Doors (TV) 77. Centennial (TV) 78. Tourist (TV) 79. Soggy Bottom USA 80. Deadly Blessing 81. Butterfly 82. The Best Little Whorehouse in Texas 82. Brass (TV) 85. Manhunt for Claude Dallas (TV) 86. Mirror, Mirror 2: Raven Dance 94, etc.
TV series: Accidental Family 67.

Neumann, Kurt (1908–1958).
German director, in Hollywood from 1925.
My Pal the King 32. The Big Cage 33. Rainbow on the River 36. Island of Lost Men 39. Ellery Queen Master Detective 40. The Unknown Guest 43. Tarzan and the Leopard Woman 46. Bad Boy 49. Rocketship XM (& w, p) 50. Son of Ali Baba 53. Carnival Story 54. Mohawk 56. Kronos 57. *The Fly* 58. Watusi 58, etc.

Neumeier, Edward (1957–).
Austrian-born screenwriter in Hollywood. Born in Vienna, and brought up in San Francisco, he studied at UCLA Film School and first worked as a script reader and as a development executive at Universal Pictures.
Robocop (co-w) 87. Frankenstein Unbound (co-w) 90. Starship Troopers (w) 97, etc.

Neuwirth, Bebe (1958–) (Beatrice Neuwirth).
American actress, born in Princeton, New Jersey. She is best known for her role in the TV series *Cheers* as Dr Lilith Sternin, who became the lover and, later, wife of Dr Frasier Crane (played by Kelsey Grammer).
Say Anything 89. Green Card 90. Bugsy 91. Painted Heart 92. Malice 93. Wild Palms (TV) 93. Jumanji 95. The Adventures of Pinocchio 96. The Associate 96. All Dogs Go to Heaven 2 (voice) 96. Celebrity 98, etc.
TV series: Cheers 86–93.

Neville, John (1925–).
British leading man, primarily on stage.
Oscar Wilde 60. Mr Topaze 61. Billy Budd 62. Unearthly Stranger 63. *A Study in Terror* (as Sherlock Holmes) 65. The Adventures of Gerard 70. The Adventures of Baron Munchausen 89. Stark (TV) 93. Baby's Day Out 94. The Road to Wellville 94. Little Women 94. Dangerous Minds 95. Swann 96. Regeneration 97. Goodbye, Lover 98. The X Files Movie 98. Urban Legend 98, etc.

Newall, Guy (1885–1937).
British stage actor who became a popular leading man in silent sentimental dramas, especially with his wife Ivy Duke. Also directed most of his films.
Comradeship 18. The Garden of Resurrection 19. The Lure of Crooning Water 20. The Duke's Son 20. Beauty and the Beast 22. Boy Woodburn 22. The Starlit Garden 23. The Ghost Train 27. The Eternal Feminine 30. The Marriage Bond 30. Grand Finale 37, etc.

Newborn, Ira.
American composer.
The Blues Brothers 80. All Night Long 81. Sixteen Candles 84. Weird Science 85. Ferris Bueller's Day Off 86. Wise Guys 86. Dragnet 87. Planes, Trains and Automobiles 87. The Naked Gun: From the Files of Police Squad 88. Uncle Buck 89. Short Time 90. My Blue Heaven 90. The Naked Gun 2½: The Smell of Fear 91. Brain Donors 92. The Opposite Sex . . . And How to Live with Them 93. Ace Ventura, Pet Detective 94. Naked Gun 33 : The Final Insult 94. Mallrats 95. The Late Shift (TV) 96. High School High 96. BASEketball 98, etc.

Newbrook, Peter (1916–).
British producer, former cinematographer.
The Yellow Teddy Bears 63. Black Torment 64. Gonks Go Beat 65. The Sandwich Man 66. Press for Time 66. Corruption 69. She'll Follow You Anywhere 70. The Asphyx 72, etc.

Newell, Mike (1943–).
British director, from TV.
The Man in the Iron Mask (TV) 77. The Awakening 80. Blood Feud (TV) 83. *Dance with a Stranger* 85. Amazing Grace and Chuck 87. *Soursweet* 88. Enchanted April 91. Into the West 92. *Four Weddings and a Funeral* 94. An Awfully Big Adventure 95. *Donnie Brasco* 97, etc.
❝ When you are dealing with the big stars, it's like being a tug that has to nudge a huge liner through a gap only just wide enough and you mustn't scrape the paint. So you don't direct them by telling them what to do, but by nudging them gently along. – *M.N.*

Newfeld, Sam (1900–1964).
American director of second features.
Reform Girl 33. Big Time or Bust 34. Northern Frontier 35. Timber War 36. Trail of Vengeance 37. Harlem on the Prairie 38. Secrets of a Model 40. Billy the Kid's Fighting Pals 41. The Mad Monster 42. Nabonga 44. Ghost of Hidden Valley 46. The Counterfeiters 48. Motor Patrol 50. Three Desperate Men 51. Thunder Over Sangoland 55. Wolf Dog 58, many others.

Newhart, Bob (1929–).
American TV and record comedian who has appeared in a few movies.
Hell Is for Heroes 62. Hot Millions 68. On a

Clear Day You Can See Forever 70. Catch 22 70. Cold Turkey 70. Thursday's Game (TV) 74. The First Family 80. Little Miss Marker 80. Marathon (TV) 80. The Rescuers Down Under (voice) 90. In & Out 97. Rudolph the Red-Nosed Reindeer: The Movie (voice) 98, etc.

TV series: The Bob Newhart Show 72–77. Newhart 82–86. George & Leo 97– .

Newland, John (1917–).
American TV actor (the host of *One Step Beyond*) who also directed a few films. He played Algy in the Tom Conway *Bulldog Drummond* films 48–49.

That Night 57. The Violators 57. The Spy with My Face 65. Hush-a-Bye Murder 70. Don't Be Afraid of the Dark (TV) 73. The Legend of Hillbilly John (TV) 74. The Suicide's Wife (TV) 79, etc.

Newland, Mary:
see Oldland, Lilian.

Newlands, Anthony (1926–).
British character actor, mainly on TV; usually plays schemers.

Beyond This Place 59. The Trials of Oscar Wilde 60. Hysteria 64. Theatre of Death 67. Universal Soldier 71. Mata Hari 84, etc.

Newley, Anthony (1931–).
Versatile but dislikeable British actor, composer, singer, comedian; former child star.

Oliver Twist 48. Vice Versa 48. Those People Next Door 53. *Cockleshell Heroes* 56. X the Unknown 56. High Flight 57. *No Time to Die* 58. Idol on Parade 59. In the Nick 61. The Small World of Sammy Lee 63. Dr Dolittle (US) 67. Sweet November (US) 68. Can Hieronymus Merkin Ever Forget Mercy Humpe and Find True Happiness? (& wd) 69. Summertree (d only) 72. Mr Quilp 75. A Good Idea at the Time (Can.) 76. Malibu (TV) 83. The Garbage Pail Kids Movie 87. Boris and Natasha: The Movie (TV) 92, etc.

TV series: The Anthony Newley Show 60–61. The Strange World of Gurney Slade 60. EastEnders 98– .

Newman, Alfred (1901–1970).
American composer, former child pianist; an eminent Hollywood musical director since early sound days, he composed over 250 film scores.

The Devil To Pay 30. Whoopee 31. *Arrowsmith* 31. Cynara 32. *The Bowery* 33. Nana 34. Dodsworth 36. *Dead End* 37. *Alexander's Ragtime Band* (AA) 38. *Gunga Din* 39. *Tin Pan Alley* (AA) 40. *The Grapes of Wrath* 40. Son of Fury 42. The Song of Bernadette (AA) 43. The Razor's Edge 46. *Mother Wore Tights* (AA) 47. Unfaithfully Yours 48. *With a Song in My Heart* (AA) 52. *Call Me Madam* (AA) 53. Love Is a Many Splendored Thing (AA) 55. *The King and I* (AA) 56. Flower Drum Song 61. The Counterfeit Traitor 62. How the West was Won 62. Nevada Smith 66, many others.

❝ Everybody here in Hollywood knows his business, plus music. – *A.N.*

Newman, Barry (1940–).
American leading actor.

Pretty Boy Floyd 60. The Moving Finger 63. *The Lawyer* 69. *Vanishing Point* 71. The Salzburg Connection 72. Fear is the Key 72. City on Fire 79. Amy 81. Fatal Vision (TV) 84. Daylight 96. Goodbye, Lover 98, etc.

TV series: Petrocelli 73–74. Nightingales 89.

Newman, David (1937–).
American screenwriter, in collaboration with Robert Benton until the early 70s, and occasionally with his wife, Leslie Newman.

■ *Bonnie and Clyde* (AAN) 67. There Was a Crooked Man 70. What's Up Doc 72. Bad Company 72. Superman 78. Superman II 80. Jinxed 82. Superman III 83. Sheena 84. Santa Claus: The Movie 85.

Newman, David.
American composer and conductor, the son of Alfred Newman.

Critters 86. The Brave Little Toaster 87. My Demon Lover 87. Throw Momma from the Train 87. Bill and Ted's Excellent Adventure 89. Disorganized Crime 89. Heathers 89. The War of the Roses 89. Madhouse 90. Fire Birds 90. The Freshman 90. Mr Destiny 90. The Marrying Man/Too Hot to Handle 91. Other People's Money 91. Bill & Ted's Bogus Journey 91. Don't Tell Mom the Babysitter's Dead 91. The Runestone 92. Honeymoon in Vegas 92. The Sandlot/The Sandlot Kids 93. Coneheads 93. Undercover Blues 93. My Father, the Hero 94. The Flintstones 94. The Air Up There 94. I Love Trouble 94. My Father, the Hero 94. Boys on the Side 95. Tommy Boy 95. Operation Dumbo Drop 95. The Phantom 96. The Nutty Professor 96. Matilda 96. Jingle All the Way 96. Out to Sea 97. Anastasia (AAN) 97, etc.

Newman, Joseph M. (1909–).
American director, in films from 1931.

Jungle Patrol 48. 711 Ocean Drive 50. The Outcast of Poker Flats 52. Red Skies of Montana 52. Pony Soldier 53. The Human Jungle 54. Dangerous Crossing 54. Kiss of Fire 55. *This Island Earth* 55. Flight to Hong Kong (& p) 56. Gunfight at Dodge City 58. The Big Circus 59. Tarzan the Ape Man 59. King of the Roaring Twenties 61. A Thunder of Drums 61. The George Raft Story 61, etc.

Newman, Lionel (1916–1989).
American composer.

The Street with No Name 48. Cheaper by the Dozen 50. Diplomatic Courier 52. Dangerous Crossing 53. Gorilla at Large 54. How to Be Very Very Popular 55. A Kiss Before Dying 56. Mardi Gras 58. Compulsion 59. North to Alaska 60. Move Over Darling 63. Do Not Disturb 65. The Salzburg Connection 72. The Bluebird 76. Alien 79. Breaking Away 79. The Final Conflict 81. Cross Creek 83. Unfaithfully Yours 83, etc.

Newman, Nanette (1934–).
British leading lady, married to Bryan Forbes.

Personal Affair 53. House of Mystery 58. Faces in the Dark 59. The League of Gentlemen 59. Twice Round the Daffodils 62. The Wrong Arm of the Law 63. Of Human Bondage 64. Séance on a Wet Afternoon 64. The Wrong Box 66. The Whisperers 66. The Madwoman of Chaillot 69. *The Raging Moon* 70. The Love Ban 72. Man at the Top 73. The Stepford Wives 75. International Velvet 78. The Mystery of Edwin Drood 93, etc.

Newman, Paul (1925–).
American leading actor who suffered initially from a similarity to Marlon Brando but later developed a lithe impertinence which served him well in his better films. He was given a special Academy Award in 1986 for 'his many memorable and compelling screen performances'. He is married to actress Joanne Woodward.

Biographies: 1975, *Paul Newman* by Charles Hamblett; 1997, *Paul Newman: A Celebration* by Eric Lax; 1998, *Paul Newman* by Lawrence J. Quirk.

The Silver Chalice 54. *Somebody Up There Likes Me* 56. The Rack 56. Until They Sail 57. The Helen Morgan Story 57. *The Long Hot Summer* 58. The Left Handed Gun 58. Rally Round the Flag Boys 58. Cat on a Hot Tin Roof (AAN) 58. The Young Philadelphians 59. From the Terrace 60. Exodus 60. *The Hustler* (AAN, BFA) 61. Paris Blues 61. Sweet Bird of Youth 62. Hemingway's Adventures of a Young Man 62. *Hud* (AAN) 63. A New Kind of Love 63. *The Prize* 63. What a Way to Go 64. The Outrage 64. Lady L 64. Torn Curtain 66. *Harper* 66. *Hombre* 67. *Cool Hand Luke* (AAN) 67. The Secret War of Harry Frigg 67. Rachel Rachel (d only) 68. Winning 69. *Butch Cassidy and the Sundance Kid* 69. W.U.S.A. 70. Sometimes a Great Notion (& d) 71. Pocket Money 72. The Effect of Gamma Rays on Man-in-the-Moon Marigolds (d only) 72. *Judge Roy Bean* 72. The Mackintosh Man 73. The Sting 73. The Towering Inferno 74. The Drowning Pool 75. Silent Movie 76. Buffalo Bill and the Indians 76. Slap Shot 77. Quintet 79. Fort Apache, the Bronx 80. When Time Ran Out 80. The Shadow Box (d only) 81. Absence of Malice (AAN) 82. *The Verdict* (AAN) 82. Harry and Son 84. The Color of Money (AA) 86. The Glass Menagerie (d only) 87. Fat Man and Little Boy/The Shadowmakers 89. Blaze 89. Mr & Mrs Bridge 90. The Hudsucker Proxy 94. Nobody's Fool (AAN) 94. Twilight 98, etc.

❝ You don't stop being a citizen just because you have a Screen Actors' Guild card. – *P.N.*

Acting is a question of absorbing other people's personalities and some of your own experience. – *P.N.*

Ever since *Slap Shot* I've been swearing more. I knew I had a problem one day when I turned to my daughter and said: 'Please pass the fucking salt.' – *P.N.*

I wasn't driven to acting by an inner compulsion. I was running away from the sporting goods business. – *P.N.*

Newman, Randy (1943–).
Witty American songwriter, musician and composer. He is the nephew of composers Lionel and Alfred Newman.

Performance (md) 70. Cold Turkey (m) 71. The Pursuit of Happiness (m) 71. Ragtime (m) (AAN) 81. The Natural (m) (AAN) 84. April Fool's Day (m) 86. Three Amigos! (a, co-w, s) 86. Huey Long (co-m) 86. Parenthood (m) 89. Avalon (m) 90. Awakenings (m) 90. The Paper (m) (AANs) 94. Maverick (m) 94. Toy Story (AANm, AANs) 95. James and the Giant Peach (AAN) 96. Michael 96. Cats Don't Dance 97. Pleasantville 98. A Bug's Life (voice) 98, etc.

Newman, Thomas.
American composer, the son of Alfred Newman, and the brother of David Newman.

Grandview, U.S.A. 84. Reckless 84. Desperately Seeking Susan 85. The Man with One Red Shoe 85. Real Genius 85. Jumpin' Jack Flash 86. Light of Day 87. The Lost Boys 87. Less than Zero 87. The Great Outdoors 88. The Prince of Pennsylvania 88. Cookie 89. Men Don't Leave 90. Welcome Back, Roxy Carmichael 91. Naked Tango 90. Fried Green Tomatoes at the Whistle Stop Café 91. Deceived 91. The Player 92. The Linguini Incident 92. Josh and S.A.M. 93. Threesome 94. The Shawshank Redemption (AAN) 94. The War 94. Little Women (AAN) 94. Unstrung Heroes (AAN) 95. How to Make an American Quilt 95. American Buffalo 96. Phenomenon 96. Up Close and Personal 96. The People vs Larry Flynt 96. Oscar and Lucinda 97. Red Corner 97. Mad City 97. The Horse Whisperer 97. Meet Joe Black 98, etc.

Newman, Walter (1916–1993).
American screenwriter.

Ace in the Hole (co-w) 51. Underwater 55. The Man with the Golden Arm (co-w) 56. The True Story of Jesse James 56. Crime and Punishment USA 59. The Interns (co-w) 62. Cat Ballou (co-w) (AAN) 65. Bloodbrothers (AAN) 78. The Champ 79. Saint Jack 79, etc.

Newmar, Julie (1930–) (Julia Newmeyer).
Tall American blonde actress.

Seven Brides for Seven Brothers 55. The Marriage Go Round 60. Mackenna's Gold 68. The Maltese Bippy 69. Hysterical 83. Streetwalkin' 85. Deep Space 87. Ghosts Can't Do It 90. Nudity Required 90. Oblivion 94, etc.

TV series: My Living Doll 64. Batman 65–67.

Newton, Robert (1905–1956).
British star character actor with a rolling eye and a voice to match; a ham, but a succulent one. Born in Shaftesbury, Dorset, he was on stage from 1920. His alcoholism hampered his career: when he made *This Happy Breed* it was written into his contract that his fee (£9,000) would be docked by £500 every time he was drunk on the set.

■ Reunion 32. Dark Journey 37. Fire Over England 37. *Farewell Again* 37. The Squeaker 37. The Green Cockatoo 37. Twenty One Days 38. Vessel of Wrath 38. Yellow Sands 38. Dead Men are Dangerous 39. Jamaica Inn 39. Poison Pen 39. Hell's Cargo 39. Bulldog Sees It Through 40. Gaslight 40. Busman's Honeymoon 40. *Major Barbara* 40. *Hatter's Castle* 41. They Flew Alone 42. *This Happy Breed* 44. *Henry V* (as Pistol) 45. Night Boat to Dublin 46. *Odd Man Out* 46. Temptation Harbour 47. Snowbound 48. *Oliver Twist* (as Bill Sikes) 48. Kiss the Blood off My Hands (US) 48. Obsession 49. *Treasure Island* (as Long John) 50. Waterfront 50. *Tom Brown's Schooldays* (as Dr Arnold) 51. Soldiers Three (US) 51. Les Misérables (US) 52. Blackbeard the Pirate (US) 52. *Androcles and the Lion* (US) 53. Desert Rats (US) 53. The High and the Mighty (US) 54. *The Beachcomber* 54. Long John Silver 55. Around the World in Eighty Days (US) 56.

TV series: *Long John Silver* 55.

✪ For being so enjoyably larger than life. *Treasure Island*.

❝ I had a great weakness for Bob Newton. He used to drink far too much, and when he had a couple of drinks, he would speak the absolute truth, which could be horrifying. – *David Lean*

Newton, Thandie.
New Zealand-born leading actress.

Flirting 90. Loaded 94. Interview with the Vampire 94. Jefferson in Paris 95. The Journey of August King 95. The Leading Man 96. Gridlock'd 96. In Your Dreams (TV) 97. Beloved 98. Besieged 98, etc.

Newton, Wayne (1942–).
Actor and singer, performing from the age of six.

80 Steps to Jonah 69. License to Kill 89. The Adventures of Ford Fairlane 90. The Dark Backward 91. Best of the Best II 93. Vegas Vacation 96, etc.

TV series: North and South, Book II 89.

Newton-John, Olivia (1948–).
English singer and actress. Born in Cambridge, she moved to Australia when she was five, and is now resident in the USA. After being diagnosed with breast cancer in the early 90s, she spent much time involved in charitable work. Married actor Matt Lattanzi in 1985.

■ Tomorrow 70. *Grease* 78. Xanadu 80. Two of a Kind 83. It's My Party 96.

Ney, Marie (1895–1981).
British stage actress in occasional films.

Escape 30. The Wandering Jew 33. Scrooge 37. Jamaica Inn 39. Seven Days to Noon 50. Simba 55. Yield to the Night 56. Witchcraft 64, etc.

Ney, Richard (1917–).
American financier who almost accidentally went into acting but appears only occasionally. Married Greer Garson.

Mrs Miniver 42. The Late George Apley 47. Joan of Arc 48. Babes in Baghdad 52. The Premature Burial 62, etc.

Ngor, Haing S. (1950–1996).
Cambodian actor in America. He was a doctor when the Khmer Rouge invaded his country and was imprisoned and tortured before leaving for America in 1980. As his French medical qualifications were not recognized, he worked in other jobs until being unexpectedly offered a role in *The Killing Fields*. Died after being shot by an unknown gunman outside his home in Los Angeles.

Autobiography: 1988, *Haing Ngor: A Cambodian Odyssey*, with Roger Warner.

The Killing Fields (AA) 84. Eastern Condors 86. The Iron Triangle 89. Vietnam, Texas 90. Ambition 91. My Life 93. Heaven and Earth 93.

Niblo, Fred (1874–1948) (Federico Nobile).
American director of silent films; had stage experience.

The Marriage Ring 18. Sex 20. *The Mark of Zorro* 20. *The Three Musketeers* 21. *Blood and Sand* 23. Thy Name is Woman 24. The Temptress 26. *Ben Hur* 27. Camille 27. Redemption 29. The Big Gamble 33. Three Sons o'Guns 41.

Niccol, Andrew (1964–).
New Zealand-born writer and director, in Hollywood; he first worked in advertising in London.

Gattaca (wd) 97. The Truman Show (w) 98.

Nichetti, Maurizio (1948–).
Italian director, screenwriter and comic actor. He studied architecture, trained in mime, and worked as a circus clown and cartoon gag writer.

Ratataplan 79 (a, wd). Ho Fatto Splash (a, wd) 80. Tomorrow We Dance/Domani Si Balla (a, wd) 82. Bertoldo, Bertoldino and Cacasenno (a) 84. The Icicle Thief/Ladri di Saponette (a, wd) 88. Volere Volare (a, co-w, co-d) 90. Stefano Quantestorie (a, co-w, d) 93. Seven Sundays/Tous les Jours Dimanche (a) 94. Snowball/Palla di Neve (a, d) 95. Luna e l'Altra (a, d) 96, etc.

TV series: Quo Vadis? 85. Pista! 86–87.

❝ Film-makers can't work today without money from television. Then our work is passed over to television and destroyed completely. It's impossible to see a story from beginning to end on television without interruption. Television is not cinema – you're at home with the lights, the telephone, the children. I want people to go to the cinema to experience film. – *M.N.*

Nicholas Brothers, The Fayard (1914–) and Harold (1921–).
American acrobatic dancers who enlivened several musicals of the 40s.
■ Calling All Stars 37. Tin Pan Alley 41. Down Argentine Way 41. The Great American Broadcast 41. Sun Valley Serenade 42. Orchestra Wives 43. Stormy Weather 43. The Pirate 48.

Nicholas, Paul (1945–).
British light leading man in all media, but especially TV.
Blind Terror 71. Stardust 74. Tommy 74. Lisztomania 75. Sergeant Pepper's Lonely Hearts Club Band 78. The World is Full of Married Men 79. Yesterday's Hero 79. The Jazz Singer 80. Nutcracker 82. Invitation to a Wedding 83.
TV series: Two Up, Two Down 79. Just Good Friends 83–86. Bust 87. Close to Home 89–90.

Nicholas, Thomas Ian (1980–).
American child actor.
Rookie of the Year 93. A Kid in King Arthur's Court 95, etc.

Nicholls, Anthony (1902–1977).
Distinguished-looking British stage actor, in occasional films.
The Laughing Lady 47. The Guinea Pig 49. The Hasty Heart 49. The Dancing Years 50. The Franchise Affair 50. The Weak and the Wicked 54. Make Me an Offer 55. The Safecracker 58. Victim 62. Mister Ten Per Cent 66, etc.

Nicholls, George (1865–1927).
Craggy American character actor.
A Romance of Happy Valley 17. Hearts of the World 18. The Eagle 25. The Wedding March 27, many others.

Nicholls, George, Jnr (1897–1939).
American director. Son of George Nicholls. Killed in a car crash.
Anne of Green Gables 34. Michael Strogoff 37. Man of Conquest 39, etc.

Nicholls, Phoebe (1958–) (Sarah Nicholls).
British actress of stage and screen, the daughter of Anthony Nicholls.
The Elephant Man 80. The Missionary 81. Party Party 83. Maurice 87. Heart of Darkness (TV) 94. Persuasion (TV) 95. Gulliver's Travels (TV) 96. Fairytale: A True Story 97, etc.

Nichols, Barbara (1929–1976).
American comedy actress, former model; adept at portraying not-so-dumb blondes.
Miracle in the Rain 56. The King and Four Queens 57. The Scarface Mob 60. The George Raft Story 61. Where the Boys Are 63. The Disorderly Orderly 64. Dear Heart 65. The Loved One 65. The Swinger 66, etc.

Nichols, Dandy (1907–1986).
British character comedienne, often seen as nervous maid or cockney char. Became famous on TV as the long-suffering Else in *Till Death Us Do Part* 64–74; appeared in the film version 68.
Hue and Cry 46. Here Come the Huggetts 49. Street Corner 52. The Deep Blue Sea 55. The Vikings 58. Help 65. The Alf Garnett Saga 72. Britannia Hospital 83, many others.

Nichols, Dudley (1895–1960).
Distinguished American screenwriter, in Hollywood from 1929.
Born Reckless 30. The Sign of the Cross 32. *The Lost Patrol* 34. Steamboat round the Bend 34. *The Informer* (AA) 35. Mary of Scotland 36. The Hurricane 37. *Bringing Up Baby* 38. *Stagecoach* 39. The Long Voyage Home (AAN) 40. For Whom the Bell Tolls 43. Air Force (AAN) 43. *It Happened Tomorrow* 44. The Bells of St Mary's 45. *And Then There Were None* 45. Scarlet Street 45. Sister Kenny (& d) 46. Mourning Becomes Electra (& p, d) 47. Pinky 49. Prince Valiant 54. The Tin Star (AAN) 57. The Hangman 59, many others.
✪ For providing the firm basis of a score of outstanding prestige films. *Stagecoach*.

Nichols, Ernest Loring 'Red' (1905–1965).
Jazz cornettist and bandleader who made a few shorts in the 30s and provided the cornet solos for *The Five Pennies* 59, a highly inaccurate version of his life in which he was played by Danny Kaye.

Nichols, Mike (1931–) (Michael Igor Peschkowsky).
German-born American cabaret entertainer and latterly film director.
■ *Who's Afraid of Virginia Woolf?* (AAN) 66. *The Graduate* (AA) 67. Catch 22 70. Carnal Knowledge 71. The Day of the Dolphin 73. The Fortune 76. Gilda Live 80. *Silkwood* (AAN) 83. Heartburn 86. Biloxi Blues 88. Working Girl (AAN) 88. Postcards from the Edge 90. Regarding Henry 91. Wolf 94. The Bird Cage 96. Designated Mourner (a) 96. Primary Colors (& p) 98.
❝ A movie is like a person. Either you trust it or you don't. – *M.N.*

Nichols, Peter (1927–).
Leading British dramatist, TV playwright and occasional screenwriter. He is a former teacher and actor.
Autobiography: 1984, *Feeling You're Behind*.
Catch Us If You Can 65. Georgy Girl (co-w) 66. A Day in the Death of Joe Egg 71. The National Health 73. Privates on Parade 84, etc.
❝ Cinema's inherent handicap is money: theatre's advantage has been that it was cheap – 'was' and 'has been' because now it's become a suburb of cinema and is cheap no longer. Cinema has raped theatre and passed on the money taint like a dose of clap. – *P.N.*

Nicholson, Jack (1937–).
American leading actor, a fashionable figure since the early 70s. Actress Anjelica Huston was his partner for 17 years, and he has a son (b. 1970) by actress Susan Anspach.
Biographies: 1991, *The Joker's Wild* by John Parker. 1991, *Jack Nicholson: An Unauthorized Biography* by Donald Shepherd. 1994, *Jack's Life: A Biography of Jack Nicholson* by Patrick McGilligan.
Book: 1997, *The Films of Jack Nicholson* by Douglas Brode.
■ Cry Baby Killer 58. Too Young to Love 59. Studs Lonigan 61. The Wild Rise 61. The Broken Land 62. The Little Shop of Horrors 62. The Raven 63. The Terror 63. Thunder Island (co-w only) 64. Back Door to Hell 64. Flight to Fury (& w) 65. Ensign Pulver 65. Ride the Whirlwind 66. The Shooting 66. Hell's Angels on Wheels 67. The St Valentine's Day Massacre 67. The Trip (w only) 67. Head (w only) 68. *Easy Rider* (AAN) 69. On a Clear Day You Can See Forever 70. Five Easy Pieces (AAN) 70. Drive He Said (d only) 70. Carnal Knowledge 71. A Safe Place 71. The King of Marvin Gardens 72. *The Last Detail* (AAN) 74. *Chinatown* (AAN) 74. Tommy 74. The Passenger 74. The Fortune 76. One Flew over the Cuckoo's Nest (AA) 76. The Missouri Breaks 76. The Last Tycoon 76. Goin' South (& d) 78. The Shining 80. The Postman Always Rings Twice 81. Reds (AAN, BFA) 81. The Border 82. Terms of Endearment (AA) 83. Prizzi's Honor (AAN) 85. Heartburn 86. The Witches of Eastwick 87. Ironweed (AAN) 87. Broadcast News (uncredited) 87. Batman 89. The Two Jakes (& d) 90. Man Trouble 92. Hoffa 92. A Few Good Men (AAN) 93. Wolf 94. The Crossing Guard 95. Blood and Wine 96. Mars Attacks! 96. The Evening Star 96. As Good as It Gets (AA) 97.
✪ For doing interesting work, *Chinatown*.
❝ As an actor, I have no desire for anybody to understand my past work. Period. – *J.N.*
I just wish every film I liked wasn't either foreign or made in America but with such terrible difficulty. It's the worst period ever for trying to do interesting work. – *J.N., 1996*
He has a fine eye for good paintings and a good ear for fine music. And he's a lovely man to drink with. – *John Huston*

Nicholson, James H. (1916–1972).
American executive, former theatre owner and distributor, who became president of American International Pictures.

Nicholson, Nora (1892–1973).
British stage character actress whose film roles have usually been fey or eccentric.
The Blue Lagoon 48. Tread Softly 48. Crow Hollow 52. Raising a Riot 54. A Town Like Alice 56. The Captain's Table 59. Diamonds for Breakfast 69, etc.

Nicholson, William (1948–).
English screenwriter and playwright.
Shadowlands (TV) (BFA) 85. *Shadowlands* (AAN) 93. Nell 94. First Knight 95. Crime of the Century (TV) 96. Firelight (& d) 97. Grey Owl 98, etc.

Nico (1938–1988) (Christa Paffgen).
Cool blonde German model, actress, and singer with the Velvet Underground. Born in Cologne, she became a model in Berlin at the age of 15 before going to work in New York, where Andy Warhol filmed her and gave her work with the Velvet Underground. She later became a solo singer but her career was not helped by her heroin addiction. She had a son by actor Alain Delon. Died of a cerebral haemorrhage after falling off a bicycle.
Biography: 1993, *Songs They Never Play on the Radio: Nico the Last Bohemian* by James Young.
La Dolce Vita 59. The Velvet Underground and Nico 66. The Chelsea Girls 66, etc.
❝ Nico was something of a celebrity in narcotic circles. Queen of the Junkies. She was famous within a limited milieu, i.e. heroin users and those who thought self-destruction a romantic vocation. – *James Young*

Nicol, Alex (1919–).
American leading man with stage experience, mainly in Universal action pictures.
The Sleeping City 50. Because of You 52. Law and Order 54. The Man from Laramie 55. Sincerely Yours 55. Under Ten Flags 60. Three Came Back (& p, d) 60. Look in Any Window 61. The Savage Guns 62. Ride and Kill 63. Gunfighters of Casa Grande 65. Bloody Mama 69. Point of Terror (d only) 71. The Night God Screamed 75. A*P*E* 76. Brandy Sheriff 78. Manila Open City 86, etc.

Nicolodi, Daria (1940–).
Italian leading actress, notably in horror movies, from the stage. Born in Florence, she studied at the National Academy of Dramatic Art in Rome. Married director Dario ARGENTO; their daughter is actress Asia ARGENTO.
Just Another War/Uomini Contro 70. La Proprieta Non E Piu un Furto 73. Deep Red/Profondo Rosso 75. Suspiria (co-w) 77. Shock 77. Inferno 80. Unsane/Tenebre 82. Phenomena 84. Creepers 85. Maccheroni 86. Terror at the Opera 87. Paganini Horror (& co-w) 88. Io Balla da Sola 96. The Word Love Exists/La Parola Amore Esiste 98, etc.

Niehaus, Lennie (1929–).
American composer and jazz alto-saxophonist, noted for his playing with the Stan Kenton orchestra in the 50s.
Tightrope 84. City Heat 84. Pale Rider 85. Never Too Young to Die 86. Ratboy 86. Heartbreak Ridge 86. Bird 88. White Hunter, Black Heart 90. The Two Jakes (md) 90. Unforgiven 92. A Perfect World 93. Lush Life 93. The Bridges of Madison County 95. Titanic (TV) 96. Crazy Horse (TV) 96. Absolute Power 97. Midnight in the Garden of Good and Evil 98. Pocahontas II: Journey to a New World 98, etc.

Nielsen, Asta (1882–1972).
Danish leading actress, from the stage, who became one of the first silent film stars with an international reputation. Married from 1912–18 to Danish director Urban Gad (1879–1947), who starred her in his films, she made her greatest impact in Germany from the 1910s, returning to the theatre with the coming of sound. She left Germany when Hitler came to power and retired to Denmark.
Der Abgrund 10. Enelein 13. Kurfürstendamm 19. Reigen 20. Hamlet 20. Fräulein Julie 21. Vanina Vanini 22. Erdgeist 23. Hedda Gabler 24. Joyless Street 25. Secrets of a Soul 26. Unmögliche Liebe 32, many others.

Nielsen, Brigitte (1963–).
Danish actress who spent some time in Hollywood. She was the second wife of actor Sylvester STALLONE (1985–87).
Red Sonja 85. Rocky IV 85. Cobra 86. Beverly Hills Cop II 87. Domino 88. Bye Bye Baby 89. 976-EVIL II 92. Mission of Justice 92. Chained Heat II 93. Terminal Force 94. Galaxis 95. Body Count 95. Snowboard Academy 96, etc.

Nielsen, Leslie (1926–).
Canadian leading man, former radio disc jockey; much TV work. He displayed an unsuspected talent for comedy in *The Naked Gun* and its sequels. In 1996, he appeared in a one-man play on the life of lawyer Clarence Darrow.
The Vagabond King 55. Forbidden Planet 56. Ransom 56. Tammy and the Bachelor 57. Harlow 65. Beau Geste 66. The Poseidon Adventure 72. Project Kill 76. Day of the Animals 77. Little Mo (TV) 78. The Amsterdam Kill 78. Backstairs at the White House (TV) 79. Institute for Revenge (TV) 79. Airplane 80. Prom Night 80. The Creature Wasn't Nice 81. Creepshow 82. Wrong Is Right 82. Soul Man 86. The Patriot 86. Home Is Where the Heart Is 87. Nightstick 87. Nuts 87. *The Naked Gun: From the Files of Police Squad* 88. Repossessed 90. The Naked Gun 2½: The Smell of Fear 91. All I Want for Christmas 91. Surf Ninjas 93. Digger 93. Naked Gun 33 : The Final Insult 94. SPQR: 2,000 and a Half Years Ago (It.) 95. Dracula: Dead and Loving It 95. Spy Hard 96. Mr Magoo 97. Wrongfully Accused 98, etc.
TV series: The New Breed 61–62. Channing 63–64. Peyton Place 65. The Protectors 69–70. Bracken's World 70. The Explorers 72–73. Police Squad 82. Shaping Up 84.

Niesen, Gertrude (1912–1975).
American singer-actress of Russian and Swedish ancestry.
Start Cheering 40. Rookies on Parade 42. He's My Guy 44. The Babe Ruth Story 48.

Nieto, José (1902–1982).
Spanish leading actor who appeared in character roles in US films made in Spain from the 50s.
That Lady 55. The Pride and the Passion 57. Solomon and Sheba 59. King of Kings 61. 55 Days at Peking 62. The Savage Guns 62. The Ceremony 63. Kid Rodeo 65. Chimes at Midnight 66. Flame over Vietnam 67. Cervantes 67. Catlow 71. Scandalous John 71, etc.

Nigh, Jane (1926–1993).
American leading lady of minor films in the 40s and 50s.
Something for the Boys 44. State Fair 45. Dragonwyck 46. Give My Regards to Broadway 48. Red Hot and Blue 49. Fighting Man of the Plains 49. County Fair 50. Blue Blood 51. Fort Osage 53. Hold That Hypnotist 57, etc.
TV series: Big Town 52.

Nigh, William (1881–1955).
American director.
Marriage Morals 23. Mr Wu 27. The Single Sin 31. Crash Donovan 35. The Ape 40. Corregidor 42. The Right to Live 45. Divorce 45, etc.

Nightingale, Florence (1820–1910).
English nurse who organized hospitals at the front during the Crimean War, with little official help and under appalling conditions. There have been two biopics of her: *The White Angel* (US) 35, with Kay Francis, and *The Lady with a Lamp* (GB) 51, with Anna Neagle. In *Sixty Glorious Years* she was briefly played by Joyce Bland.

Nilsson, Anna Q. (1889–1974).
Swedish-born actress, long in America and popular in silent films from 1919.
The Love Burglar 19. Kingdom of Dreams 20. Soldiers of Fortune 20. Hollywood 22. The Isle of Lost Ships 23. Inez of Hollywood 24. The Masked Woman 25. The Greater Glory 26. Sorrell and Son 27. The World Changes 34. Prison Farm 38. Girls' Town 42. The Farmer's Daughter 47. Sunset Boulevard 50, etc.

Nilsson, Leopold Torre:
see TORRE-NILSSON, Leopold.

Nimmo, Derek (1931–1999).
British character comedian who gets laughs from toe-twiddling and funny voices (especially of the comedy curate kind).
The Millionaires 61. The Amorous Prawn 62. The Bargee 64. Joey Boy 65. The Liquidator 65. Casino Royale 66. Mister Ten Per Cent 66. A Talent for Loving 69. One of Our Dinosaurs is Missing 75, etc.
TV series: All Gas and Gaiters 67. The World of Wooster 68. Oh Brother 70. Oh Father 73. Hell's Bells 85.

Nimoy, Leonard (1931–).
Lean-faced American character actor, best known as the Vulcan Mr Spock in the TV series *Star Trek* 66–69. He turned to directing in the 80s.

Queen for a Day 51. Rhubarb 51. The Balcony 63. Catlow 72. The Alpha Caper (TV) 73. Invasion of the Body Snatchers 78. Star Trek: The Motion Picture 79. Star Trek: The Wrath of Khan 82. A Woman Called Golda (TV) 82. Star Trek III: The Search for Spock (& d) 84. Star Trek IV: The Voyage Home (& d) 86. Transformers: The Movie 86. Three Men and a Baby (d) 87. The Good Mother (d) 88. Star Trek V: The Final Frontier 89. Funny about Love (d) 90. Star Trek VI: The Undiscovered Country 91. Holy Matrimony (d) 94. The Pagemaster (voice) 94. David (TV) 97, etc.

TV series: *Star Trek* (as Mr Spock) 66–68. Mission Impossible 70–72.

Nin, Anaïs (1903–1977).
French-born diarist and erotic novelist, of Cuban parentage. Married banker and experimental film-maker Ian HUGO. She was played by Maria DE MEDEIROS in *Henry and June* 90, the story of her relationship with Henry Miller and his wife June, directed by Philip KAUFMAN.

Biography: 1995, *Anaïs Nin* by Deirdre Bair.

❝ Mix well the sperm of four men in one day. – *A.N.'s 'recipe for happiness'*

Nishiwaki, Michiko.
Japanese actress and stuntwoman in Hong Kong and action movies, a former weightlifter; she is now resident in the USA.

My Lucky Stars 85. The Outlaw Brothers 88. In the Line of Duty 3 88. Magic Cop 89. God of Gamblers 90. The Real Me 90. Lady Cops 90. City Cops 92. Lethal Weapon 4 (US) 98. Blade (US) 98, etc.

Nissen, Greta (1906–1988) (Grethe Rutz-Nissen).
Norwegian leading lady in American films. She retired in 1937.

The Wanderer 25. The Popular Sin 26. Women of All Nations 31. Rackety Rax 32. Melody Cruise 33. Red Wagon 36, etc.

Nitzsche, Jack (1937–).
American composer.

The Exorcist 73. One Flew over the Cuckoo's Nest (AAN) 76. Cruising 81. Personal Best 82. An Officer and a Gentleman (AAN) 82. Cannery Row 82. Without a Trace 83. The Razor's Edge 84. Starman 84. Windy City 84. Jewel of the Nile 85. 8½ Weeks 86. Stand by Me 86. The Whoopee Boys 86. Streets of Gold 86. The Seventh Sign 88. Revenge 89. Next of Kin 89. The Last of the Finest 90. Mermaids 90. The Indian Runner 91. Blue Sky (made 91) 94. The Crossing Guard 95, etc.

Niven, David (1909–1983).
Debonair British leading man whose natural enthusiasm found several outlets before he accidentally arrived in Hollywood and was signed up as an extra.

His light-hearted approach to life is reflected in his 1972 autobiography *The Moon's a Balloon* and its 1975 sequel *Bring on the Empty Horses*.

Biography: 1985, *The Other Side of the Moon* by Sheridan Morley.

■ Barbary Coast 35. Without Regret 35. A Feather in Her Hat 35. Splendor 35. Rose Marie 36. *Thank You Jeeves* 36. Palm Springs 36. The Charge of the Light Brigade 36. *Dodsworth* 36. Beloved Enemy 36. We Have Our Moments 37. Dinner at the Ritz 37. *The Prisoner of Zenda* (as Fritz von Tarlenheim) 37. Four Men and a Prayer 38. Bluebeard's Eighth Wife 38. Three Blind Mice 38. The Dawn Patrol 38. Wuthering Heights 39. *Bachelor Mother* 39. The Real Glory 39. Eternally Yours 39. *Raffles* 40. The First of the Few 41. *The Way Ahead* 44. *A Matter of Life and Death* 46. The Perfect Marriage 46. Magnificent Doll 46. The Other Love 47. The Bishop's Wife 47. Bonnie Prince Charlie 47. Enchantment 48. A Kiss in the Dark 49. A Kiss for Corliss 49. The Elusive Pimpernel 50. The Toast of New Orleans 50. Soldiers Three 51. Happy Go Lovely 51. The Lady Says No 52. Appointment with Venus 52. The Moon is Blue 53. The Love Lottery 54. Happy Ever After 54. The King's Thief 55. *Carrington VC* 55. The Birds and the Bees 56. *Around The World in Eighty Days* (as Phineas Fogg) 56. Oh Men Oh Women 57. The Little Hut 57. My Man Godfrey 57. The Silken Affair 57. Bonjour Tristesse 58. *Separate Tables* (AA) 58. Ask Any Girl 59. Happy Anniversary 59. Please Don't Eat the Daisies 60. The Guns of Navarone 61. The Captive City 62. Guns of Darkness 62. The Best of Enemies 62. Road to Hong Kong (gag appearance) 63. 55 Days at Peking 63. The Pink Panther 64. Bedtime Story 64. Where the Spies Are 65. Lady L 66. Casino Royale 67. Eye of the Devil 67. The Extraordinary Seaman 68. Prudence and the Pill 68. The Impossible Years 68. Before Winter Comes 68. The Brain 69. The Statue 70. King Queen Knave 72. Vampira 74. Paper Tiger 75. Murder by Death 76. No Deposit No Return 76. Candleshoe 77. Death on the Nile 78. A Man Called Intrepid (TV) 79. Escape to Athena 79. A Nightingale Sang in Berkeley Square 80. Rough Cut 80. The Sea Wolves 80. Better Late Than Never 82. Trail of the Pink Panther 82. Curse of the Pink Panther 83.

TV series: Four Star Playhouse 56. *The David Niven Show* 59. *The Rogues* 64.

✪ For forty years as a debonair international star. *Around the World in Eighty Days*.

❝ Can you imagine being wonderfully overpaid for dressing up and playing games? – *D.N.*

He's a very, very bad actor, but he absolutely loves doing it. – *D.N. on himself*

Actors don't retire, they just get offered fewer roles. – *D.N.*

I suppose everybody becomes an actor because they want to be liked. I do enjoy being liked, but I don't work hard at it. I try to do the best I can for my age. – *D.N.*

I have a face that's a cross between two pounds of halibut and an explosion in an old-clothes closet. If it isn't mobile, it's dead. – *D.N.*

Nixon, Marian (1904–1983).
American leading lady.

What Happened to Jones? 26. Rosita 27. General Crack 29. Adios 30. After Tomorrow 32. Rebecca of Sunnybrook Farm 32. Walking Down Broadway 32.

Nixon, Marni (1931–).
American singer, former MGM messenger, who has dubbed in high notes for many stars including Margaret O'Brien in *Big City*, Deborah Kerr in *The King and I*, Natalie Wood in *West Side Story* and Audrey Hepburn in *My Fair Lady*. Has made only one film appearance, as a nun in *The Sound of Music* 65.

Mulan (voice) 98.

Nixon, Richard Milhous (1913–1994).
The American politician and president, forced to resign office over the Watergate affair, was lampooned in Emile de Antonio's documentary *Millhouse: A White Comedy* 71, and was played by Philip Baker Hall in a one-man show, *Secret Honor* 84, filmed by Robert Altman, and by Harry Spillman in *Born Again* 78, about Nixon's Special Counsel Charles Colsen's religious conversion. In two films, *Serpico* 73 and *Point Break* 91, bank robbers have been shown wearing rubber Nixon masks. In 1995, Beau Bridges played him in the made-for-TV biopic *Kissinger and Nixon*, while Anthony Hopkins played him on the big screen in *Nixon*, directed by Oliver Stone.

Noble, Peter (1917–1997).
English showbusiness journalist and biographer, a former actor. He compiled and edited the *British Film Yearbook* (later the *British Film & Television Yearbook*) from 1945 until the early 90s, and the annual *Picture Parade* in the 50s. His books included *The Negro in Films* (1948), and biographies of Orson Welles, Ivor Novello, Erich von Stroheim and Bette Davis, as well as two volumes of verse. Married actress Marianne STONE, his second wife, in 1947.

Noble, Thom.
American editor.

Fahrenheit 451 67. Joseph Andrews 77. Tattoo 81. Witness (AA) 85. The Mosquito Coast 86. Mountains of the Moon 90. Thelma and Louise (AA) 91. Final Analysis 92. Body of Evidence 93. The Hudsucker Proxy 94. The Scarlet Letter 95. The Mask of Zorro 98, etc.

Noël, Magali (1932–) (M. Guiffrais).
French leading lady.

Seul dans Paris 51. Razzia sur la Chnouf 55. Rififi 55. Elena et les Hommes 56. Desire Takes the Men 58. La Dolce Vita 59. The Man Who Understood Women 70. Amarcord 74. Season for Assassins 75. The Lost Way 79. The Death of Mario Ricci 83. Marriage 85. Pentimento 90, many others.

Noël-Noël (1897–1989) (Lucien Noel).
Dapper French character comedian.

Octave 32. A Cage of Nightingales 43. Le Père Tranquille 46. The Seven Deadly Sins 51. The Diary of Major Thompson 56. Jessica 62, etc.

Noiret, Philippe (1930–).
French leading actor in international films, from the stage.

Zazie dans le Métro 60. Les Copains 62. Cyrano and d'Artagnan 63. Lady L 65. The Night of the Generals 66. Clérambard 69. *Topaz* 69. Justine 69. Murphy's War 70. A Time for Loving 71. The Serpent 72. La Grande Bouffe 73. The Clockmaker 76. The Old Gun 76. Who Is Killing the Great Chefs of Europe? 78. Dear Detective 78. Le Grand Carnaval 83. Fort Saganne 84. Round Midnight 84. The Secret Wife 86. La Famiglia 87. *Cinema Paradiso*/Nuovo Cinema Paradiso 88. Le Cop 2/Ripoux contre Ripoux 89. To Forget Palermo/Dimenticare Palermo 89. Faux et Usage de Faux 90. Uranus 90. I Don't Kiss/J'Embrasse Pas 91. Fish Soup/Zuppa di Pesce 91. The Two of Us/Nous Deux 92. Viva i Bambini 92. Tango 93. Grosse Fatigue 94. Le Roi de Paris 94. The Postman (It.) 94. La Fille de D'Artagnan 94. Les Milles 95. Looking for Paradise (It.) 95. The Grand Dukes 95. Marianna Ucria (It.) 97. On Guard! 97, etc.

Nolan, Doris (1916–).
American leading lady who married Alexander Knox.

The Man I Married 37. Holiday 38. Irene 40. Moon over Burma 40. Follies Girl 45. Bindle 66. The Romantic Englishwoman 75, etc.

Nolan, Jeanette (1911–1998).
American character actress, much on TV. Married to John MCINTIRE.

Macbeth (as Lady Macbeth) 48. The Secret of Convict Lake 51. The Happy Time 52. The Big Heat 53. The Guns of Fort Petticoat 57. The Rabbit Trap 58. The Winds of Autumn 76. Lassie: The New Beginning (TV) 78. Cloak and Dagger 84. Street Justice 89, etc.

TV series: Hotel de Paree 59. The Richard Boone Show 63. The Virginian 67. Dirty Sally 73.

Nolan, Lloyd (1902–1985).
Dependable American character actor, with stage experience from 1927.

Stolen Harmony (film debut) 34. G Men 35. Ebb Tide 37. Gangs of Chicago 40. Michael Shayne, Private Detective 40. Blues in the Night 41. Buy Me That Town 41. Bataan 43. *A Tree Grows in Brooklyn* 44. *The House on 92nd Street* 45. The Lady in the Lake 46. The Street with No Name 48. The Last Hunt 56. Peyton Place 58. Circus World 64. Never Too Late 65. An American Dream 66. The Double Man (GB) 67. Ice Station Zebra 68. Airport 69. Isn't It Shocking? (TV) 73. Earthquake 74. The Private Files of J. Edgar Hoover 78. Hannah and Her Sisters 85, many others.

TV series: Julia 68–70.

Nolan, Mary (1905–1948) (Mary Imogene Robertson).
American leading lady, an ex-Ziegfeld girl who made a few films in Germany and Hollywood, then came to grief through drugs.

Sister Veronika 26. Sorrell and Son 27. West of Zanzibar 28. Shanghai Lady 29. Outside the Law 30. X Marks the Spot 31. Midnight Patrol 32, etc.

Nolbandov, Sergei (1895–1971).
Russian-born writer-producer, in Britain from 1926.

City of Song (w) 30. Fire over England (w) 36. Ships with Wings (wd) 42. This Modern Age (series) (p) from 1946. The Kidnappers (p) 53. Mix Me a Person (p) 62, many others.

Nolte, Nick (1940–).
Virile American leading man.

Return to Macon County 75. Death Sentence (TV) 76. The Runaway Barge (TV) 76. *Rich Man Poor Man* (TV) 76. The Deep 77. Who'll Stop the Rain? 78. North Dallas Forty 79. Heart Beat 79. Cannery Row 82. 48 Hours 82. The Ultimate Solution of Grace Quigley 84. Teachers 84. Down and Out in Beverly Hills 85. Extreme Prejudice 87. Weeds 87. Farewell to the King 89. New York Stories 89. Three Fugitives 89. Another 48 Hrs 90. Everybody Wins 90. Q & A 90. Cape Fear 91. The Prince of Tides (AAN) 91. Lorenzo's Oil 92. I'll Do Anything 94. Blue Chips 94. I Love Trouble 94. Jefferson in Paris 95. Mulholland Falls 96. Mother Night 96. U-Turn 97. After Glow 97. Affliction 98. The Thin Red Line 98, etc.

❝ If you feel you have a film that's valid, you stick your ass on the line. – *N.N.*

Noonan, Chris (1953–).
Australian director and screenwriter. He trained at the Australian Film and Television School in the early 70s and first worked as a documentary film-maker and in television.

The Chowra Breakout (TV) 85. The Riddle of the Stinson (TV) 88. *Babe* (co-w, d) 95, etc.

Noonan, Tommy (1921–1968) (Thomas Noon).
Ebullient American comedian.

Starlift 51. Gentlemen Prefer Blondes 53. A Star is Born 54. How to Be Very Very Popular 55. Bundle of Joy 56. *The Ambassador's Daughter* 56. The Rookie (& p) 60, etc.

Norden, Christine (1924–1988) (Mary Lydia Thornton).
British leading actress, a sex symbol of the late 40s. Born in London, she began as a singer and entertainer during the Second World War. In the 50s, she acted on Broadway and TV in the United States, where in 1967 she became the first topless Western actress on the legitimate stage. In the 90s, the US Geological Survey named mountains on the planet Venus after her. Married five times, including to director-cinematographer Jack CARDIFF. Her lovers included producer Alexander KORDA.

■ Night Beat 47. *Mine Own Executioner* 47. Idol of Paris 48. A Yank Comes Back 48. An Ideal Husband 48. Saints and Sinners 49. The Interrupted Journey 49. The Black Widow 50. A Case for PC 49 51. Reluctant Heroes 52. Little Shop of Horrors 87. The Wolvercote Tongue (TV) 88.

TV series: Chance in a Million 87.

Nordgren, Eric (1913–1992).
Swedish composer, associated with the early films of Ingmar Bergman.

Kvinna Utan Ansikte 47. Eva 48. Törst/Three Strange Loves 49. Sommarlek/Summer Interlude 51. Kvinnors Väntan/Secrets of Women 52. Monika 52. Sommarnattens Leende/Smiles of a Summer Night 55. The Seventh Seal 57. Wild Strawberries 57. The Magician 58. The Virgin Spring 60. Pleasure Garden 61. All These Women 64. The Emigrants 70, etc.

Noris, Assia (1912–1998) (Anastasija Noris von Gerzfeld).
Russian-born leading actress of the 30s in Italy. Born in St Petersburg, she moved with her family to France at the time of the Revolution, settling in Italy in the late 20s, and made her movie debut in 1932. She became a star playing opposite Vittorio DE SICA in the films of Mario CAMERINI, who was briefly the second of her five husbands. Retired in the mid-60s, after an undistinguished postwar career which was partly spent in Egypt.

Giallo 33. Darò un Milione 35. Ma Non E una Cosa Seria 36. Mr Max/Il Signor Max 37. I Grandi Magazzini 39. Batticuore 39. Una Romantica Avventura 40. Una Storia d'Amore 42. Le Capitaine Fracasse (Fr.) 42. Che Distinta Famiglia! 49. La Peccatrice Bianca 49. La Celestina (& co-w, story) 64, etc.

Norman, Leslie (1911–1993).
British producer-director, former editor, in films from late 20s.

Where No Vultures Fly (p) 51. The Cruel Sea (p) 54. The Night My Number Came Up (d) 56. X the Unknown (d) 57. The Shiralee (d) 58. Dunkirk (d) 58. The Long, the Short and the Tall (d) 60. Mix Me a Person (d) 61. Summer of the 17th Doll (d) 61, etc.

Normand, Mabel (1894–1930) (Mabel Fortescue).
American comedienne, a leading player of Vitagraph and Keystone comedies from 1911, and a Chaplin co-star.

Barney Oldfield's Race for Life 12. Fatty and Mabel Adrift 15. Mickey 17. Sis Hopkins 18. Molly O 21. Suzanna 22. The Extra Girl 24, many others.

Norrington, Stephen (1965–).
British director and screenwriter, a former special effects and make-up expert.

Death Machine (wd) 94. Blade (d) 98.

Norris, Chuck (1940–) (Carlos Ray Norris).
American tough-guy hero, former karate champion.
Autobiography: 1988, *The Secret of Inner Strength*, with Joe Hyams.
Good Guys Wear Black 79. An Eye for an Eye 81. Forced Vengeance 82. Silent Rage 82. *Missing in Action* 83. Lone Wolf McQuade 83. Missing in Action II 83. Code of Silence 84. Invasion USA 85. Delta Force 85. Firewalker 86. Braddock: Missing in Action III (& w) 88. Hero and the Terror 88. Delta Force 2: Operation Stranglehold 90. The Hitman 91. Sidekicks 93. Top Dog 95. Forest Warrior 95, etc.
TV series: Walker, Texas Ranger 93.
❝ Whatever luck I had, I made. I was never a natural athlete, but I paid my dues in sweat and concentration and took the time necessary to learn karate and become world champion. – *C.N.*

Norris, Edward (1910–).
American leading man of second features; former reporter. He retired from acting in the mid-50s to pursue business interests. Among his five wives were actresses Ann Sheridan and Sheila Ryan.
Queen Christina 33. Boys' Town 38. The Man with Two Lives 41. End cf the Road 44. Decoy 47. Forbidden Women 49. Inside the Walls of Folsom Prison 51. The Man from the Alamo 53. The Kentuckian 55, many others.

Norris, Frank (1870–1902).
American novelist, whose *McTeague* was the basis for Von Stroheim's *Greed*.

Norstein, Yuri (1941–)
Russian director of animated films, born in Moscow. His *Tale of Tales* has a reputation as one of the finest of animated films.
The Heron and the Crane 74. Hedgehog in the Fog 75. Tale of Tales 79.

North, Alex (1910–1991).
American composer. He was awarded an honorary Oscar in 1986.
■ *A Streetcar Named Desire* (AAN) 51. The Thirteenth Letter 51. Death of a Salesman (AAN) 51. Viva Zapata (AAN) 52. Les Misérables 52. Pony Soldier 52. The Member of the Wedding 53. Désirée 54. Go Man Go 54. The Racers 55. Unchained 55. The Man with the Gun 55. The Rose Tattoo (AAN) 55. I'll Cry Tomorrow 56. The Bad Seed 56. The Rainmaker (AAN) 56. Four Girls in Town 56. The King and Four Queens 56. The Bachelor Party 57. The Long Hot Summer 58. Stage Struck 58. Hot Spell 58. South Seas Adventure 58. The Sound and the Fury 59. The Wonderful Country 59. *Spartacus* (AAN) 60. The Children's Hour 61. Sanctuary 61. The Misfits 61. All Fall Down 62. Cleopatra (AAN) 63. The Outrage 64. Cheyenne Autumn 64. The Agony and the Ecstasy (AAN) 65. Who's Afraid of Virginia Woolf? (AAN) 66. The Devil's Brigade 68. The Shoes of the Fisherman (AAN) 68. A Dream of Kings 69. Hard Contract 69. Willard 71. Pocket Money 72. Shanks (AAN) 74. Bite the Bullet (AAN) 75. Rich Man Poor Man (TV) 76. Somebody Killed Her Husband (TV) 78. Wise Blood 79. Carny 80. Dragonslayer (AAN) 81. Under the Volcano (AAN) 84.

North, Edmund H. (1911–1990).
American screenwriter.
One Night of Love 34. I Dream Too Much 35. All the King's Horses 35. Bunker Bean 36. I'm Still Alive 40. Dishonored Lady 47. Young Man with a Horn 50. In a Lonely Place 50. Only the Valiant 51. The Day the Earth Stood Still 51. The Outcasts of Poker Flat 53. The Far Horizons 55. The Proud Ones 56. Cowboy 58. Sink the Bismarck 60. HMS Defiant 62. Patton (co-w) (AA) 70. Meteor 79, etc.

North, Jay (1952–).
American juvenile actor, popular as a child on TV in *Dennis the Menace* 59–63 and later *Maya* 67.
Pepe 60. Zebra in the Kitchen 65. The Teacher 74. Scout's Honor 80, etc.

North, Michael (1916–).
American leading man of the 40s. He gave up acting in the 50s to become an agent. Formerly known as Ted North; changed and was reintroduced for *The Unsuspected* 48.
Chad Hanna 40. Charlie Chan in Rio 41. The Oxbow Incident 43. The Devil Thumbs a Ride 47, etc.

North, Sheree (1933–) (Dawn Bethel).
Blonde American leading lady, former dancer.
Excuse My Dust 51. *How to Be Very Very Popular* 55. The Best Things in Life are Free 56. The Way to the Gold 57. No Down Payment 57. Mardi Gras 58. Destination Inner Space 66. Madigan 68. The Gypsy Moths 69. Lawman 71. Charley Varrick 73. Breakout 75. The Shootist 76. Telefon 77. *The Night They Took Miss Beautiful* (TV) 78. Maniac Cop 88. Defenceless 91. Susan's Plan 98, etc.
TV series: Big Eddie 75. But I'm a Big Girl Now 80–81. The Bay City Blues 83.

Northam, Jeremy (1962–).
English leading actor whose stage roles include Hamlet at the Royal National Theatre.
The Net (US) 95. Voices 95. Emma (US) 96. The Tribe (TV) 98. The Misadventures of Margaret 98, etc.

Norton, Edward (1971–).
American leading actor, from the theatre. Born in Boston, he studied history at Yale.
Primal Fear (AAN) 96. Everyone Says I Love You 96. The People vs Larry Flynt 96. Rounders 98. American History X 98, etc.

Norton, Jack (1889–1958) (Mortimer J. Naughton).
American character actor, invariably seen as an amiable well-dressed drunk with a sour expression; he rarely had a coherent speaking part.
Cockeyed Cavaliers 34. Thanks for the Memory 38. The Ghost Breakers 40. The Bank Dick 40. The Fleet's In 41. The Palm Beach Story 42. Hail the Conquering Hero 44. Hold that Blonde 45. Bringing Up Father 46, many others.

Norwood, Eille (1861–1948) (Anthony Brett).
British stage actor who played Sherlock Holmes in a score of 20s two-reelers and a few features.

Noseworthy, Jack (1971–).
American actor, singer and dancer. Born in Massachusetts, he studied at the Boston Conservatory and began in the musical theatre.
Encino Man 92. Alive 93. SFW 94. The Brady Bunch Movie 95. Mojave Moon 96. Barb Wire 96. The Trigger Effect 96. Event Horizon 97, etc.
TV series: Teech 91.

Nosseck, Max (1902–1972) (Alexander Norris).
Polish director in Hollywood from 1939; former stage and film actor/director in Europe.
■ AMERICAN FILMS: Girls Under Twenty-One 40. Gambling Daughters 41. *Dillinger* 45. The Brighton Strangler 45. Black Beauty 46. The Return of Rin Tin Tin 47. Kill or Be Killed 50. Korea Patrol 51. The Hoodlum 51. The Body Beautiful 53. Garden of Eden 57.

Nouri, Michael (1945–).
American leading actor.
The Last Convertible (TV) 79. Flashdance 83. Between Two Women 86. Imagemaker 86. The Hidden 87. Project: Alien 89. Thieves of Fortune 89. Total Exposure 91. Psychic 91. American Yakuza 93. To the Limit 95. Hologram Man 95. Overkill 96, etc.
TV series: Beacon Hill 75. The Curse of Dracula 79. The Gangster Chronicles 81. The Bay City Blues 83. Downtown 86–87.

Novak, Eva (1898–1988).
American silent-screen leading lady, sister of Jane. She co-starred with Tom Mix in ten films, after beginning as one of Mack Sennett's Bathing Beauties.
The Lost Trail 21. Society Secrets 21. The Man From Hells River 22. Boston Blackie 23. A Fight for Honor 24. The Forlorn Lover 25. Irene 26. Red Signals 27. Phantom of the Desert 30, etc.

Novak, Jane (1896–1990).
American silent-screen leading lady, sister of Eva.
The Barbarian 21. Colleen of the Pines 22. Jealous Husbands 23. The Lullaby 24. Lure of the Wilds 25. Whispering Canyon 26. What Price Love? 27. Free Lips 28. Redskin 29. The Boss 57, etc.

Novak, Kim (1933–) (Marilyn Novak).
Artificially-groomed American blonde star who never managed to give a natural performance, though she did try.
■ The French Line 53. *Pushover* 54. Phffft 54. Five against the House 55. Son of Sinbad 55. *Picnic* 55. The Man with the Golden Arm 56. The Eddy Duchin Story 56. *Jeanne Eagles* 57. Pal Joey 58. Vertigo 58. Bell, Book and Candle 58. Middle of the Night 59. Strangers When We Meet 60. Pépé 60. Boys' Night Out 62. The Notorious Landlady 62. Of Human Bondage 64. Kiss Me Stupid 64. The Amorous Adventures of Moll Flanders 65. The Legend of Lylah Clare 68. The Great Bank Robbery 69. Tales That Witness Madness 73. Third Girl from the Left (TV) 74. Satan's Triangle (TV) 75. The White Buffalo 77. Just a Gigolo 79. The Mirror Crack'd 80. Malibu (TV) 83. Es Hat Mich Sehr Gefreut 87. The Children 90. Liebestraum 91.
❝ When I was doing *Vertigo*, poor Kim Novak, bless her heart, said, 'Mr Hitchcock, what is my character feeling in relation to her surroundings?' There was silence on the set and Hitch said, 'It's only a movie, for God's sakes.' She never asked another question. – *James Stewart*

Novarro, Ramon (1899–1968) (Ramon Samaniegos).
Romantic Mexican leading man of the 20s in Hollywood; later came back as character actor. He was murdered in his home by two teenagers.
The Prisoner of Zenda (as Rupert) 22. Where the Pavement Ends 23. *Scaramouche* 23. The Arab 24. The Midshipman 25. *Ben Hur* 25. The Student Prince 27. Across to Singapore 28. Forbidden Hours 28. The Pagan 29. Call of the Flesh 30. Son of India 31. Mata Hari 31. The Son-Daughter 32. The Barbarian 33. The Cat and the Fiddle 34. The Night is Young 35. The Sheik Steps Out 37. *We Were Strangers* 48. The Big Steal 49. Crisis 50. Heller in Pink Tights 60, etc.

Novello, Ivor (1893–1951) (Ivor Davies).
Handsome Welsh matinée idol, composer, actor-manager, playwright and screenwriter. Born in Cardiff, he first gained fame as the composer of the First World War song 'Keep the Home Fires Burning', before becoming Britain's most popular silent film star, a stage actor and dramatist. In the early 30s he went to Hollywood, under contract to MGM, where he was unhappily employed as a writer, working uncredited on *Mata Hari* 31 and *Lovers Courageous* 32, among others. MGM also bought as a vehicle for Joan CRAWFORD his play *Party*, written during his spare time at the studio and featuring rivalries between actresses Miranda Clayfoot (based on Tallulah BANKHEAD) and Mrs MacDonald (otherwise Mrs Patrick CAMPBELL), but it was never made. He appeared in four British films on his return, but then decided to quit the cinema for the theatre, where he scored his greatest success as the star and creator of such romantic, large-scale musicals as *Glamorous Night*, which also starred Mary ELLIS, *Careless Rapture*, *The Dancing Years*, also with Mary Ellis, and *King's Rhapsody*. Died of a heart attack.
Biographies: 1951, *Ivor Novello: Man of the Theatre* by Peter Noble; 1952, *Ivor: The Story of an Achievement* by W. Macqueen Pope; 1974, *The World of Ivor Novello: Perchance to Dream* by Richard Rose; 1975, *Ivor* by Sandy Wilson; 1987, *Ivor Novello* by James Harding.
■ The Call of the Blood/L'Appel du Sang (a) 19. Miarka: The Daughter of the Bear (Fr.) (a) 20. Carnival (a) 21. The Bohemian Girl (a) 22. *The Man without Desire* (a) 23. The White Rose (US) (a) 23. Bonnie Prince Charlie (a) 23. The White Shadow (a) 24. *The Rat* (a, oa) 25. The Triumph of the Rat (a) 26. *The Lodger* (a) 26. Downhill/When the Boys Leave Home (a, oa) 27. The Vortex (a) 28. The Constant Nymph (a) 28. The Gallant Hussar (a) 28. The Return of the Rat (a) 28. A South Sea Bubble (a) 28. Elstree Calling (m) 30. Symphony in Two Flats (a, oa) 30. Once a Lady (a) (US) 31. *Tarzan the Ape Man* (co-w) (US) 31. But the Flesh Is Weak (w, from his play The Truth Game) (US) 32. The Lodger (a) 32. I Lived with You (a, oa) 33. Sleeping Car (a) 33. Autumn Crocus (a) 34. The Rat (oa) 37. Glamorous Night (oa) 37. Free and Easy (oa) (US) 41. The Dancing Years (oa) 49. King's Rhapsody (oa) 55, etc.
❝ It's just like Marie Antoinette's flight to Varennes! – *I.N. to his long-time companion, actor Bobbie Andrews, when he was collected at midnight from Wormwood Scrubs, where he had served a month's imprisonment in 1944 for misusing a wartime petrol allowance so that he could drive his Rolls-Royce at weekends*
I am an entertainer. Empty seats and good opinions mean nothing to me. – *I.N.*
On stage, every performance is an event, because you have a living, breathing audience to conquer. You *know* immediately whether you are doing something that pleases or offends, and you can adjust yourself accordingly. But the camera, which is never supposed to lie, makes no response whatsoever, and, even if the director seems pleased, he is only one man. – *I.N.*
I love seeing films, but I hate doing them. I hate the hours one has to keep. I have never been able to get up early in the morning without a feeling of impending death. – *I.N.*
He was beautiful. And he was a darling. However opinions may differ about his other attributes, on these two there is total agreement: his good looks, and his good nature. – *Sandy Wilson*
His face was his misfortune. Ivor was tripped up by his beauty. – *Phyllis Bottome*
He was mischievous and naughty and everything under the sun, but his saving grace was that he was utterly sincere. – *Mary Ellis*

Novello, Jay (1905–1982).
Wiry little American actor, familiar in films from Tenth Avenue Kid 38 to Atlantis the Lost Continent 61, usually as scruffy little crook.
TV series: McHale's Navy 65.

Noyce, Phillip (1950–).
Australian director, now working in America.
Backroads (& w, p) 77. Newsfront (wd) 78. Heatwave 82. The Dismissal (co-d) 83. The Cowra Breakout (TV) 85. Shadows of the Peacock 86. Echoes of Paradise 88. Dead Calm 89. Blind Fury 89. Patriot Games 92. Sliver 93. Clear and Present Danger 94. The Saint 97, etc.

Ntshona, Winston.
South African actor, in international films, from the stage.
The Wild Geese (GB) 78. Ashanti (US) 79. The Dogs of War (GB) 80. Marigolds in August 80. The Stick 88. A Dry White Season (US) 89. Night of the Cyclone/Perfume of the Cyclone (US) 90. Power of One 91. The Air Up There (US) 93. Tarzan and the Lost City (US) 98, etc.

Nucci, Danny (1968–).
American actor. Born in Klagenfurt, Austria, he lived in Italy until he was seven, when his family moved to the United States. He began acting in his early teens.
American Drive-In 85. Explorers 85. Book of Love 90. Alive 93. Blind Justice 94. Crimson Tide 95. The Rock 96. Eraser 96. The Big Squeeze 96. That Old Feeling 97. Titanic 97, etc.
TV series: Pryor's Place 84. Falcon Crest 88–89.

Nugent, Elliott (1899–1980).
American stage actor, producer and playwright who only dabbled in films but proved a good director of comedies.
Autobiography: 1965, *Events Leading up to the Comedy*.
AS ACTOR: So This Is College 29. The Unholy Three 30. Romance 30. The Last Flight 31, etc.
AS DIRECTOR: The Mouthpiece 32. Whistling in the Dark 33. *Three Cornered Moon* 33. She Loves Me Not 34. Love in Bloom 35. And So They Were Married 36. Professor Beware 38. *The Cat and the Canary* 39. Nothing but the Truth 40. The Male Animal (& oa) 42. The Crystal Ball 43. Up in Arms 44. My Favorite Brunette 47. *My Girl Tisa* 48. *The Great Gatsby* 49. My Outlaw Brother 51. Just for You 52, etc.

Nugent, Frank (1908–1966).
American screenwriter, former reporter and critic.
Fort Apache 48. *She Wore a Yellow Ribbon* 49. The Quiet Man (AAN) 52. Trouble in the Glen 53. *The Searchers* 56. The Last Hurrah 58. Donovan's Reef 63, etc.

Nunez, Victor (1945–).
American independent director, screenwriter and editor, a former university lecturer in film-making.
Gal Young 'Un 79. A Flash of Green 85. Ruby in Paradise 93. Ulee's Gold 97, etc.

Nunn, Trevor (1940–).
English director, artistic director of the Royal National Theatre from 1997, and former artistic director of the Royal Shakespeare Company from 1968, later becoming its chief executive, leaving in 1986 to freelance. Apart from his Shakespearian productions, he co-directed an epic and much-admired version of Dickens's *The Life and Adventures of Nicholas Nickleby*, which was shown on TV in 1982. Since the 80s, he has specialized in stage musicals, including Andrew Lloyd Webber's *Cats* and *Starlight Express*, and, in 1986, an unsuccessful version of Stephen King's *Carrie*. Formerly married to actress Janet Suzman. Married actress Imogen Stubbs in 1994. In 1998, the *Sunday Times* estimated his fortune at £40m.

Hedda 75. Comedy of Errors (TV) 78. Lady Jane 85. Twelfth Night 96.

Nureyev, Rudolf (1938–1993).
Russian ballet dancer who ventured into straight acting.
Don Quixote 73. Valentino 77. Exposed 83.
66 I love dancing. From the age of six I have not thought of anything else. – R.N.

Nutley, Colin (1947–).
British director active in Sweden. He worked in British television before moving to Sweden in the 80s. His films use improvised dialogue.

The Ninth Battalion 88. Black Jack 90. *House of Angels* 92. The Last Dance/Sista Dansen 93. Just You and Me 94. House of Angels: The Second Summer 95. Such is Life/Sånt är Livet 96, etc.

Nuyen, France (1939–).
Franco-Chinese leading lady, former model, who made some Hollywood films.

In Love and War 57. *South Pacific* 58. Satan Never Sleeps 61. The Last Time I Saw Archie 62. A Girl Named Tamiko 63. Diamond Head 62. The Man in the Middle 64. Dimension Five 66. One More Train to Rob 71. The Horror at 37,000 Feet (TV) 73. China Cry 90. The Joy Luck Club 93. A Passion to Kill 94. A Smile Like Yours 96, etc.

TV series: Knots Landing 90.

Nuytten, Bruno (1945–).
French cinematographer and director who also works in international films. He has a son by actress Isabelle Adjani.

Going Places/Les Valseuses 74. India Song 75. Barocco 76. Le Camion 77. French Postcards 79. The Brontë Sisters 79. The Best Way 80. Brubaker 80. Under Suspicion/Garde à Vue 82. Life Is a Bed of Roses/La Vie Est un Roman 83. Tchao Pantin 83. Jean de Florette 86. Manon des Sources 86. Camille Claudel (wd) 88. Albert Souffre (d) 92, etc.

Nyby, Christian (1919–1993).
American director, a former editor who began working at MGM as a carpenter. He was also a television director.
■ To Have and Have Not (ed) 45. The Big Sleep (ed) 46. Red River (ed) (AAN) 48. *The Thing* 52. Hell on Devil's Island 57. Six-Gun Law 62. Young Fury 64. Operation CIA 65. First to Fight 66. Emergency! (TV) 71.

Nye, Carrie (1937–).
American actress.
Divorce His, Divorce Hers (TV) 73. The Users (TV) 78. The Seduction of Joe Tynan 79. Creepshow 82. Too Scared to Scream 85. Hello Again 87, etc.

Nykvist, Sven (1922–).
Distinguished Swedish cinematographer.
Sawdust and Tinsel 53. Karin Mansdotter 53. *The Virgin Spring* 60. Winter Light 62. *The Silence* 64. Loving Couples 65. Persona 66. Hour of the Wolf 67. The Shame 69. The Touch 71. The Last Run 71. One Day in the Life of Ivan Denisovitch 71. Cries and Whispers (AA) 73. Scenes from a Marriage 74. Face to Face 76. King of the Gypsies 78. Pretty Baby 78. The Hurricane 79. Starting Over 79. Willie and Phil 80. The Postman Always Rings Twice 81. Cannery Row 82. Fanny and Alexander (AA) 82. Star 80 83. After the Rehearsal 84. Swann in Love/Un Amour de Swann 84. Agnes of God 85. Dream Lover 86. Another Woman 88. The Unbearable Lightness of Being (AAN) 89. New York Stories 89. Buster's Bedroom 91. The Ox/Oxen (wd) (AAN) 91. Chaplin 92. Sleepless in Seattle 93. What's Eating Gilbert Grape 93. With Honors 94. Only You 94. Mixed Nuts 94. Something to Talk About 95. Kristin Lavrandsdatter 95. Celebrity 98, etc.
66 Today we make everything so complicated. The lighting, the camera, the acting. It has taken me 30 years to arrive at simplicity. – S.N.

Nyman, Michael (1944–).
British composer, closely associated with the work of director Peter Greenaway.
The Draughtsman's Contract 82. Nelly's Version 83. A Zed and Two Noughts 85. Drowning by Numbers 88. The Cook, the Thief, His Wife and Her Lover 89. Prospero's Books 91. Mesmer 94. The Ogre 96, etc.

Nyswaner, Ron.
American screenwriter and director, from the theatre.
Smithereens (co-w) 82. Swing Shift (co-w) 83. Purple Hearts (w) 84. Mrs Soffel (w) 84. The Prince of Pennsylvania (wd) 88. Gross Anatomy (co-w) 89. Philadelphia (AANw) 93, etc.

O

Oakie, Jack (1903–1978) (Lewis D. Offield).
Cheerful American comic actor well known for a startled 'double take'; formerly in vaudeville.
Finders Keepers (debut) 27. Paramount on Parade 30. Million Dollar Legs 32. College Humor 33. If I Had a Million 33. Call of the Wild 35. The Texas Rangers 36. The Toast of New York 37. Rise and Shine 39. *The Great Dictator* (a caricature of Mussolini) (AAN) 40. Tin Pan Alley 40. Footlight Serenade 42. Song of the Islands 42. Something to Shout About 43. Hello Frisco Hello 43. *It Happened Tomorrow* 44. That's the Spirit 44. The Merry Monahans 44. On Stage Everybody 45. When My Baby Smiles at Me 48. Thieves' Highway 49. Last of the Buccaneers 50. The Battle of Powder River 52. Around the World in Eighty Days 56. The Wonderful Country 59. The Rat Race 60. Lover Come Back 62, many others.

Oakland, Simon (1922–1983).
American general-purpose actor with stage experience.
The Brothers Karamazov 58. I Want to Live 58. Psycho 60. West Side Story 61. Follow That Dream 62. Wall of Noise 63. The Satan Bug 65. The Plainsman 66. The Sand Pebbles 67. Tony Rome 67. Chubasco 68. On a Clear Day You Can See Forever 70. Chato's Land 72. Happy Mother's Day Love George 73. Emperor of the North Pole 73. Evening in Byzantium (TV) 78, etc.
TV series: Toma 73–74. Kolchak: The Night Stalker 74–75. Baa Baa Black Sheep 76–78. David Cassidy – Man Undercover 78.

Oakland, Vivian (1895–1958) (V. Anderson).
American child star and vaudeville artiste, who later became familiar as wife to the leading comic in many a two-reeler. In films from 1924.
Gold Dust Gertie 31. Only Yesterday 32. The Bride Walks Out 36. Way Out West 37. The Man in the Trunk 42. Bunco Squad 51, many others.

Oakley, Annie (1859–1926) (Phoebe Annie Oakley Mozee).
American sharpshooter who gained fame in her teens as star of Buffalo Bill's wild west show. A sharp shooter who could slice a playing card held up edgewise at thirty paces, she ended her career running a skeet range in North Carolina. Played on screen by Barbara Stanwyck in *Annie Oakley* 35, by Betty Hutton in *Annie Get Your Gun* 50, and by Reba McEntire in *Buffalo Girls* (TV) 95. A TV series in 1953–57 starred Gail Davis.

Oakman, Wheeler (1890–1949) (Vivian Eichelberger).
American silent star, later western supporting actor.
The God of Gold 12. The Spoilers 14. The Black Orchid 16. Mickey 18. The Virgin of Stamboul 20. Outside the Law 21. The Pace That Thrills 25. Lights of New York 28. Roaring Ranch 30. End of the Trail 33. G-Men 35. Mutiny in the Big House 39, etc.

Oates, Warren (1928–1982).
American supporting actor who has tended towards psychopathic heavies.
Yellowstone Kelly 59. Private Property 60. Hero's Island 61. Mail Order Bride 64. Major Dundee 65. Return of the Seven 67. In the Heat of the Night 67. The Split 68. Crooks and Coronets (GB) 69. The Wild Bunch 69. There Was a Crooked Man 70. Two Lane Blacktop 71. The Hired Hand 71. Tom Sawyer 73. Dillinger (title role) 73. The White Dawn 73. Badlands 73. 92 in the Shade 75. Race with the Devil 75. Drum 76. The Brinks Job 78. True Grit (TV) 78. My Old Man (TV) 79. Baby Comes Home (TV) 80. Stripes 81. Blue Thunder 83.
TV series: Stony Burke 62.

O'Bannon, Dan (1946–).
American science fiction and horror screenwriter and director.
Dark Star (co-w) 74. Alien (w) 79. Dead and Buried (co-w) 81. Blue Thunder (co-w) 83. Lifeforce (co-w) 85. The Return of the Living Dead (wd) 85. Invaders from Mars (co-w) 86. Total Recall (co-w) 90. Resurrected 92. Screamers (co-w) 95, etc.

Ober, Philip (1902–1982).
American general-purpose character actor.
The Secret Fury 50. From Here to Eternity 53. Tammy 56. North by Northwest 59. Let No Man Write My Epitaph 60. The Brass Bottle 64. The Ghost and Mr Chicken 66, etc.

Oberon, Merle (1911–1979) (Estelle O'Brien Merle Thompson).
British leading lady. Born in India; came to Britain 1928, worked as dance hostess until signed up by Korda. Mainly in Hollywood from 1936. The first of her four husbands was Alexander Korda (1939–45) and the second was cinematographer Lucien K. Ballard (1945–49).
■ A Warm Corner 30. Consolation Marriage 31. Flying High 31. Clara Deane 32. Strange Evidence 32. Service for Ladies 32. Ebb Tide 32. Wedding Rehearsal 32. Men of Tomorrow 32. The Private Life of Henry VIII 33. The Battle 34. The Broken Melody 34. The Private Life of Don Juan 34. *The Scarlet Pimpernel* 34. Folies Bergère 35. The Dark Angel (AAN) 35. These Three 36. Beloved Enemy 36. I Claudius (unfinished) 37. Over the Moon 37. *The Divorce of Lady X* 38. The Cowboy and the Lady 38. *Wuthering Heights* 39. The Lion Has Wings 39. 'Til We Meet Again 40. That Uncertain Feeling 41. Affectionately Yours 41. Lydia 41. Forever and a Day 43. Stage Door Canteen 43. First Comes Courage 43. The Lodger 44. Dark Waters 44. *A Song to Remember* 45. This Love of Ours 45. A Night in Paradise 46. Temptation 46. Night Song 47. Berlin Express 48. Pardon My French 51. 24 Hours of a Woman's Life 52. All is Possible in Granada 54. Désirée 54. Deep in My Heart 54. The Price of Fear 56. Of Love and Desire 63. The Oscar 66. Hotel 67. Interval 73.
TV series: Assignment Foreign Legion 56.

Oboler, Arch (1909–1987).
American writer-producer-director with a long career in radio. Made mainly gimmick films.
■ Bewitched 45. Strange Holiday 46. The Arnelo Affair 47. Five 51. Bwana Devil 52. The Twonky 53. One Plus One 61. The Bubble 67.

O'Brian, Hugh (1925–) (Hugh Krampke).
Leathery American leading man, former athlete.
Never Fear 50. On the Loose 51. Red Ball Express 52. Seminole 54. There's No Business Like Show Business 54. White Feather 55. The Brass Legend 56. The Fiend Who Walked the West 58. Come Fly with Me 62. In Harm's Way 65. Love Has Many Faces 65. Ten Little Indians 65. Ambush Bay 66. Africa Texas Style 67. Probe (TV) 72. Killer Force 75. The Shootist 76. Murder at the World Series (TV) 77. Twins 88. Doin' Time on Planet Earth 88. The Gambler Returns: The Luck of the Draw (TV) 93. Wyatt Earp: Return to Tombstone (TV) 94, etc.
TV series: *Wyatt Earp* 56–59. Search 72.

O'Brien, Dave (1912–1969) (David Barclay).
American light character actor, in Hollywood from the early 30s. Played supporting roles in innumerable films; most familiar as the hero/victim of the Pete Smith comedy shorts of the 40s.
Jennie Gerhardt 33. East Side Kids 39. Son of the Navy 40. 'Neath Brooklyn Bridge 43. Tahiti Nights 44. Phantom of 42nd Street 45. The Desperadoes are in Town 56, etc.

O'Brien, Edmond (1915–1985).
Anglo-Irish leading man of the 40s, latterly character actor; long in Hollywood.
The Hunchback of Notre Dame 39. Parachute Battalion 41. Powder Town 42, etc.; war service; *The Killers* 46. The Web 47. A Double Life 47. Another Part of the Forest 48. An Act of Murder 48. White Heat 49. *D.O.A.* 49. Between Midnight and Dawn 50. Two of a Kind 51. Denver and Rio Grande 52. Julius Caesar 53. The Hitch Hiker 53. Man in the Dark 53. The Bigamist 53. Cow Country 53. *The Barefoot Contessa* (AA) 54. Shield for Murder (& co-d) 54. 1984 (GB) 55. The Girl Can't Help It 57. *The Third Voice* 59. The Last Voyage 60. Mantrap (pd only) 61. The Great Imposter 61. The Man Who Shot Liberty Valance 62. Birdman of Alcatraz 62. *Seven Days in May* (AAN) 64. Sylvia 65. Fantastic Voyage 66. The Viscount (Fr.) 67. The Wild Bunch 69. The Love God 69. Jigsaw (TV) 72. 99 44/100 Dead 74, etc.
TV series: Johnny Midnight 60. Sam Benedict 62. The Long Hot Summer 65.

O'Brien, George (1900–1985).
American cowboy star who entered films as a stuntman.
The Iron Horse (first starring role) 24. *Sunrise* 27. Noah's Ark 28. Lone Star Ranger 30. Riders of the Purple Sage 31. The Last Trail 33. O'Malley of the Mounted 36. Daniel Boone 36. The Painted Desert 38. Stage to Chino 40. Legion of the Lawless 42. She Wore a Yellow Ribbon 49. Cheyenne Autumn 64, many others.

O'Brien, John (1960–1994).
American author whose autobiographical novel of alcoholism, *Leaving Las Vegas*, was filmed in 1995.

O'Brien, Liam (1913–1996).
American screenwriter and playwright, the brother of Edmond O'Brien. He was also a television producer and writer, on such series as *Police Story* and *Miami Vice*.
Chain Lightning (co-w) 50. Here Comes the Groom (co-w) (AAN) 51. Diplomatic Courier (co-w) 52. Young at Heart (co-w) 54. Trapeze (co-w) 56. The Remarkable Mr Pennypacker (oa) 58. The Great Imposter (w) 61. The Devil at 4 o'Clock (co-w) 61, etc.

O'Brien, Margaret (1937–) (Angela Maxine O'Brien).
Stunningly talented American child actress of the 40s; won special Academy Award in 1944. Had no luck with adult comeback.
■ Babes on Broadway 41. *Journey for Margaret* 42. Dr Gillespie's Criminal Case 43. Thousands Cheer 43. *Lost Angel* 43. Madame Curie 43. Jane Eyre 43. The Canterville Ghost 44. *Meet Me in St Louis* 44. Music for Millions 45. *Our Vines Have Tender Grapes* 45. Bad Bascomb 46. Three Wise Fools 46. The Unfinished Dance 47. Tenth Avenue Angel 47. Big City 48. *Little Women* 49. The Secret Garden 49. Her First Romance 51. Glory 56. Heller in Pink Tights 60. Split Second to an Epitaph (TV) 68. Testimony of Two Men (TV) 77. Amy 81.
✪ For being so talented up to the age of ten. *Lost Angel*.

❝ When I cry, do you want the tears to run all the way or shall I stop halfway down? – M.O'B., *aged six*
If that child had been born in the middle ages, she'd have been burned as a witch. – *Lionel Barrymore, 1943*

O'Brien, Pat (1899–1983).
Easy-going, gentle but tough-looking Irish-American character actor, a popular star of the 30s.
Autobiography: 1964, *The Wind at My Back*.
The Front Page 31. Honour among Lovers 31. Final Edition 32. Hell's House 32. American Madness 32. Air Mail 32. Bureau of Missing Persons 33. Bombshell 33. Gambling Lady 34. Here Comes the Navy 34. I Sell Anything 34. Devil Dogs of the Air 35. Oil for the Lamps of China 35. Page Miss Glory 35. The Irish in Us 35. Ceiling Zero 35. Public Enemy's Wife 36. China Clipper 36. The Great O'Malley 37. Slim 37. San Quentin 37. *Boy Meets Girl* 38. *Angels with Dirty Faces* 38. Indianapolis Speedway 39. The Fighting 69th 40. Slightly Honorable 40. Castle on the Hudson 40. Torrid Zone 40. Knute Rockne, All American 41. Submarine Zone 41. Broadway 42. The Navy Comes Through 42. Bombardier 43. The Iron Major 43. His Butler's Sister 43. Secret Command 44. Having Wonderful Crime 45. Man Alive 45. Perilous Holiday 46. Riffraff 47. Fighting Father Dunne 48. The Boy with Green Hair 48. A Dangerous Profession 49. Johnny One Eye 50. The People against O'Hara 51. Okinawa 52. Jubilee Trail 54. Inside Detroit 55. Kill Me Tomorrow (GB) 57. The Last Hurrah 58. Some Like It Hot 59. Town Tamer 65. The Phynx 69. The Over the Hill Gang (TV) 69. Welcome Home Johnny Bristol (TV) 72. The Adventures of Nick Carter (TV) 72. Joyride to Nowhere (TV) 73. Kiss Me Kill Me (TV) 76. The End 78. Ragtime 81. Scout's Honor (TV) 81, etc.
TV series: Harrigan and Son 60.

O'Brien, Richard (1942–).
Lanky British stage actor, musician, dramatist and screenwriter, the creator of the cult stage hit *The Rocky Horror Show*, which also became a cult film. Recently he has worked in TV as host of a game show, *The Crystal Maze* 91–94.
Carry On Cowboy 65. The Fighting Prince of Donegal 66. The Odd Job Man. The Rocky Horror Picture Show (a, co-w, m) 76. Flash Gordon 80. Shock Treatment (co-w) 81. Revolution 85. The Wolves of Willoughby Chase 89. Spice World: The Movie 97. Dark City 97. Ever After 98, etc.

O'Brien, Virginia (1921–).
American comedienne, the 'dead pan' singer of the 40s.
Hullaballoo 40. *The Big Store* 41. Ship Ahoy 42. Thousands Cheer 43. Dubarry Was a Lady 44. The Harvey Girls 45. Till the Clouds Roll By 46. Merton of the Movies 47. Francis in the Navy 55. Gus 76, etc.

O'Brien, Willis (1886–1962).
American specialist in the creation of monster animals for use in stop-motion techniques.
The Ghost of Slumber Mountain 20. *The Lost World* 24. *King Kong* 33. Son of Kong 33. Mighty Joe Young 49. The Animal World 56. The Black Scorpion 58, etc.

O'Brien-Moore, Erin (1902–1979).
American stage actress who made a few films.
The Life of Emile Zola 38. Little Men 39. Destination Moon 50. Phantom of the Rue Morgue 53, etc.

Obst, Lynda (1950–).
American producer.
Autobiography: 1996, *Hello, He Lied.*
Flashdance 83. Adventures in Babysitting 87. Heartbreak Hotel 88. The Fisher King 91. This Is My Life 91. Sleepless in Seattle 93. One Fine Day 96. Contact 97. Hope Floats 98. The Siege 98, etc.
❝ What hooked me, and I discovered this during the success of *Flashdance*, was having an influence on pop culture. A year after *Flashdance* came out, all over the country there were girls in torn sweatshirts following their dreams. – L.O.

O'Casey, Sean (1880–1964).
Irish playwright, much preoccupied by 'the troubles'. Works filmed include *Juno and the Paycock* and *The Plough and the Stars;* an alleged biopic, *Young Cassidy*, was made in 1964 with Rod Taylor.

O'Connell, Arthur (1908–1981).
American character actor with long Broadway experience; usually mildly bewildered roles.
Law of the Jungle 42. Countess of Monte Cristo 49. The Whistle at Eaton Falls 51. *Picnic* (AAN) 55. The Solid Gold Cadillac 56. *The Man in the Grey Flannel Suit* 56. Bus Stop 56. Operation Mad Ball 57. Operation Petticoat 59. Anatomy of a Murder (AAN) 59. Follow That Dream 61. Kissin' Cousins 64. The Monkey's Uncle 65. Your Cheating Heart 65. The Great Race 65. The Silencers 66. Fantastic Voyage 66. The Power 68. There Was a Crooked Man 70. Ben 72. The Poseidon Adventure 72. Huckleberry Finn 74. The Hiding Place 75, etc.
TV series: The Second Hundred Years 67.

O'Connell, Jerry (1974–).
American actor who began as a child.
Stand by Me 86. Ollie Hopnoodle's Haven of Bliss (TV) 88. My Secret Identity 88. Calendar Girl 93. Joe's Apartment 96. Jerry Maguire 96. Scream 2 97. Can't Hardly Wait 98, etc.
TV series: Sliders 95.

O'Connolly, Jim (1926–1987).
British director.
The Traitors (wp only) 62. Smokescreen (wd) 64. *The Little Ones* 64. Berserk 67. The Valley of Gwangi 68. Crooks and Coronets 69. Horror on Snape Island/Beyond the Fog 72. Mistress Pamela 74, etc.

O'Connor, Carroll (1922–).
Burly American character actor, often in blustery military roles.
By Love Possessed 61. Lonely are the Brave 62. Cleopatra 63. In Harm's Way 65. What Did You Do in the War, Daddy? 65. Waterhole Three 67. Point Blank 67. The Devil's Brigade 68. Marlowe 69. Doctors' Wives 70. Law and Disorder 74. Gideon's Webb 98, etc.
TV series: Rifleman 58. *All in the Family* (as Archie Bunker) 71–78. Archie Bunker's Place 79–82. In the Heat of the Night 88–90. Party of Five 96.

O'Connor, Derrick.
English character actor, now based in America.
Jabberwocky 77. Hope and Glory 87. Lethal Weapon 2 89. Dealers 89. A Question of Guilt (TV) 93. Stark (TV) 93. Soul Survivors (TV) 95. How to Make an American Quilt 95. Deep Rising 98, etc.

O'Connor, Donald (1925–).
Snappy American light comedian, singer and dancer, a teenage star of the 40s whose film career suffered with the decline of musicals.
■ *Sing You Sinners* 38. Sons of the Legion 38. Men With Wings 38. *Tom Sawyer Detective* 38. Unmarried 39. Death of a Champion 39. Boy Trouble 39. Million Dollar Legs 39. Night Work 39. On Your Toes 39. Beau Geste 39. Private Buckaroo 42. Give Out Sisters 42. Get Hep to Love 42. When Johnny Comes Marching Home 42. Strictly in the Groove 43. It Comes Up Big 43. *Mister Big* 43. Top Man 43. *Chip off the Old Block* 44. This is the Life 44. Follow the Boys 44. The Merry Monahans 44. Bowery to Broadway 44. *Patrick the Great* 45. Something in the Wind 47. Are You With It? 48. Feudin' Fussin' and a-Fightin' 48. Yes Sir That's My Baby 49. *Francis* 49. Curtain Call at Cactus Creek 50. The Milkman 50. Double Crossbones 50. Francis Goes to the Races 51. *Singin' In the Rain* 52. Francis Goes to West Point 52. *Call Me Madam* 53. I Love Melvin 53. Francis Covers Big Town 53. Walking My Baby Back Home 53. Francis Joins the WACS 54. There's No Business Like Show Business 54. Francis in the Navy 55. Anything Goes 56. *The Buster Keaton Story* 57. Cry for Happy 61. The Wonders of Aladdin 61. That Funny Feeling 65. That's Entertainment (co-narrator) 74. Ragtime 81. Pandemonium 82. A Time to Remember 90. Toys 92.
TV series: The Donald O'Connor Texaco Show 54–55.
✪ For his teenage high spirits and talent. *Patrick the Great.*

O'Connor, Glynnis (1956–).
Diminutive American leading lady of the 70s.
Jeremy 75. Ode to Billy Joe 76. California Dreaming 78. Those Lips Those Eyes 80. Night Crossing 82. Johnny Dangerously 84. Why Me? 84. Too Good to Be True (TV) 88. Past the Bleachers (TV) 95. Ellen Foster (TV) 97, etc.

O'Connor, Hazel (1955–).
English actress, singer and songwriter, of whom much was expected after *Breaking Glass.*
Girls Come First 75. Double Exposure 77. Breaking Glass (& s) 80, etc.

O'Connor, Kevin J. (1964–).
American actor.
Bogie (TV) 80. Let's Scare Jessica to Death 81. Peggy Sue Got Married 86. Candy Mountain 87. Waiting for the Moon 87. The Moderns 88. The Caine Mutiny Court-Martial (TV) 88. Signs of Life 89. Steel Magnolias 89. Love at Large 90. Hero/Accidental Hero 92. Color of Night 94. Lord of Illusions 95. Virtuosity 95. Deep Rising 98, etc.

O'Connor, Pat (1943–).
He studied film at UCLA and Ryerson Institute in Toronto and first worked in Irish television as a documentary producer and director. Married actress Mary Elizabeth MASTRANTONIO.
A Ballroom of Romance (TV) 81. Cal 84. A Month in the Country 87. The January Man 88. Stars and Bars 88. Fools of Fortune 90. Zelda (TV) 93. *Circle of Friends* 95. Inventing the Abbots 97. Dancing at Lughnasa 98, etc.

O'Connor, Robert Emmett (1885–1962).
American small-part player, often as snoop or policeman, on screen from 1909 after circus and vaudeville experience.
Public Enemy 31. A Night at the Opera 35. Tight Shoes 41. Whistling in Brooklyn 44. Boys' Ranch 46, many others.

O'Connor, Sinead (1966–).
Irish singer, composer and occasional actress. Born in Dublin.
Hush-a-Bye Baby (m) 89. O Mary This London (s) 94. The Butcher Boy (as the Virgin Mary) 98, etc.
❝ Sinead has the sex appeal of a venetian blind – *Madonna*

O'Connor, Tim (1925–).
Lean American character actor who became known as the long-lost husband in TV's *Peyton Place*.
Incident in San Francisco 70. Across 110th Street 72. Manhunter (TV) 74. Murder in Peyton Place (TV) 77. Buck Rogers in the 25th Century 79. The Golden Gate Murders (TV) 79. Naked Gun 2½: The Smell of Fear 91, etc.
TV series: Peyton Place 65–68. Wheels 78. Buck Rogers in the 25th Century 79–80.

O'Connor, Una (1880–1959).
Sharp-featured Irish character actress with stage experience before film debut in 1929; in Hollywood from 1932.
■ Dark Red Roses 29. To Oblige a Lady 30. Timbuctoo 30. Murder 30. *Cavalcade* 33. Pleasure Cruise 33. *The Invisible Man* 33. Mary Stevens MD 33. The Poor Rich 34. The Barretts of Wimpole Street 34. Orient Express 34. All Men Are Enemies 34. Stingaree 34. Chained 34. David Copperfield 35. *The Informer* 35. Father Brown Detective 35. *The Bride of Frankenstein* 35. Thunder in the Night 35. The Perfect Gentleman 35. Rose Marie 36. Little Lord Fauntleroy 36. Lloyds of London 36. Suzy 36. The Plough and the Stars 36. Call It a Day 37. Personal Property 37. The Return of the Frog 37. *The Adventures of Robin Hood* 38. We Are Not Alone 39. The Sea Hawk 40. Lillian Russell 40. He Stayed for Breakfast 40. It All Came True 40. All Women Have Secrets 40. Kisses for Breakfast 41. How Green Was My Valley 41. The Strawberry Blonde 41. Her First Beau 41. Three Girls about Town 41. Always in My Heart 42. My Favorite Spy 42. Random Harvest 42. This Land Is Mine 43. Forever and a Day 43. Holy Matrimony 43. Government Girl 43. My Pal Wolf 44. The Canterville Ghost 44. The Bells of St Mary's 45. Christmas in Connecticut 45. The Return of Monte Cristo 46. Banjo 46. Child of Divorce 46. Cluny Brown 46. Of Human Bondage 46. Unexpected Guest 46. Lost Honeymoon 47. The Corpse Came COD 47. Ivy 47. Fighting Father Dunne 48. The Adventures of Don Juan 48. *Witness for the Prosecution* 57.

O'Conor, Hugh (1975–).
Irish actor, on screen from childhood.
Lamb 86. Da 88. My Left Foot (as the young Christy Brown) 89. The Three Musketeers 93. *The Young Poisoner's Handbook* 95, etc.

O'Conor, Joseph (1916–).
British character actor, mainly on stage and TV.
Crooks in Cloisters 63. Oliver! 68. Doomwatch 72. The Black Windmill 74. Forbidden Quest 93, etc.
TV series: The Forsyte Saga (as Old Jolyon) 68.

O'Day, Anita (1919–).
Stylish American jazz singer and occasional actress who made her name singing with the Gene Krupa and Stan Kenton bands in the 40s.
Autobiography: 1981, *High Times Hard Times.*
The Gene Krupa Story (as herself) 59. Jazz on a Summer's Day (doc) 60. Zigzag/False Witness 70. The Outfit 74, etc.

O'Dea, Denis (1905–1978).
Irish stage actor who was in occasional films.
The Informer 35. The Plough and the Stars 47. Odd Man Out 47. The Fallen Idol 48. Under Capricorn 49. Treasure Island 50. Niagara 52. Mogambo 53. The Rising of the Moon 57. The Story of Esther Costello 58, etc.

O'Dea, Jimmy (1899–1965).
Irish character comedian.
■ Casey's Millions 22. Jimmy Boy 35. Blarney 38. Penny Paradise 38. Cheer Boys Cheer 39. Let's Be Famous 39. The Rising of the Moon 57. Darby O'Gill and the Little People 59. Johnny Nobody 61.

Odets, Clifford (1906–1963).
American playwright and occasional screenwriter, a former actor; associated with the left-wing Group Theatre, which established itself as an important force in the 30s through his plays *Waiting for Lefty* and *Awake and Sing!* Married actress Luise Rainer (1937–40). His lovers included actresses Frances Farmer and Fay Wray. He made intermittent visits to Hollywood to earn money and spent the last eight years of his life working there. Died of cancer.
Autobiography: 1988, *The Time Is Ripe: The 1940 Journals of Clifford Odets.*
Biography: 1982, *Clifford Odets – American Playwright* by Margaret Brenman-Gibson.
The General Died at Dawn (w) 36. *Golden Boy* (oa) 39. None But the Lonely Heart (wd) 44. Deadline at Dawn (w) 46. Humoresque (w) 46. Clash by Night (oa) 52. The Country Girl (oa) 54. *The Big Knife* (oa) 55. *Sweet Smell of Success* (w) 57. The Story on Page One (wd) 60, etc.
❝ Hollywood, like Midas, kills whatever it touches. – C.O.

Odette, Mary (1901–) (Odette Goimbault).
French actress in many British silent films from 1915, at first as juvenile.
Cynthia in the Wilderness 15. Dombey and Son 17. The Lady Clare 19. Torn Sails 20. Cherry Ripe 21. The Crimson Circle 22. Eugene Aram 24. She 25. If Youth But Knew 26. Emerald of the East 28, etc.

O'Donnell, Cathy (1923–1970) (Ann Steely).
American leading lady with brief stage experience.
■ *The Best Years of Our Lives* (debut) 46. Bury Me Dead 47. The Spiritualist 47. *They Live by Night* 48. Side Street 50. The Miniver Story 50. Detective Story 51. The Woman's Angle (GB) 52. Never Trust a Gambler 53. Eight O'Clock Walk (GB) 54. The Face that Launched a Thousand Ships 54. Mad at the World 55. The Man from Laramie 55. The Story of Mankind 58. Ben Hur 59. Terror in the Haunted House 59.

O'Donnell, Chris (1970–).
Clean-cut young American actor. Born in Chicago, he began in his early teens as a model. He has his own production company, George Street Pictures. Married teacher Caroline Fentress in 1998. His asking price: around $3m a movie.
Men Don't Leave 90. Fried Green Tomatoes 92. School Ties 92. Scent of a Woman 93. Blue Sky (made 91) 94. Circle of Friends 94. The Three Musketeers 94. Mad Love 95. Batman Forever (as Robin) 95. The Chamber 97. In Love and War 97. Batman and Robin 97, etc.

O'Donnell, Rosie (1961–).
American actress, a former stand-up comedian. She hosted a much-praised syndicated TV talk show in 1996.
A League of Their Own 92. Another Stakeout 93. Sleepless in Seattle 93. Car 54, Where Are You? 94. The Flintstones 94. Exit to Eden 94. Now and Then 95. Beautiful Girls 96. Harriet the Spy 96. A Very Brady Sequel 96. The Twilight of the Golds (TV) 97. Wide Awake 97, etc.
TV series: Gimme a Break 86–87.

O'Donnell, Walter 'Spec' (1911–1986).
Gawky American character actor, in silents from his teens, when he was a frequent foil for comedian Max DAVIDSON in his two-reelers of the 20s.
Main Street 23. Little Annie Rooney 25. The Devil's Cargo 25. Sparrows 26. Danger Street 28. The Sophomore 29. The Grand Parade 30. Young America 32. Circumstantial Evidence 35. Change of Heart 38. Gallant Lady 42. Wolf in Thief's Clothing 43, etc.
❝ To call Spec 'homely' would imply that your home was in grave need of repair. – *John Holmstrom*

O'Donovan, Fred (1889–1952).
Irish actor and director, associated with the early days of the ABBEY THEATRE.
The Food of Love 16. The Eleventh Hour (& d) 18. Willy Reilly and His Colleen (& d) 18. General John Regan 33. The House of the Spaniard 36. Ourselves Alone 36. The Vicar of Bray 37. Another Shore 48, etc.

O'Driscoll, Martha (1922–1998).
American leading lady of the 40s, mainly in second features. Born in Tulsa, Oklahoma, she was performing from the age of three and on stage at 10. She lied about her age to begin her film career at 13. Retired on her second marriage to a Chicago businessman in 1947.
The Secret of Dr Kildare 40. The Lady Eve 41. My Heart Belongs to Daddy 42. Follow the Boys 44. Ghost Catchers 44. House of Dracula 45. Carnegie Hall 47, etc.

Oedekerk, Steve.
American actor and director.
Casual Sex? (a) 88. Ace Ventura: When Nature Calls (d) 95. Nothing to Lose (wd) 97. Patch Adams (w) 98, etc.

O'Farrell, Bernadette (1926–).
British leading lady who married her director, Frank Launder.
Captain Boycott 48. The Happiest Days of Your Life 49. Lady Godiva Rides Again 51. The Story of Gilbert and Sullivan 53, etc.
TV series: Robin Hood 55–59.

O'Ferrall, George More:
see MORE O'FERRALL, George.

O'Flaherty, Liam (1896–1984).
Irish novelist whose *The Informer* was filmed twice under its own title and once as *Up Tight*.

Ogata, Ken (1937–)
Japanese leading actor, born in Tokyo.
The Sex-Check/Sekkusu Chekku-Daini No Sei 68. Farewell My Beloved/Wakare 69. Vengeance Is Mine/Fukushu Suruwa Ware Ni Ari 78. Virus/Fukkatsu No Hi 79. Eja Naika 81. The Ballad of Narayama 83. Yokiro 83. Mishima: A Life in Four Chapters (US) 85. The Pimp/Zegen 87. Shaso 89. Zato Ichi 89. Kodayu 91. The Pillow Book (Hol.) 95, etc.

Ogier, Bulle (1939–).
French leading actress, most often seen in the films of Jacques Rivette.
L'Amour Fou 68. La Salamandre 71. Rendez-vous à Bray 71. The Valley 72. The Discreet Charm of the Bourgeoisie 72. Celine and Julie Go Boating 73. Mistress/Maîtresse 75. Entire Days in the Trees 76. Duelle 76. The Third Generation 79. Navire Night 79. Le Pont du Nord (& w) 81. Aspern 81. The Cheaters/Les Tricheurs 83. Unknown Country 87. The Band of Four/La Bande des Quatre 89. North/Nord 91. Personne ne M'Aime 94. Regarde les Hommes Tomber 94. Fado, Major and Minor 95. The Carole Track 95. Irma Vep 96. Stolen Life/Voleur de Vie 98. Shattered Image (US) 98, many others.

Ogilvie, George (1931–).
English director, a former actor and drama teacher, in Australia.
Bodyline (TV) 83. Mad Max Beyond Thunderdrome (co-d) 85. Short Changed 86. The Shiralee (TV) 88. The Crossing 90. The Last of the Ryans (TV) 97, etc.

Ogilvy, Ian (1943–).
Slightly-built British leading man.
Stranger in the House 67. The Sorcerers 67. Witchfinder General 68. Wuthering Heights 70. And Now the Screaming Starts 72. No Sex Please We're British 73. Menace Unseen (TV) 88. Death Becomes Her 92. Puppet Master 5: The Final Chapter 94. The Disappearance of Kevin Johnson 95, etc.
TV series: *Return of the Saint* 78.

Ogle, Charles (1865–1940).
American silent actor, best known for being the first (in 1909) to play the Frankenstein monster.
The Honour of His Family 09. The Ironmaster 14. Joan the Woman 17. Treasure Island 20. The Covered Wagon 23. The Alaskan 24. Contraband 25. The Flaming Forest 26, many others.

O'Hagan, Colo Tavernier.
British screenwriter working in France; formerly married to director Bertrand Tavernier.
Une Semaine de Vacances (co-w) 82. Beatrice/La Passion Béatrice 87. Summer Interlude/Comédie d'Eté (co-w) 89. Story of Women (co-w) 89. These Foolish Things/Daddy Nostalgie 90. Le Petit Garçon 95. Fresh Bait/L'Appat 95, etc.

O'Hanlon, George (1912–1989) (George Rice).
American comedy actor with stage experience; played Joe McDoakes in the one-reeler *Behind the Eight Ball* series.
The Great Awakening 41. The Hucksters 47. The Tanks Are Coming 51. Battle Stations 55. Bop Girl 57. The Rookie 59. Charley and the Angel 73. Rocky 76, etc.
TV series: The Life of Riley. The Reporter. Nancy Drew.

O'Hara, Catherine (1954–).
Canadian actress and comedy writer.
Nothing Personal 80. The Last Polka (TV) 84. After Hours 85. Double Negative 86. Heartburn 86. Beetlejuice 88. Batman 89. Dick Tracy 90. Home Alone 90. Little Vegas 90. Betsy's Wedding 90. There Goes the Neighborhood/Paydirt 92. Home Alone 2: Lost in New York 92. Wyatt Earp 94. The Paper 94. A Simple Twist of Fate 94. Tall Tale: The Unbelievable Adventures of Pecos Bill 94. Waiting for Guffman 96. Last of the High Kings/Summer Fling 96. Hope (TV) 97. Home Fries 98, etc.
TV series: Second City TV 77–80. SCTV Network 90 81–82.

O'Hara, Gerry (1921–).
British director.
That Kind of Girl 61. The Pleasure Girls 64. Maroc 7 67. Amsterdam Affair 68. All the Right Noises (& w) 69. The Brute 76. The Bitch 79. Fanny Hill 83. The Mummy Lives 93, etc.

O'Hara, John (1905–1970).
American best-selling novelist who wrote chiefly about sex in suburbia. Works filmed include *Pal Joey, From the Terrace, A Rage to Live, Butterfield 8*. Also co-wrote screenplays. In 1976 a TV series was based on his *Gibbsville* stories.
I was an Adventuress 40. Moontide 42. Strange Journey 46. On Our Merry Way 48. The Best Things in Life are Free 56, etc.
❝ He lives in a perpetual state of just having discovered that it's a lousy world. – *F. Scott Fitzgerald*

O'Hara, Mary (1885–1980) (Mary Alsop).
American novelist best known for *My Friend Flicka*, which was filmed in 1943; sequels followed.

O'Hara, Maureen (1920–) (Maureen Fitzsimmons).
Striking red-haired Irish leading lady who survived in Hollywood less through acting talent than through pleasing, unassuming personality.
■ My Irish Molly 38. Kicking the Moon Around 38. Jamaica Inn 39. *The Hunchback of Notre Dame* 39. A Bill of Divorcement 40. Dance Girl Dance 40. They Met in Argentina 41. *How Green Was My Valley* 41. To the Shores of Tripoli 42. Ten Gentlemen from West Point 42. *The Black Swan* 42. The Immortal Sergeant 43. This Land is Mine 43. The Fallen Sparrow 43. Buffalo Bill 44. The Spanish Main 45. Sentimental Journey 46. Do You Love Me? 46. Sinbad the Sailor 47. The Homestretch 47. Miracle on 34th Street 47. The Foxes of Harrow 47. Sitting Pretty 48. Britannia Mews 49. A Woman's Secret 49. Father was a Fullback 49. Baghdad 49. Comanche Territory 50. Tripoli 50. Rio Grande 50. Flame of Araby 51. At Sword's Point 52. Kangaroo 52. *The Quiet Man* 52. Against All Flags 52. Redhead from Wyoming 52. War Arrow 53. Fire over Africa 54. The Long Gray Line 55. The Magnificent Matador 55. Lady Godiva 55. Lisbon 56. Everything But the Truth 56. The Wings of Eagles 57. Our Man in Havana 59. The Parent Trap 61. The Deadly Companions 61. Mr Hobbs Takes a Vacation 62. Spencer's Mountain 63. McLintock 63. The Battle of the Villa Fiorita 65. The Rare Breed 66. How Do I Love Thee? 70. Big Jake 71. The Red Pony (TV) 72. Only the Lonely 91. The Christmas Box (TV) 95.
❝ She looks as though butter wouldn't melt in her mouth – or anywhere else. – *Elsa Lanchester*
Framed in Technicolor, Miss O'Hara somehow seems more significant than a setting sun. – *New York Times, 1954*

O'Herlihy, Dan (1919–).
Irish character actor and occasional off-beat leading man, with Abbey Theatre and radio experience.
Odd Man Out (GB) 46. Hungry Hill (GB) 46. Kidnapped 48. Macbeth 48. Actors and Sin 50. Rommel, Desert Fox 51. The Blue Veil 51. The Highwayman 52. *The Adventures of Robinson Crusoe* (AAN) 52. Bengal Brigade 53. The Black Shield of Falworth 54. The Purple Mask 55. The Virgin Queen 55. That Woman Opposite (GB) 57. Home before Dark 58. Imitation of Life 59. *The Cabinet of Caligari* 62. Fail Safe 64. 100 Rifles 69. Waterloo 69. The Carey Treatment 72. QB VII (TV) 73. The Tamarind Seed 74. MacArthur 77. T. R. Sloane (TV) 79. Halloween III 82. The Last Starfighter 84. The Whoopee Boys 86. The Dead 87. Robocop 87. Robocop 2 90. Love, Cheat and Steal 94, etc.
TV series: The Travels of Jaimie McPheeters 63. The Long Hot Summer 66. A Man Called Sloane 79.

O'Herlihy, Michael (1928–1997).
Irish director in Hollywood, the brother of actor Dan O'Herlihy. Born in Dublin, he worked as a stage designer before emigrating to the US in the mid-50s to work first as a television director, on such series as *Maverick* and, especially, *Hawaii Five-O*.
The Fighting Prince of Donegal 66. The One and Only Genuine Original Family Band 68. Smith! 69. The Flame Is Love (TV) 79. Cry of the Innocent (TV) 80. I Married Wyatt Earp (TV) 83. Hoover vs the Kennedys: The Second Civil War (TV) 87, etc.

Ohmart, Carol (1928–).
American leading lady with stage experience, whose career in films did not develop.
The Scarlet Hour (debut) 55. The House on Haunted Hill 58. Born Reckless 59. The Scavengers 60. Wild Youth 60. One Man's Way 64. Caxambu 67. The Spectre of Edgar Allan Poe 72, etc.

Okada, Eiji (1920–1995).
Japanese leading actor, a former salesman and miner, in international films from the late 50s.
Until the Day We Meet Again 50. Mother 52. *Hiroshima Mon Amour* (Fr.) 59. The Ugly American (US) 63. *Woman of the Dunes* 64. The X from Outer Space 67. Alaska Monogatari 77. Dirty Hero 83. The Death of a Tea Master 89, etc.

Okamoto, Kihachi (1924–).
Japanese director and screenwriter of fast-moving action films, noted for his samurai movies. He studied at Meiji University, Tokyo, and joined Toho Studios in the mid-40s, working there for 15 years in various capacities, including as an assistant director to Mikio Naruse, before becoming a director.
Scarface 59. Independent Hooligans 59. The University Scamps 60. Warring Clans/Sengoku Yaro 63. Samurai Assassin/Samurai 65. Age of Assassins/Satsujinkyo Jidai 66. Sword of Doom/Daibosatsu Toge 66. Japan's Longest Day 67. Kill!/Kiru 68. Human Bullet/Nikudan 68. Red Lion/Akage 69. Zatoichi Meets Yojimbo 70, etc.

O'Keefe, Dennis (1908–1968) (Edward 'Bud' Flanagan).
Cheerful American leading man of the 40s; began as an extra after vaudeville experience with his parents.
Bad Man of Brimstone 38. That's Right, You're Wrong 39. La Conga Nights 40. You'll Find Out 40. Lady Scarface 41. *Topper Returns* 41. Broadway Limited 41. The Affairs of Jimmy Valentine 42. Good Morning Judge 42. The Leopard Man 43. The Fighting Seabees 43. Up in Mabel's Room 44. Abroad with Two Yanks 44. *The Affairs of Susan* 45. Brewster's Millions 45. Come Back to Me 46. Dishonoured Lady 47. T-Men 47. Mr District Attorney 47. Raw Deal 48. Walk a Crooked Mile 49. Woman on the Run 50. The Company She Keeps 51. Follow the Sun 52. The Fake (GB) 53. The Diamond Wizard (GB) (& d) 54. Angela (& d) 55. Inside Detroit 56. Dragoon Wells Massacre 57. Graft and Corruption 58. All Hands on Deck 61, many others.
TV series: The Dennis O'Keefe Show 59.

O'Keefe, Michael (1955–).
American actor.
Gray Lady Down 78. Dark Secret of Harvest Home (TV) 78. Rumor of War 80. Caddyshack 80. The Great Santini (AAN) 80. Split Image 82. Nate and Hayes 83. Finders Keepers 84. The Slugger's Wife 85. The Whoopee Boys 86. Ironweed 87. Hitchhiker II 87. Nina Takes a Lover 94. Three Wishes 95. Ghosts of Mississippi 96, etc.

O'Keeffe, Miles (1954–).
Muscular American star of sword-and-sorcery movies who played Tarzan once.
Tarzan the Ape Man 81. Ator: The Fighting Eagle 83. The Blade Master 84. S.A.S. San Salvador 84. Sword of the Valiant 84. Lone Runner 86. Campus Man 87. Iron Warrior 87. Waxwork 88. The Drifter 88. Liberty & Bash 90. Acting on Impulse 93. Silent Hunter 94. Pocahontas: The Legend 95. Marked Man 96. True Vengeance 97. Dead Tides 97, etc.

Okey, Jack (c. 1890–1963).
American art director, with Warner Brothers' First National in the 20s and 30s, and then RKO in the 40s and 50s. In 1934, he came to Britain to design Denham Studios for Sir Alexander Korda and also worked on two of Korda's films, including *The Jungle Book*.
Torment 24. Broadway Babies 29. Sally (AAN) 30. The Dawn Patrol 30. I Am a Fugitive from a Chain Gang 32. 42nd Street 33. Lydia 41. The Jungle Book 42. Experiment Perilous (AAN) 44. The Spiral Staircase 46. It's a Wonderful Life 47. Blackbeard the Pirate 51. Bengazi 55. Run of the Arrow 57, etc.

Oland, Warner (1880–1938).
Swedish character actor in Hollywood who oddly enough became the screen's most popular Chinese detective.
The Yellow Ticket 18. Witness for the Defense 19. His Children's Children 23. Don Q Son of Zorro 25. Don Juan 26. The Jazz Singer 27. Old San Francisco 27. Chinatown Nights 29. The Mysterious Dr Fu Manchu 29. The Vagabond King 30. *Charlie Chan Carries On* 31 (and 15 other episodes in this series). Shanghai Express 32. The Painted Veil 34. *Werewolf of London* 35. Shanghai 35, many others.

Olcott, Sidney (1873–1949) (John S. Alcott).
Irish-Canadian director, in Hollywood from the beginning.
Ben Hur (one reel) 07. Florida Crackers 08. Judgement 09. The Miser's Child 10. The O'Neil (Irish) 11. From the Manager to the Cross 12. Madame Butterfly 15. The Innocent Lie 17. Scratch My Back 20. Little Old New York 21. The Humming Bird 23. The Green Goddess 23. Monsieur Beaucaire 24. The Amateur Gentleman 26. The Claw 27, etc.

Oldfield, Barney (1878–1946) (Berna Eli Oldfield).
American racing driver, the first to travel a mile a minute; featured in *Barney Oldfield's Race for Life* 16.

Oldland, Lilian (1905–).
British leading lady of the silents, who later changed her name to Mary Newland. Born in Gloucester, she was on stage from the early 20s. She was the second wife of playwright and director Reginald Denham.
The Secret Kingdom 25. The Flag Lieutenant 26. Troublesome Wives 27. Jealousy 31. Ask Beccles 34. Death at Broadcasting House 34. The Silent Passenger 35. The Small Man 35. Ask Beccles 73, etc.

Oldman, Gary (1958–).
British actor of character leads. He was married to actress Uma Thurman (1990–92). His asking price: around $3m a movie.
Sid and Nancy 86. Prick Up Your Ears 87. Track 29 87. Criminal Law 88. We Think the World of You 88. Chattahoochee 89. Rosencrantz and Guildenstern Are Dead 90. State of Grace 90. JFK 91. Money 92. Bram Stoker's Dracula 92. Romeo Is Bleeding 93. True Romance 93. Leon/The Professional (Fr.) 94. Murder in the First 94. Immortal Beloved 94. The Scarlet Letter 95. Basquiat 96. *Nil by Mouth* (wd only) 97. The Fifth Element 97. Air Force One 97. Lost in Space 98. Quest for Camelot (voice) 98, etc.
❝ To be able to do this job in the first place you've got to have a bit of an ego, whether you're in a movie or on stage and say, 'Look at me, I'm interesting.' That takes a lot of ego. – G.O.

Oliansky, Joel (1935–).
American screenwriter.
The Senator (TV) 71. Masada (TV) 80. The Competition (& d) 81. Bird 88.

Olin, Lena (1956–).
Swedish actress in international films. She began by working in the theatre with Ingmar Bergman's company.
Karleken 80. Fanny and Alexander 82. After the Rehearsal 84. Friends 87. The Unbearable Lightness of Being 88. Enemies, a Love Story (AAN) 89. S/Y Joy/S/Y Glädjen 89. Havana 90. Mr Jones 93. Romeo Is Bleeding 93. The Night and the Moment 94. Mr Jones 94. Night Falls on Manhattan 97. Hamilton 98. Polish Wedding 98, etc.

Oliver, Anthony (1923–1995).
Welsh general-purpose actor, in British films and TV.
Once a Jolly Swagman 48. The Clouded Yellow 50. The Runaway Bus 54. Lost 56. The Fourth Square 61, many others.

Oliver, Barrett (1973–).
American juvenile actor.
Frankenweenie 84. The Neverending Story 84. D.A.R.Y.L. 85. Cocoon 85. The Secret Garden (TV) 87. Cocoon: The Return 88. Scenes from the Class Struggle in Beverly Hills 89, etc.

Oliver, Edna May (1883–1942) (Edna May Cox-Oliver).
American character actress, usually of acidulous but often warm-hearted spinsters; on stage from 1912. She played schoolmistress-detective Hildegard Withers in three films in the early 30s.
Icebound 23. The American Venus 26. Saturday Night Kid 29. Half Shot at Sunrise 31. Cimarron 31. *Fanny Foley Herself* 31. Penguin Pool Murder 32. Little Women 33. Alice in Wonderland 33. *David Copperfield* (as Aunt Betsy) 34. A Tale of Two Cities 35. Romeo and Juliet (as the Nurse) 36. Parnell 37. Rosalie 38. Second Fiddle 38. The Story of Vernon and Irene Castle 39. Nurse Edith Cavell 39. Drums along the Mohawk (AAN) 39.

Pride and Prejudice (as Lady Catherine de Bourgh) 40. Lydia 41, etc.

Oliver, Harry (1888–1973).
American art director who worked at Universal from 1910 to 1914, going to Fox in the 20s and MGM in the 30s. Retired in the 40s to become a hermit, living in the desert.
Face of the World 21. *Sparrows* 26. 7th Heaven (AAN) 27. *Street Angel* (AAN) 28. The Gaucho 28. Liliom 30. Scarface 32. Viva Villa! 34. Mark of the Vampire 35. The Good Earth 37, etc.

Oliver, Susan (1937–1990).
American leading TV actress whose film roles were few.
Green-Eyed Blonde 57. The Gene Krupa Story 60. Looking for Love 64. The Disorderly Orderly 65. Your Cheating Heart 66. A Man Called Gannon 68. Change of Mind 69. Ginger in the Morning 75. Hardly Working 71, etc.
TV series: Peyton Place 66.

Oliver, Vic (1898–1964) (Victor Von Samek).
Austrian-born comedian, pianist, violinist and conductor, long in Britain. Occasional films.
Autobiography: 1954, Mr *Show Business*.
Rhythm in the Air 37. Room for Two 40. He Found a Star 41. Hi Gang 41. Give Us the Moon 44. I'll Be Your Sweetheart 45, etc.

Olivera, Hector (1931–).
Argentinian director.
Psexoanalisis 67. La Patagonia Rebelde 74. El Muerto 75. A Funny Dirty Little War/No Habrá Más Penas ni Olvido 84. Wizards of the Lost Kingdom 85. Barbarian Queen 85. Cocaine Wars 86. Night of the Pencils (& co-w) 87. Two to Tango 89. Cuentos de Borges I (co-d) 91. The Maria Soledad Case/El Caso Maria Soledad 93. A Shadow You Soon Will Be/Una Sombra Ya Pronto Serás (co-w, d) 94, etc.

Olivier, Laurence (1907–1989) (Lord Olivier).
Distinguished British stage actor whose film appearances were reasonably frequent. Honorary AA 1979 'for the full body of his work, for the unique achievements of his entire career and his lifetime of contribution to the art of film'.
Autobiography: 1982, *Confessions of an Actor*.
Biographies: 1969, *Cry God for Larry* by Virginia Fairweather. 1975, *Laurence Olivier* by John Cottrell. 1992, *Laurence Olivier: A Biography* by Donald Spoto. 1996, *The Real Life of Laurence Olivier* by Roger Lewis.
■ Too Many Crooks 30. The Temporary Widow 30. Potiphar's Wife 30. The Yellow Ticket 31. Friends and Lovers 31. Westward Passage 31. No Funny Business 32. Perfect Understanding (US) 32. Conquest of the Air 35. Moscow Nights 35. As You Like It (as Orlando) 36. Fire over England 36. *The Divorce of Lady X* 38. Twenty-One Days 39. Q Planes 39. *Wuthering Heights* (US) (AAN) 39. *Rebecca* (US) (AAN) 40. *Pride and Prejudice* (US) 40. *Lady Hamilton* (US) (as Nelson) 41. 49th Parallel 41. The Demi-Paradise 43. *Henry V* (& p, co-d) (special AA) 44. *Hamlet* (& pd) (AA, AANd) 48. The Magic Box (cameo role) 51. *Carrie* (US) 52. The Beggar's Opera (as Macheath) 52. *Richard III* (& pd) (AAN) 56. The Prince and the Showgirl (& d) 58. The Moon and Sixpence (TV) 59. *The Devil's Disciple* 59. Spartacus (US) 60. *The Entertainer* (AAN) 60. The Power and the Glory (TV) 61. Term of Trial 62. Uncle Vanya (& d) 63. Bunny Lake is Missing 65. Othello (AAN) 65. Khartoum 66. The Shoes of the Fisherman 68. Oh What a Lovely War 69. The Dance of Death 69. The Battle of Britain 69. David Copperfield 69. Three Sisters (& d) 70. Nicholas and Alexandra 71. Lady Caroline Lamb 72. *Sleuth* (AAN) 72. Love Among the Ruins (TV) 74. *Marathon Man* (AAN) 76. The Seven Per Cent Solution 76. Jesus of Nazareth (TV) 77. The Betsy 77. A Bridge Too Far 77. The Boys from Brazil (AAN) 78. A Little Romance 78. Dracula 79. Clash of the Titans 81. The Jazz Singer 81. Inchon 81. Brideshead Revisited (TV) 81. A Voyage Round My Father (TV) 82. Wagner 83. A Talent for Murder (TV) 83. Mr Halpern and Mr Johnson (TV) 83. The Last Days of Pompeii (TV) 84. The Bounty 84. The Jigsaw Man 84. Wild Geese II 85. Lost Empires (TV) 86.
✪ For being consistently the most fascinating actor of his time. *Richard III*.
❝ Nothing is beneath me if it pays well. I've earned the right to damn well grab whatever I can in the time I've got left. – *L.O.*
At heart Larry was what the French call a *cabotin*. The term is difficult to translate – not exactly a ham: a performer, a vulgarian, someone who lives and dies for acting. – *Tony Richardson*
A giant, a perfectionist, a man of fantastic loyalty and abiding courage, who worked himself to a standstill for the theatre and at almost negligible material gain to himself. – *Robert Stephens*
The thing about Larry was that he was jealous of everyone, whatever they did, if he felt they did whatever they did better than he could. This gnawing dissatisfaction made him terribly unhappy all his life. – *Robert Stephens*
Famous line (*Wuthering Heights*): 'I cannot live without my life; I cannot live without my soul.'

Olivio, Bob:
see ONDINE.

Olmi, Ermanno (1931–).
Italian director noted for gentle realism.
Il Posto/The Job 61. I Fidanzati 62. And There Came a Man 65. One Fine Day 69. Diary of Summer 71. The Circumstance 74. The Tree of Wooden Clogs 77. Cammina Cammina 83. Milano '83 83. The Legend of the Holy Drinker/La Leggenda del Santo Bevitore 88. Legend of the Old Wood 93. Genesis: The Creation and the Flood/Genesi: La Creazione e il Diluvio 94, etc.

Olmos, Edward James (1947–).
American character actor who began his career as a rock singer. Married actress Lorraine Bracco.
Aloha, Bobby and Rose 75. Wolfen 81. Cannery Row 82. Blade Runner 82. Ballad of Gregorio Cortez 82. Saving Grace 86. Stand and Deliver (AAN) 88. Triumph of the Spirit 89. Maria's Story 90. Talent for the Game 91. American Me (& d) 92. Roosters 93. A Million to Juan 94. Menendez: A Killing in Beverly Hills (TV) 94. The Burning Season (TV) 94. My Family/Mi Familia 95. Roosters 95. The Disappearance of Garcia Lorca 96. Caught 96. The Limbic Region (TV) 96. Twelve Angry Men (TV) 97. Selena 97. Hollywood Confidential (TV) 97. The Wonderful Ice Cream Suit 98, etc.
TV series: Miami Vice 84–89.

O'Loughlin, Gerald S. (1921–).
American TV actor, prominent in series *The Rookies* 72–76.
Twilight's Last Gleaming 76. Frances 82. Quicksilver 86. In the Arms of a Killer (TV) 91, etc.
TV series: Storefront Lawyers 70–71. Wheels 78. Automan 83–84. Our House 86–88.

Olsen, Moroni (1889–1954).
Heavily-built American character actor, with stage experience.
The Three Musketeers (as Porthos) 36. The Witness Chair 38. The Three Musketeers (as Bailiff) 39. Kentucky 39. The Glass Key 42. Call Northside 777 48. Father of the Bride 50. The Long, Long Trailer 54, many others.

Olsen, Ole (1892–1965) (John Sigurd Olsen).
Norwegian-American comedian, in vaudeville from 1914, almost always with partner Chic Johnson.
Gold Dust Gertie 31. Fifty Million Frenchmen 31. The Country Gentleman 37. *Hellzapoppin* 42. Crazy House 44. Ghost Catchers 44. See My Lawyer 45, etc.

Olson, James (1932–).
American general-purpose actor.
The Sharkfighters 56. The Strange One 57. Rachel Rachel 67. The Andromeda Strain 70. Moon Zero Two 70. Wild Rovers 71. The Groundstar Conspiracy 72. Ragtime 81. Amityville 2 82. Commando 85. Rachel River 87, etc.

Olson, Nancy (1928–).
American leading lady who came to films from college, retired after a few years and recently reappeared in more mature roles. Formerly married to Alan Jay Lerner.
Canadian Pacific 49. Union Station 50. *Sunset Boulevard* (AAN) 50. Submarine Command 51. Force of Arms 52. So Big 52. Battle Cry 55. Pollyanna 60. The Absent-Minded Professor 61. Son of Flubber 63. Smith! 69. Snowball Express 73. Making Love 82, etc.

O'Malley, J. Pat (1901–1985).
Irish character actor in Hollywood.
The Long Hot Summer 58. Blueprint for Robbery 60. The Cabinet of Caligari 62. A House is Not a Home 67. Gunn 67. Hello Dolly 69. Willard 71. Silkwood 83, etc.
TV series: Alarm 54. My Favorite Martian 63–64. Wendy and Me 64–65. The Rounders 66–67. A Touch of Grace 73. Maude 75–77.

O'Malley, John P. (1916–1959).
Australian character actor.
Kind Lady 51. Julius Caesar 52. Desert Rats 55. The Court Jester 56. The Invisible Boy 57.

O'Malley, Pat (1891–1966).
Irish-American character actor in Hollywood.
The Papered Door 11. Happiness 26. The Fall Guy 30. Frisco Jenny 33. Hollywood Boulevard 36. A Little Bit of Heaven 40. Lassie Come Home 43. The Rugged O'Riordans 49. Invasion of the Body Snatchers 56, etc.

O'Malley, Rex (1901–1976).
American light actor who was little heard from after a promising start.
Camille 36. *Midnight* 39. Zaza 39. The Thief 52, etc.

O'Mara, Kate (1939–).
British leading lady.
Great Catherine 68. The Limbo Line 68. The Desperados 69. Horror of Frankenstein 70. The Tamarind Seed 74. Feelings 75, etc.
TV series: Dynasty 85–87.

Ondine (1937–) (Bob Olivio).
A member of Andy Warhol's entourage in the 60s who appeared in several of his films, notably as the Pope of Greenwich Village in *The Chelsea Girls*, losing his temper on-camera, attacking a woman and admitting his homosexuality. His conversation, fuelled by amphetamines, is preserved in Warhol's novel *a*. He left Warhol at the end of the 60s to work as a postman.
Vinyl 65. The Chelsea Girls 66. **** 67. Imitation of Christ 67. The Loves of Ondine 67, etc.

Ondra, Anny (1903–1987) (A. Ondrakova).
German-Czech leading lady of British silent films; her accent killed her career when sound came. Returned to Europe and appeared in a few German films.
Chorus Girls 28. The Manxman 29. Blackmail 30. Glorious Youth 31. Schön Muss Mann Sein 50. Die Zuercher Verlorung 57, etc.

Ondricek, Miroslav (1933–).
Czech cinematographer, now in international films, who has worked often with director Milos Forman.
Talent Competition 62. If . . . 68. Slaughterhouse Five 71. Taking Off 71. O Lucky Man 73. Hair 79. Ragtime (AAN) 81. The World According to Garp 82. The Divine Emma 83. Silkwood 83. Amadeus (AAN) 84. Heaven Help Us 85. F/X 86. Big Shots 87. Funny Farm 88. Valmont 89. Awakenings 90. A League of Their Own 92. Let It Be Me 95. The Preacher's Wife 97, etc.

O'Neal, Frederick (1905–1992).
Powerful American character actor, mainly on stage.
Pinky 49. No Way Out 50. Something of Value 56. Anna Lucasta 58. Take a Giant Step 59. The Sins of Rachel Cade 61. Free, White and 21 62, etc.
TV series: Car 54 Where Are You? 61–62.

O'Neal, Patrick (1927–1994).
American general-purpose actor with stage and TV experience.
The Mad Magician 54. From the Terrace 60. The Cardinal 63. In Harm's Way 65. King Rat 65. A Fine Madness 66. Chamber of Horrors 66. Alvarez Kelly 66. *Assignment to Kill* 67. Where Were You When the Lights Went Out? 68. The Secret Life of an American Wife 68. Castle Keep 69. Stiletto 69. The Kremlin Letters 69. Corky 72. The Way We Were 73. Crossfire (TV) 75. The Stepford Wives 75. The Moneychangers (TV) 76. The Deadliest Season (TV) 77. The Last Hurrah (TV) 77. To Kill a Cop (TV) 78. Like Mom Like Me (TV) 78. Make Me an Offer 80. New York Stories 89. Q & A 90. Alice 90, etc.
TV series: Dick and the Duchess 57–58. Diagnosis Unknown 60. *Kaz* 78–79. Emerald Point N.A.S. 83–84.

O'Neal, Ron (1937–).
American leading man.
Superfly 72. Superfly TNT 73. The Master Gunfighter 75. When a Stranger Calls 79. The Final Countdown 80. St Helens 81. Red Dawn 84. As Summers Die 86. Hero and the Terror 88. Mercenary Fighters 88. Up against the Wall (& d) 91. Original Gangstas 96. Hyper Space 97, etc.

O'Neal, Ryan (1941–) (Patrick Ryan O'Neal).
Bland American leading man of the 60s and 70s. Born in Los Angeles, he began as a television stuntman, found popularity on the soap opera *Peyton Place*, and became a star with *Love Story*. After *Paper Moon*, for which his daughter Tatum won an Oscar, his career faltered and forgettable films followed, apart from his title role in *The Driver*, which took advantage of his impersonality. Married actresses Joanna Moore (1963–67), Leigh TAYLOR-YOUNG (1967–73), and Farrah FAWCETT.
■ This Rugged Land (TV) 62. The Games 68. The Big Bounce 69. *Love Story* (AAN) 70. Love Hate Love (TV) 70. Wild Rovers 71. *What's Up, Doc?* 72. The Thief Who Came to Dinner 73. *Paper Moon* 73. Barry Lyndon 75. Nickelodeon 76. A Bridge Too Far 77. The Driver 78. Oliver's Story 79. The Main Event 79. So Fine 81. Green Lee 81. Partners 82. Irreconcilable Differences 84. Fever Pitch 85. Tough Guys Don't Dance 87. Chances Are 89. Small Sacrifices (TV) 89. Faithful 96. Zero Effect 98.
TV series: Empire 62. *Peyton Place* 64–68. Good Sports 91.
❝ I'm as moody and complex and private as anyone I ever knew. – *R.O'N.*
The only time I ever had steady employment was in *Peyton Place*. Once I was in control of my own destiny I found it very difficult. – *R.O'N.*

O'Neal, Shaquille (1972–).
Lofty (7 feet 1 inch) American basketball star and occasional actor, who became the highest-paid athlete in the world in 1996, when he signed a $120m seven-year contract with the Los Angeles Lakers.
CB4 93. Blue Chips 94. Kazaam 96. Steel 97, etc.

O'Neal, Tatum (1963–).
Abrasive child actress of the 70s, daughter of Ryan O'NEAL. Formerly married to tennis champion John McEnroe (1986–94), by whom she had three children. Problems with drug abuse, for which she sought treatment, hampered her attempts to resume an acting career.
Paper Moon (AA) 73. The Bad News Bears 76. Nickelodeon 76. International Velvet 78. Circle of Two 80. Little Darlings 80. Certain Fury 85. Little Noises 91. Woman on the Run: The Lawrencia Bembenek Story (TV) 93. Basquiat 96, etc.

O'Neil, Barbara (1909–1980).
American character actress who made a corner in mad wives and other neurotic roles.
■ Stella Dallas 37. Love, Honor and Behave 38. The Toy Wife 38. I Am the Law 39. The Sun Never Sets 39. *When Tomorrow Comes* 39. Tower of London 39. Gone With the Wind 39. All This and Heaven Too (AAN) 40. Shining Victory 41. The Secret Beyond the Door 48. I Remember Mama 48. Whirlpool 49. Angel Face 52. Flame of the Islands 55. The Nun's Story 59.

O'Neil, Nance (1875–1965).
American stage actress who starred in a few films.
The Kreuzer Sonata 15. Hedda Gabler 17. The Mad Woman 20. His Glorious Night 29. The Rogue Song 30. Cimarron 31. False Faces 34, etc.

O'Neil, Sally (1910–1968) (Virginia Noonan).
American leading lady of the 20s.
Sally Irene and Mary 25. Battling Butler 26. Slide Kelly Slide 27. The Lovelorn 27. The Mad Hour 28. Jazz Heaven 29. Hold Everything 30. Salvation Nell 31. Murder by the Clock 31. Sixteen Fathoms Deep 33. Kathleen 37, etc.

O'Neill, Eugene (1888–1953).
Irish-American playwright of self-pitying disposition and a tendency in his plays to tragic despair. His gloominess led Hollywood to regard his works as art, which killed many of the film versions stone dead.
Anna Christie (23 with Blanche Sweet, 30 with Garbo). Strange Interlude 32. The Emperor Jones 33. Ah Wilderness 35. The Long Voyage Home 40. The Hairy Ape 44. Summer Holiday 47. Mourning Becomes Electra 48. Desire under the Elms 57. Long Day's Journey into Night 62. The Iceman Cometh 73, etc.
~O'Neill was played by Jack Nicholson in *Reds*.

O'Neill, Henry (1891–1961).
American character actor with stage experience, in Hollywood from early 30s. Played scores of judges, guardians, fathers, lawyers, etc.
I Loved a Woman 33. Wonder Bar 34. Black Fury 35. The White Angel 36. First Lady 37. Brother Rat 38. Juarez 39. Billy the Kid 41. White Cargo 43. The Virginian 46. Alias Nick Beal 49. The Milkman 50. Untamed 55. The Wings of Eagles 57, many others.

O'Neill, James (1847–1920).
American stage actor, father of Eugene. Best film part 1913: *The Count of Monte Cristo*.

O'Neill, Jennifer (1949–).
American leading lady of the 70s.
Rio Lobo 70. *Summer of 42* 71. Such Good Friends 71. The Carey Treatment 72. Glass Houses 72. Lady Ice 73. The Reincarnation of Peter Proud 75. Whiffs 75. Caravans 78. A Force of One 79. Cloud Dancer 80. Steel 80. Scanners 81. I Love N.Y. 87. Personals 90. Committed 91. Perfect Family 92. Invasion of Privacy 92. The Cover Girl Murders 93. Bad Love 95, etc.
TV series: Cover Up 83–84.

O'Neill, Maire (1887–1952) (Maire Allgood).
Irish actress, a member of the ABBEY THEATRE, where she acted in the early 1900s with her sister Sara ALLGOOD. Her second husband was actor Arthur SINCLAIR.
Juno and the Paycock 29. Sing as We Go 34. Peg of Old Drury 35. Bulldog Drummond at Bay 37. Mountains o' Mourne 38. My Irish Molly 38. The Arsenal Stadium Mystery 39. Love on the Dole 41. Let the People Sing 42. Piccadilly Incident 46. The Hills of Donegal 47. Saints and Sinners 49. Treasure Hunt 52. The Oracle 53, etc.

Ontkean, Michael (1946–).
American leading man.
Pickup on 101 71. Necromancy 72. Slap Shot 77. Voices 79. Willie and Phil 80. Making Love 81. The Blood of Others 84. The Allnighter 87. Maid to Order 87. Clara's Heart 88. Bye Bye Blues 89. Cold Front 89. Street Justice 89. Postcards from the Edge 90. Twin Peaks: Fire Walk with Me 92. Whose Child Is This? The War for Baby Jessica (TV) 93. Swann 96. Summer of the Monkey (Can.) 98, etc.
TV series: The Rookies 73–74. Twin Peaks 90.

Ooms, Amanda.
Swedish leading actress, in international films and television.
Hotel St Pauli (Nor.) 88. The Women on the Roof 89. Karachi (Nor.) 89. Buster's Bedroom (Ger.) 91. Guinevere (Ger.) 92. Mesmer (US) 94. Black Easter (TV) 95. Wilderness (TV) 96. Seesaw (TV) 98, etc.

Opatoshu, David (1918–1996) (David Opatovsky).
American general-purpose actor, often seen as villain.
Naked City 48. Exodus 60. Guns of Darkness 63. Torn Curtain 66. The Defector 67. Enter Laughing 67. Death of a Gunfighter 69. A Walk in the Spring Rain 78. Masada (TV) 81. Forty Days of Musa Dagh 85, etc.

Ophuls, Marcel (1927–).
French director, son of Max Ophuls; mainly associated with elaborate documentaries.
Peau de Banane 63. *The Sorrow and the Pity* (AAN) 69. A Sense of Loss 73. A Memory of Justice 76. Hotel Terminus: Klaus Barbie, His Life and Times (AA) 88. The Troubles We've Seen: A History of Journalism in Wartime (doc) 94, etc.

Ophuls, Max (1902–1957) (Max Oppenheimer).
German director of international highly decorated, romantic films.
■ Dann Schon Lieber Lebertran 30. Die Lachenden Erben 31. Die Verliebte Firma 31. Der Verkaufte Braut 32. *Liebelei* 32. Une Histoire d'Amour 33. On a Volé un Homme 34. La Signora Di Tutti 34. Trouble with Money 34. Divine 35. La Tendre Ennemie 36. Yoshimara 37. Werther 38. Sans Lendemain 39. De Mayerling à Sarajevo 40. The Exile 47. *Letter from an Unknown Woman* 48. Caught 48. *The Reckless Moment* 49. *La Ronde* 50. Le Plaisir 51. *Madame De* 53. *Lola Montes* 55.
✪ For elegance of craftsmanship and knowledge of what the camera can do. *Letter from an Unknown Woman*.
❝ A shot that does not call for tracks is agony for dear old Max. – *James Mason*
If all the dollies and cranes in the world snap to attention when his name is mentioned, it is because he gave camera movement its finest hours in the history of the cinema. – *Andrew Sarris, 1968*

Oppenheimer, Alan.
Bald American character actor.
In the Heat of the Night 67. Star! 69. The Groundstar Conspiracy 73. Westworld 73. The Hindenburg 75. Freaky Friday 76. Record City 78. Private Benjamin 80. The Neverending Story (voice) 84. Trancers 4: Jack of Swords 93. Trancers 5: Sudden Death 94, etc.
TV series: The Six Million Dollar Man 74–75. Big Eddie 75. Eischied 79–80.

Oppenheimer, George (1900–1977).
American critic, screenwriter and playwright, a former publisher. Born in New York, he was educated at Williams College and Harvard University, and co-founded the Viking Press, where he worked from the mid-20s to the early 30s. He began his screenwriting career when George KAUFMAN and Robert E. SHERWOOD stopped working Eddie CANTOR's *Roman Scandals* because they found that Cantor interfered too much, and arranged for him to replace them. In Hollywood, he was most often used to improve other writers' scripts. From the mid-50s he was drama critic for *Newsday*.
Autobiography: 1966, *The View from the Sixties*.
Book: 1958, *The Passionate Playgoer*.
Roman Scandals (co-w) 33. Rendezvous (co-w) 35. Libelled Lady (co-w) 36. Man Proof (co-w) 37. I'll Take Romance (co-w) 37. London by Night (w) 37. A Day at the Races (co-w) 37. Paradise for Three (co-w) 38. A Yank at Oxford (co-w) 38. Three Loves Has Nancy (co-w) 38. Broadway Melody of 1940 (co-w) 40. Two Faced Woman (co-w) 41. A Yank at Eton (co-w) 42. Pacific Rendezvous (co-w) 42. The War against Mrs Hadley (AAN) 42. The Youngest Profession (co-w) 43. The Adventures of Don Juan (co-w) 49. Anything Can Happen (co-w) 52. Tonight We Sing (co-w) 53. Decamaron Nights (w) 53, etc.

Orbach, Jerry (1935–).
Loose-limbed American actor and musical comedy star.
The Gang That Couldn't Shoot Straight 72. The Sentinel 79. Underground Aces 81. Prince of the City 81. Street Heat (TV) 84. Brewster's Million 84. The Imagemaker 85. F/X 86. Dirty Dancing 87. I Love N.Y. 87. Someone to Watch over Me 87. Crimes and Misdemeanors 89. Last Exit to Brooklyn 89. Dead Women in Lingerie 91. Beauty and the Beast (voice) 91. Delirious 91. Out for Justice 91. Straight Talk 92. Universal Soldier 92. Mr Saturday Night 92, etc.

Orchard, Julian (1930–1979).
Lugubrious British revue comedian who enlivened a number of bit parts.
Crooks Anonymous 58. On the Beat 60. Kill or Cure 62. The Spy with a Cold Nose 66. Carry On Doctor 68. Hieronymus Merkin 69. Perfect Friday 70. The Slipper and the Rose 76, many others.

Orczy, Baroness (1865–1947) (Emma Magdalena Rosalia Marie Josefa Barbara).
Hungarian-born novelist, in London from the age of 15, and creator of that epitome of the apparently effete English aristocrat, Sir Percy Blakeney in *The Scarlet Pimpernel*. Written in 1902, it was turned into a successful play a year later and published as a novel in 1905.

Oreste:
see KIRKOP, Oreste.

Orme, Stuart (1954–).
English director, from television.
The Fear (TV) 88. The Wolves of Willoughby Chase 89. A Question of Guilt (TV) 93. The Puppet Masters (US) 94. The Sculptress (TV) 96. Ivanhoe (TV) 97, etc.

Ormond, Julia (1965–).
English leading actress, from television. Runs a production company, Indican Pictures, which has a first-look deal with Fox Searchlight Pictures. Formerly married to actor Rory Edwards.
Traffik (TV) 89. Young Catherine (TV) 91. Stalin (TV) 92. The Baby of Macon 93. Nostradamus 94. Captives 94. Legends of the Fall 94. First Knight 95. Sabrina 95. Smilla's Sense of Snow 97. The Barber of Siberia 98, etc.

Ornadel, Cyril (1924–).
British composer.
Some May Love 67. Die Screaming Marianne 71. Not Now Darling 72. Brief Encounter (TV) 75, etc.
TV series: Edward the Seventh 76.

Ornitz, Arthur J. (1916–1985).
American cinematographer.
The Goddess 58. Act One 63. The World of Henry Orient 64. Charly 68. Me Natalie 68. The Anderson Tapes 71. Serpico 73. Next Stop Greenwich Village 76. An Unmarried Woman 78. Tattoo 81. Hanky Panky 82. The Chosen 82.

O'Rourke, Brefni (1889–1945).
Irish stage actor, an Abbey player, who made some British films, usually as testy types.
The Ghost of St Michael's 41. Hatter's Castle 41. The Lamp Still Burns 43. Don't Take It to Heart 44. I See a Dark Stranger 45, etc.

O'Rourke, Heather (1975–1988).
American child star. Died during emergency surgery.
Poltergeist 82. Poltergeist II: The Other Side 86. Poltergeist III 88.
TV series: Happy Days 82–83.

Orr, Buxton (1924–1997).
Scottish composer and conductor who wrote occasional film scores, mainly for horror movies. Born in Glasgow, he studied medicine and worked as an RAF medical officer before becoming a professional composer and teaching at the Guildhall School of Music and Drama in London. He also wrote songs, chamber and orchestral music, and works for music theatre.
Fiend without a Face 57. Corridors of Blood 58. Doctor Blood's Coffin 60. The Snake Woman 61. Suddenly Last Summer (co-m) 61. The Eyes of Annie Jones 63, etc.

Orry-Kelly (1897–1964) (John Orry Kelly).
Australian designer, in Hollywood from 1923 after Broadway experience. For many years with Warner, then with Fox.
The Rich Are Always with Us 32. The Old Maid 39. The Private Lives of Elizabeth and Essex 39. Little Foxes 41. Casablanca 42. Mr Skeffington 44. An American in Paris (AA) 51. Les Girls (AA) 57. Some Like It Hot (AA) 59. Gypsy 62. Irma La Douce 63. The Cool of Day 64, etc.

Orth, Frank (1880–1962).
American small-part actor who must have played more bartenders than he could count.
Hot Money 36. Serenade 39. The Lost Weekend 45. Father of the Bride 50. Here Come the Girls 54, many others.
TV series: The Brothers 56.

Ortolani, Riz (1926–).
Italian composer. Born in Pesaro, he studied at the city's Conservatoire, and favours romantic, string-laden scores.
Mondo Cane 61. The Easy Life/Il Sorpasso 62. The Seventh Dawn (GB/US) 64. The Yellow Rolls-Royce (GB) 64. Africa Addio 65. The Glory Guys (US) 65. Maya (US) 66. Woman Times Seven 67. Buona Sera Mrs Campbell (US) 68. Anzio 68. The Bliss of Mrs Blossom (GB) 69. The Statue (GB) 70. Say Hello to Yesterday (GB) 70. Madron (AANs) 70. The Hunting Party (US) 71. Addio Zio Tom 71. The Heroes/Gli Eroi 72. The Valachi Papers 72. Le Mataf 73. Mondo Candido 75. Double Murder 78. The Fifth Musketeer (US) 78. House on the Edge of the Park 79. Christopher Columbus (TV) 85. Magnificat 93. The Voyeur/L'Uomo che Guarda 94. PO Box Tinto Brass 95, many others.

Orton, J(ohn) O. C. (1889–*).
English screenwriter and occasional director, a former editor of silents. Born in London, he served in the Army and RAF for 15 years before entering films in 1923. After working in Stockholm as a scriptwriter and editor with Swedish Biograph, he became an editor and director with British Instructional and British International before joining GAINSBOROUGH as a writer in 1932, where he collaborated on the films of Jack HULBERT and Cicely COURTNEIDGE, Will HAY, Arthur ASKEY, Tommy HANDLEY and FLANAGAN and ALLEN.
The Celestial City (& d) 29. Windjammer (d) 30. Creeping Shadows (& d) 31. Bill and Coo (& d) 31. Out of the Blue (co-d) 31. After the Ball 32. Bad Companions (& d) 32. Just Smith 33. Soldiers of the King 33. Jack Ahoy 34. Brown on Resolution 35. Bulldog Jack 35. Turn of the Tide 35. Jack of All Trades 36. Everything Is Thunder 36. Non-Stop New York 37. Old Bones of the River 38. Hey! Hey! USA! 38. Where's That Fire? 39. Goofer Trouble 40. Cottage to Let 41. Time Flies 44. For Those in Peril 44. Bon Voyage 44. Up to His Neck (story) 54, etc.

Orton, Joe (1933–1967).
English playwright of elegant iconoclasm, murdered by his lover, Kenneth Halliwell, who then committed suicide. He was the subject of a biopic, *Prick Up Your Ears* 87, in which he was played by Gary Oldman and Halliwell by Alfred Molina. He also wrote an unproduced screenplay for the Beatles, *Up Against It* 67, which was published in 1979.
Autobiography: 1986, *The Orton Diaries*, edited by John Lahr.
Biography: 1978, *Prick Up Your Ears* by John Lahr.
Entertaining Mr Sloane (oa) 69. Loot (oa) 72.
❝ The whole trouble with Western Society today is the lack of anything worth concealing. – *J.O.*
I'd never realised quite what real stars did. They light up lines and situations in an uncanny way. There's no question of a real star doing a line wrong. One accepts the most lurid interpretation of a role when a great star plays it well. – *J.O.*

Orwell, George (1903–1950) (Eric Blair).
British satirist and novelist whose chief bequests to the cinema are *Animal Farm* and *1984*.

Ory, Edward 'Kid' (1890–1973).
American jazz trombonist, bandleader and composer, in occasional films as himself. Born in La Place, Louisiana, he was the best-known exponent of the tailgate style of trombone playing in New Orleans jazz.
Crossfire 47. New Orleans 47. The Benny Goodman Story 55, etc.

Osborn, Andrew (1912–1985).
British stage and film actor. Latterly BBC TV producer: *Maigret* series, etc.
Who Goes Next? 38. Idol of Paris 48. Dark Interval 50. Angels One Five 51. The Second Mrs Tanqueray 53, etc.

Osborn, Paul (1901–1988).
American dramatist and screenwriter.
The Young in Heart 39. Madame Curie 43. The Yearling 46. East of Eden 55. Homecoming 48. Portrait of Jennie/Jennie 48. Sayonara (AAN) 57. South Pacific 58. Wild River 60, etc.

Osborne, Bud (1881–1964) (Lennie B. Osborne).
American character actor, frequently as a villain in 'B' westerns. Born in Knox County, Texas, he was a rancher and a member of Buffalo Bill's Wild West before beginning his movie career in 1915 in Thomas Ince's productions. He was noted for his skill in handling stagecoaches and any type of horse-drawn vehicle.
Casey's Border Raid 17. The Prairie Mystery 23. Ranchers and Rascals 25. The Fighting Stallion 26. Mark of the Spur 32. Deadwood Pass 33. The Crimson Trail 35. Western Gold 37. Across the Plains 39. Death Rides the Range 40. Dead or Alive 41. Six Gun Gospel 43. Range Law 44. Adventures of Mark Twain 44. Border Bandits 46. Outlaw of

the Plains 46. The Last Round-Up 47. Gun Runner 49. Winchester 73 50. Gun Glory 57. Escape from Red Rock 58, etc.

Osborne, John (1929–1994).
English dramatist, screenwriter and film producer, a former actor. He was a founder-member of Woodfall Films, begun with director Tony Richardson to film his ground-breaking play *Look Back in Anger*. His wives include actress Mary Ure, critic and writer Penelope Gilliatt, and actress Jill Bennett.

Autobiography: 1981, *A Better Class of Person*; 1991, *Almost a Gentleman*.

Look Back in Anger (oa) 59. The Entertainer (co-w from his play) 60. Tom Jones (AA, BFAw) 63. Inadmissible Evidence (w from his play) 68. Get Carter (a) 71. Tomorrow Never Comes (a) 78. England, My England (co-w, TV) 95.

❝ Some actors are little better than strolling psychopaths. – *J.O.*

Few men should be encouraged to marry actresses, and playwrights should be forcibly prevented from such self-slaughter. – *J.O.*

Theatre is theatre and has death at the heart of it, like life itself. Movies survive. Not only do they survive, but their cultural sense goes into the general memory of history in a way that no theatrical experience can. – *J.O.*

Osborne, Vivienne (1900–1961).
American leading lady who left the stage for occasional films but was relegated to supporting roles.

Over the Hill 20. Husband's Holiday 30. Luxury Liner 33. Sailor Be Good 32. Wives Never Know 36. Dragonwyck 46, etc.

Oscar, Henry (1891–1969) (Henry Wale).
British character actor, on stage from 1911, films from 1932, usually as meek or scheming fellows.

After Dark (debut) 32. I was a Spy 33. The Man Who Knew Too Much 34. Fire over England 37. *The Return of the Scarlet Pimpernel* (as Robespierre) 39. Hatter's Castle 41. They Made Me a Fugitive 47. The Greed of William Hart 48. The Black Rose 50. Private's Progress 55. Foxhole in Cairo 60, etc.

Oscarsson, Per (1927–).
Swedish leading actor.

The Doll 62. Hunger 66. My Sister My Love 66. Who Saw Him Die? 67. Dr Glas 67. A Dandy in Aspic 68. The Last Valley 71. Secrets 72. *The Emigrants* 72. Endless Night 72. Dream City 76. Sleep of Death 79. Hotel Cansino 92. Cross My Heart and Hope to Die/Ti Kniver I Hjertet 94. The Christmas Oratorio/Juloratoriet 96, etc.

O'Shea, Michael (1906–1973).
American actor with a 'good guy' personality, who, after circus and vaudeville experience, made several films in the 40s and 50s.

Jack London 42. Striptease Lady 43. The Eve of St Mark 44. It's a Pleasure 45. Circumstantial Evidence 45. The Big Wheel 49. The Model and the Marriage Broker 52. It Should Happen to You 55, etc.

TV series: It's a Great Life 54–55.

O'Shea, Milo (1926–).
Irish character actor, usually in slightly bumbling comic roles.

Never Put It in Writing 64. *Ulysses* (as Bloom) 67. Romeo and Juliet 68. Barbarella 68. The Adding Machine 69. Loot 70. The Angel Levine 70. Arabian Adventure 79. The Pilot 81. The Verdict 82. The Purple Rose of Cairo 84. The Dream Team 88. Only the Lonely 91. The Playboys 92. Murder in the Heartland (TV) 93. The Matchmaker 98, etc.

O'Shea, Tessie (1917–1995).
Amply-proportioned British music-hall singer and character actress, billed as 'Two Ton Tessie', after her signature tune.

London Town 46. The Blue Lamp 50. The Shiralee 58. The Russians Are Coming, the Russians Are Coming 66. The Best House in London 68. Bedknobs and Broomsticks 71.

Oshima, Nagisa (Nagashi) (1932–).
Japanese director.

Ai No Corrida 77. Empire of Passion 79. Merry Christmas Mr Lawrence 83. Max My Love 86. Hollywood Zen 92, etc.

Osmond, Cliff (1937–).
Heavyweight American comedy actor.

Kiss Me Stupid 64. The Fortune Cookie 67. The Front Page 74. Sharks Treasure 75. Guardian of the Wilderness 76. The Great Brain 78. The North Avenue Irregulars 80. Hangar 18 81. The Penitent (d) 88, etc.

O'Steen, Sam (1923–).
American editor and director.

As editor: Robin and the Seven Hoods 64. Who's Afraid of Virginia Woolf? 66. Cool Hand Luke 67. *The Graduate* 67. Rosemary's Baby 68. Catch 22 70. Carnal Knowledge 71. The Day of the Dolphin 73. Chinatown 74. Hurricane 79. Silkwood 83. Regarding Henry 92. Wolf 94. Night Falls on Manhattan 97, etc.

■ As director: A Brand New Life (TV) 73. I Love You Goodbye (TV) 74. Queen of the Stardust Ballroom (TV) 75. High Risk (TV) 76. Look What's Happened to Rosemary's Baby (TV) 76. Sparkle 76. The Best Little Girl in the World (TV) 81. Kids Don't Tell (TV) 85.

O'Sullivan, Maureen (1911–1988).
Irish leading lady in Hollywood, the mother of Mia Farrow, and best known for playing the scantily clad Jane to Johnny Weissmuller's Tarzan in six films. Born in Boyle, she was spotted in Dublin and offered a film role by director Frank Borzage. She made a few forgettable films for Fox, where her main function was to be used by the studio as a bargaining ploy with actress Janet Gaynor, then involved in a contractual dispute. When Fox let her go, MGM signed her to star in *Tarzan the Ape Man*; a succession of shy, reticent roles followed. From the 40s, she made fewer films following her marriage to director John Farrow (1936–63), with whom she had seven children, including actresses Tisa Farrow and Stephanie Farrow. Later, she acted mainly on stage and television. She was romantically linked with actor Robert Ryan. Apart from Jane, her best roles were as Henrietta in *The Barretts of Wimpole Street*, Dora in *David Copperfield*, Jane Bennet in *Pride and Prejudice*, and Norma in *Hannah and Her Sisters*.

■ Song of My Heart 30. So This is London 30. Just Imagine 30. The Princess and the Plumber 30. A Connecticut Yankee 31. Skyline 31. *Tarzan the Ape Man* 32 (she was his most famous Jane). The Silver Lining 32. Big Shot 32. Information Kid 32. Strange Interlude 32. Skyscraper Souls 32. Payment Deferred 32. The Fast Companions 32. Robbers Roost 33. The Cohens and Kellys in Trouble 33. Tugboat Annie 33. Stage Mother 33. Tarzan and His Mate 34. The Thin Man 34. *The Barretts of Wimpole Street* 34. Hideout 34. West Point of the Air 34. David Copperfield 34. Cardinal Richelieu 35. The Flame Within 35. Anna Karenina 35. Woman Wanted 35. The Bishop Misbehaves 35. Tarzan Escapes 36. The Voice of Bugle Ann 36. The Devil Doll 36. A Day at the Races 37. Between Two Women 37. The Emperor's Candlesticks 37. My Dear Miss Aldrich 37. A Yank at Oxford 38. Hold that Kiss 38. The Crowd Roars 38. Port of Seven Seas 38. Spring Madness 38. Let Us Live 38. Tarzan Finds a Son 39. *Pride and Prejudice* 40. Sporting Blood 40. Maisie was a Lady 41. Tarzan's Secret Treasure 41. Tarzan's New York Adventure 42. The Big Clock 48. Where Danger Lives 50. Bonzo Goes to College 52. All I Desire 53. Mission Over Korea 53. Duffy of San Quentin 54. The Steel Cage 54. The Tall T 57. Wild Heritage 58. *Never Too Late* 65. The Phynx 69. The Crooked Hearts (TV) 72. The Great Houdinis (TV) 76. Hannah and Her Sisters 85. Peggy Sue Got Married 86.

O'Sullivan, Richard (1944–).
British light leading man, formerly child actor, prominent on TV.

The Stranger's Hand 53. Dangerous Exile 56. A Story of David 60. The Young Ones 61. Wonderful Life 64. Father Dear Father 73. A Man About the House 74, etc.

TV series: *A Man About the House* 73–76. Robin's Nest 77–80. Dick Turpin 78–79.

O'Sullivan, Thaddeus.
Irish director and cinematographer. Born in Dublin, he studied in London at the Royal College of Art and worked as a photographer while making experimental films.

As cinematographer: Pigs 84. Anne Devlin 84. Rocinante 86. On the Black Hill 87. The Love Child 87, etc.

As director: The Woman Who Married Clark Gable 85. December Bride 90. *Nothing Personal* 96, etc.

Oswald, Gerd (1916–1989).
German-American director, son of Richard Oswald.

■ A Kiss before Dying 56. The Brass Legend 57. Crime of Passion 57. Fury at Sundown 57. Valerie 57. Paris Holiday 57. Screaming Mimi 58. Am Tag Als Der Regen Kam 59. Three Moves to Freedom 60. Tempesta Su Ceylon 63. Agent for H.A.R.M. 66. 80 Steps to Jonah 69. Bunny O'Hare 71. To the Bitter End 75.

Oswald, Richard (1880–1963) (R. Ornstein).
German director, father of Gerd Oswald.

Pagu 16. Round the World in Eighty Days 19. Victoria and Her Hussar 31. Der Hauptmann von Köpenick 32. I Was a Criminal (US) 41. Isle of Missing Men (US) 42. The Lovable Cheat (US) 49, etc.

Otomo, Katsuhiro (1954–).
Japanese director, screenwriter, graphic novelist and artist.

Akira 87. World Apartment Horror 91. Robot Carnival (co-d) 91. Rojin Z (w) 94, etc.

O'Toole, Annette (1953–).
American leading lady.

The Girl Most Likely To (TV) 73. Smile 75. The Entertainer (TV) 76. One on One 77. The War between the Tates (TV) 77. King of the Gypsies 78. Foolin' Around 80. Cat People 82. 48 Hours 82. Superman III 83. Best Legs in the 8th Grade 84. Copacabana (TV) 85. Cross My Heart 87. The Kennedys of Massachusetts (TV) 90. Love at Large 90. It (TV) 90. Imaginary Crimes 94. Andre 94. My Brother's Keeper (TV) 95. The Christmas Box (TV) 95, etc.

TV series: Nash Bridges 96.

O'Toole, Peter (1932–).
British leading man who after stage and TV experience had a fairly meteoric rise to stardom in films. Married actress Sian Phillips (1959–79).

Autobiographies: 1993, *Loitering with Intent*. 1996, *The Apprentice*.

Biography: 1983, by Michael Freedland.

Kidnapped (debut) 59. Savage Innocents 59. The Day They Robbed the Bank of England 60. *Lawrence of Arabia* (AAN) 62. *Becket* (AAN) 64. Lord Jim 65. What's New, Pussycat? 65. How to Steal a Million 66. The Night of the Generals 66. The Bible 66. Casino Royale 66. Great Catherine 67. *The Lion in Winter* (AAN) 68. *Goodbye Mr Chips* (AAN) 69. Country Dance 70. Murphy's War 70. Under Milk Wood 71. *The Ruling Class* (AAN) 71. Man of la Mancha 72. Rosebud 75. Man Friday 75. Foxtrot 75. Rogue Male (TV) 76. Caligula 77. Power Play 78. Zulu Dawn 79. Masada (TV) 80. Strumpet City (TV) 80. *The Stunt Man* (AAN) 80. *My Favorite Year* (AAN) 82. Svengali (TV) 82. Superman III 83. Supergirl 84. Buried Alive 84. Kim (TV) 84. Creator 84. Club Paradise 86. The Last Emperor 87. High Spirits 88. In Una Notte di Chiaro di Luna 89. Crossing to Freedom (TV) 90. The Nutcracker Prince (voice) 90. Wings of Fame 90. Isabelle Eberhardt 91. King Ralph 91. Rebecca's Daughters 91. The Seventh Coin 93. P. G. Wodehouse's Heavy Weather (TV) 95. Gulliver's Travels (TV) 96. Fairytale: A True Story 97. Phantoms 97. Coming Home (TV) 98. Molokai 98, etc.

❝ For me, life has been either a wake or a wedding. – *P.O'T.*

I can't stand light. I hate weather. My idea of heaven is moving from one smoke-filled room to another. – *P.O'T.*

Sobriety's a real turn-on for me. You can see what you're doing. – *P.O'T.*

The very prototype of the ham. – *Omar Sharif*

Ott, Fred (1860–1936).
American laboratory assistant, allegedly the first man ever to act for the cinema when he sneezed in close-up for Edison in 1893.

Ottiano, Rafaela (1894–1942).
Italian-born stage actress who went to Hollywood and played sinister housekeepers, etc.

As You Desire Me 32. Grand Hotel 32. She Done Him Wrong 33. Great Expectations 34. Maytime 37. Topper Returns 41, etc.

Otto, Barry.
Australian leading actor. He is the father of actress Miranda Otto.

Norman Loves Rose 82. *Bliss* 85. The Howling III: The Marsupials 87. The Last Voyage 88. The Punisher 89. Strictly Ballroom 92. The Custodian 93. Exile 94. Dad and Dave on Our Selection 95. Lilian's Story 95. *Cosi* 96. Mr Reliable: A True Story 96. Oscar and Lucinda 97. Kiss or Kill 97. Mr Nice Guy 98. Dead Letter Office 98, etc.

Otto, Miranda.
Australian actress, mainly on the stage. She is the daughter of actor Barry Otto.

Emnma's War 87. Initiation 87. The 13th Floor 88. Daydream Believer 91. The Last Days of Chez Nous 91. The Nostradamus Kid 93. Sex Is a Four Letter Word 95. Love Serenade 96. The Well 97. Doing Time for Patsy Cline 97. In the Winter Dark 98. Dead Letter Office 98. The Thin Red Line (US) 98, etc.

Ouédraogo, Idrissa (1954–).
African director and screenwriter, born in Burkina Faso. He studied film at the African Institute of Cinematography, and in Kiev and Paris.

The Choice/Yam Daabo 86. Yaaba 89. Tilai 90. Karim and Sala/A Karim Na Sala (TV) 91. Samba Traoré 93. Le Cri du Coeur 94.

Ouida (1839–1908) (Marie Louise de la Ramée).
Anglo-French novelist. *Under Two Flags* in 1936 was the last of her romances to be filmed, but several were used in silent days.

Oulton, Brian (1908–1992).
British stage and film comedy actor, usually in unctuous or prim roles.

Too Many Husbands 39. Miranda 48. Last Holiday 50. Castle in the Air 52. The Million Pound Note 54. Private's Progress 55. Happy is the Bride 57. The Thirty-Nine Steps 59. A French Mistress 60. Kiss of the Vampire 62. Carry on Cleo 64. The Intelligence Men 64. Carry on Camping 69. On the Buses 71. Ooh You are Awful 72.

Oury, Gérard (1919–) (Max-Gerald Tannenbaum).
Dapper French character actor, now director.

Antoine et Antoinette 46. La Belle que Voilà 49. Sea Devils (GB) 52. *Father Brown* (GB) 54. House of Secrets (GB) 56. The Journey (US) 58. The Mirror Has Two Faces 59, etc.

■ As director: La Main Chaude 60. *The Sucker/Le Corniaud* 64. The Big Spree 66. The Brain 69. Adventures of Rabbi Jacob 72. La Carapate 78. Le Coup de Parapluie 80/The Umbrella Coup 80. Ace of Aces 82. The Vengeance of the Winged Serpent 84. Levy and Goliath 86. Vanille Fraise 89. Le Grippe Sou 92. La Soif de l'Or 93. Ghost with Driver 96.

Ouspenskaya, Maria (1876–1949).
Distinguished, diminutive Russian character actress who enlivened some Hollywood films after the mid-30s.

■ Dodsworth (AAN) 36. Conquest 37. *Love Affair* (AAN) 39. *The Rains Came* 39. Judge Hardy and Son 39. Dr Ehrlich's Magic Bullet 40. Waterloo Bridge 40. The Mortal Storm 40. The Man I Married 40. Dance Girl Dance 40. Beyond Tomorrow 40. *The Wolf Man* 41. The Shanghai Gesture 41. *King's Row* 42. The Mystery of Marie Roget 42. Frankenstein Meets the Wolf Man 43. Tarzan and the Amazons 45. I've Always Loved You 46. Wyoming 47. A Kiss in the Dark 49.

Famous line (*The Wolf Man*):
'Even the man who is pure in heart
And says his prayers by night
May become a wolf when the wolf-bane blooms
And the moon is clear and bright.'

Overman, Lynne (1887–1943).
American character actor with stage experience. Memorable in cynical comedy roles for his relaxed manner and sing-song voice.

■ Midnight 34. Little Miss Marker 34. The Great Flirtation 34. She Loves Me Not 34. You Belong to Me 34. Broadway Bill 34. Enter Madame 34. Rumba 35. Paris in Spring 35. Men without Names 35. Two for Tonight 35. Collegiate 35. Poppy 36. Yours for the Asking 36. Three Married Men 36. The Jungle Princess 36. Blonde Trouble 37. Partners in Crime 37. Nobody's Baby 37. Don't Tell the Wife 37. Murder Goes to College 37. Wild Money 37. Hotel Haywire 37. Night Club Scandal 37. True Confession 37. The Big Broadcast of 1938.

Her Jungle Love 38. Hunted Men 38. Spawn of the North 38. Sons of the Legion 38. Men with Wings 38. Ride a Crooked Mile 38. Persons in Hiding 39. *Death of a Champion* 39. Union Pacific 39. Edison the Man 40. Typhoon 40. Safari 40. Northwest Mounted Police 40. Aloma of the South Seas 41. Caught in the Draft 41. New York Town 41. The Hard Boiled Canary 41. *Roxie Hart* 42. Reap the Wild Wind 42. The Forest Rangers 42. The Silver Queen 42. Star Spangled Rhythm 42. *Dixie* 43. The Desert Song 43.

Ovitz, Michael (1946–).
American agent, former chairman of CAA (Creative Artists Agency) and frequently said to be the most influential person in Hollywood. He joined the Walt Disney Company in August 1995 as President, leaving 14 months later with a severance deal said to worth $125m.
  Biography: 1997, *Ovitz: The Inside Story of Hollywood's Most Controversial Power Broker* by Robert Slater.
❝ A combination of barracuda and Mother Teresa – a crafty businessman, and I mean it in the best sense of the word. – *Paul Newman*

Owen, Bill (1914–) (Bill Rowbotham).
British character comedian, former dance-band musician and singer.
  Autobiography: 1994, *Summer Wine and Vintage Years*.
  The Way to the Stars (debut) 45. When the Bough Breaks 47. The Girl Who Couldn't Quite 49. Trottie True 49. Hotel Sahara 51. The Square

Ring 53. The Rainbow Jacket 54. Davy 57. Carve Her Name with Pride 58. The Hellfire Club 61. The Secret of Blood Island 65. Georgy Girl 66. O Lucky Man 72. In Celebration 74. The Comeback 78. Laughterhouse/Singleton's Pluck 84, etc.
  TV series: Last of the Summer Wine 74– .

Owen, Cliff (1919–).
British director, in films from 1937.
  Offbeat 61. A Prize of Arms 62. The Wrong Arm of the Law 63. A Man Could Get Killed 66. That Riviera Touch 66. The Magnificent Two 67. Steptoe and Son 72. Ooh You Are Awful 72. No Sex Please We're British 73. The Bawdy Adventures of Tom Jones 76. Get Charlie Tully 76, etc.

Owen, Clive (1966–).
English leading actor.
  Lorna Doone (TV) 90. Close My Eyes 91. Century 93. Bad Boys (TV) 94. The Turnaround (TV) 95. Bad Boy Blues (TV) 96. The Rich Man's Wife 96. Bad Boy Blues (TV) 96. Bent 97, etc.
  TV series: Chancer 90. Sharman 96.

Owen, Reginald (1887–1972).
British character actor, on stage from 1905, films (in Hollywood) from 1929.
  The Letter (debut) 29. Platinum Blonde 32. Queen Christina 33. Call of the Wild 35. Anna Karenina 35. The Great Ziegfeld 36. A Tale of Two Cities 36. *Trouble for Two* 36. Conquest 37. The Earl of Chicago 39. Florian 40. Charley's Aunt 41. Tarzan's Secret Treasure 41. *Mrs Miniver* 42. Random Harvest 42. White Cargo 42. Madame

Curie 43. Lassie Come Home 43. The Canterville Ghost 44. *Kitty* 45. The Diary of a Chambermaid 45. Cluny Brown 46. If Winter Comes 47. The Three Musketeers 48. The Miniver Story 50. Kim 51. Red Garters 54. The Young Invaders 58. Voice of the Hurricane (MRA film) 63. Mary Poppins 64. Rosie 68. Bedknobs and Broomsticks 71, many others.

Owen, Seena (1894–1966) (Signe Auen).
American silent-screen leading lady.
  Intolerance 16. The Sheriff's Son 19. Victory 19. Shipwrecked 23. Flame of the Yukon 25. The Rush Hour 28. Marriage Playground 29, many others.

Owen, Yvonne (1923–).
British actress of the 40s, wife of Alan Badel.
  The Seventh Veil 45. Girl in a Million 46. Holiday Camp 47. My Brother's Keeper 48. Quartet 48. Marry Me 49. Someone at the Door 50, etc.

Owens, Patricia (1925–).
Canadian leading lady who made films in Britain and America.
  Miss London Ltd 43. While the Sun Shines 46. The Happiest Days of Your Life 49. Mystery Junction 52. The Good Die Young 53. Windfall 55. Island in the Sun 56. Sayonara (US) 57. *No Down Payment* (US) 57. The Fly (US) 58. Five Gates to Hell (US) 59. Hell to Eternity (US) 60. Seven Women from Hell 62. Black Spurs 65. The Destructors 67, etc.

Oxley, David (c. 1929–).
British actor.
  Ill Met by Moonlight 57. Saint Joan 58. Yesterday's Enemy 58. The Hound of the Baskervilles 59. Life at the Top 64. House of the Living Dead 78, etc.

Oz, Frank (1944–) (Frank Oznowicz).
British-born director. He began as a puppeteer on the TV series *Sesame Street* and *The Muppet Show*, where he supplied the voices of Fozzie Bear, Miss Piggy and Sam the Eagle, among other characters, before becoming a director.
  The Dark Crystal (co-d) 82. The Muppets Take Manhattan 84. Little Shop of Horrors 86. Dirty Rotten Scoundrels 88. What about Bob? 91. Housesitter 92. The Indian in the Cupboard 95. Muppet Treasure Island (a) 96. In & Out 97, etc.
  TV series: The Muppet Show 76–81.

Ozep, Fedor (1893–1949).
Russian director. He was married to actress Anna Sten.
  The Crime of Dmitri Karamazov 31. The Living Dead 33. Amok 34. Gibraltar 38. She Who Dares (US) 44. Whispering City (Can.) 48, etc.

Ozu, Yasujiro (1903–1963).
Japanese director, since 1927.
  Biography: 1974, *Ozu* by Donald Ritchie.
  A Story of Floating Weeds 34. Late Spring 49. Early Summer 51. Tokyo Story 53. Early Spring 56. Late Autumn 61. Early Autumn 62, etc.

P

Pabst, G. W. (1885–1967) (George Wilhelm).
Distinguished German director who usually tackled pessimistic themes. Born in Raudnitz, he studied engineering in Vienna, toured Europe and America as an actor, and went to Berlin in the early 20s to work in films, acting and writing, before turning to directing in the mid-20s. He made an enduring star of American actress Louise Brooks in *Pandora's Box*. In the 30s, he worked in France, had an unhappy experience in Hollywood, and then returned to Germany for the remainder of his career.
■ Der Schatz 23. Gräfin Donelli 24. *Joyless Street* 25. *Secrets of a Soul* 26. Man Spielt Nicht mit der Liebe 26. *The Love of Jeanne Ney* 27. *Pandora's Box* 28. Abwege 28. *Diary of a Lost Girl* 29. The White Hell of Pitz Palu (co-d) 29. *Westfront 1918* 30. Skandal um Eva 30. *The Threepenny Opera/Die Dreigroschenoper* 31. *Kameradschaft* 31. L'Atlantide 32. Don Quixote 33. A Modern Hero (US) 34. De Haut en Bas 34. Mademoiselle Docteur 37. Le Drama de Shanghai 39. Mädchen in Uniform 39. Komödianten 41. Paracelsus 43. Der Fall Molander 45. Der Prozess 48. Geheimnisvolle Tiefen 49. The Voice of Silence 52. Cose da Pazzi 53. *Ten Days to Die* 54. Das Bekenntnis der Ina Kahr 54. Jackboot Mutiny 55. The Last Act 55. Roses for Bettina 56. Durch die Wälder 56.

Pace, Judy (1946–).
American leading actress of the 70s, born in Los Angeles.
13 Frightened Girls 63. The Thomas Crown Affair 68. Three in the Attic 68. Cotton Comes to Harlem 70. Up in the Cellar 70. The Fortune Cookie 66. Cool Breeze 72. Frogs 72. The Slams 73, etc.
TV series: The Young Lawyers 70–71.

Pacino, Al (1940–) (Alfredo Pacino).
American leading actor, of New York/Sicilian descent, from off-off-Broadway theatre. Over the years, his acting has changed from intense, tightly clenched performances to a more open, flamboyant style. Unlike many of his contemporaries, he continues to act in the theatre.
Biography: 1992, *Al Pacino: A Life on the Wire* by Andrew Yule.
■ Me Natalie 68. The Panic in Needle Park 71. *The Godfather* (AAN) 72. Scarecrow 73. Serpico (AAN) 73. The Godfather Part II (AAN) 74. *Dog Day Afternoon* (AAN) 75. Bobby Deerfield 77. And Justice for All (AAN) 79. Cruising 80. Author! Author! 82. Scarface 83. Revolution 86. Sea of Love 89. Dick Tracy (AAN) 90. The Godfather Part III 90. Frankie & Johnny 91. Scent of a Woman (AA) 92. Glengarry Glen Ross (AAN) 92. Carlito's Way 93. Two Bits 95. Heat 95. City Hall 96. Looking for Richard (& p, d) 96. *Donnie Brasco* 96. The Devil's Advocate 97.

Pack, Charles Lloyd:
see Lloyd Pack, Charles.

Pack, Roger Lloyd:
see Lloyd Pack, Roger.

Pacula, Joanna (1957–).
Polish actress in international films.
Gorky Park 83. Not Quite Jerusalem/Not Quite Paradise 86. Death before Dishonor 87. Options 88. Sweet Lies 88. The Kiss 88. Marked for Death 90. Husbands and Lovers 91. Black Ice 92. Warlock: The Armageddon 93. Tombstone 94. Kim Novak Is on the Phone (It.) 94. The Silence of the Hams (It.) 94. Last Gasp 95. Captain Nuke and the Bomber Boys 95. Not Like Us 96. The Haunted Sea 97. Virus 98. My Giant 98. Sweet Deception 99, etc.

Paderewski, Ignace (1860–1941).
Polish prime minister and classical pianist. Appeared in a few films including the British *Moonlight Sonata* 37.

Padovani, Lea (1920–1991).
Italian leading actress, in films from 1945.
Give Us This Day (GB) 49. Three Steps North (US) 51. Tempi Nostri 53. Montparnasse 19 57. The Naked Maja (US) 58. Candy 68, etc.

Pagano, Bartolomeo (1888–1947).
Italian actor who originated the role of strongman Maciste.

Page, Anthony (1935–).
British director, with stage experience.
■ *Inadmissible Evidence* 68. Alpha Beta 73. Pueblo (TV) 73. *The Missiles of October* (TV) 74. Collision Course (TV) 76. F. Scott Fitzgerald in Hollywood (TV) 76. I Never Promised You a Rose Garden 77. The Lady Vanishes 79. The Patricia Neal Story (TV) 81. Grace Kelly (TV) 83. Forbidden (TV) 85. Second Serve (TV) 85. Monte Carlo (TV) 86. Pack of Lies (TV) 87. Absolution 88. Scandal in a Small Town (TV) 88. The Nightmare Years (TV) 89. Chernobyl: The Final Warning (TV) 91. Silent Cries (TV) 93. Middlemarch (TV) 94. Human Bomb (TV) 96.

Page, Gale (1911–1983) (Sally Rutter).
American leading actress, born in Spokane, Washington. Her career was spent mainly at Warner Brothers, and most successfully in the three films about the Lemp family that began with *Four Daughters*. Died of cancer.
Crime School 38. *Four Daughters* 38. Heart of the North 38. The Amazing Dr Clitterhouse 38. Naughty but Nice 39. You Can't Get Away with Murder 39. Indianapolis Speedway 39. Four Wives 39. A Child Is Born 39. Daughters Courageous 39. They Drive by Night 40. Knute Rockne, All American 40. Four Mothers 40. The Time of Your Life 48. Anna Lucasta 49. About Mrs Leslie 54, etc.

Page, Geneviève (1931–) (G. Bonjean).
French leading lady who has made American films.
Foreign Intrigue 56. Trapped in Tangiers 60. Song without End 60. El Cid 61. L'Honorable Stanislas 63. Youngblood Hawke 64. Les Corsaires 65. Belle de Jour 67. Decline and Fall 68. The Private Life of Sherlock Holmes 70. Beyond Therapy 87. Aria 88. Stranger in the House/L'Inconnu dans la Maison 92, etc.

Page, Geraldine (1924–1987).
American leading actress, on stage from 1940. Her second husband was actor Rip Torn.
■ Taxi 53. Hondo (AAN) 54. *Summer and Smoke* (AAN) 61. Sweet Bird of Youth (AAN) 62. Toys in the Attic 63. *Dear Heart* 65. The Happiest Millionaire 67. You're a Big Boy Now (AAN) 67. Monday's Child (Arg.) 67. Trilogy (TV) 69. Whatever Happened to Aunt Alice? 69. The Beguiled 71. Pete 'n' Tillie (AAN) 72. J. W. Coop 73. The Day of the Locust 75. Nasty Habits 76. Something for Joey (TV) 77. Interiors (AAN, BFA) 78. Honky Tonk Freeway 81. Harry's War 81. I'm Dancing as Fast as I Can 82. The Pope of Greenwich Village (AAN) 84. White Nights 85. The Trip to Bountiful (AA) 85. The Bride 85. Nazi Hunter (TV) 86.

Page, Patti (1927–) (Clara Ann Fowler).
American TV singer.
■ Elmer Gantry 60. Dondi 61. Boys' Night Out 63.

Paget, Debra (1933–) (Debralee Griffin).
American leading lady with brief stage experience. The second of her three husbands was director Budd Boetticher.
Cry of the City 48. House of Strangers 49. Broken Arrow 50. Les Misérables 52. Prince Valiant 54. Love Me Tender 56. From the Earth to the Moon 58. Tales of Terror 62. The Haunted Palace 64, many others.

Pagett, Nicola (1945–) (Nicola Scott).
British leading lady of the 70s, much on TV. Born in Cairo, she studied at RADA. Her autobiography, *Diamonds Behind My Eyes* (with Graham Swannell), detailing her manic depression and breakdown in the mid-90s, was published in 1997. Married former actor and playwright Graham Swannell.
Frankenstein, the True Story (TV) 73. Operation Daybreak 76. Oliver's Story 79. Privates on Parade 83. All of You 86. Scoop (TV) 87. An Awfully Big Adventure 95, etc.
TV series: A Bit of a Do 89–90. Ain't Misbehavin' 94.

Pagnol, Marcel (1894–1974).
French writer-director noted for sprawling comedy dramas which strongly evoke country life without being very cinematic.
Autobiographies: 1960, *The Days Were Too Short*. 1962, *The Time of Secrets*.
Marius (script only) 31. *Fanny* (script only) 32. *César* 34. Joffroi 34. Regain/Harvest 37. *La Femme du Boulanger* 38. *La Fille du Puisatier* 40. La Belle Meunière 48. Manon des Sources 53. Lettres de Mon Moulin 55. Jean de Florette (oa) 86. Manon des Sources (oa) 86. My Mother's Castle/Le Château de Ma Mère (oa) 90. My Father's Glory/La Gloire de Mon Père (oa) 90, etc.
❝ The cinema and I were born on the same day, in the same place. – M.P.

Paige, Janis (1922–) (Donna Mac Jaden).
American leading lady with operatic training.
Hollywood Canteen (debut) 44. Cheyenne 46. Romance on the High Seas 48. Mr Universe 51. Remains to be Seen 53. *Silk Stockings* 57. Please Don't Eat the Daisies 61. The Caretakers 63. Welcome to Hard Times 67. Gibbsville (TV) 75. Lanigan's Rabbi (TV) 76. Angel on My Shoulder (TV) 80. Love at the Top 86. Natural Causes 94, etc.
TV series: It's Always Jan 56. Lanigan's Rabbi 77. Gun Shy 83. Baby Makes Five 83. Trapper John MD 85–86.

Paige, Mabel (1880–1954).
American character actress.
My Heart Belongs to Daddy 42. *Lucky Jordan* 43. The Good Fellows 43. *Someone to Remember* (lead role) 43. If You Knew Susie 48. The Sniper 52. Houdini 53, etc.

Paige, Robert (1910–1987) (John Arthur Page).
American leading man, former radio announcer, in many films of the 40s, little thereafter.
Cain and Mabel 37. Hellzapoppin 41. Shady Lady 42. Son of Dracula 43. Can't Help Singing 44. Red Stallion 47. The Flame 48. Raging Waters 51. Abbott and Costello Go to Mars 53. The Big Payoff 58. The Marriage Go Round 61. Bye Bye Birdie 63, etc.
TV series: Run Buddy Run 66.

Pailhas, Geraldine (1971–).
French leading actress.
La Neige et le Feu 91. IP5: L'Ile aux Pachydermes 92. La Folie Douce 94. Don Juan de Marco 95. Le Garcu 95. Suite 16 95, etc.

❝ I am very shy. I am more the convent girl type. Characters in movies help you do stuff that you would never do in life. Like having a gun, or being a whore. – G.P.

Painlevé, Jean (1902–1989).
French documentarist, famous for short naturalist studies of sea horses, sea urchins, shrimps, etc.

Paiva, Nestor (1905–1966).
American character actor of assorted foreign peasant types.
Ride a Crooked Mile 38. The Marines Fly High 40. The Falcon in Mexico 44. Fear 46. Road to Rio 46. Five Fingers 52. The Creature from the Black Lagoon 54. The Deep Six 57. The Nine Lives of Elfego Baca 59. The Spirit Is Willing 66, many others.

Pakula, Alan J. (1928–1998).
American producer who turned director. Died in a car accident, after a metal bar flew up from the road and crashed through the windscreen of his car, hitting him on the head.
■ as producer: Fear Strikes Out 57. To Kill a Mockingbird (AAN) 63. Love with the Proper Stranger 63. Baby the Rain Must Fall 65. Inside Daisy Clover 66. Up the Down Staircase 67. The Stalking Moon 68. The Nickel Ride 74. Kiss Me Goodbye 82.
■ as producer-director: The Sterile Cuckoo 69. *Klute* 71. Love, Pain and the Whole Damn Thing 73. The Parallax View 74. *All The President's Men* (AAN) 76. Comes A Horseman 78. Starting Over 80. Rollover (d only) 81. Sophie's Choice (wd only) (AANw) 82. Dream Lover 85. Orphans 87. See You in the Morning (wd, p) 89. Presumed Innocent (d) 90. Consenting Adults 92. The Pelican Brief (wd) 93. The Devil's Own 97.

Pal, George (1908–1980).
Hungarian puppeteer whose short advertising films enlivened programmes in the late 30s; went to Hollywood 1940 and produced series of 'Puppetoons'; later produced many adventure films involving trick photography. Special Academy Award 1943 'for the development of novel methods and techniques'.
Destination Moon (AA) 50. *When Worlds Collide* (AA) 51. *The War of the Worlds* (AA) 53. The Naked Jungle 55. *Tom Thumb* (AA) (& d) 58. *The Time Machine* (AA) (& d) 60. The Wonderful World of the Brothers Grimm 63. The Power 68.

Palance, Jack (1920–) (Walter Palanuik).
Gaunt American leading man with stage experience; started in films playing villains.
Panic in the Streets 50. Halls of Montezuma 51. Sudden Fear (AAN) 52. *Shane* (AAN) 53. Sign of the Pagan 54. *The Big Knife* 55. I Died a Thousand Times 56. Attack 56. The Man Inside 57. The Lonely Man 57. House of Numbers 57. Ten Seconds to Hell 58. The Mongols 60. Barabbas 62. Warriors Five 62. Le Mépris 63. Once a Thief 65. The Professionals 66. The Torture Garden (GB) 67. Kill a Dragon 67. A Professional Gun 68. Che! 69. The Desperados 69. They Came to Rob Las Vegas 69. The Companeros 70. Monte Walsh 70. The McMasters 70. The Horsemen 72. Chato's Land 72. Oklahoma Crude 73. Dracula (TV) 73. Craze 73. The Four Deuces 75. God's Gun 77. Mr Scarface 77. One Man Jury 78. The Shape of Things to Come (TV) 79. Hawk the Slayer 80. Without Warning 80. Alone in the Dark 82. Gor 87. Bagdad Café 88. Young Guns 88. Outlaw of Gor 88. Batman 89. Tango & Cash 89. Solar Crisis 90. *City Slickers* (AA) 91. Cops and Robbersons 94. City Slickers II 94. Buffalo Girls (TV) 95, etc.

TV series: The Greatest Show on Earth 63. Bronk 75. Believe It or Not 82–86.

Palca, Alfred (1920–1998).
American producer and writer who made one film before blacklisting forced him to find other means of making a living. Part of the FBI evidence of his communism, he later said, was that he had hired a black actor, Sidney Poitier, for the film; he had to remove his name from the credits in order to get it distributed. He thereafter worked as a writer and journalist.
Go Man Go 54.

Palcy, Euzhan (1955–).
Martinique director and screenwriter, a former editor and camera operator.
La Rue Cases Nègres/Sugar Cane Alley 83. A Dry White Season 89. Simeon (co-w, d) 93.

Palin, Michael (1943–).
British light actor and screenwriter, a former member of the Monty Python team. His novel, *Hemingway's Chair*, was published in 1996.
Biography: 1998, *Michael Palin* by Jonathan Margolis.
And Now for Something Completely Different (& co-w) 72. Monty Python and the Holy Grail (& co-w) 74. Monty Python's Life of Brian (& co-w) 79. The Missionary (& w, p) 81. Time Bandits (& co-w) 81. Monty Python's The Meaning of Life (& co-w) 83. A Private Function 84. Brazil 85. Consuming Passions (oa) 88. A Fish Called Wanda (BFA) 88. American Friends (& co-w) 91. The Wind in the Willows (voice, as Rat) 96. Fierce Creatures 96. You've Got Mail 98, etc.
TV series: Pole to Pole 92. Palin's Column 94. Palin's Pacific 97. Full Circle with Michael Palin 97.

Pallette, Eugene (1889–1954).
Rotund, gravel-voiced American character actor, at his peak as an exasperated father or executive in the 30s and 40s.
Intolerance 16. Alias Jimmy Valentine 20. The Three Musketeers 21. To the Last Man 23. Light of the Western Stars 25. Lights of New York 28. The Canary Murder Case 29. The Sea God 30. It Pays to Advertise 31. Shanghai Express 32. The Kennel Murder Case 33. Bordertown 34. Steamboat Round the Bend 35. *The Ghost Goes West* 36. *My Man Godfrey* 36. One Hundred Men and a Girl 37. Topper 37. *The Adventures of Robin Hood* (as Friar Tuck) 38. Mr Smith Goes to Washington 39. The Mark of Zorro 40. The Lady Eve 41. Tales of Manhattan 42. It Ain't Hay 43. Heaven Can Wait 43. Step Lively 44. Lake Placid Serenade 45. In Old Sacramento 46, many others.

Pallos, Stephen (1902–).
Hungarian producer who worked with Korda in England from 1942, later as independent.
Call of the Blood 46. The Golden Madonna 48. Jet Storm 59. Foxhole in Cairo 60. A Jolly Bad Fellow 64. Where the Spies Are 65. Captain Nemo and the Underwater City 69. Catch Me a Spy 71, etc.

Palmer, Betsy (1929–) (Patricia Brumek).
American light actress and TV panellist.
The Long Gray Line 55. Queen Bee 55. The Tin Star 57. The Last Angry Man 59. It Happened to Jane 59. Friday the Thirteenth 80. Friday the Thirteenth Part II 81. Goddess of Love (TV) 88. Still Not Quite Human 92, etc.
TV series: Number 96 80–81. Knots Landing 89–90.

Palmer, Christopher (1946–1995).
English orchestrator and arranger of film music, rescuing many classic scores so that they could be re-recorded, and author of *The Composer in Hollywood*, a study of film music. Died of AIDS.

Palmer, Ernest (1885–1978).
American cinematographer.
Ivanhoe 12. Lothar 17. Ladies Must Live 21. The Wanters 23. The Kiss Barrier 25. The Palace of Pleasure 26. Seventh Heaven 27. The River 29. City Girl 30. A Connecticut Yankee 31. The Painted Woman 32. Cavalcade 33. Berkeley Square 33. Music in the Air 34. Charlie Chan in Paris 35. Banjo on My Knee 36. Slave Ship 37. Four Men and a Prayer 38. News is Made at Night 39. The Great Profile 40. Blood and Sand (AA) 41. Song of the Islands 42. Coney Island 43. Pin Up Girl 44. The Dolly Sisters 45. Centennial Summer 46. I Wonder Who's Kissing Her Now? 47. Broken Arrow 50, many others.

Palmer, Ernest (1901–1964).
British cinematographer who began as an office boy and a laboratory assistant. He worked at Elstree in the 30s and at Ealing Studios in the early 40s and later in television, shooting *The Adventures of Sir Lancelot* 56–57.
Kiss Me Sergeant 30. What a Night! 31. Innocents of Chicago 32. Old Spanish Customers 32. The River Wolves 33. Music Hall 34. Birds of a Feather 35. The Man behind the Mask 36. The Edge of the World 37. Save a Little Sunshine 38. The Spider 39. He Found a Star 41. The Goose Steps Out 42. San Demetrio London 43. Return of the Vikings 44. 29 Acacia Avenue 45. The Lisbon Story 46. The Ghosts of Berkeley Square 47. School for Randle 49. Over the Garden Wall 50. It's a Grand Life 53. The Heart Within 57. The Crowning Touch 58, etc.

Palmer, Geoffrey (1927–).
English light leading actor, much on television.
A Prize of Arms 61. Incident at Midnight 63. O Lucky Man! 73. The Outsider 80. Retribution 81. The Honorary Consul 83. Clockwise 85. A Zed and Two Noughts 85. A Fish Called Wanda 88. Hawks 88. Smack and Thistle 91. The Madness of King George 94. Mrs Brown 97. Tomorrow Never Does 97, etc.
TV series: The Fall and Rise of Reginald Perrin 76–79. Butterflies 78–82. The Last Song 81–83. Whoops Apocalypse 82. Fairly Secret Army 84–86. Executive Stress 86–88. Blackadder Goes Forth (as Field Marshal Haig) 89. As Time Goes By 92–98. The Legacy of Reginald Perrin 96.

Palmer, Gregg (1927–) (Palmer Lee).
American 'second lead', former disc jockey.
Son of Ali Baba 51. Veils of Baghdad 53. Magnificent Obsession 54. The Creature Walks among Us 56. Forty Pounds of Trouble 62. The Undefeated 69. Big Jake 71. The Shootist 76, etc.

Palmer, Lilli (1911–1986) (Lilli Peiser).
Austrian leading actress, on stage from childhood, in films from teenage years.
Autobiography: 1975, *Change Lobsters and Dance*.
Crime Unlimited (GB) 34. Good Morning, Boys (GB) 36. Secret Agent (GB) 36. A Girl Must Live (GB) 38. The Door with Seven Locks (GB) 40. *Thunder Rock* (GB) 42. The Gentle Sex (GB) 43. English without Tears (GB) 44. *The Rake's Progress* (GB) 45. Beware of Pity (GB) 46. Cloak and Dagger (US) 46. My *Girl Tisa* (US) 47. Body and Soul (US) 48. No Minor Vices (US) 48. The Long Dark Hall (GB) 51. The Fourposter (US) 52. Is Anna Anderson Anastasia? (Ger.) 56. La Vie à Deux (Fr.) 58. But Not for Me (US) 58. Conspiracy of Hearts (GB) 60. Rendezvous at Midnight (Fr.) 60. *The Pleasure of His Company* (US) 61. The Counterfeit Traitor (US) 62. Adorable Julia (Ger.) 63. The Flight of the White Stallions (US) 64. Operation Crossbow (GB) 65. Moll Flanders (GB) 65. Sebastian (GB) 67. Oedipus the King (GB) 67. Nobody Runs Forever (GB) 68. The Dance of Death (Swe.) 68. De Sade (US) 69. Hard Contract (US) 69. Murders in the Rue Morgue (GB) 71. Night Hair Child (GB) 71. The Boys from Brazil 78. The Holcroft Covenant 85. Peter the Great (TV) 86, many others.
TV series: Lilli Palmer Theatre 54. *Zoo Gang* 73.

Palmer, Maria (1924–1981).
Austrian leading lady. Wide stage experience at home, TV and films in America.
Mission to Moscow 42. Lady on a Train 44. Rendezvous 24 46. Slightly Dishonourable 51. Three for Jamie Dawn 56, many others.

Palmer, Peter (1931–).
American actor-singer who repeated his stage role as *Li'l Abner* 59.
Deep Space 87. A Time of Destiny 88. Edward Scissorhands 90, etc.
TV series: Custer 67. The Kallikaks 77.

Palminteri, Chazz (1952–) (Calogero Palminteri).
American actor and dramatist.
Oscar 91. *A Bronx Tale* (& w, from his play) 93. Bullets over Broadway (AAN) 94. The Perez Family 95. The Usual Suspects 95. Jade 95. Faithful (& w, from his play) 96. Diabolique 96. Mulholland Falls 96. Hurlyburly 98. Falcone 98, etc.

Paltrow, Gwyneth (1973–).
American leading actress, the daughter of Blythe Danner. She was engaged to actor Brad Pitt and has been romantically linked with actor Ben Affleck.
Flesh and Bone 93. Mrs Parker and the Vicious Circle 94. Jefferson in Paris 95. Moonlight and Valentino 95. Sydney 96. The Pallbearer 96. *Emma* (title role) 96. Sliding Doors 98. Great Expectations 98. A Perfect Murder 98. Hush 98. *Shakespeare in Love* 98, etc.

Paluzzi, Luciana (1939–).
Italian leading lady in international films.
Three Coins in the Fountain 54. Sea Fury 58. Thunderball 65. The Venetian Affair 66. Chuka 67. 99 Women 69. The Green Slime 69. Black Gunn 72. War Goddess 74. The Klansman 74. The Greek Tycoon 78, etc.
TV series: Five Fingers 59.

Pampanini, Silvana (1927–).
Voluptuous Italian leading lady of the 50s, a former Miss Italy, who lent her charms to many frolics of the period; her appeal waned with the arrival of Sophia Loren and Gina Lollobrigida.
L'Apocalisse 47. Marechiaro 49. La Bisarca 50. Bellissima 51. Miracle at Viggiu/Miracolo à Viggiu 51. Scandal in the Roman Bath/OK Nerone 51. Dangerous Woman/Bufere 53. The Island Sinner/La Peccatrice dell'Isola 53. L'Allegro Squadrone 54. Il Matrimonio 54. Orient Express 54. La Schiava del Peccato 54. Roman Signorina/La Bella di Roma 55. Thirst for Love/Sed de Amor 58. Napoleoncito 63. Il Gaucho 64. Mondo Pazzo, Gente Matta 66, many others.

Pan, Hermes (1905–1990) (H. Panagiotopolous).
American dance director.
Top Hat 35. Swing Time 36. Damsel in Distress (AA) 37. Let's Dance 50. Lovely to Look At 52. Silk Stockings 57. Can Can 59. Flower Drum Song 62. Cleopatra 63. My Fair Lady 64. Finian's Rainbow 68. Lost Horizon 73, many others.

Panama, Norman (1914–).
Writer-producer-director who has long worked in collaboration with Melvin Frank (see entry for note on films). Now working solo.
Not with My Wife You Don't (wd, p) 66. How to Commit Marriage (d only) 69. The Maltese Bippy (wd) 69. Coffee, Tea or Me? (TV) 73. I Will, I Will . . . For Now (co-w, d) 76. Barnaby and Me 77.

Panfilov, Gleb (1934–).
Russian film director and screenwriter. He trained as a chemical engineer before studying direction at Mosfilm.
Across the Stream and Fire/Vogne Broda Nyet 68. The Debut/Nachalo 70. May I Have the Floor?/Proshu Slova 75. Valentina, Valentine 81. Vassa 83. The Theme 84. The Mother 88, etc.

Pangborn, Franklin (1894–1958).
American character comedian with long stage experience; in scores of films from the 20s, typically as flustered hotel clerk or organizer.
My Friend from India 27. My Man 30. International House 33. My Man Godfrey 36. Stage Door 37. Christmas in July 40. *The Bank Dick* 40. *The Palm Beach Story* 42. The Carter Case 42. Now Voyager 42. *Hail the Conquering Hero* 44. Mad Wednesday 47. Romance on the High Seas 48. The Story of Mankind 57, etc.

Panh, Rithy (1964–).
Cambodian director. Born in Phnom Penh, he now lives in France.
Rice People/Neak Sri 94. One Fine Evening after War 98, etc.

Pantoliano, Joe (1954–).
American actor.
The Idolmaker 80. Risky Business 83. The Final Terror 83. Eddie and the Cruisers 83. The Goonies 85. The Mean Season 85. Running Scared 86. La Bamba 87. The Squeeze 87. Empire of the Sun 87. Midnight Run 88. Downtown 89. The Last of the Finest 90. Short Time 90. Zandalee 91. Used People 92. Calendar Girl 93. The Fugitive 93. Three of Hearts 93. Baby's Day Out 94. Bad Boys 95. Bound 96. US Marshals 98, etc.
TV series: Free Country 78. From Here to Eternity 79. The Fanelli Boys 90–91.

Panzer, Paul (1872–1958).
American silent screen villain, an extremely hissable specimen.
The Perils of Pauline 14. The Exploits of Elaine 15. The Mystery Mind 19. The Johnstown Flood 26. Under the Red Robe 36. Casablanca 42. The Perils of Pauline 47, many others.

Papamichael, Phedon.
American cinematographer and production designer.
as cinematographer: After Midnight 89. Streets 90. Body Chemistry 90. Prayer of the Rollerboys 90. Poison Ivy 92. Cool Runnings 93. Wild Palms (TV) 93. Unstrung Heroes 95. While You Were Sleeping 95. Bio-Dome 96. Unhook the Stars 96. Phenomenon 96. The Locusts 97. Mouse Hunt 97, etc.

Papas, Irene (1926–) (I. Lelekou).
Greek stage actress who has made films at home and abroad.
Necripolitia (debut) 51. Theodora Slave Empress 54. Attila the Hun 54. Tribute to a Bad Man (US) 55. The Power and the Prize (US) 56. The Guns of Navarone 61. Electra 62. *Zorba the Greek* 64. Beyond the Mountains 66. The Brotherhood (US) 68. 'Z' 68. A Dream of Kings (US) 69. Anne of the Thousand Days 70. The Trojan Women 71. The Fifth Offensive 73. Moses (TV) 76. The Message 76. Iphigenia 77. Bloodline 79. Into the Night 84. The Assisi Underground 85. High Season 87. Sweet Country 87. Pano Kato Ke Plagios 93. Jacob (TV) 94. Party 96. The Odyssey (TV) 97. Inquietude 98, etc.

Paquin, Anna (1984–).
New Zealand juvenile actress.
The Piano (AA) 93. Jane Eyre 96. Fly Away Home 96. The Member of the Wedding (TV) 97. Amistad 97. Kiss the Sky 98. Hurlyburly 98, etc.

Paradis, Vanessa (1972–).
French pop singer and model whose film debut was much praised.
Noce Blanche 90. Elisa 95. Pleasure/Le Plaisir (voice) 98, etc.

Paradjanov, Sergei (1924–1990).
Georgian film director whose idiosyncratic films ran foul of Soviet authorities. His international reputation dates from 1968. He was imprisoned for four years in 1974 and forbidden to make films on his release. *The Bogeyman/Bobo*, a documentary on his life and work released in 1991, includes film of the heart attack that killed him when he was flying home from Paris, as well as extracts from his last, uncompleted film, *Confession*.
Andriesh 54. The First Lad/Perwyi Paren 58. Flower on the Stone/Zwetok na Kamne 63. The Ballad 64. Shadows of Our Forgotten Ancestors/Teni Zabytykh Predkov 64. *The Colour of Pomegranates*/Sayat Nova 68. The Legend of Suram Fortress (co-d) 84. Asahik Kerib 88, etc.

Paré, Michael (1959–).
American young leading actor. He trained as a chef before deciding to become an actor.
Eddie and the Cruisers 83. The Philadelphia Experiment 84. Streets of Fire 84. Undercover 84. Instant Justice 87. Space Rage 87. The Women's Club 87. World Gone Wild 88. Eddie and the Cruisers II: Eddie Lives 89. Moon 44 90. Empire City 91. The Closer 91. Into the Sun 92. Blink of an Eye 92. Dragonfight 92. Sunset Heat 92. Village of the Damned 95. Raging Angels 95. Bad Moon 96. Sworn Enemies 96. Carver's Gate 96. Strip Search 97. Hope Floats 97. The Virgin Suicides 98, etc.
TV series: The Greatest American Hero 81–83. Houston Knights 87–88.

Paredes, Marisa (1946–).
Spanish leading actress, known internationally for her roles in the films of Pedro Almodóvar.
Dark Habits 83. High Heels 91. The Flower of My Secret 95. Deep Crimson/Profundo Carmesi 96. Three Lives and Only One Death/Trois Vies et une Seule Mort 96. Life Is Beautiful (It.) 97. Preference 98. Talk of Angels (US) 98, etc.
“ I am more sure of myself if I am risking everything. I tire of people who look too much at what they are doing. – M.P.

Parer, Damien (1912–1944).
Australian cameraman whose coverage of the war in New Guinea, *Kokoda Front Line* 42, won Australia's first Oscar for the best documentary.

Parfitt, Judy.
English actress, from the stage. Born in Sheffield, she trained at RADA and was on-stage from 1954.
Hamlet 69. The Mind of Mr Soames 70. Galileo 74. Secret Orchards 80. Champions 83. Bloody Chamber 83. The Chain 84. The Jewel in the Crown (TV) 84. Maurice 87. Getting It Right 89. Diamond Skulls 89. King Ralph (US) 91. Midnight's Child (US) 92. Dolores Claiborne (US) 95. Element of Doubt 96. Wilde 97. Berkeley Square (TV) 98. Ever After 98, etc.
TV series: Diamond Crack Diamond 70. The Charmer 87.

Parillaud, Anne (1960–).
French leading actress. Married director Luc Besson.
Nikita/La Femme Nikita 91. Innocent Blood 92. Map of the Human Heart 93. Six Days, Six Nights/À la Folie 94. Frankie Starlight 95. The Man in the Iron Mask (US) 98. Shattered Image (US) 98, etc.

Paris, Jerry (1925–1986).
American supporting actor.
The Caine Mutiny 54. *Marty* 55. *Unchained* 55, many others; also played the neighbour in *The Dick Van Dyke Show* 61–66.
AS DIRECTOR: *Never a Dull Moment* 68. *Don't Raise the Bridge, Lower the River* 68. *Viva Max* 69. *The Grasshopper* 70.
Police Academy 2 84. Police Academy 3 85.

Park, Chul-Soo.
South Korean director and screenwriter.
A Bell for Nirvana 83. Mother/Omi 85. Pillar of Mist/Angae Gidung 86. The Five Year Old Buddha 91. 301,302 95. Farewell My Darling 96, etc.

Park, Nick (1959–).
English animator whose shorts starring inventor Wallace and his dog Gromit have won three Oscars.
Creature Comforts (AA) 89. A Grand Day Out 91. The Wrong Trousers (AA) 93. A Close Shave (AA) 95.

Parker, Alan (1944–).
British director with enough self-assurance to make him an international talking point.
■ Melody (w only) 70. Footsteps (& w) 73. Our Cissy (& w) 73. No Hard Feelings 73. The Evacuees (TV) 74. *Bugsy Malone* (& w) 77. *Midnight Express* (AAN, BFA) 78. Fame (& w) 79. Shoot the Moon (& w) 82. Pink Floyd the Wall 82. Birdy 85. Angel Heart 87. Mississippi Burning (AAN) 88. Come See the Paradise 90. The Commitments 91. The Road to Wellville (wd) 94. Evita 96. Angela's Ashes 98.

Parker, Barnett (1890–1941).
British character actor in Hollywood, one of the perfect butlers of the 30s.
The President's Mystery 36. Espionage 37. Wake Up and Live 37. Listen Darling 38. At the Circus 39. Love Thy Neighbour 40. The Reluctant Dragon 41, etc.

Parker, Cecil (1897–1971) (Cecil Schwabe).
British character actor with upper-class personality which could be amiable or chill.
The Silver Spoon (film debut) 33. A Cuckoo in the Nest 33. Storm in a Teacup 37. Dark Journey 37. *The Lady Vanishes* 38. The Citadel 38. *Caesar and Cleopatra* 45. Hungry Hill 46. Captain Boycott 47. *The First Gentleman* (as the Prince Regent) 47. *Quartet* 48. Dear Mr Prohack 49. *The Chiltern Hundreds* 49. Tony Draws a Horse 51. The Man in the White Suit 51. His Excellency 52. I Believe in You 52. Isn't Life Wonderful? 54. *Father Brown* 54. The Constant Husband 55. The Ladykillers 55. *The Court Jester* (US) 55. It's Great to be Young 56. The Admirable Crichton 57. Indiscreet 58. I was Monty's Double 58. Happy is the Bride 58. A Tale of Two Cities 58. The Navy Lark 59. A French Mistress 60. On the Fiddle 61. Petticoat Pirates 62. Heavens Above 63. The Comedy Man 64. Guns at Batasi 64. Moll Flanders 65. A Study in Terror 65. Circus of Fear 67. Oh What a Lovely War 69, many others.

Parker, Cecilia (1905–1993).
Canadian leading lady who played many Hollywood roles but is best remembered as Andy's sister in the *Hardy Family* series 37–44.
Young as You Feel 31. The Painted Veil 34. Naughty Marietta 35. A Family Affair (first of the Hardy films) 37. Seven Sweethearts 42. Andy Hardy Comes Home 58, etc.

Parker, Charlie 'Bird' (1920–1955).
American jazz alto saxophonist, a seminal figure in the development of modern jazz. Born in Kansas City, he played in local bands before helping to create bebop in company with Dizzy Gillespie in the mid-40s. Drink and heroin addiction led to his early death. Archive footage of him was used in the 1979 jazz documentary *The Last of the Blue Devils*. He was played by Forest Whitaker in Clint Eastwood's biopic *Bird* 88.

Parker, Clifton (1905–1990).
British composer.
The Yellow Canary 43. Johnny Frenchman 45. Blanche Fury 48. The Blue Lagoon 49. Diamond City 49. The Wooden Horse 50. Treasure Island 50. The Story of Robin Hood and His Merrie Men 52. The Gift Horse 52. The Teckman Mystery 54. Hell below Zero 54. Passage Home 55. The Feminine Touch 56. Tarzan and the Lost Safari 57. The Birthday Present 57. Campbell's Kingdom 57. Night of the Demon 57. The Secret Place 57. Sea of Sand 58. Harry Black 58. The Thirty Nine Steps 59. The House of the Seven Hawks 59. Circle of Deception 60. The Hellfire Club 60. The Big Day 60. The Treasure of Monte Cristo 60. Snowball 60. Sink the Bismarck! 60. Taste of Fear 61. Girl on Approval 62. HMS Defiant 62. Mystery Submarine 62. The Informers/Underworld Informers 63, etc.

Parker, Dorothy (1893–1967).
American short-story writer, reviewer and wit who spent some years in Hollywood as an associate scriptwriter of mainly undistinguished films. Her second husband was actor and fellow screenwriter Alan Campbell (1933–47). (In 1933 they went to Hollywood at a joint salary of $5,000 a month.) She was played by Dolores Sutton in *F. Scott Fitzgerald in Hollywood* (TV) 76, Rosemary Harris in *Julia* 77, and Jennifer Jason Leigh in *Mrs Parker and the Vicious Circle* 94.
Biography: 1971, *You Might as Well Live* by John Keats.
Paris in Spring (co-s) 35. Suzy 36. Lady Be Careful 36. *A Star Is Born* (AAN) 37. Woman Chases Man 37. Sweethearts 38. Trade Winds 38. Weekend for Three 41. Saboteur 42. Smash-Up – The Story of a Woman (co-story) (AAN) 46. The Fan 49, etc.
❝ Through the sweat and tears I shed over my first script, I saw a great truth – one of those eternal, universal truths that serve to make you feel much worse than you did when you started. And that is no writer, whether he writes from love or from money, can condescend to what he writes. – *D.P.*
Come grace this lotus-laden shore,
The isle of Do-What's-Done-Before.
Come curb the new and watch the old win,
Out where streets are paved with Goldwyn.
– *D.P.*
Scratch an actor and you'll find an actress. – *D.P.*
Hollywood money isn't money. It's congealed snow, melts in your hand. – *D.P.*
So odd a blend of Little Nell and Lady Macbeth. – *Alexander Woollcott*
The first modern American woman: she could out-talk, out-drink, out-fuck all the men. – *Alan Rudolph*
See also: ALGONQUIN ROUND TABLE.

Parker, Eddie (1900–1960).
American stuntman who doubled for most of Universal's horror stars.

Parker, Eleanor (1922–).
American leading lady with brief stage experience before a Hollywood contract; her career followed a typical pattern, with increasingly good leading roles followed by a decline, with a later comeback in character parts.
Biography: 1989, *Eleanor Parker* by Doug McClelland.
■ They Died with Their Boots On (debut as extra) 41. Buses Roar 42. Mysterious Doctor 43. Mission to Moscow 43. The Very Thought of You 44. Crime by Night 44. Between Two Worlds 44. The Last Ride 44. Pride of the Marines 45. Of Human Bondage (as Mildred) 46. Never Say Goodbye 46. Escape Me Never 47. *The Voice of the Turtle* 47. The Woman in White 48. Chain Lightning 49. Three Secrets 50. *Caged* (AAN) 50. Valentino 51. A Millionaire for Christy 51. *Detective Story* (AAN) 51. Scaramouche 52. Above and Beyond 52. Escape from Fort Bravo 53. The Naked Jungle 54. Valley of the Kings 54. Many Rivers to Cross 54. *Interrupted Melody* (AAN) 55. The Man with the Golden Arm 56. The King and Four Queens 56. Lizzie 57. The Seventh Sin 57. A Hole in the Head 59. Home from the Hill 60. Return to Peyton Place 61. Madison Avenue 62. Panic Button 64. The Sound of Music 65. The Oscar 66. An American Dream 66. Warning Shot 66. The Tiger and the Pussycat 67. How to Steal the World 68. Eye of the Cat 69. Maybe I'll Come Home in the Spring 70. Vanished (TV) 71. Home for the Holidays (TV) 72. The Great American Beauty Contest (TV) 74. *She's Dressed to Kill* (TV) 79. Sunburn 79. Madame X (TV) 81.
TV series: Bracken's World 69.

Parker, Fess (1925–).
American leading man with some stage experience. He is now a vintner and hotelier in California.
Untamed Frontier 52. *Davy Crockett* 54 (and two sequels). The Great Locomotive Chase 56. Westward Ho the Wagons 56. Old Yeller 57. The Hangman 59. Hell is for Heroes 62. Smoky 66, etc.
TV series: Mr Smith Goes to Washington 62. Daniel Boone 64–68.

Parker, Jameson (1947–).
American leading man who first appeared on the daytime soap operas *Somerset* and *One Life to Live* in the 70s.
The Bell Jar 79. A Small Circle of Friends 80. Women at West Point (TV) 80. Anatomy of a Seduction (TV) 80. White Dog 82. Who Is Julia? (TV) 86. Prince of Darkness 87. Dead before Dawn 93, etc.
TV series: Simon and Simon 81–88.

Parker, Jean (1912–) (Luis Stephanie Zelinska).
Once-demure American leading lady, popular in the 30s; latterly playing hard-boiled roles.
Rasputin and the Empress 32. *Little Women* 33. *Sequoia* 34. The Ghost Goes West (GB) 36. Princess O'Hara 37. The Flying Deuces 39. Beyond Tomorrow 40. No Hands on the Clock 42. One Body Too Many 42. Minesweeper 43. Bluebeard 44. Detective Kitty O'Day 44. Lady in the Death House 44. The Gunfighter 50. Those Redheads from Seattle 53. Black Tuesday 54. A Lawless Street 55. Apache Uprising 65. The Morning After 72, etc.

Parker, Mary-Louise (1964–).
American actress.
Signs of Life 89. Longtime Companion 90. Fried Green Tomatoes 91. Grand Canyon 91. Naked in New York 93. Mr Wonderful 93. The Client 94. Bullets over Broadway 94. Boys on the Side 95. Reckless 95. Sugartime (TV) 95. The Portrait of a Lady 96. Murder in Mind 97. The Maker 97. Goodbye, Lover 98. Legalese (TV) 98, etc.

Parker, Sarah Jessica (1965–).
American actress, a former child star who played the title role in *Annie* on Broadway in the late 70s. Married actor Matthew BRODERICK in 1997.
Rich Kids 79. Firstborn 84. Footloose 84. Girls Just Want to Have Fun 85. Flight of the Navigator 86. L.A. Story 91. Honeymoon in Vegas 92. Hocus Pocus 93. Striking Distance 93. Ed Wood 94. Miami Rhapsody 95. If Lucy Fell 96. The Substance of Fire 96. The First Wives Club 96. Mars Attacks! 96. Extreme Measures 96, etc.
TV series: Square Pegs 82–83. A Year in the Life 87–88. Equal Justice 90–91. Sex and the City 98– .

Parker, Suzy (1932–) (Cecelia Parker).
Statuesque American leading lady, former model. She married actor Bradford Dillman, her third husband, in 1963.
Kiss Them for Me (debut) 57. *Ten North Frederick* 58. The Best of Everything 59. Circle of Deception 61. The Interns 62. Chamber of Horrors 66, etc.

Parker, Trey (1972–) (Donald McKay Parker III).
American actor, writer, director and songwriter, best known as the creator of the TV cartoon series *South Park* with Matt STONE. Born in Auburn, Alabama, he began acting as a teenager, with his family relocating to Los Angeles so that he could continue his career. He studied at the Berklee School of Music before transferring to Colorado University to study film. He has also performed and recorded as part of the hip-hop group EYC (Express Yourself Clearly).
Newsies (a) 92. A Christmas Story (short) 92. Cannibal: The Musical/Alfred Packer: The Musical (p, a, wd, s) 93. BASEketball (a) 98. Orgazmo (& d) 98, etc.
TV series: Hull High 90. South Park 97– .

Parker, Willard (1912–1996) (Worster van Eps).
Tall American 'second lead', in films from 1938 after stage experience.
A Slight Case of Murder (debut) 38. The Fighting Guardsman 43. You Gotta Stay Happy 48. Sangaree 53. The Great Jesse James Raid 53. The Earth Dies Screaming 64. Waco 66, etc.
TV series: Tales of the Texas Rangers 55–57.

Parkins, Barbara (1943–).
Canadian leading lady whose major success was TV.
Valley of the Dolls 67. The Kremlin Letters 69. The Mephisto Waltz 71. Puppet on a Chain 72. Asylum 72. Captains and the Kings (TV) 76. Shout at the Devil 76. Ziegfeld: the Man and his Women (as Anna Held) (TV) 78. The Critical List (TV) 78. Bear Island 80, etc.
TV series: *Peyton Place* 64–68.

Parks, Gordon (1925–).
American director, former stills photographer, novelist and composer.
The Learning Tree 68. *Shaft* 71. Shaft's Big Score 72. Leadbelly 76. Moments without Proper Names 86, etc.

Parks, Gordon, Jnr (1948–1979).
American director, son of Gordon Parks. Killed in a plane crash.
Superfly 72. Thomasine and Bushrod 74. Three the Hard Way 74. Aaron Loves Angela 75.

Parks, Larry (1914–1975) (Sam Kleusman Lawrence Parks).
American light leading man whose career in 'B' pictures was interrupted by his highly successful impersonation of Al Jolson. He subsequently proved difficult to cast, and was forced out of Hollywood after testifying to the Unamerican Activities Committee.
■ You Belong to Me 41. Mystery Ship 41. Harmon of Michigan 41. Blondie Goes to College 42. Harvard Here I Come 42. The Boogie Man Will Get You 42. Atlantic Convoy 42. Canal Zone 42. Three Girls About Town 42. Sing for your Supper 42. Flight Lieutenant 42. Submarine Raiser 42. Honolulu Lu 42. Hello Annapolis 42. You were never Lovelier 42. A Man's World 42. North of the Rockies 42. Alias Boston Blackie 42. They All Kissed the Bride 42. Redhead from Manhattan 43. Is Everybody Happy? 43. First Comes Courage 43. Power of the Press 43. The Deerslayer 43. Destroyer 43. Reveille with Beverly 43. She's a Sweetheart 44. The Racket Man 44. The Black Parachute 44. Stars on Parade 44. Hey Rookie 44. Sergeant Mike 44. Counter Attack 45. Jealousy 45. Renegades 46. *The Jolson Story* (AAN) 46. Her Husband's Affairs 47. Down to Earth 47. The Swordsman 47. Gallant Blade 48. *Jolson Sings Again* 49. Emergency Wedding 50. Love is Better than Ever 52. Tiger by the Tail 55. *Freud* 62.

Parks, Michael (1938–).
Brooding American leading man.
Wild Seed 64. Bus Riley's Back in Town 65. The Bible (as Adam) 66. The Idol (GB) 66. The Happening 67. Can Ellen Be Saved? (TV) 73. The Last Hard Men 76. Sidewinder One 77. Love and the Midnight Auto Supply 77. The Private Files of J. Edgar Hoover 78. Breakthrough 79. Fast Friends (TV) 79. North Sea Hijack 80. Reward (TV) 81. Savannah Smiles 82. Chase (TV) 85. Club Life 86. Return of Josey Wales (& d) 86. Stamp of a Killer (TV) 87. Arizona Heat 88. Welcome to Spring Break 88. Gore Vidal's Billy the Kid 89. The Hitman 91. Storyville 92. Death Wish V: The Face of Death 94. From Dusk till Dawn 96. Julian Po 97. Niagra, Niagra 98, etc.

TV series: Then Came Bronson 69. The Colbys 87.

Parks, Van Dyke (1941–).
American composer and singer, a former child actor.
Goin' South 78. Popeye 80. Club Paradise 86. Rented Lips 88. Casual Sex? 88. The Two Jakes (& a) 90. Wild Bill 95. The Summer of Ben Tyler (TV) 96. Private Parts 96. Bastard out of Carolina (TV) 96, etc.

Parkyakarkus (1904–1958) (Harry Einstein).
American radio comedian formerly known as Harry Parke. He is the father of actor-director Albert Brooks.
Strike Me Pink 36. Night Spot 38. Glamour Boy 40. Earl Carroll's Vanities 45.

Parkyn, Leslie (–1983).
British executive producer, associated with *Sergei Nolbandov* 1951–57, subsequently with Julian Wintle.
The Kidnappers 53. Tiger Bay 59. The Waltz of the Toreadors 62. Father Came Too 64, many others.

Parlo, Dita (1906–1971) (Gerthe Kornstadt).
German star actress of the 30s.
Homecoming 28. Melody of the Heart 30. Secrets of the Orient 31. L'Atalante 34. The Mystic Mountain 36. Mademoiselle Docteur 37. La Grande Illusion 37. Ultimatum 39. Justice est Faite 50. Quand le Soleil Montera 56, etc.

Parnell, Emory (1894–1979).
American general-purpose character actor: could be villain, prison warden, weakling or kindly father.
King of Alcatraz 39. I Married a Witch 42. Mama Loves Papa 46. Words and Music 48. Call Me Madam 53. Man of the West 58, many others.

Parr-Davies, Harry (1914–1955).
Welsh composer and songwriter who contributed songs to many of Gracie Fields' films and other British musicals of the 30s and 40s. He had a big wartime hit with 'Pedro the Fisherman', from his stage show *The Lisbon Story*, which was subsequently filmed.
This Week of Grace 33. Sing as We Go 34. Queen of Hearts 36. We're Going to Be Rich 38. Keep Smiling/Smile as You Go 38. It's in the Air 38. Shipyard Sally 39. Maytime in Mayfair 49. The Lisbon Story 49, etc.

Parrish, Helen (1922–1959).
American leading lady, former baby model and child actress.
The Big Trail 31. A Dog of Flanders 34. Mad about Music 38. You'll Find Out 40. They All Kissed the Bride 42. The Mystery of the Thirteenth Guest 44. The Wolf Hunters 50, etc.

Parrish, Robert (1916–1995).
American director, former editor and child actor.
Autobiographies: 1976, *Growing Up in Hollywood*. 1988, *Hollywood Doesn't Live Here Anymore*.
■ Cry Danger 51. The Mob 51. My Pal Gus 52. The San Francisco Story 52. Rough Shoot (GB) 52. Assignment Paris 52. The Purple Plain 54. Lucy Gallant 55. Fire Down Below 57. Saddle the Wind 58. The Wonderful Country 59. In the French Style (& p) 63. Up from the Beach 65. The Bobo 67. Casino Royale (part) 67. Duffy 68. Journey to the Far Side of the Sun 69. A Town Called Bastard 71. The Marseilles Contract 74. Mississippi Blues (co-d) 84.
❝ His films belong to a director who craves anonymity. – *Andrew Sarris, 1968*

Parrondo, Gil.
American art director and production designer.
The 7th Voyage of Sinbad 58. The 3 Worlds of Gulliver 60. The Valley of Gwangi 69. The Battle of Britain 69. Patton (AA) 70. Nicholas and Alexandra (AA) 71. Travels with My Aunt (AAN) 72. Robin and Marian 76. The Boys from Brazil 78. Cuba 79. Lionheart 87. Farewell to the King 89. The Return of the Musketeers 89. Christopher Columbus: The Discovery 92. The Disappearance of Garcia Lorca 97, etc.

Parrott, James (1892–1939).
American director, mainly of two-reelers featuring Laurel and Hardy (*Blotto*, *The Music Box*, *County Hospital*, etc), Charlie Chase and Max Davidson. Features include *Jailbirds* 31, *Sing, Sister, Sing* 35.

Parry, Gordon (1908–1981).
British director of mainly secondary films: former actor, production manager, etc.
Bond Street 48. Third Time Lucky 48. Now Barabbas 49. Midnight Episode 50. Innocents in Paris 52. Women of Twilight 52. A Yank in Ermine 55. Sailor Beware 56. Tread Softly Stranger 58. The Navy Lark 60, etc.

Parry, Natasha (1930–).
British leading lady who married Peter Brook. Appears occasionally on stage and screen.
Dance Hall 49. The Dark Man 50. Crow Hollow 52. Knave of Hearts 53. Windom's Way 57. The Rough and the Smooth 59. Midnight Lace 60. The Fourth Square 62. The Girl in the Headlines 64. Romeo and Juliet 68. Oh What a Lovely War 69. La Chambre Voisine 80, etc.

Parsons, Estelle (1927–).
American character actress with stage background.
Bonnie and Clyde (AA) 67. Rachel Rachel (AAN) 68. I Never Sang for My Father 69. Don't Drink the Water 69. I Walk the Line 70. Watermelon Man 71. Two People 73. For Pete's Sake 74. Foreplay 75. Open Admissions (TV) 88. The Lemon Sisters 89. Dick Tracy 90. A Private Matter (TV) 92. That Darn Cat 96. Looking for Richard 96, etc.

Parsons, Harriet (1906–1983).
American producer, daughter of Louella Parsons.
I Remember Mama 47. Clash by Night 51. Susan Slept Here 54, etc.

Parsons, Louella (1880–1972) (L. Oettinger).
Hollywood columnist whose gossip rivalled in readership that of Hedda Hopper. In occasional films as herself, e.g. *Hollywood Hotel* 37, *Starlift* 51.
Autobiographical books: 1944, *The Gay Illiterate*. 1962, *Tell It to Louella*.
Biography: 1973, *Hedda and Louella* by George Eels.
❝ Her friends always stand by her. When she prematurely published a claim that an actress was pregnant, the actress's husband hastened to prove her correct. – *Time Magazine*
Her writings stand out like an asthmatic's gasps. – *Nunnally Johnson*
Not a bad old slob. – *James Mason*

Parsons, Milton (1904–1980).
Lugubrious American character actor often seen as undertaker.
The Hidden Hand 42. Margie 44, many others.

Parsons, Nicholas (1928–).
English light actor, also a variety and cabaret performer and quiz-game chairman, much on radio. Born in Grantham, Lincolnshire, he studied engineering at Glasgow University before beginning on stage.
Autobiography: 1994, *The Straight Man: My Life in Comedy*.
Master of Bankdam 48. Brothers in Law 57. Too Many Crooks 59. Doctor in Love 62. Don't Raise the Bridge, Lower the River 68. Spy Story 76, etc.
TV series: The Eric Barker Half Hour 51–53. Look at It This Way 52. What's It All About? 55. Here and Now 55–56. Strike a New Note 56. Get Happy 56. Four Feather Falls (voice) 60. The Arthur Haynes Show 57–62, 63–65. The Ugliest Girl in Town (US) 68–69. Sale of the Century 78–83.

Parton, Dolly (1946–).
Voluptuous American country and western singer.
Nine to Five (AANs) 81. The Best Little Whorehouse in Texas 82. Rhinestone (& m) 84. Steel Magnolias 89. Wild Texas Wind 91. Straight Talk 92, etc.
TV series: Dixie Fixin's 94.
❝ I enjoy the way I look, but it's a joke. – *D.P.*
I'm on a seafood diet – I see food, I eat it. – *D.P.*

Pascal, Christine (1952–1996).
French actress, screenwriter and director. Born in Lyon, she studied acting at the local conservatoire. Committed suicide by throwing herself from the window of a psychiatric clinic in Paris.
AS ACTRESS: The Watchmaker of Saint-Paul/L'horloger de Saint-Paul 73. La Meilleure Façon de Marcher 76. Des Enfants Gâtés (& co-w) 77. On Efface Tout 78. Panny z Wilka (Pol.) 79. Coup de Foudre 83. Elsa, Elsa 85. Round Midnight/Autour de Minuit 86. La Travestie 88. Rien que des Mensonges 91. Les Patriotes 93, etc.
AS DIRECTOR: Felicité (& a, co-w) 77. La Garce (& co-w) 83. Zanzibar (& co-w) 88. Le Petit Prince a Dit (& co-w) 92. Adultery, a User's Manual/Adultère, Mode d'Emploi 96.

Pascal, Gabriel (1894–1954) (Gabor Lehöl).
Romanian-born producer and director, a former actor, of somewhat mysterious origins. After working in Germany and Italy, he came to Britain in the 30s, won the esteem of Bernard Shaw and persuaded him to part, for a token payment, with the film rights to his plays, which many had tried to do and failed. His version of *Caesar and Cleopatra* was the most expensive British film of its time, costing around £1.25m, more than twice its original budget, which did much to damage the reputation of the Rank Organization, and grounded his career. Failed projects included a version of Shaw's *St Joan* starring Katharine Hepburn, *The Devil's Disciple* with Clark Gable and Cary Grant, and a film of the life of Gandhi. He was also a prime mover in turning *Pygmalion* into the musical *My Fair Lady*.
Biography: 1971, *The Disciple and His Devil* by Valerie Pascal.
Populi Morituri (It.) (a, co-d) 28. The Living Dead/Friedricke, Unheimliche Geschichten (Ger.) (p) 32. Café Mascot (p) 36. Reasonable Doubt (p) 36. *Pygmalion* (p) 38. Major Barbara (p, co-d) 41. Caesar and Cleopatra (p, d) 45. Androcles and the Lion (US) (p) 53, etc.
❝ I give you my word of honor as a Hungarian Cavalry Officer and an English Farmer, you are the greatest crook unhung. – *G.P., in a telegram to a Hollywood agent*
Life is a divine poem, and it is our own fault if we recite it badly. – *G.P.*
Gabriel Pascal is one of those extraordinary men who turn up occasionally, say once in a century, and may be called godsends in the arts to which they are devoted. Pascal is doing for the films what Diaghileff did for the Russian Ballet. – *George Bernard Shaw*
A marvellous gypsy rogue with incredible panache and no guile, as open as a baby and as ruthless as a tiger. – *Rex Harrison*
A Rumanian who claimed to be Hungarian and looked like a Himalayan. Architecturally he was circular and his voice had the timbre of a 78 record played at 33. – *Alan Jay Lerner*
Gabby was a showman of some magnitude, but not a director. He knew as much about directing as a cow does about playing the piano. – *Michael Powell*

Pascal, Gisèle (1923–) (Gisèle Tallone).
French leading actress of stage and screen. Born in Cannes, she was in films from the early 40s. Romantically involved with actor Yves MONTAND and Prince Rainier of Monaco, she married actor Raymond PELLEGRIN.
L'Arlésienne 42. Mademoiselle S'Amuse 47. The Naked Woman/La Femme Nue 49. Bel Amour 51. Boum sur Paris 54. Mademoiselle de Paris 55. Sylviane de Mes Nuits 57. The Iron Mask/Le Masque de Fer 62. La Femme Publique 84. Juillet en Septembre 87, etc.

Pasco, Richard (1926–).
British character actor, mainly on stage and TV.
Room at the Top 59. Yesterday's Enemy 60. The Gorgon 64. Rasputin the Mad Monk 66. The Watcher in the Woods 80. Wagner 83. Mrs Brown 97, etc.

Pasdar, Adrian (1965–).
American leading actor.
Top Gun 86. Streets of Gold 86. Solarwarriors 87. Near Dark 87. Big Time 88. Cookie 89. Torn Apart 90. Vital Signs 90. Grand Isle 91. Just Like a Woman (GB) 92. The Killing Box 93. The Last Good Time 94. The Pompatus of Love 96, etc.

Paskaljevic, Goran (1947–).
Serbian (formerly Yugoslavian) film director.
The Beach Guard in Winter/Cuvar Plaze U Zimskom Periodu 76. The Dog Who Loved Trains/Pas Koji Je Voleo Vozove 77. Twilight Time/Suton 83. Varljivo Leto '68 84. Guardian Angel/Andjeo Cuvar 87. Time of Miracles/Vreme Cuda (& p, co-w) 90. Tango Argentino (& p) 92. Someone Else's America 95. The Powder Keg/Bure Baruta (co-p, co-w, d) 98, etc.

Pasolini, Pier Paolo (1922–1975).
Italian director, novelist, poet and critic. Born in Bologna, he was expelled from the Communist Party for homosexuality, but remained passionately proletarian in his attitudes. He started in films as a writer, before becoming an increasingly controversial director and social commentator. He was beaten and run over near the seaside town of Ostia, allegedly by a homosexual prostitute, though there is evidence that his murder was committed by right-wing thugs. A documentary, *Pasolini: An Italian Crime*, made by Marco Tullio Giordana in 1995, comes to the conclusion that more than one person was involved in his death.
Biography: 1987, *Pasolini* by Enzo Siciliano.
Accattone 61. Mamma Roma 62. The Witches (part) 63. *The Gospel According to St Matthew* 64. Oedipus Rex 67. *Theorem* 68. Pigsty 69. Medea 70. Decameron 70. The Canterbury Tales 71. The Arabian Nights 74. The 120 Days of Sodom 75, etc.
❝ Life is a heap of insignificant and ironic ruins. – *P.P.P.*

Passer, Ivan (1933–).
Czech director, latterly in Hollywood.
A Boring Afternoon 64. Intimate Lighting 66. Born to Win 71. Law and Disorder 74. Silver Bears 78. Ace Up My Sleeve 78. Cutter's Way 81. Creator 85. Haunted Summer 88. Stalin (TV) 92. Kidnapped (TV) 95, etc.

Pasternak, Boris (1890–1960).
Russian novelist, author of *Dr Zhivago*.

Pasternak, Joe (1901–1991).
Hungarian producer in Hollywood during the golden years; especially identified with cheerful light musicals.
Autobiography: 1956, *Easy the Hard Way*.
Three Smart Girls 36. *One Hundred Men and a Girl* 37. Mad about Music 38. *Destry Rides Again* 39. Seven Sinners 40. It Started with Eve 41. Presenting Lily Mars 42. Song of Russia 43. Two Girls and a Sailor 44. Anchors Aweigh 45. Holiday in Mexico 46. The Unfinished Dance 47. On an Island with You 48. In the Good Old Summertime 49. The Duchess of Idaho 50. *The Great Caruso* 51. Skirts Ahoy 52. Latin Lovers 53. The Student Prince 54. Love Me or Leave Me 55. The Opposite Sex 56. Ten Thousand Bedrooms 57. Party Girl 58. Ask Any Girl 59. Please Don't Eat the Daisies 60. The Horizontal Lieutenant 61. Jumbo 62. The Courtship of Eddie's Father 63. Girl Happy 65. Penelope 66. The Sweet Ride 68, many others.

Pastorelli, Robert (1954–).
American actor.
Outrageous Fortune 87. Beverly Hills Cop II 87. Dances with Wolves 90. Folks! 92. Sister Act II: Back in the Habit 93. Striking Distance 93. Michael 96. Eraser 96. A Simple Wish 97. Scotch and Milk 98, etc.
TV series: Murphy Brown 88–94. Cracker 97.

Pastrone, Giovanni (1883–1959).
Pioneer producer and director of Italian cinema, whose spectacular *Cabiria* was one of the first, and most influential, of epic movies. He abandoned cinema in the 20s.
Giordano Bruno 08. The Fall of Troy 10. Padre 12. Cabiria 14. Tigre Real 16. Hedda Gabler 19, etc.

Patch, Wally (1888–1970) (Walter Vinicombe).
Burly British cockney character actor, in films from 1920 after varied show-business experience.
Shadows 31. The Good Companions 32. Get Off My Foot 35. Not So Dusty 36. Bank Holiday 38. Quiet Wedding 40. Gasbags 40. The Common Touch 41. Old Mother Riley at Home 45. The Ghosts of Berkeley Square 47. The Guinea Pig 49. Will Any Gentleman? 53. Private's Progress 55. I'm All Right, Jack 59. Sparrows Can't Sing 63, many others.

Pate, Michael (1920–).
Australian actor in Hollywood in the 50s and 60s, often as Red Indian chief or second-string villain.
The Rugged O'Riordans 49. The Strange Door 51. Five Fingers 52. Houdini 53. The Silver Chalice 54. The Court Jester 56. Congo Crossing

56. The Oklahoman 57. Green Mansions 59. The Canadians 61. McLintock 63. Major Dundee 65. Tim (wd) 79. Return of Captain Invincible 83. Death of a Soldier 87. Howling III: The Marsupials 87. Official Denial 94, etc.
TV series: Matlock Police 71.

Paterson, Bill (1945–).
Scottish character actor, from the stage.
Licking Hitler (TV) 71. The Ploughman's Lunch 83. Comfort and Joy 84. The Killing Fields 84. A Private Function 84. Defence of the Realm 85. The Adventures of Baron Munchausen 88. Truly Madly Deeply 90. The Witches 90. The Object of Beauty 91. Chaplin 92. Spice World: The Movie 97. Melissa (TV) 97. Hilary and Jackie 98, etc.
TV series: The Writing on the Wall 96.

Paterson, Neil (1916–).
British screenwriter and novelist.
The Kidnappers 53. High Tide at Noon 57. *Room at the Top* (AA) 59. The Spiral Road 62. Mister Moses 65.

Paterson, Pat (1911–1978).
English leading lady who went to Hollywood but gave up her career to marry Charles Boyer.
■ The Professional Guest 31. The Great Gay Road 31. Night Shadows 31. Murder on the Second Floor 32. Partners Please 32. Here's George 32. Bitter Sweet 33. Love Time 34. Bottoms Up 34. Call it Luck 34. Charlie Chan in Egypt 35. Lottery Lover 35. Spendthrift 36. 52nd Street 37. Idiot's Delight 39.

Pathé, Charles (1863–1957).
Pioneer French executive and producer, founder of Pathé Frères and later Pathé Gazette. Also credited with making the first 'long' film: *Les Misérables* (made in 1909, it ran four whole reels).

Patinkin, Mandy (1952–).
American actor.
The Big Fix 78. Ragtime 81. Daniel 83. Yentl 83. The Princess Bride 87. Alien Nation 88. The House on Carroll Street 88. Dick Tracy 90. Impromptu 91. True Colors 91. The Doctor 91. The Music of Chance 93. Broken Glass (TV) 96. The Hunchback of Notre Dame (title role, TV) 97. Lulu on the Bridge 98, etc.
TV series: Chicago Hope 94–95.

Patric, Jason (1966–).
Young American leading actor, the son of playwright Jason Miller and the grandson of actor Jackie Gleason.
Toughlove (TV) 85. Solarbabies 86. The Lost Boys 87. The Beast 88. Frankenstein Unbound 90. After Dark, My Sweet 90. Rush 91. Geronimo: An American Legend 93. The Journey of August King 95. Sleepers 96. Incognito 97. Speed 2: Cruise Control 97. Your Friends & Neighbors 98, etc.

Patrick, Dorothy (1922–1987).
Blonde American actress of the 40s.
Boy's Ranch 45. Till the Clouds Roll By 46. The Mighty McGurk 46. High Wall 47. New Orleans 47. Alias a Gentleman 47. Follow Me Quietly 49. Come to the Stable 49. 711 Ocean Drive 50. Torch Song 53. Violent Saturday 55. The View from Pompey's Head 55, etc.

Patrick, Gail (1911–1980) (Margaret Fitzpatrick).
American leading lady in Hollywood from early 30s, usually in routine smart-woman roles. Retired from acting and became a TV producer, notably of the successful *Perry Mason* series.
The Phantom Broadcast 32. Cradle Song 33. No More Ladies 35. Artists and Models 37. Reno 40. Quiet, Please, Murder 43. Women in Bondage 44. Twice Blessed 45. The Plainsman and the Lady 46. Calendar Girl 47, many others.

Patrick, John (1905–1995) (John Patrick Goggan).
American playwright. Works filmed include *The Hasty Heart*, *The Teahouse of the August Moon*. Committed suicide.
SCREENPLAYS: Educating Father 36. One Mile from Heaven 37. International Settlement 38. Mr Moto Takes a Chance 38. Enchantment 48. The President's Lady 53. Three Coins in the Fountain 54. Love Is a Many Splendored Thing 55. High Society 56. Les Girls 57. Some Came Running 58. The World of Suzie Wong 61. The Main Attraction 63. The Shoes of the Fisherman 68, etc.

Patrick, Lee (1906–1982).
American character actress with stage experience, in Hollywood from 1937, usually as hard-bitten blondes.
Strange Cargo (debut) 29. *The Maltese Falcon* 41. Now Voyager 42. Mother Wore Tights 47. Caged 50. There's No Business Like Show Business 54. Vertigo 58. Summer and Smoke 61. The New Interns 64. *The Black Bird* 75, many others.
TV series: Topper 53–55. Mr Adams and Eve 56–57.

Patrick, Nigel (1913–1981) (Nigel Wemyss).
Debonair British leading actor, on stage from 1932.
■ Mrs Pym of Scotland Yard 39. Uneasy Terms 48. *Noose* 48. Spring in Park Lane 48. Silent Dust 49. Jack of Diamonds 49. The Perfect Woman 50. *Trio* 50. Morning Departure 50. Pandora and the Flying Dutchman 51. Encore 51. The Browning Version 51. Young Wives' Tale 51. Meet Me Tonight 52. *The Pickwick Papers* (as Mr Jingle) 52. Who Goes There 52. *The Sound Barrier* 52. Grand National Night 53. Forbidden Cargo 54. The Sea Shall Not Have Them 54. All for Mary 55. A Prize of Gold 55. Raintree County 57. How to Murder a Rich Uncle 57. Count Five and Die 58. The Man Inside 58. Sapphire 59. *The League of Gentlemen* 60. The Trials of Oscar Wilde 60. Johnny Nobody (& d) 61. The Informers 63. The Virgin Soldiers 69. The Battle of Britain 69. The Executioner 70. Tales from the Crypt 72. The Great Waltz 72. The Mackintosh Man 73.
TV series: Zero One 62.

Patrick, Robert (1959–).
American actor, often in action films.
Future Hunters 86. Equalizer 2000 87. Die Hard 2 90. Terminator II: Judgment Day (as the Terminator) 91. Fire in the Sky 93. Double Dragon 94. Striptease 96. Cop Land 97. Asylum 97. The Vivero Letter 98. The Faculty 98, etc.

Patten, Luana (1938–1996).
American teenage actress of the 50s. Died of respiratory failure after a long illness.
Song of the South 46. So Dear to My Heart 48. Johnny Tremain 57. The Little Shepherd of Kingdom Come 61. A Thunder of Drums 61. Follow Me Boys 66. Grotesque 88, etc.

Patterson, Elizabeth (1876–1966).
American character actress with stage experience; in Hollywood from the late 20s, usually as kindly or shrewish elderly ladies.
Daddy Longlegs 30. A Bill of Divorcement 32. Miss Pinkerton 32. Dinner at Eight 33. So Red the Rose 36. Sing You Sinners 38. *The Cat and the Canary* 39. *Tobacco Road* 41. Hail the Conquering Hero 43. Lady on a Train 45. *Intruder in the Dust* 48. Little Women 49. Bright Leaf 50. Pal Joey 57. The Oregon Trail 59, many others.

Patterson, Lee (1929–).
Sturdy Canadian leading man of minor British and American films who spent a decade in the 60s and 70s on the soap opera *One Life to Live*.
36 Hours 51. The Passing Stranger 54. Above Us the Waves 55. Soho Incident 56. Cat and Mouse 58. Jack the Ripper 60. The Ceremony 63. Valley of Mystery 67. Chato's Land 72. Bullseye! 90, etc.
TV series: Surfside Six 60–62.

Patterson, Neva (1925–).
American character actress.
Desk Set 57. Too Much Too Soon 58. The Domino Principle 77. Women of Valor (TV) 86, etc.
TV series: The Governor and JJ 69. Nichols 71.

Patton, Will (1954–).
American actor.
Silkwood 83. After Hours 85. Desperately Seeking Susan 85. No Way Out 86. Wildfire 88. A Shock to the System 90. Dillinger 91. In the Soup 92. Cold Heaven 92. Romeo Is Bleeding 93. Natural Causes 94. The Puppet Masters 94. Judicial Consent 94. Copycat 95. The Spitfire Grill 96. Fled 96. This World, Then the Fireworks 97. The Postman 97. Inventing the Abbots 97. Armageddon 98. OK Garage 98. I Woke Up Early the Day I Died 98, etc.

Paul, Robert (1869–1943).
Pioneer British movie camera inventor (1895). The following year he invented a projector, which he called a theatrograph. Later turned showman.

Paull, Lawrence G (1943–).
American production designer. He trained as an architect and a city planner.
Little Fauss and Big Halsy 70. The Hired Hand 71. The Naked Ape 73. The Bingo Long Traveling All-Stars and Motor Kings 76. Blue Collar 78. In God We Trust 80. Blade Runner (AAN) 82. Romancing the Stone 84. Back to the Future 85. Project X 87. Cocoon: The Return 88. Harlem Nights 89. The Last of the Finest 90. Predator 2 90. City Slickers 91. Memoirs of an Invisible Man 92. Another Stakeout 93. Naked Gun 33 : The Final Insult 94. Man of the House 95. Escape from L.A. 96, etc.

Paulvé, André (1898–1982).
French producer.
La Comédie du Bonheur 39. Lumière d'Eté 42. L'Eternel Retour 43. Les Visiteurs du Soir 43. La Belle et la Bête 45. Ruy Blas 47. Orphée 49. Manèges 49. Casque d'Or 51, many others.

Pavan, Marisa (1932–) (Marisa Pierangeli).
Italian leading lady, sister of Pier Angeli. In Hollywood from 1950.
What Price Glory? (debut) 52. The Rose Tattoo (AAN) 55. The Man in the Grey Flannel Suit 56. Solomon and Sheba 59. John Paul Jones 59. The Slightly Pregnant Man (Fr.) 73. Johnny Monroe 87, etc.

Pavarotti, Luciano (1935–).
Italian tenor in international opera. Starred in one film in 1982, *Yes Giorgio*.

Pavlow, Muriel (1921–).
British leading lady, on stage and screen from 1936; her youthful appearance enabled her to continue in juvenile roles for many years.
A Romance in Flanders (debut) 36. Quiet Wedding 40. Night Boat to Dublin 45. The Shop at Sly Corner 47. Malta Story 53. Doctor in the House 54. *Reach for the Sky* 56. Tiger in the Smoke 57. Rooney 58. Murder She Said 62. Memento Mori (TV) 92. Daisies in December 95, etc.

Pawle, Lennox (1872–1936).
British character actor, mainly on stage.
The Admirable Crichton (GB) 18. The Great Adventure (GB) 21. Married in Hollywood (US) 29. The Sin of Madeleine Claudet (US) 32. *David Copperfield* (as Mr Dick) 34. Sylvia Scarlett (US) 35, etc.

Paxinou, Katina (1900–1973) (Katina Constantopoulos).
Greek actress with international experience; played in some Hollywood films.
For Whom the Bell Tolls (AA) 43. Confidential Agent 44. Uncle Silas (GB) 47. *Mourning Becomes Electra* 47. Confidential Report 55. Rocco and His Brothers 60. Zita 68, etc.

Paxton, Bill (1955–).
American leading actor. Born in Fort Worth, Texas, he studied at New York University and began as a set dresser on exploitation movies in the mid-70s.
Impulse 84. The Terminator 84. Weird Science 85. Aliens 86. Near Dark 87. Next of Kin 89. Brain Dead 89. The Last of the Finest 90. Navy SEALS 90. Predator 2 90. Hurricane 91. The Vagrant 91. One False Move 92. Monolith 93. Boxing Helena 93. Trespass 93. Indian Summer 93. Tombstone 94. True Lies 94. Apollo 13 95. The Last Supper 96. *Twister* 96. Evening Star 96. Traveller (& p) 97. Titanic 97. A Bright Shining Lie (TV) 98. A Simple Plan 98. Mighty Joe Young 98, etc.

Paxton, John (1911–1985).
American screenwriter.
■ *Murder My Sweet* 44. My Pal Wolf (co-w) 44. Cornered 46. Crack Up (co-w) 46. *Crossfire* (AAN) 47. So Well Remembered 47. Of Men and Music (co-w) 50. *Fourteen Hours* 51. The Wild One 54. A Prize of Gold (co-w) 55. The Cobweb 55. Interpol 57. How to Murder a Rich Uncle (& p) 59. On the Beach 59. Kotch 71.

Paymer, David (1954–).
American actor, born in Long Island, New York. He studied at the Professional Performing Arts School and the Lee Strasberg Theater Institute.
Airplane II: The Sequel 82. Best Defense 84. Perfect 85. Howard the Duck 86. No Way Out 87. Crazy People 90. City Slickers 91. Mr Saturday Night 92. Searching for Bobby Fischer/Innocent Moves 93. Heart and Souls 93. Quiz Show 94. Cagney & Lacey: The Return (TV) 94. Cagney & Lacey: Together Again (TV) 95. The American President 95. Get Shorty 95. Nixon 95. City Hall 96. Unforgettable 96. Carpool 96. Amistad 97. Gang Related 97. The Sixth Man 97. Mighty Joe Young 98. The Lesser Evil 98, etc.
TV series: Downtown 86. The Commish 91–92.

Payne, Jack (1899–1969).
British bandleader who appeared in two films: *Say it with Music* 32, *Sunshine Ahead* 36.

Payne, John (1912–1989).
General-purpose American leading man, mostly of 40s musicals and 50s westerns.
Dodsworth 36. Fair Warning 37. Love on Toast 38. Wings of the Navy 39. *Kid Nightingale* 39. Maryland 40. The Great Profile 40. *Tin Pan Alley* 40. *The Great American Broadcast* 41. Weekend in Havana 41. Remember the Day 41. Sun Valley Serenade 41. To the Shores of Tripoli 42. Springtime in the Rockies 42. Hello Frisco Hello 43. The Dolly Sisters 45. Sentimental Journey 46. The Razor's Edge 46. Miracle on 34th Street 47. The Saxon Charm 48. The Crooked Way 49. Captain China 49. Tripoli 50. Crosswinds 51. Caribbean 52. Kansas City Confidential 52. Raiders of the Seven Seas 53. 99 River Street 53. Rails into Laramie 54. Santa Fé Passage 55. Hell's Island 55. Slightly Scarlet 56. *The Boss* 56. Bailout at 43,000 57. Hidden Fear 57. Gift of the Nile 68, etc.
TV series: *The Restless Gun* 58–59.

Payne, Laurence (1919–).
British leading man, on stage and (occasionally) screen from 1945.
Train of Events 49. Ill Met by Moonlight 57. Ben Hur 59. The Tell Tale Heart 61. The Court Martial of Major Keller 61. Vampire Circus 72. One Deadly Owner 74, etc.

Paynter, Robert (1928–).
British cinematographer who worked on many of Michael Winner's films in the 60s and 70s.
■ Hannibal Brooks 68. The Games 69. Lawman 70. The Nightcomers 71. Chato's Land 71. The Mechanic 72. Scorpio 72. High Velocity 76. The Big Sleep 78. Firepower 79. Saturn 3 80. Superman II 80. The Final Conflict 81. An American Werewolf in London 81. Curtains 82. Superman III 83. Trading Places 83. Scream for Help 84. The Muppets Take Manhattan 84. National Lampoon's European Vacation 85. Spies Like Us 85. Into the Night 85. Little Shop of Horrors 86. When the Whales Came 89. Strike It Rich 90. Get Back 91.

Pays, Amanda (1959–).
English actress. Married actor Corbin Bernsen.
Oxford Blues 84. Cold Room/The Prisoner (TV) 84. Off Limits 87. The Kindred 87. Leviathan 89. Dead on the Money (TV) 91. Exposure 91. Solitaire for 2 95, etc.
TV series: Max Headroom 87. The Flash 90–91. Thief Takers 96.

Payton, Barbara (1927–1967).
American leading lady.
Once More My Darling 49. Dallas 50. Kiss Tomorrow Goodbye 51. Drums in the Deep South 51. Bride of the Gorilla 52. The Great Jesse James Raid 53. Four-Sided Triangle (GB) 54. The Flanagan Boy (GB) 55, etc.

Peach, Mary (1934–).
British leading lady, in films from 1957.
Follow That Horse 59. Room at the Top 59. *No Love for Johnnie* 61. A Pair of Briefs 62. A Gathering of Eagles (US) 63. Ballad in Blue 65. The Projected Man 66. Scrooge 70. Cat on a Hot Tin Roof (TV) 76. The Far Pavilions (TV) 84. Grandma's House 89. Mothers and Daughters 92. CutThroat Island 95, etc.

Pearce, Alice (1913–1966).
American character comedienne, usually in adenoidal roles.
On the Town 49. The Opposite Sex 56. The Disorderly Orderly 64. Dear Brigitte 65. The Glass Bottom Boat 66, etc.
TV series: Bewitched 65–66.

Pearce, Guy (1967–).
Australian leading actor, from the soap operas *Neighbours* and *Home and Away*.
Hunting 90. My Forgotten Man (as Errol Flynn) 93. *The Adventures of Priscilla, Queen of the Desert* 94. Dating the Enemy 96. LA Confidential 97. Woundings (GB) 98, etc.

Pearl, Jack (1894–1982).
Jewish-American comic known on radio as Baron Munchausen and famous for his catchphrase. 'Vass you dere, Sharlie?' Film appearance: *Hollywood Party* 34.

Pearson, Beatrice (1920–).
American leading lady with a brief career.
■ Force of Evil 49. Lost Boundaries 49.

Pearson, George (1875–1973).
British writer-producer-director who came to films at the age of 37 after being a schoolmaster. Hundreds of films to his credit.
Autobiography: 1957, *Flashback*.
The Fool 12. A Study in Scarlet 14. Ultus the Man from the Dead 15. The Better Ole 18. The Old Curiosity Shop 20. *Squibs* 21. Squibs Wins the Calcutta Sweep 22. Satan's Sister 25. Huntingtower 27. The Silver King 28. Journey's End (p) 30. The Good Companions (p) 32. Four Marked Men 34. The Pointing Finger 38, many others.

Pearson, Lloyd (1897–1966).
Portly British character actor, usually of bluff Yorkshire types.
The Challenge 38. Tilly of Bloomsbury 40. Kipps 41. *When We Are Married* 42. Schweik's New Adventures (leading role) 43. My Learned Friend 44. Mr Perrin and Mr Traill 49. Hindle Wakes 52. The Good Companions 57. The Angry Silence 59, etc.

Pearson, Richard (1918–).
British stage character actor in occasional films.
Love Among the Ruins (TV) 75. The Bluebird 77. She Fell Among Thieves (TV) 78. The Mirror Crack'd 80. Water 85. Pirates 86. Whoops Apocalypse 87, etc.

Peary, Harold (1908–1985) (Harold José Pereira de Faria).
American character comedian who for years in the 40s played The Great Gildersleeve on radio and in a short-lived film series, also in *Coming Round the Mountain, County Fair, Clambake*.

Peck, Bob (1945–).
English character actor, from the stage, where he was a member of the Royal Shakespeare Company and has since acted with the National Theatre Company.
Edge of Darkness (TV) 85. The Kitchen Toto 87. *On the Black Hill* 88. Ladder of Swords 88. Slipstream 89. Lord of the Flies 90. Jurassic Park 93. Seasick 96. Surviving Picasso 96. Smilla's Sense of Snow/Smilla's Feeling for Snow 97. Fairytale: A True Story 97. Deadly Summer (TV) 97. The Scold's Bridle (TV) 98, etc.

Peck, Gregory (1916–).
Durable and likeable American leading actor, with stage experience before sudden success in Hollywood.
Biography: 1980, *Gregory Peck* by Michael Freedland.
Days of Glory 43. *The Keys of the Kingdom* (AAN) 44. The Valley of Decision 44. *Spellbound* 45. The Yearling (AAN) 46. *Duel in the Sun* 46. *The Macomber Affair* 47. *Gentleman's Agreement* (AAN) 47. The Paradine Case 47. Yellow Sky 48. The Great Sinner 49. *Twelve o'Clock High* (AAN) 49. *The Gunfighter* 50. David and Bathsheba 51. Captain Horatio Hornblower (GB) 51. Only the Valiant 52. The World in His Arms 52. The Snows of Kilimanjaro 52. Roman Holiday 53. Night People 54. The Million Pound Note (GB) 54. The Purple Plain (GB) 55. *The Man in the Grey Flannel Suit* 56. Moby Dick 56. Designing Woman 57. The Bravados 58. *The Big Country* 58. Pork Chop Hill 59. Beloved Infidel (as Scott Fitzgerald) 59. On the Beach 59. The Guns of Navarone (GB) 61. Cape Fear 62. How the West was Won 62. *To Kill a Mockingbird* (AA) 63. Captain Newman 63. Behold a Pale Horse 64. Mirage 65. Arabesque 66. Mackenna's Gold 68. The Stalking Moon 68. The Most Dangerous Man in the World 69. Marooned 69. I Walk the Line 70. Shootout 71. Billy Two Hats 73. The Dove (p only) 75. *The Omen* 76. MacArthur 77. The Boys from Brazil 78. The Sea Wolves 80. The Blue and the Gray (TV) (as Lincoln) 82. The Scarlet and the Black (TV) 82. Amazing Grace and Chuck 87. Old Gringo 89. Other People's Money 91. Cape Fear 91. The Portrait (TV) 93. Moby Dick (TV) 98, etc.

Peck, Raoul (1953–).
Haitian director and screenwriter. A former minister of culture for his country, he began by making documentaries and short films.
Haitian Corner 87. Lumumba: La Mort du Prophète (Swiss/Ger.) 91. The Man by the Shore 92. Falling Bodies/Corps Plongés 98, etc.

Peckinpah, Sam (1925–1984).
American director of tough westerns.
Biography: 1994, *'If They Move . . . Kill 'Em': The Life and Times of Sam Peckinpah* by David Weddle.
■ The Deadly Companions 61. *Ride the High Country* 62. Major Dundee 65. *The Wild Bunch* (AANw) 69. The Ballad of Cable Hogue 69. Straw Dogs 71. Junior Bonner 72. The Getaway 72. Pat Garrett and Billy the Kid 73. Bring Me the Head of Alfredo Garcia 74. The Killer Elite 76. Cross of Iron 77. Convoy 78. The Osterman Weekend 83.
❝ I can shoot three people, put 'em on a cart, take 'em to the burial ground and bury 'em by the time he gets one person down to the ground.
– Howard Hawks, on Peckinpah's slow-motion approach to death

Peerce, Jan (1904–1984).
American tenor who appeared in a few films. He began as a popular singer at Radio City Music Hall, and on radio, before turning to opera and becoming a star at the Metropolitan Opera House from the 40s to the mid-60s; later, he also appeared in Broadway musicals.
Carnegie Hall 47. Something in the Wind 47. Tonight We Sing 53, etc.

Peerce, Larry (1930–).
American writer-director, son of opera singer Jan Peerce.
One Potato Two Potato 66. Goodbye Columbus 69. A Separate Peace 73. Ash Wednesday 74. The Other Side of the Mountain 76. Two Minute Warning 76. The Other Side of the Mountain Part Two 78. The Bell Jar 79. Why Would I Lie? 80. Love Child 82. Hard to Hold 84. Elvis and Me (TV) 88. The Neon Empire 89. A Woman Named Jackie (TV) 91. Child of Rage (TV) 92, etc.

Pelissier, Anthony (1912–1988).
British director with stage experience; son of Fay Compton.
The History of Mr Polly 49. The Rocking Horse Winner 50. Night without Stars 50. Meet Me Tonight 52. Meet Mr Lucifer 54, etc.

Pellegrin, Raymond (1925–).
French leading actor of stage, screen and television, also in international films. Born in Nice, of Italian parents, he specialized in brooding roles. Married actress Gisèle PASCAL.
Six Petites Filles en Blanc 41. Naïs 45. Un Flic 47. Topaze 51. Forbidden Fruit/Le Fruit Défendu 52. Manon des Sources 53. Napoléon 54. Woman of Rome/La Romana (It.) 54. Flesh and the Woman/Le Grand Jeu 54. Law of the Streets/La Loi des Rues 56. Bitter Victory 57. Le Chien de Pique 61. Horace 62 62. Venus Impériale 62. A View from the Bridge 62. Behold a Pale Horse (Fr./US) 64. Second Breath/Le Deuxième Souffle 64. Code Name Cobra/Le Saut de L'Ange 71. L'Onorata Famiglia (It.) 73. Le Rose et le Blanc 80. Louisiana (TV) 84. Maigret à New York (TV) 90, many others.

Pellonpaa, Matti (1951–1995).
Finnish leading actor, born in Helsinki, and a familiar, lugubrious presence in the films of Aki and Mika KAURISMAKI. Died of a heart attack.
Valehtelija 80. Crime and Punishment/Rikos ja Rangaistus 83. Calamari Union 85. Hamlet Goes Business/Hamlet Liikemaailmassa 87. Ariel 88. Leningrad Cowboys Go America 88. Cha Cha Cha 89. Night on Earth (US) 91. La Vie de Bohème 92. The Last Border 93. Leningrad Cowboys Meet Moses 94. Take Care of Your Scarf, Tatiana/Pida Huivista Kiini, Tatiana 94. Iron Horsemen 94, etc.

Peña, Elizabeth (1961–).
Cuban-born actress in Hollywood.
El Super 79. Times Square 80. They All Laughed 81. Crossover Dreams 85. Down and Out in Beverly Hills 86. Batteries Not Included 87. La Bamba 87. Vibes 88. Blue Steel 90. Jacob's Ladder 90. The Waterdance 92. Across the Moon 94. Dead Funny 95. Free Willy 2: The Adventure Home 95. The Invaders (TV) 95. Lone Star 96. Contagious 96. Rush Hour 98. Dee Snider's Strangeland 98, etc.

Pendleton, Austin (1940–).
Slightly built American character actor.
Skidoo 68. What's Up, Doc? 72. Every Little Crook and Nanny 72. The Thief Who Came to Dinner 73. *The Front Page* 74. The Great Smokey Roadblock 78. Starting Over 79. The First Family 80. Mr & Mrs Bridge 90. My Cousin Vinny 92. Mr Nanny 93. My Boyfriend's Back 93. Guarding Tess 94. Home for the Holidays 95. 2 Days in the Valley 96. The Proprietor 96. The Mirror Has Two Faces 96, etc.

Pendleton, Nat (1895–1967).
American character actor, formerly professional wrestler, usually seen in 'dumb ox' roles. In films from c. 1930.
You Said a Mouthful 32. The Sign of the Cross 32. *The Thin Man* 34. Manhattan Melodrama 34. The Great Ziegfeld 36. The Marx Brothers at the Circus 39. Young Dr Kildare (and series) 39. On Borrowed Time 39. Northwest Passage 40. Top Sergeant Mulligan 42. Rookies Come Home 45. Scared to Death 47. Death Valley 49, many others.

Pene Du Bois, Raoul (1914–1985).
American set and costume designer, mainly on Broadway but occasionally noticed on Hollywood credits.
Louisiana Purchase 41. Happy Go Lucky 43. Frenchman's Creek 44. Lady in the Dark 44. Kitty 45. New Faces 53, etc.

Penhaligon, Susan (1950–).
British leading lady of the late 70s.
Under Milk Wood 73. No Sex Please We're British 73. The Land that Time Forgot 75. Nasty Habits 77. The Uncanny 77. Leopard in the Snow 78. The Masks of Death (TV) 84. The Ruth Rendell Mysteries: Thornapple (TV) 97, etc.
TV series: Bouquet of Barbed Wire 76. A Fine Romance 81–84. Trouble in Mind 91.

Penn, Arthur (1922–).
American director, a former actor, who was often at odds with Hollywood. Born in Philadelphia, Pennsylvania, he studied at the Black Mountain College, in Italy at the Universities of Perugia and Florence, and at the Actors' Studio in Los Angeles. He began in television, and directed on Broadway before breaking through to wider recognition with *Bonnie and Clyde*.
■ The Left Handed Gun 58. The Miracle Worker (AAN) 62. Mickey One 65. The Chase 66. *Bonnie and Clyde* (AAN) 67. Alice's Restaurant (AAN) 69. Little Big Man 70. Night Moves 75. The Missouri Breaks 76. Four Friends 81. Target 85. Dead of Winter 87. Penn & Teller Get Killed 89. The Portrait (TV) 93. Inside 96.
❝ There hasn't been that much of a market for what I can do. I'm not into outer space epics or youth pictures. – A.P.

Penn, Chris (1966–).
Burly American actor, the son of Leo PENN and brother of Sean PENN.
Rumble Fish 83. All the Right Moves 83. Footloose 84. At Close Range 86. Made in the USA 88. Best of the Best 89. Mobsters 91. Futurekick 91. Leather Jackets 91. Reservoir Dogs 92. The Music of Chance 93. Best of the Best II 93. True Romance 93. Short Cuts 93. Josh and S.A.M. 93. Beethoven's 2nd 94. Imaginary Crimes 94. Mulholland Falls 96. The Boys Club 96. The Funeral 96. Deceiver 97. One Tough Cop 98, etc.

Penn, Leo (1921–1998).
American actor and director, the father of Sean and Christopher PENN.
Undercover Man (a) 49. The Story on Page One (a) 60. A Man Called Adam (d) 66. Murder in Music City (d) (TV) 79. Hellinger's Law (d) (TV) 81. Judgement in Berlin (d) 88, etc.
TV series: The Gertrude Berg Show 61.

Penn, Sean (1960–).
Scrawny but tough-looking American actor who has turned to writing and directing. He is the son of director Leo PENN, and the brother of Chris PENN. He was formerly married to singer MADONNA (1985–89). Married actress Robin WRIGHT, the mother of his two children, in 1996.
Taps 81. Fast Times at Ridgemont High 82. Bad Boys 83. Racing with the Moon 83. Crackers 84. The Falcon and the Snowman 84. At Close Range 85. Shanghai Surprise 86. Colors 88. Casualties of War 89. We're No Angels 89. State of Grace 90. The Indian Runner (wd) 91. Carlito's Way 93. The Crossing Guard (wd) 95. Dead Man Walking (AAN) 95. Loved 96. U-Turn 97. The Game 97. Hugo Pool 97. She's So Lovely 97. Hurlyburly 98. The Thin Red Line 98, etc.
❝ I don't like any directors. I don't get along with any of them. Mostly I think they're a bunch of whiny people without any point of view. So I don't want to be around them at 6 o'clock in the morning with make-up and bells on. And I'm probably the same way for the actors on my set – but that's their problem. – S.P.
With the Academy Awards, if you're standing there and looking out, you're not going to see many people who can find their butt with their hand. – S.P.

Pennebaker, D. A. (1930–) (Don Alan Pennebaker).
American documentary film-maker.
Don't Look Back 67. Monterey Pop 67. Town Bloody Hall (co-d) 80. Jimi 86. The Music Tells You (co-d) 93, etc.

Penner, Joe (1904–1941) (J. Pinter).
Hungarian-American radio comedian who made a few films.
College Rhythm 33. Collegiate 36. Go Chase Yourself 38. Glamour Boy 40. The Boys from Syracuse 40, etc.

Pennick, Jack (1895–1964).
American small-part actor and horse trainer, often in John Ford westerns.
Four Sons 28. Under Two Flags 36. Stagecoach 39. Northwest Mounted Police 40. My Darling Clementine 46. Fort Apache 48. Rio Grande 50. The Alamo 60.

Pennington-Richards, C. M. (1911–).
British director, former photographer.
The Oracle 54. Inn for Trouble 60. Double Bunk 62. Ladies Who Do 63. A Challenge for Robin Hood 67. Headline Hunters (co-w only) 68. The Boy with Two Heads (co-w only) 74. Sky Pirates 76, etc.

Penrose, Charles (1876–1952).
Hearty comedian and writer who played a few character roles in 30s films. He is best remembered for his recording of 'The Laughing Policeman' and similar songs. He wrote and starred, as a policeman, in the radio comedy series *The Pig and Whistle* 38–44.
Dreams Come True 36. The Crimes of Stephen Hawke 36. Calling the Tune 36. Dark Eyes of London/The Human Monster 39, etc.

Peploe, Clare.
British screenwriter and director. Married to Bernardo Bertolucci, she is the sister of writer Mark Peploe.
Zabriskie Point (co-w) 70. Luna (w) 79. High Season (co-w, d) 87. Rough Magic (co-w, d) 95. Besieged (co-w) (It.) 98, etc.

Peploe, Mark.
British screenwriter and director.
The Pied Piper (w) 72. The Passenger (w) 75. The Last Emperor (w) (AAN) 87. High Season (w) 88. The Sheltering Sky (w) 90. Afraid of the Dark (wd) 91. Little Buddha (w) 93. Victory (d) 98, etc.

Peppard, George (1928–1994).
American leading man with Broadway experience; began interestingly, but developed into an acceptable tough lead of hokum adventures.
■ *The Strange One* 57. Pork Chop Hill 59. Home from the Hill 60. The Subterraneans 60. *Breakfast at Tiffany's* 61. How the West Was Won 62. The Victors 63. *The Carpetbaggers* 64. Operation Crossbow 65. The Third Day 65. *The Blue Max* 66. Tobruk 67. Rough Night in Jericho 67. P. J. 68.

What's So Bad about Feeling Good? 68. House of Cards 68. Pendulum 68. The Executioner 69. Cannon for Cordoba 70. One More Train to Rob 70. The Bravos (TV) 71. The Groundstar Conspiracy 72. Newman's Law 74. One of Our Own (TV) 75. Guilty or Innocent: The Sam Sheppard Murder Case (TV) 75. Damnation Alley 77. Your Ticket Is No Longer Valid 79. From Hell to Victory 79. Torn between Two Lovers (TV) 79. Crisis in Mid Air (TV) 79. Battle beyond the Stars 80. Five Days from Home (& d) 80. Race For the Yankee Zephyr 81. The A-Team (TV) 83. Target Eagle 84. Man against the Mob (TV) 88. Man against the Mob: The Chinatown Murders (TV) 89. Night of the Fox (TV) 90.

TV series: *Banacek* 72–73. Doctors' Hospital 75. *The A-Team* 83–86.

Pepper, Barbara (1912–1969).
American second-lead actress who usually played tramps.

Our Daily Bread 33. Winterset 36. Lady in the Morgue 38. Brewster's Millions 45. Terror Trail 47. Inferno 53. The D.I. 57. A Child is Waiting 63. Kiss Me Stupid 64, many others.

TV series: Green Acres 65–69.

Percival, Lance (1933–).
British light comedian.

Twice Round the Daffodils 62. The VIPs 63. Carry On Cruising 63. The Yellow Rolls-Royce 64. The Big Job 65. Darling Lili 69. Up Pompeii 71. Our Miss Fred 72. The Boy with Two Heads 74. The Water Babies (voice) 75. Confessions from a Holiday Camp 77. Rosie Dixon – Night Nurse 78, etc.

TV series: It's a Living 62. Lance at Large 64. Up the Workers 74–76. Bluebirds 89.

Percy, Esmé (1887–1957).
Distinguished English stage actor, noted for his performances in the plays of George Bernard SHAW. Born in London, of French origin, he studied drama at the Brussels Conservatoire, and was also trained by Sarah BERNHARDT, having told her he would throw himself into the Seine if she did not let him join her company. He was on stage in England from 1904. As a young actor he was noted for his looks: when actor-manager Herbert Beerbohm Tree invited him to an intimate supper, Lady Tree paused on her way out and said, 'The port is on the sideboard, Herbert, and remember it's adultery just the same.' But after a dog removed one of his eyes, and he substituted a glass one, and his nose was broken in an accident, his choice of screen roles was somewhat limited.

Murder 30. Bitter Sweet 33. On Secret Service 33. The Lucky Number 33. The Unfinished Symphony 34. Nell Gwyn 34. Love, Life and Laughter 34. Lord Edgware Dies 34. Abdul the Damned 35. Invitation to the Waltz 35. Royal Cavalcade 35. It Happened in Paris 35. *The Frog* 36. The Invader 36. Land without Music 36. Song of Freedom 36. The Amateur Gentleman 36. The Return of the Scarlet Pimpernel 37. Twenty-One Days 37. Our Fighting Navy 37. Pygmalion 38. Caesar and Cleopatra 45. Dead of Night 45. Lisbon Story 46. The Ghosts of Berkeley Square 47. Death in the Hand 48, etc.

Pereira, Hal (1905–1983).
American art director, supervisor at Paramount from the 50s.

Double Indemnity 44. *Carrie* (AAN) 51. Ace in the Hole 52. Roman Holiday (AAN) 53. Sabrina (AAN) 54. *The Rose Tattoo* (AA) 55. To Catch a Thief (AAN) 55. The Proud and the Profane (AAN) 56. The Ten Commandments (AAN) 56. Funny Face (AAN) 57. *Vertigo* (AAN) 58. Career (AAN) 59. Visit to a Small Planet (AAN) 60. It Started in Naples (AAN) 60. *Breakfast at Tiffany's* (AAN) 61. Summer and Smoke (AAN) 61. The Pigeon that Took Rome (AAN) 62. Hud (AAN) 64. The Slender Thread (AAN) 65. The Spy Who Came In from the Cold (AAN) 65. The Oscar (AAN) 66. Barefoot in the Park 67. Blue 68, many others.

Perelman, S. J. (1904–1979).
Renowned American humorist whose name appeared on a few films, mostly in collaboration.

Monkey Business 31. Horse Feathers 32. Ambush 39. The Golden Fleecing 40. Around the World in Eighty Days (AA) 56, etc.

Perez, Rosie (1963–).
American actress, dancer and choreographer, born in Brooklyn.

Do the Right Thing 89. Criminal Justice (TV) 90. Night on Earth 91. White Men Can't Jump 92. Untamed Heart 93. Fearless (AAN) 93. It Could Happen to You 94. Somebody to Love 94. A Brother's Kiss 97. Perdita Durango 97. The 24-Hour Woman 98, etc.

Perez, Vincent (1965–).
Swiss-born leading actor, of German and Spanish parents, from the French stage. He studied acting in Geneva, at the Paris Conservatoire and at L'École des Amandiers.

Hôtel de France 87. The House of Jade/La Maison de Jade 88. Cyrano de Bergerac 90. Capitaine Fracasse 91. Indochine 92. Fanfan 93. Queen Margot/La Reine Margot 94. Beyond the Clouds 95. The Crow: City of Angels 96. Amy Foster 97. Le Bossu 97. Talk of Angels 98. On Guard! 97. Ceux Qui M'Aiment Prendront le Train 98. Shot through the Heart (TV) 98, etc.

Périer, Etienne (1931–).
French director.

Bobosse 59. Murder at 45 RPM 60. Bridge to the Sun 61. Swordsman of Siena 63. When Eight Bells Toll 71. Zeppelin 71. Five against Capricorn 72. A Murder is a Murder 72. The Fire's Share 77. Venetian Red 89, etc.

Périer, François (1919–) (François Pilu).
Sturdy French actor, in films from mid-30s.

Hôtel du Nord 38. Un Revenant 46. Le Silence est d'Or 48. *Orphée* 49. The Bed 53. *Gervaise* 55. Nights of Cabiria 56. Charmants Garçons 57. Weekend at Dunkirk 65. The Samurai 67. The Red Circle 70. Just Before Nightfall 73. Le Bar du Téléphone 80. Le Tartuffe 84. La Pagaille 91. Voyage à Rome 92, etc.

Perinal, Georges (1897–1965).
French cinematographer, in films from 1913.

Les Nouveaux Messieurs 28. Sous les Toits de Paris 30. *Le Sang d'un Poète* 30. *Le Million* 31. *A Nous la Liberté* 32. The Private Life of Henry VIII 32. *Rembrandt* 36. *The Thief of Baghdad* (AA) 40. *The Life and Death of Colonel Blimp* 43. *Nicholas Nickleby* 47. An Ideal Husband 47. *The Fallen Idol* 48. Lady Chatterley's Lover 55. A King in New York 57. Saint Joan 57. Bonjour Tristesse 58. Oscar Wilde 60, many others.

Perkins, Anthony (1932–1992).
Gangly American leading actor who became forever associated with the role of Norman Bates in *Psycho*, directed by Alfred HITCHCOCK. Born in New York City, the son of actor Osgood PERKINS, he was acting in summer stock at the age of 15 and made his film debut five years later. He played with success young men, troubled and unsure of themselves, but found maturer roles scarce. Married photographer and occasional actress Berry Berenson, the sister of actress Marisa BERENSON. He was romantically involved with actor Tab HUNTER. Died of AIDS.

Biographies: 1991, *Osgood and Anthony Perkins* by Laura Kay Palmer; 1995, *Anthony Perkins: A Haunted Life* by Ronald Bergan; 1996, *Split Image: The Life of Anthony Perkins* by Charles Winecoff.

■ *The Actress* 53. Friendly Persuasion (AAN) 56. The Lonely Man 57. *Desire Under the Elms* 57. *Fear Strikes Out* 57. The Tin Star 57. *This Angry Age* 58. The Matchmaker 58. Green Mansions 58. On the Beach 59. Tall Story 60. *Psycho* 60. Goodbye Again 61. Phaedra 62. Five Miles to Midnight 62. The Trial 62. Two are Guilty 64. The Fool Killer 64. A Ravishing Idiot 64. Is Paris Burning? 66. The Champagne Murders 68. Pretty Poison 68. Catch 22 70. *WUSA* 70. How Awful About Allan (TV) 70. Ten Days Wonder 71. Someone Behind the Door/Two Minds for Murder 71. Judge Roy Bean 72. Play It as It Lays 72. Lovin' Molly 73. Murder on the Orient Express 74. Mahogany 75. Remember My Name 78. First You Cry (TV) 78. Winter Kills 79. The Black Hole 79. Double Negative 79. North Sea Hijack 80. Twice a Woman 80. Les Misérables (TV) 80. For the Term of His Natural Life (TV) 82. *Psycho II* 83. Sins of Dorian Gray (TV) 83. Crimes of Passion 85. Psycho III (& d) 86. Destroyer 88. Edge of Sanity 89. I'm Dangerous Tonight (TV) 90. Psycho IV: The Beginning 90. The Naked Target 91. A Demon in My View 92. The Mummy Lives 92. In the Deep Woods (TV) 92.

Famous line (*Psycho*): 'A boy's best friend is his mother.'

Perkins, Elizabeth (1961–).
American actress.

About Last Night 86. From the Hip 87. Big 88. Sweet Hearts Dance 88. Love at Large 90. Enid Is Sleeping 90. Avalon 90. He Said, She Said 91. Indian Summer 93. The Flintstones 94. Miracle on 34th Street 94. Moonlight and Valentino 95. I'm Losing You 98, etc.

Perkins, Millie (1939–).
American leading lady who went to Hollywood from dramatic school.

The Diary of Anne Frank 59. Wild in the Country 61. Wild in the Streets 68. Lady Cocoa 75. Table for Five 83. At Close Range 85. Jake Speed 86. Slam Dance 87. Pistol: The Birth of a Legend 91. Necronomicon 93. Bodily Harm 95. The Chamber 96, etc.

TV series: Knots Landing 83–84. Elvis 90.

Perkins, Osgood (1892–1937).
American character actor, mainly on the stage, the father of Anthony PERKINS. Born in West Newton, Massachusetts, he studied French at Harvard University and turned to acting in his late 20s, first in silent films, before making his reputation on the Broadway stage, often in psychologically disturbed roles. Died from a heart attack, following the first night's performance of a new play in Washington. His one great regret was that he was passed over in favour of Adolphe MENJOU for the role of newspaper editor Walter Burns in the film of *The Front Page*, which he had originated on the Broadway stage. His best screen performance was as the gangster Johnny Lovo in *Scarface*.

Biography: 1991, *Osgood and Anthony Perkins* by Laura Kay Palmer.

The Cradle Buster 22. Puritan Passions 23. Knockout Reilly 27. Mother's Boy 29. Tarnished Lady 31. Scarface 32. Kansas City Princess 34. I Dream Too Much 35, etc.

❝ I always had the theory that heavies had beady eyes and Osgood certainly had them. – *Howard Hawks*

In every aspect of technical facility, he was peerless. – *Elia Kazan*

Perlberg, William (1899–1969).
American producer, often in conjunction with George Seaton; came from agency business, in Hollywood from mid-30s.

Golden Boy 39. The Song of Bernadette 43. Forever Amber 47. The Country Girl 54. Teacher's Pet 58. The Counterfeit Traitor 62. Thirty-Six Hours 64, many others.

Perlman, Rhea (1948–).
American actress, best known for her role as Carla in the TV series *Cheers* 82–92. Married Danny DeVito.

Intimate Strangers (TV) 77. Love Child 82. The Ratings Game (TV) 84. My Little Pony (voice) 86. Stamp of a Killer (TV) 87. Class Act 91. Enid Is Sleeping/Over Her Dead Body 91. Ted & Venus 91. There Goes the Neighborhood/Paydirt 92. Class Act 92. Canadian Bacon 95. Sunset Park 96. Matilda 96. Carpool 96, etc.

TV series: Pearl 96– .

Perlman, Ron (1951–).
American character actor, often in menacing roles, and best known for playing the lion-faced Vincent in the TV series *Beauty and the Beast*.

Quest for Fire 81. The Ice Pirates 84. The Name of the Rose 86. Blind Man's Bluff (TV) 91. Sleepwalkers 92. Cronos (Mex.) 92. The Adventures of Huck Finn 93. Double Exposure 93. Romeo Is Bleeding 93. City of Lost Children (Fr.) 95. The Island of Dr Moreau 96. Prince Valiant 97. Body Armour 97. Alien: Resurrection 97. I Woke Up Early the Day I Died 98, etc.

TV series: Beauty and the Beast 87–90. The Magnificent Seven 97– .

Perón, Eva (1919–1952) (Maria Eva Duarte).
Argentinian actress and politician. Born in Los Toldos, she worked as a radio and film actress in the 30s and 40s before becoming the influential wife of Juan Perón in 1945, a year before he was elected President of Argentina. Died of cancer. She was played by Faye DUNAWAY in the TV movie *Evita Peron* 81, and by MADONNA in the musical biopic *Evita* 96.

Autobiography: 1997, *Evita: In My Own Words*.
Biography: 1997, *Eva Peron* by Alicia Dujovne Ortiz.

■ Only the Valiant/La Carga de los Valientes 40. The Unhappiest Man in Town/El Más Infeliz del Pueblo 41. Una Novia en Apuros 42. Circus Cavalcade/La Cabalgata del Circo 45. The Prodigal Woman/La Prodiga 45.

Perreau, Gigi (1941–) (Ghislaine Perreau-Saussine).
American child actress of the 40s who seems not quite to have managed the transition to adult stardom.

Madame Curie 43. Song of Love 47. My Foolish Heart 49. Has Anybody Seen My Gal? 51. The Man in the Grey Flannel Suit 56. Wild Heritage 58. Look in Any Window 61. Journey to the Center of Time 67. Hell on Wheels 67, etc.

TV series: The Betty Hutton Show 59. Follow the Sun 69.

Perrine, Valerie (1944–).
American leading lady of the 70s.

Slaughterhouse Five 72. The Last American Hero 73. Lenny (AAN) 74. W. C. Fields and Me 76. Mr Billion 77. Ziegfeld: the Man and his Women (TV) 78. Superman 78. The Electric Horseman 79. Can't Stop the Music 80. Superman II 80. Agency 81. The Border 82. Water 85. When Your Lover Leaves (TV) 85. Maid to Order 87. Reflections in a Dark Sky/Riflessi in un Cielo Scuro 91. Bright Angel 91. Boiling Point 93. Girl in the Cadillac 95, etc.

Perrins, Leslie (1902–1962).
British character actor, often seen as a smooth crook. Born in Moseley, Birmingham, he studied at RADA and was on stage from 1922.

The Sleeping Cardinal 31. The Pointing Finger 34. Tudor Rose 36. Old Iron 39. The Woman's Angle 43. A Run for Your Money 49. Guilty 56, many others.

Perry, Eleanor (1925–1981).
American screenwriter; wrote all the scripts of her husband Frank Perry's films until their divorce in 1970. Then alone: *Diary of a Mad Housewife*, *The Lady in the Car*, *The Man Who Loved Cat Dancing*.

Perry, Frank (1930–1995).
American director, a pioneer in establishing independent film-making as commercially viable. In 1992 he made a TV documentary, *On the Bridge*, dealing with his reactions to the discovery that he had cancer of the prostate.

■ David and Lisa (AAN) 63. Ladybug, Ladybug 64. The Swimmer 68. Trilogy 68. Last Summer 69. Diary of a Mad Housewife 70. Doc 71. Play It as It Lays 72. Man on a Swing 74. Rancho de Luxe 76. Monsignor 82. Compromising Positions 85. Hello Again 87.

❝ I never really felt happy being part of the system, but it's preferable to be eaten by it than not eat. – *F.P.*

Perry, Luke (1967–).
American leading actor from TV soap operas who gained fame as Dylan McKay in the TV series *Beverly Hills, 90210* 90–93.

Buffy, the Vampire Hunter 92. Terminal Bliss 92. Lane Frost 93. 8 Seconds 94. Vacanze di Natale '95 (as himself) 95. Normal Life 96. American Strays 96. The Fifth Element 97. Lifebreath 97, etc.

TV series: Loving 87–88.

❝ I felt like I belonged on a screen. I don't know why. I guess because I related to the people up on that screen much more than the people around me. I always felt like I was one of them and in a matter of time I'd get there. – *L.P.*

Perry, Matthew (1969–).
American actor, best known for his role as Chandler in the 90s TV sitcom *Friends*. He was treated for an addiction to painkillers in 1997.

A Night in the Life of Jimmy Reardon 88. She's Out of Control 89. Fools Rush In 97. Almost Heroes 97, etc.

Perry, Paul P. (1891–1963).
Pioneer American cinematographer who experimented with colour.

Rose of the Rancho 14. The Cheat 15. Hidden

Pearls 17. The Sea Wolf 21. Rosita 23. Souls for Sables 26, many others.

Persoff, Nehemiah (1920–).
Israeli actor, long in America; trained at Actors' Studio.
On the Waterfront 54. The Harder They Fall 56. *This Angry Age* 57. The Badlanders 58. Never Steal Anything Small 58. Al Capone 59. Some Like It Hot 59. The Big Show 61. The Comancheros 62. The Hook 63. *Fate is the Hunter* 64. The Greatest Story Ever Told 65. Panic in the City 68. Red Sky at Morning 71. Psychic Killer 75. Voyage of the Damned 76. The Word (TV) 78. Yentl 83. The Last Temptation of Christ 88. An American Tail: Fievel Goes West (voice) 91, etc.

Persson, Essy (1941–).
Swedish leading lady.
I a Woman 67. Thérèse and Isabelle 68. Cry of the Banshee 70. Flourishing Times/Blomstrande Tider 80, etc.

Persson, Jörgen (1936–).
Swedish cinematographer, associated with the films of director Bille August.
The White Sport/Den Vita Sporten (co-d) 68. *Elvira Madigan* 67. Ådalen 31 69. The Ballad of Joe Hill (co-ph) 71. Visions of Eight 73. My Life as a Dog 85. The Serpent's Way/Ormens Väg På Hälleberget 86. Pelle the Conqueror/Pelle Erobreren 87. Black Jack 90. Sophie 92. The Best Intentions/Den Goda Viljan 92. House of the Spirits 93. Zorn 94. Smilla's Sense of Snow 97. Les Misérables 98, etc.

Pertwee, Jon (1919–1996).
British comic actor, brother of Michael Pertwee, son of playwright Roland.
Autobiography: 1996, *I Am the Doctor* (with David J. Howe).
Murder at the Windmill 48. Mr Drake's Duck 51. Will Any Gentleman? 53. A Yank in Ermine 56. Carry On Cleo 64. Carry On Screaming 66. The House that Dripped Blood 70. One of Our Dinosaurs is Missing 75. Adventures of a Private Eye 77, etc.
TV series: Doctor Who (title role) 70–74. Worzel Gummidge 79.

Pertwee, Michael (1916–1991).
British playwright who has been involved in many screenplays.
Autobiography: 1974, *Name Dropping*.
Silent Dust (from his play) 48. The Interrupted Journey 49. *Laughter in Paradise* 51. Top Secret 52. Now and Forever 54. *The Naked Truth* 58. In the Doghouse 62. The Mouse on the Moon 62. Ladies Who Do 63. A Funny Thing Happened on the Way to the Forum 66. Finders Keepers 66. The Magnificent Two 67. Salt and Pepper 68. One More Time 70. Digby 73, etc.

Pertwee, Roland (1885–1963).
English playwright, screenwriter, novelist and occasional director. Born in Brighton, he began as an actor, and was on-stage from 1902. He wrote his screenplays usually in collaboration with others, and was briefly contracted to Warner's in Hollywood (according to P. G. Wodehouse, 'he did a story for Marilyn Miller, and they slapped him on the back and said it was great. He returned to the studio as usual next morning, and was informed by the policeman at the gate that he could not be let in as he was fired.'). Married twice: he was the father of writer Michael Pertwee and actor Jon Pertwee.
The Ghoul 33. The Night of the Party (oa) 34. Man of the Moment 35. Without Regret (oa) 35. Non Stop New York 37. King Solomon's Mines 37. A Yank at Oxford 37. Dinner at the Ritz 37. The Ware Case 38. Kicking the Moon Around/The Playboy 38. Young Man's Fancy 39. The Four Just Men 39. The Proud Valley 39. They Came by Night 39. The Spy in Black 39. Return to Yesterday 40. Freedom Radio 41. *Pimpernel Smith/The Fighting Pimpernel* (& a) 41. Breach of Promise/Adventure in Blackmail (& d) 41. Jeannie 41. Talk about Jacqueline 42. The Lamp Still Burns 43. The Gentle Sex 43. The Night Invader 43. Madonna of the Seven Moons 44. Pink String and Sealing Wax (oa) 45. They Were Sisters (w) 45. The Magic Bow 46. Caravan (w) 46. Silent Dust (oa) 48. Night Beat 48. Diamond City 49. Not Wanted on Voyage 57, etc.

Pertwee, Sean (1965–).
English actor, the son of Jon Pertwee. He is co-founder of the production company Natural Nylon, together with actors Sadie Frost, Jude Law, Jonny Lee Miller, and Ewan McGregor.
Prick Up Your Ears 87. Swing Kids 93. Weekend 93. Leon the Pig Farmer 94. Dirty Shopping 94. Clockwork Mice 95. i.d. 95. Blue Juice 95. Bodyguards (TV) 96. Stiff Upper Lips 97. Event Horizon 97. Soldier (US) 98, etc.
TV series: Bodyguards 97.

Perugorria, Jorge (1965–).
Cuban leading actor.
Strawberries and Chocolate/Fresa y Chocolate 93. Guantanamera 95. Cachito 95. Bámbola 96. Vertical Love/Amor Vertical 97. What I Left Behind in Havana (Sp.) 98, etc.

Pesci, Joe (1943–).
Short American character actor, on radio as a child.
Death Collector 76. *Raging Bull* (AAN) 80. Easy Money 83. Eureka 83. Once upon a Time in America 84. Man on Fire 87. Lethal Weapon 2 89. Catchfire 89. Betsy's Wedding 90. Home Alone 90. *GoodFellas* (AA) 90. JFK 91. My Cousin Vinny 92. Lethal Weapon 3 92. Home Alone 2: Lost in New York 92. The Public Eye 92. A Bronx Tale 94. Jimmy Hollywood 94. With Honors 94. Casino 95. 8 Heads in a Duffel Bag 96. Gone Fishin' 97. Lethal Weapon 4 98, etc.
TV series: Half Nelson 85.

Peterman, Donald.
American cinematographer.
When a Stranger Calls 79. King of the Mountain 81. Rich and Famous 81. Young Doctors in Love 82. Kiss Me Goodbye 82. Flashdance (AAN) 83. Splash 84. Best Defence 84. Cocoon 85. American Flyers 85. Star Trek IV: The Voyage Home (AAN) 86. Planes, Trains and Automobiles 87. She's Having a Baby 88. She's Out of Control 89. Point Break 91. Mr Saturday Night 92. Addams Family Values 93. Speechless 94. Get Shorty 95. Men in Black 97. Mighty Joe Young 98, etc.

Peters, Bernadette (1948–) (B. Lazarro).
American leading lady.
Ace Eli and Rodger of the Skies 72. The Longest Yard 74. The Jerk 79. Pennies from Heaven 81. Heartbeeps 81. Annie 82. David (TV) 88. Pink Cadillac 89. Slaves of New York 89. Fall from Grace (TV) 90. Alice 90. Impromptu 92. The Odyssey (TV) 97, etc.

Peters, Brock (1927–).
American actor in international films.
To Kill a Mockingbird 62. The L-Shaped Room 62. *Heavens Above* (GB) 63. The Pawnbroker 64. Major Dundee 65. P. J. 67. The McMasters 70. Black Girl 73. Framed 75. Two Minute Warning 76. Star Trek IV: the Voyage Home 86. Star Trek VI: The Undiscovered Country 91. The Importance of Being Earnest 91. Alligator II: The Mutation 91. Ghosts of Mississippi 96. Two Weeks from Sunday 97, etc.
TV series: Star Trek: Deep Space Nine 93– .

Peters, House (1880–1967).
American silent screen leading man.
Leah Kleschna 12. The Pride of Jennico 14. The Great Divide 15. Mignon 15. The Storm 22. Held to Answer 23. Raffles 25. Head Winds 25, many others.

Peters, Jean (1926–).
Attractive American leading lady of the 50s; retired to marry Howard Hughes.
■ Captain from Castile 47. Deep Waters 48. It Happens Every Spring 49. Love That Brute 50. Take Care of My Little Girl 51. As Young as You Feel 51. Anne of the Indies 52. Viva Zapata 52. Wait Till the Sun Shines, Nellie 52. Lure of the Wilderness 52. Full House 52. Niagara 53. Pickup on South Street 53. Blueprint for Murder 53. Vicki 53. *Three Coins in the Fountain* 54. Apache 54. Broken Lance 54. *A Man Called Peter* 55. The Moneychangers (TV) 74. Peter and Paul (TV) 81.

Peters, Jon (1947–).
American producer, former hairdresser. He formed the Guber-Peters company with Peter Guber in 1982 and went with Guber to run Columbia following its takeover by Sony in 1989, before leaving to become an independent producer once more.
Book: 1996, *Hit and Run: How Jon Peters and Peter Guber Took Sony for a Ride in Hollywood* by Nancy Griffin & Kim Masters.
A Star Is Born 76. Eyes of Laura Mars 78. The Main Event 79. Die Laughing 80. Missing 82. Six Weeks 82. Flashdance 83. Sheena 84. Clue 85. The Color Purple 85. Vision Quest 85. Innerspace 87. Rain Man 88. Batman 89. Tango & Cash 89. Bonfire of the Vanities 90. Money Train 95. My Fellow Americans 96. Rosewood 97. The Wild, Wild West 99, etc.
❝ When I was in the hair business I produced huge spectacular shows. Film is just another form of production. – *J.P.*

Peters, Susan (1921–1952) (Suzanne Carnahan).
American leading lady of the 40s; badly injured in an accident, she continued her career from a wheelchair.
Santa Fé Trail 40. *Random Harvest* (AAN) 42. Assignment in Brittany 43. Song of Russia 44. Keep Your Powder Dry 45. The Sign of the Ram 48, etc.

Peters, Werner (1918–1971).
German character actor in occasional international films.
L'Affaire Blum 49. Der Untertan 51. The Girl Rosemarie 58. Scotland Yard vs. Dr Mabuse 63. The Corrupt Ones 66. Assignment K 68. Istanbul Express (TV) 68, etc.

Petersen, Colin (1946–).
British child actor of the 50s.
Smiley 56. The Scamp 57. A Cry from the Streets 57, etc.

Petersen, Paul (1945–).
American teen actor and singer who was unable to sustain his career as an adult. He began as a Mouseketeer on Disney's Mickey Mouse Club, had two hit records in the early 60s, and later became a novelist. He heads A Minor Consideration, set up to protect infant actors from exploitation.
Autobiography: 1977, *Walt, Mickey and Me*.
This Could Be the Night 57. The Monolith Monsters 57. Houseboat 58. The Happiest Millionaire 67. A Time for Killing 67. Journey to Shiloh 68, etc.
TV series: The Donna Reed Show 58–66.
❝ Fame is not a career. It's a sentence. – *P.P.*
What happens to ex-bubblegum stars? No room left for me. – *P.P.*

Petersen, Wolfgang (1941–).
German director and screenwriter, from television. His *The Boat/Das Boot* was an international hit.
Wolf 70. Einer von uns Beiden 73. The Consequence/Die Konsequenz (wd) 77. Black and White Like Night and Day/Schwarz und Weiss Wie Tage und Nächte (wd) 78. The Boat/Das Boot (wd) (AAN) 81. The Neverending Story 84. Enemy Mine 85. Shattered 91. In the Line of Fire 93. Outbreak 95. Air Force One 97, etc.

Peterson, Dorothy (c. 1900–1979).
American supporting actress of the 30s, usually in maternal roles.
Cabin in the Cotton 32. I'm No Angel 33. Treasure Island 34. The Country Doctor 36. Dark Victory 39. Lillian Russell 40. The Moon Is Down 43. The Woman in the Window 45. That Hagen Girl 47, many others.

Petit, Chris (1949–).
English critic turned director, much influenced by the films of Wim Wenders.
Radio On 79. A Suitable Job for a Woman 82. Flight to Berlin 84. Chinese Boxes 84, etc.

Petit, Jean-Claude (1943–).
French composer.
Vive la Sociale! 83. Jean de Florette 87. Manon des Sources 87. Return of the Musketeers 89. Cyrano de Bergerac 90. Uranus 90. Mother/Mayrig 91. All Out 91. 588 Rue Paradis 92. The Playboys 92. Foreign Student 94. Beaumarchais the Scoundrel 96. Desire 96, etc.

Petit, Pascale (1938–) (Anne-Marie Petit).
French leading lady.
The Witches of Salem 57. Les Tricheurs 58. Girls for the Summer 59. L'Affaire d'Une Nuit 60. Demons at Midnight 62. The Spy Who Went into Hell 65. The Sweet Sins of Sexy Susan 67. Boccaccio 72. Le Dolci Zie (It.) 75. Aggression 87, etc.

Petri, Elio (1929–1982).
Italian director, a political satirist.
The Assassin 61. The Tenth Victim 65. We Still Kill the Old Way 68. A Quiet Place in the Country 68. Investigation of a Citizen above Suspicion (AA, AANw) 69. The Working Class Goes to Heaven 71. Property is No Longer Theft 73. Todo Modo 76, etc.

Petrie, Daniel (1920–).
Canadian-born director in Hollywood, from an academic background, with stage and TV experience.
The Bramble Bush 59. A Raisin in the Sun 61. The Main Attraction 62. Stolen Hours 63. The Idol 66. The Spy with a Cold Nose 67. Silent Night Lonely Night (TV) 69. The City (TV) 71. A Howling in the Woods (TV) 71. Moon of the Wolf (TV) 72. Trouble Comes to Town (TV) 72. The Neptune Factor 73. Buster and Billie 74. The Gun and the Pulpit (TV) 74. Eleanor and Franklin (TV) 76. Lifeguard 76. Sybil (TV) 77. The Betsy 78. Resurrection 80. Fort Apache, the Bronx 81. Six Pack 82. Bay Boy 84. Square Dance 86. Rocket Gibraltar 88. Cocoon: The Return 88. Mark Twain and Me (TV) 91. Grumpy Old Men 93. Lassie 94. Kissinger and Nixon (TV) 95. Calm at Sunset (TV) 96. The Assistant 97, etc.

Petrie, Daniel, Jnr (1952–).
American screenwriter and director. A former literary agent, he is the son of Daniel Petrie.
Beverly Hills Cop (w) (AAN) 84. The Big Easy (w) 87. Shoot to Kill (w) 88. Turner & Hooch (w) 89. Toy Soldiers (wd) 91. In the Army Now (wd) 94. Dead Silence (d) (TV) 96. Maximum Risk/The Exchange (co-w) 96, etc.

Petrie, Hay (1895–1948).
Scots character actor of stage and screen, specializing in eccentrics.
Suspense 30. The Private Life of Henry VIII 32. Nell Gwyn 34. *The Old Curiosity Shop* (as Quilp) 34. The Ghost Goes West 36. *Twenty-One Days* 38. The Spy in Black 39. Q Planes 39. Jamaica Inn 39. Crimes at the Dark House 40. The Thief of Baghdad 40. One of Our Aircraft is Missing 42. A Canterbury Tale 44. Great Expectations 46. The Red Shoes 48. The Guinea Pig 48, etc.

Petrov, Vladimir (1896–1966).
Russian director.
Thunderstorm 34. *Peter the Great* 38, etc.

Petrova, Olga (1886–1977) (Muriel Harding).
British-born leading lady of Hollywood silents in which she played *femmes fatales*.
Autobiography: 1942, *Butter with My Bread*.
The Tigress 14. The Soul Market 16. The Undying Flame 17. Daughter of Destiny 18. The Panther Woman 18, etc.

Petrovic, Aleksander (1929–1994).
Yugoslavian director, a former film critic, and an influential figure in the 60s.
■ Two/Dvoje 61. The Days/Dani 63. Three/Tri (AAN) 65. I Even Met Happy Gypsies/Skuplijaci Perja (AAN) 67. The Master and Margarita 72. Group Portrait with Lady 77. Migrations 94.

Pettet, Joanna (1944–).
Anglo-American leading lady.
The Group 65. Night of the Generals 66. Robbery 67. Blue 68. The Weekend Nun (TV) 74. Welcome to Arrow Beach 75. Captains and the Kings (TV) 76. The Evil 78. The Return of Frank Cannon (TV) 80. Double Exposure 82, etc.

Pettingell, Frank (1891–1966).
British north-country character actor who dispensed rough good humour on stage from 1910; films from 1931.
Hobson's Choice (as Mossop) 31. Jealousy 31. *The Good Companions* 32. *Sing As We Go* 34. The Last Journey 36. Fame 36. Millions 36. Sailing Along 38. *Gaslight* 39. Busman's Honeymoon 40. The Seventh Survivor 41. This England 41. Kipps 41. Once a Crook 41. *When We are Married* 42. The Young Mr Pitt 42. Get Cracking 44. Gaiety George 46. The Magic Box 51. Meet Me Tonight 52. Value for Money 57. Becket 64, many others.

Petty, Lori (1965–).
American leading actress, a former graphic artist.
Cadillac Man 90. Point Break 91. A League of Their Own 92. Free Willy 93. Poetic Justice 93. In the Army Now 94. Tank Girl (title role) 95. The Glass Shield 95. Serial Bomber 96, etc.
TV series: The Thorns 88. Booker 90.

Pevney, Joseph (1920–).
American director, former stage actor.
Shakedown 50. Undercover Girl 50. Iron Man 51. The Strange Door 51. Meet Danny Wilson 51. Just across the Street 52. Because of You 54. Desert Legion 54. The Female on the Beach 55. Three Ring Circus 55. Away All Boats 56. Congo Crossing 56. Tammy 57. *Man of a Thousand Faces* 57. Twilight for the Gods 58. Cash McCall 60. Night of the Grizzly 66. Who Is the Black Dahlia? (TV) 75. Mysterious Island of Beautiful Women (TV) 77. Prisoners of the Sea 85, etc.

Pfeiffer, Dedee (1965–).
American actress, the sister of Michelle PFEIFFER.
Vamp 86. The Allnighter 87. Brothers in Arms 89. The Horror Show 89. Red Surf 90. Tune in Tomorrow/Aunt Julia and the Scriptwriter 90. Frankie & Johnny 91. Up Close and Personal 96, etc.
TV series: Cybill 95–98. For Your Love 98– .

Pfeiffer, Michelle (1957–).
Blonde American leading actress, a former beauty queen. Born in Midway City, California, she worked in a supermarket and began to train as a court stenographer before deciding to become an actress. Formerly married to actor Peter Horton (1982–88), she married TV producer and writer David Kelley in 1993. She has also been romantically linked with actors Michael KEATON, John MALKOVICH and Fisher STEVENS. Her best roles so far have been as Madame de Tourvel in *Dangerous Liaisons*, Susie Diamond in *The Fabulous Baker Boys*, Catwoman in *Batman Returns*, and Countess Ellen Olenska in *The Age of Innocence*. Her current asking price: around $6m a film.
Biography: 1994, *Michelle Pfeiffer* by Bruce Crowther.
Grease 2 82. Scarface 83. Into the Night 84. Ladyhawke 85. Sweet Liberty 86. The Witches of Eastwick 87. Married to the Mob 88. Tequila Sunrise 88. Dangerous Liaisons (AAN) 88. The Fabulous Baker Boys (AAN) 89. The Russia House 90. Frankie and Johnny 91. Love Field (AAN) 92. Batman Returns 92. The Age of Innocence 93. Wolf 94. Dangerous Minds 95. Up Close and Personal 96. One Fine Day 96. To Gillian on Her 37th Birthday 96. A Thousand Acres 97. Prince of Egypt (voice) 98. A Midsummer Night's Dream 99, etc.
TV series: Delta House 79. B.A.D. Cats 80.
❝ Hollywood is filled with beautiful, unhappy women who have shut down. – M.P.

Phifer, Mekhi (1975–).
American actor.
Clockers 95. The Tuskegee Airmen (TV) 95. High School High 96. Soul Food 97. I Still Know What You Did Last Summer 98, etc.

Philbin, Mary (1903–1993).
American leading lady of the silent screen.
The Blazing Trail 21. Merry Go Round 23. Phantom of the Opera 25. The Man Who Laughs 28. After the Fog 30, etc.

Philipe, Gérard (1922–1959).
France's leading young actor of the 50s, who alternated stage and screen activities.
Biography: 1964, *No Longer than a Sigh* by Anne Philipe.
■ La Boîte aux Rêves 43. The Children of the Flower Quay 45. Land without Stars 46. *The Idiot* 46. *Le Diable au Corps* 47. La Chartreuse de Parme 47. *Une Si Jolie Petite Plage* 49. All Roads Lead to Rome 49. La Beauté du Diable 50. La Ronde 50. Juliette ou la Clef des Songes 51. *Fanfan la Tulipe* 51. The Seven Deadly Sins 51. *Les Belles de Nuit* 52. Les Orgueilleux 53. Versailles 53. Knave of Hearts (GB) 54. Villa Borghese 54. The Red and the Black 54. Les Grandes Manoeuvres 55. La Meilleure Part 55. Si Paris Nous Était Conté 55. Till Eulenspiegel 57. Pot Bouille 57. Montparnasse 19 57. La Vie à Deux 58. The Gambler 58. Les Liaisons Dangereuses 59. La Fièvre Monte à El Pao 59.

Philips, Lee (1927–).
American leading man of the late 50s. Became TV director.
Peyton Place 57. The Hunters 58. Middle of the Night 59. Tess of the Storm Country 60. The Lollipop Cover 65. Salvage (d, TV) 79. On the Right Track (d) 81. Samson and Delilah (d) (TV) 84. Mae West (d) (TV) 84. Barnum (d) 86. Windmills of the Gods (d) (TV) 88. Silent Motive (d) 91, etc.

Philips, Mary (1900–1975).
American stage actress who made very occasional film appearances.
Life Begins 32. A Farewell To Arms 33. That Certain Woman 37. Lady in the Dark 44. Leave Her to Heaven 46. Dear Wife 47, etc.

Philliber, John (1872–1944).
Slightly-built American character actor in a few early 40s films; best remembered for *It Happened Tomorrow* 44.

Phillippe, Ryan (1974–).
American actor, brought up in New Castle, Delaware. He first came to attention playing a gay teenager on the TV soap opera *One Life to Live*.
Crimson Tide 95. Nowhere 95. White Squall 96. Lifeform 96. I Know What You Did Last Summer 97. 54 98. Dancing about Architecture 98, etc.
TV series: One Life to Live 92–93.

Phillips, Alex (1901–1977).
Canadian cinematographer who worked in Hollywood in the 20s and then went to Mexico to shoot that country's first sound film, *Santa* 31. He remained based in Mexico for the rest of his career, photographing more than 200 films, though he also returned to work in Hollywood in the 50s and 60s.
The Carnation Kid (US) 29. Divorce Made Easy (US) 29. The Mad Empress (Mex./US) 39. Pancho Villa Returns (Mex.) 50. Subida al Cielo (Mex.) 51. Adventures of Robinson Crusoe (Mex.) 52. The Proud Ones/Les Orgueilleux (Fr./Mex.) 53. The Littlest Outlaw (US) 54. The Western Story (US) 57. Last of the Fast Guns (US) 58. Villa! (US) 58. Ten Days to Tulara (US) 58. Sierra Baron (US) 58. The Wonderful Country (US) 59. For the Love of Mike (US) 60. The Last Sunset (US) 61. Geronimo (Mex./US) 62. Of Love and Desire (US) 63. Robinson Crusoe and the Tiger (Mex.) 69, many others.

Phillips, Conrad (1930–).
British leading man, mostly on TV.
The White Trap 59. Chamber of Horrors 60. The Fourth Square 61. No Love for Johnnie 62. Stopover Forever 64. Who Killed the Cat? 66, etc.
TV series: *William Tell* 58.

Phillips, Frank (1912–1994).
American cinematographer.
The Island at the Top of the World 74. Escape to Witch Mountain 75. No Deposit No Return 76. The Shaggy D.A. 76. Pete's Dragon 77. Return from Witch Mountain 78. Hot Lead and Cold Feet 78. Goin' Coconuts 78. The Apple Dumpling Gang Rides Again 79. The Black Hole (AAN) 79. Midnight Madness 80. Herbie Goes Bananas 80. Going Ape! 81, etc.

Phillips, Julia (1945–) and **Michael** (1943–).
American husband-and-wife producers, now divorced, who hit the big time with *The Sting*, *Taxi Driver* and *Close Encounters of the Third Kind*.
MICHAEL PHILLIPS AS SOLE PRODUCER: Cannery Row 81. Heartbeeps 81. The Flamingo Kid 84. Don't Tell Mom the Babysitter's Dead 91. Dick & Marge Save the World 91.
❝ Julia Phillips gained notoriety in 1991 with the publication of her acerbic, best-selling memoir, *You'll Never Eat Lunch in This Town Again*, detailing her drug-fuelled decline as a producer and notable for her low opinion of most of her former colleagues.
On John Landis:
That little megalomaniacal prick.
On Steven Spielberg:
I taught the little prick he deserved limos before he even knew what it was to travel in a first-class seat on a plane.
On François Truffaut:
Deep down I knew he was a prick.
On Donald Sutherland:
A top-ten brain fucker.
A further volume of autobiography, *Driving under the Affluence*, appeared in 1995.

Phillips, Leslie (1924–).
British light comedian, former child actor from 1935.
The Citadel 38. Train of Events 49. The Sound Barrier 52. Value for Money 57. *Carry On Nurse* 59. Carry On Constable 60. Doctor in Love 60. Watch Your Stern 60. *Very Important Person* 61. Raising the Wind 61. In the Doghouse 62. Crooks Anonymous 62. *The Fast Lady* 62. And Father Came Too 64. Doctor in Clover 66. Maroc 7 (& p) 66. Doctor in Trouble 70. The Magnificent Seven Deadly Sins 71. Not Now Darling 73. Don't Just Lie There Say Something 73. Spanish Fly 75. Not Now Comrade 76. Out of Africa 85. Empire of the Sun 87. Scandal 89. Mountains of the Moon 90. King Ralph 91. Love on a Branch Line (TV) 94. August 96. Caught in the Act 96. The Canterville Ghost (TV) 96, etc.
TV series: Honey for Tea 94. The House of Windsor 94.

Phillips, Lou Diamond (1962–).
American young leading actor. In 1996, he received rave reviews for his performance as the King of Siam in a Broadway revival of the musical *The King and I*.
Trespasses (& w) 83. Harley 85. La Bamba 87. Dakota 88. Stand and Deliver 88. Young Guns 88. Disorganized Crime 89. Renegades 89. The First Power 90. A Show of Force 90. Young Guns II 90. Harley 90. Ambition (& w) 91. Dark Wind 91. Shadow of the Wolf (& co-w) 93. Sioux City (& d) 94. Boulevard 94. Teresa's Tattoo 94. Courage under Fire 96. The Big Hit 98. Supernova 99, etc.

Phillips, Mackenzie (1959–).
American second lead of the 70s.
American Graffiti 75. Eleanor and Franklin (TV) 76. More American Graffiti 79. Love Child 82, etc.
TV series: One Day at a Time 75–83.

Phillips, Robin (1942–).
British juvenile lead, later stage director in Canada.
Decline and Fall 68. David Copperfield 69. Two Gentlemen Sharing 70. Tales From the Crypt 72. Miss Julie (d) 73. The Wars (d) 82, etc.

Phillips, Sian (1934–).
Dignified British stage actress. She was married to actor Peter O'TOOLE (1959–79).
Becket 64. Young Cassidy 64. Laughter in the Dark 69. Goodbye Mr Chips 69. Murphy's War 70. Under Milk Wood 72. I, Claudius (TV) 76. Tinker Tailor Soldier Spy (TV) 79. Nijinksy 80. Clash of the Titans 81. Dune 85. The Doctor and the Devils 85. The Two Mrs Grenvilles (TV) 86. Valmont 89. The Age of Innocence 93. Ivanhoe (TV) 97. The Scold's Bridle (TV) 98, etc.

Philo Vance:
see VAN DINE, S. S.

Philpotts, Ambrosine (1912–1980).
British character actress, mainly on stage.
This Man is Mine 46. The Franchise Affair 51. The Captain's Paradise 53. Up in the World 56. Room at the Top 59. Doctor in Love 60. Life at the Top 65, etc.

Phipps, Nicholas (1913–1980).
British light comedian often seen in cameo roles. On stage from 1932. Has also scripted or co-scripted many films, in most of which he appeared.
Piccadilly Incident 46. Spring in Park Lane 48. Doctor in the House 53. Doctor in Love 60. The Wild and the Willing 62, many others.

Phoenix, Joaquin (1974–) (aka Leaf Phoenix).
American actor, the brother of River PHOENIX. Brought up in Puerto Rico and a religious commune (the Children of God) in Venezuela, he began performing on the streets with his siblings. He is the brother of actresses Rain PHOENIX and Summer Phoenix. He has been romantically linked with actress Liv TYLER.
Parenthood 89. To Die For 95. Spacecamp 86. Russkies 87. Parenthood 89. Walking the Dog 91. To Die For 95. U-Turn 97. Inventing the Abbots 97. Return to Paradise 98. Clay Pigeons 98, etc.

Phoenix, Rain (1971–).
American actress, the sister of River and Joaquin Phoenix.
Even Cowgirls Get the Blues 93. The Thing Called Love 94. Interview with the Vampire 94, etc.

Phoenix, River (1970–1993).
American young leading actor. He also played guitar and sang with his own rock group, Aleka's Attic. Died outside a Hollywood night-club after overdosing on heroin and cocaine. His final performance was in *Dark Blood*, a film which was abandoned three weeks from completion.
Explorers 85. Mosquito Coast 86. Stand by Me 86. Little Nikita 88. A Night in the Life of Jimmy Reardon 88. Running on Empty (AAN) 88. Indiana Jones and the Last Crusade 89. I Love You to Death 90. Dogfight 91. My Own Private Idaho 91. Sneakers 92. Silent Tongue 93. The Thing Called Love 93, etc.
TV series: Seven Brides for Seven Brothers 82–83.
❝ I don't see any point or any good in drugs that are as disruptive as cocaine. – *R.P.*
There wasn't a false bone in his body. – *Sidney Lumet*

Pialat, Maurice (1925–).
French director.
L'Enfance Nue 68. We Will Not Grow Old Together 72. La Gueule Ouverte 73. Graduate First/Passe Ton Bac d'Abord 79. Loulou 79. A Nos Amours 83. Police 85. Under Satan's Sun 87. Van Gogh 91. Le Garcu 95, etc.

Piazza, Ben (1934–1991).
Canadian actor who went to Hollywood, but was little heard from.
A Dangerous Age (Can.) 58. The Hanging Tree 59. I Never Promised You a Rose Garden 77. Apocalypse Now 79. The Blues Brothers 80. Rocky V 90. Guilty by Suspicion 91, etc.
TV series: Ben Casey 65. Forever Fernwood 77. The Waverly Wonders 78. Dallas 82–83.

Picardo, Robert (1953–).
American actor, frequently hidden under elaborate make-up in horror movies.
The Howling 80. Explorers (as Wak) 85. Legend (as Meg Mucklebones) 85. Innerspace 87. Jack's Back 87. The 'burbs 88. 976-EVIL 88. Gremlins 2: The New Batch 90. Matinee 92. Wagons East 94. Revenge of the Nerds 4: Nerds in Love 94. Star Trek: First Contact 96, etc.
TV series: China Beach 88–91. Star Trek: Voyager (as the medical hologram) 95– .

Piccoli, Michel (1925–).
Franco-Italian leading man. The second of his three wives was singer Juliette GRECO.
French Cancan 55. The Witches of Salem 56. Le Bal des Espions 60. Le Mépris 63. Diary of a Chambermaid 64. De L'Amour 65. Lady L. 65. La Curée 66. The Young Girls of Rochefort 67. Un Homme de Trop 67. Belle de Jour 67. Dillinger is Dead 68. The Milky Way 69. Topaz 69. Blowout 73. The Infernal Trio 74. Mado 76. The Savage State 78. Le Sucre 78. A City 80. La Chambre Voisine 80. Leap into the Void 81. General of the Dead Army 81. Dangerous Moves 84. Revenge 84. Departure. Return 85. The Nonentity 86. Bad Blood 86. La Rumba 86. Martha und Ich 90. May Fools/Milou en Mai 90. La Belle Noiseuse 91. Le Voleur d'Enfants 91. Le Bal des Casse-Pieds 91. Archipelago/Archipel 92. Ruptures 93. Le Souper 93. La Cavale des Fous 93. Les Cent et Une Nuits 95. Beaumarchais the Scoundrel 96. Travelling Companion 96. Alors Voilà (d only) 97, etc.

Picerni, Paul (1922–).
American leading man, usually in second features.
Saddle Tramp (debut) 50. Maru Maru 52. House of Wax 53. Drive a Crooked Road 54. Hell's Island 55. Omar Khayyam 57. Strangers When We Meet 60. The Scalphunters 68. The Land Raiders 69. Kotch 71. Capricorn One 77. Beyond the Poseidon Adventure 79. The Fearmaker 89, etc.
TV series: The Untouchables 59–62.

Pichel, Irving (1891–1954).
American actor-director, in Hollywood from 1930.
AS ACTOR: The Right to Love 30. The Miracle Man 31. Oliver Twist (as Fagin) 33. Cleopatra 34. Jezebel 38. Juarez 40. Sante Fé 51, many others.
■ AS DIRECTOR: *The Most Dangerous Game* (co-

d) 32. Before Dawn 33. *She* (co-d) 35. The Gentleman from Louisiana 36. Beware of Ladies 37. Larceny of the Air 37. The Sheik Steps Out 37. The Duke Comes Back 37. The Great Commandment 39. Earthbound 40. The Man I Married 40. Hudson's Bay 40. Dance Hall 41. Secret Agent of Japan 42. The Pied Piper 42. Life Begins at 8.30 42. *The Moon is Down* 43. *Happy Land* 43. And Now Tomorrow 44. A Medal for Benny 45. Colonel Effingham's Raid 45. Tomorrow is Forever 46. The Bride Wore Boots 46. O.S.S. 46. Temptation 46. They Won't Believe Me 47. Something in the Wind 47. The Miracle of the Bells 48. Mr Peabody and the Mermaid 48. Without Honor 49. The Great Rupert 50. Quicksand 50. Destination Moon 50. Santa Fé 51. Martin Luther 53. Day of Triumph 54.

Pick, Lupu:
see LUPU-PICK.

Pickens, Slim (1919–1983) (Louis Bert Lindley).
Slow-talking American character actor, in scores of low-budget westerns from mid-40s, latterly in bigger films.

The Sun Shines Bright 53. The Great Locomotive Chase 56. One-Eyed Jacks 61. *Dr Strangelove* 63. Major Dundee 65. Rough Night in Jericho 67. The Cowboys 72. Pat Garrett and Billy the Kid 73. Blazing Saddles 74. The Apple Dumpling Gang 75. Whiteline Fever 75. The White Buffalo 77. Mr Billion 77. Wishbone Cutter 78. Beyond the Poseidon Adventure 79. Honeysuckle Rose 80. The Howling 81. Pink Motel 82, etc.

TV series: Outlaws 61. Custer 67.

Pickering, Donald (1933–).
British actor who played Holmes in the little seen 1980 TV series *Sherlock Holmes and Dr Watson*.

A Bridge Too Far 76. The Thirty-Nine Steps 78. Half Moon Street 87, etc.

Pickford, Jack (1896–1933).
American light actor, brother of Mary Pickford. He was married to actresses Marilyn Miller and Olive Thomas.

Tom Sawyer 17. Sandy 18. Just Out of College 21. The Goose Woman 25. The Bat 26. Brown of Harvard 26. Exit Smiling 26. Gang War 28, etc.

Pickford, Mary (1893–1979) (Gladys Smith).
Canadian actress who in the heyday of silent films was known as 'the world's sweetheart'; became co-founder of United Artists Films and one of America's richest women. Acting on stage from five years old; was brought into films by D. W. Griffith. Married actors Owen Moore (1911–20), Douglas Fairbanks (1920–36), and Charles 'Buddy' Rogers in 1937.

Autobiography: 1955, *Sunshine and Shadow*.

Biographies: 1974, *Sweetheart* by Robert Windeler; 1991, *Mary Pickford: America's Sweetheart* by Scott Eyman; 1997, *Pickford: The Woman Who Made Hollywood* by Eileen Whitfield.

Her First Biscuits 09. The Violin Maker of Cremona 10. The Paris Hat 13. Madame Butterfly 15. Less Than the Dust 16. The Little Princess 17. Rebecca of Sunnybrook Farm 17. Stella Maris 18. *Pollyanna* 19. Suds 20. *Little Lord Fauntleroy* 21. The Love Light 21. *Tess of the Storm Country* 22. Rosita 23. Dorothy Vernon of Haddon Hall 24. Little Annie Rooney 25. My Best Girl 27. The Taming of the Shrew 29. Secrets 29. *Coquette* (AA) 29. Kiki 31. Secrets 33, many others.

✪ For entrancing the world, and for knowing when to stop. *Little Lord Fauntleroy*.

❝ The appeal of the world's sweetheart is not well understood in the 80s. Her screen image was ever-childlike, sweet and demure, the antithesis of today's heroines. Alistair Cooke said:

She was the girl every young man wanted to have – as his sister.

Yet on first encounter D. W. Griffith told her:

You're too little and too fat, but I might give you a job.

Later, he ruefully recollected:

She never stopped listening and learning.

She was soon telling Adolph Zukor:

I can't afford to work for only ten thousand dollars a week.

And Sam Goldwyn reflected:

It took longer to make one of Mary's contracts than it did to make one of Mary's pictures.

Spoiled by success she may have been, but never blind to her own failings:

I never liked one of my pictures in its entirety.

By 1929 she was surprisingly intolerant of her screen image:

I am sick of Cinderella parts, of wearing rags and tatters. I want to wear smart clothes and play the lover.

Richard Griffith and Arthur Mayer thought the secret of her success was that:

Her sweetness and light were tempered by a certain realism. In spite of her creed, the Glad Girl knew it was no cinch to make everything come out right. Nothing could have been more in tune with an era which combined limitless optimism with a belief that 'git up and git' was necessary to make optimism come true.

But Mabel Normand at a press conference struck a sour note:

Say anything you like, but don't say I want to work. That sounds like Mary Pickford, that prissy bitch.

~Special Academy Award 1976.

Pickles, Vivian (1933–).
British character actress.

Play Dirty 68. Nicholas and Alexandra 71. Harold and Maude 71. Sunday Bloody Sunday 72. O Lucky Man 73. Candleshoe 77. Britannia Hospital 82. Suspicion 87, etc.

Pickles, Wilfred (1904–1978).
British radio personality and latterly character actor; played Yorkshiremen.

Autobiography: 1949, *Between You and Me*.

The Gay Dog 53. Billy Liar 63. The Family Way 66. For the Love of Ada 72, etc.

TV series: For the Love of Ada 70–71.

Pickup, Ronald (1940–).
British character actor, mainly on stage.

Three Sisters 68. Day of the Jackal 73. Mahler 74. Jennie (TV) (as Randolph Churchill) 75. Joseph Andrews 76. The Thirty-Nine Steps 78. Zulu Dawn 79. Nijinsky 80. The Letter (TV) 82. Ivanhoe (TV) 82. Never Say Never Again 83. Eleni 85. The Mission 86. Fortunes of War (TV) 87. Bethune: The Making of a Hero 89. Journey of Honor 91. A Time to Dance (TV) 92. Scarlett (TV) 94. Ivanhoe (TV) 97, etc.

TV series: The Riff Raff Element 94. Black Hearts in Battersea 96.

Picon, Molly (1898–1992).
American stage actress; films very occasional.

Come Blow Your Horn 63. Fiddler on the Roof 71. For Pete's Sake 74, etc.

Pidgeon, Rebecca (1963–).
Scottish-born actress and singer in Hollywood. She studied at RADA. Married writer and director David MAMET.

The Dawning 88. She's Been Away (TV) 89. Homicide (US) 91. The Water Engine (TV) 92. The Spanish Prisoner (US) 98, etc.

Pidgeon, Walter (1897–1984).
Good-looking, quiet-spoken Canadian leading man in Hollywood; during the 30s and 40s he gave gentlemanly support to several dominant leading ladies.

■ Mannequin 25. Old Loves and New 26. The Outsider 26. Miss Nobody 26. Marriage License 26. The Girl from Rio 27. The Heart of Salome 27. The Gorilla 27. The Thirteenth Juror 27. Gateway of the Moon 27. Clothes Make the Woman 28. Woman Wise 28. Turn Back the Hours 28. Melody of Love 28. A Most Immoral Lady 29. Her Private Life 29. Bride of the Regiment 30. Sweet Kitty Bellairs 30. Viennese Nights 30. Kiss Me Again 30. Going Wild 30. The Gorilla 31. The Hot Heiress 31. Rockabye 32. The Kiss Before the Mirror 33. Journal of a Crime 34. Big Brown Eyes 36. Fatal Lady 36. Girl Overboard 37. Saratoga 37. A Girl with Ideas 37. She's Dangerous 37. As Good as Married 37. My Dear Miss Aldrich 37. Man Proof 38. The Girl of the Golden West 38. Shopworn Angel 38. Too Hot to Handle 38. Listen Darling 38. *Society Lawyer* 39. Six Thousand Enemies 39. Stronger than Desire 39. Nick Carter Master Detective 39. The House across the Bay 40. It's a Date 40. Dark Command 40. Phantom Raiders 40. Sky Murder 40. Flight Command 40. *Man Hunt* 41. *Blossoms in the Dust* 41. *How Green was My Valley* 41. Design for Scandal 42. *Mrs Miniver* (AAN) 42. White Cargo 42. The Youngest Profession 43. *Madame Curie* (AAN) 43. Mrs Parkington 44. Weekend at the Waldorf 45. Holiday in Mexico 46. The Secret Heart 46. Cass Timberlane 47. If Winter Comes 47. Julia Misbehaves 48. Command Decision 48. *That Forsyte Woman* (as Young Jolyon) 49. The Red Danube 49. The Miniver Story 50. Soldiers Three 51. Calling Bulldog Drummond 51. The Unknown Man 51. The Sellout 52. Million Dollar Mermaid 52. The Bad and the Beautiful 52. Scandal at Scourie 53. Dream Wife 53. *Executive Suite* 54. Men of the Fighting Lady 54. The Last Time I Saw Paris 54. Deep in My Heart 54. Hit the Deck 55. The Glass Slipper 55. *Forbidden Planet* 56. These Wilder Years 56. The Rack 56. Voyage to the Bottom of the Sea 61. *Advise and Consent* 62. The Two Colonels 62. Big Red 62. The Shortest Day 63. Cosa Nostra (TV) 67. Warning Shot 67. Funny Girl (as Ziegfeld) 68. Rascal 69. The Mask of Sheba (TV) 69. The Vatican Affair 69. Skyjacked 72. The Neptune Factor 73. Harry in Your Pocket 73. Yellow Headed Summer 74. Live Again Die Again (TV) 75. You Lie So Deep My Love (TV) 75. The Lindbergh Kidnapping Case (TV) 76. Murder at 40,000 Feet (TV) 76. Two Minutes Warning 76. Sextette 77.

Pierce, Charles B.
American horror film screenwriter and director.

The Legend of Boggy Creek (wd) 73. Bootleggers (d) 74. Winterhawk (wd) 75. The Winds of Autumn (wd) 76. The Town that Dreaded Sundown (d) 77. Greyeagle (wd) 77. The Norsemen (wd) 78. The Evictors (wd) 79. Sacred Ground (wd) 83. Boggy Creek II (wd) 85. Hawken's Breed (d) 89, etc.

Pierce, Jack (1889–1968).
American make-up artist who worked at Universal for many years and created the familiar images of Dracula, the Wolf Man, the Mummy and the Frankenstein monster.

Pierce-Roberts, Tony.
British cinematographer.

Moonlighting 82. A Private Function 85. A Room with a View (AAN) 86. A Tiger's Tale 88. Out Cold 89. Slaves of New York 89. Mr & Mrs Bridge 90. White Fang 91. *Howards End* 92. Splitting Heirs 93. The Dark Half 93. The Remains of the Day 93. The Client 94. Haunted 95. Surviving Picasso 96. Jungle 2 Jungle 97. Paulie 98, etc.

Pierlot, Francis (1876–1955).
American character actor, usually of mild professional types.

Night Angel 31. The Captain Is a Lady 40. Night Monster 42. The Doughgirls 44. Dragonwyck 46. The Late George Apley 47. That Wonderful Urge 48. My Friend Irma 49. Cyrano de Bergerac 50. The Robe 53, many others.

Pierson, Frank L. (1945–).
American director, from TV.

Cat Ballou (co-w) 65. Cool Hand Luke (co-w, AAN) 67. The Looking Glass War 69. The Anderson Tapes (w only) 71. Dog Day Afternoon (w only) (AA) 75. A Star Is Born (d only) 76. King of the Gypsies 78. In Country (w) 89. Presumed Innocent (w) 90. Somebody Has to Shoot the Picture 91. Truman (TV) 95, etc.

TV series: *Nichols* 71.

Piesiewicz, Krzysztof.
Polish screenwriter who co-wrote the scripts of Krzysztof KIESLOWSKI's later films, including *Decalogue*, and 10 films for television based on the Ten Commandments that included the powerful *A Short Film about Killing*.

No End/Bez Konca 84. Decalogue/Dekalog 88. The Double Life of Veronique/Podwojne Zycie Weroniki 91. Three Colours: White/Trzy Kolory: Bialy 93. Three Colours: Blue/Trzy Kolory: Niebieski 93. Three Colours: Red/Trzy Kolory: Czerwony 94, etc.

Pigott, Tempe (1884–1962).
British character actress in Hollywood, usually as garrulous cockney.

Seven Days Leave 30. Cavalcade 33. One More River 34. Limehouse Blues 35. Becky Sharp 35, etc.

Piggott-Smith, Tim (1946–).
British character actor.

Sweet William 79. Richard's Things (TV) 80. Clash of the Titans 81. Victory 81. *The Jewel in the Crown* (TV) 82. A State of Emergency 86. The Bullion Boys (TV) 93. The Remains of the Day 93.

Pike, Kelvin.
Australian-born cinematographer, in Britain, from documentary films.

The Dresser 83. Gulag 84. Anna Karenina 84. Bad Medicine 85. Strong Medicine 86. Spot Marks the X 86. Apprentice to Murder 86. A New Life 87. A Dry White Season 88. Betsy's Wedding 90, etc.

Pike, Nicholas (1955–).
British-born composer and musician, in Hollywood. Born in Water Orton, Warwickshire, he was a chorister at Canterbury Choir School before studying at Boston's Berklee College of Music in the early 70s. He played flute with his own jazz group in New York before going to Hollywood.

Critters 2 88. The Prince and the Pauper 90. Stephen King's Sleepwalkers 92. Captain Ron 92. Blank Check 94. Attack of the 50 Foot Woman (TV) 94. The Sadness of Sex (co-m) 95. The Shining (TV) 97. Telling Lies in America 97. Star Kid 98, etc.

Pilbeam, Nova (1919–).
British teenage star of the 30s.

Little Friend 34. The Man Who Knew Too Much 34. *Tudor Rose* 35. *Young and Innocent* 37. Spring Meeting 40. Banana Ridge 41. This Man Is Mine 46. Counterblast 47. The Three Weird Sisters 48, etc.

Pillsbury, Sam (1946–).
American-born director, screenwriter and producer, in New Zealand from the 60s.

The Scarecrow (& co-w) 82. The Quiet Earth (p, w only) 85. Starlight Hotel 87. Zandalee 90. Into the Badlands (TV) 91. The President's Child (TV) 92. Free Willy 3: The Rescue 97, etc.

Pinchot, Bronson (1959–) (Bronson Poncharavsky).
American actor.

Risky Business 83. Beverly Hills Cop 84. The Flamingo Kid 84. Hot Resort 85. After Hours 85. Second Sight 89. Blame It on the Bellboy 92. True Romance 93. Beverly Hills Cop III 94. Courage under Fire 96. The First Wives Club 96. Courage Under Fire 96. Quest for Camelot 98, etc.

TV series: Sara 85–88. Perfect Strangers 86–92. Meego 97– .

Pine, William H. (1896–1955) and **Thomas, William C.** (1903–1984).
An American production executive and an exhibitor-writer who banded together in the early 40s to make scores of second features for Paramount. *Power Dive, Wildcat, Midnight Manhunt, They Made Me a Killer, Wrecking Crew, Torpedo Boat, I Cover Big Town*, etc. Continued into the 50s with larger-scale adventures: *Sangaree, Jamaica Run, The Far Horizons*, etc., but never managed a top-notcher. Because of their economy they were known as 'the Dollar Bills'. Thomas was almost always the director of their joint productions.

Pinelli, Tullio (1908–).
Italian dramatist and screenwriter, a former lawyer, who has worked on many of Fellini's films.

Without Pity/Senza Pietà 47. The Mill on the Po 49. The White Sheik/Lo Sceicco Bianco 52. I Vitelloni 53. La Strada 54. The Nights of Cabiria/Le Notti di Cabiria 56. La Dolce Vita (AAN) 60. Boccaccio 70 62. Eight and a Half (AAN) 63. Juliet of the Spirits 65. Ginger and Fred 86. The Voice of the Moon 90, many others.

Pinero, Sir Arthur Wing (1855–1934).
British playwright who dealt mainly with the upper middle class. Many films were made of his work in silent days; the most popular later were *The Second Mrs Tanqueray* and *The Enchanted Cottage*, though his farce *The Magistrate* had several incarnations, notably as *Those Were the Days* 34.

Pineyro, Marcelo.
Argentinian director.
Wild Tango 93. Wild Horses/Caballos Salvajes 95. Ashes from Paradise/Cenizas del Paraíso (AAN) 97, etc.

Ping, Yuen Woo.
Hong Kong actor and director of martial arts movies.
AS DIRECTOR: Snake in the Eagle's Shadow 78. Drunken Master 78. Buddhist Fist 80. Legend of a Fighter 81. Shaolin Drunkard 82. Mismatched Couples 85. Tiger Cage 88. Tiger Cage 2 89. In the Line of Duty 4 90. Tiger Cage 3 91. Tai Chi Master 93. Fire Dragons 94. Fist of Legend 94, etc.

Pink, Sidney (1916–).
American director.
Journey to the Seventh Planet 61. Reptilicus 62. Finger on the Trigger 65. The Tall Women 66.

Pink, Steve.
American screenwriter and actor, a founder of Chicago's New Crime Theater with John CUSACK and Jeremy PIVEN.
AS WRITER: Grosse Point Blank 97. High Fidelity 99, etc.
AS ACTOR: Touch and Go 86. Dangerous Curves 88. Bob Roberts 92. Grosse Pointe Blank 97, etc.

Pinkett, Jada (1971–) (aka Jada Pinkett Smith).
American actress, born in Baltimore, Maryland. Married actor Will SMITH in 1998.
Menace II Society 93. The Inkwell 94. A Low Down Dirty Shame 94. Tales from the Crypt: Demon Knight 95. The Nutty Professor 96. *Set It Off* 96. Scream 2 97. Woo 98. Return to Paradise 98, etc.

Pinsent, Gordon (1933–).
Canadian leading actor, much on TV.
The Thomas Crown Affair 68. The Forbin Project 69. Quarantined (TV) 69. The Rowdy Man 72. Newman's Law 74. Silence of the North 81. John and the Missus (& wd, from his novel) 87. Two Men (d, TV) 88. In the Eyes of the Stranger (TV) 93, etc.
TV series: *Quentin Durgens MP* 66.

Pinter, Harold (1930–).
British playwright, of menace and obscure violence, and screenwriter. A former actor, he has also occasionally appeared on screen, usually in threatening roles. Married actress Vivien MERCHANT (1956–80) and author Lady Antonia Fraser.
Biography: 1996, *The Life and Work of Harold Pinter* by Michael Billington.
The Servant (w) 63. The Caretaker (oa, w) 64. The Pumpkin Eater (w) (BFA) 64. The Quiller Memorandum (w) 67. Accident (w) 67. The Birthday Party (woa) 69. The Go Between (w) 71. The Homecoming (oa) 73. Butley (d) 73. Rogue Male (TV) (a) 76. The Last Tycoon (w) 76. The French Lieutenant's Woman (AAN) 81. Betrayal (AAN) 83. Turtle Diary 85. Reunion/L'Ami Retrouvé 89. The Handmaid's Tale 90. The Comfort of Strangers 90. The Trial 93. Breaking the Code (a) (TV) 97. Mojo (a) 98. Mansfield Park (a) 99, etc.
❝ What concerns me most is shape and structure. – *H.P.*

Pintoff, Ernest (1931–).
Modernist American cartoon maker:
Flebus 57. *The Violinist* 59. *The Interview* 60. *The Critic* 63, etc.
Also wrote and directed live-action features:
Harvey Middleman, Fireman 64. Dynamite Chicken 69. Who Killed Mary What's Her Name? 70. Blade 75. Jaguar Lives 79. Lunch Wagon 81. St Helens 81, etc.

Pinza, Ezio (1893–1957) (Fortunato Pinza).
Italian-American opera singer who graced a few films. Born in Rome, he became a star with the Metropolitan Opera in New York and, in his mid-50s, on Broadway in *South Pacific* and *Fanny*.
■ Carnegie Hall 48. Mr Imperium 50. Slightly Dishonorable 51. Tonight We Sing 53.
TV series: The RCA Victor Show 51–52. Bonino 53.
❝ I didn't know Pinza was the greatest baritone in the world. To me he was a big, unattractive, over-sexed man, the most conceited egomaniac I'd ever met. – *Debbie Reynolds.*

Pious, Minerva (1909–1979).
American radio comedienne of the 40s, famous with Fred Allen as Mrs Nussbaum.
It's In the Bag 45. The Ambassador's Daughter 56. Love in the Afternoon 57, etc.

Piovani, Nicola (1946–).
Italian composer.
Nel Nome del Padre 70. The Rebel Nun 74. Hyena's Sun 77. Il Minestrone 81. The Night of the Shooting Stars/La Notte di San Lorenzo 81. La Trace (Fr.) 84. Ginger and Fred 86. Good Morning, Babylon 87. The Voice of the Moon 90. Fiorile 93. We Don't Want to Talk about It/De Eso No Se Habla (Arg.) 93. Amok 93. Il Giovane Mussolini 93. Per Amore, Solo per Amore 94. The Tit and the Moon 94. A Month by the Lake 95, etc.

Piper, Frederick (1902–1979).
British character actor, mostly on stage: usually played the average man or police inspector.
The Good Companions 32. Jamaica Inn 39. Hue and Cry 46. Passport to Pimlico 48. The Blue Lamp 50. Doctor at Sea 55. Very Important Person 61. One Way Pendulum 64. He Who Rides a Tiger 65, etc.

Pirosh, Robert (1910–1990).
American writer-director.
The Winning Ticket (oa) 35. A Day at the Races (w) 37. I Married a Witch (w) 42. Rings on Her Fingers (w) 42. Up in Arms (w) 44. *Battleground* (w) (AA) 49. Go for Broke (wd) (AANw) 51. Washington Story (wd) 52. Valley of the Kings (wd) 54. The Girl Rush (wd) 55. Spring Reunion (wd) 57. Hell Is for Heroes (w) 62. A Gathering of Eagles (w) 63. What's So Bad about Feeling Good? (w) 68, etc.

Piscator, Erwin (1893–1966).
German director whose importance lies in his theatrical work and his theories of total theatre, a multi-media approach using newsreels, film clips and sound, which influenced Joan Littlewood's Theatre Workshop in Britain and Joseph Losey's Living Newspaper productions in New York. In the 40s, he ran a dramatic workshop at the New School for Social Research in New York, where the teachers included Lee Strasberg and Stella Adler. Marlon Brando, Maureen Stapleton, Montgomery Clift and Rod Steiger were among the students.
Hoppla! Wir Leben 28. *Revolt of the Fishermen/* Vostaniye Rybakov 35.

Pisier, Marie-France (1944–).
French leading lady of the 70s.
French Provincial 76. Love at Twenty 76. Cousin Cousine 76. The Other Side of Midnight 76. Barocco 77. Sérail 77. Love on the Run 79. French Postcards 79. La Banquière 80. Miss Right 81. Hot Touch 82. Les Nanas 84. Parking 85. Le Bal du Gouverneur (wd) 90. Blue Note/La Note Bleue 91. Pourquoi Maman Est dans Mon Lit? 94. Tous les Jours Dimanche 94. The Ice Rink/La Patinoire 98, etc.

Pistilli, Luigi (1930–1996).
Italian leading actor on stage and in films. Committed suicide shortly before he was due to go on stage in Milan in a play that had been critically savaged. He studied at Milan's Piccolo Teatro acting school in the mid-50s and was noted for his performances in the plays of Bertolt Brecht.
For a Few Dollars More 65. The Good, the Bad and the Ugly 66. Texas Addio 66. Death Rides a Horse/Da Uomo a Uomo 67. Bandidos 67. To Each His Own/A Ciascuno il Suo 67. Number One 73. Illustrious Corpses/Cadaveri Eccellenti 75. La Moglie di Mio Padre 76, etc.

Pithey, Wensley (1914–1993).
Heavily built South African-born character actor of stage and screen, in Britain from 1947.
The October Man 47. Cardboard Cavalier 49. Brandy for the Parson 52. The Titfield Thunderbolt 53. The Belles of St Trinian's 54. Moby Dick 56. Doctor at Large 57. Hell Drivers 57. Blue Murder at St Trinian's 58. The Knack 65. Oliver! 68. Oh What a Lovely War 69. The Adventurers 70. One of Our Dinosaurs Is Missing 75. Ike (as Churchill) (TV) 79. Red Monarch (TV) 83. The English Week at Dallas Texas (as Churchill) (TV) 84. White Mischief 87. American Friends 91, etc.

Pitillo, Maria (1965–).
American actress, born in Elmira, New York.
Wise Guys 86. Bright Lights, Big City 88. She-Devil 89. White Palace 91. Chaplin (as Mary Pickford) 92. I'll Do Anything 94. Natural Born Killers 94. Bye Bye Love 95. Dear God 96. Something to Believe In 97. Godzilla 98, etc.
TV series: Ryan's Hope 87–89. Partners 95–96.

Pitt, Brad (1963–) (William Bradley Pitt).
American leading actor, from television. Raised in the Ozark Mountains, Oklahoma, he left his journalism studies at the University of Missouri to seek work as an actor in Los Angeles. He was paid a reported $17.5m plus 15 per cent of the first-dollar gross to star in *Meet Joe Black*. He was engaged to actress Gwyneth PALTROW, and has been romantically involved with actresses Juliette LEWIS and Jennifer ANISTON.
Biographies: 1995, *Brad Pitt* by Chris Nickson; 1997, *Brad Pitt* by US Magazine.
Cutting Class 89. Happy Together 90. Across the Tracks 91. Thelma and Louise 91. Johnny Suede 91. A River Runs through It 92. Cool World 92. Kalifornia 93. *True Romance* 93. The Devil's Advocate 93. The Favor 94. Interview with the Vampire 94. Legends of the Fall 94. Seven 95. 12 Monkeys (AAN) 95. Sleepers 96. Devil's Own 96. Seven Years in Tibet 97. Meet Joe Black 98, etc.
TV series: Glory Days 90.
❝ The truth is, I don't want people to know me. I don't know a thing about my favourite actors. I don't think you should. Then they become personalities. – *B.P.*

Pitt, Ingrid (1944–) (Ingrid Petrov).
Polish-born leading lady in British films.
Book: 1998, *The Ingrid Pitt Bedside Companion for Vampire Lovers.*
Where Eagles Dare 69. The Vampire Lovers 70. The House that Dripped Blood 71. Countess Dracula 71. Nobody Ordered Love 72. The Wicker Man 73. Smiley's People (TV) 82. Who Dares Wins 82. Wild Geese II 86. Parker 86, etc.

Pitts, ZaSu (1898–1963).
American actress, a heroine of the 20s and a tearful comedienne of the 30s.
The Little Princess 17. Early to Wed 21. *Greed* 23. Twin Beds 27. The Wedding March 28. Seed 30. Bad Sister 31. The Guardsman 32. Back Street 32. Walking Down Broadway 32. Many two-reeler comedies with Thelma Todd (32–34): Dames 34, Mrs Wiggs of the Cabbage Patch 34. Ruggles of Red Gap 35. So's Your Aunt Emma 38. Buck Privates 39. Nurse Edith Cavell 40. Niagara Falls 41. Let's Face It 43. Life with Father 47. Francis 50. Francis Joins the WACS 55. This Could Be the Night 57. It's a Mad Mad Mad Mad World 63, many others.
TV series: Oh Susanna 56–59.
~ZaSu was originally cast as the mother in *All Quiet on the Western Front*. Her scenes were reshot after preview audiences laughed.

Piven, Jeremy (1965–).
American actor, from the stage. Born in New York and raised in Evanston, Illinois, he trained at the Piven Theatre Workshop established in Chicago by his parents, actors Byrne Piven and Joyce Hiller Piven, also studying at Drake University and New York University. He was a founder of the New Crime Theater in Chicago with John CUSACK and Steve PINK.
One Crazy Summer 86. Lucas 86. Say Anything 89. The Grifters 90. There Goes the Neighborhood 92. The Player 92. Singles 92. Bob Roberts 92. Judgment Night 93. PCU 94. Car 54, Where Are You? 94. Heat 95. Dr Jekyll and Ms Hyde 95. Miami Rhapsody 95. Larger than Life 96. Layin' Low 96. Kiss the Girls 97. Grosse Pointe Blank 97. Don King: Only in America (TV) 97. Very Bad Things 98. Just Write 98, etc.
TV series: Carol & Company 90–91. The Larry Sanders Show 92–94. Pride and Joy 95. Ellen 95–98. Cupid 98–99.

Pizer, Larry.
British cinematographer.
The Party's Over 63. Four in the Morning 65. Morgan 65. Our Mother's House 66. Isadora 68. All Neat in Black Stockings 69. Phantom of the Paradise 74. The Fury 78. The Europeans 79. Cattle Annie and Little Britches 81. The Clairvoyant/The Killing Hour 83. Phantom of the Opera (TV) 83. Grace Quigley 84. Too Scared to Scream 84. Where Are the Children 86. Blind Witness (TV) 90. Mannequin on the Move 91. Folks! 92. In Custody 93. The Proprietor 96, etc.

Placido, Michele (1946–).
Italian actor turned director.
Till Marriage Do Us Part/Dio Mio, Come Sono Caduta in Basso! 74. Corelone 78. Ernesto 79. Lulu 80. Three Brothers/Tre Fratelli 81. The Art of Love/L'Art d'Aimer 83. The Sicilian Connection 85. Forever Mary/Mery per Sempre 88. Big Business (US) 88. Private Affairs 89. Pummaro (d) 89. Le Amiche del Cuore (a, d) 91. Drug Wars (US) (TV) 92. Lamerica 94. Un Eroe Borghese (a, d) 95. Of Lost Love/Del Perduto Amore (co-w, a, d) 98, etc.

Planchon, Roger (1931–).
Leading French theatre director, actor and playwright who makes occasional films. The company he created near Lyons in the 50s became the Théâtre National Populaire in 1972.
Dandin (wd) 88. Camille Claudel (a) 88. Louis, Enfant Roi (d) 93. Lautrec (d) 98, etc.

Planck, Robert (1894–1971).
American cinematographer.
Our Daily Bread 33. *Jane Eyre* 43. Cass Timberlane 47. The Three Musketeers 48. Little Women 49. Rhapsody 54. Moonfleet 55, etc.

Planer, Franz (1894–1963).
German cinematographer, in Hollywood from 1937.
Drei von Der Tankstelle 30. *Liebelei* 33. Maskerade 34. The Beloved Vagabond (GB) 36. Holiday 38. The Face Behind the Mask 41. The Adventures of Martin Eden 42. Once Upon a Time 44. The Chase 47. *Letter from an Unknown Woman* 48. Criss Cross 48. The Scarf 51. The Blue Veil 51. *Death of a Salesman* 52. Twenty Thousand Leagues under the Sea 54. Not as a Stranger 55. The Pride and the Passion 57. *The Big Country* 58. *The Nun's Story* 59. The Unforgiven 60. The Children's Hour (AAN) 62, etc.

Plaschkes, Otto (1931–).
Austrian producer, in Britain.
Georgy Girl 66. The Bofors Gun 68. The Homecoming 73. In Celebration 74. The Sailor's Return 78. The Hound of the Baskervilles 83. The Sign of Four 83. The Holcroft Covenant 85. Shadey 85, etc.

Platt, Edward (1916–1974).
American character actor who usually plays generals, stern fathers and similar types.
The Shrike 55. Rebel Without a Cause 55. Serenade 56. The Great Man 56. Designing Woman 57. The Gift of Love 58. North by Northwest 59. Pollyanna 60. A Ticklish Affair 63, many others.
TV series: *Get Smart* 65–69.

Platt, Louise (1914–).
American leading lady who retired after a brief career. She was formerly married to producer Jed Harris.
Spawn of the North 38. *Stagecoach* 39. Forgotten Girls 40. Captain Caution 40. Street of Chance 41, etc.

Platt, Marc (1913–).
American dancer and lightweight actor: few appearances.
Tonight and Every Night 44. Tars and Spars 44. Down to Earth 47. Seven Brides for Seven Brothers 54. Oklahoma 55, etc.

Platt, Oliver (1963–).
American actor.
Married to the Mob 86. Working Girl 88. Flatliners 90. Beethoven 92. Indecent Proposal 93. The Three Musketeers (as Porthos) 93. Benny and Joon 93. Tall Tale: The Incredible Adventures of Pecos Bill 94. Funny Bones 95. A Time to Kill 96. Executive Decision 96. Dr Dolittle 98. Dangerous Beauty 98. Bulworth 98. The Imposters 98. Simon Birch 98, etc.

Platt, Polly (1941–).
American production designer who became a producer in the late 80s. Formerly married to director Peter BOGDANOVICH.
The Last Picture Show 71. What's Up, Doc? 72.

Paper Moon 73. The Thief Who Came to Dinner 73. A Star Is Born 76. Pretty Baby 78. Young Doctors in Love 82. Terms of Endearment (AAN) 83. Between Two Women (TV) 86. The Witches of Eastwick 87. Broadcast News (p) 88. The War of the Roses (p) 89. Say Anything (p) 89. I'll Do Anything 94. The Evening Star (co-p) 96, etc.

Platts-Mills, Barney (1944–).
British independent director of low-budget films.
■ Bronco Bullfrog 70. Private Road 71.

Pleasence, Donald (1919–1995).
Bald, pale-eyed British character actor usually seen in villainous or eccentric roles.
Manuela 57. A Tale of Two Cities 57. The Flesh and the Fiends 59. Hell Is a City 60. No Love for Johnnie 61. Dr Crippen 62. The Great Escape 63. *The Caretaker* 64. The Greatest Story Ever Told 65. The Hallelujah Trail 65. Fantastic Voyage 66. Cul de Sac 66. The Night of the Generals 66. Eye of the Devil 67. Will Penny 67. The Madwoman of Chaillot 69. Soldier Blue 70. Outback 71. The Jerusalem File 72. Henry VIII and His Six Wives 72. Innocent Bystanders 72. Tales That Witness Madness 73. The Mutations 73. The Black Windmill 74. Hearts of the West 75. Trial by Combat 76. The Last Tycoon 76. The Eagle has Landed (as Himmler) 76. Jesus of Nazareth (TV) 77. Oh God 77. Telefon 77. The Passover Plot 77. Halloween 78. Sergeant Pepper's Lonely Hearts Club Band 78. Dracula 79. All Quiet on the Western Front (TV) 80. Escape from New York 81. Halloween II 81. Alone in the Dark 82. The Devonsville Terror 83. Where is Parsifal? 84. Arch of Triumph (TV) 84. The Last Days of Pompeii (TV) 85. Scoop (TV) 87. Ground Zero 87. Phantom of Death 87. Deep Cover 88. Hannah's War 88. Halloween 4: The Return of Michael Myers 88. Halloween 5: The Revenge of Michael Myers 89. Casablanca Express 89. River of Death 89. Buried Alive 90. American Tiger 91. Dien Bien Phu 91. Shadows and Fog 92. The Hour of the Pig 93. Femme Fatale (TV) 93. Halloween: The Curse of Michael Myers 95, etc.
TV series: Robin Hood (as Prince John) 55–57.

Pleshette, Suzanne (1937–).
Intelligent American leading actress whose roles have been generally disappointing. She was married to actor Troy Donahue for nine months in 1964.
The Geisha Boy 58. Rome Adventure 62. Forty Pounds of Trouble 63. The Birds 63. Wall of Noise 63. A Distant Trumpet 64. Fate is the Hunter 64. Youngblood Hawke 64. A Rage to Live 65. The Ugly Dachshund 66. Nevada Smith 66. Mister Buddwing 66. The Adventures of Bullwhip Griffin 67. Wings of Fire (TV) 67. Blackbeard's Ghost 68. The Power 68. If It's Tuesday This Must Be Belgium 69. Along Came a Spider 69. Suppose They Gave a War and Nobody Came 69. Support Your Local Gunfighter 71. In Broad Daylight (TV) 71. Beyond the Bermuda Triangle (TV) 75. The Legend of Valentino (TV) 75. Return of the Pink Panther 75. The Shaggy D.A. 76. Kate Bliss and the Tickertape Kid (TV) 78. *Flesh and Blood* (TV) 79. Hot Stuff 79. Oh God Book Two 80. Help Wanted: Male (TV) 82. One Cooks, the Other Doesn't (TV) 83. Dixie: Changing Habits (TV) 83. For Love or Money (TV) 84. Kojak: The Belarus File (TV) 85. A Stranger Waits (TV) 87. The Queen of Mean (TV) 90. Battling for Baby (TV) 92, etc.
TV series: The Bob Newhart Show 72. Maggie Briggs 84. Bridges to Cross 86. The Boys Are Back 94–95.
❝ I don't sit around and wait for great parts. I'm an actress, and I love being one, and I'll probably be doing it till I'm 72, standing around the backlot doing *Gunsmokes*. – *S.P.*

Plimpton, Martha (1971–) (Martha Carradine).
American actress, the daughter of Keith Carradine.
Rollover 81. The River Rat 84. The Goonies 85. The Mosquito Coast 86. Shy People 87. Running on Empty 88. Stars and Bars 88. Parenthood 89. Silence Like Glass 90. Stanley and Iris 90. Samantha 92. Josh and S.A.M. 93. Chantilly Lace (TV) 93. Mrs Parker and the Vicious Circle 94. Last Summer in the Hamptons 95. I Shot Andy Warhol 96. Beautiful Girls 96. I'm Not Rappaport 96. Eye of God 97. Colin Fitz 97. 200 Cigarettes 98. Pecker 98, etc.

Plowright, Joan (1929–).
Leading British stage actress, widow of Laurence Olivier.
Time without Pity 58. The Entertainer 60. Equus 77. The Diary of Anne Frank (TV) 81. Britannia Hospital 82. Brimstone and Treacle 82. Wagner 82. Drowning by Numbers 88. The Dressmaker 89. I Love You to Death 90. Avalon 90. Enchanted April (AAN) 91. The Clothes in the Wardrobe/The Summer House (TV) 93. Last Action Hero 93. Dennis the Menace/Dennis 93. Widows' Peak 94. On Promised Land (TV) 94. A Pin for the Butterfly 94. Hotel Sorrento 95. A Pyromaniac's Love Story 95. The Scarlet Letter 95. Mr Wrong 96. Jane Eyre 96. Surviving Picasso 96. 101 Dalmatians 96. Tom's Midnight Garden 98. Dance with Me 98. This Could Be the Last Time (TV) 98. Tea with Mussolini 99, etc.
TV series: Encore! Encore! 98.

Plummer, Amanda (1957–).
American actress. She is the daughter of Christopher Plummer and Tammy Grimes.
Cattle Annie and Little Britches 81. The World According to Garp 82. Daniel 83. The Hotel New Hampshire 84. Courtship 86. Static 86. Made in Heaven 87. Prisoners of Inertia 89. Joe versus the Volcano 90. The Fisher King 91. The Lounge People 91. Freejack 92. So I Married an Axe Murderer 93. Last Light 93. Needful Things 93. Pulp Fiction 94. Pax (Port.) 94. Nostradamus 94. Butterfly Kiss 95. God's Army 95. Drunks 95. Freeway 96. Don't Look Back 96. A Simple Wish 97. You Can Thank Me Later 98. LA without a Map (GB/Fr./Fin.) 98, etc.

Plummer, Christopher (1927–).
Canadian leading man with stage experience including Shakespeare. His first wife was actress Tammy Grimes; their daughter is actress Amanda Plummer. In 1997 he won a Tony for his one-man show *Barrymore*, as John Barrymore.
Stage Struck 58. Wind Across the Everglades 58. *The Fall of the Roman Empire* 64. *The Sound of Music* 65. Inside Daisy Clover 65. The Night of the Generals 67. Triple Cross 67. Oedipus the King 67. Nobody Runs Forever 68. Lock Up Your Daughters 69. The Royal Hunt of the Sun 69. The Battle of Britain 69. *Waterloo* (as the Duke of Wellington) 70. The Pyx 73. Conduct Unbecoming 75. The Spiral Staircase 75. The Man Who Would Be King 75. The Return of the Pink Panther 75. The Moneychangers (TV) 75. Aces High 76. Jesus of Nazareth (TV) 77. The Day that Shook the World 77. The Assignment 77. The Disappearance 77. The Silent Partner 78. Starcrash 78. International Velvet 78. Murder by Decree 79. Hanover Street 79. Somewhere in Time 80. Highpoint 80. Eyewitness 81. Little Gloria . . . Happy at Last (TV) 82. The Amateur 82. Lily in Love 84. Dreamscape 84. The Boss's Wife 86. An American Tail (voice) 86. I Love N.Y. 87. Dragnet 87. Souvenir 88. Light Years 88. Nosferatu in Venice 88. Shadow Dancing 88. Kingsgate 89. Mind Field 89. Where the Heart Is 90. Red Blooded American Girl 90. Star Trek VI: The Undiscovered Country 91. Firehead 91. Don't Tell Mom the Babysitter's Dead 91. Rock-a-Doodle (voice) 92. Liars Edge 92. Wolf 94. Dolores Claiborne 95. 12 Monkeys 95. Skeletons 96. The Clown at Midnight 98. Winchell (TV) 98, etc.
TV series: Counterstrike 90.
❝ I'm bored with questions about acting. – C.P.
Unless you can surround yourself with as many beautiful things as you can afford, I don't think life has very much meaning. – C.P.

Plunkett, Patricia (1928–).
British leading lady of the early 50s.
It Always Rains on Sunday 47. Bond Street 48. For Them That Trespass 48. Landfall 50. Murder Without Crime 52. Mandy 53. The Crowded Day 55. Dunkirk 58, etc.

Plunkett, Walter (1902–1982).
American costume designer, at RKO 1926–39, then MGM 1947–65.
Hit the Deck 29. Rio Rita 29. Cimarron 31. *Little Women* 33. *The Gay Divorcee* 34. Of Human Bondage 34. Mary of Scotland 36. Quality Street 37. *Gone with the Wind* 39. *The Hunchback of Notre Dame* 39. Stagecoach 39. Ladies in Retirement 41. To Be or Not to Be 42. A Song to Remember 45. Duel in the Sun 46. The Three Musketeers 48. That Forsyte Woman 49. *An American in Paris* (AA) 51. *The Prisoner of Zenda* 52. *Kiss Me Kate* 53. Seven Brides for Seven Brothers 54. Lust for Life 56. Pollyanna 60. How the West was Won 63. Seven Women 66, many others.

Plympton, Bill (1946–).
Quirky American director, writer and animator. Born in Portland, Oregon, he studied at Portland State University and the School of Visual Arts in New York, beginning as a cartoonist and illustrator. He started working on animated shorts in the early 80s; *The Tune* was his first full-length animated film; he has since made live-action films, such as *J. Lyle* and *Guns on the Clackamas*. His short films have been issued on video as Plymptoons, and he is the author of the comic book *The Sleazy Cartoons of Bill Plympton*.
Your Face (AAN) 88. One of Those Days 88. How to Kiss 89. The Tune 92. J. Lyle 94. How to Make Love to a Woman 95. Guns on the Clackamas 95. Mondo Plympton 97. I Married a Strange Person 97, etc.

Podesta, Rossana (1934–).
Italian leading lady who has been in international films.
Cops and Robbers 51. La Red 53. Ulysses 54. Helen of Troy 56. Santiago 58. The Golden Arrow 65. Il Prete Sposato 70. The Sensual Man 75. Il Gatto Mammone 76. Secrets 85, etc.

Poe, Edgar Allan (1809–1849).
American poet, story-writer and manic depressive, whose tortured life as well as his strange tales have been eagerly seized upon by film-makers. Griffith made *The Life of Edgar Allan Poe* in 1909, and in 1912 another version was disguised as *The Raven*. In 1915 Charles Brabin made another film called *The Raven* with Henry B. Walthall as Poe; a few months earlier Griffith had released his own alternative version under the title *The Avenging Conscience*. The next film called *The Raven*, in 1935, starred Karloff and Lugosi and had nothing to do with Poe's life, being merely an amalgam of his stories; but in 1942 Fox brought out *The Loves of Edgar Allan Poe* starring Shepperd Strudwick; and in 1951 MGM made a curious melodrama called *Man with a Cloak*, in which the dark stranger who solved the mystery signed himself 'Dupin' and was played by Joseph Cotten in the Poe manner.
Of the stories, *The Mystery of Marie Roget* was filmed by Universal in 1931 and 1942; *The Tell-Tale Heart* was told as an MGM short directed by Jules Dassin in 1942, by a British company with Stanley Baker in 1950, by UPA as a cartoon narrated by James Mason in 1954, by an independent American company in a film known as both *Manfish* and *Calypso* in 1956 (the film also claimed to be partly based on *The Gold Bug*) and by the Danzigers in Britain in 1960. *The Fall of the House of Usher* was filmed in France by Jean Epstein in 1929, in Britain by semi-professionals in 1950, in Hollywood by Roger Corman in 1960, and in South Africa by Alan Birkinshaw in 1988. Universal released films called *The Black Cat* in 1934 and 1941, both claiming to be 'suggested' by Poe's tale; in fact, neither had anything at all to do with it, but the genuine story was told in a German film called *The Living Dead* in 1933, and in Corman's 1962 *Tales of Terror*. *The Pit and the Pendulum* was filmed in 1913 and 1961, and the central idea has been borrowed by many film-makers without credit, most recently by the 'Uncle' boys in *One Spy Too Many*. *The Premature Burial* was filmed straight in 1962, and around the same time TV's *Thriller* series presented a fairly faithful adaptation; the idea was also used in 1934 in *The Crime of Dr Crespi*, a low-budgeter starring Erich Von Stroheim. *The Murders in the Rue Morgue* was filmed in 1914 and 1932, turned up again in 3-D in 1954 under the title *Phantom of the Rue Morgue*, and was remade under the original title in 1971. Other Poe stories filmed once include *The Bells* 13, *The Facts in the Case of M. Valdemar* in *Tales of Terror* 62, *The Masque of the Red Death* 64 and 89, and *The Tomb of Ligeia* 64.

Poe, James (1918–1980).
American writer, from radio and TV.
■ Without Honor 49. Scandal Sheet (co-w) 52. Paula 52. The Big Knife 55. Around the World in 80 Days (co-w, AA) 56. *Attack!* 56. Hot Spell 58. Cat on a Hot Tin Roof (co-w) 58. Last Train from Gun Hill 59. Sanctuary 61. Summer and Smoke (co-w) 63. Toys in the Attic 63. Lilies of the Field 63. The Bedford Incident 64. They Shoot Horses Don't They? (co-w) 69.

Pogostin, S. Lee (1926–).
American writer-director.
Pressure Point (co-w) 62. Synanon (co-w) 65. Hard Contract (wd) 69. Golden Needles (co-w) 74. High Road to China (co-w) 83, etc.

Pohlmann, Eric (1903–1979).
Viennese character actor, on British stage and radio from 1948; also a familiar bald, portly villain on screen.
The Constant Husband 55. House of Secrets 56. Expresso Bongo 59. The Kitchen 62. Carry on Spying 64. The Million Dollar Collar (US) 67. The Horsemen 71, many others.
TV series: Colonel March of Scotland Yard 53.

Poiret, Paul (1879–1944).
French fashion designer who created the costumes for Sarah Bernhardt in her film debut *Queen Elizabeth* as well as her *Adrienne Lecouvreur*. He influenced many subsequent movie designers.

Poitier, Sidney (1924–).
Handsome American leading actor; his success in the late 60s helped to break the race barrier.
No Way Out 50. Cry the Beloved Country 52. Red Ball Express 52. Go Man Go 54. *The Blackboard Jungle* 55. Goodbye, My Lady 56. *Edge of the City* 57. Something of Value 57. Band of Angels 58. Mark of the Hawk 58. *The Defiant Ones* (AAN) 58. *Porgy and Bess* 59. Virgin Islands 60. All the Young Men 60. A Raisin in the Sun 61. Paris Blues 61. Pressure Point 62. *Lilies of the Field* (AA) 63. The Long Ships 64. The Greatest Story Ever Told 65. *The Bedford Incident* (for the first time his colour was not mentioned or relevant) 65. A Patch of Blue 65. The Slender Thread 65. Duel at Diablo 66. *In the Heat of the Night* 67. To Sir with Love 67. *Guess Who's Coming to Dinner* 67. For Love of Ivy 68. The Lost Man 69. They Call Me Mister Tibbs 70. The Organization 71. Brother John 71. Buck and the Preacher (& d) 72. A Warm December (& d) 73. Uptown Saturday Night (& d) 74. The Wilby Conspiracy 75. Let's Do It Again (& d) 76. A Piece of the Action (& d) 77. Stir Crazy (d only) 80. Hanky Panky (d only) 82. Fast Forward (d only) 84. Little Nikita 88. Shoot to Kill 88. Ghost Dad (d) 90. Separate but Equal (TV) 91. Sneakers 92. To Sir with Love II (TV) 96. The Jackal 97. Mandela and de Klerk (TV) 97, etc.
✪ For being the first black actor to be accepted in a romantic situation with a white girl. *Guess Who's Coming to Dinner*.

Polanski, Roman (1933–).
Polish director and screenwriter, former actor. Gained a reputation with shorts such as *Two Men and a Wardrobe* 58. He was married to actress Sharon Tate, who was murdered in 1969 by followers of Charles Manson. In 1979 he left America when awaiting sentencing on a charge of unlawful sexual intercourse, and has since worked in Europe.
Autobiography: 1984, *Roman*.
Biographies: 1982, *Polanski, the Filmmaker as Voyeur* by Barbara Leaming. 1982, *Life and Times of Roman Polanski* by Thomas Kiernan. 1994, *Polanski* by John Parker.
■ *Knife in the Water* 61. *Repulsion* 65. Cul de Sac 66. The Fearless Vampire Killers 67. *Rosemary's Baby* (AANw) 68. Macbeth 71. What? 72. *Chinatown* (AAN) 74. The Tenant 76. Tess (AAN) 80. Pirates 85. Frantic 88. Back in the USSR (a) 92. Bitter Moon 92. A Simple Formality/Una Pura Formalita (a) 94. Death and the Maiden 95.
❝ Nothing is too shocking for me. When you tell the story of a man who loses his head, you have to show the head being cut off. Otherwise it's just a dirty joke without a punchline. – *R.P.*
I know in my heart of hearts that the spirit of laughter has deserted me. – *R.P.*
The director is never wrong. – *R.P.*
His talent is as undeniable as his intentions are dubious. – *Andrew Sarris, 1968*
The four-foot Pole you wouldn't want to touch with a ten-foot pole. – *Kenneth Tynan*

Poledouris, Basil (1945–).
American composer.
Extreme Close-up 73. Big Wednesday 78. The Blue Lagoon 80. Conan the Barbarian 82. Summer Lovers 82. Conan the Destroyer 84. Red Dawn 84. Flesh and Blood 85. Iron Eagle 86. Cherry 2000 86. Robocop 87. No Man's Land 87. Split Decisions 88. Farewell to the King 89. Wired 89. Why Me?

89. The Hunt for Red October 90. Quigley Down Under 90. The Flight of the Intruder 90. Harley Davidson and the Marlboro Man 91. Wind 92. Hot Shots! Part Deux 93. Robocop 3 93. Free Willy 93. On Deadly Ground 94. Serial Mom 94. Lassie 94. Rudyard Kipling's Jungle Book 94. Free Willy 2: The Adventure Home 95. Under Siege 2: Dark Territory 95. It's My Party 96. Celtic Pride 96. Breakdown 97. Starship Troopers 97. Switchback 97. Les Misérables 98, etc.

Poletto, Piero.
Italian art director who has worked on several of Antonioni's films.
L'Avventura 60. The Minotaur/Teseo contra il Minotauro 60. The Eclipse/L'Eclisse 62. Gladiators 62. *The Red Desert*/Il Deserto Rosso 64. *More than a Miracle*/C'Era una Volta 67. The Chastity Belt 67. A Place for Lovers/Amanti 68. Sunflower/I Girasoli 69. In Search of Gregory 69. *The Passenger* 75, etc.

Polglase, Van Nest (1898–1968).
American art director, a former architect, in films from 1919. He worked for several studios before being hired as supervising art director for RKO 1932–42, when his alcoholism led to his dismissal. He later worked for Columbia, and on several films for director Allan Dwan. Although individual credit for RKO's productions is hard to establish, he was probably responsible for the Art Deco look of the Astaire-Rogers musicals.
A Kiss in the Dark 25. Stage Struck 25. Flying Down to Rio 33. *The Gay Divorcee* (AAN) 34. *Top Hat* (AAN) 35. Follow the Fleet 36. Mary of Scotland 36. Stage Door 37. Carefree (AAN) 38. *The Hunchback of Notre Dame* 39. Gunga Din 39. Love Affair (AAN) 39. My Favorite Wife (AAN) 40. *Citizen Kane* (AAN 41. Gilda 46. Cattle Queen of Montana 54. Escape to Burma 55. Slightly Scarlet 56. The River's Edge 57, many others.

Poliakoff, Stephen (1952–).
British playwright, screenwriter and director.
Hidden City 87. Close My Eyes 92. Century 93. The Tribe (wd) (TV) 98, etc.

Polito, Gene (1918–).
American cinematographer.
Prime Cut 72. Westworld 73. Five on the Black Hand Side 73. Trackdown 76. The Bad News Bears Go to Japan 78, etc.

Polito, Jon (1950–).
American character actor.
Deadly Business 86. Fire with Fire 86. Highlander 86. The Freshman 90. Miller's Crossing 90. Leather Jackets 90. Barton Fink 91. The Crow 94. Blankman 94. Bushwhacked 95. Just Your Luck 96, etc.
TV series: Homicide: Life on the Street 93.

Polito, Sol (1892–1960).
American cinematographer.
Treason 18. Hard-Boiled Haggerty 27. Five Star Final 31. *I Am a Fugitive from a Chain Gang* 32. *Forty-second Street* 33. G Men 35. *The Petrified Forest* 36. *The Charge of the Light Brigade* 36. *The Adventures of Robin Hood* 38. Confessions of a Nazi Spy 39. *The Sea Hawk* 40. The Sea Wolf 41. Now Voyager 42. Arsenic and Old Lace 44. Rhapsody in Blue 45. The Long Night 47. Sorry, Wrong Number 48. Anna Lucasta 48, many others.

Poll, Martin H. (1922–).
American producer.
Love Is a Ball 62. Sylvia 65. The Lion in Winter (AAN) 68. Night Watch 73. The Man Who Loved Cat Dancing 73. Love and Death 75. The Man Who Would Be King 75. Somebody Killed Her Husband 78. Night Hawks 81. Gimme an F 84. Haunted Summer 88. My Heroes Have Always Been Cowboys 91, etc.

Pollack, Ben (1903–1971).
American bandleader, composer and musician, in films as himself. Born in Chicago, he was a leading jazz drummer of his time; his bands, dating from the mid-20s on, featured such musicians as Benny GOODMAN, Harry JAMES, Matty MATLOCK, Glenn MILLER and Jack TEAGARDEN, and later formed the nucleus of the Bob CROSBY orchestra. He made several shorts in the late 20s and early 30s. Hanged himself.
New Faces of 1937 (s) 37. The Glenn Miller Story 54. The Benny Goodman Story 55, etc.

Pollack, Jeff.
American director and screenwriter, from television. He was co-creator of the TV sitcom *Fresh Prince of Bel Air*, which starred Will Smith.
Above the Rim (co-w, d) 94. Booty Call 96, etc.

Pollack, Sydney (1934–).
American director, screenwriter and producer, from TV.
■ *The Slender Thread* 65. This Property Is Condemned 66. The Scalphunters 68. Castle Keep 69. *They Shoot Horses Don't They?* (AAN) 69. Jeremiah Johnson 72. The Way We Were 73. The Yakusa 75. *Three Days of the Condor* 76. Bobby Deerfield 77. The Electric Horseman 79. Absence of Malice 81. Tootsie (& a) (AAN) 82. Out of Africa (AAp, AAd) 85. Bright Lights, Big City (p) 88. The Fabulous Baker Boys (p) 89. Major League (p) 89. Havana (p, d) 90. Presumed Innocent (p) 90. White Palace (p) 90. Leaving Normal (p) 91. Dead Again (p) 91. The Player (a) 92. Searching for Bobby Fischer (p) 93. Flesh and Bone (p) 93. The Firm (p, d) 93. Sabrina 95.
❝ I don't value a film I've enjoyed making. If it's good, it's damned hard work. – *S.P.*

Pollak, Kevin.
American actor.
Avalon 90. Ricochet 91. A Few Good Men 92. Indian Summer 93. Grumpy Old Men 93. Wayne's World 2 93. Clean Slate 94. Canadian Bacon 95. Casino 95. Miami Rhapsody 95. The Usual Suspects 95. House Arrest 96. Truth or Consequences, NM 97. National Lampoon's The Don's Analyst 97. Buffalo '66 97, etc.
TV series: Coming of Age 88–89.

Pollard, Daphne (1890–1978) (Daphne Trott).
Diminutive Australian actress in Hollywood; a famous sharp-tongued wife for Laurel and Hardy.
Hit of the Show 28. Big Time 29. Swing Time 30. Bright Lights 30. Lady Refuses 31. Bonnie Scotland 33. Our Relations 36. Tillie the Toiler 41. Kid Dynamite 43, etc.

Pollard, Harry (1883–1934).
American silent-screen director.
Motherhood 14. The Leather Pushers 22. Oh Doctor 24. California Straight Ahead 25. Uncle Tom's Cabin 27. Showboat (first talkie) 29. The Prodigal 31. Fast Life 32, etc.

Pollard, Michael J. (1939–) (M. J. Pollack).
Pint-sized American character actor.
Adventures of a Young Man 62. Summer Magic 62. The Stripper 64. *Bonnie and Clyde* (AAN) 67. Hannibal Brooks 69. Little Fauss and Big Halsy 70. Dirty Little Billy 72. Sunday in the Country 74. Between the Lines 77. Melvin and Howard 80. America 82. Heated Vengeance 85. The American Way 86. The Patriot 86. Roxanne 87. Scrooged 88. Fast Food 89. Season of Fear 89. Tango & Cash 89. Dick Tracy 90. Enid Is Sleeping 90. The Art of Dying 91. Motorama 92. Split Second 92. Skeeter 93. The Odyssey (TV) 97, etc.
TV series: Leo and Liz in Beverly Hills 86.

Pollard, Snub (1886–1962) (Harold Fraser).
Australian comedian, in America from early silent film days. In many silent slapstick shorts, and later continued to play bit parts, the last being in *A Pocketful of Miracles* 61.

Pollock, Channing (1926–).
Elegant American magician, notable for his act of producing a succession of white doves from, seemingly, the air, which was featured in the film *European Nights*/Europe di Notte 59. Subsequently, he had a brief movie career in Europe, before returning to America, where he made frequent TV appearances on variety shows and in dramas.
■ Musketeers of the Sea/I Moschettieri del Mare 62. The Red Sheik/Lo Sciecco Rosso 62. Rocambole (Fr.) 63. *Judex* (Fr.) 63.

Pollock, Dale (1950–).
American producer, a former journalist. He is currently president of Polygram's A & M Films and is the author of *Skywalking*, a biography of George LUCAS.
Blaze 89. A Midnight Clear 92. House of Cards 93. S.F.W. 94. Mrs Winterbourne 96. Set It Off 96. Meet the Deedles (& co-w) 98, etc.

Pollock, Ellen (1903–1997).
British stage actress, in occasional films.
Non Stop New York 37. The Street Singer 37. Sons of the Sea 39. Kiss the Bride Goodbye 44. The Galloping Major 51. The Wicked Lady 82, etc.

Pollock, George (1907–).
British director, former assistant, in films since 1933.
A Stranger in Town 56. Rooney 58. Don't Panic Chaps 60. Murder She Said 63. Murder at the Gallop 63. Murder Most Foul 64. Ten Little Indians 65, etc.

Polonsky, Abraham (1910–).
American writer and director who fell foul of the communist witch-hunt.
Body and Soul (AAN) 47. *Force of Evil* (& d) 49. I Can Get It for You Wholesale 50. Odds against Tomorrow (co-w) 59. Tell Them Willie Boy is Here (& d) 69. Romance of a Horsethief (d only) 71. Avalanche Express 78. Monsignor (co-w) 82, etc.

Pomeranc, Max (1984–).
American child actor.
Searching for Bobby Fischer/Innocent Moves 93. Journey 95. Fluke 95, etc.

Pommer, Erich (1889–1966).
German producer since 1915. During the 30s worked briefly in the US and also, with Charles Laughton, formed Mayflower Films in Britain.
Biography: 1997, *From Caligari to California: Erich Pommer's Life in the International Film Wars* by Ursula Hardt.
The Cabinet of Dr Caligari 19. Dr Mabuse 22. Die Nibelungen 24. *Variety* 25. *Metropolis* 26. *The Blue Angel* 30. Congress Dances 31. Liliom 34. Fire over England 36. Vessel of Wrath 38. Jamaica Inn 39. They Knew What They Wanted 40. Illusion in Moll 52. Kinder, Mutter und Ein General 55, etc.
✪ For his influence over a wide range of European films. *Metropolis*.

Pons, Lily (1904–1976).
French-born operatic singer who starred in some Hollywood films.
I Dream Too Much 35. That Girl from Paris 36. Hitting a New High 37. Carnegie Hall 47, etc.

Pontecorvo, Gillo (1919–).
Italian director of politically committed films with anti-colonialist themes. A former photo-journalist and documentary film-maker, he frequently uses non-professional actors in the tradition of Italian neo-realism. Recent projects having failed at the planning stages, he directs TV commercials.
Kapo 60. *The Battle of Algiers* (AAN) 66. The Wide Blue Road 68. Burn!/Queimada 70. Ogro 79, etc.
❝ I like making films because I've a certain affection for man and his condition. – G.P.
Technically, US directors keep improving. But this technical expertise hides an emptiness that keeps getting bigger. They're very good at saying nothing. – *G.P., 1995*
He has made very few films and that's very bad for our profession, for art, for the art of cinematography and for what he owes the public, what they expect of him. So it's a real pity, even a sin. – *Ennio Morricone*

Ponti, Carlo (1913–).
Italian producer, later involved in international productions. Married to Sophia Loren.
I Miserabili 47. Attila the Hun 52. Ulysses 54. War and Peace 56. Black Orchid 58. That Kind of Woman 59. Marriage, Italian Style 65. Operation Crossbow 65. Dr Zhivago (AAN) 65. Smashing Time 67. Sunflower 70. Lady Liberty 72. The Passenger 74. Massacre in Rome 74. Brief Encounter (TV) 75. Verdict 75. The Priest's Wife 75. The Cassandra Crossing 77, etc.

Ponting, Herbert G. (1870–1935).
British explorer and film-maker, a maker of quality documentaries in the cinema's early days.
With Captain Scott RN to the South Pole 13, etc.

Pontius Pilate.
The man who judged Jesus has been played on film as follows: in *King of Kings* 27 by Victor Varconi; in *The Last Days of Pompeii* 35 by Basil Rathbone; in *The Robe* 53 by Richard Boone; in *Ben Hur* 59 by Frank Thring; in *King of Kings* 61 by Hurd Hatfield; in Barabbas 62 by Arthur Kennedy; in *The Greatest Story Ever Told* by Telly Savalas; in *Jesus Christ Superstar* 75 by Barry Dennen.

Pool, Léa (1950–).
Swiss-born director and screenwriter, based in Canada, where she went in the mid-70s to study film. She has also taught film and video at the University of Quebec and worked in television. Her films often deal with the problems of artists and have homosexual protagonists.
Strass Café 79. A Woman in Transit/La Femme de L'Hôtel 84. Anne Trister 85. À Corps Perdu 88. La Demoiselle Sauvage 91. Montréal Vu par . . . (co-d) 91. Mouvements du Désir 94, etc.

Pop, Iggy (1947–) (James Newell Osterburg).
Uninhibited American rock performer and occasional actor. A seminal influence on punk rock, he was noted for his extreme behaviour on stage.
Autobiography: 1982, *I Need More*.
Rock & Rule (voice) 83. The Color of Money 86. Sid and Nancy 86. Cry-Baby 90. Coffee and Cigarettes (short) 93. The Crow: City of Angels 96. Dead Man 96. The Crow 2: City of Angels 96, etc.
❝ I like to lick girls' sweaty armpits in the summer. The smell turns me on, especially if they have hair. – *I.P.*

Pope, Angela.
British director who began in documentaries.
Sweet As You Are (TV) 88. Dream Baby (TV) 89. Children Crossing (TV) 90. Captives 94. A Man You Don't Meet Every Day (TV) 94. The Hollow Reed 96, etc.

Popkin, Harry M. (c. 1906–1991).
American independent producer.
And Then There Were None 45. Impact 48. *D.O.A.* 49. Champagne for Caesar 49. The Thief 52, etc.

Porcasi, Paul (1880–1946).
Sicilian character actor in Hollywood films; former opera singer.
The Fall of the Romanoffs 19. Say It Again 26. Broadway 29. The Criminal Code 31. The Passionate Plumber 32. Footlight Parade 32. The Gay Divorcee 34. Maytime 37. Crime School 38. It Started with Eve 41. We Were Dancing 42. Hi Diddle Diddle 43. I'll Remember April 45, many others.

Porizkova, Paulina (1965–).
Czech actress and model in American movies. Born in Prostejov, she emigrated to Sweden and then to the United States.
Covergirl 83. Anna 87. Her Alibi 89. Arizona Dream 91. Female Perversions 96. Wedding Bell Blues 97. Thursday 98. Long Time Since 98, etc.

Porten, Henny (1890–1960).
German leading lady of the silents.
Lohengrin 07. Anne Boleyn 20. Der Kaufmann von Venedig 23. Kohlhiesel's Tochter 30. Familie Buchholz 40. Das Fraulein Scuderi 55, many others.

Porter, Cole (1893–1964).
American songwriter and composer whose lyrics were probably the wittiest ever appended to popular songs. Cary Grant played Porter in a biopic, *Night and Day* 46; other films using Porter scores are: *Anything Goes* 36 and 56. *Rosalie* 38. *Broadway Melody of 1940*. *Something to Shout About* 42. *The Pirate* 48. *Kiss Me Kate* 53. *High Society* 56. *Can Can* 59, etc.
Biography: 1967, *The Life that Late He Led* by George Eels.

Porter, Don (1912–1997).
American leading man of second features, latterly character actor.
Top Sergeant 42. Night Monster 43. The Curse of the Allenbys 48. 711 Ocean Drive 50. Because You're Mine 52. The Racket 52. Our Miss Brooks 56. Bachelor in Paradise 61. Youngblood Hawke 64. The Candidate 72. Forty Carats 73. White Line Fever 75, etc.
TV series: Private Secretary 53–57. The Ann Sothern Show 59–61. Gidget 65–66.

Porter, Edwin S. (1869–1941).
America's first notable director, who later found himself in D. W. Griffith's shadow and left the industry.
The Life of an American Fireman 02. *The Great Train Robbery* 03. The Ex-Convict 05. Rescued from an Eagle's Nest 07. Alice's Adventures in Wonderland 10. The Count of Monte Cristo 12. The Eternal City 15, etc.
~A documentary about Porter, *Before the Nickelodeon*, was released in 1983.

Porter, Eric (1928–1995).
British stage actor who became nationally known as Soames in the TV version of *The Forsyte Saga*.
The Heroes of Telemark 65. Kaleidoscope 66. The Lost Continent 68. Hands of the Ripper 71. Antony and Cleopatra 71. Nicholas and Alexandra 71. The Day of the Jackal 73. The Belstone Fox 73. Callan 74. Hennessy 75. The 39 Steps 78. Why Didn't They Ask Evans? (TV) 80. Little Lord Fauntleroy (TV) 80. The Jewel in the Crown (TV) 83, etc.

Porter, Gene Stratton (1886–1924).
American novelist: her sentimental novels of country matters were once ideal film material. *Freckles*, *Laddie and Girl of the Limberlost* were among them.

Porter, Katherine Anne (1890–1980).
American novelist, author of the allegorical *Ship of Fools* which was filmed in 1963.

Porter, Nyree Dawn (1940–).
New Zealand leading lady in British films and TV.
Two Left Feet 63. The Cracksman 63. Jane Eyre 70. The House that Dripped Blood 70. From Beyond the Grave 73. The Mystery of Edwin Drood 93. Hilary and Jackie (as Dame Margot Fonteyn) 98, etc.
TV series: *The Forsyte Saga* (as Irene) 67. *The Protectors* 72.

Portman, Eric (1903–1969).
Distinguished British stage actor who appeared sporadically in films.
■ The Murder in the Red Barn (debut) 35. Abdul the Damned 35. Old Roses 35. Hyde Park Corner 35. The Cardinal 36. Hearts of Humanity 36. The Prince and the Pauper (US) 37. Moonlight Sonata 37. The Crimes of Stephen Hawke 38. *49th Parallel* 41. One of Our Aircraft is Missing 42. Uncensored 42. Squadron Leader X 43. We Dive at Dawn 43. Escape to Danger 43. *Millions Like Us* 43. A Canterbury Tale 44. Great Day 45. Men of Two Worlds 46. *Wanted for Murder* 46. Dear Murderer 47. Daybreak 48. The Mark of Cain 48. Corridor of Mirrors 48. The Blind Goddess 48. The Spider and the Fly 50. The Magic Box 51. Cairo Road 51. His Excellency 51. South of Algiers 52. The Colditz Story 54. *The Deep Blue Sea* 55. Child in the House 56. The Good Companions 57. The Naked Edge 61. The Man Who Finally Died 62. Freud 62. West Eleven 63. The Bedford Incident 65. The Whisperers 66. The Spy with a Cold Nose 67. Assignment to Kill 67. Deadfall 68.

Portman, Natalie (1981–).
American teenage actress, from the stage. Born in Jerusalem, she moved to America at the age of three.
Leon/The Professional 95. Heat 95. Beautiful Girls 96. Everyone Says I Love You 96. Mars Attacks! 96. Prince of Egypt (voice) 98, etc.

Portman, Rachel (1961–).
British composer.
Privileged 82. Life Is Sweet 90. Rebecca's Daughters 92. Used People 92. The Joy Luck Club 93. Only You 94. The War of the Buttons 94. The Road to Wellville 94. Smoke 95. A Pyromaniac's Love Story 95. To Wong Foo, Thanks for Everything! Julie Newmar 95. Palookaville 95. Emma (AA) 96. Beloved 98. Home Fries 98, etc.

Posey, Parker (1968–).
American actress, usually in independent films; appeared in the daytime soap opera *As the World Turns* in the early 90s.
Joey Breaker 93. Coneheads 93. Dazed and Confused 93. Tales of the City (TV) 94. Sleep with Me 94. Mixed Nuts 94. Amateur 94. Party Girl 95. Drunks 95. Flirt 95. Kicking and Screaming 95. The Doomed Generation 95. The Daytrippers 96. Frisk 96. Waiting for Guffman 96. Basquiat 96. Clockwatchers 97. House of Yes 97. Henry Fool 97. The Misadventures of Margaret 98. You've Got Mail 98, etc.

Post, Ted (1918–).
American director, from TV.
The Peacemaker 56. The Legend of Tom Dooley 59. Hang 'Em High 68. Beneath the Planet of the Apes 70. Yuma (TV) 70. Dr Cook's Garden (TV) 70. Night Slaves (TV) 70. The Bravos (TV) 71. Five Desperate Women (TV) 71. Do Not Fold Spindle or Mutilate (TV) 72. The Baby 73. The Harrad Experiment 73. Magnum Force 73. Whiffs 75. Good Guys Wear Black 77. Go Tell the Spartans 78. Nightkill 81. Stagecoach (TV) 86. The Human Shield 91, etc.

Posta, Adrienne (1948–) (Adrienne Poster).
British juvenile actress specializing in cheeky teenagers.
No Time for Tears 59. To Sir with Love 67. Here We Go Round the Mulberry Bush 67. Up the Junction 68. Some Girls Do 69. Percy 70. Up Pompeii 71. Percy's Progress 74, etc.

Poster, Steven B.
American cinematographer, from commercials and documentaries. Born in Chicago, he studied at Southern Illinois University, Los Angeles Art Center College of Design, and the Institute of Design at the Illinois Institute of Technology.
Blood Beach 81. Dead and Buried 81. Strange Brew 83. Testament 83. The New Kids 85. Blue City 86. The Boy Who Could Fly (& co-w) 86. Someone to Watch Over Me 87. Aloha Summer 88. Big Top Pee-Wee 88. Next of Kin 89. Opportunity Knocks 90. Rocky V 90. Life Stinks 91. The Cemetery Club 93. Roswell (TV) 94. A Midwife's Tale 96. Rocket Man 97. Half a Chance/Une Chance sur Deux (Fr.) 98, etc.

Postlethwaite, Peter (1945–).
British character actor, from the theatre.
A Private Function 84. Distant Voices, Still Lives 88. The Dressmaker 89. To Kill a Priest 89. Treasure Island 90. Hamlet 90. The Long Day Closes 92. Alien^3 92. Split Second 92. Last of the Mohicans 92. Waterland 92. *In the Name of the Father* (AAN) 93. Sharpe's Company (TV) 94. The Usual Suspects 95. Suite 16 95. James and the Giant Peach (voice) 96. When Saturday Comes 96. Brute 96. Dragonheart 96. *Brassed Off* 96. The Serpent's Kiss 97. William Shakespeare's Romeo and Juliet (as Friar Lawrence) 96. Lost World: Jurassic Park 97. Amistad 97. Among Giants 98, etc.

Poston, Tom (1927–).
American light comedian.
■ City that Never Sleeps 53. Zotz! 62. Soldier in the Rain 63. The Old Dark House 63. Cold Turkey 70. The Happy Hooker 75. Rabbit Test 78. Up the Academy 80. Carbon Copy 81.
TV series: The Steve Allen Show 56–59. On the Rocks 75–76. We've Got Each Other 77–78. Mork & Mindy 78–82. Newhart 82–90. Good Grief 90–91.

Potter, Dennis (1935–1994).
British dramatist and screenwriter, a former journalist, the pre-eminent television playwright of his time.
Biography; 1998, *Dennis Potter: The Authorized Biography* by Humphrey Carpenter.
Pennies from Heaven (AAN) 81. Brimstone and Treacle 82. Gorky Park 83. Dreamchild 85. Tender Is the Night (TV) 85. The Singing Detective (TV) 87. Track 29 88. Lipstick on Your Collar (TV) 92. Secret Friends (wd) 92. Midnight Movie 93. Mesmer 94. Karaoke (TV) 96. Cold Lazarus (TV) 96, etc.

Potter, H. C. (1904–1977).
American director with stage experience, in Hollywood from 1935; an expert at comedy.
■ Beloved Enemy 36. Wings over Honolulu 37. Romance in the Dark 38. Shopworn Angel 38. The Cowboy and the Lady 38. *The Story of Vernon and Irene Castle* 39. Blackmail 39. Congo Maisie 40. Second Chorus 40. *Hellzapoppin* 41. Mr Lucky 43. *The Farmer's Daughter* 47. A Likely Story 47. *Mr Blandings Builds His Dream House* 48. The Time of Your Life 48. You Gotta Stay Happy 48. The Miniver Story 50. Three for the Show 55. Top Secret Affair 57.

Potter, Martin (1944–).
British juvenile lead of the early 70s.
Fellini Satyricon 70. Goodbye Gemini 71. Nicholas and Alexandra 71. All Coppers Are 71. Craze 73. The Big Sleep 78. Gunpowder 84. Twinsanity 88, etc.

Potter, Monica (1971–).
American actress, a former model.
Bulletproof 96. Con Air 97. Without Limits 97. Martha, Meet Frank, Daniel and Laurence 98. Patch Adams 98. A Cool, Dry Place 98, etc.

Potter, Sally (1949–).
British director and screenwriter.
The Gold Diggers 84. *Orlando* 92. The Tango Lesson (& a) 97, etc.

Potts, Annie (1952–).
American actress, born in Nashville, Tennessee, who is frequently in television series. She studied theatre at Stephens College in Missouri.
Corvette Summer 78. Heartaches 81. Cowboy 83. Crimes of Passion 84. Ghostbusters 84. Jumpin' Jack Flash 86. Pretty in Pink 86. Ghostbusters II 89. Who's Harry Crumb? 89. Texasville 90. Breaking the Rules 92. Noises Off 92. Toy Story (voice) 95. Toy Story 2 (voice) 99, etc.
TV series: Goodtime Girls 80. Designing Woman 86–90. Love & War 93–95. Dangerous Minds 96.

Potts, Cliff (1945–).
American second lead of 70s action dramas.
Snow Job 72. The Ground Star Conspiracy 72. Face to the Wind 74. Nevada Smith (TV) 75. Once an Eagle (TV) 77. Last Ride of the Dalton Gang (TV) 79, etc.
TV series: Big Hawaii 77. Lou Grant 81–82. For Love and Honor 83.

Poujouly, Georges (1940–).
French boy-actor of the early 50s.
Jeux Interdits 52. Nous Sommes Tous des Assassins 52. Les Diaboliques 54. Lift to the Scaffold 57. Girls for the Summer 59. Une Grosse Tête 62. Peace over the Fields 70. Le Guepiot 81, etc.

Poulton, Mabel (1905–1994).
British leading lady of the 20s.
The Heart of an Actress 24. Virginia's Husband 25. The Constant Nymph 28. The Return of the Rat 28. Children of Chance 30. Star Impersonations (as Mary Pickford) 30. Number Please 31. Crown versus Stevens 36, etc.

Pounder, C. C. H. (1952–) (Carol Christine Hilaria Pounder).
Guyana-born character actress in America.
Bagdad Café 88. Postcards from the Edge 90. Psycho IV: The Beginning (TV) 90. Question of Faith 93. Sliver 93. Benny & Joon 93. Robocop 3 93. Tales from the Crypt Presents Demon Knight 95. Zooman (TV) 95. White Dwarf 95. If These Walls Could Talk 96. Face/Off 97, etc.
TV series: Women in Prison 87–88.

Powell, Anthony (1935–).
English costume designer.
Travels with My Aunt (AA) 72. Papillon 83. Death on the Nile (AA) 78. Tess (AA) 80. Indiana Jones and the Temple of Doom 84. Pirates (AAN) 86. Ishtar 87. Frantic 88. Indiana Jones and the Last Crusade 89. Hook (AAN) 91. 101 Dalmatians 96. The Avengers 98, etc.

Powell, Dick (1904–1963).
American crooning juvenile of the 30s who later suffered a sea-change and emerged as a likeable tough leading man, a competent director and an ambitious producer, the founder of Four Star Television.
Blessed Event 32. Too Busy to Work 32. The King's Vacation 33. *Forty-Second Street* 33. Gold Diggers of 1933. Footlight Parade 33. College Coach 33. Convention City 33. *Dames* 34. Wonder Bar 34. Twenty Million Sweethearts 34. Happiness Ahead 34. Flirtation Walk 34. Gold Diggers of 1935. Page Miss Glory 35. Broadway Gondolier 35. A Midsummer Night's Dream 35. Shipmates Forever 35. Thanks a Million 35. Colleen 36. Hearts Divided 36. Stage Struck 36. Gold Diggers of 1937. *On the Avenue* 37. The Singing Marine 37. Varsity Show 37. Hollywood Hotel 38. Cowboy from Brooklyn 38. Hard to Get 38. Going Places 38. Naughty but Nice 39. *Christmas in July* 40. I Want a Divorce 40. Model Wife 41. In the Navy 41. Star Spangled Rhythm 42. Happy Go Lucky 42. True to Life 43. Riding High 43. *It Happened Tomorrow* 44. Meet the People 44. *Murder My Sweet* (as Philip Marlowe) 44. Cornered 45. Johnny O'Clock 47. To the Ends of the Earth 48. Pitfall 48. Station West 48. Rogues Regiment 48. Mrs Mike 49. The Reformer and the Redhead 50. Right Cross 50. Callaway Went Thataway 51. Cry Danger 51. The Tall Target 51. You Never Can Tell 51. The Bad and the Beautiful 52. Split Second (d only) 53. Susan Slept Here 54. The Conqueror (pd only) 56. You Can't Run Away From It (d only) 56. The Enemy Below (d only) 57. The Hunters (d only) 58, etc.
TV series: *Dick Powell Theatre* 59–61.

Powell, Dilys (1901–1995).
British film critic, long with the *Sunday Times* and then with *Punch*. Her reviews have been collected in: 1989, *The Golden Screen: Fifty Years of Films*, and 1991, *The Dilys Powell Film Reader*.
Booklet: 1947, *Films Since 1939*.

Powell, Eleanor (1910–1982).
Long-legged American tap dancer whose vitality enhanced a few films. On Broadway from her late teens, she was signed by MGM, but quit in 1943 to marry actor Glenn Ford (divorced 1959). She continued to perform on stage and television.
■ George White's Scandals 35. Broadway Melody of 1936. *Born to Dance* 36. Broadway Melody of 1938. *Rosalie* 38. Honolulu 39. Broadway Melody of 1940. Lady Be Good 41. Ship Ahoy 42. I Dood It 43. Thousands Cheer 43. Sensations of 1945 44. The Duchess of Idaho 50.

Powell, Jane (1929–) (Suzanne Burce).
Diminutive American singing and dancing leading lady; former child performer. She married former child actor Dick Moore, her fifth husband, in 1988.
■ Song of the Open Road 44. Delightfully Dangerous 45. Holiday in Mexico 46. Three Daring Daughters 48. A Date with Judy 48. Luxury Liner 48. Nancy Goes to Rio 50. Two Weeks with Love 50. Royal Wedding 51. Rich Young and Pretty 51. Small Town Girl 53. Three Sailors and a Girl 53. *Seven Brides for Seven Brothers* 54. Athena 54. Deep in My Heart 54. Hit the Deck 55. The Girl Most Likely 57. The Female Animal 58. Enchanted Island 58. Wheeler and Murdoch (TV) 70. The Letters (TV) 72. Mayday at 40,000 Feet (TV) 78.

Powell, Michael (1905–1990).
Important British writer-producer-director whose highly imaginative work, especially in his collaboration with Emeric Pressburger (*The Archers* 42–57), was sometimes marred by a streak of tastelessness. His second wife was film editor Thelma Schoonmaker.
Autobiographies: 1985, *A Life in Movies*. 1992, *Million Dollar Movie*.
Book: 1996, *The Films of Michael Powell and the Archers* by Scott Salwolke.
As writer: Caste 30. 77 Park Lane 31.
As director: Two Crowded Hours 31. My Friend the King 32. Rynox 32. The Rasp 32. The Star Reporter 32. Hotel Splendide 32. C.O.D. 32. His Lordship 32. Born Lucky 33. The Fire Raisers (& co-w) 34. The Night of the Party 35. Something Always Happens 34. Red Ensign (& co-w) 35. The Girl in the Crowd 35. Lazybones 35. The Love Test 35. The Phantom Light 35. The Price of a Song 35. Someday 35. Her Last Affaire 36. The Brown Wallet 36. Crown v. Stevens 36. The Man behind the Mask 36.
■ As executive wholly or jointly in charge, including work as writer-producer-director: The Edge of the World 37. *The Spy in Black* 38. The Lion Has Wings 39. The Thief of Baghdad 39. Contraband 40. 49th Parallel/The Invaders (AA story) 41. One of Our Aircraft is Missing (AANw) 42. *The Life and Death of Colonel Blimp* 43. The Silver Fleet 43. A Canterbury Tale 44. *I Know Where I'm Going* 45. *A Matter of Life and Death* 46. Black Narcissus 46. End of the River 47. *The Red Shoes* 48. The Small Back Room 48. Gone to Earth 50. The Elusive Pimpernel 51. The Tales of Hoffman 51. Oh Rosalinda 55. The Battle of the River Plate 56. Ill Met by Moonlight 57. Peeping Tom 60. Honeymoon 61. The Queen's Guards 61. They're a Weird Mob 66. Sebastian (p only) 67. Age of Consent 69. The Boy Who Turned Yellow 72. Return to the Edge of the World 79.
✪ For being so unpredictable, and at his best so brilliant. *A Matter of Life and Death*.

❝ Of course all films are surrealist. They are making something that looks like the real world but isn't. – *M.P.*

I got my first assignment as a director in 1927. I was slim, arrogant, intelligent, foolish, shy, cocksure, dreamy and irritating. Today, I'm no longer slim. – *M.P. in 1987*

Powell, Nik (1950–).
British producer, in partnership with Steve Woolley. He was a co-founder of Palace Pictures, a distribution and production company.

Book: 1996, *The Egos Have Landed: The Rise and Fall of Palace Pictures* by Angus Finney.

The Company of Wolves 85. A Letter to Brezhnev 85. Absolute Beginners 86. Mona Lisa 86. The Courier 87. High Spirits 88. Shag 88. Scandal 89. The Big Man 90. The Miracle 91. The Pope Must Die/The Pope Must Diet 91. A Rage in Harlem 91. Waterland 92. Dust Devil 92. *The Crying Game* 92. Backbeat 93. The Neon Bible 95. Hollow Reed 96. Welcome to Woop-Woop 97. TwentyFourSeven 97. Fever Pitch 97. Divorcing Jack 98. Little Voice 98. B. Monkey 98, etc.

Powell, Robert (1944–).
Lithe, pale-eyed British leading man of the 70s.

Walk a Crooked Path 69. The Italian Job 69. Pygmalion (TV) 71. Secrets 71. Running Scared 72. Asylum 72. The Asphyx 73. Mahler 73. Tommy 75. *Jesus of Nazareth* (TV) 77. The Four Feathers (TV) 78. Beyond Good and Evil (It.) 78. The Thirty-Nine Steps 78. Harlequin 79. Jane Austen in Manhattan 79. The Survivor 80. The Jigsaw Man 83. Secrets of the Phantom Caverns 84. Shaka Zulu (TV) 86. The Mystery of Edwin Drood 93, etc.

TV series: Hannay 88–89. The Detectives 93–95.

❝ I hope Jesus Christ will be the last in my line of sensitive young men for quite a while. – *R.P., 1977*

Powell, Sandy (1898–1982) (Albert Powell).
British music-hall comedian who made some knockabout films using his radio catch-phrase 'Can you hear me, mother?'

Autobiography: 1976, *Can You Hear Me, Mother?*

The Third String 32. Leave It to Me 36. I've Got a Horse 38. Cup Tie Honeymoon 48, etc.

Powell, Sandy.
English costume designer.

Caravaggio 86. Stormy Monday 88. The Miracle 91. The Pope Must Die/The Pope Must Diet 91. *Orlando* (AAN) 93. Being Human 94. Interview with the Vampire 94. Rob Roy 95. Michael Collins 96. *The Wings of the Dove* (AAN) 97. The Butcher Boy 98. Velvet Goldmine 98. Hilary and Jackie 98. Shakespeare in Love 98, etc.

Powell, William (1892–1984).
Mature, debonair American leading man of the 30s and 40s; a pillar of MGM for many years, he began as a cowboy villain but is probably best remembered as Nick Charles in *The Thin Man*. His second wife was actress Carole Lombard (1931–33) and he was engaged to actress Jean Harlow at the time of her death.

Biography: 1984, *Gentleman, the William Powell Story*.

SELECTED SILENT FILMS: Sherlock Holmes 22. The Bright Shawl 23. Romola 24. Too Many Kisses 25. Faint Perfume 25. Desert Gold 26. Aloma of the South Seas 26. Beau Geste 26. Señorita 27. Nevada 27. Feel My Pulse 28. The Last Command 28. The Vanishing Pioneer 28, etc.

■ SOUND FILMS: Interference 29. *The Canary Murder Case* (as Philo Vance) 29. The Greene Murder Case 29. Charming Sinners 29. The Four Feathers 29. The Benson Murder Case 30. Paramount on Parade 30. Shadow of the Law 30. Pointed Heels 30. Behind the Make-up 30. *Street of Chance* 30. For the Defense 30. Man of the World 31. Ladies' Man 31. The Road to Singapore 31. High Pressure 32. Jewel Robbery 32. *One Way Passage* 32. Lawyer Man 32. Double Harness 33. Private Detective 62 33. The Kennel Murder Case 33. Fashions of 1934. The Key 34. Manhattan Melodrama 34. *The Thin Man* (AAN) 34. Evelyn Prentice 34. Reckless 35. Star of Midnight 35. Escapade 35. Rendezvous 35. *The Great Ziegfeld* 36. The Ex Mrs Bradford 36. *My Man Godfrey* (AAN) 36. Libelled Lady 36. After the Thin Man 36. The Last of Mrs Cheyney 37. The Emperor's Candlesticks 37. Double Wedding 37. The Baroness and the Butler 38. Another Thin Man 39. I Love You Again 40. Love Crazy 41. Shadow of the Thin Man 41. Crossroads 42. The Youngest Profession 43. The Heavenly Body 44. The Thin Man Goes Home 44. Ziegfeld Follies 45. The Hoodlum Saint 46. Song of the Thin Man 47. *Life With Father* (AAN) 47. The Senator was Indiscreet 47. Mr Peabody and the Mermaid 48. Take One False Step 49. Dancing in the Dark 49. Treasure of Lost Canyon 51. It's a Big Country 51. The Girl Who Had Everything 53. How to Marry a Millionaire 53. *Mister Roberts* (as Doc) 55.

✪ For spreading his cheerful suavity over 30s Hollywood; and for being so much at home in a dinner jacket. *The Thin Man*.

Famous line (*Life With Father*): 'I'm going to be baptized, damn it!'

Power, Hartley (1894–1966).
Bald-headed American character actor who settled in Britain and was often seen as general, con man or brash agent.

Friday the Thirteenth 33. Evergreen 34. A Window in London 42. The Way to the Stars 45. *Dead of Night* 45. A Girl in a Million 47. Roman Holiday 53. To Dorothy a Son 54. Island in the Sun 56, many others.

Power, Taryn (1954–).
American actress, the daughter of Tyrone Power and Linda Christian.

The Count of Monte Cristo 74. Maria 75. Tracks 76. Sinbad and the Eye of the Tiger 77. The Sea Serpent 84, etc.

Power, Tyrone (1913–1958).
American leading man, of theatrical family; in films from 1932, usually deploying smooth gentle personality. He was married three times; his wives included actresses ANNABELLA (1939–48) and Linda CHRISTIAN (1949–55), and his lovers Judy GARLAND and Lana TURNER. Died of a heart attack.

Biography: 1979, *Tyrone Power: The Last Idol* by Fred Lawrence Guiles.

■ Tom Brown of Culver 32. Girls' Dormitory 36. Ladies in Love 36. *Lloyds of London* 37. Love is News 37. Café Metropole 37. Thin Ice 37. Second Honeymoon 37. *In Old Chicago* 38. *Alexander's Ragtime Band* 38. Marie Antoinette 38. Suez 38. *Rose of Washington Square* 39. *Jesse James* 39. Second Fiddle 39. The Rains Came 39. Daytime Wife 39. Johnny Apollo 40. Brigham Young 40. *The Mark of Zorro* 40. A Yank in the RAF 41. Blood and Sand 41. This Above All 42. Son of Fury 42. *The Black Swan* 42. Crash Dive 42; war service; The Razor's Edge 46. Captain from Castile 47. Nightmare Alley 47. The Luck of the Irish 48. That Wonderful Urge 48. Prince of Foxes 49. The Black Rose 50. An American Guerilla in the Philippines 51. Rawhide 51. I'll Never Forget You 51. Diplomatic Courier 52. Pony Soldier 52. Mississippi Gambler 53. King of the Khyber Rifles 53. The Long Gray Line 54. Untamed 55. The Eddy Duchin Story 56. Seven Waves Away 57. The Rising of the Moon (narrated only) 57. *The Sun Also Rises* 57. Witness for the Prosecution 57.

❝ I've done an awful lot of stuff that's a monument to public patience. – *T.P.*

Some day I will show the motherfuckers who say I was a success just because of my pretty face. Sometimes I wish I had a really bad car accident so my face would get smashed up and I'd look like Eddie Constantine. – *T.P.*

He said that in Hollywood, the glamour and the sweet-dreamy stuff was but a façade, that it was a world of polite destruction. – *Mai Zetterling*

Power, Tyrone, Snr (1869–1931).
American stage actor, father of Tyrone Power: played heavy in a few films.

A Texas Street 15. Where are My Children? 16. Footfalls 21. The Lone Wolf 24. Bride of the Storm 26. The Big Trail 30, etc.

Powers, Mala (1931–) (Mary Ellen Powers.
American leading lady, former child actress.

Tough as They Come 41. Outrage 50. Cyrano de Bergerac 50. Rose of Cimarron 52. Rage at Dawn 55. Benghazi 55. The Storm Rider 57. Daddy's Gone A-Hunting 69. The Doomsday Machine 72, etc.

Powers, Stefanie (1942–) (Stefania Federkiewicz).
American leading lady. Married actor Gary Lockwood (1966–74).

Experiment in Terror 62. The Interns 62. Palm Springs Weekend 63. *Fanatic* (GB) 64. Stagecoach 66. Warning Shot 67. Herbie Rides Again 73. Escape to Athena 79. Family Secrets (TV) 84. Deceptions (TV) 85. She Was Marked for Murder (TV) 88. Love and Betrayal (TV) 89, etc.

TV series: *The Girl from UNCLE* 66. Washington behind Closed Doors 77. The Feather and Father Gang 78. *Hart to Hart* 79–83.

Powers, Tom (1890–1955).
American general-purpose supporting actor.

Double Indemnity 44. Two Years Before the Mast 46. Up in Central Park 48. Chicago Deadline 49. Destination Moon 50. Horizons West 52. Julius Caesar 53. The Americano 54, etc.

Prefontaine, Steve (1951–1975).
American athlete of the 70s who was undefeated in the US, holding all seven records for distances between 2,000 and 10,000 metres, although he failed to win at the Munich Olympics of 1972. Died in a car crash a year before the Montreal Games, in which he was expected to excel. Two feature films about his life were made in 1997: *Prefontaine*, directed by Steve James and starring Jared LETO, and *Without Limits*, directed by Robert TOWNE and starring Billy CRUDUP. He was also the subject of a 1995 TV documentary, *Fire on the Track*.

Preisner, Zbigniew (1955–).
Polish composer, from the theatre, especially associated with the films of Krzysztof KIÉSLOWSKI and Agnieszka HOLLAND. He studied art history at university in Krakow, and is a self-taught musician.

At Play in the Fields of the Lord (US) 91. Europa, Europa 91. The Double Life of Veronique 91. Damage 92. The Secret Garden 93. *Three Colours: Blue*/Trois Couleurs: Bleu 93. A Linha do Horizonte 93. Three Colours: Red/Trois Couleurs: Rouge 94. Three Colours: White/Trois Couleurs: Blanc 94. Mouvements du Désir 94. When a Man Loves a Woman (US) 94. Feast of July (GB/US) 95. Fairytale: A True Story (US) 97, etc.

❝ When Strauss was writing his music, it was dance music. Now it's classical music. So how can you tell that in 50 years' time film music will not turn out to be classical music? – *Z.P.*

Preiss, Wolfgang.
German character actor in international films.

The Longest Day 62. Von Ryan's Express 65. The Train 65. Hannibal Brooks 68. Raid on Rommel 71. The Salzburg Connection 72. A Bridge too Far 77. The Boys from Brazil 78. The Winds of War (TV) 83. Forget Mozart 85. The Second Victory 86, etc.

Preisser, June (1921–1984).
Vivacious teenage leading lady of the 40s.

Babes in Arms 39. Strike Up the Band 40. The Fleet's In 41. Sweater Girl 41. Babes on Swing Street 44. Sarge Goes to College 47, etc.

Préjean, Albert (1894–1979).
French light character actor who was in most of René Clair's early successes.

Le Voyage Imaginaire 25. An Italian Straw Hat 27. Sous les Toits de Paris 30. Die Dreigroschenoper/L'Opéra de Quat'Sous 31. Jenny 36. Métropolitain 40. L'Etrange Suzy 43. Les Nouveaux Maîtres 49. Les Amants du Tage 54, etc.

Prejean, Sister Helen.
American nun, a member of the Sisters of St Joseph of Medaille, Louisiana. A campaigner for the abolition of capital punishment, she was played by Susan SARANDON in *Dead Man Walking* 95, based on her book.

❝ You can be sure there are no rich people on death row. – *H.P.*

Preminger, Ingo.
Austrian/American producer, brother of Otto.

M*A*S*H (AAN) 70. The Salzburg Connection 72, etc.

Preminger, Otto (1906–1986).
Austrian/American director with theatrical background. Always a good craftsman, he latterly applied heavy-handed treatment to potentially interesting subjects.

Autobiography: 1977, *Preminger*.

Biography: 1973, *Behind the Scenes of Otto Preminger* by Willi Frischauer.

■ Die Grosse Liebe (Austrian) 32, then to US: Under Your Spell 36. Danger, Love at Work 37. The Pied Piper (a only) 42. They Got Me Covered (a only) 42. Margin for Error (& a) 43. In the Meantime, Darling 44. *Laura* 44. Royal Scandal 45. Where Do We Go from Here 45. Centennial Summer 46. Fallen Angel 46. Forever Amber 47. Daisy Kenyon 47. That Lady in Ermine (part) 48. The Fan 49. Whirlpool 50. Where the Sidewalk Ends 50. The Thirteenth Letter 51. Angel Face 52. *The Moon is Blue* 53. *Stalag 17* (a only) 53. River of No Return 54. *Carmen Jones* 54. The Court Martial of Billy Mitchell 55. *The Man with the Golden Arm* 56. Bonjour Tristesse 57. Saint Joan (GB) 57. Porgy and Bess 59. *Anatomy of a Murder* 59. Exodus 60. *Advise and Consent* 61. The Cardinal (AAN) 63. In Harm's Way 65. Bunny Lake is Missing (GB) 65. Hurry Sundown 67. Skidoo 68. Tell Me That You Love Me, Junie Moon 70. Such Good Friends 72. Rosebud 75. The Human Factor 79.

❝ A great showman who has never bothered to learn anything about making a movie . . . no one is more skilled at giving the appearance of dealing with large controversial themes in a bold way, without making the tactical error of doing so. – *Dwight MacDonald*

Otto, let my people go. – *Mort Sahl at the premiere of Exodus*

His enemies have never forgiven him for being a director with the personality of a producer. – *Andrew Sarris, 1968*

Otto was one of those directors you can't listen to because he doesn't know anything at all about the process of acting. I didn't think he was ever right. – *Faye Dunaway*

Prentiss, Paula (1939–) (Paula Ragusa).
Tall American leading lady who came almost straight from college to Hollywood. Married actor Richard Benjamin in 1961.

Where the Boys Are 61. The Honeymoon Machine 62. Bachelor in Paradise 62. The Horizontal Lieutenant 63. *Man's Favorite Sport?* 64. The World of Henry Orient 64. In Harm's Way 65. What's New, Pussycat? 65. Catch 22 69. Last of the Red Hot Lovers 72. Crazy Joe 73. The Parallax View 74. The Stepford Wives 75. Having Babies II (TV) 77. The Black Marble 80. Buddy Buddy 81. Saturday the 14th 81. M.A.D.D.: Mothers against Drunk Driving (TV) 83. Mrs Winterbourne 97, etc.

TV series: *He and She* 67.

Presle, Micheline (1922–) (Micheline Chassagne).
French leading actress with stage experience.

Jeunes Filles en Détresse 38. La Nuit Fantastique 41. Boule de Suif 45. *Le Diable au Corps* 46. Les Jeux Sont Faits 47. Under My Skin (US) 50. The Adventures of Captain Fabian (US) 51. La Dame aux Camélias 52. Villa Borghese 54. The She Wolves 57. Blind Date (GB) 59. The Prize 63. La Religieuse 65. King of Hearts 67. Peau d'Ane 70. The Slightly Pregnant Man 73. Nea: A New Woman 78. Je M'Appelle Victor 93. Fanfan 93. Pas Très Catholique 94. Casque Bleu 94, etc.

Presley, Elvis (1935–1977).
Heavy-lidded American pop singer and guitarist, once known as 'the Pelvis' because of his swivel-hipped style. His popularity with teenagers survived a host of bad movies. He remains a subject of mass interest despite his death: his home Graceland in Memphis is one of the most popular private tourist attractions in the US and is estimated to bring in $150m to the city itself. Married actress Priscilla Beaulieu, now known as Priscilla PRESLEY. His daughter Lisa Marie's marriage in May 1994 to her second husband, singer Michael Jackson, lasted 20 months.

Biography: 1977, *Elvis Presley* by W. A. Harbinson.

Book: 1997, *Elvis Film Encyclopedia* by Eric Braun.

■ Love Me Tender 56. Loving You 57. Jailhouse Rock 57. King Creole 58. G.I. Blues 60. Flaming Star 60. Wild in the Country 61. Blue Hawaii 61. Kid Galahad 62. Girls Girls Girls 62. Follow That Dream 62. Fun in Acapulco 63. It Happened at the World's Fair 63. Kissin' Cousins 64. Viva Las Vegas 64. Roustabout 64. Girl Happy 65. Tickle Me 65. Harem Scarem 65. Frankie and Johnny 66. Paradise Hawaiian Style 66. Spinout 66. Easy Come Easy Go 67. Double Trouble 67. Stay Away Joe 68. Speedway 68. Clambake 68. Live a Little Love a Little 68. Charro 69. Change of Habit 70. The Trouble with Girls 70. Elvis – that's the Way It Is 70. Elvis on Tour 72.

❝ He projects to the point where he jumps out at you from the screen. He has some of the same qualities as Rudolph Valentino. He has the same magnetism. – *Don Siegel*

Presley, Priscilla (1945–) (Priscilla Wagner aka Priscilla Beaulieu).
American light actress. She was married to Elvis PRESLEY (1967–73).
Biography: 1997, *Child Bride* by Suzanne Finstad.
Love Is Forever (TV) 83. The Naked Gun 88. The Adventures of Ford Fairlane 90. The Naked Gun 2½: The Smell of Fear 91. Naked Gun 33 : The Final Insult 94, etc.
TV series: Dallas 83.

Presnell, Harve (1933–).
American light opera singer, in occasional films.
The Unsinkable Molly Brown 64. The Glory Guys 65. Where the Boys Meet the Girls 66. Paint Your Wagon 69. Fargo 96. Larger than Life 96. The Whole Wide World 96. Julian Po 97. Face/Off 97. Everything that Rises (TV) 98, etc.

Presnell, Robert, Jnr (1914–1986).
American writer.
Meet John Doe (co-story, AAN) 41. The Man in the Attic 53. Legend of the Lost 57. Conspiracy of Hearts (GB) 59. Let No Man Write My Epitaph 60. The Third Day 65, etc.

Presnell, Robert, Snr (1894–*).
American writer, usually in collaboration.
Hi Nellie 32. My Man Godfrey 36. The Real Glory 39. Meet John Doe 41. Second Chance 53. 13 West Street 62, etc.

Pressburger, Arnold (1885–1951).
Hungarian producer who worked in Germany, Britain and Hollywood.
City of Song 30. Tell Me Tonight 32. The Return of the Scarlet Pimpernel 38. The Shanghai Gesture 41. Hangmen Also Die 43. It Happened Tomorrow 44. A Scandal in Paris 46, etc.

Pressburger, Emeric (1902–1988).
Hungarian journalist and scriptwriter in Britain from 1935. Worked on script of *The Challenge* 37 and met Michael Powell, qv for list of their joint films such as *The Archers*.
Biography: 1994, *Emeric Pressburger: The Life and Death of a Screenwriter* by Kevin Macdonald.
SOLO: Twice Upon a Time (wpd) 52. Miracle in Soho (wp) 56. Behold a Pale Horse (from his novel) 64. Operation Crossbow (w) (as Richard Imrie) 65. They're a Weird Mob (w) 66. The Boy Who Turned Yellow (w) 72.

Pressman, Edward R. (1943–).
American producer.
The Revolutionary 70. Badlands 73. Phantom of the Paradise 74. Paradise Alley 78. Heart Beat 78. Old Boyfriends 79. You Better Watch Out 80. The Hand 81. The Pirates of Penzance 83. Plenty 84. True Stories 86. Wall Street 88. Talk Radio 88. Reversal of Fortune 91. Year of the Gun 91. Storyville 92. The Crow 94. No Escape 94. Judge Dredd 95. City Hall 96. The Island of Dr Moreau 96. The Crow: City of Angels 96. The Winter Guest 97. Two Girls and a Guy 97. New Rose Hotel 98, etc.

Pressman, Michael (1950–).
American director.
The Bad News Bears in Breaking Training 77. Boulevard Nights 79. Those Lips Those Eyes 80. Some Kind of Hero 81. Doctor Detroit 83. To Heal a Nation (TV) 88. Teenage Mutant Ninja Turtles II: The Secret of the Ooze 91. To Gillian on Her 37th Birthday 96, etc.

Preston, Kelly (1962–) (Kelly Smith).
American actress. Married John TRAVOLTA.
Christine 83. Metalstorm: The Destruction of Jared-Syn 83. Mischief 85. Secret Admirer 85. 52 Pick-Up 86. Amazon Women on the Moon 87. Love at Stake 87. A Tiger's Tale 87. Spellbinder 88. Twins 88. The Experts 89. Only You 92. Cheyenne Warrior 94. Mrs Munck 95. From Dusk till Dawn 96. Precious 96. Nothing to Lose 96. Jerry Maguire 96. Citizen Ruth 96. Addicted to Love 97. Holy Man 98. Jack Frost 98, etc.

Preston, Robert (1917–1987) (Robert Preston Meservey).
American leading man who made routine films from 1938, and became a theatre star of great vitality in the 50s.
■ King of Alcatraz 38. Illegal Traffic 38. Disbarred 38. Union Pacific 39. *Beau Geste* 39. Typhoon 39. Moon over Burma 39. Northwest Mounted Police 40. New York Town 40. The Lady from Cheyenne 40. The Night of January 16th 41. Parachute Battalion 41. Pacific Blackout 41. Reap the Wild Wind 42. *This Gun for Hire* 42. Wake Island 42. Night Plane to Chungking 42; war service; Wild Harvest 47. *The Macomber Affair* 47. Variety Girl 47. Whispering Smith 47. Blood on the Moon 48. Big City 48. The Lady Gambles 48. *Tulsa* 49. The Sundowners 49. Best of the Badmen 51. My Outlaw Brother 51. When I Grow Up 51. Face to Face 52. Cloudburst (GB) 53. The Last Frontier 56. *The Dark at the Top of the Stairs* 60. *The Music Man* (his stage role) 61. Island of Love 63. *All the Way Home* 63. How the West Was Won 63. Junior Bonner 72. Child's Play 72. Mame 73. My Father's House (TV) 75. Semi-Tough 77. The Chisholms (TV) 79. S.O.B. 81. *Victor/Victoria* (AAN) 82. September Gun (TV) 83. The Last Starfighter 84. Finnegan Begin Again (TV) 85. Outrage (TV) 86.

Prévert, Jacques (1900–1977).
French screenwriter whose most memorable work was in conjunction with Marcel Carné.
Drôle de Drame 37. *Quai des Brumes* 38. *Le Jour Se Lève* 39. *Les Visiteurs du Soir* 42. *Les Enfants du Paradis* (AAN) 44. *Les Portes de la Nuit* 46. Les Amants de Vérone 48. Other scripts include L'Affaire est dans le Sac (& a) 32. *Le Crime de Monsieur Lange* 35. *Une Partie de Campagne* 36. *Lumière d'Eté* 42. Notre Dame de Paris 56, etc.

Prévert, Pierre (1906–1988).
French director, brother of Jacques Prévert.
L'Affaire est dans le Sac 32. Adieu Leonard 43. Voyage Surprise 46, etc.

Previn, André (1929–).
German composer and arranger, long in Hollywood. Settled in Britain and became orchestral conductor. He was married to Mia Farrow (1970–79).
Autobiography: 1992, *No Minor Chords: My Days in Hollywood.*
Biography: 1981, *André Previn* by Martin Bookspan and Ross Yockey.
Scene of the Crime 49. Three Little Words (AAN) 51. Bad Day at Black Rock 54. The Fastest Gun Alive 56. Designing Woman 57. Gigi (AA) 58. Porgy and Bess (AA) 59. Elmer Gantry (AAN) 60. One, Two, Three 62. Irma la Douce (AA) 63. My Fair Lady (AA) 64. Inside Daisy Clover 65. The Fortune Cookie 66. Thoroughly Modern Millie (AAN) 67. The Music Lovers 71. Jesus Christ Superstar (AAN) 73. The Elephant Man 80. Six Weeks 82. Romeo and Juliet 90, etc.

Previn, Steve (1925–1993).
American director and production executive, a former editor. The brother of André Previn, he was based in Europe from the mid-50s.
AS DIRECTOR: Almost Angels 62. Escapade in Florence 62. Waltz King 63, etc.

Prévost, Françoise (1929–1997).
French leading actress in international films. The daughter of writer Jean Prévost, she made her stage debut at the age of 18. She fell ill with cancer in the 70s, writing a book about her experience with the illness.
Virgile 53. Le Bel Age 58. The Enemy General (US) 60. Payroll (GB) 61. Bon Voyage! (US) 63. Paris Nous Appartient 63. The Condemned of Altona 63. Galia 66. Spirits of the Dead 67. Italian Secret Service 67. Le Belve 71. The Pink Telephone 75. Bonjour Amour 78. L'Amour Nu (w) 80, many others.

Prévost, Marie (1893–1937) (Marie Bickford Dunn).
Anglo-French leading lady of American silent films.
East Lynne with Variations 20. Her Night of Nights 22. The Marriage Circle 24. Red Lights 24. The Loves of Camille 25. Up in Mabel's Room 26. Getting Gertie's Garter 27. Lady of Leisure 28. Side Show 30. Sporting Blood 31. Parole Girl 33. Tango (last film) 36, etc.

Price, Alan (1942–).
British composer, singer and pianist, a founder-member of the 60s rock band The Animals.
Oh, Lucky Man 73. Alfie Darling (& a) 75. Britannia Hospital 82. The Whales of August 87.

Price, Dennis (1915–1973) (Dennistoun Franklyn John Rose-Price).
British light leading man and latterly equally light character actor; on stage from 1937.
■ No Parking (debut) 37. A Canterbury Tale 43. *A Place of One's Own* 44. The Echo Murders 45. Caravan 46. The Magic Bow 46. Hungry Hill 46. Dear Murderer 47. Jassy 47. *Holiday Camp* 47. Master of Bankdam 47. The White Unicorn 47. Easy Money 47. Snowbound 48. Good Time Girl 48. *The Bad Lord Byron* 48. *Kind Hearts and Coronets* (his best role) 49. The Lost People 49. Helter Skelter 49. The Dancing Years 50. Murder Without Crime 50. The Adventurers 50. The Magic Box 51. Lady Godiva Rides Again 51. The House in the Square 51. Song of Paris 52. The Tall Headlines 52. The Intruder 53. Noose for a Lady 53. Murder at 3 a.m. 53. Time is my Enemy 54. For Better For Worse 54. Eight Witnesses 54. That Lady 55. Oh Rosalinda 55. *Private's Progress* 55. Charley Moon 56. Port Afrique 56. A Touch of the Sun 56. Fortune is a Woman 57. *The Naked Truth* 57. Danger Within 58. Hello London 58. *I'm All Right, Jack* 59. Don't Panic Chaps 59. Dark as the Night (US) 59. School for Scoundrels 60. *Tunes of Glory* 60. Oscar Wilde 60. Piccadilly Third Stop 60. The Millionairess 60. The Pure Hell of St Trinian's 60. No Love for Johnnie 61. The Rebel 61. Five Golden Hours 61. Double Bunk 61. Watch it, Sailor 61. *Victim* 61. What A Carve Up 61. Go to Blazes 62. Play it Cool 62. Behave Yourself 62. The Pot Carriers 62. The Amorous Prawn 62. Kill or Cure 62. The Wrong Arm of the Law 62. The Cool Mikado 63. The VIPs 63. The Cracksman 63. Doctor in Distress 63. *Tamahine* 63. The Comedy Man 63. A Jolly Bad Fellow 63. The Horror of it All 64. Murder Most Foul 64. The Earth Dies Screaming 64. The Curse of Simba 65. A High Wind in Jamaica 65. Ten Little Indians 65. Just Like a Woman 66. Jules Verne's Rocket to the Moon 67. The Haunted House of Horror 69. The Magic Christian 69. She Will She Won't 70. The Horror of Frankenstein 70. The Rise and Rise of Michael Rimmer 70. Twins of Evil 71. Pulp 72. Alice's Adventures in Wonderland 72. Venus in Furs 72. Go for a Take 72. That's Your Funeral 72. The Adventures of Barry Mackenzie 72. Horror Hospital 73. Theatre of Blood 73.
TV series: *The World of Wooster* (as Jeeves) 65–68.

❝ I am a second-rate feature actor. I am not a star and never was. I lack the essential spark. – *D.P.*

Price, Nancy (1880–1970) (Lillian Maude).
Dominant British character actress with long stage experience, especially remembered as Grandma in *Whiteoaks*. Also an indefatigable traveller, naturalist and semi-mystic. Born in Kinver, Worcestershire, she was on stage from 1899. In the 30s she founded The Peoples' National Theatre company and ran it for 10 years, producing 80 plays on the London stage. She was also the author of 13 books and edited *The People's Theatre* magazine. Married actor Charles Maude (1882–1943), who was the grandson of the Swedish soprano Jenny Lind; their daughter was actress and dancer Joan MAUDE.
Autobiography: 1935, *Shadows on the Hill.*
The Lyons Mail 16. Comin' thro' the Rye 23. Bonnie Prince Charlie 24. The Price of Divorce 28. The Speckled Band 31. Down Our Street 32. The Crucifix 34. The Stars Look Down 39. Secret Mission 42. Madonna of the Seven Moons 44. I Live in Grosvenor Square 45. I Know Where I'm Going 45. Carnival 46. The Master of Bankdam 47. The Three Weird Sisters 48. Mandy 52. The Naked Earth 55, etc.

Price, Richard (1949–).
American screenwriter and novelist.
Bloodbrothers (oa) 78. The Wanderers (oa) 79. Streets of Gold 86. The Color of Money (AAN) 86. New York Stories (co-w) 89. Sea of Love 89. Night and the City 92. Mad Dog and Glory 93. Kiss of Death 95. Clockers (co-w, oa) 95. Ransom (co-w) 96, etc.

Price, Vincent (1911–1993).
Tall, gentle-voiced American character actor, lately typed in horror films. He studied art history at Yale and took a master's degree in fine arts at the University of London. He made his stage debut in London in 1935. Married actress Coral Browne, his third wife, in 1974.
Autobiography: 1959, *I Like What I Know*.
Biography: 1976, *Vincent Price Unmasked* by J. R. Parish and Steven Whitney.
Service de Luxe (debut) 38. Elizabeth and Essex 39. Green Hell 40. *Tower of London* (as Clarence) 40. Brigham Young 40. The Song of Bernadette 43. The Keys of the Kingdom 44. Laura (AAN) 44. Wilson 44. Czarina 45. *Dragonwyck* 46. Shock 46. The Long Night 47. The Three Musketeers 49. Champagne for Caesar 49. *His Kind of Woman* 51. *House of Wax* 53. The Mad Magician 54. The Ten Commandments 56. *The Story of Mankind* 57. The Fly 58. The Bat 59. The House on Haunted Hill 60. *The Fall of the House of Usher* 61. The Pit and the Pendulum 61. Tales of Terror 62. *The Raven* 63. A Comedy of Terrors 63. *The Tomb of Ligeia* 64. City under the Sea 65. Dr Goldfoot and the Sex Machine 65. House of a Thousand Dolls 67. The Oblong Box 69. Scream and Scream Again 69. Cry of the Banshee 70. The Abominable Dr Phibes 71. Dr Phibes Rises Again 72. Theatre of Blood 73. Madhouse 73. Journey into Fear 75. Scavenger Hunt 79. The Monster Club 81. The House of Long Shadows 83. Bloodbath at the House of Death 84. The Whales of August 87. Dead Heat 88. Backtrack/Catchfire 89. Edward Scissorhands 90. Arabian Knight (voice) 95, etc.
TV series: Time Express 79.

❝ I sometimes feel that I'm impersonating the dark unconscious of the whole human race. I know this sounds sick, but I love it. – *V.P.*
Doing a religious picture is a boring thing because everybody is on their best behaviour – hoping for the keys to the kingdom, I guess. – *V.P.*
~Price's was the voice on Michael Jackson's phenomenally successful 1983 video 'Thriller'.

Priestley, J. B. (1894–1984).
Prolific British novelist. There have been film versions of *The Good Companions*, *Benighted* (The Old Dark House), *Let the People Sing*, and also of his plays *Dangerous Corner*, *Laburnum Grove*, *When We Are Married* and *An Inspector Calls*. His autobiographical *Midnight on the Desert* (1937) says much about Hollywood.
Biography: 1997, *Priestley* by Judith Cook.

Priestley, Jack (1927–1993).
American cinematographer.
Naked City (TV) 61–62. The Subject Was Roses 68. No Way to Treat a Lady 68. Stiletto 69. Where's Poppa 70. The First Deadly Sin 80. Lady Blue (TV) 85. A Man Called Hawk (TV) 89. The Trials of Rosie O'Neill (TV) 92, etc.

Priestley, Jason (1969–).
Canadian-born actor in Hollywood, best known for his role as Brandon Walsh in the TV series *Beverly Hills 90210*. Born in Vancouver, he was a child actor; he has worked as an executive producer on *Beverly Hills 90210* and also directed some episodes.
Nowhere to Run 88. Calendar Girl 93. Tombstone 94. Coldblooded 95. Love and Death in Long Island 97, etc.
TV series: Sister Kate 89–90. Beverly Hills 90210 90– .

❝ The great thing about Hollywood is there's always a bigger star than you. – *J.P.*

Priestley, Tom (1932–).
British editor.
Deliverance (AAN) 72. The Great Gatsby 74. Voyage of the Damned 76. Times Square 80. Another Time, Another Place 84. Dream One 84. 1984 84. The Kitchen Toto 88. White Mischief 88. Lord of the Flies 90. Dr Jekyll and Ms Hyde 95, etc.

Priggen, Norman (1924–).
British producer, with Ealing Studios from 1939, later independent.
The Professionals 61. Payroll 61. The Servant 64. Secret Ceremony (co-p) 68. Tales That Witness Madness 73. Freddie as F.R.0.7. 92, etc.

Prima, Louis (1911–1978).
Exuberant Italian-American jazz trumpeter, singer and composer, frequently in films as himself. Born in New Orleans and much influenced by Louis ARMSTRONG, he led his own band before working in Hollywood, and as a Las Vegas cabaret act with his fourth wife, singer Keely Smith (1952–61). He wrote the 1937 Benny GOODMAN hit 'Sing, Sing, Sing', and provided the voice for the orang-utan King Louis in Disney's animated *Jungle Book* 67. The plot of Stanley TUCCI and Campbell SCOTT's *Big Night* 96 turns on a visit by Prima, at the height of his celebrity, to a struggling Italian restaurant. He died after more than two years in a coma following brain surgery.
Swing It (short) 36. Rhythm on the Range 36. Manhattan Merry-Go-Round 37. You Can't Have Everything 37. Start Cheering 38. Rose of Washington Square 39. The Benny Goodman Story 55. Senior Prom 58. Hey Boy! Hey Girl! 59. Twist All Night 61. Women by Night (It.) 62. Rafferty and the Gold Dust Twins 75, etc.

Primus, Barry (1938–).
American director, screenwriter and actor.
AS ACTOR: The Brotherhood 68. Puzzle of a Downfall Child 70. Von Richtofen and Brown 71. Been Down So Long It Looks Like Up to Me 71. Gravy Train 74. New York, New York 77. Avalanche 78. The Rose 79. Night Games 80. Heartland 81. Absence of Malice 81. Brotherly Love 85. Talking Walls 85. Jake Speed 86. The Stranger 87. Big Business 88. Cannibal Women in the Avocado Jungle of Death 89. Torn Apart 89. Guilty by Suspicion 91. Night and the City 92. Flipping 96, etc.
AS WRITER AND DIRECTOR: The Mistress 92.
TV series: Cagney & Lacey (a) 84–85.

Prince (1958–) (Prince Rogers Nelson).
American rock musician, composer and director of films built around his life and performances.
Purple Rain (AAm) 84. Under the Cherry Moon 86. Sign o' the Times (concert) 87. Graffiti Bridge 90.

Prince, Harold (1924–).
American stage producer who dabbles in films.
■ Something for Everyone 70. A Little Night Music 77. Sweeney Todd, the Demon Barber of Fleet Street (filmed theatre performance) 84.

Prince, Louis Aimé Augustin Le (1842–1890?).
French inventor, working in England, who may well have been the inventor of the first cine camera. He registered patents in England and America in 1888. In 1890, as he was preparing for a trip to America to demonstrate his camera, he boarded a train for Paris at Dijon and was never seen again.
Biography: 1990, *The Missing Reel* by Christopher Rawlence.

Prince, William (1913–1996).
American stage leading man who was less successful in films.
Destination Tokyo 44. Pillow to Post 46. Dead Reckoning 47. Carnegie Hall 48. Cyrano de Bergerac 51. The Vagabond King 55. Macabre 58. The Stepford Wives 75. Family Plot 76. The Gauntlet 77. Bronco Billy 80. Love and Money 82. Movers and Shakers 84. Spies Like Us 85. Spontaneous Combustion 90. The Taking of Beverly Hills 91. The Paper 94, etc.

Principal, Victoria (1945–).
American leading lady.
The Life and Times of Judge Roy Bean 72. The Naked Ape 73. Earthquake 74. I Will, I Will, for Now 76. Vigilante Force 76. The Night They Took Miss Beautiful (TV) 77. Fantasy Island (TV) 77. Mistress (TV) 87. Naked Lie (TV) 89. Blind Witness (TV) 89. Sparks: The Price of Passion (TV) 90, etc.
TV series: Dallas 80–91.

Prine, Andrew (1936–).
American leading man.
The Miracle Worker 62. Company of Cowards 64. The Devil's Brigade 68. Bandolero 68. A Time for Giving 69. One Little Indian 73. Grizzly 76. Amityville II: The Possession 82. Eliminators 86. Gettysburg 93. Deadly Exposure 93. Serial Killer 95. Without Evidence 96, etc.
TV series: The Wide Country 62–63. The Road West 66–67. W.E.B. 78. V: The Final Battle 84, etc.

Pringle, Aileen (1895–1989) (Aileen Bisbee).
American actress of the silent screen, best remembered for her performance in Elinor Glyn's *Three Weeks* 24.
Redhead 19. The Christian 23. Wife of a Centaur 24. Dance Madness 24. Adam and Evil 27. Soldiers and Women 30. Convicted 32. Jane Eyre 33. Piccadilly Jim 36. Nothing Sacred 37. The Girl from Nowhere 39. Happy Land 43, etc.

Pringle, Bryan (1935–).
British character actor of stage and TV.
Saturday Night and Sunday Morning 60. The Boy Friend 71. Haunted Honeymoon 86. Consuming Passions 88. Drowning by Numbers 88. Getting It Right 89. American Friends 91. P. G. Wodehouse's Heavy Weather (TV) 95. The Steal 95, etc.
TV series: Three Rousing Tinkles 66. The Dustbinmen 69–70. Room Service 79. The Management 88. Once upon a Time in the North 94.

Pringle, Ian (1953–).
Australian director, screenwriter and producer, also of documentaries.
Wronsky (co-w, p, d) 80. The Plains of Heaven 82. Celia (p) 90. Romper Stomper (p) 92. Isabelle Eberhardt 92, etc.

Printemps, Yvonne (1894–1977) (Yvonne Wigniolle).
French musical comedy star in occasional films. She was married to actors Sacha Guitry and Pierre Fresnay.
La Dame aux Camélias 34. The Paris Waltz 49. Voyage to America 52, etc.

Prinz, Le Roy (1895–1983).
American choreographer who after adventurous early life came to Hollywood and worked on many Paramount and Warner films.
The Sign of the Cross 32. The 'Road' films 39–42. Yankee Doodle Dandy 42. Night and Day 46. The Ten Commandments 56. South Pacific 58, many others. Directed short subject *A Boy and His Dog* (AA) 48.

Prinze, Freddy, Jnr (1976–).
American actor, the son of television comedian Freddie Prinze (1954–1977). Born in Albuquerque, New Mexico, he moved to Los Angeles in the mid-90s and began on television.
To Gillian on Her 37th Birthday 96. The House of Yes 97. I Know What You Did Last Summer 97. I Still Know What You Did Last Summer 98.

Prochnow, Jürgen (1941–).
German leading actor, now in American films.
The Consequence/Die Konsequenz 77. Zoff 81. The Lost Honour of Katharina Blum/Die Verlorene Ehre de Katharina Blum 75. The Boat/Das Boot 81. Comeback 82. The Keep 83. Dune 84. Forbidden (TV) 85. Killing Cars 85. Terminus 86. Beverly Hills Cop II 87. The Seventh Sign 88. A Dry White Season 89. The Fourth War 90. The Man Inside 90. Robin Hood 90. Hurricane Smith 90. Prince of Tides 91. Red Hot 92. Twin Peaks: Fire Walk with Me 92. The Last Border 93. Body of Evidence 93. The Fire Next Time (TV) 93. In the Mouth of Madness 94. Guns of Honor (TV) 94. Judge Dredd 95. The English Patient 96. Human Bomb 97. DNA 97. The Replacement Killers 98, etc.

Proctor, Elaine (1960–).
South African director and screenwriter, a former actress. Born in Johannesburg, she studied at the National Film and Television School in Britain.
On the Wire (wd) 90. Friends (wd) 93.

producer.

Proft, Pat (1947–).
American writer, actor and producer, from television.
Modern Problems (a, w) 81. Bachelor Party (a, co-w) 84. Police Academy (co-w) 84. Moving Violations (co-w) 85. Real Genius (co-w) 85. The Naked Gun (co-w) 88. Lucky Stiff (w) 89. The Naked Gun 2½: The Smell of Fear (co-w) 91. Hot Shots (p, co-w) 91. Brain Donors (w) 92. Hot Shots! Part Deux (co-w) 93. Naked Gun 33 : The Final Insult (co-w) 94. High School High (co-w) 96. Mr Magoo (co-w) 97. Wrongfully Accused (p, wd) 98, etc.

Prokoviev, Sergei (1891–1953).
Russian composer whose main film scores were *Alexander Nevsky* 39, *Lermontov* 43 and *Ivan the Terrible* 42 and 46.

Prosky, Robert (1931–) (Robert Porzuczek).
American actor.
Thief 81. The Keep 83. The Lords of Discipline 83. The Natural 84. Christine 84. Big Shots 87. Things Change 88. Funny about Love 90. Green Card 90. Hoffa 92. Far and Away 92. Last Action Hero 93. Rudy 93. Mrs Doubtfire 93. Miracle on 34th Street 94. The Scarlet Letter 95. Dead Man Walking 95. The Chamber 96. Mad City 97, etc.
TV series: Hill Street Blues 85–87. Lifestories (narrator) 90.

Prouty, Jed (1879–1956).
American character actor with stage experience, in films from the mid-20s. Best remembered as father of *The Jones Family;* he appeared in over a dozen episodes of this domestic comedy series between 1935 and 1940.
Broadway Melody 28. George White's Scandals 35. The Texas Rangers 36. Roar of the Press 41. Mug Town 43. Guilty Bystander 49, many others.

Prouty, Olive Higgins (1882–1974).
American novelist, best known to filmgoers for *Now Voyager* and *Stella Dallas*.

Provine, Dorothy (1937–).
American leading lady who became well known as nightclub entertainer in TV series *The Roaring Twenties;* also in *The Alaskans* 59.
The Bonnie Parker Story 58. Wall of Noise 63. It's a Mad Mad Mad Mad World 63. Good Neighbour Sam 64. That Darn Cat 65. The Great Race 65. One Spy Too Many 66. Kiss the Girls and Make Them Die 66. Who's Minding the Mint? 67, etc.

Prowse, Juliet (1937–1996).
South African leading lady, in Hollywood from 1958, at first as dancer.
Can Can 59. G.I. Blues 60. The Fiercest Heart 61. The Right Approach 61. The Second Time Around 61. Run For Your Wife 66, etc.
TV series: *Meet Mona McCluskey* 65.

Proyas, Alex (1961–).
Australian director, born in Alexandria, Egypt, who moved to Sydney as an infant. Now working in Hollywood.
Spirits of the Air, Gremlins of the Clouds (& p, w) 89. The Crow (US) 94. Dark City (US) 98, etc.

Pryce, Jonathan (1947–).
Saturnine British leading actor.
Voyage of the Damned 76. Breaking Glass 80. Loophole 80. The Day Christ Died (TV) 80. Praying Mantis (TV) 82. The Ploughman's Lunch 83. Something Wicked This Way Comes 83. Brazil 85. The Doctor and the Devils 86. Haunted Honeymoon 86. Jumping Jack Flash 87. Consuming Passions 88. Adventures of Baron Munchausen 89. The Rachel Papers 89. Glengarry Glen Ross 92. Barbarians at the Gate (TV) 93. Mr Wroe's Virgins (TV) 93. The Age of Innocence 93. Deadly Advice 94. A Business Affair 94. Great Moments in Aviation 94. Shopping 94. *Carrington* 95. Evita 96. Tomorrow Never Dies 97. Regeneration 97. David (TV) 97. Ronin 98, etc.

Pryor, Nicholas (1935–) (Nicholas David Probst).
American actor who sometimes plays weaklings.
The Way We Live Now 70. Man on a Swing 74. The Happy Hooker 75. Smile 75. Fear on Trial (TV) 75. *Washington behind Closed Doors* (TV) 77. The Life and Assassination of the Kingfish (TV) 77. Rainbow (TV) 78. Damien: Omen II 78. The Fish That Saved Pittsburgh 79. The Formula 80. Airplane 80. The Falcon and the Snowman 84. The Believers 86. Morgan Stewart's Coming Home 87. Less than Zero 87. Brain Dead 89. Nightbreaker (TV) 89. Pacific Heights 90. Hoffa 92. Hail Caesar 94, etc.
TV series: The Bronx Zoo 87–88.

Pryor, Richard (1940–).
American nightclub comedian and writer whose edgy and often aggressive humour made him a star, and who then teamed with Gene Wilder for a series of comedies that outstayed their initial welcome. His career declined in the 80s: he set himself on fire while free-basing cocaine and then developed multiple sclerosis which confined him to a wheelchair.
■ The Busy Body 68. The Green Berets 68. Wild in the Streets 69. The Phynx 70. You've Got to Walk It Like You Talk It or You'll Lose that Beat 71. Dynamite Chicken 72. Lady Sings the Blues 72. Wattstax 73. The Mack 73. Hit 73. Some Call It Loving 73. Blazing Saddles (co-w only) 74. Uptown Saturday Night 74. Adios Amigo 75. The Bingo Long Allstars and Travelling Motor Kings 76. Car Wash 76. Silver Streak 76. Greased Lightning 77. Which Way Is Up 77. Blue Collar 78. The Wiz 78. California Suite 78. *Richard Pryor Live in Concert* 79. The Muppet Movie 79. In God We Trust 80. Stir Crazy 80. Wholly Moses 81. Bustin' Loose 81. Some Kind of Hero 82. The Toy 82. Superman III 83. Brewster's Millions 85. Jo Jo Dancer, Your Life is Calling 85. Critical Condition 87. Moving 88. Harlem Nights 89. See No Evil, Hear No Evil 89. Look Who's Talking Too (voice) 90. Another You 91. Lost Highway 96.
TV series: The Richard Pryor Show 77.

Pryor, Roger (1901–1974).
American leading man of minor movies, also stage and radio actor.
Moonlight and Pretzels 33. Belle of the Nineties 34. Ticket to Paradise 36. Money and the Woman 40. She Couldn't Say No 41, etc.

Przygodda, Peter (1941–).
German editor and occasional director, associated with the films of Wim Wenders.
Summer in the City 70. The Goalkeeper's Fear of the Penalty Kick/Die Angst des Tormanns beim Elfmeter 71. Ludwig – Requiem for a Virgin King/ Ludwig – Requiem für einen Jungfräulichen König 72. Alice in the Cities/Alice in den Städten 73. Wrong Move/Falsche Bewegung 74. Kings of the Road/Im Lauf der Zeit 76. The Left-Handed Woman/Die Linkshändige Frau 77. The American Friend 77. Born for Diesel/Als Diesel Geboren (& wd) 79. Lightning over Water 80. Hammett 81. The State of Things/Der Stand der Dinge 82. The Man on the Wall/Der Mann auf der Mauer 83. Flight to Berlin 84. Paris, Texas 84. Wings of Desire/Der Himmel über Berlin 87. Deadline 87. Last Exit to Brooklyn 90. Until the End of the World/Bis ans Ende der Welt 91. Faraway, So Close!/In Weiter Ferne, So Nah 93. Arisha 94. Libson Story 95. The Deathmaker 95. The End of Violence 97, etc.

Pucholt, Vladimir (1942–).
Czechoslovakian actor, notably in Milos FORMAN's early films; he later became a doctor in England, before returning to the screen in the late 90s in a film by Vojtech JASNY.
Zalobnici 60. Black Peter/Cerny Petr 63. The Audition/Konkurs 63. Loves of a Blonde/Lasky Jedne Plavovlasky 65. Sign of the Virgin/Souhvezdi Panny 66. Malatesta (Ger.) 69. Return to Paradise Lost 99, etc.

Pudovkin, V. (Vsevolod) (1893–1953).
Russian film theorist, writer and actor. Best remembered as director.
Mother 26. *The End of St Petersburg* 27. *Storm over Asia* 28. The Deserter 33. General Suvorov 41, many others which have not travelled.

Puenzo, Luis (1946–).
Argentinian director and screenwriter, whose first attempt to direct a Hollywood film was a flop.
Lights of My Shoes 73. The Official Story/La Historia Oficial (AA) 85. Old Gringo 89. The Plague/La Peste 92, etc.

Puglia, Frank (1892–1975).
American character actor with vaudeville experience.
Viva Villa 34. Maisie 39. The Mark of Zorro 40. Jungle Book 42. Phantom of the Opera 43. Blood on the Sun 45. The Desert Hawk 50. The Burning Hills 56. Cry Tough 59. Say Goodbye Maggie Cole (TV) 72. Mr Ricco 75, many others.

Pullman, Bill (1954–).

Amiable American leading actor. Born in Hornell, New York, he studied at the State University of New York, the University of Massachusetts and the University of Montana and worked in several jobs, including that of a drama teacher, before becoming an actor.

Ruthless People 86. Spaceballs 87. Rocket Gibraltar 88. The Accidental Tourist 88. Cold Feet 89. Sibling Rivalry 90. Bright Angel 91. The Favor 91. Singles 91. Newsies/Newsboys 92. Sleepless in Seattle 93. Malice 93. Sommersby 93. The Favor 94. The Last Seduction 94. Wyatt Earp 94. While You Were Sleeping 95. Casper 95. Mr Wrong 96. Independence Day 96. Lost Highway 96. Mistrial (TV) 96. The End of Violence 97. Zero Effect 98. The Thin Red Line 98, etc.

Pulver, Lilo (Liselotte) (1929–).

Swiss-German leading lady.

A Time to Live and a Time to Die (US) 59. One, Two, Three (US) 61. A Global Affair (US) 63. La Religieuse (Fr.) 65. Le Jardinier d'Argentueil (Fr.) 66. Bread and Stones 79, etc.

Punch-McGregor, Angela (1953–).

Australian leading actress, from the theatre.

The Chant of Jimmy Blacksmith 78. Newsfront 78. The Island 80. The Best of Friends 82. We of the Never Never 82. Annie's Coming Out 84. A Test of Love 84. Double Deal 84. Delinquents 89. Spotswood 91. Terra Nova 98, etc.

Punsley, Bernard.

One of the original DEAD END KIDS on stage and screen who continued as a member of Universal's LITTLE TOUGH GUYS. He quit acting in the early 40s to become a doctor.

Purcell, Dick (1908–1944).

American leading man of second features.

Man Hunt 36. Navy Blues 37. Air Devils 38. Nancy Drew, Detective 39. King of the Zombies 41. Phantom Killer 42. The Mystery of the Thirteenth Guest 43. Timber Queen 44, etc.

Purcell, Gertrude.

American screenwriter, playwright and actress. Born in New York City and educated at Columbia University and Hunter College, New York, she worked in Hollywood from 1930.

Follow the Leader 30. The Royal Family of Broadway/Theatre Royal 30. The Girl Habit 31. Honor among Lovers 31. Night Mayor 32. Another Language 33. Child of Manhattan 33. Palooka 34. The Girl Friend 35. If You Could Only Cook 35. Make Way for a Lady 36. The Witness Chair 36. Music for Madame 37. Mother Carey's Chickens 38. Service de Luxe 38. The Lady and the Mob 39. Destry Rides Again 39. A Little Bit of Heaven 40. One Night in the Tropics 40. The Invisible Women 41. In Old California 42. Ice-Capades Revue 42. Follow the Boys 44. Paris Underground 45. Winter Wonderland 47. Three Husbands 50, etc.

Purcell, Noel (1900–1985).

Tall, usually bearded, Irish character actor and comedian.

Jimmy Boy 34. Blarney 38. Captain Boycott 47. The Blue Lagoon 48. Doctor in the House 53. Moby Dick 56. Watch Your Stern 60. Mutiny on the Bounty 62. Lord Jim 65. Arrivederci Baby 66. Where's Jack 69. The Mackintosh Man 73, many others.

TV series: The Buccaneer 58.

Purdell, Reginald (1896–1953) (R. Grasdorf).

British light character actor, mostly on stage and music hall.

Congress Dances 31. Q Planes 38. Many Thanks Mr Atkins 40. Pack Up Your Troubles 40. Variety Jubilee 43. We Dive at Dawn 43. 2000 Women 44. Holiday Camp 47. Captain Boycott 48, etc.

Purdom, Edmund (1924–).

British light leading man who in the 50s was given the full Hollywood treatment but failed to emerge as a star.

Titanic 53. The Student Prince 54. The Egyptian 54. The Prodigal 55. The King's Thief 55. The Cossacks 60. Herod the Great 60. Nights of Rasputin 61. The Comedy Man 63. Suleiman the Conqueror 63. The Beauty Jungle 64. The Yellow Rolls-Royce 64. The Man in the Golden Mask 69. The Black Corsair 69. Evil Fingers 72. Mr Scarface 76. Don't Open till Christmas (& d) 84. Fracchia vs Dracula 86, etc.

TV series: Sword of Freedom 57.

66 One of the symptoms of an approaching nervous breakdown is the belief that one's work is terribly important. – E.P.

Purl, Linda (1955–).

Snub-nosed American leading lady of the late 70s.

W. C. Fields and Me 76. Testimony of Two Men (TV) 77. The Flame is Love (TV) 79. Women at West Point (TV) 80. The Night the City Screamed (TV) 81. Visiting Hours 82. Pleasures (TV) 86. Viper 88. Web of Deceit (TV) 90. Body Language 92. Natural Causes 94, etc.

TV series: Happy Days 74–75. Beacon Hill 75. Happy Days 82–83. Matlock 86–87.

Purviance, Edna (1894–1958).

American leading lady of silent days.

A Night Out 15 (and other early Chaplin films including Easy Street, The Count, The Cure, The Adventurer, Shoulder Arms). Sunnyside 19. The Kid 21. The Pilgrim 23. A Woman of Paris 23. The Seagull 26. Limelight 52, many others.

Puttnam, David (1941–) (Lord Puttnam).

British producer and impresario who almost single-handedly raised the level of British film-making in the early 80s and was rewarded by a top Hollywood job which didn't last. He is the author of the 1997 book The Undeclared War, on the battle for cinematic supremacy between Europe and America. He was made a life peer by the Labour government in 1997.

Biographies: 1988, Enigma: David Puttnam by Andrew Yule. 1991, Out of Focus: David Puttnam in Hollywood by Charles Kipps.

Melody 71. That'll Be the Day 74. Mahler 74. Lisztomania 75. Bugsy Malone 76. The Duellists 77. Midnight Express 78. Chariots of Fire 80. Local Hero 82. The Killing Fields 84. The Mission (AAN) 86. Defence of the Realm 86. Memphis Belle 90. Meeting Venus 91. Being Human 94. War of the Buttons 94. The Confessional/Le Confessionale 95. My Life So Far 97, many others.

66 Nothing good will happen while there are still cinemas that are shit heaps and critics who only like popular films when they are thirty years old. – D.P., 1975

I'm not afraid to fail, providing I fail honourably. The only thing I don't want is to end up being an irrelevant 70-year-old egomaniac. – D.P.

While our technical ability to communicate grows at an exponential rate, there seems no corresponding increase in our ability to understand each other. – D.P.

In his parting comments at Columbia 10 years

ago, Puttnam told his staff, 'I am neither St George nor Don Quixote. I am just a European motion picture producer who crossed the Atlanatic to ask a few questions.' Well, he asked his questions. The answer was: 'Get lost.'
– Variety, 1997

Puzo, Mario (1920–).

American novelist whose The Godfather in 1969 was a commercial sensation and led to the equally popular film. Film rights to his 1996 novel The Last Don were sold for $2m.

■ The Godfather (co-w) (AA) 72. The Godfather Part II (co-w) (AA) 74. Earthquake (co-w) 74. Superman (co-w) 78. Superman II (co-w) 80. The Cotton Club (co-story) 84. The Godfather Part III (co-w) 90. Christopher Columbus: The Discovery 92.

Pyle, Denver (1920–1997).

American character actor, mostly in TV and big-screen westerns.

The Man from Colorado 48. To Hell and Back 55. Shenandoah 65. Bonnie and Clyde 67. Five Card Stud 68. Something Big 71. Cahill 73. Escape to Witch Mountain 75. Guardian of the Wilderness 77. Welcome to L.A. 77. Maverick 94, etc.

TV series: Wyatt Earp 56–59. The Doris Day Show 68–69. The Dukes of Hazzard 79–85.

Pyriev, Ivan (1901–1968).

Russian director.

The Functionary 30. The Party Card 36. Tractor Drivers 39. They Met in Moscow 41. Secretary of the District Committee 42. Song of Siberia 47. Kuban Cossacks 49. Test of Fidelity 54. The Idiot 58. White Nights 60. Our Mutual Friend 61. Light of a Distant Star 65. The Brothers Karamazov 68, etc.

Pyun, Albert.

American director and screenwriter of unmemorable fantasy and action films.

The Sword and the Sorcerer 82. Radioactive Dreams 86. Dangerously Close 86. Vicious Lips 87. Down Twisted/The Treasure of San Lucas 87. Alien from L.A. (w) 88. Cyborg 89. Spiderman 89. Kickboxer II 90. Arcade 92. Deceit 92. Knights (wd) 92. Nemesis 93. Brain Smasher 93. Spitfire 94. Nemesis 2: Nebula 94. Heatseeker 95. Omega Doom 96. Nemesis 3: Time Lapse 96. Blast 96. Adrenalin: Fear the Rush 96. Mean Guns 96, etc.

Q

Qissi, Michel.
Belgian tough guy in, and occasional director of, action movies, usually as the baddie.
Bloodsport 88. Kickboxer (as Tong Po) 89. Kickboxer 2: The Road Back 90. A.W.O.L./Lionheart 90. Bloodmatch 91. To the Death 91. Backlash/Terminator Woman (d) 93, etc.

Quaid, Dennis (1955–).
American actor, brother of Randy Quaid; also a musician. Married actress Meg RYAN.
Crazy Mama 75. Seniors 77. Breaking Away 78. The Long Riders 80. All Night Long 81. Caveman 81. The Night the Lights Went Out in Georgia 81. Jaws 3D 83. Tough Enough 83. The Right Stuff 83. Dreamscape 84. Enemy Mine 85. The Big Easy 86. Innerspace 87. Suspect 87. D.O.A. 88. Everybody's All-American/When I Fall in Love 88. Great Balls of Fire 89. Postcards from the Edge 90. Come See the Paradise 90. Wilder Napalm 93. Flesh and Bone 93. Undercover Blues 93. Wyatt Earp 94. Something to Talk About 95. Dragonheart 96. Switchback 97. Everything that Rises (& d) (TV) 98. The Parent Trap 98. Playing by Heart 98, etc.

Quaid, Randy (1953–).
American actor who has been seen in gangling, awkward roles.
The Last Picture Show 71. What's Up, Doc? 72. The Last Detail (AAN) 73. Lolly Madonna XXX 73. Paper Moon 73. Breakout 75. The Apprenticeship of Duddy Kravitz 75. The Missouri Breaks 76. Bound for Glory 76. The Choirboys 77. Midnight Express 78. The Raid on Coffeyville (TV) 79. Foxes 80. The Long Riders 80. Guyana Tragedy (TV) 80. Heartbeeps 81. National Lampoon's Vacation 83. Fool for Love 85. The Wraith 86. L.B.J.: The Early Years (TV) 87. No Man's Land 87. Moving 88. Caddyshack II 88. Evil in Clear River (TV) 88. Parents 89. Out Cold 89. Cold Dog Soup 89. Bloodhounds of Broadway 89. National Lampoon's Christmas Vacation 89. Martians Go Home 90. Days of Thunder 90. Quick Change 90. Texasville 90. Murder in the Heartland (TV) 93. Frankenstein (TV) 93. Freaked 93. The Paper 94. Major League II 94. Next Door (TV) 94. Curse of the Starving Class 94. Bye Bye, Love 95. Kingpin 96. Last Dance 96. Independence Day 96. Get on the Bus 96. Hard Rain 97. Bug Buster 98, etc.
TV series: Saturday Night Live 85–86. Davis Rules 90–92.

Qualen, John (1899–1987) (John Mandt Kvalen).
Canadian-born Norwegian character actor, in Hollywood from the 30s playing amiably ineffectual foreign types.
Arrowsmith (debut) 32. Black Fury 35. Seventh Heaven 37. *The Grapes of Wrath* 40. Out of the Fog 41. *All that Money Can Buy* 41. Jungle Book 42. Casablanca 42. Fairy Tale Murder 45. Adventure 46. The Fugitive 48. The Big Steal 49. Hans Christian Andersen 52. The High and the Mighty 54. The Searchers 56. Two Rode Together 60. The Man Who Shot Liberty Valance 62. The Prize 63. The Seven Faces of Dr Lao 64. Cheyenne Autumn 64. The Sons of Katie Elder 65. A Big Hand for the Little Lady 66. Firecreek 67, many others.

Quan, Ke Huy (1971–) (aka Jonathan Ke Quan).
Vietnamese-born child actor, in America from the age of six.
Indiana Jones and the Temple of Doom 84. The Goonies 85. Breathing Fire 91, etc.
TV series: Together We Stand 86.

Quantrill, Charles Clarke (1837–1865).
American guerrilla leader, the scourge of Missouri and a figure in many westerns.

Quaranta, Gianni (1943–).
Italian production designer.
La Traviata (co-pd) 83. A Room with a View (co-pd) 86. Otello 86. Dancers 87. Magdalene 89. The Comfort of Strangers 90. Farinelli/Farinelli the Castrato 95, etc.

Quarry, Robert (1923–).
American character actor who bade fair to be the horror man of the 70s.
A Kiss before Dying 56. Count Yorga Vampire 69. The Return of Count Yorga 71. Dr Phibes Rises Again 72. The Revenge of Dr Death 73. The Midnight Man 73. Rollercoaster 77. Phantom Empire 87. Warlords 88. Alienator 89. Spirits 90. Evil Spirits 91. Teenage Exorcist 93, etc.

Quay, Stephen and Timothy (1947–) (aka Brothers Quay).
American-born twin brothers and directors who came to Britain in the late 60s. They began with shorts, using stop-animation, and rock videos. Their work includes designs for opera, ballet and theatre. Their first full-length feature, using live actors, was *Institute Benjamenta* 95.

Quayle, Anna (1937–).
British comedienne.
Drop Dead Darling 67. Smashing Time 67. Chitty Chitty Bang Bang 68. Up the Chastity Belt 71. The Seven Per Cent Solution 76, etc.

Quayle, Sir Anthony (1913–1989).
Distinguished British stage actor and director, in occasional films as actor. He studied at RADA and was on stage from 1931, becoming Director of the Shakespeare Memorial Theatre at Stratford-upon-Avon 1948–56, playing many classical roles. His second wife was actress Dorothy HYSON.
Autobiography: *A Time to Heal.*
■ Hamlet 48. Saraband for Dead Lovers 48. Oh Rosalinda 55. The Battle of the River Plate 56. No Time for Tears 57. The Wrong Man (US) 57. Woman in a Dressing-Gown 57. The Man Who Wouldn't Talk 58. *Ice Cold in Alex* 58. Serious Charge 59. Tarzan's Greatest Adventure 59. The Challenge 60. The Guns of Navarone 61. Lawrence of Arabia 62. HMS Defiant 62. The Fall of the Roman Empire 64. East of Sudan 64. Operation Crossbow 64. The Poppy is also a Flower (TV) 64. A Study in Terror 65. Misunderstood 67. Mackenna's Gold 68. Before Winter Comes 69. Anne of the Thousand Days (AAN) 70. Everything You Always Wanted to Know About Sex 72. A Bequest to the Nation 73. Jarrett (TV) 73. QB VII (TV) 74. The Tamarind Seed 74. Great Expectations (TV) 75. 21 Hours at Munich (TV) 76. Moses (TV) 76. The Eagle Has Landed 76. Holocaust 2000 77. Murder by Decree 79. Masada (TV) 80. The Manions of America (TV) 81. Dial M for Murder (TV) 81. The Last Days of Pompeii (TV) 84. Lace (TV) 84. The Key to Rebecca (TV) 85. The Bourne Identity 88. The Legend of the Holy Drinker 88. Magdalene 89. Confessional 89. King of the Wind 89.
TV series: Strange Report 68.
❝ A really lovely man, untouched by any of the bitterness, or deviousness, which sometimes characterises people who have run great companies. – *Robert Stephens*

Questel, Mae (1908–1998).
American actress best known for providing the voices for cartoon characters Betty Boop 1932–39 and, in the Popeye cartoons, Olive Oyl 1933–67. She also made an impact as Woody Allen's ghostly mother in the sky in *New York Stories.*
A Majority of One 62. It's Only Money 62. Funny Girl 68. Move 70. National Lampoon's Christmas Vacation 89, etc.

Quick, Diana (1946–).
British leading lady.
Nicholas and Alexandra 71. A Private Enterprise 71. The Odd Job 78. The Duellists 78. The Big Sleep 78. The Three Hostages (TV) 78. *Brideshead Revisited* (TV) 81. Phantom of the Opera (TV) 83. Ordeal by Innocence 85. Wilt/The Misadventures of Mr Wilt 89. Nostradamus 94. Rasputin (TV) 96, etc.

Quigley, Linnea (1959–).
American actress in low-budget horror movies who has become a minor cult figure following her appearance in *The Return of the Living Dead*, dancing nearly naked in a cemetery.
Autobiography: 1991, *The Linnea Quigley Bio & Chainsaw Book.*
Stone Cold Dead 80. American Gigolo 80. Graduation Day 81. Cheech & Chong's Nice Dreams 81. The Black Room 81. Don't Go Near the Park 81. The Young Warriors 83. Cheech & Chong: Still Smokin' 83. Savage Streets 84. Silent Night, Deadly Night 84. Return of the Living Dead 85. Sorority Babes in the Slime Bowl-o-rama 87. Creepozoids 87. Hollywood Chainsaw Hookers 88. Night of the Demons 88. Vice Academy 88. Nightmare on Elm Street 4: The Dream Master 88. Assault of the Party Nerds 89. Witch Trap 89. Murder Weapon 90. Virgin High 91. Rock 'n' Roll Detective 92. Beach Babes from Beyond 93. Bachelor Jamboree 94. Pumpkinhead 2: Blood Wings 94. Jack-O 95. Assault of the Party Nerds 2: Heavy Petting Detective 95, etc.

Quillan, Eddie (1907–1990).
Bouncy, beaming American comic actor, in Hollywood from 20s.
The Godless Girl 26. Big Money 30. *Mutiny on the Bounty* 35. Young Mr Lincoln 39. *The Grapes of Wrath* 40. Dark Streets of Cairo 40. Flying Blind 41. Sideshow 50. Brigadoon 54. The Ghost and Mr Chicken 66, etc; latterly on TV.
TV series: Valentine's Day 64–65. Julia 68–71. Hell Town 85.

Quilley, Denis (1927–).
British leading actor, mostly on stage.
Anne of the Thousand Days 69. The Black Windmill 74. Murder on the Orient Express 74. Clayhanger (TV) 76. Masada (TV) 81. *Evil Under the Sun* 81. *Privates on Parade* 83. Memed My Hawk 84. Foreign Body 87. Mister Johnson 90. Sparrow/Storia di una Capinera 93, etc.

Quimby, Fred (1886–1965).
American producer, head of MGM's short subjects department 1926–56. Specially known for development of Tom and Jerry cartoons.

Quine, Richard (1920–1989).
American director, former leading man (*The World Changes* 32 as juvenile; also *Babes on Broadway* 40, *My Sister Eileen* 41, *For Me and My Gal* 42, etc.). Committed suicide.
The Sunny Side of the Street 51. Drive a Crooked Road 54. Pushover 54. My Sister Eileen 55. *The Solid Gold Cadillac* 56. Operation Mad Ball 58. Bell, Book and Candle 58. The World of Suzie Wong 60. The Notorious Landlady 62. Paris When It Sizzles 64. How to Murder Your Wife 65. Oh Dad, Poor Dad 66. Hotel 67. A Talent for Loving 69. The Moonshine War 70. 'W' 74. The Prisoner of Zenda 79, etc.

Quinlan, Kathleen (1954–).
American leading lady of the late 70s.
Can Ellen Be Saved? (TV) 74. Where Have All the People Gone? (TV) 74. The Abduction of St Anne (TV) 75. Little Ladies of the Night (TV) 77. Airport 77 77. I Never Promised You a Rose Garden 77. The Promise 79. The Runner Stumbles 79. Sunday Lovers 80. Hanky Panky 82. Twilight Zone 83. Independence Day 83. Blackout 85. Warning Sign 86. Sunset 88. Clara's Heart 88. Trapped (TV) 89. The Operation (TV) 90. The Doors 91. Trial by Jury 94. Apollo 13 (AAN) 95. Zeus and Roxanne 96. Breakdown 96. Event Horizon 97. My Giant 98. A Civil Action 98, etc.

Quinn, Aidan (1959–).
Irish-American leading man. Married actress Elizabeth Bracco in 1987.
Reckless 84. Desperately Seeking Susan 85. An Early Frost (TV) 85. The Mission 86. Stakeout 87. Crusoe 88. Perfect Witness (TV) 89. The Handmaid's Tale 90. The Lemon Sisters 90. Avalon 90. At Play in the Fields of the Lord 91. The Playboys 92. Benny & Joon 93. Blink 94. Legends of the Fall 94. Mary Shelley's Frankenstein 94. The Stars Fell on Henrietta 95. Haunted 95. Looking for Richard 96. Michael Collins 96. Commandments 96. The Assignment 97. Practical Magic 98, etc.

Quinn, Anthony (1915–).
Mexican-born leading actor, in films since 1936, latterly noted for full-blooded performances. Married actress Katherine DeMille (1937–65).
Autobiographies: 1972, *The Original Sin.* 1995, *One Man Tango.*
Parole 36. The Plainsman 37. Ghost Breakers 40. Last Train from Madrid 37. Union Pacific 39. Blood and Sand 41. The Black Swan 42. The Ox-Bow Incident 43. Buffalo Bill 44. China Sky 45. Tycoon 48. The Brave Bulls 51. *Viva Zapata* (AA) 52. The World in His Arms 52. Ride Vaquero 53. Blowing Wild 54. The Long Wait 54. *La Strada* (It.) 54. Attila the Hun (It.) 54. Ulysses 55. *Lust for Life* (AA) 56. The Man from Del Rio 56. The Hunchback of Notre Dame 56. The River's Edge 57. Wild Is the Wind (AAN) 57. Hot Spell 58. Black Orchid 58. Last Train from Gun Hill 58. Warlock 59. The Buccaneer (d only) 59. Heller in Pink Tights 60. Savage Innocents 60. The Guns of Navarone 61. Lawrence of Arabia 62. Barabbas 62. Requiem for a Heavyweight 63. The Visit 63. *Zorba the Greek* (AAN) 64. A High Wind in Jamaica 65. Lost Command 66. The Happening 67. The Twenty-Fifth Hour 67. The Rover 67. *The Shoes of the Fisherman* 68. The Magus 68. The Secret of Santa Vittoria 69. R.P.M. 69. A Walk in the Spring Rain 69. Flap 70. Across 110th Street 72. The Marseilles Contract 74. The Don is Dead 75. Mohammed/The Message 76. Jesus of Nazareth (TV) 77. Tigers Don't Cry 77. The Inheritance 78. The Children of Sanchez 78. The Greek Tycoon 78. Caravans 78. The Passage 79. Lion of the Desert 80. The Salamander 80. High Risk 81. The Con Artists 81. Man of Passion 88. Richest Man in the World: The Aristotle Onassis Story (TV) 88. The Old Man and the Sea (TV) 90. Revenge 90. Ghosts Can't Do It 90. Only the Lonely 91. Jungle Fever 91. Mobsters 91. The Magician/Il Mago 93. The Last Action Hero 93. Somebody to Love 94.

A Walk in the Clouds 95. Seven Servants (Ger.) 96. Gotti (TV) 96, etc.

TV series: *The Man and the City* 71.

66 They said all I was good for was playing Indians. – A.Q.

'I want to impregnate every woman in the world', he once told me, though I didn't realize until later how literally he meant it. – *Ruth Warrick*

Quinn, Declan (1957–).
Irish-American cinematographer, the brother of Aidan QUINN.

The Kill-Off 89. Freddy's Dead: The Final Nightmare 91. Blood and Concrete 91. Cousin Bobby 92. The Ballad of Little Jo 93. Vanya on 42nd Street 94. Leaving Las Vegas 95. Carried Away 96. Kama Sutra 96. One Night Stand 97, etc.

Quinones, Adolfo:
see SHABBA-DOO.

Quintano, Gene (1947–).
American screenwriter, director and occasional actor.

Comin' at Ya! (a, co-w) 81. Treasure of the Four Crowns (a, co-w) 83. Making the Grade (w) 84. King Solomon's Mines (co-w) 85. Police Academy 3: Back in Training (w) 86. Allan Quatermain and the Lost City of Gold (w) 87. Police Academy 4: Citizens on Patrol (w) 87. For Better or for Worse (co-w, d) 89. Honeymoon Academy (wd) 90. Why Me? (d) 90. National Lampoon's Loaded Weapon I (co-w, d) 93. Operation Dumbo Drop (co-w) 95. A Dollar for the Dead 99, etc.

R

Raab, Kurt (1941–1988).
Czechoslovakian-born actor, screenwriter, production designer and director who began in avant-garde theatre; often in the films of Rainer Werner Fassbinder. He wrote a biography of Fassbinder in 1982. Died of AIDS.

Why Does Herr R. Run Amok?/Warum Läuft Herr R. Amok? 69. Whity 70. The Tenderness of Wolves/Zärtlichkeit der Wölfe (& w) 73. Fox and his Friends/Faustrecht der Freiheit 74. Satan's Brew/Satansbraten 76. Bolwieser/The Stationmaster's Wife 77. Boarding School 83. Parker 84, etc.

Rabal, Francisco (1926–).
Leading Spanish actor, a former electrician, in international films.

La Prodiga 45. The Mighty Crusades/Gerusalemme Liberata 57. Nazarin 59. Viridiana 61. The Eclipse/L'Eclisse 62. The Nun/La Religieuse 65. Belle de Jour 67. Diary of a Rebel/El Che Guevara 68. Ann and Eve 70. The Devil Is a Woman 75. Sorcerer 77. Corleone 78. City of the Walking Dead 80. The Stilts/Los Zancos 84. La Storia 86. A Time of Destiny 88. Barroco 89. Tie Me Up, Tie Me Down/¡Atame! 90. L'Autre 91. The Man Who Lost His Shadow 93. The Lame Pigeon 95. Divine 98. Water Easy Reach/En Dag til I Solen (Nor.) 98. Talk of Angels (US) 98, etc.

Rabe, David (1940–).
American dramatist and screenwriter. He married actress Jill Clayburgh in 1979.

I'm Dancing as Fast as I Can 82. Streamers 83. Casualties of War 89. State of Grace (co-w) 90. The Firm (co-w) 93. Hurlyburly (w, oa) 98, etc.

Rabe, Pamela.
Australian actress.

A Single Life 85. Sirens 94. Cosi 95. Vacant Possession 95. Lust and Revenge 96. The Well 97. Paradise Road 97, etc.

Rabier, Jean (1927–).
French cinematographer.

Cleo de 5 à 7 61. Ophelia 62. Landru 62. La Baie des Anges 63. Les Parapluies de Cherbourg 64. Le Bonheur 65. The Champagne Murders 66. Les Biches 68. Le Boucher 70. La Rupture 70. Blood Wedding/Les Noces Rouges 73. Folies Bourgeoises 76. Violette/Violette Nozière 77. Les Fantômes du Chapelier 82. Inspector Lavardin 86. Masques 87. Une Affaire de Femmes 88. Docteur M. 90. Quiet Days in Clichy 90. Madame Bovary 91, etc.

Rackin, Martin (1918–1976).
American screenwriter.

Air Raid Wardens 43. Riff Raff 47. Fighting Father Dunne 48. Three Secrets 50. The Enforcer 51. Sailor Beware 52. The Stooge 53. Santiago (& p) 56. The Helen Morgan Story (p only) 57. The Horse Soldiers (& p) 59. North to Alaska 60. Stagecoach (p only) 66. Rough Night in Jericho (p only) 67. The Revengers (p only) 72, etc.

Radclyffe, Sarah (1950–).
English producer, co-founder with Tim Bevan of the production company Working Title.

My Beautiful Laundrette 85. Sammy and Rosie Get Laid 87. Wish You Were Here 87. A World Apart 88. Paperhouse 88. Fools of Fortune 89. Chicago Joe and the Showgirl 90. Dakota Road 90. Robin Hood 91. Edward II 91. Second Best 94. Sirens 94. Bent 97. Les Misérables 98. Cousin Bette 98, etc.

Radd, Ronald (1924–1976).
British character actor, usually in heavy roles. Much on TV.

The Camp on Blood Island 58. The Small World of Sammy Lee 63. Up Jumped a Swagman 65. Where the Spies Are 65. Mr Ten Per Cent 66. The Kremlin Letter 70. The Offence 72. The Spiral Staircase 74, etc.

Rademakers, Fons (1920–).
Dutch director, with stage experience.

Doctor in the Village 58. The Knife 61. Max Havelaar 74. Mysteries 76. The Judge's Friend 79. The Assault/De Aanslag 86. Diary of a Mad Old Man/Dagboek van een Oude Dwaas 87. The Rose Garden 89, etc.

Rader, Peter.
American screenwriter and director.

Grandmother's House (wd) 89. Hired to Kill (co-d) 90. Waterworld (w) 95, etc.

Radford, Basil (1897–1952).
British light character comedian, on stage from 1922, films from 1929 (Barnum Was Right). Became popular when he and Naunton Wayne played two imperturbable Englishmen abroad in The Lady Vanishes 38.

Just William 38. Night Train to Munich 40. Crooks Tour 40. Next of Kin 42. Millions Like Us 43. The Way to the Stars 45. Dead of Night 45. The Captive Heart 46. Girl in a Million 46. It's Not Cricket 48. Passport to Pimlico 48. The Winslow Boy 48. Quartet 48. Whisky Galore 48. Chance of a Lifetime 50. The Galloping Major 51, etc.

Radford, Michael (1946–).
British director and screenwriter. Born in New Delhi, India, he studied at Oxford University and the National Film School before working in television as a documentary director.

Another Time Another Place 83. 1984 84. White Mischief 87. The Postman/Il Postino (co-w, d) (AANw, AANd) 94. B Monkey 98. The Swedish Cavalier (Fr.) 99, etc.

66 I think of myself as the matador and the audience as the bull. – M.R.

Radner, Gilda (1946–1989).
American comedienne who gained fame in the TV series Saturday Night Live. She was married to actor and director Gene Wilder. Died of cancer.

Autobiography: 1989, It's Always Something.

Biography: 1992, Gilda: An Intimate Portrait by David Saltman; 1994, Bunny, Bunny: Gilda Radner – A Sort of Love Story by Alan Zweibel.

First Family 80. Hanky Panky 82. It Came from Hollywood 82. The Woman in Red 84. Festive Desserts 84. Movers and Shakers 85. Haunted Honeymoon 86, etc.

Radnitz, Robert B. (1925–).
American producer of 'family' films.

A Dog of Flanders 60. Misty 62. Island of the Blue Dolphins 64. Moon and Miguel 66. My Side of the Mountain 68. The Little Ark 70. Sounder 72. A Hero Ain't Nothing but a Sandwich 77. Cross Creek 83. Never Forget 91, etc.

Rafelson, Bob (1933–).
American director.

Head (co-w, d) 68. Five Easy Pieces 71. The King of Marvin Gardens 72. Stay Hungry 76. The Postman Always Rings Twice 81. Black Widow 87. Mountains of the Moon 89. Man Trouble 92. Erotic Tales (co-d) 94. Blood and Wine 96. Poodle Springs (TV) 98, etc.

Rafferty, Chips (1909–1971) (John Goffage).
Rangy Australian character actor with varied experience before coming to films.

Dad Rudd, MP 40. Forty Thousand Horsemen 40. The Rats of Tobruk 44. The Overlanders 46. The Loves of Joanna Godden (GB) 46. Eureka Stockade 47. Bitter Springs 51. Kangaroo 52. King of the Coral Sea 54. Walk into Paradise 56. The Sundowners 60. Mutiny on the Bounty 62. They're a Weird Mob 66. Kona Coast 68. Skullduggery 69. Outback 70, many others.

Rafferty, Frances (1922–).
American leading lady.

Seven Sweethearts 42. Dragon Seed 44. Abbott and Costello in Hollywood 45. The Hidden Eye 45. Lady at Midnight 48. Rodeo 52. The Shanghai Story 54. Wings of Chance 61, etc.

TV series: December Bride 54–58. Pete and Gladys 61.

Raffill, Stewart (1945–).
Anglo-American director and screenwriter.

Napoleon and Samantha 72. Adventures of the Wilderness Family 75. Shipwreck 77. High Risk 81. Ice Pirates 83. The Philadelphia Experiment 84. Mac and Me 88. Mannequin 2: On the Move 91. Passenger 57 (co-story) 92. Lost in Africa 94.

Raffin, Deborah (1953–).
American leading lady.

Forty Carats 73. Once Is Not Enough 75. Nightmare in Badham County (TV) 76. The Sentinel 77. Demon 77. Ski Lift to Death (TV) 78. How to Pick Up Girls (TV) 78. Willa (TV) 78. Touched by Love 80. Lace 2 (TV) 85. Death Wish 3 86. Noble House (TV) 87. Scanners 2: The New Order 90. Morning Glory (a, co-w) 93, etc.

Rafkin, Alan (1938–).
American director.

Ski Party 65. The Ghost and Mr Chicken 66. Nobody's Perfect 68. The Shakiest Gun in the West 68. Angel in My Pocket 69. How to Frame a Figg 71. Let's Switch (TV) 75, etc.

Raft, George (1895–1980) (George Ranft).
Smooth, rather sinister American leading man of the 30s and 40s; formerly a professional athlete, gambler, nightclub dancer and companion of gangsters. In 1961 Ray Danton appeared in the title role of The George Raft Story.

Biographies: 1973, The George Raft File by James Robert Parish. 1974, George Raft by Lewis Jablonsky.

■ Queen of the Night Clubs 29. Quick Millions 31. Hush Money 31. Palmy Days 31. Dancers in the Dark 32. Scarface 32. Night World 32. Madame Racketeer 32. Night after Night 32. If I Had a Million 32. Undercover Man 32. Pick Up 33. Midnight Club 33. The Bowery 33. All of Me 34. Bolero 34. The Trumpet Blows 34. Limehouse Blues 34. Rumba 35. Stolen Harmony 35. The Glass Key 35. Every Night at Eight 35. She Couldn't Take It 35. It Had to Happen 35. Yours for the Asking 36. Souls at Sea 37. You and Me 38. Spawn of the North 38. The Lady's from Kentucky 39. Each Dawn I Die 39. I Stole a Million 39. Invisible Stripes 40. The House across the Bay 40. They Drive by Night 40. Manpower 41. Broadway 42. Stage Door Canteen 43. Background to Danger 43. Follow the Boys 44. Nob Hill 45. Johnny Angel 45. Whistle Stop 46. Mr Ace 46. Nocturne 46. Christmas Eve 47. Intrigue 48. Race Street 48. Outpost in Morocco 49. Johnny Allegro 49. A Dangerous Profession 49. The Red Light 50. Lucky Nick Cain 51. Loan Shark 52. The Man from Cairo 53. Rogue Cop 54. Black Widow 54. A Bullet for

Joey 55. Around the World in Eighty Days 56. Some Like It Hot 59. Jet over the Atlantic 59. Ocean's Eleven 60. Ladies' Man 64. The Patsy 64. For Those Who Think Young 64. Casino Royale 67. Du Rififi à Paname 67. Five Golden Dragons 67. Skidoo 68. Madigan's Millions 69. Hammersmith is Out 72. Deadhead Miles 72. Sextette 77.

TV series: I Am the Law 52.

Raglan, Robert (1906–).
Stolid British character actor, usually seen as a police sergeant or inspector, although he made occasional appearances in the TV sitcom Dad's Army as a colonel.

Circus Boy 47. The Ringer 52. The Good Beginning 53. Brothers in Law 56. Private's Progress 56. The Crooked Sky 57. Undercover Girl 58. Gideon's Day 58. An Honourable Murder 60. A Taste of Money 60. Jigsaw 62. Where the Spies Are 65. Loot 70. The Magic Christian 70. The Rise and Fall of Michael Rimmer 70. Catch Me a Spy 71. Dad's Army 72. The Mirror Crack'd 80, etc.

TV series: Charge 69.

Ragland, Rags (1905–1946) (John Lee Ragland).
American character comedian, former boxer. Died of uremia.

■ Ringside Maisie 41. Whistling in the Dark 41. Born to Sing 42. Sunday Punch 42. Maisie Gets Her Man 42. Panama Hattie 42. The War Against Mrs Hadley 42. Somewhere I'll Find You 42. Whistling in Dixie 42. Dubarry Was a Lady 42. Girl Crazy 43. Whistling in Brooklyn 43. Meet the People 44. Three Men in White 44. The Canterville Ghost 44. Her Highness and the Bellboy 45. Anchors Aweigh 45. Abbott and Costello in Hollywood 45. Ziegfeld Follies 46. The Hoodlum Saint 46.

Railsback, Steve (1948–).
American character actor.

The Visitors 71. Cockfighter 74. Helter Skelter (TV) 76. The Stunt Man 78. From Here to Eternity (TV) 79. The Golden Seal 83. Lifeforce 85. Armed and Dangerous 86. Blue Monkey 87. The Survivalist 87. The Wind 87. Deadly Intent 88. The Assassin 89. Scissors 91. Sunstroke 92. Calendar Girl 93. Barb Wire 96. Stranger in the House 97, etc.

Raimi, Sam (1959–).
Precocious American director of horror films, noted for his extravagant camera work.

The Evil Dead 83. Crimewave 85. Evil Dead II: Dead by Dawn 87. Miller's Crossing (a) 90. Darkman 90. Army of Darkness 92. Indian Summer (a) 93. Mantis (p, story) (TV) 94. The Hudsucker Proxy (co-w) 94. The Stand (a) (TV) 94. Timecop (p) 94. The Quick and the Dead (d) 95. A Simple Plan (d) 98, etc.

Raimu (1883–1946) (Jules Muraire).
French character actor and comedian with music-hall background.

■ L'Homme Nu 12. L'Agence Cacahuète 14. Le Blanc et le Noir 31. Mam'zelle Nitouche 31. Marius 31. La Petite Chocolatière 32. Les Gaîtés de l'Escadron 32. Fanny 32. Theodore and Company 33. Charlemagne 33. Ces Messieurs de la Santé 34. Tartarin de Tarascon 34. J'ai une Idée 34. Minuit Place Pigalle 35. Faisons un Rêve 35. L'Ecole des Cocottes 35. Gaspard de Besse 35. Le Secret de Polichinelle 36. Le Roi 36. Les Jumeaux de Brighton 36. César 36. Anything to Declare 37. Les Perles de la Couronne 37. La Chaste Suzanne 37. Les Rois du Sport 37. Le Fauteuil 37. Gribouille 37. Un Carnet de Bal 37. Les Héros de la Marne 38. L'Etrange Monsieur Victor 38. Les Nouveaux Riches 38. La Femme du Boulanger 38. Noix de

Coco 39. Monsieur Brotonneau 39. Dernière Jeunesse 39. L'Homme Qui Cherche la Vérité 39. Un tel Père et Fils 40. La Fille du Puisatier 40. Le Duel 40. Parade en Sept Nuits 41. *Les Inconnus dans la Maison* 42. *L'Arlésienne* 42. *Monsieur la Souris* 42. The Benefactor 42. Les Petits Riens 42. Le Colonel Chabert 43. Les Gueux au Paradis 46. L'Homme au Chapeau Rond 46.

❝ Le plus grand comédien de tous les temps. – *Arletty*

Raine, Jack (1895–1979).
British light actor, on stage in the 20s and 30s; later in Hollywood.
The Happy Time 52. Julius Caesar 53. Rhapsody 54. My Fair Lady 64. Hello Dolly 69, etc.

Raine, Norman Reilly (1895–1971).
American screenwriter.
Tugboat Annie 33. White Woman 33. God's Country and the Woman 36. *The Life of Emile Zola* (AA) 37. The Adventures of Robin Hood 38. Elizabeth and Essex 39. The Fighting 69th 39. Captains of the Clouds 42. Ladies Courageous 44. A Bell for Adano 45. Woman of the North Country 52. Sea of Lost Ships 53, etc.

Rainer, Luise (1914–).
German leading actress, born in Dusseldorf and on stage from 1930, working with director Max Reinhardt in Berlin. In the mid-30s she went to Hollywood, where Louis B. Mayer insisted that her birthplace should be altered to Vienna and her nationality to Austrian. She was married to playwright and screenwriter Clifford Odets (1937–40).
Escapade 35. *The Great Ziegfeld* (AA) 36. *The Good Earth* (AA) 37. The Emperor's Candlesticks 37. The Big City 37. The Great Waltz 38. The Toy Wife 38. Dramatic School 38. Hostages 43. The Gambler 97, etc.

❝ For my second and third pictures I won Academy Awards. Nothing worse could have happened to me. – *L.R.*

Raines, Cristina (1954–).
American leading lady of the late 70s.
Sunshine (TV) 74. Nashville 75. The Sentinel 77. The Duellists 77. Touched by Love 80. Silver Dream Racer 83. Nightmares 83. Quo Vadis (TV) 85, etc.
TV series: Flamingo Road 80–81.

Raines, Ella (1921–1988) (Ella Raubes).
American leading lady of the 40s, with brief stage experience.
Corvette K225 43. Cry Havoc 43. Phantom Lady 43. Hail the Conquering Hero 43. Enter Arsène Lupin 44. Tall in the Saddle 44. Uncle Harry 45. The Suspect 45. The Runaround 46. Time out of Mind 47. Brute Force 47. Mr Ashton was Indiscreet 48. The Walking Hills 48. Impact 48. A Dangerous Profession 49. Ride the Man Down 53. Man in the Road (GB) 54, etc.
TV series: Janet Dean Registered Nurse 53–55.

Rainger, Ralph (1901–1942). (Ralph Reichenthal).
American song composer who usually worked with lyricist Leo Robin. Film scores include *The Big Broadcast of 1932, She Done Him Wrong, Swing High Swing Low, Paris Honeymoon, Moon Over Miami, Footlight Serenade, Coney Island.*

Rains, Claude (1889–1967).
Suave, incisive British character actor, long resident in America. Born in London, he began as a call boy at His Majesty's Theatre in London and was encouraged to become an actor by actor-manager Herbert Beerbohm Tree, who paid for him to have elocution lessons. After working as a stage manager, he concentrated on acting from 1919, and began appearing in films from 1933. His four wives included actresses Isabel Jeans, Marie Hemingway and Beatrix Thomson.
■ *The Invisible Man* 33. *Crime without Passion* 34. The Man Who Reclaimed His Head 34. The Mystery of Edwin Drood 35. The Clairvoyant (GB) 35. The Last Outpost 35. Anthony Adverse 36. Hearts Divided 36. Stolen Holiday 36. The Prince and the Pauper 37. They Won't Forget 37. Gold is Where You Find It 38. *The Adventures of Robin Hood* 38. White Banners 38. Four Daughters 38. They Made Me a Criminal 39. Juarez 39. *Mr Smith Goes to Washington* (AAN) 39. Four Wives 39. Daughters Courageous 39. Saturday's Children 39. The Sea Hawk 40. Lady with Red Hair (as David Belasco) 40. Four Mothers 40. *Here Comes Mr Jordan* 41. The Wolf Man 41. *Kings Row* 41. Moontide 42. Now Voyager 42. *Casablanca* (AAN) 42. Forever and a Day 43. Phantom of the Opera (title role) 43. Passage to Marseilles 44. *Mr Skeffington* (AAN) 44. This Love of Ours 45. *Caesar and Cleopatra* (GB) 45. Angel on My Shoulder 46. *Deception* 46. *Notorious* (AAN) 46. The Unsuspected 47. Strange Holiday 47. *The Passionate Friends* (GB) 47. Rope of Sand 49. Song of Surrender 49. The White Tower 50. Where Danger Lives 50. Sealed Cargo 51. The Man Who Watched Trains Go By (GB) 52. Lisbon 56. This Earth is Mine 59. The Lost World 60. Battle of the Worlds (It.) 61. Lawrence of Arabia 62. Twilight of Honor 63. The Greatest Story Ever Told 65.

✪ For his omnipresent urbanity. *Casablanca.*

❝ God felt sorry for actors, so he gave them a place in the sun and a lot of money. All they had to sacrifice was their talent. – *C.R., on Hollywood*

He was very short. His heels were built up and he used to backcomb his hair; that added another inch. It wasn't straight vanity. He knew how to present himself. Presenting yourself is a large part of being a star actor. – *David Lean*

He was a great influence on me. I don't know what happened to him. I think he failed and went to America. – *John Gielgud*

Famous line (*The Invisible Man*): 'We'll start with a few murders. Big men, little men – just to show that we make no distinction.'

Famous line (*Casablanca*): 'I'm only a poor corrupt official.'

Raitt, John (1917–).
American Broadway actor and singer, in films from 1940, whose only starring role was in *The Pajama Game.*
Flight Command 40. Little Nellie Kelly 40. Billy the Kid 41. Ziegfeld Girl 41. H. M. Pulham, Esq. 41. The Pajama Game 57, etc.

Raki, Laya (1927–).
Leading lady of the 50s, from New Zealand.
Up to His Neck 54. The Seekers 55. Quentin Durward 56. The Poppy is Also a Flower (TV) 65, etc.

Rakoff, Alvin (1937–).
Canadian TV director resident in Britain.
Passport to Shame 58. Treasure of San Teresa 59. On Friday at Eleven 61. The Comedy Man 64. Hoffman 70. Say Hello to Yesterday 70. Don Quixote (TV) 72. City on Fire 79. Dirty Tricks 80. A Voyage Round My Father (TV) 82. Mr Halpern and Mr Johnson (TV) 83. The First Olympics (TV) 84. Paradise Postponed (TV) 86, etc.

Raksin, David (1912–).
American composer, in Hollywood from mid-30s. Arranged Chaplin's score for *Modern Times* 36.
Laura 44. The Secret Life of Walter Mitty 47. *Force of Evil* 49. *The Bad and the Beautiful* 52. Separate Tables 58. Too Late Blues 62. Two Weeks in Another Town 62. Invitation to a Gunfighter 65. A Big Hand for the Little Lady 66. Will Penny 67. What's the Matter with Helen? 71. Glass Houses 72. The Suicide's Wife (TV) 79. Lady in a Corner 89, etc.

Rall, Tommy (1929–) (Thomas Edward Rall).
American actor, singer, dancer and choreographer.
Give Out, Sisters 42. Mr Big 43. Kiss Me Kate 53. Seven Brides for Seven Brothers 54. Invitation to the Dance 54. My Sister Eileen 55. The Second Greatest Sex 55. World in My Corner 55. Walk the Proud Land 56. Merry Andrew 58. Pennies from Heaven 81. Dancers 87, etc.

Ralli, Giovanna (1935–).
Italian leading lady.
The Children are Watching Us 43. Lights of Variety 49. La Lupa 53. The Bigamist 56. Il Generale Della Rovere 59. Deadfall 68. Cannon for Cordoba 70. We All Loved Each Other So Much 75. The Pickpocket 81. Once a Year, Every Year 94, many others.

Ralph, Jessie (1864–1944) (Jessie Ralph Chambers).
American character actress who came to Hollywood late in life and played many endearing granny roles.
■ Such a Little Queen 21. Elmer the Great 33. Cocktail Hour 33. Child of Manhattan 33. Ann Carver's Profession 33. Coming Out Party 34. One Night of Love 34. Evelyn Prentice 34. Nana 34. We Live Again 34. Murder at the Vanities 34. The Affairs of Cellini 34. *David Copperfield* (as Peggotty) 35. Enchanted April 35. Les Misérables 35. Paris in Spring 35. Vanessa 35. Mark of the Vampire 35. I Live My Life 35. Jalna 35. Metropolitan 35. I Found Stella Parish 35. Captain Blood 35. Bunker Bean 35. The Garden Murder Case 36. The Unguarded Hour 36. *San Francisco* 36. After the Thin Man 36. Camille 36. Little Lord Fauntleroy 36. Yellow Dust 36. Walking on Air 36. The Good Earth 37. Double Wedding 37. The Last of Mrs Cheyney 37. Love Is a Headache 37. Port of Seven Seas 38. Hold That Kiss 38. St Louis Blues 39. Café Society 39. Four Girls in White 39. The Kid from Texas 39. Mickey the Kid 39. Drums Along the Mohawk 39. *The Blue Bird* 40. Star Dust 40. The Girl from Avenue A 40. I Can't Give You Anything But Love Baby 40. *The Bank Dick* 40. I Want a Divorce 40. The Lady from Cheyenne 41. *They Met in Bombay* 41.

Ralston, Esther (1902–1994).
American leading lady of the 20s and 30s.
The Phantom Fortune (serial) 23. Peter Pan 24. A Kiss for Cinderella 25. Lucky Devil 26. Old Ironsides 26. Figures Don't Lie 27. The Sawdust Paradise 28. The Prodigal 31. Sadie McKee 33. Hollywood Boulevard 36. Tin Pan Alley 40, etc.

Ralston, Jobyna (1902–1967).
American leading lady of the 20s, especially with Harold Lloyd.
Why Worry 23. Girl Shy 24. The Freshman 24. For Heaven's Sake 26. Wings 27, many others.

Ralston, Vera Hruba (1921–).
Czech actress, former skating champion. In US from the late 30s, films from 1942. Married Herbert Yates, boss of Republic Studios, and appeared exclusively in his pictures. Now retired.
■ Ice Capades 41. Ice Capades Revue 42. The Lady and the Monster 44. Storm Over Lisbon 44. Lake Placid Serenade 44. Dakota 45. Murder in the Music Hall 46. The Plainsman and the Lady 46. The Flame 47. Wyoming 47. I Jane Doe 48. Angel on the Amazon 48. The Fighting Kentuckian 49. Surrender 50. Belle Le Grand 51. The Wild Blue Yonder 51. Hoodlum Empire 52. Fair Wind to Java 53. A Perilous Journey 53. Jubilee Trail 54. Timberjack 55. Accused of Murder 56. Spoilers of the Forest 57. Gunfire at Indian Gap 57. The Notorious Mr Monks 58. The Man Who Died Twice 58.

Rambeau, Marjorie (1889–1970).
American character actress.
The Dazzling Miss Davison 16. Her Man 30. Man's Castle 33. The Rains Came 39. Twenty Mule Team 40. The Primrose Path (AAN) 40. Tugboat Annie Sails Again (title role) 41. So Ends Our Night 41. Tobacco Road 41. Broadway 42. Army Wives 45. Abandoned 49. Torch Song (AAN) 53. The View from Pompey's Head 56. Man of a Thousand Faces 57, many others.

Rambo, Dack (1941–1994) (Norman Rambo).
American actor who began on television with his twin brother Dirk (1941–67), playing the sons of Loretta Young. Died of AIDS.
Which Way to the Front? 70. Nightmare Honeymoon 72. Hit Lady (TV) 74. Waikiki (TV) 80. Rich and Famous 81. Lilac Dream 87. The Spring 90. Welcome to Oblivion 90, etc.
TV series: The New Loretta Young Show 62–63. The Guns of Will Sonnett 67–69. Dirty Sally 74. Sword of Justice 78–79. Paper Dolls 84. Dallas 85–87.

Rambova, Natacha (1897–1966) (Winifred Shaunessey Hudnut).
Wealthy American designer, dance teacher and actress. Born in Salt Lake City, she was one of the first art directors and costume designers in cinema and created a sensation with her designs for *Salome*, based on Aubrey Beardsley's drawings, and starring Nazimova. She went on to marry, and have a tempestuous relationship with, Nazimova's former husband Rudolph Valentino, directing the last years of his career to his detriment. She was played by Yvette Mimieux in Melville Shavelson's *The Legend of Valentino* (TV) 75, and by Michelle Phillips in Ken Russell's *Valentino* 77.
Camille (ad) 21. The Young Rajah (ad) 22. Salome (ad, costumes) 23. Monsieur Beaucaire (ad) 24. When Love Grows Cold (a) 26, etc.

Ramis, Harold (1944–).
American director, screenwriter and actor of comedies.
National Lampoon's Animal House (w) 78. Meatballs (w) 79. Caddyshack 80. Stripes (a, w) 81. National Lampoon's Vacation 83. Ghostbusters (a, w) 84. Armed and Dangerous (w) 86. Back to School (w) 86. Ghostbusters II (a, w) 89. Groundhog Day (co-w, d) 93. Stuart Saves His Family 95. Multiplicity (p, d) 96, etc.

Rampling, Charlotte (1946–).
British leading lady.
Rotten to the Core 65. Georgy Girl 66. The Long Duel 67. The Damned 69. Corky 72. The Ski Bum 72. Henry VIII and His Six Wives 72. Asylum 72. Zardoz 73. Caravan to Vaccares 74. The Night Porter 74. Farewell My Lovely 75. Foxtrot 76. Sherlock Holmes in New York (TV) 76. Flesh of the Orchid 76. Orca 77. The Purple Taxi 78. Stardust Memories 80. The Verdict 82. The Viva la Vie 83. He Died with his Eyes Open 84. Sadness and Beauty 85. Max My Love 86. Angel Heart 87. Paris by Night 88. Hammers over the Anvil 93. Time Is Money 94. Invasion of Privacy 96, etc.

Ramsey, Anne (1929–1988).
American character actress who received an Oscar nomination for one of her last roles.
The Sporting Club 71. Up the Sandbox 72. The New Centurions 72. Goin' South 78. The Black Marble 80. Any Which Way You Can 80. The Goonies 85. Throw Momma from the Train (AAN) 88. Scrooged 88. Homer and Eddie 90, etc.

Rand, Ayn (1905–1982) (Alisa Rosenbaum).
American novelist and screenwriter. According to an American Library of Congress survey in the 90s, her novel *Atlas Shrugged* is the book that has had most influence on American lives after the Bible. Born in St Petersburg, she fled the Russian Revolution and arrived in the US in the mid-20s, finding work as an extra in Hollywood and, from the early 30s, as a script reader at Paramount. She sold an original script, *Red Pawn*, to Universal in 1932 as a vehicle for Tala Birrell; it was later acquired by Paramount for Marlene Dietrich and Joseph von Sternberg, but was never produced. In the mid-40s she briefly worked as a writer for producer Hal Wallis, but quit Hollywood after seeing a rough cut of *The Fountainhead*, declaring 'the people involved were not worthy of the assignment'. Barbara Stanwyck had persuaded Warner's to buy the screen rights to *The Fountainhead*; when the role she wanted went to Patricia Neal, Stanwyck left the studio. Producer Albert S. Ruddy announced that he was going to film *Atlas Shrugged* in 1972, but plans fell through when Rand insisted on having script approval. Later, Sterling Silliphant wrote a version for an NBC TV mini-series, but it was never made. She was a founding member of the Motion Picture Alliance for the Preservation of American Ideals. Married actor Frank O'Connor. Her works preach her Objectivist philosophy, a gospel of rational self-interest and unfettered capitalism. She was played by Helen Mirren in a TV film in 1999.
Biography: 1986, *The Passion of Ayn Rand* by Barbara Branden.
■ We the Living (It.) (oa) 42. Love Letters (w) 45. You Came Along (co-w) 45. The Fountainhead (oa, w) 49.

❝ Whoever tells you that you should exist for the collective, for the State, is, or wants to be, the State. – *A.R.*

She told us that she would blow up the Warner Brothers lot if we changed one word, and we believed her. Even Jack Warner believed her. – *producer Henry Blanke on Ayn Rand's script for The Fountainhead*

(In the event, one line was cut, the one she regarded as the most important, the hero's remark: 'I wished to come here and say that I am a man who does not exist for others.')

Rand, Sally (1904–1979) (Helen Gould Beck).
American dancer and fan dancer, in a few films.
The Dressmaker from Paris 24. Getting Gertie's Garter 27. King of Kings 27. The Fighting Eagle 28. Bolero 34, etc.

Randall, Addison 'Jack' (1906–1945).
American actor of the 30s. Born in San Fernando, California, he played romantic leads at RKO before starring, as singing cowboy Jack Randall, in 'B' westerns for Monogram from the late 30s, usually with Al St John as his sidekick. The brother of Robert Livingston, he died of a heart attack while filming a serial, *The Royal Mounted Rides Again*, for Universal.

His Family Tree 35. Another Face/It Happened in Hollywood 35. Two in the Dark 36. Don't Turn 'em Loose 36. Riders of the Dawn 37. The Gun Packer 38. Gunsmoke Trail 38. Man's Country 38. Wild Horse Canyon 39. Across the Plains 39. Covered Wagon Trails 40. High Explosive 43, etc.

Randall, Tony (1920–) (Leonard Rosenberg).
Sardonic American comedy actor, adept at light drunks, depressives and friends of the hero.
■ Oh Men Oh Women 57. Will Success Spoil Rock Hunter? 57. No Down Payment 58. The Mating Game 59. *Pillow Talk* 59. The Adventures of Huckleberry Finn 60. Let's Make Love 61. Lover Come Back 61. Boys' Night Out 62. Island of Love 63. The Brass Bottle 63. *Send Me No Flowers* 64. *Seven Faces of Dr Lao* 64. Fluffy 65. The Alphabet Murders (hilariously miscast as Hercule Poirot) 66. Our Man in Marrakesh 66. Hello Down There 68. Everything You Always Wanted to Know About Sex 72. Scavenger Hunt 79. Foolin' Around 80. Sidney Shorr: A Girl's Best Friend (TV) 81. King of Comedy 83. My Little Pony: The Movie (voice) 86. Agatha Christie's The Man in the Brown Suit (TV) 89. It Had to Be You 89. Gremlins 2: The New Batch (voice) 90. That's Adequate 90. Fatal Instinct 93.

TV series: Mr Peepers 52–55. *The Odd Couple* 70–74. Tony Randall Show 76–77. Love, Sidney 81–82.

❝ Comedy's a serious business. You've got to be true and funny, and not look as though you're trying. – *T.R.*

Randel, Tony (1956–).
American director of horror films, a former editor.

Hellbound: Hellraiser II 88. Amityville 1992: It's about Time 92. Children of the Night 92. Ticks 93. Fist of the North Star 95. One Good Turn 95. Rattled 96, etc.

Randell, Ron (1918–).
Australian leading man with radio experience; has appeared in films and TV episodes all over the world.

It Had to be You 47. Lorna Doone 50. Kiss Me Kate 53. Bulldog Drummond at Bay 54. I Am a Camera 55. Beyond Mombasa 56. The Story of Esther Costello 58. King of Kings 61. The Longest Day 62. Gold for the Caesars 63. The Seven Minutes 71. Exposed 83, many others.

TV series: O.S.S. 58.

Randle, Frank (1902–1957) (Arthur McEvoy).
Lancashire music-hall comedian of immense vulgarity; made his own slapdash but highly popular films in the 40s.

Somewhere in England 40. Somewhere in Camp 42. Somewhere in Civvies 43. School for Randle 47. Home Sweet Home 47. Holidays with Pay 48. It's a Grand Life 53, etc.

❝ The greatest character comedian that ever lived. – *Gracie Fields*

Randle, Theresa (1967–).
American actress.

Near Dark 87. King of New York 90. The Five Heartbeats 91. Jungle Fever 91. Malcolm X 92. Sugar Hill 93. Beverly Hills Cop III 94. Girl 6 96. Spawn 97, etc.

❝ I want to be Dorothy Dandridge or Marilyn Monroe walking down a red carpet looking fabulous. – *T.R.*

Randolph, Anders (1876–1930).
American character man, usually seen as heavy villain.

The Hero of Submarine D2 16. The Splendid Sinner 18. Dorothy Vernon of Haddon Hall 24. The Black Pirate 28. The Kiss 29, many others.

Randolph, Elsie (1901–1982) (Elsie Florence Killick).
British revue artiste, often teamed in the 30s with Jack Buchanan.
■ Rich and Strange 31. Brother Alfred 32. Life Goes On 32. Rise and Shine 32. Yes, Mr Brown 33. Night of the Garter 33. *That's a Good Girl* 35. *This'll Make You Whistle* 37. Smash and Grab 38. Cheer the Brave 50. Riders of the Sky (Czech.) 68. Frenzy 72. Charleston 77.

Randolph, Jane (1919–) (J. Roermer).
American leading lady of the 40s.

Highways by Night 42. Cat People 42. In the Meantime, Darling 44. Jealousy 46. T Men 48. Abbott and Costello Meet Frankenstein (last to date) 48, etc.

Randolph, John (1917–) (Emanuel Hirsch Cohen).
American character actor usually seen as pompous business man.

Naked City 48. *Seconds* 67. Pretty Poison 68. There Was a Crooked Man 70. Little Murders 71. Serpico 73. King Kong 76. Washington Behind Closed Doors (TV) 77. Blind Ambition (TV) 79. Lovely . . . but Deadly 82. Prizzi's Honor 85. As Summers Die (TV) 86. The Wizard of Loneliness 88. National Lampoon's Christmas Vacation 89. Iron Maze 91. *The Hotel Manor Inn* (as Gus) 96. A Price above Rubies 98. You've Got Mail 98, etc.

TV series: Lucas Tanner 74–75. Lucan 77–78. Angie 79–80. Annie McGuire 88. Grand 90.

Rank, J. Arthur (1888–1972) (Lord Rank).
British flour magnate who entered films in the mid-30s in the hope of promoting interest in religion. Formed or took over so many companies including production, distribution and exhibition that by the mid-40s he was accused of monopolistic tendencies. His influence was generally excellent, and he encouraged independent producers (sometimes unwisely), but his organization generally suffered from a preponderance of accountants unable to understand the ingredients of a good film. Without their financial advice, however, the empire might well have perished altogether. At its height it fostered such production companies as the Archers, Cineguild, Wessex, Individual and Two Cities. In recent years the film side of the organization has proved less important than its hotels, bowling alleys and such developments as xerox-copying; but it includes Odeon and Gaumont Theatres, Rank Film Distributors, Pinewood Studios, Denham Laboratories, etc.

Biographies: 1952, Mr Rank by Alan Wood. 1993, *J. Arthur Rank and the British Film Industry* by Geoffrey Macnab.

✪ For doing his best. *Henry V.*

❝ Methodist principles may seem a curious guide to the promotion of motion pictures, but at least they gave J. Arthur Rank a considerable start over other film promoters who had no principles at all. – *Alan Wood*

If I could recall to you some of my various adventures and experiences in the film world, it would I think be as plain to you as it is to me that I was being led by God. – *J.A.R.*

Ransford, Maurice (1896–*).
American art director at Twentieth Century-Fox, usually in collaboration with Lyle Wheeler, the studio's supervising art director. Born in Terre Haute, Indiana, and educated at the University of Illinois, he worked as an architect in the 20s and early 30s.

The Pied Piper 42. Immortal Sergeant 43. Lifeboat 44. Sweet and Lowdown 44. Hangover Square 45. Captain Eddie 45. Leave Her to Heaven (AAN) 45. 13 Rue Madeleine 47. The Foxes of Harrow (AAN) 47. Oh, You Beautiful Doll 49. Mother Is a Freshman 49. Twelve o'Clock High 49. Under My Skin 50. Panic in the Streets 50. The 13th Letter 51. The Desert Fox 51. As Young as You Feel 51. I'd Climb the Highest Mountain 51. Dreamboat 52. King of the Khyber Rifles 53. Niagara 53. Dangerous Crossing 53. Titanic (AAN) 53. Black Widow 54. Broken Lance 54. The Girl in the Red Velvet Swing 55. A Man Called Peter 55. The Left Hand of God 55. The Best Things in Life Are Free 56. 23 Paces to Baker Street 56. Desk Set 57. Kiss Them for Me 57. Oh, Men! Oh, Women! 57. The Long, Hot Summer 58. The Hunters 58. The Blue Angel 59. The Sound and the Fury 59. The Man Who Understood Women 59. Beloved Infidel 59. From the Terrace 60. The Marriage-Go-Round 60. Misty 61, etc.

Ransohoff, Martin (1927–).
American writer and producer. Longtime chairman of Filmways, producers of such TV series as *The Beverly Hillbillies* and *The Addams Family*, which was bought by Orion Pictures in 1983 and became Orion Television.

Boys' Night Out 62. The Wheeler Dealers 63. The Americanization of Emily 64. Topkapi 64. The Sandpiper 65. The Loved One 65. The Cincinnati Kid 65. Don't Make Waves 67. Ice Station Zebra 68. The Moonshine War 70. The White Dawn 73. Silver Streak 76. The Other Side of Midnight 77. Nightwing 78. The Wanderers 79. A Change of Seasons 81. Hanky Panky 82. Class 83. The Jagged Edge 85. The Big Town 87. Switching Channels 88. Physical Evidence 89. Welcome Home 89. Guilty as Sin 93. Turbulence 97, etc.

Ransome, Prunella (1943–).
British leading lady.

Far from the Madding Crowd 67. Alfred the Great 69. Man in the Wilderness 71. Who Can Kill A Child? (Sp.) 75, etc.

Rapaport, Michael (1970–).
American actor.

Zebrahead 92. Point of No Return 93. The Scout 94. Higher Learning 95. The Basketball Diaries 95. Kiss of Death 95. Mighty Aphrodite 95. Beautiful Girls 96. The Pallbearer 96. Kicked in the Head 97. Cop Land 97. Some Girls 98. The Naked Man 98. Palmetto 98, etc.

Raphael, Frederic (1931–).
British writer.

Bachelor of Hearts 58. *Nothing But the Best* 64. *Darling* (AA, BFA) 65. Two for the Road (AAN) 67. Far from the Madding Crowd 67. A Severed Head 71. Daisy Miller 74. Rogue Male (TV) 76. The King's Whore 90, etc.

Raphaelson, Samson (1896–1983).
American playwright whose best screenplays were for Lubitsch; he led the saucy, stylish European trends of the 30s.
■ The Jazz Singer (& oa) 27. Boudoir Diplomat 30. The Smiling Lieutenant 31. The Magnificent Lie 31. *One Hour with You* 32. Broken Lullaby 32. *Trouble in Paradise* 32. The Merry Widow 34. Caravan 34. Servants' Entrance 34. Queen's Affair (GB) 34. Ladies Love Danger 35. Dressed to Thrill 35. *Accent on Youth* (& oa) 35. The Last of Mrs Cheyney 37. Angel 37. *The Shop around the Corner* 40. Suspicion 41. Skylark (& oa) 41. *Heaven Can Wait* 43. The Perfect Marriage (& oa) 46. Green Dolphin Street 47. That Lady in Ermine 48. Mr Music (oa) 50. Bannerline 51. Main Street to Broadway 53. Hilda Crane (oa) 56. But Not for Me (oa) 59. The Jazz Singer (oa) 80.

Rapp, Philip (1907–1996).
American comedy writer and director. He created a popular radio series, *The Bickersons*, starring Don Ameche and Frances Langford, and worked with Eddie Cantor and on the scripts of Danny Kaye's films produced by Samuel Goldwyn. He also wrote and directed the TV series *Topper*, based on Thorne Smith's novels, in the mid-50s, and wrote for the TV sitcom *The Adventures of Hiram Holiday* 56–57, starring Wally Cox.

Strike Me Pink (w) 36. Start Cheering (co-w) 38. *Wonder Man* (co-w) 45. Ziegfeld Follies (co-w) 46. The Inspector General (co-w) 49. Ain't Misbehavin' (co-w) 55. Wild and Wonderful (co-story) 63, etc.

Rappaport, David (1951–1990).
Diminutive (3 feet 11 inches) British actor, from the stage. A former teacher, he moved to Los Angeles in the mid-80s, where he appeared in the TV series *L.A. Law*. He committed suicide there.

Cuba 79. Black Jack 79. Time Bandits 81. Sword of the Valiant 84. The Bride 85, etc.

TV series: The Wizard 86–87.

Rappeneau, Jean-Paul (1932–).
French director and screenwriter.

Zazie dans le Métro (w) 60. A Very Private Affair/La Vie Privée 62. The Man from Rio/L'Homme de Rio (w) 64. A Matter of Resistance/La Vie de Château (wd) 66. Les Mariés de l'An II (wd) 70. Le Sauvage (wd) 75. Tout Feu, Tout Flamme (wd) 82. Cyrano de Bergerac (wd) 90. Le Hussard sur le Toit 95, etc.

Rapper, Irving (1898–).
American director with stage experience, long associated with Warner films.

Shining Victory 41. One Foot in Heaven 41. The Gay Sisters 42. *Now Voyager* 42. The Adventures of Mark Twain 44. Rhapsody in Blue 45. The Corn Is Green 46. *Deception* 46. *The Voice of the Turtle* 48. The Glass Menagerie 50. Another Man's Poison (GB) 51. Forever Female 52. The Brave One 56. Strange Intruder 57. Marjorie Morningstar 58. The Miracle 59. The Christine Jorgenson Story 70. Born Again 78, etc.

Rasche, David (1944–).
American leading actor.

Honky Tonk Freeway 81. Best Defense 84. Native Son 86. Made in Heaven 87. Wedding Band 89. Wicked Stepmother 89. An Innocent Man 89. The Masters of Menace 90. Bingo 91. Silhouette 91. Delirious (TV) 91. A Million to Juan 94. Dead Weekend (TV) 95. That Old Feeling 96, etc.

TV series: Sledge Hammer! 86–88.

Rascoe, Judith (1941–).
American screenwriter, a former university teacher and short-story writer.

Road Movie 74. Who'll Stop the Rain? 78. A Portrait of the Artist as a Young Man 79. Endless Love 81. Eat a Bowl of Tea 89. Havana 91, etc.

Rasp, Fritz (1891–1976).
German character actor.

Jugend 22. Warning Shadows 23. Metropolis 27. The Loves of Jeanne Ney 27. Spione 28. Diary of a Lost Girl 29. Die Dreigroschenoper 33. Lina Braake 76, many others.

Rasputin (1869–1916).
The mysterious monk who dominated members of the Tsar's family just before the Russian revolution, has been a popular film subject. Conrad Veidt played him in *Rasputin* (Ger. 1930); Lionel Barrymore in *Rasputin and the Empress* (US 1932); Harry Baur in *Rasputin* (Fr. 1938); Edmund Purdom in *Nights of Rasputin* (It. 1960); and Christopher Lee in *Rasputin the Mad Monk* (GB 1966); while 1968 brought Gert Frobe in the role in *I Killed Rasputin*, and 1971 had Tom Baker as Rasputin in *Nicholas and Alexandra*. In 1975 Alexei Petrenko played the role in Elem Klimov's *Agony/Agonia*. He was played by Alan Rickman in the historically inaccurate biopic *Rasputin* 96, directed by Uli Edel.

Rasulala, Thalmus (1939–1991) (Jack Crowder).
American character actor.

Cool Breeze 71. Blacula 72. Willie Dynamite 73. Mr Ricco 75. Bucktown 75. Adios Amigo 76. Fun with Dick and Jane 77. Bulletproof 87. Above the Law 88. New Jack City 91, etc.

Rasumny, Mikhail (1890–1956).
Russian character actor with stage experience, long in Hollywood.

Comrade X 40. This Gun for Hire 42. For Whom the Bell Tolls 43. Saigon 47. The Kissing Bandit 49. Hot Blood 55, many others.

Rat Pack (aka the Clan).
The name given to the showbiz entourage surrounding Frank Sinatra in the 50s and 60s. Its members included Dean Martin, Sammy Davis Jnr, Joey Bishop, and Peter Lawford, though both Davis and Lawford were banished at times. The term was coined by *Time* magazine, but it had its origins in the Holmby Hills Rat Pack, who were the drinking friends of Humphrey Bogart. The Pack gathered for several films with Sinatra, in which they seemed to have more fun than the audience: *Ocean's Eleven* 60; *Sergeants 3* 62; and *Robin and the Seven Hoods* 64. The only known concert recording of the group, *Frank, Dean & Sammy: An Evening with the Rat Pack*, made on closed-circuit TV in 1965, was shown on television in 1998. A TV biopic, *The Rat Pack* 98, starred Ray Liotta as Frank Sinatra, Joe Mantegna as Dean Martin, Don Cheadle as Sammy Davis, Jnr, Angus McFayden as Peter Lawford, Bobby Slayton as Joey Bishop, Megan Dodds as May Britt, Barbara Niven as Marilyn Monroe, and Deborah Kara Unger as Ava Gardner.

Books: 1961, *Sinatra and His Rat Pack* by Richard Gehman; 1998, *Rat Pack Confidential* by Shawn Levy.

❝ In Frank's Rat Pack personal homage to their 'leader' was all important: Frank was addressed as 'the pope', 'the general', and 'el dago.' – *Kitty Kelley*

Rathbone, Basil (1892–1967).
Incisive British actor, on stage from 1911, in America from the mid-20s.

Autobiography: 1962, *In and Out of Character*.

Biography: 1972, *Basil Rathbone and His Films* by Michael B. Druxman.

■ Innocent 21. The Fruitful Vine 21. The School for Scandal 23. The Masked Bride 25. Trouping with Ellen 24. The Great Deception 24. The Last of Mrs Cheyney 29. The Bishop Murder Case 30. A Notorious Affair 30. The Lady of Scandal 30. This Mad World 30. The Flirting Widow 30. A Lady Surrenders 30. Sin Takes a Holiday 30. A Woman Commands 31. One Precious Year 33. After the Ball 33. Loyalties 33. *David Copperfield* (as Murdstone) 35. *Anna Karenina* (as Karenin) 35. The Last Days of Pompeii 35. A Feather in Her Hat 35. A Tale of Two Cities 35. *Captain Blood* 35. Kind Lady 35. Private Number 36. Romeo and Juliet (AAN) 36. The Garden of Allah 36. Confession 37. Love from a Stranger 37. Make a Wish 37. Tovarich 37. The Adventures of Marco Polo 38. *The Adventures of Robin Hood* (as Gisbourne) 38. If I Were King (AAN) 38. The Dawn Patrol 38. Son of Frankenstein 39. *The Hound of the Baskervilles* 39. The Sun Never Sets 39. The Adventures of Sherlock Holmes 39. Rio 39. Tower of London 39. Rhythm on the River 40. The Mark of Zorro 40. The Mad Doctor 41. The Black Cat 41. International Lady 41. Paris Calling 41. Fingers at the Window 41. Crossroads 42. Sherlock Holmes and the Voice of Terror 42. Sherlock Holmes and the Secret Weapon 42. Sherlock Holmes in Washington 43. Above Suspicion 43. Sherlock Holmes Faces Death 43. *Spider Woman* 44. The Scarlet Claw 44. Bathing Beauty 44. The Pearl of Death 44. Frenchman's Creek 44. The House of Fear 45. The Woman in Green 45. Pursuit to Algiers 45. Terror by Night 45. *Heartbeat* 46. Dressed to Kill 46. Casanova's Big Night 54. We're No Angels 55. *The Court Jester* 56. The Black Sleep 56. The Last Hurrah 58. The Magic Sword 62. Tales of Terror 62. Two before Zero 62. The Comedy of Terrors 64. Pontius Pilate 64. Queen of Blood 66. The Ghost in the Invisible Bikini 66. Voyage to a Prehistoric Planet 67. Autopsy of a Ghost 67. Hillbillies in a Haunted House 67.

✪ For being everybody's favourite villain and the one and only Sherlock Holmes. *The Hound of the Baskervilles*.

❝ Two profiles pasted together. – *Dorothy Parker*

∼The only time he won a screen duel was in *Romeo and Juliet*: he played Tybalt.

Rathborne, Tina (1951–).
American director.
Zelly and Me 88.

Ratoff, Gregory (1897–1960).
English-fracturing Russian actor and impresario, in Hollywood and Britain from mid-30s as actor or director.
I'm No Angel (a) 33. Under Two Flags (a) 36. Lancer Spy (d) 37. Rose of Washington Square (d) 39. Intermezzo (d) 39. I Was an Adventuress (d) 40. Adam Had Four Sons (d) 41. The Corsican Brothers (a) 41. The Men in Her Life (d) 42. Song of Russia (d) 44. Where Do We Go from Here? (d) 45. Moss Rose (d) 47. *All about Eve* (a) 50. My Daughter Joy (d) 50. Abdullah the Great (ad) 57. *Oscar Wilde* (d) 60. The Big Gamble (a) 61, many others.

Rattigan, Sir Terence (1911–1977).
Distinguished British playwright, many of whose successes have been filmed.
Biography: 1979, *Terence Rattigan, the Man and His Work* by Michael Darlow and Gillian Hodson.
French without Tears 39. While the Sun Shines 46. The Winslow Boy 48. The Browning Version 51 and 94. The Deep Blue Sea 55. Separate Tables (AAN) 58, etc.
AS SCREENWRITER: English without Tears 43. The Way to the Stars 45. The Sound Barrier (AAN) 52. The VIPs 63. The Yellow Rolls-Royce 64. Goodbye Mr Chips 69. Bequest to the Nation 73, many others.

Raven, Mike (1927–1997) (Churton Fairman).
Tall, bearded British leading actor and screenwriter, in a few horror movies of the 70s, formerly a pirate radio and BBC disc jockey, and author.
■ Lust for a Vampire 70. I, Monster 71. Crucible of Terror 71. Disciple of Death (& w, co-p) 72.

Ravera, Gina (1968–).
American actress and dancer, from commercials and television; born in San Francisco.
Five Heartbeats 91. White Mile (TV) 94. Weird World (TV) 95. Showgirls 95. Soul of the Game 96. Get on the Bus 96. Soul Food 97. Kiss the Girls 97, etc.

Ravetch, Irving (c. 1915–).
American writer who with his wife Harriet Frank has frequently worked with director Martin Ritt.
The Long Hot Summer 58. The Sound and the Fury 59. Home from the Hill 59. The Dark at the Top of the Stairs 60. Hud (AAN) 63. Hombre 67. The Reivers (& p) 69. The Cowboys 72. The Spikes Gang 74. Conrack (& co-p) 74. Norma Rae (AAN) 79. Murphy's Romance 85. Stanley & Iris 90, etc.

Rawi, Ousama (1939–).
Iranian cinematographer. Went to Canada to produce commercials.
Pulp 73. The Black Windmill 74. Gold 74. Rachel's Man 75. Alfie Darling 75. Sky Riders 76. Power Play 78. Zulu Dawn 79. The Housekeeper/A Judgement in Stone (d) 86. Parting Shots 98, etc.

Rawle, Jeff (1951–).
English actor and screenwriter, best known for his role as the nervous news editor George Dent in the 90s TV sitcom *Drop the Dead Donkey*. Born in Birmingham, he studied at LAMDA.
Home before Midnight (a) 78. Crystal Gazing (a) 82. The Doctor and the Devils (a) 85. The Young Poisoner's Handbook (co-w) 95.
TV series: Billy Liar (title role) 73–74. The Life and Times of Henry Pratt 92. Faith in the Future 97– .

Rawlings, Margaret (1906–1996).
Distinguished English stage actress in occasional films. Born in Japan, she was educated at Lady Margaret Hall, Oxford, and made her stage debut in 1927. Noted for her roles in tragedies, she had great authority on stage, once telling Donald Wolfit, when he was upstaging her as Zabina in *Tamburlaine*, 'Donald, if you do that again I shall rattle my chains all through your next speech.'
Roman Holiday 53. Beautiful Stranger 54. No Road Back 56. Hands of the Ripper 71. Follow Me! 71, etc.

Rawlings, Terence. (aka Terry Rawlings).
English editor.
Watership Down 78. Alien 79. The Awakening 80. Chariots of Fire (AAN) 81. Blade Runner 82. Yentl 83. Legend 86. F/X 86. The Lonely Passion of Judith Hearne 87. Slipstream 89. Not without My Daughter 91. Alien³ 92. No Escape 94. Trapped in Paradise 94. GoldenEye 95. The Saint 97. US Marshals 98, etc.

Rawlins, David.
American editor.
Bingo Long 76. Saturday Night Fever 77. The Last Remake of Beau Geste 78. The China Syndrome 79. Urban Cowboy 80. Soup for One 82. The Osterman Weekend 83. Firestarter 84. Girls Just Want to Have Fun 85. Back to School 86. Police Academy 4: Citizens on Patrol 87. Cold Feet 88. Life Stinks 91. Sidekicks 93. Baby's Day Out 94. Baby's Day Out 94. Mr Magoo 97, etc.

Rawlins, John (1902–1997).
American director, mainly of second features and serials. In films from 1918 as an actor, assistant director, gag-man and editor. Began directing in Britain in the early 30s at Warner's First National studio.
High Society (GB) 32. Lucky Ladies (GB) 32. Going Straight (GB) 33. Sign Please (GB) 33. They're Off (GB) 33. State Police 38. Six Lessons from Madame La Zonga 41. Halfway to Shanghai 42. Sherlock Holmes and the Voice of Terror 42. The Great Impersonation 42. Ladies Courageous 44. Sudan 45. Dick Tracy Meets Gruesome 47. Fort Defiance 52. Shark River 53. The Lost Lagoon 57, etc.

Rawlinson, Herbert (1885–1953).
English-born American circus performer, silent star and latterly character actor.
Monte Cristo 12. The Sea Wolf 13. The Black Box (serial) 15. Good Gracious, Annabelle 19. Charge It 21. Bullets or Ballots 36. Dark Victory 39. Superman (serial) 48, many others.

Rawnsley, David (1909–).
British art director and production designer, a former architect and painter with engineering training, who claimed to have worked on more than 200 films. Inventor, as head of the Rank Film Research Department, of the Independent Frame system, which was intended as a production economy. In 1947 he set up his own production company, Aquila Films, to demonstrate the advantages of the system. After its films failed at the box-office, he moved to Italy and became a potter.
AS ART DIRECTOR: Out of the Blue 31. Brother Alfred 32. Maid of the Mountains 32. Facing the Music 33. Blossom Time 34. I Give My Heart 35. The Amazing Quest of Ernest Bliss 36. Kathleen Mavourneen 37. *49th Parallel* 41. They Flew Alone 41. One of Our Aircraft Is Missing 41. *In Which We Serve* 42. The Way Ahead 44. The Rake's Progress 45. I See a Dark Stranger 45, many others.

❝ A film composer has to make his musical art fit any film line by line. Our long-haired directors must learn to do the same. – *D.R.*

Every now and then, in our extraordinary, heart-breaking, back-breaking business, a man or woman appears or disappears upon whom you look back with regret, because they were made of too fine a material to be wasted on ordinary storytelling. David Rawnsley was one of these. – *Michael Powell*

Rawsthorne, Alan (1905–1971).
British composer.
Burma Victory 45. The Captive Heart 46. Uncle Silas 47. Saraband for Dead Lovers 48. Where No Vultures Fly 51. The Cruel Sea 53. The Man Who Never Was 56. Floods of Fear 58, etc.

Ray, Aldo (1926–1991) (Aldo da Re).
Beefy American actor, in local politics before film career.
Saturday's Hero 51. *The Marrying Kind* 51. Pat and Mike 52. Let's Do It Again 53. Miss Sadie Thompson 54. We're No Angels 55. The Gentle Sergeant 56. Men in War 57. God's Little Acre 58. The Naked and the Dead 58. The Siege of Pinchgut (GB) 58. The Day They Robbed the Bank of England (GB) 60. Johnny Nobody (GB) 61. Nightmare in the Sun 64. Sylvia 65. What Did You Do in the War, Daddy? 66. Dead Heat on a Merry-Go-Round 66. Welcome to Hard Times 67. Riot on Sunset Strip 67. The Power 67. The Green Berets 68. Man Without Mercy 69. And Hope to Die 72. Inside Out 75. The Bad Bunch 76. Haunts 77. Death Dimension 78. The Glove 80. The Secret of Nimh (voice) 82. Dark Sanity 82. Evils of the Night 83. The Executioner Part II 84. Frankenstein's Great Aunt Tillie 84. Biohazard 85. Terror on Alcatraz 87. Hollywood Cop 87. The Sicilian 87. Blood Red 87. The Shooters 89. Shock 'em Dead 91. Foreign Agent 91, etc.

Ray, Andrew (1939–).
British juvenile lead, son of Ted Ray.
The Mudlark (debut) 50. The Yellow Balloon 52. Escapade 55. Woman in a Dressing-Gown 57. Serious Charge 59. Twice Round the Daffodils 62. The System 64. Great Expectations (TV) 75, etc.
TV series: Edward and Mrs Simpson (as George VI) 78.

Ray, Charles (1891–1943).
American leading man of the silent screen, often in country-boy roles. By the late 30s he was working as an extra and refusing speaking roles because 'they're too much trouble'.
SILENT FILMS: The Favorite Son 13. The Ace of Hearts 15. Bill Henry 19. The Old Swimming Hole 20. The Barnstormer 22. The Girl I Love 23. Sweet Adeline 23. The Courtship of Miles Standish (& p) 23. Vanity 25. Getting Gertie's Garter 27. The Garden of Eden 28, etc.
SOUND FILMS: Ladies Should Listen 34. By Your Leave 35. Just My Luck 37.

Ray, Fred Olen (1954–).
American director, screenwriter and producer of low-budget horror and action movies, often released direct to video. He is the author of *The New Poverty Row: Independent Filmmakers and Distributors* (1991).
Alien Dead 79. Scalps 83. Biohazard 85. Armed Response 86. The Tomb 86. Commando Squad 87. Cyclone 87. Deep Space 87. Phantom Empire 87. Star Slammer 88. Terminal Force 88. Warlords 88. Hollywood Chainsaw Hookers 88. Bulletproof (story) 88. Alienator 89. Beverly Hills Vamp 89. Mob Boss 90. Bad Girls from Mars 91. Evil Toons 91. Inner Sanctum 91. Haunting Fear 92. Wizards of the Demon Sword 92. Bikini Drive-In 94. Attack of the 60-Foot Centrefold 95. Invisible Mom 96. Nightshade 97. Invisible Dad 97, etc.

Ray, Johnnie (1927–1990).
American 'crying' singer of the 50s who played a leading role in *There's No Business Like Show Business* 54.

Ray, Man (1890–1976) (Emmanuel Rudnitsky).
American photographer, Dadaist and surrealist, long resident in France, made a few strange films.
Retour à la Raison (wd) 23. Entr'acte (a) 24. L'Etoile de Mer (wd) 28. The Mystery of the Château of the Dice (wd) 29. Dreams that Money Can Buy (oa) 46, etc.

Ray, Nicholas (1911–1979) (Raymond N. Kienzle).
American director, former writer and stage director. Acclaimed for his first film, he later seemed to lack a particular style.
Biography: 1992, *The Films of Nicholas Ray: The Poet of Nightfall* by Geoff Andrew.
■ *They Live by Night* 47. A Woman's Secret 49. Knock on Any Door 49. Born to be Bad 50. *In a Lonely Place* 50. Flying Leathernecks 51. On Dangerous Ground 51. The Lusty Men 52. Johnny Guitar 54. Run for Cover 55. *Rebel without a Cause* (AANw) 55. Hot Blood 56. Bigger than Life 56. The True Story of Jesse James 57. Bitter Victory 57. Wind Across the Everglades 58. Party Girl 58. Savage Innocents 59. King of Kings 61. 55 Days at Peking 62. Dreams of Thirteen 76. The American Friend (a only) 77.

∼In 1980, following his death from cancer, *Lightning over Water* was released, a film about himself.

Ray, René (1912–1993) (Irene Creese).
British actress, on stage from childhood; has often played downtrodden waifs. She was also a novelist and writer. Married to the Earl of Middleton (1975–79).
Young Woodley 30. *The Passing of the Third Floor Back* 35. Crime over London 36. Farewell Again 37. *The Rat* 38. Bank Holiday 38. The Return of the Frog 39. They Made Me a Fugitive 47. If Winter Comes (US) 47. Women of Twilight 52. The Good Die Young 53. Vicious Circle 57, etc.

Ray, Sandip (1954–).
Indian director, screenwriter, composer and cinematographer, the son of Satyajit Ray.
Kanchenjungha (a) 62. Fatikchand (d) 82. Satyajit Ray Presents (d) (TV) 86. The Return of Goopy and Bhaga/Goopy Bhaga Phire Elo (d) 90. Family Reunion/Sakha Prasakha (ph) 91. Target (wd) 92. Broken Journey/Jagoran (d, m) 93, etc.

Ray, Satyajit (1921–1992).
Indian director, famous for the 'Apu' trilogy of a child growing up in modern India. He was awarded an honorary Oscar in 1992.
Autobiography: 1997, My *Years with Apu*.
Pather Panchali 54. *The Unvanquished*/Aparajito 56. The Music Room 58. *The World of Apu* 59. The Goddess 60. Kanchenjunga 62. The Adventures of Goopy and Bagha 68. The Adversary 71. Company Limited 72. Distant Thunder 74. The Middle Man 76. *The Chess Players* 77. The Elephant God 79. Deliverance 82. The Home and the World 84. An Enemy of the People/Ganashatru 89. The Branches of the Tree 90. The Stranger/Agantuk 91. Broken Journey/Jagoran (w) 94, etc.

Ray, Ted (1906–1977) (Charles Olden).
British music-hall comedian and violinist who was in occasional films.
Autobiographies: 1952, *Raising the Laughs*. 1963, *My Turn Next*.
Elstree Calling 30. Radio Parade of 1935. A Ray of Sunshine 47. Meet Me Tonight 50. Escape by Night 52. My Wife's Family 54. Carry On Teacher 59. Please Turn Over 60, etc.

Raye, Carol (1923–) (Kathleen Corkrey).
Australian leading lady of British films of the 40s. She began appearing in Australian films from the 70s.
Strawberry Roan 45. Spring Song 46. While I Live 48. The Journalist 79. Relatives (TV) 85. Business as Usual 86, etc.

Raye, Martha (1916–1994) (Maggie O'Reed).
Wide-mouthed American comedienne and vocalist, popular on radio and TV. The second of her six husbands was composer David Rose.

Rhythm on the Range (debut) 36. Waikiki Wedding 37. Artists and Models 38. The Boys from Syracuse 40. Keep 'Em Flying 41. *Hellzapoppin* 41. Pin-Up Girl 43. Four Jills in a Jeep 44. *Monsieur Verdoux* 47. Jumbo 62. *Pufnstuf* 70. The Concorde – Airport 79 79, etc.

TV series: The Martha Raye Show 59. The Bugaloos 70–71. McMillan 76. Alice 82–84.

❝ I didn't have to work till I was three. But after that, I never stopped. – *M.R.*

Rayfiel, David.
American screenwriter.

Castle Keep (co-w) 69. Valdez Is Coming (co-w) 70. Three Days of the Condor (co-w) 75. Lipstick 76. Death Watch (co-w) 80. Round Midnight (co-w) 86. The Firm (co-w) 93. Intersection (co-w) 94. Sabrina (co-w) 95, etc.

Raymond, Cyril (c. 1897–1973).
British stage and screen actor often seen as the dull husband or professional man.

The Shadow 32. Mixed Doubles 33. The Tunnel 35. Dreaming Lips 37. Come On George 39. Brief Encounter 46. This was a Woman 47. Jack of Diamonds 48. Angels One Five 51. Lease of Life 53. Charley Moon 56, etc.

Raymond, Gary (1935–).
British 'second lead'.

The Moonraker 58. *Look Back in Anger* 59. Suddenly Last Summer 59. The Millionairess 61. El Cid 61. Jason and the Argonauts 63. The Greatest Story Ever Told 65. Traitors' Gate 65. The Playboy of the Western World 66. The Two Faces of Evil 82. Scarlett (TV) 94, etc.

TV series: The Rat Patrol 65.

Raymond, Gene (1908–1998) (Raymond Guion).
American leading man of the 30s, and later a character actor. Born in New York, he was on stage from the age of five, making his Broadway debut in 1920 and going to Hollywood in the early 30s, where his successes came after he was contracted to RKO from the mid-30s. After the Second World War, his career faltered, and he appeared mainly on stage and TV. Married twice; his first wife was actress and singer Jeanette MacDonald (1937–65), with whom he appeared in *Smilin' Through*. Directed one film, *Million Dollar Weekend* (& a) 48.

Personal Maid (debut) 31. *Zoo in Budapest* 33. Flying Down to Rio 33. I Am Suzanne 34. Seven Keys to Baldpate 34. That Girl from Paris 37. Stolen Heaven 38. Mr and Mrs Smith 41. Smilin' Through 41. The Locket 46. Assigned to Danger 49. Hit the Deck 55. The Best Man 64, etc.

TV series: Paris 7000 70.

Raymond, Jack (1886–1953) (John Caines).
English director and producer, mainly of lightweight comedies, in films as an actor from 1910.

Barbara Elopes (co-d) 21. French Leave 30. Up for the Cup 31. Just My Luck 33. Sorrell and Son 33. Girls Please! 34. Chick (p only) 36. The Frog 37. Blondes for Danger 38. The Mind of Mr Reeder 39. Shake Hands with Murder (a) 44. Take Me to Paris 50. Up for the Cup 50. Reluctant Heroes 51. Worm's Eye View 51. Little Big Shot 52, etc.

Raymond, Paula (1923–) (Paula Ramona Wright).
American leading lady, former model.

Devil's Doorway 49. Crisis 50. The Tall Target 51. The Beast from Twenty Thousand Fathoms 53. The Human Jungle 54. The Gun that Won the West 55. The Flight That Disappeared 62. Blood of Dracula's Castle 70. Mind Twister 94, etc.

Razatos, Spiros.
American director of action films, a former stunt expert.

Fast Getaway 91. Class of 1999 II: The Substitute 93.

Rea, Stephen.
Irish leading actor of stage, screen and television.

Angel/Danny Boy 83. Loose Connections 83. Company of Wolves 84. Four Days in July (TV) 84. The Doctor and the Devils 85. Life Is Sweet 91. *The Crying Game* (AAN) 92. Bad Behaviour 93. Angie 94. Princess Caraboo 94. Interview with the Vampire 94. The Shadow of a Gunman (TV) 95. Citizen X (TV) 95. All Men Are Mortal 95. Between the Devil and the Deep Blue Sea 95. Crime of the Century (TV) 96. Michael Collins 96. The Van 96. The Last of the High Kings 96. The Butcher Boy 97. Fever Pitch 97. Trojan Eddie 97. A Further Gesture 97. Still Crazy 98, etc.

Reader, Ralph (1903–1982).
English character actor, choreographer, composer, writer and producer, best known for staging his *The Gang Show* in more than 30 different productions from the 50s onwards. Born in Crewkerne, Somerset, he was on-stage in the United States from 1924 before returning to England, where he specialized in devising dance routines for revues and musicals and, later, in staging large-scale pageants.

Autobiographies: 1954, *It's Been Terrific*; 1960, *This Is the Gang Show*.

The Red Robe 24. I Adore You (ch) 33. Over the Garden Wall (ch) 34. The Blue Squadron (a) 34. Squibs (ch) 35. First a Girl (ch) 35. Limelight/Backstage) (ch) 35. Hello Sweetheart (ch) 35. The Gang Show (co-w, a) 37. London Melody (ch) 37. Splinters in the Air (m, ch) 37. Derby Day (a) 52. Lilacs in the Spring (a) 54. These Dangerous Years (a) 57. All for the Boys (a) 68, etc.

TV series: It's a Great Life 54–55. This Is the West 61.

Reagan, Ronald (1911–).
American leading man of the 40s, former sports reporter. Went into politics and in 1966 was elected Governor of California; in 1976 narrowly missed the Republican presidential nomination; in 1980, elected US President.

Autobiography: 1965, *Where's the Rest of Me?*

Biographies: 1987, *Early Reagan: The Rise of an American Hero* by Anne Edwards. 1994, *Ronald Reagan in Hollywood: Movies and Politics* by Stephen Vaughn.

Love Is on the Air 37. Accidents Will Happen 38. Dark Victory 39. Hell's Kitchen 39. Brother Rat and a Baby 40. Santa Fé Trail 40. International Squadron 41. Nine Lives are Not Enough 41. *Kings Row* 41. Juke Girl 42. *Desperate Journey* 42. This is the Army 43. Stallion Road 47. That Hagen Girl 47. The Voice of the Turtle 47. Night unto Night 48. John Loves Mary 49. The Hasty Heart (GB) 49. Louisa 50. Storm Warning 51. Hong Kong 52. Prisoner of War 54. Law and Order 54. Tennessee's Partner 55. Hellcats of the Navy 57. The Killers 64, etc.

TV series: Death Valley Days 62–64.

Famous line (*Kings Row*): 'Where's the rest of me?'

Famous line (*Knute Rockne, All American*): 'Win one for the Gipper!'

Reason, Rex (1928–) (formerly known as Bart Roberts).
American leading man, mainly in routine films.

Storm over Tibet 52. Salome 53. Yankee Pasha 54. This Island Earth 55. Raw Edge 56. Band of Angels 57. The Rawhide Trail 60, etc.

TV series: Man without a Gun 57–59. The Roaring Twenties 60–62.

Reason, Rhodes (1928–).
American leading man, mainly in second features. Twin of Rex Reason.

Crime against Joe 56. Jungle Heat 57. Yellowstone Kelly 59. King Kong Escapes (Jap.) 68. Cruisin' High 75, etc.

TV series: *White Hunter* 58.

Rebhorn, James.
American actor.

Deadly Business (TV) 86. Heart of Midnight 88. White Sands 92. Scent of a Woman 92. Skylark (TV) 93. Lane Frost 93. 8 Seconds 94. Blank Check 94. Guarding Tess 94. I Love Trouble 94. If Lucy Fell 96. Independence Day 96. My Fellow Americans 96. The Game 97. From the Earth to the Moon (TV) 98. A Bright Shining Lie 98, etc.

Red, Eric (1961–).
American screenwriter and director.

The Hitcher (w) 86. Near Dark (co-w) 87. Cohen & Tate (wd) 88. Blue Steel (co-w) 90. Body Parts (d) 91. The Last Outlaw (w, TV) 93. Bad Moon (wd) 96. Undertow (wd) 96, etc.

Reddy, Helen (1942–).
Australian folk singer.

Airport 75 74. Pete's Dragon 77.

Redfield, William (1927–1976).
American general-purpose actor with long stage experience; former boy actor. Author of one of the best books about acting: 1966, *Letters from an Actor*.

I Married a Woman 58. Fantastic Voyage 66. Duel at Diablo 66. A New Leaf 70. Death Wish 74. For Pete's Sake 74. One Flew Over the Cuckoo's Nest 76, etc.

❝ Movie actors learn that they must fight hard when a fight is called for lest they wake up days later no longer movie stars. – *W.R.*

Genuine success in motion pictures has not so much to do with talent as with bone structure, personality and what is called 'career management'. – *W.R.*

Movies are the swellest way to make money that ever happened in the history of the world. – *W.R.*

Redford, Robert (1937–).
Engaging, blond American leading actor and director who, although working within the studio system, has encouraged independent film-makers. Born in Santa Monica, California, he went to the University of Colorado on a baseball scholarship, but dropped out and later studied art and architecture at the Pratt Institute, New York, and at the American Academy of Dramatic Art. He began working on television and in the theatre, becoming a star with *Butch Cassidy and the Sundance Kid* in 1969. His best roles so far have been as Johnny Hooker in *The Sting* and Bob Woodward in *All the President's Men*; as a director, he scored with *Ordinary People* and *Quiz Show*. He set up the Sundance Film Institute in Utah for independent film-makers and in 1997 announced the creation of Sundance Cinemas, a venture with a major distributor to set up a chain of cinemas for the screening of independent films. Married once and divorced, he has three children.

Biography: 1977, *Robert Redford* by Donald A. Reed.

■ War Hunt 61. Situation Hopeless but not Serious 65. Inside Daisy Clover 65. *The Chase* 66. This Property is Condemned 66. Barefoot in the Park 67. Tell Them Willie Boy is Here 69. *Butch Cassidy and the Sundance Kid* 69. Downhill Racer 69. Little Fauss and Big Halsy 70. The Hot Rock 72. Jeremiah Johnson 72. *The Candidate* 72. The Way We Were 73. *The Sting* (AAN) 73. The Great Gatsby 74. The Great Waldo Pepper 75. Three Days of the Condor 75. *All the President's Men* 76. A Bridge Too Far 77. The Electric Horseman 79. Brubaker 80. Ordinary People (d only) (AA) 80. The Natural 84. Out of Africa 85. Legal Eagles 86. The Milagro Beanfield War (d) 88. Havana 90. Indecent Proposal 92. A River Runs through It (d) 92. Sneakers 92. Indecent Proposal 93. Quiz Show (AANd) 94. Up Close and Personal 96. The Horse Whisperer (p, a, d) 98.

❝ Other people have analysis. I have Utah. – *R.R.*

I often feel I'll just opt out of this rat-race and buy another hunk of Utah. – *R.R.*

A lot of what acting is, is paying attention. – *R.R.*

All my life I've been dogged by guilt because I feel there is this difference between the way I look and the way I feel inside. – *R.R.*

There's always the promise you can penetrate his cool, that you can get through to him. But you can't. – *Paul Newman*

~Redford is alleged to have turned down the leading roles in *Who's Afraid of Virginia Woolf?*, *The Graduate*, *Rosemary's Baby*, *Love Story* and *The Day of the Jackal*.

Redgrave, Corin (1939–).
British supporting actor, son of Sir Michael Redgrave. Gave up acting for a time to work in politics. In 1996, he published a biography of his father. His second wife was actress Kika Markham.

A Man for All Seasons 66. Charge of the Light Brigade 68. Oh What a Lovely War 69. David Copperfield 69. Von Richthofen and Brown 71. Serail 77. Sunday Too Far Away 77. Excalibur 81. Eureka 81. The Fool 91. In the Name of the Father 93. Four Weddings and a Funeral 94. Jane Austen's Persuasion (TV) 95. The Ice House (TV) 97, etc.

TV series: Circles of Deceit 95–96.

Redgrave, Jemma.
English actress, the daughter of Corin Redgrave.

The Dream Demon 88. The Real Charlotte 89. Howards End 92. Diana: Her True Story (TV) 93. The Buddha of Suburbia (TV) 93. Mosley (TV) 98, etc.

TV series: Bramwell 95–98.

Redgrave, Lynn (1943–).
British actress, daughter of Sir Michael Redgrave; has tended to play gauche comedy roles.

■ Tom Jones 63. Girl with Green Eyes 64. *Georgy Girl* (AAN) 66. The Deadly Affair 67. Smashing Time 67. The Virgin Soldiers 69. Blood Kin 69. Killer from Yuma 71. Every Little Crook and Nanny 72. Everything You Always Wanted to Know about Sex 72. The National Health 73. The Happy Hooker 75. The Big Bus 76. Sunday Lovers 80. Gauguin the Savage (TV) 81. Rehearsal for Murder (TV) 82. The Shooting (TV) 82. Morgan Stewart's Coming Home 87. Midnight 89. Getting It Right 89. Whatever Happened to Baby Jane? (TV) 91. Shine 96. Toothless 97. Gods & Monsters 98. Strike 98.

TV series: House Calls 80–81. Teachers Only 82. Rude Awakening 98– .

❝ Looking up at my horrible ugly bulk on a huge screen was the turning point in my life. – *L.R.* (she shed many pounds before making it big in Hollywood and on American TV game shows)

Redgrave, Sir Michael (1908–1985).
Tall, distinguished British actor, former schoolmaster, on stage from 1934. Married actress Rachel Kempson. Their children are all actors: Corin, Vanessa and Lynn Redgrave.

Autobiographies: 1958, *Mask or Face*. 1983, *In My Mind's Eye*.

Biographies: 1956, *Michael Redgrave, Actor* by Richard Findlater. 1996, *Michael Redgrave: My Father* by Corin Redgrave.

■ *The Lady Vanishes* 38. Climbing High 38. A Stolen Life 39. A Window in London 39. *The Stars Look Down* 39. *Kipps* 41. Atlantic Ferry 41. *Jeannie* 41. *Thunder Rock* 42. The Big Blockade 42. The Way to the Stars 45. *Dead of Night* 45. The Captive Heart 46. The Years Between 46. The Man Within 47. *Fame is the Spur* 47. Mourning Becomes Electra (US) (AAN) 47. The Secret beyond the Door (US) 48. *The Browning Version* 50. The Magic Box 51. *The Importance of Being Earnest* 52. The Sea Shall Not Have Them 54. The Green Scarf 54. Oh Rosalinda 55. Confidential Report 55. The Night my Number Came Up 55. *The Dam Busters* 55. Nineteen Eighty-Four 56. Time Without Pity 57. *The Quiet American* 58. Law and Disorder 58. Behind the Mask 58. Shake Hands with the Devil 59. No My Darling Daughter 60. The Innocents 61. The Loneliness of the Long Distance Runner 63. Young Cassidy 64. The Hill 65. The Heroes of Telemark 65. Assignment K 67. Oh What a Lovely War 69. Goodbye Mr Chips 69. The Battle of Britain 69. David Copperfield 69. Connecting Rooms 69. Goodbye Gemini 70. Nicholas and Alexandra 71. The Go-Between 71.

Redgrave, Vanessa (1937–).
British leading lady, daughter of Sir Michael Redgrave; as well known for her espousal of causes as for her acting. She was married to director Tony Richardson (1962–67) and has a son by actor Franco Nero.

Autobiography: 1991, *Vanessa Redgrave*.

Behind the Mask 58. *Morgan* (AAN) 66. Red and Blue 66. Sailor from Gibraltar 66. A Man for all Seasons (uncredited) 66. Blow Up 66. *Camelot* 67. The Charge of the Light Brigade 68. *Isadora* (AAN) 68. A Quiet Place in the Country (It.) 68. Dropout (It.) 69. Vacation (It.) 69. The Seagull 69. Oh What a Lovely War 69. The Trojan Women 71. The Devils 71. *Mary Queen of Scots* (AAN) 72. Murder on the Orient Express 74. Out of Season 75. The Seven Per Cent Solution 76. Julia (AA) 77. Agatha 79. Yanks 79. Bear Island 79. *Playing for Time* (TV) 81. Wagner 82. My Body My Child (TV) 83. The Bostonians (AAN) 84. Steaming 85. Wetherby 86. Three Sovereigns for Sarah (TV) 86. Peter the Great (TV) 86. Second Serve (TV) 86. Comrades 86. Prick Up Your Ears 87. Consuming Passions 88. Whatever Happened to Baby Jane? (TV) 91. The Ballad of the Sad Café 91. Howards End (AAN) 91. Di Ceria dell'Untore/The Plague Sower 92. Sparrow/Storia di una Capinera (It.) 93. Un Muro de Silencio (Arg.) 93. The House of the Spirits 94. Mother's Boys 94.

Little Odessa 94. Great Moments in Aviation 94. A Month by the Lake 95. Down Came a Blackbird (TV) 95. The Wind in the Willows (narrator) 96. Mission: Impossible 96. Vita and Virginia (TV) 97. Mrs Dalloway 97. Wilde 97. Déjà Vu 98. Deep Impact 98. Lulu on the Bridge 98. Celebrity 98, etc.

❝ America is gangsterism for the private profit of the few. – *V.R.*

I give myself to my parts as to a lover. – *V.R.*

I have a tremendous use for passionate statement. – *V.R.*

It's a kinky part of my nature – to meddle. – *V.R.*

I choose all my roles very carefully so that when my career is finished I will have covered all our recent history of oppression. – *V.R.*

The Ellen Terry of her time. – *Caryl Brahms*

Redman, Joyce (1918–).
Irish stage actress whose most memorable film role was in the eating scene in *Tom Jones* (AAN) 63.
Othello (AAN) 65. Prudence and the Pill 67. Les Misérables (TV) 77. A Different Kind of Love 85.

Redmond, Liam (1913–1989).
Irish character actor, an Abbey player.
I See a Dark Stranger 45. Captain Boycott 48. High Treason 51. The Gentle Gunman 52. The Divided Heart 54. Jacqueline 56. Night of the Demon 57. The Boy and the Bridge 59. The Ghost and Mr Chicken (US) 65. Tobruk (US) 66. The Twenty-Fifth Hour 66. The Last Safari 67. Barry Lyndon 75, etc.

Redmond, Moira.
British actress, mainly on the stage.
Doctor in Love 58. *Nightmare* 62. Jigsaw 62. The Limbo Line 66, etc.

Reece, Brian (1913–1962).
British light actor whose success was mainly on stage.
A Case for PC 49 51. Fast and Loose 54. Orders are Orders 55. Carry on Admiral 58, etc.

Reed, Alan (1907–1977) (Edward Bergman).
Burly American character actor, TV's voice of Fred Flintstone.
Days of Glory 43. Nob Hill 44. Viva Zapata 52. The Desperate Hours 55. Breakfast at Tiffany's 62, etc.

Reed, Sir Carol (1906–1976).
Distinguished British director who after a peak in the late 40s seemed to lose his way; his infrequent later films, though always civilized, were generally disappointing. Born in London, the illegitimate son of actor Herbert Beerbohm Tree, he began as an actor in the theatre, where he also directed and formed a close working relationship with Edgar WALLACE, who stimulated his interest in films: he began as a dialogue director, working under Basil DEAN at Ealing Studios. He was at his best in collaborations with writer Graham Greene on *The Fallen Idol* and *The Third Man*. Married actresses Diana Wynyard (1943–47) and Penelope Ward. His lovers included actress Jessie MATTHEWS and novelist Daphne DU MAURIER.
Biography: 1991, *The Man Between* by Nicholas Wapshott.
■ Midshipman Easy 34. Laburnum Grove 36. Talk of the Devil 36. Who's Your Lady Friend? 37. *Bank Holiday* 38. Penny Paradise 38. Climbing High 38. A Girl Must Live 39. *The Stars Look Down* 39. *Night Train to Munich* 40. The Girl in the News 40. *Kipps* 41. The Young Mr Pitt 42. *The Way Ahead* 44. The True Glory (co-d) 45. *Odd Man Out* 46. *The Fallen Idol* (AAN) 48. *The Third Man* (AAN) 49. *An Outcast of the Islands* 51. The Man Between 53. A Kid for Two Farthings 55. Trapeze 56. The Key 58. Our Man in Havana 59. The Running Man 63. The Agony and the Ecstasy 65. *Oliver!* (AA) 68. Flap 70. Follow Me 72.
✪ For the sympathy and expertise which sadly left him after the early 50s. *Kipps*.
❝ To be any good to a director, an actor or actress must either be wonderful, or know absolutely nothing about acting. A little knowledge – that's what is bad! – *C.R.*

His career demonstrates that a director who limits himself to solving technical problems quickly lapses into the decadence of the inappropriate effect. – *Andrew Sarris, 1968*

Reed, Donna (1921–1986) (Donna Mullenger).
American leading lady of the 40s, later star of long-running TV series *The Donna Reed Show*. Won screen test after a beauty contest while still at college.
The Getaway (debut) 41. Shadow of the Thin Man 42. The Courtship of Andy Hardy 42. Calling Dr Gillespie 42. The Human Comedy 43. See Here, Private Hargrove 44. The Picture of Dorian Gray 44. It's a Wonderful Life 46. Green Dolphin Street 47. Chicago Deadline 49. *From Here to Eternity* (AA) 53. The Last Time I Saw Paris 55. Ransom 56. Backlash 56. The Benny Goodman Story 56. Beyond Mombasa 57. The Best Place to Be (TV) 79. Deadly Lessons (TV) 83, etc.
TV series: Dallas 84.
❝ Forty pictures I was in, and all I remember is 'What kind of bra will you be wearing today, honey?' That was always the area of big decision – from the neck to the navel. – *D.R.*

Reed, George (1867–1952).
American character actor.
The Birth of a Nation 14. The Green Pastures 36. So Red the Rose 36. Swanee River 39. Tales of Manhattan 42. Home in Indiana 44, many others.

Reed, Les (1935–).
British composer and conductor. A former member of the John Barry Seven, he has written many popular hits and, occasionally, film scores and songs.
Girl on a Motorcycle (m) 68. Les Bicyclettes de Belsize (m) 69. One More Time (m) 69. The Lady Vanishes (s) 79. Play Misty for Me (s) 71. Creepshow 2 (m) 87, etc.

Reed, Maxwell (1920–1974).
Brooding Irish leading man in British films from 1946, after repertory experience.
The Years Between 46. Daybreak 47. *The Brothers* 48. The Dark Man 49. The Square Ring 53. Before I Wake 56. Notorious Landlady 62. Picture Mommy Dead 66, etc.
TV series: Captain David Grief 56.

Reed, Michael (1929–).
British cinematographer.
October Moth 60. Linda 61. The Gorgon 64. Dracula Prince of Darkness 66. On Her Majesty's Secret Service 69. The Mackenzie Break 71. The Groundstar Conspiracy 73. The Hireling 73. Galileo 75. Shout at the Devil 76. Loophole 80. Kim (TV) 84. Wild Geese 85, etc.

Reed, Oliver (1938–).
Burly British leading man, usually in sullen roles.
The Rebel 60. No Love for Johnnie 61. Curse of the Werewolf 61. Pirates of Blood River 62. *The Damned* 62. Paranoic 63. *The System* 64. The Scarlet Blade 64. The Party's Over 64. The Brigand of Kandahar 65. *The Trap* 66. The Shuttered Room 66. *The Jokers* 66. I'll Never Forget Whatshisname 67. The Assassination Bureau 68. Oliver! 68. Hannibal Brooks 68. *Women in Love* 69. Take a Girl Like You 69. The Lady in the Car 70. The Devils 71. The Hunting Party 71. Z.P.G. 72. Sitting Target 72. Triple Echo 72. Days of Fury 73. The Three Musketeers 73. The Four Musketeers 74. And Then There Were None 74. Royal Flash 74. Tommy 75. The Sellout 75. Great Scout and Cathouse Thursday 76. Burnt Offerings 76. The Prince and the Pauper 77. The Big Sleep 78. Tomorrow Never Comes 78. The Class of Miss MacMichael 78. The Brood 79. Lion of the Desert 81. Dr Heckyl and Mr Hype 81. Condorman 81. Venom 81. The Sting II 82 Masquerade (TV) 82. Second Chance 84. Christopher Columbus (TV) 84. Black Arrow (TV) 85. Castaway 87. The Adventures of Baron Munchausen 89. Return of the Musketeers 90. Hold My Hand I'm Dying 90. The Pit and the Pendulum 90. The House of Usher 91. Prisoners of Honor (TV) 91. The Mummy Lives 92. Return to Lonesome Dove (TV) 93. Funny Bones 95. Parting Shots 98, etc.

Reed, Pamela (1953–).
American leading actress.
The Long Riders 80. Melvin and Howard 80. Eyewitness/The Janitor 81. Young Doctors in Love 82. The Right Stuff 83. The Best of Times 86. Tanner '88 (TV) 88. Rachel River 89. Chattahoochee 89. Cadillac Man 90. Kindergarten Cop 90. Caroline? (TV) 90. Passed Away 92. The Best of Times 94. Junior 94. Santa Fe 97. Critical Choices 97. Bean 97, etc.
TV series: Andros Targets 77.

Reed, Philip (1908–1996).
American leading man with long stage experience.
Female 34. Last of the Mohicans 36. Aloma of the South Seas 41. Old Acquaintance 44. I Cover Big Town 47. Unknown Island 50. The Tattered Dress 57. Harem Scarem 67, etc.

Reed, Rex (1938–).
American interviewer and showbiz gossip columnist. Collections published include *Valentines and Vitriol, Do You Really Sleep in the Nude?, Big Screen Little Screen* and *Conversations in the Raw*. Not a great success as an actor when he played the transsexual *Myra Breckinridge*.

Reed, Robert (1932–1993) (John Robert Reitz, Jnr).
American leading actor, mainly on TV and best known for playing the ever-tolerant father of *The Brady Bunch*. Died of AIDS.
Bloodlust 59. Hurry Sundown 67. Star! 68. The Love Bug 68. The Maltese Bippy 69. Haunts of the Very Rich (TV) 72. Snatched (TV) 72. Nightmare (TV) 76. The Boy in the Plastic Bubble (TV) 76. The Hunted Lady (TV) 77. Bud and Lou (TV) 78. The Seekers (TV) 79. Love's Savage Fury (TV) 79. Casino (TV) 80. Death of a Centerfold (TV) 81. A Very Brady Christmas (TV) 88. Prime Target 91, etc.
TV series: The Defenders 61–65. *The Brady Bunch* 69–74. Mannix 69–75. Rich Man, Poor Man Book I 76. The Brady Bunch Hour 77. Roots 77. The Runaways 78. Scruples 80. Nurse 81–82. The Bradys 90.

Rees, Angharad (1949–).
Welsh leading lady, best known for her role as Demelza in the TV series *Poldark* 75–77. Formerly married to actor Christopher Cazenove.
Hands of the Ripper 72. Under Milk Wood 72. The Love Ban 73. Moments 74. The Curse of King Tut's Tomb (TV) 80, etc.

Rees, Roger (1944–).
Introspective Welsh actor and theatre director. Born in Aberystwyth, he studied art at the Slade, made his stage debut at the age of 22, and was in films from 1983. A leading member of the Royal Shakespeare Company for eight years, he played the title role in its notable production of *Nicholas Nickleby*, which was also televised.
A Bouquet of Barbed Wire (TV) 76. Star 80 83. A Christmas Carol (TV) 84. Ebony Tower (TV) 86. Mountains of the Moon 90. If Looks Could Kill 91. Stop or My Mom Will Shoot 91. Robin Hood: Men in Tights 93. Sudden Manhattan 96. The Substance of Fire 96. Titanic (TV) 96, etc.
TV series: Cheers 89–91.

Reese, Tom (1930–).
American character actor, a notable 'heavy'.
Flaming Star 60. Marines Let's Go 61. Forty Pounds of Trouble 62. Murderers' Row 66. Vanishing Point 71. The Outfit 73. The Wild Party 74. Defiance 79, etc.

Reeve, Ada (1874–1966).
British character actress and singer whose career lasted more than 80 years. Born in Whitechapel, London, she appeared in pantomime at the age of four and made her music-hall debut when she was 12. She became a star of musicals in the 1890s, touring the world until the mid-30s when she turned to acting on stage and in films.
Autobiography: 1954, *Take It for a Fact*.
They Came to a City 44. When the Bough Breaks 47. Night and the City 50. Eye Witness 56. The Passionate Stranger/A Novel Affair 57, etc.

Reeve, Christopher (1952–).
Strapping American leading man who flew to fame. He was paralysed from the neck down in a riding accident in 1995.
Autobiography: 1997, *Still Me*.
Gray Lady Down 77. *Superman* 78. Superman II 80. Somewhere in Time 80. Death Trap 82. Monsignor 82. Superman III 83. The Aviator 84. The Bostonians 84. Anna Karenina (TV) 84. Street Smart 87. Superman IV 87. Switching Channels 88. The Great Escape II: The Untold Story (TV) 88. The Rose and the Jackal (TV) 90. Bump in the Night 90. Noises Off 92. The Sea Wolf (TV) 93. Black Fox 93. Morning Glory 93. The Remains of the Day 93. Above Suspicion 94. Village of the Damned 95. Rear Window (TV) 98, etc.

Reeve, Geoffrey (1932–).
British director and producer.
Puppet on a Chain (d) 70. Caravan to Vaccares (p, d) 74. The Shooting Party (p) 84. The Far Pavilions (p) (TV) 84. Half Moon Street (p) 86. The Whistle Blower (p) 86. Souvenir (d) (TV) 88, etc.

Reeves, George (1914–1959) (George Brewer).
American leading man. Typecast as Superman, he found no parts available for him and became a wrestler. Shot himself.
Biography: 1996, *Hollywood Kryptonite: The Bulldog, the Lady and the Death of Superman* by Sam Kashner and Nancy Schoenberger.
Gone with the Wind (debut) 39. Strawberry Blonde 41. Blood and Sand 42. Bar 20 44. Jungle Jim 49. Samson and Delilah 50. Sir Galahad (serial) 50. From Here to Eternity 53.
TV series: Superman 51–57.

Reeves, Keanu (1964–).
American leading actor. Born in Beirut, Lebanon, the son of a Hawaiian father, he began acting in Canada and first came to notice on TV. He also plays bass guitar in the rock group Dogstar, which toured Europe in 1996 to indifferent reviews. The success of the thriller *Speed*, for which he was reportedly paid $1.25m, put up his asking price to $7m a film, though he turned down a sequel, *Speed II*.
Biography: 1996, *Keanu* by Sheila Johnston.
Flying 86. Youngblood 86. River's Edge 87. Dangerous Liaisons 88. The Night Before 88. Permanent Record 88. The Prince of Pennsylvania 88. Bill and Ted's Excellent Adventure 89. I Love You to Death 90. Tune in Tomorrow/Aunt Julia and the Scriptwriter 90. Point Break 91. Bill and Ted's Bogus Journey 91. My Own Private Idaho 91. Bram Stoker's Dracula 92. Much Ado about Nothing 93. Even Cowgirls Get the Blues 93. Little Buddha 93. *Speed* 94. Johnny Mnemonic 95. A Walk in the Clouds 95. Feeling Minnesota 96. Chain Reaction 96. The Devil's Advocate 97. The Last Time I Committed Suicide 97. The Matrix 99, etc.

Reeves, Kynaston (1893–1971).
British character actor of stage and screen, often seen as academic. In films from 1919.
The Lodger 32. The Housemaster 38. The Prime Minister 40. Vice Versa 48. The Guinea Pig 49. The Mudlark 50. Top of the Form 53. Brothers in Law 57. School for Scoundrels 60. The Private Life of Sherlock Holmes 70, many others.

Reeves, Michael (1944–1969).
British director whose promising career barely got started.
■ Sister of Satan/Revenge of the Blood Beast (It.) 65. The Sorcerers 67. Witchfinder General 68.

Reeves, Saskia.
British leading actress, from the stage.
December Bride 90. The Bridge 90. Close My Eyes 91. Antonia and Jane 91. Traps 94. Butterfly Kiss 95. i.d. 95. Different for Girls 96. LA without a Map 98. Heart 98, etc.
TV series: Plotlands 97.

Reeves, Steve (1926–).
American actor, formerly 'Mr World' and 'Mr Universe'; found stardom from 1953 in Italian muscleman spectacles. He retired to his Californian ranch in the late 60s.
■ Athena 54. The Labours of Hercules 57. Hercules and the Queen of Sheba/Hercules Unchained 58. The White Warrior 58. Goliath and the Barbarians 59. The Giant of Marathon 59. The White Devil 59. The Last Days of Pompeii 59. Thief of Baghdad 60. Morgan the Pirate 60. The Wooden Horse of Troy 61. Duel of the Titans/Romulus and Remus 61. Son of Spartacus 62. War of the Trojans 62. Sandokan the Great 63. The Pirates of Malaya 64. A Long Ride from Hell 68.
❝ I found acting very stressful. I never liked it. – *S.R.*

Refn, Anders (1944–).
Danish director and editor. He is the father of Nicolas REFN.
AS EDITOR: Dear Irene/Kaere Irene 71. With

Love and Kisses/Med Kaerling Hilsen 71. Carl, My Childhood Symphony/Min Finske Barndom 94, etc.
AS DIRECTOR: Prins Piwi (co-d) 74. Stromer 76. The Heritage/Slaegten 78. The Flying Devils/De Flyvende Djaevle 85. I Familiens Skod 93. Black Harvest/Sort Host (& co-w) 93, etc.

Refn, Nicolas Winding (c. 1972–).
Danish director, the son of Anders REFN. He lived in New York as a child. Turned down an offer from Hollywood to remake *Pusher*.
Pusher 97.

Regan, Phil (1906–1996).
American singer and actor of the 30s and 40s, a former policeman, who was best known for singing 'Happy Days Are Here Again' at President Truman's inauguration; later involved in politics, he was imprisoned for a time for attempted bribery in the early 70s.
The Key 34. Dames 34. We're in the Money 35. Laughing Irish Eyes 36. Manhattan Merry-Go-Round 37. She Married a Cop 39. Sweet Rosie O'Grady 43. Swing Parade of 1946 46. Three Little Words 50, etc.

Reggiani, Serge (1922–).
Slightly-built French-Italian actor with stage experience.
Les Portes de la Nuit 46. Manon 48. Les Amants de Vérone 48. La Ronde 50. Secret People (GB) 51. *Casque d'Or* 51. The Wicked Go to Hell 55. Les Misérables 57. Marie Octobre 58. Paris Blues 60. The Leopard 63. The 25th Hour 67. Les Aventuriers 67. Day of the Owl (It.) 68. The Good and the Bad 76. Cat and Mouse 76. L'Empreinte des Géantes 80. Fantastica 80. I Hired a Contract Killer 90. Under the Stars 93. Le Petit Garçon 95, etc.

Reichenbach, François (1922–1993).
French documentarist with an ironic viewpoint.
L'Amérique Insolite 59. Un Coeur Gros Comme Ça 61. Les Amoureux du France 64. Hollywood through a Keyhole 66. Love of Life (co-d) 68. F for Fake (co-d) 75. Sex O'Clock 76. Pele 77. Houston, Texas 80. François Reichenbach's Japan 83. Visages Suisses (co-d) 91, etc.

Reicher, Frank (1875–1965).
German-born character actor, long in Hollywood.
Her Man O' War 26. Mata Hari 32. *King Kong* 33. Kind Lady 36. Anthony Adverse 36. Lancer Spy 38. They Dare Not Love 41. House of Frankenstein 45. The Mummy's Ghost 46. The Secret Life of Walter Mitty 47. Samson and Delilah 50, many others.
AS DIRECTOR: The Eternal Mother 17. Behind Masks 21. Wise Husbands 21, etc.

Reid, Alastair (1939–).
British director. From the mid-70s on, working in television.
■ Baby Love 69. The Night Digger 71. Something to Hide 72. Man on the Screen (TV) 83.

Reid, Beryl (1920–1996).
British comedienne and character actress, in variety from 1936, and known for her act as a Birmingham schoolgirl, Marlene.
Autobiography: 1984, *So Much Love*.
The Belles of St Trinian's 54. The Extra Day 56. The Dock Brief 62. Star! 68. Inspector Clouseau 68. The Assassination Bureau 68. *The Killing of Sister George* (her stage role) (US) 68. Entertaining Mr Sloane 70. The Beast in the Cellar 71. Dr Phibes Rises Again 72. Psychomania 72. Father Dear Father 73. No Sex Please We're British 73. Joseph Andrews 76. Smiley's People (TV) 82. Yellowbeard 83. The Doctor and the Devils 85, etc.
TV series: The Most Likely Girl 57. Bold as Brass 64. Alcock and Gander 72. The Secret Diary of Adrian Mole Aged 13 85. The Growing Pains of Adrian Mole 87.

•

Reid, Carl Benton (1894–1973).
American character actor with stage career before settling in Hollywood.
The Little Foxes 41. In a Lonely Place 50. Convicted 50. The Great Caruso 51. Lorna Doone 51. Carbine Williams 52. The Egyptian 54. The Left Hand of God 55. The Gallant Hours 59, etc.
TV series: Amos Burke – Secret Agent 65.

Reid, Elliott (1920–).
American comedy actor who often played the dumb son of an executive.
The Story of Dr Wassell 44. Gentlemen Prefer Blondes 53. Woman's World 54. Inherit the Wind 60. Who's Been Sleeping in My Bed? 63. The Thrill of It All 63. Some Kind of a Nut 69, etc.

Reid, Kate (1930–1993).
Canadian actress.
This Property Is Condemned 66. The Andromeda Strain 71. Death Among Friends (TV) 75. Equus 77. Atlantic City USA 81. Fire with Fire 86. Sweethearts Dance 88. Bye Bye Blues 90. Deceived 91, etc.
TV series: The Whiteoaks of Jalna 72.

Reid, Wallace (1891–1923).
American leading man of the silent screen. Addiction to morphine, following an accident in 1919, and heavy drinking led to his early death. Married actress Dorothy DAVENPORT.
The Deerslayer 11. The Birth of a Nation 14. The Love Mask 16. House of Silence 18. The Dancing Fool 20. The Affairs of Anatol 21. Forever 21. The Ghost Breaker 22, many others.

Reiner, Carl (1922–).
Balding, genial American comedy writer and actor.
AS ACTOR: Happy Anniversary 59. The Gazebo 59. Gidget Goes Hawaiian 61. *It's a Mad Mad Mad Mad World* 63. The Art of Love 65. The Russians Are Coming, the Russians Are Coming 66. A Guide for the Married Man 67. The Comic 69. The End 78. Dead Men Don't Wear Plaid 82. Spirit of '76 91. The Right to Remain Silent (TV) 95. Slums of Beverly Hills 98, etc.
TV series: Good Heavens 76.
AS WRITER: The Thrill of It All 63. The Art of Love 65. Enter Laughing 67. The Comic 69. The Jerk 79. Dead Men Don't Wear Plaid 82. The Man with Two Brains (co-w) 83.
TV series: *The Dick Van Dyke Show* 61–65.
AS DIRECTOR: Enter Laughing 67. The Comic 69. Where's Poppa? 70. Oh God 77. The Jerk 79. Dead Men Don't Wear Plaid 82. The Man with Two Brains 83. Summer School 87. Bert Rigby, You're a Fool (wd) 89. Triple Indemnity 93. Fatal Instinct 93. That Old Feeling 97, etc.

Reiner, Rob (1945–).
American director, writer and former comic actor. He is the son of director Carl REINER and was formerly married to actress and director Penny MARSHALL.
This Is Spinal Tap 85. The Sure Thing 85. Stand by Me 86. The Princess Bride 87. When Harry Met Sally 89. Postcards from the Edge 90. Misery 90. Spirit of '76 90. Sleepless in Seattle (a) 93. North 94. Bullets over Broadway (a) 94. Lifesavers (a) 94. Mixed Nuts (a) 94. Bye Bye, Love (a) 95. The American President 95. Ghosts of Mississippi 97. Primary Colors (a) 98, etc.
TV series: All in the Family (a) 71–78. Free Country (a) 78.

Reinhardt, Gottfried (1911–1994).
Austrian producer, son of theatrical producer Max Reinhardt. Went to US with his father and became assistant to Walter Wanger. Produced and occasionally directed.
The Great Waltz (script) 38. Comrade X (p) 40. Two-Faced Woman (p) 41. Command Decision (p) 48. The Red Badge of Courage (p) 51. Invitation (d) 52. The Story of Three Loves (d) 53. Betrayed (d) 54. The Good Soldier Schweik (p) 59. Town without Pity (p, d) 61. Situation Hopeless but Not Serious (p, d) 65, etc.

Reinhardt, Max (1873–1943) (Max Goldman).
Austrian theatrical producer of great pageants. His only sound screen direction (with William Dieterle) was *A Midsummer Night's Dream* 35, from his stage production. He had made three German silents between 1908 and 1914.

Reinhold, Judge (1956–).
American actor.
Running Scared 79. Stripes 81. Fast Times at Ridgemont High 82. The Lords of Discipline 83. Beverly Hills Cop 84. Gremlins 84. Head Office 86. Offbeat 86. Ruthless People 86. Beverly Hills Cop II 87. Vice Versa 88. Rosalie Goes Shopping 89. Daddy's Dyin', Who's Got the Will? 90. Zandalee 90. Baby on Board 92. Bank Robber 93. Beverly Hills Cop III 94. The Santa Clause 94. The Wharf Rat (TV) 95. The Right to Remain Silent (TV) 95. As Good as Dead 95. Hostage Train 97. Teen Monster 99, etc.
TV series: Secret Service Guy 96.

Reiniger, Lotte (1899–1981).
German animator, well known for her silhouette cartoons.
The Adventures of Prince Achmed 26. Dr Dolittle (series) 28. Carmen 33. Papageno 35. The Brave Little Tailor 55, etc.

Reinking, Ann (1949–).
American dancer, from Broadway.
■ Movie Movie 78. All That Jazz 79. Annie 82. Micki & Maude 84.

Reinl, Harald (1908–1986) (Karl Reiner).
German director of popular entertainments, including a series of European westerns based on the novels of Karl MAY and starring Lex BARKER. He was killed by his wife.
Bergkristall 49. Der Schatz im Silbersee 52. The Return of Dr Mabuse/Im Stahinetz des Dr Mabuse 61. Forger of London 61. The Invisible Dr Mabuse/Die Unsichtbaren Krallen des Dr Mabuse 62. Winnetou 64. Winnetou II 64. Shatterhand 64. Winnetou III 65. Winnetou und das Halbblut Apanatschi 67. The Torture Chamber of Dr Sadism/Die Schlangengrube und das Pendel 67. Winnetou und Shatterhand im Tal der Toten 68, etc.

Reis, Irving (1906–1953).
American director, with radio experience.
■ One Crowded Night 40. I'm Still Alive 40. Weekend for Three 41. A Date with the Falcon 41. The Gay Falcon 41. The Falcon Takes Over 42. The Big Street 43. Hitler's Children 43. Crack Up 46. *The Bachelor and the Bobby-soxer* 47. *Enchantment* 48. All My Sons 48. Roseanna McCoy 49. Dancing in the Dark 49. Three Husbands 50. New Mexico 51. The Fourposter 52.

Reisch, Walter (1903–1983).
Austrian writer who in the 30s came to Britain, then Hollywood.
Men Are Not Gods (& d) 36. Ninotchka (AAN) 39. Comrade X (AAN) 40. The Heavenly Body 43. Gaslight (co-w, AAN) 44. Song of Scheherezade (& d) 46. Titanic (AA) 52. The Girl in the Red Velvet Swing 55. Journey to the Centre of the Earth 59, etc.

Reiser, Paul (1957–).
American actor and comedian. In 1998 he was paid $1m an episode for his TV series *Mad about You*.
Diner 82. Sunset Limousine 83. Beverly Hills Cop 84. From Here to Maternity (TV) 85. Odd Jobs 85. Aliens 86. Beverly Hills Cop II 87. Cross My Heart 88. Crazy People 90. Family Prayers 91. The Marrying Man 91. Mr Write 94. Bye Bye, Love 95, etc.
TV series: My Two Dads 87–90. Mad about You 92– .

Reisner, Allen.
American director, from TV.
■ All Mine to Give 56. St Louis Blues 58. To Die in Paris (TV) (co-d) 68. Your Money or Your Wife (TV) 72. Captains and the Kings (TV) 86. Mary Jane Harper Cried Last Night (TV) 77. Cops and Robin (TV) 78. The Love Tapes (TV) 80.

Reisner, Charles (1887–1962).
American director.
The Man in the Box 25. Reducing 32. The Show-Off 34. Sophie Lang Goes West 37. *The Big Store* 41. Meet the People 44. Lost in a Harem 44. The Cobra Strikes 48. The Travelling Saleswoman 50, many others, mainly second features.

Reisz, Karel (1926–).
Czech director, in Britain from childhood. Former film critic. In recent years he has been working mainly as a theatre director.
■ We are the Lambeth Boys 58. *Saturday Night and Sunday Morning* 60. Night Must Fall 63. This Sporting Life (p only) 63. *Morgan: A Suitable Case for Treatment* 66. Isadora 68. The Gambler 74. Who'll Stop the Rain? 78. The French Lieutenant's Woman 81. Sweet Dreams 86. Everybody Wins 88.

Reitherman, Wolfgang (1909–1985).
American animator, director of Disney cartoon features from the mid-60s.

Reitman, Ivan (1946–).
Canadian director and producer.
Foxy Lady 71. Cannibal Girls 73. Meatballs 79. Stripes (p, d) 81. *Ghostbusters* 84. Legal Eagles 86. Twins 88. Ghostbusters II (p, d) 89. Kindergarten Cop (p, d) 90. Stop or My Mom Will Shoot (p) 91. Beethoven (p) 92. Dave 93. Junior 94. Space Jam (p) 96. Fathers' Day 97. Six Days, Seven Nights 98, etc.

Reitz, Edgar (1932–).
German director, best known for *Homeland/Heimat*, his epic film on the life of a family over three generations, which ran for more than 15 hours. Born in Moorbach, he studied at Munich University and was a member of the Oberhausen group that announced a new German cinema in 1962. He worked as a cameraman and editor with various companies and began making short films and documentaries in the mid-50s. With Alexander KLUGE and others he set up the Institute of Film Composition in Ilum, where he taught.
Mealtimes/Mahlzeiten 67. Fussnoten 67. Cadillac 69. Stories of the Bucket Baby/Geschichten von Kubelkind (co-d) 70. Die Reise nach Wien 73. Zero Hour/Stunde Null 76. The Tailor from Ulm/Der Schneider von Ulm 78. Homeland/Heimat 84, etc.
❝ We don't believe in the 'new film' but rather in the 'new cinema'. The cinema is a place where 'film' happens. The dark room, the mystery that constitute the 'audience', a glowing screen, music, voices and sounds that fill the room, an event, a fluidity that sweeps up the audience, which needs it as an integral part of cinema . . . that's 'cinema'. – *E.R.*
The filmmaker should develop a feeling for the fact that when he is filming, what he sees, what he hears, is being transported into the past. The sorrow we feel about the transitory nature of happiness can never be greater than in the moment of filming. – *E.R.*

Reizenstein, Franz (1911–1968).
German-born composer who scored British horror movies. In films from 1951.
The Mummy 59. The White Trap 59. Jessy 60. Circus of Horrors 60, etc.

Relph, George (1888–1960).
British character actor mainly seen on stage.
Nicholas Nickleby 47. I Believe in You 52. *The Titfield Thunderbolt* (leading role as the vicar) 53. Doctor at Large 57. Davy 57, etc.

Relph, Michael (1915–).
British producer-director, son of George Relph. Former art director and production designer; from 1947 to 1969 he worked almost exclusively with Basil Dearden, usually producing while Dearden directed.
The Captive Heart 46. Frieda 47. Saraband for Dead Lovers 48. *The Blue Lamp* 50. I Believe in You (& co-w) 52. The Rainbow Jacket 54. Davy (d) 57. Rockets Galore (d) 57. Violent Playground 58. Sapphire 59. *The League of Gentlemen* 59. *Victim* 61. Life for Ruth 62. The Mind Benders 63. Woman of Straw 63. Masquerade 65. The Assassination Bureau 68. An Unsuitable Job for a Woman 82, etc.

Relph, Simon (1940–).
English producer, the son of Michael Relph.
Reds 81. The Return of the Soldier 81. Privates on Parade 82. The Ploughman's Lunch 83. Laughterhouse 84. Secret Places 85. Wetherby 85. Comrades 87. Enchanted April 91. Damage 92. Camilla 94, etc.

Remar, James (1953–).
American actor, often as a heavy.
The Warriors 79. Cruising 80. The Long Riders 80. Windwalker 81. 48 Hours 82. The Cotton Club 84. Quiet Cool 86. The Clan of the Cave Bear 86. Rent-a-Cop 88. The Dream Team 89. Drugstore Cowboy 89. Tales from the Darkside: The Movie 90. The Tigress/Die Tigerin 92. Fatal Instinct 93. Renaissance Man 94. Blink 94. Across the Moon 94. Miracle on 34th Street 94. Boys on the Side 95. The Quest 96. The Phantom 96. Mortal Kombat 2: Annihilation 97. Psycho 98, etc.
TV series: Total Security 97.

Remarque, Erich Maria (1898–1970).
German novelist.
All Quiet on the Western Front 30. The Road Back 37. Three Comrades 38. So Ends Our Night 41. Arch of Triumph 48. A Time to Love and a Time to Die (& a) 57. All Quiet on the Western Front (TV) 79, etc.

Remick, Lee (1935–1991).
American leading lady with stage and TV experience.
A Face in the Crowd (film debut) 57. The Long Hot Summer 58. *Anatomy of a Murder* 59. Sanctuary 61. Experiment in Terror 62. *Days of Wine and Roses* (AAN) 63. The Wheeler Dealers 64. Baby the Rain Must Fall 65. The Hallelujah Trail 65. No Way to Treat a Lady 68. A Severed Head 70. Loot 70. Sometimes a Great Notion 72. A Delicate Balance 73. QB VII 74. The Blue Knight (TV) 74. Hennessy 75. *Jennie* (TV) 75. The Omen 76. Telefon 77. The Medusa Touch 77. Ike (TV) 79. The Europeans 79. Torn between Two Lovers (TV) 79. The Competition 80. Tribute 80. The Women's Room (TV) 80. The Letter (TV) 82. Mistral's Daughter (TV) 84. Emma's War 85. The Vision 87, etc.
❝ It would be nice to make films for grown-ups again, and when they decide to start filming them, I'll start acting in them. – *L.R.*

Remsen, Bert (1925–).
American character actor.
Pork Chop Hill 59. Dead Ringer 64. Brewster McCloud 70. McCabe and Mrs Miller 71. California Split 74. Thieves Like Us 74. Nashville 75. Buffalo Bill and the Indians 76. Harry and Walter Go to New York 76. Borderline 80. The Sting II 83. Eye of the Tiger 86. Daddy's Dying – Who's Got the Will? 90. Only the Lonely 91. The Bodyguard 92. The Player 92. Jack the Bear 93. Maverick 94. Dillinger and Capone 95. White Man's Burden 95. Hugo Pool 97. Conspiracy Theory 97, etc.

Renaldo, Duncan (1904–1980) (Renault Renaldo Duncan).
American actor and painter with varied experience. In many films from *Trader Horn* 30 to *For Whom the Bell Tolls* 43; later more famous as The Cisco Kid in a series of second-feature westerns (1945–50). Directed some films in the 20s. Also a screenwriter under the name Renault Duncan.

Renan, Sergio.
Argentinian director, a former actor, from the stage. He went into exile in the mid-70s after receiving death threats following the release of *The Truce*.
AS ACTOR: Pasó en Mi Barrio 51. *Los Siete Locos* 72. Juan Manuel de Rosas 72, etc.
AS DIRECTOR: Growing Up Suddenly/Crecer de Golpe 70. *The Truce*/La Tregua (AAN) 73. Thanks for the Light 84. High Heels 85, etc.

Renaud, Madeleine (1903–1994).
Distinguished French stage actress, in occasional films. Married Jean-Louis Barrault, with whom she ran the post-war Compagnie Renaud-Barrault, acting in many of its notable productions.
Vent Debout 22. Jean de la Lune 31. La Maternelle 32. The Naked Heart/Maria Chapdelaine 34. Stormy Waters/Remorques 41. The Woman Who Dared/Le Ciel Est à Vous 44. Le Plaisir 52. The Longest Day 62. The Devil by the Tail/Le Diable par la Queue 69. La Mandarine 72, etc.

Rendell, Ruth.
British crime novelist who also writes under the name Barbara Vine. Her stories featuring Inspector Wexford were the basis of a successful television series, starring George BAKER.
A Judgement in Stone/La Cérémonie (oa) 86. Tree of Hands (oa) 88. Live Flesh/Carne Tremula (oa) 98, etc.
TV series: The Ruth Rendell Mysteries 87–92.

Rene, Norman (1951–1996).
American director whose films were written by Craig Lucas, with whom he also worked in the theatre. Died of AIDS.
■ Longtime Companion 90. Prelude to a Kiss 92. Reckless 95.

Renfro, Brad (1982–).
American teenage actor.
The Client 94. The Cure 95. Tom and Huck 95. Sleepers 96. Telling Lies in America 97. Apt Pupil 98, etc.

Rennahan, Ray (1896–1980).
American cinematographer, in Hollywood from 1917; an expert on colour.
Fanny Foley Herself 31. *The Mystery of the Wax Museum* 33. *Becky Sharp* 35. *Wings of the Morning* 37. *Gone with the Wind* (co-ph) (AA) 39. *The Blue Bird* 40. Down Argentine Way 40. *Blood and Sand* (co-ph) (AA) 42. *For Whom the Bell Tolls* 43. Belle of the Yukon 44. The Perils of Pauline 47. The Paleface 48. A Yankee at King Arthur's Court 49. Arrowhead 53. Terror in a Texas Town 58, many others.

Rennie, James (1890–1965).
American hero of the 20s.
Remodelling Her Husband 20. The Dust Flower 22. His Children's Children 23. Clothes Make the Pirate 25. The Girl of the Golden West 30. Illicit 31, etc.

Rennie, Michael (1909–1971).
Lean, good-looking British leading man best known as TV's *The Third Man*. Varied experience before going into repertory and film stand-in work.
Secret Agent 36. The Divorce of Lady X 38. Dangerous Moonlight 40. Ships with Wings 41. I'll be Your Sweetheart 45. *The Wicked Lady* 45. The Root of All Evil 47. Idol of Paris 48. The Black Rose 50; Then to US; Five Fingers 52. Les Misérables 52. *The Day the Earth Stood Still* 52. The Robe 53. Désirée 54. The Rains of Ranchipur 55. Island in the Sun 56. Omar Khayyam 57. Third Man on the Mountain 59. *The Lost World* 60. Mary, Mary 63. Ride beyond Vengeance 65. The Power 67. Hotel 67. The Devil's Brigade 68. The Battle of El Alamein (as Montgomery) 68. Subterfuge 69, etc.

Réno, Jean (1948–).
French leading actor, a constant presence in the films of Luc BESSON. Born in Casablanca, of Spanish parents, he studied drama there and in Paris, first working in theatre and television. Married twice.
The Last Battle/Le Dernier Combat 83. The Big Blue/Le Grand Bleu 88. Nikita/La Femme Nikita 90. Operation Corned-Beef 91. L'Homme au Masque d'Or 91. Les Visiteurs 93. Leon/The Professional 94. Beyond the Clouds 95. French Kiss 95. Two Jerks and a Pig/Les Truffes 95. Mission: Impossible 96. Roseanna's Grave/For Roseanna 96. Le Jaguar 96. Godzilla (US) 98. Ronin (US) 98. The Corridors of Time 98, etc.

Renoir, Claude (1914–1993).
French cinematographer.
Toni 34. *Une Partie de Campagne* 36. La Règle du Jeu 39. Monsieur Vincent 47. *The River* 51. The Green Glove 52. *The Golden Coach* 53. *Eléna et les Hommes* 56. Crime and Punishment 56. The Witches of Salem 56. Les Tricheurs 58. *Blood and Roses* 60. Lafayette 61. Circus World 64. The Game is Over 66. Barbarella 68. The Madwoman of Chaillot (co-ph) 69. The Horsemen 71. Paul and Michelle 74. The Spy Who Loved Me 77. Le Toubib 79, many others.

Renoir, Jean (1894–1979).
Distinguished French director, son of painter Auguste Renoir, brother of Pierre Renoir. Stage experience in productions of his own plays.
Autobiographies: 1973, *My Life and My Films*. *Letters by Jean Renoir* edited by Lorraine Lo Bianco and David Thompson.
Biographies: 1977, *Jean Renoir, the World of His Films* by Len Brandy. 1991, *Jean Renoir – a Life in Pictures* by Célia Bertin.
La Fille de L'Eau 24. Nana 26. Charleston 27. The Little Match-Seller 28. *La Chienne* 31. *Boudu Sauvé des Eaux* 32. Toni 34. Madame Bovary 34. *Le Crime de Monsieur Lange* 35. *Les Bas Fonds* 36. *Une Partie de Campagne* 36. *La Grande Illusion* 37. *La Marseillaise* 38. *La Bête Humaine* 38. *La Règle du Jeu* (& a) 39; to US; Swamp Water 41. This Land Is Mine 43. *The Southerner* (AAN) 44. Diary of a Chambermaid 45. The Woman on the Beach 47. Back to Europe. The River 51. The Golden Coach 53. French Cancan 55. Eléna et les Hommes 56. Lunch on the Grass 59. The Vanishing Corporal 61. C'est la Révolution 67. Le Petit Théâtre de Jean Renoir 69, etc.
❝ Renoir has a lot of talent, but he isn't one of us. – *Darryl F. Zanuck*
Life was not so much the subject as the *stuff* of his movies, spilling over the edges of his frames. – *Newsweek*
Only when style is confused with meaningless flourishes does Renoir's economy of expression seem inadequate for textbook critics. – *Andrew Sarris, 1968*
My dream is of a craftsman's cinema in which the author can express himself as directly as the painter in his paintings or the writer in his books. – *J.R.*
A director makes only one film in his life. Then he breaks it into pieces and makes it again. – *J.R.*
The saving grace of the cinema is that with patience, and a little love, we may arrive at that wonderfully complex creature which is called man. – *J.R.*

Renoir, Pierre (1885–1952).
French character actor, brother of Jean Renoir.
Madame Bovary 34. La Marseillaise 38. Les Enfants du Paradis 44. Doctor Knock 50, many others.

Renzi, Eva (1944–).
German leading lady in international films.
Funeral in Berlin 66. The Pink Jungle 68. Beiss Mich Liebling 70. La Chambre Voisine 80, etc.

Rescher, Gayne.
American cinematographer.
A Face in the Crowd 57. The Troublemaker 64. Rachel, Rachel 68. John and Mary 69. A New Leaf 71. Claudine 74. Olly, Olly Oxen Free 78. Star Trek II: The Wrath of Khan 82. Toughlove (TV) 85. Shooter (TV) 88. Single Women, Married Men (TV) 90, etc.

Resnais, Alain (1922–).
Controversial French director, former editor.
Statues Also Die 51. Nuit et Brouillard (short) 55. Toute la Mémoire du Monde 56. *Hiroshima Mon Amour* 59. *Last Year at Marienbad* 61. Muriel 62. The War Is Over 66. Je n'Aime, Je t'Aime 69. Stavisky 74. Providence 77. My American Uncle 80. La Vie est un Roman 83. Love unto Death 84. Mélo 86. I Want to Go Home 89. Smoking/No Smoking 93. Same Old Song/On Connaît la Chanson 97, etc.

Retford, Ella (1896–1962).
English actress, singer and dancer, from music hall, and best known as a principal boy in pantomime.
Poison Pen 39. Variety Jubilee 43. I'll Be Your Sweetheart 45. Noose 48. Paper Orchid 49. Shadow of the Past 50, etc.

Rettig, Tommy (1941–1996).
American boy actor of the 50s. Died of kidney failure.
Panic in the Streets 50. The Five Thousand Fingers of Dr T 53. The Egyptian 54. The Last Wagon 56. At Gunpoint 57, etc.
TV series: Lassie 54–57.

Reuben, Gloria (1964–).
Canadian actress, from television.
Time Cop 94. Nick of Time 95. Johnny's Girl (TV) 95, etc.
TV series: ER 94– .

Reubens, Paul (1952–).
American actor, best known for his role as Pee-Wee Herman.
The Blues Brothers 80. Cheech & Chong's Next Movie 80. Cheech & Chong's Nice Dreams 81. Meatballs Part II 84. Pee-Wee's Big Adventure 85. Flight of the Navigator 86. Big Top Pee-Wee 88. Batman Returns 92. Buffy, the Vampire Slayer 92. Tim Burton's The Nightmare before Christmas (voice) 93. Dunston Checks In 95. Mathilda 96. Buddy 97, etc.

Revel, Harry (1905–1958).
British composer in Hollywood, usually in association with Mack Gordon.
SCORES: College Rhythm 34. The Gay Divorcee 34. We're Not Dressing 34. Stowaway 36. You Can't Have Everything 37. Are You with It? 48, etc.

Revell, Graeme (1955–).
New Zealand-born composer. He studied politics and economics at the University of Auckland and turned to composing after working as a psychiatric nurse in Australia. In the early 80s he formed the experimental London-based group SPK.
Dead Calm 89. Spontaneous Combustion 90. Until the End of the World 90. Child's Play 2 90. The Hand that Rocks the Cradle 92. Hear No Evil 93. Hard Target 93. Body of Evidence 93. Boxing Helena 93. The Crush 93. Ghost in the Machine 94. The Crow 94. No Escape 94. S.F.W. 94. The Basketball Diaries 95. Tank Girl 95. Mighty Morphin Power Rangers: The Movie 95. Strange Days 95. The Tie that Binds 95. Killer: A Journal of Murder 96. From Dusk till Dawn 96. Fled 96. The Crow: City of Angels 96. The Craft 96. The Saint 97. Chinese Box 97. Suicide Kings 98. The Big Hit 98. Lulu on the Bridge 98. The Negotiator 98. Strike 98. The Siege 98, etc.

Revere, Anne (1903–1990).
American character actress, mainly on stage. Her movie career was disrupted in the early 50s when she was blacklisted for refusing to testify before the House Un-American Activities Committee.
Double Door 34. The Devil Commands 41. The Gay Sisters 42. *The Song of Bernadette* (AAN) 43. The Keys of the Kingdom 44. *National Velvet* (AA) 44. Dragonwyck 46. Body and Soul 47. *Gentleman's Agreement* (AAN) 48. A Place in the Sun 51. Macho Callahan 70. Birch Interval 76, etc.

Revier, Dorothy (1904–1993) (Doris Velagra).
American leading lady of the silents, usually as a vamp; couldn't cope with sound. Her first husband was director Harry Revier.
Broadway Madonna 22. The Wild Party 23. The Virgin 24. When Husbands Flirt 25. When the Wife's Away 26. Poor Girls 27. Sinner's Parade 28. The Iron Mask 29. The Dance of Life 29. Call of the West 30. The Black Camel 31. Sally of the Subway 32. By Candlelight 33. Unknown Blonde 34. The Cowboy and the Kid 36, many others.

Revier, Harry J.
American director, a former cameraman. He was married for a time to actress Dorothy Revier, who starred in his *Broadway Madonna*.
A Grain of Dust 18. The Return of Tarzan 20. The Revenge of Tarzan 20. Broadway Madonna 22. What Price Love 27. The Mysterious Airman (serial) 28. The Convict's Code 30. The Lost City 35. Child Bride 38, etc.

Revill, Clive (1930–).
New Zealander in Britain playing mainly comic character roles.
Bunny Lake is Missing 65. Modesty Blaise 66. Kaleidoscope 66. A Fine Madness (US) 66. The Double Man 67. Fathom 67. Nobody Runs Forever 68. The Shoes of the Fisherman 68. The Private Life of Sherlock Holmes 70. A Severed Head 71. Avanti 72. The Legend of Hell House 73. The Black Windmill 74. Galileo 75. One of Our Dinosaurs Is Missing 75. Matilda 78. T. R. Sloane (TV) 79. Moviola (as Charlie Chaplin) (TV) 80. Zorro the Gay Blade 81. The Emperor's New Clothes 87. Rumpelstiltskin 87. Mack the Knife 89. The Sea Wolf (TV) 93. Dracula: Dead and Loving It 95. Possums 97, etc.

Reville, Alma (1900–1982).
British screenwriter, married to Alfred Hitchcock; worked on many of his films.
The Ring 27. Rich and Strange 32. The Thirty-Nine Steps 35. Secret Agent 36. Sabotage 37. Young and Innocent 37. The Lady Vanishes 38. Suspicion 41. Shadow of a Doubt 43. The Paradine Case 47. Stage Fright 50, etc.

Revueltas, Rosaura (1911–1996).
Mexican actress, best known for acting in *Salt of the Earth* 53, a film about a strike in Silver City, New Mexico, which resulted in her deportation from the United States. She worked with Bertolt Brecht in Germany in the late 50s, and later taught dance and yoga. (According to official sources she was 76 years old at the time of her death.)
Marias Islands 50. Girls in Uniform 50. Soledad/El Rebozo de Soledad 52. Das Lied über dem Tal 56. Mina, Wind of Freedom/Mina, Viento de Libertad 77, etc.

Rey, Alejandro (1930–1987).
Argentinian actor in American TV and films.
The Wild Pack 72. The Stepmother 73. Money to Burn 73. Mr Majestyk 74. Breakout 75. High Velocity 76. The Swarm 78. Cuba 79. Sunburn 79. The Ninth Configuration 80. Rita Hayworth the Love Goddess (TV) 83, many others.

Rey, Fernando (1915–1994) (Fernando Arambillet).
Suave Spanish actor in international films, a favourite of Luis Buñuel.
Welcome Mr Marshall 52. Viridiana 61. Villa Rides 68. The Adventures 70. A Town Called Bastard 71. Tristana 71. *The French Connection* 72. *The Discreet Charm of the Bourgeoisie* 72. French Connection II 75. La Grande Bourgeoise 76. Jesus of Nazareth (TV) 77. *That Obscure Object of Desire* 77. Quintet 79. Monsignor 82. The Hit 84. The Knight of the Dragon 85. Saving Grace 86. My General 87. Moon over Parador 88. Naked Tango 91. L'Atlantide 92. 1492 92. Di Ceria dell'Untore/The Plague Sower 92. After the Dream 92. El Cianuro Solo o con Leche? 93. Al Otro Lado del Tunel 94, many others.

Reynolds, Adeline de Walt (1862–1961).
American character actress with long stage experience; for many years Hollywood's oldest bit player.
Come Live with Me (film debut) 41. The Human Comedy 43. Going My Way 44. A Tree Grows in Brooklyn 45. The Girl from Manhattan 48. Lydia Bailey 52. Witness to Murder 54, etc.

Reynolds, Burt (1936–).
Lithe, virile American leading man who after years in television became a 'bankable' box-office star of the early 70s, but found his popular appeal declining from the 80s. He was married to actresses Judi Carne (1963–66) and Loni Anderson.
Angel Baby 61. Armored Command 61. Operation CIA 65. Navajo Joe 67. Shark 68. Impasse 68. Skullduggery 69. Sam Whiskey 69. 100 Rifles 69. Fuzz 72. *Deliverance* 72. Shamus 72. White Lightning 73. The Man Who Loved Cat Dancing 73. The Longest Yard 74. WW and the Dixie Dancekings 75. At Long Last Love 75. Hustle 76. Lucky Lady 76. Gator (& d) 76. Nickelodeon 76. *Smokey and the Bandit* 77. Semi-Tough 77. The End (& d) 78. Hooper 78. Starting Over 79. Smokey and the Bandit II 80. Rough Cut 80. The Cannonball Run 81. Sharkey's Machine (also d) 81. The Best Little Whorehouse in Texas 82. Best Friends 82. Stroker Ace 83. The Man Who Loved Women. 83. Cannonball Run II 84. City Heat 84. Stick (& d) 85. Heat 87. Malone 87. Rent-a-Cop 88. Switching Channels 88. Physical Evidence 88. Breaking In 89. All Dogs Go to Heaven (voice) 89. Modern Love 90. Cop and a Half 93. The Maddening 95. Precious 96. Striptease 96. Frankenstein and Me 96. Citizen Ruth 96. The Cherokee Kid (TV) 96. Trigger Happy/Mad Dog Time 96. Raven 97. Meet Wally Sparks 97. Bean 97. *Boogie Nights* (AAN) 97. Stringer (Fr.) 98, etc.
TV series: Riverboat 59–60. Gunsmoke 65–67. Hawk 67. Dan August 70. Evening Shade 90–93.
❝ I think the most underrated thing in the world is a good hot bath. With bubbles. – *B.R.*
My movies were the kind they show in prisons and aeroplanes, because nobody can leave. – *B.R.*

Reynolds, Debbie (1932–) (Mary Frances Reynolds).
Petite, vivacious American leading lady of 50s musicals; later a pleasing comedienne. She now owns and performs in her own hotel in Las Vegas which also displays her collection of movie memorabilia, much of it bought when MGM sold off its warehouses of costumes and furniture. She was married to singer Eddie Fisher (1955–59) and is the mother of actress Carrie Fisher. In 1997 she and her Las Vegas hotel filed for Chapter 11 bankruptcy protection.
Autobiography: 1989, *Debbie – My Life* (with David Patrick Columba).
■ June Bride 48. The Daughter of Rosie O'Grady 50. Three Little Words 50. Two Weeks with Love 50. Mr Imperium 51. *Singin' in the Rain* 52. Skirts Ahoy 52. I Love Melvin 53. The Affairs of Dobie Gillis 53. Give a Girl a Break 53. *Susan Slept Here* 54. Athena 54. Hit the Deck 55. The Tender Trap 55. The Catered Affair 56. Bundle of Joy 56. Meet Me in Las Vegas 56. Tammy and the Bachelor 57. This Happy Feeling 58. The Mating Game 59. Say One for Me 59. It Started with a Kiss 59. The Gazebo 59. The Rat Race 60. Pépé 60. The Pleasure of His Company 61. The Second Time Around 61. How the West was Won 62. My Six Loves 63. Mary Mary 63. *The Unsinkable Molly Brown* (AAN) 64. Goodbye Charlie 64. The Singing Nun 66. Divorce American Style 67. How Sweet It Is 68. *What's the Matter with Helen?* 71. Charlotte's Web (voice only) 72. That's Entertainment! 74. Sadie and Son (TV) 87. Perry Mason: The Case of the Musical Murder (TV) 89. The Bodyguard 92. Heaven and Earth 93. Mother 96. Wedding Bell Blues (as herself) 96. In & Out 97. Rudolph the Red-Nosed Reindeer: The Movie (voice) 98.
TV series: *The Debbie Reynolds Show* 69. Aloha Paradise 81.
❝ I do twenty minutes every time the refrigerator door opens and the light comes on. – *D.R.*
I stopped making movies because I don't like taking my clothes off. – *D.R.*
When I die I'm going to have myself stuffed like Trigger. They'll put me in a museum, all stuffed. Just put a quarter in and I'll sing 'Tammy'. – *D.R.*
Some people, if they're looking for their mother, would go into the kitchen. I'd go to Vegas. – *Todd Fisher (D.R.'s son)*

Reynolds, Gene (1925–).
American boy actor who later became a producer of TV series including *The Ghost and Mrs Muir*, *Anna and the King* and *M*A*S*H*.
Thank You Jeeves 36. In Old Chicago 38. The Blue Bird 40. The Penalty 40. The Tuttles of Tahiti 42. Eagle Squadron 44. The Country Girl 54. Diane 55, many others.

Reynolds, Joyce (1924–).
Vivacious American leading lady of the 40s, usually in teenage roles.
George Washington Slept Here 42. Janie 44. Always Together 48. Dangerous Inheritance 50. Girls' School 50, etc.

Reynolds, Kevin (1952–).
American director and screenwriter whose *Robin Hood* was one of the box-office hits of 1991.
Red Dawn (co-w) 84. Fandango (wd) 85. Beast of War (d) 88. Robin Hood: Prince of Thieves (d) 91. Rapa Nui (co-w, d) 94. Waterworld 95. 187 97, etc.

Reynolds, Marjorie (1921–1997) (Marjorie Goodspeed).
American leading lady of the 40s. Former child actress.
Up in the Air 40. Holiday Inn 42. Star Spangled Rhythm 43. Ministry of Fear 43. Dixie 43. Three Is a Family 44. Bring on the Girls 45. Meet Me on Broadway 46. Heaven Only Knows 47. Home Town Story 51. The Great Jewel Robber 51. The Silent Witness 54, etc.
TV series: The Life of Riley 53–57. Our Man Higgins 62.

Reynolds, Norman.
British production designer.
The Little Prince 74. Lucky Lady 75. Mr Quilp 75. The Incredible Sarah (AAN) 76. Star Wars (AA) 77. The Empire Strikes Back (AAN) 80. Raiders of the Lost Ark (AA) 81. Return of the Jedi (AAN) 83. Young Sherlock Holmes 85. Empire of the Sun (AAN) 87. Avalon 90. Mountains of the Moon 90. Alien^3 92. Alive 93. Clean Slate 94. Mission: Impossible 96. Sphere 98, etc.

Reynolds, Peter (1926–1975) (Peter Horrocks).
British light character actor, given to shifty roles.
The Captive Heart 46. Guilt Is My Shadow 49. Smart Alec 50. Four Days 51. The Last Page 52. Devil Girl from Mars 54. You Can't Escape 55. The Delavine Affair 56. Shake Hands with the Devil 59. West Eleven 63. Nobody Runs Forever 68, etc.

Reynolds, Sheldon (1923–).
American radio and TV writer who wrote, produced and directed two films.
■ Foreign Intrigue 56. Assignment to Kill 68.
TV series: Sherlock Holmes 56. Sherlock Holmes and Dr Watson 81.

Reynolds, William H. (1910–1997).
American editor.
So Ends Our Night 41. Moontide 42. Carnival in Costa Rica 47. Come to the Stable 49. The Day the Earth Stood Still 51. Red Skies of Montana 52. Three Coins in the Fountain 54. Bus Stop 56. South Pacific 58. Compulsion 59. Fanny (AAN) 61. Kings of the Sun 63. The Sound of Music (AA) 65. Star 68. The Great White Hope 70. *The Godfather* 72. *The Sting* (AA) 73. The Great Waldo Pepper 75. The Turning Point (AAN) 77. A Little Romance 77. Heaven's Gate 80. Nijinsky 80. Author! Author! 82. Making Love 82. Yellowbeard 83. The Little Drummer Girl 84. The Lonely Guy 84. Pirates 86. Dancers 87. Ishtar 87. A New Life 88. Rooftops 89. Taking Care of Business 90. Gypsy (TV) 93, etc.

Rhames, Ving (1961–) (Irving Rhames).
American actor of threatening appearance.
Go Tell It on the Mountain (TV) 84. Patty Hearst 88. Casualties of War 89. The Long Walk Home 89. Flight of the Intruder 90. Jacob's Ladder 90. Rising Son 90. Homicide 91. The People under the Stairs 91. Stop! Or My Mum Will Shoot 92. The Saint of Fort Washington 93. Dave 93. Pulp Fiction 94. Kiss of Death 95. Mission: Impossible 96. Striptease 96. Rosewood 97. Dangerous Ground 97. Body Count 97. Con Air 97. Don King: Only in America 97. Out of Sight 98, etc.
❝ Be careful: The toes you step on today may be connected to the ass you'll be kissing tomorrow. – *V.R.*

Rhoades, Barbara (1947–).
American character actress.
The Shakiest Gun in the West 68. There Was a Crooked Man 70. Up the Sandbox 72. Harry and Tonto 74. Conspiracy of Terror (TV) 75. The Choirboys 77. Serial 80, etc.
TV series: Busting Loose 77. Soap 80.

Rhodes, Betty Jane (1921–).
American singing second lead of the early 40s.
Stage Door 37. Sweater Girl 41. The Fleet's In 42. Salute for Three 43. You Can't Ration Love 44. Practically Yours 44, etc.

Rhodes, Erik (1906–1990).
American comic actor from the musical comedy stage, best remembered as the excitable Italian in two Astaire-Rogers films, *The Gay Divorcee* 34 and *Top Hat* 35 ('Your wife is safe with Tonetti – he prefers spaghetti').
■ *The Gay Divorcee* 34. A Night at the Ritz 35. Charlie Chan in Paris 35. The Nitwits 35. Old Man Rhythm 35. *Top Hat* 35. Another Face 35. Two in the Dark 35. Chatterbox 36. One Rainy Afternoon 36. Special Investigator 36. Second Wife 36. The Smartest Girl in Town 36. Criminal Lawyer 37. Woman Chases Man 37. Music for Madame 37. Fight for Your Lady 37. Beg Borrow or Steal 37. Dramatic School 38. Say It in French 38. Meet the Girls 38. Mysterious Mr Moto 38. On Your Toes 39.

Rhodes, Marjorie (1902–1979).
Homely British character actress, on stage from 1920; usually played warm-hearted mums, nosy neighbours, etc.
Poison Pen (debut) 39. *Love on the Dole* 40. World of Plenty 41. *When We are Married* 43. Uncle Silas 47. *The Cure for Love* 50. Those People Next Door 53. Hell Drivers 58. Watch It, Sailor 62. *The Family Way* 66. Mrs Brown, You've Got a Lovely Daughter 68. Hands of the Ripper 71, many others.

Rhue, Madlyn (1934–) (Madeleine Roche).
American supporting actress.
Operation Petticoat 59. Escape from Zahrain 62. It's a Mad Mad Mad Mad World 63. He Rides Tall 64. Stand Up and Be Counted 72. Crackle of Death 76. A Mother's Justice (TV) 91, etc.
TV series: Bracken's World 69. Executive Suite 76. Houston Knights 87–88.

Rhys-Davies, John (1944–).
Heavyweight British character actor, a good roisterer.
Shogun (TV) 80. Sphinx 81. Raiders of the Lost Ark 81. Victor/Victoria 81. Ivanhoe (TV) 82. Sahara 83. Best Revenge 83. King Solomon's Mines 85. In the Shadow of Kilimanjaro 86. The Living Daylights 87. Nairobi Affair 88. Indiana Jones and the Last Crusade 89. Tusks 89. Rebel Storm 90. The Company 90. The Company II: Sacrifices 91. Canvas 92. The Unnameable Returns 92. Sunset Grill 92. Journey of Honor 92. The Seventh Coin 93. The High Crusade 94. Catherine the Great (TV) 95. The Great White Hype 96. Marquis de Sade 96. Bloodsport 3 96. Glory Daze 96. The Protector 97. Secret of the Andes 98, etc.
TV series: The Untouchables 93. Sliders 95–97. You Wish 97.

Riano, Renie (1899–1971).
American comedienne in small film roles, especially the *Jiggs and Maggie* series.
Tovarich 37. Adam Had Four Sons 41. The Time of Your Life 46. Three on a Couch 66, many others.

Ribisi, Giovanni (1976–).
American actor, born in Los Angeles. Married model and actress Mariah O'Brien.
Promised a Miracle (TV) 88. That Thing You Do! 96. Lost Highway 96. SubUrbia 97. The Postman 97. First Love, Last Rites 98. Saving Private Ryan 98. The Other Sister 98, etc.
TV series: My Two Dads 87. The Wonder Years 92–93. Davis Rules 92. Family Album 93.

Ricci, Christina (1980–).
American actress, in quirky roles. Born in Santa Monica, California, she began acting as a child and scored an early success with her performances as Wednesday in *The Addams Family*, before making a transition to parts as a troubled teenager.
Mermaids 90. *The Addams Family* 92. The Cemetery Club 93. *Addams Family Values* 93. Casper 95. Now and Then 95. Gold Diggers: The Secret of Bear Mountain 95. Bastard out of Carolina 96. That Darn Cat 96. The Last of the High Kings 96. The Ice Storm 97. Buffalo '66 97. Fear and Loathing in Las Vegas 98. 200 Cigarettes 98. Pecker 98. The Opposite of Sex 98. Small Soldiers (voice) 98. Desert Blue 98, etc.
❝ I can't imagine what kids today would be like if violence on TV and in the movies hadn't prepared us for the violence that is out there in the real world. – *C.R.*
I have life rage. What am I going to do with it? I can't kick the shit out of someone. I can't yell or be constantly rude to people, because that's unacceptable. I have a therapist on each coast. I've had a problem with that, too, because I've had a different personality when I go to different ones. – *C.R., 1998*

Rice, Anne (1941–).
American writer of vampire novels. She also writes erotic novels under the names Anne Rampling and A. N. Roquelaure.
Interview with the Vampire 94. Exit to Eden 94.

Rice, Elmer (1892–1967) (Elmer Reizenstern).
American playwright. Works filmed include *Street Scene*, *The Adding Machine*, *Dream Girl* and *Counsellor at Law*.

Rice, Florence (1907–1974).
American leading lady of the late 30s, always in sweet-tempered roles.
The Best Man Wins 34. Sweethearts 39. Miracles for Sale 39. *At the Circus* 39. Fighting Marshal 41. The Ghost and the Guest 43, etc.

Rice, Grantland (1881–1954).
American sportscaster who made innumerable one-reelers under the title *Grantland Rice Sportslights*. Father of Florence Rice.

Rice, Jack (1893–1968).
American light actor who for many years played Edgar Kennedy's useless brother-in-law in RKO shorts. Last film: *Son of Flubber* 63.

Rice, Joan (1930–1997)
British leading lady, former waitress, briefly popular in the 50s. Retired in the 70s to run an estate agency in Maidenhead, Berkshire.
Blackmailed 50. One Wild Oat 51. The Story of Robin Hood and His Merrie Men 52. A Day to Remember 54. His Majesty O'Keefe (US) 55. One Good Turn 56. Payroll 61. Horror of Frankenstein 70, etc.

Rice, Sir Tim (1944–).
English lyricist, associated with Sir Andrew Lloyd Webber's early musicals. He was knighted 'for services to music' in 1994.
Jesus Christ Superstar 73. Aladdin (AAs) 92. The Lion King (AAs, AANs) 94. Evita (AAs 'You Must Love Me').

Rich, David Lowell (1923–).
American director, from TV.
Senior Prom 58. Hey Boy, Hey Girl 59. Have Rocket Will Travel 59. Madame X 66. The Plainsman 66. Rosie 67. A Lovely Way to Die 68. *Eye of the Cat* 69. The Sex Symbol (TV) 74. The Concorde – Airport 79 79. Chu Chu and the Philly Flash 81. Thursday's Child (TV) 83. The Defiant Ones (TV) 86. Infidelity (TV) 87, etc.

Rich, Irene (1891–1988) (Irene Luther).
American silent-screen heroine, little seen after sound.
Stella Maris 18. Beau Brummell 24. Lady Windermere's Fan 25. So This is Paris 26. *Craig's Wife* 28. Shanghai Rose 29. That Certain Age 38. The Lady in Question 41. New Orleans 47. Joan of Arc 48, etc.

Rich, John (1925–).
American director. Since the 70s he has directed episodes of TV series, such as *All in the Family*, *Newhart* and *Murphy Brown*.
Wives and Lovers 63. The New Interns 64. Boeing Boeing 65. Easy Come Easy Go 67, etc.

Rich, Matty (1971–) (Matthew Richardson).
American director.
Straight out of Brooklyn 90. The Inkwell 94.

Rich, Roy (1909–1970).
British producer, director and executive, with widely varied experience including radio and TV.
My Brother's Keeper (d only) 47. It's Not Cricket (d only) 48. Double Profile (d only) 54. Phantom Caravan (d only) 54, etc.

Richard, Sir Cliff (1940–) (Harold Webb).
Boyish British pop singer who succeeded by restricting his film appearances. He was knighted in 1995 for services to charity. In 1998 the *Sunday Times* estimated his fortune at £25m.
Biography: 1993, *Cliff Richard* by Steve Turner.
■ Serious Charge 59. Expresso Bongo 60. *The Young Ones* 61. Summer Holiday 62. Wonderful Life 64. Finders Keepers 66. Two a Penny 68. Take Me High 73.

Richard, Pierre (1934–).
Leading French comic actor, director, producer and screenwriter.
Les Heures Chaudes 61. Agent 505 65. Le Distrait (& d) 70. The Tall Blond Man with One Black Shoe 72. Return of the Tall Blond 74. French Mustard (& co-w) 74. The Daydreamer 75. It's Not Me, It's Him (& d) 79. The Goat/Le Chevre 81. Les Compères 83. The Twin 84. The Fugitives 86. The Door on the Left As You Leave the Elevator 88. Nord 91. We Can Always Dream (& wd) 91. Old Rascal 92. Loonies at Large (& p, w) 93. The Chess Game 94, etc.

Richard the Lionheart (Richard I of England, 1157–1199)
was a king who has gone down into legend rather than history as a nearly wronged idealist. The truth may have been less inspiring. He was played by Wallace Beery in *Robin Hood* (1922), by Henry Wilcoxon in *The Crusades*, by Ian Hunter in *The Adventures of Robin Hood*, by Norman Wooland in *Ivanhoe*, by Patrick Barr in Disney's *Robin Hood*, by George Sanders in *King Richard and the Crusaders*, by Patrick Holt in *Men of Sherwood Forest*, by Anthony Hopkins (as a prince) in *The Lion in Winter*, by Richard Harris in *Robin and Marian*, and Sean Connery in *Robin Hood: Prince of Thieves*.

Richard III (1452–1485).
The best-known account of the life and crimes of the short-lived king of England is Laurence Olivier's version of Shakespeare's play, centring on his own performance as a charming, ruthless villain. The story was also dealt with in Rowland V. Lee's outrageous but amusing *Tower of London* 39, with Basil Rathbone as Richard and Boris Karloff as Mord the Executioner; this was remade in 1963 by Roger Corman with Vincent Price, who had played the Duke of Clarence in the earlier version, as Richard. In 1995, Ian McKellen starred in Shakespeare's play, set in a fascist Britain of the 1930s.

Richards, Addison (1887–1964).
American character actor with long stage experience; in Hollywood from early 30s, usually as professional man; later in TV series.
Riot Squad 34. Colleen 36. Black Legion 37. Boom Town 40. My Favorite Blonde 42. Since You Went Away 44. The Mummy's Curse 46. Indian Scout 50. Illegal 56. The Oregon Trail 59, many others.
TV series: Fibber McGee 59. Cimarron City 58–60.

Richards, Ann (1918–).
Australian leading lady.
Tall Timbers 38. The Rudd Family 39, etc. Then to Hollywood: Random Harvest 42. Dr Gillespie's New Assistant 43. An American Romance 44. Love Letters 45. The Searching Wind 46. Sorry, Wrong Number 48. Breakdown 52, etc.

Richards, Ariana (1979–).
American child actress, from commercials.
Into the Homeland (TV) 87. I'm Gonna Get You Sucka 88. Prancer 89. Tremors 90. Spaced Invaders 90. Switched at Birth (TV) 91. Jurassic Park 93. Come the Dawn 95. Angus 95, etc.

Richards, Beah (1926–).
American actress.
The Miracle Worker 62. In the Heat of the Night 67. *Guess Who's Coming to Dinner* (AAN) 67. Mahogany 76. Inside Out 86. Drugstore Cowboy 89. Homer & Eddie 90. Capital News (TV) 90. Out of Darkness (TV) 94. Beloved 98, etc.
TV series: Hearts Afire 92.

Richards, Denise (1972–).
American actress. Born in Downer's Grove, Illinois, she moved to Los Angeles in the late 80s to continue working as a model. She began with a recurring role on the TV series *Doogie Howser M.D.* in the early 90s.
National Lampoon's Loaded Weapon 1 93. Tammy and the T-Rex 94. In the Blink of an Eye (TV) 96. Nowhere 97. Starship Troopers 97. Wild Things 98, etc.

Richards, Dick (1936–).
American director.
■ The Culpepper Cattle Company 72. *Farewell My Lovely* 75. Rafferty and the Gold Dust Twins 75. March or Die (& w, p) 77. Death Valley 82. Tootsie (co-p only) 82. Man, Woman and Child 83. Heat 87.

Richards, Jeff (1922–1989) (Richard Mansfield Taylor).
American general-purpose actor.
Johnny Belinda 48. Kill the Umpire 50. The Strip 51. Above and Beyond 52. Seven Brides for Seven Brothers 55, many others.
TV series: Jefferson Drum 58.

Richards, Michael (1948–).
American stand-up comedian and actor, best known for his role as Cosmo Kramer in the TV sitcom *Seinfeld*. Born in Los Angeles, he studied at the California Institute of the Arts.
Young Doctors in Love 82. Transylvania 6-5000 85. Whoops Apocalypse 86. UHF 89. Problem Child 90. So I Married an Axe Murderer 93. Coneheads 93. Airheads 94. Unstrung Heroes 95. London Suite (TV) 96. Trial and Error 97, etc.
TV series: Fridays 80–82. Seinfeld 90–98.

Richards, Paul (1924–1974).
American general-purpose actor.
The Black Whip 55. Tall Man Riding 56. Battle for the Planet of the Apes 71, etc.
TV series: Breaking Point 63.

Richards, Silvia.
American screenwriter, from radio. A former communist, she was called to testify during the HUAC investigations of Hollywood; soon after, as work became scarce, she quit to become a nursery teacher. Married screenwriter A. I. Bezzerides.
Possessed (co-w) 47. Secret beyond the Door (w) 48. Tomahawk/Battle of Powder River (co-w) 51. Ruby Gentry (w) 52. Rancho Notorious (story) 52, etc.

Richardson, Ian (1934–).
Scottish character actor whose precise playing of many varied roles is an increasing delight.
The Marat/Sade 68. Man of La Mancha 72. The Darwin Adventure 73. *Ike* (TV) (as Bernard Montgomery) 79. The Sign of Four (as Sherlock Holmes) (TV) 84. The Master of Ballantrae (TV) 84. Mistral's Daughter (TV) 84. Mountbatten (TV) 85. Brazil 85. The Fourth Protocol 87. Porterhouse Blue (TV) 87. Cry Freedom 87. Burning Secret 89. The Plot to Kill Hitler (TV) 90. Rosencrantz and Guildenstern Are Dead 90. Year of the Comet 92. House of Cards (TV) 92. To Play the King (TV) 93. Foreign Affairs (TV) 93. M. Butterfly 93. Dirty Weekend 93. Words upon the Window Pane 94. Catherine the Great (TV) 95. The Final Cut (TV) 95. BAPS 97. Dark City 97. A Knight in Camelot (TV) 98, etc.

Richardson, Joely (1965–).
British actress, the daughter of Vanessa REDGRAVE and Tony RICHARDSON. Formerly married to film producer Tim Bevan.
Hotel New Hampshire 84. Wetherby 85. Drowning by Numbers 88. Heading Home 91. King Ralph 91. Rebecca's Daughters 91. Shining Through 92. Lady Chatterley's Lover (TV) 92. I'll Do Anything 94. Sister, My Sister 94. Hollow Reed 95. Loch Ness 96. 101 Dalmatians 96. Event Horizon 97. The Tribe (TV) 98. Wrestling with Alligators 99, etc.

Richardson, John (1936–).
British leading man, mainly in fancy dress.
Bachelor of Hearts 58. She 65. One Million Years BC 66. The Vengeance of She 68. The Chastity Belt 68. On a Clear Day You Can See Forever 70. Duck in Orange Sauce (It.) 75. Eyeball 78. Frankenstein 80 80. The Church/La Chiesa (It.) 88. Pistol: The Birth of a Legend 91, etc.

Richardson, Miranda (1958–).
British actress.
Dance with a Stranger 84. The Innocent 85. Underworld 85. Blackadder (TV) 86. After Pilkington (TV) 87. Empire of the Sun 87. Ball-Trap on the Côte Sauvage 89. The Mad Monkey/El Mono Loco 89. My Dear Doctor Gräsler/Mio Caro Dottore Gräsler 89. The Fool 90. Twisted Obsession 90. The Bachelor 91. Enchanted April 91. The Crying Game 92. Damage (AAN) 92. Century 93. Tom and Viv (AAN) 94. The Night and the Moment 94. Kansas City 96. Evening Star 96. Swann 96. Saint-Ex 96. Designated Mourner 97. A Dance to the Music of Time (TV) 97. The Apostle 97. Merlin (TV) 98. The Scold's Bridle (TV) 98. All for Love 98. Jacob Two Two Meets the Hooded Fang (Can.) 98, etc.

Richardson, Natasha (1963–).
British actress, the daughter of Vanessa REDGRAVE and Tony RICHARDSON. She married Liam NEESON in 1994.
Every Picture Tells a Story 84. In the Secret State 85. Gothic 86. A Month in the Country 87. Patty Hearst 88. The Handmaid's Tale 89. Fatman and Little Boy/The Shadowmakers 89. The Comfort of Strangers 90. The Favour, the Watch and the Very Big Fish/Rue Saint-Sulpice 91. Past Midnight 92. Suddenly Last Summer (TV) 93. Zelda (TV) 93. Widows' Peak 94. Nell 94. The Parent Trap 98, etc.

Richardson, Peter.
British comedy director.
■ The Supergrass 86. Eat the Rich 87. The Pope Must Die/The Pope Must Diet 91.
TV series: The Comic Strip Presents . . . (a, co-wd) 93.

Richardson, Sir Ralph (1902–1983).
Distinguished British stage actor, in occasional films. Despite his splendid theatrical voice and thespian mannerisms, he was at his best playing ordinary chaps, though his gallery included plenty of eccentrics. Born in Cheltenham, he was on stage from 1921, notably in productions at the Old Vic, in partnership with Laurence OLIVIER, at the Royal Court Theatre and the National Theatre, where first nights were marked by firing 'Ralph's Rocket', in memory of his love of fireworks. (He once destroyed Olivier's dining room with a misdirected rocket.) In private life, he was as eccentric as some of the characters he played: stopped by police late at night when walking very slowly along the gutter of an Oxford street, he explained that he was taking his pet mouse for a stroll.
Biographies: 1958, *Ralph Richardson* by Harold Hobson; 1982, *Ralph Richardson: A Celebration* by Robert Tanitch; 1995, *Ralph Richardson: the Authorised Biography* by John Miller.
■ The Ghoul 33. Friday the Thirteenth 33. The Return of Bulldog Drummond 34. Java Head 34. King of Paris 34. *Bulldog Jack* 35. Things to Come 36. The Man Who Could Work Miracles 36. Thunder in the City 37. *South Riding* 38. The Divorce of Lady X 38. The Citadel 38. *Q Planes* 39. *The Four Feathers* 39. The Lion Has Wings 39. On the Night of the Fire 39. The Day Will Dawn 42. The Silver Fleet 43. The Volunteer 43. School for Secrets 46. *Anna Karenina* 48. *The Fallen Idol* 48. *The Heiress* (AAN) 49. An Outcast of the Islands 51. Home at Seven (& d) 52. The Sound Barrier 52. The Holly and the Ivy 53. *Richard III* (as Buckingham) 56. Smiley 57. The Passionate Stranger 57. Our Man in Havana 59. *Oscar Wilde* (as Sir Edward Carson) 60. Exodus 61. The 300 Spartans 62. *Long Day's Journey into Night* 62. Woman of Straw 64. Doctor Zhivago 66. *The Wrong Box* 66. Khartoum 67. Oh What a Lovely War 69. The Midas Run 69. The Bed Sitting Room 69. The Battle of Britain 69. The Looking Glass War 69. David Copperfield (as Micawber) 69. Eagle in a Cage 71. Who Slew Auntie Roo? 71. Tales from the Crypt 71. Lady Caroline Lamb 72. Alice's Adventures in Wonderland (as the Caterpillar) 72. A Doll's House 73. O Lucky Man 73. Frankenstein: The True Story (TV) 73. Rollerball 75. Jesus of Nazareth (TV) 77. The Man in the Iron Mask (TV) 77. Time Bandits 80. Dragonslayer 81. Wagner 83. Invitation to a Wedding 83. Greystoke (AAN) 84. Witness for the Prosecution (TV) 84.
TV series: Blandings Castle (as Lord Emsworth) 67.
✪ For casting his whimsical eye over a surprisingly large range of movies, and invariably walking off with the honours. *Q Planes*.
❝ I don't like my face at all. It's always been a great drawback to me. – *R.R.*
The art of acting lies in keeping people from coughing. – *R.R.*
Actors never retire; they just get offered fewer parts. – *R.R.*
Acting on the screen is like acting under a microscope. The slightest movement becomes a gesture and therefore the discipline has to be very severe. – *R.R.*
I've never been one of those stage chaps who scoff at films. I think they're a marvellous medium, and are to the stage what engravings are to paintings. – *R.R.*
Film is a wonderful medium and I love it, but I find that I cannot increase my talent by working in pictures, any more than a painter can do so by increasing the size of his brush. – *R.R.*
I have put on so many make-ups that sometimes I have feared that when I go to wipe it off there will be nobody left underneath. – *R.R.*

Richardson, Robert.
American cinematographer, associated with the films of Oliver Stone.
Salvador 86. Platoon (AAN) 86. Dudes 87. Wall Street 87. Eight Men Out 88. Talk Radio 88. Born on the Fourth of July (AAN) 89. City of Hope 91. The Doors 91. *JFK* (AA) 91. A Few Good Men 92. Heaven and Earth 93. *Natural Born Killers* 94. Casino 95. Nixon 95. Fast, Cheap & Out of Control 97. U-Turn 97. Wag the Dog 97. The Horse Whisperer 98, etc.

Richardson, Tony (1928–1991) (Cecil Antonio Richardson).
Born in Shipley, Yorkshire, he was educated at Oxford University and worked in television before founding, with George Devine, the English Stage Company at London's Royal Court Theatre, which had a profound impact on British theatre through his production of John Osborne's *Look Back in Anger*. The collaboration with Osborne also resulted in the creation of WOODFALL FILMS. From the mid-70s, he moved to America to work. Married Vanessa REDGRAVE; their daughters, Natasha and Joely RICHARDSON, are actresses. Died of AIDS.
Autobiography: 1993, *Long Distance Runner*.
■ Momma Don't Allow (short, d) 56. Look Back in Anger (d) 59. *The Entertainer* (d) 60. A Subject of Scandal and Concern (d) (TV) 60. Saturday Night and Sunday Morning (p) 60. Sanctuary (d) 61. A Taste of Honey (p, co-w, d) 61. The Loneliness of the Long Distance Runner £ 62. *Tom Jones* (p, d) (AAp, AAd) 63. Girl with Green Eyes (p) 64. The Loved One (d) (US) 65.

Mademoiselle (d) 66. The Sailor from Gibraltar (co-w, d) 67. Red and Blue (short, co-w, d) 67. *The Charge of the Light Brigade* (d) 68. Hamlet (d) 69. Laughter in the Dark (d) 69. Ned Kelly (co-w, d) 70. A Delicate Balance (d) 73. Dead Cert (co-w, d) 74. Joseph Andrews (story, d) 77. A Death in Canaan (d) 78. The Border (d) 82. Hotel New Hampshire (wd) 84. Penalty Phase (d) (TV) 88. Shadow on the Sun (d) (TV) 88. The Phantom of the Opera (d) (TV) 90. Hills Like White Elephants (d) (TV) 90. Blue Sky (d) (made 91) 94.

❝ The most prolific and the most prosperous of the *Sight and Sound* crop, and ultimately the least respected. – *Andrew Sarris, 1968*

He convinced me (wrongly, of course) that anyone can make a movie. All Tony Richardson did was come in and ask his cameraman what he should do . . . He was a useless, unpleasant creature. – *Robert Stephens*

Richelieu, Cardinal (1585–1642).
Louis XIII's chief minister, doubtless a clever and powerful chap, was used by the movies as a schemer and often a villain, seldom on the hero's side. George Arliss gave the fullest portrait, in *Cardinal Richelieu* 35. Others who have played him include Nigel de Brulier in *The Iron Mask*, the 1935 version of *The Three Musketeers*, and the 1939 version of *The Man in the Iron Mask*; Osgood Perkins in *Madame Dubarry*; Raymond Massey in *Under the Red Robe*; Miles Mander in the 1939 version of *The Three Musketeers*; Aimé Clairond in *Monsieur Vincent*; Vincent Price in the 1948 version of *The Three Musketeers*; Paul Cavanagh in *Sword of D'Artagnan*; Christopher Logue in *The Devils*; and Charlton Heston in the 1974 versions of *The Three Musketeers* and *The Four Musketeers*.

Richert, William.
American screenwriter and director. He also played the role of a modern-day Falstaff in Gus Van Sant's *My Own Private Idaho*.
Law and Disorder (co-w) 74. The Happy Hooker (w) 75. Winter Kills (wd) 79. Success (co-w, d) 79. A Night in the Life of Jimmy Reardon (wd) 88. My Own Private Idaho (a) 91. Paradise Framed (a) 95. The Man in the Iron Mask (a, wd) 98, etc.

Richfield, Edwin (1922–1990).
English character actor, usually portraying bluff, dependable authority figures.
The Jack of Diamonds 49. The Blue Parrot 53. The Black Rider 54. X the Unknown 56. Quatermass II/Enemy from Space 57. Up the Creek 58. Further up the Creek 58. The Camp on Blood Island 58. Ben Hur 59. Tommy the Toreador 59. Sword of Sherwood Forest 60. Calculated Risk (w) 63. The Secret of Blood Island 65. Quatermass and the Pit/Five Million Miles to Earth 67. Diamonds on Wheels 72. The Champions 83, etc.
TV series: The Buccaneers 56–57. Interpol Calling 59–60. The Odd Man 62–63. 199 Park Lane 65. The Man in the Iron Mask (as D'Artagnan) 68.

Richler, Mordecai (1931–).
Canadian novelist and screenwriter on Jewish themes.
■ No Love for Johnnie (co-w) 60. Young and Willing (co-w) 62. Life at the Top 65. The Apprenticeship of Duddy Kravitz (w, oa) (AAN) 74. Fun with Dick and Jane (co-w) 77. Jacob Two-Two Meets the Hooded Fang 78. Joshua Then and Now (w, oa) 85.

Richman, Harry (1895–1972) (Harold Reichman).
American entertainer, in occasional films.
Autobiography: 1966, *A Hell of a Life*.
■ Putting on the Ritz 30. The Music Goes Round 36. Kicking the Moon Around 38.

Richman, Peter Mark (1927–).
American general-purpose actor, much on TV.
Friendly Persuasion 56. The Strange One 57. The Black Orchid 58. The Crime Busters 61. Dark Intruder 65. For Singles Only 68. Dandy in Aspic 68. The City Killer 87. Judgement Day 88. Friday the Thirteenth Part VIII: Jason Takes Manhattan 89. Naked Gun 2½: The Smell of Fear 91, etc.
TV series: *Cain's Hundred* 61–62. Longstreet 71–72. Dynasty 81–84.

Richmond, Anthony B. (1942–).
British cinematographer and occasional director, now in Hollywood.
Sympathy for the Devil 68. Only When I Larf 68. Let It Be 70. Madame Sin 72. Don't Look Now 73. Vampira 74. Stardust 74. The Man Who Fell to Earth 76. The Eagle Has Landed 76. Silver Bears 77. The Greek Tycoon 78. Love and Bullets 79. Improper Channels 79. Bad Timing 80. Nightkill 81. A Man Called Rage (d) 84. Déjà Vu (wd) 85. Blake Edwards' That's Life 86. The In Crowd 88. Sunset 88. Cat Chaser 90. The Indian Runner 91. Timebomb 91. Kryo (co-w, d) 92. Heart of Darkness (TV) 94. Full Body Massage (TV) 95. Bastard out of Carolina 96. First Kid 96. Playing God 97, etc.

Richmond, Kane (1906–1973) (Frederick W. Bowditch).
American leading man of second features.
The Leather Pushers (serial) 30. Nancy Steele is Missing 36. Hard Guy 41. Action in the North Atlantic 43. Tiger Woman 45. Black Gold 47, many others.

Richmond, Ted (1912–).
American producer, former writer.
So Dark the Night 46. The Milkman 50. The Strange Door 51. Desert Legion 53. Forbidden 54. Count Three and Pray 55. Seven Waves Away 57. Solomon and Sheba 59. Advance to the Rear 64. Return of the Seven 66. Villa Rides 68. Papillon 74, others.

Richter, Hans (1888–1976).
German Dadaist director of animated and surrealist films, most active in the 20s. His books include *The Struggle for the Film: Towards a Socially Responsible Cinema/Der Kampf um den Film*, 1976.
Prelude and Fugue 20. Film is Rhythm 20. Rhythm 23. Rhythm 25. Film Study 26. Inflation 26. Twopenny Magic 27. Vormittagspuk 28. Everything Revolves 30. Dreams That Money Can Buy 44. 8 × 8 57, etc.

❝ To varnish our lives with entertaining stories is too petty a task for this mighty technology, too petty if it is to grow to artistic maturity. Let it, on the contrary, be allowed to participate in the intellectual conflicts of the age, let us dare apply this technology to shape genuine emotions, thoughts and ideas: to shape social life; it will be stimulated as never before and manage to change from a tool for more or less elegant reproduction to an instrument of genuine imagination. – *H.R.*

Richter, Jason James (1980–).
American child actor. Born in Oregon, he was raised in Honolulu and began his career in Japanese television.
Free Willy 93. Cops and Robbersons 94. The Neverending Story III 94. Free Willy 2: The Adventure Home 95. Free Willy 3 97, etc.

Richter, W. D. (1945–).
American screenwriter and director, a former script analyst for Warner.
■ Slither 72. Peeper 75. Nickelodeon 76. Invasion of the Body Snatchers 78. Dracula 79. Brubaker (AAN) 80. All Night Long 81. Hang Tough 82. The Adventures of Buckaroo Banzai across the Eighth Dimension (d) 84. Big Trouble in Little China 86. Late for Dinner (d) 91. Needful Things (d) 93. Home for the Holidays (w) 95.

Rickert, Shirley Jean (1926–).
American actress who was on screen as a child from 1929, and appeared in the Our Gang shorts of the 30s. Later worked as a dancer and a stripper before quitting showbusiness.
How's My Baby 29. Follow Thru 30. Night Work 30. Everything's Rosie 31. Bargain Days 31. 'Neath the Arizona Skies 34, etc.

Rickles, Don (1926–).
American insult comedian.
Run Silent Run Deep 58. The Rabbit Trap 59. The Rat Race 60. Enter Laughing 67. The Money Jungle 68. Where It's At 69. Kelly's Heroes 70. Innocent Blood 92. *Casino* 95. Toy Story (voice) 95. Quest for Camelot (voice) 98, etc.
TV series: CPO Sharkey 77.

Rickman, Alan (1946–).
English classical actor from the stage, so far typecast by Hollywood as a villain, who became an actor in his mid-20s after a career as a graphic designer. He also directs plays.
Biography: 1996, *Alan Rickman* by Maureen Paton.
Shock! Shock! Shock! 87. Die Hard 88. The January Man 89. Truly Madly Deeply 90. Quigley Down Under 90. Robin Hood: Prince of Thieves 91. Close My Eyes 91. Closet Land 91. Bob Roberts 92. Mesmer 94. An Awfully Big Adventure 95. Sense and Sensibility 95. Michael Collins 96. Winter Guest (d) 97. Judas Kiss (US) 98. Dark Harbor (US) 98, etc.

❝ I do take my work seriously and the way to do that is not to take yourself too seriously. – *A.R.*

Rickman, Thomas.
American screenwriter and director.
Kansas City Bomber (co-w) 72. The Laughing Policeman (w) 73. W.W. and the Dixie Dancekings 75. The White Dawn (co-w) 76. Hooper (co-w) 78. Coal Miner's Daughter (AAN) 80. The River Rat (wd) 84. Everybody's All-American 88. Truman (TV) 95, etc.

Riddle, Nelson (1921–1985).
American composer.
A Kiss before Dying 55. St Louis Blues 58. Ocean's Eleven 60. Lolita 62. Robin and the Seven Hoods 64. Marriage on the Rocks 65. El Dorado 66. Paint Your Wagon 69. The Great Gatsby (AA) 74. Harper Valley PTA 78, etc.

Ridgeley, John (1909–1968) (John Huntingdon Rea).
American supporting actor generally cast as gangster.
Invisible Menace 38. They Made Me a Fugitive 39. Brother Orchid 40. The Big Shot 42. Destination Tokyo 44. My Reputation 46. The Big Sleep 46. Possessed 47. Command Decision 48. The Blue Veil 52, many others.

Ridges, Stanley (1892–1951).
Incisive, heavy-featured British character actor who appeared in many Hollywood films.
■ Success 23. Crime without Passion 34. The Scoundrel 35. Winterset 36. Sinner Take All 36. Internes Can't Take Money 37. Yellow Jack 38. The Mad Miss Manton 38. If I Were King 38. There's That Woman Again 38. Let Us Live 39. Confessions of a Nazi Spy 39. I Stole a Million 39. Silver on the Sage 39. Union Pacific 39. Each Dawn I Die 39. Espionage Agent 39. Dust Be My Destiny 39. Nick Carter Master Detective 39. *Black Friday* 40. The Sea Wolf 41. Mr District Attorney 41. Sergeant York 41. They Died with Their Boots On 41. The Lady Is Willing 42. The Big Shot 42. *To Be or Not to Be* 42. Eagle Squadron 42. Eyes in the Night 42. Tarzan Triumphs 43. Air Force 43. This Is the Army 43. The Master Race 44. The Story of Dr Wassell 44. Wilson 44. *The Suspect* 45. Captain Eddie 45. God Is My Co-Pilot 45. The Phantom Speaks 45. Because of Him 46. Mr Ace 46. Canyon Passage 46. Possessed 47. An Act of Murder 47. You're My Everything 49. Streets of Laredo 49. The File on Thelma Jordon 49. Task Force 49. There's a Song in My Heart 49. Paid in Full 50. No Way Out 50. The Groom Wore Spurs 51.

Ridley, Arnold (1896–1984).
English playwright, character actor and occasional director, best known for his role as the bumbling, incontinent Private Godfrey in the TV sitcom *Dad's Army* 68–77. His greatest achievement was writing the perennial comedy thriller *The Ghost Train*, which was filmed in 1927 and 1931 and was also the inspiration for Will Hay's *Oh Mr Porter* 37 and several other films, including *Back Room Boy* 42. Born in Bath, he was educated at Bristol University and made his stage debut in 1914, abandoning acting for many years from the early 20s because of wounds suffered while serving in the army during the First World War.
The Wrecker (oa) 28. The Flying Fool (oa) 31. Third Time Lucky (oa) 31. Keepers of Youth (oa) 31. Blind Justice (oa) 34. The Warren Case (oa) 34. Royal Eagle (co-d, story) 36. Seven Sinners (oa) 36. East of Ludgate Hill (story) 37. Shadowed Eyes (story) 39. Stolen Face (a) 52. Meet Mr Lucifer (oa) 53. Wings of Mystery (a) 63. Crooks in Cloisters (a) 64. Who Killed the Cat? (oa) 66. Dad's Army (a) 71. Carry On Girls (a) 73. The Amorous Milkman (a) 74, etc.

Ridley, Philip (1960–).
British director, screenwriter, dramatist, author and artist.
The Krays (w) 90. The Reflecting Skin (wd) 90. The Passion of Darkly Noon 96.

Riefenstahl, Leni (1902–).
German director, former dancer, who made brilliant propaganda films for Hitler.
Autobiography: 1993, *The Sieve of Time*.
Biographies: 1976, *Leni Riefenstahl* by Glenn B. Infield; 1998, *A Portrait of Leni Riefenstahl* by Audrey Salkeld.
The White Hell of Pitz Palu (a) 29. The Blue Light (a, d) 32. S.O.S. Iceberg (a) 33. *Triumph of the Will* (the Nuremberg Rally) (d) 34. *Olympische Spiele* 36. Tiefland 45, etc.

Riegert, Peter (1947–).
American character lead, in the George Segal tradition.
National Lampoon's Animal House 78. *Local Hero* 83. Ellis Island (TV) 85. Un Homme Amoureux 87. Crossing Delancey 88. That's Adequate 89. Beyond the Ocean 90. A Shock to the System 90. Oscar 91. Object of Beauty 91. Utz (TV) 91. The Runestone 92. Passed Away 92. Gypsy (TV) 93. The Mask 94. White Man's Burden 94. Coldblooded 95. Pie in the Sky 95. The Infiltrator (TV) 95. Infinity 96. North Shore Fish 97. Face Down 97. The Baby Dance (TV) 98. Hi-Life 98, etc.

Riesner, Dean (1918–).
American screenwriter, a former child actor under the name Dinky Dean. He also directed the curious *Bill and Coo*, with its cast of birds in hats and neckties, which won a special Oscar for 'artistry and patience'.
Bill and Coo (d) 47. The Helen Morgan Story (co-w) 57. Coogan's Bluff (co-w) 69. Dirty Harry (co-w) 71. Charlie Varrick (co-w) 73. The Enforcer (co-w) 76. Fatal Beauty (co-w) 87, etc.

Rifkin, Adam.
American director and screenwriter.
Never on Tuesday (d) 88. Tale of Two Sisters (d) 89. Invisible Maniac (d, as Rif Coogan) 90. The Dark Backward (wd) 91. The Nutt House (d) 92. Psycho Cop 2 (d, as Rif Coogan) 93. The Chase (wd) 94. Mouse Hunt (w) 97. Small Soldiers (w) 98, etc.

Rigby, Arthur (1900–1970).
Burly English character actor, mainly on stage and television. Born in London, he was on stage from 1919 and in films from 1927. He is best known for his role as Station Sergeant Flint in the long-running TV series *Dixon of Dock Green*, a role he first played on stage in a version of *The Blue Lamp*.
Q Ships 27. The Deputy Drummer 35. The Marriage of Corbal 36. Cheer Up! 36. Dangerous Cargo 54. Crossroads to Crime 60, etc.

Rigby, Edward (1879–1951).
British stage character actor; became a familiar figure in endearingly doddery roles. On stage from 1900, he appeared in two silent films in 1907 and 1910.
Lorna Doone 35. Mr Smith Carries On 37. The Proud Valley 39. *Kipps* 41. The Common Touch 41. *Let the People Sing* 42. *Salute John Citizen* 42. Get Cracking 43. *Don't Take It to Heart* 44. Quiet Weekend 47. *Easy Money* 48. It's Hard to be Good 49. *The Happiest Days of Your Life* 49. *The Mudlark* 50, many others.

Rigby, Terence (1937–).
British character actor, mostly on stage.
The Little Ones 61. West Eleven 63. Accident 67. Get Carter 71. The Homecoming 73. The Dogs of War 80. The Hound of the Baskervilles (TV) 83. Lace (TV) 84. Lace II (TV) 85. Young Americans 93. Funny Bones 95. England My England 95. Our Friends in the North (TV) 96. Tomorrow Never Dies 97. Elizabeth 98, etc.
TV series: Softly Softly 66–76. Airline 82. Crossroads 86–88. Common as Muck 97– .

Rigg, Dame Diana (1938–).
British leading actress who came to fame in *The Avengers* TV series 65–67. She won a Tony award as best actress on Broadway in *Medea* in 1994.
The Assassination Bureau 68. A Midsummer Night's Dream 68. On Her Majesty's Secret Service 69. Julius Caesar 70. The Hospital 71.

Theatre of Blood 73. In This House of Brede (TV) 75. A Little Night Music 77. Evil Under the Sun 81. The Great Muppet Caper 81. Witness for the Prosecution (TV) 84. Bleak House (TV) 85. Genghis Cohen (TV) 93. A Good Man in Africa 94. Moll Flanders (TV) 96. Samson and Delilah (TV) 96. Rebecca (TV) 97. Parting Shots 98, etc.
TV series: The Diana Rigg Show 73.

Rilla, Walter (1895–1980).
German actor on stage from 1921; to Britain in mid-30s.
Der Geiger von Florenz 26. The Scarlet Pimpernel 35. Victoria the Great 37. At the Villa Rose 39. The Adventures of Tartu 43. The Lisbon Story 46. State Secret 50. Behold the Man £ 51. Cairo 61. The Thousand Eyes of Dr Mabuse 63. The Face of Fu Manchu 65, etc.

Rilla, Wolf (1920–).
British director, son of Walter Rilla.
Noose for a Lady 53. The End of the Road 54. Pacific Destiny 56. The Scamp 57. Bachelor of Hearts 58. Witness in the Dark 59. Piccadilly Third Stop 60. *Village of the Damned* 62. Cairo 63. The World Ten Times Over (& w) 63. Secrets of a Door to Door Salesman 73, etc.

Rimmer, Shane.
American supporting actor.
S*P*Y*S 74. Twilight's Last Gleaming 77. The People That Time Forgot 77. Silver Bears 79. Arabian Adventure 79. Hanover Street 79. Gandhi 82. Crusoe 88. A Kiss before Dying 91. The Year of the Comet 92. Lipstick on Your Collar (TV) 93. A Kid in King Arthur's Court 95. Space Truckers 97, etc.

Rin Tin Tin (1916–1932).
American dog star of silent films who kept Warner Brothers solvent in its early days. He was one of five German shepherd puppies found in a trench during the First World War by Lee Duncan, then a lieutenant, who brought him back to California and earned more than $5m from his escapades. According to Jack Warner, he died with Jean Harlow cradling his head in her lap. His son Rin Tin Tin Jnr also starred in several films from the late 20s to the mid-30s.
The Man from Hell's River 22. Where the North Begins 23. Below the Line 25. A Hero of the Big Snows 26. A Dog of the Regiment 27. Jaws of Steel 27. Land of the Silver Fox 28. The Man Hunter 30. Lightning Warrior (serial) 31, etc.
❝ The dog faced one hazard after another and was grateful to get an extra hamburger for a reward. He didn't ask for a raise, or a new press agent, or an air-conditioned dressing room, or more close-ups. – *Jack Warner*

Rinehart, Mary Roberts (1876–1958).
American mystery novelist, whose plots usually involve heroines in frightening situations. *The Bat* and *Miss Pinkerton* were each filmed more than once.

Ringwald, Molly (1968–).
American teenage actress of the 80s.
Sixteen Candles 84. The Breakfast Club 85. Pretty in Pink 86. The Pick-Up Artist 87. For Keeps 88. Fresh Horses 88. Strike It Rich 90. Betsy's Wedding 90. Face the Music 92. Tous les Jours Dimanche 94. The Stand (TV) 94. Bastard Brood (Fr.) 96. Office Killer 97, etc.
TV series: The Facts of Life 79–80. Townies 96.

Rintoul, David (1948–).
Scottish leading actor, much on television and best known for his role as Dr Finlay in the TV series of the same name 92–96. Born in Aberdeen, he was educated at Edinburgh University and studied at RADA.
Legend of the Werewolf 74. The Flight of the Heron (TV) 76. Scotch Myths – the Movie 82, etc.

Ripley, Arthur (1895–1961).
American director whose films are oddly sparse.
■ I Met My Love Again 38. Prisoner of Japan 42. *A Voice in the Wind* 44. The Chase 47. Thunder Road 58.

Ripper, Michael (1913–).
British character actor, often in comic roles.
Captain Boycott 48. Treasure Hunt 52. The Belles of St Trinian's 54. Richard III 56. Quatermass II 57. The Revenge of Frankenstein 58. Brides of Dracula 60. Captain Clegg 62. The Secret of Blood Island 65. The Reptile 66. The Plague of the Zombies 66. Where the Bullets Fly 66. Scars of Dracula 70. Legend of the Werewolf 75. The Prince and the Pauper 78. No Surrender 85. Revenge of Billy the Kid 91, etc.
TV series: Butterflies 78–82.

Ripstein, Arturo (1943–).
Mexican director, influenced by Buñuel, for whom he worked as a production assistant on *The Exterminating Angel.*
A Time to Die/Tiempo de Morir 65. Children's Hour/La Hora de los Niños 69. Castle of Purity/El Castillo de la Pureza 73. The Holy Office/El Santo Oficio 73. The Black Widow/La Viuda Negra 77. Vicious Circle/Cadena Perpétua 79. Seduction/La Seducción 80. The Other/El Otro 84. Realm of Fortune/El Imperio de la Fortuna 87. White Lies/Mentiras Piadosas 88. La Mujer del Puerto 91. The Beginning and the End/Principio y Fin 93. The Queen of the Night/La Reina de la Noche 94. Profundo Carmesi 96. Divine 98, etc.
❝ In Mexico there is no such thing as a cinematic career. – *A.R.*

Riscoe, Arthur (1896–1954).
British stage comedian with rare film appearances.
Going Gay 34. Paradise for Two 38. *Kipps* (as Chitterlow) 41, etc.

Risdon, Elizabeth (1887–1958) (E. Evans).
English leading actress of early silents who in 1915 was voted the most popular British film star. On stage from 1910, she moved to America to work in the theatre in 1917 and went to Hollywood in the mid-30s, becoming a character actress. Married to director George Loane Tucker and actor Brandon Evans (1903–78).
Maria Marten 13. Idol of Paris 14. Florence Nightingale 15. A Mother of Dartmoor 16. Guard That Girl 35. Crime and Punishment 36. Tom Sawyer 38. Huckleberry Finn 39. The Roaring Twenties 39. Mexican Spitfire 40. High Sierra 41. Random Harvest 42. Mexican Spitfire at Sea 42. Reap the Wild Wind 42. The Canterville Ghost 44. The Egg and I 47. Life with Father 47. Secret Fury 50. Bannerline 51. Scaramouche 52, etc.

Risi, Dino (1917–).
Italian director.
The Sign of Venus 55. Poveri ma Belli 56. Il Sorpasso 62. Scent of a Woman 75. How Funny Can Sex Be 76. Viva Italia 78. Primo Amore 78. Caro Papa 79. Sunday Lovers 80. Ghost of Love 81. Le Bon Roi Dagobert 84. Teresa 87. Two Women (TV) 89. A Love for Living (TV) 89. Mission of Love 91, etc.

Risi, Marco (1951–).
Italian director, the son of Dino Risi.
Vado a Vivere da Solo 81. Un Ragazzo, una Ragazza 83. Soldati 86. Forever Mary 89. Ragazzi Fuori 90. The Italians/Nel Continente Nero 93. The Pack 94, etc.

Riskin, Robert (1897–1955).
Distinguished American screenwriter.
Illicit 31. The Miracle Woman 31. *Lady for a Day* (AAN) 33. *It Happened One Night* (AA) 34. Broadway Bill 34. The Whole Town's Talking 35. *Mr Deeds Goes to Town* (AAN) 36. *Lost Horizon* 37. *You Can't Take It with You* (AAN) 38. The Real Glory 39. *Meet John Doe* 41. The Thin Man Goes Home 44. Magic Town 46. Riding High 50. Mister 880 50. The Groom Wore Spurs 51. Here Comes the Groom (co-w, AAN) 51, etc.

Ritchard, Cyril (1896–1977).
Australian dancer and light comedian, mainly on stage; latterly in US.
Piccadilly 29. Blackmail 30. I See Ice 38. Half a Sixpence 67.

Ritchie, June (1939–).
British leading lady, mainly in 'realist' films.
A Kind of Loving 61. Live Now Pay Later 63. The Mouse on the Moon 63. The World Ten Times Over 63. This is My Street 64. The Syndicate (GB) 67, etc.

Ritchie, Michael (1938–).
American director. Born in Waukesha, Wisconsin, he graduated from Harvard University and worked in television, directing episodes of TV dramas, before turning to directing features in the late 60s. After an incisive beginning, his work became increasingly routine.
The Outsider (TV) 67. The Sound of Anger (TV) 69. Downhill Racer 69. Prime Cut 72. *The Candidate* 72. *Smile* 75. The Bad News Bears 76. Semi-Tough 77. An Almost Perfect Affair 79. Divine Madness 80. The Island 80. The Survivors 83. Fletch 84. Wildcats 85. The Golden Child 86. The Couch Trip 88. Fletch Lives 89. Diggstown 92. The Positively True Adventures of the Alleged Texas Cheerleader-Murdering Mom (TV) 93. Cops and Robbersons 94. The Scout 94. A Simple Wish 97, etc.

Ritt, Martin (1914–1990).
American director, a former actor. Born in New York City, and educated at St John's University, Brooklyn, he worked at the Group Theatre in the late 30s and early 40s, and, after war service with the US Army Air Force, directed and acted in plays and TV dramas. During the first half of the 50s he was blacklisted by the TV industry and taught at the Actors' Studio, where his pupils included Paul Newman and Rod Steiger.
Book: 1972, *The Films of Martin Ritt* by Sheila Whitaker.
■ *Edge of the City* 56. *No Down Payment* 57. *The Long Hot Summer* 58. The Sound and the Fury 59. The Black Orchid 59. Five Branded Women 60. Paris Blues 61. Hemingway's Adventures of a Young Man 62. *Hud* (AAN) 63. The Outrage 64. *The Spy Who Came in from the Cold* 65. Hombre 67. The Brotherhood 68. The Molly Maguires 69. The Great White Hope 71. Sounder 72. Pete 'n' Tillie 72. Conrack 74. The Front 76. The End of the Game (a only) 76. Casey's Shadow 77. Norma Rae 79. Cross Creek 83. Murphy's Romance 85. The Slugger's Wife (a only) 85. Stanley & Iris 90.
❝ I don't need a final cut. I only cut the thing once. If they're dumb enough to fool around with it, let 'em do it. – *M.R.*
As far as a Martin Ritt Production is concerned, I wouldn't embarrass myself to take that credit. What about the Ravetches? They wrote it. What about the actors who appear in it? If ever I write one, direct it and appear in it, then you can call it a Martin Ritt Production. – M.R.

Ritter, John (1948–) (Jonathan Ritter).
American actor, in comic or light romantic roles, from TV. He is the son of country singer and cowboy star Tex Ritter.
The Barefoot Executive 70. Scandalous John 71. The Other 72. Nickelodeon 76. Americathon 79. Hero at Large 80. Wholly Moses! 80. They All Laughed 81. Letting Go 85. The Last Fling 86. Real Men 87. Skin Deep 89. Problem Child 90. Problem Child 2 91. Noises Off 92. Stay Tuned 92. North 94. Sling Blade 96. Mercenary 96. A Gun, a Car, a Blonde 97. I Woke Up Early the Day I Died 98. Bride of Chucky 98, etc.
TV series: The Waltons 72–77. Three's Company 77–84. Three's a Crowd 84–85. Hearts Afire 92.

Ritter, Tex (1905–1974) (Woodward Ritter).
American singing cowboy star of innumerable second features, from the stage and radio. He sang the title song for the film *High Noon.*
Song of the Gringo 36. Sing, Cowboy, Sing 38. The Old Chisholm Trail 43. Marshal of Gunsmoke 46. Apache Ambush 55. Girl from Tobacco Road 66. What Am I Bid 67, etc.

Ritter, Thelma (1905–1969).
Wry-faced American character actress and comedienne; she provided a sardonic commentary on the antics of the principals in many 50s comedies.
■ Miracle on 34th Street 47. Call Northside 777 48. A Letter to Three Wives 49. City across the River 49. Father was a Fullback 49. Perfect Strangers 50. *All About Eve* (AAN) 50. I'll Get By 50. The Mating Season 51. As Young as You Feel 51. *The Model and the Marriage Broker* 51. With a Song in My Heart (AAN) 52. Titanic 53. The Farmer Takes a Wife 53. *Pickup on South Street* (AAN) 53. Rear Window 54. Daddy Longlegs 55. Lucy Gallant 55. The Proud and Profane 56. A Hole in the Head 59. Pillow Talk (AAN) 59. The Misfits 61. The Second Time Around 61. Birdman of Alcatraz (AAN) 62. How the West was Won 62. For Love or Money 63. A New Kind of Love 63. Move Over Darling 63. Boeing Boeing 65. The Incident 67. What's So Bad about Feeling Good? 68.
Famous line (*All About Eve*): 'What a story. Everything but the bloodhounds snapping at her rear end.'
Famous line (*Pillow Talk*): 'If there's anything worse than a woman living alone, it's a woman saying she likes it.'

The Ritz Brothers: *Al* (1901–1965), *Jim* (1903–1985) and *Harry* (the leader) (1906–1986).
Zany American nightclub comedians who made many enjoyable appearances in musicals of the 30s. Their real surname was Joachim.
■ Hotel Anchovy (short) 34. Sing Baby Sing 36. One in a Million 37. *On the Avenue* 37. You Can't Have Everything 37. Life Begins at College 37. *The Goldwyn Follies* 38. Kentucky Moonshine 38. Straight Place and Show 38. *The Three Musketeers* 39. The Gorilla 39. Pack Up Your Troubles 39. Argentine Nights 40. Behind the Eight Ball 42. Hi Ya Chum 43. Never a Dull Moment 43. Won Ton Ton (guest appearance by Harry and Jim) 76.

Riva, Emmanuele (1927–).
French leading actress, a former dressmaker.
Hiroshima Mon Amour 59. Adua et Sa Compagnie/Hungry for Love 60. Kapo 60. Leon Morin Priest 61. Climats 61. Thérèse Desqueyroux 63. Soledad 66. The Eyes, the Mouth 83. Three Colours: Blue/Trois Couleurs: Bleu 93. God, My Mother's Lover, and the Butcher's Son 95, etc.

Riva, Juan Antonio de la (1953–).
Mexican director.
Wandering Lives/Vidas Errantes 83. Pueblo de Madera 91. La Ultima Batalla 93. Una Maestra con Angel 94, etc.

Rivera, Chita (1933–) (Dolores Conchita Figueroa del Rivero).
Dynamic American dancer and singer.
Sweet Charity 69. Pippin 81. That's Singing 84. The Mayflower Madam (TV) 87, etc.

Rivers, Joan (1933–).
American cabaret comedienne with a strong line in smut.
Rabbit Test 78. Tears and Laughter: The Joan and Melissa Rivers Story (TV) 94.
❝ I'm Jewish. I don't work out. If God had intended me to bend over he'd have put diamonds on the floor. – *J.R.*

Rivette, Jacques (1928–).
French director and screenwriter, former critic.
Le Coup du Berger 56. Paris Nous Appartient 60. La Religieuse (& w) 65. L'Amour Fou (& w) 68. Celine and Julie Go Boating 74. La Vengeresse 76. Merry Go Round 83. Love on the Ground/L'Amour par Terre 84. Hurlevent 85. The Gang of Four/La Bande des Quatre 89. *La Belle Noiseuse* 91. Jeanne la Pucelle 94. Up Down Fragile/Haut Bas Fragile 95. Secret Defence 98, etc.

Rivkin, Allen (1903–1990).
American screenwriter and novelist. Born in Hayward, Wisconsin, and educated at the University of Minnesota, he worked as a journalist and publicist and in advertising before going to Hollywood in the early 30s. He later worked in television, and produced the series *Troubleshooters* 59–60. He also wrote (with Laura Kerr) *Hello Hollywood*, an anthology of reminiscences about film.
70,000 Witness 32. Meet the Baron 33. The Picture Snatcher 33. Dancing Lady 33. Cheating Cheaters 34. Our Little Girl 35. This Is My Affair 37. Love under Fire 37. Let Us Live 37. Straight, Place and Show 38. It Could Happen to You 39. Typhoon 40. Kid Glove Killer 42. Joe Smith American 42. The Guilt of Janet Ames 47. The Farmer's Daughter 47. Tension 50. Grounds for Marriage 50. Gambling House 50. The Strip 51. It's a Big Country 52. Timberjack 54. Prisoner of War 54. The Eternal Sea 55. Road to Denver 55. Live Fast, Die Young 58. The Big Operator 59, many others.

Rix, Brian (Lord Rix) (1924–).
English leading actor and producer of farce. Born in Cottingham, Yorkshire, he was on stage from 1942 and actor-manager at London's Whitehall and Garrick theatres for 30 years from 1950. He then became Secretary-General and, later, Chairman of MENCAP (The Royal Society for

Mentally Handicapped Children and Adults). He was knighted in 1986 and made a life peer in 1992. Married actress Elspet Gray in 1949.

Books: 1989, *Farce about Face*; 1992, *Tour de Farce*.

Reluctant Heroes 51. What Every Woman Wants 54. Up to His Neck 54. Dry Rot 55. The Night We Dropped a Clanger 59. And the Same to You 60. Nothing Barred 61. Don't Just Lie There, Say Something 73, etc.

TV series: Dial Rix 62–63. Laughter from Whitehall 63–64. Laughter from the Whitehall 65. Men of Affairs 73. A Roof over My Head 77.

Roach, Bert (1891–1971).
American silent screen actor.

The Millionaire 21. The Rowdy 21. The Flirt 22. Excitement 24. Don't 25. Money Talks 26. The Taxi Dancer 27. The Desert Rider 29. No No Nanette 30. Viennese Nights 30. Hallelujah I'm a Bum 33. San Francisco 36. Algiers 38. Hi Diddle Diddle 43. The Perils of Pauline 47, etc.

Roach, Hal (1892–1992).
American producer chiefly associated with gag comedies. Varied early experience before he teamed with Harold Lloyd 1916; later made films with Our Gang, Laurel and Hardy, etc.

SOUND FILMS: Sons of the Desert 33. *Way Out West* 36. *Topper* 37. *Of Mice and Men* 39. *Turnabout* 40. One Million BC 40. *Topper Returns* 41, many others.

❝ One of the few producers who knew talent when he saw it, and gave his stars, writers and directors the freedom to create great comedy.
– *Leonard Maltin*

~AA 1983 'in recognition of his distinguished contributions to the motion picture art form'.

Roach, Jay (1958?–).
American director. Born in New Mexico, he graduated from Stanford University and studied for a master's degree in film production at the University of Southern California. Married singer Susanna Hoffs.

Lifepod (co-w) (TV) 93. Blown Away (story) 94. The Empty Mirror (co-w) 96. Austin Powers: International Man of Mystery 97. Austin Powers II 99, etc.

Roache, Linus (1964–).
English leading actor, the son of William Roache (1932–), who plays Ken Barlow in the ITV soap opera *Coronation Street*.

Priest 94. The Wings of the Dove 97. Shot through the Heart (TV) 98, etc.

TV series: Seaforth 94.

Roarke, Adam (1938–1996).
American actor and occasional director. A regular in biker movies of the 60s, he is said to have turned down a leading role in *Easy Rider*. He later became an acting coach. Died of a heart attack.

Women of the Prehistoric Planet 66. Hell's Angels on Wheels 67. Psych-Out 68. The Savage Seven 68. The Losers 70. Play It as It Lays 72. How Come Nobody's on Our Side? 73. Dirty Mary, Crazy Larry 74. Four Deuces 75. The Stunt Man 80. Beach Girls 82. Trespasses (& co-d) 83, etc.

Rob Roy (1671–1734) (Robert Roy McGregor).
Scottish outlaw, a drover whose clan had been proscribed by the English as Jacobite sympathizers; like many outlaws, he became famous for his kindness to the oppressed. Sir Walter Scott immortalized him in his novel *Rob Roy*, published in 1817, and he was played by Liam Neeson in the Hollywood film *Rob Roy* 95, directed by Michael Caton-Jones.

Robards, Jason, Snr (1892–1963).
American stage actor, who made character appearances in films.

The Cohens and the Kellys 26. On Trial 28. Abraham Lincoln 30. The Crusades 35. I Stole a Million 39. Isle of the Dead 45. Bedlam 46. Riff Raff 47. Wild in the Country 61, many others.

TV series: Acapulco 61.

Robards, Jason, Jnr (1922–).
American stage actor, son of Jason ROBARDS. The second of his three wives was actress Lauren BACALL (1961–69).

The Journey 58. By Love Possessed 59. *Tender is the Night* 61. Long Day's Journey into Night 62. A Thousand Clowns 65. A Big Hand for the Little Lady 66. Any Wednesday 66. Divorce American Style 67. *The Hour of the Gun* 67. The St Valentine's Day Massacre 67. The Night They Raided Minsky's 68. Isadora 68. Once Upon a Time in the West 69. Tora! Tora! Tora! 70. Julius Caesar 70. The Ballad of Cable Hogue 70. Murders in the Rue Morgue 71. Johnny Got His Gun 71. The War Between Men and Women 72. Pat Garrett and Billy the Kid 73. Play It as It Lays 73. All The President's Men (AA) 76. Washington behind Closed Doors (TV) 77. Julia (as Dashiell Hammett) (AA) 77. Comes a Horseman 78. Hurricane 79. Melvin and Howard (as Howard Hughes) (AAN) 80. Raise the Titanic 80. Caboblanco 81. The Legend of the Lone Ranger 81. Max Dugan Returns 83. The Day After (TV) 83. Something Wicked This Way Comes 83. Sakharov (TV) 84. The Last Frontier (TV) 86. Square Dance 86. Bright Lights, Big City 88. The Good Mother 88. Black Rainbow 89. Dream a Little Dream 89. Reunion 89. Parenthood 89. Quick Change 90. Gettysburg 90. Chernobyl: The Final Warning (TV) 91. Storyville 92. The Trial 93. The Adventures of Huck Finn 93. Philadelphia 93. The Paper 94. Little Big League 94. The Enemy Within (TV) 94. My Antonia (TV) 95. Journey 95. A Thousand Acres 97. Beloved 98. The Real Macaw (Aus.) 98. Enemy of the State 98, etc.

❝ I've always played disintegrated characters.
– *J.R.*

Robbe-Grillet, Alain (1922–).
French writer, associated with Resnais in *Last Year at Marienbad* 60. Also wrote and directed: *L'Immortelle* 62. *Trans-Europe Express* 66. Glissements Progressifs du Plaisir 73. Le Jeu avec le Feu 74. La Belle Captive 83. Un Bruit Qui Rend Fou 94. The Blue Villa 95, etc.

Robbins, Brian (1964–).
American director, writer and producer, a former actor, born in Brooklyn, New York.

AS ACTOR: Crime of Innocence (TV) 85. The Gladiator (TV) 86. One Terrific Guy (TV) 86. Cellar Dweller 87. BUD/CHUD II 88. Camp Cucamonga (TV) 90, etc.

AS DIRECTOR: The Show 95. Good Burger 97.

TV series: Head of the Class 86–91.

Robbins, Gale (1922–1980).
American leading lady and singer.

In the Meantime Darling 44. My Girl Tisa 48. The Barkleys of Broadway 49. Oh You Beautiful Doll 49. Three Little Words 50. Strictly Dishonourable 51. The Belle of New York 52. Calamity Jane 53. Double Jeopardy 55. Stand Up and Be Counted 72, etc.

Robbins, Harold (1916–1997) (Francis Kane).
Best-selling American novelist and occasional screenwriter and producer. His 23 books, often based on actual events including film-world scandals, found favour for a time in Hollywood: *The Carpetbaggers*, which sold 6m copies, drew on the life of Howard HUGHES, and *Where Love Has Gone*, which was inspired by the killing of Lana TURNER's gangster lover, was filmed as *Stiletto*. Born in New York, he was a foundling, first given the name of Francis Kane and then called Harold Rubin when he was adopted at the age of 11. After a variety of jobs, and making and losing a fortune on the stock exchange, he went to work for Universal Pictures in the 40s, where he took charge of budgets and planning and began writing. Married three times.

■ Never Love a Stranger (co-w, oa) 58. King Creole (oa) 58. The Pusher (w) 59. The Carpetbaggers (oa) 63. Where Love Has Gone (oa) 64. Nevada Smith (oa) 65. Stiletto (oa) 69. The Adventurers (oa) 70. The Betsy (oa) 78. Harold Robbins' The Pirate (TV) 78. 79 Park Avenue (oa) (TV) 79. The Dream Merchants (oa) (TV) 80. The Lonely Lady (oa) 82.

TV series: The Survivors 69–70.

❝ All my characters are real. They are written as fiction to protect the guilty. – *H.R.*

Hemingway was a jerk. – *H.R.*

I'm the world's best novelist – there's nothing more to say. – *H.R.*

At best, he ranks as another King of Pulp, alongside Edgar Wallace or Mickey Spillane.
– *John Sutherland*

Robbins, Jerome (1918–1998) (Jerome Rabinowitz).
American dancer and ballet-master who has choreographed several films. Born in New York, he studied briefly at New York University and at the Dance Center in Manhattan, beginning as a dancer in the chorus of Broadway musicals. The first ballet he created, *Fancy Free*, became the basis for the musical and the movie *On the Town*. After co-directing the screen version of *West Side Story*, he turned down other offers to direct.

The King and I 56. *West Side Story* (& co-d) (AA) 61, etc.

Robbins, Matthew.
American director and screenwriter.

The Sugarland Express (co-w) 74. The Bingo Long Traveling All-Stars and Motor Kings (co-w) 76. MacArthur (co-w) 77. Corvette Summer (co-w, d) 78. Dragonslayer (co-w, d) 81. Warning Sign (co-w) 85. The Legend of Billy Jean (d) 85. Batteries Not Included (co-w, d) 87. Bingo (d) 91. Mimic (co-w) 97, etc.

Robbins, Richard.
American composer, usually for Merchant-Ivory films. His association with the company dates from 1976, when he made a short film, *Sweet Sounds*, about the children and teaching methods at the Mannes College of Music Preparatory School in New York, where he was then the director.

The Europeans 79. Jane Austen in Manhattan 80. Quartet 81. Heat and Dust 82. The Bostonians 84. Room with a View 85. Maurice 87. The Perfect Murder 88. Howards End (AAN) 92. Remains of the Day (AAN) 93. Jefferson in Paris 95. Place Vendôme (Fr.) 98, etc.

Robbins, Tim (1958–).
American leading actor, singer and songwriter who has recently turned to screenwriting and directing.

No Small Affair 84. The Sure Thing 85. Howard the Duck 86. Top Gun 86. Bull Durham 88. Erik the Viking 89. Miss Firecracker 89. Cadillac Man 90. Jacob's Ladder 90. The Player 92. Bob Roberts (& wd, s) 92. The Hudsucker Proxy 94. The Shawshank Redemption 94. Prêt-à-Porter/Ready to Wear 94. I.Q. 94. Dead Man Walking (wd) (AANd) 95. Nothing to Lose 96. Arlington Road 98, etc.

❝ Whether a movie is going to be a success or a failure, and consequently whether you're going to be a success or failure yourself, is always a crapshoot. – *T.R.*

Rober, Richard (1906–1952).
American general-purpose actor with stage experience.

Smart Girls Don't Talk 48. Deported 50. The Well 52. The Devil Makes Three 52, etc.

Robert, Yves (1920–).
French director, former actor.

The War of the Buttons 61. *Bébert et l'Omnibus* 63. *Copains* 64. *Follow the Guy with One Black Shoe* 72. Pardon Mon Affaire 76. We All Shall Go to Paradise 77. Courage Fuyons 79. Le Jumeau 84. My Father's Glory/La Gloire de Mon Père 90. My Mother's Castle/Le Château de Ma Mère 90. Le Bal des Casse-Pieds 92. Montparnasse Pondichery 94, etc.

Roberti, Lyda (1910–1938).
German-Polish leading lady, former child café singer, in several Hollywood films of the 30s.

■ Million Dollar Legs 32. The Kid from Spain 32. Dancers in the Dark 32. Torch Singers 33. Three-Cornered Moon 33. College Rhythm 34. The Big Broadcast of 1936 35. George White's Scandals 35. Pick a Star 37. Nobody's Baby 37. Wide Open Faces 37.

Roberts, Ben (1916–1984) (Benjamin Eisenberg).
American writer, almost always with Ivan GOFF.

Roberts, Eric (1956–).
American leading man. He is the brother of actress Julia Roberts.

King of the Gypsies 78. Raggedy Man 81. Star 80 83. The Pope of Greenwich Village 84. The Coca Cola Kid 85. Runaway Train (AAN) 85. Nobody's Fool 86. Dear America 87. Best of the Best 89. Options 89. Rude Awakening 89. Blood Red 89. The Ambulance 90. Descending Angel 91. Lonely Hearts 91. By the Sword 91. Final Analysis 92. Best of the Best II 93. The Hard Truth 94. Love, Cheat & Steal 94. The Specialist 94. The Grave 96. It's My Party 96. Dr Who (TV) 96. Heaven's Prisoners 96. Power 98 96. American Strays 96. The Cable Guy 96. The Glass Cage 96. In Cold Blood (TV) 96. Saved by the Light (TV) 97. The Odyssey (TV) 97. Most Wanted (TV) 97. Past Perfect 98, etc.

TV series: C16: FBI 97– .

Roberts, Ewan (1914–1983) (Thomas McEwan Hutchinson).
Scottish character actor of stage and screen.

Castle in the Air 52. The Lady Killers 55. Night of the Demon 57. The Day of the Triffids 61. The Traitors 62. Five to One 63. Hostile Witness 67. Bedevilled 71. Endless Night 72, etc.

Roberts, Florence (1860–1940).
American character actress best remembered as Granny in the Jones Family series 1936–40.

Westward Passage 32. Make Me a Star 32. Dangerously Yours 33. Torch Singer 33. Babes in Toyland 34. Les Misérables 35. Next Time We Love 36. The Life of Emile Zola 37, etc.

Roberts, Julia (1967–).
American actress, a former model who rapidly established herself as the most sought-after actress of the early 90s. She is the sister of Eric ROBERTS. Current asking price: $17m a movie.

Blood Red 88. Satisfaction 88. Baja Oklahoma (TV) 88. Mystic Pizza 88. Steel Magnolias (AAN) 89. Pretty Woman (AAN) 90. Flatliners 90. Sleeping with the Enemy 90. Dying Young 91. Hook 91. The Pelican Brief 93. I Love Trouble 94. Prêt-à-Porter/Ready to Wear 94. Something to Talk About 95. Mary Reilly 96. Michael Collins 96. Everyone Says I Love You 96. *My Best Friend's Wedding* 97. Conspiracy Theory 98. Stepmom 98, etc.

❝ I never really made it to acting school. I went to acting classes a few times, but it never seemed very conducive to what I wanted to do. – *J.R.*

Roberts, Kenneth (1885–1957).
American adventure novelist. The filming of *Northwest Passage* was never completed; the title on King Vidor's film reads *Northwest Passage, Part One: Rogers' Rangers*. *Lydia Bailey* fared better.

Roberts, Lynne (1919–1978) (Mary Hart).
American leading lady of 40s second features.

Dangerous Holiday 37. Winter Wonderland 39. Call of the Klondike 41. Quiet Please Murder 42. The Great Plane Robbery 47. The Blazing Forest 52. Port Sinister 53, many others.

Roberts, Marguerite (1908–1989).
American screenwriter of tough, masculine films, specializing in westerns. Born in Nebraska and brought up in Greeley, Colorado, she began as a journalist and then went to work at Fox in 1927 as secretary to studio head Winfield Sheehan, before becoming a script reader. She later worked for Paramount and MGM. A prominent member of the Screen Writers Guild, she was blacklisted for a decade from the early 50s and her name was removed from the credits of *Ivanhoe*, on which she was working at the time. Her second husband was novelist and occasional screenwriter John Sanford.

Sailor's Luck (w) 33. Peck's Bad Boy (w) 34. Hollywood Boulevard (w) 36. Turn of the Moon (co-w) 37. Escape (co-w) 40. Honky Tonk (co-w) 41. Ziegfeld Girl (co-w) 41. Somewhere I'll Find You (w) 42. Dragon Seed (w) 44. Desire Me (co-w) 46. If Winter Comes (co-w) 47. Sea of Grass (co-w) 47. Ambush (w) 49. The Bribe (story) 49. Soldiers Three (co-w) 51. Rampage (co-w) 62. Diamond Head (w) 63. Love Has Many Faces (w) 64. Five Card Stud (w) 68. Norwood (w) 69. *True Grit* (w) 69. Red Sky at Morning (w) 70. Shoot Out (w) 71, etc.

❝ I was weaned on stories about gunfighters and their doings, and I know all the lingo too. My grandfather came West as far as Colorado by covered wagon. He was a sheriff in the state's wildest days. – *M.R.*

She writes men with more balls than any other guy on this lot. – *Clark Gable at MGM*

Roberts, Pernell (1930–).
American general-purpose actor; became famous as one of the brothers in TV's *Bonanza*, but left after four years and never regained the limelight until

1979, when he played the title role in the series *Trapper John MD*.
Ride Lonesome 58. The Silent Gun (TV) 69. The Magic of Lassie 78. Night Train to Kathmandu (TV) 88, etc.

Roberts, Rachel (1927–1980).
Welsh character actress in leading roles. Born in Llanelli, she studied at the University of Wales and RADA and, in 1950, began working with a repertory company in Swansea (where her fellow players included Kenneth Williams and Richard Burton) and was in films from the mid-50s, coming into her own with *Saturday Night and Sunday Morning* 60 and *This Sporting Life*. Insecurity, the breakdown of her marriage to Rex Harrison (1962–71) and alcoholism bedevilled her later career and she committed suicide. Her first husband was actor Alan Dobie (1955–61).
Autobiography: *No Bells on Sunday* (edited by Alexander Walker).
Valley of Song 52. The Good Companions 57. Our Man in Havana 59. *Saturday Night and Sunday Morning* (BFA) 60. *This Sporting Life* (AAN, BFA) 63. A Flea in Her Ear 68. Doctors' Wives 71. Wild Rovers 71. *O Lucky Man* 73. The Belstone Fox 73. Murder on the Orient Express 74. Great Expectations (TV) 75. Picnic at Hanging Rock 76. Foul Play 78. When a Stranger Calls 79. Yanks (BFA) 79. Charlie Chan and the Curse of the Dragon Queen 81, etc.
TV series: The Tony Randall Show 76.
❝ Whenever I act well, my head clears. Always a bit frail I was personally, but never professionally. – *R.R.*
Day after day and night after night, I'm in this shaking fear. What am I so terribly frightened of? Life itself, I think. – *R.R.'s last entry in her journal*
She was like a ball of fire: the only trouble was, so often she had no material worthy of setting alight with her combustible energy. – *Pamela Mason*
She had good legs. How do I know? Because she was forever throwing her dress up over her head. – *Richard Gere*
That big, carnal, sensuous stage personality of hers is damn hard to find nowadays. – *Hal Prince*

Roberts, Roy (1900–1975).
American character actor who once played cops but graduated to senior executives.
Guadalcanal Diary 43. My Darling Clementine 46. Flaming Fury 49. The Big Trees 52. The Glory Brigade 53. The Boss 56, many others.
TV series: Petticoat Junction 64–68.

Roberts, Stephen (1895–1936).
American director, a former pilot and trick and exhibition flyer, in films from 1922.
■ Sky Bride 32. Lady and Gent 32. The Night of June 13th 32. If I Had a Million (part) 32. The Story of Temple Drake 33. *One Sunday Afternoon* 33. The Trumpet Blows 34. Romance in Manhattan 34. *Star of Midnight* 35. The Man Who Broke the Bank at Monte Carlo 35. The Lady Consents 36. The Ex Mrs Bradford 36.

Roberts, Tanya (1954–) (Tanya Leigh).
American actress and model, born in the Bronx, New York. She studied acting under Lee Strasberg and Uta Hagen.
The Last Victim 75. The Yum-Yum Girls 76. Fingers 78. Racquet 79. The Beastmaster 82. Sheena, Queen of the Jungle 84. A View to a Kill 85. Body Slam 87. Ladies' Game 90. Night Eyes 90. Inner Sanctum 91. Almost Pregnant 92. Sins of Desire 92. Deep Down 93, etc.
TV series: Charlie's Angels 80–81. That '70s Show 98– .

Roberts, Theodore (1861–1928).
American character actor, the grand old man of the silent screen.
Where the Trail Divides 14. The Trail of the Lonesome Pine 16. Male and Female 19. The Affairs of Anatol 21. Our Leading Citizen 22. *The Ten Commandments* (as Moses) 23. Grumpy 23. Locked Doors 25. Masks of the Devil 28, many others.

Roberts, Tony (1939–).
American light leading man.
The Beach Girls and the Monster 70. Star Spangled Girl 71. Play It Again Sam 72. Serpico 73. Le Sauvage 75. Annie Hall 77. Just Tell Me What You Want 80. A Midsummer Night's Sex Comedy 82. Amityville 3-D 83. Key Exchange 85. Hannah and Her Sisters 85. Radio Days 87. Switch 91. Popcorn 91, etc.

Robertshaw, Jerrold (1866–1941).
Gaunt British stage actor who made several film appearances.
Dombey and Son 18. She 25. Downhill 27. Kitty 29. Don Quixote (title role) 33, etc.

Robertson, Cliff (1925–).
Ambitious American leading man with long stage experience before being spotted for films. His second wife was actress Dina Merrill (1966–89).
■ *Picnic* (debut) 55. Autumn Leaves 56. The Girl Most Likely 57. The Naked and the Dead 58. Gidget 59. Battle of the Coral Sea 59. As the Sea Rages 60. All in a Night's Work 61. The Big Show 61. Underworld USA 61. The Interns 62. My Six Loves 63. *PT 109* (as President Kennedy) 63. Sunday in New York 64. *The Best Man* 64. 633 Squadron 64. Love Has Many Faces 65. Masquerade (GB) 65. Up from the Beach 65. *The Honey Pot* 67. The Devil's Brigade 68. *Charly* (AA) 68. Too Late the Hero 69. The Great Northfield Minnesota Raid 72. J. W. Coop (& p, d) 72. Ace Eli and Rodger of the Skies 73. Man on a Swing 74. My Father's House (TV) 75. Out of Season 75. Three Days of the Condor 76. Midway 76. Shoot 76. Obsession 76. *Washington behind Closed Doors* (TV) 77. Fraternity Row (narrator) 77. Dominique 78. The Pilot (& wd) 80. Two of a Kind (TV) 82. Class 83. Brainstorm 83. Star 80 83. The Key to Rebecca (TV) 85. Shaker Run 85. Wild Hearts Can't Be Broken 91. Wind 92. Renaissance Man 94. Escape from L.A. 96.
TV series: Rod Brown of the Rocket Rangers 53. Falcon Crest 83–84.
❝ As long as I get phone calls from the Museum of Modern Art, that all the film buffs love it, that's a residual. It isn't a financial residual and it isn't an artistic residual, but it's an ego residual. – *C.R.*
～In 1979 Robertson's career suffered unfairly when he accused executive David Begelman of having falsely signed a cheque in his name. The incident became a major scandal and is covered in the book *Indecent Exposure* by David McClintick.

Robertson, Dale (1923–).
American western star, former schoolteacher.
Fighting Man of the Plains (debut) 49. Two Flags West 50. Lydia Bailey 52. The Silver Whip 53. Sitting Bull 54. A Day of Fury 56. Law of the Lawless 63. Blood on the Arrow 65. Coast of Skeletons 65, etc.
TV series: Tales of Wells Fargo 57–61. The Iron Horse 66. Dynasty 80–81.

Robertson, John S. (1878–1964).
Canadian director in Hollywood, a former actor, on stage from 1890.
The Money Mill 17. Let's Elope 19. Dr Jekyll and Mr Hyde 20. Sentimental Tommy 21. Tess of the Storm Country 22. The Enchanted Cottage 24. Shore Leave 25. Annie Laurie 27. Shanghai Lady 29. Madonna of the Streets 30. One Man's Journey 33. Wednesday's Child 34. Captain Hurricane 35. Our Little Girl 35, many others.

Robertson, Michael.
Australian director and screenwriter.
The Best of Friends 82. Going Sane 85. Back of Beyond 95, etc.

Robertson, Robbie (1943–) (Jaime Robertson).
Canadian composer, songwriter, and guitarist, a member of the leading 70s rock group The Band.
The Last Waltz (doc) 78. Carny (a, co-w) 80. The King of Comedy 83. The Color of Money 86. Jimmy Hollywood 94, etc.

Robertson, Willard (1886–1948).
American character actor, often seen as lawyer or prison governor.
Skippy 31. Sky Devils 32. I Am a Fugitive from a Chain Gang 32. Doctor X 32. Tugboat Annie 33. Death on the Diamond 34. Here Comes the Navy 34. Black Fury 35. The Gorgeous Hussy 36. Exclusive 37. Men with Wings 38. Jesse James 39. Each Dawn I Die 39. My Little Chickadee 40. The Monster and the Girl 41. Juke Girl 42. Nine Girls 44. The Virginian 46. To Each His Own 46. Sitting Pretty 48, many others.

Robeson, Paul (1898–1976).
American actor and singer, on stage including concerts from mid-20s.
Biographies, all entitled *Paul Robeson*: 1958, by Marie Seton. 1968, by Edwin P. Hoyt. 1974, by Virginia Hamilton.
■ Body and Soul 24. The Emperor Jones 33. *Sanders of the River* 35. *Showboat* 36. *Song of Freedom* 36. Jericho 38. Big Fella 38. *King Solomon's Mines* 38. *The Proud Valley* 39. Tales of Manhattan 42. Native Land 42. Il Canto dei Grandi Fiumi 55.

Robey, Sir George (1869–1954) (George Edward Wade).
British music-hall comedian, 'the prime minister of mirth'. Appeared in silent farcical comedies, later in character roles.
Autobiography: 1933, *Looking Back on Life*.
Biography: 1991, *George Robey* by James Harding.
The Rest Cure 23. Don Quixote (as Sancho Panza) 23 and 33. Her Prehistoric Man 24. Chu Chin Chow 33. Marry Me 33. Birds of a Feather 36. A Girl Must Live 39. Variety Jubilee 40. Salute John Citizen 42. Henry V 44. The Trojan Brothers 45. The Pickwick Papers 52, etc.

Robin, Dany (1927–1995).
French leading lady who trained as a ballet dancer. Married French actor George Marchel and, from 1969, producer Michael Sullivan, who died with her in a fire.
Le Silence Est d'Or 46. Histoire d'Amour 52. Act of Love 54. In Six Easy Lessons 60. The Waltz of the Toreadors 62. Topaz 69, etc.

Robin, Leo (1899–1984).
American lyricist. Songs include 'Louise', 'Beyond the Blue Horizon', 'June in January', 'No Love No Nothing'.
Innocents of Paris 29. Monte Carlo 30. One Hour with You 32. Little Miss Marker 34. The Big Broadcast of 1938 (AA for 'Thanks for the Memory'). Gulliver's Travels 39. My Gal Sal 43. Meet Me after the Show 50. My Sister Eileen 55, etc.

Robinson, Andrew.
Baby-faced American character actor who has played a couple of memorable villains.
Dirty Harry 71. Charley Varrick 73. The Drowning Pool 75. Cobra 86. Shoot to Kill 88. Prime Target 91. Child's Play 3 91. Trancers III: Deth Lives 92. Pumpkinhead II 93. There Goes My Baby 94, etc.

Robinson, Bernard (1912–1970).
English art director and production designer, latterly with Hammer Films.
Tony Draws a Horse 50. Old Mother Riley Meets the Vampire 52. Albert R.N. 53. The Sea Shall Not Have Them 54. Reach for the Sky 56. Quatermass II 57. Carve Her Name with Pride 58. *Dracula* 58. The Revenge of Frankenstein 58. The Sheriff of Fractured Jaw 58. The Hound of the Baskervilles 59. The Mummy 59. Brides of Dracula 60. Watch It Sailor! 61. *The Damned* 61. Curse of the Werewolf 64. Curse of the Mummy's Tomb 64. Dracula – Prince of Darkness 65. Frankenstein Created Woman 66. The Devil Rides Out 67. Quatermass and the Pit 67, etc.

Robinson, Bill (1878–1949).
American tap-dancer and entertainer, famous for his stairway dance.
The Little Colonel 35. In Old Kentucky 36. Rebecca of Sunnybrook Farm 38. *Stormy Weather* 43, etc.

Robinson, Bruce (1946–).
British screenwriter and director, a former actor.
The Killing Fields (w) (AAN) 84. *Withnail and I* (wd) 87. How to Get Ahead in Advertising (wd) 89. Fat Man and Little Boy/The Shadow-makers (co-w) 89. Jennifer 8 92. Return to Paradise (co-w) 98. Still Crazy (a) 98, etc.
❝ There are two types of animals roaming the Hollywood jungle. Those who do the screwing, those who get screwed. You have to try to ensure you're one of the former. – *B.R.*

Robinson, Cardew (1917–1992) (Douglas Robinson).
Lanky English comic actor, best known for his act as delinquent schoolboy 'Cardew the Cad, the Bad Boy of St Fanny's', from variety and radio.
Knight without Armour 37. A Piece of Cake 48. Fun at St Fanny's 56. Happy Is the Bride 58. I'm All Right, Jack 59. The Navy Lark 59. Waltz of the Toreadors 62. Heavens Above 63. Father Came Too 64. Alfie 66. Carry On up the Khyber 67. Where's Jack 69. The Magnificent 7 Deadly Sins 71. What's Up Nurse? 75. Guess Who's Coming to Dinner? 85. Pirates 86, etc.

Robinson, Casey (1903–1979).
American screenwriter, in Hollywood from 1921.
I Love That Man 33. Captain Blood 35. Call it a Day 37. It's Love I'm After 37. Four's a Crowd 39. *Kings Row* 42. Passage to Marseilles 44. Days of Glory 44. *The Macomber Affair* 47. Under My Skin (& p) 50. Two Flags West (& p) 50. Diplomatic Courier (& p) 52. The Snows of Kilimanjaro 52. While the City Sleeps 56. This Earth is Mine (& p) 59, etc.

Robinson, David (1930–).
English critic and author, notably as the biographer of Charlie Chaplin in *Chaplin: His Life and Art* (1985). He was film critic for the *Financial Times* and *The Times*. His books include *World Cinema, The Great Funnies, Buster Keaton.*

Robinson, Dewey (1898–1950).
Burly, bristling-eyebrowed American character actor, usually in tough or gangster roles. Died of a heart attack.
Enemies of the Law 31. Blonde Venus 32. *She Done Him Wrong* (as Spider Kane) 33. A Midsummer Night's Dream (as Snug) 35. New Faces of 1937 37. The Great McGinty 40. Tin Pan Alley 40. The Big Store 41. Palm Beach Story 42. Scarlet Street 45. Dillinger 45. The Gangster 46. The Beautiful Blonde from Bashful Bend 49. My Friend Irma 49. Father of the Bride 50. Jim Thorpe – American 51, etc.

Robinson, Edward G. (1893–1973) (Emanuel Goldenberg).
Dynamic American star actor of Rumanian origin. On stage from 1913; later settled in Hollywood. Special Academy Award 1972.
Autobiography: 1973, *All My Yesterdays*.
■ The Bright Shawl 23. The Hole in the Wall 29. Night Ride 30. A Lady to Love 30. Outside the Law 30. East is West 30. Widow from Chicago 30. *Little Caesar* (which made him a star) 30. *Five Star Final* 31. Smart Money 31. The Hatchet Man 31. Two Seconds 32. Tiger Shark 32. Silver Dollar 32. The Little Giant 33. I Loved a Woman 33. Dark Hazard 34. The Man with Two Faces 34. *The Whole Town's Talking* 34. Barbary Coast 35. Bullets or Ballots 36. Thunder in the City (GB) 37. Kid Galahad 37. The Last Gangster 38. *A Slight Case of Murder* 38. *The Amazing Dr Clitterhouse* 38. I Am the Law 38. Confessions of a Nazi Spy 39. Blackmail 39. *Dr Ehrlich's Magic Bullet* 40. *Brother Orchid* 40. A Dispatch from Reuters 41. *The Sea Wolf* 41. Manpower 41. Unholy Partners 41. Larceny Inc. 42. Tales of Manhattan 42. Destroyer 43. Flesh and Fantasy 43. Tampico 44. *Double Indemnity* 44. Mr Winkle Goes to War 44. *The Woman in the Window* 44. Our Vines Have Tender Grapes 45. *Scarlet Street* 45. Journey Together (GB) 45. The Stranger 46. The Red House 47. *All My Sons* 48. *Key Largo* 48. Night Has a Thousand Eyes 48. *House of Strangers* 49. My Daughter Joy (GB) 50. Actors and Sin 52. Vice Squad 53. Big Leaguer 53. The Glass Web 53. Black Tuesday 54. The Violent Men 55. Tight Spot 55. A Bullet for Joey 55. Illegal 55. Hell on Frisco Bay 56. Nightmare 56. The Ten Commandments 56. A Hole in the Head 59. Seven Thieves 59. Pépé 60. My Geisha 62. *Two Weeks in Another Town* 62. Sammy Going South (GB) 62. The Prize 63. Good Neighbour Sam 64. Robin and the Seven Hoods 64. Cheyenne Autumn 64. The Outrage 64. *The Cincinnati Kid* 65. Who Has Seen the Wind? 65. The Biggest Bundle of Them All 66. Never a Dull Moment 67. Grand Slam 67. Mackenna's Gold 68. It's Your Move 68. Operation St Peter's 68. Blonde from Peking 68. Song of Norway 69. Operation Heartbeat (TV) 69. The Old Man Who Cried Wolf (TV) 71. Soylent Green 73.
✪ For the dynamic personality which turned many a dubious script into dramatic gold. *Double Indemnity*.
❝ Some people have youth, some have beauty – I have menace. – *E.G.R.*
Famous line (*Little Caesar*): 'Mother of mercy, is this the end of Rico?'

Robinson, Frances (1916–1971).
American supporting actress, usually in smart roles.
Forbidden Valley 25. The Last Warning 28. Tim Tyler's Luck 35. The Lone Wolf Keeps a Date 37. The Invisible Man Returns 39. Tower of London 39. Smilin' Through 41. Suddenly It's Spring 46. Keeper of the Bees 47. Backfire 50, many others.

Robinson, George (c. 1895–1958).
American cinematographer.
No Defense 21. Back to God's Country 27. Hell's Heroes 30. Her First Mate 33. The Mystery of Edwin Drood 35. Diamond Jim 35. The Invisible Ray 36. Sutter's Gold 36. Dracula's Daughter 36. The Road Back 37. *Son of Frankenstein* 39. Tower of London 39. Son of Monte Cristo 40. Frankenstein Meets the Wolf Man 43. Son of Dracula 43. *The Scarlet Claw* 44. House of Frankenstein 45. The Naughty Nineties 45. Slave Girl 47. The Creeper 48. Abbott and Costello Meet Dr Jekyll and Mr Hyde 53. Tarantula 55. Joe Dakota 57, many others.

Robinson, Jay (1930–).
American stage actor of eccentric roles.
The Robe 53. Demetrius and the Gladiators 54. The Virgin Queen 55. My Man Godfrey 57. Bunny O'Hare 71. Shampoo 75. Partners 82. The Malibu Bikini Shop 86. Transylvania Twist 89. Sinatra (TV) 92. Bram Stoker's Dracula 92. Skeeter 93. Murder between Friends (TV) 94, etc.

Robinson, Joe (1929–).
British actor and professional boxer.
Master of Bankdam 48. Daughter of Darkness 49. *A Kid for Two Farthings* 55. The Flesh Is Weak 57. The Two Faces of Dr Jekyll 58. Barabbas 62. Diamonds Are Forever 71, etc.

Robinson, John (1908–1979).
British stage actor, familiar in heavy father or tough executive roles.
The Scarab Murder Case 36. The Lion Has Wings 40. Uneasy Terms 49. Hammer the Toff 51. The Constant Husband 55. Fortune is a Woman 58. The Doctor's Dilemma 58. And the Same to You 61, etc.

Robinson, Madeleine (1916–) (Madeleine Svoboda).
French stage and film actress.
Soldats sans Uniformes 43. Douce 43. Une Si Jolie Petite Plage 48. Dieu a Besoin des Hommes 50. Le Garçon Sauvage 51. The She Wolves 57. A Double Tour 59. The Trial 64. A Trap for Cinderella 65. A New World 66. Le Voyage du Père 66. Le Petit Matin 70. Camille Claudel 88, etc.

Robinson, Phil Alden (1950–).
American director and screenwriter.
All of Me (w) 84. Rhinestone (co-w) 84. In the Mood (wd) 87. Field of Dreams (wd) (AAN) 89. Sneakers (co-w, d) 92, etc.

Robison, Arthur (1888–1935).
Chicago-born director of German films.
Warning Shadows 24. The Informer (GB) 29. The Student of Prague 35, etc.

Robson, Dame Flora (1902–1984).
Distinguished British stage actress.
Biography: 1981, *Flora: The Life of Dame Flora Robson* by Kenneth Barrow.
■ Dance Pretty Lady 31. One Precious Year 33. Catherine the Great 34. *Fire over England* 36. Farewell Again 37. Wuthering Heights 39. Poison Pen 39. We Are Not Alone 39. Invisible Stripes 39. The Sea Hawk 40. Banana Passage 41. Saratoga Trunk 43. 2000 Women 44. Great Day 45. Caesar and Cleopatra 45. The Years Between 46. *Black Narcissus* 46. Saratoga Trunk (AAN) 46. Good Time Girl 47. Frieda 47. Holiday Camp 47. Saraband for Dead Lovers 48. The Tall Headlines 52. The Malta Story 53. Romeo and Juliet 54. *Innocent Sinners* 57. High Tide at Noon 57. No Time for Tears 57. The Gypsy and the Gentleman 58. 55 Days at Peking 62. Murder at the Gallop 63. Guns at Batasi 64. Those Magnificent Men in Their Flying Machines 64. Young Cassidy 65. Seven Women 65. The Shuttered Room 66. A Cry in the Wind 66. Eye of the Devil 67. Fragment of Fear 69. The Beloved 70. The Beast in the Cellar 71. Alice's Adventures in Wonderland 72. Comedy, Tragedy and All That 72. Dominique 78. A Man Called Intrepid (TV) 79. Les Misérables (TV) 80. A Tale of Two Cities (TV) 80. Clash of the Titans 81.

Robson, Mark (1913–1978).
Canadian-born director, former editor: began with Lewton and Kramer but progressed to more solidly commercial subjects. Born in Montreal, he studied political science and economics at the University of California at Los Angeles and law at Pacific Coast University before beginning work as a prop boy at Fox.
■ *The Seventh Victim* 43. The Ghost Ship 43. Youth Runs Wild 44. Isle of the Dead 45. Bedlam 46. *Champion* 49. Home of the Brave 49. Roughshod 49. My Foolish Heart 50. Edge of Doom 50. Bright Victory 51. I Want You 51. Return to Paradise 53. Hell Below Zero (GB) 54. The Bridges at Toko-Ri 54. Phffft 54. A Prize of Gold 55. Trial 55. The Harder They Fall 56. The Little Hut (& p) 57. Peyton Place (AAN) 58. The Inn of the Sixth Happiness (GB) (AAN) 58. From the Terrace (& p) 59. Lisa/The Inspector (p only) 62. Nine Hours to Rama (GB) (& p) 63. The Prize 63. *Von Ryan's Express* (& p) 65. Lost Command (& p) 66. Valley of the Dolls (& p) 67. Daddy's Gone A-Hunting (& p) 69. Happy Birthday Wanda June 71. Limbo 73. Earthquake 74. Avalanche Express 79.

Robson, May (1858–1942) (Mary Robison).
Australian actress, in America from childhood. Long experience on stage tours before coming to Hollywood, where she played domineering but kindly old ladies.
■ How Molly Made Good 15. A Night Out 16. His Bridal Night 19. A Broadway Saint 19. The Lost Battalion 19. Pals in Paradise 26. Angel of Broadway 27. Chicago 27. A Harp in Hock 27. King of Kings 27. The Rejuvenation of Aunt Mary 27. Rubber Tires 27. Turkish Delight 27. The Blue Danube 28. Mother's Millions 31. Letty Lynton 32. Strange Interlude 32. Two against the World 32. Red Headed Woman 32. Little Orphan Annie 32. *If I Had a Million* 32. Reunion in Vienna 33. Dinner at Eight 33. Beauty for Sale 33. Broadway to Hollywood 33. Solitaire Man 33. Dancing Lady 33. *Lady for a Day* (AAN) 33. One Man's Journey 33. Alice in Wonderland 33. The White Sister 33. Men Must Fight 33. You Can't Buy Everything 34. Straight Is the Way 34. Lady by Choice 34. Vanessa, Her Love Story 35. Reckless 35. Grand Old Girl 35. Age of Indiscretion 35. Anna Karenina 35. Strangers All 35. Mills of the Gods 35. Three Kids and a Queen 36. Wife vs Secretary 36. The Captain's Kid 36. Rainbow on the River 36. Woman in Distress 37. *A Star Is Born* 37. The Perfect Specimen 37. Top of the Town 37. *The Adventures of Tom Sawyer* 38. *Bringing Up Baby* 38. The Texans 38. *Four Daughters* 38. They Made Me a Criminal 39. Yes My Darling Daughter 39. Daughters Courageous 39. Four Wives 39. The Kid from Kokomo 39. Nurse Edith Cavell 39. That's Right You're Wrong 39. Irene 39. The Texas Rangers Ride Again 40. *Granny Get Your Gun* 40. Four Mothers 41. Million Dollar Baby 41. Playmates 42. Joan of Paris 42.

Roc, Patricia (1915–) (Felicia Miriam Ursula Herold).
British leading lady of the 40s, signed for films after brief stage experience.
The Rebel Son/Taras Bulba 38. The Gaunt Stranger 39. The Mind of Mr Reeder 39. Three Silent Men 40. Let the People Sing 42. Millions Like Us 43. 2000 Women 44. Love Story 44. Madonna of the Seven Moons 44. The Wicked Lady 45. Johnny Frenchman 45. Canyon Passage (US) 46. *The Brothers* 47. Jassy 47. When the Bough Breaks 48. One Night with You 48. The Perfect Woman 49. Circle of Danger 50. The Man on the Eiffel Tower 51. Something Money Can't Buy 53. The Hypnotist 55. Bluebeard's Ten Honeymoons 60, etc.

Rocca, Daniela (1937–1995).
Voluptuous Italian actress of the early 60s, a former model who was a beauty queen (Miss Catania) at the age of 15. Her career ended after the break-up of her relationship with director Pietro GERMI, which resulted in a suicide attempt and was followed by spells in mental hospitals. She later released an album of her poetry and also featured in an Italian documentary, *The Cinema Machine* 81.
Mercanti di Donne 57. The Giant of Marathon/La Battaglia di Maratona 60. Queen of the Amazons/Colossus and the Amazon Queen/La Regina delle Amazzoni 60. *Esther and the King* 60. Head of a Tyrant/Giuditta e Oloferne 60. Revenge of the Barbarians/La Vendetta dei Barbari 61. *Divorce Italian Style*/Divorzio all'Italiana 61. The Empty Canvas 64. Behold a Pale Horse 64, etc.

Rocha, Glauber (1938–1981).
Brazilian director and screenwriter, a leader of his country's 'new cinema' movement. He went into exile 1970–76, making films in Europe, and died of pulmonary disease.
Barravento/The Turning Wind 62. Deus e o Diabo na Terra do Sol/Black God, White Devil 64. Terra em Transe/Earth Entranced 67. Antônio das Mortes 69. Le Vent d'Est/East Wind 69. O Leão Have Sete Cabeças/The Lion Has Seven Heads 70. Cabeças Cortadas/Severed Heads 71. Claro 75. A Idade da Terra/The Age of the Earth 80, etc.

Rochant, Eric (1961–).
French director and screenwriter.
Tough Life 89. Love without Pity/Un Monde sans Pitié 91. Autobus/Aux Yeux du Monde 91. Les Patriotes 94, etc.

Roche, Eugene (1928–).
American character actor with a slightly bewildered look; much on TV.
They Might Be Giants 71. Newman's Law 74. The Late Show 76. Corvette Summer 78. Foul Play 78. Oh God You Devil 84. Eternity 90. When a Man Loves a Woman 94. Roswell (TV) 94. Liz: The Elizabeth Taylor Story (TV) 95. Executive Decision 96, etc.
TV series: Lenny 90–91. Julie 92.

Rochefort, Jean (1930–).
French leading actor, often in comic roles.
Swords of Blood/Cartouche 61. Angélique 64. Angélique et le Roi 65. The Devil by the Tail/Le Diable par la Queue 69. The Tall Blond Man with One Black Shoe/Le Grand Blond avec une Chaussure Noire 72. Salut l'Artiste 74. A Happy Divorce 75. Pardon Mon Affaire/Un Eléphant Ça Trompe Enormément 76. The Clockmaker 76. Pardon Mon Affaire Too 77. Who Is Killing the Great Chefs of Europe?/Too Many Chefs 78. Till Marriage Us Do Part 79. French Postcards 79. I Hate Blondes/Odio le Bionde 83. Birgit Haas Must Be Killed/Il Faut Tuer Birgit Haas 83. My First Forty Years/I Miei Primi Quarant'anni 89. The Hairdresser's Husband/Le Mari de la Coiffeuse 91. Dien Bien Phu 91. Le Bal des Casse-Pieds 91. L'Atlantide 92. The Long Winter/El Largo Invierno 92. *Tango* 93. Wild Target/Cible Émouvante 93. Tombés du Ciel 93. La Prossima Volta il Fuoco 93. Tom Est Tout Seul 94. Palace (Sp.) 95. Ridicule 96. Wind with the Gone/El Viento Se Llevó lo Que 98, etc.

Rock, Chris. (1966–).
Fast-talking American stand-up comedian, actor and screenwriter. Born in Jamestown, South Carolina, and brought up in Brooklyn, New York, he was discovered performing in a New York club as an 18-year-old by Eddie MURPHY, and first came to notice on NBC's *Saturday Night Live* from 1990.
Book: 1998, *Rock This!*
I'm Gonna Git You Sucka (a) 88. New Jack City (a) 91. Boomerang (a) 92. Coneheads (a) 93. CB4: The Movie (a, co-w) 93. Panther 95. The Immortals (a) 95. Sgt Bilko (a) 96. Beverly Hills Ninja (a) 97. Doctor Dolittle (voice) 98. Lethal Weapon 4 (a) 98, etc.
TV series: In Living Color 93–94. The Chris Rock Show 97– .
❝ Why do famous people die of drug overdoses when they have everything in the world anyone could want? Because they have everything in the world anyone could want. And then they want more of it. And when that doesn't make them happy, they get high . . . And then next thing you know they get dead. – *C.R*

Rock, Crissy (1958–).
English actress and comedian.
Ladybird, Ladybird 94.

Rock, Joe (1891–1984).
American independent producer who, after experience in vaudeville and a brief spell in Hollywood, worked in Britain from the mid-30s, turning out quota quickies, several featuring Leslie Fuller, and also backed Michael Powell's *The Edge of the World*. He expanded his studios at Elstree to increase production but became bankrupt in 1937.
Krakatoa (US) 33. Captain Bill 35. The Stoker 35. Strictly Illegal 35. Everything Is Rhythm 36. One Good Turn 36. The Man behind the Mask 36. Boys Will Be Girls 37. Cotton Queen 37. The Edge of the World 37. Swing as You Swing 37. Reverse Be My Lot 38, etc.

Rockwell, Alexandre (1956–).
American director. He is married to actress Jennifer Beals.
Lenz 81. Hero 83. Sons 89. In the Soup 92. Somebody to Love 94. Four Rooms (co-d) 95, etc.

Rockwell, Sam (1968–).
American actor who made a breakthrough to notable starring roles with *Box of Moonlight* and *Lawn Man*. Educated at the High School for the Performing Arts in San Francisco, he began acting in the theatre from the age of 10.
Clown House (TV) 88. Last Exit to Brooklyn 89. Teenage Mutant Ninja Turtles 90. Light Sleeper 92. Jack and His Friends 92. In the Soup 92. Last Call 95. Mercy 95. The Search for One-Eyed Jimmy 96. Box of Moonlight 96. *Lawn Man* 97. Safe Men 98, etc.
❝ I actually think that no-one should be allowed to be famous until they're 30. – *S.R.*

Roddam, Franc (1946–).
British director.
Quadrophenia 79. The Lords of Discipline 82. The Bride 85. Aria (co-d) 87. War Party 89. K2 91. Moby Dick (co-w, d) (TV) 98, etc.

Roddenberry, Gene (1921–1991).
American TV producer and writer, creator of *Star Trek* and *Star Trek: The Next Generation* and executive producer of the *Star Trek* films. Wrote and produced *Pretty Maids All in a Row* 70.
Biography: 1994, *Gene Roddenberry: The Myth and the Man behind Star Trek* by Joel Engel.

Rodgers, Anton (1933–).
British comic character actor.
Rotten to the Core 65. Scrooge 70. The Day of the Jackal 73. The Fourth Protocol 87. Dirty Rotten Scoundrels 88. Impromptu 89. Son of the Pink Panther 93, etc.
TV series: Fresh Fields 83–86. May to December 92–94. Noah's Ark 97– .

Rodgers, Richard (1902–1979).
American composer who worked variously with lyricists Lorenz Hart and Oscar Hammerstein II.
Love Me Tonight 32. *Hallelujah I'm a Bum* 33. On Your Toes 38. Babes in Arms 39. The Boys from Syracuse 40. *State Fair* 45. *Oklahoma!* 55. *The King and I* 56. *Pal Joey* 57. *South Pacific* 58. *The Sound of Music* 65, many other complete scores and single songs.

Rodney, Red (1928–1994) (Robert Chudnik).
American jazz trumpeter and bandleader, best known for his association with alto saxophonist Charlie Parker. He was an adviser on Clint Eastwood's biopic of Parker, *Bird*, in which he was played by Michael Zelniker.

Rodrigues, Percy (1924–).
Canadian character actor.
The Plainsman 67. The Sweet Ride 68. The Heart is a Lonely Hunter 68. Genesis II (TV) 73. Brainwaves 82, etc.

Rodriguez, Estelita (1913–1966).
Pert Cuban-born actress and singer, mainly in Republic's musicals and westerns as a Mexican. Performing on radio in Havana from the age of nine, she went to the US in the late 20s, beginning by working in nightclubs and theatre. She was sometimes billed as Estelita. Married actor Grant WITHERS.
Along the Navajo Trail 45. Mexicana 45. Old Los Angeles 48. The Golden Stallion 49. Belle of Old Mexico 50. Federal Agent at Large 50. California Passage 50. Hit Parade of 1951 50. Cuban Fireball 51. In Old Amarillo 51. Havana Rose 51. Pals of the Old West 51. The Fabulous Senorita 52. Tropical Heat Wave 52. South Pacific Trail 52. Tropic Zone 53. Sweethearts on Parade 53. Rio Bravo 59. Jesse James Meets Frankenstein's Daughter 56, etc.

Rodriguez, Robert (1969–).
American director, screenwriter, and editor, born in San Antonio, Texas, whose first film was made in Mexico at a reported cost of $7,000 and picked up by Columbia Pictures for distribution.
Autobiography: 1995, *Rebel without a Crew*.
El Mariachi 92. Roadracers (TV) 94. Desperado 95. Four Rooms (co-d) 95. From Dusk till Dawn 95. The Faculty 98, etc.

Roeg, Nicolas (1928–).
British cinematographer and director. Married actress Theresa Russell.
AS CINEMATOGRAPHER: The System 63. Nothing but the Best 64. The Caretaker 66. Petulia 67. A Funny Thing Happened on the Way to the Forum 68. *Far from the Madding Crowd* 68, etc.
AS DIRECTOR: Performance (co-d) 72. *Walkabout* 72. *Don't Look Now* 73. The Man Who Fell to Earth 76. Bad Timing 79. Eureka 83. Insignificance 85. Castaway 87. Aria (co-d) 87. Track 29 87. The Witches 90. Cold Heaven 92. Heart of Darkness (TV) 94. Two Deaths 95. Full Body Massage (TV) 95. Samson and Delilah (TV) 96, etc.
❝ They said, even the bath water's dirty. – *N.R. on Warner's reaction to Performance*

Roemer, Michael (1928–).
German-born independent film director and academic, in America. His feature *The Plot against Harry* 69 was released to good reviews after 20 years on the shelf.
A Touch of the Times (d) 49. The Inferno (co-d) 62. *Nothing but a Man* (co-d) 65. The Plot against Harry (wd) 69 (released 89). Pilgrim Farewell (wd) 80. Haunted (d) (TV) 84, etc.

Roemheld, Heinz (1901–1985).
German musical director, long in Hollywood.
Golden Harvest 33. The Invisible Man 33. Imitation of Life 34. Dracula's Daughter 36. A Child Is Born 40. The Strawberry Blonde (AAN) 41. Blues in the Night 41. Yankee Doodle Dandy (AA) 42. Shine On, Harvest Moon 44. Heaven Only Knows 47. The Lady from Shanghai 48. Rogues of Sherwood Forest 50. Ruby Gentry 53. The 5,000 Fingers of Dr T. (co-m) 53. The Creature Walks among Us 56. The Monster that Challenged the World 57. Ride Lonesome 59. Lad: A Dog 61, many others.

Roëves, Maurice (1937–).
English character actor, stage director and television writer. Born in Sunderland, Tyne and Wear, he studied at the Royal College of Drama, Glasgow.
The Fighting Prince of Donegal 66. Ulysses 67. Oh What a Lovely War 69. A Day at the Beach 70. When Eight Bells Toll 71. Young Winston 72. The Eagle Has Landed 77. SOS Titanic 79. Escape to Victory/Victory 81. Who Dares Wins 82. North and South Book II (TV) 86. The Big Man 90. Hidden Agenda 90. The Last of the Mohicans (US) 92. Judge Dredd (US) 95. Moses (TV) 96. The Acid House 98, etc.
TV series: Tutti Frutti 87. Danger UXB 87. Rab C. Nesbitt 92.

Rogell, Albert S. (1901–1988).
American director of second features, former cameraman.
Señor Daredevil 26. Mamba 30. Riders of Death Valley 32. Argentine Nights 40. Trouble Chaser 40. The Black Cat 41. Tight Shoes 41. In Old Oklahoma 43. Heaven Only Knows 47. Northwest Stampede 48. The Admiral was a Lady (& p) 50. Men against Speed 58, etc.

Rogers, Charles (c. 1890–1960).
Diminutive English music-hall comedian who had a long association with Laurel and Hardy as gag-man, screenwriter, and director. He played bit parts in several of their films, and also co-starred with Harry Langdon in a couple of comedies.
Two Tars (a) 28. Habeas Corpus (a) 28. The Devil's Brother (co-d) 33. Me and My Pal (co-d) 33. Going Bye-Bye! (d) 34. Them Thar Hills (d) 34. Babes in Toyland (co-d) 34. The Bohemian Girl (co-d) 36. Way out West (co-w) 37. Blockheads (co-w) 38. The Flying Deuces (co-w) 39. A Chump at Oxford (co-w) 40. Saps at Sea (co-w) 40. Misbehaving Husbands (a) 40. Double Trouble (a) 41. The Dancing Masters (a) 43, etc.

Rogers, Charles 'Buddy' (1904–).
American light leading man of the 20s and 30s; married to Mary Pickford.
Fascinating Youth 26. Wings 27. Abie's Irish Rose 29. Paramount on Parade 30. Varsity 30. Young Eagles 31. This Reckless Age 32. Old Man Rhythm 35. Once in a Million 36. This Way Please 38. Golden Hooves 41. Mexican Spitfire's Baby 43. Don't Trust Your Husband 48, many others.

Rogers, Eric (*–1981).
English composer who scored many of the Carry On movies.
The Iron Maiden 62. Carry On Regardless (co-m) 62. Carry On Cabby 63. Carry On Spying 64. Carry On Cleo 64. Carry On Cowboy 65. Carry On Screaming 66. Carry On – Don't Lose Your Head 66. Carry On Doctor 68. Carry On up the Khyber 68. Carry On Again Doctor 69. Assault/In the Devil's Garden 70. Quest for Love 71. Carry On Abroad 72. Carry On Behind 75. Carry On Emmannuelle 78, etc.

Rogers, Ginger (1911–1995) (Virginia McMath).
American leading actress, comedienne and dancer, affectionately remembered for her 30s musicals with Fred ASTAIRE. Former band singer; then brief Broadway experience before being taken to Hollywood.
Biography: 1996, *Shall We Dance: The Life of Ginger Rogers* by Sheridan Morley.
■ Young Man of Manhattan 30. Queen High 30. The Sap from Syracuse 30. Follow the Leader 30. Honor among Lovers 31. The Tip Off 31. Suicide Fleet 31. Carnival Boat 32. The Tenderfoot 32. The Thirteenth Guest 32. Hat Check Girl 32. You Said a Mouthful 32. *42nd Street* (as Anytime Annie) 33. Broadway Bad 33. Gold Diggers of 1933. Professional Sweetheart 33. A Shriek in the Night 33. Don't Bet on Love 33. Sitting Pretty 33. *Flying Down to Rio* 33. Chance at Heaven 33. Rafter Romance 34. Finishing School 34. Twenty Million Sweethearts 34. Change of Heart 34. Upperworld 34. *The Gay Divorcee* 34. Romance in Manhattan 34. Roberta 35. Star of Midnight 35. *Top Hat* 35. In Person 35. *Follow the Fleet* 36. Swing Time 36. Shall We Dance 36. *Stage Door* 37. Having Wonderful Time 38. Vivacious Lady 38. Carefree 38. The Story of Vernon and Irene Castle 39. *Bachelor Mother* 39. Fifth Avenue Girl 39. The Primrose Path 40. Lucky Partners 40. *Kitty Foyle* (AA) 40. Tom Dick and Harry 41. *Roxie Hart* 42. Tales of Manhattan 42. The Major and the Minor 42. Once Upon a Honeymoon 42. Tender Comrade 43. Lady in the Dark 44. I'll Be Seeing You 44. Weekend at the Waldorf 45. Heartbeat 46. Magnificent Doll 46. It Had to Be You 47. The Barkleys of Broadway 49. Perfect Strangers 50. Storm Warning 50. The Groom Wore Spurs 51. We're Not Married 52. Monkey Business 52. Dreamboat 52. Forever Female 53. Black Widow 54. Twist of Fate/Beautiful Stranger 54. Tight Spot 55. The First Travelling Saleslady 56. Teenage Rebel 56. Oh Men Oh Women 57. The Confession 64. Harlow (electronovision) 64.
✪ For being everybody's favorite working girl of the 30s; and for being so unarguably right with Fred Astaire. *The Gay Divorcee*.
❝ He gives her class and she gives him sex. – *Katharine Hepburn of Astaire and Rogers*
They're not going to get my money to see the junk that's made today. – *G.R., 1983*
Famous line (*Young Man of Manhattan*): 'Cigarette me, big boy.'

Rogers, Jean (1916–1991) (Eleanor Lovegren).
American light leading lady of the 30s.
Eight Girls in a Boat 34. Flash Gordon 36. My Man Godfrey 36. Night Key 37. Flash Gordon's Trip to Mars 38. Hotel for Women 39. Heaven with a Barbed Wire Fence 40. Charlie Chan in Panama 40. Dr Kildare's Victory 42. Whistling in Brooklyn 43. Hot Cargo 46. Backlash 47. The Second Woman 51, etc.

Rogers, Maclean (1899–1962).
British director, mainly of low-budget features for which he often wrote his own unambitious scripts.
The Third Eye 29. Busman's Holiday 36. Old Mother Riley Joins Up 39. Gert and Daisy's Weekend 42. Variety Jubilee 43. The Trojan Brothers 45. Calling Paul Temple 48. The Story of Shirley Yorke 49. Johnny on the Spot 54. Not So Dusty 56. Not Wanted on Voyage 57. Not a Hope in Hell 60, many others.

Rogers, Mimi (1956–).
American leading actress. She was formerly married to actor Tom CRUISE.
Blue Skies Again 83. Gung Ho 86. Someone to Watch Over Me 87. Street Smart 87. Hider in the House 89. The Mighty Quinn 89. Desperate Hours 90. The Doors 91. Wedlock 91. The Rapture 92. White Sands 92. Dark Horse 92. Shooting Elizabeth 92. Monkey Trouble 94. Killer 94. Reflections on a Crime 94. Far from Home: The Adventures of Yellow Dog 95. Full Body Massage (TV) 95. Wild Bill 95. Bulletproof Heart 95. Trees Lounge 96. The Mirror Has Two Faces 96. Tricks 97. Weapons of Mass Distraction (TV) 97. Austin Powers: International Man of Mystery 97. Lost in Space 98, etc.
TV series: The Rousters 83–84. Paper Dolls 84.

Rogers, Paul (1917–).
British character actor, on stage from 1938, occasional films from 1932.
Beau Brummell 53. Our Man in Havana 59. The Trials of Oscar Wilde 60. No Love for Johnnie 61. Billy Budd 62. Life for Ruth 62. The Prince and the Pauper 62. The Wild and the Willing 63. The Third Secret 64. He Who Rides a Tiger 65. A Midsummer Night's Dream 68. The Looking Glass War 69. Three into Two Won't Go 69. The Reckoning 69. I Want What I Want 72. The Homecoming 73. The Abdication 75. Mr Quilp 75. Nothing Lasts Forever 83. The Tenth Man (TV) 88, etc.

Rogers, Peter (1916–).
British producer in films from 1942; wrote and co-produced many comedies during 40s and early 50s; conceived and produced the *Carry On* series.

Rogers, Roy (1912–1998) (Leonard Slye).
American singing cowboy star, usually seen with horse Trigger (1932–65). Varied early experience; formed 'Sons of the Pioneers' singing group; in small film roles from 1935, a star from 1938 till 1953. Married actress Dale Evans, his second wife, in 1947.
Autobiography: 1994, *Happy Trails*.
Under Western Skies 38. The Carson City Kid 40. Dark Command 40. Robin Hood of the Pecos 42. The Man from Music Mountain 44. Along the Navajo Trail 46. Roll On Texas Moon 47. Night Time in Nevada 49. Trail of Robin Hood 51. Son of Paleface 52. Pals of the Golden West 53. Mackintosh and T.J. 75. Roy Rogers, King of the Cowboys (doc) 91, etc.
TV series: The Roy Rogers Show 51–56.
❝ When my times comes, just skin me and put me right up there on Trigger, just as though nothing had ever changed. – *R.R.*

Rogers, Wayne (1933–).
American light actor.
Once in Paris 78. The Top of the Hill (TV) 80. He's Fired, She's Hired (TV) 84. The Gig 85. The Lady from Yesterday (TV) 85. American Harvest (TV) 87. The Killing Time 87. Drop-Out Mother (TV) 88. Bluegrass (TV) 88. The Goodbye Bird 93. Ghosts of Mississippi 96, etc.
TV series: Stagecoach West 60–61. M*A*S*H 72–75. City of Angels 76. House Calls 79–82. Chiefs 83. High Risk 88.

Rogers, Will (1879–1935).
American rustic comedian, ex-Ziegfeld Follies, whose crackerbarrel philosophy almost moved nations. His home in Los Angeles is the centrepiece of the Will Rogers State Park.
Autobiography: 1927, *There's Not a Bathing Suit in Russia*.
Biographies: 1953, *Our Will Rogers* by Homer Croy. 1974, *Will Rogers, the Man and His Times* by Richard M. Ketchum. 1996, *American Original: A Life of Will Rogers* by Ray Robinson.
Biopic: 1952, *The Story of Will Rogers* (starring his son).
■ Laughing Bill Hyde 18. Almost a Husband 19. Water Water Everywhere 19. *Jubilo* 19. Jes' Call Me Jim 20. The Strange Boarder 20. Scratch My Back 20. A Poor Relation 20. Cupid the Cowpuncher 20. Honest Hutch 20. Guile of Women 21. Boys Will Be Boys 21. An Unwilling Hero 21. Doubling for Romeo 21. One Glorious Day 21. The Headless Horseman 22. The Ropin' Fool 22. One Day in 365 22. Hustling Hank 22. Uncensored Movies 22. Fruits of Faith 22. Just Passing Through 23. Gee Whiz Genevieve 23. Highbrow Stuff 23. Family Fits 23. The Cake Eater 24. Big Moments from Little Pictures 24. Don't Park There 24. The Cowboy Sheik 24. Going to Congress 24. Our Congressman 24. A Truthful Liar 24. Two Wagons 24. A Texas Steer 27. Tiptoes 27. They Had to See Paris 29. Happy Days 30. So This is London 30. Lightnin' 30. A Connecticut Yankee 31. Young as You Feel 31. Ambassador Bill 31. Business and Pleasure 32. Too Busy to Work 32. *State Fair* 33. Doctor Bull 33. Mister Skitch 33. *David Harum* 34. *Handy Andy* 34. *Judge Priest* 34. County Chairman 35. *Life Begins at Forty* 35. Doubting Thomas 35. In Old Kentucky 35. *Steamboat round the Bend* 35.
✪ For establishing the wisdom of the common man. *Judge Priest*.
❝ There's only one thing that can kill the movies, and that's education. – *W.R.*
When you put down the good things you ought to have done, and leave out the bad things you did do – that's Memoirs. – *W.R.*
~When he was killed, Rogers had signed to play Dr Dafoe, who delivered the Dionne Quins, in *The Country Doctor*.

Rogosin, Lionel (1924–).
American documentarist.
On the Bowery 56. *Come Back Africa* 59. Good Times Wonderful Times 66. Black Roots 70. Woodcutters of the Deep South 73, etc.

Rohmer, Eric (1920–) (Jean Maurice Scherer).
French director of rarefied conversation pieces.
Le Signe du Lion 59. La Boulangère de Monceau 63. La Carrière de Suzanne 64. La Collectionneuse 67. Ma Nuit chez Maud (AAN) 69. Le Genou de Claire 70. Love in the Afternoon 72. The Marquise of O 76. Perceval 78. The Aviator's Wife 81. Pauline at the Beach 83. Full Moon in Paris 84. Summer 86. Girlfriends and Boyfriends/L'Ami de Mon Amie 87. Four Adventures of Reinette and Mirabelle/Quatre Aventures de Reinette et Mirabelle 87. Springtime/Conte de Printemps 90. A Winter's Tale/Conte d'Hiver 92. L'Arbre, Le Maire et La Médiathèque 93. Les Rendez-Vous de Paris 95. A Summer's Tale/Conte d'Été 96. An Autumn Tale/Conte d'Automne 98, etc.

Rohmer, Sax (1883–1959) (Arthur Sarsfield Ward).
British novelist, the creator of the much-filmed Dr Fu Manchu. A former journalist, he also wrote the lyrics for music-hall songs and the book of a musical, *Round in Fifty*, starring George ROBEY. In 1955 he sold the film, radio and TV rights in his Fu Manchu books for $4m.

Rohrig, Walter (1893–*).
German art director whose expressionist style was influential.
Cabinet of Dr Caligari/Das Cabinet des Dr Caligari 19. The Golem/Der Golem 20. Destiny/Der Müde Tod 21. The Last Laugh/Der Letzte Mann 24. Faust 26. Luther 27. Looping the Loop/Die Todesschleife 28. The Wonderful Lie of Nina Petrowna/Die Wunderbare Lüge der Nina Petrowna 29. Manolescu 29. Congress Dances/Der Kongress Tanzt 31. Refugees/Flüchtlinge 33. Capriccio 38. Rembrandt 42, etc.

Roizman, Owen (1936–).
American cinematographer.
The French Connection (AAN) 71. Play It Again Sam 72. The Exorcist (AAN) 73. The Taking of Pelham One Two Three 74. The Stepford Wives 75. Network (AAN) 76. Straight Time 78. The Electric Horseman 79. The Black Marble 80. True Confessions 81. Absence of Malice 81. Taps 81. Tootsie (AAN) 82. Vision Quest 85. I Love You to Death 90. Havana 90. The Addams Family 92. Grand Canyon 92. Wyatt Earp (AAN) 94. French Kiss 95, etc.

Roland, Gilbert (1905–1994) (Luis Antonio Damaso de Alonso).
Mexican leading man, trained as bullfighter, who gatecrashed Hollywood in the mid-20s and became immediately popular.
The Plastic Age (debut) 25. Camille 27. Men of the North 29. Call Her Savage 32. *She Done Him Wrong* 33. Last Train from Madrid 37. Juarez 39. The Sea Hawk 40. My Life with Caroline 41. Isle of Missing Men 42. Captain Kidd 45. Pirates of Monterey 47. Riding the California Trail 48. *We Were Strangers* 49. The Furies 50. The Bullfighter and the Lady 51. The Bad and the Beautiful 52. Beyond the Twelve Mile Reef 53. The Racers 54.

Treasure of Pancho Villa 56. Guns of the Timberland 58. The Big Circus 59. Cheyenne Autumn 64. The Reward 65. The Poppy is also a Flower (TV) 66. Johnny Hamlet 72. Running Wild 73. Islands in the Stream 77. The Black Pearl 77. Deadly Sunday 82. Barbarosa 82, many others.

Roland, Ruth (1893–1937).
American leading lady, a silent serial queen.
The Red Circle 15. The Neglected Wife 17. Hands Up 18. Tiger's Trail 19, etc.
FEATURES: While Father Telephoned 13. The Masked Woman 26. Reno 30. From Nine to Nine 36, many others.

Rolfe, Guy (1915–).
Lean British leading man and character actor, former racing driver and boxer.
Hungry Hill (debut) 46. Nicholas Nickleby 47. Uncle Silas 47. Broken Journey 47. Portrait from Life 49. *The Spider and the Fly* 50. Prelude to Fame 51. Ivanhoe 52. King of the Khyber Rifles 54. It's Never Too Late 56. Snow White and the Three Stooges 62. Taras Bulba 62. Mr Sardonicus 62. The Fall of the Roman Empire 64. The Alphabet Murders 65. The Land Raiders 69. Nicholas and Alexandra 71. And Now the Screaming Starts 73. Dolls 87. Puppet Master III: Toulon's Revenge 91, etc.

Rolfe, Sam (1924–1993).
American screenwriter and television producer, best known for creating the TV series *Have Gun Will Travel* 57–63 and *The Man from U.N.C.L.E.* 64–68.
The Naked Spur (AAN) 53. Target Zero 55. The McConnell Story 55. Bombers B-52 57, etc.
Features edited from episodes of The Man from U.N.C.L.E.: To Trap a Spy 66. The Spy with My Face 66. One Spy Too Many 66. The Karate Killers 67. The Spy in the Green Hat 67. One of Our Spies Is Missing 67. The Helicopter Spies 67. How to Steal the World 68.

Rollin, Jean (1940–).
French screenwriter and director, mainly of horror and exploitation movies containing scenes of sex and sadism, tinged with surrealism.
Vampire Women/Les Femmes Vampires 67. The Naked Vampire/La Vampire Nue 69. Terror of the Vampires/Les Frissons des Vampires 70. Requiem for a Vampire/Virgins and Vampires/Requiem pour une Vampire 71. La Rose de Fer 73. Lèvres de Sang 75. Once upon a Virgin/Phantasmes 76. Pesticide/Les Raisins de la Mort 78. Fascination 78. Zombie Lake/Lake of the Living Dead/El Lago de los Muertos Vivientes 80. The Living Dead Girl/La Morte Vivante 82. Les Meurtrières 83, etc.

Rollins, Howard, Jnr (1951–1996).
American leading actor.
Ragtime (AAN) 81. A Soldier's Story 84. The Children of Times Square (TV) 86. Dear America: Letters Home from Vietnam 87. Johnnie Gibson F.B.I. (TV) 87. For Us, the Living (TV) 88. On the Block 89, etc.
TV series: In the Heat of the Night 88–89.

Romain, Yvonne (1938–) (Yvonne Warren).
British leading lady.
The Baby and the Battleship 56. Seven Thunders 57. Corridors of Blood 58. Chamber of Horrors 60. Curse of the Werewolf 61. Village of Daughters 61. Devil Doll 63. The Brigand of Kandahar 65. The Swinger (US) 66. Double Trouble (US) 67. The Last of Sheila 73, etc.

Roman, Leticia (1939–).
American leading lady of the 60s.
Pirates of Tortuga 61. Gold of the Seven Saints 61. The Evil Eye (It.) 62. Fanny Hill 64, etc.

Roman, Ruth (1924–).
American actress; leading lady of the 50s, then a plumpish character player.
Ladies Courageous 44. Jungle Queen 45. You Came Along 45. A Night in Casablanca 45. The Big Clock 48. Good Sam 48. *The Window* 49. Champion 49. Barricade 50. Three Secrets 50. Lightning Strikes Twice 51. *Strangers On a Train* 51. Maru Maru 52. Blowing Wild 53. Down Three Dark Streets 54. The Far Country 55. Joe Macbeth 56. Five Steps to Danger 57. Bitter Victory 58. Desert Desperadoes 59. Look in Any Window 61. Love Has Many Faces 65. The Baby 73. Go Ask Alice (TV) 73. Day of the Animals 77. Echoes 83, etc.
TV series: *The Long Hot Summer* 65–66. Knots Landing 86.

Romance, Viviane (1912–1991) (Pauline Ortmans).
French leading lady of the 30s and 40s.
La Belle Equipe 35. Gibraltar 37. The White Slave 38. Blind Venus 39. Box of Dreams 39. Carmen 42. Panique 46. Maya 50. Flesh and Desire 53. Pleasures and Vices 56. Mélodie en Sous-Sol 63, etc.

Romanoff, Mike (1890–1972) (Harry Gerguson).
Amiable American con man who posed as a Russian prince (but 'renounced' his title in 1958). Best known as proprietor of Hollywood's most famous and expensive restaurant. Played occasional bit parts.
Arch of Triumph 48. Do Not Disturb 65. Tony Rome 67, etc.
❝ No one has ever discovered the truth about me – not even myself. – M.R.
A rogue of uncertain nationality. – *Scotland Yard*

Romberg, Sigmund (1887–1951).
Hungarian composer of light music. Scores include *The Desert Song* 29 and 43, *New Moon* 31 and 40, *Maytime* 37, *Balalaika* 39, *The Student Prince* 54. (Most of these began as stage operettas.) José Ferrer played him in a biopic, *Deep in My Heart* 54.

Rome, Stewart (1886–1965) (Septimus William Ryott).
British stage matinée idol who made several romantic films in the 20s and later appeared in character roles.
The Prodigal Son 25. Sweet Lavender 26. The Gentleman Rider 27. Thou Fool 28. Dark Red Roses 29. The Man Who Changed His Name 30. Designing Women 33. Men of Yesterday 34. Wings of the Morning 37. Banana Ridge 41. The White Unicorn 47. Woman Hater 48, etc.

Romero, Cesar (1907–1994).
Handsome Latin-American leading man, former dancer and Broadway actor. Also on TV.
The Thin Man 34. Metropolitan 35. Wee Willie Winkie 37. The Return of the Cisco Kid (and others in this series) 39. The Gay Caballero 40. Weekend in Havana 41. Tales of Manhattan 42. Orchestra Wives 42. Coney Island 43. Carnival in Costa Rica 47. That Lady in Ermine 48. Happy Go Lovely 51. Prisoners of the Casbah 53. Vera Cruz 54. The Racers 55. The Leather Saint 56. Villa 58. Two on a Guillotine 64. Marriage on the Rocks 65. Batman 66. Hot Millions 68. Crooks and Coronets (GB) 69. The Midas Run (GB) 69. A Talent for Loving 69. Now You See Him Now You Don't 72. The Strongest Man in the World 74. The Big Push 77. Mission to Glory 80. Judgement Day 88. Simple Justice 90, etc.
TV series: Passport to Danger 56. *Batman* (as the Joker) 65–67.

Romero, Eddie (1924–).
Filipino director of low-budget exploitation movies.
The Day of the Trumpet 57. Moro Witch Doctor 64. Mad Doctor of Blood Island 68. Best of the Yellow Night 70. Twilight People 72. Beyond Atlantis 73. The Woman Hunt 75. Sudden Death 77. Desire 83. The White Force 88. A Case of Honor 88, etc.

Romero, George (1940–).
American director of exploitation pictures.
Night of the Living Dead 68. The Crazies 73. Hungry Wives 73. Zombies 78. Martin 79. Knightriders 81. Creepshow 82. Day of the Dead 85. Creepshow 2 (w) 87. Monkey Shines (wd) 88. Two Evil Eyes/Due Occhi Diabolici (co-d) 89. Tales from the Darkside: The Movie (co-w) 90. Night of the Living Dead (w, p) 90. Tales from the Darkside: The Movie II (co-w) 92. The Dark Half 93, etc.
❝ Just because I'm showing somebody being disembowelled doesn't mean I have to get heavy and put a message round it. – G.R.

Romero, Manuel (1891–1954).
Prolific Argentinian director, playwright and lyricist. A former journalist, he began his career in the 30s in Paris. He was notable for his output, which included some 150 plays and as many songs, as well as more than 50 films. He made the first Argentinian gangster movie, *Outlaw*/Fuera de la Ley, in 1937.

Romm, Mikhail (1901–1971).
Russian director.
Boule de Suif 34. *Lenin in October* 37. Lenin in 1918 39. The Russian Question 48. Nine Days of One Year 61. Ordinary Fascism 64, etc.

Rommel, Field Marshal Erwin (1891–1944).
German soldier, a worthy adversary for the Eighth Army in World War II. He killed himself in 1944 after being accused of complicity in the plot against Hitler. In films he was melodramatically impersonated by Erich Von Stroheim in 1943 in *Five Graves to Cairo*, and more soberly in 1951 by James Mason in *The Desert Fox* (also in 1953 in *The Desert Rats*). Other minor portrayals were by Albert Lieven in *Foxhole in Cairo*, by Gregory Gaye in *Hitler*, by Werner Hinz in *The Longest Day*, by Christopher Plummer in *The Night of the Generals*, by Karl Michael Vogler in *Patton*, and by Wolfgang Preiss in *Raid on Rommel*.

Romney, Edana (1919–) (E. Rubenstein).
South African-born leading lady, in three British films of the 40s.
■ East of Piccadilly 41. Alibi 42. Corridor of Mirrors 48.

Ronet, Maurice (1927–1983).
French leading man.
Rendezvous de Juillet 49. La Sorcière 56. He Who Must Die 56. Lift to the Scaffold 57. Carve Her Name with Pride (GB) 58. Plein Soleil 59. Rendezvous de Minuit 61. *Le Feu Follet* 63. Enough Rope 63. The Victors 63. La Ronde 64. Three Weeks in Manhattan 65. Lost Command 66. The Champagne Murders/La Scandale 67. The Road to Corinth 68. How Sweet It Is (US) 68. L'Infidèle 69. Qui? 73. The Marseilles Contract 74. Bloodline 79. La Balance 83, etc.

Roodt, Darrell (1962–).
South African director and screenwriter.
Place of Weeping 86. City of Blood 87. Jobman (& co-w) 90. Sarafina 92. Father Hood (US) 93. Cry the Beloved Country 95. Dangerous Ground (US) 97, etc.

Rooker, Michael (1954–).
American character actor, usually as a heavy.
Eight Men Out 88. Mississippi Burning 88. Sea of Love 89. Music Box 89. Henry: Portrait of a Serial Killer 90. Days of Thunder 90. The Dark Half 91. JFK 91. Cliffhanger 93. The Dark Half 93. The Hard Truth 94. Tombstone 94. Bastard out of Carolina (TV) 96. The Trigger Effect 96. Rosewood 96. Keys to Tulsa 96. Back to Back 96. Deceiver 97. The Replacement Killers 98. Brown's Requiem 98, etc.

Rooks, Conrad (1934–).
American experimental director.
■ Chappaqua 66. Siddhartha 72.

Room, Abram (1894–1976).
Russian director, former journalist, with stage experience.
In Pursuit of Moonshine 24. The Haven of Death 26. Bed and Sofa 27. The Ghost that Never Returns 29. The Five Year Plan 30. Invasion 44. Silver Dust 53, etc.

Rooney, Mickey (1920–) (Joe Yule Jnr).
Diminutive, aggressively talented American performer, on stage from the age of two (in parents' vaudeville act). In films from 1926 (short comedies) as Mickey McGuire, then returned to vaudeville; came back as Mickey Rooney in 1932. By the late 30s and early 40s he was the most popular film star in the world, later developing into an accomplished character actor. Married eight times, his wives include actresses Ava Gardner and Martha Vickers. He was given an honorary Oscar in 1938 for 'bringing to the screen the spirit and personification of youth', and in 1982 'in recognition of his 60 years of versatility in a variety of memorable film performances'.
Autobiographies: 1965, *I.E.* 1991, *Life Is Too Short*.
My Pal the King 32. The Hide-Out 34. A *Midsummer Night's Dream* (as Puck) 35. *Ah Wilderness* 35. Little Lord Fauntleroy (not in title role) 36. Captains Courageous 37. *A Family Affair* (as Andy Hardy) 37. *Judge Hardy's Children* 38. Love Finds Andy Hardy 38. *Boys' Town* (special AA) 38. The Adventures of Huckleberry Finn 39. *Babes in Arms* (AAN) 39. Young Tom Edison 40. Strike Up the Band 40. Men of Boys' Town 41. Babes on Broadway 41. A Yank at Eton 42. Andy Hardy's Double Life 42. *The Human Comedy* (AAN) 43. Girl Crazy 43. Andy Hardy's Blonde Trouble 44. National Velvet 44. Love Laughs at Andy Hardy 46. Summer Holiday 47. The Fireball 50. A Slight Case of Larceny 53. *The Bold and the Brave* (AAN) 56. Andy Hardy Comes Home 58. Baby Face Nelson 58. The Big Operator 59. Breakfast at Tiffany's 61. It's a Mad Mad Mad Mad World 63. Twenty-Four Hours to Kill 65. Ambush Bay 66. The Extraordinary Seaman 68. Skidoo 68. The Comic 69. Pulp 72. The Domino Principle 77. Pete's Dragon 77. The Magic of Lassie 78. Arabian Adventure 79. The Black Stallion (AAN) 79. *Leave 'em Laughing* (TV) 80. *Bill* (TV) 81. The Fox and the Hound (voice) 81. La Traversée de la Pacifique 82. The Care Bears Movie (voice) 85. Lightning – the White Stallion 86. Rudolph and Frosty's Christmas in July 86. Erik the Viking 89. My Heroes Have Always Been Cowboys 91. Silent Night Deadly Night 5: The Toymaker 91. The Milky Way/La Via Lactea 92. Sweet Justice 92. The Legend of O.B. Taggart (& w) 94. Revenge of the Red Baron 94, many others.
TV series: The Mickey Rooney Show/Hey Mulligan 54. Mickey 64. One of the Boys 81, etc.
✪ For never being counted out. *Babes in Arms*.
❝ I was a fourteen-year-old boy for thirty years. – M.R.
I've been through four publics. I've been coming back like a rubber ball for years. – M.R.
I just want to be a professional. I couldn't live without acting. – M.R.
There may be a little snow on the mountain, but there's a lot of fire in the furnace. – M.R.
All the muddy waters of my life cleared up when I gave myself to Christ. – M.R.
I didn't ask to be short. I didn't want to be short. I've tried to pretend that being a short guy didn't matter. – M.R.
The guys with the power in Hollywood today, the guys with their names above the title, are thieves. They don't make movies, they make deals. Their major function is to cut themselves in for 10 per cent of the gross – off the top, of course – which is why they make movies that cost $50 million. – M.R.
His favourite exercise is climbing tall people. – *Phyllis Diller*
A rope-haired, kazoo-voiced kid with a comic strip face. – *James Agee*
Tennessee Williams once told me that he considered Rooney the best actor in the history of the movies. – *Gore Vidal*

Roope, Fay (1893–1961).
American character actress, usually as a tough old lady.
You're in the Navy Now 51. The Day the Earth Stood Still 51. Washington Story 52. Viva Zapata! 52. From Here to Eternity 53. The System 53. Naked Alibi 54. Ma and Pa Kettle at Waikiki 55. The Proud Ones 56. The F.B.I. Story 59, etc.

Roos, Don.
American screenwriter and director.
Love Field 92. Single White Female 92. Boys on the Side 95. Diabolique 96. The Opposite of Sex (& d) 98, etc.

Roosevelt, Franklin Delano (1882–1945).
American President 1933–45, exponent of the 'New Deal'. He was played by Ralph Bellamy in Dore Schary's play and film of his life, *Sunrise at Campobello* 60, by Capt. Jack Young in *Yankee Doodle Dandy* and by Godfrey Tearle in *The Beginning of the End*. In TV's *Eleanor and Franklin* (1976) he was played by Edward Herrmann, and in *Ike* (1979) by Stephen Roberts.

Roosevelt, Theodore (Teddy) (1858–1919).
American President 1901–1909. His extrovert personality and cheerful bullish manners have been captured several times on screen, notably by John Alexander in *Arsenic and Old Lace* (a parody) and *Fancy Pants*, by Wallis Clark in *Yankee Doodle Dandy*, by John Merton in *I Wonder Who's Kissing Her Now*, by Sidney Blackmer in *My Girl Tisa*, *This is My Affair* and *Buffalo Bill;* and by Brian Keith in *The Wind and the Lion*. In *The Private Files of J. Edgar Hoover* (1978) it was Howard da Silva's turn; Ralph Bellamy had a revised go in *The Winds*

of War (1982), and Edward Herrmann again in *Annie* (1982).

Root, Wells (1900–1993).
American screenwriter, a former journalist, who later wrote for television and then taught writing at UCLA.
The Storm 30. Politics (co-w) 31. The Prodigal (co-w) 31. Tiger Shark 32. I Cover the Waterfront (co-w) 33. Black Moon 34. Paris Interlude 34. Pursuit 35. Sworn Enemy 36. The Prisoner of Zenda (co-w) 37. Sergeant Madden 39. Thunder Afloat (co-w) 39. Flight Command (co-w) 40. The Bad Man 41. Mokey (co-w) 42. Tennessee Johnson 42. Salute to the Marines 43. The Man from Down Under 43. Magnificent Obsession 54. Texas across the River 66, etc.

Roquevert, Noël (1894–1973) (N. Benevent).
French character actor, usually as mean-spirited bourgeois.
The Three Must-Get-Theres 22. Cartouche 34. Entrée des Artistes 38. Les Inconnus dans la Maison 42. Le Corbeau 43. Antoine et Antoinette 47. Justice Est Faite 50. Fanfan la Tulipe 52. Les Compagnes de la Nuit 53. The Sheep Has Five Legs 54. Marie Octobre 59. A Monkey in Winter 62, many others.

Rosay, Françoise (1891–1974) (Françoise de Naleche).
Distinguished French actress in films from the mid-20s.
Autobiography: 1974, *La Traversée d'une Vie*.
Gribiche 25. *Le Grand Jeu* 33. *La Kermesse Héroïque* 35. Jenny 36. *Un Carnet de Bal* 37. Les Gens du Voyage 38. *Une Femme Disparait* 41. Johnny Frenchman (GB) 45. Macadam 46. September Affair 50. *The Red Inn* 51. The Thirteenth Letter (US) 51. That Lady (GB) 54. The Seventh Sin (US) 57. Le Joueur 58. The Sound and the Fury (US) 58. The Full Treatment (GB) 60. Up from the Beach (US) 65. Le Piétou 72, etc.

Rose, Bernard.
English director and screenwriter.
The Paperhouse 88. Chicago Joe and the Showgirl 89. Candyman 92. Immortal Beloved 94. Leo Tolstoy's Anna Karenina 97, etc.

Rose, Billy (1899–1966).
American nightclub owner and songwriter, husband of Fanny Brice. He was played in *Funny Lady* by James Caan.
Biography: 1968, *Manhattan Primitive* by Earl Rogers.

Rose, David (1910–1990).
London-born composer and pianist, in America from 1914. From the 50s he also worked in television, writing the themes for the series *Bonanza*, *The High Chaparral* and *The Little House on the Prairie*, and in the 70s and 80s scored several TV movies. He was married to Judy Garland (1941–45).
Never a Dull Moment 43. The Princess and the Pirate (AAN) 44. Winged Victory 44. The Underworld Story 50. The Clown 53. Jupiter's Darling 55. Operation Petticoat 59. Please Don't Eat the Daisies 60. Hombre 67. Sam's Son 84, etc.

Rose, David E. (1896–1992).
American producer, in films from 1930, long in charge of United Artists productions. More recently in Britain.
The End of the Affair 55. The Safecracker 58. The House of the Seven Hawks 59, etc.

Rose, George (1920–1988).
British stage and screen character actor.
Pickwick Papers 52. Grand National Night 53. The Sea Shall Not Have Them 54. The Night My Number Came Up 56. Brothers in Law 57. A Night to Remember 58. Jack the Ripper 59. The Devil's Disciple 59. Jet Storm 59. The Flesh and the Fiends 60. Hamlet 64. Hawaii (US) 66. The Pink Jungle 69. A New Leaf 71. Holocaust (TV) 78. The Pirates of Penzance 83, etc.

Rose, Helen.
American costume designer, heading MGM's department from 1942 to 1966.
Coney Island 43. Stormy Weather 43. Hello Frisco, Hello 43. The Harvey Girls 46. Two Sisters from Boston 46. Ziegfeld Follies 46. Till the Clouds Roll By 46. Take Me out to the Ball Game 48. Luxury Liner 48. Words and Music 48. East Side, West Side 49. On the Town 49. Pagan Love Song 50. Father of the Bride 50. Three Little Words 50. The Belle of New York 51. The Great Caruso (AAN) 51. The Bad and the Beautiful (AA) 52. The Merry Widow (AAN) 52. Mogambo 53. Dangerous When Wet 53. Dream Wife (AAN) 53. The Glass Slipper 54. Executive Suite (AAN) 54. It's Always Fair Weather 55. Interrupted Melody (AAN) 55. I'll Cry Tomorrow (AA) 55. Forbidden Planet 56. High Society 56. The Swan 56. The Power and the Prize (AAN) 56. Designing Woman 57. Tip on a Dead Jockey 57. Cat on a Hot Tin Roof 58. The Tunnel of Love 58. Ask Any Girl 59. The Gazebo (AAN) 59. Go Naked in the World 60. Butterfield 8 60. All the Fine Young Cannibals 60. Ada 61. Bachelor in Paradise 61. The Honeymoon Machine 61. The Courtship of Eddie's Father 63. Made in Paris 65. Mister Buddwing (AAN) 65. Made in Paris 66. How Sweet It Is! 68, many others.

Rose, Jack:
see SHAVELSON, Melville.

Rose, Reginald (1921–).
American writer who has created numerous TV plays, also a series, *The Defenders*.
Crime in the Streets 56. *Twelve Angry Men* (AAN) 57. The Man in the Net 58. Man of the West 58. The Wild Geese 78. Somebody Killed Her Husband 78. The Sea Wolves 80. Who Dares Wins 82. Wild Geese II 85, etc.

Rose, William (1918–1987).
American screenwriter who spent some years in Britain.
Once a Jolly Swagman (co-w) 48. The Gift Horse 51. I'll Get You for This 52. *Genevieve* (AAN) 53. *The Maggie* 54. The Lady Killers (AAN) 55. Touch and Go 55. Man in the Sky 56. The Smallest Show on Earth 57. *It's a Mad Mad Mad Mad World* 63. The Russians Are Coming, the Russians Are Coming (AAN) 66. The Flim Flam Man 67. *Guess Who's Coming to Dinner* (AA) 67. The Secret of Santa Vittoria 69, etc.

Rosen, Phil (1888–1951).
Russian-born American director of second features. In films from 1912 as a cameraman with Edison.
The Single Sin 21. The Young Rajah 22. Abraham Lincoln 25. Burning Up Broadway 28. Two-Gun Man 31. Beggars in Ermine 34. Two Wise Maids 37. Double Alibi 40. Forgotten Girls 40. Spooks Run Wild 41. Prison Mutiny 43. Step by Step 46. The Secret of St Ives 49, many others.

Rosenberg, Aaron (1912–1979).
American producer, in Hollywood from 1934; working for Universal from 1946.
Johnny Stool Pigeon 47. Winchester 73 50. The Glenn Miller Story 54. To Hell and Back 55. The Great Man 57. Morituri 65. The Reward 65. Tony Rome 67, many others.

Rosenberg, Philip.
American production designer, from the theatre.
The Owl and the Pussycat 70. The Anderson Tapes 71. Child's Play 72. The Gambler 74. The Sentinel 77. The Wiz (AAN) 78. All That Jazz (AA) 79. Eyewitness 80. Daniel 83. The Manhattan Project 86. Moonstruck 87. The January Man 88. Running on Empty 88. Family Business 89. Q & A 90. Other People's Money 91. A Stranger among Us 92. Guilty as Sin 93. The Pelican Brief 93. Night Falls on Manhattan 97. Critical Care 97. A Perfect Murder 98, etc.

Rosenberg, Scott.
American screenwriter.
Things to Do in Denver When You're Dead 95. Beautiful Girls 96. Con Air 97. Disturbing Behaviour 98, etc.

Rosenberg, Stuart (1928–).
American director with long TV experience.
■ Murder Inc. 60. Question 7 61. Fame Is the Name of the Game (TV) 66. Asylum for a Spy (TV) 67. *Cool Hand Luke* 67. The April Fools 69. Move 70. W.U.S.A. 70. Pocket Money 72. The Laughing Policeman 73. The Drowning Pool 75. Voyage of the Damned 76. Love and Bullets 78. The Amityville Horror 79. Brubaker 80. The Pope of Greenwich Village 84. Let's Get Harry 86. My Heroes Have Always Been Cowboys 91.

Rosenbloom, 'Slapsie' Maxie (1906–1976).
American 'roughneck' comedian, ex-boxer, in occasional comedy films as gangster or punch-drunk type.
Mr Broadway 33. Nothing Sacred 37. Louisiana Purchase 41. Hazard 48. Mr Universe 51. Abbott and Costello Meet the Keystone Kops 55. The Beat Generation 59, etc.

Rosenblum, Ralph (1925–1995).
American editor.
Mad Dog Coll 61. *Fail Safe* 64. The Pawnbroker 65. The Group 66. The Night They Raided Minsky's 67. Goodbye Columbus 69. Bananas 71. Sleeper 73. Love and Death 75. *Annie Hall* 77. The Great Bank Hoax 78. Interiors 78. Stuck on You 83. Forever Lulu 87, etc.

Rosenman, Leonard (1924–).
American composer.
The Cobweb 55. East of Eden 55. Rebel without a Cause 55. Lafayette Escadrille 58. The Chapman Report 62. Fantastic Voyage 66. Hellfighters 68. Beneath the Planet of the Apes 71. Phantom of Hollywood (TV) 74. Race with the Devil 75. *Barry Lyndon* (AAmd) 75. Bound for Glory (AAmd) 76. The Car 77. Lord of the Rings 78. Promises in the Dark 79. Hide in Plain Sight 80. Cross Creek (AAN) 83. Miss Lonelyhearts 83. Heart of the Stag 84. Sylvia 85. Star Trek IV: The Voyage Home (AAN) 86. Robocop 2 90. Ambition 91. Mrs Munck 95, etc.

Rosenthal, Jack (1931–).
British scriptwriter, mainly for television, in which medium he has won many awards.
The Lovers 72. *The Chain* 85. Captain Jack 98, etc.

Rosenthal, Laurence (1926–).
American composer and conductor who now scores TV movies and mini-series.
Yellowneck 55. Naked in the Sun 57. A Raisin in the Sun 61. The Miracle Worker 62. Becket (AAN) 64. Hotel Paradiso 66. The Comedians 67. A Gunfight 70. Man of La Mancha (AAN) 72. The Wild Party 74. Rooster Cogburn 75. The Return of a Man Called Horse 76. Who'll Stop the Rain/Dog Soldiers 78. Meteor 79. Clash of the Titans 81. Heart Like a Wheel 83. Easy Money 83, etc.

Rosher, Charles (1885–1974).
Distinguished American cinematographer.
The Clown 16. The Love Night 20. Smilin' Through 22. *Sparrows* 26. *Sunrise* (AA) 27. *Tempest* 28. What Price Hollywood? 32. Our Betters 33. The Affairs of Cellini 34. Little Lord Fauntleroy 36. White Banners 38. A Child Is Born 40. Kismet 44. *The Yearling* (co-ph) (AA) 46. *Show Boat* 51. Scaramouche 52. Kiss Me Kate 53. Young Bess 54. Jupiter's Darling 55, many others.

Rosher, Charles, Jnr.
American cinematographer.
■ Pretty Maids All in a Row 71. Semi Tough 77. Three Women 77. A Wedding 78. The Muppet Movie 79. The Onion Field 79. Heartbeeps 81. Independence Day 83. Police Academy 6: City under Siege 89.

Rosi, Francesco (1922–).
Italian director.
La Sfida 57. Salvatore Giuliano (& w) 61. Hands over the City 63. The Moment of Truth 64. More than a Miracle 68. Three Brothers (& w) 82. Christ Stopped at Eboli 82. I Tre Fratelli 80. Bizet's Carmen 84. Chronicle of a Death Foretold/Crònaca di una Morte Annunciata 87. To Forget Palermo/Dimenticare Palermo 90. The Truce 97, etc.

Rosmer, Milton (1881–1971) (Arthur Milton Lunt).
British stage actor, in many films from 1913.
General John Regan 21. The Passionate Friends 22. The Phantom Light 35. South Riding 38. Goodbye Mr Chips 39. Atlantic Ferry 41. Fame Is the Spur 47. The Monkey's Paw 48. The Small Back Room 49, etc.
AS DIRECTOR: Dreyfus 31. Channel Crossing 32. The Guvnor 36. The Challenge 37, etc.

Ross, Annie (1930–) (Annabelle Short Lynch).
British jazz singer and character actress. Brought up in America, she was a juvenile actress in Hollywood, studied drama in New York, and became a singer in England in the 50s before returning to America to form a jazz vocal trio, Lambert, Hendricks and Ross. From the 70s, she began to act on stage and TV.
Presenting Lily Mars 43. Alfie Darling 75. Superman III 83. Throw Momma from the Train 87. Witchery 88. Basket Case 2 90. Pump Up the Volume 90. Short Cuts 93. Blue Sky (made 91) 94, etc.

Ross, Benjamin (1964–).
English director and screenwriter who studied at the Columbia Film School.
The Young Poisoner's Handbook (co-w, d) 95.
❝ So often you come out of the cinema feeling soothed, patronised, morphined up to the eyeballs or given a jerk-off. It's important that people should take a journey they'd rather not take, and leave with a firecracker up their arse. – *B.R.*

Ross, Betsy King (1923–1989).
American juvenile actress, popular in western series of the 30s opposite such stars as Ken Maynard and Gene Autry. An award-winning trick rider, she later became an anthropologist and writer.
Smoke Lightning 33. Fighting with Kit Carson (serial) 33. In Old Sante Fe 34. Phantom Empire (serial) 35. Radio Ranch 35, etc.

Ross, Diana (1944–).
American singer and actress.
■ *Lady Sings the Blues* (as Billie Holiday) (AAN) 72. Mahogany 76. The Wiz 78. Out of Darkness (TV) 94.

Ross, Frank (1904–1990).
American producer, in Hollywood from early 30s.
Of Mice and Men 39. The Devil and Miss Jones 41. The Robe 53. The Rains of Ranchipur 55. Kings Go Forth 58. Mister Moses 65. Where It's At 70, etc.

Ross, Gary.
American screenwriter, director and producer.
Big (co-w) 86. Dave (w) 93. Lassie (co-w) 94. Pleasantville (p, wd) 98, etc.

Ross, Herbert (1927–).
American director and choreographer.
Doctor Dolittle 67. Funny Girl 69, etc.
AS DIRECTOR: Goodbye Mr Chips 69. The Owl and the Pussycat 70. T. R. Baskin 71. Play It Again Sam 72. The Last of Sheila (& p) 73. Funny Lady 75. The Sunshine Boys 75. The Seven Per Cent Solution 76. The Turning Point (AAN) 77. The Goodbye Girl 77. Nijinsky 80. Pennies from Heaven 81. I Ought to Be in Pictures 82. Max Dugan Returns 83. Flashdance 83. Footloose 84. Protocol 84. Dancers 87. The Secret of My Success 87. Steel Magnolias 89. My Blue Heaven 90. True Colors 91. Undercover Blues 93. Boys on the Side 95, etc.

Ross, Joe E. (1905–1982).
Short, fat American comedian with a frazzled manner, mostly on TV.
TV series: Bilko 56–59. Car 54 Where Are You? 61–62. It's about Time 64.

Ross, Katharine (1943–).
American leading lady. Married actor Sam ELLIOTT.
■ Shenandoah 65. Mr Buddwing 66. The Longest Hundred Miles (TV) 66. The Singing Nun 66. Games 67. *The Graduate* (AAN) 67. Hellfighters 68. Tell Them Willie Boy Is Here 69. Butch Cassidy and the Sundance Kid 69. Fools 70. Get to Know Your Rabbit 72. They Only Kill Their Masters 72. Le Hasard et la Violence 74. The Stepford Wives 75. Voyage of the Damned 76. Wanted, the Sundance Woman (TV) 77. The Legacy 78. The Betsy 78. The Swarm 78. Murder by Natural Causes (TV) 79. The Final Countdown 80. Murder in Texas (TV) 81. Wrong Is Right 82. The Shadow Riders (TV) 82. Travis McGee (TV) 82. Red-Headed Stranger 86. A Row of Crows 90.

Ross, Lillian (1926–).
American journalist who wrote *Picture*, a fascinating account of the production of *The Red Badge of Courage*.

Ross, Shirley (1909–1975) (Bernice Gaunt).
American pianist and singer who appeared as leading lady in a few films.
The Age of Indiscretion 35. San Francisco 36. *Thanks for the Memory* 38. Paris Honeymoon 39.

Kisses for Breakfast 41. A Song for Miss Julie 45, etc.

Ross, Steven (1927–1992) (Steven Rechnitz).
American studio executive, head of Warner from 1967 and the man who masterminded the merger of Warner and Time Inc. in 1989 to create the world's largest media and entertainment group. According to Steven Spielberg, he was the model for the portrayal of Schindler in *Schindler's List*.
Biography: 1992, *Master of the Game* by Connie Bruck.

Rossellini, Isabella (1952–).
Italian actress, daughter of Ingrid Bergman and director Roberto Rossellini.
Autobiography: 1997, *Some of Me*.
White Nights 85. Blue Velvet 86. Tough Guys Don't Dance 87. Zelly and Me 88. Cousins 89. Dames Galantes 90. Wild at Heart 90. Ivory Hunters (TV) 90. Death Becomes Her 92. The Pickle 93. The Innocent 93. Fearless 93. Wyatt Earp 94. Immortal Beloved 94. Crime of the Century 96. Big Night 96. The Funeral 96. The Odyssey (TV) 97. Left Luggage (Hol.) 98. Merlin (TV) 98. The Imposters 98, etc.

Rossellini, Roberto (1906–1977).
Italian director, in films from 1938. Started as writer; co-scripted his own films.
Autobiography: 1993, *My Method: Writings and Interviews*.
Biography: 1987, *Roberto Rossellini* by Peter Brunette.
Open City 45. *Paisa* (co-w, AAN) 46. Germany Year Zero 48. Stromboli 49. Europa 51. General Della Rovere 59. Louis XIV Seizes Power 66. Il Messia 76, many others.

Rossen, Robert (1908–1966).
American writer-producer-director, in Hollywood from 1936 after stage experience.
■ Marked Woman (w) 37. They Won't Forget (w) 37. Racket Busters (w) 38. Dust be My Destiny (w) 39. *The Roaring Twenties* (w) 39. A Child is Born (w) 39. The Sea Wolf (w) 41. Out of the Fog (w) 41. Blues in the Night (w) 41. Edge of Darkness (w) 42. *A Walk in the Sun* (w) 45. The Strange Love of Martha Ivers (w) 46. Desert Fury (w) 47. Johnny O'Clock (wd) 47. *Body and Soul* (d) 47. Treasure of the Sierra Madre (co-w, uncredited) 47. *All the King's Men* (wpd) (AAp, AANw, AANd) 49. The Brave Bulls (pd) 50. Mambo (wd) 54. Alexander the Great (wpd) 56. Island in the Sun (d) 57. They Came to Cordura (wd) 59. *The Hustler* (wpd) (AAN) 61. Billy Budd (co-w) 62. Lilith (wpd) 64.
❝ In retrospect, the dreariness of his direction is remarkably consistent. – *Andrew Sarris, 1968*

Rossi, Franco (1919–).
Italian writer-director.
I Falsari 52. Il Seduttore 54. *Amici per la Pelle*/Friends for Life 55. Morte di un Amico 60. Smog 62. Quo Vadis (TV) 85, etc.

Rossi-Drago, Eleonora (1925–) (Palmina Omiccioli).
Italian leading lady.
Pirates of Capri 48. Persiane Chiuse 50. Three Forbidden Stories 51. The White Slave 53. Le Amiche 55. Maledetto Imbroglio 59. David and Goliath 59. Under Ten Flags 60. Uncle Tom's Cabin (Ger.) 65. Camille 2000 69, etc.

Rossif, Frédéric (1922–1990).
French documentarist.
Le Temps du Ghetto 61. Mourir à Madrid 62. The Fall of Berlin 65, etc.

Rossington, Norman (1928–).
British character actor of stage, TV and films.
A Night to Remember 58. Carry On Sergeant 58. *Saturday Night and Sunday Morning* 60. Go to Blazes 62. The Comedy Man 63. A Hard Day's Night 64. Tobruk (US) 66. The Charge of the Light Brigade 68. The Adventures of Gerard 70. Deathline 72. Go for a Take 72. Let Him Have It 91, etc.

Rossio, Terry.
American scriptwriter and director, usually in collaboration with Ted Elliott.
Little Monsters 89. Aladdin (& co-d) 92. Puppet Masters 94. Godzilla (story) 98. Small Soldiers 98. The Mask of Zorro (story) 98. Antz (story consultant) 98, etc.

Rossiter, Leonard (1926–1984).
British comic actor.
Billy Liar 62. King Rat 65. Hotel Paradiso 66. The Wrong Box 66. The Whisperers 67. 2001: A Space Odyssey 68. Oliver 68. Otley 69. Barry Lyndon 75. The Pink Panther Strikes Again 77. Rising Damp 79. Britannia Hospital 82. Trail of the Pink Panther 82, etc.
TV series: Rising Damp 77–80. The Fall and Rise of Reginald Perrin 78–80. Tripper's Day 83.

Rosson, Hal (Harold) (1895–1988).
Distinguished American cinematographer. He was married to Jean Harlow (1933–35).
The Cinema Murder 19. Manhandled 24. Gentlemen Prefer Blondes 28. *Tarzan of the Apes* 32. *The Scarlet Pimpernel* 35. The Ghost Goes West 36. The Garden of Allah (AA) 36. *The Wizard of Oz* 39. Johnny Eager 42. The Hucksters 47. *On the Town* 49. *The Red Badge of Courage* 51. *Singin' in the Rain* 52. The Bad Seed 56. No Time for Sergeants 58. El Dorado 67, many others.

Rossovich, Rick (1958–).
American actor.
The Lords of Discipline 83. Streets of Fire 84. The Terminator 84. Warning Sign 85. Morning After 86. Top Gun 86. Roxanne 87. Let's Get Harry 87. Secret Ingredient 88. The Spellbinder 88. Paint It Black 89. Navy SEALS 90. Tropical Heat 93. New Crime City: Los Angeles 2020 94. Fatally Yours 95. Cover Me 95. Black Scorpion 95. Legend of the Lost Tomb (TV) 97, etc.
TV series: MacGruder & Loud 85. Sons & Daughters 91.

Rota, Nino (1911–1979) (Nino Rinalde).
Italian composer, responsible for innumerable film scores (including all of Fellini's) as well as operas. He studied at the Milan Conservatory, the Santa Cecilia Academy, and the Curtis Institute of the United States, and for many years was director of the Bari Conservatory.
The Popular Train 33. Zaza 43. Open City 46. My Son the Professor 46. Flight into France 48. *The Glass Mountain* 48. To Live in Peace 48. E Primavera 49. Anna 52. I Vitelloni 53. La Strada 54. Amici per la Pelle 56. *War and Peace* 56. Il Bidone 56. Cabiria 58. La Dolce Vita 59. Plein Soleil 60. Rocco and His Brothers 60. Boccaccio 70 62. Eight and a Half 63. Juliet of the Spirits 65. Shoot Loud, Louder, I Don't Understand 66. Romeo and Juliet 68. Satyricon 69. Waterloo 70. *The Godfather* 72. The Abdication 74. The Godfather Part II (co-m, AA) 74. Casanova 77. Death on the Nile 78. Hurricane 79, many others.

Roth, Ann.
American costume designer.
The World of Henry Orient 64. A Fine Madness 66. Up the Down Staircase 67. Midnight Cowboy 69. The Owl and the Pussycat 70. They Might Be Giants 71. Klute 71. The Day of the Locust 75. Mandingo 75. Burnt Offerings 76. The Goodbye Girl 77. Coming Home 78. California Suite 78. Hair 79. Dressed to Kill 80. Nine to Five 80. Only When I Laugh 81. Honky Tonk Freeway 81. The World According to Garp 82. Silkwood 83. Places in the Heart (AA) 84. Heartburn 86. The Unbearable Lightness of Being 87. Working Girl 88. Biloxi Blues 88. January Man 89. Family Business 89. Postcards from the Edge 90. The Bonfire of the Vanities 90. Regarding Henry 91. The Mambo Kings 92. Dave 93. Guarding Tess 94. Wolf 94. Sabrina 95. The Birdcage 96. The English Patient 96. Primary Colors 98. The Talented Mr Ripley 99, etc.

Roth, Eric.
American screenwriter.
The Nickel Ride 75. The Concorde: Airport '79 79. Suspect 87. Memories of Me (co-w) 88. *Forrest Gump* (AA) 94. The Postman 97. The Horse Whisperer 98, etc.

Roth, Gene (1903–1976) (Gene Stuttenroth).
Heavy-set American character actor.
A Game of Death 46. The Baron of Arizona 50. Pirates of the High Seas 50. Red Planet Mars 52. The Farmer Takes a Wife 53. Attack of the Giant Leeches 59, etc.

Roth, Joe (1948–).
American producer and director, former chairman of Twentieth Century-Fox. He was co-founder of the production company Morgan's Creek. In 1994 he became chairman of the Walt Disney Company.
■ As director: Streets of Gold 86. Revenge of the Nerds II 87. Coupe de Ville 90.

Roth, Lillian (1910–1980) (Lillian Rutstein).
American leading lady who began her professional career as the baby in the Educational Pictures trademark. After a few films in the early 30s, personal problems caused her retirement. Her story was filmed in 1955 as *I'll Cry Tomorrow*, with Susan Hayward.
The Love Parade 20. The Vagabond King 30. *Madame Satan* 30. Animal Crackers 30. Sea Legs 31. Ladies They Talk About 33. Take a Chance 33. Communion/Alice, Sweet Alice 77, etc.

Roth, Philip (1933–).
American novelist, somewhat excessively concerned with Jewish guilt and masturbation. *Portnoy's Complaint* and *Goodbye Columbus* were filmed. Formerly married to actress Claire Bloom.

Roth, Tim (1961–).
British character actor, from the stage.
The Hit 84. A World Apart 87. To Kill a Priest 89. The Cook, the Thief, His Wife and Her Lover 89. Rosencrantz and Guildenstern Are Dead 90. Farendj 90. Vincent and Theo 90. Backsliding 91. Jumpin' at the Boneyard 91. *Reservoir Dogs* 92. The Perfect Husband/La Mujer de Ed Medio 92. Murder in the Heartland (TV) 93. Bodies, Rest & Motion 93. Heart of Darkness (TV) 94. Pulp Fiction 94. Captives 94. Little Odessa 94. Rob Roy (AAN) 95. Four Rooms 95. No Way Home 96. Everyone Says I Love You 96. Gridlock'd 97. Animals 98. The Legend of the Pianist on the Ocean (It.) 98, etc.

Rotha, Paul (1903–1984).
British documentarist and film theorist. With GPO Film Unit in the 30s, later independent. Author of *The Film till Now*, *Documentary Film*, etc.
Shipyard 30. Contact 33. The Rising Tide 33. The Face of Britain 34. The Fourth Estate 40. *World of Plenty* 42. Land of Promise 46. The World Is Rich 48. No Resting Place 50. World without End (co-d) 52. Cat and Mouse 57. *The Life of Adolf Hitler* 62. The Silent Raid 62, etc.

Rothafel, Samuel 'Roxy' (Samuel Rothapfel).
American showman and movie exhibitor, who was among those responsible for raising the image of cinemas so that they appealed to a middle-class audience in the early 1900s. He insisted on opulence, excellent service and full-scale musical accompaniment to the films shown, as well as providing ballet and orchestral concerts for his patrons. He ran his first movie house in Forest City, Pennsylvania, and by 1914 was managing the 4,000-seater Strand Theater on Broadway, then America's largest, and, later, the Capitol, which had 26 million patrons in its first five years. In 1926, he opened the biggest movie theatre in the world, the Roxy in New York, which seated 6,000 and was built at a cost of $6m. In 1932, he left the Roxy to control the even larger Radio City Music Hall; but he was ill, its opening was a disaster, and his career never had time to recover. Died of a heart attack.
❝ My ancestors were peasants. Not one of them played the violin or eloped with a beautiful Russian opera singer. They just never did anything. – *S.R.*

Rothrock, Cynthia (1961–).
American exponent of martial arts whose mainly Hong Kong-made films tend to be released direct to video, except in Hong Kong.
No Retreat, No Surrender 2 89. China O'Brien 89. Martial Law 90. Karate Cop 91. Lady Dragon 91. Triple Cross 91. Tiger Claws 91. Fast Getaway 91. Rage and Honor 92. Angel of Fury 92. Guardian Angel 93. Fast Getaway II 94. Night Vision 97, etc.

Rothwell, Talbot (1916–1981).
English screenwriter who scripted 20 of the Carry On comedies. He also created the television series *Up Pompeii!* and wrote for TV comedies, including *Before Your Very Eyes*, *Friends and Neighbours*, *Dear Dotty*, and *The Army Game*.
Is Your Honeymoon Really Necessary 53. The Crowded Day 54. Look Before You Laugh 56. Tommy the Toreador (co-w) 59. Make Mine a Million (co-w) 59. Friends and Neighbours 60. Carry On Cabby 63. Carry On Jack 64. Carry On Spying (co-w) 64. Carry On Cleo 64. Carry On Cowboy 65. Carry On Screaming 66. Carry On – Don't Lose Your Head 66. Carry On – Follow That Camel 66. Carry On Doctor 68. Carry On up the Khyber 68. Carry On Again Doctor 69. Carry On Camping 69. Carry On up the Jungle 70. Carry On Loving 70. Carry On Henry 71. Carry On at Your Convenience 71. Carry On Abroad 72. Carry On Matron 72. Carry On Girls 73. Carry On Dick 74, etc.

Rotunno, Giuseppe (1923–).
Italian cinematographer.
Scandal in Sorrento 55. White Nights 57. Anna of Brooklyn 58. The Naked Maja 59. On the Beach 59. The Angel Wore Red 60. Rocco and His Brothers 60. The Best of Enemies 61. The Leopard 62. Yesterday, Today and Tomorrow 63. Anzio 68. The Secret of Santa Vittoria 69. Satyricon 69. Sunflower 70. Carnal Knowledge 71. Man of La Mancha 72. Amarcord 74. Casanova 77. The End of the World 78. All That Jazz (AAN, BFA) 79. Popeye 81. Five Days One Summer 82. And the Ship Sails On 84. China 9, Liberty 37 84. American Dreamer 84. The Assisi Underground 85. Red Sonja 85. Hotel Colonial 87. Julia and Julia 88. Rent-a-Cop 88. Haunted Summer 88. The Adventures of Baron Munchausen 89. Regarding Henry 91. Once upon a Crime 92. Wolf 94. Night and the Moment 94. The Stendhal Syndrome 96, etc.

Rouch, Jean (1917–).
French documentary director, cinematographer, and ethnographer who has used cinéma vérité techniques and non-professional actors, much in the style of Flaherty, to recreate the lives of ordinary people. Apart from his features, he has also made many shorts, from 1946, some of which were compiled to form *Les Fils de L'Eau* 55.
Moi, un Noir 58. Chronicle of a Summer/Chronique d'un Été (co-d) 61. Paris Vu par (co-d) 64. Jaguar 67. Petit à Petit 70. Cocorico Monsieur Poulet 77. Dionysos 84. Enigma 87. Boulevards d'Afrique 88. Cantate pour Deux Généraux 90, etc.

Roundtree, Richard (1937–).
American leading man of the 70s.
Shaft 71. Embassy 72. Charley One Eye 72. Shaft's Big Score 72. Earthquake 74. Man Friday 75. Escape to Athena 79. Game for Vultures 79. The Winged Serpent 82. One Down Two to Go 82. The Big Score 83. City Heat 84. Killpoint 84. Opposing Forces 87. Maniac Cop 88. Angel III – the Final Chapter 88. Bad Jim 89. Night Visitor 89. Cry Devil 89. Crack House 89. Bloodfist III: Forced to Fight 91. Black Heart/Nero come il Cuore 91. Deadly Rivals 92. Seven 95. Once upon a Time . . . When We Were Colored 96. Original Gangstas 96. Theodore Rex 96. Steel 97. Any Place but Home (TV) 97. George of the Jungle 97, etc.
TV series: Shaft 73. 413 Hope Street 97.

Rounseville, Robert (1914–1974).
American opera singer.
■ Tales of Hoffman 51. Carousel 56.

Rouquier, Georges (1909–1989).
French documentarist.
Le Tonnelier 42. Farrebique 46. Salt of the Earth 50. Lourdes and Its Miracles 56, etc.

Rourke, Mickey (1950–).
Tough, abrasive American actor.
■ 1941 79. Fade to Black 80. Heaven's Gate 80. Body Heat 81. Diner 81. Rumble Fish 83. Eureka 83. The Pope of Greenwich Village 84. *The Year of the Dragon* 85. Nine and a Half Weeks 86. Angel Heart 87. Barfly 87. A Prayer for the Dying 87. Homeboy 88. Johnny Handsome 89. Wild Orchid 90. Desperate Hours 90. Harley Davidson and the Marlboro Man 91. White Sands 92. F.T.W. 94. Fall Time 95. Saints and Sinners 95. Bullet 95. John Grisham's The Rainmaker 97. Buffalo '66 97. Exit in Red 97. Double Team 97. Thursday 98. Shergar 98.
❝ I always knew I'd accomplish something very special – like robbing a bank perhaps. – *M.R.*

Rouse, Russell (1916–1987).
American director and co-writer, usually in partnership with Clarence Greene.
D.O.A. 50. The Well (AANw) 51. The Thief 52. New York Confidential 55. The Fastest Gun Alive 56. Thunder in the Sun 59. A House Is Not a Home 64. The Oscar 66. Caper of the Golden Bulls 67, etc.

Rousselot, Philippe (1945–).
French cinematographer, now in international films.
Absences Répétées 72. Adam ou le Sang d'Abel 77. Peppermint Soda/Diabolo Menthe 77. Pour Clemence 77. La Drôlesse 79. Diva 82. The Moon in the Gutter/La Lune dans le Caniveau 83. Emerald Forest 85. Thérèse 86. Hope and Glory (AAN) 87. The Bear 89. Dangerous Liaisons 89. Too Beautiful for You/Trop Belle pour Toi 89. We're No Angels 89. Henry and June (AAN) 90. The Miracle 90. Merci la Vie 91. A River Runs through It (AA) 92. Sommersby 93. Queen Margot/La Reine Margot 94. Interview with the Vampire 94. Mary Reilly 96. The Serpent's Kiss (d) 97, etc.

Routledge, Patricia (1929–).
English character actress and singer, best known for her role as the fearsome social climber Hyacinth Bucket ('pronounced Bouquet') in the TV sitcom *Keeping Up Appearances* 90–95. Born in Birkenhead, she studied at the University of Liverpool and the Bristol Old Vic Theatre School and made her stage debut in 1952, subsequently appearing in dramas, musicals and revues. Won a Tony for best musical actress on the Broadway stage in 1967.
Victoria Regina (TV) 64. To Sir with Love 67. 30 Is a Dangerous Age, Cynthia 67. The Bliss of Mrs Blossom 68. If It's Tuesday, This Must Be Belgium 69. Lock Up Your Daughters 69. Girl Stroke Boy 71. Doris and Doreen (TV) 78. Talking Heads (TV) 88, etc.
TV series: Victoria Regina (as Queen Victoria) 64. Marjorie and Men 85. Victoria Wood – As Seen on TV 85–86. Hetty Wainthropp Investigates 96– .
❝ My ambition was to be a Go-Ahead headmistress. – *P.R.*

Rowan, Dan (1922–1987).
American comedian, one-half of Rowan and Martin, the other being Dick Martin (1922–). Belatedly successful on TV with *Laugh In* 1968–72, they have not been popular in films.
■ Once upon a Horse 57. The Maltese Bippy 69.

Rowland, Bruce.
Australian composer.
The Man from Snowy River 82. Phar Lap 83. Rebel 85. Les Patterson Saves the World 87. Return to Snowy River 88. Cheetah 89. Fast Getaway 91. Lightning Jack 94. Andre 94. Zeus and Roxanne 96. North Star 96, etc.

Rowland, Roy (1910–1995).
American director, mainly of routine features, in Hollywood from the mid-30s. Many shorts, including *Benchley, Pete Smith, Crime Does Not Pay*.
Lost Angel 44. *Our Vines Have Tender Grapes* 45. Killer McCoy 48. Tenth Avenue Angel 48. Scene of the Crime 49. Two Weeks with Love 50. Bugles in the Afternoon 53. The Moonlighter 53. Rogue Cop 53. The 5,000 Fingers of Doctor T 53. Affair with a Stranger 53. Many Rivers to Cross 55. Hit the Deck 55. Meet Me in Las Vegas 56. These Wilder Years 56. Gun Glory 57. Seven Hills of Rome 58. The Girl Hunters 64. Gunfighters of Casa Grande 66. They Called Him Gringo 68, many others.

Rowlands, Gena (1934–) (Virginia Rowlands).
American leading actress, mostly on stage. Married to John Cassavetes.
The High Cost of Loving 58. A Child is Waiting 62. Lonely are the Brave 62. Tony Rome 67. Faces 68. Minnie and Moskowitz 71. A Woman under the Influence (AAN) 75. Two Minute Warning 76. Opening Night 77. The Brink's Job 78. Gloria (AAN) 80. Love Streams 85. Light of Day 87. Another Woman 88. Montana (TV) 90. Once Around 91. Night on Earth 91. Crazy in Love 92. Silent Cries (TV) 93. Parallel Lives (TV) 94. The Neon Bible 95. Something to Talk About 95. Unhook the Stars 96. She's So Lovely 97. Paulie 98. The Mighty 98. Hope Floats 98. Dancing about Architecture 98, etc.
TV series: 87th Precinct 61.

Rowlands, Patsy (1934–).
British character comedienne.
In the Doghouse 61. Dateline Diamonds 65. Carry on Loving 70. Carry on Girls 73. Joseph Andrews 76. Tess 79. The Fiendish Plot of Dr Fu Manchu 80, etc.

Roxburgh, Richard.
Australian leading actor.
The Riddle of the Stinson (TV) 87. Dead to the World 90. Tracks of Glory 91. Talk 93. Billy's Holiday 95. Doing Time for Patsy Cline 97. Oscar and Lucinda 97. Passion: The Story of Percy Grainger 99, etc.

Roy, Harry (1900–1971).
British bandleader who made two films: *Everything is Rhythm* 36. *Rhythm Racketeer* 37.

Royle, Selena (1904–1983).
American character actress.
The Misleading Lady 32. Mrs Parkington 44. The Fighting Sullivans 44. Gallant Journey 47. Cass Timberlane 47. Joan of Arc 48. Branded 50. Robot Monster 53. Murder Is My Beat 55, etc.

Rozema, Patricia (1958–).
Canadian director and screenwriter.
I've Heard the Mermaids Singing 87. White Room 91. Montreal Sextet (co-d) 91. The Case of the Missing Mother 92. When Night Is Falling 95. Mansfield Park 99, etc.

Rozsa, Miklos (1907–1995).
Hungarian composer, in Hollywood from 1940.
Autobiography: 1982, *A Double Life*.
Knight without Armour 37. *The Four Feathers* 39. *The Thief of Baghdad* (AAN) 40. Lady Hamilton 41. Five Graves to Cairo 43. Double Indemnity (AAN) 44. A Song to Remember 44. The Lost Weekend 45. *Spellbound* (AA) 45. *The Killers* (AAN) 46. Brute Force 47. *A Double Life* (AA) 47. Naked City 48. Adam's Rib 49. The Asphalt Jungle 50. Quo Vadis (AAN) 51. Ivanhoe (AAN) 52. Julius Caesar 53. Moonfleet 55. Lust for Life 56. *Ben Hur* (AA) 59. King of Kings 61. El Cid (AAN) 61. Sodom and Gomorrah 62. The VIPs 63. The Power 67. The Green Berets 68. The Private Life of Sherlock Holmes 70. Providence 77. Fedora 78. The Private Files of J. Edgar Hoover 78. Time after Time 79. Last Embrace 79. Dead Men Don't Wear Plaid 82, many others.

Ruane, John (1952–).
Australian director and screenwriter, from television commercials.
Death in Brunswick 91. That Eye, the Sky 94. Dead Letter Office 98, etc.

Rub, Christian (1887–1956).
Austrian character actor, long in Hollywood. Was the model and voice for Gepetto the wood-carver in Disney's *Pinocchio*.
The Trial of Vivienne Ware 32. The Kiss behind the Mirror 33. A Dog of Flanders 35. Dracula's Daughter 36. Heidi 37. Mad about Music 38. The Great Waltz 38. The Swiss Family Robinson 40. Tales of Manhattan 42. Fall Guy 48. Something for the Birds 52, many others.

Ruben, Joseph (1951–).
American director and screenwriter.
The Sister-in-Law (wd) 75. The Pom-Pom Girls (wd) 76. Joyride (wd) 76. Our Winning Season (wd) 78. Gorp (d) 80. Dreamscape (wd) 84. The Stepfather (d) 87. True Believer (d) 89. Sleeping with the Enemy (d) 90. The Good Son (d) 93. Money Train (d) 95. Return to Paradise (d) 98, etc.

Rubens, Alma (1897–1931) (Alma Smith).
American leading lady of the silent screen; her career was prematurely ended by drug addiction.
Intolerance 15. The Firefly of Tough Luck 17. Humoresque 20. Cytherea 24. Fine Clothes 25. Siberia 26. Masks of the Devil 28. Showboat 29, etc.

Rubens, Percival.
South African director and screenwriter.
The Foster Gang 64. Three Days of Fire (It.) 67. Mister Kingstreet's War (US) 70. Saboteurs 74. Survival Zone 81. Raw Terror 85. Sweet Murder 90, etc.

Rubin, Bruce Joel (1944–).
American screenwriter and director.
Brainstorm 83. Deadly Friend 86. Ghost (co-w, AA) 90. Jacob's Ladder 90. My Life (& d) 93. Deep Impact (co-w) 98, etc.

Rubinstein, Arthur B.
American composer who also scores many TV movies and series.
Whose Life Is It Anyway? 81. Blue Thunder 83. Wargames 83. Deal of the Century 83. Lost in America 85. Stakeout 87. The Hard Way 91. Another Stakeout 93. Nick of Time 95, etc.

Rubinstein, Artur (1887–1982).
Internationally renowned classical pianist who made guest appearances in occasional films, e.g. *Carnegie Hall*.
Biography: 1996, *Artur Rubinstein: A Life* by Harvey Sachs.

Rubinstein, John (1946–).
American character actor, and occasional composer. Son of Artur Rubinstein.
Getting Straight 70. Zachariah 70. The Wild Pack 72. All Together Now (TV) 75. The Car 77. The Boys from Brazil 78. She's Dressed to Kill (TV) 79. Killjoy (TV) 81. Daniel 83. Someone to Watch over Me 87. Shadow on the Sun (TV) 88. Liberace (TV) 88. Another Stakeout 93. Mercy 95, etc.
TV series: Crazy Like a Fox 84–85.

Ruby, Harry (1895–1974).
American songwriter (with Bert Kalmar). See Kalmar, Bert for credits.

Rudd, Paul (1940–).
American actor, born in Boston, Massachusetts.
Johnny We Hardly Knew Ye (TV) 77. The Betsy 78. Beulah Land (TV) 80. Kung Fu – the Movie (TV) 86, etc.
TV series: Beacon Hill 75. Knots Landing 80–81.

Rudd, Paul (1969–) (aka Paul Stephen Rudd).
American actor. Born in Passaic, New Jersey, to an American father and an English mother, and raised in Overland Park, Kansas, he studied at the University of Kansas and the American Academy of Dramatic Arts in Los Angeles before working in the theatre in Britain.
Halloween: The Curse of Michael Myers 95. Clueless 95. William Shakespeare's Romeo and Juliet 96. The Size of Watermelons 97. The Locusts 97. Overnight Delivery 98. The Object of My Affection 98. Twelfth Night (TV) 98, etc.
TV series: Sisters 91. Wild Oats 94.

Rudd, Steele (1868–1935) (Arthur Hoey Davis).
Australian author whose tales of outback farm and family life in Queensland have enjoyed long-lasting success on stage and screen in Australia. They were first dramatized by actor Bert Bailey, who starred as Dad Rudd in the early films. Theatre director George Whaley also adapted them for the stage and directed a film version in 1995, featuring Leo McKern as Dad Rudd and Joan Sutherland as Mother Rudd.
On Our Selection 20. Rudd's New Selection 21. On Our Selection 32. Grandad Rudd 35. Dad and Dave Come to Town 38. Dave Rudd MP 40. Dad and Dave on Our Selection 95, etc.

Ruddy, Albert S. (1934–).
American producer.
The Godfather 72. The Longest Yard 74. The Mcahans (TV) 76. Matilda 78. Death Hunt 81. The Cannonball Run 81. Megaforce 82. Cannonball Run II 83. Lassiter 83. Farewell to the King 89. Speed Zone 89. Impulse 90. Bad Girls 94. The Scout 94, etc.
❝ Show me a relaxed producer and I'll show you a failure. – *A.S.R.*

Rudin, Scott (1958–).
American producer.
Mrs Soffel 84. Reckless 84. Pacific Heights 90. The Addams Family 91. Regarding Henry 91. Little Man Tate 91. Jennifer 8 92. Sister Act 92. White Sands 92. Addams Family Values 93. Sister Act 2: Back in the Habit 93. Searching for Bobby Fischer/Innocent Moves 93. Life with Mikey 93. The Firm 93. IQ 94. Nobody's Fool 94. Sabrina 95. Clueless 95. Marvin's Room 96. Ransom 96. Up Close and Personal 96. In & Out 97. The Truman Show 98, etc.

Rudkin, David (1936–).
English dramatist and occasional screenwriter, a former music teacher. Educated at Oxford University, he made his reputation in the early 60s with his play *Afore Night Come* for the Royal Shakespeare Company.
Fahrenheit 451 (dialogue) 66. Artemis 81 (TV) 81. Testimony (co-w) 87. December Bride 90. The Woodlanders 98, etc.

Rudley, Herbert (1911–).
American supporting actor.
Abe Lincoln in Illinois 39. The Seventh Cross 44. *Rhapsody in Blue* (as Ira Gershwin) 45. A Walk in the Sun 46. Joan of Arc 48. The Silver Chalice 55. The Black Sleep 56. Beloved Infidel 59. The Great Imposter 61. Falling in Love Again 80, etc.
TV series: The Californians 57. Michael Shayne 60. Meet Mona McCluskey 65. The Mothers-in-Law 67–68.

Rudnick, Paul.
American screenwriter and dramatist. He writes a witty film column for *Premiere* magazine under the pseudonym Libby Waxman-Gellner.
Addams Family Values 93. Jeffrey (w, from his play) 95. In & Out 97, etc.
❝ Movie actors are the planet's sex-education instructors: they show us how to do it right. – *P.R.*

Rudolph, Alan (1943–).
American director and screenwriter.
Premonition (wd) 72. Buffalo Bill and the Indians, or Sitting Bull's History Lesson (w) 76. Welcome to L.A. (wd) 76. Remember My Name (wd) 78. Roadie (d) 80. Endangered Species (wd) 82. Return Engagement (d) 83. Choose Me (d) 84. Songwriter (d) 84. Trouble in Mind (wd) 85. Made in Heaven (d) 87. The Moderns (co-w, d) 88. Love at Large (d) 89. Mortal Thoughts (d) 91. Equinox (d) 92. Mrs Parker and the Vicious Circle (co-w, d) 94. Afterglow (wd) 97, etc.

Ruehl, Mercedes (1954–).
American actress, from the stage.
The Warriors 79. Four Friends 81. 84 Charing Cross Road 86. Heartburn 86. Leader of the Band 87. Radio Days 87. The Secret of My Success 87. Big 88. Married to the Mob 88. Slaves of New York 89. Crazy People 90. Another You 91. The Fisher King (AA) 91. Lost in Yonkers 93. The Last Action Hero 93. Indictment: The McMartin Trial (TV) 95. Roseanna's Grave/For Roseanna 96. North Shore Fish 97. Gia 98, etc.

Ruggles, Charles (1886–1970).
American character comedian, brother of Wesley Ruggles. In films regularly from 1928 after stage experience; quickly became popular for his inimitably diffident manner.
■ Peer Gynt 15. The Majesty of the Law 15. The Reform Candidate 15. The Heart Raider 23. Gentlemen of the Press 29. The Lady Lies 29. The Battle of Paris 29. Roadhouse Nights 30. Young Man of Manhattan 30. Queen High 30. Her Wedding Night 30. *Charley's Aunt* 30. Honor among Lovers 31. The Girl Habit 31. The Smiling Lieutenant 31. Beloved Bachelor 31. Husband's Holiday 31. This Reckless Age 32. One Hour with You 32. This is the Night 32. Make Me a Star 32. *Love Me Tonight* 32. 70,000 Witnesses 32. The Night of June 13th 32. *Trouble in Paradise* 32. Evenings for Sale 32. If I Had a Million 32. Madame Butterfly 32. Murders in the Zoo 33. Terror Aboard 33. Melody Cruise 33. Mama Loves Papa 33. Girl without a Room 33. Alice in Wonderland 33. Six of a Kind 34. Goodbye Love 34. Melody in Spring 34. Murder in the Private Car 34. Friends of Mr Sweeney 34. The Pursuit of Happiness 34. *Ruggles of Red Gap* 35. People will Talk 35. No More Ladies 35. The Big Broadcast of 1936 35. Anything Goes 36. *Early to Bed* 36. Hearts Divided 36. Wives Never Know 36. Mind Your Own Business 36. Turn Off the Moon 37. Exclusive 37. *Bringing Up Baby* 38. Breaking the Ice 38. Service De Luxe 38. His Exciting Night 38. Boy Trouble 39. Sudden Money 39. Invitation to Happiness 39. Night Work 39. Balalaika 39. The Farmer's Daughter 40. Opened by Mistake 40. Maryland 40. Public Deb Number One 40. No Time for Comedy 40. Invisible Woman 41. Honeymoon for Three

41. Model Wife 41. The Parson of Panamint 41. Go West Young Lady 41. The Perfect Snob 41. Friendly Enemies 42. Dixie Dugan 43. Our Hearts Were Young and Gay 44. The Doughgirls 44. Three Is a Family 44. Bedside Manner 45. Incendiary Blonde 45. A Stolen Life 46. Gallant Journey 46. The Perfect Marriage 46. My Brother Talks to Horses 46. *It Happened on Fifth Avenue* 47. Ramrod 47. Give My Regards to Broadway 48. The Loveable Cheat 49. *Look for the Silver Lining* 49. Girl on the Subway (TV) 58. All in a Night's Work 61. *The Pleasure of His Company* 61. The Parent Trap 61. Son of Flubber 63. Papa's Delicate Condition 63. *I'd Rather Be Rich* 64. The Ugly Dachshund 66. Follow Me Boys 66.

TV series: The World of Mr Sweeney 53.

✪ For devoting a lifetime of professional experience to the presentation of dapper optimism, and for helping to cheer up several generations of filmgoers. *Trouble in Paradise*.

Ruggles, Wesley (1889–1972).
American director, in Hollywood from 1914. One of the original Keystone Kops: brother of Charles Ruggles.

Wild Honey 22. The Plastic Age 26. Silk Stockings 27. Are These Our Children? 30. *Cimarron* (AAN) 31. No Man of Her Own 32. College Humour 33. *I'm No Angel* 33. Bolero 34. The Gilded Lily 35. Valiant is the Word for Carrie 36. *I Met Him in Paris* 37. True Confession 37. *Sing You Sinners* (& p) 38. Invitation to Happiness 39. My Two Husbands 40. Arizona (& p) 40. Good Morning Doctor 41. Somewhere I'll Find You 42. See Here Private Hargrove 44. London Town (GB) 46, etc.

Rugolo, Pete (1915–).
American composer. Born in Sicily, he was first noted for his jazz arrangements for the Stan Kenton orchestra; he also wrote the music for the 60s TV series *The Fugitive*, and for TV movies.

The Sweet Ride 68. The Story of Pretty Boy Floyd (TV) 74. Chu Chu and the Philly Flash 81. This World, Then the Fireworks 97, etc.

Rühmann, Heinz (1902–1994).
German actor whose films have rarely been seen abroad.

Das Deutsche Mutterherz 26. Drei von der Tankstelle 30. Bomben auf Monte Carlo 31. The Man Who Was Sherlock Holmes 37. Die Feuerzangenbowle 44. The Captain from Kopenick 56. Menschen im Hotel 59. The Good Soldier Schweik 59. Das Schwarze Schaf (as Father Brown) 60. *Ship of Fools* (US) 65. La Bourse et la Vie (Fr.) 65. Maigret und Sein Grosster Fall 66. So Far Away, So Close/In Weiter Ferne, So Nah! 93, etc.

Ruick, Barbara (1932–1974).
American leading actress and singer of the 50s, the daughter of Lurene TUTTLE. Her husbands included actor Robert Horton and composer John WILLIAMS.

I Love Melvin 51. Invitation 52. Carousel 56. California Split 75, etc.

TV series: The College Bowl 50–51. The Jerry Colonna Show 51. The RCA Victor Show 53–54. The Johnny Carson Show 55–56.

Ruiz, Raúl (1941–).
Chilean director and screenwriter who began as a dramatist. Noted for his innovative approach, he went into exile in 1973 and is now based in Paris.

Three Sad Tigers/Tres Tristes Tigres 68. The Penal Colony/La Colonia Penal 71. The Suspended Vocation/La Vocation Suspendue 77. Games/Jeux 79. L'Or Gris 80. On Top of the Whale/Het Dak van de Walvis 82. Bérénice 84. Treasure Island 86. Richard III 86. Life Is a Dream/La Mémoire des Apparances: La Vie Est un Songe 87. The Golden Boat 90. Dark at Noon 92. The Man Who Was Thursday 92. Palomita Blanca 93. The Secret Journey: Lives of Saints and Sinners/Il Viaggio Clandestino: Vite di Santi e Peccatori (wd) 94. Fado, Major and Minor 94. Three Lives and Only One Death 96. Shattered Image (US) 98. The Stranger from Strasbourg/L'Inconnu de Strasbourg (Fr.) (co-w only) 98, many others.

Ruiz-Anchia, Juan (1949–).
Spanish cinematographer, in Hollywood.

Reborn 82. Miss Lonely Hearts 83. Valentina 83. The Stone Boy 83. Maria's Lovers 84. That Was Then . . . This Is Now 85. At Close Range 86. Where the River Runs Black 86. Surrender 87. House of Games 87. The Seventh Sign 88. Things Change 88. Lost Angels 89. The Last of the Finest 90. Naked Tango 90. Liebestraum 91. Dying Young 91. Glengarry Glen Ross 92. A Far Off Place 93. Mr Jones 93. Rudyard Kipling's Jungle Book 94. Two Bits 95. The Adventures of Pinocchio 96. The Disappearance of Garcia Lorca 97, etc.

Rule, Janice (1931–).
American leading lady with stage and TV experience. Now a psychoanalyst. Formerly married to actor Ben Gazzara.

Goodbye My Fancy 51. Holiday for Sinners 52. Rogues' March 53. Gun for a Coward 57. Bell, Book and Candle 58. The Subterraneans 60. Invitation to a Gunfighter 64. *The Chase* 66. Alvarez Kelly 66. The Ambushers 67. The Swimmer 68. Doctors' Wives 71. Gumshoe 71. Welcome to Hard Times 72. Kid Blue 73. Three Women 77. Missing 82, etc.

Ruman, Sig (1884–1967) (Siegfried Rumann).
German character actor, usually of explosive roles, in Hollywood from 1934.

The Wedding Night 35. *A Night at the Opera* 35. *A Day at the Races* 37. *Ninotchka* 39. Bitter Sweet 41. *To Be or Not To Be* 42. The Hitler Gang 44. *A Night in Casablanca* 45. On The Riviera 49. *Stalag* 17 53. The Glenn Miller Story 54. Three-Ring Circus 56. The Wings of Eagles 57. Robin and the Seven Hoods 64. Last of the Secret Agents 66, many others.

Famous line (*To Be or Not To Be*): 'So they call me Concentration Camp Erhardt!'

Runacre, Jenny (1943–).
South African character actress in Britain.

Goodbye Mr Chips 69. Dyn Amo 71. The Creeping Flesh 72. The Final Programme 73. The Mackintosh Man 73. Passenger 75. All Creatures Great and Small 75. Joseph Andrews 77. The Duellists 78. Spectre (TV) 78. The Lady Vanishes 79. The Final Programme 81. That Englishwoman 90, etc.

Runyon, Damon (1884–1946).
Inimitable American chronicler of the ways of a never-never New York inhabited by good-hearted and weirdly-named guys and dolls who speak a highly imaginative brand of English. Among the films based on his stories are *Lady for a Day* 33 (and its remake *Pocketful of Miracles* 61), *The Lemon Drop Kid* 34 and 51, *A Slight Case of Murder* 38 (and *Stop You're Killing Me* 52), *The Big Street* 42, *Guys and Dolls* 55, and *The Bloodhounds of Broadway* 52 and 89.

❝ I am frankly a hired Hessian on the typewriter and have never pretended to be anything else and when I write something I want to know in advance how much I am going to be paid for it and when. – *D.R.*

It is my observation that the rich have all the best of it in this nation and my studies of American History fail to disclose any time when this same situation did not prevail. – *D.R.*

When Damon Runyon died, Broadway wept. It had lost its first citizen, its chronicler and its glorifier. – *Don Iddon*

RuPaul (1967–).
Tall American drag performer and singer, who also became a spokesperson for the cosmetics company M.A.C.

The Brady Bunch Movie 95. Red Ribbon Blues 95, etc.

TV series: The RuPaul Show 96.

Rush, Barbara (1927–).
American leading lady who came to Hollywood from college.

The First Legion 51. When Worlds Collide 51. Flaming Feather 52. It Came from Outer Space 53. Magnificent Obsession 54. The Black Shield of Falworth 54. Captain Lightfoot 55. The World in My Corner 56. Bigger Than Life 57. Oh Men! Oh Women! 58. Harry Black 58. The Young Philadelphians/The City Jungle 59. The Bramble Bush 60. Strangers When We Meet 60. *Come Blow Your Horn* 63. Robin and the Seven Hoods 64. Hombre 67. The Eyes of Charles Sand (TV) 72. Superdad 74. The Last Day (TV) 75. Can't Stop the Music 80. Summer Lovers 82. Between Friends 83, many others.

TV series: Flamingo Road 80–81.

Rush, Geoffrey (1951–).
Australian actor, mainly on the stage, where he also works as a director. Born in Toowoomba, Queensland, he studied at the University of Queensland, and began his acting career with the Queensland Theatre Company in Brisbane. Married actress Jane Menelaus.

Starstruck 82. Twelfth Night 86. Children of the Revolution 96. On Our Selection 96. Call Me Sal 96. *Shine* (AA) 96. Oscar and Lucinda (narrator) 97. Les Misérables 98. Elizabeth 98. Shakespeare in Love 98, etc.

Rush, Richard (1930–).
American director.

■ Too Soon to Love (w, p) 60. Of Love and Desire 63. The Fickle Finger of Fate 67. Hell's Angels on Wheels 67. Thunder Alley 67. A Man Called Dagger 68. Psych-Out 68. The Savage Seven 68. Getting Straight 70. Freebie and the Bean (& p) 74. The Stunt Man (& p) (AAN) 80. Color of Night (d) 94.

Rushing, Jimmy (1902–1972).
Short, rotund American blues and jazz singer, pianist and occasional actor, nicknamed, after one of his songs, 'Mr Five by Five'. Born in Oklahoma, he gained fame working in Kansas City with the orchestras of Bennie Moten and Count Basie, making several soundies and shorts in the 40s with the latter.

Crazy House 43. Top Man 43. The Sound of Jazz (TV) 57. The Learning Tree 69. Monterey Jazz 73, etc.

Rushton, Jared (1974–).
Young American actor.

Overboard 87. Big 88. The Lady in White 88. Honey, I Shrunk the Kids 89. A Cry in the Wild 90. Pet Sematary 2 92, etc.

Rushton, William (1937–1996).
English comic actor, writer, novelist and cartoonist, one of the founders of the satirical magazine *Private Eye* in 1961. Died after complications arising from heart surgery.

AS ACTOR: Nothing but the Best 64. Those Magnificent Men in Their Flying Machines 65. The Best House in London 68. The Bliss of Mrs Blossom 68. Monte Carlo or Bust 69. Flight of the Doves 71. The Adventures of Barry McKenzie 72. Keep It Up Downstairs 76. The Adventures of a Private Eye 77. The Adventures of a Plumber's Mate 78. Consuming Passions 88, etc.

TV series: That Was the Week That Was 63. Up Pompeii 70.

Russell, Billy (1893–1971) (Adam George Brown).
English music-hall comedian and character actor, on stage from the age of seven. His music-hall experience as a tumbler led to his being hired to teach Charles LAUGHTON how to fall down a chute in *Hobson's Choice*.

Take Off That Hat 38. For Freedom 40. The Man in the White Suit 51. Judgement Deferred 52. Negatives 68. I Start Counting 69. Leo the Last 70, etc.

~Catchphrase: On behalf of the working classes.

Russell, Chuck.
American screenwriter and director.

■ Dreamscape (co-w) 84. A Nightmare on Elm Street Part 3: Dream Warriors (co-w, d) 87. The Blob (co-w, d) 88. The Mask (d) 94. Eraser 96.

Russell, Clive.
Scottish leading actor, a former teacher, from the theatre.

Tumbledown (TV) 89. The Grass Arena (TV) 91. Hancock (TV) 91. The Power of One (US) 92. Tell Tale Hearts (TV) 92. Soft Top, Hard Shoulder 92. The Hawk 93. Fatherland (TV) 94. Margaret's Museum (Can.) 95. NeverWhere (TV) 96. Oscar and Lucinda 97, etc.

Russell, Craig (1948–1990).
Canadian actor and female impersonator who had a big hit with his low-budget semi-autobiographical film *Outrageous* 77, featuring his nightclub act. Died of AIDS.

Too Outrageous 86.

Russell, Gail (1924–1961).
American leading lady of the 40s; came to Hollywood straight from dramatic training. Died from alcoholism.

Henry Aldrich Gets Glamour (debut) 43. Lady in the Dark 43. *The Uninvited* 44. Our Hearts Were Young and Gay 44. Salty O'Rourke 45. Night Has a Thousand Eyes 47. Moonrise 48. Wake of the Red Witch 49. Air Cadet 51. The Tattered Dress 57. The Silent Call 61, etc.

Russell, Harold (1914–).
Canadian paratroop sergeant who lost both hands in an explosion during World War II and demonstrated his ability not only to use hooks in their place but to act as well in *The Best Years of Our Lives* 46, for which he won two Oscars. Became a public relations executive. Appeared again 1980 in *Inside Moves*.

Autobiographies: 1949, *Victory in My Hands*. 1981, *The Best Years of My Life*.

Russell, Jane (1921–).
American leading lady who came to Hollywood when an agent sent her photo to producer Howard Hughes; he starred her in *The Outlaw* 43 but it was held up for three years by censor trouble. The publicity campaign emphasized the star's physical attributes.

Autobiography: 1985, *Jane Russell*.

■ The Young Widow 47. *The Paleface* 48. Double Dynamite 50. Macao 51. Montana Belle 51. His Kind of Woman 51. Son of Paleface 52. The Las Vegas Story 52. Gentlemen Prefer Blondes 53. The French Line 54. Underwater 55. Gentlemen Marry Brunettes 55. Foxfire 55. Hot Blood 56. The Tall Men 56. The Revolt of Mamie Stover 57. The Fuzzy Pink Nightgown 57. Fate is the Hunter (guest appearance) 64. Waco 66. Johnny Reno 66. Born Losers 67. Darker than Amber 70. The Yellow Rose (TV) 84.

❝ There are two good reasons why men will go to see her. – *Howard Hughes*

The first time I saw Jane Russell I wondered how she got her kneecaps up in her sweater. – *Fred Allen*

Russell, John (1921–1991).
American 'second lead'.

A Bell for Adano 45. The Fat Man 51. The Sun Shines Bright 53. The Last Command 55. Rio Bravo 59. Fort Utah 66. Cannon for Cordoba 70. Blood Legacy 73. The Changeling 80. The Runaways 84. Under the Gun 88, many others.

TV series: Soldiers of Fortune 55. Lawman 58–62.

Russell, Ken (1927–).
British director, a middle-aged *enfant terrible* of the 70s who after a rigorous training in BBC art films turned out to want to shock people, and did so with flair but no subtlety.

Autobiographies: 1989, *A British Picture*. 1994, *Fire Over England*.

■ French Dressing 64. Billion Dollar Brain 67. *Women In Love* (AAN) 69. *The Music Lovers* 70. The Devils 71. The Boy Friend 71. Savage Messiah 72. Mahler 74. Tommy 75. Lisztomania 75. Valentino 77. Clouds of Glory (TV) 78. Altered States 80. Crimes of Passion 84. Gothic 87. Aria (co-d) 87. The Lair of the White Worm 88. Salome's Last Dance 88. The Rainbow 89. The Russia House (a) 90. Whore 91. Prisoner of Honor (TV) 92. Lady Chatterley (a, d) (TV) 93. Erotic Tales (co-d) 94. Ken Russell's Treasure Island (TV) 95.

❝ This is not the age of manners. This is the age of kicking people in the crotch and telling them something and getting a reaction. I want to shock people into awareness. I don't believe there's any virtue in understatement. – *K.R.*

I know my films upset people. I *want* to upset people. – *K.R.*

Life is too short to make destructive films about people one doesn't like. My films are meant to be constructive and illuminating. – *K.R.*

Mr Ken Russell, the film director who now specializes in vulgar travesties of the lives of dead composers . . . – *Nicholas de Jongh, Guardian*

His originality these days seems to consist of disguising the banal behind a barrage of garish, distorted, noisy and fleeting images looted from every juvenile fantasy from Rider Haggard to *Superman*, with nods to Dali and Bosch, and strong tincture of Kubrick. – *Sunday Times, 1981*

Russell, Kurt (1951–).
American leading man, often in tough-guy roles, and former child actor, frequently in Disney films. He was married to actress Season HUBLEY and has

a son by Goldie HAWN. Current asking price: around $15m a film.

The Absent-Minded Professor 60. Follow Me Boys 66. The Horse in the Grey Flannel Suit 68. Charley and the Angel 73. Superdad 74. *Elvis* (TV) 79. Used Cars 80. Escape from New York 81. The Fox and the Hound (voice) 81. The Thing 82. Silkwood 83. Swing Shift 84. The Mean Season 84. The Best of Times 85. Big Trouble in Little China 86. Overboard 87. Tequila Sunrise 88. Tango & Cash 89. Winter People 89. Backdraft 91. Unlawful Entry 92. Captain Ron 92. Tombstone 93. Stargate 94. Executive Decision 96. Escape from LA 96. Breakdown 97. Soldier 98, etc.

TV series: The Travels of Jamie McPheeters 63–64. The New Land 74. The Quest 76.

Russell, Lillian (1861–1922) (Helen Louise Leonard).
Statuesque American singer-entertainer, highly popular around the turn of the century. Only one film, *Wildfire* (1914); was played by Alice Faye in a 1940 biopic, by Ruth Gillette in *The Great Ziegfeld*, by Andrea King in *My Wild Irish Rose*, and by Binnie Barnes in *Diamond Jim*.

Russell, Reb (1905–1978) (Fay Russell).
American star of 30s westerns, after success as a football full-back. He quit acting at the end of the 30s to become a rancher.

All-American 32. Man From Hell 34. Border Vengeance 35. Lightning Triggers 35. Rough and Tough 36. Outlaw Rule 36. Arizona Badman 42, etc.

Russell, Rosalind (1908–1976).
Dominant American leading lady of the 30s and 40s, usually as career women; later attempted character roles, but her choice was sometimes unwise.

Autobiography: 1977, *Life Is a Banquet*.

■ Evelyn Prentice 34. The President Vanishes 34. West Point of the Air 35. The Casino Murder Case 35. Reckless 35. China Seas 35. Rendezvous 35. Forsaking All Others 35. The Night is Young 35. It Had to Happen 36. Under Two Flags 36. Trouble for Two 36. Craig's Wife 36. *Night Must Fall* 37. Live Love and Learn 37. Manproof 38. *The Citadel* 38. Four's a Crowd 38. Fast and Loose 39. *The Women* 39. *His Girl Friday* 40. No Time for Comedy 40. Hired Wife 40. This Thing Called Love 41. They Met in Bombay 41. The Feminine Touch 41. Design for Scandal 41. Take a Letter Darling 42. *My Sister Eileen* (AAN) 42. Flight for Freedom 43. What a Woman 43. Roughly Speaking 45. She Wouldn't Say Yes 45. Sister Kenny (AAN) 46. The Guilt of Janet Ames 47. Mourning Becomes Electra (AAN) 48. The Velvet Touch 48. Tell it to the Judge 49. A Woman of Distinction 50. Never Wave at a WAC 52. The Girl Rush 55. Picnic 56. *Auntie Mame* (AAN) 58. A Majority of One 61. Gypsy 62. Five-Finger Exercise 62. The Trouble with Angels 66. Oh Dad, Poor Dad 67. Where Angels Go Trouble Follows 68. Rosie 68. The Unexpected Mrs Pollifax 70. The Crooked Hearts (TV) 72.

❝ At MGM there was a first wave of top stars, and a second wave to replace them in case they got difficult. I was in the second line of defence, behind Myrna Loy. – *R.R.*

Success is a public affair. Failure is a private funeral. – *R.R.*

Acting is standing up naked and turning around very slowly. – *R.R.*

Russell, Shirley (1935–).
English costume designer.

Women in Love 69. The Music Lovers 70. The Devils 71. The Boyfriend 71. Savage Messiah 72. Inserts 75. Valentino 77. Yanks 79. Agatha (AAN) 79. Reds (AAN) 81. The Razor's Edge 84. The Bride 85. Hope and Glory 87. Gulliver's Travels (TV) 96. Fairytale: A True Story 97, etc.

Russell, Theresa (1957–).
American leading lady who settled in the UK. She is married to director Nicolas Roeg.

The Last Tycoon 77. Straight Time 78. Bad Timing 80. Eureka 83. The Razor's Edge 84. Insignificance 86. Black Widow 87. Aria 87. Track 29 87. Physical Evidence 88. Impulse 90. Whore 91. Kafka 91. Cold Heaven 92. A Woman's Guide to Adultery (TV) 93. Being Human 94. The Grotesque 95. A Young Connecticut Yankee in King Arthur's Court 95. Public Enemies 96. The Proposition 96. Wild Things 98, etc.

Russell, William D. (1908–1968).
American director.

■ Our Hearts Were Growing Up 46. Ladies' Man 47. *Dear Ruth* 47. The Sainted Sisters 48. The Green Promise 49. Bride for Sale 49. Best of the Badmen 51.

Russell, Willy (1947–).
British dramatist and composer who has adapted his own plays for the screen.

■ *Educating Rita* (AAN) 83. Mr Love (m) 85. *Shirley Valentine* (& m) 89. Dancin' thru the Dark (& m) 91.

Russo, James (1953–).
American actor.

Vortex 81. Fast Times at Ridgemont High 82. Beverly Hills Cop 84. Extremities 86. China Girl 87. Blue Iguana 88. Freeway 88. We're No Angels 89. Illicit Behavior 91. Intimate Stranger 91. A Kiss before Dying 91. My Own Private Idaho 91. Cold Heaven 92. Bad Girls 94. Panther 95. Livers Ain't Cheap 96. American Strays 96. No Way Home 96. The Real Thing 97. The Postman 97. Love to Kill 97, etc.

Russo, Rene (1954–).
American leading actress, a former model.

Major League 89. Mr Destiny 90. One Good Cop 91. Freejack 92. In the Line of Fire 93. Outbreak 95. Get Shorty 95. Ransom 96. Tin Cup 96. Buddy 97. Lethal Weapon 4 98, etc.

TV series: Sable 87–88.

Rustichelli, Carlo (1916–).
Italian composer.

Gran Premio 43. Gioventu Perduta 47. In the Name of the Law 48. Behind Closed Shutters 50. The Road to Hope 50. Black 13 (GB) 53. Il Ferroviere 55. Maledetto Imbroglio 59. Queen of the Nile 61. Mamma Roma 62. Torpedo Bay 63. Blood and Black Lace 64. The Secret War of Harry Frigg 67. Alfredo, Alfredo 71. The Black Hand 73. Le Gang 76. Le Beaujolais Nouveau Est Arrivé 78. Claretta and Ben 83. Heads or Tails 83, many others.

Ruth, Babe (1895–1948).
Legendary big-hitting American baseball player who has been the subject of two biopics, *The Babe Ruth Story*, directed by Roy del Ruth in 1948, starring William Bendix, and *The Babe*, made by Arthur Hiller in 1992, starring John Goodman. He was the model for the character of Roy Hobbs in Bernard Malamud's novel *The Natural*, filmed by Barry Levinson in 1984 with Robert Redford in the role, and appears as a minor character in *The Sandlot/The Sandlot Kids*. He also appeared as himself in a few movies.

Babe Comes Home 26. Speedy 27. The Pride of the Yankees 42, etc.

Rutherford, Ann (1917–).
American leading lady of the 40s, former child stage star.

Love Finds Andy Hardy 38. The Hardys Ride High 39. Gone with the Wind 39. Pride and Prejudice 40. Happy Land 43. Two O'Clock Courage 45. *The Secret Life of Walter Mitty* 47. The Adventures of Don Juan 48. They Only Kill Their Masters 72, etc.

Rutherford, Dame Margaret (1892–1972).
Inimitable, garrulous, shapeless, endearing British comedy character actress, who usually seemed to be playing somebody's slightly dotty spinster aunt. Born in London, she studied at the Royal Academy of Music, and worked as a piano teacher; she was 33 when she began her professional career, studying at the Old Vic School and acting in various repertory theatres. The daughter of a man who had spent seven years in Broadmoor criminal asylum, for killing his father, and a mother who committed suicide, she suffered from several nervous breakdowns, fearing that she, too, might go mad. Married actor Stringer DAVIS in 1945. Her best roles were as Miss Prism in *The Importance of Being Earnest*, Madame Arcati in *Blithe Spirit*, Headmistress Miss Evelyn Whitchurch in *The Happiest Days of Your Life*, and the Duchess of Brighton in *The VIPS*, though her most popular role was probably as Agatha Christie's detective Miss Marple in four films.

Autobiography: 1972, *An Autobiography*.

Biography: 1983, *Margaret Rutherford: A Blithe Spirit* by Dawn Langley Simmons.

■ Talk of the Devil 36. Dusty Ermine 38. Beauty and the Barge 38. Catch as Catch Can 38. Missing Believed Married 38. Quiet Wedding 40. Spring Meeting 41. *The Demi Paradise* 43. Yellow Canary 43. English without Tears 44. *Blithe Spirit* (as Madame Arcati) 45. While the Sun Shines 46. Meet Me at Dawn 47. *Miranda* 47. Passport to Pimlico 48. *The Happiest Days of Your Life* 50. Her Favourite Husband 51. The Magic Box 51. Castle in the Air 51. *The Importance of Being Earnest* 52. Curtain Up 52. Miss Robin Hood 53. Innocents in Paris 53. Trouble in Store 53. The Runaway Bus 54. Mad about Men 55. Aunt Clara 55. An Alligator Named Daisy 56. The Smallest Show on Earth 57. I'm All Right Jack 59. Just My Luck 59. On the Double 61. *Murder She Said* (as Miss Marple) 62. Mouse on the Moon 63. Murder at the Gallop 63. *The VIPs* (AA) 63. Murder Most Foul 63. Murder Ahoy 64. The Alphabet Murders 65. Chimes at Midnight 66. A Countess from Hong Kong 67. Arabella 68.

✪ For being her splendidly eccentric self. *Blithe Spirit*.

❝ You never have a comedian who hasn't got a very deep strain of sadness within him or her. One thing is incidental on the other. Every great clown has been very near to tragedy. – M.R.

Ruttenberg, Joseph (1889–1983).
Russian cinematographer, in Hollywood from 1915.

Over the Hill 28. Fury 36. *The Great Waltz* (AA) 38. *Dr Jekyll and Mr Hyde* 41. *Mrs Miniver* (AA) 42. Madame Curie 43. Adventure 46. BF's Daughter 48. Side Street 49. The Forsyte Saga 49. The Great Caruso 51. Julius Caesar 53. The Last Time I Saw Paris 54. The Swan 56. *Somebody Up There Likes Me* (AA) 56. *Gigi* (AA) 58. The Reluctant Debutante 58. Butterfield 8 60. Bachelor in Paradise 61. Who's Been Sleeping in My Bed? 63. Sylvia 63. Harlow 65. Love Has Many Faces 65. The Oscar 66. Speedway 68, many others.

Ruttman, Walter (1887–1941).
German director most famous for his experimental film *Berlin* 27.

Weekend 30. Mannesmann 37. Deutsche Panzer 40, etc.

Ruven, Paul (1958–).
Dutch director and screenwriter, a former actor.

Naughty Boys 83. Max and Laura and Henk and Willie (co-d) 89. Let the Music Dance (w) 90. The Night of the Wild Donkeys (w) 91. How to Survive a Broken Heart (co-w, d) 91. Sur Place (wd) 96, etc.

Ruysdael, Basil (1888–1960).
Authoritative Russian-American character actor, former opera singer.

The Coconuts 29. Come to the Stable 49. Broken Arrow 50. My Forbidden Past 51. Carrie 52. The Blackboard Jungle 56. The Last Hurrah 58. The Story of Ruth 60, many others.

Ryan, Frank (1907–1947).
American director.

Hers to Hold 43. Can't Help Singing 44. Patrick the Great 45. A Genius in the Family 46, etc.

Ryan, Irene (1903–1973) (Irene Riordan).
Wiry American comedienne, was famous as Granny in TV's *The Beverly Hillbillies*.

Melody for Three 41. San Diego I Love You 44. Diary of a Chambermaid 45. Meet Me after the Show 51. Blackbeard the Pirate 52. Spring Reunion 57, etc.

Ryan, John P. (1938–).
American leading man.

The Tiger Makes Out 65. Five Easy Pieces 70. The King of Marvin Gardens 72. Shamus 72. Dillinger 73. Cops and Robbers 73. It's Alive 75. The Missouri Breaks 76. Futureworld 76. It Lives Again 79. The Cotton Club 84. The Runaway Train 85. Avenging Force 86. Rent-a-Cop 88. Class of 1999 89. Best of the Best 89. Delta Force 2: Operation Stranglehold 90. Eternity 90. The Inner Circle 91. Hoffa 92. Young Goodman Brown 93. CIA 2: Target Alexa 94. Bound 96, etc.

Ryan, Kathleen (1922–1985).
Irish leading lady with stage experience.

Odd Man Out (debut) 47. Captain Boycott 47. Esther Waters 48. Give Us This Day 50. The Yellow Balloon 52. Captain Lightfoot 53. Laxdale Hall 53. *Jacqueline* 56. Sail into Danger 58, etc.

Ryan, Madge (1919–1994).
Australian character actress of stage and screen, in Britain from the mid-50s. She was a member of the National Theatre in the 60s, where her roles included *Mother Courage*.

The Strange Affair 68. I Start Counting 69. A Clockwork Orange 71. Endless Night 71. Frenzy 72. Who Is Killing the Great Chefs of Europe?/Too Many Chefs 78. The Lady Vanishes 80, etc.

Ryan, Meg (1961–).
American leading actress who began acting to help pay for her university studies in journalism. She married actor Dennis Quaid in 1991. Her asking price in 1995: around $6m a film.

Rich and Famous 81. Amityville 3-D 83. Armed and Dangerous 86. Top Gun 86. Innerspace 87. Promised Land 88. DOA 88. Presidio 88. *When Harry Met Sally* 89. Joe versus the Volcano 90. The Doors 91. Prelude to a Kiss 92. *Sleepless in Seattle* 93. Flesh and Bone 93. When a Man Loves a Woman 94. I.Q. 94. French Kiss 95. Restoration 95. Courage under Fire 96. Addicted to Love 97. City of Angels 98. Hurlyburly 98. You've Got Mail 98, etc.

TV series: One of the Boys 82. Wildside 85.

Ryan, Mitchell (Mitch) (1928–).
Stalwart American character actor, mostly on TV.

Robert Kennedy & His Times (TV) 85. Northstar 86. Lethal Weapon 87. Winter People 89. Aces: Iron Eagle III 92. Dirty Work 92. Hot Shots! Part Deux 93. Speechless 94. Blue Sky 94. Halloween: The Curse of Michael Myers 95. Judge Dredd 95. Ed 96. The Devil's Own 97. Liar Liar 97. Grosse Pointe Blank 97, etc.

TV series: Chase 73–74. Executive Suite 76–77. Having Babies 78–79. The Chisholms 80. High Performance 83. All My Children 85–87. Santa Barbara 89. Dharma & Greg 97.

Ryan, Peggy (1924–).
American teenage comedienne of the early 40s, often teamed with Donald O'Connor. In vaudeville from childhood.

Top of the Town 37. Give Out Sisters 42. Top Man 43. The Merry Monahans 44. Bowery to Broadway 44. That's the Spirit 43. On Stage Everybody 45. All Ashore 52, etc.

TV series: Hawaii Five-O 69–76.

Ryan, Robert (1909–1973).
Strong-featured American leading actor who never seemed to get the roles he deserved.

Biography: 1990, *Robert Ryan* by Franklin Jarlet.

■ Golden Gloves 40. Queen of the Mob 40. Northwest Mounted Police 40. Texas Rangers Ride Again 41. The Feminine Touch 41. Bombardier 43. *Gangway for Tomorrow* 43. The Sky's the Limit 43. Behind the Rising Sun 43. The Iron Major 43. Tender Comrade 43. The Hitler Gang 44. Marine Raiders 44. The Walls Came Tumbling Down 46. Trail Street 47. The Woman on the Beach 47. *Crossfire* (AAN) 47. Berlin Express 48. Return of the Badmen 48. The Boy with Green Hair 48. Act of Violence 49. Caught 49. *The Set-Up* 49. The Woman on Pier 13 49. The Secret Fury 50. Born to be Bad 50. Best of the Badmen 51. Flying Leathernecks 51. The Racket 51. On Dangerous Ground 51. Hard Fast and Beautiful 51. *Clash by Night* 52. Beware My Lovely 52. Horizons West 52. City beneath the Sea 53. The Naked Spur 53. Inferno 53. Alaska Seas 54. About Mrs Leslie 54. Her Twelve Men 54. Bad Day at Black Rock 55. Escape to Burma 55. House of Bamboo 55. The Tall Men 55. The Proud Ones 56. Back from Eternity 56. Men in War 57. *God's Little Acre* 58. Lonelyhearts 59. Day of the Outlaw 59. *Odds against Tomorrow* 59. Ice Palace 60. The Canadians 61. King of Kings 61. The Longest Day 62. *Billy Budd* 62. The Crooked Road 65. Battle of the Bulge 65. The Dirty Game 66. The Professionals 66. The Busy Body 67. The Dirty Dozen 67. Hour of the Gun 67. Custer of the West 67. Dead or Alive 67. Anzio 68. Captain Nemo and the Underwater City 68. The Wild Bunch 69. Lawman 71. The Love Machine 71. The Man Without a Country (TV) 72. And Hope to Die 72. The Iceman Cometh 73. Executive Action 73. Lolly Madonna XXX 73. The Outfit 74.

Ryan, Sheila (1921–1975) (Katherine McLaughlin).
American leading lady in 'B' films of the 40s and
50s. Married Pat Buttram in 1952, after they met
while making Gene Autry's *Mule Train*.

The Gay Caballero 40. Sun Valley Serenade 41.
The Gang's All Here 41. Pardon My Stripes 42.
Careful, Soft Shoulders 42. Song of Texas 43.
Something for the Boys 44. Getting Gertie's
Garter 45. Lone Wolf in London 46. The Big Fix
47. Caged Fury 48. The Cowboy and the Indians
49. Mule Train 50. Mask of the Dragon 51. On
Top of Old Smoky 53. Street of Darkness 58, etc.

Ryan, Tim (1889–1956).
American comedy supporting actor, very adept at
drunks, wisecracking reporters, dumb cops, etc.

Brother Orchid 40. The Mystery of the
Thirteenth Guest 43. Crazy Knights 45. The
Shanghai Chest 48. Sky Dragon 49. Cuban Fireball
51. From Here to Eternity 53. Fighting Trouble 56,
etc.

Rydell, Bobby (1942–).
American pop star who appeared to no great
advantage in *Bye Bye Birdie* 63.

Rydell, Christopher.
American actor, the son of director Mark Rydell.

On Golden Pond 81. Gotcha! 85. Mask 85. How
I Got into College 89. Blood and Sand (Sp.) 89.

Side Out 90. For the Boys 91. Trauma 93. Flesh
and Bone 93, etc.

Rydell, Mark (1934–).
American director.
■ The Fox 68. The Reivers 69. The Cowboys (&
p) 72. Cinderella Liberty (& p) 74. Harry and
Walter Go to New York (& p) 76. The Rose 79.
On Golden Pond (AAN) 81. The River 84. For the
Boys 91. Intersection 94. Crime of the Century
(TV) 96.
AS ACTOR: Crime in the Streets 56. The Long
Goodbye 73. Punchline 88. Havana 89, etc.

Ryder, Winona (1971–) (Winona Horowitz).
American leading actress, so far at her best in
intense teenage roles. Born in Winona, Minnesota,
and raised partly in a Californian commune, she
began acting in the theatre as a 13-year-old. She
was engaged to actor Johnny DEPP, and has been
romantically linked with actor Matt DAMON.
Biographies: 1997, *Winona Ryder* by US
Magazine; 1997, *Winona Ryder* by Dave Thompson;
1997, *Winona Ryder* by Nigel Goodall.
Lucas 86. Square Dance 87. Heathers 88.
Beetlejuice 88. 1969 89. Great Balls of Fire 89.
Mermaids 90. Edward Scissorhands 90. Welcome
Home, Roxy Carmichael 91. Night on Earth 92.
Bram Stoker's Dracula 92. The Age of Innocence
(AAN) 93. The House of the Spirits 94. Reality

Bites 94. Little Women (AAN) 94. How to Make
an American Quilt 95. Looking for Richard 96.
The Crucible 96. Alien: Resurrection 97. Celebrity
98, etc.

Rylance, Mark (1960–).
English leading actor, from the Royal Shakespeare
Company. He is artistic director of London's
Globe Theatre, a re-creation of an Elizabethan
playhouse.
Love Lies Bleeding (TV) 93. The Institute
Benjamenta 95. Angels and Insects 95. Loving (TV)
96, etc.

Rymer, Michael.
Australian director and screenwriter whose first
film won seven Australian Film Institute awards,
including best film, direction and original
screenplay.
Angel Baby 95. Allie and Me 97, etc.

Ryskind, Morrie (1895–1985).
American comedy writer. Born in New York, he
studied at the Columbia School of Journalism and
collaborated with George S. KAUFMAN on the
MARX BROTHERS' early Broadway successes,
Cocoanuts and *Animal Crackers*. He shared a
Pulitzer Prize with Kaufman and Ira GERSHWIN
for the musical *Of Thee I Sing* 31. A socialist in
his earlier life, he moved to the extreme right and

gave friendly testimony at the HUAC investigation
of Hollywood in the late 40s.
Animal Crackers 30. Palmy Days 31. *A Night at
the Opera* 35. My Man Godfrey (AAN) 36. Stage
Door (AAN) 37. Room Service 38. Man about
Town 39. Penny Serenade 41. Where Do We Go
from Here? 45. Heartbeat 46, etc.

Ryu, Chishu (1906–1993).
Japanese leading actor, a regular in the films of Ozu
from 1928, often as a kindly but distracted father.
The Dreams of Youth/Wakoudo no Yume 28. I
Flunked, but . . ./Rakudai Wa Shita Keredo 30. I
Was Born but . . ./Umarete Wa Mita Keredo 32.
College Is a Nice Place/Daigaku Yoi Toko 36. The
Only Son/Hitori Masuko 36. The Brothers and
Sisters of the Toda Family/Tode-ke no Kyodai 41.
There Was a Father/Chichi Ariki 42. The Record
of a Tenement Gentleman/Nagaya no Shinshi Roku
47. A Hen in the Wind/Kaze no Naka no Mendori
48. Late Spring/Banshun 49. The Munekata
Sisters/Munekata Shimai 50. Early Summer/
Bakushu 51. Tokyo Story/Tokyo Monogatari 53.
Early Spring/Soshun 56. Twilight in Tokyo/Tokyo
Boshoku 57. Ohayo 59. Late Autumn/Akibiyori
60. An Autumn Afternoon/Samma no Aji 62. Red
Beard/Akahige 67. The Funeral 85. Tokyo-ga 85.
Akira Kurosawa's Dreams 90. Luminous Moss/
Hikarigoke 91. Until the End of the World/Bis
ans Ende der Welt 91, etc.

S

Sabatini, Rafael (1875–1950).
Anglo-Italian author of swashbuckling historical novels, several of which have been filmed more than once: *The Sea Hawk*, *Scaramouche*, *Captain Blood*, *The Black Swan*, *Bardelys the Magnificent*, etc.

Sabbatini, Enrico (1932–1998).
Italian costume designer, in international productions.
A Place for Lovers 68. Sunflowers 69. Sacco and Vanzetti 71. Giordano Bruno 73. Moses 76. A Special Day 77. Jesus of Nazareth (TV) 78. Marco Polo (TV) 82. The Mission (AAN) 86. Chronicle of a Death Foretold 86. Old Gringo 89. To Forget Palermo/Dimenticare Palermo 90. Samson and Delilah (TV) 96, etc.

Sabu (1924–1963) (Sabu Dastagir).
Boyish Indian actor, a stable lad in Mysore when he was noticed by director Robert Flaherty and appeared in *Elephant Boy* 37. Came to England, later America.
■ The Drum 38. *The Thief of Baghdad* 40. *The Jungle Book* 42. Arabian Nights 42. White Savage 43. Cobra Woman 44. Tangier 46. Black Narcissus 46. *The End of the River* 47. Maneater of Kumaon 48. Song of India 49. Hello, Elephant 52. Jaguar 56. Herrin der Welt (Ger.) 60. Rampage 63. A Tiger Walks 63.
❝ Sabu, his little brown body in nothing but a tight-fitting breech cloth, was a perfect thing of beauty. – *Frances Flaherty*
His mother died when he was a baby. His father taught his elephant to rock the baby's cradle – to rock the baby himself in his trunk. It is even said that a wild elephant came out of the forest and played with the child. – *Frances Flaherty*
Famous line (*The Thief of Baghdad*): 'I'm Abu the thief, son of Abu the thief, grandson of Abu the thief, most unfortunate of ten sons, with a hunger that yearns day and night.'

Sackheim, Jerry.
American screenwriter.
The Night Before the Divorce 42. The Last Crooked Mile 46. The Strange Door 51. Paula 52. The Black Castle 52. Young Jesse James 60, etc.

Sackheim, William B. (1919–).
American writer and producer.
Smart Girls Don't Talk 48. A Yank in Korea 51. Column South 53. Border River 54. The Human Jungle 54. Tanganyika 54. The Competition (p) 80. First Blood 82. The Survivors (p) 83. No Small Affair (p) 84. The Hard Way (p) 90. Pacific Heights (p) 90. The Hard Way (p) 91. White Sands (p) 92, etc.

Sadoul, Georges (1904–1967).
French film critic and historian; he published two useful reference works, *Dictionnaire des Films* and *Dictionnaire des Cinéastes*.

Safan, Craig.
American composer who has also scored many television movies and mini-series.
The Great Smokey Roadblock 76. The Bad News Bears in Breaking Training 77. Corvette Summer 78. Good Guys Wear Black 79. Fade to Black 80. Nightmares 83. The Last Starfighter 84. The Legend of Billie Jean 85. The Stranger 87. Nightmare on Elm Street Part 4: The Dream Warriors 88. Stand and Deliver 88. Enid Is Sleeping 90. Major Payne 95. Mr Wrong 96, etc.

Safran, Henri (1932–).
French-born director in Australia.
Elephant Boy 75. Storm Boy 76. Norman Loves Rose (wd) 82. The Wild Duck 83. Prince and the Great Race/Bush Christmas 83. The Red Crescent 87, etc.

Sagal, Boris (1923–1981).
American director, from TV.
■ Dime with a Halo 63. Twilight of Honor 64. Girl Happy 65. Made in Paris 66. The Thousand Plane Raid 69. Night Gallery (co-d) (TV) 69. Destiny of a Spy (TV) 69. U.M.C. (TV) 69. The Movie Murderer (TV) 70. Hauser's Memory (TV) 70. Mosquito Squadron 70. The Omega Man 71. Hitched (TV) 71. The Failing of Raymond (TV) 71. Deliver Us from Evil (TV) 73. A Case of Rape (TV) 74. The Greatest Gift (TV) 74. Indict and Convict (TV) 74. The Dream Makers (TV) 75. Man on the Outside (TV) 75. The Runaway Barge (TV) 75. The Oregon Trail (TV) 76. Mallory 76. Three for the Road 76. Ike (co-d) (TV) 78. Masada (TV) 81.
TV series as executive producer: T.H.E. Cat 67.

Sagan, Françoise (1935–) (F. Quoirez).
French novelist very popular in the late 50s. Works filmed include *Bonjour Tristesse*, *A Certain Smile*, *Aimez-Vous Brahms?/Goodbye Again*.

Sagan, Leontine (1899–1974) (Leontine Schlesinger).
Austrian director who emigrated to England after her first film, made one film for Korda, and spent the remainder of her life in South Africa, where she had lived as a child, working in the theatre.
■ Maedchen in Uniform 31. Men of Tomorrow 32.

Sägebrecht, Marianne (1945–).
Plump German character actress, associated with the films of director Percy Adlon; she became a star with *Bagdad Café*.
Irrsee 84. Sugarbaby/Zuckerbaby 85. Crazy Boys 87. Bagdad Café 87. Moon over Parador 88. Rosalie Goes Shopping 89. War of the Roses 89. Martha and I/Martha und Ich 91. The Milky Way/La Vida Lactea 92. Dust Devil: The Final Cut (GB) 93. Mona Must Die (US) 94. The Ogre 96. Left Luggage (Hol.) 98, etc.

Sahl, Mort (1927–).
Sardonic American political comedian fashionable in early 60s. Films untypical.
In Love and War 58. All the Young Men 60. Don't Make Waves 67. Doctor You've Got to Be Kidding 68. Nothing Lasts Forever 84, etc.
❝ My life needs editing. – M.S.

Saint, Eva Marie (1924–).
Cool, intelligent American stage actress who played heroine in a variety of films.
On the Waterfront (AA) 54. That Certain Feeling 56. *A Hatful of Rain* 57. Raintree County 57. North by Northwest 59. Exodus 60. All Fall Down 62. 36 Hours 64. The Sandpiper 65. The Russians are Coming, The Russians are Coming 66. Grand Prix 66. The Stalking Moon 68. A Talent for Loving 69. Loving 70. Cancel My Reservation 72. A Christmas to Remember (TV) 78. The Curse of King Tutankhamun's Tomb (TV) 80. The Best Little Girl in the World (TV) 82. Malibu (TV) 83. Jane Doe (TV) 83. Fatal Vision (TV) 84. The Last Days of Patton (TV) 86. Nothing in Common 86. Breaking Home Ties (TV) 87. I'll Be Home for Christmas (TV) 88. People Like Us (TV) 90. My Antonia (TV) 95. Titanic (TV) 96, etc.
TV series: How the West Was Won 76.

St Clair, Malcolm (Mal) (1897–1952).
American director with a reputation for style in the 20s; in the 40s however he almost ruined the reputation of Laurel and Hardy.
Find Your Man 24. On Thin Ice 25. A Woman of the World 25. *The Grand Duchess and the Waiter* 26. Breakfast at Sunrise 27. *Gentlemen Prefer Blondes* 28. The Canary Murder Case 29. Dangerous Nan McGrew 30. The Boudoir Diplomat 30. Olsen's Big Moment 33. She Had to Eat 37. A Trip to Paris 38 (and several other Jones Family episodes 36–40). Hollywood Cavalcade 39. Man in the Trunk 42. Over My Dead Body 42. Jitterbugs 43. The Dancing Masters 43. The Big Noise 44. The Bullfighters 45, etc.

St Cyr, Renée (1907–) (Marie-Louise Vittore).
French leading lady of the 30s.
Les Deux Orphelines 33. Le Dernier Millardaire 34. Les Perles de la Couronne 37. Strange Boarders (UK) 38. La Symphonie Fantastique 42. Pierre et Jean 43. Pamela 45. Le Chevalier de la Nuit 54. Lafayette 71. On Aura Tout Vu 76. Room Service 92, etc.

Saint-Exupéry, Antoine de (1900–1944).
French aviator and writer. His *The Little Prince* was disappointingly filmed. His *Night Freight* was the basis of *Night Flight* (1933) and also of *Only Angels Have Wings* (1939). He was played by Bruno Ganz in the biopic *Saint-Ex* 95.

St Jacques, Raymond (1930–1990) (James Johnson).
American leading man. Born in Hartford, Connecticut, he studied psychology at Yale and worked in the theatre and television before entering films. Died of cancer.
Black like Me (debut) 64. Mister Moses 65. Mister Buddwing 66. The Comedians 67. The Green Berets 68. If He Hollers Let Him Go 68. Uptight 68. Change of Mind 70. Cotton Comes to Harlem 70. The Book of Numbers (& pd) 73. Lost in the Stars 73. Born Again 78. The Private Files of J. Edgar Hoover 78. The Evil that Men Do 84. The Wild Pair 87. Glory 89. Voodoo Dawn 89. Timebomb 91, etc.
TV series: Rawhide 65–66. Roots 77. Falcon Crest 83–84.

Saint James, Susan (1946–) (Susan Miller).
American leading lady of the 70s, who is mostly seen on TV playing slightly kooky but determined young ladies.
PJ 68. Where Angels Go Trouble Follows 68. The Magic Carpet (TV) 72. Love at First Bite 79. How to Beat the High Cost of Living 80. Carbon Copy 81. Don't Cry, It's Only Thunder 81, etc.
TV series: *The Name of the Game* 68–71. *McMillan and Wife* 71–75. Kate and Allie 84–89.

St John, Al 'Fuzzy' (1893–1963).
American character comedian, best known for his enduring role as Fuzzy Q. Jones, a pop-eyed, bewhiskered sidekick in second-feature westerns, who provided comic relief alongside such clean-cut heroes of the genre as George Houston, Lash La Rue, Addison 'Jack' Randall, Fred Scott and Bob Steele. Born in Santa Ana, California, he worked in vaudeville and circus and began as a slapstick comedian in Mack Sennett's shorts in 1913, was a Keystone Kop, a rustic stooge to his uncle Fatty Arbuckle in many movies, and also wrote, directed and starred in comic shorts for Paramount and Fox, often featuring his trick cyclist act, before settling into his western groove from the late 20s to his retirement in 1950.
Mabel's Strange Predicament 13. Special Delivery 27. Dance of Life 29. Wanderer of the Wasteland 35. Call of the Yukon 37. Arizona Terrors 42. Frontier Revenge 49, many others.
TV series: Lash of the West (movies re-edited for TV) 52–53.

St John, Betta (1930–) (Betty Streidler).
American leading lady with stage experience.
Dream Wife (debut) 53. The Robe 53. The Student Prince 54. The Naked Dawn 55. High Tide at Noon (GB) 57. Tarzan the Magnificent (GB) 60. City of the Dead (GB) 61, etc.

St John, Howard (1905–1974).
American character actor on stage from 1925, films from 1948, usually as father, executive or military commander.
Born Yesterday 50. David Harding, Counterspy 50. Counterspy Meets Scotland Yard 51. The Tender Trap 55. *Li'l Abner* 59. Straitjacket 63. Sex and the Single Girl 64. Strange Bedfellows 65. Don't Drink the Water 69, many others.

St John, Jill (1940–) (Jill Oppenheim).
American leading lady. Her third husband was singer Jack Jones (1967–69) and her fourth actor Robert Wagner.
Summer Love 57. The Lost World 60. Come Blow Your Horn 62. Who's Been Sleeping in My Bed? 63. The Liquidator (GB) 65. The Oscar 66. Eight on the Lam 67. Banning 67. Tony Rome 67. Diamonds are Forever 71. Sitting Target 72. The Act 84. Out There (TV) 95, etc.
❝ I like Jill because she doesn't want to be an actress. She wants to be a movie star. – *Lance Reventlow (her husband at the time)*

St Johns, Adela Rogers (1893–1988).
Sharp-spoken American journalist who also scripted a few 30s films including *A Free Soul* and *What Price Hollywood* (AAN) 31.
Autobiography: 1978, *Love, Laughter and Tears*.

Sakall, S. Z. (1884–1955) (Eugene Gero Szakall).
Hungarian character actor with vaudeville and stage experience. In films from 1916, Hollywood from 1939; became popular comic support and was nicknamed 'Cuddles'.
Autobiography: 1953, *The Story of Cuddles*.
It's a Date 40. Ball of Fire 41. Casablanca 42. *Thank Your Lucky Stars* 43. *Wonder Man* 45. Cinderella Jones 46. Whiplash 48. Tea for Two 50. The Student Prince 54, many others.

Sakamoto, Ryuichi (1952–).
Japanese composer, rock musician, actor and leader of the 80s group Yellow Magic Orchestra.
Merry Christmas, Mr Lawrence (a, m) 83. Brand New Day (a) 87. The Last Emperor (a, m) (AAm) 87. Black Rain (s) 89. The Handmaid's Tale (m) 90. The Sheltering Sky 91. Marathon (m) 93. Little Buddha (m) 93. Snake Eyes (m) 98. New Rose Hotel (a) 98, etc.

Sakata, Harold (1920–1982).
Korean character actor who sprang to fame in *Goldfinger* 63 as the villainous Oddjob, but despite wearing the same gear around Hollywood for a number of years never got another substantial role.

Saks, Gene (1921–).
American director, from Broadway.
■ Barefoot in the Park 67. The Odd Couple 67. Cactus Flower 70. Last of the Red Hot Lovers 72. Mame 74. The Prisoner of 2nd Avenue (a only) 74. The One and Only (a) 78. Brighton Beach Memoirs 87. Tchin-Tchin 91.

Salce, Luciano (1922–1989).
Italian director.
Le Pillole d'Ercole 60. Crazy Desire/La Voglia Matta 62. The Hours of Love 63. High Infidelity (co-d) 64. Kiss the Other Sheik/Oggi, Domani e Dopodomani (co-d) 65. Slalom 65. El Greco 66. Colpo di Stato 69. Il Provinciale 71. Tragico

Fantozzi 75. Il Secondo Tragico Fantozzi 76. The Innocents Abroad 83. Quelli dell Casco 88, etc.

Sale, Charles (Chic) (1885–1936).
American character actor who specialized in grizzled old men.
Star Witness 31. Men of America 32. When a Fellow Needs a Friend 33. *Treasure Island* (as Ben Gunn) 34. Stranger in Town 36, etc.
~Sale was also the author of a best-selling small book called *The Specialist*, about a man building an outdoor lavatory, compiled from his vaudeville act.

Sale, Richard (1911–1993).
Prolific American writer of stories and screenplays, none very memorable.
Rendezvous with Annie 46. Spoilers of the North (d only) 47. A Ticket to Tomahawk 49. Meet Me after the Show 51. Half Angel (d only) 51. Let's Make It Legal (d only) 51. My Wife's Best Friend (d only) 52. Suddenly 54. Woman's World 54. Gentlemen Marry Brunettes (& wrote words and music and co-p) 55. Seven Waves Away (& d) 56. The White Buffalo 77. Assassination 87, etc.

Sales, Soupy (1926–) (Milton Hines).
American entertainer, popular on children's TV. Film debut in *Birds Do It* 66.

Salkin, Leo (1913–1993).
Canadian-born animator, writer and director for Disney and UPA, who was also the model for the cartoon character Mr Magoo.
Pigs Is Pigs (AANw) 54. The 2000 Year Old Man (d) 75, etc.

Salkind, Alexander (1915–1997).
Russian producer who moves somewhat mysteriously in international circles.
■ The Trial 62. The Light at the Edge of the World 71. The Three Musketeers 73. Superman 77. Superman 2 80. Superman 3 82. Supergirl 83. Santa Claus 84. Christopher Columbus: The Discovery 92.
❝ I don't want to meet actors, they don't impress me. – *A.S.*

Salkow, Sidney (1909–).
American director of second features from the mid-30s.
Woman Doctor 39. Café Hostess 40. The Lone Wolf Strikes 40 (and others in this series). The Adventures of Martin Eden 42. Millie's Daughter 46. Bulldog Drummond at Bay 47. Shadow of the Eagle (GB) 50. Sitting Bull 52. The Golden Hawk 52. Jack McCall, Desperado 53. Raiders of the Seven Seas 53. Chicago Confidential 57. Twice Told Tales 63. The Great Sioux Massacre 65, many others.

Sallis, Peter (1921–).
Bemused-looking British character actor, often in 'little man' roles. He is the voice of Wallace, the lugubrious hero, along with his dog Gromit, of Nick Park's animated films *The Wrong Trousers*, *A Close Shave*, etc.
Anastasia 56. The Doctor's Dilemma 58. Saturday Night and Sunday Morning 60. Charlie Bubbles 67. Inadmissible Evidence 68. Who Is Killing the Great Chefs of Europe? 78, many others.
TV series: *Last of the Summer Wine* 73–95.

Salmi, Albert (1928–1990).
Chubby American character actor, mainly on stage. Committed suicide after killing his terminally ill wife.
The Brothers Karamazov 58. The Unforgiven 59. Wild River 60. The Ambushers 67. The Deserter 70. Lawman 71. The Take 74. Empire of the Ants 77. Black Oak Conspiracy 77. Viva Knievel 77. Brubaker 80. St Helens 81. Hard to Hold 84. Born American 86. Breaking In 89, etc.
TV series: Daniel Boone 63. Petrocelli 73.

Salomon, Mikael.
Danish cinematographer, now working in Hollywood.
Fantasterne 67. Et Doegn Med Ilse 71. Welcome to the Club 71. Z.P.G. 72. De Fen 74. Why? 77. Elvis, Elvis 82. Peter von Scholten 85. The Wolf at the Door 86. Zelly and Me 88. Torch Song Trilogy 88. Stealing Heaven 89. The Abyss (AAN) 89. Always 89. Arachnophobia 90. Backdraft 91. Far and Away 92. A Far Off Place (d only) 93, etc.

Salt, Jennifer (1944–).
American leading lady, daughter of Waldo Salt.
Midnight Cowboy 69. Hi Mom 69. The Revolutionary 70. Brewster McCloud 70. Play It Again Sam 72. Sisters 73. The Great Niagara (TV) 74, etc.
TV series: Soap 78–80.

Salt, Waldo (1914–1987).
American screenwriter.
The Shopworn Angel 38. Tonight We Raid Calais 43. Mr Winkle Goes to War 44. Rachel and the Stranger 48. The Flame and the Arrow 50. Taras Bulba 62. Flight from Ashiya 64. Midnight Cowboy (AA) 68. The Gang That Couldn't Shoot Straight 72. Serpico 73. The Day of the Locust 75. Coming Home (AA) 78, etc.

Salter, Hans J. (1896–1994).
German composer in Hollywood.
Call a Messenger 39. It Started with Eve 41. The Mummy's Tomb 42. The Spoilers 42. Frankenstein Meets the Wolf Man 43. Sherlock Holmes Faces Death 44. Scarlet Street 45. The Web 47. The Reckless Moment 49. The Prince Who was a Thief 51. The Far Horizons 55. The Mole People 56. Raw Wind in Eden 58. Come September 61. Hitler 62. Bedtime Story 64. Beau Geste 66. Gunpoint 66. Return of the Gunfighter (TV) 67, many others.

Salter, James (1925–).
American director, screenwriter, and novelist. He began by making a series of television documentaries on the circus.
The Hunters (oa) 58. The Appointment (w) 65. Downhill Racer (w) 68. Three (wd) 70. Threshold (w) 83, etc.
The difficulty in the way our system works is that one often becomes committed to a completely worthless thing but pursues it with just as much ardour as it if were something good. – *J.S.*

Saltzman, Harry (1915–1994).
Canadian-born independent producer with TV experience. Very successful in Britain with *Look Back in Anger*, the James Bond films, *The Ipcress File*, *The Battle of Britain*, etc.
❝ He had a perfect mogul's figure – stocky, tubby – crinkly grey hair and the face of an eager coarse cherub. – *Tony Richardson*
See also: Woodfall Films.

Salva, Victor (1957–).
American director and screenwriter.
Clownhouse (d) 87. Nature of the Beast (d) 94. Powder (wd) 95.

Salvatores, Gabriele (1950–).
Italian director, from the theatre.
Sogno di una Notte d'Estate 82. Kamikazen – Ultima Notte a Milano 87. Marrakech Express 88. Turné 89. Mediterraneo 91. Puerto Escondido 93. Sud 93. Nirvana 97, etc.

Salzedo, Leonard (1921–).
British composer, mainly for Hammer productions.
The Glass Cage/The Glass Tomb 55. Women without Men 56. The Steel Bayonet 57. The Revenge of Frankenstein 58, etc.

Samms, Emma (1960–) (Emma Samuelson).
English starlet who went to America in 1980 and found success on TV.
Arabian Adventure 79. The Lady and the Highwayman (TV) 89. Boyfriend from Hell/The Shrimp on the Barbie 90. Fatal Inheritance 91. Illusions 91. Delirious 91. Star Quest 94. Humanoids from the Deep 96, etc.
TV series: General Hospital 80–83, 92– . Dynasty 85. The Colbys 86–89.

Samoilova, Tatania (1934–).
Russian leading actress.
The Cranes Are Flying 57. The Letter that Was Not Sent 60. Anna Karenina 67, etc.

Sampson, Will (1934–1987).
American (part Indian) character actor. Died following a heart and lung transplant.
One Flew over the Cuckoo's Nest 75. The Outlaw Josey Wales 76. Buffalo Bill and the Indians 76. The White Buffalo 77. Orca 77. Alcatraz: the Whole Shocking Story 78. Insignificance 86.
TV series: Vegas 78.

Samuelson, G. B. (1889–1947).
Pioneer British director, producer and distributor of mainly silent films. His sons David, Sydney, Anthony and Michael, three of whom worked as cameramen, developed what became the world's largest audio-visual equipment rental organization. The company's founder, Sir Sydney Samuelson (1925–), served from 1991–1997 as the first commissioner of the British Film Commission. The daughter of Michael Samuelson (1931–1998) is actress Emma Sams.
A Study in Scarlet 14. Little Women 17. Hindle Wakes 18. Quinneys 19. The Last Rose of Summer 21. Should a Doctor Tell? 23. She 25, many others.

San Giacomo, Laura (1962–).
American actress.
Miles from Home 88. sex, lies and videotape 89. Pretty Woman 89. Quigley Down Under 90. Vital Signs 90. Once Around 90. Under Suspicion 91. Where the Day Takes You 92. Nina Takes a Lover 94. The Stand (TV) 94. Stuart Saves His Family 95. The Right to Remain Silent (TV) 95. The Apocalypse 96. Suicide Kings 98, etc.

San Juan, Olga (1927–).
Vivacious American dancer and comedienne, with radio experience. She married actor Edmond O'Brien.
Rainbow Island 44. Blue Skies 46. The Beautiful Blonde from Bashful Bend 49. Countess of Monte Cristo 49. The Third Voice 60, etc.

Sanchez-Gijon, Aitana (1968–).
Spanish leading actress, in international films.
Jarrapellejos 87. Going South Shopping 89. The Monk (GB) 90. The Perfect Husband 92. The Bird of Happiness 93. Cradle Song 94. A Walk in the Clouds (US) 95. The Chambermaid/La Camarera del Titanic 98. The Naked Maja/Volaverunt 99, etc.

Sand, George (1804–1876) (Armandine Aurore Lucie Dupin).
Prolific French novelist and writer whose love affair with composer Frédéric Chopin, out of the many she had with musicians and writers, has tended to be the one to catch the fancy of film-makers. She has been played by Merle Oberon in *A Song to Remember* 45, Patricia Morison in *Song without End* 60, Lucia Bose in *Jutrzenka: A Winter in Majorca* 71, Anne Wiazemsky in *Georges Qui?* 73, Imogene Claire in *Lisztomania* 75, Judy Davis in *Impromptu* 89, and Marie-France Pisier in *Blue Note* 91.

Sand, Paul (1944–) (Paul Sanchez).
American light actor.
The Hot Rock 72. The Main Event 79. Can't Stop the Music 80. Wholly Moses 80. The Last Fling 86. Teen Wolf Too 87, etc.

Sanda, Dominique (1948–) (Dominique Varaigne).
French leading lady of the 70s.
Une Femme Douce 70. *The Garden of the Finzi-Continis* 71. The Conformist 71. Without Apparent Motive 72. Impossible Object 73. The Mackintosh Man 73. Steppenwolf 74. 1900 76. Damnation Alley 77. Cabo Blanco 81. Le Matelot 512 84. Les Mendiants 87. In una Notte di Chiaro di Luna 89. I Won't Disturb You/Tolgo il Disturbo 91. Nobody's Children 94. Green Henry/Der Grun Heinrich (Swe.) 94. Joseph (TV) 95, etc.

Sande, Walter (1906–1972).
American character actor, usually a background heavy.
The Goldwyn Follies 38. Confessions of Boston Blackie 41. To Have and Have Not 44. Wild Harvest 47. Dark City 50. Red Mountain 52. Bad Day at Black Rock 55. The Gallant Hours 60, many others.
TV series: Tugboat Annie 56.

Sandell, William.
American production designer.
The Clones 77. The Pack 77. Piranha 78. Blood Beach 81. Airplane II: The Sequel 82. St Elmo's Fire 85. Robocop 87. Big Business 88. Total Recall 90. Nothing but Trouble 91. Newsies/News Boys 92. The Flintstones 94. Outbreak 95. The Glimmer Man 96. Air Force One 97. Small Soldiers 98, etc.

Sanders, Andrew.
British production designer.
Shock Treatment 81. Merry Christmas, Mr Lawrence 83. The Hit 84. Castaway 87. The Last Temptation of Christ 88. The Witches 90. K2 92. Sense and Sensibility 95. Surviving Picasso 96. The Wings of the Dove 97, etc.

Sanders, Denis (1929–1987) and **Terry** (1931–).
American producer brothers who for many years promised great things but never quite fulfilled them.
A Time out of War (short) (AA) 54. Crime and Punishment USA 58. War Hunt 61. Shock Treatment 63. Soul to Soul 71. Invasion of the Bee Girls (d) 73, etc.

Sanders, George (1906–1972).
Suave English actor who played scoundrels, cads and crooks for 30 years. Born in St Petersburg, he was educated in England and first worked in the textile business in Manchester and as a tobacco salesman in South America. He began on the English stage in revue and as a radio actor before entering films, going to Hollywood in the mid-30s, where his first role, in *Lloyd's of London*, typed him as an elegant bounder. He also played the title role in the film series *The Saint*, which he regarded as the nadir of his career, and in its successor, *The Falcon*, before being replaced by his brother, Tom Conway. He put his name to two ghost-written mystery novels in the 40s, one of which formed the basis of the 1954 film *The Unholy Four/The Stranger Came Home*. His four wives included actresses Zsa Zsa Gabor (1949–54), Benita Hume (1959–67), and Magda Gabor (1970–71). After his film roles, and his interest in them, declined, and business ventures went wrong, he committed suicide.
Autobiography: 1960 (reissued 1993), *Memoirs of a Professional Cad*.
Biographies: 1979, *A Terrible Man* by Brian Aherne. 1991, *George Sanders – An Exhausted Life* by Richard Vanderbeets.
■ Find the Lady 36. Strange Cargo 36. The Man Who Could Work Miracles 36. Dishonour Bright 37. Slave Ship 37. Love Is News 37. Lloyds of London 37. *Lancer Spy* 37. The Lady Escapes 37. International Settlement 38. Mr Moto's Last Warning 38. Four Men and a Prayer 38. Allegheny Uprising 39. So This Is London 39. The Outsider 39. Nurse Edith Cavell 39. Confessions of a Nazi Spy 39. *The Saint* (series) 39–41. The House of Seven Gables 40. Green Hell 40. Bitter Sweet 40. Son of Monte Cristo 40. *Rebecca* 40. Foreign Correspondent 40. The Falcon (series) 41–43. Rage in Heaven 41. Man Hunt 41. Sundown 41. Her Cardboard Lover 41. Son of Fury 42. *The Moon and Sixpence* 42. The Black Swan 42. Tales of Manhattan 42. Paris after Dark 43. Quiet Please, Murder 43. They Came to Blow Up America 43. This Land Is Mine 43. Appointment in Berlin 43. Paris after Dark 43. The Lodger 44. Action in Arabia 44. Summer Storm 44. *The Picture of Dorian Gray* 44. Hangover Square 44. Uncle Harry 45. *A Scandal in Paris* 46. The Strange Woman 47. The Ghost and Mrs Muir 47. *Forever Amber* 47. Bel Ami 48. Personal Column 48. *Lady Windermere's Fan* 49. Samson and Delilah 49. *All about Eve* (AA) 50. Captain Blackjack 50. I Can Get It for You Wholesale 51. The Light Touch 51. Assignment Paris 52. Ivanhoe 52. Voyage in Italy 53. Call Me Madam 53. Witness to Murder 54. King Richard and the Crusaders 54. Jupiter's Darling 54. Moonfleet 55. The King's Thief 55. That Certain Feeling 56. The Scarlet Coat 56. Never Say Goodbye 56. While the City Sleeps 56. Death of a Scoundrel 56. The Whole Truth (GB) 57. The Seventh Sin 57. From the Earth to the Moon 58. Solomon and Sheba 59. That Kind of Woman 59. A Touch of Larceny (GB) 60. The Last Voyage 60. Bluebeard's Ten Honeymoons 60. *Village of the Damned* (GB) 60. Trouble in the Sky (GB) 61. Five Golden Hours 61. The Rebel/Call Me Genius 61. Operation Snatch 62. In Search of Castaways 62. Cairo 63. Ecco (It.) 63. The Cracksman 63. Dark Purpose 64. A Shot in the Dark 64. The Golden Head 64. Moll Flanders 65. Warning Shot 66. The Quiller Memorandum 66. Trunk to Cairo 67. Good Times 67. The Jungle Book (voice) 67. One Step to Hell 68. The Best House in London 68. The Body Stealers 69. The Kremlin Letter 69. The Candy Man 69. Endless Night 72. Doomwatch 72. Psychomania 72.
TV series: George Sanders Mystery Theatre 58.
✪ For being everybody's favourite swine, and for

adding a touch of class to some pretty unappetizing movies. *Rebecca.*

❝ I never really thought I'd made the grade. And let's face it, I haven't. – G.S.

I was beastly but never coarse. A high-class sort of heel. – G.S.

I don't ask questions. I just take their money and use it for things that really interest me. – G.S.

I am not one of those people who would rather act than eat. Quite the reverse. My own desire as a boy was to retire. That ambition has never changed. – G.S., *1950s*

One thing I know – I have never encountered a single obstacle that a sufficient quantity of money could not have overcome. I have never been faced with a problem that money could not have solved. – G.S.

I have got to the point where the lousier the part the better I like it. I would find it quite embarrassing to get a really good part nowadays, for it would call forth the feeble flames of inner fires long since banked. – G.S., *early 60s*

'I will have had enough of this earth by the time I am 65. After that I shall be having my bottom wiped by nurses and being pushed around in a wheelchair. So I shall commit suicide.' – G.S., *1937, recalled by David Niven*

Dear World, I am leaving you because I am bored. I feel I have lived long enough. I am leaving you with your worries in this sweet cesspool. Good luck. – *Suicide note left by G.S. in 1972*

Famous line (*Rebecca*): 'I say, marriage with Max is not exactly a bed of roses, is it?'

Famous line (*All About Eve*): 'I am Addison de Witt. I am nobody's fool, least of all yours.'

Famous line (*The Picture of Dorian Gray*): 'I apologize for the intelligence of my remarks, Sir Thomas. I had forgotten that you are a member of parliament.'

Famous line (*The Picture of Dorian Gray*): 'If I could get back my youth, I'd do anything in the world except get up early, take exercise or be respectable.'

Sanders-Brahms, Helma (1940–).
German producer-director. A former television presenter, she began as a documentary and TV director.
Beneath the Paving Stones Is the Beach/Unterm Pflaster Ist der Strand 75. Shirin's Wedding 76. Heinrich 77. Germany Pale Mother/Deutschland Bleiche Mutter 80. The Future of Emily 84. Laputa 86. Felix 87. Divided Love/Geteilte Liebe 88. Apple Trees/Apfelbäume 92. My Heart Is Mine Alone/Mein Herz – Niemandem! 97, etc.

Sanderson, William (1948–).
American actor.
Fight for Your Life 77. Savage Weekend 78. Coal Miner's Daughter 80. Blood Bath 81. Death Hunt 81. Raggedy Man 81. Blade Runner 82. Lone Wolf McQuade 83. City Heat 84. Black Moon Rising 85. Fletch 85. Lonesome Dove 89. Mirror, Mirror 90. Giant of Thunder Mountain 91. Man's Best Friend 93. Return to Lonesome Dove 93. Wagons East! 94. The Client 94. Last Man Standing 96. George Wallace (TV) 97, etc.

Sandford, Christopher (1939–).
Emaciated British character actor.
Half a Sixpence 67. Before Winter Comes 70. Up the Chastity Belt 71. Vampira 74, etc.

Sandford, Tiny (1894–1961) (Stanley J. Sandford).
American character actor who is best remembered as a foil for Laurel and Hardy: traffic cop or other nemesis.
The Immigrant 17. The World's Champion 22. The Circus 28. The Iron Mask 29. Our Relations 36. Modern Times 36, many others.

Sandler, Adam (1966–).
American comic actor who made his name in the TV series *Saturday Night Live* in the early 90s. Born in Brooklyn, New York, he studied at New York University. He made a breakthrough to stardom with the success of *The Wedding Singer* and, especially, *The Waterboy*, which took more than $100m at the box-office. Current asking price: $20m a movie.
Shakes the Clown 91. Coneheads 93. Airheads 94. Mixed Nuts 94. Billy Madison 95. Happy Gilmore 96. Bulletproof 97. The Wedding Singer 97. *The Waterboy* (& co-w) 98. Big Daddy 99, etc.

❝ I like working with people I've seen in just a towel. – A.S.

Sandrelli, Stefania (1946–).
Italian leading actress.
Divorce – Italian Style 62. Seduced and Abandoned/Sedotta e Abandonata 64. Partner 68. The Conformist/Il Conformista 71. Alfredo, Alfredo 72. 1900 76. We All Loved Each Other So Much/C'Eravamo Tanto Amati 75. The Lie 84. The Family/La Famiglia 87. The Sleazy Uncle/Lo Zio Indegno 89. Per Amore, Solo per Amore 94. Of Love and Shadows 94. With Closed Eyes 94. Palermo – Milan No Return 95. Stealing Beauty 95. We'll Really Hurt You/Le Faremo Tanto Male 98. Marriages/Matrimoni 98, etc.

Sandrich, Mark (1900–1945).
American director who came to Hollywood in 1927 as director of Lupino Lane two-reelers; later associated with musicals.
■ The Talk of Hollywood 30. Melody Cruise 33. Aggie Appleby, Maker of Men 33. Hips Hips Hooray 34. Cockeyed Cavaliers 34. *The Gay Divorcee* 34. *Top Hat* 35. Follow the Fleet 36. A Woman Rebels 36. Shall We Dance? 37. Carefree 38. Man About Town 39. Buck Benny Rides Again 40. Love Thy Neighbour 40. Skylark 41. *Holiday Inn* 42. So Proudly We Hail 43. I Love a Soldier 44. Here Come the Waves 44.

Sands, Diana (1934–1973).
American actress.
A Raisin in the Sun 61. Ensign Pulver 64. The Landlord 70. Georgia Georgia 72. Willie Dynamite 73, etc.

Sands, Julian (1957–).
British leading actor.
Privates on Parade 82. Oxford Blues 84. The Killing Fields 84. After Darkness 85. The Doctor and the Devils 85. Gothic 86. A Room with a View 86. The Room 87. Siesta 87. Vibes 88. Wherever You Are 88. Tennessee Nights 89. Warlock 89. Impromptu 89. Arachnophobia 90. Night Sun/Il Sole Anche di Notte 90. Wicked/Cattiva 91. Grand Isle 91. Husbands and Lovers 91. Naked Lunch 92. The Turn of the Screw 92. Warlock: The Armageddon 93. Boxing Helena 93. The Browning Version 94. Leaving Las Vegas 95. The Great Elephant Escape (TV) 95. One Night Stand 97. Circle of Passion 97. The Phantom of the Opera (It.) 98. The Loss of Sexual Innocence 98. Long Time Since 98, etc.

Sands, Tommy (1937–).
American 'teenage rave' singer. He was formerly married to singer Nancy Sinatra.
Sing Boy Sing 57. Love in a Goldfish Bowl 59. Babes in Toyland 60. The Longest Day 62. None but the Brave 65, etc.

Sanford, Erskine (1880–1950).
American character actor, playing elderly gents in the 40s.
Pop Always Pays 40. *Citizen Kane* (as flustered editor) 41. The Magnificent Ambersons 42. Ministry of Fear 44. Possessed 47. Lady from Shanghai 48. Macbeth 50, etc.

Sanford, Ralph (1899–1963).
American supporting player, usually in burly 'good guy' roles.
Give Me a Sailor 38. Thunderhead, Son of Flicka 45. Champion 49. Blackjack Ketchum Desperado 56. The Purple Gang 59, many others.

Sangster, Jimmy (1924–).
British horror screenwriter, long associated with Hammer Films.
The Trollenberg Terror 55. *The Curse of Frankenstein* 56. *Dracula* 58. *The Mummy* 59. Jack the Ripper 59. Brides of Dracula 60. Taste of Fear (& p) 61. Maniac (& p) 63. Hysteria (& p) 65. *The Nanny* (& p) 65. Deadlier than the Male 67. The Anniversary (& p) 68. Horror of Frankenstein (& pd) 70. Lust for a Vampire (& d) 70. Fear in the Night (& pd) 72, etc.

Santell, Alfred (1895–1981).
American director, former architect. With Mack Sennett as writer and director in the 20s.
Wildcat Jordan 22. Subway Sadie 26. The Patent Leather Kid 27. The Little Shepherd of Kingdom Come 28. *Daddy Long Legs* 30. The Sea Wolf 30. Tess of the Storm Country 33. A Feather in Her Hat 35. *Winterset* 36. Having Wonderful Time 38. Aloma of the South Seas 41. Beyond the Blue Horizon 42. Jack London 44. The Hairy Ape 44. That Brennan Girl 46, etc.

Santiago, Cirio H.
Filipino director of exploitation movies.
Women in Cages 72. Bamboo Gods and Iron Men 74. TNT Jackson 75. Vampire Hookers 78. Caged Fury 84. Desert Warrior 85. Naked Vengeance 86. Silk 86. The Devastator 86. Demon of Paradise 87. Equalizer 2000 87. Fast Gun 87. The Sisterhood 88. Future Hunters 88. Silk 2 89. Live by the Fist 92. One Man Army 93. Strangehold 94. Caged Heat 2 94, etc.

Santley, Joseph (1889–1971).
American director, former child actor and vaudevillian.
The Smartest Girl in Town 32. Spirit of Culver 37. Swing, Sister, Swing 41. Hitting the Headlines 42. Brazil 44. Shadow of a Woman 47. Make Believe Ballroom 49, etc.

Santo, El:
see El Santo.

Santoni, Reni (1939–).
American actor, of French-Spanish ancestry; ex TV writer.
Enter Laughing 67. Anzio 68. Dirty Harry 71. I Never Promised You a Rose Garden 77. They Went Thataway and Thataway 78. Bad Boys 83. Cobra 86. The Package 89. Private Parts 96. The Late Shift (TV) 96, etc.

Santschi, Tom (1879–1931).
American leading man of the silents.
The Sultan's Power 09. The Spoilers 14. The Garden of Allah 16. Little Orphan Annie 19. Three Bad Men 26. In Old Arizona 29. Ten Nights in a Bar-Room 31, etc.

Saperstein, David.
American director and screenwriter.
Cocoon (story) 84. A Killing Affair (wd) 86. Beyond the Stars/Personal Choice (wd) 89.

Sapper.
The pen-name of H. C. McNeile (1888–1937), creator of Bulldog Drummond. Only the first film adaptation made any attempt to convey the essential thuggishness of Drummond.

Sara, Mia (1967–) (Mia Sarapocciello).
American leading actress who began in commercials and the TV soap opera *All My Children*. She took the title role in the TV mini-series *Queenie* 87, based on the life of Merle Oberon.
Legend 85. Ferris Bueller's Day Off 86. Apprentice to Murder 88. Shadows in the Storm 88. Any Man's Death 90. A Climate for Killing 91. A Stranger among Us 92. By the Sword 93. Call of the Wild (TV) 93. Caroline at Midnight 93. Timecop 94. Undertow (TV) 95. The Set Up 95. The Pompatus of Love 95. The Maddening 95. Black Day Blue Night 95, etc.

Sarafian, Deran.
American director, the son of Richard Sarafian.
Alien Predator 87. To Die For 89. Death Warrant 91. Gunmen (& a) 93. Roadflower 93. Terminal Velocity 94, etc.

Sarafian, Richard C. (1925–).
American director, of Armenian descent; much TV experience.
■ Andy 65. Shadow on the Land (TV) 68. Run Wild Run Free 69. Fragment of Fear 70. *Vanishing Point* 71. Man in the Wilderness 71. The Man Who Loved Cat Dancing 73. Lolly Madonna XXX 73. One of Our Own (TV) 75. The Next Man 76. Sunburn 78. The Bear 84. Eye of the Tiger 86. Street Justice 89. Solar Crisis 90. Bugsy (a) 91. Gunmen (a) 93. Bound (a) 96. Bulworth (a) 98.

Sarafian, Tedi (1966–).
American screenwriter, the son of Richard C. Sarafian.
Roadflower 94. Tank Girl 95.

Sarandon, Chris (1942–).
American character actor.
Dog Day Afternoon (AAN) 75. Lipstick 76. The Sentinel 77. Cuba 79. The Day Christ Died (TV) (as Jesus) 80. A Tale of Two Cities (TV) 81. The Osterman Weekend 83. Fright Night 85. The Princess Bride 87. Child's Play 88. Tailspin (TV) 89. Slaves of New York 89. A Murderous Affair: The Carolyn Warmus Story (TV) 92. Dark Tide 93. Tim Burton's The Nightmare before Christmas (voice) 93. David's Mother (TV) 94. Just Cause 95. Tales from the Crypt Presents Bordello of Blood 96. Louisa May Alcott's Little Men 98, etc.

Sarandon, Susan (1946–) (Susan Tomaling).
American leading lady, ex-wife of Chris Sarandon. She has two sons by actor Tim Robbins.
Joe 70. The Front Page 74. The Great Waldo Pepper 75. The Rocky Horror Picture Show 75. Dragonfly 77. King of the Gypsies 78. Pretty Baby 78. Atlantic City USA (AAN) 80. Loving Couples 80. Tempest 82. The Hunger 83. The Buddy System 83. Compromising Positions 85. The Witches of Eastwick 87. Bull Durham 88. Sweet Hearts Dance 88. The January Man 89. A Dry White Season 89. Erik the Viking 89. White Palace 90. *Thelma and Louise* (AAN) 91. Light Sleeper 91. The Player 92. Lorenzo's Oil (AAN) 92. The Client (AAN) 94. Little Women 94. Dead Man Walking (AA) 95. James and the Giant Peach (voice) 96. Twilight 98. Illuminata 98. Stepmom 98. Earthly Possessions 99, etc.

❝ It's not difficult to be successful. But it is difficult to remain human. – S.S.

Acting is enforced compassion. You enter the skin of another person without judgment. – S.S.

Sarde, Alain (1952–).
French producer, associated with many leading French directors, including Godard, Blier, Tavernier, Sautet, and Doillon.
Barocco (co-p) 77. Buffet Froid 79. A Bad Son/Un Mauvais Fils 80. Hôtel des Amériques 81. Prénom Carmen 82. La Femme de Mon Pote 83. Notre Histoire 84. Détective 84. Un Dimanche à la Campagne 84. Comédie 87. A Few Days with Me/Quelques Jours avec Moi 88. La Vengeance d'une Femme 90. Le Jeune Werther 92. Wild Reed/Les Roseaux Sauvages 94, etc.

Sarde, Philippe (1945–).
Prolific French composer.
Les Choses de la Vie 69. Le Chat 71. Liza 72. La Grande Bouffe 73. Le Train 73. La Valise 73. Lancelot du Lac 74. Histoire d'O 75. Barocco 76. Madame Rosa 77. Un Taxi Mauve 77. Les Soeurs Brontë 78. Tess (AAN) 79. Le Toubib 79. Ghost Story 81. Quest for Fire 81. Lovesick 83. Stella 83. La Garce 84. Devil in the Flesh 85. Rendezvous 85. The Manhattan Project 86. Les Innocents 87. Lost Angels 89. The Music Box 89. Reunion 89. The Bear 89. A Few Days with Me 89. Lord of the Flies 90. C'est la Vie/La Baule-les-pins 90. The Voice/La Voix 92. L.627 92. La Petite Apocalypse 93. My Favourite Season/Ma Saison Préférée 93. Uncovered 94. La Fille de D'Artagnan 94. Say Yes/Dis-Moi Oui 95. Le Petit Garçon 95. Nelly & Mr Arnaud 95. Ponette 96. Thieves/Les Voleurs 96. Lucie Aubrac 97. Le Bossu 97, etc.

Sargent, Alvin (1931–).
American screenwriter.
■ The Stalking Moon 68. The Sterile Cuckoo 69. I Walk the Line 70. Love and Pain and the Whole Damn Thing 72. The Effect of Gamma Rays on Man in the Moon Marigolds 72. Paper Moon (AAN) 73. Bobby Deerfield 77. Julia (AA, BFA) 77. Straight Time 78. Ordinary People (AA) 80. Nuts 87. Dominick and Eugene 88. Other People's Money 91. What about Bob? (story) 91. Bogus 96, etc.

Sargent, Dick (1933–1994) (Richard Cox).
American screen actor who once specialized in gangling youths.
Bernardine 57. Operation Petticoat 59. That Touch of Mink 62. The Ghost and Mr Chicken 66. The Private Navy of Sergeant O'Farrell 68. Rich Man, Poor Man (TV) 76. Hardcore 79. Body Count 87. Teen Witch 89, etc.
TV series: One Happy Family 61. Broadside 64.

Sargent, Joseph (1925–) (Giuseppe Sargente).
American director.
One Spy Too Many (TV) 65. The Spy in the Green Hat (TV) 66. The Hell with Heroes 68. The Sunshine Patriot (TV) 68. The Immortal (TV) 69. The Forbin Project 69. Tribes (TV) 70. Maybe I'll Come Home in the Spring (TV) 71. White Lightning 73. Sunshine (TV) 74. The Man (TV) 74. The Taking of Pelham One Two Three 74. MacArthur 77. Goldengirl (TV) 79. Coast to

Coast 80. Jaws – the Revenge 87. Day One (TV) 88. Ivory Hunters (TV) 90. Skylark (TV) 93. The Bible: Abraham (TV) 93. My Antonia (TV) 95. Larry McMurtry's Streets of Laredo (TV) 95. Miss Evers Boys (TV) 97. Mandela and de Klerk (TV) 97, etc.

Sarin, Vic.
Canadian cinematographer.
Heartaches 82. Dancing in the Dark 86. Nowhere to Hide 87. Bye Bye Blues 90. Cold Sweat 93. The Burning Season 93. Whale Music 94. Margaret's Museum 95, etc.

Sarne, Michael (1939–).
British director, former light actor.
AS ACTOR: Sodom and Gomorrah 60. The Guns of Navarone 61. A Place to Go 64. Every Day's a Holiday 65. Two Weeks in September 67. The Hollow Men (Pol.) 93, etc.
■ AS DIRECTOR: The Road to St Tropez 66. Joanna 68. Myra Breckinridge 69. Intimade 72. Trouble with a Battery 86. The Punk (wd) 93. Glastonbury the Movie (p, co-d) 96.

Sarony, Leslie (1897–1985).
English character actor, music-hall performer, and writer of nonsense songs, including 'Ain't It Grand to Be Blooming Well Dead' and 'I Lift up My Finger and I Say "Tweet, Tweet"'. He also worked in a double act, The Two Leslies, with Leslie Holmes.
Soldiers of the King 33. Rolling in Money 34. Wedding Eve 35. Boys Will Be Boys (s) 35. Feather Your Nest (s) 37. Give My Regards to Broad Street 84, etc.

Saroyan, William (1908–1981).
American writer, mainly of fantasies about gentle people.
The Human Comedy (AA) 43. The Time of Your Life 48, etc.

Sarrazin, Michael (1940–).
Canadian leading man of the early 70s, usually seen as the young innocent.
The Doomsday Flight (TV) 66. Gunfight in Abilene 67. *The Flim Flam Man* 67. Journey to Shiloh 67. The Sweet Ride 68. A Man Called Gannon 68. Eye of the Cat 68. They Shoot Horses Don't They? 69. In Search of Gregory 70. The Pursuit of Happiness 71. Believe in Me 71. Sometimes a Great Notion 71. The Groundstar Conspiracy 72. Frankenstein: the True Story (TV) (as the creature) 73. Harry in Your Pocket 74. For Pete's Sake 74. The Reincarnation of Peter Proud 75. The Gumball Rally 76. The Loves and Times of Scaramouche 76. Caravans 78. Double Negative 80. The Seduction 82. Fighting Back 82. Joshua Then and Now 85. Kidnapped 87. Keeping Track 87. Captive Hearts 87. Mascara 87. Malarek 89. The Phone Call 90. Lena's Holiday 91. Bullet to Beijing 95. Midnight in St Petersburg 97. Hostage Train 97, etc.

Sartov, Hendrik.
American portrait photographer who joined Griffith in 1919 and was influential in soft-focus close-ups.
Way Down East 20. Orphans of the Storm 21. One Exciting Night 22. America 24. Isn't Life Wonderful 25. The Scarlet Letter 26. Quality Street 27. Under the Black Eagle 28, etc.

Sartre, Jean-Paul (1905–1980).
French existentialist writer. Works filmed include:
Huis Clos/No Exit 48. Crime Passionnel 51. La Putain Respectueuse 52. Les Jeux Sont Faits 54. The Proud and the Beautiful (AAN) 56. The Condemned of Altona 63.

Sasdy, Peter (1934–).
Hungarian director in England.
■ Taste the Blood of Dracula 69. Countess Dracula 70. Hands of the Ripper 71. Doomwatch 72. Nothing But the Night 72. I Don't Want to Be Born 75. Welcome to Blood City 76. Murder at the Wedding (TV) 79. The Lonely Lady 83. Sherlock Holmes and the Leading Lady (TV) 91.
Many television dramas.

Saslavsky, Luis (1908–1995).
Argentinian director, screenwriter and producer, much influenced by European films. In the 50s, he worked in France. He was also a novelist and film critic.
Crimen a las Tres 35. *La Fuga* 37. Historia de una Noche 41. *La Dama Duende* 45. The Stain on the Snow/La Neige Était Sale (Fr.) 54. Les Louves (Fr.) 57. Premier Mai (Fr.) 58. Historia de una Noche (Sp.) 64. Las Ratas 65. El Fausto Criollo 79, etc.

Sass, Barbara (1936–).
Polish director and screenwriter, concentrating on feminist themes, from television.
Without Love/Bez Milosci 80. The Outsider/Debiutantka 82. The Scream/Krzyk 83. Caged/W Klatce 88. An Immoral Story/Historia Niemoralna 90. Pajeczarki 93. The Fear/Tylko Strach 93. Temptation/Pokuszenie 96, etc.

Sassard, Jacqueline (1940–).
French leading lady.
Accident 67. Les Biches 68.

Sastre, Inés (c. 1974–).
Spanish leading actress, in international films. Born in Valladolid, she studied comparative literature at the Sorbonne, while alternating modelling and acting from her early teens. She became the face of Lancôme in advertisements in 1998.
El Dorado 88. Johanna d'Arc of Mongolia (Ger.) 89. Escape from Paradise/Fuga dal Paradiso (It.) 90. Beyond the Clouds/Par delà les Nuages (It.) 95. Sabrina (US) 95. The Best Man/Il Testimone dello Sposo (It.) 97, etc.

Sato, Masura (1928–).
Japanese composer.
The Lower Depths 57. Throne of Blood 57. The Hidden Fortress 58. Yojimbo 61. Sanjuro 62. Red Beard 65. Ebirah, Horror of the Deep 68. Son of Godzilla 69. Outlaws 70. Kazoku 71. Sapporo Winter Olympics 72. The Wolves 72. Godzilla vs Mecha-Godzilla 76. The Yellow Handkerchief of Happiness 78. Sensei the Teacher 83. Shogun's Shadow 89, etc.

Saunders, Charles (1904–).
English director, mainly of low-budget thrillers. In films from 1927, he was an editor with Gaumont British and Two Cities before turning to directing in the mid-40s. From the 50s, he also worked in television, on such series as *Fabian of the Yard*, and as a director of commercials.
Tawny Pipit (co-d) 44. Fly Away Peter 47. One Wild Oat 51. Meet Mr Callaghan 54. Kill Her Gently 57. Womaneater 58. Danger by My Side 62, etc.

Saunders, John Monk (1895–1940).
American screenwriter with a special interest in aviation. Married actress Fay WRAY (1928–39).
Wings 27. *Dawn Patrol* (AA) 30. *The Last Flight* 31. Devil Dogs of the Air 35. I Found Stella Parish 35.

Saura, Carlos (1932–).
Leading Spanish director and screenwriter. He worked as an engineer and a photographer before turning to film.
Biography: 1991, *The Films of Carlos Saura: The Practice of Seeing* by Marvin d'Lugo.
Cuenca (short) 59. The Hooligans/Los Golfos 59. Lament for a Bandit/Llanto por un Bandido 63. The Chase/La Caza 65. Peppermint Frappé 67. Stress es Tres, Tres 68. Honeycomb/La Madriguera 69. The Garden of Delights/El Jardín de las Delicias 70. Anna and the Wolves/Ana y los Lobos 72. Cousin Angelica 74. Cria Cuervos 75. Blindfolded/Los Ojos Vendados 78. Mama Turns a Hundred/Mama Cumple Cien Años 79. Hurry, Hurry/Deprisa, Deprisa 80. Blood Wedding/Bodas de Sangre 81. Sweet Hours/Dulces Horas 81. Antonieta 82. Carmen 83. Los Zancos 84. Love, the Magician/El Amor Brujo 86. El Dorado 87. The Dark Night/La Noche Oscura 89. ¡Ay, Carmela! 90. Sevillanas 92. Dispara (& co-w) 93. Marathon 93. Flamenco (doc) 95. Taxi 96. Tango 97, etc.

Sautet, Claude (1924–).
French director and screenwriter whose work frequently deals with the problems and difficulties of middle-class relationships. Born in Paris, he studied at IDHEC, and was a music critic before working in the 50s as an assistant to Georges FRANJU, Jacques BECKER and others.
The Big Risk 60. Head First 64. Les Choses de la Vie 69. Vincent, François, Paul and the Others 76. Mado 78. Un Mauvais Fils 80. Garçon! 83. A Few Days with Me 88. Un Coeur en Hiver 92. Haute Époque 94. Nelly & Mr Arnaud 95, etc.

Savage, Ann (1921–) (Bernie Lyon).
American leading lady of 40s seconds.
Two Señoritas from Chicago 43. Two Man Submarine 44. *Detour* 45. Scared Stiff 45. The Last Crooked Mile 46. Renegade Girl 46. Jungle Flight 47. Satan's Cradle 49. Pygmy Island 50. The Woman They Almost Lynched 53. Fire with Fire 86, many others.

Savage, John (1949–).
Baby-faced American leading man who didn't quite become another James Dean.
Bad Company 75. The Killing Kind 65. No Deposit No Return 76. The Deer Hunter 78. Hair 79. The Onion Field 80. Cattle Annie and Little Britches 81. Inside Moves 81. The Amateur 82. Brady's Escape 84. Maria's Lovers 85. Salvador 86. The Beat 87. Hotel Colonial 87. Beauty and the Beast 87. Dear America 87. Caribe 87. Do the Right Thing 89. Hunting 89. Point of View 89. Any Man's Death 90. The Godfather Part III 90. Primary Motive 92. C.I.A. 2: Target Alexa 93. A Killing Obsession 94. Red Scorpion 2 94. Tom Clancy's Op Center (TV) 95. The Crossing Guard 95. White Squall 96. Where Truth Lies 96. American Strays 96. The Mouse 96. Managua 97. Hostile Intent 97. The Thin Red Line 98, etc.
TV series: Gibbsville 76.

Saval, Dany (1940–) (Danielle Nadine Suzanne Salle).
French leading lady.
Les Tricheurs 58. The Mirror Has Two Faces 58. Nathalie 59. Les Parisiennes 61. The Seven Deadly Sins 62. Moon Pilot 62. The Devil and Ten Commandments 62. Web of Fear 64. Boeing Boeing 65. La Vie Parisienne 78, etc.

Savalas, Telly (1924–1994) (Aristotle Savalas).
Bald Greek-American character actor with TV experience; former academic.
The Young Savages 61. Birdman of Alcatraz (AAN) 62. The Interns 63. Cape Fear 63. The Man from the Diners' Club 63. The New Interns 64. Genghis Khan 65. *The Battle of the Bulge* 65. The Slender Thread 66. Beau Geste 66. The Dirty Dozen 67. *The Scalphunters* 68. Buona Sera Mrs Campbell 68. The Assassination Bureau (GB) 68. Crooks and Coronets (GB) 69. The Land Raiders 69. Mackenna's Gold 69. On Her Majesty's Secret Service 69. Kelly's Heroes 70. A Town Called Bastard 71. Pretty Maids All in a Row 71. Pancho Villa 71. The Marcus Nelson Murders (TV) 72. A Reason to Live, a Reason to Die 72. The Killer Is on the Phone 72. She Cried Murder (TV) 73. Horror Express 74. The Diamond Mercenaries 75. Inside Out 75. Capricorn One 78. The French Atlantic Affair (TV) 79. Escape to Athena 79. Beyond the Poseidon Adventure 79. The Cartier Affair (TV) 84. Kojak: The Belarus File (TV) 85. Gobots: The Battle of the Rock Lords (voice) 86. Kojak: The Price of Justice (TV) 87. The Dirty Dozen: The Next Mission (TV) 87. The Dirty Dozen: The Fatal Mission (TV) 88. Vengeance 93, etc.
TV series: Acapulco 60. *Kojak* 73–77.
~Catchphrase: Who loves ya, baby? (from *Kojak*).

Saville, Philip (1930–).
English director, mainly for television.
Stop the World – I Want to Get Off 66. Oedipus the King 68. The Best House in London 69. Secrets 71. Gangsters (TV) 75. Count Dracula 77. Boys from the Blackstuff (TV) 82. Those Glory, Glory Days 83. Shadey 86. Life and Loves of a She-Devil (TV) 86. The Fruit Machine 88. Angels (TV) 92, etc.

Saville, Victor (1897–1979).
British director who, after making some outstanding films in the 30s, went to Hollywood with very meagre results. Former film salesman and exhibitor.
The Arcadians 27. Roses of Picardy 28. *Woman to Woman* (US) 29. Hindle Wakes 31. Sunshine Susie 31. *The Good Companions* 32. I Was a Spy 33. *Friday the Thirteenth* 33. *Evergreen* 34. The Iron Duke 36. Dark Journey 37. Storm in a Teacup 37. *South Riding* 38. The Citadel (p only) 38. Goodbye Mr Chips (p only) 39. Bitter Sweet (p) 40. Dr Jekyll and Mr Hyde (p) 41. White Cargo (p) 42. Tonight and Every Night (p, d) 44. The Green Years (p, d) 46. If Winter Comes (d) 47. The Conspirator (d) 47. Kim (p) 51. I the Jury (p) 53. The Long Wait (p, d) 54. The Silver Chalice (p, d) 55. Kiss Me Deadly (p) 55. The Greengage Summer (p) 61.

Savini, Tom. (1946–).
American horror make-up specialist, director, and actor, often associated with the work of director George ROMERO. Born in Pittsburgh, Pennsylvania, he is a former journalist.
Deathdream 72. Deranged 74. Martin 77. Dawn of the Dead (& a) 78. Effects (a) 80. Maniac (a) 80. Friday the 13th 80. Midnight 81. Knightriders (a) 81. Creepshow (a) 82. Friday the 13th Part 4: The Final Chapter 84. Invasion U.S.A. 85. Day of the Dead 85. The Texas Chainsaw Massacre Part 2 86. The Ripper 86. Creepshow 2 (a) 87. Monkey Shines 88. Red Scorpion 89. Night of the Living Dead (d) 90. Two Evil Eyes 91. Necronomicon 93. From Dusk till Dawn (a) 96. Vampirates (a, d) 98, etc.

Savo, Jimmy (1896–1960).
Pint-sized American comedian who failed to repeat his Broadway success on film.
Exclusive Rights 26. Once in a Blue Moon 36. Merry Go Round of 1938, etc.

Savoca, Nancy (1960–).
American director.
True Love 89. Dogfight 91. Household Saints 93. If These Walls Could Talk (co-w, co-d) 96. The 24-Hour Woman (d) 98.

Sawalha, Julia (1968–).
English actress, much on television in teenage roles.
Martin Chuzzlewit (TV) 94. Pride and Prejudice (TV) 95. In the Bleak Midwinter 95. The Wind in the Willows 96. Ain't Misbehavin' (TV) 97, etc.
TV series: Press Gang 89–93. Second Thoughts 91–93. Absolutely Fabulous 92–94.

Sawtell, Paul (1906–1971).
Polish-born composer in America.
The Gay Falcon 41. Tarzan Triumphs 43. The Scarlet Claw 44. Dick Tracy Meets Gruesome 47. Black Magic 49. Son of Dr Jekyll 51. Inferno 53. Texas Lady 55. Stopover Tokyo 57. The Lost World 60. Five Weeks in a Balloon 62. Island of the Blue Dolphins 64. The Christine Jorgenson Story 70, many others.

Sawyer, Joseph (1901–1982) (Joseph Sauer).
American comedy actor usually seen as tough cop or army sergeant.
College Humour 33. The Marines Have Landed 36. Black Legion 37. The Roaring Twenties 40. Sergeant York 41. About Face 42. The McGuerins from Brooklyn 42. Fall In 44. Joe Palooka, Champ 46. Fighting Father Dunne 49. It Came from Outer Space 53. The Killing 56, many others.
TV series: Rin Tin Tin 55.

Saxon, John (1935–) (Carmen Orrico).
American leading man, former model.
Running Wild (debut) 55. The Unguarded Moment 56. The Reluctant Debutante 58. Portrait in Black 59. The Unforgiven 59. The Plunderers 60. Posse from Hell 61. War Hunt 62. The Cardinal 63. The Evil Eye (It.) 63. The Appaloosa 66. The Night Caller (GB) 67. Death of a Gunfighter 69. Joe Kidd 72. Enter the Dragon 73. Black Christmas 75. Mitchell 75. The Swiss Conspiracy 75. Blazing Magnum 76. Moonshine County Express 77. The Bees 78. The Electric Horseman 79. Blood Beach 81. The Glove 81. Hardcastle and McCormick (TV) 83. The Big Score 83. A Nightmare on Elm Street 84. Fever Pitch 85. My Mom's a Werewolf 89. Payoff 91. Frame-Up II: The Cover-Up 92. Jonathan of the Bears 94. A Killing Obsession 94. Beverly Hills Cop III 94. Wes Craven's New Nightmare 94. From Dusk till Dawn 96, etc.
TV series: The Bold Ones 69–72. 79 Park Avenue 77. Falcon Crest 81–82, 86–88.

Sayers, Dorothy L. (1893–1957).
British detective novelist, creator of Lord Peter Wimsey, who was personified on film by Peter Haddon in *The Silent Passenger* and Robert Montgomery in *Busman's Honeymoon*. Ian Carmichael had a long run on TV in the 70s.
❝ For her warm-hearted admirers she is still the finest detective story writer of the century; to those

less enthusiastic her work is long-winded and ludicrously snobbish. – *Julian Symons*

Sayle, Alexei (1952–).
Aggressive English character actor, comedian, writer, and newspaper columnist, a former teacher. Born in Liverpool, he was a stand-up comedian before making his reputation on TV.
Gorky Park 83. The Bride 85. Whoops Apocalypse 86. Solarbabies/Solar Warriors 86. Siesta 87. Indiana Jones and the Last Crusade 89. Reckless Kelly 93. Sorry about Last Night (& w, TV) 95, etc.
TV series: The Young Ones 82–84. Whoops Apocalypse 82. Alexei Sayle's Stuff 88–90. The All-New Alexei Sayle Show 94. Paris 94.

Sayles, John (1950–).
American independent director, producer and screenwriter; also editor, occasional actor and novelist.
Book: 1998, *Sayles on Sayles*, ed. Gavin Smith.
Piranha (w) 78. The Lady in Red (w) 79. The Return of the Secaucus Seven (a, wd, ed) (AANw) 79. Alligator (w) 80. Battle beyond the Stars (w) 80. The Howling (a, w) 80. The Challenge (w) 82. Lianna (a, wd, ed) 82. Baby, It's You (wd) 83. Enormous Changes at the Last Minute (w) 83. The Brother from Another Planet (a, wd, ed) 84. Hard Choices (a) 84. The Clan of the Cave Bear (w) 86. Something Wild (a) 86. Matewan (a, wd) 87. Wild Thing (w) 87. *Eight Men Out* (a, wd) 88. Breaking In (w) 89. Little Vegas (a) 90. *City of Hope* (a, wd, ed) 91. Straight Talk (a) 92. Matinee (a) 93. The Secret of Roan Inish (wd, e) 94. *Lone Star* (AANw) 96. Mimic (co-w) 97, etc.

Saylor, Syd (1895–1962) (Leo Sailor).
Thin American comic actor who starred in his own series of more than 50 shorts in the late 20s, was the grizzled sidekick in the first of the Three Mesquiteers westerns, and supplied comic relief in many 'B' westerns and other bigger-budget films.
Young and Beautiful 34. House of Secrets 37. Little Miss Broadway 38. Union Pacific 39. Abe Lincoln in Illinois 40. Yankee Doodle Dandy 42. Three of a Kind 44. Nob Hill 45. The Kid from Brooklyn 46. Snake Pit 48. Sitting Pretty 48. The Paleface 48. Dancing in the Dark 49. Abbott and Costello Meet Captain Kidd 52. A Cry in the Night 56. The Crawling Hand 63, etc.

Scacchi, Greta (1960–).
Italian-born leading lady in international films.
Dead on Time 81. Heat and Dust 82. Waterfront (TV) 83. The Ebony Tower (TV) 84. Camille (TV) 85. The Coca Cola Kid 85. Defence of the Realm 86. Good Morning Babylon 87. A Man in Love/L'Homme Amoureux 87. White Mischief 87. La Donna della Luna 88. Three Sisters/Paura e Amore 88. Waterfront 88. Presumed Innocent 90. Shattered 91. Fires Within 91. Turtle Beach 92. The Player 92. Salt on Our Skin 93. Country Life 94. The Browning Version 94. Jefferson in Paris 95. Cosi 96. Emma 96. The Serpent's Kiss 97. The Odyssey (TV) 97. Tom's Midnight Garden 98. The Red Violin 98, etc.
❝ When I was about eight years old, I happened to mention to my father that I wanted to be an actress and he gave me a wallop in the face. – G.S.

Scaife, Ted (1912–).
British cinematographer.
Bonnie Prince Charlie 48. An Inspector Calls 54. Sea Wife 57. *Night of the Demon* 57. 633 Squadron 64. *Khartoum* 66. The Dirty Dozen 67. Play Dirty 68. Sinful Davey 69. Forbush and the Penguins 71. Hannie Caulder 71. Sitting Target 72. Catlow 72, many others.

Scala, Gia (1934–1972) (Giovanna Scoglio).
Italian leading lady who made a few American films. Died from an overdose of drugs.
The Price of Fear 56. Four Girls in Town 56. Don't Go Near the Water 56. The Garment Jungle 57. The Two-Headed Spy (GB) 58. I Aim at the Stars 59. The Guns of Navarone 61, etc.

Scales, Prunella (1932–).
British leading actress, mainly in comedy and on TV. Married to actor and stage director Timothy West and the mother of actor Sam West.
Laxdale Hall 52. Hobson's Choice 54. Room at the Top 59. Waltz of the Toreadors 62. The Boys from Brazil 78. The Wicked Lady 84. Consuming Passions 88. A Chorus of Disapproval 88. A Question of Attribution (as the Queen) (TV) 91. Howards End 91. Second Best 94. Wolf 94. Jane Austen's Emma (TV) 96. Stiff Upper Lips 97. Breaking the Code (TV) 97, etc.
TV series: *Fawlty Towers* 75–79. After Henry 88–92.

Scarfe, Gerald.
English political cartoonist and artist. He provided the animation sequences for Pink Floyd's *Wall*, and also provided character designs for the Disney feature *Hercules* 97. Married actress Jane Asher in 1981.

Scarfiotti, Ferdinando (1941–1994).
Distinguished Italian production designer who trained as an architect and began as a protégé of Visconti, designing opera productions. He also worked on many of Bertolucci's films.
The Conformist/Il Conformista 69. *Death in Venice* (BFA) 71. Avanti! 72. Last Tango in Paris 72. Daisy Miller 74. Flash Gordon 80. American Gigolo 80. Honky Tonk Freeway 81. Cat People 82. Scarface 83. *The Last Emperor* (AA) 87. Mamba 88. *Toys* (AAN) 92. Love Affair 94, etc.
❝ The most influential film designer of the last three decades. – *Paul Schrader*

Scarwid, Diana (1955–).
American leading lady.
Pretty Baby 78. Inside Moves (AAN) 80. Mommie Dearest 81. Silkwood 83. Strange Invaders 83. Extremities 86. The Ladies Club 86. Psycho III 86. Heat 87. Brenda Starr 89. The Cure 95. If These Walls Could Talk (TV) 96. Critical Choices 97, etc.

Schaech, Johnathon.
American actor.
Sparrow (It.) 93. The Doom Generation 95. How to Make an American Quilt 95. That Thing You Do! 96. Invasion of Privacy 96. Welcome to Woop Woop (Aus.) 97. Hush 98. Finding Graceland 98. Woundings (GB) 98, etc.

Schaefer, George (1920–1997).
American director with TV experience.
■ Macbeth 61. Pendulum 68. Generation 69. Doctors' Wives 71. A War of Children (TV) 72. A Time for Love (TV) 73. F. Scott Fitzgerald and the Last of the Belles (TV) 74. In This House of Brede (TV) 75. An Enemy of the People 78. Who'll Save Our Children? (TV) 78. Right of Way (TV) 83. Laura Lansing Slept Here (TV) 88.

Schaeffer, Eric (1963–).
American independent director, screenwriter and actor.
My Life's in Turnaround 93. If Lucy Fell 96. Fall 97, etc.

Schafer, Natalie (1900–1991).
American comedienne usually seen as a dizzy rich woman. Married to actor Louis Calhern.
Marriage is a Private Affair 43. Wonder Man 45. The Snake Pit 48. Caught 49. Anastasia 56. Oh Men Oh Women 57. Susan Slade 61. Forty Carats 73. The Day of the Locust 75, etc.
TV series: *Gilligan's Island* 64–67. The Survivors 69–70.

Schaffner, Franklin (1920–1989).
Stylish American director, from TV.
■ The Stripper 63. *The Best Man* 64. *The War Lord* 65. The Double Man 67. *Planet of the Apes* 68. *Patton* (AA) 69. Nicholas and Alexandra 71. *Papillon* 73. Islands in the Stream 77. The Boys from Brazil 78. Sphinx 81. Yes Giorgio 82. Lionheart 87. Welcome Home 89.

Schallert, William (1922–).
American character actor who played a lot of dull fathers in his day. More recently president of the Screen Actors' Guild.
The Man from Planet X 52. Riot in Cell Block Eleven 55. Written on the Wind 56. Cry Terror 58. Pillow Talk 59. In the Heat of the Night 67. Will Penny 68. Charley Varrick 73. Twilight Zone – the Movie 83. Innerspace 87, many others.
TV series: The Many Loves of Dobie Gillis 59–63. The Patty Duke Show 63–66. The Nancy Walker Show 76. The Hardy Boys Mysteries 77–78. Little Women 79. The New Gidget 86–88.

Scharf, Walter (1910–).
American composer.
Chatterbox 43. Dakota 45. The Saxon Charm 48. Deported 50. Hans Christian Andersen 52. Living It Up 54. Hollywood or Bust 56. King Creole 58. A Pocketful of Miracles 61. Where Love Has Gone 64. Pendulum 69. The Cheyenne Social Club 70. Ben 72. Walking Tall 73. Final Chapter, Walking Tall 77. When Every Day Was the Fourth of July (TV) 78. This Is Elvis 81. Twilight Time 83, many others.

Schary, Dore (1905–1980).
American writer-producer with newspaper and theatrical experience. AA best screenplay *Boys' Town* 38; produced for MGM 1941–45; head of production RKO 1945–48; head of production MGM 1948–56; then independent.
Autobiography: 1979, *Heyday*.
Lonelyhearts 59. Sunrise at Campobello 60. Act One (wd, p) 63, etc.
❝ A man whose few successes were even more distasteful than his many failures. – *John Simon*

Schatzberg, Jerry (1927–).
American director, former fashion photographer.
■ Puzzle of a Downfall Child 71. The Panic in Needle Park 71. Scarecrow 73. Dandy, the All American Girl 76. The Seduction of Joe Tynan 79. Honeysuckle Rose 80. Misunderstood 83. No Small Affair 84. Street Smart 87. Clinton and Nadine (TV) 88. Reunion/L'Ami Retrouvé 89.

Schayer, Richard (1880–1956).
American scriptwriter.
Black Roses 21. The Thrill Chaser 23. Silk Stocking Sal 24. Tell It to the Marines 26. On ze Boulevard 27. The Cameraman 28. Spite Marriage 29. Free and Easy 30. Doughboys 30. Trader Horn 31. The Winning Ticket 35. The Devil Is a Sissy 36. The Black Arrow 48. Lorna Doone 51. Gun Belt 53. Lancelot and Guinevere 63, many others.

Scheider, Roy (1932–).
Lean American character actor.
The Curse of the Living Corpse 64. Star 68. Stiletto 69. Loving 70. Puzzle of a Downfall Child 70. Klute 71. L'Attentat 72. Assignment Munich (TV) 72. The Outside Man 72. *The French Connection* (AAN) 72. Sheila Levine Is Dead and Living in New York 73. The Seven-Ups 73. *Jaws* 75. Marathon Man 76. Sorcerer 77. Jaws 2 78. Last Embrace 79. *All That Jazz* (AAN) 79. Prisoner without a Name, Cell without a Number (TV) 80. Still of the Night 82. Blue Thunder 83. 2010 84. Mishima 85. Tiger Town 85. The Men's Club 86. 52 Pick-Up 86. Cohen and Tate 89. Night Game 89. Listen to Me 89. The Fourth War 90. The Russia House 90. Naked Lunch 91. Somebody Has to Shoot the Picture 91. Romeo Is Bleeding 93. Wild Justice (TV) 93. The Rage 96. The Myth of Fingerprints 97. John Grisham's The Rainmaker 97. Executive Target 97. Silver Wolf (Can.) 98. Better Living 98, etc.
TV series: SeaQuest DSV 93–96.

Schell, Catherine (1946–) (Catherine von Schell).
German character actress.
Moon Zero Two 69. Madame Sin (TV) 72. Callan 74. The Black Windmill 74. The Prisoner of Zenda 79, etc.
TV series: Space 1999 75–76.

Schell, Maria (1926–).
Austrian leading lady who has been in British and American films.
The Angle with the Trumpet 49. The Magic Box 51. So Little Time 52. The Heart of the Matter 52. Der Traumende Mund 53. The Last Bridge (Aus.) 54. Die Ratten 55. *Gervaise* 56. White Nights (It.) 57. Une Vie (Fr.) 58. The Brothers Karamazov 58. Cimarron 61. The Mark (GB) 61. 99 Women 69. The Odessa File 74. Voyage of the Damned 76. Superman 78. Just a Gigolo 79. Players 79, etc.

Schell, Maximilian (1930–).
Austrian leading man who has been in international films. Brother of Maria Schell.
Kinder, Mütter und ein General 58. The Young Lions 58. *Judgment at Nuremberg* (AA) 61. Five-Finger Exercise 62. The Condemned of Altona 63. The Reluctant Saint 63. Topkapi 64. Return from the Ashes 65. The Deadly Affair 66. Beyond the Mountains 66. Counterpoint 67. The Castle 68. Krakatoa 68. First Love (wpd only) 70. The Pedestrian (p, d) 73. The Odessa File 74. First Love (& d) 75. The Man in the Glass Booth (AAN) 75. St Ives 76. End of the Game (& d) 76. Julia (AAN) 77. Cross of Iron 77. Avalanche Express 79. The Black Hole 79. Players 79. The Diary of Anne Frank (TV) 81. The Chosen 81. Man Under Suspicion 84. Marlene (& d) 85. The Assisi Underground 85. Peter the Great (TV) 86. The Freshman 90. Labyrinth 90. A Far Off Place 93. The Bible: Abraham (TV) 93. Justiz 93. Little Odessa 94. Telling Lies in America 96. John Carpenter's Vampires 97. Left Luggage (Hol.) 98. Deep Impact (US) 98, etc.

Schenck, Aubrey (1908–).
American producer.
Shock 46. Repeat Performance 48. Beachhead 53. Up Periscope 58. Frankenstein 70 59. Robinson Crusoe on Mars 64. Don't Worry We'll Think of a Title 66. The Alpha Caper (TV) 73, etc.

Schenck, Joseph M. (1878–1961).
Russian-born executive, in America from 1900, at first as pharmacist, then as fairground showman and owner. By 1924 was chairman of United Artists and creator of its theatre chain. In 1933 he founded Twentieth Century Productions and by 1935 was head of Twentieth Century-Fox. In 1953 he created Magna Productions with Mike Todd. In 1950 he was voted a special Academy Award. Married actress Norma Talmadge.
❝ If four or five guys tell you that you're drunk, even though you know you haven't had a thing to drink, the least you can do is to lie down a little while. – J.M.S.

Schenck, Nicholas M. (1881–1969).
Russian-born executive, brother of Joseph M. Schenck, with whom after arrival in America in 1900 he ran an amusement park. Later developed theatre chain which emerged as Loew's Consolidated Enterprises; became president of Loew's and thus financial controller of MGM.
❝ There's nothing wrong with this business that good pictures can't cure. – N.M.S.
All he knows about movies you could stick in a cat's ass. – *L. B. Mayer*

Schenkel, Carl (1948–).
Swiss-born director and screenwriter who began his career in West Germany before working in North America.
Out of Order/Abwärts 84. The Mighty Quinn (US) 89. Silence Like Glass 89. Koan 91. Knight Moves (US) 92. Exquisite Tenderness (Can.) 93. The Surgeon 94. Tarzan and the Lost City 98, etc.

Schepisi, Fred (1939–).
Australian director.
The Devil's Playground 76. The Chant of Jimmie Blacksmith 78. Iceman 81. Barbarosa 81. Plenty 85. Roxanne 87. A Cry in the Dark 88. The Russia House 90. Mr Baseball 92. Six Degrees of Separation (& p) 93. Fierce Creatures 97, etc.

Scherick, Edgar J. (c. 1919–).
American independent producer.
For Love of Ivy 68. Sleuth 72. The Heartbreak Kid 72. Gordon's War 74. The Stepford Wives 74. The Taking of Pelham One Two Three 74. I Never Promised You a Rose Garden 77. Little Gloria . . . Happy at Last (TV) 82. Shoot the Moon 82. The Kennedys of Massachusetts (TV) 84. The Dakota (TV) 84. Reckless 84. Mrs Soffel 85, etc.

Schertzinger, Victor (1880–1941).
American director, former concert violinist. Wrote the first film music score, for *Civilisation* 15.
AS DIRECTOR: Forgotten Faces 29. Nothing but the Truth 31. Uptown New York 32. The Cocktail Hour 33. One Night of Love (AAN) 34. Love Me Forever 35. The Music Goes Round 36. Something to Sing About 36. The Mikado (GB) 39. Road to Singapore 40. Rhythm on the River 41. Road to Zanzibar 41. Kiss the Boys Goodbye 41, etc.

Schiaffino, Rosanna (1939–).
Italian leading lady in international films.
Two Weeks in Another Town 62. The Victors 63. El Greco 66. Arrivederci Baby 66. The Man Called Noon 73. The Heroes 75. Cagliostro 76, etc.

Schiavelli, Vincent (1947–).
American character actor with an air of lopsided menace; best known for the role of the ghost in the subway in *Ghost*.
One Flew over the Cuckoo's Nest 75. The Return 80. Fast Times at Ridgmount High 82. The Adventures of Buckaroo Banzai across the Eighth Dimension 84. Amadeus 84. Better Off Dead 85. Cold Feet 89. Valmont 89. Ghost 90. Miracle Beach 92. Batman Returns 92. Lurking Fear 94. Lord of Illusions 95. The Courtyard 95. Two Much 96. The People vs Larry Flynt 96. Back to Back 96. Tomorrow Never Dies 97, etc.

Schiff, Richard.
American actor.
Medium Straight 89. Stop! Or My Mom Will Shoot 92. Malcolm X 92. The Bodyguard 92. The Public Eye 92. Hoffa 92. My Life 93. Ghost in the Machine 93. The Hudsucker Proxy 94. Tank Girl 95. Seven 95. The Trigger Effect 96. City Hall 96. Michael 97. Touch 97. Volcano 98. The Lost World: Jurassic Park 97. The Kiss 97. Heaven 98. Living Out Loud 98. Dr Dolittle 98. Deep Impact 98, etc.

Schiffer, Claudia (1970–).
German-born model and occasional actress.
Richie Rich 94. Prêt-à-Porter/Ready to Wear 94. The Blackout 97. Friends and Lovers 98, etc.

Schiffman, Suzanne.
French screenwriter associated with the films of François Truffaut. She worked for him on continuity, became his first assistant, co-scripted his films from the mid-70s, and began directing in the late 80s.
Day for Night/La Nuit Américaine (co-w) (AAN) 74. L'Histoire d'Adèle H. (co-w) 75. Small Change/L'Argent de Poche (co-w) 76. The Man Who Loved Women (co-w) 77. The Last Metro/Le Dernier Métro (co-w) 81. The Woman Next Door/La Femme d'à Côté (co-w) 81. Vivement Dimanche (co-w) 83. L'Amour par Terre (co-w) 86. Le Moine et la Sorcière (wd) 87. La Femme de Paille (d) 89, etc.

Schifrin, Lalo (1932–).
Argentinian composer in Hollywood.
Joy House 64. The Cincinnati Kid 64. The Liquidator 66. Cool Hand Luke 67. The Brotherhood 68. Bullitt 68. Kelly's Heroes 70. The Beguiled 71. Dirty Harry 71. Prime Cut 72. The Wrath of God 72. The Four Musketeers 75. Voyage of the Damned 76. Rollercoaster 77. Telefon 77. The Cat from Outer Space 78. The Manitou 78. The Concorde – Airport 79 79. Brubaker 79. The Competition 80. When Time Ran Out 80. Caveman 81. Buddy Buddy 81. A Stranger Is Watching 82. The Osterman Weekend 83. Sudden Impact 83. Tank 84. The New Kids 85. The Mean Season 85. Bad Medicine 85. Black Moon Rising 86. The Fourth Protocol 87. The Dead Pool 88. The Neon Empire 89. FX2 – the Deadly Art of Illusion 91. The Beverly Hillbillies 93. Scorpion Spring 96. Money Talks 97. Rush Hour 98, many others.

Schildkraut, Joseph (1895–1964).
Austrian leading man and character actor, of theatrical family. On American stage from early 20s.
Autobiography: 1959, *My Father and I*.
■ Schlemiel 14. The Life of Theodore Herzl 18. Orphans of the Storm 22. The Song of Love 24. The Road to Yesterday 25. Shipwrecked 26. Young April 26. Meet the Prince 26. *King of Kings* 27. The Heart Thief 27. His Dog 27. The Forbidden Woman 27. The Blue Danube 28. Tenth Avenue 28. *Showboat* 29. The Mississippi Gambler 29. Cock o' the Walk 30. Night Ride 30. A Lady to Love (German version) 31. Carnival 31. Cleopatra 34. Viva Villa 34. Sisters Under the Skin 34. Blue Danube 34. The Crusades 35. *The Garden of Allah* 36. Slave Ship 37. *The Life of Emile Zola* (AA) (as Dreyfus) 37. Souls at Sea 37. Lancer Spy 37. Lady Behave 37. The Baroness and the Butler 38. Marie Antoinette 38. Suez 38. Idiot's Delight 39. The Three Musketeers 39. *The Man in the Iron Mask* 39. Mr Moto Takes a Vacation 39. Lady of the Tropics 39. *The Rains Came* 39. Barricade 39. Pack Up Your Troubles 39. The Shop Around the Corner 40. Phantom Raiders 40. Rangers of Fortune 40. Meet the Wildcat 40. The Parson of Panamint 41. Flame of the Barbary Coast 45. The Cheaters 45. *Monsieur Beaucaire* 46. The Plainsman and the Lady 46. Northwest Outpost 47. Old Los Angeles 48. Gallant Legion 48. *The Diary of Anne Frank* 59. King of the Roaring Twenties 60. The Greatest Story Ever Told 65.

Schilling, Gus (1908–1957).
Wry-faced American comic actor from musical comedy and burlesque.
Citizen Kane (debut; as the waiter) 41. A Thousand and One Nights 44. Lady from Shanghai 47. On Dangerous Ground 52. Glory 56, etc.

Schlamme, Thomas.
American director. Married actress Christine Lahti in 1984.
Miss Firecracker 89. Crazy from the Heart (TV) 91. So I Married an Axe Murderer 93. Kingfish (TV) 95, etc.

Schlatter, Charlie (1966–).
American leading actor.
18 Again 88. Heartbreak Hotel 88. Bright Lights, Big City 88. All-American Murder 91. Sunset Heat 92. Police Academy: Mission to Moscow 94. Ed 96, etc.
TV series: Ferris Bueller 90.

Schlesinger, John (1926–).
British director, former small-part actor and TV director. He helped finance a 35mm version of his TV film *Cold Comfort Farm* so that it could receive a US cinema release.
Terminus 60. *A Kind of Loving* 62. *Billy Liar* 63. *Darling* (AAN) 65. Far from the Madding Crowd 67. *Midnight Cowboy* (US) (AA) 69. *Sunday Bloody Sunday* (AAN) 72. Visions of Eight 73. The Day of the Locust 75. Marathon Man 76. Yanks 79. Honky Tonk Freeway 81. An Englishman Abroad (TV) 83. Separate Tables (TV) 83. The Falcon and the Snowman 85. The Believers 87. Madame Sousatzka 88. Pacific Heights 90. A Question of Attribution (TV) 91. The Lost Language of Cranes (a) (TV) 91. The Innocent 93. Cold Comfort Farm (TV) 95. Eye for an Eye 95. Sweeney Todd (TV) 97. The Twilight of the Gods (a) 97, etc.
❝ The days of dealing with one despot are over. Now it's clearly with a whole group of frightened committee people. *–J.S., 1980*
What I tend to go for, and what interests me, is not the hero but the coward . . . not the success, but the failure. *–J.S.*
Normally my films are feelbad. I don't know why, but I am attracted to dark things. *–J.S.*

Schlom, Herman (1904–1983).
American producer of 40s second features.
The Sheik Steps Out 38. The Brighton Strangler 45. Dick Tracy Meets Gruesome 48. Follow Me Quietly 50, etc.

Schlondorff, Volker (1939–).
German director. He was head of development and production at Germany's Babelsberg studios, relinquishing the post in 1997.
Young Torless 66. A Degree of Murder 67. Michael Kohlhaas 69. Baal 70. Summer Lightning 72. The Lost Honour of Katharina Blum 75. Coup de Grâce 77. *The Tin Drum* 79. Circle of Deceit 81. Hôtel de la Paix 83. Swann in Love/Un Amour de Swann 84. Death of a Salesman (TV) 85. Vermischte Nachrichten 86. The Handmaid's Tale 90. Voyager 91. The Ogre 96, etc.

Schmidt, Joseph (1906–1942).
Diminutive German opera singer who made two British films: *My Song Goes Round the World* 34. *The Singing Dream* 35.

Schmidt, Richard (1944–).
American experimental film-maker.
A Man, a Woman and a Killer 75. Showboat 1988 – the Remake 78. Emerald Cities 83.

Schnabel, Julian (1951–).
American artist, screenwriter and director whose first film dealt with the life of the graffiti artist Jean-Michael Basquiat, who died of a drug overdose at the age of 27. Born in New York, he trained at the University of Texas and had his first one-man show in 1977; his paintings have included broken crockery or have sometimes been made on velvet instead of canvas.
Basquiat (wd) 96.

Schnee, Charles (1916–1963).
American screenwriter.
I Walk Alone 47. Red River 48. The Furies 50. *The Bad and the Beautiful* (AA) 52. The Next Voice You Hear 53. Butterfield 8 60. The Crowded Sky 61. Two Weeks in Another Town 62, etc.

Schneer, Charles (1920–).
American producer, mainly of trick films using 'Superdynamation'.
The Seventh Voyage of Sinbad 58. The Three Worlds of Gulliver 60. I Aim at the Stars 61. Mysterious Island 62. *Jason and the Argonauts* 63. The First Men in the Moon 64. You Must Be Joking 65. Half a Sixpence 67. The Executioner 69. Sinbad's Golden Voyage 74. Sinbad and the Eye of the Tiger 77, etc.

Schneider, Bert (1932–) (Berton Schneider).
American producer of Hollywood's 'new wave'.
Head 68. Easy Rider 69. Five Easy Pieces 71. The Last Picture Show 71. A Safe Place 72. Drive He Said 72. The King of Marvin Gardens 73.

Schneider, John (1954–).
American actor, best known for his role as Bo in the TV series *The Dukes of Hazzard* 79–85.
Eddie Macon's Run 83. Cocaine Wars 86. Stagecoach 86. The Curse 87. Christmas Comes to Willow Creek 87. Speed Zone 88. Ministry of Vengeance 89. Texas (TV) 94. Night of the Twisters (TV) 95. True Women (TV) 97, etc.
TV series: Grand Slam 90.

Schneider, Maria (1952–).
French leading actress.
Last Tango in Paris 73. Reigen 74. The Passenger 75. Babysitter 75. A Woman Like Eve 79. Mama Dracula 80. Bunker Palace Hotel 89. Sand Screens/Ecrans de Sable 91. Au Pays des Juliets 92. Jane Eyre 96, etc.

Schneider, Rob.
American actor, a regular in the 90s on TV's *Saturday Night Live*.
Home Alone 2: Lost in New York 92. Judge Dredd 95. Down Periscope 96. The Adventures of Pinocchio 96. Knock Off 98, etc.

Schneider, Romy (1938–1982) (Rosemarie Albach-Retty).
Austrian leading lady in international films.
Wenn der Weisse Flieder Wieder Blueht 53. Sissi 55. Maedchen in Uniform 58. The Story of Vicki (Ger.) 58. Forever My Love 61. Boccaccio 70 62. The Cardinal 63. The Trial 63. The Victors 63. Good Neighbour Sam 64. What's New, Pussycat? 65. 10.30 p.m. Summer 66. Triple Cross 66. Les Choses de la Vie 69. Don't You Cry 70. Bloomfield 70. The Assassination of Trotsky 72. Ludwig 72. Qui? 73. *Un Amour de Pluie* 73. The Infernal Trio 74. Lover on a String 75. The Old Gun 76. Bloodline 79. La Banquière 80, etc.

Schneiderman, George (c. 1890–1964).
American cinematographer.
Love is Love 19. Bare Knuckles 21. Boston Blackie 23. *The Iron Horse* 24. The Johnstown Flood 26. Three Bad Men 26. Four Sons 28. Born Reckless 30. Charlie Chan Carries On 31. Young America 32. Doctor Bull 33. *Judge Priest* 34. Steamboat Round the Bend 35. The Devil is a Sissy 36. The Gladiator 38. Michael Shayne Private Detective 40, many others.

Schnitzler, Arthur (1862–1931).
Austrian playwright whose chief bequests to the cinema are *Liebelei* and *La Ronde*.

Schoedsack, Ernest B. (1893–1979).
American director, former cameraman, who with Merian C. Cooper made the following:
Grass 26. *Chang* 27. *The Four Feathers* 29. Rango 31. *The Hounds of Zaroff* 32. *King Kong* 33. Son of Kong 34. Long Lost Father 34. Outlaws of the Orient 37. Dr Cyclops 39. Mighty Joe Young 49, etc.

Schoendoerffer, Pierre (1928–).
French screenwriter and director. He is a former army photographer who was taken prisoner at the battle of Dien Bien Phu in 1954, when Vietnam was a French colony. After his release he became a war correspondent for *Life* and *Paris Match* and a documentary film-maker.
Ramuntcho 58. Pêcheurs d'Islande 59. The 317th Platoon/La 317e Section 64. Objectif 500 Millions 66. The Anderson Section (doc) (AA) 67. Le Crabe Tambour 77. A Captain's Honour/L'Honneur d'un Capitaine 82. Dien Bien Phu 92, etc.

Schofield, Johnnie (1889–1955).
Ubiquitous English character actor, almost a fixture in low-budget British movies of the 30s and 40s.
Pride of the Force 33. The Outcast 34. Mystery of the Marie Celeste 35. Song of Freedom 36. Song of the Road 37. Lassie from Lancashire 38. The Arsenal Stadium Mystery 39. Let George Do It 40. In Which We Serve 42. The Young Mr Pitt 42. We Dive at Dawn 43. Old Mother Riley, Detective 43. Tawny Pipit 44. They Came to a City 44. The Wicked Lady 45. Waterloo Road 45. The Way to the Stars 45. This Man Is Mine 46. Mr Perrin and Mr Traill 48. Appointment with Venus 51. The Browning Version 51. Home at Seven 52. The Saint Returns 53. Carrington V.C. 54. See How They Run 55, many others.

Schoonmaker, Thelma (1940–).
American film editor, often on the films of director Martin Scorsese. She married director Michael Powell in 1984.
Woodstock (AAN) 70. Raging Bull (AA) 80. The King of Comedy 83. After Hours 85. The Color of Money 86. The Last Temptation of Christ 88. New York Stories 89. GoodFellas (AAN) 90. Cape Fear 91. The Age of Innocence 93. Casino 95. Grace of My Heart 96. Kundun 97, etc.

Schrader, Paul (1946–).
American screenwriter and director, dealing almost obsessively with tough themes.
Autobiography: 1990, *Schrader on Schrader*.
The Yakuza (co-w) 75. *Taxi Driver* 76. Obsession 76. Rolling Thunder (co-w) 77. Blue Collar (& d) 78. Old Boyfriends (co-w) 79. Hardcore (& d) 79. American Gigolo (& d) 79. Raging Bull 80. Cat People (& d) 82. Mishima (& d) 85. Light of Day (& d) 87. The Last Temptation of Christ (w) 88. Patty Hearst (d) 88. The Comfort of Strangers (d) 90. Light Sleeper (wd) 91. City Hall (co-w) 96. Touch (wd) 97. Affliction (co-w, d) 98, etc.
❝ Mine was the first generation of film-makers informed by film school, just as the generation before us was informed by live television and the next generation was informed by music television. *–P.S.*

Schreck, Max (1879–1936).
German actor best known for his eerie portrayal of the vampire count in *Nosferatu* 22.

Schreiber, Liev (1967–).
American actor, mainly in independent films. Born in San Francisco, he trained at RADA and the Yale School of Drama.
Mixed Nuts 94. Party Girl 94. Buffalo Girls 95. Denise Calls Up 95. Mad Love 95. The Daytrippers 96. Big Night 96. Walking and Talking 96. Ransom 96. Scream 96. Scream 2 97. Sphere 98. Twilight 98. Since You've Been Gone (TV) 98. Phantoms 98. Kiss the Sky 98, etc.

Schroder, Rick (1970–) (aka Ricky Schroder).
American actor, a former child star.
■ *The Champ* 79. The Last Flight of Noah's Ark 80. The Earthling 80. Little Lord Fauntleroy (TV) 81. A Reason to Live (TV) 85. A Son's Promise (TV) 90. Across the Tracks 90. Call of the Wild (TV) 93. There Goes My Baby 94. Crimson Tide 95. Innocent Victims (TV) 96.
TV series: Silver Spoons 82–86. NYPD Blue 98– .

Schroeder, Barbet (1941–).
Iranian director, long in Paris, at first as producer of Eric Rohmer's films.
More 69. The Valley 72. General Idi Amin Dada 74. Maîtresse 76. Barfly 87. Reversal of Fortune (AAN) 90. Single White Female 92. Kiss of Death 95. Before and After 96. Mars Attacks! (a) 96. Shattered Image (p) 98, etc.

Schroeter, Werner (1945–).
German director, a former journalist who also worked as a stage and opera director. His films, often in a visually extravagant style on homosexual themes, have influenced his better-known contemporaries, including Fassbinder and Syberberg.
Eika Katappa 69. Bomber Pilot (TV) 70. Salome (TV) 71. Macbeth (TV) 71. The Death of Maria

Malibran/Der Tod der Maria Malibran (TV) 72. Kingdom of Naples/Neopolitanische Geschwister 78. Palermo or Wolfsburg 80. Weisse Reisse/White Journey 80. About Argentina (doc) 85. The Rose King/Der Rosenkönig 86. Malina 91. Poussières d'Amour 96, etc.

Schuck, John (1944–).
American character actor familiar as the dumb sergeant in *McMillan and Wife*.
M*A*S*H 70. Blade 73. Thieves Like Us 74. Butch and Sundance: the Early Days 79. Just You and Me Kid 79. Earthbound 81. Star Trek IV: The Voyage Home 86. Outrageous Fortune 87. The New Adventures of Pippi Longstocking 88. Dick Tracy 90. Star Trek VI: The Undiscovered Country 91, etc.
TV series: Holmes and Yo Yo 75. Turnabout 79.

Schufftan, Eugene (1893–1977).
German cinematographer. Invented the Schufftan process, a variation on the 'GLASS SHOT', by which mirror images are blended with real backgrounds.
People on Sunday 30. L'Atlantide 32. Drôle de Drame 37. *Quai des Brumes* 38. *It Happened Tomorrow* 44. Ulysses 54. Eyes without a Face 59. Something Wild 61. *The Hustler* (AA) 62. Lilith 64, etc.

Schulberg, B. P. (1892–1957).
American executive, former publicist; general manager of Paramount (1926–32), then independent producer.
❝ This is the only industry I know. I am able to work as hard as anybody in it. Sure I have made some mistakes . . . who hasn't? What is the judicial code of the industry? Life imprisonment for a misdemeanour and execution for violating a parking law? Must we always wait until a production pioneer is found dead in a Hollywood hotel room before reflecting on an 'indifferent and forgetful' industry? – *Advertisement in Variety, 1949*

Schulberg, Budd (1914–).
American novelist whose work has been adapted for the screen. Son of B. P. Schulberg.
Autobiography: 1982, *Moving Pictures*.
On the Waterfront (AA) 54. The Harder They Fall 56. A Face in the Crowd 57. Wind Across the Everglades 59. A Question of Honour (TV) 81, etc.

Schulman, Arnold (1925–).
American screenwriter and dramatist.
Wild Is the Wind 57. A Hole in the Head 59. Cimarron 60. Love with the Proper Stranger (AAN) 64. The Night They Raided Minsky's 68. Goodbye Columbus (AAN) 69. To Find a Man 71. Funny Lady 75. Won Ton Ton, the Dog Who Saved Hollywood 76. Players 79. A Chorus Line 85. Tucker: The Man and His Dream 88, etc.

Schulman, Tom.
American screenwriter.
Dead Poets Society (AA) 89. Honey, I Shrunk the Kids 89. Second Sight 89. What about Bob? 91. Medicine Man 92. 8 Heads in a Duffel Bag (& d) 97. Holy Man 98, etc.

Schultz, Carl (1939–).
Hungarian-born director, in Australia from the mid-50s.
Blue Fin 78. Goodbye Paradise 83. Bodyline (TV) 84. Travelling North 87. The Seventh Sign (US) 88. Which Way Home 90. Deadly Currents 93, etc.

Schultz, Michael (1938–).
American director.
Cooley High 75. Car Wash 76. Greased Lightning 77. Which Way Is Up? 77. Sergeant Pepper's Lonely Hearts Club Band 78. Scavenger Hunt 79. Carbon Copy 81. The Last Dragon 84. Krush Grove 85. Disorderlies 87. Rock 'n' Roll Mom (TV) 88. Livin' Large 91. The Great American Sex Scandal (TV) 94, etc.

Schumacher, Joel (1939–).
American director and screenwriter, with a liking for fantasy. Born in New York City, he studied at Parson's School of Design in Manhattan and worked as a costume designer before becoming a writer and, from the 80s, a director.
AS COSTUME DESIGNER: Play It as It Lays 72. The Last of Sheila 73. Blume in Love 73. *Sleeper* 73. The Prisoner of Second Avenue 75. Interiors 78, etc.
AS WRITER: Sparkle 76. Car Wash 76. The Wiz 78, etc.
AS DIRECTOR: The Incredible Shrinking Woman 81. D.C. Cab (& w) 83. St Elmo's Fire (& w) 85. The Lost Boys 87. Cousins 89. Flatliners 90. Dying Young 91. *Falling Down* 93. The Client 94. Batman Forever 95. A Time to Kill 96. Batman & Robin 97. Flawless 99, etc.

Schunzel, Reinhold (1886–1954).
German actor and director who came to Hollywood in the 30s.
Around the World in Eighty Days 19. Die Dreigroschenoper 31. Viktor und Viktoria 33. Amphitryon 37. Rich Man, Poor Girl (d) 38. Balalaika (d) 39. The Great Awakening (d) 41. Hostages (a) 43. The Man in Half Moon Street (a) 44. Notorious (a) 46. The Woman in Brown (a) 48. Washington Story (a) 52, etc.

Schurmann, Gerard (1928–).
Dutch composer and conductor, in British films from the late 40s. He also orchestrated the scores for *The Vikings*, *Exodus* and *Lawrence of Arabia*.
But Not in Vain 48. The Long Arm 56. The Man in the Sky 56. The Camp on Blood Island 58. Horrors of the Black Museum 59. The Two-Headed Spy 59. Cone of Silence 60. Konga 60. Day In Day Out 65. The Lost Continent 68. Claretta 84, etc.

Schuster, Harold (1902–1986).
American director, former editor.
Wings of the Morning 37. Dinner at the Ritz 37. Zanzibar 40. My Friend Flicka 43. The Tender Years 47. So Dear to My Heart 49. Kid Monk Baroni 52. Jack Slade 53. Dragoon Wells Massacre 57. The Courage of Black Beauty 58, etc.

Schwartz, Arthur (1900–1984).
American producer and composer, former lawyer.
Navy Blues (c) 42. Thank Your Lucky Stars (c) 43. Cover Girl (p) 44. The Band Wagon (c) 53. You're Never Too Young (c) 55, many others.

Schwartz, Stephen (1948–).
American composer and lyricist, from the musical theatre. Born in New York City, he studied at Carnegie-Mellon University and the Juilliard School. His stage success, *Godspell*, was turned into a film, and he later wrote the music and lyrics for two Disney films, before switching to its animation rival, Dreamworks SKG.
Godspell 73. Pocahontas (AANm, AANs 'Colours of the Wind') 95. The Hunchback of Notre Dame (AANm) 96. Prince of Egypt 98, etc.

Schwarz, Maurice (1891–1960).
American actor famous in the Yiddish theatre; many of his successes, such as *Tevye the Milkman*, were filmed for limited circulation. Appeared in Hollywood's version of *Salome* 53.

Schwarzenegger, Arnold (1947–).
Austrian-born body-builder, a former winner of many Mr Universe and Mr Olympia contests who became the biggest box-office star of the early 90s, despite his excessive musculature and heavily accented English, delivered in a monotone. He became an American citizen in 1983 and is said to harbour political ambitions. By 1993, his price per film was $15 million plus. He is one of the backers of the international theme-restaurant chain Planet Hollywood, which includes on the menu Apple Strudel from his mother's recipe. Married Maria Shriver, the niece of John F. Kennedy; they have five children.
Autobiography: 1986, *Arnold: The Education of a Bodybuilder*.
Biographies: 1990, *Arnold* by Wendy Leigh. 1995, *True Myths: The Life and Times of Arnold Schwarzenegger* by Nicholas Wapshot.
Book: 1986, *Arnold's Encyclopedia of Modern Bodybuilding*.
Stay Hungry 76. Pumping Iron 77. The Villain 79. The Jayne Mansfield Story (TV) 79. Conan the Barbarian 82. Conan the Destroyer 84. The Terminator 84. Commando 85. Red Sonja 85. Raw Deal 86. Predator 87. The Running Man 87. Red Heat 88. Twins 88. Total Recall 90. Kindergarten Cop 90. Terminator 2: Judgment Day 91. Christmas in Connecticut (d) (TV) 92. The Last Action Hero 93. True Lies 94. Junior 94. Eraser 96. Jingle All the Way 96. Batman and Robin 97, etc.
❝ He has so many muscles that he has to make an appointment to move his fingers. – *Phyllis Diller*
Famous line (*Terminator*): 'I'll be back.'

Schweiger, Til (1962–).
German leading actor.
Manta Manta 91. Ebbie's Bluff 93. Pretty Baby/Der Bewegte Mann/Maybe . . . Maybe Not 94. Mad Dogs 95. Jailbirds/Maennerpension 96. The Super-Wife 96. Knocking on Heaven's Door (& co-p, w) 97. Judas Kiss (US) 98. The Replacement Killers (US) 98. Brute 98. SLC Punk! (US) 98, etc.

Schwimmer, David (1966–).
American leading actor, best known for his role as Ross in the TV sitcom *Friends*. He studied at Northwestern University and began in theatre in Chicago.
Crossing the Bridge 92. The Pallbearer 96. Dogwater (& d) 97. Breast Men 97. Apt Pupil 98. Six Days, Seven Nights 98. Kissing a Fool 98, etc.
TV series: Monty 93–94. Friends 94– .

Schygulla, Hanna (1943–).
Blonde Polish leading actress who first gained fame in the films of Rainer Werner FASSBINDER, sealing her international reputation with *The Marriage of Maria Braun*.
The Bridegroom and the Actress 68. Katzelmacher 69. Beware of a Holy Whore 70. *The Bitter Tears of Petra von Kant* 72. Effie Briest 74. *The Marriage of Maria Braun* 79. *Berlin Alexanderplatz* 80. Lili Marleen 80. Circle of Deceit 81. La Nuit de Varenne 82. The Story of Piera 83. A Love in Germany 83. The Future is Woman 84. The Delta Force 85. Forever Lulu 87. Miss Arizona 88. El Verano de la Señora Forbes 88. Abrahams Gold 90. Dead Again 91. Warsaw Year 5703/Warszawa 92. Mavi Surgun 93. Petrified Garden 93. Aux Petits Bonheurs 94. Words/Milim 96. The Girl of Your Dreams/La Niña de Tus Ojos 98, etc.

Sciorra, Annabella (1964–).
American actress. Born in New York City, she studied at the American Academy of Dramatic Arts and began in the theatre.
True Love 89. Internal Affairs 90. Reversal of Fortune 90. Cadillac Man 90. Jungle Fever 91. The Hard Way 91. The Hand that Rocks the Cradle 92. Mr Wonderful 93. Romeo Is Bleeding 93. The Night We Never Met 93. The Addiction 95. The Cure 95. Underworld 96. The Funeral 96. Cop Land 97. Asteroid (TV) 97. What Dreams May Come 98. New Rose Hotel 98, etc.

Scofield, Paul (1922–).
Distinguished British stage actor whose films have been infrequent. Born in Hurstpierpoint, Sussex, he studied for the stage at the London Mask Theatre School and was on stage from 1940. He made his reputation in Shakespearean roles, first at the Shakespeare Memorial Theatre at Stratford-upon-Avon and later with the National Theatre. His best screen performance remains Thomas More in *A Man for All Seasons*, repeating his role from the original stage production.
That Lady 55. Carve Her Name with Pride 58. The Train 64. *A Man for All Seasons* (AA, BFA) 66. King Lear 69. Bartleby 71. Scorpio 73. A Delicate Balance 73. Anna Karenina (TV) 84. The Attic: The Hiding of Anne Frank (TV) 88. When the Whales Came 89. Henry V 89. Hamlet 90. Utz (TV) 91. Quiz Show (AAN) 94. Martin Chuzzlewit (TV) 94. The Crucible 96, etc.

Scoggins, Tracy (1953–).
American actress, much on television.
Twirl (TV) 81. Toy Soldiers 84. The Gumshoe Kid 89. One Last Run 89. Watchers II 90. Play Murder for Me 91. Timebomb 91. Demonic Toys 91. Alien Intruder 93, etc.
TV series: Renegades 83. Hawaiian Heat 84. Dynasty II: The Colbys 85–87. Lois and Clark: The New Adventures of Superman 93.

Scola, Ettore (1931–).
Italian screenwriter and director.
Two Nights with Cleopatra (w) 54. Adua et le Compagne (w) 60. The Visit (w) 63. Made in Italy (w) 65. Let's Talk About Women (w, d) 65. The Devil in Love (wd) 66. The Pizza Triangle (wd) 70. We All Loved Each Other So Much (wd) 75. A Special Day (wd) 77. Passione d'Amore (wd) 81. La Nuit de Varennes (wd) 82. Le Bal (wd) 83. Macaroni (wd) 85. What Time Is It?/Che Ora E? (co-w, d) 89. Splendour (wd) 89. Il Viaggio di Capitan Fracassa (wd, p) 90. Mario, Maria e Mario (co-w, d) 94. The Story of a Poor Young Man 95, etc.

Scorsese, Martin (1942–).
American director and screenwriter of urban life among loners, losers and gangsters. Born in Flushing, New York, and brought up in Manhattan's Little Italy, he planned to become a priest before cinema became his vocation, and he studied film at New York University. Many of his best films have featured actor Robert DE NIRO. Although he has also made musicals, period films and a biopic of the Dalai Lama, he is most at home when reflecting the uglier aspects and tensions of city living.
Biographies: 1991, *Martin Scorsese: A Journey* by Mary Pat Kelly; 1992, *The Scorsese Picture: The Art and Life of Martin Scorsese* by David Ehrenstein.
Books: 1990, *Scorsese on Scorsese* edited by David Thompson and Ian Christie; 1997, *A Personal Journey with Martin Scorsese through American Movies* by Martin Scorsese and Michael Henry Wilson.
Who's That Knocking at My Door? 70. Boxcar Bertha 72. *Mean Streets* 73. *Alice Doesn't Live Here Any More* 74. *Taxi Driver* 76. New York, New York 77. The Last Waltz 78. *Raging Bull* (AAN) 80. King of Comedy 83. After Hours 85. *The Color of Money* 86. The Last Temptation of Christ (AAN) 88. New York Stories 89. Akira Kurosawa's Dreams (a) 90. *GoodFellas* (AAN) 90. Guilty by Suspicion (a) 90. *Cape Fear* 91. The Age of Innocence (co-w, d) (AANw) 93. Quiz Show (a) 94. Casino 95. Kundun 97, etc.
❝ Cinema is a matter of what's in the frame and what's out. – M.S.

Scorupco, Izabella (1970–).
Swedish actress and singer, of Polish ancestry.
The Tears of St Peter/Petri Tarar 95. GoldenEye (US) 95, etc.

Scott, Adrian (1912–1973).
American producer who was one of the 'Hollywood Ten'. He was briefly married to actress Anne Shirley.
Murder My Sweet 44. My Pal Wolf 44. Cornered 46. So Well Remembered 47. *Crossfire* 47, etc.

Scott, Allan (Allan Shiach).
Scottish screenwriter and producer, former chairman of the Macallan Distillery. He heads the production company Rafford Films.
The Man Who Had Power over Women (co-w) 70. *Don't Look Now* (co-w) 73. The Spiral Staircase (co-w) 75. Joseph Andrews (co-w) 76. D.A.R.Y.L. (co-w) 85. Castaway (w) 86. The Witches (w) 89. Cold Heaven (p, w) 92. Shallow Grave (ex p) 94. Samson and Delilah (TV) 96. The Preacher's Wife (co-w) 96. In Love and War (w) 96. Regeneration (p) 97, etc.

Scott, Campbell (1962–).
American leading actor. He is the son of actors George C. Scott and Colleen Dewhurst.
Five Corners 87. From Hollywood to Deadwood 88. Longtime Companion 90. The Sheltering Sky 90. Dying Young 91. Dead Again 91. Singles 92. The Innocent 93. Mrs Parker and the Vicious Circle (as Robert Benchley) 94. Big Night (& co-p, co-d) 96. The Daytrippers 96. The Spanish Prisoner 98. Imposters 98. Hi-Life 98. Top of the Food Chain (Can.) 98, etc.

Scott, Dougray (c. 1967–) (Stephen Scott).
Scottish actor. Born in Fife, he trained at the Welsh College of Music and Drama and began in the theatre.
Princess Caraboo 94. Twin Town 97. Regeneration 97. Deep Impact 98. Ever After 98. This Year's Love 98. Gregory's Two Girls 99. Mission: Impossible 2 99, etc.

Scott, Fred (1902–1991).
American singer and actor, best known as a star of 'B' westerns of the mid-30s, when he was sometimes billed as 'The Silvery-Voiced Buckaroo'; his frequent sidekick was Al ST JOHN. Born in Fresno, California, he was on-screen from 1924, and also sang with the San Francisco Opera Company in the early 30s. He quit films in the 40s, but continued as a singer in revues and was later in the real estate business in Hollywood.

Bride of the Storm 26. Rio Rita 29. The Grand Parade 30. Swing High 30. Night Work 30. Beyond Victory 31. The Last Outlaw 36. Singing Buckaroo 37. Two Gun Troubador 37. The Roamin' Cowboy 37. Melody of the Plains 37. Make a Wish 37. Knight of the Plains 38. Ranger's Roundup 38. Songs and Bullets 38. Code of the Fearless 39. In Old Montana 39. Ridin' the Trail 40. Thundering Hoofs 42. Treasure Chest 45, etc.

Scott, George C. (1926–).
Distinguished but taciturn American actor; usually plays tough or sardonic characters and was the first actor to refuse an Oscar. His best roles have been as Claude Dancer in *Anatomy of a Murder*, Bert Gordon in *The Hustler*, Anthony Gethryn in *The List of Adrian Messenger*, General 'Buck' Turgidson in *Dr Strangelove*, the title role in *Patton*, and Dr Herbert Bock in *The Hospital*. His five wives included actresses Patricia Reed, Colleen Dewhurst (whom he married twice), and Trish Van Devere. He is the father of actor Campbell Scott.

The Hanging Tree 58. *Anatomy of a Murder* (AAN) 59. *The Hustler* (AAN) 62. *The List of Adrian Messenger* 63. Dr Strangelove 63. The Yellow Rolls-Royce 64. The Bible 66. Not with My Wife You Don't 66. The Flim Flam Man 67. Petulia 69. *Patton* (AA) 70. They Might Be Giants 71. The Last Run 71. *The Hospital* (AAN) 72. The New Centurions 72. Jane Eyre (TV) 72. Oklahoma Crude 73. The Day of the Dolphin 73. Rage (& d) 73. The Savage Is Loose (& d) 74. Bank Shot 75. The Hindenberg 75. This Savage Land (TV) 76. *Fear on Trial* (TV) 76. The Prince and the Pauper 77. Islands in the Stream 77. Beauty and the Beast (TV) 77. Movie Movie 78. Hardcore 79. The Changeling 80. The Formula 80. Taps 81. Oliver Twist (as Fagin) 82. China Girl (TV) 83. Firestarter 84. A Christmas Carol (TV) 84. Mussolini: The Untold Story (TV) 85. Choices (TV) 85. The Last Days of Patton (TV) 86. The Murders in the Rue Morgue (TV) 86. Pals (TV) 87. The Ryan White Story (TV) 89. The Rescuers Down Under (voice) 90. William Peter Blatty's The Exorcist III 90. Descending Angel (TV) 90. Malice 93. Tyson (TV) 95. Angus 95. Titanic (TV) 96. Twelve Angry Men (TV) 97, etc.

TV series: East Side West Side 63. Traps 94.

✪ For some of the most powerful and intense performances in the movies. *Patton*.

❝ There is no question you get pumped up by the recognition. Then a self-loathing sets in when you realize you're enjoying it. – G.C.S.

Famous line (*Dr Strangelove*): 'I don't say we wouldn't get our hair mussed, but I do say no more than ten to twenty million killed, tops – that is, depending on the break.'

Scott, Gordon (1927–) (Gordon M. Werschkul).
American leading man who after being fireman, cowboy and lifeguard was signed to play Tarzan in *Tarzan's Hidden Jungle* 55; made five further episodes, then went to Italy to make muscleman epics.

■ Tarzan's Hidden Jungle 55. Tarzan and the Trappers 55. Tarzan and the Lost Safari 56. Tarzan's Fight for Life 58. Tarzan's Greatest Adventure 59. Tarzan the Magnificent 60. Duel of the Titans 61. Samson and the Seven Miracles 61. Goliath and the Vampires 62. Zorro and the Three Musketeers 62. Battles of the Gladiators 62. A Queen for Caesar 62. The Lion of St Mark 63. Hero of Babylon 63. Hercules Attacks 63. Thunder of Battle 63. Arrow of the Avenger 63. Arm of Fire 64. Buffalo Bill 64. Hercules and the Princess of Troy 65. The Tramplers 66. Top Secret 66. Nest of Spies 67.

Scott, Gordon L. T. (1920–1991).
British producer, former production manager.

Look Back in Anger 58. Petticoat Pirates 61. The Pot Carriers 63. Crooks in Cloisters 64, etc.

Scott, Hazel (1920–1981).
American pianist and pop organist.

Something to Shout About 43. The Heat's On 43. I Dood It 43. Broadway Rhythm 44. Rhapsody in Blue 45. The Night Affair (Fr.) 61, etc.

Scott, Janette (1938–).
British leading actress, a former child star, and the daughter of actress Thora Hird. Married singer Mel Tormé (1966–78).

Autobiography: 1953, *First Act*.

Went the Day Well? 42. No Place for Jennifer 49. No Highway 50. The Magic Box 51. As Long as They're Happy 52. Now and Forever 55. The Good Companions 57. The Devil's Disciple 59. The Old Dark House 63. *The Beauty Jungle* 64. Crack in the World 65. His and Hers 68, etc.

Scott, John (1930–).
British composer and conductor. He began by creating musical arrangements for the 60s pop group The Hollies, and has also written many TV themes.

A Study in Terror 65. Doctor in Clover 66. Sumuru 66. Berserk 67. Jules Verne's Rocket to the Moon 67. The Long Duel 67. Stranger in the House 67. Loving Feeling 68. The Amsterdam Affair 68. Twinky 69. Crooks and Coronets/Sophie's Place 69. The Violent Enemy 69. Outback 70. Trog 70. Girl Stroke Boy 71. The Jerusalem File 79. *Antony and Cleopatra* 72. Doom Watch 72. England Made Me 72. Penny Gold 73. Billy Two Hats 73. Craze 73. S.P.Y.S./Whiffs 74. Symptoms/ The Blood Virgin 74. Hennessy 75. That Lucky Touch 75. Satan's Slave 76. The People that Time Forgot 77. North Dallas Forty 79. The Final Countdown 80. The Hostage Tower 80. Inseminoid 80. Greystoke: The Legend of Tarzan Lord of the Apes 84. The Shooting Party 85. King Kong Lives 86. Death of a Soldier 86. Man on Fire 87. Shoot to Kill 88. The Deceivers 88. Winter People 89. Dog Tags 90, etc.

Scott, Ken (1927–1986).
American action lead of the 60s.

The Three Faces of Eve 57. Woman Obsessed 59. Pirates of Tortuga 61. Desire in the Dust 61. Police Nurse 63. The Murder Game 65. Fantastic Voyage 66, etc.

Scott, Lizabeth (1922–) (Emma Matzo).
Sultry American leading lady of the 40s, a box-office concoction of blonde hair, defiant expression and immobile upper lip.

■ *You Came Along* 45. The Strange Love of Martha Ivers 46. Dead Reckoning 47. Desert Fury 47. I Walk Alone 47. Variety Girl 47. Pitfall 48. Too Late for Tears 49. Easy Living 49. Paid in Full 50. Dark City 50. The Racket 51. The Company She Keeps 51. Two of a Kind 51. Red Mountain 51. Stolen Face 52. Scared Stiff 53. Bad for Each Other 54. Silver Lode 54. Loving You 57. The Weapon 57. Pulp 72.

Scott, Margaretta (1912–).
British stage (from 1929) and screen (from 1934) actress who usually plays upper-middle-class women.

Dirty Work 34. Things to Come 36. Quiet Wedding 40. Sabotage at Sea 42. Fanny by Gaslight 43. The Man from Morocco 45. Mrs Fitzherbert 47. Idol of Paris 48. Where's Charley? 52. Town on Trial 56. The Last Man to Hang 56. A Woman Possessed 58. An Honourable Murder 60. Crescendo 69. Percy 71, etc.

Scott, Martha (1914–).
American actress with stage experience.

Our Town (AAN) 40. Cheers for Miss Bishop 41. The Howards of Virginia 41. One Foot in Heaven 41. Hi Diddle Diddle 43. In Old Oklahoma 43. So Well Remembered 47. The Desperate Hours 55. The Ten Commandments 56. Ben Hur 59. Airport 75 74. The Turning Point 77. The Word (TV) 78. Charleston (TV) 79. Beulah Land (TV) 80. Doin' Time on Planet Earth 88, etc.

TV series: The Bionic Woman 76. Dallas 79, 85. Secrets of Midland Heights 80–81.

Scott, Peter Graham (1923–).
British director, from TV.

Panic in Madame Tussauds 48. Sing Along with Me 52. The Headless Ghost 59. Captain Clegg 62. The Pot Carriers 63. Bitter Harvest 63. Father Came Too 64. Mister Ten Per Cent 67. The Promise 69, etc.

Scott, Pippa (1935–).
American actress.

Auntie Mame 58. Petulia 68. Cold Turkey 70. Bad Ronald 74, etc.

Scott, Randolph (1898–1987) (Randolph Crane).
Rugged American outdoor star, in films from 1931 after stage experience.

Sky Bride 31. Supernatural 32. Home on the Range 33. Roberta 34. *She* 35. So Red the Rose 35. Follow the Fleet 36. Go West Young Man 36. *Last of the Mohicans* 36. High, Wide and Handsome 37. Rebecca of Sunnybrook Farm 38. The Texans 38. Jesse James 39. Virginia City 40. My Favourite Wife 40. When the Daltons Rode 40. Western Union 41. Belle Starr 41. Paris Calling 41. To the Shores of Tripoli 42. The Spoilers 42. Pittsburgh 42. Bombardier 43. Gung Ho 43. The Desperadoes 43. Belle of the Yukon 44. China Sky 44. Captain Kidd 45. Badman's Territory 46. Abilene Town 47. Christmas Eve 47. Fighting Man of the Plains 49. Sugarfoot 51. Santa Fé 51. Hangman's Knot 53. The Stranger Wore a Gun 53. The Bounty Hunter 54. A Lawless Street 55. Seven Men from Now 56. Decision at Sundown 57. Ride Lonesome 58. *Ride the High Country* 62, many others.

Scott, Raymond (1908–1994) (Harry Warnow).
American composer, bandleader and pianist, whose compositions can be heard in many of Warner's Loony Tunes and Merrie Melodies cartoons. Born in Brooklyn, he studied at the Institute of Musical Art in New York and worked for CBS in the 30s and 40s, also leading a big band, when he was billed as 'America's Foremost Composer of Modern Music', and recording with his Quintet (which actually consisted of six musicians and included on drums Johnny Williams, father of composer John Williams). In the early 40s, Warner's licensed his compositions, which featured in many of its cartoons, as arranged by musical director Carl Stalling. In the 50s he worked as a composer and arranger, turning in the 60s to experimenting with electronic music, before retiring to Los Angeles. His composition 'Powerhouse' was used in Warner's *Hiss and Makeup* 43, *The Swooner Crooner* 44, *Little Red Riding Rabbit* 44, *The Mouse-Merized Cat* 46, *Baby Bottleneck* 46, and *Homeless Hare* 50. His 'Dinner Music for a Pack of Hungry Cannibals' featured in the cartoons *Puss 'n' Booty* 43 and *Gorilla My Dreams* 48. He also appeared on-screen with his Quintet.

Ali Baba Goes to Town (the Quintet perform his 'Twilight in Turkey') 37. Love and Hisses (the Quintet perform his 'Powerhouse') 37. Nothing Sacred (the Quintet perform 'Columbia, Gem of the Ocean') 37. Rebecca of Sunnybrook Farm (the Quintet perform his 'Toy Trumpet') 38. Happy Landing (the Quintet perform his 'War Dance for Wooden Indians') 38. Sally, Irene and Mary (a, s) 38. Not Wanted (co-m) 49. Never Love a Stranger (m) 58. The Pusher (m) 59, etc.

Scott, Ridley (1939–).
British director, from TV commercials, working in America. In 1994 he headed a consortium with his brother Tony Scott to take over Shepperton Studios.

The Duellists 78. *Alien* 79. *Blade Runner* 81. Legend 85. Someone to Watch over Me 87. Black Rain 89. *Thelma and Louise* (AAN) 91. 1492: Conquest of Paradise 92. The Browning Version (p) 94. White Squall 96. GI Jane 97, etc.

❝ I think it's remarkable that people will give you 10 million dollars to go and get your rocks off. – *R.S., 1976*

Never let yourself be seen in public unless they pay for it. – *R.S.*

Scott, Terry (1927–1994).
Plump English comic performer, from variety and the stage, where he was best known for an act as a naughty schoolboy and as a pantomime dame. Thereafter, he performed mainly in TV sitcoms and in stage farces.

Blue Murder at St Trinian's 58. A Pair of Briefs 62. Carry On Camping 68. Bless This House 72, etc.

TV series: Great Scott, It's Maynard 55–58. Hugh and I 62–70. Scott On 72. Son of the Bride 73. Happy Ever After 74. Terry and June 79–88. Danger Mouse (voice, as Penfold) 81–92.

Scott, Timothy (1938–1995).
American character actor, often in westerns.

The Way West 67. The Ballad of Josie 67. The Party 68. Butch Cassidy and the Sundance Kid 69. Vanishing Point 71. One More Train to Rob 71. Macon County Line 73. Days of Heaven 78. The Electric Horseman 79. A Chorus Line 85. Lonesome Dove (TV) 89. Chattahoochee 89. Return to Lonesome Dove (TV) 93. Clean Slate 94, etc.

Scott, Tony (1944–).
English director in Hollywood who began as a director of television commercials. He is the brother of director Ridley Scott. In 1994 he joined with Ridley in buying Shepperton Studios.

The Hunger 83. Top Gun 86. Beverly Hills Cop II 87. Days of Thunder 90. Revenge 90. The Last Boy Scout 91. True Romance 93. Crimson Tide 95. The Fan 96. Enemy of the State 98, etc.

Scott, Sir Walter (1771–1832).
Scottish novelist, mainly of period adventure stories. His *Ivanhoe*, *The Talisman* and *Rob Roy* have received most attention from film-makers.

Scott, Zachary (1914–1965).
American leading man with considerable stage experience.

The Mask of Dimitrios (film debut) 44. *The Southerner* 45. *Mildred Pierce* 46. Stallion Road 47. The Unfaithful 48. Shadow on the Wall 50. Born To Be Bad 51. Let's Make It Legal 53. Appointment in Honduras 53. Bandido 56. The Young One 60. It's Only Money 62, many others.

Scotto, Vincente (1876–1952).
French composer.

Jofroi 34. Pépé le Moko 36. La Fille du Puisatier 40. Domino 43. L'Ingénue Libertine 50, etc.

Scott Thomas, Kristin (1960–).
Coolly elegant English leading actress. Born in Redruth, Cornwall, she was brought up in Dorset. After an unhappy experience at the Central School of Speech and Drama, she left to work in Paris as an au pair, and eventually studied at the city's École Nationale des Arts et Technique de Théâtre, and first acted in French TV and films. Married French doctor François Oliviennes.

Under the Cherry Moon 86. A Handful of Dust (TV) 88. The Tenth Man (TV) 88. Le Bal du Gouverneur (Fr.) 89. The Endless Game (TV) 90. Framed (TV) 90. Autobus/Aux Yeux du Monde (Fr.) 91. Look at It This Way (TV) 92. Bitter Moon 93. Body and Soul (TV) 93. The Bachelor 93. Four Weddings and a Funeral 94. An Unforgettable Summer/Un Été Inoubliable (Fr.) 94. Angels and Insects 95. Richard III 95. The Pompatus of Love 95. Les Milles 95. Gulliver's Travels (TV) 96. The Confessional 96. Mission: Impossible 96. *The English Patient* (AAN) 96. The Horse Whisperer 98, etc.

Scourby, Alexander (1913–1985).
American stage character actor.

Affair in Trinidad 52. *The Big Heat* 53. The Silver Chalice 55. Giant 56. Seven Thieves 59. The Big Fisherman 59. Confessions of a Counterspy 60.

Screaming Mad George:
see George, Screaming Mad.

Scudamore, Margaret (1884–1958).
English character actress, mainly on the stage, the mother of Michael Redgrave. She made her stage debut in 1898 and was in films from the early 30s.

Arms and the Man 32. Double Alibi 37. Melody and Romance 37. Beauty and the Barge 37. My Wife's Family 41. A Canterbury Tale 44, etc.

❝ She had a gruff, gravelly voice which she blamed on all the Grand Guignol melodramas she had been forced to scream in as an *ingénue*, but which in fact had more to do with whisky. – *Corin Redgrave*

Seagal, Steven (1951–).
Frowning American star and producer of action films. Formerly married to actress Kelly Le Brock.

Above the Law 88. Hard to Kill 89. Marked for Death 90. Out for Justice 91. Under Siege 92. On Deadly Ground (& p, d) 94. Under Siege 2: Dark Territory 95. Executive Decision 96. The Glimmer Man 96. Executive Decision 96. Fire Down Below 97, etc.

Seagrove, Jenny (1958–).
British actress, born in Kuala Lumpur.

Tattoo 80. Moonlighting 82. Local Hero 83. Nate and Hayes 83. A Woman of Substance (TV) 85. Hold the Dream 85. Appointment with Death 88. A Chorus of Disapproval 89. The Guardian 90. Bullseye! 90. Deadly Game (TV) 91. Sherlock Holmes – the Incident at Victoria Falls (TV) 91. Don't Go Breaking My Heart 98, etc.

Seal, Elizabeth (1935–).
British dancer and occasional actress.
Town on Trial 56. Cone of Silence 60. Vampire Circus 72, etc.

Seale, John (1942–).
Australian cinematographer and director. He is noted for his work on the films of Peter WEIR, a relationship which began when he worked as camera operator to cinematographer Russell BOYD.
Alvin Purple 73. Deathcheaters 76. Fatty Finn 80. Doctors and Nurses 81. The Survivor 81. Fighting Back 82. Goodbye Paradise 82. BMX Bandits 83. Careful He Might Hear You 83. Silver City 84. The Empty Beach 85. Witness (AAN) 85. Children of a Lesser God 86. The Hitcher 86. The Mosquito Coast 86. Stakeout 87. Gorillas in the Mist 88. Rain Man (AAN) 88. Dead Poets Society 89. Till There Was You (d) 90. The Doctor 91. Lorenzo's Oil 92. The Firm 93. The Paper 94. Beyond Rangoon 95. The American President 95. *The English Patient* (AA) 96. City of Angels 98, etc.

Searle, Francis (1909–).
British director.
A Girl in a Million 46. Things Happen at Night 48. Cloudburst (& w) 51. Wheel of Fate (& w) 53, many second features.

Searle, Jackie (1920–).
American boy actor of the 30s, usually in mean roles.
Tom Sawyer 31. Skippy 31. Peck's Bad Boy 35. Little Lord Fauntleroy 36. That Certain Age 38. Little Tough Guys in Society 39. The Hard Boiled Canary 41. The Paleface 49, many others.

Sears, Fred F. (1913–1957).
American director of second features.
Desert Vigilante 49. Raiders of Tomahawk Creek 50. Snake River Desperadoes 51. Last Train from Bombay 52. Ambush at Tomahawk Gap 53. El Alamein 53. The Miami Story 54. Wyoming Renegades 55. Chicago Syndicate 55. Rock around the Clock 56. Earth versus the Flying Saucers 56. Don't Knock the Rock 56. The Giant Claw 57. The World was His Jury 58, etc.

Sears, Heather (1935–1994).
British actress with repertory experience. She later concentrated on theatre, notably at the Haymarket Theatre, Leicester.
Dry Rot 56. *The Story of Esther Costello* 57. *Room at the Top* 59. Sons and Lovers 60. Phantom of the Opera 62. Saturday Night Out 64. Black Torment 64. Great Expectations (TV) 75, etc.

Seastrom, Victor (1879–1960) (Victor Sjostrom).
Distinguished Swedish actor-director with stage experience.
Ingeborg Holm 13. Terje Vigen (ad) 16. Jerusalem (d) 18. *Ordet*/The Word (a) 21. *The Phantom Carriage*/Thy Soul Shall Bear Witness (d) 21. The Master of Man (US) (d) 23. He Who Gets Slapped (US) (d) 24. *The Scarlet Letter* (US) (d) 26. Tower of Lies (US) (d) 26. The Divine Woman (US) (d) 28. The Wind (US) (d) 28. Under the Red Robe (GB) (d) 36. Ordet (remake) (a) 43. *Wild Strawberries* (a) 57, many others.

Seaton, George (1911–1979) (George Stenius).
American writer-director. Acted and produced on stage; joined MGM writing staff 1933; later independent or working with producer William Perlberg.
A Day at the Races (co-w) 37. *The Song of Bernadette* (AANw) 43. Diamond Horseshoe (wd) 45. Junior Miss (wd) 45. The Shocking Miss Pilgrim (wd) 47. *Miracle on 34th Street* (wd) (AA) 47. The Big Lift (wd) 51. For Heaven's Sake (wd) 51. Anything Can Happen (wd) 52. Little Boy Lost (wd) 53. *The Country Girl* (wd) (AAw, AANd) 54. The Proud and Profane (wd) 56. The Tin Star (p) 57. Teacher's Pet (d) 58. The Pleasure of His Company (d) 61. The Counterfeit Traitor (wd) 63. Thirty-Six Hours (wd) 64. What's So Bad About Feeling Good? (wpd) 68. *Airport* (wd) (AANw) 69. Showdown (wpd) 73, many others.

Seberg, Jean (1938–1979).
American leading lady who won contest for role of Preminger's *Saint Joan* 57, after which her career faltered but picked up in French films. Her second husband was novelist Romain Gary. Found dead in her car. Two documentaries on her life appeared in 1995: *From the Journals of Jean Seberg*, directed by Mark Rappaport, with Mary Beth Hurt as Seberg, and *Jean Seberg, American Actress*, directed by Fosco and Donatello Dubini.
Biography: 1981, *Played Out* by David Richards.
Bonjour Tristesse 57. The Mouse That Roared 59. *Breathless*/A Bout de Souffle 60. Playtime 62. In the French Style 63. Lilith 64. Moment to Moment 65. Estouffade à la Caraïbe 66. The Road to Corinth 68. Pendulum 69. Paint Your Wagon 69. Airport 69. Macho Callahan 71. Mousey (TV) 73. The Wild Duck 76, etc.

Secchiaroli, Tazio (1925–1998).
Italian photographer who inspired the character of Paparazzo in FELLINI's *La Dolce Vita*, and so gave a name to the species of celebrity-stalking photographers. In the 50s and 60s, he cruised the streets of Rome on his Vespa scooter, taking photographs of the famous. He later became a successful portrait painter and was Sophia LOREN's personal photographer for 30 years.

Secombe, Sir Harry (1921–).
Burly Welsh comedian and singer, who apart from a number of second-feature appearances in the early 50s has filmed only rarely.
Davy 57. Jet Storm 59. *Oliver!* 68. Song of Norway 70. The Magnificent Seven Deadly Sins 71. Sunstruck 73, etc.

Sedgwick, Edie (1943–1971).
American socialite who was briefly a star in Andy Warhol's movies.
Biography: 1982, *Edie, an American Biography* by Jean Stein.
Vinyl 65. Poor Little Rich Girl 65. Kitchen 65. Beauty 2 65. Bitch 65. Death of Lupe Velez 65, etc.
“ She was the personification of the poor little rich girl – *Gerard Malanga*
She was a wonderful, beautiful blank. – *Andy Warhol*

Sedgwick, Edward (1892–1953).
American director of mainly routine films.
Live Wires 21. The First Degree 23. Two Fisted Jones 25. Spring Fever 27. *The Cameraman* 28. The Passionate Plumber 32. I'll Tell the World 34. Pick a Star 37. Beware Spooks 39. Ma and Pa Kettle Back on the Farm 50, many others.

Sedgwick, Kyra (1965–).
American leading actress, from the stage. Married actor Kevin Bacon.
War and Love 85. Kansas 88. Born on the Fourth of July 89. Mr and Mrs Bridge 90. Pyrates 91. Singles 92. Miss Rose White (TV) 92. Heart and Souls 93. Murder in the First 95. The Low Life 95. *Something to Talk About* 95. Phenomenon 96. Losing Chase (& p) (TV) 96. Critical Care 97, etc.

Seeley, Blossom (1892–1974).
American nightclub entertainer, married to Benny Fields. Played by Betty Hutton in *Somebody Loves Me* 52.
■ Broadway Through a Keyhole 33.

Segal, Alex (1915–1977).
American director, from TV.
■ Ransom 56. All the Way Home 63. Joy in the Morning 65. Harlow (electronovision) 66. My Father's House (TV) 73. The Story of David (TV) (co-d) 76.

Segal, Erich (1937–).
American university professor who unexpectedly wrote a best-selling sentimental novelette, *Love Story*, which was filmed with equal success.
■ Yellow Submarine 68. RPM 70. The Games 70. Love Story (AAN) 70. Oliver's Story (co-w) 78. A Change of Seasons (co-w) 80. Man, Woman and Child (co-w) 83.

Segal, George (1934–).
Leading American actor more at home with thought than with action, which may account for a somewhat fitful career.
The Young Doctors 61. The Longest Day 62. Act One 62. The New Interns 64. Invitation to a Gunfighter 64. Ship of Fools 65. *King Rat* 65. Lost Command 65. Who's Afraid of Virginia Woolf? (AAN) 66. The Quiller Memorandum 66. The St Valentine's Day Massacre 67. Bye Bye Braverman 68. No Way to Treat a Lady 68. The Southern Star 69. The Girl who Couldn't Say No 69. The Bridge at Remagen 69. Loving 70. *The Owl and the Pussycat* 70. Where's Poppa? 70. Born to Win 72. The Hot Rock 72. Blume in Love 73. *A Touch of Class* 73. The Terminal Man 74. California Split 75. The Black Bird 75. Russian Roulette 76. The Duchess and the Dirtwater Fox 76. Rollercoaster 77. Fun with Dick and Jane 77. Who is Killing the Great Chefs of Europe? 78. Lost and Found 79. The Last Married Couple in America 80. Carbon Copy 81. The Cold Room 81. Stick 82. Killing 'em Softly 83. The Zany Adventures of Robin Hood (TV) 84. All's Fair 89. Look Who's Talking 89. For the Boys 91. Direct Hit 93. Seasons of the Heart (TV) 94. It's My Party 96. Flirting with Disaster 96. The Feminine Touch 96. The Cable Guy 96. The Mirror Has Two Faces 96, etc.
TV series: Take Five 87. Just Shoot Me 97.
“ I have a dread of being considered bland, but I've had to reconcile myself to the fact that that's what I am. – G.S.

Segal, Peter.
American director.
Naked Gun 33: The Final Insult 94. Tommy Boy 95. My Fellow Americans 97, etc.

Segal, Vivienne (1897–1992).
American Broadway star of the early talkie period.
■ Song of the West 30. Golden Dawn 30. Bride of the Regiment 30. Viennese Nights 30. The Cat and the Fiddle 33.

Segal, Harry (1897–1975).
American writer who started the heavenly fantasies of the 40s with his play *Halfway to Heaven*.
Fatal Lady 36. Here Comes Mr Jordan (AA) 41. Angel on My Shoulder 46. For Heaven's Sake 50. Monkey Business 52, etc.

Sehr, Peter (1951–).
German director and screenwriter.
The Serbian Girl 91. Kaspar Hauser 93. Obsession 96, etc.

Seiber, Matyas (1905–1960).
Hungarian composer in London.
Animal Farm 54. The Diamond Wizard 54. A Town Like Alice 56. Chase a Crooked Shadow 58. Robbery Under Arms 58. For Better for Worse 61.

Seidelman, Susan (1952–).
American director.
■ Smithereens 82. Desperately Seeking Susan 84. Making Mr Right 87. Cookie 89. She-Devil 90. Erotic Tales (co-d) 94. The Barefoot Executive (TV) 95.

Seif, Salah Abou (1915–1996).
Egyptian film director, a former editor, whose films explored the social conditions of his country.
Raya Wa Sakina 53. Al-Futuwwa 57. No More Sleep/La Anam 59. Cairo in the Thirties/Al-Kahira Thalathin 66. Death of the Water Carrier/Al Saqa Mat 77. Al Qadisiya 81. Al-Bidaya 86. Al Moaten Al Myssri 91, etc.

Seigner, Emmanuelle (1967–).
French leading actress. She is the daughter of actress Françoise Seigner and granddaughter of actor Louis Seigner. Married director Roman POLANSKI.
Detective 85. Frantic 88. Bitter Moon 92. The Smile/Le Sourire 94. Nirvana 97. Place Vendôme 98, etc.

Seiler, Lewis (1891–1963).
American director. Many Tom Mix silents; then *Air Circus* (co-d) 28, and second features through the 30s.
Dust Be My Destiny 39. It All Came True 40. South of Suez 41. The Big Shot 42. Guadalcanal Diary 43. Molly and Me 44. If I'm Lucky 46. Whiplash 48. The Tanks are Coming 51. The Winning Team 52. The System 53. Women's Prison 55. Battle Stations 56. The True Story of Lynn Stuart 58, many others.

Seiter, William A. (1892–1964).
American director, in Hollywood from 1918, then directing shorts.
Boy Crazy 22. The Teaser 25. Skinner's Dress Suit 26. Good Morning Judge 28. The Love Racket 30. Girl Crazy 32. If I Had a Million (part) 33. Diplomaniacs 33. Professional Sweetheart 33. *Sons of the Desert* 33. Roberta 35. *The Moon's Our Home* 36. Dimples 36. *This is My Affair* 37. *Room Service* 38. It's a Date 40. *Broadway* 42. You Were Never Lovelier 42. Destroyer 43. *The Affairs of Susan* 45. I'll Be Yours 47. One Touch of Venus 48. Dear Brat 51. Make Haste to Live 54, many others.

Seitz, George B. (1888–1944).
American director, known as the serial king. A writer-director from 1913, he worked on *The Perils of Pauline*, and directed *The Fatal Ring* 17 and all subsequent Pearl White serials. In the 20s, he acted in his own serials: *Velvet Fingers*, *The Sky Ranger*, etc. Turning to features, he directed nearly forty between 1927 and 1933, then moved to MGM and kept up an even more rapid output, including episodes of the Hardy Family series.
The Woman in His Life 35. Andy Hardy Meets a Debutante 39. Kit Carson 40. Sky Murder 40. Andy Hardy's Private Secretary 41. China Caravan 42, etc.

Seitz, John F. (1893–1979).
American cinematographer, in Hollywood from 1916, brother of George B. Seitz.
SILENT FILMS: *The Four Horsemen of the Apocalypse* 21. *The Prisoner of Zenda* 22, etc.
SOUND FILMS: East Lynne 30. Over the Hill 30. She Wanted a Millionaire 32. Huckleberry Finn 39. *Sullivan's Travels* 41. The Moon and Sixpence 42. This Gun for Hire 42. The Miracle of Morgan's Creek 43. Hail the Conquering Hero 44. *Double Indemnity* 44. *The Lost Weekend* 45. *Sunset Boulevard* 50. The San Francisco Story 52. Hell on Frisco Bay 55. The Man in the Net 58. Guns of the Timberland 60, etc.

Sekely, Steve (1899–1979) (Istvan Szekely).
Hungarian director, in Hollywood from 1938.
Rhapsodie der Liebe 29. Lila Akac 34. Miracle on Main Street 40. Behind Prison Walls 43. Women in Bondage 44. The Scar 48. Stronghold 51. The Blue Camellia 54. The Day of the Triffids 68. Kenner 69. The Girl Who Liked Purple Flowers 73, etc.

Sekka, Johnny (1939–).
West African actor in London.
Flame in the Streets 61. Woman of Straw 64. Khartoum 65. The Last Safari 67. A Warm December 73. Uptown Saturday Night 75. Charlie Chan and the Curse of the Dragon Queen 81. Hanky Panky 82, etc.

Sekula, Andrzej.
Polish-born cinematographer, associated with the work of Quentin Tarantino. He first moved to London in the early 80s to study at the National Film and Television School, and then worked in commercials and music videos.
Reservoir Dogs 91. Bank Robber 93. Three of Hearts 93. Oleanna 94. Across the Moon 94. Pulp Fiction 94. Sleep with Me 94. Four Rooms 95. Cousin Bette 97, etc.

Selander, Lesley (1900–1979).
American director who made low-budget westerns and other action pictures from 1936.
Cattle Pass 37. The Round-Up 41. The Vampire's Ghost 46. Belle Starr's Daughter 48. I Was an American Spy 51. Flight to Mars 51. The Highwayman 52. Tall Man Riding 54. The Lone Ranger and the Lost City of Gold 58. Town Tamer 65. Fort Utah 67, many others.

Selick, Henry.
American director of features using stop-motion animation. He heads the San Francisco-based production company Twitching Image.
The Nightmare before Christmas 93. James and the Giant Peach 96.

Selig, William N. (1864–1948).
Pioneer American producer; many serials.
The Count of Monte Cristo 08. The Spoilers 13, etc.

Sellars, Elizabeth (1923–).
British leading actress on stage from 1941.
Floodtide (debut) 48. Madeleine 50. Cloudburst 51. The Gentle Gunman 52. The Barefoot Contessa 54. Three Cases of Murder 55. The Shiralee 57. The Day They Robbed the Bank of England 61. The Chalk Garden 64. The Mummy's Shroud 67. The Hireling 73, etc.

Selleck, Tom (1945–).
Tall, charismatic American leading man of the 80s, best known for the role of private investigator Tom Magnum in the long-running TV series. No film role has yet matched that success, though it might have done, since he was Steven Spielberg's first choice for the role of Indiana Jones. Born in Detroit, Michigan, he began acting in commercials, and then obtained small parts on television before landing his own series that mixed humour and action to considerable acclaim.

The Movie Murderer (TV) 69. Myra Breckinridge 70. The Seven Minutes 71. Daughters of Satan 72. Terminal Island 73. Returning Home (TV) 75. Most Wanted (TV) 76. Coma 77. The Sacketts (TV) 79. High Road to China 83. Lassiter 84. Three Men and a Baby 87. Her Alibi 88. An Innocent Man 89. Quigley Down Under 90. Folks! 92. Christopher Columbus: The Discovery 92. Mr Baseball 92. Broken Trust (TV) 95. In & Out 97, etc.

TV series: The Young and the Restless 75–75. The Rockford Files 79–80. Magnum, PI 80–88. The Closer 97– .

Sellers, Peter (1925–1980).
British comic actor who became an international star, then faltered. From variety stage and radio's *Goon Show*. His second wife was actress Britt Ekland (1964–68) and in 1977 he married his fourth wife, actress Lynne Frederick.

Biographies: 1969, *Peter Sellers, the Man behind the Mask* by Peter Evans. 1994, *The Life and Death of Peter Sellers* by Roger Lewis.

Book: 1993, *Peter Sellers – A Film History* by Michael Starr.

■ Penny Points to Paradise 51. Down Among the Z Men 52. Orders Are Orders 54. John and Julie 55. The Lady Killers 55. *The Smallest Show on Earth* 57. *The Naked Truth* 58. Tom Thumb 58. Up the Creek 58. Carlton-Browne of the F.O. 58. *The Mouse That Roared* 59. *I'm All Right, Jack* 59. The Battle of the Sexes 60. Two-Way Stretch 60. Never Let Go 61. The Millionairess 61. Mr Topaze (& d) 61. The Road to Hong Kong (cameo) 61. *Only Two Can Play* 62. Lolita 62. Waltz of the Toreadors 62. The Dock Brief 63. Heavens Above 63. The Wrong Arm of the Law 63. *The Pink Panther* 63. *Dr Strangelove* (AAN) 63. The World of Henry Orient 64. A Shot in the Dark 64. What's New, Pussycat? 65. The Wrong Box 66. After the Fox 66. Casino Royale 67. The Bobo 67. Woman Times Seven 67. The Party 68. *I Love You Alice B. Toklas* 68. The Magic Christian 69. Hoffman 70. There's a Girl in My Soup 70. Where Does it Hurt? 72. Alice's Adventures in Wonderland (as the March Hare) 72. The Optimists of Nine Elms 72. Soft Beds and Hard Battles 73. Ghost in the Noonday Sun 73. The Blockhouse 74. The Great McGonagall (as Queen Victoria) 74. The Return of the Pink Panther 75. Murder by Death 76. The Pink Panther Strikes Again 77. Revenge of the Pink Panther 78. The Prisoner of Zenda 79. Being There (AAN) 79. The Fiendish Plot of Dr Fu Manchu 79.

❝ There used to be a me behind the mask, but I had it surgically removed. – *P.S.*

If you ask me to play myself, I will not know what to do. I do not know who or what I am. – *P.S.*

People will swim through shit if you put a few bob in it. – *P.S.*

The only way to make a film with him is to let him direct, write and produce it as well as star in it. – *Charles Feldman*

Sellers is such an experienced impersonator that one regrets his inability to add to his list of impressions the Peter Sellers that was. – *John Simon of The World of Henry Orient*

I would squirm with embarrassment at the demeaning lengths he would go to in order to ingratiate himself with the Royal Family. – *Britt Ekland*

~In 1982 offcuts from earlier Panther films were assembled to make a tasteless sequel, The Trail of the Pink Panther.

Selten, Morton (1860–1939) (Morton Stubbs).
British stage actor who played distinguished old gentlemen in some 30s films.

Service for Ladies 32. Ten Minute Alibi 35. The Ghost Goes West 36. Fire over England 36. A Yank at Oxford 38. The Divorce of Lady X 38. The Thief of Bagdad 40, etc.

Seltzer, David (1940–).
American screenwriter who turned to directing in the mid-80s.

The Hellstrom Chronicle 71. King, Queen, Knave (co-w) 72. One Is a Lonely Number (w) 72. The Other Side of the Mountain (w) 75. The Omen (w) 76. Prophecy (w) 79. Table for Five (w) 83. Six Weeks (w) 85. Lucas (wd) 86. Punchline (wd) 88. Bird on a Wire (co-w, d) 90. Shining Through (wd) 92, etc.

Seltzer, Walter (1914–).
American producer.

One Eyed Jacks 58. The Naked Edge 61. The War Lord 65. Will Penny 67. Darker than Amber 70. Skyjacked 72, etc.

Selwyn, Edgar (1875–1944).
American director.

Night Life of New York 25. The Girl in the Show 29. War Nurse 30. The Sin of Madelon Claudet 31. Turn Back the Clock 33. The Mystery of Mr X 34. Pierre of the Plains (w, p only) 42, etc.

Selznick, David O. (1902–1965).
American independent producer, former writer. Worked for RKO from 1931, MGM from 1933; founded Selznick International Pictures in 1936. Married Irene Mayer, daughter of Louis B. Mayer, and, in 1949, actress Jennifer JONES.

Biographies: 1970, *Selznick* by Bob Thomas. 1972, *Memo from David O. Selznick*. 1993, *Showman: The Life of David Selznick* by David Thomson.

■ Roulette 24. Spoilers of the West 27. Wyoming 28. Forgotten Faces 28. Chinatown Nights 29. The Man I Love 29. The Four Feathers 29. The Dance of Life 29. Fast Company 29. Street of Chance 30. Sarah and Son 30. Honey 30. The Texan 30. For the Defense 30. Manslaughter 30. The Lost Squadron 32. Symphony of Six Million 32. State's Attorney 32. Westward Passage 32. What Price Hollywood? 32. Roar of the Dragon 32. Bird of Paradise 32. The Age of Consent 32. A Bill of Divorcement 32. The Conquerors 32. Rockabye 32. The Animal Kingdom 32. The Half Naked Truth 32. Topaze 33. The Great Jasper 33. Our Betters 33. Christopher Strong 33. Sweepings 33. The Monkey's Paw 33. *Dinner at Eight* 33. Night Flight 33. Meet the Baron 33. Dancing Lady 33. Viva Villa 34. Manhattan Melodrama 34. *David Copperfield* 35. Vanessa 35. Reckless 35. Anna Karenina 35. *A Tale of Two Cities* 35. Little Lord Fauntleroy 36. The Garden of Allah 36. *A Star Is Born* 37. *The Prisoner of Zenda* 37. Nothing Sacred 37. The Adventures of Tom Sawyer 38. The Young in Heart 38. Made for Each Other 39. Intermezzo 39. *Gone with the Wind* (AA) 39. *Rebecca* (AA) 40. Since You Went Away 44. I'll Be Seeing You 44. Spellbound 45. Duel in the Sun 46. The Paradine Case 48. Portrait of Jennie 48. *The Third Man* (co-p) 50. The Wild Heart (co-p) 52. Indiscretion of an American Wife (co-p) 54. A Farewell to Arms 57.

✪ For his integrity; for his memos; and for being a Hollywood monument. *Gone with the Wind.*

❝ Selznick was the mogul who gave up at his peak. He said in retirement:

Very few people have mastered the art of enjoying their wealth. I have mastered the art, and therefore I spend my time enjoying myself.

This was not unexpected behaviour from the man who once said:

I don't want to be normal. Who wants to be normal?

Yet his own memorable utterances were few, and on the sad side. He said of Hollywood:

Once photographed, life here is ended.

And of the house which is so central to *Gone with the Wind:*

It's somehow symbolic of Hollywood that Tara was just a façade, with no rooms inside.

An unhumorous man, intense and thorough to a fault, he was a hard taskmaster. Nunnally Johnson demurred at working for him:

I understand that an assignment with you consists of three months' work and six months' recuperation.

His creative impulse surged through his internal memos, the length of which was legendary. Alfred Hitchcock said in 1965:

When I came to America twenty-five years ago to direct *Rebecca,* David Selznick sent me a memo. (Pause.) I've just finished reading it. (Pause.) I think I may turn it into a motion picture. (Pause.) I plan to call it *The Longest Story Ever Told.*

One memo which has been quoted was to director Charles Vidor, following one of protest from him:

I don't believe I've ever used such terms with you as idiotic. I may have *thought* your excessive takes and angles were idiotic, but the most I've said was that they were a waste of my personal money.

He certainly interfered:

The way I see it, my function is to be responsible for everything.

And:

The difference between me and other producers is that I am interested in the thousands and thousands of details that go into the making of a film. It is the sum total of all these things that either makes a great picture or destroys it.

And, of the making of *A Farewell To Arms:*

In Mr Huston I asked for a first violinist and got a soloist. When I am the producer, I must produce.

His final claim was to have found a balance between God and Mammon:

I have never gone after honours instead of dollars. But I have understood the relationship between the two.

A typical Hollywood combination of oafishness and sophistication. – *John Houseman*

He wouldn't hire a secretary who could do less than 200 words per minute dictation. Otherwise it would have interrupted his train of thought. – *Irene Mayer Selznick*

The trouble with you, David, is that you did all your reading before you were twelve. – *Ben Hecht*

Selznick, Lewis J. (1870–1933) (Lewis Zeleznik).
Russian-American distributor and impresario, bankrupted in 1923.

Selznick, Myron (1898–1944).
American producer and agent, brother of David Selznick and son of Lewis.

Sembene, Ousmane (1923–).
Senegalese director, screenwriter and novelist. A former docker working in France, he studied film in Moscow.

Black Girl/La Noire 66. The Money Order/ Mandabi 68. Emitai 71. Xala 74. Ceddo 76. Camp de Thiaroye (co-d) 88, etc.

Semler, Dean (1943–).
Australian cinematographer who moved to Hollywood in the late 80s and returned home to direct his first feature.

Let the Balloon Go 76. Stepping Out 80. Hoodwink 81. Mad Max/The Road Warrior 81. Kitty and the Bagman 82. In Memory of Malawan 83. Razorback 84. Undercover 84. The Coca-Cola Kid 85. Mad Max 2: Beyond Thunderdrome 85. Bullseye 86. Going Sane 86. The Lighthorsemen 87. Cocktail 88. Young Guns 88. Dead Calm 89. Farewell to the King 89. K-9 89. Dances with Wolves (AA) 90. Impulse 90. Young Guns II 90. City Slickers 91. The Power of One 91. The Kangaroo Kid (d) 92. Super Mario Bros 93. The Three Musketeers 93. Last Action Hero 93. Waterworld 95. Firestorm (d) 97. Gone Fishin' 97, etc.

Semon, Larry (1889–1928).
American silent slapstick comedian, popular in innumerable two-reelers of the 20s; also some features.

The Simple Life 18. The Wizard of Oz 24. The Sawmill 25. Spuds 27, etc.

❝ He was so weird-looking that he could have posed either as a pinhead or a Man from Outer Space. – *Buster Keaton*

Semple, Lorenzo, Jnr.
American screenwriter.

Batman 56. Daddy's Gone a-Hunting 59. Pretty Poison 68. Marriage of a Young Stockbroker 71. The Sporting Club 71. Papillon (co-w) 73. The Parallax View 74. The Drowning Pool (co-w) 75. Three Days of the Condor (co-w) 75. King Kong 76. Hurricane 79. Flash Gordon 80. Never Say Never Again 83. Sheena (co-w) 84. Never Too Young to Die (co-w) 86, etc.

Sen, Mrinal (1923–).
Indian director and screenwriter of Marxist inclinations.

The Dawn 56. Under a Blue Sky 59. The Representative 64. Mr Shome 69. Interview 72. Calcutta 71 72. The Guerilla Fighter 73. The Royal Hunt 76. The Outsiders 77. And Quiet Rolls the Dawn 79. The Case Is Closed 81. Portrait of a New Man 84. Genesis 86. Suddenly, One Day 89. World Within, World Without/Mahaprithivi 91, etc.

Sena, Dominic (1947–).
American director and screenwriter, a former cinematographer and director specializing in music videos and commercials. He was co-founder in the mid-80s of the production company Propaganda Films.

Kalifornia 93.

Seneca, Joe (1915–1996).
American character actor and songwriter, a former song-and-dance man with the Three Riffs; on stage and screen from the late 70s. Died from an asthma attack.

The Verdict 82. Silverado 85. *Crossroads* (as Willie Brown) 87. A Gathering of Old Men (TV) 87. School Daze 88. The Blob 88. Mo' Better Blues 90. Mississippi Masala 92. Malcolm X 92. The Saint of Fort Washington 93. A Time to Kill 96, etc.

Sennett, Mack (1880–1960) (Michael Sinnott).
Canadian-born 'king of comedy' who in the 20s produced countless slapstick shorts featuring the Keystone Kops, Chester Conklin, Louise Fazenda, Charlie Chaplin, Mack Swain, Billy West, Fred Mace, Heinie Conklin, Slim Summerville and others. By the time sound came, Sennett had exhausted all the possible tricks of his 'fun factory' and found the new methods not to his taste. His output waned almost to nothing, but he was given a special Academy Award in 1937: 'For his lasting contribution to the comedy technique of the screen . . . the Academy presents a Special Award to that master of fun, discoverer of stars, sympathetic, kindly, understanding genius – Mack Sennett.'

Biography: 1955, *King of Comedy.*

Book: 1998, *The Films of Mack Sennett* by Warren Sherk.

❝ As befits the king of slapstick comedy, he was a thoughtful man.

The joke of life is the fall of dignity,

he once said. And his analysis of custard-pie-throwing was perfectly expressed:

Non-anticipation on the part of the recipient of the pastry is the chief ingredient of the recipe.

He disclaimed originality:

Anyone who tells you he has invented something new is a fool or a liar or both.

He was firm in matters of taste:

We never make fun of religion, politics, race or mothers. A mother never gets hit with a custard pie. Mothers-in-law, yes. But mothers, never!

He summed up his comedy technique very simply:

It's got to move!

And he later admitted:

I called myself king of comedy, but I was a harassed monarch. I worked most of the time. It was only in the evenings that I laughed.

Though Charlie Chaplin thought:

The secret of Mack Sennett's success was his enthusiasm. He was a great audience and laughed genuinely at what he thought funny. He stood and giggled until his body began to shake.

Serato, Massimo (1917–1989) (Giuseppe Segato).
Italian leading man, usually seen in swashbucklers.

Man of the Sea 41. Outcry 46. La Traviata 47. Sunday in August 49. The Thief of Venice 49. Shadow of the Eagle 50. Lucretia Borgia 53. The Man from Cairo 53. Madame Du Barry 54. The Naked Maja 59. David and Goliath 60. Constantine and the Cross 61. El Cid 61. 55 Days at Peking 63. The Tenth Victim 65. Wild Wild Planet 66. Camille 2000 69. Don't Look Now 73, etc.

Serbedzija, Rade.
Serbian actor and poet, a former professor of acting at Zagreb University. Married theatre director Lenka Udovicki.

Boiling Point 79. Hanna's War (US) 88. Manifesto (US) 88. Hudodelci 89. *Before the Rain* (GB/Fr./Mac.) 94. The Saint (US) 96. Broken

English (NZ) 97. Mighty Joe Young (US) 98. Eyes Wide Shut (US) 99, etc.

Seresin, Michael.
New Zealand cinematographer, based in Britain and especially associated with the films of director Alan Parker.
The Ragman's Daughter 72. Bugsy Malone 76. Sleeping Dogs 77. Midnight Express 78. Fame 80. Shoot the Moon 81. Birdy 84. Angel Heart 87. Homeboy (d) 88. Come See the Paradise 90. City Hall 96. Mercury Rising 98, etc.

Séria, Joël (1944–).
French director.
Charlie et ses Deux Nénettes 73. Les Galettes du Pont-Aven 75. Marie-Poupée 76. Comme la Lune 77, etc.

Serious, Yahoo (1954–) (Greg Pead).
Australian comic actor, screenwriter and director.
Young Einstein 88. Reckless Kelly (a, p, wd) 93. Mr Accident 99, etc.

Serling, Rod (1924–1975).
American TV playwright who contributed scores of scripts to such series as *Twilight Zone* and *Night Gallery* (which he also introduced).
Patterns of Power 56. Saddle the Wind 58. Requiem for a Heavyweight/Blood Money 63. Yellow Canary 63. *Seven Days in May* 64. Assault on a Queen 66. *Planet of the Apes* 67, etc.

Serna, Assumpta (1957–).
Spanish leading actress, in international films.
Matador 86. I, the Worst of All (Arg.) 90. Wild Orchid (US) 90. Revolver (US) (TV) 92. The Fencing Master 92. Sharpe's Rifles (GB) (TV) 93. Sharpe's Eagle (GB) (TV) 93. Nostradamus (US) 93. Havanera 93. Green Henry/Der Grun Heinrich (Swe.) 94. Shortcut to Paradise (Sp.) 94. Sharpe's Company (GB) (TV) 94. Nostradamus (GB/Ger.) 94. The Shooter 95, etc.

Sernas, Jacques (1925–).
Lithuanian-born leading man, in international films.
The Golden Salamander (GB) 50. Jump into Hell (US) 55. Helen of Troy (US/It.) 55. Maddalena (Fr.) 56. The Sign of the Gladiator (It.) 60. Son of Spartacus (It.) 62. Goliath against the Vampires 67. Hornet's Nest 70, etc.

Serra, Eduard (1943–).
Portuguese cinematographer in international films.
Le Garde du Corps 84. Tranches de Vie 85. The Hairdresser's Husband 90. Map of the Human Heart 92. Tango 93. Le Parfum d'Yvonne 94. Grosse Fatigue 94. Funny Bones 95. Jude 96. The Jew/O Judeu 96. The Disappearance of Finbar 97. *The Wings of the Dove* (AAN) 97. The Swindle/Rien Ne Va Plus 97. What Dreams May Come 98, etc.

Serra, Eric (1959–).
French composer, associated with the films of Luc Besson.
The Last Battle 83. Subway 85. The Big Blue 88. Nikita/La Femme Nikita 90. Atlantis 91. Leon/The Professional 94. GoldenEye 95. The Fifth Element 97, etc.

Serrault, Michel (1928–).
French leading actor who gained his greatest success playing a female impersonator in *La Cage aux Folles* and its sequels.
Diabolique/Les Diaboliques 55. Lovers and Thieves/Assassins et Voleurs 56. King of Hearts/Le Roi de Coeur 66. Le Viager 72. Les Gaspards 73. Holes 77. Get Out Your Handkerchiefs/Préparez Vos Mouchoirs 78. La Cage aux Folles 78. Cold Cuts/Buffet Froid 79. La Cage aux Folles II 80. Malevil 81. La Cage aux Folles III: The Wedding 86. En Toute Innocence 88. Comédie d'Amour 89. Merry Christmas, Happy New Year/Buon Natale, Buon Anno 89. Docteur Petiot 90. La Vieille qui Marchait dans la Mer 91. City for Sale/Ville à Vendre 91. Haute Époque 94. Nelly & Mr Arnaud 95. Rien Ne Va Plus 97, etc.

Serreau, Coline (1947–).
French director and screenwriter, a former actress, whose *Trois Hommes et un Couffin* was remade by Hollywood as the box-office hit *Three Men and a Baby*.
Why Not?/Pourquoi Pas! (wd) 77. Three Men and a Cradle/Trois Hommes et un Couffin (wd) 85. Romuald et Juliette (wd) 89. La Crise 92, etc.

Sersen, Fred (1890–1962).
American special-effects photographer, long with Fox, for whom he produced such spectacles as the fire in *In Old Chicago*, the storm in *The Rains Came*, and the canal-building in *Suez*.

Servais, Jean (1910–1976).
French character actor with stage experience.
Criminel 31. La Valse Eternelle 36. La Danse de Mort 47. Une Si Jolie Petite Plage 48. Le Plaisir 51. *Rififi* 55. Les Jeux Dangereux 58. That Man from Rio 64. Lost Command 66. They Came to Rob Las Vegas 69, etc.

Sessions, Almira (1888–1974).
American character actress, often seen in fluttery or eccentric bit parts.
Little Nellie Kelly 41. The Diary of a Chambermaid 46. The Fountainhead 49. The Boston Strangler 67. Rosemary's Baby 69. Everything You Always Wanted to Know about Sex 72, many others.

Seth, Roshan (1942–).
Indian character actor, from the British stage.
Juggernaut 74. Gandhi 82. Indiana Jones and the Temple of Doom 84. A Passage to India 84. My Beautiful Laundrette 85. Little Dorrit 87. 1871 89. Mountains of the Moon 89. Not without My Daughter 90. Mississippi Masala 91. London Kills Me 91. The Buddha of Suburbia (TV) 93. Solitaire for 2 95. Such a Long Journey 98, etc.

Seton, Sir Bruce (1909–1969).
British leading man, later character actor; military background.
Blue Smoke 34. Sweeney Todd 36. Love from a Stranger 38. The Curse of the Wraydons 46. Bonnie Prince Charlie 48. Whisky Galore 49. John Paul Jones (US) 59, etc.
TV series: Fabian of the Yard 54.

Seton, Marie (c. 1900–1985).
British journalist who met Eisenstein in Russia in the late 20s, wrote a biography of him, and later produced a version of his Mexican film under the title *Time in the Sun*.

Setton, Maxwell (1909–).
British independent producer, former lawyer. Held executive posts for Bryanston and Columbia.
The Spider and the Fly 50. So Little Time 52. They Who Dare 54. Footsteps in the Fog 55. Town on Trial 56. I Was Monty's Double 58, etc.

Severance, Joan (1958–).
American actress.
See No Evil, Hear No Evil 89. Worth Winning 89. No Holds Barred 89. Bird on a Wire 90. Almost Pregnant 91. Illicit Behavior 91. Write to Kill 91. The Runestone 92. Lake Consequence (TV) 92. Angel of Desire 94. Black Scorpion 95. Profile for Murder 96. Black Scorpion 2: Ground Zero 96. In Dark Places 97. The Last Seduction 2 98, etc.
TV series: Wiseguy 88.

Sevigny, Chloe (c. 1975–).
American actress and model with a cult following, born in Darien, Connecticut.
Kids 95. Trees Lounge 96. Gummo (& costumes) 97. Palmetto 98. The Last Days of Disco 98, etc.
❝ I think the designers should be influenced by the street. It's the most inspiring thing for me, fashion-wise. When I'm walking down the street and I see an old woman dressed like a mad-hatter, just like a crazy person, I think: 'Wow, she looks so amazing!' – C.S.

Sewell, George (1924–).
British character actor of tough roles, familiar on TV in *Special Branch*.
Sparrows Can't Sing 63. Robbery 67. Get Carter 71. Operation Daybreak 76. Tinker, Tailor, Soldier, Spy (TV) 80. The Fix (TV) 97, etc.
TV series: UFO 70. Home James 87. The Detectives 93–95.

Sewell, Rufus (1967–).
Dashing English leading man, from the stage.
Twenty-One 91. Middlemarch (TV) 94. A Man of No Importance 94. Carrington 95. Henry IV (TV) 95. Cold Comfort Farm (TV) 95. Hamlet 96. Dark City 97. Dangerous Beauty 98. Martha – Meet Frank, Daniel and Laurence 98. Victory 98. Vigo: A Passion for Life 98. At Sachem Farm (US) 98, etc.

Sewell, Vernon (1903–).
British director, former engineer, photographer, art director and editor.
The Silver Fleet 43. *Latin Quarter* 46. The Ghosts of Berkeley Square 47. Uneasy Terms 48. The Ghost Ship 52. Where There's a Will 55. Battle of the V1 58. House of Mystery 61. Strongroom 62. The Curse of the Crimson Altar 68. Burke and Hare 71, etc.

Seydor, Paul.
American editor; also the author of *Peckinpah – The Western Films: A Reconsideration* 97.
Turner & Hooch 89. Going Under 90. White Men Can't Jump 92. The Program 93. Major League 94. Major League II 94. Cobb 94. Tin Cup 96. The Wild Bunch: An Album in Montage (AAN) 97, etc.

Seyler, Athene (1889–1990).
British comedy actress with long stage career dating from 1908.
This Freedom 22. The Perfect Lady 32. The Citadel 38. *Quiet Wedding* 40. *Dear Octopus* 43. Nicholas Nickleby 47. Queen of Spades 48. Young Wives' Tale 51. *Pickwick Papers* 53. Yield to the Night 56. Campbell's Kingdom 58. The Inn of the Sixth Happiness 58. Make Mine Mink 59. Nurse on Wheels 63, many others.

Seymour, Anne (1909–1988) (Anne Ekert).
American character actress.
All the King's Men 49. Man on Fire 57. Home from the Hill 59. The Subterraneans 60. Sunrise at Campobello 60. Mirage 65. Blindfold 66. Never Never Land 81, etc.
TV series: Empire 62.

Seymour, Dan (1915–1993).
Burly American character actor, the scowling menace of countless films.
Casablanca 42. To Have and Have Not 44. Cloak and Dagger 46. Key Largo 48. Rancho Notorious 52. The Big Heat 53. Moonfleet 55. The Sad Sack 57. Watusi 59. Escape to Witch Mountain 75, etc.

Seymour, Jane (1951–) (Joyce Frankenberg).
British leading actress in international films, best known as *Dr Quinn, Medicine Woman* in the TV series. Her third husband is TV director and producer James Keach.
Book: 1993, *Jane Seymour's Guide to Good Loving*.
Oh What a Lovely War 70. Young Winston 72. Live and Let Die 72. Frankenstein: the True Story (TV) 73. The Hanged Man (TV) 74. Sinbad and the Eye of the Tiger 75. Captains and the Kings (TV) 76. Las Vegas Undercover (TV) 77. Seventh Avenue (TV) 77. The Four Feathers (TV) 78. Somewhere in Time 80. *East of Eden* (TV) 81. The Scarlet Pimpernel (TV) 82. Jamaica Inn (TV) 83. The Sun Also Rises (TV) 84. The Dark Mirror (TV) 85. Obsessed with a Married Woman (TV) 85. Crossings (TV) 85. War and Remembrance (TV) 87. Praying Mantis (TV) 93. Quest for Camelot (voice) 98, etc.

Seyrig, Delphine (1932–1990).
French leading actress.
Pull My Daisy 58. *Last Year in Marienbad* 61. Muriel 63. La Musica 66. Accident (GB) 67. Mr Freedom 68. *Stolen Kisses* 68. Daughters of Darkness 70. Peau d'Ane 70. *The Discreet Charm of the Bourgeoisie* 72. The Day of the Jackal 73. The Black Windmill 74. Aloise 75. Caro Michele 77. Faces of Love 77. Le Chemin Perdu 80. Chère Inconnue 80. Golden Eighties 86. Letters Home 86. Joan of Arc of Mongolia 89, etc.

Shabba-Doo (1955–) (Adolfo Quinones).
American actor, dancer, choreographer, and director.
Breakin' 84. Breakin' 2: Electric Boogaloo 84. Lambada 90. Rav'e': Dancing to a Different Beat (ch, d) 93, etc.

Shadyac, Tom (1960–).
American director and screenwriter.
Frankenstein: The College Years (TV) 91. Ace Ventura, Pet Detective 94. The Nutty Professor 96. Liar Liar 97. Patch Adams 98, etc.

Shaffer, Anthony (1926–).
British playwright and screenwriter, twin of Peter Shaffer. A former barrister, his third wife was actress Diane Cilento. He undertook an uncredited rewrite on *Murder on the Orient Express*.
Forbush and the Penguins 71. Sleuth (& oa) 72. Frenzy 73. The Wicker Man 73. Death on the Nile 78. Absolution 78. Evil under the Sun 82. Appointment with Death (co-w) 88, etc.

Shaffer, Peter (1926–).
British playwright, twin of Anthony Shaffer. Works filmed include *Five Finger Exercise*, *The Private Ear and the Public Eye*, *The Royal Hunt of the Sun*, *Equus* (AAN), *Amadeus* (AA) 84.

Shaftel, Joseph (1919–1996).
American producer, director and writer, in Britain. A former concert violinist as a youth, he was a wartime news photographer, his adventures forming the basis of the 1962 book *Star in the Wind* by Robert Nathan.
As producer: The Man Who Watched the Trains Go By 50. The Bandit 53. The Biggest Bundle of Them All (& w) 65. The Bliss of Mrs Blossom 68. Goodbye Gemini 70. The Trojan Women 71. Alice's Adventures in Wonderland 72, etc.
As director: No Place to Hide 52. The Naked Dawn 54. Potter of the Yard 56. The Great Mouthpiece 57, etc.

Shagan, Steve (1927–).
American screenwriter.
Save the Tiger (AAN) 73. Hustle (oa) 75. Voyage of the Damned 76. Nightwing 78. The Formula 80. The Sicilian 87. Primal Fear 96. Gotti (TV) 96, etc.

Shaiman, Marc (1959–).
American composer and arranger.
Big Business 88. Broadcast News (a) 88. When Harry Met Sally 89. Misery 90. Scenes from a Mall 91. City Slickers 91. Hot Shots! (a) 91. The Addams Family 91. Sister Act 92. A Few Good Men 92. Mr Saturday Night 92. Heart and Souls 93. Addams Family Values 93. A Dangerous Woman 94. North 94. Speechless 94. Stuart Saves His Family 95. Forget Paris 95. The American President (AAN) 95. The First Wives Club 96. Bogus 96. The First Wives Club (AA) 96. In and Out 97. Simon Birch 98. Patch Adams 98, etc.

Shakespeare, William (1564–1616).
British poet and dramatist whose plays have received plenty of attention from film-makers. *The Taming of the Shrew* was filmed in 1908 by D.W. Griffith; in 1929 with Douglas Fairbanks, Mary Pickford, and the immortal credit line 'additional dialogue by Sam Taylor': in 1953, more or less, as *Kiss Me Kate*; and in 1966 with Elizabeth Taylor, Richard Burton, and script credits to three writers none of whom is Shakespeare. *As You Like It* was filmed in 1912 with Rose Coghlan and Maurice Costello; the only sound filming was in 1936 by Paul Czinner, with Elisabeth Bergner and Laurence Olivier. *A Midsummer Night's Dream* was tackled in major fashion by Warners in 1935, but the elaborate Max Reinhardt production failed to please at the box office; in 1968 a 'realistic' version by Peter Hall was equally unsuccessful.
Of the tragedies, *Othello* has been frequently attempted, by Emil Jannings in 1922, Orson Welles in 1952, Sergei Bondarchuk in 1955 and Laurence Olivier in 1966; a 1961 British film called *All Night Long* was a modern up-dating of the plot, and Ronald Colman's Academy Award-winning performance in *A Double Life* 47 had him as an actor who starts playing the Moor in private life, as did Sebastian Shaw in *Men Are Not Gods* 36. *Hamlet* was played by Sir Johnston Forbes Robertson in 1913, Asta Nielsen in 1920, Olivier in 1948, and Innokenti Smoktunovsky in 1964. (Note also a 1972 western called *Johnny Hamlet* and a German modern version of 1959 called *The Rest is Silence*.) *Macbeth* is thought to be an unlucky play; but Sir Herbert Beerbohm Tree appeared in a version for Griffith in 1916; Orson Welles directed himself in the role in 1948, Paul Douglas in 1955 was an updated *Joe Macbeth*, in 1960 Maurice Evans appeared in a version originally intended for TV but shown theatrically, and in 1971 Roman Polanski presented a bloodthirsty version with Jon Finch. One should also mention *The Siberian Lady Macbeth*, the Japanese *Throne of Blood*, and a modern version, *Men of Respect*, which

turned the protagonists into gangsters. In 1969 *King Lear* was filmed with Paul Scofield; there was a one-reel Vitagraph version in 1909 and Frederic Warde starred in a 1916 production. It formed a background to *The Dresser*, starring Albert Finney as a Shakespearean actor in the manner of Donald Wolfit. Kurosawa's *Ran* was a Japanese version. *Romeo and Juliet* was also made in 1916, starring Francis X. Bushman and Beverly Bayne; this superseded several one-reel versions. In 1936 MGM produced its Leslie Howard/Norma Shearer version directed by George Cukor; in 1954 Renato Castellani directed an unsuccessful colour version with Laurence Harvey and Susan Shentall; in 1961 came the inevitable modernization in *West Side Story*; and 1968 brought another expensive production by Franco Zeffirelli. (There have also been several ballet versions.) There were early potted versions of *Julius Caesar* before the spectacular Italian production of 1914; the play was not filmed again until MGM's excellent 1953 version. The plot was used in a curious British second feature called *An Honourable Murder* 59, with the action moved to a modern executive suite; an all-star version in colour followed in 1970, starring Charlton Heston and finding more action than is normally evident in the play.

Of the histories, most of *Henry IV* has been compressed by Orson Welles into his *Chimes at Midnight*, *Henry V* was splendidly dealt with by Olivier in 1944 and by Kenneth Branagh in 1989. *Richard III* existed in several primitive versions, and John Barrymore recited a speech from it in *Show of Shows* 28; but again it was left to Olivier to do it properly. Ian McKellen more recently provided a very different, but convincing, interpretation of the role. Samuel Goldwyn Jnr financed Kenneth Branagh's bright and cheerful *Much Ado about Nothing* but turned down Ian McKellen's *Richard III* on the grounds that it was too dark. 'The public only wants Polyanna Shakespeare,' he told McKellen.

Recently, Shakespeare has become box-office material once more, following the success of Baz Luhrmann's radical treatment of *Romeo and Juliet* 92, starring Leonardo DiCaprio and Claire Danes and aimed at a teenage audience, which put the playwright's name above the title. Since then, Laurence Fishburne has played Othello to Kenneth Branagh's Iago; while Branagh, following on from Mel Gibson's 1991 treatment, has filmed an uncut *Hamlet* 96, and announced his plans to set up a new company to film the plays.

The oddest screen fate of a Shakespeare play was surely that of *The Tempest*, which in 1956 yielded its entire plot to that winning bit of science fiction, *Forbidden Planet*. Derek Jarman turned it into a punk version in 1980, and Peter Greenaway into a literary experience in *Prospero's Books*, with all the roles being spoken by Sir John Gielgud. Paul Mazursky unsuccessfully updated it in *Tempest* 82. Performances of others were put to comedy purpose in *Doubling for Romeo* and *To Be or Not to Be*.

Joseph Fiennes played him in *Shakespeare in Love* 98, Tom Stoppard's fictional treatment of the dramatist as a young man.

Books: 1971, *Shakespeare and the Film* by Roger Manvell. 1994, *Shakespeare, Cinema and Society* by John Collick. 1994, *Shakespearean Films/ Shakespearean Directors* by Peter S. Donaldson.

Shakespeare was impersonated, rather well, by Tim Curry in TV's *Will Shakespeare*; and very badly by Reginald Gardiner in *The Story of Mankind*.

Shakhnazarov, Karen (1952–).
Russian director and screenwriter. Born in Moscow, he studied at VGIK and is a former head of Courier Studios, one of Mosfilm's production companies. In 1998, he became president of Mosfilm.

Jazzmen/My Iz Dzhaza 83. A Winter Evening in Gagra/Zimnii Vecher v Gagrakh 86. Zero City/ Gorod Zero 89. Assassin of the Czar/Tsareubiitsa 91. Dreams/Sny 93. American Daughter 95. Day of the Full Moon 98, etc.

Shakur, Tupac (1971–1996).
American actor and rap performer, known as 2Pac. In 1995, he was sentenced to prison for sexual assault, and released after eight months on appeal. He died six days after being shot four times in an ambush in Las Vegas.

Biography: 1997, *Rebel for the Hell of It* by Armond White.

Juice 91. Poetic Justice 93. Above the Rim 94. Bullet 95. Gridlock'd 97. Gang Related 97, etc.

Shalhoub, Tony (1953–).
American actor. Married actress Brooke Adams in 1992.

Quick Change 90. Longtime Companion 90. Barton Fink 91. Honeymoon in Vegas 92. Searching for Bobby Fischer/Innocent Moves 93. Addams Family Values 93. IQ 94. Big Night 96. Men in Black 97. Gattaca 97. A Life Less Ordinary 97. Primary Colors 98. The Imposters 98, etc.

Shamroy, Leon (1901–1974).
Distinguished American cinematographer.

Catch as Catch Can 27. Out with the Tide 28. The Women Men Marry 31. Jennie Gerhardt 33. Three Cornered Moon 33. Thirty Day Princess 34. Private Worlds 35. Soak the Rich 36. You Only Live Once 37. *The Young In Heart* 38. The Story of Alexander Graham Bell 39. *The Adventures of Sherlock Holmes* 40. Lillian Russel 40. Tin Pan Alley 40. A Yank in the RAF 41. Roxie Hart 42. *Ten Gentlemen from West Point* (AAN) 42. *The Black Swan* (AA) 42. *Stormy Weather* 43. Buffalo Bill 44. *Wilson* (AA) 44. *A Tree Grows in Brooklyn* 45. State Fair 45. *Leave Her to Heaven* (AA) 46. Forever Amber 47. That Lady in Ermine 48. Prince of Foxes (AAN) 49. Twelve O'Clock High 49. Cheaper by the Dozen 50. On the Riviera 51. David and Bathsheba (AAN) 51. The Snows of Kilimanjaro (AAN) 53. Call Me Madam 53. *The Robe* (AAN) 53. The Egyptian (AAN) 54. Love is a Many Splendored Thing 55. *The King and I* 56. Desk Set 57. South Pacific (co-ph) (AAN) 58. Porgy and Bess (AAN) 59. North to Alaska 60. Tender is the Night 61. Cleopatra (AA) 63. The Cardinal (AAN) 63. The Agony and the Ecstasy (AAN) 65. The Glass Bottom Boat 66. Caprice (also appeared) 67. *Planet of the Apes* 67. Justine 69, many others.

❝ God was a great photographer. He'd only gotten one light. – *L.S.*

Lee Garmes will never see the day that he's as good as I am, and that goes for anybody in the motion picture business. – *L.S.*

Shane, Maxwell (1905–1983).
American writer-director, former publicist.

You Can't Beat Love (co-w) 37. One Body Too Many (w) 43. Fear in the Night (wd) 46 (remade as Nightmare 56). City across the River (wd, p) 49. The Naked Street (wd) 55, etc.

Shankar, Ravi (1920–).
Indian composer and virtuoso sitar player.

Panther Panchali 56. Aparajito 58. The World of Apu 59. Chappaqua 66. Charly 68. Raga 71. Gandhi (co-m) (AAN) 82. Genesis 86, etc.

Shanley, John Patrick (1950–).
American screenwriter, dramatist and director.

Five Corners (w) 87. Moonstruck (w) (AA) 87. The January Man (w) 89. Joe versus the Volcano (wd) 90. Alive (w) 93. We're Back!: A Dinosaur's Story (w) 93. Congo (w) 95, etc.

Shannon, Harry (1890–1964).
American character actor, often seen as sympathetic father or rustic; musical comedy experience.

Hands Up 31. Young Tom Edison 40. The Eve of St Mark 44. The Gunfighter 50. High Noon 52. Executive Suite 54. Come Next Spring 56. Hell's Crossroads 57, many others.

Shannon, Peggy (1909–1941) (Winona Sammon).
Short-lived star of the 30s who began at 15 in Ziegfeld Follies. Paramount touted her as the successor to Clara Bow, but her career had faltered by the mid-30s. Died of alcoholism.

The Secret Call 31. Silence 31. Road to Reno 31. Playing the Game 31. Second Chances/This Reckless Age 32. False Faces 32. Turn Back the Clock 33. Deluge 33. Night Life of the Gods 35. The Case of the Lucky Legs 35. Youth on Parole 37. Ellis Island 38. Fixer Dugan 39. The House across the Bay 40, etc.

Shapiro, Alan.
American director.

Tiger Town (TV) 83. The Outsiders (co-d) (TV) 90. The Crush (wd) 93. Flipper 96, etc.

Shapiro, Paul (1955–).
Canadian director, from television.

The Understudy (TV) 75. Hockey Night (TV) 84. Miracle at Moreaux (TV) 85. The Truth about Alex (TV) 87. The Lotus Eaters 93, etc.

Shapiro, Stanley (1925–1990).
American writer-producer associated with glossy comedies; long experience in radio and TV.

The Perfect Furlough (w) 58. Pillow Talk (co-w) (AA) 59. Operation Petticoat (co-w) 59. Come September (co-w) 60. That Touch of Mink (co-w) 62. Bedtime Story (w, p) 64. How to Save a Marriage (p) 68. For Pete's Sake (co-w, p) 74. Carbon Copy 81. Dirty Rotten Scoundrels 89. Running against Time 90, etc.

Sharaff, Irene (1910–1993).
American costume designer, long with Fox. She began working in the New York theatre in 1928, moving to Hollywood in 1942.

An American in Paris (AA) 51. Call Me Madam (AAN) 53. A Star Is Born (AAN) 54. Brigadoon (AAN) 54. Guys and Dolls (AAN) 56. The King and I (AA) 56. Porgy and Bess (AAN) 59. Can-Can (AAN) 60. Flower Drum Song (AAN) 61. West Side Story (AA) 61. Cleopatra (AA) 63. Who's Afraid of Virginia Woolf? (AA) 66. The Taming of the Shrew (AAN) 67. Hello Dolly (AAN) 69. The Great White Hope 70. The Other Side of Midnight (AAN) 77. Mommie Dearest 81, etc.

Sharif, Omar (1932–) (Michel Shalhouz).
Egyptian leading man now in international films.

Autobiography: 1977, *The Eternal Male*.

Goha 59. *Lawrence of Arabia* (AAN) 62. The Fall of the Roman Empire 64. Behold a Pale Horse 64. The Yellow Rolls-Royce 64. Genghis Khan 65. *Dr Zhivago* 65. The Night of the Generals 66. Marco the Magnificent 66. More Than a Miracle 67. Funny Girl 68. Mayerling 68. Mackenna's Gold 68. The Appointment 69. Che! 69. The Last Valley 70. The Horsemen 71. The Burglars 71. The Tamarind Seed 74. Juggernaut 74. The Mysterious Island of Captain Nemo 74. Funny Lady 75. Ace up My Sleeve 76. Ashanti 78. Bloodline 79. The Baltimore Bullet 80. Oh Heavenly Dog 80. Green Ice 81. Inchon! 82. Return to Eden 82. Ayoub 83. Top Secret! 84. Les Pyramides Bleues 88. Keys to Freedom 89. Mountains of the Moon 90. Journey of Love/Viaggio d'Amore 90. Memories of Midnight (TV) 91. War on the Land of Egypt/El Mowaten Masri 91. Mother/Mayrig 91. 588 rue Paradis 92. Catherine the Great (TV) 95. Gulliver's Travels (TV) 96, etc.

❝ I definitely want to do mainly theatre now. Or, two weeks in a film for a remarkable amount of money. – O.S.

Aggressive feminists scare me. – O.S.

Sharkey, Ray (1953–1993).
American leading man of the 80s. Died of AIDS, contracted through intravenous drug use.

Trackdown 76. Stunts 77. Paradise Alley 78. Who'll Stop the Rain? 78. Heart Beat 79. Willie and Phil 80. The Idolmaker 80. Love and Money 82. Body Rock 84. No Mercy 86. Wise Guys 86. Private Investigations 87. Scenes from the Class Struggle in Beverly Hills 89. Wired 89. Dead On 91. Hotel Oklahoma 91. Cop and a Half 93, etc.

TV series: Wiseguy 87. Man in the Family 91.

Sharman, Jim (1945–).
Australian director, active in the theatre.

Shirley Thompson versus the Aliens 72. Summer of Secrets 76. *The Rocky Horror Picture Show* 76. The Night the Prowler 78. Shock Treatment 81, etc.

❝ I don't believe in the art-house circuit, whether it's for plays or films: you've got to reach out. – *J.S.*

Sharp, Alan.
Scottish writer in Hollywood.

The Hired Hand 71. The Last Run 71. Ulzana's Raid 72. Billy Two Hats 74. Night Moves 75. Damnation Alley 77. The Osterman Weekend 83. Little Treasure (& d) 85. Cat Chaser 90. Descending Angel 91. Mission of the Shark 91. The Last Hit (TV) 93. Rob Roy 95, etc.

Sharp, Don (1922–).
Australian-born director, in British film industry from 1952, at first as writer.

Ha'penny Breeze (w) 52. Robbery Under Arms (w) 56. The Professionals 59. Linda 60. Kiss of the Vampire 62. Devil Ship Pirates 63. *Witchcraft* 64. Those Magnificent Men in Their Flying Machines (second unit) 65. Rasputin the Mad Monk 65. *The Face of Fu Manchu* 65. Our Man in Marrakesh 66. The Million Eyes of Su Muru 66. Rocket to the Moon 67. Psychomania 72. Callan 74. Hennessy 75. The Four Feathers (TV) 78. *The Thirty-Nine Steps* 78. Bear Island 80. A Woman of Substance (TV) 84. Tusitala (TV) 85. Hold the Dream (TV) 87. Tears in the Rain (TV) 88, etc.

Sharp, Henry (1892–1966).
American cinematographer.

Homespun Folks 20. The Hottentot 22. A Girl of the Limberlost 24. Don Q Son of Zorro 25. *The Black Pirate* 26. The Lovelorn 27. *The Crowd* 28. The Iron Mask 29. Lord Byron of Broadway 30. The False Madonna 31. The Devil is Driving 32. Duck Soup 33. Six of a Kind 34. The Glass Key 35. Lady be Careful 36. Hotel Haywire 37. Booloo 38. Geronimo 39. Dr Cyclops (co-ph) 40. Broadway Limited 41. The Hidden Hand 42. Ministry of Fear 44. Jealousy 45. It Happened on Fifth Avenue 47. Perilous Waters 48. Daughter of the West 49. The Young Land (co-ph) 59, many others.

Sharp, Ian (1946–).
British director, from TV.

The Music Machine 81. Who Dares Wins 82. Secret Weapon (TV) 90. Pleasure (TV) 94. Tess of the D'Urbervilles (TV) 98, etc.

Sharp, Lesley.
English actress.

Rita, Sue and Bob Too 86. The Love Child 87. The Rachel Papers 89. Close My Eyes 91. Naked 93. Priest 94. Prime Suspect 4: The Lost Child (TV) 95. The Moonstone (TV) 96. The Full Monty 97. Playing the Field (TV) 98, etc.

Sharpe, Albert (1885–*).
Irish character actor, in films as an old man from the mid-40s. Born in Belfast, he was on the stage in Britain, going to the US in 1947 to appear on Broadway in *Finian's Rainbow*, and thence to Hollywood.

I See a Dark Stranger/The Adventuress 45. Odd Man Out 46. Portrait of Jennie (US) 47. Up in Central Park (US) 48. Royal Wedding (US) 51. The Highwayman (US) 51. You Never Can Tell (US) 51. Face to Face (US) 52. Brigadoon (US) 54. *Darby O'Gill and the Little People* (as Darby O'Gill) (US) 59. The Day They Robbed the Bank of England 60, etc.

Sharpe, David (1910–1980).
Athletic American leading man in serials and 'B' features, and a notable stuntman, who began his career in 1924; also a second unit director. He appeared in some of Monogram's Range Busters series of westerns in the 40s, designed the action sequences in Douglas Fairbanks's *The Fighting O'Flynn* 48, and was the stunt double for the heroes in many of Republic's serials: Tom Tyler in *Adventures of Captain Marvel*, Don Barry in *Adventures of Red Ryder*, Robert Wilcox in *Mysterious Doctor Satan*, Tom Neil and Frances Gifford in *Jungle Girl*, and Tristram Coffin in *King of the Rocket Men*, etc.

The Thief of Bagdad 24. High Gear 30. Adventurous Knights 35. Social Error 35. Dick Tracy Returns (serial) 38. Daredevils of the Red Circle (serial) 39. Spy Smasher (stunts) 42. Colorado Serenade 46. The Life and Times of Judge Roy Bean 72. The Master Gunfighter (stunts) 75. Heaven Can Wait (stunts) 78, etc.

Shatner, William (1931–).
Canadian leading actor, writer and occasional director, mainly on TV, and best known for playing Captain Kirk in the *Star Trek* TV series and subsequent movies. Born in Montreal, he moved to New York in the mid-50s to begin his career on television and the Broadway stage. He has also written some science-fiction novels in the *TekWar* series, was executive producer of the subsequent *TekWar* TV series, and creator of the Marvel comic *William Shatner's TekWorld*. Married for the third time in 1997.

Autobiographies: 1993, *Star Trek Memories* (with Chris Kreshi); 1994, *Star Trek Movie Memories* (with Chris Kreshi).

The Brothers Karamazov 58. The Explosive Generation 61. The Intruder/The Stranger 61. The Outrage 64. Go Ask Alice (TV) 73. The Horror at 37,000 Feet (TV) 74. Big Bad Mama 74. Kingdom of the Spiders 77. A Whale of a Tale 77. Land of No Return 78. Star Trek: The Motion Picture 79. The Kidnapping of the President 80. Star Trek II: The Wrath of Khan 82. Visiting Hours 82. Star Trek III: The Search for Spock 84.

Star Trek IV: The Voyage Home 87. Star Trek V: The Final Frontier (& d) 89. Star Trek VI: The Undiscovered Country 91. National Lampoon's Loaded Weapon 1 93. Tekwar (d, from his novel) (TV) 94. Star Trek: Generations 94, etc.

TV series: For the People 60. *Star Trek* 66–68. Barbary Coast 75. T.J. Hooker 82–86. Rescue 911 89.

Shaughnessy, Alfred (1916–).
American-born producer, screenwriter, director and playwright, in Britain. Brought up in Nashville, Tennessee, and London, and educated at Eton and Sandhurst, he was in films from 1946 at Ealing Studios, but was best known for his work as writer and script editor for the TV series *Upstairs, Downstairs* 71–75.

Autobiography: 1978, *Both Ends of the Candle*.

Brandy for the Parson (p) 51. Laxdale Hall (p, co-w) 53. The End of the Road (p) 54. Room in the House (p, w) 55. Suspended Alibi (d) 56. A Touch of the Sun (w) 56. The High Terrace (co-w) 56. The Hostage (w) 56. Cat Girl (d) 57. Just My Luck (co-w) 57. 6.5 Special (d) 58. Heart of a Child (p) 58. Follow That Horse! (co-w) 60. The Impersonator (co-w, d) 61. Lunch Hour (p) 63. Crescendo (co-w) 70. The Flesh and Blood Show (w) 72. Tiffany Jones (w) 73, etc.

❝ The privileged have been under fire for so long now that anyone who has been to Eton is regarded as a chinless wonder. There are any number of Old Etonians of my children's generation acting in films, theatre and television who would do anything rather than admit where they were educated. These days, it's a stigma. There has been such a levelling off that the world I knew has turned upside down. – *A.S.*

Shaughnessy, Mickey (1920–1985).
Tough-looking American comic actor with stage experience.

The Last of the Comanches (debut) 52. From Here to Eternity 53. Conquest of Space 55. Jailhouse Rock 57. *Don't Go Near the Water* 57. North to Alaska 60. A Global Affair 63. A House Is Not a Home 64. Never a Dull Moment 68, etc.

TV series: Chicago Teddy Bears 71.

Shavelson, Melville (1917–).
American screenwriter, in Hollywood from the early 40s.

The Princess and the Pirate 44. Always Leave Them Laughing 50. Room for One More 52. The Seven Little Foys (& d) (AANw) 55. Beau James (& d) 57. Houseboat (& d) (AANw) 58. The Five Pennies (& d) 59. The Pigeon that Took Rome (& p, d) 62. A New Kind of Love (& p, d) 63. Cast a Giant Shadow (& p, d) 66. The War between Men and Women (co-wd) 72, many others, usually in collaboration with *Jack Rose* (1911–1995).

TV series: Ike (w, co-d) 79.

Shaver, Helen (1951–).
Canadian actress.

Shoot 76. High-Ballin' 78. In Praise of Older Women 78. The Amityville Horror 79. The Dogs of War 80. Gas 81. The Osterman Weekend 83. Harry Tracy 83. Best Defense 84. The Color of Money 86. Desert Hearts 86. The Believers 87. Bethune 89. Tree of Hands 89. Innocent Victim 90. Zebrahead 92. Morning Glory 93. Roadracers (TV) 94. Open Season 95. Born to Be Wild 95. Tremors 2: Aftershocks 96. Poltergeist: The Legacy (TV) 96. The Craft 96, etc.

TV series: United States 80. Jessica Novak 81.

Shaw, Artie (1910–) (Arthur Arschawsky).
American bandleader and clarinettist. He has married eight times, including actresses Lana Turner, Ava Gardner and Evelyn Keyes.

■ Dancing Co-Ed 39. Second Chorus 40.

Shaw, Denis (1921–1971).
Burly, heavy-featured British character actor, a former agent, usually in sinister roles. Born in Dulwich, London, he was on television from the late 30s and in films from the 50s. Died of a heart attack. He was noted in private life for his rudeness. Ned SHERRIN tells the story of a woman approaching him in Shaftesbury Avenue and asking him, after much humming and ha-ing, if he was Denis Shaw. 'Of course,' said Shaw. 'Why the hesitation?' 'Well,' she said, 'it's such an awful thing to ask anybody.'

The Case of the Frightened Lady (TV) 38. The Long Memory 52. The Colditz Story 54. The Deep Blue Sea 55. Keep It Clean 55. The Depraved 57. Blood of the Vampire 58. Jack the Ripper 58. The Mummy 59. Trouble with Eve 59. The Night We Dropped a Clanger 59. The Two Faces of Dr Jekyll 60. The Hellfire Club 60. Make Mine Mink 60. Curse of the Werewolf 61. Carry On Regardless 61. The Day of the Triffids 62. The Runaway 64. The Viking Queen 67. The File of the Golden Goose 69, etc.

Shaw, Fiona (1958–).
Irish actress.

My Left Foot 89. Mountains of the Moon 89. Three Men and a Little Lady 90. Undercover Blues 93. Jane Austen's Persuasion (TV) 95. Jane Eyre 96. Butcher Boy 97, etc.

Shaw, George Bernard (1856–1950).
Distinguished Irish playwright who for many years refused to allow film versions of his works; he was reconciled to the idea by Gabriel Pascal. The following versions have been made:

Roman Boxera (from Cashel Byron's Profession) 21. How He Lied to Her Husband 30. Arms and the Man 31. Pygmalion (Ger.) 35. Pygmalion (Hol.) 37. Pygmalion 38. Major Barbara 40. Caesar and Cleopatra 45. Androcles and the Lion 53. Saint Joan 57. The Doctor's Dilemma 58. The Devil's Disciple 59. Helden/Arms and the Man (Ger.) 59. The Millionairess 61. My Fair Lady (from Pygmalion) 64. Great Catherine 67.

❝ Owing to the fact that in filming you can select all the perfect bits from your rehearsals (every rehearsal hits off some passage to perfection) and piece them together into a perfect performance the screen can reach a point of excellence unattainable by the stage. Only, you must know which are the best bits. If, like many American producers, you prefer the worst, and piece *them* together, the result is a sustained atrocity beyond the possibilities of a penny gaff. – G.B.S.

I contemplate the popular Hollywood productions in despair. The photography is good, the acting is good, the expenditure is extravagant; but the attempt to tell a story is pitiable: the people expend tons of energy jumping in and out of automobiles, running up and downstairs, opening and shutting bedroom doors, drawing automatics, being arrested and tried for inexplicable crimes, with intervals of passionate kissing; and all this is amusing in a way; but of what it is all about neither I nor anyone else in the audience has the faintest idea. – *G.B.S., 1935*

The trouble is, Mr Goldwyn, you are interested in art, whereas I am interested in money. – *G.B.S. to Sam Goldwyn, who wanted to buy the screen rights to his plays*

As an iconoclast he is admirable, as an icon somewhat less so. – *Bertrand Russell*

Shaw, Irwin (1912–1984).
American novelist and screenwriter.

Talk of the Town (AAN) 42. I Want You 51. Fire Down Below 57. The Young Lions (& oa) 58. Tip on a Dead Jockey 58. Two Weeks in Another Town (novel only) 62. *Rich Man Poor Man* (novel only) (TV) 76. Top of the Hill (story) (TV) 79, etc.

Shaw, Martin (1945–).
British leading man who shot to fame in TV's *The Professionals*.

The Golden Voyage of Sinbad 72. Operation Daybreak 73. Cream in my Coffee (TV) 80. The Last Place on Earth (TV) 85. Ladder of Swords 88. Intrigue (TV) 88. Rhodes (title role) (TV) 96. The Scarlet Pimpernel (TV) 98, etc.

TV series: The Chief 93.

Shaw, Maxwell (1929–1985).
English supporting actor, from the stage, usually in unsympathetic roles. He was a member of Theatre Workshop, and was the company's administrator in the mid-70s.

Who, Me? (TV) 59. Once More with Feeling (US) 60. The Barber of Stamford Hill 62. Number Six 62. The Oblong Box 69. Start the Revolution without Me (US) 70, etc.

Shaw, Reta (1912–1982).
Amply proportioned American character actress.

The Pajama Game 57. Pollyanna 60. Mary Poppins 64. Escape to Witch Mountain 74.

Shaw, Robert (1927–1978).
English leading actor, novelist and playwright. He studied at RADA and began on stage in 1949. His first novel, *The Hiding Place* (1959), was turned into a comic film, *Situation Hopeless but Not Serious* 65, and his play *The Man in the Glass Booth* was filmed by Arthur Hiller in 1975. The second of his three wives was actress Mary Ure. A heavy drinker, he died of a heart attack.

Biography: 1993, *Robert Shaw: The Price of Success* by John French.

■ The Dam Busters (film debut) 55. Double Cross 55. A Hill in Korea 56. The Birthday Party 58. Libel 59. Sea Fury 59. The Valiant 61. Tomorrow at Ten 62. *From Russia with Love* 63. The Caretaker 63. The Luck of Ginger Coffey 64. The Battle of the Bulge 65. *A Man for All Seasons* (as Henry VIII) (AAN) 66. Custer of the West 67. The Battle of Britain 69. The Royal Hunt of the Sun 69. Figures in a Landscape (& w) 70. A Town Called Bastard 71. A Reflection of Fear 72. Young Winston 72. The Hireling 73. The Sting 73. The Golden Voyage of Sinbad (uncredited) 73. The Taking of Pelham One Two Three 74. Jaws 75. Robin and Marian 75. End of the Game 76. Diamonds 76. Swashbuckler 76. Black Sunday 76. The Deep 77. Force Ten from Navarone 78. Avalanche Express 79.

TV series: The Buccaneers 56.

❝ What I try to achieve in acting – flamboyance – would be self-indulgence if I tried it as a writer. – *R.S.*

I drink too much. Will you tell me one great actor who doesn't drink? – *R.S.*

Shaw, Sir Run Run (1907–) (Yifu Shao).
Prolific Chinese producer of action and kung fu movies, born in Shanghai and a dominant influence on production in Hong Kong with his brother Runme Shaw (d. 1985) in the 70s.

King Boxer 71. Valley of the Fangs 71. Death Kick 73. Five Fingers of Death 73. Blood Money 74. The Legend of the Seven Golden Vampires 74. Cannonball 76. Cleopatra Jones and the Casino of Gold 76, many others.

Shaw, Sebastian (1905–1994).
British leading man of the 30s, latterly character actor. On stage from 1913 (as child).

Caste 30. Taxi to Paradise 33. Men are not Gods 36. The Squeaker 37. The Spy in Black 39. East of Piccadilly 41. The Glass Mountain 48. It Happened Here 64. A Midsummer Night's Dream 68. High Season 87.

Shaw, Susan (1929–1978) (Patsy Sloots).
British leading lady groomed by the Rank 'charm school', whose career was hampered by alcoholism. She quit acting in the early 60s and worked in various jobs, including as a barmaid and a nightclub hostess. Died penniless, of cirrhosis of the liver. Married actors Albert LIEVEN and Bonar COLLEANO. Her son, Mark Colleano (1955–), appeared in a few films in the late 60s and early 70s.

London Town 46. The Upturned Glass 47. Holiday Camp 47. London Belongs to Me 48. The Woman in Question 50. The Intruder 51. The Good Die Young 52. Stock Car 54. Carry On Nurse 59. The Switch 63, etc.

Shaw, Victoria (1935–1988) (Jeanette Elphick).
Australian leading lady in American films. She was formerly married to actor Roger Smith.

Cattle Station (Aus.) 55. The Eddy Duchin Story 56. Edge of Eternity 59. The Crimson Kimono 60. Alvarez Kelly 66. Westworld 73, etc.

Shaw, Wini (1899–1982) (Winfred Lei Momi).
American singer of Hawaiian descent, used as voice of non-singing stars in many Warner musicals of the 30s.

Actually appeared in the following:

Three on a Honeymoon 34. Gold Diggers of 1935 35. In Caliente 35. Melody for Two 37, etc.

Shawlee, Joan (1929–1987) (formerly Joan Fulton).
American character comedienne with nightclub and stage experience.

Men in Her Diary 45. Cuban Pete 46. I'll Be Yours 47. The Marrying Kind 52. Conquest of Space 54. A Star is Born 54. *Some Like It Hot* 59. The Apartment 60. Irma La Douce 63. The Wild Angels 66. The St Valentine's Day Massacre 67. One More Time 71. Willard 71. Dead Men Tell No Tales (TV) 74. Flash and Firecat 76, etc.

TV series: Aggie 57. The Betty Hutton Show 59. Feather and Father 77.

Shawn, Dick (1928–1987) (Richard Schulefand).
American comedian, in occasional films.

Wake Me When It's Over 60. It's a Mad Mad Mad Mad World 63. A Very Special Favor 65. What Did You Do in the War, Daddy? 66. Penelope 66. The Producers 68. Looking Up 77. Love at First Bite 79, etc.

TV series: Hail to the Chief 85.

Shawn, Wallace (1943–).
American playwright and character actor of mild appearance.

All That Jazz 79. Manhattan 79. Starting Over 79. Atlantic City 80. My Dinner with André (& co-w) 81. A Little Sex 82. Lovesick 83. The Bostonians 84. Crackers 84. The Hotel New Hampshire 84. Micki and Maude 84. Heaven Help Us 85. Head Office 86. Nice Girls Don't Explode 87. Prick Up Your Ears 87. The Princess Bride 87. Radio Days 87. The Moderns 88. Scenes from the Class Struggle in Beverly Hills 89. She's Out of Control 89. We're No Angels 89. Shadows and Fog 91. Nickel & Dime 92. Mom and Dad Save the World 92. The Cemetery Club 93. Mrs Parker and the Vicious Circle 94. Vanya on 42nd Street (w) 94. The Wife 95. A Goofy Movie (voice) 95. Toy Story (voice) 95. Designated Mourner (oa) 96. House Arrest 96. Critical Care (a) 97. Just Write (a) 98, etc.

❝ Most movies promote the status quo, which I think should be changed and not accepted. They even go further by propagating particularly horrible tendencies, like lust for revenge, nauseating stereotypes, militarism, the belief that macho attitudes will solve our problems. – *W.S.*

Shaye, Robert (1939–).
American production executive and director. In 1967, he became founder and president of New Line Cinema, a company noted for low-budget films. In 1993, in a $530 million deal, the company was taken over by Ted Turner. New Line's greatest success so far has been the *Nightmare on Elm Street* series.

Book of Love (d) 90.

Shayne, Robert (1900–1992) (Robert Shaen Dawe).
American general-purpose actor.

Keep 'em Rolling 34. Shine On Harvest Moon 44. The Swordsman 47. The Neanderthal Man (lead role) 53. Spook Chasers 58. Valley of the Redwoods 61, etc.

Shayne, Tamara (1897–1983) (Tamara Nikoulin).
Russian-American character actress who played Jolson's mother in *The Jolson Story* and *Jolson Sings Again*. Also: *Ninotchka*, *Mission to Moscow*, *Anastasia*, etc.

Shbib, Bashar.
Canadian director.

Julia Has Two Lovers 90. Lana in Love 91. Love $ Greed 92. Ride Me 92. Crack Me Up 93, etc.

Shea, John (1949–).
American actor and director. Born in North Conway, New Hampshire, he studied acting at the Yale Drama School.

The Last Convertible (TV) 79. Hussy 79. Missing 82. Kennedy (TV) 83. Windy City 84. Stealing Home 88. Baby M (TV) 88. A New Life 88. Small Sacrifices (TV) 89. Freejack 92. Honey, I Blew Up the Kid 92. Backstreet Justice 93. Southie (& d) 98, etc.

TV series: Lois & Clark: The New Adventures of Superman 93.

Shea, Katt.
American director.

Stripped to Kill 87. Dance of the Damned 89. Stripped to Kill II 89. Streets 90. Poison Ivy 92.

Shea, William (1862–1918).
Scottish-born leading actor in Hollywood silents, in films from 1905.

Vanity Fair 11. The Politician's Dream 11. The Little Minister 12. The Old Rag Doll 14. The Lady of Shalott 15. A Night Out 16. Sally in a Hurry 17. A Bachelor's Children 18, etc.

Shean, Al (1868–1949) (Alfred Schoenberg).
German-born entertainer, long in American vaudeville; part of the famous 'Mr Gallagher and Mr Shean' act. After his partner's death he played character roles in Hollywood films.
Murder in the Air 35. San Francisco 36. The Great Waltz 38. Ziegfeld Girl 41. Atlantic City 44, etc.

Shear, Barry (1923–1979).
American director.
■ Wild in the Streets 68. Night Gallery (TV) (co-d) 69. Ellery Queen: Don't Look Behind You (TV) 71. The Todd Killings 71. Short Walk to Daylight (TV) 72. Across 110th Street 72. The Deadly Trackers 73. Jarrett (TV) 73. Punch and Jody (TV) 74. Strike Force (TV) 75. San Pedro Bums (TV) 77.

Shearer, Douglas (1899–1971).
American sound engineer, brother of Norma Shearer; at MGM for many years, he won twelve Academy Awards, and developed a new sound head.
The Big House 30. Naughty Marietta 35. San Francisco 36. Strike Up the Band 40. Thirty Seconds Over Tokyo 44. Green Dolphin Street 47. The Great Caruso 51, many others.

Shearer, Moira (1926–) (Moira King).
Scottish-born ballet dancer who came to films for the leading role in *The Red Shoes* 48.
■ Tales of Hoffman 52. The Story of Three Loves 53. The Man Who Loved Redheads 55. Peeping Tom 59. Black Tights 60.

Shearer, Norma (1900–1983).
Canadian actress, in Hollywood from silent days and a big MGM star of the 30s. Married to Irving THALBERG.
Biography: 1990, *Norma Shearer* by Gavin Lambert.
■ The Flapper 20. The Restless Sex 20. Way Down East 20. The Stealers 20. The Sign on the Door 20. Torchy's Millions 21. The Leather Pushers 22. The Man Who Paid 22. The Bootleggers 22. Channing of the Northwest 22. A Clouded Name 23. Man and Wife 23. The Devil's Partner 23. Pleasure Mad 23. The Wanters 23. Lucretia Lombard 23. The Trail of the Law 24. The Wolf Man 24. Blue Water 24. Broadway After Dark 24. Broken Barriers 24. Married Flirts 24. Empty Hands 24. The Snob 24. *He Who Gets Slapped* 24. Excuse Me 25. Lady of the Night 25. Waking Up the Town 25. A Slave of Fashion 25. Pretty Ladies 25. The Tower of Lies 25. His Secretary 25. The Devil's Circus 26. The Waning Sex 26. Upstage 26. The Demi-Bride 27. After Midnight 27. The Student Prince 27. The Latest from Paris 28. The Actress 28. A Lady of Chance 28. *The Trial of Mary Dugan* 29. *The Last of Mrs Cheyney* 29. Hollywood Revue 29. Their Own Desire (AAN) 29. The Divorcee (AA) 30. Let Us Be Gay 30. Strangers May Kiss 31. *A Free Soul* (AAN) 31. Private Lives 31. Strange Interlude 32. *Smilin' Through* 32. Riptide 34. *The Barretts of Wimpole Street* (AAN) 34. Romeo and Juliet (AAN) 36. Marie Antoinette (AAN) 38. Idiot's Delight 39. The Women 39. Escape 40. We Were Dancing 41. Her Cardboard Lover 42.
❝ A face unclouded by thought. – *Lillian Hellman*
It is to Irving's credit that, by expert showmanship and a judicious choice of camera angles, he made a beauty and a star out of Mrs Thalberg. – *Anita Loos*
When a critic called her 'wall-eyed', Thalberg had a renowned artist state publicly that her eyes rivalled those of any of the world's famed beauties. Another detractor observed that she had bow legs, whereupon Thalberg ordered the studio designers to dress her in long skirts and never let her be seen in a bathing suit. – *Samuel Marx*

Sheedy, Ally (1962–).
American leading lady. Married actor David Lansbury.
Bad Boys 82. War Games 83. St Elmo's Fire 85. Short Circuit 86. Maid to Order 87. Heart of Dixie 89. Betsy's Wedding 90. Fear (TV) 90. Only the Lonely 91. Chantilly Lace (TV) 93. Man's Best Friend 93. The Pickle 93. Before the Night 94. Parallel Lives (TV) 94. One Night Stand 95. High Art 98. Felons 98, etc.

Sheekman, Arthur (1891–1978).
American comedy writer, often in collaboration.
Monkey Business 31. Roman Scandals 33. Dimples 36. Wonder Man 45. Welcome Stranger 46. Saigon 47. Young Man with Ideas 52. Bundle of Joy 56. Ada 61, etc.

Sheen, Charlie (1965–) (Carlos Estevez).
American actor, son of Martin SHEEN. His personal life became headlines in 1995, when in court evidence he admitted hiring prostitutes at around $2,000 a time. He married model Donna Peel in September and sued for divorce in December. In 1996 he announced that he had become a Christian. In 1997, he was given a one-year suspended sentence and put on probation for two years after pleading no contest to beating a former girlfriend. His current asking price: around $5m a movie.
Red Dawn 84. The Boys Next Door 85. Ferris Bueller's Day Off 86. Lucas 86. The Wraith 86. Platoon 86. Wisdom 86. No Man's Land 87. Wall Street 87. Young Guns 88. Eight Men Out 88. Major League 89. Navy SEALS 90. Men at Work 90. The Rookie 90. Cadence 91. Hot Shots! 91. Hot Shots! Part Deux 93. Deadfall 93. The Three Musketeers 93. The Chase 94. Major League II 94. Terminal Velocity 94. All Dogs Go to Heaven 2 (voice) 96. The Arrival 96. Loose Women 96. Shadow Conspiracy 97. Money Talks 97. Bad Day on the Block 97, etc.
❝ How does Keanu Reeves work with Coppola and Bertolucci and I don't get a shot at that, know what I'm saying? – C.S.
Maybe I should become a heroin addict. Maybe I should roam the fucking streets at 5 a.m. and hang out at fucking coffee bars. You know, become avant-garde. Or maybe if I adopt an English accent and add a middle name, so I'm Charlie Something Sheen, I'll get there. – C.S.

Sheen, Martin (1940–) (Ramon Estevez).
American leading actor of the 70s. Father of actors Charlie SHEEN and Emilio ESTEVEZ.
The Incident 67. The Subject was Roses 68. Catch 22 69. Goodbye Raggedy Ann (TV) 71. No Drums No Bugles 71. Rage 72. Message to My Daughter (TV) 72. Pick-up on 101 72. Pursuit (TV) 73. That Certain Summer (TV) 73. Letters for Three Lovers (TV) 73. Sweet Hostage (TV) 73. *Badlands* 73. Catholics (TV) 74. The Execution of Private Slovik (TV) 74. The Missiles of October (TV) 74. The California Kid (TV) 75. The Legend of Earl Durand 75. The Little Girl Who Lives Down the Lane 76. Sweet Hostage 76. The Cassandra Crossing 77. *Apocalypse Now* 79. Eagle's Wing 79. Loophole 80. The Final Countdown 80. Gandhi 82. That Championship Season 82. Enigma 82. Man, Woman and Child 83. Kennedy (TV) 83. The Dead Zone 83. Broken Rainbow (narrator) 85. The Believers 87. Wall Street 87. Da 88. Judgement in Berlin 88. Promises to Keep 88. Walking after Midnight 88. Personal Choice 89. Beverly Hills Brats 89. Cold Front 89. Beyond the Stars 89. The Maid 91. Cadence (& d) 89. Original Intent 91. Reason to Believe 93. Queen (TV) 93. Hear No Evil 93. Gettysburg 93. Guns of Honor (TV) 94. Roswell (TV) 94. Boca 94. The American President 95. The War at Home 96. Truth or Consequences, N.M. 97. Hostile Waters 97. A Stranger in the Kingdom 98. A Letter from Death Row 98, etc.
❝ I'm a recovering alcoholic. I've been struggling with demons for about two-thirds of my life. The bottom line is surrendering to the will of God. – *M.S., 1997*

Sheen, Michael (1969–).
Welsh leading actor, from the theatre. He trained at RADA and acted with the National Theatre and Royal Shakespeare Company.
Gallowglass (TV) 93. Othello 95. Mary Reilly 96. Wilde 97, etc.

Sheffer, Craig (1960–).
American leading actor.
That Was Then . . . This Is Now 85. Fire with Fire 86. Some Kind of Wonderful 87. Babycakes (TV) 89. Night Breed 90. Instant Karma 90. Fire on the Amazon 91. Blue Desert 91. Eye of the Storm 91. A River Runs through It 92. Fire in the Sky 93. Sleep with Me 94. Roadflower 94. In Pursuit of Honor (TV) 95. Wings of Courage 95. The Grave 96. Head above Water 96. Bliss 97. Miss Evers' Boys (TV) 97. Double Take 97. Executive Power 97. Shadow of Doubt 98. The Fall 98, etc.
TV series: The Hamptons 83.

Sheffield, Johnny (1931–).
American boy actor of the 30s, especially in the *Tarzan* and later the *Bomba* series.
Babes in Arms 39. Roughly Speaking 45, etc.

Sheffield, Reginald (1901–1957).
British actor in Hollywood, father of Johnny Sheffield; formerly a child star.
David Copperfield 23. White Mice 26. The Green Goddess 30. Old English 30. Of Human Bondage 34. Cardinal Richelieu 35. Another Dawn 57. Earthbound 40. Eyes in the Night 42. Wilson 44. Kiss the Blood Off My Hands 48. The Buccaneer 58, etc.

Shefter, Bert (1904–).
Russian-born composer in Hollywood.
Danger Zone 51. M 51. No Escape 53. Kronos 57. Cattle Empire 58. The Big Circus 59. The Lost World 60. Jack the Giant Killer 62. Curse of the Fly 65. The Last Shot You Hear 69. The Christine Jorgensen Story 70, many others.

Sheldon, Gene (1909–1982).
American comedy actor.
A Thousand and One Nights 45. Where Do We Go from Here? 45. Golden Girl 52. Three Ring Circus 55. Babes in Toyland 60, etc.

Sheldon, Sidney (1917–).
American writer-director.
The Bachelor and the Bobbysoxer (w) (AA) 47. Dream Wife (co-w, d) 53. You're Never Too Young (w) 55. Pardners (w) 56. The Buster Keaton Story (wpd) 57. Jumbo (w) 62. The Other Side of Midnight (oa) 77. Bloodline (oa) 79. Rage of Angels (TV) (oa) 83. Master of the Game (TV) 84. The Naked Face (oa) TV 84. Windmills of the Gods (oa) (TV) 88. Memories of Midnight (oa) (TV) 91. Sidney Sheldon's The Sands of Time (oa) (TV) 92. Sidney Sheldon's A Stranger in the Mirror (oa) (TV) 93. Nothing Lasts Forever (oa) (TV) 95, etc.

Shelley, Barbara (1933–).
British leading lady who has filmed in Italy; latterly associated with horror films.
Cat Girl 57. Blood of the Vampire 59. Village of the Damned 61. Shadow of the Cat 62. Postman's Knock 62. The Gorgon 64. The Secret of Blood Island 65. Rasputin the Mad Monk 65. Dracula, Prince of Darkness 65. *Quatermass and the Pit* 67. Ghost Story 74, etc.

Shelley, Mary Wollstonecraft (1797–1851).
British writer (wife of the poet) who somewhat unexpectedly is remembered as the creator of *Frankenstein*, which she composed to pass the time during a wet summer. She was played in *Bride of Frankenstein* by Elsa Lanchester. Three films have dealt with the creation of her novel: Ken Russell's *Gothic* 86, in which she was played by Natasha Richardson, Ivan Passer's *Haunted Summer* 88, with Alice Krige, and Roger Corman's *Frankenstein Unbound* 90, with Bridget Fonda.

Shelly, Adrienne (1966–).
American leading actress, often in independent films.
The Unbelievable Truth 90. Trust 91. Big Girls Don't Cry . . . They Get Even/Stepkids 92. Hold Me, Thrill Me, Kiss Me 93. Hexed 93. Roadflower 94. Sleep with Me 94. Teresa's Tattoo 94. Grind 96. Sudden Manhattan (& wd) 96, etc.

Shelton, John (1917–1972) (John Price).
Rather colourless American second lead.
The Smartest Girl in Town 36. Navy Blue and Gold 37. I Take This Woman 40. Blonde Inspiration 41. Whispering Ghosts 42. The Time of Their Lives 46. Siren of Atlantis 48. Sins of Jezebel 51, etc.

Shelton, Joy (1922–).
British leading lady.
Millions Like Us 43. Waterloo Road 44. No Room at the Inn 48. A Case for PC 49 51. Impulse 54. No Kidding 60. HMS Defiant 62, etc.

Shelton, Ron (1945–).
American screenwriter and director, a former basketball player.
Under Fire (co-w) 83. The Best of Times (w) 85. Bull Durham (wd) (AAN) 88. Blaze (wd) 89. White Men Can't Jump (wd) 92. Blue Chips (w) 94. Cobb (wd) 94. The Great White Hype (co-w only) 96. Tin Cup 96, etc.

Shengeleya, Georgy (1937–).
Russian director whose *Pirosmani* 71 was widely praised.

Shenson, Walter (1919–).
American producer, former publicist; based in Britain.
Korea Patrol 53. The Mouse That Roared 59. A Matter of Who 61. *A Hard Day's Night* 64. Help! 65. A Talent for Loving 69. Welcome to the Club (d) 70. Digby 73. The Chicken Chronicles 77. Reuben Reuben 83, etc.

Shentall, Susan (1934–).
British leading lady who made a solitary appearance in *Romeo and Juliet* 54.

Shepard, Jewel (1962–).
American actress, a former stripper; a star of 'B' and sexploitation movies, she is probably best known for her self-deprecating autobiography: 1996, *If I'm So Famous, How Come Nobody's Ever Heard of Me?*
My Tutor 82. Christina 84. Hollywood Hot Tubs 84. Return of the Living Dead 84. Party Camp 87. Scenes from the Goldmine 87. Hollywood Hot Tubs II: Educating Crystal 89. Roots of Evil 91. Caged Heat II: Stripped of Freedom 94. Scanner Cop II 95, etc.
❝ There are times in this world when one must make the supreme sacrifice for one's art. – J.S.

Shepard, Sam (1943–) (Samuel Shepard Rogers).
American leading man; also screenwriter and playwright. He has two children by actress Jessica Lange.
Biography: 1986: *Sam Shepard: The Life and Work of an American Dreamer* by Ellen Oumano.
■ Zabriskie Point 70. Renaldo and Clara 78. Days of Heaven 78. Resurrection 80. Raggedy Man 81. Frances 82. The Right Stuff (AAN) 83. Paris, Texas (w only) 84. Country 84. Fool for Love (& w) 85. Crimes of the Heart 86. Baby Boom 87. Far North (wd) 88. Steel Magnolias 89. Bright Angel 91. Voyager 91. Defenseless 91. Thunderheart 92. Silent Tongue (wd) 93. The Pelican Brief 93. Curse of the Starving Class (oa) 94. The Good Old Boys (TV) 95. Lily Dale (TV) 96.
❝ I didn't go out of my way to get into this movie stuff. I think of myself as a writer. – S.S.
The most complete Renaissance Man since Sir Philip Sidney. – *Professor John Sutherland*

Shepherd, Cybill (1950–).
American leading actress and singer. Born in Memphis, she won a contest for Miss Congeniality at 16 and was a model before becoming an actress.
■ The Last Picture Show 71. The Heartbreak Kid 72. Daisy Miller 74. At Long Last Love 75. Taxi Driver 76. Special Delivery 76. Silver Bears 77. The Lady Vanishes 79. The Return 80. Chances Are 89. Alice 90. Texasville 90. Once upon a Crime 92. Married to It 93. There Was a Little Boy (TV) 93. Telling Secrets (TV) 93.
TV series: The Yellow Rose 83. Moonlighting 85–89. Cybill 95– .
❝ I've grown in spirituality and as a human being since I began to relate to Mother Earth. – C.S.

Shepherd, Elizabeth.
British actress.
The Queen's Guards 61. Blind Corner 63. *The Tomb of Ligeia* 64. Hell Boats 69. Damien: Omen II 78. Double Negative 80. The Kidnapping of the President 80. Invitation to the Wedding 85. Criminal Law 89. Mustard Bath 93. Let Me Call You Sweetheart (TV) 97, etc.
TV series: Side Effects 94. The Adventures of Shirley Holmes 96.

Shepherd, Jack (1940–).
British actor, in character roles in films and leads on stage and TV. He is also a dramatist and theatre director.
The Virgin Soldiers 69. The Bed Sitting Room 69. Ready When You Are Mr McGill (TV) 76. Count Dracula (TV) 77. The Big Man 90. Twenty-One 91. The Object of Beauty 91. Blue Ice 92. Wycliffe (TV) 93. No Escape 94. Over Here (TV) 96, etc.
TV series: Bill Brand 76. Wycliffe 94– .

Shepitko, Larissa (1938–1979).
Russian director and screenwriter. She was married to director Elem Klimov, who took over the direction of *Farewell* following her death in a car accident. He also made a documentary, *Larissa*, about her in 1980.
Heat/Znoi 63. Wings/Krylia 66. At One O'Clock/V Trinadtsatom Chasu 68. You and I/Ty i Ia 72. The Ascent/Voskhozhdenie (co-w, d) 76. Farewell/Proshchanie (co-w) 81.

Shepley, Michael (1907–1961) (Michael Shepley-Smith).
British stage actor who usually played amiable buffoons.
Black Coffee 30. Goodbye Mr Chips 39. Quiet Wedding 40. The Demi Paradise 43. Maytime in Mayfair 49. An Alligator Named Daisy 56. Don't Bother to Knock 61, etc.

Shepperd, John (1907–1983) (also known under his real name, Shepperd Strudwick).
American leading man and latterly character actor, usually in gentle, understanding roles.
Congo Maisie (debut) 40. *Remember the Day* 41. *The Loves of Edgar Allan Poe* 42. Enchantment 47. Joan of Arc 48. All the King's Men 49. A Place in the Sun 51. Autumn Leaves 56. The Sad Sack 57. The Unkillables 67. Cops and Robbers 73, etc.

Sher, Antony (1949–).
South African-born Shakespearean actor and novelist, mainly on stage in Britain.
Yanks 79. Superman II 80. Shadey 84. Erik the Viking 89. The Young Poisoner's Handbook 95. Indian Summer 96. The Wind in the Willows 96. *Mrs Brown* (as Disraeli) 97. Hornblower (TV) 98, etc.

Sher, Jack (1913–1988).
American writer-director, former columnist.
My Favorite Spy (w) 51. Off Limits (w) 53. Four Girls in Town (wd) 56. Kathy O' (wd) 58. The Wild and the Innocent (wd) 59. The Three Worlds of Gulliver (wd) 60. Paris Blues (co-w) 61. Critic's Choice (w) 63. Move Over Darling (co-w) 63, etc.

Sheridan, Ann (1915–1967) (Clara Lou Sheridan).
American leading lady at her peak in the early 40s; a cheerful beauty contest winner who developed a tough style and became known as the 'oomph' girl.
■ Search for Beauty 34. Bolero 34. Come on Marines 34. Murder at the Vanities 34. Kiss and Make Up 34. Shoot the Works 34. The Notorious Sophie Lang 34. Ladies Should Listen 34. Wagon Wheels 34. Mrs Wiggs of the Cabbage Patch 34. College Rhythm 34. You Belong to Me 34. Limehouse Blues 34. Enter Madame 35. Home on the Range 35. Rumba 35. Behold My Wife 35. Car 99 35. Rocky Mountain Mystery 35. Mississippi 35. The Glass Key 35. The Crusades 35. The Red Blood of Courage 35. Fighting Youth 35. Sing Me a Love Song 35. Black Legion 36. The Great O'Malley 37. San Quentin 37. Wine, Women and Horses 37. The Footloose Heiress 37. Alcatraz Island 37. She Loves a Fireman 38. The Patient in Room 18 38. Mystery House 38. Cowboy from Brooklyn 38. Little Miss Thoroughbred 38. Letter of Introduction 38. Broadway Musketeers 38. *Angels with Dirty Faces* 38. They Made Me a Criminal 39. Dodge City 39. Naughty but Nice 39. Winter Carnival 39. Indianapolis Speedway 39. Angels Wash Their Faces 39. Castle on the Hudson 40. It All Came True 40. *Torrid Zone* 40. *They Drive by Night* 40. City for Conquest 40. Honeymoon for Three 41. Navy Blues 41. *Kings Row* 41. *The Man Who Came to Dinner* 41. Juke Girl 42. Wings for the Eagle 42. George Washington Slept Here 42. Edge of Darkness 43. *Thank Your Lucky Stars* 43. *Shine on Harvest Moon* 44. The Doughgirls 44. One More Tomorrow 46. Nora Prentiss 47. *The Unfaithful* 47. Silver River 48. Good Sam 48. *I Was a Male War Bride* 49. Stella 50. Woman on the Run 50. Steel Town 52. Just Across the Street 52. Take Me to Town 53. Appointment in Honduras 53. *Come Next Spring* 56. The Opposite Sex 56. Woman and the Hunter 57.
TV series: Pistols and Petticoats 67.

Sheridan, Dinah (1920–) (Dinah Mec).
British leading lady. She was married to actor Jimmy Hanley and Rank chairman Sir John Davis.
Irish and Proud of It 36. Full Speed Ahead 39. Salute John Citizen 42. For You Alone 44. Hills of Donegal 47. Calling Paul Temple 48. The Story of Shirley Yorke 48. Paul Temple's Triumph 50. Where No Vultures Fly 51. *Genevieve* 53. The Railway Children 71. The Mirror Crack'd 80, etc.
TV series: All Night Long 94.

Sheridan, Jim (1949–).
Irish director, screenwriter and dramatist, from the theatre.
■ My Left Foot (AAN) 89. The Field 90. Into the West (w) 92. In the Name of the Father (p, co-w, d) (AANd, AANw) 93. Words upon the Window Pane (a) 94. Some Mother's Son (co-w) 96. The Boxer (co-w, d) 97.

Sheriff, Paul (1903–1961) (Paul Schouvaloff).
Russian art director in Britain from the mid-30s.
French without Tears 39. Quiet Wedding 40. The Gentle Sex 43. *Henry V* 44. The Way to the Stars 45. Vice Versa 48. Flesh and Blood 51. Moulin Rouge (AA) 53. Gentlemen Marry Brunettes 55. Interpol 57. The Doctor's Dilemma 58. The Grass Is Greener 60, etc.

Sherin, Edwin (1930–).
American director.
Valdez Is Coming 70. Glory Boy 71. Lena: My 100 Children (TV) 87. Daughter of the Streets (TV) 90, etc.

Sherman, Cindy (1956?–).
American photographer and director. Her best-known photographic work was called *Untitled Film Stills*, a set of 69 black-and-white photographs showing her posed in a series of ambiguous narrative situations, which was sold to New York's Museum of Modern Art for $1m. Married French video artist Michel Auder.
Office Killer 96.

Sherman, Gary A.
American director.
Death Line/Raw Meat 73. Dead and Buried 81. Vice Squad 82. Wanted Dead or Alive 86. Poltergeist III 88. Lisa 90. After the Shock (TV) 90, etc.

Sherman, George (1908–1991).
American director who graduated slowly from second-feature westerns.
Wild Horse Rodeo 37. Death Valley Outlaws 41. Outside the Law 41. Mantrap 43. Mystery Broadcast 44. The Lady and the Monster 44. *The Bandit of Sherwood Forest* 46. Renegades 46. Last of the Redskins 48. Sword in the Desert 49. Panther's Moon 50. The Golden Horde 51. Against All Flags 52. War Arrow 54. Dawn at Socorro 54. Count Three and Pray 55. Comanche 56. Son of Robin Hood 58. The Enemy General 60. Panic Button 64. Smoky 66. Big Jake 71, many others.

Sherman, Harry (1884–1952).
American producer of westerns.

Sherman, Lowell (1885–1934).
American leading man with stage experience. He was married to actress Helen Costello.
Way Down East 20. Monsieur Beaucaire 24. The Divine Woman 27. Mammy 30. The Greeks Had a Word for Them 32. False Faces 32. She Done Him Wrong (d only) 33. Morning Glory 33. Broadway Through a Keyhole 33, etc.

Sherman, Richard (1928–) and **Robert** (1925–).
American songwriting brothers who have worked mainly for Disney.
Mary Poppins (AA) 64. The Happiest Millionaire 67. The One and Only Genuine Original Family Band 68. Bedknobs and Broomsticks 71. Huckleberry Finn (& w) 74. The Slipper and the Rose (& w) 76, etc.

Sherman, Vincent (1906–) (Abram Orovitz).
American director, formerly stage actor.
The Return of Doctor X 39. *All Through the Night* 41. The Hard Way 42. Old Acquaintance 43. In Our Time 44. Mr Skeffington 45. The Unfaithful 47. The New Adventures of Don Juan 48. The Hasty Heart 49. Lone Star 51. Affair in Trinidad 52. The Garment Jungle 57. Naked Earth 57. The Young Philadelphians 59. Ice Palace 60. The Second Time Around 61. Cervantes 66. The Last Hurrah (TV) 77. Women at West Point (TV) 79. Trouble in High Timber Country (TV) 82, etc.

Sherriff, R. C. (1896–1975).
Prolific British playwright and screenwriter.
Autobiography: 1969, *No Leading Lady*.
AS PLAYWRIGHT: Journey's End 30. Badger's Green 47. Home at Seven 52.
AS SCREENWRITER: *The Invisible Man* 33. *Goodbye Mr Chips* (AAN) 39. Lady Hamilton 41. *Odd Man Out* 47. *Quartet* 48. No Highway 50. The Dam Busters 55, many others.

Sherrin, Ned (1931–).
British ex-barrister who became a BBC producer and performer, then turned to producing movies for a time, before going on to work in radio and the theatre.
Autobiography: 1983, *A Small Thing – Like an Earthquake*.
The Virgin Soldiers 69. Every Home Should Have One 70. Girl Stroke Boy 71. Up Pompeii 71. Rentadick 72. Up the Chastity Belt 72. The Alf Garnett Saga 72. Up the Front 72. The National Health 73, etc.

Sherwin, David.
English scriptwriter, associated with the films of Lindsay Anderson, who later went to Hollywood and regretted it.
Autobiography: 1996, *Going Mad in Hollywood*.
If . . . 68. *O Lucky Man!* 73. Britannia Hospital 82, etc.

Sherwin, Manning (1903–1974).
American composer, working for Paramount during the 30s; at the end of the decade he came to Britain to write for films and theatre, including many London musicals and revues. His best-known song, to Eric Maschwitz's lyrics, was 'A Nightingale Sang in Berkeley Square'.
Stolen Holiday 37. Blossoms on Broadway 37. Vogues of 1938 37. College Swing/Swing, Teacher, Swing 38. A Girl Must Live 39. He Found a Star 41. Hi, Gang! 41. King Arthur Was a Gentleman 42. Miss London Limited 43. Bees in Paradise 43. I'll Be Your Sweetheart 45, etc.

Sherwood, Bill (1952–1990).
American director. Died of AIDS.
Parting Glances 86.

Sherwood, Madeleine (1926–) (Madeleine Thornton).
Canadian character actress.
Cat on a Hot Tin Roof 58. Parrish 61. Sweet Bird of Youth 62. Hurry Sundown 67. Pendulum 69. Wicked Wicked 73, etc.
TV series: The Flying Nun 67–68.

Sherwood, Robert (1896–1955).
American dramatist. Plays filmed:
Reunion in Vienna 32. The Petrified Forest 36. Tovarich 38. Idiot's Delight 39. Abe Lincoln in Illinois 39, etc.
OTHER SCRIPTS: Waterloo Bridge 32. The Adventures of Marco Polo 38. *Rebecca* (AAN) 40. *The Best Years of Our Lives* (AA) 45. The Bishop's Wife 48. Jupiter's Darling/The Road to Rome 54.

Sheybal, Vladek (1923–1992).
Intense-looking Polish character actor in Britain.
Kanal 56. Women in Love 69. The Music Lovers 70. The Boy Friend 71. QB VII 74. The Wind and the Lion 75. Memed My Hawk 87. Strike It Rich 90, etc.

Shields, Arthur (1895–1970).
Irish character actor, an Abbey player, long in Hollywood; brother of Barry Fitzgerald. Born in Dublin, he was on stage from the age of 13.
The Plough and the Stars 37. *Drums along the Mohawk* 39. *The Long Voyage Home* 40. The Keys of the Kingdom 44. The Corn is Green 45. The River 51. The Quiet Man 52. The King and Four Queens 56. Night of the Quarter Moon 59. The Pigeon That Took Rome 62, etc.

Shields, Brooke (1965–).
American juvenile actress of the late 70s. Married tennis player Andre Agassi in 1997.
Alice Sweet Alice 78. King of the Gypsies 78. Pretty Baby 79. Just You and Me Kid 79. Tilt 79. Two of a Kind 79. Wanda Nevada 80. The Blue Lagoon 80. Endless Love 81. Sahara 82. The Muppets Take Manhattan 84. The Diamond Trap (TV) 88. Brenda Starr 89. Speed Zone 89. Backstreet Dreams 90. Brenda Starr 92. Freaked 93. Freeway 96. The Misadventures of Margaret 98, etc.
TV series: Suddenly Susan 96.

Shields, Ella (1880–1952).
British music-hall performer, as a top-hatted male impersonator, associated with the song 'Burlington Bertie'; in films as herself.
Men of Yesterday 36. Ella Shields (short) 36. Cavalcade of the Stars (short) 38, etc.

Shigeta, James (1933–).
Hawaiian leading man who usually plays Japanese in Hollywood films.
The Crimson Kimono 60. Cry for Happy 60. Walk Like a Dragon 60. Bridge to the Sun 61. Flower Drum Song 61. Paradise Hawaiian Style 66. Nobody's Perfect 68. Lost Horizon 73. Midway 76. Tomorrow's Child 82. Die Hard 88. Cage 89. China Cry 90. Blood for Blood 95. Space Marines (TV) 96. Mulan (voice) 98, etc.

Shilkret, Nathaniel (1895–1982).
American arranger and conductor.
The Plough and the Stars 36. Mary of Scotland 36. The Toast of New York 37. She Went to the Races 45. The Hoodlum Saint 46, many others.

Shimkus, Joanna (1943–).
Canadian leading lady in American and European films. She is married to actor Sidney Poitier.
Paris Vu Par 66. Les Aventuriers 67. Zita 68. Ho! 68. Boom 68. The Lost Man 69. *The Virgin and the Gypsy* 70. The Marriage of a Young Stockbroker 71. A Time for Loving 71, etc.

Shimoda, Yuki (1924–1981).
Japanese-American character actor.
Auntie Mame 59. A Majority of One 61. Midway 75. Farewell to Manzanar (TV) 76. MacArthur 77. The Last Flight of Noah's Ark 79, many others.

Shimura, Takashi (1905–1982) (Shoji Shiazaki).
Japanese leading actor, in films from 1935. He is to be seen most frequently in the films of Kurosawa.
Stray Dog 49. *Rashomon* 50. Seven Samurai 54. Godzilla 54. *Ikuru* 55. Throne of Blood 57. The Hidden Fortress 58. Yojimbo 62. Kwaidan 64. Red Beard/Akahige 65. Frankenstein Conquers the World 65. The Bullet Train/Shinkansen Daiakuha 75. Oginsama 79. Kagemusha 80. Fifth Movement/Honoo No Daigo Gakusho 81, etc.

Shindo, Kaneto (1912–).
Japanese director. Began as assistant art director and successful screenwriter, particularly in collaboration with Yoshimura, before concentrating on directing.
Children of Hiroshima 53. The Wolf 56. *The Island* 62. Ningen 63. *Onibaba* 64. Kuroncko 67. Iron Ring 72. Heart 73. Life of Chikuzan 77. The Horizon 84. Eiga Joyu 87. The Strange Story of Oyuki/Bokuto Kidan 93. Faraway Sunset/Tooki Rakujitsu (w) 93. A Last Note 95, etc.

Shine, Bill (1911–1997).
Amiable British small-part actor often seen as vacuous dandy.
The Scarlet Pimpernel 34. Farewell Again 37. Let George Do It 40. Perfect Strangers 45. Melba 53. Father Brown 54. Jack the Ripper 58. Double Bunk 61. The Pure Hell of St Trinian's 61. Left Right and Center 61. Burke and Hare 71. The Jigsaw Man 83, many others.

Shiner, Ronald (1903–1966).
British comedy actor, on stage from 1928, films from 1934, at first in bit parts, later as star.
King Arthur Was a Gentleman 42. The Way to the Stars 45. *Worm's Eye View* 50. *Reluctant Heroes* 51. Laughing Anne 53. Top of the Form 54. Up to His Neck 55. Keep It Clean 56. Dry Rot 56. Girls at Sea 58. Operation Bullshine 59. The Night We Got the Bird 60, etc.

Shingleton, Wilfrid (1914–1983).
British art director who won an Oscar for *Great Expectations* 46.

Shinoda, Masahiro (1931–).
Japanese director, part of the so-called 'New Wave' movement with Oshima. He studied drama at university before becoming an assistant director.
One Ticket for Love/Koi no Katamichi Kippu 60. Epitaph to My Love/Waga Koi no Tabiji 61. Our Marriage/Watakushi-tachi no Kekkon 62. Pale

Flower/Kawaita Hana 63. Assassination/Ansatsu 64. Captive's Island/Shokei no Shima 66. Double Suicide/Shinju Ten no Amijima 69. Silence/Chinomoku 71. Sapporo Winter Olympic Games 72. Hanare Goze Orin 77. MacArthur's Children 84. Gonza the Spearman 86. The Dancer 89. Boyhood/Shonen Jidai 91. Sharaku 95, etc.

Shire, David (1937–).
American composer.
One More Train to Rob 71. Drive He Said 71. Showdown 73. The Conversation 74. Farewell My Lovely 75. The Hindenburg 75. All the President's Men 76. Saturday Night Fever 77. Norma Rae (AA, s) 79. Only When I Laugh 81. Paternity 81. Max Dugan Returns 82. The World According to Garp 82. Oh God! You Devil 84. Return to Oz 85. Night, Mother 86. Short Circuit 86. Backfire 87. Monkey Shines 88. Vice Versa 88. The Women of Brewster Place (TV) 89. Bed and Breakfast 92. Sidekicks 93. Lily in Winter (TV) 94. One Night Stand 95. Larry McMurtry's Streets of Laredo (TV) 96. Last Stand at Saber River (TV) 96. Rear Window (TV) 98, etc.

Shire, Talia (1946–) (Talia Coppola).
American leading lady, sister of Francis COPPOLA. She is the mother of actor Jason Schwartzman.
The Wild Races 68. The Dunwich Horror 70. Un Homme Est Mort 72. *The Godfather* 72. The Godfather Part II (AAN) 74. Rocky (AAN) 76. Old Boyfriends 79. Rocky II 79. Prophecy 79. Rocky III 82. Rocky IV 85. RAD 86. From Another Star 87. New York Stories 89. The Godfather Part III 90. Rocky V 90. Bed and Breakfast 91. Cold Heaven 92. Chantilly Lace (TV) 93. Deadfall 93. One Night Stand (d) 95, etc.

Shirley, Anne (1918–1993) (Dawn Paris).
American child star of the 20s (under the name Dawn O'Day) who later graduated to leading lady roles. She retired in 1944. Married to actor John Payne (1937–43), producer Adrian Scott (1945–49), and screenwriter Charles Lederer.
So Big 32. *Anne of Green Gables* 34. Stella Dallas (AAN) 37. Vigil in the Night 39. Anne of Windy Poplars 40. West Point Widow 41. All that Money Can Buy 41. *Farewell My Lovely* 44. Murder My Sweet 45, etc.

Shoemaker, Ann (1891–1978).
American character actress with stage experience.
A Dog of Flanders 35. Alice Adams 35. Stella Dallas 37. Babes in Arms 39. Conflict 45. A Woman's Secret 49. Sunrise at Campobello 60. The Fortune Cookie 66, many others.

Sholem, Lee (c. 1900–).
American director.
Tarzan's Magic Fountain 48. Redhead from Wyoming 52. Tobor the Great 53. Emergency Hospital 56. Pharaoh's Curse 56. Sierra Stranger 57, etc.

Shore, Dinah (1917–1994) (Frances Rose Shore).
American cabaret singer, in very occasional films; latterly running a daily TV chat show for women. As a child singer, was known as Fanny Rose. Married actor George MONTGOMERY (1943–62).
■ Thank Your Lucky Stars 43. Up in Arms 44. Follow the Boys 44. Belle of the Yukon 45. Till the Clouds Roll By 46. Aaron Slick from Punkin Crick 52. Oh God 77. Health 80.

Shore, Howard (1946–).
Canadian composer, from TV.
The Brood 79. Scanners 81. Videodrome 83. Places in the Heart 84. After Hours 85. Fire with Fire 86. The Fly 86. Nadine 87. Heaven 87. Moving 88. Big 88. Dead Ringers 88. An Innocent Man 89. She-Devil 89. The Silence of the Lambs 91. Prelude to a Kiss 92. Sliver 93. Guilty as Sin 93. Mrs Doubtfire 93. M. Butterfly 93. Philadelphia 93. The Client 94. Ed Wood 94. Seven 95. White Man's Burden 95. Moonlight and Valentino 95. Looking for Richard 96. Before and After 96. The Truth about Cats and Dogs 96. Striptease 96. Heaven's Prisoners 96. Cop Land 97. The Game 97. eXistenZ 98, etc.

Shore, Pauly (1968–).
American comic actor, from television.
Encino Man/California Man 92. Son-in-Law 93. Dream Date 93. In the Army Now 94. Jury Duty 95. Bio-Dome 96. Casper: A Spirited Beginning (voice) 97, etc.
TV series: Pauly 96.

Short, Martin (1950–).
Canadian comic actor and writer. He first gained recognition with Toronto's Second City Troupe. Born in Hamilton, Ontario, he studied medicine at McMaster University.
Lost and Found 79. The Outsider 79. The Canadian Conspiracy 86. Three Amigos! 86. Cross My Heart 87. Innerspace 87. The Big Picture 88. Three Fugitives 89. Pure Luck 91. Father of the Bride 92. Captain Ron 92. We're Back! A Dinosaur's Story (voice) 93. Clifford 94. The Pebble and the Penguin (voice) 95. Father of the Bride Part II 95. Mars Attacks! 96. Jungle 2 Jungle 96. A Simple Wish 97. Merlin (TV) 98. Prince of Egypt (voice) 98, etc.
TV series: The Associates 79–80. I'm a Big Girl Now 80–81. SCTV Network 90 82–83. Saturday Night Live 84–85. The Martin Short Show 95. The Show Formerly Known as the Martin Short Show 95.

Shostakovich, Dmitri (1906–1975).
Russian composer.
The New Babylon 28. The Youth of Maxim 35. The Fall of Berlin 47. Hamlet 64. War and Peace 64.

Shotter, Winifred (1904–1996).
British leading lady of the 30s, chiefly remembered in the Aldwych farces beginning with *Rookery Nook* 30. Born in Maidenhead, she was on stage from 1918.
Rookery Nook 30. Plunder 30. Jack's the Boy 32. A Night Like This 32. Night of the Garter 33. Sorrell and Son 33. D'Ye Ken John Peel? 35. Petticoat Fever 36. Candles at Nine 44. John and Julie 55, etc.

Showalter, Max (1917–) (formerly known as Casey Adams).
American supporting actor often seen as reporter, newscaster or good-guy friend.
Always Leave Them Laughing 50. With a Song in My Heart 52. Bus Stop 56. The Naked and the Dead 58. Elmer Gantry 60. Bon Voyage 62. Fate Is the Hunter 64. The Moonshine War 70. The Anderson Tapes 71. Sergeant Pepper's Lonely Hearts Club Band 78. 10 79. Sixteen Candles 84, etc.

Shue, Elisabeth (1963–).
American leading actress. Married director Davis Guggenheim.
The Karate Kid 84. Link 86. Adventures in Babysitting 87. Cocktail 88. Back to the Future Part II 89. Back to the Future Part III 90. The Marrying Man/Too Hot to Handle 91. Soapdish 91. Twenty Bucks 93. Radio Inside 94. *Leaving Las Vegas* (AAN) 95. The Underneath 95. The Trigger Effect 96. Cousin Bette 97. The Saint 97. Deconstructing Harry 97. Palmetto 98. Molly 98, etc.
TV series: Call to Glory 84–85.

Shuken, Leo (1906–1976).
American orchestrator.
Waikiki Wedding 37. The Flying Deuces 39. *Stagecoach* (AA) 39. The Lady Eve 41. *Sullivan's Travels* 41. The Miracle of Morgan's Creek 44. The Fabulous Dorseys 47. The Greatest Story Ever Told 64, etc.

Shulman, Irving (1913–1995).
American novelist, biographer and screenwriter who introduced the theme of juvenile delinquency into 40s novels and 50s films. Born in Brooklyn, he studied at Ohio and Columbia Universities, and was a teacher before working as a contract writer at Warner's. He turned his version of the script for *Rebel without a Cause* into a novel, *Children of the Dark* 56.
City across the River (from his novel The Amboy Dukes) 49. Journey into Light (co-w) 51. The Ring (w, oa) 52. Champ for a Day (w) 53. *Rebel without a Cause* (adaptation) 55. Terror at Midnight (co-w) 56. Baby Face Nelson (co-w) 57. Cry Tough (oa) 59. College Confidential (w) 60. Harlow (oa) 65, etc.

Shumlin, Herman (1898–1979).
American stage producer who directed two films in the 40s.
■ Watch on the Rhine 43. Confidential Agent 45.

Shurlock, Geoffrey (1895–1976).
Film administrator, an Englishman who became the power behind the MPEA Production Code 1954–68.

Shusett, Ronald.
American screenwriter.
Alien (story) 79. Dead and Buried 81. Phobia 81. The Final Terror 83. King Kong Lives 86. Above the Law 88. Total Recall 90. Freejack 92, etc.

Shute, Nevil (1899–1960).
English best-selling novelist.
The Pied Piper 43. No Highway 52. Landfall 54. A Town Like Alice 56. On the Beach 59, etc.

Shyer, Charles (1941–).
American director and screenwriter. Married writer and producer Nancy Myers.
Smokey and the Bandit (co-w) 77. Goin' South (co-w) 78. House Calls (co-w) 78. Private Benjamin (co-w, AAN) 80. Irreconcilable Differences (co-w, d) 84. Baby Boom (co-w, d) 87. Father of the Bride (co-w, d) 91. I Love Trouble (co-w, d) 94. Father of the Bride 2 95. The Parent Trap (p, co-w) 98, etc.

Siao, Josephine (1947–) (Siao Fong-fong).
Chinese leading actress, a former child star. Born in Shanghai, she moved to Hong Kong as a child and became a star of family pictures and musicals from the early 50s. In 1968, after making 200 features, she stopped acting to study for a degree in communications in the US before returning to Hong Kong to act and, from the mid-70s and early 80s, to set up her own production company. She again quit acting when she moved to Australia with her second husband. On their return to Hong Kong, she scored a success as the kung-fu fighting mother of Jet LI in *Fong Sai Yuk* and its sequel. Deaf in one ear from childhood, she has lost much of her hearing in the other as an adult.
Mai Goo 55. A Purple Stormy Night 68. The True Story of a Rebellious Girl 69. Jumping Ash (& p, co-d) 76. The Spooky Bunch (& p) 80. The Wrong Couples 87. Fong Sai Yuk 93. Fong Sai Yuk II 93. Summer Snow 95. Hu-Du-Men 96. Mahjong Dragon 97, many others.

Sidney, George (1878–1945) (Sammy Greenfield).
American comedian, once popular in vaudeville.
Potash and Perlmutter 23. Millionaires 26. Clancy's Kosher Wedding 27. The Cohens and Kellys in Paris 28. Manhattan Melodrama 34. Good Old Soak 37, many others.

Sidney, George (1916–).
American director, former musician and MGM shorts director.
Free and Easy 41. Thousands Cheer 43. Bathing Beauty 44. Anchors Aweigh 45. *The Harvey Girls* 46. Cass Timberlane 47. *The Three Musketeers* 48. The Red Danube 49. Annie Get Your Gun 50. *Showboat* 51. Scaramouche 52. Young Bess 53. *Kiss Me Kate* 53. Jupiter's Darling 54. The Eddy Duchin Story 56. *Jeanne Eagels* 57. Pal Joey 57. Who Was That Lady? 59. Pepe 60. Bye Bye Birdie 62. Viva Las Vegas 63. The Swinger 66. Half a Sixpence 67, etc.

Sidney, Sylvia (1910–) (Sophia Kosow).
Fragile, dark-eyed American heroine of the 30s.
■ Thru Different Eyes 29. *City Streets* 31. Confessions of a Co-Ed 31. An American Tragedy 31. *Street Scene* 31. Ladies of the Big House 32. The Miracle Man 32. Merrily We Go to Hell 33. Madame Butterfly 33. Pick Up 33. Jennie Gerhardt 33. Good Dame 34. Thirty Day Princess 34. Behold My Wife 34. Accent on Youth 35. Mary Burns Fugitive 35. Trail of the Lonesome Pine 36. Fury 36. Sabotage (GB) 37. *You Only Live Once* 37. Dead End 37. You and Me 37. One Third of a Nation 39. The Wagons Roll at Night 41. Blood on the Sun 45. The Searching Wind 46. Mr Ace 46. Love from a Stranger 47. Les Misérables 53. Violent Saturday 55. Behind the High Wall 56. Do Not Fold Spindle or Mutilate (TV) 71. Summer Wishes, Winter Dreams (AAN) 73. Death at Love House (TV) 76. God Told Me To 76. Raid on Entebbe (TV) 77. I Never Promised You a Rose Garden 77. Siege (TV) 78. Damien: Omen II 79. The Shadow Box (TV) 80. Hammett 82. Corrupt 83. Finnegan Begin Again (TV) 85. An Early Frost (TV) 85. Pals (TV) 87. Beetlejuice 88. Mars Attacks! 96.
❝ I'd be the girl of the gangster . . . then the sister who was bringing up the gangster . . . then the mother of the gangster . . . and they always had me ironing somebody's shirt. – *S.S.*
What did Hitchcock teach me? To be a puppet and not try to be creative. – *S.S.*
Paramount paid me by the tear. – *S.S.*

Siegel, Don (1912–1991).
American director, former editor; an expert at crime thrillers, he latterly attracted the attention of highbrow critics.
Autobiography: 1993, *A Siegel Film: An Autobiography*.
■ *Hitler Lives* (short) (AA) 45. Star in the Night (short) (AA) 45. The Verdict 46. Night Unto Night 48. The Big Steal 49. Duel at Silver Creek 52. No Time for Flowers 52. Count the Hours 53. China Venture 54. *Riot in Cell Block 11* 54. Private Hell 36 55. An Annapolis Story 55. *Invasion of the Body Snatchers* 56. Crime in the Streets 57. Spanish Affair 57. *Baby Face Nelson* 57. The Line Up 58. The Gun Runners 58. The Hound Dog Man 59. Edge of Eternity 59. Flaming Star 60. Hell Is for Heroes 62. The Killers 64. The Hanged Man 64. Madigan 67. Stranger on the Run (TV) 68. *Coogan's Bluff* 68. Two Mules for Sister Sara 69. Death of a Gunfighter (co-d) 69. The Beguiled 71. Play Misty for Me (a only) 71. *Dirty Harry* 72. *Charley Varrick* 73. The Black Windmill 74. *The Shootist* 76. Telefon 77. Escape from Alcatraz 79. Rough Cut 80. Jinxed 82. Into the Night (a) 85.
❝ I once told Godard that he had something I wanted – freedom. He said: 'You have something I want – money.' – *D.S.*
Most of my pictures, I'm sorry to say, are about nothing. Because I'm a whore. I work for money. It's the American way. – *D.S.*

Siegel, Sol C. (1903–1982).
American producer, in films from 1929.
Kiss and Tell 44. Blue Skies 46. House of Strangers 49. A Letter to Three Wives 49. I Was a Male War Bride 49. Fourteen Hours 51. Monkey Business 52. Gentlemen Prefer Blondes 52. Call Me Madam 53. Three Coins in the Fountain 54. High Society 56. Les Girls 57. Home from the Hill 59. Walk Don't Run 66. Alvarez Kelly 66. No Way to Treat a Lady 68, etc.

Siemaszko, Casey (1961–) (Kazimierz Siemaszko).
American actor.
Class 83. Back to the Future 85. Secret Admirer 85. Stand by Me 86. Gardens of Stone 87. Three o'Clock High 87. Biloxi Blues 88. Young Guns 88. Back to the Future II 89. Breaking In 89. The Big Slice 91. Of Mice and Men 92. Milk Money 94. Teresa's Tattoo 94. The Phantom 95. Black Scorpion 95. Bliss 97, etc.

Sienkiewicz, Henryk (1846–1916).
Polish novelist, author of the much-filmed *Quo Vadis?* (published 1895).

Sierra, Gregory.
American supporting actor.
The Wrath of God 72. Papillon 72. The Towering Inferno 74. The Prisoner of Zenda 79. Something Is Out There (TV) 88. Honey I Blew Up The Kid 92. Deep Cover 92. Hot Shots! Part Deux 93. The Wonderful Ice Cream Suit 98, etc.
TV series: Sanford and Son 72–75. Barney Miller 75–76. Soap 80–81. Zorro and Son 83.

Sigel, Newton Thomas (aka Tom Sigel).
American cinematographer.
Latino 85. Rude Awakening 89. Salmonberries (Ger.) 91. Into the West 92. Indian Summer 93. The Usual Suspects 95. Foxfire 96. The Trigger Effect 96. Blood & Wine 96. Fallen 98. Apt Pupil 98, etc.

Signoret, Simone (1921–1985) (Simone Kaminker).
Distinguished French leading actress, married to Yves Montand.
Autobiography: 1976, *Nostalgia Isn't What It Used to Be*.
Biography: 1992, *Simone Signoret* by Catherine David.
■ Le Prince Charmant 42. Bolero 42. Les Visiteurs du Soir 42. Adieu Léonard 43. Beatrice 43. La

Boîte aux Rêves 45. The Ideal Couple 45. Les Démons de l'Aube 45. Macadam 45. Fantomas 47. Against the Wind (GB) 47. *Dédée d'Anvers* 48. L'Impasse des Deux Anges 49. *Manèges* 49. Four Days' Leave 50. *La Ronde* 50. Gunman in the Streets 50. Ombre et Lumière 51. *Casque d'Or* 52. Thérèse Raquin 53. *Les Diaboliques* 54. Le Mort en ce Jardin 56. The Witches of Salem 57. *Room at the Top* (GB) (AA) 58. Adua and Company 60. Les Mauvais Coups 61. Les Amours Célèbres 61. Term of Trial (GB) 62. The Day and the Hour 63. Dragées au Poivre 63. *Ship of Fools* (US) (AAN) 65. The Sleeping Car Murders 65. Is Paris Burning? 66. The Deadly Affair (GB) 67. Games (US) 67. The Seagull 68. L'Armée des Ombres 69. The American 69. The Confession 70. Comptes à Rebours 71. *Le Chat* 72. La Veuve Couderc 73. Rude Journée pour la Reine 73. Défense de Savoir 74. The Investigator 74. Flesh of the Orchid 74. Police Python 357 76. Madame Rosa 78. L'Adolescente 79. I Sent a Letter to My Love 81.

Siliotto, Carlo.
Italian composer.
Flight of the Innocent 94. Snowball/Palla di Neve 95, etc.

Silliphant, Sterling (1918–1996).
American writer-producer with much TV experience (*Naked City*, *Route* 66, etc.). Former advertising executive. Also a novelist, he became a Buddhist and went to live in Thailand.
The Joe Louis Story (w) 53. Five Against the House (w, co-p) 55. Nightfall (w) 56. Damn Citizen (w) 57. Village of the Damned 60. The Slender Thread (w) 66. In The Heat of the Night (w) (AA) 67. Charly 68. A Walk in the Spring Rain 69. The Liberation of L.B. Jones 70. The Poseidon Adventure 72. The Towering Inferno 74. The Killer Elite (w) 75. Telefon (co-w) 77. The Swarm (w) 78. Pearl (TV) 79. When Time Ran Out (co-w) 80. Space (TV) 85. Catch the Heat 87. Over the Top 87. The Grass Harp (co-w) 95, etc.

Sillitoe, Alan (1928–).
British north-country novelist best known to filmgoers for *Saturday Night and Sunday Morning* and *The Loneliness of the Long Distance Runner*. His less successful novel *The General* was filmed as *Counterpoint*.

Sills, Milton (1882–1930).
Stalwart American leading man of the silent screen.
The Rack 15. The Claw 17. Eyes of Youth 19. The Weekend 20. Burning Sands 22. Adam's Rib 23. Madonna of the Streets 24. The Sea Hawk 24. Paradise 26. Valley of the Giants 27. His Captive Woman 29. The Sea Wolf 30, many others.

Silva, Henry (1928–).
Pale-eyed American actor of Italian and Basque descent, often seen as sadistic villain or assorted Latin types.
Viva Zapata 52. Crowded Paradise 56. A Hatful of Rain 57. The Bravados 58. Green Mansions 59. Cinderfella 60. *The Manchurian Candidate* 62. *Johnny Cool* (leading role) 63. The Return of Mr Moto 65. The Reward 65. The Plainsman 66. The Hills Ran Red (It.) 66. Never a Dull Moment 68. Five Savage Men 70. The Kidnap of Mary Lou 75. Shoot 76. Cry of a Prostitute 76. Thirst 79. Buck Rogers 79. Alligator 80. Sharkey's Machine 81. Wrong Is Right 82. Allan Quatermain and the Lost City of Gold 86. Bulletproof 87. Above the Law 88. Dick Tracy 90. South Beach 92. The Harvest 92. Possessed by the Night 93. Trigger Happy/Mad Dog Time 96, etc.

Silver, Joan Micklin (1935–).
American director.
■ Limbo (w) 72. *Hester Street* (& w) 74. Bernice Bobs Her Hair (& w) (TV) 76. Between the Lines 78. Head over Heels (& w) 79. Crossing Delancey 88. Loverboy 89. Big Girls Don't Cry . . . They Get Even/Stepkids 92. In the Presence of Mine Enemies (TV) 97. A Fish in the Bathtub 98.

Silver, Joel (1952–).
American producer, mainly of high-budget action films.
48 Hours 82. Streets of Fire 84. Brewster's Millions 85. Commando 85. Weird Science 85. Jumpin' Jack Flash 86. Lethal Weapon 87. Predator 87. Action Jackson 88. Die Hard 88. Road House 89. Lethal Weapon 2 89. The Adventures of Ford Fairlane 90. Predator 2 90. Die Hard II 90. Hudson Hawk 91. Ricochet 91. The Last Boy Scout 92. Lethal Weapon 3 92. Demolition Man 93. Executive Decision 96. Tales from the Crypt Presents: Bordello of Blood 96. Fathers' Day 97. Conspiracy Theory 97. Lethal Weapon 4 98, etc.

Silver, Marisa (1960–).
American director and screenwriter.
Old Enough (wd) 84. Permanent Record (d) 88. Vital Signs (d) 90.

Silver, Ron (1946–).
American leading actor.
The French Connection 71. Tunnel Vision 76. Semi-Tough 77. Best Friends 82. Silent Rage 82. The Entity 82. Silkwood 83. Betrayal 83. Garbo Talks 84. Oh, God! You Devil 84. Eat and Run 86. Enemies, a Love Story 89. Fellow Traveller 89. Blue Steel 90. Reversal of Fortune 90. Trapped in Silence (TV) 90. Live Wire 92. Mr Saturday Night 92. Married to It 93. Timecop 94. A Woman of Independent Means (TV) 95. Kissinger and Nixon (TV, as Kissinger) 95. The Arrival 96. Rhapsody in Bloom 98, etc.
TV series: Rhoda 76–78. Dear Detective 79. The Stockard Channing Show 80. Baker's Dozen 82.

Silvera, Frank (1914–1970).
American general-purpose actor with stage experience. Electrocuted while repairing a kitchen appliance.
Viva Zapata 52. Killer's Kiss 55. Crowded Paradise 56. The Mountain Road 60. Mutiny on the Bounty 62. The Appaloosa 66. Che! 69. Valdez Is Coming 71, etc.
TV series: The High Chaparral 67–70.

Silverheels, Jay (1919–1980).
Canadian Red Indian actor, mainly in western films.
The Prairie 47. Fury at Furnace Creek 48. Broken Arrow 50. War Arrow 53. The Lone Ranger 55. Indian Paint 65. The Phynx 70. Santee 73, many others.
TV series: The Lone Ranger (as Tonto) 52–56.

Silvers, Louis (1889–1954).
American composer.
The Jazz Singer 27. Dancing Lady 33. It Happened One Night 34. One Night of Love (AA) 35. Lloyds of London 36. Heidi 37. In Old Chicago (AAN) 38. Suez (AAN) 38. Jesse James 39. Swanee River (AAN) 39. The Powers Girl 42, many others.

Silvers, Phil (1912–1985) (Philip Silver).
American vaudeville star comedian in occasional films from 1941.
Autobiography: 1974, *The Laugh Is on Me*.
Tom, Dick and Harry (debut) 41. *You're in the Army Now* 42. Roxie Hart 42. My Gal Sal 42. Coney Island 43. *Cover Girl* 44. A Thousand and One Nights 45. Where Do We Go from Here? 45. Summer Stock 50. Lucky Me 54. Forty Pounds of Trouble 63. *It's a Mad Mad Mad Mad World* 63. A Funny Thing Happened on the Way to the Forum 66. Follow That Camel (GB) 67. Buona Sera, Mrs Campbell 68. Deadly Tide (TV) 75. Won Ton Ton 76. The Chicken Chronicles 77. The New Love Boat (TV) 77. The Night They Took Miss Beautiful (TV) 78. There Goes the Bride 80, etc.
TV series: *You'll Never Get Rich* (as Bilko) 55–58. *The New Phil Silvers Show* 64.

Silverstein, Elliot (1927–).
American director, from TV.
■ Belle Sommers (TV) 62. *Cat Ballou* 65. The Happening 67. A Man Called Horse 69. The Car 77. Betrayed by Innocence (TV) 86. Night of Courage (TV) 87. Fight for Life (TV) 87. Rich Men, Single Women (TV) 90. Flashfire 94.

Silverstone, Alicia (1976–).
Young American leading actress, from the stage. Born in San Francisco to British parents, she attracted a teen following by appearing in Aerosmith's rock videos and, after the success of *Clueless*, signed a $10m three-picture deal with Columbia-TriStar; but the first film she produced and starred in, *Excess Baggage*, flopped at the box-office.
The Crush 93. True Crime 95. The Babysitter 95. Hideaway 95. The New World/Le Nouveau Monde 95. *Clueless* (as Cher Horowitz) 95. Excess Baggage 96. Batman and Robin (as Batgirl) 97. Excess Baggage 97. Blast from the Past 98, etc.

Silvestri, Alan.
American composer.
Romancing the Stone 84. Cat's Eye 84. Back to the Future 85. Clan of the Cave Bear 85. Outrageous Fortune 86. Predator 87. Overboard 87. Who Framed Roger Rabbit? 88. My Stepmother Is an Alien 88. The Abyss 89. Back to the Future II 89. Downtown 90. Back to the Future III 90. Predator 2 90. Young Guns II 90. Soapdish 91. Ricochet 91. Shattered 91. Father of the Bride 91. Dutch/Driving Me Crazy 91. Stop! Or My Mom Will Shoot 92. Super Mario Bros 93. Cop and a Half 93. Sidekicks 93. Judgment Night 93. Grumpy Old Men 93. Clean Slate 94. Blown Away 94. Forrest Gump (AAN) 94. Richie Rich 95. The Quick and the Dead 95. The Perez Family 95. Judge Dredd 95. Father of the Bride Part II 95. Sgt Bilko 96. Eraser 96. Volcano 97. Mouse Hunt 97. Contact 97. Fools Rush In 97. The Parent Trap 98. Holy Man 98. Practical Magic 98. The Odd Couple II 98, etc.

Sim, Alastair (1900–1976).
Lugubrious Scottish comedy actor of stage and screen; his diction and gestures were inimitable.
■ Riverside Murder 35. The Private Secretary 35. A Fire Has Been Arranged 35. Late Extra 35. The Case of Gabriel Perry 35. Troubled Waters 36. Wedding Group 36. The Big Noise 36. Keep Your Seats Please 36. The Man in the Mirror 36. The Mysterious Mr Davis 36. Strange Experiment 37. Clothes and the Woman 37. Gangway 37. The Squeaker 37. A Romance in Flanders 37. Melody and Romance 37. Sailing Along 38. *The Terror* 38. *Alf's Button Afloat* 38. *This Man is News* 38. Climbing High 38. *Inspector Hornleigh* 39. This Man in Paris 39. Inspector Hornleigh on Holiday 39. Law and Disorder 40. Inspector Hornleigh Goes to It 41. *Cottage to Let* 41. *Let the People Sing* 42. Waterloo Road 44. *Green for Danger* 46. Hue and Cry 47. Captain Boycott 47. *London Belongs to Me* 48. *The Happiest Days of Your Life* 50. Stage Fright 50. *Laughter in Paradise* 51. *Scrooge* 51. Lady Godiva Rides Again 51. Folly to be Wise 52. Innocents in Paris 53. *An Inspector Calls* 54. *The Belles of St Trinian's* 54. Escapade 55. Geordie 55. The Green Man 56. Blue Murder at St Trinian's 57. The Doctor's Dilemma 58. Left, Right and Centre 59. School for Scoundrels 60. The Millionairess 60. The Ruling Class 71. Royal Flash 75. Escape from the Dark 76. Rogue Male (TV) 76.
✪ For marvellous moments of high comedy and for the lasting comic image of his unique physiognomy. *Green for Danger*.

Sim, Gerald (1925–).
British supporting actor, often in well-bred and slightly prissy roles.
Fame is the Spur 47. The Wrong Arm of the Law 63. The Pumpkin Eater 64. King Rat 64. The Whisperers 66. Oh What a Lovely War 68. Dr Jekyll and Sister Hyde 71. No Sex Please We're British 73. The Slipper and the Rose 76. Gandhi 82. Cry Freedom 87, many others.
TV series: To the Manor Born (as the rector) 79–81.

Sim, Sheila (1922–).
English leading actress, in occasional films. Married to Lord (Richard) Attenborough.
A Canterbury Tale 43. Great Day 45. The Guinea Pig 48. Dear Mr Prohack 49. Pandora and the Flying Dutchman 51. The Magic Box 51. The Night My Number Came Up 55, etc.

Simenon, Georges (1903–1989).
Prolific French novelist, the creator of Inspector Maigret. More than 50 of his 220 novels (he wrote some 200 more under pseudonyms) have been filmed, and in the 50s his sales reached 3 million a year. He also wrote 21 volumes of memoirs. As president of the jury at the Cannes Film Festival in 1960, he ensured that Fellini's *La Dolce Vita* won the prize for best film. Years later, during an interview with Fellini to publicize the director's *Casanova*, he claimed to have had sexual relationships with 10,000 women, who included dancer and cabaret performer Josephine BAKER. In the 40s, he had moved to America for a time, though, apart from a couple of films, he was unable to interest Hollywood in his stories. He was then taking no more than 10 days to write a novel: when Alfred HITCHCOCK rang and was told Simenon was busy, having just started another book, he replied: 'All right. I'll wait.'
Biographies: 1992, *The Man Who Wasn't Maigret* by Patrick Marnham; 1997, *Simenon* by Pierre Assouline.
Les Inconnus dans la Maison 43. Panique 46. Temptation Harbour (GB) 46. La Marie du Port 50. The Man on the Eiffel Tower (US) 50. Le Fruit Défendu 52. The Brothers Rico (US) 57. Maigret Sets a Trap 58, etc.
TV series: Maigret 63. Thirteen against Fate 67.
❝ Can there be a more intimate communication between two beings than copulation? – G.S.
The artist is above all else a sick person, in any case an unstable one, if the doctors are to be believed. Why see in that some form of superiority? I would do better to ask people's forgiveness. – G.S.

Simmons, Anthony (c. 1924–).
British writer-director, known for short films.
Sunday by the Sea 53. Bow Bells 54. The Gentle Corsican 56. Your Money or Your Wife 59. Four in the Morning 65. *The Optimists of Nine Elms* 73. Black Joy 78. Little Sweetheart 88, etc.

Simmons, Jean (1929–).
Self-possessed and beautiful British leading lady who married Stewart Granger (later Richard Brooks) and settled in Hollywood to make films which have generally been unworthy of her talents.
Give Us the Moon 43. Mr Emmanuel 44. Meet Sexton Blake 44. Kiss the Bride Goodbye 44. The Way to the Stars 45. Caesar and Cleopatra 45. Hungry Hill 45. The Woman in the Hall 45. *Great Expectations* 46. *Black Narcissus* 46. Uncle Silas 47. *Hamlet* (AAN) 48. The Blue Lagoon 48. Adam and Evelyne 49. Trio 50. Cage of Gold 50. So Long at the Fair 50. The Clouded Yellow 50. Angel Face 52. Androcles and the Lion 53. Young Bess 53. Affair with a Stranger 53. The Robe 53. The Actress 53. She Couldn't Say No 54. The Egyptian 54. A Bullet is Waiting 54. Désirée 54. Footsteps in the Fog 55. Guys and Dolls 56. Hilda Crane 56. This Could Be the Night 57. Until They Sail 57. *The Big Country* 58. Home Before Dark 58. This Earth is Mine 59. *Elmer Gantry* 60. Spartacus 60. *The Grass is Greener* 61. All the Way Home 63. Life at the Top 65. Mister Buddwing 66. Rough Night in Jericho 67. Divorce American Style 67. The Happy Ending (AAN) 69. Say Hello to Yesterday 71. Mr Sycamore 75. The Dain Curse (TV) 78. Dominique 79. Beggarman Thief (TV) 79. Golden Gate (TV) 80. The Thorn Birds (TV) 82. Midas Valley (TV) 84. Perry Mason: The Case of the Lost Love (TV) 87. The Dawning 88. Great Expectations (TV) 89. Sense and Sensibility (TV) 90. Laker Girls (TV) 90. How to Make an American Quilt 95. Daisies in December (TV) 95, etc.
TV series: Dark Shadows 91.

Simms, Ginny (1916–1994) (Virginia Sims).
Glamorous American vocalist, with Kay Kyser's band.
That's Right You're Wrong 39. You'll Find Out 40. Playmates 42. Hit the Ice 43. Broadway Rhythm 44. Shady Lady 45. Night and Day 46. Disc Jockey 51, etc.

Simms, Larry (1934–).
American boy actor, notably in the *Blondie* series 1938–48. (He was Baby Dumpling.)
The Last Gangster 37. Mr Smith Goes to Washington 39. Madame Bovary 49, etc.

Simon, Adam.
American director.
Brain Dead 90. Body Chemistry II: The Voice of a Stranger 92. Carnosaur 93.

Simon, Carly (1945–).
American composer and singer.
■ Perfect (a) 85. Heartburn (m) 86. Postcards from the Edge (m) 90. This Is My Life (m) 92.

Simon, Melvin (1925–).
American independent producer, former shopping-plaza developer.
Love at First Bite 79. Scavenger Hunt 79. The Runner Stumbles 79. When a Stranger Calls 79. Cloud Dancer 80. My Bodyguard 80. The Man with Bogart's Face 80. The Stunt Man 80. Porky's 82, etc.

Simon, Michel (1895–1975) (François Simon).
Heavyweight French character actor, in films from the 20s after music-hall experience.
Feu Mathias Pascal 25. The Passion of Joan of Arc 28. La Chienne 31. *Boudu Sauvé des Eaux* 32. Lac aux Dames 34. *L'Atalante* 34. Jeunes Filles de Paris 36. Drôle de Drame 37. Les Disparus de Saint-Agil 38. Quai des Brumes 38. Fric Frac 39. *La Fin du Jour* 39. Circonstances Atténuantes 39. Vautrin 43. Un Ami Viendra Ce Soir 45. *Panique* 46. Fabiola 48. *La Beauté du Diable* 49. The Strange Desire of Monsieur Bard 53. Saadia 53. La Joyeuse Prison 56. It Happened in Broad Daylight 58. The Head 59. Austerlitz 59. Candide 60. The Devil and Ten Commandments 62. The Train 64. Two Hours to Kill 65. *The Two of Us* 67. La Maison 70. Blanche 71, many others.

Simon, Neil (1927–).
American comedy playwright whose Broadway success has been remarkable and his Hollywood follow-up diligent, either as scenarist or as original author with a watching brief.
Autobiography: 1996, *Rewrites: A Memoir*.
Come Blow Your Horn 63. After the Fox (oa) 66. Barefoot in the Park 67. The Odd Couple (AAN) 68. Sweet Charity 68. The Out of Towners 70. Plaza Suite 71. Last of the Red Hot Lovers 72. The Sunshine Boys (AAN) 75. Murder by Death 76. The Goodbye Girl (AAN) 78. California Suite (AAN) 78. Chapter Two 79. I Ought to Be in Pictures 82. Max Dugan Returns 83. The Lonely Guy 84. The Slugger's Wife 85. Brighton Beach Memoirs 87. Biloxi Blues 88. The Marrying Man 91. Lost in Yonkers 93. The Odd Couple II (& co-p) 98, etc.

Simon, Paul (1942–).
American lyricist and singer, long a team element as Simon and Garfunkel. Primarily known to the non-pop public for the music backing *The Graduate*, Simon also appeared in an unsuccessful 1980 movie, *One Trick Pony*, and can be glimpsed in *Annie Hall* 77. Married actress Carrie Fisher (1983–84).
Biography: 1995, *Simon and Garfunkel* by Victoria Kingston.

Simon, S. Sylvan (1910–1951).
American director with radio experience.
A Girl with Ideas 37. Four Girls in White 39. Whistling in the Dark 41. Rio Rita 42. Song of the Open Road 44. Son of Lassie 45. Her Husband's Affairs 47. I Love Trouble 48. The Lust for Gold 49. Born Yesterday (p) 50, etc.

Simon, Simone (1910–).
Pert French leading lady with brief stage experience.
Le Chanteur Inconnu (debut) 31. Lac aux Dames 34; to US: Girls' Dormitory 36. *Seventh Heaven* 37. Josette 38. *La Bête Humaine* 38. *All That Money Can Buy* 41. *Cat People* 42. Tahiti Honey 43. Mademoiselle Fifi 44. Temptation Harbour (GB) 47. Donna Senza Nome (It.) 49. La Ronde 50. Olivia 50. Le Plaisir 51. Double Destin 54. The Extra Day (GB) 56. The Woman in Blue 73, etc.

Simoneau, Yves (1955–).
French-Canadian director.
Les Célébrations 79. Pouvoir Intime 86. Perfectly Normal 90. Cruel Doubt (TV) 92. Mother's Boys 94. Amelia Earhart: The Final Flight (TV) 94. Larry McMurty's 'Dead Man's Walk' (TV) 96, etc.

Simpson, Alan (1929–).
British TV and film comedy writer, with Ray GALTON.

Simpson, Don (1945–1996).
American producer, in partnership with Jerry BRUCKHEIMER; also famous for his excessive life-style. Died of a drug overdose.
Biography: 1998, *High Concept: Don Simpson and the Hollywood Culture of Excess* by Charles Fleming.
Flashdance 83. Beverly Hills Cop 84. Thief of Hearts 84. Top Gun 86. Beverly Hills Cop II 87. The Big Bang 89. Days of Thunder 90. Young Guns II 90. The Ref 94. Bad Boys 95. The Rock 96, etc.
❝ In another industry, Simpson's behaviour would have made him an outcast and ensured his expulsion from the club of the powerful. – *Charles Fleming*

Simpson, Geoffrey.
Australian cinematographer in international films, from television documentaries.
Call Me Mr Brown (TV) 85. Riddle of the Stinson (TV) 88. Celia 88. *The Navigator: A Medieval Odyssey* 88. Till There Was You 90. Green Card (US) 90. Deadly 91. Fried Green Tomatoes at the Whistle Stop Café (US) 91. The Last Days of Chez Nous 92. Mr Wonderful (US) 92. The War (US) 94. Little Women (US) 94. *Shine* 96. Some Mother's Son (Ire.) 96. Oscar and Lucinda 97, etc.

Simpson, Ivan (1875–1951).
Scottish character actor in Hollywood.
The Dictator 15. The Green Goddess 23 and 30. The Man Who Played God 32. Phantom of Cresswood 33. David Copperfield 34. Maid of Salem 37. The Hour before the Dawn 43, many others.

Simpson, O. J. (1947–) (Orenthal James Simpson).
American actor and TV sportscaster, a former football star with the Buffalo Bills in the 70s, nicknamed 'The Juice'. In 1994, his arrest for the murder of his wife and a young man became headline news. The police chase of him, at a stately 45 mph along the San Diego Freeway, as he sat in a car pointing a gun at his own head, was broadcast live on television and watched by an estimated 95 million viewers; it was later released on video. He was played by Bobby Hosea in the TV movie *The O. J. Simpson Story* 95.
■ The Klansman 74. The Towering Inferno 74. The Diamond Mercenaries 75. The Cassandra Crossing 77. Roots (TV) 77. A Killing Affair (TV) 77. Capricorn One 78. Firepower 79. Detour (TV) 79. Goldie and the Boxer (TV) 79. Goldie and the Boxer Go to Hollywood (TV) 80. Hambone and Hillie 84. The Naked Gun: From the Files of Police Squad 88. The Naked Gun 2½: The Smell of Fear 91. Naked Gun 33⅓: The Final Insult 94.
TV series: Roots 77–78.

Simpson, Russell (1878–1959).
American character actor, in Hollywood from silent days.
Billy the Kid 31. Way Down East 36. Ramona 37. Dodge City 39. The Grapes of Wrath 40. Outside the Law 41. They Were Expendable 45. My Darling Clementine 46. The Beautiful Blonde from Bashful Bend 49. Seven Brides for Seven Brothers 54. Friendly Persuasion 56. The Horse Soldiers 59, many others.

Sims, Joan (1930–).
British stage, TV and film comedienne, often in cameo roles.
Colonel March Investigates 53. Meet Mr Lucifer 54. The Belles of St Trinian's 54. Dry Rot 56. The Naked Truth 58. Carry On Regardless 60. Twice Round the Daffodils 62. Strictly for the Birds 64. Follow that Camel 67. The Alf Garnett Saga 72. One of Our Dinosaurs is Missing 75. Martin Chuzzlewit (TV) 94, many others.
TV series: On the Up 93.

Sinatra, Frank (1915–1998).
American leading actor and vocalist, former band singer. A teenage rave in the 40s, he later became respected as an actor and a powerful producer. His four wives included actress Ava GARDNER (1951–54) and actress Mia FARROW (1966–68). He was the father of singer and actress Nancy SINATRA. He was played by Ray LIOTTA in the TV biopic *The Rat Pack* 98.
Biographies: 1962, *Sinatra* by Robin Douglas-Home. 1978, *Sinatra, an Unauthorized Biography* by Earl Wilson. 1980, *Frank Sinatra* by John Howlett. 1984, *Sinatra: An American Classic* by John Rockwell. 1985, *Frank Sinatra, a Celebration* by Derek Jewell. 1985, *Frank Sinatra, My Father* by Nancy Sinatra. 1986, *His Way: The Unauthorized Biography* by Kitty Kelley. 1995, *Completely Frank* by Deborah Hill. 1997, *All or Nothing at All: A Life of Frank Sinatra* by Donald Clarke.
Book: 1997, *Frank Sinatra at the Movies* by Roy Pickard.
■ Las Vegas Nights 41. Ship Ahoy 42. Reveille with Beverly 43. Higher and Higher (acting debut) 43. *Step Lively* 44. *Anchors Aweigh* 45. Till the Clouds Roll By 46. It Happened in Brooklyn 46. The Kissing Bandit 47. The Miracle of the Bells 48. *Take Me out to the Ball Game* 48. *On the Town* 49. Double Dynamite 50. Meet Danny Wilson 51. *From Here to Eternity* (AA) 53. Suddenly 54. Young at Heart 54. The Tender Trap 55. Not as a Stranger 55. *The Man with the Golden Arm* (AAN) 56. Johnny Concho 56. The Pride and the Passion 56. Around the World in Eighty Days 56. Guys and Dolls 56. *High Society* 56. *Pal Joey* 57. The Joker is Wild 57. Kings Go Forth 58. Some Came Running 58. A Hole in the Head 59. Can Can 59. Never So Few 59. Pepe 60. Ocean's Eleven 60. The Devil at Four O'Clock 61. Sergeants Three 62. *The Manchurian Candidate* 62. Four for Texas 63. The List of Adrian Messenger 63. Come Blow Your Horn 63. Robin and the Seven Hoods 64. None But the Brave (& d) 65. Von Ryan's Express 65. Marriage on the Rocks 65. Cast a Giant Shadow 66. Assault on a Queen 66. The Naked Runner (GB) 67. Tony Rome 67. *The Detective* 68. Lady in Cement 68. Dirty Dingus Magee 70. Contract on Cherry Street (TV) 77. The First Deadly Sin 80. Cannonball Run II 84.
❝ Don't tell me. Suggest. But don't tell me. – *F.S.*
I detest bad manners. If people are polite, I am. They shouldn't try to get away with not being polite to me. – *F.S.*
He's the kind of guy that, when he dies, he's going up to heaven and give God a bad time for making him bald. – *Marlon Brando*
When he dies, they're giving his zipper to the Smithsonian. – *Dean Martin*
The charm that once made him irresistible was lost in the unpredictable whims of a spoiled child. – *Roger Vadim*
I was not impressed by the creeps and Mafia types he kept about him. – *Prince Charles*
Age has softened his sinister aura. – *Newsweek, 1982*
See also: RAT PACK.

Sinatra, Nancy (1940–).
American leading lady and singer, daughter of Frank SINATRA. She was formerly married to singer Tommy SANDS.
For Those Who Think Young 64. The Last of the Secret Agents 66. Speedway 68, etc.

Sinclair, Andrew (1935–).
British director.
Before Winter Comes (w only) 69. The Breaking of Bumbo 70. Under Milk Wood 72. Blue Blood 73.

Sinclair, Arthur (1883–1951) (Arthur McDonnell).
Irish actor, often in comic roles. Born in Dublin, he was a member of the Abbey Theatre company for its first 12 years. In the 20s, he also worked in variety. Married actress Maire O'NEILL.
M'Blimey 31. Evensong 34. Irish Hearts 34. Sing as We Go 34. Wild Boy 34. Charing Cross Road 35. Peg of Old Drury 35. King Solomon's Mines 37. The Show Goes On 37. Welcome Mr Washington 44, etc.

Sinclair, Hugh (1903–1962).
British stage leading man, in occasional films.
Our Betters 33. Escape Me Never 35. A Girl Must Live 39. Alibi 42. They Were Sisters 45. Corridor of Mirrors 48. The Rocking Horse Winner 50. The Second Mrs Tanqueray 52, etc.

Sinclair, Madge (1940–1995).
Jamaican actress, a former teacher, who spent most of her working life in the US. Died of leukaemia.
Conrack 74. Cornbread, Earl and Me 75. Leadbelly 76. Convoy 78. Coming to America 88. Lion King (voice of Sarabi) 94.
TV series: Roots (as Belle) 77.

Sinclair, Robert (1905–1970).
American director. Married to Heather Angel.
Woman against Woman 38. Dramatic School 38. Mr and Mrs North 41. Mr District Attorney 46. That Wonderful Urge 48, etc.

Sinden, Sir Donald (1923–).
British leading man, on stage from mid-30s. Knighted 1997.
Autobiography: 1982, *A Touch of the Memoirs*.
The Cruel Sea (film debut) 53. Doctor in the House 54. Simba 55. Eyewitness 56. Doctor at Large 58. Operation Bullshine 59. Twice Round the Daffodils 62. Decline and Fall 68. Villain 71. Rentadick 72. The National Health 73. The Day of the Jackal 73. The Island at the Top of the World 74. That Lucky Touch 75, etc.
TV series: Our Man at St Mark's 58. Two's Company 77–80. Never the Twain 81–83.

Singer, Alexander (1932–).
American director.
■ *A Cold Wind in August* 62. Psyche 59 64. Love Has Many Faces 65. Captain Apache 71. The First 36 Hours of Dr Durant (TV) 75. The Million Dollar Rip-Off (TV) 76. Hunters of the Reef (TV) 78. The Return of Marcus Welby, MD (TV) 84.

Singer, Bryan (1967–).
American director.
Public Access 93. *The Usual Suspects* 95. Apt Pupil 98, etc.

Singer, Campbell (1909–1976).
British character actor, often seen as heavy father, commissionaire, sergeant-major or policeman.
Premiere 37. Take My Life 47. The Ringer 52. Simba 55. The Square Peg 58. The Pot Carriers 63, many others.

Singer, Lori (1962–).
Lissom leading American actress, the sister of Marc Singer.
Born Beautiful (TV) 82. Footloose 84. The Falcon and the Snowman 85. The Man with One Red Shoe 85. Trouble in Mind 86. Summer Heat 87. Warlock 91. Short Cuts 93. F.T.W. 94, etc.
TV series: Fame 82–83.

Singer, Marc (1948–).
American leading actor, frequently in bare-chested roles.
Things in Their Season 74. Journey from Darkness 75. Go Tell the Spartans 78. For Ladies Only (TV) 81. The Beastmaster 82. If You Could See What I Hear 82. Her Life as a Man (TV) 83. Born to Race 88. Body Chemistry 90. High Desert Kill (TV) 90. A Man Called Sarge 90. The Raven Red Kiss-Off 90. Watchers II 90. In the Cold of the Night 91. Dead Space 91. Beastmaster 2: Through the Portal of Time 91. Sweet Justice 92. The Sea Wolf (TV) 93, etc.
TV series: The Contender 80. Roots: The Next Generation 79–81. V 84–85. Dallas 86.

Singleton, John (1968–).
American screenwriter and director.
Boyz N the Hood (AAN) 91. Poetic Justice 93. Higher Learning 95. Rosewood 97, etc.

Singleton, Penny (1908–) (Mariana McNulty).
American leading lady who made her greatest hit as *Blondie*.
Good News 30. After the Thin Man 36. *Swing Your Lady* 38. The Mad Miss Manton 38. *Blondie* 38 (then two films in the series every year, more or less, until 1950). The Best Man 64, etc.

Sinise, Gary (1955–).
American director and actor, on stage and screen. He was a founder of Chicago's Steppenwolf Theatre.
Miles from Home (d) 88. Of Mice and Men (a, d) 92. A Midnight Clear (a) 92. Jack the Bear (a) 93. The Stand (a) (TV) 94. Forrest Gump (a) (AAN) 94. The Quick and the Dead 95. Truman (TV, title role) 95. Ransom 96. Albino Alligator 96. George Wallace (TV) 97. Snake Eyes 98, etc.

Sinyor, Gary.
British director.
Leon the Pig Farmer (co-d) 92. Solitaire for 2 95. Stiff Upper Lips 97.

Siodmak, Curt (1902–).
German writer-director, in films from 1929, Hollywood from 1937. Brother of Robert Siodmak.
People on Sunday (co-w) 29. The Tunnel (co-w) 34. Her Jungle Love (co-w) 38. Frankenstein Meets the Wolf Man (w) 42. Son of Dracula (w) 43. The Beast with Five Fingers (w) 47. Bride of the Gorilla (wd) 51. *The Magnetic Monster* (d) 51. Donovan's Brain (oa) 53. Love Slaves of the Amazon (w, d) 57. Ski Fever (w, d) 66, etc.

Siodmak, Robert (1900–1973).
American director with early experience in Germany and France.
People on Sunday 29. The Weaker Sex 32. La Vie Parisienne 35. *Pièges* 39. West Point Widow 41. Son of Dracula 43. *Phantom Lady* 44. *The Suspect* 44. Christmas Holiday 44. *The Spiral Staircase* 45. The Strange Affair of Uncle Harry 45. *The Killers* (AAN) 46. *The Dark Mirror* 46. Cry of the City 48. Criss Cross 48. The File on Thelma Jordon 49. The Great Sinner 49. Deported 50. The Whistle at Eaton Falls 51. The Crimson Pirate

52. Le Grand Jeu 53. Mein Vater der Schauspieler 56. Jatja 59. The Rough and the Smooth 59. Tunnel 28/Escape from East Berlin 62. Custer of the West 67, many others.

❝ He manipulated Hollywood's fantasy apparatus with taste and intelligence. – *Andrew Sarris, 1968*

Sirk, Douglas (1900–1987) (Detlef Sierck).
Danish director, with stage experience; in America from early 40s. Born in Hamburg, he was a theatre director before turning to film in Germany. His Hollywood films take an opulent, stylized approach to melodramatic subjects.
Books: 1994, *History, Culture and the Films of Douglas Sirk* by Barbara Klinger; 1998, *Sirk on Sirk*, ed. Jon Halliday.
SELECTED EUROPEAN FILMS: April April 35. Das Hofkonzert 36. La Habanera 37. Home Is Calling 37.
■ AMERICAN FILMS: Hitler's Madman 43. Summer Storm 44. A Scandal in Paris 46. *Lured* 47. *Sleep My Love* 48. Shockproof 49. Slightly French 49. Mystery Submarine 50. The First Legion 51. Thunder on the Hill 51. The Lady Pays Off 51. Weekend with Father 51. No Room for the Groom 52. *Has Anybody Seen My Gal?* 52. Meet Me at the Fair 52. Take Me to Town 53. All I Desire 53. Taza Son of Cochise 54. *Magnificent Obsession* 54. Sign of the Pagan 54. Captain Lightfoot 55. There's Always Tomorrow 56. All That Heaven Allows 56. *Written on the Wind* 57. Battle Hymn 57. Interlude 57. The Tarnished Angels 58. A Time to Love and a Time to Die 58. Imitation of Life 59.

Sisto, Jeremy (1974–).
American actor, from the stage. Born in Grass Valley, California, he studied at the University of California in Los Angeles.
Grand Canyon 91. The Crew 94. The Shaggy Dog (TV) 94. Hideaway 95. Clueless 95. Moonlight & Valentino 95. White Squall 96, etc.

Sitting Bull (1831–1890).
Chief of the Sioux at the time General Custer and his Seventh Cavalry were wiped out at the Little Big Horn, he later joined Buffalo Bill's Wild West. He was killed by Indian police in a raid during an uprising in which he was not a participant. On film, he is almost always on the warpath, the villain of countless westerns. He was played twice by J. Carrol Naish, in *Annie Get Your Gun* 50 and *Sitting Bull* 54. Also played by Chief Thunder Bird in *Annie Oakley* 35, Michael Granger in *Fort Vengeance* 53, John War Eagle in *Tonka* 58, Michael Pate in *The Great Sioux Massacre* 55, and Frank Kaquitts in *Buffalo Bill and the Indians* 76.

❝ Most of what he earned went into the pockets of small, ragged boys. He could not understand why all the wealth he saw in the cities wasn't divided up among the poor. Among the Indians, a man who had plenty of food shared it with those who had none. – *Annie Oakley*

Sizemore, Tom (1964–).
American leading actor.
Born on the Fourth of July 89. Lock Up 89. Where Sleeping Dogs Lie 91. Flight of the Intruder 91. Guilty by Suspicion 91. Harley Davidson & the Marlboro Man 91. Striking Distance 93. Watch It 93. Heart and Souls 93. True Romance 93. Wyatt Earp 94. Natural Born Killers 94. Strange Days 95. Devil in a Blue Dress 95. Heat 95. The Relic 96. Saving Private Ryan 98. Enemy of the State 98, etc.

Sjoberg, Alf (1903–1980).
Swedish director, former stage actor and director.
The Road to Heaven 42. *Frenzy* 44. Only a Mother 49. *Miss Julie* 51. Barabbas 53. Karin Mansdotter 54. Wild Birds 55. The Judge 60. The Island 66, many others.

Sjoman, Vilgot (1924–).
Swedish director, chiefly famous (and notorious) for '491' 66. *I Am Curious: Blue* 67, *I Am Curious: Yellow* 67, and *Blushing Charlie* 71.
Also: Troll 73. A Handful of Love 74. The Garage 74. Tabu 77. Linus Eller Tegelhusets Hemlighet 79. Malacca 86. Fallgropen 89. Alfred 95, etc.

Sjostrom, Victor:
see SEASTROM, Victor.

Skaaren, Warren (1947–1991).
American screenwriter and producer. Previously he was first commissioner of the Texas Film Commission and then ran a production services company.
Fire with Fire/Captive Hearts (co-w) 86. Top Gun (p) 86. Beverly Hills Cop II (co-w) 87. Beetlejuice (co-w) 88. Batman (co-w) 89, etc.

Skala, Lilia (1896–1994)
Austrian actress in America.
Lilies of the Field (AAN) 64. Deadly Hero 76. Roseland 77. Heartland 80. The End of August 82. Flashdance 83. House of Games 87, etc.

Skall, William V. (1898–1976).
American cinematographer.
Victoria the Great 37. The Mikado 39. Northwest Passage 40. Life with Father 47. *Joan of Arc* (AA) 48. Quo Vadis 51. The Silver Chalice 55, many others.

Skarsgard, Stellan (1951–).
Swedish actor, in international films. Born in Gothenburg, he came to notice as a teenager in Sweden in the TV series *Bombi Bitt and Me* 68. From the early 70s to the mid-80s, he acted at the Royal Dramatic Theatre in Stockholm.
Anita 73. Inkraktarna 74. Yon Sylissa 77. Den Enfaldige Mördaren 82. Bakom Jalousin 83. P&B 83. Åke and His World 84. Noon Wine (TV) 85. Hip, Hip, Hurra! 87. The Unbearable Lightness of Being (US) 87. Friends 88. The Perfect Murder (Ind.) 88. The Woman on the Roof/Kvinnorna Pa Teket 89. The Hunt for Red October (US) 90. Wind (US) 92. The Ox/Oxen 92. The Slingshot/Kadisbellan 93. Harry & Sonja 96. Breaking the Waves 96. Riget II/Kingdom II (TV) 97. Amistad (US) 97. *Insomnia* 97. Good Will Hunting 97. My Son the Fanatic (GB) 98. Ronin (US) 98, etc.

Skeggs, Roy.
British production executive, a former accountant. He worked for Hammer in the 60s and bought the company in 1985 after it went into official receivership. He announced plans to remake old Hammer features in 1994 in partnership with producer Lauren Shuler-Donner and director Richard Donner.
Frankenstein and the Monster from Hell 73. Satanic Rites of Dracula 73. To the Devil a Daughter 76, etc.

❝ Hammer was Walt Disney with a bit of blood. – *R.S.*

Skelly, Hal (1891–1934).
American character actor from Broadway.
■ *The Dance of Life* 29. Woman Trap 29. Behind the Make Up 30. Men Are Like That 30. The Struggle 31. Hotel Variety 31. Shadow Laughs 31.

Skelton, Red (1910–1997) (Richard Bernard Skelton).
American comedian of radio, film and television. Born in Vincennes, Indiana, the son of a circus clown, he began in vaudeville as a child. In the early 40s, he signed a long-term contract with MGM, but in the 50s he switched to performing on television, retiring in the early 70s. Married three times.
■ Having Wonderful Time 38. Flight Command 40. The People Versus Dr Kildare 41. Lady Be Good 41. *Whistling in the Dark* 41. Dr Kildare's Wedding Day 41. Ship Ahoy 42. Maisie Gets Her Man 42. Panama Hattie 42. Whistling in Dixie 42. *Dubarry Was a Lady* 43. I Dood It 43. Whistling in Brooklyn 43. Thousands Cheer 43. Bathing Beauty 44. Ziegfeld Follies 46. The Show Off 46. *Merton of the Movies* 47. The Fuller Brush Man 48. A Southern Yankee 48. Neptune's Daughter 49. The Yellow Cab Man 50. The Fuller Brush Girl (gag) 50. Three Little Words 50. Duchess of Idaho (gag) 50. Watch the Birdie 50. Excuse My Dust 51. Texas Carnival 51. Lovely to Look at 52. The Clown 52. Half a Hero 53. The Great Diamond Robbery 53. Susan Slept Here (gag) 54. Around the World in Eighty Days 56. Public Pigeon Number One 57. Ocean's Eleven (gag) 60. Those Magnificent Men in Their Flying Machines 65. Rudolph's Shiny New Year (voice) 79.
TV series: The Red Skelton Show 51–71.

❝ I'm nuts and I know it. But so long as I make 'em laugh, they ain't going to lock me up. – *R.S.*

I always believed God puts each one of us here for a purpose . . . and mine is to try to make people happy. – *R.S.*

Skerritt, Tom (1933–).
American actor.
War Hunt 62. One Man's Way 64. Those Callaways 65. M*A*S*H 70. Wild Rovers 71. Fuzz 72. Thieves Like Us 74. Big Bad Mama 74. The Devil's Rain 75. The Turning Point 77. Up in Smoke 78. Alien 79. Ice Castles 79. Savage Harvest 81. A Dangerous Summer 81. Silence of the North 81. Fighting Back 82. The Dead Zone 83. Top Gun 86. Wisdom 86. Opposing Force 87. Maid to Order 87. The Big Town 87. Poltergeist III 88. Big Man on Campus 89. The Heist (TV) 89. Red King, White Knight (TV) 89. Steel Magnolias 89. Child in the Night (TV) 90. The Rookie 90. Wild Orchid II: Two Shades of Blue 92. Poison Ivy 92. A River Runs Through It 92. Knight Moves 93. Divided by Hate (TV) 93. Two for Texas (TV) 98. Contact 98, etc.
TV series: Run, Run, Joe 74. Picket Fences 92–96.

Skiles, Marlin (1906–).
American composer.
The Impatient Years 44. Gilda 46. Dead Reckoning 47. Callaway Went Thataway 51. The Maze 53. Bowery to Baghdad 55. Fort Massacre 58. The Hypnotic Eye 60. The Strangler 64. The Resurrection of Zachary Wheeler 71, many others.

Skinner, Claire (1965–).
British actress, from the stage and TV.
Life Is Sweet 91. Naked 93. The Return of the Native (TV) 94. I.D. 95. Clockwork Mice 95. Smilla's Sense of Snow/Smilla's Feeling for Snow 97, etc.
TV series: Chef ! 94.

Skinner, Cornelia Otis (1901–1979).
American stage actress, daughter of Otis Skinner the tragedian. Toyed with Hollywood occasionally. Her autobiographical book *Our Hearts Were Young and Gay* (co-written with Emily Kimbrough) was filmed with Gail Russell.
The Uninvited 44. The Girl in the Red Velvet Swing 55. The Swimmer 67.

Skinner, Frank (1898–1968).
American composer.
Son of Frankenstein 39. Destry Rides Again 39. Hellzapoppin 41. Back Street 41. Saboteur 42. Gung Ho 43. The Suspect 44. The Egg and I 47. Abbott and Costello Meet Frankenstein 48. Francis 49. Harvey 50. The World in His Arms 52. Thunder Bay 53. Battle Hymn 56. Imitation of Life 58. Back Street 61. Shenandoah 65. Madame X 66, many others.

Skinner, Otis (1858–1942).
American stage actor who appeared in films only in two versions of *Kismet* 20 & 30. Charles Ruggles played him in *Our Hearts Were Young and Gay* 44.

Skipworth, Alison (1875–1952) (Alison Groom).
Chubby British character actress, long in Hollywood; a favourite foil for W. C. Fields.
Raffles 30. Outward Bound 30. Devotion 31. Night After Night 32. *If I Had a Million* 32. Song of Songs 33. *Tillie and Gus* 33. Six of a Kind 34. The Captain Hates the Sea 34. Becky Sharp 35. Shanghai 35. Satan Met a Lady 36. Stolen Holiday 37. Wide Open Faces 38, many others.

❝ *A.S., concerned that Mae West was stealing her scene:* I'll have you know I'm an actress.
Mae West: It's all right, dearie. I'll keep your secret.

Skirball, Jack H. (1896–1985).
American independent producer, former salesman.
Miracle on Main Street 38. Lady from Cheyenne 41. Saboteur 42. Shadow of a Doubt 43. It's in the Bag/The Fifth Chair 45. Guest Wife 46. Payment on Demand 51, etc.

Skjoldbjaerg, Erik (1965–).
Norwegian director.
Insomnia 97.

Skolimowski, Jerzy (1938–).
Polish director.
The Barrier 66. The Departure 67. Hands Up 67. Dialogue 69. The Adventures of Gerard 70. Deep End 71. King, Queen, Knave 72. The Shout 78. Circle of Deceit (a only) 81. Moonlighting (& w) 82. Success Is the Best Revenge 84. The Lightship 85. Torrents of Spring 89. The Hollow Men (p) 93. Mars Attacks! (a) 96. LA without a Map (a) (GB/Fr./Fin.) 98, etc.

Skouras, Spyros (1893–1971).
Greek-American executive, former hotelier. President of Twentieth Century-Fox 1943–62; instigator of CinemaScope.

❝ The only Greek tragedy I know is Spyros Skouras. – *Billy Wilder*

Skye, Ione (1971–) (Ione Skye Leitch).
British actress, working in America. She is the daughter of 60s folk singer Donovan.
The River's Edge 87. Stranded 87. A Night in the Life of Jimmy Reardon 88. Carmilla 89. The Rachel Papers 89. Say Anything 89. Mindwalk 90. Samantha 91. Gas, Food, Lodging 92. Guncrazy 92. Wayne's World 92. Four Rooms 95. Dream for an Insomniac 96. The Size of Watermelons 96. One Night Stand 97. Went to Coney Island on a Mission From God . . . Be Back by Five 98. Mascara 98, etc.
TV series: Covington Cross 92.

Slaney, Ivor (1921–).
English composer.
The Gambler and the Lady 53. Spaceways 53. The Saint's Return/The Saint's Girl Friday 53. Face the Music/The Black Glove 54. The House across the Lake/Heat Wave 54. The Stranger Came Home/The Unholy Four 54. Five Days/Paid to Kill 54. Murder by Proxy/Blackout 55. Terror 79, etc.

Slate, Jeremy (1935–).
American general-purpose actor.
Wives and Lovers 63. I'll Take Sweden 65. The Sons of Katie Elder 66. The Devil's Brigade 68. Hells Angels '69 69. The Centerfold Girls 74. Stranger in Our House (TV) 78. Mr Horn (TV) 79. Dead Pit 89. Dream Machine 91. The Lawnmower Man 92, etc.

Slater, Christian (1969–) (Christian Hawkins).
Saturnine young American leading actor. Born in New York City, the son of an actor and a casting director, he acted from childhood and was in films as a teenager. In 1997 he was jailed for 90 days after pleading no contest to charges of battery and being under the influence of a controlled substance.
The Legend of Billie Jean 85. The Name of the Rose 86. Heathers 88. Tucker: The Man and His Dream 88. The Wizard 89. Beyond the Stars 89. Gleaming the Cube 89. Tales from the Darkside: The Movie 90. Young Guns II 90. Pump Up the Volume 90. Robin Hood: Prince of Thieves 91. Mobsters 91. Star Trek VI: The Undiscovered Country 91. Where the Day Takes You (uncredited) 92. Ferngully: The Last Rainforest (voice) 92. Kuffs 92. Untamed Heart 93. True Romance 93. Jimmy Hollywood 94. Murder in the First 94. Broken Arrow 96. Bed of Roses 96. Julian Po 97. Hard Rain 97. Very Bad Things 98, etc.

❝ I have been acting since the age of eight and have been a celebrity for a long time. And when you're a celebrity, you start believing you can act off the screen any way you want without consequence. – *C.S.*

Slater, Helen (1963–).
Blonde American actress who made her debut in the title role of *Supergirl* but has since tended to play supporting roles.
Supergirl 84. The Legend of Billie Jean 85. Ruthless People 86. The Secret of My Success 87. Sticky Fingers 88. Happy Together 89. City Slickers 91. A House in the Hills 93. Chantilly Lace (TV) 93. Lassie 94. Parallel Lives (TV) 94. No Way Back 96. Toothless 97, etc.

Slater, John (1916–1975).
British cockney character actor and comedian of stage and TV, occasionally in films.
Love on the Dole (debut) 40. Went the Day Well? 42. A Canterbury Tale 44. Passport to Pimlico 48. Johnny You're Wanted 54. Violent Playground 58. Three on a Spree 61. A Place to Go 63, many others.

Slater, Ryan (1984–).
American child actor, the brother of Christian Slater.
The Little Panda 95.

Slattery, Tony (1959–).
British actor, TV presenter, and comedian, from television and the stage. Born in London, he studied at Cambridge University, where he was a member of Footlights.
How to Get a Head in Advertising 89. Peter's Friends 92, etc.
TV series: David Harper 91. Just a Gigolo 93.

Slaughter, Tod (1885–1956) (N. Carter Slaughter).
Barnstorming British actor who toured the provinces with chop-licking revivals of outrageous old melodramas, all of which he filmed after a fashion.
■ Maria Marten 35. Sweeney Todd 36. The Crimes of Stephen Hawke 36. Song of the Road 37. Darby and Joan 37. It's Never Too Late to Mend 37. The Ticket of Leave Man 37. Sexton Blake and the Hooded Terror 38. *The Face at the Window* 39. Crimes at the Dark House 40. The Curse of the Wraydons 43. The Greed of William Hart 48. King of the Underworld 52. Murder at Scotland Yard 52.

Sletaune, Pal.
Norwegian director.
Junk Mail/Budbringeren 97. Blood, Guts, Bullets and Octane 98, etc.

Slezak, Walter (1902–1983).
Austrian character actor, of theatrical family; in America from 1930. Committed suicide.
Autobiography: 1962, *What Time's the Next Swan?*
Once upon a Honeymoon (English-speaking debut) 42. *Lifeboat* 44. Step Lively 44. The Spanish Main 45. Cornered 45. Sinbad the Sailor 47. The Pirate 48. *The Inspector General* 49. Call Me Madam 53. White Witch Doctor 54. The Steel Cage 54. Come September 61. Emil and the Detectives 64. Wonderful Life (GB) 64. Twenty-Four Hours to Kill 65. A Very Special Favor 65. Caper of the Golden Bulls 67. Dr Coppelius 68. Black Beauty 71, etc.

Sloane, Everett (1909–1965).
Incisive American character actor, brought to Hollywood by Orson Welles.
■ *Citizen Kane* 41. *Journey into Fear* 42. *The Lady from Shanghai* 48. Prince of Foxes 49. *The Men* 50. Bird of Paradise 51. The Enforcer 51. Sirocco 51. The Prince Who Was a Thief 51. The Blue Veil 51. The Desert Fox 51. The Sellout 51. Way of a Gaucho 52. *The Big Knife* 55. *Patterns* 56. *Somebody Up There Likes Me* 56. Lust for Life 56. Marjorie Morningstar 58. The Gun Runners 58. Home from the Hill 60. By Love Possessed 61. Brushfire 62. The Man from the Diners Club 63. The Patsy 64. Ready for the People 64. The Disorderly Orderly 64.
TV series: Official Detective 58.
Famous line (*Citizen Kane*): 'Old age, Mr Thompson: it's the only disease you don't look forward to being cured of.'

Sloane, Olive (1896–1963).
British character actress of stage and screen whose best role was in *Seven Days to Noon* 50. Countless other small roles since film debut in *Greatheart* 21.

Sloane, Paul (1893–*).
American director, in films as a screenwriter from 1914, moving to direction for Paramount in 1925 with movies starring Richard Dix. Moved to Japan in the early 50s.
A Man Must Live 25. The Shock Punch 25. Too Many Kisses 25. The Coming of Amos 25. The Woman Accused 33. Terror Aboard 33. Lone Cowboy 34. The Texans (co-w only) 38. *Geronimo* (& w) 39. The Sun Sets at Dawn (& p, w) 50. Forever My Love/Itsu Itsu Made Mo 52, etc.

Slocombe, Douglas (1913–).
British cinematographer, former journalist.
Dead of Night 45. The Captive Heart 46. Hue and Cry 46. The Loves of Joanna Godden 47. *It Always Rains on Sunday* 47. *Saraband for Dead Lovers* 48. Kind Hearts and Coronets 49. Cage of Gold 50. The Lavender Hill Mob 51. Mandy 52. The Man in the White Suit 52. *The Titfield Thunderbolt* 53. Man in the Sky 56. The Smallest Show on Earth 57. Tread Softly Stranger 58. Circus of Horrors 59. The Young Ones 61. The L-Shaped Room 62. *Freud* 63. The Servant 63. Guns at Batasi 64. A High Wind in Jamaica 65. The Blue Max 66. Promise Her Anything 66. The Vampire Killers 67. Fathom 67. Robbery 67. Boom 68. The Lion in Winter 68. The Italian Job 69. *The Music Lovers* 70. Murphy's War 70. The Buttercup Chain 70. Travels with My Aunt (AAN) 73. The Great Gatsby 74. Love Among the Ruins (TV) 75. Rollerball 75. Hedda 76. Julia (AAN, BFA) 77. Nasty Habits 77. Caravans 78. Lost and Found 79. The Lady Vanishes 79. Nijinsky 80. Lost and Found 80. Raiders of the Lost Ark (AAN) 81. The Pirates of Penzance 83. Never Say Never Again 83. Indiana Jones and the Temple of Doom 84. Lady Jane 85. Indiana Jones and the Last Crusade 89, etc.

Sloman, Edward (1887–1972).
English director in Hollywood, mainly of silents, a former actor.
Lying Lips 16. The Eagle's Feather 23. The Foreign Legion 28. The Lost Zeppelin 29. Hell's Island 30. Puttin' on the Ritz 30. His Woman 31. There's Always Tomorrow 34. A Dog of Flanders 35. The Jury's Secret 38, etc.

Sluizer, George (1932–).
Dutch director and screenwriter, a former documentary film-maker.
Twice a Woman 79. Red Desert Penitentiary 87. The Vanishing/Spoorloos 88. Utz (GB) 91. The Vanishing (US) 93. Dark Blood (uncompleted) 94. Crimetime 96. The Commissioner 99, etc.

Small, Edward (1891–1977).
Veteran American independent producer, former actor and agent, in Hollywood from 1924.
I Cover the Waterfront 35. The Man in the Iron Mask 39. The Corsican Brothers 41. Brewster's Millions 45. Down Three Dark Streets 55. Witness for the Prosecution 57. Jack the Giant Killer 62. I'll Take Sweden 65. Forty Guns to Apache Pass 66, many others; also TV series.

Small, Michael (1939–).
American composer.
Puzzle of a Downfall Child 70. Klute 71. Child's Play 72. The Parallax View 74. Night Moves 75. Marathon Man 76. Comes a Horseman 78. Those Lips Those Eyes 80. The Postman Always Rings Twice 81. Continental Divide 81. Rollover 81. The Star Chamber 83. Firstborn 84. Target 85. Dream Lover 86. Brighton Beach Memoirs 86. Black Widow 87. Orphans 87. Jaws – the Revenge 87. 1969 88. See You in the Morning 89. Mountains of the Moon 90, etc.

Smalley, Phillips (1875–1939).
American leading actor and director of silents. He was married to director Lois Weber and was involved in some of her films as actor and co-director. From the 20s, he continued as a character actor.
The Armorer's Daughter (a) 10. The Chorus Girl (d) 12. The Jew's Christmas (a, co-d) 13. The Merchant of Venice (a, co-d) 14. Scandal (a, co-d) 15. The Dumb Girl of Portici (co-d) 15. Where Are My Children? (co-d) 15. The Flirt (co-d) 16. Flaming Youth (a) 23. Charley's Aunt (a) 25. Man Crazy (a) 27. True Heaven 29. Charley's Aunt 30. Cocktail Hour 33. A Night at the Opera 35, etc.

Smart, J. Scott (1903–1950).
Heavyweight radio actor who took his *Fat Man* character to Hollywood for one 50s film of that name.

Smart, Ralph (1908–).
British producer-director, latterly of TV series *The Invisible Man*, *Danger Man*, etc. Former editor and writer.
AS DIRECTOR: Bush Christmas 46. A Boy, a Girl and a Bike 48. Bitter Springs 50. Never Take No for an Answer (co-d) 51. Curtain Up 52. Always a Bride 54, etc.

Smeaton, Bruce.
Australian composer.
The Cars that Ate Paris 74. Picnic at Hanging Rock 75. The Devil's Playground 76. Eliza Fraser 76. The Chant of Jimmie Blacksmith 78. The Last of the Knucklemen 78. Circle of Iron 79. Double Deal 81. Barbarosa 81. Undercover 83. The Naked Country 84. Iceman 84. Plenty 85. Eleni 85. Roxanne 87. A Cry in the Dark 88, etc.

Smedley-Aston, E. M. (1912–).
British producer.
The Extra Day 56. Two-Way Stretch 60. Offbeat 61. The Wrong Arm of the Law 63. Ooh You Are Awful 72, etc.

Smethurst, Jack (1932–).
English character actor, born in Collyhurst, Manchester, and much on television.
A Kind of Loving 62. The Main Chance 64. The Agony and the Ecstasy 65. Run with the Wind 66. Night after Night after Night 70. For the Love of Ada 72. Love Thy Neighbour 73. Man about the House 74. King Ralph 91, etc.
TV series: For the Love of Ada 70–71. Love Thy Neighbour 72–76. Hilary 84.

Smight, Jack (1926–).
American director, from TV.
■ I'd Rather Be Rich 64. The Third Day 65. *Harper* 66. Kaleidoscope 66. The Secret War of Harry Frigg 67. No Way to Treat a Lady 68. The Illustrated Man 69. Strategy of Terror (TV) 69. Rabbit Run (TV) 69. The Travelling Executioner 70. The Screaming Woman (TV) 72. Detour to Nowhere (TV) 72. The Longest Night (TV) 72. Linda (TV) 73. Double Indemnity (TV) 73. Frankenstein: The True Story (TV) 73. Airport 75 74. Midway 76. Damnation Alley 77. Roll of Thunder (TV) 78. Fast Break 78. Loving Couples 80. Number One with a Bullet 87. The Favorite 89.

Smith, Albert E. (1875–1958).
British pioneer producer in America, one of the founders of the VITAGRAPH COMPANY.

Smith, Alexis (1921–1993) (Gladys Smith).
American leading lady of the 40s who won an acting contest from Hollywood high school. Married to Craig Stevens.
Lady with Red Hair 41. Dive Bomber 41. The Smiling Ghost 41. Gentleman Jim 42. The Constant Nymph 42. The Doughgirls 44. Conflict 45. Rhapsody in Blue 45. San Antonio 45. Night and Day 46. Of Human Bondage 46. Stallion Road 47. The Woman in White 47. The Decision of Christopher Blake 48. Any Number Can Play 50. Undercover Girl 52. Split Second 53. The Sleeping Tiger (GB) 55. The Eternal Sea 56. The Young Philadelphians/The City Jungle 59. Once is Not Enough 75. The Little Girl Who Lives Down the Lane 77. Casey's Shadow 78. A Death in California (TV) 85. Tough Guys 86. The Age of Innocence 93, etc.
TV series: Dallas 84. Hothouse 88.
❝ When they tell me one of my old movies is on TV, I don't look at it. – A.S.
Those films weren't very good at the time, and they haven't improved with age. – A.S.
There are so many more interesting things to think about than whether Ida Lupino or Jane Wyman got the roles I should have gotten. – A.S.

Smith, Art (1899–1973).
Bland, avuncular American character actor.
A Tree Grows in Brooklyn 44. Letter from an Unknown Woman 47. Cover Up 50. In a Lonely Place 51, etc.

Smith, Bernard (c. 1905–).
American producer, ex-publisher and story editor.
Elmer Gantry (AA) 60. How the West Was Won 62. Seven Women 65. Alfred the Great 69, etc.

Smith, Bessie (1894–1937).
America's greatest singer of classic blues, known as 'The Empress of the Blues', who made one short in 1929, singing 'St Louis Blues', which has been re-issued on video-cassette. The highest-paid black star in the 20s, she hit hard times in the 30s and died following a car crash. There are plans to make a biopic of her life.
Biography: 1972, *Bessie* by Chris Albertson.

Smith, Betty (1904–1972).
American novelist.
Works filmed include *A Tree Grows in Brooklyn*, *Joy in the Morning*.

Smith, Bubba (1945–) (Charles Smith).
Tall American actor, a former football star.
Stroker Ace 83. Police Academy 84. Police Academy 2 85. Police Academy 3 86. Police Academy 4 87. The Wild Pair 87. Police Academy 5 88. Police Academy 6 89. Gremlins 2: The New Batch 90. My Samurai 92, etc.

Smith, Sir C. Aubrey (1863–1948).
Distinguished English leading actor on stage who went to Hollywood in his 60s to play crusty, benevolent, or authoritarian old gentlemen. Born in London, he was a first-class sportsman, playing soccer for the Corinthians and cricket for Cambridge University. Nicknamed 'Round the Corner Smith' for his unusual bowling style, he captained Sussex County Cricket Club for four years, an English team that went to Australia in 1887, and the first English team to tour South Africa. A teacher and a stockbroker before becoming an actor, he was on stage from 1892, including a notable Professor Higgins in George Bernard Shaw's *Pygmalion* in 1914. He was in films from 1915 and was one of the founders of a short-lived English company, Minerva Films. Success came when he repeated for MGM his stage hit *The Bachelor Father*. A founder-member of the Hollywood Cricket Club, he was knighted in 1944. The characters of Sir Ambrose Abercrombie and, to a lesser extent, Sir Francis Hinsley in Evelyn Waugh's novel *The Loved One* are modelled on him.
Biography: 1982, *Sir Aubrey* by David Rayvern Allen.
SELECTED SILENT FILMS: The Witching Hour 16. The Bohemian Girl 23. The Rejected Woman 24.
■ SOUND FILMS: Birds of Prey (GB) 30. Such Is the Law (GB) 30. Contraband Love (GB) 31. Trader Horn 31. Never the Twain Shall Meet 31. Bachelor Father 31. Daybreak 31. Just a Gigolo 31. Son of India 31. The Man in Possession 31. Phantom of Paris 31. Guilty Hands 31. Surrender 31. Polly of the Circus 31. Tarzan the Ape Man 32. But the Flesh Is Weak 32. *Love Me Tonight* 32. Trouble in Paradise 32. No More Orchids 32. They Just Had to Get Married 32. Luxury Liner 33. Secrets 33. The Barbarian 33. Adorable 33. The Monkey's Paw 33. *Morning Glory* 33. Bombshell 33. Queen Christina 33. The House of Rothschild 34. The Scarlet Empress 34. Gambling Lady 34. Curtain at Eight 34. The Tunnel (GB) 34. Bulldog Drummond Strikes Back 34. Cleopatra 34. Madame du Barry 34. One More River 34. Caravan 34. The Firebird 34. The Right to Live 35. *Lives of a Bengal Lancer* 35. The Florentine Dagger 35. The Gilded Lily 35. Clive of India 35. China Seas 35. Jalna 35. The Crusades 35. Little Lord Fauntleroy 36. Romeo and Juliet 36. The Garden of Allah 36. Lloyds of London 36. Wee Willie Winkie 36. *The Prisoner of Zenda* 37. Thoroughbreds Don't Cry 37. The Hurricane 37. Four Men and a Prayer 38. Kidnapped 38. Sixty Glorious Years (GB) 38. East Side of Heaven 39. Five Came Back 39. *The Four Feathers* (GB) 39. The Sun Never Sets 39. Eternally Yours 39. Another Thin Man 39. The Underpup 39. Balalaika 39. *Rebecca* 40. City of Chance 40. A Bill of Divorcement 40. Waterloo Bridge 40. Beyond Tomorrow 40. A Little Bit of Heaven 40. Free and Easy 41. Maisie was a Lady 41. Dr Jekyll and Mr Hyde 41. Forever and a Day 43. Two Tickets to London 43. Flesh and Fantasy 43. Madame Curie 43. The White Cliffs of Dover 44. The Adventures of Mark Twain 44. Secrets of Scotland Yard 44. Sensations of 1945 44. They Shall Have Faith 44. *And Then There Were None* 45. Scotland Yard Investigator 45. Cluny Brown 46. Rendezvous with Annie 46. High Conquest 47. Unconquered 47. *An Ideal Husband* (GB) 47. Little Women 49.
✪ For relishing and perpetuating the stereotype of the fine old English gentleman. *The Four Feathers*.
❝ Mr Aubrey Smith has few equals in the delineation of the polished, straightforward, simple-minded English gentleman. – *The Graphic*
He was born to smell of tobacco and Harris tweeds, and to wave portentous eyebrows . . . He stands for all that is most essentially British: that queer admixture of sportsmanship, dunderheadedness and sentiment which has rendered the inhabitants of these islands the most exasperating enigma with which any other nation has ever had to cope. – *Theatre World*
The Bank of England, the cliffs of Dover, the Rock of Gibraltar and several super-dreadnoughts rolled into one. – *New York Times*
He *was* England, to a great many – perhaps an older England, but an England rich in dignity, graciousness and good will. Certainly no one could ever have known him, either in life or on the screen, without liking England better afterwards. – *James Hilton*
My God! I can't possibly act with a cricket bat!

– *Mrs Patrick Campbell, objecting to appearing with him in Pygmalion*

Aubrey, Aubrey, don't go on the stage, think of what will become of your two sisters if their brother is an actor. – *His mother*

Smith, Charles (1920–1988).
American character actor who in the 40s played Dizzy in the *Henry Aldrich* series and other amiably doltish roles.
The Shop around the Corner 40. Tom Brown's Schooldays 40. Three Little Girls in Blue 45. Two Weeks with Love 50. City of Bad Men 53, many others.

Smith, Charles Martin (1954–).
American leading actor and occasional director.
Culpepper Cattle Co. 72. Fuzz 72. American Graffiti 73. Pat Garrett and Billy the Kid 73. Law of the Land 76. The Campus Corpse 77. The Buddy Holly Story 78. More American Graffiti 79. Herbie Goes Bananas 80. Cotton Candy 82. Starman 84. Trick or Treat (& d) 86. The Untouchables 87. The Hot Spot 90. Boris & Natasha (& d) 92. Deep Cover 92. Fifty/Fifty (& d) 93. And the Band Played On (TV) 93. I Love Trouble 94. Speechless 94. Larry McMurtry's Streets of Laredo (TV) 95. Peter Benchley's The Beast (TV) 96. Dead Silence (TV) 96. The Final Cut 96. Air Bud (d only) 97. Deep Impact 98, etc.

Smith, Constance (1929–).
British leading lady.
Brighton Rock 47. Don't Say Die 50. The Thirteenth Letter (US) 51. Red Skies of Montana (US) 52. Treasure of the Golden Condor (US) 53. Tiger by the Tail 55. Cross Up 58, etc.

Smith, Cyril (1892–1963).
British character actor of stage and screen, often a hen-pecked husband but equally likely to be a grocer, dustman or policeman. On stage from 1900, films from 1908, and was in over 500 of the latter.
Friday the Thirteenth 33. School for Secrets 46. It's Hard to Be Good 48. Mother Riley Meets the Vampire 52. John and Julie 54. *Sailor Beware* (his stage role) 56, etc.

Smith, Dick (1922–).
Influential American make-up artist, noted for his work on special effects, from television.
Misty 59. The World of Henry Orient 64. Little Big Man 70. House of Dark Shadows 70. The Godfather 72. The Exorcist 73. The Godfather Part II 74. The Stepford Wives 74. Burnt Offerings 76. Exorcist II: The Heretic 77. The Sentinel 77. The Fury 78. Altered States 80. Ghost Story 81. Scanners 81. Amadeus (AA) 84. Poltergeist III 88. Tales from the Darkside: The Movie 90. Death Becomes Her 92, etc.

Smith, Dodie (1896–1990).
English dramatist and novelist, a former actress, whose children's book *The Hundred and One Dalmatians* was turned into a classic animated feature by Walt Disney in 1961. Disney made a live-action version in 1996, starring Glenn Close.
Biography: 1996, *Dear Dodie* by Valerie Grove.
Looking Forward (oa) 33. Autumn Crocus (oa) 34. Dear Octopus (oa) 43. 101 Dalmatians (oa) 96, etc.
❝ What people won't realize is that if you're separated from your dog for more than five hours, you become absolutely miserable. Five hours is the absolute maximum. – *D.S.*

Smith, G. A. (1864–1959).
British pioneer cinematographer who invented a cine-camera in 1896 and made some trick films.
The Corsican Brothers 97. The Fairy Godmother 98. Faust 98, etc.

Smith, Jack Martin (c. 1910–1993)
American art director who worked for MGM, specializing in musicals, from the late 30s to the early 50s, when he joined Twentieth Century-Fox, becoming supervising art director in 1961.
One Hundred Men and a Girl 37. Meet Me in St Louis 44. Yolanda and the Thief 45. Easter Parade 48. Madame Bovary 49. Show Boat 51. Carousel 56. Teenage Rebel (AAN) 56. An Affair to Remember 57. Voyage to the Bottom of the Sea 61. Cleopatra (AA) 63. Move Over, Darling 63. What a Way to Go (AAN) 64. The Agony and the Ecstasy 65. Fantastic Voyage (AA) 66. Batman 66. Doctor Dolittle (AAN) 67. The Detective 68. The Boston Strangler 68. Planet of the Apes 68. Hello Dolly (AA) 69. Butch Cassidy and the Sundance Kid 69. M*A*S*H 69. Justine 69. Tora! Tora! Tora! (AAN) 70. Beyond the Valley of the Dolls 70. Emperor of the North 73. Lost in the Stars 74. Pete's Dragon 77, etc.

Smith, Jaclyn (1947–).
American leading actress, mainly on television.
Goodbye Columbus 69. The Adventurers 70. Bootleggers 74. The Users 74. Nightkill 80. Jacqueline Bouvier Kennedy (TV) 81. George Washington (TV) 84. Déjà Vu 84. Rage of Angels (TV) 85. The Night They Saved Christmas (TV) 87. The Bourne Identity (TV) 88. Lies Before Kisses (TV) 92. My Very Best Friend (TV) 96, etc.
TV series: Charlie's Angels 76–81.

Smith, Jada Pinkett:
see PINKETT, Jada.

Smith, Joe (1884–1981) (Joseph Sultzer).
American vaudeville comedian in partnership with Charles DALE for 73 years and the inspiration for the play and movie *The Sunshine Boys*.
Manhattan Parade 31. The Heart of New York 32. Two Tickets to Broadway 51.

Smith, John (1931–1995) (Robert Van Orden).
Boyish American leading man.
The High and the Mighty 54. Ghost Town 56. The Bold and the Brave 57. Circus World 64. Waco 66, etc.
TV series: Cimarron City 58. Laramie 59–62.

Smith, Kate (1909–1986).
Heavyweight American singer who was popular on radio in the 30s and 40s. Made one film in 1933 (*Hello, Everybody*) and another in 1943 (*This Is the Army*).

Smith, Kent (1907–1985).
Smooth, quiet American leading man of the 40s; latterly a useful character actor.
Cat People 42. Hitler's Children 43. This Land Is Mine 43. *The Spiral Staircase* 46. *Nora Prentiss* 47. The Decision of Christopher Blake 48. The Fountainhead 49. The Damned Don't Cry 50. Paul 52. Comanche 56. Party Girl 58. Strangers When We Meet 60. Moon Pilot 62. A Distant Trumpet 64. The Trouble with Angels 66. Assignment to Kill 68. Death of a Gunfighter 69. Pete 'n' Tillie 72. Cops and Robbers 73, many others.
TV series: *Peyton Place* 64–67.

Smith, Kevin (1966–).
American director and screenwriter. His first film was made on a budget of $27,000. He runs his own production company, View Askew, from Red Bank, New Jersey, where he also owns a comic store, Jay and Silent Bob's Secret Stash.
Clerks 94. Mallrats 95. Chasing Amy 97.
❝ We need more killer shark movies. – *K.S.*
If that guy is the voice of my generation, I'll kill myself. – *Harmony Korine*

Smith, Kurtwood (1943–).
American character actor, often in sadistic roles.
Roadie 80. Staying Alive 83. Flashpoint 84. Robocop 87. Rambo III 88. Dead Poets Society 89. Heart of Dixie 89. True Believer 89. Quick Change 90. Oscar 91. Company Business 91. Star Trek VI: The Undiscovered Country 91. Shadows and Fog 92. Fortress 93. Boxing Helena 93. The Crush 93. Under Siege 2: Dark Territory 95. Last of the Dogmen 95. Time to Kill 96. Citizen Ruth 96. Prefontaine 97. Shelter 97. Deep Impact 98, etc.
TV series: That '70s Show 98.

Smith, Liz.
British character actress.
A Private Function (BFA) 84. We Think the World of You 88. High Spirits 88. Apartment Zero 89. The Cook, the Thief, His Wife and Her Lover 89. Dakota Road 92. Pretty Princess (It.) 93. Haunted 95. Karaoke (TV) 96. Keep the Aspidistra Flying 97. Tom's Midnight Garden 98, etc.
TV series: A Royle Family 98.

Smith, Lois (1930–).
American character actress.
Five Easy Pieces 70. Resurrection 80. Reckless 84. Black Widow 87. Green Card 90. Fried Green Tomatoes 91. Hard Promises 92. Skylark (TV) 93. Falling Down 93. Holy Matrimony 94. How to Make an American Quilt 95. Twister 96. Larger than Life 96, etc.

Smith, Dame Maggie (1934–).
Leading British actress with a taste for eccentric comedy. Married to actor Robert STEPHENS (1967–74) and writer Beverley Cross.
Biography: 1992, *Maggie: A Bright Particular Star* by Michael Coveney.
Nowhere to Go 58. Go to Blazes 62. *The VIPs* 63. The Pumpkin Eater 64. Young Cassidy 65. Othello (AAN) 66. *The Honey Pot* 67. Hot Millions 68. Oh What a Lovely War 69. *The Prime of Miss Jean Brodie* (AA) 69. Love Pain and the Whole Damn Thing 73. Travels with My Aunt (AAN) 73. Murder by Death 76. California Suite (AA) 78. Death on the Nile 78. Clash of the Titans 81. Quartet 81. Evil under the Sun 82. Better Late than Never 82. The Missionary 83. A Private Function (BFA) 84. A Room with a View (AAN) 85. The Lonely Passion of Judith Hearne 87. Hook 91. Memento Mori (TV) 92. Sister Act 92. The Secret Garden 93. Suddenly Last Summer (TV) 93. Sister Act 2: Back in the Habit 93. Richard III 95. The First Wives Club 96. Washington Square 97. Tea with Mussolini 99, etc.
❝ I said, 'Periods in life are sometimes like a dark tunnel but you come out into the light eventually.' She said, 'I think I'm on the Inner Circle.' – *Kenneth Williams*

Smith, Mel (1952–).
British comic actor and director.
Bullshot 83. Slayground 84. Morons from Outer Space 85. The Princess Bride 87. The Wolves of Willoughby Chase 88. The Tall Guy (d) 89. Wilt/The Misadventures of Mr Wilt 89. Brain Donors 92. Art Deco Detective 94. The Radioland Murders (d) 94. Romeo, Romeo (d) 97. Dr Bean (d) 97, etc.
TV series: Not the Nine O'Clock News 79–81. Alas Smith and Jones 84–86. Smith and Jones 95, 97– .

Smith, Oliver (1918–1994).
American production designer, mainly for the Broadway stage and the American Ballet Theatre.
Oklahoma! 55. Guys and Dolls 55. Porgy and Bess 59, etc.

Smith, Paul (1939–).
Towering American character actor who played the guard in *Midnight Express* and Bluto in *Popeye*.
Retreat, Hell! 52. Madron 70. Raiders in Action 71. Midnight Express 78. Popeye 80. Dune 84. Red Sonja 85. Crimewave 86. Haunted Honeymoon 86. Death Chase 87. Caged Fury 90. Crossing the Line 90, etc.

Smith, Paul J. (1906–1985).
American composer, almost exclusively for Disney.
Snow White and the Seven Dwarfs (AAN) 37. Pinocchio (AA) 40. Victory through Air Power (AAN) 43. The Three Caballeros (AAN) 44. Song of the South (AAN) 46. Cinderella (AAN) 50. Twenty Thousand Leagues Under the Sea 54. Perri (AAN) 57. Pollyanna 60. The Parent Trap 61. The Three Lives of Thomasina 64, etc.

Smith, Pete (1892–1979).
American producer of punchy one-reel shorts on any and every subject from 1935 to the 50s, all narrated by 'a Smith named Pete'. Former publicist. Special Academy Award 1953 'for his witty and pungent observations on the American scene'.

Smith, Roger (1932–).
American leading man. Formerly married to actress Victoria SHAW, he married actress ANN-MARGRET in 1967. Retired owing to a muscle disorder.
The Young Rebels 56. Operation Mad Ball 57. Man of a Thousand Faces (as Lon Chaney Jnr) 57. Never Steal Anything Small 59. Auntie Mame 59. Rogues' Gallery 68. The First Time (wp) 70.
TV series: 77 Sunset Strip 58–64. Mr Roberts 65.

Smith, Roy Forge.
British production designer, now working in America.
Far from the Madding Crowd 67. The Amazing Mr Blunden 72. Monty Python and the Holy Grail 74. Jabberwocky 77. The Hound of the Baskervilles 79. Running 79. Mrs Soffel 84. The Kiss 88. Bill & Ted's Excellent Adventure 89. Teenage Mutant Ninja Turtles 90. Warlock 91. Teenage Mutant Ninja Turtles II 93. Teenage Mutant Ninja Turtles III 93. Robin Hood: Men in Tights 93. The Pagemaster 94. Born to Be Wild 95. Dracula: Dead and Loving It 95. Rocket Man 97, etc.

Smith, Thorne (1892–1934).
American humorous novelist. Works filmed include *Topper, Turnabout, I Married a Witch*.

Smith, Will (1969–).
American leading actor and rap performer. Born in Philadelphia, Pennsylvania, he began as the rapper Fresh Prince, performing with DJ Jazzy Jeff, before becoming a star of his own TV sitcom. His current asking price: around $15m a movie. Married his second wife, actress Jada PINKETT, in 1997.
Where the Day Takes You 92. *Six Degrees of Separation* 93. Bad Boys 95. A Thin Line between Love and Hate 96. Independence Day 96. Men in Black 97. Enemy of the State 98. Wild Wild West 99, etc.
TV series: Fresh Prince of Bel Air 91–96.
❝ I'd be happy to just make Will Smith moves the rest of my career. – *Barry Sonnenfeld*

Smithee, Alan (1967–) (aka Allen Smithee).
Pseudonym used by members of the Director's Circle when the actual director wants his name removed from the credits. *An Alan Smithee Film: Burn, Hollywood, Burn* 97, a satire produced and scripted by Joe ESZTERHAS about a director named Smithee who disowns his own film, was in turn disowned by its actual director, Arthur HILLER, after it was recut. An earlier satirical movie, *Only in America*, featured a film director named Alan Smithee, played by Raphael Perry.
Death of a Gunfighter (d Don Siegel, Robert Totten) 67. Fade In (d Jud Taylor) 68. City in Fear (d Jud Taylor) (TV) 80. Fun and Games (d Paul Bogart) (TV) 80. Moonlight (d Jackie Cooper, Rod Holcomb) (TV) 82. Stitches (d Rod Holcomb) 82. Appointment with Fear (d Ramzi Thomas) 85. Let's Get Harry (d Stuart Rosenberg) 86. Morgan Stewart's Coming Home (d Terry Winsor, Paul Aaron) 87. Ghost Fever (d Lee Madden) 87. I Love NY (d Gianni Bozzachi) 87. Catchfire/Backtrack (d Dennis Hopper) 89. Boyfriend from Hell/The Shrimp on the Barbie (d Martin Gottlieb) 90. Starfire (d Richard Sarafian) 92. Call of the Wild (d Michael Uno, TV) 93. The Birds II: Land's End (TV) (d Rick Rosenthal) 94. Raging Angels 95. Hellraiser: Bloodline (d Kevin Yeager) 96, etc.

Smitrovich, Bill (1948–).
American actor.
Without a Trace 83. Maria's Lovers 84. Splash 84. Silver Bullet 85. Key Exchange 85. Manhunter 86. Her Alibi 89. Renegades 89. Crazy People 90. Nick of Time 95. Independence Day 96. The Great White Hype 96. Trigger Effect 96. Air Force One 97, etc.
TV series: Crime Story 86–88. Life Goes On 89–91.

Smits, Jimmy (1955–).
American leading actor.
Running Scared 86. The Believers 87. Old Gringo 89. Vital Signs 90. Fires Within 91. Switch 91. Gross Misconduct 93. The Tommyknockers (TV) 93. The Cisco Kid (title role) (TV) 94. My Family/Mi Familia 95, etc.
TV series: L.A. Law 86–92. NYPD Blue 95–98.

Smoktunovsky, Innokenti (1925–1994).
Leading Russian stage actor, seen in a few films including *Nine Days of One Year* 60. *Hamlet* 64. *Tchaikovsky* 69. Crime and Punishment 75.

Smothers, Tom (1937–).
American light leading man and comedian who with his brother Dick (1939–) was popular on American TV in the 60s. Tom himself went on to appear in a few films:
■ Get to Know Your Rabbit 74. Silver Bears 78. The Kids Are Alright 78. Serial 80. There Goes the Bride 80. Pandemonium 82. Speed Zone 88.

Snell, David.
American composer.
Madame X 37. Young Dr Kildare 38. Twenty Mule Team 40. Love Crazy 41. Pacific Rendezvous 42. The Man from Down Under 43. Keep Your Powder Dry 45. Merton of the Movies 47. The Lady in the Lake 47. Alias a Gentleman 48, etc.

Snipes, Wesley (1963–).
American leading actor.
Streets of Gold 86. Wild Cats 86. Critical Condition 87. Major League 89. Mo' Better Blues 90. King of New York 90. Jungle Fever 91. New Jack City 91. The Waterdance 92. White Men Can't Jump 92. Passenger 57 92. Rising Sun 93. Boiling Point 93. Sugar Hill 93. Demolition Man 93. Drop Zone 94. To Wong Foo, Thanks for Everything, Julie Newmar 95. Money Train 95. The Fan 96. One Night Stand 97. Murder at 1600 97. US Marshals 98. Blade 98. Down in the Delta 98, etc.
TV series: H.E.L.P. 90.

Snodgress, Carrie (1946–).
American leading lady.
The Forty-Eight Hour Mile (TV) 68. Silent Night Lonely Night (TV) 69. Rabbit Run 71. *Diary of a Mad Housewife* (AAN) 72. The Fury 78. Homework 82. Trick or Treats 82. A Night in Heaven 83. Pale Rider 85. Murphy's Law 86. Blueberry Hill 88. The Chill Factor 89. Across the Tracks 90. Mission of the Shark 91. The Ballad of Little Joe 93. 8 Seconds 94. Blue Sky (made 91) 94. White Man's Burden 95. Death Benefit (TV) 96. Wild Things 98. A Stranger in the Kingdom 98, etc.

Snyder, David L.
American production designer.
In God We Trust 80. The Idolmaker 80. Blade Runner (co-pd, AAN) 82. Brainstorm 83. The Woman in Red 84. Pee-Wee's Big Adventure 85. Armed and Dangerous 86. Summer School 87. She's out of Control 89. Cold Dog Soup 90. Bill & Ted's Bogus Journey 91. Demolition Man 93. Terminal Velocity 94. Vegas Vacation 97. An Alan Smithee Film: Burn, Hollywood, Burn 97. Soldier 98, etc.

Snyder, William (1901–1984).
American cinematographer. Noted for his colour photography in the 40s, he worked for Disney during the 60s.
Aloma of the South Seas (AAN) 41. The Bandit of Sherwood Forest 45. The Swordsman 47. The Loves of Carmen (AAN) 48. The Younger Brothers 49. Jolson Sings Again (AAN) 49. Flying Leathernecks 51. Blackbeard the Pirate 52. Second Chance 53. Creature from the Black Lagoon 54. Son of Sinbad 55. Tarzan's Fight for Life 58. Bon Voyage 62. Guns of Wyoming 63. The Tenderfoot 64. Rascal 69. Million Dollar Duck 71. Menace on the Mountain 72, etc.

Soavi, Michele (1958–).
Italian director of horror movies, a former actor, much influenced by the work of Dario Argento, for whom he worked as an assistant.
Creepers (a) 85. Demons/Demoni (a) 86. Dario Argento's World of Horror (doc) (d) 86. Stagefright/Deliria (a, d) 87. The Church/La Chiesa (a, d) 89. The Sect/La Setta (co-w, d) 91. Dellamorte Dellamore (d) 94, etc.

Sobocinski, Piotr (1958–).
Polish cinematographer, in international films. He studied at the Lodz Film School, and began in documentaries.
Draw 83. The Magnate 86. Lava 87. Three Colours: Red 94. Ransom (US) 96. Marvin's Room (US) 96, etc.

Soderbergh, Steven (1963–).
American director and screenwriter.
sex, lies and videotape (AAN) 89. Kafka 91. King of the Hill 93. The Underneath 95. Schizopolis (& a, ph) 96. Gray's Anatomy (d) 97. Out of Sight (d) 98, etc.

Soeteman, Gerard.
Dutch screenwriter, associated with the pre-Hollywood films of Paul Verhoeven.
Max Havelaar 76. Soldier of Orange 77. Spetters 80. The Fourth Man/De Vierde Man 83. Flesh and Blood 85. The Assault 86. The Bunker (& d) 92, etc.

Sofaer, Abraham (1896–1988).
Burmese actor, on British stage from 1921.
Dreyfus (debut) 31. Rembrandt 36. *A Matter of Life and Death* 46. Judgment Deferred 51. *Elephant Walk* (US) 54. The Naked Jungle (US) 54. Bhowani Junction 56. King of Kings 61. Captain Sinbad (US) 63. Head 68. Che! 69, etc.

Soffici, Mario (1900–1977).
Italian-born director who became one of the leading figures in Argentinian cinema in the 30s and 40s; his best films dealt with the effects of change on rural areas. He began as a circus clown and actor, and returned to acting late in his life. In 1974 he replaced Hugo DEL CARRIL as head of the National Film Institute.
Muñequitas Porteñas (a) 31. El Alma del Bandoneón (d) 34. Viente Norte (d) 37. *Kilómetre 111* (d) 38. *Prisoners of the Earth*/Prisioneros de la Tierra (d) 39. Besos Perdidos (d) 43. Kreutzer Sonata 46. Tierra del Fuego 48. El Hombre y la Bestia (d) 50. La Dama del Mar (d) 53. Barrio Gris (d) 54. Oro Bajo (d) 56. *Rosaura at Ten o'Clock*/ Rosaura a las Diez (d) 57. This Land Is Mine (a) 61. Maternidad sin Hombres (a) 68, etc.

Softley, Iain.
English director. Educated at Cambridge University, he began in TV documentaries and music videos.
Backbeat 94. Hackers 95. Wings of a Dove 97, etc.

Sojin (1884–1954).
Japanese actor most memorable in western films as Douglas Fairbanks' antagonist in the 1924 *Thief of Bagdad*. Back in Japan after 1930.

Sokoloff, Vladimir (1889–1962).
Russian character actor, in Hollywood from 1936.
The Loves of Jeanne Ney 27. West Front 1918 30. Die Dreigroschenoper 31. L'Atlantide 32. Mayerling 35. The Life of Emile Zola 37. Spawn of the North 38. Juarez 39. Road to Morocco 42. For Whom the Bell Tolls 43. Cloak and Dagger 46. Back to Bataan 46. Istanbul 56. Confessions of a Counterspy 60. Sardonicus 62, many others.

Solanas, Fernando (1936–).
Argentinian director and screenwriter, of revolutionary intentions. He began as a documentary film-maker, and was in exile during the late 70s and early 80s, making films in France. He was shot in the legs in 1991 after accusing the government of corruption.
The Hour of the Furnaces/La Hora de los Hornos 68. Los Hijos de Fierro 76. Tangos: The Exile of Gardel 86. Sur 88. The Voyage/El Viaje 93. The Cloud/La Nube (wd) 98, etc.

Solás, Humberto (1942–).
Cuban director.
Lucia 68. A Day in November/Un Día de Noviembre 72. Simparele 74. Cantata de Chile 75. Cecilia Valdés 82. A Successful Man/Un Hombre de Exito 87, etc.

Soldati, Mario (1906–).
Italian director.
Scandal in the Roman Bath 51. The Wayward Wife 53. The Stranger's Hand 54. Woman of the River 55, many others.

Sologne, Madeleine (1912–1995) (Madeleine Vouillon).
French leading actress, a former milliner who turned to acting after marrying cinematographer Jean Douarinou. Retired in the late 60s.
La Vie Est à Nous 36. Adrienne Lecouvreur 38. Tattooed Raphael/Raphael Le Tatoué 40. Fever/ Fièvres 41. The Eternal Return/L'Eternel Retour 43. Mademoiselle X 44. The Devil and the Angel/ La Foire aux Chimères 46. Bernadette of Lourdes/ Il Suffit d'Aimer 60. Les Temps de Loups 69, etc.

Solon, Ewen (c. 1923–1985).
New Zealand character actor in Britain, especially on TV in *Maigret* series (as Lucas).
The Sundowners 59. Jack the Ripper 60. The Hound of the Baskervilles 60. The Terror of the Tongs 61. The Wicked Lady 83, etc.

Solondz, Todd (1960–).
American director and screenwriter, born in Newark, New Jersey. *Happiness* won the International Critics' Prize at the 1998 Cannes Film Festival, but its financiers, October Films, a subsidiary of Universal, decided not to distribute it because of its content, which included scenes of paedophilia and violence.
Fear, Anxiety and Depression (& a) 89. Welcome to the Dollhouse 95. Happiness 98, etc.

Solzhenitsyn, Alexander (1918–).
Russian novelist, expelled from his own country in 1974 for too much free thought. *One Day in the Life of Ivan Denisovitch* was filmed.

Somers, Suzanne (1946–) (S. Mahoney).
American leading lady of the late 70s, especially on TV in the series *Three's Company*.
American Graffiti 73. It Happened at Lakewood Manor (TV) 77. Nothing Personal 80. Happily Ever After (TV) 82. Rich Men, Single Women (TV) 90, etc.

Somlo, Josef (1885–1974).
Hungarian producer with long experience at UFA; in Britain from 1933.
Dark Journey 37. The Mikado 39. Old Bill and Son 40. Uncle Silas 47. The Man Who Loved Redheads 55. Behind the Mask 59, etc.

Sommer, Elke (1940–) (Elke Schletz).
German leading lady now in international films.
Don't Bother to Knock (GB) 60. The Victors (GB) 63. *The Prize* (US) 63. A Shot in the Dark (US) 64. The Art of Love (US) 65. Four Kinds of Love (It.) 65. The Money Trap (US) 65. The Oscar (US) 66. Boy, Did I Get a Wrong Number (US) 66. Deadlier than the Male (GB) 66. The Venetian Affair (US) 66. The Corrupt Ones 67. The Wicked Dreams of Paula Schultz (US) 68. Zeppelin (US) 71. Percy (GB) 71. Carry On Behind (GB) 76. Lily in Love 84. Adventures beyond Belief 87, etc.

Sommer, Josef (1934–).
American character actor.
The Stepford Wives 75. Too Far to Go (TV) 78. Hide in Plain Sight 80. Still of the Night 82. Sophie's Choice 82. Hanky Panky 82. Witness 84. Dracula's Widow 88. Chances Are 89. The Bloodhounds of Broadway 89. Money, Power, Murder (TV) 89. Shadows and Fog 92. Malice 93. Hidden in America (TV) 96. The Proposition 97, etc.
TV series: Hothouse 88. Under Cover 91.

Sommers, Stephen.
American director and screenwriter.
Terroreyes (co-d) 88. Catch Me If You Can (wd) 89. Gunmen (w) 92. The Adventures of Huck Finn (wd) 93. Rudyard Kipling's The Jungle Book (wd) 94. Tom and Huck (co-w) 96. Deep Rising (wd) 98. The Mummy (wd) 99, etc.

Sondergaard, Gale (1899–1985) (Edith Sondergaard).
Tall, dark American character actress with a sinister smile. Born in Litchfield, Minnesota, and educated at the University of Minnesota, she began on stage. She went to Hollywood after marrying director Herbert BIBERMAN, her second husband and one of the 'Hollywood Ten'; as a result her career also suffered because of the anti-communist witchhunt of the early 50s.
■ *Anthony Adverse* (AA) 36. Maid of Salem 37. Seventh Heaven 37. The Life of Emile Zola 37. Lord Jeff 38. Dramatic School 38. Never Say Die 38. Juarez 38. *The Cat and the Canary* 39. The Llano Kid 40. *The Bluebird* 40. The Mark of Zorro 40. The Letter 40. The Black Cat 41. Paris Calling 41. My Favourite Blonde 42. Enemy Agent Meets Ellery Queen 42. A Night to Remember 43. Appointment in Berlin 43. Isle of Forgotten Sins 43. The Strange Death of Adolf Hitler 43. *Spider Woman* 44. Follow the Boys 44. Christmas Holiday 44. The Invisible Man's Revenge 44. Gypsy Wildcat 44. The Climax 44. Enter Arsène Lupin 44. Spider Woman Strikes Back 46. A Night in Paradise 46. Anna and the King of Siam (AAN) 46. The Time of Their Lives 46. *Road to Rio* 47. Pirates of Monterey 47. East Side West Side 49. Slaves 69. The Cat Creature (TV) 74. The Return of A Man Called Horse 76. Pleasantville 76. Echoes 83.

Sondheim, Stephen (1930–).
Celebrated American composer, lyricist and occasional screenwriter. Born in New York to an upper-middle-class family, he learned much from Oscar HAMMERSTEIN, a family friend, and, after graduating from Williams College, studied for two years with composer Milton Babbitt. He began by working on the TV series *Topper* as a writer and, after some projects collapsed, wrote the lyrics for *West Side Story*, which opened on Broadway in 1957 and later became a greater success as a film. He went on to write a dozen Broadway musicals, though few have been filmed. His love of puzzles and word-games was reflected in *The Last of Sheila*, his one screenplay, written with actor Anthony PERKINS.
Biographies: 1974, *Sondheim & Co* by Craig Zadan; 1998, *Stephen Sondheim: A Life* by Meryle Secrest.
West Side Story (ly) 61. Gypsy (ly) 62. A Funny Thing Happened on the Way to the Forum (m/ly) 66. Evening Primrose (m/ly) (TV) 66. The Last of Sheila (co-w) 73. Stavisky (m) (Fr.) 74. The Seven Percent Solution (s) 76. A Little Night Music (m/ ly) 77. Reds (m) 81, etc.
❝ I'm a lazy writer. My idea of heaven is not writing. On the other hand, I'm obviously compulsive about it. – S.S.
Without question, Steve is the best Broadway lyricist, past or present. – *Arthur Laurents*

Sonnenfeld, Barry (1953–).
American cinematographer who has turned to directing.
Blood Simple 84. Compromising Positions 85. Raising Arizona 87. Three o'Clock High 87. Throw Momma from the Train 87. Big 88. When Harry Met Sally 89. Miller's Crossing 90. Misery 90. The Addams Family (d) 91. Addams Family Values (d) 93. For Love or Money/The Concierge (d) 94. Get Shorty (d) 95. Men in Black (d) 97. Wild, Wild West (d) 99, etc.

Soo, Jack (1916–1979) (Goro Suzuki).
Japanese character actor in America, best remembered in *Flower Drum Song* 60, and as one of the gang in TV's *Barney Miller* series.

Sorbo, Kevin (1958–).
American leading actor, a former model, best known for his role as Hercules in the TV series *Hercules: The Legendary Journeys* 94–97. Born in Minneapolis, he studied at the University of Minnesota. Married actress Sam Jenkins (1964–) in 1998.
Slaughter of the Innocents 94. Hercules and the Amazon Women (TV) 94. Hercules and the Circles of Fire (TV) 94. Kull the Conqueror 97, etc.

Sordi, Alberto (1919–).
Italian leading man and comic actor who began writing and directing his films in the 80s.
I Vitelloni 53. The Sign of Venus 55. A Farewell to Arms 57. The Best of Enemies 60. Those Magnificent Men in Their Flying Machines 65. To Bed or Not To Bed 65. Le Streghe 67. Polvere di Stelle 73. Viva Italia 77. Le Témoin 78. Il Marchese del Grillo (& w) 81. Bertoldo, Bertoldino e Cacasenno 84. Tutti Dentro (a, wd) 84. The Miser/L'Avaro (& co-w) 89. Christmas Vacation '91/Vacanze di Natale '91 91. Assolto per Aver Commesso il Fatto (& co-w, d) 92. Nestore l'Ultima Corsa (& co-w, d) 94. The Story of a Poor Young Man 95. Forbidden Encounters/Incontri Proibiti (& co-w, d) 98, etc.

Sorel, Jean (1934–) (Jean de Rochbrune).
French-Canadian leading man.
The Four Days of Naples 62. A View from the Bridge 62. Vaghe Stella dell'Orsa 65. Le Bambole 66. Belle de Jour 67. A Quiet Place to Kill 70. Mil Millones para una Rubia 78, etc.

Sorel, Louise (1944–).
American leading lady of occasional films.
The Party's Over 65. B.S. I Love You 70. Plaza Suite 71. Every Little Crook and Nanny 72. When Every Day Was the Fourth of July (TV) 78. Mazes and Monsters (TV) 82, etc.
TV series: The Survivors 69–70. The Don Rickles Show 72. Curse of Dracula 79. Ladies' Man 80–81.

Sorvino, Mira.
American actress, the daughter of actor Paul SORVINO. She took a degree in East Asian studies from Harvard and worked as an assistant director before becoming an actress.
Amongst Friends 93. Barcelona 94. Parallel Lives (TV) 94. Quiz Show 94. Mighty Aphrodite (AA) 95. Sweet Nothing 95. Blue in the Face 95. Beautiful Girls 96. Romy and Michele's High School Reunion 97. Mimic 97. The Replacement Killers 98. Lulu on the Bridge 98. At First Sight 98, etc.

Sorvino, Paul (1939–).
Chubby American actor.
Where's Poppa? 70. Cry Uncle 72. A Touch of Class 72. The Gambler 74. The Day of the Dolphin 75. I Will, I Will . . . For Now 76. Oh God 77. Slow Dancing in the Big City 78. The Brink's Job 78. Bloodbrothers 78. Lost and Found 80. Cruising 80. Reds 81. Turk 182 85. A Fine Mess 86. Vasectomy, a Delicate Matter 86. Dick Tracy 90. GoodFellas 90. The Rocketeer 91. Parallel Lives (TV) 94. Escape Clause (TV) 96. Love Is All There Is 96. William Shakespeare's Romeo and Juliet 96. Most Wanted 97. Money Talks 97. Dogwatch (TV) 97. Knock Off 98. Bulworth 98, etc.
TV series: We'll Get By 75. Bert Angelo/Superstar 76. The Oldest Rookie 87–88. Law and Order 90–92.

Sothern, Ann (1909–) (Harriette Lake).
Pert American comedienne and leading lady with stage experience.
Let's Fall in Love (debut) 34. Kid Millions 35. Trade Winds 38. Hotel for Women 39. *Maisie* 39. Brother Orchid 40. Congo Maisie 40. Gold Rush Maisie 41 (and seven others in series before 1947). Lady Be Good 41. Panama Hattie 42. Cry Havoc 43. The Judge Steps Out 47. *A Letter to Three Wives* 49. Nancy Goes to Rio 50. Lady in a Cage 63. The Best Man 64. Sylvia 65. Chubasco 67. The Great Man's Whiskers (TV) 71. Golden Needles 74. Crazy Mama 75. Captains and the Kings (TV) 76. The Manitou 78. The Whales of August (AAN) 87, etc.
TV series: *Private Secretary* 52–53. The Ann Sothern Show 58–61.

Soto, Talisa (1968–) (Miriam Soto).
American actress and model.
Spike of Bensonhurst 88. License to Kill 90. Silhouette (TV) 91. Hostage (TV) 92. The Mambo Kings 92. Don Juan DeMarco 95. Mortal Kombat 95. The Sunchaser 96. Mortal Kombat 2: Annihilation 97, etc.

Soul, David (1943–) (David Solberg).
American leading man who made a killing in TV but never found the right movie; nor was singing a wise choice as a second career.
Johnny Got His Gun 71. Magnum Force 73. Dogpound Shuffle 74. The Stick Up 77. Little Ladies of the Night (TV) 77. Salem's Lot (TV) 79. Swan Song (TV) 79. Rage (TV) 80. The Hanoi Hilton 87. The Bride in Black 90. In the Cold of the Night 90. Pentathlon 94, etc.
TV series: Here Come the Brides 68–70. Owen Marshall, Counsellor at Law 74. *Starsky and Hutch* 75–80. Casablanca 83. The Yellow Rose 83.

Sousa, John Philip (1854–1932).
American composer, most notably of rousing marches. His 1928 biography, *Marching Along*, was filmed in 1953 as *Stars and Stripes Forever*.

Soutendijk, Renée (1957–).
Dutch leading actress, in international films. She is a former Olympic athlete.
Pastorale 43 76. Spetters 80. The Girl with Red Hair/Het Meisje met Rode Haar 81. Inside the Third Reich (TV) 82. The Fourth Man/De Vierde Man 83. The Cold Room 84. Out of Order/Abwarts 85. The Second Victory 87. Der Madonna-Man 87. Wherever You Are 88. Forced March 89. Grave Secrets 89. Murderers Among Us: The Simon Wiesenthal Story (TV) 90. Eve of Destruction 90. Keeper of the City 91. Heatwave/Hittegolf 93. The Betrayed/Op Afbetaling 93. House Call 94, etc.

Southern, Terry (1924–1995).
American satirist and black-comedy writer.
■ *Dr Strangelove* (co-w) (AAN) 64. The Cincinnati Kid (co-w) 65. The Loved One (co-w) 65. Barbarella 68. Easy Rider (co-w) (AAN) 69. End of the Road (co-w) 70. The Magic Christian (co-w) 70. The Telephone (co-w) 88.

Spaak, Catherine (1945–).
Belgian leading lady, daughter of Charles Spaak.
Le Trou 60. The Empty Canvas 64. Weekend at Dunkirk 65. Hotel 67. Libertine 68. Cat o' Nine Tails 71. Take a Hard Ride 75. Honey 81. Secret Scandal 89, etc.

Spaak, Charles (1903–1975).
Leading Belgian-born screenwriter of many French films. Born in Brussels, he went to Paris in the late 20s to work as secretary to director Jacques Feyder and soon began collaborating on scripts. Among the directors he worked with were Julien Duvivier, Jean Renoir and André Cayatte. His daughters, Agnès and Catherine Spaak, were both actresses.
Les Nouveaux Messieurs 28. Le Grand Jeu 34. Carnival in Flanders/*La Kermesse Héroïque* 35. They Were Five/La Belle Équipe 36. The Lower Depths/Les Bas-Fonds 36. *La Grande Illusion* 37. *La Fin du Jour* 39. The Postman Always Rings Twice/Le Dernier Tournant 39. Heart of a Nation/Untel Père et Fils 40. L'Homme au Chapeau Rond 46. Panique 46. Le Mystère Barton (& d) 49. Justice Est Faite 50. The Seven Deadly Sins 52. Are We All Murderers?/Nous Sommes Tous les Assassins 52. Adorable Creatures 52. Captain Blackjack 52. The Adulteress/Thérèse Raquin 53. Too Many Lovers/Charmants Garçons 58. The Vanishing Corporal 61. Cartouche 62. Germinal 62. Two Are Guilty/Le Glaire et la Balance 73, etc.

Space, Arthur (1908–1983).
American character actor, in many film roles and such TV series as *National Velvet* and *Lassie*.
Tortilla Flat 42. Wilson 44. Leave Her to Heaven 45. The Barefoot Mailman 52. Spirit of St Louis 57. The Shakiest Gun in the West 68. On the Nickel 80, etc.

Spacek, Sissy (1949–).
Tomboy-ish American leading lady. She is married to director Jack Fisk.
Prime Cut 71. Ginger in the Morning 72. *Badlands* 73. Katherine (TV) 75. Carrie (AAN) 76. Three Women 77. Welcome to L.A. 77. Heart Beat 79. *Coal Miner's Daughter* (AA) 80. Raggedy Man 81. Missing (AAN) 82. Country 84. The River (AAN) 84. Marie 85. Violets Are Blue 85. 'Night, Mother 86. Crimes of the Heart (AAN) 86. The Long Walk Home 90. JFK 91. Hard Promises 92. Trading Mom 94. The Good Old Boys (TV) 95. The Grass Harp 95. If These Walls Could Talk (TV) 96. Affliction 98. Blast from the Past 98, etc.

Spacey, Kevin (1959–) (Kevin Fowler).
Versatile American leading man. Born in South Orange, New Jersey, he studied drama at the Juilliard School and began acting with the New York Shakespeare Festival. In the mid-90s he began to emerge as one of the best actors of his generation, though, unlike many stars, he is one that submerges his own personality in the parts he plays.
Heartburn 86. Rocket Gibraltar 88. Working Girl 88. See No Evil, Hear No Evil 89. Dad 89. A Show of Force 90. Henry and June 90. Glengarry Glen Ross 92. Consenting Adults 92. Iron Will 94. The Ref 94. The Buddy Factor (& p) 94. Outbreak 95. *The Usual Suspects* (AAN) 95. *Seven* 95. A Time to Kill 96. Albino Alligator (d) 96. *LA Confidential* 97. Midnight in the Garden of Good and Evil 97. The Negotiator 98. Hurlyburly 98. A Bug's Life (voice) 98, etc.
TV series: Wiseguy 88.

Spade, David.
American actor and comedian, from TV's *Saturday Night Live*.
Police Academy 4: Citizens on Patrol 87. Light Sleeper 91. Coneheads 93. Tommy Boy 95. Black Sheep 96. Beavis and Butthead Do America (voice) 96. 8 Heads in a Duffel Bag 97. Jerome (ex p only) 98. The Rugrats Movie (voice) 98, etc.
TV series: Just Shoot Me 97.

Spader, James (1960–).
Youthful-appearing American actor.
Endless Love 81. Family Secrets 84. The New Kids 85. Tuff Turf 85. Pretty in Pink 86. Baby Boom 87. Jack's Back 87. Less than Zero 87. Mannequin 87. Wall Street 87. The Rachel Papers 89. sex, lies and videotape 89. Bad Influence 90. White Palace 90. True Colors 91. Bob Roberts 92. Chicago Loop 92. Storyville 92. The Music of Chance 93. Wolf 94. Crash 96. Two Days in the Valley 96. Keys to Tulsa 96. Critical Care 97, etc.
TV series: The Family Tree 83.

Spall, Timothy (1957–).
British character actor, often in grotesque roles.
Quadrophenia 79. Remembrance 82. The Missionary 83. The Bride 85. Gothic 87. Dutch Girls 87. To Kill a Priest 88. Dream Demon 88. 1871 89. The Sheltering Sky 90. White Hunter, Black Heart 90. Life Is Sweet 90. For One Night Only (as Margaret Rutherford) (TV) 93. Secrets and Lies 96. Hamlet 96. The Wisdom of Crocodiles 98. Still Crazy 98. Clandestine Marriage 99, etc.
TV series: Auf Wiedersehen Pet 83–84. Frank Stubbs Presents 93. Frank Stubbs 94. Outside Edge 94. Nice Day at the Office 94.

Spano, Vincent (1962–).
American leading actor.
The Double McGuffin 79. Over the Edge 79. Baby, It's You 83. The Black Stallion Returns 83. Rumble Fish 83. Alphabet City 84. Creator 85. Maria's Lovers 85. Good Morning Babylon 86. And God Created Woman 88. High-Frequency 88. The Heart of the Deal 90. Oscar 91. City of Hope 91. Alive 93. Indian Summer 93. The Ascent 94. The Tie that Binds 95. Downdraft 96, etc.

Spark, Dame Muriel (1918–).
British novelist feted by the intelligentsia. Two films of her work, *The Prime of Miss Jean Brodie* and *The Driver's Seat*, have both been unsatisfactory.
Nasty Habits (oa) 76. Memento Mori (oa) (TV) 92.

Sparks, Ned (1883–1957) (Edward Sparkman).
Hard-boiled, cigar-chewing Canadian comic actor often seen in Hollywood films of the 30s as grouchy reporter or agent.
The Big Noise 27. The Miracle Man 30. Forty-Second Street 33. Two's Company (GB) 37. The Star Maker 39. For Beauty's Sake 40. Magic Town 46, etc.

Sparkuhl, Theodor (1891–1945).
German cinematographer in Hollywood from the early 30s.
Carmen 18. Manon Lescaut 26. La Chienne 31. Too Much Harmony 33. Enter Madame 35. *Beau Geste* 39. *The Glass Key* 42. Star Spangled Rhythm 43. Blood on the Sun 46. Bachelor Girls 46, many others.

Sparv, Camilla (1943–).
Swedish-born leading lady in Hollywood films. She was formerly married to producer Robert Evans.
The Trouble with Angels 66. Murderers' Row 66. Dead Heat on a Merry-Go-Round 66. Department K 67. Mackenna's Gold 68. Downhill Racer 69. The Italian Job 69. Survival Zone 84, etc.

Speakman, Jeff (1957–).
American karate expert in action movies.
The Perfect Weapon 91. A.W.O.L./Lionheart 91. Street Knight 93. Deadly Takeover 95. Timelock 96. Escape from Atlantis (TV) 97. Scorpio 97, etc.

Spence, Bruce (1945–).
Lanky Australian character actor.
Stork 71. The Cars that Ate Paris 74. Newsfront 78. Dimboola 79. Mad Max 2/The Road Warrior 81. Midnight Spares 82. Buddies 83. Where the Green Ants Dream 84. Mad Max beyond Thunderdrome 85. Rikky and Pete 88. The Year My Voice Broke 88. . . . Almost 90. Boyfriend from Hell/The Shrimp on the Barbie 90. Wendy Cracked a Walnut 90. Sweet Talker 91. Ace Ventura: When Nature Calls 95, etc.

Spencer, Bud (1929–) (Carlo Pedersoli).
Italian character actor in many spaghetti westerns.
Blood River 67. Beyond the Law 68. Boot Hill 69. They Call Me Trinity 70. Four Flies on Grey Velvet 71. Watch Out We're Mad 74. Trinity Is Still My Name 75. The Knock Out Cop 78. Crime Busters 80. Aladdin 86, etc.

Spencer, Dorothy (1909–).
American editor.
The Moon's Our Home 36. Blockade 38. *Stagecoach* 39. *Foreign Correspondent* 40. To Be or Not To Be 42. Heaven Can Wait 43. Lifeboat 43. My Darling Clementine 46. The Snake Pit 48. Three Came Home 50. Fourteen Hours 51. Black Widow 54. The Man in the Grey Flannel Suit 56. The Young Lions 58. North to Alaska 60. Cleopatra (AAN) 63. Von Ryan's Express 65. Valley of the Dolls 67. Limbo 71. *Earthquake* (AAN) 74. The Concorde – Airport 79 79, many others.

Spencer, Kenneth (1912–1964).
American singer who appeared in a few 40s films including *Cabin in the Sky* and *Bataan*, both 43.

Spenser, Jeremy (1937–).
British leading man, former child actor, also on stage. He has not acted since the mid-60s and has sunk into obscurity.
Portrait of Clare 48. *Prelude to Fame* 50. Appointment with Venus 51. Summer Madness 55. The Prince and the Showgirl 57. Wonderful Things 58. Ferry to Hong Kong 58. *The Roman Spring of Mrs Stone* 61. King and Country 64. He Who Rides a Tiger 65. Fahrenheit 451 66, etc.

Sperling, Milton (1912–1988).
American producer.
Cloak and Dagger 46. Three Secrets 50. The Enforcer 51. Blowing Wild 54. The Court Martial of Billy Mitchell (& co-w) (AAN) 55. The Bramble Bush (& co-w) 59. The Battle of the Bulge 65. Captain Apache (w, p) 71, etc.

Spewack, Sam (1899–1971).
American playwright who with his wife Bella turned out several scripts for Hollywood.
The Secret Witness 31. Rendezvous 35. *Boy Meets Girl* 38. Three Loves Has Nancy 38. My Favorite Wife (AAN) 40. Weekend at the Waldorf 45. Kiss Me Kate 53. Move Over Darling 63, etc.

Spheeris, Penelope (1945–).
American director and screenwriter, concentrating mainly on themes of disaffected youth. She had her first commercial hit in 1992 with the rock-oriented comedy *Wayne's World*.
The Decline of Western Civilization (wd) 80. Suburbia (wd) 83. The Boys Next Door (d) 85. Summer Camp Nightmare (w) 86. Hollywood Vice Squad (d) 86. Dudes (d) 87. The Decline of Western Civilization Part II: The Metal Years (d) 88. Thunder & Mud (d) 89. Wayne's World (d) 92. The Beverly Hillbillies (p, d) 93. The Little Rascals (co-w, d) 94. Black Sheep 96. Senseless 98, etc.

Spiegel, Sam (1903–1985) (aka S. P. Eagle).
Polish-born producer, in Hollywood from 1941.
Biography: 1988, *Spiegel* by Andrew Sinclair.
Tales of Manhattan 42. *The Stranger* 45. *We Were Strangers* 48. *The African Queen* 51. *On the Waterfront* (AA) 54. The Strange One 57. *The Bridge on the River Kwai* (AA) 57. *Lawrence of Arabia* (AA) 62. The Chase 66. *The Night of the Generals* 66. The Happening 67. The Swimmer 68. Nicholas and Alexandra 71. The Last Tycoon 76. Betrayal 82, etc.

Spielberg, David (1939–).
American character actor.
The Effect of Gamma Rays 72. Newman's Law 74. Hustle 75. The Choirboys 77. The End 78. Stone (TV) 79. Sworn to Silence (TV) 87. Alice 90, etc.
TV series: Bob and Carol and Ted and Alice 73. The Practice 76.

Spielberg, Steven (1946–).
American director, the most commercially successful in the history of cinema so far, who in 1994 founded his own studio, DreamWorks SKG, with Jeffery Katzenberg and David Geffen. Born in Cincinnati, Ohio, he was fascinated by film from childhood, studied it at California State College, and began in television. His box-office successes, which began with *Jaws*, gave semi-adult treatment to what would once have been considered comic-strip material for children; although, with *Schindler's List* and *Saving Private Ryan*, he demonstrated that he could comprehend more serious subject-matter. With yearly earnings that have reached $335m, according to *Forbes* magazine (*Jurassic Park* alone brought him $200m), he is in a position to do precisely what he wants: judging by DreamWorks' output so far, that is to make genre movies that do not break the usual conventions of Hollywood. He was awarded a Golden Lion for Lifetime Achievement at the Venice Film Festival in 1993. Married actresses Amy Irving and Kate Capshaw.
Biographies: 1992, *Steven Spielberg* by Philip M. Taylor; 1996, *Steven Spielberg: The Unauthorized Biography* by John Baxter; 1997, *Steven Spielberg* by Joseph McBride.
■ Amblin' (short) 69. Something Evil (TV) 71. Savage (TV) 72. *Duel* (TV) 72. Sugarland Express 73. *Jaws* 75. 1941 75. Close Encounters of the Third Kind (AAN) 77. Raiders of the Lost Ark (AAN) 81. Poltergeist (p only) 82. *E.T. – the Extraterrestrial* (AAN) 82. Twilight Zone (co-d) 83. Indiana Jones and the Temple of Doom 84. Gremlins (p) 85. Back to the Future (p) 85. The

Goonies (p) 85. The Color Purple 85. An American Tail (p) 86. Empire of the Sun (& p) 87. Innerspace (p) 87. The Land before Time (p) 88. Who Framed Roger Rabbit? (p) 88. Always (p, d) 89. Back to the Future II (p) 89. Dad (p) 89. Indiana Jones and the Last Crusade (d) 89. Arachnophobia (p) 90. Back to the Future III (p) 90. Gremlins 2: The New Batch (p) 90. Joe versus the Volcano (p) 90. Hook (p, d) 91. Jurassic Park (p, d) 93. Schindler's List (AAp, AAd) 93. The Lost World: Jurassic Park 97. Amistad 97. Deep Impact (ex p only) 98. *Saving Private Ryan* 98.

❝ I've never been through psychoanalysis. I solve my problems with the pictures I make. – S.S.

Rosebud will go over my typewriter to remind me that quality in movies comes first. – *S.S. after buying (for $55,000) the sled used in Citizen Kane*

Stories don't have a middle and an end any more. They usually have a beginning that never stops beginning. – S.S.

I'd rather direct than produce. Any day. And twice on Sunday. – S.S.

What binds my films together is the concept of loneliness and isolation and being pursued by all the forces of character and nature. – S.S.

The next time you scan the movie listings only to find the neighborhood multiplex stuffed with footling Spielbergers – cartoonish action pictures, over-produced B-movie monster pictures and saccharine family fare – you're witnessing his legacy. – *Joel E. Siegel*

In many ways Spielberg is the Puccini of cinema, one of the highest compliments I can pay. He may be a little too sweet for some tastes, but what melodies, what orchestrations, what cathedrals of emotion . . . – *J. G. Ballard*

Spillane, Mickey (1918–) (Frank Morrison).
Best-selling American crime novelist of the love-'em and kill-'em variety: I the Jury 53. The Long Wait 54. Kiss Me Deadly 55. *I The Jury* was remade in 1981, with Armand Assante.

AS ACTOR: Ring of Fear 54. The Girl Hunters (as Mike Hammer) (& w) 64.

Darren McGavin played Hammer in a 1960 TV series, as did Stacy Keach in 1983 and Rob Estes in the TV film *Deader than Ever* 96.

Spilsbury, Klinton (1955–).
Mexican-born actor who played the title role in *The Legend of the Lone Ranger* 81, which was a box-office disaster, and then dropped out of sight.

Spinetti, Victor (1933–).
Italo-Welsh comic actor with stage experience.

A Hard Day's Night 64. The Wild Affair 64. Help! 65. The Taming of the Shrew 66. Hieronymus Merkin 69. The Return of the Pink Panther 76. Voyage of the Damned 76. The Krays 90. The Princess and the Goblin (voice) 92, etc.

Spinotti, Dante (1943–).
American cinematographer.

Sotto, Sotto 84. Manhunter 86. Crimes of the Heart 87. Beaches 88. Torrents of Spring 89. The Comfort of Strangers 90. True Colors 91. The Last of the Mohicans 92. La Fine è Nota 93. Blink 94. The Quick and the Dead 95. The Star Man 95. Heat 95. The Mirror Has Two Faces 96. LA Confidential (AAN) 97. Goodbye, Lover 98, etc.

Spoliansky, Mischa (1898–1985).
Russian composer, in Germany from 1930, Britain from 1934.

Don Juan 34. *Sanders of the River* 35. The Ghost Goes West 36. *King Solomon's Mines* 37. Jeannie 42. Don't Take It To Heart 44. Mr Emmanuel 44. Wanted for Murder 46. *The Happiest Days of Your Life* 50. Trouble in Store 53. Saint Joan 57. Northwest Frontier 59. The Battle of the Villa Fiorita 65. Hitler: The Last Ten Days 73, many others.

Spottiswoode, Roger (1947–).
English director and screenwriter now active in Hollywood, a former editor in television and film.

Terror Train 80. The Pursuit of D. B. Cooper 81. 48 Hours (co-w) 82. Under Fire 83. The Best of Times 86. The Last Innocent Man (TV) 87. Shoot to Kill 88. 3rd Degree Burn (TV) 89. Time Flies When You're Alive (TV) 89. Turner & Hooch 89. Air America 90. Stop! or My Mom Will Shoot 92. And the Band Played On (TV) 93. Mesmer 94. Hiroshima (co-d, TV) 95. Tomorrow Never Dies 97, etc.

Spradlin, G. D. (1926–).
American character actor.

Will Penny 67. Zabriskie Point 68. Hell's Angels '69 69. Monte Walsh 70. The Only Way Home (& d) 72. The Godfather, Part II 74. One on One 77. MacArthur 77. North Dallas Forty 79. Apocalypse Now 79. The Formula 80. The Lord of Discipline 82. Tank 84. The War of the Roses 89. Ed Wood 94. Clifford 94. Nick of Time 95. Riders of the Purple Sage (TV) 96. The Long Kiss Goodnight 96, etc.

Spriggs, Elizabeth (1929–).
English character actress, from the stage, usually in dominant or eccentric roles.

Work Is a Four Letter Word 68. Three into Two Won't Go 69. The Glittering Prizes (TV) 76. An Unsuitable Job for a Woman 82. Impromptu 89. Oranges Are Not the Only Fruit (TV) 90. Hour of the Pig 93. *Martin Chuzzlewit* (as Mrs Gamp) (TV) 94. The Secret Agent 97. Paradise Road 97, etc.

TV series: Fox 80. Shine On Harvey Moon 82, 95. A Kind of Living 88. Jeeves and Wooster (as Aunt Agatha) 92–93. Taking Over the Asylum 94.

Spring, Howard (1889–1965).
British novelist. Works filmed include *Fame Is the Spur* and My Son My Son.

Springsteen, R. G. (1904–1989).
American director who made efficient low-budget westerns from 1930.

Honeychile 48. Hellfire 49. The Enemy Within 49. The Toughest Man in Arizona 53. Track the Man Down 53. Come Next Spring 56. Cole Younger, Gunfighter 58. Battle Flame 59. Black Spurs 64. Taggart 65. Waco 66. Johnny Reno 66. Red Tomahawk 66, many others.

Squire, Ronald (1886–1958) (Ronald Squirl).
Jovial British character actor of stage (from 1909) and screen (from 1934).

Don't Take It to Heart 44. While the Sun Shines 46. Woman Hater 48. The Rocking-Horse Winner 50. Encore 52. My Cousin Rachel (US) 53. The Million Pound Note 54. Now and Forever 55. Count Your Blessings 58, etc.

Stack, Robert (1919–) (Robert Modini).
Personable, cold-eyed American leading man of the 50s, later successful in television.

■ First Love 39. The Mortal Storm 40. A Little Bit of Heaven 40. *Nice Girl* (in which he gave Deanna Durbin her first screen kiss) 41. Badlands of Dakota 41. To Be or Not To Be 42. Eagle Squadron 42. Men of Texas 42. A Date with Judy 48. Miss Tatlock's Millions 48. Fighter Squadron 48. Mr Music 50. My Outlaw Brother 51. The Bullfighter and the Lady 52. Bwana Devil 53. War Paint 53. Conquest of Cochise 53. Sabre Jet 53. The High and the Mighty 54. The Iron Glove 54. House of Bamboo 55. Good Morning Miss Dove 55. Great Day in the Morning 56. *Written on the Wind* (AAN) 56. *The Tarnished Angels* 57. The Gift of Love 58. *John Paul Jones* 59. The Last Voyage 60. The Caretakers 63. Is Paris Burning? 66. The Corrupt Ones 67. Le Soleil des Voyous 68. The Story of a Woman 70. The Action Man 70. The Strange and Deadly Occurrence (TV) 75. 1941 75. Adventures of the Queen (TV) 76. Murder on Flight 502 (TV) 76. Airplane 80. Uncommon Valour 83. Big Trouble 84. The Transformers (voice) 86. Perry Mason: The Case of the Sinister Spirit (TV) 87. Caddyshack II 88. Joe versus the Volcano 90. The Return of Eliot Ness (TV) 91. Beavis and Butthead Do America 96. BASEketball 98.

TV series: *The Untouchables* 59–62. *The Name of the Game* 68–70. Most Wanted 76. Strike Force 81–82. Falcon Crest 88.

Stafford, Frederick (1928–1979).
Austrian leading man who after many he-man roles in European movies imitating James Bond was signed by Alfred Hitchcock to play the lead in *Topaz* 69.

Stahl, Jerry (c. 1954–).
American writer who worked on such TV series as *Twin Peaks*, *thirtysomething* and *Moonlighting* and became a heroin addict. He was played by Ben STILLER in the biopic *Permanent Midnight* 98.

Dr Caligari (co-w) 89.

Stahl, John M. (1886–1950).
American director, former stage actor; in films from 1914.

Wives of Men 18. Husbands and Lovers 23. The Child Thou Gavest Me 24. The Naughty Duchess 28. Seed 31. *Back Street* 32. *Imitation of Life* 34. *Magnificent Obsession* 35. Parnell 37. Letter of Introduction 38. *When Tomorrow Comes* 39. Our Wife 41. *Holy Matrimony* 43. The Immortal Sergeant 43. The Eve of St Mark 44. *The Keys of the Kingdom* 44. Leave Her to Heaven 45. The Foxes of Harrow 47. The Walls of Jericho 47. Oh You Beautiful Doll 49, many others.

Stahl, Nick (1980–).
American child actor.

Stranger at My Door (TV) 92. The Man without a Face 93. Safe Passage (TV) 94. Tall Tale: The Unbelievable Adventures of Pecos Bill 95. Blue River 95. Eye of God 97. Disturbing Behavior 98, etc.

Stainton, Philip (1908–1961).
Rotund British actor with surprised expression; often played policemen.

Scott of the Antarctic 47. Passport to Pimlico 48. The Quiet Man 52. Angels One Five 52. Hobson's Choice 54. The Woman for Joe 56, many others.

Stalinska, Dorota (1953–).
Polish leading actress, often in the films of Barbara SASS.

Without Love/Bez Milosci 80. The Outsider/Debiutantka 82. The Scream/Krzyk 82. The Sex Mission/Saksmisja 84. An Immoral Story/Historia Niemoralna 90. Ferdydurke 91, etc.

Stalling, Carl (1888–1972).
American composer and arranger, scoring cartoons. A silent-movie pianist and conductor, he became Disney's musical director in 1928, moving to Ub Iwerks' studio and then to Warner in 1936, retiring in 1958. His scores enlivened many cartoons from *Steamboat Willie* 28 to *To Itch His Own* 58.

Stallings, Laurence (1894–1968).
American screenwriter and playwright. Born in Macon, Georgia, he lost a leg serving in the Marines in the First World War, and, after studying at Georgetown University, worked for New York newspapers while writing plays and musicals. His first play, *What Price Glory?*, was filmed, but after further success eluded him in the theatre, he turned to writing for Hollywood. He also edited and wrote the captions to a best-selling book, *The First World War: A Pictorial History* 33.

The Big Parade 25. *What Price Glory?* (co-w) 26. So Red the Rose (co-w) 35. Northwest Passage (co-w) 39. Jungle Book 42. Salome Where She Danced 45. *She Wore a Yellow Ribbon* (co-w) 49. The Sun Shines Bright 52, etc.

Stallone, Sylvester (1946–).
Beefy, solemn-looking American star who shot to the top in a modest film he wrote himself, and then became a hero of action films. He is now pondering the problem of what action stars do as they grow older. His second wife was actress Brigitte NIELSEN (1985–88). Married former model Jennifer Flavin in 1997.

Biography: 1991, *Sylvester Stallone* by Adrian Wright.

A Party at Kitty and Stud's/The Italian Stallion 70. Bananas 71. The Lords of Flatbush 73. Capone 73. The Prisoner of Second Avenue 75. Death Race 2000 75. Farewell My Lovely 75. Carquake 75. *Rocky* (AANw, AANa) 76. F.I.S.T. (& w) 78. Paradise Alley (& wd) 78. Rocky II (& wd) 79. Nighthawks 81. Victory 81. Rocky III 82. First Blood 82. Staying Alive (co-w, co-p, d) 83. Rhinestone 84. Rambo 85. Rocky IV (& d) 85. Cobra 85. Over the Top 87. Rambo III 88. Lock Up 89. Tango & Cash 89. Rocky V 90. Oscar 91. Stop! or My Mom Will Shoot 92. Demolition Man 93. Cliffhanger (& co-w) 93. The Specialist 94. Judge Dredd 95. Assassins 95. Daylight 96. Cop Land 97. Antz (voice) 98, etc.

❝ I'll just go on playing Rambo and Rocky. Both are money-making machines that can't be switched off. – S.S.

I'm not handsome in the classical sense. The eyes droop, the mouth is crooked, the teeth aren't straight, the voice sounds like a Mafioso pallbearer, but somehow it all works. – S.S.

I'd say between 3 p.m. and 8 p.m. I look great. After that it's all downhill. Don't photograph me in the morning or you're gonna get Walter Brennan. – S.S.

I'm not a genetically superior person. I built my body. – S.S.

I'm a very physical person. People don't credit me with much of a brain, so why should I disillusion them? – S.S.

I really am a manifestation of my own fantasy. – S.S.

Once in a man's life, for one mortal moment, he must make a grab for immortality. If not, he has not lived. – S.S.

All art, in this business, is an act of compromise. It's not one man's vision unless he takes very weak actors. – S.S.

Both warrior and bard, he is the author of his own myth, one of the best examples yet of how Hollywood artefacts are in the main line of Western culture and how, amid the collapse of modernism, they have inherited the traditional unifying role of high art. – *Camille Paglia*

Stamp, Terence (1939–).
British leading man.

Autobiography: 1987, *Stamp Album*, 1988, *Coming Attractions*, 1989, *Double Feature*.

Billy Budd (AAN) 62. Term of Trial 62. The Collector 65. Modesty Blaise 66. Far from the Madding Crowd 67. Poor Cow 67. Blue 68. Theorem (It.) 68. The Mind of Mr Soames 69. Superman 78. Meetings with Remarkable Men 78. The Thief of Bagdad 79. Superman II 81. The Hit 84. Company of Wolves 85. Link 86. The Sicilian 87. Wall Street 87. Young Guns 88. Alien Nation 88. Genuine Risk 90. Prince of Shadows/Beltenebros 92. The Real McCoy 93. The Adventures of Priscilla Queen of the Desert 94. Limited Edition/Tire à Part 96. Love Walked In 97, etc.

❝ I would have liked to be James Bond. – *T.S.*

Stamp-Taylor, Enid (1904–1946).
British character actress with stage experience.

Feather Your Nest 37. Action for Slander 37. The Lambeth Walk 38. Hatter's Castle 41. The Wicked Lady 45. Caravan 46, etc.

Stander, Lionel (1908–1994).
Gravel-voiced American character actor, on stage and screen from the early 30s. His career was harmed by the communist witch-hunts of the late 40s.

The Scoundrel 34. Mr Deeds Goes to Town 36. *A Star is Born* 37. Guadalcanal Diary 42. The Spectre of the Rose 46. Unfaithfully Yours 48. St Benny the Dip 51. *Cul de Sac* (GB) 66. Promise Her Anything (GB) 66. A Dandy in Aspic (GB) 68. The Gang that Couldn't Shoot Straight 72. The Con Men 73. The Black Bird 75. New York New York 77. The Cassandra Crossing 77. Matilda 78. Hart to Hart (TV) 79. The Transformers (voice) 86. Wicked Stepmother 88. Cookie 89, etc.

TV series: Hart to Hart 79.

Standing, Sir Guy (1873–1937).
British stage actor, father of Kay Hammond, in some Hollywood films.

■ The Story of Temple Drake 33. Midnight Club 33. Hell and High Water 33. The Cradle Song 33. A Bedtime Story 33. The Eagle and the Hawk 33. Death Takes a Holiday 34. Now and Forever 34. The Witching Hour 34. Double Door 34. *The Lives of a Bengal Lancer* 35. Car 99 35. Annapolis Farewell 35. The Big Broadcast of 1936 35. The Return of Sophie Lang 36. Palm Springs 36. I'd Give My Life 36. Lloyds of London 36. Bulldog Drummond Escapes 37.

Standing, John (1934–) (Sir John Leon).
British character actor, son of Kay HAMMOND.

The Wild and the Willing 62. A Pair of Briefs 63. King Rat 65. Walk Don't Run 66. The Psychopath 66. Torture Garden 67. Zee and Co. 71. Rogue Male (TV) 76. The Eagle Has Landed 77. The Elephant Man 80. The Sea Wolves 80. Night Flyers 87. Gulliver's Travels (TV) 96. A Dance to the Music of Time (TV) 97. Mrs Dalloway 97. The Man Who Knew Too Little 97, etc.

TV series: Lime Street 86.

Stanley, Kim (1921–) (Patricia Reid).
American stage actress.
■ The Goddess 58. Seance on a Wet Afternoon (AAN) 64. Three Sisters 67. Frances (AAN) 82. The Right Stuff 83.
❝ Directing Kim was as if you'd been given a piano and suddenly found you could play as well as Glenn Gould. – *Tony Richardson*

Stanley, Richard (1964–).
South-African born director and screenwriter of fantasy movies.
Hardware (wd) 90. Dust Devil (wd) 92. The Island of Dr Moreau (co-w) 96, etc.

Stannard, Don (1916–1949).
British light leading man who played Dick Barton in three serial-like melodramas 1948–49.

Stanton, Harry Dean (1926–).
American character actor.
Dragon Wells Massacre 57. How the West Was Won 62. Cool Hand Luke 67. Cisco Pike 72. Dillinger 73. Cockfighter 74. Farewell My Lovely 75. The Missouri Breaks 76. Alien 79. The Rose 79. Wise Blood 80. The Black Marble 80. Private Benjamin 80. One from the Heart 82. Christine 83. Repo Man 84. Paris, Texas 84. Pretty in Pink 86. Fool for Love 86. Slam Dance 87. Mr North 88. The Last Temptation of Christ 88. Dream a Little Dream 89. The Fourth War 90. Wild at Heart 90. Payoff 91. Twin Peaks: Fire Walk with Me 92. Man Trouble 92. Hotel Room (TV) 93. Against the Wall (TV) 94. Blue Tiger 94. Never Talk to Strangers 95. Down Periscope 96. She's So Lovely 97. Fire Down Below 97. The Mighty 98. Fear and Loathing in Las Vegas 98, etc.

Stanwyck, Barbara (1907–1990) (Ruby Stevens).
Durable American star actress, a sultry lady usually playing roles in which she is just as good as a man, if not better. Married comedian Frank FAY (1928–32) and actor Robert TAYLOR (1939–51). Her lovers included director Frank CAPRA and actor William HOLDEN. She was awarded an honorary Oscar in 1981 'for superlative creativity and unique contribution to the art of screen acting'.
Biography: 1994, *Stanwyck* by Alex Madsen.
■ Broadway Nights 27. The Locked Door 29. Mexicali Rose 29. Ladies of Leisure 30. Ten Cents a Dance 31. Illicit 31. *Miracle Woman* 31. *Night Nurse* 31. Forbidden 32. Shopworn 32. *So Big* 32. The Purchase Price 32. *The Bitter Tea of General Yen* 33. Ladies They Talk About 33. *Baby Face* 33. Ever in My Heart 33. A Lost Lady 34. Gambling Lady 34. The Secret Bride 35. The Woman in Red 35. Red Salute 35. *Annie Oakley* 35. A Message to Garcia 36. The Bride Walks Out 36. His Brother's Wife 36. Banjo on My Knee 36. The Plough and the Stars 36. Internes Can't Take Money 37. This Is My Affair 37. *Stella Dallas* (AAN) 37. Breakfast for Two 38. The Mad Miss Manton 38. Always Goodbye 38. Union Pacific 39. Golden Boy 39. Remember the Night 40. *The Lady Eve* 41. *Meet John Doe* 41. You Belong to Me 41. *Ball of Fire* (AAN) 41. The Great Man's Lady 42. The Gay Sisters 42. Lady of Burlesque 42. Flesh and Fantasy 43. *Double Indemnity* (AAN) 44. Hollywood Canteen 44. Christmas in Connecticut 45. My Reputation 45. The Bride Wore Boots 46. *The Strange Love of Martha Ivers* 46. California 46. The Other Love 47. The Two Mrs Carrolls 47. Cry Wolf 47. BF's Daughter 48. *Sorry Wrong Number* (AAN) 48. The Lady Gambles 49. East Side West Side 49. Thelma Jordon 50. No Man of Her Own 50. *The Furies* 50. To Please a Lady 50. Man with a Cloak 51. Clash by Night 52. Jeopardy 53. Titanic 53. All I Desire 53. The Moonlighter 53. Blowing Wild 53. *Executive Suite* 54. Witness to Murder 54. Cattle Queen of Montana 54. The Violent Men 55. Escape to Burma 55. There's Always Tomorrow 56. The Maverick Queen 56. These Wilder Years 56. Crime of Passion 57. Trooper Hook 57. Forty Guns 57. Walk on the Wild Side 62. Roustabout 64. The Night Walker 65. The House That Would Not Die (TV) 70. A Taste of Evil (TV) 71. The Letters (TV) 73. The Thorn Birds (TV) 83.
TV series: *The Big Valley* 65–68.
✪ For holding more than her own in comedy or melodrama, and being a match for any man. *The Lady Eve*.
❝ I want to go on until they have to shoot me. – *B.S.*
Put me in the last fifteen minutes of a picture and I don't care what happened before. I don't even care if I was IN the rest of the damned thing – I'll take it in those fifteen minutes. – *B.S.*
Attention embarrasses me. I don't like to be on display. – *B.S.*
Career is too pompous a word. It was a job, and I have always felt privileged to be paid for doing what I love doing. – *B.S.*

Stapleton, Jean (1923–) (Jeanne Murray).
American actress familiar from TV's *All in the Family*.
Damn Yankees 58. Bells are Ringing 60. Something Wild 61. Up the Down Staircase 67. Cold Turkey 70. Klute 71. The Trial 93. Michael 96. Pocahontas II: Journey to a New World (voice) 98, etc.

Stapleton, Maureen (1925–).
American character actress.
Lonelyhearts (AAN) 59. The Fugitive Kind 60. A View from the Bridge 62. Bye Bye Birdie 63. Airport (AAN) 69. Plaza Suite 70. Tell Me Where It Hurts 74. *Queen of the Stardust Ballroom* 75. The Gathering (TV) 77. Interiors (AAN) 78. Lost and Found 80. Reds (AA, BFA) 81. Johnny Dangerously 84. Cocoon 85. The Cosmic Eye 85. The Money Pit 85. Heartburn 86. Sweet Lorraine 87. Made in Heaven 87. Cocoon: The Return 88. Passed Away 92. Trading Mom 94. The Last Good Time 94. Addicted to Love 97, etc.

Stapleton, Oliver.
British cinematographer.
Restless Natives 85. My Beautiful Laundrette 86. Absolute Beginners 86. Sammy and Rosie Get Laid 87. Prick Up Your Ears 87. Chuck Berry: Hail! Hail! Rock 'n' Roll 87. Danny, the Champion of the World (TV) 89. Earth Girls Are Easy 89. Cookie 89. She-Devil 89. The Grifters 90. Let Him Have It 91. Hero/Accidental Hero 93. Kansas City 96. The Van 96. One Fine Day 96. The Designated Mourner 97. The Object of My Affection 98. The Hi-Lo Country 98, etc.

Stapley, Richard (1922–).
English leading man who went to Hollywood after wartime service in the RAF. Also known, from the late 60s, as Richard Wyler.
The Three Musketeers 48. Little Women 49. The Strange Door 51. King of the Khyber Rifles 53. Target Zero 55. The Ugly Ones 68, etc.

Stark, Graham (1922–).
British comedy actor of films and TV, mostly in cameo roles.
The Millionairess 61. Watch It, Sailor 62. A Shot in the Dark 64. Becket 64. Alfie 66. Finders Keepers 66. Salt and Pepper 68. Doctor in Trouble 70. Return of the Pink Panther 75. The Prince and the Pauper 77. Revenge of the Pink Panther 78. Hawk the Slayer 80. Trail of the Pink Panther 82. Blind Date 87. Son of the Pink Panther 93, etc.

Stark, Ray (c. 1909–).
American producer.
The World of Suzie Wong 60. Oh Dad, Poor Dad 66. This Property is Condemned 66. Funny Girl (AAN) 67. Reflections in a Golden Eye 68. The Way We Were 73. Funny Lady 75. California Suite 78. The Goodbye Girl 78. Chapter Two 79. The Electric Horseman 79. Seems Like Old Times 80. Annie 82. The Slugger's Wife 85. Brighton Beach Memoirs 86. Biloxi Blues 88. Steel Magnolias 89. Lost in Yonkers 93, etc.

Starke, Pauline (1901–1977).
American silent screen actress.
Intolerance 16. Salvation Nell 19. A Connecticut Yankee 21. Shanghai 24. Twenty Cents a Dance 26, etc.

Starr, Belle (1848–1889).
American female outlaw of the wild west period. On screen she has been glamorized by Gene Tierney in the film of that name, by Jane Russell in *Montana Belle* and by Isabel Jewell in *Badman's Territory*. Elizabeth Montgomery had an odd view of her in a 1980 TV movie.

Starr, Irving (1906–1982).
American producer, former agent.
The Crimson Trail 34. Music in My Heart 40. Swing Fever 42. Four Jills in a Jeep 44. Johnny Allegro 47. Slightly French 49, etc.

Starr, Ringo (1940–)
see THE BEATLES.

Starrett, Charles (1904–1986).
American cowboy star of innumerable second features in the 30s and 40s. Inactive after 1952. Born in Athol, Massachusetts, he was educated at Dartmouth College and studied acting at the Academy of Dramatic Arts, beginning in theatre with various stock companies. In the 30s he was contracted to Paramount; success came when he began making westerns for Columbia from the mid-30s.
The Quarterback (debut) (playing himself, a professional footballer) 26. Fast and Loose 30. Sky Bride 32. Green Eyes 34. So Red the Rose 35. Mysterious Avenger 36. Two Gun Law 37. The Colorado Trail 38. Spoilers of the Range 39. Blazing Six Shooters 40. Thunder Over the Plains 41. Pardon My Gun 42. Fighting Buckaroo 43. Sundown Valley 44. Sagebrush Heroes 45. Gunning for Vengeance 46. Riders of the Lone Star 47. Last Days of Boot Hill 48. The Blazing Trail 49. Texas Dynamo 50. The Kid from Amarillo 51. Rough Tough West 52, many others.

Starrett, Jack (1936–1989).
American director, mainly of low-budget action pieces.
Run Angel Run 69. Cry Blood Apache 70. The Strange Vengeance of Rosalie 72. Slaughter 72. Nowhere to Hide (TV) 73. Cleopatra Jones 73. Race with the Devil 75. A Small Town in Texas 76. Final Chapter Walking Tall 77. Big Bob Johnson and His Fantastic Speed Circus (TV) 78. Mr Horn (TV) 79. First Blood (a only) 82.
❝ I jump in with both feet. I figure if you ain't got balls you're in the wrong business. – *J.S., 1975*

Staudte, Wolfgang (1906–1984).
German director of socially conscious films.
The Murderers Are amongst Us (& w) 46. Der Untertan (& w) 51. Rose Bernd 56. Roses for the Prosecutor 59. Die Dreigroschenoper 63. Herrenpartie 64. Heimlichkeiten 68. Die Herren mit die Weissen Weste 70. Wolf of the Seven Seas 73. Zwischengleis (TV) 78, etc.

Staunton, Imelda (1958–).
English actress, from the stage. Trained at RADA, she has worked for the Royal Shakespeare Company and the National Theatre.
Peter's Friends 92. Much Ado about Nothing 93. Terminus (TV) 94. Deadly Advice 94. Sense and Sensibility 95, etc.
TV series: Up the Garden Path 90–93. If You See God, Tell Him 93.

Stawinksi, Jerzy Stefan (1921–).
Polish screenwriter, novelist and director. In the mid-50s he was literary head of the Kamera production unit, which also included directors Roman Polanski, Jerzy Skolimowski and Andrzej Wajda.
Kanal (& oa) 56. Man on the Track/Czlowiek Na Torze 57. *Eroica* (& oa) 57. Bad Luck/Zezowate Szczescie 60. *The Teutonic Knights*/Krzyzacy 60. Love at Twenty/L'Amour à Vingt Ans (Fr.) 61. Pingwin/Penguin (d) 65. Christmas Eve/Przedswiateczny Wieczor (co-d) 66. Who Believes in Storks/Kto Wierzy W Bociany (co-d) 71. Chasing Adam/Pogon Za Adamem (co-d) 71. Matilda's Birthday/Urodziny Matyldy (d) 74. Colonel Kwiatkowski 96, etc.

Steadman, Alison (1946–).
English actress, mainly on the stage and television. Married director Mike LEIGH.
Nuts in May (TV) 76. Abigail's Party (TV) 77. Ptang, Bang, Kipperbang 82. Number One 84. Champions 84. A Private Function 84. The Singing Detective (TV) 86. Clockwise 86. Stormy Monday 87. The Adventures of Baron Munchausen 89. Shirley Valentine 89. Wilt/The Misadventures of Mr Wilt 90. Life Is Sweet 91. Blame It on the Bellboy 92. Pride and Prejudice (TV) 95, etc.
TV series: The Wackers 75. Gone to Seed 92. No Bananas 96.

Steckler, Ray Dennis (1939–).
American director of low-budget exploitation movies that are most notable for their titles. He also acts in them under the pseudonym of Cash Flagg.
Drivers in Hell/Wild Ones on Wheels 61. Wild Guitar 62. The Incredibly Strange Creatures Who Stopped Living and Became Mixed-up Zombies 62. Rat Pfink a-Boo-Boo 62. Scream of the Butterfly 65. Lemon Grove Kids Meet the Monsters 66. Body Fever 72. The Hollywood Strangler Meets the Skid Row Slasher 79, etc.

Steege, Johanna Ter.
Dutch leading actress.
The Vanishing 77. Vincent and Theo 90. Meeting Venus 91. La Naissance de l'Amour (Fr.) 93. Goodbye 95. Paradise Road 97, etc.

Steel, Anthony (1920–).
Athletic British leading man with slight stage experience.
Saraband for Dead Lovers (film debut) 48. Marry Me 49. *The Wooden Horse* 50. Laughter in Paradise 51. The Malta Story 52. *Albert RN* 53. The Sea Shall Not Have Them 55. Storm over the Nile 56. The Black Tent 56. Checkpoint 56. A Question of Adultery 57. Harry Black 58. Honeymoon 60. The Switch 63. Hell Is Empty 67. Anzio 68. Massacre in Rome 74. The World Is Full of Married Men 79. The Mirror Crack'd 80. The Monster Club 81, etc.

Steel, Dawn (1947–1997) (Dawn Spielberg).
American production executive. She worked first for Paramount and became president of Columbia Pictures in 1987, leaving in 1990 when Sony took over the company. She then ran an independent production company, Atlas Entertainment, with her husband Charles Roven and Robert Cavallo. Died from a brain tumour.
Autobiography: 1992, *They Can Kill You . . . But They Can't Eat You*.
Flashdance 83. Footloose 84. Top Gun 86. Fatal Attraction 87. The Untouchables 87. Casualties of War 90. Cool Runnings 93. Sister Act 2: Back in the Habit 93. Angus 95. Fallen 98. City of Angels 98, etc.
❝ I was trained to be loud, passionate, direct. I didn't realise for the longest time I was intimidating. – *D.S.*

Steele, Barbara (1938–).
British leading lady who has appeared mainly in Italian horror films.
Bachelor of Hearts 58. Sapphire 59. Black Sunday/The Devil's Mask 60. The Pit and the Pendulum (US) 61. The Terror of Dr Hitchcock 62. Eight and a Half 63. The Spectre 64. Sister of Satan/The Revenge of the Blood Beast 65. Nightmare Castle 66. Renegade Girls 74. Pretty Baby 78. Silent Scream 80. Winds of War (TV) 83, etc.
TV series: Dark Shadows 91.

Steele, Bob (1907–1988) (Robert Bradbury).
American character actor, on stage from the age of two and in more than 400 second-feature westerns, appearing as Billy the Kid in a series in the early 40s. One of the 'Three Mesquiteers', he was the son of Robert N. Bradbury, who directed many westerns for Monogram and Republic Pictures and starred him and his twin brother William in his first film, *The Adventures of Bob and Bill* 14. Also played Curley in *Of Mice and Men* 39, and the villainous Canino in *The Big Sleep* 46.
Davy Crockett at the Fall of the Alamo 26. The Bandit's Son 27. Texas Cowboy 30. South of Santa Fe 32. Kid Courageous 35. Riders of the Sage 39. The Carson City Kid 40. Billy the Kid in Texas 40. Westward Ho! 42. Wildfire 45. South of St Louis 49. The Savage Horde 50. Island in the Sky 53. Drums across the River 54. Band of Angels 57. Giant from the Unknown 58. The Bonnie Parker Story 58. Atomic Submarine 59. Pork Chop Hill 59. Rio Bravo 59. McClintock! 63. Taggart 64. Requiem for a Gunfighter 65. The Great Bank Robbery 69. Rio Lobo 70. The Skin Game 71. Charley Varrick 73, many others.
TV series: F Troop 65–66.

Steele, Tom (1909–1990).
American stuntman in serials of the 40s and 50s. He was head of Republic's stunt team during its serial heyday, working as a double for the heroes and villains and also for the studio's western stars, and playing minor roles. He played the uncredited title role in *The Masked Marvel* 43.
Bound for Glory 76. The Cat from Outer Space 78. Alligator 80. The Blues Brothers 80. Scarface 83, etc.

Steele, Tommy (1936–) (Tommy Hicks).
Energetic British cockney performer and pop singer.
Kill Me Tomorrow 55. The Tommy Steele Story 57. The Duke Wore Jeans 59. Light Up The Sky 59. Tommy the Toreador 60. It's All Happening 62. *The Happiest Millionaire* (US) 67. *Half a Sixpence* 67. Finian's Rainbow (US) 68. Where's Jack? 69.

Steenburgen, Mary (1953–).
American leading actress. Married actors Malcolm McDowell (1980–90) and Ted Danson.
Going South 78. Time after Time 79. Melvin and Howard (AA) 80. Ragtime 81. A Midsummer Night's Sex Comedy 82. Cross Creek 83. Romantic Comedy 83. One Magic Christmas 85. Dead of Center 87. The Whales of August 87. End of the Line 88. Miss Firecracker 89. Parenthood 89. Back to the Future Part III 90. The Butcher's Wife 91. Gilbert Grape 93. Philadelphia 93. Clifford 94. It Runs in the Family 94. Pontiac Moon 94. Nixon 95. The Grass Harp 95. Powder 95. Gulliver's Travels (TV) 96, etc.
TV series: Ink 96–97.

Steiger, Rod (1925–).
Burly American leading character actor who became known on stage and TV after training at New York's Theatre Workshop. His four wives included actresses Sally Grace (1952–58) and Claire Bloom (1959–69).
Biography: 1998, *Rod Steiger: Memoirs of a Friendship* by Tom Hutchinson.
Teresa 51. *On the Waterfront* (AAN) 54. The Big Knife 55. Oklahoma 55. *The Court Martial of Billy Mitchell* 55. The Unholy Wife 56. Jubal 56. *The Harder They Fall* 56. Back from Eternity 57. Run of the Arrow 57. Across the Bridge (GB) 57. *Al Capone* 58. Cry Terror 58. Seven Thieves 59. The Mark 61. 13 West Street 61. On Friday at Eleven 61. The Longest Day 62. Convicts Four 62. Time of Indifference 63. Hands Over the City (It.) 63. *The Pawnbroker* (BFA, AAN) 64. A Man Called John 64. The Loved One 65. Doctor Zhivago 65. The Girl and the General 66. *In the Heat of the Night* (AA, BFA) 67. No Way to Treat a Lady 68. The Sergeant 68. The Illustrated Man 69. Three into Two Won't Go 69. Waterloo (as Napoleon) 71. A Fistful of Dynamite 71. The Heroes (It.) 72. Happy Birthday Wanda June 72. Lolly Madonna XXX 72. Lucky Luciano 73. Hennessy 74. Innocents With Dirty Hands 75. W.C. Fields and Me 76. Jesus of Nazareth (TV) 77. Jimbuck 77. The Last Four Days (as Mussolini) 77. Wolf Lake 78. Love and Bullets 78. F.I.S.T. 78. Breakthrough 79. The Amityville Horror 79. Lucky Star 80. Klondike Fever 80. Lion of the Desert (as Mussolini) 81. Cattle Annie and Little Britches 81. The Chosen 82. The Magic Mountain 82. The Glory Boys (TV) 84. Hollywood Wives (TV) 84. The Naked Face 84. The Kindred 86. Feel the Heat 87. American Gothic 87. The January Man 89. Tennessee Waltz 89. The Ballad of the Sad Café 90. Men of Respect 91. Guilty as Charged 92. That Summer of White Roses 92. The Neighbor 93. Seven Sundays/Tous les Jours Dimanche (Fr.) 94. The Specialist 94. Tom Clancy's Op Center (TV) 95. In Pursuit of Honor 95. Out There (TV) 95. Carpool 96. Mars Attacks! 96. Livers Ain't Cheap 96. Shiloh 96. Mars Attacks! 96. Incognito 97. Modern Vampires/Revenant 98, etc.

Stein, Herman (1915–).
American composer, prolific co-writer of scores at Universal in the 50s.
Back at the Front 52. Has Anybody Seen My Gal? 52. Meet Me at the Fair 52. Abbott & Costello Meet Dr Jekyll and Mr Hyde 53. Girls in the Night 53. Gunsmoke 53. The Black Shield of Falworth 54. The Creature from the Black Lagoon 54. Destry 54. Drums across the River 54. The Glenn Miller Story 54. So This Is Paris 54. The Far Country 55. This Island Earth 55. I've Lived Before 56. The Incredible Shrinking Man 57. Mister Cory 57. Slim Carter 57. Last of the Fast Guns 58. No Name on the Bullet 59. The Intruder 61, many others.

Stein, Paul (1892–1952).
Austrian director who made films in America and Britain.
Ich Liebe Dich 23. My Official Wife (US) 26. Forbidden Woman (US) 27. Sin Takes a Holiday (US) 30. One Romantic Night 30. Born to Love 31. A Woman Commands (US) 31. Lily Christine (GB) 32. The Outsider (GB) 38. The Saint Meets the Tiger (GB) 41. Talk about Jacqueline (GB) 42. Kiss the Bride Goodbye (GB) 43. Twilight Hour (GB) 44. The Lisbon Story (GB) 46. Counterblast (GB) 48. The Twenty Questions Murder Mystery (GB) 49, etc.

Steinbeck, John (1902–1968).
American novelist.
Of Mice and Men 39, 81 (TV) and 92. The Grapes of Wrath 40. Tortilla Flat 42. The Moon Is Down 43. Lifeboat (AAN) 44. A Medal for Benny (AAN) 45. The Red Pony 49. Viva Zapata! (AAN) 52. East of Eden 54. The Wayward Bus 57, etc.
❝ We bought *The Moon Is Down*, which was on the stage in New York, and when I said, 'Look, have you got any suggestions?' he said, 'Yeah, tamper with it.' – *Nunnally Johnson*

Steinberg, Michael (1959–).
American director and screenwriter.
The Waterdance (co-d) 92. Bodies, Rest and Motion 93.

Steinberg, Norman.
American screenwriter.
Blazing Saddles 73. Yes, Giorgio 82. My Favorite Year 82. Johnny Dangerously 84. Funny about Love 90, etc.

Steiner, Fred (1923–).
American composer who also scores TV movies.
Run for the Sun 56. The Man from Del Rio 56. Time Limit 57. Robinson Crusoe on Mars 64. The St Valentine's Day Massacre 67. The Sea Gypsies 78. The Color Purple (AAN) 85, etc.

Steiner, Max (1888–1971).
Austrian composer, in America from 1924; became one of Hollywood's most reliable and prolific writers of film music.
Cimarron 31. A Bill of Divorcement 32. *King Kong* 33. The Lost Patrol 34. *The Informer* (AA) 35. *She* 35. The Charge of the Light Brigade 36. A Star Is Born 37. *Gone with the Wind* 39. *The Letter* 40. *The Great Lie* 41. *Now Voyager* (AA) 42. *Casablanca* 42. *Since You Went Away* (AA) 44. Rhapsody in Blue 45. The Big Sleep 46. The Treasure of the Sierra Madre 47. Johnny Belinda 48. The Fountainhead 49. The Glass Menagerie 50. Room for One More 52. The Charge at Feather River 53. The Caine Mutiny 54. Battle Cry 55. Come Next Spring 56. Band of Angels 57. The FBI Story 59. The Dark at the Top of the Stairs 60. Parrish 61. Youngblood Hawke 64, many others.

Steinhoff, Hans (1882–1945).
German director, from the theatre. Directed features containing Nazi propaganda from the early 30s. Died in a plane crash.
Angst 28. The Alley Cat (GB) 29. The Three Kings (GB) 29. Chacun Sa Chance (Fr.) 30. Hitlerjunge Quex 33. Robert Koch, der Bekämpfer des Todes 39. Die Geierwally 40. Ohm Krüger 41. Rembrandt 42. Gabriele Dambrone 43. Shiva und die Galgenblume 45, etc.

Steinkamp, Frederic.
American editor.
Two Loves 61. Sunday in New York 64. Grand Prix (co-ed) (AA) 66. Charly 68. A New Leaf 71. Haunts of the Very Rich (TV) 72. Freebie and the Bean 74. Three Days of the Condor 75. Bobby Deerfield 77. Tootsie (AAN) 82. Against All Odds 84. White Nights 85. Out of Africa (AAN) 85. Adventures in Babysitting 87. Burglar 87. Scrooged 87. Havana 90. The Firm 93. Sabrina 95, etc.

Sten, Anna (1908–1993) (Anjuschka Stenski Sujakevitch).
Russian leading actress imported to Hollywood by Goldwyn in 1933 in the hope of rivalling Garbo; but somehow she didn't click. The first of her two husbands was director Feder Ozep.
SELECTED EUROPEAN FILMS: The Yellow Ticket 27. Storm Over Asia 28. The White Eagle 28. The Murder of Dimitri Karamazov 31. Bombs in Monte Carlo 31.
■ ENGLISH-SPEAKING FILMS: *Nana* 34. We Live Again 34. The Wedding Night 35. A Woman Alone 36. Exile Express 39. The Man I Married 40. So Ends Our Night 41. Chetniks 43. They Came To Blow Up America 43. Three Russian Girls 43. Let's Live a Little 48. Soldier of Fortune 55. Heaven Knows Mr Allison 57. The Nun and the Sergeant 62.

Steno (1915–1988) (Stefano Vanzina).
Italian screenwriter and director, mainly of comedies. Born in Rome, he began as a satirical writer and cartoonist, before working as an assistant to directors Mario Mattoli, Carlo Ludovico Bragaglia and Riccardo Freda, and writing screenplays for Mario Soldati and Alessandro Blasetti. His first films were made in collaboration with Mario Monicelli, and some of his most successful starred the comedian Toto and, later, Bud Spencer (Carlo Pedersoli).
AS DIRECTOR: Al Diavoli la Celebrità (co-d) 49. Cops and Robbers/Guardie e Ladri (co-d) 51. Toto a Colori (co-d) 52. Le Avventure di Giacomo Casanova 54. Piccola Pasta (co-d) 56. Toto nella Luna 58. Copacabana Palace 62. Toto Diabolicus 62. Gli Eroi del West 63. Love Italian Style/Amore all'Italiana 66. Transplant/Il Trapianto 70. Flatfoot/Piedone lo Sbirro 73. Piedone a Hong Kong 75. Doppio Delitto 77. Piedone l'Africano 78. Jekyll Junior/Dottor Jekyll e Gentile Signora 79. Piedone d'Egitto 80. Banana Joe 82. Il Professore – Boomerang 89. Il Professore – Polizzia Inferno 89, many others.

Stepanek, Karel (1899–1980).
Czech character actor, in Britain from 1940. Usually played Nazis or other villains.
They Met in the Dark 43. *The Captive Heart* 46. The Fallen Idol 48. State Secret 50. Cockleshell Heroes 55. *Sink the Bismarck* 60. Operation Crossbow 65. Before Winter Comes 69, many others.

Stephen, Susan (1931–).
British leading lady of the 50s. She was formerly married to director Nicolas Roeg.
His Excellency 51. The Red Beret 53. For Better For Worse 54. Golden Ivory 54. The Barretts of Wimpole Street 57. Carry On Nurse 59. Return of a Stranger 61. The Court Martial of Major Keller 63, etc.

Stephens, Ann (1931–).
British juvenile actress of the 40s.
In Which We Serve 42. Dear Octopus 43. The Upturned Glass 47. The Franchise Affair 51. Intent to Kill 58, many others.

Stephens, Martin (1949–).
British juvenile player. Later became an architect.
The Hellfire Club 61. *Village of the Damned* 62. *The Innocents* 62. Battle of the Villa Fiorita 65. The Witches 66, etc.

Stephens, Sir Robert (1931–1995).
Distinguished English classical actor, in occasional films. Born in Bristol, he studied at the Bradford Civic Theatre School and began in repertory theatre. He was a founding member of the English Stage Company at the Royal Court Theatre and of the National Theatre. In the mid-70s his career faltered through his heavy drinking, but he made a triumphant return at the Royal Shakespeare Company in the 90s as Falstaff and King Lear. Married four times: his third wife was actress Maggie Smith and his fourth actress Patricia Quinn. He was romantically involved with actresses Margaret Leighton and Tammy Grimes and writer Lady Antonia Fraser. He was knighted in 1992. His film career began when he signed a three-year contract with Twentieth Century-Fox ('the most terrible mistake') and came unstuck while he played the title role in Billy Wilder's *The Private Life of Sherlock Holmes*, an experience that led him to attempt suicide. He later replaced Peter Finch to play opposite Elizabeth Taylor in the film of *A Little Night Music*, but was fired during rehearsals by director Harold Prince. After Taylor claimed that the 'chemistry' wasn't right between them, he replied, 'Chemistry? Chemistry? We're actors, not bloody pharmacists.'
Autobiography: 1995, *Knight Errant* (with Michael Coveney).
Circle of Deception 60. Pirates of Tortuga (US) 61. A Taste of Honey 61. The Inspector 62. Cleopatra 62. The Small World of Sammy Lee 63. Morgan 66. Romeo and Juliet 68. The Prime of Miss Jean Brodie 69. *The Private Life of Sherlock Holmes* 69. The Asphyx 72. Travels with My Aunt 73. Luther 73. QB VII (TV) 73. Holocaust (TV) 78. The Shout 78. Fortunes of War (TV) 87. War and Remembrance (TV) 87. High Season 87. Testimony 87. Henry V 89. Wings of Fame 90. The Pope Must Die/The Pope Must Diet 91. Afraid of the Dark 91. Adam Bede (TV) 91. Searching for Bobby Fischer/Innocent Moves 93. Century 93. The Secret Rapture 93. England, My England (as John Dryden) (TV) 95, etc.
❝ One reason I've never chased after films is that once you become a film star, you really can't stop, because you have to be before the public's eye all the time. I wouldn't care for that. Also, in films the material can't be that good all the time. You have to make mostly bad films, or films that aren't frightfully good. That wouldn't interest me – not that I've ever been offered the opportunity. – *R.S.*
Film acting is difficult to do properly. I remember I once said to George Cukor that I think it's as difficult to be Spencer Tracy as it is to be Laurence Olivier. He said, wrong, it's much more difficult to be Spencer Tracy. – *R.S.*

Stephens, Toby (1969–).
English actor, the son of actors Robert Stephens and Maggie Smith, who made his reputation acting with the Royal Shakespeare Company in the mid-90s.
Orlando 92. The Camomile Lawn (TV) 92. Twelfth Night 96. The Tenant of Wildfell Hall (TV) 96. Sunset Heights 97. Photographing Fairies 97. Cousin Bette 98, etc.

Stephenson, Henry (1871–1956) (H. S. Garroway).
British stage actor who came to Hollywood films in his 60s and remained to play scores of kindly old men.
■ The Spreading Dawn 17. The Black Panther's Cub 21. Men and Women 25. Wild Wild Susan 25. *Cynara* 32. Red Headed Woman 32. Guilty as Hell 32. A Bill of Divorcement 32. The Animal Kingdom 32. Little Women 33. Queen Christina 33. Tomorrow at Seven 33. Double Harness 33. My Lips Betray 33. If I Were Free 33. Blind Adventure 33. Man of Two Worlds 34. The Richest Girl in the World 34. Thirty Day Princess 34. Stingaree 34. The Mystery of Mr X 34. What Every Woman Knows 34. One More River 34. Outcast Lady 34. She Loves Me Not 34. All Men Are Enemies 34. Mutiny on the Bounty 35. Vanessa, Her Love Story 35. Reckless 35. The Flame Within 35. O'Shaughnessy's Boy 35. The Night Is Young 35. Rendezvous 35. The Perfect Gentleman 35. Captain Blood 35. Beloved Enemy 36. Half Angel 36. Hearts Divided 36. Give Me Your Heart 36. Walking on Air 36. Little Lord Fauntleroy 36. *The Charge of the Light Brigade* 36. When You're in Love 37. The Prince and the Pauper 37. The Emperor's Candlesticks 37. Conquest 37. Wise Girl 37. *The Young in Heart* 38. The Baroness and the Butler 38. Suez 38. Marie Antoinette 38. Dramatic School 38. Tarzan Finds a Son 39. The Private Lives of Elizabeth and Essex 39. The Adventures of Sherlock Holmes 39. It's a Date 40. Little Old New York 40. Spring Parade 40. Down Argentine Way 41. The Man Who Lost Himself 41. The Lady from Louisiana 41. This Above All 42. Rings on Her Fingers 42. Half Way to Shanghai 42. Mr Lucky 43. *Mantrap* 43. The Hour Before the Dawn 44. Secrets of Scotland Yard 44. The Reckless Age 44. Two Girls and a Sailor 44. Tarzan and the Amazons 45. The Green Years 46. Her Sister's Secret 46. The Locket 46. Heartbeat 46. Night and Day 46. Of Human Bondage 46. The Return of Monte Cristo 46. Dark Delusion 47. The Homestretch 47. Time Out of Mind 47. Ivy 47. Song of Love 47. Julia Misbehaves 48. Enchantment 48. *Oliver Twist* (as Mr Brownlow) 48. Challenge to Lassie 48.

Stephenson, James (1888–1941).
Suave British-born stage actor, in Hollywood from 1938.
When Were You Born? (debut) 38. Boy Meets Girl 38. Confessions of a Nazi Spy 38. Beau Geste 39. Calling Philo Vance 40. The Sea Hawk 40. *The Letter* (AAN) 40. Shining Victory 41. International Squadron 41, etc.

Stephenson, Pamela (1951–).
New Zealand leading lady who has done a variety of light work on British stage and TV (especially *Not the Nine o'Clock News*).
History of the World Part One 81. Scandalous 83. Superman III 83. Bloodbath at the House of Death 83. Finders Keepers 84. Les Patterson Saves the World 87, etc.

Steppat, Ilse (1917–1969).
German character actress.
Marriage in the Shadow 47. The Bridge 51. The Confessions of Felix Krull 62. On Her Majesty's Secret Service 69, etc.

Sterling, Ford (1883–1939) (George F. Stitch).
American comic actor, a leading Keystone Kop and slapstick heavy.
Drums of the Desert 26. Gentlemen Prefer Blondes 28. Kismet 30. Alice in Wonderland 33. The Black Sheep 35, etc.

Sterling, Jan (1923–) (Jane Sterling Adriance).
Blonde American leading lady with slight stage experience.
Johnny Belinda 48. Rhubarb 51. *Ace in the Hole* 51. Split Second 52. Pony Express 53. Alaska Seas 54. The High and the Mighty (AAN) 54. Women's Prison 55. The Female on the Beach 55. 1984 56. The Harder They Fall 56. Kathy O 58. Love in a Goldfish Bowl 61. Having Babies (TV) 76. Backstairs at the White House (TV) 79. First Monday in October 81, etc.
Famous line (*Ace in the Hole*): 'I don't go to church. Kneeling bags my nylons.'
Famous line (*Ace in the Hole*): 'I've met some hard-boiled eggs in my time, but you – you're twenty minutes!'

Sterling, Robert (1917–) (William John Hart).
American leading man of the 40s, mainly in second features. Married actresses Ann Sothern and Anne Jeffreys.
Only Angels Have Wings 39. I'll Wait for You 41. Somewhere I'll Find You 42. The Secret Heart 46. Bunco Squad 48. Roughshod 50. Thunder in the Dust 51. Column South 53. Return to Peyton Place 61. Voyage to the Bottom of the Sea 62, etc.
TV series: Topper 53–54. Love That Jill 58. Ichabod and Me 61–62.

Stern, Daniel (1957–).
American leading actor and director.
Breaking Away 79. Starting Over 79. Stardust Memories 80. One Trick Pony 80. Diner 82. Blue Thunder 83. C.H.U.D. 84. Frankenweenie 84. Key Exchange 85. Hannah and Her Sisters 86. D.O.A. 88. The Milagro Beanfield War 88. Friends, Lovers and Lunatics 89. Leviathan 89. Little Monsters 89. My Blue Heaven 90. Home Alone 90. City Slickers 91. Home Alone 2: Lost in New York 92. Rookie of the Year (& d) 93. City Slickers II: The Legend of Curly's Gold 94. Bushwhacked 95. Celtic Pride 96. Very Bad Things 98, etc.
TV series: Hometown 85. The Wonder Years (voice) 88– .

Sternhagen, Frances (1930–).
American actress, from stage and television.
Up the Down Staircase 67. The Tiger Makes Out 67. The Hospital 71. Fedora 78. Starting Over 79. Outland 81. Prototype (TV) 83. Romantic Comedy 83. Bright Lights, Big City 88. Communion 89. See You in the Morning 89. Sibling Rivalry 90. Misery 90. Doc Hollywood 91. Raising Cain 92, etc.
TV series: Spencer 84–85. Stephen King's Golden Years 91.

Stevenin, Jean-François (1944–).
French leading actor and occasional director, associated with the films of François TRUFFAUT and other directors of the New Wave.
Wild Child 70. Day for Night 73. Si Je Cherche, Je Me Trouve 74. Small Change 76. Barocco 76. Merry-Go-Round 78. Le Passe Montagne (& d) 79. The Dogs of War (GB) 80. Neige 81. Passion 82. Le Pont du Nord 82. Notre Histoire 84. Tenue de Soirée 86. Double Messieurs (& p, wd) 86. Lune Froide 89. Olivier, Olivier 91. 23:58 93. Les Patriotes 93. Fast 95. Noir comme le Souvenir 95. À Vendre 98, etc.

Stevens, Andrew (1955–).
American actor, producer and director, latterly of direct-to-video thrillers. Born in Memphis, Tennessee, he is the son of actress Stella STEVENS.
Shampoo 75. Massacre at Central High 76. Day of the Animals 77. Secrets 77. The Boys in Company C 78. The Fury 78. Topper (TV) 79. Death Hunt 81. Forbidden Love (TV) 82. Ten to Midnight 83. Hollywood Wives (TV) 85. Tusks (GB) 87. The Ranch 88. The Terror Within 89. Night Eyes 90. Night Eyes 2 91. Munchie 92. The Terror Within II (& d) 92. Night Eyes 3 (& d) 93. Scorned (& d) 93. Body Chemistry 4 95. Virtual Combat (d only) 95. Grid Runners (d only) 95. Scorned 2 96. Crash Dive (d only) 96. The Corporation (& d) (TV) 96, etc.
TV series: The Oregon Trail 77. Code Red 81–82. Emerald Point NAS 83–84.

Stevens, Connie (1938–) (Concetta Ingolia).
American leading lady with mixed Italian, English, Irish and Mohican blood. She was formerly married to singer Eddie Fisher.
Eighteen and Anxious 57. Rockabye Baby 58. Parrish 61. Susan Slade 61. Two on a Guillotine 64. Never Too Late 65. Mr Jericho (TV) 70. The Grissom Gang 71. The Sex Symbol (TV) 73. Scorchy 76. Back to the Beach 87. Tapeheads 89. Love Is All There Is 96, etc.
TV series: Hawaiian Eye 59–62.

Stevens, Craig (1918–) (Gail Shekles).
American leading man, married to Alexis Smith.
Affectionately Yours 41. Since You Went Away 43. The Lady Takes a Sailor 47. The French Line 54. Abbott and Costello Meet Dr Jekyll and Mr Hyde 55. Gunn 66. The Limbo Line 68. The Snoop Sisters (TV) 72. Rich Man Poor Man (TV) 76. S.O.B. 81, etc.
TV series: *Peter Gunn* 58–60. Man of the World 62. Mr Broadway 64.

Stevens, Fisher (1963–) (Steven Fisher).
American actor of stage, screen and television, born in Chicago, Illinois.
The Burning 81. Baby It's You 83. The Brother from Another Planet 84. The Flamingo Kid 84. My Science Project 85. Short Circuit 86. Short Circuit 2 88. Bloodhounds of Broadway 89. Reversal of Fortune 90. The Marrying Kind 91. Bob Roberts 92. Super Mario Bros 93. Nina Takes a Lover 94. Only You 94. Hackers 95. Cold Fever 95. The Pompatus of Love 96, etc.

Stevens, George (1904–1975).
American director, in Hollywood from 1923. In the late 30s and early 40s he made smooth and lively entertainments, but his infrequent later productions tended towards elephantiasis.
■ The Cohens and Kellys in Trouble 33. Bachelor Bait 34. Kentucky Kernels 34. Laddie 34. The Nitwits 34. Alice Adams 34. Annie Oakley 35. Swing Time 36. A Damsel in Distress 37. *Quality Street* 37. Vivacious Lady 38. *Gunga Din* 39. Vigil in the Night 40. Penny Serenade 40. *Woman of the Year* 41. *Talk of the Town* 42. *The More the Merrier* (AAN) 43. *I Remember Mama* 47. *A Place in the Sun* (AA) 51. Something to Live For 52. *Shane* (AAN) 53. *Giant* (AA) 56. The Diary of Anne Frank (AAN) 59. The Greatest Story Ever Told 65. The Only Game in Town 69.
“ He was a minor director with major virtues before *A Place in the Sun*, and a major director with minor virtues after. – *Andrew Sarris, 1968*

Stevens, George, Jnr (1932–).
American producer, son of George Stevens, who in 1977 became head of the American Film Institute.

Stevens, Inger (1935–1970) (Inger Stensland).
Pert and pretty Swedish leading lady, in America from childhood. Died of a drug overdose.
Man on Fire (film debut) 57. Cry Terror 58. The World, the Flesh and the Devil 58. The Buccaneer 59. The New Interns 64. *A Guide for the Married Man* 67. Firecreek 67. Madigan 68. Five Card Stud 68. Hang 'Em High 68. House of Cards 68. The Borgia Stick (TV) 68. A Dream of Kings 69. Run Simon Run (TV) 70, etc.
TV series: *The Farmer's Daughter* 63–65.

Stevens, K. T. (1919–1994) (Gloria Wood).
American leading lady of a few 40s films; daughter of director Sam Wood.
Kitty Foyle 40. The Great Man's Lady 41. Address Unknown 44. Vice Squad 53. Tumbleweed 53. Missile to the Moon 58, etc.

Stevens, Leith (1909–1970).
American musical arranger and composer.
The Wild One 52. Julie 56. The Five Pennies 59. A New Kind of Love 63, many others for Fox and Paramount, including TV series.

Stevens, Leslie (1924–).
American screenwriter.
The Left-Handed Gun 58. Private Property (& p, d) 59. The Marriage-Go-Round (from his play) 60. Hero's Island (& p, d) 62. Buck Rogers 79. Sheena (story) 84. Three Kinds of Heat (w, d) 87, etc.
TV series as creator-producer-director: Stony Burke. The Outer Limits. Battlestar Galactica.

Stevens, Mark (1915–1994) (aka Stephen Richards).
American leading man with varied early experience; usually in routine roles.
Objective Burma 45. *From This Day Forward* 45. The Dark Corner 46. I Wonder Who's Kissing Her Now 47. The Snake Pit 48. The Street with No Name 48. Sand 49. Mutiny 53. Cry Vengeance (also pd) 54. Timetable (also pd) 55. September Storm 60. Fate is the Hunter 64. Frozen Alive 66. Sunscorched 66.
TV series: Big Town 52–57.

Stevens, Onslow (1902–1977) (Onslow Ford Stevenson).
American stage actor occasionally seen in film character roles. Son of Houseley Stevenson. He was murdered.
Heroes of the West (debut) 32. Counsellor at Law 33. The Three Musketeers 36. Under Two Flags 36. When Tomorrow Comes 39. Mystery Sea Raider 40. *House of Dracula* 45. O.S.S. 46. Night Has a Thousand Eyes 48. The Creeper 48. State Penitentiary 50. Them 54. Tarawa Beachhead 58. All the Fine Young Cannibals 60. Geronimo's Revenge 63, etc.

Stevens, Rise (1913–).
American opera singer, seen in a few films.
■ The Chocolate Soldier 41. Going My Way 44. Carnegie Hall 47.

Stevens, Robert (c. 1925–1989).
American director, from TV.
■ The Big Caper 57. Never Love a Stranger 58. I Thank a Fool 62. In the Cool of the Day 63. Change of Mind 69.

Stevens, Ronnie (1925–).
British comic actor with stage and TV experience.
Made in Heaven 52. An Alligator Named Daisy 55. I Was Monty's Double 58. I'm All Right, Jack 59. Dentist in the Chair 60. San Ferry Ann 65. Give a Dog a Bone 66. Some Girls Do 68. Morons from Outer Space 85. The Parent Trap 98, etc.

Stevens, Stella (1936–) (Estelle Eggleston).
American leading lady, mother of actor Andrew STEVENS.
Say One for Me (debut) 58. Li'l Abner 59. Too Late Blues 61. The Courtship of Eddie's Father 63. The Nutty Professor 63. Synanon 65. The Secret of My Success 65. The Silencers 66. How to Save a Marriage 67. The Mad Room 69. The Ballad of Cable Hogue 70. A Town Called Bastard 71. Stand Up and Be Counted 71. The Poseidon Adventure 72. Arnold 74. Cleopatra Jones and the Casino of Gold 74. Las Vegas Lady 74. Nickelodeon 76. The Night They Took Miss Beautiful (TV) 77. Cruise into Terror (TV) 78. The Manitou 78. The Terror Within II 91. Exiled 91. Mom 91. South Beach 92. The Night Caller 92. Molly & Gina 94. In Cold Blood (TV) 96. The Corporation 96, etc.
TV series: Ben Casey 65. Flamingo Road 80–81.

Stevens, Warren (1919–).
American general-purpose actor.
The Frogmen 51. The Barefoot Contessa 54. Forbidden Planet 56. Hot Spell 58. No Name on the Bullet 59. Forty Pounds of Trouble 62. An American Dream 66. Madigan 68. The Sweet Ride 68. Stroker Ace 83. Stormy Nights 96, many others.
TV series: 77th Bengal Lancers 56–57. The Richard Boone Show 63–64. Bracken's World (voice) 69–70. Behind the Screen 81–82.

Stevenson, Edward (1906–1968).
American costume designer, in Hollywood from 1922. He was chief designer at RKO from 1936–49. From the mid-50s he designed Lucille Ball's costumes for her TV series *I Love Lucy*.
The Joy of Living 38. They Knew What They Wanted 40. Citizen Kane 41. The Magnificent Ambersons 42. Journey into Fear 42, etc.

Stevenson, Houseley (1879–1953).
American character actor, latterly familiar as a gaunt, usually unshaven, old man.
Native Land 42. Somewhere in the Night 46. Dark Passage 47. Casbah 48. Moonrise 49. All the King's Men 49. The Sun Sets at Dawn 51. The Wild North 52, etc.

Stevenson, Juliet (1956–) (Juliet Stevens).
British leading actress, from classical theatre.
Drowning by Numbers 88. Ladder of Swords 88. Truly Madly Deeply 91. The Trial 93. The Secret Rapture 93. The Politician's Wife (TV) 95. Emma 96. Cider with Rosie (TV) 98, etc.
“ I'm hardly Hollywood material – they're interested in youth and perfection and I lay no claims to either. It's not a place that's particularly interested in talent. – *J.S.*

Stevenson, Robert (1905–1986).
British director, in Hollywood from 1939.
■ Happy Ever After 32. Falling for You 33. Tudor Rose 36. The Man Who Changed His Mind 36. Jack of all Trades 37. *King Solomon's Mines* 37. Non Stop New York 37. Owd Bob 38. The Ware Case 39. Young Man's Fancy 40. *Tom Brown's Schooldays* 40. *Back Street* 41. Joan of Paris 43. Forever and a Day (co-d) 43. *Jane Eyre* 43. Dishonored Lady 47. *To the Ends of the Earth* 48. The Woman on Pier 13 49. Walk Softly Stranger 50. My Forbidden Past 51. The Las Vegas Story 52. Johnny Tremain 57. Old Yeller 57. Darby O'Gill and the Little People 59. Kidnapped 60. The Absent-Minded Professor 61. In Search of the Castaways 62. Son of Flubber 63. The Misadventures of Merlin Jones 64. *Mary Poppins* (AAN) 64. The Monkey's Uncle 65. That Darn Cat 65. The Gnome-Mobile 67. Blackbeard's Ghost 67. The Love Bug 69. My Dog the Thief 70. Bedknobs and Broomsticks 71. Herbie Rides Again 73. The Island at the Top of the World 74. One of Our Dinosaurs Is Missing 75. The Shaggy D.A. 77.

Stevenson, Robert Louis (1850–1894).
British novelist and short-story writer. Works filmed include *Dr Jekyll and Mr Hyde* (many versions), *Treasure Island* (many versions), *The Body Snatcher*, *The Suicide Club*, *Kidnapped*, *The Master of Ballantrae*, *Ebb Tide*, *The Wrong Box*.

Steward, Ernest (–1990).
British cinematographer.
Appointment with Venus 51. Trouble in Store 53. Doctor in the House 54. Simon and Laura 55. Above Us the Waves 55. Doctor at Sea 55. The Secret Place 57. A Tale of Two Cities 58. The Wind Cannot Read 58. No Love for Johnnie 61. A Pair of Briefs 61. Crooks Anonymous 62. The Wild and the Willing 62. The Face of Fu Manchu 65. Circus of Fear 66. Doctor in Clover 66. Carry On Up the Khyber 68. Carry On Again Doctor 69. Carry On Camping 69. Carry On at Your Convenience 71. Percy 71. Steptoe and Son Ride Again 73. Callan 74. Carry On Dick 74. Carry On Behind 75. Hennessy 75. Carry On England 76. The Wild Cats of St Trinian's 80, etc.

Stewart, Alexandra (1939–).
Canadian leading lady who has filmed mainly in Europe.
Exodus 60. Le Feu Follet 63. Dragées au Poivre 65. Maroc 7 67. The Bride Wore Black 67. The Man Who Had Power Over Women 70. Day for Night 73. Marseilles Contract 74. In Praise of Older Women 78. Phobia 80. Chanel Solitaire 81. Your Ticket Is No Longer Valid 84. Kemek 88. Seven Servants (Ger.) 96, etc.

Stewart, Anita (1895–1961) (Anna May Stewart).
American silent screen leading lady.
A Million Bid 13. The Goddess 15. Mary Regan 19. Her Kingdom of Dreams 20. Never the Twain Shall Meet 25. Sisters of Eve 28, many others.

Stewart, Athole (1879–1940).
British stage character actor.
The Speckled Band 31. The Clairvoyant 34. Dusty Ermine 37. The Spy in Black 39. Tilly of Bloomsbury 40, etc.

Stewart, Donald.
American screenwriter.
Jackson County Jail 76. Deathsport 78. Missing (AA) 82. The Hunt for Red October 90. Patriot Games (co-w) 93. Clear and Present Danger (co-w) 94, etc.

Stewart, Donald Ogden (1894–1980).
American playwright and screenwriter.
Autobiography: 1974, *By a Stroke of Luck*.
■ Brown of Harvard 26. Laughter 30. Finn and Hattie (oa) 30. Rebound (oa) 31. Tarnished Lady (& oa) 31. Smilin' Through 32. The White Sister 33. Another Language 33. Dinner at Eight 33. The Barretts of Wimpole Street 34. No More Ladies 35. *The Prisoner of Zenda* 37. Holiday 38. Marie Antoinette 38. Love Affair 39. The Night of Nights 39. Kitty Foyle 40. *The Philadelphia Story* (AA) 40. That Uncertain Feeling 41. A Woman's Face 41. Smilin' Through 41. Tales of Manhattan 42. Without Love 45. Life with Father 47. Cass Timberlane 47. Edward My Son 49. Escapade 55. Moment of Danger 60.
NB: Some of the above were in collaboration with other writers.

Stewart, Elaine (1929–) (Elsy Steinberg).
American leading lady of a few 50s films; former usherette.
Sailor Beware 51. The Bad and the Beautiful 52. Young Bess 53. Brigadoon 54. The Tattered Dress 56. The Adventures of Hajji Baba 57. The Rise and Fall of Legs Diamond 60. The Most Dangerous Man Alive 61. The Seven Revenges 63, etc.

Stewart, Hugh (1910–).
British producer, former editor.
Trottie True 49. The Long Memory 52. Man of the Moment 55 (and all subsequent Norman Wisdom comedies). The Intelligence Men 65, etc.

Stewart, James (1908–1997).
American leading actor of inimitable slow drawl and gangly walk; portrayed slow-speaking, honest heroes for thirty-five years.
Biographies: 1984, *James Stewart* by Allen Eyles; 1994, *James Stewart: Leading Man* by Jonathan Coe; 1997, *James Stewart* by Donald Dewey; 1998, *Pieces of Time: The Life of James Stewart* by Gary Fishgall and Lisa Drew; 1998, *A Wonderful Life: The Films and Career of James Stewart* by Tony Thomas.
■ Murder Man 35. Rose Marie 36. Next Time We Love 36. Wife versus Secretary 36. Small Town Girl 36. Speed 36. The Gorgeous Hussy 36. Born to Dance 36. After the Thin Man 36. *Seventh Heaven* 37. The Last Gangster 37. Navy Blue and Gold 37. Of Human Hearts 38. Vivacious Lady 38. Shopworn Angel 38. *You Can't Take It with You* 38. Made for Each Other 38. Ice Follies of 1939. It's a Wonderful World 39. *Mr Smith Goes to Washington* (AAN) 39. *Destry Rides Again* 39. *The Shop around the Corner* 40. The Mortal Storm 40. No Time for Comedy 40. *The Philadelphia Story* (AA) 40. Come Live with Me 40. Pot O' Gold 41. Ziegfeld Girl 41; war service; *It's a Wonderful Life* (AAN) 46. Magic Town 46. *Call Northside 777* 47. On Our Merry Way 48. Rope 48. You Gotta Stay Happy 48. The Stratton Story 49. Malaya 49. *Winchester 73* 50. *Broken Arrow* 50. The Jackpot 50. *Harvey* (AAN) 50. No Highway (GB) 51. The Greatest Show on Earth 51. Bend of the River 52. Carbine Williams 52. The Naked Spur 53. Thunder Bay 53. *The Glenn Miller Story* 53. *Rear Window* 54. The Far Country 54. Strategic Air Command 55. *The Man from Laramie* 55. The Man Who Knew Too Much 56. The Spirit of St Louis 57. Night Passage 57. Vertigo 58. Bell, Book and Candle 58. *Anatomy of a Murder* (AAN) 59. The FBI Story 59. The Mountain Road 60. Two Rode Together 61. The Man Who Shot Liberty Valance 62. *Mr Hobbs Takes a Vacation* 62. How the West Was Won 62. Take Her She's Mine 63. Cheyenne Autumn 64. Dear Brigitte 65. *Shenandoah* 65. The Flight of the Phoenix 65. The Rare Breed 66. Firecreek 67. Bandolero 68. The Cheyenne Social Club 70. Fool's Parade 71. The Shootist 76. The Big Sleep 77. Airport 77 77. The Magic of Lassie 78. Right of Way (TV) 83. North and South II (TV) 86. An American Tail: Fievel Goes West (voice) 91.
TV series: The Jimmy Stewart Show 71. Hawkins on Murder 73.
✪ For becoming one of everybody's family even when playing a tough westerner. *The Philadelphia Story*.
❝ I don't act. I react. – *J.S.*
I'm the inarticulate man who tries. I don't really have all the answers, but for some reason, somehow, I make it. – *J.S.*
The big studios were an ideal way to make films – because they were a home base for people. When you were under contract, you had a chance to relax. – *J.S.*
If I had my career over again? Maybe I'd say to myself, speed it up a little. – *J.S.*
He has so many of his pictures being shown on the late show, he keeps more people up than Mexican food. – *Hal Kanter*
Famous line (*The Philadelphia Story*): 'The prettiest sight in this fine pretty world is the privileged class enjoying its privileges.'
Famous line (*Harvey*): 'I wrestled with reality for 35 years, doctor, and I'm happy. I finally won out over it.'
Famous line (*It's a Wonderful Life*): 'Well, you look about the kind of angel I'd get. Sort of a fallen angel, aren't you? What happened to your wings?
~ Special AA 1984 'for 50 years of meaningful performances, for his high ideals, both on and off the screen, with the respect and affection of his colleagues'.

Stewart, Martha (1922–) (Martha Haworth).
American actress and singer. Married comedian Joe E. Lewis (1946–48). She was played by Mitzi Gaynor in the biopic *The Joker Is Wild*.
Daisy Kenyon 47. Are You With It? 48. I Wonder Who's Kissing Her Now 47. In a Lonely Place 50. Aaron Crick from Punkin Crick 52. Surf Party 63, etc.

Stewart, Patrick (1940–).
Balding British leading actor, from classical theatre. He is now best known for his role as Captain Jean-Luc Picard in the TV series *Star Trek: The Next Generation* (1987–94).
Antony and Cleopatra 72. Hennessy 75. Hedda 75. Hamlet (TV) 79. Excalibur 81. Dune 84. Lifeforce 85. Lady Jane 86. Gunmen 93. Robin Hood: Men in Tights 93. The Pagemaster (voice) 94. Star Trek: Generations 94. Jeffrey 95. Star Trek: First Contact 96. The Canterville Ghost (TV) 96. Conspiracy Theory 97. Masterminds 97. Dad Savage 98. Moby Dick (TV) 98. Star Trek: Insurrection 98. Prince of Egypt (voice) 98, etc.
TV series: Maybury 81.

Stewart, Paul (1908–1986) (P. Sternberg).
American character actor, often in clipped, sinister roles.
Citizen Kane 41. Johnny Eager 42. Government Girl 44. *Champion* 49. *The Window* 49. Walk Softly Stranger 50. The Bad and the Beautiful 52. Prisoner of War 54. The Cobweb 55. King Creole 58. A Child Is Waiting 62. The Greatest Story Ever Told 65. In Cold Blood 67. The Day of the Locust 75. Bite the Bullet 75. W. C. Fields and Me 76. Opening Night 77. The Dain Curse (TV) 78. The Revenge of the Pink Panther 81. S.O.B. 81, many others.

Stewart, Sophie (1909–1977).
British stage and radio actress, in occasional films.
Maria Marten 35. As You Like It 36. The Return of the Scarlet Pimpernel 38. Nurse Edith Cavell 39. The Lamp Still Burns 43. Uncle Silas 47. Yangtse Incident 56, etc.

Stiers, David Ogden (1942–).
Tall, balding American comedy actor.
Drive He Said 70. Charlie's Angels (TV) 76. Oh God 77. The Cheap Detective 78. Magic 78. Better Off Dead 85. Another Woman 88. The Accidental Tourist 88. Doc Hollywood 91. Beauty and the Beast (voice) 91. Shadows and Fog 92. Iron Will 94. Bad Company 95. Mighty Aphrodite 95. Pocahontas (voice) 95. Steal Big, Steal Little 95. The Hunchback of Notre Dame (voice) 96. Everyone Says I Love You 96. Meet Wally Sparks 97. Krippendorf's Tribe 98. Pocahontas II: Journey to the New World (voice) 98, etc.
TV series: Doc 75–76. M*A*S*H 77–83.

Stigwood, Robert (1934–).
International impresario whose dominance of the pop-music field led him to produce *Saturday Night Fever* and *Grease*. In 1998, the *Sunday Times* estimated his fortune at £175m.

Stiller, Ben (1966–).
American actor and director, the son of television comedians and actors Jerry Stiller and Anne Meara.
Empire of the Sun (a) 87. Elvis Stories (a) 89. Reality Bites (a, d) 94. A Simple Plan (a, d) 95. If Lucy Fell 96. The Cable Guy (& d) 96. Happy Gilmore 96. Zero Effect 98. There's Something about Mary 98. Your Friends & Neighbors 98. Permanent Midnight 98, etc.
TV series: The Ben Stiller Show.

Stiller, Mauritz (1883–1928) (Mowscha Stiller).
Russian-Swedish director who went to Hollywood in the 20s with Garbo, but died shortly after.
Vampyren 12. *Sir Arne's Treasure* 19. Erotikon 20. *The Atonement of Gosta Berling* 24. The Blizzard (US) 26. Hotel Imperial 27. Street of Sin 28, etc.

Stillman, Whit (1952–).
American independent director, screenwriter and producer.
Metropolitan (AANw) 90. Barcelona 94. Last Days of Disco 98, etc.

Sting (1951–) (Gordon Sumner).
British musician and composer, founder-member of the rock band Police. In 1997, *Business Age* estimated his personal fortune at £97m.
Biography: 1998, *Sting: Demolition Man* by Christopher Sandford.
■ Quadrophenia 78. Radio On 79. The Secret Policeman's Other Ball 81. Brimstone and Treacle 82. Dune 84. The Bride 85. Plenty 85. Bring on the Night 86. Julia and Julia 87. Stormy Monday 88. The Adventures of Baron Munchausen 89. Resident Alien 90. The Grotesque 95. Lock, Stock and Two Smoking Barrels 98.

Stock, Nigel (1919–1986).
British character actor, former boy performer.
Lancashire Luck 38. Brighton Rock 46. Derby Day 51. The Dam Busters 55. Eye Witness 56. Victim 61. HMS Defiant 62. The Great Escape 63. The Lost Continent 68. The Lion in Winter 68. A Bequest to the Nation 73. Russian Roulette 75. A Man Called Intrepid (TV) (as Winston Churchill) 79, many others.
On TV he played Dr Watson in the 1965 *Sherlock Holmes* series.

Stockfeld, Betty (1905–1966).
Australian-born stage actress, in occasional films.
City of Song 30. The Impassive Footman 32. The Beloved Vagabond 36. Derrière la Façade (Fr.) 40. Flying Fortress 42. Edouard et Caroline (Fr.) 50. The Lovers of Lisbon 55. True As a Turtle 57, etc.

Stockwell, Dean (1935–).
American boy actor of the 40s, later leading man.
The Valley of Decision 45. Anchors Aweigh 45. Abbott and Costello in Hollywood 45. *The Green Years* 46. Home Sweet Homicide 46. The Mighty McGurk 47. The Arnelo Affair 47. Song of the Thin Man 47. The Romance of Rosy Ridge 47. Gentleman's Agreement 48. *The Boy with Green Hair* 48. Deep Waters 48. Down to the Sea in Ships 49. The Secret Garden 49. Stars in My Crown 50. The Happy Years 50. Kim 50. Cattle Drive 51. Gun for a Coward 57. The Careless Years 57. *Compulsion* 59. *Sons and Lovers* 60. Long Day's Journey into Night 62. Rapture 65. Psych-Out 68. The Dunwich Horror 70. Ecstasy 70. The Failing of Raymond (TV) 71. The Last Movie 71. The Loners 72. Another Day at the Races 73. Werewolf of Washington 73. Won Ton Ton 75. Win, Place or Steal 75. Tracks 77. Wrong Is Right 82. Human Highway 82. Paris, Texas 84. Dune 84. The Legend of Billie Jean 85. To Live and Die in L.A. 85. Blue Velvet 86. Gardens of Stone 87. The Gambler III: The Legend Continues (TV) 87. The Blue Iguana 88. Tucker: The Man and His Dream 88. Married to the Mob (AAN) 88. Limit Up 89. Backtrack/Catchfire 89. Son of the Morning Star (TV) 91. The Player 92. Chasers 94. Stephen King's The Langoliers (TV) 95. Mr Wrong 96. Twilight Man 96. Midnight Blue 96. Living in Peril 97. McHale's Navy 97. Air Force One 97, etc.
TV series: Quantum Leap 89–93.

Stockwell, Guy (1936–).
American leading actor. He is the brother of Dean Stockwell.
The War Lord 65. *Blindfold* 65. And Now Miguel 66. *Beau Geste* 66. The Plainsman 66. Tobruk 66. The King's Pirate 67. The Million Dollar Collar 67. In Enemy Country 68. The Gatling Gun 72. Airport 75 74. It's Alive 76. Grotesque 87. Santa Sangre 90, etc.
TV series: Adventures in Paradise 60. The Richard Boone Show 64.

Stoker, Bram (1847–1912).
Irish novelist, the creator of *Dracula*. Was also Henry Irving's manager.

Stokowski, Leopold (1882–1977) (Leopold Stokes or Boleslowowicz).
British-born orchestral conductor.
■ *One Hundred Men and a Girl* 37. The Big Broadcast of 1937 37. *Fantasia* 40. Carnegie Hall 47.

Stoler, Shirley (1929–1999).
Overweight American character actress, usually in unsympathetic roles and notable as the murderous nurse in *The Honeymoon Killers*.
The Honeymoon Killers 70. The Displaced Person 76. Seven Beauties 76. The Deer Hunter 78. Below the Belt 80. Splitz 84. Sticky Fingers 88. Miami Blues 90. Frankenhooker 90, etc.

Stoll, George (1905–1985).
American musical director, with MGM from 1945.
Anchors Aweigh (AA) 45. Neptune's Daughter 49. I Love Melvin 53. The Student Prince 54. Hit the Deck 55. Meet Me in Las Vegas 56, many others.

Stoloff, Ben (1895–1960).
American director. He began in comedy shorts, making his first feature for Fox in 1926.
The Canyon of Light 26. Fox Movietone Follies of 1930 30. Destry Rides Again 32. The Night Mayor 32. Palooka/The Great Schnozzle 34. Sea Devils 37. Radio City Revels 38. The Lady and the Mob 39. The Marines Fly High 40. Secret Enemies 42. Take It or Leave It 44. Johnny Comes Flying Home 46. It's a Joke, Son! 47, etc.

Stoloff, Morris (1894–1980).
American musical director, in Hollywood from 1936.
Lost Horizon 37. You Can't Take It with You 38. Cover Girl (AA) 44. A Song to Remember 45. The Jolson Story (AA) 46. The 5000 Fingers of Dr T 53. Picnic 55, many others.

Stoltz, Eric (1961–).
American leading actor.
The Grass Is Always Greener over the Septic Tank (TV) 78. Fast Times at Ridgemont High 82. Running Hot 84. The Wild Life 84. Code Name: Emerald 85. Mask 85. The New Kids 85. Lionheart 87. Sister, Sister 87. Some Kind of Wonderful 87. Haunted Summer 88. Manifesto 88. The Fly II 89. Say Anything 89. Memphis Belle 90. The Waterdance 92. Singles 92. Bodies, Rest and Motion (& p) 93. Foreign Affairs (TV) 93. Naked in New York 93. Killing Zoe 94. Pulp Fiction 94. Sleep with Me (& p) 94. Little Women 94. Rob Roy 95. God's Army 95. Kicking and Screaming 95. Inside 96. Grace of My Heart 96. Anaconda 97. Hi-Life 98, etc.

Stone, Andrew L. (1902–).
American producer-director (for a time with his wife Virginia) who made it a rule from the mid-40s not to shoot his melodramas in a studio, always on location, and with real trains, liners, airplanes, etc. Formed Andrew Stone Productions 1943.
The Great Victor Herbert 39. *Stormy Weather* (d only) 42. Hi Diddle Diddle 43. Sensations of 1945 45. Highway 301 51. The Steel Trap 52. The Night Holds Terror 54. Julie 56. *Cry Terror* 58. The Decks Ran Red 59. The Last Voyage 60. Ring of Fire 61. The Password Is Courage 62. Never Put It in Writing 64. The Secret of My Success 65. *Song of Norway* 69. *The Great Waltz* 72, etc.
❝ If the Stones had made *On the Beach*, none of us would be around now to review it. – *Andrew Sarris, 1968*

Stone, Dee Wallace (1948–) (aka Dee Wallace).
American actress who first made an impression as the mother in *E.T. – the Extraterrestrial*. She changed her name after marrying actor Christopher Stone.
The Stepford Wives 75. The Hills Have Eyes 77. 10 79. The Howling 80. E.T. – the Extraterrestrial 82. Jimmy the Kid 82. Cujo 83. Club Life 84. Secret Admirer 85. Critters 86. Shadow Play 86. Popcorn 91. Witness to the Execution (TV) 94. The Frighteners 96. Nevada 97. Black Circle Boys 97. Love's Deadly Triangle: The Texas Cadet Murder (TV) 97. Bad as I Wanna Be: The Dennis Rodman Story (TV) 98, etc.

Stone, George E. (1903–1967) (George Stein).
Short (5ft 3in) Polish-born character actor, who in Hollywood films played oppressed little men. Born in Lodz, he began as a child performer in vaudeville and silent films, first as an extra. He was best known as The Runt, the loquacious, dim-witted friend of Boston Blackie in the 'B' features of the 40s.
The Front Page 30. Little Caesar 30. Cimarron 31. Anthony Adverse 36. *The Housekeeper's Daughter* 38. His Girl Friday 40. The Boston Blackie series 41–9. Dancing in the Dark 50. The Robe 53. Guys and Dolls 55. The Man with the Golden Arm 56. Babyface Nelson 57. Some Like It Hot 59. Pocketful of Miracles 61, many others.

Stone, Harold J. (1911–).
American character actor.
The Harder They Fall 56. Garment Center 57. Man Afraid 57. Spartacus 60. The Chapman Report 62. The Man with X-Ray Eyes 63. Which Way to the Front? 70. Mitchell 75, etc.
TV series: My World and Welcome To It 68. Bridget Loves Bernie 74.

Stone, Irving (1903–1989).
American novelist whose *Lust for Life, The Agony and the Ecstasy* and *The President's Lady* were filmed.

Stone, Lewis (1879–1953).
Distinguished American stage actor, a leading man of silent films and later a respected character actor.
Honour's Altar (debut) 15. *The Prisoner of Zenda* 22. Scaramouche 23. *The Lost World* 24. The Patriot (AAN) 28. Madame X 30. The Mask of Fu Manchu 32. Mata Hari 32. Grand Hotel 33. Queen Christina 33. *David Copperfield* 34. *Treasure Island* 35. The Thirteenth Chair 37. *You're Only Young Once* 37. Judge Hardy's Children 38. Love Finds Andy Hardy 38. Out West with the Hardys 39 (and ten further episodes of this series, ending in 1947). Yellow Jack 39. The Bugle Sounds 41. Three Wise Fools 46. The State of the Union 48. Key to the City 50. Scaramouche 52. The Prisoner of Zenda 52. All the Brothers Were Valiant 53, many others.

Stone, Marianne (1923–).
British character actress, usually in bit parts. Innumerable appearances.
Angels One Five 51. The Pickwick Papers 54. The Runaway Bus 54. Yield to the Night 56. Heavens Above 63. Ladies Who Do 65. Here We Go Round the Mulberry Bush 67. The Wicked Lady 83, many others.

Stone, Matt (1971–).
American actor and writer, best known as the creator of the TV cartoon series *South Park* with Trey PARKER. Born in Houston, Texas.
Cannibal: The Musical 96. BASEketball 98. Orgazmo 98, etc.

Stone, Milburn (1904–1980).
American character actor, in Hollywood from the mid-30s; was in hundreds of low-budget action features, usually as villain or tough hero; more recently became famous as 'Doc' in the *Gunsmoke* TV series.
Ladies Crave Excitement 35. Port of Missing Girls 37. King of the Turf 39. Enemy Agent 40. The Phantom Cowboy 41. Rubber Racketeers 42. Sherlock Holmes Faces Death 43. Hat Check Honey 44. On Stage Everybody 45. Spider Woman Strikes Back 46. Train to Alcatraz 48. Snow Dog 50. The Sun Shines Bright 53. Black Tuesday 54. Drango 57, many others.

Stone, Oliver (1946–).
Combative American director, screenwriter and producer. Born in New York City, he studied film at New York University and began as a writer. His films tend to be controversial and bombastic in their re-examination of the events of America's recent past, particularly the experience of Vietnam, and how they have shaped present-day attitudes.
Biography: 1996, *Stone* by James Riordan.
Book: 1996, *The Films of Oliver Stone* by Don Kunz.
Seizure (wd) 74. The Hand (wd) 81. Midnight Express (AAw) 78. Scarface (w) 83. The Tear of the Dragon (co-w) 85. *Platoon* (wd) (AAd, AANw) 86. Salvador (wd) 86. Wall Street (wd) 87. Talk Radio (wd) 88. *Born on the Fourth of July* (wd) (AAd, AANw) 89. The Doors (wd) 91. *JFK* (wd) (AANd, AANw) 91. Heaven and Earth (wd) 93. The New Age (p) 93. Natural Born Killers (co-w, d) 94. *Nixon* (co-w, d) (AANw) 95. U-Turn 97, etc.
❝ The film business? I love film, but the film business is shit. – O.S.
I think you are really acknowledging the Vietnam veteran, and for the first time you really understand what happened out there. – O.S. *(receiving his award for Platoon)*
I do my films to take me out of where I am. The questions the movies ask – those are the questions I'm asking myself at that point in time. – O.S.
Anybody who's been through a divorce will tell you that at one point in their life they've thought of murder. No one's innocent. – O.S.
If it sometimes seems that all Hollywood is striving for the Op-Ed-page prominence that Stone has so quickly achieved, he is not necessarily the representative it would have picked. For the off-camera Stone is given to tirades and bad language, to strenuous womanizing and long, intoxicated journeys into the night. – *Stephen Schiff, New Yorker*
A Saturday night with Oliver after a long week is basically pagan Rome, 26 A.D. – *Robert Downey Jnr*

Stone, Peter (1930–) (aka Pierre Marton).
American screenwriter.
■ *Charade* 63. Father Goose 64. *Mirage* 65. Arabesque 66. The Secret War of Harry Frigg 68. The Mercenaries (as Quentin Werty) 68. Sweet Charity 69. Skin Game 71. 1776 (from his own stage musical) 72. The Taking of Pelham 123 74. Silver Bears 77. Someone Is Killing the Great Chefs of Europe 78. Why Would I Lie? 80.

Stone, Sharon (1957–).
American leading actress in sexy roles, a former model who became a star after baring all in *Basic Instinct*, with its notorious crotch shot. With *Casino*, she received critical plaudits as well. Her current asking price: around $10m a movie (less if working for Scorsese).
Biographies: 1994, *Sharon Stone: Basic Ambition* by Douglas Thompson; 1997, *The Sharon Stone Story* by Michael Munn.
Deadly Blessing 81. The Vegas Strip Wars (TV) 84. Irreconcilable Differences 84. King Solomon's Mines 85. Allan Quatermain and the Lost City of Gold 86. Cold Steel 87. Above the Law 88. Action Jackson 88. Beyond the Stars 89. Scissors 90. Total Recall 90. Year of the Gun 91. He Said, She Said 91. Where Sleeping Dogs Lie 91. Basic Instinct 92. Diary of a Hit Man 92. Sliver 93. Intersection 94. The Specialist 94. The Quick and the Dead 95. *Casino* (AAN) 95. Diabolique 96. Last Dance 96. Sphere 97. Antz (voice) 98. The Mighty 98. The Muse 99, etc.
TV series: Bay City Blues 83.
❝ I've been at this so long that I knew everyone in the business long before I became famous, and I didn't have value to many of them. Now, suddenly, the people who were coarse and rude to me before treat me as though we've never met, and now I'm fabulous, they're fabulous and isn't it fabulous we're chatting. – S.S.
In this business there is Plan A, in which you become successful by living and acting with a lot of integrity. Then there's Plan B, where you sell your soul to the devil. I still find it hard to distinguish one from the other. – S.S.
I've really given up my life to God, and I know that's why I'm OK and at peace. I've never had a conflict when I'm praying on a set. – S.S.
She is incredibly stylish and sophisticated in a somewhat self-conscious way, as if she has watched a catalogue of Grace Kelly movies a little too closely. – *Richard E. Grant*
When I suggest that Ireland is also a country of depressed and brooding writers, she is prompted to gush about one of her favorite 'Irish' authors. 'I have to say, Dylan Thomas just cuts me to the bone!' – *Lloyd Grove, Vanity Fair*

The Stooges.
A trio of American knockabout comics specializing in a peculiarly violent form of slapstick. They originally went from vaudeville to Hollywood with Ted Healy (as Ted Healy and his Stooges) but broke away to become world-famous in hundreds of two-reelers throughout the 30s, 40s and 50s. The original trio were *Larry Fine* (1911–1975), *Moe Howard* (1895–1975) and his brother *Jerry (Curly) Howard* (1906–1952). In 1947 Curly was replaced by yet another brother, *Shemp Howard (Samuel Howard)* (1891–1955). On Shemp's death he was replaced by *Joe Besser*, who in 1959 was replaced by *Joe de Rita* (1910–1993). Towards the end of their popularity the Stooges appeared in a few features. Although during their career the rights to the Three Stooges were vested in Moe Howard, a court hearing in 1996 decided that the rights were now owned by the heirs of Larry Fine and Joe de Rita. As a result, there were plans for Columbia to make a feature film on the trio's lives.
Stop Look and Laugh 61. Snow White and the Three Stooges 61. The Three Stooges Meet Hercules 63. The Outlaws Is Coming 64. The Three Stooges Go around the World in a Daze 65, etc.

Stoppa, Paolo (1906–1988).
Italian character actor, in films from 1932.
La Beauté du Diable 49. Miracle in Milan 50. The Seven Deadly Sins 52. Love Soldiers and Women 55. La Loi 59. The Leopard 63. Becket 64. After the Fox 66. Once upon a Time in the West 67, etc.

Stoppard, Sir Tom (1937–) (Thomas Strausler).
Czechoslovakian-born playwright and occasional screenwriter, in England. Born in Zlin, he arrived in England via Singapore in the mid-40s and worked as a journalist until the early 60s, when he began writing plays for radio and television. His *Rosencrantz and Guildenstern Are Dead* in the mid-60s brought him theatrical success, as did later plays produced at the National Theatre and the Royal Shakespeare Company, notable for their verbal wit, wordplay and teasing of theatrical conventions. His screenwriting has been less original. He was knighted in 1997.
Despair 78. The Human Factor 79. Brazil (AAN) 85. Empire of the Sun 87. Rosencrantz and Guildenstern Are Dead (wd) 90. The Russia House (w) 90. Billy Bathgate (w) 91. Poodle Springs (w) (TV) 98. Shakespeare in Love (w) 98, etc.

Storaro, Vittorio (1946–).
Italian cinematographer.
The Spider's Stratagem 70. The Conformist 71. Last Tango in Paris 72. 1900 77. Agatha 79. *Apocalypse Now* (AA) 79. *Reds* (AA) 81. One from the Heart 82. Ladyhawke 85. Ishtar 87. *The Last Emperor* (AA) 87. Tucker: The Man and His Dream 88. New York Stories 89. Dick Tracy 90. *The Sheltering Sky* 90. Little Buddha 93. Taxi (Sp.) 96. Bulworth (US) 98, etc.

Storch, Larry (1923–).
American comic actor.
Captain Newman MD 63. Wild and Wonderful 64. The Monitors 69. The Couple Takes a Wife (TV) 72. The Adventures of Huckleberry Finn (TV) 78. Better Late than Never 79. S.O.B. 81. Adventures beyond Belief 87, etc.
TV series: F Troop.

Storck, Henri (1907–).
Belgian documentarist.
Pour Vos Beaux Yeux 29. The Story of the Unknown Soldier 32. Symphonie Paysanne 42. Au Carrefour de la Vie 49. Les Belges de la Mer 54. Les Gestes du Silence 61. Le Musée Vivant 65, etc.

Storm, Gale (1922–) (Josephine Cottle).
American leading lady of the 40s.
Autobiography: 1981, *I Ain't Down Yet.*
Tom Brown's Schooldays 40. Foreign Agent 42. Nearly Eighteen 43. The Right to Live 45. Sunbonnet Sue 46. It Happened on Fifth Avenue 47. Abandoned 49. Underworld Story 50. The Texas Rangers 51. Woman of the North 53, etc.
TV series: My Little Margie 52–54. The Gale Storm Show 56–59.

Stormare, Peter (1953–).
Swedish actor, from the theatre, where he also works as a director and playwright, notably for the National Theatre of Sweden. Now based in America.
Fanny and Alexander 82. Awakenings 90. Damage 92. *Fargo* (as Gaer Grimsrud) 96. The Lost World: Jurassic Park 97. Playing God 97. The Big Lebowski 98. Hamilton 98. Armageddon 98. Mercury Rising 98, etc.

Stossel, Ludwig (1883–1973).
Austrian character actor in Hollywood from the mid-30s.
Four Sons 39. Man Hunt 41. Woman of the Year 42. Hilter's Madman 43. Cloak and Dagger 46. A Song Is Born 48. Call Me Madam 53. Me and the Colonel 58. G.I. Blues 60, many others.

Stothart, Herbert (1885–1949).
American composer, long with MGM, and responsible for the scores of many of the studio's most prestigious films.
Madame Satan 30. Rasputin and the Empress 33. Queen Christina 33. David Copperfield 35. Mutiny on the Bounty 35. A Night at the Opera 35. San Francisco 36. Camille 37. The Good Earth 37. Marie Antoinette 38. Idiot's Delight 39. Waterloo Bridge 40. Mrs Miniver 42. Random Harvest 42. Madame Curie 44. The Green Years 46. The Yearling 47. The Three Musketeers 48, many others.

Stout, Archie (1886–?1965).
American cinematographer in Hollywood from 1914.
Fort Apache 48. Hard Fast and Beautiful 51. *The Quiet Man* (AA) 52. The Sun Shines Bright 53. The High and the Mighty 54.

Stout, Rex (1886–1975).
American detective story writer, creator of Nero Wolfe, who appeared in two minor films of the 30s (played by Edward Arnold and Walter Connolly) and in a 70s TV movie (played by Thayer David).

Stowe, Harriet Beecher (1811–1896).
American novelist, author of the much-filmed *Uncle Tom's Cabin.*

Stowe, Madeleine (1958–).
American leading actress.
Nativity (TV) 78. The Amazons (TV) 83. Stakeout 87. Worth Winning 89. Revenge 90. The Two Jakes 90. Closet Land 91. The Last of the Mohicans 92. Unlawful Entry 92. Short Cuts 93. Another Stakeout 93. Blink 94. Bad Girls 94. China Moon 94. 12 Monkeys 95. Playing by Heart 98. The Proposition 98, etc.
TV series: The Gangster Chronicles 81.

Stradling, Harry (1901–1970).
British-born cinematographer, long in US.
La Kermesse Héroïque 35. *Knight without Armour* 37. *Pygmalion* 38. The Citadel 38. Jamaica Inn 39. Suspicion 41. *The Picture of Dorian Gray* (AA) 44. The Pirate 48. The Barkleys of Broadway (AAN) 49. *A Streetcar Named Desire* 51. Valentino 51. Hans Christian Andersen 52. Helen of Troy 55. Guys and Dolls 55. The Eddy Duchin Story 56. The Pajama Game 57. A Face in the Crowd 57. The Dark at the Top of the Stairs 60. *My Fair Lady* (AA) 64. How to Murder Your Wife 65. Moment to Moment 65. Walk, Don't Run 66. Funny Girl (AAN) 68. *Hello Dolly* 69, many others.

Stradling, Harry, Jnr (1925–).
American cinematographer, son of Harry Stradling.
Welcome to Hard Times 67. Support Your Local Sheriff 69. The Mad Room 69. Hello Dolly (AAN) 69. Something Big 71. Fools Parade 71. The Way We Were 73. McQ 74. Bite the Bullet 75. Midway 76. The Big Bus 76. Airport 77 77. Damnation Alley 77. Convoy 78. Go Tell the Spartans 78. Prophecy 79. Carny 80. S.O.B. 81. The Pursuit of D.B. Cooper 81. Buddy Buddy 81. O'Hara's Wife 82. Micki and Maude 84. A Fine Mess 86. Blind Date 87. Caddyshack II 88, etc.

Stradner, Rose (1913–1958).
Austrian actress who made a few Hollywood films.
The Last Gangster 38. Blind Alley 39. The Keys of the Kingdom 44, etc.

Straight, Beatrice (1916–).
American character actress.
Network (AA) 76. Bloodline 79. The Promise 79. Poltergeist 82. Two of a Kind 83. Power 85. Deceived 91, etc.

Strange, Glenn (1899–1973).
Giant-size American character actor, in Hollywood from 1937, mainly in cowboy roles. Also played the monster in *House of Frankenstein* 45, *Abbott and Costello meet Frankenstein* 48, etc.
TV series: Gunsmoke 56–73.

Strasberg, Lee (1899–1982).
American drama teacher; founded the Actors' Studio which in the 50s taught The Method.
■ *The Godfather Part Two* (AAN) 74. The Cassandra Crossing 77. Boardwalk 79. And Justice for All 79. Going in Style 79.
❝ I never felt Lee Strasberg could act, and I fail to see how someone who can't act can teach acting. – *Paul Henreid*

Strasberg, Susan (1938–1999).
American leading lady, daughter of Lee Strasberg, founder of the New York Actors' Studio. Stage and TV experience. Formerly married to actor Christopher Jones.
Autobiography: 1980, *Bittersweet*.
Picnic (film debut) 55. Stage Struck 57. Taste of Fear 59. Kapo 60. Hemingway's Adventures of a Young Man 62. The High Bright Sun 65. Psych-Out 68. The Brotherhood 68. Rollercoaster 77. In Praise of Older Women 78. The Returning 83. The Delta Force 85. Lambarene 90. Trauma 92, etc.
TV series: Toma 73.

Strathairn, David (1949–).
American general-purpose actor, often in the films of John SAYLES.
Return of the Secaucus 7 80. Enormous Changes at the Last Minute 83. Silkwood 83. The Brother from Another Planet 84. Iceman 84. Matewan 87. Eight Men Out 88. The Feud 90. Memphis Belle 90. Judgment (TV) 90. City of Hope 91. Big Girls Don't Cry . . . They Get Even/Stepkids 92. A League of Their Own 92. Passion Fish 92. Sneakers 92. Lost in Yonkers 93. The Firm 93. River Wild 94. Losing Isaiah 95. Dolores Claiborne 95. Home for the Holidays 95. Mother Night 96. LA Confidential 97. In the Gloaming (TV) 97. Simon Birch 98, etc.
TV series: The Days and Nights of Molly Dodd 87–88.

Stratten, Dorothy (1960–1980) (Dorothy Hoogstraten).
Canadian actress and *Playboy* pin-up whose short life, which ended when she was shot by her estranged husband, was retold in the biopic *Star 80*, starring Mariel HEMINGWAY. She was also the subject of a TV movie, *Death of a Centrefold: The Dorothy Stratten Story* 81. At the time of her death she was the lover of director Peter BOGDANOVICH.
Biography: 1984, *Death of a Unicorn* by Peter Bogdanovich.
Americathon 79. Skatetown USA 79. Galaxina 80. They All Laughed 81.

Stratton, John (1925–).
British general-purpose actor.
The Cure for Love 49. Appointment with Venus 52. The Cruel Sea 54. The Long Arm 55. Frankenstein and the Monster from Hell 74, etc.

Stratton-Porter, Gene (1863–1924).
American author of sentimental stories for girls.
A Girl of the Limberlost 34. Keeper of the Bees 35. Laddie 35. The Harvester 36. Michael O'Halloran 37 and 49. Her Father's Daughter 40. Freckles 60.

Straub, Jean-Marie (1933–).
French director in German films, in collaboration with his wife Danielle Huillet (1936–).
Machorka Muff 63. Nicht Versohnt 65. *The Chronicle of Anna-Magdalena Bach* 67. Othon 72. History Lessons 73. Moses and Aaron 75. Dalla Nube alla Resistenza 79. Too Early, Too Late 81. Class Relations/Klassenverhältnisse 84. The Death of Empedocles/Der Tod des Empedokles 86. Schwarze Sunde 89, etc.

Straus, Oscar (1870–1954).
Austrian operetta composer who also occasionally provided film music.
The Smiling Lieutenant 31. One Hour with You 32. Land Without Music 36. La Ronde 50. Madame De 52, etc.

Strauss, Helen (1909–1987).
American literary agent (for Michener and others) who became an occasional film producer: *Tom Sawyer*, *Huckleberry Finn*, *The Incredible Sarah*.
Autobiography: 1979, *A Talent for Luck*.

Strauss, Peter (1947–).
American leading man who became well known in *Rich Man Poor Man* (TV) 76.
Soldier Blue 71. The Last Tycoon 76. Young Joe the Forgotten Kennedy (TV) 77. The Jericho Mile (TV) 79. Masada (TV) 80. Spacehunter 83. Tender Is the Night (TV) 85. Kane and Abel (TV) 85. Peter Gunn (TV) 90. Nick of Time 95. Keys to Tulsa 96, etc.

Strauss, Robert (1913–1975).
American comedy actor (occasionally in menacing roles); former salesman.
Sailor Beware 52. *Stalag 17* (AAN) 53. The Seven Year Itch 54. Attack 56. The Last Time I Saw Archie 61. The Family Jewels 65, etc.

Strayer, Frank (1891–1964).
American director of second features.
Rough House Rosie 27. Enemy of Men 30. The Monster Walks 32. The Vampire Bat 33. The Ghost Walks 35. Blondie (and many others in this series) 38. The Daring Young Man 42. Messenger of Peace 50, etc.

Streep, Meryl (1949–) (Mary Louise Streep).
American leading lady of the late 70s and star actress of the 80s. Born in Summit, New Jersey, she studied drama at Vassar, Dartmouth and Yale, and began in the New York theatre. She became remarkable for the number of foreign and regional accents she displayed in her roles, and for the virtuosity of her contrasting performances. In the 90s, she has appeared in less demanding films, though once again she showed her mastery of an Irish accent in *Dancing at Lughnasa*. Married sculptor Donald Gummer.
Biography: 1988, *Meryl Streep* by Eugene E. Pfaff Jnr and Mark Emerson.
The Deadliest Season (TV) 77. Julia 77. The Deer Hunter (AAN) 78. *Holocaust* (TV) 78. Manhattan 79. The Seduction of Joe Tynan 79. *Kramer vs Kramer* (AA) 79. The French Lieutenant's Woman (BFA) 81. Sophie's Choice (AA) 82. Still of the Night 82. Silkwood (AAN) 83. Falling in Love 84. Plenty 85. Heartburn 86. Out of Africa (AAN) 86. Ironweed (AAN) 87. A Cry in the Dark (AAN) 88. She-Devil 89. Postcards from the Edge (AAN) 90. Defending Your Life 91. Death Becomes Her 92. The House of the Spirits 94. The River Wild 94. *The Bridges of Madison County* (AAN) 95. Before and After 96. One True Thing 98. Dancing at Lughnasa 98, etc.
❝ You can't get spoiled if you do your own ironing. – M.S.
The danger I'm talking about here is that she tends to sound boring because she's so perfect. – *Sydney Pollack*

Streeter, Edward (1892–1976).
American humorous novelist: *Father of the Bride* and *Mr Hobbs Takes a Vacation* were filmed.

Streisand, Barbra (1942–).
Ambitious American singer, actress, producer and director, who made a virtue of her unusual looks. Born in Brooklyn, New York, she began in the theatre and opened her movie career by repeating her show-stopping role in the Broadway musical *Funny Girl*. From the mid-70s she started to take greater control of her career by producing and directing her own films; but her choice of material has been erratic and she sometimes concentrates on her own performance to the detriment of the film as a whole. Married actor Elliott GOULD (1963–71) and, in 1998, actor James BROLIN; she was romantically involved with producer Jon PETERS. She is the mother of actor Jason GOULD.
Biographies: 1982, *Streisand: The Woman and the Legend* by James Spada with Christopher Nickens; 1994, *Her Name Is Barbra* by Randall Riese; 1995, *Streisand: The Intimate Biography* by James Spada; 1996, *Streisand: It Only Happens Once* by Anne Edwards.
Funny Girl (as Fanny Brice) (AA) 68. Hello Dolly 69. On a Clear Day You Can See Forever 70. The Owl and the Pussycat 70. What's Up, Doc? 72. Up the Sandbox 72. The Way We Were (AAN) 73. For Pete's Sake 74. Funny Lady 75. A Star Is Born (AAs) 76. The Main Event 79. All Night Long 81. Yentl (& co-w, co-p, d) 83. Nuts 87. The Prince of Tides (& d) 91. The Mirror Has Two Faces (& p, d) (AANs 'I've Finally Found Someone') 96, etc.
❝ When I sing, people shut up. – B.S.
Success to me is having ten honeydew melons and eating only the top half of each one. – B.S.
Nobody really knows me: I'm a mixture of self-confidence and insecurity. One thing's for sure – I hate talking about myself. – B.S.
This is for posterity. Everything I do will be on film for ever. – *B.S. on Funny Girl*
It's kind of a wonderful thing, to appreciate my own career. – *B.S. in 1994*
Streisand embodies everything that is tacky and cheap and hopelessly corny and unsophisticated about Middle America. – *Joe Queenan*
She really ought to be called Barbra Strident. – *Stanley Kaufmann*
To know her is not necessarily to love her. – *Rex Reed*
The most pretentious woman the cinema has ever known. – *Ryan O'Neal*
I'd love to work with her again, in something appropriate. Perhaps *Macbeth*. – *Walter Matthau*
It is given to few actresses to start out as Cinderella, pass through the fairy godmother stage and finish up as one of the ugly sisters by the time they are 50, but Streisand has managed that. – *Sheridan Morley*

Stribling, Melissa (1927–1992).
Scottish actress. Married director Basil Dearden.
The First Gentleman 48. Crow Hollow 52. Noose for a Lady 52. Wide Boy 52. Thought to Kill 53. The Safecracker 57. Dracula 58. League of Gentlemen 59. The Secret Partner 61. Only When I Larf 68. Crucible of Terror 71. Confessions of a Window Cleaner 74, etc.

Strick, Joseph (1923–).
American director.
The Savage Eye 59. The Balcony 64. *Ulysses* (AANw) 67. Ring of Bright Water (GB) (p only) 69. Tropic of Cancer 69. The Darwin Adventure (p only) 71. Janice 73. Road Movie 74. A Portrait of the Artist as a Young Man 79. Criminals (doc) 95, etc.

Strick, Wesley.
American screenwriter.
True Believer 89. Arachnophobia (co-w) 90. Cape Fear 91. Final Analysis 92. Wolf (co-w) 94. The Tie that Binds (d) 95. The Saint 97. Return to Paradise 98, etc.

Stricklyn, Ray (1930–).
American 'second lead' with stage experience.
The Proud and the Profane 56. The Last Wagon 57. Ten North Frederick 58. Young Jesse James 60. Arizona Raiders 65. Track of Thunder 68, etc.

Stride, John (1936–).
British supporting actor, much on TV.
Bitter Harvest 63. Macbeth 72. Juggernaut 74. Brannigan 75. The Omen 76. A Bridge Too Far 77, etc.
TV series: The Main Chance 69–75. The Wilde Alliance 78.

Stritch, Elaine (1925–).
Sharp, lanky American character comedienne, mainly on stage; a popular London resident during the mid-70s.
The Scarlet Hour 55. Three Violent People 57. A Farewell to Arms 57. The Perfect Furlough 58. Who Killed Teddy Bear? 65. Sidelong Glances of a Pigeon Kicker 70. The Spiral Staircase 75. Providence 77. September 87. Cocoon: The Return 88. Cadillac Man 90. Out to Sea 97. Krippendorf's Tribe 98, etc.
TV series: The Growing Paynes 49. My *Sister Eileen* 60. The Trials of O'Brien 65. Two's Company 76–78. The Ellen Burstyn Show 86–87.

Strock, Herbert L. (1918–).
American director, former publicist and editor.
The Magnetic Monster 52. Riders to the Stars 54. Battle Taxi 55. Teenage Frankenstein 57. How to Make a Monster 58. Rider on a Dead Horse 62. The Crawling Hand 63. Man on the Run 74. Monster 78. Witches' Brew (co-d) 79, etc.

Strode, Woody (Woodrow) (1914–1994).
Tall American actor.
The Lion Hunters 51. The Ten Commandments 56. *Sergeant Rutledge* 60. Spartacus 60. Two Rode Together 62. The Man Who Shot Liberty Valance 62. Genghis Khan 65. *The Professionals* 66. Shalako 68. Che! 69. The Revengers 72. The Gatling Gun 72. Winterhawk 76. Loaded Guns 76. The Black Stallion Returns 83. Vigilante 83. The Cotton Club 84. Lust in the Dust 84. Storyville 92. Posse 93, etc.

Stromberg, Hunt (1894–1968).
American producer, long with MGM, who went independent in the 40s.
Breaking into Society (as d) 24. Fire Patrol (as d) 26. Torrent 27. Our Dancing Daughters 28. Red Dust 32. *The Thin Man* 34. *The Great Ziegfeld* (AA) 36. Maytime 38. Marie Antoinette 38. Idiot's Delight 39. *The Women* 39. Northwest Passage 40. *Pride and Prejudice* 41. Guest in the House 44. Lured 47. Too Late for Tears 49. Between Midnight and Dawn 50. Mask of the Avenger 51, many others.
❝ Boys, I've an idea. Let's fill the screen with tits. – *H.S. on taking over White Shadows in the South Seas in 1928*

Stross, Raymond (1916–1988).
British producer, in films from 1933; married to Anne Heywood.
As Long as They're Happy 52. An Alligator Named Daisy 56. The Flesh is Weak 56. A Question of Adultery 58. A Terrible Beauty 59. The Very Edge 62. The Leather Boys 63. Ninety Degrees in the Shade 65. The Midas Run 69. I Want What I Want 72, etc.

Stroud, Don (1937–).
American leading man.
Madigan 68. Games 68. What's So Bad about Feeling Good 68. Coogan's Bluff 69. Bloody Mama 70. Explosion 70. Von Richthofen and Brown 70. Tick Tick Tick 70. Joe Kidd 72. Scalawag 73. The Choirboys 77. The Buddy Holly Story 78. The Amityville Horror 79. Armed and Dangerous 86. Down the Drain 89. Prime Target 91. Frogtown II 92. Sawbones (TV) 95. Dillinger and Capone 95. Hyper Space 97. The Haunted Sea 97, etc.
TV series: Kate Loves a Mystery 79. Mickey Spillane's Mike Hammer 84–87. Dragnet 89–90.

Strouse, Charles (1928–).
American composer, mainly for Broadway musicals.
The Mating Game (s) 59. Bonnie and Clyde 67. The Night They Raided Minsky's 68. There Was a Crooked Man 70. Just Tell Me What You Want 80. Annie (from musical) 82.

Strudwick, Shepperd:
see SHEPPERD, John.

Strummer, Joe (1952–) (John Mellors).
British composer, musician and occasional actor. He was a founder-member of the late-70s punk band The Clash.
Rude Boy (co-m) 80. Sid and Nancy (co-m) 86. Love Kills (co-m) 86. Straight to Hell (a) 87. Walker (m) 87. Permanent Record (m) 88. Candy Mountain (a) 88. Mystery Train (a) 89. I Hired a Contract Killer (a, s) 90. When Pigs Fly (m) 93, etc.

Struss, Karl (1891–1981).
American cinematographer.
Ben Hur 26. *Sunrise* (AA) 27. Abraham Lincoln 30. The Sign of the Cross 32. *Dr Jekyll and Mr Hyde* 32. The Great Dictator 40. Bring on the Girls 44. Suspense 46. The Macomber Affair 47. Rocketship XM 50. *Limelight* 52. Tarzan and the She-Devil 53, many others.

Struthers, Sally (1948–).
American young character actress, a hit as the daughter in TV's *All in the Family* 71–74.
Five Easy Pieces 70. The Getaway 72. Aloha Means Goodbye (TV) 76. A Gun in the House (TV) 81, etc.
❝ Acting is cheap group therapy, being a schizo fifty different ways. And we're paid! – S.S.

Stuart, Binkie (c. 1932–).
British child actress of the 30s.
Moonlight Sonata 37. Little Dolly Daydream 38. My Irish Molly 39, etc.

Stuart, Gloria (1909–) (Gloria Stuart Finch).
American leading lady of the 30s.
The Old Dark House 32. The Invisible Man 33. Roman Scandals 33. Prisoner of Shark Island 36. Rebecca of Sunnybrook Farm 38. The Three

Musketeers 39. She Wrote the Book 46. My Favorite Year 82. Titanic (AAN) 97, etc.

Stuart, Jeb.
American screenwriter.
Die Hard 88. Leviathan 89. Lock Up 89. Vital Signs 90. Another 48 Hrs 90. The Fugitive (co-w) 93. Outbreak (co-w) 95. Going West (wd) 97. Fire Down Below (co-w) 97. Switchback (& d) 97, etc.

Stuart, John (1898–1979) (John Croall).
British leading man of the 20s, character actor of the 40s and after. Born in Edinburgh, Scotland, he was on stage from 1919. The first of his two wives was actress Muriel ANGELUS.
Autobiography: 1971, *Caught in the Act*.
Her Son (debut) 20. We Women 25. The Pleasure Garden 26. Blackmail 29. Elstree Calling 30. Atlantic 30. Number Seventeen 31. Taxi for Two 32. The Pointing Finger 34. Abdul the Damned 35. Old Mother Riley's Ghost 41. The Phantom Shot 46. Mine Own Executioner 47. The Magic Box 51. Quatermass II 57. Blood of the Vampire 58. Sink the Bismarck 60. Superman 78, etc.

Stuart, Leslie (1864–1928) (Thomas Barrett).
British songwriter ('Tell Me Pretty Maiden', 'Florodora', etc.) played by Robert Morley in the 1940 biopic *You Will Remember*.

Stuart, Mel (1928–).
American director.
If It's Tuesday This Must Be Belgium 69. I Love My Wife 70. Willie Wonka and the Chocolate Factory 71. One Is a Lonely Number 72. Mean Dog Blues 78. The Chisholms (TV) 79. The White Lions 79, etc.

Stubbs, Imogen (1961–).
English leading actress, from the stage. Married director Trevor Nunn in 1994.
Privileged 82. Nanou 86. A Summer Story 88. Erik the Viking 89. Fellow Traveller 89. True Colors 91. Jack & Sarah 95. Sense and Sensibility 95. Twelfth Night 96, etc.

Studi, Wes.
American actor, usually playing an Indian. A Cherokee, he was born in Oklahoma and was formerly a teacher.
Dances with Wolves 90. The Doors 91. Last of the Mohicans 92. Geronimo: An American Legend (title role) 93. The Broken Chain (TV) 93. Street Fighter 95. Heat 95. The Killing Jar 96. Crazy Horse (TV) 96. Deep Rising 97. Soundman 98, etc.

Stuhr, Jerzy (1947–).
Polish leading actor, most closely associated with the films of Krzysztof KIESLOWSKI. Born in Cracow, he began in the theatre and turned to directing in the mid-90s.
Top Dog/Wodzirej 78. Camera Buff/Amator 79. Decalogue 88. Three Colours: White 93. Love Stories (& d) 97 etc.

Sturges, John (1911–1992).
American director of smooth if increasingly pretentious action films, former editor and documentarist.
■ The Man Who Dared 46. Shadowed 46. Alias Mr Twilight 47. For the Love of Rusty 47. Keeper of the Bees 48. The Best Man Wins 48. The Sign of the Ram 48. The Walking Hills 49. The Capture 49. Mystery Street 50. The Magnificent Yankee 50. Right Cross 50. Kind Lady 51. The People Against O'Hara 51. It's a Big Country (part) 51. The Girl in White 52. Fast Company 52. Jeopardy 53. Escape from Fort Bravo 53. *Bad Day at Black Rock* (AAN) 54. Underwater 55. The Scarlet Coat 55. Backlash 56. *Gunfight at the OK Corral* 57. The Law and Jake Wade 58. The Old Man and the Sea 58. Last Train from Gun Hill 58. Never So Few 59. *The Magnificent Seven* 60. By Love Possessed 61. Sergeants Three 62. A Girl Named Tamiko 63. *The Great Escape* 63. The Satan Bug 65. The Hallelujah Trail 65. The Hour of the Gun 67. Ice Station Zebra 68. Marooned 69. Joe Kidd 72. Valdez the Halfbreed (Sp.) 73. McQ 74. The Eagle Has Landed 77.
“ It is hard to remember why his career was ever considered meaningful. – *Andrew Sarris, 1968*

Sturges, Preston (1898–1959) (Edmund P. Biden).
American writer-director who in the early 40s was Hollywood's wonder boy who never lost the common touch despite his free-wheeling witty style and subject matter. By 1950 his talent had disappeared, and he retired unhappily to France.
Book: 1991, *Preston Sturges on Preston Sturges* edited by Sandy Sturges.
AS WRITER: *The Power and the Glory* 33. We Live Again 34. The Good Fairy 35. Diamond Jim 35. Easy Living 37. Port of Seven Seas 38. If I Were King 39. Never Say Die 39. Remember the Night 40, etc.
■ AS WRITER-DIRECTOR: *The Great McGinty* (AA) 40. *Christmas in July* 40. *Sullivan's Travels* 41. The Lady Eve 41. *The Palm Beach Story* 42. *The Great Moment* 43. *The Miracle of Morgan's Creek* (AANw) 43. *Hail the Conquering Hero* (AANw) 44. Mad Wednesday 46. Unfaithfully Yours 48. The Beautiful Blonde from Bashful Bend 49. The Diary of Major Thompson 56.
✪ For being the wonder boy of the early 40s, with his unique blend of sophisticated comedy and pratfall farce. *Sullivan's Travels*.
“ The Breughel of American comedy directors ... the absurdity of the American success story was matched by the ferocity of the battle of the sexes ... Lubitsch treated sex as the dessert of a civilized meal of manners. Sturges, more in the American style, served sex with all the courses. – *Andrew Sarris, 1968*
Jesus, he was a strange guy. Carried his own hill with him, I tell you. – *Frank Capra*
There was a desperate, hectic quality to all his films – an intense desire to believe all the Horatio Alger ideals often associated with America, intermingled with a cynical 'European' view of those ideals. – *James Ursini*
He has restored to the art of the cinema a certain graphic velocity it has missed since the turmoil of Mack Sennett's zanies. – *Bosley Crowther*
Preston is like a man from the Italian Renaissance – he wants to do everything at once. – *James Agee*
He was too large for this smelly resort, and the big studios were scared to death of him. A man who was a triple threat kept them awake nights, and I'm positive they were waiting for him to fall on his face so they could pounce and devour this terrible threat to their stingy talents. They pounced, and they got him, good. But he knew the great days when his can glowed like a port light from their kissing it. – *Earl Felton*
When the last dime is gone, I'll sit on the curb outside with a pencil and a ten-cent notebook, and start the whole thing over again. – *P.S., 1957*

Sturridge, Charles (1951–).
English director, from TV.
Runners 83. Aria (co-d) 87. A Handful of Dust 88. Where Angels Fear to Tread 91. A Foreign Field (TV) 93. Gulliver's Travels (TV) 96. Illumination 97. Fairy Tale: A True Story 97, etc.
TV series: Brideshead Revisited 81.

Styne, Jule (1905–1994) (Jules Styne).
British-born composer, in US from childhood. Former pianist and conductor. Film songs include 'There Goes That Song Again', 'Give Me Five Minutes More', 'It's Magic', 'Three Coins in the Fountain'. Shows filmed include *Gentlemen Prefer Blondes, Bells Are Ringing, Gypsy, Funny Girl*.

Subiela, Eliseo (1944–).
Argentinian director.
La Conquista del Paraiso 81. Man Facing Southeast 87. Ultimas Imágenes del Naufragio 89. El Lado Oscuro del Corazón 92. Don't You Die without Telling Me Where You Go 95. Little Miracles/Pequeños Milagros (wd) 98, etc.

Sublett, John:
see BUBBLES, John.

Subotsky, Milton (1921–1991).
American independent producer and writer.
Rock Rock Rock 56. The Last Mile 58. City of the Dead (GB) 60. It's Trad Dad (GB) 63. Dr Terror's House of Horrors (GB) 64. Dr Who and the Daleks (GB) 65. The Skull (GB) 66. The Psychopath (GB) 66. Daleks Invasion Earth 2150 AD (GB) 66. Torture Garden (GB) 67. The House That Dripped Blood (GB) 70. Tales from the Crypt (GB) 71. Asylum (GB) 72. Madhouse (GB) 73. The Land that Time Forgot (GB) 75. At the Earth's Core (GB) 76. The Monster Club 80. Cat's Eye 84. The Lawnmower Man 92, etc.

Suchet, David (1946–).
English character actor, much on stage and television. He acted with the Royal Shakespeare Company from the late 70s.
Hunchback of Notre Dame (TV) 82. Trenchcoat 82. The Missionary 83. Red Monarch (TV) 83. Greystoke: The Legend of Tarzan, Lord of the Apes 84. Little Drummer Girl 84. The Falcon and the Snowman 85. Harry and the Hendersons 87. Blott on the Landscape (TV) 85. A World Apart 87. To Kill a Priest 88. When the Whales Came 89. Secret Agent (TV) 92. Executive Decision 96. Sunday 97. Seesaw (TV) 98. A Perfect Murder 98, etc.
TV series: Poirot (title role) 88–93.

Sucksdorff, Arne (1917–).
Swedish documentarist who has normally written and photographed his own films, which vary from six minutes to feature length.
The West Wind 42. Shadows on the Snow 45. *Rhythm of a City* 47. *A Divided World* 48. The Road 48. The Wind and the River 51. *The Great Adventure* 53. The Flute and the Arrow 57. The Boy in the Tree 60. My Home is Copacabana 65. Forbush and the Penguins 71, etc.

Suhrstedt, Tim.
American cinematographer.
Forbidden World/Mutant 82. Android 82. The House on Sorority Row 82. Suburbia 84. Teen Wolf 85. Critters 86. Mystic Pizza 88. Bill & Ted's Excellent Adventure 89. Men at Work 90. Don't Tell Mom the Babysitter's Dead 91. Traces of Red/Beyond Suspicion 92. Noises Off 92. The Favor 94. Getting Even with Dad 94. To Gillian on Her 37th Birthday 96. The Wedding Singer 98, etc.

Sukowa, Barbara (1950–).
German leading actress.
Berlin Alexanderplatz (TV) 80. Lola 81. Deadly Game 83. Rosa Luxemburg 86. The Sicilian 87. Voyager 91. Europea/Zentropa 92. Johnny Mnemonic 95. Office Killer 97, etc.

Sullavan, Margaret (1911–1960) (Margaret Brooke).
American leading actress in light films of the 30s and 40s; she had a special whimsical quality which was unique. The first three of her four husbands were actor Henry FONDA (1931–33), director William WYLER (1934–36), and agent Leland HAYWARD (1936–48). Her lovers included producer Jed HARRIS. Committed suicide.
Biography: 1977, *Haywire* by Brooke Hayward (her daughter).
■ Only Yesterday 33. Little Man What Now? 34. So Red the Rose 35. *The Good Fairy* 35. Next Time We Love 36. The Moon's Our Home 36. *Three Comrades* (AAN) 38. Shopworn Angel 38. The Shining Hour 39. *The Shop around the Corner* 39. *The Mortal Storm* 40. So Ends Our Night 40. Back Street 41. Appointment for Love 41. Cry Havoc 43. No Sad Songs for Me 50.

Sullivan, Barry (1912–1994) (Patrick Barry).
American leading man with stage experience.
Lady in the Dark 43. Two Years before the Mast 44. And Now Tomorrow 44. Suspense 46. The Gangster 47. Tension 49. The Great Gatsby 49. The Outriders 50. Three Guys Named Mike 51. *The Bad and the Beautiful* 52. Jeopardy 54. Queen Bee 55. Forty Guns 57. Wolf Larsen 57. Seven Ways from Sundown 60. The Light in the Piazza 62. Stagecoach to Hell 64. My Blood Runs Cold 64. Harlow (electronovision version) 65. An American Dream/See You in Hell, Darling 66. Intimacy 66. Buckskin 68. Willie Boy 69. Earthquake 74. The Human Factor 75. Oh God 77. Casino 80, etc.
TV series: The Man Called X 55–56. Harbourmaster 57–58. The Tall Man 60–62. The Road West 67. Rich Man, Poor Man Book II 76–77.

Sullivan, C. Gardner (1885–1965).
American screenwriter.
The Battle of Gettysburg 14. The Wrath of the Gods 15. Civilization 16. The Aryan 16. The Zeppelin's Last Raid 17. Carmen of the Klondike 18. Sahara 19. Human Wreckage 23. Sparrows 26. Tempest 27. Sequoia 34. The Buccaneer 38, many others.

Sullivan, Francis L. (1903–1956).
Heavyweight British character actor, often seen as advocate. On stage from 1921, films from 1933.
The Missing Rembrandt (debut) 33. Chu Chin Chow 33. Great Expectations (US) 35. *The Mystery of Edwin Drood* (US) 35. Sabotage 36. Action for Slander 37. Dinner at the Ritz 37. Twenty-one Days 38. The Citadel 38. The Four Just Men 39. *Pimpernel Smith* 41. *Fiddlers Three* 44. Caesar and Cleopatra 45. *Great Expectations* 46. *Oliver Twist* 48. Night and the City 51. Plunder of the Sun (US) 51. The Prodigal (US) 55. Hell's Island (US) 55, many others.
TV series: Destiny (host) 57–58.

Sullivan, Pat (1887–1933).
Australian newspaper cartoonist who settled in the US and invented Felix the Cat, the most popular character in film cartoons of the 20s.

Sully, Frank (1910–1975).
American small-part actor often seen as farmer or dumb crook.
Mary Burns Fugitive 35. The Grapes of Wrath 40. Escape to Glory 41. Thousands Cheer 43. Renegades 46. With a Song in My Heart 52. The Naked Street 56, many others.

Sumac, Yma (1928–) (Emparatriz Chavarri).
Peruvian singer with five-octave range.
■ The Secret of the Incas 54. Omar Khayyam 57.

Summerfield, Eleanor (1921–).
British character comedienne, on stage from 1939.
London Belongs to Me (film debut) 47. Scrooge 51. It's Great To Be Young 56. Dentist in the Chair 59. On the Beat 62. Guns of Darkness 63. Some Will Some Won't 70. The Watcher in the Woods 80, many others.

Summers, Jeremy (1931–).
British director, from TV.
The Punch and Judy Man 62. Crooks in Cloisters 64. Ferry Cross the Mersey 64. House of a Thousand Dolls 67. Vengeance of Fu Manchu 67. Strangers and Brothers (TV) 83, etc.

Summers, Walter (1896–1973).
British director of the 20s and 30s.
Ypres 25. Mons 26. The Battle of the Coronel and Falkland Islands 31. Deeds Men Do 32. The Return of Bulldog Drummond 33. Mutiny on the Elsinore 36. Music Hath Charms (co-d) 36. At the Villa Rose 38. Dark Eyes of London 38. Traitor Spy 40, etc.

Summerville, Slim (1892–1946) (George J. Summerville).
Lanky, mournful-looking American character comedian, former gagman and director for Mack Sennett.
The Beloved Rogue 27. *All Quiet on the Western Front* 30. The Front Page 31. Life Begins at Forty 35. White Fang 36. The Road Back 37. Rebecca of Sunnybrook Farm 38. Jesse James 39. *Tobacco Road* 41. Miss Polly 41. Niagara Falls 42. The Hoodlum Saint 46, many others.

Sumner, Geoffrey (1908–1989).
British comic actor of silly-ass types.
Helter Skelter 49. The Dark Man 52. A Tale of Five Cities 53. Traveller's Joy 55, etc.

Sundberg, Clinton (1906–1987).
American character actor, former teacher; usually played flustered clerk or head-waiter.
Undercurrent 46. Living in a Big Way 47. Annie Get Your Gun 50. Main Street to Broadway 52. The Caddy 53. The Birds and the Bees 56. The Wonderful World of the Brothers Grimm 63. Hotel 67, many others.

Suo, Masayuki (1956–).
Japanese director and screenwriter. Born in Tokyo and brought up in Kawasaki, he studied French at university and began his career as an assistant director and, later, director of PINK MOVIES. *Shall We Dance?* was the sixth-most successful foreign-language film at the American box-office. Married actress and former dancer Tamiyo Kusakari, who starred in the film.
My Brother's Wife 84. A Fancy Dance/Manic Zen 89. Sumo Do, Sumo Don't/Shiko Funjatta 92. *Shall We Dance?* 97, etc.

Surtees, Bruce (1937–).
American cinematographer. He is the son of Robert L. SURTEES.
The Beguiled 71. Play Misty for Me 71. Dirty Harry 72. The Great Northfield Minnesota Raid 72. Blume in Love 73. High Plains Drifter 73. Lenny (AAN) 74. Night Moves 75. The Outlaw Josey Wales 76. Movie Movie 78. Big Wednesday 78. Escape from Alcatraz 79. Inchon 81. White Dog 82. Firefox 82. Tightrope 84. Beverly Hills Cop 84. Pale Rider 85. Out of Bounds 86. Psycho III 86. Ratboy 86. Back to the Beach 87. License to Drive 88. Men Don't Leave 90. The Super 91. Run 91. The Crush 93. The Birds II: Land's End (TV) 94. The Stars Fell on Henrietta 95. The Substitute 96, etc.

Surtees, Robert L. (1906–1985).
Distinguished American cinematographer, in Hollywood from 1927.
Thirty Seconds over Tokyo (AAN) 44. Our Vines Have Tender Grapes 45. The Unfinished Dance 47. Act of Violence 48. *Intruder in the Dust* 49. *King Solomon's Mines* (AA) 50. Quo Vadis (AAN) 51. *The Bad and the Beautiful* (AA) 52. Escape from Fort Bravo 53. Trial 55. *Oklahoma!* (AAN) 55. The Swan 56. Raintree County 57. Merry Andrew 58. *Ben Hur* (AA) 59. Mutiny on the Bounty (AAN) 62. The Hallelujah Trail 65. The Collector 65. The Satan Bug 65. Lost Command 66. Doctor Dolittle (AAN) 67. *The Graduate* (AAN) 67. *Sweet Charity* 68. The Arrangement 69. Summer of 42 (AAN) 71. The Last Picture Show (AAN) 71. The Cowboys 72. The Other 72. Oklahoma Crude 73. The Sting (AAN) 73. The Great Waldo Pepper 75. The Hindenberg (AAN) 75. A Star Is Born (AAN) 76. The Turning Point (AAN) 77. Bloodbrothers 78. Same Time Next Year (AAN) 78, etc.

Susann, Jacqueline (1921–1974).
American best-selling novelist, a former unsuccessful actress and model. Married press agent Irving Mansfield. Her lovers included actresses Carol LANDIS and Ethel MERMAN. Died of cancer. She was played by Michele Lee in the TV movie *Scandalous Me: The Jacqueline Susann Story* 98.
Biography: 1988, *Lovely Me* by Barbara Seaman.
Valley of the Dolls (oa) 67. The Love Machine (oa) 71. Once Is Not Enough (oa) 75.
❝ I write for women who read me in the goddam subways on the way home from work. I know who they are, because that's who I used to be . . . But here's the catch. All the people they envy in my books, the ones who are glamorous, or beautiful, or rich, or talented – they have to suffer, see, because that way the people who read me can get off the subway and go home feeling better about their own crappy lives. – *J.S.*
The 1960s will be remembered for three people: me, Andy Warhol and the Beatles. – *J.S.*

Suschitzky, Peter (1941–).
British cinematographer.
It Happened Here 65. Privilege 66. Charlie Bubbles 67. A Midsummer Night's Dream 68. Lock Up Your Daughters 68. Leo the Last 70. Lisztomania 76. Valentino 77. The Empire Strikes Back 80. Krull 83. Falling in Love 84. Dead Ringers 88. Where the Heart Is 90. Naked Lunch 91. M. Butterfly 93. The Vanishing 93. Crash 96. Mars Attacks! 96, etc.

Suschitzky, Wolfgang (1912–).
Austrian cinematographer in Britain.
No Resting Place 51. Cat and Mouse 57. The Small World of Sammy Lee 63. Ulysses 67. Theatre of Blood 73. Something to Hide 74, etc.

Susskind, David (1920–1987).
American TV and theatre personality and producer who also produced a few films.
Edge of the City 57. A Raisin in the Sun 61. Requiem for a Heavyweight 62. All the Way Home 63. Lovers and Other Strangers 70. Alice Doesn't Live Here Any More 74. Buffalo Bill and the Indians 76. Loving Couples 80, etc.

Sutherland, A. Edward (1895–1974).
American director, in Hollywood from 1914.
Wild Wild Susan 25. Dance of Life 29. Palmy Days 31. Mississippi 35. Diamond Jim 35. Champagne Waltz 37. Every Day's a Holiday 38. The Flying Deuces 39. *The Boys from Syracuse* 40. Beyond Tomorrow 41. Invisible Woman 41. Nine Lives Are Not Enough 42. Dixie 43. Follow the Boys 44. Abie's Irish Rose 46. Having Wonderful Crime 46. Bermuda Affair 56, many others.

Sutherland, Donald (1935–).
Gaunt Canadian actor who became very fashionable at the end of the 60s. He is the father of Kiefer SUTHERLAND.
The World Ten Times Over 63. Castle of the Living Dead 64. Dr Terror's House of Horrors 65. Fanatic 65. The Bedford Incident 65. Promise Her Anything 66. The Dirty Dozen 67. Billion Dollar Brain 67. Sebastian 68. Oedipus the King 68. Interlude 68. Joanna 68. The Split 68. Start the Revolution without Me 69. Act of the Heart 70. M*A*S*H 70. Kelly's Heroes 70. Alex in Wonderland 70. Little Murders 70. *Klute* 71. Johnny Got His Gun (as Christ) 71. Steelyard Blues 72. Lady Ice 72. Alien Thunder 73. Don't Look Now 73. S*P*Y*S 74. The Day of the Locust 75. End of the Game 76. 1900 76. Casanova 76. The Eagle Has Landed 77. The Disappearance 77. Blood Relations 78. The Kentucky Fried Movie 78. Invasion of the Body Snatchers 78. National Lampoon's Animal House 78. The First Great Train Robbery 79. Murder by Decree 79. Bear Island 79. A Man, a Woman and a Bank 80. Nothing Personal 80. Ordinary People 80. Eye of the Needle 81. Threshold 81. Gas 81. Max Dugan Returns 83. The Winter of Our Discontent (TV) 84. Crackers 84. Ordeal by Innocence 85. Heaven Help Us 85. Revolution 86. The Wolf at the Door 86. Lost Angels 89. A Dry White Season 89. Bethune: The Making of a Hero 89. Eminent Domain 90. Backdraft 91. JFK 91. Scream of Stone 91. Buster's Bedroom 91. The Railway Station Man 92. Buffy the Vampire Slayer 92. Benefit of the Doubt 93. Six Degrees of Separation 93. Shadow of the Wolf (co-w) 93. Younger and Younger 93. The Lifeforce Experiment (TV) 94. Oldest Living Confederate Widow Tells All (TV) 94. Disclosure 94. Citizen X (TV) 95. Outbreak 95. A Time to Kill 96. Hollow Point 96. Natural Enemy (TV) 96. Shadow Conspiracy 97. Without Limits 97. Fallen 97. The Assignment 97. Virus 98, etc.

Sutherland, Dame Joan (1926–).
Distinguished Australian soprano who retired in 1990 and made her feature film debut as Mother Rudd in an adaptation of the Australian stories of outback life by Steele RUDD.
Dad and Dave on Our Selection 95.

Sutherland, Kiefer (1967–).
American leading actor (born in London), the son of Donald SUTHERLAND.
The Bay Boy 85. Stand by Me 86. Crazy Moon 87. The Killing Time 87. The Lost Boys 87. Bright Lights, Big City 88. Promised Land 88. Renegades 89. Flashback 89. 1969 89. Young Guns 90. Flatliners 90. Trapped in Silence 90. Young Guns II 90. Flashback 91. Article 99 92. A Few Good Men 92. Twin Peaks: Fire Walk with Me 92. The Vanishing 93. Last Light (& d) (TV) 93. The Three Musketeers 93. The Cowboy Way 94. Eye for an Eye 95. Freeway 96. A Time to Kill 96. Truth or Consequences, N.M. 97. Dark City 97. A Soldier's Sweetheart 98, etc.

Sutton, Dudley (1933–).
British character actor.
The Leather Boys 63. Rotten to the Core 65. Crossplot 69. The Walking Stick 70. The Devils 71. The Pink Panther Strikes Again 76. Casanova 76. Valentino 77. The Big Sleep 78. Trail of the Pink Panther 82. Lamb 86. The Rainbow 88. Edward II 91. Orlando 92. Moses (TV) 96. The Tichborne Claimant 98, etc.
TV series: Lovejoy 86, 90–95.

Sutton, Grady (1908–1995).
American character comedian usually seen as vacuous country cousin; in Hollywood from 1926.
The Story of Temple Drake 32. Alice Adams 35. Stage Door 37. Alexander's Ragtime Band 38. *The Bank Dick* 40. The Great Moment 44. My Wild Irish Rose 48. White Christmas 54. The Birds and the Bees 56. My Fair Lady 64. Paradise Hawaiian Style 66. The Great Bank Robbery 69. Myra Breckinridge 70. Support Your Local Gunfighter 71. Rock 'n' Roll High School 79, many others.
TV series: The Pruitts of Southampton 66.

Sutton, John (1908–1963).
British actor with stage experience; in Hollywood from 1937, usually as second lead or smooth swashbuckling villain.
Bulldog Drummond Comes Back 37. The Adventures of Robin Hood 38. The Invisible Man Returns 40. A Yank in the RAF 41. *Ten Gentlemen from West Point* 42. Jane Eyre 43. Claudia and David 46. The Three Musketeers 48. The Golden Hawk 52. East of Sumatra 54. The Bat 59, many others.

Suzman, Janet (1939–).
South African stage actress in Britain.
■ A Day in the Death of Joe Egg 70. *Nicholas and Alexandra* (AAN) 72. The Black Windmill 74. Voyage of the Damned 76. The House on Garibaldi Street (TV) 79. Nijinsky 80. The Priest of Love 81. The Draughtsman's Contract 82. And the Ship Sailed On 84. Mountbatten (as Edwina) (TV) 85. A Dry White Season 89. Nuns on the Run 90. Leon the Pig Farmer 93.

Svankmajer, Jan (1934–).
Czechoslovakian director with a disturbing and surreal turn of mind. His reputation has been made by a series of short films that mix live action with stop-motion animation.
Alice/Neco z Alenky 88. Faust 94. The Conspirators of Pleasure 96.

Svenson, Bo (1941–).
American action lead.
The Great Waldo Pepper 75. Part Two Walking Tall 75. Special Delivery 76. Breaking Point 76. Final Chapter – Walking Tall 77. North Dallas Forty 79. Counterfeit Commandos 81. Heartbreak Ridge 86. The Delta Force 86. The Last Contract 86. Deep Space 87. Curse II: The Bite 88. The Kill Reflex 89. Soda Cracker 89. Primal Rage 90. Killer Mania 92. Three Days to a Kill 92. Savage Land 94. Private Obsession 94, etc.

Sverák, Jan (1965–).
Czech director and screenwriter who studied at FAMU (Film Academy of Music and Drama) in Prague and began as a maker of documentaries. He is the son of screenwriter and actor Zdenák Sverák. *Accumulator 1* was the most expensive Czech film so far made at a cost of $3m; he followed it with a road movie shot in two weeks at a cost of $20,000.
Elementary School/Obecná Skola (AAN) 91. Accumulator 1 94. The Ride 95. *Kolya* (AA) 96, etc.
❝ It is a mistake to fall into the view that Europe is only the ante-room of the place where the real party is. There has to be a way to do films in Europe and compete with America. Half the box-office takings come from the rest of the world. – *J.S.*

Sverák, Zdenák (1936–).
Czech screenwriter and actor, notably associated with the films of Jiri Menzel. He also wrote the semi-autobiographical script for the feature film debut of his son, director Jan SVERÁK, and starred in his second film.
The Hit/Trhak (a) 80. Like Hares/Jako Zajici (a) 82. *My Sweet Little Village* (w) 85. *Elementary School*/Obecná Skola 91. The Life and Extraordinary Adventures of Private Chonkin (w) 94. *Accumulator 1* (a, co-w) 94, etc.

Swaim, Bob (1943–).
American director and screenwriter, based in France.
La Nuit de Saint-Germain-des-Prés 77. La Balance 82. Half Moon Street 86. Masquerade 88. L'Atlantide (w) 91, etc.

Swain, Dominique (1980–).
American schoolgirl actress who made her screen debut in the title role of *Lolita*.
Lolita 97. Face/Off 97, etc.

Swain, Mack (1876–1935).
American silent actor, a Mack Sennett heavy from 1914; most memorable in *The Gold Rush* 24. Last part, *Midnight Patrol* 32.

Swank, Hilary (1975–).
American actress, from television.
Buffy the Vampire Slayer 92. The Next Karate Kid 94. Sometimes They Come Back . . . Again 96. Kounterfeit 96, etc.

Swanson, Gloria (1897–1983) (G. Svensson).
American leading lady of the silent screen who started as a Mack SENNETT bathing beauty and made many comebacks. The first of her six husbands was actor Wallace BEERY (1916–18).
Biography: 1988, *Gloria and Joe: The Star-Crossed Love Affair of Gloria Swanson and Joe Kennedy* by Axel Madsen.
Books: 1981, *Swanson on Swanson*; 1988, *The Films of Gloria Swanson* by Lawrence J. Quirk.
The Meal Ticket 15. Teddy at the Throttle 17. The Pullman Bride 17. Shifting Sands 18. Don't Change Your Husband 18. *Male and Female* 19. Why Change Your Wife? 19. *The Affairs of Anatol* 21. Adam's Rib 23. Prodigal Daughters 23. Madame Sans Gêne 25. Untamed Lady 26. *Sadie Thompson* (AAN) 28. *Queen Kelly* (unfinished) 28. The Trespasser (AAN) 29. Indiscreet 31. Perfect Understanding 33. Music in the Air 34. Father Takes a Wife 41. *Sunset Boulevard* (AAN) 50. Three for Bedroom C 52. Nero's Mistress (It.) 56. Killer Bees (TV) 73. Airport 75 74, many others.
❝ I acquired my expensive tastes from Mr De Mille. – G.S.
When I die, my epitaph should read: she paid the bills. – G.S.
Dietrich's legs may be longer, but I have seven grandchildren. – G.S.
Famous line (*Sunset Boulevard*, when told she used to be a big star): 'I *am* big. It's the pictures that got small.'

Swanson, Kristy.
American leading actress.
Deadly Friend 86. Flowers in the Attic 87. Diving In 90. Dream Trap 90. Mannequin 2: On the Move 91. Hot Shots! 91. Highway to Hell 92. Buffy the Vampire Slayer 92. The Program 93. The Ref 94. The Chase 94. Higher Learning 95. The Phantom 96. Marshal Law 96. 8 Heads in a Duffel Bag 96, etc.
TV series: Knots Landing 87–88. Nightingales 89.

Swanson, Maureen (1932–).
British leading lady who retired to marry after a brief career.
Moulin Rouge 53. A Town Like Alice 56. The Spanish Gardener 56. Robbery under Arms 57. The Malpas Mystery 63, etc.

Swarthout, Gladys (1904–1969).
American opera singer who acted in a few films.
Rose of the Rancho 35. Give Us This Night 36. Champagne Waltz 37. Romance in the Dark 38. Ambush 39, etc.

Swayze, Patrick (1952–).
American leading man, a former dancer.
Skatetown USA 79. The Outsiders 83. Uncommon Valor 83. Grandview USA 84. Red Dawn 84. Youngblood 85. *North and South* (TV) 86. Dirty Dancing 87. Steel Dawn 87. Tiger Warsaw 88. Road House 89. Next of Kin 89. Ghost 90. Point Break 91. City of Joy 92. Father Hood 93. To Wong Foo, Thanks for Everything, Julie Newmar 95. Tall Tale: The Unbelievable Adventures of Pecos Bill 95. Three Wishes 95. Black Dog 98. Letters from a Killer 98, etc.
TV series: Renegades 83.

Sweeney, D. B. (1961–) (Daniel Bernard Sweeney).
American leading actor.
Fire with Fire 86. Gardens of Stone 87. No Man's Land 87. Eight Men Out 88. Memphis Belle 90. A Day in October/En Dag i Oktober 91. Blue Desert 91. Heaven Is a Playground 91. Cutting Edge 92. Miss Rose White (TV) 92. Fire in the Sky 93. Hear No Evil 93. Roommates 95. Pawn 97, etc.
TV series: Strange Luck 95. C16: FBI 97.

Sweet, Blanche (1895–1986) (Daphne Wayne).
American silent heroine.
The Lonedale Operator 11. Judith of Bethulia 13. The Secret Sin 15. The Deadliest Sex 20. In the Palace of the King 23. Anna Christie 23. Tess of the D'Urbervilles 24. Bluebeard's Seven Wives 26. Singed 27. The Woman Racket 30. The Silver Horde 30, etc.

Sweet, Dolph (1921–1985).
Barrel-chested American character actor.
The Young Doctors 61. The Lost Man 69. Fear Is the Key 72. The Lords of Flatbush 74. Go Tell the Spartans 77. Reds 81, etc.

TV series: The Trials of O'Brien 65–66. *Gimme a Break* 81–85.

Swenson, Inga (1932–).
American actress.
■ Advise and Consent 61. The Miracle Worker 62. Earth II (TV) 71. The Betsy 78.
TV series: Soap 78. Benson 79–86. Doctor, Doctor 89–91.

Swerling, Jo (1897–) (Joseph Swerling).
Russian-American writer, long in Hollywood.
Dirigible 31. Platinum Blonde 32. Man's Castle 35. Made for Each Other 38. *The Westerner* 40. Blood and Sand 42. The Pride of the Yankees (co-w, AAN) 42. *Lifeboat* 44. Leave Her to Heaven 46. Thunder in the East 52. King of the Roaring Twenties 61, many others.
His son Jo Swerling Jnr (1931–) writes and produces for TV.

Swicord, Robin.
American screenwriter. Married Nicholas Kazan in 1984.
Shag (co-w) 88. Little Women 94. The Perez Family 95. Roald Dahl's Matilda 96. Practical Magic 98, etc.

Swift, David (1919–).
American radio and TV writer-producer-director (TV series include Mr *Peepers, Grindl*).
Pollyanna 60. The Parent Trap 61. Love is a Ball 63. The Interns 63. Under the Yum Yum Tree 64. Good Neighbour Sam 64. How to Succeed in Business without Really Trying (wd, p) 67. Candleshoe (co-w) 77, etc.

Swift, Jonathan (1667–1745).
Irish satirist best known for the much-filmed *Gulliver's Travels*, which is *not* a children's book.

Swinburne, Nora (1902–) (Elinore Johnson).
British actress on stage from 1914, screen occasionally from 1921.
Alibi 30. Potiphar's Wife 31. Fanny by Gaslight 43. *Quartet* 48. The River 51. The End of the Affair 55. Conspiracy of Hearts 59. Interlude 68. Up the Chastity Belt 71, many others.

Swinton, Tilda (1961–).
British actress in experimental and low-budget movies, most often to be seen in the films of Derek Jarman.
Caravaggio 86. Aria 87. Friendship's Death 87.

The Last of England 87. War Requiem 88. Play Me Something 89. The Garden 90. Edward II 91. The Party/Nature Morte 91. Man to Man 92. Orlando 92. Wittgenstein 93. Female Perversions 96. Love Is the Devil 98, etc.

Swit, Loretta (1937–).
American comedy actress of the 70s, familiar as Hot Lips Houlihan from TV's M*A*S*H.
■ Stand Up and Be Counted 72. Shirts/Skins (TV) 73. Freebie and the Bean 74. The Last Day (TV) 75. Race with the Devil 75. The Hostage Heart (TV) 77. The Love Tapes (TV) 79. Cagney and Lacey (TV pilot) 81. S.O.B. 81. The Kid from Nowhere (TV) 82. First Affair (TV) 83. The Execution (TV) 85. Beer 85. Whoops Apocalypse 86.

Switzer, Carl ('Alfalfa') (1926–1959).
American boy actor of the 30s, a graduate of 'Our Gang'; later in character roles. Died from a gunshot wound in an argument over a $50 debt.
General Spanky 37. The War Against Mrs Hadley 42. State of the Union 48. Track of the Cat 54. The Defiant Ones 58, many others.

Swofford, Ken.
Burly American character actor.
Father Goose 64. The Lawyer 69. One Little Indian 73. Crisis at Sun Valley (TV) 78. Black Roses 88. The Taking of Beverly Hills 91, etc.
TV series: Switch 75–76. Fame 83–85.

Syberberg, Hans-Jurgen (1935–).
German producer-director, mainly of documentaries.
Scarabea 68. Ludwig – Requiem for a Virgin King 72. Ludwig's Cook 72. Karl May 74. Confessions of Winifred Wagner 75. Our Hitler 76–77. Parsifal 82. The Night/Die Nacht 85, etc.

Sydney, Basil (1894–1968) (Basil Nugent).
British actor of heavy roles, on stage from 1911.
Romance (film debut) 20. The Midshipmaid 32. The Tunnel 35. Rhodes of Africa 36. The Four Just Men 39. Ships with Wings 41. Went the Day Well? 42. Caesar and Cleopatra 45. The Man Within 47. Hamlet 48. Treasure Island 50. Ivanhoe 52. Hell below Zero 54. The Dam Busters 55. The Three Worlds of Gulliver 60, etc.

Sykes, Eric (1923–).
British TV comedian.
Invasion Quartet 61. Village of Daughters 62. Kill or Cure 63. Heavens Above 63. The Bargee 63. One-Way Pendulum 64. Those Magnificent Men

in Their Flying Machines 65. Rotten to the Core 65. The Liquidator 65. The Spy with a Cold Nose 67. The Plank (& d) 67. Shalako 68. Monte Carlo or Bust 69. Rhubarb (& d) 70. Theatre of Blood 73. The Boys in Blue 83. Splitting Heirs 93, etc.
TV series: Dinnerladies 98.

Sylbert, Paul.
American production designer, occasional director and writer, from television.
Riot 69. The Steagle (wd) 71. Bad Company 72. The Drowning Pool 75. One Flew over the Cuckoo's Nest 76. Heaven Can Wait (AA) 78. Kramer vs Kramer 79. Resurrection 80. Wolfen 81. Gorky Park 83. The Pope of Greenwich Village 84. First Born 84. The Journey of Natty Gann 85. The Pick-Up Artist 87. Ishtar 87. Biloxi Blues 88. Fresh Horses 88. Rush 91. Career Opportunities 91. The Prince of Tides (AAN) 91. Sliver 93. Milk Money 94. The Grass Harp 95. Free Willy 2: The Adventure Home 95, etc.

Sylbert, Richard (1928–).
American art director.
Baby Doll 56. Splendor in the Grass 61. Walk on the Wild Side 62. The Manchurian Candidate 62. How to Murder Your Wife 64. Long Day's Journey into Night 64. The Pawnbroker 64. Who's Afraid of Virginia Woolf? (AA) 66. The Graduate 67. Rosemary's Baby 68. Catch 22 70. Carnal Knowledge 71. The Day of the Dolphin 73. The Fortune 75. Players 79. Reds (AAN) 81. Partners 82. Frances 82. The Cotton Club (AAN) 84. Under the Cherry Moon 86. Shoot to Kill 88. Tequila Sunrise 88. The Bonfire of the Vanities 90. Dick Tracy (AA) 90. Mobsters 91. Ruby Cairo 93. Milk Money 94. Mulholland Falls 96, etc.

Sylvester, William (1922–).
American leading man, in British films from 1949, later back in US.
Give Us This Day 50. The Yellow Balloon 52. Albert RN 53. High Tide at Noon 57. Gorgo 59. Offbeat 60. Ring of Spies 63. Devil Doll 64. Devils of Darkness 65. The Syndicate 67. The Hand of Night 67. 2001: A Space Odyssey 68. Heaven Can Wait 78, many others.
TV series: Gemini Man 76.

Sylvie (1883–1970) (Louise Sylvain).
French character actress.
Un Carnet de Bal 37. Le Corbeau 43. Le Diable au Corps 46. Dieu a Besoin des Hommes 51. Nous

Sommes Tous des Assassins 56. *The Shameless Old Lady* 64.

Syms, Sylvia (1934–).
British leading lady with brief stage and TV experience.
My Teenage Daughter (film debut) 56. Ice Cold in Alex 58. Flame in the Streets 60. Victim 61. The Quare Fellow 62. The World Ten Times Over 63. East of Sudan 64. Operation Crossbow 65. The Big Job 65. Run Wild Run Free 69. Hostile Witness 70. Asylum 72. The Tamarind Seed 74. There Goes the Bride 79. Absolute Beginners 86. Intimate Contact (TV) 87. A Chorus of Disapproval 89. Shirley Valentine 89. Shining Through 92. Dirty Weekend 93. Staggered 94, etc.

Szabó, Ildikó (1951–).
Hungarian director, screenwriter, and costume designer, a former leading actress.
Love Emilia (a) 70. The Old Time Soccer/Régi Idök Focija (a) 73. Hótréal (wd) 87. Child Murders/Gyerekgyilkosságok (wd, cost.) 93. Bitches 96, etc.

Szabó, István (1938–).
Hungarian director.
Age of Illusion 65. Father 66. A Film about Love 70. 25 Firemen's Street 74. Tales of Budapest 77. The Hungarians 78. Bizalom 79. Mephisto 81. Colonel Redl 84. Hanussen 88. Meeting Venus 91. Sweet Emma, Dear Bob/Edes Emma, Draga Bobe 92, etc.

Szasz, Janos (1958–).
Hungarian director and screenwriter; he began as a documentary film-maker in the early 50s.
Wozzeck 93. The Witman Boys/Witman Fiuk (AAN) 97, etc.

Szubanski, Magda.
Australian comedian and actress, much on television in her homeland.
The Search for Christmas (TV) 95. Babe 95. Babe: Pig in the City 98, etc.
TV series: The D Generation 86. Fast Forward 89. Bligh 92. Big Girl's Blouse 94. Something Stupid 98.

Szwarc, Jeannot (1936–).
French director in America.
Extreme Close Up 74. Bug 75. Jaws 2 78. Somewhere in Time 80. Enigma 82. Supergirl 84. Santa Claus 85. Honor Bound 91, etc.

Tabio, Juan Carlos (1943–).
Cuban director who also worked in collaboration with Tomás Gutiérrez Alea.
House for Swap/Se Permuta 84. Plaff 88. *Strawberry and Chocolate/Fresa y Chocolate* (co-d) 94. *The Elephant and the Bicycle/El Elefante y la Bicicleta* 94. Guantanamera (co-d) 95, etc.

Tabori, George (1914–).
Hungarian-born playwright, novelist and screenwriter. Married actress Viveca Lindfors.
Crisis (story) 50. I Confess (co-w) 53. The Young Lovers/Chance Meeting (co-w) 54. The Journey 59. No Exit 62. Secret Ceremony 68. Leo the Last (oa) 69. Parades 72. Frohes Fest (d) 81. Bye Bye America (a) 94. My Mother's Courage (oa) 95, etc.

Tachella, Jean-Charles (1925–).
French director and screenwriter. His *Cousin, Cousine* was remade by Joel Schumacher as *Cousins*.
Cousin, Cousine (AAN) 75. Blue Country/Le Pays Bleu 77. Il y a Longtemps que Je t'Aime 79. Croque la Vie 81. Escalier C 85. Travelling Avant 87. Gallant Ladies/Dames Galantes 91. The Man of My Life/L'Homme de Ma Vie 92. Tous les Jours Dimanche 94, etc.

Tafler, Sydney (1916–1979).
British character actor on stage from 1936. He was married to actress Joy Shelton.
The Young Mr Pitt 42. The Bells Go Down 43. The Little Ballerina 46. It Always Rains on Sunday 47. Passport to Pimlico 48. Mystery Junction 51. Venetian Bird 53. The Sea Shall Not Have Them 55. Carve Her Name with Pride 58. Sink the Bismarck 60. The Bulldog Breed 61. The Seventh Dawn 64. *The Birthday Party* 69. The Adventures 71. The Spy Who Loved Me 77, many others.

Tagawa, Cary-Hiroyuki (1950–).
Muscular American actor, mainly in action movies.
The Last Emperor 87. Spellbinder 88. The Last Warrior 89. Licence to Kill 89. LA Takedown (TV) 89. Kickboxer 2: The Road Back 91. The Perfect Weapon 91. Showdown in Little Tokyo 91. American Me 92. Rising Sun 93. Picture Bride 94. Natural Causes 94. Soldier Boyz 95. White Tiger 95. Mortal Kombat 95. The Phantom 96. John Carpenter's Vampires 97, etc.
TV series: Nash Bridges 96– .

Tait, Margaret (1919–).
Scottish director, writer, and poet. Born in Orkney, she first became a doctor, then studied film in Rome and began making short experimental films from the 50s. Her first full-length feature was released in 1993.
Blue Black Permanent 93.

Takacs, Tibor (1954–).
Canadian director of horror movies.
Metal Messiah 77. The Tomorrow Man 79. The Gate 87. Hardcover 88. I, Madman 89. The Gate 2 92. Earth Creature 92. Bad Blood 94. Sabrina the Teenage Witch (TV) 96. Redline 97, etc.

Takakura, Ken (1931–).
Japanese leading actor, in international films.
The Yakuza 75. Station 81. Antarctica 84. Black Rain 89. Mr Baseball 92. 47 Ronin 94, etc.

Takechi, Tetsuji.
Japanese director, from the stage. He began directing PINK MOVIES in the mid-60s and introduced a political element into what had been an erotic genre. He was unsuccessfully prosecuted on a charge of public indecency over *Black Snow*, when he claimed that the nude scenes in the film symbolized the defencelessness of the Japanese people in the face of the American invasion.
Daydream/Hakujitsumu 64. Black Snow/Kuroi Yuki 65. The Tale of the Genji/Genji Monogatari 66. Ukiyoe 68, etc.

Takei, George (1939–).
American character actor, best known for playing Sulu in *Star Trek*.
Ice Palace 60. Green Beret 68. Star Trek: The Motion Picture 80. Star Trek II: The Wrath of Khan 82. Star Trek III: The Search for Spock 83. Star Trek IV: The Voyage Home 86. Star Trek V: The Final Frontier 89. Star Trek VI: The Undiscovered Country 91. Prisoners of the Sun 91. Oblivion 94. Kissinger and Nixon (TV) 95. Bug Buster 98. Mulan (voice) 98, etc.
TV series: Star Trek 66–69.

Takemitsu, Toru (1930–1996).
Japanese composer.
Juvenile Passions 58. Bad Boys 60. Seppuku 63. Woman of the Dunes 64. Kwaidan 64. Rebellion 67. Double Suicide 69. Dodes'ka'dan 70. The Petrified Forest 73. Himiko 75. Empire of Passion 80. Ran 85. Arashi Ga Oka 88. Black Rain 89. Rising Sun 93, etc.

Takeshi, Beat:
see KITANO, Takeshi.

Takita, Yojiro (1955–).
Japanese director who began his career in PINK MOVIES, as an assistant director until the 80s.
Comic Magazine/Komikku Zasshi Nanika Irani 86. Yen Family 88, etc.

Talalay, Rachel.
American director and producer. A graduate of Yale University, she began as a production assistant on John Waters' *Polyester*.
AS PRODUCER: Nightmare on Elm Street 3: Dream Warriors 87. Nightmare on Elm Street 4: The Dream Master 88. Hairspray 88. Cry Baby 90. The Borrowers 97, etc.
AS DIRECTOR: Freddy's Dead: The Final Nightmare 91. Ghost in the Machine 94. Tank Girl 95, etc.

Talbot, Lyle (1902–1996) (Lysle Hollywood).
Square-built American leading man and occasional heavy, busy from the early 30s.
Love Is a Racket 32. Three on a Match 32. Havana Widows 33. The Dragon Murder Case 34. Red Hot Tyres 35. Trapped by Television 36. Three Legionnaires 37. One Wild Night 38. Second Fiddle 39. Parole Fixer 40. Mexican Spitfire's Elephant 42. Up in Arms 44. Champagne for Caesar 50. With a Song in My Heart 52. There's No Business Like Show Business 54. The Great Man 56. Sunrise at Campobello 60, many others.
TV series: The Bob Cummings Show 55–59. Ozzie and Harriet 56–66.

Talbot, Nita (1930–).
Smart, wisecracking American comedienne.
Bundle of Joy 56. Once upon a Horse 58. Who's Got the Action? 62. Girl Happy 65. That Funny Feeling 65. A Very Special Favour 65. The Cool Ones 67. Buck and the Preacher 71. The Day of the Locust 75. Serial 80. Night Shift 82. Frightmare 83. Take Two 87, etc.
TV series: Joe and Mabel 56. *Hot off the Wire* 60. *Here We Go Again* 71.

Taliaferro, Hal (1896–1980) (Floyd T. Alderson).
American stuntman who became a star of silent westerns under the name Wally Wales, then took another name for the years of his decline.
Western Hearts 21. Vanishing Hoofs 26. Saddle Mates 28. Overland Bound 29. Riders of the Cactus 31. Lone Bandit 33. Sagebrush Trail 33. Danger Trails 35. Way of the West 35. The Unknown Ranger 36. The Painted Stallion (serial) 37. Saga of Death Valley 39. Young Bill Hickok 40. The Great Train Robbery 41. Riders of the Timberline 41. Sons of the Pioneers 42. The Yellow Rose of Texas 44. Zorro's Black Whip (serial) 44. Red River 48. West of Sonora 48. Junction City 51, many others.

Tally, Ted.
American screenwriter who can command $1 million for a script.
White Palace 90. The Silence of the Lambs (AA) 90. Outbreak (co-w) 95. The Juror 96. Before and After 96, etc.

Talmadge, Constance (1898–1973).
American silent heroine and comedienne, sister of Norma Talmadge.
Biography: 1978, *The Talmadge Girls* by Anita Loos.
Intolerance 15. Matrimaniac 16. The Honeymoon 17. Happiness à la Mode 19. Lessons in Love 21. Her Primitive Lover 22. The Goldfish 24. Her Sister from Paris 25. Venus 29, many others.

Talmadge, Natalie (1899–1969).
American leading lady of a few silent comedies; retired to marry Buster Keaton. Younger sister of Norma and Constance Talmadge.

Talmadge, Norma (1893/7–1957).
American silent heroine, sister of Constance Talmadge.
Battle Cry of Peace 14. Going Straight 15. Forbidden City 18. The Sign on the Door 21. Within the Law 23. Secrets 24. The Lady 25. Camille 27. The Dove 28. Dubarry Woman of Passion (last film) 30, many others.
❝ A vision of romance as long as she kept her mouth shut. She would have made an ideal Portia until she announced in her Brooklynese, 'The quality of moicy . . .' – Anita Loos

Talmadge, Richard (1896–1981) (Ricardo Metzetti).
American stuntman of the 20s who doubled for Fairbanks, Lloyd, etc., and later became a star of action films such as *The Speed King, Laughing at Danger and Fighting Demon*. In the 30s became a director of stunt sequences, and more recently worked on *How the West Was Won, What's New Pussycat?, Hawaii* and *Casino Royale*.

Talman, William (1915–1968).
American character actor usually seen as a crook or cop: for seven years was well occupied in TV's *Perry Mason* series as the D.A. who never won a case.
Red Hot and Blue 49. The Armored Car Robbery 50. One Minute to Zero 52. The Hitch Hiker 52. City That Never Sleeps 53. This Man Is Armed 56. Two-Gun Lady 59. The Ballad of Josie 67.

Tamahori, Lee (1950–).
New Zealand director, from television, a former graphic artist and assistant director. His first feature broke box-office records in his homeland.
Once Were Warriors 94. Mulholland Falls 96. The Edge 97, etc.

Tamba, Tetsuro (c. 1929–).
Japanese actor who has appeared in occidental films.
Bridge to the Sun 61. The Seventh Dawn 64. Kwaidan 64. You Only Live Twice 67. The Five Man Army 70. Tange-Sazen 75. Tokyo Pop 88. A Taxing Woman Too 89, etc.

Tamblyn, Russ (1934–).
Buoyant American dancer and tumbler, in small film roles from 1949.
Father of the Bride 50. Father's Little Dividend 51. *Seven Brides for Seven Brothers* 54. Hit the Deck 55. Don't Go Near the Water 56. Peyton Place (AAN) 57. *Tom Thumb* 58. Cimarron 61. *West Side Story* 61. The Wonderful World of the Brothers Grimm 63. The Haunting 63. Son of a Gunfighter 65. Blood of Frankenstein 70. Win, Place or Steal 75. Black Heat 76. Human Highway 82. Phantom Empire 87. B.O.R.N. 88. Aftershock 88. Blood Screams 91. Cabin Boy 94. Invisible Mom 96. My Magic Dog 97, etc.
TV series: Twin Peaks 90, etc.

Tamiroff, Akim (1899–1972).
Russian leading character actor, in America from 1923.
Sadie McKee (film debut) 34. Lives of a Bengal Lancer 35. Naughty Marietta 35. China Seas 36. The Story of Louis Pasteur 36. *The General Died at Dawn* (AAN) 36. *The Great Gambini* 37. Spawn of the North 38. Union Pacific 39. Geronimo 40. *The Way of All Flesh* 40. The Great McGinty 40. The Corsican Brothers 41. *For Whom the Bell Tolls* (AAN) 43. The Bridge of San Luis Rey 44. A Scandal in Paris 46. The Gangster 47. My Girl Tisa 48. Outpost in Morocco 50. You Know What Sailors Are (GB) 53. Confidential Report 55. The Black Sleep 56. Me and the Colonel 57. Touch of Evil 58. Romanoff and Juliet 60. Topkapi 64. The Liquidator 65. Alphaville 65. Lord Jim 65. Lieut. Robin Crusoe 66. After the Fox 66. Great Catherine 68. Then Came Bronson (TV) 70, etc.

Tanaka, Kinuyo (1907–1977).
Leading Japanese actress and occasional director. She was in films from 1924 and appeared in many of the films of Ozu and Mizoguchi. She turned down a marriage proposal from Mizoguchi because he tried to prevent her from becoming a director in the 50s.
Woman of Genroku Era/Genroku Onna 24. I Graduated but . . ./Daigaku wa Detakeredo 29. I Flunked, but . . ./Rakudai wa Shita Keredo 30. Woman of Tokyo/Tokyo no Onna 33. The Woman of That Night/Sono Yo no Onna 34. Aisen Katsura 38. Army/Rikugun 44. The Victory of Women/Josei no Shori 46. Women of the Night/Yoru no Onnatachi 48. The Munekata Sisters/Munekata Shimai 50. Lady Musashino/Musashino Fujin 51. The Life of Oharu/Saikaku Ichidai Onna 52. Ugetsu/Ugetsu Monogatari 52. Love Letter/Koibumi (d) 53. Sansho the Bailiff/Sansho Dayu 54. Moonrise/Tsuki wa Noborinu (d) 55. Equinox Flower/Higanbana 58. The Ballad of Narayama/Narayamabushi-ko 58. Her Brother/Ototo 59. Lonely Lane/Horoki 62. Red Beard/Akahige 65. Lullaby of the Earth/Daichi no Komoriuta 76, many others.

Tandy, Jessica (1909–1994).
British-born actress. She was married to actor Jack Hawkins (1932–40) and married actor Hume Cronyn in 1942.
The Seventh Cross 44. Dragonwyck 46. The Green Years 46. Forever Amber 48. A Woman's Vengeance 48. Rommel, Desert Fox 51. The Light in the Forest 58. Hemingway's Adventures of a Young Man 62. The Birds 63. Butley 73. The World According to Garp 82. Still of the Night 82. Best Friends 82. The Bostonians 84. Cocoon 85. Batteries Not Included 87. Cocoon: The Return 88. Driving Miss Daisy (AA) 89. Fried Green Tomatoes at the Whistle Stop Café (AAN) 92.

Used People 92. Camilla 93. To Dance with the White Dog (TV) 93. Nobody's Fool 94, etc.

Tangerine Dream.
German rock band, using electronic instruments, which has contributed scores to more than 20 movies and TV films.
Sorcerer 77. Kneuss 78. Risky Business 83. The Keep 83. Flashpoint 84. Firestarter 84. Near Dark 87. Kamikaze 87. Miracle Mile 88. Catch Me If You Can 89. Rainbow 90. Highway to Hell 91, etc.

Tani, Yoko (1932–).
Japanese leading lady, in international films.
The Wind Cannot Read 57. The Quiet American 58. Savage Innocents 59. Piccadilly Third Stop 60. Marco Polo 61. Who's Been Sleeping in My Bed? 63. Invasion 66, etc.

Tanner, Alain (1929–).
Swiss director.
Jonah Who Will Be 25 in the Year 2000 76. Messidor 78. Light Years Away 81. In the White City 82. No Man's Land 85. La Vallée Fantôme 87. Une Flamme dans Mon Coeur 87. The Woman of Rose Hill/La Femme de Rose Hill 89. The Man Who Lost His Shadow/L'Homme Qui a Perdu Son Ombre 91. The Diary of Lady M/Le Journal de Lady M 93. Fourbi 96, etc.

Tanner, Peter (1914–).
British editor.
Lady from Lisbon 42. Scott of the Antarctic 48. Kind Hearts and Coronets 49. The Blue Lamp 50. Secret People 52. Lease of Life 54. The Night My Number Came Up 55. Man in the Sky 57. Light up the Sky 60. Sodom and Gomorrah 61. A Jolly Bad Fellow 64. Diamonds for Breakfast 68. The House that Dripped Blood 71. Asylum 72. Hedda 75. Nasty Habits 76. Stevie 78. The Monster Club 81. Turtle Diary 85. Sky Bandits 86. Hamburger Hill 87. Without a Clue 88. Danny, Champion of the World 89. Widow's Peak 94. A Month by the Lake 95, etc.

Tanner, Tony (1932–).
British light actor and revue artiste.
Strictly for the Birds 64. A Home of Your Own 65. The Pleasure Girls 65. Stop the World I Want to Get Off 66, etc.

Tapley, Colin (1911–).
New Zealand character actor who has played a few stalwart types in international pictures.
Search for Beauty 34. The Black Room 35. Samson and Delilah 49. Angels One Five 52. The Dam Busters 56. Fraulein Doktor 68, etc.

Taradash, Daniel (1913–).
American screenwriter.
Golden Boy 39. Rancho Notorious 48. *From Here to Eternity* (AA) 53. Désirée 54. Storm Centre (& d) 55. Picnic 55. Bell, Book and Candle 58. Morituri 65. Hawaii 66. Doctors' Wives 71. The Other Side of Midnight (co-w) 77, etc.

Tarantino, Quentin (1963–).
American director, screenwriter, and actor, with an encyclopaedic knowledge of old movies and a liking for junk culture. *Pulp Fiction* won the Palme d'Or at the Cannes Film Festival in 1994.
Biographies: 1995, *Quentin Tarantino: Shooting from the Hip* by Wensley Clarkson; 1995, *Tarantino – Inside Story* by Jeff Dawson; 1995, *Quentin Tarantino: The Man and His Movies* by Jami Bernard; 1997, *Tarantino A to Zed* by Allan Barnes and Marcus Hearn; 1998, *King Pulp* by Paul A. Woods.
Reservoir Dogs (a, wd) 91. True Romance (w) 93. Killing Zoe (p) 94. Sleep with Me (a) 94. *Pulp Fiction* (a, wd) (AAw, AANd) 94. Natural Born Killers (w) 94. Crimson Tide (co-w) 95. Destiny Turns on the Radio (a) 95. Desperado (a) 95. Four Rooms (a) 95. From Dusk till Dawn (a, ex p, w) 96. Girl 6 (a) 96. Jackie Brown (wd) 97, etc.
❝ Violence in the movies? It's fun, it's one of the coolest, funnest things for me to watch. – *Q.T.*
If you say you don't like violence in movies, it's like saying you don't like slapstick comedy or dance sequences in movies. – *Q.T.*
I've got so many movies I would like to make. I've got my western, my World War II bunch of guys on a mission, my spaghetti western, my horror film. But since I know I won't live long enough to do all the movies I want to do, with every movie the goal is to wipe out as many as I can. – *Q.T.*
I steal from every movie ever made. – *Q.T.*
I find the sensibility at work in a film like *Reservoir Dogs* absolutely appalling. – *John Duigan*

Tarkington, Booth (1869–1946).
American novelist. Films of his books include *Alice Adams, Penrod, Monsieur Beaucaire, The Magnificent Ambersons*.

Tarkovsky, Andrei (1932–1986).
Distinguished Russian director and screenwriter, with an intensely personal vision. The son of a poet, he studied at VGIK under Mikhail Romm. He suffered from censorship problems with *Andrei Rublev*, which dealt with an individual artist in conflict with the state, and retreated into metaphysics with the visually stimulating but obscure *Solaris* and *Mirror*. From the 80s, he lived and worked away from Russia. Died of lung cancer.
Book: 1989, *Tarkovsky: Cinema as Poetry* by Maya Turovskaya.
There Will Be No Leave today (short) 59. The Steamroller and the Violin/Katok i Stripa (short) 60. Ivan's Childhood/Ivanovo Destvo (d) 62. *Andrei Rublev* (co-w, d) 66. *Solaris* (co-w, d) 72. Mirror/Zerkalo (co-w, d) 74. Stalker (d, pd) 79. Nostaglia/Nostalghia (co-w, d) (It.) 83. The Sacrifice/Offret (wd, ed) (Swe.) 86.
❝ My purpose is to make films that will help people to live, even if they sometimes cause unhappiness. – *A.T.*

Tashlin, Frank (1913–1972).
American comedy writer-director, former cartoonist.
The Fuller Brush Man (w) 48. *The Paleface* (w) 48. The Good Humour Man (w) 50. Kill the Umpire (w) 51. Susan Slept Here (d) 54. Artists and Models (wd) 55. *The Girl Can't Help It* (wd, p) 57. Will Success Spoil Rock Hunter? (wd, p) 57. Rockabye Baby (wd) 58. Say One for Me (p, d) 59. Cinderfella (wd) 60. It's Only Money (d) 63. The Man from the Diners Club (d) 64. The Alphabet Murders (d) 65. The Glass Bottom Boat (d) 66. Caprice (d) 67. The Private Navy of Sgt O'Farrell (wd) 68, etc.

Tashman, Lilyan (1899–1934).
American silent screen sophisticate. Born in Brooklyn, she began her career in the Ziegfeld Follies. Married vaudevillian Al Lee and, in 1925, actor Edmund Lowe. Died of cancer.
Experience 21. Manhandled 24. Don't Tell the Wife 27. New York Nights 29. Murder by the Clock 31. Scarlet Dawn 32. Frankie and Johnny 33, etc.

Tass, Nadia (1956–) (Nadia Tassopolous).
Greek-born director and producer, in Australia.
Malcolm 86. Rikky and Pete 88. The Big Steal 90. Over the Hill 90. Pure Luck 91. Stark (TV) 93. Mr Reliable: A True Story 95, etc.

Tate, Harry (1872–1940) (Ronald MacDonald Hutchinson).
British music-hall comedian famous for motoring sketch. In occasional films.
Motoring 27. Her First Affair 32. Happy 34. Midshipman Easy 35. Hyde Park Corner 35. Keep Your Seats Please 36. Wings of the Morning 37, etc.
~Catchphrase: How's your father?

Tate, Larenz (1975–).
American actor.
Menace II Society 93. The Inkwell 94. Dead Presidents 95. Love Jones 96. The Postman 97. Why Do Fools Fall in Love (as Frankie Lymon) 98, etc.

Tate, Reginald (1896–1955).
British character actor, mainly on stage.
Riverside Murder 35. Dark Journey 37. Next of Kin 42. The Life and Death of Colonel Blimp 43. Uncle Silas 47. Robin Hood 52. King's Rhapsody 55, etc.

Tate, Sharon (1943–1969).
American leading lady, victim of a sensational murder. She was married to director Roman Polanski.
Eye of the Devil 67. The Fearless Vampire Killers 67. Valley of the Dolls 67. Don't Make Waves 67. Wrecking Crew 69, etc.

Tati, Jacques (1908–1982) (Jacques Tatischeff).
French pantomimist and actor who after years in the music halls and in small film roles began to write and direct his own quiet comedies which were really little more than strings of sight gags on a theme.
Book: 1976, *Jacques Tati* by Penelope Gilliatt.
■ *Jour de Fête* 49. *Monsieur Hulot's Holiday* (AANw) 52. Mon Oncle 58. Playtime 68. Traffic 71. Parade (TV) 74.
❝ M. Hulot is a real character, not a movie star because he's not a star. He's the opposite of the person created by Chaplin, Keaton and so on. He's not a gag man, he's not a clown; he's someone you recognise more from his back than from the front. – *J.T.*
The public always like the picture you have done before. They always see a new picture and say, his last was much funnier. – *J.T.*
I'm part of the old school. I'm the last who had the chance to learn in the music hall. That school is now closed. The singers and the sound engineers have taken over. – *J.T.*
~Tati also appeared in several shorts, and played the ghost in *Sylvie et le Fantôme* 47.

Tattersall, Gale.
British cinematographer, a former stills photographer. He began in films as camera operator for cinematographer Donald McAlpine on *The Adventures of Barry Mackenzie* 72, and also worked on commercials. He first moved to the United States to do additional photography on *The Addams Family*.
My Childhood (co-ph) 72. My Ain Folk 73. Comrades 86. Aria (co-ph) 87. Vroom 88. Homeboy 88. Wild Orchid 90. The Commitments 91. Hideaway (US) 95. Tank Girl (US) 95. Virtuosity (US) 95. From the Earth to the Moon (TV) 98, etc.

Taube, Sven-Bertil (1934–).
Swedish leading man.
The Buttercup Chain 70. Puppet on a Chain 70. The Eagle Has Landed 76. Game for Vultures 79. Handera 94. Such Is Life/Sant Ar Livet 96, etc.

Tauber, Richard (1891–1948).
Austrian operatic tenor, long in Britain where he made a number of artless but likeable musical comedy films.
Biography: 1959, *My Heart and I* by Diana Napier Tauber.
Symphony of Love 31. Blossom Time 34. Heart's Desire 35. Land without Music 35. Pagliacci 36. The Lisbon Story 45, etc.

Taurog, Norman (1899–1981).
American director, former child actor, in Hollywood from 1917.
Lucky Boy 28. *Skippy* (AA) 31. Huckleberry Finn 33. We're Not Dressing 34. Mrs Wiggs of the Cabbage Patch 35. Strike Me Pink 36. *Mad about Music* 38. The Adventures of Tom Sawyer 38. Boys' Town (AAN) 38. Broadway Melody of 1940 40. Young Tom Edison 40. A Yank at Eton 42. Girl Crazy 42. The Hoodlum Saint 46. The Bride Goes Wild 48. Please Believe Me 50. Room for One More 52. Living It Up 54. The Birds and the Bees 56. Bundle of Joy 57. Don't Give Up the Ship 59. Palm Springs Weekend 63. Tickle Me 65. Sergeant Deadhead 65. Speedway 67, many others.

Tavernier, Bertrand (1941–).
French director and screenwriter.
The Watchmaker of St Paul 74. Que la Fête Commence 75. The Judge and the Assassin 76. Spoiled Children 77. Death Watch 80. Coup de Torchon 82. A Week's Vacation 82. Mississippi Blues 83. *Sunday in the Country* 84. *'Round Midnight* 86. Beatrice/La Passion Béatrice 86. La Vie et Rien d'Autre 89. These Foolish Things/Daddy Nostalgie 90. The Undeclared War/La Guerre sans Nom (doc) 91. L.627 (wd) 92. La Fille de D'Artagnan (wd) 94. Fresh Bait/L'Appat (co-w, d) 95. Capitaine Conan (d) 96. The Other Side of the Tracks/De l'Autre Côté du Periph (co-d) 98, etc.

Taviani, Paolo (1931–) and **Vittorio** (1929–).
Italian brother directors who always work together.
■ A Man to Burn 62. Sovversivi 67. Beneath the Sign of the Scorpion 69. St Michael Had a Rooster 71. Allonsanfan 74. *Padre Padrone* 77. The Field 79. Night of the Shooting Stars 81. Kaos 84. Good Morning Babylon 87. Night Sun/Il Sole Anche di Notte 90. Wild Flower/Fiorile 93. Elective Affinities 96. You're Laughing/Tu Ridi 98.
❝ Our relationship is a very strange thing, a mystery. We don't even fully understand it ourselves; we know it works but not why. – *V.T.*

Tavoularis, Alex.
American production designer and art director, the brother of Dean Tavoularis, with whom he worked at the beginning of his career.
Peggy Sue Got Married 86. Gardens of Stone 87. Steel Dawn 87. Tucker: The Man and His Dream 88. Lost Angels 89. Scenes from the Class Struggle in Beverly Hills 89. King of New York 90. Beethoven 92. Dangerous Game 93. Jade 95. The Parent Trap 98, etc.

Tavoularis, Dean (1932–).
American production designer who trained as an architect and also worked as an animator for Disney.
Bonnie and Clyde 67. Candy 68. Zabriskie Point 70. Little Big Man 70. The Godfather 72. The Conversation 74. The Godfather Part II (AA) 74. Farewell My Lovely 75. The Missouri Breaks 76. Brinks 79. Apocalypse Now (AAN) 79. Hammett 82. One from the Heart 82. The Outsiders 83. Rumble Fish 83. Peggy Sue Got Married 86. A Man in Love 87. Gardens of Stone 87. Tucker: The Man and His Dream 88. New York Stories 89. The Godfather Part III 90. Final Analysis 92. Rising Sun 93. I Love Trouble 94. Jack 96. Bulworth 98. The Parent Trap 98, etc.

Tayback, Vic (1929–1990).
Tough-looking American supporting actor.
Bullitt 68. With Six You Get Egg Roll 68. Lepke 73. Alice Doesn't Live Here Any More 74. Thunderbolt and Lightfoot 75. No Deposit No Return 76. The Choirboys 77. The Great American Traffic Jam (TV) 80. Rage (TV) 80. Mysterious Two (TV) 82. Weekend Warriors 86. Criminal Act 88. Beverly Hills Bodysnatchers 89. Treasure Island 91, etc.
TV series: Alice 76–85.

Taylor, Alma (1895–1974).
British actress of the silent screen.
The Little Milliner and the Thief 09. Oliver Twist 12. Paying the Penalty 13. The Baby on the Barge 15. Annie Laurie 16. The American Heiress 17. Sunken Rocks 19. Alf's Button 20. The Tinted Venus 21. Comin' thro' the Rye 23. The Shadow of Egypt 24. Quinneys 27. Bachelor's Baby 32. Things are Looking Up 35. Lilacs in the Spring 54. Blue Murder at St Trinian's 57, etc.

Taylor, Deems (1886–1966).
American journalist and musician whose chief connection with films was to act as narrator for *Fantasia* 40 and to help write *A Pictorial History of the Movies* 48.

Taylor, Don (1920–1998).
American director, a former light leading man, with stage experience. His third wife is actress Hazel Court.
Naked City 48. For the Love of Mary 48. Ambush 49. Father of the Bride 50. Submarine Command 51. The Blue Veil 51. Stalag 17 53. Men of Sherwood Forest 54. I'll Cry Tomorrow 57. Savage Guns 62, etc.
AS DIRECTOR: The Savage Guns 62. Ride the Wild Surf 64. Jack of Diamonds 67. The Five Man Army 70. Escape from the Planet of the Apes 71. Tom Sawyer 73. Echoes of a Summer 75. The Great Scout and Cathouse Thursday 76. The Island of Dr Moreau 77. Damien – Omen II 78. The Final Countdown 80. My Wicked, Wicked Ways (TV) 85. Secret Weapons (TV) 85. The Diamond Trap (TV) 88, etc.

Taylor, Dub 'Cannonball' (1909–) (Walter Clarence Taylor, Jnr).
Chunky, grizzled American character actor, most frequently in 'B' westerns from the late 30s, as sidekick to the hero. Born in Richmond, Virginia, he began as a saxophonist. He was also a regular on the country music TV series *Hee Haw* in the 80s.
You Can't Take It with You 38. Taming of the West 39. Prairie Schooners 40. The Son of Davy Crockett 41. Saddles and Sagebrush 43. Wyoming Hurricane 44. Rustlers of the Badlands 45. Range Renegades 48. Roaring Westward 49. Riding High 50. The Bounty Hunter 54. The Hallelujah Trail

65. Bonnie and Clyde 67. The Shakiest Gun in the West 67. Bandolero! 68. The Undefeated 69. The Wild Bunch 69. A Man Called Horse 70. Support Your Local Gunfighter 71. The Great Smokey Roadblock 76. Gator 76. Burnt Offerings 76. Texas Guns 90. Back to the Future III 90. My Heroes Have Always Been Cowboys 91, etc.

TV series: Casey Jones 57–58. Please Don't Eat the Daisies 65–66.

Taylor, Elaine.
British leading lady.

Casino Royale 67. Half a Sixpence 68. Diamonds for Breakfast 68. The Anniversary 68. The Games 69. All the Way Up 70, etc.

Taylor, Elizabeth (1932–).
British-born leading lady with a well-publicized private life. Was evacuated to Hollywood during World War II and began as a child star. Scored nine husbands so far, including actor Michael Wilding (1952–57), producer Mike Todd (1957–58), singer Eddie Fisher (1959–64), and actor Richard Burton (1954–74 and 1975–76).

Biographies: 1981, *Elizabeth Taylor: The Last Star* by Kitty Kelley. 1991, *Elizabeth* by Alexander Walker. 1995, *Elizabeth Taylor* by Donald Spoto.

■ There's One Born Every Minute 42. Lassie Come Home 43. Jane Eyre 43. The White Cliffs of Dover 44. *National Velvet* 44. Courage of Lassie 45. Cynthia 47. Life with Father 47. A Date with Judy 48. Julia Misbehaves 48. *Little Women* 49. Conspirator 49. The Big Hangover 49. *Father of the Bride* 50. Father's Little Dividend 51. Quo Vadis 51. Love is Better Than Ever 51. *A Place in the Sun* 51. The Light Fantastic 51. Ivanhoe 52. The Girl Who Had Everything 53. Rhapsody 54. Elephant Walk 54. Beau Brummell 54. The Last Time I Saw Paris 55. *Giant* 56. *Raintree County* (AAN) 57. *Cat on a Hot Tin Roof* (AAN) 58. *Suddenly Last Summer* (AAN) 59. *Butterfield* 8 (AA) 60. Scent of Mystery 60. *Cleopatra* 62. The VIPs 63. The Sandpiper 65. *Who's Afraid of Virginia Woolf?* (AA) 66. The Taming of the Shrew 67. Doctor Faustus 67. The Comedians 67. Reflections in a Golden Eye 67. Boom 68. Secret Ceremony 68. The Only Game in Town 69. Under Milk Wood 71. Zee and Co 71. Hammersmith is Out 72. Divorce His, Divorce Hers (TV) 72. Night Watch 73. Ash Wednesday 73. The Driver's Seat 75. The Blue Bird 76. Victory at Entebbe (TV) 76. A Little Night Music 77. Repeat Performance (TV) 78. The Mirror Crack'd 80. Between Friends (TV) 82. Malice in Wonderland (TV) 84. There Must Be a Pony (TV) 86. Poker Alice (TV) 87. Sweet Bird of Youth (TV) 89. The Flintstones 94.

❝ I don't pretend to be an ordinary housewife. – *E.T.*

A pharaonic mummy, moving on tiny castors like a touring replica of the Queen Mother. – *Sunday Times on E.T. in The Mirror Crack'd*

If someone's dumb enough to offer me a million dollars to make a picture, I'm certainly not dumb enough to turn it down. – *E.T.*

I believe in mind over matter and doing anything you set your mind on. – *E.T.*

I, along with the critics, have never taken myself very seriously. – *E.T.*

Is she fat? Her favourite food is seconds. – *Joan Rivers*

She should get a divorce and settle down. – *Jack Paar*

There are three things I never saw Elizabeth Taylor do. Tell a lie; be unkind to anyone; and be on time. – *Mike Nichols*

The most astonishingly self-contained, pulchritudinous, remote, removed, inaccessible woman I had ever seen. – *Richard Burton*

Famous line (*Reflections in a Golden Eye*): 'She cut off her nipples with garden shears. You call that normal?'

Taylor, Estelle (1899–1958) (Estelle Boylan).
American stage actress who made some silent and early sound films.

While New York Sleeps 22. The Ten Commandments 23. Don Juan 26. The Whip Woman 27. When East is East 28. Liliom 30. Cimarron 31. Call Her Savage 32. The Southerner 45, etc.

Taylor, Gilbert (1914–).
British cinematographer, in films since 1929.

The Guinea Pig 48. Seven Days to Noon 50. The Yellow Balloon 52. It's Great To Be Young 55. The Good Companions 57. Ice Cold in Alex 58. The Rebel 60. Dr Strangelove 63. Repulsion 65. The Bedford Incident 65. Before Winter Comes 69. Macbeth 71. Frenzy 72. The Omen 76. *Star Wars* (AAN) 77. Dracula 79. Flash Gordon 80. Green Ice 81. Venom 82. Losin' It 82. Lassiter 84. The Bedroom Window 87. Don't Get Me Started 94, etc.

Taylor, Jud (1940–).
American director.

Weekend of Terror (TV) 70. Revenge (TV) 71. Heat of Anger (TV) 72. Say Goodbye Maggie Cole (TV) 72. Hawkins on Murder (TV) 73. Winter Kill (TV) 74. Future Cop (TV) 76. Return to Earth (TV) 76. Tail Gunner Joe (TV) 77. Mary White (TV) 77. Flesh and Blood (TV) 80. Packin' It In (TV) 83. Licence to Kill (TV) 84. Out of the Darkness (TV) 85. Foxfire (TV) 87. The Great Escape II: The Untold Story (TV) 88. The Old Man and the Sea (TV) 90. Secrets (TV) 94, etc.

Taylor, Kent (1907–1987) (Louis Weiss).
Suave American leading man of second features from the early 30s.

Two Kinds of Women 32. I'm No Angel 33. Double Door 34. Two Fisted 35. The Accusing Finger 36. The Jury's Secret 37. I Take this Woman 40. Frisco Lil 42. Bombers Moon 43. The Daltons Ride Again 45. The Crimson Key 47. Payment on Demand 51. Playgirl 54. Slightly Scarlet 56. Ghost Town 56. Harbour Lights 64. The Day Mars Invaded Earth 64. Smashing the Crime Syndicate 73, etc.

TV series: *Boston Blackie* 51–52.

Taylor, Laurette (1884–1946) (Laurette Cooney).
American leading actress of the stage who filmed her great success, *Peg o' My Heart*, which had been written for her by her second husband, J. Hartley MANNERS. She remained in Hollywood to make only two more films, also based on his plays. Born in New York, she began as a child in vaudeville and was regarded by many as America's greatest actress, despite her preference for sentimental dramas. George CUKOR attempted to interest her in returning to films, but by the 30s she was an alcoholic and unreliable; he also tried to make a biopic of her life, starring Judy GARLAND. A year before her death, she made a triumphant return to Broadway in Tennessee WILLIAMS's *The Glass Menagerie*. She had a brief affair with King VIDOR, who directed her in her first two films, and her attraction to actor John GILBERT led to the break-up of his marriage to actress Leatrice JOY. Noël COWARD took her, and her way of life, as the model for actress Judith Bliss and her family in his play *Hay Fever*.

Biography: 1955, *Laurette* by Marguerite Courtney.

■ Peg o' My Heart 22. Happiness 24. One Night in Rome 24.

❝ If they say you drink or take dope, you can get over it. But when they say you're forgetting your lines, you're *finished*. – *L.T.*

I have simply never seen anyone like her on the stage. What she did was indescribable. – *Ethel Barrymore*

Taylor, Lili (1967–).
American actress.

Mystic Pizza 88. Say Anything 89. Bright Angel 91. Dogfight 91. Watch It 93. Mrs Parker and the Vicious Circle 94. Prêt-à-Porter/Ready to Wear 94. The Addiction 95. Four Rooms 95. Cold Fever 95. Killer: A Journal of Murder 96. *Girls Town* (& co-w) 96. I Shot Andy Warhol 96. Ransom 96. Kicked in the Head 97. The Imposters 98. OK Garage 98, etc.

❝ Human life just doesn't interest Hollywood. – *L.T.*

Taylor, Noah (c. 1969–).
Australian leading actor. Born in London, he moved with his family to Australia at the age of eight. He joined a youth drama group in his early teens, and three years later played the adolescent boy in John Duigan's *The Year My Voice Broke*. His local star status was confirmed by *The Nostradamus Kid*, and his quality was recognized internationally with *Shine*.

The Year My Voice Broke 87. Flirting 89. The Prisoner of St Petersburg 90. The Nostradamus Kid 93. Dad and Dave on Our Selection 95. Shine 96. True Love and Chaos 96. There's No Fish Food in Heaven 98. Woundings (GB) 98. Simon Magus 99, etc.

❝ Career's been the least important thing in my life. All I really want is to have a child with someone I love and be reasonably sane. – *N.T.*

Taylor, Peter (1922–1997).
British editor.

Devil Girl from Mars 54. Summer Madness 55. The Man Who Never Was 55. *The Bridge on the River Kwai* (AA) 57. The Devil's Daffodil 61. Waltz of the Toreadors 62. This Sporting Life 63. Judith 66. The Taming of the Shrew 67. Monte Carlo or Bust 69. La Traviata 83. Otello 85. The Penitent 88. Becoming Colette 91, etc.

Taylor, Robert (1911–1969) (Spangler Arlington Brugh).
Handsome, durable and hard-working American leading man. His boyish good looks turned rather set and grim in middle age, but he remained a star. Born in Filley, Nebraska, he studied at Doane University. He then followed his cello teacher to study at Pomona College, California, where he began acting and was encouraged to join MGM's acting school before signing a seven-year contract with the studio at $35 a week, which is said to have made him the lowest-paid actor in the history of Hollywood; he remained at MGM for 24 years. After some unmemorable roles, he became a star in *Magnificent Obsession*, appealing especially to women; his exceptional good looks were said to alienate many men, though they won him a gay following. In 1936 he was the top male star, seen in a succession of romantic parts, but he found constant newspaper references to his 'pretty boy' looks hard to bear. His defining roles were as Bobby Merrick in *Magnificent Obsession*, Armand Duvall in *Camille*, Roy Cronin in *Waterloo Bridge*, the title role in *Ivanhoe*, and as Sir Lancelot in *Knights of the Round Table*. In the late 40s, he was one of the first friendly witnesses to testify to HUAC about Communist infiltration in Hollywood, complaining that he had been forced to make *Song of Russia*. Married actresses Barbara STANWYCK (1939–51) and, in 1959, Ursula Theiss. He was romantically involved with actresses Virginia BRUCE, Irene Harvey, Lia DiLeo, Virgina GREY, and Eleanor PARKER. Died of cancer.

■ Handy Andy 34. There's Always Tomorrow 34. Wicked Woman 34. Society Doctor 34. West Point of the Air 35. Times Square Lady 35. Murder in the Fleet 35. *Magnificent Obsession* 35. Broadway Melody of 1936 36. Small Town Girl 36. Private Number 36. His Brother's Wife 36. The Gorgeous Hussy 36. *Camille* 36. Personal Property 37. This is My Affair 37. Broadway Melody of 1938. *A Yank at Oxford* 38. Three Comrades 38. The Crowd Roars 38. Stand Up and Fight 39. Lucky Night 39. Lady of the Tropics 39. Remember 39. *Waterloo Bridge* 40. Escape 40. Flight Command 40. Billy the Kid 41. When Ladies Meet 41. Johnny Eager 42. Her Cardboard Lover 42. Stand By for Action 43. *Bataan* 43. Song of Russia 44. Undercurrent 46. High Wall 47. The Bribe 49. Ambush 49. Devil's Doorway 50. Conspirator 50. *Quo Vadis* 51. Westward the Women 51. *Ivanhoe* 52. Above and Beyond 52. Ride Vaquero 53. All the Brothers were Valiant 53. *Knights of the Round Table* 53. Valley of the Kings 54. Rogue Cop 54. Many Rivers to Cross 55. Quentin Durward 55. The Last Hunt 56. D-Day Sixth of June 56. The Power and the Prize 56. Tip on a Dead Jockey 57. Saddle the Wind 58. The Law and Jake Wade 58. Party Girl 58. The Hangman 59. The House of the Seven Hawks 59. Killers of Kilimanjaro 60. The Miracle of the White Stallions 61. Cattle King 63. A House is Not a Home 64. The Night Walker 65. Savage Pampas 66. The Return of the Gunfighter 66. Johnny Tiger 66. Where Angels Go Trouble Follows 68. The Day the Hot Line Got Hot 68. Devil May Care 68. The Glass Sphinx 68.

TV series: *The Detectives* 59–61.

❝ I was a punk kid from Nebraska who had an awful lot of the world's good things tossed in his lap. – *R.T.*

For 17 years it was Mr Mayer who guided me, and I never turned down a picture that he personally asked me to do. – *R.T.*

Acting is the easiest job in the world, and I'm the luckiest guy. All I have to do is be at the studio on time, and know my lines. The wardrobe department tells me what to wear, the assistant director tells me where to go, the director tells me what to do. What could be easier? – *R.T.*

Taylor, Rod (1930–) (Rodney Sturt Taylor).
Australian-born, Hollywood-based leading man with stage experience.

King of the Coral Sea 54. Long John Silver 55. The Catered Affair 56. Giant 56. Raintree County 57. Separate Tables 58. *The Time Machine* 60. *The Birds* 63. *The VIPs* 63. Sunday in New York 63. Fate Is the Hunter 64. *Thirty-Six Hours* 64. Young Cassidy 65. Do Not Disturb 65. The Liquidator 65. The Glass Bottom Boat 66. Hotel 67. Dark of the Sun 67. Chuka 67. Nobody Runs Forever 68. The Hell with Heroes 69. The Man Who Had Power Over Women 70. Darker than Amber 70. The Train Robbers 72. Family Flight (TV) 72. Trader Horn 73. Deadly Trackers 73. Shamus (TV) 73. The Heroes 75. The Picture Show Man 77. An Eye for an Eye 78. On the Run 82. Masquerade (TV) 83. Marbella 85. Mask of Murder 89. Open Season 95. Welcome to Woop Woop 97, etc.

TV series: Hong Kong 60. Bearcats 71. The Oregon Trail 75.

Taylor, Ronnie (1924–).
British cinematographer who won an Oscar for *Gandhi*.

Tommy 75. Circle of Iron 79. Savage Harvest 81. *Gandhi* (AA) 82. High Road to China 83. A Chorus Line 85. Foreign Body 86. Cry Freedom 87. Sea of Love 90. Popcorn 91. Age of Treason 93. The Steal 94. Redwood Curtain (TV) 95. Phantom of the Opera 98, etc.

Taylor, Sam (1895–1958).
American screenwriter of the 20s: *The Freshman*, *Exit Smiling*, etc. Remembered chiefly for the credit line to the 1928 version of *The Taming of the Shrew*: 'By William Shakespeare, with additional dialogue by Sam Taylor.'

Taylor, Samuel (1912–).
American playwright and screenwriter whose play *Sabrina Fair* has been filmed twice so far.

The Happy Time (oa) 52. *Sabrina* 54. The Eddy Duchin Story 55. The Monte Carlo Story (& d) 56. *Vertigo* (co-w) 58. Aimez-Vous Brahms? 61. The Pleasure of His Company (w, oa) 61. Three on a Couch (co-w) 66. Rosie 67. Topaz 69. Promise at Dawn (oa) 70. The Love Machine 71. Sabrina 95, etc.

Taylor-Young, Leigh (1945–).
American leading lady of the early 70s. Married actor Ryan O'NEAL (1967–73).

I Love You Alice B. Toklas 68. The Big Bounce 68. The Adventurers 69. The Buttercup Chain 70. The Horsemen 71. The Gang that Couldn't Shoot Straight 72. Soylent Green 73. Can't Stop the Music 80. Looker 81. Jagged Edge 85. Napoleon and Josephine: A Love Story (TV) 87. Who Gets the Friends (TV) 88. Accidents (Aus.) 88. Honeymoon Academy 90. Bliss 97, etc.

Tazieff, Haroun (1914–1998).
French explorer-photographer, best known for *Rendezvous du Diable/Volcano* 58, *The Forbidden Volcano* 67.

Tcherina, Ludmilla (1925–) (Monique Tchemerzine).
French ballerina.

The Red Shoes 48. Tales of Hoffman 50. Sign of the Pagan 54. Oh Rosalinda 55. Honeymoon 59. A Ravishing Idiot 63, etc.

Teagarden, Jack (1906–1964).
American jazz trombonist and singer who made occasional film appearances, among which the highlight is his performance of the Johnny Mercer song 'The Waiter and the Porter and the Upstairs Maid' with Bing Crosby and Mary Martin in *Birth of the Blues*.

Birth of the Blues 41. Glory Alley 52. The Glass Wall 53. Jazz on a Summer's Day 60.

Teague, Lewis (1941–).
American director who began as an editor for Roger Corman's productions.

The Lady in Red 79. Alligator 80. Death Vengeance 82. Fighting Back 82. Cujo 83. The Jewel of the Nile 85. Stephen King's Cat's Eye 85. Collision Course 90. Navy SEALS 90. Wedlock 90. T Bone 'n' Weasel (TV) 92. Tom Clancy's Op Center (TV) 95. Saved by the Light (TV) 97, etc.

Teal, Ray (1902–1976).
American character actor often seen as sheriff, good or bad. In films from 1938 after stage experience.
The Cherokee Strip 40. A Wing and a Prayer 44. Captain Kidd 45. Joan of Arc 48. The Men 50. *Ace in the Hole* 51. The Lion and the Horse 53. Montana Belle 53. Hangman's Knot 54. Ambush at Tomahawk Gap 54. Run for Cover 55. The Indian Fighter 55. Saddle the Wind 57. One-Eyed Jacks 61. Cattle King 63. Taggart 64. The Liberation of L. B. Jones 71, many others.
TV series: Bonanza 59–71.

Tearle, Conway (1878–1938) (Frederick Levy).
American leading actor of silent days; half-brother of Godfrey Tearle.
Stella Maris 18. The Virtuous Vamp 20. Woman of Bronze 23. Bella Donna 25. Gold Diggers of Broadway 29. Vanity Fair 32. Should Ladies Behave? 34. Klondike Annie 36. Romeo and Juliet 36, etc.

Tearle, Sir Godfrey (1884–1953).
Distinguished British stage actor, on stage from 1893; occasional films from 1906, when he played Romeo in a one-reeler.
If Youth But Knew 30. The Thirty-Nine Steps 35. *One of Our Aircraft is Missing* 42. The Rake's Progress 45. The Beginning or the End 47. Private Angelo 48. *The Titfield Thunderbolt* 53, etc.

Teasdale, Verree (1904–1987).
American comedy actress, often as sophisticated friend or suspicious wife.
■ Syncopation 29. The Sap from Syracuse 30. Skyscraper Souls 32. Payment Deferred 32. Luxury Liner 33. They Just Had to Get Married 33. Terror Aboard 33. Love Honour and Oh Baby 33. *Roman Scandals* 33. Fashions of 1934 34. Goodbye Love 34. A Modern Hero 34. Madame Du Barry 34. Desirable 34. The Firebird 34. Dr Monica 34. A Midsummer Night's Dream (as Titania) 35. The Milky Way 36. First Lady 37. Topper Takes a Trip 38. Fifth Avenue Girl 39. Turnabout 40. I Take This Woman 40. Love Thy Neighbour 40. Come Live with Me 41.

Téchiné, André (1943–).
French director, a former critic for *Cahiers du Cinéma.*
Paulina S'en Va 69. Souvenirs d'en France 75. Barocco 77. Les Soeurs Brontë 78. Hôtel des Amériques 81. L'Atelier 84. Rendez-vous 85. Les Innocents 87. I Don't Kiss/J'Embrasse Pas 91. Ma Saison Préférée 93. *The Wild Reeds*/Les Roseaux Sauvages 94. Thieves/Les Voleurs 96. Alice and Martin 98, etc.

Tellegen, Lou (1881–1934) (Isidor Van Dameler).
Dutch matinée idol who made many silent films in Hollywood. He was married to actress Geraldine Farrar. Committed suicide.
Autobiography: 1931, *Women Have Been Kind.*
Queen Elizabeth 12. The Explorer 15. The World and Its Women 19. Single Wives 23. The Redeeming Sin 25, etc.

Tempest, Dame Marie (1864–1942) (Marie Susan Etherington).
British stage actress whose very rare films included *Moonlight Sonata* 37, *Yellow Sands* 38.
❝ If you prick her, sawdust comes out. – *Mrs Patrick Campbell*
During performances, at the end of any speech of hers, she led her own applause as soon as she got into the wings. Her curtain calls were mini-masterpieces. She would get her maid to push her little white Sealyham on stage, and her sentimental reunion with the dog would guarantee there was never a dry eye in the house. – *Rex Harrison*

Temple, Julien (1953–).
English director and screenwriter who gained his experience making rock videos.
The Great Rock 'n' Roll Swindle 79. The Secret Policeman's Other Ball 81. Undercover 83. Mantrap 84. Running out of Luck 85. Absolute Beginners 86. Aria (co-d) 87. Earth Girls Are Easy 89. Bullet 95. Vigo: Passion for Life 98, etc.

Temple, Shirley (1928–).
American child star of the 30s, performing in short films at three; a genuine prodigy. Later appeared on TV in *Shirley Temple Storybook*, and in the 60s went into local Californian politics. In the 70s she was US ambassador to Ghana, and later became US Chief of Protocol. In the late 80s she was appointed US ambassador to Czechoslovakia. She was married to actor John Agar (1945–49).
Autobiography: 1988, *Child Star.*
■ The Red-Haired Alibi 32. To the Last Man 33. Out All Night 33. Carolina 34. Mandalay 34. *Stand Up and Cheer* 34. Now I'll Tell 34. Change of Heart 34. *Little Miss Marker* (her first star vehicle) 34. Baby Take a Bow 34. Now and Forever 34. Bright Eyes 34. The Little Colonel 35. Our Little Girl 35. *Curly Top* 35. The Littlest Rebel 35. Captain January 36. Poor Little Rich Girl 36. *Dimples* 36. Stowaway 36. *Wee Willie Winkie* 37. *Heidi* 37. Rebecca of Sunnybrook Farm 38. Little Miss Broadway 38. Just around the Corner 38. *The Little Princess* 39. Susannah of the Mounties 39. The Blue Bird 40. Young People 40. Kathleen 41. Miss Annie Rooney 42. Since You Went Away 44. I'll Be Seeing You 44. Kiss and Tell 45. Honeymoon 47. The Bachelor and the Bobbysoxer 47. That Hagen Girl 47. Fort Apache 48. Mr Belvedere Goes to College 49. Adventure in Baltimore 49. The Story of Seabiscuit 49. A Kiss for Corliss 49.
✪ For captivating the mass world audience and enabling it to forget the depression. *Curly Top.*
❝ I stopped believing in Santa Claus at an early age. Mother took me to see him in a department store, and he asked for my autograph. – *S.T.*

Tennant, Victoria (1950–).
British leading lady. Formerly married to actor Steve Martin.
The Ragman's Daughter 72. Sphinx 80. The Dogs of War 81. Inseminoid 81. *The Winds of War* (TV) 83. Chiefs (TV) 83. All of Me 84. The Holcroft Covenant 85. Best Seller 87. War and Remembrance (TV) 87. Flowers in the Attic 87. Dempsey (TV) 88. The Handmaid's Tale 90. Whispers 90. L.A. Story 91. The Plague 91. Edie & Pen (p, w) 96. Bram Stoker's The Mummy 97, etc.

Tenngren, Gustaf (1896–1970).
Swedish artist and illustrator who worked for the Disney studios from 1936–39. He was an art director for *Snow White* and also made the preliminary drawings that created the overall look for *Pinocchio*, which he based on the Bavarian town of Rothenburg.

Tennyson, Pen (1918–1941) (Penrose Tennyson).
British director killed in World War II.
■ There Ain't No Justice (TV) 39. *The Proud Valley* 39. Convoy 40.

Terhune, Max (1891–1973).
American small-time western star, one of the THREE MESQUITEERS in 30s second features; also appeared in the RANGE BUSTERS series. A ventriloquist and magician, he was often accompanied by his dummy, Elmer Sneezeweed.

Terriss, Ellaline (1871–1971) (Ellen Lewin).
British stage actress, widow of Sir Seymour Hicks; in a few films.
Blighty 27. Glamour 31. The Iron Duke 35. The Four Just Men 39, etc.

Terry, Alice (1899–1987) (Alice Taafe).
American leading lady of the silent screen.
Not My Sister 16. *The Four Horsemen of the Apocalypse* 21. *The Prisoner of Zenda* 22. Mare Nostrum 27. The Garden of Allah 28, etc.

Terry, Don (1902–1988) (Donald Locher).
American hero of serials and second features in the 30s.
Me Gangster 28. The Valiant 29. Whistlin' Dan 32. Paid to Dance 37. Who Killed Gail Preston? 38. The Secret of Treasure Island (serial) 38. Don Winslow of the Navy (serial) 41. Drums of the Congo 42. White Savage 43. Top Sergeant 43. Don Winslow of the Coastguard (serial) 43, etc.

Terry, Dame Ellen (1847–1928).
Distinguished English stage actress whose film appearances were few and ineffective. Born in Coventry to a family of actors, she was on stage from the age of nine and later formed a notable theatrical partnership with Henry Irving. Coming to films late in life, she is said to have found it difficult to adapt to the methods of filming, and to take direction. She was married briefly to artist George Frederick Watts in 1864, a little before her 17th birthday (though she believed she was 15 at the time), and had two children, including Edward Gordon CRAIG, by architect and designer E. W. Godwin. Her third husband was actor James CAREW, whom she married in 1907, when she was 59 and he was 30; they remained friends after the relationship foundered.
Autobiography: 1908, *The Story of My Life.*
Biography: 1968, *Ellen Terry* by Roger Manvell.
■ Her Greatest Performance 17. The Invasion of Britain 18. Pillars of Society 18. Potter's Clay 22. The Bohemian Girl 22.
❝ Ellen Terry is the most beautiful name in the world; it rings like a chime through the last quarter of the nineteenth century. – *George Bernard Shaw*
She was like a shaft of light in a dim room.
– *Edward Sheldon*

Terry, Nigel (1945–).
British actor, from the stage.
The Lion in Winter 68. Excalibur 81. Déjà Vu 85. Caravaggio 86. War Requiem 88. Christopher Columbus: The Discovery 92. Ebb-Tide (TV) 97. Far from the Madding Crowd (TV) 98, etc.
TV series: Covington Cross 92.

Terry, Paul (1887–1971).
American animator, the creator of 'Terry-toons' (starring Mighty Mouse, Heckle and Jeckle, etc.) which filled Fox supporting programmes for over 30 years.

Terry, Phillip (1909–1993).
American leading man of the 40s, mainly in second features; best remembered for briefly marrying Joan Crawford.
The Parson of Panamint 41. The Monster and the Girl 41. Bataan 43. Music in Manhattan 44. Pan-Americana 45. *The Lost Weekend* 45. Seven Keys to Baldpate 47. Born to Kill 47. Class of '74 72, etc.

Terry-Thomas (1911–1990) (Thomas Terry Hoar-Stevens).
British comedian with inimitable gap-toothed manner; became Hollywood's favourite idea of the English silly ass. Also on stage and TV. Born in Finchley, London, he was a clerk before becoming a film extra and a professional ballroom dancer. From the mid-70s he suffered from Parkinson's disease and retired to live in Ibiza and, later, Majorca. Married twice.
Autobiographies: 1959, *Filling the Gap.* 1990, *Terry-Thomas Tells Tales* (with Terry Daum).
Private's Progress 56. Blue Murder at St Trinian's 57. The Naked Truth 58. Tom Thumb 58. *Carleton Browne of the FO* 58. *I'm All Right, Jack* 59. School for Scoundrels 60. His and Hers 61. A Matter of Who 62. Bachelor Flat 62. The Wonderful World of the Brothers Grimm 63. Kill or Cure 63. It's a Mad Mad Mad Mad World 63. The Mouse on the Moon 63. *Those Magnificent Men in Their Flying Machines* 65. *How to Murder Your Wife* 65. You Must be Joking 65. Munster Go Home 66. Kiss the Girls and Make Them Die 66. Rocket to the Moon 67. The Perils of Pauline 67. Don't Look Now 68. Where Were You When the Lights Went Out? 68. 2000 Years Later 69. Monte Carlo or Bust 69. The Abominable Dr Phibes 71. Vault of Horror 73. Spanish Fly 75. The Bawdy Adventures of Tom Jones 76. The Last Remake of Beau Geste 77. The Hound of the Baskervilles 78, etc.
TV series: How Do You View? 49–53. Strictly T-T 56. The Old Campaigner 68.

Terzieff, Laurent (1935–).
French leading man.
Les Tricheurs 58. Le Bois des Amants 59. La Notte Brava 60. Kapo 60. Thou Shalt Not Kill 61. The Seven Deadly Sins 62. Ballade pour un Voyou 64. Le Triangle 65. Le Voyage du Père 66. Two Weeks in September 67. The Milky Way 68. Medea 69. Moses (TV) 75. Couleur Chair 77. Utopia 78. Red Kiss/Rouge Baiser 85. Germinal 93. Fiesta 95. The Pianist/El Pianista (Sp.) 98, etc.

Teshigahara, Hiroshi (1927–).
Japanese director. He studied painting at the Tokyo Art Institute before making documentary shorts and setting up his own production company. He stopped directing during the 70s and most of the 80s after *Summer Soldiers* failed to find an audience. Also a potter.
Pitfall 61. *Woman in the Dunes* (AAN) 64. The Face of Another 66. The Man Without a Map 68. Summer Soldiers 72. Out of Work for Years 75. Antonio Gaudi (doc) 85. Rikyu 89. Basar: The Princess Goh 92, etc.

Tesich, Steve (1942–1996) (Stoyan Tesich).
American screenwriter, playwright and novelist. Born in Yugoslavia, he emigrated to America at the age of 14, speaking no English at the time. He studied at Indiana University on a wrestling scholarship and at Columbia University before becoming a playwright in the 80s. Died of a heart attack.
■ *Breaking Away* (AA) 79. Eyewitness 81. Four Friends 81. The World According to Garp 82. American Flyers 85. Eleni 85.

Tessari, Duccio (1926–1994).
Italian director and screenwriter who began as a documentary film-maker. He scripted 'sword and sandal' epics and worked as a set designer on Sergio Leone's *For a Few Dollars More* before becoming a director, making two admired spaghetti westerns about a gunfighter called Ringo.
Kanonen-serenade (w) 59. La Vendetta di Ercole (w) 60. Carthage in Flames/Cartagine in Fiamme (co-w) 60. The Last Days of Pompeii/Gli Ultimi Giorni di Pompeii (co-w) 60. Messalina (co-w) 60. Il Colosso di Rodi 61. Samson and the Seven Miracles of the World/Maciste alla Corto del Gran Khan (co-w) 61. Il Fornaretto di Venezia (& w) 63. The Titans/Arrivano i Titani (& co-w) 63. A Pistol for Ringo/Una Pistola per Ringo (& w) 65. The Return of Ringo/Il Ritorno di Ringo (& co-w) 65. Sette Pistole per i MacGregor (co-w) 66. Kiss Kiss-Bang Bang 66. Forza G (& co-w) 70. Death Occurred Last Night/La Morte Risale a Ieri Sera (& co-w) 70. Zorro (& co-w) 75, etc.

Tester, Desmond (1919–).
British boy actor of the 30s; went to Australia.
Midshipman Easy 35. Tudor Rose 36. Sabotage 37. The Drum 38. The Stars Look Down 39. The Turners of Prospect Road 47. Barry Mackenzie Holds His Own 74. The Wild Duck 84, etc.

Tetzel, Joan (1924–1977).
American leading actress with stage experience, married to Oscar Homolka.
Duel in the Sun 46. The Paradine Case 47. The File on Thelma Jordon 50. Joy in the Morning 65, etc.

Tetzlaff, Ted (1903–).
American director, former cinematographer.
AS CINEMATOGRAPHER: Apache 28. Royal Romance 30. Hell's Island 30. Child of Manhattan 33. Paris in Spring 35. My Man Godfrey 36. Easy Living 37. Café Society 39. Road to Zanzibar 41. I Married a Witch 42. Talk of the Town (AAN) 42. Notorious 46, etc.
AS DIRECTOR: World Première 41. *Riff Raff* 46. *The Window* 48. Johnny Allegro 48. The White Tower 50. The Treasure of Lost Canyon 52. Time Bomb 53. Son of Sinbad 55. The Young Land 57, etc.

Tevis, Walter (1928–1984).
American novelist and university teacher, three of whose books have been turned into films.
The Hustler 59. The Man Who Fell to Earth 73. The Color of Money 84.

Tewkesbury, Joan (1937–).
American director.
Old Boyfriends 79. The Tenth Month (TV) 79. The Acorn People (TV) 80. Cold Sassy Tree (TV) 89. Wild Texas Wind 91. On Promised Land 94, etc.

Tewksbury, Peter (1924–).
American director, from TV (*Father Knows Best, My Three Sons*, etc.).
■ *Sunday in New York* 64. Emil and the Detectives 65. Doctor You've Got to Be Kidding 67. Stay Away Joe 68. The Trouble with Girls 69. Second Chance (TV) 71.

Tey, Josephine (1896–1952) (Elizabeth MacKintosh).
Scottish writer of plays (as Gordon Daviot) and crime novels. *A Shilling for Candles* was filmed as *Young and Innocent*, and there was also a film of *The Franchise Affair*.

Tezuka, Osamu (1926–1989).
Japanese director of animation.
Alakazam the Great/Saiyu-Ki 60. Astroboy/Tetsuwan Atom 60. Vampire 68. Adolf Ni Tsugu 86, etc.

Thackery, Bud (1903–1990).
American cinematographer, especially for Republic, where he photographed innumerable westerns and serials. Moved into TV. Born in Shawnee, Oklahoma, he began in films with First National in 1923, and became a cameraman in the early 30s.
Cheyenne Wildcat 44. Haunted Harbor 44. Saddle Pals 47. San Antone 52. Flame of the Islands 55. Jaguar 55. Accused of Murder 56. Thunder over Arizona 56. The Raiders 64. Beau Geste 66. The Plainsman 66. The Hell with Heroes 68. Coogan's Bluff 68, many others.

Thal, Eric
American actor.
The Gun in Betty Lou's Handbag 92. A Stranger among Us 92. Six Degrees of Separation 93. The Puppet Masters 94. Samson and Delilah (TV) 96, etc.

Thalberg, Irving (1899–1936).
American producer, MGM's boy wonder of the early 30s, responsible for the literary flavour of films like *The Barretts of Wimpole Street* 34, *Mutiny on the Bounty* 35, *Romeo and Juliet* 36; also for hiring the Marx Brothers. Married Norma Shearer.
Biographies: 1969, *Thalberg* by Bob Thomas. 1976, *Mayer and Thalberg* by Samuel Marx. 1994, *Thalberg: The Last Tycoon and the World of MGM* by Roland Flamini.
❝ When a man dies young, he is often underestimated. Thalberg has been lucky: the reverse proved true. Head of Universal production at 21 and of MGM at 25, his quiet efficiency and stubborn enthusiasm, coupled with his scholarly air, made him a legend even before his untimely death at 37. As early as 1925 F. L. Collins wrote:
Wherever Thalberg sits is always the head of the table.
He had apparently high aims:
I believe that although the motion picture may not live forever as a work of art, except in a few instances, it will be the most efficient way of showing posterity how we live now.
He was modest enough to keep his name off the credits of his films:
If you are in a position to give credit, you don't need it.
Charles MacArthur said:
Entertainment is Thalberg's God. He's content to serve Him without billing, like a priest at an altar or a rabbi under the scrolls.
He was a shrewd film-maker:
Movies aren't made, they're remade.
And he always had an eye for the box office. His idea of a good tag-line was:
Ladies, have you had a good cry lately? See *Imitation of Life* and cry unashamedly.
And he once said to Cedric Hardwicke:
We should all make a killing in this business: there's so much money in the pot.
Mickey Rooney had his doubts:
It seemed to me that he went out of his way to put his wife into films she didn't need and wasn't right for.
But the screenwriters were suspicious of him:
He's too good to last. The lamb doesn't lie down with the lion for long. – *Charles MacArthur*
I seriously began to question whether Thalberg ever existed, or whether he might not be a solar myth or a deity concocted by the front office to garner prestige. – *S. J. Perelman*
I think I may have once told you Irving Thalberg's classic: 'The writer? The writer is a necessary evil.' – *S. J. Perelman*
On a clear day you can see Thalberg. – *George S. Kaufman*
When he died however it was Charles MacArthur who knew the truth:
Ten years of 16-hours-a-day work had tired him. He didn't know how to rest, or play, or even breathe without a script in his hands.

Thatcher, Heather (1897–1987).
Blonde British light actress who filmed also in Hollywood.
Altar Chains 17. The Little House of Peter Wells 20. But the Flesh is Weak 32. Loyalties 33. The 13th Chair 37. Tovarich 37. Beau Geste 39. Man Hunt 41. Gaslight 44. Dear Mr Prohack 50. Will Any Gentleman 55, many others.

Thatcher, Torin (1905–1981).
Tough-looking British character actor, on stage from 1923; latterly on stage again after some years in Hollywood.
But the Flesh Is Weak 32. General John Regan 34. Major Barbara 40. The Captive Heart 45. Great Expectations 46. The Crimson Pirate 52. The Robe 53. Love is a Many-Splendored Thing 55. Witness for the Prosecution 57. The Seventh Voyage of Sinbad 58. The Canadians 60. Jack the Giant Killer 62. The Sandpiper 65. Hawaii 66. The King's Pirate 67, many others.

Thaw, John (1942–).
Rough-speaking British leading man, best known as TV's Inspector Morse. Married actress Sheila Hancock.
The Loneliness of the Long Distance Runner 62. Dead Man's Chest 65. Praise Marx and Pass the Ammunition 68. The Bofors Gun 68. The Last Grenade 69. Dr Phibes Rides Again 72. Regan (TV) 73. *Sweeney* 76. Sweeney Two 78. Cry Freedom 87. The Sign of Four (TV) 87. Business as Usual 87. Chaplin 92. Into the Blue (TV) 97, etc.
TV series: Redcap 64–66. The Sweeney 74–78. Home to Roost 85–87. A Year in Provence 93. Kavanagh QC 95– .

Thaxter, Phyllis (1921–).
American leading lady of the 40s, recently back in character roles.
Thirty Seconds over Tokyo (debut) 44. Weekend at the Waldorf 45. Bewitched 45. Tenth Avenue Angel 47. Blood on the Moon 48. Come Fill the Cup 51. Springfield Rifle 53. Women's Prison 54. The World of Henry Orient 64. The Longest Night (TV) 72. Superman 78. Three Sovereigns for Sarah (TV) 85, etc.

Theiss, William Ware.
American costume designer.
The Pink Panther 64. Harold and Maude 71. Bound for Glory (AAN) 76. Who'll Stop the Rain (aka Dog Soldiers) 78. Butch and Sundance: The Early Days (AAN) 79. Kidco 83. Heart Like a Wheel (AAN) 83. The Man with One Red Shoe 85, etc.

Theron, Charlize (1975–).
South African-born actress, in American films. Born on a farm near Benoni, she trained as a ballet dancer and became a model in her teens.
That Thing You Do! 96. Trial and Error 96. Two Days in the Valley 96. Hollywood Confidential (TV) 97. The Devil's Advocate 97. Celebrity 98. Mighty Joe Young 98, etc.

Theroux, Paul (1941–).
American novelist and travel writer.
Saint Jack (w, oa) 79. Mosquito Coast (oa) 86. Half Moon Street (oa) 86.

Thesiger, Ernest (1879–1961).
Witty, skeletal, slightly sinister aristocratic English character actor, adept at high comedy. Born in London, he was educated at Marlborough College and the Slade, and was on stage from 1909, later creating the role of the Dauphin in George Bernard Shaw's *St Joan*. He was also an accomplished watercolour artist, embroiderer and author of books on the subject, and used to do crochet-work with his great friend, 'dear Queen Mary', on whom he is said to have modelled his appearance in later life. He was given to camp gestures: he used to lay lilies at the feet of a handsome doorman at the Savoy Hotel; he enlisted as a private in the First World War, hoping to serve with a Scottish regiment as he fancied wearing a kilt. His best film performances were as Horace Femm in *The Old Dark House* and as Dr Pretorius in *The Bride of Frankenstein*, both directed by his friend and former fellow-actor James WHALE.
Autobiography: 1927, *Practically True*.
West End Wives 29. *The Old Dark House* 32. The Ghoul 33. Heart Song 34. *The Bride of Frankenstein* 35. The Man Who Could Work Miracles 36. *They Drive By Night* 38. Henry V 44. Caesar and Cleopatra 45. A Place of One's Own 46. The Ghosts of Berkeley Square 47. Quartet 48. Laughter in Paradise 51. *The Man in the White Suit* 52. *Father Brown* 54. Make Me an Offer 55. The Battle of the Sexes 59. The Roman Spring of Mrs Stone 61, many others.
❝ Anyone with a modicum of intelligence and the right kind of physique ought to make a film-actor, if they are lucky enough to be told exactly what to do, and I cannot see that the actor for the screen deserves any more credit than a schoolboy who is good at dictation should have for writing admirable prose. – *E.T.*
My dear: the noise! And the *people*! – *E.T., when asked what it had been like in the trenches in the First World War*
Famous line (*The Old Dark House*): 'Have some gin. It's my only weakness . . .'
Famous line (*The Bride of Frankenstein*). 'To a new world of gods and monsters!'
~He also published books on embroidery.

Thewlis, David (1963–).
English leading actor, from the stage.
Vroom 88. Prime Suspect 3 (TV) 93. *Naked* 93. Black Beauty 94. Total Eclipse 95. Restoration 95. James and the Giant Peach (voice) 96. Dragonheart 96. The Island of Dr Moreau 96. Seven Years in Tibet 97. The Big Lebowski 97. Divorcing Jack 98. Besieged 98, etc.

Thiele, Rolf (1918–1994).
German director.
Nachtwache (p only) 49. Mamitschka (& wp) 55. El Hakim 57. The Girl Rosemarie (& co-w) 58. Venusberg (& w) 63. Tonio Kroger 64, etc.

Thiele, William (1890–1975).
German director who went to Hollywood in the 30s but found little work.
His Late Excellency 29. Liebeswalzer 31. *Drei von der Tankstelle* 31. Le Bal 32. The Jungle Princess 36. London by Night 37. Bridal Suite 39. Tarzan Triumphs 43. Tarzan's Desert Mystery 43. The Madonna's Secret 46. The Last Pedestrian 60, etc.

Thiess, Ursula (1929–).
German leading lady, in a few American films. She was formerly married to actor Robert Taylor.
Monsoon 52. The Iron Glove 54. Bengal Brigade 55. The Americano 55, etc.
TV series: The Detectives, Starring Robert Taylor 60–61.

Thimig, Helene (1889–1974).
German character actress, widow of Max Reinhardt, in a few American films.
None But the Lonely Heart 44. Cloak and Dagger 46. The Locket 47, etc.

Thinnes, Roy (1938–).
Stocky American leading man of some successful television series: *The Long Hot Summer* 64. *The Invaders* 66–67. The Psychiatrist 70.
Journey to the Far Side of the Sun 69. Charlie One Eye 72. The Horror at 37,000 Feet (TV) 73. The Norliss Tapes (TV) 73. Airport 75 74. The Hindenburg 75. From Here to Eternity (TV) 79. Sizzle 81. Rush Week 88. The Invaders (TV) 95, etc.
TV series: From Here to Eternity 79–80. Falcon Crest 82–83. Dark Shadows 91.

Thirard, Armand (1899–).
French cinematographer.
Remorques 41. Quai des Orfèvres 47. *Manon* 49. *The Wages of Fear* 52. Act of Love 54. Les Diaboliques 54. And God Created Woman 56. The Truth 60. Guns for San Sebastian 67, etc.

Thiriet, Maurice (1906–1972).
French composer.
The Woman I Love 37. Les Visiteurs du Soir 37. Les Enfants du Paradis 44. L'Homme au Chapeau Rond 46. Une Si Jolie Petite Plage 48. Fanfan la Tulipe 51. Thérèse Raquin 53. Crime and Punishment 58, etc.

Thivisole, Victoire (1992–).
French child actor. She won a best actress award at the Venice Film Festival in 1996.
Arrow/Ponette 96.

Thomas, Betty (1948–).
American director, a former TV actress. Born in St Louis, Missouri, she worked with Chicago's Second City comedy troupe in the early 70s. She won an Emmy in 1985 for her portrayal of the tough policewoman Lucy Bates in *Hill Street Blues*.
AS ACTRESS: Tunnelvision 76. Outside Chance (TV) 78. Homework 82. When Your Lover Leaves (TV) 83. Prison for Children (TV) 87. Troop Beverly Hills 89, etc.
AS DIRECTOR: Only You 92. The Brady Bunch Movie 95. The Late Shift (TV) 96. Private Parts 97. Dr Dolittle 98, etc.
TV series: Hill Street Blues (a) 81–87.

Thomas, Billy 'Buckwheat' (1931–1980).
American child actor in the Our Gang comedies from the mid-30s until the mid-40s.

Thomas, Danny (1914–1991) (Amos Jacobs).
American nightclub comedian; star of his own TV series in the 50s and 60s. From the 60s, he was also involved in TV production (*The Andy Griffith Show, The Dick Van Dyke Show, The Mod Squad*, etc.).
Autobiography: 1991, *Make Room for Danny*.
The Unfinished Dance 47. Big City 48. Call Me Mister 51. I'll See You in My Dreams 52. The Jazz Singer 53. Looking for Love 64. Don't Worry, We'll Think of a Title 66. Journey Back to Oz (voice) 74.
TV series: *The Danny Thomas Show* 53–64. The Danny Thomas Hour 67–68. Make Room for Granddaddy 70–71. The Practice 76–77. I'm a Big Girl Now 80–81.

Thomas, Dylan (1914–1953).
Welsh poet whose drama *Under Milk Wood* has been filmed. He also worked on the scripts of a number of British films in the late 40s, including *The Three Weird Sisters*. He was portrayed by Ronald Lacey in a 1978 BBC film, *Dylan*. His *Rebecca's Daughters*, written in 1948, was filmed in 1991.

Thomas, Gerald (1920–1993).
British director, former editor, in films from 1946.
Time Lock 57. Vicious Circle 57. The Duke Wore Jeans 58. Carry On Sergeant 58 (and all the subsequent 'Carry Ons'). Watch Your Stern 60. Twice round the Daffodils 62. The Big Job 65. Don't Lose Your Head 66. Follow That Camel 67. Carry On Loving 70. Carry On Girls 73. Carry On England 76. Carry On Emmanuelle 78. That's Carry On 78. The Second Victory 87. Carry On Columbus 92, etc.

Thomas, Henry (1971–).
American child actor of the 80s.
Raggedy Man 81. E.T. – the Extraterrestrial 82. Misunderstood 83. Cloak and Dagger 84. The Quest 86. Murder One 88. Valmont 89. Psycho IV: The Beginning 90. A Taste for Killing (TV) 92. Fire in the Sky 93. Curse of the Starving Class 94. Legends of the Fall 95. Riders of the Purple Sage (TV) 96. Hijacking Hollywood 97. Niagra, Niagra 98. Suicide Kings 98. Moby Dick (TV) 98, etc.

Thomas, Jameson (1892–1939).
British actor who usually played 'the other man'. Went to Hollywood in the early 30s but did not command leading roles.
Blighty 27. A Daughter of Love 28. Piccadilly 29. High Treason 30. Hate Ship 30. Elstree Calling 30. The Phantom President 32. It Happened One Night 34. Lives of a Bengal Lancer 35. Mr Deeds Goes to Town 36. Death Goes North 38, etc.
❝ If one wants to live by playing in British films it is better to be miscast than never to be cast at all. – *J.T.*

Thomas, Jeremy (1949–).
British producer.
Mad Dog 76. The Shout 78. Bad Timing 80. Merry Christmas, Mr Lawrence 82. Eureka 83. The Hit 84. Insignificance 85. The Last Emperor (AA) 87. Everybody Wins 90. The Sheltering Sky 90. Naked Lunch 91. Little Buddha 92. Crash 96. All the Little Animals (& d) 98, etc.

Thomas, Jonathan Taylor (1981–) (Jonathan Weiss).
Young American leading actor, best known for his role as Randy in the TV sitcom *Home Improvement*. Born in Bethlehem, Pennsylvania, he began modelling at the age of four.
Man of the House 95. The Lion King (as Young Simba) 95. Tom & Huck 95. The Adventures of Pinocchio (voice) 96. Wild America 97. I'll Be Home for Christmas 98, etc.
TV series: The Bradys 90.
❝ In fifty years, I don't want to be asked, 'What have you done with your life?' and only be able to answer, 'I've been acting.' – *J.T.T.*

Thomas, Lowell (1892–1981).
American broadcaster and lecturer who partly controlled Cinerama and appeared as travelling commentator in some of its episodes.
Search for Paradise 58, etc.

Thomas, Marlo (1938–) (Margaret Thomas).
American leading lady, daughter of Danny Thomas.
The Knack 64. Jenny 70. Thieves 77. Consenting Adult (TV) 85. In the Spirit 90. The Real Blonde 97. Starf*cker 98, etc.
TV series: The Joey Bishop Show 61–62. That Girl 66–70.

Thomas, Olive (1884–1920) (Olive Elaine Duffy).
American 'Ziegfeld girl' who played a few comedy roles in films. Married actor Jack Pickford. Committed suicide.
Beatrice Fairfax 16. Limousine Life 18. The Follies Girl 19. The Glorious Lady 19. Footlights and Shadows 20, etc.

Thomas, Pascal (1945–).
French director.
Les Zozos 72. Le Chaud Lapin 74. Un Oursin dans la Poche 77. Heart to Heart/Confidences pour Confidences 78. Les Maris, les Femmes, les Amants 89. La Pagaille 91, etc.

Thomas, Philip Michael (1949–).
American leading actor, best known for his role as Detective Ricardo Tubbs in the TV series *Miami Vice* 84–89.
Stigma 73. Streetfight/Coonskin (voice) 75. Sparkle 76. Death Drug 83. The Wizard of Speed and Time 88. False Witness (TV) 89. A Fight for Jenny (TV) 90, etc.

Thomas, Ralph (1915–).
British director, former trailer maker, who with producer Betty Box has tackled some ambitious subjects in a rather stolid manner.
Helter Skelter 48. Traveller's Joy 49. The Clouded Yellow 51. Appointment with Venus 51. Venetian Bird 53. *Doctor in the House* 54. Above Us the Waves 55. The Iron Petticoat 56. *Campbell's Kingdom* 57. A Tale of Two Cities 57. The Wind Cannot Read 58. The Thirty-Nine Steps 59. No Love for Johnnie 61. The Wild and the Willing 62. Hot Enough for June 64. The High Bright Sun 65. Deadlier than the Male 66. Some Girls Do 68. Percy 71. Quest for Love 71. The Love Ban 73. Percy's Progress 74. A Nightingale Sang in Berkeley Square 80, etc.

Thomas, Richard (1951–).
American actor, best known for his role as John-Boy in *The Waltons*.
Winning 69. Last Summer 70. Cactus in the Snow 70. Red Sky at Morning 71. You'll Like My Mother 72. September 30 1955 78. The Silence (TV) 78. Battle beyond the Stars 80. Go toward the Light (TV) 88. Glory! Glory! (TV) 89. It (TV) 90. Mission of the Shark 91. Stalking Laura 93. A Thousand Heroes 94. Down, Out and Dangerous (TV) 95. A Walton Easter (TV) 97, etc.
TV series: *The Waltons* 72–76.

Thomas, Terry:
see Terry-Thomas.

Thomas, William C.:
see Pine, William H.

Thomas, Wynn (1954–).
American production designer who has worked on Spike Lee's films; from the stage.
She's Gotta Have It 86. Eddie Murphy Raw 87. Scared Stiff 87. School Daze 88. Do the Right Thing 89. Mo' Better Blues 90. Jungle Fever 91. The Five Heartbeats 91. Malcolm X 92. Crooklyn 94. To Wong Foo, Thanks for Everything, Julie Newmar 95. Mars Attacks! 96. Wag the Dog 97. He Got Game 98, etc.

Thomerson, Tim.
Laconic American leading actor, from television, where he appeared in situation comedies. On film, he is best known for his role in the *Trancers* series as Jack Deth, a tough cop from the future who models his style on Humphrey Bogart.
Car Wash 76. Terraces (TV) 87. Which Way Is Up? 77. A Wedding 78. Carny 80. Fade to Black 80. Take This Job and Shove It 81. Jekyll and Hyde . . . Together Again 82. Metalstorm: The Destruction of Jared-Syn 83. Uncommon Valor 83. Rhinestone 84. Trancers/Future Cop 85. Zone Troopers 85. Volunteers 85. Ratboy 86. Iron Eagle 86. A Tiger's Tale 87. Near Dark 87. The Wrong Guys 88. Cherry 2000 88. Who's Harry Crumb? 89. After Midnight 89. Air America 90. Vietnam, Texas 90. Trancers II: The Return of Jack Deth 91. Dollman 91. Intimate Stranger 91. The Harvest 92. Trancers III: Deth Lives 92. Nemesis 93. Natural Causes 94. Fleshtone 94. Dominion 95. Blast 96. When Time Expires (TV) 97. Fear and Loathing in Las Vegas 98, etc.
TV series: Cos 76. Quark 78. Angie 79–80. The Associates 79–80. The Two of Us 81–82. Gun Shy 83. Sirens 93. Land's End 95.

Thompson, Carlos (1916–1990) (Juan Carlos Mundanschaffter).
Argentinian stage and screen matinée idol who has made some American and German films. He was married to actress Lilli Palmer. Committed suicide.
Fort Algiers 53. The Flame and the Flesh 54. Valley of the Kings 54. Magic Fire 56. Stefanie 58. Joaquin Murietta 58. Stefanie in Rio 60, etc.
TV series: Sentimental Agent 66.

Thompson, Caroline W. (1956–).
American scriptwriter turned director.
Edward Scissorhands (w) 90. The Addams Family (co-w) 91. Homeward Bound: The Incredible Journey (w) 93. The Secret Garden (w) 93. Tim Burton's The Nightmare before Christmas (w) 93. Black Beauty (d) 94. Buddy (wd) 97, etc.

Thompson, Danièle.
French screenwriter, the daughter of director Gérard Oury.
La Grande Vadrouille (co-w) 65. The Mad Adventures of Rabbi Jacob (co-w) 73. Cousin, Cousine (co-w, AAN) 75. La Reine Margot (co-w) 94. Those Who Love Me Can Take the Train/Ceux Qui M'Aiment Prendront le Train 97, etc.

Thompson, Emma (1959–).
British actress, from TV. Her current asking price as an actress: $5m a movie. Formerly married to Kenneth Branagh, she is the daughter of actress Phyllida Law.
Biographies: 1994, *Ken & Em* by Ian Shuttleworth; 1998, *Emma: The Many Facets of Emma Thompson* by Chris Nickson.
The Tall Guy 89. Henry V 89. Impromptu 89. Dead Again 91. *Howards End* (AA) 91. Peter's Friends 92. Much Ado about Nothing 93. The Remains of the Day (AAN) 93. In the Name of the Father (AAN) 93. Junior 94. Carrington 95. *Sense and Sensibility* (AAw, AANa) 95. Winter Guest 96. Primary Colors 98. Judas Kiss 98, etc.
TV series: Tutti Frutti 87. Thompson 88.
❝ I don't want to be a Hollywood player. If I wanted to do that, I'd have a company and a four picture deal with a studio. – *E.T.*

Thompson, Fred Dalton (1943–).
American actor, a former lawyer who played himself in his first film role.
Marie: A True Story 85. No Way Out 87. Feds 88. Days of Thunder 90. Die Hard 2 90. The Hunt for Red October 90. Cape Fear 91. Curly Sue 91. Thunderheart 92. White Sands 92. Aces: Iron Eagle III 92. Born Yesterday 93. In the Line of Fire 93. Baby's Day Out 94, etc.

Thompson, J. Lee:
see Lee-Thompson, J.

Thompson, Jack (1940–) (John Pain).
Australian leading man.
Outback 70. Libido 73. Petersen 74. Sunday Too Far Away 74. Caddie 76. Mad Dog Morgan 76. The Chant of Jimmie Blacksmith 78. Breaker Morant 79. The Earthling 80. Merry Christmas Mr Lawrence 83. Burke and Wills 85. Flesh and Blood 85. Ground Zero 87. Waterfront 88. Trouble in Paradise (TV) 89. Turtle Beach 92. Wind 92. A Far Off Place 93. Ruby Cairo 93. The Sum of Us 94. Broken Arrow 96. Last Dance 96. Excess Baggage 96. Midnight in the Garden of Good and Evil 97, etc.

Thompson, Jim (1906–1977).
Pulp novelist, the author of some 29 thrillers, and occasional screenwriter whose books became unexpectedly popular as movie material in the late 80s. Died by starving himself to death after a series of strokes. At the time of his death, all his books were out of print.
Biography: 1997, *Art: A Biography of Jim Thompson* by Robert Polito.
The Killing (co-w) 56. Paths of Glory (co-w) 57. The Getaway (oa) 72. Farewell My Lovely (a) 75. The Killer Inside Me (oa) 75. Série Noire (oa) 78. Coup de Torchon (oa) 81. The Kill-Off (oa) 89. The Grifters (oa) 90. After Dark, My Sweet (oa) 90. The Getaway (oa) 94. Carried Away (from *Farmer*) 96. This World, Then the Fireworks (oa) 97, etc.

Thompson, Kay (1902–1998) (Kitty Fink).
American actress, singer, vocal arranger and author. Born in St Louis, Missouri, she began as a singer before becoming a vocal arranger at MGM in the mid-40s, but she was best known for her four books about Eloise, a precocious six-year-old girl who lived at the Plaza in New York, which were published in the mid-50s. Married bandleader Jack Jenney and producer William Spier.
Manhattan Merry-Go-Round 37. Funny Face 58. Tell Me that You Love Me, Junie Moon 69, etc.
❝ I think I've discovered the secret of life. I'll give you a few clues – a lot of hard work, a lot of sense of humour, a lot of joy and a whole lot of tra la la la. – *K.T.*

Thompson, Lea (1961–).
American leading actress.
Jaws 3-D 83. All the Right Moves 83. Going Undercover 84. Red Dawn 84. The Wild Life 84. Back to the Future 85. Howard the Duck 86. Some Kind of Wonderful 87. Casual Sex? 88. The Wizard of Loneliness 88. Nightbreaker (TV) 89. Back to the Future II 89. Back to the Future III 90. Article 99 92. Stolen Babies (TV) 93. The Substitute Wife (TV) 94, etc.
TV series: Caroline in the City 96– .

Thompson, Marshall (1925–1992) (James Marshall Thompson).
American leading man who began by playing quiet juvenile roles.
Reckless Age 44. Gallant Bess 45. The Romance of Rosy Ridge 46. Homecoming 48. Words and Music 48. Battleground 49. The Violent Hour 50. *My Six Convicts* 52. Battle Taxi 55. To Hell and Back 55. Clarence the Cross-Eyed Lion 65. Around the World under the Sea 66. The Turning Point 77, many others.
TV series: Angel 60. Daktari 66–68.

Thompson, Sada (1929–).
Gentle-looking American character actress, usually in maternal roles.
The Pursuit of Happiness 70. Desperate Characters 71. Our Town (TV) 77. The Adventures of Huckleberry Finn (TV) 85. Fear Stalk (TV) 89. Queen (TV) 93. Any Mother's Son 97. This Is My Father 98, etc.
TV series: *Family* 76–79.

Thomson, Alex (1929–).
British cinematographer.
Here We Go Round the Mulberry Bush 67. The Strange Affair 68. Alfred the Great 69. Excalibur (AAN) 81. Eureka 83. Bullshot 85. Year of the Dragon 85. Legend 86. Labyrinth 86. Duet for One 87. The Sicilian 87. Track 29 88. High Spirits 88. Leviathan 89. The Rachel Papers 89. Mr Destiny 90. Wings of Fame 90. Alien^3 92. Demolition Man 93. Cliffhanger 93. Black Beauty 94. The Scarlet Letter 95. Executive Decision 96. Hamlet 96, etc.

Thomson, Fred (1890–1928).
American cowboy star of the 20s.
Penrod 22. The Eagle's Talons 23. The Fighting Sap 24. The Wild Bull's Lair 25. Hands Across the Border 26. Arizona Nights 27. Jesse James 27. The Pioneer Scout 28. Kit Carson 28, etc.

Thorburn, June (1931–1967).
British leading lady with repertory experience.
The Pickwick Papers (debut) 53. The Cruel Sea 53. True as a Turtle 56. Tom Thumb 59. The Three Worlds of Gulliver 59. The Scarlet Blade 63, etc.

Thorin, Donald E.
American cinematographer.
Thief 81. An Officer and a Gentleman 82. Bad Boys 83. Against All Odds 84. Purple Rain 84. Mischief 85. American Anthem 86. Wildcats 86. The Golden Child 86. Collision Course 88. The Couch Trip 88. Midnight Run 88. Troop Beverly Hills 89. Lock Up 89. Tango & Cash 89. The Marrying Man/Too Hot to Handle 91. Out on a Limb 92. Undercover Blues 93. Little Big League 94. Boys on the Side 95. Ace Ventura: When Nature Calls 95. First Wives Club 96. Nothing to Lose 97, etc.

Thorndike, Andrew (1909–1979).
East German director who with his wife Annelie made the strident anti-Nazi documentary series *The Archives Testify*; also *The German Story*, *The Russian Miracle*, etc.

Thorndike, Dame Sybil (1882–1976).
Distinguished British stage actress who appeared in occasional films.
Biography: 1950, *Sybil Thorndike* by Russell Thorndike.
Moths and Rust (debut) 21. Dawn 29. To What Red Hell 30. Hindle Wakes 31. Tudor Rose 36. Major Barbara 40. *Nicholas Nickleby* 47. Stage Fright 50. The Magic Box 51. Melba 53. *Alive and Kicking* 58. Shake Hands with the Devil 59. Hand in Hand 61, etc.

Thorne, Ken.
British composer and conductor.
Master Spy 62. Help! (md) 65. A Funny Thing Happened on the Way to the Forum (AA) 66. How I Won the War 67. Sinful Davey 68. Inspector Clouseau 68. Head 68. The Magic Christian 69. The Bed-Sitting Room 69. Welcome to the Club 70. Hannie Calder 71. Brother Sun Sister Moon 72. Juggernaut 74. Royal Flash (md) 75. The Ritz 76. Power Play 78. Arabian Adventure 79. The Outsider 79. Superman II 80. Superman III 83. Lassiter 83. Finders Keepers 85. The Protector 85. The Trouble with Spies 87. Sunset Grill 93. Age of Treason 93. Diana: Her True Story (TV) 93. Return to Lonesome Dove (TV) 93. Escape Clause 96, etc.

Thornton, Billy Bob (1955–).
American leading actor, screenwriter and director. He is a former rock drummer and singer.
Hunter's Blood 87. For the Boys 91. One False Move (& co-w) 92. Indecent Proposal 93. Tombstone 93. On Deadly Ground 94. *Sling Blade* (a, wd) (AAw, AANa) 96. A Family Thing (co-w) 96. The Apostle 97. U-Turn 97. The Winner 97. An Alan Smithee Film: Burn, Hollywood, Burn 98. Armageddon 98. Homegrown 98. Primary Colors 98. A Simple Plan 98, etc.
TV series: Hearts Afire 92–95.
❝ People who've seen some of my roles are afraid that I'm this crazy, yelling-and-screaming character in real life, but outside of acting, I save that stuff for executives. – *B.B.T.*

Thornton, Frank (1921–).
British comic actor, much on TV and best known as Captain Peacock in the TV sitcom *Are You Being Served?*
Crooks and Coronets 68. All the Way Up 70. Our Miss Fred 72. Digby 73. No Sex Please We're British 73. The Three Musketeers 73. The Old Curiosity Shop (TV) 95.
TV series: Are You Being Served 74–82. Last of the Summer Wine 97–98.

Thornton, Sigrid (1959–).
Australian leading lady.
The Getting of Wisdom 80. Snap Shot 81. 1915 (TV) 82. The Man from Snowy River 82. All the Rivers Run (TV) 83. Slate, Wyn and Me 87. Return to Snowy River, Part II 88. Great Expectations – the Untold Story 90. Over the Hill 93. Trapped in Space 94. Whipping Boy 96. Love in Ambush 97, etc.

Thorpe, Jerry (1930–).
American director from TV, the son of director Richard Thorpe.
The Venetian Affair 66. The Day of the Evil Gun (& p) 68. Company of Killers/The Protectors 72. The Possessed (TV) 77. All God's Children (TV) 80. Blood and Orchids (TV) 86, etc.
TV series: *Kung Fu* 72–74.

Thorpe, Jim (1888–1953).
American Indian athlete, played by Burt Lancaster in *Jim Thorpe, All-American*. Also small-part actor, in 'B' westerns of the 30s.

Thorpe, Richard (1896–1991) (Rollo Smolt Thorpe).
American director, formerly in vaudeville.
The Feminine Touch 28. Forgotten Woman 32. The Last of the Pagans 35. *Night Must Fall* 38. Huckleberry Finn 39. Tarzan Finds a Son 39. Wyoming 40. The Earl of Chicago 40. Tarzan's New York Adventure 42. Above Suspicion 43. Her Highness and the Bellboy 45. Fiesta 47. The Sun Comes Up 48. Malaya 49. *The Great Caruso* 51. The Prisoner of Zenda 52. Ivanhoe 52. The Student Prince 54. Knights of the Round Table 54. The Prodigal 55. *The Adventures of Quentin Durward* 56. Jailhouse Rock 57. The House of the Seven Hawks 59. The Tartars 60. Fun in Acapulco 63. The Golden Head 65. That Funny Feeling 65. The Truth about Spring 65. The Scorpio Letters 67. Pistolero 67, etc.
❝ His reputation for only needing one take is why we don't remember his films. – *James Mason*

The Three Stooges:
see The Stooges.

Threlfall, David (1953–).
English actor, from the stage, notably with the Royal Shakespeare Company.
The Life and Adventures of Nicholas Nickleby (TV) 82. Red Monarch 83. When the Whales Came 89. The Russia House 90. A Casualty of War (TV) 90. A Murder of Quality (TV) 91. Patriot Games 92. Diana: Her True Story (TV, as Prince Charles) 93, etc.
TV series: Paradise Postponed 86. Nightingales 90, 92. Men of the World 94–95.

Thring, Frank (1926–1994).
Australian actor in occasional films, often as a slightly camp villain.
A Question of Adultery 58. The Vikings 58. *Ben Hur* (as Pontius Pilate) 59. King of Kings (as Herod) 61. El Cid 61. Age of Consent 69. Ned Kelly 70. Mad Max 76. Mad Max Beyond Thunderdome 85. Howling 3 87, etc.

Thulin, Ingrid (1929–).
Swedish leading actress, often in Ingmar Bergman's films.
Foreign Intrigue 55. *Wild Strawberries* 57. So Close to Life 58. The Face 59. The Four Horsemen of the Apocalypse (US) 62. Winter Light 62. *The Silence* 63. Return from the Ashes (US) 65. The War Is Over (Fr.) 66. Night Games 66. The Damned 69. The Rite 69. Cries and Whispers 72. Moses 76. The Cassandra Crossing 77. One and One/En Och En 78. After the Rehearsal 84. Il Giorno Prima 87. House of Smiles/La Casa del Sorriso 91, etc.

Thurber, James (1894–1961).
American humorist whose chief gifts to Hollywood were the original stories of *The Secret Life of Walter Mitty* and *The Male Animal*.
TV series based on his cartoons: My *World and Welcome to It* 69.

Thurman, Uma (1970–).
American leading actress, a former teenage model, born in Boston, Massachusetts. Married actor Gary Oldman (1990–92) and, in 1998, actor Ethan Hawke.
Kiss Daddy Goodnight 87. The Adventures of Baron Munchausen 88. Dangerous Liaisons 88. Johnny Be Good 88. Henry and June 90. Where the Heart Is 90. Robin Hood 90. Final Analysis 92. Jennifer 8 92. Mad Dog and Glory 93. Even Cowgirls Get the Blues 93. *Pulp Fiction* (AAN) 94. A Month by the Lake 95. Beautiful Girls 96. Batman and Robin 97. Les Misérables 98. Gattaca 98. The Avengers 98, etc.

Tianming, Wu (1939–).
Chinese director, a former actor, who became head of the Xi'an Film Studio in the mid-80s. He now lives in America.
A River without Buoys/Meiyouhangbiaode Heliu 83. Life/Rensheng 84. Old Well/Lao Jing 87. The King of Masks 96, etc.

Tibbett, Lawrence (1896–1960).
American opera star who made some films in the 30s.
■ Rogue Song (AAN) 29. New Moon 30. The Prodigal 31. Cuban Love Song 32. Metropolitan 36. Under Your Spell 37.
∼Tibbett's first movie appearance was promoted as follows: 'To bring you a new, vital figure for the further glory of your talking screen, MGM has reached into the highest realms of the Metropolitan Opera. From this renowned company of immortal voices has been picked the greatest – your new star, Lawrence Tibbett!' Louella Parsons commented: 'The long-awaited successor to Rudolph Valentino has arrived!'

Ticotin, Rachel (1958–).
American actress.
King of the Gypsies 78. Fort Apache, the Bronx 81. Critical Condition 87. Total Recall 90. FX2 – the Deadly Art of Illusion 91. Where the Day Takes You 92. Falling Down 93. Don Juan DeMarco 95. Steal Big, Steal Little 95. Turbulence 96. First Time Felon (TV) 97. Con Air 97, etc.
TV series: Crime & Punishment 93.

Tidyman, Ernest (1928–1984).
American novelist who scripted the *Shaft* films from his own novels.
The French Connection (AA) 72. High Plains Drifter 74. Report to the Commissioner (co-w) 74, etc.

Tierney, Gene (1920–1991).
Gentle-featured American leading lady of the 40s, typically a smooth socialite.
Autobiography: 1979, *Self Portrait*.
■ The Return of Frank James 40. Hudson's Bay 40. Tobacco Road 41. *Belle Starr* 41. Sundown 41. The Shanghai Gesture 41. Son of Fury 42. Rings on Her Fingers 42. Thunder Birds 42. China Girl 42. *Heaven Can Wait* 43. *Laura* 44. A Bell for Adano 45. Leave Her to Heaven (AAN) 45. Dragonwyck 46. *The Razor's Edge* 46. The Ghost and Mrs Muir 47. The Iron Curtain 48. That Wonderful Urge 48. Whirlpool 48. Night and the City 50. Where the Sidewalk Ends 50. The Mating Season 51. On the Riviera 51. The Secret of Convict Lake 51. Close to My Heart 51. Way of a Gaucho 51. The Plymouth Adventure 52. Never Let Me Go (GB) 53. Personal Affair (GB) 53. Black Widow 54. The Egyptian 54. *The Left Hand of God* 54. Advise and Consent 62. Toys in the Attic 63. The Pleasure Seekers 64. Daughter of the Mind (TV) 69.

Tierney, Harry (1890–1965).
American songwriter, usually with lyricist Joseph McCarthy. Shows filmed include *Irene*, *Kid Boots*, *Rio Rita*.

Tierney, Lawrence (1919–).
American 'tough-guy' actor, brother of Scott Brady.
The Ghost Ship 44. *Dillinger* (title role) 45. Step by Step 46. San Quentin 47. The Devil Thumbs a Ride 47. Shakedown 50. The Hoodlum 51. A Child Is Waiting 62. Custer of the West 67. Such Good Friends 71. Midnight 82. Prizzi's Honor 85. Silver Bullet 85. Murphy's Law 86. Tough Guys Don't Dance 87. The Runestone 92. Reservoir Dogs 92. A Kiss Goodnight 94, etc.

Tiffin, Pamela (1942–) (Pamela Wonso).
American leading lady, former child model.
Summer and Smoke 60. One Two Three 61. State Fair 61. The Hallelujah Trail 65. Viva Max 69, etc.

Tighe, Kevin (1944–).
American actor, on stage and television.
Matewan 87. K-9 88. Eight Men Out 89. Road House 89. Another 48 Hours 90. Bright Angel 90. Face of a Stranger (TV) 91. City of Hope 91. Newsies 92. What's Eating Gilbert Grape? 93. *I Love a Man in Uniform* 93. Double Cross 94. Geronimo 94. Jade 95. Scorpion Spring 95. Race to the Sun 96. In Cold Blood (TV) 96, etc.
TV series: Emergency 72–77.

Tilbury, Zeffie (1863–1950).
American character actress.
The Marriage of William Ashe 21. Werewolf of London 35. The Last Days of Pompeii 35. Maid of Salem 37. Balalaika 39. Tobacco Road 41. She Couldn't Say No 45, etc.

Till, Eric (1929–).
English director who moved to Canada in the 70s.
Hot Millions 68. The Walking Stick 69. A Fan's Notes 72. It Shouldn't Happen to a Vet 76. Improper Channels 81. If You Could See What I Hear 82. The Cuckoo Bride (TV) 85. Turning to Stone (TV) 85. Solomon & Sheba (TV) 95, etc.

Tiller, Nadja (1929–).
Austrian leading lady, in international films.
Rosemary 59. Portrait of a Sinner 61. The World in My Pocket 62. And So to Bed 65. The Upper Hand 67. Lady Hamilton 68. Wanted: Babysitter 75. Waiting for Sunset/Pakten 95, etc.

Tilly, Jennifer (1958–).
American leading actress, the sister of Meg Tilly.
Moving Violations 85. He's My Girl 87. Remote Control 88. Rented Lips 88. Johnny Be Good 88. High Spirits 88. Far from Home 89. Let It Ride 89. The Fabulous Baker Boys 89. Inside Out 91. Scorchers 92. Agaguk/Shadow of the Wolf 92. Made in America 93. Heads (TV) 94. The Getaway 94. Bullets over Broadway (AAN) 94. The Pompatus of Love 95. Bird of Prey 95. Man with a Gun 95. House Arrest 96. Bound 96. Edie & Penn 96. American Strays 96. Bella Mafia (TV) 97. Liar Liar 97. Bride of Chucky 98, etc.
TV series: Shaping Up 84.

Tilly, Meg (1960–).
American leading actress.
Fame 80. One Dark Night 82. Tex 82. The Big Chill 83. *Psycho II* 83. Impulse 84. Agnes of God (AAN) 85. Off Beat 85. Masquerade 88. The Girl in a Swing 88. Valmont 89. The Two Jakes 90. Leaving Normal 92. Body Snatchers 93. Sleep with Me 94, etc.

Tilton, Martha (1915–).
American singer, in occasional films.
Sunny 41. Swing Hostess 44. Crime Inc 45. The Benny Goodman Story 56, etc.

Tingwell, Charles (1923–).
Australian actor for a time in British TV and films, especially during the 50s in *Emergency Ward Ten*.
Always Another Dawn 48. Bitter Springs 50. Life in Emergency Ward Ten 58. Cone of Silence 60. Murder She Said 63. The Secret of Blood Island 65. Dracula – Prince of Darkness 65. Nobody Runs Forever 68. End Play 75. Gone to Ground 76. Eliza Fraser 76. Breaker Morant 80. Freedom 82. Windrider 86. Malcolm 86. Miracle Down Under 87. A Cry in the Dark 88. The Castle 97. Amy 98, etc.
TV series: Homicide 74–75.

Tinling, James (1889–1967).
American second-feature director.
Silk Legs 27. Arizona 30. Broadway 33. Charlie Chan in Shanghai 35. Pepper 36. 45 Fathers 37. Mr Moto's Gamble 38. Riders of the Purple Sage 41. Sundown Jim 42. The House of Tao Ling 47. Night Wind 48. Trouble Preferred 49. Tales of Robin Hood 52.

Tiomkin, Dmitri (Dimitri) (1894–1979).
Russian-American composer of innumerable film scores.
Autobiography: 1959, *Please Don't Hate Me*.
Alice in Wonderland 33. *Lost Horizon* 37. The Great Waltz 38. *The Moon and Sixpence* 42. Shadow of a Doubt 43. Duel in the Sun 46. *Portrait of Jennie* 48. The Men 50. *High Noon* (AA) 52. *The High and the Mighty* (AA) 54. Land of the Pharaohs 55. Friendly Persuasion 56. *Giant* 56. Night Passage 57. *Gunfight at the O.K. Corral* 57. The Old Man and the Sea (AA) 58. The Unforgiven 60. The Alamo 60. The Guns of Navarone 61. 55 Days at Peking 62. The Fall of the Roman Empire 64. Tchaikovsky 71, etc.
❝ I would like to thank Brahms, Bach, Beethoven, Richard Strauss, and Johann Strauss . . . – *D.T., accepting an Oscar for The High and the Mighty*

Tippett, Phil.
American special-effects expert, specializing in creatures and often using stop-motion animation.
Star Wars 77. Piranha 78. The Empire Strikes Back 80. Dragonslayer (AAN) 81. Return of the Jedi (AA) 83. Indiana Jones and the Temple of Doom 84. Howard the Duck 86. Robocop 87. Willow (AAN) 88. Robocop 2 90. Jurassic Park (AA) 93. Robocop 3 93. Coneheads 93. Dragonheart (AAN) 96. Starship Troopers (AAN) 97, etc.

Tisch, Steve (c. 1949–).
American producer.
Almost Summer 77. Outlaw Blues 77. Coast to Coast 80. Risky Business 83. Deal of the Century 83. The Burning Bed 84. Soul Man 86. Hot to Trot 88. Big Business 88. Heart of Dixie 89. Out on the Edge 89. Bad Influence 90. Heart Condition 90. Corrina, Corrina 94. Forrest Gump (AA) 94. Dear God 96. The Postman 97. American History X 98, etc.
❝ Humanity sells. – *S.T.*

Tissé, Edouard (1897–1961).
Franco-Russian cinematographer who worked closely with Eisenstein.
Strike 24. *The Battleship Potemkin* 25. *The General Line*/The Old and the New 27. *Que Viva Mexico* 32. Aerograd 36. *Alexander Nevsky* 39. *Ivan the Terrible* 42 and 46. Glinka 54, etc.

Tlatli, Moufida.
Tunisian director and screenwriter, a former script and film editor, who studied film in Paris at IDHEC.
Omar Gatlato (ed) 76. The Fertile Memory (ed) 80. Young Arab Cinema (ed) 87. Halfouine (ed) 90. The Silences of the Palace (wd, ed) 94.

Toback, James (1943–).
American writer-director.
The Gambler (w) 74. Fingers (wd) 77. Love & Money (wd) 80. Exposed (a, wd) 83. The Pick-Up Artist (wd) 87. The Big Bang (a, wd) 89. Bugsy (w) (AAN) 91. Two Girls and a Guy (wd) 98, etc.

Tobey, Kenneth (1919–).
American character actor of dependable types.
Kiss Tomorrow Goodbye 49. About Face 51. *The Thing* 52. The Beast from 20,000 Fathoms 55. The Man in the Grey Flannel Suit 56. Terror in the Sky (TV) 72. Billy Jack 73. W. C. Fields and Me 76. MacArthur 77. Strange Invaders 83. Innerspace 87. Gremlins 2: The New Batch 90. Single White Female 92. Honey, I Blew Up the Kid 92, etc.
TV series: Whirlybirds 54–58.

Tobias, George (1901–1980).
American character actor with stage experience.
Saturday's Children (debut) 40. City for Conquest 40. Sergeant York 41. Yankee Doodle Dandy 42. This is the Army 43. Thank Your Lucky Stars 43. Between Two Worlds 44. Objective Burma 45. Mildred Pierce 45. Sinbad the Sailor 47. Rawhide 50. The Glenn Miller Story 53. The Seven Little Foys 55. A New Kind of Love 63. The Glass Bottom Boat 66, many others.
TV series: Hudson's Bay 59–60. Adventures in Paradise 60–61. Bewitched 64–72.

Tobias, Oliver (1947–).
Saturnine British leading man.
Jesus of Nazareth (TV) 77. The Stud 78. Arabian Adventure 79. A Nightingale Sang in Berkeley Square 80. The Wicked Lady 83. Mata Hari 85. The Brylcreem Boys (TV) 95. Breeders 97, etc.
TV series: Arthur of the Britons 72.

Tobin, Dan (1909–1982).
Lightweight American character actor.
The Stadium Murders 38. Woman of the Year 41. Undercurrent 46. The Big Clock 48. The Velvet Touch 49. Dear Wife 52. Wedding Breakfast 56. The Last Angry Man 59. The Love Bug Rides Again 73, etc.
TV series: Perry Mason 57–65.

Tobin, Genevieve (1901–1995).
Vivacious American actress of French parentage. Mainly stage experience; made some films during the 30s. She was married to director William Keighley.
No Mother to Guide Her 23. The Lady Surrenders 31. One Hour With You 32. Easy to Wed 34. The Petrified Forest 36. The Great Gambini 37. Dramatic School 38. Zaza 39. Queen of Crime 41, etc.

Tobolowsky, Stephen (1951–).
American actor and occasional screenwriter, born in Dallas, Texas.
True Stories (co-w) 86. Nobody's Fool 86. Mississippi Burning 88. In Country 89. Great Balls of Fire 89. Bird on a Wire 90. Funny about Love 90. Thelma and Louise 91. Welcome Home, Roxy Carmichael 91. City Slickers 91. Hero/Accidental Hero 92. Memoirs of an Invisible Man 92. Sneakers 92. Single White Female 92. Josh and S.A.M. 93. Calendar Girl 93. Groundhog Day 93. My Father, the Hero 94. Murder in the First 95. Dr Jekyll and Ms Hyde 95. The Glimmer Man 96, etc.

Toch, Ernst (1887–1964).
German composer in Hollywood.
Catherine the Great 34. Little Friend 34. Peter Ibbetson 35. Four Men and a Prayer 38. *The Cat and the Canary* 39. The Ghost Breakers 40. Dr Cyclops 40. Ladies in Retirement 41. Address Unknown 44. The Unseen 45, etc.

Todd, Ann (1909–1993).
Blonde British leading actress, a big star of the 40s. Later produced and directed short travel films. She was formerly married to director David Lean.
Autobiography: 1980, *The Eighth Veil*.
■ Keepers of Youth 31. These Charming People 31. The Ghost Train 31. The Water Gypsies 31. The Return of Bulldog Drummond 34. Things to Come 36. The Squeaker 37. Action for Slander 37. *South Riding* 38. Poison Pen 39. Danny Boy 41. Ships with Wings 41. Perfect Strangers 45. *The Seventh Veil* 45. Gaiety George 46. Daybreak 47. So Evil my Love 47. The Paradine Case (US) 48. *The Passionate Friends* 48. Madeleine 49. The Sound Barrier 52. The Green Scarf 54. Time without Pity 57. Taste of Fear 61. Son of Captain Blood 62. Ninety Degrees in the Shade 65. The Friend 71. The Human Factor 79.
❝ The pattern of destiny is very strange. I sometimes wonder why I had to be an actress and achieve a well-known name – when deep down I am a private person and rather like being alone. – *A.T.*
I don't really consider myself an actress. I don't think I ever act. The parts I have played in my career that have come off best have usually been a continuation of myself. – *A.T.*

Todd, Ann (1932–) (A. T. Mayfield).
American child star of the 30s and 40s.
Zaza 39. Blood and Sand 41. Kings Row 42. The Jolson Story 46. Bomba and the Lion Hunters 52, etc.

Todd, Bob (1922–1992).
Bald British comic actor, much on TV.
The Intelligence Men 65. Hot Millions 68. The Private Life of Sherlock Holmes 70. Digby, the Biggest Dog in the World 73. The Four Musketeers 74. Superman III 83, etc.

Todd, Mike (1907–1958) (Avrom Goldenbogen).
Dynamic American producer of Broadway spectacles, a former carnival barker. His one personally produced film was in similar vein: *Around the World in Eighty Days* (AA) 56. The wide-screen system *Todd-AO* is named after him. His three wives included Joan Blondell and Elizabeth Taylor. Died in a plane crash.
Biography: 1959, *The Nine Lives of Mike Todd* by Art Cohn.
❝ I believe in giving customers a meat-and-potatoes show. Dames and comedy. – *M.K.*
Mike is the most exciting man in the world. – *Elizabeth Taylor, 1957*
This sinister dwarf who consumed nine weeks of my life has no peer in his chosen profession, which – stated very simply – is to humiliate and cheapen his fellow man, fracture one's self-esteem, convert everybody around him into lackeys, hypocrites and toadies, and thoroughly debase every relationship, no matter how casual. His enormity grows on you like some obscene fungus. – *S. J. Perelman* (screenwriter of *Around the World in Eighty Days*)

Todd, Richard (1919–).
British leading man, in repertory from 1937 until spotted by a film talent scout.
For Them that Trespass (debut) 48. *The Hasty Heart* (AAN) 49. Stage Fright 50. Lightning Strikes Twice (US) 51. *Robin Hood* 52. Venetian Bird 53. The Sword and the Rose 54. Rob Roy 54. *A Man Called Peter* 55. The Virgin Queen (US) 55. *The Dam Busters* 55. Yangtse Incident 56. Chase a Crooked Shadow 57. Danger Within 58. The Long, the Short and the Tall 59. The Hellions 60. Never Let Go 61. The Longest Day 62. The Boys 62. The Very Edge 63. Operation Crossbow 65. The Battle of the Villa Fiorita 65. Coast of Skeletons 65. Death Drums along the River 66. Last of the Long-haired Boys 68. Subterfuge 69. Dorian Gray 70. Asylum 72. The Big Sleep 78. Home Before Midnight 79. House of the Long Shadows 83. Sherlock Holmes – the Incident at Victoria Falls (TV) 91, etc.

Todd, Thelma (1905–1935).
Perky American leading blonde of the early 30s, heroine of many two-reel comedies. Died in mysterious circumstances.
Fascinating Youth 26. Rubber Heels 27. The Haunted House 28. Her Private Life 29. Aloha 30. The Hot Heiress 31. *Monkey Business* 31. The Maltese Falcon 31. *Horse Feathers* 32. Air Hostess 33. Sitting Pretty 33. Hips Hips Hooray 34. Bottoms Up 34. Two for Tonight 35. The Bohemian Girl 35, many others.

Todorovski, Valeri (1962–).
Russian director and screenwriter who studied at the Moscow Film School.
Catafalque 90. Love/Liuboc 91. *Katia Ismailova* 93, etc.

Tognazzi, Ricky (1955–).
Italian director, producer and actor, the son of Ugo Tognazzi. Born in Milan, of an Italian father and Scottish mother, he was educated partly in Britain.
Piccoli Equivoci 89. Ultra 90. *The Escort*/La Scorta 93. Sentimental Maniacs/Maniaci Sentimentali (a, p) 94. Un Eroe Borghese (a) 95. Strangled Lives/Vite Strozzate 96. Falcone 98, etc.

Tognazzi, Ugo (1922–1990).
Italian leading actor.
His Women/Il Mantenuto (& d) 61. The Fascist/Il Federale 62. Queen Bee/Ape Regina or The Conjugal Bed 63. The Magnificent Cuckold 64. An American Wife 65. A Question of Honour 66. Barbarella 68. Property Is No Longer a Theft 73. Blowout 73. Duck in Orange Sauce 75. Viva Italia 77. *La Cage aux Folles* 79. La Cage aux Folles II 80. Sunday Lovers 80. Tolerance 89, etc.

Toibin, Niall (1929–).
Irish actor who began on radio and with the Abbey Theatre.
Guns in the Heather 68. Ryan's Daughter 70. Philadelphia, Here I Come 70. Flight of the Doves 71. The Outsider (US/Hol.) 79. Tristan and Isolt (US) 79. The Ballroom of Romance (TV) 82. The Country Girls 83. Wagner (TV) 83. One of Ourselves 83. Shergar (TV) 85. Eat the Peach 86. Rawhead Rex 87. Fools of Fortune 90. Dream On 95. Far and Away 92. Frankie Starlight 95, etc.

Tokar, Norman (1920–1979).
American director, from radio; in films, worked almost exclusively for Disney.
■ Big Red 62. Savage Sam 63. Sammy the Way Out Seal 63. A Tiger Walks 64. Those Calloways 65. Follow Me Boys 65. The Ugly Dachshund 66. The Happiest Millionaire 67. The Horse in the Grey Flannel Suit 68. Rascal 69. The Boatniks 72. Snowball Express 73. The Apple Dumpling Gang 75. Where the Red Fern Grows 76. No Deposit No Return 77. Candleshoe 78. The Cat from Outer Space 78.

Toland, Gregg (1904–1948).
Distinguished American cinematographer who worked mainly with Goldwyn.
The Unholy Garden 31. Roman Scandals 33. Tugboat Annie 33. *Nana* 34. *We Live Again* 34. *Mad Love* 35. Les Misérables 35. These Three 36. *Dead End* 37. The Goldwyn Follies 38. Intermezzo 39. *Wuthering Heights* (AA) 39. Raffles 40. *The Grapes of Wrath* 40. The Long Voyage Home 40. *The Westerner* 40. *Citizen Kane* 41. *The Little Foxes* 41; war service; *The Best Years of Our Lives* 46. The Kid from Brooklyn 47. The Bishop's Wife 48. *Enchantment* 48, many others.

Toler, Sidney (1874–1947).
Chubby American character actor who in 1938 took over the part of Charlie Chan and played it twenty-two times.
Madame X 29. Is My Face Red? 32. Spitfire 35. Call of the Wild 35. Our Relations 36. Wide Open Faces 38. Charlie Chan in Honolulu 38. Law of the Pampas 39. Charlie Chan at the Wax Museum 40. Castle in the Desert 42. White Savage 43. The Scarlet Clue 45. Dark Alibi 46. The Trap 47, many others.

Tolkien, J. R. R. (1892–1973).
Donnish British novelist who created the myth of 'Middle Earth' in his trilogy *The Lord of the Rings*, which became an instant classic and was filmed in cartoon form. In 1998, plans were announced to make three live-action films of the books, to be written and directed by Peter Jackson and filmed in New Zealand.

Tolkin, Michael.
American screenwriter, director and novelist, a former journalist.
Gleaming the Cube (w) 88. *The Rapture* (wd) 91. The Player (w) 92. Deep Cover (co-w) 92. The New Age (wd) 94. The Burning Season (co-w) (TV) 94. Deep Impact (co-w) 98, etc.

Toll, John.
American cinematographer, a former camera operator during the 80s.
Wind 92. *Legends of the Fall* (AA) 94. *Braveheart* 95. Jack 96. John Grisham's The Rainmaker 97. The Thin Red Line 98, etc.

Tolstoy, Leo (1828–1910).
Russian novelist whose *Anna Karenina* and *War and Peace* have been frequently filmed.

Tomasini, George (1909–1964).
American editor.
Wild Harvest 47. Houdini 53. Elephant Walk 54. To Catch a Thief 55. The Wrong Man 57. Vertigo 58. *North By Northwest* (AAN) 59. Psycho 60. Cape Fear 62. The Birds 63. Marnie 64, etc.

Tombes, Andrew (1889–1976).
American supporting actor often seen as cop, undertaker, bartender or harassed official.
Moulin Rouge 33. Charlie Chan at the Olympics 37. Too Busy to Work 39. Phantom Lady 44. Can't Help Singing 44. Oh You Beautiful Doll 49. How to Be Very Very Popular 55, many others.

Tomei, Marisa (1964–).
American leading actress.
The Flamingo Kid 84. Oscar 91. My Cousin Vinny (AA) 92. Chaplin 92. Equinox 92. Untamed Heart 93. The Paper 94. Only You 94. The Perez Family 95. Unhook the Stars 96. Welcome to Sarajevo 96. A Brother's Kiss 97. Slums of Beverly Hills 98, etc.
TV series: A Different World 87–88.

Tomelty, Joseph (1911–1995).
Irish character actor, in British films since 1945.
Odd Man Out 46. The Sound Barrier 52. Meet Mr Lucifer 54. Simba 55. A Kid for Two Farthings 56. Bowani Junction 56. The Black Torment 64, many others.

Tomlin, Lily (1939–).
American comedy actress.
Nashville (AAN) 75. The Late Show 77. Moment by Moment 78. Nine to Five 80. The Incredible Shrinking Woman 81. All of Me 84. Big Business 88. The Search for Signs of Intelligent Life in the Universe 91. Shadows and Fog 92. The Beverly Hillbillies 93. Short Cuts 93. Blue in the Face 95. Flirting with Disaster 96. Getting Away with Murder 96. Krippendorf's Tribe 98. Tea with Mussolini 99, etc.
❝ The trouble with the rat race is that even if you win, you're still a rat. – *L.T.*

Tomlinson, David (1917–).
Amiable British leading man and comedian, a latter-day Ralph Lynn.
Quiet Wedding 40. Journey Together 45. The Way to the Stars 45. Master of Bankdam 47. *Miranda* 48. Sleeping Car to Trieste 48. *The Chiltern Hundreds* 49. Hotel Sahara 51. *Three Men in a Boat* 55. Up the Creek 58. Follow That Horse 60. Tom Jones 63. *Mary Poppins* 64. The Truth about Spring 65. City in the Sea 65. The Liquidator 66. The Love Bug 69. Bedknobs and Broomsticks 71. The Water Babies 78. The Fiendish Plot of Fu Manchu 80, many others.

Tomlinson, Ricky (1942–).
English character actor, best known for his role as Bobby Grant in the TV soap *Brookside*.
Riff-Raff 90. Raining Stones 93. Butterfly Kiss 95. Hillsborough (TV) 96. Preaching to the Perverted 97. Mojo 98, etc.
TV series: The Royle Family 98– .

Tompkinson, Stephen (1965–).
English actor, most often in comedy and best known for his TV roles as reporter Damien Day in *Drop the Dead Donkey* 90–94 and as Father Peter Clifford in *Ballykissangel* 96–98. Born in Blackpool, Lancashire, he trained at the Central School of Speech and Drama.
And a Nightingale Sang (TV) 89. *Brassed Off* 96. Oktober (TV) 98.
TV series: All Quiet on the Preston Front 94. Downwardly Mobile 94. Grafters 98– .

Tone, Franchot (1905–1968) (Stanislas Pascal Franchot Tone).
American leading man of stage and screen. The first of his four wives was Joan Crawford (1935–39).
The Wiser Sex (film debut) 32. Gabriel over the White House 33. Moulin Rouge 34. Mutiny on the Bounty (AAN) 35. Suzy 36. Quality Street 36. *They Gave Him a Gun* 37. Three Comrades 39. The Trail of the Vigilantes 40. Nice Girl 41. The Wife Takes a Flyer 42. *Five Graves to Cairo* 43. His Butler's Sister 43. *Phantom Lady* 44. Dark Waters 44. That Night with You 45. Because of Him 46. Her Husband's Affairs 47. I Love Trouble 48. Every Girl Should Be Married 48. The Man on the Eiffel Tower 50. *Advise and Consent* 62. La Bonne Soupe 64. In Harm's Way 65. Nobody Runs Forever 68, etc.

Tong, Stanley (Tony Kwai-Lai).
Chinese director of action movies, associated with the films of Jackie Chan. Born in Hong Kong, he moved to Canada as a teenager and studied at the University of Manitoba, then returning to Hong Kong in the late 70s. A martial arts expert, he began as a stuntman, before beginning to direct in the early 80s. He formed his own film company, Golden Gate, in the late 80s.
Seven Warriors 89. Police Story III: Super Cop 92. Police Story V 93. Rumble in the Bronx 95. First Strike 96. Mr Magoo (US) 97, etc.

Tonti, Aldo (1910–1988).
Italian cinematographer.
Ossessione 44. Europe 51 50. The Mill on the Po 51. War and Peace 56. Cabiria 57. Reflections in a Golden Eye 67. Ashanti 78, etc.

Toomey, Regis (1898–1991).
American character actor, on screen from 1928, usually as cop or victim in routine crime dramas.
Framed 29. Murder by the Clock 32. G-Men 35. The Big Sleep 46. The Nebraskan 53. Guys and Dolls 55. Man's Favourite Sport? 63. Peter Gunn 67. God Bless Dr Shagetz 77, many others.
TV series: Burke's Law 63–65. Petticoat Junction 68–69.

Topol (1935–) (Chaim Topol).
Israeli leading actor who gained fame with London stage run of *Fiddler on the Roof*.
Cast a Giant Shadow 65. Sallah 66. Before Winter Comes 69. *Fiddler on the Roof* (AAN) 71. Follow Me 72. Galileo 74. The House on Garibaldi Street (TV) 79. Flash Gordon 80. For Your Eyes Only 81. The Winds of War (TV) 83. Queenie (TV) 87. War and Remembrance (TV) 87. Left Luggage (Hol.) 98, etc.

Topor, Roland (1938?–1997).
Iconoclastic French artist, dramatist, writer and graphic designer, associated with the Dada-ist group Panique, which included Fernando Arrabal and Alexandro Jodorowsky. Died of a cerebral haemorrhage.
Fando y Lis (story) 68. The Tenant (story) 76. Fantastic Planet/La Planète Sauvage (design) 73. Marquis (co-w, ad) 89, etc.
TV series: Telechat 83–85.

Topper, Burt (1928–).
American director.
Diary of a High School Bride 61. The Strangler 64. The Devil's Eight 68. Wild in the Streets (p) 68. The Hard Ride 71. Lovin' Man 72. The Day the Lord Got Busted 76, etc.

Toren, Marta (1926–1957).
Swedish leading lady signed by Hollywood scout while at dramatic school.
Casbah (debut) 48. Rogues' Regiment 49. One-Way Street 50. Panthers' Moon 51. Sirocco 51. The Man Who Watched the Trains Go By 52. Maddalena 54, etc.

Tork, Peter (1944–).
American actor and musician, one of The Monkees pop group.
Head 68.

TV series: The Monkees 66–68.

Tormé, Mel (1925–).
Amiable American ballad singer who has made occasional films.
Higher and Higher 43. Let's Go Steady 45. Junior Miss 45. Good News 47. Duchess of Idaho 50. The Big Operator 59. Walk Like a Dragon 60. The Patsy 64. A Man Called Adam 66, etc.

Torn, Rip (1931–) (Elmore Torn).
American general-purpose actor, mainly on stage and TV. He was married to actress Geraldine PAGE.
Baby Doll 56. Time Limit 57. Cat on a Hot Tin Roof 58. King of Kings 61. Sweet Bird of Youth 62. The Cincinnati Kid 65. You're a Big Boy Now 66. Beach Red 67. The Rain People 69. Tropic of Cancer 69. *Payday* 73. Crazy Joe 73. Birch Interval 76. The Man Who Fell to Earth 76. Nasty Habits 77. The Private Files of J. Edgar Hoover 78. Coma 78. *Blind Ambition* (TV) (as Nixon) 79. The Seduction of Joe Tynan 79. The First Family 80. Heartland 80. One Trick Pony 80. A Stranger Is Watching 82. Cross Creek (AAN) 83. City Heat 84. Songwriter 84. Beer 85. Summer Rental 85. Nadine 87. The Telephone (d) 88. Cold Feet 89. Hit List 89. Zwei Frauen 89. Beautiful Dreamers 90. Defending Your Life 91. My Son Johnny (TV) 91. Finnegans Wake 92. Dolly Dearest 92. Where the Rivers Flow North 93. Robocop 3 93. Canadian Bacon 95. How to Make an American Quilt 95. Down Periscope 96. The Mouse 96. Men in Black 97. Senseless 98, etc.
TV series: The Larry Sanders Show 92– .

Tornatore, Giuseppe (1956–).
Italian director and screenwriter, from television.
The Professor/Il Camorrista 87. *Cinema Paradiso/Nuovo Cinema Paradiso* (AA) 88. Everybody's Fine/Stanno Tutti Bene 90. Especially on Sundays/La Domenica Specialmente (co-d) 91. A Simple Formality/Una Pura Formalita (wd, e) 94. The Star Man/L'Uomo delle Stelle 95. The Legend of the Pianist on the Ocean (wd) 98, etc.

Torrence, David (1864–1951).
Scottish silent screen actor in Hollywood.
The Inside of the Cup 21. Sherlock Holmes 22. The Abysmal Brute 23. Surging Seas 24. The Reckless Sex 25. Laddie 26. Annie Laurie 27. The Little Shepherd of Kingdom Come 28. Untamed Justice 29. Raffles 30. Voltaire 33. Mandalay 34. The Dark Angel 35, etc.

Torrence, Ernest (1878–1933).
Scottish actor, in American silent films, usually as villain; former opera singer.
Tol'able David 21. The Hunchback of Notre Dame 23. The Trail of the Lonesome Pine 23. *The Covered Wagon* 23. Peter Pan 24. King of Kings 27. The Cossacks 28. The Bridge of San Luis Rey 29. The New Adventures of Get-Rich-Quick Wallingford 31. Cuban Love Song 32. Sherlock Holmes 33, many others.

Torre-Nilsson, Leopoldo (1924–1978).
Argentinian director, usually of sharp-flavoured melodramas which he also wrote.
The House of the Angel 57. *The Fall* 59. The Hand in the Trap 60. Summer Skin 61. Four Women for One Hero 62. The Roof Garden 63. The Eavesdropper 65. Monday's Child 67. Martin Fierro 68, etc.

Torres, Raquel (1908–1987) (Paula Marie Osterman).
American leading lady who played fiery sirens in the early 30s.
White Shadows in the South Seas 28. The Bridge of San Luis Rey 29. Under a Texas Moon 30. The Woman I Stole 33. Duck Soup 33. The Red Wagon 36, etc.

Tors, Ivan (1916–1983).
Hungarian writer-producer-director, in Hollywood from 1941.
Song of Love (w) 47. The Forsyte Saga (w) 49. Storm over Tibet (w, p) 52. The Magnetic Monster (w, p) 53. Gog (w, p) 54. Riders to the Stars (p) 55. Battle Taxi (p) 56. Flipper (p) 60. Rhino (p, d) 64. Zebra in the Kitchen 65. Around the World under the Sea 65, etc.
TV series as producer include: *Sea Hunt* 57–60. *The Man and the Challenge* 59. *Flipper* 64–68. *Primus* 71.

Tosi, Mario.
Italian-American cinematographer.
Some Call It Loving 73. Report to the Commissioner 74. Hearts of the West 75. Carrie 76. The Main Event 79. Resurrection 80. The Stunt Man 80. Six Pack 82.

Totheroh, Rollie (1891–1967).
American cinematographer who worked notably for Charles Chaplin.
The Pilgrim 23. The Gold Rush 24. City Lights 31. Modern Times 36. The Great Dictator 40. Monsieur Verdoux 47, etc.

Toto (1897–1967) (Antonio Furst de Curtis-Gagliardi).
Italian comedian, from music hall and revue.
Fermo con le Mani 36. Toto Le Moko 49. Cops and Robbers 53. Gold of Naples 54. Racconti Romani 55. Persons Unknown 58. Toto of Arabia 63. The Commander 67, many others.

Totter, Audrey (1918–).
American leading lady of the 'hard-boiled' type, with stage and radio experience.
Main Street after Dark (debut) 44. Her Highness and the Bellboy 45. The Postman Always Rings Twice 45. *The Lady in the Lake* 46. Tenth Avenue Angel 47. The Unsuspected 48. Alias Nick Beal 49. The Set-Up 49. Tension 51. The Blue Veil 52. Assignment Paris 53. Women's Prison 54. A Bullet for Joey 55. The Carpetbaggers 64. Harlow (electronovision version) 65. Chubasco 68. The Apple Dumpling Gang Rides Again 79, many others.
TV series: Cimarron City 58. Our Man Higgins 62. Medical Center 72–76.

Toulouse-Lautrec, Henri (1864–1901).
French artist and lithographer of aristocratic birth and stunted growth, famous for his paintings and posters of Montmartre's cabarets, music halls, and bars and their habitués. His short, hectic, alcoholic life was the subject of two biopics: *Moulin Rouge* 52, in which he was played by José Ferrer, and *Lautrec* 98, with Regis Royer in the title role. He was also played by Jerry Bergen in *Lust for Life* 56.

Toumanova, Tamara (1919–1996).
Russian ballerina who has made occasional appearances in American films. Formerly married to producer Casey Robinson.
Days of Glory 43. Deep in my Heart 54. Invitation to the Dance 56. Torn Curtain 67. The Private Life of Sherlock Holmes 70, etc.

Tourjanksy, Victor (1891–1976) (Vyacheslav Turzhansky).
Russian-born director who had a long career in international films, also becoming a producer and screenwriter in the late 50s, when he was involved in Italian historical epics. Born in Kiev, he studied under Stanislavsky at Moscow's Academy of Dramatic Art and, after a brief period as an actor, turned to directing in 1914, leaving to live in France in 1919, where he also worked as an assistant director on Abel GANCE's epic *Napoleon*. He went to the USA to work for MGM in 1928, hired to direct *After Midnight*, starring Norma SHEARER. But he complained to producer Irving THALBERG that she was cross-eyed, not knowing that Thalberg was about to marry her. He was taken off the picture and banished to the inhospitable Mojave Desert to direct a western; he never worked in America again. He was sometimes credited as Wenceslaw Tourjansky. Married Russian actress Nathalie Kovanko.
The Brothers Karamatzov 15. Les Contes des Mille et Une Nuits (Fr.) 21. Le Chant de l'Amour Triomphant (Fr.) 23. Michel Strogoff (Fr.) 26. La Dame Masquée (Fr.) 24. The Adventurer (US) 28. Wolga-Wolga (Ger.) 28. Manolescu (Ger.) 29. Der Herzog von Reichstag (Ger.) 31. L'Ordonnance (Fr.) 33. Volga in Flames/Volga en Flammes (Fr.) 33. The World Is Mine/Die Ganze Welt Dreht Sich um Liebe (Aus.) 35. Black Eyes/Les Yeux Noirs (Fr.) 35. Fear/La Peur (Fr.) 36. The Life of Nina Petrovna/Le Mensonge de Nina Petrovna (Fr.) 37. LB 17/Geheimzeichen LB 17 (Ger.) 38. Der Blaufuchs (Ger.) 38. Der Gouverneur (Ger.) 39. Feinde (Ger.) 40. Illusion (Ger.) 41. Tonelli (Ger.) 43. Orient-Express (& w) (Ger.) 44. Arlette Erobert Paris (Ger.) 53. Salto Mortale (Ger.) 53. Konigswalzer 55. Die Toteninsel 55. Beichtgeheimnis 56. Aphrodite Goddess of Love/La Venere di Cheronea (co-d) (Fr./It.) 57. The Boatman/I Battellieri del Volga (& co-w) 58. The Cossacks/I Cosacchi (p, co-d) 59. Herod the Great/Erode il Grande (p, co-w) 59. The Pharaoh's Woman/La Donna dei Faraoni (p, co-w) 60. The Triumph of Michael Strogoff/Le Triomphe de Michel Strogoff 61. A Queen for a Caesar/Una Regina per Cesare (p only) 62, etc.

Tourneur, Jacques (1904–1977).
Franco-American director, son of Maurice Tourneur, with a special flair for the macabre.
Nick Carter, Master Detective 39. *Cat People* 42. *I Walked with a Zombie* 43. *The Leopard Man* 43. Days of Glory 44. *Experiment Perilous* 44. *Out of the Past* 47. Berlin Express 48. Stars in My Crown 50. The Flame and the Arrow 51. Appointment in Honduras 53. Wichita 55. Great Day in the Morning 56. *Night of the Demon* 57. Timbuktu 59. The Giant of Marathon 61. A Comedy of Terrors 63. City under the Sea 65, etc.

Tourneur, Maurice (1876–1961) (Maurice Thomas).
French director who made some American films.
Mother 14. Man of the Hour 15. Trilby 15. Poor Little Rich Girl 17. The Bluebird 18. The Last of the Mohicans 20. Treasure Island 20. The Christian (GB) 23. Aloma of the South Seas 26. L'Équipage 27. Mysterious Island 29. Maison de Danses 31. Koenigsmark 35. Volpone 40. The Devil's Hand 42. L'Impasse des Deux Anges 48, etc.

Tover, Leo (1902–1964).
American cinematographer in Hollywood from 1918.
Dead Reckoning 47. *The Snake Pit* 48. *The Heiress* 49. The Secret of Convict Lake 51. The President's Lady 53. Soldier of Fortune 55. The Sun Also Rises 57. *Journey to the Centre of the Earth* 59. Follow That Dream 62. Sunday in New York 63. Strange Bedfellows 64. A Very Special Favor 65, many others.

Tovoli, Luciano (1936–).
Italian cinematographer.
Bread and Chocolate/Pane e Cioccolata 74. Leonor 75. Suspiria 77. Bianca 85. La Cage aux Folles III (Fr.) 85. Love Dream 88. Reversal of Fortune (US) 90. Single White Female (US) 92. Mario, Maria e Mario 94. Before and After (US) 96. Le Jaguar (Fr.) 96. Desperate Measures (US) 98, etc.

Towb, Harry (1925–).
Irish character actor, often as comic relief, in films from 1951.
The Gift Horse 52. Knave of Hearts 54. The Sleeping Tiger 54. Above Us the Waves 55. Eye Witness 56. The 39 Steps 59. The Blue Max 66. Prudence and the Pill 68. Patton 70. Carry On at Your Convenience 71. Barry Lyndon 75. Lassiter 83. Lost Belongings (TV) 87. Moll Flanders 96, etc.
TV series: Joan and Leslie 56–58. The Army Game 58–61. Home James 87–90. So You Think You've Got Troubles 91. Comedy Nation 98.

Towers, Constance (1931–).
American actress and singer, born in Whitefish, Montana. Married actor John GAVIN, who became the US ambassador to Mexico during the Reagan administration.
Bring Your Smile Along 55. The Horse Soldiers 56. Sergeant Rutledge 60. Shock Corridor 63. Fate Is the Hunter 64. The Naked Kiss 64. Fast Forward 85. Sylvester 85. On Wings of Eagles (TV) 86, etc.

Towers, Harry Alan (1920–).
British executive producer with varied experience in films and TV. He is also a screenwriter under the name of Peter Welbeck.
Victim Five (& w) 64. Mozambique (& w) 64. The Face of Fu Manchu 65. Ten Little Indians 65. Our Man in Marrakesh/Bang, Bang, You're Dead 66. The Brides of Fu Manchu 66. Rocket to the Moon 67. Treasure Island 72. Call of the Wild 73. The Shape of Things to Come 78. Gor 85. Howling IV 89. Edge of Sanity 89. The Hitman 90. The Mangler (p, co-w) 95, etc.

Towne, Gene (1904–1979).
American screenwriter.
Little Women 33. History is Made at Night 37. The Swiss Family Robinson 40. Joy of Living 41, etc.

Towne, Robert (1936–).
American screenwriter.
The Tomb of Ligeia 64. Villa Rides 67. The Last Detail (AAN) 73. *Chinatown* (AA) 74. Shampoo (co-w) (AAN) 75. The Yakuza (co-w) 75. Personal Best (& d) 81. Greystoke: The Legend of Tarzan of the Apes 84. The Bedroom Window 87. Tequila Sunrise (& d) 88. Days of Thunder 90. The Two Jakes 90. The Firm (co-w) 93. Love Affair (co-w) 94. Mission: Impossible (co-w) 96. Without Limits (wd) 98, etc.

Townsend, Robert (1957–).
American actor, director, producer and screenwriter who began as a stand-up comedian. He made a breakthrough with *Hollywood Shuffle*, a comedy based on his own experiences as a black actor seeking work.
Willie & Phil 80. A Soldier's Story 84. Streets of Fire 84. American Flyers 85. Odd Jobs 86. Ratboy 86. Eddie Murphy Raw (d) 87. Hollywood Shuffle (& wd, p) 87. The Mighty Quinn 89. That's Adequate 89. The Five Heartbeats (& wd, p) 91. The Meteor Man (& wd) 93. B.A.P.S. (d) 97, etc.
TV series: The Parent 'Hood 95.

Townsend, Stuart (1973–).
Irish leading actor, born in Howth, from the theatre.
Trojan Eddie 97. Shooting Fish 97. Under the Skin 97. Resurrection Man 98. Simon Magus 99, etc.

Toye, Wendy (1917–).
British director, former dancer. Drew attention with two ingenious short films, *The Stranger Left No Card* 52 and *On the Twelfth Day* 55.
Features: Three Cases of Murder 54. All for Mary 55. True as a Turtle 56. We Joined the Navy 62, etc.

Toyoda, Shiro (1906–1977).
Japanese director. He began as a screenwriter in the mid-20s.
Young People/Wakai Hito 37. Spring on Lepers' Island/Kojima No Haru 40. *Wild Geese*/Gan 53. Meoto Zenzai 55. Pilgrimage at Night/Anya Koro 59. Madame Aki 63. Portrait of Hell/Jigokuhen 69. Man of Ecstasy/Kototsu No Hito 73, etc.

Tracy, Arthur (1899–1997) (Abraham Alter Tratserofski).
American singer who made his greatest success in England, especially with his rendering of 'Marta'. Born in the Ukraine, he came to America at the age of six, and performed in Yiddish theatre in New York, becoming a recording star from the early 30s. He was billed as 'The Street Singer', because that is where he began as an entertainer. His recording of 'Pennies from Heaven' was used in the BBC TV serial of that name and the subsequent Hollywood movie of 1981.
The Big Broadcast 32. Limelight (GB) 36. The Street Singer (GB) 37. Follow Your Star (GB) 38. Crossing Delancey 88, etc.

Tracy, Lee (1898–1968).
American leading actor of stage (from 1919) and screen (sporadically from 1929): had inimitable nasal delivery.
■ Big Time 29. Born Reckless 30. Liliom 30. She Got What She Wanted 30. The Strange Love of Molly Louvain 32. Love is a Racket 32. *Doctor X* 32. *Blessed Event* 32. Washington Merry Go Round 32. The Night Mayor 32. *The Half Naked Truth* 32. Clear All Wires 33. Private Jones 33. The Nuisance 33. Dinner at Eight 33. Turn Back the Clock 33. *Bombshell* 33. Advice to the Lovelorn 33. I'll Tell the World 34. You Belong to Me 34. The Lemon Drop Kid 34. Carnival 35. Two Fisted 35. Sutter's Gold 36. Wanted, Jane Turner 36. Criminal Lawyer 37. Behind the Headlines 37. Crashing Hollywood 38. Fixer Dugan 39. The Spellbinder 39. Millionaires in Prison 40. The Payoff 42. Power of the Press 43. Betrayal from the East 45. I'll Tell the World 45. High Tide 47. *The Best Man* (AAN) 64.
TV series: The Amazing Mr Malone 51. Martin Kane 53.

Tracy, Spencer (1900–1967).
Distinguished American actor with stage experience from 1922; exclusively on screen from 1930. His uneven features gained him gangster

roles to begin with, then he made a corner in priests and friends of the hero; but his chief mature image was that of a tough, humorous fellow who was also a pillar of integrity.

Biographies: 1970, *Spencer Tracy* by Larry Swindell. 1973, *Tracy and Hepburn* by Garson Kanin.

■ Up the River 30. Quick Millions 31. Six-Cylinder Love 31. Goldie 31. She Wanted a Millionaire 32. Sky Devils 32. Disorderly Conduct 32. Young America 32. Society Girl 32. Painted Woman 32. Me and My Girl 32. *Twenty Thousand Years in Sing Sing* 32. Face in the Sky 33. *The Power and the Glory* 33. Shanghai Madness 33. The Mad Game 33. *A Man's Castle* 33. Looking for Trouble 34. The Show-Off 34. Bottoms Up 34. Now I'll Tell 34. Marie Galante 34. It's a Small World 35. Dante's Inferno 35. The Murder Man 35. Whipsaw 35. Riff Raff 36. *Fury* 36. *San Francisco* (AAN) 36. *Libeled Lady* 36. *Captains Courageous* (AA) 37. They Gave Him a Gun 37. The Big City 38. Mannequin 38. Test Pilot 38. *Boys' Town* (AA) 38. *Stanley and Livingstone* 39. I Take This Woman 39. *Northwest Passage* 40. *Edison the Man* 40. Boom Town 40. Men of Boys' Town 41. Dr Jekyll and Mr Hyde 41. *Woman of the Year* 42. Tortilla Flat 42. Keeper of the Flame 43. A Guy Named Joe 43. *The Seventh Cross* 44. Thirty Seconds over Tokyo 44. Without Love 45. Sea of Grass 46. Cass Timberlane 47. *State of the Union* 48. Edward My Son (GB) 49. *Adam's Rib* 49. Malaya 49. *Father of the Bride* (AAN) 50. The People against O'Hara 51. Father's Little Dividend 51. Pat and Mike 52. Plymouth Adventure 52. The Actress 53. Broken Lance 54. *Bad Day at Black Rock* (AAN) 55. The Mountain 56. The Desk Set 57. The Old Man and the Sea (AAN) 58. *The Last Hurrah* 58. *Inherit the Wind* (AAN) 60. The Devil at Four o'Clock 61. *Judgment at Nuremberg* (AAN) 61. It's a Mad Mad Mad Mad World 63. *Guess Who's Coming to Dinner* (BFA, AAN) 67.

✪ For superb performances and for the utter reliability of his on-screen personality, which was so at odds with the insecurity of his private psyche. *Inherit the Wind*.

❝ The guy's good. There's nobody in the business who can touch him, and you're a fool to try. And the bastard knows it, so don't fall for that humble stuff!

This tribute came from Clark Gable, who suffered from co-starring with Tracy in several MGM movies of the 30s. On the other hand, Katharine Hepburn once said:

I think Spencer always thought that acting was a rather silly way for a man to make a living.

She also caught his essential strength:

He's like an old oak tree, or the summer, or the wind. He belongs to the era when men were men.

But Hepburn was exposed to his aggressive wit when they met in 1941 to make *Woman of the Year*:

I'm afraid I'm a little tall for you, Mr Tracy.
– Don't worry, I'll soon cut you down to my size.

He ranged from supreme self-confidence to abject despair. In 1931 he complained:

This mug of mine is as plain as a barn door. Why should people pay thirty-five cents to look at it?

He remembered:

There were times when my pants were so thin, I could sit on a dime and know if it was heads or tails.

Later he wondered at his own success:

The physical labour actors have to do wouldn't tax an embryo.

Perhaps this puzzlement was responsible for his attitude to the press:

Write anything you want about me. Make up something. Hell, I don't care.

But he did care, and he cared about his work. Perhaps Humphrey Bogart best summed up his appeal:

Spence is the best we have, because you don't see the mechanism at work.

Tracy, William (1917–1967).
American actor who used to play sly or dumb young fellows.

Brother Rat 38. Strike Up the Band 40. Tobacco Road 41. About Face 42. Fall In 44. The Walls of Jericho 49. Mr Walkie Talkie 54. The Wings of Eagles 56, etc.

Trang, Thuy (1974–).
Vietnamese-born, US-based actress, best known for her role as Trini the Yellow Ranger in the TV series *The Mighty Morphin Power Rangers*. She studied civil engineering at the University of California at Irvine.

The Crow: City of Angels 96.

Traubel, Helen (1899–1972).
American soprano.

■ Deep in My Heart 54. The Ladies' Man 61. Gunn 67.

Trauner, Alexander (1906–1993).
French art director who has worked on international films. Born in Budapest, he moved to Paris in the 20s as a painter, and became an assistant to Lazare MEERSON. Worked on more than 100 films.

Quai des Brumes 38. Le Jour Se Lève 39. *Les Visiteurs du Soir* 42. *Les Enfants du Paradis* 44. Les Portes de la Nuit 45. Manèges 49. Othello 52. Love in the Afternoon 56. *The Nun's Story* 58. The Apartment (AA) 60. One Two Three 61. Irma la Douce 63. Kiss Me Stupid 64. The Night of the Generals 66. *A Flea in Her Ear* 68. The Private Life of Sherlock Holmes 70. Promise at Dawn 71. The Man Who Would Be King (AAN) 75. Mr Klein 77. The Fiendish Plot of Fu Manchu 79. Don Giovanni 79. La Truite 82. Subway 85. Round Midnight 86. Reunion 89, etc.

Travanti, Daniel J. (1940–).
American character actor, mainly on TV.

St Ives 76. Adam (TV) 83. Murrow (TV) 85. Midnight Crossing 87. Millennium 89. Fellow Traveller 89. Megaville 90. Hello Stranger 92. Just Cause 95. Eyes of a Witness 94. Wasp Woman (TV) 96, etc.

TV series: *Hill Street Blues* 81–87. Missing Persons 93–94.

Traven, B. (1882–1969).
The mysterious author of *The Treasure of the Sierra Madre* was most probably an Austrian called H.A.O.M. Feige. He was a former actor and anarchist, known for a while as Ret Marut. Settling in Mexico, he became a union agitator and was listed as an enemy of the state.

Travers, Ben (1886–1980).
Long-lived British playwright responsible for the Tom Walls/Ralph Lynn Aldwych farces which were all filmed in the early 30s.

Autobiographies: 1958, *Vale of Laughter* 1979, *A-Sitting on a Gate*.

Rookery Nook 30. *A Cuckoo in the Nest* 33. A Cup of Kindness 33. Turkey Time 34. Banana Ridge 41, etc.

Also wrote filmscripts: Fighting Stock 36. Just My Luck 37. Uncle Silas 47, etc.

Travers, Bill (1922–1994).
Tall British leading man, married to Virginia McKenna; stage experience from 1947.

The Square Ring 54. Geordie 55. Bhowani Junction 56. The Barretts of Wimpole Street 57. *The Smallest Show on Earth* 57. The Seventh Sin (US) 58. The Bridal Path 59. Gorgo 60. Invasion Quartet 61. Two Living, One Dead (Swe.) 62. Born Free 66. Duel at Diablo (US) 66. A Midsummer Night's Dream 68. Ring of Bright Water 69. The Belstone Fox 73. Christian the Lion 77, etc.

Travers, Henry (1874–1965) (Travers Heagerty).
British character actor, on stage from 1894, in America from 1901. Came to films in the 30s and usually played benign old gentlemen.

■ Reunion in Vienna 32. Another Language 33. My Weakness 33. The Invisible Man 33. The Party's Over 34. Death Takes a Holiday 34. Ready for Love 34. Born to Be Bad 34. Maybe It's Love 35. After Office Hours 35. Escapade 35. Pursuit 35. Captain Hurricane 35. Seven Keys to Baldpate 35. Four Hours to Kill 35. Too Many Parents 36. The Sisters 38. Dark Victory 39. You Can't Get Away with Murder 39. Dodge City 39. On Borrowed Time 39. Remember? 39. Stanley and Livingstone 39. The Rains Came 39. The Primrose Path 40. Anne of Windy Poplars 40. Edison the Man 40. Wyoming 40. *Ball of Fire* 41. High Sierra 41. A Girl, a Guy and a Gob 41. The Bad Man 41. I'll Wait for You 41. *Mrs Miniver* (AAN) 42. Pierre of the Plains 42. Random Harvest 42. Shadow of a Doubt 42. *The Moon Is Down* 43. Madame Curie 43. Dragon Seed 44. None Shall Escape 44. The Very Thought of You 44. Thrill of a Romance 45. The Naughty Nineties 45. The Bells of St Mary's 45. Gallant Journey 46. *It's a Wonderful Life* 46. The Yearling 46. The Flame 47. Beyond Glory 48. The Girl from Jones Beach 49.

Travers, Linden (1913–) (Florence Lindon-Travers).
British leading lady of stage (from 1931), screen shortly after.

Children of the Fog 35. Double Alibi 36. The Lady Vanishes 38. The Terror 39. The Stars Look Down 39. *The Ghost Train* 41. The Missing Million 42. Beware of Pity 46. No Orchids for Miss Blandish 48. *Quartet* 48. Christopher Columbus 49, etc.

Travers, P. L. (1899–1996).
Australian-born author of children's books, creator of the magical nanny Mary Poppins, filmed by Walt Disney in 1964.

Travilla, William (1920–1990).
American costume designer who was employed by Columbia 1941–43, Warner 1946–49, and Twentieth Century Fox 1950–58, where he worked closely with Marilyn Monroe.

The Adventures of Don Juan (AA) 49. Monkey Business 52. Gentlemen Prefer Blondes 53. How to Marry a Millionaire (AAN) 53. There's No Business Like Showbusiness (AAN) 54. Bus Stop 56. The Stripper (AAN) 63. Moviola (TV) 80. The Thorn Birds (TV) 83. A Streetcar Named Desire (TV) 84, etc.

Travis, Nancy (1961–).
American actress.

Three Men and a Baby 87. Married to the Mob 88. Eight Men Out 88. Internal Affairs 90. Air America 90. Three Men and a Little Lady 90. Loose Cannons 90. Passed Away 92. The Vanishing 93. So I Married an Axe Murderer 93. Destiny Turns on the Radio 95. Bogus 96, etc.

TV series: Almost Perfect 95–96.

Travis, Neil.
American editor.

Jaws II 76. The Idolmaker 80. Second Thoughts 83. Cujo 83. Marie 85. No Way Out 87. Cocktail 88. Dances with Wolves (AA) 90. Deceived 91. Patriot Games 92. Clear and Present Danger 94. Outbreak 95. Moll Flanders 96. The Edge 97, etc.

Travis, Richard (1913–1989) (William Justice).
American leading man of 40s and 50s second features.

The Man Who Came to Dinner 41. The Big Shot 42. Buses Roar 43. Jewels of Brandenberg 44. Alaska Patrol 46. Skyliner 48. Operation Haylift 50. Mask of the Dragon 51. Fingerprints Don't Lie 51. City of Shadows 55, etc.

Travolta, John (1954–).
Long-limbed American dancing star of the late 70s. Married Kelly Preston. His career went into a decline in the 80s, and he was paid $150,000 to act in *Pulp Fiction*. His success sent his price per picture soaring to $10m and by 1996 his asking price had risen to between $17m and $21m.

Biographies: 1997, *Travolta* by Dave Thompson; 1998, *Travolta: The Life* by Nigel Andrews.

The Devil's Rain 75. Carrie 76. The Boy in the Plastic Bubble (TV) 77. *Saturday Night Fever* (AAN) 77. *Grease* 78. Moment by Moment 79. Urban Cowboy 80. Blow Out 81. Staying Alive 83. Two of a Kind 84. Perfect 85. The Experts 89. Look Who's Talking 89. Look Who's Talking Too 90. Shout 91. Look Who's Talking Now 93. *Pulp Fiction* (AAN) 94. Get Shorty 95. White Man's Burden 95. Broken Arrow 96. Phenomenon 96. Michael 96. She's So Lovely 97. Primary Colors 98. The Thin Red Line 98. A Civil Action 98, etc.

TV series: Welcome Back Kotter 75–78.

❝ I'm not an old-fashioned romantic. I believe in love and marriage, but not necessarily with the same person. –*J.T.*

I would never do anything solely for money. I have to believe in the project. –*J.T.*

My best quality? The transparency in my eyes. I have only to think a thought and it's seen. –*J.T.*

I don't think I'm very cool as a person. I'm just better than anyone else at acting cool. –*J.T.*

Treacher, Arthur (1894–1975) (A. T. Veary).
Tall British character comedian, the perfect butler for 30 years. On stage from the 20s, Hollywood from 1933.

David Copperfield 34. A Midsummer Night's Dream 35. *Thank You Jeeves* 36. The Little Princess 39. National Velvet 44. Delightfully Dangerous 45. The Countess of Monte Cristo 48. Love That Brute 50. Mary Poppins 64, many others.

Tree, David (1915–).
British comedy actor with stage experience.

Knight Without Armour 37. *Pygmalion* (as Freddy Eynsford-Hill) 38. Q Planes 39. *French Without Tears* 39. Major Barbara 40. Then war service, in which he lost an arm; subsequently retired.

∼He made a very brief reappearance as the headmaster in *Don't Look Now* 73.

Treen, Mary (1907–1989).
American comedy actress who usually played nurses, office girls, or the heroine's plain friend.

Babbitt 35. Colleen 36. First Love 40. I Love a Soldier 44. From This Day Forward 45. Let's Live a Little 48. The Caddy 53. The Birds and the Bees 56. Rockabye Baby 58. Paradise Hawaiian Style 56, many others.

TV series: Willy 54–55. The Joey Bishop Show 62–65.

Tremayne, Les (1913–).
English-born character actor, in Hollywood.

The Racket 51. Dream Wife 53. A Man Called Peter 55. The Story of Ruth 60. The Fortune Cookie 66. Strawberries Need Rain 70. Snakes 74, etc.

TV series: Shazam 74–77.

Trenchard-Smith, Brian (1946–).
British director in Australia.

The World of Kung Fu 74. Man from Hong Kong 75. Deathcheaters 76. Day of the Assassins 80. Turkey Shoot 82. BMX Bandits 83. Jenny Kissed Me 85. The Quest 86. Dead End Drive-In 86. The Day of the Panther 87. Out of the Body 88. Strike of the Panther 88. The Siege of Firebase Gloria 89. Night of the Demons 2 94. Escape Clause (US, TV) 96. Sahara 96, etc.

Trenker, Luis (1893–1990).
Italian mountain guide who played leads in several mountain films.

Peaks of Destiny 26. The Fight for the Matterhorn 28. Doomed Battalion (& wd) 31. Der Verlorene Sohn (& wd) 34. The Challenge (& wd) 37. Monte Miracolo (& wd) 43. Duell in den Bergen (& wd) 49. Sein Bester Freund (& wd) 62, many others.

Treut, Monique.
German feminist film director, screenwriter, and producer.

Seduction: The Cruel Woman/Verführung: Die Grausame Frau (p, co-w, d) 85. Virgin Machine 88. Érotique (co-d) 94. Didn't Do It for Love (d) 97, etc.

Trevelyan, John (1904–1985).
British executive, secretary of the British Board of Film Censors 1958–1970, responsible for a more liberal policy allowing such controversial films as *Saturday Night and Sunday Morning, Tom Jones, The Servant, The Silence, Repulsion* and *Who's Afraid of Virginia Woolf?*

Published memoirs 1973: *What the Censor Saw*.

Trevor, Austin (1897–1978) (A. Schilsky).
British character actor with long stage experience.

At the Villa Rose 30. *Alibi* (as Hercule Poirot) 31. Lord Edgware Dies (as Hercule Poirot) 34. Dark Journey 37. Goodbye Mr Chips 39. Champagne Charlie 44. The Red Shoes 48. Father Brown 54. The Horrors of the Black Museum 59, etc.

Trevor, Claire (1909–) (Claire Wemlinger).
American character actress on stage from childhood. Made many routine films before gaining critical notice.

Life in the Raw (debut) 33. Hold That Girl 34. Dante's Inferno 35. Career Woman 36. Dead End (AAN) 37. The Amazing Dr Clitterhouse 38. *Stagecoach* 39. I Stole a Million 39. Dark Command 40. Honky Tonk 41. Crossroads 42. Street of Chance 42. Woman of the Town 43. *Murder My Sweet* 44. Johnny Angel 45. Crack Up 46. Bachelor Girls 47. *Key Largo* (AA) 48. The Lucky Stiff 49. Best of the Badmen 50. Hard, Fast and Beautiful 51. The Stranger Wore a Gun 52. The High and the Mighty (AAN) 54. The Man without a Star 55. The Mountain 56. Marjorie Morningstar 58. Two Weeks in Another Town 62. How to Murder Your Wife 65. Capetown Affair 67. Kiss Me Goodbye 82, etc.

Trevor, Elleston (1920–1995).
English thriller writer who also used the pseudonym Adam Hall.
Wings of Danger (co-oa) 52. Mantrap (from Queen in Danger) 53. Dunkirk (from The Big Pick-up) 58. Pillars of Midnight 63. Flight of the Phoenix 65. The Berlin Memorandum (from The Quiller Memorandum) 65.

Triesault, Ivan (1898–1980).
Eastern European small-part actor in Hollywood.
Mission to Moscow 43. The Hitler Gang 44. Notorious 46. To the Ends of the Earth 48. Five Fingers 52. Fräulein 58. The 300 Spartans 62. Barabbas 62. Von Ryan's Express 65. Batman 66, many others.

Trinder, Tommy (1909–1989).
British cockney music-hall comedian, in occasional films.
Almost a Honeymoon 38. Laugh It Off 40. Sailors Three 41. The Bells Go Down 42. *The Foreman Went to France* 42. Champagne Charlie 44. *Fiddlers Three* 44. Bitter Springs 49. You Lucky People 54. The Beauty Jungle 64, etc.

Trintignant, Jean-Louis (1930–).
French leading man.
Race for Life 55. And God Created Woman 56. Austerlitz 59. Château en Suède 63. Mata Hari 64. Angélique 64. *A Man and a Woman* 66. Trans-Europe Express 66. The Sleeping Car Murders 66. The Libertine 68. Les Biches 68. 'Z' 68. Ma Nuit Chez Maud 69. The American 70. The Conformist 70. Simon the Swiss 71. Aggression 75. Faces of Love 77. The Lifeguard 79. Je Vous Aime 80. La Banquière 80. Vivement Dimanche 83. Under Fire 83. Rendez-vous 85. A Man and a Woman: Twenty Years Later/Un Homme et une Femme: Vingt Ans Déjà 86. Le Moustachu 87. Bunker Palace Hotel 89. Dr M. 90. Merci la Vie 91. L'Oeil Ecarlate 92. Regarde les Hommes Tomber 94. Three Colours: Red/Trois Couleurs: Rouge 94. Fiesta 95. Those Who Love Me Can Take the Train/Ceux Qui M'Aiment Prendront le Train 98, etc.

Tripplehorn, Jeanne (1963–).
American leading actress. Born in Tulsa, Oklahoma, she studied at New York's Juilliard School of Drama.
Basic Instinct 92. The Night We Never Met 93. The Firm 93. Waterworld 95. Old Man (TV) 97. 'Til There Was You 97. Office Killer 97. Sliding Doors 98. Very Bad Things 98, etc.

Trivas, Victor (1896–1970).
Russian writer in America.
War Is Hell (d) 31. Song of Russia 44. The Stranger 45, etc.

Trnka, Jiři (1910–1969).
Czech animator and puppeteer, many of whose short films have been shown abroad.
The Emperor's Nightingale 49. Song of the Prairie 49. The Good Soldier Schweik 54. Jan Hus 56. A Midsummer Night's Dream 57, etc.

Troell, Jan (1931–).
Swedish director.
Here Is Your Life 66. Who Saw Him Die 67. *The Emigrants* (AAN) 71. The New Land (AAN) 72. Zandy's Bride 74. Hurricane 79. Flight of the Eagle/Ingenjor Andrees Luftfard 82. Sagolandet 86. A Swedish Requiem/Il Capitano 91. Hamsun 96, etc.

Troisi, Massimo (1953–1994).
Italian actor and director, with a gentle comic style, from cabaret and television. He won a best actor award at the Venice Film Festival for his performance in *What Time Is It?* Died from a heart attack the day after he finished making *The Postman*.
Ricomincio da Tre (a, d) 81. Scusate il Ritardo (a, d) 83. Non Ci Resta Che Piangere (a, co-d) 84. Le Vie del Signore Sono Finite (a, d) 87. Splendor (a) 88. *What Time Is It?*/Che Ora È (a) 89. The Journey of Captain Fracassa (a) 90. I Thought It Was Love/Pensavo Forse Amore Invece Era un Calesse (a,d) 92. *The Postman*/Il Postino (a, co-w) (AAN) 94, etc.

Tronson, Robert (1924–).
British director, from TV.
The Man at the Carlton Tower 62. The Traitors 62. On the Run 63. Ring of Spies 64, etc.

Trotti, Lamar (1900–1952).
Prolific American scriptwriter and producer.
Judge Priest (co-w) 34. Steamboat round the Bend (co-w) 35. Ramona (w) 36. Slave Ship (w) 37. *In Old Chicago* (w) 38. *Young Mr Lincoln* (w) 39. Hudson's Bay (w) 41. *The Ox Bow Incident* (w, p) 42. Wilson (w, p) (AA) 43. The Razor's Edge (w, p) 46. Mother Wore Tights (w, p) 47. Yellow Sky (w, p) 48. *Cheaper by the Dozen* (w, p) 50. I'd Climb the Highest Mountain (w, p) 51. Stars and Stripes Forever (w, p) 52. With a Song in My Heart (w, p) 52. There's No Business Like Show Business (AAN story) 54, many others.

Troughton, Patrick (1920–1987).
British character actor, often in malevolent roles; mainly on TV (Dr Who in the late 60s).
Escape 48. Hamlet 48. Treasure Island 50. The Black Knight 52. Richard III 56. Phantom of the Opera 62. The Gorgon 64. The Omen 76, many others in small roles.

Trouncer, Cecil (1898–1953).
British stage character actor with splendidly resonant diction.
Pygmalion 38. While the Sun Shines 46. London Belongs to Me 48. *The Guinea Pig* 49. The Lady with a Lamp 51. Pickwick Papers 52. The Weak and the Wicked 54.
❝ The best heavy lead on the English stage. – *George Bernard Shaw*

Trowbridge, Charles (1882–1967).
American character actor, former architect; usually played professors or kindly fathers.
I Take This Woman 31. The Thirteenth Chair 36. Confessions of a Nazi Spy 39. The Mummy's Hand 40. Mildred Pierce 45. The Wings of Eagles 57, many others.

Trueba, Fernando (1955–).
Spanish director, a former film critic.
Opera Prima 80. Sal Gorda 83. El Año de las Luces 86. The Mad Monkey 89. Belle Époque (AA) 93. Two Much (co-w, d) 96. The Girl of Your Dreams/La Niña de Tus Ojos 98, etc.

Truex, Ernest (1890–1973).
American character actor of 'little man' roles, in films since 1918.
Whistling in the Dark 33. *The Adventures of Marco Polo* 38. Christmas in July 40. His Girl Friday 40. Always Together 48. The Leather Saint 56. Twilight for the Gods 58. Fluffy 65, many others; latterly much on TV.

Truffaut, François (1932–1984).
French 'new wave' director, former critic. Died of a brain tumour.
Autobiography: 1982, *Les Films de Ma Vie*. Also wrote *Hitchcock* (1967), a long interview with his idol.
■ Les Mistons 58. *Les Quatre Cents Coups* 59. *Shoot the Pianist* 60. *Jules et Jim* 61. Love at Twenty (part) 62. *Silken Skin* 64. Fahrenheit 451 66. The Bride Wore Black 67. Stolen Kisses 68. Mississippi Mermaid 69. L'Enfant Sauvage (& a) 69. Domicile Conjugal 70. Anne and Muriel 72. A Gorgeous Bird Like Me 72. *Day for Night/La Nuit Américaine* (AANw, AANd) 74. The Story of Adele H 75. L'Argent de Poche 76. The Man Who Loved Women 77. Close Encounters of the Third Kind (a only) 77. Love on the Run 79. Le Dernier Métro 80. Vivement Dimanche 83. Belle Epoque (co-w, TV) 96.
❝ I make films that I would like to have seen when I was a young man. – *F.T.*
To make a film is to improve on life, to arrange it to suit oneself, to prolong the games of childhood, to construct something which is at once a new toy and a vase in which one can arrange in a permanent way the ideas one feels in the morning. – *F.T.*

Truman, Michael (1916–1974).
British director, former editor.
Touch and Go 54. Go to Blazes 62. The Girl in the Headlines 63, etc.

Truman, Ralph (1900–1977).
British stage character actor who made occasional film appearances.
Henry V 44. Beware of Pity 46. Oliver Twist 48. Quo Vadis 51. The Man Who Knew Too Much 56. El Cid 61. Nicholas and Alexandra 71, many others.

Trumbo, Dalton (1905–1976).
American screenwriter, one of the 'Hollywood Ten' who were blacklisted in the 40s.
Kitty Foyle (AAN) 40. The Remarkable Andrew 42. A Guy Named Joe 43. Our Vines Have Tender Grapes 45. The Prowler (as Hugo Butler) 51. Roman Holiday (though the credit went to Ian McKellan Hunter who fronted for him) (AA) 53. The Brave One (as Robert Rich) (AA) 56. Spartacus 60. Exodus 60. The Last Sunset 61. Lonely are the Brave 62. The Sandpiper 65. Hawaii 66. The Fixer 68. Johnny Got His Gun (& d) 71. Executive Action 73. Papillon (co-w, a) 73, many others.

Trumbull, Douglas (1942–).
American special effects man. He now designs interactive entertainments and rides for theme parks.
2001: A Space Odyssey 68. Candy 68. The Andromeda Strain 71. Silent Running (& d) 72. *Close Encounters of the Third Kind* (AAN) 77. *Star Trek* (AAN) 79. Bladerunner (AAN) 82. Brainstorm (& d) 83, etc.
❝ A plain ride is a boring, plotless event. New Technology will make it a participatory art form. – *D.T.*

Trundy, Natalie (1940–).
American leading lady in occasional films.
The Careless Years 57. The Monte Carlo Story 58. Mr Hobbs Takes a Vacation 62. Conquest of the Planet of the Apes 71. Huckleberry Finn 73, etc.

Truscott, John (1936–1993).
American production and costume designer.
Camelot (AA) 67. Paint Your Wagon 69, etc.

Tryon, Tom (1926–1991).
American leading man with stage and TV experience. Later a successful novelist.
The Scarlet Hour (debut) 55. Three Violent People 56. I Married a Monster from Outer Space 57. Moon Pilot 61. Marines Let's Go 61. *The Cardinal* 63. In Harm's Way 65. The Glory Guys 65. The Horsemen 71. Johnny Got His Gun (& pd) 71. The Other (oa only) 72. Fedora (oa only) 78, etc.
TV series: Texas John Slaughter 59.

Tsu, Irene (1943–).
Chinese glamour girl in Hollywood.
Caprice 66. The Green Berets 67. Paper Tiger 75. Down and Out in Beverly Hills 85. Noble House (TV) 88. A Girl to Kill For 90. Mr Jones 93. Widow's Kiss 94. Tianmimi 96, etc.

Tsuburaya, Eiji (1901–1970).
Japanese special effects director, responsible for the effects in Toho's monster movies of the 50s and 60s. He also created the 60s TV series *Ultraman*.
Godzilla/Gojiro 54. Gigantis the Fire Monster 55. Rodan 56. King Kong versus Godzilla 62. Godzilla versus the Thing 64. Frankenstein Conquers the World 65. Son of Godzilla 67. King Kong Escapes 67. Destroy All Monsters 68. Latitude Zero 69, etc.

Tsukamoto, Shinya (1960–).
Japanese director of horror movies about the merging of man and machinery.
■ Tetsuo: The Iron Man 89. Hiruko the Goblin 90. Tetsuo II: The Body Hammer 91. Tokyo Fist 95. Bullet Ballet 98.

Tubbs, William (1909–1953).
Portly American character actor in Europe.
Paisa 46. Edward and Caroline 50. Three Steps North 50. Quo Vadis 51, etc.

Tucci, Stanley (1960–).
American actor and director.
Prizzi's Honor 85. Who's That Girl? 87. Monkey Shines 88. Billy Bathgate 91. Men of Respect 91. Beethoven 92. In the Soup 92. Prelude to a Kiss 92. The Public Eye 92. The Pelican Brief 93. Undercover Blues 93. It Could Happen to You 94. Mr 247 94. Somebody to Love 94. Big Night (& co-w, co-d) 96. The Daytrippers 96. Deconstructing Harry 97. A Life Less Ordinary 97. The Eighteenth Angel 97. The Imposters (& wd) 98. The Alarmist 98. Winchell (TV) 98, etc.
TV series: Murder One 96.
❝ I, and 15 million other Italian-Americans, suffer from stereotyping all the time. I'm always getting scripts with guys who come from Brooklyn and talk like, 'Hey, whattayadoin'?' It's the only way Italians are portrayed in American film. – *S.T.*

Tuchner, Michael (1934–).
British director.
Villain 71. Fear is the Key 72. Mister Quilp 75. The Likely Lads 76. Summer of My German Soldier (TV) 79. Haywire (TV) 80. The Hunchback of Notre Dame (TV) 81. Trenchcoat 83. Adam (TV) 83. Amos (TV) 85. Not My Kid (TV) 85. Mistress (TV) 87. Trapped in Silence (TV) 90. Rainbow Warrior (TV) 94. 30 Years to Life (TV) 98, etc.

Tuchock, Wanda (1898–1985).
American screenwriter at her peak in silent days.
Show People 27. *Hallelujah* 29. Bird of Paradise 32. Hawaii Calls 37. Silver Queen 45. The Foxes of Harrow 47. The Homestretch 49, etc.

Tucker, Chris.
Flamboyant, fast-talking leading American actor, born in Atlanta, Georgia. His current asking price: around $7m.
House Party 3 94. Friday 95. Panther 95. Dead Presidents 95. The Fifth Element 97. Money Talks 97. Jackie Brown 97. Rush Hour 98, etc.

Tucker, Forrest (1919–1986).
Rugged American leading man, mostly in routine action pictures from 1940.
The Westerner (debut) 40. Keeper of the Flame 42. The Yearling 46. The Big Cat 49. Sands of Iwo Jima 50. The Wild Blue Yonder 52. Crosswinds 53. Trouble in the Glen (GB) 54. Break in the Circle (GB) 56. *The Abominable Snowman* (GB) 57. Auntie Mame 58. The Night They Raided Minsky's 68. Cancel My Reservation 72. The Wild McCullochs 75. Final Chapter – Walking Tall 77. Thunder Run 85, many others.
TV series: Crunch and Des 55. F Troop 65–66. Dusty's Trail 73. Ghost Chasers 76. The Rebels 79.

Tucker, George Loane (1881–1921).
American silent director.
The Courting of Mary 11. Traffic in Souls 13. Called Back 14. The Prisoner of Zenda 15. Arsene Lupin 16. The Manxman 17. The Miracle Man 19. Ladies Must Live 21, many others.

Tucker, Sophie (1884–1966) (Sophia Abuza or Sonia Kalish).
Russian-born, American-oriented popular singer, the heavyweight 'red hot momma' of vaudeville.
■ Honky Tonk 29. Gay Love (GB) 34. Gay Time (GB) 34. Broadway Melody of 1937 37. Thoroughbreds Don't Cry 37. Atlantic City 44. Follow the Boys 44. Sensations of 1945 44.
❝ I have been poor and I have been rich. Rich is better. – *S.T.*

Tufts, Sonny (1911–1970) (Bowen Charleston Tufts).
Tall, good-humoured American 'second lead', in Hollywood from the early 40s.
■ So Proudly We Hail 43. Government Girl 43. In The Meantime Darling 44. I Love a Soldier 44. Here Come the Waves 45. Bring on the Girls 45. Duffy's Tavern 45. Miss Susie Slagle's 45. The Virginian 46. The Well-Groomed Bride 46. Cross My Heart 46. Easy Come Easy Go 47. Blaze Of Noon 47. Variety Girl 47. Swell Guy 47. The Untamed Breed 48. The Crooked Way 49. Easy Living 49. The Gift Horse (GB) 52. No Escape 53. Cat Women of the Moon 53. Run for the Hills 53. Serpent Island 54. The Seven Year Itch 55. Come Next Spring 56. The Parson and the Outlaw 57. Town Tamer 65. Cottonpicking Chickenpicker 67.

Tully, Montgomery (1904–1988).
British writer and director.
Murder in Reverse (wd) 45. Spring Song (wd) 47. Boys in Brown (d) 49. A Tale of Five Cities (d) 51. The Glass Cage (d) 55. The Hypnotist (d) 57. Escapement (d) 58. Clash by Night (d) 63. Who Killed the Cat? (wd) 66. Battle Beneath the Earth (d) 68, many other second features and TV episodes.

Tully, Tom (1896–1982).
American character actor with stage experience; usually tough-looking but soft-hearted roles.
Destination Tokyo 44. Adventure 45. The Town Went Wild 45. June Bride 48. Where the Sidewalk Ends 50. The Caine Mutiny (AAN) 54. Ten North Frederick 57. The Wackiest Ship in the Army 61. Coogan's Bluff 68. Charley Varrick 73. Madame X (TV) 81, etc.
TV series: The Lineup 54–59. Shane 66.

Tunberg, Karl (1907–1992).
American screenwriter, in Hollywood from 1937.
My Lucky Star 38. Down Argentine Way 40. Tall Dark and Handsome (AAN) 41. Orchestra Wives 42. Kitty 45. You Gotta Stay Happy 47. Scandal at Scourie 53. The Scarlet Coat 55. *Ben Hur* (AAN) 59. Libel 59. Taras Bulba 62. Harlow (electronovision version) 65. Where Were You When the Lights Went Out? 68, many others.

Tune, Tommy (1939–).
Lanky American dancer, choreographer, and actor, mainly on the Broadway stage.
Hello Dolly! 69. The Boy Friend 71.

Turkel, Ann (1948–).
American leading lady, former wife of Richard Harris.
99 and 44/100 Per Cent Dead 74. Matt Helm (TV) 75. The Cassandra Crossing 77. Golden Rendezvous 78. Humanoids from the Deep 80. Death Ray 2000 81. The Last Contract 86. Deep Space 87. The Fear 95, etc.

Turman, Lawrence (1926–).
American producer.
The Young Doctors 61. The Flim Flam Man 66. *The Graduate* (AAN) 67. Pretty Poison 69. The Great White Hope 70. Marriage of a Young Stockbroker (& d) 71. The Drowning Pool (co-p) 75. First Love (co-p) 77. Walk Proud 79. Tribute 80. The Thing 82. The Mean Season 85. Short Circuit 86. Full Moon in Blue Water 88. Short Circuit 2 88. Gleaming the Cube 89. The River Wild 94. The Getaway 94. Booty Call 97. American History X 98, etc.

Turner, Ann (1960–).
Australian director and screenwriter.
Celia 88. Turtle Beach (w only) 92. Hammers over the Anvil 93. Dallas Doll 94.

Turner, Florence (1887–1946).
American actress who in 1907 became the first 'movie star' known by name; also as 'the Vitagraph Girl'.
A Dixie Mother 10. Francesca da Rimini 12. The Welsh Singer (GB) 13. My Old Dutch (GB) 15. East is East (GB) 15. The Old Wives' Tale (GB) 21, etc.
Went back to Hollywood in roles of diminishing stature; retired in the mid-20s.

Turner, John (1932–).
British leading man with stage experience, also known as TV's 'Knight Errant'.
Behemoth, the Sea Monster 60. Petticoat Pirates 61. Sammy Going South 62. The Black Torment 64. The Slipper and the Rose 76. Bye Bye Columbus (TV) 91. Rasputin (TV) 96. The Ripper (TV) 97. Merlin (TV) 98, etc.

Turner, Kathleen (1954–).
Leading American actress.
Body Heat 82. Romancing the Stone 84. The Man with Two Brains 84. Prizzi's Honor 85. Crimes of Passion 85. Jewel of the Nile 86. *Peggy Sue Got Married* (AAN) 87. A Breed Apart 87. Julia and Julia 87. Switching Channels 88. Who Framed Roger Rabbit? (voice) 88. Dear America: Letters Home from Vietnam 88. The Accidental Tourist 88. The War of the Roses 89. V.I. Warshawski 91. House of Cards 93. Naked in New York 93. Undercover Blues 93. Serial Mom 94. Moonlight and Valentino 95. A Simple Wish 97. The Real Blonde 97. The Virgin Suicides 98. Legalese (TV) 98, etc.

Turner, Lana (1920–1995) (Julia Turner).
American leading lady of the 40s; began as the 'girl next door' type but became increasingly sophisticated. Married eight times, notably to actor Lex Barker.
Biography: 1976, *The Films of Lana Turner* by Lou Valentino.
They Won't Forget (debut) 37. The Great Garrick 37. Four's a Crowd 38. The Adventures of Marco Polo 38. Calling Dr Kildare 39. *Love Finds Andy Hardy* 39. Rich Man Poor Girl 39. Dramatic School 39. These Glamour Girls 39. Dancing Co-Ed 39. Two Girls on Broadway 40. We Who Are Young 40. Choose Your Partner 40. Ziegfeld Girl 41. Dr Jekyll and Mr Hyde 41. Honky Tonk 41. Johnny Eager 41. *Somewhere I'll Find You* 42. Slightly Dangerous 43. Marriage Is a Private Affair 44. Keep Your Powder Dry 44. Weekend at the Waldorf 45. The Postman Always Rings Twice 45. Green Dolphin Street 46. Cass Timberlane 47. Homecoming 48. The Three Musketeers 48. A Life of Her Own 50. Mr Imperium 51. The Merry Widow 52. The Bad and the Beautiful 52. Latin Lovers 53. The Flame and the Flesh 54. Betrayed 55. The Prodigal 55. The Rains of Ranchipur 55. The Sea Chase 55. Diane 56. Another Time Another Place (GB) 57. *Peyton Place* (AAN) 57. The Lady Takes a Flyer 58. *Imitation of Life* 59. Portrait in Black 60. By Love Possessed 61. Bachelor in Paradise 62. Who's Got the Action? 63. Love Has Many Faces 65. Madame X 66. The Big Cube 69. Persecution 74. Bittersweet Love 76, etc.
TV series: The Survivors 69. Falcon Crest 82.

Turner, Ted (1938–) (Robert Edward Turner).
Television mogul, owner of the Cable News Network and also the MGM film library. In 1993 he took over the film production and distribution companies New Line Cinema, at a cost of $53 million, and Castle Rock Entertainment, at a cost of $100 million. Married to actress Jane Fonda.
Biography: 1993, *It Ain't So Easy as It Looks: Ted Turner's Amazing Story* by Porter Bibb.

Turner, Tina (1938–) (Annie Mae Bullock).
American rhythm and blues and soul singer and actress. A biopic of her life, *What's Love Got to Do with It*, was made in 1993 starring Angela Bassett.
■ Gimme Shelter (doc) 70. Taking Off 71. Soul to Soul (concert) 71. Tommy 75. Mad Max beyond Thunderdome 85. The Last Action Hero 93.

Turney, Catherine (1906–1998).
American screenwriter, novelist and playwright, mainly for Warner Bros, who created vehicles for Barbara Stanwyck, Bette Davis and the studio's other female stars of the 40s. She later worked in television.
Mildred Pierce 45. Of Human Bondage 45. One More Tomorrow 46. A Stolen Life 46. My Reputation 46. The Man I Love 47. Cry Wolf 47. Winter Meeting 48. No Man of Her Own 50. Japanese War Bride 52. Back from the Dead (from her novel The Other One) 57, etc.

Turpin, Ben (1874–1940).
Cross-eyed American silent comedian, mainly popular in short slapstick skits of the 20s. In films from 1915 after vaudeville experience.
Uncle Tom's Cabin 19. Small Town Idol 21. Show of Shows 29. The Love Parade 30, many others.

Turpin, Dick (1706–1739)
was a seasoned criminal without too many obvious redeeming characteristics. Film-makers have seized on his ride to York and his affection for his horse as an excuse to view him through rose-tinted glasses. So he was played as a hero by Matheson Lang in 1922, Tom Mix in 1925, Victor McLaglen in 1933, Louis Hayward in 1951, and David Weston (for Walt Disney) in 1965. In the late 70s Richard O'Sullivan appeared in an ITV series, again featuring the highwayman as a kind of Robin Hood.

Turpin, Gerry (c. 1930–1997).
British cinematographer.
The Queen's Guards 61. Seance on a Wet Afternoon 64. The Whisperers 67. Deadfall 68. *Oh What a Lovely War* 69. The Man Who Had Power over Women 70. I Want What I Want 71. The Last of Sheila 73. The Doctor and the Devils 85, etc.

Turteltaub, Jon.
American director.
Think Big 90. Driving Me Crazy 91. 3 Ninjas 92. Cool Runnings 93. While You Were Sleeping 95. Phenomenon 96, etc.

Turturro, John (1957–).
American leading actor, from the stage.
Raging Bull 80. Exterminator 2 84. The Flamingo Kid 84. Desperately Seeking Susan 85. To Live and Die In L.A. 85. The Color of Money 86. Gung Ho 86. Hannah and Her Sisters 86. Off Beat 86. Five Corners 87. The Sicilian 87. Do the Right Thing 89. Catchfire/Backtrack 89. Men of Respect 90. Miller's Crossing 90. Mo' Better Blues 90. State of Grace 90. Jungle Fever 91. Barton Fink 91. Brain Donors 92. Mac (& d) 92. Fearless 93. Being Human 94. Quiz Show 94. Clockers 95. Search and Destroy 95. Unstrung Heroes 95. Sugartime (TV) 95. Girl 6. The Search for One-Eyed Jimmy (made 93) 96. Box of Moonlight 96. Grace of My Heart 96. The Truce 97. The Big Lebowski 97. He Got Game 98. Animals 98. Illuminata (& d) 98. Rounders 98. OK Garage 98, etc.

Tushingham, Rita (1940–).
British leading character actress with stage experience.
A Taste of Honey 61. The Leather Boys 63. A Place to Go 63. Girl with Green Eyes 64. *The Knack* 65. Dr Zhivago 65. The Trap 66. Smashing Time 67. Diamonds for Breakfast 68. The Guru 69. The Bed-Sitting Room 69. Straight On till Morning 72. The Human Factor 75. Rachel's Man 75. Mysteries 79. Confessions of Felix Krull (TV) 81. Judgment in Stone 86. Hem 87. Resurrected 88. Hard Days, Hard Nights 88. Paper Marriage 93. An Awfully Big Adventure 95. The Boy from Mercury 96. Under the Skin 97, etc.

Tutin, Dorothy (1930–).
Leading British actress. Occasional films.
The Importance of Being Earnest 52. The Beggar's Opera 53. A Tale of Two Cities 57. Cromwell 69. The Spy's Wife 70. *Savage Messiah* 72. The Shooting Party 85. Murder with Mirrors (TV) 85. Great Moments in Aviation 94. Alive and Kicking/Indian Summer 96. This Could Be the Last Time (TV) 98, etc.
TV series: Body and Soul 93. Jake's Progress 95.

Tuttle, Frank (1892–1963).
American director of mainly routine films; in Hollywood from the 20s.
Kid Boots 27. Roman Scandals 33. The Glass Key 35. Waikiki Wedding 37. I Stole a Million 39. *This Gun For Hire* 42. Lucky Jordan 43. Hostages 43. The Hour Before the Dawn 43. A Man Called Sullivan 45. Suspense 46. Swell Guy 47. The Magic Face 51. Gunman in the Streets 51. Hell on Frisco Bay 55. A Cry in the Night 56, etc.

Tuttle, Lurene (1906–1986).
American character actress, from radio. Married radio and stage actor Melville Ruick (1898–1972); their daughter was actress Barbara Ruick.
Mr Blandings Builds His Dream House 46. Montana Mike 47. Macbeth 48. The Whip Hand 51. The Affairs of Dobie Gillis 53. Niagara 53. The Sweet Smell of Success 57. Psycho 60. The Fortune Cookie 66. Walking Tall 73. Part Two Walking Tall/Legend of the Lawman 75. Walking Tall: Final Chapter 77. The Adventures of Huckleberry Finn 81, etc.
TV series: Life with Father 53–55. Father of the Bride 61–62. Julia 68–70.

Twain, Mark (1835–1910) (Samuel Langhorne Clemens).
Beloved American humorist and travel writer; was played by Fredric March in *The Adventures of Mark Twain* 44. Works filmed include *Tom Sawyer*, *Huckleberry Finn*. *A Connecticut Yankee*, *The Prince and the Pauper*, *The Celebrated Jumping Frog* (as *The Best Man Wins*), *The Million-Pound Banknote*.

Twelvetrees, Helen (1908–1958) (Helen Jurgens).
American leading lady of the 30s; films fairly unmemorable.
The Ghost Talks 29. Her Man 30. The Painted Desert 31. Is My Face Red? 32. King for a Night 33. Times Square Lady 35. Hollywood Round Up 37, etc.

Twiggy (1949–) (Lesley Hornby).
British fashion model of the 60s. Married actor Leigh Lawson, her second husband.
Autobiography: 1997, *Twiggy in Black and White* (with Penelope Dening).
The Boy Friend 71. 'W' 74. There Goes the Bride 80. The Doctor and the Devils 85. Club Paradise 86. The Little Match Girl (TV) 87. Madame Sousatzka 88. The Diamond Trap (TV) 88. Young Charlie Chaplin (TV) 88. Istanbul 89. Woundings 98, etc.

Twist, Derek (1905–1979).
British director, former editor and associate producer.
The End of the River 47. All over the Town 48. Green Grow the Rushes 51. Police Dog 55. Family Doctor 57, etc.

Twist, John (1895–1976).
American screenwriter.
The Toast of New York 36. The Great Man Votes 39. So Big 53. Helen of Troy 55. The FBI Story 56. Esther and the King 60. None But the Brave 64, etc.

Twitty, Conway (1934–1993) (Harold Lloyd Jenkins).
American rock singer and songwriter who appeared in a couple of films as himself and from the mid-60s became a successful country and western performer and businessman, owner of the Twitty City theme park just outside Nashville.
College Confidential 59. Platinum High School/Trouble at 16/Rich Young and Deadly 60, etc.

Twohy, David T.
American screenwriter.
Critters 2 88. Warlock 90. The Fugitive (co-w) 93. Terminal Velocity (w) 94. Waterworld (co-w) 95. The Arrival (wd) 96. GI Jane (w) 97, etc.

Tykwer, Tom (c. 1965–).
German director, screenwriter and composer. Born in Berlin, he began working as a projectionist in his early teens and was later a cinema manager before beginning by making short films. He is co-founder of the production company X-Filme.
Deadly Maria/Die Todliche Maria 94. Winterschlafer 96. Life Is a Construction Site (co-w only) 97. Run Lola Run/Lola Rennt (wd, co-m) 98, etc.

Tyler, Beverly (1924–).
American leading lady of routine 40s films.
Best Foot Forward 43. The Green Years 46. The Beginning or the End 47. The Fireball 50. Chicago Confidential 47. The Toughest Gun in Tombstone 58, etc.

Tyler, Judy (1933–1957) (Judith Mae Hess).
American actress who began as a child and starred opposite Elvis Presley in his first film, *Jailhouse Rock*.
Bob Girl Goes Calypso 57. Jailhouse Rock 57.

Tyler, Liv (1977–).
American actress and model, the daughter of rock guitarist Steven Tyler. She has been romantically linked with actor Joaquin Phoenix.
Silent Fall 94. Heavy 95. Empire Records 96. *Stealing Beauty* 96. That Thing You Do 96. U-Turn 97. Inventing the Abbotts 97. Armageddon 98. Onegin 99, etc.

Tyler, Parker (1904–974).
American highbrow film critic. Author of *The Hollywood Hallucination*, *Magic and Myth of the Movies*, *The Shadow of an Airplane Climbs the Empire State Building*, etc.

Tyler, Tom (1903–1954) (Vincent Markowsky).
American cowboy star of innumerable second features in the 30s: *The Cowboy Cop* 26. *The Sorcerer* 29. *Riding the Lonesome Trail* 34. *Pinto Rustlers* 38. *Roamin' Wild* 39, etc. Also played small roles in such films as *Gone with the Wind* 39. *Stagecoach* 39. *The Mummy's Hand* (as the mummy) 40; and had the title role in *The Adventures of Captain Marvel* (serial) 41.

Tynan, Kenneth (1927–1980).
British journalist and critic who was briefly a script editor at Ealing in the mid-50s. The character of Professor Marcus, played by Alec Guinness in *The Ladykillers*, is said to have been based on his physical appearance (though Guinness has denied it). He was film critic of the *Observer* in 1964.
Nowhere to Go (co-w) 58. Macbeth (co-w) 71.

Tyrrell, Susan (1946–).
American leading lady.
Fat City (AAN) 72. Shootout 72. Catch My Soul 73. The Killer inside Me 76. I Never Promised You a Rose Garden 77. Islands in the

Stream 77. Another Man, Another Chance 77. Andy Warhol's Bad 77. September 30, 1955 77. Lady of the House 78. Forbidden Zone 80. Loose Shoes 80. Night Warning 81. Fast-Walking 82. Tales of Ordinary Madness 83. Angel 84. Flesh and Blood 85. Avenging Angel 85. Big-Top Pee-Wee 88. Far from Home 89. Tapeheads 89. Cry-Baby 90. Rockula 90. Motorama 92. Powder 95, etc.

Tyson, Cathy (1966–).
British actress, from the stage.
Mona Lisa 86. The Serpent and the Rainbow 88. Business as Usual 88. Rules of Engagement (TV)

89. The Lost Language of Cranes (TV) 91. Priest (TV) 94, etc.
TV series: Band of Gold 95–96. Gold 97.

Tyson, Cicely (1933–).
American leading actress.
A Man Called Adam 66. The Comedians 67. The Heart Is a Lonely Hunter 68. *Sounder* (AAN) 72. *The Autobiography of Miss Jane Pittman* (TV) 74. Roots (TV) 77. A Hero Ain't Nothin' but a Sandwich 77. The Concorde – Airport '79 79. Bustin' Loose 81. Fried Green Tomatoes at the

Whistle Stop Café 91. Duplicates (TV) 92. Oldest Living Confederate Widow Tells All (TV) 94. The Road to Galveston (TV) 96. Riot (TV) 97. Hoodlum 97, etc.
TV series: East Side West Side 63.

Tyzack, Margaret (1933–).
British character actress, familiar on TV in *The First Churchills* and *The Forsyte Saga*.
Ring of Spies 64. The Whisperers 67. A Clockwork Orange 71. The Legacy 79. Mr Love 86. The King's Whore 90.

Mrs Dalloway 97. Our Mutual Friend (TV) 98, etc.
TV series: The Young Indiana Jones Chronicles 92–93. Family Money 97.

Tzelniker, Meier (1894–1982).
British character actor well known in the Yiddish theatre.
Mr Emmanuel 44. It Always Rains on Sunday 48. Last Holiday 50. The Teckman Mystery 54. Make Me an Offer 54. A Night to Remember 58. *Expresso Bongo* 60. The Sorcerers 67, etc.

U

Uchida, Tomu (1898–1970).
Japanese director, a former comic actor. He began as an assistant, working with Mizoguchi and others, and first directed comedies before turning to realistic subjects. During the Second World War, he left Japan for Manchuria and China, not returning until the mid-50s, when he specialized in period films, often remakes. His best film, *Earth*, was made in secret over a period of a year.

A Living Doll/Ikeru Ningyo 29. Hot Wind 34. *Earth/Tsuchi* 39. Outsiders/Mori To Mizuumi No Matsuri 58. Zen and Sword/Miyamoto Musashi – Ichijoji No Ketto 62. Swords of Death/Shinken Shobu 72, etc.

Uchida, Yuya.
Japanese actor and screenwriter, a former rock performer.

A Pool without Water/Mizu No Nai Puuru 82. Merry Christmas, Mr Lawrence 82. The Mosquito on the Tenth Floor/Jukai No Mosukiito 83. *Comic Magazine*/Komikku Zasshi Nanika Irani (& w) 86. Black Rain 89, etc.

Uggams, Leslie (1943–).
American revue actress.

Skyjacked 72. Roots (TV) 77. Backstairs at the White House (TV) 79. Sizzle 81. Sugar Hill 93, etc.

TV series: The Leslie Uggams Show 69. Roots 77–78.

Uhry, Alfred H. (1937–).
American dramatist and screenwriter.

Mystic Pizza 88. Driving Miss Daisy (AA) 89. Rich in Love 92.

Ullman, Daniel (1918–1979).
American scriptwriter.

The Maze 53. Seven Angry Men 54. Wichita 55. Good Day for a Hanging 59. Face of a Fugitive 59. Mysterious Island 61, etc.

Ullman, Tracey (1959–).
British actress and singer, often in comic roles, who moved to America in the mid-80s. She began her career in British theatre and television and has recorded a hit single, 'They Don't Know', and some pop albums.

Give My Regards to Broad Street 83. The Young Visitors (TV) 84. Plenty 85. Jumpin' Jack Flash 86. I Love You to Death 90. Death Becomes Her 92. Household Saints 93. Robin Hood: Men in Tights 93. I'll Do Anything 94. Bullets over Broadway 94, etc.

TV series: Three of a Kind 81. Kick Up the Eighties 81–82. Girls on Top 85–86. The Tracey Ullman Show 87–90. Tracey Takes On . . . 96.

Ullmann, Liv (1939–).
Norwegian leading actress in international films.
Autobiography: 1977, *Changing*.

The Wayward Girl 59. Persona 66. Hour of the Wolf 67. Shame 68. A Passion 70. The Night Visitor 70. Pope Joan 71. The Emigrants (AAN) 72. Lost Horizon 73. Forty Carats 73. The Abdication 74. Face to Face (AAN) 76. A Bridge Too Far 77. The Serpent's Egg 77. Leonor 77. *Autumn Sonata* 78. Players 79. Richard's Things (TV) 80. The Wild Duck 82. Bay Boy 84. Dangerous Moves 84. Ingrid 85. Let's Hope It's a Girl 85. Gaby – a True Story 87. La Amiga 88. The Rose Garden 89. Mindwalk 90. The Ox/Oxen 91. The Long Shadow 92. Sofie (co-w, d) 92.

Dreamplay/Dromspel 94. Kristin Lavransdatter (wd) 95. Private Confessions (d) (TV) 96, etc.

Ulmer, Edgar G. (1900–1972).
Austrian-born director long in Hollywood specializing in second features and exploitation subjects. In his later years somewhat mysteriously revered by French critics.

The Black Cat 34. The Singing Blacksmith 38. Isle of Forgotten Sins 43. Bluebeard 44. The Wife of Monte Cristo 46. Detour 46. Her Sister's Secret 47. Ruthless 48. The Man from Planet X 53. The Naked Dawn 55. Daughter of Dr Jekyll 57. The Amazing Transparent Man 60. Beyond the Time Barrier 61. Atlantis, the Lost Kingdom/L'Atlantide 62. The Cavern 65, many others.

Ulric, Lenore (1892–1970) (Lenore Ulrich).
American stage actress.

Tiger Rose 23. Frozen Justice 29. Camille 36. Temptation 46. Northwest Outpost 47, etc.

Ulrich, Skeet (1970–) (Brian Ulrich).
American actor. Born in Concord, he studied marine biology at the University of North Carolina, and acting under David MAMET at New York University. Married actress Georgina CATES.

Last Dance 96. The Craft 96. Boys 96. Albino Alligator 96. Touch 97. The Newton Boys 98. Ride with the Devil 98, etc.

Ultra Violet (1934–) (Isabelle Collin-Dufresne).
French-born actress who became part of the entourage that surrounded Andy Warhol and appeared in some of his films.
Autobiography: 1988, *Famous for 15 Minutes*.

I, a Man 67. Midnight Cowboy 69. Maidstone 70. Dinah East 70. Taking Off 71. Simon, King of the Witches 71. Believe in Me 71. An Unmarried Woman 78. Blackout 92, etc.

66 Nearly all of us at the Factory have had our moments of anger at Andy. He's promised us fame, money, Superstardom, and only given us walk-on parts in his home-made movies. When a film has succeeded, he's kept the profits and seized the headlines. – U.V.

She was popular with the press because she had a freak name, purple hair, an incredibly long tongue, and a mini-rap about the intellectual meaning of underground films – Andy Warhol

Umeki, Miyoshi (1929–).
Japanese leading lady who won an Academy Award for her performance in *Sayonara* 57.

Cry for Happy 61. Flower Drum Song 61. A Girl Named Tamiko 63, etc.

TV series: The Courtship of Eddie's Father 69.

Underdown, Edward (1908–1989).
British actor on stage from 1932; once a jockey. Often cast as a dull Englishman.

The Warren Case 33 (debut). Wings of the Morning 37. They Were Not Divided 50. The Voice of Merrill 52. Beat the Devil 54. The Camp on Blood Island 58. The Day the Earth Caught Fire 62. Khartoum 66. The Hand of Night 67. Running Scared 72. Digby, the Biggest Dog in the World 73. The Abdication 74, etc.

Underwood, Ron.
American director.

Tremors 90. City Slickers 91. Heart and Souls 93. Speechless 94. Mighty Joe Young 98, etc.

Unger, Deborah Kara (1966–).
Canadian actress, born in Vancouver. She studied philosophy and economics at the University of Victoria, and acting at the Australian National Institute of Dramatic Art.

Bangkok Hilton (TV) 89. Prisoners of the Sun 90. Till There Was You 90. Breakaway 90. Blood Oath 90. Whispers in the Dark 92. Highlander III: The Sorcerer 94. Crash 96. No Way Home 97. The Game 97. Luminous Motion 98. The Rat Pack (as Ava Gardner) (TV) 98, etc.

Unsworth, Geoffrey (1914–1978).
British cinematographer.

The Million Pound Note 53. Hell Drivers 57. *A Night to Remember* 58. Northwest Frontier 59. The 300 Spartans 62. *Becket* (BFA) 64. Genghis Khan 65. Half a Sixpence 67. *2001: A Space Odyssey* 68. The Bliss of Mrs Blossom 68. The Assassination Bureau 68. The Reckoning 69. Three Sisters 70. *Cabaret* (AA) 72. Alice's Adventures in Wonderland 72. Zardoz 73. Murder on the Orient Express 74. Lucky Lady 75. A Matter of Time 76. The Great Train Robbery 78. Superman 78. Tess (AA, BFA) 79, etc.

Urban, Charles (1871–1942).
American pioneer of British films. He left Edison to found his own production company in London, and developed commercial non-fiction films.

Urban, Joseph (1872–1933).
Austrian-born art director, architect, illustrator, and noted stage designer. Most famous for designing the sets for the Ziegfeld Follies on Broadway from 1915–32, he worked in films at the invitation of William Randolph Hearst to add distinction to the movies of Hearst's mistress Marion Davies.

Humoresque 20. Passionate Pilgrim 21. Enchantment 21. Beauty's Worth 22. When Knighthood Was in Flower 22. Adam and Eve 23. The Great White Way 24. Zander the Great 25. The Man Who Came Back 31. East Lynne 31, etc.

Ure, Mary (1933–1975).
British leading actress of stage and (occasionally) screen. She was married to dramatist John Osborne and later actor Robert Shaw.

■ Storm over the Nile 55. Windom's Way 59. Look Back in Anger 59. *Sons and Lovers* (AAN) 60. The Mind Benders 63. The Luck of Ginger Coffey 64. Custer of the West 67. Where Eagles Dare 68. Reflection of Fear 71.

Urecal, Minerva (1896–1966).
American character actress.

Oh Doctor 37. Boys of the City 40. The Bridge of San Luis Rey 44. Who's Guilty? 47. The Lost Moment 48. Harem Girl 52. Miracle in the Rain 56. The Seven Faces of Dr Lao 64, etc.

TV series: Tugboat Annie.

Urich, Robert (1946–).
American TV actor who has made a few films.
■ Endangered Species 82. The Ice Pirates 83. Turk 182 84. Murder by Night (TV) 89. Survive the Savage Sea 91.

TV series: S.W.A.T. 75–76. Soap 77. Tabitha 77–78. Vega$ 78–81. Gavilan 82–83. Spencer: For Hire 85–88. Crossroads 92. The Lazarus Man 96. Love Boat, the Next Wave 98– .

Urioste, Frank J.
American film editor.

Whatever Happened to Aunt Alice 69. The Grissom Gang 71. Midway 76. Damnation Alley 77. The Boys in Company C 78. Fast Break 79. Loving Couples 80. The Jazz Singer 80. The Entity 83. Trenchcoat 83. Amityville 3-D 83. Conan the Destroyer 84. Red Sonja 85. The Hitcher 86. Robocop (AAN) 87. Die Hard (AA) 88. Road House 89. Total Recall 90. Basic Instinct 92. Cliffhanger 93. Tombstone 94. CutThroat Island 95, etc.

Urquhart, Robert (1922–1995).
Scottish character actor, in films since 1951 after stage experience. He also ran a notable hotel in the Highlands of Scotland. The first of his two wives was actress Zena Walker.

You're Only Young Twice (debut) 51. Knights of the Round Table 54. You Can't Escape 56. The Curse of Frankenstein 56. Dunkirk 58. 55 Days at Peking 62. Murder at the Gallop 64. Country Dance 70. The Dogs of War 80. Restless Natives 85. The Kitchen Toto 87, etc.

TV series: The Pathfinders 72. The Amazing Mr Goodall 74.

Ustinov, Sir Peter (1921–).
Garrulous, hirsute, multi-talented British actor-director-playwright-screenwriter-raconteur.
Autobiography: 1978, *Dear Me*.
■ AS ACTOR: Hullo Fame 40. Mein Kampf 40. The Goose Steps Out 41. One of Our Aircraft is Missing 42. Let the People Sing 42. The Way Ahead 44. Private Angelo 49. Odette 50. *Hotel Sahara* 51. The Magic Box 51. *Quo Vadis* (as Nero) (AAN) 51. *Beau Brummell* (as George IV) 54. The Egyptian 54. We're No Angels 55. Lola Montez 55. The Man Who Wagged His Tail 57. The Spies 57. *The Sundowners* 60. *Spartacus* (AA) 60. *Romanoff and Juliet* 61. Billy Budd 62. *Topkapi* (AA) 64. John Goldfarb Please Come Home 65. Lady L 65. The Comedians 67. Blackbeard's Ghost 68. Hot Millions 68. Viva Max 69. Hammersmith Is Out (& d) 72. One of Our Dinosaurs Is Missing 75. Logan's Run 76. Treasure of Matecumbe 76. The Purple Taxi 77. The Last Remake of Beau Geste 77. Jesus of Nazareth (TV) 77. *Death on the Nile* (as Hercule Poirot) 78. Ashanti 78. The Thief of Baghdad (TV) 79. Charlie Chan and the Curse of the Dragon Queen 81. Evil Under the Sun 82. Memed My Hawk (& w, d) 83. Murder with Mirrors (TV) 85. Thirteen at Dinner (TV) 85. Dead Man's Folly (TV) 86. Appointment with Death 88. La Révolution Française 89. C'era un Castello con 40 Cani 90. Lorenzo's Oil 92. The Dancer 93. The Old Curiosity Shop (TV) 95. Stiff Upper Lips 97.
■ AS DIRECTOR-WRITER: School for Secrets 46. *Vice Versa* 48. *Private Angelo* 49. Romanoff and Juliet 61. Billy Budd 62. Lady L 65.

TV series: Planet Ustinov 98.

Uys, Jamie (1921–1996).
South African producer, writer and director, the first from his country to gain an international reputation, achieved with his comedy *The Gods Must Be Crazy*, the success of which he tried, but failed, to duplicate in a sequel. An Afrikaner, born in Boksburg, he studied mathematics at the University of Pretoria and worked as a teacher and farmer before becoming a film-maker, financing all his own films to retain his independence.

Rip Van Winkle 60. *Dingaka* 64. The Professor and the Beauty Queen 67. Dirkie 69. Lost in the Desert 70. *The Gods Must Be Crazy* 81. Beautiful People II 83. The Gods Must Be Crazy II 89, etc.

V

Vacano, Jost (1934–).
German cinematographer, noted for his work with director Paul Verhoeven.
The Lost Honour of Katharina Blum/Die Verlorene Ehre der Katharina Blum 75. Soldier of Orange/Soldaat van Oranje 77. Spetters 80. The Boat/Das Boot (AAN) 82. The Neverending Story 84. 52 Pick-Up 86. Robocop 87. Rocket Gibraltar 88. Total Recall 90. Untamed Heart 93. Showgirls 95. Starship Troopers 97, etc.

Vaccaro, Brenda (1939–).
American character actress.
Midnight Cowboy 69. Where It's At 69. I Love My Wife 70. Summertree 71. What's a Nice Girl Like You . . . (TV) 72. Honor Thy Father 73. Sunshine (TV) 74. Once Is Not Enough (AAN) 76. The House by the Lake 77. Airport 77 77. Capricorn One 78. Fast Charlie the Moonbeam Rider 78. Supergirl 84. Water 84. Cookie 89. Heart of Midnight 89. Masque of the Red Death 90. Lethal Games 90. Love Affair 94. The Mirror Has Two Faces 96, etc.
TV series: Sara 76. Dear Detective 79.

Vachon, Christine (1962–).
American producer of independent films.
Swoon 92. Go Fish 94. Kids 95. Safe 95. I Shot Andy Warhol 96. Office Killer 97. Kiss Me Guido 97. Velvet Goldmine 98. Happiness 98. I'm Losing You 98, etc.

Vadim, Roger (1927–) (Roger Vadim Plemiannikow).
French writer-director. His wives included Brigitte Bardot (1952–57) and Jane Fonda (1965–73). He has a son by actress Catherine Deneuve.
Autobiography: 1986, *Bardot, Deneuve and Fonda: The Memoirs of Roger Vadim*.
Futures Vedettes (w) 54. *And God Created Woman* (wd) 56. Heaven Fell That Night (wd) 57. *Les Liaisons Dangereuses* (wd) 59. Warrior's Rest (wd) 62. Vice and Virtue (wd) 62. La Ronde (wd) 64. Nutty Naughty Château/Château en Suède 64. The Game Is Over (wd) 66. Histoires Extraordinaires (part) 68. Barbarella 68. Pretty Maids All in a Row 71. Don Juan 73. Night Games 79. Rich and Famous (a) 81. Hot Touch 81. Surprise Party 82. Come Back 83. Into the Night (a) 85. And God Created Woman 88. Mad Love/ Amour Fou 94, etc.

Vague, Vera:
see Allen, Barbara Jo.

Vajna, Andrew.
Hungarian-born production executive, a co-founder of Carolco in 1976 and, following his departure, chief executive of Cinergi Pictures until that company went out of business in 1997. In 1998, following the liquidation of the company, he formed a new partnership with his former partner Mario Kassar.
First Blood 82. Rambo 85. Angel Heart 86. Red Heat 88. Total Recall 90. Tombstone 93. Renaissance Man 94. Color of Night 94. Die Hard with a Vengeance 95. Judge Dredd 95. The Scarlet Letter 95. Nixon 95. Evita 97, etc.

Valdez, Luis (1940–).
American director, screenwriter and dramatist. Of Mexican ancestry, he first worked in the theatre, and his first film was based on his own play.
Zoot Suit 81. La Bamba 87. The Cisco Kid (TV) 94.

Valens, Ritchie (1941–1959) (Ritchie Valenzuela).
American rock singer and songwriter who appeared as himself in one movie before being killed in the same plane crash as singer Buddy Holly. He was played by Lou Diamond Phillips in the biopic *La Bamba* 87.
Go Johnny Go 58. Rock and Roll – The Early Days (doc) 84.

Valenti, Jack (1921–).
American executive, dynamic president of the Motion Picture Association of America.

Valentine, Joseph (1900–1949) (Giuseppe Valentino).
Italian-American cinematographer, long in Hollywood.
Curlytop 24. Speakeasy 29. Soup to Nuts 30. Night of Terror 33. Remember Last Night 35. The Moon's Our Home 36. Three Smart Girls 36. One Hundred Men and a Girl 37. Mad About Music 38. That Certain Age 38. First Love 39. My Little Chickadee 40. Spring Parade 40. *The Wolf Man* 41. *Saboteur* 42. *Shadow of a Doubt* 43. Guest Wife 45. Tomorrow Is Forever 46. Magnificent Doll 46. Possessed 47. *Sleep My Love* 48. *Rope* 48. Joan of Arc (AA) 48. Bride for Sale 49, etc.

Valentine, Karen (1948–).
American light actress who has had most success on television.
Gidget Grows Up (TV) 69. The Daughters of Joshua Cabe (TV) 72. Coffee, Tea or Me? (TV) 73. The Girl Who Came Gift Wrapped (TV) 74. Having Babies (TV) 76. Murder at the World Series (TV) 77. Go West Young Girl (TV) 78. The North Avenue Irregulars 78. Muggable Mary: Street Cop (TV) 82. Children in the Crossfire (TV) 84. Perfect People (TV) 88. The Power Within 95, etc.
TV series: *Room 222* 69–72. Karen 75. Our Time 85.

Valentino, Rudolph (1895–1926) (Rodolpho d'Antonguolla).
Italian-American leading man, the great romantic idol of the 20s; his personality still shows. His sudden death caused several suicides and his funeral was a national event.
Biographies include: 1926, *Rudy* by his wife, Natacha Rambova. 1927, *The Real Valentino* by George S. Ullman. 1952, *Valentino* by Alan Arnold. *Rudolph Valentino* by Robert Oberfirst. 1962, *The Man behind the Myth*. 1967, *Valentino* by Irving Shulman. 1976, *Valentino the Love God* by Noel Botham and Peter Donnelly.
■ My Official Wife 14. Patria 16. Alimony 18. A Society Sensation 18. All Night 18. The Delicious Little Devil 19. A Rogue's Romance 19. The Homebreaker 19. Virtuous Sinners 19. The Big Little Person 19. Out of Luck 19. Eyes of Youth 19. The Married Virgin 20. An Adventuress 20. The Cheater 20. Passion's Playground 20. Once to Every Woman 20. Stolen Moments 20. The Wonderful Chance 20. *The Four Horseman of the Apocalypse* (the part that made him a super-star) 21. Unchained Seas 21. Camille 21. The Conquering Power 21. *The Sheik* 21. Moran of the Lady Letty 21. Beyond the Rocks 22. The Young Rajah 22. *Blood and Sand* 22. *Monsieur Beaucaire* 24. A Sainted Devil 24. Cobra 24. *The Eagle* 25. *Son of the Sheik* 26.
✪ For turning animal magnetism into at least the semblance of talent. *The Eagle*.
❝ His acting is largely confined to protruding his large, almost occult eyes until the vast areas of white are visible, drawing back the lips of his wide, sensuous mouth to bare his gleaming teeth, and flaring his nostrils.

Thus Adolph Zukor's famous put-down; but Valentino's simple technique was very effective on female audiences the world over. Yet in the year of his death, 1926, he wrote:
A man should control his life. Mine is controlling me.
And H. L. Mencken summed him up:
He was essentially a highly respectable young man; his predicament touched me. Here was one who was catnip to women . . . he had youth and fame . . . and yet he was very unhappy.
~There have been two films called *Valentino*. Anthony Dexter played him in 1951, Rudolf Nureyev in 1977. A TV movie, *The Legend of Valentino*, appeared in 1975 with Franco Nero.

Valk, Frederick (1901–1956).
Heavyweight Czech stage actor, in Britain from 1939.
Gasbags 40. *Thunder Rock* 42. *Dead of Night* 45. Latin Quarter 46. An Outcast of the Islands 51. Top Secret 52. The Colditz Story 53. Zarak 55, etc.

Vallee, Rudy (1901–1986) (Hubert Vallee).
American character comedian, the former crooning idol of the late 20s; in the early 40s Preston Sturges gave him a new lease of life.
Autobiography: 1976, *Let the Chips Fall*.
Biography: 1997, *My Vagabond Lover* by Eleanor Vallee (with Jill Amadio).
The Vagabond Lover 29. Sweet Music 34. Gold Diggers in Paris 38. Second Fiddle 39. Too Many Blondes 41. *The Palm Beach Story* 42. Happy Go Lucky 43. It's in the Bag 45. *The Bachelor and the Bobbysoxer* 47. Unfaithfully Yours 48. The Beautiful Blonde from Bashful Bend 49. Ricochet Romance 54. Gentlemen Marry Brunettes 55. The Helen Morgan Story 57. *How to Succeed in Business Without Really Trying* (his stage role) 67. Live a Little, Love a Little 68. Won Ton Ton 76, etc.
❝ People called me the guy with the cock in his voice. Maybe that's why in 84 years of life I've been with over 145 women and girls. – *R.V. in the RKO Story*
Famous line (*The Palm Beach Story*): 'That's one of the tragedies of life – that the men most in need of a beating-up are always enormous.'

Vallejo, Gerardo (1942–).
Argentinian director of documentaries of country life, a member of the radical collective Cine Liberación. He went into exile in the mid-70s, working in Panama and Spain before returning home in the mid-80s.
El Camino hacia la Muerte del Viejo Reales 69. Reflexiones de un Salvaje (Sp.) 78. El Rigor del Destino 84. Otra Historia de Amor de Buenos Aires 87, etc.

Valli, Alida (1921–) (Alida Maria Altenburger).
Beautiful Italian actress.
I Due Sergenti 36. Manon Lescaut 39. Piccolo Mondo Antico 41. Eugénie Grandet 46. The Paradine Case (US) 47. The Miracle of the Bells 48. *The Third Man* 49. Walk Softly Stranger 49. The White Tower 50. The Lovers of Toledo 52. *Senso* 53. The Stranger's Hand 53. Heaven Fell That Night 57. The Sea Wall/This Angry Age 57. Le Dialogue des Carmélites 59. Ophelia 61. Une Aussi Longue Absence 61. The Spider's Stratagem 71. 1900 76. The Cassandra Crossing 77. Suspiria 77. Aspern 82. Il Lungo Silenzio 93. A Month by the Lake 95, etc.

Valli, Virginia (1898–1968) (Virginia McSweeney).
American silent screen heroine who retired in 1932 to marry Charles Farrell.
Efficiency Edgar's Courtship 17. The Storm 22. A Lady of Quality 23. Paid to Love 27. Isle of Lost Ships 32, etc.

Vallone, Raf (1916–).
Italian leading man, former journalist.
Bitter Rice 48. Vendetta 49. Il Cristo Proibito 50. Anna 51. Thérèse Raquin 53. The Beach 53. The Sign of Venus 55. El Cid 61. *A View from the Bridge* (US) 61. Phaedra 62. The Cardinal 63. Harlow 65. Beyond the Mountains 66. The Italian Job 69. Cannon for Cordoba 70. A Gunfight 71. Rosebud 75. The Human Factor 75. The Other Side of Midnight 77. The Greek Tycoon 78. An Almost Perfect Affair 79. A Time to Die 79. Lion of the Desert 80. The Scarlet and the Black (TV) 83. Power of Evil 85. The Godfather Part III 90, etc.

Vampira (1921–) (Maila Nurmi).
Finnish-born actress in America, a former chorus girl best known as a presenter of late-night horror movies on TV, and for her role as a Ghoul Girl in Ed Wood's *Plan Nine from Outer Space*. She was played by Lisa Marie in the biopic *Ed Wood*.
The Beat Generation 59. The Big Operator 59. Plan Nine from Outer Space 59. Night of the Ghouls 59. Sex Kittens Go to College 60. The Magic Sword/Saint George and the Seven Curses 61. Vampira: About Sex, Death, and Taxes (doc) 96, etc.

Van, Bobby (1930–1980) (Robert Stein King).
American song-and-dance man who went out of fashion with musicals but found a new audience in his 40s and became a TV personality.
■ Because You're Mine 52. Small Town Girl 52. Kiss Me Kate 53. The Navy Versus the Night Monsters 66. *Lost Horizon* 73. Lost Flight (TV) 73.

Van Cleef, Lee (1925–1989).
American character actor who after years as a sneaky western villain found fame and fortune as the hero of tough Italian westerns.
High Noon 52. Arena 53. Yellow Tomahawk 54. A Man Alone 55. Joe Dakota 57. Guns Girls and Gangsters 58. The Man Who Shot Liberty Valance 62. *For a Few Dollars More* 65. Day of Anger 66. *The Good the Bad and the Ugly* 67. Death Rides a Horse 67. Sabata 69. Barquero 70. El Condor 70. Captain Apache 71. Bad Man's River 71. The Magnificent Seven Ride 72. Take a Hard Ride 75. Vendetta 76. God's Gun 77. Kid Vengeance 77. The Octagon 80. Escape from New York 81. The Squeeze 82. Jungle Raiders 84. Armed Response 86. Speed Zone 88. Thieves of Fortune 89, etc.
❝ Being born with a beady-eyed sneer was the luckiest thing that ever happened to me. – *L.V.C.*

Van Damme, Jean-Claude (1961–) (Jean-Claude Van Varenberg).
Belgian actor in Hollywood action films. A former kickboxing champion, he is sometimes known as 'The Muscles from Brussels'. So far, he has been married and divorced four times.
No Retreat, No Surrender 86. Black Eagle 88. Bloodsport 88. Kickboxer 89. Cyborg 89. Death Warrant 90. Double Impact (& co-w) 91. Universal Soldier 92. Nowhere to Run 93. Timecop 94. Streetfighter 95. Sudden Death 95. Maximum Risk 96. The Quest (& d) 96. The Exchange 96. The Colony 97. Knock Off 98, etc.
❝ He does what he does very well – kick boxing and stuff – but acting is not his forte. Neither is being humble. – *Rosanna Arquette*

Van de Sande, Theo (1947–).
Dutch cinematographer, in international films.
The Girl with the Red Hair 83. The Assault 86. Crossing Delancey 88. Rooftops 89. Once Around

91. Wayne's World 92. Erotic Tales 94. Bushwhacked 95. Volcano 97. Blade 98, etc.

Van de Ven, Monique (1952–).
Dutch leading actress, best known internationally for her role in Paul Verhoeven's *Turkish Delight*, in which she appeared after leaving acting school. Moved briefly to the United States with her then husband, cinematographer Jan DE BONT.
Turkish Delight/Turks Fruit 73. Dakota 74. A Girl Called Keetje Tippel 75. A Woman Like Eve/Een Vrouw Als Eva 79. *Dreamland*/Ademloos 82. Burning Love/Brendende Liefde 83. *The Scorpion*/De Schorpiden 84. The Assault/De Aanslag 86. Iris 87. Amsterdamned 88. *Romeo* 90. The Man Inside 90. Paint It Black (US) 90. Eline Vere 91, etc.

Van Devere, Trish (1943–) (Patricia Dressel).
American leading lady of the 70s. She married actor George C. SCOTT in 1972.
Where's Poppa? 70. The Last Run 71. One Is a Lonely Number 72. The Day of the Dolphins 73. Beauty and the Beast (TV) 76. Movie Movie 78. The Hearse 80. The Changeling 80. Uphill All the Way (TV) 85. Hollywood Vice Squad 86. Messenger of Death 88. Deadly Currents 93, etc.
❝ Barely more than a smiling hole in the air. – *Sunday Times*

Van Dien, Casper (1968–).
Square-jawed American actor, from television, who took over the role of Tarzan in 1998. Born in Ridgefield, New Jersey, he studied at the Admiral Farragut Military Academy, and at Florida State University, where he intended to study medicine; instead he began acting and moved to Los Angeles. Formerly married to actress Carrie Mitchum, daughter of Robert MITCHUM.
Night Eyes 4: Fatal Passion 95. Beastmaster 3: The Eye of Braxus 95. James Dean: Race with Destiny 95. Starship Troopers 97. On the Border 97. Tarzan and the Lost City 98. Modern Vampires/Revenant 98, etc.

Van Dine, S. S. (1888–1939) (Willard Huntingdon Wright).
American author who created the wealthy man-about-town detective Philo Vance, personified on screen by several actors. William Powell played him in *The Canary Murder Case* 29, *The Greene Murder Case* 29, *The Benson Murder Case* 30, and *The Kennel Murder Case* 33. Basil Rathbone had one attempt, *The Bishop Murder Case* 30. Warren William took over for *The Dragon Murder Case* 34 and *The Gracie Allen Murder Case* 39. Meanwhile there were Paul Lukas in *The Casino Murder Case* 35, Edmund Lowe in *The Garden Murder Case* 36, and Grant Richards in *Night of Mystery* 37. 1940 brought James Stephenson in *Calling Philo Vance;* in 1947 there was William Wright in *Philo Vance Returns;* and Alan Curtis in 1948 appeared in two poor attempts, *Philo Vance's Gamble* and *Philo Vance's Secret Mission*.

Van Doren, Mamie (1933–) (Joan Lucille Olander).
American leading lady, the blonde bombshell of the second feature, in Hollywood from 1954.
Autobiography: 1987, *Playing the Field*.
Forbidden (debut) 54. Yankee Pasha 54. The Second Greatest Sex 55. Running Wild 55. The Girl in Black Stockings 56. Teacher's Pet 58. The Navy versus the Night Monsters 66. Free Ride 85, etc.

Van Dormael, Jaco (1957–).
Belgian director and screenwriter.
In Heaven as on Earth (co-w) 91. Toto the Hero (wd) 91. The Eighth Day (wd) 96.

Van Druten, John (1901–1957).
Prolific English playwright, novelist and theatre director. Born in London, of Dutch parents, he studied law at London University, and achieved success as a writer in America, emigrating in 1938 and becoming an American citizen in 1944. His successful play, *I Am a Camera*, an adaptation of Christopher Isherwood's *Goodbye to Berlin*, has been filmed twice, the second time as the musical *Cabaret*. His long-time companion was actor and theatrical producer Walter Starke.
Autobiography: 1957, *The Widening Circle*.
■ Young Woodley 30. After Office Hours/London Wall 31. New Morals for Old/After All 32. If I Were Free/Behold We Live 33. One Night in Lisbon/There's Always Juliet 41. Old Acquaintance 43 and 81 (as Rich and Famous). Gaslight (co-w, AAN) 44. Voice of the Turtle 47. I Remember Mama 48. I Am a Camera 55. Bell, Book and Candle 58. Cabaret 72.

Van Dyke, Dick (1925–).
Lanky American TV comedian who never quite made it in movies.
■ Bye Bye Birdie 63. What a Way to Go 64. *Mary Poppins* 64. The Art of Love 65. Lt Robin Crusoe 65. Never a Dull Moment 67. Divorce American Style 67. Fitzwilly 67. Chitty Chitty Bang Bang 68. *The Comic* 69. Some Kind of a Nut 70. Cold Turkey 71. The Morning After (TV) 74. The Runner Stumbles 79. Dropout Father (TV) 82. Found Money (TV) 84. The Wrong Way Kid (TV) 84. Strong Medicine (TV) 86. Ghost of a Chance (TV) 87. Dick Tracy 90.
TV series: *The Dick Van Dyke Show* 61–66. The New Dick Van Dyke Show 71–72.

Van Dyke, W(oodbridge) S(trong) (1889–1943).
Competent, adaptable American director, at his peak in the 30s. Born in San Diego, California, he was on stage for 25 years from childhood before becoming an assistant to D. W. GRIFFITH on *Intolerance*, and soon after turned to directing. Noted for his speed in finishing films ahead of time, he was nicknamed 'One-Take Woody'. His exploits filming *Trader Horn* in Africa made him the model for film director Carl Denham in *King Kong*.
■ Men of the Desert 18. Gift of Gab 18. Land of Long Shadows 18. Open Spaces 18. Lady of the Dugout 19. Our Little Nell 20. According to Hoyle 22. Boss of Camp 4 22. Forget Me Not 22. Little Girl Next Door 23. Miracle Makers 23. Loving Lies 23. You Are In Danger 23. The Destroying Angel 23. The Battling Fool 24. Winner Take All 24. Barriers Burned Away 24. Half Dollar Bill 24. The Beautiful Sinner 25. Gold Heels 25. Hearts and Spurs 25. The Trail Rider 25. Ranger of the Big Pines 25. The Timber Wolf 25. The Desert's Price 25. The Gentle Cyclone 26. War Paint 26. Winners of the Wilderness 27. Heart of the Yukon 27. Eyes of the Totem 27. Foreign Devils 27. California 27. Spoilers of the West 27. Wyoming 28. Under the Black Eagle 28. *White Shadows in the South Seas* 28. The Pagan 29. *Trader Horn* 30. Never the Twain Shall Meet 31. Guilty Hands 31. Cuban Love Song 32. *Tarzan the Ape Man* 32. Night World 32. Penthouse 33. Eskimo 33. The Prizefighter and the Lady 33. Laughing Boy 34. Hideout 34. *Manhattan Melodrama* 34. *The Thin Man* (AAN) 34. Forsaking all Others 35. Naughty Marietta 35. I Live My Life 35. Rose Marie 36. *San Francisco* (AAN) 36. His Brother's Wife 36. The Devil is a Sissy 36. Love on the Run 36. After the Thin Man 36. Personal Property 37. They Gave Him a Gun 37. Rosalie 37. Marie Antoinette 38. *Sweethearts* 38. Stand Up and Fight 39. It's a Wonderful World 39. Andy Hardy Gets Spring Fever 39. Another Thin Man 39. I Take This Woman 40. I Love You Again 40. Bitter Sweet 40. Rage in Heaven 41. The Feminine Touch 41. Shadow of the Thin Man 41. Dr Kildare's Victory 41. I Married an Angel 42. Cairo 42. Journey for Margaret 42.
❝ Woody cut as he shot. He used his camera as though it were a six-shooter and he was the fastest gun in Hollywood. Actors rarely got more than one take on any scene, then the camera was moved rapidly to another set-up. – *Robert Taylor*

Van Enger, Charles (1890–1980).
American cinematographer.
Treasure Island 20. A Doll's House 22. The Famous Mrs Fair 23. The Marriage Circle 24. Forbidden Paradise 24. *Phantom of the Opera* 25. Kiss Me Again 25. Puppets 26. Easy Pickings 27. Port of Missing Girls 28. Fox Movietone Follies 29. High Society Blues 30. Mad Parade 31. I Was a Spy 33. The Case of Gabriel Perry 34. Seven Sinners 36. Wife Doctor and Nurse 37. Miracle on Main Street 40. Never Give a Sucker an Even Break 41. Night Monster 42. Sherlock Holmes Faces Death 43. The Merry Monahans 44. That Night with You 45. The Time of Their Lives 46. The Wistful Widow 47. Abbott and Costello Meet Frankenstein 48. Africa Screams 49. Ma and Pa Kettle Back on the Farm 51. The Magnetic Monster 53. Sitting Bull 54. Time Table 56. Gun Fever 58, many others.

Van Eyck, Peter (1911–1969).
Blond German actor, in America from mid-30s, later international.
The Moon is Down 42. Five Graves to Cairo 43. Rommel, Desert Fox 51. *The Wages of Fear* 53. Retour de Manivelle 57. The Girl Rosemarie 58. The Snorkel 58. Foxhole in Cairo 60. Station Six Sahara 63. The Spy Who Came in from the Cold 65. Million Dollar Man 67. Shalako 68. Assignment to Kill 69, many others.

Van Eyssen, John (1922–1995).
South African actor who appeared in a number of British films before turning agent. Chief production executive in Britain for Columbia 1969–73.
Quatermass II 56. Dracula 57. I'm All Right Jack 59. The Criminal 60. Exodus 60, etc.

Van Fleet, Jo (1919–1996).
American character actress who usually played older than her real age.
■ *East of Eden* (AA) 55. The Rose Tattoo 55. I'll Cry Tomorrow 55. The King and Four Queens 56. Gunfight at the OK Corral 57. This Angry Age 58. *Wild River* 60. Cool Hand Luke 67. I Love You Alice B. Toklas 67. 80 Steps to Jonah 69. The Gang that Couldn't Shoot Straight 72. The Tenant 76.

Van Gogh, Vincent (1853–1890).
The tormented Dutch post-Impressionist artist who went mad and shot himself has attracted the attention of several film-makers. In 1956 Vincente Minnelli made the big-budget biopic *Lust for Life* starring Kirk Douglas, which garnered Anthony Quinn an Oscar for his brief supporting role as Gauguin, and since then there have been several art films: Paul Cox's documentary *Vincent: The Life and Death of Vincent van Gogh* 87, with the voice of John Hurt reading from the painter's letters; Robert Altman's *Vincent and Theo* 90, starring Tim Roth and Paul Rhys, which concentrated on his relationship with his brother; and Maurice Pialat's *Van Gogh* 91, starring Jacques Dutronc, which dealt with the final three months of the artist's life.

Van Heusen, Jimmy (1913–1990).
American songwriter, usually with lyrics by Johnny Burke: 'Swinging on a Star' (AA 1944), 'Sunday, Monday or Always', 'Sunshine Cake', many others. His later partner was lyricist Sammy Cahn, with whom he wrote such songs as 'All the Way', 'High Hopes' and 'Call Me Irresponsible'.
The Tender Trap 55. The Joker Is Wild 57. Some Came Running 58. A Hole in the Head 59. The World of Suzie Wong 60. The Road to Hong Kong 62. A Walk on the Wild Side 62. Papa's Delicate Condition 63. Robin and the Seven Hoods 64 (s 'My Kind of Town'). Thoroughly Modern Millie 67. Love and Marriage 69.

Van Horn, Buddy.
American director.
Any Which Way You Can 80. Date with an Angel 87. The Dead Pool 88. Pink Cadillac 91, etc.

Van Pallandt, Nina (1932–).
Danish actress, a former singer.
The Long Goodbye 73. Guilty or Innocent (TV) 75. Quintet 78. A Wedding 79. American Gigolo 80. Cloud Dancer 80. Cutter's Way 81. Jungle Warriors 85, etc.

Van Parys, Georges (1902–1971).
French composer.
Le Million 31. Jeunesse 34. Café de Paris 38. Le Silence Est d'Or 46. Fanfan la Tulipe 51. Adorables Créatures 52. Les Diaboliques 55. French Cancan 55. Charmants Garçons 57, many others.

Van Patten, Dick (1928–).
Chubby American character actor usually in comedy roles; brother of Joyce VAN PATTEN.
Joe Kidd 72. Westworld 73. The Strongest Man in the World 75. Gus 76. Freaky Friday 77. High Anxiety 77. The New Adventures of Pippi Longstocking 88. Robin Hood: Men in Tights 93. Love Is All There Is 96. Demolition High 96. Love Is All There Is 96, etc.
TV series: Mama 49–57. The Partners 71–72. The New Dick Van Dyke Show 73–74. When Things Were Rotten 75. Eight Is Enough 77–81.

Van Patten, Joyce (1934–).
American leading lady of the 70s. Sister of Dick Van Patten. Married actors Martin Balsam and Dennis Dugan.
The Goddess 58. I Love You Alice B. Toklas 68. Something Big 71. The Bravos (TV) 72. Thumb Tripping 72. The Manchu Eagle Murder Caper Mystery 75. The Bad News Bears 76. Mikey and Nicky 76. Billy Galvin 86. Monkey Shines 88. Breathing Lessons (TV) 94, etc.
TV series: The Good Guys 68–70. The Don Rickles Show 72. The Mary Tyler Moore Hour 79.

Van Peebles, Mario (1958–).
American director, screenwriter and actor. He is the son of Melvin VAN PEEBLES.
Sweet Sweetback's Baadasss Song (a) 71. Cotton Club (a) 84. Exterminator II (a) 84. Rappin' (a, s) 85. South Bronx Heroes (a) 86. Hot Shot (a) 86. Last Resort (a) 86. Heartbreak Ridge (a) 86. Jaws 4 – the Revenge (a) 87. Identity Crisis (w) 89. New Jack City (wd) 91. Gunmen (a) 93. Posse (a, d) 93. Erotic Tales (co-d) 94. Panther (d) 95. Solo (a) 97. Gang in Blue (co-d, TV) 97. Riot (a) 97. Stag (a) 97. Los Locos (a, co-p, w) 97. Love Kills (a, wd) 98, etc.

Van Peebles, Melvin (1932–).
American director.
The Story of a Three-Day Pass 67. Watermelon Man 69. *Sweet Sweetback's Baadasss Song* 71. Identity Crisis 89. Panther (w) 95. Gang in Blue (co-d, TV) 97, etc.

Van Rooten, Luis (1906–1973).
Mexican-born American character actor.
The Hitler Gang (as Himmler) 44. Two Years before the Mast 44. To the Ends of the Earth 48. Champion 49. Detective Story 51. The Sea Chase 55, etc.

Van Runkle, Theadora.
American costume designer.
Bonnie and Clyde (AAN) 67. The Thomas Crown Affair 68. Mame 74. The Godfather Part II (AAN) 74. New York, New York 77. S.O.B. 81. The Best Little Whorehouse in Texas 82. Peggy Sue Got Married (AAN) 86. Stella 90. Butcher's Wife 91. Leap of Faith 92. Kiss of Death 95. The Last Don (TV) 97. Goodbye, Lover 98, etc.

Van Sant, Gus (1952–).
American director, screenwriter and musician, a former ad-man and assistant to Roger CORMAN.
Mala Noche 85. Drugstore Cowboy 89. My Own Private Idaho 91. Even Cowgirls Get the Blues (wd) 93. To Die For 95. *Good Will Hunting* (AAN) 97. Psycho 98, etc.
❝ I guess I'm a post-modernist. – G.V.S.

Van Sloan, Edward (1882–1964).
American character actor with stage experience; often seen as elderly professor.
Dracula 30. *Frankenstein* 31. The Mummy 33. Death Takes a Holiday 34. The Last Days of Pompeii 35. *Dracula's Daughter* 36. The Phantom Creeps 39. The Doctor Takes a Wife 40. The Conspirators 44. The Mask of Dijon 47. A Foreign Affair 47, etc.

Van Upp, Virginia (1912–1970).
American executive producer, at Columbia in the late 40s. Former writer.
Young and Willing 40. The Crystal Ball 42. Cover Girl 44. The Impatient Years (& p) 44. Together Again (& p) 45, etc.

Van Vorhees, Westbrook (1904–1968).
American commentator whose familiar stentorian voice as narrator of *The March of Time* was widely imitated.

Van Warmerdam, Alex (1952–).
Dutch director, screenwriter, and actor, an art school graduate who began as a theatre designer and writer.
Abel (a, wd) 85. *The Northerners*/De Noorderlingen (a, wd) 92. The Dress/De Jurk (wd) 96. Little Tony/Kleine Teun (a, p, wd) 98, etc.

Van Zandt, Philip (1904–1958).
Dutch character actor, in Hollywood films.
Citizen Kane 41. House of Frankenstein 45. April Showers 48. Viva Zapata 52. Knock on Wood 54. The Pride and the Passion 57, etc.

Vanbrugh, Irene (1872–1949) (Irene Barnes).
Distinguished British stage actress. Films rare.
Autobiography: 1978, *To Tell My Story*.
The Gay Lord Quex 27. Moonlight Sonata 37.

Vance, Danitra (1959–1994).
American actress, from the stage, and a regular on TV's *Saturday Night Live*. Died of cancer.
Sticky Fingers 88. Limit Up 89. Little Man Tate 91. Jumpin' at the Boneyard 92, etc.

Vance, Vivian (1911–1979).
Cheerful American character comedienne, long a partner of Lucille Ball in various TV series.
The Secret Fury 50. The Blue Veil 51. The Great Race 65, etc.

Vance-Straker, Marilyn.
American costume designer.
Fast Times at Ridgemont High 82. 48 Hrs 82. Romancing the Stone 84. Pretty in Pink 86. Predator 87. The Untouchables (AAN) 87. Die Hard 88. Road House 89. Pretty Woman 90. Die Hard 2 90. Predator 2 90. Hudson Hawk 91. The Rocketeer 91. Ricochet 91. The Last Boy Scout 91. Medicine Man 92. Sommersby 93. Judgment Night 93. Street Fighter 94. The Getaway 94. Jade 95. GI Jane 97, etc.

Vanel, Charles (1892–1989).
French character actor, with stage experience.
Les Misérables 33. Le Grand Jeu 34. La Belle Equipe 36. Légion d'Honneur 38. Carrefour 39. *La Ferme du Pendu* 45. In Nome della Legge 49. *The Wages of Fear* 53. Maddalena 54. *Les Diaboliques* 55. Rafles sur la Ville 57. Le Dialogue des Carmélites 59. La Vérité 60. Un Homme de Trop 67. La Puce et le Privé 79, many others.

Vangelis (1943–) (Vangelis Papathanassiou).
Greek composer.
Chariots of Fire (AA) 81. Missing 82. Blade Runner 82. The Bounty 84. Nosferatu a Venezia 87. Francesco 89. Bitter Moon 92, etc.

Vanity (1958–) (aka D. D. Winters) (Denise Matthews).
American leading actress and singer, in action movies.
Terror Train 80. Tanya's Island 81. The Last Dragon 85. 52 Pickup 86. Never Too Young to Die 86. Deadly Illusion/Love You to Death 87. Action Jackson 88. Memories of Murder 90. Neon City 91. DaVinci's War 92. South Beach 92, etc.

Vanna, Nina (1902–) (Nina Yarsikova).
Beautiful Russian leading actress who fled the revolution and had a brief career in English and European films.
Guy Fawkes (GB) 23. *The Man without Desire* (GB) 23. The Cost of Beauty (GB) 24. In the Night Watch/Veille d'Armes 24. We Women (GB) 25. The Woman Tempted (GB) 26. The Triumph of the Rat (GB) 27. Café Electric (Aus.) 27. Manner vor der Ehe (Ger.) 27, etc.

Varconi, Victor (1896–1976) (Mihaly Varkonyi).
Hungarian actor long in Hollywood.
Autobiography: 1976, *It's Not Enough to Be Hungarian*.
The Volga Boatmen 26. King of Kings 27. The Divine Lady (as Nelson) 29. The Doomed Battalion 31. Roberta 34. The Plainsman 36. Disputed Passage 39. Reap the Wild Wind 42. For Whom the Bell Tolls 43. Samson and Delilah 49, etc.

Varda, Agnès (1928–).
French writer-director of the 'left bank' school. She was married to Jacques Demy.
La Pointe Courte 56. Cléo de 5 à 7 62. Le Bonheur 65. Les Créatures 66. Lions Love 69. One Sings, the Other Doesn't/L'Une Chante, l'Autre Pas 77. Vagabond/Sans Toit ni Loi 85. Kung Fu Master!/Le Petit Amour 87. Jane B. par Agnes V. 88. Jacquot de Nantes 91. Les Cent et Une Nuits/A Hundred and One Nights 95. The World of Jacques Demy (doc) 95, etc.

Varden, Evelyn (1895–1958).
American stage character actress who made several films.
Pinky 49. Cheaper by the Dozen 50. Phone Call from a Stranger 52. The Student Prince 54. Night of the Hunter 55. The Bad Seed 56, etc.

Varden, Norma (1899–1989).
British character actress, usually as haughty aristocrat in comedies; went to Hollywood in the 40s.
A Night Like This 32. The Iron Duke 35. Foreign Affairs 36. Shipyard Sally 39. Random Harvest 42. The Green Years 46. Strangers on a Train 51. Gentlemen Prefer Blondes 53. *Witness for the Prosecution* 58. The Sound of Music 65. Doctor Dolittle 67, many others.

Varley, Beatrice (1896–1969).
British character actress who played worried little elderly ladies for thirty years.
Hatter's Castle 41. So Well Remembered 47. No Room at the Inn 49. Hindle Wakes 53. The Feminine Touch 55, many others.
TV series: Dick and the Duchess 57–58.

Varnel, Marcel (1894–1947).
French-born director, in Hollywood from 1924; came to England in the 30s and made some of the best comedies of Will Hay and the Crazy Gang. Died in a car crash.
The Silent Witness 32. Chandu the Magician 32. Girls will be Boys 34. No Monkey Business 35. Good Morning Boys 36. OK for Sound 37. *Oh Mr Porter* 38. Convict 99 38. *Alf's Button Afloat* 38. *Old Bones of the River* 38. *Ask a Policeman* 39. *The Frozen Limits* 39. Where's That Fire? 39. Let George Do It 40. Gasbags 40. I Thank You 41. Hi Gang 41. *The Ghost of St Michaels* 41. Much Too Shy 42. King Arthur Was a Gentleman 42. Get Cracking 43. He Snoops to Conquer 44. I Didn't Do It 45. George in Civvy Street 46. This Man is Mine 46. The First Gentleman 47, etc.
❝ The only pure comedy director we've ever had in this country. – *Basil Wright*

Varnel, Max (1925–).
British second feature director, son of Marcel Varnel.
A Woman Possessed 58. The Great Van Robbery 49. A Taste of Money 60. Return of a Stranger 61. Enter Inspector Duval 62. The Silent Invasion 63, etc.

Varney, Jim (1949–).
American comic actor, from commercials.
Ernest Goes to Camp 87. Ernest Saves Christmas 88. Ernest Goes to Jail 90. Ernest Scared Stupid 91. Wilder Napalm 93. Beverly Hillbillies 93. Ernest Rides Again 93. Toy Story (voice) 95, etc.

Varney, Reg (1922–).
Chirpy British comedian who after years of availability found fame in the 60s in TV series *The Rag Trade* and *On the Buses*.
The Great St Trinian's Train Robbery 66. On the Buses 71. Mutiny on the Buses 72. Go for a Take 72. The Best Pair of Legs in the Business 72. Holiday on the Buses 73, etc.

Varsi, Diane (1938–1992).
Slightly-built American leading lady who had a brief career in the 50s, with sporadic appearances later.
■ *Peyton Place* (AAN) 57. *Ten North Frederick* 58. From Hell to Texas 59. Compulsion 59. Sweet Love, Bitter 66. Wild in the Streets 68. Killers Three 69. Bloody Mama 70. Johnny Got His Gun 71. I Never Promised You a Rose Garden 77.

Vaughan, Frankie (1928–) (Frank Abelsohn).
Flamboyant British song-and-dance man who never really made it in movies despite a sojourn in Hollywood.
■ Ramsbottom Rides Again 56. *These Dangerous Years* 57. The Lady is a Square 58. Wonderful Things 58. Heart of a Man 59. Let's Make Love 60. The Right Approach 62. It's All Over Town 64.

Vaughan, Peter (1923–) (Peter Ohm).
British character actor of solid presence, good or evil.
Sapphire 59. Village of the Damned 60. The Punch and Judy Man 63. Fanatic 65. The Naked Runner 67. Hammerhead 68. The Bofors Gun 68. Alfred the Great 69. Eye Witness 70. Straw Dogs 71. The Pied Piper 72. 11 Harrowhouse 74. Zulu Dawn 79. Fox (TV) 80. Time Bandits 81. The French Lieutenant's Woman 81. Jamaica Inn (TV) 83. The Razor's Edge 84. Brazil 85. Haunted Honeymoon 86. Monte Carlo (TV) 86. War and Remembrance (TV) 87. The Bourne Identity (TV) 88. Prisoners of Honor (TV) 91. The Remains of the Day 93. The Crucible 96. Joseph Conrad's Secret Agent 96. Face 97. Our Mutual Friend (TV) 98. Les Misérables (US) 98. The Legend of the Pianist on the Ocean (It.) 98, etc.

Vaughan, Stevie Ray (1956–1990).
American blues guitarist. Born in Dallas, Texas, he worked with local bands before forming his own groups from the mid-70s. Died in a plane crash. A biopic of his life was announced in 1996, to be written and directed by Robert Rodriguez.
Biography: *Stevie Ray Vaughan: Caught in the Crossfire* by Joe Nick Patoski and Bill Crawford.
Gung Ho 86. Back to the Beach 87, etc.

Vaughan Williams, Ralph (1872–1958).
Distinguished English composer who scored some 40s films.
■ The 49th Parallel/The Invaders 41. Coastal Command 42. The People's Land 42. The Flemish Farm 43. Stricken Peninsula 44. The Loves of Joanna Godden 48. Scott of the Antarctic 48. Dim Little Island 49.

Vaughn, Robert (1932–).
Slight, intense American actor who didn't quite make the front rank. He is the author of *Only Victims*, 1972, a study of the effect of the HUAC investigations on Hollywood in the late 40s and the subsequent blacklisting of actors, directors and writers.
Teenage Caveman 58. No Time to Be Young 58. The Young Philadelphians (AAN) 59. *The Magnificent Seven* 60. The Big Show 61. The Caretakers 63. One Spy Too Many 66. The Venetian Affair 67. The Helicopter Spies 68. Bullitt 68. The Mind of Mr Soames 69. The Bridge at Remagen 69. The Statue 71. The Towering Inferno 74. *Washington Behind Closed Doors* (TV) 76. Brass Target 78. Good Luck Miss Wyckoff 79. Battle beyond the Stars 80. Inside the Third Reich (TV) 82. The Return of the Man from UNCLE (TV) 83. Superman III 83. Private Sessions (TV) 85. International Airport (TV) 85. The Delta Force 85. Hour of the Assassin 87. River of Death 89. Nobody's Perfect 90. Joe's Apartment 96. Milk & Money 96. BASEketball 98, etc.
TV series: The Lieutenant 63. *The Man from UNCLE* 64–67. The Protectors 72–73. Centennial 78–79. Emerald Point N.A.S. 83–84. The A-Team 86–87.

Vaughn, Vince (1970–).
American actor. Born in Minneapolis, Illinois, he began in commercials before moving to Los Angeles, where he first played small parts in TV series.
Rudy 93. At Risk 94. Swingers 96. The Lost World: Jurassic Park 97. The Locusts 97. Return to Paradise 98. Clay Pigeons 98. Psycho (as Norman Bates) 98, etc.

Veber, Francis (1937–).
French director, screenwriter and dramatist. He remade his local success as the Hollywood film *Three Fugitives*.
The Tall Blond Man with One Black Shoe/Le Grand Blond avec une Chaussure Noire (co-w) 72. A Pain in the A—/L'Emmerdeur (co-w) 73. Le Magnifique 73. Return of the Tall Blond Man with One Black Shoe/Le Retour du Grand Blond (w) 74. Peur sur la Ville (w) 75. The Toy/Le Jouet (d) 76. La Cage aux Folles (co-w) (AAN) 79. Hothead/Coup de Tête (w) 80. Sunday Lovers (co-w) 81. The Goat/La Chèvre (wd) 81. La Cage aux Folles II (w) 81. Partners (w) 82. Les Compères (wd) 83. Les Fugitifs (wd) 86. The Lover (w) 86. Three Fugitives (wd) 89. Out on a Limb (d) 92. My Father, the Hero (co-w) 94. Ghost with Driver (w) 96. Le Jaguar (wd) 96. Father's Day (oa) 97. Le Diner de Cons (wd) 98, etc.

Védrès, Nicole (1911–1965).
French director, mainly of probing documentaries.
Paris 1900 47. *La Vie Commence Demain* 50. Aux Frontières de l'Homme 53, etc.

Vee, Bobby (1943–) (Robert Velline).
American pop singer of the 60s.
Swingin' Along/Double Trouble 62. Play It Cool 62. Just for Fun 63. C'mon Let's Live a Little 67.

Veidt, Conrad (1893–1943).
Distinguished German character actor who also filmed in Britain and Hollywood.
The Cabinet of Dr Caligari 19. *Waxworks* 24. Lucrezia Borgia 25. *The Student of Prague* 26. *The Hands of Orlac* 26. The Beloved Rogue (US) 27. The Man Who Laughs 27. Rasputin 30. *Congress Dances* 31. *Rome Express* (GB) 32. I Was a Spy (GB) 33. F.P.I. 33. The Wandering Jew (GB) 33. Jew Süss (GB) 34. Bella Donna (GB) 34. *The Passing of the Third Floor Back* (GB) 35. King of the Damned (GB) 35. *Under the Red Robe* (GB) 36. *Dark Journey* (GB) 37. *The Spy in Black* (GB) 39. Contraband (GB) 40. *The Thief of Baghdad* (GB) 40. Escape (US) 40. A Woman's Face (US) 41. Whistling in the Dark (US) 41. All through the Night (US) 41. The Men in Her Life (US) 42. Nazi Agent (US) 42. Casablanca (US) 42. Above Suspicion (US) 43, etc.
✪ For his almost liquid villainy, and for a score of authentic star performances. *The Thief of Baghdad*.
❝ Women fight for Conrad Veidt! – *30s publicity*
No matter what roles I play, I can't get Caligari out of my system. – *C.V.*

Veiller, Anthony (1903–1965).
American scriptwriter, in Hollywood from 1930.
Stage Door (AAN) 37. Her Cardboard Lover 42. The Killers (AAN) 46. Along the Great Divide 51. Moulin Rouge 53. Red Planet Mars (& p) 53. Safari 56. The List of Adrian Messenger 63, many others.

Velez, Lupe (1908–1944) (Guadeloupe Velez de Villalobos).
Temperamental Mexican leading lady of the 30s; best remembered with Leon Errol in the Mexican Spitfire series. She was married to actor Johnny Weissmuller (1933–38). Committed suicide when pregnant after a love affair went wrong.
The Gaucho 27. Wolf Song 29. East is West 30. The Squaw Man 31. Kongo 32. Hot Pepper 33. Palooka 34. The Morals of Marcus (GB) 36. Gypsy Melody (GB) 37. *The Girl from Mexico* 39. *Mexican Spitfire* 39. Six Lessons from Madame La Zonga 41. Playmates 42. Mexican Spitfire's Elephant 42. Mexican Spitfire's Blessed Event 43, many others.
❝ The first time you buy a house you think how pretty it is and sign the cheque. The second time you look to see if the basement has termites. It's the same with men. – *L.V.*

Venable, Evelyn (1913–1993).
American leading lady of the 30s, usually in demure roles. She was the original model for Columbia Pictures' logo of a woman holding aloft a lamp.
Cradle Song 33. Mrs Wiggs of the Cabbage Patch 34. Alice Adams 35. The Frontiersman 38. He Hired the Boss 43, etc.

Veness, Amy (1876–1960).
British character actress who latterly played cheerful old souls.
My Wife's Family 31. Hobson's Choice 31. Lorna Doone 35. Aren't Men Beasts? 37. Yellow Sands 39. The Man in Grey 43. This Happy Breed 44. Here Come the Huggetts 49. Doctor in the House 54, etc.

Venora, Diane (1952–).
American leading actress.
Wolfen 81. Terminal Choice 82. The Cotton Club 84. F/X 85. Ironweed Bird 88. Heat 96. Surviving Picasso 96. Romeo and Juliet 97. The Jackal 97, etc.

Ventham, Wanda (1938–).
British leading lady.
My Teenage Daughter 56. The Navy Lark 59. Solo for Sparrow 62. The Cracksman 63. The Big Job 65. The Knack 65. The Spy with a Cold Nose 67. Carry On Up the Khyber 68. Captain Kronos 73. Lost Empires (TV) 86, etc.

Ventura, Lino (1919–1987) (Angelino Borrini).
Italian leading man, former boxer.
Touchez Pas au Grisbi 53. Marie Octobre 57. Crooks in Clover 63. Les Aventuriers 67. The Valachi Papers 72. Wild Horses (US) 72. La Bonne Année 73. The Pink Telephone 75. Le Silencieux 76. Sunday Lovers 80. Les Misérables 82, many others.

Venuti, Joe (1903–1978) (Giuseppe Venuti).
American jazz violinist and bandleader, in films as himself. Born on the ship taking his parents from Italy to America, and brought up in Philadelphia, he played in symphony orchestras in his early

teens before joining Paul WHITEMAN's orchestra in the 30s and later forming a long association with Bing CROSBY. He was played by Emile Levisetti in the biopic *Bix*, about Bix BEIDERBECKE. His recordings with his school-friend, guitarist Eddie Lang, formed the basis for the soundtrack of *The Fortune* 74.

King of Jazz 30. Garden of the Moon 38. Syncopation 42. Two Guys from Texas 48. Riding High 49. Disc Jockey 51. Sarge Goes to College 66, etc.

❝ I don't think my father spoke to me for seven years after he found out I was a jazz player. – *J.V.*

Vera-Ellen (1920–1981) (Vera-Ellen Westmeyr Rohe).
American dancer and songstress of 40s musicals, a former Rockette.

■ *Wonder Man* 45. The Kid from Brooklyn 46. Three Little Girls in Blue 46. Carnival in Costa Rica 47. Words and Music 48. Love Happy 49. *On the Town* 49. Three Little Words 50. Happy Go Lovely (GB) 51. The Belle of New York 52. *Call Me Madam* 53. The Big Leaguer 53. White Christmas 54. Let's Be Happy (GB) 56.

Verbong, Ben (1949–).
Dutch director.

The Girl with the Red Hair 81. De Schorpioen 84. Lily Was Here 89. De Onfatoenlijke Vrouw 91. House Call 94, etc.

Verdon, Gwen (1925–).
Vivacious American dancer and singer, once married to Bob Fosse.

On the Riviera 51. Meet Me After the Show 51. David and Bathsheba 51. The Merry Widow 52. The I Don't Care Girl 53. The Farmer Takes a Wife 53. *Damn Yankees* 58. Legs (TV) 83. The Cotton Club 84. Cocoon 85. Nadine 87. Cocoon: The Return 88. Alice 90. In Cold Blood (TV) 96. Marvin's Room 96, etc.

Verdu, Maribel (1970–).
Spanish leading actress, born in Madrid.

27 Hours/Veintisiete Horas 85. Sinatra 88. Manolo 89. Badis (Mor.) 90. Lovers/Amantes 91. Belle Epoque 92. Golden Balls/Huevos de Oro 93. Lullaby/Canción de Cuna 95. The Year of Awakening/El Año de las Luces 96. Neighborhood 98, etc.

Verdugo, Elena (1926–).
Spanish-American leading lady.

Down Argentine Way 40. The Moon and Sixpence 42. House of Frankenstein 45. Song of Scheherazade 47. Cyrano de Bergerac 50. Thief of Damascus 52. How Sweet It Is 68, etc.

TV series: Meet Millie 52. The New Phil Silvers Show 63. *Marcus Welby* M.D. 69–75.

Vereen, Ben (1946–).
American dancer.

Funny Lady 75. *Roots* (TV) 77. All That Jazz 79. Breakin' Through 84. The Zoo Gang 85. Buy and Cell 89. Once upon a Forest 93. Why Do Fools Fall in Love 98, etc.

TV series: Tenspeed and Brown Shoe 80.

Verhoeven, Michael (1938–).
German director and screenwriter, a former doctor.

Danse Macabre/Paarungen 67. Mitgift 75. Gutenbach 78. White Rose/Die Weisse Rose 82. The Nasty Girl 90. New Germany (co-d) 90. Lilli Lottofee 91. My Mother's Courage 95, etc.

Verhoeven, Paul (1938–).
Dutch director, in America from 1985. Born in Amsterdam, he studied at the University of Leiden, obtaining a doctorate in mathematics and physics, then serving with the Royal Dutch Navy as a documentary film-maker before working in television as a director of documentaries.

Biography: 1998, *Paul Verhoeven* by Rob van Scheer.

Business Is Business/Wat Zien Ik 71. *Turkish Delight*/Turks Fruit (AAN) 73. Katie's Passion/Keetje Tippel 75. Soldier of Orange/Soldaat van Oranje 77. *Spetters* 80. The Fourth Man/De Vierde Man 83. Flesh and Blood 85. *Robocop* 87. Total Recall 90. Basic Instinct 92. Showgirls 95. Starship Troopers 97, etc.

❝ My resistance to violence is less than other people's, perhaps due to my upbringing in Holland where we were occupied by the Germans and saw violence in front of our eyes. It's possible that I have more problems judging what is over the top and what is not. – *P.V.*

People seem to have this strange idea that films can influence people to be violent, but in my sincere opinion film only reflects the violence of society. – *P.V.*

It's the antagonism of American society that makes me feel alive. – *P.V.*

Vermilyea, Harold (1889–1958).
Russian-American character actor, former operatic singer.

O.S.S. 46. The Big Clock 48. Edge of Doom 50. Born to Be Bad 51, etc.

Verne, Jules (1828–1905).
French adventure novelist whose inventive science-fiction themes have latterly endeared him to Hollywood. Films of his works since 1954 include *Twenty Thousand Leagues Under the Sea, Around the World in Eighty Days, From Earth to the Moon, Journey to the Center of the Earth, Five Weeks in a Balloon, Master of the World, The Children of Captain Grant (In Search of the Castaways), Rocket to the Moon, The Light at the Edge of the World, The Southern Star* and *Michael Strogoff*.

Verne, Karen (1915–1967) (Ingabor Katrine Klinckerfuss).
German leading lady who made a number of Hollywood films.

Ten Days in Paris (GB) 39. All Through the Night 41. Kings Row 42. The Seventh Cross 44. A Bullet for Joey 55. Ship of Fools 65. Torn Curtain 67, etc.

Verneuil, Henri (1920–) (Achod Malakin).
French director, former journalist.

La Table aux Crevés 50. Forbidden Fruit 52. Public Enemy Number One 53. Paris Palace Hotel 56. The Cow and I 59. L'Affaire d'une Nuit 61. The Big Snatch/Mélodie en Sous-Sol 63. Guns for San Sebastian 68. The Burglars 71. The Serpent 72. The Night Caller 72. Le Corps de Mon Ennemi 76. Mille Milliards de Dollars 82. Les Morfalous 84. Mother/Mayrig 91. 588 rue Paradis 92, etc.

Verno, Jerry (1895–1975).
British cockney character actor.

His Lordship 32. The Thirty-Nine Steps 35. Farewell Again 37. Old Mother Riley in Paris 38. The Common Touch 41. The Red Shoes 48. The Belles of St Trinian's 54. After the Ball 57, many others.

Vernon, Anne (1925–) (Edith Vignaud).
Vivacious French leading lady who has also filmed in Britain and Hollywood.

Le Mannequin Assassiné 48. Warning to Wantons (GB) 48. Shakedown (US) 49. *Edward and Caroline* 50. Rue de l'Estrapade 52. The Love Lottery (GB) 54. Time Bomb (GB) 54. Le Long des Trottoirs 56. Les Lavandières de Portugal 57. *The Umbrellas of Cherbourg* 64. Patate 64. La Démoniaque 67. Therese and Isabelle 68, etc.

Vernon, Bobby (1897–1939).
Boyish American star comedian of the silents, usually in shorts.

Vernon, Howard (1914–1996) (Mario Lippert).
Swiss actor, in films of many nationalities, frequently as a villain. His career dipped in the 60s and 70s, when he became a regular in the mediocre films of Jesús FRANCO, though this gained him a cult following. Born in Baden, of a Swiss father and an American mother, he studied acting in Berlin and Paris and was on stage from the 40s.

Le Silence de Mer (Fr.) 41. Boule de Suif (Fr.) 45. Bob le Flambeur (Fr.) 46. Le Diable Boiteaux (Fr.) 48. The Elusive Pimpernel (GB) 50. Black Jack (Fr.) 50. The Thousand Eyes of Dr Mabuse (Ger.) 60. The Secret Ways (US) 61. The Awful Dr Orloff (Sp.) 62. Léon Morin, Priest/Léon Morin, Prêtre (Fr.) 62. The Train (US) 64. *Alphaville* (Fr.) 65. Danger Grows Wild (US) 66. Triple Cross (GB) 66. Night of the Generals (GB) 67. Mayerling (GB) 68. Le Silence de la Mer (Fr.) 68. Virgin among the Living Dead (Fr.) 71. Dracula – Prisoner of Frankenstein (Sp.) 72. The Demons (Port.) 72. La Malédiction de Frankenstein (Sp.) 73. Love and Death (US) 75. L'Assassin Musicien (Fr.) 76. Le Théâtre des Matières (Fr.) 77. Blood Bath of Dr Jekyll (Fr.) 81. The Boy Who Had Everything (Aus.) 84. Fauborg Saint-Martin (Fr.) 86. Faceless (Fr.) 88. Le Complexe de Toulon (Fr.) 91, many others.

Vernon, John (1935–).
Canadian character actor.

Point Blank 67. Topaz 69. Dirty Harry 71. One More Train to Rob 71. The Black Windmill 74. The Outlaw Josey Wales 76. A Special Day 76. National Lampoon's Animal House 78. Herbie Goes Bananas 80. Airplane II: The Sequel 82. Chained Heat 83. Jungle Warriors 85. Blue Monkey 87. Killer Klowns from Outer Space 87. Border Heat 88. Deadly Stranger 88. I'm Gonna Git You Sucka 89. Bail Out 90. Mob Story 90, etc.

TV series: Hail to the Chief 85.

Vernon, Richard (1925–1997).
British character actor of stage and TV, usually in soft-spoken aristocratic roles.

Accidental Death 63. A Hard Day's Night 64. Goldfinger 64. The Secret of My Success 65. The Satanic Rites of Dracula 73. The Pink Panther Strikes Again 76. The Human Factor 79. O Heavenly Dog 80. Evil Under the Sun 82. Gandhi 82. A Month in the Country 87, many others.

TV series: The Man in Room 17 65–66. The Lions 66. The Fellows 67. The Sandbaggers 78–80. L for Lester 82. Legacy of Murder 82. Roll Over Beethoven 85. A Gentleman's Club 88. Class Act 94–95.

Vernon, Wally (1904–1970).
American eccentric comedian.

Mountain Music 37. Alexander's Ragtime Band 38. The Gorilla 39. Tahiti Honey 43. Always Leave Them Laughing 49. What Price Glory? 52. What a Way to Go 64, many others.

Versois, Odile (1930–1980) (Militza de Poliakoff-Baidarov).
French leading lady, sister of Marina Vlady.

Les Dernières Vacances 46. Into the Blue (GB) 48. Bel Amour 51. A Day to Remember (GB) 53. *The Young Lovers*/Chance Meeting (GB) 55. To Paris with Love (GB) 55. Passport to Shame (GB) 58. Cartouche/Swords of Blood 62. Benjamin 68, etc.

Vertov, Dziga (1896–1954) (Dennis Kaufman).
Russian director and film theorist. Many documentaries.

One-Sixth of the World 27. The Man with the Movie Camera 28. Three Songs of Lenin 34. In the Line of Fire 41, etc.

Vetri, Victoria (1944–) (Angela Dorian).
Australian leading lady.

Chuka 67. Rosemary's Baby 68. When Dinosaurs Ruled the Earth 69. Invasion of the Bee Girls 73, etc.

Veysset, Sandrine.
French screenwriter and director. She studied art before working for director Leos CARAX as a set decorator and driver.

Will It Snow for Christmas? 96.

❝ People have the strangest ideas about cinema. There are so many other more complicated things – I find carpenters and sculptors a lot more impressive than film-makers. – *S.V.*

Vicas, Victor (1918–1985).
Franco-Russian director.

No Way Back 53. Double Destiny 54. Back to Kandara 57. The Wayward Bus 57. Count Five and Die (GB) 58. Les Disparus 60, etc.

Later in French TV.

Vickers, Martha (1925–1971) (M. MacVicar).
American leading lady of the 40s.

The Falcon in Mexico 44. *The Big Sleep* 46. Love and Learn 47. Ruthless 48. Bad Boy 49. Daughter of the West 51. The Burglar 57. Four Fast Guns 60, etc.

Victor, Charles (1896–1965).
British character actor with long stage experience: in films from 1938, usually in cockney roles.

The 39 Steps 35. Old Mother Riley in Society 40. Love on the Dole 41. Major Barbara 41. The Foreman Went to France 42. When We Are Married 43. San Demetrio – London 43. The Rake's Progress 45. Caesar and Cleopatra 45. The Way to the Stars 45. Gaiety George 46. The Magic Bow 47. The Cure for Love 49. The Elusive Pimpernel 50. The Magic Box 51. The Frightened Man 52. The Ringer 52. Meet Mr Lucifer 53. An Alligator Named Daisy 55. Charley Moon 56. Tiger in the Smoke 56. The Prince and the Showgirl 57. The Pit and the Pendulum 61, etc.

Victor, Henry (1898–1945).
British character actor, a silent screen star who went to Hollywood in the 30s and played villainous bit roles.

She 25. The Guns of Loos 28. The Fourth Commandment 28. The Mummy 33. Our Fighting Navy 37. Confessions of a Nazi Spy 39. Zanzibar 40. King of the Zombies 41. To Be or Not to Be 42. Sherlock Holmes and the Secret Weapon 42. They Got Me Covered 43, etc.

Victoria,
Queen of England 1837–1901, was born in 1819. Her full-length screen portraits were by Anna Neagle in *Victoria the Great* and *Sixty Glorious Years*, and by Irene Dunne, who failed rather badly, in *The Mudlark*. She was also played by Fay Compton in *The Prime Minister*, by Helena Pickard in *The Lady with the Lamp*, by Muriel Aked in *The Story of Gilbert and Sullivan*, by Sybil Thorndike in *Melba*, and by Mollie Maureen in *The Private Life of Sherlock Holmes*.

Vidal, Gore (1925–).
Elegant American novelist, essayist, dramatist, screenwriter, and occasional actor, an intellectual gadfly. In 1996, he angered Charlton Heston by claiming that there was a homosexual subtext to the film of *Ben-Hur*.

Autobiographies: 1992, *Screening History*. 1995, *Palimpsest: A Memoir*.

The Catered Affair (w) 56. I Accuse (w) 58. The Left-Handed Gun (oa) 58. The Scapegoat (co-w) 59. Visit to a Small Planet (oa) 60. Suddenly Last Summer 60. The Best Man (w, from his play) 64. Is Paris Burning? (co-w) 66. Last of the Mobile Hot-Shots (w) 70. Myra Breckinridge (oa) 70. Caligula (co-w) 79. Dress Gray (TV) 86. Gore Vidal's Lincoln (oa) (TV) 88. Gore Vidal's Billy the Kid (& a) (TV) 89. Bob Roberts (a) 92. With Honors (a) 94. The Eighth Day (a) 97. Shadow Conspiracy (a) 97, etc.

❝ As I now move, graciously, I hope, toward the door marked Exit, it occurs to me that the only thing I ever really liked to do was go to the movies. Naturally, Sex and Art always took precedence over the cinema. Unfortunately, neither ever proved to be as dependable as the filtering of present light through that moving strip of celluloid which projects past images and voices onto a screen. – *G.V.*

To write a script today means working for a committee of people who know nothing about movies, as opposed, say, to real estate or the higher art of bookkeeping. – *G.V., 1996*

Vidal, Henri (1919–1959).
Tough-looking French leading man, in films from 1940.

Les Maudits 46. Quai de Grenelle 50. Port du Désir 54. The Wicked Go to Hell 55. Porte des Lilas 56. Come Dance with Me 59, etc.

Vidgeon, Robin (1939–).
British cinematographer. He began as a second assistant cameraman in 1955 and previously worked on many films with cinematographer Douglas Slocombe and cameraman Chic Waterson.

Mr Corbett's Ghost 86. Hellraiser 87. Mr North 88. The Penitent 88. Hellbound: Hellraiser II 88. Parents 89. The Fly II 89. Nightbreed 90. Highway to Hell 92. Lady Chatterley (TV) 93. August 96, etc.

Vidor, Charles (1900–1959).
Hungarian-American director, in Hollywood from 1932.

Double Door 34. Sensation Hunters 34. The Great Gambini 37. *Blind Alley* 39. My Son My Son 40. The Lady in Question 40. Ladies in Retirement 41. The Tuttles of Tahiti 42. The Desperadoes 43. *Cover Girl* 44. Together Again 44. A Song to Remember 45. Over 21 45. *Gilda* 46. The Guilt of Janet Ames 48. Hans Christian Andersen 52. Love Me or Leave Me 55. The Swan 56. The Joker Is Wild 57. A Farewell to Arms 58. Song without End (part) 59, many others.

Vidor, Florence (1895–1977) (Florence Arto).
American leading lady of the silent screen.
Lying Lips 21. Barbara Frietchie 24. The Grand Duchess and the Waiter 26. Are Parents People? 26. The Patriot 28. Chinatown Nights 29, etc.

Vidor, King (1894–1982).
American director, formerly journalist; high style alternates with disappointing banality. Special AA 1979 'for his incomparable achievements as a cinematic creator and innovator'.
Autobiography: 1953, *A Tree Is a Tree*.
■ The Turn in the Road 18. Better Times 19. The Other Half 19. Poor Relations 19. The Jack Knife Man 19. The Family Honour 20. The Sky Pilot 21. Love Never Dies 21. Conquering the Woman 21. Woman Wake Up 21. The Real Adventure 22. Dusk to Dawn 22. Alice Adams 22. Peg O' My Heart 23. The Woman of Bronze 23. Three Wise Fools 23. Wild Oranges 23. Happiness 23. Wine of Youth 24. His Hour 24. Wife of the Centaur 24. Proud Flesh 25. *The Big Parade* 25. La Bohème 25. Bardelys the Magnificent 26. *The Crowd* (AAN) 28. *Show People* 28. *Hallelujah* (AAN) 29. Not So Dumb 30. *Billy the Kid* 30. *Street Scene* 31. *The Champ* (AAN) 31. Bird of Paradise 32. Cynara 32. The Stranger's Return 33. *Our Daily Bread* 34. The Wedding Night 34. So Red the Rose 35. The Texas Rangers 36. Stella Dallas 37. The Citadel (GB) (AAN) 38. *Northwest Passage* 39. Comrade X 40. H. M. Pulham Esq 41. An American Romance 44. Duel in the Sun 46. On Our Merry Way 47. *The Fountainhead* 49. Beyond the Forest 49. Lightning Strikes Twice 51. Japanese War Bride 52. Ruby Gentry 52. The Man without a Star 55. *War and Peace* (AAN) 56. Solomon and Sheba 59.
~In the last year of his life he acted a role in *Love and Money*.

Vierny, Sacha (1919–).
French cinematographer, associated with the films of Peter GREENAWAY.
Hiroshima Mon Amour 58. *Last Year in Marienbad* 61. Muriel 63. Do You Like Women? 64. *Belle de Jour* 67. Beau Père 81. A Zed and Two Noughts 85. The Cook, the Thief, His Wife and Her Lover 90. Drowning by Numbers 91. *Prospero's Books* 91. Rosa 92. The Baby of Macon 93. *The Pillow Book* 96, etc.

Viertel, Berthold (1885–1953).
Austrian director of stage and screen, playwright and poet. Born in Vienna, he began as an actor and stage director, then made films in Germany from the 20s. He settled in California in the late 20s, but continued for a time working in England and elsewhere in Europe. In the 50s he returned to Europe to direct plays. The first of his two wives was Salka VIERTEL, and he is the father of Peter VIERTEL. He is the model for Friedrich Bergmann in Christopher Isherwood's novel *Prater Violet*.
The Wise Sex 31. The Man from Yesterday 32. Little Friend 34. The Passing of the Third Floor Back 35. Rhodes of Africa 36, etc.

Viertel, Peter (1920–).
German-born novelist and screenwriter in Hollywood, the son of Berthold and Salka VIERTEL. Born in Dresden and raised in California, he wrote his first novel at the age of 18. Married (1944–59) Virginia Ray, one-time dancer in the Paramount chorus and former wife of writer Budd SCHULBERG, and, in 1960, actress Deborah KERR. He later moved back to live in Europe, dividing his time between Switzerland and Spain.
Autobiography: 1992, *Dangerous Friends*.
Saboteur (co-w) 42. Roughshow (oa) 49. We Were Strangers (co-w) 49. Decision before Dawn (co-w) 51. The Sun Also Rises (w) 57. The Old Man and the Sea (w) 58. Heaven Fell That Night (Fr./It.) 58. Blood and Roses (Fr./It.) (co-w) 60. Five Miles to Midnight (Fr./It.) 62. White Hunter, Black Heart (co-w, oa) 90, etc.

Viertel, Salka (1889–1978).
Polish-born actress and screenwriter, in Hollywood from the 30s and an American citizen from 1939. After acting in the Viennese theatre, she became a friend of Greta GARBO, and worked on some of the actress's films for MGM. She married director Berthold VIERTEL, and in the 30s and 40s their home was a refuge for European writers and actors; later she was the lover of Gottfried REINHARDT. In the 50s, she was blacklisted and moved back to Europe to find work. She was the mother of Peter VIERTEL.
Autobiography: 1969, *The Kindness of Strangers*.
Anna Christie (a) 30. Queen Christina (co-w) 31. The Painted Veil (co-w) 34. Anna Karenina (co-w) 35. Two-Faced Woman (co-w) 41. Deep Valley (co-w) 47. Il Battellieri del Volga (w) 58, etc.

Vigne, Daniel (1942–).
French director and screenwriter.
Les Hommes 73. The Return of Martin Guerre/Le Retour de Martin Guerre 83. One Woman or Two/Une Femme ou Deux 85. Comédie d'Eté 89. The King's Whore (co-w) 90, etc.

Vigo, Jean (1905–1934) (Jean Almereyda).
Influential French director on the strength of three semi-experimental, dream-like films.
■ *A Propos de Nice* 30. *Zéro de Conduite* 32. *L'Atalante* 34.

Vigoda, Abe (1921–).
American character actor, popular on TV in the 70s series *Barney Miller* and *Fish*.
The Godfather 71. The Don Is Dead 73. Newman's Law 74. Having Babies (TV) 76. The Cheap Detective 78. The Comedy Company (TV) 78. Vasectomy – a Delicate Matter 86. Plain Clothes 88. Look Who's Talking 89. Prancer 89. Joe versus the Volcano 90. Sugar Hill 93. Batman: Mask of the Phantasm (voice) 94. North 94. Jury Duty 95. Underworld 96. Love Is All There Is 96. A Brooklyn State of Mind 97. Underworld 97. Good Burger 97, etc.

Villa-Lobos, Heitor (1887–1959).
Brazilian composer who worked in Hollywood on *Green Mansions* 59.

Villalobos, Reynaldo.
American cinematographer.
Urban Cowboy 80. Nine to Five 80. Blame It on Rio 84. Lucas 86. Punchline 88. Major League 89. Coup de Ville 90. American Me 92. A Bronx Tale 93. Roosters 95. Romy and Michelle's High School Reunion 97. Telling Lies in America 97. Loved 97. An Alan Smithee film: Burn, Hollywood, Burn 97. Return to Paradise 98, etc.

Villard, Frank (1917–1980) (François Drouineau).
French leading man, often in shifty roles.
Le Dernier des Six 41. Gigi 48. Manèges/The Wanton 49. L'Ingénue Libertine 50. Le Garçon Sauvage 51. Huis Clos 54. Crime Passionnel 55. Mystères de Paris 57. Le Cave se Rebiffe 61. Gigot 62. Mata Hari 64, etc.

Villaverde, Teresa (1966–).
Portuguese director and screenwriter, born in Lisbon.
Alex/A Idade Maior 91. Two Brothers, My Sisters/Tres Irmaos 94. The Mutants 98, etc.

Villechaize, Herve (1943–1993).
French dwarf actor in international films. His health deteriorating, he committed suicide.
The Man with the Golden Gun 73. The One and Only 78. Forbidden Zone 80, etc.
TV series: Fantasy Island 77–82.

Villiers, James (1933–).
British actor, usually in snooty or villainous roles.
The Entertainer 60. The Damned 64. King and Country 64. The Nanny 65. Half a Sixpence 67. Some Girls Do 68. Otley 68. A Nice Girl Like Me 69. Blood from the Mummy's Tomb 70. The Ruling Class 71. Saint Jack 79. The Scarlet Pimpernel (TV) 82. Under the Volcano 84. Fortunes of War (TV) 87. Mountains of the Moon 90. King Ralph 91. Let Him Have It 91. The Tichborne Claimant 98, etc.

Villon, François (1431–c. 1470) (François de Loges).
French poet who led the life of a Robin Hood and was romanticized in *If I Were King* (in which he was played by Ronald Colman) and its musical version *The Vagabond King* (Dennis King, Oreste Kirkop).

Vilsmaier, Joseph (1939–).
German director, producer, screenwriter and cinematographer, born in Munich.
Herbstmilch 89. Rama Dama (& co-w) 91. Stalingrad (& co-w) 93. Charlie & Louise 94. Brother of Sleep/Schlafes Bruder (& co-w) 94. Comedian Harmonists 98, etc.

Vince, Pruitt Taylor (1960–).
American character actor, born in Baton Rouge, Louisiana.
Shy People 87. Angel Heart 87. Barfly 87. Mississippi Burning 88. Red Heat 88. K-9 88. Jacob's Ladder 90. Come See the Paradise 90. Wild at Heart 91. JFK 91. China Moon 94. City Slickers II: The Legend of Curly's Gold 94. Nobody's Fool 94. Natural Born Killers 94. Heavy 95. Under the Hula Moon 95. Beautiful Girls 96. A Further Gesture/The Break 97. The End of Violence 97, etc.

Vincent, Alex (1982–).
American child actor of the 80s, best known as Andy, the owner of the Chucky doll in two *Child's Play* horror movies.
Child's Play 88. Wait until Spring, Bandini 89. Child's Play 2 90. My Family Treasure 93, etc.

Vincent, Jan-Michael (1944–).
Boyish American leading man, usually in forgettable films, who first came to notice in the TV soap opera *The Survivors* 69–70. He was seriously injured in a car crash in 1996.
The Undefeated 68. Tribes (TV) 70. The Mechanic 72. The World's Greatest Athlete 73. Buster and Billie 74. Bite the Bullet 74. White Line Fever 75. Baby Blue Marine 76. Damnation Alley 77. Hooper 78. Big Wednesday 78. Defiance 80. Hard Country 81. *The Winds of War* (TV) 83. Last Plane Out 83. Born in East L.A. 87. Deadly Embrace 88. Hit List 89. Hangfire 90. Raw Nerve 91. Animal Instincts 92. Xtro II 92. Indecent Behaviour 94. Red Line 96. Orbit 96. Body Count 97. Buffalo '66 97, etc.
TV series: Airwolf 84–86.

Vincent, June (1919–).
Blond American leading lady of some 40s 'B's.
Ladies Courageous 44. The Climax 44. Can't Help Singing 44. Here Come the Co-eds 45. That's the Spirit 45. Black Angel 46. Shed No Tears 48. The Lone Wolf and His Lady 49. Mary Ryan, Detective 50. Secrets of Monte Carlo 51. Clipped Wings 53. City of Shadows 55. The Miracle of the Hills 59, etc.

Vincent, Robbie (1896–1966).
English comedian who appeared in some low-budget farces starring Frank Randle. Best known for his role as Enoch alongside Harry Korris and Cecil Frederick in the 40s radio show *Happidrome*.
Somewhere in England 40. Somewhere in Camp 42. Somewhere on Leave 42. Happidrome 43, etc.

Vincze, Ernest (1942–).
British cinematographer.
Jane Austen in Manhattan 81. A Woman of Substance (TV) 84. Biggles 85. Shanghai Surprise 85. Escape from Sobibor (TV) 86. The Nightmare Years (TV) 89. Cream in My Coffee (TV) 90. The Camomile Lawn (TV) 92. The Dance 98, etc.

Vinson, Helen (1907–) (Helen Rulfs).
Cool, aristocratic leading lady of Hollywood films of the 30s and 40s.
Jewel Robbery 31. I Am a Fugitive from a Chain Gang 32. The Power and the Glory 33. The Tunnel (GB) 35. Vogues of 1938. In Name Only 39. Torrid Zone 40. Nothing But the Truth 41. They Are Guilty 44. The Lady and the Doctor (last to date) 46, etc.

Visconti, Luchino (1906–1976) (L. V. de Modrone).
Italian writer-director, former art director.
Biography: 1982, *Luchino Visconti* by Gaia Servadio.
Book: 1998, *Visconti: Explorations of Beauty and Decay* by Henry Bacon.
Ossessione 42. *La Terra Trema* 48. Bellissima 51. Siamo Donne (part) 52. *Senso* 53. White Nights 57. *Rocco and His Brothers* 60. Boccaccio 70 62. *The Leopard* 63. *The Damned* 69. Death in Venice 70. Conversation Piece 76, etc.

Vitale, Milly (1928–).
Italian leading lady in American films.
The Juggler 53. The Seven Little Foys 55. A Breath of Scandal 60.

Vitti, Monica (1933–) (Monica Luisa Ceciarelli).
Italian leading lady in international demand in the 60s.
L'Avventura 59. La Notte 60. *L'Eclisse* 62. Dragées au Poivre 63. Nutty Naughty Château 64. *The Red Desert* 64. Modesty Blaise (GB) 65. The Chastity Belt 67. Girl with a Pistol 69. The Pacifist 71. Duck in Orange Sauce 75. An Almost Perfect Affair 79. The Mystery of Oberwald 80. Tango della Gelosia 81. When Veronica Calls 83. Secret Scandal/Scandalo Segreto (& co-w, d) 89, etc.

Viva (1941–) (Janet Sue Hoffman).
Witty, skinny American star of Andy Warhol's films, originally a painter and also a novelist. She was played by Tahnee Welch in the bio-pic *I Shot Andy Warhol* 96.
The Loves of Ondine 67. Bikeboy 67. Nude Restaurant 67. *Lonesome Cowboys* 68. Blue Movie 69. Lion's Love 69. Play It Again, Sam 72. Forbidden Zone 80. State of Things 82, etc.

Vlad, Roman (1919–).
Romanian composer.
La Beauté du Diable 49. Sunday in August 50. Three Steps North 51. Romeo and Juliet 54. Knave of Hearts 54. The Law 60. The Mighty Ursus 62. The Young Toscanini 88, etc.

Vlady, Marina (1938–) (Marina de Poliakoff-Baidarov).
French leading lady, sister of Odile Versois.
Orage d'Eté 49. Avant le Déluge 53. The Wicked Go to Hell 55. Crime and Punishment 56. Toi le Venin 59. La Steppa 61. Climats 62. Enough Rope 63. Dragées au Poivre 63. Queen Bee 64. Chimes at Midnight 66. Sapho 70. Les Jeux de la Comtesse 80. Bordello 85. Twist Again à Moscou 86. Migrations 88. Follow Me 89. Splendor 89. The Dream of Russia/Kodayu 91. The Son of Gascogne/Le Fils de Gascogne 95, etc.

Vogel, Paul C. (1899–1975).
American cinematographer.
The Lady in the Lake 46. Black Hand 49. *Battleground* (AA) 49. Rose Marie 54. High Society 56. The Wings of Eagles 56. The Time Machine 60. The Rounders 64, etc.

Vogel, Virgil (1919–1996).
American director, from TV.
The Mole People 56. Terror in the Midnight Sun 58. Son of Ali Baba 64. The Return of Joe Forrester (TV) 75. Law of the Land (TV) 76. Centennial (part) (TV) 78. Beulah Land (TV) 80. Longarm (TV) 88. Mario and the Mob (TV) 92, etc.

Vogler, Karl Michael (1928–).
German stage actor who has appeared in a few international films.
Those Magnificent Men in Their Flying Machines 65. The Blue Max 67. How I Won the War 67. Patton 69. Downhill Racer 69. Deep End 70, etc.

Voight, Jon (1938–).
American leading actor of the 70s.
The Hour of the Gun 67. Fearless Frank 68. Out of It 69. *Midnight Cowboy* (AAN) 69. The Revolutionary 70. The All American Boy 70. Catch 22 70. *Deliverance* 72. Conrack 74. The Odessa File 74. End of the Game 75. Coming Home (AA) 78. The Champ 79. Lookin' to Get Out 82. Table for Five 83. Runaway Train (AAN) 85. Desert Bloom 86. Eternity 90. Chernobyl: The Final Warning (TV) 91. Return to Lonesome Dove (TV) 93. Heat 95. Mission: Impossible 96. Anaconda 96. U-Turn 97. Most Wanted 97. Boys Will Be Boys 97. John Grisham's The Rainmaker 97. The General 98. Enemy of the State 98, etc.
Famous line (*Midnight Cowboy*): 'I'll tell you the truth now. I ain't a real cowboy, but I am one hell of a stud.'

Volk, Stephen.
British screenwriter and dramatist specializing in horror stories.
Gothic 86. The Kiss (co-w) 88. The Guardian (co-w) 90.

Volonté, Gian Maria (1933–1994).
Italian leading man of the 60s.
A Fistful of Dollars 64. For a Few Dollars More 65. We Still Kill the Old Way 68. *Investigation of a*

Citizen above Suspicion 69. Sacco and Vanzetti 71. The Working Class Go to Heaven 72. Lucky Luciano 73. Christ Stopped at Eboli 79. Chronicle of a Death Foretold/Cronaca di una Morte Annunciata 87. Tre Colonne in Cronaca 89. Open Doors/Porte Aperte 90. A Simple Story/Una Storia Semplice 91. Funes, un Gran Amor (Arg.) 93. Tirano Banderas 94, etc.

Von Bargen, Daniel.
American actor, from the stage.

Silence of the Lambs 91. Company Business 91. Shadows and Fog 92. Basic Instinct 92. Six Degrees of Separation 93. The Saint of Fort Washington 93. Philadelphia 93. Rising Sun 93. IQ 94. Crimson Tide 95. Lord of Illusions 95. Before and After 96. Looking for Richard 96. Broken Arrow 96. The Real Blonde 97. Amistad 97. GI Jane 97. The Postman 97, etc.

Von Brandenstein, Patrizia (1943–).
American production designer.

Heartland 79. Tell Me a Riddle 80. Silkwood 83. Touched 83. Amadeus (AA) 84. A Chorus Line 85. The Money Pit 86. No Mercy 87. The Untouchables (AAN) 87. Betrayed 88. Working Girl 88. The Lemon Sisters 90. State of Grace 90. Postcards from the Edge 90. Billy Bathgate 91. Sneakers 92. Leap of Faith 92. Six Degrees of Separation 93. The Quick and the Dead 95. Mercury Rising 98. A Simple Plan 98, etc.

Von Dassanowsky, Elfi (1924–).
Austrian-born actress, producer, singer and musician, now resident in the USA. She trained as a pianist and opera singer at Vienna's Academy of Music, but turned down a contract as an actress from UFA in Berlin because of its associations with the Nazi Party. She taught Curt JURGENS to play piano for his first major role in *Wen die Götter Lieben* 42. In the mid-40s, with producer Emmerich Hanus, she founded Belvedere Film, which helped kick-start the revival of the German film industry, and later worked as a casting director.

AS PRODUCER: Symphonie in Salzburg 46. Die Glücksmühle (& a) 47. Kunstschätze des Klosterneuburger Stiftes 47. The Freckle/Der Leberfleck 48. Doktor Rosin 49. Märchen vom Glück 49. Walzer von Strauss/Waltz by Strauss 52, etc.

Von Harbou, Thea (1888–1954).
German screenwriter, mainly associated with Fritz Lang's silent films.

Der Müde Tod 21. *Dr Mabuse* 22. *Nibelungen Saga* 24. Chronicles of the Grey House 25. *Metropolis* 26. The Spy 28. The Woman in the Moon 29. *The Testament of Dr Mabuse* 32. The Old and the Young King 35. Annélie 41. Fahrt ins Gluck 45. The Affairs of Dr Holl 51, many others.

Von Seyffertitz, Gustav (1863–1943).
Dignified German character actor in Hollywood films; during World War I was known as G. Butler Clonblough.

Old Wives for New 18. Moriarty (title role) 22. Sparrows 26. The Wizard 27. Docks of New York 28. The Bat Whispers 30. Shanghai Express 32.

Queen Christiana 33. She 35. In Old Chicago 38. Nurse Edith Cavell 39, many others.

Von Sternberg, Josef (1894–1969) (Jonas Sternberg).
Austrian-American director, a great pictorial stylist and the creator of Marlene Dietrich's American image.

Autobiography: 1965, *Fun in a Chinese Laundry.* A critical study by Herman G. Weinberg was published in 1967.

■ *The Salvation Hunters* 25. The Seagull (unreleased) 26. *Underworld* 27. The Last Command 28. The Dragnet 28. *Docks of New York* 28. The Case of Lena Smith 29. Thunderbolt 29. *The Blue Angel* (Ger.) 30. Morocco (AAN) 30. Dishonoured 31. An American Tragedy 31. *Shanghai Express* (AAN) 32. Blonde Venus 32. *The Scarlet Empress* 34. *The Devil is a Woman* 35. The King Steps Out 36. Crime and Punishment 36. I Claudius (unfinished) 37. Sergeant Madden 39. *The Shanghai Gesture* 41. Jet Pilot 50. Macao 51. The Saga of Anatahan (Jap.) 53.

✪ For being the kind of director who, if he didn't exist, publicists would have to invent. *The Scarlet Empress.*

66 I care nothing about the story, only how it is photographed and presented. – J.V.S.

The only way to succeed is to make people hate you. That way they remember you. – J.V.S.

A lyricist of light and shadow rather than a master of montage. – *Andrew Sarris, 1968*

He brought to the screen new horizons in the art of lighting, to the photography of shadowed and broken rays . . . His scenes seem almost always to be seen through streamers and feathers, through loose gauze, through slatted shutters or an intricate lattice wall. – *Ivan Butler*

Von Stroheim, Erich (1885–1957) (Hans Erich Maria Stroheim Von Nordenwall).
Austrian actor and director whose ruthless extravagance in Hollywood in the 20s harmed his later career. Usually played despotic villains or stiff-necked Prussians.

Biographies: 1954, *Hollywood Scapegoat* by Peter Noble. 1972, *Erich Von Stroheim* by Tom Curtis.

AS ACTOR: The Heart of Humanity 18. Blind Husbands 19. *Foolish Wives* 21. The Wedding March 27. The Great Gabbo 29. Three Faces East 30. Friends and Lovers 30. The Lost Squadron 32. As You Desire Me 32. Walking Down Broadway 32. Crimson Romance 35. The Crime of Dr Crespi 35. *La Grande Illusion* 37. Mademoiselle Docteur 37. Alibi 38. Boys' School 39. I Was an Adventuress 40. Thunder Over Parièges 40. So Ends Our Night 41. *Five Graves to Cairo* 43. North Star 43. The Lady and the Monster 44. Storm Over Lisbon 44. 32 Rue de Montmartre 44. The Great Flamarion 45. La Danse de Mort 47. *Sunset Boulevard* (AAN) 50. La Maison du Crime 52. Napoleon 54. L'Homme aux Cents Visages 56, etc.
■ AS DIRECTOR: *Blind Husbands* 19. *The Devil's Passkey* 19. *Foolish Wives* 21. Merry Go Round 22. *Greed* 23. The Merry Widow 25. *The Wedding March* 27. *Queen Kelly* 28.

✪ For taking Hollywood on and winning – for a while. *Greed.*

66 The difference between me and Lubitsch is that he shows you the king on the throne and then he shows you the king in his bedroom. I show you the king in his bedroom first. Then when you see him

on the throne you have no illusions about him. – E.V.S.

When I first saw Von Stroheim at the wardrobe tests, I clicked my heels and said, 'Isn't it ridiculous, little me directing you, when you were always ten years ahead of your time?' And he replied, 'Twenty.' – *Billy Wilder, 1942*

As to directing his own performance, Von always had an assistant to give him an opinion of his acting. Whether he listened to it or not was another matter. – *William Daniels*

One of the cinema's great enigmas . . . he conjured up a world very much in its infancy psychologically. It was a grotesque and brutal world, and the bleakness and callousness of his characters' lives were revealed with a meticulous realism. – *Claire Johnston*

He was a short man, almost squat, with a vulpine smirk that told you, as soon as his image flashed on to the screen, that no wife or bankroll must be left unguarded. – *S.J. Perelman*

Von Sydow, Max (1929–) (Carl Adolf Von Sydow).
Leading Swedish actor, a member of Ingmar BERGMAN's company.

Miss Julie 51. *The Seventh Seal* 56. Wild Strawberries 57. So Close to Life 58. *The Face* 59. The Virgin Spring 60. *Through a Glass Darkly* 61. Winter Light 62. The Mistress 62. *The Greatest Story Ever Told* (as Jesus) (US) 65. The Reward (US) 65. *Hawaii* (US) 66. The Quiller Memorandum (GB) 66. *Hour of the Wolf* 67. The Shame 68. The Kremlin Letter (US) 69. The Touch 71. Embassy 72. *The Emigrants* 72. The Exorcist (US) 73. The New Land 75. Foxtrot 76. Three Days of the Condor (US) 76. Voyage of the Damned 76. Exorcist II: The Heretic 77. March or Die 77. Brass Target 78. Hurricane 79. Flash Gordon 80. Victory 81. Never Say Never Again 83. Kojak: The Belarus File (TV) 85. Christopher Columbus (TV) 85. The Wolf at the Door 85. The Second Victory 86. Duet for One 86. Hannah and Her Sisters 86. *Pelle the Conqueror* (AAN) 88. Katinka (d) 88. My Dear Doctor Grasler/Mio Caro Dottor Gräsler 89. Awakenings 90. Father 90. A Kiss before Dying 91. Until the End of the World/Bis ans Ende der Welt 91. The Bachelor 91. The Ox/Oxen 91. The Touch 92. Best Intentions 92. Morfars Resa 93. Needful Things 93. Time Is Money 94. Judge Dredd 95. Hamsun (title role) 95. Citizen X (TV) 95. Jerusalem 96. Hostile Waters 97. What Dreams May Come 98. Private Confessions 98, etc.

Von Trier, Lars (1956–).
Danish director, screenwriter and producer. Born in Copenhagen, he studied film at the University of Copenhagen and began making short films in the mid-70s before graduating from the National Film School in the early 80s. His *Breaking the Waves* won the Grand Jury Prize at the Cannes Film Festival in 1996. In 1998 his production company Zentropa launched a new division, Pussy Power, to produce erotic films.

Element of Crime 84. Epidemic 89. *Europa*/Zentropa 91. The Kingdom/Riget 94. Breaking the Waves 96. Idiots/Idioterne 98, etc.

Von Trotta, Margarethe (1942–).
German director who married Volker Schlöndorff.

The Lost Honour of Katerina Blum (co-d) 75. The Second Awakening of Krista Clarges 77. Sisters

79. The German Sisters 81. Friends and Husbands 83. Rosa Luxemburg 85. Felix 87. The Return/Die Rückkehr 90. Three Sisters/Paura e Amore 90. The African/L'Africana 91. Anni del Muro 93. Il Lungo Silenzio (It.) 94. The Promise 95, etc.

Vonnegut, Kurt.
American novelist, often of science fiction, who gained a cult following from the 60s.

Slaughterhouse Five (oa) 72. Harrison Bergeron (TV) (oa) 95. Mother Night (oa) 96, etc.

66 I tell you, we are here on Earth to fart around, and don't let anybody tell you any different. – K.V.

Vorhaus, Bernard (c. 1898–).
German director, mostly in Britain and Hollywood.

Money for Speed (GB) 33. Broken Melody (GB) 35. Cotton Queen (GB) 37. Three Faces West (US) 40. Lady from Louisiana (US) 41. Bury Me Dead (US) 47. So Young So Bad (US) 50. The Lady from Boston (US) 51, etc.

Vorkapich, Slavko (1892–1976).
Yugoslavian writer who came to Hollywood in 1922, did a little screenwriting, tried direction in 1931 (*I Take This Woman*), then settled as a montage expert.

Viva Villa 34. *Crime without Passion* 34. San Francisco 36. Maytime 37. The Last Gangster 38. Shopworn Angel 38. Mr Smith Goes to Washington 39, etc.

Voskovec, George (1905–1981) (Jiri Voskovec).
Czech stage actor, long in US.

Anything Can Happen 52. *Twelve Angry Men* 57. The Bravados 58. Butterfield 8 60. The Spy Who Came in from the Cold 65. Mister Buddwing 66. The Boston Strangler 68. Skag (TV) 80. Somewhere in Time 80. Barbarossa 82, etc.

Vosper, Frank (1899–1937).
British stage actor and playwright who appeared in a few films.

Blinkeyes 26. The Last Post 27. Rome Express 32. Waltzes from Vienna 33. The Man Who Knew Too Much 34. Jew Süss 34. Open All Night 34. Heart's Desire 35.

Voulgaris, Pantelis (1940–).
Greek director and screenwriter. Born in Athens and a former film critic, he worked as an assistant director in the 60s.

The Engagement of Anna/To Proxenio tis Annas 72. O Megalos Erotikos 73. Happy Day 75. Venizelos 80. Stone Years/Petrina Chronia 85. The Striker with the No. 9/I Fanella Me To Ennia 98. Quiet Days in August 91. Acropole 95. It's a Long Road/Ola Ine Dromos 98, etc.

Vye, Murvyn (1913–1976).
Burly American character actor who usually played heavies.

Golden Earrings 48. A Connecticut Yankee at King Arthur's Court 49. Pick-Up 51. Road to Bali 52. Green Fire 54. Pearl of the South Pacific 55. Al Capone 58. Pay or Die 60. Andy 64, etc.

Wachowski, Andy (1967–) and **Larry** (1965–).
American directors and producers, born in Chicago, Illinois, who are billed as the Wachowski Brothers.
Assassins (co-w) 95. Bound (wd) 96. The Matrix (wd) 99.

Waddington, Patrick (1900–1987).
Elegant British character actor, mostly on stage.
Journey Together 45. School for Secrets 46. The Wooden Horse 51. A Night to Remember 56, etc.

Waddington, Steven (1968?–).
English actor, from the stage. Born in Leeds, he studied at the East 15 Acting School. After playing the role of a boxer in *Seconds Out* (TV) 92, he has become an occasional professional boxer.
Edward II 91. 1492: Conquest of Paradise 92. The Last of the Mohicans 92. The Prince of Jutland 94. Don't Get Me Started 94. Carrington 95. Ivanhoe (title role, TV) 97. Face 97. Tarzan and the Lost City 98, etc.

Wadleigh, Michael (1941–).
American director who began in TV as a documentary film-maker and director of music specials.
Woodstock 70. Wolfen 81.

Wadsworth, Henry (1902–1974).
American juvenile of the 20s and 30s.
Applause 29. Luxury Liner 33. The Thin Man 34. Ceiling Zero 35. Dr Rhythm 38. Silver Skates 43, many others.

Wager, Anthony (1933–).
British juvenile actor who played Young Pip in the 1946 *Great Expectations* and later turned up on Australian television.
The Secret Tunnel 47. Night of the Prowler 62. The Hi-Jackers 63. Shadow of Fear 63. The Night Caller/Blood Beast from Outer Space 65, etc.

Waggner, George (1894–1984).
American director, mainly of routine low-budgeters, in Hollywood from 1920.
The Wolf Man 41. The Climax (& p) 44. Cobra Woman (& p) 45. The Fighting Kentuckian (& w) 49. Operation Pacific (& w) 51. Bitter Creek 54. Destination 60,000 (& w) 57. Pale Arrow 58, many others.

Wagner, Fritz Arno (1889–1958).
German cinematographer.
Nosferatu 23. *The Loves of Jeanne Ney* 27. The Spy 28. Westfront 1918 30. *Die Dreigroschenoper* 31. Kameradschaft 31. Amphitryon 35. Ohm Krüger 41. Hotel Adlon 55, many others.

Wagner, Lindsay (1949–).
American leading lady of the 70s, a former model and singer.
The Paper Chase 73. Two People 74. The Incredible Journey of Meg Laurel (TV) 79. Scruples (TV) 81. The Two Worlds of Jennie Logan (TV) 81. Callie and Company (TV) 82. Princess Daisy (TV) 83. Martin's Day 84. Ricochet 91. Fire in the Dark 91. Danielle Steel's Once in a Lifetime (TV) 94. Contagious (TV) 96, etc.
TV series: The Bionic Woman 76–78. Jessie 84.

Wagner, Natasha Gregson (1970–).
American actress, the daughter of actress Natalie Wood and English producer Richard Gregson. She is the stepdaughter of actor Robert Wagner.
Fathers and Sons 92. Tainted Blood 93. The Substitute 93. Molly and Gina 94. Dead Beat 94. Inside the Goldmine 94. S.F.W. 94. Mind Ripper 95. Lost Highway 96. Two

Girls and a Guy 98. Another Day in Paradise 98, etc.

Wagner, Paula.
American producer, a former agent and theatre actress; partner with actor Tom Cruise in C/W Productions. She graduated in drama at Carnegie-Mellon University.
Mission Impossible 96. Without Limits 97. Mission Impossible 2 99, etc.

Wagner, Robert (1930–).
American leading man spotted by talent scout while still at college. His first wife was actress Natalie Wood and his third actress Jill St John. He is the stepfather of actress Natasha Gregson Wagner.
Halls of Montezuma (debut) 50. With a Song in My Heart 52. Titanic 53. Prince Valiant 54. Broken Lance 54. White Feather 55. The Mountain 56. A Kiss Before Dying 56. The Hunters 57. Say One for Me 58. All the Fine Young Cannibals 59. The Longest Day 62. The Condemned of Altona 63. Harper 66. The Biggest Bundle of Them All 66. Don't Just Stand There 68. Winning 69. The Streets of San Francisco (TV) 71. City Beneath the Sea (TV) 71. The Affair (TV) 73. The Towering Inferno 74. Death at Love House (TV) 76. Midway 76. The Concorde – Airport '79 79. Curse of the Pink Panther 83. I Am the Cheese 83. To Catch a King (TV) 84. This Gun for Hire (TV) 91. Dragon: The Bruce Lee Story 93. Parallel Lives (TV) 94. Austin Powers: International Man of Mystery 97. Wild Things 98, etc.
TV series: It Takes a Thief 65–69. Colditz 72–73. Switch 75–76. Hart to Hart 79–83. Lime Street 85.

Wah, Yuen.
Hong Kong star of action films, often as a villain. A former stunt double for Bruce Lee, he began with the Seven Little Fortunes performing troupe which also included Jackie Chan, Samo Hung and Yuen Biao.
Iron Finger of Death 73. To Kill a Mastermind 80. Eastern Condors 86. Dragons Forever 87. On the Run 88. Iceman Cometh 89. She Shoots Straight 90. Fist of Fury Part II 91. Kid from Tibet 91. Police Story III: Super Cop 92, etc.

Wahl, Ken (1957–).
Giant-sized American leading man.
■ The Buddy Holly Story 78. Every Which Way But Loose 79. The Champ 79. The Wanderers 79. Running Scared 79. Fort Apache, the Bronx 81. Race for the Yankee Zephyr 81. Jinxed! 82. Code Name The Soldier 82. Purple Heart 84. The Taking of Beverly Hills 91. The Favor 94, etc.
TV series: Double Dare 85. Wiseguy 87–89.

Wahlberg, Mark (1971–).
American leading actor, a former rap performer. Born in Boston, Massachusetts, he was first known as rapper Marky Mark, gaining notoriety for his on-stage antics, and for a past that included brief sentences for assault and drug dealing.
The Substitute 93. Renaissance Man 94. The Basketball Diaries 95. Fear 96. Traveller 96. *Boogie Nights* 97. The Big Hit 98, etc.

Wainwright, James (1938–).
American general-purpose actor.
The President's Plane Is Missing (TV) 71. Joe Kidd 72. Killdozer (TV) 74. The Private Files of J. Edgar Hoover 77. Mean Dog Blues 78. My Undercover Years with the Ku Klux Klan (TV) 79. Warlords of the 21st Century/Battletruck 82, etc.
TV series: Jigsaw 72. Beyond Westworld 79.

Wainwright, Rupert.
British director working in Hollywood, from television and music videos.
Dillinger (TV) 91. Blank Check 94. The Sadness of Sex 95, etc.

Waite, Ralph (1928–).
Reliable-looking American general-purpose actor.
Cool Hand Luke 67. Last Summer 69. Five Easy Pieces 70. The Grissom Gang 71. Kid Blue 72. The Stone Killer 73. On the Nickel (p, wd only) 80. OHMS (TV) 80. Angel City (TV) 81. Crash and Burn 90, etc.
TV series: The Waltons 72–78.

Waite, Ric.
American cinematographer, from TV films.
The Long Riders 80. The Border 82. Tex 82. 48 Hours 82. Class 83. Uncommon Valor 83. Footloose 84. Red Dawn 84. Brewster's Millions 85. Volunteers 85. Cobra 86. Adventures in Babysitting 87. The Great Outdoors 88. Marked for Death 90. Out for Justice 91. Rapid Fire 92. The Bodyguard 92. Cliffhanger 93. On Deadly Ground 94. Sioux City 94. Truth or Consequences, N.M. 97, etc.

Waits, Tom (1949–).
Laconic American singer-songwriter, composer and actor.
Paradise Alley (a) 78. On the Nickel (s) 80. Wolfen (a) 81. One from the Heart (a, m) (AANm) 82. Rumblefish (a) 83. The Outsiders (a) 83. The Cotton Club (a) 84. Streetwise (s) 84. Down by Law (a) 86. Ironweed (a) 87. Candy Mountain (a, m) 88. Cold Feet (a) 89. Bearskin: An Urban Fairytale (a, s) 90. The Two Jakes (a) 90. Queen's Logic (a) 90. The Fisher King (a) 91. At Play in the Fields of the Lord (a) 91. Night on Earth (m) 92. Deadfall (a) 92. Bram Stoker's Dracula (a) 92. Short Cuts (a) 93, etc.

Wajda, Andrzej (1926–).
Polish director.
A Generation 54. *Kanal* 55. *Ashes and Diamonds* 58. The Siberian Lady Macbeth 61. Love at Twenty (part only) 62. Ashes 64. Everything for Sale 67. Gates to Paradise 67. The Birch Wood 71. Landscape after a Battle 72. The Wedding 72. Promised Land 74. Shadow Line 76. *Man of Marble* 77. Without Anesthetic 79. *Man of Iron* 80. Danton 82. A Love in Germany/Eine Liebe in Deutschland 83. Chronicle of Love Affairs/Kronika Wypadkow Milosnych 86. The Possessed/Les Possédés 87. Korczak 90. The Ring with a Crowned Eagle 93. Nastazja 94. Holy Week 96. Miss Nobody 97, etc.

Wakamatsu, Koji. (1936–).
Japanese director. After working as a contract director for Nikkatsu in the early 60s, he became a leading director of PINK MOVIES, low-budget works on erotic and political themes.
History behind Walls/Kabe No Nakano Himegoto 65. The Embryo/Taji Ga Mitsuryo Suru Toki 66. Violated Angels/Okasaretabyakui 67. Sex-Jack/Sekusu-Jakku 70. Angelic Orgasm/Tenshi No Kokotsu 72. A Pool without Water/Mizu No Nai Puuru 82, etc.

Wakefield, Duggie (1899–1951).
British music-hall comedian, in character as a simpleton who always triumphed. He appeared in knockabout, low-budget comedies of the 30s with 'his Gang' (Chuck O'Neil, Billy Nelson, Jack Butler). Married variety performer Edie Stansfeld, the sister of Gracie Fields. He was the brother of Oliver Wakefield.
I'll Be Suing You 33. This Week of Grace 33.

Look Up and Laugh 35. The Penny Pool 37. Calling All Crooks 38. Spy for a Day 40, etc.

Wakefield, Hugh (1888–1971).
British character actor on stage from childhood. Usually seen in monocled roles.
City of Song 30. The Sport of Kings 31. The Man Who Knew Too Much 34. The Crimson Circle 36. The Street Singer 37. Blithe Spirit 45. One Night with You 48. Love's a Luxury 52. The Million Pound Note 54, etc.

Wakefield, Oliver (1909–1956).
English comedian and character actor, in silly-ass roles, the brother of Duggie Wakefield. His music-hall act was billed as 'The Voice of Inexperience'.
Let's Make a Night of It 37. French Leave 37. There Was a Young Man 37. Down Our Alley 39. Shipyard Sally 39. George and Margaret 40. The Briggs Family 40. Let the People Sing 42. The Peterville Diamond 42, etc.

Wakeford, Kent L.
American cinematographer.
Black Belt Jones 74. Alice Doesn't Live Here Any More 75. The Princess Academy 87. The Women's Club 87. China O'Brien 90. Total Exposure 91. The Last Hour 91. China O'Brien II 91. Night Eyes II 92. Ironheart 92. Hold Me, Thrill Me, Kiss Me 92. The Ghost Brigade 93. Some Folks Call It a Sling Blade 94. Love, Cheat & Steal (TV) 93. Boy Crazy, Girl Crazier 95. Wedding Bell Blues 96. Power 98 96. Loser 97. Last Lives 97, etc.

Wakeman, Rick (1949–).
British composer and keyboard player, a former member of the rock band Yes.
■ Lisztomania 75. White Rock 77. The Burning 82. She 83. Crimes of Passion 84. Creepshow II 87. Midnight in St Petersburg 95. Bullet to Beijing 95.

Wakhevitch, Georges (1907–1984).
Russian art director in international films.
Madame Bovary 34. La Grande Illusion 37. Prison without Bars 38. Les Visiteurs du Soir 42. L'Eternel Retour 43. L'Homme au Chapeau Rond 46. Dédée 48. The Medium 51. The Beggar's Opera 53. Don Juan 56. Marie-Octobre 59. Black Tights 60. King of Kings 61. Diary of a Chambermaid 64. Tendre Voyou 66. Mayerling 68. King Lear 70, etc.

Walas, Chris.
American designer and creator of special effects, make-up effects, and fantasy creatures, now also working as a director.
Galaxina (make-up) 80. Scanners (make-up) 81. Caveman (creature) 81. Raiders of the Lost Ark (make-up) 81. Gremlins (creatures) 84. The Fly (fx) (AA for make-up) 86. House II: The Second Story (creatures) 87. The Kiss (creatures) 88. The Fly II (d) 89. Arachnophobia (creatures) 90. Naked Lunch (creatures) 91. The Vagrant (d) 92. Jade (make-up) 95. Virtuosity (make-up) 95, etc.

Walbrook, Anton (1900–1967) (Adolf Wohlbruck).
Distinguished Austrian actor who came to Britain in the mid-30s.
Maskerade 34. The Student of Prague 35. *Michael Strogoff* (US) 37. *Victoria the Great* 37. The Rat 37. Sixty Glorious Years 38. *Gaslight* 39. Dangerous Moonlight 40. 49th Parallel 41. *The Life and Death of Colonel Blimp* 43. The Man from Morocco 44. *The Red Shoes* 48. The Queen of Spades 48. *La Ronde* 50. Vienna Waltzes 51. Oh Rosalinda 55. Lola Montes 55. Saint Joan 57. I Accuse 57, etc.

Walburn, Raymond (1887–1969).
American comedy actor with an inimitable bumbling pomposity; on stage from 1912, films from early 30s.
The Count of Monte Cristo 34. The Great Ziegfeld 36. *Mr Deeds Goes to Town* 36. Born to Dance 37. Professor Beware 38. Eternally Yours 40. Christmas in July 41. Dixie 43. *Hail the Conquering Hero* 43. The Man in the Trunk 43. The Cheaters 45. Henry the Rainmaker 48. State of the Union 48. Riding High 49. Father Takes the Air 51. Beautiful but Dangerous 53. The Spoilers 55, etc.

Walcott, Gregory (1928–).
American character actor, born in Wilson, North Carolina.
Red Skies of Montana 52. Battle Cry 54. The Lieutenant Wore Skirts 55. Strange Lady in Town 55. Texas Lady 55. Thunder over Arizona 56. The Persuader 57. Plan 9 from Outer Space 58. Badman's Country 58. The Outsider 61. On the Double 61. Man of the East 72. Joe Kidd 72. Prime Cut 72. The Last American Hero 73. Sugerland Express 74. The Eiger Sanction 75. Tilt 78. Every Which Way but Loose 78. To Race the Wind 80. House II: The Second Story 87. Ed Wood 94, etc.
TV series: 87th Precinct 61–62.

Wald, Jerry (1911–1962).
Live-wire American writer-producer, said to be the original of Budd Schulberg's novel *What Makes Sammy Run?* Former journalist, in Hollywood from early 30s.
Stars over Broadway (w) 35. Hollywood Hotel (w) 38. George Washington Slept Here (p) 42. *Mildred Pierce* 45. *Johnny Belinda* (p) 48. The Glass Menagerie (p) 50. Clash by Night (p) 52. Queen Bee (p) 55. Peyton Place (p) 57. The Sound and the Fury (p) 58. Sons and Lovers (p) 60. The Stripper (p) 63, many others.

Walden, Robert (1943–) (Robert Wolkowitz).
American character actor, best known as reporter Joe Rossi in the TV series *Lou Grant*, from the stage.
Bloody Mama 70. Pigeons/The Sidelong Glances of a Pigeon Fancier 70. The Hospital 71. Everything You Wanted to Know about Sex (but Were Afraid to Ask) 72. Larry (TV) 74. All the President's Men 76. New York, New York 77. Audrey Rose 77. Capricorn One 77. Blue Sunshine 78. Memorial Day (TV) 83. Murderer's Keep 88, etc.
TV series: The New Doctors 72–73. Lou Grant 77–82.

Waldron, Charles D. (1874–1946).
American stage actor who made a few films.
Mary Burns Fugitive 35. The Garden of Allah 36. Kentucky 38. On Borrowed Time 39. The Devil and Miss Jones 41. The Song of Bernadette 43. The Black Parachute 44. The Big Sleep 46, etc.
Famous line (*The Big Sleep*): 'You may smoke, sir. I can still enjoy the smell of it. Nice state of affairs, when a man has to indulge his vices by proxy.'

Wales, Ethel (1881–1952).
American character actress, in films from 1920.
Miss Lulu Bett 21. The Covered Wagon 23. Merton of the Movies 24. Beggar on Horseback 25. The Country Doctor 27. Blue Skies 29. Subway Express 31. Klondike 32. The Mighty Barnum 34. Barbary Coast 35. The Gladiator 38. Sudden Money 39. Young Bill Hickok 40. The Lumberjack 44. Blonde Alibi 46. The Story of a Woman 47. Fancy Pants 50, etc.

Wales, Wally:
see TALIAFERRO, Hal.

Walken, Christopher (1943–) (Ronald Walken).
American leading actor, most frequently in sinister roles. Born in New York City, he was acting on Broadway at the age of 16, and studied at Hofstra University. His early stage appearances were in musicals, and it was after his role as a disturbed prisoner-of-war in *The Deer Hunter* that he became Hollywood's favourite quietly menacing psychopath.
The Anderson Tapes 71. The Happiness Cage 72. Next Stop Greenwich Village 76. The Sentinel 77. Annie Hall 77. Roseland 77. *The Deer Hunter* (AA) 78. Last Embrace 79. Heaven's Gate 80. The Dogs of War 81. Pennies from Heaven 81. Brainstorm 83. The Dead Zone 83. A View to a Kill 85. At Close Range 86. Deadline 87. Biloxi Blues 88. The Milagro Beanfield War 88. Communion 89. King of New York 90. The Comfort of Strangers 90. McBain 91. All-American Murder 91. Day of Atonement/Le Grand Pardon 2 92. Mistress 92. Batman Returns 92. Skylark (TV) 93. God's Army 93. Scam 93. *True Romance* 93. Wayne's World 2 93. A Business Affair 94. Pulp Fiction 94. Search and Destroy 95. The Addiction 95. Things to Do in Denver When You're Dead 95. God's Army 95. Nick of Time 95. Celluloid (It.) 96. Basquiat 96. Last Man Standing 96. The Funeral 96. Excess Baggage 96. The Prophecy 2: Ashtown 97. Mouse Hunt 97. Suicide Kings 98. Illuminata 98. New Rose Hotel 98. Antz (voice) 98. Trance 98. Blast from the Past 98. Vendetta 99, etc.
❝ I'd love to do a character with a wife, a nice little house, a couple of kids, a dog, maybe a bit of singing, and no guns and no killing, but nobody offers me those kind of parts. – C.W.

Walker, Ally (1961–).
American actress, born in Tullahoma, Tennessee. She studied biology and chemistry at the University of California, and began her acting career in the early 80s in the TV soap opera *Santa Barbara*.
Universal Soldier 92. Singles 92. The Seventh Coin 93. When the Bough Breaks 93. Steal Big, Steal Little 95. Someone to Die For 95. While You Were Sleeping 95. Bed of Roses 95. The Continued Adventures of Reptile Man (and His Faithful Sidekick Tadpole) 96. Kazaam 96, etc.
TV series: True Blue 89. Moon over Miami 93. Profiler 96– .

Walker, Andrew Kevin (1964–).
American screenwriter.
Brainscan 94. Hideaway 95. Seven 95. Rendezvous with Rama 99, etc.

Walker, Charlotte (1878–1958).
American leading lady with stage experience, in silent films. Mother of Sara Haden.
Kindling 15. Trail of the Lonesome Pine 16. Eve in Exile 19. Classmates 24. The Manicure Girl 25. Paris Bound 29. Scarlet Pages 30. Millie 31, etc.

Walker, Clint (1927–) (Norman Eugene Walker).
Giant-size American leading man from TV. No acting training.
Fort Dobbs 57. Yellowstone Kelly 60. Gold of the Seven Saints 61. Send Me No Flowers 64. Night of the Grizzly 66. The Dirty Dozen 67. Sam Whiskey 68. The Great Bank Robbery 69. Yuma (TV) 70. The Bounty Man (TV) 72. Baker's Hawk 76. The White Buffalo 77. Hysterical 83. Serpent Warriors 86. The Gambler Returns: The Luck of the Draw (TV) 93, etc.
TV series: Cheyenne 55–62. Kodiak 75.

Walker, Giles (1946–).
Scottish-born director, in Canada.
Descent 75. Twice upon a Time 79. 90 Days 85. The Last Straw 87. Princess in Exile 90. Ordinary Magic 93, etc.

Walker, H. M. ('Beanie') (1887–1937).
American dialogue writer who provided most of Laurel and Hardy's classic exchanges in the early 30s, though these were usually based on Stan Laurel's gags.

Walker, Hal (1896–1972).
American director, mainly of routine films; stage experience.
■ Out of this World 45. Duffy's Tavern 45. The Stork Club 45. *Road to Utopia* 45. My Friend Irma Goes West 50. At War with the Army 50. That's My Boy 51. Sailor Beware 51. Road to Bali 52.

Walker, Helen (1921–1968).
American leading lady of the 40s.
Lucky Jordan 42. Abroad with Two Yanks 44. Murder He Says 45. Cluny Brown 46. The Homestretch 47. Nightmare Alley 47. Impact 49. My True Story 51. Problem Girls 52. The Big Combo (last role) 55, etc.

Walker, Joseph (1892–1985).
American cinematographer. On his retirement, he invented the zoom lens.
Danger 23. Flaming Fury 26. Virgin Lips 29. Dirigible 30. The Miracle Woman 31. American Madness 32. Lady for a Day 33. It Happened One Night 34. Broadway Bill 34. Mr Deeds Goes to Town 36. *Lost Horizon* 37. You Can't Take it With You 38. Mr Smith Goes to Washington 39. His Girl Friday 40. Here Comes Mr Jordan 41. *It's a Wonderful Life* 46. *The Jolson Story* 46. Born Yesterday 51, many others.

Walker, Nancy (1922–1992) (Ann Swoyer Barto).
Pint-sized American character comedienne.
Best Foot Forward 43. The World's Greatest Athlete 73. Forty Carats 73. Murder by Death 76. Can't Stop the Music (d) 80, etc.
TV series: Family Affair 70–71. McMillan and Wife 71–76. Rhoda 74–76, 77–78. The Nancy Walker Show 76. Blansky's Beauties 77. True Colors 90.

Walker, Nella (1886–1971).
American character actress, usually placid mother or socialite.
Seven Keys to Baldpate 29. Trouble in Paradise 32. Humanity 33. Four Frightened People 34. Three Smart Girls 36. The Rage of Paris 38. No Time for Comedy 40. Kitty Foyle 40. Hellzapoppin 41. Wintertime 43. In Society 44. The Locket 46. That Hagen Girl 47. Sabrina 54, many others.

Walker, Norman (1892–1963).
British director.
Tommy Atkins 27. The Middle Watch 31. Turn of the Tide 35. The Man at the Gate 40. Hard Steel 41. They Knew Mr Knight 45, etc.

Walker, Pete (1935–).
British producer-director of exploitation films.
I Like Birds 67. School for Sex 68. Cool it Carol 70. Die Screaming Marianne 71. Four Dimensions of Greta 72. Tiffany Jones 73. House of Whipcord 74. Frightmare 75. The House of Mortal Sin 76. Schizo 76. The Comeback 77. Home Before Midnight 79. House of the Long Shadows 83, etc.

Walker, Polly (1966–).
British actress, from the stage. She studied at the London Drama Centre.
Enchanted April 91. Patriot Games 92. The Trial 93. Sliver 93. Restoration 95. Emma 96. The Gambler 97. The Brute 98. Talk of Angels 98. Dark Harbor 98, etc.

Walker, Robert (1914–1951).
Slight, modest-looking American leading man of the 40s. Born in Salt Lake City, Utah, to Mormon parents, he studied at the American Academy of Dramatic Arts and had a successful career on radio before going to Hollywood to join his then wife Jennifer JONES, who left him soon after for producer David SELZNICK. An alcoholic, he became a liability on set and spent a year drying out, returning to give more controlled performances. Died from an overdose of sedatives, administered to him while he was in a drunken and violent condition, though some have insisted that he was murdered. His best role came late in his career, as Bruno Antony in *Strangers on a Train*; his last performance, as John Jefferson in *My Son John*, promised well, but he died before completing the picture.
■ Winter Carnival 39. These Glamour Girls 39. Dancing Co-Ed 39. Bataan 43. Madame Curie 43. *See Here Private Hargrove* 43. *Since You Went Away* 44. Thirty Seconds Over Tokyo 44. *The Clock* 45. Her Highness and the Bellboy 45. What Next Corporal Hargrove? 45. The Sailor Takes a Wife 45. *Till the Clouds Roll By* (as Jerome Kern) 46. The Sea of Grass 47. The Beginning or the End 47. Song of Love 47. One Touch of Venus 48. Please Believe Me 50. The Skipper Surprised His Wife 50. Vengeance Valley 51. *Strangers on a Train* 51. My Son John 52.

Walker, Robert, Jnr (1940–).
American second lead of the 60s.
The Hook 63. Ensign Pulver 64. The Ceremony 64. The Happening 67. The War Wagon 67. Easy Rider 69. Road to Salina 70. The Spectre of Edgar Allan Poe 72. God Bless Dr Shagetz 77. A Touch of Sin 83. Hambone and Hillie 84. Angkor-Cambodian Express 84, etc.

Walker, Stuart (1887–1941).
American director, former stage producer.
■ The Secret Call 31. The False Madonna 32. The Misleading Lady 32. Evenings for Sale 32. Tonight is Ours 33. *The Eagle and the Hawk* 33. White Woman 33. Romance in the Rain 34. Great Expectations 34. The Mystery of Edwin Drood 35. Werewolf of London 35. Manhattan Moon 35. Bulldog Drummond's Bride 39. Emergency Squad 40.

Walker, Syd (1887–1945).
English cockney comedian and actor, from music hall. His radio catchphrase, 'What would you do, chums?', from *Mr Walker Wants to Know*, a problem-solving spot in a weekly variety show, was the inspiration for his most successful feature.
Old Bill 24. Gift of the Gab 34. Over She Goes 37. Oh Boy 38. Hold My Hand 39. What Would You Do Chums? 39. The Gang's All Here 39, etc.

Walker, Zena (1934–).
British leading actress of the 60s, mostly on TV.
The Hellions 61. The Traitors 63. One of Those Things 69. The Dresser 83, etc.

Wall, Max (1902–1990) (Maxwell George Lorimer).
British music-hall song-and-dance performer, billed as 'The Boy with the Educated Feet', who turned comedian and became a notable character actor in his last years, especially on stage in the works of Samuel Beckett.
Autobiography: 1976, *The Fool on the Hill*.
Chitty Chitty Bang Bang 68. A Killer in Every Corner 74. One of Our Dinosaurs Is Missing 75. Jabberwocky 77. The Hound of the Baskervilles 78. Hanover Street 79. Little Dorrit 88. We Think the World of You 88. Strike It Rich 90, etc.

Wallace, Dee:
see STONE, Dee Wallace.

Wallace, Edgar (1875–1932).
Prolific British crime-story writer. Films of his books include:
The Terror 28 and 38. *The Crimson Circle* 30, 37 and 61. *The Case of the Frightened Lady* 30 and 40. *The Ringer* 32 and 52. *The Calendar* 32 and 48. *Sanders of the River* 35. The Squeaker 37. *Kate Plus Ten* 38. The Four Just Men 39. The Mind of Mr Reeder 39 (and series); and many episodes of a second-feature series made at Merton Park in the 60s.

Wallace, Irving (1916–1990) (Irving Wallechinsky).
American writer who with his son David and daughter Amy wrote encyclopaedias (*The Book of Lists*) but on his own account was a best-selling novelist. *The Chapman Report*, *The Prize*, *The Man* and *The Seven Minutes* have all been filmed.

Wallace, Jean (1923–1990) (Jean Wallasek).
American leading lady. She was married to Franchot Tone and later Cornel Wilde.
You Can't Ration Love 44. Jigsaw 48. The Good Humour Man 50. Song of India 50. Storm Fear 55. The Big Combo 55. Maracaibo 58. Lancelot and Guinevere 63. Beach Red 67. No Blade of Grass 71, etc.

Wallace, Lew (1827–1905).
American novelist who in 1880 published the much filmed *Ben Hur*.

Wallace, Nellie (1870–1948).
British character actress and music-hall performer, billed as 'The Essence of Eccentricity'. Born in Glasgow, she began as a clog-dancer when a child, emerging as a comic in the early 1900s.
The Wishbone 33. Radio Parade of 1935 35. Boys Will Be Girls 37. Cavalcade of the Stars 38, etc.

Wallace, Randall.
American screenwriter and director.
Braveheart (w) (AAN) 95. Dark Angel (w) (TV) 96. The Man in the Iron Mask (wd) 98, etc.

Wallace, Richard (1894–1951).
American director, former cutter for Mack Sennett.
MacFadden's Flats 27. Innocents of Paris 30. Seven Days' Leave 31. The Road to Reno 32. Shopworn Angel 33. The Little Minister 35. *The Young in Heart* 39. Captain Caution 40. The Navy Steps Out 41. She Knew All the Answers 41. The Fallen Sparrow 43. Bride by Mistake 44. *It's in the Bag* 45. Sinbad the Sailor 46. Tycoon 47. Let's Live a Little 48. A Kiss for Corliss 50, many others.

Wallace, Stephen (1943–).
Australian director and screenwriter, from documentaries.
Stir (d) 80. For Love Alone (wd) 86. Blood Oath (d) 90. Turtle Beach (d) 90.

Wallach, Eli (1915–).
American stage actor (from 1940) who has latterly concentrated on films, often in villainous roles which he spices with 'the method'. Married actress Anne Jackson.
■ *Baby Doll* (debut) 56. The Line Up 58. Seven Thieves 59. The Magnificent Seven 60. The Misfits 61. Hemingway's Adventures of a Young Man 62. How the West Was Won 62. The Victors 63. Act One 63. The Moonspinners 64. Kisses for My President 64. Lord Jim 65. Genghis Khan 65. How to Steal a Million 66. The Good the Bad and the Ugly (It.) 67. *The Tiger Makes Out* 67. How to Save a Marriage 68. Mackenna's Gold 68. A Lovely Way to Die 68. Revenge in El Paso (It.) 68. Ace High 69. The Brain 69. Zigzag 70. The People Next Door 70. The Angel Levine 70. The Adventures of Gerard 70. Romance of a Horsethief 71. A Cold Night's Death (TV) 72. Crazy Joe 73. Last Chance 73. Don't Turn the Other Cheek 73. Cinderella Liberty 74. Samurai 74. Indict and Convict (TV) 74. The Deep 77. Nasty Habits 77. The Sentinel 77. The Domino Principle 77. Seventh Avenue (TV) 77. Girl Friends 78. The Pirate (TV) 78. Movie Movie 78. Firepower 79. Winter Kills 79. Circle of Iron 79. The Pride of Jesse Hallam (TV) 80. The Salamander 80. The Hunter 81. The Executioner's Song (TV) 82. Anatomy of an Illness (TV) 84. Christopher Columbus (TV) 85. Sam's Son (TV) 85. Tough Guys 86. Nuts 87. The Two Jakes 90. The Godfather Part III 90. Article 99 92. Mistress 92. Two Much 96. The Associate 96.

Wallach, Ira (1912–1995).
American screenwriter, novelist and playwright.
Boys' Night Out 62. The Wheeler Dealers 63. Don't Make Waves (oa) 67. Hot Millions (AAN) 68.

Waller, Anthony (1949–).
British director, from television.
Mute Witness (wd) 95. An American Werewolf in Paris (wd) 97.

Waller, Thomas 'Fats' (1904–1943).
American jazz pianist, singer, bandleader and composer, in films as himself. Born in New York, he was a notable exponent of 'stride' piano and a prolific composer, whose songs included 'Honeysuckle Rose' and 'Black and Blue'. He gained popularity in the 30s, leading a small band in a series of hit records, many of them making fun of the songs they performed. Hard living and heavy drinking led to his death from pneumonia on a train near Kansas City, while returning from Hollywood. In films as himself, he is seen at his best in *Stormy Weather*, singing his own composition, 'Ain't Misbehavin' '. He was caricatured in several cartoons, including MGM's *The Old Mill Pond* 36, MGM's *Minnie the Moocher's Wedding Day* 37, Walt Disney's *Mother Goose Goes to Hollywood* 38, and Warner's Merrie Melodies' *Coal Black and De Sebben Dwarfs* 42 and *Tin Pan Alley Cats* 43; his organ playing was featured on the soundtrack of David Lynch's *Eraserhead* 76.
Biographies: 1966, *Ain't Misbehavin': The Story of Fats Waller* by Ed Kirkeby; 1977, *Fats Waller: His Life and Times* by J. Vance.
■ Hooray for Love 35. King of Burlesque 36. Stormy Weather 43.

Waller, Fred (1886–1954).
American research technician who invented Cinerama and saw it open successfully only two years before his death.

Walley, Deborah (1941–).
American leading actress in youth and beach movies of the 60s; later involved in film production.
Gidget Goes Hawaiian 61. Bon Voyage! 62. Summer Magic 63. Young Lovers 64. Spinout/California Holiday 65. Ski Party 65. Beach Blanket Bingo 65. Sergeant Deadhead 65. Dr Goldfoot and the Bikini Machine 65. The Bubble 66. Spinout 66. The Ghost in the Invisible Bikini 66. It's a Bikini World 67. The Severed Arm 74. Benji 74, etc.

Wallis, Hal B. (1898–1986).
American producer, latterly independent, responsible for a long line of solidly commercial films. In films from 1922.
Little Caesar 30. *The Story of Louis Pasteur* 36. Jezebel 38. *Kings Row* 42. *Casablanca* 42. The Strange Love of Martha Ivers 46. My Friend Irma 49. *Gunfight at the OK Corral* 57. G.I. Blues 60. Becket 64. Boeing-Boeing 65. The Sons of Katie Elder 65. Five Card Stud 68. True Grit 69. Anne of the Thousand Days 70. Mary Queen of Scots 72. Bequest to the Nation 73. Rooster Cogburn 75, many others (often as executive producer for major studios).

Wallis, Shani (1938–).
British cabaret singer.
■ The Extra Day 56. Ramsbottom Rides Again 56. A King in New York 67. Oliver! 68. Terror in the Wax Museum 73. Arnold 73. Round Numbers 92. The Pebble and the Penguin (narrator) 95.

Walls, Tom (1883–1949).
British actor and director, on stage from 1905 after experience as policeman, busker, jockey, etc. Associated from mid-20s with the Aldwych farces, which he produced and later transferred to the screen, as well as playing amiable philanderers in them. Subsequently in character roles.
■ *Rookery Nook* 30. On Approval 30. Canaries Sometimes Sing 30. Tons of Money 31. *Plunder* 31. A Night Like This 32. *Thark* 32. Leap Year 32. The Blarney Stone 32. Just Smith 33. Turkey Time 33. A Cuckoo in the Nest 34. A Cup of Kindness 34. Lady in Danger 34. Dirty Work 34. Fighting Stock 35. Me and Marlborough 35. Stormy Weather 35. Foreign Affaires 36. Pot Luck 36. Dishonour Bright 36. For Valour 37. Second Best Bed 38. Old Iron 38. *Strange Boarders* 38. Crackerjack 38. Undercover 43. They Met in the Dark 43. Halfway House 43. Love Story 44. Johnny Frenchman 45. This Man is Mine 46. *Master of Bankdam* 47. While I Live 47. *Spring in Park Lane* 47. Maytime in Mayfair 48. Derby Day 49. The Interrupted Journey 49.

Walpole, Sir Hugh (1884–1941).
British novelist who did some scripting in 30s Hollywood and appeared as the vicar in *David Copperfield* 34.
Vanessa: Her Love Story (oa) 35. Kind Lady (story) 35 and 51. Mr Perrin and Mr Traill (oa) 48, etc.

Walsh, Bill (1918–1976).
American producer for the Walt Disney Organization.
Mary Poppins (p, co-w) (AANw) 64, etc.

Walsh, David M.
American cinematographer.
I Walk the Line 70. The Other Side of the Mountain 75. The Silver Streak 76. Rollercoaster 77. House Calls 78. Movie Movie 78. Goldengirl 78. Seems Like Old Times 80. Only When I Laugh 81. Max Dugan Returns 83. Romantic Comedy 83. Unfaithfully Yours 84. Johnny Dangerously 84. Country 84. Teachers 84. My Science Project 85. Outrageous Fortune 87. Summer School 87. Fatal Beauty 87. Second Sight 89. Taking Care of Business 90. Brain Donors 92. Carpool 96, etc.

Walsh, Dermot (1924–).
Irish leading man, usually in second features. His first wife was actress Hazel Court (1949–63).
Bedelia 46. My Sister and I 49. The Frightened Man 52. The Floating Dutchman 53. The Night of the Full Moon 56. Woman of Mystery 57. Crash Drive 59. The Trunk 61. The Cool Mikado 63. The Wicked Lady 83, etc.
TV series: Richard the Lionheart 62.

Walsh, Dylan (1963–).
American actor, usually playing the nice guy.
Loverboy 89. Betsy's Wedding 90. Where the Heart Is 90. Nobody's Fool 94. Radio Inside 94. Congo 95. Divided by Hate (TV) 96. Changing Habits 97. Men 97. Eden 98, etc.
TV series: Brooklyn South 97.

Walsh, J. T. (1944–1998).
American character actor, from the stage; a former salesman. Died of a heart attack.
Eddie Macon's Run 83. Hard Choices 84. Hannah and Her Sisters 86. Power 86. Good Morning, Vietnam 87. House of Games 87. Tin Men 87. Tequila Sunrise 88. Things Change 88. Wired 89. The Big Picture 89. Dad 89. Crazy People 90. The Grifters 90. Narrow Margin 90. The Russia House 90. Backdraft 91. True Identity 91. Iron Maze 91. Hoffa 92. Needful Things 93. Sniper 93. Red Rock West 93. Morning Glory 93. Blue Chips 94. The Client 94. The Low Life 95. Executive Decision 96. Crime of the Century (TV) 96. Slingblade 96. The Negotiator 98. Pleasantville 98, etc.

Walsh, Kay (1914–).
British character actress, former leading lady. Trained in West End revue. She was formerly married to director David Lean.
Get Your Man (debut) 34. I See Ice 38. In Which We Serve 42. This Happy Breed 44. *The October Man* 47. Vice Versa 48. Oliver Twist 48. Stage Fright 50. Last Holiday 50. *Encore* 51. Meet Me Tonight 52. Lease of Life 54. Cast a Dark Shadow 55. The Horse's Mouth 59. *Tunes of Glory* 60. Eighty Thousand Suspects 63. The Beauty Jungle 64. A Study in Terror 65. The Witches 66. Connecting Rooms 69. The Ruling Class 71. Night Crossing 82, many others.
TV series: Sherlock Holmes and Dr Watson 80.

Walsh, M. Emmet (1935–).
Fleshy American character actor, often as a heavy.
Alice's Restaurant 69. Midnight Cowboy 69. Stiletto 69. Little Big Man 70. The Traveling Executioner 70. They Might Be Giants 71. What's Up, Doc? 72. Serpico 73. At Long Last Love 75. Nickelodeon 76. Slap Shot 77. Straight Time 78. The Jerk 79. East of Eden (TV) 80. Brubaker 80. Ordinary People 80. Reds 81. Blade Runner 82. Silkwood 83. Missing in Action 84. Blood Simple 85. Fletch 85. Back to School 86. The Best of Times 86. Harry and the Hendersons 87. The Milagro Beanfield War 88. War Party 89. The Mighty Quinn 89. Red Scorpion 89. Chattahoochee 89. Narrow Margin 90. Equinox 92. The Music of Chance 93. Bitter Harvest 93. Wilder Napalm 93. Relative Fear 94. The Glass Shield 94. Free Willy 2: The Adventure Home 95. A Time to Kill 96. Albino Alligator 96. William Shakespeare's Romeo and Juliet 96. Retroactive 97. Chairman of the Board 97. My Best Friend's Wedding 97. Albino Alligator 97. Twilight 98. Erasable You 98, etc.
TV series: The Sandy Duncan Show 72. Dear Detective 79. Unsub 89.

Walsh, Martin.
English editor.
Wolves of Willoughby Chase 88. The Krays 90. Hear My Song 91. Wild West 92. Bad Behaviour 93. Backbeat 93. Funny Bones 95. Hackers (US) 95. Feeling Minnesota (US) 96. Roseanna's Grave 97. Hilary and Jackie 98, etc.

Walsh, Raoul (1887–1980).
Veteran American director of many commercial and several distinguished pictures. In films from 1912; former actor and assistant to D. W. Griffith.
Autobiography: 1974, *Each Man in His Time*.
Carmen 15. *The Thief of Baghdad* 24. *What Price Glory?* 26. *Sadie Thompson* 28. In Old Arizona 29. *The Big Trail* 30. *The Bowery* 33. Every Night at Eight 35. Artists and Models 38. St Louis Blues 39. *They Drive by Night* 40. *High Sierra* 41. They Died with Their Boots On 41. Strawberry Blonde 41. Manpower 41. Desperate Journey 42. Gentleman Jim 43. Northern Pursuit 44. Uncertain Glory 44. The Horn Blows at Midnight 45. *Objective Burma* 45. The Man I Love 46. Pursued 47. Silver River 48. *White Heat* 49. Colorado Territory 49. Along the Great Divide 49. Captain Horatio Hornblower 50. Distant Drums 51. The World in His Arms 52. Glory Alley 52. Blackbeard the Pirate 53. A Lion is in the Streets 54. Saskatchewan 54. Battle Cry 55. The Tall Men 55. The Revolt of Mamie Stover 57. The King and Four Queens 57. Band of Angels 57. The Naked and the Dead 58. The Sheriff of Fractured Jaw (GB) 58. Esther and the King 60. Marines Let's Go 61. A Distant Trumpet 64, many others.
✪ For vigorous treatment of action subjects. *White Heat*.
❝ To Raoul Walsh, a tender love scene is burning down a whorehouse. –*Jack L. Warner*

Walston, Ray (1914–).
American character comedian with stage experience.
Kiss Them for Me 57. South Pacific 58. *Damn Yankees* 58. Say One for Me 59. The Apartment 60. Tall Story 60. Portrait in Black 60. Convicts Four 62. Wives and Lovers 63. Who's Minding the Store? 64. *Kiss Me Stupid* 64. Caprice 67. Paint Your Wagon 69. Viva Max 69. The Sting 73. Silver Streak 76. The Happy Hooker Goes to Washington 77. Popeye 81. Galaxy of Terror 81. Fast Times at Ridgemont High 82. O'Hara's Wife 82. Private School 83. Johnny Dangerously 84. O.C. and Stiggs 87. Red River (TV) 88. Blood Relations 88. Paramedics 88. Man of Passion 88. I Know My First Name Is Steven (TV) 89. Popcorn 91. Of Mice and Men 92. The Stand (TV) 94. House Arrest 96. Tricks (TV) 97. Early Bird Special 98, etc.
TV series: My Favorite Martian 63–65. Stop Susan Williams 79. Silver Spoons 85. Fast Times 86.

Walter, Harriet (1951–).
English leading actress, mainly on the stage.
The French Lieutenant's Woman 81. Amy (TV) 83. Turtle Diary 85. The Good Father 86. Milou in May 89. The Men's Room (TV) 91. The Hour of the Pig 93. The Leading Man 96, etc.

Walter, Jessica (1944–).
American leading lady of the 60s.
Lilith 64. *The Group* 66. Grand Prix 67. Bye Bye Braverman 68. Number One 69. Play Misty for Me 71. Women in Chains (TV) 71. Home for the Holidays (TV) 72. Amy Prentiss (TV) 76. Victory at Entebbe (TV) 76. Secrets of Three Hungry Wives (TV) 78. She's Dressed to Kill (TV) 79. Spring Fever 83. The Flamingo Kid 84. The Execution (TV) 85. Killer in the Mirror (TV) 86. Tapeheads 87. Aaron's Way (TV) 88. Ghost in the Machine 94. PCU 94. Temptress 95. Slums of Beverly Hills 98, etc.

Walter, Tracey (1942–).
American character actor.
Badge 373 73. Serpico 73. Blue Collar 78. Hardcore 78. Goin' South 78. Raggedy Man 81. Rumble Fish 83. Repo Man 84. Conan the Destroyer 84. At Close Range 85. Midnight Run 88. Out of the Dark 88. Married to the Mob 88. Batman 89. The Two Jakes 90. Pacific Heights 90. Young Guns 2 90. Silence of the Lambs 90. City Slickers 91. Liquid Dreams 91. Philadelphia 93. Junior 94. Destiny Turns on the Radio 95. Buffalo Girls (TV) 95. Matilda 96. Larger than Life 96, etc.
TV series: Best of the West 81–82.

Walters, Charles (1911–1982).
American director specializing in musicals. Former stage dancer and director of musical sequences in films.
Presenting Lily Mars (seq) 43. Meet Me in St Louis (seq) 44. Good News 47. *Easter Parade* 48. Summer Stock 50. Easy to Love 53. *Lili* (AAN) 53. The Glass Slipper 55. The Tender Trap 55. High Society 56. Don't Go Near the Water 57. Ask Any Girl 59. Please Don't Eat the Daisies 60. Jumbo 62. The Unsinkable Molly Brown 64. Walk, Don't Run 66, etc.

Walters, Julie (1950–).
British character actress, often in tarty roles.
Educating Rita (AAN) 83. She'll Be Wearing Pink Pajamas 84. Car Trouble 86. Prick Up Your Ears 87. Personal Services 87. Buster 88. Mack the Knife 89. Killing Dad 89. Stepping Out 91. Just Like a Woman 92. The Clothes in the Wardrobe/The Summer House (TV) 93. Wide-Eyed and Legless (TV) 93. The Wedding Gift (TV) 94. Pat and Margaret (TV) 94. Intimate Relations 96. Melissa (TV) 97. Girls' Night 98. Titanic Town 98, etc.
TV series: Wood and Walters 81–82. Boys from the Black Stuff 82. The Secret Diary of Adrian Mole Aged 13 85. Victoria Wood – As Seen on TV 85–86. Victoria Wood 89. Jake's Progess 95. Dinnerladies 98.
❝ When I think of the future I think of doing my washing so I've something to wear tomorrow. –*J.W.*

Walters, Thorley (1913–1991).
British comedy actor on stage and screen from 1934. Film parts usually cameos, as incompetent officers, etc.
They Were Sisters 45. Private's Progress 56. Carleton Browne of the FO 58. Two-Way Stretch 60. Murder She Said 62. Ring of Spies 64. Joey Boy 65. *Rotten to the Core* 65. *Dracula, Prince of Darkness* 65. The Wrong Box 66. Frankenstein Must Be Destroyed 69. Vampire Circus 72. The Adventure of Sherlock Holmes' Smarter Brother 75. The People That Time Forgot 78. The Wildcats of St Trinian's 80. The Sign of Four (TV) 83. The Little Drummer Girl 84, etc.

Walthall, Henry B. (1878–1936).
American leading man of the silent screen, in films from 1909.
In Old Kentucky 09. A Convict's Sacrifice 10. The Birth of a Nation 14. The Raven 15. Ghosts 15. His Robe of Honour 18. Single Wives 23. The Scarlet Letter 25. The Barrier 26. Abraham Lincoln 31. Police Court 32. Laughing at Life 33. Viva Villa 34. Dante's Inferno 35. A Tale of Two Cities 35. China Clipper 36, many others.

Walton, Tony (1934–).
British production designer. He was formerly married to actress Julie Andrews (1959–69).
Mary Poppins 64. Fahrenheit 451 66. A Funny Thing Happened on the Way to the Forum 66. The Seagull 68. Boy Friend 71. Murder on the Orient Express 74. The Wiz 78. All That Jazz 79. Just Tell Me What You Want 80. Prince of the City 81. Deathtrap 82. The Goodbye People 84. Heartburn 86. The Glass Menagerie 87. Regarding Henry 91, etc.

Walton, Sir William (1902–1983).
British composer whose film scores include *Henry V* 44. *Hamlet* 48. *Richard III* 56.

Wambaugh, Joseph (1937–).
American novelist, an ex-policeman who capitalized on his experience and tends to rub his readers' noses in the gutter. Films resulting include *The New Centurions, The Onion Field, The Black Marble, The Choirboys*.

Wanamaker, Sam (1919–1993).
American stage actor and director who also appeared in films; moved to Britain where he set up a trust to build a replica of Shakespeare's Globe Theatre in London.
My Girl Tisa 48. Give Us This Day 50. Mr Denning Drives North 51. The Secret 55. The Criminal 60. Taras Bulba 62. The Man in the Middle 64. Those Magnificent Men in Their Flying Machines 65. The Spy Who Came in from the Cold 65. Warning Shot 66. The Day the Fish Came Out 67. File of the Golden Goose (d only) 69. The Executioner (d only) 69. Catlow (d only) 72. Mousey (TV) 73. The Sell Out 75. Voyage of the Damned 76. Sinbad and the Eye of the Tiger (d only) 77. Holocaust (TV) 78. Death on the Nile 78. Private Benjamin 80. The Competition 80. The Aviator 84. Irreconcilable Differences 84. Raw Deal 86. Superman IV 87. Baby Boom 87. Guilty by Suspicion 91. Pure Luck 91. Wild Justice (TV) 93, etc.

Wang, Jimmy Yu.
Hong Kong leading actor, director and screenwriter of martial arts movies. He worked at the Shaw Brothers' studio until 1970, when he was replaced by an actor of similar appearance, Yu Wong.
Temple of the Red Lotus 65. The One-Armed Swordsman 67. The Chinese Boxer (& wd) 68. Escorts over Tiger Hills 69. One Armed Boxer (& wd) 71. A Man Called Tiger 72. Bronze Head Iron Fingers (& d) 72. The Magnificent Chivalry 73. Beach of the War Gods (& d) 73. Dragon Squad (& d) 75. Master of the Flying Guillotine (& wd) 75. The Man from Hong Kong (Aus.) 75. A Queen's Ransom 76. Tiger and Crane Fists (& wd) 76. Girl with the Diamond Slipper 85. The Millionaire's Express 86. Movie in Your Face (US) 90. Island of Fire/The Prisoner 92, etc.

Wang, Wayne (1949–).
Hong Kong-born director and screenwriter who studied in America and worked in Hong Kong before returning to the States to make films, mainly about the Chinese community there.
A Man, a Woman and a Killer (d) 75. Chan Is Missing (wd) 81. Dim Sum: A Little Bit of Heart (d) 85. Slam Dance (d) 87. Eat a Bowl of Tea (d) 89. Life Is Cheap . . . but Toilet Paper Is Expensive (d) 89. The Joy Luck Club (d) 93. Smoke (d) 95. Blue in the Face (co-d) 95. Chinese Box (wd) 97, etc.

Wang Yu, Jimmy.
Chinese leading man and kung fu expert.
The Legend of Seven Golden Vampires 74. The Man from Hong Kong 75. Invincible Sword 78. Fury of King Boxer 83. Kung Fu Hero II 90, etc.

Wanger, Walter (1894–1968) (W. Feuchtwanger).
American independent producer who during a long career held at various times senior executive posts with major studios.
Biography: 1994, *Walter Wanger, Hollywood Independent* by Matthew Bernstein.
Queen Christina 33. The President Vanishes 35. Private Worlds 35. Mary Burns Fugitive 35. The Trail of the Lonesome Pine 36. *You Only Live Once* 37. History is Made at Night 37. 52nd Street 38. Stand In 38. *Blockade* 38. Trade Winds 38. Algiers 38. *Stagecoach* 39. *Foreign Correspondent* 40. The Long Voyage Home 40. *Scarlet Street* 45. The Lost Moment 47. Tap Roots 48. Joan of Arc 48. Riot in Cell Block Eleven 54. *Invasion of the Body Snatchers* 55. I Want to Live 58. Cleopatra 62.
“ Nothing is as cheap as a hit, no matter how much it costs. – *W.W.*
He always wanted to be European. – *James Mason*

Warbeck, David (1941–1997) (David Mitchell).
New Zealand-born actor and model, a star of horror and exploitation movies. Born in Christchurch, of Scottish descent, he worked as a teacher before coming to London in the mid-60s to study at RADA. From the early 70s he made most of his films in Italy, often for director Antonio MARGHERITI. He was among the actors considered to replace Roger MOORE as JAMES BOND.
30 Is a Dangerous Age, Cynthia 67. Wolfshead the Legend of Robin Hood (TV) 69. Twins of Evil 71. A Fistful of Dollars (It.) 72. Blacksnake! (US) 73. Craze 73. The Sex Thief 73. Panic (It.) 80. The Last Hunter (It.) 80. The Black Cat (It.) 81. Tiger Joe (It.) 82. The Ark of the Sun God 84. The Survivors of the Dead City (It.) 84. Miami Horror (It.) 85. Arizona Road 91. Breakfast with Dracula: A Vampire in Miami (It.) 93. Dangerous Attraction (It.) 93. Razor Blade Smile 98, many others.
“ In Hollywood, everything is so psychotic, everyone's angst-ridden, everyone's visiting a shrink, but in Italy, it's just like a circus full of monkeys – so much fun! – *D.W.*

Ward, Burt (1945–) (Herbert Jervis).
American juvenile of the 60s who played Robin in TV's *Batman* series, then almost disappeared from view. He appeared in some low-budget exploitation movies in the late 80s and founded Logical Figments, a special effects, animation and video editing company, in 1994.
Batman 66. Kill Crazy 89. Robo-C.H.I.C.K. 89. Robot Ninja 89. Virgin High 90. Smooth Talker 90. Beach Babes from beyond Infinity 93. Assault of the Party Nerds 2: Heavy Petting Detectives 95, etc.

Ward, David S. (1945–).
American screenwriter and director.
Steelyard Blues (w) 72. The Sting (w) (AA) 73. Cannery Row (wd) 81. The Sting II (w) 82. Major League (wd) 89. King Ralph (wd) 90. Sleepless in Seattle (co-w, AAN) 93. The Program (co-w, d) 93. Major League II (d) 94. Down Periscope (d) 96, etc.

Ward, Edward (–1971).
American composer.
Kismet 31. Great Expectations 34. The Mystery of Edwin Drood 35. Navy Blue and Gold 37. Stablemates 38. Thunder Afloat 39. Mr and Mrs Smith 41. Phantom of the Opera (AAN) 43. The Climax 44. Salome Where She Danced 45. Copacabana 47. The Babe Ruth Story 48, etc.

Ward, Fannie (1865–1952).
American stage actress, a famous beauty of her time who in middle age began a Hollywood film career playing parts too young for her, and was the inspiration of novel and film *Mr Skeffington*.
The Marriage of Kitty 15. The Cheat 15. The Years of the Locust 16. The Yellow Ticket 18. Innocent 18. A Japanese Nightingale 18. Common Clay 19, etc.

Ward, Fred (1942–).
American leading man
■ Escape from Alcatraz 82. The Right Stuff 83. Silkwood 83. Remo Williams 85. Big Business 88. Off Limits 88. The Prince of Pennsylvania 88. Tremors 90. Miami Blues 90. Henry and June 90. The Dark Wind 91. Lovecraft/Cast a Deadly Spell (TV) 91. The Player 92. Thunderheart 92. Equinox 92. Short Cuts 93. Naked Gun 33 : The Final Insult 94. Two Small Bodies 94. The Blue Villa (Belg.) 95. Chain Reaction 96. First Do No Harm (TV) 97. Dangerous Beauty 98. The Vivero Letter 98.

Ward, Michael (1909–1997) (George Yeo).
British comic actor usually seen as nervous photographer or twee shopwalker. Born in Carnmenellis, Cornwall, he studied at the Central School of Drama in London, and worked in repertory theatre; he was on stage in London from 1945, and also appeared in many TV sitcoms and comedy shows. Retired due to ill-health in the late 70s.
An Ideal Husband 47. Sleeping Car to Trieste 48. Pool of London 50. Trio 50. What the Butler Saw 50. Calling Bulldog Drummond 51. Tom Brown's Schooldays 51. Trouble in Store 53. Man of the Moment 55. Up in the World 56. Private's Progress 56. Brothers in Law 57. I'm All Right Jack 59. Carlton-Browne of the FO 59. Doctor in Love 60. Carry On Regardless 61. Carry On Cabby 63. Carry On Cleo 64. Carry On Screaming 66. Smashing Time 67. Frankenstein and the Monster from Hell 73. Revenge of the Pink Panther 78, etc.

Ward, Nick.
English screenwriter, director and playwright. He studied at Cambridge University and film school in Bristol before working at the National Theatre Studio and in television.
Dakota Road (wd) 92. Look Me in the Eye (wd) 94, etc.

Ward, Polly (1908–) (Byno Poluski).
British-born leading lady of several 30s comedies.
Shooting Stars 28. His Lordship 32. The Old Curiosity Shop 34. Feather Your Nest 37. Thank Evans 38. It's in the Air 38. Bulldog Drummond Sees It Through 40. Women Aren't Angels 42, etc.

Ward, Rachel (1957–).
British-born leading lady, in America at first as a model. Married actor Bryan Brown.
Sharky's Machine 81. Dead Men Don't Wear Plaid 82. The Thorn Birds (TV) 83. The Good Wife 86. Hotel Colonial 87. How to Get Ahead in Advertising 89. After Dark, My Sweet 90. And the Sea Will Tell (TV) 91. Christopher Columbus: The Discovery 92. Wide Sargasso Sea 93. The Ascent 96, etc.

Ward, Simon (1941–).
British leading actor of the 70s.
■ Frankenstein Must Be Destroyed 69. Quest for Love 70. I Start Counting 71. *Young Winston* 72. Hitler – the Last Ten Days 73. Dracula (TV) 73. The Three Musketeers 74. The Four Musketeers 75. Deadly Strangers 75. All Creatures Great and Small 75. Aces High 76. Holocaust 2000 77. Children of Rage 77. Battle Flag 77. Dominique 78. Zulu Dawn 79. La Sabina 79. The Monster Club 80. Supergirl 84. The Corsican Brothers (TV) 85. Leave All Fair 85. Double X 92.

Ward, Sophie (1965–).
English actress, the daughter of Simon WARD.
Young Sherlock Holmes 85. Little Dorrit 87. Aria 88. A Summer Story 88. The Monk 90. A Demon in My View 92. Class of '61 (TV) 92. A Dark Adapted Eye (TV) 93. A Village Affair 95. The Big Fall 96. Bela Donna 98, etc.

Ward, Vincent (1956–).
New Zealand director and screenwriter.
Vigil 84. The Navigator 88. Alien^3 (story) 92. Map of the Human Heart 93. What Dreams May Come (US) 98, etc.

Ward, Warwick (1891–1967).
Elegant English leading actor of silents who also worked in French, German, and American films in the 20s. He became manager of Welwyn Studios in the mid-30s and a producer and screenwriter in the 40s.
The Silver Lining 19. Wuthering Heights 20. The Mayor of Casterbridge 21. Bulldog Drummond 23. *Variety*/Vaudeville (Ger.) 25. Madame Sans-Gêne (US) 25. The Informer 29. Stamboul 31. Ariane 34. The Man from Morocco (p, co-w) 44. Quiet Weekend (p) 46. My Brother Jonathan (p) 47. The Dancing Years (p, co-w) 49. Isn't Life Wonderful (p) 52. The Elstree Story (narrator) 52, etc.

Warde, Frederick B. (1851–1935).
English Shakespearean actor who starred in the earliest American feature film to survive to the present day, *The Life and Death of King Richard III*, released as a five-reeler running for 55m in 1912. On stage from 1867, he went to America in 1874 and toured with his own company there from the early 1880s, retiring in 1919. He was the father of silent-film actor and director Ernest C. Warde (1873–1923).
Autobiography: 1920, *Fifty Years of Make-Believe*.
King Lear 16. Hinton's Double 16. The Vicar of Wakefield 17. Silas Marner 17. Fires of Youth 18, etc.

Warden, Jack (1920–).
Burly American character actor, also on stage and TV.
From Here to Eternity 53. *Twelve Angry Men* 57. Edge of the City 57. *The Bachelor Party* 57. Escape from Zahrain 62. Mirage 65. Blindfold 65. Welcome to the Club 70. Who Is Harry Kellerman . . . ? 71. Billy Two Hats 73. The Apprenticeship of Duddy Kravitz 74. Shampoo (AAN) 75. All the President's Men 76. Voyage of the Damned 76. The White Buffalo 77. Heaven Can Wait (AAN) 78. Death on the Nile 78. The Champ 79. And Justice for All 79. Used Cars 80. So Fine 81. A Private Battle (TV) 81. The Verdict 82. Hobson's Choice (TV) 83. The Aviator 84. Crackers 84. September 87. The Presidio 88. Everybody Wins 90. Problem Child 90. Problem Child 2 91. Passed Away 92. Guilty as Sin 93. Bullets over Broadway 94. While You Were Sleeping 95. Things to Do in Denver When You're Dead 95. Mighty Aphrodite 95. Ed 96. Chairman of the Board 97. Bulworth 98, etc.
TV series: Mr Peepers 53–55. The Asphalt Jungle 60. The Wackiest Ship in the Army 65. N.Y.P.D. 67–68. The Bad News Bears 79. *Crazy Like a Fox* 84–85.

Warhol, Andy (1927–1987).
American pop artist and 'underground' film-maker of the 60s. He was played by David Bowie in *Basquiat* 96 and by Jared Harris in *I Shot Andy Warhol* 96.
Sleep 63. Blow Job 64. Harlot 65. The Chelsea Girls (shown on two screens side by side, with different images) 66. F**k, or Blue Movie 69. Trash (p only) 70. Flesh (p only) 71. Bad 76, etc.
“ Sex is the biggest nothing of all time. – *A.W.*
It would be very glamorous to be reincarnated as a giant ring on Elizabeth Taylor's finger. – *A.W.*

Warner, David (1941–).
Lanky British actor who after success in classical theatre (he was a notable Hamlet in the 60s) and in British films went to Hollywood, where he has tended to be typecast as a villain in mainly second-rate movies.
Tom Jones (as Blifil) 63. The Deadly Affair 66. *Morgan* 66. Work is a Four-Letter Word 68. A Midsummer Night's Dream 68. *The Bofors Gun* 68. The Fixer 68. The Seagull 68. Michael Kohlhaas 69. The Ballad of Cable Hogue 70. Perfect Friday 70. The Engagement 70. Straw Dogs 71. A Doll's House 73. Mr Quilp 75. Little Malcolm 75. The Omen 76. Victory at Entebbe (TV) 76. Age of Innocence 77. The Disappearance 77. Cross of Iron 77. Providence 77. The Thirty-Nine Steps 78. *Holocaust* (TV) (as Heydrich) 78. Silver Bears 78. The Concorde – Airport '79 79. Time after Time (as Jack the Ripper) 79. Nightwing 79. The Islands 80. Time Bandits 81. Iron 82. The Man with Two Brains 83. Company of Wolves 84. A Christmas Carol (TV) 84. Hansel and Gretel 87. Mr North 88. Waxwork 88. Hanna's War 88. Star Trek V: The Final Frontier 89. Office Party 89. Teenage Mutant Ninja Turtles II: The Secret of the Ooze 91. Star Trek VI: The Undiscovered Country 91. Lovecraft/Cast a Deadly Spell (TV) 91. Drive 91. Dark at Noon/La Terreur de Midi 92. The Unnameable Returns 92. Pretty Princess (It.) 93. Necronomicon 93. Seven Servants (Ger.) 96. The Leading Man 96. Titanic 97. Scream 2 97. Money Talks 97. Shergar 98. The Last Leprechaun 98. Babe: Pig in the City (voice) 98, etc.

Warner, H. B. (1876–1958) (Henry Byron Warner-Lickford).
Distinguished British actor, on stage from 1883; in Hollywood as film actor from around 1917.
The Beggar of Cawnpore 15. The Man White 19. One Hour Before Dawn 20. Zaza 23. *King of Kings* (as Jesus) 27. Sorrell and Son 27. The Divine

Lady 28. The Trial of Mary Dugan 29. Five Star Final 31. *Mr Deeds Goes to Town* 36. *Lost Horizon* (AAN) 37. *Victoria the Great* 37. You Can't Take It With You 38. Bulldog Drummond Strikes Back 39. The Rains Came 39. All That Money Can Buy 41. Topper Returns 41. The Corsican Brothers 41. It's a Wonderful Life 46. Prince of Thieves 48. Sunset Boulevard 50. Savage Drums 51. The Ten Commandments 56, many others.

✪ For bringing dignity to a wildly disparate collection of films. *Lost Horizon*.

Warner, Jack (1894–1981) (Jack Waters).
Genial British character actor, former music-hall comedian; TV's 'Dixon of Dock Green'. The success of *Holiday Camp* led to him starring as Joe Huggett in several films and a long-running radio sit-com, *Meet the Huggetts* (1953–61).

Autobiography: 1975, *Jack of All Trades*.

The Dummy Talks (debut) 43. *The Captive Heart* 46. Hue and Cry 46. It Always Rains on Sunday 47. Holiday Camp 47. *Here Come the Huggetts* 48. The Huggetts Abroad 49. *The Blue Lamp* 50. Valley of Eagles 51. Scrooge 51. The Quatermass Experiment 55. Home and Away 56. Carve Her Name with Pride 58. *Jigsaw* 62, many others.

~Catchphrase: Mind my bike (from the radio series *Garrison Theatre*).

Warner, Jack L. (1892–1978).
American executive producer, last member of the four Warner Brothers who started up a small production company in the 20s and pioneered sound pictures with *The Jazz Singer* 27. The other brothers: Albert, Harry M., and Sam.

Autobiography: 1965, *My First Hundred Years in Hollywood*.

Biography: 1990, *Clown Prince of Hollywood* by Bob Thomas.

See also: WARNER BROTHERS (Section 4).

✪ For running a studio with the discipline of a prison, and living to see the results endure. *A Midsummer Night's Dream*.

❝ You're nothing if you don't have a studio. Now I'm just another millionaire, and there are a lot of 'em around. – *J.W., in retirement in Palm Springs*

I have a theory of relatives too. Don't hire 'em. – *J.W. to Einstein*

If his brothers hadn't hired him, he'd have been out of work. – *Jack Warner Jnr*

He existed behind a self-made wall. Besides, a lot of him wasn't that nice to know. At times he gloried in being a no-good sonofabitch. – *Jack Warner Jnr*

He was a generous host, a big gambler at work and at play, and with superb confidence he put his money where his mouth was. – *David Niven*

He bore no grudge against those he had wronged. – *Simone Signoret*

I can't see what J. W. can do with an Oscar. It can't say yes. – *Al Jolson*

A man who would rather tell a bad joke than make a good movie. – *Jack Benny*

Warner, Julie (1965–).
American actress.

Flatliners 90. Doc Hollywood 91. Mr Saturday Night 92. Indian Summer 93. The Puppet Masters 94. Tommy Boy 95. Wedding Bell Blues 96, etc.

Warren, C. Denier (1889–1971).
Chubby American character comedian, in British films; vaudeville experience.

Counsel's Opinion 33. Kentucky Minstrels 34. A Fire Has Been Arranged 35. Cotton Queen 37. Trouble Brewing 39. Kiss the Bride Goodbye 44. Old Mother Riley, Headmistress 50. Bluebeard's Ten Honeymoons 60, etc.

Warren, Charles Marquis (1917–1990).
American writer-director. Moved into TV and became creator and executive producer of *Gunsmoke*, *Rawhide*, *The Virginian*, etc.

Little Big Horn 51. Hellgate 52. Arrowhead 53. Flight to Tangier 54. Seven Angry Men 55. The Black Whip 56. Charro (pd) 69, etc.

Warren, Harry (1893–1981) (Salvatore Guaragno).
American songwriter, mainly with Al Dubin; busy on many Warner musicals of the early 30s, they made a personal appearance in *42nd Street*.

Warren, Jennifer (1941–).
American general-purpose actress.

Night Moves 75. Slap Shot 77. Another Man Another Chance 77. Ice Castles 78. Paper Dolls (TV) 84. Amazons (TV) 84, etc.

Warren, Lesley Ann (1946–).
American leading lady.

The Happiest Millionaire 67. Seven in Darkness (TV) 69. Assignment Munich (TV) 72. 79 Park Avenue (TV) 77. Beulah Land (TV) 80. Victor/Victoria (AAN) 82. A Night in Heaven 83. Evergreen (TV) 84. Choose Me 84. Songwriter 84. Clue 85. Burglar 87. Cop 88. Worth Winning 89. Life Stinks 91. Color of Night 94. Bird of Prey 95. Natural Enemy 96. Going All the Way 97. Love Kills 98, etc.

Warren, Robert Penn (1905–1989).
American novelist.

All the King's Men 49. Band of Angels 57.

Warrender, Harold (1903–1953).
British stage and screen actor.

Friday the Thirteenth 33. Contraband 40. Sailors Three 41. Scott of the Antarctic 49. Pandora and the Flying Dutchman 51. Where No Vultures Fly 51. Intimate Relations 53, etc.

Warrick, Ruth (1915–).
American leading lady of the 40s. Former radio singer.

Autobiography: 1980, *The Confessions of Phoebe Tyler*.

Citizen Kane (debut) 41. The Corsican Brothers 41. Journey into Fear 42. Forever and a Day 43. Mr Winkle Goes to War 44. Guest in the House 44. China Sky 45. Swell Guy 47. Arch of Triumph 48. Three Husbands 50. Killer with a Label 50. Let's Dance 52. Ride beyond Vengeance 65. How to Steal the World 68. The Great Bank Robbery 69. The Returning 83. Deathmask 84. The Returning 90, etc.

TV series: Father of the Bride 61. Peyton Place 65.

Warwick, John (1905–1972) (John McIntosh Beattie).
Australian leading man, later character actor, in British films, including many of the 'Scotland Yard' series as police inspector.

Down on the Farm 35. Lucky Jade 37. The Face at the Window 39. Danny Boy 40. The Missing Million 42. Dancing with Crime 48. Street Corner 53. Up to His Neck 54. Just My Luck 57. Horrors of the Black Museum 59.

Warwick, Richard (1945–1997).
English actor whose bid for starring roles never recovered from the disaster of *The Breaking of Bumbo*. Died of AIDS.

If . . . 68. Romeo and Juliet 68. The Bed Sitting Room 69. The Breaking of Bumbo 70. Alice's Adventures in Wonderland 72. Confessions of a Pop Performer 75. Sebastiane 76. International Velvet 78. Black Sun (Swe.) 78. The Tempest 79. My Favorite Year (US) 82. Johnny Dangerously (US) 84. White Hunter, Black Heart (US) 90. The Lost Language of Cranes (TV) 91. Jane Eyre 96, etc.

Warwick, Robert (1878–1965) (Robert Taylor Bien).
American character actor, adept at executives and heavy fathers. A star of such silent films as *A Modern Othello*, *The Mad Lover*, *Thou Art the Man*.

So Big 32. Night Life of the Gods 35. A Tale of Two Cities 35. The Life of Emile Zola 37. The Adventures of Robin Hood 38. Sullivan's Travels 41. The Palm Beach Story 42. I Married a Witch 43. Gentleman's Agreement 47. Francis 49. Sugarfoot 51. Mississippi Gambler 53. Lady Godiva of Coventry 55. Night of the Quarter Moon 59, many others.

Washbourne, Mona (1903–1988).
British stage character actress.

Wide Boy 48. Child's Play 53. Doctor in the House 54. The Good Companions 57. Brides of Dracula 60. *Billy Liar* 63. *Night Must Fall* 63. One Way Pendulum 64. *My Fair Lady* (US) 64. The Third Day (US) 65. Mrs Brown You've Got a Lovely Daughter 68. Fragment of Fear 70. What Became of Jack and Jill? 71. O Lucky Man 73. Stevie 78. Brideshead Revisited (TV) 82, etc.

Washburn, Bryant (1889–1963).
American romantic hero of the silent screen.

The Blindness of Virtue 15. Venus in the East 18. The Parasite 25. Swing High 30. Sutter's Gold 36, many others.

Washington, Denzel (1954–).
American leading actor. Born in Mount Vernon, New York, he studied theatre at Fordham and the American Conservatory Theatre in San Francisco and began on stage, but first came to notice in the TV series *St Elsewhere*, since when he has found success in dramatic and action roles.

Biography: 1997, *Denzel Washington: His Films and Career* by Douglas Brode.

Carbon Copy 81. Licence to Kill 84. A Soldier's Story 84. Power 86. Cry Freedom (AAN) 87. For Queen and Country 88. Reunion 88. *Glory* (AA) 89. The Mighty Quinn 89. Heart Condition 90. Mo' Better Blues 90. Mississippi Masala 91. Ricochet 91. *Malcolm X* (AAN) 92. Much Ado about Nothing 93. Philadelphia 93. The Pelican Brief 93. Crimson Tide 95. Virtuosity 95. Devil in a Blue Dress 95. Courage under Fire 96. The Preacher's Wife 96. Fallen 97. He Got Game 98. The Siege 98, etc.

TV series: St Elsewhere 82–88.

Washington, Ford Lee 'Buck' (1903–1955).
American singer and musician in occasional films, usually as the duo 'Buck and Bubbles' with dancer John 'BUBBLES' Sublett. Born in Louisville, Kentucky, he played piano and trumpet, and the pair appeared in vaudeville and on Broadway from 1912 to the early 50s. He also recorded as a solo pianist and led the band that accompanied blues singer Bessie Smith on her last recordings.

Darktown Follies 30. Calling All Stars (GB) 37. Cabin in the Sky 43. Buck and Bubbles Laugh Jamboree 45. Mantan Messes Up 46. A Song Is Born 48, etc.

Washington, Fredi (1903–1994) (Fredericka Carolyn Washington).
American leading actress who made an impact in *Imitation of Life*, playing a black woman who could pass as white, but who never got another comparable role. She began as a dancer in Broadway musicals and was one of the founders of the Negro Actors Guild, working on stage until her retirement.

The Emperor Jones 33. Imitation of Life 34. One Mile from Heaven 37, etc.

Washington, George (1732–1799).
The first American President, the lad who could not tell a lie, has been impersonated in many films, including *Alexander Hamilton* (Alan Mowbray, who also had the role in *The Phantom President* and *Where Do We Go from Here?*); *America* (Arthur Dewey); *The Howards of Virginia* (George Houston); *The Remarkable Andrew* (Montagu Love); *Unconquered* (Richard Gaines); *John Paul Jones* (John Crawford); *Lafayette* (Howard St John).

Washington, Ned (1901–1976).
American composer with wide show-business experience.

Show of Shows 29. Illegal 32. A Night at the Opera 35. Romance in the Dark 38. Pinocchio 40. Dumbo 41. For Whom the Bell Tolls 43. Passage to Marseilles 44. The Uninvited 44. Green Dolphin Street 47. My Foolish Heart 50. Miss Sadie Thompson 53. The High and the Mighty 54. The Man from Laramie 55. Fire Down Below 57. Gunfight at the OK Corral 57. The Unforgiven 60. The Last Sunset 61. The Fall of the Roman Empire 64. Ship of Fools 65. Five Card Stud 68, many others.

Wasserman, Lew (1913–).
Influential American motion picture executive, head of MCA since 1946 and Universal from 1962 until the company was sold off to Seagram in 1995 by its then Japanese owners.

Wasson, Craig (1954–).
American general-purpose actor.

The Boys in Company C 77. Rollercoaster 77. Go Tell the Spartans 78. The Outsider 80. Schizoid 80. Four Friends 81. Ghost Story 81. Body Double 84. The Men's Club 86. A Nightmare on Elm Street 3: Dream Warriors 87. Midnight Fear 90. Malcolm X 92. Strapped (TV) 93. Trapped in Space 94. The Sister-in-Law 95. Harvest of Fire 95, etc.

Waterhouse, Keith (1929–).
British light journalist and novelist. His *Billy Liar* was successful also as play and film. With Willis Hall he wrote screenplays including *Whistle Down the Wind*, *A Kind of Loving*, *Pretty Polly*.

Waterman, Dennis (1948–).
British juvenile of the 60s, tough TV hero of the 70s.

Pirates of Blood River 61. *Up the Junction* 67. My Lover My Son 69. A Smashing Bird I Used to Know 69. Scars of Dracula 70. Fright 70. Man in the Wilderness 71. The Belstone Fox 73. The Sweeney 77. Sweeney Two 78. Vol-au-Vent 96, etc.

TV series: Fair Exchange 62. *The Sweeney* 74–78. Minder 79–89. On the Up 90–92. Stay Lucky 93. Circles of Deceit 95–96.

Waters, Ethel (1896–1977).
Distinguished American actress and singer.

Autobiography: 1953, *His Eye Is on the Sparrow*.

On with the Show 29. Tales of Manhattan 42. *Cabin in the Sky* 43. *Pinky* (AAN) 49. *Member of the Wedding* 52. The Sound and the Fury 59, etc.

TV series: Beulah 50–5?.

❝ Every time I tried to help her, she'd roll her eyes to the heavens and say, 'God is my director!' How can you argue with that? – *Fred Zinnemann*

Waters, John.
Australian leading actor.

End Play 75. Eliza Fraser 76. The Getting of Wisdom 77. Weekend of Shadows 78. Breaker Morant 80. Attack Force Z 82. Bushfire Moon 87. Grievous Bodily Harm 88. Boulevard of Broken Dreams 88. Which Way Home (TV) 90. Heaven Tonight 93, etc.

Waters, John (1946–).
American director and screenwriter of cult comedies in deliberately bad taste.

Autobiography: 1990, *Shock Value*.

■ Mondo Trasho 70. Multiple Maniacs 71. Pink Flamingos 72. Female Trouble 75. Desperate Living 77. Polyester 81. Something Wild 86. Hairspray 88. Cry-Baby 90. Serial Mom 94. Pecker 98.

❝ I've been called the 'King of Sleaze', the 'Pope of Trash', the 'Prince of Puke', and recently new ones have been added – the 'Duke of Dirt', the 'Ambassador of Anguish' and the 'Anal Anarchist'. All are fine by me, but I think the 'Pope of Trash' sounds more dignified. – *J.W.*

Often I wish I was a girl just so I could get an abortion. – *J.W.*

In America it doesn't matter what you've done as long as you're famous. – *J.W.*

Waters, Russell (1908–1982).
British character actor usually in meek and mild parts. The 'hero' of many of Richard Massingham's short and light-hearted instructional films.

The Woman in the Hall 47. The Happiest Days of Your Life 50. The Maggie 54. Left, Right and Centre 59, many others.

Waterston, Sam (1940–).
American general-purpose actor.

A Time for Giving 69. Savages 72. A Delicate Balance 73. *The Great Gatsby* 74. Rancho de Luxe 75. Capricorn One 78. Interiors 78. Eagle's Wing 79. Sweet William 79. Heaven's Gate 80. Hopscotch 80. Oppenheimer (TV) 81. Q.E.D. (TV) 81. Finnegan Begin Again (TV) 84. The Killing Fields (AAN) 84. September 87. Welcome Home 89. Crimes and Misdemeanors 89. Lantern Hill (TV) 90. Mindwalk 90. The Man in the Moon 91. A Captive in the Land 91. Serial Mom 94. David's Mother (TV) 94. The Journey of August King 95. The Proprietor 96. Shadow Conspiracy 97, etc.

TV series: Q.E.D. 82. I'll Fly Away 91.

Watkin, David (1925–).
British cinematographer.

The Knack 64. Help 65. The Marat/Sade 66. How I Won the War 67. The Charge of the Light Brigade 67. The Bed Sitting Room 69. Catch 22 70. The Devils 71. The Boy Friend 71. A Delicate Balance 73. The Three Musketeers 74. Robin and Marian 76. Chariots of Fire 81. Yentl 83. Out of Africa (AA) 85. Six Bandits 86. Moonstruck 87. Masquerade 88. The Good Mother 88. Last Rites 88. Journey to the Center of the Earth 89. Memphis Belle 90. Hamlet 90. Object of Beauty 91. This Boy's Life 93. Bopha! 93. Milk Money 94. Jane Eyre 96. Bogus 96. Obsession 97. Critical Care

97. Night Falls on Manhattan 97. Tea with Mussolini 99, etc.

Watkin, Pierre (1889–1960).
American character actor often seen as lawyer, doctor or kindly father.
Dangerous 35. Pride of the Yankees 41. Whistling in Dixie 43. Shanghai Chest 46. Knock On Any Door 59. The Dark Page 51. Johnny Dark 54, many others.

Watkins, Peter (1937–).
British director from TV (*Culloden*, *The War Game*), now based in Sweden.
■ Privilege 67. Punishment Park 71. Edvard Munch 75. 70-Talets 75. Fallen 75. Evening Land 77. The Journey (TV) 87.

Watling, Jack (1923–).
Boyish British character actor.
Sixty Glorious Years 38. Journey Together 45. The Courtneys of Curzon Street 47. Quartet 48. The Winslow Boy 48. Meet Mr Lucifer 54. The Sea Shall Not Have Them 55. The Admirable Crichton 57. A Night to Remember 58. Mary Had a Little 61. 11 Harrowhouse 74, many others.

Watson, Bobs (1931–).
American boy actor of the 30s and 40s; noted for his ability to weep at the drop of a hat. Now a Methodist minister.
In Old Chicago 38. Kentucky 39. *On Borrowed Time* 39. Dr Kildare's Crisis 41. Men of Boys' Town 41. The Bold and the Brave 56. First to Fight 67, etc.
TV series: The Jim Backus Show 60.

Watson, Emily (1967–).
British leading actress, born in London, from the stage.
Breaking the Waves (AAN) 96. Hilary and Jackie 98. Metroland 98. Angela's Ashes 98, etc.

Watson, Jack (1921–).
Tough-looking British general-purpose actor. He began in music hall with his father, comedian Nosmo King (Vernon Watson).
Konga 61. This Sporting Life 62. The Hill 65. Tobruk 67. *The Strange Affair* 67. Every Home Should Have One 70. The Mackenzie Break 71. Kidnapped 72. Juggernaut 76. Schizo 77. The Wild Geese 79. The Sea Wolves 80. Love and Reason (TV) 93, etc.

Watson, Lucile (1879–1962).
Canadian character actress with stage experience; usually in imperious roles.
■ What Every Woman Knows 34. The Bishop Misbehaves 35. A Woman Rebels 36. The Garden of Allah 36. Three Smart Girls 36. The Young in Heart 38. Sweethearts 38. Made for Each Other 39. The Women 39. Florian 40. *Waterloo Bridge* 40. Mr and Mrs Smith 41. Rage in Heaven 41. Footsteps in the Dark 41. The Great Lie 41. Model Wife 41. *Watch on the Rhine* (AAN) 43. Till We Meet Again 44. The Thin Man Goes Home 44. Uncertain Glory 44. My Reputation 46. Tomorrow Is Forever 46. Never Say Goodbye 46. *The Razor's Edge* 46. Song of the South 46. Ivy 47. The Emperor Waltz 48. Julia Misbehaves 48. That Wonderful Urge 48. Little Women 49. Everybody Does It 49. Harriet Craig 50. Let's Dance 50. My Forbidden Past 51.

Watson, Minor (1889–1965).
American character actor who often played lawyers or kindly fathers.
Rescuing Dave 13. No. 28 Diplomat 14. 24 Hours 31. Our Betters 33. Babbitt 34. When's Your Birthday? 37. Boys' Town 38. Moon over Miami 41. The Big Shot 42. The Virginian 46. The File on Thelma Jordon 49. Mister 880 50. My Son John 51. Trapeze 56, etc.

Watson, Moray (1928–).
British light actor.
The Grass is Greener 65. Operation Crossbow 65. Every Home should Have One 70. The Sea Wolves 80. Crazy Like a Fox (TV) 87, etc.

Watson, Robert (1888–1965).
American character actor who became famous for his resemblance to Hitler; played the lead in *The Hitler Gang* 43, and other films of this type.
Moonlight and Melody 33. Mary of Scotland 36. The Devil with Hitler 42. Nazty Nuisance 43. The Big Clock 48. Red Hot and Blue 49. Singin' in the Rain 52. The Story of Mankind 57, etc.

Watson, Wylie (1889–1966) (John Wylie Robertson).
British character actor, usually in 'little man' roles; formerly in music hall.
■ For the Love of Mike 32. Leave It to Me 33. Hawleys of the High Street 33. *The Thirty-Nine Steps* (as Mr Memory) 35. Black Mask 35. Radio Lover 36. Please Teacher 37. Why Pick on Me? 37. Paradise for Two 37. Queer Cargo 38. Yes Madam 38. Jamaica Inn 39. She Couldn't Say No 39. Pack Up Your Troubles 40. Bulldog Sees It Through 40. Danny Boy 41. My Wife's Family 41. The Saint Meets the Tiger 41. The Flemish Farm 43. The Lamp Still Burns 43. Tawny Pipit 44. Kiss the Bride Goodbye 44. Don't Take It to Heart 44. Waterloo Road 45. The World Owes Me a Living 45. Strawberry Roan 45. Don Chicago 45. Waltz Time 45. Murder in Reverse 45. The Trojan Brothers 46. The Years Between 46. Girl in a Million 46. Temptation Harbour 47. Fame Is the Spur 47. Brighton Rock 47. My Brother Jonathan 48. *London Belongs to Me* 48. No Room at the Inn 48. Things Happen at Night 48. The History of Mr Polly 49. *Whisky Galore* 49. Train of Events 49. Your Witness 50. Morning Departure 50. Shadow of the Past 50. The Magnet 50. Happy Go Lovely 51. *The Sundowners* 61.

Watt, Harry (1906–1987).
British director with varied early experience before joining GPO Film Unit as assistant in 1931.
Autobiography: 1974, *Don't Look at the Camera*.
Night Mail 36. North Sea 38. Squadron 992 40. Target for Tonight 41. *Nine Men* (& w) 44. Fiddlers Three 44. The Overlanders 46. Eureka Stockade 48. Where No Vultures Fly 51. West of Zanzibar 53. The Siege of Pinchgut 59, etc.

Wattis, Richard (1912–1975).
Bespectacled British character comedian with stage experience.
The Happiest Days of Your Life 49. The Clouded Yellow 51. Hobson's Choice 54. I Am a Camera 55. Simon and Laura 55. The Prince and the Showgirl 58. The VIPs 63. Moll Flanders 65. Up Jumped a Swagman 65. Wonderwall 68. Games that Lovers Play 69. That's Your Funeral 73. Diamonds on Wheels 73. Hot Property 73, many others.
TV series: Dick and the Duchess 59. Sykes (through 60s).

Watts, Naomi (1968–).
English-born actress who was educated in Australia and is now based in Los Angeles.
Flirting 89. Brides of Christ (TV) 91. Wide Sargasso Sea 92. Gross Misconduct 93. Matinee 93. Tank Girl 94. Bermuda Triangle (TV) 96. Children of the Corn IV: The Gathering 96. Dangerous Beauty 98, etc.

Waugh, Evelyn (1903–1966).
English novelist whose combination of snobbery and social satire has appealed to directors of period movies.
The Loved One 65. Decline and Fall 68. Brideshead Revisited (TV) 82. Scoop (TV) 87. A Handful of Dust 88.

Waxman, Franz (1906–1967) (Franz Wachsmann).
German composer, in America from 1934.
Bride of Frankenstein 35. Sutter's Gold 36. Fury 36. Captains Courageous 38. The Young in Heart 38. *Rebecca* 40. *The Philadelphia Story* 40. Dr Jekyll and Mr Hyde 41. Woman of the Year 42. Air Force 42. Mr Skeffington 44. Objective Burma 45. Humoresque 46. The Paradine Case 48. *Alias Nick Beal* 49. *Sunset Boulevard* (AA) 50. *A Place in the Sun* (AA) 51. My Cousin Rachel 53. Rear Window 54. Mister Roberts 56. Sayonara 57. The Nun's Story 59. Cimarron 60. Taras Bulba 62. Lost Command 66, etc.

Waxman, Harry (1912–1984).
British cinematographer.
Brighton Rock 46. They Were Not Divided 48. Valley of Eagles 51. The Baby and the Battleship 56. *Innocent Sinners* 57. The Secret Partner 60. The Roman Spring of Mrs Stone 61. *The Day the Earth Caught Fire* 62. Lancelot and Guinevere 63. Crooks in Cloisters 64. The Nanny 65. *Khartoum* (2nd unit) 66. The Family Way 66. The Trygon Factor 67. The Anniversary 67. Wonderwall 68. Twisted Nerve 68. There's a Girl in My Soup 70. Flight of the Doves 71. Endless Night 72. Digby 73. Blue Blood 73. Vampira 74. Journey into Fear 75. The Pink Panther Strikes Again 76, etc.

Wayans, Damon (1960–).
American comedian and actor. He is the brother of Keenen Ivory WAYANS.
Beverly Hills Cop 84. Roxanne 87. Hollywood Shuffle 87. Punchline 88. I'm Gonna Git You Sucka 88. Colors 88. Earth Girls Are Easy 89. The Last Boy Scout 91. Mo' Money (a, w, p) 92. Blankman (a, p, co-w, d) 94. Major Payne 95. Celtic Pride 96. The Great White Hype 96. Bulletproof 96, etc.
TV series: In Living Color 90–93. 413 Hope St (p, w) 97–98. Damon 98– .

Wayans, Keenen Ivory (1958–).
American director, screenwriter and actor. He is the brother of Damon WAYANS.
Hollywood Shuffle (a, co-w) 87. Eddie Murphy Raw (co-w) 87. I'm Gonna Git You Sucka (a, wd) 88. The Five Heartbeats (co-w) 91. Low Down Dirty Shame (a, d) 94. Don't Be a Menace to South Central While Drinking Your Juice in the Hood 95. The Glimmer Man 96. Most Wanted (a, w) 97, etc.
TV series: In Living Color 90–93. The Keenan Ivory Wayans Show 97– .

Wayne, Bernie (1919–1993).
American composer and songwriter whose best known song was 'Blue Velvet', used in Kenneth Anger's *Scorpio Rising* 64 and David Lynch's *Blue Velvet* 86.
Duffy's Tavern 45. Out of This World 45. Blues Busters 50. Viva Las Vegas 64, etc.

Wayne, David (1914–1995) (Wayne McKeekan).
Wiry American character actor, in films since late 40s, also stage star.
Portrait of Jennie 48. *Adam's Rib* 49. My Blue Heaven 50. Up Front 51. With a Song in My Heart 52. *Wait till the Sun Shines Nellie* 52. The I Don't Care Girl 53. Tonight We Sing 53. How to Marry a Millionaire 53. The Tender Trap 55. The Three Faces of Eve 57. The Last Angry Man 59. The Big Gamble 60. The Andromeda Strain 70. Huckleberry Finn 74. The Front Page 74. The Apple Dumpling Gang 75. Lassie: the New Beginning 79. House Calls 80. Poker Alice 87, etc.
TV series: Norby 51. The Good Life 71. Ellery Queen 74. Dallas 78. House Calls 80.

Wayne, John (1907–1979) (Marion Michael Morrison).
Tough, genial, generally inimitable American leading man of action films who after a slow start became one of the best known and most successful actors in Hollywood.
Biographies: 1974, *Shooting Star* by Maurice Zolotow; 1991, *John Wayne: Actor, Artist, Hero* by Richard D. McGhee; 1997, *John Wayne: The Politics of Celebrity* by Garry Wills; 1998, *John Wayne: American* by Randy Roberts and James S. Olson.
■ The Drop Kick 27. Hangman's House 28. Mother Machree 28. Salute 29. Words and Music 29. Men without Women 30. Rough Romance 30. Cheer Up and Smile 30. *The Big Trail* 30. Girls Demand Excitement 31. Three Girls Lost 31. Men Are Like That 31. Range Feud 31. Hurricane Express (serial) 31. Shadow of the Eagle (serial) 32. Maker of Men 32. Two Fisted Law 32. Texas Cyclone 32. Lady and Gent 32. Ride Him Cowboy 32. The Big Stampede 32. The Three Mesquiteers (serial) 33. Haunted Gold 33. Telegraph Trail 33. His Private Secretary 33. Central Airport 33. Baby Face Harrington 33. The Sagebrush Trail 33. Somewhere in Sonora 33. The Life of Jimmy Dolan 33. Baby Face 33. The Man from Monterey 33. Riders of Destiny 33. College Coach 33. West of the Divide 34. Blue Steel 34. Lucky Texan 34. The Man from Utah 34. Randy Rides Alone 34. The Star Packer 34. The Trail Beyond 34. Neath Arizona Skies 34. Texas Terror 35. The Lawless Frontier 35. New Frontier 35. Lawless Range 35. Rainbow Valley 35. Paradise Canyon 35. The Dawn Rider 35. Westward Ho 35. Desert Trail 35. The Lawless Nineties 36. King of the Pecos 36. The Oregon Trail 36. Winds of the Wasteland 36. The Sea Spoilers 36. The Lonely Trail 36. Conflict 36. California Straight Ahead 37. Cover the War 37. Idol of the Crowds 37. Adventure's End 37. Born to the West 37. Pals of the Saddle 37. I Cover the War 37. Helltown 37. Overland Stage Raiders 38. Santa Fe Stampede 38. Red River Range 38. *Stagecoach* 39. Night Riders 39. Three Texas Steers 39. Wyoming Outlaw 39. New Frontier 39. Allegheny Uprising 39. Dark Command 40. Three Faces West 40. *The Long Voyage Home* 40. *Seven Sinners* 40. A Man Betrayed 40. The Lady from Louisiana 41. The Shepherd of the Hills 41. Lady for a Night 41. Reap the Wild Wind 42. The Spoilers 42. In Old California 42. Flying Tigers 42. Reunion in France 42. Pittsburgh 42. A Lady Takes a Chance 43. In Old Oklahoma 43. The Fighting Seabees 44. Tall in the Saddle 44. Back to Bataan 44. Flame of the Barbary Coast 44. Dakota 45. They Were Expendable 45. Without Reservations 46. Angel and the Badman 47. Tycoon 47. Fort Apache 48. *Red River* 48. Three Godfathers 48. Wake of the Red Witch 48. The Fighting Kentuckian 49. *She Wore a Yellow Ribbon* 49. *Sands of Iwo Jima* (AAN) 49. Rio Grande 50. Operation Pacific 51. Flying Leathernecks 51. Big Jim McLain 52. *The Quiet Man* 52. Trouble Along the Way 53. Island in the Sky 53. Hondo 53. *The High and the Mighty* 54. The Sea Chase 55. Blood Alley 55. The Conqueror 55. I Married a Woman (gag appearance) 55. *The Searchers* 56. The Wings of Eagles 57. Jet Pilot 57. The Barbarian and the Geisha 58. *Rio Bravo* 59. The Horse Soldiers 59. North to Alaska 60. *The Alamo* (& p, d) 60. The Comancheros 61. The Man Who Shot Liberty Valance 62. Hatari 62. The Longest Day 62. How the West Was Won 63. Donovan's Reef 63. McLintock 63. Circus World 64. The Greatest Story Ever Told 65. In Harm's Way 65. The Sons of Katie Elder 65. Cast a Giant Shadow 66. El Dorado 67. The War Wagon 67. The Green Berets (& d) 68. Hellfighters 68. The Undefeated 69. *True Grit* (AA) 69. Rio Lobo 70. Chisum 70. Big Jake 71. The Cowboys 72. The Train Robbers 73. Cahill 73. McQ 74. Brannigan 75. Rooster Cogburn 75. *The Shootist* 76.
✪ For appearing in more films than any other star, and for winning respect after a lifetime of larger-than-life roles. *The Quiet Man*.
❝ I play John Wayne in every picture regardless of the character, and I've been doing all right, haven't I? – *J.W.*
I never had a goddam artistic problem in my life, never, and I've worked with the best of them. John Ford isn't exactly a bum, is he? Yet he never gave me any manure about art. – *J.W.*
Westerns are closer to art than anything else in the motion picture business. – *J.W.*
He has an endless face and he can go on forever. – *L. B. Mayer*
Famous line (*True Grit*): 'Come and see a fat old man sometime!'
Famous line (*Hondo*): 'A man oughta do what he thinks is right.'

Wayne, Michael (1934–).
American producer, son of John Wayne.
McLintock 63. The Green Berets 67. Cahill 73, etc.

Wayne, Naunton (1901–1970) (Naunton Davies).
Mild-mannered British light comedy actor, on stage from 1920, films from 1931; became well known with Basil Radford in many films as Englishmen abroad.
The First Mrs Fraser (debut) 31. Going Gay 33. For Love of You 34. *The Lady Vanishes* 38. *Night Train to Munich* 40. *Crooks' Tour* 41. Next of Kin 42. Millions Like Us 43. *Dead of Night* 45. The Calendar 47. *It's Not Cricket* 48. Quartet 48. Passport to Pimlico 48. Obsession 49. Highly Dangerous 50. *The Titfield Thunderbolt* 53. You Know What Sailors Are 53. Nothing Barred 61. Double Bunk 64, many others.

Wayne, Patrick (1939–).
American leading man, son of John Wayne.
The Searchers 56. The Alamo 60. The Comancheros 62. McLintock 63. The Bears and I 74. The People that Time Forgot 77. Sinbad and the Eye of the Tiger 77. Rustler's Rhapsody 85. Revenge 86. Young Guns 88. Her Alibi 89. Blind Vengeance 90. Chill Factor 90, etc.
TV series: The Rounders 66. Shirley 78. The Monte Carlo Show 81.

Wead, Frank 'Spig' (1895–1947).
American screenwriter of the 30s, a former navy flier whose early life was played by John Wayne in *The Wings of Eagles* (1957).

Weathers, Carl (1948–).
American actor, a former football player.
Bucktown 75. Friday Foster 75. *Rocky* 76. Close Encounters of the Third Kind 77. Semi-Tough 77. Force Ten from Navarone 78. Rocky II 79. Death Hunt 81. Rocky III 82. Rocky IV 86. Predator 87. Action Jackson 88. Hurricane Smith 92. Tom Clancy's Op Center (TV) 95. Happy Gilmore 96, etc.
TV series: Fortune Dane 86. Tour of Duty 89–90. Street Justice 91.

Weaver, Dennis (1924–).
American character actor and TV star.
The Raiders 52. War Arrow 54. Seven Angry Men 55. Touch of Evil 58. The Gallant Hours 60. Duel at Diablo 66. The Great Man's Whiskers (TV) 71. What's the Matter with Helen 71. Duel (TV) 71. The Forgotten Man (TV) 71. Rollin' Man (TV) 72. The Islander (TV) 78. Centennial (TV) 78. Pearl (TV) 78. Ishi: The Last of His Tribe (TV) 78. The Ordeal of Patty Hearst (TV) 79. The Ordeal of Dr Mudd (TV) 80. Going for the Gold: The Bill Johnson Story (TV) 85. Bluffing It (TV) 87, etc.
TV series: Gunsmoke (as Chester) 55–63. Kentucky Jones 65. McCloud 70–76. Stone 79. Navy 83.

Weaver, Doodles (1911–1983) (Winstead Sheffield Weaver).
American character comedian, often in hayseed roles. Born in Los Angeles, he was a member of Spike Jones's City Slickers in the late 40s, noted for his comic horse-race commentary to the *William Tell Overture*. He shot himself when depressed by his suffering from a heart condition. Married four times, he was the uncle of actress Sigourney Weaver.
Behind the Headlines 37. Topper 37. Another Thin Man 39. Kitty Foyle 40. A Girl, a Guy, and a Gob 41. The Pied Piper 43. San Antonio 45. Gentlemen Prefer Blondes 52. Frontier Gun 58. Hot Rod Gang 58. The Great Impostor 60. The Errand Boy 61. Ring of Fire 61. The Ladies' Man 61. Pocketful of Miracles 61. Mail Order Bride 63. A Tiger Walks 63. Tammy and the Doctor 63. The Birds 63. Quick, Before It Melts 64. Fluffy 64. The Rounders 64. The Spirit Is Willing 66. Road to Nashville 66. Rosie! 67. Cancel My Reservation 72. Macon County Line 73. Won Ton Ton, the Dog Who Saved Hollywood 75. The Great Gundown 77, etc.
TV series: Doodles Weaver 51.

Weaver, Fritz (1926–).
American stage actor.
Fail Safe 64. The Borgia Stick (TV) 68. The Maltese Bippy 69. A Walk in the Spring Rain 70. The Day of the Dolphin 73. Marathon Man 76. Demon Seed 77. Black Sunday 77. The Big Fix 78. *Holocaust* (TV) 78. Jaws of Satan 79. Creepshow 82. Power 85. Blind Spot (TV) 93. Broken Trust (TV) 95, etc.

Weaver, Marjorie (1913–1994).
American leading lady, mainly of second features.
China Clipper 36. Three Blind Mice 38. Young Mr Lincoln 39. Maryland 40. The Mad Martindales 42. We're Not Married 52, many others.

Weaver, Sigourney (1949–) (Susan Alexandra Weaver).
American leading actress, indelibly associated with the role of the tough and resourceful Ripley in the *Alien* movies. Born in New York City, she studied at Yale Drama School and began on the stage.
Alien 79. Eyewitness 81. The Year of Living Dangerously 83. Deal of the Century 83. Ghostbusters 84. Half Moon Street 86. Aliens (AAN) 86. *Gorillas in the Mist* (AAN) 88. Working Girl (AAN) 88. Ghostbusters II 89. Alien^3 92. 1492 92. Dave 93. Death and the Maiden 94. Jeffrey 95. Copycat 95. Snow White: A Tale of Terror 97. Alien: Resurrection 97. The Ice Storm 97, etc.
❝ I think I get sent the roles Meryl's not doing. – *S.W.*

Weaving, Hugo.
Australian leading actor.
The City's Edge 85. For Love Alone 86. The Right Hand Man 87. Wendy Cracked a Walnut 90. Proof 91. The Custodian 93. Reckless Kelly 93. Frauds 93. *The Adventures of Priscilla, Queen of the Desert* 94. Exile 94. Babe (voice) 95. True Love and Chaos 96. Bedrooms & Hallways 98. The Interview 98. Babe: Pig in the City (voice) 98, etc.

Webb, Alan (1906–1982).
Lean British character actor, mainly on stage.
Lease of Life 54. The Pumpkin Eater 64. Chimes at Midnight 66. The Taming of the Shrew 67. Entertaining Mr Sloane 69. Women in Love 69. Nicholas and Alexandra 71. The First Great Train Robbery 78. Rough Cut 80, etc.

Webb, Chloe (c. 1960–).
American actress, born New York.
Sid and Nancy 86. The Belly of an Architect 87. Twins 88. China Beach 88. Ghostbusters II 89. Heart Condition 90. Queens Logic 91. Lucky Day (TV) 91. A Dangerous Woman 93. Tales of the City (TV) 93. Love Affair 94. The Newton Boys 97. Practical Magic 98, etc.
TV series: Thicke of the Night 83. China Beach 88.

Webb, Clifton (1893–1966) (Webb Parmelee Hollenbeck).
American leading character actor, former dancer and stage star. In films, became in middle age well-known in waspish roles.
■ Polly with a Past 20. Let No Man Put Asunder 24. New Toys 25. The Heart of a Siren 25. The Still Alarm 26. *Laura* (AAN) 44. The Dark Corner 46. *The Razor's Edge* (AAN) 46. *Sitting Pretty* (AAN) 48. Mr Belvedere Goes to College 49. *Cheaper by the Dozen* 50. For Heaven's Sake 50. Mr Belvedere Rings the Bell 51. Elopement 51. Dreamboat 52. Stars and Stripes Forever 52. Titanic 53. Mister Scoutmaster 53. *Three Coins in the Fountain* 54. Woman's World 54. *The Man Who Never Was* 55. Boy on a Dolphin 57. The Remarkable Mr Pennypacker 58. Holiday for Lovers 59. Satan Never Sleeps 62.
Famous line (*The Dark Corner*): 'I detest the dawn. The grass always looks as though it's been out all night.'
Famous line (*The Razor's Edge*): 'The enjoyment of art is the only remaining ecstasy that's neither immoral nor illegal.'
Famous line (*The Razor's Edge*): 'If I live to be a hundred I shall never understand how any young man can come to Paris without evening clothes.'

Webb, Jack (1920–1982).
American TV star and executive: starred and directed in *Dragnet* and other series; was briefly head of Warner TV. The first of his four wives was singer Julie London.
As actor: The Men 50. Sunset Boulevard 50. You're in the Navy Now 52. Dragnet (& pd) 54. Pete Kelly's Blues (& pd) 55. The D.I. (& pd) 57. The Last Time I Saw Archie (& pd) 62, many others.

Webb, James R. (1910–1974).
American screenwriter.
The Charge at Feather River 53. Phantom of the Rue Morgue (co-w) 54. Trapeze 56. The Big Country (co-w) 58. Pork Chop Hill 59. How the West Was Won (AA) 63. Guns for San Sebastian 67. Alfred the Great (co-w) 69, many others.

Webb, Millard (1893–1935).
American director who trained as a civil engineer and, after brief experience on stage, began as an extra and writer in silent films.
Oliver Twist Jnr 21. The Dark Swan (& co-ph) 24. *The Sea Beast* 25. My Wife and I (& co-w) 25. The Drop Kick 27. Gentlemen of the Press 29. Glorifying the American Girl (& co-w) 29. Happy Ending (GB) 31, etc.

Webb, Robert D. (1903–1990).
American director, former cameraman. Married editor Barbara McLean.
White Feather 55. On the Threshold of Space 55. The Proud Ones 56. Love Me Tender 56. The Way to the Gold 57. Seven Women from Hell 61. The Agony and the Ecstasy (second unit) 65. Capetown Affair 67, etc.

Webb, Roy (1888–1982).
American composer.
Alice Adams 35. Quality Street 37. Room Service 38. Kitty Foyle 40. Cat People 42. Journey into Fear 42. Experiment Perilous 44. The Body Snatcher 45. Murder My Sweet 45. Notorious 46. The Spiral Staircase 46. Blood on the Moon 48. Mighty Joe Young 49. Flying Leathernecks 51. Houdini 53. Blood Alley 55. Top Secret Affair 57. Teacher's Pet 58, many others.

Webber, Robert (1924–1989).
American leading man with stage and TV experience.
Highway 301 51. *Twelve Angry Men* 57. The Stripper 63. Hysteria (GB) 64. The Sandpiper 65. The Third Day 65. No Tears for a Killer (It.) 65. Harper 66. The Silencers 67. The Dirty Dozen 67. Dollars 72. Bring Me the Head of Alfredo Garcia 74. Midway 76. The Choirboys 77. Casey's Shadow 78. Revenge of the Pink Panther 78. '10' 79. Private Benjamin 80. S.O.B. 81. Wrong Is Right 82. Wild Geese II 84, etc.

Weber, Bruce (1946–).
American documentary director, best known as a fashion and commercial photographer, notably for Calvin Klein's advertisements.
Broken Noses 87. Let's Get Lost 88.

Weber, Lois (1882–1939).
American director, writer, producer, and actress. After a period on stage, she went to work for the Gaumont Film Studio in New Jersey in 1908, moving to Universal in Hollywood in 1913, where her salary rose to $5,000 a week. Many of her films, which often dealt with social problems, were controversial. *Where Are My Children?*, for instance, advocated birth control (though it was opposed to abortion) and was banned in some cities. Her career declined from the mid-20s. She was married to actor and director Phillips Smalley who appeared in, and also co-directed, some of her films.
On the Brink (a) 11. The Female of the Species (a, d) 13. The Merchant of Venice (a, w, co-d) 14. Hypocrites (wd) 14. The Dumb Girl of Portici (co-d) 15. Scandal (co-d) 15. Where Are My Children? (w, co-d) 16. Shoes (wd) 16. The Hand that Rocks the Cradle (a, p, d) 17. The Price of a Good Time (w, co-d) 17. For Husbands Only (w, co-d) 18. Forbidden (co-d) 19. A Chapter in Her Life (co-w, d) 23. The Marriage Clause (wd) 26. The Angel of Broadway (d) 27. Sensation Seekers (wd) 27. White Heat (d) 34, etc.
❝ I'll never be convinced that the general public does not want serious entertainment rather than frivolous. – *L.W.*

Weber, Steven (1961–).
American leading actor, best known for his role as Brian in the 90s TV sitcom *Wings*.
Flamingo Kid 84. Hamburger Hill 87. Single White Female 92. The Temp 93. Jeffrey 95. Dracula: Dead and Loving It 95. The Shining (TV) 97. I Woke Up Early the Day I Died 98. At First Sight 98, etc.

Webster, Ben (1864–1947).
British stage character actor of the old school, married to May Whitty.
The House of Temperley 13. Enoch Arden 14. The Vicar of Wakefield 16. Because 18. The Call of Youth 20. The Only Way 25. Downhill 27. The Lyons Mail 31. The Old Curiosity Shop 34. Drake of England 35, etc.

Webster, Ferris (1916–).
American editor.
The Picture of Dorian Gray 45. If Winter Comes 47. Father of the Bride 50. Lone Star 52. Lili 53. The Blackboard Jungle 55. Forbidden Planet 56. Cat on a Hot Tin Roof 58. The Magnificent Seven 60. *The Manchurian Candidate* 62. The Great Escape 63. Seven Days in May 64. Seconds 66. Ice Station Zebra 68. Zigzag 70. High Plains Drifter 73. The Enforcer 76. The Gauntlet 77. Every Which Way But Loose 78. Escape from Alcatraz 79. Bronco Billy 80. Any Which Way You Can 80. Honkytonk Man 82. Firefox 82, many others.

Webster, Paul Francis (1907–1984).
American lyricist. Various Shirley Temple songs in the 30s; later *Love is a Many Splendored Thing* (AA) 54. *Friendly Persuasion* 56. *The Sandpiper* (AA) 65, etc.

Weegee (1899–1968) (Arthur Fellig).
Brash Austrian-born American news photographer noted for his often snatched and sensational night-time photographs, taken by flashlight on the streets of New York, of fires, gangsters, suicides, the victims of murderers and muggers, socialites, and lowlife. His book *Naked City*, published in 1945, was bought by Universal and resulted in Jules Dassin's film of the same name in 1948 ('There are eight million stories in the naked city. This has been one of them . . .'). His stark, high-contrast style can be said to have shaped the look of film noir and also influenced cinematographer Michael Chapman's work in *Raging Bull*. In 1948 he made a short film, *Weegee's New York*, worked briefly in Hollywood as a consultant, and played cameos in several films including *Every Girl Should Be Married* 48 and *The Set-Up* 49. He was a consultant and stills photographer on *Dr Strangelove*. A documentary about his work, *The Naked Eye*, was made in 1957. He was also the model for the photographer-hero of *The Public Eye* 92, directed by Howard Franklin. His nickname derived from his ability to be first on the scene of a tragedy, which was attributed to his use of a ouija board, but was more to do with the police radio he kept in his car-cum-office.
Autobiography: 1961, *Weegee by Weegee*.

Weeks, Stephen (1948–).
British director.
■ I Monster 70. Sir Gawain and the Green Knight 72. Ghost Story 74. Sword of the Valiant 84.

Wegener, Paul (1874–1948).
Distinguished German actor-writer-director.
The Student of Prague (a) 13. The Golem (ad) 14 and 20. Vanina (a) 22. Svengali (a, wd) 27. Lucrezia Borgia (a) 27. Ein Mann Will Nach Deutschland (d) 34. Der Grosse König (a) 41. Der Grosse Mandarin (a) 48, many others.

Wei, Lo (1918–1996).
Chinese director, screenwriter, producer and production designer of Hong Kong action movies, who helped make stars of Bruce Lee and Jackie Chan. He began as an actor, turning to directing in the 70s.
Red Blossom in the Snow (a) 56. The Big Boss/Fists of Fury (wd) 71. Back Alley Princes (a, wd) 72. Dragon Swamp (a, wd) 71. Fist of Fury/The Chinese Connection (p, wd) 72. Shatter (a) 74. Dragon Fist (d) 78, etc.

Weidler, Virginia (1927–1968).
American child actress who usually played a little horror. Retired in 1947, when she married. Died of a heart attack.
Surrender 31. Mrs Wiggs of the Cabbage Patch 34. Souls at Sea 37. The Women 39. *The Philadelphia Story* 40. Born to Sing 42. The Youngest Profession 43. Best Foot Forward 43, etc.

Weidman, Jerome (1913–1998).
American novelist and screenwriter. Born in New York, he began as a clerk, studying law at night, and scored a success with his first novel, *I Can Get It for You Wholesale*, published when he was 24, which later became a film and a Broadway musical.
House of Strangers (oa) 49. The Damned Don't Cry 50. I Can Get It for You Wholesale/This Is My Affair (oa) 51. Invitation (oa) 51. The Eddie Cantor Story 53. Slander 56, etc.

Weil, Samuel:
see Kaufman, Lloyd.

Weill, Claudia (1947–).
American director and screenwriter, from TV.
Joyce at 34 72. The Other Half of the Sky 75. Girlfriends 78. It's My Turn 80. Johnny Bull (TV) 86. Face of a Stranger (TV) 91. A Child Lost Forever (TV) 92. Critical Choices (TV) 96. Giving Up the Ghost (TV) 98, etc.

Weill, Cynthia (1937–).
American lyricist and singer whose songs, often written with her husband Barry Mann, have featured in several movies.
Wild in the Streets (s) 68. Cactus Flower (s) 69. I Never Sang for My Father (s) 69. An American Tail (s) 86. Summer Heat (s) 87. Harry and the Hendersons (s) 87. National Lampoon's Christmas Vacation (s) 89. Sibling Rivalry (s) 90. Muppet Treasure Island (s) 96. All Dogs Go to Heaven 2 (s) 96, etc.

Weill, Kurt (1900–1950).
German composer whose scores include *Die Dreigroschenoper*, *One Touch of Venus* and *Knickerbocker Holiday*, all filmed. Woody Allen used his music in *Shadows and Fog* 91.

Weingarten, Laurence (1898–1975).
American producer, in films from around 1917.
Broadway Melody 28. A Day at the Races 37. Escape 40. Adam's Rib 49. The Tender Trap 54. Cat on a Hot Tin Roof 58. The Unsinkable Molly Brown 64, many others.

Weinstein, Harvey and Bob.
American producers and distributors. In 1979 they founded Miramax, a company noted for its success in distributing art-house and independent features, and in the 90s Dimension Films, as a distributor of horror and action movies. They became part of the Disney empire in 1993, selling the company for a reported $100m.
❝ These guys could sell sand in the desert. – *Guillermo del Toro*

Weintraub, Fred (1928–).
American producer, formerly with Warner in the 70s, noted for, by Hollywood standards, an offbeat approach.
Woodstock 70. Klute 71. Summer of '42 71. Enter the Dragon 73. Black Belt Jones 74. Outlaw Blues 77. Tom Horn 80. High Road to China 83. Gymkata 85, etc.

Weintraub, Jerry (1938–).
American producer.
Oh God 77. 9/30/55 78. Cruising 80. All Night Long 81. Diner 82. The Karate Kid 84. The Karate Kid II 86. The Karate Kid III 89. Pure Country 92. The Specialist 94. Vegas Vacation 97. The Avengers 98. Soldier 98, etc.

Weir, Peter (1944–).
Australian director and screenwriter.
■ Homesdale 71. The Cars that Ate Paris 71. *Picnic at Hanging Rock* 75. *The Last Wave* 77. The Plumber (TV) 78. Gallipoli 81. The Year of Living Dangerously 82. *Witness* (AAN) 85. The Mosquito Coast 86. Dead Poets Society (AAN) 89. *Green Card* (AANw) 90. Fearless 93. *The Truman Show* 98.

Weis, Don (1922–).
American director; came to Hollywood from college as trainee.
Bannerline 51. I Love Melvin 53. A Slight Case of Larceny 53. Ride the High Iron 57. Critics' Choice 63. Pajama Party 63. Looking for Love 64. Billie 65. Pajama Party in a Haunted House 66. The King's Pirate 66. Zero to Sixty 78. The Munsters' Revenge (TV) 81, etc.

Weisbart, David (1915–1967).
American producer, former editor; in Hollywood from 1935.
Mara Maru 52. Rebel Without a Cause 55. Love Me Tender 56. Holiday for Lovers 59. Kid Galahad 63. Rio Conchos 64. Goodbye Charlie 65. Valley of the Dolls 67, many others.

Weisman, Sam.
American director, a former actor, from television. Born in Binghamton, New York, he graduated with a degree in music history from Yale University and has a Master of Fine Arts in acting and directing from Brandeis University.
Sunset Beat 90. D2: The Mighty Ducks 94. Bye Bye Love (& p) 95. George of the Jungle (d) 97, etc.

Weiss, Rob (1967–).
American director, a former photographer.
Amongst Friends 93.

Weissmuller, Johnny (1904–1984) (Peter John Weissmuller).
American leading man, former Olympic athlete who from 1932 played Tarzan more often than anyone else. In the late 40s and early 50s appeared in 'Jungle Jim' second features, also on TV. Only 'straight' role: *Swamp Fire* 46. The second of his five wives was actress Lupe Velez (1933–38).
Guest appearances: Glorifying the American Girl 29. Stage Door Canteen 43. The Phynx 70. Won Ton Ton 76. That's Entertainment Two 76.

Weisz, Rachel (1971–).
English actress. Born in London, of Hungarian and Austrian parents, she studied English at Cambridge University and was on-stage from 1992. She has been romantically linked with actors Neil Morrissey and Alessandro Nivola.
Advocates: Above the Law (TV) 92. Dirtysomething (TV) 93. Scarlet and Black (TV) 93. Death Machine 94. Stealing Beauty 96. Chain Reaction 96. Amy Foster 97. Land Girls 98. The Wisdom of Crocodiles 98. The Mummy 99, etc.

Welch, Elisabeth (1904–).
Singing star, born in New York but working mostly in Britain.
Song of Freedom 36. Big Fella 37. Alibi 42. Fiddlers Three 44. Dead of Night 45. Girl Stroke Boy 71. The Tempest 80, etc.

Welch, Joseph N. (1891–1960).
Real-life American judge who became famous during the army-McCarthy hearings in 1954 and was later persuaded to play the judge in *Anatomy of a Murder* 59.

Welch, Raquel (1940–) (Raquel Tejada).
Dynamic, curvaceous American sex symbol of the late 60s.
Roustabout 64. A House Is Not a Home 64. A Swinging Summer 65. Fantastic Voyage 66. One Million Years BC 66. The Biggest Bundle of Them All 66. Shoot Loud, Louder I Don't Understand 66. The Queens 67. Fathom 67. Bandolero 68. The Oldest Profession 68. Bedazzled 68. The Beloved 68. Lady in Cement 68. 100 Rifles 68. Myra Breckinridge 70. Flare Up 70. The Magic Christian 70. Hannie Caulder 71. Kansas City Bomber 72. Fuzz 72. Bluebeard 72. The Last of Sheila 73. The Three Musketeers 73. The Four Musketeers 74. The Wild Party 75. Mother Jugs and Speed 76. The Prince and the Pauper 77. The Legend of Walks Far Woman (TV) 84. Right to Die (TV) 87. Scandal in a Small Town (TV) 88. Trouble in Paradise (TV) 89. Tainted Blood 93. Naked Gun 33 : The Final Insult 94. Chairman of the Board 97. What I Did for Love 98, etc.
TV series: Central Park West 95.
❝ Being a sex symbol was rather like being a convict. – *R.W.*
If you have physical attractiveness you don't have to act. – *R.W.*

Welch, Tahnee (1961–).
American actress, the daughter of actress Raquel Welch.
Cocoon 85. Lethal Obsession 87. Cocoon: The Return 88. Sleeping Beauty 89. Improper Conduct 94. I Shot Andy Warhol (as Viva) 96, etc.

Weld, Tuesday (1943–) (Susan Ker Weld).
American leading actress, a model from childhood. She was married to actor Dudley Moore (1975–80).
Biography: 1996, *Pretty Poison: Tuesday Weld Story* by Floyd Conner.
Rock Rock Rock 56. Rally round the Flag Boys 57. The Five Pennies 59. Return to Peyton Place 61. Wild in the Country 62. Bachelor Flat 63. I'll Take Sweden 65. *The Cincinnati Kid* 65. Lord Love a Duck 66. *Pretty Poison* 68. I Walk the Line 70. A Safe Place 71. Play It as It Lays 73. Looking for Mr Goodbar (AAN) 77. Who'll Stop the Rain? 78. A Question of Guilt (TV) 78. Serial 80. Thief 81. Author! Author! 82. Once upon a Time in America 84. Heartbreak Hotel 88. Falling Down 93. Feeling Minnesota 96, etc.

Welden, Ben (1901–1997).
British character actor who moved to Hollywood.
The Missing Rembrandt 32. The Triumph of Sherlock Holmes 34. Marked Woman 37. Crime Ring 38. Hollywood Cavalcade 39. Angel on My Shoulder 45. The Lemon Drop Kid 51, many others.

Welland, Colin (1934–).
British actor-writer, mostly for television.
AS ACTOR: Kes 69. Villain 71. Straw Dogs 71. The Sweeney 77. Femme Fatale (TV) 93, etc.
■ AS WRITER: Yanks 79. Chariots of Fire (AA) 81. Twice in a Lifetime 86. A Dry White Season (co-w) 89. War of the Buttons 94.

Weller, Michael.
American dramatist and screenwriter.
Hair 79. Ragtime (AAN) 81. Lost Angels 89. Spoils of War (TV) 94.

Weller, Peter (1947–).
Gaunt American leading man, from the stage.
Butch and Sundance: The Early Days 79. Just Tell Me What You Want 80. Shoot the Moon 81. Of Unknown Origin 83. The Adventures of Buckaroo Banzai across the Eighth Dimension 84. Firstborn 84. The Dancing Princesses (TV) 84. Two Kinds of Love (TV) 85. A Killing Affair 85. Apology (TV) 86. My Sister's Keeper 86. Robocop 87. Shakedown/Blue Jean Cop 88. The Tunnel 88. Cat Chaser 89. Leviathan 89. Robocop 2 90. Rainbow Drive (TV) 90. Naked Lunch 91. Grill 92. The Substitute Wife (TV) 94. The New Age 94. Mighty Aphrodite 95. Beyond the Clouds 95. Screamers 95. The Decoy 95. Top of the World 97, etc.

Welles, Gwen (1949–1993).
American actress. She was married to actor Harris Yulin. *Angel on My Shoulder*, a documentary about her struggle against cancer, was made by her friend, director Donna Deitch, and shown in 1997.
A Safe Place 71. California Split 74. Nashville 75. Desert Hearts 86. The Men's Club 86. Sticky Fingers 88. New Year's Day 89, etc.

Welles, Orson (1915–1985).
Ebullient American actor-writer-producer-director with stage and radio experience (in 1938 he panicked the whole of America with a vivid radio version of *The War of the Worlds*). His extravagance and unconventionality in Hollywood forced him to Europe, where his projects continued interesting and ambitious but generally undisciplined; he never again achieved the standard of his first two films. The second of his three wives was actress Rita Hayworth (1943–48). A documentary, *Orson Welles: One-Man Band*, released in 1995, contains scenes from his uncompleted *Don Quixote* as well as TV interviews.
Biographies: 1956, *The Fabulous Orson Welles* by Peter Noble. 1973, *Orson Welles* by Peter Bogdanovich. 1973, *A Ribbon of Dreams* by Peter Cowie. 1985, *Orson Welles* by Barbara Leaming. 1989, *Citizen Welles* by Frank Brady. 1996, *Rosebud* by David Thomson.
Book: 1993, *This Is Orson Welles* by Orson Welles and Peter Bogdanovich, ed. Jonathan Rosenbaum.
■ This list of Welles' films assumes his presence as actor unless otherwise stated: *Citizen Kane* (& d) (AA script, co-w with Herman J. Mankiewiez, AANa, AANd) 41. *The Magnificent Ambersons* (wd only) 42. *Journey into Fear* 42. *It's All True* (unreleased) (wd only) 42. Jane Eyre 43. Follow the Boys 44. Tomorrow Is Forever 44. *The Stranger* (& d) 45. *The Lady from Shanghai* (& d) 47. Black Magic 47. Macbeth (& d) 48. Prince of Foxes 49. *The Third Man* 49. The Black Rose 50. Othello (& d) 51. Trent's Last Case 53. Trouble in the Glen 53. Si Versailles m'Etait Conté 53. Man Beast and Virtue 53. Napoleon 54. Three Cases of Murder 55. Confidential Report (& d) 55. Moby Dick 56. Man in the Shadow 57. Touch of Evil (& d) 58. The Long Hot Summer 58. Roots of Heaven 58. Ferry to Hong Kong 58. David and Goliath 59. Compulsion 59. Crack in the Mirror 60. The Mongols 60. The Tartars 60. Lafayette 61. *The Trial* (& d) 62. The VIPs 63. Chimes at Midnight (& d) 66. Is Paris Burning? 66. A Man For All Seasons 66. Marco the Magnificent 66. I'll Never Forget Whatshisname 67. Casino Royale 67. Sailor from Gibraltar 67. Oedipus the King 67. House of Cards 68. The Immortal Story (& d) 68. Start the Revolution without Me 69. The Southern Star 69. The Kremlin Letter 70. The Battle of Neretva 70. Waterloo 70. Catch 22 70. Safe Place 71. Malpertuis 72. Necromancy 72. Rogopag 72. Treasure Island (as Long John) 72. Ten Days Wonder 72. Get to Know Your Rabbit 72. F for Fake 73. The Other Side of the Wind (unfinished) 76. Voyage of the Damned 76. The Muppet Movie 79. It Happened One Christmas (TV) 79. The Man Who Saw Tomorrow 81. Genocide 81. History of the World Part I 82. Butterfly 82. Almonds and Raisins 83. In Our Hands 83. Where Is Parsifal? 84. Transformers 86. Someone to Love 87.
✪ For starting as big as could be, and not minding about the inevitable tailing-off (and even encouraging it). *Citizen Kane*.
❝ There, but for the grace of God, goes God.
So snapped Herman Mankiewiez during the making of *Citizen Kane*. There must have been something infuriatingly godlike about Orson the young Messiah from New York, brought out with his troupe to play with what he called:
The biggest toy train set any boy ever had.
Unfortunately, as he later admitted.
I started at the top and worked down.
It was indeed the only way to go: he could not, either by temperament or ability, make the films Hollywood wanted. The end of his reign came when:
They let the studio janitor cut *The Magnificent Ambersons* in my absence.
The years that followed saw an amassment of unfinished projects and haphazard wanderings over Europe, with flashes of acting genius in between. Paul Holt called him:
The oldest enfant terrible in the world.
Jean Cocteau saw him as:
An active loafer, a wise madman.
Ken Tynan called him:
A superb bravura director, a fair bravura producer, and a limited bravura writer; but an incomparable bravura personality.
John Simon opined:
The sad thing is that he has consistently put his very real talents to the task of glorifying his imaginary genius.
Charles Higham adds a reason:
His genius fed on Hollywood's marvellous machinery.
Pauline Kael was revolted:
By the 60s he was encased in make-up and his own fat, like a huge operatic version of W. C. Fields.
Perhaps he best summed up his own career:
Everybody denies I am a genius – but nobody ever called me one!
By 1982 the *Sunday Times* would state:
His talents now seem as deeply buried as a sixpence in a Christmas pudding.
Gluttony is not a secret vice. – O.W.
I'm not bitter about Hollywood's treatment of me, but over its treatment of Griffith, Von Sternberg, Von Stroheim, Buster Keaton and a hundred others. – O.W.
When you're down and out, something always turns up – usually the noses of your friends. – O.W.
Movie directing is a perfect refuge for the mediocre. – O.W.
There is nothing about him to convince us that he has ever felt humility or love anywhere but in front of a mirror. – *John Simon*
Famous line (*Citizen Kane*): 'I run a couple of newspapers. What do you do?'
Famous line (*The Third Man*): 'In Italy for thirty years under the Borgias they had warfare, terror, murder, bloodshed – they produced Michelangelo, Leonardo da Vinci and the Renaissance. In Switzerland they had brotherly love, five hundred years of democracy and peace, and what did that produce? The cuckoo clock.'

Wellington, David.
Canadian director and screenwriter, from the stage.
Zombie Nightmare (w) 86. The Carpenter (d) 88. I Love a Man in Uniform (wd) 93. Long Day's Journey into Night (d) 96, etc.

Wellman, William (1896–1975).
American director, former pilot, actor and Foreign Legionary; in Hollywood from 1921.
Autobiography: 1977, *A Short Time for Insanity*.
The Man Who Won 23. You Never Know Women 26. *Wings* 27. Beggars of Life 28. *Public Enemy* 31. The Conquerors 32. Central Airport 33. Looking for Trouble 34. Small Town Girl 35. Call of the Wild 35. Robin Hood of Eldorado 36. *Nothing Sacred* 37. *A Star Is Born* (AAw, AANd) 37. Men with Wings (& p) 38. Beau Geste 39. The Light that Failed 39. The Great Man's Lady 42. *The Ox Bow Incident* 42. *Roxie Hart* 42. Buffalo Bill 43. *The Story of G.I. Joe* 45. Magic Town 46. Yellow Sky 48. The Iron Curtain 48. Battleground (AAN) 49. The Next Voice You Hear 50. Westward the Women 50. Across the Wide Missouri 51. My Man and I 52. *The High and the Mighty* (AAN) 54. *Track of the Cat* 54. Blood Alley 55. Darby's Rangers 57. Lafayette Escadrille 58, many others.
❝ He was a tough little bastard but I liked him . . . he shot real bullets and stuff. – *James Mason*
What is at issue is not the number of bad films he has made, but a fundamental deficiency in his direction of good projects. – *Andrew Sarris, 1968*

Wells, George (1909–).
American screenwriter, at MGM from 1944. Born in New York City, he studied at New York University and began as a writer for radio.
Take Me Out to the Ball Game/Everybody's Cheering 48. Three Little Words 50. Everything I Have is Yours (& p) 52. Jupiter's Darling (p only) 55. Designing Woman (AA) 57. Ask Any Girl 59. The Honeymoon Machine 62. The Horizontal Lieutenant 63. Penelope 66. The Impossible Years 68, etc.

Wells, H. G. (1866–1946).
Distinguished British author, several of whose novels have been filmed.
The Island of Dr Moreau/Island of Lost Souls 32. The Invisible Man 33. The Man Who Could Work Miracles 35. Things To Come 36. Kipps 41. The History of Mr Polly 49. The War of the Worlds 53. The Time Machine 60. The Island of Dr Moreau 77, etc.

Welsh, John (1904–1985).
Lean British character actor adept at professors, fathers, scientists, barristers etc.

Wenders, Wim (1945–).
German director.
Autobiography: 1998, *The Art of Seeing*.
■ The Goalkeeper's Fear of the Penalty Kick 71. The Scarlet Letter 72. *Alice in the Cities* 74. Wrong Movement 75. Kings of the Road 76. The American Friend 77. Lightning over Water 80. Hammett 82. The State of Things 83. Tokyo-Ga 84. Aus der Familie der Panzereschen 84. Paris, Texas (BFA) 84. Wings of Desire/Himmel über Berlin 87. Until the End of the World/Bis ans Ende der Welt 91. The Heavenly Twins (a) 92. Faraway, So Close!/In Weiter Ferne, So Nah 93. Beyond the Clouds (co-d) 95. Les Lumières de Berlin 96. The End of Violence 97.

Wendkos, Paul (1922–).
American director.
The Burglar 57. Tarawa Beachhead 58. Gidget 59. Face of a Fugitive 59. Because They're Young 60. *Angel Baby* 60. Gidget Goes to Rome 63. 52 Miles to Terror 66. Guns of the Magnificent Seven 69. Cannon for Cordoba 70. The Mephisto Waltz 71. *Haunts of the Very Rich* (TV) 72. Honor Thy Father (TV) 73. Special Delivery 76. The Death of Richie (TV) 77. Good Against Evil (TV) 77. 79 Park Avenue (TV) 78. A Woman Called Moses (TV) 78. The Ordeal of Patty Hearst (TV) 79. A Cry for Love (TV) 80. The Bad Seed (TV) 85. Blood Vows: The Story of a Mafia Wife (TV) 87. The Taking of Flight 847: The Uli Derickson Story (TV) 88, etc.

Wendt, George (1948–).
Stocky American character actor, from Chicago's Second City company; he is best known for his role as Norm Peterson in the TV sitcom *Cheers* 83–93.
My Bodyguard 80. Somewhere in Time 80. Dreamscape 83. Thief of Hearts 84. Fletch 85. Gung Ho 86. House 86. Plain Clothes 88. Never Say Die (NZ) 88. Masters of Menace 90. Guilty by Suspicion 91. Forever Young 92. The Little Rascals 94. Man of the House 95. Spice World: The Movie 97. Outside Providence 99, etc.
TV series: Making the Grade 82. The George Wendt Show 94.

Wengraf, John (1897–1974) (Johann Wenngraft).
Lean Austrian actor, mainly in Hollywood; played a lot of Nazis in his time.
Homo Sum 22. Night Train To Munich 39. Mission To Moscow 43. Sahara 43. The Seventh Cross 44. Weekend at the Waldorf 45. T Men 47. Five Fingers 51. Call Me Madam 53. The Pride and The Passion 57. The Return of Dracula 58. Judgment at Nuremberg 60. The Prize 63, etc.

Wenham, Jane (Jane Figgins).
English actress whose career has been mainly on the stage. Born in Southampton, she trained at the Central School of Speech and Drama and made her theatrical debut at the Old Vic in 1945. Formerly married to actor Albert Finney.
Make Me an Offer 54. The Teckman Mystery 54. An Inspector Calls 54, etc.

Werker, Alfred (1896–1975).
American director, in Hollywood from 1917.
Little Lord Fauntleroy 21. Nobody's Children 28. Bachelor's Affairs 32. *The House of Rothschild* 34. Kidnapped 38. *The Adventures of Sherlock Holmes* 39. Moon over Her Shoulder 41. The Mad Martindales 42. Whispering Ghosts 42. A Haunting We Will Go 42. Shock 45. Lost Boundaries 46. Repeat Performance 47. Pirates of Monterey 48. Sealed Cargo 51. Walk East on Beacon 52. Devil's Canyon 53. Canyon Crossroads 55. At Gunpoint 58, many others.

Werner, Gosta (1908–).
Swedish director, mainly of shorts.
Midvinterblot 46. *The Train* 48. The Street 49. Meeting Life 50. To Kill a Child 52. Matrimonial Announcement 55. The Forgotten Melody 57. A Glass of Wine 60. Human Landscape 65. When People Meet 66, many others.

Werner, Oskar (1922–1984) (Josef Schliessmayer).
Austrian leading actor with international stage and screen credits.
■ Eroica 49. Angel with a Trumpet 49. The Wonder Kid (GB) 50. Ruf aus dem Aether (Aus.) 51. Ein Laecheln in Sturm (Aus.) 51. Das Gestohlene Jahr (Ger.) 51. *Decision before Dawn* 51. The Last Act (Ger.) 55. Lola Montes 55. Spionage (Aus.) 55. Der Letzte Akt (Aus.) 55. The Life of Mozart 56. *Jules et Jim* 61. *Ship of Fools* (AAN) 65. The Spy Who Came in from the Cold 65. *Fahrenheit 451* 66. Interlude 68. The Shoes of the Fisherman 68. Voyage of the Damned 76.

Wertmuller, Lina (1928–) (Angela Wertmuller von Elg).
Italian director, whose favourite theme is the little man.
The Lizards 63. Rita la Zanzarra 66. Mimi the Metalworker 72. Swept Away 74. *Seven Beauties* (AAN) 76. The End of the World 77. Blood Feud 80. A Joke of Destiny 83. Sotto, Sotto 84. Camorra 86. Summer Night with Greek Profile, Almond Eyes and Scent of Basil 86. Crystal or Ash, Fire or Wind, as Long as It's Love/In una Notte di Chiaro di Luna 89. Saturday, Sunday and Monday/Sàbato, Doménica e Lunedí 90. Me Let's Hope I Make It/Io Speriamo che Me la Cavo 93. The Nymph 96, etc.

Wessel, Dick (1910–1965).
American supporting actor, usually in comedy roles.
Arson Racket Squad 38. They Made Me a Criminal 39. Action in the North Atlantic 42. Slattery's Hurricane 48. Texas Carnival 51. Calamity Jane 53. The Gazebo 60. The Ugly Dachshund 65, many others.
TV series: Riverboat 59–61.

Wessely, Paula (1908–).
Austrian leading actress.
Maskerade 34. Julika 36. Spiegel des Lebens 38. Die Kluge Marianne 43. Maria Theresa 51. The Third Sex 57. Die Unvollkommene Ehe 59, many others.

Wesson, Dick (1922–1979).
American character actor.
Destination Moon 49. Breakthrough 50. Inside the Walls of Folsom Prison 51. About Face 52. The Desert Song 53. Calamity Jane 54, etc.
TV series: The People's Choice 60. The Bob Cummings Show 62. Friends and Lovers 78.

West, Adam (1928–) (William Anderson).
American light leading man.
The Young Philadelphians 59. Geronimo 62. Robinson Crusoe on Mars 64. Mara of the Wilderness 65. Batman 66. The Girl Who Knew Too Much 68. Marriage of a Young Stockbroker 71. The Specialist 75. Partisan 75. Hooper 78. Swamp Thing 82. Hellriders 84. Doin' Time on Planet Earth 88. Mad about You 90. Maximum Xul 91. Night of the Kickfighters 91. The New Age 94. The Size of Watermelons 96. Joyride 97, etc.
TV series: The Detectives 59–61. *Batman* 65–68.

West, Billy (1893–1975) (Roy B. Weissberg).
American silent screen comedian, a successful imitator of Charlie Chaplin; later a Hollywood restaurateur.

West, Claudine.
English-born screenwriter in Hollywood. Born in Nottingham, she began writing fiction for magazines before moving to Hollywood, where she spent her career at MGM, always working in collaboration with other writers.
The Last of Mrs Cheyney 29. A Lady's Morals/Jenny Lind 30. Just a Gigolo 31. The Guardsman 31. Payment Deferred 32. Smilin' Through 32. The Son-Daughter 32. Reunion in Vienna 33. The Barretts of Wimpole Street 34. The Good Earth 37. Marie Antoinette 38. On Borrowed Time 39. Goodbye Mr Chips (AAN) 39. The Mortal Storm 40. Random Harvest (AAN) 42. We Were Dancing 42. Mrs Miniver (AA) 42. Forever and a Day 43. The White Cliffs of Dover 44, etc.

West, Con (1891–*).
English comedy screenwriter and dramatist, working with comedians like Ernie Lotinga, Arthur Lucan, and Max Miller, and writing screen versions of Fred Karno's music-hall sketches. He also worked for radio, co-writing in 1944 a series for Will Hay, and co-wrote a biography of Karno.
P.C. Josser (co-w from his music-hall sketch) 31. Up for the Cup (co-w) 31. The Bad Companions 32. Letting in the Sunshine (co-w) 33. Oh, What a Duchess! (co-w) 34. Birds of a Feather (co-w) 35. Jimmy Boy (story) 35. Charing Cross Road (co-w) 35. Strictly Illegal (oa) 35. Sunshine Ahead (story) 35. Things Are Looking Up (co-w) 35. The Small Man (story) 35. Smith's Wives (co-w) 35. Don't Rush Me (co-w) 36. Love up the Pole (story) 36. Why Pick on Me? (story) 37. Old Mother Riley (w) 37. Old Mother Riley in Paris (w) 38. Old Mother Riley Joins Up (co-w) 39. Old Mother Riley, M.P. (co-w) 39. Jailbirds (co-w) 39. What Would You Do Chums? 39. Up for the Cup (co-w) 50, etc.

West, Lockwood (1905–1989).
English character actor, frequently in gentle, avuncular roles. Born in Birkenhead, he was on-stage from 1926. He was the father of actor Timothy West.
A Song for Tomorrow 48. Celia 49. No Place for Jennifer 50. Single-Handed 53. Privates Progress 56. Tunes of Glory 60. The Leather Boys 63. Rotten to the Core 65. Life at the Top 65. Up the Junction 68. Loot 71. I, Claudius (TV) 77. The Dresser 83. The Shooting Party 84. Young Sherlock Holmes 85. Porterhouse Blue (TV) 87, etc.

West, Mae (1892–1980).
American leading lady of the 30s, the archetypal sex symbol, splendidly vulgar, mocking, overdressed and endearing. Wrote most of her own stage plays and filmscripts, which bulge with double meanings. She was played by Ann Jillian in the TV biopic *Mae West* 84.
Autobiographies: 1959, *Goodness Had Nothing to Do with It*. 1975, *Life, Sex and ESP*.
Biographies: 1988, *Mae West Entertainer* by Carol Bergman; 1991, *Mae West: Empress of Sex* by Maurice Leonard; 1997, *Becoming Mae West* by Emily Wortis Leider.
■ Night After Night 32. *She Done Him Wrong* 33. *I'm No Angel* 33. Going to Town 34. Belle of the Nineties 34. Klondike Annie 36. Go West Young Man 37. Every Day's a Holiday 37. My Little Chickadee 39. The Heat's On 43. *Myra Breckinridge* 70. Sextet 77.
✪ For enjoying the sensations she caused in the 30s, and for having the talent to exploit them to the full. *She Done Him Wrong*.
❝ Whole books of Mae West's wit have been published. A much cleverer woman than she was usually given credit for being, she seemed to talk in epigrams. In her 70s on TV, when someone gushed:
Oh, Miss West, I've heard so much about you
the reply was:
Yeah, but you can't prove a thing.
When a lifejacket was named after her during World War II, her reaction had the appearance of spontaneity:
I've been in *Who's Who* and I know what's what, but it's the first time I ever made the dictionary.
However, she never did say:
Come up and see me sometime . . .
At least, not quite, and not in the film she was supposed to. She did however say:
Beulah, peel me a grape,
which for some reason has passed into the language. Her first screen appearance is also legendary:
Goodness, what beautiful diamonds!
– Goodness had nothing to do with it, dearie.
For the rest, one can only list a few sparklers:
She's one of the finest women who ever walked the streets.
It's not the men in my life, it's the life in my men that counts.
I wouldn't let him touch me with a ten foot pole.
How tall are you son?
– Ma'am, I'm six feet seven inches.
Let's forget the six feet and talk about the seven inches.
On arriving at her office and being greeted by a score of virile young men:
I'm feeling a little tired today. One of those fellows'll have to go home.
In a Broadway costume play, when the romantic lead got his sword so tangled in his braid that it stuck up at an unfortunate angle:
Is that your sword, or are you just pleased to see me?
I wouldn't even lift my veil for that guy.
When I'm good I'm very good, but when I'm bad I'm better.
It isn't what I do, but how I do it. It isn't what I say, but how I say it. And how I look when I do it and say it.
On the mirrored ceiling over her bed:
I like to know what I'm doing.
Whenever I'm caught between two evils, I take the one I've never tried.
Small wonder that her first co-star, George Raft, remarked of her debut:
She stole everything but the cameras.
In a non-permissive age, she made remarkable inroads against the taboos of her day, and did so without even lowering her neckline. Indeed, her most effective moment may have been in a scene in which she drove a funfair crowd wild with a dance that did nothing but tease. As she disappears into the tent, she wraps up years of experience, enjoyment and disapproval of the sex war into one word:
Suckers!

West, Morris (1916–).
Australian best-selling novelist, internationally popular; usually on religious themes. Films include *The Devil's Advocate*, *The Shoes of the Fisherman*.

West, Nathanael (1904–1940) (Nathan Weinstein).
American novelist and screenwriter. His novel *Miss Lonelyhearts* was filmed, poorly, as *Advice to the Lovelorn* 33 and his *A Cool Million* was sold to Columbia but never produced. He wrote scathingly about Hollywood in *The Day of the Locust*, published in 1939 and filmed in 1975 by John Schlesinger. His screenplays give little indication of his unsettling talent, being routine 'B' pictures for the most part, for companies like Republic and RKO. He and his wife Eileen (heroine of the book *My Sister Eileen*, 1938, by her sister Ruth McKenney, which was filmed in 1942) were killed in a car crash.
Biography: 1970, *Nathanael West: The Art of His Life* by Jay Martin. Also: 1976, *Sometime in the Sun* by Tom Dardis. 1990, *Writers in Hollywood 1915–51* by Ian Hamilton.
Ticket to Paradise 36. The President's Mystery 36. It Could Happen to You 37. Five Came Back 39. The Spirit of Culver 39. Men against the Sky 40. Let's Make Music 40, etc.
❝ My hours are from ten in the morning to six at night with a full day on Saturday. They gave me a job to do five minutes after I sat down in my office – a scenario about a beauty parlour – and I'm expected to turn out pages and pages a day. There's no fooling here. – *N.W. on his first Hollywood job at Columbia*
He left two books more finished and complete as works of art than almost anything else produced by his generation. – *Edmund Wilson*
He was ahead of his time in knowing that Hollywood was impermanent and literature lasting, and in never confusing the two. – *Milton Spurling*
Honesty and hard work will buy you pain, disgrace and death – *Columbia Pictures' reader's report on the theme of West's A Cool Million*

West, Roland (1887–1952).
American director of the late silent period.
■ De Luxe Annie 18. The Silver Lining 21. Nobody 22. The Unknown Purple 23. The Monster 25. *The Bat* 26. The Dove 27. Alibi 29. *The Bat Whispers* 31. Corsair 31.

West, Sam (1966–).
English actor on stage and screen. The son of actors Timothy West and Prunella Scales, he studied physics at Oxford University before becoming an actor.
Chronicles of Narnia (TV) 90. Howards End 92. Carrington 95. Jane Austen's Persuasion (TV) 95. P. G. Wodehouse's Heavy Weather (TV) 95. Over Here (TV) 96. Stiff Upper Lips 97, etc.

West, Simon (1961–).
American director, from commercials and music videos.
Con Air 97.

West, Timothy (1934–).
British character actor who became famous as TV's *Edward the Seventh* 75.
Autobiography: 1994, *I'm Here I Think, Where Are You?*
Twisted Nerve 68. Nicholas and Alexandra 71. The Day of the Jackal 74. Hedda 76. Agatha 78. The 39 Steps 78. Churchill and the Generals (TV) 80. Rough Cut 80. Murder Is Easy (TV) 82. Oliver Twist (as Bumble) (TV) 82. Tender Is the Night (TV) 84. Cry Freedom 87. Consuming Passions 88. Eleven Men against Eleven (TV) 96. Over Here (TV) 96. Ever After 98, etc.
TV series: Big Breadwinner Hog 69. Brass 83–84, 90. A Very Peculiar Practice 86–88.

West, Vera (c.1900–1947).
American costume designer at Universal 1927–47. Committed suicide.
Showboat 36. Mad about Music 38. Destry Rides Again 39. The Spoilers 42. Cobra Woman 44, etc.

Westcott, Gordon (1903–1935).
American support actor of the 30s, almost always for Warners and usually the other man.
Love Me Tonight 32. The Working Man 33. Heroes for Sale 33. Footlight Parade 33. Fog Over Frisco 34. Registered Nurse 34. Go into Your Dance 35. Bright Lights 35. Two Fisted 35, etc.

Westcott, Helen (1928–1998) (Myrthas Helen Hickman).
American leading lady, former child actress.
A Midsummer Night's Dream 35. The New Adventures of Don Juan 48. The Gunfighter 50. With a Song in My Heart 52. The Charge at Feather River 53. Hot Blood 55. The Last Hurrah 58. I Love My Wife 71.

Westerby, Robert (1909–1968).
British screenwriter, in films from 1947.
Broken Journey 48. The Spider and the Fly 50. They Who Dare 54. War and Peace (co-w) 56. Town on Trial 56. Cone of Silence 60. Greyfriars Bobby 60. The Three Lives of Thomasina 64, etc.

Westerfield, James (1912–1971).
Heavyweight American character actor.
Undercurrent 46. The Whistle at Eaton Falls 51. On the Waterfront 54. Chief Crazy Horse 55. Three Brave Men 57. The Shaggy Dog 59. Wild River 60. Birdman of Alcatraz 62. Blue 68. True Grit 69, many others.

Westlake, Donald E. (1933–).
American screenwriter and crime novelist who also writes as Richard Stark.
The Hot Rock/How to Steal a Diamond in Four Uneasy Lessons (oa) 72. Cops and Robbers 73. The Bank Shot (oa) 74. Hot Stuff (co-w) 79. The Stepfather 87. Why Me? (co-w, from his novel) 90. *The Grifters* (AAN) 90. Two Much (oa) 96, etc.

Westley, Helen (1879–1942) (Henrietta Conroy).
American character actress of stage and screen; usually played crotchety but kind-hearted dowagers.
Death Takes a Holiday 34. The House of Rothschild 34. Moulin Rouge 34. Anne of Green Gables 34. Roberta 35. Showboat 36. *Dimples* 36. Banjo on My Knee 36. Stowaway 36. Heidi 37. Rebecca of Sunnybrook Farm 38. Zaza 39. Lady with Red Hair 40. Lillian Russell 40. Adam Had Four Sons 41. Sunny 41. My Favorite Spy 42, etc.

Westman, Nydia (1902–1970).
American character comedienne, usually in fluttery, nervous roles.
King of the Jungle 33. The Invisible Ray 36. *The Cat and the Canary* 39. When Tomorrow Comes 40. The Late George Apley 47. The Velvet Touch 49. The Ghost and Mr Chicken 66, many others.

Westmore.
The famous family of Hollywood make-up artists was headed by George Westmore (1879–1931), English by birth but a West Coast success from the moment he changed Valentino's hairstyle. The sons all worked for different studios, and most had health and emotional problems. They were *Mont* (1902–1940), *Perc* (1904–1970), *Ern* (1904–1968), *Wally* (1906–1973), *Bud* (1918–1973) and *Frank* (1923–1985) who, in 1976, wrote a book about the family, *The Westmores of Hollywood*.

Weston, David (1938–).
British actor of TV and films.
Doctor in Distress 63. Becket 64. The Legend of Young Dick Turpin 65. The Red Baron 70. Go for a Take 73. The Incredible Sarah 75. A Man Called Intrepid (TV) 79, etc.

Weston, Jack (1925–1996) (Jack Weinstein).
American roly-poly character actor, often an incompetent minor villain.
Stage Struck 58. It's Only Money 62. *Mirage* 65. *Wait until Dark* 67. The Thomas Crown Affair 68. The April Fools 69. Fuzz 72. A New Leaf 72. Marco 73. Gator 76. The Ritz 77. Cuba 79. Can't Stop the Music 80. The Four Seasons 81. High Road to China 83. The Longshot 86. RAD 86. Dirty Dancing 87. Ishtar 87. Short Circuit 2 88, etc.
TV series: The Hathaways 61.

Wettig, Patricia (1951–).
American actress, from theatre and television. She is a former dresser to Shirley MacLaine. Married actor Ken Olin.
Guilty by Suspicion 91. City Slickers 91. Parallel Lives (TV) 94. City Slickers 2: The Legend of Curly's Gold 94. Stephen King's The Langoliers 95, etc.
TV series: thirtysomething 88–91. Courthouse 95.

Wexler, Haskell (1926–).
American cinematographer.
The Savage Eye 59. Angel Baby 60. The Hoodlum Priest 61. A Face in the Rain 62. America America 63. *The Best Man* 64. The Loved One (co-ph) 65. Who's Afraid of Virginia Woolf? (AA) 66. *In the Heat of the Night* 67. *The Thomas Crown Affair* 68. Medium Cool (& d) 69. The Conversation 73. American Graffiti 73. One Flew over the Cuckoo's Nest (AAN) 75. Bound for Glory (AA) 76. Coming Home 78. Days of Heaven 78. No Nukes 80. Second Hand Hearts 80. The Man Who Loved Women 83. Latino (& wd) 85. Matewan (AAN) 87. Colors 88. Three Fugitives 89. Blaze (AAN) 89. Through the Wire 90. Other People's Money 91. The Babe 92. The Secret of Roan Inish 94. Canadian Bacon 95. Mulholland Falls 96. The Rich Man's Wife 96, etc.

Wexler, Norman (1926–).
American screenwriter and dramatist.
Joe (AAN) 70. Serpico (AAN) 73. Mandingo 75. Drum 76. Saturday Night Fever 77. Staying Alive 83. Raw Deal 86, etc.

Whale, James (1896–1957).
Enigmatic English director who brought a fresh touch to Hollywood films of the macabre. Born in Dudley, Worcestershire, he trained as an artist and began acting in a German prison camp in the First World War, later working as a repertory actor and set designer before becoming an in-demand director following the unexpected success of his production of R. C. SHERRIFF's *Journey's End*. He went to Hollywood to film the play and stayed, working for Universal. After Carl LAEMMLE lost control of the studio in the mid-30s, his career declined under unsympathetic producers and he turned to painting and directing plays. He drowned himself in his swimming pool, after suffering a stroke. His lovers included former actor and producer David LEWIS, with whom he lived for many years. He was played by Ian MCKELLEN in the 1998 biopic *Gods and Monsters*.
Biographies: 1982, *James Whale* by James Curtis; 1995, *James Whale: A Biography or the Would-be Gentleman* by Mark Gatiss.
■ Waterloo Bridge 30. *Frankenstein* 31. The Impatient Maiden 32. *The Old Dark House* 32. The Kiss before the Mirror 33. *The Invisible Man* 33. By Candlelight 33. One More River 34. *Bride of Frankenstein* 35. *Remember Last Night* 35. *Showboat* 36. The Road Back 37. The Great Garrick 37. Sinners in Paradise 37. Wives under Suspicion 38. Port of Seven Seas 38. *The Man in the Iron Mask* 39. Green Hell 40. They Dare Not Love 40. Hello Out There 49.
✪ For contriving to make four classics of the macabre before his enthusiasm ran out. *Bride of Frankenstein*.
❝ A director must be pretty bad if he can't get a thrill out of war, murder, robbery. – *J.W.*
The future is just old age and pain. Goodbye all and thank you for all your love. I must have peace and this is the only way. – *J.W., in his suicide note*
Jimmy Whale was the first guy who was blackballed because he refused to stay in the closet. – *Robert Aldrich*

Whalen, Michael (1899–1974) (Joseph Kenneth Shovlin).
American leading man of the 30s.
Country Doctor 36. Time Out for Murder 38. Sign of the Wolf 41. Tahiti Honey 43. Gas House Kids in Hollywood 48. Mark of the Dragon 51. The Phantom from Ten Thousand Leagues 56, many others.

Whaley, Frank (1963–).
American actor.
Ironweed 87. Field of Dreams 89. Born on the Fourth of July 89. The Freshman 90. Career Opportunities/One Wild Night 91. The Doors 91. A Midnight Clear 91. Back in the USSR 92. Swing Kids 93. Pulp Fiction 94. I.Q. 94. Broken Arrow 96. Retroactive 97. Café Society 97. Bombshell 97. Went to Coney Island on a Mission from God . . . Be Back by Five 98, etc.
TV series: Buddy Faro 98– .

Whalley, Joanne (1964–).
British leading actress, from stage and TV, now in America. She was credited as Joanne Whalley-Kilmer during her marriage to actor Val KILMER.
A Kind of Loving (TV) 82. Pink Floyd the Wall 82. Edge of Darkness (TV) 85. Dance with a Stranger 85. The Good Father 86. The Singing Detective (TV) 86. No Surrender 86. Willow 88. Kill Me Again 89. Scandal 89. To Kill a Priest 89. The Big Man 90. Navy SEALS 90. Shattered 91. Storyville 92. The Secret Rapture 93. Mother's Boys 94. A Good Man in Africa 94. Trial by Jury 94. Scarlett (as Scarlett O'Hara) (TV) 94. The Man Who Knew Too Little 97, etc.

Whatham, Claude.
British director.
■ That'll Be the Day 72. Swallows and Amazons 74. Sweet William 80. Hoodwink 82. Murder Is Easy (TV) 82. Murder Elite (TV) 85. Jumping the Queue (TV) 87. Buddy's Song 90.

Wheatley, Alan (1907–1991).
Suave British character actor best known as the Sheriff of Nottingham in TV's *Robin Hood*.
Inn for Trouble 60. Shadow of the Cat 61. Tomorrow at Ten 63. A Jolly Bad Fellow 64, etc.

Wheatley, David.
British director.
The Magic Toyshop 86. Nobody's Children 94. The Wingless Bird (TV) 97. Imogen's Face (TV) 98, etc.

Wheatley, Dennis (1897–1977).
Prolific best-selling English author, a former wine merchant who turned to writing fiction at the age of 36 and enjoyed immediate success. There were moves to ban *Forbidden Territory*, about an Englishman who escapes from a Siberian prison, on the grounds that it was anti-Russian. His occult thrillers have been made into some forgettable films.
■ Forbidden Territory (oa) 34. The Secret of Stamboul (from novel The Eunuch of Stamboul) 36. An Englishman's Home (co-w) 39. The Devil Rides Out/The Devil's Bride 68. The Lost Continent (from novel Uncharted Seas) 68. To The Devil a Daughter (oa) 76.
❝ Writing is a profession, and you don't succeed if you wait for inspiration. – *D.W.*
James Agate reported the following exchange. Humbert Wolfe:
Dennis Wheatley told me his novels have been translated into every European language except one. I can't think which.
Pamela Frankau:
English!

Wheaton, Wil (1972–).
American actor, in films as a juvenile.
The Secret of NIMH (voice) 82. The Buddy System 83. The Last Starfighter 84. Long Time Gone (TV) 86. Stand by Me 86. The Curse 87. December 91. Toy Soldiers 91. The Last Prostitute (TV) 91. Pie in the Sky 95. Mr Stitch 95. Flubber 97. Fag Hag 98, etc.
TV series: Star Trek: The Next Generation 87–90.

Whedon, Joss (1964–).
American screenwriter, a former television story editor, who gained a reputation for rewriting, uncredited, the hit thriller *Speed* during production.
Buffy the Vampire Slayer 92. Waterworld (co-w) 95. Toy Story (co-w) (AAN) 95. Alien: Resurrection 97, etc.

Wheeler, Anne (1946–).
Canadian director and screenwriter.
A War Story 81. Loyalties 86. Cowboys Don't Cry 88. Bye Bye Blues 89. Angel Street 91. The War between Us 96, etc.

Wheeler, Bert (1895–1968).
American comedian who teamed as double act with Robert WOOLSEY.
Rio Rita 29. Half Shot at Sunrise 30. Hook Line and Sinker 30. Cracked Nuts 30. Caught Plastered 32. Hold 'em Jail 32. Diplomaniacs 33. Hips Hips Hooray 34. The Nitwits 35. The Rainmakers 35. Mummy's Boys 37. High Flyers 37. On Again Off Again 37. The Gay City (solo) 41, etc.
TV series: Brave Eagle 55.

Wheeler, Charles F.
American cinematographer.
Tora! Tora! Tora! (AAN) 70. Cold Turkey 70. The Cat from Outer Space 78. Condorman 81. The Best of Times 86, etc.

Wheeler, Lyle (1905–1990).
American art director. Born in Woburn, Massachusetts, he studied at the University of Southern California and was an architect, magazine illustrator and industrial designer before entering films in 1929, when the financial depression put him out of work. He began at MGM, then was hired by David SELZNICK to work under production designer William Cameron MENZIES on *Gone with the Wind*, and was responsible for suggesting setting on fire the *King Kong* and *King of Kings* sets on the backlot to represent the burning of Atlanta. He then ran Twentieth Century-Fox's art department from 1944 to 1960, working on some 500 films during his career.
A Tale of Two Cities 36. A Star Is Born 37. *The Prisoner of Zenda* 37. *Tom Sawyer* 38. *Gone with the Wind* (AA) 39. *Rebecca* (AAN) 40. *Laura* (AAN) 44. Leave Her to Heaven (AAN) 45. *Anna and the King of Siam* (AA) 46. The Foxes of Harrow (AAN) 47. Come to the Stable (AAN) 49. All about Eve (AAN) 50. Fourteen Hours (AAN) 51. House on Telegraph Hill (AAN) 51. Fourteen Hours 51. David and Bathsheba (AAN) 51. On the Riviera (AAN) 51. My Cousin Rachel (AAN) 52. Viva Zapata! (AAN) 52. The Snows of Kilimanjaro (AAN) 52. *The Robe* (AA) 53. The President's Lady (AAN) 53. Titanic (AAN) 53. Desiree (AAN) 54. Daddy Longlegs (AAN) 55. Love Is a Many Splendored Thing (AAN) 55. Teenage Rebel (AAN) 56. *The King and I* (AA) 56. A Certain Smile (AAN) 58. *The Diary of Anne Frank* (AA) 59. *Journey to the Center of the Earth* (AAN) 59. The Cardinal (AAN) 63. The Swimmer 68. Tell Me that You Love Me, Junie Moon 69. The Love Machine 71. Posse 75. Flight to Holocaust (TV) 77, many others.

Whelan, Albert (1875–1962).
Dapper Australian character actor and music-hall entertainer, in Britain from the early 1900s.
An Intimate Interlude 28. The Man from Chicago 30. Matinee Idol 33. Stars on Parade 36. Educated Evans 36. The Green Cockatoo 37. Thank Evans 38. Danny Boy 41. English without Tears 44. Keep It Clean 56, etc.

Whelan, Arleen (1916–1993).
American leading lady of the 40s.
Kidnapped 38. Young Mr Lincoln 39. Charley's American Aunt 42. Ramrod 47. The Sun Shines Bright 52. The Badge of Marshal Brennan 57, etc.

Whelan, Tim (1893–1957).
American director who often filmed in Britain.
Safety Last 23. It's a Boy (GB) 33. Murder Man 35. The Mill on the Floss (GB) 36. *Farewell Again* (GB) 37. The Divorce of Lady X (GB) 37. *St Martin's Lane* (GB) 38. *Q Planes* (GB) 39. Ten Days in Paris (GB) 39. *The Thief of Bagdad* (GB) (co-d) 40. A Date with Destiny 40. International Lady 41. Twin Beds 42. Nightmare 42. Seven Days'

Leave 42. Higher and Higher 42. Step Lively 44. Badman's Territory 46. This Was a Woman (GB) 47. Texas Lady 55. Rage at Dawn 55, etc.

Whiley, Manning (1915–1975).
British actor, usually in sinister roles.
Consider Your Verdict 38. The Trunk Crime 39. The Ghost of St Michael's 41. The Seventh Veil 45. Teheran 47. The Shop at Sly Corner 50. Little Big Shot (last to date) 52, etc.

Whipper, Leigh (1877–1975).
American character actor.
Of Mice and Men 39. The Ox Bow Incident 42. Mission to Moscow 43, etc.

Whitaker, Forest (1961–).
Plump American character actor, producer and director, born in Longview, Texas.
Fast Times at Ridgemont High 82. Vision Quest 85. The Color of Money 86. Platoon 86. Stakeout 87. Good Morning Vietnam 87. Bird 88. Bloodsport 88. Johnny Handsome 89. Downtown 90. A Rage in Harlem (& p) 91. Article 99 92. The Crying Game 92. Diary of a Hit Man 92. Consenting Adults 92. Strapped (d) (TV) 93. Last Light (TV) 93. Body Snatchers 93. Bank Robber 93. Lush Life 93. Blown Away 94. Jason's Lyric 94. Prêt-à-Porter/Ready to Wear 94. Waiting to Exhale (d) 95. Smoke 95. Species 95. Phenomenon 96. Body Count 97. Hope Floats (d) 98, etc.

White, Alice (1907–1983) (Alva White).
American leading lady of 'B' features who played flappers and gangsters' molls from the 20s to the 40s. Born in Patterson, New Jersey, she was discovered while working as a script girl.
The Thief of Bagdad 24. Hot Stuff 27. The Sea Wolf 30. Gentlemen Prefer Blondes 31. The Picture Snatcher 33. Big City 38. Annabel Takes a Tour 39. Flamingo Road 48, many others.

White, Barbara (1924–).
British leading lady of the 40s.
It Happened One Sunday 44. The Voice Within 45. Quiet Weekend 46. While the Sun Shines 46. Mine Own Executioner 47. This Was a Woman 48, etc.

White, Carol (1941–1991).
British leading lady, in films as a child, who went to Hollywood and failed to become a star there, with an over-indulgence in drink and drugs causing her early death. She first attracted attention on TV in the plays *Up the Junction* 65 and *Cathy Come Home* 66.
Autobiography: 1982, *Carol Comes Home*.
Linda 60. Never Let Go 60. Slave Girls 66. *Poor Cow* 67. I'll Never Forget Whatshisname 68. Daddy's Gone a-Hunting 69. The Man Who Had Power over Women 70. Dulcima 71. Something Big 71. Made 72. The Squeeze 77. Nutcracker 82, etc.

White, Chrissie (1895–1989).
British leading lady of the silent screen, especially popular when teamed with her husband Henry Edwards. Films include *Broken Threads, David Garrick, Barnaby Rudge, Sweet Lavender, Trelawny of the Wells, The City of Beautiful Nonsense, Possession;* last appearance in *General John Regan* 34.

White, Jesse (1918–1997) (Jesse Wiedenfeld).
American comic character actor, usually seen as nervous cigar-chewing crook. Wide stage experience.
Harvey (debut) 50. Death of a Salesman 52. Not as a Stranger 55. Designing Woman 57. The Rise and Fall of Legs Diamond 59. It's Only Money 62. A House Is Not a Home 64. Dear Brigitte 65. The Reluctant Astronaut 67. The Brothers O'Toole 73. The Cat from Outer Space 78. Monster in the Closet 86, many others.
TV series: *Make Room for Daddy* 53–57.

White, Jules (1900–1985).
American (originally Hungarian) shorts director in charge of The Three Stooges from 1945 to 1957.

White, Merrill (c. 1895–1959).
American editor.
The Love Parade 29. *Love Me Tonight* 32. Nell Gwyn 34. The Frog 37. Victoria the Great 37. The Red House 47. Blaze of Glory 50. One Girl's Confession 53. Carnival Story 54. The Fly 58. Crime and Punishment USA 59, many others.

White, Michael Jai.
American actor and martial arts expert; he holds black belts in six different styles of karate.
Universal Soldier 92. Tyson (TV) 95. Captive Heart: The James Mink Story (TV) 96. City of Industry 96. 2 Days in the Valley 96. Spawn 97. Ringmaster 98, etc.

White, Onna.
Canadian choreographer.
The Music Man 62. Bye Bye Birdie 63. *Oliver* (AA) 68. 1776 72. The Great Waltz 72. Mame 73, etc.

White, Pearl (1889–1938).
American leading lady, 'queen of the silent serials'. On stage from six years old. At first a stunt woman, then in such serials as *The Perils of Pauline* 14 and *The Exploits of Elaine* 15, involving circus-like thrills. Later in features: *The White Moll* 20. *Know Your Men* 21. *A Virgin Paradise* 21, etc.; retired 1921. A pseudo-biography, *The Perils of Pauline*, was filmed with Betty Hutton in 1947.
Autobiography: 1919, *Just Me*.

White, Ruth (1914–1969).
American character actress.
To Kill a Mockingbird 63. Up the Down Staircase 67. The Tiger is Out 68. Charly 69. Midnight Cowboy 69, etc.

White, Valerie (1916–1975).
British character actress.
Halfway House 43. My Learned Friend 44. Hue and Cry 46. Travels with My Aunt 73, etc.

Whitehead, Geoffrey (1939–).
British light actor who in 1980 played Holmes in the Anglo-Polish TV series *Sherlock Holmes and Dr Watson*.
Inside the Third Reich (TV) 82. Peter the Great (TV) 85. War and Remembrance (TV) 87.

Whitehead, O(othout) Z(abriskie) (1911–1998).
Gawky American character actor, usually in eccentric roles, and playwright. Born in New York, he studied at Harvard and was on-stage from 1933. In the late 60s, he moved to Dublin to live and work.
The Scoundrel 35. The Grapes of Wrath 40. The Romance of Rosy Ridge 47. My Brother Talks to Horses 47. A Song Is Born 48. Road House 48. Ma and Pa Kettle 49. The Hoodlum 51. Beware My Lovely 52. The San Francisco Story 52. Rally round the Flag Boys 58. The Last Hurrah 58. The Horse Soldiers 59. Chartroose Caboose 60. Two Rode Together 61. The Man Who Shot Liberty Valance 62. Ulysses 67. Summer Magic 68. The Lion in Winter 68. Philadelphia, Here I Come 75, etc.

Whitelaw, Billie (1932–).
British leading actress of stage and TV, also in occasional films. She began as an 11-year-old on radio.
Autobiography: 1995, *Billie Whitelaw – Who He?*
The Fake 54. Make Mine Mink 59. Bobbikins 59. Hell is a City 60. *No Love for Johnnie* 61. Payroll 61. The Comedy Man 63. *Charlie Bubbles* (BFA) 68. Twisted Nerve 68. The Adding Machine 69. Gumshoe 71. Eagle in a Cage 71. Frenzy 72. Night Watch 73. *The Omen* 76. The Water Babies 78. An Unsuitable Job for a Woman 82. Jamaica Inn (TV) 83. Camille (TV) 84. The Chain 86. Shadey 86. Maurice 87. The Dressmaker 88. Joyriders 89. The Krays 90. Freddie as F.R.O.7. (voice) 92. Deadly Advice 94. Skallagrigg (TV) 94. Jane Eyre 96. Merlin (TV) 98, etc.
TV series: Firm Friends 92–94.

Whiteley, Jon (1945–).
British boy actor. He quit acting in his early 20s to follow a business career.
Hunted 52. *The Kidnappers* (special AA) 53. Moonfleet 55. The Weapon 56. The Spanish Gardener 56. Capetown Affair 67, etc.

Whiteman, Paul (1890–1967).
Tall, portly American bandleader who made several film appearances.
King of Jazz 30. Thanks a Million 35. Strike Up the Band 40. Atlantic City 44. Rhapsody in Blue 45. The Fabulous Dorseys 47, etc.

Whitfield, June (1925–).
British character actress, in comic roles. She first became known on radio, as Eth in The Glums on *Take It from Here* 53–60, and was on TV from the 50s, as support to Tony Hancock and Arthur Askey.
Carry On Nurse 58. Friends and Neighbours 59. The Spy with a Cold Nose 66. The Magnificent Seven Deadly Sins 71. Bless This House 72. Carry On Abroad 72. Carry On Girls 73. Not Now, Comrade 76. Carry On Columbus 92. Jude 96. Family Money (TV) 97, etc.
TV series: Beggar My Neighbour 67–68. Scott On . . . 69. The Fossett Saga 69. The Best Things in Life 69–70. Happy Ever After 74–78. Terry and June 79–87. Absolutely Fabulous 92–94. Common as Muck 97.

Whiting, Leonard (1950–)
British juvenile lead.
The Legend of Young Dick Turpin 66. *Romeo and Juliet* (as Romeo) 68. The Royal Hunt of the Sun 69. Young Casanova 70. Say Hello to Yesterday 71. Frankenstein: The True Story 73 (TV), etc.

Whiting, Richard (1891–1938).
American composer and songwriter who went to Hollywood in 1929 to write for Maurice Chevalier, an assignment that produced 'Louise'. Other hits followed: 'On the Good Ship Lollipop' for Shirley Temple, 'Beyond the Blue Horizon', 'Hooray for Hollywood' and 'Too Marvellous for Words'. His daughter is the singer Margaret Whiting.
Innocents of Paris 29. Monte Carlo 30. Playboy of Paris 30. One Hour with You 32. My Weakness 33. Adorable 33. Take a Chance 33. Bright Eyes 34. Transatlantic Merry-Go-Round 34. The Big Broadcast of 1936 35. Coronado 35. Hollywood Hotel 37. Ready Willing and Able 37. Cowboy from Brooklyn 38, etc.

Whitley, Ray (1902–1979).
American character actor and songwriter, usually as a singing cowboy.
Hopalong Cassidy Returns 36. Gun Law 38. Wagon Train 40. Along the Rio Grande 41. Thundering Hoofs 41. Robbers of the Range 41. Riders of the Santa Fe 44. Trail to Gunsight 44. West of the Alamo 46. Giant 56, etc.

Whitlock, Albert (1915–).
British special effects technician.
The Birds 63. Marnie 64. Torn Curtain 66. Diamonds Are Forever 70. Frenzy 73. The Sting 73. *Earthquake* (AA) 74. *The Hindenburg* (AA) 75. Family Plot 75. The Car 77. High Anxiety 77. Dracula 79. Heartbeeps 81. History of the World Part One 81. Missing 82. Dune 84. Clue 85. Red Sonja 85. Millennium 89, etc.

Whitman, Ernest (1893–1954).
American character actor of sizeable presence.
Prisoner of Shark Island 36. The Green Pastures 36. Nothing Sacred 37. Gone with the Wind 39. Congo Maisie 40. Road to Zanzibar 41. Cabin in the Sky 43. *Stormy Weather* 43. The Sun Shines Bright 53, many others.

Whitman, Stuart (1926–).
American leading man, former boxer and stage and TV actor.
When Worlds Collide 52. Rhapsody 54. Darby's Rangers 57. *Ten North Frederick* 58. The Decks Ran Red 58. The Story of Ruth 60. Murder Inc. 61. *The Mark* (AAN) 62. The Comancheros 62. Reprieve 63. Shock Treatment 64. Signpost to Murder 64. Rio Conchos 64. Those Magnificent Men in Their Flying Machines 65. Sands of the Kalahari 65. An American Dream 66. The Invincible Six 68. The Only Way Out is Dead 70. Captain Apache 71. City Beneath the Sea (TV) 71. Night of the Lepus 73. Mean Johnny Barrows 76. Strange Shadows in an Empty Room 77. Eaten Alive 77. The White Buffalo 77. Run for the Roses 78. Guyana 80. Sweet Dirty Tony 81. Butterfly 82. Stillwatch (TV) 87. Deadly Reactor 89. Moving Target 89. Mob Boss 90. Omega Cop 90. The Color of Evening 91. Smooth Talker 91. Trial by Jury 94, etc.
TV series: Cimarron Strip 67. The Men from Shiloh 70.

Whitmore, James (1921–).
Craggy American character actor.
Undercover Man 49. Battleground (AAN) 49. The Asphalt Jungle 50. Across the Wide Missouri 51. Kiss Me Kate 53. *Them* 54. Battle Cry 55. Oklahoma 55. The Eddy Duchin Story 56. Who Was That Lady? 60. Black Like Me 64. Chuka 67. Planet of the Apes 68. Madigan 68. The Split 68. Guns of the Magnificent Seven 69. Tora! Tora! Tora! 70. Chato's Land 71. If Tomorrow Comes (TV) 71. The Harrad Experiment 73. Give 'em Hell Harry (AAN) 75. Where the Red Fern Grows 75. The Serpent's Egg 77. The Word (TV) 78. Bully 78. The First Deadly Sin 80. The Adventures of Mark Twain (voice) 85. Favorite Son (TV) 88. The Shawshank Redemption 94. The Relic 96, etc.
TV series: *The Law and Mr Jones* 60–61. My Friend Troy 69. Temperature Rising 72–73.

Whitney, Peter (1916–1972) (Peter King Engle).
Portly American character player.
Reunion in France 42. *Murder He Says* (as twins) 45. Hotel Berlin 45. The Iron Curtain 48. The Big Heat 53. Great Day in the Morning 56. Sword of Ali Baba 65. Chubasco 67. The Ballad of Cable Hogue 70, etc.

Whitrow, Benjamin (1939–).
British light actor, mostly on stage and radio.
Quadrophenia 78. Brimstone and Treacle 82. Clockwise 85. Personal Services 86. Pride and Prejudice (TV) 95. Tom Jones (TV) 97, etc.

Whitsun-Jones, Paul (1923–1974).
Rotund British character actor, usually in comedy.
The Constant Husband 55. *The Moonraker* 57. Room at the Top 59. Tunes of Glory 60, etc.

Whittingham, Jack (1910–1972).
British screenwriter.
Q Planes 39. Kiss the Bride Goodbye 44. Twilight Hour 45. I Believe in You 51. Hunted 52. The Divided Heart 54. The Birthday Present (& p) 57, etc.

Whitty, Dame May (1865–1948).
Distinguished character actress, on stage from 1881. Settled in Hollywood in the mid-30s and played dozens of indomitable but kindly old ladies. Married actor Ben Webster.
Biography: 1969, *The Same Only Different* by her daughter, Margaret Webster.
■ Enoch Arden 14. The Little Minister 15. Colonel Newcombe 20. The Thirteenth Chair 37. *Night Must Fall* (AAN) 37. Conquest 37. I Met My Love Again 37. *The Lady Vanishes* (GB) 38. Return to Yesterday (GB) 40. Raffles 40. A Bill of Divorcement 40. One Night in Lisbon 41. Suspicion 41. Mrs Miniver (AAN) 42. Thunder Birds 42. Slightly Dangerous 42. Forever and a Day 43. Crash Dive 43. The Constant Nymph 43. Lassie Come Home 43. Flesh and Fantasy 43. Madame Curie 43. Stage Door Canteen 43. The White Cliffs of Dover 44. Gaslight 44. *My Name Is Julia Ross* 45. Devotion 46. This Time for Keeps 47. Green Dolphin Street 47. If Winter Comes 47. The Sign of the Ram 48. The Return of October 48.
❝ So long as I can do my bit, I'll keep right on doing it. – M.W.

Whorf, Richard (1906–1966).
Sullen-looking American actor-director.
As actor: Midnight 34. *Blues in the Night* 41. Yankee Doodle Dandy 42. Keeper of the Flame 43. Christmas Holiday 44. Chain Lightning 50, etc.
As director: The Hidden Eye 45. Till the Clouds Roll By 46. It Happened in Brooklyn 47. Love from a Stranger 47. Luxury Liner 48. Champagne for Caesar 50, etc.
Lots of TV half-hours and hours, especially *Rawhide* and *The Beverly Hillbillies*.

Wickes, David.
British director and producer, working mainly in television.
Sweeney! 76. Silver Dream Racer (& p, w) 80. Jack the Ripper (TV) 88. Jekyll and Hyde (TV) 90. Frankenstein (TV) 93.

Wickes, Mary (1910–1995) (Mary Wickenhauser).
American character comedienne.
The Man Who Came to Dinner (as the nurse) 41. Now Voyager 42. Higher and Higher 43. June Bride 48. Young Man with Ideas 52. The Actress 54.

Good Morning, Miss Dove 56. It Happened to Jane 59. The Music Man 62. How to Murder Your Wife 64. The Trouble with Angels 66. Where Angels Go Trouble Follows 68. Snowball Express 73. Postcards from the Edge 90. Sister Act 92. Sister Act 2: Back in the Habit 93. Little Women 94. The Hunchback of Notre Dame (voice) 96, etc.

TV series: The Peter Lind Hayes Show 50. Bonino 50. Halls of Ivy 54. Dennis the Menace 59–61. The Gertrude Berg Show 61–62. Julia 68–71. Doc 75.

Famous line (*The Man Who Came to Dinner*): 'If Florence Nightingale had ever nursed you, Mr Whiteside, she would have married Jack the Ripper instead of founding the Red Cross!'

Wicki, Bernhard (1919–).
Austrian actor-director.

AS ACTOR: Der Fallende Stern 50. The Last Bridge 54. Kinder, Mütter und ein General 54. Jackboot Mutiny 55. The Face of the Cat 57. La Notte 61. Paris, Texas 84. Killing Cars 85. Marie Ward 85. Das Geheimnis 92, etc.

AS DIRECTOR: The Bridge 59. The Miracle of Malachias 61. The Longest Day (co-d) 62. The Visit (US) 63. The Saboteur 65. Karpfs Karriere 72. Die Eroberung der Zitadelle 77. Die Grunstein-Variante 85. The Spider's Web/Das Spinnennetz 89. Success/Erfolg 91, etc.

Wicking, Christopher (1943–).
English screenwriter, mainly of horror movies. Born in London, he studied at St Martin's School of Art.

Scream and Scream Again 69. The Oblong Box 69. Cry of the Banshee 70. Blood from the Mummy's Tomb 71. Murders in the Rue Morgue 71. Venom 71. To the Devil a Daughter 76. Lady Chatterley's Lover 81. Absolute Beginners 86. Dream Demon 88, etc.

Widdoes, Kathleen (1939–).
American actress with stage experience.

The Group 66. Petulia 68. The Seagull 68. The Mephisto Waltz 71. Savages 72. Mafia Princess (TV) 86. Courage under Fire 96, etc.

Widerberg, Bo (1930–1997).
Swedish writer-director and editor, much influenced by the French New Wave. Born in Malmö, he began as a journalist, short-story writer, novelist and film critic, first making a local reputation with a 1962 pamphlet, *Visions of Swedish Film*, attacking postwar Swedish cinema and the work of Ingmar BERGMAN. In films dealing with Sweden's past, intended to throw light on contemporary life, he often worked with non-professional actors, though his best-known films starred Thommy BERGGREN.

Raven's End (AAN) 63. Karlek 63. Thirty Times Your Money 66. *Elvira Madigan* 67. *Adalen 31* (AAN) 69. The Ballad of Joe Hill 69. The Man on the Roof 75. Victoria 79. The Man from Majorca 85. The Serpent's Way 87. Up the Naked Rock 88. *End All Things Fair* (AAN) 95, etc.

Widerberg, Johan (1974–).
Swedish actor, the son of Bo WIDEBERG.

Tango in August/Augustitango 93. Love Lessons/All Things Fair/Lust och Fägring Stor 95. Svart, Vitt 96, etc.

Widmark, Richard (1914–).
American leading actor; once typed as cold-eyed killer, he fought successfully for more varied roles. Born in Sunrise, Minnesota, he taught drama at Lake Forest College, where he graduated in Speech and Political Science, and worked in radio and theatre in the early 40s. Married former actress and occasional screenwriter Jean Hazelwood in 1942.

■ *Kiss of Death* (AAN) 47. Road House 48. The Street with No Name 48. Yellow Sky 49. Down to the Sea in Ships 49. Slattery's Hurricane 49. Night and the City 50. Panic in the Streets 50. No Way Out 50. Halls of Montezuma 50. The Frogmen 51. Full House 52. Don't Bother to Knock 52. Red Skies of Montana 52. My Pal Gus 52. Destination Gobi 53. Pickup on South Street 53. Take the High Ground 53. Hell and High Water 54. Garden of Evil 54. Broken Lance 54. The Cobweb 55. A Prize of Gold 55. Backlash 56. Run for the Sun 56. The Last Wagon 56. Saint Joan 57. Time Limit 57. The Law and Jake Wade 58. The Tunnel of Love 58. The Trap 59. Warlock 59. The Alamo 60. The Secret Ways 61. Two Rode Together 61. Judgment at Nuremberg 61. How the West Was Won 63. Flight from Ashiya 64. The Long Ships 64. Cheyenne Autumn 64. *The Bedford Incident* 65. Alvarez Kelly 66. The Way West 67. *Madigan* 68. Death of a Gunfighter 69. A Talent for Loving 69. The Moonshine War 70. Brock's Last Case (TV) 71. Vanished (TV) 71. When the Legends Die 72. Murder on the Orient Express 74. To the Devil a Daughter 75. The Sellout 76. Twilight's Last Gleaming 76. Rollercoaster 77. The Domino Principle 77. Mr Horn (TV) 78. Coma 78. The Swarm 78. Bear Island 79. All God's Children (TV) 80. A Whale for the Killing (TV) 81. Who Dares Wins 82. Hanky Panky 82. National Lampoon's Movie Madness 82. The Final Option 82. Against All Odds 83. Blackout 85. A Gathering of Old Men (TV) 87. Once upon a Texas Train/Texas Guns (TV) 88. Cold Sassy Tree (TV) 89. True Colors 91.

TV series: *Madigan* 72.

❝ It is clear that murder is one of the kindest things he is capable of. – *James Agee*

Wieck, Dorothea (1908–1986).
German character actress.

Mädchen in Uniform 31. Cradle Song (US) 33. The Student of Prague 35. Der Vierte Kommt Nicht 39, etc.

Wiene, Robert (1881–1938).
German director of expressionist films.

The Cabinet of Dr Caligari 19. Genuine 20. Raskolnikov 23. The Hands of Orlac 24, etc.

The Wiere Brothers.
German eccentric comedians, long in America: *Harry* (1908–1992), *Herbert* (1909–), *Sylvester* (1910–1970). Films very occasional.

The Great American Broadcast 41. Swing Shift Maisie 44. *Road to Rio* 47. Double Trouble 68, etc.

TV series: *Oh Those Bells* 62.

Wiest, Dianne (1948–).
American character actress.

Footloose 84. Falling in Love 84. The Purple Rose of Cairo 85. *Hannah and Her Sisters* (AA) 86. Radio Days 87. September 87. The Lost Boys 87. Bright Lights, Big City 88. Cookie 89. Parenthood (AAN) 89. Edward Scissorhands 90. Little Man Tate 91. Cops and Robbersons 94. Bullets over Broadway (AA) 94. The Scout 94. Drunks 95. The Bird Cage 96. The Associate 96. The Horse Whisperer 98. Practical Magic 98, etc.

Wilbur, Crane (1887–1973).
American writer-director.

Canon City 48. The Story of Molly X 49. Outside the Wall 49. Inside the Walls of Folsom Prison 50. House of Wax (script only) 53. The Bat 59. Solomon and Sheba (script only) 59, etc.

Wilby, James (1958–).
Elegant British actor (born in Burma), from the stage.

Dreamchild 85. A Room with a View 85. Maurice 87. A Handful of Dust 88. A Summer Story 88. Conspiracy 90. Adam Bede (TV) 91. Howards End 91. Immaculate Conception 92. Lady Chatterley (TV) 93. Regeneration 97. Tom's Midnight Garden 98, etc.

Wilcox, Frank (1907–1974).
Tall American character actor, a bit player who was always seen in Warner films of the 40s – sometimes in two parts in the same film.

The Fighting 69th 39. River's End 40. Highway West 41. Across the Pacific 42. Juke Girl 43. The Adventures of Mark Twain 44. Conflict 45. Gentleman's Agreement 47. Samson and Delilah 49. Those Redheads from Seattle 53. Dance with Me Henry 56. A Majority of One 61, many others.

Wilcox, Fred M. (1905–1964).
American director, former publicist; films mainly routine.

Lassie Come Home 43. Blue Sierra 46. Courage of Lassie 46. Hills of Home 48. Three Daring Daughters 48. The Secret Garden 49. Shadow in the Sky 50. Code Two 53, Tennessee Champ 54. *Forbidden Planet* 56. I Passed for White 60.

Wilcox, Herbert (1892–1977).
British independent producer-director in films from 1919 (as salesman); married to Anna Neagle.

The Wonderful Story 20. The Dawn of the World 21. Chu Chin Chow 23. *Nell Gwyn* 24. *Dawn* 26. Wolves 28. Rookery Nook 30. Good Night Vienna 32. Carnival 32. *Bitter Sweet* 33. *Nell Gwyn* 34. Peg of Old Drury 35. Limelight 36. The Three Maxims 36. The Frog 37. *Victoria the Great* 37. Sixty Glorious Years 38. Our Fighting Navy 38. *Nurse Edith Cavell* (US) 39. Sunny (US) 39. *No No Nanette* (US) 40. Irene (US) 40. They Flew Alone 42. Yellow Canary 43. I Live in Grosvenor Square 45. *Piccadilly Incident* 46. The Courtneys of Curzon Street 47. *Spring in Park Lane* 48. Elizabeth of Ladymead 49. Maytime in Mayfair 49. *Odette* 50. The Lady with a Lamp 51. Trent's Last Case 52. Laughing Anne 53. Lilacs in the Spring 55. King's Rhapsody 56. Yangtse Incident 56. My Teenage Daughter 56. Those Dangerous Years 57. The Lady Is a Square 58. Heart of a Man 59. To See Such Fun (ex p only) 77, etc.

❝ Mr Herbert Wilcox proceeds on his appointed course. As slow and ponderous and well protected as a steamroller, he irons out opposition. We get from his films almost everything except life, character, truth. – *Graham Greene reviewing Nurse Edith Cavell*

Wilcox, Jack (John) (1905–1984).
British cinematographer.

Mr Topaz 61. Where's Jack? 68. The Chairman 68. The Last Valley 70. Legend of the Werewolf 75, etc.

Wilcox, Larry (1946–).
American actor and producer, best known for his role as Officer Jon Baker in the TV series *CHiPS* 77–82. A former professional rodeo roper, he also runs his own network marketing company.

Sky Hei$t (TV) 75. The Last Hard Men 76. The Last Ride of the Dalton Gang (TV) 79. The Love Tapes (TV) 80. Death of a Centerfold: The Dorothy Stratten Story (p) (TV) 81. Deadly Lessons (TV) 83. The Dirty Dozen: The Next Mission (TV) 85. National Lampoon's Loaded Weapon 93, etc.

Wilcoxon, Henry (1905–1984).
British leading man with stage experience, in Hollywood from early 30s, latterly as executive for Cecil B. de Mille.

The Perfect Lady 31. The Flying Squad 32. Cleopatra 34. The Crusades 35. The Last of the Mohicans 36. Mrs Miniver 42. Samson and Delilah 49. Scaramouche 52. The Greatest Show on Earth 53. The Ten Commandments (& co-p) 56. The Buccaneer (& p) 59. The Private Navy of Sergeant O'Farrell 69. Man in the Wilderness 71. Against a Crooked Sky 75. Pony Express Rider 76. F.I.S.T. 78. Caddyshack 80. Sweet Sixteen 81, etc.

Wild, Jack (1952–).
British juvenile, popular around 1970.

Oliver (AAN) 68. Melody 70. Flight of the Doves 71. The Pied Piper 72. The Fourteen 73. Robin Hood: Prince of Thieves 91, etc.

TV series: *H. R. Pufnstuf* 69.

Wilde, Cornel (1915–1989).
American leading man of the 40s; later produced and directed some interesting films, but never equalled his 1944 impact as Chopin. His second wife was actress Jean Wallace (1951–81).

■ Lady with Red Hair 40. Kisses for Breakfast 41. High Sierra 41. Right to the Heart 41. The Perfect Snob 42. Life Begins at 8.30 42. Manila Calling 42. Wintertime 43. *A Song to Remember* (AAN) 45. A Thousand and One Nights 45. Leave Her to Heaven 45. *The Bandit of Sherwood Forest* 46. Centennial Summer 46. The Homestretch 46. Forever Amber 47. It Had to be You 47. Roadhouse 48. The Walls of Jericho 48. Shockproof 49. Four Days' Leave 50. Two Flags West 50. At Sword's Point 52. Operation Secret 52. The Greatest Show on Earth 52. California Conquest 52. Treasure of the Golden Condor 53. Main Street to Broadway 53. Saadia 53. Passion 54. *Woman's World* 54. The Scarlet Coat 55. Storm Fear (& d) 55. The Big Combo 55. Star of India 55. Hot Blood 56. The Devil's Hairpin (& w) 57. Omar Khayyam 57. Beyond Mombasa 57. Maracaibo (& d) 58. Edge of Eternity 59. Constantine and the Cross 60. Sword of Lancelot (& d) 63. *The Naked Prey* (& d) 66. Beach Red (& d) 67. The Comic 69. No Blade of Grass (& d) 71. Gargoyles (TV) 72. Shark's Treasure (& d) 75. The Fifth Musketeer 78. The Norseman 78.

Wilde, Hagar (1904–1971).
American screenwriter.

Bringing Up Baby 38. Carefree 39. Fired Wife 43. Guest in the House 44. The Unseen 45. I Was a Male War Bride 49. This is My Love 54, etc.

Wilde, Marty (1939–) (Reginald Smith).
British pop singer who appeared in a film or two.

Jetstorm 59. The Hellions 61. What a Crazy World 63. Stardust 74, etc.

Wilde, Oscar (1854–1900).
British playwright, poet and wit, the subject in 1960 of two film biographies: *Oscar Wilde* starring Robert Morley and *The Trials of Oscar Wilde* starring Peter Finch. The former was directed by Gregory Ratoff from a script by Jo Eisinger, and had Ralph Richardson as Carson, John Neville as Lord Alfred, and Edward Chapman as the Marquess of Queensberry. The latter, written and directed by Ken Hughes, had James Mason, John Fraser and Lionel Jeffries respectively in these roles. Films have been made of several of Wilde's works including *The Importance of Being Earnest*, *An Ideal Husband*, *Lady Windermere's Fan*, *The Picture of Dorian Gray*, *Lord Arthur Savile's Crime* (in *Flesh and Fantasy*) and *The Canterville Ghost*. In 1997, the biopic *Wilde*, which put much emphasis on him as a married man and father, was directed by Brian Gilbert and starred Stephen Fry in the title role, Jude Law as his nemesis Lord Alfred Douglas, and Tom Wilkinson as the Marquess of Queensberry.

❝ One needs misfortunes to live happily. – *O.W.*

Wilder, Billy (1906–) (Samuel Wilder).
Austro-Hungarian writer-director, in Hollywood from 1934. A specialist for years in bitter comedy and drama torn from the world's headlines, he has lately concentrated on rather heavy-going bawdy farce.

Biographies: 1970, *The Brighter Side of Billy Wilder, Primarily* by Tom Wood; 1976, *Billy Wilder in Hollywood* by Maurice Zolotow; 1996, *Wilder Times* by Kevin Lally.

■ AS WRITER: People on Sunday 30; followed by ten other German films; Adorable (Fr.) 34. Music in the Air (co-w) 34. Lottery Lover (co-w) 35. Bluebeard's Eighth Wife (co-w) 38. *Midnight* (co-w) 39. What a Life (co-w) 39. *Ninotchka* (co-w, AAN) 39. *Arise My Love* (co-w) 40. Ball of Fire (co-w, AAN) 41. Hold Back the Dawn (co-w, AAN) 41.

■ AS WRITER-DIRECTOR (script always in collaboration): Mauvaise Graine (Fr.) 33. *The Major and the Minor* 42. *Five Graves to Cairo* 43. *Double Indemnity* (AAN) 44. *The Lost Weekend* (AA) 45. The Emperor Waltz 47. *A Foreign Affair* (co-w, AAN) 48. *Sunset Boulevard* (AAN) 50. *Ace in the Hole* 51. *Stalag 17* (AAN) 53. Sabrina (AAN) 54. *The Seven Year Itch* 55. The Spirit of St Louis 57. Love in the Afternoon 57. *Witness for the Prosecution* (AAN) 57. *Some Like It Hot* (AAN) 59. *The Apartment* (AA) 60. *One Two Three* 61. Irma La Douce 63. Kiss Me Stupid 64. The Fortune Cookie 66. *The Private Life of Sherlock Holmes* 70. Avanti 72. The Front Page 74. Fedora 78. Buddy Buddy 81.

✪ For being Hollywood's most mischievous immigrant. *Sunset Boulevard*.

❝ The pixie wit of this Hollywood Viennese has sporadically brightened the film scene for more than thirty years. Nor does he save all his wit for his scripts; he is the most quotable of film-makers:

I have ten commandments. The first nine are, thou shalt not bore. The tenth is, thou shalt have right of final cut.

On critical prejudice:

What critics call dirty in our movies, they call lusty in foreign films.

On fashion:

You watch, the new wave will discover the slow dissolve in ten years or so.

On messages:

In certain pictures I do hope they will leave the cinema a little enriched, but I don't make them pay a buck and a half and then ram a lecture down their throats.

On direction:

The best director is the one you don't see

On technique:

The close-up is such a valuable thing – like a trump at bridge.

On finances:

No one says, 'Boy I must see that film – I hear it came in under budget.'

A man with such waspish wit naturally invites retaliation, even from his wife:

Long before Billy Wilder was Billy Wilder, he thought he was Billy Wilder.

That may have been in response to a cable he sent her from Paris just after the war. She had requested him to buy and send a bidet. After a vain search he sent the message:

Unable obtain bidet. Suggest handstand in shower.

Wilder is the kind of man who can scarcely observe anything without being funny about it. For instance:

France is a country where the money falls apart in your hands and you can't tear the toilet paper.

But he could be just as ornery as anybody else. As Harry Kurnitz said:

Billy Wilder at work is two people: Mr Hyde and Mr Hyde.

Andrew Sarris summed up accurately:

Wilder is a curdled Lubitsch, romanticism gone sour, 78rpm played at 45 an old-worldling from Vienna perpetually sneering at Hollywood as it engulfs him.

Wilder wouldn't be listening – too busy constructing scenarios:

An actor enters through a door, you've got nothing. But if he enters through a window, you've got a situation.

Wilder, Gene (1934–) (Jerry Silberman).
American comic actor. Married Gilda Radner.
Bonnie and Clyde 67. *The Producers* (AAN) 68. Start the Revolution Without Me 69. Quackser Fortune has a Cousin in the Bronx 70. Willy Wonka and the Chocolate Factory 71. Everything You Always Wanted to Know about Sex 72. Rhinoceros 73. The Little Prince 73. Blazing Saddles 74. Young Frankenstein (AANw) 74. The Adventure of Sherlock Holmes' Smarter Brother (& p, d) 75. Silver Streak 76. The World's Greatest Lover (& wd, p) 77. The Frisco Kid 79. Stir Crazy 80. Sunday Lovers 80. Hanky Panky 82. The Woman in Red (& d) 84. Haunted Honeymoon (& d) 86. See No Evil, Hear No Evil 89. Funny about Love 90. Another You 91, etc.

Wilder, Robert (1901–1974).
American novelist and screenwriter.
Flamingo Road (& oa) 48. *Written on the Wind* (& oa) 56. The Big Country 58. Sol Madrid 66, etc.

Wilder, Thornton (1897–1975).
American playwright and novelist. Works filmed include *Our Town*, *The Bridge of San Luis Rey* (several times), *The Matchmaker;* also wrote screenplay of Hitchcock's *Shadow of a Doubt*.

Wilder, W. Lee (1904–).
Austro-Hungarian producer in America, brother of Billy Wilder. Films mainly low-budget oddities.
The Great Flamarion 44. Phantom from Space 53. The Snow Creature 54. Bluebeard's Ten Honeymoons 60, etc.

Wilding, Michael (1912–1979).
British leading man of the 40s. His four wives included actresses Elizabeth Taylor and Margaret Leighton.
Posthumous autobiography: 1982, *Apple Sauce*.
Wedding Group 35. Tilly of Bloomsbury 40. *Sailors Three* 40. Kipps 41. Cottage To Let 41. *In Which We Serve* 42. Dear Octopus 43. *English Without Tears* 44. Carnival 46. *Piccadilly Incident* 46. The Courtneys of Curzon Street 47. An Ideal Husband 47. *Spring in Park Lane* 48. Maytime in Mayfair 50. Under Capricorn 50. Stage Fright 50. Into the Blue 51. The Law and the Lady (US) 52. Derby Day 52. Trent's Last Case 53. The Egyptian 54. The Glass Slipper 55. Zarak 56. Danger Within 57. The World of Suzie Wong 60. The Naked Edge 61. The Best of Enemies 61. A Girl Named Tamiko 63. The Sweet Ride 68. Waterloo 69. Lady Caroline Lamb 72. Frankenstein: The True Story (TV) 73, etc.

❝ I was the worst actor I ever came across. – M.W.

He was a man who should never have become an actor because his nerves were so terrible that every appearance was an ordeal. – *Hermione Baddeley*

Wildman, John (1961–).
Canadian actor. Won a Genie (the Canadian equivalent of an Oscar) for his performance in *My American Cousin*.
Humongous 81. My *American Cousin* 85. Sorority Babes in the Slimeball Bowl-A-Rama 87. Lethal Pursuit 88. American Boyfriends 89, etc.

Wilke, Robert J. (1911–1989).
American character actor, usually in mean, shifty or villainous roles.
San Francisco 36. Sheriff of Sundown 44. The Last Days of Boot Hill 47. Kill the Umpire 50. Twenty Thousand Leagues under the Sea 54. Night Passage 57. The Gun Hawk 63. The Hallelujah Trail 65. Tony Rome 67. A Gunfight 71. Days of Heaven 78. Stripes 81, etc.

Wilkinson, Tom (1948–).
English character actor.
Wetherby 85. Paper Mask 90. Martin Chuzzlewit (as Pecksniff) (TV) 94. *Priest* 94. A Very Open Prison (TV) 95. Crossing the Floor (TV) 96. Smilla's Sense of Snow/Smilla's Feeling for Snow 96. *The Full Monty* 96. Wilde 97. Oscar and Lucinda 97. The Governess 98. Rush Hour 98. Shakespeare in Love 98. Molokai 98, etc.

William, Warren (1895–1948) (Warren Krech).
Suave American leading man with stage experience.
The Perils of Pauline 14. The Woman from Monte Carlo 32. The Mouthpiece 33. *Lady for a Day* 33. *Imitation of Life* 34. Cleopatra (as Julius Caesar) 34. The Case of the Lucky Legs 35. Satan Met a Lady 36. The Firefly 37. *The Lone Wolf's Spy Hunt* 39 (and others in this series). The Man in the Iron Mask 39. Lillian Russell 40. The Wolf Man 41. Counter Espionage 42. One Dangerous Night 43. Fear 46. Bel Ami 47, etc.

Williams, Adam (1929–).
American 'second lead'.
Queen for a Day 50. Without Warning 52. Crashout 55. Garment Centre 57. Darby's Rangers 58. North by Northwest 59. The Last Sunset 61. The Glory Guys 67, etc.

Williams, Bill (1916–1992) (William Katt).
American leading man, an innocent-type hero of the 40s. Former professional swimmer and singer.
Murder in the Blue Room (debut) 44. Those Endearing Young Charms 45. Till the End of Time 46. Deadline at Dawn 47. The Great Missouri Raid 51. The Outlaw's Daughter 53. Wiretapper 56. A Dog's Best Friend 61. Tickle Me 65, etc.
TV series: Kit Carson 52–54. Assignment Underwater 61.

Williams, Billy (1929–).
British cinematographer.
Just Like a Woman 66. Billion Dollar Brain 67. *Women in Love* 69. Two Gentlemen Sharing 70. Tam Lin 70. *Sunday Bloody Sunday* 72. Night Watch 73. The Wind and the Lion 75. Eagle's Wing 79. Saturn Three 80. *On Golden Pond* 81. *Gandhi* (AA) 82. Monsignor 82. The Survivors 83. Dreamchild 85. Eleni 85. The Manhattan Project 86. Suspect 87. The Rainbow 89. Stella 90. Diamond's Edge 90. Shadow of the Wolf 92. Reunion (TV) 94. Driftwood 95, etc.

Williams, Billy Dee (1937–).
American leading man.
Brian's Song (TV) 71. Lady Sings the Blues 72. Hit 73. The Take 74. Mahogany 75. Bingo Long and the Travelling All Stars 76. *Scott Joplin* 78. The Empire Strikes Back 80. Nighthawks 81. Marvin and Tige 83. Number One with a Bullet 87. Deadly Illusion 87. The Impostor 88. Batman 89. Dangerous Passion (TV) 90. Alien Intruder 93. TripleCross 95. Dangerous Passion 95. Moving Target 96. Steel Sharks 97. Mask of Death 97, etc.

Williams, Bransby (1870–1961) (Bransby William Pharez).
British actor and mimic, a former clerk. Born in Hackney, London, he was on stage from the 1890s and in silent films from 1911, but was best known for his music-hall performances from the mid-1890s which made him a star, imitating popular actors of the time, including Henry Irving and Beerbohm Tree, reciting monologues to music, including 'The Green Eye of the Yellow God', and presenting characters from Dickens. In later life, he was much on radio and also appeared on television. He made an early talkie appearance in an experimental Lee de Forest Phonofilm.
Royal England 11. Grimaldi 14. Hard Times 15. Adam Bede 18. The Adventures of Mr Pickwick 21. The Cold Cure 25. Jungle Woman 26. Scrooge 28. Troublesome Wives 28. Hearts of Humanity 36. *Song of the Road* 37. The Common Touch 41. Tomorrow We Live 42. The Trojan Brothers 46. Judgment Deferred 52, etc.

Williams, Cara (1925–) (Bernice Kamiat).
American TV and radio comedienne. She was formerly married to John Drew Barrymore.
Happy Land 43. Don Juan Quilligan 45. Sitting Pretty 48. The Girl Next Door 53. The Defiant Ones (AAN) 58. The Man from the Diners Club 63. The White Buffalo 77.
TV series: Pete and Gladys 60–61. The Cara Williams Show 64. Rhoda 74–75.

Williams, Charles (1893–*).
English composer and musical director. Born in London, he studied at the Royal Academy of Music and began by composing scores for silent pictures. He worked for Gaumont-British for much of the 30s. His best-known composition was 'The Dream of Olwyn', the theme for *While I Live*, which became so popular that the film was later reissued under the tune's title.
Kipps 41. The Night Has Eyes/Terror House 42. The Young Mr Pitt 42. The Life and Death of Colonel Blimp (md) 43. Twilight Hour (md) 44. Quiet Weekend 46. While I Live/The Dream of Olwen 47. Noose 48. The Romantic Age 49, etc.

Williams, Cindy (1948–).
American leading lady.
Drive He Said 71. American Graffiti 73. Travels with My Aunt 73. The Conversation 74. Mr Ricco 75. More American Graffiti 79. The Creature Wasn't Nice 81. Rude Awakening 89. Bingo! 91. Meet Wally Sparks 97, etc.
TV series: Laverne and Shirley 76–82. Normal Life 90. Getting By 93–94.

Williams, Derick (1906–).
English cinematographer and producer. Born in Nottingham, he studied at Nottingham University and began his career as assistant cameraman on Alfred Hitchcock's *Blackmail* 29. In the early 30s he became head of Gainsborough's camera department, then spent a year in Hollywood before returning to Britain. He set up his own production company in the 50s.
The Lucky Number (co-ph) 33. Inspector Hornleigh 38. Ask a Policeman 38. Ghost of St Michael's 41. The Way Ahead (co-ph) 44. The Way to the Stars/Johnny in the Clouds 45. Beware of Pity 46. White Cradle Inn/High Fury 47. My Brother Jonathan 47. For Them that Trespass 48. Don't Talk to Strange Men (p) 62. Seventy Deadly Pills (p) 63. On the Run (p) 69, etc.

Williams, Elmo (1913–).
American editor and producer. Produced, edited and directed *The Cowboy* 54; worked as editor on several major productions; became head of Twentieth Century-Fox British productions.

Williams, Emlyn (1905–1987).
Welsh leading actor, dramatist, screenwriter and director. Born in Mostyn, he was a poor boy from a mining village who, encouraged by his teacher, won a scholarship to Oxford, a subject that formed the basis of his most successful play, *The Corn Is Green*. On stage from 1927, and a prolific playwright in the 30s and 40s, he began in films repeating one of his stage successes, later becoming an occasional screenwriter and director. Two projects that never came to fruition were the role of Caligula in Alexander Korda's abandoned *I, Claudius* and a screenplay, *Gala Night*, based on Arthur Machen's *The Terror*. From the early 50s, he gained a new fame for his one-man shows based on the work of Charles Dickens, Dylan Thomas and Saki. His best film roles were as Lord Lebanon in *The Frightened Lady*, Shorty Matthews in *They Drive by Night*, Dennis in *Hatter's Castle*, Maxwell Bard in *Three Husbands*, and William Collyer in *The Deep Blue Sea*. He is the father of actor Brook Williams (1938–).
Autobiographies: 1972, *George*. 1974, *Emlyn*.
Biography: 1992, *Emlyn Williams* by James Harding.
The Frightened Lady 32. Sally Bishop 32. Men of Tomorrow 32. Friday the Thirteenth (& w) 34. My Song for You 34. Evensong 34. The Iron Duke 34. Evergreen (co-w only) 34. The Man Who Knew Too Much (co-w only) 34. The Love Affair of a Dictator 35. Roadhouse 35. The Divine Spark (co-w only) 35. The City of Beautiful Nonsense 35. Broken Blossoms (& w) 36. Night Must Fall (oa) 37. Night Alone 38. Dead Men Tell No Tales 39. The Citadel 39. *They Drive by Night* 39. Jamaica Inn 39. The Stars Look Down 40. You Will Remember 41. The Girl in the News 41. Major Barbara 41. This England (& w) 41. *Hatter's Castle* 42. The Corn Is Green (oa) 45. *The Last Days of Dolwyn* (& wd) 49. *Three Husbands* (US) 51. Another Man's Poison 51. The Scarf (US) 51. The Magic Box 52. Ivanhoe 52. *The Deep Blue Sea* 55. I Accuse 57. Time without Pity (oa) 57. Beyond This Place 59. The Wreck of the Mary Deare 59. The L-Shaped Room 62. Night Must Fall (oa) 64. The Eye of the Devil 66. David Copperfield (TV) 69. The Walking Stick 70. The Corn Is Green (oa) (TV) 78. The Deadly Game (TV) 82. Past Caring (TV) 85. King Ralph (oa) 91, etc.

Williams, Esther (1923–).
Aquatic American leading lady, former swimming champion. She married Fernando Lamas, her third husband, in 1967.
■ Andy Hardy's Double Life (debut) 42. A Guy Named Joe 43. *Bathing Beauty* 44. Ziegfeld Follies 44. Thrill of a Romance 45. Easy to Wed 45. This Time for Keeps 46. Till the Clouds Roll By 46. Fiesta 47. On an Island with You 48. *Take Me Out to the Ball Game* 48. Neptune's Daughter 49. Pagan Love Song 50. Duchess of Idaho 51. Callaway Went Thataway 51. Texas Carnival 52. Skirts Ahoy 52. Million Dollar Mermaid 52. *Dangerous When Wet* 53. Easy to Love 54. Jupiter's Darling 54. The Unguarded Moment 56. Raw Wind in Eden 57. The Big Show 61. The Magic Fountain (Sp.) 61.

❝ All they ever did for me at MGM was change my leading men and the water in my pool. – *E.W.*

Wet she was a star. – *Joe Pasternak*

Williams, Grant (1930–1985).
American leading man who never quite made the big time.
Written on the Wind 56. *The Incredible Shrinking Man* 57. The Monolith Monsters 58. PT 109 63. Doomsday 72, etc.
TV series: Hawaiian Eye 59–63.

Williams, Guinn 'Big Boy' (1900–1962).
American character actor, usually in amiably tough roles. In Hollywood 1919 as an extra.
Noah's Ark 29. Dodge City 39. Mr Wise Guy 42. The Desperadoes 43. Thirty Seconds Over Tokyo 44. Bad Men of Tombstone 49. Hangman's Knot 53. The Outlaw's Daughter 55. The Comancheros 62, many others.
TV series: Circus Boy 56–57.

Williams, Guy (1924–1989) (Armand Catalano).
American leading man, the 'Zorro' of Walt Disney's TV series and films.
The Prince and the Pauper 62. Captain Sinbad 63, etc.
TV series: Lost in Space 65–68.

Williams, Hank (1923–1953).
Influential American country singer and songwriter who had a short, unruly life. In the biopic *Your Cheatin' Heart* 64, he was played by George Hamilton, with his songs dubbed by his son, Hank Williams Jnr.

Williams, Harcourt (1880–1957).
Distinguished British stage actor.
Henry V 44. *Brighton Rock* 47. Hamlet 48. Third Time Lucky 48. *The Late Edwina Black* 51. Roman Holiday 53. Around the World in Eighty Days 56.

Williams, Hugh (1904–1969) (Brian Williams).
British leading man and playwright on stage from 1921.
Charley's Aunt (film debut) 30. In a Monastery Garden 31. Rome Express 33. Sorrell and Son 34. *David Copperfield* (US) 34. The Amateur Gentleman 36. Dark Eyes of London 38. Wuthering Heights (US) 39. A Girl in a Million 46. *An Ideal Husband* 47. Take My Life 47. The Blind Goddess 48. Elizabeth of Ladymead 49. The Gift Horse 52. The Fake 53. Twice Upon a Time 53. Khartoum 66, etc.

Williams, Jo Beth (1953–).
American leading lady.
Kramer vs Kramer 79. The Dogs of War 80. Stir Crazy 80. Poltergeist 82. Endangered Species 82. The Big Chill 83. American Dreamer 84. Teachers 84. Desert Bloom 85. Poltergeist II 86. Memories of Me 88. Welcome Home 89. Victim of Love 91. Switch 91. Dutch/Driving Me Crazy 91. Stop! or My Mom Will Shoot 92. Chantilly Lace (TV) 93. Wyatt Earp 94. Parallel Lives (TV) 94. Ruby Jean and Joe 96. Jungle 2 Jungle 96. When Danger Follows You Home 97. Just Write 98, etc.
TV series: The Client 95–96.

Williams, John (1903–1983).
Suave British stage actor, usually in polished comedy roles.
Emil and the Detectives 35. Next of Kin 42. A Woman's Vengeance 48. Dick Turpin's Ride 51. *Dial M for Murder* 54. Sabrina Fair 54. To Catch a Thief 55. *The Solid Gold Cadillac* 56. Island in the Sun 56. Witness for the Prosecution 57. Visit to a Small Planet 60. Last of the Secret Agents 66. The Secret War of Harry Frigg 67. A Flea in Her Ear 68. The Hound of the Baskervilles (TV) 72. No Deposit No Return 76. Hot Lead and Cold Feet 78, etc.

Williams, John (1932–).
Prolific American composer and pianist, the creator of sweeping scores, and best known for the music to the *Star Wars* films. Born in Floral Park, New York, the son of a musician, he studied at the Juilliard School and worked as a studio musician and arranger before turning to composition. During the 80s and early 90s he was also conductor of the Boston Pops Orchestra.
The Secret Ways 61. Diamond Head 62. None but the Brave 65. How to Steal a Million 66. Valley of the Dolls (AAN) 67. Goodbye Mr Chips (AAN) 69. The Reivers (AAN) 69. The Cowboys 71. *Fiddler on the Roof* (AA) 71. The Poseidon Adventure (AAN) 72. Images (AAN) 72. Tom Sawyer (AAN) 73. Cinderella Liberty (AANm, AANs) 73. Earthquake 74. The Towering Inferno (AAN) 74. *Jaws* (AA) 75. The Eiger Sanction 75. *Star Wars* (AA) 77. Close Encounters of the Third Kind (AAN) 77. Jaws 2 78. Superman (AAN) 78. The Fury 78. 1941 79. Dracula 79. Superman 2 80. The Empire Strikes Back (AAN, BFA) 80. Raiders of the Lost Ark (AAN) 81. E.T. – the Extraterrestrial (AA, BFA) 82. Yes, Giorgio (AANs) 82. Return of the Jedi (AAN) 83. Monsignor 83. Indiana Jones and the Temple of Doom (AAN) 84. The River (AAN) 84. Spacecamp 85. The Witches of Eastwick (AAN) 87. Empire of the Sun (AAN) 87. Jaws: The Revenge 87. Superman IV: The Quest for Peace 87. The Accidental Tourist (AAN) 88. Always 89. Born on the Fourth of July (AAN) 89. Indiana Jones and the Last Crusade (AAN) 89. *Home Alone* (AANm, AANs) 90. Stanley and Iris 90. JFK (AAN) 91. Hook (AAN) 91. Far and Away 92. Jurassic Park 93. Schindler's List (AA) 93. Nixon (AAN) 95. Sabrina (AANm, AANs) 95. Sleepers (AAN) 96. Seven Years in Tibet 97. Amistad (AAN) 97. Stepmom 98, etc.

Williams, Kathlyn (1888–1960).
American leading lady of silent films: one of the first serial queens.
Witch of the Everglades 11. Driftwood 12. The Adventures of Kathlyn 13. Sweet Alyssum 15. The Highway of Hope 17. Just a Wife 20. Morals 23. The Enemy Sex 24. Our Dancing Daughters 28. Blood Money 33, many others.

Williams, Kenneth (1926–1988).
British comic actor adept at 'small boy' characters and a variety of outrageous voices. Also on stage, radio and TV. He starred in 22 'Carry On' films.
Autobiography: 1985, *Just Williams*. Also: 1993, *The Diaries of Kenneth Williams*, edited by Russell Davies. 1994, *The Letters of Kenneth Williams*, edited by Russell Davies.
The Beggar's Opera 52. The Seekers 54. *Carry On Sergeant* 58 (and most other 'Carry Ons'). Raising the Wind 61. Twice Round the Daffodils 62. Don't Lose Your Head 67. Follow That Camel 68. Carry On Dick 74, etc.
❝ The thing to do, in any circumstance, is to appear to know exactly what you are doing and at the same time convey casual doubts about the abilities of everybody else and undermine their confidence. – *K.W.*
It is not as an actor that he will be remembered, but as a voice veering between posh and rough-trade and all of it laced with camp. And as a look too: beady eyes, cavernous nostrils and pursed mouth. – *George Melly*

Williams, Michelle (1980–).
American teenaged actress, born in Kalispell, Montana, who began appearing in commercials at the age of 10, when her family moved to San Diego. She is best known for her role as Jennifer in the TV series *Dawson's Creek*.
Lassie 94. Species 95. A Thousand Acres 97. Halloween H20: Twenty Years Later 98. Dick 99, etc.
TV series: Dawson's Creek 98– .

Williams, Olivia (c. 1969–).
English actress, from the theatre. Born in London, she studied English at Cambridge University and acting at the Bristol Old Vic school.
The Postman 97. Emma (TV) 97. Rushmore 98, etc.

Williams, Patrick (1939–).
American composer who has also scored many TV movies and series.
How Sweet It Is! 68. Don't Drink the Water 69. Evel Knievel 72. Framed 74. The Cheap Detective 78. Breaking Away (AAN) 79. Butch and Sundance: The Early Days 79. Cuba 79. Wholly Moses 80. Some Kind of Hero 82. Swing Shift 83. Best Defense 84. Just Between Friends 86. Worth Winning 89. Cry-Baby 90. In the Spirit 90. Geronimo (TV) 94. Kingfish (TV) 95. The Grass Harp 95, etc.

Williams, Paul (1940–).
Diminutive American singer, composer and actor.
The Chase (a) 65. Phantom of the Paradise (a, m) (AANm) 74. Bugsy Malone (m) 76. A Star Is Born (AAs) 76. Smokey and the Bandit (a) 77. The End (m) 78. The Muppet Movie (a, m) (AANm) 79. The Wild Wild West Revisited (a) (TV) 79. Rooster (a) (TV) 82. Smokey and the Bandit III 83. Headless Body in a Topless Bar 95, etc.

Williams, Paul (1943–).
American director of quirky films.
Out of It 69. The Revolutionary 70. Dealing: Or the Berkeley-to-Boston Forty-Brick Lost-Bag Blues 72. A Light in the Afternoon 86. The November Men 93. Mirage 95, etc.

Williams, Rhys (1892–1969).
Welsh character actor, long in Hollywood; former technical adviser.
How Green Was My Valley 40. The Spiral Staircase 45. Scandal at Scourie 53. There's No Business Like Show Business 54. The Kentuckian 55. The Fastest Gun Alive 56. The Sons of Katie Elder 65. Skullduggery 69, many others.

Williams, Richard (1933–).
Canadian animator in England who has been working on his animated feature *The Thief and the Cobbler* for more than 20 years. After he lost control of it, it was finally released in 1995 as *Arabian Knight*.
The Little Island 58. *The Charge of the Light Brigade* (titles) 67. *A Christmas Carol* 73, etc.
Designed title sequences for *What's New Pussycat*, *The Liquidator*, *Casino Royale*, *Sebastian*, etc.

Williams, Robert (1899–1931).
Slow-speaking American leading man of the early 30s.
The Common Law 31. Rebound 31. Devotion 31. *Platinum Blonde* 31, etc.

Williams, Robin (1952–).
Eccentric American nightclub comedian who became a TV star as Mork from Ork in *Mork and Mindy*. He has a claim as the biggest box-office attraction from the mid-80s: since 1986, he has starred in seven films that have each taken more than $100m at the US box-office, putting him ahead of Tom Hanks, who has appeared in five $100m films, and Tom Cruise, who has appeared in six. Current asking price: around $15m. In 1998 *Fortune* magazine estimated his personal wealth at $100m.
Popeye 80. The World According to Garp 82. The Survivors 83. Moscow on the Hudson 84. The Best of Times 85. Club Paradise 86. Good Morning Vietnam (AAN) 87. Dear America: Letters Home from Vietnam 88. The Adventures of Baron Munchausen (uncredited) 89. Dead Poets Society (AAN) 89. Cadillac Man 90. Awakenings 90. Dead Again (uncredited) 91. The Fisher King (AAN) 91. Shakes the Clown (uncredited) 91. Hook 91. Ferngully . . . the Last Rainforest (voice) 92. Toys 92. Mrs Doubtfire 93. Being Human 94. Nine Months 95. Jumanji 95. The Bird Cage 96. Jack 96. Hamlet 96. Father's Day 96. Joseph Conrad's Secret Agent 96. Flubber 97. *Good Will Hunting* (AA) 97. Deconstructing Harry 97. What Dreams May Come 98. Patch Adams 98, etc.
❝ Cocaine is God's way of saying you're making too much money. – *R.W.*
You're only given a little madness. You mustn't lose it. – *R.W.*

Williams, Simon (1946–).
British light leading man, son of Hugh Williams, who became a TV star in *Upstairs Downstairs*.
The Incredible Sarah 75. Jabberwocky 76. The Odd Job 77. The Prisoner of Zenda 79. The Fiendish Plot of Fu Manchu 80. The Return of the Man from UNCLE (TV) 83.

Williams, Tennessee (1911–1983) (Thomas Lanier Williams).
Popular American playwright whose work, usually concerned with strong sexual emotions, has often been translated to the screen, despite the fact that in the process it has been so watered down as to lose much of its power. Born in Columbus, Mississippi, the son of a shoe salesman, he studied at the University of Iowa and found success with his autobiographical *The Glass Menagerie* 45, the only one of his plays not to have been distorted by the film studios. The Broadway production of *A Streetcar Named Desire* 47 made a star of Marlon Brando, who repeated his role in the film directed by Elia Kazan. Williams was not often happy with the films of his work: he thought *Baby Doll* lacked the right wanton hilarity; that *Suddenly, Last Summer* ('It made me throw up,' he said) suffered from the miscasting of Elizabeth Taylor in the part of a woman used by her homosexual cousin to attract youths. He was no happier with her performance in *Boom*, based on *The Milk Train Doesn't Stop Here Anymore*, thinking her too young for her role, and Richard Burton too old for his, though he thought the result 'an artistic success'. His later plays, which were written under the stimulus of alcohol and drugs, have not attracted film-makers. He died choking on a bottle-cap in a New York hotel room.
Autobiography: 1976, *Memoirs*.
Biography: 1993, *Tennessee Williams: Everyone Else Is an Audience* by Ronald Hayman.
■ *The Glass Menagerie* 50. *A Streetcar Named Desire* (AA) 52. The Rose Tattoo 56. Baby Doll (AAN) 56. Cat on a Hot Tin Roof 58. Suddenly Last Summer 59. The Fugitive Kind 60. Summer and Smoke 61. The Roman Spring of Mrs Stone 61. Period of Adjustment 62. Sweet Bird of Youth 63. *The Night of the Iguana* 64. This Property Is Condemned 66. Boom 68. Blood Kin 70.
❝ Why did I write? Because I found life unsatisfactory. – *T.W.*

Williams, Treat (1952–) (Richard Williams).
American leading actor of heavy presence, from Broadway.
The Ritz 76. The Eagle Has Landed 77. *Hair* 79. 1941 79. Why Would I Lie? 80. The Pursuit of D. B. Cooper 81. Prince of the City 81. Flashpoint 84. Once upon a Time in America 84. Dempsey (TV) 85. Smooth Talk 85. The Men's Club 86. Dead Heat 88. Heart of Dixie 89. Russicum 89. Sweet Lies 89. Beyond the Ocean/Oltre l'Oceano (a, co-w, d) 89. Max and Helen (TV) 90. Bonds of Love (TV) 93. Where the Rivers Flow North 93. Handgun 94. Parallel Lives (TV) 94. Things to Do in Denver When You're Dead 95. Mulholland Falls 96. The Phantom 96. The Late Shift 96. The Devil's Own 97. Deep Rising 98, etc.
TV series: Eddie Dodd 91.

Williams, Vanessa (1963–).
American actress and singer. Born in Tarrytown, New York, she studied at Syracuse University.
New Jack City 91. Harley Davidson and the Marlboro Man 91. Another You 91. Candyman 92. DROP Squad 94. Hoodlum 96, etc.
TV series: Melrose Place 92–93. Murder One 95. Chicago Hope 96– .

Williamson, David (1942–).
Australian dramatist and screenwriter.
Stork 71. Petersen 74. The Removalists 75. Don's Party 76. Eliza Fraser 76. The Club 80. Gallipoli 81. Duet for Four 82. The Year of Living Dangerously 82. Phar Lap 83. Sanctuary 95. Brilliant Lies 96, etc.

Williamson, Fred (1938–).
American action hero.
M*A*S*H 70. The Legend of Nigger Charley 72. Hammer 72. Black Caesar 72. Crazy Joe 73. That Man Bolt 74. Boss Nigger 75. Darktown 75. Take a Hard Ride 75. Mr Mean (& p, d) 77. Fist of Fear, Touch of Death 80. Vigilante 83. The Big Score (& d) 83. Foxtrap (& d) 86. The Messenger (& d) 87. Soda Cracker (& d) 89. Black Cobra 3: Manila Connection 91. Three Days to a Kill (& story, p, d) 92. South Beach (& p, d) 92. The Night Caller (& p, d) 92. From Dusk till Dawn (a) 95. Original Gangstas (a) 96. Night Vision (a) 97. Blackjack (a) 97, etc.
TV series: Julia 70–71. Wheels 79. Half Nelson 85.

Williamson, James A. (1855–1933).
British production pioneer.
The Big Swallow 01. Fire! 01, etc.

Williamson, Kevin (1965–).
American screenwriter of horror movies, born in Oriental, North Carolina. He is the creator of the TV series *Dawson's Creek*.
Scream 96. I Know What You Did Last Summer 97. Scream 2 97. The Faculty 98, etc.

Williamson, Lambert (1907–).
British composer.
Edge of the World 38. End of the River 48. One Night With You 48. Cosh Boy 53. The Spaniard's Curse 58, etc.

Williamson, Malcolm (1931–).
Australian-born composer, pianist, and organist, in Britain from 1953. Composer of operas, ballets, choral and orchestral music, he was made Master of the Queen's Music in 1975.
The Brides of Dracula 60. The Horror of Frankenstein 70. Crescendo 72. Nothing but the Night 75. Watership Down (co-m) 76, etc.

Williamson, Nicol (1938–).
British leading actor of stage and screen; tends to play bulls in china shops. In 1994 he starred in a one-man play on the life of actor John Barrymore.
Six Sided Triangle 64. *Inadmissible Evidence* 67. *The Bofors Gun* 68. Laughter in the Dark 68. *The Reckoning* 69. Hamlet 69. The Jerusalem File 72. The Wilby Conspiracy 75. Robin and Marian 76. The Seven Per Cent Solution 76. The Word (TV) 78. The Cheap Detective 78. The Human Factor 79. Venom 81. Excalibur 81. I'm Dancing as Fast as I Can 82. Sakharov (TV) 85. Return to Oz 85. Black Widow 87. The Exorcist III 90. The Hour of the Pig 93. The Wind in the Willows 96. Spawn 97, etc.
❝ I don't even notice competition. I'm a centre-forward. I don't watch them. Let them watch me. – *N.W.*
I can understand people's pain, passion, fear, hurt, and I can mirror it and set it up for them to look at. – *N.W.*
The greatest actor since Marlon Brando. – *John Osborne*

Willingham, Calder (1922–1995).
American novelist and screenwriter.
The Strange One/End as a Man (w, oa) 57. Paths of Glory (co-w) 57. The Bridge on the River Kwai (co-w, uncredited) 57. The Vikings 58. One-Eyed Jacks (co-w) 61. *The Graduate* (co-w) (AAN) 67. Little Big Man (w) 70. Thieves Like Us (co-w) 74. *Rambling Rose* (w, oa) 91, etc.

Willis, Bruce (1955–).
American leading man. Married Demi Moore. He is one of the backers of the restaurant chain Planet Hollywood.
Biography: 1997, *Bruce Willis: The Unauthorised Biography* by John Parker.
Blind Date 87. Sunset 88. Die Hard 88. In Country 89. That's Adequate 89. Look Who's Talking (voice) 90. Die Hard 2 90. The Bonfire of the Vanities 90. Look Who's Talking Too (voice) 90. Hudson Hawk (& co-story) 91. Mortal Thoughts 91. Billy Bathgate 91. Last Boy Scout

91. Death Becomes Her 92. The Player 92. Striking Distance 93. Pulp Fiction 94. North 94. Color of Night 94. Nobody's Fool 94. Die Hard with a Vengeance 95. Four Rooms 95. 12 Monkeys 95. Last Man Standing 96. The Jackal 97. The Fifth Element 97. Armageddon 98. Mercury Rising 98. The Siege 98, etc.

TV series: Moonlighting 85–89.

Willis, Gordon.
American cinematographer.

Loving 70. The Landlord 70. The People Next Door 70. Klute 71. Little Murders 71. Bad Company 72. *The Godfather* 72. Up the Sandbox 72. The Paper Chase 73. The Godfather Part Two 74. The Parallax View 74. The Drowning Pool 75. All the President's Men 76. Annie Hall 77. Comes a Horseman 78. Manhattan 79. Stardust Memories 80. Windows 80. Pennies from Heaven 81. A Midsummer Night's Sex Comedy 82. Zelig (AAN) 83. Broadway Danny Rose 84. The Purple Rose of Cairo 85. Perfect 85. The Money Pit 86. The Pick-Up Artist 87. Bright Lights, Big City 88. Presumed Innocent 90. The Godfather Part III (AAN) 90. Malice 93. The Devil's Own 97, etc.

Willis, Ted (1918–1992) (Lord Willis).
Influential British writer who set the scene for television's preoccupation with low life via such items as *Dixon of Dock Green* and *Woman in a Dressing Gown*. Dixon was derived from his filmscript *The Blue Lamp*; *Hot Summer Night* was later filmed as *Flame in the Streets*.

Willman, Noel (1918–1988).
British actor and stage director whose film roles were often coldly villainous.

Pickwick Papers 52. The Net 53. Beau Brummell 54. Cone of Silence 60. The Girl on the Boat 62. *Kiss of the Vampire* 63. The Reptile 65. Doctor Zhivago 65. The Vengeance of She 68, etc.

Willock, Dave (1909–1990).
American light actor, usually the hero's friend.

Legion of Lost Flyers 39. Let's Face It 43. Pin Up Girl 44. The Runaround 46. Chicago Deadline 49. Call Me Mister 51. It Came from Outer Space 53. The Buster Keaton Story 57. Wives and Lovers 63. Send Me No Flowers 64, many others.

TV series: Boots and Saddles 57. Margie 61.

Wills, Brember (1883–1948).
Slightly built British character actor best remembered for playing the mad arsonist Saul Femm in *The Old Dark House* (1932).

Wills, Chill (1903–1978).
Gravel-voiced American character actor, in films from 1934, mainly low-budget westerns. Also the voice of the talking mule in the 'Francis' series.

Boom Town 40. Best Foot Forward 43. The Harvey Girls 46. Raw Deal 48. High Lonesome 50. Bronco Buster 52. City That Never Sleeps 53. Timberjack 55. Giant 56. The Alamo (AAN) 60. The Deadly Companions 62. The Cardinal 63. The Over the Hill Gang Rides Again (TV) 71. Mr Billion 77, etc.

TV series: Frontier Circus 61. The Rounders 67.

Wills, J. Elder (1900–*).
English director, art director, screenwriter, and producer. Born in London and educated at London University, he was a scenic artist in Drury Lane before entering films in 1927 and working as an art director on more than 200 movies. He began directing in the early 30s, including two films for Hammer (of which he was then a director), and, after serving in the Second World War, worked as a producer and production designer for Rank before returning to art directing for Hammer. The Ealing spy thriller *Against the Wind* 47 was based on his own war experiences.

Biography: *Sabotage* by Leslie Bell.

AS DIRECTOR: Tiger Bay (& ad, co-story) 33. Song of Freedom 36. Everything in Life 36. Sporting Love 36. Big Fella 37.

AS ART DIRECTOR: The Informer 29. Alf's Carpet 29. Holiday Lovers 32. Money Mad 34. Sing as We Go 34. Honeymoon for Three 35. It Happened in Paris 35. No Limit 35. Look Up and Laugh 35. The Stoker 35. Queen of Hearts 36. Against the Wind 47. Mantrap 52. Spaceways 53. Blood Orange/Three Stops to Murder 53. Face the Music/The Black Glove 54. Break in the Circle 55. The Quatermass Experiment/The Creeping Unknown 55, etc.

Wills, Mary (1914–1997).
American costume designer, often in collaboration with Charles LeMaire at Twentieth Century-Fox in the 50s.

Song of the South 46. Hans Christian Anderson (AAN) 52. The Virgin Queen (AAN) 55. Carousel 56. Teenage Rebel (AAN) 56. A Certain Smile (AAN) 58. The Diary of Anne Frank (AAN) 59. The Wonderful World of the Brothers Grimm (AA) 62. Cape Fear 62. Camelot 67. The Passover Plot (AAN) 76, etc.

Willson, Meredith (1902–1984) (Robert Meredith Reiniger).
American song composer and lyricist whose chief bequests to the cinema are *The Music Man* and *The Unsinkable Molly Brown*.

Wilmer, Douglas (1920–).
British character actor of stage, screen and TV.

Richard III 56. An Honourable Murder 60. El Cid 61. Cleopatra 62. The Fall of the Roman Empire 64. One Way Pendulum 65. Brides of Fu Manchu 66. Unman Wittering and Zigo 71. The Golden Voyage of Sinbad 73. The Adventure of Sherlock Holmes' Smarter Brother 75. Sarah 76. The Revenge of the Pink Panther 78. Rough Cut 80. Octopussy 83, many others.

Wilson, Andy.
English film director, from television. Born in London, he studied drama at Birmingham University and also worked with Circus Lumière and Archaos as a clown.

Dread Poets Society (TV) 92. An Evening with Gary Lineker (TV) 94. Playing God (US) 97, etc.

❝ Films should be iconic, mythic and have a moral. – *A.W.*

Wilson, Bridgette (1973–).
American actress and singer, born in Gold Beach, Oregon. She was Miss Teen USA 1990, and began on the daytimne TV soap opera *Santa Barbara* 92–93.

Last Action Hero 93. Higher Learning 95. Billy Madison 95. Mortal Kombat 95. Nixon 95. Unhook the Stars 96. I Know What You Did Last Summer 97. The Real Blonde 97, etc.

Wilson, Carey (1889–1962).
American screenwriter of the 20s and 30s, for Goldwyn and MGM, who wrote more than 80 films, usually in collaboration. He was said to be Louis B. MAYER's favourite writer. In the 40s, he turned to producing for MGM, and was executive producer of films in the Dr Kildare and Andy Hardy series. Born in Philadelphia, Pennsylvania, he studied at the city's Industrial Art School.

AS WRITER: He Who Gets Slapped 24. Wine of Youth 24. The Masked Bride 25. Monte Carlo 26. Ben-Hur 27. Oh Kay! 28. The Cardboard Lover 28. Diamond Handcuffs 28. Footlights and Fools 29. Gabriel over the White House 33. Murder at the Vanities 34. Mutiny on the Bounty 35. Dangerous Number 36. Between Two Women 37. Judge Hardy and Son 39, many more.

AS PRODUCER: The Postman Always Rings Twice 46. Dark Delusion 47. Green Dolphin Street 47. The Red Danube 49. The Happy Years 50. Scaramouche 52. This Is Russia (narrator) 57, etc.

❝ Wilson was a catch-all of information, a gusher of trivia and some profundity, an unstoppable chatterbox who was described by a friend, 'Ask him what time it is and he'll tell you how they make a watch.' – *Samuel Marx*

Wilson, Don 'The Dragon'.
American leading actor in martial arts and action movies, a former kick-boxing champion.

Bloodfist 89. Bloodfist 2 90. Bloodfist 3: Forced to Fight 91. Ring of Fire 91. Futurekick 91. Ninja Dragons 92. Ring of Fire 2: Blood and Steel 92. Cyber-Tracker 93. Bloodfist 7: Manhunt 95. Manhunt: Bloodfist 8 96, etc.

Wilson, Dooley (1894–1953).
American character actor.

Casablanca (as Sam, who played it again) 42. Stormy Weather 43. Come to the Stable 49. Passage West 51, etc.

~It is alleged that Elliot Carpenter played the piano for Wilson in *Casablanca* . . . and some say Wilson didn't sing either.

Wilson, Flip (1932–1998) (Clerow Wilson).
American actor and entertainer.

Uptown Saturday Night 74. Pinocchio (TV) 76. Skatetown USA 79.

Wilson, Georges.
French leading actor and occasional director, the father of actor Lambert WILSON.

The Green Mare/La Jument Verte 59. The Joker/Le Farceur 60. Une Aussi Longue Absence 61. The Longest Day 62. The Stranger (It.) 67. Beatrice Cenci (It.) 69. Blanche 71. The Three Musketeers/The Queen's Diamonds 73. Tendre Poulet 77. La Vouivre (wd) 89. Cache-Cash 94. Marquise 97. From the Earth to the Moon (TV) 98, etc.

Wilson, Harry Leon (1867–1939).
American comedy novelist; chief works filmed are *Ruggles of Red Gap* and *Merton of the Movies*.

Wilson, Hugh (1943–).
American director and screenwriter.

Police Academy 84. Rustler's Rhapsody 85. Burglar 87. Guarding Tess 94. Down Periscope (co-w) 96. The First Wives Club (d) 96. Rough Riders (w) (TV) 97. Blast from the Past (wd) 98, etc.

Wilson, Ian.
British cinematographer.

Tell Me Lies 67. Bartelby 70. Up Pompeii 71. Captain Kronos Vampire Hunter 72. The House in Nightmare Park 73. Privates on Parade 84. Wish You Were Here 87. Dream Demon 88. Checking Out 89. Erik the Viking 89. Edward II 91. The Crying Game 92. The Secret Rapture 93. Backbeat 94. Emma 96. A Midsummer Night's Dream 96. Savior 98, etc.

Wilson, Janis.
American child actress, long retired, who made an impressive debut in *Now Voyager*.

Now Voyager 42. Watch on the Rhine 43. Snafu/Welcome Home 45. The Strange Love of Martha Ivers 46, etc.

Wilson, Lambert (1956–).
French leading actor, the son of actor and director Georges WILSON.

From Hell to Victory 79. Chanel Solitaire 81. Five Days One Summer 82. Sahara (US) 83. The Blood of Others 84. Red Kiss/Rouge Baiser 85. Rendez-Vous 85. The Possessed 87. The Belly of an Architect 87. El Dorado 88. A Man and Two Women/Un Homme et Deux Femmes 91. Frankenstein: The Real Story (TV) 92. Jefferson in Paris (US) 95. The Leading Man (US) 96. Same Old Song/On Connaît la Chanson 97. Marquise 97, etc.

Wilson, Lois (1895–1988).
American leading lady of the silent screen.

The Dumb Girl of Potici 16. Why Smith Left Home 19. The Covered Wagon 23. Miss Lulu Bett 24. Monsieur Beaucaire 24. What Every Woman Knows 24. Icebound 24. The Show Off 26. Seed 28. Manslaughter 28. The Crash 32. Laughing at Life 33. Bright Eyes 34. The Girl from Jones Beach 49, etc.

Wilson, Mara (1987–).
American child actress.

Mrs Doubtfire 93. A Time to Heal (TV) 94. Miracle on 34th Street 94. Matilda 96. A Simple Wish 97, etc.

TV series: Melrose Place 93.

Wilson, Margery (1896–1986).
American star of silent films, and occasional director. With the coming of sound, she turned to writing self-help books, including *Get the Most out of Life* and *The Woman You Want to Be*.

Bred in the Bone 15. *Intolerance* 16. The Clodhopper 17. The Gun Fighter 17. The Hand at the Window 18. Venus in the East 19. That Something (& d) 21. Insinuation (& d) 22. The Offenders 24, etc.

Wilson, Marie (1916–1972) (Katherine Elizabeth White).
American leading lady often seen as 'dumb blonde'.

Satan Met a Lady 36. Fools for Scandal 38. *Boy Meets Girl* 40. Broadway 42. The Young Widow 47. Linda Be Good 48. *My Friend Irma* (title role) 49. A Girl in Every Port 51. Marry Me Again 54. Mr Hobbs Takes a Vacation 62, etc.

TV series: My Friend Irma 52.

Wilson, Michael (1914–1978).
American screenwriter whose career was interrupted by the communist witch-hunt of the late 40s.

The Men in Her Life 42. It's a Wonderful Life (co-w) 46. Salt of the Earth 51. Five Fingers (AAN) 52. *A Place in the Sun* (AA) 52. Friendly Persuasion (uncredited) 56. *The Bridge on the River Kwai* (uncredited) 57. Lawrence of Arabia 62. The Sandpiper 65. *Planet of the Apes* 67. Che! 69, etc.

Wilson, Owen.
American actor and screenwriter, often in collaboration with Wes Anderson. Born in Austin, Texas, he studied at the University of Texas.

Bottle Rocket (& w) 96. The Cable Guy 96. Anaconda 97. Armageddon 98. Rushmore (co-w only) 98. Permanent Midnight 98, etc.

Wilson, Richard (1915–1991).
American producer and director, former radio actor.

The Golden Blade (p) 54. Man with a Gun (wd, p) 55. Raw Wind in Eden (d) 58. Al Capone (d) 59. Pay or Die (p, d) 60. Invitation to a Gunfighter (p, d) 64. Three in an Attic (p, d) 68, etc.

Wilson, Richard (1936–).
Sardonic Scottish actor and director, mainly on stage and television, best known for his role as Victor Meldrew in the TV series *One Foot in the Grave*. Born in Greenock, he was a research scientist before deciding to become an actor at the age of 27. He studied at RADA and first worked in repertory theatre. As a director he has been associated with the Oxford Playhouse and the Stables Theatre, Manchester.

Biography: 1996, *One Foot on the Stage* by James Roose Evans.

A Sharp Intake of Breath (TV) 77. Virginia Fly Is Drowning (TV) 82. A Passage to India 84. Whoops Apocalypse 86. Prick Up Your Ears 87. A Dry White Season 89. Fellow Traveller 89. How to Get Ahead in Advertising 89. The Vision Thing (TV) 93. One Foot in the Algarve (TV) 93. Gulliver's Travels (TV) 96. The Man Who Knew Too Little 97, etc.

TV series: My Good Woman 72. A Sharp Intake of Breath 78–80. Only When I Laugh 79–82. Room at the Bottom 86–88. Tutti Frutti 87. High and Dry 87. Hot Metal 88. One Foot in the Grave 90–95. Under the Hammer 94. Duck Patrol 98.

Wilson, Sandy (1924–).
British songwriter and lyricist whose best show, *The Boy Friend*, reached the screen in mangled form through the intervention of Ken Russell.

Wilson, Sandy (1947–).
Canadian director.

My American Cousin 85. Mama's Going to Buy You a Mocking Bird 88. American Boyfriends 89. Harmony Cats 93, etc.

Wilson, Scott (1942–).
American general-purpose actor, usually in tough roles.

In Cold Blood 67. The Grissom Gang 71. The New Centurions 72. Lolly Madonna XXX 73. The Great Gatsby 74. The Passover Plot 77. The Ninth Configuration 80. On the Line 83. The Right Stuff 83. A Year of the Quiet Sun 84. The Aviator 85. Blue City 86. Malone 87. The Tracker 88. Johnny Handsome 89. The Exorcist III 90. Lethal Weapon 3 92. Teenage Mutant Ninja Turtles 3 93. Judge Dredd 95. Dead Man Walking 95. Shiloh 97. GI Jane 97. Pride/Unmei No Toki (Jap.) 98, etc.

Wilson, Stuart.
English character actor.

Dulcima 71. The Strauss Family (TV) 73. The Prisoner of Zenda 79. Wetherby 85. Wallenberg: A Hero's Story (TV) 85. Nonni (Nor.) 88. Lionheart/AWOL 91. Lethal Weapon 3 92. Teenage Mutant Ninja Turtles III 93. The Age of Innocence 93. No Escape 94. Exit to Eden 94. Death and the Maiden 95. Edie and Pen 95. Crosswords 96. The Mask of Zorro 98. Enemy of the State 98, etc.

Wilson, Trey (1949–1989).
American character actor. Died of a cerebral haemorrhage.

A Soldier's Story 84. F/X 85. Raising Arizona 87. The House on Carroll Street 88. Bull Durham

88. Married to the Mob 88. Twins 88. Miss Firecracker 89. Great Balls of Fire 89. Welcome Home 89, etc.

Wilson, Whip (1915–1964) (Charles Meyer).
American cowboy actor who appeared in a great number of second features in the 30s and 40s.

Wilton, Penelope (1946–).
British actress, mainly on stage and TV. Married actor Ian Holm in 1990.
Joseph Andrews 77. The French Lieutenant's Woman 81. Othello 82. Laughterhouse/Singleton's Pluck 84. Clockwise 86. Cry Freedom 87. Blame It on the Bellboy 92. The Secret Rapture 93. Carrington 95. This Could Be the Last Time (TV) 98, etc.
TV series: Ever Decreasing Circles 84.

Wilton, Robb (1882–1957).
Much admired English music-hall and radio comedian and character actor. His act, notably as a muddled policeman, fireman, or member of the Home Guard, has been preserved in several films.
The Fire Brigade 28. Stars on Parade 35. Chips 38. Don't Rush Me 36. Servants All 36. Pathé Radio Music Hall 45. The Love Match 55, etc.
~Catchphrase: The day war broke out . . .

Wimperis, Arthur (1874–1953).
British librettist and screenwriter, usually in collaboration.
The Private Life of Henry VIII 32. Sanders of the River 35. The Four Feathers 39. Mrs Miniver (AA) 42. Random Harvest (AAN) 43. The Red Danube 48. Calling Bulldog Drummond 51. Young Bess 53, many others.

Wincer, Simon (1943–).
Australian director, from TV.
The Day after Halloween 79. Harlequin 79. Phar Lap 83. D.A.R.Y.L 85. The Lighthorsemen 87. Blue Grass (TV) 88. Lonesome Dove (TV) 89. Quigley Down Under 90. Harley Davidson and the Marlboro Man 91. Free Willy 93. Lightning Jack 94. Operation Dumbo Drop 95. The Phantom 96, etc.

Winchell, Walter (1897–1972).
Fast-talking American newspaper columnist with a keen eye for crime and showbusiness, in movies as himself. A vaudeville song-and-dance performer from the age of 15, he became the highest-paid and most widely read gossip columnist of his time from the mid-20s, and also had a vast radio audience in the 30s and 40s, doing much to create a public appetite for celebrity-led journalism. His film performances in the 30s are said to have influenced the urban tough-guy approach of such actors as James Cagney and George Raft. He was the model for J. J. Hunsecker, the Broadway columnist played by Burt Lancaster in *Sweet Smell of Success* 57, and was played by Michael T. Wright in the TV biopic *The Rat Pack* 98, and by Stanley Tucci in the TV biopic *Winchell* 98.
Autobiography: 1975, *Winchell Exclusive: 'Things that Happened to Me – And Me to Them'*.
Biographies: 1971, *Winchell* by Bob Thomas; 1976, *Winchell, His Life and Times* by Herman Klurfeld; 1994, *Walter Winchell: Gossip, Power and the Culture of Celebrity* by Neal Gabler.
Broadway through a Keyhole (story) 33. Wake Up and Live 37. Love and Kisses 37. The Private Lives of Adam and Eve 59. College Confidential 60. Dondi 61. Wild in the Streets 68, etc.
TV series: The Walter Winchell Show 52–56. The Walter Winchell File 57–58. The Untouchables (as narrator) 59–63. The Walter Winchell Show 60.

Wincott, Jeff (1957–).
Canadian leading man of action movies.
Happy Birthday, Gemini 80. Prom Night 80. Deadly Bet 91. Martial Law 2: Undercover 91. Mission of Justice 92. Martial Outlaw 93. The Killing Man 94. Last Man Standing 95. When the Bullet Hits the Bone 96. Fatal Combat 96. The Undertaker's Wedding 97. Future Fear 97, etc.
TV series: Night Heat 85–91.

Windom, William (1923–).
American leading man, usually in minor film roles.
To Kill a Mockingbird 62. For Love or Money 63. One Man's Way 64. The Americanization of Emily 64. The Detective 68. Brewster McCloud 70. Fool's Parade 71. Now You See Him Now You Don't 72. Echoes of a Summer 75. Mean Dog Blues 78. Grandview USA 84. Planes, Trains and Automobiles 87. She's Having a Baby 88. Funland 89. Sommersby 93. Miracle on 34th Street 94. Fugitive X 96. Children of the Corn 4: The Gathering 96, etc.
TV series: The Farmer's Daughter 63–66. My World and Welcome to It 69. The Girl with Something Extra 73–74. Brothers and Sisters 79. Murder She Wrote 85–91.

Windsor, Barbara (1937–) (Barbara Deeks).
British cockney actress specializing in dumb blondes.
Lost 55. Too Hot to Handle 59. Sparrows Can't Sing 64. Carry On Spying 64. Crooks in Cloisters 64. The Boy Friend 71. Carry On Abroad 72. Carry On Girls 73. Comrades 87, etc.
TV series: Worzel Gummidge 78–81. EastEnders 94– .

Windsor, Claire (1898–1972) (Olga Cronk).
American leading lady of the silent screen. Her second husband was actor Bert Lytell (1925–27).
To Please a Woman 20. Rich Men's Wives 22. Nellie the Beautiful Cloak Model 24. Money Talks 26. Captain Lash 29, etc.

Windsor, Marie (1923–) (Emily Marie Bertelson).
American leading lady with stage and radio experience; films mainly routine.
All American Co-Ed 41. Song of the Thin Man 47. Force of Evil 48. Outpost in Morocco 49. Dakota Lil 50. *The Narrow Margin* 51. The Tall Texan 53. City that Never Sleeps 53. Abbott and Costello Meet the Mummy 55. *The Killing* 56. The Unholy Wife 57. Bedtime Story 64. Chamber of Horrors 66. The Good Guys and the Bad Guys 69. Support Your Local Gunfighter 71. Cahill 73. Hearts of the West 75. Lovely . . . but Deadly 82, many others.

Windust, Bretaigne (1906–1960).
American director, from the New York stage.
Winter Meeting 47. June Bride 48. Pretty Baby 50. *The Enforcer* 51. Face to Face 52. The Pied Piper of Hamelin 59, etc.

Winfield, Paul (1941–).
American leading actor.
The Lost Man 69. RPM 70. Brother John 71. *Sounder* (AAN) 72. Gordon's War 73. Conrack 74. Hustle 75. Damnation Alley 77. Twilight's Last Gleaming 77. The Greatest 77. Backstairs at the White House (TV) 79. King (TV) 80. Angel City (TV) 81. Star Trek II: The Wrath of Khan 82. On the Run 82. Mike's Murder 82. Go Tell It on the Mountain 84. The Terminator 84. Blue City 85. The Serpent and the Rainbow 88. Presumed Innocent 90. Dennis the Menace/Dennis 93. Cliffhanger 93. Scarlett (TV) 94. Breathing Lessons (TV) 94. Tyson (TV) 95. Original Gangstas 96. The Legend of Gator Face 96. The Assassination File 96. Mars Attacks! 96, etc.

Winfrey, Oprah (1954–).
American actress, a former newsreader who became rich, successful and powerful airing topical problems on her syndicated TV talk show from 1986. In the 90s she donated $2m to Atlanta's Morehouse College.
The Color Purple (AAN) 85. Native Son 86. Throw Momma from the Train 87. The Women of Brewster Place (TV) 89. There Are No Children Here (TV) 93. Beloved (& p) 98, etc.
❝ Arguably has more influence in the culture than any university president, politician, or religious leader, except perhaps the Pope. – *Vanity Fair*

Winger, Debra (1955–).
American leading lady of the early 80s, in increasingly strong roles. She was married to actor Timothy Hutton (1986–89).
Thank God It's Friday 78. French Postcards 79. Urban Cowboy 80. Cannery Row 82. An Officer and a Gentleman (AAN) 82. Terms of Endearment (AAN) 83. Mike's Murder 84. Legal Eagles 85. Black Widow 87. Made in Heaven 87. Betrayed 88. Everybody Wins 90. The Sheltering Sky 90. Wilder Napalm 93. Shadowlands (AAN) 93. A Dangerous Woman 93. Forget Paris 95, etc.

Winkler, Henry (1946–).
Extrovert American actor best known as Fonz in TV's *Happy Days* 74–83. He began directing in the mid-80s.
The Lords of Flatbush 72. Heroes 77. The One and Only 78. Night Shift 82. A Smokey Mountain Christmas (d) 86. Memories of Me (d) 88. Absolute Strangers (TV) 91. Cop and a Half (d) 93. Scream (a) 96. National Lampoon's Dad's Week Off (a) 97. The Waterboy (a) 98, etc.
TV series: Monty 94.

Winkler, Irwin (1931–).
American producer who began directing in the 90s.
The Split 68. They Shoot Horses Don't They? 69. The Strawberry Statement 70. The Mechanic 72. Up the Sandbox 72. Peeper 75. The Gambler 75. Nickelodeon 76. Rocky (AA) 76. New York New York 77. Comes a Horseman 78. Rocky II 79. Raging Bull (AAN) 81. True Confessions 81. Author! Author! 82. Rocky III 82. The Right Stuff (AAN) 83. Revolution 85. Rocky IV 85. Round Midnight 86. Betrayed 88. Music Box 90. GoodFellas (AAN) 90. Rocky V 90. Guilty by Suspicion (wd) 90. Night and the City (d) 92. The Net (d) 95. At First Sight (d) 98, etc.

Winn, Godfrey (1908–1971).
British journalist who made rare film appearances.
Blighty 27. Very Important Person 61. Billy Liar 63. The Great St Trinian's Train Robbery 66. Up the Chastity Belt 71, etc.

Winner, Michael (1935–).
Ebullient British director who never shoots in a studio. His own best publicist. Also a restaurant columnist.
Climb Up the Wall 57. The Clock Strikes Eight 57. Man with a Gun 58. Shoot to Kill 59. Some Like It Cool 61. Haunted England 61. Play It Cool 62. The Cool Mikado 63. West Eleven 63. *The System* 64. You Must be Joking 65. *The Jokers* 66. *I'll Never Forget Whatshisname* 67. Hannibal Brooks 69. The Games 69. *Lawman* 70. The Night Comers 71. Chato's Land 72. The Mechanic 72. Scorpio 72. The Stone Killer 73. *Death Wish* 74. Won Ton Ton 76. The Sentinel 77. The Big Sleep 78. Firepower 79. Death Wish II 81. The Wicked Lady 83. Scream for Help 84. Death Wish 3 85. Appointment with Death 87. A Chorus of Disapproval (p, wd) 89. Bullseye! (story, d, ed) 91. Dirty Weekend (wd) 93. Decadence (a) 94. Parting Shots (p, d) 98, etc.
TV series: Michael Winner's True Murders 92–93. Michael Winner's True Crimes 93–94.
❝ In a time when diffidence is fashionable, it is refreshing to find a British director who seems deliberately to court comparison with Erich Von Stroheim:
A team effort is a lot of people doing what I say.
Original? It seems so. It is also true; and unlike Von Stroheim Mr Winner does get his films out on time and below budget, facts which tend to atone for his arrogance. He knows that:
In this business, disaster is always just around the corner.
And that:
Every film is a great success until it is released.
He remembers the days when:
You could make a film for £100,000 and get your money back from people sheltering from the rain.
He won't make the mistake of imagining that those days are still here. He enjoys the big money:
Success has gone to my stomach.
And he finds that:
The hardest part of directing is staying awake for nine weeks at a stretch.
He has no qualms about what he purveys:
There's no moralistic side to *Death Wish:* it's a pleasant romp.
And he is proud of his prowess:
Being in the movie business is like being a tennis player. You have to keep your total concentration and your mind on the ball. The minute you fall in love with Tatum O'Neal or get flabby, you've had it.

Winninger, Charles (1884–1969) (Karl Winninger).
Chubby, lovable American character actor, in films from 1916 as vaudeville appearances permitted. His catchphrase: '*Happ-y* new year . . .'
■ Pied Piper Malone 24. The Canadian 24. Summer Bachelors 26. Soup to Nuts 30. Bad Sister 31. Night Nurse 31. Flying High 31. God's Gift to Women 31. Fighting Caravans 31. Gun Smoke 31. Children of Dreams 31. The Sin of Madelon Claudet 31. Husband's Holiday 31. Social Register 34. *Show Boat* (as Captain Andy) 36. White Fang 36. *Three Smart Girls* 36. You're a Sweetheart 37. Woman Chases Man 37. *Nothing Sacred* 37. Café Metropole 37. You Can't Have Everything 37. The Go-Getter 37. Every Day's a Holiday 37. Goodbye Broadway 38. Hard to Get 38. Three Smart Girls Grow Up 39. *Destry Rides Again* 39. *Babes in Arms* 39. Barricade 39. If I Had My Way 40. My Love Came Back 40. Beyond Tomorrow 40. Little Nellie Kelly 40. When Ladies Meet 41. *Ziegfeld Girl* 41. The Getaway 41. My Life with Caroline 41. Pot o' Gold 41. Friendly Enemies 42. Coney Island 43. A Lady Takes a Chance 43. Flesh and Fantasy 43. Hers to Hold 43. Broadway Rhythm 44. Belle of the Yukon 44. Sunday Dinner for a Soldier 44. She Wouldn't Say Yes 45. *State Fair* 45. Lover Come Back 46. Living in a Big Way 47. Something in the Wind 47. The Inside Story 48. *Give My Regards to Broadway* 48. Father Is a Bachelor 50. *The Sun Shines Bright* 53. Torpedo Alley 53. A Perilous Journey 53. Champ for a Day 53. Las Vegas Shakedown 55. Raymie 60.
TV series: The Charlie Farrell Show 56.

Winningham, Mare (1959–) (Mary Winningham).
American actress.
One-Trick Pony 80. Threshold 81. Single Bars, Single Women (TV) 84. St Elmo's Fire 85. Nobody's Fool 86. Shy People 87. Made in Heaven 87. Miracle Mile 89. Turner & Hooch 89. Eye on the Sparrow (TV) 91. Fatal Exposure (TV) 91. Hard Promises 92. Wyatt Earp 94. Georgia (AAN) 95. The Boys Next Door (TV) 96. George Wallace (TV) 97. Everything that Rises (TV) 98, etc.

Winslet, Kate (1975–).
English leading actress whose rise to stardom benefited from being the love of Leonardo DiCaprio in James Cameron's record-breaking *Titanic*. Born in Reading, Berkshire, she studied from the age of 11 at Redroofs Theatre School, Maidenhead, and began appearing in commercials when she was 16. Married assistant director James Threapleton in 1998.
Heavenly Creatures 94. *Sense and Sensibility* (AAN) 95. A Kid in King Arthur's Court 95. Jude 96. Hamlet (as Ophelia) 96. *Titanic* (AAN) (US) 97. Hideous Kinky 98, etc.
TV series: Get Back 92.

Winslow, George (1946–) (George Wenzlaff).
American boy actor whose throaty voice earned him the nickname 'Foghorn'.
Room for One More 52. My Pal Gus 52. Mr Scoutmaster 53. Gentlemen Prefer Blondes 53. Artists and Models 55. Wild Heritage 58, etc.

Winston, Stan (1946–).
American make-up special effects and creature creator, and occasional director.
Blacula 72. The Wiz 78. The Exterminator 80. Heartbeeps 81. Parasite 82. The Terminator 84. Aliens (AA) 86. Predator 87. The Monster Squad 87. Pumpkinhead (co-story, d) 88. Leviathan 89. Predator 2 90. Edward Scissorhands (AAN) 90. Terminator 2: Judgment Day (AA) 91. Batman Returns (AAN) 92. Jurassic Park (AA) 93. Interview with the Vampire 94. The Island of Dr Moreau 96. *The Lost World: Jurassic Park* (AAN) 97. Mouse Hunt 97. Paulie 98. Creature (TV) 98. Small Soldiers 98, etc.

Winstone, Ray (1957–).
Burly English character actor, born in Hackney, London, often in violent or criminal roles.
Scum 79. That Summer! 79. Quadrophenia 79. Ladies and Gentlemen, the Fabulous Stains (US) 82. Tank Malling 88. Underbelly (TV) 91. Black and Blue (TV) 92. Ladybird Ladybird 94. *Nil by Mouth* 97. Face 97. Final Cut 97. Darkness Falls 98. Woundings 98. The Sea Change 98. Martha, Meet Frank, Daniel and Laurence 98, etc.
TV series: Fox 80. Robin of Sherwood 84–86. Get Back 92–93. Ghostbusters of East Finchley 95.

Winter, Alex (1965–).
English-born leading actor, in America from the early 70s, from the stage.
Death Wish 3 85. The Lost Boys 87. Haunted Summer 88. Rosalie Goes Shopping 89. Bill and Ted's Excellent Adventure 89. Bill and Ted's Bogus Journey 92. Freaked (& co-w, co-d) 93, etc.

Winter, Donovan.
British director of eccentric low-budgeters.
The Trunk 60. A Penny for Your Thoughts 65. Promenade 68. Come Back Peter 69. Give Us Tomorrow 77, etc.

Winter, Vincent (1947–1998)
Scottish juvenile actor, born in Aberdeen, who gave a remarkable performance at the age of five in *The Kidnappers*. He became unhappy with the roles offered him as he grew up, and later worked as an assistant director, production manager and production supervisor on various films.
The Dark Avenger 55. Time Lock 56. Beyond This Place 59. Gorgo 60. Greyfriars Bobby 61. Almost Angels 63. The Three Lives of Thomasina 63. The Horse Without a Head 64, etc.

Winterbottom, Michael (1961–).
English director and screenwriter. He studied English at Oxford University before working in television.
Forget about Me 90. Under the Sun 92. Love Lies Bleeding (TV) 92. Cracker: The Mad Woman in the Attic (TV) 93. Family (TV) 94. Butterfly Kiss (& co-w) 94. Go Now (TV) 95. Jude 96. Welcome to Sarajevo 97. I Want You 98, etc.

Winters, Jonathan (1925–).
American comedian with TV and nightclub experience.
It's a Mad Mad Mad Mad World 63. *The Loved One* 65. The Russians Are Coming, the Russians Are Coming 66. Penelope 66. Oh Dad Poor Dad 67. Viva Max 69. The Fish that Saved Pittsburgh 79. The Longshot 86. Moon over Parador 88. The Flintstones 94. The Shadow 94, etc.
TV series: The Jonathan Winters Show 56–57, 67–69. The Wacky World of Jonathan Winters 72–74. Mork & Mindy 81–82. Hee Haw 83–84. Davis Rules 91–92.

Winters, Ralph.
American film editor. He was on the staff of MGM for more than 30 years and edited 13 of Blake Edwards' films.
Mr and Mrs North 41. Eyes in the Night 42. Cry Havoc 43. Gaslight 44. Boy's Ranch 46. Tenth Avenue Angel 47. Hills of Home 48. Any Number Can Play 49. Little Women 49. On the Town 49. King Solomon's Mines (AA) 50. Quo Vadis? (AAN) 51. Kiss Me Kate 53. Young Bess 53. Executive Suite 54. Seven Brides for Seven Brothers (AAN) 54. Love Me or Leave Me 55. High Society 56. Jailhouse Rock 57. The Sheepman 58. Ben Hur (AA) 59. Butterfield 8 60. Soldier in the Rain 63. The Pink Panther 64. The Great Race (AAN) 65. What Did You Do in the War, Daddy? 66. How to Succeed in Business without Really Trying 67. The Party 68. The Thomas Crown Affair 68. Gaily Gaily 69. Kotch (AAN) 71. Avanti 72. The Outfit 73. The Front Page 74. Mr Majestyk 74. King Kong 75. Orca 77. 10 79. S.O.B. 81. Victor/Victoria 82. The Curse of the Pink Panther 83. Micki and Maude 84. Let's Get Harry 87. Moving 88. CutThroat Island 95, etc.
❝ The general public doesn't understand a thing about editing and I don't think they should. – *R.W.*

Winters, Roland (1904–1989).
Heavily built American character actor with stage and radio experience, in Hollywood from 1946; played Charlie Chan in six Monogram features 1948–52.
13 rue Madeleine 46. Inside Straight 52. So Big 53. Loving 70, etc.
TV series: Meet Millie 52–55. The Smothers Brothers Show 65.

Winters, Shelley (1922–) (Shirley Schrift).
American leading character actress with vaudeville and stage experience, in Hollywood from 1943.
Autobiographies: 1980, *Shelley*. 1987, *Also Known as Shirley*. 1989, *The Middle of My Century/The Best of Times, the Worst of Times*.
■ What a Woman 43. Sailor's Holiday 44. The Racket Man 44. Two Man Submarine 44. She's a Soldier Too 44. Nine Girls 44. Cover Girl 44. Knickerbocker Holiday 44. 1001 Nights 45. Tonight and Every Night 45. Living in a Big Way 47. The Gangster 48. Red River 48. Larceny 48. *A Double Life* 48. Cry of the City 48. Take One False Step 49. Johnny Stool Pigeon 49. The Great Gatsby 49. Winchester 73 50. East of Java 51. He Ran All The Way 51. Frenchie 51. Behave Yourself 51. The Raging Tide 51. A Place in the Sun (AAN) 51. My Man and I 52. Phone Call from a Stranger 52. Meet Danny Wilson 52. Untamed Frontier 52. Tennessee Champ 54. Saskatchewan 54. Playgirl 54. Executive Suite 54. To Dorothy a Son 54. *The Big Knife* 55. *The Night of the Hunter* 55. Mambo 55. I Am a Camera 55. I Died a Thousand Times 56. Treasure of Pancho Villa 56. Odds Against Tomorrow 58. *The Diary of Anne Frank* (AA) 59. Let No Man Write My Epitaph 60. The Young Savages 61. Lolita 62. Wives and Lovers 63. The Chapman Report 63. The Balcony 63. A House is Not a Home 64. Time of Indifference 64. The Greatest Story Ever Told 65. *A Patch of Blue* (AA) 65. Alfie (GB) 66. Harper 66. Enter Laughing 67. The Scalp Hunters 67. Wild in the Streets 68. Buona Sera Mrs Campbell 68. The Mad Room 69. Arthur! Arthur! 69. Flap 70. Bloody Mama 70. How Do I Love Thee 70. What's the Matter with Helen 70. Who Slew Auntie Roo? 71. Revenge! (TV) 71. The Poseidon Adventure (AAN) 72. Something to Hide 72. The Devil's Daughter (TV) 72. Blume in Love 73. Cleopatra Jones 73. Big Rose (TV) 74. Diamonds 75. That Lucky Touch 75. Journey Into Fear 75. Next Stop Greenwich Village 76. The Tenant 76. Pete's Dragon 77. Tentacles 77. Black Journey 77. King of the Gypsies 78. City on Fire 79. The Magician of Lublin 79. Redneck County Rape 79. The Visitor 79. Elvis (TV) 79. S.O.B. 81. Over the Brooklyn Bridge 83. Déjà Vu 84. Delta Force 85. Purple People Eater 88. Rudolph & Frosty's Christmas in July 88. An Unremarkable Life 89. Touch of a Stranger 90. Stepping Out 91. The Pickle 93. Heavy 95. Jury Duty 95. Mrs Munck 95. Raging Angels 95. The Portrait of a Lady 96.
❝ I did a picture in England one winter and it was so cold I almost got married. – *S.W.*
I'm more comfortable playing victims. I feel ashamed to reveal nasty aspects of myself. I was afraid to play an unsympathetic character in *A Patch of Blue*. I thought I was lousy, and I won the Oscar. – *S.W.*

Wintle, Julian (1913–1980).
British producer, former editor, in films from 1934. Co-founder of Independent Artists 1958.
Hunted 51. High Tide at Noon 57. Tiger Bay 59. Very Important Person 61. This Sporting Life 63. And Father Came Too 64, many others.

Winwood, Estelle (1882–1984) (Estelle Goodwin).
British stage character actress who played in many American films, usually as eccentric ladylike flutterers. Married actor Arthur Chesney, the brother of Edmund Gwenn.
The House of Trent 34. Quality Street 37. The Glass Slipper 55. *The Swan* 56. Twenty-three Paces to Baker Street 56. *Alive and Kicking* (GB) 58. Darby O'Gill and the Little People 59. Notorious Landlady 62. Dead Ringer 64. Camelot 67. Games 67. The Producers 68. Murder by Death 76, etc.

Wisbar, Frank (1899–1967).
German director in America; made one memorable low-budgeter, *Strangler of the Swamp* 46.

Wisberg, Aubrey (1909–1990).
British-born writer-producer of Hollywood films, mainly second features.
So Dark the Night (w) 41. The Man from Planet X (wp) 51. The Neanderthal Man (wp) 53. Captain Kidd and the Slave Girl (wp) 54. Son of Sinbad (w) 55, many others.

Wisdom, Norman (1920–).
British slapstick comedian, also on stage and TV.
Biography: 1991, *Trouble in Store* by Richard Dacre.
■ *Trouble in Store* (film debut) 53. One Good Turn 54. Man of the Moment 55. Up in the World 56. Just My Luck 58. The Square Peg 58. Follow a Star 59. There Was a Crooked Man 60. The Bulldog Breed 61. The Girl on the Boat 61. On the Beat 62. A Stitch in Time 63. The Early Bird 65. Press for Time 66. The Sandwich Man 66. The Night They Raided Minsky's (US) 68. What's Good for the Goose 69. Going Gently (TV) 81. Double X 92.

Wise, Ernie:
see Morecambe, Eric.

Wise, Robert (1914–).
American director, former editor (worked on *Citizen Kane, All That Money Can Buy, The Magnificent Ambersons*).
■ Mademoiselle Fifi 44. Curse of the Cat People 44. *The Body Snatcher* 45. A Game of Death 46. Criminal Court 46. Born to Kill 47. Mystery in Mexico 47. Blood on the Moon 48. *The Set-Up* 49. Three Secrets 50. Two Flags West 50. The House on Telegraph Hill 51. *The Day the Earth Stood Still* 51. Captive City 52. Destination Gobi 52. Something for the Birds 52. Desert Rats 52. So Big 53. *Executive Suite* 54. Helen of Troy 55. Tribute to a Bad Man 56. Somebody Up There Likes Me 56. Until They Sail 57. This Could Be the Night 57. Run Silent Run Deep 58. I Want to Live (AAN) 58. Odds Against Tomorrow 59. *West Side Story* (AA) 61. Two for the Seesaw 62. The Haunting (GB) 63. *The Sound of Music* (AA) 65. The Sand Pebbles 66. Star! 68. The Andromeda Strain 70. Two People 73. The Hindenberg 75. Audrey Rose 77. Star Trek 79. Rooftops 89.

Wiseman, Frederick (1931–).
American documentarist, former law professor.
Titicut Follies 67. High School 68. Law and Order 69. Hospital 70. Basic Training 71. Essene 72. Juvenile Court 73. Primate 74. Welfare 75. Meat 76. Model 80. Racetrack 85. Blind 87. Near Death 89. Aspen 91. Zoo 93. La Comédie Française, ou l'Amour Joue 96. Public Housing 97, etc.

Wiseman, Joseph (1918–).
American stage actor who has made several film appearances.
Detective Story 51. Viva Zapata 52. Les Misérables 52. The Prodigal 55. The Garment Jungle 57. The Unforgiven 60. *Dr No* (title role) 62. *The Night They Raided Minsky's* 68. Bye Bye Braverman 68. Stiletto 69. The Valachi Papers 72. The Apprenticeship of Duddy Kravitz 74. Buck Rogers 79. Rage of Angels (TV) 83. The Ghost Writer 84. Seize the Day 86, etc.

Wister, Owen (1860–1938).
American western novelist whose *The Virginian*, published in 1902, was the basis of several films and a television series.

Withers, Googie (1917–) (Georgette Withers).
English leading actress of stage, screen and television. Born in Karachi, of English and Dutch parents, she trained at the Italia Conti School, studied dancing with Buddy Bradley, and was on stage from the age of 13, beginning in the chorus. Given a small part in her first film, *Girl in the Crowd*, she took over the star role when the leading lady walked out, going on to make more than 60 films. Married actor-producer John McCallum, and moved to Australia, though she returned to Britain to appear on stage and television.
Biography: 1979, *Life with Googie* by John McCallum.
Girl in the Crowd 34. Accused 36. Strange Boarders 37. The Lady Vanishes 38. Trouble Brewing 39. Back Room Boy 41. *One of Our Aircraft Is Missing* 42. *On Approval* 44. They Came to a City 44. Dead of Night 45. The Loves of Joanna Godden 46. Pink String and Sealing Wax 46. *It Always Rains on Sunday* 47. Miranda 48. Once Upon a Dream 49. Traveller's Joy 50. Night and the City 50. *White Corridors* 51. Derby Day 52. Devil on Horseback 54. Port of Escape 55. The Nickel Queen 70. Time after Time 85. Country Life 94. Shine 96, etc.
TV series: Within These Walls 74–77.

Withers, Grant (1904–1959).
Rugged American general-purpose actor, a former salesman and reporter who began in silent films as an extra. Born in Pueblo, Colorado, he found success first as a leading man in the 20s, then as an action hero of low-budget movies and serials of the 30s, and later as a character actor. Married actresses Loretta Young (1930–31) and Estelita Rodriguez. Committed suicide.
The Gentle Cyclone 26. Tiger Rose 29. Red Haired Alibi 32. The Red Rider (serial) 34. Tailspin Tommy (serial) 34. Fighting Marines (serial) 35. Society Fever 35. Jungle Jim (serial) 37. Radio Patrol (serial) 37. The Secret of a Treasure Island 38. Mr Wong, Detective 38. Mexican Spitfire 39. Billy the Kid 41. Woman of the Year 42. The Fighting Seabees 44. The Yellow Rose of Texas 44. Bring On the Girls 45. My Darling Clementine 46. Fort Apache 48. Rio Grande 50. Springfield Rifle 52. Fair Winds to Java 53. Lady Godiva 55. The Hired Gun 57. I, Mobster 58, many others.

Withers, Jane (1926–).
American child star of the 30s, more mischievous and less pretty than Shirley Temple.
Bright Eyes 34. Ginger 35. The Farmer Takes a Wife 35. The Mad Martindales 42. North Star 43. Faces in the Fog 44. Affairs of Geraldine 46. Giant 56. The Right Approach 62. Captain Newman 63, etc.

Witherspoon, Cora (1890–1957).
American character comedienne often seen as shrewish wife; on stage from 1910.
Libeled Lady 36. Madame X 38. The Bank Dick 40. This Love of Ours 45. The Mating Season 50. The First Time 52, etc.

Witherspoon, John.
American character actor.
Ratboy 86. Hollywood Shuffle 87. Bird 88. I'm Gonna Git You, Sucka 88. House Party 90. Killer Tomatoes Strike Back 90. The Five Heartbeats 91. Talkin' Dirty after Dark 91. Boomerang 92. Friday 95. Vampire in Brooklyn 95, etc.

Witherspoon, Reese (1976–).
American leading actress.
Wildflower (TV) 91. The Man in the Moon 91. The Crush 93. A Far Off Place 93. Jack the Bear 93. Return to Lonesome Dove (TV) 93. SFW 94. Fear 96. Freeway 96. Overnight Delivery 97. Twilight 98. Pleasantville 98. Election 98, etc.

Witney, William (1910–).
American director, mainly of routine westerns for Republic.
Roll On Texas Moon 46. Night Time in Nevada 49. The Fortune Hunter 52. City of Shadows 54. Stranger at My Door 56. The Bonnie Parker Story 58. Paratroop Command 59. Master of the World 61. Girls on the Beach 65. Arizona Raiders 66. I Escaped from Devil's Island 73. Darktown Strutters 75, many others.

Wixted, Michael James (1961–).
American child actor of the 70s.
Lost in the Stars 74. Where Have All the People Gone? (TV) 74. Islands in the Stream 77, etc.
TV series: The Smith Family 71. The Swiss Family Robinson 75.

Wizan, Joe (1935–).
American producer.
Jeremiah Johnson 72. Junior Bonner 72. Prime Cut 72. The Last American Hero 73. Audrey Rose 77. And Justice for All 79. Voices 79. Best Friends 82. Unfaithfully Yours 83. Iron Eagle 85. Tough Guys 86. Spellbinder 88. Split Decisions 88. Short Time 90. The Nanny 90. Stop, or My Mom Will Shoot 91. Wrestling Ernest Hemingway 93. Fire in the Sky 93. Dunston Checks In 96. Kiss the Girls 97, etc.

Wodehouse, Sir P(elham) G(ranville) (1881–1975).
Prolific English comic novelist, lyricist and screenwriter. Born in Guildford, Surrey, he was educated at Dulwich College, published his first novel in 1902, and wrote some 120 books. He also worked as a journalist and moved to America to become drama critic of *Vanity Fair*. He adapted his work as plays and musicals, often in collaboration with Guy Bolton, and spent a year in Hollywood from 1929, under contract to MGM at $2,000, where he also gained a reputation as Beverly Hills' only pedestrian, always walking the six miles from his home to the studio. He returned to the studio in 1936, at $2,500 a week for six months, and, as previously, found that he was given little work to do. His best-known lyrics, to Jerome Kern's music, were 'Bill' for the three-times-filmed musical *Showboat*, which also featured in *The Man I Love* 47 and *The Helen Morgan Story/Both Ends of the Candle* 57, and the title song for a biopic of Kern, *Till the Clouds Roll By* 46. His broadcasts to America during the Second World War from Germany, where he had been detained, caused a scandal in Britain, which resulted in him returning to live in America and becoming an American citizen in 1955. He was knighted in 1975, shortly before his

death. His work has been somewhat neglected by the cinema, though it has proved more popular on television, with the series *Blandings Castle* 67, starring Ralph RICHARDSON as the pig-obsessed Lord Emsworth; *Ukridge* 68, starring Anton RODGERS; and *Wodehouse Playhouse* 75–78, based on his short stories, with John ALDERTON and Pauline COLLINS. Two American films were made about the perfect manservant Jeeves, starring Arthur TREACHER, though neither bore much resemblance to the original. In the 30s, MGM considered buying the rights to the character, but Irving THALBERG decided against it when he asked his chauffeur if he had ever hear of anyone called Jeeves, and the driver replied that he thought it was the name of his wife's butcher. Faithful to the spirit of the stories were two British TV series about the ineffectual, upper-class Bertie Wooster and his impeccable valet: *The World of Wooster* 65–67, starring Ian CARMICHAEL and Dennis PRICE, and *Jeeves and Wooster* 90–93, with Stephen FRY and Hugh LAURIE.

Autobiographies: 1953, *Bring On the Girls* (with Guy Bolton); 1953, *Performing Flea/Author! Author!*; 1957, *America, I Like You/Over Seventy*.

Biographies: 1975, P. G. *Wodehouse: A Portrait of a Master* by David Jasen; 1982, P. G. *Wodehouse* by Frances Donaldson.

Oh Lady, Lady! (oa) 20. A Gentleman of Leisure (oa) 23. Those Three French Girls (co-w) 30. The Man in Possession (co-w) 31. Piccadilly Jim (oa) 36. Thank You Jeeves (oa) 36. Anything Goes (co-w) 36. Step Lively, Jeeves (oa) 37. A Damsel in Distress (co-w) 37, etc.

❝ I suppose the secret of writing is to go through your stuff until you come on something you think is particularly good, and then cut it out. – *P.G.W.*

I get much more kick out of a place like Droitwich, which has no real merits, than out of something like the Taj Mahal. – *P.G.W.*

As a rule pictures are a bore. – *P.G.W.*

Wolfe, Ian (1896–1992).
American character actor who usually played worried, grasping or officious roles. He appeared in more than 150 films.

The Barretts of Wimpole Street 33. Clive of India 35. Hudson's Bay 40. The Moon is Down 43. The Invisible Man's Revenge 44. Mr Blandings Builds His Dream House 48. The Great Caruso 50. Gaby 56. The Lost World 60. Games 67. The Fortune 74. Jinxed 82, many others.

TV series: Soap 78–80.

Wolff, Lothar (1909–1988).
German producer-director, former editor; with 'The March of Time' for many years, and still associated with Louis de Rochemont.

Lost Boundaries (p) 45. Martin Luther (co-wp) 53. Windjammer (p) 57. Question Seven (pd) 61. Fortress of Peace (p) 63, etc.

Wolfit, Sir Donald (1902–1968).
Distinguished British thespian who, having brought Shakespeare to the provinces, gave some enjoyably hammy performances in films.

Autobiography: 1954, *First Interval*.

Biography: 1971, *The Knight Has Been Unruly* by Ronald Harwood.

■ Death at Broadcasting House 34. Drake of England 35. The Silent Passenger 35. Sexton Blake and the Bearded Doctor 35. Checkmate 35. Late Extra 35. Hyde Park Corner 35. Calling the Tune 36. *The Ringer* 52. Pickwick Papers 53. Isn't Life Wonderful? 53. Svengali 54. A Prize of Gold 55. Guilty 56. The Man in the Road 56. The Man on the Beach 56. Satellite in the Sky 56. The Traitor 57. I Accuse 57. Blood of the Vampire 58. *Room at the Top* 59. The House of Seven Hawks 59. The Angry Hills 59. The Rough and the Smooth 59. The Hands of Orlac 60. The Mark 61. Lawrence of Arabia 62. Dr Crippen 63. Becket 64. Ninety Degrees in the Shade 65. Life at the Top 65. The Sandwich Man 66. *Decline and Fall* 68. The Charge of the Light Brigade 68.

Wolfman, Jack (1938–1995) (Robert Smith).
American rock disc jockey, noted for his extrovert style, who gained national fame after playing himself in *American Graffiti*.

Autobiography: 1995, *Have Mercy: The Confession of the Original Party Animal*.

The Committee 68. The Seven Minutes 71. American Graffiti 73. Deadman's Curve (TV) 78. Hanging on a Star 78. Motel Hell 80. Midnight 89. Mortuary Academy 91, etc.

Wolfson, P. J. (1903–1979).
American screenwriter.

Madison Square Garden 31. The Picture Snatcher 33. Mad Love 35. Public Enemy's Wife 37. Shall We Dance? (co-w) 37. Vivacious Lady (co-w) 38. Allegheny Uprising (& p) 39. They All Kissed the Bride (co-w) 42. Saigon (co-w & p) 48, many others.

Wolheim, Louis (1880–1931).
German-born character actor, often of semi-brutish roles, with American stage experience; in Hollywood from 1919. He was a former mathematics teacher at Cornell University.

Dr Jekyll and Mr Hyde 20. Little Old New York 22. America 24. *Two Arabian Knights* 27. The Racket 28. Tempest 28. Frozen Justice 29. *All Quiet on the Western Front* 31. Sin Ship (& d) 31, etc.

Wolper, David L. (1928–).
American documentarist who turned feature film producer and TV executive.

If It's Tuesday This Must Be Belgium 69. The Bridge at Remagen 69. The Hellstrom Chronicle 71. Roots (TV) 77. The Man Who Saw Tomorrow 80. This Is Elvis 81. Imagine: John Lennon 88. Murder in Mississippi (TV) 90. Murder in the First 95. Surviving Picasso 96. LA Confidential 97, etc.

Wolski, Dariusz.
Polish-born cinematographer, in America.

Heart 87. The Land of Little Rain 88. Nightfall 88. Romeo Is Bleeding 94. The Crow 94. Crimson Tide 95. The Fan 96. Dark City 98. A Perfect Murder 98, etc.

Wolsky, Albert (1930–).
American costume designer.

The Turning Point 77. An Unmarried Woman 78. Grease 78. All That Jazz (AA) 79. Manhattan 79. The Jazz Singer 80. Sophie's Choice (AAN) 82. Star 80 83. The Journey of Natty Gan (AAN) 85. Moon over Parador 88. Scenes from a Mall 91. Bugsy (AA) 91. Toys (AAN) 92. The Pickle 93. Striptease 96. Red Corner 97. The Jackal 97. You've Got Mail 98, etc.

Wong, Anna May (1907–1961) (Wong Liu Tsong).
Chinese-American actress popular in the 30s.

Red Lantern 19. The Thief of Bagdad 24. *Piccadilly* (GB) 29. On the Spot 30. Shanghai Express 32. *Chu Chin Chow* (GB) 33. *Java Head* (GB) 34. Limehouse Blues 36. Bombs Over Burma 42. Impact 49. Portrait in Black 60, etc.

Wong, Faye (1969–) (Wong Fei).
Beijing-born, Hong Kong-based Chinese singer and actress.

Chungking Express 94. Summer in Beijing 98.

Wong, Kirk (aka Che-Kirk Wong, Kirk Wong Chi-keung).
Hong Kong director, best known for his trio of police procedural thrillers based on actual cases.

The Club 81. True Colours 86. Gunmen 90. Crime Story/Chung On Tsou 92. Organized Crime and Triad Bureau 94. Rock'n'Roll Cop/Sang Gong Yatho Tungchap Fan 95. *The Big Hit* (US) 98, etc.

Wong, Victor.
Affable Chinese-American character actor.

Dim Sum: A Little Bit of Heart 85. Big Trouble in Little China 86. Shanghai Surprise 86. The Golden Child 86. The Last Emperor 87. Prince of Darkness 87. Eat a Bowl of Tea 89. 3 Ninjas 92. The Joy Luck Club 93. 3 Ninjas Kick Back 94. 3 Ninjas Knuckle Up 95. The Stars Fell on Henrietta 95. Jade 95. Paper Dragons 96. The Devil Takes a Holiday 96. Search 97. Seven Years in Tibet 97. 3 Ninjas: High Noon at Mega Mountain 98, etc.

Wontner, Arthur (1875–1960).
Gaunt British character actor of stage and screen; a splendid, if elderly, Sherlock Holmes.

Frailty 16. Bonnie Prince Charlie 23. Eugene Aram 24. The Infamous Lady 28. The Sleeping Cardinal 31. *The Sign of Four* 32. *The Triumph of Sherlock Holmes* 35. Dishonour Bright 36. Silver Blaze 36. Storm in a Teacup 37. Kate Plus Ten 38. The Terror 38. The Life and Death of Colonel Blimp 43. Blanche Fury 47. Brandy for the Parson 52. *Genevieve* 53, etc.

Woo, John (1946–) (Ng Ya-sum).
Chinese director, screenwriter and occasional actor who moved to the USA in the early 90s. Born in China, he lived in Hong Kong as a child. He began as script supervisor at Cathay Studios in the late 60s, then became an assistant director at Shaw Brothers studios in the early 70s, later becoming a production manager. International recognition came with *The Killer*, with its violent, elaborately choreographed action sequences.

The Young Dragons 73. Money Crazy 77. Last Hurrah for Chivalry 78. Laughing Times 81. The Time You Need a Friend 84. Run Tiger, Run 85. A Better Tomorrow 86. The Killer 89. Bullet in the Head 90. Once a Thief 91. Hard Boiled 92. Hard Target (US) 93. Broken Arrow (US) 96. *Face/Off* (US) 97. Replacement Killers (ex p) (US) 98. The Big Hit (ex p) (US) 98. Blackjack (TV) 98, etc.

AS ACTOR: Starry Is the Night 88. Rebel from China 90. Twin Dragons 92, etc.

❝ I hate violence. – *J.W.*

The most exciting director to emerge in action cinema since Sergio Leone. – *Quentin Tarantino*

Wood, Charles (1932–).
British playwright with a penchant for military matters.

Help 65. The Knack 65. How I Won the War 67. The Charge of the Light Brigade 68. The Long Day's Dying 68. The Bed Sitting Room 69. Cuba 79. The Red Monarch (TV) 83. Wagner 83. Sharpe's Company (TV) 94. An Awfully Big Adventure 95, etc.

Wood, Edward D., Jnr (1924–1978).
American film director and screenwriter generally regarded as making the worst films in the history of the cinema. Most starred Bela Lugosi, at the sad and drug-addicted end of his career, and the bulky Tor Johnson. A cult has grown around the worst of his worst, *Plan 9 from Outer Space*, which was even the inspiration for a computer game in 1992. A biopic, *Ed Wood*, directed by Tim Burton and starring Johnny Depp in the title role, was released in 1994. A documentary, *The Haunted World of Edward J. Wood Jnr*, directed by Brett Thompson, was released in 1995. A restored and re-edited version of his first 20-minute western, *Crossroads at Laredo*, which was made in 1948, was also released in 1995.

Biography: 1992, *Nightmare of Ecstasy: The Life and Art of Edward D. Wood Jnr* by Rudolph Grey.

■ Glen or Glenda (a, wd) 53. Jail Bait (a, wd) 54. Bride of the Monster (wd) 55. The Violent Years (w) 56. The Bride and the Beast (w) 58. Plan 9 from Outer space (a, wd) 59. The Sinister Urge (a, wd) 60. Night of the Ghouls/Revenge of the Dead (wd) 60. Shotgun Wedding (w) 63. Orgy of the Dead (w) 65. 1,000,000 AC/DC (w) 69. Take It Out in Trade (a, wd) 71. Class Reunion (w) 73. Fugitive Girls (a, w) 74. The Cocktail Hostess (w) 74. Necromancy/Necromania (wd) 75. I Woke Up Early the Day I Died (oa) 98.

Wood, Elijah (1981–).
American child actor, a former model.

Avalon 90. Radio Flyer 92. Forever Young 92. The Adventures of Huck Finn 93. The Good Son 93. North 94. Flipper 96. Oliver Twist 97. The Ice Storm 97. Deep Impact 98. The Faculty 98. The Bumblebee Flies Anyway 98, etc.

Wood, 'Wee Georgie' (1895–1979).
Diminutive, squeaky-voiced English music-hall comedian, on stage from the age of five.

Convict 99 19. Two Little Drummer Boys 28. The Black Hand Gang 30. Stepping Toes 38. The Visit 61, etc.

Wood, Mrs Henry (1814–1887).
British Victorian novelist whose *East Lynne* has been filmed several times.

Wood, John (1937–).
British stage actor usually seen in intellectual roles.

The Rebel 60. Nicholas and Alexandra 72. Slaughterhouse Five 72. Somebody Killed Her Husband 77. War Games 83. Ladyhawke 85. The Purple Rose of Cairo 85. Jumpin' Jack Flash 86. Memento Mori (TV) 92. Orlando 92. Young Americans 93. Shadowlands 93. Uncovered 94. Citizen X (TV) (US) 95. Sabrina 95. Richard III 95. Jane Eyre 96. Family Money (TV) 97. The Avengers 98, etc.

Wood, Lawson (1878–1957).
British artist and illustrator, noted for his humorous drawings of animals. He was the creator of *Gran' Pop Monkey*, a short-lived cartoon series about an artful chimpanzee, animated by Ub Iwerks.

A Busy Day 40. Beauty Shoppe 40. Baby Checkers 40.

Wood, Natalie (1938–1981) (Natasha Gurdin).
Former American child actress who became a top star of the 60s. Born in San Francisco, she began to dance almost before she could walk and was on screen from the age of five. Married actor Robert WAGNER (1957–62, 1972–81) and British producer Richard Gregson (1969–71). Drowned after falling from a yacht. Mother of actress Natasha Gregson WAGNER.

Happy Land 43. Tomorrow Is Forever 45. The Bride Wore Boots 46. Miracle on 34th Street 47. No Sad Songs for Me 50. The Blue Veil 52. Rebel without a Cause (AAN) 55. A Cry in the Night 56. The Searchers 56. *Marjorie Morningstar* 58. Kings Go Forth 59. Cash McCall 60. *Splendor in the Grass* (AAN) 61. *West Side Story* 61. Gypsy 62. *Love with the Proper Stranger* (AAN) 64. Sex and the Single Girl 64. *The Great Race* 65. Inside Daisy Clover 66. This Property is Condemned 66. Penelope 66. *Bob and Carol and Ted and Alice* 69. The Affair (TV) 73. Peeper 74. *From Here to Eternity* (TV) 79. Meteor 79. Brainstorm 83 (release), etc.

TV series: Pride of the Family 53.

Wood, Oliver.
American cinematographer.

The Honeymoon Killers 69. Don't Go in the House 79. Q the Winged Serpent/The Winged Serpent 82. Maya 82. Alphabet City 84. Body Rock 84. Joey 85. Hoosiers/Best Shot 86. The Adventures of Ford Fairlane 90. Die Hard 2 90. Rudy 93. Sister Act 2: Back in the Habit 93. Terminal Velocity 94. Mr Holland's Opus 95. 2 Days in the Valley 96. Celtic Pride 96. SwitchBack 97. Face/Off 97, etc.

Wood, Peggy (1894–1978).
American character actress, former opera singer.

Almost a Husband 19. Handy Andy 34. The Housekeeper's Daughter 39. The Story of Ruth 60. *The Sound of Music* (AAN) 65, etc.

TV series: Mama 49–56.

Wood, Sam (1883–1949).
American director, in business before becoming assistant to Cecil B. De Mille *c.* 1915; directing from 1920.

The Beloved Villain 20. Under the Lash 22. Bluebeard's Eighth Wife 23. One Minute to Play 26. The Latest from Paris 28. Within the Law 30. Stamboul Quest 32. The Late Christopher Bean 33. Get-Rich-Quick Wallingford 34. *A Night at the Opera* 35. The Unguarded Hour 36. *A Day at the Races* 37. Madame X 37. Lord Jeff 38. *Goodbye Mr Chips* (AAN) 39. Raffles 39. *Our Town* 40. Kitty Foyle (AAN) 40. *The Devil and Miss Jones* 41. The Pride of the Yankees 42. *Kings Row* (AAN) 42. Saratoga Trunk 43 (released 46). *For Whom the Bell Tolls* (& p) 43. Casanova Brown 44. Guest Wife 45. Heartbeat 46. Ivy 47. Command Decision 48. Ambush 49, etc.

Woodard, Alfre (1953–).
American actress.

Remember My Name 78. Health 80. Cross Creek (AAN) 83. Go Tell It on the Mountain 84. Extremities 86. Scrooged 88. Miss Firecracker 89. Grand Canyon 91. Passion Fish 92. Rich in Love 93. Heart and Souls 93. Bopha! 93. Crooklyn 94. Blue Chips 94. How to Make an American Quilt 95. Primal Fear 96. Star Trek: First Contact 96. Miss Evers' Boys (TV) 97. The Member of the Wedding (TV) 97. Down in the Delta (& co-p) 98, etc.

TV series: Tucker's Witch 82–83. St Elsewhere 85–87. Sara 85–88.

Woodbridge, George (1907–1973).
Portly British character actor, often seen as tavern-keeper or jovial policeman.

Tower of Terror 42. Green for Danger 46. Bonnie Prince Charlie 48. The Story of Gilbert and Sullivan 53. The Constant Husband 55. Dracula 58. Two-Way Stretch 60. Dracula Prince of Darkness 65, many others.

Woodbury, Joan (1915–1989).
American leading lady of 40s second features.
Without Children 35. Forty Naughty Girls 38. The Mystery of the White Room 39. The Desperadoes 43. Flame of the West 46. Here Comes Trouble 49. The Ten Commandments 56, many others.

Woodlawn, Holly (1947–) (Harold Ajzenberg).
Puerto Rico-born transvestite star of Andy Warhol's movies.
Trash 69. Scarecrow in a Garden of Cucumbers 72. Women in Revolt 72. Night Owl 93, etc.
❝ We tried to be women so much. I think that basically Andy loved glamorous women and around that time he just didn't know any. – *H.W.*

Woods, Arthur B. (1904–1942).
British director.
On Secret Service 34. Radio Parade 35. Drake of England 35. The Dark Stairway 37. The Return of Carol Deane 38. *They Drive by Night* 38. The Nursemaid Who Disappeared 39. Busman's Honeymoon 40, etc.

Woods, Aubrey (1928–).
British character actor.
Nicholas Nickleby 47. Queen of Spades 48. Father Brown 54. School for Scoundrels 59. Spare the Rod 61. Just Like a Woman 66. The Abominable Dr Phibes 71. The Darwin Adventure 72. That Lucky Touch 75, etc.

Woods, Donald (1906–1998) (Ralph L. Zink).
Canadian leading man of the 30s and 40s.
Sweet Adeline 33. *A Tale of Two Cities* 35. *Anthony Adverse* 36. Forgotten Girls 40. Love, Honour and Oh Baby 41. I Was a Prisoner on Devil's Island 41. Watch on the Rhine 43. Roughly Speaking 45. Wonder Man 45. Barbary Pirate 49. Undercover Agent 54. Thirteen Ghosts 60. Kissing Cousins 64. Moment to Moment 65. True Grit 69, many others.
TV series: Craig Kennedy, Criminologist 52. Damon Runyon Theatre (host) 55–56. Tammy 65–66.

Woods, Eddie (1905–1989).
American leading man of the early 30s. He seemed to lose heart after swapping roles with Cagney for *The Public Enemy* (he was originally cast for the top role and elected to take the less interesting role of the brother).

Woods, Harry Macgregor (1896–1970).
American songwriter. Educated at Harvard, he lacked any fingers on his left hand and played the piano one-handed. He came to Britain in the 30s to work for Gaumont British Pictures and wrote, among other hits, 'Over My Shoulder' and 'When You've Got a Little Springtime in Your Heart' for Jessie Matthews to sing in *Evergreen*. He returned to America in the 40s and wrote no more.
Aunt Sally 33. Jack Ahoy! 34. Evergreen 35. It's Love Again 36.

Woods, James (1947–).
Lean American actor, in roles of increasing stature. Born in Vernal, Utah, he studied politcal science at the Massachusetts Institute of Technology and began as an actor on the stage.
The Way We Were 72. Alex and the Gypsy 76. The Choirboys 78. The Onion Field 79. The Black Marble 80. Eyewitness 80. Split Image 82. Videodrome 83. Against All Odds 83. Once upon a Time in America 84. Cat's Eye 84. *Salvador* (AAN) 85. Joshua Then and Now 87. Best Seller 87. Cop 88. The Boost 88. True Believer 89. Immediate Family 89. The Hard Way 91. Straight Talk 92. Chaplin 92. Diggstown/Midnight Sting 92. The Getaway 94. Curse of the Starving Class 94. Next Door (TV) 94. The Specialist 94. Casino 95. Nixon 95. Indictment: The McMartin Trial (TV) 95. Killer: A Journal of Murder 96. The Summer of Ben Tyler (TV) 97. *Ghosts of Mississippi* (AAN) 97. Kicked in the Head 97. Contact 97. John Carpenter's Vampires 98. Another Day in Paradise 98. The Virgin Suicides 98, etc.

Woodward, Edward (1930–).
British stage actor who achieved popularity on TV as *Callan* 67–73.
Where There's a Will 54. Becket 64. The File of the Golden Goose 69. Sitting Target 72. The Wicker Man 73. Young Winston 73. Callan 74. Stand Up Virgin Soldiers 77. Breaker Morant 79. Winston Churchill, the Wilderness Years (TV) 81. Who Dares Wins 82. A Christmas Carol (TV) 84. King David 85. Mister Johnson 90. Deadly Advice 94. Gulliver's Travels (TV) 96, etc.
TV series: The Equalizer 85–89. Over My Dead Body 90–91. Common as Muck 94–97.

Woodward, Joanne (1930–).
Tomboyish American leading actress, married to Paul Newman.
■ Count Three and Pray 55. A Kiss before Dying 56. *The Three Faces of Eve* (AA) 57. *No Down Payment* 57. The Long Hot Summer 58. Rally round the Flag Boys 58. The Sound and the Fury 59. The Fugitive Kind 59. From the Terrace 60. Paris Blues 61. The Stripper 63. A New Kind of Love 63. Signpost to Murder 64. *A Big Hand for the Little Lady* 66. A Fine Madness 66. *Rachel Rachel* (AAN) 68. Winning 69. W.U.S.A. 70. They Might Be Giants 71. The Effect of Gamma Rays on Man-in-the-Moon Marigolds 72. Summer Wishes, Winter Dreams (AAN) 73. The Drowning Pool 75. Sybil (TV) 77. The End 78. See How She Runs (TV) 78. A Christmas to Remember (TV) 78. The Shadow Box (TV) 80. Harry and Son 84. Passions (TV) 84. Do You Remember Love 85. The Glass Menagerie 87. Mr & Mrs Bridge (AAN) 90. Foreign Affairs (TV) 93. Blind Spot (TV) 93. The Age of Innocence (narrator) 93. Philadelphia 93. Breathing Lessons (TV) 94.

Woof, Emily (1970–).
British leading actress, from the stage. Born in Newcastle, she studied English at Oxford University and first came to notice writing and performing experimental one-woman shows.
The Full Monty 97. Photographing Fairies 97. The Woodlanders 97. Killer Net (TV) 98. Velvet Goldmine 98. Fast Food 98. Passion: The Story of Percy Grainger 99, etc.

Wooland, Norman (1905–1989).
British actor, former radio announcer.
Hamlet (film debut) 48. All over the Town 48. Escape 49. Romeo and Juliet 53. The Master Plan 55. Richard III 56. Guilty 56. The Rough and the Smooth 59. The Fall of the Roman Empire 64. Saul and David 65. The Projected Man 66, etc.

Wooldridge, Susan.
English leading actress, from the stage and television, daughter of actress Margaretta Scott.
Butley 74. The Shout 78. The Jewel in the Crown (TV) 84. Loyalties 85. Hope and Glory 87. Bye Bye Blues 89. How to Get Ahead in Advertising 89. Twenty-One 91. Afraid of the Dark 92. Just Like a Woman 92. Bad Company (TV) 93, etc.
TV series: Underworld 97.

Woolf, James (1919–1966).
British producer. With brother, *Sir John Woolf* (1913–), founded Romulus Films 1949. Both are sons of leading producer-distributor C. M. Woolf, who died in 1942.
Pandora and the Flying Dutchman 51. The African Queen 52. Moulin Rouge 53. Three Men in a Boat 56. Room at the Top 59, etc.
James only: The L-Shaped Room 62. The Pumpkin Eater 64. Life at the Top 65. King Rat 65.
John only: Oliver! (AA) 68. Day of the Jackal 73. No Sex Please We're British 73. The Odessa File 74.

Woolf, Virginia (1882–1941).
British novelist whose introspection and sensitivity, rather than her themes, were used as symbols in the title *Who's Afraid of Virginia Woolf?* *Orlando* was successfully filmed by Sally Potter in 1992. *Mrs Dalloway* followed in 1998.

Woolfe, H. Bruce (1880–1965).
British producer, best known for his war reconstructions of the 20s (*Armageddon, Ypres, The Battle of the Somme*, etc.) and for the *Secrets of Nature* series begun in 1919. Head of British Instructional Films from 1926; later in charge of production for children.

Woollcott, Alexander (1887–1943).
Waspish American columnist and critic, the original inspiration for Kaufman and Hart's *The Man Who Came to Dinner*. He was played by Tom McGowan in *Mrs Parker and the Vicious Circle* 94.
Biography: 1976, *Smart Aleck* by Howard Teichmann.
■ Gift of Gab 34. *The Scoundrel* 35. Babes on Broadway 41.
❝ He spoke the English language with all the style of a prose writer; his wit was devastating and original; he was a man of great but deviating loyalty to his friends; and, if he chose, could make an evening come brightly to light. – *George Oppenheimer*
He was petty, shockingly vindictive in a feminine fashion, given to excesses when expressing his preferences or his prejudices. He probably endorsed more second-rate books than any man of his time. – *Tallulah Bankhead*
See also: Algonquin Round Table.

Woolley, Monty (1888–1963) (Edgar Montillion Woolley).
American comedy character actor of ebullient personality, a former Yale professor who came to movie stardom via a big hit as Alexander Woollcott on the Broadway stage.
Live, Love and Learn 37. Nothing Sacred 37. Arsène Lupin Returns 38. Girl of the Golden West 38. Everybody Sing 38. Three Comrades 38. Lord Jeff 38. Artists and Models Abroad 38. Young Dr Kildare 38. Vacation from Love 38. Never Say Die 39. Midnight 39. Zaza 39. Man about Town 39. Dancing Co-Ed 39. *The Man Who Came to Dinner* 41. The Pied Piper (AAN) 42. Life Begins at 8.30 42. *Holy Matrimony* 43. Since You Went Away (AAN) 44. Irish Eyes Are Smiling 44. Molly and Me 45. *Night and Day* 46. The Bishop's Wife 47. *Miss Tatlock's Millions* 48. As Young as You Feel 51. Kismet 55, etc.
Famous line (*The Man Who Came to Dinner*): 'Gentlemen, will you all now leave quietly, or must I ask Miss Cutler to pass among you with a baseball bat?'
Famous line (*The Man Who Came to Dinner*) (to his nurse who has reproved him for eating chocolates): 'My great aunt Elizabeth ate a box of chocolates every day of her life. She lived to be a hundred and two, and when she had been dead three days, she looked healthier than you do now.'

Woolley, Stephen (1956–).
British producer. With Nik Powell, he was a co-founder of Palace Pictures, a distribution and production company.
Book: 1996, *The Egos Have Landed: The Rise and Fall of Palace Pictures* by Angus Finney.
The Company of Wolves 85. A Letter to Brezhnev 85. Absolute Beginners 86. Mona Lisa 86. The Courier 87. High Spirits 88. Shag 88. Scandal 89. The Big Man 90. The Miracle 91. The Pope Must Die/The Pope Must Diet 91. A Rage in Harlem 91. Interview with the Vampire 94. Michael Collins 96. Hollow Reed 96. Welcome to Woop-Woop 97. Downtime 97. TwentyFourSeven 97. Fever Pitch 97. The Lost Son 98. Little Voice 98. *The Butcher Boy* 98. B. Monkey 98. Divorcing Jack 98, etc.

Woolrich, Cornell (1903–1968).
American mystery writer also known as William Irish. A recluse, he handed some interesting ideas to Hollywood, but most were ineptly handled.
Street of Chance (from The Black Curtain) 42. The Leopard Man (from Black Alibi) 43. Phantom Lady 44. Deadline at Dawn 46. Black Angel 46. Fear in the Night 47. Night Has a Thousand Eyes 48. The Window 49. No Man of Her Own 50. Rear Window 54. The Bride Wore Black 67. Union City 79. Cloak and Dagger 84. Mrs Winterbourne (from I Married a Dead Man) 96, etc.

Woolsey, Ralph.
American cinematographer.
The Culpeper Cattle Company 72. The New Centurions 72. The Mack 73. The Iceman Cometh 73. Black Eye 74. 99 44/100 Per Cent Dead 74. Rafferty and the Gold Dust Twins 75. Mother, Jugs and Speed 76. The Promise 79. The Great Santini 80. The Last Married Couple in America 80. Oh God! Book II 80, etc.

Woolsey, Robert:
see Wheeler, Bert.

Worden, Hank (1901–1992) (Norton Earl Worden).
American western character actor.
The Plainsman 36. Northwest Passage 40. The Bullfighters 45. The Secret Life of Walter Mitty 47. Yellow Sky 48. Fort Apache 48. Red River 48. Wagon Master 50. The Searchers 56. McLintock 63. Scream 82, many others.

Wordsworth, Richard (1915–1993).
Lanky English character actor, on stage, frequently in Shakespearian roles, from 1938. Also a director of plays and the great-great-grandson of the poet William Wordsworth, whom he impersonated in his one-man show, *The Bliss of Solitude*. His most memorable screen role was as the astronaut who turned to fungus in *The Quatermass Experiment/The Creeping Unknown* 55.
The Man Who Knew Too Much 56. Time without Pity 57. The Camp on Blood Island 58. Revenge of Frankenstein 58. Curse of the Werewolf 61. The Moving Toyshop (as detective Professor Gervase Fen) 64. Lock Up Your Daughters! 69. Song of Norway 70, etc.
TV series: R3 64. The Regiment 72.

Worlock, Frederick (1886–1973).
British character actor in Hollywood after long stage career.
Miracles for Sale 39. The Sea Hawk 40. Rage in Heaven 41. The Black Swan 43. Sherlock Holmes Faces Death 44. Terror by Night 46. Joan of Arc 48. Notorious Landlady 62. Spinout 66, etc.

Worsley, Wallace (1880–1944).
American director of the 20s.
Honor's Cross 18. The Little Shepherd of Kingdom Come 19. *The Penalty* 20. A Blind Bargain 21. Rags to Riches 22. *The Hunchback of Notre Dame* 23. The Man Who Fights Alone 24. The Shadow of Law 26. The Power of Silence 28, etc.

Worth, Brian (1914–1978).
British light leading man.
The Lion Has Wings 39. One Night with You 48. Hindle Wakes 52. An Inspector Calls 54. Ill Met by Moonlight 57. Peeping Tom 60. On Her Majesty's Secret Service 69, etc.

Worth, Irene (1916–).
American leading actress, in recent years mainly on British stage.
■ One Night with You 48. Another Shore 48. Secret People 51. *Orders to Kill* (BFA) 58. The Scapegoat 59. Seven Seas to Calais (as Elizabeth I) 63. King Lear 69. Nicholas and Alexandra 71. Rich Kids 79. Deathtrap 82. Forbidden 85. Lost in Yonkers 93.

Worth, Marvin (1925–1998).
American producer and screenwriter. Born in Brooklyn, he began as a jazz promoter while still in his teens, then becoming a writer for TV shows, and of special material for comedians, and manager of Lenny Bruce.
As writer: Boys Night Out 62. Three on a Couch (co-w) 66. Promise Her Anything 66. Malcolm X (& d) (doc) 72, etc.
As producer: Where's Poppa? 70. Lenny 74. The Rose 79. Up the Academy 80. Soup for One 82. Unfaithfully Yours 83. Rhinestone 84. Falling in Love 84. Less than Zero 87. Patty Hearst 88. Flashback 90. Diabolique 96. Norman Jean & Marilyn (TV) 96. Goa (TV) 98, etc.

Wotruba, Michael:
see D'Amato, Joe.

Wouk, Herman (1915–).
American best-selling novelist.
The Caine Mutiny 54. Marjorie Morningstar 58. Youngblood Hawke 64. The Winds of War (TV) 83. The Caine Mutiny Court-Martial (TV) 88. War and Remembrance (TV) 89, etc.
TV series: Troubleshooters 59–60. Dallas 79–80. Call to Glory 84–85. The Last Precinct 86.

Wray, Fay (1907–).
American leading lady of the 30s, a great screamer. Born in Canada, she moved to America as a child. The first and second of her three husbands were screenwriters John Monk Saunders (1928–40) and Robert Riskin.
Autobiography: 1989, *On the Other Hand.*
Street of Sin 28. The Wedding March 28. The Four Feathers 29. The Texan 30. Dirigible 30. Doctor X 31. *The Most Dangerous Game* 32. The Vampire Bat 33. The Mystery of the Wax Museum 33. *King Kong* 33. The Bowery 33. Madame Spy 34. The Affairs of Cellini 34. The Clairvoyant 35. They Met in a Taxi 36. Murder in Greenwich

Village 37. The Jury's Secret 38. Adam Had Four Sons 41. Small Town Girl 53. Queen Bee 55. Crime of Passion 56. Tammy and the Bachelor 57. Gideon's Trumpet (TV) 80, etc.

TV series: Pride of the Family 53.

❝ At the premiere of *King Kong* I wasn't too impressed. I thought there was too much screaming . . . I didn't realize then that King Kong and I were going to be together for the rest of our lives, and longer . . . – *F.W.*

Wray, John (1890–1940) (John Malloy).
American general-purpose actor.

All Quiet on the Western Front 30. Doctor X 32. I Am a Fugitive from a Chain Gang 32. The Defence Rests 34. The Whole Town's Talking 35. Valiant is the Word for Carrie 36. You Only Live Once 37. The Cat and the Canary 39. The Man from Dakota 40, etc.

Wrede, Caspar (1929–1998).
Finnish director, in British TV.
■ The Barber of Stamford Hill 62. Private Potter 64. One Day in the Life of Ivan Denisovich 71. Ransom 74.

Wren, P. C. (1885–1941) (Percival Christopher Wren).
British adventure novelist who after a military life wrote the much filmed *Beau Geste*, followed by *Beau Sabreur* and *Beau Ideal*.

Wright, Basil (1907–1987).
British producer-director. In films from 1929; worked with John Grierson in creation of 'documentary'.

Film history: 1975, *The Long View*.

Windmill in Barbados (d) 30. Song of Ceylon (p, d) 34. Night Mail (co-d) 36. Waters of Time (p, d) 51. World without End (d) 53. The Immortal Land (p, d) 58. A Place for Gold (p, d) 61, etc.

Wright, Cobina, Jnr (1921–).
American actress of the 40s, a slinky blonde.

Charlie Chan in Rio 41. Weekend in Havana 41. Moon over Miami 41. Footlight Serenade 42. Something to Shout About 43, etc.

Wright, Geoffrey.
Australian director and screenwriter, a former journalist.

Romper Stomper 92. Metal Skin 94.

Wright, Robin (1966–) (aka Robin Wright Penn).
American leading actress. Married actor Sean Penn, by whom she has a son and a daughter, in 1996.

Hollywood Vice Squad 86. The Princess Bride 87. State of Grace 90. The Playboys 92. Toys 92. Forrest Gump 94. The Crossing Guard 95. Moll Flanders 96. Loved 96. She's So Lovely 97. Hurlyburly 98, etc.

Wright, Teresa (1918–).
American leading actress with stage experience.
■ *The Little Foxes* (debut) (AAN) 41. *Mrs Miniver* (AA) 42. The Pride of the Yankees (AAN) 42. *Shadow of a Doubt* 43. Casanova Brown 44. *The Best Years of Our Lives* 46. Pursued 47. The Imperfect Lady 47. The Trouble with Women 47. Enchantment 48. *The Men* 50. The Captive 50. The Steel Trap 52. Something to Live For 52. Count the Hours 53. The Actress 53. Track of the Cat 54. *The Search for Bridey Murphy* 56. Escapade in Japan 57. The Wonderful Years 58. Hail Hero 69. The Happy Ending 69. Crawlspace (TV) 71. The Elevator (TV) 73. Flood (TV) 76. *Roseland* 77. Somewhere in Time 80. Bill: On His Own (TV) 83. The Good Mother 88.

Wright, Tony (1925–1986).
British light leading man, with stage experience.

The Flanagan Boy (film debut) 51. Jumping for Joy 54. Jacqueline 56. Seven Thunders 57. Faces in the Dark 60. Journey to Nowhere 62. All Coppers Are 72, etc.

Wright, Will (1894–1962).
Lugubrious American character actor.

China Clipper 36. World Première 41. Bewitched 45. *The Blue Dahlia* (his best role, as the murderer) 46. Adam's Rib 49. Excuse My Dust 51. The Wild One 52. The Deadly Companions 62. Cape Fear 62. Fail Safe 64, many others.

Wrightsman, Stan (1910–1975).
American jazz pianist. Born in Gotebo, Oklahoma, he worked in New Orleans before settling in the late 30s in Los Angeles, where he often played for films and television. He dubbed the piano playing of Richard Whorf in *Blues in the Night* 41, and of Bonita Granville in *Syncopation* 42. He is seen on-screen backing guitarist Tony Romano in *The Man I Love* 46. He also played on the soundtracks of *The Time, the Place and the Girl* 46, *Young Man with a Horn* 49, *Picnic* 55, and *The Five Pennies* 59.

Wrixon, Maris (1917–).
American light leading lady of the 30s.

Broadway Musketeers 38. The Ape 41. The Man Who Talked Too Much 42. Bullets for O'Hara 43. As You Were 51, etc.

Wrubel, Allie (1905–1973).
American composer. A big-band saxophonist and bandleader, he went to Hollywood in the 30s to write songs for Warner's movies.

Dames 34. Housewife 34. Flirtation Walk 34. Happiness Ahead 34. The Key 34. Sweet Music 35. Broadway Hostess 35. I Live for Love 35. In Caliente 35. Bright Lights 35. Life of the Party 37. Radio City Revels 38. Sing Your Way Home 45. Song of the South (AA for song 'Zip-a-Dee-Doo-Dah') 46. Never Steal Anything Small 58, etc.

Wu, Vivian (1966–) (Wu Jun Mei).
Chinese actress, now based in Los Angeles. Married to producer-director Oscar Costo.

The Last Emperor 87. Iron and Silk 90. Shadow of China 91. The Guyver 91. Teenage Mutant Turtles III 92. Man Tseung (HK) 93. Heaven and Earth 93. The Joy Luck Club 93. Vanishing Son (TV) 94. The Pillow Book 95. Blindness 98. A Bright Shining Lie (TV) 98, etc.

Wuhl, Robert (1951–).
American comedian and actor.

The Hollywood Knights 80. Good Morning, Vietnam 87. Bull Durham 88. Tales from the Crypt (TV) 89. Wedding Band 89. Blaze 89. Batman 89. Mistress 92. The Bodyguard 92. Blue Chips 94. Cobb 94. Open Season (& wd) 95. The Last Don (TV) 97. Good Burger 97. The Last Don II (TV) 98, etc.

Wurlitzer, Rudy.
American screenwriter and occasional director, often of quirky, individualistic road movies.

Glen and Randa 71. Two Lane Blacktop (co-w) 71. Pat Garrett and Billy the Kid 73. Walker 87. Candy Mountain (& co-d) 87. Voyager 91. Little Buddha (co-w) 93. Shadow of the Wolf (co-w) 93. Fearless 94, etc.

Wyatt, Jane (1912–).
Pleasing American leading lady of the 30s and 40s, with stage experience.

One More River 34. The Luckiest Girl in the World 36. *Lost Horizon* 37. Kisses for Breakfast 41. The Kansan 42. The Iron Road 43. None but the Lonely Heart 44. Boomerang 47. Gentleman's Agreement 47. Pitfall 48. Bad Boy 49. Task Force 49. Our Very Own 50. The Man Who Cheated Himself 51. Never Too Late 65. Tom Sawyer (TV) 73. Treasure of Matecumbe 76. Star Trek IV: The Journey Home 86. Amityville 4: The Evil Escapes (TV) 89, many others.

TV series: Father Knows Best 54–59 (reunion show 77).

Wycherly, Margaret (1881–1956).
British-born character actress with American stage experience.

The Thirteenth Chair 29. Sergeant York (AAN) 41. Keeper of the Flame 43. The Yearling 46. *White Heat* 49. Man with a Cloak 51. That Man from Tangier 53, many others.

Wyler, Richard:
see Stapley, Richard.

Wyler, William (1902–1981).
Distinguished German-American director, former film publicist, in Hollywood from 1920. Director from 1925, starting with low-budget silent westerns.

Biography: 1996, *A Talent for Trouble: The Life of Hollywood's Most Acclaimed Director, William Wyler* by Jan Herman.

■ TALKIES: Hell's Heroes 30. The Storm 30. A House Divided 31. Tom Brown of Culver 32. Her First Mate 33. Counsellor at Law 33. Glamour 34. *The Good Fairy* 35. The Gay Deception 35. These Three 36. Come and Get It (co-d) 36. *Dodsworth* (AAN) 36. *Dead End* 37. *Jezebel* 38. *Wuthering Heights* (AAN) 39. *The Letter* (AAN) 40. *The Westerner* 40. *The Little Foxes* (AAN) 41. *Mrs Miniver* (AA) 42. The Memphis Belle (doc) 44. The Fighting Lady (doc) 44. *The Best Years of Our Lives* (AA) 46. *The Heiress* (AAN) 49. *Detective Story* (AAN) 51. Carrie 52. Roman Holiday (AAN) 53. The Desperate Hours 55. The Friendly Persuasion (AAN) 56. *The Big Country* 58. *Ben Hur* (AA) 59. The Children's Hour 62. The Collector (AAN) 65. How to Steal a Million 66. Funny Girl 68. The Liberation of L.B. Jones 70.

❝ Doing a picture with Willie is like getting the works at a Turkish bath. You damn near drown, but you come out smelling like a rose. – *Charlton Heston*

Wyman, Jane (1914–) (Sarah Jane Faulks).
American leading lady of the 40s, at first in dumb blonde roles, later as serious actress. The second of her three husbands was Ronald Reagan (1940–48).

My Man Godfrey 36. Brother Rat 38. Flight Angels 40. Bad Men of Missouri 41. The Body Disappears 41. You're in the Army Now 41. My Favourite Spy 42. Princess O'Rourke 43. Crime by Night 44. The Doughgirls 44. Make Your Own Bed 44. *The Lost Weekend* 45. Night and Day 46. Magic Town 46. The Yearling (AAN) 46. *Johnny Belinda* (AA) 48. Three Guys Named Mike 49. Here Comes the Groom 51. The Blue Veil (AAN) 52. Just for You 53. So Big 53. *Magnificent Obsession* (AAN) 54. All that Heaven Allows 55. Miracle in the Rain 56. Pollyanna 60. Bon Voyage 63. How to Commit Marriage 69. The Failing of Raymond (TV) 71. The Incredible Journey of Dr Meg Laurel (TV) 79, etc.

TV series: The Jane Wyman Theater 56–60. Falcon Crest 81– .

~When asked why she divorced Ronald Reagan, she said: 'He talked too much.'

Wymark, Patrick (1920–1970) (Patrick Cheesman).
British TV actor, in occasional films. The voice of Churchill in *The Finest Hours* 64, *A King's Story* 65.

The Criminal 60. Repulsion 65. The Secret of Blood Island 65. The Psychopath 66. Where Eagles Dare 68. Cromwell 69. Satan's Skin 70, etc.

Wymore, Patrice (1926–).
American leading lady. She married Errol Flynn in 1953.

Tea for Two 50. Rocky Mountain 50. The Big Trees 52. She's Working Her Way through College 52. She's Back on Broadway 53. Chamber of Horrors 66, etc.

Wyndham, John (1903–1969) (John Wyndham Harris).
British science fiction novelist. Works filmed include *Village of the Damned/The Midwich Cuckoos* and *The Day of the Triffids*.

Wynn, Ed (1886–1966) (Isaiah Edwin Leopold).
American vaudeville, radio and TV comic who after initial film failure returned to Hollywood in the 50s as a character actor of fey old gentlemen.
■ Rubber Heels 27. Follow the Leader 30. Manhattan Mary 30. The Chief 33. Stage Door Canteen 43. *The Great Man* 56. Marjorie Morningstar 58. *The Diary of Anne Frank* (AAN) 59. The Absent Minded Professor 60. Cinderfella 60. Babes in Toyland 61. Son of Flubber 63. Those Calloways 64. *Mary Poppins* 64. That Darn Cat 65. Dear Brigitte 65. The Greatest Story Ever Told 65. The Gnome-Mobile 67.

TV series: The Ed Wynn Show 58.

Wynn, Keenan (1916–1986).
American character actor, son of Ed Wynn. In Hollywood from early 40s after stage experience.

Autobiography: 1960, *Ed Wynn's Son*.

See Here Private Hargrove 44. Under the Clock 45. Weekend at the Waldorf 45. The Hucksters 47. Annie Get Your Gun 50. Kiss Me Kate 53. The Glass Slipper 55. The Great Man 57. A Hole in the Head 59. The Absent-Minded Professor 60. Man in the Middle 63. Dr Strangelove 63. The Americanization of Emily 65. The Great Race 65. The War Wagon 67. Mackenna's Gold 68. Smith 69. Once upon a Time in the West 69. Five Savage Men 70. Pretty Maids all in a Row 71. Herbie Rides Again 73. Hit Lady (TV) 75. Nashville 75. The Devil's Rain 75. Orca 77. High Velocity 77. Coach 78. Piranha 78. Sunburn 79. Just Tell Me What You Want 80. The Glove 81. Best Friends 82, many others.

TV series: The Trouble Shooters 59.

❝ He's the fellow who, when Esther Williams jumps into the pool, gets splashed. – *Ed Wynn of Keenan Wynn*

Wynn, May (1931–) (Donna Lee Hickey).
American leading lady of the 50s.
■ 3 The Caine Mutiny 54. The Violent Men 54. They Rode West 55. Hong Kong Affair 59.

Wynn, Tracy Keenan (1945–).
American screenwriter, son of Keenan Wynn.

The Glass House (TV) 70. Tribes (TV) 71. *The Autobiography of Miss Jane Pittman* (TV) 73. The Longest Yard 74. The Drowning Pool (co-w) 75. The Deep (co-w) 77, etc.

Wynorski, Jim (1950–).
American director and screenwriter of exploitation movies. He began as a writer for Roger Corman's productions.

Sorceress (w) 83. Screwballs (co-w) 83. The Lost Empire (wd) 84. Chopping Mall/Killbots (co-w, d) 86. Deathstalker II: Duel of the Titans (d) 87. Big Bad Mama 2 (co-w, d) 87. Not of This Earth (d) 88. The Return of the Swamp Thing (d) 89. Transylvania Twist (d) 89. The Haunting of Maurella (wd) 90. 976 Evil: The Return (d) 91. Sins of the Flesh (d) 92. Tough Cookies (co-w, d) 93. Munchie Strikes Back 94. Attack of the 60 Foot Centerfold (a) 94. Body Chemistry 4: Full Exposure (d) 95. Demolition High (d) 96. Wasp Woman (d) (TV) 96. Vampirella (d) (TV) 96, etc.

❝ I got into this business for two reasons – chicks and money. Art has nothing to do with it. – *J.W.*

Wynter, Dana (1927–) (Dagmar Wynter).
British leading lady.

White Corridors 51. Colonel March Investigates 53. *Invasion of the Body Snatchers* (US) 56. D Day Sixth of June 56. Value 57. Shake Hands with the Devil 59. *Sink the Bismarck* 60. The List of Adrian Messenger 63. If He Hollers Let Him Go 68. Airport 69. Santee 73. Backstairs at the White House (TV) 79. The Royal Romance of Charles and Diana (TV) 82. The People from Another Star 86. Dead Right 88, etc.

TV series: The Man Who Never Was 66.

Wynyard, Diana (1906–1964) (Dorothy Isobel Cox).
Distinguished British stage actress who began her film career with MGM in Hollywood, returning to Britain to act on the stage. Married to director Carol Reed.
■ Rasputin and the Empress 32. *Cavalcade* (AAN) 33. Men Must Fight 33. Reunion in Vienna 33. Where Sinners Meet 34. Let's Try Again 34. One More River 34. On the Night of the Fire 39. Freedom Radio 40. *Gaslight* 40. The Prime Minister 40. *Kipps* 41. An Ideal Husband 47. Tom Brown's Schooldays 51. The Feminine Touch 56. Island in the Sun 57.

Xiaowen, Zhou (1954–).
Chinese director. Born in Beijing, he studied at
the Film Academy there and then worked at the
Xi'an Film Studio.

In Their Prime (co-d) 86. Desperation 87.
Obsession 89. No Regrets about Youth 92. Ermo 94.
The Emperor's Shadow 96, etc.

Yablans, Frank (1935–).
American independent producer.
The Other Side of Midnight 77. The Silver Streak 77. The Fury 78. North Dallas Forty (& w) 80. Mommie Dearest 81. Monsignor 82. The Star Chamber 83. Buy & Cell 89. Lisa 90. Congo 95, etc.

Yablans, Irwin (1934–).
American independent producer.
Badge 373 73. Halloween 78. Roller Boogie 79. Fade to Black 80. The Seduction 82. Parasite 82. Halloween III: Season of the Witch 83. Tank 84. Prison 88. Men at Work 90. Arena 91, etc.

Yagher, Kevin.
American special effects and make-up expert; also an occasional director.
A Nightmare on Elm Street 3: Dream Warriors 87. A Nightmare on Elm Street 4: The Dream Master 88. Child's Play 88. Child's Play 3 91. The Borrower 91. Hellraiser III: Hell on Earth (d credited to Allan Smithee) 92. Radio Flyer 92. Honey, I Blew Up the Kid 92. Dr Jekyll and Ms Hyde 96. The Fan 96. Starship Troopers 97. Face/Off 97. Bride of Chucky 98, etc.

Yakin, Boaz (1966–).
American director and screenwriter.
The Punisher (w) 89. Rookie (w) 90. *Fresh* (wd) 94. A Price above Rubies (wd) 98, etc.

Yakusho, Koji (1956–) (Koji Hashimoto).
Japanese leading actor, from the theatre. After working in an office for four years, he began acting in 1981.
Tampopo 86. Kamikaze Taxi 95. The Eel 96. Shall We Dance? 96. Cure/Kyua 97. Shitsurakuen 97, etc.

Yamada, Isuzu (1917–) (Mitsu Yamada).
Japanese leading actress, best known for her role as Lady Washizu (an oriental Lady Macbeth) in Kurosawa's *Throne of Blood*. She began her career at the age of 14 and married director Teinosuke Kinusaga, with whom she set up a short-lived production company in the 50s.
Osaka Elegy/Niniwa Hika 36. Sisters of the Gion/Gion No Shimai 36. Throne of Blood/Kumonosujo 57. Buddha/Shaka 61. Yojimbo 61, etc.

Yamada, Yoji (1931–).
Japanese director of working-class comedies. He is best known for the popular series of *Tora-san* movies, about the adventures of an itinerant pedlar. So far, he has directed more than 40 of them at the rate of two a year since 1969.

Yamamoto, Satsuo (1910–1983).
Japanese director, a former actor, in films as an assistant director from 1933. His own anti-authoritarian films were influenced by his wartime experiences, fighting in Manchuria. In the 50s, when he was one of the many sacked by Toho in trade union disputes, he ran his own independent production company.
La Symphonie Pastorale 37. Street of Violence/Boryoku No Machi 50. Storm Clouds over Mount Hakone/Hakone Fuun Roku 51. *Vacuum Zone*/Shinku Chitai 52. War of the Sun/Hi No Hate 54. Duckweed Story/Ukigusa Nikki 55. Tycoon/Kizu Darake No Sanga 64. Hyoten 66. The Bride from Hades/Botandoro 68. *The Family*/Kareinaru Ichizoku 74. Solar Eclipse/Kinkanshoku 75. The Barren Zone/Fumo Chitai 76, etc.

Yamanaka, Sadeo (1909–1938).
Japanese director whose promising career, which began in 1932, was cut short by his early death. He was sent to fight on the Chinese front by a government unhappy with his depiction of samurai as less than heroic, and died there. Only two of his 12 films survive.
The Pot Worth a Million Ryo/Hyaku-Man Ryono Tsubo 35. *Humanity and Paper Balloons*/Ninjo Kai Fusen 37.

Yanagimachi, Mitsuo (1944–).
Japanese director.
Farewell to the Land 82. Himatsuri 85. Shadow of China 91. About Love, Tokyo 92, etc.

Yang, Edward (1947–) (Yang Dechang).
Chinese-born director, working in Taiwan.
In Our Time (co-d) 82. That Day on the Beach 83. Taipei Story 85. The Terrorizers 86. A Brighter Summer Day 91. A Confucian Confusion/Duli Shidai 94. Mahjong 96, etc.

Yanne, Jean (1933–) (J. Gouye).
Heavy-set French actor.
Life Upside Down 65. Weekend 67. *Le Boucher* 69. Cobra 73. The Accuser 75. The Pink Telephone 76. Hanna K 83. Quicker than the Eye 88. Madame Bovary 91. Indochine 92. Chacun pour Toi 93. Fausto 93. Pétain 93. Regarde les Hommes Tomber 94. The Horseman on the Roof 95. News from the Good Lord 96. Desire 96. Des Nouvelles du Bon Dieu 96. La Belle Verte 96. Tenue Correcte Exigée 97, etc.

Yarbrough, Jean (1900–1975).
American director of second features, former prop man.
Devil Bat 41. Lure of the Islands 42. Good Morning Judge 43. In Society 44. The Naughty Nineties 45. The Brute Man 46. Curse of the Allenbys 47. The Creeper 48. Abbott and Costello Lost in Alaska 52. Jack and the Beanstalk 52. Women of Pitcairn Island 57. Saintly Sinners 61. Hillbillies in a Haunted House 67. The Over-the-Hill Gang (TV) 69, many others.

Yared, Gabriel (1949–).
Lebanese-born composer, resident in Paris.
Every Man for Himself/Sauve Qui Peut la Vie 80. Invitation au Voyage 82. Hanna K. 83. Dream One 84. Red Zone/Zone Rouge 86. Betty Blue/37.2 Degrés le Matin 86. Beyond Therapy 87. Clean and Sober 88. Camille Claudel 88. Romero 89. The King's Whore 90. The Lover/L'Amant 92. Map of the Human Heart 93. Les Feux Mal Éteints 94. Profil Bas 94. Black for Remembrance 96. *The English Patient* (AA) 96. The Wings of the Dove 97. City of Angels 98, etc.

Yates, Herbert (1880–1966).
American executive, ex-president of Republic Pictures, where his word was law in the 40s. Many of his productions starred his wife, Vera Hruba Ralston.

Yates, Marjorie (1941–).
English character actress, mainly in theatre and TV.
The Optimists of Nine Elms 73. Stardust 74. The Black Panther 77. Priest of Love 81. Wetherby 85. The Long Day Closes 92, etc.

Yates, Peter (1929–).
British director. He trained at the Royal Academy of Dramatic Arts and was an actor with repertory companies, then worked at the Royal Court Theatre.
Summer Holiday 62. One Way Pendulum 64.

Robbery 67. *Bullitt* (US) 68. John and Mary (US) 69. Murphy's War 70. The Hot Rock (US) 72. *The Friends of Eddie Coyle* 73. For Pete's Sake 74. Mother Jugs and Speed 76. The Deep 77. Breaking Away (AAN) 79. Eyewitness 81. Krull 83. *The Dresser* (& p) (AAN) 83. Eleni 85. Suspect 87. The House on Carroll Street 88. Hard Rain 89. Year of the Comet 92. Roommates 95. The Run of the Country 95, etc.
66 I've given American culture the car chase and the wet T-shirt. – P.Y.

Yen, Donnie (1966–) (Yan Chi Tan).
American-born star of Hong Kong action movies. He spent three years in China from the age of 16 studying martial arts.
Drunken Tai-Chi 85. Mismatched Couples 87. Tiger Cage 88. Tiger Cage 2 90. Holy Virgin versus the Evil Dead 90. Once upon a Time in China 91. Butterfly and Sword 93. Iron Monkey 93. Circus Kid 94. High Voltage 94, etc.

Yeoh, Michelle (1963–) (Yeo Chu-Kheng).
Leading Malaysian-born actress, in action films, also known as Michelle Khan earlier in her career. Born in Ipoh, she trained as a ballet dancer and studied at the Royal Academy of Dance in London. She was Miss Malaysia of 1983 and then moved to Hong Kong, where she began making films. Formerly married to producer Dickson Poon.
Yes, Madam 85. Royal Warriors 86. Twinkle Twinkle Lucky Stars 86. In the Line of Duty 87. In the Line of Duty II 87. Police Assassins II 87. Police Story III: Super Cop 92. The Heroic Trio 92. Police Story V 93. Tai Chi Master 93. Wing Chun 93. Ah Kam 96. Tomorrow Never Dies 97, etc.
66 The young *grande dame* of Hong Kong films. – Oliver Stone

Yeung, Bolo (Yang Sze).
Hong Kong martial arts actor, often as a villain.
Enter the Dragon 73. Young Dragon 77. Bolo 78. Bloodsport 88. Bloodfight 90. Tiger Claws 91. Double Impact 91. Iron Heart 92. TC 2000 93. Shootfighter: Fight to the Death 93. Fearless Tiger 94. Shootfighter 2: Kill or Be Killed 96, etc.

Yimou, Zhang (1950–).
Chinese director of the so-called Fifth Generation, a former cinematographer and actor. His more recent films have been banned in China. In 1994, the authorities forbade him from making films in China for five years.
AS ACTOR: Old Well 87. The Terra-Cotta Warrior 90.
AS CINEMATOGRAPHER: Yellow Earth 83. The Big Parade 85.
AS DIRECTOR: Red Sorghum/Hong Gaoliang 87. Operation Cougar 89. Jou Dou 90. Raise the Red Lantern/Dahong Denglong Gaogao Gua 91. *The Story of Qiu Jou* 92. To Live 94. The Great Conqueror's Concubine/Xi Chu Bawang (p) 94. Shanghai Triad 95. Breaking Up Is Hard to Do 97, etc.
66 To survive is to win. – Z.Y.

Yoda, Yoshikata (1909–).
Japanese screenwriter who collaborated with Kenji Mizoguchi on the scripts of many of the director's films from the mid-30s.
Osaka Elegy/Niniwa Hika 36. Sisters of the Gion/Gion No Shimai 36. Roei No Uta 38. Zangiku Monogatari 39. The Woman of Osaka/Naniwa Onna 40. The Loyal 47 Ronin I and II 41. Woman of the Night/Yoru No Onnatachi 48. The Life of Oharu/Saikaki Ichidai Onna 52. Ugetsu 53. Sansho the Bailiff/Sansho Dayu 54. A Story from Chikamatsu/Chikamatsu Monogatari 54. Shin Heike Monogatari 55, etc.

Yordan, Philip (1913–).
Prolific American writer-producer.
SCREENPLAYS: Syncopation 42. Dillinger (AAN) 45. House of Strangers 49. Detective Story (AAN) 51. Johnny Guitar 54. Broken Lance (AA story) 54. El Cid 61. 55 Days at Peking 62. The Fall of the Roman Empire 64, many others.
WROTE AND PRODUCED: The Harder They Fall 56. Men in War 57. God's Little Acre 58. Day of the Outlaw 59. Studs Lonigan 60. The Thin Red Line 64. The Battle of the Bulge 65. Captain Apache 71. Savage Journey 83. Night Train to Terror 85. Bloody Wednesday 87. Cry Wilderness 87. The Unholy 88, etc.
66 People would rather go and see a big bad picture than a good small one. – P.Y.

Yorick, John (1969–).
Polish actor, director, and screenwriter, the son of Jerzy Skolimowski. He co-wrote, co-directed and co-starred in *The Hollow Men* with his brother Joseph Kay (1971–).
Success Is the Best Revenge (as Michael Lyndon) 84. The Lightship (as Michael Lyndon) 85. The Hollow Men (a, co-w, co-d) 93.

York, Dick (1928–1992).
American actor.
My Sister Eileen 55. Operation Mad Ball 57. They Came to Cordura 58. Inherit the Wind 60, etc.
TV series: Going My Way 62–63. Bewitched 64–69.

York, Michael (1942–) (Michael Hugh Johnson).
English leading actor, often in sensible, clean-cut roles. Born in Fulmer, Buckinghamshire, he began acting as a schoolboy with Croft's Youth Theatre and continued at Oxford University, where he studied English. He began his professional career with the Dundee Repertory before joining the National Theatre, where he worked with Zeffirelli, who gave him his first screen role.
Autobiography: 1991, *Travelling Player*.
The Taming of the Shrew 67. *Accident* 67. Red and Blue 67. Smashing Time 67. Romeo and Juliet 68. The Strange Affair 68. The Guru 69. Alfred the Great 69. Justine 69. Something for Everyone 70. Zeppelin 71. *Cabaret* 72. England Made Me 72. *Lost Horizon* 73. The Three Musketeers 74. The Four Musketeers 74. Murder on the Orient Express 74. Conduct Unbecoming 75. Great Expectations 75. Logan's Run 76. *Jesus of Nazareth* (TV) 77. The Last Remake of Beau Geste 77. Seven Nights in Japan 77. The Island of Dr Moreau 77. Fedora 78. The Riddle of the Sands 79. A Man Called Intrepid (TV) 79. The White Lions 80. Final Arrangement 80. Phantom of the Opera (TV) 82. The Master of Ballantrae (TV) 83. Success Is the Best Revenge 84. Space (TV) 85. The Dawn 85. The Far Country (TV) 86. Sword of Gideon (TV) 86. Phantom of Death 87. Midnight Cop 88. Till We Meet Again (TV) 89. The Lady and the Highwayman (TV) 89. The Return of the Musketeers 89. Eline Vere 91. The Heat of the Day (TV) 91. Duel of Hearts (TV) 92. Wide Sargasso Sea 93. Our Lady/Gospa 94. Fall from Grace 94. A Young Connecticut Yankee in King Arthur's Court 95. Not of This Earth 96. True Women 97. The Ripper (TV) 97. Dark Planet 97. Austin Powers: International Man of Mystery 97. Wrongfully Accused 98. 54 98. Merchants of Venus 98. A Knight in Camelot (TV) 98, etc.
66 Cinema, it has always seemed to me, is essentially filmed thought. – M.Y.

York, Susannah (1941–) (Susannah Yolande Fletcher).
British leading lady of stage and screen.
■ *Tunes of Glory* (debut) 60. There Was a Crooked Man 60. *The Greengage Summer* 61. Freud 62. Tom Jones 63. The Seventh Dawn 64. Scene Nun Take One. 64. Scruggs 64. Sands of the Kalahari 65. Kaleidoscope 66. A Man For All Seasons 66. Sebastian 67. The Killing of Sister George 68. Duffy 68. Oh What a Lovely War 69. The Battle of Britain 69. Lock Up Your Daughters 69. *They Shoot Horses Don't They?* (US) (AAN) 69. Country Dance 70. Jane Eyre 70. Zee and Co. 71. Happy Birthday Wanda June (US) 71. *Images* 72. The Maids 73. Gold 74. Conduct Unbecoming 75. That Lucky Touch 75. Sky Riders 76. Eliza Frazer 76. Superman 78. The Golden Gate Murders (TV) 79. The Silent Partner 79. The Shout 79. Falling in Love Again 80. Superman II 80. The Awakening 80. Loophole 81. Yellowbeard 83. A Christmas Carol (TV) 84. Prettykill 87. Superman IV: The Quest for Peace (voice) 87. The Land of Faraway 87. American Roulette 88. A Summer Story 88. Just Ask for Diamond 88. Bluebeard Bluebeard/ Barbablu Barbablu 89. Melancholia 89. A Handful of Time/En Handfull Tid 90. Fate 90. Pretty Princess (It.) 93.
TV series: Second Chance 80. We'll Meet Again 81.

Yorkin, Bud (1926–) (Alan Yorkin).
American director, from TV.
Come Blow Your Horn 63. Never Too Late 65. Divorce American Style 67. Inspector Clouseau 68. Start the Revolution without Me 69. The Thief Who Came to Dinner 73. Twice in a Lifetime 85. Arthur 2: On the Rocks 88. Love Hurts 90. Intersection (p) 93, etc.

Yoshida, Yoshishige (1933–).
Japanese director and screenwriter, a member of the 'New Wave' of the 60s. He studied French literature at Tokyo University before becoming an assistant director. In the 70s, he was in Europe making TV documentaries.
Good for Nothing/Rokudenashi 60. Blood Is Dry/ Chi Wa Kawaite Iru 60. Akitsu Onsen 62. 18 Roughs/Arashi o Yobu Juhachinim 63. Woman of the Lake/Onna no Mizumi 66. Honoo To Onna 67. Affair in the Snow/Juhyo no Yorumeki 68. Eros and Massacre/Eros Purasu Gyakusatsu 69. Rengoku Eroica 70. Coup d'Etat/Kaigenre 73. Wuthering Heights/Arashi ga Oka 89, etc.

Yoshimura, Kozaburo (1911–).
Japanese director. Many of his most successful films were scripted by Kaneto Shindo, with whom he set up his own production company in the 50s.
Tomorrow's Dancers 39. Blossom 41. Temptation 48. Spring Snow 50. A Tale of Genji 51. Before Dawn 53. Beauty and the Dragon 55. Undercurrent 56. Design for Dying 61. The Bamboo Doll 63. A Fallen Woman 67. A Hot Night/Atsui Yoru 68. A Ragged Flag 74, etc.

Youmans, Vincent (1898–1946).
American song composer of the 20s. Shows filmed include *No No Nanette* and *Hit the Deck*.

Young, Aden.
Australian leading actor.
The Great Pretender 91. Black Robe 91. Over the Hill 92. Sniper (US) 92. Broken Highway 93. Shotgun Wedding 93. Love in Limbo 93. Metal Skin 94. Exile 94. *River Street* 96. Hotel de Love 97. Cousin Bette 97. The Girl of Your Dreams/La Niña de Tus Ojos 98, etc.

Young, Alan (1919–) (Angus Young).
British-born comic actor, in Canada since childhood.
Margie (debut) 46. Mr Belvedere Goes to College 49. Aaron Slick from Punkin Crick 52. *Androcles and the Lion* 53. Gentlemen Marry Brunettes 55. Tom Thumb 58. The Time Machine 60. The Cat from Outer Space 78. Duck Tales: The Movie (voice) 90. Beverly Hills Cop 3 94, etc.
TV series: Mister Ed 60–65.

Young, Arthur (1898–1959).
Portly British stage actor; film appearances usually in self-important roles.
No Limit 35. Victoria the Great 37. My Brother Jonathan 48. The Lady with a Lamp 51. An Inspector Calls 54. The Gelignite Gang 56, etc.

Young, Burt (1940–).
American supporting actor.
The Gambler 74. The Killer Elite 75. Rocky (AAN) 76. The Choirboys 77. Twilight's Last Gleaming 77. Convoy 78. Rocky II 79. Murder Can Hurt You (TV) 79. All the Marbles 81. Blood Beach 81. Once upon a Time in America 84. Rocky III 85. Back to School 86. Blood Red 88. Beverly Hills Brats 89. Last Exit to Brooklyn 89. Betsy's Wedding 90. Diving In 90. Rocky V 90. Red American/Americano Rosso 91. Club Fed 91. Bright Angel 91. Excessive Force 93. North Star 96. The Mouse 96. The Undertaker's Wedding 97. Kicked in the Head 97, etc.

Young, Carleton (1906–1971).
American character actor, from radio; father of Tony Young.
The Glory Brigade 53. The Court Martial of Billy Mitchell 55. The Horse Soldiers 59. Sergeant Rutledge 60, many others.

Young, Christopher (1958–).
American composer, born in Redbank, New Jersey; often scoring horror movies and dark thrillers.
The Dorm that Dripped Blood 81. Barbarian Queen 85. Wizards of the Lost Kingdom 85. A Nightmare on Elm Street Part 2: Freddy's Revenge 85. Trick or Treat 86. Invaders from Mars 86. Flowers in the Attic 87. Hellraiser 87. Hellbound: Hellraiser II 88. The Fly II 89. Jennifer Eight 92. Rapid Fire 92. Vagrant 92. The Dark Half 93. Sliver 93. The Dark Half 93. Judicial Consent 94. Dream Lover 94. Virtuosity 95. Species 95. Murder in the First 95. Copycat 95. Unforgettable 96. Set It Off 96. Head above Water 96. The Man Who Knew Too Little 97. Hard Rain 98. Judas Kiss 98. Rounders 98, etc.

Young, Clara Kimball (1890–1960).
Popular American heroine of the silent screen.
Cardinal Wolsey (debut) 12. Beau Brummell 13. Goodness Gracious 16. Eyes of Youth 19. Cheating Cheaters 19. Forbidden Woman 20. Hush 21. Charge It 21. Lying Wives 25. Kept Husbands 31. Love Bound 33. Romance in the Rain 34. The Frontiersman 39. Mr Celebrity 42, etc.

Young, Collier (1908–1980).
American writer-producer.
The Hitch-Hiker 53. The Bigamist 54. Mad at the World 55. Huk! 56, etc.
TV series: One Step Beyond 58–60. Ironside 67, etc.

Young, Dan.
British character actor, from music hall, most often seen supporting comedian Frank Randle.
The New Hotel 32. Off the Dole 35. Dodging the Dole 36. Calling All Crooks 38. Somehwere in England 40. Somewhere in Camp 42. Somewhere on Leave 42. Demobbed 44. Under New Management 46. Cup-Tie Honeymoon 48. Holidays with Pay 48. School for Randle 49. Over the Garden Wall 50. It's a Grand Life 53, etc.

Young, Freddie (1902–1998).
Distinguished British cinematographer, best known for his work on David Lean's epic films. He was in movies from silents and received his first credit as an assistant cameraman on *Rob Roy* 22.
Bitter Sweet 33. Nell Gwyn 34. When Knights Were Bold 36. Victoria the Great 37. Sixty Glorious Years 38. Goodbye Mr Chips 39. The Young Mr Pitt 41. 49th Parallel 41; war service; Bedelia 46. So Well Remembered 47. Edward My Son 49. Treasure Island 50. *Ivanhoe* (AAN) 52. *Lust for Life* 56. *Invitation to the Dance* 56. Bhowani Junction 56. Island in the Sun 56. *Lawrence of Arabia* (AA) 62. The Seventh Dawn 64. Lord Jim 65. Rotten to the Core 65. *Doctor Zhivago* (AA) 65. The Deadly Affair 67. You Only Live Twice 67. The Battle of Britain 69. *Ryan's Daughter* (AA) 70. Nicholas and Alexandra (AAN) 71. The Tamarind Seed 74. The Blue Bird 76. Seven Nights in Japan 77. Stevie 78. Bloodline 79. Rough Cut 80. Richard's Things 81. Sword of the Valiant 84. Invitation to the Wedding 84, etc.
~In 1985, at the age of 82, he directed his first film, *Arthur's Hallowed Ground*.

Young, Gig (1913–1978) (Byron Barr; aka Bryant Fleming).
American light comedy leading man with a pleasantly bemused air. Committed suicide after killing his fifth wife. He was previously married to actress Elizabeth Montgomery.
Misbehaving Husbands 40. They Died With Their Boots On 41. Dive Bomber 41. The Gay Sisters (in which he played a character called Gig Young and thereafter used the name) 41. Old Acquaintance 43. Air Force 43; war service; Escape Me Never 46. The Woman in White 47. Wake of the Red Witch 48. The Three Musketeers 49. *Come Fill the Cup* (AAN) 51. City That Never Sleeps 54. Young at Heart 55. Desk Set 57. Teachers Pet (AAN) 58. The Story on Page One 59. Ask Any Girl 59. *That Touch of Mink* 62. For Love or Money 63. Strange Bedfellows 65. The Shuttered Room 67. *They Shoot Horses, Don't They?* (AA) 69. *Lovers and Other Strangers* 70. The Neon Ceiling (TV) 71. A Son-in-Law for Charlie McReady 73. Bring Me the Head of Alfredo Garcia 74. The Hindenburg 75. The Killer Elite 75. Sherlock Holmes in New York (TV) 77. Spectre (TV) 78.
TV series: *The Rogues* 64. *Gibbsville* 76.
Famous line (*They Shoot Horses, Don't They?*): 'There can only be one winner, folks, but isn't that the American way?'

Young, Harold (1897–1970).
American director who made distinguished British films for Korda but was little heard from on his return to Hollywood.
The Scarlet Pimpernel 35. 52nd Street 38. Code of the Streets 39. Juke Box Jenny 42. The Frozen Ghost 43. I'll Remember April 44, etc.

Young, Loretta (1913–) (Gretchen Young).
American leading lady whose career in films began when she accidentally, at 15, answered a studio call meant for her elder sister, Polly Ann Young. Her three husbands included actor Grant Withers (1930–31) and costume designer Jean Louis (1993–97).
Autobiography: 1962, *The Things I Had to Learn*.
Laugh Clown Laugh (debut) 28. Loose Ankles 29. The Squall 30. Kismet 30. *The Devil to Pay* 30. I Like Your Nerve 31. Platinum Blonde 32. The Hatchet Man 32. Big Business Girl 32. Life Begins 32. Zoo in Budapest 33. *Man's Castle* 33. The House of Rothschild 34. Midnight Mary 35. The Crusaders 35. Clive of India 35. Call of the Wild 35. Shanghai 36. *Ramona* 36. Ladies in Love 37. Wife, Doctor and Nurse 37. Second Honeymoon 38. Four Men and a Prayer 38. Suez 38. Kentucky 38. Three Blind Mice 38. The Story of Alexander Graham Bell 39. The Doctor Takes a Wife 39. He Stayed for Breakfast 40. Lady from Cheyenne 41. The Men in Her Life 41. *A Night to Remember* 42. China 43. Ladies Courageous 44. And Now Tomorrow 44. The Stranger 45. Along Came Jones 46. The Perfect Marriage 46. *The Farmer's Daughter* (AA) 47. The Bishop's Wife 48. Rachel and the Stranger 48. Come to the Stable (AAN) 49. Cause for Alarm 51. Half Angel 51. Paula 52. Because of You 52. It Happens Every Thursday 53. Christmas Eve (TV) 86, many others.
TV show of anthology dramas 53–60.

Young, Ned (1914–1968).
American actor and screenwriter.
AS ACTOR: The Devil's Playground 46. Border Incident 49. Gun Crazy 49. Captain Scarlett 52. House of Wax 53. Terror in a Texas Town 58. Seconds 66, etc.
AS WRITER: Joe Palooka in the Knockout (w) 47. Passage West (story) 51. Jailhouse Rock (story) 57. *The Defiant Ones* (co-w) 58. Inherit the Wind (co-w) 60, etc.

Young, Otis (1932–).
American actor.
The Last Detail 73. The Capture of Bigfoot 79. Blood Beach 81, etc.
TV series: The Outcasts 68.

Young, Robert (1907–1998).
American leading actor invariably cast in amiable, dependable roles, at his best on television, in the title roles of *Father Knows Best* and *Marcus Welby, MD.* Born in Chicago, he was brought up in Los Angeles and worked in various jobs as well as acting at the Pasadena Community Playhouse, before beginning in small roles in silents. He was contracted to MGM in the early 30s, staying with the studio until the mid-40s. He appeared in 125 movies: his best roles were out of his usual range, as the spy Robert Marvin in *Secret Agent* and in the title role in *H. M. Pulham Esq.* For much of his career he suffered from alcoholism and also depression, attempting suicide in 1991. He was married for 61 years to his high-school sweetheart Elizabeth Henderson (d. 1994); they had four daughters.
The Sin of Madelon Claudet 31. Strange Interlude 31. The Kid from Spain 32. Hell Below 32. Tugboat Annie 33. Lazy River 34. The House of Rothschild 34. Spitfire 34. Whom the Gods Destroy 35. West Point of the Air 35. It's Love Again (GB) 36. *Secret Agent* (GB) 36. Stowaway 36. The Emperor's Candlesticks 37. I Met Him in Paris 37. The Bride Wore Red 37. Josette 38. Frou Frou 38. Three Comrades 39. Rich Man, Poor Girl 39. Honolulu 39. Miracles for Sale 39. Maisie 39. Northwest Passage 40. The Mortal Storm 40. Florian 40. Western Union 41. The Trial of Mary Dugan 41. Lady Be Good 41. *H. M. Pulham Esq.* 41. Joe Smith American 42. Cairo 42. Journey for Margaret 42. Sweet Rosie O'Grady 43. *Claudia* 43. The Canterville Ghost 44. The Enchanted Cottage 44. Those Endearing Young Charms 45. Lady Luck 46. Claudia and David 46. The Searching Wind 46. They Won't Believe Me 47. *Crossfire* 47. Sitting Pretty 48. The Forsyte Woman 49. And Baby Makes Three 50. The Second Woman 51. Goodbye My Fancy 51. The Half-Breed 52. The Secret of the Incas 54. Vanished (TV) 71. All My Darling Daughters (TV) 72. My Darling Daughters' Anniversary (TV) 73. Little Women (TV) 78. The Return of Marcus Welby MD 84. Mercy or Murder (TV) 86. Conspiracy of Love (TV) 87. A Holiday Affair (TV) 88. Talent for the Game 91, etc.
TV series: Father Knows Best 54–60. Window on Main Street 61. Marcus Welby MD 69–75.
❝ I was an introvert in an extrovert profession. – *R.Y.*

Young, Robert M. (1924–).
American director.
Nothing but a Man (co-d) 65. Alambrista! 77. Short Eyes 78. Rich Kids 79. One-Trick Pony 80. The Ballad of Gregorio Cortez (& co-w) 83. Saving Grace 86. Extremities 86. Dominick and Eugene 88. Triumph of the Spirit 89. Talent for the Game 91. Roosters 93. Solomon & Sheba (TV) 95. Slave of Dreams (TV) 95. Caught 96, etc.

Young, Roland (1887–1953).
British character actor with stage experience; made a screen career in Hollywood and is affectionately remembered for a gallery of whimsical or ineffectual types.
Sherlock Holmes (debut) 22. Moriarty 22. The Unholy Night 29. Madame Satan 30. New Moon 30. *One Hour with You* 32. Wedding Rehearsal (GB) 32. The Guardsman 32. His Double Life 33. *David Copperfield* (as Uriah Heep) 34. Ruggles of Red Gap 34. One Rainy Afternoon 36. *The Man Who Could Work Miracles* (GB) 36. Call It a Day 37. King Solomon's Mines (GB) 37. *Topper* (title role) (AAN) 37. Ali Baba Goes to Town 38. Sailing Along (GB) 38. *The Young in Heart* 39. Topper Takes a Trip 39. No No Nanette 40. *The Philadelphia Story* 40. Flame of New Orleans 41. Topper Returns 41. The Lady Has Plans 42. They All Kissed the Bride 42. Tales of Manhattan 42. Forever and a Day 43. Standing Room Only 44. And Then There Were None 45. Bond Street (GB) 47. The Great Lover 49. Let's Dance 50. St Benny the Dip 51. That Man from Tangier 53, many others.
✪ For his inimitable diffidence; and for becoming quite a character actor whenever he shaved off his moustache. *The Young in Heart*.
Famous line (*The Philadelphia Story*): 'Oh, this is one of those days that the pages of history teach us are best spent lying in bed.'

Young, Sean (1959–).
American leading actress, a former model.
Jane Austen in Manhattan 80. Stripes 81. Blade Runner 82. Young Doctors in Love 82. Baby: The Secret of the Lost Legend 85. Dune 85. Under the Biltmore Clock (TV) 85. No Way Out 87. Wall Street 87. The Boost 88. Cousins 89. Fire Birds 90. A Kiss before Dying 91. Once upon a Crime 92. Love Crimes 92. Hold Me, Thrill Me, Kiss Me 92. Blue Ice 92. Fatal Instinct 93. Ace Ventura, Pet Detective 94. Witness to the Execution (TV) 94.

Dr Jekyll and Ms Hyde 95. The Proprietor 96. The Invader 96. Evil Has a Face 96, etc.

Young, Stephen (1939–) (Stephen Levy).
Canadian leading man, former extra.

Cleopatra 63. Patton 70. Soylent Green 73. Lifeguard 75. Breaking Point 76. Between Friends 83. Who's Harry Crumb? 89. The Gumshoe Kid 90, etc.

TV series: Seaway 64. Judd for the Defence 66–68.

Young, Terence (1915–1994).
British screenwriter who became a successful director.

AS WRITER: On the Night of the Fire 39. Dangerous Moonlight 40, etc.

■ AS DIRECTOR: Corridor of Mirrors 48. One Night with You 48. Woman Hater 49. They Were Not Divided 50. Valley of Eagles 51. The Tall Headlines 52. The Red Beret 53. That Lady 55. Storm Over the Nile (co-d) 55. Safari 56. Zarak 56. Action of the Tiger 57. No Time to Die 57. Serious Charge 59. Too Hot to Handle 60. Black Tights 60. *Doctor No* 62. *From Russia with Love* 63. The Amorous Adventures of Moll Flanders 65. Thunderball 65. The Poppy Is Also a Flower 66. Secret War 66. Triple Cross 66. The Rover (It.) 66. *Wait until Dark* 67. Mayerling 68. The Christmas Tree 69. Cold Sweat 70. Red Sun 71. The Valachi Papers 72. War Goddess 73. The Klansman 74. Bloodline 79. Inchon 80. The Jigsaw Man 83. Sweet Revenge 86.

Young, Tony (1938–).
American leading man, from TV series *Gunslinger*.

He Rides Tall 63. Taggart 64. Charro 69. The Outfit 73.

Young, Victor (1900–1956).
American composer with over 300 film scores to his credit.

Fatal Lady 36. Wells Fargo 37. Golden Boy (AAN) 39. Raffles 40. The Way of All Flesh 40. Caught in the Draft 41. The Outlaw 41. Reap the

Wild Wind 42. Beyond the Blue Horizon 42. The Glass Key 42. The Palm Beach Story 42. For Whom the Bell Tolls (AAN) 43. Frenchman's Creek 44. Ministry of Fear 44. *The Uninvited* 44. Love Letters (AAN) 45. The Blue Dahlia 46. To Each His Own 47. Unconquered 47. Golden Earrings 47. The Big Clock 48. The Paleface 48. My Foolish Heart 49. Samson and Delilah (AAN) 49. Our Very Own 50. September Affair 50. My Favorite Spy 51. The Greatest Show on Earth 52. The Quiet Man 52. *Shane* 53. The Country Girl 54. Knock on Wood 54. Strategic Air Command 55. *Around the World in Eighty Days* (AA) 56. Omar Khayyam 57. Run of the Arrow 57. China Gate 57, many others.

Youngson, Robert (1917–1974).
American producer specializing in compilation films. Started as writer-director of short films, including *World of Kids* (AA) 50, *This Mechanical Age* (AA) 51. Later released omnibus editions of silent comedy snippets:

The Golden Age of Comedy 58. *When Comedy Was King* 59. Days of Thrills and Laughter 60. Thirty Years of Fun 62, etc.

Yu, Ronny.
Hong Kong director and screenwriter. He studied at the University of Ohio, after spending some time at school in England.

The Servants 79. The Saviour 80. The Trail 83. Legacy of Rage (& w) 87. China White 90. The Bride with White Hair/Jiang-Hu: Between Love and Glory 93. The Phantom Lover/Yebun Gosing (& co-w) 96. Bride of Chucky (US) 98, etc.

Yuan, Zhang (1963–).
Chinese director, a graduate of the Beijing Film Academy, from rock videos. The Chinese government has tried to prevent his films being shown outside the country.

Mama 91. Beijing Bastards/Beijing Zazhong 93. Sons/Erzi 96. East Palace, West Palace 97, etc.

Yuen, Anita (1971–) (Yuen Wing Yi).
Hong Kong leading actress.

C'est la Vie, Mon Chéri 93. Crossings 94. He's a Woman, She's a Man/Gam Tsi Yuk Yip 95. The Chinese Feast/Gamyuk Muntong 95. Hu-Du-Men 96. God of Gamblers 3 97, etc.

Yuen, Corey (Yuen Kuei).
Hong Kong director, martial arts expert, and actor. A contemporary of Jackie Chan and Sammo Hung at the Peking Opera, he is a former stuntman who has made two action films in Hollywood.

Ninja in the Dragon's Den 82. No Retreat No Surrender (US) 82. Yes, Madam 85. No Retreat No Surrender II 89. Fong Sai Yuk 93. Fong Sai Yuk II 93, etc.

Yule, Joe (1894–1950).
Scottish-born vaudeville comedian and actor who was best known on screen as Jiggs in the *Jiggs and Maggie* series, based on a popular comic strip about a working-class couple who win a sweepstake. He is the father of Mickey Rooney.

Sudden Money 39. Judge Hardy and Son 39. The Secret of Dr Kildare 39. Broadway Melody of 1940 40. New Moon 40. The Big Store 41. Billy the Kid 41. Born to Sing 42. Air Raid Wardens 43. The Thin Man Goes Home 44. Kismet 44. Two Girls and a Sailor 44. Bringing Up Father 46. Jiggs and Maggie in Jackpot Jitters 49. Jiggs and Maggie Out West 50, etc.

Yulin, Harris (1937–).
American general-purpose actor.

Doc 71. The Midnight Man 74. Night Moves 75. The Last Ride of the Dalton Gang (TV) 79. Steel 80. Scarface 83. The Believers 87. Fatal Beauty 87. Another Woman 88. Bad Dreams 88. Ghostbusters II 89. Tailspin 89. Narrow Margin 90. Final Analysis 92. The Last Hit (TV) 93. Stuart Saves His Family 95. CutThroat Island 95. Looking for Richard 96. Loch Ness 96. Multiplicity 96. If These Walls Could Talk 96. Murder at 1600 96. Hostile Waters 97. Bean 97, etc.

TV series: WIOU 90–91.

Yun-fat, Chow (Zhao Runfa).
Hong Kong leading actor, associated with the work of director John WOO. He began as a 17-year-old in television.

A Better Tomorrow 86. An Autumn's Tale/Qiutiande Tonghua 87. City on Fire 87. A Better Tomorrow III 89. The Killer/Diexue Shuang Xiong 89. All about Ah-Long 89. Triads – The Inside Story 90. Wild Search 90. Once a Thief 91. Hard-Boiled 92. Full Contact 93. The Replacement Killers (US) 98, many others.

Yung, Sen (1915–1980) (aka Victor Sen Yung).
Chinese-American character actor familiar 1938–48 as Charlie Chan's number-one son.

The Letter 40. Across the Pacific 42. The Breaking Point 50. The Left Hand of God 55. Flower Drum Song 61. A Flea in Her Ear 68, etc.

TV series: Bonanza 59–72. Bachelor Father 61.

Yurka, Blanche (1887–1974).
Czech-American character actress.

Autobiography: 1970, *Bohemian Girl*.

■ *A Tale of Two Cities* 36. Queen of the Mob 40. Escape 40. City for Conquest 40. Ellery Queen and the Murder Ring 41. Lady for a Night 42. Pacific Rendezvous 42. A Night to Remember 42. Keeper of the Flame 43. Tonight We Raid Calais 43. Hitler's Madman 43. The Bridge of San Luis Rey 44. Cry of the Werewolf 44. One Body Too Many 44. The Southerner 45. 13 rue Madeleine 46. The Flame 47. The Furies 50. At Sword's Point 51. Taxi 53. Thunder in the Sun 57.

Yuzna, Brian (1949–).
American producer and director of horror movies, born in the Philippines.

Re-Animator (p) 84. From Beyond (p) 86. Dolls (p) 87. Honey, I Shrunk the Kids (p, co-story) 89. Society (d) 89. Bride of Re-Animator (d) 89. Return of the Living Dead 3 (p, d) 93. Necronomicon (p, co-d) 93. Crying Freeman (p) 95. The Dentist (d) 96, etc.

Zadok, Arnon (1949–).
Israeli leading actor, and director.
Stigma 82. Beyond the Walls 84. War Zone/
Deadline 87. Unsettled Land 88. Torn Apart (US)
90. White Knight/Laila Lavin (& wd) 95, etc.

Zadora, Pia (1954–) (Pia Schipani).
American actress, usually in exaggeratedly sexy
roles, and singer, on screen as a juvenile.
Santa Claus Conquers the Martians 64. Butterfly
81. Fake-Out 82. The Lonely Lady 83. Pajama Tops
83. Voyage of the Rock Aliens 87. Hairspray 88,
etc.

Zaentz, Saul (1921–).
Independent producer who, unusually, tends to
finance films with his own money. He owned the
record label Fantasy Records, which published the
hit group Creedence Clearwater Revival in the
mid-60s.
Payday 72. One Flew over the Cuckoo's Nest
(AA) 75. The Lord of the Rings 78. Amadeus
(AA) 84. Mosquito Coast 86. The Unbearable
Lightness of Being 88. At Play in the Fields of the
Lord 91. *The English Patient* (AA) 96, etc.
66 The question is why does Hollywood go on
making crap they pass off as movies? The answer is
money. – S.Z.

Zahn, Steve (c. 1968–).
American actor. Born in Marshall, Minnesota, he
began in the theatre and spent two years training
with the American Repertory Theater in
Cambridge, Massachusetts. Married actress Robyn
Peterman.
Rain without Thunder 92. Reality Bites 94.
Armed Response 95. Crimson Tide 95. Race the
Sun 96. That Thing You Do! 96. SubUrbia 97.
Subway Stories: Tales from the Underground
(TV) 97. The Object of My Affection 98. From
the Earth to the Moon (TV) 98. Out of Sight 98,
etc.

Zaillian, Steve (1951–).
American screenwriter and director, a former
editor.
The Falcon and the Snowman (w) 85.
Awakenings (AANw) 90. Jack the Bear (w) 93.
Searching for Bobby Fischer/Innocent Moves (wd)
93. *Schindler's List* (AAw) 94. Clear and Present
Danger (co-w) 94. A Civil Action (wd) 98, etc.

Zamachowski, Zbigniew (1961–).
Polish leading actor, born in Brzeziny.
The Big Picnic/Wielka Majowka 81. Pierscien I
Roza 86. Ten Commandments, Part 10 (TV) 89.
Dr Kurczak 89. Seychelles/Seszele 90. Kanalia 91.
Ferdydurke 91. Ptak 91. Sauna 92. Three Colours:
White/Trzy Kolory: Bialy 93. Three Colours: Blue/
Trzy Kolory: Niebieski 93. Turned Back/Zawrocony
93. Three Colours: Red/Trzy Kolory: Czerwony 94.
Once Upon a Dream (Swiss) 95. Merry Christmas
and a Happy New York/Szczesliwego Nowego Jorku
98, etc.

Zampa, Luigi (1905–1991).
Italian director, formerly scriptwriter. Films, all on
neo-realist lines, include:
To Live in Peace 46. City on Trial 52. *The Woman
of Rome* 54.

Zampi, Mario (1903–1963).
Italian director, long in Britain, mainly involved
in semi-crazy comedies which he usually wrote
and produced.
The Fatal Night 48. *Laughter in Paradise* 50. Top
Secret 52. Happy Ever After 54. The Naked Truth
56. Too Many Crooks 58. Five Golden Hours 61,
etc.

Zane, Billy (1965–).
American actor.
Dead Calm 88. The Hillside Strangler (TV) 89.
Back to the Future II 89. Memphis Belle 90. Billions/
Miliardi 91. Blood and Concrete 91. Femme Fatale
91. Millions 91. Orlando 92. Sniper 93. Posse 93.
Tombstone 94. Flashfire 94. Reflections on a Crime
94. The Silence of the Hams (It.) 94. Only You 94.
Tales from the Crypt Presents the Demon Knight
95. The Phantom (title role) 96. Head above Water
96. This World, Then the Fireworks 97. Titanic
97. Pocahontas II: Journey to a New World (voice)
98. I Woke Up Early the Day I Died (& p) 98.
Susan's Plan 98, etc.

Zanuck, Darryl F. (1902–1979).
American production executive. Started career in
the 20s, writing stories for Rin Tin Tin.
Production chief for Warners 1931. Co-founder
Twentieth-Century Productions 1933; merged
with Fox 1935. Vice-president in charge of
production for Twentieth Century-Fox 1935–52,
then independent; returned in 1962 as executive
president. He was romantically involved with
actresses Dolores COSTELLO, Linda DARNELL,
Carol LANDIS and Gene TIERNEY. He also
attempted unsuccessfully to make stars of his lover
Bella DARVI and of French singer Juliette
GRECO.
Biography: 1998, *Twentieth Century's Fox* by
George F. Custen.
Book: 1993, *Memo from Darryl Zanuck: The
Golden Years at Twentieth Century Fox*, edited by
Rudy Behlmer.
Clive of India 35. Lloyds of London 37. *In Old
Chicago* 38. Drums along the Mohawk 40. *The
Grapes of Wrath* 40. How Green Was My Valley 42.
Wilson 45. Gentleman's Agreement 47. All about
Eve 50. Twelve o'Clock High 51. Viva Zapata 52.
Island in the Sun 57. Roots of Heaven 58. *The
Longest Day* (& d scenes) 62.
Under the name Mark Canfield wrote the
screenplay of Crack in the Mirror 60.
✪ For being Hollywood's most efficient mogul,
and for making very good films. *The Grapes of
Wrath*.
66 The hardiest and longest-lived of the moguls
of Hollywood's golden age was somehow the most
disappointing in terms of colour and personality.
His most personal trait was his allegedly avid
sexual appetite, though he himself said:
Any of my indiscretions were with people,
not actresses.
He was a tough employer:
There was only one boss I believed in, and
that was me.
As his biographer Mel Gussow said:
He couldn't stand stubbornness in anybody
but himself.
He spent 35 years, more or less, as boss of
Twentieth Century-Fox, and before that for 10
years was production head of Warners. His ideas
for remakes were legendary:
I want to do Air Force in a submarine.
Another of his credos is now outdated:
When you get a sex story in biblical garb,
you can open your own mint.
He produced many worthy films, perhaps for
rather stodgy reasons:
We are in the business primarily to provide
entertainment, but in doing so we do not dodge
the issue if we can also provide enlightenment.
Or, more pithily:
I know audiences feed on crap, but I cannot
believe we are so lacking that we cannot dish it
up to them with some trace of originality.
On another occasion, however, he was
optimistic:
Public taste is an ascending spiral.

But his final production philosophy was:
Take a chance and spend a million dollars
and hope you're right.
Time summed him up in 1950:
He is richly endowed with tough-mindness,
talent, an outsized ego, and a glutton's craving for
hard work.
And his son has the last word:
He had guts. He was willing to take the
responsibility and the blame. He would say yes or
no. They would ask is it any good, and if he
thought it was, that was enough to put it into
production.
Don't say yes until I finish talking! – D.F.Z. (also
the title of his biography by Mel Gussow)
I decided to become a genius. – D.F.Z.
As I see it today, the boss of the Studio is actually
no longer a boss – he has a title but that is all. He
is the slave of agents and actors with their own
corporations and insane competition from
independent operators and promoters. – D.F.Z.,
1961
Success in movies boils down to three things:
story, story, story. – D.F.Z.
From Poland to Polo in one generation. – Arthur
Mayer on D.F.Z.
A narrow bastard with only two interests in life,
making movies and satisfying his cock. – Henry
Fonda on D.F.Z.

Zanuck, Lili Fini (1954–).
American producer and director, married to
producer Richard ZANUCK.
AS PRODUCER: Cocoon 84. Cocoon II 88.
Driving Miss Daisy (AA) 89. Clean Slate 94. Wild
Bill 95. Mulholland Falls 96, etc.
AS DIRECTOR: Rush 91.

Zanuck, Richard (1934–).
American producer who started career as assistant
to his father, Darryl F. ZANUCK. Solo ventures:
Compulsion 59. Sanctuary 61. The Chapman
Report 62, etc.
Was vice-president in charge of production for
Twentieth Century-Fox; moved to Warner 1971.
In 1972 he founded the independent production
company Zanuck/Brown with David Brown. That
partnership ended in 1988 when he formed the
Zanuck Company with his wife Lili Fini ZANUCK.
■ The Sting 73. Jaws (AAN) 75. MacArthur 77.
The Island 80. Neighbors 81. The Verdict 82.
Cocoon 84. Target 84. Cocoon: The Return 88.
Driving Miss Daisy (AA) 89. Rush 91. Clean Slate
94. Wild Bill 95. Deep Impact 98.

Zanussi, Krzystof (1939–).
Polish director.
Illumination 73. The Spiral 78. Night Paths 79.
The Constant Factor 80. Imperative 82. The Year
of the Quiet Sun 84. Power of Evil 85. Wherever
You Are 88. Life for a Life – Maximilian Kolbe
90. The Touch/Dotkniecie 92. At Full Gallop 96,
etc.

Zappa, Frank (1940–1993).
American composer, bandleader, and director,
whose extended concert performances were
occasionally filmed. In the 60s, he scored some 'B'
movies.
Book: 1994, *Frank Zappa: The Negative Dialectics
of Poodle Play* by Ben Watson.
The World's Greatest Sinner (m) 62. Run Home
Slow (m) 65. Head (a) 68. 200 Motels (a, co-d,
m) 71. Baby Snakes (a, d, m) 79, etc.

Zavattini, Cesare (1902–1989).
Italian scriptwriter and film theorist.
Shoeshine (AAN) 46. Bicycle Thieves (AAN) 48.
Miracle in Milan 51. First Communion 51. Umberto

D (AAN) 52. Gold of Naples 55. The Roof 56.
Two Women 61. Marriage Italian Style 64. A
Brief Vacation 75, etc.

Zaza, Paul.
Canadian composer, frequently for the films of
director Bob Clark.
Title Shot 79. Prom Night (co-m) 80. My Bloody
Valentine 81. Porky's (co-m) 81. Curtains 83.
Turk 182 85. From the Hip 87. Meatballs III 87.
Loose Cannons 90. Popcorn 91. Cold Sweat 93.
It Runs in the Family 94. Iron Eagle IV 95. Salt
Water Moose 96. The Rage 96. No Contest II 97.
Misbegotten 97. A Brooklyn State of Mind 97.
Stag 97, etc.

Zecca, Ferdinand (1864–1947).
French pioneer producer.
The Prodigy 01. Catastrophe in Martinique 04.
Vendetta 05. Whence Does He Come? 06. Mutiny
in Odessa 07. The Dreyfus Affair 08. The Dissolute
Woman 10, etc.

Zeffirelli, Franco (1922–).
Italian stage director turning to films.
The Taming of the Shrew 66. Romeo and Juliet
(AAN) 68. Brother Sun and Sister Moon 73. Jesus
of Nazareth (TV) 77. The Champ 79. Endless Love
81. *La Traviata* 82. Otello 86. Young Toscanini
88. Hamlet 90. Sparrow/Storia di una Capinera 93.
Jane Eyre 96. Tea with Mussolini 99, etc.

Zegers, Kevin (1984–).
Canadian child actor, born in St Mary's, Ontario.
Life with Mickey 93. Thicker than Blood: The
Larry McLinden Story 93. In the Mouth of
Madness 95. Air Bud 97. Nico the Unicorn 97. A
Call to Remember (TV) 97. Shadowbuilder 98. Air
Bud: Golden Receiver 98, etc.
TV series: Traders 96.

Zehetbauer, Rolf.
German production designer.
Cabaret (AA) 72. The Serpent's Egg 77.
Twilight's Last Gleaming 77. Brass Target 78.
From the Life of the Marionettes 80. The Boat/
Das Boot (Ger.) 80. Lili Marleen 81. Lola 82. The
Neverending Story 84. Enemy Mine 85. Brother
of Sleep 95. Comedian Harmonists 97, etc.

Zellweger, Renée (1969–).
American leading actress, of Swiss and Norwegian
parents. Born in Katy, Texas, she studied at the
University of Texas, where her experience on a
drama course persuaded her to become an actress.
A Taste for Killing (TV) 92. My Boyfriend's Back
93. Dazed and Confused 93. Love and a.45 94.
Reality Bites 94. The Return of the Texas
Chainsaw Massacre/The Texas Chainsaw
Massacre: The Next Generation 94. The Low Life
95. Empire Records 95. Jerry Maguire 96. The Whole
Wide World 96. Liar 97. One True Thing 98, etc.

Zelnik, Fred (1885–1950).
Rumanian director of English films in the 30s.
Happy 32. Mr Cinders 34. The Lilac Domino
37. I Killed the Count 39. Give Me the Stars (p
only) 44. The Glass Mountain (p only) 49, etc.

Zelniker, Michael.
Canadian actor.
Hog Wild 80. Pick Up Summer 80. Heartaches
81. The Terry Fox Story (TV) 83. Bird 88. Queens
Logic 91. The Naked Lunch 91. Glory Enough for
All: The Discovery of Insulin (TV) 92. Within the
Rock 96. Stuart Bliss (& p, co-w) 98, etc.

Zeman, Karel (1910–1989).
Czech producer-director of trick and fantasy films of which the best known internationally are *Journey to Primeval Times* 55 and *Baron Münchausen* 61.

Zemeckis, Robert (1952–).
American director and screenwriter, one of the brightest of the movie brats. He set up his own production company, Image-Movers, in 1997. In 1998 he gave $5m to the University of Southern California for the creation of a digital arts studio.
I Wanna Hold Your Hand 78. Used Cars 80. Romancing the Stone 84. *Back to the Future* (wd) (AANw) 85. *Who Framed Roger Rabbit?* (d) 88. Back to the Future II (d, story) 89. Back to the Future III (d, story) 90. Looters (co-w) 92. Death Becomes Her (d) 92. *Forrest Gump* (AA) 94. Contact 97, etc.
❝ When I showed Twentieth Century-Fox the finished cut of *Romancing the Stone*, they fired me from *Cocoon*. It's the great mystery of my career. – *R.Z.*

Zerbe, Anthony (1936–).
American character actor.
Will Penny 67. The Liberation of L. B. Jones 69. The Omega Man 71. The Life and Times of Judge Roy Bean 72. The Laughing Policeman 73. Farewell My Lovely 75. The Turning Point 77. The First Deadly Sin 80. The Dead Zone 83. North and South (TV) 86. Opposing Force 87. Private Investigations 87. Licence to Kill 89. See No Evil, Hear No Evil 89. Touch 96. Asteroid (TV) 97, etc.
TV series: Harry O 74–76. Centennial 78–80. North and South, Book II 89. The Young Riders 89–92.

Zeta-Jones, Catherine (1969–).
Welsh leading actress, born in Swansea, from the musical theatre.
1001 Nights/Les Mille et Une Nuits (Fr.) 89. Out of the Blue (TV) 91. Christopher Columbus: The Discovery 92. Splitting Heirs 93. The Cinder Path (TV) 94. The Return of the Native (TV) 94. Catherine the Great (TV) 95. Blue Juice 95. The Phantom 96. Titanic (TV) 96. The Mask of Zorro (US) 98. Entrapment (US) 99, etc.
TV series: The Darling Buds of May 91–93.

Zetterling, Mai (1925–1994).
Swedish director, screenwriter and leading actress who first gained fame in Britain. She is also a novelist. Born in Vasteras, she trained at the National Theatre School in Stockholm. Her second husband was the novelist David Hughes. Her lovers included Herbert Lom, Peter Finch, and Tyrone Power.
Autobiography: 1985, *All Those Tomorrows*.
■ *Frenzy* 44. Frieda 47. The Bad Lord Byron 48. Portrait from Life 48. *Quartet* 48. The Romantic Age 49. Blackmailed 50. Hell is Sold Out 51. The Tall Headlines 53. The Ringer 52. Desperate Moment 53. Dance Little Lady 54. Knock on Wood 54. A Prize of Gold 55. Seven Waves Away 56. The Truth about Women 58. Jetstorm 59. Faces in the Dark 60. Piccadilly Third Stop 60. Offbeat 61. The Man Who Finally Died 62. *Only Two Can Play* 62. The Main Attraction 62. The Bay of St Michel 63. The Vine Bridge 65. The Witches 90. Hidden Agenda 90. Morfars Resa 93.
■ AS DIRECTOR: The War Game 62. Loving Couples 64. Night Games 66. Doctor Glas 68. Visions of Eight (part) 73. Scrubbers 83. Amarosa 86.
❝ I have been a child, a girl, a party doll, a mistress, a wife, a mother, a professional woman, a virgin, a grandmother. I have been a woman for more than fifty years and yet I have never been able to discover precisely what it is I am, how real I am. I ask myself – perhaps my femaleness is just a human disease. – *M.Z.*

Zhuangzhuang, Tian (1952–).
Chinese director, a former cameraman who graduated from the Beijing Film Academy in the early 80s. His films have caused controversy in his homeland and post-production work on *The Blue Kite* had to be done outside the country.
September/Jiuyue 84. On the Killing Ground/ Liechang Zhasa 85. Horse Thief/Daoma Zei 86. The Travelling Players/Gushu Yiren 87. Rock Kids/ Yaogun Qingnian 88. Li Lianying, the Imperial Eunuch/Da Taijian Li Lianying 91. The Blue Kite/ Lan Fengzheng 93, etc.

❝ Sometimes I think how silly I am: knowing that making films in China is probably the most difficult thing I could do, and still wanting to do it. But the first time I stood behind a camera and heard it rolling, I got so excited. – *T.Z.*

Zidi, Claude (1934–).
French director and producer, a former cinematographer.
Stuntwoman 81. Le Cop/My New Partner/Les Ripoux 85. Le Cop 2/Ripoux contre Ripoux 89. La Totale 91. Profil Bas 94. True Lies (oa) 94. Ma Femme Me Quitte 95. Arlette 96. Astérix et Obélix 98, etc.

Zieff, Howard (1943–).
American director.
■ Hearts of the West 75. Slither 76. House Calls 78. The Main Event 79. Private Benjamin 80. Unfaithfully Yours 83. The Dream Team 89. My Girl 91. My Girl 2 94.

Ziegfeld, Florenz (1867–1932).
American Broadway impresario who had three films named after him (*The Great Ziegfeld, Ziegfeld Girl, Ziegfeld Follies*). He was impersonated in two of them by William Powell and in *Funny Girl* by Walter Pidgeon. He also 'supervised' 1929's *Glorifying the American Girl*.
Biography: 1973, *Ziegfeld* by Charles Higham.

Ziegler, William (c. 1909–1977).
American editor.
The Housekeeper's Daughter 39. No Hands on the Clock 41. Minesweeper 43. Abie's Irish Rose 46. Rope 49. *Strangers on a Train* 51. The Desert Song 53. Rebel without a Cause 55. Auntie Mame 58. Ice Palace 60. *The Music Man* 62. My Fair Lady 64. A Fine Madness 66. Firecreek 68. Topaz 69. The Omega Man 71, many others.

Zielinski, Jerzy (1950–).
Polish-born cinematographer, in international films.
Aria for an Athlete/Aria dla Atlety 80. Shivers/ Dreszcze 81. Cal (GB) 84. The Flight of the Spruce Goose (US) 86. Valentino Returns (US) 87. Stars and Bars (US) 88. The January Man (US) 89. Fools of Fortune (US) 90. Escape from the Liberty Cinema/Ucieczka Z Kina Wolnosc 91. Paradise (US) 91. Swing Kids (US) 93. Houseguest (US) 95. Powder (US) 95. Washington Square (US) 97. That Darn Cat (US) 97, etc.

Ziemann, Sonja (1926–).
German leading actress.
Ein Windstoss 42. Girl of the Black Forest 50. Made in Heaven (GB) 52. My Sister and I 54. Menschen im Hotel 59. A Matter of Who 62. The Bridge at Remagen 69. De Sade 70, etc.

Zimbalist, Efrem, Jnr (1918–).
American leading man with stage experience; plays characters who inspire confidence.
House of Strangers 49. Band of Angels 57. Too Much Too Soon 58. By Love Possessed 61. A Fever in the Blood 61. The Chapman Report 62. The Reward 65. Wait until Dark 67. Airport 75 74. A Family Upside Down (TV) 78. Terror out of the Sky 78. Hot Shots! 91. Batman: Mask of the Phantasm (voice) 94, etc.
TV series: 77 Sunset Strip 58–63. The F.B.I. 65–73. Scruples 80. Hotel 86.

Zimbalist, Sam (1904–1958).
American producer.
The Crowd Roars 38. Boom Town 40. King Solomon's Mines 50. Quo Vadis 51. Mogambo 53. Beau Brummell 54. Ben Hur 59 (died during production), etc.

Zimbalist, Stephanie (1956–).
American actress, mainly on television. Born in New York City, she is the daughter of Efrem ZIMBALIST, Jnr.
The Gathering (TV) 77. Forever 78. The Magic of Lassie 78. The Best Place to Be (TV) 79. The Awakening 80. The Babysitter (TV) 80. Elvis and the Beauty Queen (TV) 81. Tommorrow's Child (TV) 82. Love on the Run (TV) 85. Personals (TV) 90. The Story Lady (TV) 91. Jericho Fever (TV) 93. The Great Elephant Escape (TV) 95. Stop the World, I Want to Get Off (TV) 96. Dead Ahead (TV) 96, etc.
TV series: Centennial 78–79. Remington Steele 82–86.

Zimmer, Hans (1958–).
German-born musician and composer, now working in Hollywood. He was a member of the British pop group The Buggles, who had a hit with 'Video Killed the Radio Star' 79, and collaborated with composer Stanley Myers on several films before his first solo score for *A World Apart*.
Moonlighting (co-m) 82. Success Is the Best Revenge (co-m) 84. Insignificance (co-m) 85. A World Apart 87. Double Exposure 87. The Nature of the Beast (co-m) 88. Burning Secret 88. Paperhouse 88. The Fruit Machine 88. Rain Man (AAN) 88. Driving Miss Daisy 89. Diamond Skulls 89. Black Rain 89. Twister 89. Bird on a Wire 90. Chicago Joe and the Showgirl 90. Days of Thunder 90. Fools of Fortune 90. Pacific Heights 90. Green Card 90. The Neverending Story II: The Next Chapter 90. Backdraft 91. Regarding Henry 91. Thelma and Louise 91. Where Sleeping Dogs Lie 91. Radio Flyer 92. A League of Their Own 92. Point of No Return 93. Younger and Younger 93. True Romance 93. Calendar Girl 93. Cool Runnings 93. The House of the Spirits 94. I'll Do Anything 94. Renaissance Man 94. The Lion King (AA) 94. Crimson Tide 95. Beyond Rangoon 95. Nine Months 95. Something to Talk About 95. Two Deaths 95. Broken Arrow 96. The Fan 96. The Rock 96. Muppet Treasure Island 96. The Preacher's Wife (AAN) 96. The Peacemaker 97. *As Good as It Gets* (AAN) 97. The Thin Red Line 98, etc.

Zimmerman, Enrique.
Venezuelan director who directed, with Lucas Manzano, that country's first feature film, *La Dama de las Cayenas* 13, based on Alexander Dumas's *Camille*.

Zinnemann, Fred (1907–1997).
Austrian-born director with varied experience before going to Hollywood in 1929. Born in Vienna, he first planned to be a musician, then studied law at the University of Vienna, and worked as an assistant cameraman in France and Germany. In the USA, he began as an extra in *All Quiet on the Western Front*, became a script clerk, and directed shorts, including *That Mothers Might Live* (AA) 38, and episodes of *Crime Does Not Pay* in the late 30s and early 40s. After a tentative start as a director, he scored a box-office success with *High Noon* in the early 50s, and a succession of well-crafted, popular movies followed. He was conscious of his own worth: when one gauche young movie executive summoned him to his office and said to him, 'Tell me about a few things you've done,' Zinnemann paused and said, 'You first.'
Autobiography: 1992, *A Life in Movies*.
■ Kid Glove Killer 42. Eyes in the Night 42. *The Seventh Cross* 44. Little Mister Jim 46. My Brother Talks to Horses 47. The Search (AAN) 48. *Act of Violence* 49. *The Men* 50. Teresa 51. *High Noon* (AAN) 52. The Member of the Wedding 53. *From Here to Eternity* (AA) 53. Oklahoma 55. A Hatful of Rain 57. *The Nun's Story* (AAN) 58. *The Sundowners* (AAN) 60. Behold a Pale Horse 64. *A Man for All Seasons* (AAp, AAd) 66. The Day of the Jackal 73. Julia (AAN) 77. Five Days One Summer 82.
❝ I'm not in pictures to promote my private personality. I'm in it for the joy of it. – *F.Z.*
John Ford told me, 'Don't give them too much extra film, then they can't cut it a different way.' – *F.Z.*

Zinner, Peter (1919–).
Austrian-born film editor in Hollywood.
The Professionals 60. Gunn 67. In Cold Blood 67. Changes 69. Darling Lili 70. The Red Tent 71. The Godfather (AAN) 71. The Godfather Part II 74. Mahogany 75. Foxtrot 76. A Star Is Born 76. The Deer Hunter (AA) 78. Foolin' Around 80. An Officer and a Gentleman (AAN) 82. The Salamander (& d) 82. Saving Grace 86. The Hunt for Red October (AAN) 90. Eternity 90. Gladiator 92. Motel Blue 97, etc.

Zito, Joseph (1946–).
American director of horror and action movies.
The Abduction 81. The Prowler 82. Friday the 13th: The Final Chapter 84. Missing in Action 84. Invasion USA 85. Red Scorpion 88. Barr Sinister 90, etc.

Zola, Emile (1840–1902).
Prolific French novelist of the seamy side. Works filmed include *Nana, La Bête Humaine* and *Thérèse Raquin*. A 1937 biopic, *The Life of Emile Zola*, starred Paul Muni and centred on Zola's participation in the Dreyfus case.

Zorina, Vera (1917–) (Eva Brigitta Hartwig).
Norwegian ballet dancer and actress in American films. Now retired. She was married to choreographer George Balanchine (1938–46).
The Goldwyn Follies 39. On Your Toes 39. *I Was an Adventuress* 40. Star Spangled Rhythm 43. Follow the Boys 44.

Zsigmond, Vilmos (1930–).
Hungarian cinematographer.
Deliverance 72. Images 72. The Long Goodbye 73. Scarecrow 73. Cinderella Liberty 73. The Sugarland Express 74. The Girl from Petrovka 74. Obsession 76. Close Encounters of the Third Kind (AA) 77. The Deer Hunter (AAN) 78. Flesh and Blood (TV) 79. Winter Kills 79. The Rose 79. Heaven's Gate 80. Blow Out 81. Jinxed 82. Table for Five 83. The River (AAN) 84. Real Genius 85. The Witches of Eastwick 87. Journey to Spirit Island 88. Fat Man and Little Boy/The Shadowmakers 89. Bonfire of the Vanities 90. The Two Jakes 90. The Long Shadow (d) 92. Stalin (TV) 93. Sliver 93. Intersection 93. Maverick 94. The Crossing Guard 95. Assassins 95. The Ghost and the Darkness 96, etc.

Zucco, George (1886–1960).
Sepulchral-toned British stage actor, long in Hollywood and typecast in horror films in which he admirably exuded upper-bracket malignancy.
Autumn Crocus 30. Dreyfus 31. The Good Companions 32. The Man Who Could Work Miracles 35. Marie Antoinette 38. *The Cat and the Canary* 39. The Hunchback of Notre Dame 39. Arise My Love 40. *The Mummy's Hand* 40. *The Adventures of Sherlock Holmes* (as Moriarty) 40. Sherlock Holmes in Washington 42. The Black Swan 42. Dead Men Walk 43. The Black Raven 43. The Mad Ghoul 43. House of Frankenstein 45. Fog Island 45. Dr Renault's Secret 46. The Pirate 47. Joan of Arc 48. Madame Bovary 49. Let's Dance 50. David and Bathsheba 51. The First Legion 51, many others.

Zucker, David (1947–).
American director and screenwriter who began collaborating with his brother Jerry and Jim Abrahams on a series of broad and sometimes satirical comedies.
The Kentucky Fried Movie (co-wd) 77. Airplane! (co-wd) 80. Top Secret! (co-wd) 84. Ruthless People (co-d) 86. The Naked Gun: From the Files of Police Squad (d) 88. The Naked Gun 2½: The Smell of Fear (co-w, d) 91. Naked Gun 33 : The Final Insult (p, co-w) 94. High School High (co-p, co-w) 96. BASEketball (co-p, co-w, d) 98, etc.
TV series: Police Squad 82.

Zucker, Jerry (1950–).
American director and screenwriter, usually in collaboration with his brother David and Jim Abrahams. His first solo effort as a director was *Ghost*, the biggest box-office success of 1990.
The Kentucky Fried Movie (co-wd) 77. Airplane! (co-wd) 80. Top Secret! (co-wd) 84. Ruthless People (co-d) 86. The Naked Gun: From the Files of Police Squad (co-w) 88. Ghost (d) 90. My Life (p) 93. First Knight (d) 95. My Best Friend's Wedding (p) 97, etc.
TV series: Police Squad 82.

Zuckmayer, Carl (1896–1977).
German playwright whose *The Captain from Koepenick* has been much filmed. His screenplays include:
The Blue Angel 30. Escape Me Never 35. *Rembrandt* 36. Mayerling 40. I Was a Criminal 41.

Zugsmith, Albert (1910–).
American producer-director with a taste for exploitation subjects.
Written on the Wind (p) 57. The Tattered Dress (p) 57. The Incredible Shrinking Man (p) 58. Touch of Evil (p) 58. High School Confidential (d) 60. Teacher Was a Sexpot (d) 60. The Private Life of Adam and Eve (d) 61. Confessions of an Opium Eater (d) 63. Fanny Hill (p) 64. Movie Star

American Style (or LSD I Hate You) (d) 66. The Incredible Sex Revolution (d) 67, etc.

Zukor, Adolph (1873–1976).

Hungarian-born film pioneer. Emigrated to America, became film salesman, nickelodeon owner, and independent producer (in 1913), by persuading New York stage stars James O'Neill, James K. Hackett and Minnie Maddern Fiske to appear in productions of, respectively, *The Count of Monte Cristo*, *The Prisoner of Zenda* and *Tess of the D'Urbervilles*. This was the start of 'Famous Players', which in 1916 merged with Jesse Lasky's production interests and later became Paramount Pictures. He remained board chairman of the latter from 1935.

Autobiography: 1945, *The Public Is Never Wrong*.

✪ For being the industry's first centenarian. *The Covered Wagon*.

66 Fish stinks from the head. – A.Z.

If I'd known I was going to live this long, I'd have taken better care of myself. – A.Z.

~Special Academy Award 1948 'for his services to the industry over a period of 40 years'.

Zulawski, Andrzej (1940–).

Polish-born director of bleak dramas that blossom into fantasy. Born in the Ukraine, he studied film at IDHEC, political science in Paris, and philosophy at the University of Warsaw. He began as an assistant to Andrzej WAJDA in the early 60s and made his first films for television. He left Poland after his second film, *The Devil*, was banned by the authorities, and moved to France. He is also a novelist and theatre director. He has a son by his partner, actress Sophie MARCEAU.

The Third Part of the Night/Trzecia Czesc Nocy 71. The Devil/Diabel 72. The Main Thing Is to Love/L'Important C'Est d'Aimer 75. The Silver Globe/Na Srebrnym Globie 77. Possession 80. The Public Woman/La Femme Publique 84. Mad Love/L'Amour Braque 85. My Nights Are More Beautiful than Your Days/Mes Nuits Sont Plus Belles que Vos Jours 88. Boris Godunov 89. Blue Note/La Note Bleue 91. Szamanka 96, etc.

Zurinaga, Marco.

Puerto Rican director and screenwriter.

Step Away 79. La Gran Fiesta 86. Tango Bar 88. A Flor de Piel (TV) 90. The Disappearance of Garcia Lorca 96, etc.

Zweig, Stefan (1881–1942).

Austrian novelist. Films of his books include *Beware of Pity*, *Twenty-Four Hours of a Woman's Life*, *Letter from an Unknown Woman*.

Zwick, Edward (1952–).

American director and screenwriter who began as a magazine journalist. He also created the hit TV series *thirtysomething* 87–91.

Having It All (TV) 82. Special Bulletin (TV) 83. About Last Night . . . 86. Glory 89. Leaving Normal 92. Legends of the Fall 94. Courage under Fire 96. The Siege 98, etc.

TV series: Family 76–80.

Last Words

A few favourite unclassifiable moments.

Bette Davis, on having pointed out to her a starlet who had allegedly slept her way to the top:
" I see – she's the original good time that was had by all.

Billy Wilder to his cinematographer during the filming of *Sunset Boulevard:*
" Johnny, keep it out of focus. I want to win the foreign picture award.

An anonymous wartime crack:
" In case of an air raid, go directly to RKO: they haven't had a hit in years.

Will Rogers, philosophizing:
" What's the salvation of the movies? I say, run 'em backwards. It can't hurt, and it's worth a trial.

King Vidor, evaluating one of his own movies:
" The picture was so bad they had to do retakes before they could put it on the shelf.

Carole Lombard, refusing a role in an Orson Welles film:
" I can't win working with Welles. If the picture's a hit he will get the credit, and if it's a flop, I'll be blamed.

John Grierson, evaluating the decline of Josef Von Sternberg:
" When a director dies, he becomes a photographer.

Sir Cedric Hardwicke on judgement by sneak preview:
" On Hollywood's theory that the audience knows best, the schoolboy's 'lousy' becomes the last word in dramatic criticism.

Jean Renoir, leaving Hollywood after an enforced wartime sojourn:
" Goodbye, Mr Zanuck: it certainly has been a pleasure working at 16th Century Fox.

Howard Hawks, commenting on his penchant for remaking films with similar characters and situations:
" When you find out a thing goes pretty well, you might as well do it again.

Victor Mature, when Rita Hayworth deserted him for Orson Welles, with whom she had been working in a charity magic act:
" Apparently the way to a girl's heart is to saw her in half.

Walter Wanger on Hollywood gossip columnists:
" This is the only industry that finances its own blackmail.

Robert Lord on the film city:
" It's such nonsense, this immorality of Hollywood. We're all too tired.

Robert Benchley after viewing an arty film:
" There's less in this than meets the eye.

And Spencer Tracy, on finding himself working for a director with 'artistic' ideas who tried to turn every gesture into a symbol:
" I'm too tired and old and rich for all this, so let's do the scene.

Wilson Mizner on Hollywood egos:
" Some of the greatest love affairs I've known involved one actor, unassisted.

And Graham Greene on actors' shelf-life:
" For an actor, success is simply delayed failure.

Although Will Rogers thought differently:
" The movies are the only business where you can go out front and applaud yourself.

Billy Wilder, setting up Gloria Swanson's attempted suicide in *Sunset Boulevard:*
" Johnny, it's the usual slashed-wrist shot.

Robert Mitchum perhaps put it all into perspective:
" What's history going to say about the movies? All those rows of seats facing a blank screen. Crazy!

A final thought from Auguste Lumière, pioneer of cinematography, in 1895:
" Young man, you can be grateful that my invention is not for sale, for it would undoubtedly ruin you. It can be exploited for a certain time as a scientific curiosity, but apart from that it has no commercial value whatsoever.

2

Movie Remakes, Series, Themes and Genres

Abie's Irish Rose.

Anne Nichols' long-running Broadway comedy of 1927, about a Catholic girl marrying into a Jewish family, has twice been filmed: by Victor Fleming in 1928 and by Edward Sutherland in 1946. The theme has frequently been borrowed, as in the 1973 TV series *Bridget Loves Bernie*.

abortion,

unmentionable on the screen for many years save in Continental dramas like *Carnet de Bal* 37, and officially ostracized exploitation pictures like *Amok* 34, was first permitted as a Hollywood plot point in *Detective Story* 51. Six years later, *Blue Denim* concerned an abortion that was prevented; and the later abortion scenes in *The Best of Everything* 59, *Sweet Bird of Youth* 62, *The Interns* 62, and *Love with the Proper Stranger* 64 scarcely displayed an obsession with the subject. Meanwhile however the British gave it full rein in *Saturday Night and Sunday Morning* 60, *The L-Shaped Room* 62, *Alfie* 66, and *Up the Junction* 68; by which time it had certainly lost its shock value. By 1969 Hollywood felt confident enough to use it as the plot point of a commercial thriller, *Daddy's Gone A-Hunting*, and in 1972 it became the specific subject of *To Find A Man*.

Accent on Youth.

Samson Raphaelson's successful Broadway play about a lazy playwright spurred to success by his young secretary has been filmed three times. In 1935 Herbert Marshall and Sylvia Sidney were directed by Wesley Ruggles. In 1950 it turned up as *Mr Music*, with Bing Crosby and Nancy Olson, directed by Richard Haydn; and in 1959 it emerged again as *But Not for Me*, with Clark Gable and Carroll Baker, directed by Walter Lang.

actors

have seldom been the subject of biopics. Anna Neagle appeared as Peg Woffington, with Cedric Hardwicke as David Garrick, in *Peg of Old Drury* 35, and Garrick was played by Brian Aherne in *The Great Garrick* 37. Miriam Hopkins was Mrs Leslie Carter in *Lady with Red Hair* 41. Charlie Ruggles (of all people) played Otis Skinner in *Our Hearts Were Young and Gay* 44, Richard Burton was Edwin Booth in *Prince of Players* 54, and Kim Novak was *Jeanne Eagels* 56. The 60s brought Julie Andrews and Daniel Massey as Gertie Lawrence and Noël Coward in *Star!* Of the idols of its own creation, Hollywood has so far given us biographics of Valentino, Jean Harlow, Lon Chaney, Diana and John Barrymore, Lillian Roth, Buster Keaton, Pearl White, W.C. Fields and Gable and Lombard.

adaptations.

A high proportion of feature films have been adapted from other media. A poem was the basis of *The Set-Up*, but mostly the studios have raided novels and plays for their material. The cost of such rights used to be minimal, but can now run into millions of dollars, the rights to *Annie* having allegedly cost a quarter of the film's $35m budget. A bonus however has appeared in the form of television mini-series, which thirty or forty years after the film version, when the original material would be unfashionable with film audiences, have started the money flowing again for such items as *My Cousin Rachel*, *The Citadel* and *How Green Was My Valley*.

At one time Hollywood had the reputation of using only the title of the items it bought. Certainly the Bulldog Drummond and Sherlock Holmes series bore little relation to the stories on which they were allegedly based: it seemed to be a point of honour with screenwriters to do better (if they could). *The Grapes of Wrath* was given an upbeat ending. *Pride and Prejudice* had its period advanced fifty years to a time when the fashions were more alluring. *Wuthering Heights* lost its second half. *Rebecca* reduced its hero from a murderer to an accessory after the fact. *Foreign Correspondent* took not a single incident from its alleged basis, *Personal History* by Vincent Sheean. *Forever Amber's* heroine became far more sinned against than sinning. *These Three* was adapted by Lillian Hellman from her own play *The Children's Hour*, but she had to change the central relationship from lesbian to heterosexual. *The Killers* wore out Hemingway's short story in the first ten minutes, and filled out the next ninety with new material. *Forbidden Planet* placed the plot of Shakespeare's *The Tempest* in outer space. Graham Greene's *The Quiet American* saw its point exactly reversed. Bernard Shaw was persuaded to add a happy ending (now the accepted one) to his anti-romantic *Pygmalion*. And Noël Coward's *Design for Living* saw the light of day in Hollywood with only one line intact, allegedly 'Kippers on toast'.

It has to be admitted that some excellent films have resulted from this tampering, and 'rearrangement' may seem in many cases preferable to the too-literal transcriptions in recent years of such properties as *Sleuth*, *The Best Whorehouse in Texas*, the Neil Simon comedies, and *Death Trap*, in which last case a new twist ending was added, but so lamely that the audience failed to grasp it.

Among the most skilled adapters from the 'golden age' are Dudley Nichols, Ben Hecht, Jules Furthman, Lamar Trotti, Philip Dunne, Casey Robinson, Samson Raphaelson, R. C. Sherriff, John Balderston and Donald Ogden Stewart.

addresses

which have formed film titles include *13 West Street*, *13 Rue Madeleine*, *13 East Street*, *13 Demon Street* (TV), *Ten North Frederick*, *10 Rillington Place*, *15 Maiden Lane*, *26 Acacia Avenue*, *99 River Street* and *711 Ocean Drive*. Then there were *42nd Street*, *52nd Street* and *The House on 92nd Street*, not to mention *Flamingo Road*, *Stallion Road*, *Madison Avenue*, *Rue de l'Estrapade*, *Montparnasse 19*, *Quai des Orfèvres*, *Piccadilly*, *Bond Street*, *St Martin's Lane*, etc. Nor should one forget Anna Neagle's London series: *Piccadilly Incident*, *The Courtneys of Curzon Street*, *Spring in Park Lane*, *I Live in Grosvenor Square* and *Maytime in Mayfair*. A clever scheme for disposing of an enemy was worked out in *Address Unknown*.

The Admirable Crichton.

J. M. Barrie's comedy, about master and man reversing roles after being shipwrecked on a desert island, has long fascinated film-makers. (Goldwyn is said to have lost interest after discovering that it was not what it sounded, a naval drama.) De Mille filmed it in 1919 as *Male and Female*, with Thomas Meighan and Gloria Swanson; a musical version, *We're Not Dressing*, turned up in 1934 with Bing Crosby and Carole Lombard; a further variation, *Our Girl Friday*, was filmed by Noel Langley in 1953 starring Kenneth More and Joan Collins; and in 1957 Kenneth More and Diane Cilento appeared in a more or less straight version of the play, under its original title, directed by Lewis Gilbert. More also appeared on the stage in a musical adaptation, *Our Man Crichton*.

advertising

appears seldom as a background to movies, but when it does, satire is usually in the air, as in *Christmas in July*, *The Hucksters*, *Mr Blandings Builds His Dream House*, *It Should Happen To You*, *Lover Come Back*, *Good Neighbor Sam*, *How to Succeed in Business without Really Trying*, *Putney Swope*, *How to Get Ahead in Advertising*, *Every Home Should Have One/Think Dirty* and *Crazy People*. It was played fairly straight in *Madison Avenue* and *The Narrowing Circle*.

aeroplanes:

see AIRPLANES.

Ah, Wilderness!

Eugene O'Neill's gentle comedy of growing up in a small American town was produced on Broadway in 1933. In 1935 it was filmed by Clarence Brown, with Eric Linden, Lionel Barrymore, Wallace Beery and Mickey Rooney. In 1947 Rouben Mamoulian remade it as a semi-musical, *Summer Holiday*: in the same roles were Mickey Rooney, Walter Huston, Frank Morgan and Jackie Jenkins.

AIDS,

a deficiency of the immune system caused by infection with HIV (human immunodeficiency virus), became headline news in July 1985 when Rock Hudson, seriously ill in a Paris clinic, issued a statement to the press to the effect that he had 'acquired immune deficiency syndrome'. He died later that year. Since that time many more performers and others involved in showbusiness have died from AIDS – the American magazine *Premiere* reported in its February 92 issue that AIDS deaths in Hollywood were 'climbing into the thousands' – and Hollywood personalities have been involved in fund-raising to combat the disease. That concern has so far not resulted in many films on the subject, though Larry Kramer, producer and screenwriter of *Women in Love* and other films, has written a play, *The Normal Heart*, and a book about it, and Oscar Moore, editor of the trade paper *Screen International*, published a novel, *A Matter of Life and Sex*, in which the central character dies of AIDS. The first was a low-budget film, *Parting Glances* 86, directed by Bill Sherwood, who died of AIDS four years later aged 37; it was followed by a mainstream movie, *Longtime Companion* 90; an Oscar-winning documentary, *Common Threads: Stories from the Quilt* 89; a Spanish comedy, *Love in the Time of Hysteria/ Solo con Tu Pareja* 92, directed by Alfonso Cuaron, and Israeli director Amos Guttman's *Amazing Grace* 92. Since then, it was been dealt with in *Savage Nights/Les Nuits Fauves* 92, written and directed by its star Cyril Collard, who died of AIDS shortly after completing it; Derek Jarman's *Blue* 93, made shortly before he died of AIDS; *Philadelphia* 93, which won an Oscar for its star, Tom Hanks, but annoyed many activists with its timid treatment of homosexuality; and in the TV film *And the Band Played On* 94. Independent film-makers have treated the subject with greater irreverence, notably in Gregg Araki's *The Living End* 92, and John Greyson's *Zero Patience* 94, the first AIDS musical. It remains a subject avoided by mainstream Hollywood, though providing subject-matter for TV films, of the 'disease of the week' variety, and independent films, such as *Green Plaid Shirt* (wd Richard Natale) 96, *Chocolate Babies* (wd Stephen Winter) 96, and *It's My Party* (d Randal Kleiser) 96. *The Velocity of Gary* 98, directed by Dan Ireland, starred Vincent D'Onofrio as a bisexual porn star who succumbs to the disease, and *Long Live Life/Zindagi Zindabad* 98, directed by Sumitra Bhave and Sunil Sukthankar, dealt with the impact of AIDS on Indian society.

air balloons,

of the spherical type with a hanging basket, have provided picturesque climaxes in films as diverse as *Trottie True*, *The Wizard of Oz* and *Charlie Bubbles*, while the initial part of the journey in *Around the World in Eighty Days* was accomplished in a splendidly ornate example of the species, and a dramatically styled version was used in *Five Weeks in a Balloon*. Balloons were popular for comic gags in silent films, notably Buster Keaton's *Balloonatic*. The most charming adaptation of the idea was in *The Red Balloon*, at the end of which a group of toy balloons carried the boy hero off into the sky; and the director of that film next made *Stowaway in the Sky*, which was about an air balloon over France. Balloons also featured in *Those Magnificent Men in Their Flying Machines*, *Mysterious Island*, *The Great Bank Robbery*, *Chitty Chitty Bang Bang*, *The Great Race*, *Black Sunday*.

Barrage balloons, a familiar sight in the Britain of World War II, seldom featured in films apart from the Crazy Gang's *Gasbags* and *Map of the Human Heart* 93, where a couple make love on top of one; but zeppelins or dirigibles were featured in *Dirigible* itself, *Hell's Angels*, *Madame Satan*, *The Assassination Bureau*, *The Red Tent*, *Zeppelin*, and of course in *The Hindenburg*.

airplanes,

one of the most exciting inventions of the twentieth century, have naturally been a popular source of cinematic thrills. Films about aviation itself began with the newsreel shots of attempts by early birdmen, some of them with tragic results: these have been well preserved in a Robert Youngson one-reeler of the early 50s, *This Mechanical Age*. In the 20s began the long series of spectacular aerial dramas: *Wings*, *Hell's Angels*, *Dawn Patrol*, *Lucky Devils*, *Devil Dogs of the Air*, *F.P.1*, *Wings of the Navy*, *Men with Wings*, *Test Pilot*, *Only Angels Have Wings*. British films on aviation were rare, exceptions being the exciting *Q Planes* and Korda's ill-fated documentary *Conquest of the Air*; but 1939 brought a need to show the nation's strength, and this was done superbly in such films as *The Lion Has Wings*, *Squadron Leader X*, *Target for Tonight*, *The First of the Few*, *Coastal Command*, *Flying Fortress*, *Journey Together* and *The Way to the Stars*. When America entered the war we were deluged with aerial melodramas, mostly with high-sounding titles and high propagandist content: *Eagle Squadron*, *International Squadron*, *I Wanted Wings*, *Winged Victory*, *A Wing and a Prayer*, *The Wild Blue Yonder*, *Bombardier*, *God Is My Co-Pilot*, *Flying Tigers*, *Captains of the Clouds*, *Dive Bomber*, *Air Force*, *Flight Command*, *Thirty Seconds over Tokyo*, and many others. Even Disney weighed in with the instructional *Victory Through Air Power*.

During the 40s began the still-continuing stream of biographies of aviation pioneers and air aces: *They Flew Alone* (Amy Johnson), *Gallant Journey* (John Montgomery), *Flight for Freedom* (Amelia Earhart), *Captain Eddie* (Eddie Rickenbacker), *The McConnell Story*, *Reach for the Sky* (Douglas Bader), *The Dam Busters* (Dr Barnes Wallis and Guy Gibson), *The Spirit of St Louis* (Lindbergh), *The One That Got Away* (Franz von Werra), *Wings of the Eagle* (Spig Wead), *Von Richthofen and Brown*, etc. Fictional additions to this cycle include *Ace Eli and Rodger of the Skies* and *The Great Waldo Pepper*.

Post-war air dramas from Hollywood showed a considerable increase in thoughtfulness. The responsibility of power was examined in *Command Decision*, *Twelve O'Clock High*, *The Beginning or the End*, *Strategic Air Command* and others, while the future of aviation was the subject of such films as *On the Threshold of Space*, *Towards the Unknown* and *X-15*. But there has also been room for spectaculars like *Lafayette Escadrille*, *Bombers B-52*, *The Longest Day* and *The Blue Max*, for such romantic dramas as *Blaze of Noon*, *Chain Lightning*, *Tarnished Angels* and *The Bridges at Toko-Ri*, and even for the more routine melodramatics of *Sky Commando*, *Battle Taxi*, *633 Squadron*, *Sky Tiger*, *Jet Pilot*, *Flight from Ashiya* and *The Flight of the Phoenix*. Britain too has turned out routine recruiting thrillers like *The Red Beret* and *High Flight*, with a nod to civil aviation in *Out of the Clouds*; against these can be set the earnest probing of *The Sound Barrier* and *The Man in the Sky*, the affectionate nostalgia of *Angels One Five* and *Conflict of Wings*. *Airport* and its all-star sequels are in a category of their own, that of aerial multi-drama, inspired by *The High and the Mighty*, *Jet Over the Atlantic* and *Jetstorm* and continuing into the 70s with *Skyjacked*.

In films where aviation itself is not the main subject, planes can be used for a wide variety of dramatic purposes. In *Triumph of the Will* Hitler's arrival at Nuremberg was made to seem godlike by clever photography of his plane descending through the clouds. A very different effect was given in *The Best Years of Our Lives* which began with three war veterans being given a lift home in the nose of a bomber; and in the same film, in the scene when Dana Andrews walks through a scrapyard full of the planes he has so recently been flying in the war, produced a ruefully moving sense of waste and futility. Godlike again was Raymond Massey's fleet of futuristic planes in *Things to Come*; and impeccable trick photography gave memorable punch to a musical, *Flying Down to Rio*, in which chorus girls apparently performed on the wings of planes in mid-air.

Any list of the most spectacular plane sequences should include Cary Grant being chased through the cornfield in *North by Northwest*; Claudette Colbert and Ray Milland escaping from Spain in *Arise My Love*; King Kong being cornered on the Empire State Building; the plane crashing into the sea in *Foreign Correspondent*; the climax of *Murphy's War*, and, of course, the climactic sequences of films already mentioned, such as *Hell's Angels*, *The Blue Max*, *The Sound Barrier* and *Dawn Patrol*. Comedy flying sequences can be equally thrilling, as shown by George Formby in *It's in the Air*, Abbott and Costello in *Keep 'Em Flying*, the Marx Brothers in *A Night in Casablanca*, Laurel and Hardy in *The Flying Deuces*, Duggie Wakefield in *Spy for a Day*, Buddy Hackett and Mickey Rooney in *It's a Mad Mad Mad Mad World*, Jimmy Edwards in *Nearly a Nasty Accident*, Pat Boone in *Never Put It In Writing*, W. C. Fields in *Never Give a Sucker an Even Break*, Spencer Tracy in *State of the Union*, Jack Lemmon in *The Great Race*, Fred MacMurray (flying a Model T) in *The Absent-minded Professor*, James Stewart in *You Gotta Stay Happy*, and practically the whole cast of *Those Magnificent Men in Their Flying Machines*. Air hostesses were featured in *Come Fly With Me* and *Boeing-Boeing*.

Plane crashes have been the dramatic starting point of many films including *Lost Horizon*, *Five Came Back*, *Back from Eternity*, *Fate Is the Hunter*, *The Night My Number Came Up*, *Broken Journey*, *SOS Pacific*, *The Flight of the Phoenix*, *Sands of the Kalahari*, *Survive!*, *Hey I'm Alive* (TV) and *Family Flight* (TV). The *fear* that a plane will crash has also been a potent source of screen melodrama, especially in such films as *No Highway*, *The High and the Mighty*, *Julie*, *Zero Hour*, *Jet Storm*, *Jet over the Atlantic*, *The Night My Number Came Up*, the *Airport* series, and *Skyjacked*, which focus on the emotional reactions of passengers. The proximity of planes to heaven has been useful in fantasies like *Here Comes Mr Jordan*, *A Guy Named Joe*, *A Matter of Life and Death* and *The Flight That Disappeared*. Finally, plane-building was used as a symbol of power in *The Carpetbaggers*; and symbols of a more fearsome kind are the atomic bombers which figured so largely in *Dr Strangelove* and *Fail Safe*.

In 1980 the airplane crash or near-crash genre, which had been done to death in such TV movies as *SST: Disaster in the Sky* and *Murder on Flight 502*, was effectively parodied in *Airplane!*, which took its thread of plot from *Zero Hour* and hung on to it every airplane joke that anybody could think of. 1983's *Airplane II: The Sequel* was far less funny, and just to show that parody doesn't harm the chances of the jut-jawed stuff, along on TV soon after came *Starflight: The Plane That Couldn't Land*. *Firefox* dealt with Soviet state-of-the-art fighter planes, with Clint Eastwood having to 'think Russian' in order to fly the one he steals; *Top Gun* gave us Tom Cruise as an élite naval aviator and was followed by the lower-budget *Iron Eagle* series of derring-do in the skies, a genre that was mercilessly mocked by *Hot Shots!*

See also: DOCUMENTARIES; HELICOPTERS.

airships

were historically short-lived, and being expensive to reconstruct appeared in few films and never very good ones. Some of the atmosphere can however be gained from *Madam Satan*, *Hell's Angels*, *The Assassination Bureau*, *Zeppelin* and *The Hindenburg*.

The Alamo,

originally a cottonwood tree, gave its name to a Franciscan mission in San Antonio, where in 1836 180 Americans were overpowered and slaughtered by 4,000 Mexicans. As those who died included such legendary figures as Jim Bowie and Davy Crockett, the siege of the Alamo has figured in many a film, notably *Man of Conquest* 39, *The Last Command* 55 and *The Alamo* 60; while in *San Antonio* 45, Errol Flynn and Paul Kelly had a non-historic fight in the mission ruins.

alcoholics

have been familiar screen figures since movies began: Jack Norton and Arthur Housman made a living playing little else, and other comic inebriates include James Stewart in *Harvey*, William Powell in *The Thin Man* and its successors, Wallace Beery in *Ah Wilderness* (followed by Frank Morgan in *Summer Holiday*), Dean Martin in *Rio Bravo* (followed by Robert Mitchum in *El Dorado*), Jackie Gleason in *Papa's Delicate Condition*, and Dudley Moore in *Arthur*.

More serious studies of alcoholism include Fredric March (followed by James Mason) in *A Star is Born*, Bing Crosby in *The Country Girl*, James Cagney and Gig Young in *Come Fill The Cup*, Spencer Tracy in *The People Against O'Hara*, Michael Redgrave in *Time Without Pity*, Claude Rains in *The White Tower*, Ingrid Bergman in *Under Capricorn*, Chester Morris in *Blind Spot*, Ray Milland in *The Lost Weekend* and *Night into Morning*, Jack Lemmon and Lee Remick in *Days of Wine and Roses*, Julie London in *The Great Man*, Van Johnson in *The Bottom of the Bottle*, Henry Fonda in *The Fugitive*, Lars Hanson in *The Atonement of Gosta Berling*, Susan Hayward in *Smash Up* and *I'll Cry Tomorrow*, Burt Lancaster in *Come Back Little Sheba*, Thomas Mitchell (followed by Bing Crosby) in *Stagecoach*, David Farrar in *The Small Back Room*, Bette Davis in *Dangerous*, Jason Robards in *Long Day's Journey Into Night*, Gregory Peck in *Beloved Infidel*, Donald O'Connor in *The Buster Keaton Story*, George Murphy in *Show Business*, Charles Laughton (followed by Robert Newton) in *Vessel of Wrath* (US, *The Beachcomber*), James Dunn in *A Tree Grows in Brooklyn*, Joan Fontaine in *Something to Live For*, Myrna Loy in *From the Terrace*, Maurice Ronet in *Le Feu Follet*, Kenneth More in *Dark Of The Sun*, Frank Sinatra in *The Joker is Wild*, Claire Bloom in *Red Sky At Morning*, Dick Van Dyke in *The Morning After* (TV), and Meg Ryan in *When a Man Loves a Woman*.

See also: DRUNK SCENES.

Aldwych farces

were plays presented at the Aldwych Theatre in London, starting in 1925 with *Cuckoo in the Nest*, up to 1933's *A Bit of a Test*. Most were written by BEN TRAVERS, and starred Tom WALLS, Ralph LYNN, Robertson HARE and Mary BROUGH. With the exception of *A Bit of a Test*, they were transferred virtually intact to the screen, retaining members of the original cast and usually directed by Walls. As cinema they are often stilted, but they form a valuable record of popular entertainment of the era and display some admirably skilled comic acting. According to producer Herbert Wilcox, *Rookery Nook* cost £14,000 to make and grossed £150,000 in Britain alone. Travers also wrote original screenplays for Walls and company in a similar style.

Rookery Nook 30. Plunder 31. Mischief 31. Thark 32. A Night Like This 32. A Cuckoo in the Nest 33. Turkey Time 33. A Cup of Kindness 34. Dirty Work 34.

Algonquin Round Table.

A meeting-place in the dining-room of the Algonquin Hotel of New York journalists, columnists, writers and actors during the 20s. They included Franklin P. Adams, Heywood Broun, Robert Benchley, George S. Kaufman, Marc Connelly, Alexander Woollcott, Robert E. Sherwood, Ring Lardner, Dorothy Parker, Ben Hecht, Deems Taylor, Charles MacArthur, Harpo Marx and Tallulah Bankhead. Noted for its wit, reported in newspaper and magazine columns by many of the participants, it was commemorated in Alan Rudolph's film *Mrs Parker and the Vicious Circle* 94, as well as in two books – *The Vicious Circle* by Margaret Case Harriman (1951) and *The Algonquin Wits* (1968), edited by Robert E. Drennen – and a novel, Grace Atherton's *Black Oxen*, published in 1932.

Among its witticisms:

What is so rare as a Woollcott first edition?

asked Alexander Woollcott as he autographed one of his books.

A Woollcott second edition,

said Franklin P. Adams. Woollcott also complained:

Everything I like is either illegal, immoral, or fattening.

Robert Benchley remarked:

Let's get out of these wet clothes and into a dry martini.

Dorothy Parker said:

That woman speaks eighteen languages and can't say 'No' in any of them

and, when a guest boasted of the longevity of her marriage by saying 'I've kept him for seven years', replied:

Keep him long enough and he'll come back in style.

After listening to the recitation of a work by a dead poet, Ring Lardner asked:

Did he write that before or after he died?

“ The Round Table was made up of a motley and nondescript group of people who wanted to eat lunch, and that's about it. – *George S. Kaufman*

The Round Table was also a kind of obstetrics ward and testing and development laboratory for some of the best humor and best humorists the United States has ever produced. – *Scott Meredith*

Ali Baba.

The *Arabian Nights* story, of a poor camel-driver who outwits 40 thieves by trailing them to their magic cave which opens to a password, has been a favourite with film-makers. Edison made a version in 1902, William Fox in 1919. In 1944 Jon Hall starred in *Ali Baba and the Forty Thieves*, while in 1952 Tony Curtis was *Son of Ali Baba*. (The 1944 film was remade, with much use of footage from the original, in 1964 as *Sword of Ali Baba*, starring Peter Mann.) Meanwhile in 1954 Fernandel appeared in a French comedy version under Jacques Becker's direction. Eddie Cantor dreamed he was Ali Baba in *Ali Baba Goes to Town* 37, and the character has appeared in many other *Arabian Nights* films. A superior spelling was adopted for *The Adventures of Hajji Baba* 56, in which John Derek played the role.

Alice in Wonderland.

This Victorian nonsense classic was written by Lewis Carroll (C. L. Dodgson) and published in 1865. Most film versions – and there have been several silent ones – have included material from *Through the Looking Glass*, published in 1871. Since sound there have been two American productions using actors (in 1931 with little-known players and in 1933 with Charlotte Henry and an all-star Paramount cast); a 1950 French version with Carol Marsh and Bunin's puppets; a rather stiff and unimaginative Disney cartoon in 1951; a stolid British live-action version in 1972; and a disturbingly surrealist production, using live-action and stop-motion animation, by Jan Svankmajer in 1988. In 1985 EMI brought out Dennis Potter's *Dreamchild*, in which the aged Alice Liddell, played by Coral Browne, goes to New York and is questioned about her relationship with Lewis Carroll.

Alien/Aliens.

Ridley Scott's science-fiction thriller, made in 1979 and scripted by Dan O'Bannon, about an alien intruder aboard a spaceship, was memorable for its brooding atmosphere, its creation of one of the screen's few tough heroines, played by Sigourney Weaver, its publicity tag ('In space, no one can hear you scream') and the complex life-cycle of its alien, created by Swiss artist Hans GIGER. A similar plot had already done service in *It! The Terror from Beyond Space* 58, written by Jerome Bixby. Three sequels followed: the all-action *Aliens* 86, directed by James Cameron, the downbeat *Alien³* 92, directed by David Fincher, and *Alien Resurrection* 97.

all-star films.

The phrase usually connotes giant musicals of the kind which started in the early days of talkies, when each studio put on an extravaganza displaying the talents of all its contract artistes, often to little effect.

Titles included *Movietone Follies*, *Paramount on Parade*, *The Hollywood Revue of 1929* (MGM), *Show of Shows* (Warner), *King of Jazz* (Universal) and *Elstree Calling*. The practice was revived during World War II: *Star Spangled Rhythm* (Paramount), *Thank Your Lucky Stars* (Warner), *Follow the Boys* (Universal), *Hollywood Canteen* (Warner) and *Stage Door Canteen* helped to cheer up the armed forces. Paramount continued into the later 40s with *Variety Girl* and *Duffy's Tavern*, and Warner came up with *It's a Great Feeling* and *Starlift*. *Carnegie Hall* applied the technique to classical music.

Meanwhile dramatic films had found the value of an occasional all-star cast. *Grand Hotel*, *If I Had a Million*, *Dinner at Eight* in the early 30s were followed ten years later by *Tales of Manhattan*, *Forever and a Day* and *Flesh and Fantasy*, while the adoption of particular authors later in the 40s produced all-star episodic films such as Somerset Maugham's *Quartet* and O'Henry's *Full House*. From the 50s, an occasional giant-screen epic would pack itself with stars: *Around the World in Eighty Days*, *How the West Was Won*, *The Greatest Story Ever Told*, *The Longest Day* and *A Bridge Too Far* were perhaps the most significant of these. Robert Altman's film about Hollywood, *The Player*, featured 69 stars, mainly playing themselves.

The American Civil War,

despite the peaks of *The Birth of a Nation* and *Gone with the Wind*, was long thought to be an uncommercial subject for film-makers, and certainly this was confirmed by the cool reception of *The General*, *So Red the Rose*, and *The Red Badge of Courage*, among others: the cry 'Fort Sumter has been fired upon' became a guaranteed laugh with any audience. Many westerns considered the after-effects of the war, but the conflict itself was dealt with only occasionally, perhaps because of budget problems. *Drums in the Deep South*, *Alvarez Kelly*, *Prince of Players*, *Prisoner of Shark Island*, *Escape from Fort Bravo*, *The Outlaw Josey Wales* and *The Good the Bad and the Ugly* were among those to touch on the subject, while *Shenandoah* dealt thoroughly with the resulting problems for one family. In the 80s, television took up the subject with vigour but no style, in such mini-series as *Beulah Land*, *The Blue and the Gray*, and *North and South*, the story having been previously told in such longer serials as *The Americans* and *Centennial*. In 89, the Oscar-winning *Glory* dealt with the first black soldiers recruited to fight under a young white officer. *Gettysburg*, 94, dealt with the war's decisive battle, in a film originally made for television which ran for 4½ hours.

The American Revolution.

Because the subject means no sale in several international markets, this has not been a popular subject with film-makers. D. W. Griffith's *America* in 1924 was the most thoroughgoing reconstruction. A year later, *Janice Meredith* covered some of the same ground. *Alexander Hamilton* (31) starred George Arliss and had Alan Mowbray as George Washington. Walt Disney's *Johnny Tremain* showed revolutionary figures through the eyes of an apprentice silversmith. John Paul Jones, the sailor patriot, was played in 1959 by Robert Stack in the film of the same name. In 1959 Bernard Shaw's *The Devil's Disciple* was filmed with Burt Lancaster, Kirk Douglas and Laurence Olivier. *Lafayette* (1962) showed the war from the viewpoint of the French soldiers sent to assist. *1776* (72) is a musical version from the Broadway stage, with Howard da Silva as Ben Franklin. In the mid-70s public broadcasting viewed the revolutionary years through a serial drama, *The Adams Chronicles*. 1984 brought an 8-hour mini-series with Barry Bostwick as George Washington.

amnesia

has been a favourite theme of the movies, and the line 'Who am I?' long since become immortal. Heroes and heroines who have suffered memorably from the affliction include Ronald Colman in *Random Harvest*, John Hodiak in *Somewhere in the Night*, Greta Garbo in *As You Desire Me*, George Peppard in *The Third Day*, Cornell Borchers in *Istanbul*, Gregory Peck in *Spellbound* and *Mirage*,

Phyllis Calvert in *The Woman With No Name*, Genevieve Page in *The Private Life of Sherlock Holmes*, Jennifer Jones in *Love Letters*, Laird Cregar in *Hangover Square*, William Powell in *I Love You Again* and *Crossroads*, Joan Fontaine in *The Witches* and James Garner in *Mister Buddwing*. In *While I Live* Carol Raye was the archetypal film amnesiac, emerging out of the mist complete with theme tune. In *Portrait of Jennie* Jennifer Jones played a ghost who forgot she was dead, and the same might be said of the passengers in *Outward Bound* (remade as *Between Two Worlds*) and *Thunder Rock*. The prize for audacity was won by the scriptwriters of *The Mummy's Curse*, with its dainty modern maiden who managed to forget that she was really a 3000-year-old mummy! Perhaps the cutest twist of all was suffered by Dan Duryea in *Black Angel* and Boris Karloff in *Grip of the Strangler*: having spent the film's running time tracking down a murderer, each discovered himself to be the culprit. The theme was taken probably as far as it can go in *Clean Slate* 94, in which Dana Carvey wakes up each morning unable to remember anything from the day before.

See: PSYCHOLOGY.

Amos 'n' Andy.

The original blackface double act, immensely popular for many years on American radio, consisted of Freeman F. Gosden (1899–1982) and Charles Correll (1890–1972). They made one film in 1930, *Check and Double Check*.

anachronisms

are fun to spot, but the ones involving language are easy to defend: ancient Romans may not have used modern slang phrases such as 'nuts to you', but nor did they speak in English anyway. Rarely indeed do the studios let through such gaffes as the extra who wore a wristwatch in *The Viking Queen*, or the TV aerials in 'Victorian' London in *The Wrong Box*. Mistakes we did enjoy include the use of dynamite in *Tap Roots*, which was set in 1860 (dynamite was not invented until 1867); the British Railways signs in *Cockleshell Heroes*, set during World War II (British Railways was formed in 1948); the death of Laird Cregar by Tower Bridge in *The Lodger*, set several years before Tower Bridge was built; and the modern lounge suits sported by Colin Clive in James Whale's Frankenstein films, otherwise apparently set in nineteenth-century Europe. Even TV movies are not immune: *The Triangle Factory Fire Scandal* includes a Chaplin movie visit but is set in 1909 before Chaplin made a film. But then, even Shakespeare put a striking clock in *Julius Caesar*.

ancient Egypt

has not been a popular stopping place for movie-makers. Several films based on the BIBLE, notably *The Ten Commandments*, have stayed awhile, and there were detailed reconstructions in *The Egyptian*, *Land of the Pharaohs*, and Kawalerowicz's *Pharaoh*. Otherwise it has been most frequently seen in flashbacks in *The Mummy* and its sequels.

angels

made appearances in many silent films: *Intolerance*, *The Four Horsemen of the Apocalypse*, *The Sorrows of Satan*, and the many versions of *Uncle Tom's Cabin* and *Faust* were among them. Since sound they have remained a favourite Hollywood device, but have naturally tended to lose their wings and become more whimsical, less awesome and often of somewhat ambiguous reality, to be explained away in the last reel as a result of the hero's bump on the head. The last completely serious angels were probably those in the all-Negro *Green Pastures* 37; since then they have been played by Claude Rains in *Here Comes Mr Jordan*, Jeanette MacDonald in *I Married an Angel*, Kenneth Spencer (and others) in *Cabin in the Sky*, Jack Benny (and others) in *The Horn Blows at Midnight*, Clifton Webb and Edmund Gwenn in *For Heaven's Sake*, Henry Travers in *It's a Wonderful Life*, Leon Ames in *Yolanda and the Thief*, Kathleen Byron and a great many extras in *A Matter of Life and Death*, Robert Cummings in *Heaven Only Knows*, Cary Grant in *The Bishop's Wife*, several actors in *Angels in the Outfield*, James Mason in *Forever Darling*, Diane Cilento in *The Angel Who Pawned Her Harp*, John Phillip Law in *Barbarella*, and Harry Belafonte in *The Angel Levine*. In 1978 Warren Beatty remade *Here Comes Mr Jordan* as *Heaven Can Wait* and spawned several ineffective TV imitations including Ray Bolger in *Heaven Only Knows*.

Used in a figurative sense, the word 'angel' has continued to be a favourite title component: *I'm No Angel*, *Angel*, *The Dark Angel*, *Angels with Dirty Faces*, *Angels Wash Their Faces*, *Angel and the Badman*, *Angel Face*, *Angel Baby*, *Angels in Disguise*, *The Angel Wore Red*, *Angels One Five*, *Angels in Exile*, etc.

See also: FANTASY.

animals,

as Walt Disney knew, are a sure way to success at the box office, with dogs well established as number-one providers. Dog stars of the movies have included Rin Tin Tin, Strongheart (his closest rival), Ben (Mack Sennett's comedy dog), Pete (of 'Our Gang'), Asta (of the 'Thin Man' series), Daisy (so popular in the 'Blondie' films that he starred in his own movies), and of course the immortal Lassie. Less publicized canines have successfully taken on dramatic roles in such films as *The Voice of Bugle Ann*, *Oliver Twist*, *Umberto D*, *Greyfriars Bobby*, *Owd Bob*, *Old Yeller*, *Savage Sam*, *The Ugly Dachshund* and *The Spy with a Cold Nose*; while Dick Powell was reincarnated as a very handsome Alsatian in *You Never Can Tell*. Rhubarb has been the only 'starred' cat, though felines have played important roles in *The Cat and the Canary*, *The Cat Creeps*, *Cat Girl*, *Shadow of the Cat*, *Breakfast at Tiffany's*, *The Incredible Journey*, *A Walk on the Wild Side*, *The Three Lives of Thomasina*, *That Darn Cat*, *The Torture Garden* (with its diabolical pussy), *The Wrong Box*, *The Goldwyn Follies* (in which the Ritz Brothers were memorably assisted by hundreds of cats to sing 'Hey Pussy Pussy'), *The Bluebird* (in which a sleek black feline was humanized very satisfyingly into Gale Sondergaard), *The Tomb of Ligeia*, *Eye of the Cat*, and several versions of *The Black Cat*.

Other animals to achieve something like stardom have included Balthasar the donkey, Flipper the dolphin, Gentle Ben the bear, Cheta the chimp (in the Tarzan films), Slicker the seal (in *Spawn of the North*), the chimp in *The Barefoot Executive*, Clarence the Cross-eyed Lion (not to mention Fluffy), the *Zebra in the Kitchen*, and a great many horses including Rex (*King of the Wild Horses*), Tarzan (with Ken Maynard), Fritz (with William S. Hart), Tony (with Tom Mix), Silver (with Buck Jones), Champion (with Gene Autry) and Trigger (with Roy Rogers). *Born Free* and its sequels made stars of lions; *Ring of Bright Water* and *Tarka the Otter* did the same for otters, and *Benji* for a little dog; then there was *The Belstone Fox*; the deer in *The Yearling*; the dolphins in *The Day of the Dolphin*; the bear in *Grizzly*; the host of assorted animals in *Doctor Dolittle*; the bear cub in *The Bear*; the kitten and puppy in *Milo and Otis*; and the killer whale in *Free Willy*. Perhaps one shouldn't count the anthropoids in *Planet of the Apes*.

anti-Semitism

was understandably not a popular subject with film-makers when the function of movies was simply to entertain. Amiable comic Jews were permitted, in *Abie's Irish Rose*, *Potash and Perlmutter*, and the Cohen and Kelly series; and it was readily acknowledged that Jewry provided a flow of star talent without which show business could not continue. But thoughtful movies on the Jewish plight were almost non-existent, unless one counts such epics as *The Wandering Jew* 33 and *Jew Süss* 34. Occasionally came a cry from Europe, as in *Professor Mamlock* 36, but it was not really until *The Great Dictator* 40 that the film-going public was made aware of what was happening to the Jews in Germany. For propaganda purposes the Nazis put out a number of anti-Semitic films such as *Der Ewige Jude* and another version of *Jew Süss*; the only real reply during World War II was a gentle British movie called *Mr Emmanuel*. In *Tomorrow the World* 44, from the play about an ex-Nazi youth in America, the subject was touched on; but not till the reconstruction days of 1947 could a spade really be called a spade. In a taut murder thriller called *Crossfire*, the victim was changed from a homosexual to a Jew; then came *Gentleman's Agreement*, in which a gentile reporter posed as a Jew to expose anti-Semitism in America. Perhaps this interest was stimulated by the immense popularity of *The Jolson Story*, with its sympathetic portrait of a Jewish home; but the confusion in American minds is demonstrated by the fact that David Lean's *Oliver Twist* was banned in 1948 because of Alec Guinness's 'caricature' of Fagin!

During the last decade or so there seems to have been sporadic interest in the subject. The birth of Israel generated such movies as *Sword in the Desert*, *Exodus*, *Judith* and *Cast a Giant Shadow*, and Christopher Isherwood's Berlin stories of the early 30s became first a play and film called *I Am a Camera* and later a musical and film called *Cabaret*. Poignant recollections of World War II by a girl who died in Auschwitz produced a book, play and film called *The Diary of Anne Frank*, and a little British film called *Reach for Glory*, which took a swipe at the consequences of intolerance. In 1971 the world's most successful stage musical, *Fiddler on the Roof*, was filmed; dealing with the Russian pogroms, the story has been filmed many times before in Yiddish, usually under the title *Tevye the Milkman*. The 70s saw the pendulum swinging to the extent that we were almost swamped by films and actors proclaiming their Jewishness: Barbra Streisand, Bette Midler, Woody Allen, Elliott Gould, George Segal. The plight of the Jews under Hitler was again explored in a dozen television epics including *Inside the Third Reich*, *Blood and Honour*, *The Winds of War*, *The Wall* and *The House on Garibaldi Street* and in the cinema in Steven Spielberg's *Schindler's List*; while feature films on the subject of Jewishness were *The Pawnbroker* and *The Chosen*.

Antoine Doinel.

A character who served as an alter ego for director François Truffaut in a series of semi-autobiographical films, each starring over a period of 20 years Jean-Pierre Léaud, who was 13 when he was picked to play the role in *The 400 Blows/Les Quatre Cents Coups* 59, the first of the sequence. It was followed by *Antoine et Colette*, part of the compilation film *Love at Twenty/L'Amour à 20 Ans* 62, *Stolen Kisses/Baisers Volés* 68, *Bed and Board/Domicile Conjugal* 70, and *Love on the Run/Amour en Fuite* 79, a series which follows Doinel from his unhappy adolescence and dead-end jobs to his becoming a writer, a lover, an unhappy husband and a father. Truffaut once wrote, 'The character of Antoine Doinel is always on the run, always late, a young man in a hurry.'

army comedies

have always been popular, and most well-known comedians have at least one to their credit. Laurel and Hardy were in *Pack Up Your Troubles* and *Blockheads* and *Great Guns*; Abbott and Costello in *Buck Privates*; Wheeler and Woolsey in *Half Shot at Sunrise*; Buster Keaton in *The Dough Boys*; Charlie Chaplin in *Shoulder Arms*; Harry Langdon in *A Soldier's Plaything*; Larry Semon in *Spuds*; George Jessel in *Private Izzy Murray*; Joe E. Brown in *Sons of Guns*; Jimmy Durante and Phil Silvers in *You're in the Army Now*; The Ritz Brothers in *We're in the Army Now*; Norman Wisdom in *The Square Peg*; Jerry Lewis in *The Sad Sack*; Martin and Lewis in *At War With The Army*; Bob Hope in *Caught In the Draft*; Frank Randle in *Somewhere In England*; Arthur Lucan in *Old Mother Riley Joins Up*; George K. Arthur and Karl Dane in *Rookies*; Wallace Beery and Raymond Hatton in *Behind The Front*; Alan Carney and Wally Brown in *Adventures of A Rookie* and *Rookies In Burma*; Joe Sawyer and William Tracy in several comedies including *Tanks a Million*, *About Face* and *Fall In*; Tom Wilson and Heimie Conklin in *Ham And Eggs At The Front*; George Sidney and Charlie Murray in *Lost At The Front*.

Other American successes in the genre include: *What Did You Do In The War, Daddy?*; *Two Arabian Knights*; *What Price Glory?*; *The Cockeyed World*; *Top Sergeant Mulligan*; *The Teahouse of The August Moon*; *The Wackiest Ship In the Army*; *Operation Mad Ball*, and above all *M*A*S*H*. Britain has provided *Carry On Sergeant*; *Private's Progress*; *On The Fiddle*; *I Only Arsked*; *Idol On Parade* and *Reluctant Heroes*.

Outstanding TV series: Britain's *The Army Game* and Hollywood's *Bilko* series with Phil Silvers; *Hogan's Heroes*; *McHale's Navy*; *Gomer Pyle U.S.M.C.*; *M*A*S*H*.

Arsène Lupin.

The gallant French jewel thief and part-time detective, created at the beginning of the century by Maurice Leblanc, has been the subject of many films, the first being a Vitagraph 1917 version starring Earle Williams. In 1932 the Barrymore brothers were in *Arsène Lupin*, John taking the title role; in 1938 Melvyn Douglas was in *Arsène Lupin Returns*; Charles Korvin took over in 1944 for *Enter Arsène Lupin*; in 1957 there was Robert Lamoureux in *The Adventures of Arsène Lupin*; and in 1962 Jean-Claude Brialy starred in *Arsène Lupin Contre Arsène Lupin*. A French TV series ran during the 70s.

Arthur.

The legendary British king of the 5th or 6th century, central figure of the courtly love tradition and alleged creator not only of the democratic Round Table but of the idyllic city and palace of Camelot, has figured in several movies, especially in recent years when we seem to have had need to cherish our legends. There have been three sound versions, to begin with, of *A Connecticut Yankee at King Arthur's Court*; in the 1949 version Cedric Hardwicke played the King as having a perpetual cold. In 1942, Arthur Askey dreamed he was a member of the Round Table in *King Arthur Was a Gentleman*. In 1964 Disney presented in cartoon form the childhood of Arthur in *The Sword in the Stone*. In slightly more serious vein, Mel Ferrer was Arthur in *Knights of the Round Table* 54, with Robert Taylor as Lancelot and Ava Gardner as Guinevere. Anthony Bushell had the role in *The Black Knight* 54 and Mark Dignam took over in *Siege of the Saxons* 64. In the 1963 *Lancelot and Guinevere*, the three roles were taken respectively by Brian Aherne, Cornel Wilde and Jean Wallace; in the 1967 musical *Camelot*, by Richard Harris, Franco Nero, and Vanessa Redgrave. In the 70s there came Bresson's *Lancelot du Lac* and Rohmer's *Perceval*. In 1980 John Boorman gave us a noisy, violent version of the legend, *Excalibur*. In *First Knight* 95, Sean Connery played Arthur to Juliet Ormond's Guinevere and Richard Gere's Lancelot (who remained a modern Yankee at King Arthur's court) but the film failed to find much of a public. It has become harder to take the legends seriously since they were treated with much irreverence in *Monty Python and the Holy Grail* 75.

TV series on the subject have included *Sir Lancelot*, an Australian cartoon series called *Arthur!*, and a Welsh serial called *Arthur of The Britons*. There is also a TV movie, *Arthur the King*.

assassination

has not been a favourite film subject, though historical incidents have been examined in *Julius Caesar*, *Sarajevo*, *Nicholas and Alexandra*, *Nine Hours to Rama*, *The Assassination of Trotsky*, *Gandhi*, *The Parallax View* and *JFK*. Assassination attempts have figured in *Suddenly*, *The Man Who Knew Too Much*, *Foreign Correspondent*, *The Manchurian Candidate* and *The Day of the Jackal*. The assassination of President Kennedy, and its aftermath, was the subject of Oliver Stone's *JFK* 91, while *The Day of the Jackal* was remade as *The Jackal* 97, in which the target was the First Lady.

Asterix.

Cunning, diminutive, moustachioed Gaul, the hero of strip cartoons created by Alberto Uderzo and René Goscinny. The stories, about a village of Gauls that the invading Romans are unable to defeat, satirize many aspects of contemporary life. Less successful are the series of animated films based on the books. In 1999 came *Asterix and Obelix vs Caesar*, starring Gérard Depardieu, a live-action version of the stories that was the most expensive French film so far made.

Asterix the Gaul 67. Asterix and Cleopatra 70. The Twelve Labours of Asterix 75. Asterix in Britain 86. Asterix and the Big Fight 89, etc.

authors as actors

are few. Alexander Woollcott once had fun playing opposite Noël Coward in *The Scoundrel*; Irvin S. Cobb tried to take over the mantle of Will Rogers on the latter's death; Mickey Spillane played his own hero Mike Hammer in *The Girl Hunters* and also appeared in *Ring of Fear*. Otherwise literary lions have aspired only to bit parts, such as Compton Mackenzie in *Whisky Galore* and Hugh Walpole in *David Copperfield*. Somerset Maugham did contribute lengthy introductions to three compendiums of his short stories, but they were virtually eliminated from the release prints. Jacqueline Susann and Peter Benchley appeared as interviewers in *Valley of the Dolls* and *Jaws* respectively. Writer-director Bryan Forbes did become a popular juvenile in the 50s, and John Osborne turned villain in *Get Carter*, while Truman Capote was the sinister host of *Murder by Death*. Actors who became authors include David Niven, Dirk Bogarde, Ruth Chatterton, Mary Astor, Elissa Landi, Errol Flynn and Corinne Griffith; and many others wrote autobiographies, more or less unaided.

automobiles
with personality enough to become movie titles include *Genevieve*, *The Fast Lady*, *La Belle Américaine*, *The Solid Gold Cadillac*, *The Yellow Rolls-Royce*, *Chitty Chitty Bang Bang*, *The Gnome-Mobile* and *The Love Bug*. Other cars with individuality were James Bond's tricksy Aston Martin in *Goldfinger* and the one that ran on two wheels in *Diamonds are Forever*; the Flying Wombat in *The Young at Heart*; the gadget-filled limousine in *Only Two Can Play*; the airborne Model T in *The Absent-minded Professor*. The Model T was also Laurel and Hardy's favourite car, and they wrecked a great many in their time; other old cars were featured in *The Reivers* and TV's *The Beverly Hillbillies*. Multitudes of old and strange cars were featured in *The Great Race*, *It's a Mad Mad Mad Mad World*, *Monte Carlo or Bust*.

Comic car chases have been featured by Mack Sennett, Abbott and Costello, W. C. Fields and countless other comedians, and a new car was splendidly wrecked in *Tobacco Road*. Realistic chases became more and more violent in the 70s. *Bullitt* and *The French Connection* were box-office hits almost for this reason alone, and imitations included *Robbery*, *Vanishing Point*, *Freebie and the Bean*, *The Car*, *The Driver*, *The Blues Brothers*, *Smokey and the Bandit*, *Every Which Way But Loose*, *The Gauntlet* and *The Hunter*. The best television film of the genre was undoubtedly *Duel*, but series from *The Dukes of Hazzard* to *T. J. Hooker* based their appeal on the number of cars crashed each week. The ultimate spoof was probably *Knight Rider*, in which the car became a secondary hero, talking back to its master and making most of his decisions.

See: MOTOR RACING.

The Avengers.
Camp English television series, created by Sydney Newman and Leonard White, and featuring John Steed, a suave, bowler-hatted, tightly-rolled-umbrella-wielding secret agent with a tough female sidekick. Patrick McNEE starred, and his assistants were played by Honor BLACKMAN, as Cathy Gale, Diana RIGG, as Emma Peel (whose name derived from the search for something with 'man appeal', which was then shortened to 'M appeal'), Linda Thorsen, as Tara King, and Joanna LUMLEY, as Purdey. It ran from 1961 to 1969, and, as *The New Avengers*, from 1976 to 1977, and appeared on American TV for three series from 1966. A film version was released in 1998, starring Ralph FIENNES and Uma THURMAN, and intended to be the start of a series, but it was a critical and financial failure.

Book: 1997, *The Avengers* by Toby Miller.

babies
who have achieved screen stardom include Baby Parsons and Baby Peggy in silent days, Baby Le Roy in the early 30s and Baby Sandy in the early 40s. Shirley Temple and the Our Gang cast were scarcely weaned when they hit the big time. Other films about particular babies include *Bachelor Mother*, *Bobbikins*, and *A Diary for Timothy*. *Baby's Day Out* 94 proved that a small child was more than a match for incompetent kidnappers.

There was a shortlived TV series about a talking baby called *Happy*, a trend that reached the cinema with *Look Who's Talking* 89, *Look Who's Talking Too* 90, and *Look Who's Talking Now* 93, and Lucille Ball worked her own confinement into her weekly half-hour. More recently there has been a lamentable fashion for diabolical infants: *Rosemary's Baby*, *It's Alive*, *I Don't Want to be Born*, *The Devil within Her*, *The Exorcist*, *The Omen* and *Damien: Omen II*.

Back Street.
Fanny Hurst's novel about a married man and his suffering mistress has been filmed three times: in 1932, directed by John Stahl, 1941, directed by Robert Stevenson, and 1961, directed by David Miller.

backstage
is a term suggesting musicals about putting on a show. But other types of film have taken place mainly or climactically in this area. Thrillers: *The Velvet Touch*, *Stage Fright*, *The Phantom of the Opera*, *Charlie Chan at the Opera*, *Cover Girl Killer*, *Murder at the Vanities*, *The G-String Murders*, *Theatre of Death*. Dramas: *A Double Life*, *Applause*, *The Blue Angel*, *Limelight*, *Les Enfants du Paradis*, *Act One*. Comedies: *A Night at the Opera*, *Hellzapoppin*, *The Guardsman*, *The Royal Family of Broadway*, *Curtain Up*, etc. Musicals themselves got off to a pretty good start in the early 30s, best and most typical of them being *42nd Street*, which was amiably spoofed in *Movie Movie* 78.

ballet
sequences have been a boon to many indifferent films, permitting a brief glimpse into a world that is strange, alarming, but graceful and glamorous. From the time of *The Goldwyn Follies* 38, any Hollywood musical with aspirations had to have a ballet sequence, some of the most memorable being in *The Pirate*, *On the Town*, *An American in Paris*, *Singin' in the Rain*, and *The Band Wagon*. The custom died out in the 50s, since when there has been an over-abundance of unimaginatively presented full-length stage ballets with famous dancing stars. These, filmed at low cost, have found a market, but expensive film ballets like *Tales of Hoffman*, *Invitation to the Dance* and *Black Tights* had tougher going. Dramatic films set in the ballet world have included *La Mort du Cygne* (remade in Hollywood as *The Unfinished Dance*), *The Red Shoes* and *The Spectre of the Rose*; lighter stories in which the heroine is a ballerina (usually a novice) include *Waterloo Bridge*, *Carnival*, *Dance Little Lady*, *On Your Toes* and *St Martin's Lane*. Several comedians have found themselves pursued by plot complications on to a stage and forced to take part clumsily in the ballet in progress: Jack Buchanan in *That's a Good Girl*, Danny Kaye in *Knock on Wood*, Morecambe and Wise in *The Intelligence Men*; even Laurel and Hardy donned tutus in *The Dancing Masters*.

By the 70s, ballet had lost its general popularity. *Nijinsky* accentuated the homosexual element. Rudolf Nureyev, on film in several straight ballets, turned actor as *Valentino*. Following him came fellow Russian Mikhail Baryshnikov who, in *The Turning Point* 77, not only danced but was nominated for an Oscar as best supporting actor. With the same director, Herbert Ross, he tried for something similar ten years later in *Dancers*, but without the same impact. Perhaps the boldest attempt to bring ballet to the big screen so far has been Carroll Ballard's *Nutcracker: The Motion Picture* in 86.

balloons:
see AIR BALLOONS.

Barney Bear.
Ponderous, affable, dim-witted grizzly who was a star of MGM cartoons from 1939–54. His voice was supplied by Bill Bletcher, Rudolph Ising and Paul Frees.

The Bear that Couldn't Sleep 39. The Fishing Bear 40. The Flying Bear 41. Barney Bear's Victory Garden 42. Bah Wilderness 43. Bear Raid Warden 44. Busybody Bear 52. Heir Bear 53. Bird-Brain Bird Dog 54, etc.

baseball
has been the subject for occasional films since 1899, when *Casey at the Bat* was first made. (It turned up again in 1927 with Wallace Beery.) Biopics of famous baseball personalities include *The Stratton Story* (James Stewart), *The Babe Ruth Story* (William Bendix), *The Pride of the Yankees* (Gary Cooper as Lou Gehrig), *The Winning Team* (Ronald Reagan as G. C. Alexander), *The Pride of St Louis* (Dan Dailey as Dizzy Dean), *Fear Strikes Out* (Anthony Perkins as Jim Piersall), *The Jackie Robinson Story*, *Babe*, with John Goodman as Babe Ruth, and *Cobb*, with Tommy Lee Jones as Ty Cobb. Serious dramatic films about the sport include *The Bush Leaguer*, *Slide Kelly Slide*, *The Big Leaguer*, *The Natural* and *Field of Dreams*. Baseball's biggest scandal, involving the Chicago White Sox of 1919, was treated sympathetically in *Eight Men Out*. There has been a fantasy, *Angels in the Outfield*, and a who-done-it, *Death on the Diamond*. Musicals are led by *Take Me Out to the Ball Game* and *Damn Yankees*. Comedies include *Elmer the Great*, *Alibi Ike*, *Fast Company*, *Rhubarb*, *It Happens Every Spring*, *Speedy* (Harold Lloyd), *College* (Buster Keaton), *Ladies' Day*, *The Bad News Bears* and its sequels, *Major League* and *A League of Their Own*, about a female team. Baseball stadiums have provided memorable scenes in films on other subjects: *The FBI Story*, *Beau James*, *The Satan Bug*, *Experiment in Terror*, etc.

bathtubs,
though especially associated with Cecil B. De Mille, have been a favourite Hollywood gimmick from early silent days. But De Mille undressed his heroines with the most showmanship, whether it was Gloria Swanson in *Male and Female*, Claudette Colbert in her asses' milk in *The Sign of the Cross* (emulated years later by Frances Day in *Fiddlers Three*) or Paulette Goddard in *Unconquered*. Other ladies who have bathed spectacularly include Joan Crawford in *The Women*, Deanna Durbin in *Can't Help Singing*, Jean Harlow in *Red Dust*, Phyllis Haver in *The Politic Flapper*, Joan Collins in *The Wayward Bus*, Elke Sommer in *The Wicked Dreams of Paula Schultz*, Gina Lollobrigida in *Belles de Nuit*, Carroll Baker in *Harlow* and Sophia Loren (who had Gregory Peck hiding in her shower) in *Arabesque*. Not that the men have had it all their own way: Roger Livesey in *Colonel Blimp* and Gary Cooper in *Love in the Afternoon* suffered in the steamroom; and all the actors who have played coal miners, including Trevor Howard in *Sons and Lovers* and Donald Crisp in *How Green Was My Valley*, know how it feels to be scrubbed all over. Marat in *Marat/Sade* spent the whole film in a tub. The most bathed male star is probably Cary Grant, who had a tub in *The Howards of Virginia*, a shower in *Mr Blandings Builds His Dream House*, another shower, fully clothed this time, in *Charade*, and a Japanese geisha bath in *Walk, Don't Run*. And Hitchcock, with *Psycho*, still takes the prize for the most memorable shower scene.

Batman.
An American comic strip character created in 1939 by Bob Kane, Batman was a personable millionaire who, with his young helper Robin, donned fancy dress to fight the evil forces in society, and zoomed about in a 'batmobile' with many a pow and a splat. His chief enemies were the Riddler, the Penguin, the Joker and Catwoman. He came to the big screen in two serials, and was played in 1943 by Lewis Wilson and in 1949 by Robert Lowery. A TV series in 1965–67 starred Adam West with Burt Ward, and the villains were played by Frank Gorshin, Burgess Meredith, Cesar Romero and Lee Meriwether. A feature version emerged in 1966. In 1989 a new version transformed him into a semi-psychotic character, with Michael Keaton in the title role. A sequel, *Batman Returns*, followed in 1992, and *Batman Forever*, with Val Kilmer replacing Keaton, in 1995. Kilmer left to play the Saint and, in 1997, the role was taken over by George CLOONEY in *Batman and Robin*.

Ben Hur.
There were several silent versions of Lew Wallace's semi-biblical adventure novel. Best known is MGM's lavish spectacular of 1926, directed by Fred Niblo with Ramon Navarro and Francis X. Bushman; it was reissued with sound effects in 1931. In 1959 it was remade by MGM and William Wyler, with Charlton Heston and Stephen Boyd: the greatest praise went to the chariot race sequence directed by Andrew Marton with the assistance of Yakima Canutt.

Berlin
has seemed to film-makers a grim grey city, and history provides obvious reasons for this. Standard attitudes are shown in *The Murderers Are Amongst Us*, *Germany Year Zero*, *Four Men in a Jeep*, *Hotel Berlin*, *Berlin Express*, *The Man Between*, *Night People*, *The Big Lift*, *I Am a Camera*, *The Spy Who Came in from the Cold*, *The Man Who Finally Died*, *A Prize of Gold*, *The Quiller Memorandum*, *Cabaret*, *Escape from East Berlin*, *Funeral in Berlin*. But some people have found fun there, notably Billy Wilder in *People on Sunday*, *A Foreign Affair* and *One Two Three*; and in 1928 Walter Ruttman's stylishly kaleidoscopic documentary, *Berlin: Symphony of a Great City*, showed the place and its people to be just as sympathetic as anywhere else if they are understandingly portrayed.

Betty Boop.
Doll-like cartoon creation, a wide-eyed gold-digging flapper created by animator Grim Natwick for Max Fleischer in the 1932 cartoon *Any Rags*. She was censored by Will H. Hays in 1935. She was developed from a dog who appeared in *Dizzy Dishes* in 1930, in which she was chased by Fleischer's dog star Bimbo, who first appeared in the early 20s. The cartoons she featured in were wildly imaginative and usually made comments on the social follies of their time; in the 70s they became popular through compilation features. She was based on the 'boop-a-doop' singer Helen Kane, with her voice being provided by Mae Questel.

Beverly Hills.
Residential area of Los Angeles, home to many of Hollywood's seriously rich. It has come to be synonymous with wealth, excess and conspicuous consumption. Since the 80s, it has gained wider fame through its use in movie titles and from the teenage sitcom *Beverly Hills 90210*.

Dawn to Dark in Beverly Hills (doc) 59. The Beverly Hills Call Boys 70. Beverly Hills Cop 84. Down and Out in Beverly Hills 86. Beverly Hills Madam (TV) 86. Beverly Hills Cop II 87. Beverly Hills Vamp 89. Beverly Hills Bodysnatchers 89. Scenes from the Class Struggle in Beverly Hills 89. Beverly Hills Knockouts 89. Beverly Hills Brats 89. The Taking of Beverly Hills 91. The Beverly Hillbillies 93. Beverly Hills Cop III 94. Pterodactyl Woman of Beverly Hills 94, etc.

“ With an area of less than 6 square miles and a population barely exceeding 30,000 – only 20,000 of whom are old enough to vote – Beverly Hills supports 35 banks, 299 beauty salons, 651 medical doctors and psychoanalysts, and 761 gardeners.
– David McClintick

The Bible.
The extravaganza which claimed to be the 'film of the book' was conceived by Dino de Laurentiis as a nine-hour survey by several directors. It turned up in 1966 as a slow plod through Genesis by and with John Huston. Of the hundreds of films which have been inspired by the Old Testament stories, some of the most memorable are *The Private Life of Adam and Eve*, *Sodom and Gomorrah*, *Green Pastures*, *A Story of David*, *David and Bathsheba*, *Samson and Delilah*, *The Prodigal*, *The Ten Commandments* (two versions), *Salome*, *Esther and the King* and *The Story of Ruth*. For the New Testament, see under *Christ*; the immediate effects of whose life have been treated in such assorted films as *The Robe*, *Demetrius and the Gladiators*, *The Sign of the Cross*, *The Big Fisherman*, *Quo Vadis*, *Ben Hur*, *Spartacus*, *Fabiola*, *Barabbas*, *The Silver Chalice*, and *The Fall of the Roman Empire*, not to mention Lord Grade's six-hour *Jesus of Nazareth* for TV (a 'sequel' to his *Moses*). All this activity sparked off in 1978 a rather naive American TV series, *Greatest Heroes of the Bible*.

big business
was outside the range of silent movie-makers, but in the 30s, usually personified by Edward Arnold, it became a useful villain for the comedies and dramas of social conscience. A switch was made in *Dodsworth*, in which the businessman became an innocent abroad; but not until the growing affluence of the 50s did Hollywood think it worth while to probe into the personal lives of those who occupy the corridors of power. Then in quick succession we had *Executive Suite*, *Woman's World*, *Patterns of Power*, *The Power and the Prize* and *The Man in the Grey Flannel Suit*; while the inevitable knocking process began as early as *The Man in the White Suit* and continued with *The Solid Gold Cadillac*, *Cash McCall*, *Ice Palace*, *The Apartment*, *The Wheeler Dealers*, *Wall Street*, *Other People's Money* and *The Hudsucker Proxy*.

bigamists
have been prevented by the censorship codes from achieving hero status in more than a few films; perhaps it is significant that although the Italian film called *The Bigamist* is a comedy, the American one is a solemn affair. Over the years, however, scriptwriters have achieved some sympathy and humour for the characters played by William Bendix in *Don Juan Quilligan*, Alec Guinness in *The Captain's Paradise*, Clifton Webb in *The Remarkable Mr Pennypacker*, Rex Harrison in *The Constant Husband*, Jean-Claude Drouot in *Le Bonheur* and Leo McKern in *Decline and Fall*.

birds
fit nicely into the glamorous romantic backgrounds of which Hollywood used to be so fond, but a few particular examples have been malevolent, including *The Vulture*, the owner of *The Giant Claw*, the carnivorous birds which nearly pecked *Barbarella* to death, and of course *The Birds* which turned on the human race in Hitchcock's 1963 movie. (In the various versions of Edgar Allan Poe's *The Raven*, the title character has been almost irrelevant.) Other notable birds have been seen

in *Treasure Island*, *Birdman of Alcatraz*, *The Pigeon That Took Rome*, *Run Wild Run Free*, *The Bluebird*, *Kes*, *Doctor Dolittle*, and *Bill and Coo*; and in the cartoon field one must remember with affection Donald and Daffy Duck, Tweetie Pie, the Road Runner, and an assortment of other feathered friends. The heroes of *Brewster McCloud* and several other films thought they were birds; *Jonathan Livingston Seagull* was. *Mr Drake's Duck* and his Disney lookalike *The Million Dollar Duck* laid extremely valuable eggs. The pelican in *Storm Boy* stole the show from the hero; and the birds in *Tawny Pipit* and *Conflict of Wings* upset whole countrysides.

The Bishop's Wife

was based on Robert Nathan's novel about an angel who improves a bishop's attitude to his neglected wife and parishioners. A light comedy, it was directed by Henry Koster in 1947 after William A. Seiter was removed halfway through shooting, and starred Cary Grant, Loretta Young and David Niven, winning four Oscar nominations, including those for best film and best director. In 1996, it was remade by Penny Marshall and retitled *The Preacher's Wife*, starring Denzel Washington as the angel, and Whitney Houston.

black comedy

finds humour in serious matters such as death, neurosis and sex perversion. In recent years it has become almost normal, though such films as *A Clockwork Orange* still cause controversy. We were once less sophisticated: in the early 30s, for instance, the comedy element in horror films such as James Whale's *The Bride of Frankenstein* and *The Old Dark House* was not understood, and even now is difficult to maintain on the same level, though Hammer films make sporadic attempts in this direction, and Roger Corman was rather more successful in *The Raven*. (Roman Polanski failed spectacularly in *The Fearless Vampire Killers*.) Comedies of murder date back to *The Front Page* and *Boudu Sauvé des Eaux*, with a progression through *Drôle de Drame*, *A Slight Case of Murder*, *Arsenic and Old Lace*, *Monsieur Verdoux*, *Kind Hearts and Coronets*, *The Red Inn*, *The Criminal Life of Archibaldo de la Cruz*, *The Naked Truth*, *She'll Have to Go*, *Candy* and *The Assassination Bureau*. Death and funerals have been the subject of jest in *Here Comes Mr Jordan*, *Too Many Crooks*, *The Loved One*, *The Wrong Box*, *Loot*, and *Harold and Maude*. On the level of social behaviour, there is black humour in *Who's Afraid of Virginia Woolf?*, *The Anniversary* and *The Honey Pot*, while Luis Buñuel castigates society through similar means in most of his films, notably *El*, *The Exterminating Angel* and *The Diary of a Chambermaid*. *Dr Strangelove* managed to laugh at the destruction of the world. Finally, Laurel and Hardy understood one aspect of the genre in their many grotesque jokes involving physical distortion. Elements of black comedy are to be found in an increasing number of modern films, notably those of Billy Wilder, John Huston and Alfred Hitchcock, and in the adventures of James Bond.

blacks

in films have only slowly attained equal status with whites. In early silents they were invariably depicted as slaves, a fact encouraged by the several popular versions of *Uncle Tom's Cabin*. If a film had a black role of consequence, it was usually played by a white man in blackface. But blacks began to make their own films for their own audiences, and still do, though these seldom get a general showing. The first all-black film was *Darktown Jubilee* in 1914 . . . the year that Griffith made *The Birth of a Nation*, with its strong anti-black bias. Griffith atoned for this in *The Greatest Thing in Life* 18, in which a white soldier and a black embraced, but in 1922 he again incurred the wrath of colour-sensitive critics by making *One Exciting Night*, the first film to boast the quickly stereotyped figure of the terrified black manservant. Early talkies included such all-black films as *Hearts in Dixie* and Vidor's *Hallelujah*, and in 1933 Paul Robeson appeared in a version of Eugene O'Neill's *The Emperor Jones*. Much of the interest of *Imitation of Life* 34 centred on the problems of black servant Louise Beavers and her half-white daughter. In 1936 the screen version of *Green Pastures*, depicting the simple black's idea of the Bible, was widely acclaimed but tended to perpetuate a patronizing attitude. The feeling of the South for its blacks was strongly outlined in *They Won't Forget* 37 and *Gone with the Wind* 39. *Stormy Weather* 42 and *Cabin in the Sky* 43 were all-black musicals in Hollywood's best manner, but *Tales of Manhattan* 42 was retrogressive in showing blacks as inhabitants of a vast shanty town. In *Casablanca* 42, however, Dooley Wilson was accepted on equal terms by Humphrey Bogart. Disney's *Song of the South* 46, despite an engaging performance by James Baskett, brought back the old Uncle Remus image. The post-war period generally permitted the emergence of serious black actors like James Edwards and Sidney Poitier, and films on racial themes such as *Intruder in the Dust* and *Pinky*. At last, in 1965, came films in which a black could play a straight part utterly unrelated to his colour. Poitier did so in *The Bedford Incident*, then used colour defiantly in *In the Heat of the Night* and *Guess Who's Coming to Dinner*. Remakes of well known 'white' movies were one way to bring in a wide range of coloured actors: *The Lost Man (Odd Man Out)*, *Uptight (The Informer)*, *Cool Breeze (The Asphalt Jungle)*. Even *Barefoot in the Park* became a black TV series. The subject was rather self-consciously aired in such films as *Change of Mind*, *Watermelon Man*, *The Landlord* and *Medium Cool*. In 1970 came *Cotton Comes to Harlem*, perhaps the first black thriller with no chip on its shoulder; in 1972 the seal of approval was set up by *Shaft*, a violent private-eye thriller with an all-black cast which proved not only acceptable to all audiences but highly commercial. The floodgates opened and before 1972 was out we even had *Blacula* and *Blackenstein*. Wholly black films which followed included *Sounder*, *The Autobiography of Miss Jane Pittman* (TV), *Uptown Saturday Night*, *Let's Do It Again*; and in 1977 a sensational impact was achieved by a TV serialization of Alex Haley's *Roots*, by watching which half of America sought to atone for centuries of bad white behaviour towards the blacks. Redd Foxx, a nightclub comedian, became a TV star in the 70s in *Sanford and Son*, based on the British series *Steptoe and Son*, followed by *Sanford and the Redd Foxx Show* in the 80s. At the same time, another comedian, Richard Pryor, was making a similar impact in films, particularly when teamed with Gene Wilder in *Silver Streak* and *Stir Crazy*. Following him came the fast-talking, self-confident Eddie Murphy, a hit on the TV show *Saturday Night Live* while still in his teens. The film *48 Hours* established him as a Hollywood star, and *Beverly Hills Cop* confirmed his position as a big box-office attraction, although *Harlem Nights*, his attempt at writing and directing as well as acting, was not a success. Robert Townsend, also a comedian, turned his frustrations in Hollywood to comic account in *Hollywood Shuffle*, which also featured the talents of Keenan Wayans, who wrote, directed and starred in *I'm Gonna Git You Sucka*, a send-up of the 'blaxploitation' movies of the 70s, a genre which still lives on in the films of actor-director Fred Williamson. From the mid-80s the talented director, actor and writer Spike Lee created a series of provocative, socially-conscious films dealing with uneasy relationships between white and black: *She's Gotta Have It*, *School Daze*, *Do The Right Thing*, *Mo' Better Blues*, *Jungle Fever*, *Malcolm X*, and *Crooklyn*. Lee's cinematographer, Ernest Dickerson, turned director with the powerful *Juice*, and the young John Singleton became the first director to be nominated for an Oscar for his first film with *Boyz N the Hood*, which probed into the reasons for the wasted lives of members of Los Angeles street gangs. Director Melvin Van Peebles had made one of the earliest and most significant films of black experience with *Sweet Sweetback's Baadasssss Song* in 1971. Twenty years later, his son Mario directed *New Jack City*, a violent anti-drug thriller that may have made a new star of rap performer Ice T. Actor Bill Duke returned to a Chester Himes novel to direct *A Rage in Harlem* in 1991, and followed it with *Deep Cover* in 92. Actors escaping from stereotyped roles include Wesley Snipes, Forest Whitaker, Danny Glover, Whoopi Goldberg and Morgan Freeman.

Britain, less affected by black problems, moved in parallel fashion: in the early 30s, films of *The Kentucky Minstrels*; then Paul Robeson dominating somewhat insulting material in *Sanders of the River* and subsequently earning three or four serious film vehicles of his own; the post-war attempt to understand in *Men of Two Worlds*; and problem pictures like *Simba*, about the Mau-Mau, and *Flame in the Streets*, about the prospect of a black in an East End family. The racism of British movies of the 30s is visible in the 90s on afternoon and late-night television screenings, where actors can still be seen putting coal-dust on their faces to pass as black, and you can still hear dialogue such as 'Whitemail? What's whitemail?' 'Blackmailing a nigger.' Comedian Lenny Henry is Britain's nearest equivalent to Eddie Murphy, though his success is so far confined to television. Director and writer Isaac Julien dealt with black experience in Britain in *Young Soul Rebels*.

See also: BLAXPLOITATION.

blaxploitation

was a word coined to describe action movies of the 70s featuring black stars and intended for black audiences, though they enjoyed a wider public. The originator of the genre was Melvin van Peebles with his *Sweet Sweetback's Baadasssss Song* 71, which he produced, directed, wrote and starred in. The films that followed were less angry, more frivolous and often produced by the big studios or exploitation experts such as AIP. The most successful were those featuring Richard Roundtree (as Shaft), Ron O'Neal (as Superfly), Tamara Dobson (as Cleopatra Jones), Jim Brown (as Slaughter), Fred Williamson and Pam Grier. Music was sometimes provided by Isaac Hayes, who wrote the theme for *Shaft*. The genre also included horror movies, such as *Blackula*, and was later parodied by *I'm Gonna Git You Sucka* 88, written and directed by Keenen Ivory Wayans, while many of the 70s stars appeared together in *Original Gangstas* 96. In the 90s came a cycle of films about the toughness of black inner-city life, often involving rap performers such as Ice-T and Tupac Shakur, including *Boyz N The Hood* 91, *New Jack City* 91, directed by Mario van Peebles, *Juice* 92, and *Menace II Society* 93; these in turn were parodied by *Fear of the Black Hat* 93 and *Don't Be a Menace to South Central While Drinking Your Juice in the Hood* 96. In the mid-90s, the success of *Waiting to Exhale*, directed by Forest Whitaker from Terry McMillan's novel, gave producers a new market to target: black women.

Book: 1995, *That's Blaxploitation! Roots of the Baadasssss 'Tude (Rated X by an All-Whyte Jury)* by Darius James.

blindness,

a tragic affliction, has generally been treated by film-makers with discretion, though not without sentimentality. Typical is Herbert Marshall as the blind pianist in *The Enchanted Cottage*, dispensing words of wisdom with piano music in the background and the sounds of nature through the open door. Other sympathetic blind roles include Cary Grant in *Wings in the Dark*; Irene Dunne (later Jane Wyman) in *Magnificent Obsession*; Ronald Colman (later Fredric March) in *The Dark Angel*; Colman also in *The Light That Failed*; Ralph Richardson (later Laurence Harvey) in *The Four Feathers*; James Cagney in *City for Conquest*; Ida Lupino in *On Dangerous Ground*; Arthur Kennedy in *Bright Victory*; Patricia Neal in *Psyche 59* 64; John Garfield in *Pride of the Marines*; Michele Morgan in *La Symphonie Pastorale*; Virginia Cherrill in *City Lights*; Elizabeth Hartman in *A Patch of Blue*; Michael Wilding in *Torch Song*; and Nicol Williamson in *Laughter in the Dark*. More sinister blind characters came in *Saboteur* and *Victim*; while blind detectives, not forgetting TV's *Longstreet*, include Edward Arnold in *Eyes in the Night* and *The Hidden Eye*, Van Johnson in *23 Paces to Baker Street*, Dick Powell (briefly blinded by cordite fumes) in *Murder My Sweet*; and Karl Malden in *Cat o' Nine Tails*.

In thrillers, terrified blind heroines have been useful: Patricia Dainton in *Witness in the Dark*, Audrey Hepburn in *Wait Until Dark* and Mia Farrow in *Blind Terror*. Other tricks with blind characters were played in *Faces in the Dark* and *Silent Dust*, in both of which the hero's condition helped him to outwit his assailants; and *Tread Softly Stranger*, where the murderer gave himself away through fear of the only witness – who turned out to be blind. *Afraid of the Dark* had a blind woman threatened by a serial killer while *Blink* dealt with a woman who may have witnessed a murder as she regained her sight. Genuinely blind actors include Esmond Knight (temporarily) playing a sighted role in *The Silver Fleet*, and Ray Charles in *Ballad in Blue*. A nice ironic point was made in *Bride of Frankenstein*, where O. P. Heggie as a blind hermit was the only human being who did not fear the monster.

Other films involving blindness include *Night Song*, *Destiny*, *Man in the Dark*, *Afraid of the Dark* and *Blink*. Finally, in *The Day of the Triffids*, almost everyone on earth was blinded.

boffins

are research scientists working on hush-hush government projects. Their problems have been dramatized in such films as *The Small Back Room*, *School for Secrets*, *Suspect*, *The Man in the Moon*, *The Satan Bug*, *The Andromeda Strain*, *The Atomic City* and *The Forbin Project*.

boo-boos:

see CONTINUITY ERRORS AND BOO-BOOS.

Boston Blackie

was a jewel thief who became an upholder of law and order in 14 'B' features for Columbia in the 40s. They starred Chester MORRIS, with George E. STONE providing comic relief as his dim-witted friend The Runt, and Richard LANE as a suspicious detective inspector. Directors of the movies included Edward DMYTRYK and Robert FLOREY. The character, created by writer Jack Boyle in stories dating from 1910, also featured in several silent movies from 1918 on, a radio series, and in a TV series from 1951 to 1953, starring Kent TAYLOR.

Meet Boston Blackie 41. Confessions of Boston Blackie 41. Alias Boston Blackie 42. Boston Blackie Goes to Hollywood 42. After Midnight with Boston Blackie 43. The Chance of a Lifetime 43. One Mysterious Night 44. Boston Blackie Booked on Suspicion 45. Boston Blackie's Rendezvous 45. A Close Call for Boston Blackie 46. The Phantom Thief 46. Boston Blackie and the Law 46. Trapped by Boston Blackie 48. Boston Blackie's Chinese Venture 49.

The Bowery Boys.

A gang of ageing, street-smart Brooklyn kids, who had their origins in *Dead End*, Sidney Kingsley's Broadway hit of 1935, and the subsequent 1937 film of the same name, directed by William Wyler. The popularity of the boys led to a series for Warner featuring the DEAD END KIDS. Some members then went to Universal to appear in LITTLE TOUGH GUYS and a series of half a dozen movies until the early 40s. Meanwhile others went to Monogram to create the EAST SIDE KIDS, who made 22 films between 1940 and 1945. In 1946, Monogram merged the remaining members of the groups to create The Bowery Boys, who featured in 48 films between 1946 and 1958. The original members were Leo Gorcey (as Slip Mahoney), Huntz Hall (as Sach Jones), Gabriel Dell (as Gabe), Bobby Jordan – all original Dead End Kids – David Gorcey (aka David Condon), Bill Benedict and Bennie Bartlett. Jordan left the series after *News Hounds* in 1947, Dell quit in 1950, and Benedict a year later. The films also featured the Gorcey brothers' father, Bernard Gorcey.

■ In Fast Company 46. Bowery Bombshell 46. Live Wires 46. Spook Busters 46. Mr Hex 46. Bowery Buckaroo 47. Hard Boiled Mahoney 47. News Hounds 47. Angels' Alley 47. Jinx Money 48. Smuggler's Cove 48. Trouble Makers 48. Angels in Diguise 49. Fighting Fools 49. Hold That Baby 49. Master Minds 49. Blonde Dynamite 50. Blues Busters 50. Lucky Losers 50. Triple Trouble 50. Bowery Battalion 51. Crazy over Horses 51. Ghost Chasers 51. Let's Go Navy 51. Feudin' Fools 52. Here Come the Marines 52. Hold That Line 52. No Holds Barred 52. Clipped Wings 53. Jalopy 53. Loose in London 53. Private Eyes 53. The Bowery Boys Meet the Monsters 54. Jungle Gents 54. Paris Playboys 54. Bowery to Bagdad 55. High Society 55. Jail Busters 55. Spy Chasers 55. Dig That Uranium 56. Crashing Las Vegas 56. Fighting Trouble 56. Hot Shots 56. Spook Chasers 57. Hold That Hypnotist 57. Looking for Danger 57. Up in Smoke 58. In the Money 58.

boxing.

Actual prizefighters whose lives have been fictionalized on film include Jim Corbett (Errol Flynn in *Gentleman Jim*), John L. Sullivan (Greg McClure in *The Great John L*), Joe Louis (Coley Wallace in *The Joe Louis Story*), Rocky Graziano (Paul Newman in *Somebody Up There Likes Me*), and Jack Johnson (James Earl Jones in *The Great White Hope*). Purely fictional boxing films have tended to emphasize the corruption of the fight game: *The Ring*, *The Square Ring*, *The Square Jungle*, *Iron Man*, *Kid Galahad*, *Kid Nightingale*, *The Champ*, *The Crowd Roars*, *Body and Soul*, *The Set Up*, *Champion*, *Golden Boy*, *No Way Back*, *The*

Good Die Young, Run With the Wind, The Harder They Fall*, and from Europe *Walkover* and *Boxer*. Boxing comedy is rare once one discounts the Joe Palooka series, but most comedians have taken part in boxing sequences: Abbott and Costello in *Meet the Invisible Man*, Harold Lloyd in *The Milky Way*, Danny Kaye in *The Kid from Brooklyn*, Chaplin in *The Champion*, etc. The only boxing fantasy was *Here Comes Mr Jordan*, in which Robert Montgomery's soul was transferred into that of a prizefighter. The most violent boxing film was undoubtedly *Raging Bull*, in which Robert de Niro put on fifty pounds to play the ageing Jake La Motta.

The Brady Bunch.

Relentlessly cheerful American sitcom, running from 1969 to 1974, about a happy middle-class family in which a widow with three daughters married a widower with three sons. It was followed by the less successful *The Brady Bunch Hour* (1977) and the bleaker *The Bradys* (1990), all of which retained most of the original cast, including Robert Reed and Florence Henderson as husband and wife Mike and Carol Brady. A spin-off series, *The Brady Brides*, was seen briefly in 1981, and the animated *The Brady Kids* ran from 1972 to 1974. A film version in 1995 put the wholesome family, unchanged from the 70s, into a decidedly grungy 90s setting, with Shelley Long and Gary Cole as Mike and Carol Brady. It was followed by *A Very Brady Sequel* in 1996.

The British Empire

has provided a useful background for innumerable movies: some comic, some tragic, but most of them plain adventurous. The Elizabethan Adventurers roistered through films like *The Sea Hawk*, *The Virgin Queen* and *Seven Seas to Calais;* the westward voyage occupied *Plymouth Adventure;* Australia provided the canvas for *Under Capricorn*, *Robbery Under Arms*, and *Botany Bay; Mutiny on the Bounty* showed the British in the South Seas; Africa was the subject of *Zulu*, *The Four Feathers*, *Khartoum*, *Sundown*, *Rhodes of Africa*, *The Sun Never Sets* and (for the anti-British view) *Ohm Krüger;* and favourite of all far-flung outposts, India provided splendid terrain for such adventures as *The Drum*, *Northwest Frontier*, *Gunga Din*, *King of the Khyber Rifles*, *The Rains Came*, *Charge of the Light Brigade* and *Lives of a Bengal Lancer*. When the Empire was at its height, one could view the British influence as benevolent (*Pacific Destiny*), maiden-auntish (*Sanders of the River*), or merely acquisitive (*Victoria the Great*).

The inevitable break-up was rather less well covered. Even American independence has been played down by Hollywood producers with an eye on the British market, though of course it comes into such films as *Last of the Mohicans*, *Lafayette*, *Daniel Boone*, and even Disney's *Ben and Me*. Emergent Africa was the theme of *Men of Two Worlds* as long ago as 1946, but between that and the independent state depicted in *Guns at Batasi* came the Mau Mau period shown in *Simba*, *Safari* and *Something of Value*. *The High Bright Sun* dealt with Cyprus; *The Planter's Wife* and *The Seventh Dawn* with Malaya; *Exodus*, *Judith* and *Cast a Giant Shadow* with Israel; scores of films with the Irish troubles; *Bhowani Junction* and *Nine Hours to Rama* with India. But the emergence of new states is a painful business as a rule, and most of these films give the impression of so much tasteless picking at sore points. The unexpected 1982 success of *Gandhi* may, however, begin a more serious process of revaluing imperial history. *Rhodes*, a TV series on Cecil Rhodes, the South African statesman, was broadcast in 1996.

See also: IRELAND.

brothels

were reasonably prominent in silent films, but the Hays Code banished them and for many years one had to look to the French for such revelations as were to be found in *Le Plaisir* and *Adua et sa Compagnie*. In the 60s, however, the doors opened. Comic Victorian brothels were shown in *The Assassination Bureau* and *The Best House in London*, and a French version in *Lady L. Ulysses* showed the Dublin version. *A House is not a Home* told the 'true' story of Polly Adler. The brothel in *The Balcony* was symbolic, in *House of a Thousand Dolls* fantastic, in *How Sweet It Is* charming, in *Games That Lovers Play* whimsical, in *The Last Detail* grimly realistic. *Walk on the Wild Side* concentrated on the depressing aspects and even sported a lesbian madam. *Pretty Baby* had a young girl growing up in a brothel and being sold for the night to the highest bidder. Nowadays every western has one, notably *Waterhole Three*, *Five Card Stud*, *Hang 'em High*, *McCabe and Mrs Miller*, *Dirty Dingus Magee*, *The Cheyenne Social Club*, *The Ballad of Cable Hogue*, and *Unforgiven;* nor are police thrillers such as *Badge 343* complete without them.

Bugs Bunny.

Warners' famous cartoon character, the wise-cracking Brooklynesque rabbit who maintained his aplomb in all situations. Voiced by Mel Blanc.

Catchphrase: 'What's up Doc?' First appearance in *A Wild Hare* 40, although he evolved from a rabbit seen earlier in *Porky's Hare Hunt* 37; 'retired' 1963; reappeared in 70s as 'compère' of TV specials grouping his old cartoons.

Biography: 1990, *Bugs Bunny: Fifty Years and Only One Grey Hare* by Joe Adamson.

AA 1958: *Knightly Knight Bugs*.

~One of Bugs' creators claimed that the character was inspired by the sight of Clark Gable eating a carrot in *It Happened One Night*.

Bulldog Drummond.

'Sapper' (Herman Cyril McNeile) created this famous character, an amateur James Bond of the 20s with old-fashioned manners and an army background, based on his friend Gerard FAIRLIE. First portrayed on screen by Carlyle Blackwell in 1922; later by Jack Buchanan (1925 and 1940), Ronald Colman (1928 and 1934), Kenneth McKenna (1930), Ralph Richardson (1934), Atholl Fleming in Jack Hulbert's *Bulldog Jack* (1935), John Lodge (1937), Ray Milland (1937), John Howard, in eight films (1937–39), Ron Randell, in two films (1947), Tom Conway, in two films (1948), Walter Pidgeon in *Calling Bulldog Drummond* (1951) and Richard Johnson in *Deadlier than the Male* (1966) and *Some Girls Do* (1968).

bullfights

have understandably not been a popular ingredient of English-speaking films, apart from the romanticism of the two versions of *Blood and Sand* and the cynicism of *The Last Flight* 31 and *The Sun Also Rises*. Several Continental films, including *The Moment of Truth*, have tried to convey the mystique of bullfighting, but it has more often been seen as a background for suspense films (*The Caper of the Golden Bulls*) and comedy (*The Kid from Spain*, Laurel and Hardy in *The Bullfighters* and *Tommy the Toreador*, Abbott and Costello in *Mexican Hayride*, Peter Sellers in *The Bobo*, etc.). The three more recent American attempts to make a serious drama on the subject (*The Bullfighter and the Lady*, *The Brave Bulls* and *The Magnificent Matador*) were notably unpopular, while *Arruza* by Budd Boetticher (himself an ex-bullfighter) was never properly finished.

burlesque.

A word of Italian origin which came to mean an acted 'spoof' of a serious subject. In America it was applied to what the British would call music hall or variety, and eventually connoted striptease and low comedians. It died out as an institution in the 30s: Mamoulian's film *Applause* 29 gives a vivid picture of its latter days. George Watters and Arthur Hopkins' play *Burlesque*, popular in the 20s, concerns a comedian who leaves his long-suffering wife for other women and the demon rum. It was filmed three times, most recently as *When My Baby Smiles at Me* 48, with Betty Grable and Dan Dailey. The heyday of burlesque was also evoked in *The Night They Raided Minsky's* 68, in *Lady of Burlesque* and in *Gypsy*.

buses

have often provided a dramatic background for film plots. In *Speed*, Sandra Bullock had to drive a booby-trapped bus at more than 50 mph to prevent the vehicle exploding. *Man-Made Monster* and *The October Man* began with bus accidents, and one of the stories in *Dead of Night* ended with one. Strangers met on a bus in *Friday the Thirteenth*, *It Happened One Night*, *San Diego I Love You* (in which Buster Keaton defied regulations by driving his bus along the seashore), *Bus Stop* and *The Wayward Bus*. Parting at the bus station was featured in *Orchestra Wives*, *Dark Passage*, *Two Tickets to Broadway*, and *Rattle of a Simple Man;* romances were conducted on a bus in *Violent Playground* and *Underground;* a trap was set for a criminal in a bus station in *Down Three Dark Streets*. Passengers on buses broke into song in *Keep Your Seats Please*, *Ride 'Em Cowboy* and *Summer Holiday*. As for comedy effects using buses, there was the little boy whose head stuck in the bus wheel in *Monsieur Hulot's Holiday*, Will Hay driving a bus round a race-track in *Ask a Policeman*, Bob Hope wrecking an Irish bus outing in *My Favourite Blonde*, Frankie Howerd losing his way in the fog in *The Runaway Bus*, Richard Burton escorting his matrons on a bus tour in *The Night of the Iguana*, and Laurel and Hardy driving a bus on to a roller coaster in *The Dancing Masters* . . . among others. The only comedies about bus crews were the spinoffs from the British TV series *On the Buses*. *The Big Bus* was a spoof on disaster movies. *Speed* 94 made a runaway bus big box-office.

butlers.

Hollywood has always been fascinated by butlers, especially those who give an impression of British imperturbability. Actors notably benefiting from this penchant include Arthur Treacher (who played Jeeves on film in the 30s), Robert Greig, Charles Coleman, Aubrey Mather, Melville Cooper, Halliwell Hobbes, Barnett Parker, Alan Mowbray and Eric Blore (whose butlers usually had a kind of suppressed malevolence). The catch-phrase 'the butler did it' was, however, seldom true of murder mysteries, though Bela Lugosi played some very sinister servants in the 40s, Richard Haydn was guilty of at least one murder in *And Then There Were None;* the butler in *The Hound of the Baskervilles* certainly had something to hide. Another villainous 'man's man' was Philip Latham in *Dracula Prince of Darkness:* he lured the count's victims. Comedy butlers are led by Charles Laughton as *Ruggles of Red Gap* and by Edward Brophy, who often played an American imitation of the real thing, John Gielgud in *Arthur* and its sequel, Richard Hearne in *The Butler's Dilemma*, Edward Rigby in *Don't Take It to Heart*, and Laurel and Hardy who in *A Chump at Oxford* took literally an instruction to 'serve the salad undressed'. Jack Buchanan pretended to be his own butler in *Lord Richard in the Pantry*, and William Powell and David Niven, who both played *My Man Godfrey*, had their own reasons for going into service. Other butlers with something to hide were found in *White Tie and Tails* and *The Baroness and the Butler*, and in *Spring in Park Lane* Michael Wilding was a mysterious footman. In *The Fallen Idol* Ralph Richardson's butler was almost arrested for a murder he didn't commit. Perhaps television gave us the most famous butler of all: Gordon Jackson as Hudson in *Upstairs Downstairs*.

cable cars

have added excitement to the climax of many a film adventure, notably *Night Train to Munich*, *The Trollenberg Terror*, *Edge of Eternity*, *Second Chance*, *Where Eagles Dare*, *Hannibal Brooks* and *The Double Man*. In 1979 Irwin Allen made a four-hour TV suspenser, *Hanging by a Thread*, entirely about a cable car accident; but it failed to thrill.

cannibalism

has been featured in such documentaries as *The Sky Above*, *The Mud Below*, but it is rare in fiction films, although it is becoming much more common. Apart from the Swedish short *Midvinterblot*, the main examples are from the 70s: *Welcome to Arrow Beach* and *Survive!*, a low-budget film based on the true story of the cannibalistic survivors of a South American plane crash. It was remade in 92 as *Alive!* By then, the films *Manhunter* 86 and *The Silence of The Lambs* 91 had made a popular bogeyman of Dr Hannibal Lecter, a serial killer who feasted on his victims. Cannibalism also featured in the climax of Peter Greenaway's art-house hit *The Cook, the Thief, His Wife and Her Lover* 89. From the 60s onwards, eaters of human flesh had become a familiar ingredient of horror movies, notably in the cult success *Texas Chainsaw Massacre* 74 and its sequels. But it also found its way into more mainstream films, including *The 'burbs* and *Parents*, showing that no taboo is proof against the predations of producers.

Carl Hamilton

is a Swedish secret agent, the hero of a sequence of novels by Jan Guillou. So far, six have been filmed, starring in the role Peter Haber and Stefan Sauk; Stellan SKARSGARD in two films, *Töcknam Coq Rouge* 89 and *Den Demokratiske Terroristen* 92; and Peter STORMARE in *Hamilton* 98, a film based on two of the books.

Carmen.

Prosper Mérimée's high-romantic tale of a fatal gypsy whose worthless attractions wreck men's lives was promptly turned by Bizet into an opera which has been filmed many times, notably as *Carmen Jones* 54. The straight dramatic story, however, probably holds the record for the number of film versions it has spawned:

France	1909	with Victoria Lepanto
Spain	1910	actress unknown
US	1913	Marguerite Snow
US	1913	Marion Leonard
Spain	1914	actress unknown
US	1915	Geraldine Farrar
US	1915	Edna Purviance (*Burlesque on Carmen*)
US	1916	Theda Bara
US	1918	Pola Negri
US	1921	Raquel Meller
US	1927	Dolores del Rio
France	1942	Viviane Romance
US	1948	Rita Hayworth
US/WG	1966	Uta Levke

carnivals:

see FUNFAIRS.

Carry On films.

This long-running series that became as much a British institution as fish and chips began with an army farce, *Carry On Sergeant*, scripted by Norman Hudis from an unpublished play by R. F. Delderfield, and directed by Gerald Thomas. Among the cast were Kenneth Williams, Charles Hawtrey and Kenneth Connor, who were to become Carry On regulars. Over the years the plots gradually disappeared under an accumulation of old jokes which grew steadily bluer, especially when, after the first six, Talbot Rothwell replaced Hudis as the writer; after his death the last four were written by various hands but failed to recapture the flavour of the earlier movies. An amalgam of music-hall humour and end-of-pier farces, the films' makeshift construction was evident even with the later use of colour, and they never raised their sights as high as satire. All were directed by Thomas and produced by Peter Rogers on as low a budget as possible. A Sussex beach stood in for the Sahara in *Carry On, Follow That Camel* and a Welsh mountainside for the Khyber Pass. Apart from Williams, Hawtrey and Connor, the regulars included Sid James, Bernard Bresslaw, Jim Dale, Joan Sims, Barbara Windsor, Hattie Jacques, Terry Scott, Patsy Rowlands, Jack Douglas and Peter Butterworth, with occasional guests such as Harry H. Corbett, Fenella Fielding, Juliet Mills and even Phil Silvers. The music for the first four was written by Bruce Montgomery and for the remainder, apart from the final film, by Eric Rogers.

The sequence was: Carry On Sergeant 58; Carry On Nurse (a surprising hit in the US) 59; Carry On Teacher 59; Carry On Constable 60; Carry On Regardless 60; Carry On Cruising (the first in colour) 62; Carry On Cabby (bw) 63; Carry On Jack (colour, the first by Talbot Rothwell) 64; Carry On Spying (bw) 64; Carry On Cleo (colour, as were all subsquent films) 64; Carry On Cowboy 65; Carry On Screaming 66; Carry On – Don't Lose Your Head 66; Carry On – Follow That Camel 66; Carry On Doctor 68; Carry On up the Khyber 68; Carry On Again Doctor 69; Carry On Camping 69; Carry On up the Jungle 70; Carry On Loving 70; Carry On Henry 71; Carry On at Your Convenience 71; Carry On Abroad 72; Carry On Matron 72; Carry On Girls 73; Carry On Dick (Rothwell's last) 74; Carry On Behind (scripted by Dave Freeman) 75; Carry On England (scripted by Jack Seddon and David Pursall) 76; Carry On Emmannuelle (scripted by Lance Peters) 78; Carry On Columbus (scripted by Dave Freeman) 92.

“ I am convinced that audiences do not like change; they like the same thing over and over again. – *Peter Rogers*

They were all alike, weren't they? We made 31 films out of one gag. – *Peter Rogers*

This is v. odd, the way that Carry Ons are just starting to get mentioned: why are they suddenly fashionable? They're even trying to justify the bad scripts now! and talk about the classlessness of them. What hogwash! You can only call a mess a mess. – *Kenneth Williams, 1964*

The film was *Carry On Abroad* and I was featured doing all the old crap. Looking at this rubbish you realise that nothing has changed! British sit-coms all consist of the same routines, jokes, and dirt. Very depressing. – *Kenneth Williams, 1988*

If I had to think of one reason why the Carry Ons matter so much, it's because they really aren't recuperable for proper culture. Like the Crazy Gang, like George Formby, like Frank Randle, they display a commitment to bodily functions and base desires that will always render them irreducibly vulgar, inescapably Not Art. – *Andy Medhurst, Sight and Sound, 1992*

case histories

from medical files, which would once have been considered pretty dull plot material, have recently been presented quite starkly to paying audiences who appear to have relished them. In the 40s, *Lady in the Dark* was a richly decorated trifle, and even *The Snake Pit* and *Mandy* had subsidiary love interest, but in more recent years we have had such unvarnished studies as *El* (paranoiac jealousy), *Pressure Point* (fascist tendencies), *A Child is Waiting* (mentally handicapped children), *Life Upside Down* (withdrawal), *The Collector* (sex fantasies), *Repulsion*, *In Cold Blood*, *10 Rillington Place* and *The Boston Strangler* (homicidal mania), *Bigger Than Life* (danger from drugs). *The Three Faces of Eve* and *Lizzie* (split personality), *Marnie* (frigidity), *Morgan* (infantile regression), and *Family Life*. At least the pretence of studying a case history relieves writers of the responsibility of providing a dramatic ending.

See also: DREAMS; FANTASY; AMNESIA.

Casper, the Friendly Ghost.

The happy baby ghost created by producer Joseph Oriolo and animator Seymour Wright in 1945 was popular through the 50s and as a star of children's television in the 60s. A live action feature starring Christina Ricci and Eric Idle was released in 1995.

The Friendly Ghost 45. There's Good Boos Tonight 48. A-Haunting We Will Go 49. Casper Comes to Clown 51. Deep Boo Sea 52. Frightday the 13th 53. Zero the Hero 54. Casper Genie 54. Hide and Shriek 55. Ground Hog Play 56. Ghost of Honor 57. Heir Restorer 58. Not Ghoulty 59. Casper's Birthday 59, etc.

catchphrases

Although Garbo got into the act with 'I want to be alone' and Boyer impersonators have had a ball with a line Boyer never spoke, 'Come with me to the Casbah', it is comedians who devise and need readily identifiable catchphrases, so that audiences have something to laugh at without even being warmed up. Here are a few which should be immediately recognized:

Diminutive Arthur Askey came up with

I thank you (pronounced Ay Theng Yow)

and was annoyed when Cyril Fletcher used the slight variation

Thanking you . . .

as well as:

Dreaming oh my darling love of thee.

Sandy Powell had

Can you hear me, mother?

George Formby contracted this, in moments of stress, to

Ohh, muvver!

when he wasn't telling everyone that it had

Turned out nice again!

Flanagan and Allen's most notable trade mark was simply

Oi!

while Will Hay perfected a sniff, Max Miller however told his audiences:

There'll never be another!

and when they laughed at his floral suit, asked:

Well, what if I am?

When Old Mother Riley needed help, she screamed:

Mrs Ginocchi, SOS!

and of her errant daughter she inevitably demanded:

Where've you been, who've you been with, what've you been doing, and why?

Robb Wilton reminisced about

The day war broke out

and Tommy Trinder called his audience

You lucky people!

Bruce Forsyth also gets on chummily with his audience, asking for applause with

Didn't he do well?

Jack Warner was worried for his property:

Mind my bike . . .

and Robertson Hare always anticipated disaster:

Oh, calamity!

Schoolmasterish Jimmy Edwards told his audience to

Wake up at the back there!

While Ben Lyon was constantly afraid that his mother-in-law in the audience might take umbrage at any insulting lines from the stage:

Not you, momma, sit down!

The famous radio series *It's That Man Again* practically consisted of catchphrases, including

Can I do you now, sir?

Don't forget the diver . . .

After you, Claude . . . no, after you, Cecil . . .

I go, I come back.

Good morning, nice day.

I don't mind if I do.

Boss, boss, sumpn terrible's happened . . .

This is Funf speaking . . .

After *ITMA*'s demise, other radio shows caught on to the idea, Arthur Askey producing

Hello, playmates!

Before your very eyes.

Don't be filthy.

and

These jokes are free for pantomime!

Sam Costa was recognized by:

Good morning, sir, was there something?

While *Take It from Here* also added its share of phrases to the language:

Gently, Bentley.

A *mauve* one.

Clumsy clot.

Oh, Eth . . . oh, Ron . . .

More recently, Frankie Howerd has wished his audiences:

And the best of luck!

Max Bygraves has asserted himself:

I've arrived, and to prove it, I'm here.

Tough heroes have been getting in on the act. Clint Eastwood's

Make my day

has become a cliché that has even found its way on to T-shirts. And there's Arnold 'The Terminator' Schwarzenegger with:

I'll be back.

Cenobites.

Demons from hell that feature in the work of author Clive Barker and which have appeared in three films: *Hellraiser*; *Hellbound: Hellraiser II*; *Hellraiser III*. The best known is Pinhead, so called because the contours of his face are marked out by pins stuck in his flesh.

Charley's Aunt.

There have been at least ten film versions, of various nationalities, of the farce by English actor and playwright Walter Brandon Thomas (1856–1914), which has been rarely absent from the stage since its first production in 1892, when it ran for four years. Its comedy stems from undergraduate Lord Fancourt Babberley having to impersonate his friend's aunt from Brazil, 'where the nuts come from'. It was made as a silent in 1925, starring Sydney CHAPLIN. Other notable versions came in 1930, with Charles RUGGLES; in 1940, with Arthur ASKEY in *Charley's Big Hearted Aunt*; in 1941, with Jack BENNY in what was known in Britain as *Charley's American Aunt*; in 1952, when Ray BOLGER repeated his Broadway success in *Where's Charley?*, a musical version by George ABBOTT and Frank LOESSER.

❝ It's pleasing to think that probably the two most famous plays throughout the entire world are *Hamlet* and *Charley's Aunt*. – *John Chapman*

Charlie Chan.

Earl Derr Biggers' polite oriental detective with the large family and an even more plentiful supply of wise and witty sayings was first featured by Hollywood in a 1926 serial; George Kuwa played him.

Kamiyama Sojin played him once in 1928, E. L. Park once in 1929, Warner Oland sixteen times (1931–37), Sidney Toler twenty-two times (1938–47) and Roland Winters six times (1948–52). J. Carrol Naish then took over for thirty-nine TV films (1957), and in 1971 Ross Martin appeared as Chan in a TV feature. 1972 brought an animated TV cartoon series, *Charlie Chan and the Chan Clan*: Chan was voiced by Keye Luke, who had played Chan's number two son so often in the 30s. A veil is best drawn over the so-called spoof of 1981's *Charlie Chan and the Curse of the Dragon Queen*, in which Peter Ustinov took over the role of the famous detective.

The 'classic' Chan films were as follows:

1929	*Behind That Curtain*
1931	*Charlie Chan Carries On*, *The Black Camel*
1932	*Charlie Chan's Chance*, *Charlie Chan's Greatest Case*
1934	*Charlie Chan's Courage*, *Charlie Chan in London*
1935	Charlie Chan in Paris, Charlie Chan in Egypt, Charlie Chan in Shanghai
1936	*Charlie Chan's Secret*, *Charlie Chan at the Circus*, *Charlie Chan at the Racetrack*, *Charlie Chan at the Opera*
1937	*Charlie Chan at the Olympics*, *Charlie Chan on Broadway*
1938	*Charlie Chan at Monte Carlo* (last Oland), *Charlie Chan in Honolulu*
1939	*Charlie Chan in Reno*, *Charlie Chan at Treasure Island*, *Charlie Chan in the City of Darkness*
1940	*Charlie Chan in Panama*, *Charlie Chan's Murder Cruise*, *Charlie Chan in the Wax Museum*, *Murder over New York*
1941	*Dead Men Tell*, *Charlie Chan in Rio*
1942	*Castle in the Desert* (after which the series moved from Fox to Monogram and consequently lower budgets)

Charters and Caldicott

were two imperturbable, cricket-loving Englishmen played by Basil Radford and Naunton Wayne respectively in Hitchcock's *The Lady Vanishes* 38, which was written by Frank Launder and Sidney Gilliat. They turned up again in the same writers' thriller *Night Train to Munich* 40, directed by Carol Reed, and were heard in BBC radio serials. One such, *Crook's Tour* 40, was turned into a low-budget film by John Baxter, with a script by John Watt and Max Kester. Launder and Gilliat wrote and directed the wartime *Millions Like Us* 43, in which Charters and Caldicott appeared in uniform. A remake of *The Lady Vanishes* 79 had the duo played by Arthur Lowe and Ian Carmichael, and they also featured in a short-lived TV series, *Charters and Caldicott* 85, featuring Robin Bailey and Michael Aldridge.

the chase

has always been a standard ingredient of film-making, providing a foolproof way of rounding off a comedy or thriller in good style. In silent days it was necessary to every comedian, from the Keystone Kops to Buster Keaton, while westerns inevitably concluded with the goodies chasing the baddies, and even *Intolerance* has a four-stranded chase finale. Sound comedies began by using the chase more sparingly, but René Clair's *Le Million* 32 was a superbly sustained example of the fuller orchestration now possible, and later sophisticated comedies like *It Happened One Night*, *Sullivan's Travels*, *The Runaround*, *Sex and the Single Girl*, *Good Neighbour Sam* and *What's Up Doc?* have not disdained using the chase as a basic theme; nor of course have broader comedians such as Harold Lloyd, W.C. Fields, Laurel and Hardy and Abbott and Costello, and Stanley Kramer devised a super chase in the marathon *It's a Mad Mad Mad Mad World* 63, to be rivalled in 1965 by *The Great Race*. Most of the old chase gags were crammed into the finale of *A Funny Thing Happened on the Way to the Forum* 67. Ealing comedies of the late 40s and early 50s (*The Lavender Hill Mob*, *Whisky Galore*, *The Man in the White Suit*, *A Run For Your Money*) also used chases brilliantly to broaden their shafts of satire.

More serious films using the chase theme include: *You Only Live Once*, *Stagecoach*, *Out of the Past*, *High Sierra*, *They Live By Night*, *Odd Man Out*, *The Capture*, *The Chase*, *Tell Them Willie Boy Is Here*, *Figures in a Landscape*, and the innumerable versions of *Les Misérables*, which also sparked off five television series: *The Fugitive*, *Run For Your Life*, *Branded*, *Run Buddy Run*, and *Kung Fu*. Thrillers which have featured exciting chases include the Bond adventures, many Hitchcocks including *The 39 Steps* and *North by Northwest*, *The Naked City*, *Robbery*, *Bullitt*, *Vanishing Point*, *The French Connection*, *Puppet on a Chain*, *Dirty Mary Crazy Larry*, *Race with the Devil*, *Escape from Zahrain* and *The Seven-Ups*.

child stars

have been popular with every generation of filmgoers. Throughout the 20s Mary Pickford stayed at the top by remaining a child as long as, and after, she could; with only slight competition from Baby Peggy, Madge Evans, Dawn O'Day (later Anne Shirley) and Wesley Barry. Stronger competitors, perhaps, were Junior Coghlan and, around 1930, Junior Durkin; strongest of all was Jackie Coogan, immortalized by Chaplin as *The Kid* in 1920 and subsequently cast in all the standard juvenile roles. The child comedians who composed *Our Gang* for Hal Roach started in the 20s and went on, with cast changes, into the 40s: best remembered of them are Joe Cobb, Jean Darling, Johnny Downs, Mickey Daniels, Farina, Spanky McFarland, Alfalfa Switzer, Darla Hood and Buckwheat Thomas.

Jackie Cooper also started in *Our Gang* but became a star in his own right after playing in *The Champ* and *Skippy*. In the early 30s his main rival was Dickie Moore, a lad of somewhat gentler disposition. Soon both were displaced in popular favour by Freddie Bartholemew in *David Copperfield*; but no boy could hold a candle to the multi-talented prodigy Shirley Temple, a star in 1933 at the age of five. She captivated a generation in a dozen or more hurriedly-produced sentimental comedies, and neither the angelic British Binkie Stuart nor the mischievous Jane Withers could cast the same spell.

Noting a splendid performance by twelve-year-old Robert Lynen in the French *Poil de Carotte*, we next encounter the still irrepressible Mickey Rooney, who popped up variously as Puck, Andy Hardy or a one-man-band. Then in 1937, the year that the Mauch twins appeared in *The Prince and the Pauper*, an MGM short called *Every Sunday* introduced two singing teenage girls, Deanna Durbin and Judy Garland, who went on to achieve enormous popularity in maturing roles until both were overtaken by personal difficulties. Another child who went on to musical stardom was vaudeville-bred Donald O'Connor, first seen in *Sing You Sinners*. But little more was seen of Tommy Kelly, who played *Tom Sawyer*, or Ann Gillis, or Terry Kilburn, or even Roddy McDowall until he re-emerged as a character actor twenty-five years later.

The early 40s saw Edith Fellows as a good girl and Virginia Weidler, so marvellous in *The Philadelphia Story*, as a bad one. Baby Sandy appeared in a few comedies, as had Baby Le Roy ten years earlier; neither was seen on screen after the toddler stage. Two infant Dead End Kids, Butch and Buddy, roamed mischievously through several Universal comedies. Margaret O'Brien and Peggy Ann Garner were two truly remarkable child actresses who never quite managed the transition to adult stardom. Teenagers Ann Blyth and Peggy Ryan partnered Donald O'Connor in many a light musical. Other child actors of the period were Ted Donaldson, Diana Lynn, Darryl Hickman and Sharyn Moffett, while Skippy Homeier gave an electrifying performance as the young Nazi in *Tomorrow the World*. In the post-war years Europe contributed Ivan Jandl in *The Search*; Britain had George Cole and Harry Fowler for cockney roles, Jeremy Spenser for well-bred ones, Anthony Wager and Jean Simmons in *Great Expectations*, and very memorable performances from Bobby Henrey in *The Fallen Idol* and John Howard Davies in *Oliver Twist*. Hollywood responded with thoughtful Claude Jarman, tearful Bobs Watson, spunky Bobby Driscoll and Tommy Rettig, and pretty little misses Gigi Perreau and Natalie Wood.

The 50s brought William (now James) Fox in *The Magnet*, Brigitte Fossey and Georges Poujouly in *Les Jeux Interdits*, Mandy Miller in *Mandy*, Vincent Winter and Jon Whiteley in *The Kidnappers*, Brandon de Wilde in *Shane*, and Patty McCormack as the evil child in *The Bad Seed*. In 1959 Hayley Mills embarked on a six-year reign (somewhat outshone in *Whistle down the Wind* by Alan Barnes); the similar and equally capable American actress Patty Duke confined herself principally to stage and TV apart from *The Miracle Worker*. Then there have been Disney's over-wholesome Tommy Kirk and Annette Funicello, Fergus McClelland in *Sammy Going South*, Jean-Pierre Léaud in *The Four Hundred Blows*, William Dix in *The Nanny*, Matthew Garber and Karen Dotrice in *Mary Poppins*, Deborah Baxter in *A High Wind in Jamaica*, Mark Lester and Jack Wild in *Oliver*, Tatum O'Neal in *Paper Moon*, Linda Blair in *The Exorcist*, Ando in *Paper Tiger*, Kim Richards and Ike Eisenmann in *Escape to Witch Mountain*, Ricky Schroder in *The Champ* . . . and more moppets are inevitably waiting in the wings, though the recent tendency has been for them to make one appearance and disappear from the boards.

One exception has been Bonnie Bedelia's nephew Macaulay Culkin, who starred in the most successful of all comedies, *Home Alone*, which was his fourth film, and commanded a fee of $5 million for the sequel. Lukas Haas, who played the wide-eyed seven-year-old boy in *Witness*, has gone on to make another eight or so films with great success. Perhaps it is significant that Jodie Foster, one of the few to have made the successful transition from child star to adult actress, chose to make her début as a director in 91 with *Little Man Tate*, a film about the problems of gifted children.

❝ Being a child actor is not something I'd allow my child to choose. Why? Because I'm in the business. I know you have to become an adult far too quickly. You're working. You're not being a kid. It's a giant responsibility. But there are all kinds of child actors out there, and if we didn't have them we'd have to hire a lot of midgets. – *Craig Baumgarten*

childhood portrayed by grown-ups

was instanced by Joan Fontaine in *Letter from an Unknown Woman*; by Ginger Rogers in *The Major and the Minor*; by Ginger Rogers and Alan Marshal in *Tom Dick and Harry*; by Ginger Rogers and Cary Grant in *Monkey Business*; and by Jack Buchanan, Fred Astaire and Nanette Fabray in the 'Triplets' number in *Band Wagon*. One might also add Judy Garland in *The Wizard of Oz*: she was seventeen when she played Dorothy.

Chilly Willy.

Cheerful, quick-witted penguin who starred in 35 cartoons from 1953–72, produced by Walter Lanz and released by Universal. He enjoyed his greatest success when animated briefly by Tex Avery.

Chilly Willy 53. I'm Cold (AAN) 54. Hot and Cold 55. The Big Snooze 57. Polar Pests 58. Clash and Carry 61. Fish and Chips 63. Snow Place Like Home 66. Hot Time on Ice 67. Chilly's Cold War 70. The Rude Intruder 72, etc.

Christ

on the screen was for many years a controversial subject: film-makers have usually preferred to imply his presence by a hand, a cloak, or simply reactions of onlookers. However, even in the first ten years of cinephotography there were several versions of his life, and in 1912 Robert Henderson played the role in a 'super' production of *From the Manger to the Cross*. In 1916 came *Civilisation*, with George Fisher as Christ on the battlefields, and in the same year *Intolerance*, in which Howard Gaye was Jesus. In 1927 Cecil B. de Mille's *King of Kings* had H. B. Warner in the role; any offence was minimized by having his first appearance a misty fade-in as the blind girl regains her sight. In 1932 Duvivier made *Golgotha*, with Robert le Vigan; twenty years then went by before Christ's next appearance on the screen, played by a non-professional, Robert Wilson, in a sponsored movie called *Day of Triumph*. In 1961 Jeffrey Hunter appeared as Christ in *King of Kings*, which was unfortunately tagged by the trade *I Was a Teenage Jesus*. George Stevens' disappointing 1965 colossus, *The Greatest Story Ever Told*, cleverly cast Swedish Max von Sydow in the part; in the same year came Pasolini's *The Gospel According to St Matthew*, with Enrique Irazoqui; and in 1969 Buñuel cast Bernard Verley as Christ in *The Milky Way*. Christ-like figures of various kinds have been found in such films as *The Passing of the Third Floor Back*, *The Fugitive*, *Strange Cargo* and *The Face*; while films about the direct influence of Christ's life include *Quo Vadis*, *The Last Days of Pompeii*, *Ben Hur*, *Barabbas*, *The Wandering Jew* and *The Robe*, in which the voice of Christ was provided by Cameron Mitchell. The most recent Christs have been in the modernized pop-operas *Godspell* and *Jesus Christ Superstar*; a TV series, *Jesus of Nazareth*; a TV movie with a literal slant, *The Day Christ Died*; and Martin Scorsese's *The Last Temptation of Christ*. Alessandro D'Alatri's *The Garden of Eden* 98 covered the childhood and adolescence of Jesus, who was played by Kim Rossi Stuart.

Christmas

has provided a favourite sentimental climax for many a film. Films wholly based on it include *The Holly and the Ivy*, *Tenth Avenue Angel*, *Miracle on 34th Street*, *White Christmas*, *Christmas Eve*, *Christmas in Connecticut*, *The Bishop's Wife*, *I'll Be Seeing You*, and the many versions of *Scrooge*. There were happy Christmas scenes in *The Bells of St Mary*, *The Inn of the Sixth Happiness*, *The Man Who Came to Dinner*, *Holiday Inn*, *Since You Went Away*, *Three Godfathers*, *It's a Wonderful Life*, *Young at Heart*, *Meet Me in St Louis*, *On Moonlight Bay*, *Little Women*, *The Cheaters*, *Desk Set* and *Young at Heart* among others; while unhappy Christmases were spent in *Things to Come*, *Full House* ('The Gifts of the Magi'), *The Apartment*, *Meet John Doe*, *The Glenn Miller Story*, *The Christmas Tree*, *Christmas Holiday*, and *The Victors*. (Nor was there much for the characters in *The Lion in Winter* to celebrate at the Christmas court of 1189.)

Santa Claus himself put in an appearance in *Miracle on 34th Street* (played by Edmund Gwenn and, in the remake, Richard Attenborough), *The Lemon Drop Kid* (played by Bob Hope), *The Light at Heart* (played by Monty Woolley), and *Robin and the Seven Hoods* (played by the Sinatra clan). Disney features him in *Babes in Toyland* and a short cartoon, *The Night Before Christmas*; and in their 1934 version of *Babes in Toyland* Laurel and Hardy found him an irate employer. Tim Allen substitutes for him in *The Santa Clause*.

Christmas was celebrated in unlikely settings in *Knights of the Round Table*, *Conquest of Space*, *Scott of the Antarctic*, *Encore* ('Winter Cruise'), *Destination Tokyo* (in a submarine), *The Nun's Story* (in a Congo Mission), and *Black Narcissus* (in an Indian nunnery).

churches

have provided a setting for many pretty secular-minded films, from the various versions of *The Hunchback of Notre Dame* to the use of a church as a refuge during a flood in *When Tomorrow Comes*. Other memorable moments include Bogart confessing the plot of *Dead Reckoning* to a priest; Robert Donat's sermon in *Lease of Life* and Orson Welles' in *Moby Dick*; the scandalous confessions in *Les Jeux Interdits* and the dramatic one in *I Confess*; the murder of Becket; the bombed but well-used churches in *Mrs Miniver* and *Sundown*; the thing in the rafters of Westminster Abbey in *The Quatermass Experiment*; the attempted murder in Westminster Cathedral in *Foreign Correspondent* and the fall from the church tower in *Vertigo*; the spies in the mission chapel in *The Man Who Knew Too Much*; the arrest of *Pastor Hall*; Arturo de Cordova going mad during a service in *El*; the church-tower climax of *The Stranger*; the Russian services in *Ivan the Terrible* and *We Live Again*; Cagney dying on the church steps in *The Roaring Twenties*; the church used as refuge against the Martians in *The War of the Worlds*; the church used for a town meeting in *High Noon*; the Turkish mosque and espionage rendezvous in *From Russia with Love*; the comic rifling of offertory boxes in *Heaven Sent*; the finale of *Miracle in the Rain* in the church porch; the meeting in church of the protagonists of *The Appaloosa*; the characters finally trapped in a church in *The Exterminating Angel*; the churches swept away by the elements in *The Hurricane* and *Hawaii*; the church rendezvous in *Alice's Restaurant*; the church with the moving statue in *The Miracle of the Bells*; and all the many films in which the protagonists are PRIESTS, MONKS and NUNS.

the cinema

A few fragments of thought:

The cinema, like the detective story, makes it possible to experience without danger all the excitement, passion and desirousness which must be suppressed in a humanitarian ordering of society. – *C.G. Jung*

It has no boundary . . . it is a ribbon of dream. – *Orson Welles*

The most collaborative of the arts. – *Dore Schary*

Truth twenty-four times a second. – *Jean-Luc Godard*

Of all the arts, the cinema is the most important for us. – *V.I. Lenin*

That temple of sex, with its goddesses, its guardians and its victims . . . – *Jean Cocteau*

An uncomfortable way of watching television. – *Sheila Black*

The film is not an art but a super tabloid for young and old, moron and genius. Her sister muses are the comic strips, the pulp magazines, the radio and all other forms of entertainment based on democratic rather than aesthetic principles. – *Howard Collins (manager in 1953 of Roxy Theatre, NY)*

Of course a film should have a beginning, a middle and an end. But not necessarily in that order. – *Jean-Luc Godard*

I always think that watching films is very like dreaming. – *John Boorman*

Whoever it was who first thought the cinema was an art, he should have kept his mouth shut. Not that it isn't, but there are so many terrible instances of films made specifically to be art which come perilously close to making us doubt the whole proposition. – *John Russell Taylor*

The film does best when it concentrates on a single character. It does *The Informer* superbly. It tends to lose itself in the ramifications of *War and Peace*. – *Budd Schulberg*

The finished product is not finished when the actor is. The work is completed by a pair of shears. – *Josef von Sternberg*

Editing is the foundation of the film art. – *Pudovkin*

Get a director and a writer and leave them alone. That's how the best pictures get made. – *William Wellman*

Any attempt in America to make a film a work of art must be hailed. Usually, in the same breath, it must be farewelled. – *John Simon*

The American film mind, though it can deal competently enough with the stupendous, cannot help vulgarizing any scene which approaches the intimate. – *James Agate*

Collectively the audience is, in the matter of aesthetic, totally uneducated. They gape before the screen today as the thirteenth-century play-goer gaped at the morality play. – *James Agate again, in 1921*

Most Hollywood comedies are so vulgar, witless and dull that it is preposterous to write about them in any publication not meant to be read while chewing gum. – *Wolcott Gibbs*

Cinema is an improvement on life. – *François Truffaut*

If you want art, don't mess about with movies. Buy a Picasso. – *Michael Winner*

The movies languish as a fine art because the men who determine what is to get into them haven't the slightest visible notion that such a thing as a fine art exists. – *H. L. Mencken, 1927*

Film-making has now reached the same stage as sex – it's all technique and no feeling. – *Penelope Gilliatt* in the 80s

cinemas

have only rarely provided a background for film situations. A Hollywood première and a sneak preview were shown in *Singin' in the Rain*, and *The Oscar* revealed all about the Academy Awards ceremony. Characters in *Sherlock Junior*, *Borderlines* and *Merton of the Movies* (Red Skelton version) clambered on to the stage while a film was showing. Projectionists were featured in *Clash by Night*, *The Blob*, *The Great Morgan*, and *Hellzapoppin*; also in *The Smallest Show on Earth*, the only film concerned with the running of a cinema as its main plot unless one counts *The Last Picture Show* in which the small-town cinema is an essential background to the character development. Fred Allen in *It's in the Bag* had a terrible time trying to find a seat in a full house; Dillinger was killed coming out of a cinema in *The F.B.I. Story*; Bogart was nearly shot in a Chinese cinema in *Across the Pacific*, and Anthony Perkins met Valli in a Siamese one in *This Angry Age/The Sea Wall*. A cinema was used as a rendezvous for spies in *The Traitors* and *Sabotage*; a church was used as a cinema in *Sullivan's Travels* when chain-gang convicts watched Mickey Mouse. Mark Stevens and Joan Fontaine in *From This Day Forward* visited a news cinema but were too much in love to heed the warnings of impending war. Louis Jourdan and Linda Christian watched Valentino at the local in *The Happy Time*, and astronauts watched Bob Hope in a space station in *Conquest of Space*. Deanna Durbin got a murder clue in a cinema in *Lady on a Train*; and in *Bullets or Ballots* Humphrey Bogart took Barton MacLane to see a documentary about his nefarious career. Ray Danton in *The Rise and Fall of Legs Diamond* excused himself during a performance to rob the shop next door. The monster in *The Tingler* escapes into a silent cinema. Linda Hayden in *Baby Love* was accosted in a cinema. Robert Cummings in *Saboteur* started a riot in Radio City Music Hall, on the stairs of which Danny Kaye sang in *Up in Arms*. Fredric March watched a Thomas Ince silent at the local nickelodeon in *One Foot in Heaven*. In *Brief Encounter*, Celia Johnson and Trevor Howard thought the organist was the best part of the programme. Polly Bergen in *The Caretakers* went crazy and climbed up in front of the screen. *Bonnie and Clyde* found time between robberies to see a *Gold Diggers* movie. In *Eye Witness* a cinema manager was killed during the Saturday night performance; and in *Targets* a killer was apprehended by Boris Karloff at a drive-in. A drive-in was used as a rendezvous in *White Heat* and a 42nd Street cinema was a homosexual rendezvous in *Midnight Cowboy*. *Cinema Paradiso* was a love-letter to a small-town cinema and its projectionist. Home movies figured most notably in *Rebecca* and *Adam's Rib*.

See also: EXCERPTS, THEATRES.

circuses,

according to the cinema, are full of drama and passion behind the scenes. So you would think if you judged from *Variety*, *Freaks*, *The Wagons Roll at Night*, *The Greatest Show on Earth*, *The Big Show*, *The Big Circus*, *Sawdust and Tinsel*, *Circus of Horrors*, *Tromba*, *Four Devils*, *The Three Maxims*, *Trapeze*, *Captive Wild Woman*, *Ring of Fear*, *Charlie Chan at the Circus*, *A Tiger Walks*, *Circus World*, *The Trojan Brothers*, *Circus of Fear*, *Berserk*, *The Dark Tower*, *He Who Gets Slapped*, *Flesh and Fantasy*, *Man on a Tightrope*, *Chad Hanna*, *Pagliacci*, *Far From the Madding Crowd*, and *Vampire Circus*. But there is a lighter side, as evidenced by *Doctor Dolittle*, *Yo Yo*, *Jumbo*, *High Wide and Handsome*, *Lady in the Dark*, *Life is a Circus*, *The Marx Brothers at the Circus*, *Three Rings Circus*, Chaplin's *The Circus*, *The Great Profile*, *You Can't Cheat an Honest Man*, *Road Show*, *Merry Andrew*, and *Toby Tyler*.

TV series have included *Circus Boy*, *Frontier Circus* and *The Greatest Show on Earth*.

The Cisco Kid

was a Mexican outlaw of the 1890s, created by O. Henry in a short story, *The Caballero's Way*. The character died in his first, silent-screen appearance in 1914, and owed his later longevity to the early talkie *In Old Arizona* 29, in which he was played as a dashing rogue by Warner BAXTER. The role made Baxter a star and earned him an Oscar, after he took over the part from an injured Raoul WALSH; he followed it with three lesser sequels. Cesar ROMERO played the role in seven 'B' features from 1939, and was followed by Duncan RENALDO, who appeared in eight films from 1945, and Gilbert ROLAND, who clocked up six appearances in the late 40s. Renaldo also starred in a popular TV series, *The Cisco Kid* 50–56, with Leo CARRILLO as his sidekick, Pancho. A TV film, *The Cisco Kid* 94, starred Jimmy SMITS, with Cheech MARIN as Pancho.

clairvoyance

on the screen seems to have caused a remarkable amount of suffering to Edward G. Robinson: he was haunted by the effects of a prophecy in *Flesh and Fantasy*, *Nightmare* and *Night Has a Thousand Eyes*. Other frightened men for similar reasons were Claude Rains in *The Clairvoyant*, Dick Powell in *It Happened Tomorrow*, George Macready in *I Love a Mystery*, Mervyn Johns in *Dead of Night*, and Michael Hordern in *The Night My Number Came Up*. Rosanna Arquette suffers more than most as a medium able to foretell the violent deaths of those around her in *Black Rainbow* 89.

coal mines

and the bravery of the men who work in them formed a theme which commanded the respect of cinema audiences for many years. Apart from *Kameradschaft* (the French-German border), *Black Fury* (US), and *The Molly Maguires* (US), all the major films on this subject have been about Britain: *The Proud Valley*, *The Stars Look Down*, *How Green Was My Valley*, *The Citadel*, *The Corn is Green*, *The Brave Don't Cry*, *Sons and Lovers*, *Women in Love*.

Cobra (1986):

see FAIR GAME.

the Cold War
has occupied the cinema right from Churchill's Fulton speech in 1948. For three years diehard Nazis had been the international villains par excellence, but a change was required, and Russians have been fair game ever since, in films like *The Iron Curtain, Diplomatic Courier, I Was a Communist for the FBI, I Married a Communist, The Big Lift, Red Snow, The Red Danube, Red Menace, Red Planet Mars, The Journey, From Russia With Love* and innumerable pulp spy thrillers, as well as such classier productions as *The Third Man, The Man Between* and *The Spy Who Came in from the Cold*. Rather surprisingly none of these caused much escalation of tension between the nations, and cooler feelings have permitted comedies like *One Two Three, Dr Strangelove* and *The Russians are Coming, The Russians are Coming*; while such terrifying panic-button melodramas as *Fail Safe* and *The Bedford Incident* are probably our best guarantee that the dangers are realized on both sides.

colleges:
see UNIVERSITIES.

comedy:
see COMEDY TEAMS; CRAZY COMEDY; LIGHT COMEDIANS; SATIRE; SEX; SOCIAL COMEDY; SLAPSTICK.

comedy teams
in the accepted sense began in vaudeville, but, depending so much on the spoken word, could make little headway in films until the advent of the talkies. Then they all tried, and many (Amos 'n Andy, Gallagher and Shean, Olsen and Johnson) didn't quite make it, at least not immediately. Laurel and Hardy, who had been successful in silents by the use of mime, adapted their methods very little and remained popular; during the 30s they were really only challenged by Wheeler and Woolsey, whose style was more frenetic, and briefly by Burns and Allen. From 1940 the cross-talking Abbott and Costello reigned supreme, with an occasional challenge from Hope and Crosby and the splendid *Hellzapoppin* from Olsen and Johnson. Then came Martin and Lewis, who didn't appeal to everybody, Rowan and Martin, who in 1957 didn't appeal to anybody, and sporadic attempts to popularize such teams as Brown and Carney and Allen and Rossi. In Britain, comedy teams were popular even in poor films: the best of them were Jack Hulbert and Cicely Courtneidge, Tom Walls and Ralph Lynn, Lucan and MacShane ('Old Mother Riley'), Arthur Askey and Richard Murdoch, and the Crazy Gang, a bumper fun bundle composed of Flanagan and Allen, Naughton and Gold, and Nervo and Knox. One should also mention Basil Radford and Naunton Wayne, not cross-talkers but inimitable caricaturists of the Englishman abroad; and others, not strictly comedians, who raised a lot of laughs together: Edmund Lowe and Victor McLaglen, Slim Summerville and ZaSu Pitts, Joan Blondell and Glenda Farrell, George Sidney and Charlie Murray, Marie Dressler and Polly Moran, Wallace Beery and Raymond Hatton, James Cagney and Pat O'Brien, Jack Lemmon and Walter Matthau. Recent teams include Morecambe and Wise and Cannon and Ball.

See: 1970, *Movie Comedy Teams* by Leonard Maltin.

Of larger groups, among the most outstanding are Our Gang, the Keystone Kops, the Marx Brothers, the Three Stooges, the Ritz Brothers, Will Hay with Moore Marriott and Graham Moffat, the 'Carry On' team, the Beatles and the Monty Python team.

See also: ROMANTIC TEAMS.

œ

Nobody should try to play comedy unless they have a circus going on inside. – *Ernst Lubitsch*

comic strips
in newspapers have always been avidly watched by film producers with an eye on the popular market. Among films and series so deriving are the following:

Gertie the Dinosaur (cartoon series) 19; The Gumps (two-reelers) 23–28; *Bringing Up Father* 16 (drawn), 20 (two-reeler), 28 (feature with J. Farrell MacDonald and Marie Dressler), 45 (series of 'Jiggs and Maggie' features with Joe Yule and Renée Riano); *The Katzenjammer Kids* (cartoon series) 17 and 38, *Krazy Kat* (various cartoons 16–38); *Ella Cinders* (with Colleen Moore) 22; *Tillie the Toiler* (with Marion Davies) 27; *Skippy* (with Jackie Cooper) 30; *Little Orphan Annie* 32 (with Mitzi Green) and 38 (with Ann Gillis); *Joe Palooka* 34 (with Stu Erwin) and 47–51 (with Joe Kirkwood); *Blondie* (with Penny Singleton) 38–48; *Gasoline Alley* (with James Lydon) 51; *L'il Abner; Popeye; Jungle Jim* 49–54; Prince Valiant 54; *Up Front* 51–53; *Felix the Cat; Old Bill* (GB) 40; *Dick Barton* (GB) in various personifications; *Jane* (GB) in an abysmal 1949 second feature; and, of course, *Modesty Blaise* 66, *Batman* 66, *Barbarella* 68, and *Fritz the Cat* 71.

Strip characters whose adventures were turned into Hollywood serials during the 30s and 40s include *Tailspin Tommy, Mandrake the Magician, Don Winslow of the Navy, Jet Jackson Flying Commando, Flash Gordon, Batman, Buck Rogers in the 25th century, Brick Bradford* ('in the centre of the earth'), *Chandu, Superman, Dick Tracy* (also in 40s features), *The Lone Ranger* and *Red Ryder*. The re-emergence of Superman and Batman as heroes of big-budget films from the late 70s led to a search for similar fantastic figures to appeal to a mass audience. The Shadow and The Phantom both made unsuccessful appearances in the 90s, together with such recent and ambivalent comic-book creations as Judge Dredd and Tank Girl, where the distinctions between good and evil are more blurred. With the successful marketing on video of Japanese ANIME, derived from their comic books, and MANGA, featuring fantastic heroes, came an attempt to turn Crying Freeman, a Chinese hitman, into an action movie hero.

In the late 70s comic strip characters became popular TV action heroes, and until the balloon burst audiences were overwhelmed by the antics of *The Incredible Hulk, Wonder Woman, Buck Rogers in the 25th Century*, etc., following on the success of TV's own creations in this vein, *The Six Million Dollar Man, Bionic Woman* and *The Man from Atlantis*.

communism
has always been treated by Hollywood as a menace. In the 30s one could laugh at it, in *Ninotchka* and *He Stayed for Breakfast*. Then in World War II there was a respite during which the virtues of the Russian peasantry were extolled in such films as *Song of Russia* and *North Star*. But with the Cold War, every international villain became a Commie instead of a Nazi, and our screens were suddenly full of dour dramas about the deadliness of 'red' infiltration: *I Married a Communist, I Was a Communist for the FBI, The Red Menace, The Iron Curtain, Trial, My Son John, Walk East on Beacon, The Red Danube, Red Snow, Red Planet Mars, Blood Alley, Big Jim McLain, The Manchurian Candidate*. In the early 60s a documentary compilation of red aggression was released under the title *We'll Bury You*. The British never seemed to take the peril seriously, though the agitator in *The Angry Silence* was clearly labelled red.

Famous line: 'Communism,' said the butler in *Soak the Rich*, 'is the growing pains of the young.'

compilation films
have become commonplace on TV through such series as *Twentieth Century, Men of Our Time* and *The Valiant Years*, all using library material to evoke a pattern of the past. Thanks to the careful preservation of original documentary material, film-makers have been able, over the last thirty years or so, to give us such films on a wide variety of subjects and to develop an exciting extra dimension of film entertainment which also serves a historical need.

The first outstanding efforts in this direction were made by H. Bruce Woolfe in his 20s documentaries of World War I, mixing newsreel footage with reconstructed scenes. In 1940 Cavalcanti assembled his study of Mussolini, *Yellow Caesar*; and in 1942 Frank Capra, working for the US Signal Corps, gave a tremendous fillip to the art of the compilation film with his 'Why We Fight' series. Paul Rotha's *World of Plenty* 43 was a clever study of world food shortages using all kinds of film material including animated diagrams and acted sequences. In 1945 Carol Reed and Garson Kanin, in *The True Glory*, gave the story of D-Day to Berlin an unexpected poetry, and in 1946 Don Siegel in his short *Hitler Lives* showed all too clearly what a frightening potential the compilation form had as propaganda. Nicole Védrès in 1947 turned to the more distant past and in *Paris 1900* produced an affectionate portrait of a bygone age; Peter Baylis followed this with *The Peaceful Years*, covering the period between the two wars. In 1950 Stuart Legg's *Powered Flight* traced the history of aviation.

The Thorndikes, working in East Germany, started in 1956 their powerful series *The Archives Testify*, attributing war crimes to West German officials; this aggressive mood was followed in their *Du und Mancher Kamerad* ('The German Story') and *The Russian Miracle*, though in the latter case they seemed somewhat less happy in praising than in blaming. In 1959 George Morrison's *Mise Eire* graphically presented the truth of the much-fictionalized Irish troubles; and in 1960 came the first of the films about Hitler, Erwin Leiser's *Mein Kampf*, to be sharply followed by Rotha's *The Life of Adolf Hitler* and Louis Clyde Stoumen's rather fanciful *Black Fox*. Jack Le Vien, producer of the last-named, went on to make successful films about Churchill (*The Finest Hours*) and the Duke of Windsor (*A King's Story*). Now every year the compilations come thick and fast. From France, *Fourteen-Eighteen*; from BBC TV, twenty-six half-hours of *The Great War*; from Granada TV, *The Fanatics* (suffragettes), *The World of Mr Wells* (H. G., that is) and a long-running weekly series, *All Our Yesterdays*, which consisted entirely of old newsreels; from Associated-British, *Time to Remember*, a series devoting half an hour to each year of the century; from Italy, *Allarmi Siam' Fascisti*, a history of the fascist movement; from Japan, *Kamikaze*, about the suicide pilots; from France, Rossif's *Mourir à Madrid* and *The Fall of Berlin*. The list will be endless, because even though every foot of old newsreel were used up, one could begin again, using different editing, juxtapositions and commentary to achieve different effects.

Best book on the subject: Jay Leyda's *Films Beget Films*.

In the late 50s there began a pleasing fashion for compilations of scenes from fictional films on a theme. This began with Robert Youngson's masterly evocations of silent slapstick: *The Golden Age of Comedy, When Comedy Was King*, etc. TV series such as *Silents Please* and *Hollywood and the Stars* followed suit. In the 70s MGM had an immense success with *That's Entertainment*, compiled from its past successes, and also brought out *The Big Parade of Comedy*. Twentieth-Century-Fox turned its backlog into a television series, *That's Hollywood*; and for a while wherever one looked in Hollywood there was at least one studio cutting room devoted to turning over and reassembling highlights of the past.

See also: DOCUMENTARY (Section 5).

composers
have frequently been lauded on cinema screens, usually in storylines which bore little relation to their real lives, and the films were not often box-office successes. Here are some of the subjects of musical biopics:

~George Frederick Handel (1685–1759): Wilfred Lawson, *The Great Mr Handel* 42.
~Wolfgang Amadeus Mozart (1756–91): Stephen Haggard, *Whom the Gods Love* 36; Hannes Steltzer, *Die Kleine Nachtmusik* 39; Gino Cervi, *Eternal Melody* 39; Oskar Werner, *The Life of Mozart* 56; Tom Hulce, *Amadeus* (84).
~Ludwig van Beethoven (1770–1827): Albert Basserman, *New Wine* 41; Ewald Balser, *Eroica* 49; Karl Boehm, *The Magnificent Rebel* 60; Gary Oldman, *Immortal Beloved* 95.
~Niccolò Paganini (1782–1840): Stewart Granger, *The Magic Bow* 47.
~Franz Schubert (1797–1828): Nils Asther, *Love Time* 34; Richard Tauber, *Blossom Time* 34; Hans Jaray, *Unfinished Symphony* 35; Alan Curtis *New Wine* 41; Tino Rossi, *La Belle Meunière* 47; Claude Laydu, *Symphony of Love* 54; Karl Boehm, *Das Dreimaederlhaus* 58.
~Vincenzo Bellini (1801–35): Phillips Holmes, *The Divine Spark* 35.
~Hector Berlioz (1803–69): Jean-Louis Barrault, *La Symphonie Fantastique* 40.
~Frederic Chopin (1810–49): Jean Servais, *Adieu* 35; Cornel Wilde, *A Song to Remember* 44; Czeslaw Wollejko, *The Young Chopin* 52; Alexander Davion, *Song Without End* 60; Hugh Grant, *Impromptu* 89; Janusz Olejniczak, *La Note Bleue* 91.
~Robert Schumann (1810–56): Paul Henreid, *Song of Love* 47.
~Franz Liszt (1811–86): Stephen Bekassy, *A Song to Remember* 44; Henry Daniell, *Song of Love* 47; Will Quadflieg, *Lola Montez* 55; Dirk Bogarde, *Song Without End* 60; Henry Gilbert, *Song of Norway* 70; Roger Daltrey, *Lisztomania* 75.
~Richard Wagner (1813–83): Alan Badel, *Magic Fire* 56; Trevor Howard, *Ludwig* 73; Richard Burton, *Wagner* 83.
~Johann Strauss Jnr (1825–99): Esmond Knight, *Waltzes from Vienna* 33; Anton Walbrook, *Vienna Waltzes* 34. Fernand Gravey, *The Great Waltz* 38; Kerwin Matthews, *The Waltz King* 60; Horst Buchholz, *The Great Waltz* 72.
~Stephen Foster (1826–64): Don Ameche, *Swanee River* 39; Bill Shirley, *I Dream of Jeannie* 52.
~Johannes Brahms (1833–97): Robert Walker, *Song of Love* 47.
~W. S. Gilbert (1836–1911) and Arthur Sullivan (1842–1900): Nigel Bruce and Claud Allister, *Lillian Russell* 41; Robert Morley and Maurice Evans, *The Story of Gilbert and Sullivan* 53.
~Peter Ilich Tchaikovsky (1840–93): Frank Sundstrom, *Song of My Heart* 47; Innokenti Smoktunovsky, *Tchaikovsky* 69; Richard Chamberlain, *The Music Lovers* 70.
~Edvard Grieg (1843–1907): Toralv Maurstad, *Song of Norway* 70.
~Nikolai Rimsky-Korsakov (1844–1908): Jean-Pierre Aumont, *Song of Scheherezade* 47.
~John Philip Sousa (1854–1932): Clifton Webb, *Stars and Stripes Forever* 52.
~Victor Herbert (1859–1924): Walter Connolly, *The Great Victor Herbert* 39; Paul Maxey, *Till the Clouds Roll By* 46.
~Gustav Mahler (1860–1911): Robert Powell, *Mahler* 74.
~Leslie Stuart (1866–1928): Robert Morley, *You Will Remember* 40.
~W. C. Handy (1873–1948): Nat King Cole, *St Louis Blues* 58.
~Jerome Kern (1885–1945): Robert Walker, *Till the Clouds Roll By* 46.
~Sigmund Romberg (1887–1951): Jose Ferrer, *Deep in My Heart* 54.
~Irving Berlin (1888–1989): Tyrone Power, *Alexander's Ragtime Band* 38.
~Cole Porter (1892–1964): Cary Grant, *Night and Day* 45.
~George Gershwin (1898–1937): Robert Alda, *Rhapsody in Blue* 45.

The list of biopics of lesser modern composers would be long indeed.

computers
from the mid-70s became so commonplace as barely to rate a mention, forming the basis of such films as *Rollover* and *War Games* and TV series such as *Knight Rider* and *Whiz Kids*. Some of their earlier uses in film, however, were in Disney's *The Computer Wore Tennis Shoes*; in the unpleasant *Demon Seed*; in space fiction such as *The Forbin Project, 2001* and *Dark Star*; in *Billion Dollar Brain*; and in a rather advanced TV movie of 1971 called *Paper Man*. In the beginning, computers tended to be regarded as evil, machines that wanted to control people, as in *Superman III* or *Electric Dreams*. But as computers became familiar objects in many homes, and computer and video games grew in popularity, and in turn were often based on hit movies, attitudes changed. Disney's *Tron* tried to capitalize on computer games, as did *Interface*, in which a game turned into reality. The appeal of *The Lawnmower Man* depended on its stunning computer graphics and its simulation of the latest technology of 'virtual reality', a computer-generated world with which people can interact. Androids – half-men, half-computers – emerged as popular heroes in such films as *Robocop* and *The Terminator 2*. By 1992, the tail was beginning to wag the dog, with computer games on compact disk incorporating film clips, and the Nintendo game *Super Mario Brothers* being turned into a movie starring Bob Hoskins. Computers continued to be seen as dangerous devices in *Sneakers* 92, *Hackers* 95, *Strange Days* 95, *Lawnmower Man 2: Beyond Cyberspace* 95, and *The Net* 95. In *Virtuosity* 95, a computerized composite of the world's worst serial killers was let loose in real life. It was not until *You've Got Mail* 98, in which Tom Hanks and Meg Ryan conducted a romance via e-mail, that computers became cuddly.

Conan the Barbarian.
A warrior from the land of Cimmeria in the Hyborian Age who was created in the 30s by pulp writer Robert E. HOWARD for the magazine *Weird Tales*. The stories were later re-edited and rewritten by other hands, and the thick-headed hero gained

an increasing popularity from his appearance in Marvel comic-books in the 70s, which culminated in two films, *Conan the Barbarian* 82 and *Conan the Destroyer* 84, both starring Arnold SCHWARZENEGGER in the title role. A TV series, starring Ralf Moeller, followed in 1997. Many of the SWORD-AND-SORCERY films of the 70s and 80s unfortunately show the influence of Howard's hero.

concentration camps,

until long after World War II, were thought too harrowing a subject for film treatment; but a few serious reconstructions have emerged, notably *The Last Stage* (Poland) 48, *Kapo* (Italy) 60, *Passenger* (Poland) 61, and *One Day in the Life of Ivan Denisovich* 71, while the shadow of Auschwitz hangs over *The Diary of Anne Frank* 59 and *The Pawnbroker* 64. An alleged British concentration camp in South Africa was depicted in the Nazi film *Ohm Krüger* 42. The best documentary on the subject was probably RESNAIS' *Night and Fog*. In 1978 TV included much footage on the subject in *Holocaust*, which was quickly followed by *Playing for Time*. *Shoah* (1986) used no archive footage at all, but spent its nine hours in long interviews with survivors. *Triumph of the Spirit* told the true story of a boxer's survival in Auschwitz. Steven SPIELBERG's stirring *Schindler's List* 93 told the true story of how one man saved many Jews from the camps, while *Paradise Road* 97 showed how women imprisoned by the Japanese kept their spirits high by forming a choir. Robert BENIGNI's *Life Is Beautiful* 98 was a tragi-comedy in a concentration camp setting.

concerts

of serious music naturally figure largely in films about the lives of COMPOSERS, and also in those concerned to show off living musicians: *They Shall Have Music*, *Music for Millions*, *Battle for Music*, *Tonight We Sing*, *Carnegie Hall*, *A Hundred Men and a Girl*, *Rhapsody in Blue*. In the 40s a string of romantic films were centred on classical musicians and had concert climaxes: *Dangerous Moonlight*, *Love Story*, *The Seventh Veil*, *Intermezzo*, *The Great Lie*; this style later returned in *Interlude*. Other dramatic and comic concerts were featured in *Unfaithfully Yours*, *Tales of Manhattan*, *The Man Who Knew Too Much*, *The World of Henry Orient*, *The Bride Wore Black*, *Counterpoint* and *Deadfall*. The most influential film concert was certainly *Fantasia*, and the most poignant probably Myra Hess's recital in the blitz-beset National Gallery in *Listen to Britain*.

confidence tricksters

have figured as minor characters in hundreds of films, but full-length portraits of the breed are few and choice. Harry Baur in *Volpone* and Rex Harrison in *The Honey Pot*; Roland Young, Billie Burke, Janet Gaynor and Douglas Fairbanks Jnr in *The Young in Heart*; Gene Tierney, Laird Cregar and Spring Byington in *Rings on Her Fingers*; Tyrone Power in *Nightmare Alley* and *Mississippi Gambler*; Mai Zetterling in *Quartet*; Paul Newman in *The Hustler*; Charles Coburn and Barbara Stanwyck in *The Lady Eve*; David Niven and Marlon Brando in *Bedtime Story*; George C. Scott in *The Flim Flam Man*; Richard Attenborough and David Hemmings in *Only When I Larf*; James Garner in *The Skin Game*; Newman and Robert Redford in *The Sting*; Ryan and Tatum O'Neal in *Paper Moon*; James Coburn in *Dead Heat on a Merry-go-Round*; Joe Mantegna in *House of Games*, demonstrating how to do it to a bemused Lindsay Crouse; Steve Martin and Michael Caine in *Dirty Rotten Scoundrels*; John Cusack, Annette Bening and Angelica Huston in *The Grifters*.

continuity errors and boo-boos

occur even in the best-regulated movies; sometimes they pass the eagle eye of editor and director and find their way into the release version. Here are a few which have delighted me.

~In *Carmen Jones*, the camera tracks with Dorothy Dandridge down a shopping street, and the entire crew is reflected in the windows she passes.

~In *The Invisible Man*, when the naked but invisible hero runs from the police but is given away by his footprints in the snow, the footprints are of shoes, not feet.

~In *The Wrong Box*, the roofs of Victorian London are disfigured by TV aerials.

~In *The Viking Queen*, one character is plainly wearing a wrist watch.

~In *One Million Years BC*, all the girls wear false eyelashes.

~In *The Group*, set in the 30s, there are several shots of the Pan Am building in New York, built in the 60s.

~In *Stagecoach*, during the Indian chase across the salt flats one can see the tracks of rubber tyres.

~In *Decameron Nights*, Louis Jourdan as Paganino the Pirate stands on the deck of his fourteenth-century ship . . . and down a hill in the distance trundles a large white truck.

~In *Camelot*, the character played by Lionel Jeffries first meets King Arthur about an hour into the movie; yet twenty minutes earlier he is plainly visible at the king's wedding.

~In *Son of Frankenstein*, Basil Rathbone during a train journey draws attention to the weirdly stunted trees . . . one of which passes by three times during the conversation.

~In *Castle of Fu Manchu*, one of the leading characters is referred to in the film as Ingrid, in the synopsis as Anna, and in the end credits as Maria.

~In *Tea and Sympathy*, a pair of china dogs are back to back in a general view of the scene, but face to face in the close-ups.

~In *Dracula*, Bela Lugosi refers to Whitby as 'so close to London'. It is in fact 243 miles away.

~In *The Yellow Mountain* and *A Man Alone*, both westerns set in the last century, aeroplane vapour trails can be seen in the sky.

~In *The King and I*, while Yul Brynner is singing 'Puzzlement' he is wearing an earring in some shots but not in others.

~In *Emma Hamilton* (1969) Big Ben is heard to strike in 1804, fifty years before it was built.

~In *The Lodger* (1944) London's Tower Bridge is shown, ten years before it was built.

~In *Hello Dolly*, set at the turn of the century, a modern car lies derelict by the side of the railway track.

~In *Anatomy of a Murder*, Lee Remick in the café scene wears a dress, but when she walks outside she is wearing slacks.

~In *Hangover Square*, the introductory title gives the date of the action as 1899, but shortly thereafter a theatre programme shows 1903.

~In *Queen Christina*, the famous final close-up apparently has the wind blowing in two directions at once, one to get the boat under way and the other to arrange Garbo's hair to the best advantage.

~In *The Desk Set*, Katharine Hepburn leaves her office carrying a bunch of white flowers. By the time she reaches the pavement they are pink.

~In *Knock on Wood*, Danny Kaye turns a corner in London's Oxford Street, and finds himself in Ludgate Hill, three miles away.

~In *23 Paces to Baker Street*, Van Johnson has an apartment in Portman Square, with a river view which seems to be that of the Savoy Hotel two miles away.

~In *Triple Cross*, a World War II newspaper bears a headline about the cost of Concorde going up again.

~In *The Lady Vanishes*, Miss Froy writes her name in the steam on a train window, but two or three shots later the writing is quite different and in another place.

~In *The Eddie Cantor Story*, the scene is set in 1904, but Eddie sings 'Meet Me Tonight in Dreamland' which was not written till 1909.

~Similarly, in *Thoroughly Modern Millie*, clearly set in 1922 per the song title, one of the big numbers is 'Baby Face', written in 1926.

~In *Miracle on 34th Street*, a camera shadow follows Edmund Gwenn and John Payne as they walk across a square.

~In *Broken Lance*, Katy Jurado's dress changes colour in alternate shots as she stands in a doorway talking to Spencer Tracy at the gate.

~In *North by Northwest*, Cary Grant's only suit during his stay in Chicago is a different colour out in the prairie from back at the hotel. Hitchcock said this was because of different kinds of lighting which were used.

~In *Mysterious Island*, set in 1860, an air balloon rises above a nest of TV aerials.

~In *The Alamo*, mobile trailers are clearly seen in the battle sequences, and a falling stuntman lands on a mattress.

~In *North to Alaska* during a fistfight, John Wayne loses his toupee and then regains it.

~In *The Green Berets*, the sun sets in the east during the final shot.

~In *The Scalphunters*, set in the 1800s, Ossie Davis mentions the planet Pluto, which was not discovered until 1930.

~In *Annie*, set in 1933, characters go to Radio City Music Hall and see *Camille*, which was not made until 1937.

~In *Yankee Doodle Dandy*, the *Lusitania* is sunk and there is a newspaper picture showing a ship with two funnels. The *Lusitania* had four funnels.

~In the same film a luggage label with a picture of Nelson's Column bears the legend 'Nelson Square Hotel'.

~In *Brief Encounter*, Celia Johnson runs through a downpour but remains dry.

~In *National Lampoon's Animal House*, the word Satan written on a blackboard looks totally different in adjacent shots.

~In *Quadrophenia*, clearly set in 1964, a cinema is showing Warren Beatty in *Heaven Can Wait*, made fourteen years later.

~In *Carrie*, the final dream was projected backwards to achieve the right effect. But in the background a car is also moving backwards . . .

~In *Halloween*, which is set in Illinois, all the cars have California number plates.

~In *The Birds*, the creatures which pursue the children cast no shadows.

~In *Cain and Mabel*, a workman walks across a sound stage during a production number.

~In *The Band Wagon*, during the train ride to Baltimore, the scenery is dark on one side and light on the other.

~In *Knock on Wood*, a policeman rushes upstairs wearing a helmet, and into a room wearing a peaked cap.

~In *Silk Stockings*, a typewriter shown on a table vanishes in the reverse shot taken from the balcony.

~In *Fire Maidens from Outer Space*, Sidney Tafler in a T-shirt glances down at his watch, and we get an insert of a watch on a fully-sleeved arm.

~In *Genevieve*, Kenneth More comes out of a pub carrying a pint of beer, which has become a half pint by the time he reaches his table.

~In *The Band Wagon*, a theatre is shown on its canopy as the Alcott; but on the programme it says the Stratton.

~In *Meet Me In St Louis*, during the Trolley Song, one of the extras calls 'Hi, Judy!' Judy Garland's character name is Esther.

~In *The Adventures of Robin Hood*, Errol Flynn takes a bite at a complete leg of mutton. In the next shot, only a bone is left.

~In *Round Midnight*, which is set in the 50s, there is a shot of New York's World Trade Center towers, which were built much later.

~In *Camelot*, Richard Harris plays one scene with a Band-Aid on his neck.

~In *North by Northwest*, a small boy (who has obviously been to rehearsal) puts his fingers in his ears *before* Eva Marie Saint picks up a gun to shoot Cary Grant.

~In *Mysterious Island*, during the air balloon sequence, it is raining *above* the clouds.

~In *The Smallest Show on Earth*, although the cinema is supposedly in the north of England, a taxi arriving at it stops outside Hammersmith station.

~In *The Corn Is Green*, the villagers are all said to be illiterate, but they cluster round to read a poster.

~In *The Bridges of Madison County*, as Clint Eastwood drives Meryl Streep to Roseman Bridge, they twice pass the same house and a field containing some black cows.

~In *Conspiracy Theory*, Mel Gibson plays a paranoid taxi driver called Jerry Fletcher. But his identity card displayed in the cab shows the name Raffi Paloulian.

~In James Cameron's *Titanic*, when the officer of the watch orders 'full starboard rudder' on sighting the iceberg, the helmsman puts the wheel smartly to port. Perhaps (as Rear Admiral J. F. Perowne pointed out) the confusion was caused by the officers wearing their shoulder boards back to front, which is known in the Royal Navy as 'going astern'.

courtesans

have always been viewed by the cinema through rose-coloured glasses. There have been innumerable films about Madame du Barry, Madame Sans Gêne and Nell Gwyn; Garbo played Camille and Marie Walewska as well as Anna Christie; even Jean Simmons had a shot at Napoleon's *Désirée*, and Vivien Leigh was a decorative Lady Hamilton. Martine Carol played Lola Montes in the Max Ophüls film, Yvonne de Carlo in *Black Bart* (in which she became involved in western villainy during an American tour).

See also: PROSTITUTES.

courtroom scenes

have been the suspenseful saving grace of more films than can be counted; and they also figure in some of the best films ever made.

British courts best preserve the ancient aura of the law; among the films they have figured in are *London Belongs to Me*, *The Paradine Case*, *Eight O'Clock Walk*, *Life for Ruth*, *Twenty-one Days*, *Brothers in Law*, *The Winslow Boy*, *Witness for the Prosecution*, *The Blind Goddess* and *The Dock Brief*. The last four are based on stage plays, as are the American *Madame X*, *Counsellor at Law*, and *The Trial of Mary Dugan*. Other American films depending heavily on courtroom denouements include *They Won't Believe Me*, *The Unholy Three*, *The Mouthpiece*, *Boomerang*, *They Won't Forget*, *The Missing Juror*, *Trial*, *The Young Savages*, *The Criminal Code*, *To Kill a Mockingbird*, *Criminal Lawyer*, *Fury*, *The Lawyer*, *A Free Soul*, *The Seven Minutes*, *The People Against O'Hara*, *The Lady from Shanghai*, *Twilight of Honour*, *An American Tragedy* (and its remake *A Place in the Sun*), the several Perry Mason films, *Young Mr Lincoln*, and *Philadelphia*. These, even the last-named, were fictional: genuine cases were reconstructed in *I Want to Live*, *Cell 2455 Death Row*, *Compulsion*, *Inherit the Wind*, *Dr Ehrlich's Magic Bullet*, *The Witches of Salem*, *The Trials of Oscar Wilde*, *Judgment at Nuremberg*, *The Life of Emile Zola*, *Dr Crippen*, *Captain Kidd*, *Landru* and *The Case of Charles Peace*. Comedy courtroom scenes have appeared in *I'm No Angel*, *Mr Deeds Goes to Town*, *You Can't Take It With You*, *Roxie Hart*, *My Learned Friend*, *Adam's Rib*, *Pickwick Papers*, *Brothers in Law*, *What's Up Doc?*, *Star!* and *A Pair of Briefs*.

Films in which special interest has centred on the jury include *Twelve Angry Men*, *Murder (Enter Sir John)*, *Perfect Strangers (Too Dangerous to Love)*, *Justice est Faite* and *The Monster and the Girl* (in which the criminal brain inside the gorilla murders the jurors at his trial one by one). Ghostly juries figured in *All That Money Can Buy* and *The Remarkable Andrew*. The judge has been the key figure in *The Judge Steps Out*, *Talk of the Town*, *The Bachelor and the Bobbysoxer*, and *Destry Rides Again*; and we are constantly being promised a film of Henry Cecil's *No Bail for the Judge*. *Anatomy of a Murder* remains the only film in which a real judge (Joseph E. Welch) has played a fictional one. A lady barrister (Anna Neagle) had the leading role in *The Man Who Wouldn't Talk*.

Specialized courts were seen in *M* (convened by criminals), *Saint Joan* and *The Hunchback of Notre Dame* (church courts), *Black Legion* (Ku Klux Klan), *The Devil's Disciple* (18th-century military court), *Kind Hearts and Coronets* (a court of the House of Lords), *The Wreck of the Mary Deare* (mercantile), *Cone of Silence* (civil aviation), *A Tale of Two Cities* and *The Scarlet Pimpernel* (French Revolutionary courts). Courts in other countries were shown in *The Lady in Question*, *The Count of Monte Cristo*, *Crack in the Mirror*, *A Flea in Her Ear*, *La Vérité*, and *Can Can* (French); *The Purple Heart* (Japanese); *The Fall of the Roman Empire* (ancient Roman); *The Spy Who Came in from the Cold* (East German); and *Shoeshine* (Italian). Coroners' courts were featured in *Inquest*, *My Learned Friend* and *Rebecca*.

Courts martial figured largely in *The Caine Mutiny*, *Time Limit*, *The Man in the Middle*, *Across the Pacific*, *The Rack*, *Carrington VC*, *The Court Martial of Billy Mitchell* and *A Few Good Men*. There was also a TV series called *Court Martial/ Counsellors at War*.

Heavenly courts were convened in *A Matter of Life and Death*, *Outward Bound* and *The Flight That Disappeared*; while other fantasy courts appeared in *Rashomon*, *Morgan*, *One Way Pendulum*, *Alice in Wonderland*, *The Balcony*, *The Wonderful World of the Brothers Grimm*, *The Trial*, *All That Money Can Buy*, and *The Remarkable Andrew*. The court in *Planet of the Apes* is perhaps best classed as prophetic, along with that in *1984*.

TV series based on trials and lawyers include *The Law and Mr Jones*, *Harrigan and Son*, *Sam Benedict*, *The Trials of O'Brien*, *Perry Mason*, *Arrest and Trial*, *The Defenders*, *The D.A.*, *The Verdict is Yours*, *Judd for the Defense*, *Owen Marshall*, *Petrocelli*, *Adam's Rib* and *L.A. Law*.

crazy comedy
has two distinct meanings in the cinema. On one hand it encompasses the Marx Brothers, *Hellzapoppin* and custard pies; for this see *Slapstick*. On the other it means the new kind of comedy which came in during the 30s, with seemingly adult people behaving in what society at the time thought was a completely irresponsible way. The Capra comedies, for instance, are vaguely 'agin' the government', upholding Mr Deeds' right to give away his money and play the tuba, the Vanderhofs' right not to work, and Mr Smith's right to be utterly honest. This endearing eccentricity permeated many of the funniest and most modern comedies of the period. William Powell and Myrna Loy in *The Thin Man* were a married couple who upheld none of the domestic virtues. In *Libeled Lady* four top stars behaved like low comedians. In *My Man Godfrey* a rich man pretended to be a tramp and so reformed a party of the idle rich who found him during a 'scavenger hunt'. *Theodora Goes Wild, I Met Him in Paris* and *Easy Living* had what we would now call 'kooky' heroines. In *True Confession* Carole Lombard confessed to a murder she hadn't done, and was told by John Barrymore that she would 'fry'; in *Nothing Sacred* she pretended to be dying of an obscure disease and was socked on the jaw by Fredric March. Hal Roach introduced comedy ghosts, played by two of Hollywood's most sophisticated stars, in *Topper*, and followed it up with two sequels as well as three individual and endearingly lunatic comedies called *The Housekeeper's Daughter* (a battle of fireworks), *Turnabout* (a husband and wife exchange bodies) and *Road Show* (an asylum escapee runs a travelling circus). *The Awful Truth* had no respect for marriage; *You Can't Take It With You* had no respect for law, business, or the American way of life. A film called *Bringing Up Baby* turned out to be about a leopard and a brontosaurus bone; *Boy Meets Girl* was a farcical send-up of Hollywood; and *A Slight Case of Murder* had more corpses than characters. *The Women* had its all-female cast fighting like tiger-cats. *Road to Singapore* began as a romantic comedy but degenerated into snippets from Joe Miller's gag-book; and any Preston Sturges film was likely to have pauses while the smart and witty hero and heroine fell into a pool. In *Here Comes Mr Jordan* the hero was dead after five minutes or so and spent the rest of the film trying to get his body back.

The genre was by this time well established, and although America's entry into the war modified it somewhat it has remained fashionable and popular ever since. A 1966 film like *Morgan* may seem rather startling, but in fact it goes little further in its genial anarchy than *You Can't Take It With You*; only the method of expression is different. What modern crazy comedies lack is the clear pattern which produced so many little masterpieces within a few years: even direct imitations like *What's Up Doc?* fail to produce the same results.

Crime Doctor
was a series of 'B' features, based on a popular CBS radio show created by Max Marcin, and made by Columbia. They starred Warner Baxter as Dr Robert Ordway, a former gangster who, after a blow on the head caused amnesia, became a criminologist and psychiatrist specializing in solving mysteries.

Crime Doctor 43. Crime Doctor's Strangest Case 43. Shadows in the Night 44. The Crime Doctor's Courage 45. Crime Doctor's Warning 45. Crime Doctor's Man Hunt 46. Just Before Dawn 46. The Millerson Case/The Crime Doctor's Vacation 47. The Crime Doctor's Gamble 47. Crime Doctor's Diary 49.

criminals
– real-life ones – whose careers have been featured in films include Burke and Hare (*The Flesh and the Fiends, Burke and Hare*), Cagliostro (*Black Magic*), Al Capone (*Little Caesar, The Scarface Mob, Al Capone*), Caryl Chessman (*Cell 2455 Death Row*), Crippen (*Dr Crippen*), John Wilkes Booth (*Prince of Players*), Jack the Ripper (*The Lodger, A Study in Terror, Jack the Ripper*, many others), Landru (*Landru, Bluebeard, Monsieur Verdoux, Bluebeard's Ten Honeymoons*), Leopold and Loeb (*Rope* and *Compulsion*), Christie (*10 Rillington Place*), Charles Peace (*The Case of Charles Peace*), Dick Turpin, Jesse James, Vidocq (*A Scandal in Paris*), Robert Stroud (*Birdman of Alcatraz*), Barbara Graham (*I Want to Live*), Rasputin, Eddie Chapman (*Triple Cross*), the Kray brothers (*The Krays*), and the various American public enemies of the 30s: *Bonnie and Clyde, Dillinger, Baby Face Nelson, Bloody Mama* (Barker), *A Bullet for Pretty Boy* (Floyd), etc. The clinical 60s also brought accounts of the motiveless murderers of *In Cold Blood* and of *The Boston Strangler*. Criminal movements have been very well explored in fictional films, especially the Mafia, the Thugs, Murder Inc. and the racketeers and bootleggers of the 20s.

critics
Very little film criticism is quotable: at its best it is an expression of personality rather than wit. The reviews one remembers tend to be the scathing ones, especially those dismissive one-liners which are really unforgivable but linger over the arch of years:

No Leave, No Love. No comment.
I Am a Camera. Me no Leica.
Lost in a Harem. But with Abbott and Costello.
Aimez-vous Brahms? Brahms, oui.
Ben Hur. Loved Ben, hated Hur.
Samson and Delilah. A movie for de Millions.
Bill and Coo. By conservative estimate, one of the God-damnedest things ever seen.

The authors of these pearls are now, by me, forgotten, with the exception of the last, which came from the pen of James Agee, a lamented American writer whose economical, literate reviews delighted all film enthusiasts in the 40s and established a few Hollywood reputations. His collected reviews should all be read with affection; here we can spare room for five of his more waspish put-downs:

Random Harvest. I would like to recommend this film to those who can stay interested in Ronald Colman's amnesia for two hours and who could with pleasure eat a bowl of Yardley's shaving soap for breakfast.

During the making of *Pin Up Girl* Betty Grable was in an early stage of pregnancy – and everyone else was evidently in a late stage of paresis.

Tycoon. Several tons of dynamite are set off in this picture – none of it under the right people.

You Were Meant For Me. That's what you think.

Star Spangled Rhythm. A variety show including everyone at Paramount who was not overseas, in hiding or out to lunch.

A few more moments of invective. First, *Variety* on Hedy Lamarr's independent production *The Strange Woman*:

Hedy bit off more than she could chew, so the chewing was done by the rest of the cast, and what was chewed was the scenery.

And Pamela Kellino on *The Egyptian*:

One of those great big rotten pictures Hollywood keeps on turning out.

And Stanley Kauffmann on *Isadora*:

This long but tiny film . . .

And the *New Statesman* (Frank Hauser) on *Another Man's Poison*:

Like reading Ethel M. Dell by flashes of lightning.

And the *Saturday Evening Post on Macabre*:

It plods along from its opening scene in a funeral parlor to its dénouement in a graveyard, unimpeded by the faintest intrusion of good taste, literacy, or sense.

And Don Herold on *The Bride Walks Out*:

You've seen this a million times on the screen, but they keep on making it, and folks keep asking me why I am so dyspeptic regarding the cinema. Because I have judgment, is the answer.

And John Simon on *Camelot*:

This film is the Platonic idea of boredom, roughly comparable to reading a three-volume novel in a language of which one knows only the alphabet.

And David Lardner on *Panama Hattie*:

This film needs a certain something. Possibly burial.

And Judith Crist on *Five Card Stud*:

So mediocre that you can't get mad at it.

And Charles Champlin on *The Missouri Breaks*:

A pair of million dollar babies in a five and ten cent flick.

Now for some self-criticism. Joseph L. Mankiewicz on his own movie *Cleopatra*:

This picture was conceived in a state of emergency, shot in confusion, and wound up in blind panic.

He also called it:

The toughest three pictures I ever made.

Ethel Barrymore, when asked her opinion of *Rasputin and the Empress*, in which she co-starred with her brothers Lionel and John, replied:

I thought I was pretty good, but what those two boys were up to I'll never know.

Erich Von Stroheim, reminiscing on his own much-mutilated picture *Greed*:

When ten years later I saw the film myself, it was like seeing a corpse in a graveyard.

Otto Preminger on *Saint Joan*:

My most distinguished flop. I've had much less distinguished ones.

And Victor Fleming, director of *Gone with the Wind*, refusing David O. Selznick's offer of a percentage of the profits instead of salary:

Don't be a damn fool, David. This picture is going to be one of the biggest white elephants of all time.

Philip French on *Carry on Emmanuelle*:

Put together with an almost palpable contempt for its audience, this relentless sequence of badly written, badly timed dirty jokes is surely one of the most morally and aesthetically offensive pictures to emerge from a British studio.

Similarly misguided was Adolph Zukor when he first read the script of *Broken Blossoms*:

You bring me a picture like this and want money for it? You may as well put your hand in my pocket and steal it. It isn't commercial. Everyone in it dies.

I can recall only three memorable items of praise. Cecilia Ager on *Citizen Kane*:

It's as though you had never seen a movie before.

Terry Ramsaye on *Intolerance*:

The only film fugue.

And Woodrow Wilson on *The Birth of a Nation*:

Like writing history with lightning. And it's all true.

My own favourite critiques also include Sarah Bernhardt's enthusiastic remark when she saw her 1912 version of *Queen Elizabeth*:

Mr Zukor, you have put the best of me in pickle for all time.

And the comment of macabre New Yorker cartoonist Charles Addams, when asked his opinion after the première of *Cleopatra*:

I only came to see the asp.

And the anonymous reviewer of a Jack Benny violin concert:

Jack Benny played Mendelssohn last night. Mendelssohn lost.

Come to that, another anonymous gentleman had a pretty good definition of critics:

Yawning as a profession.

Channing Pollock defined a critic as:

A legless man who teaches running.

To Whitney Balkett he was:

A bundle of biases held together by a sense of taste.

And to Ken Tynan:

A man who knows the way but can't drive a car.

Mel Brooks was scathing:

Critics can't even make music by rubbing their back legs together.

R. W. Emerson was dismissive:

Taking to pieces is the trade of those who cannot construct.

Perhaps the wisest reflection on the critics was made by Rouben Mamoulian:

The most important critic is Time.

Cry the Beloved Country.
Alan Paton's novel of racial tension in South Africa, as a Zulu Christian pastor searches Johannesburg for his missing son, has been filmed twice: in 1951, directed by Zoltan Korda, starring Canada Lee, and in 1995, starring James Earl Jones and Richard Harris and directed by South African Darrell James Roodt.

Crying Freeman.
Heroic and lachrymose hitman of Japanese Manga and Anime, created by Kazuo Koike and Ryoichi Ikegami, the basis of two live-action movies made in Hong Kong, in which the character was played by Simon Yam and Sam Hui, and a European production in 1995 in which the role was taken by Mark Dacascos. Three animated Japanese films of the early 90s, which have been released on video dubbed into English, retain the narrative of the original comic books.

Killers Romance 89. Dragon from Russia 90. Crying Freeman Chapter One: Portrait of a Killer 92. Crying Freeman Chapter Two: The Enemy Within 92. Crying Freeman Chapter Three: Retribution 92. Crying Freeman 95.

custard pies
as a comic weapon were evolved in music hall by Fred Karno and at the Keystone studio around 1915, and most silent comedians relied heavily on them. In the 30s Mack Sennett staged a splendid one for a nostalgic farce called *Keystone Hotel*. Other notable pie fighters have included Laurel and Hardy in *The Battle of the Century* 28; the whole cast of *Beach Party* 63; and most of the cast of *The Great Race* 64 and *Smashing Time* 65.

Daffy Duck.
Witty, manic duck who was a star of Warner Looney Tunes and Merrie Melodies cartoons from 1937 and evolved into a mischief-making foil to Bugs Bunny and Porky Pig. He is said to have been modelled on Harpo Marx, although he was far more loquacious and developed a spluttering speech impediment in the 50s. He was voiced by Mel Blanc.

Porky's Duck Hunt 37. The Daffy Doc 38. A Coy Decoy 41. To Duck or Not to Duck 43. The Stupid Cupid 44. Ain't That Ducky 45. Birth of a Notion 47. Wise Quackers 49. Rabbit Fire 51. Rabbit Seasoning 52. Duck Dodgers in the 24½th Century 53. A Star Is Bored 56. Robin Hood Daffy 58. The Abominable Snow-Rabbit 61. The Iceman Ducketh 64. Moby Duck 65. Daffy's Diner 67. The Duckorcist 87. Night of the Living Duck 88, etc.

dance bands.
in the 30s and 40s were so popular as to be stars in their own films: Henry Hall's in *Music Hath Charms*, Kay Kyser's in half a dozen films including *That's Right You're Wrong*, Paul Whiteman's in *King of Jazz*, Tommy and Jimmy Dorsey's in *The Fabulous Dorseys*. Also frequently on hand to assist the stars were the bands of Glenn Miller, Xavier Cugat, Woody Herman and Harry James, to name but a few. In the 50s bands became too expensive to maintain, but *The Glenn Miller Story* and *The Benny Goodman Story* reawakened interest.

The Dead End Kids
were Gabriel Dell, Huntz Hall, Billy Halop, Bobby Jordan, Leo Gorcey and Bernard Punsley, a group of young actors who appeared in Sidney Kingsley's Broadway play of slum life, *Dead End*, and were hired by Sam Goldwyn to repeat their roles on film in 1937. They went on to make six other gangster films for Warner, and some also appeared in a series for Universal, *The Dead End Kids and Little Tough Guys*. The group reformed in various combinations as the East Side Kids and The Bowery Boys, turning out 'B' features that soon emphasized comedy rather than crime.

Angels with Dirty Faces 38. Crime School 38. They Made Me a Criminal 39. Hell's Kitchen 39. The Angels Wash Their Faces 39. On Dress Parade 39.

deaf mutes
have been movingly portrayed by Jane Wyman in *Johnny Belinda*, Mandy Miller in *Mandy*, Harry Bellaver in *No Way Out*, and Alan Arkin *The Heart Is a Lonely Hunter*. Dorothy McGuire in *The Spiral Staircase* was mute but not deaf; Patty Duke in *The Miracle Worker* was deaf but could make sounds.

death
has always fascinated film-makers, though the results have often appeared undergraduate-ish, as fantasy tends to look when brought down to a mass-appeal level. Death has been personified in *Death Takes a Holiday* by Fredric March and in the 1971 TV remake by Monte Markham, in *On Borrowed Time* by Cedric Hardwicke, in *Here Comes Mr Jordan* by Claude Rains, in *Orphée* by Maria Casares, in *The Seventh Seal* by Bengt Ekerot, by Richard Burton in *Boom*, by George Jessel in *Hieronymous Merkin* and by several actors in *The Masque of the Red Death*. In *Devotion*, Ida Lupino as Emily Brontë dreamed of death on horseback coming to sweep her away; in *The Bluebird* Shirley Temple ventured into the land of the dead to see her grandparents. Most of the characters in *Thunder Rock*, and all in *Outward Bound* (remade as *Between Two Worlds* and later varied for TV as *Haunts of the Very Rich*) were already dead at the start of the story. Other films to involve serious thought about death include *Dark Victory, Jeux Interdits, All the*

Way Home, *Sentimental Journey*, *No Sad Songs for Me*, *One Way Passage*, *Paths of Glory*, *Wild Strawberries*, and *Ikuru*. *Flatliners* and *The Rapture* both dealt with experiences after death.

Comedies taking death lightly included *A Slight Case of Murder*, *Kind Hearts and Coronets*, *The Trouble with Harry*, *Too Many Crooks*, *The Criminal Life of Archibaldo de la Cruz*, *Send Me No Flowers*, *The Assassination Bureau*, *The Loved One*, *The Wrong Box*, *Arrivederci Baby*, *Kiss the Girls and Make Them Die*, *Arsenic and Old Lace*, *Une Journée Bien Remplie*, and *Weekend at Bernie's*.

dentists

are seldom popular chaps, but Preston Sturges made a film about one of them, the inventor of laughing gas: *The Great Moment*. *The Counterfeit Traitor* had a spy dentist. Sinister dentists were found in *The Man Who Knew Too Much* (original version), *The Secret Partner*, and *Footsteps in the Dark*, and a comic one, in the person of Bob Hope, in *The Paleface*. Dentistry is the subject of two British farces: *Dentist in the Chair* and *Dentist on the Job*. W. C. Fields once made a film of his sketch *The Dentist*; and Laurel and Hardy in *Leave 'Em Laughing* were overcome by laughing gas. The most notable dentist hero was in the twice remade *One Sunday Afternoon*; and the most villainous dentist is certainly Laurence Olivier in *Marathon Man*. The dentist with the most hectic private life was Walter Matthau in *Cactus Flower*. The oddest was Daniel Day-Lewis as a motorcycling enthusiast for dental hygiene in *Eversmile, New Jersey*.

department stores

have usually been a background for comedy. New York store backgrounds have often shown the native superiority of the working girl to snobbish shopwalkers and obtuse management, as in *Bachelor Mother* and its remake *Bundle of Joy*, *The Devil and Miss Jones* and *Manhandled* 24. Broader comedy elements were to the fore in *Miracle on 34th Street*, *Modern Times*, *The Big Store*, *Who's Minding the Store?*, *Fitzwilly* and *How to Save a Marriage*. British comedies with store settings included *Kipps*, *The Crowded Day*, *Laughter in Paradise*, *Keep Fit*, and *Trouble in Store*.

desert islands

have provided the locale of many a film adventure. *Robinson Crusoe* has been filmed several times, with two recent variations in *Robinson Crusoe on Mars* and *Lt Robin Crusoe USN*. *Treasure Island* too has survived three or four versions, to say nothing of imitations like *Blackbeard the Pirate* and parodies such as *Abbott and Costello Meet Captain Kidd* and *Old Mother Riley's Jungle Treasure*. *The Admirable Crichton* is perhaps the next most overworked desert island story, with *The Swiss Family Robinson* following on. Dorothy Lamour found a few desert islands in films like *Typhoon* and *Aloma of the South Seas*; the inhabitants of *The Little Hut* had one nearly to themselves; Joan Greenwood and co. were marooned on a rather special one in *Mysterious Island*. *Our Girl Friday* played the theme for sex; *Dr Dolittle* found educated natives on one; Cary Grant lived on one as a reluctant spy in *Father Goose*; *Sea Wife*, *Lord of the Flies* and *The Day the Fish Came Out* were three recent but not very successful attempts to take the theme seriously: *Hell in the Pacific* was one that did work. *The Blue Lagoon* was treated decorously in the 50s and sexily in the 80s.

A comic TV series on the subject was *Gilligan's Island* 64–66; a serious one, *The New People* 69.

deserts

have figured in many a western, from *Tumbleweed* to *Mackenna's Gold*. Other films which have paid particularly respectful attention to the dangers that too much sand can provide include *The Sheik* and *Son of the Sheik*, *Greed*, *The Lost Patrol*, *The Garden of Allah*, *Sahara*, *Five Graves to Cairo*, *Ice Cold in Alex*, *Sea of Sand*, *Desert Rats*, *Play Dirty*, *An Eye for an Eye*, *Inferno*, *Zabriskie Point*, *The Sabre and the Arrow*, *Legend of the Lost*, *The Ten Commandments*, *She*, *Lawrence of Arabia*, *The Black Tent*, *Oasis*, *Sands of The Kalahari*, *The Flight of the Phoenix*, *Garden of Evil* and *The Professionals*.

the devil

has made frequent appearances in movies. There were versions of *Faust* in 1900, 1903, 1904, 1907, 1909, 1911, 1921 and 1925, the last of these featuring Emil Jannings as Mephistopheles. Later variations on this theme include *The Sorrows of Satan* 27, with Adolphe Menjou; *All That Money Can Buy* 41, with Walter Huston as Mr Scratch; *Alias Nick Beal* 49, with Ray Milland; *La Beauté du Diable* 50 with Gérard Philipe; *Damn Yankees* 58 with Ray Walston; *Bedazzled* 67 with Peter Cook; and *Doctor Faustus* 68 with Andreas Teuber. In other stories, Satan was played by Helge Nissen in *Leaves From Satan's Book* 20, Jules Berry in *Les Visiteurs du Soir* 42, Alan Mowbray in *The Devil with Hitler* 42, Rex Ingram in *Cabin in the Sky* 43, Laird Cregar in *Heaven Can Wait* 43, Claude Rains in *Angel on My Shoulder* 46, Stanley Holloway in *Meet Mr Lucifer* 53, Richard Devon in *The Undead* 56, Vincent Price in *The Story of Mankind* 57, Cedric Hardwicke in *Bait* 54, Vittorio Gassman in *The Devil in Love* 67, Stig Järrel in *The Devil's Eye* 60, Donald Pleasence in *The Greatest Story Ever Told* 65, Burgess Meredith in *Torture Garden* 68, Pierre Clementi in *The Milky Way* 68, Ralph Richardson in *Tales From the Crypt* 71. In the Swedish *Witchcraft through the Ages* 21, the devil was played by the director, Benjamin Christensen. Devil worship has been the subject of *The Black Cat* 34, *The Seventh Victim* 43, *Night of the Demon* 57, *Back from the Dead* 57, *The Witches* 66, *Eye of the Devil* 66, *The Devil Rides Out* 68, *Rosemary's Baby* 68; while the last-named presaged a rash of diabolically-inspired children in *The Exorcist*, *I Don't Want to be Born*, *It's Alive*, *Devil Within Her* and *The Omen*.

Devil's Island,

the French Guianan penal colony, has intermittently fascinated film-makers. Apart from the versions of the Dreyfus case (*Dreyfus*, *The Life of Emile Zola*, *I Accuse*), there have been Ronald Colman in *Condemned to Devil's Island*, Donald Woods in *I Was a Prisoner on Devil's Island*, Boris Karloff in *Devil's Island*, Clark Gable in *Strange Cargo*, Humphrey Bogart in *Passage to Marseilles*, Bogart and company in *We're No Angels*, Eartha Kitt in *Saint of Devil's Island*, Steve McQueen in *Papillon*, and Jim Brown in *I Escaped From Devil's Island*. The prison colony opened in 1852 and closed in 1946.

Dick Barton.

Tough British special agent, created by Edward J. Mason, who was the hero of a popular radio programme 1946–51, and three low-budget films starring Don Stannard. In 1978, Tony Vogel played him in an unsuccessful television series.

Dick Barton, Special Agent 48. Dick Barton Strikes Back 49. Dick Barton at Bay 50.

Dick Tracy.

The lantern-jawed detective of the comic strips made sporadic film appearances, notably when impersonated by Ralph Byrd or Morgan Conway in a number of 40s second features and serials. In 1951 Byrd starred in a TV series. Tracy also appeared in a TV cartoon series in the 50s, in *TV Funnies* in 1971, and in the big-budget film of 1990, starring Warren Beatty.

Die Hard.

The film starring Bruce Willis as a tough cop outwitting a group of terrorists who had taken his wife and others hostage in a skyscraper was followed by two sequels that repeated the formula, first in an airport and then in various New York locations. The popularity of the series led to similar movies of lone heroes battling against overwhelming odds in claustrophobic situations, which were usually defined in terms of the original: *Passenger 57* ('Die Hard on a plane'), *Under Siege* ('Die Hard on a boat'), *On Lonely Ground* ('Die Hard on ice'), *Speed* ('Die Hard on a bus'), etc. In similar fashion, the *Die Hard* sequels were adapted from already existing scripts. The addition of Samuel L. Jackson as Willis's sidekick in the third film seemed an attempt to emulate the *Lethal Weapon* series which coupled Mel Gibson with Danny Glover. The first and third films were directed by John McTiernan, the second by Renny Harlin. A fourth film in the series is likely.

Die Hard 88. Die Hard 2/Die Hard: Die Harder 90. Die Hard with a Vengeance 95.

dinosaurs

have been a cinematic favourite since the earliest days of cinema, when Winsor McCay appeared with his cartoon creation Gertie in 1909. But it was *The Lost World* 25 which proved to be the template for virtually all the succeeding dinosaur films. This silent movie adaptation of Conan Doyle's novel of an isolated plateau where prehistoric monsters survived improved on the original. Where that had a pterodactyl loose in London, the film sent a brontosaurus rampaging through the streets, attacking Tower Bridge (special effects by Willis O'Brien). It was a scene that became a standard in most subsequent movies, from the Japanese series that began with *Godzilla, King of the Monsters!* 54, in which Tokyo was flattened, to *Gorgo*, which brought a monster swimming up the Thames to rescue its offspring; *Behemoth the Sea Monster* 58, which was just another *Beast from Twenty Thousand Fathoms*, also gave London a going-over. The GODZILLA movies, in which the beast progressed from ravening monster to a saviour of mankind, also drew on the dinosaur battles from *King Kong* 33, in which O'Brien refined the stop-motion techniques he used in *The Lost World*. The problem of getting man and dinosaur into the same setting was solved in many ways: *One Million BC* simply ignored the anachronism, using lizards optically enlarged and a stuntman in a suit for its creatures, and covering elephants with fur to pass as mastodons; its footage was to turn up in later, low-budget efforts, such as Bert I. Gordon's *King Dinosaur* 55. *Unknown Island* 48, *The Land that Time Forgot* and its sequel *The People that Time Forgot* used a similar amnesiac low-budget approach. Hammer's remake *One Million Years BC* used stop-motion for the beasts, although the film is remembered, if at all, for Raquel Welch in a fur bikini. Hammer also made *When Dinosaurs Ruled the Earth* 70, which again relied on the sex appeal of its leading lady. Others used nuclear power to revive the long-dead creatures, including *The Beast from Twenty Thousand Fathoms*, with special effects by Ray Harryhausen. *The Land Unknown* 57 put them in a lost, underground world beneath the Pole, as did *Journey to the Center of the Earth* 59, which again used real lizards (ignoring modern thinking which believes that dinosaurs are related to birds rather than reptiles), and *The Last Dinosaur* 77. Lizards again turn up in the 60s remake of *The Lost World*. *Jurassic Park* was scientifically more advanced, using modern techniques of DNA cloning to bring the creatures back; it once again made dinosaurs monster box-office (special effects by Stan Winston and others), although the mutated creatures of *Super Mario Bros* proved that special effects were not enough on their own to make a successful film, and Roger Corman's attempt to cash in on the craze with *Carnosaur* proved to be no more than a throwback to 50s monster films. There have been two dinosaur westerns, *The Beast of Hollow Mountain* 56 and *The Valley of the Gwangi* 68. Only one animated film has used dinosaurs to good effect: Walt Disney's *Fantasia*, although they were also to be found in Steven Spielberg's jokey *We're Back: A Dinosaur's Story*, and *The Land before Time*.

Books: 1988, *Beasts and Behemoths: Prehistoric Creatures in the Movies* by Roy Kinnard. 1992, *When Dinosaurs Ruled the Screen* by Marc Shapiro. 1993, *The Illustrated Dinosaur Movie Guide* by Stephen Jones.

directors' appearances

in films are comparatively few. Hitchcock remains the unchallengeable winner, with moments in over thirty of his fifty-odd films, including the confined *Rope* (in which his outline appears on a neon sign) and *Lifeboat* (in which he can be seen in a reducing ad. in a newspaper). Preston Sturges can be glimpsed in *Sullivan's Travels*, and in *Paris Holiday*, as a French resident, gets a whole scene to himself. John Huston, uncredited, plays a tourist in *The Treasure of the Sierra Madre* and a master of foxhounds in *The List of Adrian Messenger*; he later began to take sizeable credited roles, e.g. in *The Cardinal* and *The Bible*. The Paramount lot became a familiar scene in many 40s pictures, with notable guest appearances by Mitchell Leisen in *Hold Back the Dawn* and Cecil B. de Mille in *Sunset Boulevard*, *The Buster Keaton Story*, *Star-Spangled Rhythm*, *Variety Girl*, *Son of Paleface* and others. Jean Cocteau played an old woman in *Orphée* and appeared throughout *The Testament of Orphée*. Nicholas Ray was the American ambassador in *55 Days in Peking*. Jules Dassin played major roles in *Rififi* (as Perlo Vita) and *Never on Sunday*, as did Jean Renoir in *La Règle du Jeu*. Hugo Fregonese was a messenger in *Decameron Nights*, Samuel Fuller a Japanese cop in *House of Bamboo*. Others who can be glimpsed in their own work include Tony Richardson in *Tom Jones*, Michael Winner in *You Must Be Joking*, George Marshall in *The Crime of Dr Forbes*, Frank Borzage in *Jeanne Eagels*, Robert Aldrich in *The Big Knife*, Ingmar Bergman in *Waiting Women*, King Vidor in *Our Daily Bread*, William Castle (producer) in *Rosemary's Baby*, Claude Chabrol in *Les Biches* and *The Road to Corinth*, and Joseph Losey in *The Intimate Stranger* (which he made under the name of Joseph Walton). Huston, Polanski, Truffaut and Bondarchuk are among those who have played major roles in their own and other films.

Dirty Harry:

see HARRY CALLAHAN.

disaster films

have always been popular. In the 30s large crowds flocked to see *Tidal Wave*, *San Francisco*, *The Last Days of Pompeii*, *In Old Chicago* and *The Rains Came*. World War II was disaster enough for the 40s, but the 50s brought *Titanic*, *A Night to Remember*, and *Invasion USA*, and the 60s *The Devil at Four O'Clock* and *Krakatoa East of Java*. It was the 70s, however, that found the killing of large numbers of people to be really top box office. *Earthquake* and *The Towering Inferno* were giants of their kind, and even though *The Hindenburg* was not clever enough to attract, there were plenty of successful imitators: *The Swarm*, *Avalanche*, *Meteor*, etc. A new cycle began in the mid-90s, featuring such large-scale natural disasters as hurricanes (*Twister*), erupting volcanoes (*Dante's Peak*; *Volcano*) and looming asteroids (*Deep Impact*; *Armageddon*). TV contributions include *Smash-up on Interstate Five*, *Hanging by a Thread*, *The Death of Ocean View Park* and *Disaster on the Coastliner*.

disguise

has featured in many hundreds of films, and was in the 20s the perquisite of Lon Chaney, all of whose later films featured it. Lon Chaney Jnr has also had a tendency to it, as had John Barrymore; while most of the Sherlock Holmes films involved it. Other notable examples include Henry Hull in *Miracles for Sale*; Donald Wolfit in *The Ringer*; Marlene Dietrich in *Witness for the Prosecution*; Jack Lemmon and Tony Curtis in *Some Like It Hot*; Alec Guinness in *Kind Hearts and Coronets*; Peter Sellers in *The Naked Truth* and *After the Fox*; Rod Steiger in *No Way to Treat a Lady*; Tony Randall in *Seven Faces of Dr Lao*; John Barrymore in *Bulldog Drummond Comes Back*; Michael Caine in *Sleuth*; Dustin Hoffman in *Tootsie*; and practically the entire cast of *The List of Adrian Messenger*. Extensions of disguise are the split personality films: *Dr Jekyll and Mr Hyde*, *Lizzie*, *The Three Faces of Eve*, *Sybil*, *Darkman*.

See also: TRANSVESTISM; MULTIPLE ROLES.

Django.

Eponymous machinegun-toting hero of a spaghetti western that spawned many sequels, including several that had no connection with the original, but were simply renamed outside Italy in order to cash in on the international success of a film that was banned for many years in Britain. The ploy worked because the genre so often featured a dark, morose, lone gunfighter. The first in the series, directed by Sergio CORBUCCI in 1966, starred Franco NERO, who also appeared in a sequel, *Django 2: The Big Comeback*, in 1987.

Dr Christian

was the kindly country doctor hero, played by Jean Hersholt, of a number of unambitious little films which came out between 1938 and 1940, based on a radio series and inspired by the publicity surrounding Dr Dafoe, who delivered the Dionne Quins in 1934. In 1956 Macdonald Carey featured in a TV series of the same name, but he played the nephew of the original Dr Christian.

Dr Mabuse.

The criminal mastermind was created by novelist Norbert Jacques and first filmed in 1922 by Fritz Lang in the two-part *Doctor Mabuse, the Gambler/Doktor Mabuse, der Spieler*, starring Rudolf Klein-Rogge, who repeated the role in Lang's 1933 sound film *The Testament of Dr Mabuse/Das Testament des Dr Mabuse*, which was banned by the Nazis and led to Lang fleeing to America. He returned to West Germany in 1960 to make the less successful *The Thousand Eyes of Dr Mabuse/Die Tausend Augen des Dr Mabuse* with Wolfgang Preiss in the role. In 1990, Claude Chabrol updated Jacques' original novel in *Docteur M/Club Extinction*, starring Alan Bates, but the story no longer seemed plausible.

Dr Who.
Ageless time traveller with a time machine, the Tardis, disguised as a police box. Created by producer Sydney Newman as a science-fiction TV series in 1963, its mixture of fantasy, adventure and comedy captured the imagination of the nation and became almost required viewing in the 60s, especially in adventures involving the Daleks, aliens encased in what looked like mobile pepperpots, whose conversation consisted mainly of 'Exterminate! Exterminate!' Also featuring men in rubber suits as aliens, its popularity waned as some odd choices were made in casting the title role, and its run of 695 episodes ended in 1989. It gave rise to a stage play and two dull films starring Peter Cushing as the Doctor. On TV the role was played by William Hartnell (with Richard Hurndall substituting for him after his death in one episode featuring five incarnations of the Doctor), Patrick Troughton, Jon Pertwee, Tom Baker, Peter Davison, Colin Baker, and Sylvester McCoy. A pilot for a television series produced by Steven Spielberg was shown in 1996, starring Paul McGann in the title role, but it lacked the charm of the original.

Dr Who and the Daleks 65. Daleks: Invasion Earth 2150 AD 66.

doctors
(in the medical sense) have been crusading heroes of many movies: fictional epics that come readily to mind include *Arrowsmith, The Citadel, Magnificent Obsession, Private Worlds, Men in White, The Green Light, Disputed Passage, Yellow Jack, The Last Angry Man, Not as a Stranger, Johnny Belinda, The Girl in White, The Doctor and the Girl, Green Fingers, The Outsider, The Crime of Dr Forbes, The Interns, The New Interns, The Young Doctors, Behind the Mask, Doctor Zhivago,* and *White Corridors*. A few have even commanded whole series to themselves: *Dr Kildare, Dr Christian, Dr Gillespie, The Crime Doctor*. Once-living doctors have received the accolade of a Hollywood biopic: *The Story of Louis Pasteur, Dr Ehrlich's Magic Bullet, Prisoner of Shark Island* (Dr Mudd), *L'Enfant Sauvage* (Dr Jean Retard), *The Story of Dr Wassell, Il Est Minuit Dr Schweitzer*. Many less single-minded films have had a background of medicine and doctors as leading figures: *The Nun's Story, Kings Row, No Way Out, People Will Talk, The Hospital*. More or less villainous doctors were found in *The Flesh and the Fiends, Frankenstein, Dr Socrates, Dr Jekyll and Mr Hyde, Green for Danger, Dr Cyclops, The Hands of Orlac, Dr Goldfoot, The Amazing Dr Clitterhouse,* and *Malice*.

TV series on medical subjects have included *Medic* 54–55. *Ben Casey* 60–65. *Dr Kildare* 61–66. *Dr Christian* 56. *Dr Hudson's Secret Journal* 55–56. *The Nurses* 62–63. *The Doctors and the Nurses* 64. *Marcus Welby MD* 69. *The Bold Ones* 68–72. *Police Surgeon* 72. *St Elsewhere* 82–88. *Ryan's Four* 83. And, in the 90s, *Casualty* and *ER*.

See also: HOSPITALS.

Don Juan.
The amorous adventures of this legendary rascal, a heartless seducer created in stories by Gabriel Tellez (1571–1641), have been filmed several times, notably with John Barrymore in 1927, Douglas Fairbanks Snr in 1934, Errol Flynn in 1948 and (of all people) Fernandel in 1955. Versions of the opera, *Don Giovanni*, are legion: the most elaborate was directed by Joseph Losey in 1979.

Don Quixote.
There have been many screen versions of Cervantes' picaresque novel about the adventures of the addled knight and his slow but faithful lieutenant Sancho Panza . . . but none have been entirely successful because the genius of the book is a purely literary one. There was a French production in 1909; an American one in 1916 directed by Edward Dillon; a British one in 1923 directed by Maurice Elvey and starring Jerrold Robertshaw with George Robey. In 1933 Pabst made a British film of the story with Chaliapin and (again) George Robey; meanwhile a Danish director, Lau Lauritzen, had done one in 1926. The next batch of Quixotes began in 1947 with Rafael Gil's Spanish version; but the Russian production of 1957, directed by Kozintsev with Cherkassov in the title role, was probably the best of all. Orson Welles filmed sections of his own version, which it looks as though we may never see, though edited versions are being screened at festivals; a Jugoslavian cartoon version appeared in 1961; in 1962 Finland, of all nations, contributed its own Quixote, directed by Eino Ruutsalo; and in 1972 the BBC and Universal made a TV film with Rex Harrison. The popular stage musical *Man of la Mancha*, filmed in 1972, is based on the life of author Miguel de Cervantes (1547–1616) and its correlation with that of his hero. There followed in 1973 a ballet version with Rudolph Nureyev.

Donald Duck.
Belligerent Disney cartoon character who was introduced in 1934 in *The Wise Little Hen*, was quickly streamlined and became more popular than Mickey Mouse. Still going strong.

Dracula.
The Transylvanian vampire count created by Bram Stoker in his novel published 1897 has been on the screen in many manifestations. Max Schreck played him in Murnau's German silent *Nosferatu* 23. Bela Lugosi first donned the cloak for Universal's *Dracula* 31, was not in *Dracula's Daughter* 36 but reappeared as one of Dracula's relations in *Return of the Vampire* 44 and played the Count in *Abbott and Costello Meet Frankenstein* 48. Lon Chaney starred in *Son of Dracula* 43; John Carradine took over in *House of Frankenstein* 45 and *House of Dracula* 45; Francis Lederer had a go in *The Return of Dracula* 58. Also in 1958 came the British remake of the original *Dracula* (*Horror of Dracula*) with Christopher Lee; David Peel was one of the Count's disciples in *Brides of Dracula* 60 and Noel Willman another in *Kiss of the Vampire* 63; while Lee ingeniously reappeared in 1965 as *Dracula Prince of Darkness*, in 1968 in *Dracula Has Risen from the Grave*, in 1969 in *Taste the Blood of Dracula*, and in 1970 in *Scars of Dracula*. In the same year Ingrid Pitt was *Countess Dracula* and 1972 brought *Vampire Circus*. Meanwhile the Count had American rivals in Count Yorga, in *The House of Dark Shadows* and in *Blacula*. (Hollywood in 1957 had produced a lady vampire in *Blood of Dracula*, and in 1965 *Billy the Kid Meets Dracula*. Polanski's failed satire of 1967, *The Fearless Vampire Killers*, had Ferdy Mayne as Von Krolock, who was Dracula in all but name.) *Dracula AD 1972* and *The Satanic Rites of Dracula* were further variations on the main theme, both with Mr Lee; while Jack Palance in 1973 did a TV film version of the original story for Dan Curtis. It seemed that the Count, though officially dead, was unlikely ever to lie down for long; but no one could have been prepared for the profusion of Dracula variations of the late 70s, by which time Hammer had given up participating. Klaus Kinski aped Schreck in a remake of *Nosferatu*. George Hamilton appeared in a sexy spoof, *Love at First Bite*. Laurence Olivier played Van Helsing to Frank Langella's *Dracula*. Would it never end? No, it wouldn't. Francis Ford Coppola's *Bram Stoker's Dracula* in 1992 began another frenzied cycle of vampire movies.

Books: 1987, *The Dracula Scrapbook* by Peter Haining. 1990, *Hollywood Gothic* by David J. Skal.

See also: VAMPIRES.

drag:
see TRANSVESTISM.

dreams,
with their opportunities for camera magic and mystery, are dear to Hollywood's heart. The first film with dream sequences followed by a psychological explanation was probably Pabst's *Secrets of a Soul*; the trick caught on very firmly in such later pictures as *Lady in the Dark, A Matter of Life and Death, Spellbound, Dead of Night, Fear in the Night, Farewell My Lovely, The Secret Life of Walter Mitty, Possessed, Dream Girl, Three Cases of Murder* and *The Night Walker*. In *Vampyr* and *Wild Strawberries* the hero dreamed of his own funeral; and in *Devotion* Ida Lupino dreamed of death as a man on horseback coming across the moor to sweep her away. Recently, flashbacks have become less fashionable than a story told as in a series of daydreams by the main character, the past mingling with the present, as in *Death of a Salesman* and *I Was Happy Here*. *Roman Scandals, A Connecticut Yankee at the Court of King Arthur, Ali Baba Goes to Town, Fiddlers Three* and *Dreaming* are but five examples of the many comedies in which a character has been knocked on the head and dreams himself back in some distant time.

In the mid-40s such films as *The Woman in the Window, The Strange Affair of Uncle Harry* and *The Horn Blows at Midnight* set the fashion for getting the hero out of some impossible situation by having him wake up and find he'd been dreaming. This was scarcely fair in adult films, though it had honourable origins in *Alice in Wonderland* and *The Wizard of Oz*. Nor is there much excuse for the other favourite script trick of having one's cake and eating it, as in *Portrait of Jennie* and *Miracle in the Rain*, when some ghostly occurrence to the hero is passed off as a dream until he finds some tangible evidence – a scarf, a coin or some other memento – that it was real.

The closest a film dream came to coming true was in *The Night My Number Came Up*, when the foreseen air crash was narrowly averted. In the brilliantly clever frame story of *Dead of Night*, the hero dreams he will commit a murder, and does, only to wake up and find the whole sequence of events beginning again: he is caught in an endless series of recurring nightmares. *A Nightmare on Elm Street* developed the idea of dreams becoming real, with its sadistic child murderer haunting the horrific dreams of a group of teenagers who burned him to death, only to find that the power of their emotions brings him back to life. Its many sequels continued the nightmare until it became quite soporific. The notion was developed with more subtlety in *Paperhouse*, in which a young girl dreams her drawings into existence.

See also: FANTASY.

Droopy.
Stony-faced, lugubrious bloodhound star of MGM cartoons. Created by Tex Avery, he was inspired by Wallace Wimple, of the popular radio comedy *The Fibber McGee and Molly Show*, played by Bill Thompson, who first supplied the voice for Droopy.

Dumb Hounded 43. The Shooting of Dan McScrew 45. Señor Droopy 49. Caballero Droopy 52. Dixieland Droopy 54. Millionaire Droopy 56. One Droopy Knight (AAN) 57. Sheep Wrecked 58, etc.

drug addiction,
long forbidden by the Hays Code, even in Sherlock Holmes films (though it featured in Chaplin's *Easy Street* in 1917), has recently been the subject of many intense reforming movies such as *The Man with the Golden Arm, A Hatful of Rain, Bigger than Life, Monkey on My Back* and *Synanon*. *Confessions of an Opium Eater*, on the other hand, is a throwback to the Hollywood films of the 20s, when almost every adventure involved a chase through a Chinatown opium den. The addiction has provided plots for many thrillers about the tireless efforts of agents of the US Narcotics Bureau: *Johnny Stool Pigeon, To the Ends of the Earth, Sol Madrid, The Poppy is Also a Flower, The French Connection*, etc. In the late 60s drugs began to be advocated as a permissible opting out, or to be freely and seriously discussed, in such films as *The Trip, Chappaqua* and *Beyond the Valley of the Dolls; Panic in Needle Park; Born to Win; Believe in Me; Jennifer on my Mind;* and *Lenny*.

drunk scenes
have been the delight of many actors as well as audiences. Who can judge between the charms of the following? Greta Garbo in *Ninotchka*; Robert Montgomery in *June Bride*; Jean Arthur in *Mr Smith Goes to Washington*; Laurel and Hardy in *The Bohemian Girl* and *Scram*; Lionel Barrymore in *A Free Soul*; Eva Marie Saint in *That Certain Feeling*; Errol Flynn in *The Sun Also Rises*; Katharine Hepburn in *The Desk Set*; Leslie Caron in *Father Goose*; Fredric March in *There Goes My Heart*; Lee Marvin in *Cat Ballou* (accompanied by a drunken horse); Albert Finney in *Saturday Night and Sunday Morning*; Alan Bates in *A Kind of Loving*; Bette Davis in *Dark Victory*; Claudia Cardinale in *The Pink Panther*; Charles Laughton in *Hobson's Choice*; Katharine Hepburn in *The Philadelphia Story* and *State of the Union*; Lucille Ball in *Yours Mine and Ours*; Arthur Askey in *The Love Match*; Dan Dailey in *It's Always Fair Weather*; Vanessa Redgrave in *Isadora*; Julie Andrews in *Star!*; Dudley Moore in *Arthur*; Dean Martin and Tony Curtis in *Who Was That Lady?* Martin indeed deliberately built himself an off-screen alcoholic reputation, as did W. C. Fields.

See also: ALCOHOLICS.

duels
are fought in hundreds of low-budget action dramas, but the well-staged ones are rare enough to be recounted. Basil Rathbone fought Errol Flynn in *The Adventures of Robin Hood* (and later spoofed the occasion in *The Court Jester*). He also lost to Tyrone Power in *The Mark of Zorro*; Flynn also encountered Rathbone in *Captain Blood* and Henry Daniell in *The Sea Hawk*. Douglas Fairbanks Snr fought duels in *The Mark of Zorro, The Black Pirate* and others; Douglas Fairbanks Jnr was a memorable opponent for Ronald Colman in *The Prisoner of Zenda* (later restaged for James Mason and Stewart Granger and mimicked by Tony Curtis and Ross Martin in *The Great Race*) and duelled again in *The Corsican Brothers*. Granger also duelled with Mason in *Fanny by Gaslight*, but used pistols this time; it was back to foils again for *Scaramouche* and *Swordsman of Siena*. John Barrymore fought splendid duels in his silent films, notably *Don Juan* and *General Crack*, later opposing Rathbone in *Romeo and Juliet*. In the 40s Cornel Wilde became fencer in chief, in such films as *Bandit of Sherwood Forest, Forever Amber* and *Sons of the Musketeers*. All the versions of *The Three Musketeers* involved duelling, but Gene Kelly turned it into a splendid series of acrobatic feats. Paul Henreid duelled in *The Spanish Main*, Larry Parks in *The Swordsman*, Fredric March in *The Buccaneer*, Charlton Heston in *El Cid*, Louis Hayward in half a dozen low-budgeters. In more serious films Ferrer duelled in *Cyrano de Bergerac* and Olivier in *Hamlet*, and there was a pistol duel in the Russian *War and Peace* and the Italian *Colpi di Pistola*. The most recent major films to feature duels are *Barry Lyndon, Royal Flash* and the ultimate *The Duellists*.

The East Side Kids.
Set up in 1939 by Monogram as a Poverty Row challenge to the Dead End Kids, the original team consisted of Hally Chester, Harris Berger, Frankie Burke, Donald Hines, Eddie Brian and Sam Edwards. They were later joined by Bobby Jordan and Leo Gorcey from Dead End, and within a few years elements of both rival gangs were absorbed into the Bowery Boys.

El Santo.
Silver-masked Mexican wrestler who was a star of the ring and of more than 50 cheap, popular and profitable adventure movies in which he defeated crooks, monsters, vampires, werewolves and extra-terrestrials. He first appeared in films in *Santo – El Enmascarado de Plata* 52, but the series proper began in 1961 with *Santo versus the Diabolic Brain* and ended in 1982 with *Santo versus the Television Assassin*. It was probably not always the same actor behind the mask. Most often, it was Rodolfo Guzmán HUERTA, but Eric del Castillo may have taken the role in some of the films. Occasionally El Santo was paired with a rival masked wrestler, Blue Demon (El Demonio Azul), played by Alejandro Cruz. In versions of the films dubbed into English, the character is sometimes renamed Samson.

the electric chair
has figured prominently in innumerable gangster and prison movies, notably *Two Seconds, Twenty Thousand Years in Sing Sing, Angels with Dirty Faces* and *The Last Mile*. *Front Page Woman* concentrated on the reporters ushered in to watch. The death cell scenes in *Double Indemnity* were deleted before the film's release. The most horrific sequence of this kind was the gas chamber climax of *I Want To Live*.

elephants
have come closest to starring roles in *Zenobia, Elephant Boy* and *Hannibal Brooks*; but they were the subject of concern in *Chang, Where No Vultures Fly, Elephant Walk, Maya,* and *Roots of Heaven*, and Tarzan and Dorothy Lamour (in her jungle days) usually had one around as a pet. (*Tarzan Goes to India* had a splendid elephant stampede.) Circus elephants were stars of *Jumbo*, and above all of *Dumbo*.

elevators:
see LIFTS.

Ellery Queen.
The fictional American detective was played by four actors between 1935 and 1943: Donald Cook, Eddie Quillan, Ralph Bellamy and William Gargan. The name is a pseudonym for two authors: Frederick Dannay (1905–82) and Manfred Lee (1905–71). In 1971 Peter Lawford turned up in a TV movie, *Don't Look Behind You*, and in 1975 there was a TV series with Jim Hutton, following a 1954 one with George Nader.

Elmer Fudd.
Warner Brother's cartoon star. An adversary of Bugs Bunny, Elmer is a constantly frustrated wabbit-hunter noted for his deer-stalker hat, double-barrelled shotgun, and his inability to pronounce the letter 'r'. He made his debut in 1939 in a Tex Avery cartoon.

Dangerous Dan McFoo 39. Wabbit Twouble 41. An Itch in Time 43. Hare Remover 46. Hare Do 49. Rabbit Fire 51. Rabbit Seasoning 52. Robot Rabbit 53. Hare Brush 55. Pre-Hysterical Hare 58. What's My Lion? 61, etc.

the end of the world
has been fairly frequently considered in movies, and not only in panic button dramas like *Dr Strangelove*, *The Bedford Incident* and *Fail Safe*. Movement of the earth was threatened in *The Day the Earth Stood Still* and stopped (by Roland Young) in *The Man Who Could Work Miracles*. Plague very nearly ended everything in *Things to Come*. Danger from other planets looming perilously close was only narrowly averted in *Red Planet Mars*, while in *When Worlds Collide* and *The Day the Earth Caught Fire* the worst happened. Another kind of danger was met in *Crack in the World*. The Martians nearly got us in *The War of the Worlds*. In *Five* there were only five people left alive, in *The World, the Flesh and the Devil* only three, and in *On the Beach* none at all. The world was saved at the last moment from being pulverized by huge asteroids in two disaster movies of 1998, *Deep Impact* and *Armageddon*.

Enoch Arden
was a character in a Tennyson poem who came back to his family after having been long supposed dead. Films with an 'Enoch Arden' theme include *Tomorrow Is Forever* (with Orson Welles), *The Years Between* (with Michael Redgrave), *My Two Husbands* (with Fred MacMurray) and its remake *Three for the Show* (with Jack Lemmon), *My Favourite Wife* (with Irene Dunne) and its remake *Move Over Darling* (with Doris Day), *Piccadilly Incident* (with Anna Neagle), *Return from the Ashes* (with Ingrid Thulin), *Desire Me* (with Robert Mitchum), *Laura* (with Gene Tierney), *Man Alive* (with Pat O'Brien), and *The Man from Yesterday* (with Clive Brook). D. W. Griffith in 1910 and 1911 made short versions of the original story.

entertainers,
including actors and impresarios, have frequently been the subject of biopics, and if all their stories have seemed much the same, that is Hollywood's fault rather than theirs. Here is a reasonably comprehensive list:

Always Leave Them Laughing Milton Berle, *After the Ball* Pat Kirkwood as Vesta Tilley, *Bound for Glory* David Carradine as Woody Guthrie, *The Buddy Holly Story* Gary Busey, *The Buster Keaton Story* Donald O'Connor, *Champagne Charlie* Tommy Trinder as George Leybourne and Stanley Holloway as the Great Vance, *Chaplin* Robert Downey Jnr as Charlie Chaplin, *The Dolly Sisters* Betty Grable & June Haver, *The Doors* Val Kilmer as Jim Morrison, *The Eddie Cantor Story* Keefe Brasselle, *The Fabulous Dorseys* Tommy and Jimmy Dorsey, *W. C. Fields and Me* Rod Steiger as W. C. Fields, *The Five Pennies* Danny Kaye as Red Nichols, *Frances* Jessica Lange as Frances Farmer, *Funny Girl* Barbra Streisand as Fanny Brice, *Gable and Lombard* James Brolin and Jill Clayburgh, *The Gene Krupa Story* Sal Mineo, *The Glenn Miller Story* James Stewart, *Great Balls of Fire* Dennis Quaid as Jerry Lee Lewis, *The Great Caruso* Mario Lanza, *The Great Ziegfeld* William Powell, *Gypsy* Natalie Wood as Gypsy Rose Lee, *Harlow* Carroll Baker/Carol Lynley, *The Helen Morgan Story* Ann Blyth, *Houdini* Tony Curtis, *The I Don't Care Girl* Mitzi Gaynor as Eva Tanguay, *Incendiary Blonde* Betty Hutton as Texas Guinan, *Interrupted Melody* Eleanor Parker as Marjorie Lawrence, *Jeanne Eagels* Kim Novak, *The Joker is Wild* Frank Sinatra as Joe E. Lewis, *The Jolson Story* Larry Parks, *La Bamba* Lou Diamond Phillips as Richie Valens, *A Lady's Morals* Grace Moore as Jenny Lind, *Lady Sings the Blues* Diana Ross as Billie Holiday, *Lady With Red Hair* Miriam Hopkins as Mrs Leslie Carter and Claude Rains as David Belasco, *Leadbelly* Roger E. Mosley, *Lenny* Dustin Hoffman as Lenny Bruce, *Lillian Russell* Alice Faye, *Look for the Silver Lining* June Haver as Marilyn Miller, *Love Me or Leave Me* Doris Day as Ruth Etting, *Man of a Thousand Faces* James Cagney as Lon Chaney, *Melba* Patrice Munsel, *Peg of Old Drury* Anna Neagle as Peg Woffington, *Prince of Players* Richard Burton as Edwin Booth, *The Seven Little Foys* Bob Hope as Eddie Foy, *Shine on Harvest Moon* Ann Sheridan as Nora Bayes, *Somebody Loves Me* Betty Hutton as Blossom Seeley, *So This Is Love* Kathryn Grayson as Grace Moore, *Star!* Julie Andrews as Gertrude Lawrence and Daniel Massey as Noël Coward, *The Story of Vernon and Irene Castle* Fred Astaire and Ginger Rogers, *The Story of Will Rogers* Will Rogers Jnr, *Tonight We Sing* David Wayne as Sol Hurok, *Too Much Too Soon* Dorothy Malone as Diana Barrymore and Errol Flynn as John Barrymore, *With a Song in My Heart* Susan Hayward as Jane Froman, *Yankee Doodle Dandy* James Cagney as George M. Cohan, *Young Man With a Horn* Kirk Douglas as Bix Beiderbecke, *Your Cheatin' Heart* George Hamilton as Hank Williams.

Movies made for TV include: *Bud and Lou* Buddy Hackett and Harvey Korman as Abbott and Costello, *Elvis* Kurt Russell as Presley, *Elvis and Me* Dale Midkiff as Elvis, *James Dean* Stephen McHattie, *The Jayne Mansfield Story* Loni Anderson with Arnold Schwarzenegger as Mickey Hargitay, *The Legend of Valentino* Franco Nero, *Liberace* Andrew Robinson, *Liberace: Behind the Music* Victor Garber, *Marilyn: The Untold Story* Catherine Hicks as Monroe, *Rainbow* Andrea McArdle as the young Judy Garland, *Rita Hayworth: The Love Goddess* Lynda Carter, *Sophia Loren: Her Own Story* Sophia Loren as herself and her mother, John Gavin as Cary Grant, Edmund Purdom as Vittorio De Sica.

epidemics
featured memorably in *Jezebel*, *Yellow Jack*, *Arrowsmith*, *The Rains Came*, *Forever Amber*, *Panic in the Streets*, *The Killer that Stalked New York*, *Elephant Walk No Blade of Grass*, *The Andromeda Strain*, *Eighty Thousand Suspects*, *The Omega Man*, *Things to Come*, *Isle of the Dead*, *The Satan Bug*, *The Seventh Seal* and *Outbreak*.

episodic films
in a sense have always been with us – *If I Had a Million*, after all, came out in 1932, and *Intolerance* in 1916 – but it was in the 40s, possibly spurred by the all-star variety films intended to help the war effort, that they achieved their greatest popularity. Julien Duvivier, who had made *Un Carnet de Bal* in Paris, remade it in Hollywood as *Lydia* and followed it with *Tales of Manhattan* which was linked by a tailcoat and *Flesh and Fantasy* which was linked by the ramblings of a club bore. The stories in *Forever and a Day* were held together by a house, *Easy Money* by football pools, *Train of Events* by a railway accident, *Meet Mr Lucifer* by television. Then came the author complex: *Quartet* (Somerset Maugham), *Le Plaisir* (Maupassant), *Meet Me Tonight* (Noël Coward). The French took over with films like *The Seven Deadly Sins*, *The Devil and Ten Commandments*, *Life Together*; and the Italians were at it with *Four Kinds of Love*, *Made in Italy* and *The Queens*. For English-speaking markets the form was killed in the mid-50s by the advent of the half-hour TV play, but the 60s saw a brief revival with *How the West Was Won* and *The Yellow Rolls-Royce*. The 80s showed signs: the Italians were at it again with *Sunday Lovers* and Hollywood assigned four directors to one story each for *Twilight Zone*.

epitaphs
Over the years, a few stars have been nudged by the press into composing their own epitaphs. Herewith a selection of this grave humour.

~*W. C. Fields:* On the whole, I'd rather be in Philadelphia.

~*Cary Grant:* He was lucky – and he knew it.

~*Edward Everett Horton:* A nice part – only four 'sides', but good company and in for a long run.

~*Lionel Barrymore:* Well, I've played everything but a harp.

~*Hedy Lamarr:* This is too deep for me.

~*Dorothy Parker:* Excuse my dust.

~*Warner Baxter:* Did you hear about my operation?

~*William Haines:* Here's something I want to get off my chest.

~*Lewis Stone:* A gentleman farmer goes back to the soil.

~*Constance Bennett:* Do not disturb.

~*Wallace Ford:* At last I get top billing.

~*Preston Sturges:*
Now I've laid me down to die
I pray my neighbours not to pry
Too deeply into sins that I
Not only cannot here deny
But much enjoyed as time flew by . . .

Eskimos
have seldom been seriously tackled by the cinema. Documentaries abound, from *Nanook of the North* to *Eskimo*, and *Ukaliq* is a charming cartoon of Eskimo folklore, but the fictional stuff such as *Savage Innocents* and *The White Dawn* has been dull and unsympathetic. The most authentic was probably *Igloo* 32, starring CHEE-AK, but it failed to attract audiences, as did the more recent *Shadows of the Wolf/Agaguk* 93.

excerpts
from films are sometimes incorporated into other films in which characters go to a cinema or watch television. So in *Hollywood Cavalcade* Don Ameche watched a rough-cut of *The Jazz Singer*, just as ten years later Larry Parks in *Jolson Sings Again* watched a rough-cut of himself in *The Jolson Story*; an unidentified silent comedy was being played in the room below when the first murder took place in *The Spiral Staircase*; Linda Christian and Louis Jourdan saw *Son of the Sheik* at their local in *The Happy Time*, and Fredric March and his son watched a William S. Hart film in *One Foot in Heaven*. Prisoners watched *Wings of the Navy* during *Each Dawn I Die* and *The Egg and I* during *Brute Force*; and the chain gang in *Sullivan's Travels* roared with laughter at a Mickey Mouse cartoon. Footage from *Phantom of the Opera* was shown in *Hollywood Story*, from *Comin' thru' the Rye* in *The Smallest Show on Earth*, from *Tol'able David* in *The Tingler*, from *Queen Kelly* in *Sunset Boulevard*, from *Camille* in *Bridge to the Sun*, from *Destination Tokyo* in *Operation Pacific*, and from *Boom Town* in *Watch the Birdie*. Other movies shown in 'cinemas' in later films include: *Uncle Tom's Cabin* in *Abbott and Costello Meet the Keystone Kops*; *Gold Diggers of 1933* in *Bonnie and Clyde*; *Crossroads* in *The Youngest Profession*; *Casablanca* in *First to Fight*; *Red River* in *The Last Picture Show*; *Hell Divers* in *The Wings of Eagles*; *Task Force* in *White Heat*; *The Walking Dead* in *Ensign Pulver*; *Tin Pan Alley* in *Wing and a Prayer*; *Now Voyager* in *Summer of '42*; *Red Dust* in *Heavy Traffic*; various Bogart films in *Play It Again Sam*; *Caprice* in *Caprice* (Doris Day went to the movies, saw herself on the screen, and didn't like it). In *Two Weeks in Another Town*, which had a plot pretty close to that of *The Bad and the Beautiful*, Kirk Douglas watched himself in – *The Bad and the Beautiful!* The Bette Davis character in *Whatever Happened to Baby Jane?* was criticized as a bad actress on the strength of clips from early Bette Davis movies, *Ex-Lady* and *Parachute Jumper*. In the same film Joan Crawford watched herself on TV in *Sadie McKee*; and in *Walk Don't Run* there was a flash of James Stewart dubbed in Japanese in *Two Rode Together*. Finally the cosmonauts on their space station in *Conquest of Space* were entertained by a showing of *Here Come the Girls* . . . thus showing, as one critic remarked, that in 50 years' time TV will still be relying on old movies!

Other uses for old footage in new films include such gags as Bob Hope in *Road to Bali* meeting up with Humphrey Bogart in *The African Queen*; and economy dictates such measures as the ten-minute chunk of *The Mummy* at the beginning of *The Mummy's Hand* and the use in *Singin' in the Rain*, as part of a 'new' picture in production, of sequences from Gene Kelly's version of *The Three Musketeers*. Similarly bits of *The Sheik* were in *Son of the Sheik*, and *Topper* in *Topper Takes a Trip*. Great chunks of the *Joan of Arc* battles turned up in *Thief of Damascus*, as did *The Black Knight* in *Siege of the Saxons* and *The Four Feathers* in *Storm Over the Nile* and *East of Sudan*. Universal's *Sword of Ali Baba* used so much footage from their *Ali Baba and the Forty Thieves* that one actor had to be engaged to replay his original part! It was, however, wit rather than economy that persuaded Preston Sturges to open *Mad Wednesday* with the last reel of *The Freshman* and the Boris Karloff clips were central to the concept of *Targets*. As for *Dead Men Don't Wear Plaid*, the new footage was constructed entirely to fit in with clips from old movies, so that the hero appeared to be taking part in 40s scenes with the likes of Dorothy Lamour and Alan Ladd.

explorers
have inspired many documentaries but surprisingly few features except wholly fictitious ones like *Trader Horn*, *She* and *The Lost World*. *Marco Polo* has thrice been dealt with, and *Christopher Columbus* got the full Rank treatment as well as featuring in the satirical *Where Do We Go from Here?* The Pilgrim Fathers were the heroes of *Plymouth Adventure*, and Drake of *Seven Seas to Calais*. Lewis and Clark in *The Far Horizons* were played by Fred MacMurray and Charlton Heston. *Scott of the Antarctic* was played by John Mills, and Amundsen in *The Red Tent* by Sean Connery; Pierre Radisson in *Hudson's Bay* by Paul Muni; Cortez in *Captain from Castile* by César Romero; Pizarro in *The Royal Hunt of the Sun* by Robert Shaw; Junipero Serra in *Seven Cities of Gold* by Michael Rennie. *Penn of Pennsylvania* and *Stanley and Livingstone* were in the practical sense explorers, though driven by other motives; *Aguirre Wrath of God* seemed to be driven chiefly by greed.

Fair Game.
Paula Gosling's thriller about a cop who uses a female witness as bait to catch a serial killer was filmed as *Cobra* in 1986, directed by George Pan Cosmatos and starring Sylvester Stallone. The emphasis was on the cop. In 1995 it was remade under its original title, the emphasis now being on the woman, who was played by leading model Cindy Crawford in her first film role. Neither movie enjoyed much critical or commercial success.

fairy tales:
see FANTASY.

The Fall of the House of Usher.
This grisly tale by Edgar Allan Poe was filmed by Jean Epstein in 1928, by Americans Melville Webber and James Watson in the same year, by British semi-professionals in 1950, by Roger Corman in 1960, and by Allan Burkinshaw in 1988.

falling
is, of all man's inherited fears, the one most spectacularly played on by Hollywood, where the shot of the villain's hand slipping away from the hero's frenzied grasp, followed by a quick-fading scream, has become a screen stereotype. Harold Lloyd's skyscraper comedies played on this fear, as have the films of many comedians since; in *The Horn Blows at Midnight*, for instance, Jack Benny is only one of six people hanging on to each other's coat-tails from the top of a high building. All circus films, and that includes *The Marx Brothers at the Circus*, base one or two of their thrills on trapeze acts that might go wrong. And whenever a villain starts climbing upwards, as Ted de Corsia did in *Naked City*, or along a ledge, as the same accident-prone Ted de Corsia did in *The Enforcer*, the audience grits its teeth and waits for the inevitable. The whole action of *Fourteen Hours* was based on the question whether a potential suicide would or would not jump from a ledge.

Some of the screen's most spectacular falls include Walter Abel's in *Mirage*, the key to the whole action; Agnes Moorehead's (through a window) in *Dark Passage*; Charlotte Henry's in *Alice in Wonderland*; Cedric Hardwicke's in *Hunchback of Notre Dame*; W. C. Fields' (from an aeroplane) in *Never Give a Sucker an Even Break*; Alan Ladd's (through a roof) in *The Glass Key*; Slim Pickens' (on the bomb) in *Dr Strangelove*; Eleanor Parker's in *An American Dream*; *King Kong's* (from the top of the Empire State Building); William Bendix's from a skyscraper in *The Dark Corner*. To Alfred Hitchcock, falls are a speciality: Edmund Gwenn fell from Westminister Cathedral in *Foreign Correspondent*, Norman Lloyd from the torch of the Statue of Liberty in *Saboteur*, while *Vertigo* not only boasted three falls but based its entire plot on the hero's fear of heights. Falls under trains and buses are legion, but in *The Well* a little girl fell down an old wellshaft, in *The List of Adrian Messenger* a victim fell to his death in a lift (as did characters in *Hotel* and *House of Wax*, while in *Ivy* Joan Fontaine fell down a lift shaft), in Somerset Maugham's *Encore* an acrobat hoped to fall safely into a water tank; and an unnamed gentleman was pushed out of *The High Window* by Florence Bates.

the family
is the centre of most people's lives, so naturally there have been many memorable film families. Those popular enough to have warranted a series include the Joneses, the Hardys, the Huggetts, the Wilkinses of *Dear Ruth*, *The Cohens and the Kellys*, the Bumsteads of *Blondie* and the *Four Daughters* saga. World War II brought a sentimental attachment to the family which in Hollywood expressed itself in *Happy Land*, *The Human Comedy*, *Our Town*, *The Happy Time*, *Since You*

Went Away, *Meet Me in St Louis*, *A Genius in the Family*, *The Sullivans* and *The Best Years of Our Lives*; in Britain, *Salute John Citizen*, *The Holly and the Ivy*, *Dear Octopus*, *Quiet Wedding*, *This Man is Mine*. Semi-classical treatments of the theme include *Cavalcade*, *The Swiss Family Robinson*, *Pride and Prejudice*, *Little Women*, *Scrooge* and *Whiteoaks*. Odd families, ranging from the merely sophisticated to the downright bizarre, were seen in *Three Cornered Moon*, *The Old Dark House*, *The Royal Family of Broadway*, *My Man Godfrey*, *You Can't Take It With You*, *The Young in Heart*, *The Little Foxes*, *Tobacco Road*, *The Bank Dick*, *House of Strangers*, *An Inspector Calls*, *Sweethearts*, *Treasure Hunt*, *Holiday*, *The Philadelphia Story*, *The Anniversary*, and *The Lion in Winter*. Vaudeville families were seen in *Yankee Doodle Dandy*, *The Merry Monahans*, *The Seven Little Foys*, *The Buster Keaton Story* and *There's No Business Like Show Business*. There has been a fashion for the large family, started by *Cheaper by the Dozen* and *Chicken Every Sunday* in 1949 and reprised by *With Six You Get Egg Roll* and *Yours Mine and Ours* in 1968 and a TV series *The Brady Bunch* in 1969. Other charming families have included those in *Our Vines Have Tender Grapes*, *Background*, *The Happy Family*, *Four Sons*, *The Holly and the Ivy*, *Made in Heaven*, *29 Acacia Avenue*, *Little Murders*, *Never Too Late*, *This Happy Breed* and *My Wife's Family*; but the most memorable family of all is likely to remain the Joads in *The Grapes of Wrath*, unless it is one of the real families put under the microscope by American and British TV.

Fanny.
Originally one of Marcel Pagnol's 1932–34 trilogy (the others: *Marius* and *César*) about the Marseilles waterfront, this tale of a girl left pregnant by a sailor was almost unrecognizable in the MGM version *Port of Seven Seas* 38. The film was subsequently turned into a stage musical, and in 1960 Joshua Logan filmed this – but deleted the songs. The stars were Leslie Caron, Maurice Chevalier, and Charles Boyer.

fans
have been with us as long as the star system. One way of describing them is as people who adore an actor whatever he's doing and whether he's good or not. Another definition is: 'People who tell an actor he's not alone in the way he feels about himself.' Judy Garland once played a fan when she sang 'Dear Mr Gable'; and MGM made a whole movie about them, called *The Youngest Profession*. *The Fan* who pursued Lauren Bacall was quite another matter, a homicidal lunatic; and Eve in *All About Eve* was another fan who didn't do her star any good. The baseball fan in *The Fan* 96 became so upset that he kidnapped a player's son and threatened to murder him.

fantasy
has always been a popular form of cinema entertainment because the camera can lie so well, and trick work is most easily used in an unrealistic or fanciful story. The early films of Méliès and his innumerable imitators set a high standard and were still popular when the sombre German classics of the 20s – *The Golem*, *Nosferatu*, *Faust*, *Warning Shadows*, *The Niebelungen Saga*, *Metropolis* – awakened filmgoers to the possibilities of the medium for sustaining impossible situations throughout a whole serious feature.

Although Ince's *Civilisation* showed Christ on the battlefields, and the 20s brought such films as *The Four Horsemen of the Apocalypse*, *The Lost World* and *The Sorrows of Satan*, Hollywood did not fully explore the possibilities of fantasy until sound. Then in quick succession picturegoers were startled by *Outward Bound*, *Dracula*, *Frankenstein*, *Berkeley Square*, *King Kong* and *The Invisible Man*. *The Scoundrel*, with Noël Coward, was the forerunner of the few serious ghost films: *The Uninvited*, *The Return of Peter Grimm*, *Earthbound*, *The Ghost and Mrs Muir*, *Portrait of Jennie*, *The Haunting*, etc. Comic ghosts have, of course, been legion, notably in the *Topper* films, *The Ghost Breakers*, *I Married a Witch*, *The Canterville Ghost*, *The Man in the Trunk*, *The Remarkable Andrew*, *Thirteen Ghosts*, *The Spirit Is Willing*, *Blackbeard's Ghost*, *Wonder Man*, and so on. There were even singing ghosts in *Maytime*, *Bitter Sweet* and *Carousel*. Britain's contributions to the genre were few but choice: *The Ghost Goes West*, *Blithe Spirit*, *Things to Come*, *The Man Who Could Work Miracles*, *A Matter of Life and Death*, *Dead of Night*.

In 1936 *Green Pastures* showed the Negro view of heaven, and *On Borrowed Time* three years later paved the way for the heavenly comedies of the 40s: *Here Comes Mr Jordan*, *That's the Spirit*, *A Guy Named Joe*, *Heaven Can Wait*, *Down to Earth*, *The Horn Blows at Midnight*, *You Never Can Tell*, even *Ziegfeld Follies* (in which Ziegfeld's shade wrote in his diary 'Another *heavenly* day . . .'). For many years the last in this vein was *Carousel* 56; but 1968 brought *Barbarella* with its slightly tarnished angel, and *The Adding Machine* had its own perverse view of the hereafter. Meanwhile objects with magical properties were well served in *Alf's Button Afloat*, *A Thousand and One Nights*, *The Thief of Baghdad*, *Turnabout* and *The Picture of Dorian Gray*.

Among the many fairy tales filmed are *The Bluebird*, *The Wizard of Oz*, *Alice in Wonderland*, *The Glass Slipper*, *Tom Thumb*, *Mary Poppins* and a selection in *Hans Christian Andersen* and *The Wonderful World of the Brothers Grimm*. Disney's cartoon versions included *Pinocchio*, *Dumbo*, *The Sleeping Beauty*, *Cinderella*, *Peter Pan*, and, of course, *Snow White and the Seven Dwarfs*, which was cannily adapted for grown-ups by Billy Wilder as *Ball of Fire*. *Lost Horizon* was a kind of grown-up fairy tale too; and *The Red Shoes* as shown was certainly not for children. Original fairy tales for both categories were *The Luck of the Irish*, with Cecil Kellaway as a leprechaun, and *Miracle on 34th Street*, with Edmund Gwenn as Santa Claus. Modern fairy tales adapted for the screen include: *Chitty Chitty Bang Bang*, *Mary Poppins*, *Bedknobs and Broomsticks* and *Willy Wonka and the Chocolate Factory*.

In France during the occupation Marcel Carné made *Les Visiteurs du Soir*, a medieval fantasy with allegorical overtones, and after the war poet Jean Cocteau once again turned his attention to the cinema with such results as *La Belle et la Bête*, *Love Eternal*, *Orphée*, and *The Testament of Orphée*. More recently Albert Lamorisse has produced fantasies like *Crin Blanc* and *The Red Balloon*. Japan electrified the world with *Rashomon* and other strange, fanciful, stylized entertainments; Russia contributed many solidly-staged versions of old legends like *Sadko* and *Epic Hero and the Beast/Ilya Muromets*.

Since 1950, when in Hollywood Dick Powell played an Alsatian dog in *You Never Can Tell* and James Stewart in *Harvey* had a white rabbit six feet high which the script could never quite categorize as fact or hallucination, fantastic elements have been infiltrating into supposedly realistic films to such an extent that it is now difficult to separate them, especially in the films of Fellini, Antonioni, Tony Richardson, Richard Lester and Robert Altman.

See also: DREAMS; HORROR; PROPHECY; SPACE EXPLORATION.

farce
was once called 'tragedy with its trousers down'. Like melodrama, it presents exaggerated accounts of things that might happen in life. Comedy is more plausible than farce, but farce is often more enjoyable, involving more happenings, more chases, more doors slamming, more misunderstandings and mistaken identities. Good farce must be played with great style, and no lapses are permitted until the curtain comes down. Major exponents in Britain have been the Aldwych team of Tom Walls, Ralph Lynn and Robertson Hare and the Whitehall team headed by Brian Rix. In Hollywood good farce has been more occasional, but one might highlight *Nothing Sacred*, *To Be or Not to Be*, *Topper Returns*, *Love Crazy* and *The Palm Beach Story* (or almost anything else by Preston Sturges, who so delighted in controlled disorder). France gave us Fernandel and Pierre Etaix. The real trouble with farce on film is that it needs an audience: watched cold, it can often seem merely silly, and great stage farces such as Feydeau's *Hotel Paradiso* don't really translate.

Farewell, My Lovely.
Raymond Chandler's thriller of private eye Philip Marlowe searching for the girlfriend of an ex-convict was first filmed as vehicle for George Sanders' suave detective The Falcon (based on a character created by Michael Arlen) in *The Falcon Takes Over* 42. It was more faithfully and successfully remade two years later as *Murder, My Sweet/Farewell, My Lovely*, starring Dick Powell. In 1975, Dick Richards made another good version with Robert Mitchum in the lead.

A Farewell to Arms.
Hemingway's tough-romantic anti-war novel has been filmed twice: in 1932 by Frank Borzage, with Gary Cooper and Helen Hayes, and in 1957 by Charles Vidor, with Rock Hudson and Jennifer Jones. Neither version was a triumph artistically, but the first proved more popular than the second, which was badly inflated by David O. Selznick into a pseudo-epic.

fashions
were the basis of many a woman's film of the 30s: *Roberta*, *Fashions of 1934*, *Vogues of 1938*. Later attempts to recapture this interest had an air of *déjà vu*: *Maytime in Mayfair*, *It Started in Paradise*, *Lucy Gallant*, *Designing Woman*. But the wheel turns, and the 70s brought *Mahogany* and the 80s *Chanel Solitaire*.

fastest money-making movies:
Independence Day holds the record, taking $104m at the US box-office in six days in 1996. It beat *Jurassic Park*, which took $100m in nine days in 1993. *Independence Day* reached $200m in 20 days, while *Jurassic Park* took 23. In 1989, *Batman* took 10 days to reach that mark, while *Batman Returns* took 11 days in 1992.

Father Brown.
The only British attempt to film the adventures of G. K. Chesterton's tubby detective in 1958 was a civilized comedy with all concerned on the same wavelength. A quietly witty script by Thelma Schnee, polished direction by Robert Hamer, and high-comedy acting by Alec Guinness, Peter Finch, Joan Greenwood, and Ernest Thesiger made it a film with a rare flavour. On television, Kenneth More played the role in a 1974 series. In 1934 Walter Connolly played the role in a Hollywood second feature, *Father Brown Detective*. In West Germany, Heinz Ruhmann played the role in two 60s films, and Josef Meinrad in a 1969 TV series. In 1980 Barnard Hughes played the priest on TV in *The Girl in the Park*.

FBI.
The US governmental crime-fighting agency was set up in 1924 by J. Edgar Hoover and became famous for its heroic stand against the public enemies of the 30s, when its agents became known as G-Men. Surface glamour concealed an immensely painstaking organization relying heavily on science, but only the glamour was shown in such films as *Show 'Em No Mercy*, *G-Men*, *Persons in Hiding*, *Let 'Em Have It*, *The FBI Story*, *FBI Girl*, *Parole Fixer*, *Confessions of a Nazi Spy*, *FBI Code 98*, *Walk East on Beacon* and *Queen of the Mob*. *The House on 92nd Street* in 1945 gave the best impression of the FBI at work, but its sequel *The Street with No Name* reverted to stereotype, which was maintained by Quinn Martin's nine-year TV series. In 1978, *The Private Files of J. Edgar Hoover* provided a rather superficial exposé.

Felix (the Cat).
Cartoon creation of Pat Sullivan, a perky and indestructible character highly popular in the 20s; in the 50s revived for TV by other hands in more streamlined style. An unsuccessful full-length feature, directed by Tibor Hernadi, was released in 89.

female impersonation:
see TRANSVESTISM.

fights
provide the climax to many a film, but only the outstandingly staged ones remain in the mind. The slugging match between the two heroes of *The Spoilers* became a tradition, as each of the five versions tried to outdo the previous one. John Wayne had many fighting triumphs, notably against Victor McLaglen in *The Quiet Man*; *McLintock* and *North to Alaska* seemed at times to have more brawling than dialogue. Spoof fights were probably topped by the saloon brawl in *The Great Race*; serious ones by the solemn allegorical punch-up in *The Big Country*. Other good western fights are found in *Shane*, *The Sheepman*, and (between Dietrich and Una Merkel) in *Destry Rides Again*. For viciousness within a serious picture the waterfront fights in *Edge of the City* and *On the Waterfront* take some beating.

film-making
is not too frequently used as a background for movies, as movies about movies are thought to be bad box office. Certainly not too many of the following were big hits: *OK for Sound*, *The Best Pair of Legs in the Business*, *Go for a Take*, *The Comedy Man*, *The Bad and the Beautiful*, *Two Weeks in Another Town*, *It's a Great Feeling*, *Shooting Stars*, *Pick a Star*, *A Star is Born*, *The Carpetbaggers*, *Eight and a Half*, *Hellzapoppin*, *Day for Night*, *Stand In*, *Singin' In The Rain*, *Abbott and Costello Meet the Keystone Kops*, *Gable and Lombard*, *Harlow*, *W.C. Fields and Me*, *The Big Knife*, *Once in a Lifetime*, *Wonderful Life*, *Hollywood Cavalcade*, *Hollywood Boulevard*, *Hollywood Story*, *Nickelodeon*, *The Last Tycoon*, *Everything for Sale*, *The Stunt Man*, *Crimes and Misdemeanors*, *The Big Picture*, *The Player*, *Living in Oblivion*, *Swimming with Sharks*.

films à clef
are those which appear to be fiction but are really based on factual cases with the names changed. The obvious example is *Citizen Kane*, which parallels the career of William Randolph Hearst. Others are *The Great Dictator*, in which Hynkel is obviously Hitler; *Compulsion*, based on the Leopold and Loeb murder; *Inherit the Wind*, about the Scopes monkey trial; *The Moon and Sixpence*, in which Charles Strickland stands in for Paul Gauguin; *The Man Who Came to Dinner*, in which Sheridan Whiteside is Alexander Woollcott, Banjo is Harpo Marx, and Beverly Carlton is Noël Coward; *Young Cassidy*, drawn from the early life of Sean O'Casey; *All About Eve*, in which Margo Channing was said to be Tallulah Bankhead and Addison de Witt George Jean Nathan; *Twentieth Century*, in which Oscar Jaffe is an amalgam of Jed Harris and David Belasco; *All the King's Men* and *A Lion is in the Streets*, both essentially about Huey Long; *The Lost Moment*, in which the old lady is allegedly Claire Clairemont, the aged mistress of Byron; *The Adventurers*, in which the characters are supposedly based on Porfirio Rubirosa, Barbara Hutton, Aristotle Onassis and Maria Callas; *The Carpetbaggers*, plainly about Howard Hughes; *Little Caesar*, who was clearly Al Capone; *Major Barbara*, in which Adolphus Cusins was Gilbert Murray; *Call Me Madam*, based on the exploits of Perle Mesta; *The Winslow Boy*, based on the Archer–Shee case, with Sir Robert Morton standing in for Sir Edward Carson; *An American Tragedy*, from the real life Chester Gillette murder case; *Monsieur Verdoux*, who was Landru; *Death of a Scoundrel*, from the career of Charles Rubenstein; *The Prisoner*, inspired by the sufferings of Cardinal Mindzenty; *Fame is the Spur*, in which Homer Radshaw was Ramsay MacDonald; and if you like, *Dr Jekyll and Mr Hyde*, whose story was inspired by the burglarious second life of Deacon William Brodie; or even any Sherlock Holmes story, as Holmes was modelled on Dr Joseph Bell. *Where Love Has Gone* was modelled on the Lana Turner case in which her daughter murdered her lover; and *Imitation of Life* also reflected the Turner career, as *Dancing Lady* and *Torch Song* reflected Joan Crawford's. *The Barefoot Contessa* was vaguely drawn from Rita Hayworth's international goings-on, though the star who played her, Ava Gardner, was also no slouch in the fun department. *Bombshell* was an obvious echo of Jean Harlow's own troubles with hangers-on. *I Could Go on Singing* featured Judy Garland clearly playing herself; *The Devil Is a Woman* can be seen as Sternberg's farewell to Dietrich (with Lionel Atwill playing himself), just as Orson Welles cast himself as bedevilled by his then wife Rita Hayworth in *The Lady from Shanghai*. The leading roles in *Will Success Spoil Rock Hunter?*, *After the Fox*, *The Band Wagon*, *Blondie of the Follies* and *Kiss Me Stupid* were clearly based on those who played them: Jayne Mansfield, Victor Mature, Fred Astaire, Marion Davies and Dean Martin. The same can be said of Gloria Swanson in *Sunset Boulevard*, Bette Davis in *The Star*, Errol Flynn in *The Sun Also Rises*, Hedy Lamarr in *The Female Animal*, Marlene Dietrich in *No Highway*, John Wayne in *The Shootist*, John Barrymore in *The Great Profile* and Zero Mostel in *The Front*. *The Goddess* reflected Marilyn Monroe's marriage with Joe Di Maggio. *Flight for Freedom*, though not using Amelia Earhart's name, gave a fictional solution to the aviatrix's real-life disappearance. *Funny Girl* was the official biography of Fanny Brice, but *Rose of Washington Square* also had lots of similarities. *All About Eve*'s leading character, Margo Channing, according to its creator, was based on Elisabeth Bergner. *New York*

New York seemed to be taken from Doris Day's autobiography. *Smash-Up* was allegedly based on the drinking problems of Bing Crosby's first wife Dixie Lee, just as *Written on the Wind* had connections with the suicide of Libby Holman's first husband. Evangelist Aimee Semple McPherson was clearly impersonated by Barbara Stanwyck in *The Miracle Woman* and by Jean Simmons in *Elmer Gantry*. Columnist Walter Winchell was parodied in several Lee Tracy vehicles – Tracy even looked like him – and also by Burt Lancaster in *Sweet Smell of Success*. The Robert Ryan character in *Caught* was allegedly based on Howard Hughes. Bette Midler in *The Rose* is obviously Janis Joplin. *The Greek Tycoon* is clearly inspired by Aristotle Onassis and Jackie Kennedy. In *It's Tough to Be Famous*, Douglas Fairbanks Jnr could only be Charles Lindbergh. James Cagney and Pat O'Brien in *Boy Meets Girl* were inspired by Charles MacArthur and Ben Hecht. In *The Last Tycoon*, Robert de Niro was Irving Thalberg. Anne Baxter in *You're My Everything* was Clara Bow. The sliding marriage in *A Star Is Born* could have been based on Al Jolson and Ruby Keeler, or on John Gilbert and Greta Garbo. Patty Duke in *Valley of the Dolls* was Judy Garland. And so on.

fire
is a standard part of the melodramatist's equipment, whether it be used for disposing of country houses with too many memories (*Dragonwyck*, *Rebecca*, *The Lost Moment*, *The Fall of the House of Usher*, *The Tomb of Ligeia*, *Gone with the Wind*) or whole cities (*Forever Amber*, *In Old Chicago*, *Quo Vadis*, *City on Fire*). Sometimes, as in *House of Wax*, it makes a splendid starting point; though to judge from *She* one can't rely on its life-prolonging qualities. Its use in realistic films is rare, though cases of arson were seriously studied in *On the Night of the Fire* and *Violent Playground*. The fires of hell were most spectacularly recreated in the 1935 version of *Dante's Inferno*. Comedies about firemen include *Where's That Fire?* (Will Hay), *Fireman Save My Child*, *Harvey Middleman Fireman*, and *Go to Blazes* (Dave King); and firemen who start fires instead of putting them out are prophesied in *Fahrenheit 451*. Oil fires were spectacularly depicted in *Tulsa*, *Wildcat*, and *Hellfighters*. The classic study of conventional firemen remains *Fires Were Started*; TV series which took up the theme include *Emergency*, *Firehouse* and *London's Burning*. For many, the greatest screen fire will be the burning of Atlanta in *Gone with the Wind*, but *The Towering Inferno* was probably the most spectacular. *Backdraft* is another where the flames stole the picture. *Endless Love* was brought to an end by a pyromaniac, *Firestarter* dealt with a psychic who could set anything ablaze, while *Quest for Fire* dealt with a Stone Age tribe who weren't able to set anything alight after their fire went out. Finally, fire was always a splendid aid for serial producers, as the oft-used title 'Next Week: Through the Flames' may suggest.

See also: FOREST FIRES.

firing squads
have figured chiefly in films about World War I (*Paths of Glory*, *King and Country*) or those telling the lives of spies (*Mata Hari*, *Nurse Edith Cavell*, *Carve Her Name With Pride*). Other uses have been in *Dishonoured*, *The Fugitive*, *Custer of the West*, *The Victors*, *The Long Ride Home*, *Reach for Glory*, *The Counterfeit Traitor* and *The Ceremony*; and firing squads were given a comic effect in *The Captain's Paradise*, *Casino Royale*, *Morgan* and *The Ambushers*.

The Flag Lieutenant.
The stiff-upper-lip stage melodrama by W. P. Drury and Lee Trevor, about the intrepid exploits of a naval officer in an outpost of empire, was filmed as a silent in 1919 with George Wynn, and in 1926 with Henry Edwards. In 1932 Edwards appeared in a sound remake with Anna Neagle as his leading lady.

Flash Gordon.
American newspaper strip hero whose exploits were featured in three famous Hollywood serials starring Buster Crabbe. In the original *Flash Gordon* 36 our hero and his friends saved the Earth from collision with another planet at the cost of being stranded there at the mercy of the wicked Emperor Ming. *Flash Gordon's Trip to Mars* 38 and *Flash Gordon Conquers the Universe* 40 were compounded of similar elements. The directors respectively were Frederick Stephani; Ford Beebe and Robert Hill; and Ray Taylor. A softcore spoof, *Flesh Gordon*, appeared in 1974. In 1980 Dino de Laurentiis presented a lavish but empty remake of the original, and in the following year came a cartoon remake from Filmation.

The Flintstones.
An animated TV suburban situation comedy set in the Stone Age, created by Bill Hanna and Joe Barbera, was turned into a feature film using actors in 1994. In the cartoon version, Fred Flintstone was voiced by Alan Reed, his wife Wilma by Jean Vanderpyl, and their pet dinosaur, Dino, by Mel Blanc, who also supplied the voice for their neighbour Barney Rubble. Broadcast from 1960–66 and often repeated, it owed much to an earlier TV sitcom, *The Honeymooners*, starring Jackie Gleason, and became the longest-running animated show on television; its spin-offs included *The Flintstone Kids*, broadcast in the late 80s. In the feature film, John Goodman appeared as Fred, Rosie O'Donnell as Wilma, and Rick Moranis as Barney.

fog
has been a godsend to many a cinematic entertainment, whether it's the genuine pea-souper inseparable from Hollywood's idea of London, or the ankle-high white mist which used to distinguish heaven and dream sequences. Fog can provide a splendid dramatic background, especially in horror-thrillers like *Dracula*, *The Wolf Man* and *The Cat and the Canary*; but too often it is simply imposed on a film to force a particular atmosphere, as in *Footsteps in the Fog*, *Fog over Frisco*, *Fog Island*, *Winterset*, *Out of the Fog* and *The Notorious Landlady*. *Barbary Coast* seemed to be permanently enveloped in fog, as did the village in *Sherlock Holmes and the Scarlet Claw*: while in *The Adventures of Sherlock Holmes* London had fog in May! Fog was dramatically used in *The VIPs* and *The Divorce of Lady X* (for bringing people together in a hotel); in *The Runaway Bus* (for bringing people together in an abandoned village); in *Midnight Lace* (for masking the identity of the voice threatening Doris Day); in *Twenty-Three Paces to Baker Street* (for hampering the villain but not the blind hero); in *Alias Nick Beal* (as a background for the devil's materialization); in *The Lost Continent* (as a nauseous yellow background for the weird community); in *Random Harvest* (as a means for the hero's escape); and in the various versions of *The Sea Wolf* (for causing the accident that brings hero and heroine together on Wolf Larsen's boat). Even comedies find it useful: the chase through fog in *After the Fox* results in happy confusion. Oddly enough John Carpenter's film *Fog* made insufficient use of its titular commodity.

Foghorn Leghorn.
Boastful rooster from the Deep South, a star of Warner Brothers' Merrie Melodies and Looney Tunes cartoons. His voice was supplied by Mel Blanc.

Walky Talky Hawky (AAN) 46. The Foghorn Leghorn 48. Leghorn Swoggled 51. All Fowled Up 55. The High and the Flighty 56. Fox Terror 57. A Broken Leghorn 59. Strangled Eggs 61. Banty Raids 63, etc.

Folies Bergère.
This innocuous 1935 musical comedy was written by Bess Meredith and Hal Long as a vehicle for Maurice Chevalier, who played a dual role; at the climax his double had to masquerade to his wife as himself. It was too good an idea not to be used again. In 1941 came *That Night in Rio* with Don Ameche; in 1951, there was *On the Riviera* with Danny Kaye. Kaye apparently liked it so much that he had it altered a little and it served for *On the Double* 61 as well.

the Foreign Legion
has been taken reasonably seriously in the three versions of *Beau Geste*, the two versions of *Le Grand Jeu*, *Beau Sabreur*, *China Gate*, *Rogue's Regiment*, *Ten Tall Men*, and *The Legion's Last Patrol*. It was sent up something wicked by Laurel and Hardy in *Beau Hunks* and *The Flying Deuces*; by Abbott and Costello *In the Foreign Legion*; and by the Carry On gang in *Follow That Camel*.

forest fires
have made a roaring climax for many films including *The Blazing Forest*, *Red Skies of Montana*, *Guns of the Timberland*, *The Bluebird*, *The Big Trees* and *Ring of Fire*. None was more dramatic than the cartoon version in *Bambi*.

The Fox.
Name of an actor-detective played by Red Skelton in three films directed by S. Sylvan Simon. He plays an actor who plays The Fox, hero of a radio series, and finds himself called upon to solve crimes in the real world. The character Skelton plays resembles that projected by Bob Hope in many of his films of the period – a wisecracking coward who nevertheless comes good and gets the girl (played in Skelton's films by Ann Sothern).

Whistling in the Dark 41. Whistling in Dixie 42. Whistling in Brooklyn 43.

Fox and the Crow.
Stars of Columbia Pictures' (1941–47) and UPA's (1948–50) cartoons. Created by Frank Tashlin, Fox was voiced by Frank Graham and Crow by Paul Frees.

The Fox and the Grapes 41. Woodman Spare That Tree 42. Slay It with Flowers 43. The Dream Kids 44. Treasure Jest 45. Tooth or Consequences 47. Robin Hoodlum (AAN) 48. Magic Fluke (AAN) 49. Punchy De Leon 50, etc.

Francis.
The talking mule of several Universal comedies (1950–56) was the direct ancestor of TV's talking palomino *Mister Ed*, also produced by Arthur Lubin. Francis' first master was Donald O'Connor, but later Mickey Rooney took over the reins. Francis was 'voiced' by Chill Wills, Ed by Allan Lane.

Frankenstein.
The man/monster theme was explored in American movies of 1908 (with Charles Ogle) and 1916 (*Life Without Soul*); also in Italy in 1920 (*Master of Frankenstein*). The 1931 Hollywood film, written by Robert Florey and directed by James Whale, borrowed as much from Wegener's *The Golem* 22 as from Mary Shelley's early 19th-century novel; but despite censorship problems the elements jelled, with Boris Karloff a great success as the monster composed from dead bits and pieces, and a legend was born. Sequels included *Bride of Frankenstein* 35. *Son of Frankenstein* 39. *Ghost of Frankenstein* 41. *Frankenstein Meets the Wolf Man* 43. *House of Frankenstein* 45. *House of Dracula* 45. *Abbott and Costello Meet Frankenstein* 48; among those who took over from Karloff were Lon Chaney, Bela Lugosi and Glenn Strange. In 1956 the original story was remade in Britain's Hammer Studios under the title *The Curse of Frankenstein*; colour and gore were added, and sequels, with various monsters, came thick and fast: *The Revenge of Frankenstein* 58. *The Evil of Frankenstein* 63. *Frankenstein Created Woman* 67. *Frankenstein Must Be Destroyed* 69. *Horror of Frankenstein* 70. *Frankenstein and the Monster from Hell* 73. A variation on the original monster make-up was used by Fred Gwynne in the TV comedy series, *The Munsters* 64–65. There have also been several recent American, Japanese and Italian attempts to cash in on the name of Frankenstein in cheap exploitation pictures: *I Was a Teenage Frankenstein* 57. *Frankenstein 1970* 58. *Frankenstein Versus the Space Monsters* 65. *Frankenstein Conquers the World* 68. *Lady Frankenstein* 70, etc. In 1973 a four-hour TV version called *Frankenstein: The True Story* (which it could scarcely be) was co-authored by Christopher Isherwood but proved merely a laborious reworking of the earlier films, with occasional references back to the book, but no humour. Films about Mary Shelley's creation of Frankenstein appeared towards the end of the 80s: *Haunted Summer*, *Gothic* and *Frankenstein Unbound*, and *Mary Shelley's Frankenstein*, directed by Kenneth Branagh with Robert De Niro as the monster, appeared in 1994.

Book: 1994, *The Illustrated Frankenstein Movie Guide* by Stephen Jones.

Friday the 13th.
A series of low-budget horror movies about serial killer Jason Vorhees, who wears a hockey mask and, in the style of such films, murders teenagers. The first, produced and directed by Sean S. Cunningham, became a cult hit among young audiences and was turned into a computer game. The later films were low on quality and inspiration. In 1995 there were plans to team Jason and New Line's other horror creation, Freddy Kruger (of *Nightmare on Elm Street*), together in a film.

Fritz the Cat.
Randy feline, created by cartoonist Robert CRUMB, who appeared in various magazines of the 60s and was the star of two animated adult features:

Fritz the Cat 72. The Nine Lives of Fritz the Cat 74.

The Front Page.
Ben HECHT and Charles MACARTHUR's indestructible, fast-moving, witty and cynical play about journalists and politicians has been filmed four times: in 1931, directed by Lewis MILESTONE with Pat O'BRIEN as reporter Hildy Johnson and Adolphe MENJOU as editor Walter Burns; in 1940, as the superlative *His Girl Friday*, directed by Howard HAWKS, with Rosalind RUSSELL as Hildy and Cary GRANT as Burns; in 1974, directed by Billy WILDER, with Jack LEMMON as Hildy and Walter MATTHAU as Burns; and in 1988, as *Switching Channels*, directed by Ted KOTCHEFF, with Kathleen TURNER and Burt REYNOLDS. Hecht thought the best performance of Hildy was by Lee TRACY in the original 1928 Broadway production, in which Osgood PERKINS also triumphed as Walter Burns.

Fu Manchu.
Sax Rohmer's oriental master-criminal was played by Harry Agar Lyons in a series of British two-reelers in the 20s. Warner Oland played him in *The Mysterious Fu Manchu* 29, *The Return of Fu Manchu* 30 and *Daughter of the Dragon* 31; Boris Karloff in *Mask of Fu Manchu* 32, and Henry Brandon in *Drums of Fu Manchu* 41. Otherwise he was oddly neglected until the 60s series starring Christopher Lee, beginning with *The Face of Fu Manchu* 65 and *Brides of Fu Manchu* 66: it degenerated into shambling nonsense.

funerals
provided a starting point for *The Third Man*, *Frankenstein*, *The Great Man*, *Death of a Salesman*, *The Bad and the Beautiful*, *Citizen Kane*, and *Keeper of the Flame*; figured largely in *The Premature Burial*, *The Mummy*, *The Egyptian*, *The Fall of the House of Usher*, *The Counterfeit Traitor*, *Funeral in Berlin*, *The Godfather*, *The Glass Key*, *I Bury the Living*, *Miracle in Milan*, *Doctor Zhivago* and *Hamlet*; and formed a climax for *Our Town* and *Four Weddings and a Funeral*. In *Vampyr* and *Wild Strawberries* the hero dreamed of his own funeral; and in *Holy Matrimony* Monty Woolley attended his own funeral, having arranged to have his valet's body mistaken for his. Funerals were taken lightly in *I See a Dark Stranger*, *Little Caesar*, *Kind Hearts and Coronets*, *Too Many Crooks*, *A Comedy of Terrors*, *Charade*, *The Wrong Box*, *I Love You Alice B. Toklas*, *Robin and the Seven Hoods*, *Monsieur Hulot's Holiday*, *Entr'acte*, *Ocean's Eleven*, *Comrade X*, *What a Way to Go*, *The Private Life of Sherlock Holmes*, and above all *The Loved One*.

funfairs
have provided fascinating settings for many a bravura film sequence. *The Wagons Roll at Night*, *Nightmare Alley*, *Dante's Inferno*, *Rollercoaster* and *The Ring* were set almost entirely on fairgrounds. Tawdry or 'realistic' funfairs were shown in *Jeanne Eagels*, *Saturday Night and Sunday Morning*, *East of Eden*, *Picnic*, and *Inside Daisy Clover*; glamorized or sentimentalized ones cropped up in *The Wolf Man*, *My Girl Tisa*, *State Fair*, *Roseanna McCoy*, *The Great Ziegfeld* and *Mr and Mrs Smith*. Musicals like *On the Town*, *On the Avenue*, *Coney Island*, *Centennial Summer*, *State Fair* and *Down to Earth* had funfair sequences and they are also used to excellent advantage in thrillers:

Brighton Rock, *Spider Woman*, *Horrors of the Black Museum*, *Gorilla at Large*, *The Third Man*, *Lady from Shanghai*, *Strangers on a Train*. Naturally funfairs are also marvellous places for fun: though not for Eddie Cantor in *Strike Me Pink*, Tony Curtis in *Forty Pounds of Trouble*, Laurel and Hardy in *The Dancing Masters*, or Bob Hope (fired from a cannon) in *Road to Zanzibar*. *The Beast from 20,000 Fathoms* was finally cornered in a funfair; *Dr Caligari* kept his cabinet in one. The star who made the most of a funfair sequence was undoubtedly Mae West as the carnival dancer in *I'm No Angel*, in which she delivered her famous line: 'Suckers!'

gambling,
in the indoor sport sense, is quite a preoccupation of film-makers. Gregory Peck in *The Great Sinner* played a man who made a great career of it, as did James Caan in *The Gambler* and George Segal in *California Split;* while in *The Queen of Spades* Edith Evans learnt the secret of winning at cards from the devil himself. Other suspenseful card games were played in *The Cincinnati Kid, Lucky Jordan, The Lady Eve, Hazard,* and *Big Hand for a Little Lady;* snooker pool was the game in *The Hustler* and *The Color of Money;* old-time Mississippi riverboats were the setting for *Mississippi Gambler, The Naughty Nineties, Frankie and Johnny* and a sequence in *The Secret Life of Walter Mitty.* Roulette, however, is the most spectacular and oft-used film gambling game, seen in *The Shanghai Gesture, Robin and the Seven Hoods, Ocean's Eleven, The Big Snatch, Doctor No, La Baie des Anges, Quartet* (the 'Facts of Life' sequence), *Seven Thieves, The Las Vegas Story, The Only Game in Town, The Big Sleep, Gilda, Kaleidoscope,* and many others. Second features with such titles as *Gambling House, Gambling Ship* and *Gambling on the High Seas* were especially popular in the 40s. Musically, the filmic high-point was undoubtedly the 'oldest established permanent floating crap game in New York' number in *Guys and Dolls.* This stemmed from the writings of Damon Runyon, also adapted in such films as *Sorrowful Jones* and *The Lemon Drop Kid.* The most comic game on film was perhaps the hand of poker played between Judy Holliday and Broderick Crawford in *Born Yesterday.*

gangsters,
a real-life American menace of the 20s, provided a new kind of excitement for early talkies like *Little Caesar* and *Public Enemy,* which told how their heroes got into criminal activities but didn't rub in the moral very hard. The pace of the action, however, made them excellent movies, and critics defended them against religious pressure groups. *Quick Millions, Scarface, Lady Killer, The Little Giant* and *Public Enemy's Wife* were among the titles which followed; then Warner Brothers cleverly devised a way of keeping their thrills while mollifying the protesters: they made the policeman into the hero, in films like *G-Men, I Am the Law, Bullets or Ballots.* By 1938 it seemed time to send up the whole genre in *A Slight Case of Murder,* with its cast of corpses, and in the later *Brother Orchid* the gangster-in-chief became a monk; yet in 1939 the heat had cooled off sufficiently to allow production of *The Roaring Twenties,* one of the most violent gangster movies of them all. The war made gangsters old-fashioned, but in the late 40s Cagney starred in two real psychopathic toughies, *White Heat* and *Kiss Tomorrow Goodbye.* After that the fashion was to parody gangsterism, in *Party Girl, Some Like It Hot,* and a couple of Runyon movies; but the success of a French film called *Rififi* and a TV series called *The Untouchables* left the field wide open for redevelopment. Successes in the 60s included *Bonnie and Clyde, The St Valentine's Day Massacre, Pay or Die, The Rise and Fall of Legs Diamond, King of the Roaring Twenties,* and from the French *Borsalino* and various *Rififi* sequels. The 70s brought British gang violence in *Get Carter, Villain, The Squeeze* and *Sweeney,* and in 1972 the gigantic success of *The Godfather* spawned sequels, rivals (*The Valachi Papers*) and parodies (*The Gang That Couldn't Shoot Straight*). Britain showed that it could make gangster movies in the American style with *The Long Good Friday,* but there were few successors, although *The Krays* followed the fortunes of its most notorious criminals. Alan Parker's *Bugsy Malone* parodied the Chicago gangster movies by having one acted by kids armed with pop guns, but the era continued to fascinate film-makers. Sergio Leone's epic *Once Upon a Time in America,* hacked about by its producers on its first release, became available on video-cassette in an uncut version. Brian De Palma remade *Scarface* as a film about Hispanic gangsters and turned *The Untouchables* into a big-screen success. Coppola's examination of the Mafia was extended into *The Godfather II* and *III,* while Marlon Brando parodied his title role in *The Freshman.* Martin Scorsese had a hit with *GoodFellas* while Shakespeare's *Macbeth* was turned into a gangland movie in *Men of Respect.* Jonathan Demme found some humour in the subject of a Mafia widow fleeing the gangs in *Married to the Mob.* In the 90s, the hot subject became the gangs' involvement in drug-dealing. Abel Ferrera's *The King of New York* traced the rise of a white drug baron and his black confederates taking over from the Mafia, while *New Jack City* showed a gang turning an apartment block into a fortified drug factory. It was almost a relief to return to the simpler antics of the 50s in Bill Duke's *A Rage in Harlem.*

The Garden of Allah.
Robert Hichen's novel, about a sophisticated woman whose husband turns out to be an escaped Trappist monk, was filmed as a silent in 1917, with Tom Santschi and Helen Ware, and again in 1927 with Ivan Petrovich and Alice Terry. The 1936 sound remake had excellent early colour, elegant direction by Richard Boleslawski, and exotic performances from Charles Boyer and Marlene Dietrich.

Gaslight.
Patrick Hamilton's stage suspense thriller, about a Victorian wife deliberately being driven insane by her murderous husband, was perfectly filmed in Britain in 1940 by Thorold Dickinson with Anton Walbrook, Diana Wynyard, and Frank Pettingell. MGM promptly bought and destroyed the negative, and in 1944 produced an opulent and inferior remake with Charles Boyer, Ingrid Bergman (AA), and Joseph Cotten, directed by George Cukor. In Britain this version was known as *The Murder in Thornton Square;* prints of the original did survive and have been shown in America as *Angel Street.*

Gentlemen Prefer Blondes.
Anita Loos's comic novel about a gold-digging 20s chorus girl on the make in the millionaire set was filmed in 1928 by Mal St Clair, with Ruth Taylor and Alice White, then in 1953 by Howard Hawks with Marilyn Monroe and Jane Russell. Hawks's film was followed in 1955 by a sequel of sorts, *Gentlemen Marry Brunettes,* directed by Richard Sale and starring Jane Russell and Jeanne Crain.

Gerald McBoing Boing.
A smiling little boy who could only make sounds, created by author Dr Seuss and the hero of four UPA cartoons. The spareness of line and sharpness of wit, particularly in the first of the series, contrasted happily with Disney's chocolate-box period.

Gerald McBoing Boing (AA) 51. Gerald McBoing Boing's Symphony 53. How Now Boing Boing 54. Gerald McBoing Boing on the Planet Moo (AA) 56.

Gertie the Dinosaur.
Early American cartoon character created by Winsor McKay in 1909.

The Ghost Breaker.
This American stage thriller by Paul Dickey and Charles W. Goddard, about an heiress's voodoo-haunted castle, was filmed in 1915 with H. B. Warner and in 1922, directed by Alfred E. Green, with Wallace Reid. In 1940 George Marshall directed a talkie version as a vehicle for Bob Hope, and the result was an oddly successful combination of laughs and horror, with contributions from Willie Best, Paulette Goddard and Paul Lukas. (The title, incidentally, was made plural.) In 1953 Marshall remade it, with remarkable fidelity to the 1940 script, as a vehicle for Dean Martin and Jerry Lewis under the title *Scared Stiff,* with Lizabeth Scott and Carmen Miranda; the results were hardly stimulating.

The Ghost Train.
This hugely successful British stage comedy-thriller by Arnold Ridley (also an actor best known for playing Private Godfrey in the long-running television series *Dad's Army*), about stranded passengers at a lonely Cornish station being used by gun-runners, was first filmed in 1928, directed by Geza Bolvary, with Guy Newall as the silly-ass hero who turns out to be a policeman. A talkie version followed in 1931 with Jack Hulbert, directed by Walter Forde, who also directed the 1941 remake in which the leading role was split between Arthur Askey and Richard Murdoch.

ghosts:
see FANTASY.

giants
are infrequently encountered in films, but Harold Lloyd met one in *Why Worry?,* as did Abbott and Costello in *Lost in a Harem.* Costello also met *The Thirty Foot Bride of Candy Rock,* not to be confused with *The Attack of the Fifty Foot Woman.* Then there was *The Giant of Marathon,* and Glenn Langan played *The Amazing Colossal Man* in two films. Back to Abbott and Costello again: it was they who appeared with Buddy Baer in *Jack and the Beanstalk.*

Gidget.
An American teenager of the early 60s, a kind of female Andy Hardy. The first film was released in 1959 and starred Sandra Dee. Then in 1961 came *Gidget Goes Hawaiian* with Deborah Walley, and in 1963 *Gidget Goes to Rome* with Cindy Carol. In 1969 and 1971 there were TV movies called *Gidget Grows Up* with Karen Valentine, and *Gidget Gets Married* with Monie Ellis; in 1972 came a cartoon version, *Gidget Makes the Wrong Connection.* In 1965 there was also a TV series with Sally Field.

gigolos
are figures from another age, when women could be imposed on, but they were memorably played by David Niven in *Dodsworth,* Montgomery Clift in *The Heiress,* Fred MacMurray in *The Lady is Willing,* Burt Lancaster in *Sorry Wrong Number,* William Holden in *Sunset Boulevard,* Van Johnson in *Invitation,* Bekim Fehmiu in *The Adventurers,* Jon Voight in *Midnight Cowboy,* Charles Grodin in *The Heartbreak Kid,* Helmut Berger in *Ash Wednesday,* David Bowie in *Just a Gigolo* and Richard Gere in *American Gigolo.*

gimmicks.
There are those who would classify such developments as 3-D, CinemaScope and even talkies under this heading. The genuine gimmick however is a more fleeting affair, a momentary method for getting audiences into cinemas for reasons that have little to do with the quality of the film. William Castle is the established master. For *Macabre* he offered free insurance if one died of heart failure. For *Homicidal,* a fright break before the climax when cowards could leave – and even get their money back if they could stand to go home without learning the awful secret. For *The House on Haunted Hill,* 'Emergo', in which a skeleton on wires shot above the audience's head at a suitable point in the film. For *The Tingler,* a device which wired up certain seats to give people a small electric shock. In competition, the producers of *Chamber of Horrors* thought up the fear flasher and the horror horn to warn weak spirits when a nasty moment was coming.

The Glass Key.
Dashiell Hammett's novel of a politician saved from a murder charge has been turned into two lively thrillers, in 1935 with George Raft and Claire Dodd and directed by Frank Tuttle, and in 1942 with Alan Ladd and Veronica Lake, directed by Stuart Heisler.

Godzilla.
A Japanese monster creation first seen in the film of that name in 1955.

Apparently closely related to *Tyrannosaurus rex,* he has since suffered at the hands of King Kong and the Thing in inferior sequels. He remained rather plainly a man in a rubber suit. The Japanese killed off Godzilla in 1995, but the lizard king was revived by the US in 1997, with Roland EMMERICH's *Godzilla,* a big-budget movie that failed to generate much excitement.

Book: 1996, *Godzilla, King of the Monsters* by Robert Marrero.

Godzilla's screen appearances:
Godzilla 54
Gigantis the Fire Monster 55
King Kong vs Godzilla 62
Godzilla vs the Thing 64
Ghidrah the Three Headed Monster 64
Monster Zero 65
Godzilla vs the Sea Monster 66
Son of Godzilla 67
Destroy all Monsters 68
Godzilla's Revenge 69
Godzilla vs the Smog Monster 71
Godzilla on Monster Island 72
Godzilla vs Megalon 73
Godzilla vs the Cosmic Monster 74
Terror of Mechagodzilla 75
Godzilla '85 85
Godzilla vs Biollante 89
Godzilla vs King Ghidorah 91
Godzilla vs Mothra 92
Godzilla vs Destroyer 95

The Golem.
This legend of a clay monster being brought to life by a rabbi to save persecuted Jews was first filmed in 1914; a classic version followed in 1920, written and directed by Henrik Galeen and Paul Wegener, who also played the Golem. Brilliant Grimm-like medieval sets, photographed by Karl Freund, make the second part of the film still fresh and both in detail and general development it was closely copied in *Frankenstein* 31. The story was remade in France in 1936 (with Harry Baur) and in Czechoslovakia in 1953, and in 1922 a British film called *It* borrowed the idea.

The Good Companions.
J. B. Priestley's sprawling comic novel of English life was filmed by Victor Saville in rather primitive style in 1932, but its very naiveté remains infectious, and there are attractive performances by Edmund Gwenn, Jessie Matthews, Max Miller and others. It was remade in 1957 by J. Lee-Thompson, with Eric Portman and Janette Scott, with only fair success. A nine-hour TV version with music in 1980 missed the bus at every stop.

Goodbye Mr Chips.
This sentimental biography of a schoolmaster, from James Hilton's novel, was a highly successful product of MGM's short-lived British studio under Michael Balcon (1937–39), directed by Sam Wood and enhanced by a brilliant performance from Robert Donat (AA). It was remade in 1969 as an overlong and lifeless semi-musical starring Peter O'Toole (AAN), directed by Herbert Ross; and in 1983 as a six-part BBC TV serial, with Roy Marsden.

Goofy.
Dim-witted, optimistic, enthusiastic dog created by Walt Disney's animators in the 30s, with Art Babbitt contributing most to the development of his character. For much of his career, his voice was supplied by Pinto Colvig.

Goofy and Wilbur 39. The Art of Skiing 41. How to Swim 42. How to Play Football (AAN) 44. Hockey Homicide 45. Foul Hunting 47. Goofy Gymnastics 47. How to Ride a Horse 50. Two-Gun Goofy 52. How to Sleep 53. Aquamania 61. Goofy's Freeway Trouble 65. *A Goofy Movie* 95, etc.

governesses
have most frequently been personified by Deborah Kerr: in *The King and I, The Innocents,* and *The Chalk Garden.* Julie Andrews runs a close second with *Mary Poppins* and *The Sound of Music;* as does Bette Davis with *All This and Heaven Too* and *The Nanny.* Joan Fontaine's contribution to the gallery was *Jane Eyre,* and Susannah York later trod in her footsteps. She was followed by Charlotte Gainsbourg in 1996, while Minnie Driver played a slight and not very interesting variation on the theme of the governess in love with her master in *The Governess* 98.

Grand Hotel.
The Hollywood all-star film *par excellence* and an Oscar-winner as best film of 1932, from Vicki Baum's novel. Directed by Edmund Golding, it allowed effective parts for Garbo, the Barrymore brothers, Joan Crawford, and Wallace Beery. It was remade in 1945 as *Weekend at the Waldorf* with no impact whatsoever. A 1959 West German remake, *Menschen im Hotel,* had Michele Morgan in Garbo's role and O. W. Fischer in John Barrymore's.

The Great Adventure.
Arnold Bennett's play and novel, *Buried Alive,* about a famous painter who assumes the identity of his valet and falls in love, was first filmed in England in 1915 with Henry Ainley in the lead. It was remade in America in 1921 with Lionel Barrymore; in 1933 came *His Double Life* with Roland Young and Lillian Gish as the lovers. The best version, emphasizing the comedy and retitled *Holy Matrimony,* came in 1943, directed by John Stahl, with a script by Nunnally Johnson, and pairing Monty Woolley with Gracie Fields.

The Great Gatsby.
F. Scott Fitzgerald's mordant story of an ex-gangster who meets his death among the Long Island high-livers was filmed in 1926 with Warner Baxter, in 1949 with Alan Ladd, and in 1974 with Robert Redford. The first was by all accounts the most successful, the second being merely surprising for biting off more than it could chew, and the third swamped by decoration and overlength.

The Great Impersonation.
E. Phillips Oppenheim's cunningly constructed spy thriller was filmed in 1921 with James Kirkwood; in 1935 with Edmund Lowe; and in 1942 with Ralph Bellamy.

Green Hornet, The.
A masked crime-fighter, who used a gas gun to incapacitate criminals, on US radio 36–52, and hero of the film serials *The Green Hornet* 40, starring Gordon Jones, and *The Green Hornet Strikes Again* 41, starring Warren Hull. A TV series 66–67 starred Van Williams and featured Bruce Lee as his Japanese assistant, Kato. The Green Hornet, otherwise Britt Reid, was the nephew of John Reid, better known as The Lone Ranger; both were creations of radio producer George W. Trendle and writer Fran Striker.

the guillotine,
that French instrument of execution, cast its shadow over a variety of films including *Marie Antoinette*, *A Tale of Two Cities*, *Uncertain Glory*, *The Scarlet Pimpernel*, and *Mad Love*. The Carry On gang managed to make fun with it in *Don't Lose Your Head*. Private guillotines were employed for diabolical purposes in *The Mystery of the Wax Museum*, *House of Wax*, *Chamber of Horrors* and *Two on a Guillotine*.

Gulliver's Travels.
Jonathan Swift's savage allegory was naturally seen by Hollywood as merely a child's fantasy. Max Fleischer's 1939 feature cartoon seemed at the time to have as much charm and skill as a Disney production, but it has worn disappointingly. Jack Sher's 1960 live-action version, *The Three Worlds of Gulliver*, had neat trick-work but a less than absorbing screenplay. Peter Hunt's 1977 version had Richard Harris as Gulliver in an otherwise lacklustre animated film. A big-budget TV mini-series, starring Ted Danson and many special effects, was broadcast in 1995.

Gunfight at the OK Corral.
The celebrated, if semi-legendary, confrontation between Wyatt Earp and the Clanton Gang in 1881 at Tombstone, Arizona has been filmed several times, notably in the film of the same name in 1957, with Burt Lancaster as Earp and Kirk Douglas as Doc Holliday, roles played in *My Darling Clementine* 46 by Henry Fonda and Victor Mature, in *Tombstone* 94 by Kurt Russell and Val Kilmer, and in *Wyatt Earp* 94 by Kevin Costner and Dennis Quaid. Randolph Scott also played Earp in an earlier version, *Frontier Marshal* 39, and the TV series *Wyatt Earp* starred Hugh O'Brian.

Gunga Din.
Rudyard Kipling's narrative poem of the north-west frontier was rewritten in 1939 by Joel Sayre and Fred Guiol as a rousing combination of high adventure and barrack-room comedy, directed by George Stevens and starring Douglas Fairbanks Jnr, Cary Grant, and Victor McLaglen. In 1951, *Soldiers Three*, directed by Tay Garnett with Stewart Granger, David Niven, and Walter Pidgeon, amounted almost to a remake; while in 1961 John Sturges directed Frank Sinatra, Dean Martin, and Peter Lawford in a pastiche called *Sergeants Three*, set in the American West.

gypsies
have not been a favourite subject for movies but glamorized versions have turned up in *Gypsy Wildcat*, *Golden Earrings*, *Caravan*, *Hot Blood*, and *The Man in Grey*. Something closer to the real thing, perhaps, was on view in *Sky West and Crooked*, *The Gypsy and the Gentleman*, and *Alex and the Gypsy*, while TV failed to get going a gypsy detective series called *Roman Grey*. The screen's most memorable gypsy was probably Maria Ouspenskaya as Maleva in *The Wolf Man* and *Frankenstein Meets the Wolf Man*. The most authentic were probably in Hungary's *I Even Met Happy Gypsies*.

Hamlet.
William Shakespeare's play of an enigmatic prince slow to revenge his father's death has been filmed many times. Among the 19 silent versions are two female Hamlets, from Sarah Bernhardt in 1900, and from Asta Nielsen in 1920, as well as one by the leading Shakespearean actor of his time, Johnston Forbes-Robertson, in 1913. Laurence Olivier's 1948 version remains the most celebrated, winning Oscars for the best film, for him as best actor, for Roger Furse's art direction and costume design, and for Carmen Dillon's set decoration. A powerful Russian version appeared in 1964, starring Innokenti Smoktunovsky, directed by Grigori Kozintsev, and with music by Shostakovich. Nicol Williamson starred in an uneven version, directed by Tony Richardson, in 1969, and Mel Gibson took the role under Franco Zeffirelli's direction, in a version aimed at a young audience, in 1991. The role has been notably played on TV by Richard Chamberlain 70, Ian McKellen 72, and Derek Jacobi 80. The play's plot also turns up in Akira Kurosawa's *The Bad Sleep Well* 60, a story of corporate corruption, a western, *Johnny Hamlet* 72, and Aki Kaurismäki's *Hamlet Goes Business* 87, set in the rubber duck industry.

❝ It's undoubtedly the greatest part ever written, but it's so complex. You can't really play it, you just give an opinion of it. – *Robert Stephens*

hands.
The clutching hand was long a staple of melodrama; usually hairy, with long fingernails, it came out of shadowed panelling and menaced the heroine in hundreds of thrillers such as *The Cat and the Canary*. Severed hands were also a favourite: passing fancies in most of the mummy films, they received more detailed attention in *The Beast with Five Fingers*, *Chamber of Horrors*, *The Hand*, and the various versions of *The Hands of Orlac*.

The Hands of Orlac.
Maurice Renard's novel about a concert pianist whose hands are crushed in an accident and replaced by those of a murderer has been filmed three times, the first as a German silent in 1926. The best version is *Mad Love*, directed by Karl Freund for MGM in 1935, starring Colin Clive. It was remade by Edmond T. Gréville as *The Hands of Orlac* in 1960, starring Mel Ferrer.

Harry Callahan.
The tough, maverick cop who imposes his own law and order on the world has been played by Clint Eastwood in five films: *Dirty Harry* 71, *Magnum Force* 73, *The Enforcer* 76, *Sudden Impact* 83, *The Dead Pool* 88. He made famous the phrase 'Make my day', addressed as a dare to a crook about to go for his gun. Other dialogue, from *Dirty Harry* (uncredited addition by John Milius to the script by Harry Julian Fink, Rita M. Fink, Dean Riesner):

'I know what you're thinking, punk. You're thinking, Did he fire six shots or only five? Now to tell you the truth I've forgotten myself in all this excitement. But being this is a.44 Magnum, the most powerful handgun in the world, and will blow your head clean off, you've got to ask yourself a question: Do I feel lucky? Well, do you, punk?'

heaven:
see FANTASY.

Heckle and Jeckle.
Crafty twin magpies, created by Paul Terry, the heroes of more than 50 Terrytoons cartoons. Although identical in appearance, Heckle spoke with a New York accent and Jeckle with a British one. Their voices were supplied by Dayton Allen, Ned Sparks, and Roy Halee.

The Talking Magpies 46. Flying South 47. Magpie Madness 48. Dancing Shoes 49. King Tut's Tomb 50. Movie Madness 52. Bargain Daze 53. Blue Plate Symphony 54. Miami Maniacs 56. Wild Life 59. Trapeze Please 60. Sappy New Year 61. Messed Up Movie Madness 66, etc.

helicopters,
restricted in scope, have been put to sound dramatic use in two films about helicopter services, *Battle Taxi* and *Flight from Ashiya*; while their potential for thrill sequences was well explored in *The Bridges at Toko-Ri*, *Experiment in Terror*, *From Russia with Love*, *Arabesque*, *Caprice*, *You Only Live Twice*, *The Satan Bug*, *Fathom*, *The Las Vegas Story*, *Where Eagles Dare*, *Masquerade*, *Tarzan in the Valley of Gold*, *That Riviera Touch*, *The Wrecking Crew*, *Figures in a Landscape*, *Birds of Prey*, *Breakout*, *Russian Roulette* and *Apocalypse Now*. TV series on the subject include *Chopper One*, *Chopper Squad*, *Riptide*, *Blue Thunder* and *Air Wolf*.

See also: AIRPLANES.

hell
has been used more figuratively than realistically in movies; but what passed for the real thing did appear in *Dante's Inferno*, *Heaven Can Wait*, *Hellzapoppin* and *Angel on My Shoulder*, not to mention a Sylvester cartoon called *Satan's Waitin'*.

Henry Aldrich.
The accident-prone American teenager of the 40s series derived from Clifford Goldsmith's play *What a Life*, which was filmed in 1939 with Jackie Cooper in the role. *Life with Henry*, again with Cooper, followed in 1941, owing to the popularity of the radio series featuring Ezra Stone, who had played the part on Broadway. The series proper starred Jimmy Lydon, with Charles Smith as his friend Dizzy. Goldsmith then created *The Aldrich Family*, a TV situation comedy that ran from 1949–53, in which Henry was played by Robert Casey, Richard Tyler, Henry Girard, Kenneth Nelson and Bobby Ellis.

What a Life 39. Life with Henry 41. Henry Aldrich for President 41. Henry and Dizzy 42. Henry Aldrich, Editor 42. Henry Aldrich Gets Glamour 43. Henry Aldrich Swings It 43. Henry Aldrich Haunts a House 43. Henry Aldrich, Boy Scout 44. Henry Aldrich Plays Cupid 44. Henry Aldrich's Little Secret 44.

Hercule Poirot.
Agatha Christie's short, fussy, fiercely moustachioed Belgian detective was first played by the tall, clean-shaven Austin Trevor in *Alibi* 31, *Black Coffee* 31, *Lord Edgware Dies* 34; Tony Randall was closer to Christie's creation in the otherwise dull *The Alphabet Murders* 66; Albert Finney received an Oscar nomination for his performance in the big-budget *Murder on the Orient Express* 74, which was the best of the Poirot films; Peter Ustinov took the role in *Death on the Nile* 78 and *Evil under the Sun* 82. He was first portrayed on stage by Francis L. Sullivan in 1940. On television, David Suchet has made the role his own in the series *Poirot* since 1989.

hillbillies
became a stereotype of the 30s cinema, and subsequently made infrequent appearances before the enormous success of the TV series *The Real McCoys* 57–62 and *The Beverly Hillbillies* 62–70. Notable hillbillies through the years include the Kettles, Lum and Abner, the Weaver Brothers and Elviry; the Ritz Brothers in *Kentucky Moonshine*; Annie in *Annie Get Your Gun*; and the characters in *Roseanna McCoy*, *Thunder Road*, *Li'l Abner*, *Guns in the Afternoon*, *Feudin' Fussin' and A-Fightin'*, *The Moonshine War*, *I Walk the Line*, and *Coming Round the Mountain*; while the denizens of *Tobacco Road*, geographically not hillbillies, splendidly personified the image. Cartoon-wise, Elmer Fudd in the Bugs Bunny series is an old-fashioned hillibilly, and Disney produced a twenty-minute version of *The Martins and the McCoys*, followed in 1975 by a TV movie, *The Hatfields and the McCoys*. In 1980 *Coal Miner's Daughter* brought to general notice the rags-to-riches story of singer Loretta Lynn, and in 1983 Cheryl Ladd plumbed a similar milieu in a TV movie, *Kentucky Woman*.

Hollywood.
The American film city, nominally a suburb of Los Angeles, was founded in 1912 when a number of independent producers headed west from New York to avoid the effects of a patents trust. The site was chosen because of its nearness to the Mexican border in case of trouble, and because the weather and location possibilities were excellent. By 1913 Hollywood was established as the film-maker's Mecca, and continued so for forty years. Several factors combined in the late 40s to affect its unique concentration. Actors transformed themselves into independent producers and reduced the power of the 'front office'; stars now made the films they liked instead of the ones to which they were assigned. The consequent break-up of many big studios, which now simply sold production space to independent outfits, weakened continuity of product. Each production now had to start from scratch; there was no longer a training ground for new talent, nor was the old production gloss always in evidence. The communist witch-hunt unfortunately drove many leading talents to Europe, and some found they preferred Shepperton or Cinecitta to California. The coming of CinemaScope, a device to halt the fall in box-office returns which resulted from the beginning of commercial TV, meant that real locations were now necessary, as studio sets would show up on the screen. So began the world-wide trekking now evident in American production: generally speaking only routine product and TV episodes are made in the film city itself, but each distribution set-up will have up to a dozen films being made in various parts of the globe.

Books about Hollywood include *Hello Hollywood* (1962) by Allen Rivkin and Laura Kerr; *Hollywood* (1974) by Garson Kanin: *The Hollywood Exiles* (1976) by John Baxter; *Hollywood and the Great Fan Magazines* (1970) by Martin Levin; *Hollywood the Haunted House* (1969) by Paul Mayersberg; *Flesh and Fantasy* (1978) by Penny Stallings; *This Was Hollywood* (1960) by Beth Day; *Gone Hollywood* (1979) by Christopher Finch and Linda Rosenkrantz; *The Pink Palace* (1978) by Sandra Lee Stuart; *The Garden of Allah* (1971) by Sheilah Graham; *The Shattered Silents* (1978) by Alexander Walker; *Some Time in the Sun* (1976) by Tom Dardis; *Hollywood the Dream Factory* (1951) by Hortense Powdermaker; *The Hollywood Studios* (1978) by Roy Pickard; *Hollywood Babylon* (1975) by Kenneth Anger. And some classics: *Hollywood, The Movie Colony, The Movie Makers* (1939) by Leo Rosten; *America at the Movies* (1945) by Margaret Farrand Thorp; *Picture* (1951) by Lillian Ross; *The Studio* (1968) by John Gregory Dunne; *Hollywood, the Pioneers* (1979) by Kevin Brownlow and John Kobal; *The Parade's Gone By* (1968) by Kevin Brownlow; *The Real Tinsel* (1970) by Bernard Rosenberg and Harry Silverstein; *The Fifty Year Decline and Fall of Hollywood* (1961) by Ezra Goodman; *City of Nets* (1986) by Otto Friedrich; *You'll Never Eat Lunch in This Town Again* (1991) by Julia Phillips; *Naked Hollywood: Money and Power in the Movies Today* (1990) by Nicholas Kent. Plus all the books about individual stars, directors, studios and producers, especially: *King Cohn* (1967) by Bob Thomas; *Memo from David O. Selznick* (1972) by Rudy Behlmer; and *David O. Selznick's Hollywood* (1980) by Ronald Haver; *Showman: The Life of David O. Selznick* (1993) by David Thomson; *Goldwyn* (1989) by A. Scott Berg; *Frank Capra: The Catastrophe of Success* (1992) by Joseph McBride; *Merchant of Dreams: Louis B. Mayer, M.G.M., and the Secret Hollywood* (1993) by Charles Higham.

❝ The legendary film city – sometimes referred to as Sodom-by-the-Sea – seems far from glamorous to the casual visitor. Geographically, it is not a city at all but a mere suburban segment of a forty-mile-square jigsaw puzzle of dormitory areas which all run into each other. James Gleason, Dorothy Parker, and several other people are credited with calling Los Angeles:

Seventy-two suburbs in search of a city.

No matter who said it, it's still true. L.A. also remains a supreme example of man's inhumanity to man, the promised land that only humans have polluted. Even before the glorious climate was filtered through several layers of smog, the values were all wrong. The residents were almost all on the run from somewhere else, and tended to idle their lives away under the sun, pursuing the buck when they could and taking the biggest for the best. Ethel Barrymore's first impressions, in 1932, were vivid:

The people are unreal. The flowers are unreal, they don't smell. The fruit is unreal, it doesn't taste of anything. The whole place is a glaring, gaudy, nightmarish set, built up in the desert.

The heat, the richness and the sweet smells are certainly enervating. Shirley Maclaine, hot from Broadway, saw the difference at once:

The most important deals in the movie industry are finalized on the sun-drenched turf of golf courses or around turquoise swimming pools, where the smell of barbecue sauce is borne on gentle breezes and wafts over the stereo system of houses that people seldom leave.

Cedric Hardwicke felt the danger:

God felt sorry for actors, so he gave them a place in the sun and a swimming pool. The price they had to pay was to surrender their talent.

There's always a price tag. Fred Allen knew it when he said:

California is a great place . . . if you happen to be an orange.

Someone else called it 'Siberia with palms'. Raymond Chandler aptly summed up L.A. as:

A city with all the personality of a paper cup.

Joe Frisco thought of it as:

The only town in the world where you can wake up in the morning and listen to the birds coughing in the trees.

Stephen Vincent Benet was even more picturesque:

Of all the Christbitten places in the two hemispheres, this is the last curly kink in the pig's tail.

Hollywood is superior to other parts of L.A. only by virtue of the dusty hills into which it nestles on its northern side. The fact that most comments on it are cynical seems inevitable in an industrial area where the product is an intangible dream. Human beings must get injured in the process, their souls bruised by the struggle for fame, their bodies tossed onto the junkheap the minute they pass their prime. Hollywood has always sought, and then misused, the services of great talent. In the early 30s so many New York actors and writers made the four-day train journey and shortly returned in dejection that a saying sprang up on Broadway:

Never buy anything in Hollywood that you can't put on the Chief.

Billie Burke, a longtime resident, declared that:

To survive there, you need the ambition of a Latin-American revolutionary, the ego of a grand opera tenor, and the physical stamina of a cow pony.

Moss Hart called Beverly Hills:

The most beautiful slave quarters in the world.

Nelson Algren had a brief but unhappy experience:

I went out there for a thousand a week, and I worked Monday and I got fired Wednesday. The fellow who hired me was out of town Tuesday.

Walter Pidgeon liked the system:

It was like an expensive, beautifully-run fan club. You didn't need to carry money. Your face was your credit card – all over the world.

But Dorothy Parker saw its dangers:

Hollywood money isn't money. It's congealed snow.

Hedda Hopper put it another way:

Our town worships success, the bitch goddess whose smile hides a taste for blood.

John Huston saw through the illusion:

Hollywood has always been a cage . . . a cage to catch our dreams.

George Jean Nathan gave the most all-embracing description:

Ten million dollars worth of intricate and ingenious machinery functioning elaborately to put skin on baloney.

Oscar Levant was bitter:

Strip the phoney tinsel off Hollywood and you'll find the real tinsel underneath.

Wilson Mizner thought it:

A trip through a sewer in a glass-bottomed boat,

and varied this thought as:

A sewer with service from the Ritz Carlton.

Dudley Field Malone found it:

A town where inferior people have a way of making superior people feel inferior.

Elinor Glyn in 1927 wondered:

Where else in the world will you find a coloured cook bursting into the dining room to say 'You folks better hustle to dinner if you don't want the stuff to get cold'?

H.L. Mencken marvelled at its reputation:

Immorality? Oh, my God, Hollywood seemed to me to be one of the most respectable towns in America. Even Baltimore can't beat it.

Leo Rosten saw its lotus-land attraction:

Fortunes were made overnight, and along with the speculators, the oil men and the real estate promoters, another group came to the promised land – the old, the sick and the middle-aged, who came not to woo Mammon but to sit out their savings in the sun and die in the shadow of an annuity and an orange tree.

Herman Weinberg saw the dangers:

Whatever goes into the Hollywood grist mill, it comes out the same way. It is a meat-grinder that will take beef and suet, pheasant and turnips, attar of roses and limburger and turn it all into the same kind of hash that has served so many so well for so long.

To Ginger Rogers,

Hollywood is like an empty wastebasket.

To John Schlesinger,

An extraordinary kind of temporary place.

To Carrie Fisher,

You can't find true affection in Hollywood because everyone does the fake affection so well.

To Sylvester Stallone,

The only way to be a success in Hollywood is to be as obnoxious as the next guy.

To Rod Steiger,

A community of lonely people searching for even the most basic kind of stimulation in their otherwise mundane lives.

To Groucho Marx,

It provided the kind of luxury that exists today only for the sons of Latin-American dictators.

To Marilyn Monroe,

A place where they pay you 50,000 dollars for a kiss and 50 cents for your soul.

To Rex Reed,

A place where, if you don't have happiness, you send out for it.

Elinor Glyn was waspish about it:

When I arrived, spittoons were still being placed in rows down the centre of a set which was supposed to be the baronial hall of an old English castle.

Lana Turner survived the dream:

It was all beauty and it was all talent, and if you had it they protected you.

Josef Von Sternberg was downright cynical:

You can seduce a man's wife there, rape his daughter and wipe your hands on his canary, but if you don't like his movie, you're dead.

Lauren Bacall spoke from other people's experience:

The only place in the world where an amicable divorce means that each gets fifty per cent of the publicity.

Evelyn Keyes recalled:

The big studios were each headed by a Big Daddy who reigned supreme.

Louis Sherwin remembered:

They knew only one word of more than one syllable, and that was FILLUM.

Wilson Mizner, in similar vein:

What I like about Hollywood is that you can get along knowing only two words of English: swell and lousy.

He added:

I spent several years there, and I think all the heroes are in the audience.

An anonymous wag called it:

Paradise with a lobotomy.

But for Joseph L. Mankiewicz it had saving graces, in the 30s at least:

The old moguls were really impressed to know that Lion Feuchtwanger and Aldous Huxley and Thomas Mann were living in Pacific Palisades. They reached for things in those days. Even Bernard Shaw came out to look around. I don't think he'd come today.

Ernst Lubitsch saw another danger, that the dream might be dangerously more attractive than reality:

I've been to Paris France and I've been to Paris Paramount. Paris Paramount is better.

Some failed to relish the easy life. After a short stay in 1932 Sergei Eisenstein packed his bags. When asked at the station 'Are you coming back?' he replied:

❝ No, I'm *going* back.

And an anonymous wag complained:

In Hollywood you can be forgotten while you're out of the room going to the toilet.

F. Scott Fitzgerald was whimsical about it:

I accepted the assignment with the resignation of a ghost assigned to a haunted house.

A character in Gavin Lambert's *The Slide Area* had a different slant:

The past is out of place here, mister. You don't feel it, you only feel the future.

To Grover Jones it was:

The only asylum run by the inmates.

Walter Winchell called it:

A town that has to be seen to be disbelieved.

And Marlon Brando dismissed it as:

A cultural boneyard.

Ken Murray loved it, but admitted it to be:

A place where you spend more than you make, on things you don't need, to impress people you don't like.

Ethel Barrymore was finally repelled:

It looks, it feels, as though it had been invented by a Sixth Avenue peepshow man.

And Sonny Fox summed it all up:

Hollywood is like a world's fair that's been up a year too long.

All such remarks spring mainly from the system. But perhaps the people were partly to blame.

I'll miss Hollywood. Of the twenty friends I thought I had, I'll miss the six I really had,

remarked Lauren Bacall wryly on her way to Broadway. And Errol Flynn once said:

They've great respect for the dead in Hollywood, but none for the living.

Richard Burton responded frankly to a question about Hollywood morals:

Certainly most movie executives were making love to starlets. But then, so were most of us actors.

Alfred Hitchcock, on the other hand, maintained:

We lead a very suburban life here. We're in bed by nine o'clock every night.

And that reminds one of the anonymous 30s complaint about Hollywood's fabled social life:

No matter how hot it gets during the day, there's nothing to do at night.

Anonymous too was the mogul-hater who averred:

There's nothing wrong with the place, that six first-class funerals wouldn't cure.

Nepotism was of course rife. When Louis B. Mayer appointed his daughter's husband William Goetz to a key position at MGM, someone cracked:

The son-in-law also rises.

And Ogden Nash devised a famous couplet about the head of Universal:

Uncle Carl Laemmle
Has a very large faemmle.

Ethics were out, as Dorothy Parker knew:

The only-ism Hollywood believes in is plagiarism.

Glamour and insincerity gave it the atmosphere of a luxury liner, as someone said in the 30s:

I have this terrible apprehension that suddenly the boat is going to dock and I shall never see any of you again.

Phyllis Batelli called it:

A place where great-grandmothers dread to grow old.

And there's an old saying:

In Hollywood the eternal triangle consists of an actor, his wife and himself.

(There is another version which runs 'an actor, his wife and his agent'. Take your choice.) Walter Winchell thought:

They shoot too many pictures and not enough actors.

One can hardly be surprised that people are false when the movies themselves were sham for so many years. Arthur Freed produced the Scottish fantasy *Brigadoon* on the MGM lot and defended himself by saying:

I went to Scotland and found nothing there that looks like Scotland.

A wise saying of Hollywood's heyday, by David O. Selznick:

Nothing here is permanent. Once photographed, life here is ended.

But the system had its rueful supporters. Orson Welles:

Hollywood's all right: it's the pictures that are bad.

Raymond Chandler:

If my books had been any worse I should not have been invited to Hollywood, and if they had been any better I should not have come.

An anonymous writer:

They ruin your stories. They trample on your pride. They massacre your ideas. And what do you get for it? A fortune.

Typically, Hollywood was often ignorant of the talent it had bought. Bert Lahr didn't make it until his third trip, and said wryly:

If you want to be a success in Hollywood, be sure and go to New York.

Richard Dyer McCann wrote truthfully:

The most familiar, solid, bedrock certainty in Hollywood is sudden change.

Certainly, the town depended on fashion, and its well-set ways were in themselves a mere fashion. By 1956, David Selznick found the place to be:

Like Egypt, full of crumbled pyramids.

Fred Allen had said in 1941 that:

Hollywood is a place where people from Iowa mistake each other for stars.

In the 50s the mistake became pardonable: male leads were required to look less like matinée idols and more like the slob next door, or the fellow at the gas station. Humphrey Bogart was heard to remark:

I came out here with one suit and everybody said I looked like a bum. Twenty years later Marlon Brando comes out with only a sweatshirt and the town drools over him. That shows you how much Hollywood has progressed.

Hollywood was desperate in the face of TV and better living standards. One trend followed another: in the 60s, for instance, English actors became more fashionable than ever before, and Bob Hope quipped:

There'll always be an England, even if it's in Hollywood.

By the end of the 60s the old complaints were being repeated with a new veneer of resigned cynicism. Paul Mayersberg:

The desert of Southern California cannot be said to have created a religion, but it has contributed greatly to the development of a way of life that operates at the extremity of our civilization. When you reach Los Angeles you are as far West as you can go.

An anonymous agent:

You fail upwards here. A guy makes a ten-million-dollar picture, the thing is not that he's made a bomb [i.e. disaster] but that he's made a ten-million-dollar picture. So next time out, they give him a twelve-million-dollar picture.

David Mamet thought that only one rule governed the place:

Hollywood is the city of the modern gold rush, and money calls the turn. That is the first and last rule, as we know, of Hollywood – we permit ourselves to be treated like commodities in the hope that we may, one day, be treated like *valuable* commodities.

Whether Hollywood finally succeeds or goes under, it has had a fair run, long enough to confound two doubting remarks of 1915, by Carl Laemmle:

I hope I didn't make a mistake coming out here.

And D. W. Griffith:

It's a shame to take this country away from the rattlesnakes. Perhaps the rattlesnakes are just biding their time.

Hollywood on film
has generally been shown as the brassy, gold-digging, power-conscious society which, in the nature of things, it can hardly fail to be. There was a somewhat sentimental period in the 20s and 30s, with *Ella Cinders*, *Hollywood*, *Going Hollywood*, *Hollywood Cavalcade*, and *Hollywood Boulevard*; but satire had already struck in such films as *The Last Command*, *Merton of the Movies*, *Show People*, *The Lost Squadron*, *What Price Hollywood*, *LadyKiller*, *Something to Sing About*, *Once in a Lifetime*, *Stardust*, *Hollywood Hotel*, *Stand In*, *A Star Is Born* and *Boy Meets Girl*. The moguls didn't seem to mind the film city being shown as somewhat zany, as in *The Goldwyn Follies*, Disney's *Mother Goose Goes Hollywood*, *The Cohens and Kellys in Hollywood*, *Abbott and Costello in Hollywood*, *The Jones Family in Hollywood*, *Movie Crazy*, *Never Give a Sucker an Even Break*, and *Hellzapoppin*; but they preferred the adulatory attitude best expressed in *The Youngest Profession*, which concerned the autograph hunters who lay in wait at the studio exits.

During the 40s Paramount was the studio most addicted to showing itself off, though the front office can't have relished watching Preston Sturges bite the hand that fed him in *Sullivan's Travels*. The story of *Hold Back the Dawn* was supposedly told to sentimental Mitchell Leisen during a lunch break on the studio floor; Crosby and Hope based a score of gags on Paramount; and the studio was the setting for *Star Spangled Rhythm*, an all-star musical which encouraged other studios to emulate it, with Warner's *Thank Your Lucky Stars* and *It's a Great Feeling*, Universal's *Follow the Boys*, the independent *Stage Door Canteen*, and later Paramount's less successful reprise, *Variety Girl*.

In 1950 *Sunset Boulevard* took a really sardonic look at the film city, and set a fashion for scathing movies like *The Star*, *The Bad and the Beautiful*, *The Barefoot Contessa* and *The Big Knife*. As though to atone, almost every studio threw in a light-hearted, nostalgic look at Hollywood's golden era: *Singin' in the Rain*, *The Perils of Pauline*,

Jolson Sings Again, The Eddie Cantor Story. But in the last few years the only really affectionate review of Hollywood's past has been in the Cliff Richard musical *Wonderful Life*, though Jerry Lewis continued to paint zany pictures of studio life in *The Errand Boy, The Ladies' Man* and *The Patsy*. The rest was all denunciation and bitterness: *Hollywood Boulevard, Hollywood Story, The Wild Party, The Day of the Locust, Inserts, The Goddess, Two Weeks in Another Town, The Carpetbaggers, Harlow, Inside Daisy Clover, The Loved One, Whatever Happened to Baby Jane, The Legend of Lylah Clare, Myra Breckinridge, The Oscar* and the satiric *The Player*. A 1969 TV series, *Bracken's World*, was set in a film studio (Twentieth Century-Fox) and saw it as a kind of valley of the dolls – and the studio scenes in *that* movie were none too convincing.

See the book by Rudy Behlmer and Tony Thomas: 1975, *Hollywood's Hollywood, the Movies about the Movies*.

❝ Hollywood is full of multiple conspiracies. There's more back-stabbing and cross purposes going on than they had in the Roman senate. – *Mel Gibson*

homosexuality

can be said to have arrived during the late 60s as a fit subject for the western cinema, producers having toyed gingerly with it for the previous three decades. During the 40s, there were clear intimations of it in *The Maltese Falcon, Victory*, and *Rope*. The 50s brought *Strangers on a Train, I Vitelloni, Serious Charge*, Germany's *The Third Sex*, and *Suddenly Last Summer*, and the decade was rounded off with two productions of the life of Oscar Wilde. *Cat on a Hot Tin Roof* 58 and *Spartacus* 60 were probably the last Hollywood movies to have homosexual inferences deliberately removed from the original. In 1962 the subject came right out into the open with *Victim*, a well-intentioned thriller about the blackmail of homosexuals; *A Taste of Honey* featured a sympathetic homosexual; and both *Advise and Consent* and *The Best Man* concerned allegations of homosexuality against American politicians. On the other hand *Lawrence of Arabia* was so reticent about its hero's sexual make-up that it was difficult to know what estimate was being made; but for good measure Peter O'Toole was raped a second time in *Lord Jim*. Universal romantic comedies now began to make fun of the subject: in *That Touch of Mink* Gig Young's psychiatrist thought he was in love with Cary Grant, and in *A Very Special Favour* Rock Hudson deliberately made Leslie Caron think him effeminate so that she would 'rescue him'. The floodgates were now open: in rapid succession we had *A View From the Bridge*, with its male kiss; *The Servant*, with its odd relationship between master and man; *The Leather Boys; Stranger in the House; The Fearless Vampire Killers*, with its young homosexual bloodsucker; the miscast and unhappy *Staircase; The Detective*, which made New York appear to be a very gay city; *The Gay Deceivers*, in which two young men avoided the draft by pretending to be queer; *Reflections in a Golden Eye; Midnight Cowboy; The Boys in the Band*, the first sympathetic homosexual comedy; *The Boston Strangler* and *Funeral in Berlin*, with scenes in transvestite bars; *If, Young Woodley, Tea and Sympathy, Riot, The Sergeant* and *Villain*, which revealed camp goings-on in school, prison, the army and gangland. *Girl Stroke Boy* revealed the plight of parents who could not tell whether their son was engaged to a girl or a boy. In *Myra Breckinridge* homosexuality was almost lost in a welter of more spectacular perversions. Historical figures such as Richard the Lionheart and Tchaikovsky had their sexual pecadilloes explored in *The Lion in Winter* and *The Music Lovers*, and Billy Wilder jokingly investigated *The Private Life of Sherlock Holmes*. TV movies invaded the territory in 1973 with *That Certain Summer*. There wasn't much further to go, especially as 'gays' had their own porno films. 1978 brought the last curiosity: *A Different Story*, the love affair of a homosexual and a lesbian. There was a celebration of extraordinary individuals in TV's *The Naked Civil Servant, Kiss of the Spider Woman*, based on Manuel Puig's novel steeped in 40s Hollywood, and Harvey Fierstein's semi-autobiographical stage-hit *Torch Song Trilogy*, which had less impact in the cinema. It went hand in hand with the camp sensibility and frivolity of *The Rocky Horror Picture Show, La Cage aux Folles* and its sequels, some of Andy Warhol's films, like *Lonesome Cowboys*, and the work of John Waters. There was the particularly British repression and love across social classes exemplified by *A Month in the Country, Maurice*, based on E.M. Forster's long-unpublished novel, and *We Think the World of You*. The mood changed towards the end of the 80s as AIDS (not, of course, restricted to homosexuals) became more prevalent and began to kill many young and talented performers. *Early Frost*, made for TV, dealt with the problems of a lawyer explaining to his family that he is gay and dying from AIDS. Bill Sherwood made the much-praised *Parting Glances* on a similar theme, and the bigger-budget *Longtime Companion* explored the subject sympathetically. British director Derek Jarman reacted by making his films more militantly homosexual, culminating in his modern-dress version of Christopher Marlowe's *Edward II*. Younger directors, working outside the mainstream, proclaimed a 'New Queer Cinema', making films aimed at gay audiences or attempting to reclaim themes from mainstream cinema: Tom Kalin's *Swoon* ('Puts the Homo back in Homicide' according to its publicity) dealt with the Leopold-Loeb murder, tackled in *Rope and Compulsion*, from a specifically homosexual viewpoint; Todd Haynes's *Poison* contemplated sexual and social deviance with the equanimity of Jean Genet; Gregg Araki's *The Living End* had two HIV-positive homosexuals taking revenge on the straight world; Christopher Münch's *The Hours and the Times* dealt with Beatles manager Brian Epstein's love for John Lennon; Mark Rappaport's *Rock Hudson's Home Movies* took a witty look at the actor's performances from a gay perspective. Gus Van Sant enjoyed success with *My Private Idaho*, about a narcoleptic hustler; British director Isaac Julien's *Young Soul Rebels* had a black and white male couple as its protagonists; Spanish director Pedro Almodóvar's films, displaying a camp sensibility, were box-office hits around the world; and Jonathan Demme's *Philadelphia* was an Oscar-winner in 1993, though it managed to upset many AIDS activists. Stephen Fry in *Wilde* 97, reminded audiences of past persecutions, while Rupert Everett concentrated on present pleasures in his scene-stealing performance as Julia Roberts's gay companion in *My Best Friend's Wedding* 97.

❝ I would really like to find a single actor whose career was harmed by playing gay. They usually end up winning Oscars and Tony awards. – *Paul Rudnick*

Actors like playing gay roles because they haven't played those characters before and they get to have fun in a new way. Or, for a lot of them, a way they're very familiar with. – *Paul Rudnick*

See also: AIDS; LESBIANISM.

Hopalong Cassidy,

the genial black-garbed hero of scores of western second features since 1935, was created by novelist Clarence E. Mulford. William BOYD was his only screen and TV personification.

Book: 1992, *Hopalong Cassidy* by Bernard A. Drew.

horror

as a staple of screen entertainment really emanates from Germany (although Edison shot a picture of *Frankenstein* as early as 1908). Before World War I Wegener had made a version of *The Golem*, which he improved on in 1920: it was this second version which directly influenced the Hollywood horror school stimulated by James Whale. What is surprising is that Hollywood took so long to catch on to a good idea, especially as the Germans, in depressed postwar mood, relentlessly turned out such macabre films as *The Cabinet of Dr Caligari* (with Veidt as a hypnotically-controlled monster), *Nosferatu* (Murnau's brilliantly personal account of Bram Stoker's 'Dracula'), *Waxworks* (Leni's three-part thriller about Ivan the Terrible, Haroun-al-Raschid and Jack the Ripper); *The Hands of Orlac* and *The Student of Prague*. Most of the talents involved were exported to Hollywood by 1927; but the only horror film directly resulting was Leni's *The Cat and the Canary*, which was a spoof. California did encourage Lon Chaney, but his films were grotesque rather than gruesome; and John Barrymore had already been allowed in 1921 to impersonate *Dr Jekyll and Mr Hyde* (a role to be played even more for horror by Fredric March in 1932). By the end of the 20s, the European horror film was played out except for Dreyer's highly individual *Vampyr;* the ball was in Hollywood's court.

In 1930 Tod Browning filmed the stage version of *Dracula*, using a Hungarian actor named Bela Lugosi; shortly after, Robert Florey wrote and James Whale directed a version of *Frankenstein* that borrowed freely from *The Golem*. Both films (see individual entries) were wildfire successes, and the studio involved, Universal, set out on a steady and profitable progress through a series of sequels. In 1932 Karloff appeared in *The Mummy*, and in 1933 Claude Rains was *The Invisible Man;* these characters were added to the grisly band. In 1935 the studio made *Werewolf of London*, which led five years later to *The Wolf Man* giving Lon Chaney Jnr a useful sideline. By 1945, despite the upsurge in supernatural interest during the war, these characters were thought to be played out, and in the last two 'serious' episodes they appeared *en masse*. In 1948 they began to meet Abbott and Costello, which one would have thought might ensure their final demise; but more of that later.

Meanwhile other landmarks had been established. Browning made the outlandish *Freaks*, and in 1935 the spoof *Mark of the Vampire*. James Whale in 1932 made *The Old Dark House*, an inimitably entertaining mixture of disagreeable ingredients. Warners in 1932 came up with *Doctor X* and *The Mystery of the Wax Museum* (remade as *House of Wax*) and later got some mileage out of *The Walking Dead*. Paramount went in for mad doctors, from *The Island of Dr Moreau* (*Island of Lost Souls*) to *Doctor Cyclops*, and at the beginning of World War II produced scary remakes of *The Cat and the Canary* and *The Ghost Breakers*. RKO was busy with *King Kong* and *She*, MGM with *The Devil Doll*. In the early 40s Universal began a listless anthology series under the title *Inner Sanctum*, and later failed in *The Creature from the Black Lagoon* to add another intriguing monster to their gallery. By far the most significant extension of the genre was the small group of depressive but atmospheric thrillers produced by Val Lewton at RKO in 1942–45, the best of them being *The Body Snatcher, The Cat People* and *I Walked with a Zombie*.

After the war, little was heard of horror until the advent of science fiction in 1950. After this we heard a very great deal of nasty visitors from other planets (*The Thing, Invasion of the Body Snatchers*), mutations (*The Fly, This Island Earth*), robots (*The Day the Earth Stood Still, Forbidden Planet*) and giant insects (*Them, Tarantula*). To please the teenage audience, fly-by-night producers thought up fantastic horror-comic variations and came up with titles like *The Blob, I Married a Monster from Outer Space* and *I Was a Teenage Werewolf;* such crude and shoddy productions cheapened the genre considerably. The Japanese got into the act with rubber-suited monsters like *Godzilla* and *Rodan;* then, surprisingly, it was the turn of the British. Hammer Films, a small independent outfit with an old Thames-side house for a studio, impudently remade the sagas of Frankenstein, Dracula *et alia*, and the results have been flooding the world's screens for more than twenty years now, marked by a certain bold style, lack of imagination, and such excess of blood-letting that several versions have to be made for each film (the bloodiest for Japan, the most restrained for the home market). Britain also produced commendable screen versions of *The Quatermass Experiment* and other TV serials.

Since 1955 horror has been consistently in fashion, at least in the world's mass markets, and film-makers have been busy capping each other by extending the bounds of how much explicit physical shock and horror is permissible. (This, of course, does not make for good films.) If Franju was revolting in the detail of *Eyes Without a Face*, Hitchcock certainly topped him in *Psycho* and was himself outdone by William Castle in *Homicidal*, and by the perpetration in the 70s of films like *Blood Feast* and *Death Line*. (*Psycho* also gave the screen an inventive horror-writing talent in Robert Bloch, who has since been kept as busy as he could wish.) And the cheapjack American nasties at least provided a training ground for producer-director Roger Corman, who between 1960 and 1964 made a series of Poe adaptations much admired for style and enthusiasm if not for production detail. The trend in the early 70s was towards the compendiums of graveyard horror typified by *Tales from the Crypt* and *The House that Dripped Blood*, and towards such combinations of spoof and nastiness as *Theatre of Blood, Shivers* and *Squirm*.

The video craze of the early 80s revealed a significant and rather worrying minority of people who doted on excesses of horror, not only on the recent wave of teenage assassination thrillers like *Friday the Thirteenth, Hell Night* and *Terror Train*, but on 'nasties' such as *Driller Killer* and *I Spit on Your Grave*, which seemed to have been made explicitly for the new medium. This cheap rubbish, with neither style nor imagination, had nothing at all to do with the great achievements of the genre, though indications of talent were found by some in the work of John Carpenter (*Halloween*, etc.) and David Cronenberg (*The Brood*, etc.). The success of George Romero's *Night of the Living Dead* in 68 encouraged many similar low-budget horrors, some made by Romero himself. From the time of *An American Werewolf in London* 81, with its startling transformations from man to beast, make-up and special effects experts such as Rick Baker and Rob Bottin have grown in importance and some, like Chris Walas (*The Fly 2*) and Tom Savini (a remake of *Night of the Living Dead*), have even become directors. From the 80s, though, the predominant influence was that of novelist Stephen King. His first novel, *Carrie*, became a successful film in 74 and his second novel, *Salem's Lot*, became a TV movie in 79. After Stanley Kubrick made *The Shining*, based on his third novel, in 80, the pace quickened so that by the 90s even a seven-page short story was being turned into a full-length film, *The Lawnmower Man*, and King's name was above the titles and usually in bigger type than those of the stars. His British rival, novelist Clive Barker, turned director with *Hellraiser*, a film that has so far spawned two sequels and turned one of his hellish characters, Pinhead, into something of a cult figure – though nothing so far to rival the extraordinary and outlandish appeal for many of Freddy (Robert Englund), the child murderer of the *A Nightmare on Elm Street* series that ran through most of the 80s and into the 90s. By the mid-90s, Hammer was promising to remake its greatest hits and the genre was attracting notable actors and directors, with Francis Ford Coppola's big-budget and overblown *Bram Stoker's Dracula*, Mike Nichols directing *Wolf* with Jack Nicholson and Michelle Pfeiffer, and Kenneth Branagh making *Mary Shelley's Frankenstein*, which had Robert De Niro surprisingly stepping into Boris Karloff's built-up shoes.

Best books: 1968, *An Illustrated History of Horror Films* by Carlos Clarens; 1973, *A Pictorial History of Horror Films* by Denis Gifford; 1980, *Caligari's Children* by S. S. Prawer; 1988, *Nightmare Movies* by Kim Newman; 1994, *The Monster Show* by David J. Skal.

horses

have in several cases risen to the rank of star. All the great cowboy heroes had their familiar steed: Trigger for Roy Rogers, Topper for Hopalong Cassidy, Fritz for William S. Hart, Tarzan for Ken Maynard, Tony for Tom Mix, Silver for Buck Jones, Blackjack for Allan Rocky Lane, Koko for Rex Allen, White Flash for Tex Ritter, Champion for Gene Autry. Other movies strongly featuring horses have included *National Velvet, The Red Pony, Red Stallion, The Black Stallion, Crin Blanc, King of the Wild Horses, My Friend Flicka, Green Grass of Wyoming, Thunderhead Son of Flicka, Sand, Fury, Black Beauty*.

hospitals

have been the setting of many films. *Life Begins* and its remake *A Child is Born* were set in the maternity wards, *No Time for Tears* in the children's wards. *Young Dr Kildare* started a whole series about a general hospital, and soon they were *Calling Dr Gillespie*. Other general hospital dramas include *White Corridors, The Lamp Still Burns, Behind the Mask, Life in Emergency Ward Ten, Emergency Hospital;* thrillers set among the wards include *Intent to Kill, The Sleeping City, Green for Danger* (the best of all), *Eye Witness* and *The Carey Treatment*, which last is in the vein of savage black humour evidenced in the early 70s by such films as *The Hospital* and *Where Does It Hurt?* Gentler hospital comedy has been found in *Doctor in the House, Twice Round the Daffodils, Trio*, and several episodes of the *'Carry On'* series which have specialized in bedpan humour.

TV series on the subject include *Medic, The Nurses, The Doctors and the Nurses, Doctor Kildare, Ben Casey, Dr Hudson's Secret Journal, Dr Christian, General Hospital, West Side Medical, Trapper John, Quincy, St Elsewhere*.

hotels

have frequently formed a useful setting for films wanting to use the 'slice of life' technique. Thus *Grand Hotel*, *Hotel for Women*, *Stage Door*, *Hotel Berlin*, *Weekend at the Waldorf*, *Separate Tables* and *Hotel* itself; while *Ship of Fools* is a variation on the same theme. The hotel background was a valuable dramatic asset to films as varied as *The Last Laugh*, *The October Man*, *Don't Bother to Knock*, *Hotel du Nord*, *Pushover*, *Honeymoon Hotel*, *Room Service* (and its remake *Step Lively*), *Hotel Reserve*, *Hotel Sahara*, *The Horn Blows at Midnight*, *Hotel for Women*, *Hollywood Hotel*, *Paris Palace Hotel*, *Bedtime Story*, *The Best Man*, *The Greengage Summer*, *A Hole in the Head*, and *The Silence*. Hotel security did not prevent attempts on the hero's life in *Journey into Fear* and *Foreign Correspondent*. The most bewildering hotel was certainly that in *So Long at the Fair*; the most amusing hotel sequences may have been in *Ninotchka*, *The Bellboy*, *Hotel Paradiso*, *A Flea in Her Ear* or *The Perfect Woman*. And hotels which had no accommodation to offer sparked off quite a few comedies during World War II, including *Government Girl*, *Standing Room Only* and *The More the Merrier* (later remade as *Walk Don't Run*). The hotel format endeared itself to television, which brought forth such variations as *Love Boat*, *Fantasy Island* and *Paradise Cove*; 1983 brought back *Hotel* itself, with shooting in San Francisco's Fairmont. The hotels no one would wish to revisit are those which sheltered Janet Leigh in *Psycho* and Jack Nicholson in *The Shining*.

The Hound of the Baskervilles

has been filmed more times than any other of Conan Doyle's stories featuring Sherlock Holmes. V. Gareth Gundrey directed a dull version for Gainsborough in 1931, starring Robert Rendel as Sherlock Holmes and Frederick Lloyd as Watson, with John Stuart as Sir Henry Baskerville and Heather Angel as Beryl Stapleton. Twentieth Century-Fox did better in 1939, when Sidney Lanfield directed the classic teaming of Basil Rathbone and Nigel Bruce as Holmes and Watson. Hammer offered a Gothic verison 20 years later, directed by Terence Fisher, with Peter Cushing as Holmes, André Morell as Watson and Christopher Lee as Sir Henry. A lamentable comic variation was made by Paul Morrissey in 1977, with Peter Cook as Holmes and Dudley Moore as Watson. Denholm Elliott was also among the cast and popped up in a more faithful retelling in 1983, directed by Douglas Hickox, with Ian Richardson as Holmes and Donald Churchill as Watson.

houses

have been the dramatic center of many films: there was even one, *Enchantment*, in which the house itself told the story. The films of Daphne du Maurier's novels usually have a mysterious old house at the crux of their plots, as in *Rebecca*, *Frenchman's Creek*, *Jamaica Inn*, *My Cousin Rachel*. So in *Dragonwyck*; so in *House of Fear*; so, of course, in *Jane Eyre* and *Wuthering Heights*. Both *Citizen Kane* and *The Magnificent Ambersons* are dominated by unhappy houses, as is *Gaslight*. Thrillers set in lonely houses full of secret panels and hidden menace are exemplified by *The Spiral Staircase*, *The Black Cat*, *Night Monster*, *The House on Haunted Hill*, *The Cat and the Canary*, *The Ghost Breakers*, *The House that Dripped Blood*, *Whatever Happened to Baby Jane?* *The Beast with Five Fingers*, *Ladies in Retirement* and *And Then There Were None*. Haunted houses are rarer, but those in *THe Uninvited*, *The Unseen*, *The Innocents*, *The Enchanted Cottage* and *The Haunting* linger vividly in the memory. So for a different reason does the Bates's house in *Psycho*: happier houses of note include the rose-covered cottage in *Random Harvest*, the family mansions of *Forever and a Day* and *Enchantment*, the red-decorated Denver house in *The Unsinkable Molly Brown*, the laboriously built country seat of *Mr Blandings Builds His Dream House*, the labour-saving modern house of *Mon Oncle*, the broken-down houses of *George Washington Slept Here* and *Father Came Too*, and dear old *Rookery Nook*. And filmgoers have various reasons to remember *The House on 92nd Street*, *The House on Telegraph Hill*, *House of Strangers*, *House of Horrors*, *House of Bamboo*, *House of Numbers*, *House of the Damned*, *House of the Seven Hawks*, *House of Women*, *House by the River*, *House of Dracula*, *House of Frankenstein*, *House of Wax*, *Sinister House*, *The Red House*, *Crazy House*, *The Old Dark House*, *The House of Usher*, *The House of the Seven Gables* and the house in *House* and *House II*. The house in *Malpertius* brought little comfort; come to that, nor did the noble pile in *Brideshead Revisited*, or the crumbling property in *The Money Pit*.

Hubie and Bertie.

Cartoon mice created by Chuck Jones. Their voices were supplied by Mel Blanc and Stan Freberg.

The Aristo Cat 43. House-Hunting Mice 48. Mouse Wreckers (AAN) 49. Cheese Chasers 51. Mouse Warming 52, etc.

The Huggetts.

Cheerful cockney family first featured in the film *Holiday Camp* 47. Its success inspired a radio series, *Meet the Huggetts*, featuring the film's two stars, Jack Warner and Kathleen Harrison, as Joe and Ethel Huggett, which ran from 1953–61, as well as three further films: *Here Come the Huggetts* 48, *Vote for Huggett* 48, *The Huggetts Abroad* 49.

The Hunchback of Notre Dame.

Victor Hugo's novel, *Notre-Dame de Paris*, about the cathedral's deformed bell-ringer Quasimodo and his love for the gypsy Esmerelda during the reign of Louis XI, has proved a potent source of inspiration to film-makers. Lon Chaney, giving one of his best performances, starred in a silent version in 1923, while William Dieterle directed the definitive Hollywood version in 1939, with Charles Laughton rampant in the title role. A crude remake appeared in 1956, starring Anthony Quinn and Gina Lollobrigida. Walt Disney made an animated version in 1996 which tried to turn it into a Broadway musical with Gothic overtones, and a TV film was in production for 1997 starring Mandy Patinkin. Other versions include two French silents, in 1906 and 1911, an English silent in 1906, an Italian in 1911 and an American in 1917, *The Darling of Paris*, with Glenn White and Theda Bara. Parodies include *The Hunchback Hairball of L.A.* 89, and *The Halfback of Notre Dame* 96, an updated teen TV movie about a clumsy football player.

hypnosis

on the screen has mainly been a basis for melodrama. *Svengali* was its most demonic exponent, but others who followed in his footsteps were Jacques Bergerac in *The Hypnotic Eye*, Boris Karloff in *The Climax*, Bela Lugosi in *Dracula*, Charles Gray in *The Devil Rides Out*, Erich Von Stroheim in *The Mask of Dijon*, Christopher Lee in *The Face of Fu Manchu*, Orson Welles in *Black Magic*, and José Ferrer in *Whirlpool* (in which, immediately after major surgery, he hypnotized himself into leaving his bed and committing a murder). In *Fear in the Night* and its remake *Nightmare*, De Forrest Kelley and Kevin McCarthy were hypnotized into becoming murderers. Comic uses are legion, the perpetrators including Lugosi in *Abbott and Costello Meet Frankenstein*, Karloff in *The Secret Life of Walter Mitty*, Gale Sondergaard in *Road to Rio*, the cast of *How to be Very Very Popular*, Yves Montand in *On a Clear Day You Can See Forever*, Alan Badel in *Will Any Gentleman*, Mildred Natwick in *The Court Jester*, and Pat Collins in *Divorce American Style*. The chief serious study of the subject has been *Freud*, though one might also count *The Search for Bridey Murphy*.

impresarios

presented on film include Sol Hurok, by David Wayne in *Tonight We Sing*; Rupert D'Oyly Carte, by Peter Finch in *The Story of Gilbert and Sullivan*; Walter de Frece, by Laurence Harvey in *After the Ball*; David Belasco, by Claude Rains in *Lady With Red Hair*; Lew Dockstatter, by John Alexander in *The Jolson Story*; Noël Coward by Daniel Massey, and André Charlot by Alan Oppenheimer, in *Star!*; and Florenz Ziegfeld, by William Powell in *The Great Ziegfeld* and by Walter Pidgeon in *Funny Girl*. Of fictional impresarios, the most memorable were those played by John Barrymore in *Maytime* and Anton Walbrook in *The Red Shoes*.

in-jokes

were especially frequent when Hollywood was a parochial society, and many must have been so private as to escape the general eye. The following, however, seem reasonably typical. *The Black Cat* (34): Boris Karloff as a devil worshipper has to be heard reciting an invocation to Satan, which to please the Hays Code is made up of such Latin phrases as 'cave canem' (beware of the dog), 'cum grano salis' (with a grain of salt), 'in vino veritas' (in wine is truth) and 'reductio ad absurdum est' (it is shown to be impossible). *Bride of Frankenstein:* Ernest Thesiger repeats a line ('It's my only weakness') from his previous role for the same director in *The Old Dark House*. *Mad Love:* a statue apparently comes to life, and a frightened onlooker says 'It went for a little walk', which is a line used of the monster in *The Mummy*, the same director's previous film. *His Girl Friday:* Cary Grant refers to the execution of a fellow named Archie Leach, which is Grant's own real name.

Hellzapoppin: Olsen and Johnson see a sledge on a film set and remark 'I thought they burned that', a reference to Rosebud in *Citizen Kane*. *Song of the Thin Man:* William Powell finds a razor blade and remarks 'Somerset Maugham has been here', a reference to the author's current best-seller *The Razor's Edge*. *The Maltese Falcon* and *In This Our Life:* Walter Huston plays uncredited bit parts under his son John's direction (one of innumerable similar instances). *On the Town:* Frank Sinatra is subjected to good-nature joshing about his real-life marriage to Ava Gardner. *Arise My Love:* Ray Milland, asked whether he was a test pilot, replies 'No, that was Clark Gable', referring to the recently released *Test Pilot*. *Northern Pursuit:* Errol Flynn, then in the middle of a real-life rape case, tells the heroine she is the only girl he has ever loved, then looks at the audience and says: 'What am I saying?' *How to Marry a Millionaire:* Lauren Bacall, then married to Humphrey Bogart, says in conversation 'That old man in *The African Queen*, I'm crazy about him'. *The Big Store:* Groucho tells the audience: 'This scene should have been in Technicolor but Mr Mayer said it was too expensive'. (Again, many similar instances exist, notably in the *Road* films, which are full of studio gags such as 'Paramount will protect us 'cause we're signed for five more years'.) *Another Dawn:* in the 30s, whenever a cinema canopy was shown, it usually advertised a non-existent film under this title; but in 1938 Warners were stuck for a title for their new Errol Flynn film, so they irrelevantly and cynically called it *Another Dawn*. *Some Like It Hot:* Tony Curtis has to impersonate a millionaire and as part of the disguise gives a devastatingly accurate impression of Cary Grant's voice, only to be told scathingly by Jack Lemmon 'Nobody talks like that!' In the same movie, and also in *Singin' in the Rain*, a gangster tosses a coin in imitation of George Raft in *Scarface*. *The VIPs:* asked for her home phone number, Elizabeth Taylor gives 'Grosvenor 7060', which is the number of MGM's London office. *Star Spangled Rhythm:* the harassed and excitable producer played by Walter Abel is named G. B. de Soto, in imitation of B. G. de Sylva, then a Paramount producer. *The Wings of Eagles:* the film director, John Dodge, is played by Ward Bond as an imitation of John Ford, who directed *The Wings of Eagles*. *Irma La Douce:* the pimps' union is called the Mecs' Paris Protective Association, or MPPA, which also stands for Motion Picture Producers Association, an organization which gave director Billy Wilder some trouble. *Caprice:* heroine Doris Day goes to the movies and sees a Doris Day movie. *One Two Three:* James Cagney threatens a girl with a grapefruit, mimicking his own action thirty years before in *Public Enemy:* he also steals from *Little Caesar* the line 'Mother of mercy, is this the end of Rico?' *The Entertainer:* reference is made to Sergeant Ossie Morris; the film was photographed by Ossie Morris. *Finian's Rainbow:* Fred Astaire has a short speech which consists, with different emphasis, of the words of one of his old songs. *The House that Dripped Blood:* Geoffrey Bayldon as a mad scientist is made up to look like Ernest Thesiger in *Bride of Frankenstein*. *How to Marry a Millionaire:* Betty Grable fails to recognize a Harry James recording (she was married to him at the time). *For the First Time:* there is reference to a convict named Cocozza, which happens to be star Mario Lanza's real name. *Connecting Rooms:* Bette Davis passes a poster mentioning stage star Margo(t) Channing, the name of the character she played in *All About Eve*. (The name is also used for one of the unseen characters in *Sleuth*.) *Pete 'n' Tillie:* Walter Matthau takes his girl to a cinema showing *Lonely Are the Brave*, one of his own earlier films. *Aaron Slick From Punkin Crick:* a waiter in a café scene calls 'Give that Perlberg-Seaton order special attention'. (Perlberg and Seaton produced and directed the film.) *Road to Utopia:* Bob Hope says Bing Crosby's voice is 'just right for selling cheese', a reference to Bing's then-current radio show, *Kraft Music Hall*. *Godfather II:* Troy Donahue plays a character called Merle Johnson, which is his own real name. *Dames:* Dick Powell is told 'Miss Warren, Miss Dubin and Miss Kelly are outside', a reference to songwriters Al Dubin and Harry Warren and dress designer Orry-Kelly. *Strange Boarders:* Tom Walls sees a picture of Disraeli and says 'Good old George, what a make-up', a reference to George Arliss' penchant for playing historical characters. *What's New Pussycat:* a stranger who bumps into Peter O'Toole in a nightclub turns out to be Richard Burton, who asks 'Don't you know me from someplace?' *West of the Divide:* in this 1934 quickie western John Wayne assumes the identity of a bandit whose image (i.e. his own) he sees on a wanted poster. The poster appeared in two other Wayne films that year. *A Chump at Oxford:* Laurel and Hardy foil a raid on the Finlayson National Bank, a clear reference to their favourite supporting player, James of that ilk. *The Lady in the Lake:* Crystal Kingsley, the character who never appears because she is dead, is listed as being played by Ellay Mort ('elle est morte'). *Gold Diggers of 1933:* a songwriter is told, 'Dubin and Warren are out! You're writing the score!' (Dubin and Warren wrote the score.) *Weekend at the Waldorf:* Walter Pidgeon imitates John Barrymore and Ginger Rogers says, 'Why, that's right out of *Grand Hotel!*' (from which *Weekend at the Waldorf* was adapted). *Trent's Last Case:* Orson Welles, who had played Othello in London a year previously, says: 'I saw *Othello* in London last year, but the fellow was not very good.' *The Howling:* most of the characters bear the names of horror film directors. *Quo Vadis:* Peter Ustinov as Nero says as he dies 'Is this the end of Nero?', echoing Edward G. Robinson's line at the end of *Little Caesar*, 'Is this the end of Rico?' In Paul Cox's *Lust and Revenge*, photographs displayed of Baba Thomas, the leader of an eccentric religious sect, are actually those of fellow director Rolf de Heer.

incest

has scarcely been fashionable film fare, though the theatrical acceptance of it goes back to *Oedipus Rex* (filmed in 1969) and one supposes *The Bible* (filmed in 1966) which fails to explain how else Adam and Eve's two sons propagated the species. It has been implied in a handful of American films from *Scarface* to *Toys in the Attic*, and more or less clearly stated in *Mourning Becomes Electra*, *A View from the Bridge* and *Chinatown*. Its full flowering came with the British *Country Dance*, but as expected the French had beaten us to it with *Souffle au Coeur*, though it became more explicit in *La Luna*. *My Lover My Son* is another example. *Close My Eyes* deals with an affair between a brother and sister, as does *The Cement Garden*, *The Miracle* with a son unwittingly attracted to his mother, and *U-Turn* a daughter abused by her violent father.

The Incredible Journey.

Sheila Burnford's story of two dogs and a cat who are left with a friend and make a journey of 250 miles across the Canadian wilderness to their old home was first filmed by Disney in 1963 with a voice-over narration by Rex Allen. It was remade in 1993 with the animals being voiced by Don Ameche as a labrador, Michael J. Fox as a terrier, and Sally Field as the cat. A sequel followed in 1996.

Indians:

see Red Indians.

insanity

in the cinema has usually been of the criminal kind: Robert Montgomery (and Albert Finney) in *Night Must Fall*, Keir Dullea in *Bunny Lake is Missing*, Bette Davis in *Whatever Happened to Baby Jane?* and *The Nanny*, Franchot Tone in *Phantom Lady*, George Brent in *The Spiral Staircase*, Joseph Cotten in *Shadow of a Doubt*, Edward G. Robinson in *The Sea Wolf*, Robert Ryan in *Beware My Lovely*, Ivan Kirov in *Spectre of the Rose*, Robert Mitchum in *Night of the Hunter*, Douglass Montgomery in *The Cat and the Canary*, Anthony Perkins in *Psycho*, Hywel Bennett in *Twisted Nerve*, Oliver Reed in *Paranoiac*, Brember Wills in *The Old Dark House* and hundreds of others. Indeed, most screen villains have been, if not psychopathic, at least subject to an *idée fixe:* and many a tortured hero has had a mad wife in the attic. Insanity has however been played quite frequently for comedy, notably in *Harvey*, *Miss Tatlock's Millions*, *The Criminal Life of Archibaldo de la Cruz* and *Drôle de*

Drame. Serious studies of insanity and its effects are on the increase, not only through fictitious situations as shown in *A Bill of Divorcement*, *The Shrike*, *Suddenly Last Summer*, *Of Mice and Men*, *David and Lisa*, *Shock Corridor*, *Shock Treatment*, *Diary of a Madman*, *One Flew over the Cuckoo's Nest* and *Cul de Sac*, but also in more clinical investigations such as *The Snake Pit*, *El*, *Labyrinth*, *La Tête contre les Murs*, *Morgan*, *Pressure Point*, *A Child Is Waiting*, *Lilith* and *Repulsion*. A mixture of attitudes is found in the scientific fantasy of *Charly;* while *Bedlam* was a curious attempt at a horror film set entirely in an asylum, a setting later used by *The Marat/Sade*. In *King of Hearts* the insane are shown to be wiser than the rest, like Mr Dick in *David Copperfield*.

insects
on the screen have generally been of the monstrous kind: *Tarantula*, *The Black Scorpion*, *The Wasp Woman*, *The Fly*, *Them*, and *The Monster That Challenged the World* come to mind. Of course, normal-sized ants can be monstrous enough if seen in quantity, as in *The Naked Jungle*, or if you are as small as *The Incredible Shrinking Man*. Giant spiders are perhaps the most popular breed: there was a particularly loathsome one in *The Thief of Baghdad*. But even normal-sized ones caused trouble in *Arachnophobia*. Friendly insects have included those who went to the 'ugly bug ball' in *Summer Magic;* and the dancing caterpillar of *Once upon a Time*. The most symbolic insect was certainly the butterfly in *All Quiet on the Western Front;* the most abundant, the locust in *The Good Earth*. A documentary feature about insects of the most dramatic kind was *The Hellstrom Chronicle*. Another documentary, *Microcosmos* 96, showed in startling detail a day in the insect life of a French meadow. And in 1998 came two computer-animated features, DreamWorks' *Antz* and Disney's *A Bug's Life*, in which the heroes, for once, were ants.

Inspector Hornleigh.
A detective whose interrogation of witnesses always led to a slip that gave away the criminal. Created by Hans Priwin (aka John P. Wynn), he was first featured on radio in 1937, which led to magazine stories and a stage play, followed by three films starring Gordon Harker in the title role: *Inspector Hornleigh* 39; *Inspector Hornleigh on Holiday* 39; *Inspector Hornleigh Goes to It* 41. A later radio series in the late 50s and early 60s from the same writer featured an identical detective except that he was now called Inspector Scott, but he failed to make the transition to the cinema.

insults.
A choice selection, from scripts and from life.

Tony Curtis, about having to make love to Marilyn Monroe:

It's like kissing Hitler.

George Sanders to Anne Baxter in *All About Eve:*

That I should want you at all suddenly seems to me the height of improbability.

Louis B. Mayer to Greta Garbo's agent:

Tell her that in America men don't like fat women.

Monty Woolley to Mary Wickes in *The Man Who Came to Dinner:*

You have the touch of a sex-starved cobra.

Charles Winninger to Fredric March in *Nothing Sacred:*

The hand of God reaching down into the mire couldn't elevate you to the depths of degradation.

And in the same movie, Walter Connolly to Fredric March:

I am sitting here, Mr Cook, toying with the idea of removing your heart and stuffing it – like an olive!

Billy Wilder, after listening to Cliff Osmond singing for a part:

You have Van Gogh's ear for music.

Jan Sterling to Kirk Douglas in *Ace in the Hole:*

I've met a lot of hard-boiled eggs in my time, but you – you're twenty minutes!

Walter Matthau to Barbra Streisand on the set of *Hello Dolly:*

I have more talent in my smallest fart than you have in your entire body.

And later:

I have no disagreement with Barbra Streisand. I was merely exasperated by her tendency towards megalomania.

Mae West of W. C. Fields during the filming of *My Little Chickadee:*

There's no one in the world quite like Bill – thank God.

inventors
have been the subject of many screen biographies; indeed, Don Ameche had to live down his invention of the telephone in *The Story of Alexander Graham Bell* and of the sub-machine gun in *A Genius in the Family*. Mickey Rooney appeared as *Young Tom Edison* and Spencer Tracy as *Edison the Man;* James Stewart was *Carbine Williams;* Robert Donat played William Friese-Greene, inventor of the movie camera, in *The Magic Box*. Joel McCrea in *The Great Moment* invented laughing gas; *The Sound Barrier* covered Sir Frank Whittle's invention of the jet engine, and *The Dam Busters* has Michael Redgrave as the inventor of the bouncing bomb, Dr Barnes Wallis. That prolific inventor Galileo was played in an Italian film by Cyril Cusack and more recently by Topol. In *I Aim At the Stars* Curt Jurgens was Wernher von Braun. Benjamin Franklin was portrayed not by an actor but by Disney's cartoonists in *Ben and Me*. Charles Coburn later took over in *John Paul Jones* and Howard da Silva in *1776*.

The Island of Dr Moreau.
H. G. Wells's novella, published in 1896, about a shipwrecked scientist operating on animals to give them human characteristics, was filmed by Erle C. Kenton in 1932 under the title *Island of Lost Souls*, with Charles Laughton giving a rip-roaring performance as the mad naturalist, Bela Lugosi as his mutant servant, and Kathleen Burke as the Panther Woman, who was chosen after the stunt of a nationwide search for an actress to play the role. With its heated publicity – 'Out of the dark fantastic madness of his science he created her – the panther woman – throbbing to the hot flush of new-found love!' – it was banned in England, on the grounds that it was 'against nature', and in some parts of America. It was remade in 1977 by Don Taylor, with Burt Lancaster as a somewhat stolid doctor, and in 1996 by John Frankenheimer, with Marlon Brando.

Jack the Ripper.
The unknown murderer of London prostitutes in 1888–9 has stimulated several flights of film fancy. Pabst brought him in to carry off the heroine of *Pandora's Box* 28. Two years earlier Alfred Hitchcock had directed the first film adaptation of Mrs Belloc Lowndes' novel *The Lodger*, but in this version Ivor Novello was found not to be the Ripper after all. Further versions were offered by Maurice Elvey in 1932 (Ivor Novello), John Brahm in 1944 (Laird Cregar) and Hugo Fregonese in 1953 (Jack Palance as *The Man in the Attic*). Further slight variations were posed in *The Phantom Fiend* 35 and *The Strangler* 64, while the long-standing puzzle was 'solved' in *Jack the Ripper* 58, *A Study in Terror* 65 and a TV 'Thriller' episode called *Yours Truly Jack the Ripper*. The Ripper was used as an alibi by *Dr Jekyll and Sister Hyde* 71, and the sins of the fathers were passed on in *Hands of the Ripper* 72, with Angharad Rees as the Ripper's daughter. In the 70s there was a German variation with Klaus Kinski, and in *Time after Time* the Ripper landed in modern San Francisco via H. G. Wells' time machine. In 1988, a TV film starred Michael Caine as a policeman on the track of the killer.

James Bond,
the over-sexed one-man spy machine created by Ian Fleming, first came to the screen in the guise of Sean Connery in *Dr No* 62. Connery continued in *From Russia with Love* 63, *Goldfinger* 64, *Thunderball* 65, *You Only Live Twice* 67; David Niven appeared as 'Sir James' in *Casino Royale* 67. George Lazenby took over for *On Her Majesty's Secret Service* 69; Connery came back for *Diamonds Are Forever* 71; Roger Moore signed on for *Live and Let Die*, *The Man with the Golden Gun*, *The Spy Who Loved Me*, *Moonraker*, *For Your Eyes Only* and *Octopussy*. In 1983 Connery returned as Bond in *Never Say Never Again*. Moore's last outing, in 1985, was *A View to a Kill*. Timothy Dalton took over for 1987's *The Living Daylights* and 1989's *Licence to Kill*. Pierce Brosnan took over the role in *GoldenEye*. In terms of admissions, *Thunderball* in 1975 was the most successful Bond film, being seen by more than 74 million and taking $63.6m at the box-office, followed by *Goldfinger*, seen by more than 66 million, *You Only Live Twice*, *From Russia with Love*, *Diamonds Are Forever*, *Moonraker*, *Octopussy*, *Dr No*, *The Spy Who Loved Me*, *Live and Let Die*. The least successful, in terms of admissions, was *The Man with the Golden Gun*, seen by an audience of just over 11 million.

Books: 1996, *The Complete James Bond Movie Encyclopedia* by Steven Jay Rubin; 1989, *The New Official James Bond Movie Book* by Sally Hibbin; 1998, *The Essential Bond: The Authorized Guide to the World of 007* by Lee Pfeiffer and Dave Worrall.

❝ James Bond is a blunt instrument wielded by a government department. He is quiet, hard, ruthless, sardonic, fatalistic. – *Ian Fleming*

Jane Eyre.
Charlotte Bronte's novel of a governess who falls in love with her master, Rochester, a man with a guilty secret, has been popular with film-makers from the early years of the century, although no version has yet captured the romantic spirit of the original. Christy Cabanne tried in 1934 with a cast that included Virginia Bruce as Jane Eyre and Colin Clive as Rochester; it was followed in 1943 by a classier version starring Orson Welles and Joan Fontaine, directed by Robert Stevenson and with Aldous Huxley among its scriptwriters. In 1970 came another lacklustre attempt destined for TV showing and directed by Delbert Mann, with George C. Scott and Susannah York heading the cast. The newest version was directed by Franco Zeffirelli, with a script by Hugh Whitemore. Novelist Jean Rhys wrote a prequel, *Wide Sargasso Sea*, explaining how Rochester met and married his first wife, which was lushly filmed in 1992 by John Duigan. The theme was also explored earlier, in Jacques Tourneur's 1943 film *I Walked with a Zombie*.

jazz
has been featured in American movies since the earliest days, with the first jazz band to record, the Original Dixieland Jazz Band, appearing in the silent *The Good-for-Nothing* in 1917; the word 'jazz' began to appear in the titles of many films of the period, used to evoke an atmosphere of fast living. Most famously, it was used in the title of the innovative semi-talkie *The Jazz Singer* 27, starring the vaudevillean style of the blackface singer Al JOLSON. The first films to feature jazz proper were shorts: *St Louis Blues*, featuring Bessie SMITH with James P. Johnson, and *Black and Tan Fantasy*, featuring Duke ELLINGTON and his Orchestrra with Fredi Washington. The coming of sound and the popularity of big bands, heard nationwide on radio and records, led to their appearances in many musicals, or movies with nightclub settings, typified by Paul WHITEMAN in the late 20s, and Benny GOODMAN and other exponents of what came to be called 'swing' in the late 30s. 'Swing' featured in many movie titles of that period, as 'Rock' would in the late 50s and 60s when rock 'n' roll became the popular music. During the 40s many bands also appeared in short movies and 'soundies', brief films shown in special juke-boxes. As the swing era passed, nostalgic biopics of leading figures of that time began to be made, and occasional films about the lives of fictional musicians became popular. Many composers of film music have their roots in jazz, including Terence BLANCHARD, Quincy JONES, Lennie NIEHAUS, Nelson RIDDLE, and Pete RUGOLO.

Jazz biopics include: *The Benny Goodman Story*, *Bird* (Charlie Parker), *Bix* (Bix Beiderbecke), *The Fabulous Dorseys* (Tommy and Jimmy Dorsey), *The Five Pennies* (Loring 'Red' Nichols), *The Gene Krupa Story*, *The Glenn Miller Story*, *Is Everybody Happy?* (Ted Lewis), *Lady Sings the Blues* (Billie Holiday), *Sven Klangs Kvintett* (fictionalized account of the life of Swedish saxophonist Lars Gullin), *St Louis Blues* (W. C. Handy), *Scott Joplin*, *Young Man with a Horn* (a fictional version of the life of Bix Beiderbecke, with soundtrack trumpet by Harry James).

Films with jazz interest include: *Atlantic City* (Louis Armstrong, Dorothy Dandridge, Paul Whiteman), *Ballad in Blue* (Ray Charles), *Birth of the Blues* (Bing Crosby, Jack Teagarden), *Blues in the Night* (Jimmy Lunceford), *Cabin in the Sky* (Louis Armstrong, Duke Ellington *et al*), *Carnegie Hall* (Harry James), *The Connection* (Freddie Red, Jackie McLean *et al*), *The Cotton Club* (Bob Wilbur), *The Gig* (Warren Vache), *Hellzapoppin'* (Rex Stewart, Slim Gaillard, Slam Stewart), *Hollywood Hotel* (Benny Goodman), *Jam Session* (Louis Armstrong, Charlie Barnet *et al*), *Jazz on a Summer's Day* (Jimmy Guiffre, Anita O'Day, Thelonious Monk *el al*), *Kansas City* (Joshua Redman, James Carter), *King of Jazz* (Paul Whiteman), *Make Believe Ballroom* (Jimmy Dorsey, Charlie Barnet *et al*), *New Orleans* (Louis Armstrong, Billie Holiday), *New York, New York* (Georgie Auld), *Orchestra Wives* (Glenn Miller), *Paris Blues* (Duke Ellington, Louis Armstrong), *Pete Kelly's Blues* (Peggy Lee, Ella Fitzgerald), *Round Midnight* (Dexter Gordon), *Stormy Weather* (Fats Waller, Cab Calloway *et al*), *A Song Is Born* (Louis Armstrong, Benny Goodman *et al*), *Sweet and Low-Down* (Benny Goodman), *Syncopation* (Rex Stewart and Bunny Berigan on the soundtrack), *Sun Valley Serenade* (Glenn Miller), *Top Man* (Count Basie, Bob Crosby *et al*).

Films with notable jazz or jazz-influenced soundtracks include: *Alfie* (Sonny Rollins), *Anatomy of a Murder* (Duke Ellington), *Assault on a Queen* (Duke Ellington), *Blow-Up* (Herbie Hancock), *The Cool World* (Mal Waldron), *Le Départ* (Krzysztof Komeda), *I Want to Live* (Johnny Mandel), *Jack Johnson* (Miles Davis), *Last Tango in Paris* ('Gato Barbieri), *Lift to the Scaffold/L'Ascenseur pour l'Échafaud* (Miles Davis), *The Man with the Golden Arm* (Elmer Bernstein, Shorty Rogers), *Odds against Tomorrow* (John Lewis), *Too Late Blues* (David Raksin), *The Sweet Smell of Success* (Elmer Bernstein, Chico Hamilton), *Les Valseuses/Going Places* (Stéphane Grappelli), *When the Devil Drives/Saît-on Jamais?* (John Lewis).

Book: 1981, *Jazz in the Movies* by David Meeker.

jewel thieves
were fashionable with Hollywood film-makers in the 30s, the heyday of Raffles, the Lone Wolf, and Arsène Lupin; they were the subject of Lubitsch's best comedy, *Trouble in Paradise*. In the 60s they seemed to come into their own again, with *To Catch a Thief*, *The Greengage Summer*, *Topkapi*, *The Pink Panther* and *Jack of Diamonds*.

Jews
and their plight in Europe under the Nazis were the subject of *So Ends Our Night*, *The Great Dictator*, *Professor Mamlock*, *Mr Emmanuel*, *The Diary of Anne Frank*, *M. Klein*, *Docteur Petiot* and *Schindler's List*. The problems of the new state of Israel were treated in *Sword in the Desert*, *Exodus*, *The Juggler*, *Judith* and *Cast a Giant Shadow;* while looking further back in history we find many versions of *Jew Süss* and *The Wandering Jew*, also *The Fixer* and the *Fiddler on the Roof*. American films about Jews used to show them as warm-hearted comic figures: *Kosher Kitty Kelly*, *Abie's Irish Rose*, *The Cohens and the Kellys*. Gertrude Berg continued this tradition on TV in the 50s. Recently films set in Jewish milieux have treated their characters more naturally, if with a touch of asperity: *No Way to Treat a Lady*, *I Love You Alice B. Toklas*, *Bye Bye Braverman*, *Funny Girl*, *The Night They Raided Minsky's*, *Goodbye Columbus*, *Portnoy's Complaint*, *Hester Street*, *Lies My Father Told Me*, *The Apprenticeship of Duddy Kravitz*, *The Chosen;* while TV revived for the world the plight of Jews under Hitler in *Holocaust* and *Playing for Time*, and Woody Allen has found a vein of internationally appreciated mordant humour in the foibles and follies of Jewishness.

See also: ANTI-SEMITISM.

Joe Palooka.
The dumb boxer hero of the famous American comic strip was first on screen in 1934, played by Stuart Erwin. Ten years later Joe Kirkwood, an amateur golfer, played him in a Monogram series, with Leon Errol (later James Gleason) as his manager Knobby Walsh.

The Jones Family.
A 1936 second feature called *Every Saturday Night* started off a series of 17 about a small-town American family in which Pa was Jed Prouty and Ma was Spring Byington. They had four years of popularity without ever quite equalling MGM's Hardy family, which had more sentimentality.

Judge Dredd.
Comic-book hero, a tough, shoot-first-ask-questions-after cop who also operates as judge and jury in Mega-City One. The creation of artist Brian Bolland and writer John Wagner, he first appeared in *2000 AD* magazine in 1977. In 1995 he made it to the big screen played by Sylvester Stallone.

The Jungle Book.
Rudyard Kipling's story of Mowgli, a boy able to converse with animals, was a role that might have been written for Sabu who played it in Zoltan Korda's version in 1942. Disney turned it into one of its most popular animated features in 1967, using to good effect the voices of George Sanders, Phil Harris, and Louis Prima. In 1995 came another live-action version starring Jason Scott Lee as Mowgli.

Jungle Jim.
This sub-Tarzan character began as a comic strip, and in 1937 Forde Beebe directed a serial on his exploits. In 1948 began the rather tired series tossed off for Columbia, with a paunchy Johnny Weismuller in the title role; it started ineptly and quickly became ridiculous.

Ma and Pa Kettle.
Hillbilly couple played in *The Egg and I* 47, and in a subsequent long-running series of comedy second features, by Marjorie Main and Percy Kilbride. Highly successful in US, less so in Britain.

The films were as follows:

1949 *Ma and Pa Kettle*
1950 *Ma and Pa Kettle Go To Town*
1951 *Ma and Pa Kettle Back on the Farm*
1952 *Ma and Pa Kettle at the Fair*
1953 *Ma and Pa Kettle on Vacation*
1954 *Ma and Pa Kettle at Home*
1955 *Ma and Pa Kettle at Waikiki*
1956 *The Kettles in the Ozarks*
1957 (with Parker Fennelly replacing Percy Kilbride) *The Kettles on Old MacDonald's Farm*

The Keystone Kops.
A troupe of slapstick comedians led by Ford Sterling who, from 1912–20 under the inspiration of Mack Sennett at Keystone Studios, made innumerable violent comedies full of wild chases and trick effects. *Abbott and Costello Meet the Keystone Kops* 55 was a somewhat poor tribute.

Kid Galahad.
A boxing drama, thought at the time of its release to be one of the best of its kind, directed by Michael Curtiz, starring Edward G. Robinson and Bette Davis and introducing Wayne Morris. It was remade in a disguised form as *The Wagons Roll at Night* 41, with Humphrey Bogart; then it turned up again in 1962 as an Elvis Presley vehicle, directed by Phil Karlson.

kidnapping
has been the subject of a great number of films; apart from the various versions of Robert Louis Stevenson's *Kidnapped*, examples include *Nancy Steele Is Missing, No Orchids for Miss Blandish, Ransom, The Kidnappers, A Cry in the Night, Cry Terror, Tomorrow at Ten, High and Low, My Name Is Julia Ross, Seance on a Wet Afternoon, The Collector, The Happening, Bunny Lake Is Missing, Bonnie and Clyde, Big Jake, The Night of the Following Day, The Grissom Gang, Murder on the Orient Express, The Man Who Loved Cat Dancing, Night People, Funeral in Berlin, Sugarland Express, The Wind and the Lion*, and on TV *The Longest Night* and *The Lindbergh Kidnapping Case*.

King Arthur:
see ARTHUR.

King Kong.
The most famous screen monster remains after more than 50 years the most impressive in the 1933 production. Willis O'Brien's trick photography created a believable great ape and the film, produced and directed by Merian Cooper and Ernest Schoedsack, holds together as a splendid adventure, with suitably throbbing music by Max Steiner. The same production team made a further visit to the mysterious island for *Son of Kong* 33, but the giant gorilla was played for laughs and the trick effects were skimpy, as they were for the similar *Mighty Joe Young* 49. The 1976 remake of the original story totally lacked charisma, as did its sequel and Japanese versions that have pitted Kong against robots and Godzilla. A remake was announced in 1996, to be directed by Peter Jackson, using his special effects facilities in New Zealand, which Universal also hoped would provide new attractions for its theme parks.

King Solomon's Mines.
Rider Haggard's African adventure novel was less than adequately filmed in Britain in 1937, directed by Robert Stevenson, with Cedric Hardwicke as Allan Quartermain. MGM's 1951 remake with Stewart Granger was an unsatisfactory mishmash; there was so much spare location footage that a semi-remake, *Watusi*, used it up in 1959. Harry Alan Tower's 1975 version, *King Solomon's Treasure*, makes its predecessors look like classics. A 1985 version, directed by J. Lee Thompson and starring Richard Chamberlain, was little better, and was followed by a lamentable sequel, shot at the same time, *Allan Quatermain and the Lost City of Gold*.

kings and queens,
of England at least, have been lovingly if not very accurately chronicled in the cinema. We still await an epic of the Norman Conquest, but in 1925 Phyllis Neilson-Terry went still further back to play *Boadicaea*, and in 1969 David Hemmings played *Alfred the Great*. Henry II, played by Peter O'Toole, was protagonist of *Becket* and *The Lion in Winter*. Richard I (Lionheart), also in the latter, was a shadowy figure of do-goodery in scores of films from *Robin Hood* to *King Richard and the Crusaders*; his brother John was just as frequently the villain of the piece, as in *The Adventures of Robin Hood*. Edward IV made an appearance in *Tower of London* and *Richard III*, but only as a pawn in the scheming hands of Richard III (Crookback). Henry IV appeared in *Chimes at Midnight*; *Henry V* was a notable role for Laurence Olivier; Henry VII-to-be was played in *Richard III* by Stanley Baker. Henry VIII was for long personified by Charles Laughton, who played him in 1933, but there have been other contenders: Montagu Love in *The Prince and the Pauper*, Robert Shaw in *A Man for All Seasons*, Richard Burton in *Anne of the Thousand Days*, Keith Michell in *Henry VIII and his Six Wives*, and James Robertson Justice in *The Sword and the Rose*. Similarly Elizabeth I was identified with Bette Davis (*Elizabeth and Essex*, *The Virgin Queen*) until Glenda Jackson played her on TV and in *Mary Queen of Scots*, though she was also personified by Flora Robson (*Fire over England*, *The Sea Hawk*), Florence Eldridge (*Mary of Scotland*), Irene Worth (*Seven Seas to Calais*) and others. The unfortunate *Mary of Scotland* was notably played by Katharine Hepburn and Vanessa Redgrave. Young Edward VI was in *The Prince and the Pauper*. The early Stuarts were a dour lot, but Charles I was impersonated by Alec Guinness in *Cromwell*; Charles II, the merry monarch, has been personified by a number of actors including Cedric Hardwicke (*Nell Gwyn*), George Sanders (*Forever Amber*), Vincent Price (*Hudson's Bay*), Douglas Fairbanks Jnr (*The Exile*) and Sam Neill (*Restoration*). Of the Hanoverians, George I was played by Eric Pohlmann in *Rob Roy* and Peter Bull in *Saraband for Dead Lovers*, George III by Raymond Lovell in *The Young Mr Pitt*, by Robert Morley in *Beau Brummell* and Nigel Hawthorne in *The Madness of King George*. Prinny, the Prince Regent, later George IV, was undertaken by Cecil Parker in *The First Gentleman* and Peter Ustinov in *Beau Brummell*. Victoria to many people still looks like Anna Neagle, who played her three times; other actresses in the role have included Irene Dunne (*The Mudlark*), Fay Compton (*The Prime Minister*) and Mollie Maureen (*The Private Life of Sherlock Holmes*). James Robertson Justice played Edward VII in *Mayerling*, and Richard Chamberlain Edward VIII in a TV film, *The Woman I Love*. In 1982 two American TV movies about the romance of Prince Charles cast well-known actors as the current royal family: neither was shown in the U.K.

Foreign monarchs who have been notably impersonated include Catherine the Great of Russia (Pola Negri, Elisabeth Bergner, Tallulah Bankhead, Bette Davis, Marlene Dietrich); Russia's last Czar and Czarina, *Nicholas and Alexandra* (Michael Jayston and Janet Suzman); *Peter the Great*; *Ivan the Terrible*; *Queen Christina* of Sweden (Greta Garbo, and Liv Ullmann in *The Abdication*); Louis XI of France (Harry Davenport in *The Hunchback of Notre Dame*, Basil Rathbone in *If I Were King*); Charles VII of France, by Jose Ferrer in *Joan of Arc*; *Marie Antoinette* (Norma Shearer); Louis XIV, by John Barrymore in *Marie Antoinette*; Louis XVI, by Robert Morley in *Marie Antoinette* and by Pierre Renoir in *La Marseillaise*; Louis XIII, by Jean-Pierre Cassel in *The Three Musketeers*; Philip II of Spain (Paul Scofield in *That Lady*, Raymond Massey in *Fire over England*).

Kismet.
Edward Knoblock's rather stolid Arabian Nights play has been filmed five times. In 1920 Louis Gesnier directed Otis Skinner; in 1931 William Dieterle directed Gustav Frölich in a German version; also in 1931 Otis Skinner played in a talkie version directed by John Francis Dillon; in 1944 Dieterle had another crack at it, with Roland Colman in the lead; and in 1955 the stage musical with themes from Borodin was filmed by Vincente Minnelli, with Howard Keel.

The Ku Klux Klan
was sympathetically portrayed in Griffith's *The Birth of a Nation*, a fact which has never ceased to provoke controversy. The villainous actuality has, however, been displayed in *Black Legion* 36, *Legion of Terror* 37, *The Burning Cross* 47, *Storm Warning* 51, *The FBI Story* 59, *The Cardinal* 63 and *The Klansman* 74, among others.

See also: LYNCH LAW.

labour relations
is too downbeat a subject to be very popular on the screen; but strikes have been treated with seriousness in *Strike*, *The Crime of Monsieur Lange*, *Black Fury*, *How Green Was My Valley*, *The Agitator*, *Love on the Dole*, *Chance of a Lifetime*, *The Whistle at Eaton Falls*, *The Angry Silence*, *F.I.S.T.* and *Last Exit to Brooklyn*; with humour in *A Nous la Liberté*, *Modern Times*, *Carry On at Your Convenience*, *The Pajama Game*, and *I'm All Right Jack*. The classical comical strike of women against their husbands, led by Lysistrata, was depicted in the French *Love, Soldiers and Women* and Americanized in *The Second Greatest Sex*.

Lady for a Day.
Robert Riskin wrote and Frank Capra directed, in 1933, this Runyonesque fantasy about an old flower seller who is helped by gangster friends to deceive her visiting daughter into believing that she is comfortably placed. In 1961 Capra remade it as *Pocketful of Miracles*, but not even Bette Davis could save it from tedium, and Capra's direction seemed tired.

Lassie.
The first film featuring this intelligent collie (actually a laddie, as were his successors) was *Lassie Come Home* 42, based on Eric Knight's novel; the dog was called Pal (1941–59), and continued his masquerade in *Son of Lassie* 45 and *Courage of Lassie* 46. The original was remade as *Gypsy Colt* 54, which substituted a horse for the dog; *The Magic of Lassie* 78; and *Lassie* 94. Other films in the series include *Lassie's Great Adventure* 62 and *Lassie: Adventures of Neeka* 68. A radio series ran from 1947–50 and a television series from 1954–71, in which the dog was the only constant factor with its owner changing periodically; by the end of the series Lassie had no owner at all. An animated version, *Lassie's Rescue Rangers*, was produced for children's television from 1973–75 and *The New Lassie*, which put the dog in a suburban setting, was shown on television from 1989–91.

The Last Days of Pompeii.
Lord Lytton's novel climaxing in the catastrophic eruption of Vesuvius was filmed in Italy in 1912 ('10,000 people, 260 scenes'), 1925 and 1960. In 1935 Cooper and Schoedsack filmed it in Hollywood, with a cast including Basil Rathbone and Preston Foster. The 1960 Italian version is barely worth mentioning and the 1985 TV mini-series is good for a laugh.

The Last of the Mohicans.
Fenimore Cooper's adventure novel of American colonization was filmed in 1920 by Maurice Tourneur, with George Hackathorne; in 1936 by George Seitz, with Randolph Scott; in 1952 as *The Last of the Redskins* by George Sherman, with Jon Hall; and in 1992 by Michael Mann, with Daniel Day-Lewis. A Canadian TV series in 1956 starred John Hart.

Leave It to Beaver
was a long-running US TV sitcom about family life as experienced by a young boy, Theodore 'Beaver' Cleaver, played by Jerry Mathers, who was seven when the series began in 1957 and a teenager when it finished its run in 1963. His parents were played by Hugh BEAUMONT and Barbara BILLINGSLEY. The series was popular enough 20 years on to spawn a TV movie, *Still the Beaver* 83, with Mathers and most of the original cast still in the same roles; Beaver was now an unemployed father with two unruly children and a wife wanting a divorce. It was followed by two sitcoms, *Still the Beaver* 85–86 and *The New Leave It to Beaver* 86–89. In 1997 came a film version starring Chris MacDonald and Janine Turner with Cameron Finley as the eight-year-old Beaver.

legends.
Over the years a number of Hollywood legends have built up, never proved or disproved. Here is a selection: George Raft was a protégé of the Mafia. James Dean is not really dead but on a life support machine. Walt Disney is cryonically preserved. Louella Parsons witnessed the murder of Thomas Ince by W. R. Hearst. Marilyn Monroe was killed by the CIA because of her association with John Kennedy. Cary Grant and Randolph Scott were lovers. Ida Lupino is bald.

Lemmy Caution.
Tough private eye, created by British novelist Peter Cheyney in imitation of American models in the 30s and 40s, who was incarnated on screen by Eddie Constantine in a series of French films, culminating in Jean-Luc Godard's futuristic *Alphaville* 65.

leprechauns
have made rare but effective screen appearances in the persons of Cecil Kellaway (*Luck of the Irish*), Jimmy O'Dea (*Darby O'Gill and the Little People*), Don Beddoe (*Jack the Giant Killer*) and Tommy Steele (*Finian's Rainbow*). A murderous one appeared in the horror movie *Leprechaun*.

lesbianism
came fully into its own with the filming of *The Killing of Sister George*; but for many years it was unthinkable as a screen subject. *These Three* in 1936 had to be so changed that it was almost unrecognizable as a version of *The Children's Hour*; and the matter was scarcely broached again until the 50s, when the French brought it up in *Olivia* and *The Girl with the Golden Eyes*.

The first Hollywood film to bring the subject to our notice was *A Walk on the Wild Side* 62; since then there have been more or less discreet references in *The Haunting*, *The Balcony*, *Lilith*, *The Silence*, *Alyse and Chloe*, *The Vampire Lovers*, *Beyond the Valley of the Dolls*, *La Religieuse*, *The Group*, *Tony Rome*, *The Fox*, *Therese and Isabelle*, *Baby Love*, *The Smashing Bird I Used to Know*, and *Once Is Not Enough*; while *The Children's Hour* was filmed again, this time with its full force. In 1982 *Personal Best* again brought the subject into the open, as did *Desert Hearts* in 1985. The 90s brought some straightforwardly romantic films, such as *Go Fish* and *The Incredible Story of Two Girls in Love*, as well as lesbianism on skates in *Thin Ice*. There were also darker movies of repression and murder, including *Butterfly Kiss* and Claude Chabrol's *A Judgement in Stone/La Cérémonie*, and a move into genre films with a thriller, *Bound*, and even a fairy story, *The Midwives' Tale*.

letters
have provided a starting point or climax for several films. Undelivered ones for *Address Unknown*, *The Postman Didn't Ring*; misdelivered ones for *Dear Ruth*, *The Go-Between*, *A Letter for Evie*; an incriminating one in *Suspicion*; lost ones for *Cause for Alarm*, *Never Put It In Writing*; indiscreet ones for *A Letter To Three Wives*, *So Evil My Love*, *The Last of Mrs Cheyney*, *The Letter*; posthumous ones for *Letter from an Unknown Woman*, *Love Letters*, *The Lost Moment*, *Mister Roberts*; anonymous ones for *Poison Pen* and *Le Corbeau*.

lifts
(or elevators) provided a convenient means of murder in *Garment Center*, *The List of Adrian Messenger* and *House of Wax*, and of unwitting suicide in *Ivy*. In *The Lift*, the machine was the murderer. Sean Connery in *Diamonds Are Forever* had a spectacular fight in a lift. People were trapped in lifts in *Cry Terror*, *A Night in Casablanca*, *Love Crazy*, *Sweet Charity*, *Towering Inferno* and *Lady in a Cage*, in which last the lift was of the domestic variety used by Katharine Hepburn in *Suddenly Last Summer*. Michael Rennie had more trouble in lifts than any other actor – in *The Power*, *The Day the Earth Stood Still*, and *Hotel*.

Invalid chair-lifts were sported by Ethel Barrymore in *The Farmer's Daughter*, Charles Laughton in *Witness for the Prosecution*, and Eugenie Leontovich in *Homicidal*.

light comedians,

the lithe and dapper heroes who can be funny and romantic at the same time, have added a great deal to the mystique and nostalgia of the screen. Linder and Chaplin both partly belong to this debonair tradition, and indeed did much to mould it; but only sound could enable its full realization. Maurice Chevalier had the field pretty well to himself in Hollywood during the early 30s, with strong support from such stalwarts as Roland Young, Edward Everett Horton and Charles Butterworth. Soon Cary Grant entered the lists along with David Niven, William Powell, Louis Hayward, Melvyn Douglas and Ronald Colman when he felt in lighter mood. Britain scored with Jack Buchanan, Jack Hulbert, and the ineffable Aldwych team of Tom Walls and Ralph Lynn; while Leslie Howard scored a major hit in *Pygmalion* and Rex Harrison, who was to play the same role twenty-five years later in *My Fair Lady*, was already demonstrating his talent in less important comedies.

Back in Hollywood *The Philadelphia Story* was a milestone in light comedy and set Katharine Hepburn firmly on the road she later followed in her splendid series with Spencer Tracy. Bette Davis, too, had her moments in this field, and so did Rosalind Russell. Bob Hope and Danny Kaye both clowned around a good deal but still got the girl in the end . . . but Britishers Basil Radford and Naunton Wayne were bachelors born and bred. The more realistic approach of the 50s was stifling the genre, but Dennis Price managed a notable performance in *Kind Hearts and Coronets* before Ian Carmichael cornered the diminishing market. In more recent years actors have had to turn comic or tragic at the drop of a hat: among those best able to manage the light touch are Jack Lemmon, Tony Curtis, Frank Sinatra, Peter O'Toole, Jack Nicholson, Warren Beatty, Shirley Maclaine, Diane Keaton, Jane Fonda and Anne Bancroft.

lighthouses

formed dramatic settings for such movies as *Thunder Rock, The Seventh Survivor, The Phantom Light* and *Back Room Boy*, and dominated key scenes of *Portrait of Jennie, A Stolen Life, The Beast from 20,000 Fathoms* and *Pete's Dragon*.

Li'l Abner.

Al Capp's comic strip about the hillbilly inhabitants of Dogpatch was first filmed, unsuccessfully, in 1940 with Granville Owen; masks were rather oddly used for some characters. In 1957 Panama and Frank made a successful musical version with Peter Palmer, based on the Broadway show. Paramount made a few Li'l Abner cartoons in the late 40s.

Liliom.

Ferenc Molnar's play about the here and the hereafter was filmed in Hollywood in 1930 by Frank Brozage and in Germany in 1934 by Fritz Lang. In 1956 it turned up again, via a stage musical, as *Carousel*, directed by Henry King. There had also been a 1921 silent under the title *A Trip to Paradise*.

Little Lord Fauntleroy.

The well-known children's novel by Frances Hodgson Burnett, about an American boy who becomes a British earl, was filmed in 1922 as a transvestite vehicle for Mary Pickford; direction appears to have been shared between Alfred E. Green, Jack Pickford, and Alfred Werker. In 1936 it was remade by John Cromwell for Selznick, with Freddie Bartholomew in the title role. In 1980 there was a TV version with Ricky Schroder.

Little Miss Marker.

Damon Runyon's story of a small girl with a belief in chivalry reforming a hard-bitten gambler made an ideal vehicle for Shirley Temple and Adolphe Menjou in 1934; it was remade as *Sorrowful Jones* in 1949 with the emphasis on its male lead, Bob Hope. Norman Jewison's *Forty Pounds of Trouble* in 1962 updated the story to little effect. Walter Bernstein tried the original story again in 1980 with *Little Miss Marker*, featuring Walter Matthau, but by then the tale seemed tired and dated.

Little Rascals:

see: 'OUR GANG'.

Little Tough Guys.

A gang of young actors who were a spin-off from the success of The DEAD END KIDS and were sometimes indistinguishable from them, appearing in low-budget films and serials for Universal. They included Gabriel Dell (as String), Hally Chester (as Dopey), David Gorcey (as Sniper), Billy Halop (as Johnny), Huntz Hall (as Pig), and Bernard Punsley (as Ape).

Little Tough Guy 38. Little Tough Guys in Society 38. Call a Messenger 39. Sea Raider (serial) 40. Junior G-Men (serial) 40. You're Not So Tough 40. Give Us Wings 40. Mob Town 41. Hit the Road 41. Junior G-Men of the Air (serial) 42. Tough as They Come 42. Mug Town 43. Keep 'Em Slugging 43, etc.

See also: The EAST SIDE KIDS, The BOWERY BOYS.

Little Women.

Louisa M. Alcott's cosy 19th-century saga of a nice mother's even nicer daughters was twice filmed as a silent, in 1917 in Britain and 1918 in America, and became a major success when filmed in 1933 by George Cukor, with Katharine Hepburn and Paul Lukas. Remade in 1949 with June Allyson and Rossano Brazzi, it seemed calculated and coy. Another remake came in 1994, directed by Gillian Armstrong and starring Winona Ryder, Samantha Mathis, Trini Alvarado, Susan Sarandon, and Gabriel Byrne. A 1978 TV series got nowhere. A sequel, *Little Men*, was filmed in 1940 as a vehicle for Kay Francis.

The Lodger:

see: JACK THE RIPPER.

London

has provided a background, usually highly inaccurate, for innumerable movies, but few have really explored it, though *The Ipcress File* and *The Pumpkin Eater* found some unusual angles. *London Town* was a half-hearted musical; twenty years later *Three Hats for Lisa* captured the mood better but managed to seem old-fashioned. *Pygmalion* and *My Fair Lady* embodied the spirit of London in some theatrical sets. *Indiscreet* prowled lovingly around the Embankment, and *A Run for Your Money* made good use of the Paddington area as well as suburban Twickenham. The City was the venue of part of *You Must Be Joking*, while *Morgan* used Hampstead to good advantage. The East End, especially the street markets and the railway sidings, were exploited in *Waterloo Road, A Kid for Two Farthings* and *It Always Rains on Sunday*. The docks had *Pool of London* to themselves. Hollywood's idea of London in geography can be pretty weird, as in *Knock on Wood*, when Paramount went to the trouble of having special location material shot with Jon Pertwee doubling for Danny Kaye, but showed the star turning off Marble Arch into Fleet Street two miles away. Similarly in *Twenty-three Paces to Baker Street* the river frontage of the Savoy Hotel could be entered from Portman Square, in actuality another two-mile jaunt. London fog has been a useful cover for many a scrappy set, especially in films presenting the Victorian London associated with Sherlock Holmes. Going further back, *Henry V* presented in model form the London of 1600, and attempts at historical recreation were also made in *Tower of London, Fire over England, Elizabeth and Essex, Nell Gwyn, Forever Amber, Mrs Fitzherbert, The First Gentleman, Victoria the Great, Cromwell* and *The Mudlark*. It was probably Hitchcock who began the fashion of making London a stately background for thrillers, with his East End mission in *The Man Who Knew Too Much*, the music hall in *The Thirty-nine Steps*, the bus journey and the Lord Mayor's Show in *Sabotage*, the fall from Westminister Cathedral in *Foreign Correspondent*, the theatrical garden party in *Stage Fright*, and Covent Garden in *Frenzy*. Others in this tradition have included *Brannigan, Hennessy, Villain, Robbery*, and innumerable TV series such as *The Sweeney*.

See also: SWINGING LONDON.

The Lone Ranger.

This western Robin Hood originally featured in a radio serial and later became a comic strip in 1935; 20 years later Clayton Moore played the hero in a successful TV series and a couple of feature films, with Jay Silverheels as Tonto. The 1981 attempt to retell the tale half seriously, *The Legend of the Lone Ranger*, met with disaster: Klinton Spilsbury was the Lone Ranger and has not been heard of since.

The Lone Rider

was Tom Cameron, a cowboy who rode the West on a white horse righting wrongs in 'B' westerns starring George HOUSTON, who found time in each feature to sing a couple of songs as well as the stirring title song ('I'm the Lone Rider on the Great Divide/All alone, roamin' far and wide/ When a helpin' hand is needed/I am ready without fail/I'm the Lone Rider on the trail'). Despite his nickname, he was always accompanied by sidekick Fuzzy Jones, played by Al ST JOHN. The films were directed by Sam NEWFELD.

The Lone Rider Ambushed 41. The Lone Rider Crosses the Rio 41. The Lone Rider Fights Back 41. The Lone Rider in Frontier Fury 41. The Lone Rider in Ghost Town 41. The Lone Rider in Texas Justice 41. The Lone Rider Rides On 41. The Lone Rider and the Bandit 42. The Lone Rider in Cheyenne 42. Outlaws of Boulder Pass 42. The Lone Rider in Border Roundup 43.

The Lone Wolf,

a gentleman thief (Michael Lanyard), was created by Louis Joseph Vance and reached the screen in silent days played by H. B. Warner, Jack Holt, and Bert Lytell; in the 30s Melvyn Douglas and Francis Lederer each played him once and then Warren William took over for eight episodes, usually with Eric Blore as his manservant. In 1946 Gerald Mohr played in the first of three episodes, and in 1949 Ron Randell personified him for the last time on the big screen. In 1954 Louis Hayward played him in a TV series, *The Lone Wolf/Streets of Danger*.

lookalikes.

The old studios would frequently hire less talented performers who looked rather like their main stars, simply to keep the latter in order. Also, if a star with a certain style proved fashionable, a rival might try to repeat the dose. Whatever the reason, Gloria Jean was designed to remind filmgoers of Deanna Durbin; John Carroll of Clark Gable; Anna Sten of Marlene Dietrich; Brian Aherne of Ronald Colman; Patric Knowles of Errol Flynn; Dane Clark of John Garfield; Antonio Moreno and Ricardo Cortez of Rudolph Valentino; Viveca Lindfors of Ingrid Bergman; Roddy McDowall of Freddie Bartholomew; John Gavin of Rock Hudson; Gig Young of Cary Grant; Lizabeth Scott of Lauren Bacall; Mary Beth Hughes of Lana Turner; Yvonne de Carlo of Maria Montez; Mamie Van Doren and Sheree North of Marilyn Monroe; Joel McCrea of Gary Cooper; Tippi Hedren of Grace Kelly. Not too surprisingly, lightning never struck in the same place twice.

Looney Tunes/Merrie Melodies

are the umbrella titles under which Warners have long released their cartoon shorts featuring such characters as Bugs Bunny, Daffy Duck, Porky Pig, Pepe le Pew, Sylvester and Tweetie Pie. They have won Academy Awards for *Tweetie Pie* 47, *For Scentimental Reasons* 49, *Speedy Gonzales* 55, *Birds Anonymous* 57, *Knighty Knight Bugs* 58.

Los Angeles,

being the home of the film studios, was the anonymous background of ninety per cent of Hollywood films from the very beginning. Only more recently, however, has the actual city been explored, usually in a cynical Chandleresque manner as in *The Long Goodbye* and *Marlowe*, or as a vivid sunlit background for police thrillers with their screaming car chases, especially in such TV series as *Police Story, The Blue Knight, Police Woman, The Rookies, Chase, Emergency, The Smith Family* and *Dragnet*. The city's seamy side was shown in M and *The Savage Eye*, its future in *The Omega Man*, its sophisticated present in *Divorce American Style, L.A. Story* and *Grand Canyon*, its sewers in *Them*, and its past in *Chinatown*. Perhaps the most vivid picture of the growing sprawl is to be found as background to the comedies of the Keystone Kops and Laurel and Hardy; and *Earthquake* finally destroyed it.

One positive approach to Tinseltown was expressed in *The Model Shop*: 'How could you find this place ugly? It's pure poetry.'

❝ Perhaps there are more haunted houses in Los Angeles than in any other city in the world. They are haunted by the fears of their former owners. They smell of divorce, broken contracts, studio politics, bad debts, false friendships, adultery, extravagance, whisky and lies. Every closet hides the poor little ghost of a stillborn reputation.
– *Christopher Isherwood*

It's the most stunningly vulgar town in the world. There's a free gas escape of nonsense that prevails, and people, if they go on breathing it, become brain-damaged. – *Jonathan Miller*

Lost Horizon.

James Hilton's novel about a Tibetan Utopia was turned into an uneven but attractive film in 1937 by Frank Capra, which made Shangri-La a household word. In 1973 Ross Hunter remade the story as a semi-musical with unhappy results.

Lost in Space

was a TV series of the mid-60s featuring the Robinson family who wandered from planet to planet trying to find their way home after their spaceship was sabotaged. It was notable for its cheap special effects. It became a big-budget movie in 1997, but, despite its technical excellence, failed to find an audience.

Lost Patrol.

Philip MacDonald's story, about a British desert patrol being picked off one by one by Arabs until rescuers find one survivor raving mad, has inspired many war films since John Ford's 1934 version with heavily overacted but enjoyable performances from Victor McLaglen, Boris Karloff, and Reginald Denney. A Russian version, *The Thirteen*, was made in 1937, and Zoltan Korda's 1943 *Sahara*, starring Humphrey Bogart, gave the story a cast of Allied soldiers facing an overwhelming Nazi force. It was also the inspiration for *Bataan* 46 and *Last of the Comanches* 51. In 1996 came *Sahara*, an Australian-US remake of Korda's treatment, directed by Brian Trenchard-Smith and starring James Belushi, which flopped at the box-office.

Love Affair.

The story of two people agreeing, and failing, to meet at the top of the Empire State Building after six months apart to discover if their love remains strong was first filmed by Leo McCarey in 1939 with Irene Dunne and Charles Boyer; in 1957, again directed by Leo McCarey, it became the weepie *An Affair to Remember*, with Cary Grant and Deborah Kerr (which also featured in the 1993 hit *Sleepless in Seattle*); in 1994, as *Love Affair*, it became a vehicle for the husband and wife team of Warren Beatty and Annette Bening.

The Lower Depths.

Gorki's doss-house study has had two notable filmings. As *Les Bas Fonds*, directed by Jean Renoir, it provided memorable roles for Jean Gabin and Louis Jouvet in 1936. In 1958, Akira Kurosawa directed Toshiro Mifune in a surprisingly faithful Japanese adaptation.

lumberjacks

have figured in comparatively few movies: here are some of them: Conflict 36. Come and Get It 36. God's Country and the Woman 36. The Big Trees 52. Timberjack 55. Guns of the Timberland 60. Freckles 60. Sometimes a Great Notion 71.

lynch law

has been condemned in many outstanding dramatic movies from Hollywood.

Fury 36. They Won't Forget 37. Young Mr Lincoln 39. The Ox-Bow Incident 43. Storm Warning 51. The Sound of Fury 51. The Sun Shines Bright 52. Rough Night in Jericho 68.

See also: KU KLUX KLAN.

M.

Fritz Lang was the first, in 1931, to film this story of a child-murderer finally hunted down by the city's organized criminal element, and Peter Lorre had his first great success as the psychopath. In 1950 Joseph Losey directed an almost scene-for-scene American remake starring David Wayne, but it generated no particular atmosphere. Woody Allen was more successful in creating Lang's air of decadence and despair in his comic-tinged *Shadows and Fog* 92.

Macbeth.

Among many attempts to film Shakespeare's Scottish tragedy, none of them wholly successful, have been the following: in 1915 John Emerson directed and D. W. Griffith produced a straightforward version starring Sir Herbert Beerbohm Tree and Constance Collier; in 1948 Orson Welles directed and starred in his own adaptation shot in 21 days for Republic; in 1956 Ken Hughes wrote and directed a modernized version, *Joe Macbeth*, in which the kings and princes became rival gangsters; in 1957 Akira Kurosawa directed *Throne of Blood*, a stylized Japanese version; in 1960 George Schaefer directed an honest school exam-style rendering in colour with Maurice Evans and Judith Anderson which was shown on US television but released theatrically in Britain; in 1971 Jon Finch and Francesca Annis starred in a blood-spattered version by Roman Polanski; in 1991 William Reilly again tried a gangster Macbeth in *Men of Respect*, starring John Turturro, which even included Lady M's sleep-walking scene in an attempt to keep its audience awake.

Maciste.

A legendary hero of the Italian cinema, a strong man originating in *Cabiria* 14. Such of his adventures as have been dubbed into English usually translate him as Samson. The role in *Cabiria* was played by Bartolomeo Pagano (1888–1947), who continued in the part, billed as Maciste, in many films until 1928. In the 60s cycle of Italian 'sword and sandal' epics, Maciste was played by a succession of interchangeable musclemen, including South African Reg Park and Americans Gordon Scott, Reg Lewis, Mark Forest and Gordon Mitchell.

Maciste the Mighty/Maciste nella Valle dei Re 60. Goliath against the Vampires/Maciste contro il Vampiro 61. Atlas in the Land of the Cyclops/ Maciste nella Terra dei Ciclopi 61. Samson and the Seven Miracles of the World/Maciste alla Corte del Gran Khan 62. Goliath and the Sins of Babylon/ Maciste, l'Eroe Più Grande del Mondo 63. Maciste vs the Stone Men/Maciste contro gli Uomini Luna 64. Maciste and the Hundred Gladiators/ Maciste, Gladiatore di Sparta 65, etc.

Madame Bovary.

Gustave Flaubert's 1857 novel of the bored wife of a provincial doctor, who seeks escape from her stifling environment in romantic fantasies and affairs, and finds it only in suicide, has been filmed at least eight times, though no version is entirely successful. Jean RENOIR made a three-hour version in 1933, with stage actress Valentine Tessier in the title role, but before its release it was drastically cut by an hour; Gerhard Lamprecht directed a version in Germany in 1937, starring Pola NEGRI, trying to re-establish herself after the coming of sound had finished her Hollywood career; Vincente MINNELLI made a Hollywood version in 1949, starring Jennifer JONES (though Minnelli had wanted Lana TURNER for the role), with the censors insisting that adultery must not be seen as attractive; and Claude CHABROL directed a dull version in 1991, with Isabelle HUPPERT starring. A low-budget adaptation had been filmed in 1932 by Albert Ray under the title *Unholy Love*, with silent star Lila LEE; a loose, erotic version, *The Naked Bovary*, was made in 1969 by Hans Schott-Schöbinger, with Edwige Fenech; Ketan Mehta made *Maya*, a version set in modern-day India in 1992 with Deepa Sahi; and Aleksandr Sokhurov directed a Russian version in 1994 with Cecile Zervoudaki.

The Mafia.

A Sicilian secret society which emerged spectacularly in the urban Italian sections of the US and is believed to control most organized crime and rackets in that country. Films which have seized on the subject with glee include *The Godfather* (and sequels), *The Black Hand, The Don Is Dead, Pay or Die, The Sicilian Clan, The Brotherhood, Johnny Cool, New York Confidential, The Brothers Rico, Honor Thy Father, The Valachi Papers, Charley Varrick, GoodFellas* and *Mobsters*. In America the Mafia is sometimes known as Cosa Nostra ('our thing' or 'our cause'): the word is an acronym for Morte Alla Francia Italia Anela ('Death to the French is Italy's cry').

❝ Let's show those asshole Hollywood fruitcakes that they can't get away with it as if nothing's happened. Let's hit Sinatra. Or I could whack out a couple of those other guys, Lawford and Martin, and I could take the nigger and put his other eye out. – *Johnny Formosa to his boss, gangster Sam Giancana, after Dean Martin had ignored a demand that he perform in Chicago, as recorded by an FBI wiretap*

magicians

have always had a fascination for film-makers, who on the whole preferred to have their tricks finally discredited, as with Cesar Romero in *Charlie Chan on Treasure Island* and *Two on a Guillotine*, Dante in *A-Haunting We Will Go*, Vincent Price in *The Mad Magician*, Jules Berry in *Le Jour Se Lève*, Harold Lloyd in *Movie Crazy* and Tony Curtis in *Houdini*. The most splendidly genuine magician was the sorcerer in *Fantasia*, but Cecil Kellaway was an amiable warlock in *I Married a Witch*, and Edmund Lowe was chilling as *Chandu*. The 1927 version of Somerset Maugham's book *The Magician* contributed a caricature of Aleister Crowley; *The Magician* is also the title of a 1973 TV series starring Bill Bixby. The best 'live' act on film may be Orson Welles sawing Marlene Dietrich in half in *Follow the Boys*.

Magnificent Obsession.

The tear-jerking novel by Lloyd C. Douglas, about an irresponsible playboy who becomes a surgeon and not only cures but falls in love with the woman he accidentally blinded, was filmed in 1935 by John M. Stahl, with Robert Taylor and Irene Dunne, and again in 1954 by Douglas Sirk, with Rock Hudson and Jane Wyman.

Maigret.

The police commissioner created by French novelist Georges Simenon has been played by many actors on screen and television since 1932: Pierre Renoir, Harry Baur, Abel Tarride, Albert Prejean, Michel Simon, Maurice Manson, and Jean Gabin in French films, Heinz Ruhmann in a German film, and Charles Laughton in the American *The Man on the Eiffel Tower* 49. On television, the role has been taken by Basil Sydney, Rupert Davies, and Michael Gambon.

Maisie.

The hard-boiled (but soft-centred) gold-digging showgirl was played by Ann Sothern in 10 MGM comedy-dramas: *Maisie* 39; *Congo Maisie* 40; *Gold Rush Maisie* 40; *Maisie Was a Lady* 41; *Ringside Maisie* 41; *Maisie Gets Her Man* 42; *Swing Shift Maisie* 43; *Maisie Goes to Reno* 44; *Up Goes Maisie* 46; *Undercover Maisie* 47. Sothern survived the type-casting to go on to bigger and better films.

male impersonation:

see TRANSVESTISM.

The Maltese Falcon.

Dashiell Hammett's brilliantly written crime story was filmed three times by Warner. In 1931 it starred Bebe Daniels and Ricardo Cortez and was directed by Roy del Ruth; in 1936 it appeared as *Satan Met a Lady*, directed by William Dieterle, with Bette Davis and Warren William. The definitive version, however, did not come until 1941, when John Huston wrote and directed it with Humphrey Bogart and a rogues' gallery that included Mary Astor, Sydney Greenstreet, Peter Lorre, and Elisha Cook Jnr. A low-budget rip-off, *Target Harry/How to Make It* 68, was made by Roger Corman, understandably hiding his identity under the pseudonym of Harry Neill. Huston spoofed it unsuccessfully in his *Beat the Devil* 54, and David Giler wrote and directed an altogether witless parody, *The Black Bird* 75.

The Man in the Iron Mask.

No one knows what mixture of fact and fiction exists in the famous story of Louis XIV's mysterious prisoner who languished for years in the Bastille, his face always covered (actually with velvet). Some said it was Louis' bastard brother, others an Italian diplomat. Anyway, Dumas wrote an exciting novel on the subject, and it has been filmed twice: in 1929 as *The Iron Mask* with Douglas Fairbanks, and in 1939 by James Whale with Louis Hayward. A TV movie with Richard Chamberlain was made in 1976 and in the following year *The Fifth Musketeer* trod much the same ground. A 1998 version enjoyed some popularity, mainly owing to the presence of Leonardo DiCaprio in twin roles of hero and villain.

The Man Who Knew Too Much.

Alfred Hitchcock twice filmed this thriller about a child held hostage by a gang planning to assassinate an international political figure: in 1934 in Britain, with Leslie Banks, Edna Best, and Peter Lorre; and in America in 1956, with James Stewart, Doris Day, and Bernard Miles. The first version, despite (or, perhaps, because of) its curious studio sets, made incomparably better entertainment. A spoof, *The Man Who Knew Too Little*, starring Bill Murray, was released in 1998, but did poorly at the box-office.

The March of Time.

A highly influential series of two-reelers on current affairs, started and financed in 1935 by the founders of *Time* magazine and film-maker Louis de Rochemont. The raucous American commentary by Westbrook van Voorhis marred it for European consumption, but its contents were a first-class, in-depth examination of what was happening in the world. It ran with great success until the late 40s, when it was gradually replaced by television coverage of world events. Its history was chronicled by Raymond Fielding in his 1977 book *The March of Time*.

Matt Helm.

The laconic hero of a number of self-spoofing secret agent dime novels by Donald Hamilton was personified on screen by a droopy-eyed Dean Martin. Over-sexed and witless, the series represents a rather miserable but commercial 60s blend of high camp, self-indulgence, and comic strip. *The Silencers* 66, *Murderers' Row* 66, *The Ambushers* 67, and *Wrecking Crew* 69 were the titles, and it seemed a point of honour with the producer that the title should have no relevance whatever to the movie. A TV movie, *Matt Helm* 75, starred Tony Franciosa, but the resulting series was brief.

Mau Mau.

The terrorist activities in Kenya during the 50s were the subject of three very savage movies: *Simba* 55, *Safari* 56, *Something of Value* 56.

Merrie Melodies:

see LOONEY TUNES.

The Merry Widow.

Franz Lehar's operetta has been filmed at least four times: in 1925 as a silent by Erich Von Stroheim with John Gilbert, Mae Murray, and Roy D'Arcy; in 1934 by Ernest Lubitsch with Maurice Chevalier and Jeanette MacDonald, with added lyrics by Gus Kahn and Lorenz Hart; in 1952 by Curtis Bernhardt with Fernando Lamas, Lana Turner, and Richard Haydn, with added lyrics by Paul Francis Webster; in 1962, in an Austrian version with Karin Huebner and Peter Alexander.

Merton of the Movies.

The comic American novel by Harry Leon Wilson, about an innocent in Hollywood in the early silent days, has been filmed three times: in 1924 with Glenn Hunter; in 1932, as *Make Me a Star*, with Stuart Erwin; and in 1947 with Red Skelton.

Mexican Spitfire.

A series of American second-feature comedies, concerning a young businessman (Donald Woods) with a temperamental wife (Lupe Velez), a scheming uncle, and a drunken English client, both played by Leon Errol. The films were only tolerably well made, but always managed a hectic finale of impersonation and mistaken identity which allowed full play to Errol's jerky convulsions.

The Girl from Mexico 39. Mexican Spitfire 39. Mexican Spitfire Out West 40. Mexican Spitfire's Baby 41. Mexican Spitfire at Sea 42. Mexican Spitfire Sees a Ghost 42. Mexican Spitfire's Elephant 42. Mexican Spitfire's Blessed Event 43.

Michael Shayne.

The American private eye created by Brett Halliday in a string of 30s novels was a lightly shaded character at best, but sufficed for a number of 'B' features with Lloyd Nolan as star. In 1960 Richard Denning played the lead in a television series.

Michael Shayne, Private Detective 40. Sleepers West 41. Dressed to Kill 41. Blue, White and Perfect 41. The Man Who Wouldn't Die 42. Just off Broadway 42. Time to Kill (adapted from Raymond Chandler's The High Window, not from a Halliday original) 42.

Later, Hugh Beaumont took over the role in some forgettable low-budget mysteries:

Murder Is My Business 46. Larceny in Her Heart 46. Blonde for a Day 46. Three on a Ticket 47. Too Many Winners 47.

Mickey Mouse.

Walt Disney's most famous cartoon character began in the 20s as Mortimer Mouse. By the early 30s his outlines had been simplified and he was perhaps the most certain box-office lure in the world. His voice was supplied by Disney himself (later by Jim MacDonald and Wayne Allwine); his finest hour, perhaps, was in the 'Sorcerer's Apprentice' segment of *Fantasia* 40.

❝ The best known and most popular international figure of his day. – *New York Times, 1935*

A Midsummer Night's Dream.

Shakespeare's fairy play was filmed in America in 1929 by J. Stuart Blackton, starring Maurice Costello, and there is a Czech puppet version by Jiri Trnka. But the best-known version is Max Reinhardt's lavish production for Warner in 1935, directed by Reinhardt and William Dieterle, with a surprising cast including James Cagney as Bottom, Mickey Rooney as Puck, Hugh Herbert, Arthur Treacher, Dick Powell, Anita Louise, Victor Jory, and Olivia de Havilland. Peter Hall's muddy version of 1968, aimed primarily at American television, lacked magic.

Mighty Joe Young

was an oversized gorilla, dreamt up by producer Merian C. COOPER in 1949 to try to repeat his success with King Kong. He re-emerged in 1998 as a 15-foot-tall mountain gorilla with an ecological message for the world: kept for safety in a Californian game reserve, he is threatened by poachers, runs amok through Los Angeles, and proves to be a noble, self-sacrificing beast.

Mighty Mouse.

Rodent superhero of Terrytoons cartoons from the 40s to the 60s and known in his earliest cartoons as Super Mouse. His voice was supplied by Tom Morrison.

The Mouse of Tomorrow 42. Down with Cats 43. Wreck of Hesperus 44. Mighty Mouse and the Pirates 45. Svengali's Cat 46. Swiss Cheese Family Robinson 47. The Catnip Gang 49. A Cat's Tale 51. When Mousehood Was in Flower 53. Outer Space Visitor 59. Cat Alarm 61, etc.

Mike Hammer.

The tough, immoral private eye created by Mickey Spillane.

miniaturization.

Making people small is a theme obviously likely to appeal to the cinema's trick photographers. Characters were reduced by 'scientific' or magic means in *The Devil Doll, Dr Cyclops, The Incredible Shrinking Man*, and *Fantastic Voyage*. *Land of the Giants* showed the other side of the coin. Laurel and Hardy were miniaturized into their own children in *Brats*; other small humans were in *Darby O'Gill and the Little People, The Adventures of Mark Twain* and *The Bride of Frankenstein*. *The Borrowers* 97, based on Mary Norton's children's books, featured a race of tiny people living beneath the floorboards of houses, making use of human rubbish and discarded objects.

mirrors

have a clear psychological fascination, and cameramen have frequently derived dramatic compositions from the use of them. Innumerable characters have talked to their reflections, and *The Man in the Mirror* changed places with his. *Dracula* and his kind cast no reflection; a switch on this was provided in *The Gorgon*, where looking at the monster turned one to stone, but looking at her through a mirror was OK. In *The Lady in the Lake* Robert Montgomery played the lead from the position of the camera lens, so the only time we saw him was when he looked in a mirror. Eric Portman in *Corridor of Mirrors* was surrounded by them: the hero of *The Student of Prague* shot his reflection in one. Then there was the magic mirror in *Snow White and the Seven Dwarfs*, which told the queen all she wanted to hear; and the more evil magic mirror in *Dead of Night*, which had belonged to a murderer and caused Ralph Michael when he looked in it to strangle his wife. Two-way mirrors are now familiar, especially since *From Russia With Love*; but they were used as long ago as 1946 in *The House on 92nd Street*. In *Orphée* a full-length mirror proved liquid to the touch and was the doorway to the other world. *The Lady from Shanghai* had a splendidly confusing finale in a mirror maze which was gradually shot to pieces; *Up Tight* made dramatic use of a distorting mirror arcade. The most-used mirror joke is that in which the glass is broken and a 'double' tries to take the place of the reflection: Max Linder performed it in 1919 in *Seven Years Bad Luck*, and it was superbly reprised by the Marx Brothers in *Duck Soup* 44, and by Abbott and Costello in *The Naughty Nineties* 45.

Les Misérables.

Victor HUGO's novel about Jean Valjean, a reformed convict who is relentlessly pursued by the police chief Jarvet, has been filmed more than 20 times from silent days on, as well as becoming a long-running stage musical (known to its English adherents as *The Glums*). Richard BOLESLAWSKI made the definitive version starring Charles LAUGHTON and Fredric MARCH for United Artists in 1935; Lewis MILESTONE directed a dull adaptation for Twentieth Century-Fox in 1952, with Robert NEWTON and Michael RENNIE; Bille AUGUST did somewhat better with his version in 1998 with Liam NEESON and Geoffrey RUSH. The best French version was made by Raymond BERNARD in 1934, with Harry BAUR and Charles VANEL; it was originally shown in three parts, and later cut to the two-part *Jean Valjean* and *Cosette* (which dealt with the romance between Valjean's adopted daughter and a young student). It was superior to a 1958 version, directed by Jean-Paul LE CHANOIS, despite the fact that the latter starred Jean GABIN and Bernard BLIER. Claude LELOUCH directed an intriguing update on the original in 1995, starring Jean-Paul BELMONDO as a modern-day Valjean.

misnomers

A title has to appeal to the greatest possible number of people. Sometimes it loses its relevance in the progress; sometimes, as in metaphors like *Straw Dogs* and *A Clockwork Orange*, the film-maker is too arrogant to explain it. Here are one or two examples where the irrelevance is still traceable:

The Black Cat. Hardly any of the several films under this title have much to do with Poe's story, and although a black cat may have casually strolled across the scene it has had little bearing on the plot. In Britain the 1934 version was retitled *House of Doom*, which is a little more to the point of the story.

Son of Dracula, like many other horror films, soon proved to have an inapposite label: the protagonist is none other than the old Count himself in disguise. In *Bride of Frankenstein*, the title role is a minor one, played by Valerie Hobson; the real bride is that of the monster. In *Frankenstein Created Woman*, he doesn't: he merely performs some brain-switching. In *Abbott and Costello Meet Frankenstein*, the Baron doesn't appear at all: it's the monster they meet, and he has much less to do with the plot than Dracula or the Wolf Man.

Abbott and Costello were never careful about titles. In *Abbott and Costello Go to Mars*, they go to Venus. And *Abbott and Costello Meet the Killer, Boris Karloff* seems devised purely for equality of billing; it is doubly misleading, for not only is Boris Karloff not a killer, he does not even play a killer in the movie.

The original title *The Thin Man* referred to a minor character in the murder plot. As sequel followed sequel, and continuity had to be maintained, the tag gradually attached itself to the investigator played by William Powell.

The films of W. C. Fields were noted for the studied irrelevance of their titles, the crowning glory being *Never Give a Sucker an Even Break*. Laurel and Hardy were not far behind, as anyone knows who has tried to explain the relevance of *Hog Wild, You're Darn Tootin', Be Big, Wrong Again, Double Whoopee* or *They Go Boom*. Woody Allen is plainly in the great tradition: when asked why he called his movie *Bananas*, he replied, 'Because there are no bananas in it'.

The Glass Bottom Boat is seen in the first sequence of the film titled after it, but it is not essential to that sequence and has no relevance at all to the rest of the movie.

It Happened One Night. Which night? The film covers several, and none is central to the plot.

Big Deal at Dodge City is the British title for *Big Hand for a Little Lady*. It is not only less attractive but wildly inaccurate, as the action is clearly denoted as taking place in Laredo! It was the work of a title fiend operating in Warner's London office, who also turned *An American Dream* into the weirdly irrelevant *See You In Hell, Darling*.

Halls of Montezuma is set in the Pacific, and *To the Shores of Tripoli* never leaves a California training camp. All the titles tell you is that the characters are Marines, from whose marching song the labels are taken.

In *Northwest Passage*, the passage is barely mentioned and never explored. MGM started to film Kenneth Roberts' historical novel in 1939. The script was too long, so they decided to make two films, the first to deal with the training of Rogers' Rangers and the second with their exploits. The second film was never made; the one that exists does have a subtitle, 'Part One: Rogers' Rangers'.

The Silencers, Murderers' Row, The Ambushers: Any reader who can link these Matt Helm titles to their plots deserves a small prize.

Miss Marple.

Agatha Christie's spinster detective Jane Marple, who first appeared in the 1930 mystery *The Murder at the Vicarage*, was played by Margaret Rutherford in four films: *Murder She Said* (from *4.50 from Paddington*) 61, *Murder at the Gallop* (from *After the Funeral*) 63, *Murder Most Foul* (from *Mrs McGinty's Dead*) 64, *Murder Ahoy!* 64 (not based on a Christie original). Angela Lansbury played her in the glossy *The Mirror Crack'd* 80, and her sleuth in the television series *Murder, She Wrote* owes much to the example of Miss Marple. On television, she was first played by Gracie Fields in *A Murder Is Announced* 58 and subsequently by Helen Hayes in *A Caribbean Mystery* 83 and *They Do It with Mirrors* 85, and by Joan Hickson in an 80s BBC-TV series.

missionaries

have not been popular cinema heroes: the most lauded real-life ones were David Livingstone in *Stanley and Livingstone* and Gladys Aylward in *The Inn of the Sixth Happiness*. Over-zealous ones appeared in *Zulu, Hawaii, Seven Women*, the various versions of *Rain, At Play in the Fields of the Lord*, and *The Missionary* itself.

Mr Belvedere.

An acerbic, self-styled genius played by the waspish Clifton Webb in three comedies: *Sitting Pretty* 48, based on Gwen Davenport's novel *Belvedere, Mr Belvedere Goes to College* 49, *Mr Belvedere Rings the Bell* 51.

Mr Magoo.

Myopic, bumbling cartoon character created by UPA in the early 50s and voiced by Jim Backus. He quickly became a bore, but some of the early shorts were outstandingly funny. A live-action version, directed by Stanley Tong and starring Leslie Nielsen, was released in 1997, but it passed by unseen.

Ragtime Bear 49. Spellbound Hound 50. Trouble Indemnity (AAN) 50. Bare Faced Flatfoot 51. Fuddy Duddy Buddy 51. Grizzly Golfer 51. Pink Blue Plums (AAN) 52. When Magoo Flew (AA) 55. Magoo's Puddle Jumper (AA) 56. Meet Mother Magoo 56. Magoo's Private War 57. Terror Faces Magoo 59. Mr Magoo's Christmas Carol (TV) 62, etc.

TV series: The Famous Adventures of Mr Magoo 64–65.

Mr Moto.

A mild-mannered Japanese detective and master of disguise created by novelist John P. Marquand and played in nearly a dozen films by Peter Lorre: from *Think Fast Mr Moto* in 1937 to *Mr Moto Takes a Vacation* in 1939. In 1965 Henry Silva played the role in an unsuccessful second feature.

❝ I wrote about him to get shoes for the baby. – *John P. Marquand*

Mr Wong.

A Chinese detective, James Lee Wong, created by author Hugh Wiley and brought to the screen by Monogram as a counter to Mr Moto who was doing so well for Fox. Boris Karloff, who was not physically suited to the role, played him in five rather feeble second features directed by William Nigh: *Mr Wong, Detective* 38; *Mystery of Mr Wong* 39; *Mr Wong in Chinatown* 39; *The Fatal Hour* 40; *Doomed to Die*/*The Mystery of the Wentworth Castle* 40. Keye Luke took over the role for *Phantom of Chinatown* 41.

Mrs Wiggs of the Cabbage Patch.

Alice Hegan Rice's sentimental shanty-town novel was filmed three times: in 1919 with Mary Carr, in 1934 with Pauline Lord, and in 1943 with Fay Bainter.

Moby Dick.

Herman Melville's allegorical novel about an obsessed sea captain's pursuit of a white whale has been filmed at least three times: *The Sea Beast* 26, directed by Millard Webb with John Barrymore, Dolores Costello, and George O'Hara; *Moby Dick* 30, directed by Lloyd Bacon with John Barrymore, Joan Bennett, and Lloyd Hughes; *Moby Dick* 56, directed by John Huston with Gregory Peck, Richard Basehart, and no female lead. A similar story was served up in *The White Buffalo* 77, directed by J. Lee-Thompson and starring Charles Bronson as Wild Bill Hickok chasing the eponymous beast.

See also: MELVILLE, Herman.

Modesty Blaise.

Dauntless heroine with a shady background and martial arts skills, created by Peter O'Donnell (1920–) for a newspaper comic strip and, subsequently, novels. She was played by Monica Vitti in a camp film, with pop-art decor, directed by Joseph Losey in 1966, and by Ann Turkel in a pilot for a television series. In 1994, rights to the character were bought by Miramax Films with the intention of producing a series of action adventures from 1996.

monks

in films have usually been caricatures of the Friar Tuck type; Tuck himself turned up, personified by Eugene Pallette or Alexander Gauge, in most of the versions of Robin Hood. The funny side of monastery life was presented in *Crooks in Cloisters*, while milder humour came from Edward G. Robinson's conversion to the simple life in *Brother Orchid*. *The Monk*, based on a classic Gothic novel, treated the monastery as a place of demonic passion and sin. Serious crises of the monastic spirit have been treated in two American films, *The Garden of Allah* and *The First Legion*; but on the whole monks have appealed less than priests to film-makers in search of an emotional subject.

See also: NUNS; PRIESTS; CHURCHES.

Monsieur Beaucaire.

Booth Tarkington's light novel about a barber who impersonates the King of France was filmed as a straight romantic vehicle for Rudolph Valentino and Bebe Daniels in 1924, directed by Sidney Olcott. In 1946 Bob Hope had his way with it in a version directed by George Marshall.

monster animals.

The 1924 version of *The Lost World* set a persisting fashion for giant animals operated by technical ingenuity. The supreme achievement in the genre was of course *King Kong*, who carried on in *Son of Kong* and (more or less) in *Mighty Joe Young*. Many films concentrated on normal species which had been giantized by radiation or some other accident of science: *The Black Scorpion, Them, The Deadly Mantis, The Giant Claw, Tarantula, Mysterious Island, Bug, Night of the Lepus, Squirm, Jaws, Food of the Gods*. More fanciful giant animals were created for *Jason and the Argonauts, Jack the Giant Killer* and *The Seventh Voyage of Sinbad*. The 1976 *King Kong* remake mainly featured a man in a gorilla suit, and the fashion of the late 70s and early 80s was for ordinary animals which turned savage, such as *Alligator, Piranha* and *Cujo*.

See also: DINOSAURS.

Monty Python.

An ensemble name for a group of British nonsense comedians who had much influence on television comedy of the 60s and 70s. They include John Cleese, Michael Palin, Terry Gilliam, Eric Idle, Terry Jones and Graham Chapman. Apart from Graham Chapman, who died early, each went on to a successful solo career: Gilliam and Jones as directors, Cleese as a writer and actor, Idle as an actor, and Palin as an actor, writer and a televised explorer.

Book: 1998, *The Monty Python Encyclopedia* by Robert Ross.

■ And Now for Something Completely Different 71. *Monty Python and the Holy Grail* 75. *The Life of Brian* 79. Monty Python Live at the Hollywood Bowl 82. Monty Python's Meaning of Life 83.

❝ What were we trying to achieve? Silliness. We tried to create something that was unpredictable, that had no parameters. Perhaps the fact that Pythonic is now in the dictionary is a measure of our failure. – *Terry Jones*

morticians:

see UNDERTAKERS.

'The Most Dangerous Game'.

Richard Connell's well-known short story concerned a mad sportsman who trapped human beings on a tropical island in order to hunt them and display their heads in the trophy room. The first film version (GB: *The Hounds of Zaroff*) was produced in 1932 by Merian C. Cooper, directed by Ernest Schoedsack and Irving Pichel, starring Leslie Banks. In 1945 it was remade as *Game of Death*, with Edgar Barrier; in 1948 Johnny Allegro borrowed liberally from it, with George Macready shooting arrows at George Raft; *Kill or Be Killed* in 1950 had George Coulouris as the menace; *The Black Castle* in 1952, directed by Nathan Juran with Boris Karloff, set the story in the 18th century. In 1954 *The Black Forest*, directed by Gene Martel, was a dull 'B' feature; *Run for the Sun* in 1956 made Trevor Howard a refugee Nazi in the Brazilian jungle, pursuing unwary intruders with savage hounds. In 1961, *Bloodlust*, directed by Ralph Brooks, was an even worse remake, aimed at the market for teenage horror; 1966 found Cornel Wilde on the run from African headhunters in *The Naked Prey*, which used basically the same story; in 1973 *To Kill a Clown* proved to be yet another retread, as was the TV movie *Maneater*. It cropped up again in 1993 as *Hard Target*, with Jean-Claude Van Damme in the lead, and in 1994 as *Surviving the Game*, directed by Ernest Dickerson with Ice-T as the intended victim. A variation of the plot has become constant in many martial arts movies of the 80s and 90s: a mad entrepreneur kidnaps or blackmails a fighter, forcing him to engage in gladiatorial contests to the death with experts at kick-boxing and other esoteric disciplines.

mother love

has been the driving force of many of the screen's most popular, and therefore most remade, melodramas, such as *Imitation of Life, Madame X, Stella Dallas, Over the Hill, Mrs Wiggs of the Cabbage Patch* and *To Each His Own*. Britain chipped in with *The Woman in the Hall, The White Unicorn*, and *When the Bough Breaks*. Some say that Hitchcock made *Psycho* as the ultimate riposte to this sentimental tendency; but *The Anniversary* came a close second. Nor should mother-motivated gangsters such as those in *White Heat, Villain* and *The Krays* be forgotten, while Melina Mercouri in *Promise at Dawn* and Rosalind Russell in *Gypsy* were perhaps the most sinister mothers of all.

motor-cycles,

hideous and unbearably noisy machines, have become a badge of aggressive youth, and since *The Wild Angels* in 1966 American drive-in screens have been filled with a host of cheap movies extolling the pleasures of leather-jacketed speed with a bird on the back. All of these appear to have been banned in Britain, as was *The Wild One*, an early example of the genre, in 1954. But we did let through Elvis Presley in *Roustabout*, and Steve McQueen doing his own stunt sequence in *The Great Escape*, and *Easy Rider*, and *Coogan's Bluff*, and *Little Fauss and Big Halsy*, and we even made *The Leather Boys*, about our own ton-up teenagers. As for *Girl on a Motorcycle*, in which the bike becomes the ultimate sex symbol, words fail one. There was a good British film about speedway racing, *Once a Jolly Swagman*, and one about the fairground called *Wall of Death*. Comedian George Formby went in for the TT races in *No Limit*, and rode a motor-bike also in *It's In the Air*. Groucho Marx used one to comic effect in *Duck Soup*, as did Horst Buchholz in *One, Two, Three*. In American films, the motor-cycle cops are too familiar to warrant individual attention but *Electra Glide in Blue* took one seriously. *Easy Rider*, almost an *hommage* to the machine, is also the most successful film to feature it.

motor racing

has been the subject of many a routine melodrama, and always seems to reduce the writer to banalities, even in a spectacular like *Grand Prix*. Some other examples of the genre include *The Crowd Roars*,

Indianapolis Speedway, *Checkpoint*, *The Green Helmet*, *The Devil's Hairpin*, *Red Line 7000*, *Le Mans*, *Winning* and *Days of Thunder*. The funniest comedy use of the sport was probably in *Ask a Policeman*, when Will Hay accidentally drove a bus on to Brooklands racetrack in the middle of a race.

mountains

have provided a challenge in innumerable movies including *The Challenge*, *The White Tower*, *The Mountain*, *The White Hell of Pitz Palu*, *The Gold Rush*, *Trail of 98*, *The Eiger Sanction*, *The Snows of Kilimanjaro*, *The Abominable Snowman*, *Lost Horizon*, *Goodbye Mr Chips*, *K2* and *Scream of Stone*.

movies

The cinema is an art. Movies are . . . well, movies. Are they a good thing? To Cecil B. de Mille they were:

The new literature.

To Barbara Streisand, starting to shoot *Funny Girl*:

This is for posterity. Everything I do will be on film forever.

To Sarah Bernhardt they were:

My one chance for immortality.

Darryl F. Zanuck called them:

The greatest political fact in the world today.

Sam Spiegel was careful in his commendation:

The best motion pictures are those which reach you as entertainment, and by the time you leave have provoked thoughts. A picture that provokes no thoughts is usually not well conceived and does not entertain one anyway.

Warren Beatty gave a verbal shrug:

Movies are fun, but they're not a cure for cancer.

In Ava Gardner's experience:

It's the kissiest business in the world. You have to keep kissing people.

Ben Hecht took the money and ran:

Movies are one of the bad habits that have corrupted our century.

and:

They have slipped into the American mind more misinformation in one evening than the Dark Ages could muster in a decade.

and:

A movie is never any better than the stupidest man connected with it.

David O. Selznick was thoughtful:

There might have been good movies if there had been no movie industry.

St John Ervine had little time for them:

American movies are written by the half-educated for the half-witted.

H. L. Mencken similarly called them:

Entertainment for the moron majority. And added:

The kind of jackass who likes the movies as they are is the kind who keeps them as they are.

And again:

No one ever went broke underestimating the taste of the American public.

Stephen Longstreet knew the root of the trouble:

In the Hollywood studios, the mass attack of a mob of halfwits in sport shirts and fifty-dollar shoes stamps any real idea to death before it leaves the studio.

S. J. Perelman summed up his own experiences:

Movie scriptwriting is no worse than playing piano in a call house.

Pare Lorentz was a shade more hopeful:

There's no trick to movies. All the businessman needs to do is to employ a fine playwright, a group of good actors, a skilful cameraman, and put them all under the direction of a man who understands the possibilities of the camera and who has besides a comic gift, charm, and dramatic skill – leave them to work unchecked – and he'll get popular entertainment almost every time.

Ivan Butler despaired:

Whoever has the original idea for a movie, it is soon taken away from him.

E. B. White in 1956 saw a gleam of light:

The movies long ago decided that a wider commercial exploitation could be achieved by a deliberate descent to a lower level, and they walked downhill till they found the cellar. Now they are groping for the light switch, looking for the way out.

Robert E. Sherwood was scathing in 1922:

Who invented hokum? Think how much money he'd have made from the film producers if he'd sold his invention on a royalty basis!

Will Rogers was satirical:

There's only one thing that can kill the movies, and that's education.

Maybe Robert Mitchum has the last word:

What's history going to say about the movies? All those rows of seats facing a blank screen? Crazy!

Meanwhile, a few tips on the making of movies:

You should think of each shot as you make it as the most important one in the film. – *Henry Blanke*

Don't act, think! – *F.W. Murnau*

Making a film is like going down a mine – once you've started you bid a metaphorical goodbye to the daylight and the outside world for the duration. – *John Schlesinger*

In a good movie, the sound could go off and the audience would still have a perfectly clear idea of what was going on. – *Alfred Hitchcock*

If we can make films that are useful as well as entertaining, marvellous. But cinema must reflect the temper of the times. We must choose material not only on the basis of whether we feel deeply, but on whether or not anyone's bloody well going to see it. – *Richard Lester*

Me, if I can't blow up the world in the first ten seconds, the show is a flop. – *Irwin Allen*

You can't overthrow regimes through movies, but it can help. – *J.A. Bardem*

I believe that although the motion picture may not live forever as a work of art, except in a few instances, it will be the most efficient way of showing posterity how we live now. – *Irving Thalberg*

Ninety-five per cent of films are born of frustration, of self-despair, of ambition for survival, for money, for fattening bank accounts. Five per cent, maybe less, are made because a man has an idea, an idea which he must express. – *Samuel Fuller*

The movie is a reflector and not an innovator. – *Jack Valenti*

The cinema is not a slice of life, it's a piece of cake. – *Alfred Hitchcock*

Movies, like detective stories, make it possible to experience without danger all the excitement, passion and desirousness which must be suppressed in a humanitarian ordering of society. – *Carl Jung*

They may cost a lot, but none of the money is wasted. All my pictures can be reissued again and again. They stand up pretty well, and they retain their residual values, both financial and prestige-wise. – *Sam Spiegel*

Messages are for Western Union. – *Sam Goldwyn*

There's too much pretentious nonsense talked about the artistic problems of making pictures. I've never had a goddam artistic problem in my life, never, and I've worked with the best of them. – *John Wayne*

Let me tell you what this business is about. It's cunt and horses! – *Harry Cohn*

Some critics say that people complain about the movies because the movies do not reflect reality. It is this writer's suspicion that more people lament the fact that reality does not reflect the movies. – *Leo Rosten*

I know audiences feed on crap, but I can't believe we are so lacking that we cannot dish it up to them with some trace of originality. – *Darryl F. Zanuck*

The public is never wrong. – *Adolph Zukor*

multiple roles.

The record for the number of characters played by one actor in a film is held not by Alec Guinness in *Kind Hearts and Coronets* but (probably) by Lupino Lane, who played twenty-four parts in a 1929 comedy called *Only Me*, by Buster Keaton in *The Playhouse*, or by George S. Melies in his 1900 film *The One Man Band*. Others with high scores, apart from Guinness' eight, include Robert Hirsch's dozen in *No Questions on Saturday*, Rod Steiger's seven in *No Way to Treat a Lady*, Paul Muni's seven in *Seven Faces*, Jerry Lewis' seven in *The Family Jewels*, Tony Randall's seven in *The Seven Faces of Dr Lao*, Hugh Herbert's six in *La Conga Nights*, Peter Sellers' six in *Soft Beds, Hard Battles*, Fernandel's six in *The Sheep Has Five Legs*, Anna Neagle's four in *Lilacs in the Spring*, Françoise Rosay's four in *Une Femme Disparait*, Louis Jourdan's and Joan Fontaine's four each in *Decameron Nights*, Rod Steiger's and Claire Bloom's four each in *The Illustrated Man*, Lionel Jeffries' four in *The Secret of My Success*, Alan Young's four in *Gentlemen Prefer Brunettes*, Terry Kilburn's four generations of boy in *Goodbye Mr Chips*, Moira Shearer's three in *The Man Who Loved Redheads*, Deborah Kerr's three in *The Life and Death of Colonel Blimp*, Peter Sellers' three in *The Mouse That Roared* and *Dr Strangelove*, Leon Errol's three in some episodes of the *Mexican Spitfire* series, Joanne Woodward's three in *The Three Faces of Eve* and Eleanor Parker's three in *Lizzie*. One should perhaps also count Danny Kaye's various dream selves in *The Secret Life of Walter Mitty*.

Dual roles have frequently been of the schizophrenic type of which *Dr Jekyll and Mr Hyde* is the most obvious example. This category includes Henry Hull in *Werewolf of London* and Lon Chaney Jnr in *The Wolf Man*, Phyllis Calvert in *Madonna of the Seven Moons*, Phyllis Thaxter in *Bewitched*, Jerry Lewis in *The Nutty Professor*, Alec Guinness in *The Captain's Paradise* and Jeremy Irons in *Dead Ringers*. Two-character roles include Ronald Colman in *The Masquerader* and *The Prisoner of Zenda*, Lon Chaney in *London After Midnight*, Edward G. Robinson in *The Man with Two Faces*, Laurel and Hardy in *Our Relations*, Allan Jones and Joe Penner in *The Boys from Syracuse*, Chaplin in *The Great Dictator*, Louis Hayward in *The Man in the Iron Mask*, Olivia de Havilland in *The Dark Mirror*, Boris Karloff in *The Black Room*, Herbert Lom in *Dual Alibi*, George M. Cohan in *The Phantom President*, Jack Palance in *House of Numbers*, Peter Whitney in *Murder He Says*, Elisabeth Bergner (and later Bette Davis) in *Stolen Life*, Bette Davis in *Dead Ringer*, Yul Brynner in *The Double Man*, Stanley Baxter in *Very Important Person*, Peter Lawford in *One More Time*, George Arliss in *His Lordship*, Alain Delon in *The Black Tulip*, John McIntire in *The Lawless Breed*, Valentino in *Son of the Sheik*, Jack Mulhall in *Dark Streets* (allegedly the first to use the split-image technique), Larry Parks (playing Jolson *and* himself) in *Jolson Sings Again*, Douglas Fairbanks Jnr in *The Corsican Brothers*, Jessie Matthews in *Evergreen* and Julie Christie in *Fahrenheit 451*.

multiple-story films

probably began in 1916 with *Intolerance*, which audiences rejected as too complicated. Later attempts made sure that the stories were clearly woven into a common thread; *The Bridge of San Luis Rey* in 1929, *Grand Hotel* in 1932, *Friday the Thirteenth* and *Dinner at Eight* in 1933, *Un Carnet de Bal* (also known as *Christine*) in 1936, *Tales of Manhattan* in 1942, *Forever and a Day* in 1942, *Flesh and Fantasy* in 1943, *Weekend at the Waldorf* and *Dead of Night* in 1945. In 1948–50 three Somerset Maugham compendiums, introduced by the author, emerged as *Quartet*, *Trio* and *Encore*; this inspired O. Henry's *Full House* in 1952. In 1963 we had *The VIPs* and in 1964 *The Yellow Rolls-Royce*, the stories in the latter being very casually linked. Meanwhile horror compendiums were becoming popular, 1962's *Tales of Terror* being followed between 1967 and 1972 by *Dr Terror's House of Horrors*, *The Torture Garden*, *The House that Dripped Blood*, *Tales From the Crypt*, *Asylum*, *Vault of Horror*, *Tales that Witness Madness*, *From Beyond the Grave*, *The Monster Club*, *Creepshow* and *Cat's Eyes*.

multi-screen techniques

are nothing new, but the Montreal Exhibition of 1967 made them fashionable again, so that in such films as *The Boston Strangler*, *Grand Prix* and *The Thomas Crown Affair* the audience was supposed to look at up to a dozen different images at the same time, which became mighty exhausting. Mercifully, the fashion soon wore off.

The Mummy.

Interest in avenging mummies was aroused during the 20s by the widespread stories of the curse of Tutankhamen whose tomb had recently been discovered and opened. In 1932 Karl Freund directed a rather strange romantic film on the subject with Boris Karloff as a desiccated but active three-thousand-year-old still on the track of his lost love. Despite good box office it was not reprised until 1940, when *The Mummy's Hand*, a pure hokum thriller, appeared with Tom Tyler in the role. Between 1942 and 1944 there were three increasingly foolish sequels starring (if it really *was* him under the bandages) Lon Chaney Jnr: they were *The Mummy's Tomb*, *The Mummy's Ghost* and *The Mummy's Curse*. In 1959 Hammer took over the character and remade *The Mummy* with an English Victorian setting: Christopher Lee was the monster. There have been two poor sequels, *The Curse of the Mummy's Tomb* 64 and *The Mummy's Shroud* 66. *Blood From The Mummy's Tomb* 71 did not feature a monster; it was based on a Bram Stoker story. The lighter side of the subject was viewed by Wheeler and Woolsey in *Mummy's Boys* 35, the Three Stooges in *Mummie's Dummies* 38, and Abbott and Costello in *Meet the Mummy* 54. Bram Stoker's novel *The Jewel of Seven Stars* was revived in the cheap and shoddy *Bram Stoker's Legend of the Mummy* 97.

Muppets.

An American cross between marionettes and puppets which came in all sizes and shapes and were stars of the TV series *Sesame Street* from 1969, and their own British TV series *The Muppet Show* 76–80, before moving on to the big screen. The best known characters were Kermit the Frog, Miss Piggy and Fozzie Bear.

The Muppet Movie 79. The Great Muppet Caper 81. The Muppets Take Manhattan 84. A Muppet Christmas Carol 92.

See also: HENSON, Jim; Oz, Frank.

murderers

abound in fictional films, but only a handful of real-life cases have been analysed with any seriousness. There have been several 'lives' of Charlie Peace and Landru, and fantasies about the earlier French 'Bluebeard'. More recently a cold clinical eye was applied to Barbara Graham in *I Want to Live* 57, *Dr Crippen* 64, *The Boston Strangler* 68, John Christie in *Ten Rillington Place* 71. Ruth Ellis was said to have inspired *Yield to the Night* 56 and Leopold and Loeb were plainly the subject of *Compulsion* 58 as well as *Rope* 48. More recent years have brought such case histories as *In Cold Blood* 67, *The Executioner's Song* 82, *Let Him Have It* 91 and *The Young Poisoner's Handbook* 95. TV has done its bit with *Kill Me If You Can* (Caryl Chessman) 77, *The Lindbergh Kidnapping Case* (Bruno Hauptmann) 75 and *Helter Skelter* (Charles Manson) 76.

musical remakes

are becoming thicker on the ground than musical originals. All the following had been filmed at least once before, as straight dramas or comedies with music:

Where's Charley? as *Charley's Aunt*; *Three for the Show* as *My Two Husbands*; *Living It Up* as *Nothing Sacred*; *Carmen Jones* as *Carmen*; *Scrooge* as *A Christmas Carol*; *Step Lively* as *Room Service*; *In the Good Old Summertime* as *The Shop Around The Corner*; *Meet Me After The Show* as *He Married His Wife*; *Annie Get Your Gun* as *Annie Oakley*; *Kismet* as *Kismet*; *The King and I* as *Anna and the King of Siam*; *Carousel* as *Liliom*; *High Society* as *The Philadelphia Story*; *Silk Stockings* as *Ninotchka*; *Gigi* as *Gigi*; *My Fair Lady* as *Pygmalion*; *The Sound of Music* as *The Trapp Family*; *Funny Girl* as *Rose of Washington Square*; *Sweet Charity* as *Nights of Cabiria*; *Camelot* as *Lancelot and Guinevere*; *Oliver!* as *Oliver Twist*; *Hello Dolly* as *The Matchmaker*; *Cabaret* as *I Am a Camera*; *Fiddler on the Roof* as *Tevye the Milkman*; *Mame* as *Auntie Mame*; *Lost Horizon* as *Lost Horizon*; *Goodbye Mr Chips* as *Goodbye Mr Chips*; *A Star Is Born* as *What Price Hollywood?* (and in 1937 as *A Star is Born*).

musicals

obviously could not exist before Al Jolson sang 'Mammy', in 1927. During the first two or three years of talkies, however, Hollywood produced so many gaudy back-stage stories and all-star spectacles that the genre quickly wore out its welcome:

Broadway Melody, *The Singing Fool*, *The Desert Song*, *Showboat*, *Chasing Rainbows*, *Show of Shows*, *Hollywood Revue*, *Lights of New York*, *On with the Show*, *King of Jazz*, *Gold Diggers of Broadway*, *Sunny Side Up* . . . all these before the end of 1930, and there were many poorer imitations. Discipline was needed, and the disciplinarian who emerged was Broadway dance director Busby Berkeley. His kaleidoscopic ensembles first dazzled the eye in Goldwyn–Cantor extravaganzas like *Whoopee* and *Palmy Days*, and came to full flower in the Warner musicals which brought to the fore stars like Joan Blondell, Ruby Keeler and Dick Powell, filling the years from 1933 to 1937 with such shows as *Footlight Parade*, *Forty-Second Street*, *Dames*, *Wonder Bar*, *Flirtation Walk* and the annual *Gold Digger* comedies. Meanwhile at Paramount Lubitsch had been quietly establishing a quieter style, using recitative, with *The Love Parade* and *One Hour with*

You; Mamoulian was equally successful with *Love Me Tonight*; and the Marx Brothers contributed their own brand of musical anarchy. From 1933 to 1939 at RKO Fred Astaire and Ginger Rogers were teamed in an affectionately-remembered series of light comedy-musicals. MGM made sporadic efforts with creaky vehicles like *Cuban Love Song* but did not come into their own until 1935, when they started the Jeanette MacDonald/Nelson Eddy series of operettas; these were followed by a dramatic musical, *The Great Ziegfeld*, by the Eleanor Powell spectaculars like *Rosalie*, by a revived *Broadway Melody* series, and by *The Wizard of Oz* and the early Judy Garland/Mickey Rooney teenage extravaganzas, *Babes in Arms* and *Strike Up the Band*. Fox had Shirley Temple, Sonja Henie and Alice Faye; Goldwyn contributed Cantor and *The Goldwyn Follies*. Paramount concentrated on Maurice Chevalier, Bing Crosby and the all-star *Big Broadcast* series.

The popularity of musicals continued into the war-torn 40s, when escapism was *de rigueur*. Universal, whose only major pre-war musical was *Showboat*, continued to build up Deanna Durbin and threw in Donald O'Connor and Gloria Jean for good measure. Warners had *This Is the Army* and several musical biopics: *Yankee Doodle Dandy*, *Night and Day*, *Rhapsody in Blue*. RKO had a young man named Sinatra. Fox found goldmines in Carmen Miranda and Betty Grable, but their vehicles were routine; Columbia did slightly better by Rita Hayworth, and then surprised everyone with *The Jolson Story*, which set the musical back on top just when it was flagging. Paramount was doing very nicely with Bing Crosby and Bob Hope. Everybody did at least one big morale-building musical with all the stars on the payroll blowing kisses to the boys out there: *Star-Spangled Rhythm*, *Thank Your Lucky Stars*, *Hollywood Canteen*, *Thousands Cheer* and so on.

Top dog in the 40s and 50s was undoubtedly MGM. Specialities like *Ziegfeld Follies*, *Till the Clouds Roll By* and *Words and Music* came side by side with more routine productions starring Gene Kelly, Judy Garland, and Esther Williams (in aqua-musicals, of course). The decade ended in a blaze of glory with *On the Town*, which led to the even more spectacular heights of *An American in Paris* and *Singin' in the Rain*. By this time Mario Lanza and Howard Keel were needing new vehicles for themselves, *The Great Caruso* and *Seven Brides for Seven Brothers* being outstanding productions in their own right. But by the mid-50s the demand, or the fashion, for musicals was dying. It lasted longest at Metro, who doggedly remade pictures like *The Belle of New York* and *Rose Marie*, added music to *Ninotchka* and *The Philadelphia Story* and *Gigi*. Warners plugged on until their bright star of 1948, Doris Day, signed with another studio and turned dramatic; Fox had two mammoth tries in *Call Me Madam* and *There's No Business Like Show Business*; Paramount came up with *White Christmas*, the enterprising *Red Garters* and *Funny Face*, and even *Li'l Abner*. But the risk was becoming too great in a chancy market, with expenses growing by the minute; and in the 60s no original musicals were written in Hollywood, with the exception of the family-aimed *Mary Poppins*, *Thoroughly Modern Millie* and the twenty-odd look-alike vehicles of Elvis Presley. Copper-bottomed Broadway hits like *Pal Joey*, *Oklahoma*, *Carousel*, *The Pajama Game*, *South Pacific*, *The King and I*, *West Side Story*, *Guys and Dolls*, *Hello Dolly*, *On a Clear Day You Can See Forever*, *Fiddler on the Roof*, *Man of La Mancha*, *The Sound of Music* and *My Fair Lady* were still filmed, at gargantuan cost, but as cinema they all too often disappointed filmgoers with memories of Berkeley and Kelly and Donen. Amongst the most inventive screen musicals have been Bob Fosse's *Sweet Charity* and *Cabaret*. In the 90s, the success of the Disney animated features *The Little Mermaid*, *Aladdin*, *The Lion King* and, especially, *Beauty and the Beast* promised to revive the musical in a different form. Indeed, Disney turned *Beauty and the Beast* into a successful Broadway musical in 1994.

In Britain, the 30s were a highpoint of the light musical, starring such talents as Jack Buchanan, Jessie Matthews, Gracie Fields, George Formby and Anna Neagle; Miss Neagle indeed carried on, dauntless, into the less favourable climate of the 50s. The 40s were pretty barren apart from the Rank spectacular *London Town*, which flopped; and it wasn't until the 60s that Elstree struck something like the right note with its energetic though derivative series starring Cliff Richard. In 1968 the old-fashioned though energetic *Oliver!* proved that Britain can handle a really big musical. The 70s brought little but rock operas and one or two curiously old-fashioned stagings of such as *Mame* and *1776*, until John Travolta spurred a new trend with *Saturday Night Fever* and a nostalgic one with *Grease*. *Flashdance* and *Breaking* started new forms, and *A Chorus Line*, long promised, was finally made in 1984, by which time most Broadway musicals had become too expensive to film. A disastrous attempt to revive the film musical was made in 1994 with *I'll Do Anything*, directed by James L. Brooks and starring Nick Nolte. Eleven of its 12 songs were removed during previews, after some of the audience walked out. The form survived only in Alan Menken and Howard Ashman's songs for Disney's animated features such as *The Little Mermaid* 89, *Beauty and the Beast* 91, which in a reversal of the usual trend was turned into a Broadway musical, and *Aladdin* 92, and, with various songwriters, *The Lion King* 94 and *Pocahontas* 95. Whether there is any long-term future for the musical other than as an accompaniment to animation may depend on the success or otherwise of Andrew Lloyd Webber's *Evita*, directed by Alan Parker, which has taken 19 years from its first stage performance in 1978 to reach the cinema.

Books: *Gotta Sing Gotta Dance* by John Kobal. *The Hollywood Musical* by John Russell Taylor. *All Singing, All Dancing* by John Springer. 1987, *The American Film Musical* by Rick Altman.

See also: ENTERTAINERS.

Mutiny on the Bounty.

Three films have been made of this semi-historical account of how Captain Bligh was cast adrift in an open boat in 1787: the first was directed in 1935 by Frank Lloyd with Clark Gable and Charles Laughton, in a performance that launched a thousand impersonations; the second, in 1962, was directed by Carol Reed (who resigned) and Lewis Milestone, with Marlon Brando and Trevor Howard; the most recent, *The Bounty*, was directed by Roger Donaldson in Australia in 1984, with Anthony Hopkins and Mel Gibson.

My Man Godfrey.

The crazy comedy about a family of bored millionaires brought to heel by a butler they pick up in the gutter has been filmed twice: in 1936 by Gregory La Cava with William Powell and Carole Lombard; and in 1957 by Kenry Koster with David Niven and June Allyson.

My Sister Eileen.

The stories by Ruth McKenney about two sisters on the hunt for fame and men in New York was turned first into a play and then a film by Joseph Fields and Jerome Chodorov; directed by Alexander Hall, it starred Rosalind Russell and Janet Sherwood as the sisters; Richard Quine remade it in 1955 as a semi-musical with Betty Garrett and Janet Leigh. A Broadway musical of 1953, *Wonderful Town*, was also based on the stories, and there was a TV series with Elaine Stritch and Shirley Bonne, 1960–61. (In real life, Eileen McKenney married writer Nathanael West and died with him in a car crash.)

mystery

has always been a popular element of motion picture entertainment. Always providing scope for sinister goings-on and sudden revelations, mystery films divide themselves into two basic genres: who done it, and how will the hero get out of it? Silent melodramas like *The Perils of Pauline* were full of clutching hands and villainous masterminds, devices adopted by the German post-war cinema for its own purposes: *The Cabinet of Dr Caligari*, *Dr Mabuse* and *Warning Shadows* are all mysteries, peopled by eccentrics and madmen. American silent who-done-its like *The Cat and the Canary*, *The Thirteenth Chair* and *One Exciting Night* set a pattern for thrillers which could not come fully into their own until music and sound were added. In the 30s the 'thunderstorm mystery', with its spooky house and mysterious servants (the butler usually did it) quickly became a cliché; but this is not to denigrate the entertainment value of such movies as *The Bat*, *The Terror*, *Murder by the Clock*, *The Gorilla*, *Seven Keys to Baldpate*, *Double Door*, *You'll Find Out*, *Topper Returns*, *The House on Haunted Hill*, and the Bob Hope remakes of *The Cat and the Canary* and *The Ghost Breakers*.

The 30s also saw a movement to relegate the puzzle film to the detective series, a genre later taken over eagerly by TV. These films were built around such protagonists as Charlie Chan, Sherlock Holmes, Hercule Poirot, Inspector Hanaud, Ellery Queen, Perry Mason, Inspector Hornleigh, Nero Wolfe, Philo Vance, Nick Carter, The Crime Doctor, The Saint, The Falcon, Bulldog Drummond, Mrs Pym, the 'Thin Man' (the thin man was actually the victim of the first story, but the tag stuck to William Powell), Mr Moto, Michael Shayne, Hildegarde Withers, Mr Wong, Arsène Lupin, Dick Barton, The Baron, The Toff, Gideon, Slim Callaghan, Lemmy Caution and Maigret . . . all soundly spoofed by Groucho Marx as Wolf J. Flywheel in *The Big Store*. The best of these fictional detectives were the creations of Dashiell Hammett (Sam Spade in *The Maltese Falcon*) and Raymond Chandler (Philip Marlowe in *The Big Sleep*, *Farewell My Lovely* and *The High Window*); and after a twenty-year hiatus the threads were picked up by Ross MacDonald's *Harper*, Craig Stevens as *Gunn*, Frank Sinatra as *Tony Rome*, films of Chandler's *Marlowe* and J.D. MacDonald's *Darker Than Amber*, and Richard Roundtree as *Shaft*. Single who-done-its of great merit were *Gaslight*, *Laura*, *Green for Danger* (one ached for a whole series starring Alastair Sim as Inspector Cockrill), *The Spiral Staircase*, *Crossfire*, *Boomerang*, *Bad Day at Black Rock*, *Les Diaboliques*, *Charade*, *Mirage*, *Taste of Fear*, *The List of Adrian Messenger*, and the two versions of *Ten Little Niggers*. Two gentler detectives were provided by Alec Guinness' *Father Brown* and Margaret Rutherford's Miss Marple.

The other type of mystery, with a hero on the run, usually suspected of murder, finally uncovering the real villain after many narrow escapes from death, was developed by Alfred Hitchcock in such films as *The Thirty-Nine Steps*, *The Lady Vanishes*, *Saboteur*, *Spellbound*, *Strangers on a Train*, *North by Northwest* and *Torn Curtain*. But stars as various as Alan Ladd, Bob Hope, Danny Kaye, Robert Mitchum and Paul Newman have also found the device useful.

The recent vogue for tongue-in-cheek spy thrillers is to all intents and purposes a reversion to the Pearl White school, with the hero menaced at every turn but, of course, finally triumphant.

Useful books: *The Detective in Film* by William K. Everson. *The Detective in Hollywood* by Jon Tuska.

See also: SPIES; PRIVATE EYES.

The Mystery of the Wax Museum.

This badly structured but interesting shocker in two-colour Technicolor, with sets by Anton Grot and direction by Michael Curtiz, survives as a milestone of its era, with Lionel Atwill as a mad sculptor who uses a wax face to disguise his hideously burned features. In 1953, the story was remade in 3-D as *House of Wax*, starring Vincent Price, and in 1966 most of it turned up again in *Chamber of Horrors*.

Nana.

Zola's novel of the Paris demi-monde in the 1860s has been seen in four major film versions: a silent French film directed by Jean Renoir in 1926, with Catherine Hessling and Werner Krass; an American version, sometimes known as *The Lady of the Boulevards*, directed by Dorothy Arzner in 1934, with Anna Sten, Lionel Atwill, and Phillips Holmes; a second French version, directed by Christian-Jaque in 1955, with Martine Carol and Charles Boyer; a Franco-Swedish version, *Take Me, Love Me*, directed by Mac Ahlberg, with Anna Gael.

Nancy Drew.

The teenage heroine, created by Carolyn Keene (one of many pseudonyms used by the team of Edward Stratemeyer and Harriet Adams), appeared in a series of second features made by Warner, directed by William Clemens and starring Bonita Granville: *Nancy Drew, Detective* 38; *Nancy Drew – Reporter* 39; *Nancy Drew – Troubleshooter* 39; *Nancy Drew and the Hidden Staircase* 39. A television series, *The Nancy Drew Mysteries*, ran from 1977–78, starring Pamela Sue Martin.

narrators

are heard at the beginning of many important movies. Well-known actors are normally used, but sometimes take no credit. Here is a selected checklist to silence nagging doubts:

Arizona Bushwhackers: James Cagney.
Barry Lyndon: Michael Hordern.
The Big Knife: Richard Boone.
Casablanca: Lou Marcelle.
The Curse of King Tutankhamun's Tomb: Paul Scofield.
Desert Rats: Michael Rennie.
Dragon Seed: Lionel Barrymore.
Duel in the Sun: Orson Welles.
The Hallelujah Trail: John Dehner.
How Green Was My Valley: Irving Pichel.
How the West Was Won: Spencer Tracy.
The Human Comedy: Ray Collins.
An Ideal Husband: Ralph Richardson.
It's a Big Country: Louis Calhern.
Khartoum: Leo Genn.
King of Kings: Orson Welles.
Kings of the Sun: James Coburn.
A Letter to 3 Wives: Celeste Holm.
Mackenna's Gold: Victor Jory.
The Master of Ballantrae: Robert Beatty.
Mother Wore Tights: Anne Baxter.
The Mummy's Shroud: Peter Cushing.
The Night They Raided Minsky's: Rudy Vallee.
The Picture of Dorian Gray: Cedric Hardwicke.
Quo Vadis: Walter Pidgeon.
The Red Badge of Courage: James Whitmore.
The Reivers: Burgess Meredith.
Repeat Performance: John Ireland.
Romeo and Juliet (1968): Laurence Olivier.
The Secret Heart: Hume Cronyn.
The Solid Gold Cadillac: George Burns.
The Story of Jacob and Joseph: Alan Bates.
Summer of 42: Robert Mulligan.
The Swiss Family Robinson: Orson Welles.
The Third Man: Wilfrid Thomas.
Those Magnificent Men in Their Flying Machines: James Robertson Justice.
To Hell and Back: John McIntire.
To Kill a Mockingbird: Kim Stanley.
Tom Jones: Micheal MacLiammoir.
The Unseen: Ray Collins.
The Vikings: Orson Welles.
The Wild Heart: Joseph Cotten.
The War of the Worlds: Cedric Hardwicke.
Zulu: Richard Burton.

naval comedy

in British movies usually has a 30s look about it, may well be written by Ian Hay, and almost always concerns the officers; as in *The Middle Watch*, *Carry On Admiral*, *The Midshipmaid*, *The Flag Lieutenant* and *Up the Creek* (though the other ranks had their look in with *The Bulldog Breed*, *The Baby and the Battleship* and *Jack Ahoy*). In Hollywood movies the focus of interest is set firmly among the other ranks: *Follow the Fleet*, *Abbott and Costello in the Navy*, *Anchors Aweigh*, *Operation Petticoat*, *Mr Roberts*, *South Pacific*, *Ensign Pulver*, *On the Town*, *You're in the Navy Now*, *The Fleet's In*, *Onion-Head*, *Don't Go Near the Water*, *Don't Give Up the Ship*, *The Honeymoon Machine*, *Down Periscope*.

nepotism.

Hollywood moguls were at one time well known for promoting within the family. Hence the quip: the son-in-law also rises. Hence the rhyme:

Uncle Carl Laemmle
Has a very large faemmle.

Of an untalented Warner relative, Julius Epstein once commented that he had set the son-in-law business back twenty years. And when another gentleman of similar ilk taunted Oscar Levant with 'Oscar, play us a medley of your hit', Oscar came back with 'Okay, play us a medley of your father-in-law.' Of Louis B. Mayer's brother, Irving Brecher remarked: 'Jerry has a very important job and he has to have that big corner office. He's supposed to watch Washington Boulevard and warn everybody to evacuate the studio if icebergs are spotted coming down the street.' Similarly in London, after Alexander Korda's rise to fame and power, it was said that in order to get a job in British films you had to be Hungarian. These days, nepotism seems limited to directors giving their children roles in their films, sometimes with disastrous results.

New York

has provided a vivid backcloth for films of many types, and its skyscrapers allegedly gave Fritz Lang the inspiration for *Metropolis*. Studio re-creations provided the period flavour of *Little Old New York*, *New York Town*, *One Sunday Afternoon*, *A Tree Grows in Brooklyn*, *Incendiary Blonde*, *My Girl Tisa*, and *The Bowery*; and it was a studio city which was wrecked by *King Kong*. But the camera has also explored the real article, notably in thrillers like *Saboteur*, *Naked City*, *Union Station*, *The FBI Story* and *North by Northwest*; in realistic comedy dramas like *From This Day Forward*, *So This is New York*, *Miracle on 34th Street*, *Lovers and Lollipops*, *Marty*, *It Should Happen to You*, *Sunday in New York*, *Breakfast at Tiffany's*, *The Lost Weekend*, *The Bachelor Party*, *A Man Ten Feet Tall*, *A Fine Madness*, *Love with the Proper Stranger*, *The World of Henry Orient*, *Midnight Cowboy*, *The Pawnbroker*, *Barefoot in the Park*, *Beau James*, *The French Connection*, *Cotton Comes to Harlem*, *Shaft*, *The Out-of-Towners*, *Any Wednesday*, *Serpico*, *Bye Bye Braverman*, *Sweet Charity*, *The Seven-Ups*, *The Taking of Pelham One Two Three*, *The Prisoner of Second Avenue*, *Mean Streets*, *Taxi Driver*, *Death Wish* and *Three Days of the Condor*; in hard-hitting social melodramas like *On the Waterfront*, *Sweet Smell of Success*, and *The Young Savages*; and in musicals like *On the Town* and *West Side Story*. Other films which concern the effect of New York without showing much of the actuality include *Mr Deeds Goes to Town*, *Bachelor Mother*, *Lady on a Train*, *Bell, Book and Candle*, *Portrait of Jennie*, *Kid Millions*, *Dead End*, *The Apartment*, *Patterns of Power*, *The Garment Jungle*, *Mr Blandings Builds His Dream House* and *America, America*. Finally Manhattan Island was bought from the Indians by Groucho Marx in *The Story of Mankind*, *Knickerbocker Holiday* pictured the city in its Dutch colonial days as New Amsterdam and *Godspell* used it as a novel background for its revised version of the Life of Christ. Television series with authentic New York locations include *Naked City*, *The Defenders*, *East Side West Side*, *N.Y.P.D.*, *Madigan*, *McCloud*, *Kojak*, *Eischied*.

Nick and Nora Charles.

Married detectives created by Dashiell Hammett in his novel *The Thin Man* 34. In the book, the thin man is the murderer's first victim. Oddly enough, the tag stuck to William Powell (not all that thin), who played Nick Charles and starred in five sequels: *After the Thin Man* 37, *Another Thin Man* 38, *Shadow of the Thin Man* 42, *The Thin Man Goes Home* 44, *Song of the Thin Man* 46. Myrna Loy played Nora in all the features, and it was said that her domestic scenes with Powell in the original film marked the first time a sophisticated, affectionate marriage had been realistically portrayed on the screen. A later TV series, 57–59, starred Peter Lawford and Phyllis Kirk.

Nick Carter.

The tough young American detective, the occidental answer to Sexton Blake, was created in 1886 by Ormond G. Smith (1860–1933) and John Russell Coryell (1848–1924) for the *New York Weekly*. Dozens of hack writers later authored the stories under pseudonyms. Four French films starring André Liabel were made in 1912; Thomas Carrigan appeared in some shorts in 1920; Edmund Lowe had a series in 1924; Walter Pidgeon was in three in 1940; Eddie Constantine in two (French) in 1963 and 1965. From 1943 the character was very popular on radio, but television has made one poorish attempt in 1972, *The Adventures of Nick Carter* starring Robert Conrad.

Nightmare on Elm Street.

A series of low-budget horror movies starring Robert Englund as Freddy Kruger, a child killer who returns from the dead through dreams to kill again. The first, written and directed by Wes Craven, was made for $1.3m and took more than $26m at the American box-office. The sequels were of diminishing interest, although a TV series was spun off from the films. The series seemingly came to an end with the sixth film, *Freddy's Dead: The Final Nightmare* 91, but was revived by the self-referential *Wes Craven's New Nightmare* 94. There are plans, yet to come to fruition, to team Freddy with another killer-hero, the hockey-masked Jason, from the Friday the 13th series.

No Man of Her Own

was the film, starring Barbara STANWYCK, of Cornell WOOLRICH's novel *I Married a Dead Man*. It was also filmed by the French as *I Married a Shadow*, and as *Mrs Winterbourne* by Richard BENJAMIN in 1996, starring Ricki LAKE.

Norman Bates.

The mother-obsessed killer, based on the real-life murderer Ed GEIN, was memorably portrayed by Anthony PERKINS in Alfred HITCHCOCK's *Psycho* and three sequels. Although in the first film his sexual orientation seemed ambiguous, he became more heterosexual in outlook with each sequel. In a 1998 remake of Hitchcock's original, directed by Gus VAN SANT, the role was played by Vince VAUGHN.

Nothing but the Truth.

James Montgomery's Broadway comedy about a man who takes a bet that he can tell the absolute truth for 24 hours was filmed in 1920, with Taylor Holmes; in 1929, with Richard Dix; and in 1941, with Bob Hope.

numbered sequels.

This rather offhand practice probably began in 1956 with *Quatermass II*, but did not really become fashionable until the 70s. Among the successes to label their sequels so casually are *The French Connection*, *Jaws*, *The Sting*, *Mad Max*, *Walking Tall*, *Superman*, *Halloween*, *Death Wish*, *Grease*, *That's Entertainment*, *Piranha*, *Friday the 13th*, *La Cage aux Folles*, *The Amityville Horror*, *Porky's*, *Rocky*, *Airplane*, *The Howling*, *Die Hard*, *The Terminator*, *Predator* and *The Naked Gun*, which spoofed the process, going to 2½ and 33 .

nuns

have been popular figures on the screen, though only in *The Nun's Story* and the Polish *The Devil and the Nun* has any real sense of dedication been achieved; the French *Dialogue des Carmélites* tried hard but failed. Sentimentalized nuns were seen in *The Cradle Song*, *Bonaventure*, *The White Sister*, *Conspiracy of Hearts*, *The Bells of St Mary's*, *Come to the Stable*, *Portrait of Jennie*, *Heaven Knows Mr Allison*, *Black Narcissus*, *Lilies of the Field*, *The Miracle*, *The Song of Bernadette* and *The Sound of Music;* while nuns who combined modern sophistication with sweetness and light afflicted us in *The Singing Nun* and *The Trouble with Angels*, and in *Two Mules for Sister Sara* Shirley Maclaine played a prostitute disguised as a nun. A nun was raped in *Five Gates to Hell*. The most sinister nun was perhaps Catherine Lacey, with her high heels, in *The Lady Vanishes*, but the nuns in *The Trygon Factor* also count. The most agonized nuns were in *The Devils*, *La Religieuse*, and *The Awful Story of the Nun of Monza*. The weirdest was TV's *The Flying Nun*. More recently, they have been a source of amusement: *Dark Habits/Entre Tinieblas*, *Nuns on the Run* and *Sister Act*.

nurses

have inspired biopics (*Sister Kenny*, *The White Angel*, *The Lady with a Lamp*, *Nurse Edith Cavell*); sentimental low-key studies of the profession (*The Lamp Still Burns*, *The Feminine Touch*, *Vigil in the Night*, *No Time for Tears*, *White Corridors*, *Prison Nurse*, *Private Nurse*, *Night Nurse*); even comedies (*Carry On Nurse*, *Twice Round the Daffodils*, *Nurse on Wheels*). *Green for Danger* is probably still the only thriller in which both victim and murderer were nurses. The best satire has been *The National Health* (or *Nurse Norton's Affair*). There was a popular TV series called *Janet Dean Registered Nurse* 53, and later *The Nurses* 62–64. See also HOSPITALS; DOCTORS.

nymphomaniacs

are still fairly rare in normal commercial movies. The fullest studies have been by Suzanne Pleshette in *A Rage to Live*, Françoise Arnoul in *La Rage au Corps*, Claire Bloom in *The Chapman Report*, Merle Oberon in *Of Love and Desire*, Sue Lyon in *Night of the Iguana*, Lee Remick in *The Detective*, Melina Mercouri in *Topkapi*, Maureen Stapleton in *Lonelyhearts*, Jean Seberg in *Road to Corinth*, Elizabeth Taylor in *Butterfield 8*, and Sandra Jullien in *I Am a Nymphomaniac;* but one should not forget Myrna Loy's comic nympho in *Love Me Tonight*.

Of Mice and Men.

John Steinbeck's spare little morality tale about a gentle but homicidal giant who has to be killed by his best friend has been filmed twice: in 1939, directed by Lewis Milestone with Lon Chaney Jnr, Burgess Meredith, and Betty Field; and in 1992, directed by Gary Sinise, starring himself, John Malkovich, and Sherilyn Fenn.

offices

have provided the setting for many a film. *The Crowd* in 1926 and *The Rebel* in 1961 chose pretty much the same way of stressing the dreariness of daily routine; but *Sunshine Susie* in 1931 and *How to Succeed in Business without Really Trying* in 1967 both saw the office as a gay place full of laughter and song. Satyajit Ray in *Company Limited* and Ermanno Olmi in *Il Posto* and *One Fine Day* took a realistic look at office life. Billy Wilder took a jaundiced view of it in *The Apartment*, as did the makers of *Patterns of Power*, *Executive Suite*, *Bartleby* and *The Power and the Prize*. Romantic comedies of the 30s like *Wife versus Secretary*, *After Office Hours* and *Take a Letter Darling* saw it as ideal for amorous intrigue, and in 1964 *The Wild Affair* took pretty much the same attitude. Orson Welles in *The Trial* made it nightmarish; Preston Sturges in *Christmas in July* made it friendly; *The Desk Set* made it computerized; *The Bachelor Party* made it frustrating. Perhaps the best film office is that of Philip Marlowe in the Raymond Chandler films: there's seldom anyone in it but himself. The most spectacular was that of Alfred Abel in *Metropolis*.

Oh God!

Avery Corman's novel of God coming to Earth to ask a supermarket manager for help in promulgating his message was filmed in 1977 by Carl Reiner with the veteran comedian George Burns as the deity and was followed by two lacklustre sequels: *Oh God! Book II*, directed by Gilbert Cates in 1980, and *Oh God! You Devil*, directed by Paul Bogart from Andrew Bergman's script.

oil

and its procurement from the earth have been the subjects of a number of films including *High Wide and Handsome* 38, *Boom Town* 40, *The Big Gusher* 51, *Tulsa* 49, *Thunder Bay* 53, *Lucy Gallant* 55, *Giant* 56, *The Houston Story* 56, *Maracaibo* 58, *Black Gold* 60, *Hellfighters* 68 and *Oklahoma Crude* 73.

old age

on the screen has seldom been explored, and the commercial reasons for this are obvious. Among the serious studies are *The Whisperers*, with Edith Evans; *Umberto D*, with Carlo Battisti; *The Shameless Old Lady*, with Sylvie; *Ikuru*, with Takashi Shimura; *The End of the Road*, with Finlay Currie; *I Never Sang for My Father*, with Melvyn Douglas; *Make Way for Tomorrow*, with Beulah Bondi; *Alive and Kicking*, with Sybil Thorndike and Estelle Winwood; *Kotch* with Walter Matthau; *Harry and Tonto* with Art Carney; *Tokyo Story* with Chishu Ryu and Chieko Higashiyama; *On Golden Pond* with Henry Fonda and Katharine Hepburn; *The Gin Game* with Jessica Tandy and Hume Cronyn (a video version of their stage hit); *The Whales of August* with Bette Davis and Lillian Gish; and *Driving Miss Daisy* with Jessica Tandy and Morgan Freeman. Sentimentality crept in in *Mr Belvedere Rings the Bell;* and *The Old Man and the Sea* was merely pretentious.

There was an element of black comedy in the attitudes expressed towards the old people in *Grapes of Wrath*, *Tobacco Road* and *Nights of the Iguana;* and more melodramatic caricatures were presented in *The Lost Moment* (Agnes Moorehead), *The Queen of Spades* (Edith Evans), *Little Big Man* (Dustin Hoffman), and *The Old Dark House* (John Dudgeon). Fantasy crept in with *Lost Horizon*, in which the lamas grew incredibly old by natural processes, and *The Man in Half Moon Street*, in which Nils Asther was assisted by science. Other actors who have specialized in geriatric portraits include A. E. Matthews, Edie Martin, Clem Bevans, Andy Clyde, Maria Ouspenskaya, Jessie Ralph, Nancy Price and Adeline de Walt Reynolds, who did not become an actress until she was eighty. Perhaps the Screen's most delightful senior citizens were the capering Harbottle, played by Moore Marriott in Will Hay comedies, and Barry Fitzgerald in *Broth of a Boy;* the most horrific was Cathleen Nesbitt in *Staircase;* the most commercially successful were George Burns and Walter Matthau in *The Sunshine Boys*. Katie Johnson became a star at 78 in *The Lady Killers:* Ruth Gordon played capering old dames well into her 80s, and in *Harold and Maude*, when she was 75, played an 80-year-old who had an affair with an immature young boy.

Stars who donned ageing make-up include Hope, Crosby and Lamour in *Road to Utopia;* Barbara Stanwyck in *The Great Man's Lady;* Tyrone Power in *The Long Gray Line;* Anna Neagle in *Victoria the Great;* Madeleine Carroll in *The Fan;* Gable and Shearer in *Strange Interlude;* Rosalind Russell and Alexander Knox in *Sister Kenny;* Joel McCrea in *Buffalo Bill;* Fredric March in *The Adventures of Mark Twain;* Dustin Hoffman in *Little Big Man*. The most tasteless treatment of old age was surely that offered in *The Ultimate Solution of Grace Quigley;* the most graceful that of *Going in Style*.

Old Mother Riley.

The vociferous, anarchic Irish washerwoman was created by Arthur Lucan on the music halls and in many films, with daughter Kitty played by the resistible Kitty McShane, Lucan's wife. Most of the films were atrociously made but all of them made a sizeable profit from British provincial showings.

For a complete list, see LUCAN, Arthur.

Oliver Twist.

Dickens's novel was filmed many times in the early silent period: in 1909 by Pathé, in 1910 by Vitagraph, in 1912 by an independent company with Nat C. Goodwin as Fagin. A famous American version of 1916 had Tully Marshall as Fagin and Marie Doro as Oliver; in 1922 the roles were played by Lon Chaney and Jackie Coogan, and in 1933 by Irving Pichel and Dickie Moore. The definitive version so far, however, is the British one directed by David Lean in 1948, with John Howard Davies in the title role. Alec Guinness's brilliant performance as Fagin caused a hold-up in American distribution as it was accused of anti-Semitism. *Oliver!*, a 1968 musical version directed by Carol Reed, with Ron Moody as Fagin and Mark Lester as Oliver, won six Oscars. *Twisted*, an updated version, set among New York's homosexuals, was made in 1996 by Seth Michael Donsky, with William Hickey in the role of a Fagin-like pimp.

One Million B.C.

This highly unscientific account of the tribulations of primitive man has been filmed several times. The 1939 version featured Carole Landis and Victor Mature and was produced and directed by Hal Roach with assistance from D. W. Griffith, upon whose 1912 *Man's Genesis* it was based. The dialogue consisted largely of grunts and there were a variety of prehistoric monsters which were rather obviously normal reptiles crudely decorated and magnified. Hammer remade it in 1960 with Don Chaffey directing Raquel Welch and John Richardson; this time the monsters were plastic animations. A kind of sequel, *When Dinosaurs Ruled the Earth*, directed by Val Guest, came out in 1970, and *Creatures the World Forgot* followed in 1971. Another all-grunting caveman epic followed in 1981, with *Quest for Fire*, directed by Jean-Jacques Annaud. This, however, aimed for accuracy, with the cast using a prehistoric language created by novelist Anthony Burgess and gestures devised by zoologist Desmond Morris, and was consequently much less fun.

One Way Passage.

A popular tear-jerker of 1932, written and directed by Tay Garnett, about a dying beauty (Kay Francis) and a convicted murderer (William Powell) who meet on an ocean liner and fall in love while keeping their secrets, it was remade in 1940 by Edmund Goulding as *Till We Meet Again*, with Merle Oberon and George Brent.

opera

has never been a successful commodity on the screen, although many operas have been filmed as from the stalls, and appear to have succeeded with minority audiences. The occasional big opera production such as *Porgy and Bess*, *Pagliacci* or *Carmen Jones*, however, can expect to meet with only moderate success. Opera does, however, make an excellent background for thrillers (*Charlie Chan at the Opera*), farces (*A Night at the Opera*) and melodramas (*Metropolitan*). Opera singers who have succeeded as film stars include Grace Moore, Lily Pons, Mario Lanza, Tito Gobbi, Richard Tauber, Lauritz Melchior, Ezio Pinza and Gladys Swarthout. Oddly enough the singer Mary Garden was a big hit in *silent* films. In a comprehensive reference guide, *Opera on Screen*, published in 1997, Ken Wlaschin lists the best operas on film as Francesco Rosi's *Carmen* 84, Ingmar Bergman's *The Magic Flute* 74, Franco Zeffirelli's *La Traviata* 82, Joseph Losey's *Don Giovanni* 78, Max Ophuls' *The Bartered Bride* 32, Michael Powell and Emeric Pressburger's *The*

Tales of Hoffman 51, and Gian Carlo Menotti's *The Medium* 51. The title of best operetta goes to Ernst Lubitsch's *The Merry Widow* 32. The worst opera on film is said to be Albert Hopkins's version of *Faust* 36, made in Britain and starring Anne Ziegler and Webster Booth.

orchestral conductors
have figured as leading men in *Intermezzo, Interlude, Once More with Feeling, Unfaithfully Yours, Song of Russia, Break of Hearts, Prelude to Fame, Counterpoint;* Charles Laughton cut a tragi-comic figure in *Tales of Manhattan.* Real conductors who have played dramatic roles in movies include Leopold Stokowski, José Iturbi and many swing and jazz figures such as Paul Whiteman, Tommy Dorsey, Henry Hall, Glenn Miller, Benny Goodman, Xavier Cugat.

oriental roles.
It never seems a good idea, but occidental actors have often been tempted by the wish to play Eastern. Among the less fortunate results are Lee J. Cobb in *Anna and the King of Siam;* John Wayne in *The Conqueror;* Katharine Hepburn in *Dragon Seed;* Alec Guinness in *A Majority of One;* Mickey Rooney in *Breakfast at Tiffany's;* George Raft in *Limehouse Blues;* Edward G. Robinson in *The Hatchet Man.* Those who more or less got away with it include Robert Donat in *Inn of the Sixth Happiness;* Boris Karloff in *The Mask of Fu Manchu;* and Luise Rainer and Paul Muni in *The Good Earth.*

Oswald the Rabbit.
Cute cartoon star who survived the transition from silent to talking pictures. Originated by Walt Disney, he was taken over by Universal Pictures and animator Walter Lantz from 1929 and appeared in many cartoons until 1938. He was voiced by Mickey Rooney and Bernice Hansen. His finest moment was an appearance in 1930 in *The King of Jazz* with bandleader Paul Whiteman.

Othello.
Shakespeare's tragedy of a jealous lover was filmed many times as a silent and on three notable occasions in more recent times. Orson Welles starred in and directed an uneven version in 1952, which was beset by financial problems and inspired a hilarious account of its travails, *Put Money in Thy Purse,* by Michael MacLiammoir, who played Iago. Sergei Yutkevich made a Russian version in 1955, starring Sergei Bondachuk, and Laurence Olivier's astonishing National Theatre performance as a West Indian Othello, with Maggie Smith as Desdemona and Frank Finlay as Iago, was preserved in Stuart Burge's unsatisfactory screen version in 1965. A musical version, *Catch My Soul,* was filmed in 1972, and murderous actors playing the role of Othello have also turned up in *Men Are Not Gods* 36, directed by Walter Reisch and starring Sebastian Shaw, and *A Double Life* 47, directed by George Cukor and starring Ronald Colman. Basil Dearden's *All Night Long* 61 updated the play as a tale of a jealous jazz musician (Patrick McGoohan), and a western, *Jubal* 56, had Ernest Borgnine as a jealous rancher being urged to commit murder by Rod Steiger.

'Our Gang'.
A collection of child actors first gathered together in short slapstick comedies by producer Hal Roach in the mid-20s. They remained popular through the 30s and 40s, though the personnel of the team naturally changed. The originals included 'Fat' Joe Cobb, Jackie Condon, Mickey Daniels, Mary Kornman and Ernie 'Sunshine Sammy' Morrison, said to be the highest-paid member at $12 a week in 1927. Later cast members, joining in the late 20s, were Matthew 'Stymie' Beard, Norman 'Chubby' Chaney, Jackie Cooper, Johnny Downs and Bobby 'Wheezer' Hutchins, who were followed by, among others, Scotty Beckett, Tommy 'Butch' Bond, Dorothy De Borba, Mary Anne Jackson, Darla Hood, Dickie Moore, Carl 'Alfalfa' Switzer, Billy 'Buckwheat' Thomas and Spanky McFarland, who became leader of the gang in the early 30s. Roach sold the series to MGM in 1938 and production continued until 1944. Many of Roach's Our Gang shorts have appeared on television and have been released on video under the title 'The Little Rascals', since MGM hold copyright in the original name. One, *Bored of Education,* won an Oscar in 1936 and a feature, *General Spanky,* directed by Fred Newmeyer, was made in 1938. More than 90 of their short films were restored for television showing in the 90s, and Steven Spielberg produced a new feature film, *The Little Rascals,* based on the series, in 1994, directed by Penelope Spheeris.

Book 1977: *Our Gang* by Leonard Maltin.

painters
have frequently had their lives glamorized to provide film-makers with drama to counterpoint art. Among the most notable are Charles Laughton as *Rembrandt,* George Sanders as Gauguin in *The Moon and Sixpence,* José Ferrer as Toulouse-Lautrec in *Moulin Rouge,* Anthony Franciosa as Goya in *The Naked Maja,* Kirk Douglas as Van Gogh and Anthony Quinn as Gauguin in *Lust for Life,* Gérard Philipe as Modigliani in *Montparnasse 19,* Cecil Kellaway as Gainsborough in *Kitty,* Charlton Heston as Michelangelo in *The Agony and the Ecstasy,* and Mel Ferrer as *El Greco.*

The Paleface.
Bob Hope's western romp with Jane Russell as Calamity Jane, directed by Norman Z. McLeod in 1948, was followed by an even crazier extravaganza, *Son of Paleface,* which also featured Roy Rogers. In 1968 the original was revamped for Don Knotts as *The Shakiest Gun in the West.*

Paris
has usually figured in films as the centre of sophistication, romance and luxury: thus *Ninotchka, I Met Him in Paris, The Last Time I Saw Paris, Innocents in Paris, April in Paris, How to Steal a Million, To Paris with Love, Paris When It Sizzles, A Certain Smile, Funny Face, Paris Holiday, Can Can, Parisienne, Paris Palace Hotel, Two for the Road* and innumerable others. The bohemian aspect is another favourite, as depicted in *An American in Paris, Latin Quarter, Paris Blues, What's New, Pussycat?, Svengali, French Cancan, Moulin Rouge, What a Way to Go, The Moon and Sixpence,* etc. The tourists' Paris has provided a splendid backcloth for films as diverse as *The Great Race, The Man on the Eiffel Tower, Charade, Those Magnificent Men in Their Flying Machines, Zazie dans le Métro, Pig Across Paris, The Red Balloon, Father Brown, Take Her She's Mine, Dear Brigitte, Bon Voyage,* and *Paris Nous Appartient.* French film-makers seem particularly fond of showing the city's seamy side in thrillers about vice, murder and prostitution: *Quai de Grenelle, Quai des Orfèvres, Les Compagnes de la Nuit, Le Long des Trottoirs, Rififi,* etc. René Clair has always had his own slightly fantastic view of Paris, from *Paris Qui Dort* through *Sous les Toits de Paris, A Nous la Liberté, Le Million, Le Quatorze Juillet,* and *Porte des Lilas.* Rouben Mamoulian recreated this vision in *Love Me Tonight,* and *The Mad Woman of Chaillot* lived in a city of similar nuances. Historical Paris has been recreated for *The Hunchback of Notre Dame, The Scarlet Pimpernel, The Three Musketeers, Camille, A Tale of Two Cities, Marie Antoinette, So Long at the Fair* and *Les Enfants du Paradis;* while Paris under fire in World War II was depicted in *Is Paris Burning?* As for *Last Tango in Paris,* its emphasis was hardly on the city.

parody
without satire was never prominent among film genres until the 70s, when the easy-going talents of such as Mel Brooks and Gene Wilder produced films such as *Blazing Saddles, Sherlock Holmes' Smarter Brother, Young Frankenstein, Murder by Death, The Black Bird, The Big Bus, Phantom of the Paradise, High Anxiety* and *The Cheap Detective.* The Zucker brothers and Jim Abrahams have made a speciality of the form with *Kentucky Fried Movie, Airplane, The Naked Gun* and their sequels, and *Hot Shots!* (Abrahams only). Short films in this vein are headed by *Six-Sided Triangle, The Dove* and *Cry Wolf.*

parties
in movies have often been wild, as for instance in *The Wild Party,* also *The Party's Over, I'll Never Forget What's 'is Name, Breakfast at Tiffany's, I Love You Alice B. Toklas, The Impossible Years, Skidoo, Beyond the Valley of the Dolls, Camille 2000, The Pursuit of Happiness, The Party Crashers,* and *The Party* itself, which started out sedately but finished with an elephant in the swimming pool. Some of the more amusing film parties, however, were better behaved, as in *The Apartment, Only Two Can Play, All About Eve* and *Citizen Kane.*

The Passing of the Third Floor Back.
Jerome K. Jerome's popular novel and play, about a Christ-like stranger who has a benign influence on the down-at-heel inhabitants of a boarding house, has been filmed twice. Sir Johnston Forbes-Robertson, who had a lasting success on stage in the role from 1908 ('Chr-r-rist! Will they never let me give up this *bloody* part?' he once exclaimed before going on as the saintly figure), starred in a silent film in 1918, two years after he had retired from the stage, and Conrad Veidt appeared in a version, also British, in 1935.

The Passing Parade.
A series of one-reel films, mostly historical cameos enacted in corners of MGM's great sets, devised and produced by John Nesbitt in the 30s and 40s.

Penrod.
Booth Tarkington's American boy character, in his mid-west small-town setting, was for many years a favourite Hollywood subject. Marshall Neilan directed Gordon Griffith in a 1922 version. In 1923 William Beaudine directed Ben Alexander in the role in *Penrod and Sam,* which was remade by Beaudine in 1931 with Leon Janney, and again by William McGann in 1937 with Billy Mauch. Mauch and his twin brother Bobby appeared in two sequels: *Penrod's Double Trouble* 38, directed by Lewis Seiler, and *Penrod and His Twin Brother* 38, directed by McGann. Two Doris Day musicals, *On Moonlight Bay* 51 and *By the Light of the Silvery Moon* 53, were also lightly based on the Tarkington stories: Penrod, unaccountably disguised as 'Wesley', was played by Billy Gray.

Pepe Le Pew.
Smooth, romantic French skunk, the star of 14 Warner Brothers cartoons. Based on Charles Boyer's Pepe Le Moko in *Algiers,* he was created by writer Michael Maltese and animator Chuck Jones and voiced by Mel Blanc.

Scent-Imental over You 47. For Scent-Imental Reasons (AA) 49. Scent-Imental Romeo 51. Cat's Bah 54. Heaven Scent 56. Really Scent 59. Who Scent You? 60. Louvre Come Back to Me 62, etc.

The Perils of Pauline.
Pearl White's famous 1914 serial was directed by Donald Mackenzie, co-starred Crane Wilbur, and concerned the heroine's evasion of attempts on her life by her dastardly guardian. The 1947 film of the same name was a lightly fictionalized biography of Pearl White, directed by George Marshall, with Betty Hutton in the title role. The 1967 film was vaguely based on the original serial, with Pamela Austin as the heroine, directed by Herbert Leonard and Joshua Shelley.

Perry Mason,
a crime-solving lawyer who wins all his cases, usually during a court-room cross-examination, was created by Erle Stanley Gardner in *The Case of the Velvet Claws* 33, the first of more than 80 novels in which he was the hero. On film, he has been played by Warren William, Ricardo Cortez and Donald Woods, but it was Raymond Burr who became closely identified with the character in the TV series of 245 hour-long episodes that ran 1957–66. Monte Markham took over the part in the unsuccessful *The New Adventures of Perry Mason* 73–74; then in 1985 Burr returned to the role in a continuing series of TV movies.

The Case of the Howling Dog 34. The Case of the Curious Bride 35. The Case of the Lucky Legs 35. The Case of the Velvet Claws 36. The Case of the Black Cat 36. The Case of the Stuttering Bishop 37. Perry Mason Returns (TV) 85. Perry Mason: The Case of the Notorious Nun (TV) 86. Perry Mason: The Case of the Lost Love (TV) 87. Perry Mason: The Case of the Lady in the Lake (TV) 88. Perry Mason: The Case of the All-Star Assassin (TV) 89. Perry Mason: The Case of the Ruthless Reporter (TV) 91, etc.

Peyton Place.
The 1957 film version of Grace Metalious's novel started a fashion for small-town sex exposés on the screen, and was followed by a sequel, *Return to Peyton Place,* in 1961. A TV series of two half-hours a week followed in 1964 and proved so popular that in 1965 it was given three half-hours and lasted until 1969, bringing to public notice Mia Farrow and Ryan O'Neal.

The Phantom of the Opera.
Gaston Leroux's melodramatic tale of the embittered, disfigured composer who haunts the sewers beneath the Paris Opéra and takes a pretty young singer as his protégée has been filmed several times: in 1925 Rupert Julian directed a version with Lon Chaney and Mary Philbin; in 1943 Arthur Lubin directed Claude Rains and Susanna Foster; in 1962 came a British version, directed by Terence Fisher, with Herbert Lom and Heather Sears; in 1989 Dwight H. Little directed Robert Englund, better known as Freddy from *A Nightmare on Elm Street,* in a version set in London. In 1977 Brian DePalma made a rock version, *Phantom of the Paradise,* and there have been two TV movies, one in 1983 starring Maximilian Schell and Jane Seymour, and another in 1990, directed by Tony Richardson from a script by Arthur Kopit, with Charles Dance and Teri Polo. Andrew Lloyd-Webber's highly successful stage musical, premiered in 1986, will no doubt be filmed in the future.

Philip Marlowe
was the weary but incorruptible private-eye creation of Raymond Chandler, treading the seamier streets of Los Angeles in a dogged hunt for suspects. On television he was played in a poor series by Phil Carey, on screen by Humphrey Bogart, Robert Montgomery, George Montgomery, Dick Powell, James Garner, Robert Mitchum and (very badly) by Elliott Gould. In 1983 he was portrayed in a British television series, *Chandlertown,* by Powers Boothe. He was played by James Caan in *Poodle Springs* (TV) 98.

The Pink Panther.
Blake Edwards' 1964 film of an unequal battle of wits between an aristocratic jewel thief (David Niven) and an accident-prone French policeman, Inspector Clouseau (Peter Sellers), spawned several sequels: *A Shot in the Dark* 64; *Inspector Clouseau* 68, in which Alan Arkin took the title role; *The Return of the Pink Panther* 74, which brought back Sellers; *The Pink Panther Strikes Again* 76; and *Revenge of the Pink Panther* 78. Sellers' widow, Lynne Frederick, objected to *The Trail of the Pink Panther* 82, which cobbled together outtakes of Sellers from earlier films and new linking material. It was followed by *Curse of the Pink Panther* 83, in which Ted Wass starred as the world's worst detective, and *Son of the Pink Panther* 93, with Italian comedian Robert Benigni in the title role, but neither was a success. The animated credits of the original film, featuring a pink panther and Henry Mancini's catchy title song, inspired a long-running cartoon series, beginning with the Oscar-winning *The Pink Phink* 64, and a comic book that was published from 1971–84.

pirates
have regularly appeared on the screen. Stories with some claim to historical authenticity, or at least based on the exploits of a pirate who once lived, include *Captain Blood* (and its various sequels), *The Black Swan, Morgan the Pirate, Seven Seas to Calais, Blackbeard the Pirate, Captain Kidd, The Buccaneer,* and *Anne of the Indies* (a rare female pirate: one other was depicted in *The Pirate Queen*). Totally fictitious stories are of course headed by *Treasure Island* in its various versions; other swashbuckling yarns included *The Sea Hawk, The Black Pirate, The Crimson Pirate, The Golden Hawk, Fair Wind to Java, A High Wind in Jamaica, Pirates of Tortuga, Yankee Buccaneer, The Spanish Main, Pirates of Tripoli, Devil Ship Pirates, Pirates of Blood River, Prince of Pirates,* and *Raiders of the Seven Seas.* The only notable musical pirate was Gene Kelly in *The Pirate;* comic pirates are also rare, but they do include *The Princess and the Pirate, Blackbeard's Ghost, Double Crossbones, The Dancing Pirate* and *Old Mother Riley's Jungle Treasure.* 1983's *Yellowbeard* was a sad spoof of the genre. *Pirates* in 1985 didn't even seem to know whether it was a spoof or not. *Hook* 91 put the pirate captain of *Peter Pan* centre-galleon.

The Plainsman.
Cecil B. De Mille's 1937 western starred Gary Cooper as Wild Bill Hickok, James Ellison as Buffalo Bill, and Jean Arthur as Calamity Jane. It was poorly remade in 1966 with Don Murray, Guy Stockwell, and Abby Dalton.

Planet of the Apes.

Pierre Boulle's novel of an astronaut who lands on a planet where the humans have degenerated and the apes rule with wisdom was adapted by Paul Dehn and stylishly directed by Franklin Schaffner in 1967; Charlton Heston played the hero who discovers, in a twist at the end, that the planet is Earth, and John Chambers provided the splendidly flexible ape make-up. It spawned four sequels of increasing violence and decreasing interest: *Beneath the Planet of the Apes* 69; *Escape from the Planet of the Apes* 70; *Conquest of the Planet of the Apes* 72; and *Battle for the Planet of the Apes* 73. They were followed by a short-lived television series in 1974, and an animated series, *Beyond the Planet of the Apes*, in 1975–76.

plastic surgery

was long a staple of horror films, but improved techniques have made it a subject for 'woman's pictures' such as *Ash Wednesday* and *Once is not Enough*. *Arsenic and Old Lace* made a comedy point of it, and *Seconds* took it seriously. Other examples: *Dark Passage, False Faces, A Woman's Face, Eyes without a Face, Johnny Handsome*.

police

in the 40s and earlier were offered in British films only for our admiration; in the 50s they began to have human frailties; and in the 60s many of them were shown, truthfully or not, to be corrupt. The *Blue Lamp, The Long Arm* and *Gideon of Scotland Yard* are only three of many of the first kind; *Violent Playground* one of the second; and *The Strange Affair* a corking example of the last. But the *Z Cars* series on British TV will long uphold the best traditions of the force . . . as will *Maigret* for France.

American cops have always been tougher, but even so a gradual change can be traced through *Naked City, The Big Heat, Detective Story, Shield for Murder, Experiment in Terror, Madigan, The Detective, The French Connection, Fuzz* and *The New Centurions*.

TV series which have been influential include *Dragnet* 52–59 and 67–69, *Naked City* 58–62, *87th Precinct* 61, *M Squad* 57–60, *The Detectives* 60–61, *The Line-up* 54–59, *Hawk* 66, *The New Breed* 61, *Adam 12* 68–75, *Hawaii Five O* 68–80, *The Rookies* 72, *Police Story* 73–77, *Police Woman* 74–76, *Starsky and Hutch* 75–78, *Miami Vice* 84–88, *Hill Street Blues* 81–87, *NYPD Blue* 93–95, *Homicide: Life on the Streets* 93–.

Comic policemen go right back to the Keystone Kops. Other examples: Will Hay in *Ask a Policeman*, George Formby in *Spare a Copper*, Norman Wisdom in *On the Beat*, Alastair Sim in *Green for Danger*, Peter Sellers in *The Pink Panther*, Lionel Jeffries in *The Wrong Arm of the Law*, 'Officer Krupke' in *West Side Story*, Donald McBride in *Topper Returns*, Dennis Hoey as Inspector Lestrade in the Sherlock Holmes films, Sidney James and crew in *Carry On Constable*, Laurel and Hardy in *Midnight Patrol*, Buster Keaton's cast in *Cops*, Charles Chaplin in *Easy Street*, the cast of *Police Academy* and, on TV, *Car 54 Where are You?*

politics,

as any exhibitor will tell you, is the kiss of death to a film as far as box office is concerned. Nevertheless many films with serious political themes have been made. Among those presenting biographies of actual political figures, the American ones include *Young Mr Lincoln, Abe Lincoln in Illinois, Tennessee Johnson, The Man with Thirty Sons* (Oliver Wendell Holmes), *Magnificent Doll* (Dolly Madison and Aaron Burr), *The President's Lady* (Andrew Jackson), *Wilson*, Teddy Roosevelt (in *My Girl Tisa* and others), Franklin Roosevelt (in *Sunrise at Campobello*), *Beau James* (Jimmy Walker) and John Kennedy (*PT 109*). *JFK* (Kennedy again) and *Nixon*, while *All the King's Men* and *A Lion Is in the Streets* are clearly based on Huey Long, and there was a real-life original for the idealistic young senator from Wisconsin in *Mr Smith Goes to Washington*. Fictional presidencies have been involved in *Gabriel over the White House, First Lady, The Tree of Liberty* (*The Howards of Virginia*), *Advise and Consent, The Manchurian Candidate, Seven Days in May, Dr Strangelove, Kisses for My President*, and *Fail Safe*. Among the many films alleging political graft and corruption in the US are *Mr Smith Goes to Washington, Confessions of a Nazi Spy, Louisiana Purchase, Alias Nick Beal, State of the Union, Li'l Abner, The Great McGinty, The Glass Key, Citizen Kane, All the King's Men, Bullets*

or *Ballots, A Lion Is in the Streets, The Last Hurrah, The Best Man, The Senator was Indiscreet* and *The Candidate*. The witch-hunts of 1948 produced a series of right-wing melodramas like *I Was a Communist for the FBI, I Married a Communist* and *My Son John . . .* a striking contrast to 1942, when *Mission to Moscow* could be made. In 1971 TV produced a four-hour thriller called *Vanished* about a president with doubtful motives. The mid-70s brought a number of TV drama-documentaries about political matters: *Eleanor and Franklin, Collision Course* (Truman and MacArthur), *The Missiles of October, Fear On Trial, Tail Gunner Joe* (McCarthy), *Meeting at Potsdam*.

The British House of Commons and its characters have been involved in many a film with DISRAELI coming out as favourite. Pitt the Younger was impersonated by Robert Donat, and Charles James Fox by Robert Morley, in *The Young Mr Pitt*; Gladstone was played by Ralph Richardson in *Khartoum*, Malcolm Keen in *Sixty Glorious Years* and Stephen Murray in *The Prime Minister*; *Cromwell* by Richard Harris; Canning by John Mills and William Lamb by Jon Finch in *Lady Caroline Lamb*; while Ramsay MacDonald was allegedly pictured in *Fame is the Spur*. MPs were also the leading figures of the fictional *No Love for Johnnie, Three Cases of Murder* and *The Rise and Rise of Michael Rimmer*.

Political films from other countries abound; one might almost say that every Soviet film is political. But politics do not export well, so that for the life of Villa, Zapata, Juarez and Che Guevara we have to turn to glamorized Hollywood versions of the truth; ditto for Parnell, Richelieu and even Hitler. Lenin has been pictured in innumerable Soviet films, and Richard Burton starred in *The Assassination of Trotsky*.

That politics is not entirely a serious matter can be seen from the number of comedies about it. The best of them is the already mentioned *State of the Union*, but one can also instance the *Don Camillo* series, *Old Mother Riley MP, Angelina MP, Dad Rudd MP, Louisiana Purchase, Kisses for My President, The Great Man Votes, Left Right and Centre, Vote for Huggett*, and *The American President*.

Popeye.

Tough sailorman hero of over 250 cartoon shorts produced by Max Fleischer c. 1933–50. Other characters involved were girlfriend Olive Oyl and tough villain Bluto, against whose wiles Popeye fortified himself with tins of spinach. The films were so popular on TV that a newly-drawn series was produced c. 1959 by King Features – but the old vulgar panache was missing.

In 1980 Robert Altman directed a live-action version, but it was a sad affair.

Porky Pig.

Stammering, nervous pig whose cry of 'Th-th-th-th-that's all, folks' brought to an end many Warner Brothers cartoons. Created by Bob Clampett, for the first two years he was voiced by Joe Dougherty (who did stutter), after which Mel Blanc took over.

I Haven't Got a Hat 35. *Gold Diggers of '49* 36. *Porky's Pet* 36. *Porky's Duck Hunt* 37. *The Case of the Stuttering Pig* 37. *Porky and Daffy* 38. *The Lone Stranger and Porky* 39. *Prehistoric Porky* 40. *Porky's Ant* 41. *My Favorite Duck* 42. *Swooner Crooner* (AAN) 44. *The Pest that Came to Dinner* 48. *Porky's Chops* 49. *Cracked Quack* 52. *Deduce, You Say* 56. *China Jones* 59. *Daffy's Inn Trouble* 61, many others.

poverty

in America and Britain is rare enough now to be little discussed, but in the days when film-makers began to have a social conscience a number of films memorably examined the problem in different milieux. American hoboes and shanty-town dwellers were revealed in *Sullivan's Travels, Hallelujah I'm a Bum, Man's Castle, My Man Godfrey, One More Spring*; the rural poor were the subject of *Our Daily Bread, The Grapes of Wrath, Tobacco Road*. Hollywood's regretful gaze wandered to China for *The Good Earth* and for *Tortilla Flat* to Mexico, which was more memorably covered by Buñuel in *Los Olvidados*. Poverty in Italy was the subject of *Bicycle Thieves*, and in England of *Love on the Dole, Doss House* and *The Whisperers*.

priests

have been a godsend to film-makers. Most male stars have played them occasionally: the combination of masculine attractiveness and non-availability apparently works at the box office. Thus Frank Sinatra in *The Miracle of the Bells*; William Holden and Clifton Webb in *Satan Never Sleeps*; Bing Crosby in *Going My Way, The Bells of St Mary's* and *Say One for Me*; Richard Dix in *The Christian*; Pat O'Brien in a dozen films including *Angels with Dirty Faces, The Fighting 69th* and *Fighting Father Dunne*; ditto Spencer Tracy, in *Boys' Town, San Francisco, The Devil at Four O'Clock*, and others; George Arliss in *Cardinal Richelieu*; Don Murray in *The Hoodlum Priest*; Karl Malden in *On the Waterfront* and *The Great Impostor*; Pierre Fresnay in *Monsieur Vincent*; Claude Laydu in *Diary of a Country Priest*; Jean-Paul Belmondo in *Leon Morin Priest*; John Mills in *The Singer Not the Song*; Tom Tryon in *The Cardinal*; Gregory Peck in *The Keys of the Kingdom*; Geoffrey Bayldon in *Sky West and Crooked*; Richard Burton in *Becket*; , David Warner in *The Ballad of Cable Hogue*; Ward Bond in *The Quiet Man*; Mickey Rooney in *The Twinkle in God's Eye*; Montgomery Clift in *I Confess*; Alec Guinness in *Father Brown* and *The Prisoner*; Trevor Howard in *Ryan's Daughter*; Donald Sutherland in *Act of the Heart*; and Marcello Mastroianni in *The Priest's Wife*.

Protestant priests included Anthony Quayle in *Serious Charge*; Richard Burton in *The Sandpiper*; Robert Donat in *Lease of Life*; Wilfred Lawson in *Pastor Hall*; Peter Sellers in *Heavens Above*; Richard Todd in *A Man Called Peter*; Fredric March in *One Foot in Heaven*; David Niven in *The Bishop's Wife*. Actors who have got to play pope include Anthony Quinn and John Gielgud in *The Shoes of the Fisherman*, Rod Steiger in *A Man Called John*, Paolo Stoppa in *Becket* and Rex Harrison in *The Agony and the Ecstasy*.

False priests were Humphrey Bogart in *The Left Hand of God*, Rod Steiger in *No Way to Treat a Lady*, Dennis Price in *Kind Hearts and Coronets*, and Peter Sellers in *After the Fox*; while priestly villains were Ralph Richardson in *The Ghoul*, George Arliss in *Dr Syn* (followed by Peter Cushing in *Captain Clegg*), Keenan Wynn in *Johnny Concho*, Cedric Hardwicke in *The Hunchback of Notre Dame* and Robert Mitchum in *Night of the Hunter*. Classifiable as fallen priests were Henry Fonda in *The Fugitive*, Richard Burton in *Night of the Iguana*, Max Von Sydow in *Hawaii*, Burt Lancaster in *Elmer Gantry*, Lars Hanson in *The Scarlet Letter*, and Pierre Fresnay in *Le Défroqué* and *Dieu a Besoin des Hommes*.

Priests came into their own again in a spate of diabolical thrillers: Max Von Sydow and Jason Miller in *The Exorcist*, Patrick Troughton in *The Omen*, Oliver Reed in *The Devils*. Other troubled priests have included Rod Steiger (and various successors) in *The Amityville Horror* series Christopher Reeve in *Monsignor*, and the protagonists of *True Confessions*.

The Prince and the Pauper.

Mark Twain's novel, about the young King Edward VI changing places with a street urchin who happens to be his double, has been a favourite with film-makers, though it has transferred unsatisfactorily to the screen so far. There were at least five silent versions before William Keighley made it into a moderate swashbuckler in 1937, starring Errol Flynn and with twins Billy and Bobby Mauch as the prince and the beggar-boy. Don Chaffey directed a dull television version for Disney in 1962 which was released in cinemas elsewhere with a cast headed by TV's Zorro, Guy Williams, and young Sean Scully in the title roles. (Disney also turned the tale into an animated short with Mickey Mouse and Donald Duck.) In 1977, Richard Fleischer directed a lacklustre version in the US retitled *Crossed Swords*, starring Oliver Reed and Raquel Welch, and with Mark Lester taking both roles. It was then updated and given a sex change in 1995 as *It Takes Two*, starring twins Mary-Kate and Ashley Olsen, Steve Guttenberg and Kirstie Alley. A British TV version, with Keith Michell as Henry VIII and Philip Sarson in the two roles, was shown in 1996.

prison films

have always had an audience, but did not reach their full potential until sound. Then and through the 30s, film-makers took us on a conducted tour of American prisons. *The Big House, The Last Mile, I Was a Fugitive from a Chain Gang, Twenty*

Thousand Years in Sing Sing, Front Page Woman (with its gas chamber scene), *Angels with Dirty Faces, San Quentin, Blackwell's Island, Each Dawn I Die, Invisible Stripes, King of Alcatraz, Prison Ship, Prison Doctor, Mutiny in the Big House* and many others. During the war prison films were surpassed in excitement, but they came back with a bang in *Brute Force*, the toughest of them all, and *White Heat*. The 50s brought *Behind the High Wall, Duffy of San Quentin, Riot in Cell Block Eleven, Inside the Walls of Folsom Prison, Black Tuesday, I Want to Live, Cell 2455 Death Row*, and a remake of *The Last Mile*. More recently Burt Lancaster appeared in the factual *Bird Man of Alcatraz*; and in the second half of the 60s the subject became popular again with *The Brig, The Ceremony, Reprieve, Point Blank, The Dirty Dozen, Triple Cross, Riot, There was a Crooked Man, A Clockwork Orange* and *Fortune* and *Men's Eyes*.

British studios have produced few prison films until the realist wave of the 60s which brought with it *The Criminal, The Pot Carriers*, and the army prison film *The Hill*.

Unusual prisons were shown in *Sullivan's Travels, Devil's Canyon, One Day in the Life of Ivan Denisovich*, and *Nevada Smith*; while among the films poking fun at prison life are *Up the River, Pardon Us* (Laurel and Hardy), *Convict 99* (Will Hay), *Jailhouse Rock*, and *Two-Way Stretch*.

Prisons for women crop up quite regularly in such films as *Prison without Bars, Caged* (US), *Caged* (It.), *Au Royaume des Cieux, Women's Prison, Girls behind Bars, So Evil So Young, The Weak and the Wicked, Yield to the Night, The Smashing Bird I Used to Know* and *Women in Chains* (TV).

The Prisoner of Zenda.

At least four versions have been made of Anthony Hope's classic Ruritanian romance about a great impersonation, all in Hollywood: Rex Ingram directed a version in 1922 with Lewis Stone and Ramon Novarro; in 1937 John Cromwell directed Ronald Colman and Douglas Fairbanks Jnr in a version that was a model of its kind; Richard Thorpe made a mechanical scene-by-scene remake in 1952 with Stewart Granger and James Mason; in 1979 Peter Sellers appeared in an unsatisfactory half-humorous version by Dick Clement and Ian La Frenais. Comic variations on the story were included in *The Great Race* 65 and *Royal Flash* 75.

prisoners of war

were featured in many films after World War II. The British examples often made the camps seem almost too comfortable, despite the possibility of being shot while attempting to escape; this was perhaps because they were all filled with the same familiar faces. *Albert RN, The Captive Heart, The Colditz Story, The Betrayal, Danger Within, Reach for the Sky* and *The Password is Courage* all found humour in the situation at any rate; whereas the American counterparts, *The Purple Heart, Prisoner of War, Stalag 17* and *The Mackenzie Break* saw the harsher side which doubtless existed. The co-production, *The Bridge on the River Kwai*, gave a mixed picture of a Japanese camp; Britain's Hammer horror studio then produced *The Camp on Blood Island*, a fictitious record of atrocity, followed some years later by *The Secret of Blood Island*. Meanwhile the British in *The One That Got Away* paid tribute to the one German to escape from a British camp; and more recently *The Great Escape* showed the Americans coming some way towards the British idea of how jolly life in a camp can be. The ultimate absurdity was reached by an American TV series, *Hogan's Heroes*, which has a camp almost entirely controlled by the prisoners. The best serious film about prisoners of war remains undoubtedly Renoir's *La Grande Illusion*, made in 1937; though *King Rat* in 1965 made a fair bid to reveal the squalor and futility of the life, as did *The Empire of the Sun* 87, from the perspective of a young boy. Comic adventure stories about the escape of POWs have included *Very Important Person, The Secret War of Harry Frigg, Where Eagles Dare, Hannibal Brooks* and *Situation Hopeless but Not Serious*.

Women's camps were shown in *Two Thousand Women* (GB 1944), *Three Came Home* (US 1950), *A Town Like Alice* (GB 1956) and *Kapo* (It. 1960). Vietnam made a horrifying start to its quota of prisoner-of-war films with *The Deer Hunter*, and brought it to its nadir with *Rambo: First Blood Part II*.

private eyes:
see MYSTERY.

prizefighting:
see BOXING.

prophecy

has interested film-makers only occasionally, but at least two outstanding films have resulted: *Metropolis* and *Things to Come*. *Just Imagine* painted a light-hearted picture, and *Seven Days in May* was not too frightening about what might be happening politically a few years from now; but one hopes not to take too seriously the predictions in *1984*, *The Time Machine*, *Fahrenheit 451*, *Alphaville*, *When Worlds Collide*, *The World, the Flesh and the Devil*, *The War Game*, *Dr Strangelove*, *Punishment Park*, *Beyond the Time Barrier*, *No Blade of Grass*, *Barbarella*, *A Clockwork Orange*, *Planet of the Apes*, *Westworld*, *Futureworld*, *Logan's Run*, *Star Wars*, *The Final Programme*, *Death Race 2000*, *Soylent Green*, *The Ultimate Warrior*, *Robocop* and *Terminator 2*.

prostitutes

for many years could not be so labelled in Hollywood films, which featured a surprising number of 'café hostesses'. It was however fairly easy to spot the real profession of the various ladies who played Sadie Thompson in *Rain*, of Marlene Dietrich in *Dishonoured* and *Shanghai Express*, of Clara Bow in *Call Her Savage*, of Greta Garbo in *Anna Christie*, of Miriam Hopkins in *Dr Jekyll and Mr Hyde*, of Tallulah Bankhead in *Faithless*, of Bette Davis in *Of Human Bondage*, of Vivien Leigh in *Waterloo Bridge*, and of Joan Bennett in *Man Hunt*, to name but a few. The French, who have always called a spade a spade, flaunted the calling in hundreds of films including *Dedée D'Anvers*, *La Ronde*, *Le Plaisir*, *Boule de Suif*, *Le Long des Trottoirs*, *La Bonne Soupe*, *Adua et sa Compagnie* and *Les Compagnons de la Nuit*; Italy chipped in with *Mamma Roma* and Japan with *Street of Shame*. In the 50s Britain moved into the field with surprising eagerness – every other movie seemed to feature Dora Bryan in a plastic mac – and there were several alleged exposés of Soho corruption under such titles as *The Flesh is Weak*, *Passport to Shame* and *The World Ten Times Over*. Hollywood half-heartedly followed with some double-talking second features about call girls – *Why Girls Leave Home*, *Call Girl*, *Girls in the Night* – and some 'medical case histories' such as *The Three Faces of Eve*, *Girl of the Night*. Around 1960 the floodgates opened, eased by the sensationally successful Greek comedy *Never on Sunday* (and some continental imitators like *Always on Saturday* and *Every Night of the Week*). Among English-speaking stars who have played prostitutes are Shirley Maclaine in *Some Came Running* and *Irma La Douce*, Sophia Loren in *Lady L*, *Yesterday, Today and Tomorrow*, *Marriage Italian Style*, *Boccaccio 70* and *Man of La Mancha*, Anna Karina in *Vivre sa Vie*, Lee Grant in *Divorce American Style* and *The Balcony*, Catherine Deneuve in *Belle de Jour*, Carroll Baker in *Sylvia*, Shirley Jones in *Elmer Gantry*, Nancy Kwan in *The World of Suzie Wong*, Elizabeth Taylor in *Butterfield 8*, Diane Cilento in *Rattle of a Simple Man*, Carol White in *Poor Cow*, Inger Stevens in *Five Card Stud*, Margot Kidder in *Gaily, Gaily*, Kitty Wynn in *Panic in Needle Park*, Jane Fonda in *Klute*, Julia Roberts in *Pretty Woman*. Brothels have been shown in *Lady L*, *A Walk on the Wild Side*, *The Revolt of Mamie Stover*, *A House is not a Home*, *Ulysses*, *The Balcony*, *A Funny Thing Happened on the Way to the Forum*, *The Assassination Bureau*, *The Best House in London*, *Games That Lovers Play*, *The Reivers*, *Gaily, Gaily*, and an increasing number of westerns. In *Our Man Flint*, girls were described as 'pleasure units' . . .

See also: COURTESANS.

psychology

is featured most prominently in American films – quite naturally since the United States is the home of the psychiatrist. However, one of the best serious psychological films, *Mine Own Executioner*, did come from Britain and showed the doctor to be more in need of help than the patient; while two other notable British films, *Thunder Rock* and *Dead of Night*, centred on the depiction of psychological states.

Although films about psychology can be firmly traced back to *The Cabinet of Dr Caligari* and *Secrets of a Soul*, the subject took its firmest hold in the

middle of World War II, when so many people needed reassurance; the recounting of dreams to an analyst could even take the place of musical numbers in a romantic trifle like *Lady in the Dark*. Soon we were inundated with melodramas like *Spellbound*, *The Dark Mirror* and *Possessed*, in which the question to be answered was not so much who or how but why; and it wasn't until about 1950, with *Harvey*, that analysts could be laughed at; they were still being analysed in the 70s in such films as *Taking Off*. In the 50s the schizophrenic drama took on a new lease of life (*The Three Faces of Eve*, *Lizzie*, *Vertigo*), as did the tendency to guy individual psychiatrists while still claiming to respect the profession (*Oh Men Oh Women*, *Mirage*, *A Fine Madness*, *The Group*, *What a Way to Go*, *Marriage of a Young Stockbroker*, *The Couch Trip*). Of course, films were still made which took the whole matter with deadly seriousness, as in *The Cobweb*, *The Mark*, *Captain Newman MD*, *The Third Secret* and *Pressure Point*. John Huston's underrated film on the life of *Freud* may have been unlucky to arrive at a time of change: the fashion is now for case histories in which no solution is offered (*Repulsion*, *Morgan*, *Cul-de-Sac*) or psychological horror comics such as *Psycho*, *Homicidal*, and *The Night Walker*, while in *Promise Her Anything* we were finally shown a psychiatrist (Robert Cummings) who doesn't believe in psychiatry. The subject turned romantic in 1991 with Barbra Streisand as an analyst who falls in love with her patient's brother in *The Prince of Tides*, and sinister in *What about Bob?*, in which the patient drives the analyst crazy, the same year.

See also DREAMS; FANTASY; AMNESIA; CASE HISTORIES.

publicity

No right minded film-maker believes his own publicity . . . but he surely hopes it works. The tag-line devised for a film can have a make-or-break effect on its box-office record. Seldom can such lines be claimed as an honest distillation of truth, and very often they hint at more sensations than can be found in the film to which they are attached. But for sheer ingenuity some are unbeatable, and a few have even passed into the language.

● *The Twenties:*

The dangerous age for women is from three to seventy! – *Adam's Rib* (1922)

A photoplay of tempestuous love between a madcap English beauty and a bronzed Arab chief! – *The Sheik*

A cast of 125,000! – *Ben Hur*

The mightiest dramatic spectacle of all the ages! – *The Ten Commandments* (1923)

The epic of the American doughboy! – *The Big Parade*

A thrill a minute! A laugh a second! A comedy cyclone! – *Feet First*

Love of tender girlhood! Passionate deeds of heroes! A rushing, leaping drama of charm and excitement! – *America*

A thing of beauty is a joy forever . . . – *Street Angel*

● *The Thirties:*

The knockout picture of the year! – *The Champ*

The most startling drama ever produced! – *Strange Interlude*

Mothered by an ape – he knew only the law of the jungle – to seize what he wanted! – *Tarzan of the Apes*

Strange Desires! Loves and hates and secret yearnings . . . hidden in the shadows of a man's mind. – *Dr Jekyll and Mr Hyde*

The picture that will make 1933 famous! – *Gabriel over the White House*

The dance-mad musical triumph of two continents! – *The Gay Divorcee*

The love affair that shook the world! – *Cleopatra*

The most glorious musical romance of all time! – *One Night of Love*

His love challenged the flames of revolution! – *A Tale of Two Cities*

Love as burning as Sahara's sands! – *Under Two Flags*

The march of time measured by a human heart – a mother's heart! – *Cavalcade*

Romance aflame through dangerous days and nights of terror! In a land where anything can happen – most of all to a beautiful girl alone! – *Gunga Din* (in which the girl was very dispensable indeed)

The picture made behind locked doors! – *Dr Cyclops*

The strangest love a man has ever known! – *Dracula*

More sensational than her unforgettable father! – *Dracula's Daughter*

A love story that lived for three thousand years! – *The Mummy*

He's just as funny as his old man was fierce! – *Son of Kong*

Three centuries in the making! – *A Midsummer Night's Dream*

He plucked from the gutter a faded rose and made an immortal masterpiece! – *The Life of Emile Zola*

135 women – with men on their minds! – *The Women*

He treated her rough – and she loved it! – *Red Dust* .

A story so momentous it required six Academy Award stars and a cast of 1,186 players! – *Juarez*

Only the rainbow can duplicate its brilliance! – *The Adventures of Robin Hood*

Don't pronounce it – see it! – *Ninotchka*

A monster in form but human in his desire for love! – *Bride of Frankenstein*

Boiling passions in the burning sands! – *The Lost Patrol*

Six sticks of dynamite that blasted his way to freedom – and awoke America's conscience! – *I Am a Fugitive from a Chain Gang*

● *The Forties:*

No one is as good as Bette when she's bad! – *In This Our Life*

If she were yours, would you forgive? – *The Unfaithful*

The relentless drama of a woman driven to the depths of emotion by a craving beyond control! – *The Lady Gambles*

The thousands who have read the book will know why WE WILL NOT SELL ANY CHILDREN TICKETS to see this picture! – *The Grapes of Wrath*

Half men, half demons, warriors such as the world has never known – they lived with death and danger for the women who hungered for their love! – *Northwest Passage*

You can't keep a good monster down! – *The Ghost of Frankenstein*

A romantic gentleman by day – a love-mad beast by night! – *Dr Jekyll and Mr Hyde*

The minx in mink with a yen for men! – *Lady in the Dark*

The immortal thriller . . . – *Orpheus*

How'd you like to tussle with Russell? – *The Outlaw*

Gable's back and Garson's got him! – *Adventure*

There never was a woman like . . . – *Gilda*

It tells ALL about those Brontë sisters! – *Devotion*

More thrilling than the deeds of man . . . more beautiful than the love of woman . . . more wonderful than the dreams of children! – *The Jungle Book*

The picture they were born for! – *The Big Sleep*

The picture that helped to win the war! – *Mrs Miniver* (reissue)

He's as fast on the draw as he is in the drawing room! – *The Maltese Falcon*

We're going to see Jennifer Jones AGAIN in . . . – *The Song of Bernadette*

The sum total of all human emotion! – *Leave Her to Heaven*

The truth about the Nazis from the cradle to the battlefront! – *Hitler's Children*

A peek into the other woman's male! – *A Letter to Three Wives*

She knows all about love potions and lovely motions! – *I Married a Witch*

Paramount proudly brings to the screens of America one of the three great love stories of all time! – *To Each His Own* (which were the others?)

'I bought this woman for my own . . . and I'll kill the man who touches her!' – *Unconquered*

A thousand miles of danger with a thousand thrills a mile! – *Santa Fé Trail*

168 minutes of breathless thrills and romance! – *For Whom the Bell Tolls*

The girl of the moment in the wonderful picture of America's hey! hey! day! – *Margie*

The kind of woman most men want – but shouldn't have! – *Mildred Pierce*

They had a date with fate in . . . – *Casablanca*

The flaming drama of a high-born beauty who

blindly loved the most icy-hearted big shot gangland ever knew! – *Johnny Eager*

Whisper her name! – *The Strange Love of Martha Ivers*

A mouth like hers is just for kissing . . . not for telling! – *Nora Prentiss*

She insulted her soul! – *Dishonored Lady*

She's got the biggest six-shooters in the west! – *The Beautiful Blonde from Bashful Bend*

The private lady of a public enemy! – *The Damned Don't Cry*

It was the look in her eyes that did it! How could he know it meant murder? – *The Woman in the Window*

A love story every woman would die a thousand deaths to live! – *Jane Eyre*

'The men in her life sometimes lived to regret it!' – *Temptation*

● *The Fifties:*

Greater than IVANHOE! – *Julius Caesar*

First they moved (1895)! Then they talked (1927)! Now they smell! – *Scent of Mystery*

The butler did it! He made every lady in the house oh so very happy! – *My Man Godfrey*

Sing, Judy! Dance, Judy! The world is waiting for your sunshine! – *A Star Is Born*

Even in the first wild joy of her arms, he realized that she would be . . . an unfit mother! – *Because of You*

A lion in your lap! – *Bwana Devil* (the first 3-D film)

In making this film, MGM feel privileged to add something of permanent value to the cultural treasure house of mankind . . . – *Quo Vadis*

Ancient Rome is going to the dogs, Robert Taylor is going to the lions, and Peter Ustinov is going crazy! – *Quo Vadis* (revived for TV in the 70s)

You have never really seen Gregory Peck until you see him in CinemaScope! – *Night People*

We didn't say nice people, we said – *Night People*

Their story is not in the history books. It has never been seen on the screen – until now! – *Désirée*

A hard cop and a soft dame! – *The Big Heat*

A completely new experience between men and women! – *The Men* (about paraplegics)

He faced a decision that someday may be yours to make! – *Ransom* (the hero's son was kidnapped)

The colossus who conquered the world! The most colossal motion picture of all time! – *Alexander the Great*

When the hands point straight up . . . the excitement starts! – *High Noon*

That streetcar man has a new desire! – *The Wild One*

Her treachery stained every stone of the pyramid! – *Land of the Pharaohs*

The supreme screen achievement of our time! – *Salome*

Of what a girl did . . . what a boy did . . . of ecstasy and revenge! – *East of Eden*

If a woman answers . . . hang on for dear life! – *Dial M For Murder*

Body of a boy! Mind of a monster! Soul of an unearthly thing! – *I Was a Teenage Frankenstein*

The story of a family's ugly secret and the stark moment that thrust their private lives into public view! – *Written on the Wind*

'She was too hungry for love to care where she found it!' – *The Female on the Beach*

● *The Sixties:*

If you miss the first five minutes you miss one suicide, two executions, one seduction and the key to the plot! – *The Kremlin Letter*

The motion picture with something to offend everybody! – *The Loved One*

Beware the beat of the cloth-wrapped feet! – *The Mummy's Shroud*

The world's most uncovered undercover agent! – *Fathom*

Don't give away the ending – it's the only one we have! – *Psycho*

The birds is coming! – *The Birds*

Every time a woman turns her face away because she's tired or unwilling, there's someone waiting like me . . . – *The Dark at the Top of the Stairs*

The hot line suspense comedy! – *Dr Strangelove*

A thousand thrills . . . and Hayley Mills! – *In Search of the Castaways*

A picture that goes beyond what men think about – because no man ever thought about it in quite this way! – *Eight and a Half*

You may not believe in ghosts, but you cannot deny terror . . . – *The Haunting*

There are many kinds of love, but are there any without guilt? – *Five Finger Exercise*

You can expect the unexpected! – *Charade*

Now . . . add a motion picture to the wonders of the world! – *Taras Bulba*

One man . . . three women . . . one night! – *The Night of the Iguana*

You'll laugh your pants off! – *Laurel and Hardy's Laughing Twenties*

£10,000 if you die of fright! – *Macabre*

The picture with the fear flasher and the horror horn! – *Chamber of Horrors*

Meet the girls with the thermo-nuclear navels! The most titillating time bombs you've ever been tempted to trigger! – *Dr Goldfoot and the Girl Bombs*

Keep the children home! And if you're squeamish, stay home with them! – *Witchfinder General*

A side of life you never expected to see on the screen! – *Walk on the Wild Side*

You are cordially invited to George and Martha's for an evening of fun and games! – *Who's Afraid of Virginia Woolf?*

Why the crazy title? If we told you, you'd only laugh! – *The Russians are Coming, The Russians are Coming*

Every father's daughter is a virgin! – *Goodbye Columbus*

They're young . . . they're in love . . . and they kill people. – *Bonnie and Clyde*

'What we've got here is a failure to communicate.' – *Cool Hand Luke*

The big comedy of nineteen-sexty-sex! – *Boeing Boeing*

He is a shy schoolmaster. She is a music hall star. They marry and immediately have 283 children . . . all boys! – *Goodbye Mr Chips*

● *The Seventies:*

Love means never having to say you're sorry . . . – *Love Story*

Hope never dies for a man with a good dirty mind! – *Hoffman*

The story of a homosexual who married a nymphomaniac! – *The Music Lovers*

Like the act of love, this film must be experienced from beginning to end . . . – *The Sailor Who Fell from Grace with the Sea*

They stand side by side. Young and old. Rich and poor. They gather together for a single purpose. Survival. – *The Seagull*

We don't love – we just make love. And damn little of that! – *The Happy Ending*

She gave away secrets to one side and her heart to the other! – *Darling Lili*

For the price of a movie you'll feel like a million! – *The Sunshine Boys*

The damnedest thing you ever saw. – *Nashville*

1953 was a good year for leaving home. – *Next Stop Greenwich Village*

The epic love story in which everybody has a great role and a big part. – *Joseph Andrews*

You have nothing to lose but your mind. – *Asylum*

A degenerate film with dignity! – *Inserts*

In space no one can hear you scream. – *Alien*

We are not alone. – *Close Encounters of the Third Kind*

Just when you thought it was safe to go back into the water. – *Jaws 2*

It was a line which spawned such imitations as:

Now you're not safe OUT of the water. – *Piranha II – Flying Killers*

Just when you thought it was safe to go back into the departure lounge. – *Airplane II*

Just when he thought it was safe to go back into the water. – *10*

● *The Eighties:*

He was D. H. Lawrence. She was his Lady Chatterley. Their extraordinary romance was more tempestuous than any he wrote. – *Priest of Love*

The film where you hiss the villain and cheer the hero. – *The Legend of the Lone Ranger*

As brutal, beautiful, vicious and vast as America itself! – *Heaven's Gate*

Breaking out is impossible. Breaking in is insane! – *Escape from New York*

The most exciting pair in the jungle! – *Tarzan the Ape-Man* (starring Bo Derek)

From the very beginning, they knew they'd be friends to the very end. What they didn't count on was everything in between. – *Rich and Famous*

The last word about the first time. – *Losin' It*

To the valley of beauty came the shadow of death! – *Deadly Blessing*

Every great love leaves its mark. – *Tattoo*

The third dimension is terror. – *Jaws 3-D*

It's 22 years later. And Norman Bates is coming home. – *Psycho II*

Trust me, I'm a doctor. – *Shock Treatment* (a line that turned up a decade later for *Paper Mask*)

The good news is Jonathan's having his first affair. The bad news is she's his roommate's mother. – *Class*

I'd been shot so many times you could use my shirt as a tea strainer. – *Dead Men Don't Wear Plaid*

Forged by a god. Foretold by a wizard. Found by a King. – *Excalibur*

What they wanted most wasn't on the menu. – *Diner*

He is afraid. He is totally alone. He is 3 million light years from home. – *E.T. – the Extraterrestrial*

She was the woman of Allen's dreams. She had large dark eyes, a beautiful smile and a great pair of fins. – *Splash*

When the going gets tough, the tough get going! – *Jewel of the Nile*

They left for war as boys, never to return as men. – *All Quiet on the Western Front*

The tenant in room seven is very small, very twisted and very mad. – *Basket Case*

Be afraid. Be very afraid. – *The Fly*

When he pours, he reigns. – *Cocktail*

Just when he was ready for mid-life crisis, something unexpected came up. Puberty. – *Vice Versa*

Dying is easy. Comedy is hard. – *Punchline*

Somewhere under the sea and beyond your imagination is an adventure in fantasy. – *The Little Mermaid*

Can two friends sleep together and still love each other in the morning? – *When Harry Met Sally*

● *The Nineties:*

Their love was as dangerous as the secrets they kept. – *The Russia House*

Paul Sheldon used to write for a living . . . Now he's writing to stay alive. – *Misery*

There was a time when the only way to uphold justice was to break the law. – *Robin Hood: Prince of Thieves*

He's coming to town with a few days to kill. – *Predator 2*

Having a wonderful time. Wish I were here. – *Postcards from the Edge*

Eight legs, two fangs and an attitude. – *Arachnophobia*

Once in a lifetime comes a motion picture that makes you feel like falling in love all over again. This is not that picture. – *The War of the Roses*

How many times can you die for love? – *Dead Again*

There is nothing in the dark that isn't there in the light. Except fear. – *Cape Fear*

He'd be the perfect criminal if he wasn't the perfect cop. – *Deep Cover*

He was a man who couldn't care less . . . until he met a man who couldn't care more. – *City of Joy*

The fountain of youth. The secret of eternal life. The power of an ancient potion. Sometimes it works . . . Sometimes it doesn't. – *Death Becomes Her*

An adventure 65 million years in the making – *Jurassic Park*

63 million years ago they ruled the Earth. They're back, and it's no theme park! – *Carnosaur*

No one would take on his case . . . until one man was willing to take on the system – *Philadelphia*

Just your average Girl meets Girl, Girl loses Girl, Girl hires Boy to get Girl back story. With a twist. – *Three of Hearts*

Stealing . . . Cheating . . . Killing . . . Who says romance is dead? – *True Romance*

Houston, we have a problem. – *Apollo 13*

When intimacy is forbidden and passion is a sin, love is the most defiant crime of all – *The Scarlet Letter*

Leave your inhibitions at the door – *Showgirls*

NB: In 1972 a New York magazine ran a competition, inviting readers to invent way-out and hilarious tag-lines for non-existent movies. The results were indeed hilarious, but not so way-

out that one can't imagine them being used. Here are some of the winners:

Makes Myra Breckinridge look like Snow White!

It took guts to film. Have you the guts to see it?

There were four men in her life. One to love her. One to marry her. One to take care of her. And one to kill her . . .

They lived a lifetime in 24 crowded hours!

The picture that could change your life – or save it!

If you scoff at the powers of darkness, do not see this film alone!

The book they said could never be written has become the movie they said could never be filmed!

put-downs

Waspish comments about other people always make good reading. Here are a few for starters:

Let's face it, Billy Wilder at work is two people – Mr Hyde and Mr Hyde. – *Harry Kurnitz*

I loved it – particularly the ideas he took from me. – *D.W. Griffith on Citizen Kane*

Jack Lemmon's Hildy Johnson is like a mortuary assistant having a wild fling. – *New Yorker review of The Front Page*

Mae West, playing a ghastly travesty of the travesty of womanhood she once played, has a Mae West face painted on the front of her head and moves to and fro like the Imperial Hotel during the 1923 Tokyo earthquake. – *Joseph Morgenstern reviewing Myra Breckinridge*

As a pompous middle-European intellectual Kenneth Mars mugs and drools in a manner that Jerry Lewis might find excessive. – *Jay Cocks reviewing What's Up, Doc?*

To insinuate that Leslie Bricusse's plodding score is merely dreadful would be an act of charity. – *Rex Reed on Goodbye Mr Chips*

Miss Martin, I notice, is playing Jean Arthur, a tendency which even Miss Arthur should learn to curb. – *James Agee on True To Life*

Mr Muni seemed intent on submerging himself so completely in make-up that he disappeared. – *Bette Davis on Juarez*

Which is he playing now? – *W. Somerset Maugham while watching Spencer Tracy on the set of Dr Jekyll and Mr Hyde*

Ryan O'Neal is so stiff and clumsy that he can't even manage a part requiring him to be stiff and clumsy. – *Jay Cocks on What's Up Doc?*

He has a gift for butchering good parts while managing to look intelligent, thus constituting Hollywood's abiding answer to the theatre. – *Wilfred Sheed of Jack Lemmon*

Just how garish her commonplace accent, squeakily shrill voice, and the childish petulance with which she delivers her lines are, my pen is neither scratchy nor leaky enough to convey. – *John Simon of Elizabeth Taylor in The Taming of the Shrew*

George Raft and Gary Cooper once played a scene in front of a cigar store, and it looked like the wooden Indian was overacting. – *George Burns*

Quiller.

Code name of a tough British secret agent, able to take any amount of torture, who is the hero of a series of novels by Adam Hall (Elleston Trevor). United Artists acquired the film rights to them in 1993 with the intention of producing a series of movies featuring what the company called 'the thinking man's James Bond'. A film of the first novel, *The Quiller Memorandum*, was directed by Michael Anderson in 1966 starring George Segal, and Michael Jayston played the role in a BBC TV series, *Quiller*, in 1975.

Quo Vadis?

The biblical epic by Henryk Sienkiewicz has been filmed three times: in Italy in 1912 and 1924, and in America in 1951. The third version, though less impressive as a product of its period than the others, was certainly the most spectacular. Robert Taylor and Deborah Kerr suffered under Peter Ustinov's Nero; Mervyn Le Roy directed.

radio,

being a competitor, was largely ignored by serious movies in the 30s, but radio stars featured in a number of musicals, especially the *Big Broadcast* series and the British *Radio Parade*, *Music Hath Charms*, etc.; in the 40s, a number of low-budgeters such as *Reveille with Beverly* had a radio background.

Popular radio series to be filmed included *Dr Christian*, *Fibber McGee and Molly*, *Charlie McCarthy Detective*, *The Great Gildersleeve*, *Hi Gang*, *Band Waggon* and *It's That Man Again*. Mysteries set in radio stations included *Who Done It* and *Death at Broadcasting House*; *Helter Skelter* was a slapstick comedy set at the BBC. In the 70s, *Play Misty for Me* revolved around a disc jockey, as did the TV movie *A Cry for Help*; while *WUSA* was undoubtedly the most serious drama on the subject unless one counts the sharply satirical *A Face in the Crowd* and *Talk Radio*, highlighting the potential dangers of chat shows.

Raffles.

The sophisticated burglar who returns to crime to help an old friend was created by E. W. Hornung and has attracted the attentions of several suave leading men. There were half a dozen silent Raffles, including one from House Peters in 1925, directed by King Baggot; Ronald Colman played the role in 1930, and a shot-by-shot remake in 1939 starred David Niven.

railway stations

have provided a major setting for some memorable films including *The Ghost Train*, *Doctor Zhivago*, *Knight without Armour*, *I'll Never Forget Whatshisname* (with its white 'dream' station), *Union Station*, *3.10 to Yuma*, *Last Train from Madrid*, *Bhowani Junction*, *Northwest Frontier*, *100 Rifles*, *The Mercenaries*, *Waterloo Road*, *Anna Karenina*, *Grand Central Station*, *Under the Clock*, *Brief Encounter*, *Oh Mr Porter*, *The Titfield Thunderbolt*, *High Noon*, *In the Heat of the Night* and *The Train* . . . while Orson Welles made *The Trial* almost entirely within a deserted station, and de Sica made *Indiscretion* among the crowds of Rome's Stazione Termini.

See also: TRAINS.

rain

has been put to many uses by film scenarists. It was the direct cause of dramatic situations in *Rebecca* (a shower flattened Joan Fontaine's hair-do just as she arrived at Manderley); in *The Loneliness of the Long Distance Runner* (it revealed evidence which the hero was trying to conceal); in *Floods of Fear* (it permitted the escape of three convicts, one of whom then rescued the heroine); in *The African Queen* (it raised the water level and so released the boat from the reeds which held it captive); in *Desk Set* (it persuaded Spencer Tracy to accept Katharine Hepburn's offer of hospitality); in *Pygmalion* (it caused the meeting of Higgins and Eliza); in *Sands of the Kalahari* (it flooded a pit in which Stuart Whitman was imprisoned and permitted his escape); in *When Tomorrow Comes* (it stranded Charles Boyer and Irene Dunne in a remote church for the night); and in many others. Two splendid symbolic uses were in *Saraband for Dead Lovers* (a raindrop made a stained-glass madonna appear to weep at the ill-fated wedding) and *The Stars Look Down* (as the hero and heroine make love, two raindrops intertwine on the window-pane).

Rain has often been used symbolically as a relief from tension and heat, in films as diverse as *Night of the Iguana*, *Passport to Pimlico*, *The Long Hot Summer*, *Key Largo*, *Twelve Angry Men*, *Black Narcissus*, *The Good Earth* and *Rain* itself. It has provided a solemn or ominous background in *Psycho*, *Term of Trial*, *Rashomon*, *It Always Rains on Sunday*, *Room at the Top*, *The Robe*, *Fires on the Plain*, *The Collector* and many others. It has a particularly depressing effect at a funeral, as was shown in *The Glass Key* and *Our Town*; or at an assassination (*Foreign Correspondent*). But it can also be used for farcical purposes: in *Three Men in a Boat*, *The Silencers*, *Fraternally Yours*, *Oh Mr Porter*, etc. And it can provide a comedy twist, as at the end of *The Lady Vanishes*, when the English travellers so eager to get back to the test match find that rain has stopped play.

It can produce a decorative effect (*Les Parapluies de Cherbourg*, *Miracle in the Rain*, *Breakfast at Tiffany's*). It can be spectacular (the climax of *Journey into Fear*, the glistening streets in *The Third Man*, the downpours in *The Rains Came*, and *Pather Panchali*, the battles in the rain in *Tower of London* and *Seven Samurai*). And it can provide a cue for song: 'Isn't it a Lovely Day to be Caught in the Rain' in *Top Hat*, the title songs of *Singin' in the Rain* and *Stormy Weather*, 'The Rain in Spain' in *My Fair Lady*, 'April Showers' in *The Jolson Story*, 'Little April Shower' in *Bambi*. In fact, it seems to be by far the most versatile of all the film-maker's effects. It has even featured as the subject of a disaster movie, *Hard Rain* 98, in which a town was flooded, and its cast, wet, no longer seemed stars.

Rain.

Somerset Maugham's story of the conflict between a missionary and a woman of highly doubtful character has been filmed three times in Hollywood: in 1928 with Gloria Swanson and Lionel Barrymore; in 1932 with Joan Crawford and Walter Huston; and in 1957 (as *Miss Sadie Thompson*) with Rita Hayworth and José Ferrer. In each case the Production Code made you guess what the lady's actual profession was.

The Rains Came.

Louis Broomfield's novel of the high days of British India was filmed in 1939 with Myrna Loy and Tyrone Power, and, as *The Rains of Ranchipur*, in 1955 with Lana Turner and Richard Burton.

Rambo.

The disgruntled former Green Beret has been played by Sylvester Stallone in three increasingly violent films: *First Blood* 82, directed by Ted Kotcheff; *Rambo: First Blood Part II* 85, directed by George P. Cosmatos, in which he had become a comic-strip hero, destroying enemies in Vietnam; and *Rambo III* 88, directed by Peter MacDonald, in which he continued as a one-man army, this time defeating the Russians in Afghanistan, most of which he blew up. The series was spoofed in *Hot Shots! Part Deux* 93, with Charlie Sheen as a dim mercenary with big muscles and bigger guns.

Ramona.

Helen Hunt Jackson's novel about an Indian girl was filmed four times: by D. W. Griffith in 1910, with Mary Pickford and Henry B. Walthall; by Donald Crisp in 1916, with Adda Gleason and Monroe Salisbury; by Edwin Carewe in 1928, with Dolores del Rio and Warner Baxter; and by Henry King in 1936, with Loretta Young and Don Ameche.

The Range Busters.

A series of 'B' westerns produced for seven years from 1940 by Monogram Pictures in imitation of Republic's THREE MESQUITEERS series. It starred two of the Mesquiteers, Ray 'Crash' CORRIGAN and Mex TERHUNE, together with John 'Dusty' KING. Many were directed by S. Roy Luby, who churned out dozens of westerns from the mid-30s to the late 40s.

rape

was virtually unmentionable in English-speaking films until Warner's got away with it in *Johnny Belinda* in 1947. Then it became the centre of attention in *Outrage, Peyton Place, Wicked as They Come, A Streetcar Named Desire, Last Train from Gun Hill, Two Women, To Kill a Mockingbird, Satan Never Sleeps, Shock Corridor, Assault, Trial, Five Gates to Hell, The Chapman Report, The Mark, Anatomy of a Murder, Town without Pity, The Party's Over* (in which the victim proved to be dead), and *The Penthouse*. In *Waterhole Three* James Coburn, accused of the crime, shrugged it off as 'assault with a friendly weapon'. There was much talk of rape in *The Knack* and *Lock Up Your Daughters*, threat of rape in *Experiment in Terror* and *Cape Fear*, and an accusation of rape in *Term of Trial*. Foreign language films on the subject have included *Rashomon, The Virgin Spring, Two Women, Viridiana* and the Greek *Amok*. In 70s films it became too commonplace to be worth mentioning, outstanding fictional instances being *Straw Dogs, A Clockwork Orange, Lipstick*, and *Death Wish*, with *Cry Rape* and *A Case of Rape* adopting a documentary treatment. *The Accused* 88 caused controversy with its depiction of the gang-rape of a provocative woman and subsequent court-room trial – it also brought an Oscar for Jodie Foster as best actress. And some cheered in *Thelma & Louise* 91 when a would-be rapist was shot and killed.

Rashomon.

Akira Kurosawa's 1951 masterpiece, featuring the different accounts by four people concerned in a moment of violence, re-opened Western cinemas to Japanese films and established his international reputation. It was remade by Martin Ritt in 1964 and given a western setting, starring Paul Newman as a Mexican bandit.

The Rat

began as a film script written by Ivor NOVELLO for director Adrian BRUNEL, following their success in the film *The Man without Desire*. When Brunel was unable to finance it, Novello collaborated with actress Constance COLLIER to turn it into a lurid melodrama, which they wrote under the pseudonym of David L'Estrange and subtitled 'The Story of an Apache'. It starred Novello as Pierre Boucheron, a French crook who is reformed by the love of a poor but honest woman. It was a surprising success on the stage, as was the subsequent film in 1925, which was followed by two sequels: *The Triumph of the Rat* 26, in which he goes from riches to rags, and *The Return of the Rat* 28, in which he is suspected of murdering his philandering wife. In 1937, Herbert WILCOX directed a remake of the original, starring Anton WALBROOK, but it failed to repeat its earlier success.

Rebecca of Sunnybrook Farm.

The American children's classic by Kate Douglas Wiggin was filmed in 1917 by Marshall Neilan, with Mary Pickford; in 1932 by Alfred Santell, with Marian Nixon; and in 1938, much changed, by Allan Dwan, with Shirley Temple.

Red Dust.

This rubber-plantation drama by Wilson Collinson is remembered for the electric teaming of Clark Gable and Jean Harlow in the 1932 version, directed by Victor Fleming, and for the scene in which Harlow takes a primitive shower. It was remade in 1939 as *Congo Maisie*, with Ann Sothern and John Carroll; and in 1954 Gable himself appeared opposite Ava Gardner in a lavish restyling under the title *Mogambo*, directed by John Ford.

Red Indians (native Americans),

it is generally thought, were always portrayed as villains on screen until *Broken Arrow* in 1950, when Jeff Chandler played Cochise. But in fact there were many silent films in which Indians were not only on the side of right but the leading figures in the story. In 1911 one finds titles like *An Indian Wife's Devotion, A Squaw's Love, Red-Wing's Gratitude; Ramona* had already been made once and was to survive three remakes; 1913 brought *Heart of an Indian* and *The Squaw Man*. Later there were versions of *In the Days of Buffalo Bill* 21, *The Vanishing American* 25, and *Redskin* 28. It seems to have been sound that made the Indians villainous, and kept them that way for twenty-two years.

After *Broken Arrow* there was a deluge of pro-Indian films. *Devil's Doorway, Across the Wide Missouri, The Savage, Arrowhead, The Big Sky, Apache, Taza – Son of Cochise, Chief Crazy Horse, Sitting Bull, White Feather, Navajo, Hiawatha*, all came within four years. There were even biopics of modern Indians: *The Outsider* (Ira Hayes) and *Jim Thorpe, All American*. In recent years the Indians have been slipping back into villainy: but the 60s brought *Flaming Star, Cheyenne Autumn, Tell them Willie Boy is Here, A Man called Horse, Flap, Little Big Man, The Stalking Moon*; and TV in 1966 boasted a series based on a Red Indian cop in New York (the name is *Hawk*) as well as comic Indians in *F Troop*; and Elvis Presley played a Red Indian hero in *Stay Away Joe*. In the 90s, *Dances with Wolves* established the Indians as heroes and the American cavalry as the villains.

Other whites who have played red include Boris Karloff in *Tap Roots*; Victor Mature in *Chief Crazy Horse*; Charlton Heston in *The Savage*; Burt Lancaster in *Apache*; Paul Newman in *Hombre*; Robert Taylor in *Devil's Doorway*; Don Ameche in *Ramona*.

~The Jacarillo tribe financed *A Gunfight* in 1971.

reincarnation

has seldom been seriously tackled in the cinema: *The Search for Bridey Murphy, I've Lived Before* and *The Reincarnation of Peter Proud* are almost the only examples. Many characters of farce and melodrama have *thought* they were reincarnated, including the hero of *She* and heroine of *The Vengeance of She*. The real thing happened to Oliver Hardy in *The Flying Deuces* (he came back as a horse); to a dog in *You Never Can Tell* (he came back as Dick Powell); and to the luckless heroine of *The Bride and the Beast*, who found that in a former existence she had been a gorilla. Reincarnation was also the basis of *Here Comes Mr Jordan*, and of *The Mummy*. A man came back as Debbie Reynolds in *Goodbye Charlie*, and in *Quest for Love* there were parallel love stories two centuries apart. In 1968 a version was made of Elmer Rice's *The Adding Machine*, with its celestial laundry for souls; and in 1970 there was even a musical on the subject, *On a Clear Day You Can See Forever*.

rejuvenation

is not a theme the cinema has frequently explored. *She* tried it several times with unhappy results, as did Laurel and Hardy in *Dirty Work* (Olly came back as a chimpanzee). *The Man in Half Moon Street* and *Countess Dracula* both kept young on the blood of others; *Dorian Gray* did it by keeping a picture of himself in the attic. Most successful were *Lost Horizon*'s inhabitants of Shangri-La, but once the cold winds of the outside world blew they were done for. Rock Hudson had worse luck in *Seconds*. *Cocoon* introduced alien aid to staying young, although *Cocoon: The Return* showed that there was no permanent solution to the problems of age.

religion

has inspired film-makers from the beginning – as a commercial trump card. In the early years of the century it was the Italians who produced vast semi-biblical spectacles like *Quo Vadis* and *Cabiria*, but Hollywood was not slow to catch on, and producers soon found that religious shorts gave them extra prestige. There were several versions of *From the Manger to the Cross*; Griffith, in *Judith of Bethulia* and *Intolerance*, contributed his share; *Ben Hur* was the biggest spectacular of all; but it was Cecil B. de Mille in the 20s who brought the Bible to full commercial flower with *The Ten Commandments* and *King of Kings*. (His 1932 *The Sign of the Cross*, 1950 *Samson and Delilah* and 1956 remake of *The Ten Commandments* show that for him at least time continued to stand still.) In 1929, though *Noah's Ark* was spectacle pure and simple, Vidor's *Hallelujah* at least partially transmitted Negro religious fervour. In the 30s Hollywood was seeking fresh ways to combine religion with sentiment or spectacle, in *The Cradle Song, Dante's Inferno, The Garden of Allah, The Green Light* and *Boys' Town*. One result was a new characterization of PRIESTS as jolly good fellows: stars like Spencer Tracy and Pat O'Brien were eager to play them. Yet none had the quiet dignity of Rex Ingram as De Lawd in *Green Pastures*, a Negro version of the Scriptures.

The war naturally brought a religious revival. Every film set in England seemed to end with a service in a bombed church, and religious figures became big time in films like *The Song of Bernadette, Going My Way, The Keys of the Kingdom* and *The Bells of St Mary's*. Savage war films masqueraded under such titles as *God Is My Co-Pilot* and *A Wing and a Prayer*. And heaven was used as a background for light-hearted fantasy films about death and judgement day, such as *Here Comes Mr Jordan, Heaven Can Wait*, and *The Horn Blows at Midnight*. The only film of this period to question religion at all was the British *Major Barbara*: 'What price salvation now?'

In the cynical post-war years religion was at a low ebb. An expensive *Joan of Arc* in 1948 failed disastrously, and an attempt to bring God into our everyday life, *The Next Voice You Hear*, fared no better. A sincere performance by Robert Donat could not bring people to see *Lease of Life*. Indeed, the only religious films to break even at the box office were those with a direct Roman Catholic appeal, such as *Monsieur Vincent* and *The Miracle of Fatima*. True religion, to Hollywood, was out, and the Bible became once more a source book for a string of tawdry commercial epics: *Quo Vadis, Salome, The Prodigal, The Robe*, a remake of *Ben Hur, Barabbas, The Silver Chalice, Sodom and Gomorrah* and many cut-rate dubbed Italian spectacles of a similar kind (most with Hollywood stars). Occasionally a spark of sincerity would flash through, as in the otherwise dull *David and Bathsheba*; while small independent companies could produce interesting films like *The First Legion*. Towards the end of the 50s there were occasional attempts to see religion afresh: *A Man Called Peter, The Nun's Story, Inn of the Sixth Happiness, Whistle Down the Wind*. Otto Preminger, despite a 1957 failure with *Saint Joan*, tried again in 1963 with *The Cardinal*. In 1965 George Stevens unveiled *The Greatest Story Ever Told*, a tepid life of Jesus which found little box-office favour, being overtaken in some quarters by Pasolini's *The Gospel According to St Matthew*. 1966 brought the long-promised Italian-American epic known as *The Bible*: in fact it dealt only with the Book of Genesis, and that at such a dull pace and inordinate length that it is doubtful whether sequels will be called for. 1969 offered a drama of modern popes, *The Shoes of the Fisherman*, but it died. The most fashionable film interpretations of religion in the early 70s were the pop operas exemplified by *Godspell* and *Jesus Christ Superstar*; but in 1977 Lew Grade's mammoth six-hour *Jesus of Nazareth*, directed by Franco Zeffirelli, achieved record viewing figures and pointed to a benighted world's requirement to believe in *something*.

Martin Scorsese's *The Last Temptation of Christ* 88 focused on Jesus's self-doubts as he faced his crucifixion, while Michael Tolkin's *The Rapture* 91 dealt in fundamentalist terms with the end of the world, complete with the Four Horsemen of the Apocalypse.

remakes in disguise.

Hollywood studios were famous for squeezing every drop of value from a literary property, even if it meant changing the locale, switching the sexes and generally bamboozling the audience, which hopefully would not get that I-have-been-here-before feeling until they were half-way home. Here are just a few movies which went through a change of title but used up the same old plot:

~*Sentimental Journey; The Gift of Love*
~*Libelled Lady; Easy to Wed*
~*Here Comes Mr Jordan; Heaven Can Wait*
~*Love Is News; Sweet Rosie O'Grady; That Wonderful Urge*
~*The Bowery; Coney Island; Wabash Avenue*
~*The Greeks Had a Word for Them; Ladies in Love; Three Blind Mice; Moon over Miami; Three Little Girls in Blue; How to Marry a Millionaire; Three Coins in the Fountain; The Pleasure Seekers*
~*Kentucky; Down Argentine Way*
~*Folies Bergère; That Night in Rio; On the Riviera; On the Double*
~*The Front Page; His Girl Friday; Torrid Zone; Switching Channels*
~*Gunga Din; Sergeants Three*
~*My Favorite Wife; Move Over Darling*
~*Grand Hotel; Weekend at the Waldorf*
~*It Happened One Night; You Can't Run Away From It*
~*Tiger Shark; Slim; Manpower*
~*House of Strangers; Broken Lance*
~*High Sierra; I Died a Thousand Times*
~*20,000 Years in Sing Sing; Castle on the Hudson*
~*Mystery of the Wax Museum; House of Wax*
~*One Way Passage; Till We Meet Again*
~*Bordertown; They Drive by Night*
~*Dangerous; Singapore Woman*
~*The Petrified Forest; Escape in the Desert*
~*Four Daughters; Young at Heart*
~*Dr Socrates; King of the Underworld*
~*The Butter and Egg Man; The Tenderfoot; Dance Charlie Dance; An Angel from Texas*
~*The Most Dangerous Game; A Game of Death; Run for the Sun*
~*The Kennel Murder Case; Calling Philo Vance*
~*The Letter; The Unfaithful*
~*The Mouthpiece; The Man Who Talked Too Much; Illegal*
~*Oil for the Lamps of China; Law of the Tropics*
~*The Sea Wolf; Wolf Larsen; Barricade; Wolf of the Seven Seas*
~*Kid Galahad; The Wagons Roll at Night*
~*Casablanca; Far East*
~*The Man Who Played God; Sincerely Yours*
~*The Millionaire; That Way with Women*
~*The Miracle of Morgan's Creek; Rock-a-bye Baby*
~*Anna and the King of Siam; The King and I*
~*London After Midnight; Mark of the Vampire*
~*Love Affair; An Affair to Remember*
~*Morning Glory; Stage Struck*
~*The Lady Eve; The Birds and the Bees*
~*The Marriage Circle; One Hour with You*
~*Nothing Sacred; Living It Up*
~*Dark Victory; Stolen Hours*
~*One Sunday Afternoon; The Strawberry Blonde*
~*A Slight Case of Murder; Stop! You're Killing Me*
~*The Paleface; The Shakiest Gun in the West*
~*Le Jour Se Lève; The Long Night*
~*The Women; The Opposite Sex*
~*The Asphalt Jungle; The Badlanders; Cairo; Cool Breeze*
~*The Four Feathers; Storm over the Nile*
~*It Started with Eve; I'd Rather Be Rich*
~*Rome Express; Sleeping Car to Trieste*
~*This Gun for Hire; Short Cut to Hell*

∾*The Informer; Uptight*
∾*Against All Flags; The King's Pirate*
∾*Red Dust; Congo Maisie; Mogambo*
∾*An American Tragedy; A Place in the Sun*
∾*Outward Bound; Between Two Worlds*
∾*Ebb Tide; Adventure Island*
∾*Ah, Wilderness; Summer Holiday*

reporters
in American films have since the beginning of the sound era been pictured as trench-coated, trilby-hatted, good-looking guys with a smart line in wisecracks. Among the outstanding examples of this tradition are Pat O'Brien in *The Front Page*, Robert Williams in *Platinum Blonde*, Clark Gable in *It Happened One Night* and *Teacher's Pet*, Fredric March in *Nothing Sacred*, Lee Tracy in *Doctor X*, Joel McCrea in *Foreign Correspondent*, David Janssen in *The Green Berets*, James Stewart in *The Philadelphia Story*, Lynne Overman in *Roxie Hart*, Gene Kelly in *Inherit the Wind;* while on the distaff side one can't overlook Glenda Farrell in *The Mystery of the Wax Museum*, Bette Davis in *Front Page Woman*, Jean Arthur in *Mr Deeds Goes to Town*, Rosalind Russell in *His Girl Friday* or Barbara Stanwyck in *Meet John Doe*. Presented somewhat more realistically were William Alland in *Citizen Kane*, James Stewart in *Call Northside 777*, Burgess Meredith as Ernie Pyle in *The Story of G.I. Joe*, Kirk Douglas in *Ace in the Hole*, and Arthur Kennedy in *Lawrence of Arabia*. The apotheosis of the reporter as hero was *All the President's Men*, with Robert Redford and Dustin Hoffman as Bob Woodward and Carl Bernstein of *The Washington Post* investigating Watergate.

British films have used their newshawks more flippantly, especially in the case of *This Man Is News* with Barry K. Barnes and *A Run for Your Money* with Alec Guinness. Just as well; for Edward Judd in *The Day the Earth Caught Fire*, Jack Hawkins in *Front Page Story*, Sidney James in *Quatermass II* and Norman Wooland in *All Over the Town* were a pretty dull lot, and Colin Gordon's imitation of the American model in *Escapade* was hardly convincing. Television series, of course, have found the reporter a convenient peg, as in the British *Deadline Midnight* and the American *Saints and Sinners* and *The Reporter*.

The Ringer.
Edgar Wallace's thriller about a vengeful master of disguise has been filmed three times in Britain: as a silent directed by Arthur Maude in 1928, starring Leslie Faber and Lawson Butt; and two versions directed by Walter Forde: the first with Gordon Harker and Franklin Dyall in 1931; and, under the title *The Gaunt Stranger*, with Sonnie Hale and Wilfred Lawson in 1938.

road movie.
A genre in which the main characters are on the move, usually in a car. The journey is more important than the destination, and puts its protagonists among unfamiliar people and situations. The form was best defined in a novel, Jack Kerouac's *On the Road* (1957), which, with its travellers looking for some kind of fulfilment, has influenced many subsequent movies. The form, in which cars often seem to be the main characters and the emphasis is on action, had an immediate appeal to the young of America and, to an extent, replaced the western as popular entertainment. Sub-genres that grew out of road movies include car race movies, such as *The Cannonball Run* and *Deathrace 2000*, the biker movies of the 60s, which reached a peak with *Easy Rider* 69, and the young outlaw movies, such as *Badlands, Natural Born Killers, Love and a.45*. The emphasis was on male bonding until the 90s, when *Thelma and Louise* and *The Adventures of Priscilla, Queen of the Desert* added feminist and gay interest.

Book: 1982, *Road Movies* by Mark Williams.

Road Runner.
Long-necked bird who whizzes along Arizona desert roads with a cry of 'Beep! Beep!' and gets the better of its pursuer Wile E. Coyote in Warner Brothers' Looney Tunes and Merrie Melodies cartoons. Its creators were Chuck Jones and writer Michael Maltese and its beep was supplied by the ubiquitous Mel Blanc.

Fast and Furry-Ous 49. Beep, Beep 52. There They Go-Go-Go 56. Fastest with the Mostest 60. Beep Prepared (AAN) 61. Tired and Feathered 65. Shot and Bothered 66. Run, Run, Sweet Road Runner 65. Out and Out Rout 66, etc.

robberies
have been a commonplace of film action fare since *The Great Train Robbery* itself; but of late there has been a fashion for showing the planning and execution of robberies through the eyes of the participants. Perhaps this started in 1950 with *The Asphalt Jungle* (and its two remakes *The Badlanders* and *Cairo*); anyway, some of the films built in this mould are *Rififi, Five against the House, Seven Thieves, The Killing, Payroll, Piccadilly Third Stop, The Day They Robbed the Bank of England, A Prize of Gold, On Friday at Eleven, Once a Thief, He Who Rides a Tiger, Robbery, Charley Varrick, Cops and Robbers, The Taking of Pelham One Two Three, The Getaway, 11 Harrowhouse, The Bank Shot, Gambit, Dog Day Afternoon* and *Inside Out;* while films treating the same subject less seriously included *The Lavender Hill Mob, The Lady Killers, Ocean's Eleven, Persons Unknown, The League of Gentlemen, Topkapi, The Big Job, Assault on a Queen, The Biggest Bundle of Them All, Grand Slam, They Came to Rob Las Vegas, The Italian Job, The Hot Rock* and *The Anderson Tapes*. The biggest attempted robbery of all was probably the raid on Fort Knox in *Goldfinger*. Sometimes one longs for a return to the days of the dapper jewel thieves: Ronald Colman or David Niven in *Raffles*, Herbert Marshall in *Trouble in Paradise*, John Barrymore or even Charles Korvin as Arsène Lupin, Cary Grant in *To Catch a Thief*. The closest we have come to this style for many years, apart from William Wyler's *How to Steal a Million*, is 1973's *The Thief Who Came to Dinner* with Ryan O'Neal. In 1964 TV made a gallant effort with *The Rogues*.

Robin Hood.
The legendary outlaw leader of Plantagenet England is one of literature's most oft-filmed characters. There were film versions in 1909 (GB), 1912 (GB), 1912 (US), 1913 (US), and 1913 (GB). Douglas Fairbanks made his big-scale *Robin Hood* in 1922, with Wallace Beery as King Richard. In 1938 came *The Adventures of Robin Hood*, one of Hollywood's most satisfying action adventures, with Errol Flynn as Robin, Claude Rains as Prince John and Basil Rathbone as Guy of Gisbourne; directed by William Keighley and Michael Curtiz, from a script by Norman Reilly Raine and Seton I. Miller. Its exhilaration has not diminished with time. In 1946 (US) Cornel Wilde played Robin's son in *Bandit of Sherwood Forest;* in 1948 (US) Jon Hall was Robin in *Prince of Thieves;* in 1950 (US) John Derek was Robin's son in *Rogues of Sherwood Forest;* Robert Clarke played Robin in an odd concoction called *Tales of Robin Hood* (US 1952). Also in 1952, in Britain, Disney filmed Richard Todd in *The Story of Robin Hood and His Merrie Men*, with only fair success, though the real Sherwood Forest was used for the first time. Robin also appeared briefly (played by Harold Warrender) in *Ivanhoe* 52. *Men of Sherwood Forest* (GB 1956) had Don Taylor as Robin; *Son of Robin Hood* (GB 1959) turned out to be a daughter, played by June Laverick. Most durable Robin is Richard Greene, who played the role not only in 165 half-hour TV films but in a feature, *Sword of Sherwood Forest* (GB 1961). In 1967 Barrie Ingham took over in *A Challenge for Robin Hood*, in 1973 the Disney studios produced a cartoon version, and in 1976 came *Robin and Marian*, which traced the sad fortunes of the protagonists twenty years later. A new television series, *Robin of Sherwood*, appeared in 1984. Patrick Bergin played the role, with Uma Thurman as a petulant Maid Marian, in the downbeat *Robin Hood* 91. It was swiftly eclipsed by the dour Kevin Costner in *Robin Hood: Prince of Thieves* which was, surprisingly, one of the box-office successes of 1991 – though the acting honours went to Alan Rickman as a dastardly Sheriff of Nottingham.

Robinson Crusoe.
There have been many film variations on Defoe's novel. The closest to the original have been Luis Buñuel's *The Adventures of Robinson Crusoe* (Mexico, 1953), with Dan O'Herlihy, and oddly enough Byron Haskin's *Robinson Crusoe on Mars* (US, 1954), with Paul Mantee. *Lt Robin Crusoe, U.S.N.* (US, 1966) had a shipwrecked mariner teaming up with a chimpanzee and a Girl Wednesday. *Man Friday* (GB, 1975), with Peter O'Toole and Richard Roundtree, tried to be satirical by showing the situation from Friday's viewpoint. *Crusoe* (US, 1988), with Aidan Quinn, turned him into a slave trader.

Robocop.
A cyborg created from the remains of a cop shot by drug-dealers in a future Detroit, and turned into an invincible upholder of law and order, who has been the hero of three films so far. The first, directed by Paul Verhoeven, is by far the best. Peter Weller played the role in the first two films. In *Robocop 3*, Robert Burke took over. Richard Eden played the role in a 1994 television series.

robots
have been sparingly used in movies. Brigitte Helm memorably played one in *Metropolis;* so did Patricia Roc in *The Perfect Woman*. Robby the Robot featured sympathetically in *Forbidden Planet* and *Invisible Boy;* then there was *Kronos*, and Gort in *The Day the Earth Stood Still*. *Westworld, Futureworld* and *Star Wars* brought in a whole race of robots, one of whom looked like Yul Brynner; while in TV, *The Avengers* have frequently encountered the Cybernauts and *Dr Who* the Daleks.

Rocky Balboa.
Dim but enduring, and even endearing, boxer created by Sylvester Stallone, as actor and screenwriter, in the Oscar-winning film *Rocky* 75, directed by John Avildsen, and four sequels (1979–90), in which he wins and loses championships and ends up brain-damaged, but training a protégé to succeed him.

Roger Rabbit.
Madcap rabbit with a sexy human wife and the troublesome Baby Herman to look after. Following the success of the Walt Disney feature *Who Framed Roger Rabbit*, combining animated characters and live actors, he has appeared in shorts noted for their fast, slapstick action. Created by novelist Gary Wolf, he is voiced by Charles Fleischer and his wife Jessica by Kathleen Turner.

Who Framed Roger Rabbit 88. Tummy Trouble 89. Rollercoaster Rabbit 90.

Rogue Male.
Geoffrey Household's adventure melodrama about a big-game hunter stalking Hitler has been filmed twice: by Fritz Lang as *Manhunt* 41, with Walter Pidgeon and George Sanders in hilariously foggy London settings, and as a TV movie in 1976 under its original title, starring Peter O'Toole.

romantic teams
who have been popular enough to make several films together are headed by William Powell and Myrna Loy, who made 12 joint appearances. Runners-up include Janet Gaynor and Charles Farrell (11 appearances); Dick Powell and Joan Blondell (10); Fred Astaire and Ginger Rogers (10); Spencer Tracy and Katharine Hepburn (9); Richard Burton and Elizabeth Taylor (9); Judy Garland and Mickey Rooney (8); Clark Gable and Joan Crawford (8); Nelson Eddy and Jeanette Macdonald (8); Greer Garson and Walter Pidgeon (8); Errol Flynn and Olivia de Havilland (8); Bette Davis and George Brent (7); Clark Gable and Jean Harlow (6); James Cagney and Joan Blondell (6). Even though most of these teamings began because both stars happened to be under contract to the same studio, they would not have continued had they not been felicitous. Other teams who struck notable sparks off each other but have fewer films to their credit include Humphrey Bogart and Lauren Bacall; Ronald Colman and Greer Garson; Cary Grant and Irene Dunne; Greta Garbo and John Gilbert; Greta Garbo and Melvyn Douglas; Bob Hope and Paulette Goddard; Danny Kaye and Virginia Mayo; Alan Ladd and Veronica Lake; Donald O'Connor and Peggy Ryan; Marie Dressler and Wallace Beery; Rita Hayworth and Glenn Ford; John Barrymore and Carole Lombard; Charlie Ruggles and Mary Boland; Rock Hudson and Doris Day; Jack Hulbert and Cicely Courtneidge; John Payne and Betty Grable; James Dunn and Sally Eilers; David Niven and Loretta Young; Van Johnson and June Allyson; Louis Hayward and Patricia Medina; Bob Hope and Dorothy Lamour; John Wayne and Maureen O'Hara; Tom Hanks and Meg Ryan.

Rome
in its ancient days was reconstructed for *Quo Vadis, The Sign of the Cross, Ben Hur, The Last Days of Pompeii, Androcles and the Lion, The Fall of the Roman Empire, The Robe, I Claudius, Julius Caesar, Cleopatra and Spartacus*. The funny side of its life was depicted in *Roman Scandals, Fiddlers Three, Carry On Cleo, Scandal in the Roman Bath* and *A Funny Thing Happened on the Way to the Forum*. Modern Rome has been seen hundreds of times in Italian movies, notably *Bicycle Thieves, Paisa, La Dolce Vita, The Girls of the Spanish Steps, Sunday in August, Rome Eleven o'Clock* and the American co-production *Indiscretion* which was shot entirely within Rome's railway station. American views of Rome include *Three Coins in the Fountain, Seven Hills of Rome, Roman Holiday, Two Weeks in Another Town, The Pigeon That Took Rome* and *The Roman Spring of Mrs Stone;* while the Colosseum was used for the finale of films as various as *House of Cards* and *Twenty Million Miles to Earth*. The Vatican was well shown in *Never Take No for an Answer*, about the small boy who persists in getting an audience with the Pope.

Romeo and Juliet.
Shakespeare's tragedy of star-crossed lovers has been a director's favourite ever since it was first filmed in 1900, and many more silent versions followed. There have been three major straight versions since sound: in 1936 George Cukor directed Leslie Howard and Norma Shearer in a lavish, genteel, studio-bound, semi-pop version for MGM; in 1953 Renato Castellani came to Britain and made for Rank a more sober, but duller film in colour, with Laurence Harvey and Susan Shentall; and in 1968 came Franco Zeffirelli's youthful version with Leonard Whiting and Olivia Hussey. In the late 40s, a French film noir, *Les Amants de Verone*, transposed the story to a modern setting. The musical *West Side Story* 61 is a violent modernization of Shakespeare's tale, and Peter Ustinov's *Romanoff and Juliet* 61 a satirical rendering. The oddest so far is Armando Acosta's 1990 Belgian version played by a cast of cats (Juliet is a white Angora, Romeo a grey Persian), dubbed with the voices of, among others, Robert Powell, Francesca Annis, Ben Kingsley, Vanessa Redgrave, and Maggie Smith. A grunge version, *Tromeo and Juliet*, was released in 1996 by Troma Films, directed by Lloyd Kaufman and written by James Gunn. Set in the future ('What light from yonder Plexiglas breaks?' asked Tromeo), it featured Tromeo proposing to Juliet while seated on the toilet. A more conventional contemporary adaptation, set in a US resort called Verona Beach, also appeared in 1996, starring Leonardo DiCaprio and Claire Danes and directed by Baz Luhrmann.

Rose Marie.
The Rudolph Friml/Oscar Hammerstein operetta about the Mounties getting their man was first filmed in 1928 by Lucien Hubbard as a silent; Joan Crawford has the title role. In 1936 W. S. Van Dyke made the well-remembered version with Jeanette MacDonald and Nelson Eddy, and in 1954 Mervyn LeRoy directed a remake with Ann Blyth and Howard Keel.

Rosebud.
The enigmatic last word of *Citizen Kane*, referring back to Kane's childhood sled. It is also said to be the pet name William Randolph Hearst gave to his mistress Marion Davies's private parts, which may help explain that tycoon's implacable hostility to the film. Several sleds were said to have been used in the film, in addition to the one burned at the end. One of them was bought at auction for $55,000 by Steven Spielberg in 1982, although its authenticity has since been questioned.

Ruggles of Red Gap.
The story by Harry Leon Wilson, about a British butler exported to the American midwest, was filmed with Edward Everett Horton in 1923 and with Charles Laughton in 1935. Bob Hope's *Fancy Pants* 50 bore more than a passing resemblance to it.

Sabrina.
Billy Wilder's romantic comedy, made in 1954, about an up-tight businessman who falls in love with his chauffeur's daughter, who, in turn, is attracted by his high-living brother, starred Humphrey Bogart, Audrey Hepburn and William Holden. Sydney Pollack's less successful remake in 1995 starred Harrison Ford in the Bogart role, Julia Ormond and Greg Kinnear.

Sahara:
see Lost Patrol.

sailors
of whom screen accounts have been given include Christopher Columbus (1446–1506), by Fredric March in *Christopher Columbus* 49, Gérard Depardieu in *1492: Discovery of Paradise* 92, and George Corraface in *Christopher Columbus: The Discovery* 92; Horatio Nelson; Captain Bligh, by Charles Laughton, and later by Trevor Howard, in *Mutiny on the Bounty;* John Paul Jones (1747–92), by Robert Stack in *John Paul Jones* 59; Francis Drake (1540–96), by Matheson Lang in *Drake of England* 35 and by Rod Taylor in *Seven Seas to Calais* 62; Walter Raleigh by Richard Todd in *The Virgin Queen* 55; and Admiral Halsey, by James Cagney in *The Gallant Hours* 61 and by Robert Mitchum in *Midway*.

The Saint.
Among the actors who have played Leslie Charteris' 'Robin Hood of crime' in both British and American films since 1937 are Louis Hayward, Hugh Sinclair and George Sanders. One feels that 'the Falcon', a series character played in the 40s by George Sanders and later Tom Conway, was heavily indebted to the Saint, who made a strong comeback on television in the person of Roger Moore in the 60s. In France, a barely recognizable 'Saint' has been played in several films by Jean Marais. In 1995, Val Kilmer was signed for the role, which prevented him from continuing to play Batman; he was replaced by George Clooney. Other actors approached for the role of the Saint included Ralph Fiennes, Mel Gibson, Hugh Grant and Arnold Schwarzenegger.

St Trinian's.
This school full of little female horrors was originally conceived by cartoonist Ronald Searle. From his formula Frank Launder and Sidney Gilliat made four commercially successful if disappointing farces: *The Belles of St Trinian's* 54, *Blue Murder at St Trinian's* 57, *The Pure Hell of St Trinian's* 60, *The Great St Trinian's Train Robbery* 66. In 1980 Launder alone produced yet another.

Salome.
Oscar Wilde's play of Salome's Dance of the Seven Veils before King Herod for the head of John the Baptist was filmed at least seven times in silent days, notably by Nazimova in 1923 against backgrounds inspired by the drawings of Aubrey Beardsley. It was remade in 1953 with Rita Hayworth as Salome and Charles Laughton as Herod, while Ken Russell's *Salome's Last Dance* 87 had Wilde watching a performance of his play in a brothel.

San Francisco,
replete with cable cars, steep streets, Golden Gate Bridge and Alcatraz out there in the bay, has provided a picturesque location for innumerable movies, outstandingly *Vertigo, What's Up Doc?, The Glenn Miller Story, The Well Groomed Bride, Bullitt, Guess Who's Coming to Dinner, Point Blank, Yours Mine and Ours, The House on Telegraph Hill, Sudden Fear, Experiment in Terror, Flower Drum Song, The Maltese Falcon, The Conversation, Daddy's Gone a-Hunting, Dirty Harry, Pete 'n' Tillie, The Laughing Policeman, Dark Passage, Foul Play* and *Petulia*. The Barbary Coast days were well caught in *San Francisco, Nob Hill, Barbary Coast, Flame of the Barbary Coast*, and many other movies.

TV series have also used it *ad nauseam*: *The Line Up, Sam Benedict, Ironside, McMillan and Wife, Streets of San Francisco, Phyllis*.

satire,
being defined in theatrical circles as 'what closes Saturday night', has seldom been encouraged by Hollywood, and the few genuinely satirical films have not been commercially successful, from *A Nous la Liberté* through *American Madness, Nothing Sacred* and *Roxie Hart* to *The Loved One*. However, the odd lampoon in the middle of an otherwise straightforward comedy has often brought critical enthusiasm for films as diverse as *Modern Times, Boy Meets Girl, I'm All Right, Jack, The President's Analyst* and *The Groove Tube;* and in future it looks as though one can at least expect that the range of permissible targets will become even wider. The spotty but considerable success in 1976 of *Network*, the screen's most hysterical satire of all, was at least partly due to its sexy scenes and uninhibited language.

Scarface.
Armitage Trail's novel, about the rise of a thinly disguised Al Capone, made an exciting gangster movie under the direction of Howard Hawks in 1932, with Paul Muni in the title role and George Raft flipping a coin at moments of stress. Brian DePalma remade it as an exercise in excess in 1983, starring Al Pacino as a modern-day Latin American thug, thriving in Miami.

The Scarlet Letter.
Nathaniel Hawthorne's story of puritanical 18th-century New England was filmed in 1917 with Mary Martin as the adulteress and Stuart Holmes as her priest-lover forced to accuse her. In 1926 came Victor Sjostrom's more famous version with Lillian Gish and Lars Hanson; 1934 brought a talkie remake with Colleen Moore and Hardie Albright; and Wim Wenders made a German version in 1973, starring Senta Berger. Demi Moore starred in a version directed by Roland Jaffe which took many liberties with the original, but even so flopped at the box-office in 1995.

The Scarlet Pimpernel.
Baroness Orczy's foppish hero of the French Revolution has been filmed three times in Britain since sound: in 1935, directed by Harold Young, with Leslie Howard opposing Raymond Massey as Chauvelin; in 1938, directed by Hans Schwarz, with Barry K. Barnes winning out over Francis Lister; in 1950, directed by Michael Powell and Emeric Pressburger, with David Niven as Sir Percy. There has also been a TV series starring Marius Goring. Silent versions included one in 1917 starring Dustin Farnum and one in 1929 starring Matheson Lang. The idea was modernized in Leslie Howard's *Pimpernel Smith* 41. In 1982, the original was remade for television with Anthony Andrews, Jane Seymour, and Ian McKellen.

Scattergood Baines,
an amiable small-town busybody created by Clarence Buddington Kelland, was personified by Guy Kibbee in six second features (41–42), all directed by Christy Cabanne.

schooldays
have often been depicted in films with a thick sentimental veneer, as in *Goodbye Mr Chips, Good Morning Miss Dove* and *Blossoms in the Dust*. But more usually the pupils have serious problems to worry about, as in *Young Woodley, The Guinea Pig, Friends for Life, Tea and Sympathy* and *Tom Brown's Schooldays;* while with at least equal frequency our sympathies are elicited on behalf of the staff: *The Housemaster, Bright Road, The Blackboard Jungle, The Browning Version, Spare the Rod, Edward My Son, The Blue Angel, The Children's Hour, The Corn Is Green, Term of Trial, To Sir with Love, Spinster, The Prime of Miss Jean Brodie, Please Sir, Unman Wittering and Zigo*. More light-hearted treatment of the whole business is evident in *The Trouble with Angels* and *Margie*, and in some cases the treatment has undeniably been farcical: *Boys Will Be Boys, The Ghost of St Michael's, Good Morning Boys, A Yank at Eton, Vice Versa, Bottoms Up* and *The Happiest Days of Your Life;* with the St Trinian's saga wildest of all. The strangest schools on film are those depicted in *Zéro de Conduite* and its semi-remake *If . . .* while very special schools were seen in *Battement de Coeur* (for pickpockets), *School for Secrets* (for 'boffins'), *Old Bones of the River* (for African tiny tots), *The Goose Steps Out* (for young Nazis), *Orders to Kill, The House on 92nd Street, 13 rue Madeleine, Carve Her Name with Pride* and *From Russia with Love* (for spies).

science fiction,
a term incapable of precise definition, may perhaps be taken as that kind of fantasy which depends not on legend only, like Dracula, but involves the work of man. Thus King Kong and the 'natural' monsters would not qualify, but Frankenstein and the Invisible Man would. Space exploration and prophecy, considered elsewhere, are branches of it, as are all the films about mad doctors and colliding worlds.

scientists
have been the subject of many films, though few real-life ones have led sufficiently dramatic lives to warrant filming. Warners led the way in the 30s with *The Story of Louis Pasteur* and *Dr Ehrlich's Magic Bullet*. In 1939 Mickey Rooney played *Young Tom Edison*, followed by Spencer Tracy as *Edison the Man*. Then, in 1943, Greer Garson played *Madame Curie*. At this point the movie fan's thirst for scientific knowledge died out, and John Huston's *Freud* in 1962 did not revive it. In the 80s, the lives of Oppenheimer and Sakharov have been filmed.

See also: inventors.

The Sea Wolf.
Jack London's stark psychological novel of an obsessed sea captain, Wolf Larsen, has been filmed at least seven times: in 1913 it starred Hobart Bosworth, in 1920 Noah Beery, in 1925 Ralph Ince, in 1930 Milton Sills, and in 1941 Edward G. Robinson. A disguised western version, *Barricade*, with Raymond Massey, appeared in 1950, and in 1957 yet another straight version, under the title *Wolf Larsen*, was made with Barry Sullivan. In 1974 Chuck Connors starred in a European version, *Wolf of the Seven Seas*.

seances
on the screen have often been shown to be fake, as in *Seance on a Wet Afternoon, Bunco Squad, Palmy Days, The Spiritualist, Houdini*, and *The Medium*. But just occasionally they do result in something being called up from over there. It happened in *Blithe Spirit, The Haunting, The Uninvited, Night of the Demon, Thirteen Ghosts, Hands of the Ripper*, and *The Legend of Hell House*.

seaside resorts
have provided lively settings for many British comedies: Douglas in *No Limit*, Brighton in *Bank Holiday*, Blackpool in *Sing As We Go*, and a variety of south coast resorts in *The Punch and Judy Man, French Dressing, All Over the Town, Barnacle Bill*. Sometimes the resort has provided a contrast to more serious goings-on, as in *The Entertainer, Brighton Rock, Room at the Top, The Dark Man, A Taste of Honey, I Was Happy Here, Family Doctor, The System, The Damned*. Hollywood usually comes a cropper when depicting British resorts, either comically as in *The Gay Divorcee* or seriously as in *Separate Tables;* its own resorts have a monotonous look, whether viewed romantically in *Moon Over Miami* and *Fun in Acapulco*, nostalgically in *Some Like It Hot*, trendily in *Beach Party* and its many sequels, or morosely in *Tony Rome*. The French Riviera has never been notably well captured on film since Vigo's *A Propos de Nice*, but among the movies to have a go with the aid of back projection are *On the Riviera, That Riviera Touch* and *Moment to Moment*. Hitchcock got some picture-postcard views but little else out of *To Catch a Thief*, while the French had a go for themselves in *St Tropez Blues* and others. A Mediterranean resort was the setting of the climax of *Suddenly Last Summer;* other European watering-places featured memorably in *Une Si Jolie Petite Plage, Sunday in August* and *The Lady with the Little Dog*. The most ingenious use of the seaside for purposes of film fantasy was certainly in *Oh What a Lovely War*.

Seaside settings of the 70s and 80s have included *Out of Season, Atlantic City USA* and *The King of Marvin Gardens*.

Sergeant Ernie Bilko.
Wisecracking, loquacious, conniving army sergeant played by Phil Silvers in his TV show from 1955 to 1959. Stationed at Fort Baxter, Kansas, Bilko tried to get rich quick, aided and also hindered by his platoon, and at war with his superior officer, Colonel Hall (Paul Ford). A feature film version, directed by Jonathan Lynn and starring Steve Martin as Bilko and Dan Aykroyd as Colonel Hall, appeared in 1996. It contained the credit: 'The filmmakers gratefully acknowledge the total lack of cooperation from the US Army.'

serial killers.
Mass murderers have long held a fascination for film-makers and audiences alike, as is demonstrated by Charlie Chaplin's *Monsieur Verdoux* 47, and the many *Bluebeard* films from the 40s onwards, based on the activities of the French murderer Henri Landru, and such comedies as *Kind Hearts and Coronets* 49 and *No Way to Treat a Lady* 68. But a specific genre emerged after the term serial killer was coined by the FBI in the 60s and following the success of Alfred Hitchcock's *Psycho*, from Robert Bloch's novel based on Ed Gein. A succession of slasher movies ensued featuring fictional murderers, including *Halloween* and its successors, and two long-drawn-out series featuring killers returning from the dead: Jason in *Friday the Thirteenth* (eight films so far) and Freddy in *Nightmare on Elm Street*. Terrence Malick's *Badlands*, based on teenagers Charley Starkweather and Caril Fugate's killing spree which left 10 dead, was followed by a series of murderous road movies which includes *True Romance* 93, *Kalifornia* 93, and *Natural Born Killers* 94. The latter two made much of public fascination with serial killers, as did John McNaughton's chilling *Henry: Portrait of a Serial Killer* and the Belgian film *Man Bites Dog* 92, in which a film crew begin to record a murderer at work and end by helping him with his crimes. Certainly Thomas Harris's fictional creation, the cannibalistic Hannibal Lecter, has become a favourite ogre following the performances of Brian Cox in *Manhunter* 86 and Anthony Hopkins in *The Silence of the Lambs* 90. Real-life serial killers on film include the Boston Strangler, Peter Kurten (M and *The Vampire of Dusseldorf*), and Fritz Haarman (*The Tenderness of Wolves*).

❝ The serial killer has become our debased, condemned, yet eerily glorified Noble Savage, the vestiges of the frontier spirit. *– Joyce Carol Oates*

serials
demand a book to themselves. They began in the early years of the century and continued until the early 50s, their plethora of adventurous and melodramatic incident being usually divided into fifteen or twenty chapters of about twenty minutes each. They were the domain of mad doctors, space explorers, clutching hands, mysterious strangers, diabolical villains and dewy-eyed heroines. Each chapter ended with a 'cliffhanger' in which the hero or heroine was left in some deadly danger from which it was plain he could not escape; but at the beginning of the next chapter, escape he did. A few favourite serials are *Fantomas, The Perils of Pauline, Batman, Flash Gordon's Trip to Mars* and *Captain Marvel*. Almost all of them were American. They were finally killed by the advent of TV and by the increasing length of the double-feature programme.

Books on the subject include *To Be Continued* by Weiss and Goodgold; *Days of Thrills and Adventure* by Alan Barbour; and *The Great Movie Serials* by Harmon and Glut.

series
of feature films used to be popular enough, and many are individually noted in this book; in recent years the series concept has been taken over by TV, and in any case low-budget movies featuring cut-to-pattern characters could no longer be made to pay their way in theatres. When one looks back over these old heroes, who flourished chiefly in the 30s and 40s, most of them turn out to be sleuths of one kind or another. They included *Sherlock Holmes, The Saint, The Lone Wolf, Father Brown, Nero Wolfe, Duncan McLain, The Crime Doctor, Sexton Blake, Mr Moto, Perry Mason, Bulldog Drummond, Nancy Drew, Mr Wong, Charlie Chan, Ellery Queen, Boston Blackie, The Falcon, Hildegarde Withers, Hercule Poirot, Dick Tracy, Torchy Blane, Michael Shayne, Philip Marlowe* and, more recently, *Inspector Clouseau, Tony Rome, Virgil Tibbs, Coffin Ed Johnson* and *Shaft*. Nor should one forget crime anthologies like *Inner Sanctum* and *The Whistler*. The spy vogue, a recent happening, is naturally headed by *James Bond:* in his wake you may discern *Counterspy, Coplan, Flint, The Tiger, The Man from UNCLE, Harry Palmer*, and *Superdragon*. Among the more masculine outdoor heroes may be counted *Hopalong Cassidy, The Three Mesquiteers, The Lone Ranger, Captain Blood, Zorro, Robin Hood, Tarzan, Jungle Jim, The Cisco Kid, Bomba, The Man with No Name* and the Italian giants who go under such names as *Maciste, Goliath, Hercules* and *Ursus*. The longest surviving series villain is certainly *Fu Manchu*. As for monsters, take your pick from *Frankenstein, Dracula, The Mummy, The Creature from the Black Lagoon, The Invisible Man, The Wolf Man, Dr X;* while if you prefer comedy freaks there are *Topper* and *Francis*. There have been a goodly number of domestic comedies and dramas, including *Squibs, The Jones Family, The Hardy Family, The Cohens and the Kellys, Blondie, Ma and Pa Kettle, Maisie, Henry Aldrich, Scattergood Baines, Lum and Abner, Jeeves, Mr Belvedere, Gidget* and the *Four Daughters* saga. Other comedy series have ranged from the subtleties of *Don Camillo* to the pratfalls of *Old Mother Riley, Mexican Spitfire*, the

Doctor series, *Carry On* films, the *Police Academy* series, and the *Naked Gun* movies. Animals have had series to themselves, as for instance *Rin Tin Tin*, *Flicka*, *Lassie*, *Rusty* and *Flipper*. So have children of various ages: *Our Gang*, *Gasoline Alley*, *The Dead End Kids*, *The East Side Kids*, *The Bowery Boys*. The best-established musical series were *Broadway Melody* and *The Big Broadcast*. And three cheers for *Dr Kildare*, *Dr Christian*, *Dr Mabuse* and *Dr Goldfoot* . . . to say nothing of Professor *Quatermass*.

servants
in movies have provided great pleasure, mainly because the vast majority of the audience has been unlikely to encounter the breed in person. Actors who spent their lives playing stately butlers include Eric Blore, Charles Coleman, Robert Greig, Barnett Parker, Halliwell Hobbes and Arthur Treacher. Louise Beavers and Hattie McDaniel were the leading coloured maids, and many black comedians played frightened valets: Mantan Moreland, Stepin Fetchit, Willie Best. Sinister housekeepers are led by Gale Sondergaard and Judith Anderson. Even more eccentric servants were played by Edward Rigby in *Don't Take it to Heart*, Cantinflas in *Around the World in Eighty Days*, Seymour Hicks in *Busman's Honeymoon*, Edward Brophy in the Falcon series; and downright villainous ones by Dirk Bogarde in *The Servant*, Philip Latham in *Dracula Prince of Darkness*, Boris Karloff in *The Old Dark House* and Bela Lugosi in *The Body Snatcher*. Romantic comedies in which servants have had liaisons with their masters (or mistresses) include *History is Made at Night*, *When Tomorrow Comes*, *Common Clay*, *What Price Hollywood?*, *The Farmer's Daughter*, *If You Could Only Cook*, *Lord Richard in the Pantry* and *Upstairs Downstairs*; while 30s comedies in which Russian exiles and new poor took jobs as servants are exemplified by *Tovarich* and *My Man Godfrey*. One should not forget *The Admirable Crichton* in any of his forms; but other servants less admirable were James Mason in *Five Fingers*, and Glenda Jackson and Susannah York in *The Maids*. Anthony Hopkins in *The Remains of the Day* was a butler whose loyalty to his master is his undoing.

Seven Keys to Baldpate.
The famous stage comedy-thriller by Earl Derr Biggers and George M. Cohan has been filmed five times: with Cohan himself in 1917, Douglas MacLean in 1926, Richard Dix in 1929, Gene Raymond in 1935, and Philip Terry in 1947. The most recent version, in 1983, was *House of Long Shadows*, with Christopher Lee and Peter Cushing.

Seventh Heaven.
Austin Strong's play, a simple garret love story set in Paris at the time of World War I, from which the hero returns blinded, was successfully filmed by Frank Borzage, with Janet Gaynor and Charles Farrell; Henry King remade it in 1937 with Simone Simon and James Stewart.

sewers
have figured in several thrillers, most notably *The Third Man* with its exciting final chase; its sewer complex was recently spoofed in *Carry On Spying*. In 1948 in *He Walked by Night* Richard Basehart played a criminal who invariably escaped through the sewers; and our old friend *The Phantom of the Opera* was similarly skilled, as was Lee Marvin in *Point Blank*. As recently as the British thriller *Invasion* a sewer detour was used; while the Frankenstein monster was saved from the burning windmill by falling through to the sewer, where he was found at the beginning of *Bride of Frankenstein*. As for more serious films, sewers are of course featured in the many versions of *Les Misérables*, while the Polish resistance film *Kanal* takes place entirely – and nauseatingly – in the sewers of Warsaw. Fred MacMurray had a comic sewer escape in *Bon Voyage*, and the giant ants of *Them!* were cornered in the sewers of Los Angeles, while the mutant beast of *Alligator* and *Alligator II* emerged from the sewers and the pizza-loving *Teenage Mutant Ninja Turtles* lived in them.

sex.
This was once called 'romance': the beginnings of corruption set in with de Mille's silent comedies such as *Why Change Your Wife?* and Lubitsch's classics *Forbidden Paradise* and *The Marriage Circle*. These gentlemen carried their sophistication into the early sound period, assisted by such stars as Valentino, Harlow, Dietrich, Clara Bow and Ginger Rogers; and there was considerable help from a film called *The Private Life of Henry VIII*, a lady named Mae West and a director named Josef Von Sternberg; but around 1934 the Hays Code and the Legion of Decency forced innocence upon Hollywood to such an extent that the smart hero and heroine of 1934's *It Happened One Night* just wouldn't dream of sharing a bedroom without a curtain between them. The later 30s, perforce, were the heyday of the boy-next-door and the *ingénue*: nice people all, personified by such stars as Gary Cooper, Dick Powell, Ray Milland, David Niven, Ruby Keeler, Janet Gaynor, Deanna Durbin and Irene Dunne. Meanwhile a strong rearguard action was being fought by actors like William Powell, Myrna Loy, Melvyn Douglas, Ann Sheridan and Cary Grant, but usually the blue pencil had been wielded so heavily on their scripts that it was difficult to tell what was really being implied. The best way out was found in such comedies as *The Philadelphia Story*, which were basically earthy but gave every appearance of keeping it all in the mind. The war years produced a certain slackening of restrictions; for instance, the pin-up girl became not only permissible but desirable as a way of building up military morale. Preston Sturges brought sex out into the open in *The Palm Beach Story* and *The Miracle of Morgan's Creek*; Spencer Tracy and Katharine Hepburn started (in *Woman of the Year*) a series of films portraying the battle of the sexes in a recognizably human way. The 'love goddesses' became progressively more blatant in their appeal: Jane Russell, Marilyn Monroe, Jayne Mansfield. (But in the 50s it turned out that one of the earthiest of them, Sophia Loren, was also the best actress.) By now the production code had been broken down to the extent of permitting words like 'virgin' and 'mistress'(*The Moon is Blue*), the recognition of adultery and prostitution as human facts (*Wives and Lovers*, *Kiss Me Stupid*), depiction of the lustfulness of males (*Tom Jones*, *Alfie*), 'realistic' dramas like *Room at the Top*, erotic romances like *Les Amants*, and the presentation, albeit in a fantasy, of girls as 'pleasure units' (*Our Man Flint*). Indeed, after *Georgy Girl*, *Night Games* and *Who's Afraid of Virginia Woolf?*, it seemed that public frankness could go very little further; but along came *Blow Up*, *Midnight Cowboy*, *Satyricon*, *Flesh*, *The Music Lovers*, *Percy*, *Last Tango in Paris* and *Deep Throat* to prove the opposite. There even emerged an X-rated cartoon *Fritz the Cat*; and by the mid-70s pornographic films on view in most cities outnumbered the other kind.

sex changes
have not been a profitable line of inquiry for the cinema, though the gimmick thriller *Homicidal* depended on one, as did *Myra Breckinridge*. *The Christine Jorgenson Story* was an account of a genuine case, and *I Want What I Want* presented a fictitious case history. The most amusing film on the subject is certainly *Turnabout*. In Blake Edwards' *Switch*, a male chauvinist is reincarnated as a woman.

Sexton Blake.
The lean, ascetic detective hero of several generations of British boys was the creation of Harry Blyth ('Hal Meredith') (1852–98). On screen he was first portrayed in 1914 in *The Clue of the Wax Vesta*. He was played in the 20s by Langhorne Burton, in the 30s by George Curzon, in the 40s by David Farrar and in the 50s by Geoffrey Toone; while 1962's *Mix Me a Person* was taken from a Blake story but cast Anne Baxter in the role.

Shaft.
Ernest Tidyman's tough Harlem private eye was played by Richard Roundtree in three films: *Shaft* 71; *Shaft in Africa* 73; and *Shaft's Big Score* 73.

She.
Seven silent versions were made of Rider Haggard's adventure fantasy about a lost tribe, an ageless queen, and a flame of eternal life in darkest Africa. Only the last remains, made in London and Berlin by G. B. Samuelson, with Betty Blythe and Carlyle Blackwell. In 1934 in Hollywood, Merian Cooper and Ernest Schoedsack remade the story in a North Pole setting, with Helen Gahagan and Randolph Scott. In 1965 came a lifeless Hammer version directed by Robert Day, with Ursula Andress and John Richardson; this was followed in 1968 by a sequel, *The Vengeance of She*, which was more than slightly potty.

She Loves Me Not.
The story of a night-club singer taking refuge in a men's college and disguising herself as an undergraduate after witnessing a murder has been filmed three times: in 1934, directed by Elliott Nugent, with Bing Crosby and Miriam Hopkins; in 1942, as *True to the Army*, in which Judy Canova pretends to be a soldier; in 1955, as *How to Be Very, Very Popular*, in which strippers Betty Grable and Sheree North hide in a college. The notion also served Whoopi Goldberg well in *Sister Act* 92, as a singer fleeing from the Mob who takes refuge in a convent and disguises herself as a nun.

The Sheik.
Rudolph Valentino first appeared as a romantic Arab in 1922, with Agnes Ayres as his willing co-star, in an adaptation of E. M. Hull's novelette. It was one of his most successful roles, and *Son of the Sheik* came out in 1926, with Vilma Banky partnering him. His death prevented further episodes, but in 1937 Ramon Novarro made fun of the idea in *The Sheik Steps Out*, and in 1962 came an Italian spoof called *The Return of the Son of the Sheik*, with Gordon Scott.

Sherlock Holmes,
Conan Doyle's classic fictional detective, around whom a detailed legend has been created by ardent followers, has a long screen history. There were American one-reel films featuring him in 1903, 1905 and 1908. Also in 1908 there began a series of twelve Danish one-reelers starring Forrest Holger-Madsen. In 1910 there were two German films and in 1912 six French. A second French series began in 1913; also in this year an American two-reel version of *The Sign of Four* featured Harry Benham. British six-reelers were made of *A Study in Scarlet* 14, and *Valley of Fear* 16; also in 1916 the famous stage actor William Gillette put his impersonation of Holmes on film for Essanay. In 1917 came a German version of *The Hound of the Baskervilles*; then nothing till 1922, when John Barrymore played Holmes and Roland Young was Watson in Goldwyn's *Sherlock Holmes*, based on Gillette's stage play. In Britain in the same year Maurice Elvey directed a full-length version of *The Hound of the Baskervilles* and followed it with over 25 two-reelers starring Eille Norwood, remaining faithful to the original stories. In 1929 Carlyle Blackwell played Holmes in a German remake of *The Hound of the Baskervilles*; and in the same year Clive Brook played in a talkie, *The Return of Sherlock Holmes*, with H. Reeves-Smith as Watson. Arthur Wontner, a perfect Holmes, first played the role in *Sherlock Holmes' Final Hour* (GB) 31, later appearing in *The Sign of Four* 32, *The Missing Rembrandt* 33, *The Triumph of Sherlock Holmes* 35, and *The Silver Blaze* 36 (Ian Fleming was Watson). Raymond Massey was Holmes in *The Speckled Band* (GB) 31, with Athole Stewart as Watson; in 1932 Robert Rendel was in *The Hound of the Baskervilles* (GB). Clive Brook again appeared in *Sherlock Holmes* (US) 32, with Reginald Owen as Watson; Owen then played Holmes in *A Study in Scarlet* (US) 33. The Germans made three more Holmes films in the mid-30s, including yet another remake of *The Hound*, which in 1939 was again tackled by Fox in Hollywood, this time with Basil Rathbone as the detective and Nigel Bruce as Watson. Its success led to a hurried remake of the Gillette play under the title *The Adventures of Sherlock Holmes* 39; two years later the same two actors began a series of twelve films in which the settings were modernized and most of the stories unrecognizable, although the acting and much of the writing were well in character. The titles were *Sherlock Holmes and the Voice of Terror* 41, *Sherlock Holmes and the Secret Weapon* 42, *Sherlock Holmes in Washington* 42, *Sherlock Holmes Faces Death* 43, *Spider Woman* 44, *The Scarlet Claw* 44, *Pearl of Death* 44, *House of Fear* 45, *Woman in Green* 45, *Pursuit to Algiers* 45, *Terror by Night* 46, *Dressed to Kill/Sherlock Holmes and the Secret Code* 46. Then a long silence was broken by Peter Cushing and André Morell in the leads of a British remake of *The Hound of the Baskervilles* 59. In 1962 Christopher Lee and Thorley Walters played Holmes and Watson in a German film, *Sherlock Holmes and the Deadly Necklace*; and in 1965 John Neville and Donald Houston appeared in an original story involving the famous pair with Jack the Ripper: *A Study in Terror*. Also in 1965 a BBC TV series featured Douglas Wilmer and Nigel Stock, with Peter Cushing later taking over as Holmes; the period atmosphere was carefully sought but the stories suffered from being padded out to the standard TV length. (There was also a Franco-American TV series in 1954 with Ronald Howard and Howard Marion-Crawford.) In 1969 Billy Wilder made *The Private Life of Sherlock Holmes* with Robert Stephens, apparently intending a send-up but producing only a further pleasant variation. In 1970 George C. Scott thought he was Sherlock Holmes in *They Might Be Giants*, so did Larry Hagman in a 1976 TV movie, *The Return of the World's Greatest Detective*. Nicol Williamson as Holmes was treated by Sigmund Freud in 1976's *The Seven Per Cent Solution*, and in the same year Gene Wilder tried a spoof, *The Adventure of Sherlock Holmes' Smarter Brother*. The same year brought a TV movie called *Sherlock Holmes in New York*, with Roger Moore and Patrick MacNee. In 1978 there was a perfectly ghastly, supposedly comic *Hound of the Baskervilles* with Peter Cook and Dudley Moore, while Christopher Plummer starred in a TV half-hour of *Silver Blaze* and a feature called *Murder by Decree*, which again linked Holmes with Jack the Ripper. A stage revival of the William Gillette version was followed by other adaptations. 1979 brought another TV series with Geoffrey Whitehead and Donald Pickering; but *Sherlock Holmes and Doctor Watson* was barely seen outside Poland, where it was shot. In 1983 Sy Weintraub made TV movies of *The Sign of Four* and *The Hound of the Baskervilles*, with Ian Richardson an excellent Holmes; and Tom Baker starred in a BBC serial of *The Hound of the Baskervilles*. In 1984 Granada TV had a 13-hour series starring Jeremy Brett and David Burke, and this continues. Brett also starred in a full-length 1987 version of *The Sign of Four*. Christopher Lee played the role in TV versions made in South Africa in the 90s.

ships,
of the modern passenger kind, have provided a useful setting for many films, most recently in *Ship of Fools*. Four notable versions of the *Titanic* disaster were *Atlantic* 30, *Titanic* 53, *A Night to Remember* 58 and *Titanic* 97; while sinking ships also figured in *We're Not Dressing* 34, *Souls at Sea* 37, *History Is Made at Night* 37, *The Blue Lagoon* 48, *Our Girl Friday* 52, *The Admirable Crichton* 57 (and earlier versions), *The Last Voyage* 60 and *The Poseidon Adventure* 72. A sinister time was had on board ship in *Journey into Fear*, *Across the Pacific*, *King Kong*, *My Favorite Blonde*, *The Ghost Ship*, *The Mystery of the Marie Celeste*, *The Sea Wolf*, *The Hairy Ape*, *Dangerous Crossing*, *Ghost Breakers*, *The Wreck of the Mary Deare*, *Juggernaut*, and *Voyage of the Damned*; laughter, however, was to the fore in *Monkey Business* 31, *The Lady Eve* 41, *Luxury Liner* 48, *Doctor at Sea* 55, *The Captain's Table* 58, *A Countess from Hong Kong* 66, and *A Night at the Opera* 35 with its famous cabin scene. The romance of a cruise was stressed in *Dodsworth* 36, *The Big Broadcast of 1938*, *Now Voyager* 42, and the two versions of *Love Affair* 39 (the second being *An Affair to Remember* 56); while in the 'Winter Cruise' section of *Encore* 51, it was almost forced on Kay Walsh. In *Assault on a Queen* 66 the leading characters plan to hijack the *Queen Mary*. The weirdest ship was the ship of the dead in *Outward Bound* 30, and its remake *Between Two Worlds* 44.

Mississippi riverboats have featured in *Mississippi*, *Rhythm on the River*, *Mississippi Gambler*, *The Secret Life of Walter Mitty*, *The Naughty Nineties*, *The Adventures of Mark Twain*, *Four for Texas*, *Frankie and Johnny*, and the several versions of *Showboat*; also in the TV series *Riverboat*.

Sailing ships of olden days are too numerous to detail.

The Shop around the Corner.
Nikolaus Laszlo's play about two Budapest shop assistants who are unaware that they are pen pals was filmed by Ernst Lubitsch in 1940, with Margaret Sullavan and James Stewart, as a charming piece of Hollywood schmaltz. In 1949 Robert Z. Leonard remade it as a musical, *In the Good Old Summertime*, with Judy Garland and Van Johnson.

The Shopworn Angel.
This comedy-drama about a Hollywood gold-digger who gives up her rich provider for a poor soldier has been filmed four times: as *Pettigrew's Girl*, a silent in 1919, with Ethel Clayton and Monte

Blue; in 1929, with Nancy Carroll, Paul Lukas, and Gary Cooper; in 1938, with Margaret Sullavan, Walter Pidgeon, and James Stewart; and in 1959, as *That Kind of Woman*, with Sidney Lumet directing Sophia Loren, George Sanders, and Tab Hunter.

Show Boat.
Jerome Kern and Oscar Hammerstein II's operetta from Edna Ferber's novel was filmed by Harry Pollard in 1929 with Laura La Plante and Joseph Schildkraut; by James Whale in 1936 with Irene Dunne, Allan Jones, and Paul Robeson; and by George Sidney in 1951 with Kathryn Grayson, Howard Keel, and William Warfield.

Silly Symphony.
The name given by Walt Disney to all his short cartoon fables of the 30s which did not feature Mickey Mouse, Pluto or Donald Duck.

A Sister to Assist'er.
George Dewhurst wrote, from John le Breton's play, and directed three versions of this comedy about a poor tenant who pretends to be her rich sister in order to trick her landlady into giving her back her possessions: in 1930, starring Barbara Gott; in 1938, starring Muriel George; and again in 1948, with Muriel George. The definitive performance as the hard-up Mrs May, though, was given on the stage by Fred Emney (1866–1917), father of the film and stage comic actor Fred Emney.

Sitting Pretty.
The 1947 comedy starring Clifton Webb as Lynn Belvedere, babysitter extraordinary, brought two sequels: *Mr Belvedere Goes to College* 49, and *Mr Belvedere Rings the Bell* 51. The title was also used for a 1933 comedy featuring Jack Oakie and Jack Haley as two songwriters hitch-hiking their way to Hollywood.

skiing
has formed a pleasant background in many romantic comedies including *I Met Him in Paris* and *Two-Faced Woman*; in farces including *The Pink Panther* and *Snowball Express*; dramas including *Last of the Ski Bums*, *Ski Fever* and *Downhill Racer*; and in a plethora of spy stories, including *Caprice*, *The Double Man* and a couple of Bonds. The most musical ski sequence was provided by The Beatles in *Help!*

slapstick.
One of the earliest (1895) Lumière shorts, *L'Arroseur Arrosé*, was a knockabout farce, and in 1966 *A Funny Thing Happened on the Way to the Forum* was keeping the tradition going. Out of simple slapstick developed the great silent clowns, each with his own brand of pathos: Harold Lloyd, Charlie Chaplin, Buster Keaton, Fatty Arbuckle, Harry Langdon, Mabel Normand, Larry Semon, Laurel and Hardy. Pure destructive slapstick without humanity was superbly dispensed by Mack Sennett, especially in his Keystone Kops shorts. France had produced Max Linder; Britain lagged behind, but in the 20s Betty Balfour, Monty Banks and Lupino Lane kept the flag flying. Many of these names survived in some degree when sound came, but cross-talk was an added factor in the success of Wheeler and Woolsey, Charlie Chase, Edgar Kennedy, Leon Errol, Hugh Herbert, Joe E. Brown, W. C. Fields, Eddie Cantor, Abbott and Costello and above all the Marx Brothers. Similarly in Britain there was an influx of stage comics with firm music-hall traditions: George Formby, Will Hay, Max Miller, Gracie Fields, Leslie Fuller, the Crazy Gang, Arthur Askey, Gordon Harker, Sandy Powell, Frank Randle and Old Mother Riley. The 40s in Hollywood brought the more sophisticated slapstick of Danny Kaye, writer-director Preston Sturges, and the Bob Hope gag factory, with extreme simplicity keeping its end up via Olsen and Johnson and Jerry Lewis. In the 50s, TV finally brought a female clown, Lucille Ball, to the top; though competition was thin. France since the war has had Fernandel, Louis de Funes, Jacques Tati and Pierre Etaix; Britain, Norman Wisdom and Morecambe and Wise; Italy, Toto and Walter Chiari. In Hollywood the fashion over the last thirty years has been for epic comedies of violence and destruction, such as *It's a Mad Mad Mad Mad World*, *The Great Race*, *Those Magnificent Men in Their Flying Machines* and *The Blues Brothers*.

Slaughter.
A Vietnam veteran out for revenge on those who killed his parents and friend was played by Jim Brown in two films: *Slaughter* 72 and *Slaughter's Big Rip-Off* 73.

slogans
All kinds of claims have been made over the years for all kinds of products. Here are a few of the most memorable.

Famous Players in Famous Plays

is certainly the longest lasting, all the way from 1912. The films hardly lived up to it, any more than it was true that:

Selznick Pictures Create Happy Homes

Or that Warners fooled anybody by linking:

Good Films – Good Citizenship

Or MGM by claiming that their spur was:

Ars Gratia Artis (art for its own sake)

MGM's secondary claim:

More Stars than there are in Heaven

was simply a slight exaggeration. When talkies came in, two favourite lines were:

All Talking, All Singing, All Dancing

And, from Vitaphone:

Pictures that Talk Like Living People!

The whole industry sometimes gets together on a propaganda campaign. In the 30s, it was:

Go to a Motion Picture – and Let Yourself Go!

In the 40s, simply:

Let's go to a movie!

In the 50s, in face of the arch-enemy television:

Don't be a Living Room Captive! Go Out and See a Great Movie!

And a few years later:

Movies are Your Best Entertainment!

The one I like best was concocted by the proprietors of CinemaScope in the face of 3-D. Originally it ran:

You see it without the use of glasses!

This not unnaturally brought a few complaints from bespectacled patrons who thought they were being guaranteed a new freedom, so hurriedly and rather lamely it was changed to:

You see it without the use of special glasses!

small towns
were for many years the staple of the American cinema. Most audiences were small-town folk, and wanted to see slightly idealized versions of themselves. Thus the popularity of the happy families, the Hardys and the Joneses; thus *Our Town*, *The Human Comedy*, *Ah Wilderness*, *The Music Man* and *The Dark at the Top of the Stairs*. The darker side of small-town life was shown in *The Chase*, *Kings Row*, *Peyton Place* and *Invasion of the Body Snatchers*. British small towns did not have the same aura; most of the comparable stories were set against industrial backgrounds.

Smilin' Through.
The popular sentimental stage play by Jane Cowl and June Murfin, about a tragedy affecting the romances of two generations, was filmed in 1922 by Sidney Franklin, with Norma Talmadge, Wyndham Standing, and Harrison Ford; in 1932, again by Sidney Franklin, with Norma Shearer, Leslie Howard, and Fredric March. In 1941 Frank Borzage remade it with Jeanette MacDonald, Brian Aherne, and Gene Raymond.

smoking
has served as the springboard of a few plots. *No Smoking* and *Cold Turkey* concerned cures for it, and one also figured in *Taking Off*. In *On a Clear Day You Can See Forever* Barbra Streisand launched the plot by taking psychiatric advice about it. The most fashionable smoking habit was Paul Henreid's in *Now Voyager*, lighting two cigarettes and passing one to Bette Davis; this was mimicked with eight cigarettes by Bob Hope in *Let's Face It*. The longest cigarette holder was sported by Harpo Marx in *A Night in Casablanca*. In the 90s there was a concerted campaign to stop stars smoking on-screen, on the grounds that it encouraged the young and impressionable to take up the habit. Perhaps as a reaction came *Smoke* and *Blue in the Face* 95, two films set in a Brooklyn cigar store.

smugglers
of the old-fashioned type are almost entirely a British concern, figuring in *Fury at Smugglers' Bay*, *Jamaica Inn*, *The Ghost Train*, *Oh Mr Porter*, *Ask a Policeman*, *I See a Dark Stranger*, *Moonfleet*, and others. Smuggling in American films has been a much more modern and less picturesque affair.

social comedy.
Silent romantic comedies were completely unrealistic, though they sometimes found it prudent to pretend satirical intent to cloak their lowbrow commercialism. Social comedy really came in as a substitute for sex comedy when the Hays Office axe fell in 1934. Frank Capra took by far the best advantage of it, with his series of films showing an America filled to bursting point with good guys who only wanted a simple and comfortable home life in some small town where corruption never raised its ugly head. The best of these films were *Mr Deeds Goes to Town*, *You Can't Take It with You* and *Mr Smith Goes to Washington*; by the time *Meet John Doe* came along in 1941 war had soured the mood again. There was no British equivalent to Capra, unless one counts a few attempts by Priestley (*The Good Companions*, *Let the People Sing*) and such amusing depictions of the middle class as *Quiet Wedding* and *Dear Octopus*; but in the late 40s came the Ealing comedies, delightful and apparently realistic, but presenting a picture of England just as false as Capra's America. In both countries the 50s saw the development of an affluent society in which cynicism was fashionable and few reforms seemed worth urging except in bitterly serious fashion.

social conscience
has long been a feature of Hollywood film production. Other countries have presented the odd feature pointing to flaws in their national make-up, but America has seemed particularly keen to wash its own dirty linen on screen, perhaps because this is rather easier than actually cleaning up the abuses.

The evolution of this attitude can be traced back as far as 1912 and Griffith's *The Musketeers of Pig Alley*, showing slum conditions, a theme developed in *Intolerance* 16; and, of course, Chaplin was a master at devising humour and pathos out of the unpleasant realities of poverty, a fact which endeared him to poor people all over the world. But it was not till the late 20s that the flood of socially conscious films began in earnest. Vidor's *The Crowd* investigated the drabness of everyday life for a city clerk. John Baxter's British *Dosshouse* was a lone entry on the lines of *The Lower Depths*. *City Streets* and *One-Third of a Nation* treated slum conditions; Vidor's *Our Daily Bread* concerned a young couple driven out of the city by poverty only to find farming just as precarious. *Little Caesar* and the gangster dramas which followed always assumed a crusading moral tone deploring the lives of vice and crime which they depicted; there was a somewhat more honest ring to *I Was a Fugitive from a Chain Gang*, which showed how circumstance can drive an honest man into anti-social behaviour. Capra sugared his pill with comedy: *American Madness* (the madness was money) and the popular comedies which followed all pitted common-man philosophy against urban sophistication and corruption.

In the mid-30s there were certainly many abuses worth fighting. *Black Legion* began Hollywood's campaign against the Ku Klux Klan, later followed up in *The Flaming Cross*, *Storm Warning* and *The Cardinal*. Lynch law, first tackled in *Fury*, was subsequently the subject of *They Won't Forget*, *The Ox Bow Incident* and *The Sound of Fury*. Juvenile delinquency was probed in *Dead End*, *Angels with Dirty Faces* and *They Made Me a Criminal*, but the 'Dead End Kids' were later played for comedy. Prison reform was advocated in *Each Dawn I Die*, *Castle on the Hudson*, and many other melodramas of questionable integrity. *The Good Earth* invited concern for the poor of other nations; *Mr Smith Goes to Washington* and *The Glass Key* were among many dramas showing that politicians are not incorruptible; *Love on the Dole* depicted the poverty of industrial Britain; *The Grapes of Wrath* and *Tobacco Road* pondered the plight of farming people deprived of a living by geographical chance and thoughtless government. In *Sullivan's Travels*, Preston Sturges came to the curious conclusion that the best thing you can do for the poor is make them laugh.

During World War II the nations were too busy removing the abuse of Nazidom to look inward, and indeed much poverty was alleviated by conscription and a fresh national awareness which, together with the increased need for industrial manpower, greatly improved the lot of the lower classes. But with victory came a whole crop of films, led by *The Best Years of Our Lives* and *Till the End of Time*, about the rehabilitation of war veterans. Concern about mental illness was shown in *The Snake Pit*, about paraplegia in *The Men*, and about labour relations in *The Whistle at Eaton Falls*. Alcoholism was treated in *The Lost Weekend* and *Smash-Up*, and the racial issues were thoroughly aired in *Lost Boundaries*, *Crossfire*, *Home of the Brave*, *No Way Out*, *Gentleman's Agreement* and *Pinky*. A plea for nations to help and understand each other was made in the French *Race for Life*.

With the development in the 50s of the affluent society, the number of reforms worth urging was drastically reduced. Teenage hoodlums figured largely in a score of films of which the best were *The Wild One* and *Rebel without a Cause*. Mentally handicapped children were sympathetically portrayed in *A Child is Waiting*. In the 1960s, however, it was one world issue which dominated the film-makers' social consciousness, that of the panic button; and this manifested itself in films as diverse as *On the Beach*, *Dr Strangelove*, *Fail Safe* and *The Bedford Incident*.

Social consciousness was apparent in almost every drama of the 70s, but used as a top dressing, sometimes to permit the exploitation of violence. In films like *A Clockwork Orange* and *O Lucky Man* it is difficult enough to discover what point is being made.

soldiers
depicted at length in films include Alexander the Great (by Richard Burton), Hannibal (by Victor Mature), Genghis Khan (by John Wayne and Omar Sharif), Alexander Nevsky (by Cherkassov), Clive of India (by Ronald Colman), Napoleon (by Charles Boyer, Marlon Brando, Herbert Lom, and others), Bonnie Prince Charlie (by David Niven), Wellington (by George Arliss), General Gordon (by Charlton Heston), Custer (by Errol Flynn and Robert Shaw), La Fayette (by Michel le Royer), Davy Crockett (by Fess Parker and others), Sergeant York (by Gary Cooper), Audie Murphy (by Audie Murphy), Rommel (by Erich von Stroheim and James Mason), Che Guevara (by Omar Sharif), General Patton (by George C. Scott), and General Macarthur (by Gregory Peck).

space exploration
on screen began in 1899 with Méliès; in the 20s Fritz Lang made *The Woman in the Moon* and in the 30s there was *Buck Rogers in the Twenty-Fifth Century*, but not until 1950 did the subject seem acceptable as anything but fantasy. In that year an adventure of the comic-strip type, *Rocketship XM*, competed for box-office attention with George Pal's semi-documentary *Destination Moon*, and suddenly the floodgates were opened. During the years that followed we were offered such titles as *Riders to the Stars*, *Fire Maidens from Outer Space*, *Satellite in the Sky*, *From the Earth to the Moon*, *Conquest of Space*, *Forbidden Planet*, *It!*, *The Terror from Beyond Space*, *Robinson Crusoe on Mars*, *The First Men in the Moon*, *2001: A Space Odyssey*, *Saturn Three*, *Outland* and the *Star Wars* saga. Nor was the traffic all one way: Earth had many strange visitors from other planets, notably in *The Thing From Another World*, *The Day the Earth Stood Still*, *Devil Girl from Mars*, *Stranger from Venus*, *It Came from Outer Space*, *Invasion of the Body Snatchers* (the best and subtlest of them all), *The War of the Worlds*, *The Quatermass Experiment*, *Quatermass II*, *Visit to a Small Planet*, *This Island Earth*, and *The Man Who Fell to Earth*. On television, the most imaginative exploits have been in *Star Trek*, *Space 1999*, *Buck Rogers* and *Galactica*.

spaghetti westerns.
A dismissive name for the blood-spattered Italian imitations of American westerns which became popular in the 60s, using such actors as Lee Van Cleef and Clint Eastwood. They gained an international reputation, and incidentally made Eastwood into a star, through the work of Sergio Leone in the mid-60s, beginning with his *A Fistful of Dollars*. Leone orchestrated the action around dramatic close-ups, with a slow build to moments of extreme action, to the accompaniment of Ennio Morricone's plangent, percussive music. Eastwood set the pattern for the protagonist: a taciturn, laconic wanderer who was deadly with a gun. While he was 'the man with no name', other recurring heroes of the genre were Sartana, Django and Ringo. Other US actors who found employment

in the films included Charles BRONSON. Italian actors also found a role, including Franco NERO as Django, Tomas MILIAN and, as the genre encompassed more comedy, Bud SPENCER and Terence HILL. By the beginning of the 70s, the genre has lost most of its impetus, though it influenced later westerns such as Sam PECKINPAH's *The Wild Bunch*.

Books: 1975, *Italian Western: The Opera of Violence* by Laurence Staig and Tony Williams; 1998, *Spaghetti Westerns: Cowboys and Europeans from Karl May to Sergio Leone* by Christopher Frayling.

The Spanish Civil War

featured in a few Hemingway picturizations, notably *For Whom the Bell Tolls* and *The Snows of Kilimanjaro*; in *The Fallen Sparrow*, *Blockade*, *The Angel Wore Red*, *Love under Fire*, *Last Train from Madrid*, *Arise My Love*, *Confidential Agent* and (remotely) *The Prime of Miss Jean Brodie*. In more documentary style were *L'Espoir*, *Spanish Earth*, *Guernica*, *To Die in Madrid*, *¡Ay, Carmela!* and *Land and Freedom*, while British television has produced two extended assemblies of newsreel footage.

speeches

of any length are the antithesis of good film-making, but sometimes a long monologue has been not only an actor's dream but absolutely right, memorable and hypnotic in its context. The record (20 minutes) is probably held by Edwige Feuillère in *The Eagle Has Two Heads*, but more effective, and somewhat shorter, were Sam Jaffe in *Lost Horizon*, Alec Guinness in *The Mudlark*, Orson Welles in *Compulsion*, Spencer Tracy in *Inherit the Wind*, Anne Baxter in *The Walls of Jericho*, James Stewart in *Mr Smith Goes to Washington*, Paul Muni in *The Life of Emile Zola*, Don Murray in *One Man's Way*, Orson Welles in *Moby Dick*, and Charles Chaplin in *The Great Dictator*.

Speedy Gonzales.

Fast-moving Mexican mouse who was the hero of Warner Brothers cartoons. Created by Friz Freleng and animator Hawley Pratt, he was voiced by Mel Blanc.

Speedy Gonzales (AA) 55. Tabasco Road (AAN) 57. The Pied Piper of Guadalupe (AAN) 61. Mexican Cat Dance 63. Chili Corn Corny 66. Speedy Ghost to Town 67. See Ya Later, Gladiator 67, etc.

spies

enjoyed enormous popularity as the heroes of over-sexed, gimmick-ridden melodramas. Real-life spies have been less frequently depicted, the world of James Bond being much livelier than those of Moyzich (*Five Fingers*), Odette Churchill (*Odette V.C.*), *Nurse Edith Cavell*, Violette Szabo (*Carve Her Name with Pride*), *Mata Hari*, or the gangs in *The House on 92nd Street*, *13 Rue Madeleine*, and *Ring of Spies*.

Fictional spy films first became popular during and after World War I: they added a touch of glamour to an otherwise depressing subject, even though the hero often faced the firing squad in the last reel. Right up to 1939 romantic melodramas on this theme were being made: *I Was a Spy*, *The Man Who Knew Too Much*, *The Thirty-Nine Steps*, *Lancer Spy*, *The Spy in Black*, *Dark Journey*, *British Agent*, *Secret Agent*, *The Lady Vanishes*, *Espionage Agent*, *Confessions of a Nazi Spy*. The last-named brought the subject roughly up to date, and with the renewed outbreak of hostilities new possibilities were hastily seized in *Foreign Correspondent*, *Night Train to Munich*, *Casablanca*, *The Conspirators*, *They Came to Blow Up America*, *Berlin Correspondent*, *Across the Pacific*, *Escape to Danger*, *Ministry of Fear*, *Confidential Agent*, *Sherlock Holmes and the Secret Weapon*, *Hotel Reserve*, and innumerable others. (It was fashionable during this period to reveal that the villains of comedy-thrillers and who-done-its were really enemy agents.) During the post-war years two fashions in film spying became evident: the downbeat melodrama showing spies as frightened men and women doing a dangerous job (*Notorious*, *Cloak and Dagger*, *Hotel Berlin*, *Orders to Kill*) and the 'now it can be told' semi-documentary revelation (*O.S.S.*, *Diplomatic Courier*, *The Man Who Never Was*, *The Two-Headed Spy*, *The Counterfeit Traitor*, *Operation Crossbow*). In the late 40s Nazis and Japs were replaced by reds, and we had a spate of melodramas under such titles as *I Married a Communist*, *I Was a Communist for the FBI*, *I Was an American Spy*, *Red Snow* and *The Red Danube*.

There had always been spy comedies. Every comedian made one or two: the Crazy Gang in *Gasbags*, Duggie Wakefield in *Spy for a Day*, Jack Benny in *To Be or Not To Be*, Bob Hope in *They Got Me Covered*, Radford and Wayne in *It's Not Cricket*, George Cole in *Top Secret*, right up to the *Carry On* Team in *Carry On Spying* and Morecambe and Wise in *The Intelligence Men*. There were also occasional burlesques like *All Through the Night* and sardonic comedies like *Our Man in Havana*. But it was not until the late 50s that the spy reasserted himself as a romantic figure who could be taken lightly; and not until 1962 was the right box-office combination of sex and suspense found in *Dr No*. Since then we have been deluged with pale imitations of James Bond to such an extent that almost every leading man worth his salt has had a go. Cary Grant in *Charade*, David Niven in *Where the Spies Are*, Rod Taylor and Trevor Howard in *The Liquidator*, Dirk Bogarde in *Hot Enough for June*, Michael Caine in *The Ipcress File*, Paul Newman in *Torn Curtain*, James Coburn in *Our Man Flint*, Gregory Peck in *Arabesque*, Yul Brynner in *The Double Man*, George Peppard in *The Executioner*, Stephen Boyd in *Assignment K*, Frank Sinatra in *The Naked Runner*, Anthony Hopkins in *When Eight Bells Toll*, Kirk Douglas in *Catch Me a Spy*, Tom Adams in *Licensed to Kill*. There have also been elaborations such as the extreme sophistication of *The Manchurian Candidate*, the cold realism of *The Spy Who Came in from the Cold*, the op-art spoofing of *Modesty Blaise*, even the canine agent of *The Spy with a Cold Nose* and spies from outer space in *This Island Earth*. And the TV screens of 1970 were filled with such tricky heroes as those in *Danger Man* (Secret Agent), *The Man from U.N.C.L.E.*, *Amos Burke Secret Agent*, *The Baron*, *I Spy* and *The Avengers*. The trend of the 70s was towards sour and disenchanted looks at the whole business, such as *Callan*, *The Killer Elite*, *Permission to Kill* and *Three Days of the Condor*.

The Spoilers.

Rex Beach's action novel has been filmed five times, with interest centring on its climactic fight scene between the two male leads, who were as follows: 1914, William Farnum and Tom Santschi; 1922, Milton Sills and Noah Beery; 1930, William Boyd and Gary Cooper; 1942, John Wayne and Randolph Scott; 1956, Jeff Chandler and Rory Calhoun.

sportsmen

who have been the subject of biopics include Babe Ruth (William Bendix) in *The Babe Ruth Story* and *Babe* (John Goodman); Grover Cleveland Alexander (Ronald Reagan) in *The Winning Team*; Lou Gehrig (Gary Cooper) in *The Pride of the Yankees*; Monty Stratton (James Stewart) in *The Stratton Story*; Jim Piersall (Anthony Perkins) in *Fear Strikes Out*; Jim Corbett (Errol Flynn) in *Gentleman Jim*; John L. Sullivan (Greg McClure) in *The Great John L.*; Knute Rockne (Pat O'Brien) in *Knute Rockne All-American*; Jim Thorpe (Burt Lancaster) in *Jim Thorpe All-American/Man of Bronze*; Ben Hogan (Glenn Ford) in *Follow the Sun*; Annette Kellerman (Esther Williams) in *Million Dollar Mermaid*. American athlete Steve Prefontaine, who died young, was the subject of two competing biopics in 1997: *Prefontaine*, starring Jared Leto, and *Without Limits*, starring Billy Crudup. He was also the subject of a 1995 TV documentary, *Fire on the Track*.

Squibs.

The cockney flower-seller heroine of George Pearson's silent comedy put in her first successful appearance in 1921. Public acclaim produced three sequels: *Squibs Wins the Calcutta Sweep* 22, *Squibs MP* 23, *Squibs' Honeymoon* 23. Pearson then grew tired of the tomboyish character and cast Betty Balfour in other roles, but she reappeared in a not-too-successful talkie version in 1936, with Gordon Harker and Stanley Holloway.

staircases

have provided dramatic backgrounds for many films. Martin Balsam was murdered on one in *Psycho*; the climax of *The Spiral Staircase* took place just there; Vivien Leigh was carried up one by a lustful Clark Gable in *Gone with the Wind*; Jerry Lewis danced down one in *Cinderfella*; Errol Flynn and Basil Rathbone duelled on one in *The Adventures of Robin Hood*; Ann Todd rode a horse up one in *South Riding*; Joan Fontaine in *Rebecca* descended one in delight and ascended it in tears; Raymond Massey ascended a particularly shadowy one in *The Old Dark House*, and later a very sinister character came down it; the entire cast of *Ship of Fools* came down one at the end, like a musical finale; a severed head bumped down one in *Hush Hush Sweet Charlotte*; Gene Tierney threw herself down one in *Leave Her to Heaven*; an old lady was tossed down one in a wheelchair in *Kiss of Death*; Bela Lugosi in *Dracula* passed through the cobwebs on one without breaking them; Laurel and Hardy in *Blockheads* had to descend and ascend innumerable flights of stairs in pursuit of a lost ball; Anna Sten was killed on one in *The Wedding Night*; the lighthouse staircase was a dramatic feature of *Thunder Rock*; James Cagney danced down the White House staircase in *Yankee Doodle Dandy*; and the main feature of *A Matter of Life and Death* was a moving stairway to heaven. In his last film, *Greystoke*, Ralph Richardson slid down a staircase on a tea-tray. Universal and Paramount both had very striking and oft-used staircase sets in the 40s; the latter was most dramatically used for Kirk Douglas' death in *The Strange Love of Martha Ivers*. Oddly enough in the film called *Staircase* the staircase was not an essential feature.

A Star Is Born.

Dorothy Parker, Alan Campbell, and Robert Carson's screenplay for the 1937 film has become a Hollywood legend and in some cases a reality: the marriage of two stars goes on the rocks because one of them is on the way up and the other on the way down. It was first tailored for Janet Gaynor and Fredric March and directed by William Wellman. In 1954 George Cukor directed Judy Garland and James Mason in the star roles. In 1976 it was revamped for Barbra Streisand and Kris Kristofferson. The theme can be traced back to a 1930 film, *What Price Hollywood?*, from a story by Adela Rogers St Johns.

Star Wars.

George LUCAS's immensely popular science-fiction romp of 1977 was swiftly followed by two sequels: *The Empire Strikes Back* 80 and *The Return of the Jedi* 83. In 1999 came *Star Wars: The Phantom Menace*, the first of a projected trilogy of prequels to the original three films, detailing the earlier history of the protagonists. It was preceded, in 1997, by a re-release of *Star Wars* and its two sequels, featuring enhanced special effects. The films proved as popular the second time around.

State Fair.

Philip Strong's novel of small-town virtues, champion hogs, and bucolic romance has been filmed three times: in 1933, directed by Henry King, with Will Rogers and Janet Gaynor; in 1945, as a musical, directed by Walter Lang, with Jeanne Crain, Dana Andrews, Dick Haymes, Vivian Blane, and songs by Oscar Hammerstein II; and in 1962, directed by José Ferrer, with Pat Boone, Bobby Darin, Pamela Tiffin, and Ann-Margret, and new songs added by Richard Rodgers.

statesmen

who have frequently been depicted in films include Disraeli (most often), Gladstone, Melbourne, Ramsay Macdonald (disguised in *Fame is the Spur*), Woodrow Wilson, Churchill, Roosevelt (notably in *Sunrise at Campobello*), LINCOLN and Parnell. Fleeting glimpses of famous leaders were also given in *Mission to Moscow* and some Russian wartime films.

statues

have come to life in *Night Life of the Gods*, *Animal Crackers*, *Turnabout* and *One Touch of Venus*. They were central to the plots of *The Light that Failed*, *Latin Quarter*, *Song of Songs* and *Mad Love*, while *A Taste of Honey* involved them in an attractive title sequence. In horror films, they came murderously alive in *Night of the Eagle*, *The Norliss Tapes* (TV) and that grand-daddy of them all, *The Golem*.

Stella Dallas.

The weepy novel of frustrated mother love, written by Olive Higgins Prouty, was filmed by Henry King in 1925, with Belle Bennett and Ronald Colman; by King Vidor in 1937, with Barbara Stanwyck and John Boles; and by John Erman in 1990, as *Stella*, with Bette Midler and John Goodman.

storms

of one kind or another have been brilliantly staged in *The Hurricane*, *The Wizard of Oz*, *When Tomorrow Comes*, *Reap the Wild Wind*, *Typhoon*, *Lord Jim*, *A High Wind in Jamaica*, *The Blue Lagoon*, *Sunrise*, *Key Largo*, *Ryan's Daughter*, *Portrait of Jennie*, *Noah's Ark* and *The Bible*, to name but a handful; they have also been essential situation-builders in such films as *Five Came Back*, *Hatter's Castle*, *Our Man Flint*, *The Card*, *Storm Fear* and *The Blue Lagoon*. A whole genre of films, known as the 'thunderstorm mystery', grew up in the 30s when every screen murder took place in a desolate mansion during a terrifying storm with no means of communication with the outside world; typical of these are *The Black Cat*, *The Cat and the Canary*, *The Ghost Breakers*, *Night Monster*, *Hold That Ghost*, *You'll Find Out* and *The Spiral Staircase*. Finally there is nothing like a good electrical storm for breathing life into a monster, as evidenced in a score of films from *Frankenstein* to *The Electric Man* and after.

strikes:

see LABOUR RELATIONS.

striptease.

The staple of burlesque and Las Vegas finally made it to the screen with no holds barred and no breasts bra'ed in Paul Verhoeven's *Showgirls* 95, a film about the lives of two 'lap dancers'. It also brought Demi Moore $12m, the most money ever paid to a Hollywood actress, to play the role of a stripper in *Striptease* 96, based on Carl Hiassen's thriller. Strippers also featured in Atom Egoyan's award-winning art film *Exotica* 94. The first known stripper was Lady Godiva, whose legend formed the basis for the updated British movie *Lady Godiva Rides Again* 51, and *Lady Godiva* 55, a US historical recreation set in Saxon times. The most famous artiste remains Gypsy Rose Lee whose autobiography of her early life was filmed as *Gypsy* 62; she was played by Natalie Wood, a guarantee that proceedings remained genteel. Gypsy Rose Lee's novel *G-String Murders* was filmed as *Lady of Burlesque/Striptease Lady* 43, featuring Barbara Stanwyck as a stripper who solves a number of backstage murders, and her play *Doll Face/Come Back to Me*, about a burlesque queen who goes to Broadway, was filmed in 1945. From the 30s onwards, she also appeared in Hollywood films, including *The Stripper* 63, but that had little to do with taking off clothes to music. Roger Corman produced a couple of exploitation movies on the theme, with *Stripped to Kill* 87 and *Stripped to Kill II* 89. Other strippers have included Britt Ekland in *The Night They Raided Minsky's* 68; Melanie Griffith in *Fear City* 84; Lolita Davidovitch, bringing about politician Earl Long's downfall in *Blaze* 89; Sherilyn Fenn in *Ruby* 92; and Goldie Hawn as a hard-working mother in *CrissCross* 92. Male strippers have been less popular so far, though Christopher Atkins appeared as one in *A Night in Heaven* 83, and Mel Chionglo's *Midnight Dancers* 94 was set in a nightclub featuring little else. *The Full Monty* 97 focused on a group of unemployed men who try stripping to earn some cash.

The Student of Prague.

The old German legend, about a man who sold his soul to the devil and bought it back only at the expense of his life, was filmed in 1913 by Stellan Rye, with Paul Wegener; in 1926 by Henrik Galeen, with Conrad Veidt; and in 1936 by Arthur Robison, with Anton Walbrook.

The Student Prince.

The Sigmund Romberg/Dorothy Donnelly operetta about a Ruritanian prince who loves a barmaid was filmed by Lubitsch in 1927 with Ramon Novarro and Norma Shearer. There was no sound version until 1954, when Richard Thorpe directed Ann Blyth and Edmund Purdom (the latter using Mario Lanza's voice).

student protest

was a feature of a few films of the late 60s. They were not successful, with the exception of *If*. For the record the other main titles were *Flick*, *The Strawberry Statement*, *Getting Straight*, *R.P.M.* and *The Revolutionary*.

stuntmen,

who risk their lives doubling for the stars when the action gets too rough, have been featured in remarkably few movies: *Hollywood Stunt Men*,

Lucky Devils, The Lost Squadron, Sons of Adventure, Callaway Went Thataway, Singin' in the Rain and *Hooper, Hell's Angels* was said to be the film on which most stuntmen were killed; more recently Paul Mantz lost his life while stunt-flying for *The Flight of the Phoenix*, which was subsequently dedicated to him. Most famous stuntmen are probably Yakima Canutt, who later became a famous second-unit director; Richard Talmadge, who doubled for Douglas Fairbanks and also directed a few films himself; and Cliff Lyons, who stood in for most of the western stars. Stuntmen who became famous in their own right include George O'Brien, Jock Mahoney, Rod Cameron and George Montgomery. In the early 80s a film called *The Stunt Man* took a wry view of the matter and a TV series called *The Fall Guy* was popular for a while.

submarines
have been the setting for so many war action films that only a few can be noted. Pure entertainment was the object of *Submarine Patrol, Submarine Command, Torpedo Run, Destination Tokyo, Run Silent Run Deep, Crash Dive, The Deep Six* and *Ice Station Zebra*. Somewhat deeper thoughts were permitted in *Morning Departure, The Silent Enemy, Les Maudits,* and *We Dive at Dawn*. Submarines became objects of farce in *Jack Ahoy, Let's Face It*, and *Operation Petticoat*.

More unusual submarine vehicles appeared in *Voyage to the Bottom of the Sea, Around the World Under the Sea, Twenty Thousand Leagues Under the Sea, Thunderball, You Only Live Twice, Above Us the Waves* and *The Beast from 20,000 Fathoms*.

subways:
see UNDERGROUND RAILWAYS.

suicide
became the central subject of two 60s films, *Le Feu Follet* and *The Slender Thread*, in which the motives for it in two particular cases are examined. It has, of course, been part of countless other plots, including factual or legendary ones such as *Cleopatra, Romeo and Juliet* and *Scott of the Antarctic*. Innumerable melodramas have begun with apparent suicides which have been proved by the disbelieving hero to be murder; the least likely of these may be *The Third Secret*. In *An Inspector Calls* a girl's suicide caused guilt complexes in an entire family for different reasons. In *An American Dream* the hero virtually commits suicide by walking into a room full of gangsters out to kill him. In *Leave Her to Heaven* the leading character commits suicide in such a way that her husband will be blamed for her murder. Several Japanese films have been based on the suicide pilots or kamikaze, and there has also been a graphic account of the principles of *hara kiri*. Suicide has often been the way out for villains in mystery pictures: drowning for Herbert Marshall in *Foreign Correspondent*, shooting for Leo G. Carroll in *Spellbound*, poison for Rosamund John in *Green for Danger* and Barry Fitzgerald in *And Then There Were None*. And one could not begin to count the films in which characters have been narrowly saved from suicide, like Ray Milland in *The Lost Weekend*. Attempted suicide was even played for comedy by Laurel and Hardy in *The Flying Deuces*, by Graham Chapman in *The Odd Job*, by Jack Lemmon in *Buddy Buddy* and *Luv*, by Burt Reynolds in *The End*, while in *It's a Wonderful Life* James Stewart was dissuaded from suicide by a friendly angel. In *The Long Goodbye*, Elliott Gould finds a presumed suicide alive, and shoots him.

Superman.
A comic strip character of the 30s, a being of giant powers from the planet Krypton; until they are needed he masquerades as Clark Kent, a timid newspaperman. Superman has never been out of fashion – 1978 brought a multi-million-dollar live version to follow the various cartoons and serials which have been popular over the years – and along the way he has inspired Batman, Spiderman, Doc Savage, the Six Million Dollar Man, the Bionic Woman, etc, etc. In 1984, after two further sequels, *Superman* gave way to *Supergirl*. The role has been played by Kirk ALYN in two serials, George REEVES, who took over for one serial before playing the part on television, Christopher REEVE in the big-budget films of the 70s and 80s, and Dean Cain in a 90s TV series.

Superman (serial) 48. Atom Man vs Superman (serial) 50. Superman and the Mole Men (serial) 51. Superman 78. Superman II 80. Superman III 83. Superman IV: The Quest for Peace 87.

TV series: Superman (with George Reeves) 53–57. Lois and Clark: The New Adventures of Superman 93–97.

Svengali,
the evil genius of George du Maurier's Victorian romance *Trilby*, has been seen at least five times on-screen. In 1915 Wilton Lackaye and Clara Kimball Young appeared in a version under the title *Trilby*. There was a British one-reeler in 1922 in the 'Tense Moments with Great Authors' series, and in 1923 James Young directed a second Hollywood version with Arthur Edmund Carewe and Andrée Lafayette. In 1931, under the title *Svengali*, Archie Mayo directed a sound remake with John Barrymore as the hypnotist to Marian Marsh's heroine, and in 1954 Donald Wolfit and Hildegarde Neff appeared in a British version directed by Noel Langley. (Robert Newton had proved incapable of playing the lead.) In 1982 Peter O'Toole and Jodie Foster were in a dismal TV modernization set in New York.

swashbucklers
are films of period adventure in which the hero and villain usually settle the issue by a duel to the death. The greatest screen swashbucklers of all are probably Douglas Fairbanks Snr and Errol Flynn, but one should also be grateful for the efforts of Tyrone Power (*The Mark of Zorro*), Douglas Fairbanks Jnr (*Sinbad the Sailor*), Ronald Colman (*The Prisoner of Zenda*), Stewart Granger (*Scaramouche*), Rudolph Valentino (*The Eagle*), Gene Kelly (*The Three Musketeers*), Robert Donat (*The Count of Monte Cristo*), Louis Hayward (*The Man in the Iron Mask*), Cornel Wilde (*The Bandit of Sherwood Forest*), Tony Curtis (*The Purple Mask*) and their numerous imitators. The 1976 attempt to revive (or spoof) the genre in *Swashbuckler* was a sorry failure.

swinging London
was a myth, a creation of *Time* Magazine which rebounded through the world's press and lasted for several silly seasons from 1965. It also helped British production finances by persuading American impresarios that London was where the action was, and its influence was felt in scores of trendy and increasingly boring films, including *Georgy Girl, Alfie, The Jokers, Kaleidoscope, Smashing Time, Help!, The Knack, Blow Up, Casino Royale, I'll Never Forget Whatshisname, To Sir with Love, Up the Junction, Bedazzled, Poor Cow, The Strange Affair, Salt and Pepper, Joanna, Darling* and *Otley*.

The Swiss Family Robinson.
The classic children's novel by Johann Wyss was filmed in Hollywood in 1940 by Edward Ludwig, with Thomas Mitchell, Edna Best, Freddie Bartholomew, and Terry Kilburn. In 1960 Ken Annakin remade it as a Disney spectacular, with John Mills, Dorothy McGuire, James Macarthur, and Tommy Kirk as the desert island castaways.

sword and sorcery
is the term used to describe stories set in mythic fantasy worlds, where muscular heroes cleave their way through a landscape filled with monsters and magic. The most influential author in the genre has been Robert E. HOWARD, creator of Conan the Barbarian. In the mid-90s, the genre found its home on television in the series *Hercules: the Legendary Journeys*, starring Kevin Sorbo, and *Xena: Warrior Princess*, starring Lucy Lawless, which put the emphasis on spectacle and camp humour.

Hawk the Slayer 80. Conan the Barbarian 81. Fire and Ice 82. The Beastmaster 82. Sword and the Sorcerer 82. Ator the Fighting Eagle 83. Deathstalker 83. Krull 83. Blade Master/Ator the Invincible 84. Conan the Destroyer 84. Red Sonja 85. Wizards of the Lost Kingdom 85. Highlander 86. Deathstalker 2: Duel of the Titans 87. Deathstalker 3: The Warriors from Hell 89. Wizards of the Lost Kingdom 2 89. Highlander II: The Quickening 90. Beastmaster 2: Through the Portals of Time 91. Deathstalker 4: Match of the Titans 92. Highlander III: The Sorcerer 94. Wizards of the Demon Sword 94. Beastmaster 3: The Eye of Braxus 95. Kull the Conqueror 97, etc.

Sylvester.
The celebrated cartoon cat with the lisping Bronx accent, always in pursuit of Tweetie Pie but never quite managing to win, appeared from the 40s to the 60s in Warner shorts, voiced by the inimitable Mel Blanc.

Life with Feathers (AAN) 45. Tweetie Pie (AA) 47. Little Red Rodent Hood 52. Claws for Alarm 54. Speedy Gonzales (AA) 55. Tabasco Road (AAN) 57. Mouse-Taken Identity 57. Birds Anonymous (AA) 57. Trip for Tat 60. The Pied Piper of Guadalupe (AAN) 61. Freudy Cat 64, etc.

A Tale of Two Cities.
Apart from three very early one-reel versions, Dickens's novel of the French Revolution was filmed in 1917, with William Farnum, in 1926 with Maurice Costello and (as *The Only Way*) with Sir John Martin-Harvey, in 1935, with Ronald Colman, and in 1958, with Dirk Bogarde.

Tales of Manhattan.
Julien Duvivier's 1942 film, a string of anecdotes linked by the travels of one tail-coat, can be credited with starting or revivifying the short-story compendium form, later developed in such movies as *Flesh and Fantasy, Quartet, Full House, The Story of Three Loves, It's a Great Country*, and many others. The film's inspiration was Duvivier's own *Un Carnet de Bal*, made in 1937, which gave him his ticket to Hollywood.

talkies
caused the biggest revolution the film industry has known, and provoked critical resentment difficult to understand until one sees a very early talkie and realizes what a raucous and unpleasant experience it must have been until Hollywood caught up with itself. The main steps of development were as follows. In 1923 Lee DE FORREST made primitive shorts. In 1926 Warners created Vitaphone, a disc process, and Fox pioneered sound on film with Movietone. Also in 1926 came *Don Juan*, the first film with synchronized music and effects. The first speaking and singing came in 1927 with Al Jolson in *The Jazz Singer*. In 1928 the first all-talking film, *Lights of New York*, set the seal of popular success on the new medium.

❛❛ The addition of sound to the movies was ridiculed and frantically opposed; but the industry needed the fresh impetus and at great expense the revolution was achieved.

> No closer approach to resurrection has ever been made by science,

said Professor M. Pupin of the American Institute of Electrical Engineers. But it was years before he could claim perfect reproduction.

> The tinkle of a glass, the shot of a revolver, a footfall on a hardwood floor, and the noise of a pack of cards being shuffled, all sounded about alike,

said Gilbert Seldes in 1929. And Tallulah Bankhead complained:

> They made me sound as if I'd been castrated.

E.V. Lucas complained:

> They are doing away with the greatest boon that has ever been offered to the deaf.

The distinguished documentarist Paul Rotha joined in the dismay:

> A film in which the speech and sound effects are perfectly synchronized and coincide with their visual images on screen is absolutely contrary to the aims of the cinema. It is a degenerate and misguided attempt to destroy the real use of the film.

Nor was the prestige of the industry helped by claims of mathematical impossibility such as:

> 100% talking! 100% singing! 100% dancing!

But the public forgave all: the novelty value was tremendous, even though they missed a number of favourite stars whose voices proved unsuitable. As Jack Warner said:

> Men and women whose names were known throughout the land disappeared as though they had been lost at sea.

And *Variety* summed up:

> Talkies didn't do more to the industry than turn it upside down, shake the entire bag of tricks from its pocket, and advance Warner Brothers from last place to first in the league.

But Ernst Lubitsch took a more cynical view:

> You could name the great stars of the silent screen who were finished; the great directors, gone; the great title writers who were washed up. But remember this, as long as you live: the producers didn't lose a man. They all made the switch. That's where the great talent is.

Tammy.
Cid Ricketts Sumner's romantic novel of a cheerful country girl was filmed in 1957 with Debbie Reynolds in the title role; two sequels, *Tammy Tell Me True* and *Tammy and the Doctor*, followed in 1961 and 1963 starring Sandra Dee; they were followed by a fourth film, *Tammy and the Millionaire*, in 1967, starring Debbie Watson.

Tarzan.
The brawny jungle hero, an English milord lost in Africa as a child and who grew up with the apes, was a creation of novelist Edgar Rice Burroughs (1875–1950); the first Tarzan story was published in 1913. The films quickly followed. *Tarzan of the Apes* 18 starred Elmo Lincoln with Enid Markey as Jane; so did *Romance of Tarzan* 18. *The Return of Tarzan* 20 had Gene Pollar and Karla Schramm. *Son of Tarzan* 20 was a serial with Kamuela C. Searle in the title role; Tarzan was P. Dempsey Tabler, Elmo Lincoln returned in another serial, *The Adventures of Tarzan* 21, with Louise Lorraine. *Tarzan and the Golden Lion* 27 starred James Pierce and Dorothy Dunbar. Another serial, *Tarzan the Mighty* 28, had Frank Merrill and no Jane; a runner-up, *Tarzan the Tiger* 30, had the same crew. In 1932 came Johnny Weissmuller in the first of MGM's long line of Tarzan pictures: *Tarzan the Ape Man*, with Maureen O'Sullivan as Jane. There followed *Tarzan and His Mate* 34, *Tarzan Escapes* 36, *Tarzan Finds a Son* 39, *Tarzan's Secret Treasure* 41, and *Tarzan's New York Adventure* 42. Meanwhile in 1935 an independent company had made a serial starring Herman Brix which was later released as two features, *Tarzan and the Green Goddess* and *New Adventures of Tarzan*; and in 1933 producer Sol Lesser had started his Tarzan series with *Tarzan the Fearless*, starring Buster Crabbe; he followed this up with *Tarzan's Revenge* 38 starring Glenn Morris. In 1943 Lesser took over Weissmuller (but not O'Sullivan or any other Jane) for *Tarzan Triumphs*, followed by *Tarzan's Desert Mystery* 44, *Tarzan and the Amazons* (reintroducing Jane in the shape of Brenda Joyce) 45, *Tarzan and the Leopard Woman* 46, *Tarzan and the Huntress* 47, and *Tarzan and the Mermaids* 48. Then Weissmuller was replaced by Lex Barker for *Tarzan's Magic Fountain* 48, *Tarzan and the Slave Girl* 49, *Tarzan's Peril* 50, *Tarzan's Savage Fury* 51, and *Tarzan and the She-Devil* 52. Gordon Scott next undertook the chore in *Tarzan's Hidden Jungle* 55, *Tarzan and the Lost Safari* 57, *Tarzan's Fight for Life* 58, *Tarzan's Greatest Adventure* 59 and *Tarzan the Magnificent* 60. MGM now remade *Tarzan the Ape Man* 60 starring Denny Miller; and, with Jock Mahoney, *Tarzan Goes to India* 62 and National General presented *Tarzan's Three Challenges* 64. There followed *Tarzan and the Valley of Gold* 66, *Tarzan and the Great River* 67, and *Tarzan and the Jungle Boy* 68, all with Mike Henry. A 1982 remake of *Tarzan the Ape Man* had Miles O'Keeffe in the role but concentrated on the charms of Bo Derek as Jane; however, in 1984 *Greystoke* set the record straight by remaining slightly more faithful to Burroughs' original legend. A 1966–67 TV series starred Ron Ely. Joe Lara played him in a TV movie, *Tarzan in Manhattan* 89, and a subsequent TV series, *Tarzan – The Epic Adventures*. In production at Walt Disney is an animated feature. Casper Van Dien was a live-action ape-man in *Tarzan and the Lost City* 98, but failed to interest a new generation in his antics.

teachers
have been notably played by Robert Donat in *Goodbye Mr Chips;* Jennifer Jones in *Good Morning Miss Dove;* Greer Garson in *Her Twelve Men;* Michael Redgrave and Albert Finney in *The Browning Version;* Aline MacMahon in *Back Door to Heaven;* Claudette Colbert in *Remember the Day;* Bette Davis in *The Corn Is Green;* Jack Hawkins in *Mandy;* Judy Garland in *A Child Is Waiting;* Anne Bancroft in *The Miracle Worker;* Shirley Maclaine in *Spinster;* Glenn Ford in *The Blackboard Jungle;* Sidney Poitier in *To Sir With Love;* Sandy Dennis in *Up the Down Staircase;* Dorothy Dandridge in *Bright Road;* Max Bygraves in *Spare the Rod;* Otto Kruger in *The Housemaster;* Cecil Trouncer in *The Guinea Pig;* Maggie Smith in *The Prime of Miss Jean Brodie;* Joanne Woodward in *Rachel, Rachel;* Robert Mitchum in *Ryan's Daughter;* Laurence Olivier in *Term of Trial;* Richard Todd in *The Love-Ins;* James Whitmore

in *The Harrad Experiment*; David Hemmings in *Unman, Wittering and Zigo*; Per Oscarsson in *Who Saw Him Die?* James Mason in *Child's Play*; Glenda Jackson in *The Class of Miss MacMichael*; Michael Ontkean in *Willie and Phil*; Perry King in *Class of 1984*, harassed by his pupils; Robin Williams in *Dead Poets Society*; Danny DeVito in *Renaissance Man*; and Michelle Pfeiffer in *Dangerous Minds*. In *Class of 1999*, the teachers got their revenge – they turned out to be androids equipped with military hardware. J. Eddie Peck taught by day and danced all night in *Lambada* so he could teach maths to his slum students. In the more inspiring *Stand and Deliver*, based on a true story, Edward James Olmos forced his pupils to succeed against the odds. So did Danny De Vito in *Renaissance Man 94*, Michelle Pfeiffer in *Dangerous Minds 95*, and Richard Dreyfuss in the tear-jerking *Mr Holland's Opus 95*. The genre was mocked in *High School High 96*.

Comic teachers were to the fore in *Boys Will Be Boys* (Will Hay, the best of them all); the *St Trinian's* films; *Carry On Teacher*; *Old Mother Riley Headmistress*; *Bottoms Up* (Jimmy Edwards); *Fun at St Fanny's* (Fred Emney); *The Happiest Days of Your Lives*; *Please Sir*; and *Vice Versa* (James Robertson Justice).

See also: SCHOOLDAYS.

teams:

see ROMANTIC TEAMS.

Teenage Mutant Ninja Turtles.

Comic-book heroes created by Kevin Eastman and Peter Laird in 1984. There are four, each named after a European artist – Leonardo, Raphael, Donatello and Michelangelo – because their creators thought that Japanese names would sound silly. Their transformation into humanoids came about in the way of 50s movie monsters: they were contaminated by radioactivity while babies. They were featured in animated TV cartoons (rechristened by BBC-TV *Teenage Mutant Hero Turtles*) in 1988, and a live-action film, directed by Steve Barron in 1990, became the most successful independent movie so far released. Sequels followed in 1991 and 1993.

the telephone

has been a very useful instrument to film scenarists. The saga of its invention was told in *The Story of Alexander Graham Bell*. It brought sinister, menacing and threatening calls in *Sorry – Wrong Number*, *The Small World of Sammy Lee*, *Midnight Lace*, *I Saw What You Did*, *Experiment in Terror*, *Sudden Fear*, *Strangers on a Train*, and *Dirty Harry*. *Chicago Calling* and *The Slender Thread* were among the films based entirely on someone trying to contact another character by telephone. *Bells Are Ringing*, *The Glenn Miller Story* and *Bye Bye Birdie* had musical numbers based on telephones. Shelly Berman, Jeanne de Casalis and Billy de Wolfe are among the revue artists famous for telephone sketches. Single phone calls were of high dramatic significance in *The Spiral Staircase*, *Little Caesar*, *Fail Safe*, *Dr Strangelove*, *Murder Inc.*, *Dial M for Murder*, *The Silencers*, *2001: A Space Odyssey*, *No Way to Treat a Lady*, *Call Northside 777*, and *Phone Call from a Stranger*, while the phone had a special inference in several call-girl pictures including *Butterfield 8*, *Our Man Flint*, *Indiscreet*, *Strange Bedfellows*, *Come Blow Your Horn* and *It's a Mad Mad Mad Mad World* are among the many films deriving comedy from the telephone . . . while the most chilling moment in many a thriller has been the discovery that the phone is disconnected. In *The President's Analyst* the telephone company turned out to be the supreme enemy of civilization. In *Julia Has Two Lovers*, a crossed line led to the beginning of a romantic involvement with a gentleman caller.

television,

arch-enemy of the film-makers, was used during the 50s as an object of derision (*The Titfield Thunderbolt*, *Happy Anniversary*, *It's Always Fair Weather*, *My Blue Heaven*, *Simon and Laura*, *Callaway Went Thataway*, *No Down Payment*, *Meet Mr Lucifer*), or totally ignored. Yet it had featured in films even before World War II: *International House*, *Television Spy*, *Murder by Television*, *Raffles*, and a host of science fiction serials. More recently, television studios have provided a useful background for comedy (*You Must Be Joking*, *A Hard Day's Night*), for thrillers (*The Glass Web*, *Arabesque*, *The Barefoot Executive*) and for

melodramas (*Seven Days in May*, *The Third Secret*, *The Love Machine*). The only serious movie study of the effects of television is *A Face in the Crowd*; and the funniest scenes about television programmes are probably those in *The Apartment*. Closed circuit TV is extensively used in *The Forbin Project*, *The Andromeda Strain*, *Loving* and *The Anderson Tapes*. In *THX 1138* television is used as a mass opiate for the workers of the subterranean world of the future. A wild but fairly barbed satire on television was *The Groove Tube*, and *Network* took a lofty view of it before pitching into hysterical melodrama. *Stay Tuned* was an inept satire about a husband and wife sucked into a TV hell.

  Some definitions, mostly jaundiced:
The bland leading the bland. – *Anon*
Chewing gum for the eyes. – *Frank Lloyd Wright*
The longest amateur night in history. – *Robert Carson*
A medium, so called because it is neither rare nor well done. – *Ernie Kovacs*
A twenty-one-inch prison. I'm delighted with it because it used to be that films were the lowest form of art. Now we have something to look down on. – *Billy Wilder*
Why should people go out and pay money to see bad films when they can stay at home and see bad television for nothing? – *Samuel Goldwyn*
A TV commercial was defined as:
The opening and closing quarter-hours of a half-hour show.
Though Cedric Hardwicke thought the ads were:
The last refuge of optimism in a world of gloom.
Irving Allen had his problems working in the medium:
I've tried to take the lunacy that exists in television and reduce it to a quiet panic.
John Simon was dismissive:
It is inconceivable what trash would be put on film these days if TV had not been invented, and the TV writers were functioning as scenarists.
Fred Allen saw it as:
A triumph of equipment over people. The minds that control it are so small that you could put them in the navel of a flea and still have room for a network vice-president's heart.
Billy Wilder was apprehensive:
A bad play folds and is forgotten, but in pictures we don't bury our dead. When you think it's out of your system your daughter sees it on TV and says: 'My father is an idiot.'
Groucho Marx as usual had a smart answer:
I find television very educational. Every time someone switches it on I go into another room and read a good book.
And it was an anonymous wit who had perhaps the best answer of all:
I prefer television. It's not so far to the bathroom.
Bob Hope as so often had the last word:
The other night I saw a Road picture so cut to make room for forty-five commercials that Bing and I weren't even in it.

television movies

became prevalent in the late 60s. For four or five years mediocre movies had failed to get theatrical release and were seen first on television; from this it was a short step to making feature films specifically for television exposure. Aaron Spelling and Universal were the main providers; costs were kept low by assembly-line methods, and it soon became just like the old days at the big studios, with stars making fast appearances in superficially glossy vehicles tailored to a specific time requirement. The quality obtained was roughly that of a Universal co-feature of the 50s. Middle-aged or elderly stars who still meant something to the home-viewing circle were coaxed back to the studios: Barbara Stanwyck, Susan Hayward, Ray Milland, Bette Davis, Shelley Winters, Broderick Crawford, Myrna Loy, Milton Berle and their peers all starred again in the new forms, some in two-hour slots (97 minutes actual) but most successfully in 90-minute slots (73 minutes actual). By 1972 such films were appearing at the rate of two or three a week, more if one includes long-form series such as *Mystery Movie*, which gave new life to George Peppard, Rock Hudson, Richard Boone, Peter Falk and others. Crime was the most popular element of these films, with a strong flavouring of the supernatural, an occasional western or sob story, and a modicum of comedy. Art was not sought

after, but as the touch became more assured, a few films received critical acclaim, notably *Brian's Song*, *Short Walk to Daylight*, *Duel*, and *That Certain Summer*. One such film, *My Sweet Charlie*, was sent on theatrical release after its TV exposure, but the experiment failed. In Britain, several of the films went out on theatrical release before TV exposure, and one of them, *Duel*, received rave reviews. By the mid-70s the trend in TV movies had turned to drama documentaries (*Eleanor and Franklin*, *Fear On Trial*) and to character drama, with an unfortunate stress on heroes and heroines dying of leukaemia, tumours and similar afflictions. Then the success of two serialized novels (*Rich Man, Poor Man* and *Roots*) started a stampede to climb on this new bandwagon.

A useful guide by Alvin H. Marill was published in 1981 under the title *Movies Made for Television*.

television series

based on motion picture originals almost outnumber the other kind. They include *The Thin Man*, *The Whistler*, *Kings Row*, *Casablanca*, *My Friend Flicka*, *How to Marry a Millionaire*, *Margie*, *The Roaring Twenties*, *I Remember Mama*, *Blondie*, *Claudia*, *Jungle Jim*, *Hawkeye*, *The Invisible Man*, *Hudson's Bay*, *The Asphalt Jungle*, *Mr Smith Goes to Washington*, *Father of the Bride*, *Life with Father*, *National Velvet*, *Bus Stop*, *No Time for Sergeants*, *Going My Way*, *The Greatest Show on Earth*, *Les Girls*, *Peyton Place*, *The Naked City*, *Rin Tin Tin*, *Topper*, *The Virginian*, *Hopalong Cassidy*, *The Munsters* (indirectly), *The Wackiest Ship in the Army*, *Mr Roberts*, *Gidget*, *Please Don't Eat the Daisies*, *Twelve O'Clock High*, *Dr Kildare*, *The Farmer's Daughter*, *The Long Hot Summer*, *Tarzan*, *The Rounders*, *The Saint*, *Gideon's Way*, *The Man Who Never Was*, *Batman*, *Mr Deeds Goes to Town*, *The Courtship of Eddie's Father*, *The Odd Couple*, *Barefoot in the Park*, *Anna and the King*, *Perry Mason*, *M*A*S*H*, *Shane*, *Lassie*, *Bob and Carol and Ted and Alice*, *Shaft*, *Adam's Rib*, *How the West Was Won*, *Planet of the Apes*, *Alice Doesn't Live Here Any More*, *Bagdad Café*, *Party Girl*.

The Ten Commandments.

Cecil B. De Mille made two films under this title. The 1923 version divided its time between the biblical story and a tale of what happens when moral laws are broken nowadays. It starred Richard Dix, Rod La Rocque, and Estelle Taylor. The 1956 version spent nearly four hours on the Bible story alone, and with less cinematic flair than the silent picture. Charlton Heston was Moses and Yul Brynner Pharaoh.

tennis

has accounted for some memorable scenes in the cinema, among them the suspenseful match in *Strangers on a Train* and the hilarious one in *Monsieur Hulot's Holiday*. Professional tennis was the subject of *Hard Fast and Beautiful* and *Jocks*. Nor should one forget the championship between Tom and Jerry in *Tennis Chumps*, or the weird game with no ball in *Blow Up*. Other tennis sequences figured in *The System*, *Nobody Runs Forever*, *Come to the Stable*, *Pat and Mike*, and *Players*; while there was a TV movie about Little Mo.

The Texas Chainsaw Massacre,

directed, produced and co-written by Tobe Hooper in 1974, has become a cult horror film and spawned several sequels. Its narrative, about teenagers who stumble across a family of deranged cannibalistic killers, was made memorable by its visual qualities, notably Gunnar Hansen as Leatherface, who owed something to real-life serial killer Ed GEIN. It also had an intellectual appeal, being shown at the 1975 London Film Festival, though the BBFC refused it a certificate. The sequels were inferior: Hooper made Part 2 in 1986; the third followed in 1990, directed by Jeff Burr; the fourth, in 1995, featured Matthew McConaughey shortly before *A Time to Kill* made him Hollywood's newest heartthrob.

theatres

have provided an effective setting for many films apart from the countless putting-on-a-show musicals. Films concerned exclusively with matters theatrical include *The Royal Family of Broadway*, *Twentieth Century*, *The Great Profile*, *The Country Girl*, *Stage Door*, *Morning Glory*, *Queen of Hearts*, *Heller in Pink Tights*, *Take the Stage*, *To Be or Not To Be*, *Main Street to Broadway*, *Les Enfants du*

Paradis, *Prince of Players*, *The Velvet Touch*, *All About Eve*, *Curtain Up*, *Kiss Me Kate*, *The Producers*, *The Boyfriend*, *Variety Jubilee*, *A Chorus Line* and *Noises Off*, while a theatre was also the principal setting for *Those Were the Days*, *Henry V*, *Occupe-Toi d'Amélie*, *The Lost People*, *The High Terrace*, *Four Hours to Kill*, *The Phantom of the Opera* and *The Climax*. Thrillers with climaxes in a theatre include *The Thirty-Nine Steps*, *Torn Curtain*, *Charlie Chan at the Opera*, *Cover Girl Killer*, *The Westerner*, *Stage Fright*, *Charade*, *Scaramouche*, *The Deadly Affair*, *No Way to Treat a Lady* and *King Kong*; comedies include *A Night at the Opera*, *A Haunting We Will Go*, *Knock On Wood*, *The Intelligence Men*, *Trouble in Paradise*, *The Secret of My Success*, *My Learned Friend* and *Meet Mr Lucifer*. Less frequent are uses of the theatre as a setting for romance, but it served this purpose in *All This and Heaven Too*, *The Lady with a Little Dog*, and *Letter from an Unknown Woman*. The scariest theatre was *Theatre of Blood*, with Vincent Price as an actor murdering all the critics who had given him bad notices.

See: CINEMAS.

The Thief of Bagdad.

This Arabian Nights tale was superbly filmed with Douglas Fairbanks in 1924, and again in 1940 with Sabu and some remarkable trick photography, directed by Michael Powell, Tim Whelan, and Ludwig Berger. An Italian version with a much-altered plot, starring Steve Reeves, followed in 1961, and there was a TV movie version in 1978, directed by Clive Donner with Roddy McDowell and Peter Ustinov.

The Thin Man.

In Dashiell Hammett's crime novel, the thin man was the murderer's first victim, but the tag stuck to William Powell as Nick Charles the detective in the film, the success of which led to him starring, with Myrna Loy as Nora Charles, in five sequels: *After the Thin Man 37*; *Another Thin Man 38*; *Shadow of the Thin Man 42*; *The Thin Man Goes Home 44*; and *Song of the Thin Man 46*. A TV series starring Peter Lawford and Phyllis Kirk ran from 1957–59.

The Thing (from Another World).

The original, in 1951, was one of the first films to combine the horror genre with science fiction. It was produced by Howard Hawks (and some say directed by him, despite the credit to Christian Nyby; there were also rumours that Orson Welles had a hand in it). In John Carpenter's 1982 remake, the emphasis was on visceral special effects.

The Thirty-Nine Steps.

The first two film versions of John Buchan's spy yarn bore little resemblance to the novel, apart from the hero's original predicament and the Scottish setting: Hitchcock's version in 1935, working from Charles Bennett's pacy script, starred Robert Donat, Madeleine Carroll, and Godfrey Tearle; Ralph Thomas remade it in more stolid fashion in 1959 with Kenneth More, Taina Elg, and Barry Jones. Don Sharp's 1978 version with Robert Powell restored the original period and some of the plot.

This Gun for Hire.

Graham Greene's novel, *A Gun for Sale*, has been filmed twice: the first version, in 1942, directed by Frank Tuttle, catapulted Alan Ladd into the front rank of box-office attractions; the second, retitled *Short Cut to Hell*, was directed by James Cagney and starred Robert Ivers as the gunman, but both he and the movie passed without comment.

This Modern Age.

A series of current-affairs two-reelers sponsored in 1946 by Rank as the British answer to *The March of Time*. Although decently produced by Sergei Nolbandov, the monthly issues were not a popular addition to already overlong programmes, and the attempt was given up in 1949.

Three Coins in the Fountain.

Jean Negulesco's highly commercial romantic 1954 film, from John Secondari's novel, taught Hollywood the travelogue possibilities of CinemaScope in terms of freshening up a tired story. Ten years later, he attempted a disguised remake under the title *The Pleasure Seekers*, but the picture crept by almost unnoticed.

Three Men in a Boat.

Jerome K. Jerome's comic novel of three friends on a boat trip up the Thames has been filmed twice in the sound era: in 1933, directed by Graham Cutts, with William Austin, Edmund Breon, and Billy Milton; and in 1957, directed by Ken Annakin, with Laurence Harvey, Jimmy Edwards, and David Tomlinson.

The Three Mesquiteers.

A series of 'B' feature westerns released by Republic and featuring characters created by western novelist William Colt MacDonald. The first, in 1936, starred Ray 'Crash' Corrigan as Tucson Smith, Robert Livingston as Stony Brooke, and Syd Saylor, who was replaced thereafter by ventriloquist Max Terhune, as comic relief Lullaby Joslin with his dummy, Elmer Sneezeweed. The series was among the most popular westerns of the time, peaking in the late 30s but continuing into the 40s. John Wayne replaced Livingston as Stony Brooke in eight of the series, from *Pals of the Saddle* 38 to *New Frontier/Frontier Horizon* 39, making his first four films in five months, then taking a break before filming another four in order to appear in *Stagecoach* 38. Terhune left after making 21 movies in the series, Corrigan after 24, Livingston after 29. The later films starred Duncan Renaldo, Raymond Hatton, Tom Tyler, and Bob Steele. Corrigan and Terhune went on to appear with John 'Dusty' King in the similar Range Busters series for Monogram in the early 40s.

The Three Musketeers.

Apart from the numerous European versions, Alexandre Dumas's classic swashbuckler has been a Hollywood favourite too. Edison made a version in 1911; so did Edward Laurillard in 1913, C. V. Heinkel in 1914, and Fred Niblo in 1921, with Douglas Fairbanks and Eugene Pallette, Leon Barry and George Siegmann as the musketeers. Walter Abel was D'Artagnan in a 1935 version for RKO, with Paul Lukas, Moroni Olsen, and Onslow Stevens; Rowland V. Lee directed. Don Ameche sang in a 1939 musical comedy version (sometimes known as *The Singing Musketeer*) with the Ritz Brothers, no less, as lackeys impersonating the famous trio. Directed by Allan Dwan, it was very, very funny. Gene Kelly made an acrobatic D'Artagnan for MGM in 1948, with Van Heflin, Gig Young, and Robert Coote; and 1973 brought an all-star international version, directed by Richard Lester, with Michael York, Oliver Reed, Frank Finlay, and Richard Chamberlain. A sequel, *The Four Musketeers*, came the following year, but *The Fifth Musketeer*, a multi-national 1978 adventure directed by Ken Annakin, told in fact the story of the man in the iron mask. A 1993 version starred Charlie Sheen, Kiefer Sutherland, Chris O'Donnell, and Oliver Platt, a cast that looked ill at ease in a period setting. Bertrand Tavernier's *The Daughter of D'Artagnan* (*La Fille de D'Artagnan*) 94 was an original sequel to Dumas's story and a tribute to swashbucklers, with Sophie Marceau in the title role and Philippe Noiret as D'Artagnan leading the ageing musketeers, played by Jean-Luc Bideau, Raoul Billeray, and Sami Frey, on one last adventure.

Three Smart Girls.

A minor domestic comedy about three teenagers, directed by Henry Koster in 1937, was the first feature appearance of Deanna Durbin and was followed by a sequel in 1939, *Three Smart Girls Grow Up*. In 1943 followed a third film on the adventures of the Durbin character only, *Hers to Hold*.

tinting

has plainly gone out of fashion now that virtually all films are in colour, but in black-and-white days the use of single colours could lead to interesting effects. In the 20s and earlier it was common practice to tint night scenes blue, sunlit scenes yellow, etc.; I saw one Russian film made in 1917 in which the only scene in black-and-white was that in which the hero hanged himself! When talkies came in these colour effects were forgotten, but towards the mid-30s when colour was threatening, a tint seemed better than nothing. Films released wholly in sepia included *The Ghost Goes West*, *Bad Man of Brimstone*, *The Firefly*, *Maytime*, *The Girl of the Golden West*, *The Oklahoma Kid*, *Of Mice and Men* and *The Rains Came*; while the 'real' scenes of *The Wizard of Oz* were also sepia, leaving full colour until we landed over the rainbow. *A Midsummer Night's Dream* was released with a blue rinse, as were the water-ballet reels of *A Day at the Races*. Other colours have been used for short sequences. Green for *Portrait of Jennie* (the storm), *Luck of the Irish* (the leprechaun forest) and *Lost Continent* (to obscure the poor monster animation). Red for the *Hell's Angels* battle scenes and for the flash at the end of *Spellbound* when the villain turns a gun on himself. Even monochrome has its effectiveness, as shown in *A Matter of Life and Death* and *Bonjour Tristesse*.

The Titanic.

The sinking of the 'unsinkable' passenger liner in 1912 has attracted many film-makers, though most have preferred to surround the event with a great deal of unimaginative fiction. The first was *Saved from the Titanic*, a silent one-reeler starring a survivor, which was shown a month after the actual event. In 1929 E. A. Dupont directed German- and English-language versions of the story. The Germans remade it as *Titanic* in 1940 as anti-British propaganda. It was followed by *Titanic* 53, directed by Jean Negulesco and starring Clifton Webb and Barbara Stanwyck among a shipload of American passengers. Its invented story won an Oscar for the scriptwriters Charles Brackett, Walter Reisch and Richard Breen. A more faithful documentary approach was taken by the reticent British film *A Night to Remember* 58, directed by Roy Ward Baker from Eric Ambler's script and Walter Lord's book, and starring Kenneth More and David McCallum. A dull TV film, *SOS Titanic* 77, starred David Janssen and Susan Saint James, to be followed by an even duller TV *Titanic* 96, with a cast that included George C. Scott, Eva Marie Saint and Tim Curry. In 1997, James Cameron's epic *Titanic* combined a brilliant recreation of the event with a trivializing romance, starring Kate Winslet and Leonardo DiCaprio, to become one of the most commercially successful films made so far. The great ship was also used for a passing joke in *Time Bandits* 80, and surfaced in the costly flop *Raise the Titanic* 80, of which its producer Lew Grade quipped that it would have been cheaper to lower the Atlantic.

To Have and Have Not.

Ernest Hemingway's tough, soft-hearted adventure novel has been filmed three times: in 1944 by Howard Hawks, with Bogart, Bacall, and not much left of the plot; in 1951 by Michael Curtiz, as *The Breaking Point*, with John Garfield and Patricia Neal; and in 1958, as *The Gun Runner*, with Audie Murphy.

The Toff.

John Creasey's aristocratic investigator was the hero of two British films, in which he was played by John Bentley, both directed by Maclean Rogers: *Salute the Toff* 51 and *Hammer the Toff* 52.

Tol'able David.

Joseph Hergesheimer's novel was first, and most successfully, filmed in 1921, with Richard Berthelmess as the gentle youth making good in the tough outdoor life. In 1931 John G. Blystone directed a disappointing sound remake with Richard Cromwell.

Tom and Jerry.

Short cartoons featuring the mean-minded, accident-prone cat and his inventive and likeable little adversary were in production at MGM, with a break in the 50s, from 1941, with Fred Quimby as executive producer until his death. They have been much criticized for their excessive violence, but their humour, coupled with the impossibility of the situations, has won the day. The Academy Award-winning titles are *The Milky Way* 40, *Yankee Doodle Mouse* 43, *Mouse Trouble* 44, *Quiet Please* 45, *Cat Concerto* 46, *The Little Orphan* 48, *The Two Mouseketeers* 51, *Johann Mouse* 52. The original cartoons were drawn by William Hanna and Joe Barbera.

Book: 1991, *Fifty Years of Cat and Mouse* by T. R. Adams.

Tom Brown's Schooldays.

The famous Victorian story of life at Rugby School exists in two major film versions: the first directed in America in 1939 by Robert Stevenson, with Cedric Hardwicke as Dr Arnold and Jimmy Lydon as Tom; the second made in Britain in 1951, directed by Gordon Parry, with Robert Newton and John Howard Davies.

Tom Sawyer.

Mark Twain's boy hero has been played on film by Jack Pickford in 1917 and, in *Huck and Tom*, in 1918; Jackie Coogan in 1920; Tommy Kelly in the Selznick production in 1938; Billy Cook in 1938 in *Tom Sawyer, Detective*; Johnnie Whitaker in 1973 in a musical version; and Josh Albee in a TV movie in 1973.

Tony Rome.

The down-market private eye created by Marvin H. Albert was played by Frank Sinatra in two films directed by Gordon Douglas: *Tony Rome* in 1967, and *Lady in Cement* in 1968.

Topper.

Thorne Smith's story of a dull banker haunted by two fun-loving ghosts was filmed in 1937, directed by Norman Z. McLeod, with Roland Young, Constance Bennett, and Cary Grant; two sequels followed: *Topper Takes a Trip* in 1939, and *Topper Returns* in 1941. A TV series ran from 1953–56.

Torchy Blane.

A series of second features, mostly starring Glenda Farrell as a wisecracking girl reporter and Barton MacLane as her boyfriend, a puzzled policeman who gets the comeback for her zany ideas.

Smart Blonde 36. Fly-Away Baby 37. Adventurous Blonde 37. Blondes at Work 38. Torchy Blane in Panama (with Lola Lane replacing Farrell for one film) 38. Torchy Gets Her Man 38. Torchy Blane in Chinatown 39. Torchy Runs for Mayor 39. Torchy Plays with Dynamite (with Jane Wyman as the star) 39.

torture

has figured in *Arabian Nights*, *Thief of Bagdad*, and others of this genre; in witchcraft dramas such as *Witchfinder General*, *The Devils* and *Day of Wrath*; in medieval epics such as *El Cid*, *Ivanhoe* and *Tower of London*; further back to Roman times, in *The Robe*, *Barabbas*, *Spartacus* and *Demetrius and the Gladiators*; in World War II yarns such as *13 Rue Madeleine*, *OSS*, *Carve Her Name with Pride*, *The Seventh Cross* and *633 Squadron*; in Cold War melodramas such as *Treason*, *The Prisoner*, and *The Manchurian Candidate*; in historical mysteries such as *The Man in the Iron Mask* and in documentary adventures such as *A Man Called Horse*.

Trail of the Lonesome Pine.

This backwoods melodrama was first filmed in 1916 with Charlotte Walker and Earle Fox; in 1923 it was remade with Mary Miles Minter, Antonio Moreno, and Ernest Torrence. In 1936 Henry Hathaway made a sound version with Sylvia Sidney, Henry Fonda, and Fred MacMurray, which was the first outdoor film in the newly perfected three-colour Technicolor.

trains

have above all served film-makers as a splendid background for suspense thrillers. Scores of sequences crowd to mind, all enhanced by the dramatic background of a speeding train: *The Lady Vanishes*, *North by Northwest*, *From Russia with Love*, *The Narrow Margin*, *The Tall Target*, *How the West Was Won*, *3.10 to Yuma*, *Lady on a Train*, *Cat Ballou*, *Jesse James*, *Bad Day at Black Rock*, *Night of the Demon*, *Time Bomb*, *Rome Express*, *Sleeping Car to Trieste*, *Northwest Frontier*, *Man without a Star*, *The Thirty-Nine Steps*, *Secret Agent*, *Shanghai Express*, *Number 17*, *Last Train from Madrid*, *Last Train to Bombay*, *Ministry of Fear*, *Von Ryan's Express*, *Across the Bridge*, *Double Indemnity*, *Strangers on a Train*, *The Iron Horse*, *Union Pacific*, *Canadian Pacific*, *Next of Kin*, *Berlin Express*, *The Great Locomotive Chase*, *Terror by Night*, *Crack-Up*, *Rampage*, *Fool's Parade*, *The Train*, *Breakheart Pass*, *Murder on the Orient Express* . . . the list could be almost endless. More serious films using trains include *La Bête Humaine* (and its remake *Human Desire*), *Metropolitan* (and its remake *A Window in London*), *Brief Encounter*, *The Last Journey*, *Sullivan's Travels*, *Indiscretion of an American Wife*, *Anna Karenina*, *Terminus*, *Night Mail*, *The Manchurian Candidate*, *The Railway Children*, *Doctor Zhivago*, *Boxcar Bertha*, and *Emperor of the North*; while spectacular crashes were featured in *The Greatest Show on Earth*, *Hatter's Castle*, *Seven Sinners*, *The Young in Heart*, *Mad Love*, *The Wrong Box*, *Lawrence of Arabia*, *Crack in the World*, *The Ghost Train*, and *King Kong*. Murder was seen from a train in *Metropolitan* and *Lady in a Train* (happening in a second passing train in *Murder She Said*), and *through* a train in *Twelve Angry Men*. The subway, elevated or underground railway was featured in *Practically Yours*, *On the Town*, *The Bachelor Party*, *Boys' Night Out*, *Union Station*, *The FBI Story*, *The Young Savages*, *Underground*, *Bulldog Jack*, *Daleks Invasion Earth 2150 AD*, *The French Connection*, *Beneath the Planet of the Apes*, and *The Liquidator*. The back platforms of American trains have become familiar, especially in political films like *Abe Lincoln in Illinois*, *Wilson* and *All the King's Men*; but also in *Hail the Conquering Hero*, *Double Indemnity*, *The Merry Monahans* and *Mr Deeds Goes to Town*. Comedy train sequences include the Marx Brothers chopping up moving carriages for fuel in *Go West*, the Ale and Quail Club in *The Palm Beach Story*, Buster Keaton's splendidly inventive *Our Hospitality* and *The General*, *The Great St Trinian's Train Robbery*, Laurel and Hardy going to sleep in the same bunk in *The Big Noise*, Hal Roach's *Broadway Limited*, John Barrymore in *Twentieth Century*, Peter Sellers in *Two-Way Stretch*, the western sequence of *Around the World in Eighty Days*, the Pullman car sequence of *Some Like It Hot*, Monty Banks in *Play Safe*, Morecambe and Wise in *The Magnificent Two*, *The Private Life of Sherlock Holmes*, the whole of *The Titfield Thunderbolt* and *Oh Mr Porter* . . . and many scenes of jaywalking on top of moving carriages, including *Professor Beware*, *The Merry Monahans* and *Fancy Pants*. Musical sequences with a train motif or setting are found in *A Hard Day's Night*, *Monte Carlo*, *Some Like It Hot*, *The Harvey Girls* ('The Atchison, Topeka and the Santa Fe'), *At the Circus* ('Lydia the Tattooed Lady'), *Sun Valley Serenade* ('Chattanooga Choo Choo'), *Dumbo* ('Casey Junior'), *The Jazz Singer* ('Toot Toot Tootsie, Goodbye'), *Easter Parade* ('When the Midnight Choo Choo Leaves for Alabam'), *Forty-second Street* ('Shuffle off to Buffalo').

TV series involving trains as a regular motif include *Casey Jones*, *The Wild Wild West*, *The Iron Horse*, *Petticoat Junction*, *Union Pacific* and *Supertrain*.

tramps

or hoboes who have figured largely in films include those played by William Powell in *My Man Godfrey*, Joel McCrea in *Sullivan's Travels*, George Arliss in *The Guv'nor*, Jean Gabin in *Archimède le Clochard*, practically the whole cast of *Hallelujah I'm a Bum*, and of course Charlie Chaplin in all his earlier comedies.

transvestism.

There have been many films, mostly lightweight ones, making effective use of situations in which men dress up as women. *Charley's Aunt* has proved a perennial, and in silent days Julian Eltinge, a female impersonator, made several popular films: his 1972 successor was Danny la Rue, in *Our Miss Fred*. Well-known actors in female attire have included Wallace Beery as 'Swedy' in a series of silent comedies, Lon Chaney in *The Unholy Tree*, Lionel Barrymore in *The Devil Doll*, William Powell in *Love Crazy*, Cary Grant in *I Was a Male War Bride*, Joe E. Brown as his own grandma in *The Daring Young Man*, Cook and Moore as leaping nuns in *Bedazzled*, Alec Guinness in *The Comedians*, Brian Deacon in *Triple Echo*, Alec Guinness in *Kind Hearts and Coronets*, Peter Sellers in *The Mouse That Roared*, William Bendix and Dennis O'Keefe in *Abroad with Two Yanks*, Jimmy Durante in *You're in the Army Now*, Lee J. Cobb in *In Like Flint*, Ray Walston in *Caprice*, Jerry Lewis in *Three on a Couch*, Stan Laurel in *That's My Wife* and *Jitterbugs*, Bing Crosby in *High Time*, Bob Hope in *Casanova's Big Night*, Tony Curtis and Jack Lemmon in *Some Like It Hot*, Tony Perkins in *Psycho*, Dick Shawn in *What Did You Do in the War, Daddy?* Phil Silvers and Jack Gilford in *A Funny Thing Happened on the Way to the Forum*, Jerry Lewis in *At War with the Army*, Jack Oakie in *Let's go Native*, Lou Costello in *Lost in a Harem*, Eddie Cantor in *Ali Baba Goes to Town*, Joe E. Brown in *Shut my Big Mouth*, Billy de Wolfe in *Isn't it Romantic?*, William Powell in *Love Crazy*, Melvyn Douglas in *The Amazing Mr Williams*, James Coco in *The Wild Party*, Preston Foster in *Up the River*, Oscar Levant and David Wayne in *The I Don't Care Girl*, Alastair Sim in *The Belles of St Trinian's*, Helmut Berger in *The Damned*, Tim Curry in *The Rocky Horror Movie*, Dustin Hoffman in *Tootsie*, Denis Quilley in *Privates on Parade*, Michel Serrault in *La Cage aux Folles* and its sequels, and Divine in *Pink Flamingos* and other

John Waters films; while the device became in the 60s a standard device of spy stories, including *The Kremlin Letter, Thunderball, Licensed to Kill, Where the Bullets Fly*, and *Gunn*. *Myra Breckinridge* also fits in somewhere, as do *Glen or Glenda* and *Dr Jekyll and Sister Hyde*. In the 90s, cross-dressing became almost fashionable. Robin Williams had a box-office success disguised as a nannie in *Mrs Doubtfire*, Quentin Crisp became a believable Queen Elizabeth I in *Orlando*, Leslie Cheung was a specialist in female roles at the Peking Opera in *Farewell My Concubine*, Terence Stamp was among the drag queens tramping around the Australian outback in *The Adventures of Priscilla, Queen of the Desert*, Johnny Depp put on women's clothes as the angora-sweater-loving transvestite director Ed Wood – star of *Glen or Glenda* – in Tim Burton's affectionate biopic of the world's worst film director, and Wesley Snipes and others donned frocks in *To Wong Foo, Thanks for Everything, Julie Newmar*. *La Cage aux Folles* became a hit again in 1995, remade and Americanized as *The Bird Cage*, starring Nathan Lane and Robin Williams.

Women disguised as men are rarer; but one can instance such notable examples as Katharine Hepburn in *Sylvia Scarlett*, Annabella in *Wings of the Morning*, Signe Hasso in *The House on 92nd Street*, Nita Talbot in *A Very Special Favor*, Marlene Dietrich in *Morocco*, Greta Garbo in *Queen Christina*, Mary Pickford in *Kiki*, Debbie Reynolds in *Goodbye Charlie*, Jessie Matthews in *Gangway*, Miriam Hopkins in *She Loves Me Not*, Marlene Dietrich in *Seven Sinners*, Louise Brooks in *Beggars of Life*, Doris Day in *Calamity Jane*, Frances Farmer in *Badlands of Dakota*, Veronica Lake in *Sullivan's Travels*, Jean Peters in *Anne of the Indies*, Maureen O'Hara in *At Sword's Point*, Merle Oberon in *A Song to Remember*, Lupe Velez in *Honolulu Lu*, Julie Andrews in *Victor/Victoria*, and the ambiguous hero-heroine of *Homicidal*. In *Turnabout* a husband and wife exchanged bodies, with dire results. In *Switch*, a murdered male chauvinist returned to earth as Ellen Barkin in search of salvation. And in *Orlando* Tilda Swinton went from Elizabethan man to modern woman. In two 1996 films, actresses appeared in male roles: Pam Grier in *Escape from L.A.*, and a black-bearded Wendy Hughes in *Lust and Revenge*.

Treasure Island.

Robert L. Stevenson's adventure classic was filmed four times as a silent and even more often in the sound era. In 1935, in a splendid production for MGM, Victor Fleming directed Wallace Beery as Long John Silver and Jackie Cooper as the cabin-boy Jim Hawkins; in 1950, in Britain for Disney, Byron Haskins directed Robert Newton, who was born to play the one-legged pirate, and Bobby Driscoll. Newton afterwards played the role in a feature, *Long John Silver* 54, and 26 TV half-hours filmed in Australia. In 1972 Orson Welles starred in a European remake, using such a thick accent that he had to be dubbed, in which he was shown from the waist up for much of the film since he was too fat to bend back his leg; in 1973 Kirk Douglas appeared in *Scallawag*, which borrowed the plot for a modern story; in 1989 Fraser Heston directed his father Charlton in a TV movie; and in 1991 Chilean director Raúl Ruiz turned the story into a deliriously experimental movie, in which its characters act out roles from the story.

trends

R. D. McCann said that in Hollywood the only familiar, solid, bedrock certainty is sudden change. That goes for the entire industry, which throughout its history has been subject to the whims of fashion and has moved in a gingerly way from one crisis to another. In the midst of such uncertainty the industry's leaders can only comfort themselves with the incontrovertible adage:

> There's nothing wrong with this business that a few good movies can't cure.

The trouble has been to find out what kind of movies, at any given time, are good ones in the eyes of the public. As Adolph Zukor said long ago:

> The public is never wrong.

And Bryan Forbes said:

> Nobody can be a prophet in an industry which is entirely dependent on the public whim.

Walter Wanger knew that:

> Nothing is as cheap as a hit, no matter how much it cost.

Unfortunately the public has not always been in the forefront of good taste. When close-ups were first introduced, many audiences felt cheated and yelled:

> Show us their feet!

But without an advance in technical quality the film could hardly have survived. Billy Bitzer, the famous cameraman, said:

> The fade-out gave us a really dignified touch – we didn't have a five cent movie any more.

It is true that the moguls have sometimes taken a long time to answer the public's call. Ted Willis said in 1966:

> The film business is like that prehistoric monster the dinosaur, which apparently had two brains, one in its head and one in its rear.

It was not always thus: in the golden years they knew a thing or two. At Warners, for instance, Bette Davis said:

> We had the answer, the sequel and the successor to everything.

But even imitation did not always pay. Darryl Zanuck knew:

> Only the first picture of a cycle really succeeds: all the imitators dwindle.

Cesare Zavattini in 1945 had a similar idea:

> The world is full of people thinking in myths.

Iris Barry in 1926 scorned film clichés:

> Why must all American movie mothers be white-haired and tottery even though their children are mere tots? Does the menopause not operate in the US?

Reality was entirely shunned. Wilson Mizner in the early talkie era commented:

> The public doesn't want to know what goes on behind the scenes. It prefers to believe that a cameraman hung in the clouds, mid-Pacific, the day Barrymore fought the whale.

Samuel Goldwyn is credited with the tersest capsuling of the tradition that audiences wanted to be soothed and not stimulated:

> Messages are for Western Union.

Even Terry Ramsaye, editing a trade journal in 1936, complained:

> If they want to preach a sermon, let them hire a hall.

This was the day of the formula:

> Boy meets girl, boy loses girl, boy gets girl.

The public paid to see it and demanded more of the same. A 1943 exhibitor said:

> You could open a can of sardines and there'd be a line waiting to get in.

Momentary turns of fashion could of course be allowed for, so many movies were being made. When *Variety* headlined:

> STICKS NIX HICK PIX

it was a simple matter to discontinue the movies about poor hillbillies to which the midwestern audiences had shown such antipathy. Towards the 50s, however, there were signs of growing unease: no kind of film, and no star, could be absolutely relied on to make money. Hollywood had previously regarded the international market as a pleasant source of extra revenue; now film-making had to be geared to it. Alfred Hitchcock, however, felt that no change of style was necessary:

> When we make films for the United States, we automatically make them for the world, for the United States is full of foreigners.

But Hitch did note a change of emphasis:

> In the old days, villains had moustaches and kicked the dog. Audiences are smarter today. They don't want their villain to be thrown at them with green limelight on his face. They want an ordinary human being with failings.

The studio conveyor belt was outdated: everyone was bitten by the location bug. Rouben Mamoulian said in 1957:

> We have forsaken the magic of the cinema. We have gotten too far away from the cinematic effects achievable by camera angles and creative editing.

There was another increasing danger:

> You have to offer the public something a helluva lot better than they can get for free on TV.

What was offered was 3-D, which failed. As Hitch said:

> A nine-days' wonder – and I came in on the ninth day.

Then came CinemaScope and the other wide-screen processes, but the extra size only rarely contributed towards a better entertainment. Content was what mattered. The only reliable regular audience was for cheap horror films. Said Vincent Price in 1965:

> The cinemas have bred a new race of giant popcorn-eating rats.

At last the English came back into fashion as film-makers, chiefly on the strength of their actors and their 'X' subjects. This success had its drawbacks, according to Tony Garnett:

> To be an Englishman in the film business is to know what it's like to be colonialized.

Sex had come to stay. Said Shelagh Delaney:

> The cinema has become more and more like the theatre: it's all mauling and muttering.

Said Billy Wilder:

> Titism has taken over the country. But Audrey Hepburn single-handed may make bozooms a thing of the past. The director will not have to invent shots where the girl leans forward for a glass of scotch and soda.

Said Adolphe Menjou:

> The Brando school are grabbers, not lovers. If it wasn't that the script says they get the girl, they wouldn't.

Said Bob Hope in 1960:

> Our big pictures this year have had some intriguing themes: sex, perversion, adultery and cannibalism. We'll get those kids away from their TV sets yet.

Said Bob Hope in 1968:

> Last year Hollywood made the first pictures with dirty words. This year we made the pictures to go with them.

And in 1971:

> The line 'I love you' is no longer a declaration but a demonstration.

In the same year Candice Bergen admitted:

> I may not be a great actress but I've become the greatest at screen orgasms. Ten seconds of heavy breathing, roll your head from side to side, simulate a slight asthma attack and die a little.

And Frank Capra snorted:

> Hollywood film-making of today is stooping to cheap salacious pornography in a crazy bastardization of a great art.

The system had crumbled, the studios were empty, every movie was a new enterprise, usually shot in some far-flung corner of the earth. Bob Hope again, in 1968:

> This year is a good one for Hollywood. Some of the movies nominated for Oscars were even made here.

Hal Wallis had another complaint:

> In the old days we had the time and money to give prospective stars a slow build-up. Today, an actor makes it fast or he just doesn't make it at all.

Orson Welles realized that:

> The trouble with a movie these days is that it's old before it's released. It's no accident that it comes in a can.

And Billy Wilder:

> Today we spend eighty per cent of our time making deals and twenty per cent making pictures.

Otto Preminger remembers when:

> There were giants in the industry. Now it is an era of midgets and conglomerates.

The watchword for the 70s was violence. Hear the producer of *The Strawberry Statement*:

> We live in a time when revolution is a very saleable commodity.

Hear Roman Polanski in 1971:

> Nothing is too shocking for me. When you tell the story of a man who loses his head, you have to show the head being cut off. Otherwise it's just a dirty joke without a punch line.

Hear Ken Russell, middle-aged enfant terrible of the same year:

> This is not the age of manners. This is the age of kicking people in the crotch and telling them something and getting a reaction. I want to shock people into awareness. I don't believe there's any virtue in understatement.

Hear the redoubtable Sam Peckinpah:

> You can't make violence real to audiences today without rubbing their noses in it. We've all been anaesthetized by the media.

Hear producer Steve Krantz defending his 'adult cartoon' *Heavy Traffic*:

> Mary Poppins is OK, but when did you last date her?

Hear Peter Cook:

> I don't like watching rape and violence at the cinema. I get enough of that at home!

And finally:

> America's a new country and we have very little history. We have the American Indian and we have Superman. Don't fuck with either.
> – *R. Donner*

Trilby:

see SVENGALI.

Tugboat Annie.

This aggressive, middle-aged lady of the waterfront was devised by Norman Reilly Raine and personified in the 1933 film by Marie Dressler. Subsequent films include *Tugboat Annie Sails Again* 40 with Marjorie Rambeau and *Captain Tugboat Annie* 45 with Jane Darwell. A 1956 TV series featured Minerva Urecal.

Tweety Pie.

Baby-voiced canary, the adversary of Sylvester the cat in Warner Brothers cartoons. A song based on its cry, 'I Tawt I Saw a Putty Cat', was a hit in 1950. Its creator was Bob Clampett and Mel Blanc supplied the voice.

A Tale of Two Kitties 42. Tweetie Pie (AA) 47. Bad Ol' Putty Cat 49. Sandy Claws (AAN) 54. Birds Anonymous (AA) 57. The Jet Cage 62, etc.

Uncle Tom's Cabin.

The anti-slavery story of excellent intentions and unabashed sentimentality was written in 1852 by American novelist Harriet Beecher Stowe. It features the dastardly white villain Simon Legree, the cheerful black Uncle Tom (whose name has entered the American language as an insulting description of obsequiousness to whites), and poor little Eva, who is taken to heaven by an angel. The main film versions include a 1903 one-reeler by Edwin S. Porter, a Pathé three-reeler of 1910, and an American three-reeler of 1913. In 1914 came a longer American version with Marie Eline as Little Eva, and 1918 brought a full-length version with Marguerite Clark in the dual role of Topsy and Eva. Then in 1927 Harry Pollard directed a full-blown silent spectacle which was frequently revived with sound effects in later years; Virginia Gray was Eva. The subject might have been thought too dated for sound treatment, but in 1965 a colour and wide-screen European co-production was directed by Geza von Radvanyi and featured Herbert Lom as Simon Legree. A television version followed in 1987, directed by Stan Lathan.

uncredited appearances

by well-known stars are usually intended as gags to liven up a film which can do with an extra laugh. Thus the brief cameos of Cary Grant and Jack Benny in *Without Reservations*; Lana Turner in *Du Barry Was a Lady*; Robert Taylor in *I Love Melvin*; Bing Crosby in *My Favourite Blonde*, *The Princess and the Private* and other Bob Hope films; Alan Ladd in *My Favourite Brunette*; Peter Lorre in *Meet Me in Las Vegas*; Myrna Loy in *The Senator was Indiscreet*; Peter Sellers and David Niven in *Road to Hong Kong*; Vincent Price in *Beach Party*; Boris Karloff in *Bikini Beach*; Groucho Marx in *Will Success Spoil Rock Hunter?*; Elizabeth Taylor in *Scent of Mystery*, *What's New Pussycat?* and *Anne of the Thousand Days*; Richard Burton in *What's New Pussycat?* Jack Benny and Jerry Lewis in *It's a Mad Mad Mad Mad World*; Robert Vaughn in *The Glass Bottom Boat*; Bob Hope and others in *The Oscar*; Rock Hudson in *Four Girls in Town*; Jack Benny and Jimmy Durante in *Beau James*; Red Skelton in *Susan Slept Here*; Bing Crosby and Bob Hope in *Scared Stiff*; Martin and Lewis, Humphrey Bogart and Jane Russell in *Road to Bali*; Lauren Bacall in *Two Guys from Milwaukee*; Gene Kelly in *Love is Better Than Ever*; Clark Gable and Robert Taylor in *Callaway Went Thataway*; Peter O'Toole in *Casino Royale*; Yul Brynner in *The Magic Christian*; Edward G. Robinson in *Robin and the Seven Hoods*; Humphrey Bogart in *Always Together*, *Two Guys from Milwaukee* and *The Love Lottery*; Jack Benny in *The Great Lover*; Ray Milland in *Miss Tatlock's Millions*; John Wayne in *I Married a Woman*; Tony Curtis in *Chamber of Horrors*; Sammy Davis Jnr in *A Raisin in the Sun*; Shirley Maclaine in *Ocean's Eleven*; Margaret Rutherford in *The ABC Murders*; Jack Nicholson in *Broadcast News*; Macaulay Culkin in *Jacob's Ladder*; Sean Connery in *Robin Hood: Prince of Thieves*; Kenneth Branagh in *Swing Kids*.

Sometimes a sequel not featuring the star of the first story will have a brief reminiscence of him with no credit: this happened to Cary Grant in *Topper Takes a Trip* and to Simone Signoret in *Life at the Top*. Then there are deliberate in-jokes like Walter Huston playing bit parts in his son John's movies, Peter Finch playing a messenger in *The First Men in the Moon* because he happened to be there when the hired actor failed to turn up, Joseph

Cotten playing a small part in *Touch of Evil* because he dropped in to watch the location shooting and Orson Welles sent a make-up man over for old times' sake, Helen Hayes playing a small role in *Third Man on the Mountain* because her son James MacArthur was in the cast. Occasionally when stars are replaced during production, long shots of them remain in the completed film: thus Vivien Leigh in *Elephant Walk* and George Brent in *Death of a Scoundrel*. The best gag was played by Al Jolson who, determined to get into *The Jolson Story* at all costs, played himself in the theatre runaway long shots during 'Swanee'.

There remain a few mysteries. In *The Great Ziegfeld*, 'A Pretty Girl is Like a Melody' was apparently sung by Stanley Morner, soon to become quite famous as Dennis Morgan. He was not credited (perhaps because the voice finally used on the soundtrack was that of Allan Jones). Nor were the following who had important roles to play and were well-known at the time: Constance Collier in *Anna Karenina*, Marlene Dietrich in *Touch of Evil*, Henry Daniell in *Mutiny on the Bounty*, Audrey Totter in *The Carpetbaggers*, Dorothy Malone and John Hubbard in *Fate is the Hunter*, Wilfrid Lawson in *Tread Softly Stranger*, Ava Gardner in *The Band Wagon*, Edmond O'Brien in *The Greatest Show on Earth*, David Warner in *Straw Dogs*, Henry Daniell in *My Fair Lady*, Edmond O'Brien in *The Greatest Show on Earth*, Mercedes McCambridge in *Touch of Evil*, Glenda Jackson in *The Boy Friend*, Leo McKern in *The High Commissioner*. And in *Those Magnificent Men in Their Flying Machines*, Cicely Courtneidge and Fred Emney had roughly equal dialogue in their one scene; yet he was credited and she was not. The reasons surely can't have anything to do with modesty.

See also: DIRECTORS' APPEARANCES.

Under Two Flags.

Ouida's romantic melodrama about the Foreign Legion was filmed in 1916 by J. Gordon Edwards, with Theda Bara as Cigarette; in 1922 by Tod Browning, with Priscilla Dean and Jack Kirkwood; and in 1936 by Frank Lloyd, with Claudette Colbert and Ronald Colman.

underground railways

have been used remarkably little in films considering their dramatic possibilities. There were chases through them in *Underground* itself, *Bulldog Jack*, *Waterloo Road*, *The French Connection*, *The Taking of Pelham One Two Three*, *Death Line* and *Death Wish*; they were also used for a comedy scene in *Rotten to the Core*, a murder in *Man Hunt*, *Otley*, and *The Liquidator*, and a musical number in *Three Hats for Lisa*, and *Death Line/Raw Meat* exploited the unease that can be felt in underground stations by putting cannibals in a deserted tunnel. The New York subway was the setting for musical numbers in *Dames* ('I Only Have Eyes for You') and *On the Town* ('Miss Turnstiles' ballet), and it also featured in a romantic comedy (*Practically Yours*) and was the scene of a brutal beating-up in *The Young Savages* and a nasty accidental death in *P.J.*; while the whole of *Dutchman* took place on it, and *Short Walk To Daylight* began with an earthquake trapping passengers in it.

The New York elevated railway, on the other hand, was most dramatically used in *King Kong*, and provided effective backing in *The Lost Weekend*, *Union Station*, *The Bachelor Party*, *The FBI Story*, *Beneath the Planet of the Apes*, *Cry of the City* and *The French Connection*.

undertakers,

or morticians, have provided comedy relief in many a western, relying on frequent shootings to bring in business: perhaps this theme was first explored in *The Westerner* 39. The comedy elements of the profession were also presented by Vincent Price and Peter Lorre in *A Comedy of Terrors*, by Terry-Thomas in *Strange Bedfellows*, by almost the entire cast of *The Loved One*, by Paul Lynde in *Send Me No Flowers*, and by J. Pat O'Malley in *Willard*. Literature's most famous undertaker is perhaps Mr Sowerberry in *Oliver Twist*, played by Gibb McLaughlin in the 1948 version and by Leonard Rossiter in *Oliver!*

underwater sequences

of note were found in *Reap the Wild Wind*, *The Silent Enemy*, *The Beast from 20,000 Fathoms*, *The Golden Mistress*, *Twenty Thousand Leagues under the Sea*, *Around the World under the Sea*, *Voyage to the Bottom of the Sea*, *Thunderball*, *Shark*, *Lady in Cement*, and *The Big Blue*. Two fantasies of alien life, *The Abyss* 89 and *Alien: Resurrection* 98, were most effective in underwater sequences, while James CAMERON's *Titanic* 98 gained much from the undersea explorations of the liner's rusting hulk and its submerged cabins.

See also: SUBMARINES.

unemployment

in Britain was the somewhat unpopular subject of *Doss House*, *Love on the Dole*, and *The Common Touch*; in Europe, *Joyless Street*, *Little Man What Now?* and *Berliner Ballade*. America has seemed almost to boast about its unemployed, who were featured in *The Crowd*, *Our Daily Bread*, *Grapes of Wrath*, *Hallelujah I'm a Bum*, *Sullivan's Travels*, *I Am a Fugitive from a Chain Gang*, *The Great McGinty*, *One More Spring*, *Mr Deeds Goes to Town*, *Man's Castle*, *My Man Godfrey* and *Tobacco Road*, among many others.

Unfaithfully Yours.

Preston Sturges' vintage satirical comedy, about a jealous orchestral conductor who suspects his wife of infidelity and plots three revenges during a concert, was made in 1948, starring Rex Harrison; 1983 brought a tolerable remake with Dudley Moore.

unfinished films.

Among the productions which ran out of money halfway, or were terminated for other reasons, are Josef Von Sternberg's *I Claudius*; Errol Flynn's *William Tell*; Orson Welles' *Don Quixote*, *The Other Side of the Moon* and *It's All True*; Eisenstein's *Que Viva Mexico*; Brecht's *Mother Courage*; Zinnemann's *Man's Fate*; David Miller's *The Bells of Hell go Ting-a-ling-a-ling*; Marilyn Monroe in *Something's Got to Give*; Willis O'Brien's *Creation*; and George Sluizer's *Dark Blood*, abandoned after the death of its star, River Phoenix. Films which had troubles but were completed in scrappy fashion include Michael Caine in *The Jigsaw Man*, James Caan in *Man Without Mercy*, Natalie Wood in *Brainstorm*, Bela Lugosi in *Plan 9 from Outer Space*, and Bruce Lee in *Game of Death* (in which nearly ninety per cent of his role was played by doubles). Bruce Lee's son, Brandon Lee, was accidentally killed during the filming of *The Crow*, but that film was completed with the aid of doubles and sophisticated computer techniques to create new scenes for Lee from existing footage.

unfinished performances.

Here are some cases of actors who began to film roles but then either walked off the set or were let go because of unhappiness, inadequacy or just plain cussedness. Replacements are in brackets.

George Segal in '*10*' (Dudley Moore); John Travolta in *American Gigolo* (Richard Gere); Richard Dreyfuss in *All that Jazz* (Roy Scheider); Marlon Brando in *Child's Play* (Robert Preston); Robert Mitchum in *Rosebud* (Peter O'Toole); Richard Harris in *Flap* (Anthony Quinn); Rip Torn in *Easy Rider* (Jack Nicholson); George C. Scott in *How to Steal a Million* (Eli Wallach); Judy Garland in *Valley of the Dolls* (Susan Hayward); Elvis Presley in *A Star is Born* (Kris Kristofferson); Lana Turner in *Anatomy of a Murder* (Lee Remick); Christopher Plummer in *Dr Dolittle* (Rex Harrison); Judy Garland in *Annie Get Your Gun* (Betty Hutton); Joan Crawford in *Hush Hush Sweet Charlotte* (Olivia de Havilland); Charles Laughton in *David Copperfield* (W. C. Fields); Tyrone Power in *Solomon and Sheba* (he died during filming) (Yul Brynner); Buddy Ebsen in *The Wizard of Oz* (Jack Haley); Bela Lugosi in *Frankenstein* (Boris Karloff); River Phoenix in *Dark Blood* (he died from a drug overdose during filming).

Performers unavailable to play roles for which they were badly wanted include Cary Grant for *My Fair Lady* (Rex Harrison); Joan Crawford for *From Here to Eternity* (Deborah Kerr); Boris Karloff for *Arsenic and Old Lace* (Raymond Massey); Basil Radford and Naunton Wayne for *I See a Dark Stranger* (Garry Marsh and Tom Macaulay); Gary Cooper and Barbara Stanwyck for *Saboteur* (Robert Cummings and Priscilla Lane); Robert Newton for *The Paradine Case* (Louis Jourdan); Jessie Matthews for *A Damsel in Distress* (Joan Fontaine); Claude Rains for *Bride of Frankenstein* (Ernest Thesiger); Burt Lancaster for *Ben Hur* (Charlton Heston); Lon Chaney for *Dracula* (Bela Lugosi); Robert Donat for *Captain Blood* (Errol Flynn); Frank Sinatra for *Carousel* (Gordon Macrae); Jack Benny for *The Sunshine Boys* (George Burns); Jeff Chandler for *Operation Petticoat* (Cary Grant); Bette Davis and Errol Flynn for *Gone with the Wind* (Vivien Leigh and Clark Gable); W. C. Fields for *The Wizard of Oz* (Frank Morgan); Claude Rains for *The Day the Earth Stood Still* (Michael Rennie); George Raft for *High Sierra* and *The Maltese Falcon* (Humphrey Bogart).

universities

have scarcely been studied seriously by movie-makers. Of Britain's most venerable, Cambridge has served as a background for one light comedy, *Bachelor of Hearts*, and Oxford for another, *A Yank at Oxford*, which was subsequently parodied by Laurel and Hardy in *A Chump at Oxford*. *Charley's Aunt* was also set among dreaming spires. Dramas with Oxford settings include *Accident* and *The Mind Benders*. Provincial universities score one comedy (*Lucky Jim*) and one drama (*The Wild and the Willing*). American campuses used to feature in films of the *Hold That Co-Ed* type, the pleasantest to remember being *The Freshman* and *Horse Feathers*, with *How to Be Very Very Popular* a poor third; but in the late 60s student protest held sway in *The Strawberry Statement*, *Getting Straight*, *R.P.M.*, *Drive He Said*, and *The Activist*. Other views of the American higher learning came in *Paper Chase*, *The Group*, *The Male Animal*, *Class of 44*, and *The Magic Garden of Stanley Sweetheart*.

vampires

in the cinema began under the influence of Bram Stoker's *Dracula* but have developed into a genre of their own, often set in the present day. These deviate from the lore as set down by Stoker and folk tradition: 'Don't believe everything you read,' says a pony-tailed vampire as he wrenches a cross from the grasp of a man in the otherwise unremarkable *Vampire Cop* 93, and George Romero created in *Martin* 78 a person who was far removed from the tradition, simply driven by a craving for blood. There is also a tradition of female vampire films, sometimes lesbian, which provide exploitation film-makers with plenty of opportunities for sex scenes. It has respectable origins in Sheridan Le Fanu's Victorian novel *Carmilla*, which has been filmed by Roger Vadim as *Blood and Roses/Et Mourir de Plaisir* 60, Camillo Matrocinque as *Terror in the Crypt* 63, and Roy Ward Baker as *The Vampire Lovers* 70. Lesbian vampires also turn up in *Vampyres* 74, directed by Joseph LARRAZ, while the female vampires in the films of Jean ROLLIN seem to be more interested in sex than blood.

Books: 1993, *The Illustrated Vampire Movie Guide* by Stephen Jones. 1994, *The Vampire Film: From Nosferatu to Bram Stoker's Dracula* by Alain Silver and James Ursini.

See also DRACULA.

Venice

has been most persuasively caught by the movie camera in *Summertime*, *Venetian Bird*, and (for the depressed view) *Death in Venice* and *Don't Look Now*.

ventriloquists

rarely stray from music hall to cinema, but Michael Redgrave played a demented one in *Dead of Night*, and very similar themes were explored in 1929's *The Great Gabbo*, in 1964's *Devil Doll* and in 1978's *Magic*. A vent's dummy was used for comedy in *Knock on Wood*, for satire in *How I Won the War*, and for mystery in *The Dummy Talks* and *The Thirty-Nine Steps* (1959 version). The most movie-exposed performing ventriloquist is certainly Edgar Bergen, who with his dummies Charlie McCarthy and Mortimer Snerd appeared in a dozen or more films between 1937 and 1944.

Victory.

Joseph CONRAD's novel has been filmed three times. The best version was probably the first, made in 1919 by Maurice TOURNEUR and starring Lon CHANEY as Mr Jones. John CROMWELL remade it in 1940, with Cedric HARDWICKE in the role of Mr Jones. Mark PEPLOE made a version in 1994, with Sam NEILL in the role, and also starring Willem DAFOE and Irène JACOB, which was released to lukewarm reviews in 1998. William WELLMAN directed a loose treatment of the story, *Dangerous Paradise*, in 1930.

Vienna

was frequently pictured in pre-war films such as *The Great Waltz*, *Bitter Sweet* and *Vienna Waltzes*, but the myths were always perpetuated on a studio backlot. The post-war reality was caught vividly in *Four in a Jeep* and *The Third Man*.

The Vietnam War

stunned America to such an extent that few films were made about it until long after its end. An exception was John Wayne's gung-ho *The Green Berets* 68. *Go Tell the Spartans* followed in 1978, rapidly followed by *The Deer Hunter* and *Apocalypse Now*. *Coming Home* 82 and *Born on the Fourth of July* 89 covered the effect on veterans. In 1987 there was a deluge: *Hamburger Hill*, *Platoon*, and *Full Metal Jacket*. Director Oliver Stone returned to the subject with *Heaven and Earth* in 1993.

vigilantes

were originally groups of honest citizens who formed together to rid San Francisco's Barbary Coast of some of its villains. In the early 70s it became fashionable to make films about citizens who took the law of our violent cities into their own hands, notably in *Death Wish*, *Walking Tall* and *Law and Disorder*.

violence

caused little concern until the 50s. Even the makers of the horror and gangster films of the 30s were comparatively subtle in their approach; they delighted in machine guns and clutching hands, but would not have dreamed of showing fist connect against flesh or suggesting the sight of actual blood. The rot began to set in in 1952 with films like *The Wild One*, which still showed little but pointed out that *imitable* forms of violence were on the streets of our cities; location shooting was inviting greater realism than had been necessary in the studio. In 1956, when Hammer began to remake the great horror stories, a new ghoulishness was found to have set in, especially in the versions prepared for the Far East. Still the censor held sway until the late 60s, when he gave up the ghost. *Witchfinder General* was a sadistic piece of Grand Guignol, *The Wild Bunch* a blood-spattered western, *Get Carter* and *Villain* new-fashioned gangster films in which the killing was merciless and explicit. *Soldier Blue* has as its high point a mutilation scene which its director seemed to claim as a protest against Vietnam; *Straw Dogs* featured an irrelevant but thoroughly detailed rape. As for *A Clockwork Orange* and *The Devils*, our eyes were spared no conceivable atrocity. According to one's point of view, the cinema had either come of age or ventured beyond the pale. By the 80s, much more violence was being accepted in a family film like *Raiders of the Lost Ark* than would have been passed twenty years earlier for adults only; but the excesses of Brian de Palma's remake of *Scarface* caused most critical hands to be thrown up in horror. A cycle of horror films featuring spectacularly gory make-up effects in the late 80s and 90s revived concerns about screen violence, from politicians at least, as did the emergence of Quentin Tarantino as a director of note with such films as *Reservoir Dogs* and *Pulp Fiction*, and as screenwriter of *True Romance*. Oliver Stone's *Natural Born Killers*, based on Tarantino's script, investigated media concern with violence in an extremely violent manner. In Britain, the result was to add extra confusion to the already arbitrary methods of the Board of Film Classification through government legislation designed to prevent violent films being given a video release, a policy that has lengthened the cinematic life of *Reservoir Dogs*.

The Virginian.

Owen Wister's western novel was filmed in 1914 with Dustin Farnum, in 1930 with Gary Cooper, and in 1945 with Joel McCrea; in 1964 it turned up as a long-running TV series with James Drury. *Spawn of the North* 38 borrowed the basic plot, and in its turn was remade as *Alaska Seas* 54.

volcanoes

in the late 30s seemed to belong mostly to Paramount, which used them as the climax of most of Dorothy Lamour's jungle pictures and of odd adventures like *Cobra Woman* and *Mysterious Island*. They more recently turned up in *The Devil at Four O'Clock*, and in *Journey to the Centre of the Earth* in which the way was down an extinct Icelandic crater and back on a fountain of lava up the inside of Etna. The famous eruption of Vesuvius was staged for the various versions of *The Last Days of Pompeii* (and for *Up Pompeii*), and *Krakatoa, East of Java* featured another historical disaster. An extinct volcano formed a lair for giant monsters in *The Black Scorpion*. A volcano was also the climax of Hal Roach's *Man and His Mate* and of its recent remake *One Million Years BC*; *Joe versus the Volcano* featured a man with a terminal illness who agreed to jump into a volcano after six months of rich living; but the most spectacular pictures were obtained for the documentary compilation simply called *Volcano*. When disaster films proved popular again, volcanoes erupted in *Dante's Peak* 97 and *Volcano* 97, which rained its lava down on Los Angeles, thus saving its makers a journey to the more usual exotic locations.

The Wages of Fear.
Henri-Georges Clouzot's superlative thriller featuring four drivers with a cargo of nitroglycerine was made from Georges Arnaud's novel in 1953, starring Yves Montand, Charles Vanel, and Peter Van Eyck. William Friedkin's 1977 remake, *Sorcerer*, was an artistic and commercial disaster.

War and Peace.
The main film versions of Tolstoy's epic novel were a Russian one of 1916; King Vidor's of 1955, with Henry Fonda and Audrey Hepburn, photographed by Jack Cardiff and Aldo Tonti; and Sergei Bondarchuk's seven-hour colossus of 1964, photographed by Anatole Petrinsky.

war heroes
who have become the subject of biopics include Eddie Rickenbacker (Fred MacMurray, *Captain Eddie*); Audie Murphy (himself, *To Hell and Back*); Guy Gabaldon (Jeffrey Hunter, *Hell to Eternity*); Alvin York (Gary Cooper, *Sergeant York*); Douglas Bader (Kenneth More, *Reach for the Sky*); Guy Gibson (Richard Todd, *The Dam Busters*); Ernie Pyle (Burgess Meredith, *The Story of G.I. Joe*); John Hoskins (Sterling Hayden, *The Eternal Sea*).

The War of the Worlds.
H. G. Wells's novel of an alien invasion, published in 1898, has been the uncredited inspiration behind many science-fiction movies featuring violent, bug-eyed monsters. It was filmed set in present-day America in 1953, produced by George Pal and directed by Byron Haskins, winning an Oscar for its special effects. A new though uncredited version of the story was *Independence Day* 96, which involved the destruction of the White House and used spectacular computer-generated effects. In 1938, Orson Welles's radio version for the Mercury Theatre of the Air, adapted by Howard Koch in the style of an on-the-spot news report, caused widespread fear and was itself the subject of a TV film, *The Night that Panicked America* 75.

The Ware Case.
George Bancroft's play, about a murderer who gets away with his crime but then does the decent thing and kills himself when he discovers his wife and lawyer are in love, has been filmed three times in Britain: in 1917, with Matheson Lang in the lead; in 1928, with Stewart Rome; and in 1938, with Clive Brook.

Washington Square,
Henry JAMES's novel of a plain heiress pursued by a fortune hunter was first filmed as *The Heiress* in 1949, with Olivia DE HAVILLAND and Montgomery CLIFT. It was remade less effectively in 1997, under its original title, by Agnieszka HOLLAND, with Jennifer Jason LEIGH and Ben CHAPLIN.

water,
in inconvenient quantity, played a dramatic part in *Way Down East*; *Noah's Ark*; *The Rains Came* and its remake *The Rains of Ranchipur*; *The Bible*; *Floods of Fear*; *The Hurricane*; *Campbell's Kingdom*; *When Worlds Collide*; *Rain*; *Whistling in Dixie*; *Foreign Correspondent*; *Who Was That Lady?*; and no doubt a hundred others.

See also: RAIN.

waterfront
films have turned up frequently. Among the more seriously-intended are *On the Waterfront*, *Anna Christie*, *Waterfront*, and *Slaughter on Tenth Avenue*; melodramas include *The Mob*, the *Tugboat Annie* films, and *I Cover the Waterfront*. Laurel and Hardy worked the milieu in *The Live Ghost*. TV series include yet another *Waterfront*.

Waterloo Bridge.
Robert Sherwood's sentimental drama, about a ballerina who heads for the gutter after her wealthy lover is reported killed in action and commits suicide when he returns, has been filmed three times: James Whale directed a version in 1931 starring Mae Clark and Kent Douglass; Mervyn Le Roy remade it in 1940 with Vivien Leigh and Robert Taylor; and a lesser version, *Gaby*, updating the story to the Second World War, followed in 1956, directed by Curtis Bernhardt, with Leslie Caron, John Kerr, and a happy ending.

waxworks
have featured from time to time in horror films and other thrillers, notably *The Mystery of the Wax Museum*, *House of Wax*, *Nightmare in Wax*, *Terror in the Wax Museum*, *The Florentine Dagger*, *Charlie Chan in the Wax Museum*, *Midnight at Madame Tussaud's* and the original German *Waxworks*.

weddings
have formed a happy ending for innumerable films, and an unhappy start for others, but some are more memorable than the rest. Weddings on a lavish scale were seen in *Camelot*, *Royal Wedding*, *The Scarlet Empress*, *Ivan the Terrible (Part One)*, *The Private Life of Henry VIII*. More domestic occasions were in *Quiet Wedding*, *The Member of the Wedding*, *The Catered Affair*, *Father of the Bride*, *June Bride*, *A Kind of Loving*, *Lovers and Other Strangers*, *Brigadoon*, *Four Weddings and a Funeral*. Weddings were interrupted in *The Philadelphia Story*, *The Bride Wasn't Willing*, *I Married a Witch*, *The Runaround*, *You Gotta Stay Happy*, *The Bride Went Wild*, *The Lion in Winter*, *The Graduate* and *I Love You Alice B. Toklas*. Macabre weddings were found in *The Night Walker*, *The Bride Wore Black*, *The Bride of Frankenstein*, *The Bride and the Beast*, *Chamber of Horrors*. The wedding night was the center of interest in *The Man in Grey*, *The Wicked Lady*, *Wedding Night*, *The Family Way* and *My Little Chickadee*. And the funniest wedding still remains that in *Our Wife*, when cross-eyed justice of the peace Ben Turpin married Mr Hardy to his best man Mr Laurel.

westerns
have been with us almost as long as the cinema itself; and although Britain supplied *Carry On Cowboy* and a number of Continental countries are now making passable horse operas of their own, it is natural enough that almost all westerns should have come from America.

The Great Train Robbery was a western, and two of the most popular stars of the early silent period, Bronco Billy Anderson and William S. Hart, played western heroes, establishing the conventions and the legends still associated with the opening of America's west – Hollywood style. The attractions of western stories included natural settings, cheapness of production, ready-made plots capable of infinite variation, and a general air of tough simplicity which was saleable the world over. Many of Hollywood's most memorable films of the teens and 20s were westerns: *The Squaw Man*, *The Spoilers*, *The Vanishing American*, *The Covered Wagon*, *The Iron Horse*, *The Virginian*, *In Old Arizona*, *The Cisco Kid*, *Cimarron*. The western adapted itself to sound with remarkable ease, and throughout the 30s provided many entertainments of truly epic stature: *Wells Fargo*, *Arizona*, *The Texas Rangers*, *Union Pacific*, *The Plainsman*, *Drums Along the Mohawk*, *Jesse James*, *The Westerner*, *Destry Rides Again*, *Stagecoach*. By now the major directorial talents in the field were established: they included John Ford, William Wyler, Howard Hawks, King Vidor, Victor Fleming, Michael Curtiz, Henry King, Frank Lloyd. And each year brought in the wake of epics scores of cheap but entertaining second features, usually running in familiar series with such stars as Buck Jones, Tom Mix, Tim McCoy, John Wayne, Bob Steele, William Boyd ('Hopalong Cassidy'), Ken Maynard, Tom Tyler, Gene Autry, and 'The Three Mesquiteers'. The singing cowboy familiarized by Autry led to the arrival of other practitioners in the 40s: Roy Rogers, Eddie Dean, Lee 'Lasses' White. The 40s also based westerns more firmly on historical events, telling such stories as *Brigham Young*, *Northwest Passage*, *My Darling Clementine*, *Santa Fe Trail*, *They Died with Their Boots On*. But by the end of the decade this genre had worn itself out except in the case of Ford, whose films became increasingly stylish and personal. Elsewhere westerns deteriorated into routine action adventures starring actors a little past their best: Gary Cooper, Errol Flynn, Dennis Morgan, Alan Ladd. Howard Hawks' *Red River* was a useful move towards realism, and was followed in the early 50s by films like *The Gunfighter* and *Shane*, intent on proving how unpleasant a place the real West must have been. Side by side with realism came the 'message' western, given its impetus by *Broken Arrow* 50, the first western since silent days to sympathize with the Indians. It was followed by western allegories like *High Noon* and *3.10 to Yuma*, in which the action elements were restricted or replaced by suspense in taut stories of good versus evil. In these ways the western became a highly respectable form, attracting actors of the calibre of James Stewart, Marlon Brando, Glenn Ford, Henry Fonda, Burt Lancaster, Richard Widmark and Kirk Douglas, all of whom tended to play half-cynical heroes who preserved their sense of right by indulging in violent action in the last reel. The later 50s brought many spectacular western productions including *Gunfight at the OK Corral*, *Last Train from Gun Hill*, *One-Eyed Jacks*, *Warlock* and *The Magnificent Seven;* but no new ground was broken. Second features continued to prosper in the capable hands of Randolph Scott, Joel McCrea and Audie Murphy. Comedy westerns were seldom successful, though exceptions include *Go West* (Keaton and Marx versions), Laurel and Hardy's *Way Out West*, and *Blazing Saddles*.

The galloping success of TV made potted westerns so familiar that even the biggest epics made for the cinema found it hard to attract a paying audience. Ford persevered with *The Man Who Shot Liberty Valance* and *Cheyenne Autumn*, both rehashes of earlier and better work; Cinerama made a patchy spectacle called *How the West Was Won;* novelty westerns have tried violence, horror and sentimentality as gimmicks.

In the 60s westerns came from an unexpected source: Italy, where directors took the conventions and added a baroque twist or two of their own. At their worst, the spaghetti westerns were ponderous and violent; at their best, they had a style and verve that re-invented the genre. Sergio Leone emerged as the leading director, his films aided by the atmospheric scores of Ennio Morricone and their reticent, almost blank hero, played in appropriate fashion by Clint Eastwood. But the revival was not long-lived. Hollywood directors seemed to have lost faith in the western's mythic qualities, preferring to stick to comedies such as *Cat Ballou*. Sam Peckinpah's *The Wild Bunch* 69 and George Roy Hill's *Butch Cassidy and the Sundance Kid* 69 were almost the last flourishes before the form went into what seemed like a terminal decline. Clint Eastwood was the last cowboy, but his moody outcasts seemed pale before his *Dirty Harry*. It was Eastwood who showed that there was life left in the western with *Unforgiven*, the success of which sparked off another cycle. But none of the succeeding films, including two on the life of Wyatt Earp, did particularly well at the box-office, leaving the future of the genre again in doubt.

Books: 1969, *Horizons West* by Jim Kitses. 1977, *Westerns* by Philip French. 1988, *The BFI Companion to the Western*, edited by Edward Buscombe. 1993, *Encyclopedia of Western Movies*, edited by Phil Hardy (revised edition).

❝ An adult western is where the hero still kisses his horse at the end, only now he worries about it. – *Milton Berle*

wheelchairs
have usually had sinister connotations in the cinema. The Spanish film *The Wheelchair* was a very black comedy indeed, and villains who have operated from wheelchairs include Lionel Atwill in *The Mystery of the Wax Museum*, Vincent Price in *House of Wax*, Ralph Morgan in *Night Monster*, and Francis L. Sullivan in *Hell's Island*. General 'heavies' confined to wheelchairs include Eleanor Parker in *The Man with the Golden Arm* and *Eye of the Cat*, cantankerous Dame May Whitty (and later Mona Washbourne) in *Night Must Fall*, and crusty old Lionel Barrymore in the *Dr Kildare* series and every other film he made after 1939 (he was confined to a chair after twice breaking his hip). Wheelchair victims included Estelle Winwood in *Notorious Landlady*, careering away over the countryside, and the old lady who was pushed downstairs in a wheelchair in *Kiss of Death*. Perhaps the most fearsome wheelchair occupant was Monty Woolley, of the barbed tongue, in *The Man Who Came to Dinner*. Electric staircase chairs were used by 'invalids' Ethel Barrymore in *The Farmer's Daughter*, Eugenie Leontovich in *Homicidal* and Charles Laughton in *Witness for the Prosecution*.

The Whistler.
Based on a popular American radio show, this crime anthology ran as a film series from 1944 to 1947, with Richard Dix playing the hero of each. The only other connection between episodes was the whistled theme at the beginning. The first story was the old chestnut about the man who hires someone to kill him and then changes his mind.

The Whistler 44. Mark of the Whistler 44. Power of the Whistler 45. Voice of the Whistler 45. Mysterious Intruder 46. Secret of the Whistler 46. The 13th Hour 47. The Return of the Whistler 48.

Whistling in the Dark.
This crime-comedy play by Lavinia Cross and Edward Carpenter was first filmed by Elliott Nugent, with Ernest Truex as the little man who beats the crooks in the end. In 1940 it was revamped as a vehicle for Red Skelton, directed by S. Sylvan Simon, who also handled the two sequels: *Whistling in Dixie* 42 and *Whistling in Brooklyn* 43.

White Cargo.
Leon Gordon's much-caricatured play was based on a book by Ida Vera Simonton called *Hell's Playground*; it dealt with the difficulties of acclimatization for Malayan rubber planters, and in particular with a shapely native distraction called Tondelayo. It was filmed in Britain by J. B. Williams in 1929, with Leslie Faber and Gypsy Rhouma; and in Hollywood in 1942 with Walter Pidgeon and Hedy Lamarr.

Why We Fight.
A brilliant series of World War II documentaries using all the resources of the cinema, compiled by Frank Capra and the US Signal Corps Film Unit from material shot by Allied cameramen and from pre-war newsreel material. Each lasted just over an hour, and was kept absorbingly entertaining as well as instructive by the use of music, diagrams, and optical work. Titles were *Prelude to War*, *The Nazis Strike*, *Divide and Conquer*, *The Battle of Britain*, *The Battle of Russia*, *The Battle of China*.

The Wicked Lady.
Magdalen King-Hall's novel of an aristocratic woman who turns to highway robbery made a star of Margaret Lockwood in 1945, directed by Leslie Arliss. Michael Winner's remake in 1983 did nothing for Faye Dunaway's career.

Wile E. Coyote.
Dumb but cunning cartoon character, forever in pursuit of Road Runner, created by Chuck Jones and Michael Maltese.

❝ The coyote is victimized by his own ineptitude. I never understood how to use tools and that's really the coyote's problem. – *Chuck Jones*

See ROAD RUNNER for list of movies.

William.
The argumentative small boy created in over thirty novels by Richmal Crompton had several British film incarnations, none very satisfactory, in the 30s and 40s.

witchcraft
has not been frequently tackled by film-makers, usually for censorship reasons, and *Witchcraft through the Ages* remains the most comprehensive cinematic treatise on the subject. Dreyer's *Day of Wrath* took it seriously, as did *The Witches of Salem*, *Maid of Salem*, *Witchfinder General*, *The Dunwich Horror*, *The Devils* and *Il Demonio*, but all were chiefly concerned with the morals of witch-hunting. Witch doctors are familiar figures from African adventure films like *King Solomon's Mines* and *Men of Two Worlds*; more lightheartedly, witches featured in *The Wizard of Oz*, *I Married a Witch* and *Bell, Book and Candle*, as well as in TV's *Bewitched* and all the films featuring Merlin. A nasty cannibalistic coven was seen in Gosta Werner's *Midvinterblot* and several recent thrillers (*Night of the Demon*, *City of the Dead*, *Night of the Eagle*, *Witchcraft*, *The Witches*, *Rosemary's Baby*, *Satan's Skin*, *Cry of the Banshee*, *The Illustrated Man*,

The Mephisto Waltz, The Brotherhood of Satan, The Sentinel) purported to believe in the effects of witchcraft. Angela Lansbury in *Bedknobs and Broomsticks* played a kindly witch. Paul Schrader's *Witch Hunt* showed a world where magic was real and a witch conjured up Shakespeare to write for the movies. *The Craft* 96 had teenage girls using witchcraft on their enemies.

See also: THE DEVIL.

The Wolf Man.

The werewolf or lycanthrope, a man who turns into a ravaging beast at full moon, is a fairly ancient Central European mythological figure. Hollywood did not develop the idea until *Werewolf of London* 34, a one-shot in which Henry Hull, a victim of his own well-intentioned research, was firmly despatched before the end. Not until 1941 was the possibility of a series character envisaged. *The Wolf Man* had a splendid cast: Claude Rains, Warren William, Patric Knowles, Bela Lugosi, Maria Ouspenskaya, and Lon Chaney Jnr as Lawrence Talbot, heir to a stately English home but unlucky enough to be bitten by a werewolf and thus condemned to monstrous immortality until despatched by a silver bullet. In this film he was battered to apparent death by Claude Rains, but arose from the family crypt for *Frankenstein Meets the Wolf Man* 43, which ended with him and the Frankenstein Monster being swept away in a flood. In *House of Frankenstein* he was discovered in a block of ice and promptly thawed out, only to be shot with the requisite silver bullet by a gipsy girl. The producers, however, played so unfair as to revive him for *House of Dracula* 45, in which he lived to be the only movie monster with a happy ending: brain surgery cured him and he even got the girl. Years later, however, in *Abbott and Costello Meet Frankenstein* 48, it seemed that his affliction was again tormenting him: this time we last saw him falling into a rocky and turbulent sea. Mr Chaney had by now done with the character apart from a spoof appearance in an episode of TV's *Route* 66. But Hammer Films revived the basic plot in *Curse of the Werewolf* 61, with Oliver Reed as the mangy hero. To date this has provoked no sequels. One should also mention: *The Werewolf* 56, *I Was a Teenage Werewolf* 57, *La Casa del Terror* (Mex.) 59, *Werewolf in a Girl's Dormitory* (with its theme song 'The Ghoul in School') 61, and *Legend of the Werewolf* 74, but the less said about these the better.

There was a werewolf in *Dr Terror's House of Horrors* 65, and in *The Beast Must Die* 74, while the 80s brought a whole slew of hairy monsters in *Wolfen, An American Werewolf in London, Werewolf of Washington, Teen Wolf* and *The Howling*. In 1994 Jack Nicholson brought a touch of class to the role in *Wolf*, directed by Mike Nichols.

Woman to Woman.

Michael Morton's tear-jerking play, about a doomed love affair between a British officer and a French dancer, was first filmed by Graham Cutts in 1923, and achieved some renown as one of the better examples of British silent cinema. Clive Brooks and Betty Compson had the leads, and Miss Compson appeared with Georges Barraud in the talkie remake of 1929, directed by Victor Saville. In 1946 Maclean Rogers directed an updated version with Douglas Montgomery and Joyce Howard.

The Women.

Clare Boothe Luce's venomous comedy was filmed twice by MGM: in 1939 with an all-woman cast headed by Norma Shearer, Rosalind Russell, Paulette Goddard, and Joan Crawford; and in 1956, in a semi-musical version called *The Opposite Sex*, with June Allyson and Ann Sheridan. There are plans to film a new version.

Woody Woodpecker.

A cartoon character with an infectious laugh, created in the 30s by Walter Lantz for Universal, and still going strong in 1973 via a new TV incarnation.

World War I (1914–1918).

now a remote and comparatively concentrated event, was seen by film-makers of the next four decades chiefly as an opportunity for pacifist propaganda arising from horror and disillusion. This is the kind of attitude struck in *Civilisation, War Brides, The Battle Cry of Peace, All Quiet on the Western Front* (and its sequel *The Road Back*), *Westfront 1918, J'Accuse, The Man Who Reclaimed His Head, Journey's End, La Grande Illusion, The Man I Killed, The Road to Glory, They Gave Me a Gun, Sergeant York*, and *Paths of Glory*. *Oh What a Lovely War* made the same points by use of bitter comedy. The romantic aspect of war, however, was not neglected by *The White Sister, A Farewell to Arms, Hearts of the World, The Four Horsemen of the Apocalypse, The Big Parade, Lilac Time, Hell's Angels, Seventh Heaven, The Dark Angel, Waterloo Bridge, Lawrence of Arabia*, and many others. *What Price Glory?* was pure cynicism, *The Fighting 69th* pure jingoism. The spy element was to the fore in *I Was a Spy, Dark Journey, The Spy in Black, Mata Hari, Nurse Edith Cavell* and *Darling Lili*; aviation in *Hell's Angels, Wings, The Red Baron* and *The Blue Max*. Comedy aspects of the war were depicted in *Shoulder Arms, Spy for a Day, Pack Up Your Troubles, We're in the Army Now, Half Shot at Sunrise* and *Up the Front*. Rehabilitation problems were dealt with in *The Sun Also Rises, The Last Flight, Isn't Life Wonderful?, The Lost Squadron, The Roaring Twenties* and the 'Forgotten Man' number in *Gold Diggers of 1933*. *Regeneration* 97 dealt with the shell-shocked victims of trench warfare, including poets Siegfried Sassoon and Wilfred Owen.

writers

depicted in films include the following: Rod Taylor as Sean O'Casey in *Young Cassidy*, John Shepperd as Edgar Allan Poe in *The Loves of Edgar Allan Poe*, Beau Bridges as Ben Hecht in *Gaily Gaily*, James Mason as Gustave Flaubert in *Madame Bovary*, Herbert Marshall as Somerset Maugham in *The Moon and Sixpence* and *The Razor's Edge*, Reginald Gardiner as Shakespeare in *The Story of Mankind*, Turhan Bey as Aesop in *A Night in Paradise*, Michael O'Shea as Jack London in *Jack London*, Dean Stockwell as Eugene O'Neill in *Long Day's Journey into Night*, Daniel Massey as Noël Coward in *Star!*, Frederick Jaeger as Henrik Ibsen in *Song of Norway*, Danny Kaye as *Hans Christian Andersen*, Paul Muni in *The Life of Emile Zola*, Gregory Peck as F. Scott Fitzgerald in *Beloved Infidel*, Burgess Meredith as Ernie Pyle in *The Story of G.I. Joe*, Michael Redgrave as W.B. Yeats in *Young Cassidy*, Laurence Harvey and Karl Boehm in *The Wonderful World of the Brothers Grimm*, Dennis Price in *The Bad Lord Byron*, Richard Chamberlain as Byron in *Lady Caroline Lamb*, Fredric March (later Bill Travers) as Robert Browning in *The Barretts of Wimpole Street*, Olivia de Havilland, Nancy Coleman and Ida Lupino as the Brontë Sisters in *Devotion*, Arthur Kennedy as Branwell Brontë in *Devotion*, Sydney Greenstreet as Thackeray in *Devotion*, Robert Morley in *Oscar Wilde*, Peter Finch in *The Trials of Oscar Wilde*, Cornel Wilde in *Omar Khayyam*, Fredric March in *The Adventures of Mark Twain*, Ian McKellen as D.H Lawrence in *Priest of Love*. Henry Miller was played by David Brandon and Anais Nin by Martine Brochard in *Room of Words* 89, and by Fred Ward and Maria de Medeiros in *Henry and June* 90. The film with the most writers gathered together is Alan Rudolph's 1994 film *Mrs Parker and the Vicious Circle*, about Dorothy Parker and friends gathering for battles of wits at the ALGONQUIN ROUND TABLE. The cast includes Jennifer Jason Leigh as Parker, Matthew Broderick as Charles MacArthur, Campbell Scott as Robert Benchley, Lili Taylor as Edna Ferber, Nick Cassavetes as Robert Sherwood, David Thornton as George S. Kaufman, Tom McGowan as Alexander Woollcott, Chip Zien as Franklin P. Adams, Gary Basaraba as Heywood Broun, and David Gow as Donald Ogden Stewart.

❝ Despite the greater reputations of stars and directors, no Hollywood film could begin to be made without a writer, and it is often the dialogue which lingers most effectively in the mind, bringing life even to corny old yarns which were anonymously satirized as follows:

Arizona. Indians thronging.
Arrows pinging. Pistols ponging.
Something smelly – old and hoary.
Not to worry: it's the story.

A bad story can be salvaged by a good director, just as vice versa. Richard Corliss remarked:

While these two functions can be distinguished for research purposes, they are really the inseparable halves of a work of art.

What happens, of course, isn't always art; Mr Corliss was referring to *Citizen Kane*. And some writers give up trying soon after they get to Hollywood with its compromises. As William Holden remarked in *Sunset Boulevard*:

Audiences don't know anybody writes a picture. They think the actors just make it up as they go along.

Other cynics have claimed that there are only six basic plots. As Mr Holden said in another film, *Paris When It Sizzles*:

Frankenstein and *My Fair Lady* are really the same story.

He was right. But of all the arts, the screen is most capable of transforming old sows' ears into shining new silk purses. It can be tremendously subtle in its effects, as Dudley Nichols knew:

The stage is a medium of action, but the screen is a medium of reaction.

Leading those who made screencraft their own was Preston Sturges.

Among the handful of screenwriters whose influence was critical to the craft, Sturges deserves at least two fingers and a thumb.

That's the view of Richard Corliss, who also admires Samson Raphaelson:

Style may be said to comprise his theme: the way people embody it, employ it.

Wuthering Heights.

Emily Brontë's brooding romantic novel was filmed in Britain in the silent era, but the best version was made in America in 1939, directed by William Wyler, with Laurence Olivier, as Heathcliff, and Merle Oberon. (It is said that Goldwyn's original casting preferences for Heathcliff were Ronald Colman, Douglas Fairbanks Jnr, and Robert Newton.) A subsequent Mexican version of the story by Luis Buñuel, *Abismos de Pasión* 50, has not been widely seen. Robert Fuest remade it in 1970 with Timothy Dalton and Anna Calder-Marshall, and a lacklustre treatment came in 1992, with Ralph Fiennes and Juliette Binoche.

Yojimbo,

Akira Kurosawa's 1961 movie, with Toshiro Mifune as a wandering samurai who tricks two rival gangs of cutthroats into destroying one another, was one of the inspirations for Italy's 'spaghetti westerns' when it was remade by Sergio Leone in 1964 as *A Fistful of Dollars*, starring Clint Eastwood. In 1996 came an American version, *Last Man Standing*, directed by Walter Hill and starring Bruce Willis.

Yosemite Sam.

Bad-tempered, loud-mouthed, long-moustachioed cartoon cowboy, the self-styled 'roughest, toughest hombre', usually to be seen chasing Bugs Bunny in Warner Brothers' Merrie Melodies and Loony Tunes cartoons. Created by Fritz Freleng, he was voiced by Mel Blanc.

Hare Trigger 45. Buccaneer Bunny 48. Mutiny on the Bunny 50. 14 Carrot Rabbit 52. Captain Hareblower 54. Rabbitson Crusoe 56. Knighty-Knight Bugs (AA) 58. Prince Violent 61. Shishkabugs 62. Devil's Feud Cake 63, etc.

Zatoichi

was a blind masseur with superb abilities as a swordsman, the hero of a series of 24 popular Japanese films that ran for a decade from 1962, many of them directed by Kenji Misumi. In 1964, *Zatoichi and the Scoundrels*, the sixth film in the series and the first to be made in colour, was dubbed into English and retitled *Zatoichi the Blind Swordsman*, but it failed to find an international audience, though some later films, including *Zatoichi Meets Yojimbo* 70, were released in America and elsewhere. The character was created by writer Kan Shimozawa and all the films starred Shintaro Katsu in the title role. He also produced and directed the last movie in the series, *Zatoichi in Desperation* 73. The success of the films led to a short-lived rival blind swordsman called Oichi or the Crimson Bat, who lasted for four films.

zombies

originate from Haitian legend, and are generally held to be dead people brought back to life by voodoo. In movies they invariably shamble along with sightless eyes, looking pretty awful but doing no real damage. They were most convincingly displayed in Victor Halperin's 1932 *White Zombie*; other examples of the species turned up in *Revolt of the Zombies, The Zombies of Mora Tau, I Walked With a Zombie, King of the Zombies, The Ghost Breakers* (and its remake *Scared Stiff*), and *Dr Terror's House of Horrors*. The species gave its name to a strong rum punch, and one treasured memory is a movie in which the Ritz Brothers walked up to a bar and said: 'Three zombies.' 'I can see that,' said the barman, 'but what'll you have to drink?' In the 70s George Romero adopted the theme in such repellent films as *Night of the Living Dead* and *Dawn of the Dead*; but the most fearsome undead of all appeared in the dream scene of Hammer's 1965 *Plague of the Zombies*.

Zorro (Don Diego de Vega).

The black-garbed Robin Hood of Spanish California originated as the hero of a 1919 strip cartoon by Johnston McCulley. (Zorro, incidentally, is Spanish for fox.) Films featuring the devil-may-care righter of wrongs include *The Mark of Zorro* 20 with Douglas Fairbanks, and its 1925 sequel *Don Q, Son of Zorro*; *The Bold Caballero* 37 with Robert Livingston; *Zorro Rides Again* 37, a serial with John Carroll; *Zorro's Fighting Legion* 39, a serial with Reed Hadley; Mamoulian's splendid remake of *The Mark of Zorro* 40, with Tyrone Power; *The Ghost of Zorro* 49, a serial with Clayton Moore; Walter Chiari in *The Sign of Zorro* 52; *Zorro the Avenger* 60 and other Disney TV films with Guy Williams; Sean Flynn in *The Sign of Zorro* 62; Frank Latimore in *Shadow of Zorro* 62; Pierre Brice in *Zorro versus Maciste* 63; George Ardisson in *Zorro at the Court of Spain* 63; Gordon Scott in *Zorro and the Three Musketeers* 63; and Alain Delon in *Zorro* 75. Almost inevitably the 80s brought a spoof version, *Zorro the Gay Blade* 82, featuring a limp-wristed avenger. A return to the swashbuckling style of the original came in 1998 with *The Mask of Zorro*, directed by Martin Campbell and starring Anthony Hopkins as an ageing Zorro and Antonio Banderas as his virile replacement, after director Robert Rodriguez and his star Andy Garcia had dropped out of the project.

3
An Alphabetical Listing of Remakes, Series, Themes and Genres

Abie's Irish Rose
abortion
Accent on Youth
actors
adaptations
addresses
The Admirable Crichton
advertising
aeroplanes
Ah, Wilderness!
AIDS
air balloons
airplanes
airships
The Alamo
alcoholics
Aldwych farces
Algonquin Round Table
Ali Baba
Alice in Wonderland
Alien/Aliens
all-star films
The American Civil War
The American Revolution
amnesia
Amos 'n' Andy
anachronisms
ancient Egypt
angels
animals
anti-Semitism
Antoine Doinel
army comedies
Arsène Lupin
Arthur
assassination
Asterix
authors as actors
automobiles
The Avengers
babies
Back Street
backstage
ballet
balloons
Barney Bear
baseball
bathtubs
Batman
Ben Hur
Berlin
Betty Boop
Beverly Hills
The Bible
big business
bigamists
birds
The Bishop's Wife
black comedy
blacks
blaxploitation

blindness
boffins
boo-boos
Boston Blackie
The Bowery Boys
boxing
The Brady Bunch
The British Empire
brothels
Bugs Bunny
Bulldog Drummond
bullfights
burlesque
buses
butlers
cable cars
cannibalism
Carl Hamilton
Carmen
carnivals
Carry On films
case histories
Casper, the Friendly Ghost
catchphrases
Cenobites
Charley's Aunt
Charlie Chan
Charters and Caldicott
the chase
child stars
childhood portrayed by grown-ups
Chilly Willy
Christ
Christmas
churches
the cinema
cinemas
circuses
The Cisco Kid
clairvoyance
coal mines
Cobra
the Cold War
colleges
comedy
comedy teams
comic strips
communism
compilation films
composers
computers
Conan the Barbarian
concentration camps
concerts
confidence tricksters
continuity errors
courtesans
courtroom scenes
crazy comedy
Crime Doctor
criminals

critics
Cry the Beloved Country
Crying Freeman
custard pies
Daffy Duck
dance bands
The Dead End Kids
deaf mutes
death
dentists
department stores
desert islands
deserts
the devil
Devil's Island
Dick Barton
Dick Tracy
Die Hard
dinosaurs
directors' appearances
Dirty Harry
disaster films
disguise
Django
Dr Christian
Dr Mabuse
Dr Who
doctors
Don Juan
Don Quixote
Donald Duck
Dracula
drag
dreams
Droopy
drug addiction
drunk scenes
duels
The East Side Kids
El Santo
the electric chair
elephants
elevators
Ellery Queen
Elmer Fudd
the end of the world
Enoch Arden
entertainers
epidemics
episodic films
epitaphs
Eskimos
excerpts
explorers
Fair Game
fairy tales
The Fall of the House of Usher
falling
the family
Fanny
fans

fantasy
farce
Farewell, My Lovely
A Farewell to Arms
fashions
fastest money-making movies
Father Brown
FBI
Felix (the Cat)
female impersonation
fights
film-making
films à clef
fire
firing squads
The Flag Lieutenant
Flash Gordon
The Flintstones
fog
Foghorn Leghorn
Folies Bergère
the Foreign Legion
forest fires
The Fox
Fox and the Crow
Francis
Frankenstein
Friday the 13th
Fritz the Cat
The Front Page
Fu Manchu
funerals
funfairs
gambling
gangsters
The Garden of Allah
Gaslight
Gentlemen Prefer Blondes
Gerald McBoing Boing
Gertie the Dinosaur
The Ghost Breaker
The Ghost Train
ghosts
giants
Gidget
gigolos
gimmicks
The Glass Key
Godzilla
The Golem
The Good Companions
Goodbye Mr Chips
Goofy
governesses
Grand Hotel
The Great Adventure
The Great Gatsby
The Great Impersonation
Green Hornet, The
the guillotine
Gulliver's Travels

Gunfight at the OK Corral
Gunga Din
gypsies
Hamlet
hands
The Hands of Orlac
Harry Callahan
heaven
Heckle and Jeckle
helicopters
hell
Henry Aldrich
Hercule Poirot
hillbillies
Hollywood
Hollywood on film
homosexuality
Hopalong Cassidy
horror
horses
hospitals
hotels
The Hound of the Baskervilles
houses
Hubie and Bertie
The Huggetts
The Hunchback of Notre Dame
hypnosis
impresarios
in-jokes
incest
The Incredible Journey
Indians
insanity
insects
Inspector Hornleigh
insults
inventors
The Island of Dr Moreau
Jack the Ripper
James Bond
Jane Eyre
jazz
jewel thieves
Jews
Joe Palooka
The Jones Family
Judge Dredd
The Jungle Book
Jungle Jim
Ma and Pa Kettle
The Keystone Kops
Kid Galahad
kidnapping
King Arthur
King Kong
King Solomon's Mines
kings and queens
Kismet
The Ku Klux Klan
labour relations
Lady for a Day
Lassie
The Last Days of Pompeii
The Last of the Mohicans
Leave It to Beaver
legends
Lemmy Caution
leprechauns
lesbianism
letters
lifts
light comedians
lighthouses

Li'l Abner
Liliom
Little Lord Fauntleroy
Little Miss Marker
Little Rascals
Little Tough Guys
Little Women
The Lodger
London
The Lone Ranger
The Lone Rider
The Lone Wolf
lookalikes
Looney Tunes
Los Angeles
Lost Horizon
Lost in Space
Lost Patrol
Love Affair
The Lower Depths
lumberjacks
lynch law
M
Macbeth
Maciste
Madame Bovary
The Mafia
magicians
Magnificent Obsession
Maigret
Maisie
male impersonation
The Maltese Falcon
The Man in the Iron Mask
The Man Who Knew Too
    Much
The March of Time
Matt Helm
Mau Mau
Merrie Melodies
The Merry Widow
Merton of the Movies
Mexican Spitfire
Michael Shayne
Mickey Mouse
A Midsummer Night's Dream
Mighty Joe Young
Mighty Mouse
Mike Hammer
miniaturization
mirrors
Les Misérables
misnomers
Miss Marple
missionaries
Mr Belvedere
Mr Magoo
Mr Moto
Mr Wong
Mrs Wiggs of the Cabbage
    Patch
Moby Dick
Modesty Blaise
monks
Monsieur Beaucaire
monster animals
Monty Python
morticians
'The Most Dangerous Game'
mother love
motor-cycles
motor racing
mountains
movies

multiple roles
multiple-story films
multi-screen techniques
The Mummy
Muppets
murderers
musical remakes
musicals
Mutiny on the Bounty
My Man Godfrey
My Sister Eileen
mystery
The Mystery of the Wax Museum
Nana
Nancy Drew
narrators
naval comedy
nepotism
New York
Nick and Nora Charles
Nick Carter
Nightmare on Elm Street
No Man of Her Own
Norman Bates
Nothing but the Truth
numbered sequels
nuns
nurses
nymphomaniacs
Of Mice and Men
offices
Oh God!
oil
old age
Old Mother Riley
Oliver Twist
One Million B.C.
One Way Passage
opera
orchestral conductors
oriental roles
Oswald the Rabbit
Othello
'Our Gang'
painters
The Paleface
Paris
parody
parties
The Passing of the Third Floor
    Back
The Passing Parade
Penrod
Pepe Le Pew
The Perils of Pauline
Perry Mason
Peyton Place
The Phantom of the Opera
Philip Marlowe
The Pink Panther
pirates
The Plainsman
Planet of the Apes
plastic surgery
police
politics
Popeye
Porky Pig
poverty
priests
The Prince and the Pauper
prison films
The Prisoner of Zenda
prisoners of war

private eyes
prizefighting
prophecy
prostitutes
psychology
publicity
put-downs
Quiller
Quo Vadis?
radio
Raffles
railway stations
rain
Rain (Somerset Maugham)
The Rains Came
Rambo
Ramona
The Range Busters
rape
Rashomon
The Rat
Rebecca of Sunnybrook Farm
Red Dust
Red Indians (native Americans)
reincarnation
rejuvenation
religion
remakes in disguise
reporters
The Ringer
road movie
Road Runner
robberies
Robin Hood
Robinson Crusoe
Robocop
robots
Rocky Balboa
Roger Rabbit
Rogue Male
romantic teams
Rome
Romeo and Juliet
Rose Marie
Rosebud
Ruggles of Red Gap
Sabrina
Sahara
sailors
The Saint
St Trinian's
Salome
San Francisco
satire
Scarface
The Scarlet Letter
The Scarlet Pimpernel
Scattergood Baines
schooldays
science fiction
scientists
The Sea Wolf
seances
seaside resorts
Sergeant Ernie Bilko
serial killers
serials
series
servants
Seven Keys to Baldpate
Seventh Heaven
sewers
sex
sex changes

Sexton Blake
Shaft
She
She Loves Me Not
The Sheik
Sherlock Holmes
ships
The Shop around the Corner
The Shopworn Angel
Show Boat
silent films
Silly Symphony
A Sister to Assist'er
Sitting Pretty
skiing
slapstick
Slaughter
slogans
small towns
Smilin' Through
smoking
smugglers
social comedy
social conscience
soldiers
space exploration
spaghetti westerns
The Spanish Civil War
speeches
Speedy Gonzales
spies
The Spoilers
sportsmen
Squibs
staircases
A Star Is Born
Star Wars
State Fair
statesmen
statues

Stella Dallas
storms
strikes
striptease
The Student of Prague
The Student Prince
student protest
stuntmen
submarines
subways
suicide
Superman
Svengali
swashbucklers
swinging London
The Swiss Family Robinson
sword and sorcery
Sylvester
A Tale of Two Cities
Tales of Manhattan
talkies
Tammy
Tarzan
teachers
teams
Teenage Mutant Ninja Turtles
the telephone
television
television movies
television series
The Ten Commandments
tennis
The Texas Chainsaw Massacre
theatres
The Thief of Bagdad
The Thin Man
The Thing (from Another World)
The Thirty-Nine Steps
This Gun for Hire
This Modern Age

Three Coins in the Fountain
Three Men in a Boat
The Three Mesquiteers
The Three Musketeers
Three Smart Girls
tinting
The Titanic
To Have and Have Not
The Toff
Tol'able David
Tom and Jerry
Tom Brown's Schooldays
Tom Sawyer
Tony Rome
Topper
Torchy Blane
torture
Trail of the Lonesome Pine
trains
tramps
transvestism
Treasure Island
trends
Trilby
Tugboat Annie
Tweety Pie
Uncle Tom's Cabin
uncredited appearances
Under Two Flags
underground railways
undertakers
underwater sequences
unemployment
Unfaithfully Yours
unfinished films
unfinished performances
universities
vampires
Venice
ventriloquists

Victory
Vienna
The Vietnam War
vigilantes
violence
The Virginian
volcanoes
The Wages of Fear
War and Peace
war heroes
The War of the Worlds
The Ware Case
Washington Square
water
waterfront
Waterloo Bridge
waxworks
weddings
westerns
wheelchairs
The Whistler
Whistling in the Dark
White Cargo
Why We Fight
The Wicked Lady
Wile E. Coyote
William
witchcraft
The Wolf Man
Woman to Woman
The Women
Woody Woodpecker
World War I
writers
Wuthering Heights
Yojimbo
Yosemite Sam
Zatoichi
zombies
Zorro

4

Movie Studios and Production Companies, etc.

Abbey Theatre.
Significant Irish theatre, founded in Dublin in 1904, which presented the first performances of plays by W. B. Yeats, J. M. Synge and Sean O'Casey. Over the years, many of its actors went on to film careers, though the theatre discouraged them and often refused to ever employ them again as a result. They included J. M. Kerrigan, who also directed some now-lost silent films, Fred O'Donovan, also a director of some silents, Sara ALLGOOD, Maire O'NEILL, Arthur SINCLAIR, W. G. FAY, F. J. MCCORMICK, Dudley DIGGES, Barry FITZGERALD, Cyril CUSACK, Liam REDMOND, Dan O'HERLIHY, Denis O'DEA, Jack MACGOWRAN, Niall TOIBIN, T. P. MCKENNA, and Ray MCANALLY. John FORD drew on Abbey actors for his two Irish films, *The Informer* 35 and *The Plough and the Stars* 36, and some, like Arthur SHIELDS and Una O'CONNOR, became familiar players in Hollywood. In the 50s, six Abbey plays were filmed at the newly opened Ardmore Studios, including *Broth of a Boy* 58, directed by George POLLOCK from the play by Hugh LEONARD, and *This Other Eden* 60, directed by Muriel BOX from Louis D'Alton's play, but they were not commercially successful.

Books: 1958, *The Abbey Theatre* by Gerard Fay; 1967, *The Story of the Abbey Theatre*, ed. Sean McCann.

The Actors' Studio.
Drama school established in 1947 by Elia Kazan, Cheryl Crawford and Robert Lewis at West 48th Street, Manhattan (later West 44th Street). It is especially associated with Lee Strasberg, who ran it for 30 years from 1949, and The Method, a style of acting that owed much to the teachings of Stanislavsky and which revolutionized American acting, becoming the predominant film style, from Marlon Brando to Robert de Niro and Al Pacino. In its earlier days, the Studio gained much publicity through Marilyn Monroe's involvement. Among those who studied there were Brando (though he credits Stella Adler with teaching him how to act), Rod Steiger, James Dean, Geraldine Page, Karl Malden, Shelley Winters, Steve McQueen and Paul Newman.

Books: 1980, *A Player's Place: The Story of the Actors Studio* by David Garfield; 1984, *A Method to Their Madness* by Foster Hirsch.

Documentary: 1981, *Lee Strasberg and The Actors' Studio* (d. Herbert Kline).

❝ I am very proud to announce that I am a member of The Actors' Studio. The greatest school of the theatre . . . It is the best thing that can happen to an actor. – *James Dean*

That whole Strasberg school was created by the idiosyncrasies and genius of one man, Marlon Brando. From him, not Strasberg, came the likes of James Dean and Paul Newman and Monty Clift and John Cassavetes. It was a mind fuck: Go off in your head somewhere to find some other reality for what you were doing, regardless of what the script intended. – *Tony Curtis*

Method acting is anything that gets you involved personally in the part, so that you can communicate in human terms with an audience. Despite all the obstacles, the American actor changed the acting of the world. – *Rod Steiger*

Allied Artists Corporation.
An American production company, more recently involved in TV, which flourished throughout the 30s and 40s as a purveyor of routine crime and comedy second features. Its policy was to put out the poorer product under the banner of its subsidiary, *Monogram Pictures Corporation*; the 'quality' AA product was little in evidence until the 50s, when films like *Love in the Afternoon*, *Friendly Persuasion* and *Al Capone* came from this stable. Meanwhile the Monogram films, boasting such attractions as Frankie Darro, the East Side Kids, the Bowery Boys, Bela Lugosi and Charlie Chan, had their faithful following, and in France attracted highbrow cinéastes to such an extent that Jean-Luc Godard dedicated his film *A Bout de Souffle* to Monogram.

Amalgamated Dynamics, Inc.
Visual effects and creature design company established in 1988 by Tom Woodruff, Jnr, and Alec Gillis, who formerly worked with Stan WINSTON. Woodruff played a monster in *Monster Squad* 87, and the title role in *Pumpkinhead* 88.

Tremors 90. Death Becomes Her (AA) 92. Alien 3 (AAN) 92. Demolition Man 93. Wolf 94. The Santa Clause 94. Tremors 2: Aftershocks 95. Mortal Kombat 95. Jumanji 95. Michael 96. Alien: Resurrection 97. Starship Troopers 97. The X Files Movie 98, etc.

American International Pictures.
Independent production company founded in 1955 by Samuel Z. ARKOFF and James H. NICHOLSON. After a profitable splurge of Z pictures churned out mainly by Roger Corman the company began to set its sights on the big time. In 1980 the ailing company was taken over by Filmways, which in 1982 was in its turn taken over by Orion.

The Archers.
British production company set up in 1943 by Michael POWELL and Emeric PRESSBURGER. Its films were produced, directed and written by the pair. The partnership lasted until 1956.

Book: 1985, *Arrows of Desire* by Ian Christie.

■ The Silver Fleet 43. *The Life and Death of Colonel Blimp* 43. The Volunteer 43. A Canterbury Tale 44. I Know Where I'm Going 45. *A Matter of Life and Death* 46. *Black Narcissus* 47. The End of the River 47. *The Red Shoes* 48. The Small Back Room 49. Gone to Earth 50. The Elusive Pimpernel 50. The Tales of Hoffman 51. Oh Rosalinda! 55. The Battle of the River Plate 56. Ill Met by Moonlight 56.

Associated British
was the only British complex of companies which had power comparable to that of the RANK Organization. Its history is tied up with Elstree Studios, originally owned by British International Pictures, which after many mergers emerged as Associated British in 1933. The men involved in the story are producer Herbert Wilcox, John Maxwell, a lawyer who turned film distributor and later founded the ABC cinema chain, and J. D. Williams, a wealthy exhibitor. Distribution was arranged through Pathé Pictures, which became a powerful partner. Elstree was the first British studio to wire for sound (*Blackmail*) and the first to produce a bilingual talkie (*Atlantic*). Throughout the thirties it turned out fifteen films a year, usually unambitious but competent; and unmistakably British. In 1940 a great number of shares were sold to Warner Brothers, and in 1956 the distribution arm became known as Warner-Pathé. Other associated companies include Pathé News, Pathé Laboratories, Pathé Equipment, and ABC Television. In 1969, after several years of comparative inactivity, the complex was taken over by EMI. In the 80s Cannon took over all the companies, but promptly sold the library to Jerry Weintraub.

Boreham Wood.
A British studio fourteen miles north of London, a site originally chosen by John M. East (1860–1924), a stage and silent screen actor. It opened in 1914 as Neptune Films, which folded in 1921; the stages were later taken over by Ideal, Rock, British National, and Associated Television. MGM and ABPC also had studios in nearby Elstree.

Bray Studios
became the home of Hammer Films in the late 40s, with many of its horror movies being shot in the grounds and in its mansion, Down Place, which dated from the 17th century. After Hammer ceased production in the late 60s, the studios continued to provide facilities for various films and television series.

British Lion Film Corporation.
A film production company of the 20s which, in the 30s, became mainly a distributor of cheap American product but was revived after World War II by the control of Alexander Korda, then by Michael Balcon, the Boulting Brothers and Frank Launder and Sidney Gilliat. It merged in 1976 with EMI.

Carolco.
American production company founded by Mario Kassar and Andrew Vajna in 1982 and noted for its big-budget approach to film-making. Vajna left later to found another production company, Cinergi. Carolco filed for bankruptcy in 1995 and its assets were sold to Twentieth Century-Fox.

First Blood 82. Rambo: First Blood Part Two 85. Angel Heart 87. Red Heat 88. Total Recall 90. Terminator 2: Judgment Day 91. Basic Instinct 91. Cliffhanger 93. CutThroat Island 95, etc.

Castle Rock Entertainment.
Hollywood production company co-founded by director Rob Reiner. Now a subsidiary of the Turner Broadcasting System, it has plans to become a distributor also.

Children's Film Foundation.
British company formed in 1951 to produce and distribute specially devised entertainment films for children's Saturday matinées. Sponsored by trade organizations.

Cine Liberación
was a radical film collective founded in Argentina in the late 60s by Fernando SOLANAS and Octavio GETINO. Its manifesto, *Toward a Third Cinema*, argued for a cinema based on collective, and even clandestine, production, distribution that involved its audience in discussion of the film and the issues raised, and opposition to the country's military dictatorship. (The first two cinemas were defined as the Hollywood studio system and the *auteur* approach.) The two founders put their theories into practice in *The Hour of the Furnaces* 68, a revolutionary documentary clandestinely distributed in Argentina, while a third member of the group, Gerardo Vallejo, made *El Camino hacia la Muerte del Viejo Reales* 70, about three years he spent with a rural family.

Cinecittà.
Large film studios in Rome, built in 1935, that have been at the centre of the Italian film industry and have also housed such international blockbusters as *Ben Hur* 59 and *Cleopatra* 63.

Cineguild.
A short-lived British production company set up in 1943 by David LEAN, Ronald NEAME and Anthony HAVELOCK-ALLAN following their success working together on Noël COWARD's *In Which We Serve*. After filming versions of Coward's plays, the trio moved on to create classic adaptations of two of DICKENS's novels. Associated with the Rank Organization, the company came to an end when Rank cut back on its production plans in 1949.

This Happy Breed 44. Blithe Spirit 45. *Brief Encounter* 45. *Great Expectations* 46. *Oliver Twist* 48. The Passionate Friends 49. Madeleine 50, etc.

Columbia Pictures.
American production and distribution company long considered one of the 'little two' (the other being Universal) against the 'big five' (MGM, RKO, Fox, Warner and Paramount). Columbia originated with one man, Harry Cohn, who founded it in 1924 after a career as a salesman and shorts producer. Throughout the 30s and 40s he turned out competent co-features and second features, apart from prestige pictures such as the Capra comedies and an ill-fated Kramer deal; he was also prepared to spend big money on certainties such as Rita Hayworth and *The Jolson Story*. From the late 40s, with films like *All the King's Men*, *Born Yesterday* and *From Here to Eternity*, the company began to pull itself into the big-time, and when Cohn died in 1958 it was one of the leaders of international co-production, with such major films to its credit as *On the Waterfront* and *The Bridge on the River Kwai*, with *Lawrence of Arabia* and *A Man For All Seasons* to come. It also produces and distributes TV films through its subsidiary Screen Gems (Columbia Television). In 1990, the Japanese company Sony paid $3.4 billion for the company. Peter Guber and Jon Peters were installed to run the organization, but Peters soon left to resume life as an independent producer. Since then, the studio has had mixed fortunes. It has had moderate successes, such as *A League of Their Own*, *A Few Good Men*, *In The Line of Fire* and *Philadelphia*, but it also had many misses, culminating in the disaster of *The Last Action Hero* starring Arnold Schwarzenegger, which turned out to be not the expected blockbuster but a dismal flop. In 1994 Peter Guber followed Jon Peters' example and quit to become an independent producer. Many of its recent films were less successful than expected, including *City Hall*, with Al Pacino, *Cable Guy*, with the seemingly impregnable Jim Carrey, *Striptease* with Demi Moore, and *Multiplicity* with Michael Keaton in several roles. Lisa Henson, president of Columbia, and Marc Platt, president of TriStar, were among the executives who left the company in 1996. Under John Calley, who joined the studio from MGM in 1996, it has enjoyed better times. In 1997, Sony announced box-office revenues of $1.3 billion, a figure reached in record time. The company absorbed its sister company TriStar in 1998. Its recent hits have included *Jerry Maguire*, *Anaconda*, *The Fifth Element*, *My Best Friend's Wedding*, *Men in Black*, *Airforce One*, *Starship Troopers*, and *As Good as It Gets*.

Books: 1967, *King Cohn* by Bob Thomas; *Hail Columbia* by Rochelle Larkin; 1989, *The Columbia Story* by Clive Hirschhorn; 1991, *The Columbia Checklist* by Leo D. Martin; 1996, *Hit & Run: How Jon Peters and Peter Guber Took Sony for a Ride in Hollywood* by Nancy Griffin & Kim Masters.

DEFA (Deutsche Film Aktiengesellschaft).
The East German party line film production company which absorbed UFA in 1946.

Denham.
An English village north of London where in 1936 Korda opened a huge film studio which was later taken over by the Rank Organisation but closed in the 50s so that production could be concentrated at Pinewood a few miles away. The studio was designed by American art director Jack OKEY. Originally intended to be relatively small, with three sound stages, it grew under construction to have seven sound stages and to be the best-equipped studio in Europe; but it was too large to be profitable in the long term.

DreamWorks SKG.
Hollywood studio set up in 1994 by Steven SPIELBERG, Jeffrey KATZENBERG and David GEFFEN. Its plans to set up the first fully electronic studios have been held up by an environmental dispute. Its first releases were lacklustre, and it was not until 1998 that it enjoyed hits, with Spielberg's *Saving Private Ryan* and the computer-animated feature *Antz*. So far, the studio has stuck to offering familiar Hollywood fare, and most of its ambitions appear to be channelled into challenging Disney's dominance of animated features.

Ealing Studios
In its heyday in the 40s and 50s this famous little studio in suburban west London was the independent home of scores of well-paced comedies featuring the likes of Will Hay and George Formby, and from 1948 on aspired a little higher, to quiet comedies of the English character, usually featuring a downtrodden group who rebelled against authority. The resulting films, including *The Lavender Hill Mob*, *Whisky Galore!* and *The Titfield Thunderbolt*, became known the world over. The credit for these films is largely due to Michael BALCON as impresario, and often to T. E. B. CLARKE as writer and Alec GUINNESS as actor; but the results were less happy when the studio tackled epic themes such as *Scott of the Antarctic* and *The Cruel Sea*, though it certainly brought off non-comic subjects like *Dead of Night* and *Mandy*. The studios were bought by the BBC in 1955, when Balcon put up a plaque: 'Here films were made projecting Britain and the British character.' The BBC sold them in 1992 to a film company which went into receivership, and the studios were acquired as a home for the National Film and Television School, though continuing to provide production facilities. In 1998 the School decided it needed premises near London and put the studio up for sale.

Books: 1977 (revised 1995), *Ealing Studios* by Charles Barr; 1981, *Forever Ealing* by George Perry; 1983, *Projecting Britain* edited by David Wilson was a collection of Ealing posters.

Come On George 39. Let George Do It 40. Convoy 40. Sailors Three 40. The Ghost of St Michael's 41. The Black Sheep of Whitehall 42. The Foreman Went to France 42. The Goose Steps Out 42. Went the Day Well? 43. They Came to a City 44. Champagne Charlie 44. *Dead of Night* 45. The Captive Heart 46. The Overlanders 46. Nicholas Nickleby 47. *It Always Rains on Sunday* 47. Scott of the Antarctic 48. Passport to Pimlico 49. *Whisky Galore!* 49. *Kind Hearts and Coronets* 49. The Blue Lamp 50. *The Lavender Hill Mob* 51. *The Man in The White Suit* 51. Mandy 52. The Cruel Sea 53. *The Ladykillers* 55. Dunkirk 58, etc.

❝ Everything about Ealing was defiantly small, and glorified the small at the expense of the big, the conventional, the pompous. – *Peter Ustinov*

Elstree Studios.
Production complex at Borehamwood, north of London, started in the 20s by British International, which later became ASSOCIATED BRITISH. After many vicissitudes the facilities and library passed into the hands of Thorn-EMI, who sold out in the 80s to Cannon, who sold off the library to Weintraub. The studio was deemed unprofitable and shut down in 1993, but went back into production in 1996 after it was bought by Hertsmere Council.

Book: 1982, *Elstree, the British Hollywood* by Patricia Warren.

Essanay.
A production company formed in 1907 by G. K. Spoor and G. M. Anderson (S and A). Mainly remembered for enormous output of early westerns and for Chaplin's first comedies.

Famous Players.
A production company founded by Adolph Zukor in New York in 1912, following his success in distributing Sarah Bernhardt in *Queen Elizabeth*. The motif was 'famous players in famous plays' which could not work too well as the films were silent; but the tag caught on and the company did well enough. It was later absorbed into Paramount.

First National
was a Hollywood company founded in 1917. During the next 12 years it was very active, with films featuring Chaplin, Pickford, Milton Sills and Richard Barthelmess. In 1929 it was taken over by Warner Brothers, who however kept the name going for certain product until the mid-30s.

Free Cinema.
A term applied to their own output by a group of British documentarists of the 50s, e.g. Lindsay Anderson, Karel Reisz. Their aim was to make 'committed' films which cared about the individual and the significance of the everyday. The resulting films were not always better than those produced by professional units with more commercial intent. The most notable were *O Dreamland*, *Momma Don't Allow*, *The March to Aldermaston*, *Every Day Except Christmas* and *We Are the Lambeth Boys*, the two latter films being sponsored by commercial firms.

❝ As film-makers we believe that:
No film can be too personal.
The image speaks. Sound amplifies and comments. Size is irrelevant.
Perfection is not an aim.
An attitude means a style. A style means an attitude.
– *statement of belief, signed by the members of Free Cinema and written by Lindsay Anderson in 1956*

Gainsborough.
A British film company of the 30s, associated with costume drama and Aldwych farces. Subsequently merged with Rank. Its trademark showed actress Glennis Lorrimer as Mrs Siddons in Thomas Gainsborough's portrait, turning to smile at the audience. She was the daughter of Harry Ostrer, co-founder of the company.

Group Theatre.
A left-wing company founded in New York in 1931 by Harold Clurman, Cheryl Crawford and Lee Strasberg, it fostered and encouraged many talents who went on to have careers in Hollywood, though some were later damaged by blacklisting in the 50s. Those involved included writer Clifford Odets, and Luther Adler, Lee J. Cobb, Morris Carnovsky, Frances Farmer, John Garfield, Elia Kazan, Robert Lewis, Ruth Nelson, Franchot Tone, and Sylvia Sidney. Two other members, Stella ADLER and Sanford MEISNER, both became influential teachers from the 40s. The Group Theatre was disbanded in 1940.

Book: 1945, *The Fervent Years* by Harold Clurman.

See also: The ACTORS' STUDIO.

Group 3.
A British production company set up in 1951 by the National Film Finance Corporation. In charge were John Baxter, John Grierson and Michael Balcon, and their aim was to make low-budget films employing young talent. The venture was regarded with suspicion by the trade, and the results were not encouraging – a string of mildly eccentric comedies and thrillers lucky to get second-feature circuit bookings. Some of the titles: *Judgement Deferred*, *Brandy for the Parson*, *The Brave Don't Cry*, *You're Only Young Twice*, *The Oracle*, *Laxdale Hall*, *Time Gentlemen Please*.

Hammer Films.
British production company set up in 1947 which gained fame and fortune from its cycle of horror films, beginning in 1955 with *The Quatermass Experiment/The Creeping Unknown*. It revived the Frankenstein myth with *The Curse of Frankenstein* 56, and followed it with the first of its Dracula series a year later, making stars of Christopher Lee and Peter Cushing. The company grew out of Exclusive Films, a distribution company formed by Will Hammer and Enrique Carreras, a Spaniard who had opened cinemas in London in 1913. Enrique's son, Sir James Carreras, and his grandson Michael, were the main forces behind Hammer's success, together with Hammer's son Tony Hinds, who produced and wrote scripts under the name of John Elder, and director Terence Fisher. Hammer announced its return to film production in 1994, planning to remake some of its previous successes. Among the films in development were *The Day the Earth Caught Fire*, to be directed by Renny Harlin, *The Devil Rides Out*, *The Quatermass Xperiment* and *Vlad the Impaler*. In 1997, British investors, including Charles Saatchi, bought a 50 per cent stake in the company for $9m, with plans to use the brand name in theme parks, restaurants and video games, and to remake old movies, including *The Day the Earth Caught Fire* and *Quatermass and the Pit*. A series of short animated horror films for children's television, *Hammer Horror Zone*, appeared in 1998.

Book: 1973, *The House of Horror* edited by Allen Eyles, Robert Adkinson and Nicholas Fry.

HandMade Films.
British production company formed by Denis O'Brien and former Beatle George Harrison. Among its successes have been *Monty Python's Life of Brian* 79, *The Long Good Friday* 80, *Time Bandits* 81, *A Private Function* 84, *Mona Lisa* 86, and *Withnail and I* 87.

Hecht-Hill-Lancaster:
see HECHT-LANCASTER.

Hecht-Lancaster
was an independent production company set up by former agent Harold HECHT and actor Burt LANCASTER. They had earlier formed Hecht-Norma (named after Lancaster's wife) to make films with Warner's. When that arrangement came to an end, Hecht-Lancaster was formed in 1954, to make films in partnership with United Artists, a studio then in decline which, anxious to secure Lancaster's services, agreed a deal that offered the two full financing and 75 per cent of the profits as well as other sweeteners. In 1956, it became Hecht-Hill-Lancaster with the addition, at Lancaster's insistence, of writer James HILL. The company was wound up in 1960, when the partners began to disagree more often and it was overspending after too rapid an expansion.

AS HECHT-NORMA: Kiss the Blood Off My Hands 48. The Flame and the Arrow 50. Ten Tall Men 51. The Crimson Pirate 52. His Majesty O'Keefe 54, etc.

AS HECHT-LANCASTER: Apache 54. Vera Cruz 54. The Kentuckian 55. Trapeze 56, etc.

AS HECHT-HILL-LANCASTER: Marty (AA) 55. *Sweet Smell of Success* 57. Run Silent, Run Deep 58. Separate Tables 58. The Devil's Disciple 59. The Unforgiven 60, etc.

Hecht-Norma:
see HECHT-LANCASTER.

IDHEC,
Institut des Hautes Études Cinématographiques, the leading French film school founded in Paris in the early 40s by Marcel L'HERBIER, where many French and foreign directors, producers, cinematographers and other production staff have studied. It closed in 1968, reopening two years later.

Industrial Light and Magic.
Special effects company formed by producer-director George LUCAS when making *Star Wars*. It was headed by John DYKSTRA, who later left to form his own special effects company. It is part of Lucas's production company Lucasfilm, which also includes a software company that produces computer games which are often based on the company's movies. Since its beginnings working on Lucas's own projects, it has established itself as the leading special effects company, employed by many other producers and directors, including Steven SPIELBERG.

Book: 1996, *Industrial Light and Magic: Into the Digital Realm* by Mark Cotta Vaz and Patricia Rose Duignan.

Star Wars (AA) 77. The Empire Strikes Back (AA) 80. Raiders of the Lost Ark (AA) 81. Dragonslayer (AAN) 81. Poltergeist 82. Star Trek II: The Wrath of Khan 82. E.T. – the Extra-Terrestrial (AA) 82. Return of the Jedi (AA) 83. Indiana Jones and the Temple of Doom (AA) 84. Star Trek III: The Search for Spock 84. The Neverending Story 84. Starman 84. The Goonies 85. Cocoon (AA) 85. Back to the Future 85. Explorers 85. Mishima 85. Young Sherlock Holmes (AAN) 85. Enemy Mine 85. Out of Africa 85. Howard the Duck 86. Star Trek IV: The Voyage Home 86. The Golden Child 86. The Witches of Eastwick 87. Innerspace 87. Batteries Not Included 87. Star Trek: The Next Generation 87. Empire of the Sun 87. Willow (AAN) 88. Who Framed Roger Rabbit? (AA) 88. Caddyshack II 88. Cocoon: The Return 88. The Last Temptation of Christ 88. The Burbs 89. Field of Dreams 89. Indiana Jones and the Last Crusade 89. Ghostbusters II 89. The Abyss (AA) 89. Back to the Future, Part II (AAN) 89. Always 89. Joe versus the Volcano 90. The Hunt for Red October 90. Back to the Future, Part III 90. Die Hard 2 90. Ghost 90. Switch 91. The Doors 91. Hudson Hawk 91. Backdraft (AAN) 91. The Rocketeer 91. Terminator 2: Judgement Day (AA) 91. Hook (AAN) 91. Memoirs of an Invisible Man 92. Death Becomes Her 92. Alive 92. The Meteor Man 93. Jurassic Park (AA) 93. Schindler's List 93. Rising Sun 93. Manhattan Murder Mystery 93. Baby's Day Out 94. Star Trek VII: Generations 94. Disclosure 94. The Flintstones 94. Forrest Gump (AA) 94. The Mask (AAN) 94. Congo 95. In the Mouth of Madness 95. Casper 95. Jumanji 95. Dragonheart (AAN) 96. Star Trek: First Contact 96. 101 Dalmatians 96. Mars Attacks! 96. Daylight 96. Twister 96. Mission: Impossible 96. Eraser 96. The Lost World: Jurassic Park (AAN) 97. Men in Black 97. Titanic 97. Speed 2: Cruise Control 97. Contact 97. Spawn 97. Starship Troopers 97. Flubber 97. Saving Private Ryan 98. Deep Impact 98. Small Soldiers 98. Meet Joe Black 98. Mercury Rising 98. Deep Rising 98. Mighty Joe Young 98. Jack Frost 98. Star Wars: The Phantom Empire 99, etc.

International Pictures.
Independent production company set up by Nunnally JOHNSON, William Goetz and Leo Spitz, formerly head of RKO, to distribute their films. In 1946 it was merged with Universal, which became Universal-International, and Goetz and Spitz took over the new company's production duties for a time.

Casanova Brown 44. The Woman in the Window 44. It's a Pleasure 45. Along Came Jones 45. Tomorrow Is Forever 46. The Stranger 46, etc.

Kalem.
An early American production company founded in 1907, taking its name from the initials of its three principals, George Klein, Sam Long and Frank Marion (K-L-M). Its most famous production is *From the Manger to the Cross* 12.

Keystone.
A company established in 1912 to produce comedies. Run by Mack Sennett, who also directed and edited most of the films, the company's early films featured Mabel Normand and created a fast and furious slapstick comedy. Its star performers included Fatty Arbuckle, Charlie Chaplin, Chester Conklin and Mack Swain. Sennett's second innovation came in 1915 when he introduced his Bathing Beauties to add some glamour. Sennett left Keystone in 1917 to work for Paramount and the company soon foundered without him.

Leavesden.
English studio complex sited on an aerodrome formerly owned by Rolls-Royce. It was first used in 1994 to house the James Bond movie *GoldenEye* and then bought, at a cost of £42.75m, by Third Millennium Studios, a Malaysian-owned company.

Lexington.
Production company set up in 1996 by producer-director Don BOYD to make distinctive British films.
Lucia 98.

Liberty Films.
Independent production company set up in 1946 by Frank CAPRA, William WYLER, George STEVENS and Sam Briskin. It made only one feature, *It's a Wonderful Life*, directed by Capra in 1946, before it ran into financial problems and was taken over by Paramount in 1947.

London Films.
Production company founded by Alexander KORDA and associated with his own major films of the 30s and later with other leading names operating under his banner. Others associated with the company included the Hungarian screenwriter Lajos BIRO and actor George GROSSMITH, who was its first chairman.

Mancunian Films.
A small but dauntless little British studio which throughout the 40s and early 50s earned its keep locally with a stream of wild farces starring home-grown music-hall talent: Frank Randle, Harry Korris, Sandy Powell, Tessie O'Shea, Betty Jumel, Nat Jackley, Josef Locke, Jewel and Warriss, Suzette Tarri and Norman Evans. Neither art nor craft entered into the matter.

Merton Park.
A small, independent south London studio. Founded in 1930 to make advertising films, it later housed Radio Luxembourg. Training films were made there during the war, and in the 50s it turned to the production of Edgar Lustgarten's *Scotland Yard* shorts, the Edgar Wallace supports, and *Scales of Justice*. It closed in the mid-60s.

Metro-Goldwyn-Mayer.
For many years the undoubted leader of the industry, this famous American production company has lately suffered most from the lack of 'front office' control and the proliferation of independent productions: now that it doesn't own the racecourse, it can't seem to pick the winners. The company stems from Loew's Inc., an exhibiting concern which in 1920 bought into Metro Pictures, which then produced two enormous money-spinners, *The Four Horsemen of the Apocalypse* and *The Prisoner of Zenda*. In 1924 Metro was merged with the Goldwyn production company (though Samuel Goldwyn himself promptly opted out and set up independently); and the next year Louis B. Mayer Pictures joined the flourishing group to add further power. Mayer himself became studio head and remained the dominant production force for over twenty-five years. Ideas man and executive producer in the early years was young Irving Thalberg, whose artistic flair provided a necessary corrective to Mayer's proletarian tastes, and who, before his death in 1936, had established a lofty pattern with such successes as *Ben Hur*, *The Big Parade*, *Anna Christie*, *Grand Hotel*, *The Thin Man*, *David Copperfield* and *Mutiny on the Bounty*, and stars like Garbo, Gable, Beery, Lionel Barrymore, Joan Crawford, John Gilbert, Lon Chaney, William Powell, Jean Harlow, Spencer Tracy, Lewis Stone, Nelson Eddy, Jeanette MacDonald, Laurel and Hardy and the Marx Brothers. (MGM's motto was in fact 'more stars than there are in heaven . . .') The success story continued through the 40s with *Goodbye Mr Chips*, Greer Garson, *The Wizard Of Oz*, Judy Garland, the Hardy Family, Gene Kelly and Esther Williams. Such continuity of product is a thing of the past, but MGM keep its end up in the 60s and 70s with occasional big guns like *Dr Zhivago*, *Where Eagles Dare* and *Network;* while reissues of *Gone with the Wind*, which it did not produce, kept the image of Leo the Lion fresh on cinema screens. In the 70s MGM gave up movie-making to concentrate on its huge Las Vegas hotel. A comeback attempt failed, and it was taken over by United Artists and Ted Turner. The 80s were a troubled time for the new MGM-UA; production fell and many of the films were lacklustre. There were some successes: *My Favorite Year*, *Moonstruck*, *A Fish Called Wanda* (MGM), *Rainman* (UA) and *Rocky III* (UA) and its sequels, as well as some failures: *Yes Giorgio*, an attempt to make a star of opera singer Luciano Pavarotti, and *2010*, a poor sequel to *2001: A Space Odyssey*. At the beginning of the 90s, the situation worsened as MGM was taken over by Italian Giancarlo Paretti, of Pathé Communications, to become MGM-Pathé. But Paretti turned out to lack the necessary financial resources, and legal complications between him and his bankers were not sorted out until mid-1992, when the company was auctioned off to its biggest creditor, Crédit Lyonnais of Paris. The dispute had held up production plans, but the future looked brighter as Alan Ladd Jnr, former president of Twentieth Century-Fox, became MGM's chairman and CEO. Ladd left in mid-1993, to be replaced by Frank Mancuso, former chairman and CEO of Paramount. Under him, its fortunes revived with such hits as *GoldenEye* and *The Birdcage*. Credit Lyonnais, the French bank, put it up for sale in mid-1996, when the studio was bought for $1.3 billion by a group headed by Mancuso, with finance coming from Kirk Kerkorian and the Australian television company Seven Network. Its progress has remained unpredictable; the long-term aim seems to be a merger with, or takeover of, a distribution company. In 1997 few films were in production; those that were released included the dull family film *Zeus and Roxanne*, about dolphins, and *Turbulence*, a disaster movie that did poor business. Its one critical success was *Ulee's Gold*, with Peter Fonda, but that earned little more than $4m at the US box-office. In 1998 it scored with its James Bond movie, *Tomorrow Never Dies*, but its flops included *Disturbing Behavior*, *Species 2* and *Dirty Work*. It had ambitious plans for 1999, including the release of around a dozen films, involving such stars as Arnold Schwarzenegger, Richard Gere and Robert De Niro.

Books: 1991, *Fade Out* by Peter Bart details MGM's collapse in the 80s. 1992, *When the Lion Roars* by Peter Hay. *The MGM Story* by John Douglas Eames is an excellent illustrated film-by-film history of the studio 1924–89.

❝ Beautiful pictures for beautiful people. – *Louis B. Mayer*

MGM was my mother and father, mentor and guide, my all-powerful and benevolent crutch. – *June Allyson*

Mayer's Ganz Mispochen (Mayer's whole family). – *Anon*

More stars than there are in the heavens. – *publicity slogan coined by Howard Dietz*

Minerva Films.
A British production company set up in 1920 by Leslie Howard, C. Aubrey Smith, Adrian Brunel, A. A. Milne, and Nigel Playfair. Its shareholders included H. G. Wells. It made four comedy shorts, directed by Brunel from Milne's stories, before running out of money.

Miramax Films
is a distribution and production company founded in 1979 by Bob and Harvey Weinstein. It first became noted for its ability to attract audiences to foreign art-house and American independent films such as *Pelle the Conqueror*, *Cinema Paradiso*, *sex, lies and videotape*, and *The Crying Game*. After a decade of success as a distributor, in 1989 it also began to produce films. In 1993 the Disney company acquired it for $100m. Recent successes have included *Good Will Hunting*, the horror movies *Scream* and *Scream 2*, and *Sliding Doors*.

Monogram Pictures:
see ALLIED ARTISTS.

New Line Cinema Corporation
was founded in 1967 by Robert SHAYE and began as a distributor of movies for college audiences. It moved into production later, and had its greatest hits with two film series, *A Nightmare on Elm Street*, which began in 1984, and *Teenage Mutant Ninja Turtles*, which became one of the most commercially successful independent movies following its release in 1990, and spawned two sequels. In 1991, Fine Line Features was formed, catering for more adult tastes, and also had critical successes with *My Own Private Idaho* 92, *The Player* 92, *Menace II Society* 93, and *Short Cuts* 93. In 1993 the companies were taken over by Ted TURNER. Since then, major hits have been scored with *The Mask* 94, *Dumb and Dumber* 94, *Seven* 95 (which took more than $320m around the world), and *Mortal Kombat* 95, which took around $120m. But in 1996 the companies had a series of flops, including *Long Kiss Goodnight*, which earned not much more than the $25m spent on marketing it, *The Island of Dr Moreau* (cost: $50m; US earnings: $28m), and *Last Man Standing*, which took less than half of its $57m cost. More recently, it has done better with such hits as the Jackie Chan film *Rush Hour* and the vampire movie *Blade*.

Oberhausen Group
was a collection of 26 young West German film-makers who, at the Short Film Festival at Oberhausen in 1962, announced the birth of a new German cinema: 'We declare our intention of creating the new German feature film. This new film needs new freedoms: freedom from influence by commercial partners, freedom from domination by special interest groups. We have concrete artistic, formal, and economic conceptions about the production of the new German film. We are collectively prepared to bear the economic risks. The old film is dead. We believe in the new.' The signatories included Alexander KLUGE and Edgar REITZ. It was followed in 1967 by the Mannheim Declaration, also signed by Kluge and Reitz, among others, which noted 'Six years have passed since the Oberhausen Declaration. The renewal of German film has not yet taken place', and called again for that renewal.

Paramount Pictures Corporation
was basically the creation of Adolph ZUKOR, a nickelodeon showman who in 1912 founded Famous Players, with the intention of presenting photographed versions of stage successes. In 1914 W. W. Hodkinson's Paramount Pictures took over distribution of Famous Players and Lasky products, and in the complex mergers which resulted, Zukor came out top man. Through the years his studio more than any other gave a family atmosphere, seldom producing films of depth but providing agreeable light entertainment with stars like Valentino, Maurice Chevalier, the Marx Brothers, Mary Pickford, Claudette Colbert, Bob Hope, Bing Crosby, Dorothy Lamour, Alan Ladd, and directors like Lubitsch, de Mille and Wilder. Notable films include *The Sheik*, *The Covered Wagon*, *The Ten Commandments* (both versions), *Trouble in Paradise*, *The Crusades*, *Union Pacific*, the Road films, *Going My Way*, *The Greatest Show on Earth*, etc. In recent years, since Zukor's retirement, the company had many difficulties, but was helped by a takeover by Gulf and Western Industries which spurred the commercial instinct, and produced two enormous winners in *Love Story* and *The Godfather*, followed in 1977 by *Saturday Night Fever*, in 1978 by *Grease*, in 1979 by *Star Trek* and in 1981 by *Raiders of the Lost Ark*. The latter's two sequels, *Indiana Jones and the Temple of Doom* and *Indiana Jones and the Last Crusade*, were box-office successes in 1984 and 1989 respectively. *Beverly Hills Cop* 84 and its sequel in 1987 also brought box-office rewards and established Eddie Murphy as a star, while *Top Gun* was among the top films of 1986, as were, in their respective years, *The Hunt for Red October* 90, *The Addams Family* 91 and *Wayne's World* 92. But all that paled besides the phenomenal success of *Forrest Gump* in 1994, a film that became the company's biggest box-office success and among the top ten grossing films so far produced. In mid-1994 the studio was taken over by Viacom, an entertainment conglomerate that includes MTV, Nickelodeon and Showtime television channels. The company enjoyed great success with *Forrest Gump*, but its following films were less popular; while *Mission: Impossible* was a hit, the studio had to write off some $30m when *The Phantom* flopped at the box-office. The studio, along with Twentieth Century-Fox, enjoyed a spectacular success with *Titanic*, a film that went wildly over budget before becoming a worldwide success, taking more than $1 billion at box-offices. The thriller *Face/Off* was also one of the hits of 1997, and, in 1998, *The Truman Show* was a critical and financial success.

Pinewood Studios,
seventeen miles northwest of London, was built in 1935 and opened in 1936 by a millionaire named Charles Boot as Britain's reply to Hollywood. It rapidly came under the control of the Rank Organisation, and its fortunes have fluctuated, but on the whole it has been fairly well used.

History published 1976: *Movies from the Mansion* by George Perry.

Pixar.
Computer animation company that created *Toy Story*, the first feature-length computer-generated film, and plans to make more. Founded by George LUCAS, it was bought by Steve Jobs, former head, and co-founder, of Apple Computers. *Toy Story* was directed by John LASSETER, and distributed by Walt Disney.

Polygram.
A subsidiary of the electronics company Philips, Polygram Filmed Entertainment was established in 1991, producing films through Propaganda, Interscope and the British company Working Title. In 1995, it acquired ITC Entertainment and set up an American distribution company. It also owns half of Gramercy Pictures with Universal. It was acquired in 1998, together with the remainder of the Polygram Group, by Seagram, whose interests include Universal Studios, and put up for sale. When no buyer for the company was forthcoming, Polygram Filmed Entertainment was absorbed by Universal.

Republic Pictures Corporation.
A small Hollywood production and distribution company founded in 1935 by a former tobacco executive named Herbert J. YATES, who had spent some years building up a film laboratory. Republic continued as a one-man concern, producing innumerable competently-made second-feature westerns and melodramas with such stars as Roy Rogers, Vera Hruba Ralston (Yates' wife), John Carroll, Constance Moore. The studio also churned out the majority of Hollywood's serials. Very occasionally there would be a major production such as *Rio Grande* or *The Quiet Man*. Production stopped in the mid-50s, when 'bread and butter' pictures were no longer needed, and the company's interests moved into TV.

RKO Radio Pictures Inc.
was for many years one of Hollywood's 'big five' production companies, with its own distribution arm. It started in 1921 as a joint enterprise of the Radio Corporation of America and the Keith-Orpheum cinema circuit. Despite severe financial vicissitudes, it struggled on for twenty-seven years, buoyed by a generally decent production standard; stars like Cary Grant, Katharine Hepburn, Wheeler and Woolsey, Leon Errol; individual films such as *Cimarron*, *King Kong*, *The Informer*, *Suspicion*, *Mr Blandings Builds His Dream House* and *Fort Apache;* and the participation of Goldwyn, Disney and Selznick, all released through RKO at its peak. In 1948 Howard HUGHES acquired a large share of the stock; but after a period of uncertainty RKO ceased production in 1953 and the studio was sold to Desilu TV.

A glossy book by Richard B. Jewell and Vernon Harbin, *The RKO Story*, came out in 1982 and was a valuable research tool.

Saturday Night Live.
The late-night US TV comedy series that began in 1975 has spawned several films based on the programme's characters, though only two so far have been successful. It has also provided a showcase for many comic talents who have gone on to movie careers, including Chevy CHASE, John BELUSHI, Dan AYKROYD, Bill MURRAY, Eddie MURPHY, Billy CRYSTAL, Martin SHORT, Jon LOVITZ, Damon WAYANS, Chris FARLEY, David SPADE and Chris ROCK.

The Blues Brothers 80. Wayne's World 92. Wayne's World 2 93. Coneheads 93. It's Pat 94. Stuart Saves His Family 95. Blues Brothers 2000 98, etc.

Silicon Graphics Inc.
is a computer company whose workstations are used extensively in the film industry to provide special effects in movies. *Toy Story*, the first computer-generated animated feature, was created on SGI computers. Other films such as *Men in Black*, *Jurassic Park*, *The Peacemaker*, *Starship Troopers*, *Alien: Resurrection* and the remake of *Flubber* also relied on SGI equipment.

Sony Pictures Entertainment
was formed in 1991, after the Japanese electronics company had bought COLUMBIA PICTURES and TRISTAR PICTURES from Coca-Cola in 1989. At the time, SPE's executives believed that it was an advantage to have two studios because it was difficult for any one company to produce and market more than a dozen or so movies a year. But in 1998, TriStar was merged into Columbia Pictures.

Tempean Films.
British production company founded by Monty BERMAN and Robert S. BAKER, who were active in the 40s and 50s making second features, mainly low-budget thrillers and horror movies.

Theatre Workshop
was a co-operative, populist, left-wing company formed in 1945, with Joan LITTLEWOOD as its director. After years of touring, in 1953 the company took over and transformed the derelict Theatre Royal in Stratford, East London, doing much to revolutionize British theatre in the process. Littlewood left the company for a time in the early

60s, and it had a sporadic existence thereafter, finally breaking up in 1974. Its plays dealing with working-class experience influenced the mood of British films of the 60s. Actors associated with the company included Avis BUNNAGE, Harry H. CORBETT, Howard GOORNEY, Stephen LEWIS, Murray MELVIN, Brian MURPHY and Maxwell SHAW. Among the writers it introduced to cinema were Brendan BEHAN and Shelagh DELANEY. Plays filmed, though few resembled the stage productions, included *A Taste of Honey* 61, *The Quare Fellow* 62, *Sparrows Can't Sing* 62, and *Oh, What a Lovely War* 69.

Book: 1981, *The Theatre Workshop Story* by Howard Goorney.

Triangle Film Corporation.

Company formed by D. W. Griffith, Thomas Ince, and Mack Sennett in 1915 to produce and release films made by the three directors, who left the company in 1917.

TriStar Pictures

was a movie production and distribution company founded in 1982 by CBS, the cable TV company Home Box Office, and Columbia Pictures. Columbia bought out CBS in 1985, and HBO also reduced its stake in the company. In 1987 TriStar was merged with Columbia to become Columbia Pictures Entertainment, although it retained its separate identity. In 1998 it was absorbed into Columbia Pictures.

Troma.

Company specializing in the production and distribution of low-budget exploitation movies, usually combining kitsch and gore, many produced and directed by the company's president, Lloyd KAUFMAN, and vice-president, Michael HERZ. It is best known for its *Toxic Avenger* series, which has spawned dolls and other novelty merchandising.

Squeeze Play! 80. Waitress! 82. Stuck on You 83. The First Turn-On! 84. The Toxic Avenger 84. Nuke 'em High 85. The Toxic Avenger: Part II 88. Troma's War 88. The Toxic Avenger III: The Last Temptation of Toxie 90. Def by Temptation 90. Class of Nuke 'em High II: Subhumanoid Meltdown 91. Sgt Kabukiman N.Y.P.D. 94, etc.

❝ When watching a Troma movie, you must not only suspend your disbelief: you must lock it up in a small iron crate and torture it. – *Lloyd Kaufman*

Although I feel as if I've been lucky on a few occasions, many of the movies in the Troma library are, to use a technical term, goat shit. – *Lloyd Kaufman*

Twentieth Century-Fox Film Corporation.

An American production and distribution company formed in 1935 by a merger of Joseph Schenck's Twentieth Century Pictures with William Fox's Fox Film Corporation. Fox had started in nickelodeon days as a showman, then a distributor.

Putting his profits into production, he started the careers of several useful stars including Theda Bara, and pioneered the Movietone sound-on-film process; but in the early 30s, after a series of bad deals, he lost power. The new company had Darryl F. Zanuck as production head from 1935 to 1952; he returned in 1962 as president after the resignation of Spyros Skouras, who had reigned from 1942. These two men are therefore largely responsible for the Fox image, which usually gave the impression of more careful budget-trimming and production-processing than did the films of the rest of the 'big five'. Fox's successful personality stars include Shirley Temple, Alice Faye, Don Ameche, Betty Grable and Marilyn Monroe; its best westerns include *The Big Trail*, *Drums along the Mohawk*, *My Darling Clementine* and *The Gunfighter*; in drama it can claim *What Price Glory?*, *Dante's Inferno*, *The Grapes of Wrath*, *How Green Was My Valley*, *The Ox Bow Incident*, *The Song of Bernadette*, *Wilson*, *The Snake Pit*, and *Gentlemen's Agreement*. In 1953 Spyros Skouras successfully foisted the new screen shape, CinemaScope, on to world markets, but Fox have not used it with greater success than anyone else, their most elaborate 'spectaculars' being *The Robe*, *There's No Business Like Show Business*, *The King and I*, *South Pacific*, *The Diary of Anne Frank*, *The Longest Day*, *Cleopatra*, *Those Magnificent Men in Their Flying Machines*, *The Sound of Music*, *Star!*, *Hello Dolly*, and *Tora! Tora! Tora!*

On his return, Darryl Zanuck appointed his son Richard as vice-president in charge of production and, in 1965, the company enjoyed one of its greatest successes with the musical *The Sound of Music*. Darryl and Richard Zanuck, who went on to become a successful independent producer, left at the beginning of the 70s after a succession of big-budget flops (*Hello Dolly* and *Tora! Tora! Tora!* among them). The fashion for disaster films brought the company successes with *The Towering Inferno* (made with Warners) and *The Poseidon Adventure*. Alan Ladd Jnr became President in the mid-70s, leaving in 1979 to become an independent producer; during his time Fox hit the jackpot in 1977 with *Star Wars* and its sequels. In 1981, the company was bought by oil billionaire Marvin Davis; he in turn sold it in 1985 to publishing tycoon Rupert Murdoch, who took over personal control following the resignation of its chairman and CEO Barry Diller in 1992. In recent years, the company has enjoyed hits with *Big*, *Aliens*, *Die Hard* and *Die Hard 2*, *Sleeping with the Enemy* and *Home Alone*, the most financially successful of comedies. In 1996, in a summer of blockbuster movies, it produced the biggest hit of the year: *Independence Day*, which took more than $286m at the US box-office and more than $435m worldwide. The company had a poor 1997: two blockbusters, *Volcano* and *Speed 2: Cruise Control*, did not do as well as expected, and James Cameron was going way over budget with *Titanic*; its greatest success came with the re-release of the 20-year-old *Star Wars*, which went on to become the fifth most popular film at the box-office, auguring well for its prequel, *Star Wars: The Phantom Empire*, which was among the most eagerly awaited releases of 1999. *Titanic* proved to be a massive hit, and the company had surprise hits in 1998 with the comedies *Doctor Dolittle* and *There's Something about Mary*.

❝ Leaving Fox was like leaving home at 28; I'd been there since I was 16. – *Linda Darnell*

Two Cities Films.

A British company set up in the early days of World War II by the expatriate Italian Filippo del Giudice. It was responsible for many of Britain's most famous films, including *In Which We Serve*, *The Way Ahead*, *Henry V*, *Blithe Spirit* and *Odd Man Out*.

UFA.

Universum Film Aktien Gesellschaft: the main German film production company since 1917, owning its studio and linked in the 20s with Paramount and MGM. In the 30s it was brought under state control and in the 40s, with the end of the war, it ceased to exist.

United Artists Corporation

was founded in 1919 by Mary Pickford, Douglas Fairbanks, Charlie Chaplin and D. W. Griffith, the object being to make and distribute their own and other people's quality product. Among the company's early successes were *His Majesty the American*, *Pollyanna* (the first film sold on a percentage basis), *Broken Blossoms*, *Way Down East*, and *A Woman of Paris*. In the mid-20s Joe Schenck was brought in to run the company, and he in turn gained Valentino, Goldwyn, Keaton and Swanson; but later all were bought out by various syndicates. Howard Hughes contributed *Hell's Angels* and *Scarface*, but in the 30s the UA product began to thin out, partly because the company was purely a distributor and financer of independent producers, without any studio of its own or any large roster of stars under contract. The hardest times, with only inferior product to sell, were between 1948 and 1953; but after that a new board of directors, through careful choice of product, fought its way back to the top; despite the defection of half its executives to Orion, UA was again riding high with *The Magnificent Seven*, *The Battle of Britain*, *Tom Jones*, *One Flew Over the Cuckoo's Nest*, *Rocky* and the James Bond films. The 80s however brought the 40-million-dollar calamity of *Heaven's Gate* (book: *Final Cut* by Steven Bach) and a takeover by MGM to become MGM-UA. Once MGM's problems were sorted out and the company was sold in a management buyout in 1996, studio executives began planning to spend more money than in the past, intending to make expensive films, such as the volcano disaster movie *Dante's Peak*, budgeted at more than $110m, and a costly remake of *King Kong*, to be produced, written and directed by Peter Jackson. The company, like its parent MGM, has been suffering from uncertainty and lack of direction. But its *The Man in the Iron Mask* gained from the backwash of the success of *Titanic*, since, like that massive hit, it also starred the hottest actor in Hollywood, Leonardo DiCaprio.

Book: 1986, *The United Artists Story* by Ronald Bergen.

❝ The lunatics have taken over the asylum. – *Robert Lord, 1919*

We maniacs had fun and made good pictures and a lot of money. In the early years United Artists was a private golf club for the four of us. – *Mary Pickford*

Universal Pictures

was founded in 1912 by Carl Laemmle, an exhibitor turned producer. Universal City grew steadily and included among its output many of the most famous titles of Von Stroheim, Valentino and Lon Chaney. In 1930 came *All Quiet on the Western Front*, and soon after *Dracula* and *Frankenstein*, the precursors of a long line of horror pictures. Laemmle lost power in the mid-30s and the studio settled down to be one of Hollywood's 'little two', producing mainly modest, low-budget co-features without too many intellectual pretensions. The Deanna Durbin series saved it from receivership, and there were occasional notable pictures: *Destry Rides Again*, *Hellzapoppin*, *Flesh and Fantasy*. The stars under contract were durable: Boris Karloff, Lon Chaney Jnr, Donald O'Connor, Abbott and Costello, Jeff Chandler, Audie Murphy. More ambition was noted in the 50s, when the era of the bread-and-butter picture was ended by TV. Decca Records gained a large measure of control, but in 1962 a merger gave the ultimate power to the Music Corporation of America, ex-agents and TV producers. The 1960s saw a steady resumption of prestige, with films like *Spartacus*, the Doris Day – Rock Hudson sex comedies, *Charade*, *The War Lord*, Ross Hunter's soapily sentimental but glossy remakes of Hollywood's choicest weepies, *Thoroughly Modern Millie*, *The Day of the Jackal*, *Earthquake*, *Airport* and *The Seven Per Cent Solution*. The company, now a division of MCA Inc. is currently one of Hollywood's most powerful sources of box-office films and television series, though its venture into 'enlightened' European production was fairly disastrous. In the 80s the company enjoyed its biggest-ever hit, *E.T. – the Extraterrestrial*, courtesy of Steven Spielberg, who had also scored for them in the mid-70s with *Jaws*. Spielberg also produced Universal's other big winners, *Back to the Future* and its sequels, while it enjoyed Oscar successes with *Out of Africa*. His contribution remained important to the company when his *Jurassic Park* was a monster hit around the world. Science fact also met with approval in *Apollo 13*, a story of a space flight that went wrong. The studio found success by recycling familiar subject-matter, such as the TV favourites *The Flintstones* and *Casper*, and an updating of the old Jerry Lewis comedy *The Nutty Professor*, which brought Eddie Murphy a much-needed hit. Its only box-office successes in 1997 were the disaster movie *Dante's Peak* and, especially, the comedy *Liar Liar*, starring Jim Carrey. The studio's more recent record has been poor. It announced a $65m loss for the third quarter of 1998, owing to the failure of its $100m-budgeted *Meet Joe Black*, starring Brad Pitt, *Babe: Pig in the City*, and Gus van Sant's remake of Alfred Hitchcock's *Psycho*. As a result, several top executives left the company.

Clive Hirschhorn's splendidly illustrated book *The Universal Story* (1983) is an excellent critical history. Also: 1991, *The Best of Universal* by Tony Thomas.

UPA (United Productions of America)

was a cartoon factory which in the early 50s received generous critical plaudits for a hundred or so shorts and even pushed the Disney studio into a more sophisticated style. Its creations included Mr Magoo, Gerald McBoing Boing and Pete Hothead, and it specialized in a stylish economy of line and in an appeal to a much higher intelligence bracket than any cartoon had aspired to in the past.

VGIK

is the acronym for the All-Union State Cinema Institute (Vsesoyuznyi Gosudarstvennyi Institut Kinematografii), the leading film school in Russia. Its founders in 1919 included Vladimir Gardin and Lev Kuleshov.

Vitagraph.

An early American production company which had great success but was taken over in the 20s by Warner's.

Walt Disney Productions,

the studio founded and controlled by Walt DISNEY, has dominated animated features since the release of the first, *Snow White and the Seven Dwarfs*, in 1937. The company began in Kansas City as Laugh-O-Gram films, with Disney in partnership with Ub IWERKS. Disney moved to Hollywood in the early 20s, and set up a studio with his brother Roy. After his death, its features declined in quality for a time, and many leading animators, including Don BLUTH, quit the studio in the late 70s over the issue of deteriorating standards. In the 90s, under the chairmanship of Michael EISNER, its animated films improved and the company had deserved hits with *Beauty and the Beast* 91, *Aladdin* 92, *The Lion King* 94, and *Toy Story* 95, which was the first computer-animated feature. Both *Beauty and the Beast* and *The Lion King* were turned into successful stage musicals. The studio's live-action films have continued to be bland family entertainment, many of them remakes of earlier movies, including *That Darn Cat*, *Flubber* and *The Parent Trap*, although it did have an unexpected success with the comic *George of the Jungle* in 1997. Other studios have challenged Disney's domination of animated features, including Don Bluth's, but so far without success. The strongest challenge has come from Jeffrey KATZENBERG, who left Disney to become a co-founder of the new Hollywood studio DREAMWORKS SKG. DreamWorks' computer-generated feature *Antz* was a hit in 1998, taking around $90m at the US box-office, but it had little effect on the success of Disney's similarly themed *A Bug's Life*, which was released later.

Warner Brothers Pictures Inc.

is a family affair started in 1923 by four American exhibitor brothers. After a very shaky start it soared to pre-eminence through their gamble on talking pictures in the shape of *The Jazz Singer* and *The Singing Fool*. Through the 30s and 40s the company kept its popularity through tough gangster films starring James Cagney, Edward G. Robinson and Humphrey Bogart, and musicals with Dick Powell and Ruby Keeler; and its prestige by exposés like *Confessions of a Nazi Spy* and *Mission to Moscow* and biographies of Zola, Pasteur, Ehrlich and Reuter. Other Warner stars included Bette Davis and Errol Flynn, both enormously popular with all classes. Warner films were not usually over-budgeted but contrived to look immaculate through solid production values and star performances. Since 1950 the company's product has been more variable, as deals have had to be done with independent producers, and there has been a patchy flirtation with TV; yet on the serious side directors like Kazan have been encouraged, popular taste is taken care of by spectaculars like *My Fair Lady* and *The Great Race*, and the company took a calculated risk (which paid off in spades) with *Who's Afraid of Virginia Woolf?* In the mid-60s came a merger with Seven Arts, and in 1969 the company was taken over by a conglomerate. In 1989 the company merged with the publishing group Time Inc. to become Time-Warner.

During the 80s the famous production company seemed to be kept solvent by Clint Eastwood toughies, although it had a success with the fast-paced action film *Lethal Weapon* and immediately repeated the process with satisfying results: the movie had reached its second sequel by 1992. *Gremlins*, a hit in 1984, begat *Gremlins II: The New Batch*, which did less well. Its dark fantasy *Batman* was the top box-office attraction of 1989, and *Batman Returns* became a hit in 1992. *Robin Hood: Prince of Thieves* was a surprise success in 1991. Fortunately, there has so far been no attempt to repeat it. The company also had a monumental flop with the costly *Hudson Hawk*, which brought Bruce Willis's career to a temporary halt. But the company was soon enjoying great success, with a succession of hit films, including *Batman Returns*, *Lethal Weapon 3*, *The Bodyguard*, *Sommersby* and *The Fugitive*. Time Warner is the world's largest media company, a title it briefly lost to the Walt Disney organization, and then regained when it took over Turner Broadcasting Systems for $7.3 billion in 1996. Its hits that year included *Twister* and *A Time to Kill*. Its blockbuster for 1997, *Batman and Robin*, was a disappointment, although it took more than $100m at the box-office and was the ninth most successful film of the year. But its thriller *LA Confidential* was among the critically acclaimed films of the year. *Lethal Weapon 4*, the latest instalment of the thriller series, was its biggest hit in 1998.

Various books have been published about its glory days, including: 1986, *Inside Warner Brothers 1935–51* by Rudy Behlmer (a collection of memos).

66 Working for Warner Brothers is like fucking a porcupine. It's a hundred pricks against one. – *Wilson Mizner*

I would rather take a fifty-mile hike than crawl through a book. I prefer to skip the long ones and get a synopsis from the story department. – *Jack Warner*

This studio has more suspensions than the Golden Gate Bridge. – *Humphrey Bogart*

Woodfall Films.
British production company set up in the late 50s by director Tony Richardson and playwright John Osborne together with financier Harry Saltzman (though it turned out he didn't actually have any money). They first produced a screen version of Osborne's *Look Back in Anger* 59. Productions that helped change the nature of British films included *The Entertainer* 60, *Saturday Night and Sunday Morning* 60, *A Taste of Honey* 61, *The Loneliness of the Long Distance Runner* 62, *Tom Jones* 63, *Girl with Green Eyes* 64, *The Knack* 65. Other productions included *One Way Pendulum* 65, *Mademoiselle* 66, *The Sailor from Gibraltar* 67, *Red and Blue* (short) 67, *Hamlet* 69, *Laughter in the Dark* 69, *Ned Kelly* 70, *Dead Cert* 74, *Joseph Andrews* 77.

5

Movie Talk – *An A–Z of Technical and Critical Terms*

'A' picture.

A term used to indicate the most important film in the days of double-feature programmes, one that used the talents of a studio's top actors, directors and technicians. The distinction between 'A' pictures and supporting films, or 'B' pictures, disappeared with the demise of double features in the 1950s.

above-the-line costs

refer to the expenses contracted before filming begins: on obtaining film rights, where necessary, and accounting for the cost of the principal talents involved, such as producer, screenwriter, director and actors.

above the title.

Credits that appear on posters or the screen before the title of a film. At one time, such billing was an indication of star status, though that no longer necessarily holds; these days it is more to do with deal-making and the massaging of egos than with the ability to draw an audience to a film. Only a few producers and directors, such as Cecil B. De Mille, Alfred Hitchcock and Steven Spielberg, have achieved above the title billing, and even fewer writers have managed it, of whom the most prominent is Stephen King.

abstract film.

One in which the images are not representational but fall into visually interesting or significant patterns: e.g. Disney's *Fantasia*, Norman McLaren's hand-drawn sound films, etc.

Academy Awards.

Merit prizes given annually since 1927 by the American Academy of Motion Picture Arts and Sciences. The award is in the form of a statuette known in the trade – for reasons variously explained – as Oscar, and each April the ABC network televises the award ceremonies as an increasingly pretentious spectacular: Johnny Carson in 1979 called it 'two hours of sparkling entertainment spread out over a four-hour show'. See Appendix for full list of awards.

Books: *The Academy Awards* by Paul Michael (1968), *Inside Oscar* by Mason Wiley and Damien Bona (1985), *60 Years of the Oscar* by Robert Osborne (1989), *The Oscars: The Secret History of Hollywood's Academy Awards* by Anthony Holden (1993), *The Academy Awards Handbook* by John Harkness (1994).

66 The Oscar means one thing – an added million-dollar gross for the picture. It's a big publicity contest. Oh, the voting is legitimate, but there's the sentimentality. One year when I was a candidate, when Elizabeth Taylor got a hole in her throat, I cancelled my plane. – *Shirley Maclaine*

In the myth of the cinema, Oscar is the supreme prize. – *Federico Fellini*

As you danced, you saw the most important people in Hollywood whirling past you. – *Joan Crawford at first Oscar ceremony*

The statuette is a perfect symbol of the picture business – a powerful athletic body clutching a gleaming sword, with half of his head, the part that holds his brains, completely sliced off. – *Frances Marion, 1928*

Academy Frame.

The standard film frame in a ratio of 4 to 3, more usually referred to as 1.33 to 1.

Academy Leader.

Regulation length of film attached to the front of a reel about to be projected, bearing a 'countdown' and various standard images to facilitate focusing.

accelerated motion.

An effect obtained by running the camera more slowly than usual: when the resulting film is projected at normal speed, the movements seem faster because they occupy fewer frames than would normally be the case. The opposite of SLOW MOTION.

ACE.

Initials that indicate membership of the American Cinema Editors, a professional society for film and TV editors.

acetate.

Another word for safety base, which replaced nitrate stock in the 50s and is much slower to burn.

acting

A short selection of attitudes.

Acting is like roller-skating. Once you know how to do it, it is neither stimulating nor exciting. – *George Sanders*

In Europe an actor is an artist. In Hollywood, if he isn't working, he's a bum. – *Anthony Quinn*

The secret of my success? I speak in a loud clear voice and try not to bump into the furniture. – *Alfred Lunt*

We who play, who entertain for a few years, what can we leave that will last? – *Ethel Barrymore*

Actors are cattle. – *Alfred Hitchcock* (NB. When attacked for this remark Hitch claimed he had been misquoted: what he really said was: 'Actors should be *treated* like cattle.')

Film acting is unquestionably a director's medium. – *Charles Chaplin* (NB. Chaplin used to advise his silent actors: 'Don't sell it. Remember they're *peeking* at you.')

Scratch an actor – and you'll find an actress. – *Dorothy Parker*

Acting is a question of absorbing other people's personalities and adding some of your own experience. – *Paul Newman*

Don't act – think! – *F.W. Murnau*

Actors and burglars work better at night. – *Cedric Hardwicke*

I always had one ear offstage, listening for the call from the bookie. – *Walter Matthau*

The only thing you owe the public is a good performance. – *Humphrey Bogart*

Joan Crawford is the only actress to read the whole script. Most actresses just read their own lines to find out what clothes they're going to wear. – *Anita Loos*

You spend all your life trying to do something they put people in asylums for. – *Jane Fonda*

The best actors in the world are those who feel the most and show the least. – *Jean-Louis Trintignant*

I'm afraid to look, because I'm probably awful. – *George Raft*

There are lots of methods. Mine involves a lot of talent, a glass, and some cracked ice. – *John Barrymore*

The main problem of the actor is not to let the audience go to sleep, then wake up and go home feeling they've wasted their money. – *Laurence Olivier*

Acting is a way to overcome your own inhibitions and shyness. The writer creates a strong, confident personality, and that's what you become – unfortunately, only for the moment. – *Shirley Booth*

The movies are the only business where you can go out front and applaud yourself. – *Will Rogers*

I learn the lines and pray to God. – *Claude Rains*

Talk low, talk slow, and don't say too much. – *John Wayne*

First wipe your nose and check your flies. – *Alec Guinness*

See also: THE METHOD.

action film

is one where movement and events, usually of a violent nature such as explosions, fist- and gunfights, take precedence over characterization and, increasingly, intelligible narrative.

action still.

A photograph of a scene as it actually appears in the film as opposed to one specially posed for publicity purposes. Sometimes called a frame blow-up. In TV, an 'action stills' programme has come to mean one consisting of still photographs given a semblance of life by camera movement.

ACTT.

The Association of Cinematograph, Television and Allied Technicians, a British trade union, founded 1931. Now renamed BECTU.

ADR

stands for Automatic Dialogue Replacement, the term used to describe the re-recording of dialogue to improve the quality of a soundtrack.

See also: LOOPING.

agent.

An intermediary who acts on behalf of talent and takes a percentage of the rewards. Agents played little part in the early years of Hollywood when studios controlled the system and signed actors to long-term contracts. With the decline of the studios, agents became more powerful by acting as packagers, putting together director, stars and script and selling the result to the studios. A few, such as Irving 'Swifty' LAZAR, became almost as famous as the stars they represented; the power became concentrated not with individuals but with the large agencies who were able to put together deals in which they represented all the major talent involved. William Morris founded the talent agency named after him in 1898, and in the 50s and 60s, as the studios relinquished control, represented many of Hollywood's leading stars and directors. Its later rivals include International Creative Management (ICM), founded in 1975 from a merger of Creative Management Associates and International Famous Agency, and Creative Artists Agency (CAA), also founded in 1975. Michael OVITZ, until 1995 head of CAA, was said to be the most important man in Hollywood, and agents have even moved on to run studios. Agents were partly blamed for the rising cost of Hollywood movies because many were too concerned with increasing their client's income, and therefore their own, at the expense of sound economic film-making. Some also became producers, though few succeeded.

œ

Only in Hollywood will an agent betray a client one year and cozy up to him the next as if nothing had happened. – *David McClintick*

~When agent Leland Hayward married his client Margaret Sullavan, a friend cabled him: 'Congratulations on getting the other ninety per cent.'

66 An agent is a guy who is sore because an actor gets ninety per cent of what he makes. – *Alva Johnston*

Agfacolor.

German multilayer colour process, widely used in Europe and basically the same as Russian Sovcolor and American Anscocolor (which became Metrocolor). Noted for softness and often lack of sharpness.

aka.

A 70s abbreviation for 'also known as'.

'also known as':

see AKA.

American Film Institute.

Government-sponsored body rather belatedly founded in 1967. Based in Washington, its comprehensive catalogue will provide full detail on every American film ever made. Its first director was George Stevens, Jnr.

See Section 7 for its choice of best American films.

American Society of Cinematographers:

see ASC.

anaglyph.

A simple system for making three-dimensional films. The two slightly differing images are printed in different colours, usually red and green, and viewed through similarly coloured lenses to sort them out into a single image. (The alternative is to use polaroid, which distinguishes the two images through lenses invisibly stripped in different directions.)

anamorphic lens.

One which, in a camera, 'squeezes' a wide picture on to standard film; in a projector, 'unsqueezes' the image to fill a wide screen (usually of a 2.45:1 aspect ratio); e.g. CinemaScope, Panavision, TohoScope, HammerScope, WarnerScope, DyaliScope, which are not essentially different from each other.

See also: ASPECT RATIO.

animation.

The filming of static drawings, puppets or other objects in sequence so that they give an illusion of movement. Sometimes called 'stop-frame animation' because only one frame of film is exposed at a time.

Leading figures in the history of animation include Winsor McKAY, who in 1909 introduced Gertie the Dinosaur, Emile COHL, Len LYE, Max FLEISCHER, Walt DISNEY, the UPA Group, Norman McLAREN, William HANNA and Joe BARBERA, HALAS AND BATCHELOR, Ralph BAKSHI and Richard WILLIAMS.

Best books on the subject are *The Technique of Film Animation* by John Halas and Roger Manvell; *The Art of Walt Disney* by Christopher Finch; *The Animated Film* by Ralph Stephenson.

Anime.

A Japanese term for animated films, applied particularly to its own tradition, which differs from the American style, as exemplified in the work of the Walt Disney studios. Japanese animation is often based on comic books and features more adult fantasies, often marked by an excess of sex and violence and drawing on local legends and myths. The graphic techniques are often stylized: the heroes and heroines tend to cuteness, with large round eyes. The best film so far is Otomo Katsuhiro's *Akira* 87, though many others are gaining a cult following in the West owing to their release on video and there are several magazines devoted to Anime. The Anime style has influenced some action films, such as *Gunhed*, and other live-action films are being based on animated originals, such as the gangster epic *Crying Freeman*. The process is likely to quicken with the trend for computer games inspiring movies, since these also are influenced by Japanese comic-book styles.

Books: 1993, *Anime! A Beginner's Guide to*

Japanese Animation by Helen McCarthy; 1996, *The Anime! Movie Guide* by Helen McCarthy.
See also: MANGA.

Anscocolor.
American process derived from AGFACOLOR.

answer print.
The first complete combined print supplied by the laboratory, usually with no very careful attempt to grade colour or contrast.

arc.
A high-powered lamp used in projectors and studio lighting, its illumination consisting of an electrical discharge between two carbon rods.

archive.
A vault, usually government-sponsored, containing a selection of films to be preserved for research and for posterity.

Aromarama.
A process that linked smells to sequences in a movie, the perfume being pumped through the air-conditioning system into the auditorium. It was first used for the screening of a documentary, *The Great Wall of China* 59, but, like the similar SMELL-O-VISION, was never more than a short-lived gimmick.

art director.
Technician responsible for designing sets, sometimes also costumes and graphics. 'Production designer' is a more pretentious way of saying much the same thing. The importance of this work to the finished product first became noticeable in *Intolerance* and the German expressionist films of the 20s, then in such diverse talking films as *The Old Dark House*, *Things to Come*, *The Cat and the Canary* (both versions), *Citizen Kane*, *Trouble in Paradise*, *The Mystery of the Wax Museum*, *A Matter of Life and Death*, *Les Enfants du Paradis*, and *Kings Row*. Important figures include William Cameron MENZIES, Anton GROT, Cedric GIBBONS, Ken ADAM, Vincent KORDA, Hans DREIER, Alfred JUNGE, Carmen DILLON.

art house.
American term (now displacing 'specialized hall' in GB) for cinema showing classic revivals and highbrow or off-beat new films of limited commercial appeal.

ASC.
Often seen on credit titles after the names of cinematographers, these initials stand for the American Society of Cinematographers, a professional association, membership of which is by invitation only. Its aims since its foundation in 1918 have been 'to advance the art and science of cinematography'. The Society publishes a monthly periodical, *American Cinematographer*.

aspect ratio.
Relative breadth and height of screen. Before 1953 this was 4:3 or 1.33:1. 'Standard' wide screen varies from 1.66:1 to 1.85:1. Anamorphic processes are wider: SuperScope 2:1, CinemaScope and most others 2.35:1 (or 2.55:1 with magnetic stereophonic sound). Vista-Vision, a printing process, was shot in 1.33:1 but recommended for screening at up to 2:1, i.e. with top and bottom cut off and the rest magnified. The TV screen is fixed at 1.33:1, therefore all wide-screen films lose something when played on it.

assistant director.
More properly 'assistant to the director', being concerned with details of administration rather than creation.

associate producer.
Usually the actual producer or supervisor of the film, the title of 'executive producer' having been taken by the head of the studio.

Association of Cinematograph, Television and Allied Technicians:
see ACTT.

auteur.
A term used in the 60s and 70s by egghead critics to denote directors whom they judge to have a discernible message or attitude which runs throughout their work. Oddly enough the term is not applied to authors.

authenticator.
Studio researcher responsible for establishing accuracy of all script details, ensuring use of 'clear' telephone numbers, etc.

avant-garde.
An adjective generally used to describe artists 'in advance of their time'; especially used of French surrealists in the 20s, e.g. Kirsanoff, Buñuel, Germaine Dulac.

Avid Media Composer
is a digital editing system, based on the Apple Macintosh computer. It was first used in film in 1992 by Steve Cohen when editing *Lost in Yonkers*. His success led other editors to adopt the method. The advantage of digital editing is that it is non-linear, providing swift access to all raw film footage and allowing multiple versions of each edited sequence. Some editors prefer a rival system, LIGHTWORKS.

'B' picture.
A low-budget production usually designed as part of a double bill or to support a more important feature. There are four excellent books on the subject: *B Movies* by Don Miller, *The Wonderful World of B Films* by Alan G. Barbour, *Kings of the Bs* by Todd McCarthy and Charles Flynn and *The Big Book of B Movies* by Robin Cross.

back projection.
A method of producing 'location' sequences in the studio: the players act in front of a translucent screen on which the scenic background is projected.

ballyhoo.
An expressive term, allegedly Irish in origin, used in show business to denote the kind of publicity that has nothing to do with the merits, or indeed the actual contents, of the film in question.

barring clause.
The part of an exhibitor's contract with a renter preventing him from showing new films before other specified cinemas in the area. The showing of a film in London may thus prevent its exhibition elsewhere within a radius of fifty miles or more.

BECTU
is the Broadcasting, Entertainment, Cinematograph and Theatre Union, which replaced the ACTT.

below-the-line costs
are the expenses that cover the cost of filming and post-production work.

best boy.
Term used to describe the assistant to the chief electrician, or gaffer, on a film set.

bicycling.
A trade term for the sharing, usually illegally, of one print between two theatres: the manager had to make frequent bicycle trips!

billing.
The official credits for a film, usually stating the relative sizes of type to be accorded to title, stars, character actors, etc.

biograph.
(1) An old name for a cinema projector. (2) The name of Britain's first public cinema, near Victoria Station, London, opened 1905. (3) The name of D. W. Griffith's New York studios, 1903–10.

biopic.
A contraction of 'biographical picture', i.e. a film about the life of a real person. For examples see under COMPOSERS, COURTESANS, ENTERTAINERS, EXPLORERS, INVENTORS, KINGS AND QUEENS, PAINTERS, POLITICIANS, SCIENTISTS, SOLDIERS, SPIES, SPORTSMEN, WRITERS.

Black Maria.
In the history of film this evocative phrase for a police van has a secondary meaning, being the nickname given to Edison's first portable studio.

blackface.
A vaudeville adjective for comedians or singers who found their best appeal in 'Negro' disguise, i.e. with faces entirely blacked save for thick lips. Among the singers Al Jolson was perhaps the most famous exponent of this art, with Eddie Cantor a close second; the style derived from the minstrel shows which toured America from the mid-nineteenth century and which are clearly depicted in Jolson's *Mammy* and *Swanee River*. Dockstader's minstrels are recreated in *The Jolson Story*, and Dan Emmet's in *Dixie*; while Judy Garland and Mickey Rooney created their own blackface troupe in *Babes in Arms*. Among blackface comics there were Moran and Mack, the 'two black crows'; and others who made themselves black for comic effect were Betty Grable and June Haver in *The Dolly Sisters*, Myrna Loy in *Ham and Eggs at the Front*, Gene Wilder in *Silver Streak*, Buster Keaton in *College*, Marion Davies in *Going Hollywood*, Fred Astaire in *Swing Time*, Dan Dailey in *You're My Everything*, and Chick Chandler in *The Big Shot*. In *Watermelon Man*, on the other hand, Godfrey Cambridge appeared in whiteface, as did Lenny Henry in *True Identity*.

blacklisting:
see THE HOLLYWOOD TEN.

blimp.
A soundproof cover fixed over a camera during shooting to absorb running noise.

block booking.
A system supposedly illegal but still practised, whereby a renter forces an exhibitor to book a whole group of mainly mediocre films in order to get the one or two he wants.

bloop.
To cover a splice in the sound track, usually with thick 'blooping ink'.

blow up.
To magnify an image, either a photograph for background purposes, or a piece of film (e.g. from 16mm to 35mm).

boom.
A 'long arm' extending from the camera unit and carrying a microphone to be balanced over the actors so that sound can be picked up in a semi-distant shot. A 'camera boom' is a high movable platform strong enough to support the entire camera unit.

break figure.
A specified amount of takings after which an exhibitor pays a greater percentage to the renter. For the protection of both parties many contracts are on a sliding scale, with the exhibitor paying anything from 25% to 50% of the gross according to the business he does.

breakaway furniture
is specially constructed from balsa wood for those spectacular saloon brawls in which so much damage is apparently done to stars and stunt men.

British Film Academy.
An organization founded in 1946 'for the advancement of the film'. Since 1959 it has been amalgamated with the Society of Film and Television Arts. Its award statuette is noted in this book by the letters BFA. See Section 8 for full listing.

British Film Commission.
An organization set up in 1992 and funded by the British government to provide information and services to international film and television companies to encourage the use of British technicians, artists, facilities and locations. The first British Film Commissioner was Sir Sydney Samuelson, who began working in the cinema industry in 1939.

British Film Institute.
Partly government-subsidized organization founded in 1933 'to encourage the use and development of cinema as a means of entertainment and instruction'. Includes the National Film Archive (founded 1935) and the National Film Theatre (founded after the 1951 Festival of Britain). Also library, information section, stills collection, film distribution agency, lecture courses, etc. Chief publication: *Sight and Sound*.

B.S.C.
British Society of Cinematographers, a professional society founded in the 50s, similar in aims to the A.S.C.

burned out.
Cinematographer's jargon for 'over-exposed'.

cable.
A method of disseminating television programmes by underground cable whose fibres can accommodate a great many channels, none of them subject to interference from the others. From the mid-70s it became highly popular in America because of poor airwave reception in many areas; as a subscription service it also screened fewer commercials and most of its movies were uncut. These advantages however did not apply in most other countries, where it had a slower start.

cameo.
A word coined (in its cinematic sense) by Mike Todd when persuading famous stars to accept walk-on parts for *Around the World in Eighty Days*.

cartoon:
a film composed of animated drawings, carefully varied to give the appearance of motion. Gertie the Dinosaur, who appeared in 1909, is thought to be the first cartoon character; Mutt and Jeff followed soon after. In the 20s, Pat Sullivan's Felix the Cat and Max Fleischer's Out of the Inkwell series vied for popularity until both were ousted by Walt Disney, who with Ub Iwerks created Mickey Mouse and his familiar friends. In the 30s, Disney went on to Silly Symphonies, Fleischer to Popeye. Other creations were Woody Woodpecker (Walter Lantz), Mighty Mouse, Heckle and Jeckle, Tom and Jerry (Hanna-Barbera for MGM) and Bugs Bunny. Disney's Donald Duck became more popular than Mickey. In the 40s, David Hand made British cartoons for the Rank Organisation, but they were not commercially successful. The 50s brought U.P.A. with their new refined lines, intellectual conceptions and sophisticated jokes; Mr Magoo and Gerald McBoing Boing led the new characters but quickly palled. Then the needs of television led to innumerable cartoon series which for the sake of economy had to be only semi-animated and had little vitality; the best of them were The Flintstones and Yogi Bear. These series proliferated into hundreds and not until 1972 did anyone try an adult cartoon series, Hanna-Barbera's *Wait Till Your Father Gets Home*.
■ Feature-length cartoons were started by Disney in 1937 with *Snow White and the Seven Dwarfs;* Fleischer responded in 1939 with *Gulliver's Travels*. Disney's outstanding serious cartoon was *Fantasia* 40, an interpretation of classical music. Later, French and Japanese cartoons flooded the market, but inspiration was lacking in most of them. Halas and Batchelor's British *Animal Farm* was a fair summation of Orwell's fable, but their later attempts to interpret Gilbert and Sullivan failed. In recent years the cartoon has been put to every kind of serious and comic purpose, including propaganda and advertising, and many prizewinners have come from Europe. Ralph Bakshi's ruderies of Fritz the Cat were startling, but he atoned with his careful rendering of *Lord of the Rings*.

cast.
The actors in a movie.

casting.
To the old Hollywood, casting usually meant type-casting, or bending the character to suit the star. In the 70s, stars became less important, and leading actors became more chameleon-like. Even so, many best-remembered performances have been given by actors who were second or third choice. The original requirement for *Dracula* was Paul Muni, not Bela Lugosi. Clark Gable was thought of for Tarzan. Greta Garbo was asked to play Dorian Gray as a woman. Gloria Swanson's role in *Sunset Boulevard* was first offered to Mae West. Humphrey Bogart got *High Sierra* and *The Maltese Falcon* only because George Raft turned them down. Robert Montgomery, Fredric March, Carole Lombard and Myrna Loy all turned down *It Happened One Night* before Gable and Colbert accepted. Carole Lombard however benefited when Miriam Hopkins turned

down *Twentieth Century*. Olivier's role as Maxim de Winter in *Rebecca* was first offered to William Powell and Ronald Colman. Doris Day was offered Mrs Robinson in *The Graduate*. Lana Turner gave way to Lee Remick on *Anatomy of a Murder*. Bette Davis would have been Scarlett O'Hara if she hadn't thought Errol Flynn was to play Rhett. George Jessel would have starred in *The Jazz Singer* if his demands had been less outrageous. Danny Thomas would have starred in *The Jolson Story* if he had agreed to have his nose shortened. Marlon Brando, Montgomery Clift and Paul Newman were all sought for *East of Eden* before James Dean got the role. Bette Davis played Margo in *All About Eve* only because Claudette Colbert gave it up. Ingrid Bergman was second choice to Vera Zorina for *For Whom the Bell Tolls*. Jack Nicholson took over from Rip Torn in *Easy Rider*, Marlon Brando from Montgomery Clift in *On The Waterfront*. Bette Davis turned down *Mildred Pierce* and Joan Crawford grabbed it. Olivia de Havilland, not Vivien Leigh, was first choice for *A Streetcar named Desire*. Ingrid Bergman won Oscars for *Gaslight*, first offered to Hedy Lamarr, and *Anastasia*, intended for Jennifer Jones; but she turned down *The Farmer's Daughter* and *To Each His Own*, which won Oscars for Loretta Young and Olivia de Havilland. If Grace Kelly hadn't become Princess of Monaco, she would have played in *Cat on a Hot Tin Roof* and *Designing Woman*, not Elizabeth Taylor or Lauren Bacall. William Holden got *Sunset Boulevard* after Montgomery Clift said no. Frank Sinatra walked out of *Carousel*: Gordon MacRae took over. Ginger Rogers replaced the ailing Judy Garland in *The Barkleys of Broadway*. Deborah Kerr got *From Here to Eternity* when Joan Crawford withdrew. Vivien Leigh thought herself too young to play the role in *Suddenly Last Summer* which went to Katharine Hepburn. Shirley Temple was wanted for Judy Garland's role in *The Wizard of Oz*; W. C. Fields was to have been the wizard, but argued over money. Fields himself only got Micawber in *David Copperfield* because Charles Laughton walked out after two days of filming.

❝ Casting: deciding which of two faces the public is least tired of. – *Anonymous definition*

I couldn't go on forever being Little Miss Fixit who burst into song. – *Deanna Durbin*

No matter what roles I play, I can't get Caligari out of my system. – *Conrad Veidt*

I was a thirteen-year-old boy for thirty years. – *Mickey Rooney*

After *The Wizard of Oz* I was typecast as a lion, and there aren't all that many parts for lions. – *Bert Lahr*

If I made *Cinderella*, the audience would be looking for the body in the coach. – *Alfred Hitchcock*

They get to know your face too well out there in Hollywood, and you're finished. – *Ethel Griffies*

Aren't you tired, Spence, of always playing Spencer Tracy?

– What am I supposed to do, play Bogart?

CD-ROM

stands for Compact Disc – Read Only Memory. It is a computer-compatible means of storing a mass of information (up to 630 megabytes of data, enough to hold an entire encyclopedia) on one compact disc. It has been used as an alternative method to video cassette and laser disc for making films available at home, but has so far failed to gain a large consumer base and is likely to be superseded by DVD. As it can contain high-quality sound, animation and text, CD-ROM is now the preferred method of distributing computer programs, including games, many of which are derived from successful films. It has also been used as a method of publishing film guides: see Section 10.

cel.

The sheet of celluloid on which cartoon animators draw their foreground actions, one cel per film frame.

censorship.

Each country has found it necessary to apply its own rules for film producers; in Britain and America at least these rules were drawn up and enforced at the request of the industry itself. The British Board of Film Censors was founded in 1912. It has now changed its name to the British Board of Film Classification and covers material released on video-cassette as well as films. For many years films were classified as 'U' (for universal exhibition), 'A' (adults and accompanied children only) or (from 1933) 'H' (horrific; prohibited for persons under 16). In 1951, with the growing emphasis on sex, 'H' was replaced by 'X', which includes sex *and* horror. In the 60s 'X' came to mean over 18, 'AA' no one under 14, and 'A' was simply a warning to parents (children could still get in unaccompanied). The current ratings system is 'U', suitable for children; 'PG', parental guidance advised; '12', suitable for persons over the age of 12; '15', only suitable for persons over the age of 15; and '18', only suitable for adults. In America, the Arbuckle scandal of 1921 precipitated the founding of the 'Hays Office' (named after its first paid president) by the Motion Picture Producers and Distributors of America. The first Production Code was issued in 1930 and has undergone constant amendment especially since *The Moon is Blue* 53, and very rapidly indeed since *Room at the Top* 59; in 1966 *Who's Afraid of Virginia Woolf?* almost swamped it completely and a revised, broadened code was issued. In 1968 this was replaced by a new rating system: 'X', 'R' (restricted), 'PG' (parental guidance advised) and 'G' (general audience). In the 90s the 'X' rating was replaced by an 'NC-17' rating. The independent and very strict Catholic Legion of Decency was founded in 1934 and issues its own classifications; it recently changed its name to the National Catholic Office for Motion Pictures.

Best books: Murray Schumach's *The Face on the Cutting Room Floor*, Doug McClelland's *The Unkindest Cuts*, Leonard J. Leff and Jerold L. Simmons's *The Dame in the Kimono: Hollywood's Censorship and the Production Code* (1990), and Tom Dewe Mathews' *Censored* (1994).

❝ We are paid to have dirty minds. – *John Trevelyan, British censor, 1968*

Any film that isn't fit to be shown to my youngest child isn't fit to be shown to anybody. – *Chicago Chief of Police, 1936*

The Seashell and the Clergyman is apparently meaningless. If it has any meaning, it is doubtless objectionable. – *British Board of Film Censors, 1929*

Travesties of religious rites . . . references to royalty . . . hangings or executions either serious or comic . . . political propaganda . . . too much shooting . . . intoxication . . . cruelty . . . companionate marriage . . . free love . . . immodesty . . . vamping . . . vulgar noises . . . harsh screams . . . the divinity . . . life after death . . . British officers shown in an unflattering light . . . – *themes banned by the British censor, 1930*

The cinema needs continual repression of controversy if it is to stave off disaster. – *Lord Tyrrell, Chairman of British Board of Film Censors, 1936*

They can't censor the gleam in my eye. – *Charles Laughton, told that incest had been removed from his role in The Barretts of Wimpole Street*

The inanities blessed by the Hays Office are more genuinely corrupting than any pornography. – *Joseph Wood Krutch*

It is in the interest of producers to maintain a certain moral standard since, if they don't do this, the immoral films won't sell. – *Jean Renoir*

Hollywood buys a good story about a bad girl and changes it to a bad story about a good girl. – *Anon, 1930s*

The Hays Office warned us that we couldn't show the heroine as a prostitute. We had to put a sewing machine in her apartment, so in that way she was not a whore but a seamstress. – *Fritz Lang on Man Hunt*

The industry must have towards that sacred thing, the mind of a child, towards that clean virgin thing, that unmarked slate, the same responsibility, the same care about the impressions made on it, that the best clergyman or the most inspired teacher of youth would have. – *Will Hays, 1930s*

Will Hays is my shepherd, I shall not want, He maketh me to lie down in clean postures. – *Gene Fowler*

Hollywood must never permit censorship to collapse. It's far too good for the box office. – *Claude Binyon*

What critics call dirty in our movies, they call lusty in foreign films. – *Billy Wilder*

In a novel a hero can lay ten girls and marry a virgin for the finish. In a movie, this is not allowed. The hero, as well as the heroine, has to be a virgin. The villain can lay anyone he wants, have as much fun as he wants cheating and stealing, getting rich and whipping the servants. But you have to shoot him in the end. When he falls with a bullet in his forehead, it is advisable that he clutch at the Gobelin tapestry on the library wall and bring it down over his head like a symbolic shroud. Also, covered by such a tapestry, the actor does not have to hold his breath while being photographed as a dead man. – *Herman J. Mankiewicz, 1930s*

I don't like censorship, but nor do I like the absence of it. – *Robert Rossen, 1950s*

The trouble with censors is they worry if a girl has cleavage. They ought to worry if she hasn't any. – *Marilyn Monroe, 1950s*

Nowadays when a film is awarded the production seal the producer cries: 'Where have we failed?' – *Bob Hope, 1962*

They are doing things on the screen now that I wouldn't do in bed. If I could. – *Bob Hope, 1965*

They are doing things on the screen now that the French don't even put on postcards. – *Bob Hope, 1970*

The Americans are nice people, but right now they're behaving like small boys who've just discovered what sex is. – *John Trevelyan, British Board of Film Censors, 1970*

The only censor is the audience, which will decide whether it wants it and how soon it gets fed up with it. – *Lord Eccles, Minister for the Arts, 1972*

Central Casting.

The talent agency through whose doors passed many unknowns who stayed that way. In the 30s the Hollywood office had a sign above the door: DON'T TRY TO BECOME AN ACTOR. FOR EVERY ONE WE EMPLOY, WE TURN AWAY THOUSANDS.

chambara

is the term for a genre of samurai films, which could be described as the Japanese equivalent of westerns.

chanchada.

Term used to describe a genre of popular Brazilian films that mixes love stories with comedy and colourfully staged musical numbers, usually involving the samba. The form was created by Watson Macedo (1918–81), a Brazilian director, screenwriter and art director, in his musicals of the 40s and 50s, particularly *Carnaval No Fogo* 49. It includes parodies of Hollywood movies, such as Carlos Manga's *Matar ou Correr*, based on *High Noon*.

change-over.

Transition from one reel of film to another during projection. A reel originally lasted ten minutes but most 35mm projectors now take 20 or 30 minutes. Change-over cues are given in the form of dots which appear on the top right-hand corner of the screen a standard number of seconds before the end of the reel.

character actor.

Usually thought of as one who does not play romantic leads.

Cinecolor.

A two-colour process that was a cheaper alternative to Technicolor and so was used on many 'B' pictures in the 30s and 40s. The film had an orange-red emulsion on one side and a blue-green emulsion on the other.

cinéma vérité

A fashionable term of the 60s for what used to be called candid camera. A TV-style technique of recording life and people as they are, in the raw, using handheld cameras, natural sound and the minimum of rehearsal and editing. Chiefly applied to *Chronique d'un Eté* 61, *Le Joli Mai* 62, and the documentaries of Richard Leacock and the Maysles brothers.

CinemaScope

Wide-screen process copyrighted by Fox in 1953 and first used in *The Robe*; invented many years earlier by Henri Chrétien. Other companies either adopted it or produced their own trade name: WarnerScope, SuperScope, etc. Basically, the camera contains an anamorphic lens which 'squeezes' a wide picture on to a standard 35mm frame (which has a breadth/height ratio of 4:3 or 1.33:1). This, when projected through a complementary lens, gives a picture ratio on screen of 2.55:1 with stereophonic magnetic sound, or 2.35:1 with optical sound. Directors found the new shape awkward to compose for, the easiest way of handling it being to park the camera and let the actors move, a reversion to early silent methods. Although wide screens are said to have helped the box office, they have effectively prevented the full use of cinematic techniques. Oddly enough Fox in the mid-60s quietly dropped their own system and moved over to Panavision. The last word belongs to writer Nunnally Johnson, who, when asked how he would cope with the demands of CinemaScope, replied: 'Easy. What I'm going to do from now on is put the paper in my typewriter sideways.'

❝ The wide, wide screen may have saved the industry, but it came close to killing the art. Hear these justified cries of woe.

The worst shape ever devised. – *Rouben Mamoulian*

It's fine if you want a system that shows a boa constrictor to better advantage than a man. – *George Stevens*

A wide screen makes a bad film twice as bad. – *Samuel Goldwyn*

It is a formula for a funeral, or for snakes, but not for human beings. – *Fritz Lang*

It wrecked the art of film for a decade. – *Leon Shamroy*

Why not keep the screen the same size and reduce the size of the audience? – *Irving Brecher*

There was a time when all I looked for was a good story, but nowadays everything has to look the size of Mount Rushmore, and the actors in close-up look as though they belong there. – *Fritz Lang*

Processed by De Luxe, it made all films look like very cheap colour advertisements in magazines. – *James Mason*

It resulted in a collapse of visual quality even more disastrous than that which accompanied the dawn of sound. – *Charles Higham*

cinematographer.

Lighting cameraman or chief photographer.

Cinemobile.

A massive truck into which everything necessary for location shooting, including dressing rooms and toilets, can be packed.

Cinerama.

Extra-wide-screen system, invented by Fred Waller. Three projectors, electronically synchronized, were used to put the picture on the screen in three sections: this gave a disturbing wobble at the joins, though the range of vision was sometimes magnificently wide, as in the aerial shots and roller coaster sequence in *This is Cinerama* 52. After ten years of scenic but cinematically unremarkable travelogues (*Cinerama Holiday*, *Seven Wonders of the World*, *Search for Paradise*, etc.), the first story film in the process, *How the West Was Won*, was made in 1962. Shortly afterwards the three-camera system was abandoned in favour of 'single-lens Cinerama' which is virtually indistinguishable from CinemaScope except for the higher definition resulting from using wider film. 'Cinemiracle', a similar process, was short-lived. In 1997 the Cinerama Preservations Society was set up in the US to save the films made using the process. At that time, there were two cinemas in the world still capable of showing the films, one in the United States – the New Neon in Dayton, Ohio – and the other in England, at the National Museum of Photography, Film and Television in Bradford.

The released Cinerama features were:

This is Cinerama 52. Cinerama Holiday 55. Seven Wonders of the World 56. Search for Paradise 57. South Seas Adventure 58. The Wonderful World of the Brothers Grimm 62. How the West Was Won 62. It's a Mad Mad Mad Mad World (single lens) 63. Circus World 64. The Best of Cinerama 64. Battle of the Bulge 65. Grand Prix 66. Cinerama's Russian Adventure 66. Ice Station Zebra 68. Custer of the West 68. 2001: A Space Odyssey 68. Krakatoa – East of Java 69.

circuit.

A chain of cinemas under the same ownership, often playing the same release programme.

clapperboard.

A hinged board recording film details. At the beginning of each 'take' it is held before the camera for identification and then 'clapped' to make a starting point in the sound track. This point is then synchronized with the image of the closed board.

cliffhanger.
Trade name for a serial, especially an episode ending in an unresolved situation which keeps one in suspense till next time.

close-up.
Generally applied to a head-and-shoulders shot of a person or any close shot of an object. The first close-up is said to be that of Fred Ott sneezing in an Edison experimental film of 1900. See: LONG SHOT.

co-feature.
A moderate-budget production designed (or fated) to form equal half of a double bill.

cokuloris.
A palette with random irregular holes, placed between lights and camera to prevent glare and give a better illusion of real-life light and shadow.

colour
prints of a primitive kind were made as long ago as 1898. During the next few years many films were hand-coloured by stencil, and two unsatisfactory processes. KinemaColor and Gaumont colour, were tried out. D. W. Griffith in *The Birth of a Nation* 14 developed the French practice of tinting scenes for dramatic effect: blue for night, orange for sunshine, etc. In 1918 red-and-green Technicolor was tried out along with half a dozen other processes. 1921: Prizmacolour was used for the British historical film *The Great Adventure*. 1923: de Mille used a colour sequence in *The Ten Commandments*. 1926: *The Black Pirate* was shot in two-colour Technicolor. 1932: first three-colour Technicolor film, Disney cartoon *Flowers and Trees* (AA). 1934: colour used in dramatic sequences of *La Cucaracha* and *The House of Rothschild*. 1935: first feature film entirely in three-strip colour, *Becky Sharp*. 1937: first British Technicolor feature, *Wings of the Morning*. 1939: two-colour Cinecolor, very cheap, became popular for low-budget westerns. 1942: Technicolor introduced monopack process, using one negative instead of three and making equipment less cumbersome and more flexible. 1948: Republic adopted Trucolor. 1949: Anscocolor, later to become Metrocolor, used on *The Man on the Eiffel Tower*. 1951: Supercinecolor (3 colours) adopted by Columbia in *Sword of Monte Cristo*. 1952: Eastmancolor used in *Royal Journey;* Warners adopted it as Warnercolor. 1954: Fox adopted De Luxe Color.

Today, with new colours springing up all the time, effectiveness seems to depend not on the trademark but on how well the film is shot, processed and printed.

colour sequences
in otherwise black-and-white movies were used at first experimentally (see above) but have also been employed for dramatic effect. Early examples include *The Ten Commandments* 23, *Ben Hur* 26, *The Wedding March* 28, *Chasing Rainbows* 30; many of the early sound musicals went into colour for their final number, and this went on as late as *Kid Millions* 35. *Victoria the Great* 37 had colour for the final 'Empress of India' scenes. *The Wizard of Oz* 39 had the Oz scenes in colour and the Kansas scenes in sepia. *Irene* 40 went into colour for the 'Alice Blue Gown' number – which made the second half of the film anti-climactic. *The Moon and Sixpence* 42 blazed into colour for the fire at the end . . . and the same director, Albert Lewin, used a similar trick whenever the picture was shown in *The Picture of Dorian Gray* 44. *A Matter of Life and Death* 45 had earth in colour, heaven in a rather metallic monochrome. *Task Force* 49 went into colour for its final battle reels, most of which consisted of blown-up 16mm war footage. *The Secret Garden* 49 played the same trick as *The Wizard of Oz*. *The Solid Gold Cadillac* 56 had a few final feet of colour to show off the irrelevant car of the title. In 1958 *I Was a Teenage Frankenstein* revived the old dodge of colour for the final conflagration. In *Cleo de 5 à 7* only the ominous tarot cards were in colour; in *The House of Rothschild* only the court finale. In *If*, nobody was ever able to work out why black-and-white alternated with colour until someone guessed that the producers kept on running out of money as shooting progressed. And *Is Paris Burning?* 66 used colour for the climactic victory sequence, having been forced into black-and-white for the rest of the movie by the necessity of using old newsreel footage. In few of the above cases has reissue printing maintained the original intention: printing short sequences in colour is time-consuming. See also: TINTING.

combined print.
One on which both sound and picture (always produced separately) have been 'married', i.e. a standard print as shown in cinemas.

See also: DOUBLE-HEADED PRINT.

composite print:
see COMBINED PRINT for which it is an alternative term.

continuity.
The development of cinematic narrative from beginning to end of a film. If continuity is good the audience will be carried smoothly from one scene to another without disturbing breaks or lapses of detail.

contrast.
The tone range in a print. Heavy contrast results in 'soot and whitewash', i.e. blurry blacks and burnt-out whites.

copyright.
British law relating to film copyright is notably vague, but in practice the owner of a film is protected against piracy for fifty years. In America copyright must be renewed in the 28th year, which has resulted in some fatal errors: e.g. MGM now have no control over *Till the Clouds Roll By* because they forgot to renew it, and Chaplin renewed only the version of *The Gold Rush* including his specially composed 40s music track.

coverage.
All the shots that comprise the photography from various angles of a particular scene in a film.

crane shot.
A high-angle shot in which the camera travels up, down or laterally while mounted on a travelling crane.

credits.
Titles at beginning or end of film (nowadays very often five minutes *after* the beginning) listing the names of the creative talents concerned.

creeping title.
One which moves up (or sometimes across) the screen at reading pace. Also known as *roller title*.

cross cutting.
Interlinking fragments of two or more separate sequences so that they appear to be taking place at the same time. One of the most famous examples is the climax of *Intolerance* which intertwines four stories; and in more modern times *The Godfather* crosscut a murder with a baptism.

cut.
Noun: abrupt transition from one shot to another, the first being instantaneously replaced by the second (as opposed to a wipe or a dissolve). Verb: to edit a film, or (during production) to stop the camera running on a scene.

cutaway.
An intervening shot allowing an editor to change the focus of action, e.g. clouds or a clock face.

cutting copy.
The first print assembled from the 'rushes'. When this is deemed satisfactory, the negative will be cut to match it, and release prints made.

cyclorama.
A smooth, curved giant screen at the back of the set, cunningly lit to give the impression of daylight.

dailies:
see RUSHES.

day for night,
which is often abbreviated to D/N, is the technique of shooting in daylight but making the result look as if it was shot at night. This can be achieved by using filters, underexposing the film, or by printing. Its advantage is that it is both easier and cheaper to film during daylight hours.

DeLuxe Color
is the Twentieth Century-Fox version of Eastmancolor but usually comes out decidedly blue.

deep focus.
Dramatic camera technique which brings both foreground and background objects into equal focus and clarity; notably used in *Citizen Kane* and *Hamlet*.

definitions
A selection, chosen for entertainment rather than instruction.

Agent: A guy who is sore because an actor gets ninety per cent of what he makes.

Casting: Deciding which of two faces the public is least tired of.

Disneyland: The biggest people trap ever built by a mouse.

Double feature: A show that enables you to sit through a picture you don't care to see, so you can see one you don't like. – *Henry Morgan*

Epic: The easiest kind of picture to make badly. – *Charlton Heston*

It: The indefinable something. – *Elinor Glyn*, creator of 'It'

Musicals: A series of catastrophes ending with a floor show. – *Oscar Levant*

Oomph: The sound a fat man makes when he bends over to tie his laces in a phone booth. – *Ann Sheridan*

Romanoff's Restaurant: A place where a man can take his wife and family and have a lovely seven-course meal for $3,400. – *George Jessel*

Starlet: Any woman under thirty not actively employed in a brothel.

Television: A medium, so called because it is neither rare nor well done. – *Ernie Kovacs*

digital distribution
is a method of distributing and projecting on a screen an image transmitted from elsewhere, either by cable or from a satellite. Technically, it is possible to provide instant distribution of a film simultaneously to hundreds of individual cinemas, by digitally transmitting a movie from one central computer. All that is holding back such developments at the moment is the very high cost of the necessary equipment. The long-term effect of such technology may be the disappearance of independent or art movies and the cinemas that show such films.

director.
Normally the most influential creator of a film, who may not only shoot scenes on the studio floor but also supervise script, casting, editing, etc., according to his standing. In more routine films these functions are separately controlled.

❝ A selection of directional attitudes:

I feel very strongly that the director is supposed to be the boss. Art was never created by democracy. – *Charlton Heston*

Don't get excited. Obstacles make a better picture. – *Victor Fleming*

You can have all the philosophy you like: if a film doesn't come across in graphic terms, it falls short. – *Rouben Mamoulian*

There is no suspense like the suspense of a delayed coition. – *D. W. Griffith*

I don't try to guess what a million people will like. It's hard enough to know what I like. – *John Huston*

Always cast against the part and it won't be boring. – *David Lean*

Film-making has become a kind of hysterical pregnancy. – *Richard Lester*

I am never quite sure whether I am one of the cinema's elder statesmen or just the oldest whore on the beat. – *Joseph L. Mankiewicz*

The best films are best because of nobody but the director. – *Roman Polanski*

I renew myself at the fountain of the past. – *François Truffaut*

I regard actors as marionettes, as pieces of colour in my canvas. – *Josef von Sternberg*

You should think of each shot you make as the most important one in the film. – *Henry Blanke*

I have never made a picture to please me. Do you imagine I'd make a film like *Tammy* for me? – *Ross Hunter*

The director is the channel through which a motion picture reaches the screen. – *King Vidor*

The director is the only man besides your husband who can tell you how many of your clothes to take off. – *Betty Blythe*

No one can pretend to be a film director unless he also does his own editing. – *Orson Welles*

Shooting a film is like taking a stagecoach ride in the old west. At first you look forward to a nice trip. Later you just hope to reach your destination. – *François Truffaut*

It's the best job in picture business because when you're a director, you're God. And you know, that's the best job in town. – *Burt Lancaster*

It's not a film-maker's job to explain his technique, but to tell his story the best way he can. – *Mike Nichols*

Each picture has some sort of rhythm which only the director can give it. He has to be like the captain of a ship. – *Fritz Lang*

Am I a cult director? Yeah, I love all of that. I want to join the cult of the 100 to 200 million grossers and still make an artistic picture. – *Samuel Fuller*

I like stylization. I try to get away with as much as possible until people start laughing at it. – *Brian de Palma*

dissolve (or mix).
A change of scene accomplished by gradually exposing a second image over the first while fading the first away.

distributor (or renter).
A company which, for a percentage of the profits or a flat fee, undertakes to rent a film to exhibitors on the producing company's behalf. Originally major producers like MGM, Warner and Paramount distributed their own films exclusively, but with the rise of independent producers the situation has become much more fluid, with distributors bidding for the films they consider most likely to succeed at the box office and tying up successful producers to long-term contracts.

❝ It's easy enough to make fun of a distributor today, but how can you help but feel sorry for the poor bastard? He's faced with the daily decision whether or not to commit large sums of capital to producers who want to make pictures for release a year from now. Now, we all realize that exhibitors haven't a clue about what the kids want to see today. How can anyone possibly know what kids will want to see a year from now? – *Arthur Mayer*

documentary
was not coined as a word until 1929, but several famous films, including Ponting's *With Scott to the Antarctic*, Lowell Thomas' *With Allenby in Palestine*, and Flaherty's *Nanook of the North*, had before 1921 brought an attitude to their reportage which made them more than mere travel films. In Britain during the 20s, H. Bruce Woolfe made a series of painstaking and still evocative reconstructions of the battles of World War I; while Cooper and Schoedsack went even further afield for the exciting material in *Grass* and *Chang*. 1928 brought Eisenstein's *The General Line*, a brilliant piece of farming propaganda, and Turin's *Turksib*, a showy account of the building of the Turko-Siberian railway. John Grierson, who invented the term 'documentary', made in 1929 a quiet little two-reeler about Britain's herring fleet, and called it *Drifters;* for the next ten years Britain's official and sponsored film units produced such brilliant results as *Shipyard*, *Coalface*, *Housing Problems*, *Song of Ceylon*, *North Sea* and *Night Mail*. In 1931 Vigo made his satirical documentary *A Propos de Nice*, and shortly afterwards Eisenstein was at work on his never-finished *Thunder over Mexico*, brilliant fragments of which survive as *Time in the Sun*. Travel films by explorers like the Martin Johnsons proliferated during the 30s; Flaherty spent two uncomfortable years off the Irish coast to make his *Man of Aran*, and later produced in India the semi-fictional *Elephant Boy*. Pare Lorenz produced cinematic poetry out of America's geographical problems in *The Plow that Broke the Plains* and *The River*.

World War II stimulated documentarists to new urgency and new techniques, brilliantly exemplified by Frank Capra's *Why We Fight* series for the US Signal Corps, turning unpleasant facts into breathtaking entertainment. With a predictably understated approach the British units produced a more sober but equally stirring series of reports on the war (*Western Approaches*, *Desert Victory*, *Target for Tonight*) and the home front (*Listen to Britain*, *Fires Were Started*, *A Diary for Timothy*), many of them directed by Britain's first documentary poet, Humphrey Jennings. The two countries combined resources to present a brilliant, high-flying compilation film about the last year of war, *The True Glory*.

Since 1945 the use of documentary for advertising (often very subtly) and teaching has so proliferated that no simple line of development can be shown. Television has relentlessly explored and elaborated every technique of the pioneers, with special attention to 'action stills', compilation films, and hard-hitting popular journalist approaches such as NBC's White Paper series and Granada's *World in Action*. Entertainment films devised a popular blend of fact and fiction in such neo-classics as *Boomerang*, *The House on 92nd Street* and *Naked City*. At last documentary was accepted as an agreeable blend of instruction and pleasure; and in the changed environment Flaherty's lyrical *Louisiana Story* seemed slow and solemn.

Book: *Documentary, a History of the Non-fiction film*, by E. Barnouw, was published by OUP in 1974.

❝ The story of the documentary movement is the story of how, not without a scar or two, we got by. – *John Grierson*

Dolby system.
A method of improving the sound quality of optical sound tracks by reducing background noise and hiss, first used for tape recordings. The Dolby stereo system creates four sound tracks.

dolly.
A trolley on which a camera unit can be soundlessly moved about during shooting: can usually be mounted on rails. A 'crab dolly' will move in any direction.

dope sheet.
A list of the contents of a piece of film, usually applied to newsreel libraries.

double exposure.
This occurs when two or more images are recorded on the same piece of film. Used for trick shots when two characters played by the same actor have to meet; also for dissolves, dream sequences, etc.

double-headed print.
One in which sound and picture are recorded on separate pieces of film, usually at cutting copy stage or before OK is received to make combined negative.

double take.
A form of comic reaction to a piece of news or situation. The subject at first fails to take it in, and after a few moments the penny drops with a start. Cary Grant and Oliver Hardy were among the prime exponents of the device, but the comedian who really brought it to the point of art was James Finlayson, who not only had the most pronounced reactions but added a slow withdrawal of the head, calling the entire effect a 'double take and fade away'.

drive-in.
A cinema in the open air, with loudspeakers relaying the sound track into your car.

dry ice.
A chemical substance which in water produces carbon dioxide gas and gives the effect of a low-hanging white ground mist, very effective in fantasy sequences.

DTS
stands for Digital Theatre Systems, a new sound recording and playback system launched by Universal Pictures and used first for *Jurassic Park* in 1993. The sound is stored on a compact disk which is synchronized with the film.

dubbing
has several shades of meaning within the general one of adding sound (effects, music, song, dialogue) to pictures already shot. It can mean re-recording; or replacing original language dialogue by a translation; or having someone else provide top notes for a star who can't sing. Here is an incomplete list of singers who provided uncredited voice-overs for actors who couldn't quite measure up.

Band Wagon India Adams for Cyd Charisse, *The Belle of New York* Anita Ellis for Vera-Ellen, *Brigadoon* Carole Richards for Cyd Charisse, *Call Me Madam* Carole Richards for Vera-Ellen, *Cover Girl* Nan Wynn for Rita Hayworth, *Down to Earth* Anita Ellis for Rita Hayworth, *Gigi* Betty Wand for Leslie Caron, *Gilda* Nan Wynn for Rita Hayworth, *The Great Ziegfeld* Allan Jones for Dennis Morgan, *Gypsy* Lisa Kirk for Rosalind Russell, *Happy Go Lovely* Eve Boswell for Vera-Ellen, *The Helen Morgan Story* Gogi Grant for Ann Blyth, *Interrupted Melody* Eileen Farrell for Eleanor Parker, *The Jolson Story* Al Jolson for Larry Parks, *The King and I* Marni Nixon for Deborah Kerr, *Meet Me in St Louis* Arthur Freed for Leon Ames, *The Merry Widow* Trudy Erwin for Lana Turner, *My Fair Lady* Marni Nixon for Audrey Hepburn, *Orchestra Wives* Pat Friday for Lynn Bari, *Pal Joey* Jo Ann Greer for Rita Hayworth, *South Pacific* Muriel Smith for Juanita Hall, *South Pacific* Giorgio Tozzi for Rossano Brazzi, *Showboat* Annette Warren for Ava Gardner, *A Song Is Born* Jeri Sullivan for Virginia Mayo, *The Sound of Music* Bill Lee for Christopher Plummer, *State Fair* (1945) Lorraine Hogan for Jeanne Crain, *To Have and Have Not* (believe it or not) Andy Williams for Lauren Bacall, *Torch Song* India Adams for Joan Crawford, *West Side Story* Marni Nixon for Natalie Wood, *West Side Story* Jim Bryant for Richard Beymer, *West Side Story* Betty Wand for Rita Moreno, *White Christmas* Trudy Stevens for Vera-Ellen, *With a Song in My Heart* Jane Froman for Susan Hayward.

Dubbing of speaking parts is comparatively rare, but note Joan Barry for Anny Ondra in *Blackmail* and Angela Lansbury for Ingrid Thulin in *The Four Horsemen of the Apocalypse*.

dupe negative.
One made from the original negative (via a lavender print) to protect it from wear by producing too many copies.

duping (lavender) print.
A high-quality print made from the original negative. From it dupe negatives can be made.

DVD
stands for digital video disc, a compact disc format that is capable of containing on a single disc a feature film in several different formats and languages, with stereo sound. Movies released on DVD became generally available in 1996/97, though some film companies were initially reluctant to release their productions in this format because of the problems of piracy, and of films becoming available on disc before they reached cinemas, because of their staggered release around the world. These problems have been overcome, from the studios' point of view, by dividing the world into six areas and making DVD releases in one area incompatible with DVD players in another area. Despite DVD's improvement in picture quality and sound over videocassettes, sales of discs and players were initially lower than anticipated. It remains to be seen whether DVD will gain mass acceptance.

dynamic frame.
A concept invented in 1955 by an American, Glenn Alvey: the screen was maximum size, i.e. CinemaScope, but individual scenes were to be masked down to whatever ratio suited them best, e.g. rather narrow for a corridor. Only one experimental British film, a version of H. G. Wells' *The Hole in the Wall*, was made in dynamic frame, which proved distracting and has in any case been overtaken by multiscreen experiments of the 60s.

edge numbers.
Serial numbers printed along the edge of all film material to assist identification when re-ordering sections.

editor.
Technician who assembles final print of film from various scenes and tracks available; works closely under director's control except in routine pictures. Conventional editing involved cutting scenes of the film in sequence to produce first a rough cut, and then the final result. Technical developments have led to the use of digital or non-linear editing with computer-based systems such as the AVID MEDIA COMPOSER and LIGHTWORKS.

❝ Editing is crucial. Imagine James Stewart looking at a mother nursing her child. You see the child, then cut back to him. He smiles. Now Mr Stewart is a benign old gentleman. Take away the middle piece of film and substitute a girl in a bikini. Now he's a dirty old man. – *Alfred Hitchcock*

8mm.
A substandard gauge introduced in 1932 and used mostly by amateurs, though from the early 60s, often with sounded recorded on an added magnetic strip, it also found use in schools and similar institutions. From the mid-60s, Super-8 was introduced which allowed a larger area to be used for film and provided better soundtrack reproduction. Both have now been superseded by the advent of cam-corders using video-cassettes or digital means for recording, and providing an instant playback of, sound and images.

electronovision.
A much-touted form of transfer from videotape to film, thought likely to save money in putting great stage performances on to the big screen.

Unfortunately it proved technically and aesthetically unacceptable, and the two features shot in it in 1965 are only interesting if one can ignore the technical shortcomings. They are *Harlow* with Carol Lynley and *Hamlet* with Richard Burton.

Elektrotachyscope.
A device for displaying motion pictures, patented in 1887 by the Polish inventor Ottomar Anschutz, who also took the photographs of the movement of people and animals it showed.

epic film.
Term used to describe a film directed and designed on a spectacular scale, focusing on the actions of a great hero and featuring a cast of thousands. The style has fallen out of favour in recent times, mainly due to the fiasco of *Cleopatra* 63 and the increasing cost of elaborate sets and large casts, so that the continuing appetite for spectacle is now supplied by movies that concentrate on violent action, such as car chases and crashes, and special effects. Favourite settings for epic films have included Rome (*Ben Hur*, *Spartacus* and dozens of movies from Italian directors) and Biblical times, in the productions of Cecil B. De Mille. More modern history featured in D. W. Griffith's *Birth of a Nation* 15 and in the work of the last master of the epic form, David Lean's, *Lawrence of Arabia* 62 and *Dr Zhivago* 65.

Books: 1984, *The Epic Film* by Derek Elley. 1992, *Epic Films: Casts, Credits and Commentary on over 250 Historical Spectacle Movies* by Gary A. Smith.

establishing shot.
Opening shot of sequence, showing location of scene or juxtaposition of characters in action to follow.

exchange.
An American enterprise: a middleman business which for a commission deals with the small exhibitors of an area on behalf of major renters.

exploitation.
A trade word covering all phases of publicity, public relations and promotion.

exploitation film.
A term used to describe low-budget movies of a sensational kind that either focus on some headline-making social phenomenon or attempt to cash in on a current box-office success. Sex, horror and fantasy are the predominant subject matters. Sometimes the title or the poster comes first, and the movie is made to match it. Such films flourished from the early 60s when drive-in cinemas provided double-bills and there was a new youthful audience for rock 'n' roll and biker movies. One of the most successful companies in the field was AIP, run by Samuel Arkoff and Jack Nicholson. The most notable exponent of the form has been producer and director Roger Corman, who began by supplying films for AIP to distribute before setting up his own production companies. Many of today's most successful directors, writers and cinematographers began by making films for Corman. That may, in part, be the reason why in recent years Hollywood studios have been turning out what are in effect big-budget exploitation movies, such as *Terminator 2*, and have also followed the exploitation movie-makers' habit of recycling their successes, as witness the seemingly endless succession of sequels to *A Nightmare on Elm Street*, *Halloween*, etc. As the subject matter of exploitation movies is now part of mainstream cinema, and there are fewer cinemas in which to show such movies, the likelihood is that the day of the exploitation film is nearly over. Its main market is now video, with films bypassing the cinema entirely, or being given very restricted releases in the hope of garnering publicity for their video-release. It is possible, however, that the growth in soft-core pornography for satellite and cable TV will provide its practitioners with a continuing market.

expressionism.
A term indicating the fullest utilization of cinematic resources to give dramatic larger-than-life effect, as in *Citizen Kane* or, in a different way, *The Cabinet of Dr Caligari*. In a secondary sense it also allows the fullest expression to be given, by the above means, to states of emotion.

exterior.
A shot taken in normal lighting outside the studio.

extra.
A crowd player with no lines to speak.

fade in.
Gradual emergence of a scene from blackness to full definition; opposite of *fade out*.

FAMU
stands for Film Faculty of the Academy of Music and Drama, the Prague Film School that was established in 1947 and where the majority of Czech and Slovak film-makers trained. Graduates of the school include Agnieszka HOLLAND, Vojtech JASNY and Emir KUSTURICA.

fast motion:
see ACCELERATED MOTION.

feature film.
Normally accepted to mean a (fictional) entertainment film of more than 3000 feet in length (approx. 34 minutes). Anything less than this is technically a 'short'. *NB:* In journalism and television a 'feature' usually means a *non*-fiction article or documentary.

featured players.
Those next in importance to the stars: usually billed after the title.

Federation of Film Societies.
British organization which issues information and arranges screening for film societies; also publishes magazine *Film*.

festivals.
Since World War II a great many cities round the world have derived excellent publicity from annual film festivals. Producers, distributors and actors in search of accolades now diligently trek each year to Cannes, Venice, Berlin, Mar del Plata, Cork, Edinburgh, Karlovy Vary, San Sebastian, Moscow, etc., while London and New York offer résumés in October.

F.I.D.O.
The Film Industry Defence Organization, a body formed by British renters and exhibitors to prevent old feature films being sold to television. It collapsed in 1964 after five years during which no renter dared sell his product for fear of reprisals.

film noir.
A French phrase meaning *dark film*. It was probably first applied to the moody, downbeat character melodramas of the late 30s, such as *Quai des Brumes* and *Le Jour se Lève*, but it soon came to be thought of as applying chiefly to the American urban crime film of the 40s, for instance *Double Indemnity*, *Laura*, *Scarlet Street* (based on a French original) and the versions of Raymond Chandler novels.

Books: 1980 (revised 1988), *Film Noir: An Encyclopedic Reference Guide*, edited by Alain Silver and Elizabeth Ward. 1984, *Dark City: The Film Noir* by Spencer Selby.

Films include:

The Maltese Falcon 41. Johnny Eager 42. The Glass Key 42. Double Indemnity 44. Laura 44. Murder, My Sweet/Farewell My Lovely 44. Ministry of Fear 44. Mildred Pierce 45. Scarlet Street 45. Gilda 46. The Big Sleep 46. The Blue Dahlia 46. The Chase 46. Notorious 46. The Postman Always Rings Twice 46. Crossfire 47. Lady in the Lake 47. He Walked by Night 48. The Big Clock 48. Key Largo 48. The Naked City 48. White Heat 49. Follow Me Quietly 49. The Asphalt Jungle 50. D.O.A. 50. Gun Crazy 50. Ace in the Hole 51. M 51. The Prowler 51. Beware, My Lovely 52.

Clash by Night 52. Angel Face 53. The Big Heat 53. The Hitch-Hiker 53. Drive a Crooked Road 54. Witness to Murder 54. The Big Knife 55. Kiss Me Deadly 55. The Killing 56. Sweet Smell of Success 57. Touch of Evil 58. The Crimson Kimono 59. Odds against Tomorrow 59. Underworld USA 61. Cape Fear 62. The Manchurian Candidate 62. The Servant 63. Marlowe 69. The Friends of Eddie Coyle 73. Chinatown 74. Farewell My Lovely 75. Taxi Driver 76. The Driver 78. Body Heat 81. The Postman Always Rings Twice 81. Blood Simple 84. Backfire 88. Miller's Crossing 90. The Grifters 90. The Two Jakes 90. Cape Fear 91. The Last Seduction 94.

film society.
A club formed to show high-quality revivals and new films not normally found in public cinemas.

fine grain print.
One of high quality stock (avoiding the coarseness of silver salt deposit); used for making dupe negatives.

first dollar-gross
is a contractual agreement in which the participants receive a percentage of a film's gross receipts without any deductions for distribution fees or production costs. It was once limited to a few top stars, but these days there are also producers, directors and writers who command it. As a result, studios complain that they can make little profit on films involving several such talents, and as a result more films will be made featuring no more than one star name. According to the studios, the system also means that producers and directors do not care whether they bring a movie in on budget as their payment depends not on the film's profitability but on box-office receipts. Around 15 producers, including Arnold KOPELSON, Jerry BRUCKHEIMER, Brian GRAZIER and Scott RUDIN, directors such as Steven SPIELBERG, Chris COLUMBUS and Sydney POLLACK, and writers such as Michael CRICHTON and Tom CLANCY are among those who can command first dollar-gross.

flashback.
A break in chronological narrative during which we are shown events of past time which bear on the present situation. The device is as old as the cinema: you could say that *Intolerance* was composed of four flashbacks. As applied to more commonplace yarns, however, with the flashback narrated by one of the story's leading characters, the convention soared into popularity in the 30s until by 1945 or so a film looked very dated indeed if it was not told in retrospect. In the 50s flashbacks fell into absolute disuse, but are now creeping back into fashion again. Some notable uses are:

The Power and the Glory 33, which was advertised as being in 'Narratage' because Ralph Morgan spoke a commentary over the action. *Bride of Frankenstein* 35, which was narrated by Elsa Lanchester as Mary Shelley; the gag was that she also played the monster's mate. *The Great McGinty* 40, in which the flashback construction revealed the somewhat corrupt leading figures finally as penniless, thus mollifying the Hays Office. *Rebecca* 40, in which the introductory narrative, while revealing that Manderley was to go up in flames, also comforted in the knowledge that the hero and heroine would be saved. *Citizen Kane* 41, the complex structure of which was so influential that a whole host of pictures followed in which we tried to get at the truth about a character already dead, by questioning those who knew him: cf. *The Killers*, *The Rake's Progress*, *The Moon and Sixpence*, *The Bridge of San Luis Rey*, *The Woman in Question*, *Letter from an Unknown Woman*, *Rashomon*, *The Great Man*, even *Doctor Zhivago*. *Hold Back the Dawn* 41, in which Charles Boyer as a penniless refugee visited Paramount Studios and sold his story to Mitchell Leisen. *The Mummy's Hand* 41, in which the ten-minute chunk telling how the mummy came to be buried alive was lifted straight from the 1932 film *The Mummy*. (Such economies have become commonplace.) *Roxie Hart* 42, in which George Montgomery told a twenty-year-old tale about a notorious lady who at the end of the film was revealed as the mother of his large family. *Ruthless* 48, a tortuous Zachary Scott melodrama, reviewed as follows by the British critic C. A. Lejeune:

Beginning pictures at the end
Is, I'm afraid, a modern trend;
But I'd find *Ruthless* much more winning
If it could end at the beginning.

Road to Utopia 45, in which Hope and Lamour appeared as old folks telling the story; as a pay-off their 'son' appeared, looking just like Crosby, and Hope told the audience: 'We adopted him.' *Passage to Marseilles* 44, a complex melodrama ranging from Devil's Island to war-torn Britain; it has flashbacks within flashbacks *within flashbacks*. In *Dead of Night* 45, all the characters told supernatural experiences to a psychiatrist, who was then murdered by one of them; the murderer then woke up with no recollection of his nightmare, and proceeded to meet all the other characters again as though for the first time, being caught in an endless series of recurring dreams. *Enchantment* 47, and later *Death of a Salesman* 52, and many films up to *I Was Happy Here* 66, in which characters walk straight out of the present into the past, dispensing with the boring 'I remember' bit. *Edward My Son* 49 and *Teahouse of the August Moon* 56, in which characters step out of the play to tell the story to the audience. *Dead Reckoning* 47, in which Humphrey Bogart confesses the entire plot to a priest. *Kind Hearts and Coronets* 49, in which the story springs from the memoirs of a murderer being written on the night before his execution. *Sunset Boulevard* 50, in which the story is told by the dead hero. *An Inspector Calls* 54, in which a supernatural figure visits a family to make them remember their harsh treatment of a girl who has committed suicide. *Repeat Performance* 47, in which a desperate husband relives the events of the year, leading up to his predicament, and gets a chance to change the outcome. *A Woman's Face* 41, in which the story was based on the recollections of eight courtroom witnesses. *The Locket* and *Lust for Gold*, in which complex flashbacks framed and divided the action.

If the format is to catch on again it will have to be more deftly used than in two 60s films: *Ride Beyond Vengeance*, with its completely irrelevant framing story about a census-taking, and *Lady L*, in which the framing story with the characters as old folks is only marginally less inept than the basic one. Two big-scale musicals, *Star!* and *Funny Girl*, have flashbacks with style but little purpose, and *Little Big Man* barely used its framework except to show that Dustin Hoffman can play a 121-year-old.

fleapit.
An affectionate British term for the kind of tatty little cinema in which, it was sometimes alleged, the management loaned a hammer with each ticket.

floor effects
is the term used to describe special effects that occur live, in-camera, during filming rather than being added later; it covers such effects as explosions, bullet impacts, and many types of mechanical effect.

Foley artist.
A sound effects specialist, named after Jack Foley, who is credited for creating the techniques for adding post-production sound effects to enhance the action on the screen.

footage.
Length of a film expressed in feet.

foyer cards.
Elaborate, oversized stills with coloured borders bearing credits, all designed for lobby display. A collection of them by John Kobal was published in 1983: it bore the wince-making title *Foyer Pleasure*.

frame.
A single picture on a strip of film. At normal sound projection speed, 24 frames are shown each second.

franchise.
A term used to describe a film that provides opportunities for more of the same: that lends itself to sequels or features a character who can appear in several more films, often virtually indistinguishable from the original. There are low-rent franchises, such as *Nightmare on Elm Street* or *Friday the 13th*, and big-budget ones such as *James Bond*, *Superman*, *Batman* and *Lethal Weapon*. Such series have been around since the early days of films, beginning with serials like *The Perils of Pauline* and such series as *Tarzan*, but they used to be largely confined to the low-budget end of film-making; these days creating a franchise seems to be the main preoccupation of mainstream Hollywood producers and directors. Apart from the films themselves, franchises also lend themselves to MERCHANDISING. The term derives from business, and results from films being seen as the artistic equivalent of fast food.

freeze frame.
A printing device whereby the action appears to 'freeze' into a still, this being accomplished by printing one frame many times.

frost
on movie windows is usually produced from a mixture of Epsom salts and stale beer.

Fujicolor.
Japanese colour film first used in 1955. Fuji's ultra-high-speed colour negative film was given an Academy Award of Merit in 1981, and was used to film the international success *Das Boot*, directed by Wolfgang Petersen.

gaffer.
The chief electrician on a film, responsible for operating the lights under the instructions of the cinematographer or director of photography.

gaffer tape
is a heavy-duty adhesive tape, backed with canvas, which is used to secure objects on film sets.

genny
is a mobile electric generator used to supply power while working on location.

ghosting.
Another word for dubbing, especially when a star apparently singing is actually miming to the voice of the real artist.

See also: DUBBING.

glass shot.
Usually a scenic shot in which part of the background is actually painted on a glass slide held in front of the camera and carefully blended with the action. In this way castles, towns, etc. may be shown on a location where none exist, without the expense of building them.

grading:
the laboratory process of matching the density and brightness of each shot to the next.

grip.
A technician who builds or arranges the film set; a specialized labourer. The chief grip on a picture is usually credited as 'Key Grip'.

Book: 1997, *Grip Book: How to Become a Motion Picture Film Technician* by Michael G. and Sabrina Uva.

Hale's Tours.
In 1902 at the St Louis Exposition, George C. Hale, ex-chief of the Kansas City Fire Department, had the bright idea of shooting a film from the back of a moving train and screening the result in a small theatre decorated like an observation car. During the screening bells clanged, train whistles sounded and the 'coach' rocked slightly. The idea was so successful that it toured for several years in the United States.

hard ticket.
A phrase used in the 60s to describe film exhibition of the type once called 'road show': separate performances, reserved seats, long runs and high prices.

HDTV,
High Definition Television, the latest development in television technology, which provides a better picture by increasing the resolution to 1,125 lines and having a screen with a similar ratio to the cinema. Future development may be held up by the failure of interested parties to agree on a standard; it seems likely that Europe will set a standard that differs from America and Japan in order to protect European manufacturers of electronic equipment. Japan began HDTV broadcasts in 1991, using an analog system. In the long term, as computers grow in importance in entertainment, it is more likely that the HDTV of the future will be digital. It has already attracted the attention of film-makers: Peter Greenaway used HDTV editing facilities to create the rich imagery of *Prospero's Books* 91, his version of Shakespeare's *The Tempest*, and Wim Wenders used it for his *Until the End of the World/Bis ans Ende der Welt* 92.

hokum.
A word allegedly derived from an Indian word for a stodgy food, it came to mean pure entertainment of a routine kind, usually involving fast action. From it came the adjective 'hokey'. It was not always applied in the pejorative sense: many of most people's favourite films are basically hokum, in that they do not advance the art, but they may show it at its professional best.

❝ Who invented hokum? Think how much money he'd have made from the film producers if he'd sold his invention on a royalty basis. – *Robert Sherwood*

The Hollywood Ten.
Alvah Bessie, Herbert Biberman, Lester Cole, Edward Dmytryk, Ring Lardner Jnr, John Howard Lawson, Albert Maltz, Sam Ornitz, Adrian Scott and Dalton Trumbo were the famous band of writers, producers and directors who in 1947 refused to tell the Unamerican Activities Committee whether or not they were communists. All served short prison sentences and had difficulty getting work in Hollywood for several years.

Imax.
A large-screen technology, developed in Canada, that provides an image three times bigger than 70mm systems, and which uses six magnetic soundtracks to drive loudspeakers surrounding its audience. So far there are some 80 cinemas in the world capable of utilizing the system. There is one in Britain, at the National Museum of Photography, Film and Television in Bradford, with a screen 52 x 64 feet, and the British Film Institute plans to open another in London in the near future. Imax was first shown at Expo '70 in Japan, but attracted wider interest following the release in 1992 of a concert film, *At the Max*, directed by Julien Temple and featuring the rock band The Rolling Stones. The system's name is derived from a combination of the words Image and Maximum.

impressionism.
Generally understood to mean contriving an effect or making a point by building up a sequence from short disconnected shots or scenes.

independent film
is the term applied to a film made outside the Hollywood studio system. It can be used of uncommercial films intended for a specialized audience, or of films made by talent that wishes to keep creative control of the project, though many such productions do tend to involve the financial participation of studio-distributors, so that the term is often used indiscriminately to describe small-scale movies. With the breakdown of the old studio system in the late 40s, following the US Supreme Court decision that forced the major studios to get rid of their cinema chains, there has been a plethora of independent producers, though many work within the system. Some directors, such as Hal HARTLEY, Jim JARMUSCH and Shane MEADOWS, have preferred to work outside the mainstream, and others have done so when major studios have rejected them: Orson Welles raised the finance for his later films, and, in 1997, Robert Duvall used his own money to direct and star in *The Apostle* after many years of trying to obtain studio backing.

❝ Independent film is a misnomer. Who cares if you're an independent? You want to be an independent? Sharpen your pencil, write a poem. You want to spend 20 million? Get real. – *James Schamus*

Independent Frame
was a technique devised in the mid-40s for the Rank Organization by art director David RAWNSLEY to save costs on location shooting by using back and front projection and a stylized, mass production approach to film-making. Rawnsley believed that it would also increase production and free directors' imaginations from literal representations. It was championed by Michael POWELL, but in practice its factory

methods proved constricting, and involved working out a production in every detail, including camera placements, before filming began. Hailed by *Kinematograph Weekly* as 'one of the greatest technical advances since the advent of commercial colour photography', it was abandoned when films made by the method were critical and box-office failures. They included *Warning to Wantons* 49, *Floodtide* 49, *Stop Press Girl* 49, and *Poet's Pub* 49.

independent producer.

One not employed by a studio or distributor, who raises his own finance and makes his own deals. For many years independent productions tended to lack big studio expertise, and Tallulah Bankhead is said to have remarked, after viewing one of them, 'I don't see what that producer has got to be so independent about.' Since the breakup of the big studios in the 50s, however, most productions have been 'independent', and as Billy Wilder remarked, 'You now spend eighty per cent of your time making deals and only twenty per cent making pictures.'

insert shot.

One inserted into a dramatic scene, usually for the purpose of giving the audience a closer look at what the character on screen is seeing, e.g. a letter or a newspaper headline.

interactive films

are a goal towards which many seem to be working, though few agree on what is exactly meant by the term. At the moment, it is used to describe computer games on CD-ROM which incorporate filmed sequences using actors, who usually do little more than set the scene or tell the player what to do next. Interaction by the player is usually limited to choosing between one of several alternative actions. In the future, as technology progresses, it may be possible for an audience to interact more directly with what is happening, by altering the outcome of the story to suit its own tastes or by taking over the role of director to give instructions to the participants.

❝ The interaction between two people communicating enriches while interactive storytelling is like masturbation as opposed to love-making – *Krzystof Zanussi*

iris.

An adjustable diaphragm in the camera which opens or closes from black like an expanding or contracting circle, giving a similar effect on the screen. So called because it resembles the iris of the human eye.

jump-cutting.

Moving abruptly from one scene to another to make a dramatic point, e.g. from cause to effect.

Kaiju eiga

is the term used by the Japanese to describe its genre of monster movies, of which the best known are the GODZILLA series.

Kinematograph Renters' Society (KRS).

This British organization was founded by film distributors in 1915 for their own protection and collective bargaining power, chiefly against exhibitors.

Kinescope.

American term for what the British call a telerecording, i.e. a live or tape show transferred for convenience on to tape. The technical quality is seldom satisfactory, and the process was gradually discontinued in favour of electronic tape conversion from one line standard to another.

Kinetoscope.

An early film viewing apparatus (1893) in which a continuous loop of film could be viewed by one person only.

lavender print.

A high-quality fine-grain master positive film, struck from the original negative for the purpose of making duplicates, so called because the emulsion was coated with a lavender-tinted base to reduce halation and scatter in the image.

leader.

Length of blank film joined to the beginning of a reel for lacing up in projector. 'Academy' leaders give a numbered countdown to the start of action.

library shot:

see STOCK SHOT.

Lightwave 3D

is a relatively low-cost computer graphics program, originally developed by NewTek for the Amiga computer in conjunction with the Video Toaster hardware, which is used to create animation and special effects in TV programmes and movies. It has been used in *Men in Black* (for the opening sequence of the dragonfly), *Contact*, *The Jackal*, *Titanic*, *The Fifth Element*, *Mortal Kombat II*, *Spawn*, and *Tomorrow Never Dies*.

Lightworks

is a computer-based digital editing system, one of the two, with AVID MEDIA COMPOSER, that is rapidly becoming the preferred method of editing film. It was first used in 1992 by David Brenner and Sally MENKE on *Heaven and Earth*, directed by Oliver STONE.

The Lion's Share,

by Bosley Crowther. A lively history of the Metro-Goldwyn-Mayer company, written in 1957 by the critic of the *New York Times*.

location.

A shooting site away from the studio, not encouraged in the days of the moguls, but considered essential in the cause of realism as soon as the studio system broke up.

❝ A rock is a rock, a tree is a tree, shoot it in Griffith Park. – *Anon*

long shot.

One taken from a distance, usually to establish a scene or a situation but sometimes for dramatic effect. Opposite of close-up.

looping

is the term used to describe the process of dubbing dialogue onto the soundtrack of a film, usually because the original sound was not of sufficiently good quality, owing to extraneous noises caused by shooting on location. The scene to be dubbed is contained on a short loop of film joined together so that it can be projected continuously in order that the actors can match exactly their speaking of the new dialogue with the old. The method is also used for adding dialogue in another language to a foreign film. The process is also known as DUBBING, POST-SYNCHRONIZATION or post-synching and, more recently, as ADR, a recent technical improvement that does away with the need for actual looping.

❝ My idea of hell when you die is they make you loop your entire life. – *Anthony Perkins*

losing the light.

What happens during outdoor shooting when the natural light of the sun is obscured and filming comes to a stop.

lot.

A term used to cover all areas of a studio where filming takes place, and also where sets are built and stored.

m and e track.

A sound track giving music and effects but not dialogue, necessary in dubbing stages.

Macguffin (aka McGuffin).

Term invented by writer Angus MacPhail, and associated with the films of Alfred HITCHCOCK, to describe a plot device of little intrinsic interest, such as stolen papers, that triggers the action.

make-up.

A general term for the cosmetic application to the body of materials intended to enhance or change the appearance, from glamorization to the creation of monsters.

❝ The relationship between the make-up man and the film actor is that of accomplices in crime. – *Marlene Dietrich*

Manga.

Japanese term for comics, which translates as 'irresponsible pictures'. The word has come to be applied in the West to Japanese animated films owing to the release of such films on the Manga video label and the appearance of fan magazines devoted to the style. Many of the best-selling comic books have been turned into animated films, which are more properly known as ANIME.

mask.

A technical device for blocking out part of the image. *Masking* is the black cloth which surrounds the actual cinema screen: these days it has to be electrically adjustable to encompass the various screen sizes.

matt or matte.

A technique (sometimes known as *travelling matt*) for blending actors in the studio with location or trick scenes. The actor is photographed against a non-reflective background (e.g. black velvet) and a high-contrast negative of this image is combined with the desired background. Thus men can move among animated monsters, and ghosts can slowly disappear.

medium shot.

One taking in the full body of the actor, not so close as a close-up, not so far off as a long shot.

merchandising.

The means of exploiting films and personalities through souvenirs, toys and other consumable items has always brought in considerable revenue to canny film-makers, often more than the film itself. Film editions of novels, illustrated with stills from the movie, and novelizations of film scripts were being published from the early 20s onwards, but Walt Disney was among the first to realize the commercial possibilities of exploiting his animated characters, with such goods as a Mickey Mouse watch, a trend culminating in the opening of an international chain of shops selling Disney goods from the mid-80s onwards. Television accelerated the process, with such personalities as Hopalong Cassidy appearing on everything from lunch boxes to pillow cases. Disney's shops were followed in the 90s by Warner opening a store merchandising Bugs Bunny and other cartoon heroes. But it is only in comparatively recent times that films have been primarily designed to sell a range of toys or to advertise particular products. Product placement, in which cameras linger on a particular range of footwear or obtrusively feature a certain type of soft drink, has become a means of gaining as much income as possible from a film. It was no accident that E.T. munched on M&Ms rather than, say, jelly-babies. E.T. still remains one of the most successful merchandising operations – in Britain alone, the wholesaler of E.T. merchandise guaranteed sales of £1 million – together with the *Star Wars* movies, which shifted around $2 billion of toys and other paraphernalia now gathering dust in cupboards. Occasionally, merchandisers do get caught short. The makers of *Forrest Gump* did not believe that the film lent itself to merchandising opportunities. Once it was a runaway hit in America, they changed their minds and began producing Forrest Gump goods, including a book of Gump sayings. In 1995, the toy company Mattel sold $450m of Disney products. The amount of money involved was revealed in a proposed deal in 1996 between the fast-food chain McDonald's and Disney, in which McDonald's would pay Disney $100m a year for the rights to 14 to 17 film and television features, a sponsorship of Disney's projected Animal Kingdom theme park, and video promotions. It was estimated that the cost of the deal, including promotional advertising, would amount to $2 billion over a 10-year period.

❝ There is a staunch refusal to admit that anything needs to be taken so seriously as to get in the way of its marketing, and a confidence that anything can be marketed, anything can be made appealing, if it is packaged well enough and given the right advertising spin. – *David Rieff on American popular culture*

The Method

is a style of acting derived initially from the teachings and writings of the Russian actor and director Konstantin Stanislavsky, as refracted through the Actors' Studio in New York, which was co-founded by director Elia KAZAN and later dominated by the teaching of Lee STRASBERG.

❝ I once asked two old Russian actors about the Method, because I'd seen American actors in New York using their version of it and it was so awful, amateur and inept and stupid. And they said to me, if you have a copy of Stanislavsky's *My Life in Art* or *An Actor Prepares* just take it out and throw it in the river. If it was bilge to them, it was certainly no use to me. – *Robert Stephens*

See also: The ACTORS' STUDIO.

moguls.

The name given half-affectionately to the men who ran Hollywood in the golden days of the studios: Mayer, Thalberg, Selznick, Goldwyn, Warner, Zanuck, Zukor, Cohn, etc. The best capsule guide to them is Philip French's *The Movie Moguls* (1970).

❝ They were monsters and pirates and bastards right down to the bottom of their feet but they loved movies. Some of the jerks running the business today don't even have faces. – *Richard Brooks, c. 1970*

I was impressed by the moral potentialities of the screen. – *Adolph Zukor*

Those of us who became film producers hailed from all sorts of occupations – furriers, magicians, butchers, boilermakers – and for this reason highbrows have often poked fun at us. Yet one thing is certain: every man who succeeded was a born showman. And once in the show business he was never happy out of it. – *Adolph Zukor*

There's nothing wrong with Hollywood that six first-class funerals couldn't cure. – *Anon, 1930*

Don't make these pictures any better. Just keep them the way they are. – *Louis B. Mayer on the Hardy Family series*

We should all make a killing in this business. There's so much money in the pot. – *Irving Thalberg*

It's better than being a pimp. – *Harry Cohn*

montage.

In the most general sense, the whole art of editing or assembling scenes into the finished film. Specifically, 'a montage' is understood as an impressionistic sequence of short dissolve-shots either bridging a time gap, setting a situation or showing the background to the main story. Classic montages which come to mind are in *The Battleship Potemkin*, *The Roaring Twenties* and *Citizen Kane*.

MOS

Mysterious Hollywood script abbreviation indicating a silent shot. Allegedly it derived from the early 30s, when one of the many immigrant German directors called for a scene 'mit out sound'.

motion capture

is a method of capturing in real time the actual movements of a person and transferring them to a computer-generated character, from a rabbit to Godzilla.

Motion Picture Alliance for the Preservation of American Ideals

was an organization set up in 1943 in opposition to the unionization of the film industry and the promulgation of left-wing opinions. Its founding members included directors Sam WOOD, Clarence BROWN and King VIDOR, actors Clark GABLE, Gary COOPER, Adolphe MENJOU, Charles COBURN, Barbara STANWYCK, Robert TAYLOR and Ward BOND, and writers Hedda HOPPER and Ayn RAND, who wrote for it *A Screen Guide for Americans*. Later members included Irene DUNNE and Ginger ROGERS, and it had the support of the anti-union Walt DISNEY and the newspaper tycoon William Randolph HEARST. Its statement of principles was: 'we resent the growing impression that this industry is made up of, and dominated, by communists, radicals and crackpots'. The Alliance asked for a congressional investigation of communism in Hollywood and also invited HUAC (the House Un-American Activities Committee) to come to Hollywood, which resulted in the interrogation of many film-makers, the imprisonment of what became known as The HOLLYWOOD TEN, and the blacklisting by the studios of those suspected of left-wing opinions. It had lost all influence and ceased to exist by the mid-50s.

❝ My *Screen Guide for Americans* . . . was reproduced on the front page of the Drama Section of the New York *Times*, and several other papers ran it. All the points I had made, particularly about the attacks on businessmen as villains, disappeared from the screen. I take credit for that. – *Ayn Rand*

The purpose of the Communists in Hollywood is *not* the production of political movies openly advocating Communism. Their purpose is to *corrupt our moral premises by corrupting non-political movies* – by introducing small, casual bits of propaganda into innocent stories – thus making people absorb the basic principles of Collectivism *by indirection and implication*. – *Ayn Rand, Screen Guide for Americans*

Motion Picture Association of America
A trade guild in which distributors meet to set tariffs and deal with complaints, also set a censorship code.

Moviola.
A portable editing machine which enables the user to run film backwards and forwards at various speeds and to examine it frame by frame while viewing it on a small screen.

MOW.
Acronym for a movie made for television, deriving from ABC's Movie of the Week, consisting of 90-minute dramas, which ran from 1968 to 1975. The first TV movie was probably *See How They Run*, made by Universal TV and aired on NBC in October 1964, directed by David Lowell Rich and starring John Forsythe, Leslie Nielsen, George Kennedy, Franchot Tone and Jane Wyatt. Some earlier TV dramas from the 50s, when television was live, were later remade as films, the most notable example being *Marty*.

MPEG
stands for the Motion Picture Experts Group and is a standard for the digital compression of images. The method compares and saves only the changes between one frame of a film or animation and another, thus enabling 72 minutes of film to be recorded on a five-inch compact disk. A refinement of the system, MPEG II, is being prepared.

multiplane.
A word introduced by Walt Disney to explain his new animation process for *The Old Mill* 37. Instead of building up a drawing by laying 'cells' directly on top of each other, a slight illusion of depth was obtained by leaving space between the celluloid images of foreground, background, principal figure, etc. Special Academy Award 1938.

mute print.
One with only the picture, no sound track.

National Film Archive.
A government-financed museum of films of artistic and historical value. Operated by the British Film Institute.

The National Film Board of Canada
was set up in 1939, with John Grierson at its head, to show Canada's face to the world. Many excellent documentaries ensued, not to mention the brilliant animation films of Norman McLaren, but by the end of the 60s the Board's fortunes were at a lower ebb and its reputation declined.

The National Film Finance Corporation
was founded in 1949 to provide loans for film production, but began to withdraw its facilities in the early 70s, at a time when financial encouragement had never been more needed for British production.

The National Film Theatre
on London's South Bank is an extension of the British Film Institute; founded in 1951, it runs a daily repertory in three theatres of films of all nationalities and types.

neo-realism
is a term mainly applied to the Italian post-war films which seemed to present a fresh and vivid kind of social realism. The essentials were real locations and at least a proportion of amateur actors. The most famous neo-realist film is *Bicycle Thieves*.

'new wave'/'nouvelle vague'.
Term used (by themselves) for a group of new, exploring young French directors towards the end of the 50s: François Truffaut, Jean-Luc Godard, Louis Malle, Alain Resnais, etc. As their talents were widely divergent, the term meant very little. It was coined by Françoise Giroud.

❝ There is no new wave, only the sea. – *Claude Chabrol*

newsreels
were part of the very earliest cinema programme, and the nine-minute round up of topical events filmed by roving cameramen was a feature of programmes in cinemas throughout the world until the mid-60s, when it was clear that the newsreel had been replaced by television. Most newsreel companies have looked after their libraries, and the result is a vivid history of the twentieth century, frequently plundered by producers of compilation films.

nickelodeon.
A humorous term applied to early American cinemas once they had become slightly grander than the converted stores which were used for the purpose at the turn of the century.

The Nine Old Men
was the name Walt Disney gave to his most trusted animators, who had joined the studio by the mid-30s, before it began feature film production. They were: Les Clark, Marc Davis, Ollie Johnson, Milt Kahl, Ward Kimball, Eric Larson, John Lounsbery, Wolfgang Reitherman, Frank Thomas.

nitrate.
Until 1950 film stock had a nitrate base, which helped give a splendid sheen, but was very inflammable. The change was made to safety stock, which burns much more slowly, but black-and-white films at least never looked so good again.

non-theatrical.
A descriptive adjective usually applied to film showings at which there is no paid admission on entrance, e.g. schools, clubs, etc. Some distributors apply the term to all 16mm showings.

opticals.
A general term indicating all the visual tricks such as wipes, dissolves, invisibility, mattes, etc., which involve laboratory work.

original version.
In European countries, this indicates a foreign language film which is sub-titled and not dubbed.

'Oscar'.
An affectionate name given to the Academy Award statuette; reputedly because when the figure was first struck in 1927 a secretary said: 'It reminds me of my Uncle Oscar.'

pan.
A shot in which the camera rotates horizontally. Also used as a verb.

Panavision.
A wide-screen system which outdistanced CinemaScope because of its improved anamorphic lens. Super-Panavision and Panavision 70 are 'road show' processes involving projection on wide film: in the first case the film is shot on 65mm, in the second blown up after photography. Great confusion was caused in the 70s by the company insisting on the credit 'filmed with Panavision equipment' even on non-anamorphic films.

paparazzi
is the term used to describe freelance photographers who stalk celebrities to take unposed photographs of them. It is derived from the character of the photographer Paparazzo in Fellini's *La Dolce Vita*, who was based on the Italian photographer Tazio Secchiaroli.

paper prints
were made of most films between 1895 and 1912 because the US Copyright Act did not allow for celluloid. This quirk of the law meant the preservation of hundreds of early titles which could otherwise have been lost, and in the 60s they were all copied for the archives of the Motion Picture Academy on to 16mm film.

Patsy Awards
are annual awards given to the top animal performers in movies and, from 1958, television by the American Humane Association, in co-operation with the Hollywood studios. The title is an acronym for Picture Animal Top Star of the Year. The first winner, in 1951 at a ceremony with Ronald Reagan as the master of ceremonies, was FRANCIS the mule, who also won awards in 1952, 1954, 1955, 1956 and 1957.

peplum.
Term to describe Italian historical epics, which are also known as 'sword and sandal'. Both expressions relate to the costumes of the participants, 'peplum' referring to the short skirts worn by both the men and the women. Such films were at their height in the early 60s, sparked off by the success in the US of *Ben-Hur* and of *Hercules*, made in 1957 by Pietro Francisci and starring Steve Reeves, which was promoted heavily by Joseph E. Levine. The genre in Italy goes back to *Cabiria*, made in 1914, starring Bartolomeo Pagano as MACISTE. The 60s cycle was notable for using mainly American muscle-men to play its heroes and for employing many talents, such as Sergio Leone, who went on to make the even more popular spaghetti westerns.

See also: EPIC FILM.

persistence of vision.
The medical explanation for our being able to see moving pictures. Twenty-four ordered still pictures are shown to us successively each second, and our sense of sight is slow enough to merge them into one continuous action. The retina of the eye retains each still picture just long enough for it to be replaced by another only slightly different.

pilot:
in television terminology, a film which is made as a trial, to see whether a series on the same premise will be ordered.

pin screen animation:
a curious and short-lived means of animation by photographing pins pushed through a rubber sheet. The shadows caused by the varying height of the pins gives the single picture. The best example is Alexieff's *Night on Bald Mountain* 33.

pink movies
— *pinku eiga* — was the name given to the genre of low-budget erotic films that emerged in Japan during the mid-60s and became extremely popular, accounting for as much as half the studios' output. The most controversial director was Tetsuji Takechi, whose *Black Snow/Kuroi Yuki* in 1965 was the subject of a failed prosecution for public indecency. Other directors included Seijun Suzuki and Koji Wakamatsu. The films were notable for scenes of rape, torture and voyeurism.

See also: ROMAN PORNO.

Pixelvision.
Title given to films made by a group of experimental film-makers using a Fisher-Price PXL 2000 video camera. Made of moulded plastic, with a fixed lens or 'image receptor', and recording on standard audio cassettes, the camera produces images that tend to fade rapidly, are composed of easily visible pixels, like an over-enlarged computer image, and blur if the camera is moved. It was made as a toy for Christmas 1987 and discontinued soon after; working cameras are now much sought after. So far, Michael ALMEREYDA has made a 56-minute feature, *Another Girl Another Planet*, using the camera; shorts made with it include *Glass Jaw* 91, directed by Michael O'Reilly, *Don from Lakewood* 91, directed by Pat Tierney and Eric Saks, *Elegy* 91, directed by Joe Gibbons, *It Wasn't Love* 91, directed by Sadie Benning, and *Black and White/Grain* 93, directed by Stuart Sherman.

Pixilation.
A method of stop-motion animation applied to real objects or people. The shots are taken in a camera that exposes one frame at a time, with the person moving slightly between each shot. Animating people frame by frame can be a simple way of achieving special effects, such as flying, or to produce jerky, comic results. It was used to good effect in *The Secret Adventures of Tom Thumb* 93, a feature-length film by Dave Borthwick which combined animated and human figures, and by Japanese director Shinya Tsukamoto in his fantasies *Tetsuo: The Iron Man* 91 and *Tetsuo II: Bodyhammer* 91. The effect can also be achieved by editing normally photographed action.

post-synchronization.
Adding sound, by dubbing, to visuals already shot. Sound can only rarely be recorded at the time of shooting because of extraneous noise and requirements of volume, pitch, etc.; actors must usually repeat their lines in accordance with their image on screen.

pratfall.
Something in which all silent comedians were skilled: the art of falling on one's fundament without getting hurt.

pre-credits sequence.
It has recently become fashionable to start films with an explosive opening scene, sometimes running seven or eight minutes, before the titles appear. This now over-worked device, used by almost all American TV series, is generally traced back to *Rommel, Desert Fox* 51, which had a long pre-credits sequence showing a commando raid; but the titles come quite late in *The Egg and I* 47, and even in *Destry Rides Again* 39 there is nearly a minute of shooting before they appear; while in *The Magnificent Ambersons* 42 they are not seen at all, only spoken at the end of the picture.

More recently, *Cruising* and *Papillon* are among the movies to place all their credits at the end.

prequel.
The opposite of a sequel, i.e. a film showing events which happened *before* one already known. The first film prequel may have been *Another Part of the Forest*, which came after *The Little Foxes* but described events before it. The word came into being in the late 70s with the production of *Butch and Sundance: The Early Days*. A game rapidly sprang up in which one had to supply prequel titles for famous films. Among them were *Mr Blandings Applies for Planning Permission; The Boy Who Would Be Prince; Friday Night Slight Temperature; Destry Dismounts;* and *Hello Mr Chips*.

preview:
see SNEAK PREVIEW.

Prizmacolour.
An early American colour process used for *The Glorious Adventure* 21. Crude in effect, in using orange and turquoise filters, it anticipated Cinecolor.

Producer.
On the stage this term may be equivalent to 'director', i.e. the man who actually marshals the actors and whose conception of the show is supreme. In the film world it almost always indicates the man in control of the budget, whether an independent or working for a big studio. He controls all personnel including the director, and though the film may originally be his overall conception, he normally delegates his artistic responsibilities, remaining responsible chiefly for the film's ultimate commercial success or failure.

❝ The producer must be a prophet and a general, a diplomat and a peacemaker, a miser and a spendthrift. He must have vision tempered by hindsight, daring governed by caution, the patience of a saint and the iron of a Cromwell. – *Jesse L. Lasky*

Movie production requires producers, men who can orchestrate the sound and the fury of which pictures are made. – *Joseph Kennedy*

The job of turning good writers into movie hacks is the producer's chief task. – *Ben Hecht*

A producer is a clever man whose brain starts working the moment he gets up in the morning and doesn't stop until he reaches the studio. – *Martin Ragaway*

Producers are men who will keep their heads in the noisy presence of writers and directors and not be carried away by art in any of its subversive guises. Their task is to guard against the unusual. They are the trusted loyalists of cliché. – *Ben Hecht*

A producer shouldn't get ulcers, he should give them. – *Sam Goldwyn*

Producing is a thankless task akin to hotel management. Unfortunately there are not too many good hotel managers. – *David Hemmings*

The director is the fellow who directs the picture and his status is that of an artist, whereas the producer is the big-shot but his real function, outside of prodigious cigar-smoking, has never been discovered. – *George Sanders*

production designer.
Technician responsible for the overall 'look' of a film, ranging from actual set design to photographic style.

production manager.
The person responsible for administrative details of a production, e.g. salaries, transport, departmental expenditure.

programmer.
Trade term for a routine feature of only moderate appeal, likely to form half a bill; similar to 'co-feature'.

propaganda:
see DOCUMENTARY.

quota.
By Act of Parliament renters were obliged to sell, and exhibitors to show, a varying proportion of British-made films. There has not always been enough British talent to fill the necessary number of releases: hence the notorious 'quota quickies' of the 20s and 30s, and much second-feature material, which however bad could invariably get a circuit booking providing it had a British quota ticket. The normal quota which an exhibitor has to fill is 30% for features, 25% for supporting programmes. This contrasts markedly with independent television contractors, whose programmes must be 86% British.

ratio (screen):
see ASPECT RATIO.

reduction print:
one optically reduced from 35mm to 16mm.

reel.
A loose term generally taken to mean 1,000 feet of 35mm film, i.e. the amount which would fit on to a reel of the old-fashioned kind, running about ten minutes. Thus short films were spoken of as two-reelers, three-reelers, etc., and charged accordingly. But modern 35mm projector spools will take 2,000 feet and sometimes 3,000 feet, so the term is slowly falling into disuse . . . especially as 16mm projectors have always taken spools of either 400, 800 or 1,600 feet.

road show.
A term which used to mean a travelling show; latterly in cinema terms it indicates the special, prolonged pre-release at advanced prices of a big-screen attraction, e.g. *My Fair Lady* or *The Sound of Music*, which may in this way run for years in a big city before being released to local theatres.

roman porno
is the term used to describe Japanese erotic films of the 70s, which grew out of PINK MOVIES. While the showing of pubic hair is forbidden, the films are sadistic in tone, marked by scenes of rape and cruelty to women.

rough cut.
The first assembly of shots in the order in which they will be seen in the finished film, used to show those involved what work still needs to be done.

running shot.
One in which the camera, mounted on wheels, keeps pace with its subject, a moving actor or vehicle.

running speed.
In silent days, 35mm ran through the projector at 16 frames per second or 60 feet per minute. When sound came, this was amended for technical reasons to 24 frames per second or 90 feet per minute. No normal 35mm projector can now operate at silent speed, which is why silent films look jerky when you see them (unless a special and very expensive laboratory process is adopted). It is said that many films made in the later silent period were in fact intended for showing at about 20 frames per second, and as machines were variable this was easily accomplished: such films now seem unduly slow when projected at 16 frames per second.

See: SLOW MOTION, ACCELERATED MOTION.

running time.
The length of a film, usually expressed in minutes; if in feet, one must say whether 35mm or 16mm. In European television, for technical reasons, films run faster by one frame in 25, so a 75m film runs only 72m, a 100m film only 96m, etc. Films tended to be shorter and crisper in the 30s, especially when double bills came in; but now nobody seems to have control over self-indulgent directors.

œ

The length of a film should be directly related to the endurance of the human bladder. – *Alfred Hitchcock*

How long should the film be? – *An MGM director*
How long is it good? – *Nicholas Schenck*

rushes.
A day's shooting on film when it comes back from the laboratories and is ready for viewing by those involved.

safety film
took over from nitrate stock in 1950–51. It burns much more slowly and therefore reduces fire risk, but its acetate base also reduces the possibility of gleaming black-and-white photography, tending instead to a matt look.

scenario:
see SHOOTING SCRIPT.

score.
The music composed for a film.

scream queen
is a term used to describe an actress who is frequently cast as the glamorous heroine of horror movies, from her accustomed reaction to peril. The first was Fay Wray in *King Kong*. Notable ones since have been Barbara Steele and Linnea Quigley.

screenplay:
see SHOOTING SCRIPT.

second unit director.
One who directs not the actors but the spectacular location sequences, stunt men, scenic backgrounds, etc., and is thus sometimes responsible for a film's most striking effects; e.g. Andrew Marton's (and Yakima Canutt's) chariot race sequence in *Ben Hur* 59.

Sensurround.
A system evolved in 1975 for *Earthquake*, this dispensable gimmick involved the augmentation of violent action on screen by intense waves of high decibel sound, enough almost to crack the ribs. It never caught on except as a big city come-on.

sequence:
a film paragraph, usually starting and ending with a fade to black.

Sequence.
Cinema magazine of the Oxford University Film Society, which flourished briefly in the mid-40s and early 50s. Its leading lights included Lindsay Anderson, Penelope Houston, Gavin Lambert, and Karel Reisz. Many of its aesthetic ideas influenced FREE CINEMA, which involved many of the same participants.

❛❛ It's no exaggeration to say that the *Sequence* group changed the whole way of feeling and thinking about film in England – at any rate for a few inspiring years, before the British sank once again into complacency and philistinism. – *Tony Richardson*

shooting script.
This differs from a screenplay, which concentrates on dialogue, in that it includes camera directions and breaks up the script into shots; it is an instruction manual for technicians rather than a work of art.

shorts
are officially any films running less than 3000 feet (about 33 minutes). In the 30s most programmes consisted of a feature and several one-reelers, but the big studios first found shorts uneconomic and then closed down altogether. Shorts fell into the hands of independent producers, who found that the longer they made them the more money they could demand, even if the quality was not high. Double-feature programmes also contributed to their demise.

silent films
began to grow unfashionable during 1927, though for eighteen months or so producers continued to put out so-called 'silent versions' of their talkies: these versions were unspeakably bad, as the new talkies used very little camera movement and a great deal of dialogue which had to be given in sub-titles. By 1930 silents had all but disappeared, with exceptions such as Flaherty's *Tabu* 32, Chaplin's *City Lights* 31, and *Modern Times* 36, and an unsuccessful 1952 experiment called *The Thief*, which eschewed dialogue though it did have a music and effects track. In 1976 Mel Brooks produced *Silent Movie*, a comic extravaganza with no dialogue.

❛❛ There never was a silent film. We'd finish a picture, show it in one of our projection rooms and come out shattered. It would be awful. Then we'd show it in a theatre with a girl pounding away at a piano and there would be all the difference in the world. Without that music there wouldn't have been a movie industry at all. – *Irving Thalberg*

It will never be possible to synchronize the voice with the pictures. Music – fine music – will always be the voice of the silent drama . . . There will never be speaking pictures. – *D.W. Griffith, 1924*

16mm.
A 'sub-standard' gauge to which feature films are reduced for private hire and in many countries for television. Many sponsored documentaries not intended for cinema showing are filmed in 16mm, as are television news and features. The smaller frame and greater magnification do not always lead to unsatisfactory results, but the dangers are obvious.

sleeper:
a trade term for a film which suddenly does much better at the box office than was expected.

slides
A feature of film-going in nickelodeon days was the decorative slides used between the brief entertainments. Here is a nostalgic selection:

Please Read the Titles to Yourself. Loud Reading Annoys Your Neighbours.

Just a Moment Please While the Operator Changes Reels.

If Annoyed When Here Please Tell the Management.

Ladies and Gentlemen May safely visit this Theatre as no Offensive Films are ever Shown Here.

We Aim to Present the Pinnacle of Motion Picture Perfection.

Ladies, We Like your Hats, but Please Remove Them.

You Wouldn't Spit on the Floor at Home, so Please Don't do it Here.

slow motion.
An effect obtained by running the camera faster than usual. When the film passes through the projector at normal speed, each movement appears slower, as it occupies more frames of film. For scientific purposes (e.g. recording the growth of plants) cameras are so arranged that a single frame of film is exposed at regular intervals, thus giving an impression of accelerated growth.

Smell-O-Vision.
A process initiated in 1960 by which evocative smells were pumped to the cinema audience through pipes leading to individual seats in the auditorium. Bottles of scent were held on a rotating drum, and the process triggered by a signal on the film itself. *Scent of Mystery* was the only film to be made in Smell-O-Vision.

sneak preview.
An unheralded tryout of a film at a public performance, usually in place of a second feature. Intended to gauge audience reaction, it is often followed by considerable re-editing before the official première.

❛❛ Let one dim-witted adolescent schoolboy scrawl 'Lousy' on his card, and the entire studio may be stampeded the following morning in executive meeting to discuss slicing and revising the picture to shreds. On Hollywood's theory that the customer must know best, the schoolboy's 'Lousy' is regarded as the last word in dramatic criticism. – *Cedric Hardwicke*

If you're working for a studio, you're at the mercy of market testing. You end up cutting your movie according to what a bunch of people in Baltimore said on their little test cards. – *John Sayles*

The whole idea of trying something on an audience until you find what works is first nature to me. I don't think it's first nature to the kind of film people who think it's somehow corrupt or depraved to allow an audience to influence your version of the film. If you're Kurosawa, you can think that way; the rest of them are just pompous oafs. – *John Cleese*

snow,
when needed for a movie scene, has been known to consist of a variety of ingredients including bleached cornflakes, soapflakes, chopped feathers, shredded asbestos, balsa chips, sawdust, and a wide range of plastic products.

soap opera.
A term used disparagingly of TV domestic drama serials. Originated because such offerings were invariably sponsored by the big soap companies who needed to attract the housewife.

soft focus.
A diffused effect used in photographing ageing leading ladies who can't stand good definition; also frequently used for exotic shots in musical numbers, etc.

Sony Dynamic Digital Sound.
A system for recording and playing back sound digitally, launched in 1993. It is one of three competing digital sound systems, the others being Dolby SR-D and Universal's DTS.

sound.
The first really successful experiments with synchronized sound had the track on gramophone discs; cylinders were also employed. These systems obviously led to maddening breakdowns, and editing was next to impossible. Fox, using the De Forrest Phonofilm system combined with a German process called Tri-Ergon, contrived in 1926 to record sound directly on to film next to the picture, forming the first soundtrack. It was this system which by 1930 had superseded the others and is still with us. In a reversion to the past, though, some modern systems feature soundtracks recorded on compact discs synchronized with the film to provide better-quality sound.

soundies
were short, musical films lasting around three minutes that were made for playing in juke-boxes equipped with a screen. In the early 40s, the Mills Panoram Soundies machines were to be found in thousands of American bars and hotel lobbies. Some five films a week were made, usually featuring the latest recordings by popular entertainers and jazz singers and musicians. Their popularity waned by the mid-40s, and many soundies were acquired by television companies or issued on 16mm film.

special effects:
a general term covering the many tricks of film-making which cannot be achieved by direct photography: optical wipes, dissolves, sub-titles, invisibility, mattes, etc.

star
is a word coined by some forgotten publicist in the early years of the century who presumably touted his leading actors as twinkling heavenly lights. It came in the 30s to mean any actor who was billed above the title; but nowadays real stars are hard to find, and the word is generally applied only to those thought likely actually to draw patrons to the box office.

❛❛ Stars may shine so brightly that they dazzle, but the glory of the movie variety is transient. Marie Dressler put it succinctly:

You're only as good as your last picture.

Myron Selznick expressed the same thought:

Stars should get as much money as they can, while they can. They don't last long.

On the other hand Bette Davis, taking it easy in the 70s, was able to rely on her past:

My price for putting my name on that marquee is two hundred thousand dollars and ten per cent of the gross and I won't even talk to anybody for less because when they see me on a screen they're seeing thirty-seven years of sweat.

It didn't work quite as well for Stewart Granger:

I haven't aged into a character actor. I'm still an old leading man.

And Shirley Temple was disillusioned early:

I stopped believing in Santa Claus when I was six. Mother took me to see him in a department store and he asked for my autograph.

Paul Mayersberg thought that:

The star is Hollywood's gift to the twentieth century. Great actors are not the same as stars. A star must depend on some system of reproduction since to become a star you must be available to a large number of people.

Jerry Wald knew that the real trick was to find smart executives:

There's no shortage of talent. There's only a shortage of talent that can recognize talent.

Robert Redford was suspicious:

They throw that word 'star' at you loosely, and they take it away equally loosely. You take the responsibility for their crappy movie, that's what that means.

An anonymous wit classically detailed the five stages in a star's life, as seen by a casting director:

1 Who is Hugh O'Brian?
2 Get me Hugh O'Brian.
3 Get me a Hugh O'Brian type.
4 Get me a young Hugh O'Brian.
5 Who is Hugh O'Brian?

While you're at the top, it can be pleasant. Robert Stack says:

If you're a star you go through the front door carrying the roses, instead of through the back door carrying the garbage.

Gloria Swanson:

I have decided that while I am a star I will be every inch and every moment the star. Everyone from the studio gateman to the highest executive will know it.

Dustin Hoffman:

One thing about being successful is that I stopped being afraid of dying. Once you're a star you're dead already. You're embalmed.

Billie Burke:

By the time you get your name up in lights you have worked so hard and so long, and seen so many names go up and down, that all you can think of is: 'How can I keep it here?'

George Sanders was equally cynical:

The important thing for a star is to have an interesting face. He doesn't have to move it very much. Editing and camerawork can always produce the desired illusion that a performance is being given.

Ethel Barrymore took a different view:

To be a success an actress must have the face of Venus, the brain of Minerva, the grace of Terpsichore, the memory of Macaulay, the figure of Juno and the hide of a rhinoceros.

Katharine Hepburn put it more simply:

Show me an actress who isn't a personality and I'll show you a woman who isn't a star.

Jean Arthur found the going tough:

It's a strenuous job every day of your life to live up to the way you look on the screen.

The temptation to try remains great. Director Michael Winner remarked recently:

Hitchcock said actors are cattle, but show me a cow who can earn one million dollars per film.

But as Harry Cohn said:

After a while the stars believe their own publicity. I've never met a grateful performer in the film business.

Likewise Sam Spiegel:

You make a star, you sometimes make a monster.

So in the 50s the top stars gained control over their own careers, setting up their own independent companies. Jack Warner did not like the result:

In the old days you called the actor and made the deal with him. Now, they bring an army.

At the same time, as Vincent Price noted:

One of the deaths of Hollywood is that they tried to make everyone look normal. Some of the actresses who are around today look and sound like my niece in Scarsdale. I love my niece in Scarsdale, but I wouldn't pay to see her act.

People began to realize that they had been deceived by the apparent effortlessness of the old stars, who had lasted so long and given such good service. When Ronald Colman played a bit part in *Around the World in Eighty Days*, he was asked:

Did you really get a Cadillac for one day's work? – No, he replied – for the work of a lifetime.

In the end, as Sam Goldwyn knew from experience of changing fashions, it is not the actors or the moguls who decide who is a star:

Producers don't make stars. God makes stars, and the public recognizes His handiwork.

And Ellen Terry had the simplest definition of star quality:

That little something extra.

Or as Humphrey Bogart said when asked why he was worth two hundred thousand dollars a picture:

Because I can get it.

Or as Barbra Streisand said:

The real, real reason I like to be in movies is because it's an easy place to have my hems done. There's always a seamstress on the set. And if you break a chair, they can fix it – they have people who can do anything. Chair people, hem people.

Or as Louis Armstrong said:

A lotta cats copy the Mona Lisa, but people still line up to see the original.

Or as David Hemmings said:

I quite like being mobbed. After all it is extremely nice to be recognized. That's what acting is all about – being recognized.

Producer Sam Spiegel had a jaundiced view:

You make a star, you make a monster.

Let Humphrey Bogart have the last word:

You're not a star till they can spell your name in Karachi.

stereophony:
hearing sound from more than one source at the same time, a gimmick used to 'put you in the picture' by surrounding you with loudspeakers when CinemaScope was first introduced.

stereoscopy:
viewing in three dimensions, usually accomplished by watching through polaroid glasses, two films projected one on top of the other after being photographed from slightly different angles corresponding to one's two eyes.

stock shot.
One not made at the time of filming but hired from a library. It can be either newsreel, specially shot material such as planes landing at an airport, views of a city, etc., or spectacular material lifted from older features (e.g. *Storm over the Nile* 55 had a large proportion of action footage from the original *Four Feathers* 39, and the same shots have turned up in several other films including *Master of the World* 61 and *East of Sudan* 64).

stop motion.
The method by which much trick photography is effected: the film is exposed one frame at a time, allowing time for rearrangement of models, etc. between shots, and thus giving the illusion in the completed film of motion by something normally inanimate. The monsters in *King Kong* 33 are the supreme example of this method. The best-known practitioners of the art have been Willis O'BRIEN and Ray HARRYHAUSEN. The method is being supplanted these days by a mix of animatronics (electronically controlled puppets) and computer-generated graphics.

See also: TIME-LAPSE PHOTOGRAPHY.

storyboard.
A means of pre-planning a sequence of individual shots for a film by means of a series of drawings, somewhat like a comic-strip. Some directors, notably Alfred Hitchcock, prepare an entire film, and the necessary camera set-ups, by means of a storyboard. Others use it to work out in advance the likely problems, or the best positions for the camera, in action sequences. Storyboard artists can play a creative role in movie-making by suggesting shots or camera angles and movements that may not have occurred to the director.

stretch-printing.
The reason silent films look jerky is that they were shot at 16 frames a second whereas modern sound projectors operate at 24, making everything move half as fast again as normal. One means of overcoming this jerkiness is stretch-printing in the lab: every second frame is printed twice. This still gives a curious effect, as for every two frames slower than normal sound speed we still get one frame faster.

sub-titles
in silent days came *after* the scene in which the actors mouthed the dialogue. When talkies came the less cumbersome method was evolved of superimposing the dialogue at the foot of the screen, which considerably sharpened up the audience's reading speed.

superdynamation.
A term coined by Ray Harryhausen for his method of animating rubber monsters.

Super-8.
Improved 8mm film which can take a soundtrack, therefore replacing the old 9.5mm.

superimpose:
to place one image on top of another, usually during a dissolve when one is fading out and the other fading in.

supervisor.
In Hollywood in the early 30s, a studio name for the assigned producer.

synchronization.
The arranging of sound and picture to match. Only rarely is this done by shooting them simultaneously; the normal process involves re-recording and much laboratory work to give the optimum results.

Synthespian:
a term to describe computer-generated actors, copyrighted by the special effects company Kleiser-Walczak Construction Co.

take.
A take is a single recording of a scene during the making of a film. Sometimes one take is enough; but directors have been known to shoot as many as 50 before they are satisfied with the results.

teaser.
A poster, trailer, or other piece of publicity which whets the appetite for a forthcoming film without giving full details about it, sometimes not even the title. The term was also applied to early pornographic films 1900–05, e.g. *Lovers Interrupted*, *Making Love in a Hammock*, etc.

Technicolor.
Colour process which existed from 1915, though the various improvements virtually amounted to completely new versions. The first had separate red and green films projected simultaneously; the second combined them on panchromatic film; the third used dye transfer. In 1932 came the three-strip process which gave the rich full tones familiar to filmgoers of the 40s, but a link with Eastmancolor in 1951 made it difficult to pick out Technicolor from any other process. In 1997, the company announced that it was bringing out a new photomechanical, or dye transfer, system which would improve the quality of prints. The method was used for the prints of *Becky Sharp* in 1935 but was discontinued in the 70s when it was thought that the photochemical process was better.

Technirama.
A process similar to Vistavision for producing extreme clarity of image.

Techniscope.
A process saving money by printing two wide images one below the other on the old 4 x 3 frame, then blowing them up to CinemaScope size; the results were awful.

telecine:
the machine which enables film to be 'projected' electronically on television. Theoretically it is capable of panning from side to side across the CinemaScope image, picking out the optimum sections of each scene, but the results are usually dire unless the process has been carefully rehearsed.

telephoto lens.
One which brings far-off objects apparently very close, but has the disadvantage of distorting and flattening perspective.

temp track
is an existing musical track sometimes used by a director while preparing a rough cut of a film, before specially composed music is available.

tentpole movie.
One that can support many other commercial activities, such as toys and clothes associated with the film. Among the most successful have been the *Star Wars* trilogy and the two *Jurassic Park* movies, whose merchandising profits exceeded one billion dollars. The greatest exponent of such an approach to film-making is Disney, whose animated features and characters have inspired theme parks and a vast variety of merchandise sold in its own stores.

35mm.
The standard commercial film gauge or width.

3-D.
Three-dimensional film-making had been tried in 1935 by MGM, as a gimmick involving throwaway paper glasses with one red and one green eyepiece to match the double image on the screen. In 1953, Hollywood really got the idea that this device would save an ailing industry, and a number of cheap exploitation pictures were shot in 3-D before anyone got down to the practical problem of renting out and collecting the necessary polaroid spectacles, which threw cinema managers into fits. *Bwana Devil* was an awful picture; *Man in the Dark* and *Fort Ti* were a shade better, except that the action kept stopping for something to be hurled at the audience; *House of Wax*, a Warner horror remake of *The Mystery of the Wax Museum*, had better production values and seemed to catch on with the public. All the studios began to make 3-D films – *Kiss Me Kate*, *The Charge at Feather River*, *Dial M for Murder*, *Miss Sadie Thompson*, *Sangaree* – but by the time these were ready, interest had shifted to Fox's new CinemaScope process, which although it gave no illusion of depth was at least a different shape and didn't need glasses. Nor did it entail such problems as running both projectors at once, with consequent intervals every twenty minutes; or long pauses when the film broke in order to mutilate the second copy in precisely the same way; or one machine running a little slower than the other, with gradual loss of synchronization. The remaining 3-D films were released 'flat', and the industry breathed a sigh of relief. So did the critics, who had wondered whether they would ever again see a film which did not involve frequent violent action. The Russians did claim at the time that they were inventing a 3-D process which would not require the use of glasses, but we are still waiting for that. In 1967 Arch Oboler made *The Bubble* in 3-D and in 1970–71 there was a brief revival of interest in the process as a promotion gimmick for cheap pornographic films. It flared up again in the early 80s as a medium for horror films and such shockers as *Jaws 3-D*, while Hitchcock's 1954 *Dial M for Murder* was shown for the first time in the process.

Books: 1983, *Amazing 3-D* by Hal Morgan and Dan Symmes. 1989, *3-D Movies* by R. M. Hayes.

tilt.
An upward or downward camera movement.

time-lapse photography.
The method by which one can obtain such fascinating results as a flower growing and blooming before one's eyes. The camera is set up and regulated to expose one frame of film at pre-arranged intervals.

See also: STOP MOTION.

tracking shot.
One taken with a moving camera, usually forwards or backwards, and often on an actual track.

travelling matte:
a masking film overlaid with another in the optical printer so as to produce a trick effect.

treatment.
The first expansion of a script idea into sequence form, giving some idea of how the story is to be told, i.e. with examples of dialogue, camera angles, etc.

turnaround
is what happens to a film project when a studio decides that it is no longer a commercial proposition, a situation that the trade paper *Variety* has defined as 'the development purgatory where projects go when studios want to dump them'.

Turnaround happens not only when producers grow disenchanted with a script, but also when new executives replace old and ritually kill off all the projects approved by their predecessors, or when a star or director decides to drop out. One studio will occasionally buy from another a script in turnaround, sometimes when executives move studios and want to take some pet project with them. Among subsequent hit movies put into turnaround are E.T. – the Extra-Terrestrial, which was picked up by Universal from Columbia, Jaws, which went from MGM to Universal, Star Wars, which went from Universal to Twentieth Century-Fox, Home Alone, which went from Warner to Twentieth Century-Fox, The Addams Family, which went from Orion to Paramount, Forrest Gump, which went from Warner to Paramount, and Speed, which went from Paramount to Twentieth Century-Fox.

underground films

are generally thought of as those made cheaply to espouse a cause or experimentally at a director's whim, commercial success being a secondary consideration. The most successful underground film-maker, breaking through into box-office success, was Andy Warhol, with Paul Morrissey directing the later films that capitalized on Warhol's name. Other influential American underground film-makers include Kenneth Anger, Stan Brakhage, Ed Emshwiller, Gregory Markopoulos, Jonas Mekas, Jack Smith.

Book: 1969, Underground Film: A Critical History by Parker Tyler.

variable area, variable density.

Types of soundtrack. Variable area appears as a spiky symmetrical line (like a long folded ink blot). Variable density is the same width throughbutbut with horizontal bars of varying light andshade.

vaudeville

is the American equivalent of the British music hall. Eight or ten variety acts, booked separately, formed a two-hour bill for the family. Burlesque was different, being for adults only.

videocassettes

are a means of recording and watching movies and programmes by means of a video recorder linked to a television set. During the 70s, they were regarded as equipment with little popular appeal, as it was thought that nobody would want to buy or rent old movies. Their widespread acceptance, particularly in the United States of America, came about because they provided a cheap way to make and distribute pornographic films, which people could watch in the privacy and comfort of their own homes. As the cost of video recorders dropped, they became standard equipment in homes next to the television set, and by the mid-80s films could be hired for a few dollars, or a pound, a night, and even bought for little more than the cost of a cinema seat. There was a great deal of fuss about porn and video nasties, but the great surge in their popularity was due to the fact that people simply wanted to see newish movies at home. Film studios at first regarded videocassettes with suspicion, concerned about piracy and losing audiences. But they have proved to be a way of making money from old movies that would otherwise be left rotting on shelves. Box-office hits can recoup much extra income from the sales of videocassettes: the amount of money made on video sales of Disney's Toy Story covered its production costs. In recent times, videocassettes have faced competition from newer and more advanced technologies, such as laser discs and DVD (Digital Video Discs). So far they have survived, because they also provide a means, lacking in rival systems, of recording programmes, including old movies, from television broadcasts. In mid-1998 (before the video release of James Cameron's Titanic), the best-selling videocassettes in the United States were mainly of animated and children's films. The best-seller was Disney's The Lion King, released in 1994, with sales of 28.8m copies, followed by Disney's 1937 animated movie Snow White and the Seven Dwarfs, with sales of 25.1m.

video discs

operate similarly to video cassettes, but instead of being stored on tape the information is mounted on a disc similar to a gramophone record.

VistaVision.

In 1953, when some companies were reluctant to follow Fox's lead and adopt CinemaScope, Paramount introduced VistaVision, a non-anamorphic, deep-focus process retaining the old frame ratio of 4 × 3. The chief innovation was that none of the essential action took place at the top or bottom of the picture, so that exhibitors with appropriate lens and aperture plates could choose their own screen ratio (from 4 × 3 to 2 × 1). At 2 × 1 on a big screen, VistaVision did not look very different from CinemaScope.

Vitaphone.

The sound-on-disc process introduced in 1926 by Warner's.

W.A.M.P.A.S. (Western Association of Motion Picture Advertisers).

A group of publicity executives who, from 1922 to 1934, gave annual certificates of merit to promising female starlets, known as 'Wampas baby stars'. Among those who succeeded were Bessie Love (nominated 1922), Laura la Plante 23, Clara Bow 24. Mary Astor 26, Joan Crawford 26, Dolores del Rio 26, Janet Gaynor 26, Lupe Velez 28, Jean Arthur 29, Loretta Young 29, Jean Blondell 31, Anita Louise 31, Ginger Rogers 32.

Warnercolor.

Actually Eastmancolor, though it always looked as though it had had a blue rinse.

wide screen.

Strictly speaking this does not mean anamorphic processes such as CinemaScope, which requires a wide, wide screen, but the now-standard 1:1.65 ratio which was achieved by projecting the old

1.3:1 image, cutting the top and bottom from it, and magnifying the result.

wild track:

one recorded in situ, not prepared in the studio.

wipe.

A wipe is an optical device used for quick changes of scene: a line appears at one edge or corner of the screen and 'wipes' across, bringing the new picture with it. Wipes can also be devised in complex patterns or as expanding images, etc.

work print:

the same as cutting copy, the first edited print from which, when it is satisfactory, the negative will be cut accordingly.

Zoetrope.

A device, invented by Englishman William George Horner, that created an illusion of motion. It consisted of a strip of paper, containing a series of drawings of simple actions, wrapped around the inside of a rotating drum. The spectator viewed the drawings through a slit in the side of the drum, where the successive pictures seemed to move due to the persistence of vision.

zoom.

A lens of variable focal length, normally used for swiftly magnifying a distant object or moving rapidly away from a close one.

Zoopraxiscope.

A projector for showing motion pictures, designed by photographer Eadweard MUYBRIDGE. It was a natural development from his photographic sequence demonstrating the movement of horses in 1878. He first called his device the Zoogyroscope, renaming it in 1881. It projected a sequence of 12 images derived from his photographs and painted on a glass disc. He demonstrated it on a lecture tour of Europe in 1881–82. A working replica is on display at the Museum of the Moving Image in London.

6
World Movies

Argentina

has been producing films since 1897, when Frenchman Eugenio Py made *The Argentine Flag*, though the first dramatic short, *Dorrego's Execution*, was not made until 1908, by Mario Gallo, an Italian. The first feature-length film, *Amalia*, followed in 1914, directed by Enrique Garcia Velloso. The burgeoning local industry collapsed in the 20s when US studios set up their own distribution companies and filled the cinemas with American movies. The coming of sound increased the popularity of local films, which found outlets in other Spanish-speaking countries, but lack of raw film stock during the Second World War soon led to a rapid decline in production, with the result that Mexico replaced Argentina as the main supplier of films to the Latin American countries. One leading director, Hugo FREGONESE, went to work in Hollywood in 1945, and many others left the country after Perón was elected president in 1946 and encouraged films that supported his ideology. The first films to receive worldwide distribution and acclaim were those of Leopoldo TORRE-NILSSON in the 50s. This breakthrough was not maintained, due to the unsettled political situation following the military coup that overthrew Perón in 1955, the rising cost of production, and harsh government censorship. In the late 60s, Fernando Solanas and Octavio Getino demanded a political cinema and made *The Hour of the Furnaces*/La Hora de los Hornos 68, a vivid documentary of national oppression, dedicated to Che Guevara and those 'who have died fighting to liberate Latin America'; the film was distributed clandestinely. Perón's return to power in the early 70s was marked by a resurgence of film-making and a liberalization: Getino was named as film censor and Héctor Olivera emerged as a notable director. But it was short-lived; in 1974, following the death of Perón, Getino was replaced by a censor who banned more than 150 films in the following two years, including Torre-Nilsson's *Home Free*/Piedra Libre 76. Sergio Renán, whose *The Truce*/La Tregua 73 was nominated for an Oscar, was forced to leave the country after receiving death threats, and actor Julio Troxler, who had appeared in two of Solanas's films and in Jorge Cedrón's *Operation Massacre* 72, was shot and killed by neo-fascists; many directors and writers left in the period leading up to the military coup of 1976 and others were later imprisoned or were never heard of again. In the 80s, with a return to democracy and the abolition of censorship, a few films reached an international audience, including Héctor Olivera's *Funny Dirty Little War*, Luis Puenzo's *The Official Story*, an Oscar-winner as best foreign film in 1986, and Fernando Solanas's *Tangos – The Exile of Gardel* 85, *South*/Sur 88, which won him the award as best director at the Cannes Film Festival, and *The Voyage*/El Viaje 93. But the country remains a difficult one for film-makers: Solanas was shot and wounded in 1991 after accusing the government of corruption.

Book: 1986, *Argentine Cinema*, ed. Tim Barnard.

Australia

has long had a vigorous cinema movement, but it did not suit the rest of the world to take much note of it until the 70s. Now many of its outstanding directors, actors and cinematographers have migrated to Hollywood. In the 30s and 40s, producer and director Ken G. Hall at the Cinesound Studios turned out popular local films, but J. Arthur Rank's investment in the company after the Second World War ended its involvement in production. The continent's best-known director until the 50s was Charles Chauvel, but even his films have travelled remarkably little. The archetypal Australian actor was Chips Rafferty, a tough, no-nonsense performer surviving hazardous adventures. In the 50s and 60s, many films with an Australian theme were made by the British, particularly Ealing Studios (including *The Overlanders*, *The Shiralee*, and *Eureka Stockade*), and the Americans, with such films as *On the Beach* and *Summer of the Seventeenth Doll* (with Ernest Borgnine and John Mills cast as Australian cane-cutters). That trend reached its nadir in 1970 with Tony Richardson's *Ned Kelly*, starring Mick Jagger as the legendary outlaw, and its apogee in 1971 with Nicolas Roeg's *Walkabout*. In the early 70s Australia's traditional rough-edged action adventures gave way on the one hand to Barry Mackenzie-style smut and on the other to macabre, stylish curiosities such as *The Cars That Ate Paris* and *Picnic At Hanging Rock*; there developed from these a new, serious Australian school including such internationally well-regarded general movies as *Newsfront* and *The Chant of Jimmie Blacksmith*. Peter Weir and Fred Schepisi became OK directorial names; such films as *Breaker Morant* and *Gallipoli* were given international fanfares; *The Man from Snowy River* broke all records in Australia; Helen Morse, Mel Gibson, Bryan Brown and Judy Davis showed that Australia had skilled actors; *Mad Max* showed that Australia could dispense stylish violence with the best of them. In 1982, however, the bubble seemed about to burst. Hollywood began to steal the best talents, and the Australian unions became greedy for the kind of salaries that only Hollywood could afford to pay, while at home a valuable tax concession was withdrawn, making finance for home-grown movies more difficult. In the mid-80s, the affable comedian Paul Hogan scored an international success with his comedy *Crocodile Dundee*, but has so far failed to repeat it with his later films. By that time, much Australian talent was working in America. Directors George Miller, Peter Weir, Fred Schepisi, Bruce Beresford, Phillip Noyce, Russell Mulcahy and Simon Wincer were busy in international films, along with cinematographers Ian Baker and Dean Semler. Jane Campion, who although born in New Zealand regards herself as an Australian director, scored with *The Piano* 93. Directors John Duigan and the Dutch-born Paul Cox kept alive Australia's reputation for intelligent, thoughtful movies, while Geoffrey Wright, with *Romper Stomper* and *Metal Skin*, and Rolf de Heer, with *Bad Boy Bubby*, showed that there was still plenty of high-tension talent around.

Meanwhile Australian television doggedly aped Hollywood, grinding out soap operas such as *The Sullivans*, *Cop Shop*, *Country Practice* and *Sons and Daughters*, with occasional mini-series ranging from the poverty-stricken *Sara Dane* to the more smoothly ambitious *A Town Like Alice* and *For the Term of His Natural Life*. The main problem turned out to be the lack of native subject matter, once producers had exhausted World War I, Botany Bay and sheep shearing.

Brazil

has had a very patchy production history. One of its best directors, Alberto Cavalcanti, spent most of his career abroad, and failed in the 50s to spark local production. Despite subsequent attempts, the best-known Brazilian film is still 1953's *O'Cangaceiro*/*The Bandit*. Its only rival is Hector Babenco's *Pixote* 81. The country's film production came to a virtual stop in 1990 with the abolition of Emrafilme, the state finance board, but resumed on a smaller scale in 1994 when government grants were resumed and tax incentives offered to film-makers. Walter Salles is the newest director to reach an international audience, with his third feature, *Central Station*, about a young boy's search for his father, being awarded an Oscar in 1998 as the best foreign film.

Canada

has made strenuous efforts through the years to promote a native film industry, but the trouble has been that its best talents are easily siphoned off to Hollywood or Britain, and few genuinely Canadian films have earned world acclaim; among those to raise interest have been *Mon Oncle Antoine* and *The Apprenticeship of Duddy Kravitz*.

The National Film Board of Canada, however, has had a stimulating effect on world documentary, especially when under the leadership of John Grierson: and Norman McLaren's experimental cartoons are enjoyed the world over.

Films wholly or largely set in Canada have included *Saskatchewan*, *Quebec*, *Northwest Mounted Police*, *The Canadians*, *River's End*, *The Naked Heart*, *Northern Pursuit*, *Island in the Sky*, *Hudson's Bay*, *Rose Marie* and *Jalna*. Until the end of the 70s the best of them was probably the wartime *49th Parallel*, but the 80s brought new efforts in the direction of international co-production, and although the first fruits seemed heavily influenced by current Hollywood fashion, signs of a new vitality have undoubtedly emerged.

The Canadian government has made half-hearted attempts to encourage the local industry to escape American domination, but with little success. Some excellent talents, however, emerged towards the end of the 80s. The French-Canadian director Denys Arcand attracted international attention with his *The Decline of the American Empire* 86 and, especially, *Jesus of Montreal* 89. And Atom Egoyan's more experimental *Family Viewing* 87, *Speaking Parts* 89, and *The Adjuster* 91 have found appreciative art-house audiences. Egoyan's *The Sweet Hereafter*, based on Russell Bank's novel about the effects on a small town of the aftermath of an accident that killed many of its children, broke through to a wider, more mainstream audience, winning many awards in Canada as well as an Oscar nomination for its director.

China

was making films of a kind early in the century, but development of the industry was sporadic until the 50s, when the communists churned out many propaganda dramas. In recent years, though, the so-called Fifth Generation of Chinese directors has produced films of world class, notably Chen Kaige's *Yellow Earth*, *King of the Children* and *Life on a String*, and Zhang Yimou's *Red Sorghum*, *Jou Dou* and *Raise the Red Lantern*, which starred Gong Li. These films came from the Xi'an Studios, which were under the direction of Wu Tianming, himself a director (*The Old Well*), but most of the directors' best efforts were either given a very restricted release in China or banned altogether. Zhang Yimou turned to Japan and Taiwan to finance his films, and Wu Tianming and Chen Kaige left for America at the end of the 80s, so the blossoming of an indigenous Chinese cinema may have been a short one.

It is too early to know what effect will result from the absorption of the Hong Kong film industry, although many of the actors and directors of Hong Kong's internationally appealing action films have moved on to seek their fortunes in North America. There, John Woo scored a hit with *Face/Off*, teaming Nicolas Cage and John Travolta in a thriller of identity confusion; Jackie Chan, after several attempts, had an American hit with *Rush Hour*; and Sammo Hung began a US TV series. It was perhaps significant that the only Chinese film to make an international impact in 1998 was *Xiu Xiu: The Sent Down Girl*, which, although financed by Chinese and Taiwanese money, was produced and directed by actress Joan CHEN, who is based in the United States.

Cuba

produced its first film in 1897, but native film-making was swamped by American imports until the Communist revolution of 1959, when a politically conscious programme was begun under the auspices of ICAIC (the Cuban Institute of Film Art and Industry). Until then, the only films that reached an international market had been pornographic, and directors concentrated on churning out musicals and comedies attuned to local tastes. Some local talent, such as cinematographer Nestor ALMENDROS, moved away after the revolution. The first director to emerge from the new regime with an international reputation was Tomás Gutiérrez ALEA with his satirical *Death of a Bureaucrat* 66, followed by *Memories of Underdevelopment* 68. Perhaps inevitably, he found himself at odds with official policy-makers, and his *Strawberry and Chocolate* 93, which showed homosexuality in a positive light, met with much local opposition. As Gutiérrez Alea became ill with cancer, the film was co-directed by Juan Carlos TABIO, who went on to make the diverting *The Elephant and the Bicycle* 95, about the transforming power of art.

Czech Republic:

see CZECHOSLOVAKIA.

Czechoslovakia

had a movie industry from the earliest days of cinema, with its first film being made in 1898. But it was not until Hedy LAMARR, then Hedy Kiesler, caused a sensation by appearing naked in *Extase* 33 that it came to international notice. Its heyday was in the early 60s with the emergence of a new wave of directors who included Vera CHYTILOVA, Milos FORMAN, Jaromil JIRES, Jiri MENZEL, Jan NEMEC and Ivan PASSER. Most were soon forced to contend with problems of censorship, and Chytilova's playful *Daisies* 66, and Nemec's biting political allegory *The Party and the Guests* 66, were both banned outright. After the Soviet invasion of 1968, many leading talents went into exile and those that remained were frequently stifled. The most interesting director to emerge after the political situation eased was Jan Sverak with *The Elementary School* 91 and *Kolya* 96, which was an international hit. By then, of course, Czechoslovakia had been divided in two, becoming the Czech Republic and Slovakia, the effects of which are still to be felt. One problem for the Republic is that the future of Prague's important Barrandov Studios is uncertain – and the studio holds the copyright in Czech feature films made over the last 30 years or so. So far, little of international interest has come out of Slovakia, though it is early days.

Denmark

was one of the first countries to start film production. Nordisk studios were founded in 1906 and from 1910 to 1915 Danish films were as internationally popular as those of any country in the world. But the talent was all drained away, first by the merger with Germany's UFA studios in 1917 and later by a steady trek to Hollywood. Carl Dreyer, one of the wanderers, later returned to Denmark and made there such major films as *Day of Wrath* and *Order;* but no Danish school ever emerged again. In recent years some Danish directors have gained international recognition, notably Bille August with *Pelle the Conqueror*,

Gabriel Axel with *Babette's Feast* – both Oscar winners for the best foreign film in consecutive years – and Lars von Trier with *Europa*, *Breaking the Waves* and *Idiots*. Von Trier is one of the signatories to Dogma 95, a credo for film-makers which states, among other tenets, that genre movies are to be avoided and that films must be shot on location using hand-held cameras. Another signatory is director Thomas Vinterberg, who was true to his own precepts in *The Celebration*, about a 60th birthday party for a father who, it is revealed, sexually abused his son and daughter; it aroused much interest at film festivals around the world.

Finland
has produced many films for internal consumption, but its films have not enjoyed the international success of its neighbours Sweden and Denmark. Until the mid-80s, the best-known Finnish film was probably Edvin Laine's *The Unknown Soldier* 55, although Jorn Donner's *A Sunday in September* 63 also found an audience outside Finland. Then the Kaurismaki Brothers, Mika and Aki, began to attract attention with their output. Both make at least a film a year, taking it in turns to use the same crew. Aki Kaurismaki has filmed in America and England, attracting an art-house audience for his *The Match Girl* 89, *Leningrad Cowboys Go America* 89 and *I Hired a Contract Killer* 90. But perhaps the best-known Finnish director is Renny Harlin, who works in Hollywood.

France's
national film history falls into a pattern of clearly-defined styles. First of note was that of Louis Feuillade, whose early serials had tremendous panache. In the 20s came René Clair, with his inimitable touch for fantastic comedy, and a little later Jean Renoir, whose view of the human comedy was wider but equally sympathetic. Sacha Guitry contributed a series of rather stagey but amusing high comedies; Jean Vigo in his brief career introduced surrealism. Marcel Pagnol made a number of self-indulgent regional comedies which were hugely enjoyable but had little to do with cinema. Then beginning in the 30s came an unsurpassed group of adult entertainments from the writer-director team of Jacques Prévert and Marcel Carné; these were widely copied by less talented hands and the resulting stream of sex dramas, seldom less than competent, preserved the legend of the naughty French. Other notable directors were Julien Duvivier, the romantic; Jacques Becker, at his happiest in comedy; and Jacques Feyder, who generally made melodramas with flashes of insight. Henri-Georges Clouzot developed into the French Hitchcock, and Cocteau's art films reached a wide public. In the 40s Robert Bresson, René Clément and Jacques Tati all began to make themselves felt. The 50s were in danger of becoming a dull period, with no new talent of note, when the 'NEW WAVE' changed the whole direction of French film-making and made some of the older hands look suddenly and undeservedly old-fashioned. Directors well-regarded in the 60s include Jacques Demy, François Truffaut, Jean-Luc Godard, Louis Malle, Jean-Pierre Melville, Claude Chabrol, Claude Lelouch and Georges Franju; in the 70s, Eric Rohmer, Jacques Deray, Yves Boisset, Costa-Gavras, Bertrand Blier and Jacques Rivette; in the 80s, Maurice Pialat, though he had been making films since the 60s, Claude Berri, influential as a producer as well as a director, Diane Kurys, Bertrand Tavernier, Jean-Jacques Annaud and Patrice Leconte. Coline Serreau, a former actress, demonstrated a gift for comedy that attracted the attention of Hollywood. Younger talents include Jean-Jacques Beineix, Leos Carax, and Luc Besson.

Among French male stars of note are Raimu, Michel Simon, Harry Baur, Fernandel, Louis Jouvet, Jean Gabin, Pierre Fresnay, Jean-Louis Barrault, Gérard Philipe, Pierre Brasseur, Maurice Chevalier, Charles Boyer, Yves Montand, Jean-Paul Belmondo, Alain Delon, Patrick Dewaere, Philippe Noiret, Michel Blanc and Gérard Depardieu. Of the women, the most influential have been Ginette Leclerc, Michèle Morgan, Danielle Darrieux, Arletty, Simone Signoret, Brigitte Bardot, Jeanne Moreau, Françoise Dorléac, Catherine Deneuve, Miou Miou, Annie Girardot, Isabelle Adjani and Isabelle Huppert. The new generation of actresses emerging in the 90s includes Charlotte Gainsbourg, Emmanuelle Béart, Juliette Binoche and Julie Delpy.

German cinema
had its most influential period in the years following World War I, when depression and despair drove directors into a macabre fantasy world and produced films like *The Golem*, *The Cabinet of Dr Caligari*, *Nosferatu*, *Warning Shadows* and *Waxworks;* it is also notable that many of the makers of these films later went to Hollywood and exerted a strong influence there. G. W. Pabst was somewhat more anchored to reality, apart from the stylish *Die Dreigroschenoper;* Fritz Lang seemed primarily interested in the criminal mentality, though he produced masterworks of prophecy and Teutonic legend. With the advent of Hitler most of Germany's genuine creative talent was forced abroad; the main achievements of the 30s were Leni Riefenstahl's colossal propaganda pieces *Triumph of the Will* and *Olympische Spiele*. The anti-British war-time films have their interest, but the post-war German cinema was not producing competent thrillers and comedies for the home market. In the 70s however a new realistic school developed in the hands of Rainer Fassbinder, Werner Herzog, etc. Other notable directors who emerged at this time included Alexander Kluge, Jean-Marie Straub, Volker Schlöndorff, Wim Wenders and Hans Jürgen Syberberg. Margarethe von Trotta was one of the few women directors to come to the fore, although she was joined in the 80s by Doris Dörrie. Commercial success was enjoyed in the 80s by Wolfgang Petersen with *The Boat* and by Percy Adlon with his English-language film *Bagdad Café*, featuring Marianne Sägebrecht, who had starred in his earlier *Sugarbaby*. Another German director fascinated by America was Uli Edel with his *Last Exit to Brooklyn*. Michael Verhoeven received international acclaim for *The Nasty Girl*. Notable German players include Werner Krauss, Conrad Veidt, Emil Jannings, Marlene Dietrich, Anton Walbrook, Gert Frobe and, in the 70s, Hanna Schygulla, star of many of Fassbinder's films. The Austrian-born actor Klaus Maria Brandauer, who trained in Germany, became an international star in the 80s following his performance as the Nazis' favourite actor in *Mephisto* 81.

The best-known directors, Wim Wenders and Volker Schlondorff, both made movies with American actors in 1997: Wenders with a Los Angeles setting for *The End of Violence*, with a cast headed by Bill Pullman and Andie MacDowell, and Schlondorff with a thriller, *Palmetto*, starring Woody Harrelson and Elisabeth Shue; neither did well at the box-office. The most successful film of recent years has been Josef Vilsmaier's lavish and nostalgic *Comedian Harmonists*, about a popular vocal group of the 20s and 30s who were forced to disband by the Nazis because some of its members were Jewish.

Great Britain
had been making films for more than 50 years when finally a 'British school' emerged capable of influencing world production. Hollywood films had invaded British cinemas during World War I, and British audiences liked them; so the battle for power was won with only faint stirrings of resistance. British films were tepid, shoddy, stilted, old-fashioned in acting and production; and for many years they were kept that way by short-sighted government legislation, intended to help the industry, ensuring that at least a proportion (usually a third) of local product must be shown in every British cinema. Thus began the long list of 'quota quickies', deplorable 'B' pictures whose producers knew they could not fail to get their money back. In the mid-30s, Britain was producing 200 films a year, but they reflected nothing of life and offered little in the way of entertainment.

Exceptions to this general rule were the suspense thrillers of Alfred Hitchcock; a couple of promising dramas from Anthony Asquith; some well-produced entertainments from Victor Saville, such as *The Good Companions* and *South Riding;* Herbert Wilcox's popular view of such historical figures as Nell Gwyn and Queen Victoria; and the ambitious and often masterly, but not particularly British, productions of Alexander Korda, whose *Rembrandt* and *Things to Come* could still justify their inclusion in any list of the world's ten best. The British music-hall tradition also survived remarkably well in skilful low-budget productions with such stars as Gracie Fields, George Formby, Will Hay and the Crazy Gang; the two directors most concerned, Marcel Varnel and Walter Forde, had much to tell anyone who cared to listen about the art of screen comedy, as had writers Val Guest, Frank Launder and Sidney Gilliat.

In 1939 MGM had achieved three notable British productions – *A Yank at Oxford*, *Goodbye Mr Chips* and *The Citadel* – but the war swept away all plans and British studios started anew. Their renaissance began through the splendid documentaries of Humphrey Jennings, Harry Watt and Basil Wright, graduates of the GPO Film Unit which had been turning out excellent short films in the 30s but failing to secure cinema bookings for them. The strong feelings of national pride and urgency percolated to the fiction film, first in stories of social comment (*The Proud Valley*, *The Stars Look Down*, *Love on the Dole*), then in topical entertainments like Carol Reed's *Night Train to Munich* and Thorold Dickinson's *Next of Kin*. Noël Coward's *In Which We Serve* came as a revelation of style and substance, and what it did for the navy was done for the army by Reed's *The Way Ahead* and for the air force by Asquith's *The Way to the Stars*. The home front was covered with equal sensitivity by Launder and Gilliat's *Millions Like Us*, Leslie Howard's *The Gentle Sex*, and Coward's *This Happy Breed*.

Even non-war films had a fresh impetus. Gabriel Pascal made an excellent *Major Barbara* to follow the success of his 1938 *Pygmalion*. Dickinson's *Gaslight*, Reed's *Kipps*, and Asquith's *Quiet Wedding* were all excellent of their kind. The new team of Michael Powell and Emeric Pressburger brought a fresh command and insight to some unlikely but ambitious themes in *The Life and Death of Colonel Blimp* and *A Matter of Life and Death*. Korda supplied *The Thief of Baghdad*, *Lady Hamilton* and *Perfect Strangers*. The Boulting Brothers followed up *Pastor Hall* with the thoughtful *Thunder Rock*. Launder and Gilliat followed the realistic *Waterloo Road* with sparkling comedy-dramas (*The Rake's Progress*, *I See a Dark Stranger*), and a classic who-done-it (*Green for Danger*). Gainsborough Studios turned out several competent costume dramas on the Hollywood model. In 1945 the future of British films seemed bright indeed with Olivier's *Henry V*, Coward and Lean's *Blithe Spirit*, and Ealing Studios' supernatural omnibus *Dead of Night* earning popular approval, and such films as *Brief Encounter* and *Odd Man Out* in the works.

In the next few years the industry was beset by financial problems and diminishing audiences. Then Britain's leading film magnate, J. Arthur Rank, set out to conquer by means which proved regrettable. Originally attracted to the cinema as a means for spreading the Methodist religion, he now determined to impress world markets by a series of enormously expensive and generally arty productions, few of which recovered their costs: *Caesar and Cleopatra* is the most notorious. The more modestly-budgeted pictures proved to have little to say now that the end of the war had removed their main subject; and with exceptions like *Mine Own Executioner*, *The Red Shoes*, and *The Third Man* the field was thin until the celebrated Ealing comedies (*Passport to Pimlico*, *Whisky Galore*, *The Man in the White Suit*, *Kind Hearts and Coronets*) began to attract world audiences. But these too had their day, and all through the 50s British studios were trying in vain to find subjects to replace them. During this period many stars found their way to Hollywood, and then gradually began to drift back as kingpins of international co-productions, ventures which seldom turned out very happily. It was not till the relaxed hand of censorship permitted *Room at the Top*, *Saturday Night and Sunday Morning*, *The Leather Boys*, *Tom Jones*, *Georgy Girl*, *Blow Up*, James Bond and *Alfie* that British films at last set the world afire by showing just what you could get away with if you did it with sufficient skill and truth. Unfortunately even sex and violence must pall . . . so what next? The stopgap answer of the late 60s and early 70s was low comedy, much of it borrowed from TV; but that couldn't last, and didn't. By 1980 so many cinemas had closed that it was impossible to make ends meet on films for English consumption alone, and British studios and unions had priced themselves out of the international market. It remained for enterprising financiers such as Goldcrest to stimulate international palates with what would once have seemed very unlikely themes (*Chariots of Fire*, *Gandhi*); between these occasional high-spots good reviews were achieved for a number of outspoken low-budget realistic dramas, most of them partly financed by the new television Channel Four, which aired them after a usually brief run in cinemas. Cinema was no longer a mass entertainment, but a means of attracting specific minorities.

With the local film industry worsening each year, and the government giving only grudging help, much British talent settled for Hollywood. The British directors there included Alan Parker, Ridley Scott, Tony Scott, Franc Roddam, Adrian Lyne, Mike Figgis and Mike Jackson. British actors like Jeremy Irons and Anthony Hopkins were winning Oscars, but in American films. The few directors left in Britain made low-budget films, with Ken Russell turning out some cheap horrors. The will seemed to have gone. John Boorman's essentially English *Hope and Glory* was mainly financed by foreign money. Even when some notable local films were made, like Ken Loach's *Riff-Raff* and Peter Chelsom's *Hear My Song*, British distributors could hardly be bothered to show them in the cinemas. Only Richard Attenborough, with his biopic of Charlie Chaplin (with an American star, Robert Downey, in the title role), seemed to be able to continue to work on a large scale. Yet, against the odds, some distinctive films did emerge, including Kenneth Branagh's *Henry V*, Peter Greenaway's *The Cook, the Thief, His Wife and Her Lover* and *Prospero's Books*, Christine Edzard's *Little Dorrit*, Peter Medak's *The Krays*, with a script by Philip Ridley, Derek Jarman's *Edward II* and Terence Davies's *Distant Voices, Still Lives* and *The Long Day Closes*.

In the mid-90s, Mike Newell directed *Four Weddings and a Funeral* 94, which became the most successful British film ever made and established Hugh Grant as a new star. As ever, no sooner did promising young directors appear, such as Paul Anderson and Danny Cannon, than they were tempted to Hollywood to direct big-budget films. But some notable talents began to emerge from Scotland, including Gillies MacKinnon with *Small Faces*, and, especially, the producer-director-writer team of Andrew Macdonald, John Hodge and Danny Boyle with *Shallow Grave* and *Trainspotting*. And still very much active was an older generation of directors, working in a realist tradition: Mike Leigh scoring with his *Secrets and Lies*, and Ken Loach continuing to make memorable films, notably *Raining Stones* and *Land and Freedom*. The renaissance continued with the international hit *The Full Monty*, directed by Peter Cattaneo, and other films which, if not particularly original in subject-matter, still found appreciative audiences: they included *Mrs Brown*, with Judi Dench as Queen Victoria and Billy Connolly as her Highland manservant John Brown; *Bean*, featuring the slapstick comedy and mugging of Rowan Atkinson; the romantic comedy *Sliding Doors*, pairing the Scottish John Hannah with the American Gwyneth Paltrow; and a violent thriller, *Lock, Stock and Two Smoking Barrels*. The engaging talent of director Shane Meadows emerged from independent, low-budget film-making with *TwentyFourSeven*, while actor Gary Oldman returned from Hollywood to his South London haunts to write and direct the abrasive, autobiographical *Nil by Mouth*.

Greece
has had a film industry since 1912, but its development has been affected by political upheavals, and the results have had little international appeal, the best known directors being Michael Cacoyannis and Greg Tallas. The personality of Melina Mercouri and the music of Mikis Theodorakis were, however, more successfully exported. In the 80s, the only new director to emerge to international acclaim was Theodorous Angelopoulos, a former critic, with *The Beekeeper* and *Landscape in the Mist*. Angelopoulos went on to win the Palme d'Or at the 1998 Cannes Film Festival with *Eternity and a Day*, in which a dying writer confronts his past.

Holland
has produced two major documentarists: Joris Ivens and Bert Haanstra. At one time, Fons Rademakers was the only Dutch director to be known outside his home country. But Holland has produced one of the most controversial directors of the 90s in Paul Verhoeven, especially since his move to America in the mid-80s to make films like *Robocop*, *Total Recall* and *Basic Instinct*. Even before, with such films as *Spetters* and *The Fourth Man*, he attracted interest. His films have helped make international actors of Dutch stars Rutger Hauer,

Jeroen Krabbé and Renée Soutendijk, and have also drawn attention to the talents of cinematographers Jost Vacano (German-born) and Jan de Bont. Maruschka Detmers is another whose talent has taken her away from her home country. Verhoeven is not the only Dutch director to have made an impact in recent years: Dick Maas, a busy producer-director, scored with his thriller *Amsterdamned*, and George Sluizer went to Hollywood to remake his chilling *The Vanishing*.

Hungary

has had one of the most flourishing film histories in Europe, and many of its talents found their way to Hollywood, including Michael Curtiz, Alexander Korda and Bela Lugosi. The native films were seldom exported, oddly enough, until after a strong Soviet influence made itself felt: Zoltan Fabri and Miklos Jancso are now respected names. Marta Meszaros, Jancso's former wife, has made some impressive semi-autobiographical films. Karoly Makk came to the fore in the mid-70s, while Istvan Szabo has transcended national boundaries to become a truly European director.

India

has provided the setting for English-speaking films mainly of the military kind: *King of the Khyber Rifles*, *The Drum*, *Lives of a Bengal Lancer*, *Gunga Din*, *Soldiers Three*, *The Charge of the Light Brigade* (1936 version), *Bengal Brigade*, and *Conduct Unbecoming*. Civilian interests were the concern of *They Met in Bombay*, *The Rains Came*, *Elephant Boy*, *Bhowani Junction*, *Monsoon*, *The River Song of India*, *Calcutta*, *Thunder in the East*, *Northwest Frontier*, *Nine Hours to Rama* and *The Guru*. Of native Indian films only a few have percolated to Western cinemas, mostly directed by Mehboob, Satyajit Ray, or James Ivory. In the 80s there was a sudden flowering of interest in the last days of the Raj, especially on television: thus *The Jewel in the Crown*, *The Far Pavilions*, *Mountbatten the Last Viceroy*, and in the cinema *Heat and Dust* and *A Passage to India*. Director Shekhar Kapur, best known for *Bandit Queen* 94, moved on to the international scene in 1998 by directing the British costume drama *Elizabeth*, which concerned itself with the Tudor Queen's flirtation with Robert Dudley, Earl of Leicester.

Ireland

to film-makers has rather too often meant 'the troubles', which were celebrated in *Beloved Enemy*, *The Informer*, *The Gentle Gunman*, *Shake Hands with the Devil*, and the films of Sean O'Casey's plays, including *Juno and the Paycock* and *The Plough and the Stars*. (Rod Taylor played O'Casey, lightly disguised, in *Young Cassidy*.) More romantic or whimsical views of Eire were expressed in *The Luck of the Irish*, *The Rising of the Moon*, *Top of the Morning*, *Broth of a Boy*, *Home is the Hero*, *The Quiet Man*, *I See a Dark Stranger*, *Happy Ever After*, *Hungry Hill*, *The Search for Bridey Murphy*, *Jacqueline*, *Rooney*, *Never Put It In Writing* and *Ulysses*; realism was sought in *Odd Man Out*, *Parnell*, *Captain Boycott*, *No Resting Place*, *A Terrible Beauty*, and *Ryan's Daughter*. The number of Irish characters on the screen is of course legion, the most numerous and memorable varieties being priests, drunks, New York cops, and Old Mother Riley. The new 'troubles' of the early 70s and 80s have been, at the time of writing, too horrifying to provoke much response from makers of fiction films, apart from a TV movie called *War of Children* and a low-budget American exploiter called *The Outsider*. Ken Loach's controversial *Hidden Agenda* is the best film so far to grapple with the political realities of the present situation. Some talented Irish directors and writers have come to the fore in the 80s, including Neil Jordan, Jim Sheridan and Pat O'Connor. But aspects of 'the troubles', in one form or another, continue to dominate the local agenda. Neil Jordan tackled the controversial

subject of *Michael Collins*, the IRA hero and villain, and in *The General*, John Boorman dealt perceptively, in the style of a Warner's gangster movie, with Martin Cahill, a violent thief who turned the present-day conflict to his own advantage; the film won him the Best Director award at the 1998 Cannes Film Festival. But the best film of recent years has been Neil Jordan's *The Butcher Boy*, a darkly humorous, devastating portrait of small-town repression with an astonishing performance from 13-year-old Eamonn Owens in the title role.

Book: 1996, *Irish Film: 100 Years* by Arthur Flynn.

Israel's

native films have been few owing to problems of finance and language: *Hill 24 Does Not Answer* 55 is still the most notable, though a few comedies have been exported. The country's problems however have been aired in *Exodus*, *Judith*, *Cast a Giant Shadow*, *QB VII* and *Raid on Entebbe*, while Ingrid Bergman appeared as *Golda Meir* in a mini series.

Italy

was an international force in the early years of cinema with spectaculars like *Quo Vadis?* 12 and *Cabiria* 14. It later succumbed to the power of Hollywood and was little heard from until the post-war realist movement brought de Sica to world eminence. *Bicycle Thieves* was the high-water mark of achievement; afterwards came a slow slide into the commercialism of the 50s, which however re-established Rome – and Cinecittà Studios – as a world force in film-making, together with the idiosyncratic fancies of Fellini and Antonioni. Many big Hollywood films were made on Italian locations, the familiar cut-rate spectaculars peopled by mythical strong-men along with the 'spaghetti westerns' which aped Hollywood traditions but added an extra helping of violence. Dario Argento gained a following for his baroque thrillers and horror films. New life was signalled by Bernardo Bertolucci's *Before the Revolution* 64 and Marco Bellocchio's *Fist in His Pocket* 65. Bellocchio's later films have not travelled as well as Bertolucci's, who soon established himself as an international director with a series of films on sex and politics and sexual politics: *The Conformist* 70, *Last Tango in Paris* 72, *1900* 76, *La Luna* 79. More recently, he has made films of great beauty and less message. Other notable directors include Paolo and Vittorio Taviani, whose best work so far is *Padre Padrone* 77, and Ermanno Olmi. Among film composers, few can match the output or the style of Ennio Morricone, while Roberto Benigni has an international reputation as a comic actor, despite the failure of his *Son of the Pink Panther*. Benigni's *Life Is Beautiful/La Vita è Bella*, a comedy in the unlikely setting of a concentration camp, won him many international awards both as director and actor.

Japan

has a cinema tradition all of its own, based on No plays and samurai epics, both with a style quite alien to the West. The first breakthrough was made in the 50s by the vivid films of Kurosawa, such as *Rashomon* and *Seven Samurai*; other directors who came to be respected if not entirely understood are Gosho, Ozu, Mizoguchi, Ichikawa, Kinugasa, Kobayashi, Naruse and Kinoshita. In the 60s Japan produced a new wave of directors including Imamura, Oshima and Shinoda. Since then the former actor Juzo Itami has gained an international reputation for his comedies of Japanese life and customs. Some innovative animators, who have learned their craft working on popular comic-books, have displayed an approach far removed from the Disney tradition in animated films like *Akira* and *Barefoot Gen*. Younger Japanese directors are now incorporating the style in their live-action films. What the future holds, though, is uncertain now that many Japanese companies have been

investing heavily in Hollywood following Sony's acquisition of Columbia Pictures. The greatest success so far at the Japanese box-office has been an animated film, Hiyao Miyazaki's *Princess Mononoke*, which Disney is to release around the world. The suicide of Juzo Itami in 1997 ended the career of a director with an international reputation. Actor-director Takeshi Kitano enhanced his cult reputation in the West by winning the Golden Lion award at the Venice Film Festival with his *Fireworks/Hana-bi*.

Mexico

was a late starter in the feature film market, but made a few from about 1920, hampered by competition from Hollywood, which also plundered most of its best actors. The late 30s saw an improvement, with Emilio Fernandez as leading director, and in the 40s Buñuel settled there and made some small, stylish films. More recent productions have varied between cheap Hollywood-aping hokum and dour politically conscious social dramas. Mexican cinema has continued to stagger from crisis to crisis. Perhaps the most interesting director to emerge is Paul Leduc with his films *Reed: Mexico Insurgente* 73 and *Frida* 86, but his opportunities and output remain limited.

Norway

took many years to produce distinctive movies, having been overshadowed by both Sweden and Denmark for most of this century. Audiences, which were, of necessity, tiny in such a small country, were happy to watch foreign films or those made by their Scandinavian neighbours. Few production companies lasted more than a year or so, and it was not until the 20s that the country produced, in Rasmus Breistein (1890–1976), a director whose films reflected national preoccupations. Norwegian movies began to reach an international audience in the mid-80s, with Ola Solum's *Orion's Belt*, a somewhat plodding cold war thriller. Rather better was Nils Gaupe's *Pathfinder* 87, a tense thriller based on a Lapp legend, though Gaupe's next films were less interesting. More recently, Pal Sletaune's *Junk Mail*, in which a postman becomes involved in the affairs of a young woman, has shown that there is still some life in Norwegian cinema to interest an international audience.

Poland

had a vigorous cinema school from the earliest days, but subjects were dominated by Russian influence. After World War II Alexander Ford led a new vigorous group of film-makers including Wajda and Munk, whose films of post-war problems became world famous. Later directors of note include Polanski, Kawalerowicz and Skolimowski in the 50s and 60s. That era also produced the charismatic actor Zbigniew Cybulski, star of Wajda's *Ashes and Diamonds*. Like James Dean, with whom he was often compared, he died young, falling beneath a train. In the 70s, more fine directors emerged, including Krzysztof Kieslowski and Krzysztof Zanussi. More recently, Agnieszka Holland, a screenwriter and former assistant to Zanussi, has become an accomplished director. As in the past, Polish directors often work away from their home country where there are no problems of censorship. The government banned Ryszard Bugajski's 1982 film *The Interrogation*, and it was not seen until the 1990 Cannes Festival, by which time he had long emigrated in order to continue working.

Russia

has been one of the greatest influences on world cinema, thanks chiefly to a small group of highly talented men. Before the Revolution, Russian films were old-fashioned and literary; but the Bolsheviks saw the great potential of the film as propaganda

and actively encouraged the maturing talents of such men as Eisenstein (*Battleship Potemkin*, *October*, *The General Line*, *Alexander Nevsky*, *Ivan the Terrible*), Pudovkin (*Mother*, *The End of St Petersburg*, *The Deserter*, *General Suvorov*), Dovzhenko (*Arsenal*, *Earth*), Turin (*Turksib*) and Petrov (*Peter the Great*). Donskoi in *The Childhood of Maxim Gorki* and its two sequels was allowed to be nostalgic, but this vein only occasionally comes to the surface, most recently in *The Lady with a Little Dog*. The light touch comes hard to Russian film-makers, but Alexandrov achieved it in *Volga Volga*, and recently there have been signs of greater effort in this direction, at least for home consumption. The stolidity of most Russian films since World War II should not blind anyone to the enormous influence which the best Soviet work has had on film-makers the world over, especially in its exploration of the potentialities of camera movement, editing and sound; all these techniques were seen at their best in the mid-60s in a seven-hour version of *War and Peace*.

Slovakia:

see CZECHOSLOVAKIA.

Spain

produced few distinguished films before the Civil War, Buñuel having settled in France, and afterwards the product was dictated by politics apart from a few pleasing comedies and melodramas by such directors as Berlanga and Bardem. Buñuel made a few visits in the 60s. Following the death of the dictator General Franco in 1975, Spanish cinema underwent a renaissance, although some talented directors had emerged in the 60s and 70s, notably Carlos Saura. They were followed by a new generation of directors that included Victor Erice and Pedro Almodóvar, whose films made international stars of Carmen Maura and Antonio Banderas.

Sweden

was at the forefront of world film production as early as 1910. Famous directors such as Victor Sjostrom and Mauritz Stiller were well known by 1912, and tended to make films of Swedish legends, which appealed by their very strangeness. *Sir Arne's Treasure* 19, *Thy Soul Shall Bear Witness* 20, *The Atonement of Gosta Berling* 24, are among the best-known titles of the Swedish silent period; but in the mid-20s all Sweden's best talent – including the newly discovered Greta Garbo – moved towards Hollywood and the home industry was eclipsed until the late 40s saw the appearance of talents like Werner (*Midvinterblot*), Sucksdorff (*Rhythm of a City*) and Sjoberg (*Frenzy*). In the 50s the Swedish vein of romantic pessimism was developed to its ultimate in the semi-mystic but commercial films of Ingmar Bergman, who remains the most significant name in Scandinavian cinema. In the 60s and 70s, Bo Widerberg, Vilgot Sjoman and Jan Troell established international reputations with widely differing styles. In the 80s and 90s, Lasse Hallstrom went to America to work following the success of his *My Life as a Dog*, and Bille August won the top prize at the Cannes Film Festival with *Pelle the Conqueror* and *Best Intentions*, from an autobiographical screenplay by Ingmar Bergman, both starring the distinguished Swedish actor Max von Sydow. Swedish actors, notably Stellan Skarsgard and Peter Stormare, have also achieved international reputations by appearing in Hollywood movies while continuing to act in local films: Skarsgard in Anders Grönros's *The Glassblower's Children* and Stormare in the title role in Harald Zwart's thriller *Hamilton*. But Ingmar Bergman still remains the most potent force: although he has said that he will direct no more films, he nevertheless made a powerful TV film, *In the Presence of a Clown*.

United States of America:

see HOLLYWOOD (Section 2).

7
Movie Lists

American Film Institute's Best American Movies

In 1977, the AFI polled its 35,000 members to select the greatest American films. From this, the AFI produced a list of the 50 Greatest American Films. Members then voted again to produce a list of the Top Ten.

In 1998, to celebrate 100 years of movies, a similar exercise was carried out. Four hundred films were listed by AFI historians. Criteria used included critical recognition, popularity over time, historical significance, cultural impact and major award-winners. A panel of experts then voted for films from this list to produce a Top 100.

Both lists are noteworthy for the preponderance of recent films over older ones.

AFI's Top 50 Best American Films 1977 (in chronological order)

The Birth of a Nation (D. W. Griffith, 1915)
Intolerance (D. W. Griffith, 1916)
The General (Buster Keaton, Clyde Bruckman, 1926)
It Happened One Night (Frank Capra, 1934)
All Quiet on the Western Front (Lewis Milestone, 1930)
City Lights (Charles Chaplin, 1931)
King Kong (Merian C. Cooper, Ernest Schoedsack, 1933)
Modern Times (Charles Chaplin, 1936)
Snow White and the Seven Dwarfs (David Hand, 1938)
Gone with the Wind (Victor Fleming, 1939)
The Wizard of Oz (Victor Fleming, 1939)
Wuthering Heights (William Wyler, 1939)
Fantasia (Samuel Armstrong, James Algar, Bill Roberts et al, 1940)
The Grapes of Wrath (John Ford, 1940)
Citizen Kane (Orson Welles, 1941)
The Maltese Falcon (John Huston, 1941)
Casablanca (Michael Curtiz, 1942)
The Best Years of Our Lives (William Wyler, 1946)
It's a Wonderful Life (Frank Capra, 1946)
The Treasure of the Sierra Madre (John Huston, 1948)
All About Eve (Joseph Mankiewicz, 1950)
Sunset Boulevard (Billy Wilder, 1950)
The African Queen (John Huston 1951)
A Streetcar Named Desire (Elia Kazan, 1951)
Singin' in the Rain (Gene Kelly, Stanley Donen, 1952)
High Noon (Fred Zinnemann, 1952)
On the Waterfront (Elia Kazan, 1954)
The Bridge on the River Kwai (David Lean, 1957)
Ben-Hur (William Wyler, 1959)
Psycho (Alfred Hitchcock, 1960)
West Side Story (Robert Wise, Jerome Robbins, 1961)
Lawrence of Arabia (David Lean, 1962)
To Kill a Mockingbird (Robert Mulligan, 1962)
The Sound of Music (Robert Wise, 1965)
Dr Strangelove (Stanley Kubrick, 1967)

The Graduate (Mike Nichols, 1967)
2001: A Space Odyssey (Stanley Kubrick, 1968)
Midnight Cowboy (John Schlesinger, 1969)
Butch Cassidy and the Sundance Kid (George Roy Hill, 1969)
Cabaret (Bob Fosse, 1972)
The Godfather (Francis Ford Coppola, 1972)
The Sting (George Roy Hill, 1973)
The Godfather, Part II (Francis Ford Coppola, 1974)
Chinatown (Roman Polanski, 1974)
Nashville (Robert Altman, 1975)
One Flew over the Cuckoo's Nest (Milos Forman, 1975)
Jaws (Steven Spielberg, 1975)
All the President's Men (Alan J. Pakula, 1976)
Rocky (John Avildsen, 1976)
Star Wars (George Lucas, 1977)

AFI's Top 10 American Films 1977

1 *Gone with the Wind* (Victor Fleming, 1939)
2 *Citizen Kane* (Orson Welles, 1941)
3 *Casablanca* (Michael Curtiz, 1942)
4 *The African Queen* (John Huston, 1952)
5 *The Grapes of Wrath* (John Ford, 1940)
6 *One Flew over the Cuckoo's Nest* (Milos Forman, 1975)
7 *Singin' in the Rain* (Gene Kelly, Stanley Donen, 1952)
8 *Star Wars* (George Lucas, 1977)
9 *2001: A Space Odyssey* (Stanley Kubrick, 1968)
10 *The Wizard of Oz* (Victor Fleming, 1939)

The AFI's 400 Greatest American Films 1998 (in chronological order)

Richard III (Andre Calmettes, James Keane, 1912)
The Birth of a Nation (D. W. Griffith, 1915)
The Cheat (Cecil B. De Mille, 1915)
Intolerance (D. W. Griffith, 1916)
The Poor Little Rich Girl (Maurice Tourneur, 1917)
Within Our Gates (Oscar Micheaux, 1920)
The Four Horsemen of the Apocalypse (Rex Ingram, 1921)
The Kid (Charles Chaplin, 1921)
Safety Last (Sam Taylor, Fred Newmeyer, 1923)
The Thief of Bagdad (Raoul Walsh, 1924)
Greed (Erich von Stroheim, 1925)
The Big Parade (King Vidor, 1925)
The Gold Rush (Charles Chaplin, 1925)
The Phantom of the Opera (Rupert Julian, 1925)
Ben-Hur (Fred Niblo, 1926)
The General (Buster Keaton, Clyde Bruckman, 1926)
The Jazz Singer (Alan Crosland, 1927)
Sunrise (F. W. Murnau, 1927)
Wings (William Wellman, 1927)
The Crowd (King Vidor, 1928)
The Wind (Victor Sjostrom, 1928)
Broadway Melody (Harry Beaumont, 1929)
All Quiet on the Western Front (Lewis Milestone, 1930)

Morocco (Josef von Sternberg, 1930)
Cimarron (Wesley Ruggles, 1930)
Little Caesar (Mervyn Le Roy, 1931)
City Lights (Charles Chaplin, 1931)
Frankenstein (James Whale, 1931)
The Public Enemy (William Wellman, 1931)
Freaks (Tod Browning, 1932)
Grand Hotel (Edmund Goulding, 1932)
I am a Fugitive from a Chain Gang (Mervyn Le Roy, 1932)
Scarface: The Shame of a Nation (Howard Hawks, 1932)
Trouble in Paradise (Ernst Lubitsch, 1932)
Cavalcade (Frank Lloyd, 1933)
Duck Soup (Leo McCarey, 1933)
42nd Street (Lloyd Bacon, 1933)
King Kong (Merian C. Cooper, Ernest Schoedsack, 1933)
She Done Him Wrong (Lowell Sherman, 1933)
Sons of the Desert (William A. Selter, 1934)
It Happened One Night (Frank Capra, 1934)
The Scarlet Empress (Josef von Sternberg, 1934)
The Thin Man (W. S. Van Dyke, 1934)
David Copperfield (George Cukor, 1935)
The Little Colonel (David Butler, 1935)
Mutiny on the Bounty (Frank Lloyd, 1935)
A Night at the Opera (Sam Wood, 1935)
Top Hat (Mark Sandrich, 1935)
Dodsworth (William Wyler, 1936)
Fury (Fritz Lang, 1936)
The Great Ziegfeld (Robert Z. Leonard, 1936)
Mr Deeds Goes to Town (Frank Capra, 1936)
Modern Times (Charles Chaplin, 1936)
My Man Godfrey (Gregory La Cava, 1936)
Swing Time (George Stevens, 1936)
The Awful Truth (Leo McCarey, 1937)
Camille (George Cukor, 1937)
The Life of Emile Zola (William Dieterle, 1937)
Lost Horizon (Frank Capra, 1937)
Snow White and the Seven Dwarfs (David Hand, 1937)
A Star Is Born (William Wellman, 1937)
The Adventures of Robin Hood (William Keighley, Michael Curtiz, 1938)
Boys' Town (Norman Taurog, 1938)
Bringing Up Baby (Howard Hawks, 1938)
You Can't Take It with You (Frank Capra, 1938)
Babes in Arms (Busby Berkeley, 1939)
Beau Geste (William Wellman, 1939)
Destry Rides Again (George Marshall, 1939)
Gone with the Wind (Victor Fleming, 1939)
Goodbye, Mr Chips (Sam Wood, 1939)
Gunga Din (George Stevens, 1939)
Mr Smith Goes to Washington (Frank Capra, 1939)
Ninotchka (Ernst Lubitsch, 1939)
Only Angels Have Wings (Howard Hawks, 1939)
Stagecoach (John Ford, 1939)
The Wizard of Oz (Victor Fleming, 1939)
Wuthering Heights (William Wyler, 1939)
Young Mr Lincoln (John Ford, 1939)
The Bank Dick (Eddie Cline, 1940)

Fantasia (Samuel Armstrong, James Algar, Bill Roberts et al, 1940)
The Grapes of Wrath (John Ford, 1940)
His Girl Friday (Howard Hawks, 1940)
The Mark of Zorro (Rouben Mamoulian, 1940)
The Philadelphia Story (George Cukor, 1940)
Pinocchio (Ben Sharpsteen, Hamilton Luske, 1940)
Rebecca (Alfred Hitchcock, 1940)
Citizen Kane (Orson Welles, 1941)
How Green Was My Valley (John Ford, 1941)
The Lady Eve (Preston Sturges, 1941)
The Little Foxes (William Wyler, 1941)
The Maltese Falcon (John Huston, 1941)
Sergeant York (Howard Hawks, 1941)
Sullivan's Travels (Preston Sturges, 1941)
Bambi (David Hand, 1942)
Casablanca (Michael Curtiz, 1942)
Cat People (Jacques Tourneur, 1942)
The Magnificent Ambersons (Orson Welles, 1942)
Mrs Miniver (William Wyler, 1942)
Now, Voyager (Irving Rapper, 1942)
The Pride of the Yankees (Sam Wood, 1942)
Road to Morocco (David Butler, 1942)
To Be or Not to Be (Ernst Lubitsch, 1942)
Woman of the Year (George Stevens, 1942)
Yankee Doodle Dandy (Michael Curtiz, 1942)
Bataan (Tay Garnett, 1943)
Cabin in the Sky (Vincente Minnelli, 1943)
The Ox-Bow Incident (William Wellman, 1943)
Shadow of a Doubt (Alfred Hitchcock, 1943)
Miracle of Morgan's Creek (Preston Sturges, 1943)
Double Indemnity (Billy Wilder, 1944)
Going My Way (Leo McCarey, 1944)
Hail the Conquering Hero (Preston Sturges, 1944)
Laura (Otto Preminger, 1944)
Meet Me in St Louis (Vincente Minnelli, 1944)
Thirty Seconds over Tokyo (Mervyn Le Roy, 1944)
To Have and Have Not (Howard Hawks, 1945)
The Lost Weekend (Billy Wilder, 1945)
The Best Years of Our Lives (William Wyler, 1946)
The Big Sleep (Howard Hawks, 1946)
Gilda (Charles Vidor, 1946)
It's a Wonderful Life (Frank Capra, 1946)
My Darling Clementine (John Ford, 1946)
Notorious (Alfred Hitchcock, 1946)
The Yearling (Clarence Brown, 1946)
Gentleman's Agreement (Elia Kazan, 1947)
Miracle on 34th Street (George Seaton, 1947)
Out of the Past (Jacques Tourneur, 1947)
Force of Evil (Abraham Polonsky, 1948)
Red River (Howard Hawks, 1948)
Treasure of the Sierra Madre (John Huston, 1948)
Adam's Rib (George Cukor, 1949)
All the King's Men (Robert Rossen, 1949)
The Heiress (William Wyler, 1949)
Intruder in the Dust (Clarence Brown, 1949)
A Letter to Three Wives (Joseph Mankiewicz, 1949)
Sands of Iwo Jima (Allan Dwan, 1949)
The Third Man (Carol Reed, 1949)
Twelve o'Clock High (Henry King, 1949)
White Heat (Raoul Walsh, 1949)
All about Eve (Joseph Mankiewicz, 1950)
Cinderella (Wilfred Jackson, Hamilton Luske, Clyde Geronimi, 1950)
Gun Crazy (Joseph H. Lewis, 1950)
The Gunfighter (Henry King, 1950)
Sunset Boulevard (Billy Wilder, 1950)
Winchester '73 (Anthony Mann, 1950)
The African Queen (John Huston, 1951)
An American in Paris (Vincente Minnelli, 1951)
The Day the Earth Stood Still (Robert Wise, 1951)
A Place in the Sun (George Stevens, 1951)
Strangers on a Train (Alfred Hitchcock, 1951)
A Streetcar Named Desire (Elia Kazan, 1951)

The Greatest Show on Earth (Cecil B. De Mille, 1952)
High Noon (Fred Zinnemann, 1952)
The Quiet Man (John Ford, 1952)
Singin' in the Rain (Gene Kelly, Stanley Donen, 1952)
The Band Wagon (Vincente Minnelli, 1953)
From Here to Eternity (Fred Zinnemann, 1953)
Gentlemen Prefer Blondes (Howard Hawks, 1953)
Shane (George Stevens, 1953)
Stalag 17 (Billy Wilder, 1953)
The War of the Worlds (Byron Haskin, 1953)
The Caine Mutiny (Edward Dmytryk, 1954)
Carmen Jones (Otto Preminger, 1954)
On the Waterfront (Elia Kazan, 1954)
Rear Window (Alfred Hitchcock, 1954)
Salt of the Earth (Herbert Biberman, 1954)
A Star Is Born (George Cukor, 1954)
20,000 Leagues under the Sea (Richard Fleischer, 1954)
The Blackboard Jungle (Richard Brooks, 1955)
East of Eden (Elia Kazan, 1955)
Lady and the Tramp (Hamilton Luske, Clyde Geronimi, Wilfred Jackson, 1955)
Marty (Delbert Mann, 1955)
Mister Roberts (John Ford, Mervyn Le Roy, 1955)
The Night of the Hunter (Charles Laughton, 1955)
Oklahoma! (Fred Zinnemann, 1955)
Rebel without a Cause (Nicholas Ray, 1955)
The Seven Year Itch (Billy Wilder, 1955)
Invasion of the Body Snatchers (Don Siegel, 1955)
Around the World in 80 Days (Michael Anderson, 1956)
Giant (George Stevens, 1956)
The Searchers (John Ford, 1956)
The Ten Commandments (Cecil B. De Mille, 1956)
An Affair to Remember (Leo McCarey, 1957)
The Bridge on the River Kwai (David Lean, 1957)
Paths of Glory (Stanley Kubrick, 1957)
12 Angry Men (Stanley Lumet, 1957)
The Defiant Ones (Stanley Kramer, 1958)
Gigi (Vincente Minnelli, 1958)
Run Silent, Run Deep (Robert Wise, 1958)
Touch of Evil (Orson Welles, 1958)
Vertigo (Alfred Hitchcock, 1958)
Anatomy of a Murder (Otto Preminger, 1959)
Ben-Hur (William Wyler, 1959)
The Diary of Anne Frank (George Stevens, 1959)
Imitation of Life (Douglas Sirk, 1959)
North by Northwest (Alfred Hitchcock, 1959)
On the Beach (Stanley Kramer, 1959)
Pillow Talk (Michael Gordon, 1959)
Shadows (John Cassavetes, 1959)
Some Like It Hot (Billy Wilder, 1959)
The Apartment (Billy Wilder, 1960)
Elmer Gantry (Richard Brooks, 1960)
Psycho (Alfred Hitchcock, 1960)
Spartacus (Stanley Kubrick, 1960)
Breakfast at Tiffany's (Blake Edwards, 1961)
El Cid (Anthony Mann, 1961)
The Hustler (Robert Rossen, 1961)
Judgment at Nuremberg (Stanley Kramer, 1961)
101 Dalmatians (Wolfgang Reitherman, Hamilton Luske, Clyde Geronimi, 1961)
A Raisin in the Sun (Daniel Petrie, 1961)
Splendor in the Grass (Elia Kazan, 1961)
West Side Story (Robert Wise, Jerome Robbins, 1961)
Days of Wine and Roses (Blake Edwards, 1962)
Lawrence of Arabia (David Lean, 1962)
The Longest Day (Andrew Marton, Ken Annakin, Bernhard Wicki, 1962)
The Manchurian Candidate (John Frankenheimer, 1962)
To Kill a Mockingbird (Robert Mulligan, 1962)

Whatever Happened to Baby Jane? (Robert Aldrich, 1962)
The Birds (Alfred Hitchcock, 1963)
Cleopatra (Joseph Mankiewicz, 1963)
From Russia with Love (Terence Young, 1963)
Hud (Martin Ritt, 1963)
It's a Mad Mad Mad Mad World (Stanley Kramer, 1963)
The Pink Panther (Blake Edwards, 1963)
Tom Jones (Tony Richardson, 1963)
Dr Strangelove (Stanley Kubrick, 1963)
The Americanization of Emily (Arthur Hiller, 1964)
Goldfinger (Guy Hamilton, 1964)
Mary Poppins (Robert Stevenson, 1964)
My Fair Lady (George Cukor, 1964)
Cat Ballou (Eliot Silverstein, 1965)
Doctor Zhivago (David Lean, 1965)
The Sound of Music (Robert Wise, 1965)
Fantastic Voyage (Richard Fleischer, 1966)
A Man for All Seasons (Fred Zinnemann, 1966)
Who's Afraid of Virginia Woolf? (Mike Nichols, 1966)
Two for the Road (Stanley Donen, 1966)
Barefoot in the Park (Gene Saks, 1967)
Bonnie and Clyde (Arthur Penn, 1967)
Cool Hand Luke (Stuart Rosenberg, 1967)
The Graduate (Mike Nichols, 1967)
Guess Who's Coming to Dinner (Stanley Kramer, 1967)
In Cold Blood (Richard Brooks, 1967)
In the Heat of the Night (Norman Jewison, 1967)
The Jungle Book (Wolfgang Reitherman, 1967)
The Producers (Mel Brooks, 1968)
Bullitt (Peter Yates, 1968)
Funny Girl (William Wyler, 1968)
Night of the Living Dead (George A. Romero, 1968)
Oliver! (Carol Reed, 1968)
Planet of the Apes (Franklin Schaffner, 1968)
Rosemary's Baby (Roman Polanski, 1968)
2001: A Space Odyssey (Stanley Kubrick, 1968)
Butch Cassidy and the Sundance Kid (George Roy Hill, 1969)
Easy Rider (Dennis Hopper, 1969)
Medium Cool (Haskell Wexler, 1969)
Midnight Cowboy (John Schlesinger, 1969)
The Wild Bunch (Sam Peckinpah, 1969)
Patton (Franklin Schaffner, 1970)
Five Easy Pieces (Bob Rafelson, 1970)
Little Big Man (Arthur Penn, 1970)
Love Story (Arthur Hiller, 1970)
*M*A*S*H* (Robert Altman, 1970)
A Clockwork Orange (Stanley Kubrick, 1971)
Dirty Harry (Don Siegel, 1971)
Fiddler on the Roof (Norman Jewison, 1971)
The French Connection (William Friedkin, 1971)
The Last Picture Show (Peter Bogdanovich, 1971)
McCabe and Mrs Miller (Robert Altman, 1971)
Cabaret (Bob Fosse, 1972)
Deliverance (John Boorman, 1972)
The Godfather (Francis Ford Coppola, 1972)
Sounder (Martin Ritt, 1972)
Last Tango in Paris (Bernardo Bertolucci, 1972)
American Graffiti (George Lucas, 1973)
Badlands (Terrence Malick, 1973)
The Exorcist (William Friedkin, 1973)
Mean Streets (Martin Scorsese, 1973)
The Sting (George Roy Hill, 1973)
The Way We Were (Sydney Pollack, 1973)
Blazing Saddles (Mel Brooks, 1974)
Chinatown (Roman Polanski, 1974)
The Conversation (Francis Ford Coppola, 1974)
The Godfather Part II (Francis Ford Coppola, 1974)
Dog Day Afternoon (Sidney Lumet, 1975)
Jaws (Steven Spielberg, 1975)
The Man Who Would Be King (John Huston, 1975)

Nashville (Robert Altman, 1975)

One Flew over the Cuckoo's Nest (Milos Forman, 1975)

The Rocky Horror Picture Show (Jim Sharman, 1975)

All the President's Men (Alan J. Pakula, 1976)

Carrie (Brian de Palma, 1976)

Network (Sidney Lumet, 1976)

The Outlaw Josey Wales (Clint Eastwood, 1976)

Rocky (John G. Avildsen, 1976)

Taxi Driver (Martin Scorsese, 1976)

Annie Hall (Woody Allen, 1977)

Close Encounters of the Third Kind (Steven Spielberg, 1977)

The Goodbye Girl (Herbert Ross, 1977)

Saturday Night Fever (John Badham, 1977)

Star Wars (George Lucas, 1977)

Coming Home (Hal Ashby, 1978)

Days of Heaven (Terrence Malick, 1978)

The Deer Hunter (Michael Cimino, 1978)

Grease (Randal Kleiser, 1978)

National Lampoon's Animal House (John Landis, 1978)

Alien (Ridley Scott, 1979)

All That Jazz (Bob Fosse, 1979)

Apocalypse Now (Francis Ford Coppola, 1979)

Breaking Away (Peter Yates, 1979)

Kramer vs Kramer (Robert Benton, 1979)

Manhattan (Woody Allen, 1979)

The Empire Strikes Back (Irvin Kirschner, 1980)

Melvin and Howard (Jonathan Demme, 1980)

Ordinary People (Robert Redford, 1980)

Raging Bull (Martin Scorsese, 1980)

Return of the Secaucus 7 (John Sayles, 1980)

Atlantic City (Louis Malle, 1981)

Chariots of Fire (Hugh Hudson, 1981)

On Golden Pond (Mark Rydell, 1981)

Raiders of the Lost Ark (Steven Spielberg, 1981)

Reds (Warren Beatty, 1981)

Blade Runner (Ridley Scott, 1982)

E.T. – the Extra-Terrestrial (Steven Spielberg, 1982)

Fast Times at Ridgemont High (Amy Heckerling, 1982)

Gandhi (Richard Attenborough, 1982)

Missing (Costa-Gavras, 1982)

Sophie's Choice (Alan J. Pakula, 1982)

Tootsie (Sydney Pollack, 1982)

The Big Chill (Lawrence Kasdan, 1983)

Local Hero (Bill Forsyth, 1983)

El Norte (Gregory Nava, 1983)

Return of the Jedi (Richard Marquand, 1983)

The Right Stuff (Philip Kaufman, 1983)

Risky Business (Paul Brickman, 1983)

Terms of Endearment (James L. Brooks, 1983)

Amadeus (Milos Forman, 1984)

Beverly Hills Cop (Martin Brest, 1984)

Ghostbusters (Ivan Reitman, 1984)

The Killing Fields (Roland Joffe, 1984)

Stranger than Paradise (Jim Jarmusch, 1984)

Back to the Future (Robert Zemeckis, 1985)

Brazil (Terry Gilliam, 1985)

The Color Purple (Steven Spielberg, 1985)

Out of Africa (Sydney Pollack, 1985)

Witness (Peter Weir, 1985)

Blue Velvet (David Lynch, 1986)

Children of a Lesser God (Randa Haines, 1986)

Ferris Bueller's Day Off (John Hughes, 1986)

Hannah and Her Sisters (Woody Allen, 1986)

Platoon (Oliver Stone, 1986)

Broadcast News (James L. Brooks, 1987)

Fatal Attraction (Adrian Lyne, 1987)

The Last Emperor (Bernardo Bertolucci, 1987)

Lethal Weapon (Richard Donner, 1987)

Moonstruck (Norman Jewison, 1987)

The Untouchables (Brian de Palma, 1987)

Big (Penny Marshall, 1988)

Dangerous Liaisons (Stephen Frears, 1988)

Die Hard (John McTiernan, 1988)

The Last Temptation of Christ (Martin Scorsese, 1988)

Rain Man (Barry Levinson, 1988)

Batman (Tim Burton, 1989)

Born on the Fourth of July (Oliver Stone, 1989)

Dead Poets Society (Peter Weir, 1989)

Do the Right Thing (Spike Lee, 1989)

Driving Miss Daisy (Bruce Beresford, 1989)

Field of Dreams (Phil Alden Robinson, 1989)

Glory (Edward Zwick, 1989)

sex, lies and videotape (Steven Soderberg, 1989)

Dances with Wolves (Kevin Costner, 1990)

GoodFellas (Martin Scorsese, 1990)

Pretty Woman (Garry Marshall, 1990)

Silence of the Lambs (Jonathan Demme, 1990)

Beauty and the Beast (Gary Trousdale, Kirk Wise, 1991)

Rambling Rose (Martha Coolidge, 1991)

Terminator 2: Judgement Day (James Cameron, 1991)

Thelma & Louise (Ridley Scott, 1991)

The Player (Robert Altman, 1992)

Unforgiven (Clint Eastwood, 1992)

The Fugitive (Andrew Davis, 1993)

The Joy Luck Club (Wayne Wang, 1993)

Jurassic Park (Steven Spielberg, 1993)

Philadelphia (Jonathan Demme, 1993)

Schindler's List (Steven Spielberg, 1993)

Sleepless in Seattle (Nora Ephron, 1993)

Forrest Gump (Robert Zemeckis, 1994)

The Lion King (Roger Allers, Rob Minkoff, 1994)

Pulp Fiction (Quentin Tarantino, 1994)

The Shawshank Redemption (Frank Darabont, 1994)

Apollo 13 (Ron Howard, 1995)

Babe (Chris Noonan, 1995)

Braveheart (Mel Gibson, 1995)

Casino (Martin Scorsese, 1995)

Leaving Las Vegas (Mike Figgis, 1995)

Sense and Sensibility (Ang Lee, 1995)

Toy Story (John Lasseter, 1995)

The English Patient (Anthony Minghella, 1996)

Fargo (Joel Coen, 1996)

Jerry Maguire (Cameron Crowe, 1996)

AFI's Top 100 American Films 1998

1 Citizen Kane (Orson Welles, 1941)

2 Casablanca (Michael Curtiz, 1942)

3 The Godfather (Francis Ford Coppola, 1972)

4 Gone with the Wind (Victor Fleming, 1939)

5 Lawrence of Arabia (David Lean, 1962)

6 The Wizard of Oz (Victor Fleming, 1939)

7 The Graduate (Mike Nichols, 1967)

8 On the Waterfront (Elia Kazan, 1954)

9 Schindler's List (Steven Spielberg, 1993)

10 Singin' in the Rain (Gene Kelly, Stanley Donen, 1952)

11 It's a Wonderful Life (Frank Capra, 1946)

12 Sunset Boulevard (Billy Wilder, 1950)

13 The Bridge on the River Kwai (David Lean, 1957)

14 Some Like It Hot (Billy Wilder, 1959)

15 Star Wars (George Lucas, 1977)

16 All About Eve (Joseph Mankiewicz, 1950)

17 The African Queen (John Huston, 1951)

18 Psycho (Alfred Hitchcock, 1960)

19 Chinatown (Roman Polanski, 1974)

20 One Flew over the Cuckoo's Nest (Milos Forman, 1975)

21 The Grapes of Wrath (John Ford, 1940)

22 2001: A Space Odyssey (Stanley Kubrick, 1968)

23 The Maltese Falcon (John Huston, 1941)

24 Raging Bull (Martin Scorsese, 1980)

25 E.T. – the Extra-Terrestrial (Steven Spielberg, 1982)

26 Dr Strangelove (Stanley Kubrick, 1964)

27 Bonnie and Clyde (Arthur Penn, 1967)

28 Apocalypse Now (Francis Ford Coppola, 1979)

29 Mr Smith Goes to Washington (Frank Capra, 1939)

30 The Treasure of the Sierra Madre (John Huston, 1948)

31 Annie Hall (Woody Allen, 1977)

32 The Godfather Part II (Francis Ford Coppola, 1974)

33 High Noon (Fred Zinnemann, 1952)

34 To Kill a Mockingbird (Robert Mulligan, 1962)

35 It Happened One Night (Frank Capra, 1934)

36 Midnight Cowboy (John Schlesinger, 1969)

37 The Best Years of Our Lives (William Wyler, 1946)

38 Double Indemnity (Billy Wilder, 1944)

39 Doctor Zhivago (David Lean, 1965)

40 North by Northwest (Alfred Hitchcock, 1959)

41 West Side Story (Robert Wise, Jerome Robbins, 1961)

42 Rear Window (Alfred Hitchcock, 1954)

43 King Kong (Merian C. Cooper, Ernest Schoedsack, 1933)

44 The Birth of a Nation (D. W. Griffith, 1915)

45 A Streetcar Named Desire (Elia Kazan, 1951)

46 A Clockwork Orange (Stanley Kubrick, 1971)

47 Taxi Driver (Martin Scorsese, 1976)

48 Jaws (Steven Spielberg, 1975)

49 Snow White and the Seven Dwarfs (David Hand, 1938)

50 Butch Cassidy and the Sundance Kid (George Roy Hill, 1969)

51 The Philadelphia Story (Geroge Cukor, 1940)

52 From Here to Eternity (Fred Zinnemann, 1953)

53 Amadeus (Milos Forman, 1984)

54 All Quiet on the Western Front (Lewis Milestone, 1930)

55 The Sound of Music (Robert Wise, 1965)

56 M*A*S*H (Robert Altman, 1970)

57 The Third Man (Carol Reed, 1949)

58 Fantasia (Samuel Armstrong, James Algar, Bill Roberts et al, 1940)

59 Rebel without a Cause (Nicholas Ray, 1955)

60 Raiders of the Lost Ark (Steven Spielberg, 1981)

61 Vertigo (Alfred Hitchcock, 1958)

62 Tootsie (Sydney Pollack, 1982)

63 Stagecoach (John Ford, 1939)

64 Close Encounters of the Third Kind (Steven Spielberg, 1977)

65 Silence of the Lambs (Jonathan Demme, 1991)

66 Network (Sidney Lumet, 1976)

67 The Manchurian Candidate (John Frankenheimer, 1962)

68 An American in Paris (Vincente Minnelli, 1951)

69 Shane (George Stevens, 1953)

70 The French Connection (William Friedkin, 1971)

71 Forrest Gump (Robert Zemeckis, 1994)

72 Ben-Hur (William Wyler, 1959)

73 Wuthering Heights (William Wyler, 1939)

74 The Gold Rush (Charles Chaplin, 1925)

75 Dances with Wolves (Kevin Costner, 1990)

76 City Lights (Charles Chaplin, 1931)

77 American Graffiti (George Lucas, 1973)

78 Rocky (John G. Avildsen, 1976)

79 The Deer Hunter (Michael Cimino, 1978)

80 The Wild Bunch (Sam Peckinpah, 1969)

81 Modern Times (Charles Chaplin, 1936)

82 *Giant* (George Stevens, 1956)
83 *Platoon* (Oliver Stone, 1986)
84 *Fargo* (Joel Coen, 1996)
85 *Duck Soup* (Leo McCarey, 1933)
86 *Mutiny on the Bounty* (Frank Lloyd, 1935)
87 *Frankenstein* (Frank Whale, 1931)
88 *Easy Rider* (Dennis Hopper, 1969)
89 *Patton* (Franklin Schaffner, 1970)
90 *The Jazz Singer* (Alan Crosland, 1927)
91 *My Fair Lady* (George Cukor, 1964)
92 *A Place in the Sun* (George Stevens, 1951)
93 *The Apartment* (Billy Wilder, 1960)
94 *GoodFellas* (Martin Scorsese, 1990)
95 *Pulp Fiction* (Quentin Tarantino, 1994)
96 *The Searchers* (John Ford, 1956)
97 *Bringing Up Baby* (Howard Hawks, 1938)
98 *Unforgiven* (Clint Eastwood, 1992)
99 *Guess Who's Coming to Dinner* (Stanley Kramer, 1967)
100 *Yankee Doodle Dandy* (Michael Curtiz, 1942)

Top 20 Box-Office Films in America

According to figures published in the trade newspaper *Variety*, the following are the films that have taken the most money at the US box-office. The year of release and the names of the director and distributor are given in brackets.

1 *Star Wars* (1977, George Lucas, Twentieth Century-Fox) $461m.
2 *Titanic* (1997, James Cameron, Paramount) $407.3m.
3 *E.T. – The Extra-Terrestrial* (1982, Steven Spielberg, Universal) $399.8m.
4 *Jurassic Park* (1993, Steven Spielberg, Universal) $357.1m.
5 *Forrest Gump* (1994, Robert Zemeckis, Paramount) $329.7m.
6 *The Lion King* (1994, Roger Allers, Rob Minkoff, Buena Vista) $312.8m.
7 *Return of the Jedi* (1983, Richard Marquand, Twentieth Century-Fox) $309.2m.
8 *Independence Day* (1996, Roland Emmerich, Twentieth Century-Fox) $306.2m.
9 *The Empire Strikes Back* (1980, Irvin Kershner, Twentieth Century-Fox) $290.3m.
10 *Home Alone* (1992, Chris Columbus, Twentieth Century-Fox) $285.8m.
11 *Jaws* (1975, Steven Spielberg, Universal) $260m.
12 *Batman* (1989, Tim Burton, Warner) $251.2m.
13 *Men in Black* (1997, Barry Sonnenfeld, Sony) $250.1m.
14 *Raiders of the Lost Ark* (1981, Steven Spielberg, Paramount) $242.4m.
15 *Twister* (1996, Jan de Bont, Warner) $241.7m.
16 *Ghostbusters* (1981, Ivan Reitman, Columbia) $238.6m.
17 *Beverly Hills Cop* (1984, Martin Brest, Paramount) $234.8m.
18 *Lost World: Jurassic Park* (1997, Steven Spielberg, Universal) $229.1m.
19 *Mrs Doubtfire* (1993, Chris Columbus, Twentieth Century-Fox) $219.2m.
20 *Ghost* (1990, Jerry Zucker, Paramount) $217.6m.

However, if the money taken by older releases is adjusted for inflation to 1998 values, a different top 20 emerges:
1 *Gone with the Wind* (1939, Victor Fleming, MGM) $1,299.4m.
2 *Snow White and the Seven Dwarfs* (1937, David Hand, Buena Vista) $1,034.3m.
3 *Star Wars* (1977, George Lucas, Twentieth Century-Fox) $812m.

4 *E.T. – the Extra-Terrestrial* (1982, Steven Spielberg, Universal) $725.4m.
5 *101 Dalmatians* (1961, Wolfgang Reitherman, Hamilton Luske, Clyde Geronimi, Buena Vista) $656.6m.
6 *Bambi* (1942, David Hand, Buena Vista) $646.1m.
7 *Jaws* (1975, Steven Spielberg, Universal) $590.3m.
8 *The Sound of Music* (1965, Robert Wise, Twentieth Century-Fox) $568.8m.
9 *The Ten Commandments* (1956, Cecil B. De Mille, Paramount) $547.6m.
10 *Return of the Jedi* (1983, Richard Marquand, Twentieth Century-Fox) $540.5m.
11 *Mary Poppins* (1964, Robert Stevenson, Buena Vista) $517.4m.
12 *Cinderella* (1949, Wilfred Jackson, Hamilton Luske, Clyde Geronimi, Buena Vista) $503.3m.
13 *The Empire Strikes Back* (1980, Irvin Kershner, Twentieth Century-Fox) $451.5m.
14 *Fantasia* (1940, Samuel Armstrong, James Algar, Bill Roberts *et al*, Buena Vista) $450.7m.
15 *Raiders of the Lost Ark* (1981, Steven Spielberg, Paramount) $442.4m.
16 *The Exorcist* (1973, William Friedkin, Warner) $436.4m.
17 *Ben-Hur* (1959, William Wyler, MGM) $434.2m.
18 *Ghostbusters* (1981, Ivan Reitman, Columbia) $427.6m.
19 *Doctor Zhivago* (1965, David Lean, MGM) $423.2m.
20 *Beverly Hills Cop* (1984, Martin Brest, Paramount) $420.7m.

The Guardian's Top 100 Contemporary Films 1980–1993

In 1993, the *Guardian* newspaper asked its readers to vote for the best films made since 1980. Depending on how you count, there are either 98 or 108 films in the resulting Top 100, since Ridley Scott's *Blade Runner* appears twice, at No. 9 in its original release and at No. 65 in its later *Director's Cut*, and Kieslowski's *A Short Film about Killing*, at No. 34, was part of his sequence of 10 films made originally for television – *Decalogue*, at No. 24. The results, with the dates of release and the directors' names, were:

1 *Cinema Paradiso*, 1989 (Giuseppe Tornatore).
2 *Blue Velvet*, 1986 (David Lynch).
3 *Raging Bull*, 1980 (Martin Scorsese).
4 *GoodFellas*, 1990 (Martin Scorsese).
5 *Fanny and Alexander*, 1982 (Ingmar Bergman).
6 *Heimat*, 1984 (Edgar Reitz).
7 *Wings of Desire*, 1987 (Wim Wenders).
8 *Babette's Feast*, 1987 (Gabriel Axel).
9 *Blade Runner*, 1982 (Ridley Scott).
10 *E.T.*, 1982 (Steven Spielberg).
11 *Paris, Texas*, 1984 (Wim Wenders).
12 *Reservoir Dogs*, 1991 (Quentin Tarantino).
13 *The Dead*, 1987 (John Huston).
14 *Brazil*, 1985 (Terry Gilliam).
15 *Once upon a Time in America*, 1984 (Sergio Leone).
16 *Unforgiven*, 1992 (Clint Eastwood).
17 *The Sacrifice*, 1986 (Andrei Tarkovsky).
18 *Cyrano de Bergerac*, 1990 (Jean-Paul Rappeneau).
19 *Jean de Florette*, 1986 (Claude Berri).
20 *Do the Right Thing*, 1989 (Spike Lee).
21 *Withnail and I*, 1987 (Bruce Robinson).
22 *Distant Voices, Still Lives*, 1988 (Terence Davies).
23 *Betty Blue*, 1986 (Jean-Jacques Beineix).

24 *Decalogue*, 1988 (Krzysztof Kieslowski).
25 *Ran*, 1985 (Akira Kurosawa).
26 *Field of Dreams*, 1989 (Phil Alden Robinson).
27 *Raise the Red Lantern*, 1991 (Zhang Yimou).
28 *Aliens*, 1986 (James Cameron).
29 *The King of Comedy*, 1983 (Martin Scorsese).
30 *Delicatessen*, 1990 (Jean-Pierre Jeunet, Marc Caro).
31 *Witness*, 1985 (Peter Weir).
32 *Rumble Fish*, 1983 (Francis Ford Coppola).
33 *Salvador*, 1986 (Oliver Stone).
34 *A Short Film about Killing*, 1986 (Krzysztof Kieslowski).
35. *Jesus of Montreal*, 1989 (Denys Arcand).
36 *Come and See*, 1985 (Elem Klimov).
37 *Local Hero*, 1983 (Bill Forsyth).
38 *Manon des Sources*, 1986 (Claude Berri).
39 *The Player*, 1992 (Robert Altman).
40 *The Blues Brothers*, 1980 (John Landis).
41 *Blood Simple*, 1983 (Joel and Ethan Coen).
42 *Gregory's Girl*, 1980 (Bill Forsyth).
43 *My Life as a Dog*, 1985 (Lasse Hallström).
44 *Diva*, 1981 (Jean-Jacques Beineix).
45 *Dances with Wolves*, 1990 (Kevin Costner).
46 *Raiders of the Lost Ark*, 1981 (Steven Spielberg).
47 *The Right Stuff*, 1983 (Philip Kaufman).
48 *The Commitments*, 1991 (Alan Parker).
49 *Nostalgia*, 1983 (Andrei Tarkovsky).
50 *The Cook, the Thief, His Wife and Her Lover*, 1989 (Peter Greenaway).
51 *Hannah and Her Sisters*, 1986 (Woody Allen).
52 *Heaven's Gate*, 1980 (Michael Cimino).
53 *Life Is Sweet*, 1990 (Mike Leigh).
54 *Les Amants du Pont-Neuf*, 1991 (Leos Carax).
55 *Miller's Crossing*, 1990 (Joel and Ethan Coen).
56 *A Room with a View*, 1985 (James Ivory).
57 *Au Revoir les Enfants*, 1988 (Louis Malle).
58 *Atlantic City*, 1981 (Louis Malle).
59 *Amadeus*, 1984 (Milos Forman).
60 *JFK*, 1991 (Oliver Stone).
61 *The Last Emperor*, 1987 (Bernardo Bertolucci).
62 *The Fisher King*, 1991 (Terry Gilliam).
63 *Truly Madly Deeply*, 1990 (Anthony Minghella).
64 *The Killing Fields*, 1984 (Roland Joffé).
65 *Blade Runner: The Director's Cut*, 1991 (Ridley Scott).
66 *Bagdad Café*, 1988 (Percy Adlon).
67 *One from the Heart*, 1982 (Francis Ford Coppola).
68 *Chariots of Fire*, 1981 (Hugh Hudson).
69 *House of Games*, 1987 (David Mamet).
70 *My Own Private Idaho*, 1991 (Gus Van Sant).
71 *Mona Lisa*, 1986 (Neil Jordan).
72 *Down by Law*, 1986 (Jim Jarmusch).
73 *Midnight Run*, 1988 (Martin Brest).
74 *Wild at Heart*, 1990 (David Lynch).
75 *Salaam Bombay!*, 1988 (Mira Nair).
76 *Company of Wolves*, 1984 (Neil Jordan).
77 *Wall Street*, 1987 (Oliver Stone).
78 *The Unbearable Lightness of Being*, 1987 (Philip Kaufman).
79 *Strictly Ballroom*, 1992 (Baz Luhrmann).
80 *Good Morning Vietnam*, 1987 (Barry Levinson).
81 *My Left Foot*, 1989 (Jim Sheridan).
82 *Shirley Valentine*, 1989 (Lewis Gilbert).
83 *Gandhi*, 1982 (Richard Attenborough).
84 *Videodrome*, 1982 (David Cronenberg).
85 *Silence of the Lambs*, 1990 (Jonathan Demme).
86 *Sophie's Choice*, 1982 (Alan J. Pakula).
87 *Educating Rita*, 1983 (Lewis Gilbert).
88 *Europa, Europa*, 1991 (Agnieszka Holland).

89 *Someone to Watch over Me*, 1987 (Ridley Scott).
90 *Full Metal Jacket*, 1987 (Stanley Kubrick).
91 *Orlando*, 1992 (Sally Potter).
92 *Prick Up Your Ears*, 1987 (Stephen Frears).
93 *Pretty Woman*, 1990 (Garry Marshall).
94 *Eureka*, 1982 (Nicolas Roeg).
95 *Edward Scissorhands*, 1990 (Tim Burton).
96 *Platoon*, 1986 (Oliver Stone).
97 *This Is Spinal Tap*, 1984 (Rob Reiner).
98 *Kiss of the Spider Woman*, 1985 (Hector Babenco).
99 *Koyaanisqatsi*, 1983 (Godfrey Reggio).
100 *The Hairdresser's Husband*, 1990 (Patrice Leconte).

Royal Film Performances

A charity function begun in London in 1946 with *A Matter of Life and Death*. The Queen usually attends, but the film is chosen, usually on the basis of what is least offensive rather than best, by executives of the Cinema & Television Benevolent Fund, for whose financial benefit the evening is staged. Subsequent films have been:

1947 *The Bishop's Wife*
1948 *Scott of the antarctic*
1949 *That Forsyte Woman*
1950 *The Mudlark*
1951 *Where No Vultures Fly*
1952 *Because You're Mine*
1953 *Rob Roy*
1954 *Beau Brummell*
1955 *To Catch a Thief*
1956 *The Battle of the River Plate*
1957 *Les Girls*
1958 no performance
1959 *The Horse's Mouth*
1960 *The Last Angry Man*
1961 *The Facts of Life*
1962 *West Side Story*
1963 *Sammy Going South*
1964 *Move Over Darling*
1965 *Lord Jim*
1966 *Born Free*
1967 *The Taming of the Shrew*
1968 *Romeo and Juliet*
1969 *The Prime of Miss Jean Brodie*
1970 *Anne of the Thousand Days*
1971 *Love Story*
1972 *Mary Queen of Scots*
1973 *Lost Horizon*
1974 *The Three Musketeers*
1975 *Funny Lady*
1976 *The Slipper and the Rose*
1977 *Silver Streak*
1978 *Close Encounters of the Third Kind*
1979 *California Suite*
1980 *Kramer vs Kramer*
1981 *Chariots of Fire*
1982 *Evil Under the Sun*
1983 *Table for Five*
1984 *The Dresser*
1985 *A Passage to India*
1986 *White Nights*
1987 *84 Charing Cross Road*
1988 *Empire of the Sun*
1989 *Madame Sousatzka*
1990 *Always*
1991 *Hot Shots!*
1992 *Chaplin*
1993 *The Man Without a Face*
1994 *34th Street*
1995 *French Kiss*
1996 *True Blue*
1997 *Titanic*
1998 *The Parent Trap*

The Longest Feature Films

1 *Die Zweite Heimat* (Edgar Reitz, 1992) at 1,532m
2 *Heimat* (Edgar Reitz, 1984) at 940m
3 *Little Dorrit* (Christine Edzard, 1987) at 357m
4 *Cleopatra* (Joseph Mankiewicz, 1963) at 243m
5 *Hamlet* (Kenneth Branagh, 1996) at 238m
6 *Once Upon a Time in America* (Sergio Leone, 1984) at 228m
7 *The Greatest Story Ever Told* (George Stevens, 1965) at 225m
8 *Gone with the Wind* (Victor Fleming, 1939) at 220m
8 *Exodus* (Otto Preminger, 1960) at 220m
10 *Heaven's Gate* (Michael Cimino, 1980) at 219m

Erich Von Stroheim's *Foolish Wives* 21 was released in Latin America in a version that ran for 408m, though the US version was cut to 85m; his *Greed* 24 originally ran at more than eight hours, but exists now in a version that lasts 110m.

8
Movie Awards

Academy Awards

The Academy of Motion Picture Arts and Sciences was formed in 1927 with Douglas Fairbanks as its first president. Qualification for membership, which remains by invitation, is achievement in one or other areas of film production. Its first awards were held on 16 May 1929 for films that had been released in Los Angeles between the beginning of August 1927 and the end of July 1928. The Academy's gold-plated statuette was designed by Cedric Gibbons, MGM's art director. Its nickname, Oscar, which, like Academy Awards, is now registered as a trademark, is said to have been due to a secretary who remarked that it looked just like her uncle Oscar, although several people have claimed to have invented the term. Over the years, the categories have altered, and in 1937 the Irving Thalberg Memorial Award was added to commemorate MGM's former production chief who died in 1936; it is presented to producers who achieve a consistently high level of work. An Oscar remains the cinema's most sought-after award and is the only one that can give a considerable financial boost to the career of an individual or a film. Its main prizewinners are:

1927/28
Picture: *Wings*
Unique and Artistic Picture: *Sunrise*
Director: Frank Borzage (*Seventh Heaven*)
Comedy Director: Lewis Milestone (*Two Arabian Knights*)
Actor: Emil Jannings (*The Last Command, The Way of All Flesh*)
Actress: Janet Gaynor (*Seventh Heaven, Street Angel, Sunrise*)
Original Screenplay: Ben Hecht (*Underworld*)
Adapted Screenplay: Benjamin Glazer (*Seventh Heaven*)
Title Writing: Joseph Farnham (*Telling the World*)
Cinematography: Charles Rosher, Karl Struss (*Sunrise*)
Art Direction: William Cameron Menzies (*The Dove, Tempest*)
Engineering Effects: Roy Pomeroy (*Wings*)
Special Awards: Warner Bros for *The Jazz Singer*; Charles Chaplin for acting, writing, directing and producing *The Circus*

1928/29
Picture: *The Broadway Melody*
Director: Frank Lloyd (*The Divine Lady, Weary River, Drag*)
Actor: Warner Baxter (*Old Arizona*)
Actress: Mary Pickford (*Coquette*)
Writing Achievement: Hans Kraly (*The Patriot*)
Cinematography: Clyde De Vinna (*White Shadows in the South Seas*)
Art Direction: Cedric Gibbons (*The Bridge of San Luis Rey*)

1929/30
Picture: *All Quiet on the Western Front*
Director: Lewis Milestone (*All Quiet on the Western Front*)
Actor: George Arliss (*Disraeli*)
Actress: Norma Shearer (*The Divorcee*)
Writing Achievement: Frances Marion (*The Big House*)
Cinematography: Joseph T. Rucker, Willard Van Der Veer (*With Byrd at the South Pole*)
Art Direction: Herman Rosse (*King of Jazz*)
Sound: Douglas Shearer (*The Big House*)

1930/31
Picture: *Cimarron*
Director: Norman Taurog (*Skippy*)
Actor: Lionel Barrymore (*A Free Soul*)
Actress: Marie Dressler (*Min and Bill*)
Original Screenplay: John Monk Saunders (*The Dawn Patrol*)
Adapted Screenplay: Howard Estabrook (*Cimarron*)
Cinematography: Floyd Crosby (*Tabu*)
Art Direction: Max Ree (*Cimarron*)
Sound: Paramount Sound Dept

1931/32
Picture: *Grand Hotel*
Director: Frank Borzage (*Bad Girl*)
Actor: Wallace Beery (*The Champ*); Frederick March (*Dr Jekyll and Mr Hyde*)
Actress: Helen Hayes (*The Sin of Madelon Claudet*)
Original Screenplay: Francis Marion (*The Champ*)
Adapted Screenplay: Edwin Burke (*Bad Girl*)
Cinematography: Lee Garmes (*Shanghai Express*)
Art Direction: Gordon Wiles (*Transatlantic*)
Sound: Paramount Sound Dept
Cartoon: *Flowers and Trees*
Comedy Short: *The Music Box*
Novelty Short: *Wrestling Swordfish*
Special Award: Walt Disney for the creation of Mickey Mouse

1932/33
Picture: *Cavalcade*
Director: Frank Lloyd (*Cavalcade*)
Actor: Charles Laughton (*The Private Life of Henry VIII*)
Actress: Katharine Hepburn (*Morning Glory*)
Original Screenplay: Robert Lord (*One Way Passage*)
Adapted Screenplay: Victor Heerman, Sarah Y. Mason (*Little Women*)
Cinematography: Charles Bryant (*A Farewell to Arms*)
Art Direction: William S. Darling (*Cavalcade*)
Sound: Harold C. Lewis (*A Farewell to Arms*)
Cartoon: *Three Little Pigs*
Comedy Short: *So This Is Harris*
Novelty Short: *Krakatoa*

1934
Picture: *It Happened One Night*
Director: Frank Capra (*It Happened One Night*)
Assistant Director: John Waters (*Viva Villa*)
Actor: Clark Gable (*It Happened One Night*)
Actress: Claudette Colbert (*It Happened One Night*)
Original Screenplay: Arthur Caesar (*Manhattan Melodrama*)
Adapted Screenplay: Robert Riskin (*It Happened One Night*)
Cinematography: Victor Milner (*Cleopatra*)
Art Direction: Cedric Gibbons, Frederic Hope (*The Merry Widow*)
Original Song: 'The Continental' from *The Gay Divorcee* (m Con Conrad, ly Herb Magidson)
Original Score: Victor Schertziner, Gus Kahn (*One Night of Love*)
Sound: John Livadary (*One Night of Love*)
Editing: Conrad Nevig (*Eskimo*)
Cartoon: *The Tortoise and the Hare*
Comedy Short: *La Cucaracha*
Novelty Short: *City of Wax*
Special Award: Shirley Temple

1935
Picture: *Mutiny on the Bounty*
Director: John Ford (*The Informer*)
Assistant Director: Clem Beauchamp (*Lives of a Bengal Lancer*)
Dance Direction: Dave Gould (*Broadway Melody of 1936* and *Folies Bergère*)
Actor: Victor McLaglen (*The Informer*)
Actress: Bette Davis (*Dangerous*)
Original Screenplay: Ben Hecht, Charles MacArthur (*The Scoundrel*)
Adapted Screenplay: Dudley Nichols (*The Informer*)
Cinematography: Hal Mohr (*A Midsummer Night's Dream*)
Art Direction: Richard Day (*The Dark Angel*)
Original Song: 'Lullaby of Broadway' from *Gold Diggers of 1935* (m Harry Warren, ly Al Dubin)
Original Score: Max Steiner (*The Informer*)
Sound: Douglas Shearer (*Naughty Marietta*)
Editing: Ralph Dawson (*A Midsummer Night's Dream*)
Cartoon: *Three Orphan Kittens*
Comedy Short: *How to Sleep*
Novelty Short: *Wings over Mt Everest*
Special Award: David Wark Griffith

1936
Picture: *The Great Ziegfeld*
Director: Frank Capra (*Mr Deeds Goes to Town*)
Assistant Director: Jack Sullivan (*The Charge of the Light Brigade*)
Dance Direction: Seymour Felix (*The Great Ziegfeld*)
Actor: Paul Muni (*The Story of Louis Pasteur*)
Actress: Luise Rainer (*The Great Ziegfeld*)

Supporting Actor: Walter Brennan (*Come and Get It*)

Supporting Actress: Gale Sondergaard (*Anthony Adverse*)

Original Screenplay: Pierre Collings, Sheridan Gibney (*The Story of Louis Pasteur*)

Cinematography: Gaetano Gaudio (*Anthony Adverse*)

Art Direction: Richard Day (*Dodsworth*)

Original Song: 'The Way You Look Tonight' from *Swingtime* (m Jerome Kern, ly Dorothy Fields)

Original Score: Erich Wolfgang Korngold (*Anthony Adverse*)

Sound: Douglas Shearer (*San Francisco*)

Editing: Ralph Dawson (*Anthony Adverse*)

Cartoon: *Country Cousins*

One-Reel Short: *Bored of Education*

Two-Reel Short: *The Public Pays*

Colour Short: *Give Me Liberty*

Special Award: *March of Time* for revolutionizing the newsreel; W. Howard Greene and Harold Rosson for colour cinematography (*The Garden of Allah*)

1937

Picture: *The Life of Emile Zola*

Director: Leo McCarey (*The Awful Truth*)

Assistant Director: Robert Webb (*In Old Chicago*)

Dance Direction: Hermes Pan (*Damsel in Distress*)

Actor: Spencer Tracy (*Captains Courageous*)

Actress: Luise Rainer (*The Good Earth*)

Supporting Actor: Joseph Schildkraut (*The Life of Emile Zola*)

Supporting Actress: Alice Brady (*In Old Chicago*)

Original Story: William A. Wellman, Robert Carson (*A Star Is Born*)

Original Screenplay: Heinz Herald, Geza Herczeg, Norman Reilly Raine (*The Life of Emile Zola*)

Cinematography: Karl Freund (*The Good Earth*)

Art Direction: Stephen Goosson (*Lost Horizon*)

Original Song: 'Sweet Leilani' from *Waikiki Wedding* (m/ly Harry Owens)

Original Score: Charles Previn (*100 Men and a Girl*)

Sound: Thomas T. Moulton (*The Hurricane*)

Editing: Gene Havlick, Gene Milton (*Lost Horizon*)

Cartoon: *The Old Mill*

One-Reel Short: *Private Life of the Gannets*

Two-Reel Short: *Torture Money*

Colour Short: *Penny Wisdom*

Special Awards: Mack Sennett for his contribution to comedy technique; Edgar Bergen for *Charlie McCarthy*; The Museum of Modern Art Film Library; W. Howard Greene for colour photography (*A Star Is Born*)

Irving Thalberg Memorial Award: Darryl Zanuck

1938

Picture: *You Can't Take It with You*

Director: Frank Capra (*You Can't Take It with You*)

Actor: Spencer Tracy (*Boys' Town*)

Actress: Bette Davis (*Jezebel*)

Supporting Actor: Walter Brennan (*Kentucky*)

Supporting Actress: Fay Bainter (*Jezebel*)

Original Story: Eleonore Griffin, Dore Schary (*Boys' Town*)

Screenplay: George Bernard Shaw, adapted by Ian Dalrymple, Cecil Lewis, W. P. Liscomb (*Pygmalion*)

Cinematography: Joseph Ruttenberg (*The Great Waltz*)

Art Direction: Carl J. Weyl (*The Adventures of Robin Hood*)

Sound: Thomas Moulton and United Artists Sound Dept (*The Cowboy and the Lady*)

Editing: Ralph Dawson (*The Adventures of Robin Hood*)

Song: 'Thanks for the Memory' from *Big Broadcast of 1938* (m Ralph Rainger, ly Leo Robin)

Scoring: Alfred Newman (*Alexander's Ragtime Band*)

Original Score: Erich Wolfgang Korngold (*The Adventures of Robin Hood*)

Cartoon: *Ferdinand the Bull*

One-Reel Short: *That Mothers Might Live*

Two-Reel Short: *Declaration of Independence*

Special Awards: Deanna Durbin and Mickey Rooney; Harry M. Warner; Walt Disney; Oliver Marsh and Allen Davey for colour photography (*Sweethearts*); Gordon Jennings, Farciot Edouart, Loren Ryder and others for special effects (*Spawn of the North*); J. Arthur Ball for advancing the use of colour

Irving Thalberg Memorial Award: Hal B. Wallis

1939

Picture: *Gone with the Wind*

Director: Victor Fleming (*Gone with the Wind*)

Actor: Robert Donat (*Goodbye Mr Chips*)

Actress: Vivien Leigh (*Gone with the Wind*)

Supporting Actor: Thomas Mitchell (*Stagecoach*)

Supporting Actress: Hattie McDaniel (*Gone with the Wind*)

Original Story: Lewis R. Foster (*Mr Deeds Goes to Washington*)

Screenplay: Sidney Howard (*Gone with the Wind*)

B/w Cinematography: Gregg Toland (*Wuthering Heights*)

Colour Cinematography: Ernest Haller, Ray Rennahan (*Gone with the Wind*)

Art Direction: Lyle Wheeler (*Gone with the Wind*)

Sound: Bernard B. Brown and Universal Sound Dept (*When Tomorrow Comes*)

Editing: Hal C. Kern, James E. Newcom (*Gone with the Wind*)

Special Effects: E. H. Hansen, Fred Sersen (*The Rains Came*)

Song: 'Over the Rainbow' from *The Wizard of Oz* (m Harold Arlen, ly E. Y. Harburg)

Scoring: Richard Hageman, Frank Harling, John Leipold, Leo Shuken (*Stagecoach*)

Original Score: Herbert Stothart (*The Wizard of Oz*)

Cartoon: *The Ugly Duckling*

One-Reel Short: *Busy Little Bears*

Two-Reel Short: *Sons of Liberty*

Special Awards: Douglas Fairbanks; Motion Picture Relief Fund; Judy Garland; William Cameron Menzies for the use of colour (*Gone with the Wind*); Technicolor Company

Irving Thalberg Memorial Award: David O. Selznick

1940

Picture: *Rebecca*

Director: John Ford (*The Grapes of Wrath*)

Actor: James Stewart (*The Philadelphia Story*)

Actress: Ginger Rogers (*Kitty Foyle*)

Supporting Actor: Walter Brennan (*The Westerner*)

Supporting Actress: Jane Darwell (*The Grapes of Wrath*)

Original Story: Benjamin Glazer, John S. Toldy (*Arise, My Love*)

Original Screenplay: Preston Sturges (*The Great McGinty*)

Screenplay: Donald Ogden Stewart (*The Philadelphia Story*)

B/w Cinematography: George Barnes (*Rebecca*)

Colour Cinematography: George Perinal (*The Thief of Bagdad*)

Art Direction: Cedric Gibbons, Paul Groesse (*Pride and Prejudice*)

Sound: Douglas Shearer and MGM Sound Dept (*Strike Up the Band*)

Editing: Anne Bauchens (*North West Mounted Police*)

Special Effects: Lawrence Butler, Jack Whitney (*The Thief of Bagdad*)

Song: 'When You Wish upon a Star' from *Pinocchio* (m Leigh Harline, ly Ned Washington)

Scoring: Alfred Newman (*Tin Pan Alley*)

Original Score: Leigh Harline, Paul J. Smith, Ned Washington (*Pinocchio*)

Cartoon: *Milky Way*

One-Reel Short: *Quicker'n a Wink*

Two-Reel Short: *Teddy, the Rough Rider*

Special Awards: Bob Hope; Col. Nathan Levinson

1941

Picture: *How Green Was My Valley*

Director: John Ford (*How Green Was My Valley*)

Actor: Gary Cooper (*Sergeant York*)

Actress: Joan Fontaine (*Suspicion*)

Supporting Actor: Donald Crisp (*How Green Was My Valley*)

Supporting Actress: Mary Astor (*The Great Lie*)

Original Story: Harry Segall (*Here Comes Mr Jordan*)

Original Screenplay: Herman J. Mankiewicz, Orson Welles (*Citizen Kane*)

Screenplay: Sidney Buchman, Seton I. Miller (*Here Comes Mr Jordan*)

B/w Cinematography: Arthur Miller (*How Green Was My Valley*)

Colour Cinematography: Ernest Palmer, Ray Rennahan (*Blood and Sand*)

B/w Art Direction: Richard Day, Nathan Duran (*How Green Was My Valley*)

Colour Art Direction: Cedric Gibbons, Joseph C. Wright (*Blood and Sand*)

Sound: Jack Whitney (*That Hamilton Woman*)

Editing: William Holmes (*Sergeant York*)

Special Effects: Farciot Edouart, Gordon Jennings, Louis Mesenkop (*I Wanted Wings*)

Song: 'The Last Time I Saw Paris' from *Lady Be Good* (m Jerome Kern, ly Oscar Hammerstein II)

Scoring of a Drama: Bernard Herrmann (*All that Money Can Buy*)

Scoring of a Musical: Frank Churchill, Oliver Wallace (*Dumbo*)

Documentary: *Churchill's Island*

Cartoon: *Led a Paw*

One-Reel Short: *Of Pups and Puzzles*

Two-Reel Short: *Main Street on the March*

Special Awards: Rey Scott for producing *Kukan*; British Ministry of Information for producing *Target for Tonight*; Leopold Stokowski for *Fantasia*; Walt Disney, William Garity, John A. Hawkins, RCA for the sound in *Fantasia*

Irving Thalberg Memorial Award: Walt Disney

1942

Picture: *Mrs Miniver*

Director: William Wyler (*Mrs Miniver*)

Actor: James Cagney (*Yankee Doodle Dandy*)

Actress: Greer Garson (*Mrs Miniver*)

Supporting Actor: Van Heflin (*Johnny Eager*)

Supporting Actress: Teresa Wright (*Mrs Miniver*)

Original Story: Emeric Pressburger (*The Invaders*)

Original Screenplay: Michael Kanin, Ring Lardner Jnr (*Woman of the Year*)

Screenplay: George Froeschel, James Hilton,

Claudine West, Arthur Wimperis (Mrs Miniver)
B/w Cinematography: Joseph Ruttenberg (Mrs Miniver)
Colour Cinematography: Leon Shamroy (The Black Swan)
B/w Art Direction: Richard Day, Joseph Wright (This Above All)
Colour Art Direction: Richard Day, Joseph Wright (My Gal Sal)
Sound: Nathan Levinson and Warner Sound Dept (Yankee Doodle Dandy)
Editing: Daniel Mandell (The Pride of the Yankees)
Special Effects: Farciot Edouart, Gordon Jennings, William L. Pereira, Louis Mesenkop (Reap the Wild Wind)
Song: 'White Christmas' from Holiday Inn (m/ly Irving Berlin)
Scoring of a Drama or Comedy: Max Steiner (Now Voyager)
Scoring of a Musical: Ray Heindorf, Heinz Roemheld (Yankee Doodle Dandy)
Documentary: US Navy, TCF (Battle of Midway)
Cartoon: Der Fuehrer's Face
One-Reel Short: Speaking of Animals and Their Families
Two-Reel Short: Beyond the Line of Duty
Special Awards: Charles Boyer; Noël Coward; MGM for the Andy Hardy films
Irving Thalberg Memorial Award: Sidney Franklin

1943

Picture: Casablanca
Director: Michael Curtiz (Casablanca)
Actor: Paul Lukas (Watch on the Rhine)
Actress: Jennifer Jones (Song of Bernadette)
Supporting Actor: Charles Coburn (The More the Merrier)
Supporting Actress: Katina Paxinou (For Whom the Bell Tolls)
Original Story: William Saroyan (The Human Comedy)
Original Screenplay: Norman Krasna (Princess O'Rourke)
Screenplay: Julius J. Epstein, Philip G. Epstein, Howard Koch (Casablanca)
B/w Cinematography: Arthur Miller (The Song of Bernadette)
Colour Cinematography: Hal Mohr, W. Howard Greene (The Phantom of the Opera)
B/w Art Direction: James Basevi, William Darling (The Song of Bernadette)
Colour Art Direction: Alexander Golitzen, John B. Goodman (The Phantom of the Opera)
Sound: Stephen Dunn and RKO Sound Dept (This Land Is Mine)
Editing: George Amy (Air Force)
Special Effects: Fred Sersen, Roger Heman (Crash Dive)
Song: 'You'll Never Know' from Hello, Frisco, Hello (m Harry Warren, ly Mack Gordon)
Scoring of a Drama or Comedy: Alfred Newman (The Song of Bernadette)
Scoring of a Musical: Ray Heindorf (This Is the Army)
Documentary: December 7th
Cartoon: Yankee Doodle Mouse
One-Reel Short: Amphibious Fighters
Two-Reel Short: Heavenly Music
Special Award: George Pal
Irving Thalberg Memorial Award: Hal B. Wallis

1944

Picture: Going My Way
Director: Leo McCarey (Going My Way)
Actor: Bing Crosby (Going My Way)
Actress: Ingrid Bergman (Gaslight)
Supporting Actor: Barry Fitzgerald (Going My Way)
Supporting Actress: Ethel Barrymore (None but the Lonely Heart)
Original Story: Leo McCarey (Going My Way)
Original Screenplay: Lamar Trotti (Wilson)
Screenplay: Frank Butler, Frank Cavett (Going My Way)
B/w Cinematography: Joseph LaShelle (Laura)
Colour Cinematography: Leon Shamroy (Wilson)
B/w Art Direction: Cedric Gibbons, William Ferrari (Gaslight)
Colour Art Direction: Wiard Ihnen (Wilson)
Sound: E. H. Hansen and TCF Sound Dept (Wilson)
Editing: Barbara McLean (Wilson)
Special Effects: Arnold Gillespie, Donald Jahraus, Gordon Jennings, Douglas Shearer (Thirty Seconds over Tokyo)
Song: 'Swinging on a Star' from Going My Way (m James Van Heusen, ly Johnny Burke)
Scoring of a Drama or Comedy: Max Steiner (Since You Went Away)
Scoring of a Musical: Carmen Dragon, Morris Stoloff (Cover Girl)
Documentary: With the Marines at Tarawa
Cartoon: Mouse Trouble
One-Reel Short: Who's Who in Animal Land
Two-Reel Short: I Won't Play
Special Awards: Margaret O'Brien; Bob Hope
Irving Thalberg Memorial Award: Darryl F. Zanuck

1945

Picture: The Lost Weekend
Director: Billy Wilder (The Lost Weekend)
Actor: Ray Milland (The Lost Weekend)
Actress: Joan Crawford (Mildred Pierce)
Supporting Actor: James Dunn (A Tree Grows in Brooklyn)
Supporting Actress: Anne Revere (National Velvet)
Original Story: Charles G. Booth (The House on 92nd Street)
Original Screenplay: Richard Schweizer (Marie-Louise)
Screenplay: Charles Brackett, Billy Wilder (The Lost Weekend)
B/w Cinematography: Harry Stradling (The Picture of Dorian Gray)
Colour Cinematography: Leon Shamroy (Leave Her to Heaven)
B/w Art Direction: Wiard Ihnen (Blood on the Sun)
Colour Art Direction: Hans Dreier, Ernst Fegte (Frenchman's Creek)
Sound: Stephen Dunn and RKO Sound Dept (The Bells of St Mary's)
Editing: Robert J. Kern (National Velvet)
Special Effects: John Fulton, A. W. Jones (Wonder Man)
Song: 'It Might as Well Be Spring' from State Fair (m Richard Rodgers, ly Oscar Hammerstein II)
Scoring of a Drama or Comedy: Miklos Rozsa (Spellbound)
Scoring of a Musical: Georgie Stoll (Anchors Aweigh)
Documentary: The True Glory
Cartoon: Quiet Please
One-Reel Short: Stairway to Light
Two-Reel Short: Star in the Night

Special Awards: Walter Wanger; Peggy Ann Garner

1946

Picture: The Best Years of Our Lives
Director: William Wyler (The Best Years of Our Lives)
Actor: Fredric March (The Best Years of Our Lives)
Actress: Olivia De Havilland (To Each His Own)
Supporting Actor: Harold Russell (The Best Years of Our Lives)
Supporting Actress: Anne Baxter (The Razor's Edge)
Original Story: Clemence Dane (Vacation from Marriage)
Original Screenplay: Muriel Box, Sydney Box (The Seventh Veil)
Screenplay: Robert E. Sherwood (The Best Years of Our Lives)
B/w Cinematography: Arthur Miller (Anna and the King of Siam)
Colour Cinematography: Charles Rosher, Leonard Smith, Arthur Arling (The Yearling)
B/w Art Direction: Lyle Wheeler, William Darling (Anna and the King of Siam)
Colour Art Direction: Cedric Gibbons, Paul Groesse (The Yearling)
Sound: John Livadary and Columbia Sound Dept (The Jolson Story)
Editing: Daniel Mandell (The Best Years of Our Lives)
Special Effects: Thomas Howard (Blithe Spirit)
Song: 'On the Atchison, Topeka and the Santa Fe' from The Harvey Girls (m Harry Warren, ly Johnny Mercer)
Scoring of a Drama or Comedy: Hugo Friedhofer (The Best Years of Our Lives)
Scoring of a Musical: Morris Stoloff (The Jolson Story)
Documentary: Seeds of Destiny
Cartoon: The Cat Concerto
One-Reel Short: Facing Your Danger
Two-Reel Short: A Boy and His Dog
Special Awards: Laurence Olivier; Harold Russell; Ernest Lubitsch; Claude Jarman Jnr
Irving Thalberg Memorial Award: Samuel Goldwyn

1947

Picture: Gentleman's Agreement
Director: Elia Kazan (Gentleman's Agreement)
Actor: Ronald Colman (A Double Life)
Actress: Loretta Young (The Farmer's Daughter)
Supporting Actor: Edmund Gwenn (Miracle on 34th Street)
Supporting Actress: Celeste Holm (Gentleman's Agreement)
Original Story: Valentine Davies (Miracle on 34th Street)
Original Screenplay: Sidney Sheldon (The Bachelor and the Bobby-Soxer)
Screenplay: George Seaton (Miracle on 34th Street)
B/w Cinematography: Guy Green (Great Expectations)
Colour Cinematography: Jack Cardiff (Black Narcissus)
B/w Art Direction: John Bryan (Great Expectations)
Colour Art Direction: Alfred Jung (Black Narcissus)
Sound: Gordon Sawyer and Goldwyn Sound Dept (The Bishop's Wife)
Editing: Francis Lyon, Robert Parrish (Body and Soul)
Special Effects: A. Arnold Gillespie, Warren

Newcombe, Douglas Shearer, Michael Steinore (*Green Dolphin Street*)
Song: 'Zip-a-Dee-Doo-Dah' from *Song of the South* (*m* Allie Wrubel, *ly* Roy Gilbert)
Scoring of a Drama or Comedy: Miklos Rozsa (*A Double Life*)
Scoring of a Musical: Alfred Newman (*My Mother Wore Tights*)
Documentary Short: *First Steps*
Documentary Feature: *Design for Death*
Cartoon: *Tweetie Pie*
One-Reel Short: *Goodbye Miss Turlock*
Two-Reel Short: *Climbing the Matterhorn*
Special Awards: James Baskett; Bill and Coo; *Shoe-Shine* (foreign film)

1948

Picture: *Hamlet*
Director: John Huston (*The Treasure of the Sierra Madre*)
Actor: Laurence Olivier (*Hamlet*)
Actress: Jane Wyman (*Johnny Belinda*)
Supporting Actor: Walter Huston (*The Treasure of the Sierra Madre*)
Supporting Actress: Claire Trevor (*Key Largo*)
Motion Picture Story: Richard Sweizer, David Wechsler (*The Search*)
Screenplay: John Huston (*The Treasure of the Sierra Madre*)
B/w Cinematography: William Daniels (*The Naked City*)
Colour Cinematography: Joseph Valentine, William V. Skall, Winton Hoch (*Joan of Arc*)
B/w Art Direction: Roger K. Furse (*Hamlet*)
Colour Art Direction: Hein Heckroth, Arthur Lawson (*The Red Shoes*)
B/w Costume Design: Roger K. Furse (*Hamlet*)
Colour Costume Design: Dorothy Jeakins, Karinska (*Joan of Arc*)
Sound: TCF Sound Dept (*The Snake Pit*)
Editing: Paul Weatherwax (*The Naked City*)
Special Effects: Paul Eagler, J. McMillan Johnson, Russell Shearman, Clarence Slifer, Charles Freeman, James G. Stewart (*Portrait of Jennie*)
Song: 'Buttons and Bows' from *The Paleface* (*m/ly* Jay Livingstone, Ray Evans)
Scoring of a Drama or Comedy: Brian Easdale (*The Red Shoes*)
Scoring of a Musical: Johnny Green, Roger Edens (*Easter Parade*)
Documentary Short: *Toward Independence*
Documentary Feature: *The Secret Land*
Cartoon: *The Little Orphan*
One-Reel Short: *Symphony of a City*
Two-Reel Short: *Seal Island*
Special Awards: Ivan Jandl; Sid Grauman; Adolph Zukor; Walter Wanger; *Monsieur Vincent* (foreign film)
Irving Thalberg Memorial Award: Jerry Wald

1949

Picture: *All the King's Men*
Director: Joseph L. Mankiewicz (*A Letter to Three Wives*)
Actor: Broderick Crawford (*All the King's Men*)
Actress: Olivia De Havilland (*The Heiress*)
Supporting Actor: Dean Jagger (*Twelve O'Clock High*)
Supporting Actress: Mercedes McCambridge (*All the King's Men*)
Motion Picture Story: Douglas Morrow (*The Stratton Story*)
Screenplay: Joseph L. Mankiewicz (*A Letter to Three Wives*)
Story & Screenplay: Robert Pirosh (*Battleground*)

B/w Cinematography: Paul C. Vogel (*Battleground*)
Colour Cinematography: Winton Hoch (*She Wore a Yellow Ribbon*)
B/w Art Direction: John Meehan, Harry Horner (*The Heiress*)
Colour Art Direction: Cedric Gibbons, Paul Groesse (*Little Women*)
B/w Costume Design: Edith Head, Gile Steele (*The Heiress*)
Colour Costume Design: Leah Rhodes, Travilla, Marjorie Best (*Adventures of Don Juan*)
Sound: TCF Sound Dept (*Twelve O'Clock High*)
Editing: Harry Gerstad (*Champion*)
Special Effects: *Mighty Joe Young*
Song: 'Baby It's Cold Outside' from *Neptune's Daughter* (*m/ly* Frank Loesser)
Scoring of a Drama or Comedy: Aaron Copland (*The Heiress*)
Scoring of a Musical: Roger Edens, Lennie Hayton (*On the Town*)
Documentary Short: *A Chance to Live*
Documentary Feature: *Daybreak in Udi*
Cartoon: *For Scent-imental Reasons*
One-Reel Short: *Aquatic House Party*
Two-Reel Short: *Van Gogh*
Special Awards: Bobby Driscoll; Fred Astaire; Cecil B. De Mille; Jean Hersholt; *The Bicycle Thief* (foreign film)

1950

Picture: *All About Eve*
Director: Joseph L. Mankiewicz (*All About Eve*)
Actor: José Ferrer (*Cyrano de Bergerac*)
Actress: Judy Holliday (*Born Yesterday*)
Supporting Actor: George Sanders (*All About Eve*)
Supporting Actress: Josephine Hull (*Harvey*)
Motion Picture Story: Edna Anhalt, Edward Anhalt (*Panic in the Streets*)
Screenplay: Joseph L. Mankiewicz (*All About Eve*)
Story & Screenplay: Charles Brackett, Billy Wilder, D. M. Marshman Jnr (*Sunset Boulevard*)
B/w Cinematography: Robert Krasker (*The Third Man*)
Colour Cinematography: Robert Surtees (*King Solomon's Mines*)
B/w Art Direction: Hans Dreier, John Meehan (*Sunset Boulevard*)
Colour Art Direction: Hans Dreier, Walter Tyler (*Samson and Delilah*)
B/w Costume Design: Edith Head, Charles LeMaire (*All About Eve*)
Colour Costume Design: Edith Head, Dorothy Jeakins, Elois Jenssen, Gile Steele, Gwen Wakeling (*Samson and Delilah*)
Sound: TCF Sound Dept (*All About Eve*)
Editing: Ralph E. Winters, Conrad A. Nervig (*King Solomon's Mines*)
Special Effects: *Destination Moon*
Song: 'Mona Lisa' from *Captain Carey* (*m/ly* Ray Evans, Jay Livingston)
Scoring of a Drama or Comedy: Franz Waxman (*Sunset Boulevard*)
Scoring of a Musical: Adolph Deutsch, Roger Edens (*Annie Get Your Gun*)
Documentary Short: *Why Korea?*
Documentary Feature: *The Titan: Story of Michelangelo*
Cartoon: *Gerald McBoing Boing*
One-Reel Short: *Grandad of Races*
Two-Reel Short: *Beaver Valley*
Honorary Awards: George Murphy; Louis B. Mayer; *The Walls of Malapaga* (foreign film)
Irving Thalberg Memorial Award: Darryl F. Zanuck

1951

Picture: *An American in Paris*
Director: George Stevens (*A Place in the Sun*)
Actor: Humphrey Bogart (*The African Queen*)
Actress: Vivien Leigh (*A Streetcar Named Desire*)
Supporting Actor: Karl Malden (*A Streetcar Named Desire*)
Supporting Actress: Kim Hunter (*A Streetcar Named Desire*)
Motion Picture Story: Paul Dehn, James Bernard (*Seven Days to Noon*)
Screenplay: Michael Wilson, Harry Brown (*A Place in the Sun*)
Story & Screenplay: Alan Jay Lerner (*An American in Paris*)
B/w Cinematography: William C. Mellor (*A Place in the Sun*)
Colour Cinematography: Alfred Gilks, John Alton (*An American in Paris*)
B/w Art Direction: Richard Day (*A Streetcar Named Desire*)
Colour Art Direction: Cedric Gibbons, Preston Ames (*An American in Paris*)
B/w Costume Design: Edith Head (*A Place in the Sun*)
Colour Costume Design: Orry-Kelly, Walter Plunkett, Irene Sharaff (*An American in Paris*)
Sound: Douglas Shearer (*The Great Caruso*)
Editing: William Hornbeck (*A Place in the Sun*)
Special Effects: *When Worlds Collide*
Song: 'In the Cool, Cool, Cool of the Evening' from *Here Comes the Groom* (*m* Hoagy Carmichael, *ly* Johnny Mercer)
Scoring of a Drama or Comedy: Franz Waxman (*A Place in the Sun*)
Scoring of a Musical: Johnny Green, Saul Chaplin (*An American in Paris*)
Documentary Short: *Benjy*
Documentary Feature: *Kon-Tiki*
Cartoon: *Two Mouseketeers*
One-Reel Short: *World of Kids*
Two-Reel Short: *Nature's Half Acre*
Honorary Awards: Gene Kelly; *Rashomon* (foreign film)
Irving Thalberg Memorial Award: Arthur Freed

1952

Picture: *The Greatest Show on Earth*
Director: John Ford (*The Quiet Man*)
Actor: Gary Cooper (*High Noon*)
Actress: Shirley Booth (*Come Back, Little Sheba*)
Supporting Actor: Anthony Quinn (*Viva Zapata!*)
Supporting Actress: Gloria Grahame (*The Bad and the Beautiful*)
Motion Picture Story: Frederic M. Frank, Theodore St John, Frank Cavett (*The Greatest Show on Earth*)
Screenplay: Charles Schnee (*The Bad and the Beautiful*)
Story & Screenplay: T. E. B. Clarke (*The Lavender Hill Mob*)
B/w Cinematography: Robert Surtees (*The Bad and the Beautiful*)
Colour Cinematography: Winton C. Hoch, Archie Stout (*The Quiet Man*)
B/w Art Direction: Cedric Gibbons, Edward Carfagno (*The Bad and the Beautiful*)
Colour Art Direction: Paul Sheriff (*Moulin Rouge*)
B/w Costume Design: Helen Rose (*The Bad and the Beautiful*)
Colour Costume Design: Marcel Vertes (*Moulin Rouge*)
Sound: London Film Sound Dept (*Breaking the Sound Barrier*)

Editing: Elmo Williams, Harry Gerstad (*High Noon*)
Special Effects: *Plymouth Adventure*
Song: 'High Noon' from *High Noon* (m Dimitri Tiomkin, ly Ned Washington)
Scoring of a Drama or Comedy: Dimitri Tiomkin (*High Noon*)
Scoring of a Musical: Alfred Newman (*With a Song in My Heart*)
Documentary Short: *Neighbors*
Documentary Feature: *The Sea around Us*
Cartoon: *Johann Mouse*
One-Reel Short: *Light in the Window*
Two-Reel Short: *Water Birds*
Honorary Awards: George Alfred Mitchell; Joseph M. Schenck; Merian C. Cooper; Harold Lloyd; Bob Hope; *Forbidden Games* (foreign film)
Irving Thalberg Memorial Award: Cecil B. De Mille

1953

Picture: *From Here to Eternity*
Director: Fred Zinnemann (*From Here to Eternity*)
Actor: William Holden (*Stalag 17*)
Actress: Audrey Hepburn (*Roman Holiday*)
Supporting Actor: Frank Sinatra (*From Here to Eternity*)
Supporting Actress: Donna Reed (*From Here to Eternity*)
Motion Picture Story: Ian McLellan Hunter, fronting for the blacklisted Dalton Trumbo (*Roman Holiday*)
Screenplay: Daniel Taradash (*From Here to Eternity*)
Story & Screenplay: Charles Brackett, Walter Reisch, Richard Breen (*Titanic*)
B/w Cinematography: Burnett Guffey (*From Here to Eternity*)
Colour Cinematography: Loyal Griggs (*Shane*)
B/w Art Direction: Cedric Gibbons, Edward Carfagno (*Julius Caesar*)
Colour Art Direction: Lyle Wheeler, George W. Davis (*The Robe*)
B/w Costume Design: Edith Head (*Roman Holiday*)
Colour Costume Design: Charles LeMaire, Emile Santiago (*The Robe*)
Sound: J. P. Livadary and Columbia Sound Dept (*From Here to Eternity*)
Editing: William Lyon (*From Here to Eternity*)
Special Effects: *The War of the Worlds*
Song: 'Secret Love' from *Calamity Jane* (m Sammy Fain, ly Paul Francis Webster)
Scoring of a Drama or Comedy: Bronislau Kaper (*Lili*)
Scoring of a Musical: Alfred Newman (*Call Me Madam*)
Documentary Short: *The Alaskan Eskimo*
Documentary Feature: *The Living Desert*
Cartoon: *Toot, Whistle, Plunk and Boom*
One-Reel Short: *The Merry Wives of Windsor Overture*
Two-Reel Short: *Bear Country*
Honorary Awards: Pete Smith; Joseph I. Breen; Twentieth Century-Fox for Cinemascope
Irving Thalberg Memorial Award: George Stevens

1954

Picture: *On the Waterfront*
Director: Elia Kazan (*On the Waterfront*)
Actor: Marlon Brando (*On the Waterfront*)
Actress: Grace Kelly (*The Country Girl*)
Supporting Actor: Edmond O'Brien (*The Barefoot Contessa*)

Supporting Actress: Eva Marie Saint (*On the Waterfront*)
Motion Picture Story: Philip Yordan (*Broken Lance*)
Screenplay: George Seaton (*The Country Girl*)
Story & Screenplay: Budd Schulberg (*On the Waterfront*)
B/w Cinematography: Boris Kaufman (*On the Waterfront*)
Colour Cinematography: Milton Krasner (*Three Coins in the Fountain*)
B/w Art Direction: Richard Day (*On the Waterfront*)
Colour Art Direction: John Meehan (*20,000 Leagues under the Sea*)
B/w Costume Design: Edith Head (*Sabrina*)
Colour Costume Design: Sanzo Wada (*Gate of Hell*)
Sound: Leslie I. Carey (*The Glenn Miller Story*)
Editing: Gene Milford (*On the Waterfront*)
Special Effects: *20,000 Leagues under the Sea*
Song: 'Three Coins in the Fountain' from *Three Coins in the Fountain* (m Jule Styne, ly Sammy Cahn)
Scoring of a Drama or Comedy: Dimitri Tiomkin (*The High and the Mighty*)
Scoring of a Musical: Adolph Deutsch, Saul Chaplin (*Seven Brides for Seven Brothers*)
Documentary Short: *Thursday's Children*
Documentary Feature: *The Vanishing Prairie*
Cartoon: *When Magoo Flew*
One-Reel Short: *This Mechanical Age*
Two-Reel Short: *A Time out of War*
Honorary Awards: Greta Garbo; Danny Kaye; Jon Whiteley; Vincent Winter; *Gate of Hell* (foreign film)

1955

Picture: *Marty*
Director: Delbert Mann (*Marty*)
Actor: Ernest Borgnine (*Marty*)
Actress: Anna Magnani (*The Rose Tattoo*)
Supporting Actor: Jack Lemmon (*Mister Roberts*)
Supporting Actress: Jo Van Fleet (*East of Eden*)
Motion Picture Story: Daniel Fuchs (*Love Me or Leave Me*)
Screenplay: Paddy Chayevsky (*Marty*)
Story & Screenplay: William Ludwig, Sonya Levien (*Interrupted Melody*)
B/w Cinematography: James Wong Howe (*The Rose Tattoo*)
Colour Cinematography: Robert Burks (*To Catch a Wife*)
B/w Art Direction: Hal Pereira, Tambi Larsen (*The Rose Tattoo*)
Colour Art Direction: William Flannery, Jo Mielziner (*Picnic*)
B/w Costume Design: Helen Rose (*I'll Cry Tomorrow*)
Colour Costume Design: Charles LeMaire (*Love Is a Many-Splendored Thing*)
Sound: Fred Hynes and Todd-AO Sound Dept (*Oklahoma!*)
Editing: Charles Nelson, William A. Lyon (*Picnic*)
Special Effects: *The Bridges at Toko-Ri*
Song: 'Love Is a Many-Splendored Thing' from *Love Is a Many-Splendored Thing* (m Sammy Fain, ly Paul Francis Webster)
Scoring of a Drama or Comedy: Alfred Newman (*Love Is a Many-Splendored Thing*)
Scoring of a Musical: Robert Russell Bennett, Jay Blackton, Adolph Deutsch (*Oklahoma!*)
Documentary Short: *Men against the Arctic*
Documentary Feature: *Helen Keller in Her Story*
Cartoon: *Speedy Gonzales*

One-Reel Short: *Survival City*
Two-Reel Short: *The Face of Lincoln*
Honorary Awards: *Samurai, the Legend of Musashi* (foreign film)

1956

Picture: *Around the World in Eighty Days*
Foreign-Language Film: *La Strada* (Federico Fellini)
Director: George Stevens (*Giant*)
Actor: Yul Brynner (*The King and I*)
Actress: Ingrid Bergman (*Anastasia*)
Supporting Actor: Anthony Quinn (*Lust for Life*)
Supporting Actress: Dorothy Malone (*Written on the Wind*)
Motion Picture Story: Dalton Trumbo (as Robert Rich) (*The Brave One*)
Original Screenplay: Albert Lamorisse (*The Red Balloon*)
Adapted Screenplay: James Poe, John Farrow, S. J. Perelman (*Around the World in Eighty Days*)
B/w Cinematography: Joseph Ruttenberg (*Somebody Up There Likes Me*)
Colour Cinematography: Lionel Lindon (*Around the World in Eighty Days*)
B/w Art Direction: Cedric Gibbons, Malcolm F. Brown (*Somebody Up There Likes Me*)
Colour Art Direction: Lyle Wheeler, John DeCuir (*The King and I*)
B/w Costume Design: Jean Louis (*The Solid Gold Cadillac*)
Colour Costume Design: Irene Sharaff (*The King and I*)
Sound: Carl Faulkner and TCF Sound Dept (*The King and I*)
Editing: Gene Ruggiero, Paul Weatherwax (*Around the World in Eighty Days*)
Special Effects: John Fulton (*The Ten Commandments*)
Song: 'Whatever Will Be, Will Be' from *The Man Who Knew Too Much* (m/ly Jay Livingston, Ray Evans)
Scoring of a Drama or Comedy: Victor Young (*Around the World in Eighty Days*)
Scoring of a Musical: Alfred Newman, Ken Darby (*The King and I*)
Documentary Short: *The True Story of the Civil War*
Documentary Feature: *The Silent World*
Cartoon: *Mister Magoo's Puddle Jumper*
One-Reel Short: *Crashing the Water Barrier*
Two-Reel Short: *The Bespoke Overcoat*
Honorary Award: Eddie Cantor
Irving Thalberg Memorial Award: Buddy Adler

1957

Picture: *The Bridge on the River Kwai*
Foreign-Language Film: *The Nights of Cabiria* (Federico Fellini)
Director: David Lean (*The Bridge on the River Kwai*)
Actor: Alec Guinness (*The Bridge on the River Kwai*)
Actress: Joanne Woodward (*The Three Faces of Eve*)
Supporting Actor: Red Buttons (*Sayonara*)
Supporting Actress: Miyoshi Umeki (*Sayonara*)
Original Story & Screenplay: George Wells (*Designing Woman*)
Adapted Screenplay: Pierre Boulle, Michael Wilson, Carl Foreman (*The Bridge on the River Kwai*)
Cinematography: Jack Hildyard (*The Bridge on the River Kwai*)
Art Direction: Ted Hayworth (*Sayonara*)
Costume Design: Orry-Kelly (*Les Girls*)

Sound: George Groves and Warner Sound Dept (*Sayonara*)
Editing: Peter Taylor (*The Bridge on the River Kwai*)
Special Effects: Walter Rossi (*The Enemy Below*)
Song: 'All the Way' from *The Joker Is Wild* (m James van Heusen, ly Sammy Cahn)
Music Scoring: Malcolm Arnold (*The Bridge on the River Kwai*)
Documentary Feature: *Albert Schweitzer*
Cartoon: *Birds Anonymous*
Live-Action Short: *The Wetback Hound*
Honorary Awards: Charles Brackett; B. B. Kahane; Gilbert 'Bronco Billy' Anderson

1958
Picture: *Gigi*
Foreign-Language Film: *My Uncle* (Jacques Tati)
Director: Vincente Minnelli (*Gigi*)
Actor: David Niven (*Separate Tables*)
Actress: Susan Hayward (*I Want to Live!*)
Supporting Actor: Burl Ives (*The Big Country*)
Supporting Actress: Wendy Hiller (*Separate Tables*)
Original Story & Screenplay: Nathan E. Douglas (the blacklisted Ned Young), Harold Jacob Smith (*The Defiant Ones*)
Adapted Screenplay: Alan Jay Lerner (*Gigi*)
B/w Cinematography: Sam Leavitt (*The Defiant Ones*)
Colour Cinematography: Joseph Ruttenberg (*Gigi*)
Art Direction: William A. Horning, Preston Ames (*Gigi*)
Costume Design: Cecil Beaton (*Gigi*)
Sound: Fred Hynes and the Todd-AO Sound Dept (*South Pacific*)
Editing: Adrienne Fazan (*Gigi*)
Special Effects: Tom Howard (*Tom Thumb*)
Song: 'Gigi' from *Gigi* (m Frederick Loewe, ly Alan Jay Lerner)
Scoring of a Drama or Comedy: Dimitri Tiomkin (*The Old Man and the Sea*)
Scoring of a Musical: André Previn (*Gigi*)
Documentary Short: *Ama Girls*
Documentary Feature: *White Wilderness*
Cartoon: *Knighty Knight Bugs*
Live-Action Short: *Grand Canyon*
Honorary Award: Maurice Chevalier
Irving Thalberg Memorial Award: Jack L. Warner

1959
Picture: *Ben-Hur*
Foreign-Language Film: *Black Orpheus* (Marcel Camus)
Director: William Wyler (*Ben-Hur*)
Actor: Charlton Heston (*Ben-Hur*)
Actress: Simone Signoret (*Room at the Top*)
Supporting Actor: Hugh Griffith (*Ben-Hur*)
Supporting Actress: Shelley Winters (*The Diary of Anne Frank*)
Original Story & Screenplay: Russell Rouse, Clarence Greene, Stanley Shapiro, Maurice Richlin (*Pillow Talk*)
Adapted Screenplay: Neil Paterson (*Room at the Top*)
B/w Cinematography: William C. Mellor (*The Diary of Anne Frank*)
Colour Cinematography: Robert L. Surtees (*Ben-Hur*)
B/w Art Direction: Lyle R. Wheeler, George W. Davis (*The Diary of Anne Frank*)
Colour Art Direction: William A. Horning, Edward Carfagno (*Ben-Hur*)
B/w Costume Design: Orry-Kelly (*Some Like It Hot*)

Colour Costume Design: Elizabeth Haffenden (*Ben-Hur*)
Sound: Franklin E. Milton and MGM Sound Dept (*Ben-Hur*)
Editing: Ralph E. Winters, John D. Dunning (*Ben-Hur*)
Special Effects: Arnold Gillespie, Robert MacDonald, Milo Lory (*Ben-Hur*)
Song: 'High Hopes' from *A Hole in the Head* (m James Van Heusen, ly Sammy Cahn)
Scoring of a Drama or Comedy: Miklos Rosza (*Ben-Hur*)
Scoring of a Musical: André Previn, Kim Darby (*Porgy and Bess*)
Documentary Short: *Glass*
Documentary Feature: *Serengeti Shall Not Die*
Cartoon: *Moonbird*
Live-Action Short: *The Golden Fish*
Honorary Awards: Lee De Forest; Buster Keaton

1960
Picture: *The Apartment*
Foreign-Language Film: *The Virgin Spring* (Ingmar Bergman)
Director: Billy Wilder (*The Apartment*)
Actor: Burt Lancaster (*Elmer Gantry*)
Actress: Elizabeth Taylor (*Butterfield 8*)
Supporting Actor: Peter Ustinov (*Spartacus*)
Supporting Actress: Shirley Jones (*Elmer Gantry*)
Original Story & Screenplay: Billy Wilder, I. A. L. Diamond (*The Apartment*)
Adapted Screenplay: Richard Brooks (*Elmer Gantry*)
B/w Cinematography: Freddie Francis (*Sons and Lovers*)
Colour Cinematography: Russell Metty (*Spartacus*)
B/w Art Direction: Alexander Trauner (*The Apartment*)
Colour Art Direction: Alexander Golitzen, Eric Orbom (*Spartacus*)
B/w Costume Design: Edith Head, Edward Stevenson (*The Facts of Life*)
Colour Costume Design: Valles, Bill Thomas (*Spartacus*)
Sound: Gordon E. Sawyer and Samuel Goldwyn Sound Dept (*The Alamo*)
Editing: Daniel Mandell (*The Apartment*)
Special Effects: Gene Warren, Tim Baar (MGM) (*The Time Machine*)
Song: 'Never on Sunday' from *Never on Sunday* (m/ly Manos Hadjidakis)
Scoring of a Drama or Comedy: Ernest Gold (*Exodus*)
Scoring of a Musical: Morris Stoloff, Harry Sikman (*Song without End*)
Documentary Short: *Giuseppina*
Documentary Feature: *The Horse with the Flying Tail*
Cartoon: *Munro*
Live-Action Short: *Day of the Panther*
Honorary Awards: Gary Cooper; Stan Laurel; Hayley Mills

1961
Picture: *West Side Story*
Foreign-Language Picture: *Through a Glass Darkly* (Ingmar Bergman)
Director: Jerome Robbins, Robert Wise (*West Side Story*)
Actor: Maximilian Schell (*Judgment at Nuremberg*)
Actress: Sophia Loren (*Two Women*)
Supporting Actor: George Chakiris (*West Side Story*)
Supporting Actress: Rita Moreno (*West Side Story*)

Original Story & Screenplay: William Inge (*Splendor in the Grass*)
Adapted Screenplay: Abby Mann (*Judgment at Nuremberg*)
B/w Cinematography: Eugene Schufftan (*The Hustler*)
Colour Cinematography: Daniel L. Fapp (*West Side Story*)
B/w Art Direction: Harry Horner (*The Hustler*)
Colour Art Direction: Boris Leven (*West Side Story*)
B/w Costume Design: Piero Gherardi (*La Dolce Vita*)
Colour Costume Design: Irene Sharaff (*West Side Story*)
Sound: Fred Hynes and Samuel Goldwyn Sound Dept, Gordon E. Sawyer (*West Side Story*)
Editing: Thomas Stanford (*West Side Story*)
Special Effects: Bill Warrington, Vivian C. Greenham (*The Guns of Navarone*)
Song: 'Moon River' from *Breakfast at Tiffany's* (m Henry Mancini, ly Johnny Mercer)
Scoring of a Drama or Comedy: Henry Mancini (*Breakfast at Tiffany's*)
Scoring of a Musical: Saul Chaplin, Johnny Green, Sid Ramin, Irwin Kostal (*West Side Story*)
Documentary Short: *Project Hope*
Documentary Feature: *Le Ciel et la Boue*
Cartoon: *Ersatz*
Live-Action Short: *Seawards the Great Ships*
Honorary Awards: William L. Hendricks; Fred L. Metzler; Jerome Robbins
Irving Thalberg Memorial Award: Stanley Kramer

1962
Picture: *Lawrence of Arabia*
Foreign-Language Film: *Sundays and Cybele* (Serge Bourgignon)
Director: David Lean (*Lawrence of Arabia*)
Actor: Gregory Peck (*To Kill a Mockingbird*)
Actress: Anne Bancroft (*The Miracle Worker*)
Supporting Actor: Ed Begley (*Sweet Bird of Youth*)
Supporting Actress: Patty Duke (*The Miracle Worker*)
Original Story & Screenplay: Ennio De Concini, Alfredo Gianetti, Pietro Germi (*Divorce Italian Style*)
Adapted Screenplay: Horton Foote (*To Kill a Mockingbird*)
B/w Cinematography: Jean Bourgoin, Walter Wottitz (*The Longest Day*)
Colour Cinematography: Fred A. Young (*Lawrence of Arabia*)
B/w Art Direction: Alexander Golitzen, Henry Bumstead (*To Kill a Mockingbird*)
Colour Art Direction: John Box, John Stoll (*Lawrence of Arabia*)
B/w Costume Design: Norma Koch (*What Ever Happened to Baby Jane?*)
Colour Costume Design: Mary Wills (*The Wonderful World of the Brothers Grimm*)
Sound: John Cox, Shepperton Studio Sound Dept (*Lawrence of Arabia*)
Editing: Anne Coates (*Lawrence of Arabia*)
Special Effects: Robert MacDonald, Jacques Maumont (*The Longest Day*)
Song: 'Days of Wine and Roses' from *Days of Wine and Roses* (m Henry Mancini, ly Johnny Mercer)
Original Score: Maurice Jarre (*Lawrence of Arabia*)
Adapted Score: Ray Heindorf (*The Music Man*)
Documentary Short: *Dylan Thomas*
Documentary Feature: *Black Fox*
Cartoon: *The Hole*
Live-Action Short: *Happy Anniversary*

1963

Picture: *Tom Jones*
Foreign-Language Film: 8½ (Federico Fellini)
Director: Tony Richardson (*Tom Jones*)
Actor: Sidney Poitier (*Lilies of the Field*)
Actress: Patricia Neal (*Hud*)
Supporting Actor: Melvyn Douglas (*Hud*)
Supporting Actress: Margaret Rutherford (*The VIPs*)
Original Story & Screenplay: James R. Webb (*How the West Was Won*)
Adapted Screenplay: John Osborne (*Tom Jones*)
B/w Cinematography: James Wong Howe (*Hud*)
Colour Cinematography: Leon Shamroy (*Cleopatra*)
B/w Art Direction: Gene Callahan (*America America*)
Colour Art Direction: John DeCuir, Jack Martin Smith, Hilyard Brown, Herman Blumenthal, Elven Webb, Maurice Pelling, Boris Juraga (*Cleopatra*)
B/w Costume Design: Piero Gherardi (8½)
Colour Costume Design: Irene Sharaff, Vittorio Nino Novarese, Renie (*Cleopatra*)
Visual Effects: Emil Kosa Jnr (*Cleopatra*)
Sound Effects: Walter G. Elliott (*It's a Mad, Mad, Mad, Mad World*)
Sound: Franklin E. Milton, MGM Sound Dept (*How the West Was Won*)
Editing: Harold F. Cress (*How the West Was Won*)
Song: 'Call Me Irresponsible' from *Papa's Delicate Condition* (m James Van Heusen, ly Sammy Cahn)
Original Score: John Addison (*Tom Jones*)
Adapted Score: André Previn (*Irma La Douce*)
Documentary Short: *Chagall*
Documentary Feature: *Robert Frost: A Lover's Quarrel with the World*
Cartoon: *The Critic*
Live-Action Short: *An Occurrence at Owl Creek Bridge*
Irving Thalberg Memorial Award: Sam Spiegel

1964

Picture: *My Fair Lady*
Foreign-Language Film: *Yesterday, Today and Tomorrow* (Vittorio De Sica)
Director: George Cukor (*My Fair Lady*)
Actor: Rex Harrison (*My Fair Lady*)
Actress: Julie Andrews (*Mary Poppins*)
Supporting Actor: Peter Ustinov (*Topkapi*)
Supporting Actress: Lila Kedrova (*Zorba the Greek*)
Original Story & Screenplay: S. H. Barnett, Peter Stone, Frank Tarloff (*Father Goose*)
Adapted Screenplay: Edward Anhalt (*Becket*)
B/w Cinematography: Walter Lassally (*Zorba the Greek*)
Colour Cinematography: Harry Stradling (*My Fair Lady*)
B/w Art Direction: Vassilis Fotopoulos (*Zorba the Greek*)
Colour Art Direction: Gene Allen, Cecil Beaton (*My Fair Lady*)
B/w Costume Design: Dorothy Jeakins (*The Night of the Iguana*)
Colour Costume Design: Cecil Beaton (*My Fair Lady*)
Visual Effects: Peter Ellenshaw, Hamilton Luske, Eustace Lycett (*Mary Poppins*)
Sound Effects: Norman Wanstall (*Goldfinger*)
Sound: George R. Groves, Warner Sound Dept (*My Fair Lady*)
Editing: Cotton Warburton (*Mary Poppins*)
Song: 'Chim Chim Cheree' from *Mary Poppins* (m/ly Richard M. Sherman, Robert B. Sherman)

Original Score: Richard M. Sherman, Robert B. Sherman (*Mary Poppins*)
Adapted Score: André Previn (*My Fair Lady*)
Documentary Short: *Nine from Little Rock*
Documentary Feature: *Jacques-Yves Cousteau's World without Sun*
Cartoon: *The Pink Phink*
Live-Action Short: *Casals Conducts: 1964*
Honorary Award: William Tuttle (for make-up on *Seven Faces of Dr Lao*)

1965

Picture: *The Sound of Music*
Foreign-Language Film: *The Shop on Main Street* (Jan Kadar)
Director: Robert Wise (*The Sound of Music*)
Actor: Lee Marvin (*Cat Ballou*)
Actress: Julie Christie (*Darling*)
Supporting Actor: Martin Balsam (*A Thousand Clowns*)
Supporting Actress: Shelley Winters (*A Patch of Blue*)
Original Story & Screenplay: Frederic Raphael (*Darling*)
Adapted Screenplay: Robert Bolt (*Dr Zhivago*)
B/w Cinematography: Ernest Laszlo (*Ship of Fools*)
Colour Cinematography: Freddie Young (*Dr Zhivago*)
B/w Art Direction: Robert Clatworthy (*Ship of Fools*)
Colour Art Direction: John Box, Terry Marsh (*Dr Zhivago*)
B/w Costume Design: Julie Harris (*Darling*)
Colour Costume Design: Phyllis Dalton (*Dr Zhivago*)
Visual Effects: John Stears (*Thunderball*)
Sound Effects: Tregoweth Brown (*The Great Race*)
Sound: James P. Corcoran, TCF Sound Dept, Fred Hynes, Todd-AO Sound Dept (*The Sound of Music*)
Editing: William Reynolds (*The Sound of Music*)
Song: 'The Shadow of Your Smile' from *The Sandpiper* (m Johnny Mandel, ly Paul Francis Webster)
Original Score: Maurice Jarre (*Dr Zhivago*)
Adapted Score: Irwin Kostal (*The Sound of Music*)
Documentary Short: *To Be Alive!*
Documentary Feature: *The Eleanor Roosevelt Story*
Cartoon: *The Dot and the Line*
Live-Action Short: *The Chicken*
Honorary Award: Bob Hope
Irving Thalberg Memorial Award: William Wyler

1966

Picture: *A Man for All Seasons*
Foreign-Language Film: *A Man and a Woman* (Claude Lelouch)
Director: Fred Zinnemann (*A Man for All Seasons*)
Actor: Paul Scofield (*A Man for All Seasons*)
Actress: Elizabeth Taylor (*Who's Afraid of Virginia Woolf?*)
Supporting Actor: Walter Matthau (*The Fortune Cookie*)
Supporting Actress: Sandy Dennis (*Who's Afraid of Virginia Woolf?*)
Original Story & Screenplay: Claude Lelouch, Pierre Uytterhoeven (*A Man and a Woman*)
Adapted Screenplay: Robert Bolt (*A Man for All Seasons*)
B/w Cinematography: Haskell Wexler (*Who's Afraid of Virginia Woolf?*)
Colour Cinematography: Ted Moore (*A Man for All Seasons*)
B/w Art Direction: Richard Sylbert (*Who's Afraid of Virginia Woolf?*)

Colour Art Direction: Jack Martin Smith, Dale Hennesy (*Fantastic Voyage*)
B/w Costume Design: Irene Sharaff (*Who's Afraid of Virginia Woolf?*)
Colour Costume Design: Elizabeth Haffenden, Joan Bridge (*A Man for All Seasons*)
Visual Effects: Art Cruickshank (*Fantastic Voyage*)
Sound Effects: Gordon Daniel (*Grand Prix*)
Sound: Franklin E. Milton, MGM Sound Dept (*Grand Prix*)
Editing: Frederic Steinkamp, Henry Berman, Stewart Linder, Frank Santillo (*Grand Prix*)
Song: 'Born Free' from *Born Free* (m John Barry, ly Don Black)
Original Score: John Barry (*Born Free*)
Adapted Score: Ken Thorne (*A Funny Thing Happened on the Way to the Forum*)
Documentary Short: *A Year toward Tomorrow*
Documentary Feature: *The War Game*
Cartoon: *Herb Alpert and the Tijuana Brass Double Feature*
Live-Action Short: *Wild Wings*
Honorary Award: Yakima Canutt
Irving Thalberg Memorial Award: Robert Wise

1967

Picture: *In the Heat of the Night*
Foreign-Language Film: *Closely Observed Trains* (Jiri Menzel)
Director: Mike Nichols (*The Graduate*)
Actor: Rod Steiger (*In the Heat of the Night*)
Actress: Katharine Hepburn (*Guess Who's Coming to Dinner*); Barbra Streisand (*Funny Girl*)
Supporting Actor: George Kennedy (*Cool Hand Luke*)
Supporting Actress: Estelle Parsons (*Bonnie and Clyde*)
Original Story & Screenplay: William Rose (*Guess Who's Coming to Dinner*)
Adapted Screenplay: Sterling Silliphant (*In the Heat of the Night*)
Cinematography: Burnett Guffey (*Bonnie and Clyde*)
Art Direction: John Truscott, Edward Carrere (*Camelot*)
Costume Design: John Truscott (*Camelot*)
Special Effects: L. B. Abbott (*Doctor Dolittle*)
Sound Effects: John Poyner (*The Dirty Dozen*)
Sound: Samuel Goldwyn Studio Dept (*In the Heat of the Night*)
Editing: Hal Ashby (*In the Heat of the Night*)
Song: 'Talk to the Animals' from *Doctor Dolittle* (m/ly Leslie Bricusse)
Original Score: Elmer Bernstein (*Thoroughly Modern Millie*)
Adapted Score: Alfred Newman, Ken Darby (*Camelot*)
Documentary Short: *The Redwoods*
Documentary Feature: *The Anderson Platoon*
Cartoon: *The Box*
Live-Action Short: *A Place to Stand*
Honorary Award: Arthur Freed
Irving Thalberg Memorial Award: Alfred Hitchcock

1968

Picture: *Oliver!*
Director: Carol Reed (*Oliver!*)
Actor: Cliff Robertson (*Charly*)
Actress: Katharine Hepburn (*The Lion in Winter*)
Supporting Actor: Jack Albertson (*The Subject Was Roses*)
Supporting Actress: Ruth Gordon (*Rosemary's Baby*)

Original Story & Screenplay: Mel Brooks (*The Producers*)
Adapted Screenplay: James Goldman (*The Lion in Winter*)
Cinematography: Pasqualino De Santis (*Romeo and Juliet*)
Art Direction: John Box, Terence Marsh (*Oliver!*)
Costume Design: Danilo Donati (*Romeo and Juliet*)
Sound: Shepperton Sound Dept (*Oliver!*)
Editing: Frank P. Keller (*Bullitt*)
Special Effects: Stanley Kubrick (*2001: A Space Odyssey*)
Song: 'The Windmills of Your Mind' from *The Thomas Crown Affair* (m Michel Legrand, ly Alan and Marilyn Bergman)
Original Score: John Barry (*The Lion in Winter*)
Scoring of a Musical: John Green (*Oliver!*)
Documentary Short: *Why Man Creates*
Documentary Feature: *Journey into Self*
Cartoon: *Winnie the Pooh and the Blustery Day*
Live-Action Short: *Robert Kennedy Remembered*
Honorary Awards: John Chambers (make-up for *Planet of the Apes*); Onna White (choreography for *Oliver!*)

1969

Picture: *Midnight Cowboy*
Foreign-Language Film: *Z* (Costa-Gavras)
Director: John Schlesinger (*Midnight Cowboy*)
Actor: John Wayne (*True Grit*)
Actress: Maggie Smith (*The Prime of Miss Jean Brodie*)
Supporting Actor: Gig Young (*They Shoot Horses, Don't They?*)
Supporting Actress: Goldie Hawn (*Cactus Flower*)
Original Story & Screenplay: William Goldman (*Butch Cassidy and the Sundance Kid*)
Adapted Screenplay: Waldo Salt (*Midnight Cowboy*)
Cinematography: Arthur Ibbetson (*Anne of the Thousand Days*)
Art Direction: John DeCuir, Jack Martin Smith, Herman Blumenthal (*Hello, Dolly!*)
Costume Design: Margaret Furse (*Anne of the Thousand Days*)
Sound: Jack Solomon, Murray Spivack (*Hello, Dolly!*)
Editing: Françoise Bonnot (*Z*)
Special Effects: Robbie Robertson (*Marooned*)
Song: 'Raindrops Keep Fallin' on My Head' from *Butch Cassidy and the Sundance Kid* (m Burt Bacharach, ly Hal David)
Original Score: Burt Bacharach (*Butch Cassidy and the Sundance Kid*)
Scoring of a Musical: Lennie Hayton, Lionel Newman (*Hello, Dolly!*)
Documentary Short: *Czechoslovakia 1968*
Documentary Feature: *Arthur Rubinstein – the Love of Life*
Cartoon: *It's Tough to Be a Bird*
Live-Action Short: *The Magic Machines*
Honorary Award: Cary Grant

1970

Picture: *Patton*
Foreign-Language Film: *Investigation of a Citizen above Suspicion* (Elio Petri)
Director: Franklin J. Schaffner (*Patton*)
Actor: George C. Scott (*Patton*)
Actress: Glenda Jackson (*Women in Love*)
Supporting Actor: John Mills (*Ryan's Daughter*)
Supporting Actress: Helen Hayes (*Airport*)
Original Story & Screenplay: Francis Ford Coppola, Edmund H. North (*Patton*)

Adapted Screenplay: Ring Lardner Jnr (*M*A*S*H*)
Cinematography: Freddie Young (*Ryan's Daughter*)
Art Direction: Urie McCleary, Gil Parrondo (*Patton*)
Costume Design: Nino Novarese (*Cromwell*)
Sound: Douglas Williams, Don Bassman (*Patton*)
Editing: Hugh S. Fowler (*Patton*)
Special Effects: A. D. Flowers, L. B. Abbott (*Tora! Tora! Tora!*)
Song: 'For All We Know' from *Lovers and Other Strangers* (m Fred Karlin, ly Robb Royer, James Griffin)
Original Score: Francis Lai (*Love Story*)
Original Song Score: The Beatles (*Let It Be*)
Documentary Short: *Interviews with My Lai Veterans*
Documentary Feature: *Woodstock*
Cartoon: *Is It Always Right to Be Right*
Live-Action Short: *The Resurrection of Bronco Billy*
Honorary Awards: Lillian Gish; Orson Welles
Irving Thalberg Memorial Award: Ingmar Bergman

1971

Picture: *The French Connection*
Foreign-Language Film: *The Garden of the Finzi-Continis* (Vittorio De Sica)
Director: William Friedkin (*The French Connection*)
Actor: Gene Hackman (*The French Connection*)
Actress: Jane Fonda (*Klute*)
Supporting Actor: Ben Johnson (*The Last Picture Show*)
Supporting Actress: Cloris Leachman (*The Last Picture Show*)
Original Story & Screenplay: Paddy Chayevsky (*The Hospital*)
Adapted Screenplay: Ernest Tidyman (*The French Connection*)
Cinematography: Oswald Morris (*Fiddler on the Roof*)
Art Direction: John Box, Ernest Archer, Jack Maxsted, Gil Parrondo (*Nicholas and Alexandra*)
Costume Design: Yvonne Blake, Antonio Castillo (*Nicholas and Alexandra*)
Sound: Gordon K. McCallum, David Hildyard (*Fiddler on the Roof*)
Editing: Jerry Greenberg (*The French Connection*)
Special Effects: Alan Maley, Eustace Lycett, Danny Lee (*Bedknobs and Broomsticks*)
Song: Theme from *Shaft* (m/ly Isaac Hayes)
Original Dramatic Score: Michel Legrand (*Summer of '42*)
Adaptation and Original Song Score: John Williams (*Fiddler on the Roof*)
Documentary Short: *Sentinels of Silence*
Documentary Feature: *The Hellstrom Chronicle*
Animated Film: *The Crunch Bird*
Live-Action Short: *Sentinels of Silence*
Honorary Award: Charles Chaplin

1972

Picture: *The Godfather*
Foreign-Language Film: *The Discreet Charm of the Bourgeoisie* (Luis Buñuel)
Director: Bob Fosse (*Cabaret*)
Actor: Marlon Brando (*The Godfather*)
Actress: Liza Minnelli (*Cabaret*)
Supporting Actor: Joel Grey (*Cabaret*)
Supporting Actress: Eileen Heckart (*Butterflies Are Free*)
Original Story & Screenplay: Jeremy Larner (*The Candidate*)

Adapted Screenplay: Mario Puzo, Francis Ford Coppola (*The Godfather*)
Cinematography: Geoffrey Unsworth (*Cabaret*)
Art Direction: Rolf Zehetbauer, Jurgen Kiebach (*Cabaret*)
Costume Design: Anthony Powell (*Travels with My Aunt*)
Sound: Robert Knudson, David Hildyard (*Cabaret*)
Editing: David Bretherton (*Cabaret*)
Song: 'The Morning After' from *The Poseidon Adventure* (m/ly Al Kasha, Joel Hirschhorn)
Original Dramatic Score: Charles Chaplin, Raymond Rasch, Larry Russell (*Limelight*)
Adaptation and Original Song Score: Ralph Burns (*Cabaret*)
Documentary Short: *This Tiny World*
Documentary Feature: *Marjoe*
Animated Film: *A Christmas Carol*
Live-Action Short: *Norman Rockwell's World . . . An American Dream*
Special Achievement Award: L. B. Abbott, A. D. Flowers (for visual effects, *The Poseidon Adventure*)
Honorary Award: Edward G. Robinson

1973

Picture: *The Sting*
Foreign-Language Film: *Day for Night* (François Truffaut)
Director: George Roy Hill (*The Sting*)
Actor: Jack Lemmon (*Save the Tiger*)
Actress: Glenda Jackson (*A Touch of Class*)
Supporting Actor: John Houseman (*The Paper Chase*)
Supporting Actress: Tatum O'Neal (*Paper Moon*)
Original Story & Screenplay: David S. Ward (*The Sting*)
Adapted Screenplay: William Peter Blatty (*The Exorcist*)
Cinematography: Sven Nykvist (*Cries and Whispers*)
Art Direction: Henry Bumstead (*The Sting*)
Costume Design: Edith Head (*The Sting*)
Sound: Robert Knudson, Chris Newman (*The Exorcist*)
Editing: William Reynolds (*The Sting*)
Song: 'The Way We Were' from *The Way We Were* (m Marvin Hamlisch, ly Alan and Marilyn Bergman)
Original Dramatic Score: Marvin Hamlisch (*The Way We Were*)
Adaptation and Original Song Score: Marvin Hamlisch (*The Sting*)
Documentary Short: *Princeton: A Search for Answers*
Documentary Feature: *The Great American Cowboy*
Animated Film: *Frank Film*
Live-Action Short: *The Bolero*
Honorary Awards: Henri Langlois; Groucho Marx
Irving Thalberg Memorial Award: Lawrence Weingarten

1974

Picture: *The Godfather Part II*
Foreign-Language Film: *Amarcord* (Federico Fellini)
Director: Francis Ford Coppola (*The Godfather Part II*)
Actor: Art Carney (*Harry and Tonto*)
Actress: Ellen Burstyn (*Alice Doesn't Live Here Any More*)
Supporting Actor: Robert De Niro (*The Godfather Part II*)
Supporting Actress: Ingrid Bergman (*Murder on the Orient Express*)

Original Story & Screenplay: Robert Towne (*Chinatown*)
Adapted Screenplay: Francis Ford Coppola, Mario Puzo (*The Godfather Part II*)
Cinematography: Fred Koenekamp, Joseph Biroc (*The Towering Inferno*)
Art Direction: Dean Tavoularis, Angelo Graham (*The Godfather Part II*)
Costume Design: Theoni V. Aldredge (*The Great Gatsby*)
Sound: Ronald Pierce, Melvin Metcalfe Snr (*Earthquake*)
Editing: Harold F. Kress, Carl Kress (*The Towering Inferno*)
Song: 'We May Never Love Like This Again' from *The Towering Inferno* (m/ly Al Kasha, Joel Hirshhorn)
Original Dramatic Score: Nino Rota, Carmine Coppola (*The Godfather Part II*)
Adaptation and Original Song Score: Nelson Riddle (*The Great Gatsby*)
Documentary Short: *Don't*
Documentary Feature: *Hearts and Minds*
Animated Film: *Closed Mondays*
Live-Action Short: *One-Eyed Men Are Kings*
Honorary Awards: Howard Hawks; Jean Renoir
Special Achievement Award: Frank Brendel, Glen Robinson, Albert Whitlock (for visual effects, *Earthquake*)

1975

Picture: *One Flew over the Cuckoo's Nest*
Foreign-Language Film: *Dersu Uzala* (Akira Kurosawa)
Director: Milos Forman (*One Flew over the Cuckoo's Nest*)
Actor: Jack Nicholson (*One Flew over the Cuckoo's Nest*)
Actress: Louise Fletcher (*One Flew over the Cuckoo's Nest*)
Supporting Actor: George Burns (*The Sunshine Boys*)
Supporting Actress: Lee Grant (*Shampoo*)
Original Screenplay: Frank Pierson (*Dog Day Afternoon*)
Adapted Screenplay: Lawrence Hauben, Bo Goldman (*One Flew over the Cuckoo's Nest*)
Cinematography: John Alcott (*Barry Lyndon*)
Art Direction: Ken Adam, Roy Walker (*Barry Lyndon*)
Costume Design: Britt Soderland, Milena Canonero (*Barry Lyndon*)
Sound: Robert L. Hoyt, Roger Heman, Earl Madery, John Carter (*Jaws*)
Editing: Verna Fields (*Jaws*)
Song: 'I'm Easy' from *Nashville* (m/ly Keith Carradine)
Original Score: John Williams (*Jaws*)
Adaptation and Original Song Score: Leonard Rosenman (*Barry Lyndon*)
Documentary Short: *The End of the Game*
Documentary Feature: *The Man Who Skied Down Everest*
Animated Film: *Great*
Live-Action Short: *Angel and Big Joe*
Honorary Award: Mary Pickford
Special Achievement Awards: Peter Berkos (sound effects, *The Hindenburg*); Albert Whitlock and Glen Robinson (visual effects, *The Hindenburg*)
Irving Thalberg Memorial Award: Mervyn Le Roy

1976

Picture: *Rocky*
Foreign-Language Film: *Black and White in Colour* (Jean-Jacques Annaud)

Director: John G. Avildsen (*Rocky*)
Actor: Peter Finch (*Network*)
Actress: Faye Dunaway (*Network*)
Supporting Actor: Jason Robards (*All the President's Men*)
Supporting Actress: Beatrice Straight (*Network*)
Original Screenplay: Paddy Chayevsky (*Network*)
Adapted Screenplay: William Goldman (*All the President's Men*)
Cinematography: Haskell Wexler (*Bound for Glory*)
Art Direction: George Jenkins (*All the President's Men*)
Costume Design: Danilo Donati (*Fellini's Casanova*)
Sound: Arthur Piantadosi, Les Fresholtz, Dick Alexander, Jim Webb (*All the President's Men*)
Editing: Richard Halsey, Scott Conrad (*Rocky*)
Song: 'Evergreen' from *A Star Is Born* (m Barbra Streisand, ly Paul Williams)
Original Score: Jerry Goldsmith (*The Omen*)
Adaptation and Original Song Score: Leonard Rosenman (*Bound for Glory*)
Documentary Short: *Number Our Days*
Documentary Feature: *Harlan County, USA*
Animated Film: *Leisure*
Live-Action Short: *In the Region of Ice*
Special Achievement Awards: Carlo Rambaldi, Glen Robinson, Frank Van Der Veer (visual effects, *King Kong*); L. B. Abbott, Glen Robinson, Matthew Yuricich (visual effects, *Logan's Run*)
Irving Thalberg Memorial Award: Pandro S. Berman

1977

Picture: *Annie Hall*
Foreign-Language Film: *Madame Rosa* (Moshe Mizrahi)
Director: Woody Allen (*Annie Hall*)
Actor: Richard Dreyfuss (*The Goodbye Girl*)
Actress: Diane Keaton (*Annie Hall*)
Supporting Actor: Jason Robards (*Julia*)
Supporting Actress: Vanessa Redgrave (*Julia*)
Original Screenplay: Woody Allen, Marshall Brickman (*Annie Hall*)
Adapted Screenplay: Alvin Sargent (*Julia*)
Cinematography: Vilmos Zsigmond (*Close Encounters of the Third Kind*)
Art Direction: John Barry, Norman Reynolds, Leslie Dilley (*Star Wars*)
Costume Design: John Mollo (*Star Wars*)
Sound: Don MacDougall, Ray West, Bob Minkler, Derek Ball (*Star Wars*)
Editing: Marcia Lucas, Richard Chew (*Star Wars*)
Visual Effects: John Stears, John Dystra, Richard Edlund, Grant McCune, Robert Black (*Star Wars*)
Song: 'You Light Up My Life' from *You Light Up My Life* (m/ly Joseph Brooks)
Adaptation and Original Song Score: Jonathan Tunick (*A Little Night Music*)
Documentary Short: *Gravity Is My Enemy*
Documentary Feature: *Who Are the DeBolts? And Where Did They Get Nineteen Kids?*
Animated Film: *Sand Castle*
Live-Action Short: *I'll Find a Way*
Honorary Award: Margaret Booth (for contribution to the art of film editing)
Special Achievement Awards: Frank Warner (sound effects editing, *Close Encounters of the Third Kind*); Benjamin Burtt Jnr (sound effects, *Star Wars*)
Irving Thalberg Memorial Award: Walter Mirisch

1978

Picture: *The Deer Hunter*
Foreign-Language Film: *Get Out Your Handkerchiefs* (Bertrand Blier)
Director: Michael Cimino (*The Deer Hunter*)
Actor: Jon Voight (*Coming Home*)
Actress: Jane Fonda (*Coming Home*)
Supporting Actor: Christopher Walken (*The Deer Hunter*)
Supporting Actress: Maggie Smith (*California Suite*)
Original Screenplay: Nancy Dowd, Waldo Salt, Robert C. Jones (*Coming Home*)
Adapted Screenplay: Oliver Stone (*Midnight Express*)
Cinematography: Nestor Almendros (*Days of Heaven*)
Art Direction: Paul Sylbert, Edwin O'Donovan (*Heaven Can Wait*)
Costume Design: Anthony Powell (*Death on the Nile*)
Sound: Richard Portman, William McCaughey, Aaron Rochin, Darrin Knight (*The Deer Hunter*)
Editing: Peter Zinner (*The Deer Hunter*)
Song: 'Last Dance' from *Thank God It's Friday* (m/ly Paul Jabara)
Original Score: Giorgio Moroder (*Midnight Express*)
Adaptation and Original Song Score: Joe Renzetti (*The Buddy Holly Story*)
Documentary Short: *The Flight of the Gossamer Condor*
Documentary Feature: *Scared Straight*
Animated Film: *Special Delivery*
Live-Action Short: *Teenage Father*
Honorary Awards: Walter Lantz (for his animated pictures); Laurence Olivier (for the full body of his work); King Vidor (for his incomparable achievements)
Special Achievement Award: Les Bowie, Colin Chilvers, Denys Coop, Roy Field, Derek Meddings, Zoran Perisic (visual effects, *Superman*)

1979

Picture: *Kramer vs Kramer*
Foreign-Language Film: *The Tin Drum* (Volker Schlöndorff)
Director: Robert Benton (*Kramer vs Kramer*)
Actor: Dustin Hoffman (*Kramer vs Kramer*)
Actress: Sally Field (*Norma Rae*)
Supporting Actor: Melvyn Douglas (*Being There*)
Supporting Actress: Meryl Streep (*Kramer vs Kramer*)
Original Screenplay: Steve Tesich (*Breaking Away*)
Adapted Screenplay: Robert Benton (*Kramer vs Kramer*)
Cinematography: Vittorio Storaro (*Apocalypse Now*)
Art Direction: Philip Rosenberg, Tony Walton (*All That Jazz*)
Costume Design: Albert Wolsky (*All That Jazz*)
Sound: Walter Murch, Mark Berger, Richard Beggs, Nat Boxer (*Apocalypse Now*)
Editing: Alan Heim (*All That Jazz*)
Visual Effects: H. R. Giger, Carlo Rambaldi, Brian Johnson, Nick Allder, Denys Ayling (*Alien*)
Song: 'It Goes Like It Goes' from *Norma Rae* (m David Shire, ly Norman Gimbel)
Original Score: Georges Delerue (*A Little Romance*)
Adaptation and Original Song Score: Ralph Burns (*All That Jazz*)
Documentary Short: *Paul Robeson: Tribute to an Artist*
Documentary Feature: *Best Boy*

Animated Film: *Every Child*
Live-Action Short: *Board and Care*
Honorary Award: Alec Guinness (for advancing the art of screen acting)
Special Achievement Award: Alan Splet (sound editing, *The Black Stallion*)
Irving Thalberg Memorial Award: Ray Stark

1980

Picture: *Ordinary People*
Foreign-Language Film: *Moscow Does Not Believe in Tears* (Vladimir Menshov)
Director: Robert Redford (*Ordinary People*)
Actor: Robert De Niro (*Raging Bull*)
Actress: Sissy Spacek (*Coal Miner's Daughter*)
Supporting Actor: Timothy Hutton (*Ordinary People*)
Supporting Actress: Mary Steenburgen (*Melvin and Howard*)
Original Screenplay: Bo Goldman (*Melvin and Howard*)
Adapted Screenplay: Alvin Sargent (*Ordinary People*)
Cinematography: Geoffrey Unsworth, Ghislain Cloquet (*Tess*)
Art Direction: Pierre Guffroy, Jack Stephens (*Tess*)
Costume Design: Anthony Powell (*Tess*)
Sound: Bill Varney, Steve Maslow, Gregg Landacker, Peter Sutton (*The Empire Strikes Back*)
Editing: Thelma Schoonmaker (*Raging Bull*)
Song: 'Fame' from *Fame* (m Michael Gore, ly Dean Pitchford)
Original Score: Michael Gore (*Fame*)
Documentary Short: *Karl Hess: Towards Liberty*
Documentary Feature: *From Mao to Mozart: Isaac Stern in China*
Animated Film: *The Fly*
Live-Action Short: *The Dollar Bottom*
Honorary Award: Henry Fonda (in recognition of his brilliant accomplishments)
Special Achievement Award: Brian Johnson, Richard Edlund, Dennis Muren, Bruce Nicholson (visual effects, *The Empire Strikes Back*)

1981

Picture: *Chariots of Fire*
Foreign-Language Film: *Mephisto* (Istvan Szabo)
Director: Warren Beatty (*Reds*)
Actor: Henry Fonda (*On Golden Pond*)
Actress: Katharine Hepburn (*On Golden Pond*)
Supporting Actor: John Gielgud (*Arthur*)
Supporting Actress: Maureen Stapleton (*Reds*)
Original Screenplay: Colin Welland (*Chariots of Fire*)
Adapted Screenplay: Ernest Thompson (*On Golden Pond*)
Cinematography: Vittorio Storaro (*Reds*)
Art Direction: Norman Reynolds, Leslie Dilley (*Raiders of the Lost Ark*)
Costume Design: Milena Canonero (*Chariots of Fire*)
Make-Up: Rick Baker (*An American Werewolf in London*)
Sound: Bill Varney, Steve Maslow, Gregg Landaker, Roy Charman (*Raiders of the Lost Ark*)
Editing: Michael Kahn (*Raiders of the Lost Ark*)
Song: 'Arthur's Theme' from *Arthur* (m/ly Burt Bacharach, Carole Bayer Sager, Christopher Cross, Peter Allen)
Original Score: Vangelis (*Chariots of Fire*)
Documentary Short: *Close Harmony*
Documentary Feature: *Genocide*
Animated Film: *Crac*
Live-Action Short: *Violet*
Honorary Award: Barbara Stanwyck

Special Achievement Awards: Ben Burtt, Richard L. Anderson (sound effects editing, *Raiders of the Lost Ark*)
Irving Thalberg Memorial Award: Albert R. Broccoli

1982

Picture: *Gandhi*
Foreign-Language Picture: *To Begin Again* (José Luis Garci)
Director: Richard Attenborough (*Gandhi*)
Actor: Ben Kingsley (*Gandhi*)
Actress: Meryl Streep (*Sophie's Choice*)
Supporting Actor: Louis Gossett Jnr (*An Officer and a Gentleman*)
Supporting Actress: Jessica Lange (*Tootsie*)
Original Screenplay: John Briley (*Gandhi*)
Adapted Screenplay: Costa-Gavras, Donald Stewart (*Missing*)
Cinematography: Billy Williams, Ronnie Taylor (*Gandhi*)
Art Direction: Stuart Craig, Bob Lang (*Gandhi*)
Costume Design: John Mollo, Bhanu Athaiya (*Gandhi*)
Make-Up: Sarah Monzani, Michele Burke (*Quest for Fire*)
Sound: Robert Knudson, Robert Glass, Don Digirolamo, Gene Cantemassa (*ET*)
Sound Effects Editing: Charles L. Campbell, Ben Burtt (*ET*)
Editing: John Bloom (*Gandhi*)
Visual Effects: Carlo Rambaldi, Dennis Muren, Kenneth F. Smith (*ET*)
Song: 'Up Where We Belong' from *An Officer and a Gentleman* (m Jack Nitzsche, Buffy Sainte-Marie, ly Will Jennings)
Original Score: John Williams (*ET*)
Original Song Score or Adaptation: Henry Mancini, Leslie Bricusse (*Victor/Victoria*)
Documentary Short: *If You Love This Planet*
Documentary Feature: *Just Another Missing Kid*
Animated Film: *Tango*
Live-Action Short: *A Shocking Accident*
Honorary Award: Mickey Rooney

1983

Picture: *Terms of Endearment*
Foreign-Language Film: *Fanny and Alexander* (Ingmar Bergman)
Director: James L. Brooks (*Terms of Endearment*)
Actor: Robert Duvall (*Tender Mercies*)
Actress: Shirley MacLaine (*Terms of Endearment*)
Supporting Actor: Jack Nicholson (*Terms of Endearment*)
Supporting Actress: Linda Hunt (*The Year of Living Dangerously*)
Original Screenplay: Horton Foote (*Tender Mercies*)
Adapted Screenplay: James L. Brooks (*Terms of Endearment*)
Cinematography: Sven Nykvist (*Fanny and Alexander*)
Art Direction: Anna Asp (*Fanny and Alexander*)
Costume Design: Marik Vos (*Fanny and Alexander*)
Sound: Mark Berger, Tom Scott, Randy Thom, David MacMillan (*The Right Stuff*)
Sound Effects Editing: Jay Boekelheide (*The Right Stuff*)
Editing: Glenn Farr, Lisa Fruchtman, Stephen A. Rotter, Douglas Stewart, Tom Rolf (*The Right Stuff*)
Song: 'Flashdance' from *Flashdance* (m Giorgio Moroder, ly Keith Forsey, Irene Cara)
Original Score: Bill Conti (*The Right Stuff*)
Original Song Score or Adaptation: Michel

Legrand, Alan and Marilyn Bergman (*Yentl*)
Documentary Short: *Flamenco at 5:15*
Documentary Feature: *He Makes Me Feel Like Dancin'*
Animated Film: *Sundae in New York*
Live-Action Short: *Boys and Girls*
Honorary Award: Hal Roach
Special Achievement Awards: Richard Edlund, Dennis Muren, Ken Ralston, Phil Tippett (visual effects, *Return of the Jedi*)

1984

Picture: *Amadeus*
Foreign-Language Film: *Dangerous Moves* (Richard Dembo)
Director: Milos Forman (*Amadeus*)
Actor: F. Murray Abraham (*Amadeus*)
Actress: Sally Field (*Places in the Heart*)
Supporting Actor: Haing S. Ngor (*The Killing Fields*)
Supporting Actress: Peggy Ashcroft (*A Passage to India*)
Original Screenplay: Robert Benton (*Places in the Heart*)
Adapted Screenplay: Peter Shaffer (*Amadeus*)
Cinematography: Chris Menges (*The Killing Fields*)
Art Direction: Patrizia Von Brandenstein (*Amadeus*)
Costume Design: Theodor Pistek (*Amadeus*)
Make-Up: Paul LeBlanc, Dick Smith (*Amadeus*)
Sound: Mark Berger, Tom Scott, Todd Boekelheide, Chris Newman (*Amadeus*)
Editing: Jim Clark (*The Killing Fields*)
Visual Effects: Dennis Muren, Michael McAlister, Lorne Petersen, George Gibbs (*Ghostbusters*)
Song: 'I Just Called to Say I Love You' from *The Woman in Red* (m/ly Stevie Wonder)
Original Score: Maurice Jarre (*A Passage to India*)
Original Song Score or Adaptation: Prince (*Purple Rain*)
Documentary Short: *The Stone Carvers*
Documentary Feature: *The Times of Harvey Milk*
Animated Film: *Charade*
Live-Action Short: *Up*
Honorary Award: James Stewart
Special Achievement Award: Kay Rose (sound effects editing, *The River*)

1985

Picture: *Out of Africa*
Foreign-Language Film: *The Official Story* (Luis Puenzo)
Director: Sydney Pollack (*Out of Africa*)
Actor: William Hurt (*Kiss of the Spider Woman*)
Actress: Geraldine Page (*The Trip to Bountiful*)
Supporting Actor: Don Ameche (*Cocoon*)
Supporting Actress: Anjelica Huston (*Prizzi's Honor*)
Original Screenplay: William Kelley, Pamela Wallace, Earl W. Wallace (*Witness*)
Adapted Screenplay: Kurt Luedtke (*Out of Africa*)
Cinematography: David Watkin (*Out of Africa*)
Art Direction: Stephen Grimes (*Out of Africa*)
Costume Design: Emi Wada (*Ran*)
Make-Up: Michael Westmore, Zoltan Elek (*Mask*)
Sound: Chris Jenkins, Gary Alexander, Larry Stensvold, Peter Handford (*Out of Africa*)
Sound Effects Editing: Charles L. Campbell, Robert Rutledge (*Back to the Future*)
Editing: Thom Noble (*Witness*)
Visual Effects: Ken Ralston, Ralph McQuarrie, Scott Farrar, David Berry (*Cocoon*)
Song: 'Say You, Say Me' from *White Nights* (m/ly Lionel Richie)
Original Score: John Barry (*Out of Africa*)

Documentary Short: *Witness to War*
Documentary Feature: *Broken Rainbow*
Animated Film: *Anna & Bella*
Live-Action Short: *Molly's Pilgrim*
Honorary Awards: Paul Newman; Alex North

1986

Picture: *Platoon*
Foreign-Language Film: *The Assault* (Fons Rademakers)
Director: Oliver Stone (*Platoon*)
Actor: Paul Newman (*The Color of Money*)
Actress: Marlee Matlin (*Children of a Lesser God*)
Supporting Actor: Michael Caine (*Hannah and Her Sisters*)
Supporting Actress: Dianne Wiest (*Hannah and Her Sisters*)
Original Screenplay: Woody Allen (*Hannah and Her Sisters*)
Adapted Screenplay: Ruth Prawer Jhabvala (*A Room with a View*)
Cinematography: Chris Menges (*The Mission*)
Art Direction: Gianni Quaranta, Brian Ackland-Snow (*A Room with a View*)
Costume Design: Jenny Beavan, John Bright (*A Room with a View*)
Make-Up: Chris Walas, Stephan Dupuis (*The Fly*)
Sound: John K. Wilkinson, Richard Rogers, Charles Grenzbach, Simon Kaye (*Platoon*)
Sound Effects Editing: Don Sharpe (*Aliens*)
Editing: Claire Simpson (*Platoon*)
Visual Effects: Robert Skotak, Stan Winston, John Richardson, Suzanne Benson (*Aliens*)
Song: 'Take My Breath Away' from *Top Gun* (m Giorgio Moroder, ly Tom Whitlock)
Original Score: Herbie Hancock (*Round Midnight*)
Documentary Short: *Women – For America, For the World*
Documentary Feature: *Artie Shaw: Time Is All You've Got*
Animated Film: *A Greek Tragedy*
Live-Action Short: *Precious Images*
Honorary Award: Ralph Bellamy
Irving Thalberg Memorial Award: Steven Spielberg

1987

Picture: *The Last Emperor*
Foreign-Language Film: *Babette's Feast* (Gabriel Axel)
Director: Bernardo Bertolucci (*The Last Emperor*)
Actor: Michael Douglas (*Wall Street*)
Actress: Cher (*Moonstruck*)
Supporting Actor: Sean Connery (*The Untouchables*)
Supporting Actress: Olympia Dukakis (*Moonstruck*)
Original Screenplay: John Patrick Shanley (*Moonstruck*)
Adapted Screenplay: Mark Peploe, Bernardo Bertolucci (*The Last Emperor*)
Cinematography: Vittorio Storaro (*The Last Emperor*)
Art Direction: Ferdinando Scarfiotti (*The Last Emperor*)
Costume Design: James Acheson (*The Last Emperor*)
Make-Up: Rick Bajer (*Harry and the Hendersons*)
Sound: Bill Rowe, Ivan Sharrock (*The Last Emperor*)
Editing: Gabriella Cristiani (*The Last Emperor*)
Visual Effects: Dennis Muren, William George, Harley Jessup, Kenneth Smith (*Innerspace*)
Song: 'The Time of My Life' from *Dirty Dancing*

(m Franke Previte, John DeNicola, Donald Markowitz, ly Franke Previte)
Original Score: Ryuichi Sakamoto, David Byrne, Cong Su (*The Last Emperor*)
Documentary Short: *Young at Heart*
Documentary Feature: *The Ten-Year Lunch: The Wit and Legend of the Algonquin Round Table*
Animated Film: *The Man Who Planted Trees*
Live-Action Short: *Ray's Male Heterosexual Dance Hall*
Special Achievement Awards: Stephen Flick, John Pospisil (sound effects, *Robocop*)
Irving Thalberg Memorial Award: Billy Wilder

1988

Picture: *Rain Man*
Foreign-Language Film: *Pelle the Conqueror* (Bille August)
Director: Barry Levinson (*Rain Man*)
Actor: Dustin Hoffman (*Rain Man*)
Actress: Jodie Foster (*The Accused*)
Supporting Actor: Kevin Kline (*A Fish Called Wanda*)
Supporting Actress: Geena Davis (*The Accidental Tourist*)
Original Screenplay: Ronald Bass, Barry Morrow (*Rain Man*)
Adapted Screenplay: Christopher Hampton (*Dangerous Liaisons*)
Cinematography: Peter Biziou (*Mississippi Burning*)
Art Direction: Stuart Craig (*Dangerous Liaisons*)
Costume Design: James Acheson (*Dangerous Liaisons*)
Make-Up: Ve Neill, Steve LaPorte, Robert Short (*Beetlejuice*)
Sound: Les Fresholtz, Dick Alexander, Vern Poore, Willie D. Burton (*Bird*)
Sound Effects Editing: Charles L. Campbell, Louis L. Edelman (*Who Framed Roger Rabbit?*)
Editing: Arthur Schimdt (*Who Framed Roger Rabbit?*)
Visual Effects: Ken Ralston, Richard Williams, Edward Jones, George Gibbs (*Who Framed Roger Rabbit?*)
Song: 'Let the River Run' from *Working Girl* (m/ly Carly Simon)
Original Score: Dave Grusin (*The Milagro Beanfield War*)
Documentary Short: *You Don't Have to Die*
Documentary Feature: *Hotel Terminus: The Life and Times of Klaus Barbie*
Animated Film: *Tin Toy*
Live-Action Short: *The Appointments of Dennis Jennings*
Special Achievement Award: Richard Williams (animation direction, *Who Framed Roger Rabbit?*)

1989

Picture: *Driving Miss Daisy*
Foreign-Language Film: *Cinema Paradiso* (Giuseppe Tornatore)
Director: Oliver Stone (*Born on the Fourth of July*)
Actor: Daniel Day-Lewis (*My Left Foot*)
Actress: Jessica Tandy (*Driving Miss Daisy*)
Supporting Actor: Denzel Washington (*Glory*)
Supporting Actress: Brenda Fricker (*My Left Foot*)
Original Screenplay: Tom Schulman (*Dead Poets Society*)
Adapted Screenplay: Alfred Uhry (*Driving Miss Daisy*)
Cinematography: Freddie Francis (*Glory*)
Art Direction: Anton Furst (*Batman*)
Costume Design: Phyllis Dalton (*Henry V*)
Make-Up: Manlio Rocchetti, Lynn Barber, Kevin Haney (*Driving Miss Daisy*)

Sound: Donald O. Mitchell, Kevin O'Connell, Greg P. Russell, Keith A. Wester (*Black Rain*)
Sound Effects Editing: Ben Burtt, Richard Hymns (*Indiana Jones and the Last Crusade*)
Editing: David Brenner, Joe Hutshing (*Born on the Fourth of July*)
Visual Effects: John Bruno, Dennis Muren, Hoyt Yeatman, Dennis Skotak (*The Abyss*)
Song: 'Under the Sea' from *The Little Mermaid* (m Alan Menken, ly Howard Ashman)
Original Score: Alan Menken (*The Little Mermaid*)
Documentary Short: *The Johnstown Flood*
Documentary Feature: *Common Threads: Stories from the Quilt*
Animated Film: *Balance*
Live-Action Short: *Work Experience*
Honorary Award: Akira Kurosawa

1990

Picture: *Dances with Wolves*
Foreign-Language Film: *Journey of Hope* (Xavier Koller)
Director: Kevin Costner (*Dances with Wolves*)
Actor: Jeremy Irons (*Reversal of Fortune*)
Actress: Kathy Bates (*Misery*)
Supporting Actor: Joe Pesci (*GoodFellas*)
Supporting Actress: Whoopi Goldberg (*Ghost*)
Original Screenplay: Bruce Joel Rubin (*Ghost*)
Adapted Screenplay: Michael Blake (*Dances with Wolves*)
Cinematography: Dean Semler (*Dances with Wolves*)
Art Direction: Richard Sylbert (*Dick Tracy*)
Costume Design: Franca Squarciapino (*Cyrano de Bergerac*)
Make-Up: John Caglione Jnr, Doug Drexler (*Dick Tracy*)
Sound: Russell Williams II, Jeffrey Perkins, Bill W. Benton, Greg Watkins (*Dances with Wolves*)
Sound Effects Editing: Cecelia Hall, George Watters II (*The Hunt for Red October*)
Editing: Neil Travis (*Dances with Wolves*)
Song: 'Sooner or Later' from *Dick Tracy* (m/ly Stephen Sondheim)
Original Score: John Barry (*Dances with Wolves*)
Documentary Short: *Days of Waiting*
Documentary Feature: *American Dream*
Animated Film: *Creature Comforts*
Live-Action Short: *The Lunch Date*
Honorary Awards: Sophia Loren; Myrna Loy
Special Achievement Awards: Eric Brevig, Rob Bottin, Tim McGovern, Alex Funke (visual effects, *Total Recall*)
Irving Thalberg Memorial Award: Richard Zanuck and David Brown

1991

Picture: *Silence of the Lambs*
Foreign-Language Film: *Mediterraneo* (Gabriele Salvatores)
Director: Jonathan Demme (*Silence of the Lambs*)
Actor: Anthony Hopkins (*Silence of the Lambs*)
Actress: Jodie Foster (*Silence of the Lambs*)
Supporting Actor: Jack Palance (*City Slickers*)
Supporting Actress: Mercedes Ruehl (*The Fisher King*)
Original Screenplay: Callie Khouri (*Thelma and Louise*)
Adapted Screenplay: Ted Tally (*Silence of the Lambs*)
Cinematography: Robert Richardson (*JFK*)
Art Direction: Dennis Gassner (*Bugsy*)
Costume Design: Albert Wolsky (*Bugsy*)
Make-Up: Stan Winston, Jeff Dawn (*Terminator 2*)

Sound: Tom Johnson, Gary Rydstrom, Gary Summers, Lee Orloff (*Terminator 2*)
Sound Effects Editing: Gary Rydstrom, Gloria S. Borders (*Terminator 2*)
Editing: Joe Hutshing, Pietro Scalia (*JFK*)
Visual Effects: Dennis Muren, Stan Winston, Gene Warren Jnr, Robert Skotak (*Terminator 2*)
Song: 'Beauty and the Beast' from *Beauty and the Beast* (m Alan Menken, ly Howard Ashman)
Original Score: Alan Menken (*Beauty and the Beast*)
Documentary Short: *Deadly Deception*
Documentary Feature: *In the Shadow of the Stars*
Animated Film: *Manipulation*
Live-Action Short: *Session Man*
Honorary Award: Satyajit Ray
Irving Thalberg Memorial Award: George Lucas

1992
Picture: *Unforgiven*
Foreign-Language Film: *Indochine* (Régis Wargnier)
Director: Clint Eastwood (*Unforgiven*)
Actor: Al Pacino (*Scent of a Woman*)
Actress: Emma Thompson (*Howards End*)
Supporting Actor: Gene Hackman (*Unforgiven*)
Supporting Actress: Marisa Tomei (*My Cousin Vinny*)
Original Screenplay: Neil Jordan (*The Crying Game*)
Adapted Screenplay: Ruth Prawer Jhabvala (*Howards End*)
Cinematography: Philippe Rousselot (*A River Runs through It*)
Art Direction: Luciana Arrighi (*Howards End*)
Costume Design: Eiko Ishioka (*Bram Stoker's Dracula*)
Make-Up: Greg Cannom, Michele Burke, Matthew W. Mungle (*Bram Stoker's Dracula*)
Sound: Chris Jenkins, Doug Hemphill, Mark Smith, Simon Kaye (*The Last of the Mohicans*)
Sound Effects Editing: Tom C. McCarthy, David E. Stone (*Bram Stoker's Dracula*)
Editing: Joel Cox (*Unforgiven*)
Visual Effects: Ken Ralston, Doug Chiang, Doug Smythe, Tom Woodruff (*Death Becomes Her*)
Song: 'A Whole New World' from *Aladdin* (m Alan Menken, ly Tim Rice)
Original Score: Alan Menken (*Aladdin*)
Documentary Short: *Educating Peter*
Documentary Feature: *The Panama Deception*
Animated Film: *Mona Lisa Descending a Staircase*
Live-Action Short: *Omnibus*
Honorary Award: Federico Fellini

1993
Picture: *Schindler's List*
Foreign-Language Film: *Belle Époque* (Fernando Trueba)
Director: Steven Spielberg (*Schindler's List*)
Actor: Tom Hanks (*Philadelphia*)
Actress: Holly Hunter (*The Piano*)
Supporting Actor: Tommy Lee Jones (*The Fugitive*)
Supporting Actress: Anna Paquin (*The Piano*)
Original Screenplay: Jane Campion (*The Piano*)
Adapted Screenplay: Steve Zaillian (*Schindler's List*)
Cinematography: Janusz Kaminski (*Schindler's List*)
Art Direction: Allan Starski (*Schindler's List*)
Costume Design: Gabriella Pescucci (*The Age of Innocence*)
Make-Up: Greg Cannom, Ve Neill, Yolanda Toussieng (*Mrs Doubtfire*)
Sound: Gary Summers, Gary Rydstrom, Shawn Murphy, Rod Judkins (*Jurassic Park*)

Sound Effects Editing: Gary Rydstrom, Richard Hymns (*Jurassic Park*)
Editing: Michael Kahn (*Schindler's List*)
Visual Effects: Dennis Muren, Stan Winston, Phil Tippett, Michael Lantieri (*Jurassic Park*)
Song: 'Streets of Philadelphia' from *Philadelphia* (m/ly Bruce Springsteen)
Original Score: John Williams (*Schindler's List*)
Documentary Short: *Defending Our Lives*
Documentary Feature: *I Am a Promise*
Animated Film: *The Wrong Trousers*
Live-Action Short: *Black Rider*
Honorary Award: Deborah Kerr

1994
Picture: *Forrest Gump*
Foreign-Language Film: *Burnt By the Sun* (Nikita Mikhalkov)
Director: Robert Zemeckis (*Forrest Gump*)
Actor: Tom Hanks (*Forrest Gump*)
Actress: Jessica Lange (*Blue Sky*)
Supporting Actor: Martin Landau (*Ed Wood*)
Supporting Actress: Dianne Wiest (*Bullets Over Broadway*)
Original Screenplay: Quentin Tarantino, Roger Avary (*Pulp Fiction*)
Adapted Screenplay: Eric Roth (*Forrest Gump*)
Cinematography: John Toll (*Legends of the Fall*)
Art Direction: Ken Adam, Carolyn Scott (*The Madness of King George*)
Costume Design: Lizzy Gardiner, Tim Chappel (*The Adventures of Priscilla, Queen of the Desert*)
Make-up: Rick Baker, Ve Neill, Yolanda Toussieng (*Ed Wood*)
Sound: Gregg Landaker, Steve Maslow, Bob Beemer, David R.B. MacMillan (*Speed*)
Sound Effects Editing: Stephen Hunter Flick (*Speed*)
Editing: Arthur Schmidt (*Forrest Gump*)
Visual Effects: Ken Ralston, George Murphy, Stephen Rosenbaum, Allen Hall (*Forrest Gump*)
Song: 'Can You Feel the Love Tonight' from *The Lion King* (m Elton John, ly Tim Rice)
Original Score: Hans Zimmer (*The Lion King*)
Documentary Short: *A Time For Justice*
Documentary Feature: *Maya Lin: A Strong Clear Vision*
Animated film: *Bob's Birthday*
Live-Action Short: *Franz Kafka's It's A Wonderful Life*
Honorary Award: Michelangelo Antonioni
Irving G. Thalberg Memorial Award: Clint Eastwood

1995
Picture: *Braveheart*
Foreign-Language Film: *Antonia's Line* (Marleen Gorris)
Director: Mel Gibson (*Braveheart*)
Actor: Nicolas Cage (*Leaving Las Vegas*)
Actress: Susan Sarandon (*Dead Man Walking*)
Supporting Actor: Kevin Spacey (*The Usual Suspects*)
Supporting Actress: Mira Sorvino (*Mighty Aphrodite*)
Original Screenplay: Christopher McQuarrie (*The Usual Suspects*)
Adapted Screenplay: Emma Thompson (*Sense and Sensibility*)
Cinematography: John Toll (*Braveheart*)
Art Direction: Eugenio Zanetti (*Restoration*)
Costume Design: James Acheson (*Restoration*)
Make-up: Peter Frampton, Paul Pattison, Lois Burwell (*Braveheart*)

Sound: Rick Dior, Steve Pederson, Scott Millan, David MacMillan (*Apollo 13*)
Sound Effects Editing: Lon Bender, Per Hallberg (*Braveheart*)
Editing: Michael J. Hill, Daniel P. Hanley (*Apollo 13*)
Visual Effects: Scott E. Anderson, Charles Gibson, Neal Scanlan, John Cox (*Babe*)
Song: 'Colours of the Wind' from *Pocahontas* (m Alan Menken, ly Stephen Schwartz)
Original Dramatic Score: Luis Enriquez Bacalov (*Il Postino*)
Original Musical or Comedy Score: *Pocahontas* (Alan Menken, Stephen Schwartz)
Documentary Short: *One Survivor Remembers*
Documentary Feature: *Anne Frank Remembered*
Animated film: *A Close Shave*
Live-Action Short: *Lieberman in Love*
Honorary Awards: Kirk Douglas, Chuck Jones

1996
Picture: *The English Patient* (Saul Zaentz)
Foreign-Language Film: *Kolya* (Jan Sverák)
Director: Anthony Minghella (*The English Patient*)
Actor: Geoffrey Rush (*Shine*)
Actress: Frances McDormand (*Fargo*)
Supporting Actor: Cuba Gooding, Jnr (*Jerry Maguire*)
Supporting Actress: Juliette Binoche (*The English Patient*)
Original Screenplay: *Fargo* (Ethan Coen, Joel Coen)
Adapted Screenplay: *Sling Blade* (Billy Bob Thornton)
Cinematography: John Seale (*The English Patient*)
Art Direction: Stuart Craig (*The English Patient*)
Costume Design: Ann Roth (*The English Patient*)
Make-up: David Leroy Anderson, Rick Baker (*The Nutty Professor*)
Sound: Mark Berger, Walter Murch, Chris Newman, David Parker (*The English Patient*)
Sound Effects Editing: Bruce Stambler (*The Ghost and the Darkness*)
Editing: Walter Murch (*The English Patient*)
Visual Effects: Volker Engel, Clay Pinney, Douglas Smith, Joseph Viskocil (*Independence Day*)
Song: 'You Must Love Me' from *Evita* (m Andrew Lloyd Webber, ly Tim Rice)
Original Dramatic Score: Gabriel Yared (*The English Patient*)
Original Musical or Comedy Score: Rachel Portman (*Emma*)
Documentary Short: *Breathing Lessons: The Life And Work of Mark O'Brien* (Jessica Yu)
Documentary Feature: *When We Were Kings* (Leon Gast, David Sonenberg)
Animated Film: *Quest* (Tyron Montgomery, Thomas Stellmach)
Live-Action Short: *Dear Diary* (David Frankel, Barry Jossen)
Honorary Award: Michael Kidd
Irving G. Thalberg Memorial Award: Saul Zaentz

1997
Picture: *Titanic* (James Cameron, Jon Landau)
Foreign-Language Film: *Character* (Mike Van Diem)
Director: James Cameron (*Titanic*)
Actor: Jack Nicholson (*As Good as It Gets*)
Actress: Helen Hunt (*As Good as It Gets*)
Supporting Actor: Robin Williams (*Good Will Hunting*)
Supporting Actress: Kim Basinger (*LA Confidential*)

Original Screenplay: Ben Affleck, Matt Damon (*Good Will Hunting*)
Adapted Screenplay: Curtis Hanson, Brian Helgeland (*LA Confidential*)
Cinematography: Russell Carpenter (*Titanic*)
Art Direction: Peter Lamont (*Titanic*)
Costume Design: Deborah L. Scott (*Titanic*)
Make-up: David Leroy Anderson, Rick Baker (*Men in Black*)
Sound: Tom Johnson, Gary Rydstrom, Gary Summers, Mark Ulano (*Titanic*)
Sound Effects Editing: Tom Bellfort, Christopher Boyes (*Titanic*)
Editing: Conrad Buff, James Cameron, Richard A. Harris (*Titanic*)
Visual Effects: Thomas L. Fisher, Michael Kanfer, Mark Lasoff, Robert Legato (*Titanic*)
Song: 'My Heart Will Go On' from *Titanic* (m James Horner, ly Will Jennings)
Original Dramatic Score: James Horner (*Titanic*)
Original Musical or Comedy Score: Anne Dudley (*The Full Monty*)
Documentary Short: *A Story of Healing* (Donna Dewey, Carol Pasternak)
Documentary Feature: *The Long Way Home* (Rabbi Marvin Hier, Richard Trank)
Animated Film: *Geri's Game* (Jan Pinkava)
Live-Action Short: *Visas and Virtue* (Chris Donahue, Chris Tashima)
Honorary Award: Stanley Donen

Books
60 Years of The Oscar: The Official History of the Academy Awards, Robert Osborne (Abbeville Press, 1989).
The Oscars: The Secret History of Hollywood's Academy Awards, Anthony Holden (Little, Brown, 1993).

BAFTA Awards
The British Academy of Film and Television Arts began in 1947 as the British Film Academy, becoming the Society of Film and Television Arts in 1959, and changing its name to its present title in 1975. The BAFTA award, a bronze theatrical mask, was originally nicknamed a Stella. At the beginning, there were two awards for feature films – one for the best film from any source and one for the best British film. Over the years, the awards have widened. The film winners in the major categories are listed below.

1947
Film: *The Best Years of Our Lives* (William Wyler)
British Film: *Odd Man Out* (Carol Reed)

1948
Film: *Hamlet* (Laurence Olivier)
British Film: *The Fallen Idol* (Carol Reed)

1949
Film: *The Bicycle Thief* (Vittorio De Sica)
British Film: *The Third Man* (Carol Reed)

1950
Film: *All About Eve* (Joseph L. Mankiewicz)
British Film: *The Blue Lamp* (Basil Dearden)

1951
Film: *La Ronde* (Max Ophuls)
British Film: *The Lavender Hill Mob* (Charles Crichton)

1952
Film: *The Sound Barrier* (US: *Breaking the Sound Barrier*) (David Lean)
British Film: *The Sound Barrier* (David Lean)
Actor: Ralph Richardson (*The Sound Barrier*)
Actress: Vivien Leigh (*A Streetcar Named Desire*)
Foreign Actor: Marlon Brando (*Viva Zapata!*)
Foreign Actress: Simone Signoret (*Casque d'Or*)
Newcomer: Claire Bloom (*Limelight*)

1953
Film: *Forbidden Games* (René Clément)
British Film: *Genevieve* (Henry Cornelius)
Actor: John Gielgud (*Julius Caesar*)
Actress: Audrey Hepburn (*Roman Holiday*)
Foreign Actor: Marlon Brando (*Julius Caesar*)
Foreign Actress: Leslie Caron (*Lili*)
Newcomer: Norman Wisdom (*Trouble in Store*)

1954
Film: *The Wages of Fear* (Henri-Georges Clouzot)
British Film: *Hobson's Choice* (David Lean)
Actor: Kenneth More (*Doctor in the House*)
Actress: Yvonne Mitchell (*The Divided Heart*)
Foreign Actor: Marlon Brando (*On the Waterfront*)
Foreign Actress: Cornell Borchers (*The Divided Heart*)
Newcomer: David Kossoff (*Chance Meeting*)
Screenplay: Robin Estridge, George Tabori (*Young Lovers* aka *Chance Meeting*)

1955
Film: *Richard III* (Laurence Olivier)
British Film: *Richard III* (Laurence Olivier)
Actor: Laurence Olivier (*Richard III*)
Actress: Katie Johnson (*The Ladykillers*)
Foreign Actor: Ernest Borgnine (*Marty*)
Foreign Actress: Betsy Blair (*Marty*)
Newcomer: Paul Scofield (*That Lady*)
Screenplay: William Rose (*The Ladykillers*)

1956
Film: *Gervaise* (René Clément)
British Film: *Reach for the Sky* (Lewis Gilbert)
Actor: Peter Finch (*A Town Like Alice* aka *The Rape of Malaya*)
Actress: Virginia McKenna (*A Town Like Alice* aka *The Rape of Malaya*)
Foreign Actor: François Périer (*Gervaise*)
Foreign Actress: Anna Magnani (*The Rose Tattoo*)
Newcomer: Eli Wallach (*Baby Doll*)
Screenplay: Nigel Balchin (*The Man Who Never Was*)

1957
Film: *The Bridge on the River Kwai* (David Lean)
British Film: *The Bridge on the River Kwai* (David Lean)
Actor: Alec Guinness (*The Bridge on the River Kwai*)
Actress: Heather Sears (*The Story of Esther Costello*)
Foreign Actor: Henry Fonda (*Twelve Angry Men*)
Foreign Actress: Simone Signoret (*The Witches of Salem*)
Newcomer: Eric Barker (*Brothers in Law*)
Screenplay: Pierre Boulle (*The Bridge on the River Kwai*)

1958
Film: *Room at the Top* (Jack Clayton)
British Film: *Room at the Top* (Jack Clayton)
Actor: Trevor Howard (*The Key*)
Actress: Irene Worth (*Orders to Kill*)
Foreign Actor: Sidney Poitier (*The Defiant Ones*)
Foreign Actress: Simone Signoret (*Room at the Top*)
Newcomer: Paul Massie (*Orders to Kill*)
Screenplay: Paul Dehn (*Orders to Kill*)

1959
Film: *Ben-Hur* (William Wyler)
British Film: *Sapphire* (Basil Dearden)
Actor: Peter Sellers (*I'm All Right Jack*)
Actress: Audrey Hepburn (*The Nun's Story*)
Foreign Actor: Jack Lemmon (*Some Like It Hot*)
Foreign Actress: Shirley MacLaine (*Ask Any Girl*)
Newcomer: Hayley Mills (*Tiger Bay*)
Screenplay: John Boulting, Frank Harvey, Alan Hackney (*I'm All Right Jack*)

1960
Film: *The Apartment* (Billy Wilder)
British Film: *Saturday Night and Sunday Morning* (Karel Reisz)
Actor: Peter Finch (*The Trials of Oscar Wilde*)
Actress: Rachel Roberts (*Saturday Night and Sunday Morning*)
Foreign Actor: Jack Lemmon (*The Apartment*)
Foreign Actress: Shirley MacLaine (*The Apartment*)
Newcomer: Albert Finney (*Saturday Night and Sunday Morning*)
Screenplay: Bryan Forbes (*The Angry Silence*)

1961
Film: *Ballad of a Soldier* (Grigori Chukrai); *The Hustler* (Robert Rossen)
British Film: *A Taste of Honey* (Tony Richardson)
Actor: Peter Finch (*No Love for Johnnie*)
Actress: Dora Bryan (*A Taste of Honey*)
Foreign Actor: Paul Newman (*The Hustler*)
Foreign Actress: Sophia Loren (*Two Women*)
Newcomer: Rita Tushingham (*A Taste of Honey*)
Screenplay: Shelagh Delaney, Tony Richardson (*A Taste of Honey*); Val Guest, Wolf Mankowitz (*The Day the Earth Caught Fire*)

1962
Film: *Lawrence of Arabia* (David Lean)
British Film: *Lawrence of Arabia* (David Lean)
Actor: Peter O'Toole (*Lawrence of Arabia*)
Actress: Leslie Caron (*The L-Shaped Room*)
Foreign Actor: Burt Lancaster (*Birdman of Alcatraz*)
Foreign Actress: Anne Bancroft (*The Miracle Worker*)
Newcomer: Tom Courtenay (*The Loneliness of the Long Distance Runner*)
Screenplay: Robert Bolt (*Lawrence of Arabia*)

1963
Film: *Tom Jones* (Tony Richardson)
British Film: *Tom Jones* (Tony Richardson)
Actor: Dirk Bogarde (*The Servant*)
Actress: Rachel Roberts (*This Sporting Life*)
Foreign Actor: Marcello Mastroianni (*Divorce Italian Style*)
Foreign Actress: Patricia Neal (*Hud*)
Newcomer: James Fox (*The Servant*)
Screenplay: John Osborne (*Tom Jones*)
Cinematography: b/w Douglas Slocombe (*The Servant*); colour Ted Moore (*From Russia with Love*)

1964
Film: *Dr Strangelove* (Stanley Kubrick)
British Film: *Dr Strangelove* (Stanley Kubrick)
Actor: Richard Attenborough (*Séance on a Wet Afternoon*; *Guns at Batasi*)
Actress: Audrey Hepburn (*Charade*)

Foreign Actor: Marcello Mastroianni (*Yesterday, Today and Tomorrow*)

Foreign Actress: Anne Bancroft (*The Pumpkin Eater*)

Newcomer: Julie Andrews (*Mary Poppins*)

Screenplay: Harold Pinter (*The Pumpkin Eater*)

Cinematography: b/w Oswald Morris (*The Pumpkin Eater*); colour Geoffrey Unsworth (*Becket*)

Production Design: b/w Ken Adam (*Dr Strangelove*); colour John Bryan (*Becket*)

1965

Film: *My Fair Lady* (George Cukor)

British Film: *The Ipcress File* (Sidney J. Furie)

Actor: Dirk Bogarde (*Darling*)

Actress: Julie Christie (*Darling*)

Foreign Actor: Lee Marvin (*Cat Ballou*; *The Killers*)

Foreign Actress: Patricia Neal (*In Harm's Way*)

Newcomer: Judi Dench (*Four in the Morning*)

Screenplay: Frederic Raphael (*Darling*)

Cinematography: b/w Oswald Morris (*The Hill*); colour Otto Heller (*The Ipcress File*)

Production Design: b/w Ray Simm (*Darling*); colour Ken Adam (*The Ipcress File*)

1966

Film: *Who's Afraid of Virginia Woolf?* (Mike Nichols)

British Film: *The Spy Who Came in from the Cold* (Martin Ritt)

Actor: Richard Burton (*Who's Afraid of Virginia Woolf?*; *The Spy Who Came in from the Cold*)

Actress: Elizabeth Taylor (*Who's Afraid of Virginia Woolf?*)

Foreign Actor: Rod Steiger (*The Pawnbroker*)

Foreign Actress: Jeanne Moreau (*Viva Maria!*)

Newcomer: Vivien Merchant (*Alfie*)

Screenplay: David Mercer (*Morgan – A Suitable Case for Treatment*)

Cinematography: b/w Oswald Morris (*The Spy Who Came in from the Cold*); colour Christopher Challis (*Arabesque*)

Production Design: b/w Tambi Larsen (*The Spy Who Came in from the Cold*); colour Wilfred Shingleton (*The Blue Max*)

1967

Film: *A Man for All Seasons* (Fred Zinnemann)

British Film: *A Man for All Seasons* (Fred Zinnemann)

Actor: Paul Scofield (*A Man for All Seasons*)

Actress: Edith Evans (*The Whisperers*)

Foreign Actor: Rod Steiger (*In the Heat of the Night*)

Foreign Actress: Anouk Aimée (*A Man and a Woman*)

Newcomer: Faye Dunaway (*Bonnie and Clyde*)

Screenplay: Robert Bolt (*A Man for All Seasons*)

Cinematography: b/w Gerry Turpin (*The Whisperers*); colour Ted Moore (*A Man for All Seasons*)

Production Design: John Box (*A Man for All Seasons*)

1968

Film: *The Graduate* (Mike Nichols)

Director: Mike Nichols (*The Graduate*)

Actor: Spencer Tracy (*Guess Who's Coming to Dinner?*)

Actress: Katharine Hepburn (*Guess Who's Coming to Dinner?*)

Supporting Actor: Ian Holm (*The Bofors Gun*)

Supporting Actress: Billie Whitelaw (*The Twisted Nerve*; *Charlie Bubbles*)

Newcomer: Dustin Hoffman (*The Graduate*)

Screenplay: Buck Henry, Calder Willingham (*The Graduate*)

Cinematography: Geoffrey Unsworth (*2001: A Space Odyssey*)

Music: John Barry (*The Lion in Winter*)

Production Design: Tony Masters, Harry Lange, Ernie Archer (*2001: A Space Odyssey*)

1969

Film: *Midnight Cowboy* (John Schlesinger)

Director: John Schlesinger (*Midnight Cowboy*)

Actor: Dustin Hoffman (*Midnight Cowboy*; *John and Mary*)

Actress: Maggie Smith (*The Prime of Miss Jean Brodie*)

Supporting Actor: Laurence Olivier (*Oh! What a Lovely War*)

Supporting Actress: Celia Johnson (*The Prime of Miss Jean Brodie*)

Newcomer: Jon Voight (*Midnight Cowboy*)

Screenplay: Waldo Salt (*Midnight Cowboy*)

Cinematography: Gerry Turpin (*Oh! What a Lovely War*)

Music: Mikis Theodorakis (*Z*)

Production Design: Don Ashton (*Oh! What a Lovely War*)

1970

Film: *Butch Cassidy and the Sundance Kid* (George Roy Hill)

Director: George Roy Hill (*Butch Cassidy and the Sundance Kid*)

Actor: Robert Redford (*Butch Cassidy and the Sundance Kid*; *Tell Them Willie Boy Is Here*; *Downhill Racer*)

Actress: Katharine Ross (*Butch Cassidy and the Sundance Kid*; *Tell Them Willie Boy Is Here*)

Supporting Actor: Colin Welland (*Kes*)

Supporting Actress: Susannah York (*They Shoot Horses, Don't They?*)

Newcomer: David Bradley (*Kes*)

Screenplay: William Goldman (*Butch Cassidy and the Sundance Kid*)

Cinematography: Conrad Hall (*Butch Cassidy and the Sundance Kid*)

Music: Burt Bacharach (*Butch Cassidy and the Sundance Kid*)

Production Design: Mario Garbuglia (*Waterloo*)

1971

Film: *Sunday, Bloody Sunday* (John Schlesinger)

Director: John Schlesinger (*Sunday, Bloody Sunday*)

Actor: Peter Finch (*Sunday, Bloody Sunday*)

Actress: Glenda Jackson (*Sunday, Bloody Sunday*)

Supporting Actor: Edward Fox (*The Go-Between*)

Supporting Actress: Margaret Leighton (*The Go-Between*)

Newcomer: Dominic Guard (*The Go-Between*)

Screenplay: Harold Pinter (*The Go-Between*)

Cinematography: Pasqualino De Santis (*Death in Venice*)

Music: Michel Legrand (*Summer of '42*)

Production Design: Ferdinando Scarfiotti (*Death in Venice*)

1972

Film: *Cabaret* (Bob Fosse)

Director: Bob Fosse (*Cabaret*)

Actor: Gene Hackman (*The French Connection*; *The Poseidon Adventure*)

Actress: Liza Minnelli (*Cabaret*)

Supporting Actor: Ben Johnson (*The Last Picture Show*)

Supporting Actress: Cloris Leachman (*The Last Picture Show*)

Newcomer: Joel Grey (*Cabaret*)

Screenplay: Peter Bogdanovich, Larry McMurtry (*The Last Picture Show*)

Cinematography: Geoffrey Unsworth (*Cabaret*; *Alice's Adventures in Wonderland*)

Music: Nina Rota (*The Godfather*)

Production Design: Rolf Zehetbauer (*Cabaret*)

1973

Film: *Day for Night* (François Truffaut)

Director: François Truffaut (*Day for Night*)

Actor: Walter Matthau (*Pete 'n' Tillie*; *Charley Varrick*)

Actress: Stéphane Audran (*The Discreet Charm of the Bourgeoisie*; *Just before Nightfall*)

Supporting Actor: Arthur Lowe (*O Lucky Man!*)

Supporting Actress: Valentina Cortese (*Day for Night*)

Newcomer: Peter Egan (*The Hireling*)

Screenplay: Luis Buñuel, Jean-Claude Carrière (*The Discreet Charm of the Bourgeoisie*)

Cinematography: Anthony Richmond (*Don't Look Now*)

Music: Alan Price (*O Lucky Man!*)

Production Design: Natasha Kroll (*The Hireling*)

1974

Film: *Lacombe Lucien* (Louis Malle)

Director: Roman Polanski (*Chinatown*)

Actor: Jack Nicholson (*Chinatown*; *The Last Detail*)

Actress: Joanne Woodward (*Summer Wishes, Winter Dreams*)

Supporting Actor: John Gielgud (*Murder on the Orient Express*)

Supporting Actress: Ingrid Bergman (*Murder on the Orient Express*)

Newcomer: Georgina Hale (*Mahler*)

Screenplay: Robert Towne (*Chinatown*; *The Last Detail*)

Cinematography: Douglas Slocombe (*The Great Gatsby*)

Music: Richard Rodney Bennett (*Murder on the Orient Express*)

Production Design: John Box (*The Great Gatsby*)

1975

Film: *Alice Doesn't Live Here Any More* (Martin Scorsese)

Director: Stanley Kubrick (*Barry Lyndon*)

Actor: Al Pacino (*The Godfather Part II*; *Dog Day Afternoon*)

Actress: Ellen Burstyn (*Alice Doesn't Live Here Any More*)

Supporting Actor: Fred Astaire (*The Towering Inferno*)

Supporting Actress: Diane Ladd (*Alice Doesn't Live Here Any More*)

Newcomer: Valerie Perrine (*Lenny*)

Screenplay: Robert Getchell (*Alice Doesn't Live Here Any More*)

Cinematography: John Alcott (*Barry Lyndon*)

Music: John Williams (*Jaws*; *The Towering Inferno*)

Production Design: John Box (*Rollerball*)

1976

Film: *One Flew over the Cuckoo's Nest* (Milos Forman)

Director: Milos Forman (*One Flew over the Cuckoo's Nest*)

Actor: Jack Nicholson (*One Flew over the Cuckoo's Nest*)

Actress: Louise Fletcher (*One Flew over the Cuckoo's Nest*)

Supporting Actor: Brad Dourif (*One Flew over the Cuckoo's Nest*)
Supporting Actress: Jodie Foster (*Taxi Driver; Bugsy Malone*)
Newcomer: Jodie Foster (*Taxi Driver; Bugsy Malone*)
Screenplay: Alan Parker (*Bugsy Malone*)
Cinematography: Russell Boyd (*Picnic at Hanging Rock*)
Music: Bernard Herrmann (*Taxi Driver*)
Production Design: Geoffrey Kirkland (*Bugsy Malone*)

1977
Film: *Annie Hall* (Woody Allen)
Director: Woody Allen (*Annie Hall*)
Actor: Peter Finch (*Network*)
Actress: Diane Keaton (*Annie Hall*)
Supporting Actor: Edward Fox (*A Bridge Too Far*)
Supporting Actress: Jenny Agutter (*Equus*)
Newcomer: Isabelle Huppert (*The Lacemaker*)
Screenplay: Woody Allen, Marshall Brickman (*Annie Hall*)
Cinematography: Geoffrey Unsworth (*A Bridge Too Far*)
Music: John Addison (*A Bridge Too Far*)
Production Design: Danilo Donati (*Fellini's Casanova*)

1978
Film: *Julia* (Fred Zinnemann)
Director: Alan Parker (*Midnight Express*)
Actor: Richard Dreyfuss (*The Goodbye Girl*)
Actress: Jane Fonda (*Julia*)
Supporting Actor: John Hurt (*Midnight Express*)
Supporting Actress: Geraldine Page (*Interiors*)
Newcomer: Christopher Reeve (*Superman*)
Screenplay: Alvin Sargent (*Julia*)
Cinematography: Douglas Slocombe (*Julia*)
Music: John Williams (*Star Wars*)
Production Design: Joe Alves (*Close Encounters of the Third Kind*)

1979
Film: *Manhattan* (Woody Allen)
Director: Francis Ford Coppola (*Apocalypse Now*)
Actor: Jack Lemmon (*The China Syndrome*)
Actress: Jane Fonda (*The China Syndrome*)
Supporting Actor: Robert Duvall (*Apocalypse Now*)
Supporting Actress: Rachel Roberts (*Yanks*)
Newcomer: Dennis Christopher (*Breaking Away*)
Screenplay: Woody Allen, Marshall Brickman (*Manhattan*)
Cinematography: Vilmos Zsigmond (*The Deer Hunter*)
Music: Ennio Morricone (*Days of Heaven*)
Production Design: Michael Seymour (*Alien*)

1980
Film: *The Elephant Man* (David Lynch)
Director: Akira Kurosawa (*Kagemusha*)
Actor: John Hurt (*The Elephant Man*)
Actress: Judy Davis (*My Brilliant Career*)
Newcomer: Judy Davis (*My Brilliant Career*)
Screenplay: Jerzy Kozinski (*Being There*)
Cinematography: Giuseppe Rotunno (*All That Jazz*)
Music: John Williams (*The Empire Strikes Back*)
Production Design: Stuart Craig (*The Elephant Man*)

1981
Film: *Chariots of Fire* (Hugh Hudson)
Director: Louis Malle (*Atlantic City*)
Actor: Burt Lancaster (*Atlantic City*)

Actress: Meryl Streep (*The French Lieutenant's Woman*)
Supporting Artist: Ian Holm (*Chariots of Fire*)
Newcomer: Joe Pesci (*Raging Bull*)
Screenplay: Bill Forsyth (*Gregory's Girl*)
Cinematography: Geoffrey Unsworth, Ghislain Cloquet (*Tess*)
Music: Carl Davis (*The French Lieutenant's Woman*)
Production Design: Norman Reynolds (*Raiders of the Lost Ark*)

1982
Film: *Gandhi* (Richard Attenborough)
Foreign-Language Film: *Christ Stopped at Eboli* (Francesco Rosi)
Director: Richard Attenborough (*Gandhi*)
Actor: Ben Kingsley (*Gandhi*)
Actress: Katharine Hepburn (*On Golden Pond*)
Supporting Actor: Jack Nicholson (*Reds*)
Supporting Actress: Maureen Stapleton (*Reds*); Rohini Hattangadi (*Gandhi*)
Newcomer: Ben Kingsley (*Gandhi*)
Screenplay: Costa-Gavras, Donald Stewart (*Missing*)
Cinematography: Jordan Cronenweth (*Blade Runner*)
Music: John Williams (*ET*)
Production Design: Lawrence G. Paull (*Blade Runner*)

1983
Film: *Educating Rita* (Lewis Gilbert)
Foreign-Language Film: *Danton* (Andrzej Wajda)
Director: Bill Forsyth (*Local Hero*)
Actor: Michael Caine (*Educating Rita*)
Actress: Julie Walters (*Educating Rita*)
Supporting Actor: Denholm Elliott (*Trading Places*)
Supporting Actress: Jamie Lee Curtis (*Trading Places*)
Newcomer: Phyllis Logan (*Another Time, Another Place*)
Adapted Screenplay: Ruth Prawer Jhabvala (*Heat and Dust*)
Original Screenplay: Paul D. Zimmerman (*King of Comedy*)
Cinematography: Sven Nykvist (*Fanny and Alexander*)
Music: Ryuichi Sakamoto (*Merry Christmas, Mr Lawrence*)
Production Design: Franco Zeffirelli, Gianni Quaranta (*La Traviata*)

1984
Film: *The Killing Fields* (Roland Joffe)
Foreign-Language Film: *Carmen* (Carlos Saura)
Director: Wim Wenders (*Paris, Texas*)
Actor: Haing S. Ngor (*The Killing Fields*)
Actress: Maggie Smith (*A Private Function*)
Supporting Actor: Denholm Elliott (*A Private Function*)
Supporting Actress: Liz Smith (*A Private Function*)
Newcomer: Haing S. Ngor (*The Killing Fields*)
Adapted Screenplay: Bruce Robinson (*The Killing Fields*)
Original Screenplay: Woody Allen (*Broadway Danny Rose*)
Cinematography: Chris Menges (*The Killing Fields*)
Music: Ennio Morricone (*Once Upon a Time in America*)
Production Design: Roy Walker (*The Killing Fields*)

1985
Film: *The Purple Rose of Cairo* (Woody Allen)
Foreign-Language Film: *Colonel Redl* (Istvá Szabó)
Actor: William Hurt (*Kiss of the Spider Woman*)
Actress: Peggy Ashcroft (*A Passage to India*)
Supporting Actor: Denholm Elliott (*Defence of the Realm*)
Supporting Actress: Rosanna Arquette (*Desperately Seeking Susan*)
Adapted Screenplay: Richard Condon, Janet Roach (*Prizzi's Honor*)
Original Screenplay: Woody Allen (*The Purple Rose of Cairo*)
Cinematography: Miroslav Ondricek (*Amadeus*)
Music: Maurice Jarre (*Witness*)
Production Design: Norman Garwood (*Brazil*)

1986
Film: *A Room with a View* (James Ivory)
Foreign-Language Film: *Ran* (Akira Kurosawa)
Director: Woody Allen (*Hannah and Her Sisters*)
Actor: Bob Hoskins (*Mona Lisa*)
Actress: Maggie Smith (*A Room with a View*)
Supporting Actor: Ray McAnally (*The Mission*)
Supporting Actress: Judi Dench (*A Room with a View*)
Adapted Screenplay: Kurt Luedtke (*Out of Africa*)
Original Screenplay: Woody Allen (*Hannah and Her Sisters*)
Cinematography: David Watkin (*Out of Africa*)
Music: Ennio Morricone (*The Mission*)
Production Design: Gianni Quaranta, Brian Ackland-Snow (*A Room with a View*)

1987
Film: *Jean de Florette* (Claude Berri)
Foreign-Language Film: *The Sacrifice* (Andrei Tarkovsky)
Director: Oliver Stone (*Platoon*)
Actor: Sean Connery (*The Name of the Rose*)
Actress: Anne Bancroft (*84 Charing Cross Road*)
Supporting Actor: Daniel Auteuil (*Jean de Florette*)
Supporting Actress: Susan Wooldridge (*Hope and Glory*)
Adapted Screenplay: Gérard Brach, Claude Berri (*Jean de Florette*)
Original Screenplay: David Leland (*Wish You Were Here*)
Cinematography: Bruno Nuytten (*Jean de Florette*)
Music: Ennio Morricone (*The Untouchables*)
Production Design: Santo Loquasto (*Radio Days*)

1988
Film: *The Last Emperor* (Bernardo Bertolucci)
Foreign-Language Film: *Babette's Feast* (Gabriel Axel)
Director: Louis Malle (*Au Revoir les Enfants*)
Actor: John Cleese (*A Fish Called Wanda*)
Actress: Maggie Smith (*The Lonely Passion of Judith Hearne*)
Supporting Actor: Michael Palin (*A Fish Called Wanda*)
Supporting Actress: Judi Dench (*A Handful of Dust*)
Adapted Screenplay: Jean-Claude Carrière, Philip Kaufman (*The Unbearable Lightness of Being*)
Original Screenplay: Shawn Slovo (*A World Apart*)
Cinematography: Allen Daviau (*Empire of the Sun*)
Music: John Williams (*Empire of the Sun*)
Production Design: Dean Tavoularis (*Tucker: The Man and His Dream*)

1989

Film: *Dead Poets Society* (Peter Weir)
Foreign-Language Film: *Life and Nothing But* (Bertrand Tavernier)
Director: Kenneth Branagh (*Henry V*)
Actor: Daniel Day-Lewis (*My Left Foot*)
Actress: Pauline Collins (*Shirley Valentine*)
Supporting Actor: Ray McAnally (*My Left Foot*)
Supporting Actress: Michelle Pfeiffer (*Dangerous Liaisons*)
Adapted Screenplay: Christopher Hampton (*Dangerous Liaisons*)
Original Screenplay: Nora Ephron (*When Harry Met Sally*)
Cinematography: Peter Biziou (*Mississippi Burning*)
Music: Maurice Jarre (*Dead Poets Society*)
Production Design: Dante Ferretti (*Adventures of Baron Munchausen*)

1990

Film: *GoodFellas* (Martin Scorsese)
Foreign-Language Film: *Nuovo Cinema Paradiso* (Giuseppe Tornatore)
Director: Martin Scorsese (*GoodFellas*)
Actor: Philippe Noiret (*Nuovo Cinema Paradiso*)
Actress: Jessica Tandy (*Driving Miss Daisy*)
Supporting Actor: Salvatore Cascio (*Nuovo Cinema Paradiso*)
Supporting Actress: Whoopi Goldberg (*Ghost*)
Adapted Screenplay: Nicholas Pileggi, Martin Scorsese (*GoodFellas*)
Original Screenplay: Giuseppe Tornatore (*Nuovo Cinema Paradiso*)
Cinematography: Vittorio Storaro (*The Sheltering Sky*)
Music: Ennio and Andrea Morricone (*Nuovo Cinema Paradiso*)
Production Design: Richard Sylbert (*Dick Tracy*)

1991

Film: *The Commitments* (Alan Parker)
Foreign-Language Film: *The Nasty Girl* (*Das Schreckliche Mädchen*) (Michael Verhoeven)
Director: Alan Parker (*The Commitments*)
Actor: Anthony Hopkins (*The Silence of the Lambs*)
Actress: Jodie Foster (*The Silence of the Lambs*)
Supporting Actor: Alan Rickman (*Robin Hood: Prince of Thieves*)
Supporting Actress: Kate Nelligan (*Frankie and Johnnie*)
Adapted Screenplay: Dick Clement, Ian La Frenais, Roddy Doyle (*The Commitments*)
Original Screenplay: Anthony Minghella (*Truly Madly Deeply*)
Cinematography: Pierre Lhomme (*Cyrano de Bergerac*)
Music: Jean-Claude Petit (*Cyrano de Bergerac*)
Production Design: Bo Welch (*Edward Scissorhands*)

1992

Film: *Howards End* (James Ivory)
Foreign-Language Film: *Raise the Red Lantern* (Zhang Zimou)
Director: Robert Altman (*The Player*)
Actor: Robert Downey Jnr (*Chaplin*)
Actress: Emma Thompson (*Howards End*)
Supporting Actor: Gene Hackman (*Unforgiven*)
Supporting Actress: Miranda Richardson (*Damage*)
Adapted Screenplay: Michael Tolkin (*The Player*)
Original Screenplay: Woody Allen (*Husbands and Wives*)
Cinematography: Dante Spinotti (*The Last of the Mohicans*)
Music: David Hirschfelder (*Strictly Ballroom*)

Production Design: Catherine Martin (*Strictly Ballroom*)

1993

Film: *Schindler's List* (Steven Spielberg)
Foreign-Language Film: *Farewell My Concubine* (Chen Kaige)
British Film: *Shadowlands* (Richard Attenborough)
Director: Steven Spielberg (*Schindler's List*)
Actor: Anthony Hopkins (*The Remains of the Day*)
Actress: Holly Hunter (*The Piano*)
Supporting Actor: Ralph Fiennes (*Schindler's List*)
Supporting Actress: Miriam Margolyes (*The Age of Innocence*)
Adapted Screenplay: Steven Zaillian (*Schindler's List*)
Original Screenplay: Danny Rubin, Harold Ramis (*Groundhog Day*)
Cinematography: Janusz Kaminski (*Schindler's List*)
Music: John Williams (*Schindler's List*)
Production Design: Andrew McAlpine (*The Piano*)

1994

Film: *Four Weddings and a Funeral* (Mike Newell)
Foreign-Language Film: *To Live* (Zhang Yimou)
British Film: *Shallow Grave* (Danny Boyle)
Director: Mike Newell (*Four Weddings and a Funeral*)
Actor: Hugh Grant (*Four Weddings and a Funeral*)
Actress: Susan Sarandon (*The Client*)
Supporting Actor: Samuel L. Jackson (*Pulp Fiction*)
Supporting Actress: Kristin Scott Thomas (*Four Weddings and a Funeral*)
Adapted Screenplay: Paul Attanasio (*Quiz Show*)
Original Screenplay: Quentin Tarantino and Roger Avary (*Pulp Fiction*)
Cinematography: Philippe Rousselot (*Interview with the Vampire*)
Music: Don Was (*Backbeat*)
Production Design: Dante Ferretti (*Interview with the Vampire*)

1995

Film: *Sense and Sensibility* (Ang Lee)
Foreign-Language Film: *The Postman/Il Postino* (Michael Radford)
British Film: *The Madness of King George* (Nicholas Hytner)
Director: Michael Radford (*The Postman/Il Postino*)
Actor: Nigel Hawthorne (*The Madness of King George*)
Actress: Emma Thompson (*Sense and Sensibility*)
Supporting Actor: Tim Roth (*Rob Roy*)
Supporting Actress: Kate Winslet (*Sense and Sensibility*)
Adapted Screenplay: John Hodge (*Trainspotting*)
Original Screenplay: Christopher McQuarrie (*The Usual Suspects*)
Cinematography: John Toll (*Braveheart*)
Music: Luis Bacalov (*Il Postino*)
Production Design: Michael Corenblith (*Apollo 13*)

1996

Film: *The English Patient* (Anthony Minghella)
Foreign-Language Film: *Ridicule* (Patrice Leconte)
British Film: *Secrets and Lies* (Mike Leigh)
Director: Joel Coen (*Fargo*)
Actor: Geoffrey Rush (*Shine*)
Actress: Brenda Blethyn (*Secrets and Lies*)
Supporting Actor: Paul Scofield (*The Crucible*)
Supporting Actress: Juliette Binoche (*The English Patient*)
Adapted Screenplay: Anthony Minghella (*The English Patient*)

Original Screenplay: Mike Leigh (*Secrets and Lies*)
Cinematography: John Seale (*The English Patient*)
Music: Gabriel Yard (*The English Patient*)
Production Design: Tony Burrough (*Richard III*)

1997

Film: *The Full Monty* (Peter Cattaneo)
Foreign-Language Film: *L'Appartement* (Gilles Mimouni)
British Film: *Nil by Mouth* (Gary Oldman)
Director: Baz Luhrmann (*William Shakespeare's Romeo & Juliet*)
Actor: Robert Carlyle (*The Full Monty*)
Actress: Judi Dench (*Mrs Brown*)
Supporting Actor: Tom Wilkinson (*The Full Monty*)
Supporting Actress: Sigourney Weaver (*The Ice Storm*)
Adapted Screenplay: Baz Luhrmann, Craig Pearce (*William Shakespeare's Romeo & Juliet*)
Original Screenplay: Gary Oldman (*Nil by Mouth*)
Audience Award: *The Full Monty* (Peter Cattaneo)
Cinematography: Eduardo Serra (*The Wings of the Dove*)
Music: Nellee Hooper (*William Shakespeare's Romeo & Juliet*)
Production Design: Catherine Martin (*William Shakespeare's Romeo & Juliet*)

Cannes Film Festival Awards

The Cannes Film Festival, held each year in May, has established itself as the world's leading festival. The first, in 1939, was abandoned when Hitler invaded Poland and it resumed in 1946. There was no festival in 1948 and 1950, and the one in 1968 was disrupted by the nationwide demonstrations. In 1946, there was a multitude of prizes, one for each participating nation, although there was an International Jury Prize, which went to *The Battle of the Rails* (*La Bataille du Rail*), directed by René Clément. In 1947, six prizes were given for various vague genres of film. In 1949, a Grand Prize was given to the best film, together with other prizes for direction, acting, writing, composing, and set design. A special Jury Prize was added in 1951, and the Palme d'Or (Golden Palm) for best film was inaugurated in 1955. Over the years the juries have varied the nature of the awards, according to whim, although always retaining a prize for the best film. The main prizewinners since 1949 are:

1949

Grand Prix: *The Third Man* (Carol Reed)
Director: René Clément (*The Walls of Malapaga* (*Le Mura di Malapaga*))
Actor: Edward G. Robinson (*House of Strangers*)
Actress: Isa Miranda (*The Walls of Malapaga* (*Le Mura di Malapaga*))

1951

Grand Prix: *Miracle in Milan* (*Miracolo a Milano*) (Vittoria De Sica); *Miss Julie* (Alf Sjöberg)
Director: Luis Buñuel (*Los Olvidados*)
Actor: Michael Redgrave (*The Browning Version*)
Actress: Bette Davis (*All About Eve*)

1952

Grand Prix: *Two Pennyworth of Hope* (*Due Soldi di Speranza*) (Renato Castellani); *Othello* (Orson Welles)
Director: Christian-Jaque (*Fanfan la Tulipe*)
Actor: Marlon Brando (*Viva Zapata*)
Actress: Lee Grant (*Detective Story*)

1953
Grand Prix: *The Wages of Fear* (Henri-Georges Clouzot)
Actor: Charles Vanel (*The Wages of Fear*)

1954
Grand Prix: *Gate of Hell* (*Jigoku-Mon*) (Teinosuke Kinugasa)

1955
Palme d'Or: *Marty* (Delbert Mann)
Director: Sergei Vasiliev (*The Heroes of Shipka* (*Geroite Na Shipka*)); Jules Dassin (*Rififi*)
Performance: Spencer Tracy

1956
Palme d'Or: *The Silent World* (*Le Monde du Silence*) (Jacques Yves Cousteau, Louis Malle)
Director: Sergei Yutkevich (*Othello*)
Performance: Susan Hayward (*I'll Cry Tomorrow*)

1957
Palme d'Or: *Friendly Persuasion* (William Wyler)
Director: Robert Bresson (*A Man Escaped* (*Un Condamné à Mort S'Est Échappé*))
Actor: John Kitzmiller (*Valley of Peace* (*Dolina Miru*))
Actress: Giulietta Masina (*Cabiria* (*Nights of Cabiria*))

1958
Palme d'Or: *The Cranes Are Flying* (*Letiat Zhuravli*) (Mikhail Kalatozov)
Director: Ingmar Bergman (*So Close to Life* (*Nara Livet*))
Actor: Paul Newman (*The Long Hot Summer*)
Actress: Bibi Andersson, Eva Dahlbeck, Barbro Hiortas-Ornas, Ingrid Thulin (*So Close to Life* (*Nara Livet*))

1959
Palme d'Or: *Black Orpheus* (*Orfeu Negro*) (Marcel Camus)
Director: François Truffaut (*The 400 Blows* (*Les Quatre Cents Coups*))
Actor: Dean Stockwell, Bradford Dillman, Orson Welles (*Compulsion*)
Actress: Simone Signoret (*Room at the Top*)

1960
Palme d'Or: *La Dolce Vita* (Federico Fellini)
Actress: Melina Mercouri (*Never on Sunday*); Jeanne Moreau (*Moderato Cantabile*)

1961
Palme d'Or: *Viridiana* (Luis Buñuel); *Une Aussi Longue Absence* (Henri Colpi)
Director: Julia Solntseva (*The Flaming Years* (*Povest' Plamennykh Ket*))
Actor: Anthony Perkins (*Goodbye Again*)
Actress: Sophia Loren (*Two Women* (*La Ciociara*))

1962
Palme d'Or: *The Given Word* (*O Pagador de Promessas*) (Anselmo Duarte)
Actor: Ralph Richardson, Jason Robards Jnr, Dean Stockwell (*Long Day's Journey into Night*); Murray Melvin (*A Taste of Honey*)
Actress: Katharine Hepburn (*Long Day's Journey into Night*); Rita Tushingham (*A Taste of Honey*)

1963
Palme d'Or: *The Leopard* (*Il Gattopardo*) (Luchino Visconti)
Actor: Richard Harris (*This Sporting Life*)

Actress: Marina Vlady (*Queen Bee*, aka *The Conjugal Bed* (*Una Storia Moderna: L'Ape Regina*))

1964
Palme d'Or: *The Umbrellas of Cherbourg* (*Les Parapluies de Cherbourg*) (Jacques Demy)
Actor: Saro Urzi (*Seduced and Abandoned* (*Sedotta e Abbandonata*)); Antal Pager (*The Lark* (*Pacsirta*))
Actress: Anne Bancroft (*The Pumpkin Eater*); Barbara Barrie (*One Potato, Two Potato*)

1965
Palme d'Or: *The Knack . . . And How to Get It* (Richard Lester)
Director: Liviu Ciulei (*The Forest of the Hanged* (*Padurea Spinzuratilor*))
Actor: Terence Stamp (*The Collector*)
Actress: Samantha Eggar (*The Collector*)

1966
Palme d'Or: *A Man and a Woman* (*Un Homme et une Femme*) (Claude Lelouch); *The Birds, the Bees, and the Italians* (*Signore et Signori*) (Pietro Germi)
Director: Sergei Yutkevich (*Lenin in Poland* (*Lenin en Poland*))
Actor: Per Oscarrson (*Hunger* (*Sult*))
Actress: Vanessa Redgrave (*Morgan!*)

1967
Palme d'Or: *Blow Up* (Michelangelo Antonioni)
Director: Ferenc Kósa (*Ten Thousand Suns* (*Tízezer Nap*))
Actor: Odded Kotier (*Three Days and a Child*)
Actress: Pia Degermark (*Elvira Madigan*)

1969
Palme d'Or: *If . . .* (Lindsay Anderson)
Director: Glauber Rocha (*Antonio das Mortes*); Vojtech Jasn (*All My Good Countrymen* (*Vsichni Dobri Rodaci*))
Actor: Jean-Louis Trintignant (*Z*)
Actress: Vanessa Redgrave (*Isadora*)

1970
Palme d'Or: *M*A*S*H* (Robert Altman)
Director: John Boorman (*Leo the Last*)
Actor: Marcello Mastroianni (*Jealousy, Italian Style* (*Dramma della Gelosia . . . Tutti i Particolari in Cronaca*))
Actress: Ottavia Piccolo (*Metello*)

1971
Palme d'Or: *The Go-Between* (Joseph Losey)
Actor: Riccardo Cucciolla (*Sacco e Vanzetti*)
Actress: Kitty Winn (*Panic in Needle Park*)

1972
Palme d'Or: *The Mattei Affair* (*Il Caso Mattei*) (Francesco Rossi); *The Working Class Go to Heaven*, aka *Lulu the Tool* (*La Classe Operaia Va in Paradiso*) (Elio Petri)
Director: Miklós Jancsó (*Red Psalm* (*Még Kér A Nép*))
Actor: Jean Yanne (*We Will Not Grow Old Together* (*Nous Ne Vieillirons Pas Ensemble*))
Actress: Susannah York (*Images*)

1973
Palme d'Or: *Scarecrow* (Jerry Schatzberg); *The Hireling* (Alan Bridges)
Actor: Giancarlo Giannini (*Love and Anarchy* (*Film d'Amore e d'Anarchia*))

Actress: Joanne Woodward (*The Effect of Gamma Rays on Man-in-the-Moon Marigolds*)

1974
Palme d'Or: *The Conversation* (Francis Ford Coppola)
Actor: Jack Nicholson (*The Last Detail*)
Actress: Marie-José Nat (*Les Violons du Bal*)

1975
Palme d'Or: *Chronicle of the Burning Years* (*Ahdat Sanawouach Eldjamr*) (Mohammed Lakhdar Hamina)
Director: Michel Brault (*The Orders* (*Les Ordres*)); Costa-Gavras (*Special Section* (*Section Spéciale*))
Actor: Vittorio Gassman (*Scent of a Woman* (*Profumo di Donna*))
Actress: Valerie Perrine (*Lenny*)

1976
Palme d'Or: *Taxi Driver* (Martin Scorsese)
Director: Ettore Scola (*Down and Dirty* (*Brutti, Sporchi e Cattivi*))
Actor: José Luis Gomez (*Pascual Duarte*)
Actress: Mari Töröcsic (*Where Are You, Mrs Dery?* (*Deryne, Hol Van?*)); Dominique Sanda (*The Inheritance* (*L'Eredità Ferramonti*))

1977
Palme d'Or: *Padre Padrone* (Paolo and Vittorio Taviani)
Actor: Fernando Rey (*Elisa, My Life* (*Elisa, Vida Mia*))
Actress: Shelley Duvall (*Three Women*); Monique Mercure (*J. A. Martin Photographe*)

1978
Palme d'Or: *The Tree of Wooden Clogs* (*L'Albero degli Zoccoli*) (Ermanno Olmi)
Director: Nagisa Oshima (*The Empire of Passion* (*Ai No Borei*))
Actor: Jon Voight (*Coming Home*)
Actress: Jill Clayburgh (*An Unmarried Woman*); Isabelle Huppert (*Violette* (*Violette Nozière*))

1979
Palme d'Or: *The Tin Drum* (*Die Blechtrommel*) (Volker Schlöndorff); *Apocalypse Now* (Francis Ford Coppola)
Director: Terrence Malick (*Days of Heaven*)
Actor: Jack Lemmon (*The China Syndrome*)
Actress: Sally Field (*Norma Rae*)

1980
Palme d'Or: *Kagemusha* (Akira Kurosawa); *All That Jazz* (Bob Fosse)
Actor: Michel Piccoli (*Leap into the Void* (*Salto nel Vuoto*))
Actress: Anouk Aimée (*Leap into the Void* (*Salto nel Vuoto*))

1981
Palme d'Or: *Man of Iron* (*Czolowieck z Zelaza*) (Andrzej Wajda)
Actor: Ugo Tognazzi (*Tragedy of a Ridiculous Man* (*La Tragedia di un Uomo Ridicolo*))
Actress: Isabelle Adjani (*Quartet; Possession*)

1982
Palme d'Or: *Missing* (Costa-Gavras); *Yol* (Yilmaz Güney, Serif Gören)
Director: Werner Herzog (*Fitzcarraldo*)
Actor: Jack Lemmon (*Missing*)
Actress: Jadwiga Jankowska-Cieslak (*Another Way* (*Egymásra Nézve*))

1983
Palme d'Or: *The Ballad of Narayama (Narayama Bushi Ko)* (Shohei Imamura)
Actor: Gian Maria Volonte (*The Death of Mario Ricci (La Mort de Mario Ricci)*)
Actress: Hanna Schygulla (*Story of Piera (Storia di Piera)*)

1984
Palme d'Or: *Paris, Texas* (Wim Wenders)
Director: Bertrand Tavernier (*A Sunday in the Country (Un Dimanche à la Campagne)*)
Actor: Alfredo Landa, Francisco Rabal (*The Holy Innocents (Los Santos Innocentes)*)
Actress: Helen Mirren (*Cal*)

1985
Palme d'Or: *When Father Was Away on Business (Otak Na Sluzbenom Putu)* (Emir Kusturica)
Director: André Téchiné (*Rendezvous*)
Actor: William Hurt (*Kiss of the Spider Woman*)
Actress: Cher (*Mask*); Norma Aleandro (*The Official Story (La Historia Oficial)*)

1986
Palme d'Or: *The Mission* (Roland Joffe)
Director: Martin Scorsese (*After Hours*)
Actor: Michel Blanc (*Menage (Tenue de Soirée)*); Bob Hoskins (*Mona Lisa*)
Actress: Barbara Sukowa (*Rosa Luxemburg*); Fernanda Torres (*I Love You (Eu Sei Que Vou Te Amar)*)

1987
Palme d'Or: *Under Satan's Sun (Sous le Soleil de Satan)* (Maurice Pialat)
Director: Wim Wenders (*Wings of Desire (Der Himmel über Berlin)*)
Actor: Marcello Mastroianni (*Dark Eyes (Ocie Ciornie)*)
Actress: Barbara Hershey (*Shy People*)

1988
Palme d'Or: *Pelle the Conqueror (Pell Erobreren)* (Bille August)
Director: Fernando E. Solanas (*South (Sur)*)
Actor: Forest Whitaker (*Bird*)
Actress: Barbara Hershey, Johdi May, Linda Mvusi (*A World Apart*)

1989
Palme d'Or: *sex, lies and videotape* (Steven Soderbergh)
Director: Emir Kusturica (*The Time of the Gypsies*)
Actor: James Spader (*sex, lies and videotape*)
Actress: Meryl Streep (*A Cry in the Dark, aka Evil Angels*)

1990
Palme d'Or: *Wild at Heart* (David Lynch)
Director: Pavel Lounguine (*Taxi Blues*)
Actor: Gérard Depardieu (*Cyrano de Bergerac*)
Actress: Krystyna Janda (*Interrogation (Przesluchanie)*)

1991
Palme d'Or: *Barton Fink* (Joel and Ethan Coen)
Director: Joel Coen (*Barton Fink*)
Actor: John Turturro (*Barton Fink*)
Actress: Irene Jacob (*The Double Life of Veronique (La Double Vie de Véronique)*)

1992
Palme d'Or: *Best Intentions (Den Goda Vilijan)* (Bille August)
Director: Robert Altman (*The Player*)
Actor: Tim Robbins (*The Player*)
Actress: Pernilla August (*Best Intentions (Den Goda Vilijan)*)

1993
Palme d'Or: *Farewell My Concubine* (Chen Kaige); *The Piano* (Jane Campion)
Director: Mike Leigh (*Naked*)
Actor: David Thewlis (*Naked*)
Actress: Holly Hunter (*The Piano*)

1994
Palme d'Or: *Pulp Fiction* (Quentin Tarantino)
Director: Nanni Moretti (*Dear Diary*)
Actor: Ge You (*To Live*)
Actress: Virna Lisi (*Queen Margaret (La Reine Margot)*)

1995
Palme d'Or: *Underground* (Emir Kusturica)
Director: Mathieu Kassovitz (*La Haine*)
Actor: Jonathan Pryce (*Carrington*)
Actress: Helen Mirren (*The Madness of King George*)

1996
Palme d'Or: *Secrets and Lies* (Mike Leigh)
Director: Joel Coen (*Fargo*)
Actor: Daniel Auteuil, Pascal Duquenne (*The Eighth Day*)
Actress: Brenda Blethyn (*Secrets and Lies*)

1997
Palme d'Or: *The Eel* (Shohei Imamura); *The Taste of Cherries* (Abbas Kiorostami)
Director: Wong Kar-Wai (*Happy Together*)
Actor: Sean Penn (*She's So Lovely*)
Actress: Kathy Burke (*Nil by Mouth*)

1998
Palme d'Or: *Eternity and a Day* (Theo Angelopoulos)
Director: John Boorman (*The General*)
Actor: Peter Mullen (*My Name Is Joe*)
Actress: Élodie Bouchez, Natacha Régnier (*Dream Life of Angels/(Vie Rêve des Anges)*)

Books
Hollywood on the Riviera: The Inside Story of the Cannes Film Festival, Cari Beauchamp and Henri Béhar (1992).
Hype and Glory, William Goldman (Macdonald, 1990).

Golden Bear Awards
The Berlin Film Festival began in 1951. Its main prize is the Golden Bear for best feature, which was inaugurated in 1956. The Golden Bear winners are:

1956
Invitation to the Dance (Gene Kelly)

1957
Twelve Angry Men (Sidney Lumet)

1958
Wild Strawberries/Smultonstället (Ingmar Bergman)

1959
The Cousins/Les Cousins (Claude Chabrol)

1960
Lazarillo/El Lazarillo de Tormes (Cesar Ardavin)

1961
The Night/La Notte (Michelangelo Antonioni)

1962
A Kind of Loving (John Schlesinger)

1963
Bushido/Bushido Zankoku Monogatari (Tadashi Imai); *The Devil/II Diavolo* (US: *To Bed . . . Or Not to Bed*) (Gian Luigi Polidoro)

1964
Dry Summer aka *I Had My Brother's Wife/Süsuz Yaz* (Ismail Metin)

1965
Alphaville (Jean-Luc Godard)

1966
Cul-de-Sac (Roman Polanski)

1967
Le Départ (Jerzy Skolimowski)

1968
Ole Dole Doff (Jan Troell)

1969
Early Years/Rani Radovi (Zelimir Zilnik)

1970
No prize awarded

1971
The Garden of the Finzi Contini (Vittorio de Sica)

1972
The Canterbury Tales (Pier Paolo Pasolini)

1973
Distant Thunder (Satyajit Ray)

1974
The Apprenticeship of Duddy Kravitz (Ted Kotcheff)

1975
Adoption/Orökbefogadás (Márta Mészáros)

1976
Buffalo Bill and the Indians (Robert Altman)

1977
The Ascent/Voskhozhdenie (Larisa Sheptiko)

1978
The Trout/Las Truchas (José Luis Garcia Sánchez); *The Words of Max/Las Palabras de Max* (Emilio Martinez-Lazaro)

1979
David (Peter Lilienthal)

1980
Heartland (Richard Pearce); *Palermo Oder Wolfsberg* (Werner Schroeter)

1981
Fast, Fast/Depiesa, Deprisa (Carlos Saura)

1982
Veronika Voss/Die Sehnsucht der Veronica Voss (Rainer Werner Fassbinder)

1983
Ascendancy (Edward Bennett); *The Beehive/La Colmena* (Mario Camus)

1984
Love Streams (John Cassavetes)

1985
Wetherby (David Hare); *The Woman and the Stranger/Die Frau und Der Fremde* (Rainer Simon)

1986
Stammheim (Reinhard Hauff)

1987
The Theme/Thema (Gleb Panfilov)

1988
Red Sorghum/Hong Gao Liang (Zhang Yimou)

1989
Rain Man (Barry Levinson)

1990
Music Box (Costa-Gavras); *Larks on a String* (Jiri Menzel)

1991
House of Smiles (Marco Ferreri)

1992
Grand Canyon (Lawrence Kasdan)

1993
The Woman from the Lake of Scented Souls/Xiang Hun N (Xei Fei); *The Wedding Banquet/Xiyan* (Ang Lee)

1994
In The Name of the Father (Jim Sheridan)

1995
Fresh Bait/L'Appat (Bertrand Tavernier)

1996
Sense and Sensibility (Ang Lee)

1997
The People vs Larry Flynt (Milos Forman)

1998
Central Station (Walter Salles)

1999
The Thin Red Line (Terence Malick)

Golden Lion Awards
The Venice Film Festival, held every September, began in 1934, was suspended in 1942, and started again in 1946. Its main award is the Golden Lion of St Mark, which since 1980 has been given to the best feature film. The Golden Lion winners are:

1980
Gloria (John Cassavetes); *Atlantic City* (Louis Malle)

1981
The German Sisters/Die Bleierne Zeit (Margarethe Von Trotta)

1982
The State of Things (Wim Wenders)

1983
First Name Carmen Prénom: Carmen (Jean-Luc Godard)

1984
The Year of the Quiet Sun/Rok Spokojnego Slonca (Krzysztof Zanussi)

1985
Vagabonde/aka Sans Toit Ni Loi (Agnès Varda)

1986
The Green Ray US: Summer/Le Rayon Vert (Eric Rohmer)

1987
Au Revoir les Enfants (Louis Malle)

1988
The Legend of the Holy Drinker/La Leggenda del Santo Bevitore (Ermanno Olmi)

1989
A City of Sadness/Beiqing Chengshi (Hou Hsiao-hsien)

1990
Rosencrantz and Guildenstern Are Dead (Tom Stoppard)

1991
Urga (Nikita Mikhalkov)

1992
The Story of Qiu Ju/Qiu Ju de Guansi (Yang Zimou)

1993
Short Cuts (Robert Altman); *Three Colours: Blue/Trois Couleurs: Bleu* (Krzysztof Kiéslowski)

1994
Before the Rain (Milcho Manchevski); *Vive l'Amour/Aiqing Wansui* (Tsai Ming-liang)

1995
Cyclo (Tran Anh Hung)

1996
Michael Collins (Neil Jordan)

1997
Fireworks/Hana-Bi (Takeshi Kitano)

1998
They All Laughed/Cosi Ridevano (Gianni Amelio)

European Film Awards
The European Film Awards, known as Felixes, were inaugurated in 1988. The European Film Academy announced in 1995 that it would no longer administer the award, partly because of financial problems, but also because it was impossible 'to put a single name on something as multifaceted and complicated as European cinema.' However, after a rethink and new sources of finance, the awards are continuing, though they were privatized from 1997. The main prizewinners were:

1988
Film: *A Short Film about Killing* (Krzysztof Kiéslowski)
Director: Wim Wenders (*Wings of Desire*)
Actor: Max Von Sydow (*Pelle the Conqueror*)
Actress: Carmen Maura (*Women on the Verge of a Nervous Breakdown*)
Supporting Actor: Curt Bois (*Wings of Desire*)
Supporting Actress: Johnna Ter Steege (*The Vanishing*)
Screenplay: Louis Malle (*Au Revoir, les Enfants*)

1989
Film: *Landscape in the Mist* (Theo Angelopoulos)
Director: Géza Bereményi (*The Midas Touch*)
Actor: Philippe Noiret (*Life and Nothing But; Cinema Paradiso*)
Actress: Ruth Sheen (*High Hopes*)
Supporting Performance: Edna Doré (*High Hopes*)
Screenplay: Maria Khmelik (*Little Vera*)

1990
Film: *Open Doors* (*Porte Aperte*) (Gianni Amelio)
Actor: Kenneth Branagh (*Henry V*)
Actress: Carmen Maura (*Ay! Carmela*)
Supporting Actor: Dimitri Pevsov (*Mother* (*Matj*))
Supporting Actress: Malin Ek (*The Guardian Angel* (*Skyddsanglen*))
Screenplay: Vitaly Kanevsky (*Don't Move, Die and Rise Again* (*Zamri Umi Voskresni*))

1991
Film: *Riff-Raff* (Ken Loach)
Actor: Michel Bouquet (*Toto le Héros*)
Actress: Clotilde Courau (*Le Petit Criminel*)
Supporting Actor: Ricky Memphis (*Ultrè*)
Supporting Actress: Marta Keler (*Virginia*)
Screenplay: Jaco Van Dormael (*Toto le Héros*)

1992
Film: *Il Ladro di Bambini* (Gianni Amelio)
Actor: Matti Pellonpää (*La Vie de Bohème*)
Actress: Juliette Binoche (*Les Amants du Pont-Neuf*)
Supporting Actor: André Wilms (*La Vie de Bohème*)
Supporting Actress: Ghita Norby (*Freud Flyttar Hemifran*)
Screenplay: István Szabó (*Edes Emma, Draga Böbe*)

1993
Film: *Urga* (Nikita Mikhalkov)
Actor: Daniel Auteuil (*Un Coeur en Hiver*)
Actress: Maia Morgenstern (*Balanta*)

1994
Film: *Lamerica* (Gianni Amelio)
Lifetime achievement: Robert Bresson

1995
Film: *Land and Freedom* (Ken Loach)

1996
Film: *Breaking the Waves* (Lars von Trier)
Young Film: *Some Mother's Son* (Terry George)
Actress: Emily Watson (*Breaking the Waves*)
Actor: Ian McKellen (*Richard III*)

Screenwriter: Arief Aliev, Sergai Bodrov, Boris Giler (*The Prisoner of the Mountains*)

1997
Film: *The Full Monty* (Peter Cattaneo)
Actor: Bob Hoskins (*TwentyFourSeven*)
Actress: Juliette Binoche (*The English Patient*)
Screenwriter: Chris Vander Stappen, Alain Berline (*Ma Vie en Rose*)

1998
Film: *Life Is Beautiful* (Roberto Begnini)
Actor: Roberto Begnini (*Life Is Beautiful*)
Actress: Élodie Bouchez, Natacha Régnier (*Dream Life of Angels/Vie Rêve des Anges*)
Screenwriter: Peter Howitt (*Sliding Doors*)
Cinematographer: Adrian Biddle (*The Butcher Boy*)
Oustanding European Achievement in World Cinema: Stellan Skarsgard (*Amistad, Good Will Hunting*)
Audience Awards: actor: Antonio Banderas (*Godzilla*); actress: Kate Winslet (*Titanic*); director: Roland Emmerich (*Godzilla*)

American Society of Cinematographers' Annual Awards
This professional association gives an award for the best cinematography of the year. Its winners are:
1986 Jordan Cronenweth (*Peggy Sue Got Married*)
1987 Allen Daviau (*Empire of the Sun*)
1988 Conrad L. Hall (*Tequila Sunrise*)
1989 Haskell Wexler (*Blaze*)
1990 Dean Semler (*Dances with Wolves*)
1991 Allen Daviau (*Bugsy*)
1992 Stephen H. Burum (*Hoffa*)
1993 Conrad L. Hall (*Searching for Bobby Fischer*)
1994 Roger Deakins (*The Shawshank Redemption*)
1995 John Toll (*Braveheart*)
1996 John Seale (*The English Patient*)
1997 Russell Carpenter (*Titanic*)

The Directors Guild of America Awards
The national union of directors presents annual awards for feature film direction, which also usually provide an indication of the likely Oscar winner for best direction. Its winners are:
1948 Joseph Mankiewicz (*A Letter to Three Wives*)
1949 Robert Rossen (*All the King's Men*)
1950 Joseph Mankiewicz (*All About Eve*)
1951 George Stevens (*A Place in the Sun*)
1952 John Ford (*The Quiet Man*)
1953 Fred Zinnemann (*From Here to Eternity*)
1954 Elia Kazan (*On the Waterfront*)
1955 Delbert Mann (*Marty*)
1956 George Stevens (*Giant*)
1957 David Lean (*Bridge on the River Kwai*)
1958 Vincente Minnelli (*Gigi*)
1959 William Wyler (*Ben-Hur*)
1960 Billy Wilder (*The Apartment*)
1961 Robert Wise, Jerome Robbins (*West Side Story*)
1962 David Lean (*Lawrence of Arabia*)
1963 Tony Richardson (*Tom Jones*)
1964 George Cukor (*My Fair Lady*)
1965 Robert Wise (*The Sound of Music*)
1966 Fred Zinnemann (*A Man for All Seasons*)
1967 Mike Nichols (*The Graduate*)
1968 Anthony Harvey (*The Lion in Winter*)
1969 John Schlesinger (*Midnight Cowboy*)
1970 Franklin J. Schaffner (*Patton*)
1971 William Friedkin (*The French Connection*)
1972 Francis Ford Coppola (*The Godfather*)
1973 George Roy Hill (*The Sting*)
1974 Francis Ford Coppola (*The Godfather, Part II*)

1975 Milos Forman (*One Flew over the Cuckoo's Nest*)
1976 John G. Avildsen (*Rocky*)
1977 Woody Allen (*Annie Hall*)
1978 Michael Cimino (*The Deer Hunter*)
1979 Robert Benton (*Kramer vs Kramer*)
1980 Robert Redford (*Ordinary People*)
1981 Warren Beatty (*Reds*)
1982 Richard Attenborough (*Gandhi*)
1983 James L. Brooks (*Terms of Endearment*)
1984 Milos Forman (*Amadeus*)
1985 Steven Spielberg (*The Color Purple*)
1986 Oliver Stone (*Platoon*)
1987 Bernardo Bertolucci (*The Last Emperor*)
1988 Barry Levinson (*Rain Man*)
1989 Oliver Stone (*Born on the Fourth of July*)
1990 Kevin Costner (*Dances with Wolves*)
1991 Jonathan Demme (*Silence of the Lambs*)
1992 Clint Eastwood (*Unforgiven*)
1993 Steven Spielberg (*Schindler's List*)
1994 Robert Zemeckis (*Forrest Gump*)
1995 Ron Howard (*Apollo 13*)
1996 Anthony Minghella (*The English Patient*)
1997 James Cameron (*Titanic*)

London Critics' Circle Awards (ALFS)
The Critics' Circle was founded in 1913. The Film Critics' Circle, based in London, has more than 80 members, and began presenting awards, known as ALFS (Awards of the London Film Critics' Circle), in 1980. Its prizes include the Dilys Powell Award for lifetime achievement. Until 1991, there was no separate award for actress of the year; the term 'actor' applied to men and women.

1980
Film: *Apocalypse Now* (Francis Ford Coppola)
Foreign Film: *Agni Vera* (Pal Gabor); *The Marriage of Maria Braun* (Rainer Werner Fassbinder)
Director: Nicolas Roeg (*Bad Timing*)
Screenwriter: Steve Tesich (*Breaking Away*)
Special Award: Gillian Armstrong (*My Brilliant Career*); Peter Sellers (*Being There*)

1981
Film: *Chariots of Fire* (Hugh Hudson)
Foreign Film: *Man of Iron* (Andrzej Wajda)
Director: Andrzej Wajda (*Man of Iron*)
Screenwriter: Colin Welland (*Chariots of Fire*)
Special Award: Freddie Francis (*The Elephant Man*); Bill Forsyth (*Gregory's Girl; That Sinking Feeling*)

1982
Film: *Missing* (Costa-Gavras)
Foreign Film: *Mephisto* (Istvan Szabo)
Director: Costa-Gavras (*Missing*)
Screenwriter: Costa-Gavras, Donald Stewart (*Missing*)
Special Award: David Puttnam; Lawrence Paull, Douglas Trumbull, Syd Mean (*Blade Runner*)

1983
Film: *King of Comedy* (Martin Scorsese)
Foreign Film: *Yol* (Serif Goren)
Director: Andrzej Wajda (*Danton*)
Actor: Ben Kingsley (*Gandhi*)
Screenwriter: Ruth Prawer Jhabvala (*Heat and Dust*)
Special Award: Artifical Eye; Jonathan Hodgson (*Night Club*)

1984
Film: *Paris, Texas* (Wim Wenders)
Foreign Film: *A Sunday in the Country* (Bertrand Tavernier)
Director: Neil Jordan (*The Company of Wolves*)
Actor: Albert Finney (*Under the Volcano*); Harry Dean Stanton (*Paris, Texas*)
Screenwriter: Philip Kaufman (*The Right Stuff*)
Special Award: Iain McCall (animation: *Christmas for Sale*)

1985
Film: *The Purple Rose of Cairo* (Woody Allen)
Foreign Film: *Heimat* (Edgar Reitz)
Director: Roland Joffe (*The Killing Fields*)
Actor: Richard Farnsworth (*The Grey Fox*); James Mason (*The Shooting Party*)
Screenwriter: Alan Bennett (*A Private Function*)
Special Award: Palace Pictures

1986
Film: *A Room with a View* (James Ivory)
Foreign Film: *Ran* (Akira Kurosawa)
Director: Akira Kurosawa (*Ran*)
Actor: Bob Hoskins (*Mona Lisa*); William Hurt (*Kiss of the Spider Woman*)
Screenwriter: Woody Allen (*Hannah and Her Sisters*)
Special Award: Lillian Gish; Alexandre Trauner; John Barry (*Out of Africa*)

1987
Film: *Hope and Glory* (John Boorman)
Foreign Film: *Jean de Florette* (Claude Berri)
Director: Stanley Kubrick (*Full Metal Jacket*)
Actor: Sean Connery (*The Untouchables*); Gary Oldman (*Prick Up Your Ears*)
Screenwriter: Alan Bennett (*Prick Up Your Ears*)
Special Award: Pinewood Studios; Tommie Manderson (make-up); David Rose; Ennio Morricone

1988
Film: *House of Games* (David Mamet)
Foreign Film: *Babette's Feast* (Gabriel Axel)
Director: John Huston (*The Dead*)
Actor: Leo McKern (*Travelling North*); Stéphane Audran (*Babette's Feast*)
Screenwriter: David Mamet (*House of Games*)
Special Award: Leslie Halliwell; Leslie Hardcastle, David Francis (Museum of Moving Image); Dilys Powell; Miklos Rozsa

1989
Film: *Distant Voices, Still Lives* (Terence Davies)
Foreign Film: *Au Revoir, les Enfants* (Louis Malle)
Director: Terence Davies (*Distant Voices, Still Lives*)
Actor: Daniel Day-Lewis (*My Left Foot*)
Screenwriter: Christopher Hampton (*Dangerous Liaisons*)
Special Award: Alec Guinness, Charles Crichton; Artifical Eye

1990
Film: *Crimes and Misdemeanors* (Woody Allen)
Foreign Film: *Cinema Paradiso* (Giuseppe Tornatore)
Director: Woody Allen (*Crimes and Misdemeanors*)
Actor: Philippe Noiret (*Cinema Paradiso*)
Screenwriter: Woody Allen (*Crimes and Misdemeanors*)
Special Award: Penelope Houston

1991
Film: *Thelma and Louise* (Ridley Scott)
British Film: *Life Is Sweet* (Mike Leigh)
Foreign Film: *Cyrano de Bergerac* (Jean-Paul Rappeneau)
Director: Ridley Scott (*Thelma and Louise*)
British Director: Alan Parker (*The Commitments*)
Actor: Gérard Depardieu (*Cyrano de Bergerac*)
British Actor: Alan Rickman (*Close My Eyes, Truly Madly Deeply, Robin Hood: Prince of Thieves, Quigley Down Under*)
Actress: Susan Sarandon (*Thelma and Louise, White Palace*)
Screenwriter: David Mamet (*Homicide*)
British Screenwriter: Dick Clement, Ian La Frenais, Roddy Doyle (*The Commitments*)
British Producer: Lynda Myles, Roger Randall-Cutler (*The Commitments*)
British Technical Achievement: Peter Greenaway (*Prospero's Books*)
International Newcomer: Annette Bening (*The Grifters, Guilty by Suspicion, Regarding Henry, Postcards from the Edge, Valmont*)
Dilys Powell Award: Dirk Bogarde
Special Award: John Sayles

1992
Film: *Unforgiven* (Clint Eastwood)
British Film: *Howards End* (James Ivory)
Foreign Film: *Raise the Red Lantern* (Zhang Zimou)
Director: Robert Altman (*The Player*)
British Director: Neil Jordan (*The Crying Game*)
Actor: Robert Downey, Jnr (*Chaplin*)
British Actor: Daniel Day-Lewis (*Last of the Mohicans*)
Actress: Judy Davis (*Husbands and Wives, Barton Fink, Naked Lunch*)
Screenwriter: Michael Tolkin (*The Player*)
British Screenwriter: Neil Jordan (*The Crying Game*)
British Producer: Stephen Woolley (*The Crying Game*)
British Technical Achievement: Roger Deakins (*Barton Fink*)
International Newcomer: Baz Luhrmann (*Strictly Ballroom*)
British Newcomer: Peter Chelsom (*Hear My Song*)
Dilys Powell Award: Frederick Young
Special Award: Freddie Francis

1993
Film: *The Piano* (Jane Campion)
British Film: *The Remains of the Day* (James Ivory)
Foreign Film: *Un Coeur en Hiver* (Claude Sautet)
Director: James Ivory (*The Remains of the Day*)
British Director: Ken Loach (*Raining Stones*)
Actor: Anthony Hopkins (*The Remains of the Day*)
British Actor: David Thewlis (*Naked*)
Actress: Holly Hunter (*The Piano*)
British Actress: Miranda Richardson (*Damage*)
Screenwriter: Harold Ramis, Danny Rubin (*Groundhog Day*)
British Screenwriter: Roddy Doyle (*The Snapper*)
British Producer: Kenneth Branagh (*Much Ado about Nothing*)
British Technical Achievement: Ken Adam (*Addams Family Values*)
International Newcomer: Quentin Tarantino (*Reservoir Dogs*)
British Newcomer: Vadim Jean, Gary Sinyor (*Leon, the Pig Farmer*)
Dilys Powell Award: Christopher Lee
Special Award: Kate Maberly (*The Secret Garden*)

1994
Film: *Schindler's List* (Steven Spielberg)
British Film: *Four Weddings and a Funeral* (Mike Newell)
Foreign Film: *Farewell My Concubine* (Chen Kaige)
Director: Steven Spielberg (*Schindler's List*)
British Director: Mike Newell (*Four Weddings and a Funeral*)
Actor: John Travolta (*Pulp Fiction*)
Actress: Linda Fiorentino (*The Last Seduction*)
British Actress: Crissy Rock (*Ladybird Ladybird*)
Screenwriter: Quentin Tarantino (*Pulp Fiction*)
British Screenwriter: Richard Curtis (*Four Weddings and a Funeral*)
British Producer: Duncan Kenworthy (*Four Weddings and a Funeral*)
British Technical Achievement: Roger Deakins (*The Hudsucker Proxy*)
International Newcomer: Jim Carrey (*The Mask, Ace Ventura Pet Detective*)
British Newcomer: Iain Softley (*Backbeat*)
Dilys Powell Award: Richard Attenborough
Special Award: Hugh Grant (*Four Weddings and a Funeral*); Barry Norman

1995
Film: *Babe* (Chris Noonan)
British Film: *The Madness of King George* (Nicholas Hytner)
Foreign Film: *Il Postino* (Michael Radford)
Director: Peter Jackson (*Heavenly Creatures*)
British Director: Michael Radford (*Il Postino*)
Actor: Johnny Depp (*Ed Wood, Don Juan de Marco*)
British Actor: Nigel Hawthorne (*The Madness of King George*)
Actress: Nicole Kidman (*To Die For*)
British Actress: Kate Winslet (*Heavenly Creatures*)
Screenwriter: Paul Attanasio (*Quiz Show, Disclosure*)
British Screenwriter: Alan Bennett (*The Madness of King George*)
British Producer: Simon Fields, Peter Chelsom (*Funny Bones*)
British Technical Achievement: Ken Adam (*The Madness of King George*)
International Newcomer: Chris Noonan (*Babe*)
British Newcomer: Danny Boyle (*Shallow Grave*)
Dilys Powell Award: Wendy Hiller
Special Award: Peter Rogers; John Gielgud

1996
Film: *Fargo* (Joel Coen)
British Film: *Secrets and Lies* (Mike Leigh)
Foreign Film: *Les Misérables* (Claude Lelouch)
Director: Joel Coen (*Fargo*)
British Director: Mike Leigh (*Secrets and Lies*)
Actor: Morgan Freeman (*Seven*)
British Actor: Ewan McGregor (*Trainspotting, Brassed Off, The Pillow Book, Emma*)
Actress: Frances McDormand (*Fargo*)
British Actress: Brenda Blethyn (*Secrets and Lies*)
Screenwriter: Joel and Ethan Coen (*Fargo*)
British Screenwriter: Emma Thompson (*Sense and Sensibility*)
British Producer: Andrew Macdonald (*Trainspotting*)
British Newcomer: Emily Watson (*Breaking the Waves*)
Dilys Powell Award: John Mills
Special Award: Fred Zinnemann; Jack Cardiff; Norman Wisdom

1997
Film: *LA Confidential* (Curtis Hanson)
British Film: *The Full Monty* (Peter Cattaneo)
Foreign Film: *Ridicule* (Patrice Leconte)
Director: Curtis Hanson (*LA Confidential*)
British Director: Anthony Minghella (*The English Patient*)
Actor: Al Pacino (*Donnie Brasco, Looking for Richard*)
British Actor: Robert Carlyle (*The Full Monty*)
Actress: Claire Danes (*William Shakespeare's Romeo & Juliet*)
British Actress: Judi Dench (*Mrs Brown*)
British Supporting Actress: Minnie Driver (*Big Night, Grosse Pointe Blank, Sleepers*)
Screenwriter: Brian Helgeland, Curtis Hanson (*LA Confidential*)
British Screenwriter: Simon Beaufoy (*The Full Monty*)
British Producer: Uberto Pasolini (*The Full Monty*)
British Newcomer: Peter Cattaneo (*The Full Monty*)
Dilys Powell Award: Michael Caine
Special Award: Woody Allen; Paul Scofield; Martin Scorsese; Kevin Spacey

The National Society of Film Critics' Awards

Formed in 1966, this American organization comprises around 40 critics from publications across the United States. Their main awards are as follows:

1966
Film: *Blow Up* (Michelangelo Antonioni)
Director: Michelangelo Antonioni (*Blow Up*)
Actor: Michael Caine (*Alfie*)
Actress: Sylvie (*The Shameless Old Lady*)

1967
Film: *Persona* (Ingmar Bergman)
Director: Ingmar Bergman (*Persona*)
Actor: Rod Steiger (*In the Heat of the Night*)
Actress: Bibi Andersson (*Persona*)
Supporting Actor: Gene Hackman (*Bonnie and Clyde*)
Supporting Actress: Marjorie Rhodes (*The Family Way*)
Screenplay: David Newman, Robert Benton (*Bonnie and Clyde*)
Cinematography: Haskell Wexler (*In the Heat of the Night*)

1968
Film: *Shame* (Ingmar Bergman)
Director: Ingmar Bergman (*Shame, Hour of the Wolf*)
Actor: Per Oscarsson (*Hunger*)
Actress: Liv Ullmann (*Shame*)
Supporting Actor: Seymour Cassel (*Faces*)
Supporting Actress: Billie Whitelaw (*Charlie Bubbles*)
Screenplay: John Cassavetes (*Faces*)
Cinematography: William A. Fraker (*Bullitt*)

1969
Film: *Z* (Costa-Gavras)
Director: François Truffaut (*Stolen Kisses*)
Actor: Jon Voight (*Midnight Cowboy*)
Actress: Vanessa Redgrave (*The Loves of Isadora*)
Supporting Actor: Jack Nicholson (*Easy Rider*)
Supporting Actress: Sian Phillips (*Goodbye, Mr Chips*)
Screenplay: Paul Mazursky and Larry Tucker (*Bob & Carol & Ted & Alice*)

Cinematography: Lucien Ballard (*The Wild Bunch*)

1970

Film: *M*A*S*H* (Robert Altman)
Director: Ingmar Bergman (*The Passion of Anna*)
Actor: George C. Scott (*Patton*)
Actress: Glenda Jackson (*Women in Love*)
Supporting Actor: Chief Dan George (*Little Big Man*)
Supporting Actress: Lois Smith (*Five Easy Pieces*)
Screenplay: Eric Rohmer (*My Night at Maud's*)
Cinematography: Nestor Almendros (*The Wild Child, My Night at Maud's*)

1971

Film: *Claire's Knee* (Eric Rohmer)
Director: Bernardo Bertolucci (*The Conformist*)
Actor: Peter Finch (*Sunday, Bloody Sunday*)
Actress: Jane Fonda (*Klute*)
Supporting Actor: Bruce Dern (*Drive, He Said*)
Supporting Actress: Ellen Burstyn (*The Last Picture Show*)
Screenplay: Penelope Gilliatt (*Sunday, Bloody Sunday*)
Cinematography: Vittorio Storaro (*The Conformist*)

1972

Film: *The Discreet Charm of the Bourgeoisie* (Luis Buñuel)
Director: Luis Buñuel (*The Discreet Charm of the Bourgeoisie*)
Actor: Al Pacino (*The Godfather*)
Actress: Cicely Tyson (*Sounder*)
Supporting Actor: Joel Grey (*Cabaret*); Eddie Albert (*The Heartbreak Kid*)
Supporting Actress: Jeannie Berlin (*The Heartbreak Kid*)
Screenplay: Ingmar Bergman (*Cries and Whispers*)
Cinematography: Sven Nykvist (*Cries and Whispers*)

1973

Film: *Day for Night* (François Truffaut)
Director: François Truffaut (*Day for Night*)
Actor: Marlon Brando (*Last Tango in Paris*)
Actress: Liv Ullmann (*The New Land*)
Supporting Actor: Robert De Niro (*Mean Streets*)
Supporting Actress: Valentina Cortese (*Day for Night*)
Screenplay: George Lucas, Gloria Katz, Willard Huyck (*American Graffiti*)
Cinematography: Vilmos Zsigmond (*The Long Goodbye*)

1974

Film: *Scenes from a Marriage* (Ingmar Bergman)
Director: Francis Ford Coppola (*The Godfather, Part II, The Conversation*)
Actor: Jack Nicholson (*Chinatown, The Last Detail*)
Actress: Liv Ullmann (*Scenes from a Marriage*)
Supporting Actor: Holger Löwenadler (*Lacombe, Lucien*)
Supporting Actress: Bibi Andersson (*Scenes from a Marriage*)
Screenplay: Ingmar Bergman (*Scenes from a Marriage*)
Cinematography: Gordon Willis (*The Godfather, Part II, The Parallax View*)
Special Award: Jean Renoir

1975

Film: *Nashville* (Robert Altman)
Director: Robert Altman (*Nashville*)

Actor: Jack Nicholson (*One Flew over the Cuckoo's Nest*)
Actress: Isabelle Adjani (*The Story of Adèle H*)
Supporting Actor: Henry Gibson (*Nashville*)
Supporting Actress: Lily Tomlin (*Nashville*)
Screenplay: Robert Towne, Warren Beatty (*Shampoo*)
Cinematography: John Alcott (*Barry Lyndon*)
Special Award: Ingmar Bergman (*The Magic Flute*)

1976

Film: *All the President's Men* (Alan J. Pakula)
Director: Martin Scorsese (*Taxi Driver*)
Actor: Robert De Niro (*Taxi Driver*)
Actress: Sissy Spacek (*Carrie*)
Supporting Actor: Jason Robards (*All the President's Men*)
Supporting Actress: Jodie Foster (*Taxi Driver*)
Screenplay: Alan Tanner, John Berger (*Jonah Who Will Be 25 in the Year 2000*)
Cinematography: Haskell Wexler (*Bound for Glory*)

1977

Film: *Annie Hall* (Woody Allen)
Director: Luis Buñuel (*That Obscure Object of Desire*)
Actor: Art Carney (*The Late Show*)
Actress: Diane Keaton (*Annie Hall*)
Supporting Actor: Edward Fox (*A Bridge Too Far*)
Supporting Actress: Ann Wedgeworth (*Handle with Care*)
Screenplay: Woody Allen, Marshall Brickman (*Annie Hall*)
Cinematography: Thomas Mauch (*Aguirre, Wrath of God*)

1978

Film: *Get Out Your Handkerchiefs* (Bertrand Blier)
Director: Terrence Malick (*Days of Heaven*)
Actor: Gary Busey (*The Buddy Holly Story*)
Actress: Ingrid Bergman (*Autumn Sonata*)
Supporting Actor: Richard Farnsworth (*Comes a Horseman*); Robert Morley (*Who Is Killing the Great Chefs of Europe?*)
Supporting Actress: Meryl Streep (*The Deer Hunter*)
Screenplay: Paul Mazursky (*An Unmarried Woman*)
Cinematography: Nestor Almendros (*Days of Heaven*)

1979

Film: *Breaking Away* (Peter Yates)
Director: Robert Benton (*Kramer vs Kramer*); Woody Allen (*Manhattan*)
Actor: Dustin Hoffman (*Kramer vs Kramer, Agatha*)
Actress: Sally Field (*Norma Rae*)
Supporting Actor: Frederic Forrest (*Apocalypse Now, The Rose*)
Supporting Actress: Meryl Streep (*Kramer vs Kramer, The Seduction of Joe Tynan, Manhattan*)
Screenplay: Steve Tesich (*Breaking Away*)
Cinematography: Caleb Deschanel (*Being There, The Black Stallion*)

1980

Film: *Melvin and Howard* (Jonathan Demme)
Director: Martin Scorsese (*Raging Bull*)
Actor: Peter O'Toole (*The Stunt Man*)
Actress: Sissy Spacek (*Coal Miner's Daughter*)
Supporting Actor: Joe Pesci (*Raging Bull*)
Supporting Actress: Mary Steenburgen (*Melvin and Howard*)
Screenplay: Bo Goldman (*Melvin and Howard*)
Cinematography: Michael Chapman (*Raging Bull*)

1981

Film: *Atlantic City* (Louis Malle)
Director: Louis Malle (*Atlantic City*)
Actor: Burt Lancaster (*Atlantic City*)
Actress: Marilia Pera (*Pixote*)
Supporting Actor: Robert Preston (*S.O.B.*)
Supporting Actress: Maureen Stapleton (*Reds*)
Screenplay: John Guare (*Atlantic City*)
Cinematography: Gordon Willis (*Pennies from Heaven*)

1982

Film: *Tootsie* (Sydney Pollack)
Director: Steven Spielberg (*E.T. – the Extra-Terrestrial*)
Actor: Dustin Hoffman (*Tootsie*)
Actress: Meryl Streep (*Sophie's Choice*)
Supporting Actor: Mickey Rourke (*Diner*)
Supporting Actress: Jessica Lange (*Tootsie*)
Screenplay: Murray Schisgal, Larry Gelbart (*Tootsie*)
Cinematography: Philippe Rousselot (*Diva*)

1983

Film: *The Night of the Shooting Stars* (Paolo and Vittorio Taviani)
Director: Paolo and Vittorio Taviani (*The Night of the Shooting Stars*)
Actor: Gérard Depardieu (*Danton, The Return of Martin Guerre*)
Actress: Debra Winger (*Terms of Endearment*)
Supporting Actor: Jack Nicholson (*Terms of Endearment*)
Supporting Actress: Sandra Bernhard (*King of Comedy*)
Screenplay: Bill Forsyth (*Local Hero*)
Cinematography: Hiro Narita (*Never Cry Wolf*)

1984

Film: *Stranger than Paradise* (Jim Jarmusch)
Director: Robert Bresson (*L'Argent*)
Actor: Steve Martin (*All of Me*)
Actress: Vanessa Redgrave (*The Bostonians*)
Supporting Actor: John Malkovich (*Places in the Heart, The Killing Fields*)
Supporting Actress: Melanie Griffith (*Body Double*)
Screenplay: Babaloo Mandel, Lowell Ganz, Bruce Jay Friedman (*Splash*)
Cinematography: Chris Menges (*Comfort and Joy, The Killing Fields*)
Documentary: *Stop Making Sense* (Jonathan Demme)

1985

Film: *Ran* (Akira Kurosawa)
Director: John Huston (*Prizzi's Honor*)
Actor: Jack Nicholson (*Prizzi's Honor*)
Actress: Vanessa Redgrave (*Wetherby*)
Supporting Actor: John Gielgud (*Plenty, The Shooting Party*)
Supporting Actress: Anjelica Huston (*Prizzi's Honor*)
Screenplay: Albert Brooks, Monica Johnson (*Lost in America*)
Cinematography: Takao Saito (*Ran*)
Documentary: *Shoah* (Claude Lanzmann)

1986

Film: *Blue Velvet* (David Lynch)
Director: David Lynch (*Blue Velvet*)
Actor: Bob Hoskins (*Mona Lisa*)
Actress: Chloe Webb (*Sid and Nancy*)
Supporting Actor: Dennis Hopper (*Blue Velvet*)
Supporting Actress: Dianne Wiest (*Hannah and Her Sisters*)

Screenplay: Hanif Kureishi (*My Beautiful Laundrette*)
Cinematography: Frederic Elmes (*Blue Velvet*)
Documentary: *Marlene* (Maximilian Schell)

1987
Film: *The Dead* (John Huston)
Director: John Boorman (*Hope and Glory*)
Actor: Steve Martin (*Roxanne*)
Actress: Emily Lloyd (*Wish You Were Here*)
Supporting Actor: Morgan Freeman (*Street Smart*)
Supporting Actress: Kathy Baker (*Street Smart*)
Screenplay: John Boorman (*Hope and Glory*)
Cinematography: Philippe Rousselot (*Hope and Glory*)

1988
Film: *The Unbearable Lightness of Being* (Philip Kaufman)
Director: Philip Kaufman (*The Unbearable Lightness of Being*)
Actor: Michael Keaton (*Beetlejuice, Clean and Sober*)
Actress: Judy Davis (*High Tide*)
Supporting Actor: Dean Stockwell (*Married to the Mob, Tucker: The Man and His Dream*)
Supporting Actress: Mercedes Ruehl (*Married to the Mob*)
Screenplay: Ron Shelton (*Bull Durham*)
Cinematography: Henri Alekan (*Wings of Desire*)
Documentary: *The Thin Blue Line* (Errol Morris)

1989
Film: *Drugstore Cowboy* (Gus Van Sant)
Director: Gus Van Sant (*Drugstore Cowboy*)
Actor: Daniel Day-Lewis (*My Left Foot*)
Actress: Michelle Pfeiffer (*The Fabulous Baker Boys*)
Supporting Actor: Beau Bridges (*The Fabulous Baker Boys*)
Supporting Actress: Anjelica Huston (*Enemies: A Love Story*)
Screenplay: Gus Van Sant, Daniel Yost (*Drugstore Cowboy*)
Cinematography: Michael Ballhaus (*The Fabulous Baker Boys*)
Documentary: *Roger and Me* (Michael Moore)

1990
Film: *GoodFellas* (Martin Scorsese)
Foreign Film: *Ariel* (Aki Kaurismaki)
Director: Martin Scorsese (*GoodFellas*)
Actor: Jeremy Irons (*Reversal of Fortune*)
Actress: Anjelica Huston (*The Grifters, The Witches*)
Supporting Actor: Bruce Davison (*Longtime Companion*)
Supporting Actress: Annette Bening (*The Grifters*)
Screenplay: Charles Burnett (*To Sleep with Anger*)
Cinematography: Peter Suschitzky (*Where the Heart Is*)
Documentary: *Berkeley in the Sixties* (Mark Kitchell)

1991
Film: *Life Is Sweet* (Mike Leigh)
Foreign Film: *The Double Life of Véronique* (Krzysztof Kiéslowski)
Director: David Cronenberg (*Naked Lunch*)
Actor: River Phoenix (*My Own Private Idaho*)
Actress: Alison Steadman (*Life Is Sweet*)
Supporting Actor: Harvey Keitel (*Bugsy, Thelma & Louise, Mortal Thoughts*)
Supporting Actress: Jane Horrocks (*Life Is Sweet*)
Screenplay: David Cronenberg (*Naked Lunch*)

Cinematography: Roger Deakins (*Barton Fink*)
Experimental Film: *Archangel* (Guy Maddin)
Documentary: *Paris Is Burning* (Jennie Livingston)

1992
Film: *Unforgiven* (Clint Eastwood)
Foreign Film: *Raise the Red Lantern* (Zhang Yimou)
Director: Clint Eastwood (*Unforgiven*)
Actor: Stephen Rea (*The Crying Game*)
Actress: Emma Thompson (*Howards End*)
Supporting Actor: Gene Hackman (*Unforgiven*)
Supporting Actress: Judy Davis (*Husbands and Wives*)
Screenplay: David Webb Peoples (*Unforgiven*)
Cinematography: Zhao Fei (*Raise the Red Lantern*)
New Director: Allison Anders (*Gas Food Lodging*)
Documentary: *American Dream* (Barbara Kopple)

1993
Film: *Schindler's List* (Steven Spielberg)
Foreign Film: *The Story of Qiu Ju* (Zhang Yimou)
Director: Steven Spielberg (*Schindler's List*)
Actor: David Thewlis (*Naked*)
Actress: Holly Hunter (*The Piano*)
Supporting Actor: Ralph Fiennes (*Schindler's List*)
Supporting Actress: Madeleine Stowe (*Short Cuts*)
Screenplay: Jane Campion (*The Piano*)
Cinematography: Janusz Kaminski (*Schindler's List*)
Documentary: *Visions of Light, the Art of Cinematography* (Arnold Glassman, Todd McCarthy, Stuart Samuels)

1994
Film: *Pulp Fiction* (Quentin Tarantino)
Foreign Film: *Red* (Krzysztof Kiéslowski)
Director: Quentin Tarantino (*Pulp Fiction*)
Actor: Paul Newman (*Nobody's Fool*)
Actress: Jennifer Jason Leigh (*Mrs Parker and the Vicious Circle*)
Supporting Actor: Martin Landau (*Ed Wood*)
Supporting Actress: Dianne Wiest (*Bullets over Broadway*)
Screenplay: Quentin Tarantino (*Pulp Fiction*)
Cinematography: Stefan Czapsky (*Ed Wood*)
Documentary: *Hoop Dreams* (Steve James)

1995
Film: *Babe* (Chris Noonan)
Foreign Film: *Wild Reeds* (André Téchiné)
Director: Mike Figgis (*Leaving Las Vegas*)
Actor: Nicolas Cage (*Leaving Las Vegas*)
Actress: Elisabeth Shue (*Leaving Las Vegas*)
Supporting Actor: Don Cheadle (*Devil in a Blue Dress*)
Supporting Actress: Joan Allen (*Nixon*)
Screenplay: Amy Heckerling (*Clueless*)
Cinematography: Tak Fujimoto (*Devil in a Blue Dress*)
Documentary: *Crumb* (Terry Zwigoff)

1996
Film: *Breaking the Waves* (Lars Von Trier)
Foreign Film: *La Cérémonie* (Claude Chabrol)
Director: Lars Von Trier (*Breaking the Waves*)
Actor: Eddie Murphy (*The Nutty Professor*)
Actress: Emily Watson (*Breaking the Waves*)
Supporting Actor: Martin Donovan (*The Portrait of a Lady*); Tony Shalhoub (*Big Night*)
Supporting Actress: Barbara Hershey (*The Portrait of a Lady*)
Screenplay: Albert Brooks, Monica Johnson (*Mother*)
Cinematography: Robby Muller (*Breaking the Waves, Dead Man*)
Documentary: *When We Were Kings* (Leon Gast)

1997
Film: *LA Confidential* (Curtis Hanson)
Foreign Film: *La Promesse* (Jean-Pierre Dardenne, Luc Dardenne)
Director: Curtis Hanson (*LA Confidential*)
Actor: Robert Duvall (*The Apostle*)
Actress: Julie Christie (*Afterglow*)
Supporting Actor: Burt Reynolds (*Boogie Nights*)
Supporting Actress: Julianne Moore (*Boogie Nights*)
Screenplay: Brian Helgeland, Curtis Hanson (*LA Confidential*)
Cinematography: Roger Deakins (*Kundun*)
Documentary: *Fast, Cheap & Out of Control* (Errol Morris)

1998
Film: *Out of Sight* (Steven Soderbergh)
Foreign Film: *Taste of Cherry* (Abbas Kiarostami)
Director: Steven Soderbergh (*Out of Sight*)
Actor: Nick Nolte (*Affliction*)
Actress: Ally Sheedy (*High Art*)
Supporting Actor: Bill Murray (*Rushmore*)
Supporting Actress: Judi Dench (*Shakespeare in Love*)
Screenplay: Scott Frank (*Out of Sight*)
Cinematography: John Toll (*The Thin Red Line*)
Documentary: *The Farm: Angola USA* (Liz Garbus, Jonathan Stack)

New York Film Critics' Circle Awards
The New York Film Critics' Circle was formed in 1935, and consists of around 30 critics from the city's publications. Its main awards have been:

1935
Film: *The Informer* (John Ford)
Director: John Ford (*The Informer*)
Actor: Charles Laughton (*Mutiny on the Bounty, Ruggles of Red Gap*)
Actress: Greta Garbo (*Anna Karenina*)

1936
Film: *Mr Deeds Goes to Town* (Frank Capra)
Director: Rouben Mamoulian (*The Gay Desperado*)
Actor: Walter Huston (*Dodsworth*)
Actress: Luise Rainer (*The Great Ziegfeld*)
Foreign Film: *Carnival in Flanders/La Kermesse Héroïque* (Jacques Feyder)

1937
Film: *The Life of Emile Zola* (William Dieterle)
Director: Gregory La Cava (*Stage Door*)
Actor: Paul Muni (*The Life of Emile Zola*)
Actress: Greta Garbo (*Camille*)
Foreign Film: *Mayerling* (Anatole Litvak)

1938
Film: *The Citadel* (King Vidor)
Director: Alfred Hitchcock (*The Lady Vanishes*)
Actor: James Cagney (*Angels with Dirty Faces*)
Actress: Margaret Sullavan (*Three Comrades*)
Foreign Film: *La Grande Illusion* (Jean Renoir)
Special Award: *Snow White and the Seven Dwarfs* (Walt Disney)

1939
Film: *Wuthering Heights* (William Wyler)
Director: John Ford (*Stagecoach*)
Actor: James Stewart (*Mr Smith Goes to Washington*)
Actress: Vivien Leigh (*Gone with the Wind*)
Foreign Film: *Harvest* (Marcel Pagnol)

1940

Film: *The Grapes of Wrath* (John Ford)
Director: John Ford (*The Grapes of Wrath, The Long Voyage Home*)
Actor: Charles Chaplin (*The Great Dictator*: award refused)
Actress: Katharine Hepburn (*The Philadelphia Story*)
Foreign Film: *The Baker's Wife* (Marcel Pagnol)
Special Award: *Fantasia* (Walt Disney)

1941

Film: *Citizen Kane* (Orson Welles)
Director: John Ford (*How Green Was My Valley*)
Actor: Gary Cooper (*Sergeant York*)
Actress: Joan Fontaine (*Suspicion*)

1942

Film: *In Which We Serve* (Noël Coward, David Lean)
Director: John Farrow (*Wake Island*)
Actor: James Cagney (*Yankee Doodle Dandy*)
Actress: Agnes Moorehead (*The Magnificent Ambersons*)

1943

Film: *Watch on the Rhine* (Herbert Shumlin)
Director: George Stevens (*The More the Merrier*)
Actor: Paul Lukas (*Watch on the Rhine*)
Actress: Ida Lupino (*The Hard Way*)

1944

Film: *Going My Way* (Leo McCarey)
Director: Leo McCarey (*Going My Way*)
Actor: Barry Fitzgerald (*Going My Way*)
Actress: Tallulah Bankhead (*Lifeboat*)

1945

Film: *The Lost Weekend* (Billy Wilder)
Director: Billy Wilder (*The Lost Weekend*)
Actor: Ernest Borgnine (*Marty*)
Actress: Ingrid Bergman (*Spellbound, The Bells of St Mary's*)
Special Awards: *The True Glory* (Garson Kanin, Carol Reed); *The Fighting Lady* (William Wyler)

1946

Film: *The Best Years of Our Lives* (William Wyler)
Director: William Wyler (*The Best Years of Our Lives*)
Actor: Laurence Olivier (*Henry V*)
Actress: Celia Johnson (*Brief Encounter*)
Foreign Film: *Open City* (Roberto Rossellini)

1947

Film: *Gentleman's Agreement* (Elia Kazan)
Director: Elia Kazan (*Gentleman's Agreement, Boomerang*)
Actor: William Powell (*Life with Father, The Senator Was Indiscreet*)
Actress: Deborah Kerr (*Black Narcissus, The Adventuress*)
Foreign Film: *To Live in Peace* (Luigi Zampa)

1948

Film: *The Treasure of the Sierra Madre* (John Huston)
Director: John Huston (*The Treasure of the Sierra Madre*)
Actor: Laurence Olivier (*Hamlet*)
Actress: Olivia de Havilland (*The Snake Pit*)
Foreign Film: *Paisan* (Roberto Rossellini)

1949

Film: *All the King's Men* (Robert Rossen)
Director: Carol Reed (*The Fallen Idol*)
Actor: Broderick Crawford (*All the King's Men*)
Actress: Olivia de Havilland (*The Heiress*)
Foreign Film: *The Bicycle Thief* (Vittorio De Sica)

1950

Film: *All About Eve* (Joseph L. Mankiewicz)
Director: Joseph L. Mankiewicz (*All About Eve*)
Actor: Gregory Peck (*Twelve o'Clock High*)
Actress: Bette Davis (*All About Eve*)
Foreign Film: *Ways of Love* (Roberto Rossellini)

1951

Film: *A Streetcar Named Desire* (Elia Kazan)
Director: Elia Kazan (*A Streetcar Named Desire*)
Actor: Arthur Kennedy (*Bright Victory*)
Actress: Vivien Leigh (*A Streetcar Named Desire*)
Foreign Film: *Miracle in Milan* (Vittorio De Sica)

1952

Film: *High Noon* (Fred Zinnemann)
Director: Fred Zinnemann (*High Noon*)
Actor: Ralph Richardson (*Breaking the Sound Barrier*)
Actress: Shirley Booth (*Come Back, Little Sheba*)
Foreign Film: *Forbidden Games* (René Clément)

1953

Film: *From Here to Eternity* (Fred Zinnemann)
Director: Fred Zinnemann (*From Here to Eternity*)
Actor: Burt Lancaster (*From Here to Eternity*)
Actress: Audrey Hepburn (*Roman Holiday*)
Foreign Film: *Justice Is Done* (André Cayette)

1954

Film: *On the Waterfront* (Elia Kazan)
Director: Elia Kazan (*On the Waterfront*)
Actor: Marlon Brando (*On the Waterfront*)
Actress: Grace Kelly (*The Country Girl, Rear Window, Dial M for Murder*)
Foreign Film: *Gate of Hell* (Teinosuke Kinugaza)

1955

Film: *Marty* (Delbert Mann)
Director: David Lean (*Summertime*)
Actor: Ernest Borgnine (*Marty*)
Actress: Anna Magnani (*The Rose Tattoo*)
Foreign Film: *Umberto D* (Vittorio De Sica)

1956

Film: *Around the World in 80 Days* (Michael Anderson)
Director: John Huston (*Moby Dick*)
Actor: Kirk Douglas (*Lust for Life*)
Actress: Ingrid Bergman (*Anastasia*)
Foreign Film: *La Strada* (Federico Fellini)
Screenplay: S. J. Perelman (*Around the World in 80 Days*)

1957

Film: *The Bridge on the River Kwai* (David Lean)
Director: David Lean (*The Bridge on the River Kwai*)
Actor: Alec Guinness (*The Bridge on the River Kwai*)
Actress: Deborah Kerr (*Heaven Knows, Mr Allison*)
Foreign Film: *Gervaise* (René Clément)

1958

Film: *The Defiant Ones* (Stanley Kramer)
Director: Stanley Kramer (*The Defiant Ones*)
Actor: David Niven (*Separate Tables*)
Actress: Susan Hayward (*I Want to Live!*)

Screenplay: Nathan E. Douglas, Harold Jacob Smith (*The Defiant Ones*)
Foreign Film: *My Uncle* (Jacques Tati)

1959

Film: *Ben-Hur* (William Wyler)
Director: Fred Zinnemann (*The Nun's Story*)
Actor: James Stewart (*Anatomy of a Murder*)
Actress: Audrey Hepburn (*The Nun's Story*)
Screenplay: Wendell Mayes (*Anatomy of a Murder*)
Foreign Film: *The 400 Blows* (François Truffaut)

1960

Film: *The Apartment* (Billy Wilder); *Sons and Lovers* (Jack Cardiff)
Director: Billy Wilder (*The Apartment*); Jack Cardiff (*Sons and Lovers*)
Actor: Burt Lancaster (*Elmer Gantry*)
Actress: Deborah Kerr (*The Sundowners*)
Screenplay: Billy Wilder, I. A. L. Diamond (*The Apartment*)
Foreign Film: *Hiroshima, Mon Amour* (Alain Resnais)

1961

Film: *West Side Story* (Robert Wise, Jerome Robbins)
Director: Robert Rossen (*The Hustler*)
Actor: Maximilian Schell (*Judgement at Nuremberg*)
Actress: Sophia Loren (*Two Women*)
Foreign Film: *La Dolce Vita* (Federico Fellini)

1962

No awards were made, because of a newspaper strike

1963

Film: *Tom Jones* (Tony Richardson)
Director: Tony Richardson (*Tom Jones*)
Actor: Albert Finney (*Tom Jones*)
Actress: Patricia Neal (*Hud*)
Foreign Film: *8½* (Federico Fellini)

1964

Film: *My Fair Lady* (George Cukor)
Director: Stanley Kubrick (*Dr Strangelove*)
Actor: Rex Harrison (*My Fair Lady*)
Actress: Kim Stanley (*Seance on a Wet Afternoon*)
Screenplay: Harold Pinter (*The Servant*)
Foreign Film: *That Man from Rio* (Philippe De Broca)

1965

Film: *Darling* (John Schlesinger)
Director: John Schlesinger (*Darling*)
Actor: Oskar Werner (*Ship of Fools*)
Actress: Julie Christie (*Darling*)
Foreign Film: *Juliet of the Spirits* (Federico Fellini)

1966

Film: *A Man for All Seasons* (Fred Zinnemann)
Director: Fred Zinnemann (*A Man for All Seasons*)
Actor: Paul Scofield (*A Man for All Seasons*)
Actress: Elizabeth Taylor (*Who's Afraid of Virginia Woolf?*); Lynn Redgrave (*Georgy Girl*)
Screenplay: Robert Bolt (*A Man for All Seasons*)
Foreign Film: *The Shop on Main Street* (Jan Kadar, Elmar Klos)

1967

Film: *In the Heat of the Night* (Norman Jewison)
Director: Mike Nichols (*The Graduate*)
Actor: Rod Steiger (*In the Heat of the Night*)
Actress: Edith Evans (*The Whisperers*)

Screenplay: David Newman, Robert Benton
  (*Bonnie and Clyde*)
Foreign Film: *La Guerre Est Finie* (Alain Resnais)

1968
Film: *The Lion in Winter* (Anthony Harvey)
Director: Paul Newman (*Rachel, Rachel*)
Actor: Alan Arkin (*The Heart Is a Lonely Hunter*)
Actress: Joanne Woodward (*Rachel, Rachel*)
Screenplay: Lorenzo Semple, Jnr (*Pretty Poison*)
Foreign Film: *War and Peace* (Sergei Bondarchuk)

1969
Film: *Z* (Costa-Gavras)
Director: Costa-Gavras (*Z*)
Actor: Jon Voight (*Midnight Cowboy*)
Actress: Jane Fonda (*They Shoot Horses, Don't
  They?*)
Supporting Actor: Jack Nicholson (*Easy Rider*)
Supporting Actress: Dyan Cannon (*Bob & Carol
  & Ted & Alice*)
Screenplay: Larry Tucker, Paul Mazursky (*Bob &
  Carol & Ted & Alice*)

1970
Film: *Five Easy Pieces* (Bob Rafelson)
Director: Bob Rafelson (*Five Easy Pieces*)
Actor: George C. Scott (*Patton*)
Actress: Glenda Jackson (*Women in Love*)
Supporting Actor: Chief Dan George (*Little Big
  Man*)
Supporting Actress: Karen Black (*Five Easy Pieces*)
Screenplay: Eric Rohmer (*My Night at Maud's*)

1971
Film: *A Clockwork Orange* (Stanley Kubrick)
Director: Stanley Kubrick (*A Clockwork Orange*)
Actor: Gene Hackman (*The French Connection*)
Actress: Jane Fonda (*Klute*)
Supporting Actor: Ben Johnson (*The Last Picture
  Show*)
Supporting Actress: Ellen Burstyn (*The Last Picture
  Show*)
Screenplay: Peter Bogdanovich, Larry McMurtry
  (*The Last Picture Show*); Penelope Gilliatt
  (*Sunday, Bloody Sunday*)

1972
Film: *Cries and Whispers* (Ingmar Bergman)
Director: Ingmar Bergman (*Cries and Whispers*)
Actor: Laurence Olivier (*Sleuth*)
Actress: Liv Ullmann (*Cries and Whispers, The
  Emigrants*)
Supporting Actor: Robert Duvall (*The Godfather*)
Supporting Actress: Jeannie Berlin (*The Heartbreak
  Kid*)
Screenplay: Ingmar Bergman (*Cries and Whispers*)
Special Citation: *The Sorrow and the Pity* (Marcel
  Ophuls)

1973
Film: *Day for Night* (François Truffaut)
Director: François Truffaut (*Day for Night*)
Actor: Marlon Brando (*Last Tango in Paris*)
Actress: Joanne Woodward (*Summer Wishes,
  Winter Dreams*)
Supporting Actor: Robert De Niro (*Bang the Drum
  Slowly*)
Supporting Actress: Valentina Cortese (*Day for
  Night*)
Screenplay: George Lucas, Gloria Katz, Willard
  Huyck (*American Graffiti*)

1974
Film: *Amarcord* (Federico Fellini)
Director: Federico Fellini (*Amarcord*)
Actor: Jack Nicholson (*Chinatown, The Last Detail*)
Actress: Liv Ullmann (*Scenes from a Marriage*)
Supporting Actor: Charles Boyer (*Stavisky*)
Supporting Actress: Valerie Perrine (*Lenny*)
Screenplay: Ingmar Bergman (*Scenes from a
  Marriage*)

1975
Film: *Nashville* (Robert Altman)
Director: Robert Altman (*Nashville*)
Actor: Jack Nicholson (*One Flew over the Cuckoo's
  Nest*)
Actress: Isabelle Adjani (*The Story of Adele H.*)
Supporting Actor: Alan Arkin (*Hearts of the West*)
Supporting Actress: Lily Tomlin (*Nashville*)
Screenplay: François Truffaut, Jean Gruault,
  Suzanne Schiffman (*The Story of Adele H.*)

1976
Film: *All the President's Men* (Alan J. Pakula)
Director: Alan J. Pakula (*All the President's Men*)
Actor: Robert De Niro (*Taxi Driver*)
Actress: Liv Ullmann (*Face to Face*)
Supporting Actor: Jason Robards (*All the President's
  Men*)
Supporting Actress: Talia Shire (*Rocky*)
Screenplay: Paddy Chayefsky (*Network*)

1977
Film: *Annie Hall* (Woody Allen)
Director: Woody Allen (*Annie Hall*)
Actor: John Gielgud (*Providence*)
Actress: Diane Keaton (*Annie Hall*)
Supporting Actor: Maximilian Schell (*Julia*)
Supporting Actress: Sissy Spacek (*Three Women*)
Screenplay: Woody Allen, Marshall Brickman
  (*Annie Hall*)

1978
Film: *The Deer Hunter* (Michael Cimino)
Director: Terrence Malick (*Days of Heaven*)
Actor: Jon Voight (*Coming Home*)
Actress: Ingrid Bergman (*Autumn Sonata*)
Supporting Actor: Christopher Walken (*The Deer
  Hunter*)
Supporting Actress: Colleen Dewhurst (*Interiors*)
Screenplay: Paul Mazursky (*An Unmarried Woman*)
Foreign Film: *Bread and Chocolate* (Franco Brusati)

1979
Film: *Kramer vs Kramer* (Robert Benton)
Director: Woody Allen (*Manhattan*)
Actor: Dustin Hoffman (*Kramer vs Kramer*)
Actress: Sally Field (*Norma Rae*)
Supporting Actor: Melvyn Douglas (*Being There*)
Supporting Actress: Meryl Streep (*Kramer vs
  Kramer, The Seduction of Joe Tynan*)
Screenplay: Steve Tesich (*Breaking Away*)
Foreign Film: *The Tree of Wooden Clogs* (Ermanno
  Olmi)

1980
Film: *Ordinary People* (Robert Redford)
Director: Jonathan Demme (*Melvin and Howard*)
Actor: Robert De Niro (*Raging Bull*)
Actress: Sissy Spacek (*Coal Miner's Daughter*)
Supporting Actor: Joe Pesci (*Raging Bull*)
Supporting Actress: Mary Steenburgen (*Melvin and
  Howard*)
Screenplay: Bo Goldman (*Melvin and Howard*)
Cinematography: Geoffrey Unsworth, Ghislain
  Cloquet (*Tess*)

Foreign Film: *Mon Oncle d'Amérique* (Alain
  Resnais)
Documentary: *Best Boy* (Ira Wohl)

1981
Film: *Reds* (Warren Beatty)
Director: Sidney Lumet (*Prince of the City*)
Actor: Burt Lancaster (*Atlantic City*)
Actress: Glenda Jackson (*Stevie*)
Supporting Actor: John Gielgud (*Arthur*)
Supporting Actress: Mona Washbourne (*Stevie*)
Screenplay: John Guare (*Atlantic City*)
Cinematography: David Watkin (*Chariots of Fire*)
Foreign Film: *Pixote* (Hector Babenco)
Special Prize: *Napoleon* (Abel Gance); Andrzej
  Wajda, Krzysztof Zanussi

1982
Film: *Gandhi* (Richard Attenborough)
Director: Sydney Pollack (*Tootsie*)
Actor: Ben Kingsley (*Gandhi*)
Actress: Meryl Streep (*Sophie's Choice*)
Supporting Actor: John Lithgow (*The World
  According to Garp*)
Supporting Actress: Jessica Lange (*Tootsie*)
Screenplay: Murray Schisgal, Larry Gelbart
  (*Tootsie*)
Cinematography: Nestor Almendros (*Sophie's
  Choice*)
Foreign Film: *Time Stands Still* (Peter Gothar)

1983
Film: *Terms of Endearment* (James L. Brooks)
Director: Ingmar Bergman (*Fanny and Alexander*)
Actor: Robert Duvall (*Tender Mercies*)
Actress: Shirley MacLaine (*Terms of Endearment*)
Supporting Actor: Jack Nicholson (*Terms of
  Endearment*)
Supporting Actress: Linda Hunt (*The Year of Living
  Dangerously*)
Screenplay: Bill Forsyth (*Local Hero*)
Cinematography: Gordon Willis (*Zelig*)
Foreign Film: *Fanny and Alexander* (Ingmar
  Bergman)

1984
Film: *A Passage to India* (David Lean)
Director: David Lean (*A Passage to India*)
Actor: Steve Martin (*All of Me*)
Actress: Peggy Ashcroft (*A Passage to India*)
Supporting Actor: Ralph Richardson (*Greystoke:
  The Legend of Tarzan, Lord of the Apes*)
Supporting Actress: Christine Lahti (*Swing Shift*)
Screenplay: Robert Benton (*Places in the Heart*)
Cinematography: Chris Menges (*The Killing Fields*)
Foreign Film: *A Sunday in the Country* (Bertrand
  Tavernier)
Documentary: *The Times of Harvey Milk* (Robert
  Epstein)

1985
Film: *Prizzi's Honor* (John Huston)
Director: John Huston (*Prizzi's Honor*)
Actor: Jack Nicholson (*Prizzi's Honor*)
Actress: Norma Aleandro (*The Official Story*)
Supporting Actor: Klaus Maria Brandauer (*Out of
  Africa*)
Supporting Actress: Anjelica Huston (*Prizzi's
  Honor*)
Screenplay: Woody Allen (*The Purple Rose of
  Cairo*)
Cinematography: David Watkin (*Out of Africa*)
Foreign Film: *Ran* (Akira Kurosawa)
Documentary: *Shoah* (Claude Lanzmann)

1986

Film: *Hannah and Her Sisters* (Woody Allen)
Director: Woody Allen (*Hannah and Her Sisters*)
Actor: Bob Hoskins (*Mona Lisa*)
Actress: Sissy Spacek (*Crimes of the Heart*)
Supporting Actor: Daniel Day-Lewis (*My Beautiful Laundrette, A Room with a View*)
Supporting Actress: Dianne Wiest (*Hannah and Her Sisters*)
Screenplay: Hanif Kureishi (*My Beautiful Laundrette*)
Cinematography: Tony Pierce-Roberts (*A Room with a View*)
Foreign Film: *The Decline of the American Empire* (Denys Arcand)
Documentary: *Marlene* (Maximilian Schell)

1987

Film: *Broadcast News* (James L. Brooks)
Director: James L. Brooks (*Broadcast News*)
Actor: Jack Nicholson (*The Witches of Eastwick, Ironweed, Broadcast News*)
Actress: Holly Hunter (*Broadcast News*)
Supporting Actor: Morgan Freeman (*Street Smart*)
Supporting Actress: Vanessa Redgrave (*Prick Up Your Ears*)
Screenplay: James L. Brooks (*Broadcast News*)
Cinematography: Vittorio Storaro (*The Last Emperor*)
Foreign Film: *My Life as a Dog* (Lasse Hallstrom)

1988

Film: *The Accidental Tourist* (Lawrence Kasdan)
Director: Chris Menges (*A World Apart*)
Actor: Jeremy Irons (*Dead Ringers*)
Actress: Meryl Streep (*A Cry in the Dark*)
Supporting Actor: Dean Stockwell (*Married to the Mob, Tucker: The Man and His Dream*)
Supporting Actress: Diane Venora (*Bird*)
Screenplay: Ron Shelton (*Bull Durham*)
Cinematography: Henri Alekan (*Wings of Desire*)
Foreign Film: *Women on the Verge of a Nervous Breakdown* (Pedro Almodóvar)
Documentary: *The Thin Blue Line* (Errol Morris)

1989

Film: *My Left Foot* (Jim Sheridan)
Director: Paul Mazursky (*Enemies – a Love Story*)
Actor: Daniel Day-Lewis (*My Left Foot*)
Actress: Michelle Pfeiffer (*The Fabulous Baker Boys*)
Supporting Actor: Alan Alda (*Crimes and Misdemeanors*)
Supporting Actress: Lena Olin (*Enemies – a Love Story*)
Screenplay: Gus Van Sant, Daniel Yost (*Drugstore Cowboy*)
Cinematography: Ernest Dickerson (*Do the Right Thing*)
Foreign Film: *The Story of Women* (Claude Chabrol)
New Director: Kenneth Branagh (*Henry V*)
Documentary: *Roger and Me* (Michael Moore)

1990

Film: *GoodFellas* (Martin Scorsese)
Director: Martin Scorsese (*GoodFellas*)
Actor: Robert De Niro (*GoodFellas, Awakenings*)
Actress: Joanne Woodward (*Mr and Mrs Bridge*)
Supporting Actor: Bruce Davison (*Longtime Companion*)
Supporting Actress: Jennifer Jason Leigh (*Miami Blues, Last Exit to Brooklyn*)
Screenplay: Ruth Prawer Jhabvala (*Mr and Mrs Bridge*)

Cinematography: Vittorio Storaro (*The Sheltering Sky*)
Foreign Film: *The Nasty Girl* (Michael Verhoeven)
New Director: Whit Stillman (*Metropolitan*)

1991

Film: *Silence of the Lambs* (Jonathan Demme)
Director: Jonathan Demme (*Silence of the Lambs*)
Actor: Anthony Hopkins (*Silence of the Lambs*)
Actress: Jodie Foster (*Silence of the Lambs*)
Supporting Actor: Samuel L. Jackson (*Jungle Fever*)
Supporting Actress: Judy Davis (*Naked Lunch, Barton Fink*)
Screenplay: David Cronenberg (*Naked Lunch*)
Cinematography: Roger Deakins (*Barton Fink*)
Foreign Film: *Europa, Europa* (Agnieszka Holland)
New Director: John Singleton (*Boyz N the Hood*)
Documentary: *Paris Is Burning* (Jennie Livingston)

1992

Film: *The Player* (Robert Altman)
Director: Robert Altman (*The Player*)
Actor: Denzel Washington (*Malcolm X*)
Actress: Emma Thompson (*Howards End*)
Supporting Actor: Gene Hackman (*Unforgiven*)
Supporting Actress: Miranda Richardson (*The Crying Game, Damage, Enchanted April*)
Screenplay: Neil Jordan (*The Crying Game*)
Cinematography: Jean Lapine (*The Player*)
Foreign Film: *Raise the Red Lantern* (Zhang Yimou)
New Director: Allison Anders (*Gas Food Lodging*)
Documentary: *Brother's Keeper* (Joe Berlinger, Bruce Sinofsky)

1993

Film: *Schindler's List* (Steven Spielberg)
Director: Jane Campion (*The Piano*)
Actor: David Thewlis (*Naked*)
Actress: Holly Hunter (*The Piano*)
Supporting Actor: Ralph Fiennes (*Schindler's List*)
Supporting Actress: Gong Li (*Farewell, My Concubine*)
Screenplay: Jane Campion (*The Piano*)
Cinematography: Janusz Kaminski (*Schindler's List*)
Foreign Film: *Farewell, My Concubine* (Chen Kaige)
Documentary: *Visions of Light, the Art of Cinematography* (Arnold Glassman, Todd McCarthy, Stuart Samuels)

1994

Film: *Quiz Show* (Robert Redford)
Director: Quentin Tarantino (*Pulp Fiction*)
Actor: Paul Newman (*Nobody's Fool*)
Actress: Linda Fiorentino (*The Last Seduction*)
Supporting Actor: Martin Landau (*Ed Wood*)
Supporting Actress: Dianne Wiest (*Bullets over Broadway*)
Screenplay: Quentin Tarantino (*Pulp Fiction*)
Cinematography: Stefan Czapsky (*Ed Wood*)
Foreign Film: *Red* (Krzysztof Kiéslowski)
New Director: Darnel Martin (*I Like It Like That*)
Documentary: *Hoop Dreams* (Steve James)
Special Award: Jean-Luc Godard

1995

Film: *Leaving Las Vegas* (Mike Figgis)
Director: Ang Lee (*Sense and Sensibility*)
Actor: Nicolas Cage (*Leaving Las Vegas*)
Actress: Jennifer Jason Leigh (*Georgia*)
Supporting Actor: Kevin Spacey (*Seven, The Usual Suspects, Swimming with Sharks*)
Supporting Actress: Mira Sorvino (*Mighty Aphrodite*)

Screenplay: Emma Thompson (*Sense and Sensibility*)
Cinematography: Le Yue (*Shanghai Triad*)
Foreign Film: *Shanghai Triad* (Zhang Yimou)
New Director: Chris Noonan (*Babe*)
Documentary: *Crumb* (Terry Zwigoff)

1996

Film: *Fargo* (Joel Coen)
Director: Lars Von Trier (*Breaking the Waves*)
Actor: Geoffrey Rush (*Shine*)
Actress: Emily Watson (*Breaking the Waves*)
Supporting Actor: Harry Belafonte (*Kansas City*)
Supporting Actress: Courtney Love (*The People vs Larry Flynt*)
Screenplay: Albert Brooks, Monica Johnson (*Mother*)
Cinematography: Robby Muller (*Breaking the Waves, Dead Man*)
Foreign Film: *The White Balloon* (Jafar Panahi)
First Film: *Big Night* (Stanley Tucci, Campbell Scott)
Documentary: *When We Were Kings* (Leon Gast)

1997

Film: *LA Confidential* (Curtis Hanson)
Director: Curtis Hanson (*LA Confidential*)
Actor: Peter Fonda (*Ulee's Gold*)
Actress: Julie Christie (*Afterglow*)
Supporting Actor: Burt Reynolds (*Boogie Nights*)
Supporting Actress: Joan Cusack (*In and Out*)
Screenplay: Curtis Hanson, Brian Helgeland (*LA Confidential*)
Cinematography: Roger Deakins (*Kundun*)
Foreign Film: *Ponette* (Jacques Doillon)
First Film: *In the Company of Men* (Neil LaBute)
Documentary: *Fast, Cheap and Out of Control* (Errol Morris)

1998

Film: *Saving Private Ryan* (Steven Spielberg)
Director: Terrence Malick (*The Thin Red Line*)
Actor: Nick Nolte (*Affliction*)
Actress: Cameron Diaz (*There's Something about Mary*)
Supporting Actor: Bill Murray (*Rushmore*)
Supporting Actress: Lisa Kudrow (*The Opposite of Sex*)
Screenplay: Tom Stoppard, Marc Norman (*Shakespeare in Love*)
Cinematography: John Toll (*The Thin Red Line*)
Foreign Film: *Celebration/Festen* (Thomas Vinterberg)
First Film: *Love and Death in Long Island* (Richard Kwietniowski)
Documentary: *The Farm* (Jonathan Stack, Liz Garbus, Wilbert Rideau)

Los Angeles Film Critics Association Awards

The Los Angeles film critics, who work close to Hollywood, formed an association in 1975. Their main awards have been:

1975

Film: *Dog Day Afternoon* (Sidney Lumet); *One Flew over the Cuckoo's Nest* (Milos Forman)
Foreign Film: *And Now My Love* (Claude Lelouch)
Actor: Al Pacino (*Dog Day Afternoon*)
Actress: Florinda Bolkan (*A Brief Vacation*)
Director: Sidney Lumet (*Dog Day Afternoon*)
Screenplay: Joan Tewkesbury (*Nashville*)
Cinematography: John Alcott (*Barry Lyndon*)
Special Award: *Love among the Ruins* (George Cukor)

1976

Film: *Network* (Sidney Lumet); *Rocky* (John G. Avildsen)
Foreign Film: *Face to Face* (Ingmar Bergman)
Actor: Robert De Niro (*Taxi Driver*)
Actress: Liv Ullmann (*Face to Face*)
Director: Sidney Lumet (*Network*)
Screenplay: Paddy Chayefsky (*Network*)
Cinematography: Haskell Wexler (*Bound for Glory*)
Music: Bernard Herrmann (*Taxi Driver*)
Special Award: Marcel Ophuls (*The Memory of Justice*)
Life Award: Allan Dwan
New Generation: Martin Scorsese, Jodie Foster (*Taxi Driver*)

1977

Film: *Star Wars* (George Lucas)
Foreign Film: *That Obscure Object of Desire* (Luis Buñuel)
Actor: Richard Dreyfuss (*The Goodbye Girl*)
Actress: Shelley Duvall (*3 Women*)
Supporting Actor: Jason Robards (*Julia*)
Supporting Actress: Vanessa Redgrave (*Julia*)
Director: Herbert Ross (*The Turning Point*)
Screenplay: Woody Allen, Marshall Brickman (*Annie Hall*)
Cinematography: Douglas Slocombe (*Julia*)
Music: John Williams (*Star Wars*)
Special Award: Barbara Kopple (*Harlan County, USA*)
Life Achievement: King Vidor
New Generation: Joan Micklin Silver (*Between the Lines*)

1978

Film: *Coming Home* (Hal Ashby)
Foreign Film: *Madame Rosa* (Moshe Mizrahi)
Actor: Jon Voight (*Coming Home*)
Actress: Jane Fonda (*Coming Home, Comes a Horseman, California Suite*)
Supporting Actor: Robert Morley (*Who Is Killing the Great Chefs of Europe?*)
Supporting Actress: Maureen Stapleton (*Interiors*); Mona Washbourne (*Stevie*)
Director: Michael Cimino (*The Deer Hunter*)
Screenplay: Paul Mazursky (*An Unmarried Woman*)
Cinematography: Nestor Almendros (*Days of Heaven*)
Music: Giorgio Moroder (*Midnight Express*)
Life Achievement: Orson Welles
New Generation: Gary Busey (*The Buddy Holly Story*)

1979

Film: *Kramer vs Kramer* (Robert Benton)
Foreign Film: *Soldier of Orange* (Paul Verhoeven)
Actor: Dustin Hoffman (*Kramer vs Kramer*)
Actress: Sally Field (*Norma Rae*)
Supporting Actor: Melvyn Douglas (*Being There, The Seduction of Joe Tynan*)
Supporting Actress: Meryl Streep (*Kramer vs Kramer, Manhattan, The Seduction of Joe Tynan*)
Director: Robert Benton (*Kramer vs Kramer*)
Screenplay: Robert Benton (*Kramer vs Kramer*)
Cinematography: Caleb Deschanel (*The Black Stallion*)
Music: Carmine Coppola (*The Black Stallion*)
Life Achievement: John Huston
New Generation: John Carpenter (*Halloween*)

1980

Film: *Raging Bull* (Martin Scorsese)
Foreign Film: *The Tin Drum* (Volker Schlöndorff)
Actor: Robert De Niro (*Raging Bull*)
Actress: Sissy Spacek (*Coal Miner's Daughter*)
Supporting Actor: Timothy Hutton (*Ordinary People*)
Supporting Actress: Mary Steenburgen (*Melvin and Howard*)
Director: Roman Polanski (*Tess*)
Screenplay: John Sayles (*Return of the Secaucus 7*)
Cinematography: Ghislain Cloquet, Geoffrey Unsworth (*Tess*)
Music: Ry Cooder (*The Long Riders*)
Experimental/Independent Film: *Journeys from Berlin* (Yvonne Rainer); *Demon Lover Diary* (Joel Demot)
Life Achievement: Robert Mitchum
New Generation: Carroll Ballard (*The Black Stallion*)

1981

Film: *Atlantic City* (Louis Malle)
Foreign Film: *Pixote* (Hector Babenco)
Actor: Burt Lancaster (*Atlantic City*)
Actress: Meryl Streep (*The French Lieutenant's Woman*)
Supporting Actor: John Gielgud (*Arthur*)
Supporting Actress: Maureen Stapleton (*Reds*)
Director: Warren Beatty (*Reds*)
Screenplay: John Guare (*Atlantic City*)
Cinematography: Vittorio Storaro (*Reds*)
Music: Randy Newman (*Ragtime*)
Experimental/Independent Film: *The Art of Worldly Wisdom* (Bruce Elder)
Special Award: Kevin Brownlow (*Napoleon*)
Life Achievement: Barbara Stanwyck
New Generation: John Guare (*Atlantic City*)

1982

Film: *E.T. – the Extra-Terrestrial* (Steven Spielberg)
Foreign Film: *The Road Warrior/Mad Max 2* (George Miller)
Actor: Ben Kingsley (*Gandhi*)
Actress: Meryl Streep (*Sophie's Choice*)
Supporting Actor: John Lithgow (*The World According to Garp*)
Supporting Actress: Glenn Close (*The World According to Garp*)
Director: Steven Spielberg (*E.T. – the Extra-Terrestrial*)
Screenplay: Larry Gelbart, Murray Schisgal (*Tootsie*)
Cinematography: Jordan Cronenweth (*Blade Runner*)
Music: James Horner & the Busboys (*48 Hrs*)
Experimental/Independent Film: *Chan Is Missing* (Wayne Wang)
Special Award: Carlo Rimbaldi (*E.T. – the Extra-Terrestrial*)
Life Achievement: Robert Preston
New Generation: Melissa Mathison (*E.T. – the Extra-Terrestrial*)

1983

Film: *Terms of Endearment* (James L. Brooks)
Foreign Film: *Fanny and Alexander* (Ingmar Bergman)
Actor: Robert Duvall (*Tender Mercies*)
Actress: Shirley MacLaine (*Terms of Endearment*)
Supporting Actor: Jack Nicholson (*Terms of Endearment*)
Supporting Actress: Linda Hunt (*The Year of Living Dangerously*)
Director: James L. Brooks (*Terms of Endearment*)
Screenplay: James L. Brooks (*Terms of Endearment*)
Cinematography: Sven Nykvist (*Fanny and Alexander*)
Music: Philip Glass (*Koyaanisqatsi*)
Experimental/Independent Film: *So Is This* (Michael Snow)
Life Achievement: Myrna Loy
New Generation: Sean Penn (*Bad Boys, Fast Times at Ridgemont High*)

1984

Film: *Amadeus* (Milos Forman)
Foreign Film: *The Fourth Man* (Paul Verhoeven)
Actor: F. Murray Abraham (*Amadeus*); Albert Finney (*Under the Volcano*)
Actress: Kathleen Turner (*Crimes of Passion, Romancing the Stone*)
Supporting Actor: Adolph Caesar (*A Soldier's Story*)
Supporting Actress: Peggy Ashcroft (*A Passage to India*)
Director: Milos Forman (*Amadeus*)
Screenplay: Peter Shaffer (*Amadeus*)
Cinematography: Chris Menges (*The Killing Fields*)
Music: Ennio Morricone (*Once Upon a Time in America*)
Experimental/Independent Film: George Kuchar (oeuvre)
Life Achievement: Rouben Mamoulian
New Generation: Alan Rudolph (*Choose Me*)
Special Award: Andrew Sarris; François Truffaut

1985

Film: *Brazil* (Terry Gilliam)
Foreign Film: *Ran* (Akira Kurosawa); *The Official Story* (Luis Puenzo)
Actor: William Hurt (*Kiss of the Spider Woman*)
Actress: Meryl Streep (*Out of Africa*)
Supporting Actor: John Gielgud (*Plenty, The Shooting Party*)
Supporting Actress: Anjelica Huston (*Prizzi's Honor*)
Director: Terry Gilliam (*Brazil*)
Screenplay: Terry Gilliam, Charles McKeown, Tom Stoppard (*Brazil*)
Cinematography: David Watkin (*Out of Africa*)
Music: Toru Takemitsu (*Ran*)
Experimental/Independent Film: *Fear of Emptiness* (Rosa Von Praunheim)
Life Achievement: Akira Kurosawa
New Generation: Laura Dern (*Mask, Smooth Talk*)
Special Award: Claude Lanzmann (*Shoah*)

1986

Film: *Hannah and Her Sisters* (Woody Allen)
Foreign Film: *Vagabond* (Agnès Varda)
Actor: Bob Hoskins (*Mona Lisa*)
Actress: Sandrine Bonnaire (*Vagabond*)
Supporting Actor: Dennis Hopper (*Blue Velvet, Hoosiers*)
Supporting Actress: Cathy Tyson (*Mona Lisa*)
Director: David Lynch (*Blue Velvet*)
Screenplay: Woody Allen (*Hannah and Her Sisters*)
Cinematography: Chris Menges (*The Mission*)
Music: Herbie Hancock, Dexter Gordon (*Round Midnight*)
Experimental/Independent Film: *Magdalena Criaga* (Nina Menkes); *He Stands in the Desert Counting the Seconds of His Life* (Jonas Mekas)
Life Achievement: John Cassavetes
New Generation: Spike Lee

1987

Film: *Hope and Glory* (John Boorman)
Foreign Film: *Au Revoir, les Enfants* (Louis Malle)

Actor: Steve Martin (*Roxanne*); Jack Nicholson (*Ironweed, The Witches of Eastwick*)
Actress: Holly Hunter (*Broadcast News*); Sally Kirkland (*Anna*)
Supporting Actor: Morgan Freeman (*Street Smart*)
Supporting Actress: Olympia Dukakis (*Moonstruck*)
Director: John Boorman (*Hope and Glory*)
Screenplay: John Boorman (*Hope and Glory*)
Cinematography: Vittorio Storaro (*The Last Emperor*)
Music: David Byrne, Ryuichi Sakamoto, Cong Su (*The Last Emperor*)
Experimental/Independent Film: *Mala Noche* (Gus Van Sant)
Life Achievement: Joel McCrea; Samuel Fuller
New Generation: Pedro Almodóvar
Special Award: Pierre Sauvage (*Weapons of the Spirit*)

1988

Film: *Little Dorrit* (Christine Edzard)
Foreign Film: *Wings of Desire* (Wim Wenders)
Actor: Tom Hanks (*Big, Punchline*)
Actress: Christine Lahti (*Running on Empty*)
Supporting Actor: Alec Guinness (*Little Dorrit*)
Supporting Actress: Geneviève Bujold (*Dead Ringers, The Moderns*)
Director: David Cronenberg (*Dead Ringers*)
Screenplay: Ron Shelton (*Bull Durham*)
Cinematography: Henri Alekan (*Wings of Desire*)
Music: Mark Isham (*The Moderns*)
Documentary: *Hotel Terminus: The Life and Times of Klaus Barbie* (Marcel Ophuls)
Experimental/Independent Film: *The Last of England* (Derek Jarman); *Amerika* (Al Razutis)
Life Achievement: Don Siegel
New Generation: Mira Nair
Special Award: *Who Framed Roger Rabbit?* (Robert Zemeckis)

1989

Film: *Do the Right Thing* (Spike Lee)
Foreign Film: *Distant Voices, Still Lives* (Terence Davies); *The Story of Women* (Claude Chabrol)
Actor: Daniel Day-Lewis (*My Left Foot*)
Actress: Andie MacDowell (*sex, lies and videotape*); Michelle Pfeiffer (*The Fabulous Baker Boys*)
Supporting Actor: Danny Aiello (*Do the Right Thing*)
Supporting Actress: Brenda Fricker (*My Left Foot*)
Director: Spike Lee (*Do the Right Thing*)
Screenplay: Gus Van Sant, Daniel Yost (*Drugstore Cowboy*)
Cinematography: Michael Ballhaus (*The Fabulous Baker Boys*)
Music: Bill Lee (*Do the Right Thing*)
Documentary: *Roger & Me* (Michael Moore)
Animation: *The Little Mermaid* (John Musker, Ron Clements)
Experimental/Independent Film: *The Long Weekend (o' Despair)* (Gregg Araki)
Life Achievement: Stanley Donen
New Generation: Laura San Giacomo (*sex, lies and videotape*)
Special Award: Margaret Herrick Library of the Academy of Motion Film Arts & Sciences

1990

Film: *GoodFellas* (Martin Scorsese)
Foreign Film: *Life and Nothing But* (Bertrand Tavernier)
Actor: Jeremy Irons (*Reversal of Fortune*)
Best Actress: Anjelica Huston (*The Grifters, The Witches*)

Supporting Actor: Joe Pesci (*GoodFellas*)
Supporting Actress: Lorraine Bracco (*GoodFellas*)
Director: Martin Scorsese (*GoodFellas*)
Screenplay: Nicholas Kazan (*Reversal of Fortune*)
Cinematography: Michael Ballhaus (*GoodFellas*)
Music: Richard Horowitz, Ryuichi Sakamoto (*The Sheltering Sky*)
Documentary: *Paris Is Burning* (Jennie Livingston)
Animation: *The Rescuers Down Under* (Hendel Butoy, Mike Gabriel)
Experimental/Independent Film: *Tongues Untied* (Marlon Riggs)
Life Achievement: Chuck Jones; Blake Edwards
New Generation: Jane Campion (*Sweetie*)
Special Award: Charles Burnett (*To Sleep with Anger*)

1991

Film: *Bugsy* (Barry Levinson)
Foreign Film: *La Belle Noiseuse* (Jacques Rivette)
Actor: Nick Nolte (*Prince of Tides*)
Actress: Mercedes Ruehl (*The Fisher King*)
Supporting Actor: Michael Lerner (*Barton Fink*)
Supporting Actress: Jane Horrocks (*Life Is Sweet*)
Director: Barry Levinson (*Bugsy*)
Screenplay: James Toback (*Bugsy*)
Cinematography: Roger Deakins (*Barton Fink, Homicide*)
Music: Zbigniew Preisner (*The Double Life of Véronique, At Play in the Fields of the Lord, Europa, Europa*)
Documentary: *American Dream* (Barbara Kopple)
Animation: *Beauty and the Beast* (Gary Trousdale, Kirk Wise)
Experimental/Independent Film: *All the Vermeers in New York* (Jon Jost, Henry Rosenthal)
Special Award: National Film Board of Canada
Life Achievement: Budd Boetticher
New Generation: Carl Franklin (*One False Move*)

1992

Film: *Unforgiven* (Clint Eastwood)
Foreign Film: *The Crying Game* (Neil Jordan)
Actor: Clint Eastwood (*Unforgiven*)
Actress: Emma Thompson (*Howards End*)
Supporting Actor: Gene Hackman (*Unforgiven*)
Supporting Actress: Judy Davis (*Husbands and Wives*)
Director: Clint Eastwood (*Unforgiven*)
Screenplay: David Webb Peoples (*Unforgiven*)
Cinematography: Zhao Fei (*Raise the Red Lantern*)
Music: Zbigniew Preisner (*Damage*)
Documentary: *Black Harvest* (Bob Connolly, Robin Anderson); *Threat* (Stefan Jarl)
Animation: *Aladdin* (John Musker, Ron Clements)
Experimental/Independent Film: *It Wasn't Love* (Sadie Benning)

1993

Film: *Schindler's List* (Steven Spielberg)
Foreign Film: *Farewell My Concubine* (Chen Kaige)
Actor: Anthony Hopkins (*Shadowlands, Remains of the Day*)
Actress: Holly Hunter (*The Piano*)
Supporting Actor: Tommy Lee Jones (*The Fugitive*)
Supporting Actress: Rosie Perez (*Fearless*); Anna Paquin (*The Piano*)
Director: Jane Campion (*The Piano*)
Screenplay: Jane Campion (*The Piano*)
Cinematography: Janusz Kaminski (*Schindler's List*); Stuart Dryburgh (*The Piano*)
Music: Zbigniew Preisner (*Three Colours: Blue, The Secret Garden, Olivier, Olivier*)
Production Design: Allan Starski (*Schindler's List*)

Documentary: *It's All True* (Orson Welles, Myron Meisel, Bill Krohn, Richard Wilson)
Animation: *The Mighty River* (Frederic Back)
Experimental/Independent Film: *Silverlake Live: The View from Here* (Tom Joslin, Peter Friedman)
Life Achievement: John Alton
New Generation: Leonardo DiCaprio (*What's Eating Gilbert Grape?*)

1994

Film: *Pulp Fiction* (Quentin Tarantino)
Foreign Film: *Three Colours: Red* (Krzysztof Kiéslowski)
Actor: John Travolta (*Pulp Fiction*)
Actress: Jessica Lange (*Blue Sky*)
Supporting Actor: Martin Landau (*Ed Wood*)
Supporting Actress: Dianne Wiest (*Bullets over Broadway*)
Director: Quentin Tarantino (*Pulp Fiction*)
Screenplay: Quentin Tarantino, Roger Avary (*Pulp Fiction*)
Cinematography: Stefan Czapsky (*Ed Wood*)
Music: Howard Shore (*Ed Wood*)
Production Design: Dennis Gassner (*The Hudsucker Proxy*)
Documentary: *Hoop Dreams* (Steve James, Peter Gilbert)
Animation: Roger Allers, Rob Minkoff (*The Lion King*)
Experimental/Independent Film: *Remembrance of Things Fast* (John Maybury)
Special Award: Pauline Kael
Life Achievement: Billy Wilder
New Generation: John Dahl (*The Last Seduction*)

1995

Film: *Leaving Las Vegas* (Mike Figgis)
Foreign Film: *Wild Reeds* (André Téchiné)
Actor: Nicolas Cage (*Leaving Las Vegas*)
Actress: Elisabeth Shue (*Leaving Las Vegas*)
Supporting Actor: Don Cheadle (*Devil in a Blue Dress*)
Supporting Actress: Joan Allen (*Nixon*)
Director: Mike Figgis (*Leaving Las Vegas*)
Screenplay: Emma Thompson (*Sense and Sensibility*)
Cinematography: Lu Yue (*Shanghai Triad*)
Music: Patrick Doyle (*A Little Princess*)
Production Design: Bo Welch (*A Little Princess*)
Documentary: *Crumb* (Terry Zwigoff)
Animation: John Lasseter (*Toy Story*)
Experimental/Independent Film: *From the Journals of Jean Seberg* (Mark Rappaport)
Life Achievement: André De Toth
New Generation: Alfonso Cuaron (*A Little Princess*)

1996

Film: *Secrets and Lies* (Mike Leigh)
Foreign Film: *La Cérémonie* (Claude Chabrol)
Actor: Geoffrey Rush (*Shine*)
Actress: Brenda Blethyn (*Secrets and Lies*)
Supporting Actor: Edward Norton (*Everyone Says I Love You, The People vs Larry Flynt, Primal Fear*)
Supporting Actress: Barbara Hershey (*The Portrait of a Lady*)
Director: Mike Leigh (*Secrets and Lies*)
Screenplay: Ethan and Joel Coen (*Fargo*)
Cinematography: Chris Menges (*Michael Collins*); John Seale (*The English Patient*)
Music: Hal Willner and the Hey Hey Club Musicians (*Kansas City*)

Production Design: Brian Morris (*Evita*); Janet Patterson (*The Portrait of a Lady*)

Documentary: *When We Were Kings* (Leon Gast)

Animation: Nick Park (*Creature Comforts, A Grand Day Out, The Wrong Trousers, A Close Shave*)

Experimental/Independent Film: *Sonic Outlaws* (Craig Baldwin)

Life Achievement: Roger Corman

New Generation: Emily Watson (*Breaking the Waves*)

1997

Film: *LA Confidential* (Curtis Hanson)

Foreign Film: *La Promesse* (Jean-Pierre Dardenne, Luc Dardenne)

Actor: Robert Duvall (*The Apostle*)

Actress: Helena Bonham Carter (*The Wings of the Dove*)

Supporting Actor: Burt Reynolds (*Boogie Nights*)

Supporting Actress: Julianne Moore (*Boogie Nights*)

Director: Curtis Hanson (*LA Confidential*)

Screenplay: Curtis Hanson, Brian Helgeland (*LA Confidential*)

Cinematography: Dante Spinotti (*LA Confidential*)

Music: Philip Glass (*Kundun*)

Production Design: Peter Lamont (*Titanic*)

Animation: *The Spirit of Christmas* (Trey Parker, Matt Stone); *Hercules* (John Musker, Ron Clements)

Documentary: *Riding the Rails* (Michael Uys, Lexy Lovell)

Special Award: Peter Bogdanovich

New Generation: Paul Thomas Anderson (*Hard Eight, Boogie Nights*)

1998

Film: *Saving Private Ryan* (Steven Spielberg)

Foreign Film: *Celebration/Festen* (Thomas Vinterberg)

Actor: Ian McKellen (*Gods and Monsters*)

Actress: Ally Sheedy (*High Art*); Fernanda Montenegro (*Central Station*)

Supporting Actor: Billy Bob Thornton (*A Simple Plan*); Bill Murray (*Rushmore, Wild Things*)

Supporting Actress: Joan Allen (*Pleasantville*)

Director: Steven Spielberg (*Saving Private Ryan*)

Screenplay: Warren Beatty, Jeremy Pisker (*Bulworth*)

Cinematography: Janusz Kaminski (*Saving Private Ryan*)

Music: Elliot Goldenthal (*The Butcher Boy*)

Production Design: Jeannine Oppewall (*Pleasantville*)

Animation: *A Bug's Life* (John Lasseter, Andrew Stanton); *T.R.A.N.S.I.T.* (Piet Kroon)

Documentary: *The Farm* (Jonathan Stack, Liz Garbus, Wilbert Rideau)

Experimental/Independent Film: Elizabeth Subrin (*Shuttle*)

New Generaton: Wes Anderson (*Rushmore, Bottle Rocket*)

9
Movie Books and Periodicals

This is given because it has been requested; but it is given with some diffidence. The best books for you will depend upon your particular interest. As autobiographies, biographies, and other relevant books are covered in the *Companion*'s individual entries, what follows is a basic list of books and periodicals covering more general aspects of cinema. Those that are starred are particularly recommended as encapsulating a feeling about the movies wider than their own particular subject.

Many will be out of print, so the publisher and publication date (usually taken from my own copies and therefore not necessarily the first edition) are given in most instances to assist in tracking them down. There are specialist bookshops that can, at some cost, supply second-hand copies, and many will attempt to find out-of-print books for customers for a nominal service charge. Probably the best bookshops are the Cinema Bookshop in London's Great Russell Street, the BFI and MOMI bookshops in London's National Film Theatre and Museum of the Moving Image, and Larry Edmunds' Bookshop on Los Angeles's Hollywood Boulevard, but there are many other general shops with a good selection of new and second-hand film books.

Annual Guides

BFI Film and Television Handbook (British Film Institute). Digest of film and television production in Britain, produced by the British Film Institute.

Film Review, F. Maurice Speed and (since 1989) James Cameron Wilson (W. H. Allen). Reviews and credits of films released in Britain during the year, together with general essays, film books of the year, obituaries, etc. First published 1945.

Halliwell's Film Guide, ed. John Walker (HarperCollins). Reviews and star ratings for 20,000 films, together with technical and creative production credits and critics' comments, UK and US video, laser disc, video CD, and soundtrack availability, and index to four-star films. First published 1977.

International Motion Picture Almanac (Quigley Publications). Provides a who's who and information on the movie industry, from a US perspective. First published 1930.

Leonard Maltin's Movie and Video Guide (Plume). Reviews and star ratings for around 20,000 films, with details of director and cast, US video and laser disc availability, and index of leading directors and stars. First published 1969.

Projections, ed. John Boorman and Walter Donohue (Faber & Faber). Essays by 'film-makers on film-making'. First published 1992.

Screen World, ed. John Willis (Applause). A pictorial and statistical record, together with credits, of the year's releases in the USA. First published 1949.

Variety International Film Guide, ed. Peter Cowie (Hamlyn). Reports on film-making around the world. First published 1964.

Variety Movie Guide, ed. Derek Elley (Hamlyn). Reprints edited reviews from the trade newspaper for around 7,500 films, including key technical and creative credits, UK and US video and laser disc availability, and an index of directors. First published 1992.

Virgin Film Guide, ed. James Monaco and the editors of *Baseline* (Virgin). Reviews and star ratings for around 3,500 films, together with technical and production credits, classification by genre, the Motion Picture Association of America rating and the British Board of Film Classification certificate, and an index of directors. First published 1992.

Reference

A–Z of Movie Directors, Ronald Bergan (Proteus, 1982).

The American Film Institute Catalog: Feature Films 1921–1930, ed. Kenneth W. Munden (Bowker, 1971).

The American Movies Reference Book: The Sound Era, ed. Paul Michael (Prentice Hall, 1969).

A Biographical Dictionary of the Cinema, David Thomson (Secker & Warburg, 1980).

British Film Actors' Credits, 1895–1987, Scott Palmer (St James Press, 1988).

The British Film Catalogue, Denis Gifford (David & Charles, 1985).

Character People, Ken D. Jones, Arthur F. McClure, and Alfred E. Twomey (Citadel Press, 1976).

Cinema: A Critical Dictionary Vols 1–2, ed. Richard Roud (Secker & Warburg, 1980).

The Complete Film Dictionary, Ira Konigsberg (Bloomsbury, 1988).

Cult Movie Stars, Danny Peary (Simon & Schuster, 1991).

Dictionary of Film Makers, Georges Sadoul, translated and updated by Peter Morris (University of California, 1972).

The Encyclopedia of Animated Cartoons, Jeff Lenburg (Facts on File, 1991).

Encyclopedia of European Cinema, ed. Ginette Vincendeau (Cassell/BFI, 1995).

The Encyclopedia of Film, James Monaco and the editors of *Baseline* (Perigee, 1991).

The Encyclopedia of Hollywood, Scott Siegel and Barbara Siegel (Avon Books, 1990).

The Encyclopedia of Monsters, Jeff Rovin (Facts on File, 1989).

The Encyclopedia of the Musical Film, Stanley Green (OUP, 1981).

Fashion in Film, ed. Regine and Peter W. Engelmeier (Prestel, 1997).

Film Fanatics' Guide, David Jones (Merlin, 1988).

Filmmaking on the Fringe: The Good, the Bad and the Deviant Directors, Maitland McDonagh (Citadel, 1995).

Focal Encyclopaedia of Film Techniques (Focal Press, 1969).

The Guinness Book of Movie Facts and Feats, Patrick Robinson (Guinness Publishing, fifth edition, 1993).

The Great Movie Stars Vols 1–3, David Shipman (various, 1970/1991).

Hollywood Musicals Year by Year, Stanley Green (Hal Leonard, 1990).

The Illustrated Directory of Film Character Actors, David Quinlan (Batsford, 1985).

The Illustrated Encyclopedia of Cartoon Animals, Jeff Rovin (Prentice Hall, 1991).

The International Dictionary of Films and Filmmakers Vols 1–4, ed. Nicholas Thomas (St James Press, 1992).

The International Encyclopedia of Film, ed. Roger Manvell (Rainbird, 1972).

The International Film Encyclopedia, Ephraim Katz (Macmillan, 1980).

Leonard Maltin's Movie Encyclopedia (Plume, 1994).

The Movie Directors Story, Joel W. Finler (Octopus, 1985).

Movie Parade, Paul Rotha (Studio, 1936).

Nonfiction Film: A Critical History (Indiana University Press, 1993).

The Oxford Companion to Film, ed. Liz-Anne Bawden (OUP, 1976).

The Oxford History of World Cinema, ed Geoffrey Nowell-Smith (OUP, 1996).

The Picturegoer's Who's Who and Encyclopaedia of the Screen Today (Odhams Press, 1933).

Quinlan's Illustrated Directory of Film Comedy Stars, David Quinlan (Batsford, 1992).

Quinlan's Illustrated Directory of Film Stars, David Quinlan (Batsford, third edition, 1991).

Quinlan's Illustrated Guide to Film Directors, David Quinlan (Batsford, 1983).

Reel Women: Pioneers of the Cinema, 1896 to the Present, Ally Acker (Batsford, 1991).

Variety's Who's Who in Showbusiness, ed. Mike Kaplan (Bowker, revised edition, 1989).

Who Played Who on the Screen, Roy Pickard (Batsford, 1988).

Who Was Who on Screen, Evelyn Mack Truitt (Bowker, 1984).

Who's Who in Hollywood Vols 1–2, David Ragan (Facts on File, 1992).

Who's Who of the Horrors and Other Fantasy Films, David J. Hogan (Barnes, 1980).

Women in Film: An International Guide, ed. Annette Kuhn with Susannah Radstone (Fawcett Columbine, 1990).

World Film Encyclopedia: A Universal Screen Guide, ed. Clarence Winchester (Amalgamated Press, 1933).

Histories

The American Film Industry: An Historical Dictionary, Anthony Slide (Limelight, 1990).

The American Movie, William K. Everson (Atheneum, 1963).

The American Silent Film, William K. Everson (OUP, 1978).

Archaeology of the Cinema, C. W. Ceram (Thames & Hudson, 1965).

Archaeology of the Cinema, K. W. Marek (Harcourt, Brace, 1965).

The Best Remaining Seats, Ben M. Hall (Da Capo Press, 1988).

The British Film Collection 1896–1984, Patricia Warren (Elm Tree Books, 1984).

The Chronicle of the Movies, ed. Julian Brown (Hamlyn, 1991).

Cinema: The First Hundred Years, David Shipman (Weidenfeld & Nicolson, 1993).

A Concise History of the Cinema Vols 1–2, ed. Peter Cowie (Zwemmer/Barnes, 1971).

The Contemporary Cinema, Penelope Houston (Penguin, 1963).

Early American Cinema, Anthony Slide (Zwemmer, 1971).

Film: An International History of the Medium, Robert Sklar (Thames & Hudson, 1993).

The Film Till Now, Paul Rotha and Richard Griffith (Spring Books, 1967).

Flashback: A Brief History of Film, Louis Giannetti and Scott Eyman (Prentice Hall, 1986).

The History of Movie Photography, Brian Coe (Eastview, 1981).

The History of the British Film 1896–1906, Rachael Low and Roger Manvell (Allen & Unwin, 1948).

The History of the British Film 1906–1914, Rachael Low (Allen & Unwin).

The History of the British Film 1914–1918, Rachael Low (Allen & Unwin).

The History of the British Film 1918–1929, Rachael Low (Allen & Unwin).

The History of the British Film: Documentary and Educational Films of the 30s, Rachael Low (Allen & Unwin).

The History of the British Film: Film Making in 1930s Britain, Rachael Low (Allen & Unwin, 1985).

The History of the British Film: Films of Comment and Persuasion of the 30s, Rachael Low (Allen & Unwin).

Hollywood: 60 Great Years, 1930–1990, Jack Lodge, John Russell Taylor, Adrian Turner, Douglas Jarvis, David Castell, Mark Kermode (Prion, 1992).

The Hollywood Story, Joel W. Finler (Octopus, 1988).

The Illustrated History of the Cinema, ed. Ann Lloyd, consultant ed. David Robinson (Orbis, 1986).

The International Film Industry: An Historical Dictionary, Anthony Slide (Greenwood, 1989).

The Liveliest Art, Arthur Knight (Macmillan, 1957).

The Long View: An International History of Cinema, Basil Wright (Secker & Warburg, 1974).

A Million and One Nights, Terry Ramsaye (Simon & Schuster, 1964).

The Miracle of the Movies, Leslie Wood (Burke, 1947).

Movie Parade, Paul Rotha (The Studio, 1936).

Movie-Made America: A Cultural History of American Movies, Robert Sklar (Random House, 1975).

The Movies, Raymond Griffith and Arthur Mayer (Simon & Schuster, 1970).

A Pictorial History of the Silent Screen, Daniel Blum (Spring Books, 1953).

A Pictorial History of the Talkies, Daniel Blum (Grosset & Dunlap, 1958).

A Short History of the Movies, Gerald Mast (Bobbs-Merrill, third edition, 1981).

Speed of Sound: Hollywood and the Talkie Revolution, Scott Eyman (Simon & Schuster, 1997).

Spellbound in Darkness: A History of the Silent Film, George C. Pratt (N.Y. Graphic Society, 1973).

The Story of Cinema Vols 1–2, David Shipman (Hodder and Stoughton, 1982).

Variety History of Show Business (Hamlyn, 1993).

World Cinema 1895–1980, David Robinson (Eyre Methuen, 1981).

Movie Music

Music and the Silent Film: Contexts and Case Studies 1895–1924, Martin Miller Marks (OUP, 1998).

Music for the Movies, Tony Thomas (2nd ed., Gazelle, 1998).

Twenty-Four Frames Under: A Buried History of Film Music, Russell Lack (Quartet, 1997).

Studio Histories

COLUMBIA

The Columbia Story, Clive Hirshhorn (Pyramid, 1989).

Frank Capra: The Catastrophe of Success, Joseph McBride (Simon & Schuster, 1992).

Hail Columbia, Rochelle Larkin (Arlington House, 1975).

Hit & Run: How Jon Peters and Peter Guber Took Sony For a Ride in Hollywood, Nancy Griffin & Kim Masters (Simon & Schuster, 1996).

Indecent Exposure – A True Story of Hollywood and Wall Street, David McClintick (Columbus, 1982).

King Cohn, Bob Thomas (Barrie & Rockliff, 1967).

The Name above the Title, Frank Capra (Macmillan, 1971).

Out of Focus: Power, Pride and Prejudice – David Puttnam in Hollywood, Charles Kipps (Century, 1989).

DISNEY

The Art of Walt Disney, Christopher Finch (Abrams, 1973).

The Disney Studio Story, Richard Holliss and Brian Sibley (Octopus, 1988).

The Disney Version, Richard Schickel (Pavilion, 1986).

The Walt Disney Biography, Bob Thomas (Simon & Schuster, 1977).

FOX

Don't Say Yes until I Finish Talking, Mel Gussow (Doubleday, 1971).

The Films of 20th Century-Fox, Tony Thomas and Aubrey Solomon (Citadel, 1985).

Skouras, King of the Fox Studios, Carlo Curti (Holloway House, 1967).

The Studio, John Gregory Dunne (W. H. Allen, 1970).

Upton Sinclair Presents William Fox (Upton Sinclair, 1933).

Zanuck: The Rise and Fall of Hollywood's Last Tycoon, Leonard Mosley (Granada, 1984).

The Zanucks of Hollywood: The Dark Legacy of a Movie Dynasty, Marlys J. Harris (Crown, 1989).

MGM

Fade Out: The Calamitous Final Days of MGM, Peter Bart (Simon & Schuster, 1990).

Heyday: An Autobiography, Dore Schary (Little, Brown, 1979).

The Lion's Share: The Story of an Entertainment Empire, Bosley Crowther (Dutton, 1957).

Merchant of Dreams: Louis B. Mayer, MGM and the Secret Hollywood (Sidgwick & Jackson, 1993).

The MGM Story, John Douglas Eames (Pyramid, 1990).

MGM: When the Lion Roars, Peter Hay (Turner, 1993).

Picture, Lillian Ross (Rinehart, 1952).

Thalberg: Life and Legend, Bob Thomas (Doubleday, 1969).

PARAMOUNT

Mountain of Dreams, Leslie Halliwell (Stonehill, 1976).

The Paramount Story, John Douglas Eames (Octopus, 1985).

The Public Is Never Wrong, Adolph Zukor with Dale Kramer (Putnam, 1953).

RKO

Empire: The Life, Legend and Madness of Howard Hughes, Donald L. Bartlett and James B. Steele (Norton, 1979).

The RKO Story, Richard Jewell and Vernon Harbin (Arlington House, 1982).

UNITED ARTISTS

Final Cut: Dreams and Disaster in the Making of Heaven's Gate, Steven Bach (Jonathan Cape, 1985).

The United Artists Story, Ronald Bergan (Octopus, 1986).

United Artists: The Company Built by the Stars, Tino Balio (University of Wisconsin, 1976).

UNIVERSAL

The Horror Factory: The Horror Films of Universal 1931–55, Bruce Dettman and Michael Bedford (Gordon Press, 1976).

Universal Pictures: A Panoramic History, Michael G. Fitzgerald (Arlington House, 1977).

The Universal Story, Clive Hirshhorn (Octopus, 1983).

WARNER BROS

The Devil's Candy: The Bonfire of the Vanities Goes to Hollywood, Julie Salamon (Jonathan Cape, 1992).

Here's Looking at You Kid: 50 Years of Fighting, Working and Dreaming at Warner Bros, James R. Silke (Little, Brown, 1976).

Inside Warner Brothers 1935–1951, Rudy Behlmer (Viking, 1985).

The Warner Bros Story, Clive Hirshhorn (Octopus, 1979).

Warner Brothers, Charles Higham (Scribner, 1976).

National Cinemas

AUSTRALIA

Australian Cinema, ed. Scott Murray (Allen & Unwin, 1994).

Australian Cinema 1970–1985, Brian McFarlane (Secker & Warburg, 1987).

The Australian Film Book 1930–Today, Simon Brand (Dreamweaver, 1985).

Australian Film: The Inside Story, Ken G. Hall (Summit, 1980).

BRITAIN

The Age of the Dream Palace: Cinema and Society

in Britain 1930–1939, Jeffrey Richards (Routledge & Kegan Paul, 1984).

All Our Yesterdays: 90 Years of British Cinema, ed. Charles Barr (BFI, 1986).

Arrows of Desire: The Films of Michael Powell and Emeric Pressburger, Ian Christie (Waterstone, 1985).

An Autobiography of British Cinema, Brian McFarlane (Methuen/BFI, 1996).

The Beginnings of the Cinema in England, John Barnes (David & Charles, 1976).

Black in the British Frame, Stephen Bourne (Cassell, 1998).

British Cinema History, ed. James Curran and Vincent Porter (Weidenfeld & Nicolson, 1983).

British Cinema: The Lights that Failed, James Park (Batsford, 1990).

British Cinemas and Their Audiences, J. P. Mayer (Dobson, 1948).

British Film Music, John Huntley (Skelton Robinson, 1947).

British Film Studios, Patricia Warren (Batsford, 1995).

The Carry On Companion, Robert Ross (Batsford, 1996).

A Critical History of British Cinema, Roy Armes (OUP, 1978).

Ealing Studios, Charles Barr (David & Charles, 1977).

Elstree: The British Hollywood, Patricia Warren (Elm Tree, 1983).

Fifty Classic British Films, 1932–1982: A Pictorial Record, Anthony Slide (Dover, 1985).

The Film Business: A History of British Cinema 1896–1972, Ernest Betts (Allen & Unwin, 1973).

The Finest Years: British Cinema of the 1940s, Charles Drazin (André Deutsch, 1998).

Forever Ealing, George Perry (Pavilion, 1981).

Gainsborough Pictures, ed. Pam Cook (Cassell, 1998).

The Golden Gong: Fifty Years of the Rank Organization, Its Films and Its Stars, Quentin Falk (Columbus, 1987).

The Great British Picture Show, George Perry (Hart-Davis, MacGibbon, 1974).

The Hammer Story, Marcus Hearn, Alan Barnes (Titan, 1998).

Hollywood England: The British Film Industry in the Sixties, Alexander Walker (Michael Joseph, 1974).

The House of Horror: The Complete Story of Hammer Films, ed. Allen Eyles, Robert Adkinson, and Nicholas Frey (Lorrimer, 1973).

In Search of Gandhi, Richard Attenborough (The Bodley Head, 1982).

J. Arthur Rank and the British Film Industry, Geoffrey Macnab (Routledge, 1993).

Kiss Kiss Bang Bang: The Unofficial James Bond Film Companion, Alan Barnes and Marcus Hearn (Batsford, 1996).

Mass Observation at the Movies, ed. Jeffrey Richards and Dorothy Sheridan (Routledge, 1987).

A Mirror for England: British Movies from Austerity to Affluence, Raymond Durgnat (Faber & Faber, 1970).

Monty Python Encyclopedia, Robert Ross (Batsford, 1998).

My Indecision Is Final: The Rise and Fall of Goldcrest Films, Jake Eberts and Terry Ilott (Faber & Faber, 1990).

National Heroes: British Cinema in the Seventies and Eighties, Alexander Walker (Harrap, 1985).

The Once and Future Film: British Cinema in the Seventies and Eighties, John Walker (Methuen, 1985).

The Rise of the Cinema in Great Britain, John Barnes (Bishopsgate, 1983).

Sex, Class and Realism: British Cinema 1956–1963, John Hill (BFI, 1986).

Travels in Greeneland: The Cinema of Graham Greene, Quentin Falk (Quartet, 1990).

Twenty Years of British Films, Michael Balcon, Ernest Lindgren, Forsyth Hardy, Roger Manvell (Falcon Press, 1947).

CHINA

Hong Kong Babylon, Fredric Dannen and Barry Long (Faber & Faber, 1997).

Hong Kong Cinema, Stephen Teo (BFI, 1997).

Sex and Zen and a Bullet in the Head, Stefan Hammond and Mike Williams (Titan, 1997).

EASTERN EUROPE

The Czechoslovak New Wave, Peter Hames (University of California Press, 1985).

Directory of Eastern European Filmmakers and Films, ed. Keith Shiri (Flicks Books, 1992).

The Most Important Art: East European Film after 1945, Miura Leihm and Antonin J. Leihm (University of California Press, 1977).

World Cinema 1: Poland, Frank Bren (Flicks Books, 1990).

FRANCE

The Cinema in France After the New Wave, Jill Forbes (BFI/Macmillan, 1992).

Fifty Classic French Films, 1912–1982: A Pictorial Record, Anthony Slide (Dover, 1987).

French Cinema in the 80s: Nostalgia and the Crisis of Masculinity, Phil Powrie (OUP, 1997).

French Cinema Since 1946: Vol 1: The Great Tradition, Roy Armes (Tantivy/Barnes, 1970).

French Cinema Since 1946: Vol 2: The Personal Style, Roy Armes (Tantivy/Barnes, 1970).

The Golden Age of French Cinema 1929–1939, John W. Martin (Columbus, 1983).

The Great French Films, James Reid Paris (Citadel, 1983).

The New Wave, James Monaco (OUP, 1976).

GERMANY

From Caligari to Hitler, Siegfried Kracauer (Princeton University Press, 1947).

From Caligari to Hitler: A Psychological History of the German Film, Siegfried Kracauer (Noonday Press, 1960).

From Hitler to Heimat, Anton Kaes (Harvard University Press, 1989).

The Great German Films, Frederick W. Ott (Citadel, 1986).

The Haunted Screen: Expressionism in German Cinema and the Influence of Max Reinhardt, Lotte H. Eisner (University of California Press, 1969).

The New German Cinema, John Sandford (Oswald Wolff, 1980).

New German Cinema: A History, Thomas Elsaesser (BFI/Macmillan, 1989).

IRELAND

Cinema and Ireland, Kevin Rockett, Luke Gibbons, John Hill (Croom Helm, 1987).

World Cinema 4: Ireland, Brian McIlroy (Flicks Books, 1989).

ITALY

Italian Cinema from Neorealism to the Present, Peter Bonadella (Ungar, 1985).

Italian Films, Robin Buss (Batsford, 1989).

Off Screen: Women and Film in Italy, ed. Giuliana Bruno and Maria Nadotti (Routledge, 1988).

Spaghetti Nightmares: Italian Fantasy-Horrors as Seen through the Eyes of Their Protagonists, Luca M. Palmerini and Gaetano Misretta (Fantasma, 1996).

Spaghetti Westerns: The Good, the Bad and the Violent, Thomas Weisser (McFarland, 1992).

JAPAN

Eros Plus Massacre: An Introduction to Japanese New Wave Cinema, David Desser (Indiana University Press, 1988).

Japan: Screen Guide, Arne Svensson (Barnes, 1970).

The Japanese Film: Art and Industry, Joseph Anderson and Donald Richie (Grove Press, 1960).

Japanese Film Directors, Audie Bock (Kodansha, 1985).

Japanese Films: A Filmography and Commentary, 1921–1989, Beverley Bare Buehrer (St James Press, 1990).

The Japanese Movie: An Illustrated History, Donald Ritchie (Kodansha, 1966).

Monsters Are Attacking Tokyo: The Incredible World of Japanese Fantasy Films, Stuart Galbraith IV (Feral House, 1998).

MEXICO

Mexican Cinema: Reflections of a Society 1986–1988, Carl J. Mora (University of California Press, 1989).

Mexican Cinema, ed. Paulo Antonio Paranagua (BFI/IMCINE, 1995).

RUSSIA

Kino: A History of the Russian and Soviet Film, Jay Leda (Allen & Unwin, 1983).

Silent Witness: Russian Films 1908–1919, ed. Paolo Cherchi Usai, Lorenzo Codelli, Carlo Montanaro, David Robinson (BFI, 1989).

SCANDINAVIA

Scandinavian Cinema: Films and Film-makers in Denmark, Finland, Iceland, Norway and Sweden, Peter Cowie (Tantivy, 1992).

Sweden Vols 1–2, Peter Cowie (Zwemmer/Barnes, 1970).

World Cinema 2: Sweden, Brian McIlroy (Flicks Books, 1986).

SOUTH AMERICA

Argentine Cinema, ed. Tim Barnard (Nightwood, 1986).

Magical Reels: A History of Cinema in Latin America, John King (Verso, 1990).

Mexican Cinema, ed. Paulo Antonio Paranagua (BFI, 1996).

Mexican Cinema: Reflections of a Society 1986–1988, Carl J. Mora (University of California Press, 1989).

South American Cinema: Dictionary of Film Makers, Luis Trelles Plazaola (University of Puerto Rico, 1989).

Twenty-Five Years of the New Latin American Cinema, ed. Michael Chanan (BFI, 1983).

SPAIN

New Cinema in Spain, Vicente Molina Foix (BFI, 1977).

Out of the Past: Spanish Cinema after Franco, John Hopewell (BFI, 1986).

Spanish Film under Franco, Virginia Higginbotham (University of Texas Press, 1988).

The World of Luis Buñuel, ed. Joan Mellen (OUP, 1978).

UNITED STATES

*A Personal Journey with Martin Scorsese through American Movies, Martin Scorsese, Michael Henry Wilson (Faber, 1997).

*Adventures in the Screen Trade: A Personal View of Hollywood and Screenwriting, William Goldman (Macdonald, 1983).

*America at the Movies, Margaret Farrand Thorp (Yale University Press, 1939).

American Cinema: Directors and Directions 1929– 1968, Andrew Sarris (Dutton, 1968).

American Film Music, William Darby and Jack Du Bois (McFarland, 1990).

Behind the Scenes, Rudy Behlmer (Samuel French, 1990).

Canned Goods as Caviar: American Film Comedies of the 1930s, Gerald Weales (University of Chicago Press, 1985).

The Chaplin Encyclopedia, Glenn Mitchell (Batsford, 1997).

The Citizen Kane Book, Pauline Kael (Secker & Warburg, 1971).

*City of Nets: A Portrait of Hollywood in the 1940s, Otto Friedrich (Headline, 1987).

Close Encounters of the Third Kind Diary, Bob Balaban (Paradise Press, 1978).

David I. Selznick's Hollywood, Ronald Haver (Secker & Warburg, 1980).

*Easy Riders, Raging Bulls: How the Sex-Drugs-and-Rock'n'Roll Generation Saved Hollywood, Peter Biskind (Simon & Schuster, 1998).

An Empire of Their Own: How the Jews Invented Hollywood, Neal Gabler (W. H. Allen, 1988).

Hanging On in Paradise, Fred Lawrence Guiles (McGraw-Hill, 1975).

Hollywood at Sunset, Charles Higham (Saturday Review Press, 1972).

Hollywood in the Twenties, David Robinson (Zwemmer, 1968).

Hollywood in the Thirties, John Baxter (Zwemmer, 1968).

Hollywood in the Forties, Charles Higham and Joel Greenberg (Zwemmer, 1968).

Hollywood in the Fifties, Charles Higham and Joel Greenberg (Zwemmer, 1972).

Hollywood in the Sixties, John Baxter (Zwemmer, 1972).

Hollywood in the Seventies, Les Keyser (Zwemmer, 1984).

Hollywood the Dream Factory, Hortense Powdermaker (Secker & Warburg, 1950).

Hollywood the Haunted House, Paul Mayersberg (Allen Lane, 1967).

Hollywood: The Movie Colony, the Movie Makers, Leo Rosten (Harcourt, Brace, 1941).

Hollywood: The Pioneers, Kevin Brownlow and John Kobal (Collins, 1979).

Hollywood Talks Turkey: The Screen's Greatest Flops, Doug McClelland (Faber & Faber, 1989).

Hollywood: The Years of Innocence, John Kobal (Thames & Hudson, 1985).

Hollywood Tycoons, Norman Zierold (Hamish Hamilton, 1969).

The Laurel and Hardy Encyclopedia, Glenn Mitchell (Batsford, 1995).

*The Making of the Wizard of Oz, Aljean Harmetz (Pavilion, 1989).

The Marx Brothers Encyclopedia, Glenn Mitchell (Batsford, 1996).

Masters of Starlight: Photographers in Hollywood, David Fahey and Linda Rich (Columbus, 1988).

Medium Cool: The Movies of the 1960s, Ethan Mordden (Knopf, 1990).

*The Movie Moguls, Philip French (Weidenfeld & Nicolson, 1969).

*My Life with Cleopatra, Walter Wanger and Joe Hyams (Bantam, 1963).

Naked Hollywood: Money and Power in the Movies Today, Nicolas Kent (BBC Books, 1991).

*Of Mice and Magic: A History of American Animated Cartoons, Leonard Maltin (Plume, 1987).

Offscreen Onscreen: Inside Stories of 60 Great Films, Peter van Gelder (Aurum, 1990).

*The Parade's Gone By . . ., Kevin Brownlow (Secker & Warburg, 1960).

The Rise of the American Film, Lewis Jacobs (Harcourt, Brace, 1939).

Round Up the Usual Suspects: The Making of Casablanca – Bogart, Bergman, & World War II, Aljean Harmetz (Weidenfeld & Nicolson, 1993).

Seeing Is Believing: How Hollywood Taught Us to Stop Worrying and Love the Fifties, Peter Biskind (Pantheon, 1983).

Sometime in the Sun: The Hollywood Years of Fitzgerald, Faulkner, Nathanael West, Aldous Huxley, and James Agee, Tom Dardis (Scribner, 1976).

A Star Is Born: The Making of the 1954 Movie and its 1983 Restoration, Ronald Haver (Knopf, 1988).

Strangers in Paradise: The Hollywood Emigrés 1933–1950, John Russell Taylor (Faber & Faber, 1983).

Tales from the Hollywood Raj: The British in California, Sheridan Morley (Weidenfeld & Nicolson, 1983).

*The War, the West and the Wilderness, Kevin Brownlow (Secker & Warburg, 1979).

We're in the Money: Depression America and Its Films, Andrew Bergman (New York University Press, 1979).

Writers in Hollywood, Ian Hamilton (Heinemann, 1989).

Censorship and Related Issues

Behind the Mask of Innocence, Kevin Brownlow (Jonathan Cape, 1990).

Brief Encounters: Lesbians and Gays in British Cinema 1930–1971, Stephen Bourne (Cassell, 1996).

The British Board of Film Censors: Film Censorship in Britain 1896–1950, James C. Robertson (Croom Helm, 1985).

The Celluloid Closet: Homosexuality in the Movies, Vito Russo (HarperCollins, 1987).

Censored, Tom Dewe Mathews (Chatto & Windus, 1994).

*Cinema, Censorship and Sexuality 1909–1925, Annette Kuhn (Routledge, 1989).

The Dame in the Kimono: Hollywood Censorship and the Production Code from the 1920s to the 1960s, Leonard J. Leff and Jerold L. Simmons (Weidenfeld & Nicolson, 1990).

*The Face on the Cutting Room Floor: The Story of Movie and Television Censorship, Murray Schumach (Morrow, 1964).

Film Censorship, Guy Phelps (Gollancz, 1975).

From Reverence to Rape: The Treatment of Women in the Movies, Molly Haskell (Holt, Rinehart & Winston, 1974).

The Hidden Cinema: British Film Censorship in Action 1913–1972, James Robertson (Routledge, 1993).

Hollywood Censored, Gregory D. Black (Cambridge University Press, 1994).

Hollywood Lolitas: The Nymphet Syndrome in the Movies, Marianne Sinclair (Henry Holt, 1988).

Images in the Dark: An Encyclopedia of Gay and Lesbian Film and Video, Raymond Murray (Plume, 1996).

Sex in the Movies: The Celluloid Sacrifice, Alexander Walker (Penguin, 1986).

Sin and Censorship, Frank Walsh (Yale, 1996).

What the Censor Saw, John Trevelyan (Michael Joseph, 1973).

The Critics

*Agee on Film: Reviews and Comments, James Agee (Beacon Press, 1964).

Around Cinemas, James Agate (Home and Van Thal, 1946).

Before My Eyes: Film Criticism and Comment, Stanley Kauffmann (Harper & Row, 1980).

*The C. A. Lejeune Film Reader, ed. Anthony Lejeune (Carcanet, 1991).

*Chestnuts in Her Lap, C. A. Lejeune (Phoenix House, 1947).

Cruising the Movies: A Sexual Guide to 'Oldies' on TV, Boyd McDonald (Gay Presses of New York, 1985).

Deadline at Dawn: Film Writings 1980–1990, Judith Williamson (Marion Boyars, 1992).

*The Dilys Powell Film Reader, ed. Christopher Cook (OUP, 1991).

Dilys Powell – The Golden Screen: Fifty Years of Films, ed. George Perry (Pavilion, 1989).

Drawn and Quartered, Richard Winnington (Saturn Press, 1948).

Durgnat on Film, Raymond Durgnat (Faber & Faber, 1976).

Film Criticism and Caricatures 1943-53, Richard Winnington (Elek, 1975).

Halliwell's Hundred: A Nostalgic Choice of Films from the Golden Age, Leslie Halliwell (Granada, 1982).

Let's Go to the Pictures, Iris Barry (Chatto & Windus, 1936).

Movies into Film: Film Criticism 1967–1970, John Simon (Delta, 1971).

*On Movies, Dwight Macdonald (Prentice Hall, 1969).

100 Best Films of the Century, Barry Norman (Chapmans, 1992).

Pauline Kael's *New Yorker* reviews have been collected in the following volumes:

I Lost It at the Movies, 1964; *Kiss Kiss Bang Bang*, 1968; *Going Steady*, 1970; *Deeper into Movies*, 1974; *Reeling*, 1976; *When the Lights Go Down*, 1980; *Taking It All In*, 1984; *State of the Art*, 1986; *Hooked*, 1990; *Movie Love*, 1992.

Her capsule reviews were collected in *5001 Nights at the Movies*, 1982.

*The Pleasure Dome: The Collected Film Criticism 1935–1940, Graham Greene (Secker & Warburg, 1972).

The Private Eye, the Cowboy and the Very Naked Girl, Judith Crist (Paperback Library, 1970).

Private Screenings: Views of the Cinema of the Sixties, John Simon (Macmillan, 1967).

*Produced and Abandoned: The National Society of Film Critics Write on the Best Films You've Never Seen, ed. Michael Sragow (Mercury House, 1990).

Shots in the Dark, ed. Edgar Anstey, Roger

Manvell, Ernest Lindgren, Paul Rotha (Allan Wingate, 1951).

Three-Quarter Face, Penelope Gilliatt (Secker & Warburg, 1980).

Violent Screen: A Critic's 13 Years on the Front Lines of Movie Mayhem, Stephen Hunter (Bancroft Press, 1996).

You Ain't Heard Nothin' Yet: The American Talking Film: History and Memory 1927–1949, Andrew Sarris (OUP, 1998).

Film Theory and Practice

The Art of the Film, Ernest Lindgren (Allen & Unwin, 1948).

Celluloid: The Film Today, Paul Rotha (Longman, 1931).

Concepts in Film Theory, Dudley Andrew (OUP, 1984).

A Discovery of Cinema, Thorold Dickinson (OUP, 1970).

Documentary Film, Paul Rotha (Faber & Faber, 1936).

*Film, Roger Manvell (Pelican, 1944).

Film as Art, Rudolph Arnheim (Faber & Faber, 1969).

Film as Film, V. F. Perkins (Penguin, 1972).

Film Form, Sergei Eisenstein (Harcourt, Brace, 1947).

Film Language: A Semiotics of the Cinema, Christian Metz (OUP, 1974).

Film Sense, Sergei Eisenstein (Harcourt, Brace, 1949).

Film Technique and Film Acting, V. L. Pudovkin (Vision/Mayflower, 1958).

Footnotes to the Film, ed. Charles Davy (Lovat Dickson, 1938).

A Grammar of Film, Raymond Spottiswoode (Jonathan Cape, 1937).

Grierson on Documentary, ed. Forsyth Hardy (Faber & Faber, 1966).

The Immediate Experience, Robert Warshow (Doubleday, 1962).

Independent Filmmaking, Lenny Lipton (Straight Arrow, 1972).

Kino-Eye: The Writing of Dziga Vertov, ed. Annette Michelson (Pluto Press, 1984).

The Major Film Theories, J. Dudley Andrew (OUP, 1976).

Movies and Methods Vols 1–2, ed. Bill Nichols (University of California Press, 1985).

Rotha on the Film, Paul Rotha (Faber & Faber, 1958).

The Secret Language of Film, Jean-Claude Carrière (Faber & Faber, 1994).

Signs and Meanings in the Cinema, Peter Wollen (Secker & Warburg, 1974).

The Struggle for the Film, Hans Richter (Scolar Press, 1986).

The Technique of Film Editing, Karel Reisz (Focal Press, 1968).

What Is Cinema? Vols 1–2, André Bazin (University of California Press, 1971).

Individual Movies

The Devil's Candy: The Bonfire of the Vanities Goes Hollywood, Julie Salamon (Jonathan Cape, 1992).

Ultimate Porno, Pier Nico Solinas (Eyecontact, 1981). On the making of *Caligula*.

Casablanca: As Time Goes By, Frank Miller (Turner, 1992).

Round Up the Usual Suspects: The Making of Casablanca – Bogart, Bergman, & World War II, Aljean Harmetz (Weidenfeld & Nicolson, 1995).

Meeting at the Sphinx: Gabriel Pascal's Production

of Bernard Shaw's Caesar and Cleopatra, Marjorie Deans (Macdonald, 1945).

My Life with Cleopatra, Walter Wanger and Joe Hyams (Corgi, 1963).

Close Encounters of the Third Kind Diary, Bob Balaban (Paradise Press, 1978).

The Citizen Kane Book, Pauline Kael (Secker & Warburg, 1971).

The Making of Citizen Kane, Robert L. Carringer (John Murray, 1985).

The Godfather Book, Peter Cowie (Faber, 1997).

How It Happened Here, Kevin Brownlow (Secker & Warburg, 1968). On the making of *It Happened Here*.

Killer Instinct, Jane Hamsher (Orion, 1997). On the making of *Natural Born Killers*.

The Making of King Kong, Orville Goldner and George E. Turner (Ballantine, 1975). On the 1933 film.

The Creation of Dino De Laurentiis's King Kong, Bruce Bahrenburg (Star, 1976).

By Any Means Necessary: The Trials and Tribulations of the Making of Malcolm X, Spike Lee with Ralph Wiley (Vintage, 1993).

Making Priscilla, Al Clarke (Penguin, 1994). On the making of *The Adventures of Priscilla, Queen of the Desert*.

Picture, Lillian Ross (Gollancz, 1953). On the making of *The Red Badge of Courage*.

A Star Is Born: The Making of the 1954 Movie and its 1983 Restoration, Ronald Haver (Harper & Row, 1990).

Scott of the Antarctic: The Film and Its Production, David James (Convoy, 1948).

The Story of The Fifth Element, Luc Besson (Titan, 1998).

The Lost Worlds of 2001, Arthur C. Clarke (Sidgwick and Jackson, 1972).

Monster: Living Off the Big Screen, John Gregory Dunne (Random House, 1997). On the writing of *Up Close and Personal*.

The Making of The Wizard of Oz, Aljean Harmetz (Pavilion, 1989).

Titanic and the Making of James Cameron, Paula Parisi (Orion, 1998).

Types of Film

ANIMATED

The Encyclopedia of Walt Disney's Animated Characters: From Mickey Mouse to Hercules, John Grant (Hyperion, 1997).

Looney Tunes and Merrie Melodies: A Complete Illustrated Guide to the Warner Bros Cartoons, Jerry Beck, Will Friedwald (Henry Holt, 1989).

Of Mice and Magic: A History of American Animated Cartoons, Leonard Maltin (Plume, 1987).

B MOVIES

B Movies, Don Miller (Curtis, 1973).

Kings of the B's: Working within the Hollywood System, ed. Todd McCarthy and Charles Flynn (E. P. Dutton, 1975).

Second Feature: The Best of the 'B' Films, John Cocchi (Citadel, 1991).

COMEDY

Canned Goods as Caviar: American Film Comedies of the 1930s, Gerald Weales (University of Chicago Press, 1985).

The Carry-On Book, Kenneth Eastaugh (David & Charles, 1978).

The Comic Mind, Gerald Mast (University of Chicago Press, 1979).

The Great Funnies: A History of Film Comedies, David Robinson (Studio Vista/Dutton, 1969).

Monty Python: Complete and Utter Theory of the Grotesque, ed. John O. Thompson (BFI, 1982).

Screwball: Hollywood's Madcap Romantic Comedies, Ed Sikov (Crown, 1989).

CRIME

The BFI Companion to Crime, ed. Phil Hardy (Cassell/BFI, 1997).

Dark City: The Lost World of Film Noir, Eddie Muller (Titan, 1998).

The Great Cop Pictures, James Robert Parish (Scarecrow, 1989).

Crime Movies, Carlos Clarens (W. W. Norton, 1980).

Dark City: The Film Noir, Spencer Selby (St James Press, 1984).

Film Noir: An Encyclopedic Reference Guide, ed. Alain Silver and Elizabeth Ward (Bloomsbury, 1988).

The Great Detective Pictures, James Robert Parish and Michael R. Pitts (Scarecrow, 1990).

A Pictorial History of Crime Films, Ian Cameron (Hamlyn, 1975).

Prison Pictures from Hollywood, James Robert Parish (McFarland, 1990).

CULT

Cult Movies Vols 1–3, Danny Peary (Delacorte, 1981)

The Incredibly Strange Film Book, Jonathan Ross (Simon & Schuster, 1993).

Incredibly Strange Films, ed. V. Vale and Andrea Juno (Re/Search, 1986).

The Official Splatter Movie Guide Vols 1–2, John McCarty (St Martin's Press, 1989/1992).

The Psychotronic Encyclopedia of Film, Michael Weldon (Plexus, 1989).

Shock Xpress – the Essential Guide to Exploitation Cinema Vols 1–2, ed. Stefan Jaworzyn (Titan, 1993/1994).

Splatter Movies, John McCarty (Columbus, 1984).

FANTASY AND SCIENCE FICTION

The A–Z of Science Fiction & Fantasy Film, Howard Maxford (Batsford, 1998).

Aurum Film Encyclopedia: Science Fiction, ed. Phil Hardy (Aurum, 1984).

Fantastic Cinema: An Illustrated Survey, Peter Nicholls (Ebury Press, 1984).

The Film Fantasy Scrapbook, Ray Harryhausen (Titan Books, 1984).

The Illustrated Dinosaur Movie Guide, Stephen Jones (Titan, 1993).

Keep Watching the Skies, Brian J. Robb (Shelwing/McFarland, 1998)

The Primal Screen: A History of Science Fiction Film, John Brosnan (Orbit, 1991).

The Science Fiction Image: The Illustrated Encyclopedia of Science Fiction in Film, Television, Radio and the Theater, Gene Wright (Columbus, 1983).

HISTORY

Epic Film: Myth and History, Derek Elley (Routledge & Kegan Paul, 1984).

Epic Films: Casts, Credits and Commentary on Over 250 Historical Spectacle Movies, Gary A. Smith (McFarland, 1991).

The Hollywood History of the World, George Fraser MacDonald (William Morrow, 1988).

Hollywood Holyland, Ken Darby (Scarecrow, 1992).

Religion in the Cinema, Ivan Butler (Barnes, 1979).

Past Imperfect: History According to the Movies, ed Mark C.Carnes (Henry Holt, 1995).

Visions of Yesterday, Jeffrey Richards (Routledge & Kegan Paul, 1973).

HORROR

A–Z of Horror Films, Howard Maxford (Batsford, 1996).

Aurum Film Encyclopedia: Horror, ed. Phil Hardy (Aurum Press, revised edition, 1993).

The BFI Companion to Horror, ed. Kim Newman (Cassell, 1997).

Caligari's Children: The Film as Tale of Terror, S. S. Prawer (OUP, 1980).

The Dracula Centenary Book, Peter Haining (Souvenir Press, 1987).

The Frankenstein File, ed. Peter Haining (New English Library, 1977).

Hammer, House of Horror: Behind the Screams, Howard Maxford (Batsford, 1996).

A Heritage of Horror: The English Gothic Cinema 1946–1972, David Pirie (Gordon Fraser, 1973).

Hollywood Gothic, David J. Skal (W. W. Norton, 1990).

Horror Film Directors 1931–1990, Dennis Fischer (McFarland, 1991).

Horror Movies, Carlos Clarens (Secker & Warburg, 1967).

The Illustrated Frankenstein Movie Guide, Stephen Jones (Titan, 1994).

The Illustrated Vampire Movie Guide, Stephen Jones (Titan, 1993).

Immoral Tales: Sex and Horror Cinema in Europe 1956-1984, Cathal Tohill and Pete Tombs (Primitive, 1994).

Let's Scare 'Em, Rick Atkins (Shelwing/McFarland, 1998).

Movie Monsters, Denis Gifford (Studio Vista, 1969).

Necronomican Book 1, ed. Andy Black (Creation, 1997).

Nightmare Movies: A Critical Guide to Contemporary Horror Films, Kim Newman (Harmony Books, 1988).

Nightwalkers: Gothic Horror Movies – The Modern Era, Robert Lanier Wright (Taylor Publishing, 1997).

The Vampire Cinema, David Pirie (Galley Press, 1977).

The Vampire Film, Alan Silver and James Ursini (Barnes, 1976).

MUSICALS

All Singing! All Talking! All Dancing! A Pictorial History of the Movie Musical, John Springer (Cadillac, 1966).

The American Film Musical, Rick Altman (BFI/Indiana University Press, 1989).

Encyclopedia of Rock Music on Film, Linda J. Sandahl (Blandford Press, 1986).

Gotta Sing! Gotta Dance!: A Pictorial History of Film Musicals, John Kobal (Hamlyn, 1971).

The Hollywood Musical, Jane Feuer (BFI, 1982).

The Hollywood Musical, Clive Hirshhorn (Crown, 1981).

Hollywood Sings: An Inside Look at Sixty Years of Academy Award-Nominated Songs, Susan Sackett (Billboard, 1995).

The Rock and Roll Movie Encyclopedia of the 1950s, Mark Thomas McGee (McFarland, 1990).

A Song in the Dark: The Birth of the Musical Film, Richard Barrios (OUP, 1995).

The World of Entertainment! Hollywood's Greatest Musicals, Hugh Fordin (Doubleday, 1975).

WAR

Hollywood at War, Ken D. Jones and Arthur F. McClure (Barnes, 1973).

Hollywood's Vietnam: From the Green Berets to Apocalypse Now, Gilbert Adair (Proteus, 1981).

A Pictorial History of War Films, Clyde Jeavons (Hamlyn, 1974).

War Movies, Jay Hyams (Gallery Books, 1984).

WESTERN

B Western Actors Encyclopedia, Ted Holland (Shelwing/McFarland, 1998).

The Film Encyclopedia of Westerns, ed. Phil Hardy (Octopus, 1985).

The BFI Companion to the Western, ed. Edward Buscombe (BFI/André Deutsch, 1988).

The Golden Corral, Ed Andreychuk (Shelwing/McFarland, 1998).

Horizons West, Jim Kitses (Thames & Hudson, 1969).

The Life and Times of the Western Movie, Jay Hyams (Columbus, 1983).

The Movie Book of the Western, ed. Ian Cameron and Douglas Pye (Studio Vista/Cassell, 1996)

A Pictorial History of the Western Film, William K. Everson (Citadel, 1969).

Shoot 'Em Ups, Les Adams and Buck Rainey (Arlington House, 1978).

The Western, Allen Eyles (Tantivy, 1975).

The Western from Silents to the Seventies, William K. Everson and George N. Fenin (Penguin, 1973).

Westerns, Philip French (Secker & Warburg, 1977).

Wild West Movies, Kim Newman (Bloomsbury, 1990).

OTHER

Black Action Films, James Robert Parish and George H. Hill (McFarland, 1989).

Martial Arts Movies: From Bruce Lee to the Ninjas, Richard Meyers, Amy Harlib, Bill and Karen Palmer (Citadel, 1985).

Road Movies: A Complete Guide to Cinema on Wheels, Mark Williams (Proteus, 1982).

The Samurai Film, Alain Silver (Columbus, 1983).

Sports in the Movies, Ronald Bergen (Proteus, 1982).

Journalism and Gossip

Do You Sleep in the Nude?, Rex Reed (W. H. Allen, 1969).

*The 50-Year Decline and Fall of Hollywood, Ezra Goodman (Simon & Schuster, 1961).

*Hollywood Babylon, Kenneth Anger (Straight Arrow, 1975).

Hollywood Babylon II, Kenneth Anger (Arrow Books, 1986).

Hollywood Confidential, Coral Amende (Plume, 1997).

Hollywood Revisited, Sheilah Graham (St Martin's Press, 1985).

Hollywood's Unsolved Mysteries, John Austin (SPI Books, 1992).

If You're Talking to Me, Your Career Must Be in Trouble: Movies, Mayhem and Malice, Joe Queenan (Picador, 1994).

Opening Shots: The Unusual, Unexpected, Potentially Career-Threatening First Roles that Launched the Careers of 70 Hollywood Stars, Damine Bona (Workman Publishing, 1994).

People Will Talk, John Kobal (Aurum, 1986).

The Prince, The Showgirl and Me: The Colin Clark Diaries, Colin Clark (HarperCollins, 1995).

Rolling Breaks and Other Movie Business, Aljean Harmetz (Alfred A. Knopf, 1983).

Scratch an Actor: The Intimate Lowdown on Hollywood Nightlife, Sheilah Graham (W. H. Allen, 1969).

Self-Creations: 13 Impersonalities, Thomas B. Morgan (Michael Joseph, 1966). Includes profiles of Gary Cooper, Sammy Davis Jnr, Elia Kazan, Teenage Heroes (Frankie Avalon, Edd Byrnes), John Wayne.

Travolta to Keaton, Rex Reed (William Morrow, 1979).

Fiction

Beggar's Cup, Eric Blau (Knopf, 1993). A Hollywood producer of horror movies decides to make a biopic of Zionist leader Theodor Herzl.

Blue Movie, Terry Southern (Calder and Boyars, 1973). A leading director attempts to make a film covering every aspect of love and desire.

Boy Wonder, James Robert Baker (NAL, 1988). Friends and enemies remember the dazzling career of Shark Trager, the quintessential Hollywood producer of the last quarter of the twentieth century.

By Design, Richard E. Grant (Picador, 1998). In Hollywood, an interior designer and a masseuse are involved with stars making the disaster movie to end all disaster movies.

Cannes: The Movie, Ian Johnstone (Chatto and Windus, 1990). The director of the 50th Cannes Film Festival in 1995 tries to come to terms with political, commercial and criminal pressures.

The Carpetbaggers, Harold Robbins (1949). A millionaire playboy and plane-maker (who resembles Howard Hughes) moves to Hollywood in the 20s and 30s; filmed by Edward Dmytryk in 1954.

Concerning a Woman of Sin, ed. Daniel Talbot (Consul, 1960). Anthology of nine stories set in Hollywood: Ben Hecht's title story; John O'Hara's 'Brother'; Christopher Isherwood's 'The World in the Evening'; F. Scott Fitzgerald's 'Crazy Sunday'; William Saroyan's 'The Brokenhearted Comedian and the Girl Who Took the Place of His Unfaithful Wife'; Irwin Shaw's 'The City Was in Total Darkness'; Budd Schulberg's 'A Table at Ciro's'; Ring Lardner's 'The Love Nest'.

The Day of the Locust, Nathanael West (1939). An account of Hollywood's dispossessed; filmed by John Boorman in 1975.

The Deer Park, Norman Mailer (Allan Wingate, 1957). A young writer compromises his talent as he becomes involved in the lives of a movie director, a temperamental Hollywood star, and a sleazy producer.

Dirty Eddie, Ludwig Bemelmans (1947). Farcical fun at the expense of Hollywood.

The Disenchanted, Budd Schulberg (Random House, 1950). A young screenwriter in Hollywood witnesses the final collapse of an alcoholic writer (who resembles Scott Fitzgerald).

The Distant Laughter, Bryan Forbes (Collins, 1972). A film director with a failing marriage to an actress embarks on his new film, a love story.

The Dream Merchants, Harold Robbins (1961). A film director becomes successful in the early days of Hollywood; made into a TV movie in 1980 by Vincent Sherman.

The Ecstasy Business, Richard Condon (William Heinemann, 1967). The world's greatest director of thrillers makes a new film starring a

British superstar, whose ambition is to sleep with every female in the world between the ages of eighteen and twenty-four, and his voluptuous former wife, whom he keeps remarrying.

The Englishman's Boy, Guy Vanderheaghe (Doubleday, 1997). A hack is hired by a sleazy producer to write an epic western.

The Errol Flynn Movie, Geoff Nicholson (Hodder and Stoughton, 1993). An unknown actor cast as Errol Flynn in a biopic by an Australian director begins to realize how much he has in common with the late hell-raiser.

The Film Explainer, Gert Hoffman (Secker & Warburg, 1995). An elderly man who is the film explainer and pianist at a village cinema faces an uncertain future as his employer considers showing talkies. Filmed as *Kinoerzähler*, directed by Bernhard Sinkel and starring Armin Muller-Stahl in 1993.

Flicker, Theodore Roszak (Summit, 1991). A film buff is drawn into a conspiracy to control the world through cinema as he investigates the disappearance of a horror-movie director.

Fowler's End, Gerald Kersh (Heinemann, 1957). A young man takes over as manager of a dingy flea-pit of a cinema in darkest North London.

Get Shorty, Elmore Leonard (Delacorte Press, 1990). A Miami debt collector for the mob goes to Los Angeles and discovers that he has the requisite talents to be a movie producer. Filmed in 1995 by Barry Sonnenfeld, starring John Travolta, Gene Hackman and Rene Russo.

Gone Tomorrow, Gary Indiana (Hodder and Stoughton, 1993). An actor goes to Colombia to appear in a film financed by a drug dealer and made by a disciple of a dead, drug-addicted, homosexual German director (who resembles Rainer Werner Fassbinder).

Inside Daisy Clover, Gavin Lambert (1959). The problems of a young actress in 30s Hollywood; filmed by Robert Mulligan in 1965.

In The Beauty of the Lilies, John Updike (Hamish Hamilton, 1996). In a history of four generations of an American family in the 20th century, a beauty queen – Miss Delaware Peach of 1947 – becomes a Hollywood star.

Jimmy Dean Prepares, Sam Toperoff (Granta, 1998). A re-creation of the life of James Dean, using actual events, but told as a novel.

Keystone, Peter Lovesey (Arrow, 1984). An English vaudeville comedian joins Mack Sennett's studio in 1915, becomes a Keystone Kop and is framed for murder.

The Last Tycoon, Scott Fitzgerald (1941). The travails of a film producer (who resembles Irving Thalberg); filmed by Elia Kazan in 1976.

The Little Sister, Raymond Chandler (Hamish Hamilton, 1949). A thriller that touches on life in Los Angeles.

Loser Takes All, Graham Greene (Bodley Head, 1955). Not strictly a novel about film, but it does feature Herbert Drethter, the boss of a large organisation, who is based on Alexander Korda. The story of an accountant who spends his honeymoon gambling in Monte Carlo, it was filmed in 1956 by Ken Annakin, starrring Glynis Johns, Rossano Brazzi and Robert Morley, and in 1990 by James Scott, starring Molly Ringwald, Robert Lindsay and John Gielgud. Greene wrote that the earlier film was 'a disaster of miscasting, with a middle-aged actress as the twenty-year old heroine, a romantic Italian star as the English assistant accountant, and Robert Morley playing Robert Morley'.

The Loved One, Evelyn Waugh (Little, Brown,

1948). An English poet in Hollywood shocks the crusty expatriate community by going to work in a pet's funeral parlour. Described by its author as 'a little nightmare produced by the unaccustomed high living of a brief visit to Hollywood'; filmed by Tony Richardson in 1965.

Maybe the Moon, Armistead Maupin (Bantam, 1993). A diminutive actress who once played an elf in a hit movie longs for her chance of stardom. The book is dedicated to the late Tamara DeTreaux, who played ET in some scenes of the film.

Merton of the Movies, Harry Leon Wilson (1922). An innocent becomes a Hollywood star in the early silent days; filmed in 1924, in 1932 (as *Make Me a Star*) by William Beaudine, and in 1947 by Robert Alton.

Most Likely to Succeed, John Dos Passos (Prentice-Hall, 1954). A Marxist playwright goes to Hollywood.

A Mouse Is Born, Anita Loos (Jonathan Cape, 1951). A film star known as 'The Bust' tells of her rise to fame, fortune, and pregnancy.

Moving Pictures, Terry Pratchett (Victor Gollancz, 1990). In the Discworld, moving pictures come into being in Holy Wood, threatening the fabric of reality.

Nobody Ordered Wolves, Jeffrey Dell. A satire on the film business.

One Hell of An Actor, Garson Kanin (Harper & Row, 1977). The author investigates the career of a man some claim to have been America's greatest actor, and probes the mystery of his son, a Hollywood film director.

Pink, Gus Van Sant (Faber, 1997). A middle-aged homosexual TV director becomes involved with two young men who use sex to enter into another dimension.

The Player, Michael Tolkin (Atlantic Monthly Press, 1988). A film producer gets away with murder; filmed by Robert Altman in 1992.

Playland, John Gregory Dunne (Granta, 1994). The life and times of a child star as she grows up in the Hollywood of the 1940s and 50s.

Popcorn, Ben Elton (Simon & Schuster, 1996). An award-winning Hollywood director of violent films confronts the realities of his fiction when two serial killers break into his home.

Postcards from the Edge, Carrie Fisher (Simon & Schuster, 1987). A film actress tries to deal with her drug addiction and her overbearing showbiz mother; filmed by Mike Nichols in 1990.

Prater Violet, Christopher Isherwood (Methuen, 1946). In London in the mid-30s, a novelist is hired to work on the script of an historical romance with a Viennese film director.

The Producer, Richard Brooks (Simon & Schuster, 1961). An independent producer (who resembles Mark Hellinger) risks everything on one film.

Queen of Desire, Sam Toperoff (HarperCollins, 1992). Variations on the life of Marilyn Monroe.

Queenie, Michael Korda (Linden/Simon & Schuster, 1985). A half-caste girl from Calcutta (who resembles Merle Oberon) becomes a glamorous film star.

The Rewrite Man, Bryan Forbes (Michael Joseph, 1983). A scriptwriter goes to the South of France to try to salvage an historical epic that has run into trouble on- and off-screen.

Screen, Barry Malzberg (Olympia Press, 1970). A New York City Welfare Department investigator fantasizes about being married to

Sophia Loren, seducing Elizabeth Taylor, and being seduced by Brigitte Bardot.

The Silver Castle, Clive James (Jonathan Cape, 1997). A Bombay street urchin is obsessed with Bollywood and its stars.

The Slide Area, Gavin Lambert (Penguin, 1959). Short stories about life in Hollywood.

A Slightly Used Woman, Peter Kortner (W. H. Allen, 1973). Scandal threatens to ruin for the second time the career of a Hollywood film star, trying to make a comeback in a TV series aimed at a family audience.

Still, Adam Thorpe (Secker, 1995). A failed middle-aged director ponders his film covering the great events of the 20th century.

The Symbol, Alva Bessie (Bodley Head, 1967). A voluptuous small-town girl (who resembles Marilyn Monroe) becomes a Hollywood star but fails to find love.

To See Ourselves, Rachel Field and Arthur Pederson (Collins, 1939). A small-town furniture salesman, together with his wife and dog, leaves Idaho to try, and fail, to become a screenwriter in Hollywood.

A Voyage to Puerilia, Elmer Rice (1930). A satire on Hollywood.

What Makes Sammy Run, Budd Schulberg (1961). Classic story of a producer (who resembles Jerry Wald) on the make.

White Hunter, Black Heart, Peter Viertel (W. H. Allen, 1954). A film director (who resembles John Huston) is more interested in shooting big game than his movie in Africa; filmed in 1990 by Clint Eastwood.

Film Periodicals

American Cinematographer: The International Journal of Film and Electronic Production Techniques, established 1920. Covers current cinema from the point of view of the cinematographer. Published monthly in Hollywood.

American Film: Film, Video and Television Arts. News and features on current cinema. Published bi-monthly, six times a year, from New York.

The Dark Side: The Magazine of the Macabre and Fantastic. British magazine covering horror films, video, and books. Published monthly.

Empire. British magazine, with news and features on current cinema, and reviews of new cinema, video, laser disc, and soundtrack releases. Published monthly.

Entertainment Weekly. American magazine covering all aspects of show-business: movies, television, books, music, and video.

Fangoria. Long-established American magazine covering horror, including films and books. Published monthly, except February and December.

Film Comment. Magazine covering current and past cinema. Published bi-monthly, six times a year, by the Film Society of Lincoln Center, New York.

Film Dope. British magazine providing biographical information and credits of actors, directors, and others involved in films. Published at irregular intervals, two or three times a year.

Film Review. British magazine with features and reviews of current cinema and video releases. Published monthly with special extra issues, including a video movie guide and a yearbook.

Films in Review. American magazine with reviews of new releases and features on past and current cinema. Published bi-monthly.

The Hollywood Reporter. US trade daily and weekly.

Impact. British magazine covering action movies and stars from around the world. Published monthly.

The Independent Film & Video Monthly. US magazine published by the Foundation for Independent Video and Film, covering all aspects of independent film-making. Published monthly except February and September.

Monthly Film Bulletin 1934–91. Monthly magazine containing reviews and complete credits for all feature films released in Britain. From May 1991, it was incorporated into *Sight and Sound*.

Movieline. Los Angeles-based magazine, with news and features on current cinema. Published monthly except February.

Moving Pictures International. Trade publication covering the business of movies, television and the new media. Published ten times a year.

Premiere. US magazine, with news and features on current cinema. Published monthly.

Premiere (UK edition). Magazine containing a mix of original features and material originating in the US edition. Published monthly.

Screen International. British trade weekly.

Shivers. British magazine covering horror films, videos, and personalities. Published monthly.

Sight and Sound. Magazine with an academic approach to current and past films, published by the British Film Institute. Quarterly from 1935 until May 1991, when it became a monthly, incorporating the *Monthly Film Bulletin*. Now includes reviews and complete credits of all current cinema releases, and short reviews of new videos.

Starburst. British magazine covering science fiction in all its forms, including film and television. Published monthly.

US. American magazine featuring interviews and news on current show-business stars. Published monthly.

Variety. US trade daily and weekly.

10
Movie Guides on CD-ROM

General Guides

• *Blockbuster Entertainment Guide to Movies and Videos*, 2nd Edition (Creative Multimedia, £27.99).

Minimum system requirements: IBM-compatible PC 486DX2/66, Windows 3.1, 8 Mb of RAM, 7 Mb available hard drive space, double-speed CD-ROM drive, 256-colour display, Sound Blaster or compatible sound card.

Now that many rivals have ceased publication, including Microsoft's *Cinemania* (the 1997 edition was, unfortunately, the last), *VideoHound Multimedia* and the *Mega Movie Guide*, this is the best general-purpose CD-ROM-based guide available, and a great improvement on the first edition. It gives cast and credits for more than 23,000 films and includes 5,500 photographs. There are brief clips from 30 or so classic films, such as *Casablanca*, *Chinatown*, *Lawrence of Arabia* and *Psycho*. Films are given star ratings, and there are 11,000 reviews taken from the *Time Out Film Guide*, and biographies of stars and directors from David Thomson's *Biographical Dictionary of Film*. You can click on the names of many stars and directors and get a list of their films, though not of other talents, such as composers and cinematographers. Free monthly updates to the guide can be downloaded via the Internet.

• *The Cannes Film Festival* (EMME Interactive, £30 or $24.95).

Minimum system requirements: IBM-compatible PC 386 or 486 with Windows 3.1 with 4 Mb of RAM, SVGA display.

A history of the first 50 years of the Cannes Film Festival from 1939 to 1990, providing details of all award-winners, together with 2,000 film stills, and some grainy and not very interesting newsreel footage of past festivals.

• *Corel/AMG All-Movie Guide 2.0* (Corel, £20 or $19.95).

Minimum system requirements: IBM-compatible PC 486SX 66 MHz, Windows 3.x, MS-DOS 5.0, with 8 Mb RAM and 6 Mb (9 Mb for Windows 95) hard drive space, SVGA display. Macintosh LCIII, System 7.1, with 8 Mb RAM, and 19.5 Mb hard drive space.

This remains potentially an excellent guide, with details of 100,000 movies and some 170,000 filmographies/biographies. You can annotate entries, and there's a useful glossary of film terms. But, like the first edition, it has many inaccuracies and the same films are included under different titles. More information at AMG's Web site (www.allmusic.com/AMGCorel.htm).

• *Halliwell's Film & Video Guide* (Palmtop, £40).

Minimum system requirements: Psion series 5 with 8 Mb RAM and a computer with a CD-ROM drive that can transfer files to the Psion.

Our companion volume, the comprehensive *Halliwell's Film & Video Guide*, a bulky book of 918 pages, fits happily into a hand-held Psion computer, providing plot synopses, critical evaluations and credits for more than 20,000 films, filmographies for more than 36,300 actors, directors and writers, and information on video, laser disc and soundtrack availability. The computer version adds sophisticated search facilities and the ability to annotate the entries. More information can be found at Palmtop's Web site (www.palmtop.nl/).

Specialist Guides

• *The Complete Index to World Film* by Alan Goble (Bowker Saur, £495).

Minimum system requirements: IBM-compatible PC 486 with a VGA or SVGA colour monitor with 4 Mb RAM.

The second edition of Alan Goble's guide is even more comprehensive than the first and almost half the price. It covers films from 1895 to 1998, includes 300,154 titles from 173 countries, including more than 100,000 silent films, 13,000 animated films and 8,000 TV films. There are filmographies for 45,075 directors, and credits for 1,085,827 actors. There are 63,850 films with cinematographer credits, 27,906 with composer credits, 91,757 with production credits, and 17,137 with their literary source.

• *Film Index International* (British Film Institute/Chadwyck-Healey, £1,295 with annual updates costing £350; £1,095 plus updates at £295 for universities and public libraries).

Minimum system requirements: IBM-compatible PC 386 with MS-DOS 3.1 or Windows 3.1, with 4 Mb of RAM.

Based on SIFT (Summary of Information on Film and Television), a database compiled by the Library and Information Services Department of the British Film Institute, it provides detailed production details on 98,000 films, with basic biographical information on more than 41,000 personalities, as well as references to articles on films and people from various periodicals. It now includes details of Oscars and other awards. For more information see Chadwyck-Healey's Web site (www.chadwyck.co.uk).

11
Movie Resources on the Internet

The Internet is a great source of movie information, gossip and reviews. More than other media, it is also in a constant state of flux, with publications appearing and disappearing with great speed. For that reason, I have listed just the most useful websites, ones that are likely to stay around, and which also provide the best starting points, by classifying current sources of information.

The World Wide Web

The World Wide Web often seems more of a maze, in which you can easily become lost in a series of dead ends. Search engines can save a lot of wasted effort. These days simple search engines are built into the latest operating systems of both Windows and Macintosh computers. Also available are some excellent commercial search engines that reside on your computer's hard disk; there are at least two useful free ones that can be downloaded to your computer from the Internet: Webferret (at http://www.ferretsoft.com) and Copernic (http://www.copernic.com). If you are searching for information on a new movie, particularly if it's a blockbuster, then frequently you'll be able to reach it by typing: 'http://www.nameofthemovie.com'. *Godzilla*, for instance, could be found at http://www.godzilla.com. The addresses (or Universal Resource Locators) below are not given in full. You'll need to add 'http://' to the beginning of each one.

Fan Pages

These range from those originated by enthusiastic and usually uncritical fans of a particular personality to official fan clubs and pages organized by the actors and actresses themselves – everyone from yesterday's sex symbol Mamie Van Doren to today's hottest stars, such as Leonardo DiCaprio, have their own official sites. The best places to begin a search for a favourite is at sites that provide alphabetical lists of fan sites:
- Celebsite (www.celebsite.com) has links to celebrity sites for actors, actresses, directors, comedians, producers and musicians.
- Fan Links (www.tnef.com/stars/) provides links to actors and actresses.
- Fan Sites (www.fansites.com) provides links to more than 2,500 sites for actors and actresses. Oddly, it indexes them by first names.
- Star Seeker (www.starseeker.com/index.com) is a collection of links to fan pages, news, and movies.

Film Reference
- All Movie Guide (www.allmovie.com/) provides casts and production information for many movies.
- Internet Movie Database (uk.imdb.com or us.imdb.com) details more than 170,479 films with some 2.4m filmography entries, and includes links to other sites of interest.

- Motion Picture Guide (www.tvgen.com/movies/) has full production details, cast credits and reviews for 35,000 movies, with biographical information from Ephraim Katz's *Movie Encyclopedia*.

Movie Publications
- Boxoffice Magazine (www.boxoff.com/) is a monthly trade publication with an on-line site featuring news stories and interviews with directors and stars.
- Bright Lights Film Journal (www.slip.net/gmm/bright.html) is a quarterly magazine of movie analysis, history and commentary.
- Cinescape (www.cinescape.com/) has news and features on science-fiction and fantasy movies.
- The Dark Side (www.ebony.co.uk/darkside/) is an on-line site for the British monthly horror magazine.
- Entertainment Weekly (cgi.pathfinder.com/ew//) has star interviews, reviews and celebrity gossip.
- Empire Magazine (www.futurenet.com) is the on-line version of the best-selling British film monthly.
- Film Comment (www.interactive.line.com/film/cover.html) is an on-line version of the bimonthly publication of the Film Society of Lincoln Center.
- Film Review (www.visimag.com) is designed to persuade people to buy the monthly British film magazine, but includes a few features.
- FilmScore Monthly (www.filmscoremonthly.com) covers film music and composers.
- Film Threat (www.filmthreat.com) has information on independent film-makers.
- Hollywood Reporter (www.hollywoodreporter.com) is a trade publication providing free news and a subscription service for those who want to know more.
- Movieline (www.movieline.mag.com) is the on-line version of the American movie monthly.
- Motion Picture (www.motionpicture.com) offers news and gossip, as well as reviews of movies currently in cinemas, and on video and television.
- People (cgi.pathfinder.com/people) has celebrity gossip and interviews.
- Premiere Magazine (www.premieremag.com) is the on-line version of the American movie monthly.
- Total Film (www.futurenet.com) is the on-line version of the British movie monthly.
- Variety (www.variety.com): the showbusiness trade paper provides news and has a subscription service for those who want *Daily Variety* on-line.
- White's Guide to the Movies

(www.whitesguidetomovies.com) is an on-line version of an American monthly magazine giving lots of ratings, lists and statistics.

Movie News and Features
- Ain't It Cool News (www.aint-it-cool-news.com) has gossip and advance information on audiences' reactions to previews of new films. The film studios don't like it, but they're doing their best to co-opt it.
- E! Online (www.eonline.com/) for celebrity gossip and features.
- Film.com (www.film.com) is an independent voice of film criticism on the Internet, providing news, reviews, features and previews, and bringing together critics, writers and movie buffs everywhere.
- Hollywood Online (www.hollywood.com) for trailers, photos and information.
- Jam! (www.canoe.ca/JamMovies/home.html) for news, interviews and reviews on current movies and personalities.
- Movie Snapshot (www.moviesnapshot.com/) has news-service reviews, features, interviews and photographs on Hollywood.
- Movieweb (www.movieweb.com/) has previews of, and information on, current and upcoming movies.
- Film Scouts (www.filmscouts.com/) has news about film and leading festivals, including Cannes, Sundance and Toronto.
- Rough Cut (www.roughcut.com) has movie news, reviews and features.
- Mr Showbiz (www.mrshowbiz.com/) provides news, features, interviews on current movies and personalities.
- Showbizwire (www.showbizwire.com) is an entertainment news resource.

Search Engines and Links
- Cinema Crawler (www.cinemacrawler.com/movies) is a search engine indexing cinema and movie sites.
- Cinema Sites (www.cinema-sites.com/) has links to reviews, previews, screenings, fan pages, magazines, journals, festivals and more.
- CineMedia's Cinema Sites (www.gu.edu.au/cinemedia/CineMedia.cinema.htm) provides an index to movie sites in various categories.
- Excite (www.excite.com.entertainment/movies) has the latest entertainment news.
- Intertainment Cybercenter (hollywoodnetwork.com/hn/directory/hec/index.html) provides links to film studios, TV networks and news sources.
- The Mining Co. (www.miningco.com/arts/movies) has features and links to such subjects as anime, classic movies, cult movies, film buffs, Hollywood movies, home video, independent movies and box-office reports.
- Movie Review Query Engine (www.mrqe.com/

lookup?) will search the Web for reviews of particular films.

- Movie Thing (www.moviething.com) has quizzes, information and links on movies and celebrities.
- Movies Net (www.movies.net/index.html) has links to stars and celebrities, studios, films, festivals, reviews, gossip, databases, archives, and movie memorabilia.
- Ultimate Movies (www.ultimatemovies.com) has links to the official sites for current movie releases.
- Yahoo! (www.yahoo.com/entertainment/ movies_and_films/) provides links to everything from actors and actresses, awards, box-office reports to news, reviews, screenplays and more, classified under 40 headings.

Specialist Sites

- Absolute Horror (www.smackem.com/horror/ horror.htm) provides information on, and reviews of, many horror movies.
- American Movie Classics Company (www.amctv.com/home.html) has features on classic movies and video releases.
- Cyber Film School (www.cyberfilmschool.com/) is an on-line film learning environment to assist student and professional film-makers to improve their craft.
- Film Festivals (www.filmfestivals.com) has information on the world's leading film festivals.
- The Film 100 (www.film100.com) gives a ranking of the 100 most influential people in the history of the cinema, with biographies, interactive demos and links to other websites.
- Films: Research and Resources (www.gen.umn.edu/faculty_staff/yahnke/film/ Default.htm), compiled by Professor Robert E. Yahnke, includes a work-in-progress, *Cinema History*, an on-line book beginning with silents and, when last viewed, discussing 60s films.
- Greatest Films (www.filmsite.org/) contains plot summaries, commentary and film posters of classic films, compiled by Tim Dirks.
- Horror Movies (www.horrormovies.com/) provides a classified guide.
- The Movie Times (www.the-movie-times.com/) provides movie box-office information, movie release schedules, reviews, and information on actors and actresses.
- Red Flower Society (www.geocities.com/ Tokyo/9667/) for links to Hong Kong movies, actors and actresses, film companies and picture archives.
- Roger Ebert on Movies (www.suntimes.com/ ebert/) has reviews by an influential critic.
- The Silents Majority (www.mdle.com/ ClassicFilms/) is devoted to silent films.
- Silver Screen Legends (www.cowboypal.com/ cowboy2.html) links to old-time cowboy film stars, such as Rex Allen, Monte Hale and Tex Ritter.
- The Ultimate Science Fiction Web Guide (magicdragon.com/UltimateSF/SF-index.html) has information on sf movies and links to associated sites.
- Women in Cinema (www.people.virginia.edu/ pm9k/libsci/womFilm.html) is just what it says it is.
- The World of Bollywood (www.indopak.com/ bolly/home.htm) has information on Indian movies.

Professional Organizations

- Academy of Motion Picture Arts and Sciences (www.oscars.org/ampas/) for everything you want to know about the Oscars and AMPAS's other activities.
- American Film Institute (www.afionline.org/ home.html) includes the AFI OnLine Cinema (www.afionline.org/cinema/archive/ lobby.html) showing classic movies.
- The British Film Institute (www.bfi.org.uk/) is a dull site about BFI activities, although improvements are promised.
- The Bill Douglas Centre at the University of Exeter (www.ex.ac.uk/bill.douglas/) has information on the beginnings of cinema.
- Directors Guild of America (www.dga.org/) includes interviews with its distinguished members.
- US National Film Registry (www.cs.cmu.edu/ afs/cs.cmu.edu/user/clamen/misc/movies/NFR-Titles.html) lists the 'culturally, historically, or esthetically important' films selected by the Library of Congress for preservation.

Studios and Production Companies

- Aardman Animations (bchannel.avonibp.co.uk/productioncos/ aardman/aardman.html) is the home of Wallace and Gromit.
- Buena Vista (bvp.wdp.com/BVI/) has information on upcoming and current releases.
- Disney Pictures (www.disney.com/ DisneyPictures/index.html) has information on upcoming and current releases, and merchandise to buy.
- Fine Line Features (www.flf.com) details its current and upcoming releases.
- Fox Searchlight (www.foxsearchlight) has information on upcoming and current releases.
- Jim Henson Company (www.henson.com) has movie information and Muppets galore.
- MCA/Universal Studios (www.mca.com) has information on upcoming and current releases.
- MGM/UA Pictures (www.mgmua.com) has information on upcoming and current releases.
- Miramax Films (www.miramax.com) has information on upcoming and current releases.
- New Line Cinema (www.newline.com/) has details of its releases.
- October Films (www.octoberfilms.com) details its art-house releases (like *Hilary and Jackie* and *Touch of Evil*).
- Paramount Pictures (www.paramount.com/ BronsonGate.htm) has information on upcoming and current releases.
- Sony (www.music.sony.com/ index.alternate.html) has information on upcoming and current releases.
- Star Wars (www.starwars.com) has information on the current and upcoming films in the series.
- Troma (www.troma.com/) has information about the studio responsible for the Toxic Avenger.
- Twentieth Century-Fox (www.fox.com) has information on upcoming and current releases.
- UIP (www.uip.com/lingos/uk/uk_index.html) has information on the films it distributes in English, Dutch, French, German and Spanish.
- Universal (www.universalstudios.com) has information on upcoming and current releases.
- View Askew (www.viewaskew.com/) for

information on the films of director Kevin Smith.
- Warner's (www.warnerbros.com) has information on upcoming and current releases.

Usenet

Newsgroups provide the opportunity to share news, gossip and information with like-minded people. You can subscribe directly to groups, or access them through the World Wide Web by way of Deja News (http://www.dejanews.com). There are newsgroups devoted to individuals, such as Woody Allen, Alfred Hitchcock and Stanley Kubrick. But the more general discussion groups include:

- alt.celebrities has gossip about the famous, though curiosity is often focused on the sexual proclivities of the stars.
- alt.fan.actors has discussion of the current favourite male performers.
- alt.fan.actors.dead deals with stars of the past.
- alt.fan.british-actors discusses British actors.
- alt.fan-james.bond discusses in minute detail every aspect of the films.
- alt.movies discusses all aspects of movies and movie-going.
- alt.asian-movies deals mainly with Hong Kong movies and their stars.
- alt.movies.cinematography holds discussions of techniques and equipment.
- alt.cult-movies deals with a wide variety of movies, some seemingly with a cult of only one fan.
- alt.movies.monster finds Godzilla endlessly fascinating.
- alt.movies.independent discusses movies that you might otherwise miss, or never hear of.
- alt.movies.silent has often erudite discussions on the silent era.
- alt.movies.uk deals with British films and releases.
- alt.showbiz.gossip is similar in style to alt.celebrities.
- alt.movies.visual-effects discusses how film-makers achieve their spectacular effects.
- rec.arts.movies.announce has birthday lists and box-office grosses.
- rec.arts.movies.current-films has opinions and discussions on the latest films, and the critical response to them.
- rec.arts.movies.international discusses and reviews foreign films.
- rec.arts.movies.misc discusses all aspects of movies, much as does alt.movies.
- rec.arts.movies.movie-going discusses the physical pleasures and discomforts of cinemas and their audiences.
- rec.arts.movies.past-films deals with classic genres.
- rec.arts.movies.people has discussion and opinion on those in front of, and behind, the camera.
- rec.arts.movies.production deals with technical matters, and questions and discussions on movie-making equipment.
- rec.arts.movies.reviews has reviews and often heated discussions on the worth of particular movies.
- rec.arts.sf.movies deals with sf and fantasy movies and their stars.
- rec.music.movies concerns itself with movie music, composers and soundtrack releases.
- uk.media.films discusses British films and personalities.

12
A Brief History of the Cinema

1873
America: Eadweard Muybridge, an English photographer, uses cameras spaced along a racetrack to capture the movement of a galloping horse.

1878
America: Muybridge improves his method of taking photographs of animals in motion. He begins work on a projector.

1881
America: Muybridge perfects his Zoopraxiscope, which uses rotating glass disks containing painted images based on his photographs. He lectures on his work in America and, from 1892, in Europe, inspiring others.

1884
America: American artist Thomas Eakins, one of Muybridge's assistants, creates a single-motion picture camera.
Britain: John Rudge, an inventor living in Bath, patents a means of showing animations with a magic lantern. William Friese-Greene later demonstrates it as his own invention.
Germany: Ottomar Anschütz photographs animals and men in motion which can be viewed on his Tachyscope.

1885
America: George Eastman markets film on a roll, made of sensitized paper.
Britain: William Friese-Greene, a Bath photographer, exhibits the results of his experiments in film: an image of a girl moving her eyes.

1887
Germany: Ottomar Anschütz demonstrates his Electro-Tachyscope, which uses a sequence of still photographs fitted on a large wheel and viewed through a small hole to produce the effect of motion. His machines are shown around the world, as penny-in-the-slot novelties.

1888
Britain: French inventor Louis Augustin Le Prince patents a machine to film and project a sequence of images.

1889
America: Eastman's company, now named Eastman Kodak, begins to manufacture roll-film on celluloid.
Thomas Edison takes out a patent on perforated film.
Britain: William Friese-Greene obtains a patent for a moving picture camera.

1890
France: Louis Augustin Le Prince boards a train for Paris at Dijon and vanishes. He is never seen again.

1891
America: Edison applies for a patent on the Kinetoscope, a cabinet for displaying film to one spectator at a time, designed by his assistant William Dickson.

1892
France: Émile Renaud exhibits his Praxinoscope, which projects brief animations of hand-drawn images onto a screen.

1893
Britain: Friese-Greene patents a rapid-sequence camera.

1894
America: Fred Ott, one of Edison's workers, is recorded sneezing on film shot in the inventor's 'Black Maria' studio. Edison's assistant Dickson makes films to show in the Kinetoscope. They last around 20 seconds and feature vaudeville acts and famous personalities, including Buffalo Bill Cody.
Edison begins to manufacture Kinetoscopes but doubts whether 'there is any commercial future in it'. The first Kinetoscope parlour opens in New York. More follow in other cities, although the glimpse of a Spanish dancer's ankle upsets some.
Britain: In October, Edison's Kinetoscope goes on show in Oxford Street, London.
Robert W. Paul, a London scientific instrument maker, is asked to copy Edison's Kinetoscope and discovers that Edison has not patented his invention in England. He works on improving it, by projecting images on a screen and by incorporating a wheel shaped like a Maltese cross to stop each frame of film for a moment in order to make the image seem less jerky.
Germany: Ottomar Anschütz demonstrates a projection system in Berlin.

1895
Films average between 40 to 80 feet in length, running for little more than a minute at most.
America: The American Mutoscope Company is set up to manufacture peep-show machines. It soon goes into film production proper and is renamed the Biograph Company.
Britain: Robert W. Paul and photographer Birt Acres begin to collaborate on designing a motion picture camera. Acres films sporting events, including the Derby.
France: Louis and Auguste Lumière, partners in a photographic business, patent the Cinématographe, a camera and projector, in

February. In March, they demonstrate the system with a film of their workers leaving the factory and go on to hold other demonstrations. The brothers open Le Cinématographe, the first-ever public film show, in the basement of the Grand Café in Paris on 28 December. Twelve films are shown during the half-hour show.
Germany: In Berlin, Max Skladanowsky patents his Bioskop projector and gives a public show of films in November.

1896
America: Edison demonstrates the new Vitascope, a projector designed by Thomas Armat. The first public show is held in a New York music hall on 23 April.
In June, the Lumière show opens in New York.
Britain: In January, Birt Acres demonstrates motion picture projection in London and founds the Northern Photographic Works.
On 20 February, the Lumière show opens in London. It transfers in March to the Empire Music Hall, Leicester Square.
On 21 February, Robert W. Paul demonstrates his method of motion picture projection, the Theatrograph. Shortly after, his films open at Olympia and become a special attraction at music halls, including the Alhambra, Leicester Square.
Paul makes the first British fiction film, *The Soldier's Courtship*, on the roof of the Alhambra in April. He films the Derby winners and screens it the next day to appreciative audiences. The Derby is later shown in colour, with the tints added by hand.
In Kingston-upon-Thames, the first cinema opens in a converted shop. It fails. But film flourishes as an attraction at fairground sideshows.
Denmark: Peter Elfelt shoots the first Danish film, a fake short of huskies pulling a sledge in the snows of Greenland.
France: Charles and Émile Pathé found the Pathé Frères, mainly to sell phonographs, but soon become involved in film production.
In Paris, George Méliès begins to make films with trick effects.
Auguste Baron begins working on a process of adding sound to film. He also invents a system of multi-screen cinema, Cinématorama, without attracting much interest.
Germany: Oskar Messter develops a motion picture camera and projection system.
India: The Lumière show opens in Bombay.
South Africa: Carl Hertz, a magician, shows as part of his stage act films bought, together with a projector, from Paul. He then takes them to Australia.
Spain: The first public film show of Lumière's films takes place in Madrid to an audience mainly of schoolgirls.

1897

France: In Paris, Alexander Rapoutat opens the first cinema devoted to newsreels.

One hundred and fifty people die in a Paris cinema fire caused by a burning projector, creating widespread concern about the safety of cinemas and equipment.

Spain: Fructuoso Gelabert makes the country's first fictional film, *Riña en un Café*.

1898

America: Biograph cameramen film war in Cuba.

Britain: Cecil M. Hepworth, son of a magic-lantern lecturer, writes *Animated Photography*, the first handbook on cinema.

In Brighton, G. A. Smith becomes the first Englishman to use double exposure for trick effects in *Cinderella and the Fairy Godmother* and other films.

The French Gaumont company opens a London office and begins making films at Dulwich.

American Charles Urban forms the Warwick Trading Company, which soon becomes a major producer and distributor.

1899

Films average around 70 feet in length, running for just over a minute.

Britain: Supply of American films dries up as Edison tries to combat what he regards as piracy. R. W. Paul opens one of Britain's earliest studios at New Southgate, North London, consisting of a stage, similar to that of a theatre, with a camera platform running on wheels in front of it. Among the first films produced is Dickens's *A Christmas Carol*.

Cecil M. Hepworth begins film production.

France: Auguste Baron perfects his system of sound cinema, but can find no one interested in exploiting his method.

Méliès' *Cinderella* is one of the first films to approach a narrative style.

1900

Australia: Joseph Perry directs films for the Salvation Army, including *Soldiers of the Cross*, mixing brief movies, lantern slides, and music.

Britain: The Warwick Trading Company's Joseph Rosenthal becomes the most celebrated of war cameramen with his film of the Boer War, which he follows with action from the Boxer Rebellion in China.

France: Léon Gaumont demonstrates synchronized sound and pictures.

1901

Britain: Will Barker founds the Autoscope Company and erects a rudimentary open-air studio at Stamford Hill, London.

G. H. Cricks and H. M. Sharp open a studio at Mitcham, Surrey, and make *Saved from the Burning Wreck* and a series of shorts featuring music-hall comedian Fred Evans.

1902

Films begin to reach a length of 250 feet or so, running for around four minutes.

Britain: Gaumont's Chronophone, by which gramophone recordings are synchronized to films of music-hall performers, is installed at the London Pavilion.

France: Charles Pathé opens a studio and begins turning out a film a day.

Méliès makes *A Trip to the Moon*, the first science-fiction film.

Germany: Oskar Messter establishes a production company in Berlin and begins to make films using cabaret artists and actors.

Spain: Segundo de Chomón begins to make films full of trick effects, but finds it hard to attract finance. He is later to work in Italy on *Cabiria* and in France on *Napoleon*.

1903

America: Edwin S. Porter makes *Life of an American Fireman*, mixing real-life and staged action to tell a story. He follows it with *Uncle Tom's Cabin* and *The Great Train Robbery*, an exciting western drama which causes a sensation and influences future directors.

Britain: Cecil Hepworth builds an indoor studio at Walton-on-Thames and films scenes from *Alice in Wonderland*.

Denmark: Peter Elfelt makes the country's first fiction film, *Capital Punishment* (Henrettelsen).

France: Méliès makes another science-fiction film full of trick effects, *Impossible Voyage*.

1904

America: At the St Louis Exhibition, George C. Hale presents Hale's Tours: travelogues shown in a mock-up of a railway carriage with train sound-effects and a swinging floor to simulate movement. Similar shows open in other American cities.

Cinema owner William Fox founds a distribution company.

German inventor Oskar Messter demonstrates sound films at the St Louis World Exposition.

Britain: The Clarendon Film Company opens a studio in Croydon.

1905

America: The first nickelodeon, a simple cinema where the price of admission is five cents, opens in Pittsburgh.

Vitagraph, which will become the most successful production company of its day, opens its own studio in Brooklyn. Its stars include Florence Turner and plump comedian John Bunny.

Variety begins publication.

Britain: Cecil Hepworth, using his family as actors, makes *Rescued by Rover* at the cost of £7 and sells 400 copies of it at £8 a time. Actors who are to begin their careers at his studio include Chrissie White, Alma Taylor, Helen Mathers, and Ronald Colman.

The first purpose-built cinemas open in London: the New Gallery in Regent Street and the Rialto in Coventry Street.

Italy: *La Presa di Roma* is the country's first feature film.

1906

Films are reaching 850 feet in length, running for around 14 minutes.

America: Cartoonist Winsor McCay incorporates an animated cartoon into his vaudeville act.

Carl Laemmle opens a nickelodeon in Chicago.

Pennsylvania cinema owner S. L. Rothafel adds the scent of roses to the showing of the Pasadena Rose Bowl game, the first use of smells in the cinema.

Australia: Charles Tait makes *The Story of the Kelly Gang*, one of the longest narrative films so far, running for more than 40 minutes.

Britain: In Ealing, Will Barker opens the Barker Motion Picture Company, which amalgamates with the Warwick Trading Company. He shoots a film of Shakespeare's *Hamlet* in a day.

Hale's Tours opens in Oxford Street, London.

The first news cinema, the Daily Bioscope, opens in London.

G. A. Smith patents his Kinemacolor colour process.

Denmark: Ole Olsen, a former fairground operator, establishes Nordisk Films, which soon becomes one of Europe's biggest production companies.

France: Charles Pathé signs music-hall performer André Deed to make comic films.

Sweden: Inventor Sven Berglund works on a system of recording sound on film by an optical process.

1907

America: Gilbert M. Anderson and George K. Spoor form Essanay production company in Chicago.

Finland: Apollo Studios release the first Finnish feature, *The Moonshiners*.

France: Actor Charles Le Bargy and other people from the Comédie Française form Film d'Art to make artistic films. Camille Saint-Saëns is to write the scores for its first production, *The Assassination of the Duke de Guise*.

1908

America: Anderson moves Essanay to California, away from Edison's law suits, and begins starring as 'Bronco Billy' in more than 300 westerns in eight years, despite the fact that he can hardly sit on a horse.

D. W. Griffith, an actor and writer, directs his first film, *The Adventures of Dollie*, for Biograph.

Hale's Tours goes into liquidation.

Argentina: Mario Gallo makes *El Fusilamiento de Dorrego*, the country's first feature film using professional actors.

Brazil: Portuguese-born director and cinematographer Antonio Leal makes *Os Estranguladores* and *Os Guaranis*.

Britain: The Gaumont Company hold the first Trade Show. Sir Geoffrey Tearle plays Romeo for Gaumont's version of *Romeo and Juliet*.

Colour films are shown for the first time at London's Palace Theatre.

The British Cinephone system of recorded sound synchronized to pictures begins to be installed in cinemas.

Electric Theatres becomes the first British cinema chain.

France: Max Linder becomes Pathé's leading comedian when André Deed leaves to make films in Italy.

1909

America: Edison, with seven leading film production companies and France's Pathé and Méliès, forms the Motion Picture Patents Company, claiming a monopoly on film production, and attempting to control distribution and license exhibition.

Distributors William Fox and Carl Laemmle decide to fight the monopoly by making their own films.

In December, D. W. Griffith directs his 100th one-reel film for Biograph. His films for the year include *The Violin Maker of Cremona*, starring Mary Pickford, who had begun her career months earlier as an extra. She becomes known as 'The Biograph Girl with the Curls'.

Australia: A 4,000-seater cinema opens in Melbourne. In Sydney, the Colonial cinema shows films non-stop from 11 a.m. to 11 p.m.

Ireland: Irish novelist James Joyce opens Dublin's first cinema, with the aid of Swiss financiers.

1910
America: *Pathé's Weekly* becomes the first newsreel.
Britain: Montague Pyke opens a cinema chain offering greater comfort and luxury.
Paul closes his studio and returns to making scientific instruments.
Denmark: Actress Asta Nielsen creates a sensation in *The Abyss*, as a man-hungry circus performer.

1911
America: *Photoplay* and *Motion Picture Story Magazine* are the world's first fan magazines.
Britain: London's Scala Theatre begins a two-year run of showing colour films.
France: The lavish Gaumont Palace opens in Paris as the world's biggest and best cinema.
Italy: Giovanni Pastrone's *The Fall of Troy*, with its cast of thousands, is the first epic movie.

1912
America: Dorothy and Lillian Gish begin their careers in films by Griffith.
Mack Sennett forms Keystone with two partners and begins making slapstick comedies.
Carl Laemmle founds Universal Pictures.
Adolph Zukor founds the Famous Players Film Company and begins by importing the French *Queen Elizabeth*, starring Sarah Bernhardt.
Britain: The British Board of Film Censors is established.
Fred Karno decides to make a second tour of America's music halls. Among his troupe are Charlie Chaplin and Stan Laurel, who will not return.
France: Film d'Art releases Louis Mercanton's *Les Amours de la Reine Élizabeth*, starring an ageing Sarah Bernhardt, thus helping cinema gain respectability.
Auguste Baron invents a new multi-screen process, Multirama, but can find no backers.
Gaumont gives the first public show in Paris of its Chronophone, synchronizing sound and pictures.
Germany: Shooting begins at Babelsberg studios of Asta Nielsen in *The Death Dance*.
Italy: Enrico Guazzoni's *Quo Vadis?*, a 12-reel epic of Roman life with a spectacular chariot race, is a box-office hit around the world.
Sweden: Inventor Sven Berglund claims to be the first to perfect a system of recording sound on film by an optical process.

1913
America: Mary Pickford signs a five-year contract with Adolph Zukor to become one of the first female film stars.
Fatty Arbuckle signs to make comedies for Mack Sennett.
Charlie Chaplin is spotted by Mack Sennett and goes to Hollywood.
The Adventures of Kathlyn, starring Kathlyn Williams, is the first serial, in 13 parts, to reach the cinemas.
Edison demonstrates his Kinetophone for synchronizing sound and pictures.
Orlando Kellum develops his system of synchronizing sound and pictures.
Vitagraph opens a studio in Santa Monica, California.
Jesse Lasky sets up the Jesse Lasky Feature Play Company.
Britain: Cinema attendance in Britain reaches an average of 10 visits a year.
Will Barker films *Jane Shore*.

Hepworth makes Dickens's *Barnaby Rudge*, restaging the Gordon Riots.
Eugene Lauste invents a method of recording sound on film, but fails to arouse any interest as war approaches. He emigrates to America.
India: Dadasaheb Phalke makes the first feature, *Raja Harishchandra*.
Sweden: Actor Victor Sjöström turns director with *Ingeborg Holm*.
Mauritz Stiller's *The Vampire* runs into censorship problems.
Venezuela: Lucas Manzano and Enrique Zimmerman direct the country's first feature film, *La Dama de las Cayenas*, based on Alexandre Dumas's *Camille*.

1914
America: Cecil B. De Mille shoots *The Squaw Man* in Los Angeles, converting a barn into a studio.
Mack Sennett makes the first comedy feature, *Tillie's Punctured Romance*, starring Chaplin, Mabel Normand, and Marie Dressler.
Pearl White stars in the serial *The Perils of Pauline*.
Winsor McCay creates the cartoon *Gertie the Dinosaur*.
William Fox produces his first feature.
Paramount Pictures is formed as a distribution company.
Poet Vachel Lindsay writes *Art of the Moving Picture*, one of the first critical studies of the new medium.
Britain: George Pearson directs *A Study in Scarlet*, the first major screen treatment of Sherlock Holmes.
Gaumont opens its new studio at Lime Grove, Shepherd's Bush.
France: Méliès runs out of money. His films are sold and many are destroyed to recover the celluloid.
Germany: Oskar Messter begins a weekly newsreel which is distributed around the world.
Italy: Giovanni Pastrone finishes the influential epic *Cabiria*.

1915
America: D. W. Griffith's *The Birth of a Nation*, 12 reels long and photographed by Bill Bitzer, causes a sensation when it opens in New York. It becomes the first film to be screened at the White House.
Cecil B. De Mille makes *The Cheat*, influential for its style and sexually suggestive content.
Chaplin goes to work for Essanay at $1,000 a week.
Douglas Fairbanks makes his film debut.
Triangle Films is set up by D. W. Griffith, Thomas Ince, and Mack Sennett.
Metro Pictures is founded and soon becomes a leading, though not particularly profitable, production company.
Edwin S. Porter retires from films.
Britain: A million people vote the six most popular British film stars as Alma Taylor, Elizabeth Risdon, Charlie Chaplin, Stewart Rome, Chrissie White, and Fred Evans.
Denmark: Nordisk releases more than 140 films during the year.

1916
America: D. W. Griffith releases the spectacular epic *Intolerance*, but audiences stay away.
Chaplin signs with Mutual for $10,000 a week. Mary Pickford demands and gets more from Zukor.
Zukor and Lasky acquire an interest in Paramount Pictures and merge their production companies.

Samuel Goldfish and his partners Archibald and Edgar Selwyn found Goldwyn Pictures. Goldfish soon takes the name as his own.
Britain: Hepworth's *Coming through the Rye* is seen by Queen Alexandra as the first film to have a Royal Command Performance.
Italy: Leading stage actress Eleanora Duse makes her only film, *Cenere*, but is disappointed with the result.

1917
America: Charlie Chaplin makes the first of his two-reel comedies, *The Cure* and *Easy Street*.
Fatty Arbuckle founds his own studio. Vaudeville performer Buster Keaton appears in many of his films.
After beginning as a Chaplin imitator, Harold Lloyd begins to define his own distinctive personality as a bespectacled, shy young man.
Erich Von Stroheim makes the first of his many appearances as a vicious Prussian officer in *For France*.
Douglas Fairbanks's earnings are more than $750,000 a year.
Britain: Cinema attendances reach 20 million a week.
Germany: The German High Command forms UFA to make propaganda films.

1918
America: Chaplin makes his first film, *A Dog's Life*, in his own studio, which resembles a British village. His *Shoulder Arms*, parodying war films, is a success.
Oscar Micheaux makes *The Homesteader*, from his novel, establishing the best-known production company making films for black audiences.
Warner Bros releases its first major feature, *My Four Years in Germany*.

1919
America: Lon Chaney becomes a star with *The Miracle Man*.
D. W. Griffith shoots *Broken Blossoms* with Richard Barthelmess and Lillian Gish.
Charlie Chaplin, D. W. Griffith, Mary Pickford, and Douglas Fairbanks form United Artists. *Hollywood* quips, 'The lunatics have taken charge of the asylum.'
Hal Roach opens his own studio and begins to make comedy films with such stars as Harold Lloyd, Laurel and Hardy, and Charley Chase.
Australia: Raymond Longford makes *The Sentimental Bloke*, the country's best-regarded silent.
Germany: Ernst Lubitsch establishes himself as a leading director with *Madame Dubarry*, starring Pola Negri and Emil Jannings as Louis XV.
Sweden
: Yearly attendances reach eight million.
USSR: The film industry is nationalized.

1920
America: Douglas Fairbanks marries Mary Pickford. He begins his swashbuckling career with *The Mark of Zorro*.
Fatty Arbuckle is arrested on charges of rape and manslaughter following the death of Virginia Rappe at a party. His films are withdrawn from cinemas and the scandal ends his Hollywood career, despite his acquittal.
Britain: Paramount opens a London studio, but it soon folds.
Denmark: Nordisk's output falls to eight films a year.

Germany: Robert Weine directs the expressionist *The Cabinet of Dr Caligari*.

Paul Wegner directs *The Golem*, an influential monster movie.

Norway
: Rasmus Breistein makes the first feature, *Anna, the Gypsy Girl*.

Sweden
: Mauritz Stiller's comedy *Erotikon* excites audiences with its sexual innuendo.

1921

America: Charlie Chaplin's feature *The Kid* makes Jackie Coogan a star at the age of six.

Rudolph Valentino stars in *The Four Horsemen of the Apocalpyse* and creates a sensation. His appeal to women is increased by his next film, *The Sheik*.

Max Linder makes two features, *Seven Years Bad Luck* and *Be My Wife*.

D. W. Griffith makes *Dream Street*, with sound synchronized on disk at the film's beginning, using Orlando Kellum's system. It is a hit, but exhibitors remain unconvinced that talking pictures have a future.

Britain: *The Glorious Adventure* is the first feature in colour to be made in England.

At a meeting called to save the British film industry, William Friese-Greene makes a passionate speech in favour of the continuance of British production, sits down, and dies, penniless. A monument erected over his grave in Highgate Cemetery reads, 'The Inventor of Kinematography. His Genius Bestowed Upon Humanity The Boon of Commercial Cinematography Of Which He Was The First Inventor And Patentee.'

Germany: UFA is privatized and soon becomes a leading company with large studios, laboratories, and cinemas.

Japan: Actor Teinosuke Kinugasa turns director with *The Death of My Sister* and soon exerts a powerful influence on the development of Japanese cinema.

Sweden: Benjamin Christensen directs the sexually explicit *Witchcraft through the Ages*.

Greta Garbo makes her debut as an extra in *A Fortune Hunter*.

Sven Berglund demonstrates his sound system in Stockholm.

1922

America: Harold Lloyd's *Grandma's Boy* establishes him as a gifted and original comedian.

Robert Flaherty makes *Nanook of the North*.

The Toll of the Sea, with Anna May Wong, is the first feature to be made using Technicolor's two-colour process.

The Power of Love, with Noah Beery, is the first feature to be made in 3-D.

Rin Tin Tin makes his debut in *The Man from Hell's River* and becomes the greatest dog star, saving Warner from bankruptcy during the 20s.

Irving Thalberg fires Erich Von Stroheim as director of *Merry Go Round* at Universal.

Director William Desmond Taylor is murdered and scandal follows with revelations of his involvement with Mabel Normand and others. Producers and distributors get together to form an association to 'maintain the highest possible moral and artistic standards'. The righteous Will Hays is chosen to head it.

The Cohn Brothers start C. B. C. Film Sales Corporation, which is to become Columbia Pictures in 1924.

Walt Disney founds Laugh-O-Gram Films in Kansas City with Ub Iwerks.

Samuel Goldwyn is forced out of Goldwyn Pictures.

Britain: The first British serial is released: *The Great London Mystery*, in 16 episodes, starring Lady Doris Stapleton and David Devant, the magician.

Germany: Fritz Lang makes *Dr Mabuse the Gambler*, about a master criminal.

F. W. Murnau directs the vampire film *Nosferatu*.

Ernst Lubitsch leaves to work in Hollywood.

Sven Berglund demonstrates his sound system in Berlin.

1923

America: Lon Chaney stars in *The Hunchback of Notre Dame*.

Harold Lloyd makes *Safety Last*, performing its dangerous stunts.

Cecil B. De Mille turns from sex to religion with *The Ten Commandments*

. James Cruze makes an epic western, *The Covered Wagon*, for Paramount.

Eric Von Stroheim turns Frank Norris's novel *McTeague* into an eight-hour epic which he cuts to four hours. Thalberg orders it reduced to two hours and finally releases it as *Greed*, a flawed masterpiece. Stroheim hardly works in Hollywood again.

The high-living Mabel Normand survives the scandal of William Desmond Taylor's death but her career falters when her chauffeur kills a millionaire at a party with her pistol.

Wallace Reid, Paramount's leading actor, dies of drug addiction at the age of 30. Mrs Wallace Reid stars in the anti-drug film *Human Wreckage*, as part of Hollywood's new moral crusade.

Disney goes to Hollywood to start his own studio.

Britain: The British National Film League is formed to promote local movies with 'British Film Week', in which exhibitors are urged to show British films. The audiences stay away.

Victor McLaglen and others campaign for protection of British films.

After becoming a star in America in *The White Rose*, directed by D. W. Griffith, Ivor Novello offers a solution to the problem of English films in America: 'What we must do is establish our stars in the States. It is to see certain actors that the people in America go to the pictures.'

Germany: The government attempts to protect its film industry by allowing only German producers to import foreign films. American companies open German production offices to overcome the problem.

Hans Dreier leaves UFA for Hollywood where he joins Paramount to become head of its art department.

Italy: Guazzoni's epic *Messalina* captures the imagination with its climactic chariot race.

Sweden: Victor Sjöström leaves for Hollywood, where he will be known as Seastrom and direct for MGM.

1924

America: Buster Keaton's comic skills show to advantage in *Sherlock Jr* and the *Navigator*.

Douglas Fairbanks stars in *The Thief of Bagdad*.

English romantic novelist Elinor Glyn supervises the filming of her *Three Weeks*, about love on a tiger-skin rug. Two years later she will proclaim Clara Bow the 'It' girl.

Metro-Goldwyn-Mayer is formed from Metro Pictures, Louis B. Mayer's production company, and the Goldwyn Company. In charge of production is Irving Thalberg.

Scandal and rumours of murder follow the sudden death of producer and director Thomas Ince aboard William Randolph Hearst's yacht.

Britain: British film-making falters: Ideal Studios, British and Colonial, Stoll and Samuelson close. Broadwest and Hepworth cut production. But Michael Balcon and partners found Gainsborough Pictures at Islington Studios.

Germany: F. W. Murnau directs *The Last Laugh*, starring Emil Jannings.

Fritz Lang makes the epic *Die Nibelungen*.

Sweden: Mauritz Stiller directs *The Atonement of Gösta Berling* with Greta Garbo.

1925

America: Charlie Chaplin makes *The Gold Rush*.

Lon Chaney stars in *The Phantom of the Opera*.

MGM release *Ben Hur*, directed by Fred Niblo, after production problems.

Willis O'Brien creates the special effects for *The Lost World*, which include a dinosaur rampaging through London.

Joan Crawford makes her screen debut.

Stiller and Garbo sign contracts with MGM.

Warner Bros buys Vitagraph.

Britain: *The Lost World* becomes the world's first in-flight movie when it is shown on an Imperial Airways flight from London to France, but it is not until the 60s that in-flight movies become routine.

Lee De Forest Phonofilms opens a studio in Clapham, London to make films with integral sound, which are shown in music halls.

The British Empire Exhibition cinema at Wembley is the first in the UK to be equipped for showing talkies.

France: Leading comedian Max Linder and his wife are found dead in their hotel rooms, apparent suicides.

Germany: Ewald-André Dupont directs *Variety* starring Emil Jannings and English actor Warwick Ward.

Sweden: Mauritz Stiller and Greta Garbo leave for Hollywood, as does Benjamin Christensen.

USSR: Eisenstein makes *Strike* and *The Battleship Potemkin*, which are to influence all film-makers who see them.

1926

America: Buster Keaton makes his comic masterpiece, *The General*.

Ronald Colman stars in *Beau Geste*.

Stiller leaves MGM without making a film. He makes *Hotel Imperial* for Paramount.

The first all-sound film programme is shown at the Warner in New York in August using the Vitaphone method, with music recorded on heavy disks played at 33[fr1/3] rpm.

Rudolph Valentino dies.

Britain: Alfred Hitchcock directs *The Lodger*, about Jack the Ripper.

France: Jean Renoir makes *Nana*.

Japan: Kinugasa's *A Page of Madness* almost does away with the need for titles.

USSR: Pudovkin's *Mother* is a brilliantly edited social melodrama.

1927

America: On 6 October *The Jazz Singer* opens at the Warner, and Al Jolson's cry of 'you ain't heard nothin' yet' ushers in the era of sound. It takes $3.5m at the box-office.

On 28 October, the first Fox Movietone newsreel

with sound is shown at the Roxy, New York.

Cecil B. De Mille makes *The King of Kings*, on the life of Christ.

Garbo and John Gilbert are a romantic pair in *Flesh and the Devil*.

New York's lavish Roxy Theater, dubbed 'The Cathedral of the Motion Picture', opens, seating nearly 6,000.

William Fox shows his first sound-on-film short in January and in May shows *Seventh Heaven* with a synchronized musical accompaniment.

Will Hays draws up a production code for the industry, emphasizing morality.

Britain: Alfred Hitchcock directs the boxing drama *The Ring*.

The Cinematograph Films Act makes it compulsory for British cinemas to show seven and a half per cent local films, rising to 20 per cent by 1936. British studios begin to turn out 'quota quickies', low-budget films made with little finesse to satisfy the law.

Victor McLaglen decides to go to Hollywood.

British Lion Film Corporation opens studios at Beaconsfield.

George Tootell, organist of London's Stoll Theatre, publishes *How to Play the Cinema Organ*.

France: Abel Gance's epic five-hour *Napoleon* uses three screens to cinematic effect. It will be shown in the US in a 70-minute version in 1929.

Germany: Fritz Lang directs his futuristic, spectacular *Metropolis*.

F. W. Murnau leaves for Hollywood, where he makes *Sunrise*.

Sweden: Mauritz Stiller leaves Hollywood and returns to Stockholm to direct for the theatre.

1928

America: King Vidor's *The Crowd* tackles the impersonal nature of modern life.

Victor Sjöström directs *The Wind*, starring Lillian Gish.

Warner produce the first all-talking film, *The Lights of New York*.

Walt Disney makes the first Mickey Mouse cartoon and follows it with the first sound cartoon, *Steamboat Willie*, again starring Mickey Mouse.

RKO Radio Pictures is founded.

Frank Capra is hired by Columbia. His involvement, together with the acumen of Harry Cohn, is to take the studio from poverty row to the status of a major.

Britain: *The Jazz Singer* causes a sensation when it opens in London in September.

Alfred Hitchcock makes *Blackmail*, Britain's first all-talking feature film. Joan Barry speaks the dialogue for its Polish-born star Anny Ondra.

Herbert Wilcox directs *Dawn*, with Sybil Thorndike as Nurse Edith Cavell.

Opposition to sound remains strong. Edward Wood, editor of *Picture Show* annual, writes: 'True progress in picture plays must be based on maintaining the silence of the screen'. British distributors predict failure for the development.

In a poll for *Picturegoer*, the public vote Ivor Novello the most popular male actor, followed by Ronald Colman, Ramon Novarro, Matheson Lang, Harold Lloyd and Milton Sills.

France: Carl Theodor Dreyer's *The Passion of Joan of Arc* stars Maria Falconetti in her only screen role. It will be banned by the British censors.

Luis Buñuel makes *Le Chien Andalou* with Salvador Dali.

Germany: The Germans try to set up a European

---

union to compete with Hollywood on equal terms. It fails.

Sweden: Mauritz Stiller dies.

USSR: Eisenstein makes a propaganda masterpiece, *October*.

Pudovkin makes *Storm over Asia*, about a Mongolian trapper who becomes a puppet emperor.

Dovzhenko makes *Arsenal*, set in World War I.

Dziga Vertov makes the abstract documentary *The Man with the Movie Camera*.

Kinugasa travels to Moscow from Japan to meet Eisenstein and Pudovkin.

1929

America: Cinema attendances reach 95 million in the second year of talkies, an increase of 38 million since 1927.

King Vidor makes *Hallelujah* with an all-black cast.

MGM's *Broadway Melody* is the first film musical with an original score.

The Marx Brothers make their debut in *The Cocoanuts*.

Douglas Fairbanks and Mary Pickford make their first sound film, Shakespeare's *The Taming of the Shrew*, 'with additional dialogue by Sam Taylor'.

The coming of sound ends many careers; Constance and Norma Talmadge retire. Those soon to return to Europe include Emil Jannings, Pola Negri, and Vilma Banky.

Warner Bros buy First National Pictures.

Fox develop a wide-screen system, Fox Grandeur, but it fails to catch on.

The first Academy Awards ceremony is held.

The Reverend William H. Short, head of the Motion Picture Research Council, recruits a team of social psychologists to investigate the effect of films on children, hoping to prove that they are damaging.

Britain: New studios, occupied by producer Archibald Nettlefold, open at Walton-on-Thames on the site of Hepworth's original studio.

France: Charles Pathé retires.

Méliès is found running a sweet-stall at a Paris station and is belatedly honoured for his contribution to cinema.

Germany: G. W. Pabst makes *Pandora's Box*, aka *Lulu*, with American actress Louise Brooks.

Karl Freund, leading German cinematographer, moves to Hollywood, as does director William Dieterle.

1930

America: Lewis Milestone makes the anti-war *All Quiet on the Western Front*.

Romantic star John Gilbert disappoints in his sound film *Redemption*.

The Marx Brothers star in *Animal Crackers*.

MGM publicize *Anna Christie* with the line 'Garbo Talks!'

The Motion Picture Producers and Distributors of America agree to a production code largely drawn up by the Reverend Daniel A. Lord, a Jesuit moralist. Its central principle is that 'no picture shall be produced which will lower the moral standards of those who see it'.

William Fox loses control of his company. Upton Sinclair, in his biography published in 1933, is to charge that Fox was forced out 'by a criminal conspiracy of Wall Street bankers'.

Monogram Productions opens, and will become one of the more successful 'Poverty Row' companies, turning out low-budget genre movies.

Britain: Tom Walls directs and stars in Ben Travers's Aldwych farce *Rookery Nook*, with most of its original cast, including Ralph Lynn and Robertson Hare.

Basil Dean founds the New Ealing Studios.

Denmark: George Schéevoigt makes the first talkie, *Eskimo*.

France: Demonstrators wreck a Paris cinema showing Luis Buñuel's surrealist *L'Age d'Or*, made in collaboration with Salvador Dali.

Germany: Joseph Von Sternberg makes *The Blue Angel*, starring Emil Jannings and Marlene Dietrich. Von Sternberg and Dietrich leave for Hollywood.

USSR: Alexander Dovzhenko makes the lyrical *Earth*.

1931

America: Chaplin stars in his sentimental comedy *City Lights*.

Cimarron, about the Oklahoma land rush, is a rugged epic.

Warner begins its gritty gangster films with *The Public Enemy* and *Little Caesar*, a cycle which is to make stars of Edward G. Robinson, James Cagney, and Humphrey Bogart.

Horror movies also catch the public imagination: Tod Browning makes *Dracula*, starring Bela Lugosi, and James Whale directs *Frankenstein*, starring Boris Karloff, for Universal, beginning that studio's long involvement with horror.

David O. Selznick becomes production chief at RKO.

Britain: Basil Dean produces Gracie Fields' first film, *Sally in Our Alley*.

Top films at the box-office include Ben Travers's farce *Plunder* and the American films *Hell's Angels*, *One Heavenly Night*, and *Trader Horn*.

Alexander Korda founds London Films.

France: René Clair makes the satirical *À Nous la Liberté*, which is to inspire Chaplin's *Modern Times* and the equally influential *Le Million*, an example of the possibilities of the film musical.

Jean Cocteau's experimental *The Blood of a Poet* excites admiration and derision.

Maurice Pagnol founds a film company and writes and produces film versions of his stage hit *Marius* and its successor *Fanny*, starring Raimu.

Germany: Fritz Lang directs *M*, starring Peter Lorre as a child murderer.

Leontine Sagan's all-female *Mädchen in Uniform*, about a schoolgirl's love for her female teacher, causes a sensation. The Nazis will ban it as an attack on authoritarianism.

India: *Alam Ara*, the first Indian talking picture, includes six songs and sets a lasting fashion.

Japan: Heinosuke Gosho's *The Neighbour's Wife and Mine* is the first talkie.

Norway: Tancred Ibsen makes the first talkie, *The Big Baptism*.

1932

America: MGM's star-studded *Grand Hotel* is the hit of the year.

Mervyn Le Roy's *I Am a Fugitive from a Chain Gang*, starring Paul Muni, epitomizes the Depression.

Howard Hawks directs *Scarface*, inspired by Al Capone.

Mae West makes her screen debut at the age of 40 in *Night after Night*.

Rouben Mamoulian directs Frederic March in *Dr Jekyll and Mr Hyde* for Paramount.

Johnny Weismuller as *Tarzan the Ape Man* provides

escapist fare in the first of a series that will keep him occupied until the late 40s.

Marie Dressler tops the first *Motion Picture Herald-Fame* poll of US distributors for the top money-making stars, followed by Janet Gaynor, Joan Crawford, Charles Farrell, and Greta Garbo.

Australia: Ken G. Hall makes the first talkie, *On Our Selection*, which becomes the most successful Australian film of the 30s and 40s.

Britain: Walter Forde directs an exciting and influential train thriller, *Rome Express*.

The Sunday Entertainments Act allows cinemas to open on Sundays.

Gaumont opens a bigger and better studio at Lime Grove, one that will be able to handle the production of four films at the same time.

Britain produces 141 features, which is a little less than France (143) and Germany (164).

France: Jean Renoir makes *Boudu Saved from Drowning*.

Danish director Carl Dreyer makes his first sound movie, *Vampyr*.

Germany: Leni Riefenstahl directs and stars in *The Blue Light*.

Spain: José Buchs makes the first talkie, *Carceleras*.

1933

America: The average time for making a film is now 22 days. The average cost is $70,000. Production rises to 547 films.

Roman Scandals and *42nd Street* are the big hits of the year.

King Kong is the sensation of the year.

Fred Astaire dances for the first time with Ginger Rogers in *Flying Down to Rio*. They are to make nine more films together.

The Marx Brothers reach new heights of delirium in *Duck Soup*.

Garbo insists on John Gilbert as her co-star in *Queen Christina*. It is his last film.

Frank Capra directs *Lady for a Day* for Columbia.

James Whale makes *The Invisible Man* for Universal.

Selznick leaves RKO to join MGM. Merian C. Cooper takes over, following the success of his *King Kong* (co-director) for the studio. He lasts only a year.

Warner's production chief, Darryl F. Zanuck, leaves the studio.

Mae West has two box-office hits with *She Done Him Wrong* and *I'm No Angel*.

Mary Pickford retires and refuses to let her films be seen. She is to become ever more reclusive until her death in 1979.

Marie Dressler tops the box-office poll, followed by Will Rogers, Janet Gaynor, Eddie Cantor, and Wallace Beery.

The Reverend William Short's team reports, in *Our Movie Made Children*, that films are 'extremely likely to create a haphazard, promiscuous and undesirable national consciousness', though the research findings, on closer examination, prove to be much more inconclusive, and are ignored.

Australia: Errol Flynn makes his film debut as Fletcher Christian in Charles Chauvel's *In the Wake of the Bounty*.

Britain: Average cost of a British film is £20,000. Production reaches 169 films.

Alexander Korda directs *The Private Life of Henry VIII* with Charles Laughton. Its success brings him financial backing.

Victor Savile's *The Good Companions*, starring Jessie Matthews, brings J. B. Priestley's bestselling novel to the screen.

Czechoslovakia: Gustav Machaty's *Ecstasy* becomes notorious for a scene with its star, Hedy Kiesler, naked. Five years later she goes to Hollywood, where she is renamed Hedy Lamarr.

France: Erich Von Stroheim stars in Jean Renoir's *La Grande Illusion* and makes his home in Paris.

Raymond Bernard directs an epic version of *Les Misérables* starring Harry Baur.

Jean Vigo makes his rebellious *Zero for Conduct*, which is immediately banned.

Germany: As the Nazis come to power, Dr Joseph Goebbels assumes control of the arts. He bans Fritz Lang's *The Testament of Dr Mabuse*, but offers to make him head of film production. Lang leaves for France and then goes to Hollywood. Many other producers, directors, and actors are to follow him into exile.

1934

America: Frank Capra directs *It Happened One Night* with Clark Gable and Claudette Colbert, and helps create a genre of screwball comedies.

W. C. Fields establishes himself in five films, including *Six of a Kind*.

Bette Davis seizes her opportunity in *Of Human Bondage*, from Somerset Maugham's novel.

Astaire and Rogers are together again in *The Gay Divorcee*.

The Production Code Administration is established under Joseph Breen to clean up films. Producers put the emphasis on family films and turn to Dickens and Victorian authors.

Will Rogers is voted America's top money-making star, followed by Clark Gable, Janet Gaynor, Wallace Beery, and Mae West.

Britain: Hitchcock directs the spy drama *The Man Who Knew Too Much*.

Anna Neagle flirts in *Nell Gwynn*, directed by future husband Herbert Wilcox.

Jessie Matthews stars in one of the few successful local musicals, *Evergreen*.

Basil Dean directs *Sings as We Go*, starring Gracie Fields.

J. Arthur Rank, heir to a flour and milling fortune, founds the Religious Film Society to make evangelical films and also the commercial British National Films. Its first film is *Turn of the Tide*, about Yorkshire fishing families.

France: Jean Vigo makes his masterpiece, *L'Atalante*. Its producers recut it and it flops at the box-office. Vigo dies at the age of 29 shortly after.

1935

America: George Cukor's *David Copperfield*, with W. C. Fields as Mr Micawber, is perfect family entertainment.

Charles Laughton's Captain Bligh in *Mutiny on the Bounty*, directed by Frank Lloyd, becomes the most memorable, and most often imitated, of screen villains.

Jeanette MacDonald and Nelson Eddy are together for the first of many times in *Naughty Marietta*.

Victor McLaglen stars in John Ford's *The Informer*.

Max Reinhardt transfers Shakespeare to the screen in *A Midsummer Night's Dream*, with James Cagney as Bottom and Mickey Rooney as Puck.

James Whale makes *The Bride of Frankenstein* for Universal, with the electric-haired Elsa Lanchester in the title role.

Becky Sharp, based on Thackeray's *Vanity Fair*, is the first feature to be made in three-colour Technicolor.

Fox merges with Twentieth Century Pictures to become Twentieth Century-Fox, with Darryl F.

Zanuck in charge of production and Joseph Schenck as chairman.

Herbert Yates founds Republic Studios, which is to become the most successful producer of 'B' movies.

David O. Selznick forms Selznick Independent Pictures, his own production company.

Shirley Temple tops the list of America's money-making stars, followed by Will Rogers, Clark Gable, Fred Astaire and Ginger Rogers, and Joan Crawford.

Britain: Alfred Hitchcock makes the comedy thriller *The Thirty-Nine Steps* with Robert Donat and Madeleine Carroll.

Harold Young directs *The Scarlet Pimpernel*, starring Leslie Howard and Merle Oberon.

France: Jacques Feyder directs *Carnival in Flanders*, inspired by Old Master paintings.

Germany: Leni Riefenstahl directs *Triumph of the Will*, a documentary about Hitler's 1934 Nuremberg Rally.

The government sets up a censorship board, which is to ban many European and American films. It will also ban film criticism in the coming year.

1936

America: *San Francisco*, with Clark Gable, Spencer Tracy, Jeanette MacDonald, and a spectacular earthquake, is the box-office hit of the year.

Frank Capra directs for Columbia *Mr Deeds Goes to Town*, starring Gary Cooper.

Chaplin mocks the mechanical aspects of society in *Modern Times*.

Fritz Lang makes his first Hollywood film, *Fury*, about a lynch mob.

Douglas Fairbanks retires.

Irving Thalberg dies.

Carl Laemmle is ousted from Universal. But the company does well with Deanna Durbin's *Three Smart Girls*.

Selznick's first independent production is *Little Lord Fauntleroy*.

Shirley Temple remains America's top money-making star, followed by Clark Gable, Fred Astaire and Ginger Rogers, Robert Taylor, and Joe E. Brown.

Britain: Charles Laughton is at his best as *Rembrandt*, directed by Alexander Korda.

Korda produces H. G. Wells's futuristic *Things to Come*, directed by William Cameron Menzies, and the intriguing *The Man Who Could Work Miracles*.

René Clair makes *The Ghost Goes West*, starring Robert Donat.

Alfred Hitchcock directs the brooding *Sabotage*.

Basil Wright and Harry Watt make *Night Mail*, a documentary about a mail train with music by Benjamin Britten and words by W. H. Auden.

J. Arthur Rank opens the company's new Pinewood studios in Buckinghamshire.

Vigo's *Zero for Conduct* gets a British release and is disliked by critics. 'Nought for direction. Nought for acting,' writes the *Observer*'s C. A. Lejeune.

France: Pagnol directs *César*, the last of his Marius trilogy.

Jean Renoir makes the charming 40-minute *A Day in the Country*, although it is not seen until 1946.

Anatole Litvak, who left Germany when the Nazis came to power, directs the romantic *Mayerling*. He is invited to Hollywood.

Sweden: Ingrid Bergman stars in Gustaf Molander's *Intermezzo*, which she will remake in Hollywood for David O. Selznick three years later, bringing her international stardom.

1937

America: Garbo stars as *Camille*, directed by George Cukor.

Roland Colman and Douglas Fairbanks Jnr add distinction to the romantic, swashbuckling fantasy *The Prisoner of Zenda*.

Frank Capra provides more escapism in *Lost Horizon* for Columbia.

Laurel and Hardy reach comic perfection in *Way Out West*.

Disney's first animated feature, *Snow White and the Seven Dwarfs*, is a huge success.

America's top five money-making stars are Shirley Temple, Clark Gable, Robert Taylor, Bing Crosby, and Joan Withers.

Britain: Will Hay stars in his best comedy, *Oh, Mr Porter*, with help from Moore Marriott and Graham Moffat.

Flora Robson stars as Elizabeth I in *Fire over England*.

Anna Neagle takes the title role in Herbert Wilcox's successful *Victoria the Great*.

Wings of the Morning is the first British film to be made in Technicolor.

MGM open a British offshoot at Denham Studios.

France: Jean Renoir directs a prison-camp drama, *La Grande Illusion*, with Jean Gabin and Erich Von Stroheim, promoting tolerance between nations. It is banned in Nazi Germany and Fascist Italy.

Jean Gabin stars as the romantic gangster in Julien Duvivier's *Pépé Le Moko*. At Von Stroheim's suggestion, MGM acquire the rights to remake it. Duvivier and his female star Mireille Balin leave for Hollywood, but Gabin turns down the trip. Balin is back in France without making a film within a year.

Germany: Director Detlef Sierck makes *La Habanera*, attacking US colonialism, and leaves for Hollywood, where he becomes Douglas Sirk.

Goebbels puts film production under state control.

USSR: Eisenstein's *Bezhin Meadow* is banned.

1938

America: Errol Flynn brings new panache to swashbucklers in *The Adventures of Robin Hood*.

James Cagney stars as the doomed gangster in *Angels with Dirty Faces*, directed by Michael Curtiz.

Walter Wanger acquires the rights to *Pépé Le Moko* and remakes it as *Algiers*, with Charles Boyer and Hedy Lamarr.

Mickey Rooney and Judy Garland star in *Love Finds Andy Hardy*, the first of a wholesome series.

Shirley Temple still has the public enthralled, again topping the list of America's money-making stars, followed by Clark Gable, Sonja Henie, Mickey Rooney, and Spencer Tracy.

Britain: Hitchcock makes *The Lady Vanishes* with its very English chorus of Caldicott and Charters, played by Naughton Wayne and Basil Radford.

Bernard Shaw's *Pygmalion* is filmed with Wendy Hiller in the role of Eliza and earns the author a shared Oscar for best screenplay.

Michael Balcon becomes head of production at Ealing Studios.

France: Marcel Pagnol writes and directs *The Baker's Wife* with Raimu.

Marcel Carné's *Port of Shadows*, starring Jean Gabin and Michèle Morgan, establishes him as a leading director.

Méliès dies.

Germany: Leni Riefenstahl's *Olympia*, a film of the 1936 Olympic Games in Berlin, is released.

USSR: Eisenstein makes *Alexander Nevsky*, a patriotic epic about a German defeat, with a score by Prokoviev.

1939

America: David O. Selznick's *Gone with the Wind*, despite its production problems, swiftly becomes a Hollywood classic and a box-office phenomenon.

Judy Garland stars in *The Wizard of Oz* with Ray Bolger, Bert Lahr, and Jack Haley.

Garbo stars in *Ninotchka*, directed by Ernst Lubitsch and with Billy Wilder among the contributors to its witty script.

John Ford makes *Stagecoach*, giving John Wayne a boost to stardom and reviving the western.

Marlene Dietrich mocks western conventions in *Destry Rides Again*.

Charles Laughton stars as Quasimodo in *The Hunchback of Notre Dame*.

Laurence Olivier scores as Heathcliff in *Wuthering Heights*, directed by William Wyler.

Frank Capra makes the populist *Mr Smith Goes to Washington*, with James Stewart.

In a national poll, 22 million people vote Jeanette MacDonald America's most popular actress. But the professionals' poll of top money-makers is headed by Mickey Rooney, followed by Tyrone Power, Spencer Tracy, Clark Gable, and Shirley Temple, whose appeal is slipping as she grows older.

Britain: As the Second World War begins, cinemas are closed, briefly. Directors are urged to make films to raise morale – and to encourage America to enter the war. Pinewood Studios is used for food storage.

Zoltan Korda makes the rousing *The Four Feathers* with John Clements, Ralph Richardson, and C. Aubrey Smith.

Robert Donat and Greer Garson star in *Goodbye Mr Chips*, directed by Sam Wood at MGM's British studio.

Hitchcock directs the dull *Jamaica Inn* and then heads for Hollywood.

France: Marcel Carné's *Le Jour Se Lève* consolidates his reputation. Hollywood is to remake it eight years later with a happy ending as *The Long Night*.

Jean Renoir's *The Rules of the Game* is banned by the government soon after its release. He leaves for Italy.

Spain: As Franco is triumphant in the civil war, Luis Buñuel moves to New York.

1940

America: Walt Disney's *Pinocchio* builds on the success of *Snow White*; the studio's ambitious *Fantasia* marries animations to classical music and is the first feature to use stereo sound.

Rebecca, Hitchcock's first Hollywood film for David O. Selznick, combines mystery and romance with an impeccable cast headed by Laurence Olivier and Joan Fontaine.

Hitchcock also makes the suspenseful *Foreign Correspondent*, which encourages the US to enter the war.

George Cukor directs the sparkling *The Philadelphia Story*, teaming Katharine Hepburn, Cary Grant, and James Stewart.

Howard Hawks scores with the snappy newspaper comedy *His Girl Friday*.

Chaplin mocks Hitler and Mussolini, but also becomes sententious in *The Great Dictator*.

John Ford makes the sombre, populist *The Grapes of Wrath*.

Writer Preston Sturges turns director with *The Great McGinty*, the first of his exuberant comedies.

W. C. Fields writes (as Mahatma Kane Jeeves) and stars in his best comedy, *The Bank Dick*.

Mickey Rooney heads the list of top money-making stars, followed by Spencer Tracy, Clark Gable, singing cowboy Gene Autry, and Tyrone Power.

Australia: Charles Chauvel's First World War film *Forty Thousand Horsemen* is the first movie to attract attention outside the country for more than a decade.

Britain: Korda produces, Michael Powell and others direct, the great fantasy *The Thief of Bagdad*, pitting Sabu against the wicked Conrad Veidt.

Thorold Dickinson makes the suspenseful *Gaslight* with Anton Walbrook and Diana Wynyard.

Carol Reed directs the comedy thriller *Night Train to Munich*.

Quentin Reynolds narrates the documentary *London Can Take It*, directed by Harry Watt, designed to persuade the US to take up arms.

1941

America: Howard Hawks's *Sergeant York*, about a hero of the First World War, is the hit of the year.

Orson Welles, playing with 'the biggest electric train set a boy ever had', directs and stars in *Citizen Kane*. The film is attacked by the newspapers of William Randolph Hearst, the model for Kane.

Preston Sturges's *Sullivan's Travels* emphasizes the value of comedy.

Laurence Olivier and Vivien Leigh star in Alexander Korda's *That Hamilton Woman*, a mixture of sex and patriotism.

Writer John Huston turns director with the thriller *The Maltese Falcon*, with Humphrey Bogart, Mary Astor, Sidney Greenstreet, and Peter Lorre.

William Dieterle remakes the Faust story as *All that Money Can Buy*, with Walter Huston as the Devil.

Walt Disney releases another classic animated feature, *Dumbo*.

After starring in George Cukor's *Two-Faced Woman*, Garbo retires.

Jean Renoir makes his home in Hollywood.

Mickey Rooney remains America's top money-making star, testifying to the enduring appeal of the sentimental small-town Andy Hardy series, followed by Clark Gable, Abbott and Costello, Bob Hope, and Spencer Tracy.

Britain: Michael Powell's *The Forty-Ninth Parallel* stars Eric Portman as a German trying to escape from Canada to the US.

Dangerous Moonlight combines romance and the war with the music of Richard Addinsell's 'Warsaw Concerto' to provide some welcome escapism.

Leslie Howard brings *The Scarlet Pimpernel* up to date by directing and starring in *Pimpernel Smith*.

Humphrey Jennings directs the documentary *Listen to Britain*, about the effects of the war.

Harry Watt's *Target for Tonight* effectively tells the story of an RAF raid over Germany.

J. Arthur Rank acquires the Odeon cinema chain.

USSR: *Land of Youth* is a 3-D film that does away with the requirement for the audience to wear glasses.

1942

America: Michael Curtiz overcomes severe production problems to deliver, surprisingly, a Hollywood classic, *Casablanca*, with Humphrey Bogart and Ingrid Bergman.

Mervyn Le Roy's *Random Harvest*, with Ronald Colman and Greer Garson, is the weepie of the year, though running it close is *Now, Voyager*, with Bette Davis and Paul Henreid.

Orson Welles's *The Magnificent Ambersons* is re-edited without his approval.

Walt Disney scores again with the animated feature *Bambi*.

Ernst Lubitsch's *To Be or Not to Be*, starring Jack Benny, is fun at the expense of the Nazis.

Sam Wood's *Kings Row*, with Ann Sheridan and Robert Cummings, is gripping melodrama.

Jacques Tourneur's *Cat People* begins another cycle of horror movies, under producer Val Lewton.

Olsen and Johnson star in the anarchic comedy *Hellzapoppin*.

William Wyler's *Mrs Miniver* shows the plucky British coping with the war and scores heavily at the box-office.

Abbott and Costello head the poll of top money-making stars, followed by Clark Gable, Gary Cooper, Mickey Rooney, and Bob Hope.

Britain: David Lean and Noël Coward direct *In Which We Serve*, the archetypal British war film.

Went the Day Well?, directed by Alberto Cavalcanti from a Graham Greene story, shows German paratroopers invading an English village.

Thorold Dickinson's propaganda film *The Next of Kin* is a popular success.

Robert Donat as *Young Mr Pitt*, directed by Carol Reed, provides more wartime propaganda.

Italy: Luchino Visconti's first film, *Ossessione*, based on James M. Cain's *The Postman Always Rings Twice*, begins the flowering of neo-realist films.

1943

America: Howard Hughes's aerodynamic bra lifts Jane Russell to stardom in *The Outlaw*.

The Warner production of Irving Berlin's musical *This Is the Army* and Sam Wood's ponderous version of Ernest Hemingway's *For Whom the Bell Tolls* are the hits of the year.

Stormy Weather, a black musical with Bill Robinson, Lena Horne, and Fats Waller, is the liveliest film of the year.

The forces' pin-up Betty Grable heads the list of top money-making stars, followed by Bob Hope, Abbott and Costello, Bing Crosby, and Gary Cooper.

Britain: Frank Launder and Sidney Gilliat's *Millions Like Us* deals effectively with a family's wartime difficulties.

Gainsborough Films hit on what was to be a successful formula of historical romances with *The Man in Grey*, directed by Leslie Arliss and starring James Mason and Margaret Lockwood.

Michael Powell and Emeric Pressburger make *The Life and Death of Colonel Blimp*.

David MacDonald's *Desert Victory* is a classic war documentary.

Leslie Howard dies when his plane is shot down by Nazis.

R. W. Paul dies.

Denmark: Carl Theodor Dreyer makes the spellbinding melodrama with a message, *Day of Wrath*.

Germany: Josef Von Baky directs *Münchausen*, commemorating the 25th anniversary of UFA.

1944

America: Leo McCarey's *Going My Way*, with Bing Crosby, is the hit of the year.

Billy Wilder's *Double Indemnity*, with Fred MacMurray and Barbara Stanwyck, is a classic film noir.

Otto Preminger's *Laura*, with Dana Andrews and Clifton Webb, is another early example of film noir.

Preston Sturges's *Hail the Conquering Hero* is a deft comedy of small-town attitudes to returning heroes.

Producer Arthur Freed makes MGM the home of the lavish musical, beginning with Vincente Minnelli's *Meet Me in St Louis*, with Judy Garland.

Luis Buñuel heads for Mexico to make films.

Bing Crosby is the top money-making star in America, followed by Gary Cooper, Bob Hope, Betty Grable, and Spencer Tracy.

Britain: Laurence Olivier makes Shakespeare's *Henry V* into a rousing patriotic boost to wartime spirits.

Carol Reed's semi-documentary *The Way Ahead*, with David Niven and Stanley Holloway, is a hit with audiences.

Sidney Gilliat's wartime story of romance and revenge, *Waterloo Road*, catches the mood of the moment.

Sweden: Alf Sjöberg makes *Frenzy*, scripted by Ingmar Bergman, and starring Mai Zetterling and Alf Kjellin.

1945

America: *The Bells of St Mary's* and Hitchcock's *Spellbound*, both starring Ingrid Bergman, are the hits of the year.

Billy Wilder makes an alcoholic classic, *The Lost Weekend*, starring Ray Milland.

Bing Crosby remains the top money-making star, followed by Van Johnson, Greer Garson, Betty Grable, and Spencer Tracy.

Britain: The documentary *True Glory* provides an uplifting account of the last years of the war.

David Lean has audiences laughing and weeping with *Brief Encounter* and *Blithe Spirit*, both written by Noël Coward.

Anthony Asquith's *The Way to the Stars*, written by Terence Rattigan, successfully recreates the wartime mood.

Robert Hamer makes a classic compendium of spooky stories, *Dead of Night*.

Leslie Arliss directs another successful piece of period hokum for Gainsborough, *The Wicked Lady*, with Margaret Lockwood and James Mason.

France: Marcel Carné makes his masterpiece *Les Enfants du Paradis* with Arletty and Jean-Louis Barrault.

Vigo's 12-year-old *Zero for Conduct* is seen for the first time.

Italy: Roberto Rossellini's *Rome, Open City*, using mainly amateur actors, electrifies audiences with its realistic approach.

USSR: Eisenstein makes *Ivan the Terrible, Part II*.

1946

America: Film audiences reach 100 million a week.

William Wyler's *The Best Years of Our Lives*, produced by Sam Goldwyn, is the box-office hit of the year with its stories of servicemen returning to civilian life.

Larry Parks stars as Al Jolson in *The Jolson Story*, another of the year's hits.

Duel in the Sun, produced by David O. Selznik and

directed mainly by King Vidor, brings passion and profit back to the western.

Hitchcock does some of his best work in *Notorious*, with Cary Grant and Ingrid Bergman.

Howard Hawks's *The Big Sleep*, with Humphrey Bogart and Lauren Bacall, is a classic tough thriller.

Frank Capra's optimistic *It's a Wonderful Life* is received coolly, although it goes on to become a Christmas-time classic.

Universal merge with International Pictures to become Universal-International.

Bing Crosby is the American box-office favourite, followed by Ingrid Bergman, Van Johnson, Gary Cooper, and Bob Hope.

Australia: Harry Watt's *The Overlanders*, starring Chips Rafferty, is the first and best result of Ealing Studio's involvement in Australian film.

Britain: 25 million Britons go to the cinema each week.

Humphrey Jennings's documentary *A Diary for Timothy* encapsulates feelings about the war and the future.

David Lean makes a superb adaptation of Dickens's *Great Expectations*.

Michael Powell and Emeric Pressburger's *A Matter of Life and Death* (aka *Stairway to Heaven*) is a witty, stylish fantasy.

Caesar and Cleopatra, with Claude Rains and Vivien Leigh, is, at more than £1m, the most expensive British film so far, but no one cares for it.

Margaret Lockwood becomes Britain's favourite female star.

Feature-film production resumes at Pinewood.

Sir Alexander Korda says that discussions about the British film industry 'succeed only in betraying the sad fact that we have not got one – as yet.'

France: Jean Cocteau's austere and poetic *Beauty and the Beast* is an artistic success.

Italy: Roberto Rossellini consolidates his reputation with his war film *Paisa*.

Vittorio de Sica's *Shoeshine* is another key film in the neo-realist movement, with its story of two boys trying to survive in Nazi-occupied Rome.

1947

America: Edward Dmytryk's tense thriller *Crossfire* confronts racial bigotry.

The House Un-American Activities Committee, chaired by J. Parnell Thomas, holds its first hearings in Los Angeles, at which friendly witnesses condemn Communist subversion in Hollywood. HUAC subpoenas witnesses to appear at further hearings. Writers, directors, and producers who refuse to answer HUAC's questions on their political affiliations, known as the Hollywood Ten, are sentenced to prison (where some find as a fellow inmate J. Parnell Thomas, sentenced for misappropriation of funds). Blacklisting by the studios of those with left-wing sympathies begins and is to continue throughout the 50s. Carl Foreman, Joseph Losey, and Jules Dassin are among those who are to leave the US for Britain.

The top five money-making stars are the bland Bing Crosby, Betty Grable, Ingrid Bergman, Gary Cooper, and Humphrey Bogart.

Britain: Ronald Hamer's *It Always Rains on Sunday*, starring Googie Withers and John McCallum, is a sensational low-life melodrama.

Carol Reed directs *Odd Man Out*, starring James Mason, a performance that takes him to Hollywood.

The Boulting Brothers film *Brighton Rock*, Graham Greene's tale of a petty criminal, starring Richard Attenborough.

Michael Powell and Emeric Pressburger's heady *Black Narcissus* is one of the cinema's most beautiful films.

American studios embargo their films being shown, following a tax imposed on export. As Rank gears up to fill the cinemas with British films, the embargo is lifted, causing Rank financial problems. Managing director John Davis, who regards producers and directors as extravagant, wields the axe.

France: Claude Autant-Lara's *Devil in the Flesh* makes Gérard Philipe a star.

1948

America: Jules Dassin's *The Naked City* adopts a semi-documentary approach to a murder mystery.

Fred Astaire returns to dancing in *Easter Parade*, with Judy Garland.

The melodramatic *Johnny Belinda*, directed by Jean Negulesco, makes Jane Wyman a star.

The Supreme Court rules that the five major studios can no longer own cinemas, so breaking their monopoly of the industry.

Millionaire Howard Hughes buys RKO.

America's top five money-making stars are Bing Crosby, Betty Grable, Abbott and Costello, Gary Cooper, and Bob Hope.

Britain: David Lean's *Oliver Twist* is another successful Dickens adaptation, notable for Alec Guinness's performance as Fagin.

Michael Powell and Emeric Pressburger's *The Red Shoes*, with Moira Shearer, makes ballet box-office.

Carol Reed's *The Fallen Idol*, with Ralph Richardson, is a near-perfect piece of small-scale cinema.

Iceland: Loftur Gudmundsson makes the first talkie, *Between the Mountains and the Sea*.

Italy: Vittorio De Sica's *The Bicycle Thief* is hailed as a neo-realist classic.

Luchino Visconti takes neo-realism to its limits with *La Terra Trema*, about a Sicilian fisherman and his family.

Giuseppe De Santis's *Bitter Rice* attacks American corruption of Italian culture, but it is Silvano Mangano at work in the rice fields who attracts international attention.

USSR: Eisenstein dies less than three weeks after his 50th birthday.

1949

America: William Dieterle's glossy *Portrait of Jennie*, with Jennifer Jones and Joseph Cotten, is David O. Selznick's last production with his company, which he folds soon after.

James Cagney is back at his energetic best as a brutal gangster in the searing *White Heat*.

Cecil B. De Mille's *Samson and Delilah*, with Victor Mature and Hedy Lamarr in the title roles, is a hit despite derisive reviews.

Gene Kelly and Stanley Donen's *On the Town*, produced by Arthur Freed and with a cast that includes Kelly, Frank Sinatra, and Vera-Ellen, is one of the best-ever musicals.

Larry Parks scores another hit with *Jolson Sings Again*.

The top five money-making stars are Bob Hope, Bing Crosby, Abbott and Costello, John Wayne, and Gary Cooper.

Britain: Carol Reed directs the thrilling *The Third Man*, starring Orson Welles and with Anton Karas's haunting zither music.

Three Ealing comedies make the studio's reputation: Henry Cornelius's *Passport to Pimlico*, Alexander Mackendrick's *Whisky Galore*, and Robert Hamer's *Kind Hearts and Coronets*.

Rank sells its Shepherd's Bush studios to BBC-TV.

France: Jacques Tati's *Jour de Fête* introduces his gentle humour to the world.

1950

America: Billy Wilder's *Sunset Boulevard* is a tart classic, with William Holden as the innocent who becomes involved with ageing star Gloria Swanson.

Joseph Mankiewicz's *All about Eve* gives Bette Davis the best role of her career as a bitchy actress.

Delmer Daves's *Broken Arrow* is the first revisionist western, on the side of the Indians.

Judy Holliday scores as the not-so-dumb chorus girl in *Born Yesterday*, directed by George Cukor.

Disney's live-action film *Treasure Island* provides Robert Newton with the opportunity for an eye-rolling, lip-smacking performance as Long John Silver.

The top five money-making stars are John Wayne, Bob Hope, Bing Crosby, Betty Grable, and James Stewart.

Britain: Basil Dearden directs the crime drama *The Blue Lamp*, starring Dirk Bogarde and Jack Warner, which is to inspire the long-running television series *Dixon of Dock Green*.

The Boulting Brothers make a tense and influential thriller, *Seven Days to Noon*.

Frank Launder's *The Happiest Days of Your Life* is a sprightly comedy, sparked by the performances of Alastair Sim and Margaret Rutherford.

The prison-camp drama, *The Wooden Horse*, is a success, as nostalgia for recent heroics continues.

France: Jean Cocteau's *Orpheus* is a fantastic success and a successful fantasy.

Max Ophuls makes the stylish and sexy *La Ronde*. Its banning in New York leads to a court case that eventually frees films from local censorship.

Robert Bresson directs the austere *The Diary of a Country Priest*.

Italy: Ingrid Bergman stars in *Stromboli*, directed by Roberto Rossellini, and scandalizes many when she has a child by him, an event that is to keep her away from Hollywood for much of the decade.

Mexico: Luis Buñuel signals his re-emergence with *The Young and the Damned*.

Sweden: Alf Sjöberg directs Anita Björk and Ulf Palme in an exemplary version of Strindberg's *Miss Julie*.

1951

America: Vincente Minnelli scores with *An American in Paris*, culminating in a ballet sequence for Gene Kelly and Leslie Caron.

Marlon Brando makes his film debut in the role that brought him fame on Broadway: Stanley Kowalski in *A Streetcar Named Desire*, directed by Elia Kazan.

Montgomery Clift is at his best in the steamy *A Place in the Sun*, also starring Elizabeth Taylor and directed by George Stevens.

Hitchcock makes the quirky *Strangers on a Train*, with Farley Granger and Robert Walker.

Dean Martin and Jerry Lewis star in *Sailor, Beware* to become the top comedy act.

Howard Hawks's *The Thing* begins a cycle of

monster movies, based on fear of the atom bomb.

Larry Parks admits to having been a Communist at the HUAC hearings. His contract with Columbia, and his film career, ends.

Louis B. Mayer is forced out of MGM, to be replaced by Dore Schary.

The box-office favourites are John Wayne, Dean Martin and Jerry Lewis, Betty Grable, Abbott and Costello, and Bing Crosby.

Britain: Ealing comedies keep audiences happy with Charles Crichton's *The Lavender Hill Mob* and Alexander Mackendrick's *The Man in the White Suit*, starring Alec Guinness.

John Huston's *The African Queen* delights, with the antagonistic Humphrey Bogart and Katharine Hepburn.

Michael Powell and Emeric Pressburger's *The Tales of Hoffman* combines operetta and ballet in a remarkable way.

John Boulting directs the pageant-like *The Magic Box*, on the life of William Friese-Greene, as part of the Festival of Britain celebrations.

France: Robert Bresson's *Diary of a Country Priest* gains him international fame.

Japan: Kurosawa's *Rashomon* opens Western eyes to Japanese cinema.

Yashujiro Ozu makes the complex family drama *Early Summer*.

1952

America: Cecil B. De Mille's circus film, *The Greatest Show on Earth*, is a smash hit.

This Is Cinerama, a film using stereo sound and a wide-screen process that requires three projectors, causes a sensation with its opening roller-coaster ride, but the system is cumbersome and there are no more than 40 cinemas equipped to show its films by the early 60s.

Fred Zinnemann makes a classic western, *High Noon*, with Gary Cooper, which can be read as a condemnation of blacklisting in Hollywood.

Gene Kelly stars in *Singin' in the Rain*, a brilliant musical about Hollywood at the time the talkies arrived.

Charlie Chaplin's *Limelight* seems a sentimental farewell to his own past.

Arch Oboler's *Bwana Devil* revives interest in 3-D films.

Charlie Chaplin leaves to visit Britain and is told by the Attorney-General not to return.

John Garfield dies of a heart attack. Friends claim it was caused by the stress of his appearance as an unfriendly witness before HUAC and his subsequent blacklisting.

Decca Records takes over Universal.

Dean Martin and Jerry Lewis are tops at the box-office, followed by Gary Cooper, John Wayne, Bing Crosby, and Bob Hope.

Britain: David Lean directs the topical *The Sound Barrier*, with Ralph Richardson and Nigel Patrick.

Anthony Asquith's version of Oscar Wilde's *The Importance of Being Earnest* captures Edith Evans's definitive performance as Lady Bracknell.

The National Film Theatre is created from a cinema built for the Festival of Britain.

France: René Clément directs *Forbidden Games*, a sombre film of childhood trauma.

Jacques Becker's *Casque d'Or*, with Simone Signoret and Serge Reggiani, is an impeccable piece of film-making.

Brigitte Bardot lands her first significant role in

The Lighthouse Keeper's Daughter and marries her mentor, Roger Vadim.

Fernandel becomes an international star in *The Little World of Don Camillo*.

Italy: Vittorio De Sica makes the deeply pessimistic *Umberto D*, a study of neglected old age.

Federico Fellini directs the satirical *The White Sheik*.

Japan: Kenji Mizoguchi directs *The Life of Oharu*, about a samurai's daughter's ill-fated love for a servant.

1953

America: In an attempt to combat falling audiences and the influence of television, Twentieth Century-Fox shows off CinemaScope, its new wide-screen process, with *The Robe*, which becomes the most successful film of the year and one of the big hits of the decade.

From Here to Eternity, with Burt Lancaster and Deborah Kerr rolling in the sand and sea, is also a box-office success.

Vincente Minnelli makes another classic musical for MGM, *The Band Wagon*, with Fred Astaire and his English equivalent, Jack Buchanan.

George Stevens's western *Shane* pits Alan Ladd against Jack Palance.

Joseph Mankiewicz's *Julius Caesar* combines the classical English acting of John Gielgud and the Method of Marlon Brando.

The horror film *The House of Wax*, starring Vincent Price, gives 3-D films a further fillip. It is directed by the one-eyed André de Toth.

Chaplin sells his Hollywood studio and settles in Switzerland.

Gary Cooper is the top money-making star followed by Dean Martin and Jerry Lewis, John Wayne, Alan Ladd, and Bing Crosby.

Britain: Cosy comedy predominates, exemplified by Henry Cornelius's *Genevieve*, with Kenneth More.

The Cruel Sea, with its stiff-upper-lipped officers still fighting the war, is a good representative of the alternative, and audiences flock to it.

Cecil Hepworth dies.

France: Jacques Tati's *Monsieur Hulot's Holiday* develops his concept of comedy without stars.

Henri-Georges Clouzot's thriller *The Wages of Fear* electrifies audiences and provides Yves Montand with his first serious role.

Italy: Federico Fellini's *I Vitelloni*, in the neo-realist tradition, focuses on the aimless young.

Jean Renoir, having left the US, makes the unsuccessful *The Golden Coach* with Anna Magnani.

Japan: Yashujiro Ozu's *Tokyo Story* is an austere and moving drama of disappointments.

Teinosuke Kinugasa's 12th-century saga *Gate of Hell* wins the top prize at Cannes and an Oscar.

Kenji Mizoguchi's 16th-century story *Ugetsu Monogatari* is hailed at the Venice Film Festival.

Mexico: Luis Buñuel makes a brilliantly faithful version of *The Adventures of Robinson Crusoe* with Dan O'Herlihy.

1954

America: Elia Kazan's *On the Waterfront*, with Marlon Brando and Rod Steiger at their best, can be read as his apologia for naming names to HUAC; it is powerfully convincing on its own terms.

Brando also plays a somewhat elderly rebel in *The Wild One*, a biker movie that causes controversy.

Hitchcock's teasing thriller *Rear Window* stars Grace Kelly and James Stewart as a voyeuristic photographer.

Judy Garland and James Mason bring passion to the remake of *A Star Is Born*, but it at first fails to find an audience and is drastically cut.

Gordon Douglas's *Them!*, with its giant ants, is the first of a cycle of post-atomic monster movies.

Paramount's VistaVision wide-screen process makes its debut in *White Christmas*, a cosy musical with Bing Crosby. The process fades by the end of the 50s.

Samuel Z. Arkoff and James H. Nicholson found American International Pictures (AIP), the low-budget film company that includes Roger Corman among its producers.

John Wayne is America's top money-making star, followed by Dean Martin and Jerry Lewis, Gary Cooper, James Stewart, and Marilyn Monroe.

Britain: David Lean's *Hobson's Choice* features Charles Laughton at his best.

Alexander Mackendrick's Ealing comedy *The Maggie* comes perilously close to *Whisky Galore* but manages to amuse.

Frank Launder's *The Belles of St Trinian's*, with Alastair Sim in drag, is a commercial success and brings three sequels.

Ralph Thomas's *Doctor in the House*, with Dirk Bogarde and James Robertson Justice, is a comic success, but unfortunately results in several sequels.

The BBFC bans *The Wild One*, which will not be seen in Britain until 1968.

Italy: Vittorio De Sica makes Sophia Loren a star in *The Gold of Naples*, the first of their six collaborations.

Federico Fellini's *La Strada*, with Giulietta Masina and Anthony Quinn, infuses neo-realism with poetry in its story of an ill-used simpleton.

Japan: Akira Kurosawa directs the exciting and action-filled epic *The Seven Samurai* with Toshiro Mifune.

Poland: Andrzej Wajda directs *A Generation* starring Zbigniew Cybulski.

1955

America: A new star is born, and quickly dies: James Dean makes *East of Eden* and *Rebel without a Cause* – before crashing his sports car and becoming an enduring screen icon.

Spencer Tracy stars with Robert Ryan in John Sturges's seminal suspense thriller, *Bad Day at Black Rock*.

Paddy Chayevsky's TV play *Marty* transfers successfully to the screen, bringing stardom to Ernest Borgnine.

Billy Wilder's *The Seven Year Itch* makes the most of Marilyn Monroe's comic talents.

Charles Laughton directs *The Night of the Hunter*; its reputation is to grow with the years.

Rock 'n' roll arrives with Bill Haley and the Comets singing 'Rock around the Clock' behind the credits of *The Blackboard Jungle*, about life in a slum school. Within months, Haley and others will be starring in cheap exploitation movies, such as *Rock around the Clock* and *Don't Knock the Rock*, and popular music will never be the same.

Robert Aldrich's *Kiss Me Deadly* announces the arrival of an overwrought talent.

Oklahoma is shown in Todd-AO, a new wide-screen process promoted by showman Mike Todd.

Disney opens the first Disneyland, extending the appeal of its films and characters.

Hitchcock luminaries James Stewart and Grace Kelly head America's money-making stars, followed by John Wayne, William Holden, and Gary Cooper.

Britain: Yet another war film, Michael Anderson's *The Dam Busters*, does well, thanks to R. C. Sherriff's script and the acting of Michael Redgrave and others.

Alexander Mackendrick's *The Ladykillers* is almost the last of the Ealing comedies.

John Halas and Joy Batchelor direct Britain's first animated feature, George Orwell's *Animal Farm*.

Brigitte Bardot stars with Dirk Bogarde in *Doctor at Sea*.

Hammer Films, a small production company recycling TV programmes, strikes it rich with *The Quatermass Experiment*, a horror movie based on a BBC serial written by Nigel Kneale.

France: Jean Renoir makes a frothy musical, *French Cancan*, with Jean Gabin.

Henri-Georges Clouzot's *Les Diaboliques* is a grim suspense story.

Henri Verneuil's *The Sheep Has Five Legs* gives comedian Fernandel the six roles of his life.

Jules Dassin's film *Rififi*, with its tense safe-cracking sequence, captures audiences' imaginations around the world.

Max Ophuls directs the sumptuous *Lola Montes*.

India: Satyajit Ray's *Pather Panchali* is an art-house hit in the West.

Sweden: Bergman's comedy Smiles of a Summer Night brings him international recognition.

1956

America: Cecil B. De Mille's *The Ten Commandments* tops the box-office.

George Stevens's family saga *Giant* also does well, owing in part to the growing cult around James Dean.

Mike Todd's star-packed *Around the World in Eighty Days*, in Todd-AO, is a hit.

John Ford's *The Searchers* provides John Wayne with his best, most complex role.

Forbidden Planet, starring Leslie Nielsen, gives a science-fiction twist to Shakespeare's *The Tempest*.

The blacklisted Dalton Trumbo, writing under a pseudonym, wins an Oscar for *The Brave One*.

Fox experiment with CinemaScope 55, using 55mm film, for *Carousel*, but the process is not a success.

Dore Schary is sacked from MGM.

Darryl F. Zanuck leaves Twentieth Century-Fox.

Dean Martin and Jerry Lewis split.

Fritz Lang decides he has had enough of Hollywood.

William Holden is the top money-making star, followed by John Wayne, James Stewart, Burt Lancaster, and Glenn Ford.

Britain: Jack Lee's war film *A Town Like Alice*, with Virginia McKenna and Peter Finch, is a hit.

Hammer Films switches its attention to horror, reviving a Universal favourite with *The Curse of Frankenstein*, starring Christopher Lee and Peter Cushing and directed by Terence Fisher.

Lindsay Anderson, Karel Reisz, and others issue the Free Cinema manifesto.

The BBC buys Ealing Studios.

France: Robert Bresson's *A Man Escaped* details an escape by a Resistance fighter imprisoned by the Nazis.

India: Satyajit Ray makes *Aparajito*, a sequel to *Pather Panchali*.

Italy: Fellini's *Cabiria* (aka *The Nights of Cabiria*) is a life-enhancing look at Roman low-life.

Japan: Kon Ichikawa directs the horrifying war film *The Burmese Harp*.

Poland: Andrzej Wajda directs *Kanal*, starring Zbigniew Cybulski as one of the Polish partisans trapped in the sewers of Warsaw by the Nazis.

1957

America: Stanley Kubrick directs the overpowering *Paths of Glory*, set in the First World War.

Don Siegel's *The Invasion of the Body Snatchers* is a brilliantly effective paranoid parable.

Sidney Lumet makes *Twelve Angry Men*, a TV play that transfers successfully to the screen.

Alexander Mackendrick makes the moody, brilliant *Sweet Smell of Success*, with Burt Lancaster and Tony Curtis.

Mark Robson's *Peyton Place*, from a bestselling novel, is a hit; in the 60s it will become a long-running TV soap opera.

William Hanna and Joseph Barbera found Hanna-Barbera Productions to make family entertainment for television, including such animated series as *The Flintstones*.

Rock Hudson becomes America's top star at the box-office, followed by John Wayne, Pat Boone, Elvis Presley, and Frank Sinatra.

Argentina: Leopold Torre Nilsson gains international recognition with *The House of the Angel*.

Britain: David Lean's *The Bridge on the River Kwai*, produced by Sam Spiegel and starring William Holden and Alec Guinness, is the box-office success of the year.

Hammer Films remake *Dracula*, with Christopher Lee in the title role, and *The Revenge of Frankenstein*, with Peter Cushing.

France: Brigitte Bardot becomes an international star as Roger Vadim's *And God Created Woman* is released around the world.

Japan: Akira Kurosawa's *Throne of Blood* re-invents Shakespeare's *Macbeth*.

Sweden: Ingmar Bergman's reputation is made with *The Seventh Seal*, with the gaunt Max Von Sydow as a knight returning from the Crusades, and the gentler *Wild Strawberries*, starring Victor Sjöström.

USSR: Mikhail Kalatozov makes the sleek love story *The Cranes Are Flying*.

1958

America: Rodgers and Hammerstein's musical *South Pacific*, despite its old-fashioned air and airs, is the hit of the year.

Orson Welles stars in, and directs, the brooding thriller *Touch of Evil*.

Hitchcock's dizzying thriller *Vertigo* stars James Stewart as a man trying to remake the past.

Harry Cohn, head of Columbia, dies.

Mike Todd is killed in a plane crash.

The top five money-making stars are Glenn Ford, Elizabeth Taylor, Jerry Lewis, Marlon Brando, and Rock Hudson.

Britain: Gerald Thomas's *Carry On Sergeant*, an army farce produced by Peter Rogers, is a surprising hit; it begins a sequence of low-budget Carry On comedies that are to become a profitable staple of British cinema.

Mark Robson directs *The Inn of the Sixth Happiness* starring Ingrid Bergman, with Wales standing in for its Chinese locations.

France: Louis Malle's *Lift to the Scaffold* (aka *Frantic*) and *The Lovers*, both starring Jeanne

Moreau, announce the arrival of the French 'New Wave'.

Mexico: Luis Buñuel directs *Nazarin*, about a priest who tries to follow Christ's example.

Poland: Andrzej Wajda makes the compelling *Ashes and Diamonds*, starring Zbigniew Cybulski as a man confused about killing after the end of war.

Sweden: Ingmar Bergman's startling *The Face* stars Max Von Sydow as a 19th-century magician.

1959

America: William Wyler's *Ben Hur* takes epic amounts of money at the box-office.

Hitchcock makes his chase thriller *North by Northwest*, with Cary Grant doing the running.

Billy Wilder directs his comic masterpiece *Some Like It Hot*.

Behind the Great Wall is the first film to be shown in Aromarama. It is also the last.

Joseph E. Levine buys US rights to *Hercules*, a cheap Italian film, and spends $1.2m on promoting it; it becomes a hit, making body-builder Steve Reeves a star and starting a cycle of muscle-man movies.

Herbert Yates resigns as president of Republic Pictures and production ceases.

Cecil B. De Mille dies.

Rock Hudson is America's top money-making star, along with Cary Grant, James Stewart, Doris Day, and Debbie Reynolds.

Brazil: French director Marcel Camus's *Black Orpheus* uses myth and carnival to impressive effect.

Britain: Jack Cardiff's *Room at the Top* claims to bring sex and the industrial north into British films.

Tony Richard and John Osborne form Woodfall Films with producer Harry Saltzman to film Osborne's *Look Back in Anger*, a play that helped bring a new realism to British theatre.

Young Hayley Mills becomes a star in *Tiger Bay*, directed by J. Lee-Thompson.

Peter Cushing and Christopher Lee star in *The Mummy* for Hammer, directed by Terence Fisher.

Rank backs Richard Attenborough, Bryan Forbes, and others in founding Allied Film Makers.

France: Claude Chabrol's *The Cousins* rides the New Wave.

Cocteau's final masterpiece is *Testament of Orpheus*.

François Truffaut's *The 400 Blows* is the first of his semi-autobiographical films to track the life of Antoine Doinel, played by Jean-Pierre Léaud.

Alain Resnais directs *Hiroshima, Mon Amour*, written by Marguerite Duras.

Germany: Bernard Wicki directs *The Bridge*, about boy soldiers in the last days of the war.

Greece: Jules Dassin makes *Never on Sunday*, with Melina Mercouri and a hummable score by Monos Hadjidakis.

India: Satyajit Ray makes *The World of Apu*, the third film in his trilogy.

USSR: Grigori Chukrai's *Ballad of a Soldier* focuses on the detail of everyday life.

1960

America: Alfred Hitchcock's creepy *Psycho*, with a twitchy Anthony Perkins, scores at the box-office.

John Sturges remakes *The Seven Samurai* as a western, *The Magnificent Seven*. It results in three sequels.

Roger Corman's *The House of Usher* for AIP,

starring Vincent Price, starts a new horror cycle.

John Cassavetes makes the semi-improvised *Shadows*, which is to influence many independent film-makers.

Scent of Mystery is the first feature to be shown in Smell-o-Vision. It is also the last.

Joseph E. Levine repeats his success with *Hercules Unchained*, again starring Steve Reeves.

New York's Roxy Theater, once the largest and grandest cinema in the world, is demolished 33 years after it was opened.

Doris Day and Rock Hudson, a double act in innocuous comedies, are America's top stars at the box-office, followed by Cary Grant, Elizabeth Taylor, and Debbie Reynolds.

Australia: Fred Zinnemann makes *The Sundowners*, with Robert Mitchum, Deborah Kerr, and the ubiquitous Chips Rafferty.

Britain: Karel Reisz's gritty, anti-authoritarian *Saturday Night and Sunday Morning*, with Albert Finney, is to transform British cinema, for a time.

Michael Powell's voyeuristic *Peeping Tom* upsets audiences and critics.

Richard Attenborough and Bryan Forbes produce, and Guy Green directs, the topical *The Angry Silence*.

Jack Cardiff directs D. H. Lawrence's *Sons and Lovers*, with Dean Stockwell and Trevor Howard.

France: Jean-Luc Godard's *Breathless* is a New Wave hit in art cinemas and makes a star of Jean-Paul Belmondo.

Louis Malle directs the inventive comedy *Zazie dans le Métro*.

François Truffaut makes *Shoot the Pianist*, starring Charles Aznavour.

Italy: Fellini's *La Dolce Vita*, starring Marcello Mastroianni and Anita Ekberg, is a worldwide hit, with its depiction of the wasted lives of the rich in Rome.

Visconti directs *Rocco and His Brothers*, with Alain Delon, about a peasant family in Milan.

Michelangelo's *L'Avventura*, with Monica Vitti, and *La Notte*, starring Marcello Mastroianni, Jeanne Moreau, and Monica Vitti, make the emptiness of life seem attractive.

Vittorio De Sica's *Two Women* gives Sophia Loren her best screen role.

1961

America: Robert Wise and Jerome Robbins make a successful film of the stage hit *West Side Story*.

Robert Rossen directs the brilliantly handled *The Hustler*, with Paul Newman and Jackie Gleason.

Disney releases *One Hundred and One Dalmatians*, which is to be its last splendid animated feature for 30 years.

Elizabeth Taylor becomes the top money-making star, followed by Rock Hudson, Doris Day, John Wayne, and Cary Grant.

Britain: Tony Richardson directs another 'kitchen sink' drama, *A Taste of Honey*, with Rita Tushingham, Dora Bryan, and Murray Melvin.

Basil Dearden's *Victim*, starring Dirk Bogarde, is one of the first films to deal sympathetically with homosexuality.

Joseph Losey makes the science-fiction *The Damned* for Hammer Films.

Pop singer Cliff Richard stars in the innocuous musical *The Young Ones*, directed by Sidney J. Furie.

France: Alain Resnais directs the enigmatic *Last Year at Marienbad*.

Italy: Poet and novelist Pier Paolo Pasolini directs his first film, the low-life *Accatone*.

Francesco Rosi makes *Salvatore Giuliano*, about a Sicilian bandit.

Pietro Germi's *Divorce Italian Style* mocks the country's divorce laws.

Ermanno Olmi makes the social comedy *The Job*.

Japan: Kurosawa directs *Yojimbo*, with Toshiro Mifune as a wandering samurai.

Spain: Luis Buñuel returns to Spain at the government's invitation and makes the sacrilegious *Viridiana*; it is promptly banned.

Sweden: Max Von Sydow goes to Hollywood to play Christ in *The Greatest Story Ever Told*.

1962

America: John Frankenheimer directs the brilliantly plotted thriller *The Manchurian Candidate*.

Robert Aldrich shocks by casting Bette Davis and Joan Crawford as two ageing, homicidal harridans in *Whatever Happened to Baby Jane?*

Darryl F. Zanuck returns to Twentieth Century-Fox as president with his son Richard as head of production as the company runs into difficulties over the out-of-control *Cleopatra*, starring Richard Burton and Elizabeth Taylor. His production of *The Longest Day*, about the Allied landings at Normandy, is a hit.

MCA acquire Universal.

Doris Day and Rock Hudson bounce back as the top money-makers, followed by Cary Grant, John Wayne, and Elvis Presley.

Britain: Tony Richardson directs the anti-authoritarian *The Loneliness of the Long Distance Runner*, starring Tom Courtenay.

John Schlesinger makes *A Kind of Loving*, with Alan Bates, June Ritchie, and Thora Hird.

David Lean's painstaking epic *Lawrence of Arabia* brings stardom to the lanky Peter O'Toole in the title role as the short, enigmatic hero.

Sean Connery plays James Bond in *Dr No*, a role that elevates him to stardom and begins a profitable cycle of films.

France: François Truffaut directs *Jules and Jim*, starring Jeanne Moreau as the woman shared by two friends.

Germany: 26 film-makers issue a manifesto for a new German feature film.

Japan: Yashujiro Ozu makes his last film, *An Autumn Afternoon*, on the loneliness of old age.

Mexico: Luis Buñuel directs *The Exterminating Angel*, about dinner guests who find themselves unable to leave the room.

Poland: Roman Polanski's *Knife in the Water* is attacked by the authorities and he soon leaves to work elsewhere.

USSR: Andrei Tarkovsky makes the tragic *Ivan's Childhood*, about a boy who joins the partisans.

1963

America: Martin Ritt directs the incisive character drama *Hud*, well acted by Paul Newman, Patricia Neal, and Melvyn Douglas.

Cleopatra is released but fails to make a profit.

Andy Warhol and his entourage begin making films at his Factory.

AIP's *Beach Party*, with Annette Funicello and Frankie Avalon, begins a cycle of beach movies.

Doris Day remains the top money-making star, followed by John Wayne, Rock Hudson, Jack Lemmon, and Cary Grant.

Brazil: Glauber Rocha gains an international

reputation with his grim and violent *Black God, White Devil*.

Britain: Joseph Losey directs *The Servant*, scripted by Harold Pinter and starring Dirk Bogarde and James Fox.

Lindsay Anderson makes the tough *This Sporting Life*, written by David Storey and starring Richard Harris and Rachel Roberts.

Tony Richardson and John Osborne bring sex and exuberance to the cinema in *Tom Jones*, portrayed by Albert Finney.

John Schlesinger's *Billy Liar*, starring Tom Courtenay and Julie Christie, is another seminal film in the revival of British cinema, taken from Keith Waterhouse's novel of adolescent fantasy.

Italy: Fellini's brilliantly self-indulgent *8[fr1/2]*, with Marcello Mastroianni, depicts an artist suffering from a creative block.

Visconti makes a perfect adaptation of Giuseppe de Lampedusa's *The Leopard*, about the decline of the Sicilian aristocracy.

1964

America: Disney's *Mary Poppins*, with Julie Andrews, is the hit of the year.

Franklin Schaffner's *The Best Man*, starring Henry Fonda, is a brilliant political melodrama, as is John Frankenheimer's *Seven Days in May*, with Kirk Douglas.

Sidney Lumet's *Fail Safe* deals frighteningly with the threat of nuclear war.

Doris Day is still the most bankable star, followed by Jack Lemmon, Rock Hudson, John Wayne, and Cary Grant.

Britain: Stanley Kubrick makes the blackly comic *Dr Strangelove*, with Peter Sellers and George C. Scott.

Richard Lester finds a way to make the Beatles funny in *A Hard Day's Night*

. Guy Hamilton directs the Bond film *Goldfinger*.

Michael Winner makes *The System*, about sex at the seaside.

France: Jacques Demy's musical *The Umbrellas of Cherbourg*, written by Michel Legrand, charms audiences everywhere.

Greece: Michael Cacoyannis's *Zorba the Greek*, with Anthony Quinn and the music of Mikis Theodorakis, is an international hit.

Italy: Sergio Leone borrows the plot of Kurosawa's *Yojimbo* for his western *A Fistful of Dollars*, starring a young American television actor, Clint Eastwood. Its success is helped by the evocative music of Ennio Morricone.

Antonioni's *The Red Desert*, with Monica Vitti and Richard Harris, revels in the possibilities for colour in film.

Bernardo Bertolucci's *Before the Revolution* heralds the arrival of a new, politicized talent.

Japan: Masaki Kobayashi's *Kwaidan* is a collection of perfectly composed ghost stories.

USSR: Innokenti Smoktunovsky is an impressive Hamlet in a version of Shakespeare's tragedy directed by Grigori Kozintsev.

1965

America: Robert Wise's *The Sound of Music*, starring Julie Andrews, is a massive hit.

Daniel Mann directs *Our Man Flint*, starring James Coburn, in an attempt to duplicate the success of the Bond movies. It fails.

David Lean's romantic *Dr Zhivago*, starring Omar Sharif and Julie Christie, is a worldwide box-office hit.

The Bond movies take British actor Sean Connery to the top of the list of money-making stars,

followed by John Wayne, Doris Day, Julie Andrews, and Jack Lemmon.

Britain: The new Bond movie, *Thunderball*, is another big hit.

Sidney J. Furie's *The Ipcress File*, with Michael Caine as a shabby agent, attempts to cash in on the Bond phenomenon.

Richard Lester's comic *The Knack* gives impetus to the image of what is soon to be called 'Swinging London'.

John Schlesinger's *Darling*, with Julie Christie, catches the mood of the moment.

Roman Polanski makes the psychological horror film *Repulsion*, with Catherine Deneuve.

Czechoslovakia: Milos Forman directs *A Blonde in Love* (aka *Loves of a Blonde*).

France: Jean-Luc Godard directs the futuristic *Alphaville*, starring Eddie Constantine.

Hungary: Miklós Jancsó's *The Round-Up* gains him international recognition.

Italy: Fellini makes his first film in colour, the exuberant *Juliet of the Spirits*.

Sergio Leone's *For a Few Dollars More* establishes spaghetti westerns and Clint Eastwood as forces to be reckoned with.

1966

America: Sidney Lumet's *The Group*, from Mary McCarthy's novel, is the most talked-about film of the year with its cast of unknowns, who mostly remain so.

Mike Nichols films Edward Albee's *Who's Afraid of Virginia Woolf?* with Hollywood's most famous couple, Richard Burton and Elizabeth Taylor, as the embattled husband and wife.

Roger Corman's *The Wild Angels* for AIP begins a cycle of biker and youthful-protest movies.

Charles Bluhdorn's Gulf Western acquire Paramount Pictures.

Seven Arts Productions acquires Warner Bros.

Two British talents, Julie Andrews and Sean Connery, head the poll of money-making stars, followed by Elizabeth Taylor, Jack Lemmon, and Richard Burton.

Britain: Fred Zinnemann directs an impeccable version of Robert Bolt's play *A Man for All Seasons*, finely performed by Paul Scofield and Robert Shaw.

Michael Caine becomes an international star as the raffish *Alfie*, directed by Lewis Gilbert from Bill Naughton's play.

Antonioni comes to London to make *Blow-Up* with David Hemmings as a fashionable fashion photographer.

Karel Reisz directs the anarchic *Morgan*, which gives David Warner his best role before he goes to Hollywood to become a fixture in horror movies.

Silvio Narrizano's *Georgy Girl*, with James Mason and Lynn Redgrave, gives further impetus to the image of London as the place to be.

Universal Pictures establish a London office and other American companies step up local productions.

Czechoslovakia: Vera Chytilova makes the lively comedy *Daisies*, which runs into censorship problems.

Jiri Menzel directs the mainly comic *Closely Observed Trains*.

France: Claude Lelouch directs the romantic *A Man and a Woman*, with Jean-Louis Trintignant and Anouk Aimée and the music of Francis Lai.

Robert Bresson directs *Balthazar*, about the life of a donkey, with a non-professional cast.

Italy: Gillo Pontecorvo's *The Battle of Algiers* uses a documentary style to great effect.

Sergio Leone's spaghetti western *The Good, the Bad and the Ugly* not only confirms Clint Eastwood as a star but also elevates former bit-player Lee Van Cleef.

Spain: Orson Welles finishes his Shakespeare adaptation, *Chimes at Midnight*, with himself as Falstaff.

Sweden: Ingmar Bergman directs the intense *Persona*, with Liv Ullmann and Bibi Andersson.

USSR: Andrei Tarkovsky's masterly historical work *Andrei Rublev* is banned.

1967

America: Mike Nichols' *The Graduate*, with Dustin Hoffman, hits a nerve with the young and is the hit of the year, followed by the safer inter-racial *Guess Who's Coming to Dinner*, starring Spencer Tracy, Katharine Hepburn, and Sidney Poitier.

Norman Jewison's thriller *In the Heat of the Night* is a better examination of racial prejudice, excellently acted by Sidney Poitier and Rod Steiger.

Arthur Penn's *Bonnie and Clyde* sets a new style for gangster films and brings stardom to Warren Beatty and Faye Dunaway.

Robert Aldrich establishes his own film studio following the success of his war film *The Dirty Dozen*.

Julie Andrews retains her appeal at the box-office, followed by Lee Marvin, Paul Newman, Dean Martin, and Sean Connery.

Britain: Joseph Losey directs *Accident*, scripted by Harold Pinter and starring Michael York and Dirk Bogarde.

Czechoslovakia

: Milos Forman directs the comic *The Foreman's Ball*. In France the next year when the Russians invade, he subsequently goes to America, as does his colleague Ivan Passer.

France: Luis Buñuel directs the elegant, teasing *Belle de Jour*, starring Catherine Deneuve.

Jean-Luc Godard makes the ferocious *Weekend*.

Hungary: Miklós Jancsó makes the epic *The Red and the White*.

Italy: Pasolini directs a version of Sophocles's tragedy *Oedipus Rex*.

Poland: Jerzy Skolimowski's *Hands Up* is banned and he leaves the country, later working in Britain.

Leading actor Zbigniew Cybulski dies in an accident.

Sweden: Bo Widerberg's ravishing *Elvira Madigan* is an international success.

Vilgot Sjöman's *I Am Curious – Yellow* is a worldwide sensation and begins a cycle of indifferent sexploitation movies.

USSR: Sergei Bondarchuk makes an epic version of *War and Peace*, with spectacular battle scenes.

1968

America: *Funny Girl*, with Barbra Streisand repeating her Broadway performance as Fanny Brice, is the box-office success of the year.

Stanley Kubrick's *2001: A Space Odyssey* is a trip that finds favour with the young and begins a new cycle of science-fiction films.

Franklin J. Schaffner's *Planet of the Apes* is also a hit; its success results in several inferior sequels.

Andy Warhol's underground film *Flesh*, about a day in the life of a male prostitute, played by Joe Dallesandro, surfaces as a surprise hit. In a small part is Maurice Braddell, once a promising English actor and writer of the 30s.

British director Peter Yates makes *Bullitt*, with Steve McQueen, notable for its car chases.

Sidney Poitier becomes the first black actor to head the poll of money-making stars, followed by Paul Newman, Julie Andrews, John Wayne, and Clint Eastwood.

Britain: Lindsay Anderson directs *If . . .*, a powerful film about schoolboy rebellion, starring Malcolm McDowell.

Carol Reed makes the best British musical film, *Oliver!*, from Lionel Bart's stage success.

Ralph Thomas's *Carry On up the Khyber* is the best of the series, with Kenneth Williams, Charles Hawtrey and company.

Cuba: Tomás Gutiérrez Alea's *Memories of Underdevelopment* explores life under Castro.

France: Claude Chabrol's *Les Biches*, starring Stéphane Audran, deals with a bisexual love triangle.

Italy: Franco Zeffirelli makes Shakespeare box-office with his version of *Romeo and Juliet*, starring Leonard Whiting and Olivia Hussey.

Sergio Leone, with US backing, makes *Once upon a Time in the West*, with Henry Fonda as a ruthless killer.

1969

America: Dennis Hopper and Peter Fonda add social relevance to the biker movie in *Easy Rider*, a surprise hit that has Hollywood attempting to repeat its success by hiring other young directors.

British director John Schlesinger makes a quintessential American movie, *Midnight Cowboy*, starring Dustin Hoffman and Jon Voight.

George Roy Hill's *Butch Cassidy and the Sundance Kid*, with its memorable pairing of Paul Newman and Robert Redford, and Sam Peckinpah's elegiac *The Wild Bunch*, show there is life left in the western.

Sidney Pollack directs the dark *They Shoot Horses, Don't They?*, with Gig Young and Jane Fonda.

George Romero's relentless, low-budget *Night of the Living Dead* revives the horror genre.

Kinney takes over Warner Bros. The company is renamed Warner Communications and takes in Kinney's other entertainment interests, including publishing, video, and record companies.

Paul Newman, Sidney Poitier, and Barbra Streisand form a major new production company, First Artists.

Darryl Zanuck resigns from Twentieth Century-Fox.

Paul Newman becomes the top box-office star, followed by John Wayne, Steve McQueen, Dustin Hoffman, and Clint Eastwood.

Brazil: Glauber Rocha's brooding *Antonio das Mortes* is banned and he leaves the country.

Britain: Ken Russell's adaptation of D. H. Lawrence's *Women in Love*, starring Glenda Jackson, is a success, gaining notoriety for its nude wrestling scene between Alan Bates and Oliver Reed.

Richard Attenborough directs *Oh, What a Lovely War*, from Joan Littlewood's stage show.

George Lazenby replaces Sean Connery as James Bond, but *On Her Majesty's Secret Service* does poorly at the box-office.

Ken Loach's *Kes*, produced by Tony Garnett, brings socially conscious talents to the cinema.

Bryan Forbes is appointed head of production by EMI at Elstree and announces an ambitious programme.

Egypt: Shadi Abdelsalam gains international notice with *The Night of Counting the Years*, about tomb robbers.

France: Costa-Gavras's political thriller *Z*, with Yves Montand, is a worldwide hit, but it is banned in Greece and Spain.

Jean-Pierre Melville's *The Army in the Shadows* is a gripping documentary-style film about the French Resistance.

Eric Rohmer's civilized *My Night at Maud's* is an international success.

Germany: Rainer Werner Fassbinder, working in experimental theatre, turns to films with his troupe and makes *Love Is Colder than Death*.

India: Satyajit Ray directs *Days and Nights in the Forest*, about the impact of rural life on some city boys.

1970

America: Woodstock, the great hippie gathering of 'love, peace and music' in 1969, is captured on film by Michael Wadleigh.

Robert Altman's anti-establishment *M*A*S*H*, with Elliott Gould and Donald Sutherland, is a hit, as is the three-handkerchief weepie *Love Story*, directed by Arthur Hiller.

George C. Scott scores as *Patton*, directed by Franklin Schaffner.

Roger Corman founds his own production and distribution company, New World Pictures.

Paul Newman remains the top money-making star, followed by Clint Eastwood, Steve McQueen, John Wayne, and Elliott Gould.

Australia: After years of procrastination, the government decides to support the local film industry, including the establishment of a film and television school.

Britain: Nicolas Roeg and Donald Cammel direct the complex *Performance*, with James Fox and Mick Jagger, which seems the last gasp of 60s permissiveness.

Joseph Losey turns to the past in his continuing dissection of the class system in *The Go-Between*.

Ken Russell courts controversy with *The Music Lovers*, starring Richard Chamberlain as Tchaikovsky, with Glenda Jackson.

David Lean's epic *Ryan's Daughter* is not liked, and he loses his confidence in directing.

France: Claude Chabrol makes the Hitchcockian thrillers *The Butcher* and *La Rupture*, with Stéphane Audran.

Hong Kong: King Hu makes the martial arts epic *A Touch of Zen*.

Italy: Pasolini directs the Greek tragedy *Medea*, starring Maria Callas.

Japan: The wide-screen process Imax is shown for the first time.

Spain: Luis Buñuel makes *Tristana*, a complex black comedy with Catherine Deneuve and Fernando Rey.

Sweden: Jan Troell's *The Emigrants*, about Swedes leaving their homeland for America, is a hit in the two countries.

1971

America: William Friedkin's gritty thriller *The French Connection*, with Gene Hackman, is a hit.

Peter Bogdanovich makes the impressive, nostalgic *The Last Picture Show*, with Ben Johnson.

Milos Forman's first US film, *Taking Off*, is a gentle satire on America.

Alan J. Pakula directs the adult thriller *Klute*, with Jane Fonda and Donald Sutherland.

Don Siegel makes *Dirty Harry*, starring Clint Eastwood as a maverick cop, a role he is to play often.

Steve McQueen joins Newman, Poitier, and Streisand in First Artists. The company's first production is *Pocket Money*, starring Newman and directed by Stuart Rosenberg.

John Wayne takes over as the top box-office attraction, followed by Clint Eastwood, Paul Newman, Steve McQueen, and George C. Scott.

Australia: Nicolas Roeg makes the eerily effective *Walkabout*, with Jenny Agutter and David Gulpilil.

Britain: Stanley Kubrick's controversial *A Clockwork Orange*, based on Anthony Burgess's novel, is the first film to use Dolby sound.

Ken Russell shocks with his exuberant *The Devils*, starring Vanessa Redgrave and Oliver Reed.

John Schlesinger makes the stylish *Sunday, Bloody Sunday*, with Peter Finch and Glenda Jackson as two people in love with the same man.

Roman Polanski emphasizes the violence in his version of Shakespeare's *Macbeth*.

Mike Hodges makes the tough thriller *Get Carter*, with Michael Caine.

Bryan Forbes quits as head of production for EMI at Elstree a year early.

The National Film School opens.

Hungary: Miklós Jancsó makes the colourful *Red Psalm*, about a workers' strike.

Italy: Pasolini's *Decameron* brings him an international hit. He is to follow it with the similar *Canterbury Tales* and *Arabian Nights*.

Yugoslavia: Dusan Makavejev's *WR: Mysteries of the Organism* is an international hit; after it is banned, he leaves the country.

1972

America: Francis Ford Coppola's brilliant *The Godfather*, with Marlon Brando and Al Pacino, treats the Mafia as a normal family business.

Bob Fosse gives bite and style to *Cabaret*, with Liza Minnelli, Joel Grey, and Michael York.

John Boorman's *Deliverance* is a superior thriller.

The success of Ronald Neame's *The Poseidon Adventure* begins a cycle of disaster movies.

Dustin Hoffman joins First Artists. It releases the muddled *Up the Sandbox*, starring Barbra Streisand.

Clint Eastwood is the top box-office star, followed by George C. Scott, Gene Hackman, John Wayne, and Barbra Streisand.

Britain: Lindsay Anderson directs the satirical *O Lucky Man!*, starring Malcolm McDowell.

Ken Loach makes *Family Life*, from David Mercer's play of a dysfunctional family.

Bill Douglas's *My Childhood* wins an award for the best first feature at the Venice Film Festival.

Lord (J. Arthur) Rank dies.

France: Luis Buñuel makes the hilarious and savage *The Discreet Charm of the Bourgeoisie*, with Fernando Rey, Delphine Seyrig, and Stéphane Audran.

Germany: Werner Herzog directs the startling *Aguirre, Wrath of God*, starring Klaus Kinski.

Rainer Werner Fassbinder makes *The Bitter Tears of Petra Von Kant*, about lesbian jealousies, with Hanna Schygulla.

Italy: Marlon Brando stars in Bertolucci's *Last Tango in Paris*, an explicit exploration of lust.

Francesco Rosi investigates political corruption in *The Mattei Affair*.

Sweden: Ingmar Bergman's *Cries and Whispers*, with Harriet Andersson and Liv Ullmann, is tough but important viewing.

1973

America: William Friedkin's horror movie *The Exorcist* becomes a controversial hit.

George Roy Hill's *The Sting* re-unites Robert Redford and Paul Newman to become a big hit, helped by Marvin Hamlisch's use of Scott Joplin's ragtime tunes.

Terrence Malick's seminal *Badlands*, with Sissy Spacek and Martin Sheen, follows two young lovers on a killing spree.

Martin Scorsese's *Mean Streets* reveals him as a major talent.

Bruce Lee kicks his way to stardom in Robert Clouse's *Enter the Dragon* and begins a Western fashion for martial arts films. Lee himself dies suddenly, but becomes a continuing cult.

Clint Eastwood is the top box-office star, followed by Ryan O'Neal, Steve McQueen, Burt Reynolds, and Robert Redford.

Britain: Nicolas Roeg directs the chilling *Don't Look Now*, with Donald Sutherland and Julie Christie.

Roger Moore takes over as James Bond in *Live and Let Die*.

Cinema admissions keep falling and are now down to 142 million a year.

France: François Truffaut's *Day for Night*, about the world of cinema, is an international hit.

Germany: Rainer Werner Fassbinder's *Ali: Fear Eats the Soul* brings him international recognition.

India: Satyajit Ray makes *Distant Thunder*, about the breakdown of traditional values.

Italy: Marco Ferreri scandalizes audiences with *Blow-Out*, in which four men indulge in a prolonged and terminal orgy of food and sex.

Netherlands: Paul Verhoeven's *Turkish Delight*, starring Rutger Hauer, is an international success.

1974

America: Francis Ford Coppola's *The Godfather II*, with Robert De Niro, is a rare sequel that matches the original.

Roman Polanski makes the complex thriller *Chinatown*, with Jack Nicholson.

John Guillermin's *The Towering Inferno* reveals the public's voracious appetite for disaster movies.

Michael Winner directs the vigilante movie *Death Wish*, starring Charles Bronson, which is to be followed by several sequels.

Universal Pictures introduces Sensurround, low-frequency sound effects, to add to the impact of *Earthquake*. The system gains a limited acceptance and is used in some other of its features.

Australia: Peter Weir's *The Cars that Ate Paris* gives notice of the stirrings of new and exciting talents.

Britain: Sidney Lumet directs the glossy *Murder on the Orient Express*, from Agatha Christie's novel.

Michael Apted directs the pop musical *Stardust*, with Adam Faith and David Essex.

Lew Grade announces that he will spend millions of dollars on film production in the coming year.

British Lion announce a new slim-line Shepperton Studios.

France: Louis Malle's delicate exploration of collaboration in *Lacombe, Lucien* is attacked by many and he decides to move to America.

Bertrand Blier's *Going Places* features two bright young stars, Gérard Depardieu and Patrick Dewaere.

Germany: Werner Herzog directs the disturbing and affecting *The Enigma of Kaspar Hauser*.

Italy: Fellini directs the nostalgic *Amarcord*.

Senegal: Ousmane Sembène's exuberant satire *Xala* is one of the first films from Africa to gain international attention.

1975

America: Steven Spielberg's *Jaws* is a monster hit and will spawn several sequels.

Milos Forman's anti-authoritarian *One Flew over the Cuckoo's Nest* gives Jack Nicholson one of his best roles.

Robert Redford is the top box-office star, followed by Barbra Streisand, Al Pacino, Charles Bronson, and Paul Newman.

Australia: Peter Weir makes the enigmatic *Picnic at Hanging Rock*.

Britain: Jim Sharman's *The Rocky Horror Picture Show*, from Richard O'Brien's stage hit, starring Tim Curry as a transvestite transsexual from Transylvania, becomes a cult phenomenon.

The Monty Python team make fun of Arthurian legends in *Monty Python and the Holy Grail*, directed by Terry Gilliam and Terry Jones.

Ken Russell directs *Tommy*, The Who's rock opera, starring Ann-Margret.

EMI cut back at Elstree Studios.

Lew Grade announces the formation of Associated General Films with the General Cinema chain in America, to finance films on an equal basis, with the cinemas providing a US release.

Charlie Chaplin receives a knighthood.

Italy: Pasolini's *Salo*, based on the Marquis de Sade's writings, causes controversy. Britain is one of the countries that bans it. Pasolini himself is murdered soon afterwards.

USSR: Andrei Tarkovsky's *Mirror* upsets the authorities and he leaves the country.

1976

America: Alan J. Pakula's exciting *All the President's Men*, with Dustin Hoffman and Robert Redford, dramatizes the *Washington Post*'s investigation into the Watergate affair.

Martin Scorsese's coruscating *Taxi Driver*, starring Robert De Niro, is concerned with the malaise of urban violence.

Sidney Lumet's *Network* is a brilliantly melodramatic satire on the excesses of television, written by Paddy Chayevsky; its star Peter Finch dies soon after its release.

Sylvester Stallone writes and stars in the old-fashioned boxing drama *Rocky*, directed by John G. Avildsen; it brings him stardom and is to be followed by four sequels.

Brazil: Bruno Barreto's erotic *Dona Flor and Her Two Husbands* becomes an international success.

Britain: Nicolas Roeg makes the science-fiction *The Man Who Fell to Earth*, starring David Bowie.

Alan Parker directs the gangster film *Bugsy Malone* with a cast of children.

Derek Jarman makes *Sebastiane*, about homosexual desire in the Roman empire, in Latin.

Germany: Wim Wenders' leisurely road movie *Kings of the Road* is admired by many.

Italy: Bertolucci's *1900* tracks Italian history through the first half of the 20th century.

Japan: Nagisa Oshima's controversial *In the Realm of the Senses* is a claustrophobic examination of sexual obsession. Britain and other countries ban it.

Sweden: Ingmar Bergman's *Face to Face*, made for

television, is edited down for cinema release; it is among his best films.

1977

America: The success of Woody Allen's comedy *Annie Hall*, with Diane Keaton, makes them both stars.

George Lucas's *Star Wars* gives fantasy and science fiction a spectacular box-office boost. It is followed by another fantasy, Steven Spielberg's *Close Encounters of the Third Kind*.

John Travolta becomes a star in the disco-dancing hit *Saturday Night Fever*, a film that also dominates the pop charts with the Bee Gees' songs.

Burt Reynolds scores a surprising hit in Hal Needham's coarse chase comedy *Smokey and the Bandit*.

Sylvester Stallone is the top box-office star, followed by Barbra Streisand, Clint Eastwood, Burt Reynolds, and Robert Redford.

Australia: Bruce Beresford makes the period piece *The Getting of Wisdom*. Within five years, he will be in Hollywood.

Peter Weir directs *The Last Wave*, with Richard Chamberlain.

Britain: Richard Attenborough directs the ambitious *A Bridge Too Far*, the story of the Allied defeat at Arnhem.

Alan Parker makes the successful *Midnight Express*, from a script by Oliver Stone.

Lord (Lew) Grade announces plans to spend $125m on film production. His partnership with Boston's General Cinema Corporation is ended.

Goldcrest Films is founded. It becomes a leading production company, producing films that include *Gandhi* and *The Killing Fields*.

Herbert Wilcox dies.

Sir Michael Balcon dies.

France: Philippe de Broca's comedy thriller *Dear Inspector* is a popular success.

Germany: Wim Wenders makes the art-house hit *The American Friend*.

Rainer Werner Fassbinder's English-language *Despair*, written by Tom Stoppard and starring Dirk Bogarde, is expected to be his popular breakthrough, but it fails.

Italy: The Taviani brothers, Paolo and Vittorio, score with *Padro Padrone*, about a son's problems with a violent father.

1978

America: *Grease*, a celebration of 50s music starring John Travolta and Olivia Newton-John, is the hit of the year, followed by the youthful comedy *National Lampoon's Animal House*.

Michael Cimino's *The Deer Hunter* makes the Vietnam war box-office.

John Carpenter's *Halloween* scares cinema audiences, fuelling the horror revival.

Walter Hill directs the existential thriller *The Driver*.

Terrence Malick's *Days of Heaven* is the second film from an exciting talent. But audiences do not respond, and he withdraws from film-making.

Louis Malle directs his first American film, *Pretty Baby*, with Brooke Shields as a young prostitute.

Orion Pictures is founded by former executives of United Artists and becomes, for a while, an important producer.

Burt Reynolds is the top money-making star,

followed by John Travolta, Richard Dreyfuss, Warren Beatty, and Clint Eastwood.

Australia: Fred Schepisi's aboriginal tragedy *The Chant of Jimmy Blacksmith* is a success, and soon takes him to Hollywood, together with his cinematographer, Ian Baker. Other directors who will go to Hollywood include Graeme Clifford, Simon Wincer, and Richard Franklin.

Philip Noyce makes *Newsfront*, a valediction to newsreel cameramen. He, too, will be in Hollywood by the 90s.

Britain: Joan Collins stars in *The Stud*, based on Jackie Collins's novel, which is a surprising box-office hit.

Martin Rosen's *Watership Down* is an animated version of Richard Adams's bestselling novel about rabbits.

Lew Grade announces $120m productions. He renames his company Associated Communication Corporation and, with EMI, forms a new distribution company in North America.

France: Eduardo Molinaro's screen version of *La Cage aux Folles* makes this transvestite comedy an international hit, one that spawns two sequels.

Bertrand Blier's *Get Out Your Handkerchiefs* reunites Gérard Depardieu and Patrick Dewaere.

Germany: Rainer Werner Fassbinder directs *The Marriage of Maria Braun*, starring Hanna Schygulla.

Italy: Ermanno Olmi makes *The Tree of Wooden Clogs* with a non-professional cast.

Japan: Nagisa Oshima directs the award-winning *Empire of Passion*, about adultery and murder.

Turkey: Yilmaz Güney supervises from prison the shooting of *The Herd*.

1979

America: Richard Donner's *Superman*, starring Christopher Reeve, is the hit of the year.

Robert Benton's *Kramer vs Kramer*, a domestic drama with Dustin Hoffman and Meryl Streep, also scores at the box-office.

Francis Ford Coppola's ambitious *Apocalypse Now* casts the Vietnam war as America's heart of darkness.

Woody Allen makes *Manhattan*, a film in love with New York.

Blake Edwards's *10* brings brief stardom to the unlikely pairing of Dudley Moore and Bo Derek.

Hal Ashby's comedy *Being There* stars Peter Sellers as a dim gardener who becomes a political savant.

Menahem Golan and Yoram Globus take over Cannon Films and announce ambitious production plans.

First Artists runs into financial problems.

Burt Reynolds remains the leading box-office attraction, followed by Clint Eastwood, Jane Fonda, Woody Allen, and Barbra Streisand.

Australia: Gillian Armstrong's *My Brilliant Career* makes Judy Davis a star.

George Miller's apocalyptic road movie *Mad Max* brings Mel Gibson to the fore.

Britain: Ridley Scott directs the science-fiction thriller *Alien*.

Franc Roddam makes the Mods and Rockers musical *Quadrophenia*, with music by The Who.

John Schlesinger's *Yanks* deals with American GIs in Britain during World War II.

Joan Collins tries to repeat her success with *The Bitch*, directed by Gerry O'Hara from a story by sister Jackie.

HandMade Films is formed to finance *Monty Python's Life of Brian* after Lord (Bernard) Delfont disapproves of the script and withdraws EMI's backing.

Thorn take over EMI.

Lord (Lew) Grade buys the Classic Cinema chain.

France: François Truffaut's cycle of films about Antoine Doinel starring Jean-Pierre Léaud comes to an end after 20 years with *Love on the Run*.

Germany: Volker Schlöndorff's *The Tin Drum* is an international success.

Werner Herzog remakes *Nosferatu*, with Klaus Kinski.

Hong Kong: Tsui Hark directs the martial arts fantasy *The Butterfly Murders*.

Poland: Andrzej Wajda's *The Conductor* stars John Gielgud as a man returning to his country.

Krzysztof Kieslowski's *Camera Buff* is a lively political allegory.

Turkey: Yilmaz Güney supervises from prison the shooting of *The Enemy*.

1980

America: Martin Scorsese's *Raging Bull*, with a devastating performance by an overweight Robert De Niro, is to become the critics' favourite movie of the decade.

The failure of Michael Cimino's profligate western epic *Heaven's Gate* virtually destroys United Artists, which is taken over by MGM.

Robert Redford directs *Ordinary People*, about an unhappy family, with Donald Sutherland, Mary Tyler Moore, and Timothy Hutton; it succeeds at the box-office.

George Lucas continues his science-fiction saga with *The Empire Strikes Back*.

David Lynch makes *The Elephant Man*, with John Hurt in the title role.

Burt Reynolds still attracts crowds at the box-office, followed by Robert Redford, Clint Eastwood, Jane Fonda, and Dustin Hoffman.

Australia: Bruce Beresford makes the anti-colonial *Breaker Morant*.

Britain: John Mackenzie makes the tough thriller *The Long Good Friday*, with Bob Hoskins and Helen Mirren.

Bill Forsyth's low-budget comedy *Gregory's Girl* is a hit.

Derek Jarman directs a low-budget version of Shakespeare's *The Tempest*.

Rank announces a £12m production package at the Cannes Film Festival – and a month later decides to cancel it.

Kevin Brownlow's five-hour reconstruction of Abel Gance's *Napoleon* is shown in London.

Alfred Hitchcock, who is knighted this year, dies.

Canada: Louis Malle makes the elegiac *Atlantic City*, with Burt Lancaster as an ageing petty crook.

France: François Truffaut's *The Last Metro* is to become the French critics' favourite film of the 80s.

Alain Resnais's *My American Uncle* is a meticulous, pessimistic dissection of human life.

Hungary: Imre Gyöngyössy, Katalin Petényi, and Barna Kabay make *The Revolt of Job*.

Japan: Akira Kurosawa makes the medieval epic *Kagemusha* with American backing.

Mozambique: Brazilian director Ruy Guerra makes the country's first feature, *Mueda, Memory and Massacre*.

Netherlands: Paul Verhoeven directs the controversial *Spetters*, full of sex and violence and with a cast that includes Rutger Hauer and

Jeroen Krabbé, who will both become international stars.

Spain: Pedro Almodóvar makes the sexually delirious *Labyrinth of Passion*.

1981

America: Steven Spielberg hits the jackpot with the adventure *Raiders of the Lost Ark*, starring Harrison Ford.

Warren Beatty directs and stars in the epic *Reds*, about the life of John Reed.

Walter Hill makes a tense thriller, *Southern Comfort*, which is also an allegory of Vietnam.

Mark Rydell's nostalgic *On Golden Pond* is a hit, with the pairing of Henry Fonda and Katharine Hepburn.

Burt Reynolds scores in Hal Needham's coarse chase comedy *The Cannonball Run*.

Dudley Moore enjoys his brief moment of stardom in the comedy *Arthur*, although John Gielgud steals all the notices.

Oil multi-millionaire Marvin Davis buys Twentieth Century-Fox.

First Artists releases its final film, *An Enemy of the People*, starring Steve McQueen.

Burt Reynolds continues to dominate at the box-office, followed by Clint Eastwood, Dudley Moore, Dolly Parton, and Jane Fonda.

Australia: Peter Weir's *Gallipoli* brings Mel Gibson international recognition.

George Miller's *Mad Max II*, aka *The Road Warrior*, confirms Gibson's status.

Brazil: Hector Babenco makes *Pixote*, about street-wise, homeless kids.

Britain: Rank closes 27 cinemas. Audiences fall to 86 million.

Hugh Hudson directs *Chariots of Fire*, which is an international success and is hailed as a revitalization of the local industry. Its writer, Colin Welland, shouts 'The British are coming!' at the Oscar ceremonies.

Karel Reisz makes *The French Lieutenant's Woman*, scripted by Harold Pinter and starring Meryl Streep and Jeremy Irons.

Leading film-makers write a letter pleading for help to save the industry as fewer than ever British movies reach the cinemas.

Lord Grade's big-budget production *Raise the Titanic* is a flop. He comments that it would have been cheaper to have lowered the Atlantic. His losses on film production are more than £26m.

France: Jean-Jacques Beineix's *Diva* becomes a cult hit.

Germany: Wolfgang Petersen directs *The Boat*, an international success.

Czech director Istvan Szabo's *Mephisto* makes Klaus Maria Brandauer a star.

Poland: Andrzej Wajda directs *Man of Iron*, about the emergence of Solidarity.

1982

America: Steven Spielberg makes the box-office smash *E.T.*, with its ugly but lovable alien.

Dustin Hoffman dons drag for the comedy *Tootsie*.

Ridley Scott designs an unpalatable future in his thriller *Blade Runner*.

Costa-Gavras makes the tense *Missing*, about American involvement in the overthrow of Allende's government in Chile; Jack Lemmon and Sissy Spacek star.

Barry Levinson's *Diner* is a little masterpiece of observation.

Walter Hill's *48 Hours* makes the fast-talking Eddie Murphy a star.

Coca-Cola acquires Columbia Pictures.

Burt Reynolds remains the box-office favourite, followed by Clint Eastwood, Sylvester Stallone, Dudley Moore, and Richard Pryor.

Britain: Lindsay Anderson's savage *Britannia Hospital* divides the critics and does badly at the box-office. It will be his last British feature.

James Ivory directs Ruth Prawer Jhabvala's novel of colonial India, *Heat and Dust*, produced by Ismail Merchant.

Peter Greenaway's *The Draughtsman's Contract* is an art-house success.

Cannon buy the Classic Cinema chain.

France: Daniel Vigne makes *The Return of Martin Guerre*, starring Gérard Depardieu.

Depardieu also stars as *Danton*, a vivid historical re-creation directed by Andrzej Wajda.

Patrick Dewaere commits suicide.

Germany: Werner Herzog makes the strange *Fitzcarraldo* with Klaus Kinski as an obsessive.

Fassbinder makes the teasing *Veronika Voss*, about the troubles of an ageing star. He dies soon afterwards of a drug overdose.

Hungary: Marta Mészáros makes the autobiographical *Diary for My Children* about the country's recent history.

Italy: Paolo and Vittorio Taviani make the nostalgic *The Night of San Lorenzo*.

Mali: Souleymane Cissé directs *The Wind*, about romance and repression in Africa.

Poland: Ryszard Bugajski's harrowing and uplifting *Interrogation*, starring Krystyna Janda, is banned. It will not be seen until 1990. Bugajski leaves for North America.

Spain: Pedro Almodóvar directs *Dark Habits*, set in a decadent convent.

Sweden: Ingmar Bergman's final cinema film, *Fanny and Alexander*, is one of his best.

Turkey: Having escaped from prison, Yilmaz Güney edits in Switzerland *The Way*, made by Serif Gören under his supervision.

1983

America: Richard Marquand directs *Return of the Jedi*, the third of George Lucas's *Star Wars* movies, and it is a box-office smash.

John Landis's *Trading Places*, with Dan Aykroyd and Eddie Murphy, does well at the box-office.

James L. Brooks's *Terms of Endearment*, with Jack Nicholson and Shirley MacLaine, is another popular success.

Martin Scorsese's *King of Comedy*, with Robert De Niro and Jerry Lewis, takes an uncomfortable look at show-business and the people it attracts.

Clint Eastwood is the box-office champion, followed by Eddie Murphy, Sylvester Stallone, Burt Reynolds, and John Travolta.

Britain: Lewis Gilbert's *Educating Rita*, starring Julie Walters and Michael Caine, is a hit.

Bill Forsyth makes the quirky comedy *Local Hero*, with Burt Lancaster.

Richard Eyre's *The Ploughman's Lunch*, starring Jonathan Pryce, is an incisive social drama.

Richard Attenborough's *Gandhi*, which he spent more than a decade setting up, is finally released to plaudits.

Sean Connery returns one last time as James Bond in *Never Say Never Again*.

France: Euzhan Palcy's *Sugar Cane Alley* is an evocative account of colonial life.

Spain: Carlos Saura makes the dance drama *Carmen*.

1984

America: Ivan Reitman's comic fantasy *Ghostbusters* is the biggest hit of the year.

Martin Brest's *Beverly Hills Cop* is another hit for Eddie Murphy, mixing comedy and violence.

Joe Dante's *Gremlins*, a comic horror movie, also does well at the box-office.

Sergio Leone directs the complex gangster film *Once upon a Time in America*, which its producers recut.

Rob Reiner's *This Is Spinal Tap* makes fun of the pretensions of rock.

Milos Forman directs *Amadeus*, with Tom Hulce as Mozart and F. Murray Abraham as his rival, Salieri.

Disney creates Touchstone Films to give it a brand name for films not intended for a family audience. Its first release is *Splash*, a fantasy about a mermaid.

James Cameron uses body-builder Arnold Schwarzenegger to good effect as a bad cyborg in *The Terminator*.

Marvin Davis sells half of Twentieth Century-Fox to Rupert Murdoch.

Clint Eastwood remains the box-office favourite, followed by Bill Murray, Harrison Ford, Eddie Murphy, and Sally Field.

Argentina: Maria Luisa Bemberg's *Camila* is a powerful period piece about a woman who defies Church and government.

Britain: Cinema admissions reach their lowest-ever level of 55 million.

Roland Joffe directs the ambitious and harrowing *The Killing Fields*, with Sam Waterston and Haing S. Ngor.

Peter Yates directs the delightful *The Dresser*, with Albert Finney as a Donald Wolfit-like actor and Tom Courtenay as his dresser.

Hugh Hudson attempts to take Tarzan seriously in *Greystoke*, starring Christopher Lambert.

Bill Forsyth makes a comedy about a Glaswegian ice-cream war, *Comfort and Joy*. It is his last local feature before he leaves for Hollywood.

The Video Recordings Act establishes censorship for video cassettes.

China: Chen Kaige's *Yellow Earth*, photographed by Yang Zimou, makes the most of vast landscapes in its story of a peasant family.

France: Claude Zidi's *Le Cop*, with Philippe Noiret as a corrupt policeman, is a domestic hit.

Germany: Wolfgang Petersen directs the fantasy *The Neverending Story* and goes to Hollywood.

Wim Wenders' English-language *Paris, Texas* brings him international acclaim.

Edgar Reitz makes the 15-hour saga *Heimat*.

Hungary: Istvan Szabo makes *Colonel Redl*, about an officer forced to commit suicide, starring Klaus Maria Brandauer.

India: Satyajit Ray directs *Home and the World*, about a man who brings his wife out of purdah.

1985

America: Robert Zemeckis's comedy *Back to the Future*, with Michael J. Fox, is the hit of the year.

Australian director Peter Weir directs the tense *Witness*, starring Harrison Ford; Hollywood is to remain Weir's future base.

Sydney Pollack's *Out of Africa* meets with critical and popular success.

Martin Scorsese directs the sprightly urban fable *After Hours*.

Paul Verhoeven makes his first English-language film *Flesh Blood*, with Rutger Hauer; it fails.

Rupert Murdoch acquires Twentieth Century-Fox.

Sylvester Stallone is the box-office favourite, followed by Eddie Murphy, Clint Eastwood, Michael J. Fox, and Chevy Chase.
Argentina: Luis Puenzo's *The Official Version* is an international hit.
Britain: Stephen Frears makes *My Beautiful Laundrette*, with Daniel Day-Lewis and Gordon Warnecke as an unlikely couple.
Miranda Richardson attracts attention as Ruth Ellis, the last woman to be hanged, in *Dance with a Stranger*, directed by Mike Newell.
David Lean makes *A Passage to India*, with Peggy Ashcroft, Alec Guinness, and Victor Banerjee.
Malcolm Mowbray directs Alan Bennett's comedy *A Private Function*, with Michael Palin and Denholm Elliott, and then leaves for Hollywood.
Terry Gilliam's satirical *Brazil* receives mixed notices.
Hugh Hudson's *Revolution* flops at the box-office and causes financial problems for Goldcrest, ending its powerful production role.
Roger Moore makes his last Bond film, *A View to a Kill*. He is replaced by Timothy Dalton.
British Film Year is held, to revive interest in the cinema.
Brazil: Hector Babenco makes *Kiss of the Spider Woman*, with William Hurt and Raul Julia and American money. Insisting that Brazilian cinema is dead, he moves to Hollywood.
France: Maurice Pialat's *Police*, about a tough, bigoted cop and starring Gérard Depardieu, is a domestic hit.
François Truffaut dies.
Germany: Percy Adlon directs the witty romantic comedy *Sugarbaby* with Marianne Sagebrecht.
Hong Kong: Actor and director Jackie Chan does well with his mix of martial arts, comedy and spectacular stunts in *Police Story*.
Japan: Akira Kurosawa, out of favour in his own country, makes *Ran*, based on Shakespeare's *King Lear*, with foreign finance.
Taiwan: Hou Hsiao-hsien explores the tensions with mainland China in *The Time to Live and the Time to Die*.
Yugoslavia: Emir Kusturica directs *When Father Was Away on Business*, a child's-eye view of politics.

1986
America: Tony Scott's *Top Gun*, starring Tom Cruise as a naval fighter pilot, is the hit of the year.
Woody Allen is near his wittiest in *Hannah and Her Sisters*, with Michael Caine and Mia Farrow.
David Cronenberg remakes the 50s horror *The Fly*, starring Jeff Goldblum and Geena Davis, with gruesome special effects.
David Lynch directs the elegantly perverse *Blue Velvet*.
Bill Sherwood's independently made *Parting Glances* is the first feature to deal with AIDS.
Ted Turner takes over MGM/UA.
Tom Cruise is now America's top box-office star, followed by Eddie Murphy, Paul Hogan, Rodney Dangerfield, and Bette Midler.
Australia: *Crocodile Dundee* makes Paul Hogan an international star and becomes the country's most successful film.
Britain: The Merchant-Ivory *A Room with a View*, starring Maggie Smith and Helena Bonham Carter, is a hit.
Derek Jarman makes *Caravaggio*, on the life of the painter.

Producer David Puttnam leaves for Hollywood to become production head of Columbia Pictures.
Canada: Denys Arcand makes the witty conversation piece *The Decline of the American Empire*.
China: Tian Zhuangzhuang makes the stunningly visual *Horse Thief*.
Chen Kaige directs *The Big Parade*, about army volunteers training for a march-past in Beijing's Tiananmen Square. The army force him to make changes.
Finland: Aki Kaurismäki makes *Hamlet Goes Business*, updating Shakespeare's play.
France: Claude Berri's versions of Marcel Pagnol's novels, *Jean de Florette* and *Manon des Sources*, with Yves Montand, Daniel Auteuil, and Emmanuelle Béart, are international hits.
Mexico: Jaime Humberto Hermosillo makes the gay comedy *Dona Herlinda and Her Son*.
Spain: Pedro Almodóvar sets out to shock with *Matador*, full of images of sex and death.
Sweden: Andrei Tarkovsky makes his last film, *Sacrifice*, dying soon afterwards at the age of 54.

1987
America: Eddie Murphy's appeal makes *Beverly Hills Cop II* a success at the box-office.
Adrian Lyne's *Fatal Attraction*, with Michael Douglas and Glenn Close, is a talking point and a box-office hit.
Oliver Stone's study of corporate corruption, *Wall Street*, also stars Michael Douglas, with Charlie Sheen.
Mel Gibson stars as a reckless cop with Danny Glover in Richard Donner's *Lethal Weapon*; its success brings several sequels.
Paul Verhoeven directs the science-fiction *Robocop* with wit, pace, and plenty of violence.
Brian De Palma's *The Untouchables* has the incorruptible Kevin Costner and Sean Connery battling against Robert De Niro's Al Capone.
John Huston's final film, *The Dead*, is one of his best.
David Mamet makes the tricky *House of Games*.
David Puttnam leaves Columbia, to be replaced by Dawn Steel.
Eddie Murphy is the box-office favourite, followed by Michael Douglas, Michael J. Fox, Arnold Schwarzenegger, and Paul Hogan.
Australia: John Duigan directs the charming *The Year My Voice Broke*.
Britain: John Boorman's *Hope and Glory* focuses on a young boy's experience of the Blitz.
David Leland's *Wish You Were Here* benefits from the assured performance of Emily Lloyd as a rebellious teenager. She soon heads for Hollywood.
Stephen Frears directs *Prick Up Your Ears*, about murdered playwright Joe Orton, with Gary Oldman and Alfred Molina.
Richard Attenborough makes *Cry Freedom*, about the death of black activist Steve Biko in South Africa.
Canada: Jean-Claude Lauzon's *Night Zoo* is an international art-house hit.
China: Zhang Yimou gains an international reputation with *Red Sorghum*, starring Gong Li.
Denmark: Gabriel Axel makes the art-house hit, the ironic and elegant *Babette's Feast*.
Germany: Wim Wenders directs *Wings of Desire*, with Bruno Ganz and Otto Sander as two angels visiting Berlin.
Italy: Bernardo Bertolucci makes the visually splendid *The Last Emperor*, about the life of China's last imperial ruler.

Mali: Souleymane Cissé's *Yeelen* concerns a battle between magicians.
Norway: Nils Gaup finds an international audience for his *Pathfinder*, based on a Lapp legend.
Sweden: Bille August makes *Pelle the Conqueror*, an epic about Swedish workers in 19th-century Denmark, starring Max Von Sydow.
Lasse Hallström's *My Life as a Dog* is an international success and takes the director to Hollywood.

1988
America: Robert Zemeckis's *Who Framed Roger Rabbit*, with Bob Hoskins, combines live action and animation in a remarkable way and is a box-office hit.
Barry Levinson's successful *Rain Man* teams Tom Cruise as a slick salesman with Dustin Hoffman as his autistic brother.
Martin Brest directs *Midnight Run*, an action-filled comedy with Robert De Niro and Charles Grodin.
Tim Burton's ghostly *Beetlejuice*, with Michael Keaton, is a hit.
The Museum of the Moving Image opens in New York.
Tom Cruise is top gun at the box-office, followed by Eddie Murphy, Tom Hanks, Arnold Schwarzenegger, and Paul Hogan.
Argentina: Fernando Solanas's *South*, about a political prisoner returning home, is an international art-house hit.
AustraliaThe government establishes a Film Finance Corporation to invest in films and TV miniseries. The first film it backs, *The Delinquents*, starring American Charlie Schlatter and local Kylie Minogue, upsets local producers by its emphasis on commerce and US sales rather than quality.
Britain: *A Fish Called Wanda*, directed by veteran Ealing hand Charles Crichton and written by its star, John Cleese, is the most successful British comedy for years.
Terence Davies makes his autobiographical *Distant Voices, Still Lives*.
The Museum of the Moving Image opens in London.
France: Louis Malle's *Au Revoir les Enfants*, concerned with inadvertent betrayal during the German occupation, is much admired in France and liked elsewhere.
Germany: Percy Adlon's *Bagdad Café* is an international hit. He is to go to America with his star Marianne Sagebrecht to make *Rosalie Goes Shopping*, which fails to repeat the success.
India: Mira Nair's lively *Salaam Bombay!* focuses on a tea-boy's adventures on the streets of the city, using a non-professional cast.
Italy: Giuseppe Tornatore's *Cinema Paradiso*, a nostalgic celebration of cinema, is a much-loved international hit, with sympathetic performances from Philippe Noiret and the young Salvatore Cascio.
JapanCinemas achieve their smallest-ever attendance.
Poland: Krzysztof Kieslowski's bleakly unforgettable *A Short Film about Killing* and the equally memorable *A Short Film about Love* are the cinema versions of two of the Decalogues, on the Ten Commandments, that he made for television.
Senegal: Ousmane Sembène and Thierno Faty Sow's *Camp de Thiaroye* is a powerful indictment of colonialism.
South Africa: Oliver Schmitz's *Mapantsula*, written

by, and starring, Thomas Mogotlane, is a lively look at life in a black township.

Spain: Pedro Almodóvar's *Women on the Verge of a Nervous Breakdown*, with Carmen Maura, is an international hit.

USSR: Vasili Pichul's 'kitchen sink' drama *Little Vera* is an international hit.

1989

America: Rob Reiner directs the witty romantic comedy *When Harry Met Sally*, with Billy Crystal and Meg Ryan.

Tim Burton's *Batman*, with Michael Keaton in the title role and Jack Nicholson as The Joker, breaks US box-office records by taking $100m in 10 days.

Steven Spielberg's *Indiana Jones and the Temple of Doom*, with Harrison Ford, is another romping hit.

Spike Lee directs the witty and passionate *Do the Right Thing*, about racism.

Steven Soderberg has an unexpected critical hit with his independently made *sex, lies and videotape*, with James Spader and Andie MacDowell.

Peter Weir makes *Dead Poets Society*, with Robin Williams as a charismatic teacher.

Phil Alden Robinson directs a successful fantasy, *Field of Dreams*, with Kevin Costner.

Oliver Stone makes the rousing anti-war drama *Born on the Fourth of July*, with Tom Cruise.

Sony buys Columbia Pictures from Coca-Cola.

Time Inc. buy Warner Communications to become Time Warner.

Jack Nicholson ousts Tom Cruise as the box-office favourite, both ahead of Robin Williams, Michael Douglas, and Tom Hanks.

Australia: Yahoo Serious's *Young Einstein* is the second-most successful Australian film so far.

Britain: Kenneth Branagh's impressive *Henry V* stresses the futility of war.

Philip Savile's *Fellow Traveller* probes the effect of the 50s blacklist on an American screenwriter.

Michael Caton-Jones makes *Scandal*, starring Joanne Whalley-Kilmer as Christine Keeler.

Pauline Collins scores as *Shirley Valentine*, directed by Lewis Gilbert.

Mike Newell directs *Sour-Sweet*, about a Chinese family in London.

Peter Greenaway's *The Cook, the Thief, His Wife and Her Lover* is an art-house hit.

Burkina Faso: Idrissa Ouedraogo directs *Yaaba*, a riveting account of African village life.

Canada: Deny Arcand's *Jesus of Montreal*, starring Lothaire Bluteau, is an international success.

China: Zhang Yimou directs *Ju Dou*, starring Gong Li as an adulterous wife at the mercy of an impotent old husband. The authorities ban it.

France: Bertrand Tavernier's *Life and Nothing But* is a complex story of disillusion, set at the time of World War I and starring Philippe Noiret.

Luc Besson's love affair with the sea results in *The Big Blue*.

Jean-Jacques Annaud's charming *The Bear* focuses on an orphaned cub.

Patrice Leconte makes the stylish *M. Hire*, with Michel Blanc.

Germany: Uli Edel makes the English-language *Last Exit to Brooklyn*, from Hubert Selby's grim novel of Brooklyn street life.

Hong Kong: John Woo's violent *The Killer*, starring Chow Yun-Fat, is an international hit.

Ireland: Jim Sheridan directs *My Left Foot* with a remarkable performance from Daniel Day-Lewis as the writer Christy Brown, a sufferer from cerebral palsy.

New Zealand: Peter Jackson attracts attention with the gross *Bad Taste*.

1990

America: Kevin Costner directs, as well as starring in, *Dances with Wolves*, an epic revisionist western on the side of the Indians.

Macaulay Culkin becomes the most popular child star since Shirley Temple in Chris Columbus's *Home Alone*, produced and written by John Hughes, which also becomes the most popular comedy yet made.

Martin Scorsese's *GoodFellas*, with Robert De Niro, Ray Liotta, and Joe Pesci, is a chilling Mafia movie.

Bruce Beresford's nostalgic *Driving Miss Daisy* is a hit.

Jerry Zucker's romantic fantasy *Ghost*, starring Patrick Swayze, Demi Moore, and Whoopi Goldberg, is a hit.

Julia Roberts becomes a star in Garry Marshall's *Pretty Woman*, as a tart with a heart of gold.

Stephen Frears directs *The Grifters*, with John Cusack and Annette Bening.

Paul Verhoeven makes the science-fiction *Total Recall*, with Arnold Schwarzenegger.

Brian De Palma's *The Bonfire of the Vanities* is a flop.

Steve Barron's *Teenage Mutant Ninja Turtles* becomes the most successful independent movie so far.

Matsushita acquires Universal when it buys parent company MCA.

Arnold Schwarzenegger is the top money-making star, followed by Julia Roberts, Bruce Willis, Tom Cruise, and Mel Gibson.

Australia: John Duigan's *Flirting* is a successful sequel to *The Year My Voice Broke*.

Belgium: Gerard Corbiau's *The Music Teacher* is an art-house hit.

Britain: Peter Medak directs a home-grown true-life gangster movie, *The Krays*, starring Gary and Martin Kemp.

Michael Caton-Jones makes *Memphis Belle*, a throwback to the war films of the 50s.

Burkina Faso: Idrissa Ouedraogo directs *Tilai*, an African tragedy.

France: Jean-Paul Rappeneau makes the definitive *Cyrano de Bergerac*, with Gérard Depardieu in the title role.

Luc Besson directs the chic thriller *Nikita*, with Anne Parillaud.

Louis Malle makes the elegiac *Milou in May*.

Germany: Michael Verhoeven's *The Nasty Girl*, about a schoolgirl who digs into her hometown's Nazi past, is an international hit.

Italy: Maurizio Nichetti's *The Icicle Thief* attacks television's treatment of films.

Netherlands: George Sluizer directs the chilling *The Vanishing*, which he is later to remake in Hollywood with a happy ending.

Spain: Pedro Almodóvar's *Tie Me Up! Tie Me Down!* with Victoria Abril is a hit.

1991

America: James Cameron's *Terminator 2: Judgment Day*, with Arnold Schwarzenegger as a good cyborg, is the hit of the year.

Jonathan Demme's violent thriller *The Silence of the Lambs* boosts Anthony Hopkins, as a cannibalistic killer, to stardom.

Kevin Reynolds's glum *Robin Hood: Prince of Thieves*, starring Kevin Costner, is also a box-office success.

Ridley Scott makes a feminist road movie, *Thelma and Louise*, with Susan Sarandon and Geena Davis.

Ron Underwood's *City Slickers*, with Billy Crystal and Jack Palance, is a superior comedy.

Joel and Ethan Coen make the surreal Hollywood comedy *Barton Fink*, starring John Turturro.

Disney produces its best animated feature for years with *Beauty and the Beast*, the first to receive an Oscar nomination as best picture.

Oliver Stone mixes technical wizardry and paranoid conspiracies to create *JFK*, on the assassination of Kennedy.

John Singleton makes his directing debut with the deeply felt *Boyz N the Hood*.

Orion runs into financial problems.

Kevin Costner heads the box-office stars, followed by Arnold Schwarzenegger, Robin Williams, Julia Roberts, and young Macaulay Culkin.

Belgium: Jaco Von Dormael's *Toto the Hero* is an international success.

Britain: Ken Loach's *Hidden Agenda*, about British brutality in Ireland, is given limited distribution. Also briefly seen is his *Riff-Raff*, about life and death on a building site.

Mike Newell's period piece *Enchanted April* does better in the US than in Britain.

Peter Greenaway's *Prospero's Books* is a variation on Shakespeare's *The Tempest*, with John Gielgud.

Derek Jarman directs *Edward II*, a modern-dress version of Marlowe's tragedy.

Canada: Bruce Beresford makes the historical *Black Robe*, starring Lothaire Bluteau.

China: Zhang Yimou directs *Raise the Red Lantern*, an allegory of sexual politics.

Denmark: Lars Von Trier makes *Europa* (US: *Zentropa*).

France: Patrice Leconte directs *The Hairdresser's Husband*, with Jean Rochefort.

Yves Roberts' *My Father's Glory*, about Maurice Pagnol's early life, is an art-house hit.

Italy: Robert Benigni's Mafia comedy *Johnny Stecchino* breaks box-office records.

Mexico: Alfonso Arau's *Like Water for Chocolate* is the most successful Mexican film so far, an international hit.

Poland: Krzysztof Kieslowski makes the enigmatic *The Double Life of Veronique*.

Spain: Vicente Aranda makes the erotic *The Lovers*, starring Victoria Abril.

Taiwan: Edward Yang's *A Brighter Summer Day* deals with social tensions through a story of young love.

1992

America: Clint Eastwood revives the western with the stark *Unforgiven*.

Paul Verhoeven's sex-laden thriller *Basic Instinct*, with Michael Douglas and Sharon Stone, is a controversial hit.

Tim Burton scores again with *Batman Returns*, taking $100m at the US box-office in 11 days.

Disney's *Aladdin*, using Robin Williams's voice to clever effect, is another animated classic.

Robert Altman's sly satire on Hollywood, *The Player*, has stars lining up to play themselves.

Mick Jackson's *The Bodyguard*, starring Kevin Costner and Whitney Houston, is a smash hit.

Penelope Spheeris's *Wayne's World*, with Mike Myers and Dana Carvey, is a surprise hit.

Quentin Tarantino makes his directing debut with the startling *Reservoir Dogs*.

Tom Cruise tops the list of American money-making stars, followed by Mel Gibson, Kevin Costner, Jack Nicholson, and Macaulay Culkin.

Australia: Baz Luhrmann's *Strictly Ballroom* is a comedy hit and its star, Paul Mercurio, goes to Hollywood to star in the erotic thriller *Exit to Eden*.

Geoffrey Wright makes the violent *Romper Stomper*, about racist skinheads.

Belgium: Rémy Belvaux, André Bonzel, and Benoît Poelvoorde make the provocative *Man Bites Dog*, about a serial killer.

Britain: Cinema admissions top 102 million.

The Merchant-Ivory version of E. M. Forster's *Howards End*, with Anthony Hopkins and Emma Thompson, is an impeccable period piece.

Richard Attenborough makes the biopic *Chaplin*, with Robert Downey Jnr as the great clown.

Kenneth Branagh makes the comedy *Peter's Friends*, about a reunion.

Terence Davies directs another slice of his life, *The Long Day Closes*.

China: Zhang Yimou's tale of a peasant seeking justice, *The Story of Qiu Ju*, starring Gong Li, gets official approval.

France: Jacques Rivette releases *La Belle Noiseuse*, about an artist, in both a long and a short version.

Hong Kong: John Woo scores with the violent gangster movie *Hard-Boiled*, with Chow Yun-Fat.

Ireland: Neil Jordan directs the intriguing thriller *The Crying Game*, with Stephen Rea, Forest Whitaker, and Jaye Davidson.

Mexico: Maria Novaro's *Danzon* is an art-house hit.

Sweden: Bille August directs *The Best Intentions*, from a script by Ingmar Bergman, about his parents.

1993

America: Steven Spielberg makes the juvenile *Jurassic Park*, which takes $100m at the box-office in nine days, and, in black and white, the adult *Schindler's List*.

Jonathan Demme's *Philadelphia*, starring Tom Hanks and Denzil Washington, is the first Hollywood film to deal with AIDS. It is a hit.

Harold Ramis directs the smart comedy *Groundhog Day* with Bill Murray.

John McTiernan's *Last Action Hero*, starring Arnold Schwarzenegger, costs $100m and takes under $30m at the US box-office.

Blake Edwards's *Son of the Pink Panther*, starring Italian comic actor Roberto Benigni, flops.

John Woo's first Hollywood film, *Hard Target*, is a pale shadow of his Hong Kong movies.

Whoopi Goldberg briefly becomes the highest-paid actress in history, with a fee of $8.5m for making a sequel to *Sister Act*. It is topped by the $9m paid to Julia Roberts to star in *Mary Reilly*.

A survey shows that many old films are decaying faster than they can be preserved. Fewer than one in 10 of films made in the 1910s survives in a complete form, and one in five of the features of the 20s. Deterioration is even prevalent in post-50s films on acetate, with colours fading and the film itself turning to brown sludge.

Paramount is taken over by the entertainment conglomerate Viacom.

Clint Eastwood reigns as top star at the box-office, followed by Tom Cruise, Robin Williams, Kevin Costner and Harrison Ford.

Australia: Jane Campion's *The Piano*, starring Holly Hunter, Harvey Keitel, and Sam Neill, is both an art-house and popular hit.

Britain: Richard Attenborough directs the understated *Shadowlands*, with Anthony Hopkins and Debra Winger.

Sally Potter makes the exotic *Orlando*, starring Tilda Swinton.

Gary Sinyor and Vadim Jean's low-budget comedy *Leon the Pig Farmer* amuses some.

Derek Jarman completes *Blue*, dealing with his illness, shortly before dying of AIDS.

The *Guardian* readers vote *Cinema Paradiso* their favourite contemporary film.

The biggest films of the year are *Jurassic Park*, *The Bodyguard* and *Home Alone 2*. The most popular British films are two from Kenneth Branagh – *Much Ado About Nothing* (which just squeezes into the UK's top 20 box office successes) and *Peter's Friends*.

Canada: Jean-Claude Lauzon makes the tragi-comic *Léolo*.

China: Tian Zhuangzhuang's *The Blue Kite*, about recent Chinese history, is banned, but is seen in the West.

Chen Kaige makes the epic *Farewell My Concubine*.

France: Claude Berri's downbeat *Germinal* becomes the most expensive French film made so far; but the box-office hit is Jean-Marie Poire's knockabout comedy *Les Visiteurs*.

Japan: Takeshi Kitano gains a cult following by directing, and starring in, the thriller *Sonatine*.

New Zealand: Peter Jackson attracts attention with the gross *Braindead*.

Spain: Bigas Luna's *Jamón, Jamón* is an art-house hit.

Sweden: Cinematographer Sven Nykvist turns director with the austere *The Ox*.

Taiwan: Ang Lee's *The Wedding Banquet* is an international success.

Hou Hsiao-hsien's *The Puppetmaster* is an art-house hit.

1994

America: *Forrest Gump*, with its retarded hero, becomes a box-office phenomenon, the fourth most popular US film yet.

Disney's *The Lion King* becomes the most successful of all its animated features.

Keanu Reeves stars in *Little Buddha*, directed by Bernardo Bertolucci, and *Speed*, directed by Dutch former cinematographer Jan De Bont; the latter boosts his bankability.

Tom Cruise and Brad Pitt become immortal in Neil Jordan's *Interview with the Vampire*.

Quentin Tarantino scores with *Pulp Fiction*, reviving the career of John Travolta.

Oliver Stone makes *Natural Born Killers*, a satire on the media treatment of serial killers.

The Mask, starring Jim Carrey, is the comedy hit of the year.

Bill Forsyth's *Being Human*, with Robin Williams, flops at the box-office and he expresses disillusion with Hollywood.

Sony report a loss, due to Columbia's poor performance.

Universal's heads complain that Matsushita's management is cramping their style.

Steven Spielberg, David Geffen, and Jeffrey Katzenberg announce the formation of a major new studio.

Cinematographer Jan De Bont makes an exciting debut as director with *Speed*, a film that turns Keanu Reeves into an action hero and catapults Sandra Bullock to stardom.

Hollywood dominates the world's screens, with *The Lion King* grossing $358m at foreign box offices, with

followed by *Schindler's List* ($221m), *True Lies* ($218m), and *The Flintstones* ($210m).

Tom Hanks is the top star at the box office, followed by newcomer Jim Carrey, Arnold Schwarzenegger, Tom Cruise and Harrison Ford.

Australia: Stephan Elliott's drag comedy *The Adventures of Priscilla, Queen of the Desert*, starring Terence Stamp, is a hit.

Rolf de Heer's *Bad Boy Bubby*, about an unbalanced man's first contact with the world, is liked and reviled in equal measure.

Britain: Mike Newell's *Four Weddings and a Funeral*, written by Richard Curtis, becomes the most successful British film yet and catapults Hugh Grant to stardom.

Ken Loach's controversial *Ladybird, Ladybird* is his biggest success since *Kes*.

Kenneth Branagh makes an epic version of *Mary Shelley's Frankenstein*.

Franco Zeffirelli begins his version of *Jane Eyre* at Ealing, as the studios' directors, facing debts of £6.5m, call in the receivers.

Ridley and Tony Scott head a syndicate that announces its intention of buying Shepperton Studios.

A tough new censorship law will prevent the video release of many films. The BBFC dithers about granting Stone's *Natural Born Killers* a certificate.

China: Zhang Yimou directs *To Live*, with Gong Li. The authorities forbid him to make films in China for five years and ban Gong Li from visiting the West.

Cuba: Tomás Gutiérrez Alea and Juan Carlos Tabio's *Strawberry and Chocolate* examines homosexuality in Castro's Cuba.

France: The government resists a US trade agreement that would have removed protection for local film-makers.

Readers of a French trade magazine vote as the top three films ever made Marcel Carne's *Les Enfants du Paradis*, Milos Forman's *One Flew Over the Cuckoo's Nest* and Robert Wise and Jerome Robbins' *West Side Story*.

Italy: Roberto Benigni's *The Monster* breaks box-office records.

Poland: As his *Three Colours: Red* opens in Europe, Kieslowski announces that he will make no more films.

Spain: Fernando Trueba's *Belle Époque* is an art-house hit.

The governments plan a tax on dubbed films to protect local producers.

1995

America: Presidential hopeful Bob Dole accuses Hollywood of producing 'nightmares of depravity drenched in violence and sex'.

Batman Forever, directed by Joel Schumacher, with Val Kilmer taking over as Batman and Jim Carrey as The Riddler breaks box-office records by taking $53.3m in its opening weekend.

Waterworld, starring Kevin Costner and directed by Kevin Reynolds (though he left during post-production) becomes the most expensive film so far made, costing around $175m, which was $100m over budget. It takes $88m at the US box-office.

Toy Story, directed by John Lasseter, the first computer-generated feature, makes conventional animated films look old-fashioned.

After *Dumb and Dumber* follows *Ace Ventura: Pet Detective* and *The Mask* by earning more than $100m at the box-office, Jim Carrey is paid $20m to make a darker comedy, *The Cable Guy*.

Ed Wood, by general consent America's worst

director, is celebrated in a biopic starring Johnny Depp that also brings Martin Landau an Oscar for his supporting role as Bela Lugosi.

After much re-editing and re-shooting, *Mary Reilly*, which brought Julia Roberts a record fee, is released and flops at the box-office.

Demi Moore becomes the highest paid actress in history, receiving $12m to make the thriller *Striptease*, which also fails to excite audiences.

Paul Verhoeven's controversial *Showgirls*, a film about Las Vegas' lap-dancers, is greeted with critical disdain and audience indifference.

Antonia Bird's British film *Priest*, about a homosexual priest, is condemned by the Catholic League for Civil and Religious Rights and its American release is delayed.

Scottish heroes figure in two rousing nationalistic US-financed epics: *Rob Roy*, starring Liam Neeson and directed by Michael Caton-Jones, and *Braveheart* (filmed mainly in Ireland) with star and director Mel Gibson as William Wallace.

Hollywood films take $5.1 billion from foreign cinemas, at least as much as they earn in the US. Some, such as the dire *First Knight* take $85 million in foreign revenue, compared to $38 million in the US. The biggest foreign earner of the year is *Die Hard With a Vengeance*, with $254 million.

Australia: *Babe*, a film about a talking pig who wants to be a sheepdog, directed by Chris Noonan and produced by George Miller (of 'Mad Max' fame) is a surprising international hit.

Belgium: Jan Bucquoy's *The Sexual Life of the Belgians 1950-1978* enjoys some international success, though it does little for the reputation of the Belgians as lovers.

Britain: The National Heritage Select Committee reports that despite the growth in cinema audiences – up from an all-time low of 58m in 1984 to 124m in 1994 – British films managed to capture 2.5 per cent of British box-office receipts in 1993, while American films took a 94.2 per cent share.

The government announces that the National Lottery will contribute at least £80m to film production and distribution over five years.

Ken Loach's impassioned political *Land and Freedom*, set in the Spanish Civil War, emphasises his lonely pre-eminence among British directors.

Theatre director Nicholas Hytner makes an impressive debut with *The Madness of King George*, starring Nigel Hawthorne.

Danny Boyle's energetic Scottish thriller *Shallow Grave*, written by John Hodge and produced by Andrew Macdonald announces the arrival of excellent new talents, including its stars Christopher Eccleston and Ewan McGregor.

France: the Prime Minister insists that his Cabinet watch *La Haine*, Mathieu Kassovitz's passionate film about life and racism on a rundown housing estate, which also wins him the best director award at the Cannes Film Festival.

Luc Besson reaches an international audience with his thriller *Leon* (US: *The Professional*), with a cast that includes Gary Oldman, Nathalie Portman and Danny Aiello alongside French star Jean Reno.

Jean-Pierre Jeunet follows his quirky *Delicatessen* with another extraordinary, though flawed, movie *The City of Lost Children*.

Hong Kong: Wong Kar-Wai's *Chungking Express* establishes him as an director of great individuality.

Italy: Michael Radford directs Italian star Massimo Troisi in the romantic *Il Postino*. Troisi dies of a heart attack within days of finishing the film.

Macedonia: Milo Manchevski's *Before the Rain* explores, in a circular narrative, the roots of nationalistic hatred of the kind that destroyed Yugoslavia.

New Zealand: Peter Jackson turns from gross horror to true crime, with the disturbing, sensitively directed *Heavenly Creatures*, about two schoolgirl murderers.

Lee Tamahori's *Once Were Warriors* is a powerful film about Maori life in an Auckland slum. He leaves for Hollywood to make a thriller, *Mulholland Falls*.

Russia: Nikita Mikhalkov's *Burnt By The Sun* deals movingly with the horrors and personal betrayals of a totalitarian system.

1996

America: Sensation and spectacular special effects, become the defining mark of Hollywood films: *Independence Day*, *Twister* and *Mission Impossible* all become runaway hits at the box office, with *Independence Day* becoming the fastest grossing film so far, taking $104.3m in its first week.

Jim Carrey's box-office appeal falters with the release of *The Cable Guy*.

Eddie Murphy revives his career in a remake of the Jerry Lewis vehicle *The Nutty Professor*.

Steven Spielberg begins shooting *The Lost World*, a sequel to his *Jurassic Park*, starring Jeff Goldblum.

Hugh Wilson's *The First Wives Club*, starring Goldie Hawn, Bette Midler and Diane Keaton as deserted women who take revenge on errant husbands, becomes the most talked-about movie of the autumn.

Fox Family Films and producer John Hughes begin a search to find a new child actor to replace Macaulay Culkin, too old at 16, in *Home Alone III*.

Matthew McConaughey is hailed as a new star following his performance in the courtroom drama *A Time to Kill*, based on John Grisham's novel.

Meanwhile Grisham claims Oliver Stone's *Natural Born Killers* was responsible for the shooting of a friend and suggests that artists should take responsibility for the effect of their works.

MGM/UA is put up for sale by Credit Lyonnais, the French bank, and acquired in a management buyout for $1.3 billion by its current chairman Frank Mancuso, backed by Kirk Kerkorian, a former owner, and the Australian television company Seven Network.

Time Warner takes over the Turner Broadcasting System for $7.3 billion to become once again the world's largest media company.

John Calley, president of United Artists, leaves to head Sony Pictures Entertainment, which includes Columbia and TriStar Pictures, following the departure of several leading executives.

The recently discovered *The Life and Death of King Richard III*, released in 1912 and the earliest American feature film to survive in a complete form, is shown at Los Angeles County Museum of Art. Running for 55 minutes and based on Shakespeare's play, it stars the British-born Frederick Warde and is directed by James Keane.

William Shakespeare's Romeo and Juliet, an updated treatment by director Baz Luhrmann, starring Claire Danes and Leonardo DiCaprio, is a hit at the box-office.

Il Postino becomes the highest-grossing foreign-language film shown in the US, taking more than $21m at the box-office.

After heavy lobbying by US companies, the European Parliament rejects its Culture Committee's recommendation that it increase the protection of European film and television from American imports.

Ted Turner says that he is 'personally appalled' by David Cronenberg's *Crash*, but will not stop the release of the film by his company Fine Line Features. But the release date, originally set for October, is put back to March 1997.

The box-office success of Wes Craven's *Scream*, with a self-referential script from Kevin Williamson, starts a new cycle of teenage horror and slasher movies.

A survey by *Variety* finds that films with budgets greater than $60m are more likely to make profits than cheaper movies.

Australia: After the killing of 35 people by a gunman in Port Arthur, Tasmania, the government announces tougher censorship laws for film, video, and television, including electronic filters on all new TV sets to prevent children from watching violent programmes.

Scott Hicks's *Shine* enjoys international acclaim and he signs a deal with new Hollywood studio DreamWorks SKG.

Britain: The first weekend in January is the best-ever for British cinemas, with £7,240,081 taken at the box office. The most popular films are *Seven* and *GoldenEye*, starring Pierce Brosnan as the new James Bond.

Director Danny Boyle, writer John Hodge and producer Andrew Macdonald have a hit with *Trainspotting*, based on Irvine Welsh's novel of drug addiction, which takes more than $18m at the British box office. The film is cut by four seconds and has some of its dialogue re-dubbed for its American release.

Mike Leigh's *Secrets and Lies* is his most accessible film so far, and a winner of the Palme D'Or at the Cannes Film Festival. But local audiences show little interest, though it does well in France.

The Jane Austen cycle reaches its peak with *Sense and Sensibility*, directed by Ang Lee and winning an Oscar for Emma Thompson as screenwriter.

Liam Neeson switches from Scottish hero Rob Roy to Irish patriot Michael Collins in a controversial biopic directed by Neil Jordan.

Rank, which stopped fully financing films in the late 1960s, announces that it will finance films costing less than $7m, rather than its previous policy of investing no more than half the budget in films that already had an American distributor. But it is rumoured that the company has plans to sell Pinewood studios and Rank Film Distributors.

ITV announces that it plans to invest at least £100m in British production over five years, producing at least 10 films a year.

Top films at the British box-office are *Independence Day*, which took $61m, *Toy Story*, *Seven*, *Mission: Impossible*, *Twister*, *Sense and Sensibility*, *Jumanji* and *Trainspotting*.

The Arts Council announces that it will award up to six franchises to production companies for six years, allowing them access to lottery cash to develop and finance British films.

The Home Office, claiming widespread public concern about violence on television and films, demands that the BBFC reports on how it proposes to reduce the level of violence on videos, adding that significant cuts must be made. James Ferman, director of the BBFC, says that censorship cannot change 'the culture of violence which permeates much mainstream filmmaking'. In the past three years, the Board had made cuts to 369 videos, amounting to six hours, and banned a further 14 from distribution. He adds that several recent films were likely to receive significant cuts when classified for video release in 1997. 'The real solution is for Hollywood to wake up with a conscience. But I have my doubts. There is too much money at stake.'

As the BBFC takes its time in granting a certificate to David Cronenberg's *Crash*, the Conservative government's Heritage Secretary calls for local authorities to use their powers under the Cinemas Act to ban its showing.

Jeremy Irons says that he will leave Britain if *Lolita* fails to find a distributor.

France: Producers campaign for curbs on American films.

David Cronenberg's *Crash* is shown uncut with a 16 certificate and enjoys a successful run.

Italy: TV and film producers demand production and distribution quotas to protect the ailing local industry against American imports.

Japan: The lowest number of admissions (119.6m) for 46 years and the second-worst box-office figures are recorded, despite an increase in the number of screens by more than 50 over the previous year.

Romania: The government-owned Romaniafilm announces that it will sell off around 300 of its 400 cinemas.

Ukraine: Local producers are worried that, since the country's independence in 1991, its feature film production has fallen from 40 films in 1992 to six in 1995.

1997

America: Cinema admissions reach 1.388 billion, the highest figure since 1959.

The average cost of a Hollywood movie is $75.6m ($53.4m on production and $22.2 on publicity and advertising), an increase of 166 per cent in the last ten years and a 34 per cent rise since 1996.

Studios, led by Fox and Universal, develop 'off-balance-sheet financing', in which three years of films are owned by outside investors and, after five years, when revenues have been collected, they are bought back from the investors. The studios collect fees from the investors for marketing and distribution and also retain most of the net profits. *Business Week* reported that Fox's New Millennium Investors had $40m in equity and $960m in debt, while Universal's Galaxy Investors had $44m in equity from outside investors and $1.06 billion in debt, none of which shows up in the studios' balance sheets.

Universal Studios buy independent distributor and producer October Films, the last remaining independent studio, for $15m.

Oklahoma City Police seize videos of *The Tin Drum* after a judge declares the film obscene. MPAA President Jack Valenti says that he is 'deeply troubled' by their action.

American distributors show no interest in Adrian Lyne's film *Lolita*.

The National Federation of the Blind ask Disney to stop production on a live-action version of the cartoon character *Mr Magoo*, starring Leslie Nielsen, on the grounds that there is nothing funny in watching 'an ill-tempered and

incompetent blind man stumble into things and misunderstand his surroundings'. Production continues: the film flops at the box-office.

The Peacemaker, the first release from the new studio DreamWorks, underwhelms critics and audiences, and does nothing to enhance George Clooney's reputation as Hollywood's rising star.

Sony Pictures enjoys its best year with hits *Men in Black*, *My Best Friend's Wedding*, *Jerry Maguire* and *The Fifth Element*.

James Cameron's *Titanic* becomes the most expensive film yet made, as it goes over budget to reach a cost of $200m.

According to a Harris poll, the most popular movie actors are Clint Eastwood, Mel Gibson, Tom Cruise, John Wayne, Kevin Costner, Arnold Schwarzenegger, Richard Gere and Sean Connery. The most popular actress is Demi Moore. Those whose popularity is slipping include Steven Seagal, Tom Hanks, Paul Newman and Sylvester Stallone.

Britain: *The Full Monty* becomes the highest-grossing movie so far in Britain.

Cinema attendances reach their highest figure – 138.9m – since the late 60s.

Mike Leigh, after receiving the BAFTA award for best British film for *Secrets and Lies*, reveals that he had resigned from the Academy in protest after being ignored in the past.

Polygram announces continuing losses from its film business in the first quarter of the year and arranges a £50m loan from the European Investment Bank to help finance its future production and distribution.

The BBFC pass David Cronenberg's *Crash* without cuts, but it is banned by three councils, including Westminster, which covers many London cinemas.

The Labour government's first budget provides improved tax relief that is likely to boost local film production.

After three consortia are given lottery money to make films, Mick Southworth, managing director of Film Four Distributors, warns, 'The depressing reality is that more than 50 per cent of British films fail to get a domestic UK theatrical release.'

Labour Home Secretary Jack Straw criticizes James Ferman for passing two sexually explicit films for sale in licensed sex shops. He blocks the appointment of Lord Birkett as chairman of the British Board of Film Classification, and appoints Andreas Whittam Smith, the former editor of the *Independent* newspaper, as chairman. Whittam Smith says that one of the first things he will look at is pornography on video.

David Aukin, Channel 4's head of film, objects to the Broadcasting Standards Commission censure of the channel for showing Ken Loach's *Ladybird, Ladybird* for violence and language that goes 'beyond acceptable boundaries'. He leaves to set up Hal Films, part of the growing Miramax empire.

Alan Parker is appointed chairman of the British Film Institute, an organization he once claimed was '28 intellectuals in a library'.

Rank sells its film distribution business and film library to Carlton TV for £65m.

The government's Film Policy Review Group proposes a voluntary levy on film revenues to create a basis for a fund to support the distribution and development of British films. Companies that choose not to contribute to the fund will be barred from receiving any subsidies. Also suggested is a relaxation of the definition

of British films to include Hollywood-financed films made in the UK and using British talent.

Denmark: Sydney Pollack sues Danish state television for screening one of his films in a cut version, claiming damage to his professional reputation.

France: Cannes celebrates its 50th Film Festival, but the films on show are less worthy of acclaim: it opens with Luc Besson's fantasy *The Fifth Element*, which critics hate but which goes on to top the US box-office.

Cinema attendance passes the 140m mark for the first time in ten years, as film production reaches its highest level of the last decade.

A French economist, Professor Patrick Messerlin, says that the system of subsidies and quotas designed to protect the French film industry is both costly and useless, with the quality and number of locally made films falling as subsidies have grown. He adds that the tax on cinema tickets affects box-office successes more than flops. French producers, he says, tend to make quasi-American films to the detriment of local culture.

Germany: Producer Artur Brauner denounces as scandalous the local complaints over naming a street or square after Marlene Dietrich. 'She was the only major German entertainer who maintained her integrity during the Third Reich,' he says.

India: Four leading film industry figures are shot dead in daytime in three months of the summer, including Gulshan Kumar, a producer who refused to pay extortion money to local gangsters.

Japan: After a 14-year-old boy is arrested for killing an 11-year-old and leaving his severed head by his school gates, Japanese police and politicians blame the crime on American horror films.

Hayao Miyazaki's anime *Princess Mononoke* beats *E.T. – the Extra-Terrestrial* to become Japan's biggest box-office success. Masayuki Suo's *Shall We Dance?*, about the exotic rituals of ballroom dancing, becomes an international success.

South Korea: Censors ban Wong Kar-Wai's Cannes award-winning movie *Happy Together*, objecting to its homosexual theme.

1998

America: Despite critical misgivings, James Cameron's *Titanic* becomes a massive hit, with a worldwide gross of more than $1 billion, and elevates Leonardo DiCaprio to superstardom. 'So does this prove, once and for all, that size does matter?' asks Cameron. The film goes on to win 11 Oscars, including best film and best director, and be nominated for three more.

A video store offers to edit *Titanic* for its customers, removing scenes that contain nudity or references to sexual activity, claiming 2,000 people have asked for the service. Paramount threatens to sue for copyright violation. The Artists Rights Foundation asks it to stop, on the grounds that 'the protection of American cultural heritage for future generations depends upon our ability to protect the work of artists from any alteration that seeks to "improve" the efforts of the original artists'.

The paraplegic Christopher Reeve stars as the crippled photographer in a well-received TV movie remake of *Rear Window*. But Gus Van Sant's colour remake of Alfred Hitchcock's *Psycho* opens to lukewarm reviews.

Jim Carrey maintains his star status with *The Truman Show*, which attracts audiences and rave reviews.

Jackie Chan finally cracks the American market with *Rush Hour*, teaming him with Chris Tucker.

The unexpected success of *Waterboy* allows Adam Sandler to command a $20m-a-movie pay cheque.

Despite being released after the similar *Deep Impact*, the disaster movie *Armageddon* becomes the year's big hit, taking more than $200m at the US box-office.

DreamWorks SKG enjoys its first hits with Steven Spielberg's *Saving Private Ryan*, which takes more than $360m at the world's box-offices, and the animated feature *Antz*.

Universal's poorly performing movies at the box-office, including the big-budget *Meet Joe Black* and *Babe: Pig in the City*, result in the departure of top executives.

Britain: Only three British-made films – *Sliding Doors*, *Spiceworld: The Movie* and *Lock, Stock and Two Smoking Barrels*, feature in the year's Top 20. The list is dominated by *Titanic*, which takes more than three times as much as the next most popular film, *Doctor Dolittle*.

The government scraps plans for a voluntary levy on companies involved in British films, which was to raise £15m to help distribution and development.

The National Film and Television School puts Ealing Studios up for sale, while the Rank Organization considers whether to sell off Pinewood Studios.

Sean Connery announces plans to set up a film studio in Scotland.

The government announces the formation of a Film Council, which will combine the activities of the BFI, British Screen, the British Film Commission and the film-funding activities of the Arts Council.

Indian director's Yash Johar's Bollywood film *Kuch Kuch Kotai Hai* is a hit with Asian audiences in London, and becomes for a time one of the top 10 movies showing in the city.

Polygram is sold for $10.4 billion to Seagram, owners of Universal Studios, who want it for its music division: the future of its film production business remains undecided.

France: Cinema attendance reaches 175m, but the numbers watching French-made films go down from 51m in 1997 to 44m. The French share of the box-office drops to 27 per cent, against 68 per cent for American films.

Gérard Depardieu stars in the most expensive French film so far made, *Asterix and Obelix vs Caesar*, which is budgeted at $48m.

Enduring star Alain Delon announces his retirement, adding, 'The Americans have completed their conquest. We are outflanked, shrivelled and completely chewed up.'

Italy: Robert Benigni scores as writer, director and star of *Life Is Beautiful*, which goes on to win 28 international awards, including the Grand Jury prize at the Cannes Film Festival, and European Film and Actor of the Year.

Netherlands: Ben Sombogaert's family film *Abeltje*, based on a popular book about a flying lift boy, is the most expensive Dutch film so far made, with a budget of $4.6m.

Singapore: *Money No Enough*, a low-budget film directed by Tay Teck-lock, becomes the highest-grossing Chinese-language film, taking $3m in its first two months.

South Korea: The government resists the USA's demands that it scrap its quota system which makes cinemas show local movies for 106 days a year. Local producers, directors and actors claim that the abolition of the system would erase 'the soul of Korean cinema'.

Halliwell's Film & Video Guide
2000 Edition

EDITED BY JOHN WALKER

'Heavy enough to be authoritative, light enough to be idosyncratic'
The Times

The 2000 edition of *Halliwell's Film & Video Guide* is perennially entertaining, comprehensive and indispensable. The best known of British film guides, *Halliwell's* is the undisputed bible for film enthusiasts and trivia buffs – a must-have for every movie-goer. Fully revised and updated for the millennium to include hundreds of new films, it is packed full with cast and credit information and pithy comment. It also includes:

★ Plot synopses and critical evaluations; video cassette, laser disc and DVD availability; quotes from contemporary reviews; alternative titles and original publicity tags

★ Easy-to-follow icons denoting films suitable for family viewing, Academy Award winners and nominees, soundtrack availability, computer-coloured versions and video format compatibility

★ Lists of four-star and three-star films by title and year, and a list of all the Academy Award winners for best picture and director, best actor and actress, best supporting actor and actress, and best original and adapted screenplays

'retains its crown as the king of the guides'
Film Review

£19.99
0 00 653165 2
Publication: 4 October 1999